2020
STANDARD POSTAGE
STAMP CATALOGUE

ONE HUNDRED AND SEVENTY-SIXTH EDITION IN SIX VOLUMES

VOLUME 6B

THAI-Z

EDITOR-IN-CHIEF	Jay Bigalke
EDITOR-AT-LARGE	Donna Houseman
EDITOR	Charles Snee
MANAGING EDITOR	Timothy A. Hodge
EDITOR EMERITUS	James E. Kloetzel
SENIOR EDITOR /NEW ISSUES & VALUING	Martin J. Frankevicz
ADMINISTRATIVE ASSISTANT/CATALOGUE LAYOUT	Eric Wiessinger
PRINTING AND IMAGE COORDINATOR	Stacey Mahan
SENIOR GRAPHIC DESIGNER	Cinda McAlexander
SALES DIRECTOR	David Pistello
SALES DIRECTOR	Eric Roth

Released September 2019

Includes New Stamp Listings through the July 2019 *Linn's Stamp News Monthly* Catalogue Update

Copyright© 2019 by

AMOS MEDIA

911 S. Vandemark Road, Sidney, OH 45365-4129
Publishers of *Linn's Stamp News, Linn's Stamp News Monthly, Coin World* and *Coin World Monthly*.

Table of Contents

See the following volumes for other country listings:
Volume 1A: United States, United Nations, Abu Dhabi-Australia; Volume 1B: Austria-B
Volume 2A: C-Cur; Volume 2B: Cyp-F
Volume 3A: G; Volume 3B: H-I
Volume 4A: J-L; Volume 4B: M
Volume 5A: N-Phil; Volume 5B: Pit-Sam
Volume 6A: San-Tete

Scott Catalogue Mission Statement

The Scott Catalogue Team exists to serve the recreational,
educational and commercial hobby needs of stamp collectors and dealers.

We strive to set the industry standard for philatelic information and products by developing and
providing goods that help collectors identify, value, organize and present their collections.

Quality customer service is, and will continue to be, our highest priority.
We aspire toward achieving total customer satisfaction.

SCOTT

What's new for 2020 Scott Standard Volume 6B?

Another catalog season is upon us as we continue the journey of the 151-year history of the Scott catalogs. The 2020 volumes are the 176th edition of the Scott *Standard Postage Stamp Catalogue*. Vol. 6A includes listings for countries of the world San Marino through Tete. Listings for countries of the world Thailand through Z can be found in Vol. 6B.

Frequent users of the catalogs may notice a new look for the covers. Highlighted are single stamps from a postal entity found in that catalog. The Vol. 6B catalog shows the 2016 Uruguay $20 stamp illustrating a poster for 1915-16 Summer Festival and Carnival (Scott 2543).

Both Portuguese colonies found in Volume 6B, Timor and Zambezia, were reviewed. Slightly more than 800 value changes were made, mostly in an upward direction due to a thriving market.

Values increased for two no-comma varieties of the overprinted Vatican City stamps of 1934 (Scott 37a and 38u). Shown here is a normal example of the 1.30-lira on 1.25-lira Pope Pius XI stamp (36), which is not known without the comma.

The stamps of Timor are doing quite well. The most substantial increase was for the 1894 light blue 50-rupee King Carlos stamp with gauge 13½ perforations (Scott 27a). It soared in value from $160 unused and $125 used to $575 and $425, respectively.

The 1913 Timor varieties featuring the "REPUBLICA" overprint on the 1902 provisional issue misspelled as "REUBPLICA" and "REPBLICAU" (Scott 133a and 133b, respectively) increased from $19 in both unused and used condition to $40 unused and $35 used.

A careful review of Zambezia yielded approximately 170 value changes, most of which were increases. By far the most substantial increase was for the 1894 dark blue on blue 200-rupee King Carlos stamp that is perforated gauge 11½ (Scott 11a). This minor-letter variety increased from $250 unused and $175 used to $1,350 and $1,000, respectively. The new values are in italics.

The stamps of Turkey were thoroughly reviewed, and more than 2,000 changes were made. The 1901 50-piaster yellow brown stamp with perforations that gauge 13½ (Scott 117) increased in value from $37.50 to $60 unused, and from $5 to $6 used. Many minor-letter varieties issued prior to 1940 saw increases in value.

More modern Turkish stamps saw a mix of increases and decreases. One of the issues that increased in value was the 2005 Galatasaray Sports Club Centenary sheet

The 2005 Galatasaray Sports Club centenary sheet of four from Turkey (Scott 2974) increased in value from $5 to $6 in unused condition. Additionally, a footnote was added to point out the existence of an imperforate variety.

of four (Scott 2974). It moved from $5 unused and $2.50 used to $6 and $3, respectively. A footnote was also added to indicate this sheet's existence in imperforate condition. This variety is valued at $40 mint.

Russian stamps of 1907-17 that were overprinted for the Transcaucasian Federated Republic were among the stamps reviewed by the editors. The 25-kopeck green and gray violet stamp overprinted in black (Scott 3) increased from $4 to $10 in unused condition.

Substantial increases were made for two no-comma varieties of the 1934 Vatican City surcharges. The 2.05-lira on 2-lira Pope Pius XI stamp without the comma between the "2" and the "0" (Scott 37a) increased from $550 unused and $40 used to $1,000 and $800, respectively. The 2.55-lira on 2.50-lira stamp without the comma between the "2" and the "5" (Scott 38a) increased from $200 to $800 unused, and from $300 to $900 used.

Editorial enhancements for Vol. 6B

Because of a lack of evidence of its existence, the Vatican City 3.70-lira on 10-lira stamp without the comma between the "3" and the "7" (Scott 40a) was delisted. The editors welcome any feedback from collectors who might have this variety or additional information about it.

And lastly, we encourage you to pay special attention to the Number Additions, Deletions & Changes found on page 968 in this volume. We also suggest reading the catalog introduction, which includes an abundance of useful information.

Best wishes in your stamp collecting pursuits!

Jay Bigalke, Scott catalog editor-in-chief

Acknowledgments

Our appreciation and gratitude go to the following individuals who have assisted us in preparing information included in this year's Scott Catalogues. Some helpers prefer anonymity. These individuals have generously shared their stamp knowledge with others through the medium of the Scott Catalogue.

Those who follow provided information that is in addition to the hundreds of dealer price lists and advertisements and scores of auction catalogues and realizations that were used in producing the catalogue values. It is from those noted here that we have been able to obtain information on items not normally seen in published lists and advertisements. Support from these people goes beyond data leading to catalogue values, for they also are key to editorial changes.

A special acknowledgment to Liane and Sergio Sismondo of The Classic Collector for their assistance and knowledge sharing that have aided in the preparation of this year's Standard and Classic Specialized Catalogues.

Roland Austin (United States Stamp Society)
Michael & Cecilia Ball (A To Z Stamps)
Anthony Bard
Jim Bardo (Bardo Stamps)
Jules K. Beck (Latin American Philatelic Society)
John Birkinbine II
Helmut Blaschczyk
James A. Booth
Les Bootman
Federico Brid
Roger S. Brody
Peter Bylen
Tina & John Carlson (JET Stamps)
Carlson Chambliss
Tony L. Crumbley (Carolina Coin and Stamp, Inc.)
Christopher Dahle
Ubaldo Del Toro
Bob and Rita Dumaine (Sam Houston Duck Co.)
Mark Eastzer
Paul G. Eckman
Robert Finder (Korea Stamp Society)
Jeffrey M. Forster
Robert S. Freeman
Ernest E. Fricks (France & Colonies Philatelic Society)
Bob Genisol (Sultan Stamp Center)
Stan Goldfarb
Dan Harding
Bruce Hecht (Bruce L. Hecht Co.)
Peter Hoffman
John M. Hotchner
Armen Hovsepian (ArmenStamp)
Eric Jackson

John I. Jamieson (Saskatoon Stamp and Coin)
Peter C. Jeannopoulos
William A. (Bill) Jones
Allan Katz (Ventura Stamp Co.)
Patricia A. Kaufmann (Confederate Stamp Alliance)
Jon Kawaguchi (Ryukyu Philatelic Specialist Society)
William V. Kriebel (Brazil Philatelic Association)
George Krieger
John R. Lewis (The William Henry Stamp Co.)
Ulf Lindahl (Ethiopian Philatelic Society)
Ignacio Llach (Filatelia Llach, S.L.)
Dennis Lynch (Eire Philatelic Association)
Kevin MacKeown (Korea Stamp Society)
Marilyn Mattke
William K. McDaniel
Pat McElroy
Gary Morris (Pacific Midwest Co.)
Peter Mosiondz, Jr.
Bruce M. Moyer (Moyer Stamps & Collectables)
Scott Murphy
Leonard Nadybal
Dr. Tiong Tak Ngo
Nik & Lisa Oquist
Dr. Everett L. Parker
John E. Pearson
Don Peterson (International Philippine Philatelic Society)
Stanley M. Piller (Stanley M. Piller & Associates)
Virgil Pirvulescu

Todor Drumev Popov
Dr. Charles Posner
Bob Prager (Gary Posner, Inc.)
Ed Reiser (Century Stamp Co.)
Ghassan D. Riachi
Peter A. Robertson
Omar Rodriguez
Mehrdad Sadri (Persiphila)
Dennis W. Schmidt
Michael Schreiber
Christian Schunck
Guy Shaw (Mexico-Elmhurst Philatelic Society International)
Jeff Siddiqui (Pakistan Philatelic Study Circle)
Sergio & Liane Sismondo (The Classic Collector)
Jay Smith
Telah Smith
Ivo Spanjersberg (Korea Stamp Society)
Earl Toops
Dan Undersander
Steven Unkrich
Philip T. Wall
Yong S. Yi (Korea Stamp Society)
Ralph Yorio
Val Zabijaka (Zabijaka Auctions)
Dr. Michal Zika (Album)
Steven Zirinsky (Zirinsky Stamps)
Alfonso G. Zulueta, Jr.

Addresses, Telephone Numbers, Web Sites, E-Mail Addresses of General & Specialized Philatelic Societies

Collectors can contact the following groups for information about the philately of the areas within the scope of these societies, or inquire about membership in these groups. Aside from the general societies, we limit this list to groups that specialize in particular fields of philately, particular areas covered by the Scott Standard Postage Stamp Catalogue, and topical groups. Many more specialized philatelic society exist than those listed below. These addresses are updated yearly, and they are, to the best of our knowledge, correct and current. Groups should inform the editors of address changes whenever they occur. The editors also want to hear from other such specialized groups not listed. Unless otherwise noted all website addresses begin with http://

General Societies

American Philatelic Society
100 Match Factory Place
Bellefonte, PA 16823-1367
(814) 933-3803
https://stamps.org
apsinfo@stamps.org

International Society of Worldwide Stamp Collectors
Joanne Berkowitz, M.D.
P.O. Box 19006
Sacramento, CA 95819
www.iswsc.org
executivedirector@iswsc.org

Royal Philatelic Society of Canada
P.O. Box 69080
St. Clair Post Office
Toronto, ON M4T 3A1
CANADA
(888) 285-4143
www.rpsc.org
info@rpsc.org

Royal Philatelic Society, London
41 Devonshire Place
London W1G 6JY
UNITED KINGDOM
020 7486 1044
www.rpsl.org.uk
secretary@rpsl.org.uk

Libraries, Museums, and Research Groups

American Philatelic Research Library
Scott Tiffney
100 Match Factory Place
Bellefonte, PA 16823
(814) 933-3803
www.stamplibrary.org
library@stamps.org

V. G. Greene Philatelic Research Foundation
P.O. Box 69100
St. Clair Post Office
Toronto, ON M4T 3A1
CANADA
(416) 921-2073
info@greenefoundation.ca

Aero/Astro Philately

American Air Mail Society
Stephen Reinhard
P.O. Box 110
Mineola, NY 11501
www.americanairmailsociety.org
sreinhard1@optonline.net

Postal History

Auxiliary Markings Club
Jerry Johnson
6621 W. Victoria Ave.
Kennewick, WA 99336
www.postal-markings.org
membership-2016@postal-markings.org

Cover Collectors Circuit Club
P.O. Box 316
Clallam Bay, WA 98326-0316
www.covercollectors.org
adirondack.stamps@gmail.com

Postage Due Mail Study Group
Bob Medland
Camway Cottage
Nanny Hurn's Lane
Cameley, Bristol BS39 5AJ
UNITED KINGDOM
01761 45959
www.postageduemail.org.uk
secretary.pdmsg@gmail.com

Postal History Society
Yamil Kouri
405 Waltham St. #347
Lexington, MA 02421
www.postalhistorysociety.org
yhkouri@massmed.org

Post Mark Collectors Club
Bob Milligan
7014 Woodland Oaks Drive
Magnolia, TX 77354
(281) 259-2735
www.postmarks.org
bob.milligan@gmail.com

Precancel Stamp Society
Dick Kalmbach
2658 Ironworks Drive
Buford, GA 30519-7070
www.prooancels.com
promo@precancels.com

U.S. Cancellation Club
Roger Curran
20 University Ave.
Lewisburg, PA 17837
rcurran@dejazzd.com

Postal Stationery

United Postal Stationery Society
Stuart Leven
1659 Branham Lane, Suite F-307
San Jose, CA 95118-2291
www.upss.org
postat@gmail.com

Revenues & Cinderellas

American Revenue Association
Lyman Hensley
473 E. Elm St.
Sycamore, IL 60178-1934
www.revenuer.org
ilrno2@netzero.net

Christmas Seal & Charity Stamp Society
John Denune Jr. & Sr.
234 E. Broadway
Granville, OH 43023
(740) 814-6031
www.seal-society.org
john@christmasseals.net

National Duck Stamp Collectors Society
Anthony J. Monico
P.O. Box 43
Harleysville, PA 19438-0043
www.ndscs.org
ndscs@ndscs.org

State Revenue Society
Kent Gray
P.O. Box 67842
Albuqueque, NM 87193
www.staterevenue.org
srssecretary@comcast.net

Thematic Philately

Americana Unit
Dennis Dengel
17 Peckham Road
Poughkeepsie, NY 12603-2018
www.americanaunit.org
ddengel@americanaunit.org

American Topical Association
Vera Felts
P.O. Box 8
Carterville, IL 62918-0008
(618) 985-5100
www.americantopicalassn.org
americantopical@msn.com

Astronomy Study Unit
Leonard Zehr
1009 Treverton Crescent
Windsor, ON N8P 1K2
CANADA
(416) 833-9317
www.astronomystudyunit.net
lenzehr@gmail.com

Bicycle Stamps Club
Steve Andreasen
2000 Alaskan Way, Unit 157
Seattle, WA 98121
www.bicyclestampsclub.org
steven.w.andreasen@gmail.com

Biology Unit
Chris Dahle
1401 Linmar Drive NE
Cedar Rapids, IA 52402-3724
www.biophilately.org
chris-dahle@biophilately.org

Bird Stamp Society
Mr. S. A. H. (Tony) Statham
Ashlyns Lodge
Chesham Road
Berkhamsted, Herts HP4 2ST
UNITED KINGDOM
www.bird-stamps.org/bss
tony.statham@sky.com

Captain Cook Society
Jerry Yucht
8427 Leale Ave.
Stockton, CA 95212
www.captaincooksociety.com
us@captaincooksociety.com

The CartoPhilatelic Society
Marybeth Sulkowski
2885 Sanford Ave., SW, #32361
Grandville, MI 49418-1342
www.mapsonstamps.org
secretary@mapsonstamps.org

Casey Jones Railroad Unit
Jeff Lough
2612 Redbud Land, Apt. C
Lawrence, KS 66046
www.uqp.de/cjr
jeffydplaugh@gmail.com

Cats on Stamps Study Unit
Robert D. Jarvis
2731 Teton Lane
Fairfield, CA 94533
www.catstamps.info
bobmarci@aol.com

Chemistry & Physics on Stamps Study Unit
Dr. Roland Hirsch
20458 Water Point Lane
Germantown, MD 20874
(301) 903-9009
www.cpossu.org
rfhirsch@cpossu.org

Chess on Stamps Study Unit
Barry Keith
555 Rolling Valley Court
Charlottesville, VA 22902-8257
www.chessonstamps.org
keithfam@embarqmail.com

Cricket Philatelic Society
A. Melville-Brown
11 Weppons, Ravens Road
Shorham-by-Sea
West Sussex BN43 5AW
UNITED KINGDOM
www.oriolcricketstamp.net
mel.cricket.100@googlemail.com

Ebony Society of Philatelic Events and Reflections (ESPER)
Don Neal
P.O. Box 5245
Somerset, NJ 08875-5245
www.esperstamps.org
esperdon@verizon.net

Earth's Physical Features Study Group
Fred Klein
515 Magdalena Ave.
Los Altos, CA 94024
http://epfsu.jeffhayward.com
epfsu@jeffhayward.com

Europa Study Unit
Tonny E. Van Loij
3002 S. Xanthia St.
Denver, CO 80231-4237
(303) 752-0189
www.europastudyunit.org
tvanloij@gmail.com

Fire Service in Philately
John Zaranek
81 Hillpine Road
Cheektowaga, NY 14227-2259
(716) 668-3352
jczaranek@roadrunner.com

Gay & Lesbian History on Stamps Club
Joe Petronie
P.O. Box 190842
Dallas, TX 75219-0842
www.glhsonline.org
glhsc@aol.com

Gems, Minerals & Jewelry Study Unit
Fred Haynes
10 Country Club Drive
Rochester, NY 14618-3720
fredmhaynes55@gmail.com

Graphics Philately Association
Larry Rosenblum
1030 E. El Camino Real
PMB 107
Sunnyvale, CA 94087-3759
www.graphics-stamps.org
larry@graphics-stamps.org

Journalists, Authors and Poets on Stamps
Christopher D. Cook
7222 Hollywood Rd.
Berrien Springs, MI 49103
cdcook2@gmail.com

Lighthouse Stamp Society
Dalene Thomas
1805 S. Balsam St., #106
Lakewood, CO 80232
(303) 986-6620
www.lighthousestampsociety.org
dalene@lighthousestampsociety.org

Lions International Stamp Club
David McKirdy
s-Gravenwetering 248
3062 SJ Rotterdam
NETHERLANDS
31(0) 10 212 0313
www.lisc.nl
davidmckirdy@aol.com

Masonic Study Unit
Gene Fricks
25 Murray Way
Blackwood, NJ 08012-4400
genefricks@comcast.net

Mathematical Study Unit
Monty J. Strauss
4209 88th Street
Lubbock, TX 79423-2941
www.mathstamps.org
montystrauss@gmail.com

Medical Subjects Unit
Dr. Frederick C. Skvara
P.O. Box 6228
Bridgewater, NJ 08807
fcskvara@optonline.net

Napoleonic Age Philatelists
Ken Berry
4117 NW 146th St.
Oklahoma City, OK 73134-1746
(405) 748-8646
www.nap-stamps.org
krb4117@att.net

Old World Archaeological Study Unit
Caroline Scannell
14 Dawn Drive
Smithtown, NY 11787-1761
www.owasu.org
editor@owasu.org

Petroleum Philatelic Society International
Feitze Papa
922 Meander Drive
Walnut Creek, CA 94598-4239
www.ppsi.org.uk
oildad@astound.net

Rotary on Stamps Fellowship
Gerald L. Fitzsimmons
105 Calle Ricardo
Victoria, TX 77904
www.rotaryonstamps.org
glfitz@suddenlink.net

Scouts on Stamps Society International
Woodrow (Woody) Brooks
498 Baldwin Road
Akron, OH 44312
(330) 612-1294
www.sossi.org
secretary@sossi.org

Ships on Stamps Unit
Erik Th. Matzinger
Voorste Havervelden 30
4822 AL Breda
NETHERLANDS
www.shipsonstamps.org
erikships@gmail.com

Space Topic Study Unit
David Blog
P.O. Box 174
Bergenfield, NJ 07621
www.space-unit.com
davidblognj@gmail.com

Stamps on Stamps Collectors Club
Michael Merritt
73 Mountainside Road
Mendham, NJ 07945
www.stampsonstamps.org
stampsonstamps@yahoo.com

Windmill Study Unit
Walter J. Hallien
607 N. Porter St.
Watkins Glenn, NY 14891-1345
(607) 229-3541
www.windmillworld.com

Youth Philately
Young Stamp Collectors of America
100 Match Factory Place
Bellefonte, PA 16823
(814) 933-3803
https://stamps.org/stamps/Learn/
youth-in-philately
ysca@stamps.org

United States

American Air Mail Society
Stephen Reinhard
P.O. Box 110
Mineola, NY 11501
www.americanairmailsociety.org
sreinhard1@optonline.net

American First Day Cover Society
Douglas Kelsey
P.O. Box 16277
Tucson, AZ 85732-6277
(520) 321-0880
www.afdcs.org
afdcs@afdcs.org

American Plate Number Single Society
Rick Burdsall
APNSS Secretary
P.O. BOX 1023
Palatine, IL 60078-1023
www.apnss.org
apnss.sec@gmail.com

American Revenue Association
Lyman Hensley
473 E. Elm St.
Sycamore, IL 60178-1934
www.revenuer.org
ilrno2@netzero.net

American Society for Philatelic Pages and Panels
Ron Walenciak
P.O. Box 1042
Washington TWP, NJ 07676
www.asppp.org
rwalenciak@aol.com

Auxiliary Markings Club
Jerry Johnson
6621 W. Victoria Ave.
Kennewick, WA 99336
www.postal-markings.org
membership-2016@postal-markings.org

Canal Zone Study Group
Mike Drabik
P.O. Box 281
Bolton, MA 01740
www.canalzonestudygroup.com
czsgsecretary@gmail.com

Carriers and Locals Society
John Bowman
14409 Pentridge Drive
Corpus Christi, TX 78410
(361) 933-0757
www.pennypost.org
jbowman@stx.rr.com

Christmas Seal & Charity Stamp Society
John Denune Jr. & Sr.
234 E. Broadway
Granville, OH 43023
(740) 814-6031
www.seal-society.org
john@christmasseals.net

Confederate Stamp Alliance
Patricia A. Kaufmann
10194 N. Old State Road
Lincoln, DE 19960-3644
(302) 422-2656
www.csalliance.org
trishkauf@comcast.net

Cover Collectors Circuit Club
P.O. Box 316
Clallam Bay, WA 98326-0316
www.covercollectors.org
adirondack.stamps@gmail.com

Error, Freaks, and Oddities Collectors Club
Scott Shaulis
P.O. Box 549
Murrysville, PA 15668-0549
(724) 733-4134
www.efocc.org
scott@shaulisstamps.com

National Duck Stamp Collectors Society
Anthony J. Monico
P.O. Box 43
Harleysville, PA 19438-0043
www.ndscs.org
ndscs@ndscs.org

Plate Number Coil Collectors Club (PNC3)
Gene Trinks
16415 W. Desert Wren Court
Surprise, AZ 85374
(623) 322-4619
www.pnc3.org
gctrinks@cox.net

Post Mark Collectors Club
Bob Milligan
7014 Woodland Oaks Drive
Magnolia, TX 77354
(281) 259-2735
www.postmarks.org
bob.milligan@gmail.com

Souvenir Card Collectors Society
William V. Kriebel
1923 Manning St.
Philadelphia, PA 19103-5728
www.souvenircards.org
kriebewv@drexel.edu

U.S. Cancellation Club
Roger Curran
20 University Ave.
Lewisburg, PA 17837
rcurran@dejazzd.com

U.S. Philatelic Classics Society
Rob Lund
2913 Fulton
Everett, WA 98201-3733
www.uspcs.org
membershipchairman@uspcs.org

US Possessions Philatelic Society
Daniel F. Ring
P.O. Box 113
Woodstock, IL 60098
http://uspps.tripod.com
danielfring@hotmail.com

United States Stamp Society
Larry Ballantyne
P.O. Box 6634
Katy, TX 77491-6634
www.usstamps.org
webmaster@usstamps.org
North America (excluding United States)

Bermuda Collectors Society
John Pare
405 Perimeter Road
Mount Horeb, WI 53572
(608) 852-7358
www.bermudacollectorssociety.com
pare16@mhtc.net

British Caribbean Philatelic Study Group
Bob Stewart
7 West Dune Lane
Long Beach Township, NJ 08008
(941) 379-4108
www.bcpsg.com
bcpsg@comcast.net

British North America Philatelic Society
Andy Ellwood
10 Doris Ave.
Gloucester, ON K1T 3W8
CANADA
www.bnaps.org
secretary@bnaps.org

British West Indies Study Circle
John Seidl
4324 Granby Way
Marietta, GA 30062
(404) 229-6863
www.bwisc.org
john.seidl@gmail.com

Haiti Philatelic Society
Ubaldo Del Toro
5709 Marble Archway
Alexandria, VA 22315
www.haitiphilately.org
u007ubi@aol.com

Hawaiian Philatelic Society
Gannon Sugimura
P.O. Box 10115
Honolulu, HI 96816-0115
www.stampshows.com/hps.html
hiphilsoc@gmail.com

Latin America

Brazil Philatelic Association
William V. Kriebel
1923 Manning St.
Philadelphia, PA 19103-5728
www.brazilphilatelic.org
info@brazilphilatelic.org

Canal Zone Study Group
Mike Drabik
P.O. Box 281
Bolton, MA 01740
www.canalzonestudygroup.com
czsgsecretary@gmail.com

Colombia-Panama Philatelic Study Group
Thomas P. Myers
P.O. Box 522
Gordonsville, VA 22942
www.copaphil.org
tpmphil@hotmail.com

Association Filatelic de Costa Rica
Giana Wayman (McCarty)
#SJO 4935
P.O. Box 025723
Miami, FL 33102-5723
011-506-2-228-1947
scotland@racsa.co.cr

International Cuban Philatelic Society (ICPS)
Ernesto Cuesta
P.O. Box 34434
Bethesda, MD 20827
(301) 564-3099
www.cubafil.org
ecuesta@philat.com

Falkland Islands Philatelic Study Groups
Morva White
42 Colton Road
Shrivenham
Swindon SN6 8AZ
UNITED KINGDOM
44(0) 1793 783245
www.fipsg.org.uk
morawhite@supanet.com

International Society of Guatemala Collectors
Jaime Marckwordt
449 St. Francis Blvd.
Daly City, CA 94015-2136
(415) 997-0295
www.guatemalastamps.com
president@guatemalastamps.com

Federacion Filatelica de la Republica de Honduras
Mauricio Mejia
Apartado Postal 1465
Tegucigalpa, D.C.
HONDURAS
504 3399-7227
www.facebook.com/filateliadehonduras
ffrh@hotmail.com

Asociacion Mexicana de Filatelia (AMEXFIL)
Alejandro Grossmann
Jose Maria Rico, 129
Col. Del Valle
3100 Mexico City, DF
MEXICO
www.amexfil.mx
amexfil@gmail.com

Mexico-Elmhurst Philatelic Society International
Eric Stovner
P.O. Box 10097
Santa Ana, CA 92711-0097
www.mepsi.org
treasurer@mepsi.org

Nicaragua Study Group
Erick Rodriguez
11817 S. W. 11th St.
Miami, FL 33184-2501
nsgsec@yahoo.com

Asociación Filatélica de Panamá
Edward D. Vianna B
ASOFILPA
0819-03400
El Dorado, Panama
PANAMA
http://asociacionfilatelicadepanama.
blogspot.com
asofilpa@gmail.com

Associated Collectors of El Salvador
Joseph D. Hahn
301 Rolling Ridge Drive, Apt. 111
State College, PA 16801-6149
www.elsalvadorphilately.org
joehahn100@hotmail.com

Africa

Bechuanalands and Botswana Society
Otto Peetoom
Roos
East Yorkshire HU12 0LD
UNITED KINGDOM
44(0)1964 670239
www.bechuanalandphilately.com
info@bechuanalandphilately.com

Egypt Study Circle
Mike Murphy
11 Waterbank Road
Bellingham
London SE6 34DJ
UNITED KINGDOM
(44) 0203 6737051
www.egyptstudycircle.org.uk
secretary@egyptstudycircle.org.uk

Ethiopian Philatelic Society
Ulf Lindahl
21 Westview Place
Riverside, CT 06878
(203) 722-0769
https://ethiopianphilatelicsociety.weebly.com
ulindahl@optonline.net

Liberian Philatelic Society
Travis Searls
P.O. Box 1570
Parker, CO 80134
www.liberiastamps.org
liberiastamps@comcast.net

Society for Moroccan and Tunisian Philately
S.P.L.M.
206, Bld Pereire
75017 PARIS
FRANCE
http://splm-philatelie.org
splm206@aol.com

Sudan Study Group
Andy Neal
Bank House, Coedway
Shrewsbury SY5 9AR
UNITED KINGDOM
www.sudanstamps.org
andywneal@gmail.com

Orange Free State Study Circle
J. R. Stroud, RDPSA
24 Hooper Close
Burnham-on-sea
Somerset TA8 1JQ
UNITED KINGDOM
44 1278 782235
www.orangefreestatephilately.org.uk
richard@richardstroud.plus.com

Rhodesian Study Circle
William R. Wallace
P.O. Box 16381
San Francisco, CA 94116
(415) 564 6060
www.rhodesianstudycircle.org.uk
bwall8rscr@earthlink.net

Philatelic Society for Greater Southern Africa
Alan Hanks
34 Seaton Drive
Aurora, ON L4G 2K1
CANADA
www.psgsa.org
alan.hanks@sympatico.ca

South Sudan Philatelic Society
William Barclay
1370 Spring Hill Road
South Londonderry, VT 05155
barclayphilatelics@gmail.com

Transvaal Study Circle
c/o 9 Meadow Road
Gravesend, Kent DA11 7LR
UNITED KINGDOM
www.transvaalstamps.org.uk
transvaalstudycircle@aol.co.uk

West Africa Study Circle
Martin Bratzel
1233 Virginia Ave.
Windsor, ON N8S 2Z1
CANADA
www.wasc.org.uk
marty_bratzel@yahoo.ca

Europe

Andorran Philatelic Study Circle
David Hope
17 Hawthorn Drive
Stalybridge
Cheshire SK15 1UE
UNITED KINGDOM
www.andorranpsc.org.uk
andorranpsc@btinternet.com

Austria Philatelic Society
Ralph Schneider
P.O. Box 978
Iowa Park, TX 76376
(940) 213-5004
www.austriaphilatelicsociety.com
rschneiderstamps@att.net

Channel Islands Specialists Society
Richard Flemming
Burbage, 64 Falconers Green
Hinckley
Leicestershire LE102SX
UNITED KINGDOM
www.ciss1950.org.uk
secretary@ciss1950.org.uk

Cyprus Study Circle
Rob Wheeler
47 Drayton Ave.
London W13 0LE
UNITED KINGDOM
www.cyprusstudycircle.org
robwheeler47@aol.com

Society for Czechoslovak Philately
Tom Cossaboom
P.O. Box 4124
Prescott, AZ 86302
(928) 771-9097
www.csphilately.org
klfck1@aol.com

Danish West Indies Study Unit of Scandinavian Collectors Club
Arnold Sorensen
7666 Edgedale Drive
Newburgh, IN 47630
(812) 480-6532
www.scc-online.org
valbydwi@hotmail.com

Eire Philatelic Association
John B. Sharkey
1559 Grouse Lane
Mountainside, NJ 07092-1340
www.eirephilatelicassoc.org
jsharkeyepa@me.com

Estonian Philatelic Society
Eo Vaher
39 Clafford Lane
Melville, NY 11747
www.eestipost.com

Faroe Islands Study Circle
Norman Hudson
40 Queen's Road
Vicar's Cross
Chester CH3 5HB
UNITED KINGDOM
www.faroeislandssc.org
jntropics@hotmail.com

France & Colonies Philatelic Society
Edward Grabowski
111 Prospect St., 4C
Westfield, NJ 07090
(908) 233-9318
www.franceandcolsps.org
edjjg@alum.mit.edu

Germany Philatelic Society
P.O. Box 6547
Chesterfield, MO 63006-6547
www.germanyphilatelicusa.org
info@germanyphilatelicsocietyusa.org

Gibraltar Study Circle
Susan Dare
22, Byways Park, Strode Road
Clevedon
North Somerset BS21 6UR
UNITED KINGDOM
www.gibraltarstudycircle.wordpress.com
smldare@yahoo.co.uk

Great Britian Collector's Club
Steve McGill
10309 Brookhollow Circle
Highlands Ranch, CO 80129
(303) 594-7029
www.gbphilately.org
steve.mcgill@comcast.net

Society for Hungarian Philately
Alan Bauer
P.O. Box 3024
Andover, MA 01810
(978) 682-0242
www.hungarianphilately.org
alan@hungarianstamps.com

Italy and Colonies Study Circle
Richard Harlow
7 Duncombe House
8 Manor Road
Teddington, Middlesex TW118BE
UNITED KINGDOM
44 208 977 8737
www.icsc-uk.com
richardharlow@outlook.com

Liechtenstudy USA
Paul Tremaine
410 SW Ninth St.
Dundee, OR 97115-9731
(503) 538-4500
www.liechtenstudy.org
tremaine@liechtenstudy.org

Lithuania Philatelic Society
Audrius Brazdeikis
9915 Murray Landing
Missouri City, TX 77459
(281) 450-6224
www.lithuanianphilately.com/lps
audrius@lithuanianphilately.com

Luxembourg Collectors Club
Gary B. Little
7319 Beau Road
Sechelt, BC V0N 3A8
CANADA
(604) 885-7241
http://lcc.luxcentral.com
gary@luxcentral.com

American Society for Netherlands Philately
Hans Kremer
50 Rockport Court
Danville, CA 94526
(925) 820-5841
www.asnp1975.com

Plebiscite-Memel-Saar Study Group of the German Philatelic Society
Clayton Wallace
100 Lark Court
Alamo, CA 94507
claytonwallace@comcast.net

Polonus Polish Philatelic Society
Daniel Lubelski
P.O. Box 2212
Benicia, CA 94510
(419) 410-9115
www.polonus.org
info@polonus.org

International Society for Portuguese Philately
Clyde Homen
1491 Bonnie View Road
Hollister, CA 95023-5117
www.portugalstamps.com
ispp1962@sbcglobal.net

Rossica Society of Russian Philately
Alexander Kolchinsky
1506 Country Lake Drive
Champaign, IL 61821-6428
www.rossica.org
alexander.kolchinsky@rossica.org

Scandinavian Collectors Club
Steve Lund
P.O. Box 16213
St. Paul, MN 55116
www.scc-online.org
steve88h@aol.com

Spanish Study Circle
Edith Knight
www.spaincircle.wixsite.com/
spainstudycircle
spaincircle@gmail.com

American Helvetia Philatelic Society
Richard T. Hall
P.O. Box 15053
Asheville, NC 28813-0053
www.swiss-stamps.org
secretary2@swiss-stamps.org

Ukrainian Philatelic & Numismatic Society
Martin B. Tatuch
5117 8th Road N.
Arlington, VA 22205-1201
www.upns.org
treasurer@upns.org
hkremer@usa.net

Vatican Philatelic Society
Joseph Scholten
1436 Johnston St. SE
Grand Rapids, MI 49507-2829
www.vaticanphilately.org
jscholten@vaticanphilately.org

Yugoslavia Study Group
Michael Chant
1514 N. Third Ave.
Wausau, WI 54401
0208-748-9919
www.yugosg.org
membership@yugosg.org

Middle East

Aden & Somaliland Study Group
Gary Brown
P.O. Box 106
Briar Hill, VIC 3088
AUSTRALIA
www.stampdomain.com/aden
garyjohn951@optushome.com.au

Iran Philatelic Study Circle
Nigel Gooch
Marchwood, 56, Wickham Ave.
Bexhill-on-Sea
East Sussex TN39 3ER
UNITED KINGDOM
www.iranphilately.org
nigelmgooch@gmail.com

Society of Israel Philatelists, Inc.
Jacqueline Baca
100 Match Factory Place
Bellefonte, PA 16823-1367
(814) 933-3803 ext. 212
www.israelstamps.com
israelstamps@gmail.com

Pakistan Philatelic Study Circle
Jeff Siddiqui
P.O. Box 7002
Lynnwood, WA 98046
jeffsiddiqui@msn.com

Ottoman and Near East Philatelic Society
Rolfe Smith
201 SE Verada Ave.
Port St. Lucie, FL 34983
(772) 240-8937
www.oneps.org
xbow2@mac.com

Asia

Burma (Myanmar) Philatelic Study Circle
Michael Whittaker
1, Ecton Leys, Hillside
Rugby
Warwickshire CV22 5SL
UNITED KINGDOM
https://burmamyanmarphilately.
wordpress.com/burma-myanmar-
philatelic-study-circle
manningham8@mypostoffice.co.uk

Ceylon Study Circle
Rodney W. P. Frost
42 Lonsdale Road
Cannington
Bridgwater, Somerset TA5 2JS
UNITED KINGDOM
01278 652592
www.ceylonsc.org
rodney.frost@tiscali.co.uk

China Stamp Society
H. James Maxwell
1050 W. Blue Ridge Blvd.
Kansas City, MO 64145-1216
www.chinastampsociety.org
president@chinastampsociety.org

Hong Kong Philatelic Society
John Tang
G.P.O. Box 446
HONG KONG
www.hkpsociety.com
hkpsociety@outlook.com

Hong Kong Study Circle
Robert Newton
www.hongkongstudycircle.com/index.html
newtons100@gmail.com

India Study Circle
John Warren
P.O. Box 7326
Washington, DC 20044
(202) 488-7443
https://indiastudycircle.org
jw-kbw@earthlink.net

Society of Indo-China Philatelists
Ron Bentley
2600 N. 24th St.
Arlington, VA 22207
(703) 524-1652
www.sicp-online.org
ron.bentley@verizon.net

International Society for Japanese Philately
William Eisenhauer
P.O. Box 230462
Tigard, OR 97281
(503) 496-2634
www.isjp.org
secretary@isjp.org

Korea Stamp Society
John E. Talmage, Jr.
P.O. Box 6889
Oak Ridge, TN 37831
(865) 482-5226
https://koreastampsociety.org
jtalmage@usit.net

Nepal & Tibet Philatelic Study Group
Colin T. Hepper
2238 Greiner St.
Eugene, OR 97405
www.fuchs-online.com/ntpsc
ntpsc@fuchs-online.com

International Philippine Philatelic Society
James R. Larot, Jr.
4990 Bayleaf Court
Martinez, CA 94553
(925) 260-5425
www.theipps.info
jlarot@ccwater.com

Australasia and Oceana

Australian States Study Circle of the Royal Sydney Philatelic Club
Ben Palmer
G.P.O. 1751
Sydney, NSW 2001
AUSTRALIA
http://club.philas.org.au/states

Society of Australasian Specialists / Oceania
David McNamee
P.O. Box 37
Alamo, CA 94507
www.sasoceania.org
treasurer@sosoceania.org

Malaya Study Group
David Tett
4 Amenbury Court
Harpenden Herts
Wheathampstead, Herts AL5 2BU
UNITED KINGDOM
www.m-s-g.org.uk
davidtett@aol.com

New Zealand Society of Great Britain
Michael Wilkinson
121 London Road
Sevenoaks
Kent TN13 1BH
UNITED KINGDOM
01732 456997
www.nzsgb.org.uk
mwilkin799@aol.com

Pacific Islands Study Circle
John Ray
24 Woodvale Ave.
London SE25 4AE
UNITED KINGDOM
www.pisc.org.uk
secretary@pisc.org.uk

Papuan Philatelic Society
Steven Zirinsky
P.O. Box 49, Ansonia Station
New York, NY 10023
(718) 706-0616
www.papuanphilatelicsociety.com
szirinsky@cs.com

Pitcairn Islands Study Group
Dr. Everett L. Parker
207 Corinth Road
Hudson, ME 04449-3057
(207) 573-1686
www.pisg.net
eparker@hughes.net

Ryukyu Philatelic Specialist Society
Laura Edmonds
P.O. Box 240177
Charlotte, NC 28224-0177
(336) 509-3739
www.ryukyustamps.org
secretary@ryukyustamps.org

Fellowship of Samoa Specialists
Trevor Shimell
18 Aspen Drive, Newton Abbot
Devon TQ12 4TN
UNITED KINGDOM
www.samoaexpress.org
trevor.shimell@gmail.com

Sarawak Specialists' Society
Stephen Schumann
2417 Caballo Drive
Hayward, CA 94545
(510) 785-4794
www.britborneostamps.org.uk
vpnam@s-s-s.org.uk

Western Australia Study Group
Brian Pope
P.O. Box 423
Claremont, WA 6910
AUSTRALIA
(61) 419 843 943
www.wastudygroup.com
wastudygroup@hotmail.com

Interregional Societies

American Society of Polar Philatelists
Alan Warren
P.O. Box 39
Exton, PA 19341-0039
(610) 321-0740
www.polarphilatelists.org
alanwar@att.net

First Issues Collector's Club
Kurt Streepy
3128 E. Mattatha Drive
Bloomington, IN 47401
www.firstissues.org
secretary@firstissues.org

France & Colonies Philatelic Society
Edward Grabowski
111 Prospect St., 4C
Westfield, NJ 07090
(908) 233-9318
www.franceandcolsps.org
edjjg@alum.mit.edu

Former French Colonies Specialist Society
Col.fra
BP 628
75367 PARIS Cedex 08
FRANCE
www.colfra.org
postmaster@colfra.org

International Society of Reply Coupon Collectors
Peter Robin
P.O. Box 353
Bala Cynwyd, PA 19004
peterrobin@verizon.net

Italy and Colonies Study Circle
Richard Harlow
7 Duncombe House
8 Manor Road
Teddington, Middlesex TW118BE
UNITED KINGDOM
44 208 977 8737
www.icsc-uk.com
richardharlow@outlook.com

Joint Stamp Issues Society
Richard Zimmermann
29A, Rue Des Eviats
67220 LALAYE
FRANCE
www.philarz.net
richard.zimmermann@club-internet.fr

The King George VI Collectors Society
Brian Livingstone
21 York Mansions
Prince of Wales Drive
London SW11 4DL
UNITED KINGDOM
www.kg6.info
livingstone484@btinternet.com

St. Helena, Ascension & Tristan Da Cunha Philatelic Society
Dr. Everett L. Parker
207 Corinth Road
Hudson, ME 04449-3057
(207) 573-1686
www.shatps.org
eparker@hughes.net

United Nations Philatelists
Blanton Clement, Jr.
P.O. Box 146
Morrisville, PA 19067-0146
www.unpi.com
bclemjunior@gmail.com

Stamp Dealer Associations

American Stamp Dealers Association, Inc.
P.O. Box 692
Leesport, PA 19553
(800) 369-8209
www.americanstampdealer.com
asda@americanstampdealer.com

National Stamp Dealers Association
Sheldon Ruckens, President
3643 Private Road 18
Pinckneyville, IL 62274-3426
(618) 357-5497
www.nsdainc.org
nsda@nsdainc.org

Expertizing Services

The following organizations will, for a fee, provide expert opinions about stamps submitted to them. Collectors should contact these organizations to find out about their fees and requirements before submitting philatelic material to them. The listing of these groups here is not intended as an endorsement by Amos Media Co.

General Expertizing Services

American Philatelic Expertizing Service (a service of the American Philatelic Society)
100 Match Factory Place
Bellefonte PA 16823-1367
(814) 933-3803 ext. 206
https://stamps.org/stamp-authentication
twhorn@stamps.org
Areas of Expertise: Worldwide

B. P. A. Expertising, Ltd.
P.O. Box 1141
Guildford
Surrey, GU5 0WR
UNITED KINGDOM
www.bpaexpertising.com
sec@bpaexpertising.org
Areas of Expertise: British Commonwealth, Great Britain, Classics of Europe, South America and the Far East

Philatelic Foundation
22 E. 35th St., 4th Floor
New York, NY 10016
(212) 221-6555
www.philatelicfoundation.org
philatelicfoundation@verizon.net
Areas of Expertise: U.S. & Worldwide

Philatelic Stamp Authentication and Grading, Inc.
P.O. Box 41-0880
Melbourne, FL 32941-0880
(305) 345-9864
www.psainc.com
info@psainc.com
Areas of Expertise: U.S., Canal Zone, Hawaii, Philippines, Canada & Provinces

Professional Stamp Experts
P.O. Box 539309
Henderson, NV 89053-9309
(702) 776-6522
www.gradingmatters.com
www.psestamp.com
info@gradingmatters.com
Areas of Expertise: Stamps and covers of U.S., U.S. Possessions, British Commonwealth

Royal Philatelic Society Expert Committee
41 Devonshire Place
London, W1N 1PE
UNITED KINGDOM
44 (0) 20 7935 7332
www.rpsl.limited/experts.aspx
experts@rpsl.limited
Areas of Expertise: Worldwide

Specialized Expertizing Services

China Stamp Society Expertizing Service
1050 W. Blue Ridge Blvd.
Kansas City, MO 64145
(816) 942-6300
www.chinastampsociety.org/expertization-and-identification-procedure
expertizing@chinastampsociety.org
Areas of Expertise: China

Confederate Stamp Alliance Authentication Service
John L. Kimbrough
P.O. Box 278
Capshaw, AL 35742-0396
(302) 422-2656
www.csalliance.org/CSAAS.shtml
authentication@csalliance.org
Areas of Expertise: Confederate stamps and postal history

Estonian Philatelic Society Expertizing Service
39 Clafford Lane
Melville NY 11747
(516) 421-2078
esto4@aol.com
Areas of Expertise: Estonia

Hawaiian Philatelic Society Expertizing Service
P.O. Box 10115
Honolulu HI 96816-0115
Areas of Expertise: Hawaii

International Association of Philatelic Experts
United States Associate members:

Paul Buchsbayew
119 W. 57th St.
New York, NY 10019
Ph: (212) 977-7734
paulb@cherrystoneauctions.com
Areas of Expertise: Russia, Soviet Union

William T. Crowe
P.O. Box 2090
Danbury CT 06813-2090
E-mail: wtcrowe@aol.com
Areas of Expertise: United States

Robert Odenweller
P.O. Box 401
Bernardsville NJ 07924-0401
(908) 766-5460
odenwelleraiep@verizon.net
Areas of Expertise: New Zealand, Samoa to 1900

Sergio Sismondo
The Regency Tower, Suite 1109
770 James Street
Syracuse NY 13203
Ph: (315) 422-2331
Fax: (315) 422-2956
Areas of Expertise: British East Africa, Camerouns, Cape of Good Hope, Canada, British North America

International Society for Japanese Philately Expertizing Committee
Florian Eichhorn
Adolfsallee 17
D-65185 Wiesbaden
GERMANY
www.isjp.org/expertizing
minatobay@t-online.de
Areas of Expertise: Japan and related areas, except WWII Japanese Occupation issues

International Society for Portuguese Philately Expertizing Service
P.O. Box 43146
Philadelphia PA 19129-3146
(215) 843-2106
www.portugalstamps.com/expert.html
s.s.washburne@worldnet.att.net
Areas of Expertise: Portugal and Colonies

Mexico-Elmhurst Philatelic Society International Expert Committee
Expert Committee Administrator
Marc E. Gonzales
P.O. Box 29040
Denver CO 80229-0040
www.mepsi.org/expertization
Areas of Expertise: Mexico

Ukrainian Philatelic & Numismatic Society Expertizing Service
Jerry G. Tkachuk
7266 Dibrova Drive
Brighton, MI 48116
www.upns.org/expertization
Areas of Expertise: Ukraine, Western Ukraine

V. G. Greene Philatelic Research Foundation
P.O. Box 69100, St. Clair Post Office
Toronto, ON, M4T 3A1
CANADA
(416) 921-2073
www.greenefoundation.ca
info@greenefoundation.ca
Areas of Expertise: British North America

Information on Catalogue Values, Grade and Condition

Catalogue Value

The Scott Catalogue value is a retail value; that is, an amount you could expect to pay for a stamp in the grade of Very Fine with no faults. Any exceptions to the grade valued will be noted in the text. The general introduction on the following pages and the individual section introductions further explain the type of material that is valued. The value listed for any given stamp is a reference that reflects recent actual dealer selling prices for that item.

Dealer retail price lists, public auction results, published prices in advertising and individual solicitation of retail prices from dealers, collectors and specialty organizations have been used in establishing the values found in this catalogue. Amos Media Co. values stamps, but Amos Media is not a company engaged in the business of buying and selling stamps as a dealer.

Use this catalogue as a guide for buying and selling. The actual price you pay for a stamp may be higher or lower than the catalogue value because of many different factors, including the amount of personal service a dealer offers, or increased or decreased interest in the country or topic represented by a stamp or set. An item may occasionally be offered at a lower price as a "loss leader," or as part of a special sale. You also may obtain an item inexpensively at public auction because of little interest at that time or as part of a large lot.

Stamps that are of a lesser grade than Very Fine, or those with condition problems, generally trade at lower prices than those given in this catalogue. Stamps of exceptional quality in both grade and condition often command higher prices than those listed.

Values for pre-1900 unused issues are for stamps with approximately half or more of their original gum. Stamps with most or all of their original gum may be expected to sell for more, and stamps with less than half of their original gum may be expected to sell for somewhat less than the values listed. On rarer stamps, it may be expected that the original gum will be somewhat more disturbed than it will be on more common issues. Post-1900 unused issues are assumed to have full original gum. From breakpoints in most countries' listings, stamps are valued as never hinged, due to the wide availability of stamps in that condition. These notations are prominently placed in the listings and in the country information preceding the listings. Some countries also feature listings with dual values for hinged and never-hinged stamps.

Grade

A stamp's grade and condition are crucial to its value. The accompanying illustrations show examples of Very Fine stamps from different time periods, along with examples of stamps in Fine to Very Fine and Extremely Fine grades as points of reference. When a stamp seller offers a stamp in any grade from fine to superb without further qualifying statements, that stamp should not only have the centering grade as defined, but it also should be free of faults or other condition problems.

FINE stamps (illustrations not shown) have designs that are quite off center, with the perforations on one or two sides very close to the design but not quite touching it. There is white space between the perforations and the design that is minimal but evident to the unaided eye. Imperforate stamps may have small margins, and earlier issues may show the design just touching one edge of the stamp design. Very early perforated issues normally will have the perforations slightly cutting into the design. Used stamps may have heavier than usual cancellations.

FINE-VERY FINE stamps will be somewhat off center on one side, or slightly off center on two sides. Imperforate stamps will have two margins of at least normal size, and the design will not touch any edge. For perforated stamps, the perfs are well clear of the design, but are still noticeably off center. *However, early issues of a country may be printed in such a way that the design naturally is very close to the edges. In these cases, the perforations may cut into the design very slightly.* Used stamps will not have a cancellation that detracts from the design.

VERY FINE stamps will be just slightly off center on one or two sides, but the design will be well clear of the edge. The stamp will present a nice, balanced appearance. Imperforate stamps will be well centered within normal-sized margins. *However, early issues of many countries may be printed in such a way that the perforations may touch the design on one or more sides. Where this is the case, a boxed note will be found defining the centering and margins of the stamps being valued.* Used stamps will have light or otherwise neat cancellations. This is the grade used to establish Scott Catalogue values.

EXTREMELY FINE stamps are close to being perfectly centered. Imperforate stamps will have even margins that are slightly larger than normal. Even the earliest perforated issues will have perforations clear of the design on all sides.

Amos Media Co. recognizes that there is no formally enforced grading scheme for postage stamps, and that the final price you pay or obtain for a stamp will be determined by individual agreement at the time of transaction.

Condition

Grade addresses only centering and (for used stamps) cancellation. *Condition* refers to factors other than grade that affect a stamp's desirability.

Factors that can increase the value of a stamp include exceptionally wide margins, particularly fresh color, the presence of selvage, and plate or die varieties. Unusual cancels on used stamps (particularly those of the 19th century) can greatly enhance their value as well.

Factors other than faults that decrease the value of a stamp include loss of original gum, regumming, a hinge remnant or foreign object adhering to the gum, natural inclusions, straight edges, and markings or notations applied by collectors or dealers.

Faults include missing pieces, tears, pin or other holes, surface scuffs, thin spots, creases, toning, short or pulled perforations, clipped perforations, oxidation or other forms of color changelings, soiling, stains, and such man-made changes as reperforations or the chemical removal or lightening of a cancellation.

Grading Illustrations

On the following two pages are illustrations of various stamps from countries appearing in this volume. These stamps are arranged by country, and they represent early or important issues that are often found in widely different grades in the marketplace. The editors believe the illustrations will prove useful in showing the margin size and centering that will be seen on the various issues.

In addition to the matters of margin size and centering, collectors are reminded that the very fine stamps valued in the Scott catalogues also will possess fresh color and intact perforations, and they will be free from defects.

Examples shown are computer-manipulated images made from single digitized master illustrations.

Stamp Illustrations Used in the Catalogue

It is important to note that the stamp images used for identification purposes in this catalogue may not be indicative of the grade of stamp being valued. Refer to the written discussion of grades on this page and to the grading illustrations on the following two pages for grading information.

Fine-Very Fine

SCOTT
CATALOGUES
VALUE
STAMPS IN
THIS GRADE

Very Fine

Extremely Fine

Fine-Very Fine

SCOTT
CATALOGUES
VALUE
STAMPS IN
THIS GRADE

Very Fine

Extremely Fine

Fine-Very Fine →

SCOTT
CATALOGUES
VALUE
STAMPS IN
THIS GRADE

Very Fine →

Extremely Fine →

Fine-Very Fine →

SCOTT
CATALOGUES
VALUE
STAMPS IN
THIS GRADE

Very Fine →

Extremely Fine →

For purposes of helping to determine the gum condition and value of an unused stamp, Scott presents the following chart which details different gum conditions and indicates how the conditions correlate with the Scott values for unused stamps. Used together, the Illustrated Grading Chart on the previous pages and this Illustrated Gum Chart should allow catalogue users to better understand the grade and gum condition of stamps valued in the Scott catalogues.

Gum Categories:	MINT N.H.	ORIGINAL GUM (O.G.)				NO GUM
	Mint Never Hinged *Free from any disturbance*	**Lightly Hinged** *Faint impression of a removed hinge over a small area*	**Hinge Mark or Remnant** *Prominent hinged spot with part or all of the hinge remaining*	**Large part o.g.** *Approximately half or more of the gum intact*	**Small part o.g.** *Approximately less than half of the gum intact*	**No gum** *Only if issued with gum*
Commonly Used Symbol:	★★	★	★	★	★	(★)
Pre-1900 Issues (Pre-1881 for U.S.)	*Very fine pre-1900 stamps in these categories trade at a premium over Scott value*			Scott Value for "Unused"		Scott "No Gum" listings for selected unused classic stamps
From 1900 to breakpoints for listings of never-hinged stamps	Scott "Never Hinged" listings for selected unused stamps	Scott Value for "Unused" (Actual value will be affected by the degree of hinging of the full o.g.)				
From breakpoints noted for many countries	Scott Value for "Unused"					

Never Hinged (NH; ★★): A never-hinged stamp will have full original gum that will have no hinge mark or disturbance. The presence of an expertizer's mark does not disqualify a stamp from this designation.

Original Gum (OG; ★): Pre-1900 stamps should have approximately half or more of their original gum. On rarer stamps, it may be expected that the original gum will be somewhat more disturbed than it will be on more common issues. Post-1900 stamps should have full original gum. Original gum will show some disturbance caused by a previous hinge(s) which may be present or entirely removed. The actual value of a post-1900 stamp will be affected by the degree of hinging of the full original gum.

Disturbed Original Gum: Gum showing noticeable effects of humidity, climate or hinging over more than half of the gum. The significance of gum disturbance in valuing a stamp in any of the Original Gum categories depends on the degree of disturbance, the rarity and normal gum condition of the issue and other variables affecting quality.

Regummed (RG; (★)): A regummed stamp is a stamp without gum that has had some type of gum privately applied at a time after it was issued. This normally is done to deceive collectors and/or dealers into thinking that the stamp has original gum and therefore has a higher value. A regummed stamp is considered the same as a stamp with none of its original gum for purposes of grading.

Understanding the Listings

On the opposite page is an enlarged "typical" listing from this catalogue. Below are detailed explanations of each of the highlighted parts of the listing.

1 Scott number — Scott catalogue numbers are used to identify specific items when buying, selling or trading stamps. Each listed postage stamp from every country has a unique Scott catalogue number. Therefore, Germany Scott 99, for example, can only refer to a single stamp. Although the Scott catalogue usually lists stamps in chronological order by date of issue, there are exceptions. When a country has issued a set of stamps over a period of time, those stamps within the set are kept together without regard to date of issue. This follows the normal collecting approach of keeping stamps in their natural sets.

When a country issues a set of stamps over a period of time, a group of consecutive catalogue numbers is reserved for the stamps in that set, as issued. If that group of numbers proves to be too few, capital-letter suffixes, such as "A" or "B," may be added to existing numbers to create enough catalogue numbers to cover all items in the set. A capital-letter suffix indicates a major Scott catalogue number listing. Scott generally uses a suffix letter only once. Therefore, a catalogue number listing with a capital-letter suffix will seldom be found with the same letter (lower case) used as a minor-letter listing. If there is a Scott 16A in a set, for example, there will seldom be a Scott 16a. However, a minor-letter "a" listing may be added to a major number containing an "A" suffix (Scott 16Aa, for example).

Suffix letters are cumulative. A minor "b" variety of Scott 16A would be Scott 16Ab, not Scott 16b.

There are times when a reserved block of Scott catalogue numbers is too large for a set, leaving some numbers unused. Such gaps in the numbering sequence also occur when the catalogue editors move an item's listing elsewhere or have removed it entirely from the catalogue. Scott does not attempt to account for every possible number, but rather attempts to assure that each stamp is assigned its own number.

Scott numbers designating regular postage normally are only numerals. Scott numbers for other types of stamps, such as air post, semi-postal, postal tax, postage due, occupation and others have a prefix consisting of one or more capital letters or a combination of numerals and capital letters.

2 Illustration number — Illustration or design-type numbers are used to identify each catalogue illustration. For most sets, the lowest face-value stamp is shown. It then serves as an example of the basic design approach for other stamps not illustrated. Where more than one stamp use the same illustration number, but have differences in design, the design paragraph or the description line clearly indicates the design on each stamp not illustrated. Where there are both vertical and horizontal designs in a set, a single illustration may be used, with the exceptions noted in the design paragraph or description line.

When an illustration is followed by a lower-case letter in parentheses, such as "A2(b)," the trailing letter indicates which overprint or surcharge illustration applies.

Illustrations normally are 70 percent of the original size of the stamp. Oversized stamps, blocks and souvenir sheets are reduced even more. Overprints and surcharges are shown at 100 percent of their original size if shown alone, but are 70 percent of original size if shown on stamps. In some cases, the illustration will be placed above the set, between listings or omitted completely. Overprint and surcharge illustrations are not placed in this catalogue for purposes of expertizing stamps.

3 Paper color — The color of a stamp's paper is noted in italic type when the paper used is not white.

4 Listing styles — There are two principal types of catalogue listings: major and minor.

Major listings are in a larger type style than minor listings. The catalogue number is a numeral that can be found with or without a capital-letter suffix, and with or without a prefix.

Minor listings are in a smaller type style and have a small-letter suffix or (if the listing immediately follows that of the major number) may show only the letter. These listings identify a variety of the major item. Examples include perforation and shade differences, multiples (some souvenir sheets, booklet panes and se-tenant combinations), and singles of multiples.

Examples of major number listings include 16, 28A, B97, C13A, 10N5, and 10N6A. Examples of minor numbers are 16a and C13Ab.

5 Basic information about a stamp or set — Introducing each stamp issue is a small section (usually a line listing) of basic information about a stamp or set. This section normally includes the date of issue, method of printing, perforation, watermark and, sometimes, some additional information of note. *Printing method, perforation and watermark apply to the following sets until a change is noted.* Stamps created by overprinting or surcharging previous issues are assumed to have the same perforation, watermark, printing method and other production characteristics as the original. Dates of issue are as precise as Scott is able to confirm and often reflect the dates on first-day covers, rather than the actual date of release.

6 Denomination — This normally refers to the face value of the stamp; that is, the cost of the unused stamp at the post office at the time of issue. When a denomination is shown in parentheses, it does not appear on the stamp. This includes the non-denominated stamps of the United States, Brazil and Great Britain, for example.

7 Color or other description — This area provides information to solidify identification of a stamp. In many recent cases, a description of the stamp design appears in this space, rather than a listing of colors.

8 Year of issue — In stamp sets that have been released in a period that spans more than a year, the number shown in parentheses is the year that stamp first appeared. Stamps without a date appeared during the first year of the issue. Dates are not always given for minor varieties.

9 Value unused and Value used — The Scott catalogue values are based on stamps that are in a grade of Very Fine unless stated otherwise. Unused values refer to items that have not seen postal, revenue or any other duty for which they were intended. Pre-1900 unused stamps that were issued with gum must have at least most of their original gum. Later issues are assumed to have full original gum. From breakpoints specified in most countries' listings, stamps are valued as never hinged. Stamps issued without gum are noted. Modern issues with PVA or other synthetic adhesives may appear ungummed. Unused self-adhesive stamps are valued as appearing undisturbed on their original backing paper. Values for used self-adhesive stamps are for examples either on piece or off piece. For a more detailed explanation of these values, please see the "Catalogue Value," "Condition" and "Understanding Valuing Notations" sections elsewhere in this introduction.

In some cases, where used stamps are more valuable than unused stamps, the value is for an example with a contemporaneous cancel, rather than a modern cancel or a smudge or other unclear marking. For those stamps that were released for postal and fiscal purposes, the used value represents a postally used stamp. Stamps with revenue cancels generally sell for less.

Stamps separated from a complete se-tenant multiple usually will be worth less than a pro-rated portion of the se-tenant multiple, and stamps lacking the attached labels that are noted in the listings will be worth less than the values shown.

10 Changes in basic set information — Bold type is used to show any changes in the basic data given for a set of stamps. These basic data categories include perforation gauge measurement, paper type, printing method and watermark.

11 Total value of a set — The total value of sets of three or more stamps issued after 1900 are shown. The set line also notes the range of Scott numbers and total number of stamps included in the grouping. The actual value of a set consisting predominantly of stamps having the minimum value of 25 cents may be less than the total value shown. Similarly, the actual value or catalogue value of se-tenant pairs or of blocks consisting of stamps having the minimum value of 25 cents may be less than the catalogue values of the component parts.

SCOTT NUMBER ➊

ILLUS. NUMBER ➋

PAPER COLOR ➌

LISTING STYLES ➍
MAJORS
MINORS

King George VI
A7

5 BASIC INFORMATION ON STAMP OR SET

6 DENOMINATION

7 COLOR OR OTHER DESCRIPTION

8 YEAR OF ISSUE

9 CATALOGUE VALUES
UNUSED
USED

10 CHANGES IN BASIC SET INFORMATION

11 TOTAL VALUE OF SET

1938-44			**Engr.**	**Perf. 12½**	
54	A6	½p	green	.25	2.00
54A	A6	½p	dk brown ('42)	.25	2.25
55	A6	1p	dark brown	2.50	.35
55A	A6	1p	green ('42)	.25	1.75
56	A6	1½p	dark carmine	5.00	6.00
56A	A6	1½p	gray ('42)	.25	5.75
57	A6	2p	gray	5.00	1.25
57A	A6	2p	dark car ('42)	.25	2.00
58	A6	3p	blue	.60	1.00
59	A6	4p	rose lilac	1.75	2.00
60	A6	6p	dark violet	2.00	2.00
61	A6	9p	olive bister	2.00	5.25
62	A6	1sh	orange & blk	2.10	3.25

Typo.
Perf. 14
Chalky Paper

63	A7	2sh	ultra & dl vio, *bl*	7.00	17.50
64	A7	2sh6p	red & blk, *bl*	9.00	24.00
65	A7	5sh	red & grn, *yel*	35.00	30.00
a.		5sh dk red & dp grn, *yel* ('44)		55.00	140.00
66	A7	10sh	red & grn, *grn*	35.00	70.00

Wmk. 3

67	A7	£1	blk & vio, *red*	30.00	52.50
		Nos. 54-67 (18)		138.20	228.85
		Set, never hinged		220.00	

Catalogue Listing Policy

It is the intent of Amos Media Co. to list all postage stamps of the world in the *Scott Standard Postage Stamp Catalogue*. The only strict criteria for listing is that stamps be decreed legal for postage by the issuing country and that the issuing country actually have an operating postal system. Whether the primary intent of issuing a given stamp or set was for sale to postal patrons or to stamp collectors is not part of our listing criteria. Scott's role is to provide basic comprehensive postage stamp information. It is up to each stamp collector to choose which items to include in a collection.

It is Scott's objective to seek reasons why a stamp should be listed, rather than why it should not. Nevertheless, there are certain types of items that will not be listed. These include the following:

1. Unissued items that are not officially distributed or released by the issuing postal authority. If such items are officially issued at a later date by the country, they will be listed. Unissued items consist of those that have been printed and then held from sale for reasons such as change in government, errors found on stamps or something deemed objectionable about a stamp subject or design.

2. Stamps "issued" by non-existent postal entities or fantasy countries, such as Nagaland, Occusi-Ambeno, Staffa, Sedang, Torres Straits and others. Also, stamps "issued" in the names of legitimate, stamp-issuing countries that are not authorized by those countries.

3. Semi-official or unofficial items not required for postage. Examples include items issued by private agencies for their own express services. When such items are required for delivery, or are valid as prepayment of postage, they are listed.

4. Local stamps issued for local use only. Postage stamps issued by governments specifically for "domestic" use, such as Haiti Scott 219-228, or the United States non-denominated stamps, are not considered to be locals, since they are valid for postage throughout the country of origin.

5. Items not valid for postal use. For example, a few countries have issued souvenir sheets that are not valid for postage. This area also includes a number of worldwide charity labels (some denominated) that do not pay postage.

6. Egregiously exploitative issues such as stamps sold for far more than face value, stamps purposefully issued in artificially small quantities or only against advance orders, stamps awarded only to a selected audience such as a philatelic bureau's standing order customers, or stamps sold only in conjunction with other products. All of these kinds of items are usually controlled issues and/or are intended for speculation. These items normally will be included in a footnote.

7. Items distributed by the issuing government only to a limited group, club, philatelic exhibition or a single stamp dealer or other private company. These items normally will be included in a footnote.

8. Stamps not available to collectors. These generally are rare items, all of which are held by public institutions such as museums. The existence of such items often will be cited in footnotes.

The fact that a stamp has been used successfully as postage, even on international mail, is not in itself sufficient proof that it was legitimately issued. Numerous examples of so-called stamps from non-existent countries are known to have been used to post letters that have successfully passed through the international mail system.

There are certain items that are subject to interpretation. When a stamp falls outside our specifications, it may be listed along with a cautionary footnote.

A number of factors are considered in our approach to analyzing how a stamp is listed. The following list of factors is presented to share with you, the catalogue user, the complexity of the listing process.

Additional printings — "Additional printings" of a previously issued stamp may range from an item that is totally different to cases where it is impossible to differentiate from the original. At least a minor number (a small-letter suffix) is assigned if there is a distinct change in stamp shade, noticeably redrawn design, or a significantly different perforation measurement. A major number (numeral or numeral and capital-letter combination) is assigned if the editors feel the "additional printing" is sufficiently different from the original that it constitutes a different issue.

Commemoratives — Where practical, commemoratives with the same theme are placed in a set. For example, the U.S. Civil War Centennial set of 1961-65 and the Constitution Bicentennial series of 1989-90 appear as sets. Countries such as Japan and Korea issue such material on a regular basis, with an announced, or at least predictable, number of stamps known in advance. Occasionally, however, stamp sets that were released over a period of years have been separated. Appropriately placed footnotes will guide you to each set's continuation.

Definitive sets — Blocks of numbers generally have been reserved for definitive sets, based on previous experience with any given country. If a few more stamps are issued in a set than originally expected, they often have been inserted into the original set with a capital-letter suffix, such as U.S. Scott 1059A. If it appears that many more stamps than the originally allotted block will be released before the set is completed, a new block of numbers will be reserved, with the original one being closed off. In some cases, such as the U.S. Transportation and Great Americans series, several blocks of numbers exist. Appropriately placed footnotes will guide you to each set's continuation.

New country — Membership in the Universal Postal Union is not a consideration for listing status or order of placement within the catalogue. The index will tell you in what volume or page number the listings begin.

"No release date" items — The amount of information available for any given stamp issue varies greatly from country to country and even from time to time. Extremely comprehensive information about new stamps is available from some countries well before the stamps are released. By contrast some countries do not provide information about stamps or release dates. Most countries, however, fall between these extremes. A country may provide denominations or subjects of stamps from upcoming issues that are not issued as planned. Sometimes, philatelic agencies, those private firms hired to represent countries, add these later-issued items to sets well after the formal release date. This time period can range from weeks to years. If these items were officially released by the country, they will be added to the appropriate spot in the set. In many cases, the specific release date of a stamp or set of stamps may never be known.

Overprints — The color of an overprint is always noted if it is other than black. Where more than one color of ink has been used on overprints of a single set, the color used is noted. Early overprint and surcharge illustrations were altered to prevent their use by forgers.

Personalized Stamps — Since 1999, the special service of personalizing stamp vignettes, or labels attached to stamps, has been offered to customers by postal administrations of many countries. Sheets of these stamps are sold, singly or in quantity, only through special orders made by mail, in person, or through a sale on a computer website with the postal administrations or their agents for which an extra fee is charged, though some countries offer to collectors at face value personalized stamps having generic images in the vignettes or on the attached labels. It is impossible for any catalogue to know what images have been chosen by customers. Images can be 1) owned or created by the customer, 2) a generic image, or 3) an image pulled from a library of stock images on the stamp creation website. It is also impossible to know the quantity printed for any stamp having a particular image. So from a valuing standpoint, any image is equivalent to any other image for any personalized stamp having the same catalogue number. Illustrations of personalized stamps in the catalogue are not always those of stamps having generic images.

Personalized items are listed with some exceptions. These include:

1. Stamps or sheets that have attached labels that the customer cannot personalize, but which are nonetheless marketed as "personalized," and are sold for far more than the franking value.

2. Stamps or sheets that can be personalized by the customer, but where a portion of the print run must be ceded to the issuing country for sale to other customers.

3. Stamps or sheets that are created exclusively for a particular commercial client, or clients, including stamps that differ from any similar stamp that has been made available to the public.

4. Stamps or sheets that are deliberately conceived by the issuing authority that have been, or are likely to be, created with an excessive number of different face values, sizes, or other features that are changeable.

5. Stamps or sheets that are created by postal administrations using the same system of stamp personalization that has been put in place for use by the public that are printed in limited quantities and sold above face value.

6. Stamps or sheets that are created by licensees not directly affiliated or controlled by a postal administration.

Excluded items may or may not be footnoted.

Se-tenants — Connected stamps of differing features (se-tenants) will be listed in the format most commonly collected. This includes pairs, blocks or larger multiples. Se-tenant units are not always symmetrical. An example is Australia Scott 508, which is a block of seven stamps. If the stamps are primarily collected as a unit, the major number may be assigned to the multiple, with minors going to each component stamp. In cases where continuous-design or other unit se-tenants will receive significant postal use, each stamp is given a major Scott number listing. This includes issues from the United States, Canada, Germany and Great Britain, for example.

Special Notices

Classification of stamps

The *Scott Standard Postage Stamp Catalogue* lists stamps by country of issue. The next level of organization is a listing by section on the basis of the function of the stamps. The principal sections cover regular postage, semi-postal, air post, special delivery, registration, postage due and other categories. Except for regular postage, catalogue numbers for all sections include a prefix letter (or number-letter combination) denoting the class to which a given stamp belongs. When some countries issue sets containing stamps from more than one category, the catalogue will at times list all of the stamps in one category (such as air post stamps listed as part of a postage set).

The following is a listing of the most commonly used catalogue prefixes.

Prefix .... Category

C	Air Post
M	Military
P	Newspaper
N	Occupation - Regular Issues
O	Official
Q	Parcel Post
J	Postage Due
RA	Postal Tax
B	Semi-Postal
E	Special Delivery
MR	War Tax

Other prefixes used by more than one country include the following:

H	Acknowledgment of Receipt
I	Late Fee
CO	Air Post Official
CQ	Air Post Parcel Post
RAC	Air Post Postal Tax
CF	Air Post Registration
CB	Air Post Semi-Postal
CBO	Air Post Semi-Postal Official
CE	Air Post Special Delivery
EY	Authorized Delivery
S	Franchise
G	Insured Letter
GY	Marine Insurance
MC	Military Air Post
MQ	Military Parcel Post
NC	Occupation - Air Post
NO	Occupation - Official
NJ	Occupation - Postage Due
NRA	Occupation - Postal Tax
NB	Occupation - Semi-Postal
NE	Occupation - Special Delivery
QY	Parcel Post Authorized Delivery
AR	Postal-fiscal
RAJ	Postal Tax Due
RAB	Postal Tax Semi-Postal
F	Registration
EB	Semi-Postal Special Delivery
EO	Special Delivery Official
QE	Special Handling

New issue listings

Updates to this catalogue appear each month in the *Linn's Stamp News* monthly magazine. Included in this update are additions to the listings of countries found in the *Scott Standard Postage Stamp Catalogue* and the *Specialized Catalogue of United States Stamps and Covers*, as well as corrections and updates to current editions of this catalogue.

From time to time there will be changes in the final listings of stamps from the *Linn's Stamp News* magazine to the next edition of the catalogue. This occurs as more information about certain stamps or sets becomes available.

The catalogue update section of the *Linn's Stamp News* magazine is the most timely presentation of this material available. Annual subscriptions to *Linn's Stamp News* are available from Linn's Stamp News, Box 926, Sidney, OH 45365-0926.

Number additions, deletions & changes

A listing of catalogue number additions, deletions and changes from the previous edition of the catalogue appears in each volume. See Catalogue Number Additions, Deletions & Changes in the table of contents for the location of this list.

Understanding valuing notations

The *minimum catalogue value* of an individual stamp or set is 25 cents. This represents a portion of the cost incurred by a dealer when he prepares an individual stamp for resale. As a point of philatelic-economic fact, the lower the value shown for an item in this catalogue, the greater the percentage of that value is attributed to dealer mark up and profit margin. In many cases, such as the 25-cent minimum value, that price does not cover the labor or other costs involved with stocking it as an individual stamp. The sum of minimum values in a set does not properly represent the value of a complete set primarily composed of a number of minimum-value stamps, nor does the sum represent the actual value of a packet made up of minimum-value stamps. Thus a packet of 1,000 different common stamps — each of which has a catalogue value of 25 cents — normally sells for considerably less than 250 dollars!

The *absence of a retail value* for a stamp does not necessarily suggest that a stamp is scarce or rare. A dash in the value column means that the stamp is known in a stated form or variety, but information is either lacking or insufficient for purposes of establishing a usable catalogue value.

Stamp values in *italics* generally refer to items that are difficult to value accurately. For expensive items, such as those priced at $1,000 or higher, a value in italics indicates that the affected item trades very seldom. For inexpensive items, a value in italics represents a warning. One example is a "blocked" issue where the issuing postal administration may have controlled one stamp in a set in an attempt to make the whole set more valuable. Another example is an item that sold at an extreme multiple of face value in the marketplace at the time of its issue.

One type of warning to collectors that appears in the catalogue is illustrated by a stamp that is valued considerably higher in used condition than it is as unused. In this case, collectors are cautioned to be certain the used version has a genuine and contemporaneous cancellation. The type of cancellation on a stamp can be an important factor in determining its sale price. Catalogue values do not apply to fiscal, telegraph or non-contemporaneous postal cancels, unless otherwise noted.

Some countries have released back issues of stamps in canceled-to-order form, sometimes covering as much as a 10-year period. The Scott Catalogue values for used stamps reflect canceled-to-order material when such stamps are found to predominate in the marketplace for the issue involved. Notes frequently appear in the stamp listings to specify which items are valued as canceled-to-order, or if there is a premium for postally used examples.

Many countries sell canceled-to-order stamps at a marked reduction of face value. Countries that sell or have sold canceled-to-order stamps at *full* face value include United Nations, Australia, Netherlands, France and Switzerland. It may be almost impossible to identify such stamps if the gum has been removed, because official government canceling devices are used. Postally used examples of these items on cover, however, are usually worth more than the canceled-to-order stamps with original gum.

Abbreviations

Scott uses a consistent set of abbreviations throughout this catalogue to conserve space, while still providing necessary information.

COLOR ABBREVIATIONS

amb. amber	crim. crimson	ol ..... olive
anil.. aniline	cr ..... cream	olvn . olivine
ap.... apple	dk .... dark	org... orange
aqua aquamarine	dl ..... dull	pck .. peacock
az .... azure	dp.... deep	pnksh pinkish
bis ... bister	db.... drab	Prus. Prussian
bl ..... blue	emer emerald	pur... purple
bld... blood	gldn. golden	redsh reddish
blk... black	gryshgrayish	res ... reseda
bril... brilliant	grn... green	ros ... rosine
brn... brown	grnsh greenish	ryl .... royal
brnsh brownish	hel ... heliotrope	sal ... salmon
brnz. bronze	hn .... henna	saph sapphire
brt.... bright	ind... indigo	scar . scarlet
brnt . burnt	int .... intense	sep .. sepia
car... carmine	lav ... lavender	sien . sienna
cer ... cerise	lem.. lemon	sil..... silver
chlky chalky	lil ..... lilac	sl...... slate
chamchamois	lt ...... light	stl .... steel
chnt . chestnut	mag. magenta	turq.. turquoise
choc chocolate	man. manila	ultra ultramarine
chr ... chrome	mar.. maroon	Ven.. Venetian
cit .... citron	mv ... mauve	ver ... vermilion
cl...... claret	multi multicolored	vio ... violet
cob.. cobalt	mlky milky	yel ... yellow
cop .. copper	myr.. myrtle	yelsh yellowish

When no color is given for an overprint or surcharge, black is the color used. Abbreviations for colors used for overprints and surcharges include: "(B)" or "(Blk)," black; "(Bl)," blue; "(R)," red; and "(G)," green.

Additional abbreviations in this catalogue are shown below:

Adm.	Administration
AFL.................	American Federation of Labor
Anniv.............	Anniversary
APS	American Philatelic Society
Assoc.	Association
ASSR.	Autonomous Soviet Socialist Republic
b.	Born
BEP...............	Bureau of Engraving and Printing
Bicent............	Bicentennial
Bklt.	Booklet
Brit................	British
btwn.	Between
Bur................	Bureau
c. or ca..........	Circa
Cat.	Catalogue
Cent.	Centennial, century, centenary
CIO	Congress of Industrial Organizations
Conf.	Conference
Cong.............	Congress
Cpl.	Corporal
CTO	Canceled to order
d.	Died
Dbl.	Double
EDU..............	Earliest documented use
Engr.	Engraved
Exhib.............	Exhibition
Expo.............	Exposition
Fed.	Federation
GB	Great Britain
Gen.	General
GPO..............	General post office
Horiz.	Horizontal
Imperf.	Imperforate
Impt...............	Imprint

Intl.	International
Invtd..............	Inverted
L	Left
Lieut., lt..........	Lieutenant
Litho.	Lithographed
LL	Lower left
LR	Lower right
mm.................	Millimeter
Ms.	Manuscript
Natl................	National
No..................	Number
NY	New York
NYC	New York City
Ovpt.	Overprint
Ovptd.............	Overprinted
P	Plate number
Perf................	Perforated, perforation
Phil................	Philatelic
Photo.............	Photogravure
PO	Post office
Pr.	Pair
P.R..................	Puerto Rico
Prec...............	Precancel, precanceled
Pres...............	President
PTT	Post, Telephone and Telegraph
R	Right
Rio.................	Rio de Janeiro
Sgt.................	Sergeant
Soc................	Society
Souv...............	Souvenir
SSR...............	Soviet Socialist Republic, see ASSR
St...................	Saint, street
Surch.	Surcharge
Typo.	Typographed
UL..................	Upper left
Unwmkd.	Unwatermarked
UPU	Universal Postal Union
UR	Upper Right
US	United States
USPOD	United States Post Office Department
USSR	Union of Soviet Socialist Republics
Vert................	Vertical
VP..................	Vice president
Wmk...............	Watermark
Wmkd.	Watermarked
WWI	World War I
WWII.............	World War II

Examination

Amos Media Co. will not comment upon the genuineness, grade or condition of stamps, because of the time and responsibility involved. Rather, there are several expertizing groups that undertake this work for both collectors and dealers. Neither will Amos Media Co. appraise or identify philatelic material. The company cannot take responsibility for unsolicited stamps or covers sent by individuals.

All letters, E-mails, etc. are read attentively, but they are not always answered due to time considerations.

How to order from your dealer

When ordering stamps from a dealer, it is not necessary to write the full description of a stamp as listed in this catalogue. All you need is the name of the country, the Scott catalogue number and whether the desired item is unused or used. For example, "Japan Scott 422 unused" is sufficient to identify the unused stamp of Japan listed as "422 A206 5y brown."

Basic Stamp Information

A stamp collector's knowledge of the combined elements that make a given stamp issue unique determines his or her ability to identify stamps. These elements include paper, watermark, method of separation, printing, design and gum. On the following pages each of these important areas is briefly described.

Paper

Paper is an organic material composed of a compacted weave of cellulose fibers and generally formed into sheets. Paper used to print stamps may be manufactured in sheets, or it may have been part of a large roll (called a web) before being cut to size. The fibers most often used to create paper on which stamps are printed include bark, wood, straw and certain grasses. In many cases, linen or cotton rags have been added for greater strength and durability. Grinding, bleaching, cooking and rinsing these raw fibers reduces them to a slushy pulp, referred to by paper makers as "stuff." Sizing and, sometimes, coloring matter is added to the pulp to make different types of finished paper.

After the stuff is prepared, it is poured onto sieve-like frames that allow the water to run off, while retaining the matted pulp. As fibers fall onto the screen and are held by gravity, they form a natural weave that will later hold the paper together. If the screen has metal bits that are formed into letters or images attached, it leaves slightly thinned areas on the paper. These are called watermarks.

When the stuff is almost dry, it is passed under pressure through smooth or engraved rollers - dandy rolls - or placed between cloth in a press to be flattened and dried.

Wove   Laid   Granite

Quadrille   Oblong Quadrille   Laid Batonne

Stamp paper falls broadly into two types: wove and laid. The nature of the surface of the frame onto which the pulp is first deposited causes the differences in appearance between the two. If the surface is smooth and even, the paper will be of fairly uniform texture throughout. This is known as *wove paper*. Early papermaking machines poured the pulp onto a continuously circulating web of felt, but modern machines feed the pulp onto a cloth-like screen made of closely interwoven fine wires. This paper, when held to a light, will show little dots or points very close together. The proper name for this is "wire wove," but the type is still considered wove. Any U.S. or British stamp printed after 1880 will serve as an example of wire wove paper.

Closely spaced parallel wires, with cross wires at wider intervals, make up the frames used for what is known as *laid paper*. A greater thickness of the pulp will settle between the wires. The paper, when held to a light, will show alternate light and dark lines. The spacing and the thickness of the lines may vary, but on any one sheet of paper they are all alike. See Russia Scott 31-38 for examples of laid paper.

Batonne, from the French word meaning "a staff," is a term used if the lines in the paper are spaced quite far apart, like the printed ruling on a writing tablet. Batonne paper may be either wove or laid. If laid, fine laid lines can be seen between the batons.

Quadrille is the term used when the lines in the paper form little squares. *Oblong quadrille* is the term used when rectangles, rather than squares, are formed. Grid patterns vary from distinct to extremely faint. See Mexico-Guadalajara Scott 35-37 for examples of oblong quadrille paper.

Paper also is classified as thick or thin, hard or soft, and by color. Such colors may include yellowish, greenish, bluish and reddish.

Brief explanations of other types of paper used for printing stamps, as well as examples, follow.

Colored — Colored paper is created by the addition of dye in the paper-making process. Such colors may include shades of yellow, green, blue and red. *Surface-colored papers*, most commonly used for British colonial issues in 1913-14, are created when coloring is added only to the surface during the finishing process. Stamps printed on surface-colored paper have white or uncolored backs, while true colored papers are colored through. See Jamaica Scott 71-73.

Pelure — Pelure paper is a very thin, hard and often brittle paper that is sometimes bluish or grayish in appearance. See Serbia Scott 169-170.

Native — This is a term applied to handmade papers used to produce some of the early stamps of the Indian states. Stamps printed on native paper may be expected to display various natural inclusions that are normal and do not negatively affect value. Japanese paper, originally made of mulberry fibers and rice flour, is part of this group. See Japan Scott 1-18.

Manila — This type of paper is often used to make stamped envelopes and wrappers. It is a coarse-textured stock, usually smooth on one side and rough on the other. A variety of colors of manila paper exist, but the most common range is yellowish-brown.

Silk — Introduced by the British in 1847 as a safeguard against counterfeiting, silk paper contains bits of colored silk thread scattered throughout. The density of these fibers varies greatly and can include as few as one fiber per stamp or hundreds. U.S. revenue Scott R152 is a good example of an easy-to-identify silk paper stamp.

Silk-thread paper has uninterrupted threads of colored silk arranged so that one or more threads run through the stamp or postal stationery. See Great Britain Scott 5-6 and Switzerland Scott 14-19.

Granite — Filled with minute cloth or colored paper fibers of various colors and lengths, granite paper should not be confused with either type of silk paper. Austria Scott 172-175 and a number of Swiss stamps are examples of granite paper.

Chalky — A chalk-like substance coats the surface of chalky paper to discourage the cleaning and reuse of canceled stamps, as well as to provide a smoother, more acceptable printing surface. Because the designs of stamps printed on chalky paper are imprinted on what is often a water-soluble coating, any attempt to remove a cancellation will destroy the stamp. *Do not soak these stamps in any fluid.* To remove a stamp printed on chalky paper from an envelope, wet the paper from underneath the stamp until the gum dissolves enough to release the stamp from the paper. See St. Kitts-Nevis Scott 89-90 for examples of stamps printed on this type of chalky paper.

India — Another name for this paper, originally introduced from China about 1750, is "China Paper." It is a thin, opaque paper often used for plate and die proofs by many countries.

Double — In philately, the term double paper has two distinct meanings. The first is a two-ply paper, usually a combination of a thick and a thin sheet, joined during manufacture. This type was used experimentally as a means to discourage the reuse of stamps.

The design is printed on the thin paper. Any attempt to remove a cancellation would destroy the design. U.S. Scott 158 and other Banknote-era stamps exist on this form of double paper.

The second type of double paper occurs on a rotary press, when the end of one paper roll, or web, is affixed to the next roll to save time feeding the paper through the press. Stamp designs are printed over the joined paper and, if overlooked by inspectors, may get into post office stocks.

Goldbeater's Skin — This type of paper was used for the 1866 issue of Prussia, and was a tough, translucent paper. The design was printed in reverse on the back of the stamp, and the gum applied over the printing. It is impossible to remove stamps printed on this type of paper from the paper to which they are affixed without destroying the design.

Ribbed — Ribbed paper has an uneven, corrugated surface made by passing the paper through ridged rollers. This type exists on some copies of U.S. Scott 156-165.

Various other substances, or substrates, have been used for stamp manufacture, including wood, aluminum, copper, silver and gold foil, plastic, and silk and cotton fabrics.

Watermarks

Watermarks are an integral part of some papers. They are formed in the process of paper manufacture. Watermarks consist of small designs, formed of wire or cut from metal and soldered to the surface of the mold or, sometimes, on the dandy roll. The designs may be in the form of crowns, stars, anchors, letters or other characters or symbols. These pieces of metal - known in the paper-making industry as "bits" - impress a design into the paper. The design sometimes may be seen by holding the stamp to the light. Some are more easily seen with a watermark detector. This important tool is a small black tray into which a stamp is placed face down and dampened with a fast-evaporating watermark detection fluid that brings up the watermark image in the form of dark lines against a lighter background. These dark lines are the thinner areas of the paper known as the watermark. Some watermarks are extremely difficult to locate, due to either a faint impression, watermark location or the color of the stamp. There also are electric watermark detectors that come with plastic filter disks of various colors. The disks neutralize the color of the stamp, permitting the watermark to be seen more easily.

Multiple watermarks of Crown Agents and Burma

Watermarks of Uruguay, Vatican City and Jamaica

WARNING: Some inks used in the photogravure process dissolve in watermark fluids (Please see the section on Soluble Printing Inks). Also, see "chalky paper."

Watermarks may be found normal, reversed, inverted, reversed and inverted, sideways or diagonal, as seen from the back of the stamp. The relationship of watermark to stamp design depends on the position of the printing plates or how paper is fed through the press. On machine-made paper, watermarks normally are read from right to left. The design is repeated closely throughout the sheet in a "multiple-watermark design." In a "sheet watermark," the design appears only once on the sheet, but extends over many stamps. Individual stamps

may carry only a small fraction or none of the watermark.

"Marginal watermarks" occur in the margins of sheets or panes of stamps. They occur on the outside border of paper (ostensibly outside the area where stamps are to be printed). A large row of letters may spell the name of the country or the manufacturer of the paper, or a border of lines may appear. Careless press feeding may cause parts of these letters and/or lines to show on stamps of the outer row of a pane.

Soluble Printing Inks

WARNING: Most stamp colors are permanent; that is, they are not seriously affected by short-term exposure to light or water. Many colors, especially of modern inks, fade from excessive exposure to light. There are stamps printed with inks that dissolve easily in water or in fluids used to detect watermarks. Use of these inks was intentional to prevent the removal of cancellations. Water affects all aniline inks, those on so-called safety paper and some photogravure printings - all such inks are known as fugitive colors. *Removal from paper of such stamps requires care and alternatives to traditional soaking.*

Separation

"Separation" is the general term used to describe methods used to separate stamps. The three standard forms currently in use are perforating, rouletting and die-cutting. These methods are done during the stamp production process, after printing. Sometimes these methods are done on-press or sometimes as a separate step. The earliest issues, such as the 1840 Penny Black of Great Britain (Scott 1), did not have any means provided for separation. It was expected the stamps would be cut apart with scissors or folded and torn. These are examples of imperforate stamps. Many stamps were first issued in imperforate formats and were later issued with perforations. Therefore, care must be observed in buying single imperforate stamps to be certain they were issued imperforate and are not perforated copies that have been altered by having the perforations trimmed away. Stamps issued imperforate usually are valued as singles. However, imperforate varieties of normally perforated stamps should be collected in pairs or larger pieces as indisputable evidence of their imperforate character.

PERFORATION

The chief style of separation of stamps, and the one that is in almost universal use today, is perforating. By this process, paper between the stamps is cut away in a line of holes, usually round, leaving little bridges of paper between the stamps to hold them together. Some types of perforation, such as hyphen-hole perfs, can be confused with roulettes, but a close visual inspection reveals that paper has been removed. The little perforation bridges, which project from the stamp when it is torn from the pane, are called the teeth of the perforation.

As the size of the perforation is sometimes the only way to differentiate between two otherwise identical stamps, it is necessary to be able to accurately measure and describe them. This is done with a perforation gauge, usually a ruler-like device that has dots or graduated lines to show how many perforations may be counted in the space of two centimeters. Two centimeters is the space universally adopted in which to measure perforations.

Perforation gauge

perce en arc   perce en lignes

perce en points   oblique roulette

perce en scie   perce serpentin

To measure a stamp, run it along the gauge until the dots on it fit exactly into the perforations of the stamp. If you are using a graduated-line perforation gauge, simply slide the stamp along the surface until the lines on the gauge perfectly project from the center of the bridges or holes. The number to the side of the line of dots or lines that fit the stamp's perforation is the measurement. For example, an "11" means that 11 perforations fit between two centimeters. The description of the stamp therefore is "perf. 11." If the gauge of the perforations on the top and bottom of a stamp differs from that on the sides, the result is what is known as *compound perforations*. In measuring compound perforations, the gauge at top and bottom is always given first, then the sides. Thus, a stamp that measures 11 at top and bottom and 10½ at the sides is "perf. 11 x 10½." See U.S. Scott 632-642 for examples of compound perforations.

Stamps also are known with perforations different on three or all four sides. Descriptions of such items are clockwise, beginning with the top of the stamp.

A perforation with small holes and teeth close together is a "fine perforation." One with large holes and teeth far apart is a "coarse perforation." Holes that are jagged, rather than clean-cut, are "rough perforations." *Blind perforations* are the slight impressions left by the perforating pins if they fail to puncture the paper. Multiples of stamps showing blind perforations may command a slight premium over normally perforated stamps.

The term *syncopated perfs* describes intentional irregularities in the perforations. The earliest form was used by the Netherlands from 1925-33, where holes were omitted to create distinctive patterns. Beginning in 1992, Great Britain has used an oval perforation to help prevent counterfeiting. Several other countries have started using the oval perfs or other syncopated perf patterns.

A new type of perforation, still primarily used for postal stationery, is known as microperfs. Microperfs are tiny perforations (in some cases hundreds of holes per two centimeters) that allows items to be intentionally separated very easily, while not accidentally breaking apart as easily as standard perforations. These are not currently measured or differentiated by size, as are standard perforations.

ROULETTING

In rouletting, the stamp paper is cut partly or wholly through, with no paper removed. In perforating, some paper is removed. Rouletting derives its name from the French roulette, a spur-like wheel. As the wheel is rolled over the paper, each point makes a small cut. The number of cuts made in a two-centimeter space determines the gauge of the roulette, just as the number of perforations in two centimeters determines the gauge of the perforation.

The shape and arrangement of the teeth on the wheels varies. Various roulette types generally carry French names:

Perce en lignes - rouletted in lines. The paper receives short, straight cuts in lines. This is the most common type of rouletting. See Mexico Scott 500.

Perce en points - pin-rouletted or pin-perfed. This differs from a small perforation because no paper is removed, although round, equidistant holes are pricked through the paper. See Mexico Scott 242-256.

Perce en arc and *perce en scie* - pierced in an arc or saw-toothed designs, forming half circles or small triangles. See Hanover (German States) Scott 25-29.

Perce en serpentin - serpentine roulettes. The cuts form a serpentine or wavy line. See Brunswick (German States) Scott 13-18.

Once again, no paper is removed by these processes, leaving the stamps easily separated, but closely attached.

DIE-CUTTING

The third major form of stamp separation is die-cutting. This is a method where a die in the pattern of separation is created that later cuts the stamp paper in a stroke motion. Although some standard stamps bear die-cut perforations, this process is primarily used for self-adhesive postage stamps. Die-cutting can appear in straight lines, such as U.S. Scott 2522, shapes, such as U.S. Scott 1551, or imitating the appearance of perforations, such as New Zealand Scott 935A and 935B.

Printing Processes

ENGRAVING (Intaglio, Line-engraving, Etching)

Master die — The initial operation in the process of line engraving is making the master die. The die is a small, flat block of softened steel upon which the stamp design is recess engraved in reverse.

Master die

Photographic reduction of the original art is made to the appropriate size. It then serves as a tracing guide for the initial outline of the design. The engraver lightly traces the design on the steel with his graver, then slowly works the design until it is completed. At various points during the engraving process, the engraver hand-inks the die and makes an impression to check his progress. These are known as progressive die proofs. After completion of the engraving, the die is hardened to withstand the stress and pressures of later transfer operations.

Transfer roll

Transfer roll — Next is production of the transfer roll that, as the name implies, is the medium used to transfer the subject from the master die to the printing plate. A blank roll of soft steel, mounted on a mandrel, is placed under the bearers of the transfer press to allow it to roll freely on its axis. The hardened die is placed on the bed of the press and the face of the transfer roll is applied to the die, under pressure. The bed or the roll is then rocked back and forth under increasing pressure, until the soft steel of the roll is forced into every engraved line of the die. The resulting impression on the roll is known as a "relief" or a "relief transfer." The engraved image is now positive in appearance and stands out from the steel. After the required number of reliefs are "rocked in," the soft steel transfer roll is hardened.

Different flaws may occur during the relief process. A defective relief may occur during the rocking in process because of a minute piece of foreign material lodging on the die, or some other cause. Imperfections in the steel of the transfer roll may result in a breaking away of parts of the design. This is known as a relief break, which will show up on finished stamps as small, unprinted areas. If a damaged relief remains in use, it will transfer a repeating defect to the plate. Deliberate alterations of reliefs sometimes occur. "Altered reliefs" designate these changed conditions.

Plate — The final step in pre-printing production is the making of the printing plate. A flat piece of soft steel replaces the die on the bed of the transfer press. One of the reliefs on the transfer roll is positioned over this soft steel. Position, or layout, dots determine the correct position on the plate. The dots have been lightly marked on the plate in advance. After the correct position of the relief is determined,

the design is rocked in by following the same method used in making the transfer roll. The difference is that this time the image is being transferred from the transfer roll, rather than to it. Once the design is entered on the plate, it appears in reverse and is recessed. There are as many transfers entered on the plate as there are subjects printed on the sheet of stamps. It is during this process that double and shifted transfers occur, as well as re-entries. These are the result of improperly entered images that have not been properly burnished out prior to rocking in a new image.

Modern siderography processes, such as those used by the U.S. Bureau of Engraving and Printing, involve an automated form of rocking designs in on preformed cylindrical printing sleeves. The same process also allows for easier removal and re-entry of worn images right on the sleeve.

Transferring the design to the plate

Following the entering of the required transfers on the plate, the position dots, layout dots and lines, scratches and other markings generally are burnished out. Added at this time by the siderographer are any required *guide lines*, *plate numbers* or other *marginal markings*. The plate is then hand-inked and a proof impression is taken. This is known as a plate proof. If the impression is approved, the plate is machined for fitting onto the press, is hardened and sent to the plate vault ready for use.

On press, the plate is inked and the surface is automatically wiped clean, leaving ink only in the recessed lines. Paper is then forced under pressure into the engraved recessed lines, thereby receiving the ink. Thus, the ink lines on engraved stamps are slightly raised, and slight depressions (debossing) occur on the back of the stamp. Prior to the advent of modern high-speed presses and more advanced ink formulations, paper had to be dampened before receiving the ink. This sometimes led to uneven shrinkage by the time the stamps were perforated, resulting in improperly perforated stamps, or misperfs. Newer presses use drier paper, thus both *wet* and *dry printings* exist on some stamps.

Rotary Press — Until 1914, only flat plates were used to print engraved stamps. Rotary press printing was introduced in 1914, and slowly spread. Some countries still use flat-plate printing.

After approval of the plate proof, older *rotary press plates* require additional machining. They are curved to fit the press cylinder. "Gripper slots" are cut into the back of each plate to receive the "grippers," which hold the plate securely on the press. The plate is then hardened. Stamps printed from these bent rotary press plates are longer or wider than the same stamps printed from flat-plate presses. The stretching of the plate during the curving process is what causes this distortion.

Re-entry — To execute a re-entry on a flat plate, the transfer roll is re-applied to the plate, often at some time after its first use on the press. Worn-out designs can be resharpened by carefully burnishing out the original image and re-entering it from the transfer roll. If the original impression has not been sufficiently removed and the transfer roll is not precisely in line with the remaining impression, the resulting double transfer will make the re-entry obvious. If the registration is true, a re-entry may be difficult or impossible to distinguish. Sometimes a stamp printed from a successful re-entry is identified by having a much sharper and clearer impression than its neighbors. With the advent of rotary presses, post-press re-entries were not possible. After a plate was curved for the rotary press, it was impossible to make a re-entry. This is because the plate had already been bent once (with the design distorted).

However, with the introduction of the previously mentioned modern-style siderography machines, entries are made to the preformed cylindrical printing sleeve. Such sleeves are dechromed and softened. This allows individual images to be burnished out and re-entered on the curved sleeve. The sleeve is then rechromed, resulting in longer press life.

Double Transfer — This is a description of the condition of a transfer on a plate that shows evidence of a duplication of all, or a portion of the design. It usually is the result of the changing of the registration between the transfer roll and the plate during the rocking in of the original entry. Double transfers also occur when only a portion of the design has been rocked in and improper positioning is noted. If the worker elected not to burnish out the partial or completed design, a strong double transfer will occur for part or all of the design.

It sometimes is necessary to remove the original transfer from a plate and repeat the process a second time. If the finished re-worked image shows traces of the original impression, attributable to incomplete burnishing, the result is a partial double transfer.

With the modern automatic machines mentioned previously, double transfers are all but impossible to create. Those partially doubled images on stamps printed from such sleeves are more than likely re-entries, rather than true double transfers.

Re-engraved — Alterations to a stamp design are sometimes necessary after some stamps have been printed. In some cases, either the original die or the actual printing plate may have its "temper" drawn (softened), and the design will be re-cut. The resulting impressions from such a re-engraved die or plate may differ slightly from the original issue, and are known as "re-engraved." If the alteration was made to the master die, all future printings will be consistently different from the original. If alterations were made to the printing plate, each altered stamp on the plate will be slightly different from each other, allowing specialists to reconstruct a complete printing plate.

Dropped Transfers — If an impression from the transfer roll has not been properly placed, a dropped transfer may occur. The final stamp image will appear obviously out of line with its neighbors.

Short Transfer — Sometimes a transfer roll is not rocked its entire length when entering a transfer onto a plate. As a result, the finished transfer on the plate fails to show the complete design, and the finished stamp will have an incomplete design printed. This is known as a "short transfer." U.S. Scott No. 8 is a good example of a short transfer.

TYPOGRAPHY (Letterpress, Surface Printing, Flexography, Dry Offset, High Etch)

Although the word "Typography" is obsolete as a term describing a printing method, it was the accepted term throughout the first century of postage stamps. Therefore, appropriate Scott listings in this catalogue refer to typographed stamps. The current term for this form of printing, however, is "letterpress."

As it relates to the production of postage stamps, letterpress printing is the reverse of engraving. Rather than having recessed areas trap the ink and deposit it on paper, only the raised areas of the design are inked. This is comparable to the type of printing seen by inking and using an ordinary rubber stamp. Letterpress includes all printing where the design is above the surface area, whether it is wood, metal or, in some instances, hardened rubber or polymer plastic.

For most letterpress-printed stamps, the engraved master is made in much the same manner as for engraved stamps. In this instance, however, an additional step is needed. The design is transferred to another surface before being transferred to the transfer roll. In this way, the transfer roll has a recessed stamp design, rather than one done in relief. This makes the printing areas on the final plate raised, or relief areas.

For less-detailed stamps of the 19th century, the area on the die not used as a printing surface was cut away, leaving the surface area raised. The original die was then reproduced by stereotyping or electrotyping. The resulting electrotypes were assembled in the required number and format of the desired sheet of stamps. The plate used in printing the stamps was an electroplate of these assembled electrotypes.

Once the final letterpress plates are created, ink is applied to the raised surface and the pressure of the press transfers the ink impression to the paper. In contrast to engraving, the fine lines of letterpress are impressed on the surface of the stamp, leaving a debossed surface. When viewed from the back (as on a typewritten page), the corresponding line work on the stamp will be raised slightly (embossed) above the surface.

PHOTOGRAVURE (Gravure, Rotogravure, Heliogravure)

In this process, the basic principles of photography are applied to a chemically sensitized metal plate, rather than photographic paper. The design is transferred photographically to the plate through a halftone, or dot-matrix screen, breaking the reproduction into tiny dots. The plate is treated chemically and the dots form depressions, called cells, of varying depths and diameters, depending on the degrees of shade in the design. Then, like engraving, ink is applied to the plate and the surface is wiped clean. This leaves ink in the tiny cells that is lifted out and deposited on the paper when it is pressed against the plate.

Gravure is most often used for multicolored stamps, generally using the three primary colors (red, yellow and blue) and black. By varying the dot matrix pattern and density of these colors, virtually any color can be reproduced. A typical full-color gravure stamp will be created from four printing cylinders (one for each color). The original multicolored image will have been photographically separated into its component colors.

Modern gravure printing may use computer-generated dot-matrix screens, and modern plates may be of various types including metal-coated plastic. The catalogue designation of Photogravure (or "Photo") covers any of these older and more modern gravure methods of printing.

For examples of the first photogravure stamps printed (1914), see Bavaria Scott 94-114.

LITHOGRAPHY (Offset Lithography, Stone Lithography, Dilitho, Planography, Collotype)

The principle that oil and water do not mix is the basis for lithography. The stamp design is drawn by hand or transferred from engraving to the surface of a lithographic stone or metal plate in a greasy (oily) substance. This oily substance holds the ink, which will later be transferred to the paper. The stone (or plate) is wet with an acid fluid, causing it to repel the printing ink in all areas not covered by the greasy substance.

Transfer paper is used to transfer the design from the original stone or plate. A series of duplicate transfers are grouped and, in turn, transferred to the final printing plate.

Photolithography — The application of photographic processes to lithography. This process allows greater flexibility of design, related to use of halftone screens combined with line work. Unlike photogravure or engraving, this process can allow large, solid areas to be printed.

Offset — A refinement of the lithographic process. A rubber-covered blanket cylinder takes the impression from the inked lithographic plate. From the "blanket" the impression is *offset* or transferred to the paper. Greater flexibility and speed are the principal reasons offset printing has largely displaced lithography. The term "lithography" covers both processes, and results are almost identical.

EMBOSSED (Relief) Printing

Embossing, not considered one of the four main printing types, is a method in which the design first is sunk into the metal of the die. Printing is done against a yielding platen, such as leather or linoleum. The platen is forced into the depression of the die, thus forming the design on the paper in relief. This process is often used for metallic inks.

Embossing may be done without color (see Sardinia Scott 4-6); with color printed around the embossed area (see Great Britain Scott 5 and most U.S. envelopes); and with color in exact registration with the embossed subject (see Canada Scott 656-657).

HOLOGRAMS

For objects to appear as holograms on stamps, a model exactly the same size as it is to appear on the hologram must be created. Rather than using photographic film to capture the image, holography records an image on a photoresist material. In processing, chemicals eat away at certain exposed areas, leaving a pattern of constructive and destructive interference. When the photoresist is developed, the result is a pattern of uneven ridges that acts as a mold. This mold is then coated with metal, and the resulting form is used to press copies in much the same way phonograph records are produced.

A typical reflective hologram used for stamps consists of a reproduction of the uneven patterns on a plastic film that is applied to a reflective background, usually a silver or gold foil. Light is reflected off the background through the film, making the pattern present on the film visible. Because of the uneven pattern of the film, the viewer will perceive the objects in their proper three-dimensional relationships with appropriate brightness.

The first hologram on a stamp was produced by Austria in 1988 (Scott 1441).

FOIL APPLICATION

A modern technique of applying color to stamps involves the application of metallic foil to the stamp paper. A pattern of foil is applied to the stamp paper by use of a stamping die. The foil usually is flat, but it may be textured. Canada Scott 1735 has three different foil applications in pearl, bronze and gold. The gold foil was textured using a chemical-etch copper embossing die. The printing of this stamp also involved two-color offset lithography plus embossing.

THERMOGRAPHY

In the 1990s stamps began to be enhanced with thermographic printing. In this process, a powdered polymer is applied over a sheet that has just been printed. The powder adheres to ink that lacks drying or hardening agents and does not adhere to areas where the ink has these agents. The excess powder is removed and the sheet is briefly heated to melt the powder. The melted powder solidifies after cooling, producing a raised, shiny effect on the stamps. See Scott New Caledonia C239-C240.

COMBINATION PRINTINGS

Sometimes two or even three printing methods are combined in producing stamps. In these cases, such as Austria Scott 933 or Canada 1735 (described in the preceding paragraph), the multiple-printing technique can be determined by studying the individual characteristics of each printing type. A few stamps, such as Singapore Scott 684-684A, combine as many as three of the four major printing types (lithography, engraving and typography). When this is done it often indicates the incorporation of security devices against counterfeiting.

INK COLORS

Inks or colored papers used in stamp printing often are of mineral origin, although there are numerous examples of organic-based pigments. As a general rule, organic-based pigments are far more subject to varieties and change than those of mineral-based origin.

The appearance of any given color on a stamp may be affected by many aspects, including printing variations, light, color of paper, aging and chemical alterations.

Numerous printing variations may be observed. Heavier pressure or inking will cause a more intense color, while slight interruptions in the ink feed or lighter impressions will cause a lighter appearance. Stamps printed in the same color by water-based and solvent-based inks can differ significantly in appearance. This affects several stamps in the U.S. Prominent Americans series. Hand-mixed ink formulas (primarily from the 19th century) produced under different conditions (humidity and temperature) account for notable color variations in early printings of the same stamp (see U.S. Scott 248-250, 279B, for example). Different sources of pigment can also result in significant differences in color.

Light exposure and aging are closely related in the way they affect stamp color. Both eventually break down the ink and fade colors, so that a carefully kept stamp may differ significantly in color from an identical copy that has been exposed to light. If stamps are exposed to light either intentionally or accidentally, their colors can be faded or completely changed in some cases.

Papers of different quality and consistency used for the same stamp printing may affect color appearance. Most pelure papers, for example, show a richer color when compared with wove or laid papers. See Russia Scott 181a, for an example of this effect.

The very nature of the printing processes can cause a variety of differences in shades or hues of the same stamp. Some of these shades are scarcer than others, and are of particular interest to the advanced collector.

Luminescence

All forms of tagged stamps fall under the general category of luminescence. Within this broad category is fluorescence, dealing with forms of tagging visible under longwave ultraviolet light, and phosphorescence, which deals with tagging visible only under shortwave light. Phosphorescence leaves an afterglow and fluorescence does not. These treated stamps show up in a range of different colors when exposed to UV light. The differing wavelengths of the light activates the tagging material, making it glow in various colors that usually serve different mail processing purposes.

Intentional tagging is a post-World War II phenomenon, brought about by the increased literacy rate and rapidly growing mail volume. It was one of several answers to the problem of the need for more automated mail processes. Early tagged stamps served the purpose of triggering machines to separate different types of mail. A natural outgrowth was to also use the signal to trigger machines that faced all envelopes the same way and canceled them.

Tagged stamps come in many different forms. Some tagged stamps have luminescent shapes or images imprinted on them as a form of security device. Others have blocks (United States), stripes, frames (South Africa and Canada), overall coatings (United States), bars (Great Britain and Canada) and many other types. Some types of tagging are even mixed in with the pigmented printing ink (Australia Scott 366, Netherlands Scott 478 and U.S. Scott 1359 and 2443).

The means of applying taggant to stamps differs as much as the intended purposes for the stamps. The most common form of tagging is a coating applied to the surface of the printed stamp. Since the taggant ink is frequently invisible except under UV light, it does not interfere with the appearance of the stamp. Another common application is the use of phosphored papers. In this case the paper itself either has a coating of taggant applied before the stamp is printed, has taggant applied during the papermaking process (incorporating it into the fibers), or has the taggant mixed into the coating of the paper. The latter method, among others, is currently in use in the United States.

Many countries now use tagging in various forms to either expedite mail handling or to serve as a printing security device against counterfeiting. Following the introduction of tagged stamps for public use in 1959 by Great Britain, other countries have steadily joined the parade. Among those are Germany (1961); Canada and Denmark (1962); United States, Australia, France and Switzerland (1963); Belgium and Japan (1966); Sweden and Norway (1967); Italy (1968); and Russia (1969). Since then, many other countries have begun using forms of tagging, including Brazil, China, Czechoslovakia, Hong Kong, Guatemala, Indonesia, Israel, Lithuania, Luxembourg, Netherlands, Penrhyn Islands, Portugal, St. Vincent, Singapore, South Africa, Spain and Sweden to name a few.

In some cases, including United States, Canada, Great Britain and Switzerland, stamps were released both with and without tagging. Many of these were released during each country's experimental period. Tagged and untagged versions are listed for the aforementioned countries and are noted in some other countries' listings. For at least a few stamps, the experimentally tagged version is worth far more than its untagged counterpart, such as the 1963 experimental tagged version of France Scott 1024.

In some cases, luminescent varieties of stamps were inadvertently created. Several Russian stamps, for example, sport highly fluorescent ink that was not intended as a form of tagging. Older stamps, such as early U.S. postage dues, can be positively identified by the use of UV light, since the organic ink used has become slightly fluorescent over time. Other stamps, such as Austria Scott 70a-82a (varnish bars) and Obock Scott 46-64 (printed quadrille lines), have become fluorescent over time.

Various fluorescent substances have been added to paper to make it appear brighter. These optical brightners, as they are known, greatly affect the appearance of the stamp under UV light. The brightest of these is known as Hi-Brite paper. These paper varieties are beyond the scope of the Scott Catalogue.

Shortwave UV light also is used extensively in expertizing, since each form of paper has its own fluorescent characteristics that are impossible to perfectly match. It is therefore a simple matter to detect filled thins, added perforation teeth and other alterations that involve the addition of paper. UV light also is used to examine stamps that have had cancels chemically removed and for other purposes as well.

Gum

The Illustrated Gum Chart in the first part of this introduction shows and defines various types of gum condition. Because gum condition has an important impact on the value of unused stamps, we recommend studying this chart and the accompanying text carefully.

The gum on the back of a stamp may be shiny, dull, smooth, rough, dark, white, colored or tinted. Most stamp gumming adhesives use gum arabic or dextrine as a base. Certain polymers such as polyvinyl alcohol (PVA) have been used extensively since World War II.

The *Scott Standard Postage Stamp Catalogue* does not list items by types of gum. The *Scott Specialized Catalogue of United States Stamps and Covers* does differentiate among some types of gum for certain issues.

Reprints of stamps may have gum differing from the original issues. In addition, some countries have used different gum formulas for different seasons. These adhesives have different properties that may become more apparent over time.

Many stamps have been issued without gum, and the catalogue will note this fact. See, for example, United States Scott 40-47. Sometimes, gum may have been removed to preserve the stamp. Germany Scott B68, for example, has a highly acidic gum that eventually destroys the stamps. This item is valued in the catalogue with gum removed.

Reprints and Reissues

These are impressions of stamps (usually obsolete) made from the original plates or stones. If they are valid for postage and reproduce obsolete issues (such as U.S. Scott 102-111), the stamps are *reissues*. If they are from current issues, they are designated as *second, third,* etc., *printing*. If designated for a particular purpose, they are called *special printings*.

When special printings are not valid for postage, but are made from original dies and plates by authorized persons, they are *official reprints*. *Private reprints* are made from the original plates and dies by private hands. An example of a private reprint is that of the 1871-1932 reprints made from the original die of the 1845 New Haven, Conn., postmaster's provisional. *Official reproductions* or imitations are made from new dies and plates by government authorization. Scott will list those reissues that are valid for postage if they differ significantly from the original printing.

The U.S. government made special printings of its first postage stamps in 1875. Produced were official imitations of the first two stamps (listed as Scott 3-4), reprints of the demonetized pre-1861 issues (Scott 40-47) and reissues of the 1861 stamps, the 1869 stamps and the then-current 1875 denominations. Even though the official imitations and the reprints were not valid for postage, Scott lists all of these U.S. special printings.

Most reprints or reissues differ slightly from the original stamp in some characteristic, such as gum, paper, perforation, color or watermark. Sometimes the details are followed so meticulously that only a student of that specific stamp is able to distinguish the reprint or reissue from the original.

Remainders and Canceled to Order

Some countries sell their stock of old stamps when a new issue replaces them. To avoid postal use, the *remainders* usually are canceled with a punch hole, a heavy line or bar, or a more-or-less regular-looking cancellation. The most famous merchant of remainders was Nicholas F. Seebeck. In the 1880s and 1890s, he arranged printing contracts between the Hamilton Bank Note Co., of which he was a director, and several Central and South American countries. The contracts provided that the plates and all remainders of the yearly issues became the property of Hamilton. Seebeck saw to it that ample stock remained. The "Seebecks," both remainders and reprints, were standard packet fillers for decades.

Some countries also issue stamps *canceled-to-order (CTO)*, either in sheets with original gum or stuck onto pieces of paper or envelopes and canceled. Such CTO items generally are worth less than postally used stamps. In cases where the CTO material is far more prevalent in the marketplace than postally used examples, the catalogue value relates to the CTO examples, with postally used examples noted as premium items. Most CTOs can be detected by the presence of gum. However, as the CTO practice goes back at least to 1885, the gum inevitably has been soaked off some stamps so they could pass as postally used. The normally applied postmarks usually differ slightly from standard postmarks, and specialists are able to tell the difference. When applied individually to envelopes by philatelically minded persons, CTO material is known as *favor canceled* and generally sells at large discounts.

Cinderellas and Facsimiles

Cinderella is a catch-all term used by stamp collectors to describe phantoms, fantasies, bogus items, municipal issues, exhibition seals, local revenues, transportation stamps, labels, poster stamps and many other types of items. Some cinderella collectors include in their collections local postage issues, telegraph stamps, essays and proofs, forgeries and counterfeits.

A *fantasy* is an adhesive created for a nonexistent stamp-issuing authority. Fantasy items range from imaginary countries (Occusi-Ambeno, Kingdom of Sedang, Principality of Trinidad or Torres Straits), to non-existent locals (Winans City Post), or nonexistent transportation lines (McRobish & Co.'s Acapulco-San Francisco Line).

On the other hand, if the entity exists and could have issued stamps (but did not) or was known to have issued other stamps, the items are considered *bogus* stamps. These would include the Mormon postage stamps of Utah, S. Allan Taylor's Guatemala and Paraguay inventions, the propaganda issues for the South Moluccas and the adhesives of the Page & Keyes local post of Boston.

Phantoms is another term for both fantasy and bogus issues.

Facsimiles are copies or imitations made to represent original stamps, but which do not pretend to be originals. A catalogue illustration is such a facsimile. Illustrations from the Moens catalogue of the last century were occasionally colored and passed off as stamps. Since the beginning of stamp collecting, facsimiles have been made for collectors as space fillers or for reference. They often carry the word "facsimile," "falsch" (German), "sanko" or "mozo" (Japanese), or "faux" (French) overprinted on the face or stamped on the back. Unfortunately, over the years a number of these items have had fake cancels applied over the facsimile notation and have been passed off as genuine.

Forgeries and Counterfeits

Forgeries and counterfeits have been with philately virtually from the beginning of stamp production. Over time, the terminology for the two has been used interchangeably. Although both forgeries and counterfeits are reproductions of stamps, the purposes behind their creation differ considerably.

Among specialists there is an increasing movement to more specifically define such items. Although there is no universally accepted terminology, we feel the following definitions most closely mirror the items and their purposes as they are currently defined.

Forgeries (also often referred to as *Counterfeits*) are reproductions of genuine stamps that have been created to defraud collectors. Such spurious items first appeared on the market around 1860, and most old-time collections contain one or more. Many are crude and easily spotted, but some can deceive experts.

An important supplier of these early philatelic forgeries was the Hamburg printer Gebruder Spiro. Many others with reputations in this craft included S. Allan Taylor, George Hussey, James Chute, George Forune, Benjamin & Sarpy, Julius Goldner, E. Oneglia and L.H. Mercier. Among the noted 20th-century forgers were Francois Fournier, Jean Sperati and the prolific Raoul DeThuin.

Forgeries may be complete replications, or they may be genuine stamps altered to resemble a scarcer (and more valuable) type. Most forgeries, particularly those of rare stamps, are worth only a small fraction of the value of a genuine example, but a few types, created by some of the most notable forgers, such as Sperati, can be worth as much or more than the genuine. Fraudulently produced copies are known of most classic rarities and many medium-priced stamps.

In addition to rare stamps, large numbers of common 19th- and early 20th-century stamps were forged to supply stamps to the early packet trade. Many can still be easily found. Few new philatelic forgeries have appeared in recent decades. Successful imitation of well-engraved work is virtually impossible. It has proven far easier to produce a fake by altering a genuine stamp than to duplicate a stamp completely.

Counterfeit (also often referred to as *Postal Counterfeit or Postal Forgery*) is the term generally applied to reproductions of stamps that have been created to defraud the government of revenue. Such items usually are created at the time a stamp is current and, in some cases, are hard to detect. Because most counterfeits are seized when the perpetrator is captured, postal counterfeits, particularly used on cover, are usually worth much more than a genuine example to specialists. The first postal counterfeit was of Spain's 4-cuarto carmine of 1854 (the real one is Scott 25). Apparently, the counterfeiters were not satisfied with their first version, which is now very scarce, and they soon created an engraved counterfeit, which is common. Postal counterfeits quickly followed in Austria, Naples, Sardinia and the Roman States. They have since been created in many other countries as well, including the United States.

An infamous counterfeit to defraud the government is the 1-shilling Great Britain "Stock Exchange" forgery of 1872, used on telegraph forms at the exchange that year. The stamp escaped detection until a stamp dealer noticed it in 1898.

Fakes

Fakes are genuine stamps altered in some way to make them more desirable. One student of this part of stamp collecting has estimated that by the 1950s more than 30,000 varieties of fakes were known. That number has grown greatly since then. The widespread existence of fakes makes it important for stamp collectors to study their philatelic holdings and use relevant literature. Likewise, collectors should buy from reputable dealers who guarantee their stamps and make full and prompt refunds should a purchased item be declared faked or altered by some mutually agreed-upon authority. Because fakes always have some genuine characteristics, it is not always possible to obtain unanimous agreement among experts regarding specific items. These students may change their opinions as philatelic knowledge increases. More than 80 percent of all fakes on the philatelic market today are regummed, reperforated (or perforated for the first time), or bear forged overprints, surcharges or cancellations.

Stamps can be chemically treated to alter or eliminate colors. For example, a pale rose stamp can be re-colored to resemble a blue shade of high market value. In other cases, treated stamps can be made to resemble missing color varieties. Designs may be changed by painting, or a stroke or a dot added or bleached out to turn an ordinary variety into a seemingly scarcer stamp. Part of a stamp can be bleached and reprinted in a different version, achieving an inverted center or frame. Margins can be added or repairs done so deceptively that the stamps move from the "repaired" into the "fake" category.

Fakers have not left the backs of the stamps untouched either. They may create false watermarks, add fake grills or press out genuine grills. A thin India paper proof may be glued onto a thicker backing to create the appearance an issued stamp, or a proof printed on cardboard may be shaved down and perforated to resemble a stamp. Silk threads are impressed into paper and stamps have been split so that a rare paper variety is added to an otherwise inexpensive stamp. The most common treatment to the back of a stamp, however, is regumming.

Some in the business of faking stamps have openly advertised fool-proof application of "original gum" to stamps that lack it, although most publications now ban such ads from their pages. It is believed that very few early stamps have survived without being hinged. The large number of never-hinged examples of such earlier material offered for sale thus suggests the widespread extent of regumming activity. Regumming also may be used to hide repairs or thin spots. Dipping the stamp into watermark fluid, or examining it under longwave ultraviolet light often will reveal these flaws.

Fakers also tamper with separations. Ingenious ways to add margins are known. Perforated wide-margin stamps may be falsely represented as imperforate when trimmed. Reperforating is commonly done to create scarce coil or perforation varieties, and to eliminate the naturally occurring straight-edge stamps found in sheet margin positions of many earlier issues. Custom has made straight-edged stamps less desirable. Fakers have obliged by perforating straight-edged stamps so that many are now uncommon, if not rare.

Another fertile field for the faker is that of overprints, surcharges and cancellations. The forging of rare surcharges or overprints began in the 1880s or 1890s. These forgeries are sometimes difficult to detect, but experts have identified almost all. Occasionally, overprints or cancellations are removed to create non-overprinted stamps or seemingly unused items. This is most commonly done by removing a manuscript cancel to make a stamp resemble an unused example. "SPECIMEN" overprints may be removed by scraping and repainting to create non-overprinted varieties. Fakers use inexpensive revenues or pen-canceled stamps to generate unused stamps for further faking by adding other markings. The quartz lamp or UV lamp and a high-powered magnifying glass help to easily detect removed cancellations.

The bigger problem, however, is the addition of overprints, surcharges or cancellations - many with such precision that they are very difficult to ascertain. Plating of the stamps or the overprint can be an important method of detection.

Fake postmarks may range from many spurious fancy cancellations to a host of markings applied to transatlantic covers, to adding normally appearing postmarks to definitives of some countries with stamps that are valued far higher used than unused. With the increased popularity of cover collecting, and the widespread interest in postal history, a fertile new field for fakers has come about. Some have tried to create entire covers. Others specialize in adding stamps, tied by fake cancellations, to genuine stampless covers, or replacing less expensive or damaged stamps with more valuable ones. Detailed study of postal rates in effect at the time a cover in question was mailed, including the analysis of each handstamp used during the period, ink analysis and similar techniques, usually will unmask the fraud.

Restoration and Repairs

Scott bases its catalogue values on stamps that are free of defects and otherwise meet the standards set forth earlier in this introduction. Most stamp collectors desire to have the finest copy of an item possible. Even within given grading categories there are variances. This leads to a controversial practice that is not defined in any universal manner: stamp *restoration*.

There are broad differences of opinion about what is permissible when it comes to restoration. Carefully applying a soft eraser to a stamp or cover to remove light soiling is one form of restoration, as is washing a stamp in mild soap and water to clean it. These are fairly accepted forms of restoration. More severe forms of restoration include pressing out creases or removing stains caused by tape. To what degree each of these is acceptable is dependent upon the individual situation. Further along the spectrum is the freshening of a stamp's color by removing oxide build-up or the effects of wax paper left next to stamps shipped to the tropics.

At some point in this spectrum the concept of *repair* replaces that of restoration. Repairs include filling thin spots, mending tears by reweaving or adding a missing perforation tooth. Regumming stamps may have been acceptable as a restoration or repair technique many decades ago, but today it is considered a form of fakery.

Restored stamps may or may not sell at a discount, and it is possible that the value of individual restored items may be enhanced over that of their pre-restoration state. Specific situations dictate the resultant value of such an item. Repaired stamps sell at substantial discounts from the value of sound stamps.

Terminology

Booklets — Many countries have issued stamps in small booklets for the convenience of users. This idea continues to become increasingly popular in many countries. Booklets have been issued in many sizes and forms, often with advertising on the covers, the panes of stamps or on the interleaving.

The panes used in booklets may be printed from special plates or made from regular sheets. All panes from booklets issued by the United States and many from those of other countries contain stamps that are straight edged on the sides, but perforated between. Others are distinguished by orientation of watermark or other identifying features. Any stamp-like unit in the pane, either printed or blank, that is not a postage stamp, is considered to be a *label* in the catalogue listings.

Scott lists and values booklet panes. Modern complete booklets also are listed and valued. Individual booklet panes are listed only when they are not fashioned from existing sheet stamps and, therefore, are identifiable from their sheet stamp counterparts.

Panes usually do not have a used value assigned to them because there is little market activity for used booklet panes, even though many exist used and there is some demand for them.

Cancellations — The marks or obliterations put on stamps by postal authorities to show that they have performed service and to prevent their reuse are known as cancellations. If the marking is made with a pen, it is considered a "pen cancel." When the location of the post office appears in the marking, it is a "town cancellation." A "postmark" is technically any postal marking, but in practice the term generally is applied to a town cancellation with a date. When calling attention to a cause or celebration, the marking is known as a "slogan cancellation." Many other types and styles of cancellations exist, such as duplex, numerals, targets, fancy and others. See also "precancels," below.

Coil Stamps — These are stamps that are issued in rolls for use in dispensers, affixing and vending machines. Those coils of the United States, Canada, Sweden and some other countries are perforated horizontally or vertically only, with the outer edges imperforate. Coil stamps of some countries, such as Great Britain and Germany, are perforated on all four sides and may in some cases be distinguished from their sheet stamp counterparts by watermarks, counting numbers on the reverse or other means.

Covers — Entire envelopes, with or without adhesive postage stamps, that have passed through the mail and bear postal or other markings of philatelic interest are known as covers. Before the introduction of envelopes in about 1840, people folded letters and wrote the address on the outside. Some people covered their letters with an extra sheet of paper on the outside for the address, producing the term "cover." Used airletter sheets, stamped envelopes and other items of postal stationery also are considered covers.

Errors — Stamps that have some major, consistent, unintentional deviation from the normal are considered errors. Errors include, but are not limited to, missing or wrong colors, wrong paper, wrong watermarks, inverted centers or frames on multicolor printing, inverted or missing surcharges or overprints, double impressions, missing perforations, unintentionally omitted tagging and others. Factually wrong or misspelled information, if it appears on all examples of a stamp, are not considered errors in the true sense of the word. They are errors of design. Inconsistent or randomly appearing items, such as misperfs or color shifts, are classified as freaks.

Color-Omitted Errors — This term refers to stamps where a missing color is caused by the complete failure of the printing plate to deliver ink to the stamp paper or any other paper. Generally, this is caused by the printing plate not being engaged on the press or the ink station running dry of ink during printing.

Color-Missing Errors — This term refers to stamps where a color or colors were printed somewhere but do not appear on the finished stamp. There are four different classes of color-missing errors, and the catalog indicates with a two-letter code appended to each such listing what caused the color to be missing. These codes are used only for the United States' color-missing error listings.

FO = A *foldover* of the stamp sheet during printing may block ink from appearing on a stamp. Instead, the color will appear on the back of the foldover (where it might fall on the back of the selvage or perhaps on the back of the stamp or another stamp). FO also will be used in the case of foldunders, where the paper may fold underneath the other stamp paper and the color will print on the platen.

EP = A piece of *extraneous paper* falling across the plate or stamp paper will receive the printed ink. When the extraneous paper is removed, an unprinted portion of stamp paper remains and shows partially or totally missing colors.

CM = A misregistration of the printing plates during printing will result in a *color misregistration*, and such a misregistraion may result in a color not appearing on the finished stamp.

PS = A *perforation shift* after printing may remove a color from the finished stamp. Normally, this will occur on a row of stamps at the edge of the stamp pane.

Measurements – When measurements are given in the Scott catalogues for stamp size, grill size or any other reason, the first measurement given is always for the top and bottom dimension, while the second measurement will be for the sides (just as perforation gauges are measured). Thus, a stamp size of 15mm x 21mm will indicate a vertically oriented stamp 15mm wide at top and bottom, and 21mm tall at the sides. The same principle holds for measuring or counting items such as U.S. grills. A grill count of 22x18 points (B grill) indicates that there are 22 grill points across by 18 grill points down.

Overprints and Surcharges — Overprinting involves applying wording or design elements over an already existing stamp. Overprints can be used to alter the place of use (such as "Canal Zone" on U.S. stamps), to adapt them for a special purpose ("Porto" on Denmark's 1913-20 regular issues for use as postage due stamps, Scott J1-J7) or to commemorate a special occasion (United States Scott 647-648).

A *surcharge* is a form of overprint that changes or restates the face value of a stamp or piece of postal stationery.

Surcharges and overprints may be handstamped, typeset or, occasionally, lithographed or engraved. A few hand-written overprints and surcharges are known.

Personalized Stamps — In 1999, Australia issued stamps with se-tenant labels that could be personalized with pictures of the customer's choice. Other countries quickly followed suit, with some offering to print the selected picture on the stamp itself within a frame that was used exclusively for personalized issues. As the picture used on these stamps or labels vary, listings for such stamps are for any picture within the common frame (or any picture on a se-tenant label), be it a "generic" image or one produced especially for a customer, almost invariably at a premium price.

Precancels — Stamps that are canceled before they are placed in the mail are known as precancels. Precanceling usually is done to expedite the handling of large mailings and generally allow the affected mail pieces to skip certain phases of mail handling.

In the United States, precancellations generally identified the point of origin; that is, the city and state. This information appeared across the face of the stamp, usually centered between parallel lines. More recently, bureau precancels retained the parallel lines, but the city and state designations were dropped. Recent coils have a service inscription that is present on the original printing plate. These show the mail service paid for by the stamp. Since these stamps are not intended to receive further cancellations when used as intended, they are considered precancels. Such items often do not have parallel lines as part of the precancellation.

In France, the abbreviation *Affranchts* in a semicircle together with the word *Postes* is the general form of precancel in use. Belgian precancellations usually appear in a box in which the name of the city appears. Netherlands precancels have the name of the city enclosed between concentric circles, sometimes called a "lifesaver." Precancellations of other countries usually follow these patterns, but may be any arrangement of bars, boxes and city names.

Precancels are listed in the Scott catalogues only if the precancel changes the denomination (Belgium Scott 477-478); if the precanceled stamp is different from the non-precanceled version (such as untagged U.S. precancels); or if the stamp exists only precanceled (France Scott 1096-1099, U.S. Scott 2265).

Proofs and Essays — Proofs are impressions taken from an approved die, plate or stone in which the design and color are the same as the stamp issued to the public. Trial color proofs are impressions taken from approved dies, plates or stones in colors that vary from the final version. An essay is the impression of a design that differs in some way from the issued stamp. "Progressive die proofs" generally are considered to be essays.

Provisionals — These are stamps that are issued on short notice and intended for temporary use pending the arrival of regular issues. They usually are issued to meet such contingencies as changes in government or currency, shortage of necessary postage values or military occupation.

During the 1840s, postmasters in certain American cities issued stamps that were valid only at specific post offices. In 1861, postmasters of the Confederate States also issued stamps with limited validity. Both of these examples are known as "postmaster's provisionals."

Se-tenant — This term refers to an unsevered pair, strip or block of stamps that differ in design, denomination or overprint.

Unless the se-tenant item has a continuous design (see U.S. Scott 1451a, 1694a) the stamps do not have to be in the same order as shown in the catalogue (see U.S. Scott 2158a).

Specimens — The Universal Postal Union required member nations to send samples of all stamps they released into service to the International Bureau in Switzerland. Member nations of the UPU received these specimens as samples of what stamps were valid for postage. Many are overprinted, handstamped or initial-perforated "Specimen," "Canceled" or "Muestra." Some are marked with bars across the denominations (China-Taiwan), punched holes (Czechoslovakia) or back inscriptions (Mongolia).

Stamps distributed to government officials or for publicity purposes, and stamps submitted by private security printers for official approval, also may receive such defacements.

The previously described defacement markings prevent postal use, and all such items generally are known as "specimens."

Tete Beche — This term describes a pair of stamps in which one is upside down in relation to the other. Some of these are the result of intentional sheet arrangements, such as Morocco Scott B10-B11. Others occurred when one or more electrotypes accidentally were placed upside down on the plate, such as Colombia Scott 57a. Separation of the tete-beche stamps, of course, destroys the tete beche variety.

Pronunciation Symbols

ə .... banana, collide, abut

ˈə, ˌə .... humdrum, abut

ə .... immediately preceding \l\, \n\, \m\, \ŋ\, as in battle, mitten, eaten, and sometimes open \ˈō-pᵊm\, lock and key \-ᵊŋ-\; immediately following \l\, \m\, \r\, as often in French table, prisme, titre

ər .... further, merger, bird

ˈər-
ˈə-r } .... as in two different pronunciations of hurry \ˈhər-ē, ˈhə-rē\

a .... mat, map, mad, gag, snap, patch

ā .... day, fade, date, aorta, drape, cape

ä .... bother, cot, and, with most American speakers, father, cart

à .... father as pronounced by speakers who do not rhyme it with bother, French patte

aù .... now, loud, out

b .... baby, rib

ch .... chin, nature \ˈnā-chər\

d .... did, adder

e .... bet, bed, peck

ˈē, ˌē .... beat, nosebleed, evenly, easy

ē .... easy, mealy

f .... fifty, cuff

g .... go, big, gift

h .... hat, ahead

hw .... whale as pronounced by those who do not have the same pronunciation for both whale and wail

i .... tip, banish, active

ī .... site, side, buy, tripe

j .... job, gem, edge, join, judge

k .... kin, cook, ache

ḵ .... German ich, Buch; one pronunciation of loch

l .... lily, pool

m .... murmur, dim, nymph

n .... no, own

ⁿ .... indicates that a preceding vowel or diphthong is pronounced with the nasal passages open, as in French un bon vin blanc \œⁿ-bōⁿ-vaⁿ-bläⁿ\

ŋ .... sing \ˈsiŋ\, singer \ˈsiŋ-ər\, finger \ˈfiŋ-gər\, ink \ˈiŋk\

ō .... bone, know, beau

ȯ .... saw, all, gnaw, caught

œ .... French boeuf, German Hölle

œ̄ .... French feu, German Höhle

ȯi .... coin, destroy

p .... pepper, lip

r .... red, car, rarity

s .... source, less

sh .... as in shy, mission, machine, special (actually, this is a single sound, not two); with a hyphen between, two sounds as in grasshopper \ˈgras-ˌhä-pər\

t .... tie, attack, late, later, latter

th .... as in thin, ether (actually, this is a single sound, not two); with a hyphen between, two sounds as in knighthood \ˈnīt-ˌhu̇d\

th .... then, either, this (actually, this is a single sound, not two)

ü .... rule, youth, union \ˈyün-yən\, few \ˈfyü\

u̇ .... pull, wood, book, curable \ˈkyu̇r-ə-bəl\, fury \ˈfyu̇r-ē\

ᵫ .... German füllen, hübsch

ᵫ̄ .... French rue, German fühlen

v .... vivid, give

w .... we, away

y .... yard, young, cue \ˈkyü\, mute \ˈmyüt\, union \ˈyün-yən\

ʸ .... indicates that during the articulation of the sound represented by the preceding character the front of the tongue has substantially the position it has for the articulation of the first sound of yard, as in French digne \dēnʸ\

z .... zone, raise

zh .... as in vision, azure \ˈa-zhər\ (actually, this is a single sound, not two); with a hyphen between, two sounds as in hogshead \ˈhȯgz-ˌhed, ˈhägz-\

\ .... slant line used in pairs to mark the beginning and end of a transcription: \ˈpen\

ˈ .... mark preceding a syllable with primary (strongest) stress: \ˈpen-mən-ˌship\

ˌ .... mark preceding a syllable with secondary (medium) stress: \ˈpen-mən-ˌship\

- .... mark of syllable division

( ) .... indicate that what is symbolized between is present in some utterances but not in others: factory \ˈfak-t(ə-)rē\

÷ .... indicates that many regard as unacceptable the pronunciation variant immediately following: cupola \ˈkyü-pə-lə, ÷-ˌlō\

Currency Conversion

Country	Dollar	Pound	S Franc	Yen	HK $	Euro	Cdn $	Aus $
Australia	1.4193	1.8543	1.3967	0.0127	0.1809	1.5938	1.0589	–
Canada	1.3404	1.7512	1.3190	0.0120	0.1709	1.5052	–	0.9444
European Union	0.8905	1.1634	0.8763	0.0080	0.1135	–	0.6644	0.6274
Hong Kong	7.8446	10.249	7.7195	0.0704	–	8.8092	5.8524	5.5271
Japan	111.41	145.56	109.63	–	14.202	125.11	83.117	78.496
Switzerland	1.0162	1.3277	–	0.0091	0.1295	1.1412	0.7581	0.7160
United Kingdom	0.7654	–	0.7532	0.0069	0.0976	0.8595	0.5710	0.5393
United States	–	1.3065	0.9841	0.0090	0.1275	1.1230	0.7460	0.7046

Country	Currency	U.S. $ Equiv.
Thailand	baht	.0313
Timor	U.S. dollar	1.0000
Togo	Community of French Africa (CFA) franc	.0017
Tokelau	New Zealand dollar	.6652
Tonga	pa'anga	.4392
Niuafoíou	pa'anga	.4392
Trinidad & Tobago	dollar	.1476
Tristan da Cunha	British pound	1.3065
Tunisia	dinar	.3312
Turkey	lira	.1681
Turk. Rep. of Northern Cyprus	lira	.1681
Turkmenistan	manat	.2857
Turks & Caicos Islands	U.S. dollar	1.0000
Tuvalu	Australian dollar	.7046
Uganda	shilling	.0003
Ukraine	hryvnia	.0379
United Arab Emirates	dirham	.2723
Uruguay	peso	.0289
Uzbekistan	sum	.0001
Vanuatu	vatu	.0087
Vatican City	euro	1.1230
Venezuela	bolivar	.1001
Viet Nam	dong	.00004
Virgin Islands	U.S. dollar	1.0000
Wallis & Futuna Islands	Community of French Pacific (CFP) franc	.0094
Yemen	rial	.0040
Zambia	kwacha	.0786
Zaire (Congo Dem. Rep.)	franc	.0006
Zimbabwe	U.S. dollar	1.0000

Source: **xe.com** *May 1, 2019. Figures reflect values as of May 1, 2019.*

COMMON DESIGN TYPES

Pictured in this section are issues where one illustration has been used for a number of countries in the Catalogue. Not included in this section are overprinted stamps or those issues which are illustrated in each country. Because the location of Never Hinged breakpoints varies from country to country, some of the values in the listings below will be for unused stamps that were previously hinged.

EUROPA
Europa, 1956

The design symbolizing the cooperation among the six countries comprising the Coal and Steel Community is illustrated in each country.

Belgium	496-497
France	805-806
Germany	748-749
Italy	715-716
Luxembourg	318-320
Netherlands	368-369

Nos. 496-497 (2)	9.00	.50
Nos. 805-806 (2)	5.25	1.00
Nos. 748-749 (2)	7.40	1.10
Nos. 715-716 (2)	9.25	1.25
Nos. 318-320 (3)	65.50	42.00
Nos. 368-369 (2)	25.75	1.50
Set total (13) Stamps	122.15	47.35

Europa, 1958

"E" and Dove — CD1

European Postal Union at the service of European integration.

1958, Sept. 13

Belgium	527-528
France	889-890
Germany	790-791
Italy	750-751
Luxembourg	341-343
Netherlands	375-376
Saar	317-318

Nos. 527-528 (2)	3.75	.60
Nos. 889-890 (2)	1.65	.55
Nos. 790-791 (2)	2.95	.60
Nos. 750-751 (2)	1.05	.60
Nos. 341-343 (3)	1.35	.90
Nos. 375-376 (2)	1.25	.75
Nos. 317-318 (2)	1.05	2.30
Set total (15) Stamps	13.05	6.30

Europa, 1959

6-Link Enless Chain — CD2

1959, Sept. 19

Belgium	536-537
France	929-930
Germany	805-806
Italy	791-792
Luxembourg	354-355
Netherlands	379-380

Nos. 536-537 (2)	1.55	.60
Nos. 929-930 (2)	1.40	.80
Nos. 805-806 (2)	1.35	.60
Nos. 791-792 (2)	.80	.50
Nos. 354-355 (2)	2.65	1.00
Nos. 379-380 (2)	2.10	1.85
Set total (12) Stamps	9.85	5.35

Europa, 1960

19-Spoke Wheel CD3

First anniverary of the establishment of C.E.P.T. (Conference Europeenne des Administrations des Postes et des Telecommunications.) The spokes symbolize the 19 founding members of the Conference.

1960, Sept.

Belgium	553-554
Denmark	379
Finland	376-377
France	970-971
Germany	818-820
Great Britain	377-378
Greece	688
Iceland	327-328
Ireland	175-176
Italy	809-810
Luxembourg	374-375
Netherlands	385-386
Norway	387
Portugal	866-867
Spain	941-942
Sweden	562-563
Switzerland	400-401
Turkey	1493-1494

Nos. 553-554 (2)	1.25	.55
No. 379 (1)	.55	.50
Nos. 376-377 (2)	1.70	1.80
Nos. 970-971 (2)	.50	.50
Nos. 818-820 (3)	1.90	1.35
Nos. 377-378 (2)	8.00	5.00
No. 688 (1)	5.00	2.00
Nos. 327-328 (2)	1.30	1.85
Nos. 175-176 (2)	47.50	27.50
Nos. 809-810 (2)	.50	.50
Nos. 374-375 (2)	1.00	.80
Nos. 385-386 (2)	2.00	2.00
No. 387 (1)	1.00	.80
Nos. 866-867 (2)	3.00	1.75
Nos. 941-942 (2)	1.50	.75
Nos. 562-563 (2)	1.05	.55
Nos. 400-401 (2)	1.75	.75
Nos. 1493-1494 (2)	2.10	1.35
Set total (34) Stamps	81.60	50.30

Europa, 1961

19 Doves Flying as One — CD4

The 19 doves represent the 19 members of the Conference of European Postal and Telecommunications Administrations C.E.P.T.

1961-62

Belgium	572-573
Cyprus	201-203
France	1005-1006
Germany	844-845
Great Britain	382-384
Greece	718-719
Iceland	340-341
Italy	845-846
Luxembourg	382-383
Netherlands	387-388
Spain	1010-1011
Switzerland	410-411
Turkey	1518-1520

Nos. 572-573 (2)	.75	.50
Nos. 201-203 (3)	2.10	1.20
Nos. 1005-1006 (2)	.50	.50
Nos. 844-845 (2)	.60	.75
Nos. 382-384 (3)	.75	.75
Nos. 718-719 (2)	.80	.50
Nos. 340-341 (2)	1.10	1.60
Nos. 845-846 (2)	.50	.50
Nos. 382-383 (2)	.55	.55
Nos. 387-388 (2)	.50	.50
Nos. 1010-1011 (2)	.70	.55
Nos. 410-411 (2)	1.90	.60
Nos. 1518-1520 (3)	1.55	.90
Set total (29) Stamps	12.30	9.40

Europa, 1962

Young Tree with 19 Leaves CD5

The 19 leaves represent the 19 original members of C.E.P.T.

1962-63

Belgium	582-583
Cyprus	219-221
France	1045-1046
Germany	852-853
Greece	739-740
Iceland	348-349
Ireland	184-185
Italy	860-861
Luxembourg	386-387
Netherlands	394-395
Norway	414-415
Switzerland	416-417
Turkey	1553-1555

Nos. 582-583 (2)	.65	.65
Nos. 219-221 (3)	76.25	6.75
Nos. 1045-1046 (2)	.60	.50
Nos. 852-853 (2)	.65	.75
Nos. 739-740 (2)	2.25	1.15
Nos. 348-349 (2)	.85	.85
Nos. 184-185 (2)	2.00	.50
Nos. 860-861 (2)	1.00	.55
Nos. 386-387 (2)	.75	.55
Nos. 394-395 (2)	1.35	.90
Nos. 414-415 (2)	1.75	1.70
Nos. 416-417 (2)	1.65	1.00
Nos. 1553-1555 (3)	2.05	1.10
Set total (28) Stamps	91.80	16.95

Europa, 1963

Stylized Links, Symbolizing Unity — CD6

1963, Sept.

Belgium	598-599
Cyprus	229-231
Finland	419
France	1074-1075
Germany	867-868
Greece	768-769
Iceland	357-358
Ireland	188-189
Italy	880-881
Luxembourg	403-404
Netherlands	416-417
Norway	441-442
Switzerland	429
Turkey	1602-1603

Nos. 598-599 (2)	1.60	.55
Nos. 229-231 (3)	64.00	9.40
No. 419 (1)	1.25	.55
Nos. 1074-1075 (2)	.60	.50
Nos. 867-868 (2)	.50	.55
Nos. 768-769 (2)	5.25	1.90
Nos. 357-358 (2)	1.20	1.20
Nos. 188-189 (2)	4.75	3.25
Nos. 880-881 (2)	.50	.50
Nos. 403-404 (2)	.75	.55
Nos. 416-417 (2)	1.30	1.00
Nos. 441-442 (2)	2.60	2.40
No. 429 (1)	.90	.60
Nos. 1602-1603 (2)	1.20	.50
Set total (27) Stamps	86.40	23.45

Europa, 1964

Symbolic Daisy — CD7

5th anniversary of the establishment of C.E.P.T. The 22 petals of the flower symbolize the 22 members of the Conference.

1964, Sept.

Austria	738
Belgium	614-615
Cyprus	244-246
France	1109-1110
Germany	897-898
Greece	801-802
Iceland	367-368
Ireland	196-197
Italy	894-895
Luxembourg	411-412
Monaco	590-591
Netherlands	428-429
Norway	458
Portugal	931-933
Spain	1262-1263
Switzerland	438-439
Turkey	1628-1629

No. 738 (1)	1.20	.80
Nos. 614-615 (2)	1.40	.60
Nos. 244-246 (3)	32.25	5.10
Nos. 1109-1110 (2)	.50	.50
Nos. 897-898 (2)	.50	.50
Nos. 801-802 (2)	5.00	1.90
Nos. 367-368 (2)	1.40	1.15
Nos. 196-197 (2)	17.00	4.25
Nos. 894-895 (2)	.50	.50
Nos. 411-412 (2)	.75	.55
Nos. 590-591 (2)	2.50	.70
Nos. 428-429 (2)	.75	.60
No. 458 (1)	3.50	3.50
Nos. 931-933 (3)	10.00	2.00
Nos. 1262-1263 (2)	1.30	.80
Nos. 438-439 (2)	1.65	.50
Nos. 1628-1629 (2)	2.00	.80
Set total (34) Stamps	82.20	24.75

Europa, 1965

Leaves and "Fruit" CD8

1965

Belgium	636-637
Cyprus	262-264
Finland	437
France	1131-1132
Germany	934-935
Greece	833-834
Iceland	375-376
Ireland	204-205
Italy	915-916
Luxembourg	432-433
Monaco	616-617
Netherlands	438-439
Norway	475-476
Portugal	958-960
Switzerland	469
Turkey	1665-1666

Nos. 636-637 (2)	.50	.50
Nos. 262-264 (3)	25.35	6.00
No. 437 (1)	1.25	.55
Nos. 1131-1132 (2)	.70	.55
Nos. 934-935 (2)	.50	.50
Nos. 833-834 (2)	2.25	1.15
Nos. 375-376 (2)	2.50	1.75
Nos. 204-205 (2)	16.00	3.35
Nos. 915-916 (2)	.50	.50
Nos. 432-433 (2)	.75	.55
Nos. 616-617 (2)	3.25	1.65
Nos. 438-439 (2)	.55	.50
Nos. 475-476 (2)	2.40	1.90
Nos. 958-960 (3)	10.00	2.75
No. 469 (1)	1.15	.50
Nos. 1665-1666 (2)	2.00	1.25
Set total (32) Stamps	69.65	23.95

Europa, 1966

Symbolic Sailboat — CD9

1966, Sept.

Andorra, French	172
Belgium	675-676
Cyprus	275-277
France	1163-1164
Germany	963-964

Greece		862-863
Iceland		384-385
Ireland		216-217
Italy		942-943
Liechtenstein		415
Luxembourg		440-441
Monaco		639-640
Netherlands		441-442
Norway		496-497
Portugal		980-982
Switzerland		477-478
Turkey		1718-1719

No. 172 (1)	3.00	3.00
Nos. 675-676 (2)	.80	.55
Nos. 275-277 (3)	4.75	2.75
Nos. 1163-1164 (2)	.55	.50
Nos. 963-964 (2)	.50	.55
Nos. 862-863 (2)	2.25	1.05
Nos. 384-385 (2)	4.50	3.50
Nos. 216-217 (2)	6.75	2.00
Nos. 942-943 (2)	.50	.50
No. 415 (1)	.40	.35
Nos. 440-441 (2)	.70	.55
Nos. 639-640 (2)	2.00	.65
Nos. 441-442 (2)	.85	.50
Nos. 496-497 (2)	2.35	2.15
Nos. 980-982 (3)	9.75	2.25
Nos. 477-478 (2)	1.40	.60
Nos. 1718-1719 (2)	3.35	1.75
Set total (34) Stamps	44.40	23.15

Europa, 1967

Cogwheels CD10

1967

Andorra, French		174-175
Belgium		688-689
Cyprus		297-299
France		1178-1179
Germany		969-970
Greece		891-892
Iceland		389-390
Ireland		232-233
Italy		951-952
Liechtenstein		420
Luxembourg		449-450
Monaco		669-670
Netherlands		444-447
Norway		504-505
Portugal		994-996
Spain		1465-1466
Switzerland		482
Turkey		B120-B121

Nos. 174-175 (2)	10.75	6.25
Nos. 688-689 (2)	1.05	.55
Nos. 297-299 (3)	1.25	2.50
Nos. 1178-1179 (2)	.55	.50
Nos. 969-970 (2)	.55	.55
Nos. 891-892 (2)	3.75	1.00
Nos. 389-390 (2)	3.00	2.00
Nos. 232-233 (2)	5.90	2.30
Nos. 951-952 (2)	.60	.50
No. 420 (1)	.45	.40
Nos. 449-450 (2)	1.00	.70
Nos. 669-670 (2)	2.75	.70
Nos. 444-447 (4)	2.70	2.05
Nos. 504-505 (2)	2.00	1.80
Nos. 994-996 (3)	9.50	1.85
Nos. 1465-1466 (2)	.50	.50
No. 482 (1)	.60	.30
Nos. B120-B121 (2)	2.50	2.00
Set total (38) Stamps	52.40	26.45

Europa, 1968

Golden Key with C.E.P.T. Emblem CD11

1968

Andorra, French		182-183
Belgium		705-706
Cyprus		314-316
France		1209-1210
Germany		983-984
Greece		916-917
Iceland		395-396
Ireland		242-243
Italy		979-980

Liechtenstein		442
Luxembourg		466-467
Monaco		689-691
Netherlands		452-453
Portugal		1019-1021
San Marino		687
Spain		1526
Switzerland		488
Turkey		1775-1776

Nos. 182-183 (2)	16.50	10.00
Nos. 705 706 (2)	1.25	.50
Nos. 314-316 (3)	2.90	2.50
Nos. 1209-1210 (2)	.85	.55
Nos. 983-984 (2)	.50	.55
Nos. 916-917 (2)	3.75	1.65
Nos. 395-396 (2)	3.00	2.20
Nos. 242-243 (2)	3.30	2.25
Nos. 979-980 (2)	.50	.50
No. 442 (1)	.45	.40
Nos. 466-467 (2)	.80	.70
Nos. 689-691 (3)	5.40	.95
Nos. 452-453 (2)	1.05	.70
Nos. 1019-1021 (3)	9.75	2.10
No. 687 (1)	.55	.35
No. 1526 (1)	.25	.25
No. 488 (1)	.40	.25
Nos. 1775-1776 (2)	2.50	1.25
Set total (35) Stamps	53.70	27.65

Europa, 1969

"EUROPA" and "CEPT" CD12

Tenth anniversary of C.E.P.T.

1969

Andorra, French		188-189
Austria		837
Belgium		718-719
Cyprus		326-328
Denmark		458
Finland		483
France		1245-1246
Germany		996-997
Great Britain		585
Greece		947-948
Iceland		406-407
Ireland		270-271
Italy		1000-1001
Liechtenstein		453
Luxembourg		475-476
Monaco		722-724
Netherlands		475-476
Norway		533-534
Portugal		1038-1040
San Marino		701-702
Spain		1567
Sweden		814-816
Switzerland		500-501
Turkey		1799-1800
Vatican		470-472
Yugoslavia		1003-1004

Nos. 188-189 (2)	18.50	12.00
No. 837 (1)	.65	.30
Nos. 718-719 (2)	.75	.50
Nos. 326-328 (3)	3.00	2.25
No. 458 (1)	.75	.75
No. 483 (1)	3.50	.75
Nos. 1245-1246 (2)	.55	.50
Nos. 996-997 (2)	.70	.50
No. 585 (1)	.25	.25
Nos. 947-948 (2)	5.00	1.50
Nos. 406-407 (2)	4.20	2.40
Nos. 270-271 (2)	3.50	2.00
Nos. 1000-1001 (2)	.50	.50
No. 453 (1)	.45	.45
Nos. 475-476 (2)	.95	.50
Nos. 722-724 (3)	10.50	2.00
Nos. 475-476 (2)	1.35	1.00
Nos. 533-534 (2)	2.20	1.95
Nos. 1038-1040 (3)	17.75	2.40
Nos. 701-702 (2)	.90	.90
No. 1567 (1)	.25	.25
Nos. 814-816 (3)	4.00	2.85
Nos. 500-501 (2)	1.85	1.00
Nos. 1799-1800 (2)	2.50	1.65
Nos. 470-472 (3)	.75	.75
Nos. 1003-1004 (2)	4.00	4.00
Set total (51) Stamps	89.30	43.90

Europa, 1970

Interwoven Threads CD13

1970

Andorra, French		196-197
Belgium		741-742
Cyprus		340-342
France		1271-1272
Germany		1018-1019
Greece		985, 987
Iceland		420-421
Ireland		279-281
Italy		1013 1014
Liechtenstein		470
Luxembourg		489-490
Monaco		768-770
Netherlands		483-484
Portugal		1060-1062
San Marino		729-730
Spain		1607
Switzerland		515-516
Turkey		1848-1849
Yugoslavia		1024-1025

Nos. 196-197 (2)	20.00	8.50
Nos. 741-742 (2)	1.10	.55
Nos. 340-342 (3)	2.70	2.75
Nos. 1271-1272 (2)	.65	.50
Nos. 1018-1019 (2)	.60	.50
Nos. 985,987 (2)	7.75	2.00
Nos. 420-421 (2)	6.00	4.00
Nos. 279-281 (3)	7.50	2.50
Nos. 1013-1014 (2)	.50	.50
No. 470 (1)	.45	.45
Nos. 489-490 (2)	.80	.55
Nos. 768-770 (3)	6.35	2.10
Nos. 483-484 (2)	1.30	1.15
Nos. 1060-1062 (3)	9.75	2.35
Nos. 729-730 (2)	.90	.55
No. 1607 (1)	.25	.25
Nos. 515-516 (2)	1.85	.70
Nos. 1848-1849 (2)	2.50	1.50
Nos. 1024-1025 (2)	.80	.80
Set total (40) Stamps	71.75	32.20

Europa, 1971

"Fraternity, Cooperation, Common Effort" CD14

1971

Andorra, French		205-206
Belgium		803-804
Cyprus		365-367
Finland		504
France		1304
Germany		1064-1065
Greece		1029-1030
Iceland		429-430
Ireland		305-306
Italy		1038-1039
Liechtenstein		485
Luxembourg		500-501
Malta		425-427
Monaco		797-799
Netherlands		488-489
Portugal		1094-1096
San Marino		749-750
Spain		1675-1676
Switzerland		531-532
Turkey		1876-1877
Yugoslavia		1052-1053

Nos. 205-206 (2)	20.00	7.75
Nos. 803-804 (2)	1.30	.55
Nos. 365-367 (3)	2.60	3.25
No. 504 (1)	5.00	.75
No. 1304 (1)	.45	.40
Nos. 1064-1065 (2)	.60	.50
Nos. 1029-1030 (2)	4.00	1.80
Nos. 429-430 (2)	5.00	3.75
Nos. 305-306 (2)	4.50	1.50
Nos. 1038-1039 (2)	.65	.50
No. 485 (1)	.45	.45
Nos. 500-501 (2)	1.00	.65
Nos. 425-427 (3)	.80	.80
Nos. 797-799 (3)	15.00	2.80
Nos. 488-489 (2)	1.20	.95
Nos. 1094-1096 (3)	9.75	1.75
Nos. 749-750 (2)	.65	.55
Nos. 1675-1676 (2)	.75	.55
Nos. 531-532 (2)	1.85	.65
Nos. 1876-1877 (2)	2.50	1.25
Nos. 1052-1053 (2)	.50	.50
Set total (43) Stamps	78.55	31.65

Europa, 1972

Sparkles, Symbolic of Communications CD15

1972

Andorra, French		210-211
Andorra, Spanish		62
Belgium		825-826
Cyprus		380-382
Finland		512-513
France		1341
Germany		1089-1090
Greece		1049-1050
Iceland		439-440
Ireland		316-317
Italy		1065-1066
Liechtenstein		504
Luxembourg		512-513
Malta		450-453
Monaco		831-832
Netherlands		494-495
Portugal		1141-1143
San Marino		771-772
Spain		1718
Switzerland		544-545
Turkey		1907-1908
Yugoslavia		1100-1101

Nos. 210-211 (2)	21.00	7.00
No. 62 (1)	60.00	60.00
Nos. 825-826 (2)	.95	.55
Nos. 380-382 (3)	5.95	4.25
Nos. 512-513 (2)	7.00	1.40
No. 1341 (1)	.50	.35
Nos. 1089-1090 (2)	1.10	.50
Nos. 1049-1050 (2)	2.00	1.55
Nos. 439-440 (2)	2.90	2.65
Nos. 316-317 (2)	13.00	4.50
Nos. 1065-1066 (2)	.55	.50
No. 504 (1)	.45	.45
Nos. 512-513 (2)	.95	.65
Nos. 450-453 (4)	1.05	1.40
Nos. 831-832 (2)	5.00	1.40
Nos. 494-495 (2)	1.20	.90
Nos. 1141-1143 (3)	9.75	1.50
Nos. 771-772 (2)	.70	.50
No. 1718 (1)	.50	.40
Nos. 544-545 (2)	1.65	.60
Nos. 1907-1908 (2)	4.00	2.00
Nos. 1100-1101 (2)	1.20	1.20
Set total (44) Stamps	141.40	94.25

Europa, 1973

Post Horn and Arrows CD16

1973

Andorra, French		219-220
Andorra, Spanish		76
Belgium		839-840
Cyprus		396-398
Finland		526
France		1367
Germany		1114-1115
Greece		1090-1092
Iceland		447-448
Ireland		329-330
Italy		1108-1109
Liechtenstein		528-529
Luxembourg		523-524
Malta		469-471
Monaco		866-867
Netherlands		504-505
Norway		604-605
Portugal		1170-1172
San Marino		802-803
Spain		1753
Switzerland		580-581
Turkey		1935-1936
Yugoslavia		1138-1139

Nos. 219-220 (2)	20.00	11.00
No. 76 (1)	1.25	.85
Nos. 839-840 (2)	1.00	.65
Nos. 396-398 (3)	4.25	3.85
No. 526 (1)	1.25	.55
No. 1367 (1)	1.25	.75
Nos. 1114-1115 (2)	.85	.50
Nos. 1090-1092 (3)	2.10	1.40
Nos. 447-448 (2)	6.65	3.35

Nos. 329-330 (2)	5.25	2.00
Nos. 1108-1109 (2)	.50	.50
Nos. 528-529 (2)	.60	.60
Nos. 523-524 (2)	.90	.75
Nos. 469-471 (3)	.90	1.20
Nos. 866-867 (2)	15.00	2.40
Nos. 504-505 (2)	1.20	.95
Nos. 604-605 (2)	4.00	1.80
Nos. 1170-1172 (3)	13.00	2.15
Nos. 802-803 (2)	1.00	.60
No. 1753 (1)	.35	.25
Nos. 580-581 (2)	1.55	.60
Nos. 1935-1936 (2)	4.15	2.25
Nos. 1138-1139 (2)	1.15	1.10
Set total (46) Stamps	88.15	40.05

Europa, 2000

CD17

2000

Albania	2621-2622
Andorra, French	522
Andorra, Spanish	262
Armenia	610-611
Austria	1814
Azerbaijan	698-699
Belarus	350
Belgium	1818
Bosnia & Herzegovina (Moslem)	358
Bosnia & Herzegovina (Serb)	111-112
Croatia	428-429
Cyprus	959
Czech Republic	3120
Denmark	1189
Estonia	394
Faroe Islands	376
Finland	1129
Aland Islands	166
France	2771
Georgia	228-229
Germany	2086-2087
Gibraltar	837-840
Great Britain (Jersey)	935-936
Great Britain (Isle of Man)	883
Greece	1959
Greenland	363
Hungary	3699-3700
Iceland	910
Ireland	1230-1231
Italy	2349
Latvia	504
Liechtenstein	1178
Lithuania	668
Luxembourg	1035
Macedonia	187
Malta	1011-1012
Moldova	355
Monaco	2161-2162
Poland	3519
Portugal	2358
Portugal (Azores)	455
Portugal (Madeira)	208
Romania	4370
Russia	6589
San Marino	1480
Slovakia	355
Slovenia	424
Spain	3036
Sweden	2394
Switzerland	1074
Turkey	2762
Turkish Rep. of Northern Cyprus	500
Ukraine	379
Vatican City	1152

Nos. 2621-2622 (2)	11.00	11.00
No. 522 (1)	2.00	1.00
No. 262 (1)	1.75	.80
Nos. 610-611 (2)	4.75	4.75
No. 1814 (1)	1.40	1.40
Nos. 698-699 (2)	6.00	6.00
No. 350 (1)	1.75	1.75
No. 1818 (1)	1.40	.60
No. 358 (1)	4.75	4.75
Nos. 111-112 (2)	110.00	110.00
Nos. 428-429 (2)	6.25	6.25
No. 959 (1)	2.10	1.40
No. 3120 (1)	1.20	.40
No. 1189 (1)	3.50	2.25
No. 394 (1)	1.25	1.25
No. 376 (1)	2.40	2.40
No. 1129 (1)	2.00	.60
No. 166 (1)	2.00	1.10
No. 2771 (1)	1.25	.40
Nos. 228-229 (2)	9.00	9.00
Nos. 2086-2087 (2)	4.35	2.10
Nos. 837-840 (4)	5.50	5.30

Nos. 935-936 (2)	2.40	2.40
No. 883 (1)	1.75	1.75
No. 363 (1)	1.90	1.90
Nos. 3699-3700 (2)	6.50	2.50
No. 910 (1)	1.60	1.60
Nos. 1230-1231 (2)	4.35	4.35
No. 2349 (1)	1.50	.40
No. 504 (1)	5.00	2.40
No. 1178 (1)	2.25	1.75
No. 668 (1)	1.50	1.50
No. 1035 (1)	1.40	.85
No. 187 (1)	3.00	3.00
Nos. 1011-1012 (2)	4.35	4.35
No. 355 (1)	3.50	3.50
Nos. 2161-2162 (2)	2.80	1.40
No. 3519 (1)	1.25	.75
No. 2358 (1)	1.25	.65
No. 455 (1)	1.25	.50
No. 208 (1)	1.25	.50
No. 4370 (1)	2.50	1.25
No. 6589 (1)	2.00	.85
No. 1480 (1)	1.00	1.00
No. 355 (1)	1.60	.80
No. 424 (1)	3.25	3.25
No. 3036 (1)	.75	.40
No. 2394 (1)	3.00	2.25
No. 1074 (1)	2.10	1.05
No. 2762 (1)	2.75	2.00
No. 500 (1)	2.50	2.50
No. 379 (1)	4.50	3.00
No. 1152 (1)	1.25	1.25
Set total (68) Stamps	261.60	230.15

The Gibraltar stamps are similar to the stamp illustrated, but none have the design shown above. All other sets listed above include at least one stamp with the design shown, but some include stamps with entirely different designs. Bulgaria Nos. 4131-4132, Guernsey Nos. 802-803 and Yugoslavia Nos. 2485-2486 are Europa stamps with completely different designs.

PORTUGAL & COLONIES
Vasco da Gama

Fleet Departing
CD20

Fleet Arriving at
Calicut — CD21

Embarking at
Rastello
CD22

Muse of
History
CD23

San Gabriel,
da Gama and
Camoens
CD24

Archangel
Gabriel, the
Patron Saint
CD25

Flagship San
Gabriel — CD26

Vasco da
Gama — CD27

Fourth centenary of Vasco da Gama's discovery of the route to India.

1898

Azores	93-100
Macao	67-74
Madeira	37-44
Portugal	147-154
Port. Africa	1-8
Port. Congo	75-98
Port. India	189-196
St. Thomas & Prince Islands	170-193
Timor	45-52

Nos. 93-100 (8)	122.00	76.25
Nos. 67-74 (8)	136.00	96.75
Nos. 37-44 (8)	44.55	34.00
Nos. 147-154 (8)	155.00	50.25
Nos. 1-8 (8)	27.00	17.75
Nos. 75-98 (24)	41.50	34.45
Nos. 189-196 (8)	20.25	12.95
Nos. 170-193 (24)	38.75	34.30
Nos. 45-52 (8)	39.75	27.25
Set total (104) Stamps	624.80	383.95

Pombal
POSTAL TAX
POSTAL TAX DUES

Marquis de
Pombal — CD28

Planning
Reconstruction
of Lisbon,
1755 — CD29

Pombal Monument,
Lisbon — CD30

Sebastiao Jose de Carvalho e Mello, Marquis de Pombal (1699-1782), statesman, rebuilt Lisbon after earthquake of 1755. Tax was for the erection of Pombal monument. Obligatory on all mail on certain days throughout the year. Postal Tax Dues are inscribed "Multa."

1925

Angola	RA1-RA3, RAJ1-RAJ3
Azores	RA9-RA11, RAJ2-RAJ4
Cape Verde	RA1-RA3, RAJ1-RAJ3
Macao	RA1-RA3, RAJ1-RAJ3
Madeira	RA1-RA3, RAJ1-RAJ3
Mozambique	RA1-RA3, RAJ1-RAJ3
Nyassa	RA1-RA3, RAJ1-RAJ3
Portugal	RA11-RA13, RAJ2-RAJ4
Port. Guinea	RA1-RA3, RAJ1-RAJ3
Port. India	RA1-RA3, RAJ1-RAJ3
St. Thomas & Prince Islands	RA1-RA3, RAJ1-RAJ3
Timor	RA1-RA3, RAJ1-RAJ3

Nos. RA1-RA3, RAJ1-RAJ3 (6)	6.60	6.60
Nos. RA9-RA11, RAJ2-RAJ4 (6)	6.60	9.30
Nos. RA1-RA3, RAJ1-RAJ3 (6)	4.50	3.90
Nos. RA1-RA3, RAJ1-RAJ3 (6)	21.25	10.50
Nos. RA1-RA3, RAJ1-RAJ3 (6)	4.35	12.45
Nos. RA1-RA3, RAJ1-RAJ3 (6)	2.40	2.55
Nos. RA1-RA3, RAJ1-RAJ3 (6)	52.50	38.25
Nos. RA11-RA13, RAJ2-RAJ4 (6)	5.95	5.20
Nos. RA1-RA3, RAJ1-RAJ3 (6)	3.30	2.70
Nos. RA1-RA3, RAJ1-RAJ3 (6)	3.45	3.45
Nos. RA1-RA3, RAJ1-RAJ3 (6)	3.75	3.60
Nos. RA1-RA3, RAJ1-RAJ3 (6)	2.10	3.90
Set total (72) Stamps	116.75	102.40

Vasco da Gama
CD34

Mousinho de
Albuquerque
CD35

Dam
CD36

Prince Henry
the Navigator
CD37

Affonso de
Albuquerque
CD38

Plane over
Globe
CD39

1938-39

Angola	274-291, C1-C9
Cape Verde	234-251, C1-C9
Macao	289-305, C7-C15
Mozambique	270-287, C1-C9
Port. Guinea	233-250, C1-C9
Port. India	439-453, C1-C8
St. Thomas & Prince Islands	302-319, 323-340, C1-C18
Timor	223-239, C1-C9

Nos. 274-291,C1-C9 (27)	132.90	22.85
Nos. 234-251,C1-C9 (27)	87.00	27.15
Nos. 289-305,C7-C15 (26)	589.45	145.25
Nos. 270-287,C1-C9 (27)	63.45	11.20
Nos. 233-250,C1-C9 (27)	88.05	30.70
Nos. 439-453,C1-C8 (23)	74.75	25.50
Nos. 302-319,323-340,C1-C18 (54)	316.25	191.35
Nos. 223-239,C1-C9 (26)	193.55	94.50
Set total (237) Stamps	1,545.	548.50

Lady of Fatima

Our Lady of the
Rosary, Fatima,
Portugal — CD40

1948-49

Angola	315-318
Cape Verde	266
Macao	336
Mozambique	325-328
Port. Guinea	271
Port. India	480
St. Thomas & Prince Islands	351
Timor	254

Nos. 315-318 (4)	68.00	17.25
No. 266 (1)	8.50	4.50
No. 336 (1)	42.50	12.00
Nos. 325-328 (4)	73.25	16.85
No. 271 (1)	3.25	3.00
No. 480 (1)	2.50	2.25
No. 351 (1)	7.25	6.50
No. 254 (1)	6.00	6.00
Set total (14) Stamps	211.25	68.35

A souvenir sheet of 9 stamps was issued in 1951 to mark the extension of the 1950 Holy Year. The sheet contains: Angola No. 316, Cape Verde No. 266, Macao No. 336, Mozambique No. 325, Portuguese Guinea No. 271, Portuguese India Nos. 480, 485, St. Thomas & Prince Islands No. 351, Timor No. 254. The sheet also contains a portrait of Pope Pius XII and is inscribed "Encerramento do

Ano Santo, Fatima 1951." It was sold for 11 escudos.

Holy Year

Church Bells and Dove CD41 — Angel Holding Candelabra CD42

Holy Year, 1950.

1950-51

Angola	331-332
Cape Verde	268-269
Macao	339-340
Mozambique	330-331
Port. Guinea	273-274
Port. India	490-491, 496-503
St. Thomas & Prince Islands	353-354
Timor	258-259

Nos. 331-332 (2)	7.60	1.35
Nos. 268-269 (2)	5.50	3.50
Nos. 339-340 (2)	60.00	11.00
Nos. 330-331 (2)	3.00	1.10
Nos. 273-274 (2)	3.50	2.60
Nos. 490-491,496-503 (10)	12.80	5.40
Nos. 353-354 (2)	7.75	4.90
Nos. 258-259 (2)	8.00	4.00
Set total (24) Stamps	108.15	36.85

A souvenir sheet of 8 stamps was issued in 1951 to mark the extension of the Holy Year. The sheet contains: Angola No. 331, Cape Verde No. 269, Macao No. 340, Mozambique No. 331, Portuguese Guinea No. 275, Portuguese India No. 490, St. Thomas & Prince Islands No. 354, Timor No. 258, some with colors changed. The sheet contains doves and is inscribed 'Encerramento do Ano Santo, Fatima 1951.' It was sold for 17 escudos.

Holy Year Conclusion

Our Lady of Fatima — CD43

Conclusion of Holy Year. Sheets contain alternate vertical rows of stamps and labels bearing quotation from Pope Pius XII, different for each colony.

1951

Angola	357
Cape Verde	270
Macao	352
Mozambique	356
Port. Guinea	275
Port. India	506
St. Thomas & Prince Islands	355
Timor	270

No. 357 (1)	5.25	1.50
No. 270 (1)	1.50	1.25
No. 352 (1)	45.00	10.00
No. 356 (1)	2.25	1.00
No. 275 (1)	1.00	.65
No. 506 (1)	1.60	1.00
No. 355 (1)	3.00	1.00
No. 270 (1)	5.75	2.40
Set total (8) Stamps	65.35	19.80

Medical Congress

CD44

First National Congress of Tropical Medicine, Lisbon, 1952. Each stamp has a different design.

1952

Angola	358
Cape Verde	287
Macao	364

Mozambique	359
Port. Guinea	276
Port. India	516
St. Thomas & Prince Islands	356
Timor	271

No. 358 (1)	1.50	.50
No. 287 (1)	.75	.60
No. 364 (1)	10.00	6.00
No. 359 (1)	1.25	.55
No. 276 (1)	.45	.35
No. 516 (1)	4.75	2.00
No. 356 (1)	.35	.30
No. 271 (1)	2.50	1.30
Set total (8) Stamps	21.55	11.60

Postage Due Stamps

CD45

1952

Angola	J37-J42
Cape Verde	J31-J36
Macao	J53-J58
Mozambique	J51-J56
Port. Guinea	J40-J45
Port. India	J47-J52
St. Thomas & Prince Islands	J52-J57
Timor	J31-J36

Nos. J37-J42 (6)	4.05	3.15
Nos. J31-J36 (6)	2.80	2.30
Nos. J53-J58 (6)	17.45	6.85
Nos. J51-J56 (6)	1.80	1.55
Nos. J40-J45 (6)	2.55	2.55
Nos. J47-J52 (6)	6.10	6.10
Nos. J52-J57 (6)	3.85	3.85
Nos. J31-J36 (6)	6.20	3.50
Set total (48) Stamps	44.80	29.85

Sao Paulo

Father Manuel da Nobrega and View of Sao Paulo — CD46

Founding of Sao Paulo, Brazil, 400th anniv.

1954

Angola	385
Cape Verde	297
Macao	382
Mozambique	395
Port. Guinea	291
Port. India	530
St. Thomas & Prince Islands	369
Timor	270

No. 385 (1)	.80	.50
No. 297 (1)	.70	.60
No. 382 (1)	15.00	6.00
No. 395 (1)	.40	.30
No. 291 (1)	.35	.25
No. 530 (1)	.80	.40
No. 369 (1)	.70	.50
No. 279 (1)	3.00	1.25
Set total (8) Stamps	21.75	9.80

Tropical Medicine Congress

CD47

Sixth International Congress for Tropical Medicine and Malaria, Lisbon, Sept. 1958. Each stamp shows a different plant.

1958

Angola	409
Cape Verde	303
Macao	392
Mozambique	404
Port. Guinea	295
Port. India	569
St. Thomas & Prince Islands	371

Timor	289

No. 409 (1)	3.50	1.10
No. 303 (1)	5.50	2.10
No. 392 (1)	10.00	5.00
No. 404 (1)	2.50	.85
No. 295 (1)	2.75	1.10
No. 569 (1)	1.75	.75
No. 371 (1)	2.75	2.00
No. 289 (1)	3.50	2.75
Set total (8) Stamps	32.25	15.65

Sports

CD48

Each stamp shows a different sport.

1962

Angola	433-438
Cape Verde	320-325
Macao	394-399
Mozambique	424-429
Port. Guinea	299-304
St. Thomas & Prince Islands	374-379
Timor	313-318

Nos. 433-438 (6)	5.50	3.20
Nos. 320-325 (6)	15.25	5.20
Nos. 394-399 (6)	68.65	14.60
Nos. 424-429 (6)	5.70	2.45
Nos. 299-304 (6)	4.95	2.15
Nos. 374-379 (6)	6.75	3.20
Nos. 313-318 (6)	9.15	5.05
Set total (42) Stamps	115.95	35.85

Anti-Malaria

Anopheles Funestus and Malaria Eradication Symbol — CD49

World Health Organization drive to eradicate malaria.

1962

Angola	439
Cape Verde	326
Macao	400
Mozambique	430
Port. Guinea	305
St. Thomas & Prince Islands	380
Timor	319

No. 439 (1)	1.75	.90
No. 326 (1)	1.40	.90
No. 400 (1)	7.00	2.25
No. 430 (1)	1.40	.40
No. 305 (1)	1.25	.45
No. 380 (1)	2.25	1.25
No. 319 (1)	1.50	1.00
Set total (7) Stamps	16.55	7.15

Airline Anniversary

Map of Africa, Super Constellation and Jet Liner — CD50

Tenth anniversary of Transportes Aereos Portugueses (TAP).

1963

Angola	490
Cape Verde	327
Mozambique	434
Port. Guinea	318
St. Thomas & Prince Islands	381

No. 490 (1)	1.00	.35
No. 327 (1)	1.10	.70
No. 434 (1)	.40	.25

No. 318 (1)	.65	.35
No. 381 (1)	.80	.50
Set total (5) Stamps	3.95	2.15

National Overseas Bank

Antonio Teixeira de Sousa — CD51

Centenary of the National Overseas Bank of Portugal.

1964, May 16

Angola	509
Cape Verde	328
Port. Guinea	319
St. Thomas & Prince Islands	382
Timor	320

No. 509 (1)	.90	.30
No. 328 (1)	1.10	.75
No. 319 (1)	.65	.40
No. 382 (1)	.70	.50
No. 320 (1)	1.50	.85
Set total (5) Stamps	4.85	2.80

ITU

ITU Emblem and the Archangel Gabriel — CD52

International Communications Union, Cent.

1965, May 17

Angola	511
Cape Verde	329
Macao	402
Mozambique	464
Port. Guinea	320
St. Thomas & Prince Islands	383
Timor	321

No. 511 (1)	1.25	.65
No. 329 (1)	2.10	1.40
No. 402 (1)	6.00	2.25
No. 464 (1)	.45	.25
No. 320 (1)	1.90	.75
No. 383 (1)	2.00	1.00
No. 321 (1)	1.50	.90
Set total (7) Stamps	15.20	7.20

National Revolution

CD53

40th anniv. of the National Revolution. Different buildings on each stamp.

1966, May 28

Angola	525
Cape Verde	338
Macao	403
Mozambique	465
Port. Guinea	329
St. Thomas & Prince Islands	392
Timor	322

No. 525 (1)	.50	.25
No. 338 (1)	.60	.45
No. 403 (1)	9.00	2.25
No. 465 (1)	.50	.30
No. 329 (1)	.55	.35
No. 392 (1)	.80	.50
No. 322 (1)	1.75	.95
Set total (7) Stamps	13.70	5.05

Navy Club

CD54

Centenary of Portugal's Navy Club. Each stamp has a different design.

1967, Jan. 31

Angola	527-528
Cape Verde	339-340
Macao	412-413
Mozambique	478-479
Port. Guinea	330-331
St. Thomas & Prince Islands	393-394
Timor	323-324

Nos. 527-528 (2)	1.75	.75
Nos. 339-340 (2)	2.00	1.40
Nos. 412-413 (2)	11.25	4.00
Nos. 478-479 (2)	1.40	.65
Nos. 330-331 (2)	1.20	.90
Nos. 393-394 (2)	3.30	1.30
Nos. 323-324 (2)	4.65	1.90
Set total (14) Stamps	25.55	10.90

Admiral Coutinho

CD55

Centenary of the birth of Admiral Carlos Viegas Gago Coutinho (1869-1959), explorer and aviation pioneer. Each stamp has a different design.

1969, Feb. 17

Angola	547
Cape Verde	355
Macao	417
Mozambique	484
Port. Guinea	335
St. Thomas & Prince Islands	397
Timor	335

No. 547 (1)	.85	.35
No. 355 (1)	.50	.25
No. 417 (1)	5.00	1.75
No. 484 (1)	.25	.25
No. 335 (1)	.35	.25
No. 397 (1)	.60	.35
No. 335 (1)	2.50	1.05
Set total (7) Stamps	10.05	4.25

Administration Reform

Luiz Augusto Rebello da Silva — CD56

Centenary of the administration reforms of the overseas territories.

1969, Sept. 25

Angola	549
Cape Verde	357
Macao	419
Mozambique	491
Port. Guinea	337
St. Thomas & Prince Islands	399
Timor	338

No. 549 (1)	.35	.25
No. 357 (1)	.50	.25
No. 419 (1)	6.00	1.00
No. 491 (1)	.25	.25
No. 337 (1)	.25	.25
No. 399 (1)	.45	.45
No. 338 (1)	1.25	.50
Set total (7) Stamps	9.05	2.95

Marshal Carmona

CD57

Birth centenary of Marshal Antonio Oscar Carmona de Fragoso (1869-1951), President of Portugal. Each stamp has a different design.

1970, Nov. 15

Angola	563
Cape Verde	359
Macao	422
Mozambique	493
Port. Guinea	340
St. Thomas & Prince Islands	403
Timor	341

No. 563 (1)	.45	.25
No. 359 (1)	.55	.35
No. 422 (1)	2.00	1.00
No. 493 (1)	.40	.25
No. 340 (1)	.35	.25
No. 403 (1)	.75	.40
No. 341 (1)	1.00	.35
Set total (7) Stamps	5.50	2.85

Olympic Games

CD59

20th Olympic Games, Munich, Aug. 26-Sept. 11. Each stamp shows a different sport.

1972, June 20

Angola	569
Cape Verde	361
Macao	426
Mozambique	504
Port. Guinea	342
St. Thomas & Prince Islands	408
Timor	343

No. 569 (1)	.65	.25
No. 361 (1)	.85	.30
No. 426 (1)	4.25	1.00
No. 504 (1)	.30	.25
No. 342 (1)	.45	.25
No. 408 (1)	.45	.25
No. 343 (1)	1.60	.80
Set total (7) Stamps	8.55	3.10

Lisbon-Rio de Janeiro Flight

CD60

50th anniversary of the Lisbon to Rio de Janeiro flight by Arturo de Sacadura and Coutinho, March 30-June 5, 1922. Each stamp shows a different stage of the flight.

1972, Sept. 20

Angola	570
Cape Verde	362
Macao	427
Mozambique	505
Port. Guinea	343
St. Thomas & Prince Islands	409
Timor	344

No. 570 (1)	.35	.25
No. 362 (1)	1.50	.30
No. 427 (1)	22.50	8.50
No. 505 (1)	.25	.25
No. 343 (1)	.25	.25
No. 409 (1)	.50	.25
No. 344 (1)	1.40	.60
Set total (7) Stamps	26.75	10.40

WMO Centenary

WMO Emblem — CD61

Centenary of international meterological cooperation.

1973, Dec. 15

Angola	571
Cape Verde	363
Macao	429
Mozambique	509
Port. Guinea	344
St. Thomas & Prince Islands	410

Timor	345

No. 571 (1)	.45	.25
No. 363 (1)	.65	.30
No. 429 (1)	6.00	1.75
No. 509 (1)	.30	.25
No. 344 (1)	.45	.35
No. 410 (1)	.60	.50
No. 345 (1)	4.25	2.50
Set total (7) Stamps	12.70	5.90

FRENCH COMMUNITY
Upper Volta can be found under Burkina Faso in Vol. 1
Madagascar can be found under Malagasy in Vol. 3
Colonial Exposition

People of French Empire CD70

Women's Heads CD71

France Showing Way to Civilization CD72

"Colonial Commerce" CD73

International Colonial Exposition, Paris.

1931

Cameroun	213-216
Chad	60-63
Dahomey	97-100
Fr. Guiana	152-155
Fr. Guinea	116-119
Fr. India	100-103
Fr. Polynesia	76-79
Fr. Sudan	102-105
Gabon	120-123
Guadeloupe	138-141
Indo-China	140-142
Ivory Coast	92-95
Madagascar	169-172
Martinique	129-132
Mauritania	65-68
Middle Congo	61-64
New Caledonia	176-179
Niger	73-76
Reunion	122-125
St. Pierre & Miquelon	132-135
Senegal	138-141
Somali Coast	135-138
Togo	254-257
Ubangi-Shari	82-85
Upper Volta	66-69
Wallis & Futuna Isls.	85-88

Nos. 213-216 (4)	23.00	18.25
Nos. 60-63 (4)	22.00	22.00
Nos. 97-100 (4)	26.00	26.00
Nos. 152-155 (4)	22.00	22.00
Nos. 116-119 (4)	19.75	19.75
Nos. 100-103 (4)	18.00	18.00
Nos. 76-79 (4)	30.00	30.00
Nos. 102-105 (4)	19.00	19.00
Nos. 120-123 (4)	17.50	17.50
Nos. 138-141 (4)	19.00	19.00
Nos. 140-142 (3)	12.00	11.50
Nos. 92-95 (4)	22.50	22.50
Nos. 169-172 (4)	7.90	5.00
Nos. 129-132 (4)	21.00	21.00
Nos. 65-68 (4)	22.00	22.00
Nos. 61-64 (4)	20.00	18.50
Nos. 176-179 (4)	24.00	24.00
Nos. 73-76 (4)	20.50	20.50
Nos. 122-125 (4)	22.00	22.00
Nos. 132-135 (4)	24.00	24.00
Nos. 138-141 (4)	20.00	20.00
Nos. 135-138 (4)	22.00	22.00
Nos. 254-257 (4)	22.00	22.00

Nos. 82-85 (4)	21.00	21.00
Nos. 66-69 (4)	19.00	19.00
Nos. 85-88 (4)	31.00	35.00
Set total (103) Stamps	547.15	541.50

Paris International Exposition
Colonial Arts Exposition

"Colonial Resources"
CD74   CD77

Overseas Commerce CD75

Exposition Building and Women CD76

"France and the Empire" CD78

Cultural Treasures of the Colonies CD79

Souvenir sheets contain one imperf. stamp.

1937

Cameroun	217-222A
Dahomey	101-107
Fr. Equatorial Africa	27-32, 73
Fr. Guiana	162-168
Fr. Guinea	120-126
Fr. India	104-110
Fr. Polynesia	117-123
Fr. Sudan	106-112
Guadeloupe	148-154
Indo-China	193-199
Inini	41
Ivory Coast	152-158
Kwangchowan	132
Madagascar	191-197
Martinique	179-185
Mauritania	69-75
New Caledonia	208-214
Niger	77-83
Reunion	167-173
St. Pierre & Miquelon	165-171
Senegal	172-178
Somali Coast	139-145
Togo	258-264
Wallis & Futuna Isls.	89

Nos. 217-222A (7)	18.80	20.30
Nos. 101-107 (7)	23.60	27.60
Nos. 27-32, 73 (7)	28.10	32.10
Nos. 162-168 (7)	22.50	24.50
Nos. 120-126 (7)	24.00	28.00
Nos. 104-110 (7)	21.15	36.50
Nos. 117-123 (7)	58.50	75.00
Nos. 106-112 (7)	23.60	27.60
Nos. 148-154 (7)	19.55	21.05
Nos. 193-199 (7)	17.70	19.70
No. 41 (1)	21.00	27.50
Nos. 152-158 (7)	22.20	26.20
No. 132 (1)	9.25	11.00
Nos. 191-197 (7)	19.25	21.75
Nos. 179-185 (7)	19.95	21.70
Nos. 69-75 (7)	20.50	24.50
Nos. 208-214 (7)	39.00	50.50
Nos. 73-83 (11)	40.60	45.10
Nos. 167-173 (7)	21.70	23.20
Nos. 165-171 (7)	49.60	64.00
Nos. 172-178 (7)	21.00	23.80
Nos. 139-145 (7)	25.60	32.60
Nos. 258-264 (7)	20.40	20.40
No. 89 (1)	19.00	37.50
Set total (154) Stamps	606.55	742.10

Curie

Pierre and Marie Curie CD80

40th anniversary of the discovery of radium. The surtax was for the benefit of the Intl. Union for the Control of Cancer.

1938

Cameroun	B1
Cuba	B1-B2
Dahomey	B2
France	B76
Fr. Equatorial Africa	B1
Fr. Guiana	B3
Fr. Guinea	B2
Fr. India	B6
Fr. Polynesia	B5
Fr. Sudan	B1
Guadeloupe	B3
Indo-China	B14
Ivory Coast	B2
Madagascar	B2
Martinique	B2
Mauritania	B3
New Caledonia	B4
Niger	B1
Reunion	B4
St. Pierre & Miquelon	B3
Senegal	B3
Somali Coast	B2
Togo	B1

No. B1 (1)	10.00	10.00
Nos. B1-B2 (2)	12.00	3.35
No. B2 (1)	9.50	9.50
No. B76 (1)	21.00	12.50
No. B1 (1)	24.00	24.00
No. B3 (1)	13.50	13.50
No. B2 (1)	8.75	8.75
No. B6 (1)	10.00	10.00
No. B5 (1)	20.00	20.00
No. B1 (1)	12.50	12.50
No. B3 (1)	11.00	10.50
No. B14 (1)	12.00	12.00
No. B2 (1)	11.00	7.50
No. B2 (1)	11.00	11.00
No. B2 (1)	13.00	13.00
No. B3 (1)	7.75	7.75
No. B4 (1)	16.50	17.50
No. B1 (1)	16.50	16.50
No. B4 (1)	14.00	14.00
No. B3 (1)	21.00	22.50
No. B3 (1)	10.50	10.50
No. B2 (1)	7.75	7.75
No. B1 (1)	20.00	20.00
Set total (24) Stamps	313.25	294.60

Caillie

Rene Caillie and Map of Northwestern Africa — CD81

Death centenary of Rene Caillie (1799-1838), French explorer. All three denominations exist with colony name omitted.

1939

Dahomey	108-110
Fr. Guinea	161-163
Fr. Sudan	113-115
Ivory Coast	160-162
Mauritania	109-111
Niger	84-86
Senegal	188-190
Togo	265-267

Nos. 108-110 (3)	1.20	3.60
Nos. 161-163 (3)	1.20	3.20
Nos. 113-115 (3)	1.20	3.20
Nos. 160-162 (3)	1.05	2.55
Nos. 109-111 (3)	1.05	3.80
Nos. 84-86 (3)	2.35	2.35
Nos. 188-190 (3)	1.05	2.90
Nos. 265-267 (3)	1.05	3.30
Set total (24) Stamps	10.15	24.90

New York World's Fair

Natives and New York Skyline CD82

1939

Cameroun	223-224
Dahomey	111-112
Fr. Equatorial Africa	78-79
Fr. Guiana	169-170
Fr. Guinea	164-165
Fr. India	111-112
Fr. Polynesia	124-125
Fr. Sudan	116-117
Guadeloupe	155-156
Indo-China	203-204
Inini	42-43
Ivory Coast	163-164
Kwangchowan	133-134
Madagascar	209-210
Martinique	186-187
Mauritania	112-113
New Caledonia	215-216
Niger	87-88
Reunion	174-175
St. Pierre & Miquelon	205-206
Senegal	191-192
Somali Coast	179-180
Togo	268-269
Wallis & Futuna Isls.	90-91

Nos. 223-224 (2)	2.80	2.40
Nos. 111-112 (2)	1.60	3.20
Nos. 78-79 (2)	1.60	3.20
Nos. 169-170 (2)	2.60	2.60
Nos. 164-165 (2)	1.60	3.20
Nos. 111-112 (2)	3.00	8.00
Nos. 124-125 (2)	4.80	4.80
Nos. 116-117 (2)	1.60	3.20
Nos. 155-156 (2)	2.50	2.50
Nos. 203-204 (2)	2.05	2.05
Nos. 42-43 (2)	7.50	9.00
Nos. 163-164 (2)	1.50	3.00
Nos. 133-134 (2)	2.50	2.50
Nos. 209-210 (2)	1.50	2.50
Nos. 186-187 (2)	2.35	2.35
Nos. 112-113 (2)	1.40	2.80
Nos. 215-216 (2)	3.35	3.35
Nos. 87-88 (2)	1.60	2.80
Nos. 174-175 (2)	2.80	2.80
Nos. 205-206 (2)	4.80	6.00
Nos. 191-192 (2)	1.40	2.80
Nos. 179-180 (2)	1.40	2.80
Nos. 268-269 (2)	1.40	2.80
Nos. 90-91 (2)	5.00	6.00
Set total (48) Stamps	62.65	86.65

French Revolution

Storming of the Bastille CD83

French Revolution, 150th anniv. The surtax was for the defense of the colonies.

1939

Cameroun	B2-B6
Dahomey	B3-B7
Fr. Equatorial Africa	B4-B8, CB1
Fr. Guiana	B4-B8, CB1
Fr. Guinea	B3-B7
Fr. India	B7-B11
Fr. Polynesia	B6-B10, CB1
Fr. Sudan	B2-B6
Guadeloupe	B4-B8
Indo-China	B15-B19, CB1
Inini	B1-B5
Ivory Coast	B3-B7
Kwangchowan	B1-B5
Madagascar	B3-B7, CB1
Martinique	B2-B6
Mauritania	B4-B8
New Caledonia	B5-B9, CB1
Niger	B2-B6
Reunion	B5-B9, CB1
St. Pierre & Miquelon	B4-B8
Senegal	B4-B8, CB1
Somali Coast	B3-B7
Togo	B2-B6
Wallis & Futuna Isls.	B1-B5

Nos. B2-B6 (5)	60.00	60.00
Nos. B3-B7 (5)	47.50	47.50
Nos. B4-B8,CB1 (6)	120.00	120.00
Nos. B4-B8,CB1 (6)	79.50	79.50
Nos. B3-B7 (5)	47.50	47.50
Nos. B7-B11 (5)	28.75	32.50
Nos. B6-B10,CB1 (6)	122.50	122.50
Nos. B2-B6 (5)	50.00	50.00
Nos. B4-B8 (5)	50.00	50.00
Nos. B15-B19,CB1 (6)	85.00	85.00
Nos. B1-B5 (5)	80.00	100.00
Nos. B3-B7 (5)	43.75	43.75
Nos. B1-B5 (5)	46.25	46.25
Nos. B3-B7,CB1 (6)	65.50	65.50
Nos. B3-B7 (5)	52.50	52.50
Nos. B4-B8 (5)	42.50	42.50
Nos. B5-B9,CB1 (6)	101.50	101.50
Nos. B2-B6 (5)	60.00	60.00
Nos. B5-B9,CB1 (6)	87.50	87.50
Nos. B4-B8 (5)	67.50	72.50
Nos. B4-B8,CB1 (6)	56.50	56.50
Nos. B3-B7 (5)	45.00	45.00
Nos. B2-B6 (5)	42.50	42.50
Nos. B1-B5 (5)	80.00	110.00
Set total (128) Stamps	1,562.	1,621.

Plane over Coastal Area CD85

All five denominations exist with colony name omitted.

1940

Dahomey	C1-C5
Fr. Guinea	C1-C5
Fr. Sudan	C1-C5
Ivory Coast	C1-C5
Mauritania	C1-C5
Niger	C1-C5
Senegal	C12-C16
Togo	C1-C5

Nos. C1-C5 (5)	4.00	4.00
Nos. C1-C5 (5)	4.00	4.00
Nos. C1-C5 (5)	4.00	4.00
Nos. C1-C5 (5)	3.80	3.80
Nos. C1-C5 (5)	3.50	3.50
Nos. C1-C5 (5)	3.50	3.50
Nos. C12-C16 (5)	3.50	3.50
Nos. C1-C5 (5)	3.15	3.15
Set total (40) Stamps	29.45	29.45

Defense of the Empire

Colonial Infantryman — CD86

1941

Cameroun	B13B
Dahomey	B13
Fr. Equatorial Africa	B8B
Fr. Guiana	B10
Fr. Guinea	B13
Fr. India	B13
Fr. Polynesia	B12
Fr. Sudan	B12
Guadeloupe	B10
Indo-China	B19B
Inini	B7
Ivory Coast	B13
Kwangchowan	B7
Madagascar	B9
Martinique	B9
Mauritania	B14
New Caledonia	B11
Niger	B12
Reunion	B11
St. Pierre & Miquelon	B8B
Senegal	B14
Somali Coast	B9
Togo	B10B
Wallis & Futuna Isls.	B7

No. B13B (1)	1.60
No. B13 (1)	1.20
No. B8B (1)	3.50
No. B10 (1)	1.40
No. B13 (1)	1.40
No. B13 (1)	1.25
No. B12 (1)	3.50
No. B12 (1)	1.40
No. B10 (1)	1.00
No. B19B (1)	1.60
No. B7 (1)	1.75
No. B13 (1)	1.25
No. B7 (1)	.85
No. B9 (1)	1.50
No. B9 (1)	1.40
No. B14 (1)	.95
No. B12 (1)	1.40
No. B11 (1)	1.60
No. B8B (1)	4.50
No. B14 (1)	1.25
No. B9 (1)	1.60
No. B10B (1)	1.10
No. B7 (1)	1.75
Set total (23) Stamps	38.75

Each of the CD86 stamps listed above is part of a set of three stamps. The designs of the other two stamps in the set vary from country to country. Only the values of the Common Design stamps are listed here.

Colonial Education Fund

CD86a

1942

Cameroun	CB3
Dahomey	CB4
Fr. Equatorial Africa	CB5
Fr. Guiana	CB4
Fr. Guinea	CB4
Fr. India	CB3
Fr. Polynesia	CB4
Fr. Sudan	CB4
Guadeloupe	CB3
Indo-China	CB5
Inini	CB3
Ivory Coast	CB4
Kwangchowan	CB4
Malagasy	CB5
Martinique	CB3
Mauritania	CB4
New Caledonia	CB4
Niger	CB4
Reunion	CB4
St. Pierre & Miquelon	CB3
Senegal	CB5
Somali Coast	CB3
Togo	CB3
Wallis & Futuna	CB3

No. CB3 (1)	1.10	
No. CB4 (1)	.80	5.50
No. CB5 (1)	.80	
No. CB4 (1)	1.10	
No. CB4 (1)	.40	5.50
No. CB3 (1)	.90	
No. CB4 (1)	2.00	
No. CB4 (1)	.40	5.50
No. CB3 (1)	1.10	
No. CB5 (1)	1.10	
No. CB3 (1)	1.25	
No. CB4 (1)	1.00	5.50
No. CB4 (1)	1.00	
No. CB5 (1)	.65	
No. CB3 (1)	1.00	
No. CB4 (1)	.80	
No. CB4 (1)	2.25	
No. CB4 (1)	.35	
No. CB4 (1)	.90	
No. CB3 (1)	7.00	
No. CB5 (1)	.80	6.50
No. CB3 (1)	.70	
No. CB3 (1)	.35	
No. CB3 (1)	2.00	
Set total (24) Stamps	29.75	28.50

Cross of Lorraine & Four-motor Plane CD87

1941-5

Cameroun	C1-C7
Fr. Equatorial Africa	C17-C23
Fr. Guiana	C9-C10
Fr. India	C1-C6
Fr. Polynesia	C3-C9
Fr. West Africa	C1-C3
Guadeloupe	C1-C2
Madagascar	C37-C43

Martinique.................................. C1-C2
New Caledonia C7-C13
Reunion C18-C24
St. Pierre & Miquelon............... C1-C7
Somali Coast........................ C1-C7

Nos. C1-C7 (7)	6.30	6.30
Nos. C17-C23 (7)	10.40	6.35
Nos. C9-C10 (2)	3.80	3.10
Nos. C1-C6 (6)	9.30	15.00
Nos. C3-C9 (7)	13.75	10.00
Nos. C1-C3 (3)	9.50	3.90
Nos. C1-C2 (2)	3.75	2.50
Nos. C37-C43 (7)	5.60	3.80
Nos. C1-C2 (2)	3.00	1.60
Nos. C7-C13 (7)	8.85	7.30
Nos. C18-C24 (7)	7.05	5.00
Nos. C1-C6 (6)	11.60	9.40
Nos. C1-C7 (7)	13.95	11.10
Set total (71) Stamps	106.85	85.35

Somali Coast stamps are inscribed "Djibouti".

Transport
Plane
CD88

Caravan
and Plane
CD89

1942

Dahomey................................. C6-C13
Fr. Guinea C6-C13
Fr. Sudan............................... C6-C13
Ivory Coast............................ C6-C13
Mauritania............................. C6-C13
Niger..................................... C6-C13
Senegal C17-C25
Togo...................................... C6-C13

Nos. C6-C13 (8)	7.15
Nos. C6-C13 (8)	5.75
Nos. C6-C13 (8)	8.00
Nos. C6-C13 (8)	11.15
Nos. C6-C13 (8)	9.75
Nos. C6-C13 (8)	6.20
Nos. C17-C25 (9)	9.45
Nos. C6-C13 (8)	6.75
Set total (65) Stamps	64.20

Red Cross

Marianne
CD90

The surtax was for the French Red Cross and national relief.

1944

Cameroun.................................. B28
Fr. Equatorial Africa B38
Fr. Guiana B12
Fr. India B14
Fr. Polynesia B13
Fr. West Africa B1
Guadeloupe B12
Madagascar B15
Martinique B11
New Caledonia B13
Reunion B15
St. Pierre & Miquelon.................... B13
Somali Coast............................ B13
Wallis & Futuna Isls. B9

No. B28 (1)	2.00	1.60
No. B38 (1)	1.60	1.20
No. B12 (1)	1.75	1.25
No. B14 (1)	1.50	1.25
No. B13 (1)	2.00	1.60
No. B1 (1)	6.50	4.75
No. B12 (1)	1.40	1.00
No. B15 (1)	.90	.90
No. B11 (1)	1.20	1.20
No. B13 (1)	1.50	1.50
No. B15 (1)	1.60	1.10
No. B13 (1)	2.60	2.60
No. B13 (1)	1.75	2.00
No. B9 (1)	3.00	3.00
Set total (14) Stamps	29.30	24.95

Eboue

CD91

Felix Eboue, first French colonial administrator to proclaim resistance to Germany after French surrender in World War II.

1945

Cameroun...............................296-297
Fr. Equatorial Africa 156-157
Fr. Guiana 171-172
Fr. India.............................210-211
Fr. Polynesia 150-151
Fr. West Africa 15-16
Guadeloupe...........................187-188
Madagascar...........................259-260
Martinique............................196-197
New Caledonia........................274-275
Reunion 238-239
St. Pierre & Miquelon................322-323
Somali Coast.........................238-239

Nos. 296-297 (2)	2.40	1.95
Nos. 156-157 (2)	2.55	2.00
Nos. 171-172 (2)	2.45	2.00
Nos. 210-211 (2)	2.20	1.95
Nos. 150-151 (2)	3.60	2.85
Nos. 15-16 (2)	2.40	2.40
Nos. 187-188 (2)	2.05	1.60
Nos. 259-260 (2)	2.00	1.45
Nos. 196-197 (2)	2.05	1.55
Nos. 274-275 (2)	3.40	3.00
Nos. 238-239 (2)	2.40	2.00
Nos. 322-323 (2)	4.40	3.45
Nos. 238-239 (2)	2.45	2.10
Set total (26) Stamps	34.35	28.30

Victory

Victory — CD92

European victory of the Allied Nations in World War II.

1946, May 8

Cameroun.................................. C8
Fr. Equatorial Africa C24
Fr. Guiana C11
Fr. India C7
Fr. Polynesia C10
Fr. West Africa C4
Guadeloupe C3
Indo-China.............................. C19
Madagascar C44
Martinique C3
New Caledonia C14
Reunion C25
St. Pierre & Miquelon.................... C8
Somali Coast............................ C8
Wallis & Futuna Isls. C1

No. C8 (1)	1.60	1.20
No. C24 (1)	1.60	1.25
No. C11 (1)	1.75	1.25
No. C7 (1)	1.00	4.00
No. C10 (1)	2.75	2.00
No. C4 (1)	1.60	1.20
No. C3 (1)	1.25	1.00
No. C19 (1)	1.00	.55
No. C44 (1)	1.00	.35
No. C3 (1)	1.30	1.00
No. C14 (1)	1.50	1.25
No. C25 (1)	1.10	.90
No. C8 (1)	2.10	2.10
No. C8 (1)	1.75	1.40
No. C1 (1)	2.25	1.90
Set total (15) Stamps	23.55	21.35

Chad to Rhine

Leclerc's Departure from
Chad — CD93

Battle at Cufra Oasis — CD94

Tanks in Action, Mareth — CD95

Normandy Invasion — CD96

Entering Paris — CD97

Liberation of Strasbourg — CD98

"Chad to the Rhine" march, 1942-44, by Gen. Jacques Leclerc's column, later French 2nd Armored Division.

1946, June 6

Cameroun................................ C9-C14
Fr. Equatorial Africa C25-C30
Fr. Guiana C12-C17
Fr. India C8-C13
Fr. Polynesia C11-C16
Fr. West Africa C5-C10
Guadeloupe.......................... C4-C9
Indo-China.......................... C20-C25
Madagascar......................... C45-C50
Martinique.......................... C4-C9
New Caledonia C15-C20
Reunion C26-C31
St. Pierre & Miquelon.............. C9-C14
Somali Coast....................... C9-C14
Wallis & Futuna Isls. C2-C7

Nos. C9-C14 (6)	12.05	9.70
Nos. C25-C30 (6)	14.70	10.80
Nos. C12-C17 (6)	12.65	10.35
Nos. C8-C13 (6)	12.80	15.00
Nos. C11-C16 (6)	17.55	13.40
Nos. C5-C10 (6)	16.05	11.95
Nos. C4-C9 (6)	12.00	9.60
Nos. C20-C25 (6)	6.40	6.40
Nos. C45-C50 (6)	10.30	8.40
Nos. C4-C9 (6)	8.85	7.30
Nos. C15-C20 (6)	13.40	11.90
Nos. C26-C31 (6)	10.25	6.55
Nos. C9-C14 (6)	17.30	14.35

Nos. C9-C14 (6)	18.10	12.65
Nos. C2-C7 (6)	13.75	10.45
Set total (90) Stamps	196.15	158.80

UPU

French Colonials, Globe and
Plane — CD99

Universal Postal Union, 75th anniv.

1949, July 4

Cameroun.................................. C29
Fr. Equatorial Africa C34
Fr. India C17
Fr. Polynesia C20
Fr. West Africa C15
Indo-China.............................. C26
Madagascar C55
New Caledonia C24
St. Pierre & Miquelon.................... C18
Somali Coast............................ C18
Togo..................................... C18
Wallis & Futuna Isls. C10

No. C29 (1)	8.00	4.75
No. C34 (1)	16.00	12.00
No. C17 (1)	11.50	8.75
No. C20 (1)	20.00	15.00
No. C15 (1)	12.00	8.75
No. C26 (1)	4.75	4.00
No. C55 (1)	4.00	2.75
No. C24 (1)	7.50	5.00
No. C18 (1)	20.00	12.00
No. C18 (1)	14.00	10.50
No. C18 (1)	8.50	7.00
No. C10 (1)	11.00	8.25
Set total (12) Stamps	137.25	98.75

Tropical Medicine

Doctor
Treating
Infant
CD100

The surtax was for charitable work.

1950

Cameroun.................................. B29
Fr. Equatorial Africa B39
Fr. India B15
Fr. Polynesia B14
Fr. West Africa B3
Madagascar B17
New Caledonia B14
St. Pierre & Miquelon.................... B14
Somali Coast............................ B14
Togo..................................... B11

No. B29 (1)	7.25	5.50
No. B39 (1)	7.25	5.50
No. B15 (1)	6.00	4.00
No. B14 (1)	10.50	8.00
No. B3 (1)	9.50	7.25
No. B17 (1)	5.50	5.50
No. B14 (1)	6.75	5.25
No. B14 (1)	16.00	15.00
No. B14 (1)	7.75	6.25
No. B11 (1)	5.00	3.50
Set total (10) Stamps	81.50	65.75

Military Medal

Medal, Early Marine
and Colonial
Soldier — CD101

Centenary of the creation of the French Military Medal.

1952

Cameroun...................................322
Comoro Isls. 39
Fr. Equatorial Africa 186

Fr. India 233
Fr. Polynesia 179
Fr. West Africa 57
Madagascar 286
New Caledonia 295
St. Pierre & Miquelon 345
Somali Coast 267
Togo 327
Wallis & Futuna Isls. 149

No. 322 (1)	7.25	3.25
No. 39 (1)	45.00	37.50
No. 186 (1)	8.00	5.50
No. 233 (1)	5.50	7.00
No. 179 (1)	13.50	10.00
No. 57 (1)	8.75	6.50
No. 286 (1)	3.75	2.50
No. 295 (1)	6.50	6.00
No. 345 (1)	16.00	15.00
No. 267 (1)	9.00	8.00
No. 327 (1)	5.50	4.75
No. 149 (1)	7.25	7.25
Set total (12) Stamps	136.00	113.25

Liberation

Allied Landing, Victory Sign and Cross
of Lorraine — CD102

Liberation of France, 10th anniv.

1954, June 6

Cameroun C32
Comoro Isls. C4
Fr. Equatorial Africa C38
Fr. India C18
Fr. Polynesia C22
Fr. West Africa C17
Madagascar C57
New Caledonia C25
St. Pierre & Miquelon C19
Somali Coast C19
Togo C19
Wallis & Futuna Isls. C11

No. C32 (1)	7.25	4.75
No. C4 (1)	32.50	19.00
No. C38 (1)	12.00	8.00
No. C18 (1)	11.00	8.00
No. C22 (1)	10.00	8.00
No. C17 (1)	12.00	5.50
No. C57 (1)	3.25	2.00
No. C25 (1)	7.50	5.00
No. C19 (1)	19.00	12.00
No. C19 (1)	10.50	8.50
No. C19 (1)	7.00	5.50
No. C11 (1)	11.00	8.25
Set total (12) Stamps	143.00	94.50

FIDES

Plowmen
CD103

Efforts of FIDES, the Economic and Social
Development Fund for Overseas Possessions
(Fonds d' Investissement pour le Developpe-
ment Economique et Social). Each stamp has
a different design.

1956

Cameroun 326-329
Comoro Isls. 43
Fr. Equatorial Africa 189-192
Fr. Polynesia 181
Fr. West Africa 65-72
Madagascar 292-295
New Caledonia 303
St. Pierre & Miquelon 268-269
Somali Coast 331

Nos. 326-329 (4)	6.90	3.20
No. 43 (1)	2.25	1.60
Nos. 189-192 (4)	3.20	1.65
No. 181 (1)	4.00	2.00
Nos. 65-72 (8)	16.00	6.35
Nos. 292-295 (4)	2.25	1.20
No. 303 (1)	1.90	1.10
No. 350 (1)	6.00	4.00

Nos. 268-269 (2)	5.35	3.15
No. 331 (1)	4.25	2.10
Set total (27) Stamps	52.10	26.35

Flower

CD104

Each stamp shows a different flower.

1958-9

Cameroun 333
Comoro Isls. 45
Fr. Equatorial Africa 200-201
Fr. Polynesia 192
Fr. So. & Antarctic Terr. 11
Fr. West Africa 79-83
Madagascar 301-302
New Caledonia 304-305
St. Pierre & Miquelon 357
Somali Coast 270
Togo 348-349
Wallis & Futuna Isls. 152

No. 333 (1)	1.60	.80
No. 45 (1)	5.25	4.25
Nos. 200-201 (2)	3.60	1.60
No. 192 (1)	6.50	4.00
No. 11 (1)	8.75	7.50
Nos. 79-83 (5)	10.45	5.60
Nos. 301-302 (2)	1.60	.60
Nos. 304-305 (2)	8.00	3.00
No. 357 (1)	4.50	2.25
No. 270 (1)	4.25	1.40
Nos. 348-349 (2)	1.10	.50
No. 152 (1)	3.25	3.25
Set total (20) Stamps	58.85	34.75

Human Rights

Sun, Dove
and U.N.
Emblem
CD105

10th anniversary of the signing of the Universal Declaration of Human Rights.

1958

Comoro Isls. 44
Fr. Equatorial Africa 202
Fr. Polynesia 191
Fr. West Africa 85
Madagascar 300
New Caledonia 306
St. Pierre & Miquelon 356
Somali Coast 274
Wallis & Futuna Isls. 153

No. 44 (1)	9.00	9.00
No. 202 (1)	2.40	1.25
No. 191 (1)	13.00	8.75
No. 85 (1)	2.40	2.00
No. 300 (1)	.80	.40
No. 306 (1)	2.00	1.50
No. 356 (1)	3.50	2.50
No. 274 (1)	3.50	2.10
No. 153 (1)	4.50	4.50
Set total (9) Stamps	41.10	32.00

C.C.T.A.

CD106

Commission for Technical Cooperation in
Africa south of the Sahara, 10th anniv.

1960

Cameroun 339
Cent. Africa 3
Chad 66
Congo, P.R. 90
Dahomey 138
Gabon 150
Ivory Coast 180
Madagascar 317

Mali 9
Mauritania 117
Niger 104
Upper Volta 89

No. 339 (1)	1.60	.75
No. 3 (1)	1.60	.75
No. 66 (1)	1.90	.50
No. 90 (1)	1.00	1.00
No. 138 (1)	.50	.25
No. 150 (1)	1.40	1.10
No. 180 (1)	1.10	.50
No. 317 (1)	.60	.30
No. 9 (1)	1.20	.50
No. 117 (1)	.75	.40
No. 104 (1)	.85	.45
No. 89 (1)	.65	.40
Set total (12) Stamps	13.15	6.90

Air Afrique, 1961

Modern and Ancient Africa, Map and
Planes — CD107

Founding of Air Afrique (African Airlines).

1961-62

Cameroun C37
Cent. Africa C5
Chad C7
Congo, P.R. C5
Dahomey C17
Gabon C5
Ivory Coast C18
Mauritania C17
Niger C22
Senegal C31
Upper Volta C4

No. C37 (1)	1.00	.50
No. C5 (1)	1.00	.65
No. C7 (1)	1.00	.25
No. C5 (1)	1.75	.90
No. C17 (1)	.80	.40
No. C5 (1)	11.00	6.00
No. C18 (1)	2.00	1.25
No. C17 (1)	2.50	1.25
No. C22 (1)	1.75	.90
No. C31 (1)	.80	.30
No. C4 (1)	3.50	1.75
Set total (11) Stamps	27.10	14.15

Anti-Malaria

CD108

World Health Organization drive to eradicate malaria.

1962, Apr. 7

Cameroun B36
Cent. Africa B1
Chad B1
Comoro Isls. B1
Congo, P.R. B3
Dahomey B15
Gabon B4
Ivory Coast B15
Madagascar B19
Mali B1
Mauritania B16
Niger B14
Senegal B16
Somali Coast B15
Upper Volta B1

No. B36 (1)	1.00	.45
No. B1 (1)	1.40	1.40
No. B1 (1)	1.25	.50
No. B1 (1)	3.50	3.50
No. B3 (1)	1.40	1.00
No. B15 (1)	.75	.75
No. B4 (1)	1.00	1.00
No. B15 (1)	1.25	1.25
No. B19 (1)	.75	.50
No. B1 (1)	1.25	.60
No. B16 (1)	.80	.80
No. B14 (1)	.75	.75

No. B16 (1)	1.10	.65
No. B15 (1)	7.00	7.00
No. B1 (1)	.75	.70
Set total (15) Stamps	23.95	20.85

Abidjan Games

CD109

Abidjan Games, Ivory Coast, Dec. 24-31,
1961. Each stamp shows a different sport.

1962

Cent. Africa 19-20, C6
Chad 83-84, C8
Congo, P.R. 103-104, C7
Gabon 163-164, C6
Niger 109-111
Upper Volta 103-105

Nos. 19-20,C6 (3)	4.15	2.85
Nos. 83-84,C8 (3)	6.30	1.55
Nos. 103-104,C7 (3)	3.85	1.80
Nos. 163-164,C6 (3)	5.00	3.00
Nos. 109-111 (3)	2.60	1.25
Nos. 103-105 (3)	2.80	1.75
Set total (18) Stamps	24.70	12.20

African and Malagasy Union

Flag of
Union
CD110

First anniversary of the Union.

1962, Sept. 8

Cameroun 373
Cent. Africa 21
Chad 85
Congo, P.R. 105
Dahomey 155
Gabon 165
Ivory Coast 198
Madagascar 332
Mauritania 170
Niger 112
Senegal 211
Upper Volta 106

No. 373 (1)	2.00	.75
No. 21 (1)	1.25	.75
No. 85 (1)	1.25	.25
No. 105 (1)	1.50	.50
No. 155 (1)	1.25	.90
No. 165 (1)	1.60	1.25
No. 198 (1)	2.10	.75
No. 332 (1)	.80	.80
No. 170 (1)	.75	.50
No. 112 (1)	.80	.50
No. 211 (1)	.80	.50
No. 106 (1)	1.10	.75
Set total (12) Stamps	15.20	8.20

Telstar

Telstar and Globe Showing Andover
and Pleumeur-Bodou — CD111

First television connection of the United
States and Europe through the Telstar satellite, July 11-12, 1962.

1962-63

Andorra, French 154
Comoro Isls. C7
Fr. Polynesia C29
Fr. So. & Antarctic Terr. C5
New Caledonia C33
St. Pierre & Miquelon C26
Somali Coast C31
Wallis & Futuna Isls. C17

No. 154 (1)	2.00	1.60
No. C7 (1)	4.50	2.75
No. C29 (1)	11.50	8.00

No. C5 (1)	29.00	21.00
No. C33 (1)	25.00	18.50
No. C26 (1)	7.25	4.50
No. C31 (1)	1.00	1.00
No. C17 (1)	3.75	3.75
Set total (8) Stamps	84.00	61.10

Freedom From Hunger

World Map and Wheat Emblem CD112

U.N. Food and Agriculture Organization's "Freedom from Hunger" campaign.

1963, Mar. 21

Cameroun	B37-B38
Cent. Africa	B2
Chad	B2
Congo, P.R.	B4
Dahomey	B16
Gabon	B5
Ivory Coast	B16
Madagascar	B21
Mauritania	B17
Niger	B15
Senegal	B17
Upper Volta	B2

Nos. B37-B38 (2)	2.25	.75
No. B2 (1)	1.25	1.25
No. B2 (1)	2.00	.50
No. B4 (1)	1.40	1.00
No. B16 (1)	.80	.80
No. B5 (1)	1.00	1.00
No. B16 (1)	1.50	1.50
No. B21 (1)	.60	.45
No. B17 (1)	.80	.80
No. B15 (1)	.75	.75
No. B17 (1)	.80	.50
No. B2 (1)	.75	.70
Set total (13) Stamps	13.90	10.00

Red Cross Centenary

CD113

Centenary of the International Red Cross.

1963, Sept. 2

Comoro Isls.	55
Fr. Polynesia	205
New Caledonia	328
St. Pierre & Miquelon	367
Somali Coast	297
Wallis & Futuna Isls.	165

No. 55 (1)	7.50	6.00
No. 205 (1)	15.00	12.00
No. 328 (1)	8.00	6.75
No. 367 (1)	12.00	5.50
No. 297 (1)	6.25	6.25
No. 165 (1)	4.00	4.00
Set total (6) Stamps	52.75	40.50

African Postal Union, 1963

UAMPT Emblem, Radio Masts, Plane and Mail CD114

Establishment of the African and Malagasy Posts and Telecommunications Union.

1963, Sept. 8

Cameroun	C47
Cent. Africa	C10
Chad	C9
Congo, P.R.	C13

Dahomey	C19
Gabon	C13
Ivory Coast	C25
Madagascar	C75
Mauritania	C22
Niger	C27
Rwanda	36
Senegal	C32
Upper Volta	C9

No. C47 (1)	2.25	1.00
No. C10 (1)	1.90	.90
No. C9 (1)	2.40	.60
No. C13 (1)	1.40	.75
No. C19 (1)	.75	.25
No. C13 (1)	1.90	.80
No. C25 (1)	2.50	1.50
No. C75 (1)	1.25	.80
No. C22 (1)	1.50	.60
No. C27 (1)	1.25	.60
No. 36 (1)	1.00	.75
No. C32 (1)	1.75	.50
No. C9 (1)	1.50	.75
Set total (13) Stamps	21.35	9.80

Air Afrique, 1963

Symbols of Flight — CD115

First anniversary of Air Afrique and inauguration of DC-8 service.

1963, Nov. 19

Cameroun	C48
Chad	C10
Congo, P.R.	C14
Gabon	C18
Ivory Coast	C26
Mauritania	C26
Niger	C35
Senegal	C33

No. C48 (1)	1.25	.40
No. C10 (1)	2.40	.60
No. C14 (1)	1.60	.60
No. C18 (1)	1.40	.65
No. C26 (1)	1.00	.50
No. C26 (1)	.70	.25
No. C35 (1)	1.00	.55
No. C33 (1)	2.00	.65
Set total (8) Stamps	11.35	4.20

Europafrica

Europe and Africa Linked — CD116

Signing of an economic agreement between the European Economic Community and the African and Malagasy Union, Yaounde, Cameroun, July 20, 1963.

1963-64

Cameroun	402
Cent. Africa	C12
Chad	C11
Congo, P.R.	C16
Gabon	C19
Ivory Coast	217
Niger	C43
Upper Volta	C11

No. 402 (1)	2.25	.60
No. C12 (1)	2.50	1.75
No. C11 (1)	2.00	.50
No. C16 (1)	1.60	1.00
No. C19 (1)	1.40	.75
No. 217 (1)	1.10	.35
No. C43 (1)	.85	.50
No. C11 (1)	1.50	.80
Set total (8) Stamps	13.20	6.25

Human Rights

Scales of Justice and Globe CD117

15th anniversary of the Universal Declaration of Human Rights.

1963, Dec. 10

Comoro Isls.	56
Fr. Polynesia	206
New Caledonia	329
St. Pierre & Miquelon	368
Somali Coast	300
Wallis & Futuna Isls.	166

No. 56 (1)	7.50	6.00
No. 205 (1)	15.00	12.00
No. 329 (1)	7.00	6.00
No. 368 (1)	7.00	3.50
No. 300 (1)	8.50	8.50
No. 166 (1)	7.00	7.00
Set total (6) Stamps	52.00	43.00

PHILATEC

Stamp Album, Champs Elysees Palace and Horses of Marly CD118

Intl. Philatelic and Postal Techniques Exhibition, Paris, June 5-21, 1964.

1963-64

Comoro Isls.	60
France	1078
Fr. Polynesia	207
New Caledonia	341
St. Pierre & Miquelon	369
Somali Coast	301
Wallis & Futuna Isls.	167

No. 60 (1)	4.00	3.50
No. 1078 (1)	.25	.25
No. 206 (1)	15.00	10.00
No. 341 (1)	6.50	6.50
No. 369 (1)	11.00	8.00
No. 301 (1)	7.75	7.75
No. 167 (1)	3.00	3.00
Set total (7) Stamps	47.50	39.00

Cooperation

CD119

Cooperation between France and the French-speaking countries of Africa and Madagascar.

1964

Cameroun	409-410
Cent. Africa	39
Chad	103
Congo, P.R.	121
Dahomey	193
France	1111
Gabon	175
Ivory Coast	221
Madagascar	360
Mauritania	181
Niger	143
Senegal	236
Togo	495

Nos. 409-410 (2)	2.50	.50
No. 39 (1)	.90	.50
No. 103 (1)	1.00	.25
No. 121 (1)	.80	.35
No. 193 (1)	.80	.35
No. 1111 (1)	.25	.25
No. 175 (1)	.90	.60
No. 221 (1)	1.10	.35

No. 360 (1)	.60	.25
No. 181 (1)	.60	.35
No. 143 (1)	.80	.40
No. 236 (1)	1.60	.85
No. 495 (1)	.70	.25
Set total (14) Stamps	12.55	5.25

ITU

Telegraph, Syncom Satellite and ITU Emblem CD120

Intl. Telecommunication Union, Cent.

1965, May 17

Comoro Isls.	C14
Fr. Polynesia	C33
Fr. So. & Antarctic Terr.	C8
New Caledonia	C40
New Hebrides	124-125
St. Pierre & Miquelon	C29
Somali Coast	C36
Wallis & Futuna Isls.	C20

No. C14 (1)	18.00	9.00
No. C33 (1)	80.00	52.50
No. C8 (1)	200.00	160.00
No. C40 (1)	10.00	8.00
Nos. 124-125 (2)	40.50	34.00
No. C29 (1)	24.00	11.50
No. C36 (1)	15.00	9.00
No. C20 (1)	16.00	16.00
Set total (9) Stamps	403.50	300.00

French Satellite A-1

Diamant Rocket and Launching Installation — CD121

Launching of France's first satellite, Nov. 26, 1965.

1965-66

Comoro Isls.	C16a
France	1138a
Reunion	359a
Fr. Polynesia	C41a
Fr. So. & Antarctic Terr.	C10a
New Caledonia	C45a
St. Pierre & Miquelon	C31a
Somali Coast	C40a
Wallis & Futuna Isls.	C23a

No. C16a (1)	9.00	9.00
No. 1138a (1)	.65	.65
No. 359a (1)	3.50	3.00
No. C41a (1)	14.00	14.00
No. C10a (1)	29.00	24.00
No. C45a (1)	7.00	7.00
No. C31a (1)	14.50	14.50
No. C40a (1)	7.00	7.00
No. C23a (1)	8.50	8.50
Set total (9) Stamps	93.15	87.65

French Satellite D-1

D-1 Satellite in Orbit — CD122

Launching of the D-1 satellite at Hammaguir, Algeria, Feb. 17, 1966.

1966

Comoro Isls.	C17
France	1148

Fr. Polynesia.................................C42
Fr. So. & Antarctic Terr. C11
New Caledonia.............................C46
St. Pierre & Miquelon....................C32
Somali Coast................................C49
Wallis & Futuna Isls. C24

No. C17 (1)	4.00	4.00
No. 1148 (1)	.25	.25
No. C42 (1)	7.00	4.75
No. C11 (1)	57.50	40.00
No. C46 (1)	2.25	2.00
No. C32 (1)	9.00	6.00
No. C49 (1)	4.25	2.75
No. C24 (1)	3.50	3.50
Set total (8) Stamps	87.75	63.25

Air Afrique, 1966

Planes and Air Afrique
Emblem — CD123

Introduction of DC-8F planes by Air Afrique.

1966

Cameroun.......................................C79
Cent. Africa C35
Chad C26
Congo, P.R....................................C42
Dahomey C42
Gabon...C47
Ivory Coast C32
Mauritania C57
Niger...C63
Senegal C47
Togo C54
Upper Volta..................................C31

No. C79 (1)	.80	.25
No. C35 (1)	1.00	.50
No. C26 (1)	1.00	.25
No. C42 (1)	1.00	.25
No. C42 (1)	.75	.25
No. C47 (1)	.90	.35
No. C32 (1)	1.00	.60
No. C57 (1)	.80	.30
No. C63 (1)	.70	.35
No. C47 (1)	.80	.30
No. C54 (1)	.80	.25
No. C31 (1)	.75	.50
Set total (12) Stamps	10.30	4.15

African Postal Union, 1967

Telecommunications Symbols and Map
of Africa — CD124

Fifth anniversary of the establishment of the
African and Malagasy Union of Posts and
Telecommunications, UAMPT.

1967

Cameroun.......................................C90
Cent. Africa C46
Chad C37
Congo, P.R....................................C57
Dahomey C61
Gabon...C58
Ivory Coast C34
Madagascar..................................C85
Mauritania C65
Niger...C75
Rwanda C1-C3
Senegal C60
Togo C81
Upper Volta..................................C50

No. C90 (1)	2.40	.65
No. C46 (1)	2.25	.85
No. C37 (1)	2.00	.60
No. C57 (1)	1.60	.60
No. C61 (1)	1.75	.95
No. C58 (1)	2.25	.95
No. C34 (1)	3.50	1.50
No. C85 (1)	1.25	.60
No. C65 (1)	1.25	.60
No. C75 (1)	1.40	.60

Nos. C1-C3 (3)	2.30	1.25
No. C60 (1)	1.75	.50
No. C81 (1)	1.90	.30
No. C50 (1)	1.80	.70
Set total (10) Stamps	27.40	10.65

Monetary Union

Gold Token of the
Ashantis, 17-18th
Centuries — CD125

West African Monetary Union, 5th anniv.

1967, Nov. 4

Dahomey 244
Ivory Coast 259
Mauritania 238
Niger...204
Senegal 294
Togo 623
Upper Volta..................................181

No. 244 (1)	.65	.65
No. 259 (1)	.85	.40
No. 238 (1)	.45	.25
No. 204 (1)	.55	.25
No. 294 (1)	.60	.25
No. 623 (1)	.60	.25
No. 181 (1)	.65	.35
Set total (7) Stamps	4.35	2.40

WHO Anniversary

Sun,
Flowers
and WHO
Emblem
CD126

World Health Organization, 20th anniv.

1968, May 4

Afars & Issas...............................317
Comoro Isls. 73
Fr. Polynesia...............................241-242
Fr. So. & Antarctic Terr. 31
New Caledonia.............................367
St. Pierre & Miquelon....................377
Wallis & Futuna Isls. 169

No. 317 (1)	3.00	3.00
No. 73 (1)	2.40	1.75
Nos. 241-242 (2)	22.00	12.75
No. 31 (1)	62.50	47.50
No. 367 (1)	4.00	2.25
No. 377 (1)	12.00	9.00
No. 169 (1)	5.75	5.75
Set total (8) Stamps	111.65	82.00

Human Rights Year

Human Rights
Flame — CD127

1968, Aug. 10

Afars & Issas...............................322-323
Comoro Isls. 76
Fr. Polynesia...............................243-244
Fr. So. & Antarctic Terr. 32
New Caledonia.............................369
St. Pierre & Miquelon....................382
Wallis & Futuna Isls. 170

Nos. 322-323 (2)	6.75	4.00
No. 76 (1)	3.25	3.25
Nos. 243-244 (2)	24.00	14.00
No. 32 (1)	55.00	47.50
No. 369 (1)	2.75	1.50
No. 382 (1)	8.00	5.50
No. 170 (1)	3.25	3.25
Set total (9) Stamps	103.00	79.00

2nd PHILEXAFRIQUE

CD128

Opening of PHILEXAFRIQUE, Abidjan, Feb.
14. Each stamp shows a local scene and
stamp.

1969, Feb. 14

Cameroun.......................................C118
Cent. Africa C65
Chad C48
Congo, P.R....................................C77
Dahomey C94
Gabon...C82
Ivory Coast C38-C40
Madagascar..................................C92
Mali C65
Mauritania C80
Niger...C104
Senegal C68
Togo C104
Upper Volta..................................C62

No. C118 (1)	3.25	1.25
No. C65 (1)	1.75	1.75
No. C48 (1)	2.40	1.00
No. C77 (1)	2.00	1.75
No. C94 (1)	2.25	2.25
No. C82 (1)	2.25	2.25
Nos. C38-C40 (3)	14.50	14.50
No. C92 (1)	1.70	.05
No. C65 (1)	1.75	1.00
No. C80 (1)	1.90	.75
No. C104 (1)	3.00	1.90
No. C68 (1)	2.00	1.40
No. C104 (1)	2.25	.45
No. C62 (1)	4.00	3.25
Set total (16) Stamps	45.05	34.35

Concorde

Concorde in
Flight
CD129

First flight of the prototype Concorde supersonic plane at Toulouse, Mar. 1, 1969.

1969

Afars & Issas...............................C56
Comoro Isls. C29
France..C42
Fr. Polynesia...............................C50
Fr. So. & Antarctic Terr. C18
New Caledonia.............................C63
St. Pierre & Miquelon....................C40
Wallis & Futuna Isls. C30

No. C56 (1)	26.00	16.00
No. C29 (1)	18.00	12.00
No. C42 (1)	.75	.35
No. C50 (1)	55.00	35.00
No. C18 (1)	55.00	37.50
No. C63 (1)	27.50	20.00
No. C40 (1)	32.50	11.00
No. C30 (1)	15.00	10.00
Set total (8) Stamps	229.75	141.85

Development Bank

Bank
Emblem — CD130

African Development Bank, fifth anniv.

1969

Cameroun.......................................499
Chad 217
Congo, P.R....................................181-182

Ivory Coast 281
Mali 127-128
Mauritania 267
Niger...220
Senegal 317-318
Upper Volta..................................201

No. 499 (1)	.80	.25
No. 217 (1)	.70	.25
Nos. 181-182 (2)	.80	.50
No. 281 (1)	.70	.40
Nos. 127-128 (2)	1.00	.50
No. 267 (1)	.60	.25
No. 220 (1)	.70	.30
Nos. 317-318 (2)	1.55	.50
No. 201 (1)	.65	.30
Set total (12) Stamps	7.50	3.25

ILO

ILO Headquarters, Geneva, and
Emblem — CD131

Intl. Labor Organization, 50th anniv.

1969-70

Afars & Issas...............................337
Comoro Isls. 83
Fr. Polynesia...............................251-252
Fr. So. & Antarctic Terr. 35
New Caledonia.............................379
St. Pierre & Miquelon....................396
Wallis & Futuna Isls. 172

No. 337 (1)	2.75	2.00
No. 83 (1)	1.25	.75
Nos. 251-252 (2)	24.00	12.50
No. 35 (1)	15.00	10.00
No. 379 (1)	2.25	1.10
No. 396 (1)	10.00	5.50
No. 172 (1)	2.75	2.75
Set total (8) Stamps	58.00	34.60

ASECNA

Map of
Africa,
Plane and
Airport
CD132

10th anniversary of the Agency for the
Security of Aerial Navigation in Africa and
Madagascar (ASECNA, Agence pour la
Securite de la Navigation Aerienne en Afrique
et a Madagascar).

1969-70

Cameroun.......................................500
Cent. Africa 119
Chad 222
Congo, P.R....................................197
Dahomey 269
Gabon...260
Ivory Coast 287
Mali 130
Niger...221
Senegal 321
Upper Volta..................................204

No. 500 (1)	2.00	.60
No. 119 (1)	2.00	.80
No. 222 (1)	1.00	.25
No. 197 (1)	2.00	.40
No. 269 (1)	.90	.55
No. 260 (1)	1.75	.75
No. 287 (1)	.90	.40
No. 130 (1)	.90	.40
No. 221 (1)	1.40	.70
No. 321 (1)	1.60	.50
No. 204 (1)	1.75	1.00
Set total (11) Stamps	16.20	6.35

U.P.U. Headquarters

CD133

New Universal Postal Union headquarters,
Bern, Switzerland.

1970

Afars & Issas	342
Algeria	443
Cameroun	503-504
Cent. Africa	125
Chad	225
Comoro Isls.	84
Congo, P.R.	216
Fr. Polynesia	261-262
Fr. So. & Antarctic Terr.	36
Gabon	258
Ivory Coast	295
Madagascar	444
Mali	134-135
Mauritania	283
New Caledonia	382
Niger	231-232
St. Pierre & Miquelon	397-398
Senegal	328-329
Tunisia	535
Wallis & Futuna Isls.	173

No. 342 (1)	2.50	1.40
No. 443 (1)	1.10	.40
Nos. 503-504 (2)	2.60	.55
No. 125 (1)	1.75	.70
No. 225 (1)	1.00	.25
No. 84 (1)	5.50	2.00
No. 216 (1)	.80	.25
Nos. 261-262 (2)	20.00	10.00
No. 36 (1)	40.00	27.50
No. 258 (1)	.90	.55
No. 295 (1)	1.10	.50
No. 444 (1)	.55	.25
Nos. 134-135 (2)	1.05	.50
No. 283 (1)	.60	.30
No. 382 (1)	3.00	1.50
Nos. 231-232 (2)	1.50	.60
Nos. 397-398 (2)	34.00	16.25
Nos. 328-329 (2)	1.55	.55
No. 535 (1)	.60	.25
No. 173 (1)	3.25	3.25
Set total (26) Stamps	123.35	67.55

De Gaulle

CD134

First anniversay of the death of Charles de Gaulle, (1890-1970), President of France.

1971-72

Afars & Issas	356-357
Comoro Isls.	104-105
France	1325a
Fr. Polynesia	270-271
Fr. So. & Antarctic Terr.	52-53
New Caledonia	393-394
Reunion	380a
St. Pierre & Miquelon	417-418
Wallis & Futuna Isls.	177-178

Nos. 356-357 (2)	12.50	7.50
Nos. 104-105 (2)	9.00	5.75
No. 1325a (1)	3.00	2.50
Nos. 270-271 (2)	51.50	29.50
Nos. 52-53 (2)	40.00	29.50
Nos. 393-394 (2)	23.00	11.75
No. 380a (1)	9.25	8.00
Nos. 417-418 (2)	56.50	31.00
Nos. 177-178 (2)	20.00	16.25
Set total (16) Stamps	224.75	141.75

African Postal Union, 1971

UAMPT Building, Brazzaville, Congo — CD135

10th anniversary of the establishment of the African and Malagasy Posts and Telecommunications Union, UAMPT. Each stamp has a different native design.

1971, Nov. 13

Cameroun	C177
Cent. Africa	C89
Chad	C94

Congo, P.R.	C136
Dahomey	C146
Gabon	C120
Ivory Coast	C47
Mauritania	C113
Niger	C164
Rwanda	C8
Senegal	C105
Togo	C166
Upper Volta	C97

No. C177 (1)	2.00	.50
No. C89 (1)	2.25	.85
No. C94 (1)	1.50	.50
No. C136 (1)	1.60	.75
No. C146 (1)	1.75	.80
No. C120 (1)	1.75	.70
No. C47 (1)	2.00	1.00
No. C113 (1)	1.20	.65
No. C164 (1)	1.25	.60
No. C8 (1)	2.75	2.50
No. C105 (1)	1.60	.50
No. C166 (1)	1.25	.40
No. C97 (1)	1.50	.70
Set total (13) Stamps	22.40	10.45

West African Monetary Union

African Couple, City, Village and Commemorative Coin — CD136

West African Monetary Union, 10th anniv.

1972, Nov. 2

Dahomey	300
Ivory Coast	331
Mauritania	299
Niger	258
Senegal	374
Togo	825
Upper Volta	280

No. 300 (1)	.65	.25
No. 331 (1)	1.00	.50
No. 299 (1)	.75	.25
No. 258 (1)	.65	.30
No. 374 (1)	.50	.30
No. 825 (1)	.60	.25
No. 280 (1)	.60	.25
Set total (7) Stamps	4.75	2.10

African Postal Union, 1973

Telecommunications Symbols and Map of Africa — CD137

11th anniversary of the African and Malagasy Posts and Telecommunications Union (UAMPT).

1973, Sept. 12

Cameroun	574
Cent. Africa	194
Chad	294
Congo, P.R.	289
Dahomey	311
Gabon	320
Ivory Coast	361
Madagascar	500
Mauritania	304
Niger	287
Rwanda	540
Senegal	393
Togo	849
Upper Volta	297

No. 574 (1)	1.75	.40
No. 194 (1)	1.25	.75
No. 294 (1)	1.75	.40
No. 289 (1)	1.60	.50
No. 311 (1)	1.25	.55
No. 320 (1)	1.40	.75
No. 361 (1)	2.50	1.00
No. 500 (1)	1.10	.35
No. 304 (1)	1.10	.40
No. 287 (1)	.90	.60
No. 540 (1)	4.00	2.00
No. 393 (1)	1.60	.50

No. 849 (1)	1.00	.35
No. 297 (1)	1.25	.70
Set total (14) Stamps	22.45	9.25

Philexafrique II — Essen

CD138

CD139

Designs: Indigenous fauna, local and German stamps. Types CD138-CD139 printed horizontally and vertically se-tenant in sheets of 10 (2x5). Label between horizontal pairs alternately commemoratives Philexafrique II, Libreville, Gabon, June 1978, and 2nd International Stamp Fair, Essen, Germany, Nov. 1-5.

1978-1979

Benin	C286a
Central Africa	C201a
Chad	C239a
Congo Republic	C246a
Djibouti	C122a
Gabon	C216a
Ivory Coast	C65a
Mali	C357a
Mauritania	C186a
Niger	C292a
Rwanda	C13a
Senegal	C147a
Togo	C364a

No. C286a (1)	9.00	8.50
No. C201a (1)	7.50	7.50
No. C239a (1)	8.00	4.00
No. C246a (1)	7.00	7.00
No. C122a (1)	8.50	8.50
No. C216a (1)	6.50	4.00
No. C65a (1)	9.00	9.00
No. C357a (1)	5.00	3.00
No. C186a (1)	4.50	4.00
No. C292a (1)	6.00	6.00
No. C13a (1)	4.00	4.00
No. C147a (1)	10.00	4.00
No. C364a (1)	3.00	1.50
Set total (13) Stamps	88.00	71.00

BRITISH COMMONWEALTH OF NATIONS

The listings follow established trade practices when these issues are offered as units by dealers. The Peace issue, for example, includes only one stamp from the Indian state of Hyderabad. The U.P.U. issue includes the Egypt set. Pairs are included for those varieties issued with bilingual designs se-tenant.

Silver Jubilee

Windsor Castle and King George V CD301

Reign of King George V, 25th anniv.

1935

Antigua	77-80
Ascension	33-36
Bahamas	92-95
Barbados	186-189
Basutoland	11-14

Bechuanaland Protectorate	117-120
Bermuda	100-103
British Guiana	223-226
British Honduras	108-111
Cayman Islands	81-84
Ceylon	260-263
Cyprus	136-139
Dominica	90-93
Falkland Islands	77-80
Fiji	110-113
Gambia	125-128
Gibraltar	100-103
Gilbert & Ellice Islands	33-36
Gold Coast	108-111
Grenada	124-127
Hong Kong	147-150
Jamaica	109-112
Kenya, Uganda, Tanzania	42-45
Leeward Islands	96-99
Malta	184-187
Mauritius	204-207
Montserrat	85-88
Newfoundland	226-229
Nigeria	34-37
Northern Rhodesia	18-21
Nyasaland Protectorate	47-50
St. Helena	111-114
St. Kitts-Nevis	72-75
St. Lucia	91-94
St. Vincent	134-137
Seychelles	118-121
Sierra Leone	166-169
Solomon Islands	60-63
Somaliland Protectorate	77-80
Straits Settlements	213-216
Swaziland	20-23
Trinidad & Tobago	43-46
Turks & Caicos Islands	71-74
Virgin Islands	69-72

The following have different designs but are included in the omnibus set:

Great Britain	226-229
Offices in Morocco (Sp. Curr.)	67-70
Offices in Morocco (Br. Curr.)	226-229
Offices in Morocco (Fr. Curr.)	422-425
Offices in Morocco (Tangier)	508-510
Australia	152-154
Canada	211-216
Cook Islands	98-100
India	142-148
Nauru	31-34
New Guinea	46-47
New Zealand	199-201
Niue	67-69
Papua	114-117
Samoa	163-165
South Africa	68-71
Southern Rhodesia	33-36
South-West Africa	121-124

Nos. 77-80 (4)	20.25	23.25
Nos. 33-36 (4)	58.50	127.50
Nos. 92-95 (4)	25.00	46.00
Nos. 186-189 (4)	30.00	50.30
Nos. 11-14 (4)	11.60	21.25
Nos. 117-120 (4)	15.75	36.00
Nos. 100-103 (4)	16.80	58.50
Nos. 223-226 (4)	18.35	35.50
Nos. 108-111 (4)	15.25	16.35
Nos. 81-84 (4)	21.60	24.50
Nos. 260-263 (4)	10.40	21.60
Nos. 136-139 (4)	39.75	34.40
Nos. 90-93 (4)	18.85	19.85
Nos. 77-80 (4)	55.00	14.75
Nos. 110-113 (4)	20.25	34.00
Nos. 125-128 (4)	12.20	25.25
Nos. 100-103 (4)	28.75	42.75
Nos. 33-36 (4)	36.80	67.00
Nos. 108-111 (4)	25.75	78.10
Nos. 124-127 (4)	16.70	40.60
Nos. 147-150 (4)	59.00	18.75
Nos. 109-112 (4)	17.00	39.00
Nos. 42-45 (4)	8.75	11.00
Nos. 96-99 (4)	35.75	49.60
Nos. 184-187 (4)	22.00	33.70
Nos. 204-207 (4)	47.60	58.25
Nos. 85-88 (4)	10.25	30.25
Nos. 226-229 (4)	17.50	12.05
Nos. 34-37 (4)	17.50	70.00
Nos. 18-21 (4)	17.00	15.00
Nos. 47-50 (4)	39.75	80.25
Nos. 111-114 (4)	31.15	33.25
Nos. 72-75 (4)	10.80	18.65
Nos. 91-94 (4)	16.00	20.80
Nos. 134-137 (4)	9.45	21.25
Nos. 118-121 (4)	15.75	40.00
Nos. 166-169 (4)	23.60	50.35
Nos. 60-63 (4)	29.00	38.00
Nos. 77-80 (4)	17.00	48.25
Nos. 213-216 (4)	15.00	25.10
Nos. 20-23 (4)	6.80	18.25
Nos. 43-46 (4)	14.05	27.75
Nos. 71-74 (4)	8.40	14.50
Nos. 69-72 (4)	25.00	55.25
Nos. 226-229 (4)	5.15	4.40

Nos. 67-70 (4)	14.35	26.10
Nos. 226-229 (4)	8.20	28.90
Nos. 422-425 (4)	3.90	2.00
Nos. 508-510 (3)	18.80	23.85
Nos. 152-154 (3)	49.50	45.35
Nos. 211-216 (6)	23.85	10.35
Nos. 98-100 (3)	9.65	12.00
Nos. 142-148 (7)	28.85	14.00
Nos. 31-34 (4)	9.90	9.90
Nos. 46-47 (2)	4.35	1.70
Nos. 199-201 (3)	23.00	28.50
Nos. 67-69 (3)	11.80	26.50
Nos. 114-117 (4)	9.20	17.50
Nos. 163-165 (3)	4.40	6.50
Nos. 68-71 (4)	57.50	153.00
Nos. 33-36 (4)	27.75	45.25
Nos. 121-124 (4)	13.00	36.10
Set total (245) Stamps	1,335.	2,142.

Coronation

Queen Elizabeth and King George VI
CD302

1937

Aden	13-15
Antigua	81-83
Ascension	37-39
Bahamas	97-99
Barbados	190-192
Basutoland	15-17
Bechuanaland Protectorate	121-123
Bermuda	115-117
British Guiana	227-229
British Honduras	112-114
Cayman Islands	97-99
Ceylon	275-277
Cyprus	140-142
Dominica	94-96
Falkland Islands	81-83
Fiji	114-116
Gambia	129-131
Gibraltar	104-106
Gilbert & Ellice Islands	37-39
Gold Coast	112-114
Grenada	128-130
Hong Kong	151-153
Jamaica	113-115
Kenya, Uganda, Tanzania	60-62
Leeward Islands	100-102
Malta	188-190
Mauritius	208-210
Montserrat	89-91
Newfoundland	230-232
Nigeria	50-52
Northern Rhodesia	22-24
Nyasaland Protectorate	51-53
St. Helena	115-117
St. Kitts-Nevis	76-78
St. Lucia	107-109
St. Vincent	138-140
Seychelles	122-124
Sierra Leone	170-172
Solomon Islands	64-66
Somaliland Protectorate	81-83
Straits Settlements	235-237
Swaziland	24-26
Trinidad & Tobago	47-49
Turks & Caicos Islands	75-77
Virgin Islands	73-75

The following have different designs but are included in the omnibus set:

Great Britain	234
Offices in Morocco (Sp. Curr.)	82
Offices in Morocco (Fr. Curr.)	439
Offices in Morocco (Tangier)	514
Canada	237
Cook Islands	109-111
Nauru	35-38
Newfoundland	233-243
New Guinea	48-51
New Zealand	223-225
Niue	70-72
Papua	118-121
South Africa	74-78
Southern Rhodesia	38-41
South-West Africa	125-132

Nos. 13-15 (3)	2.70	5.65
Nos. 81-83 (3)	1.85	8.00
Nos. 37-39 (3)	2.75	2.75
Nos. 97-99 (3)	1.05	3.05
Nos. 190-192 (3)	1.10	1.95
Nos. 15-17 (3)	1.15	3.00
Nos. 121-123 (3)	.95	3.35
Nos. 115-117 (3)	1.25	5.00
Nos. 227-229 (3)	1.45	3.05
Nos. 112-114 (3)	1.20	2.40
Nos. 97-99 (3)	1.10	2.70
Nos. 275-277 (3)	8.25	10.35

Nos. 140-142 (3)	3.75	6.50
Nos. 94-96 (3)	.85	2.40
Nos. 81-83 (3)	2.90	2.30
Nos. 114-116 (3)	1.35	5.75
Nos. 129-131 (3)	.95	3.95
Nos. 104-106 (3)	2.25	6.45
Nos. 37-39 (3)	.85	2.15
Nos. 112-114 (3)	3.10	10.00
Nos. 128-130 (3)	1.00	.85
Nos. 151-153 (3)	23.00	12.50
Nos. 113-115 (3)	1.25	1.25
Nos. 60-62 (3)	1.00	2.35
Nos. 100-102 (3)	1.55	4.00
Nos. 188-190 (3)	1.25	1.60
Nos. 208-210 (3)	2.05	3.75
Nos. 89-91 (3)	1.00	3.35
Nos. 230-232 (3)	7.00	2.80
Nos. 50-52 (3)	3.25	8.50
Nos. 22-24 (3)	.95	2.25
Nos. 51-53 (3)	1.05	1.30
Nos. 115-117 (3)	1.45	2.05
Nos. 76-78 (3)	.95	2.15
Nos. 107-109 (3)	1.05	2.05
Nos. 138-140 (3)	.80	4.75
Nos. 122-124 (3)	1.20	1.90
Nos. 170-172 (3)	1.95	5.65
Nos. 64-66 (3)	.90	2.00
Nos. 81-83 (3)	1.10	3.50
Nos. 235-237 (3)	3.25	1.60
Nos. 24-26 (3)	.75	2.70
Nos. 47-49 (3)	1.00	1.00
Nos. 75-77 (3)	1.30	1.15
Nos. 73-75 (3)	2.20	6.90

No. 234 (1)	.25	.25
No. 82 (1)	.80	.80
No. 439 (1)	.35	.25
No. 514 (1)	.55	.55
No. 237 (1)	.35	.25
Nos. 109-111 (3)	.85	.80
Nos. 35-38 (4)	1.10	5.50
Nos. 233-243 (11)	41.90	30.40
Nos. 48-51 (4)	1.40	7.90
Nos. 223-225 (3)	1.75	2.25
Nos. 70-72 (3)	.80	2.05
Nos. 118-121 (4)	1.60	5.25
Nos. 74-78 (5)	7.60	9.35
Nos. 38-41 (4)	3.55	15.50
Nos. 125-132 (8)	5.00	8.40
Set total (189) Stamps	170.90	262.15

Peace

King George VI and Parliament Buildings, London
CD303

Return to peace at the close of World War II.

1945-46

Aden	28-29
Antigua	96-97
Ascension	50-51
Bahamas	130-131
Barbados	207-208
Bermuda	131-132
British Guiana	242-243
British Honduras	127-128
Cayman Islands	112-113
Ceylon	293-294
Cyprus	156-157
Dominica	112-113
Falkland Islands	97-98
Falkland Islands Dep.	1L9-1L10
Fiji	137-138
Gambia	144-145
Gibraltar	119-120
Gilbert & Ellice Islands	52-53
Gold Coast	128-129
Grenada	143-144
Jamaica	136-137
Kenya, Uganda, Tanzania	90-91
Leeward Islands	116-117
Malta	206-207
Mauritius	223-224
Montserrat	104-105
Nigeria	71-72
Northern Rhodesia	46-47
Nyasaland Protectorate	82-83
Pitcairn Islands	9-10
St. Helena	128-129
St. Kitts-Nevis	91-92
St. Lucia	127-128
St. Vincent	152-153
Seychelles	149-150
Sierra Leone	186-187
Solomon Islands	80-81
Somaliland Protectorate	108-109
Trinidad & Tobago	62-63
Turks & Caicos Islands	90-91
Virgin Islands	88-89

The following have different designs but are included in the omnibus set:

Great Britain	264-265

Offices in Morocco (Tangier)	523-524
Aden	
Kathiri State of Seiyun	12-13
Qu'aiti State of Shihr and Mukalla	12-13
Australia	200-202
Basutoland	29-31
Bechuanaland Protectorate	137-139
Burma	66-69
Cook Islands	127-130
Hong Kong	174-175
India	195-198
Hyderabad	51-53
New Zealand	247-257
Niue	90-93
Pakistan-Bahawalpur	O16
Samoa	191-194
South Africa	100-102
Southern Rhodesia	67-70
South-West Africa	153-155
Swaziland	38-40
Zanzibar	222-223

Nos. 28-29 (2)	.95	2.50
Nos. 96-97 (2)	.50	.80
Nos. 50-51 (2)	.80	2.00
Nos. 130-131 (2)	.50	1.40
Nos. 207-208 (2)	.50	1.10
Nos. 131-132 (2)	.55	.55
Nos. 242-243 (2)	1.05	1.40
Nos. 127-128 (2)	.50	.50
Nos. 112-113 (2)	.80	.80
Nos. 293-294 (2)	.60	2.10
Nos. 156-157 (2)	.90	.70
Nos. 112-113 (2)	.50	.50
Nos. 97-98 (2)	.90	1.35
Nos. 1L9-1L10 (2)	1.30	1.00
Nos. 137-138 (2)	.75	1.75
Nos. 144-145 (2)	.50	.95
Nos. 119-120 (2)	.75	1.00
Nos. 52-53 (2)	.50	1.10
Nos. 128-129 (2)	1.85	3.75
Nos. 143-144 (2)	.50	.95
Nos. 136-137 (2)	.80	12.50
Nos. 90-91 (2)	.65	.65
Nos. 116-117 (2)	.60	1.50
Nos. 206-207 (2)	.65	2.00
Nos. 223-224 (2)	.50	1.05
Nos. 104-105 (2)	.50	.50
Nos. 71-72 (2)	.70	2.75
Nos. 46-47 (2)	1.25	2.00
Nos. 82-83 (2)	.50	.50
Nos. 9-10 (2)	1.40	1.40
Nos. 128-129 (2)	.65	.70
Nos. 91-92 (2)	.50	.50
Nos. 127-128 (2)	.50	.60
Nos. 152-153 (2)	.50	.50
Nos. 149-150 (2)	.55	.50
Nos. 186-187 (2)	.50	.50
Nos. 80-81 (2)	.50	1.50
Nos. 108-109 (2)	.70	.50
Nos. 62-63 (2)	.50	.50
Nos. 90-91 (2)	.50	.50
Nos. 88-89 (2)	.50	.50

Nos. 264-265 (2)	.50	.50
Nos. 523-524 (2)	1.50	3.00
Nos. 12-13 (2)	.50	.90
Nos. 12-13 (2)	.50	1.25
Nos. 200-202 (3)	1.60	1.25
Nos. 29-31 (3)	2.10	2.60
Nos. 137-139 (3)	2.05	4.75
Nos. 66-69 (4)	1.50	1.25
Nos. 127-130 (4)	2.00	1.85
Nos. 174-175 (2)	6.75	3.15
Nos. 195-198 (4)	5.60	5.50
Nos. 51-53 (3)	1.50	1.70
Nos. 247-257 (11)	3.35	3.65
Nos. 90-93 (4)	1.70	2.20
No. O16 (1)	5.50	7.00
Nos. 191-194 (4)	2.05	1.00
Nos. 100-102 (3)	1.00	3.25
Nos. 67-70 (4)	1.40	1.75
Nos. 153-155 (3)	1.85	3.25
Nos. 38-40 (3)	2.40	5.50
Nos. 222-223 (2)	.65	1.00
Set total (151) Stamps	74.55	114.15

Silver Wedding

King George VI and Queen Elizabeth

CD304   CD305

1948-49

Aden	30-31
Kathiri State of Seiyun	14-15
Qu'aiti State of Shihr and Mukalla	14-15

Antigua	98-99
Ascension	52-53
Bahamas	148-149
Barbados	210-211
Basutoland	39-40
Bechuanaland Protectorate	147-148
Bermuda	133-134
British Guiana	244-245
British Honduras	129-130
Cayman Islands	116-117
Cyprus	158-159
Dominica	114-115
Falkland Islands	99-100
Falkland Islands Dep.	1L11-1L12
Fiji	139-140
Gambia	146-147
Gibraltar	121-122
Gilbert & Ellice Islands	54-55
Gold Coast	142-143
Grenada	145-146
Hong Kong	178-179
Jamaica	138-139
Kenya, Uganda, Tanzania	92-93
Leeward Islands	118-119
Malaya	
Johore	128-129
Kedah	55-56
Kelantan	44-45
Malacca	1-2
Negri Sembilan	36-37
Pahang	44-45
Penang	1-2
Perak	99-100
Perlis	1-2
Selangor	74-75
Trengganu	47-48
Malta	223-224
Mauritius	229-230
Montserrat	106-107
Nigeria	73-74
North Borneo	238-239
Northern Rhodesia	48-49
Nyasaland Protectorate	85-86
Pitcairn Islands	11-12
St. Helena	130-131
St. Kitts-Nevis	93-94
St. Lucia	129-130
St. Vincent	154-155
Sarawak	174-175
Seychelles	151-152
Sierra Leone	188-189
Singapore	21-22
Solomon Islands	82-83
Somaliland Protectorate	110-111
Swaziland	48-49
Trinidad & Tobago	64-65
Turks & Caicos Islands	92-93
Virgin Islands	90-91
Zanzibar	224-225

The following have different designs but are included in the omnibus set:

Great Britain	267-268
Offices in Morocco (Sp. Curr.)	93-94
Offices in Morocco (Tangier)	525-526
Bahrain	62-63
Kuwait	82-83
Oman	25-26
South Africa	106
South-West Africa	159

Nos. 30-31 (2)	45.40	56.50
Nos. 14-15 (2)	17.85	16.00
Nos. 14-15 (2)	18.55	12.50
Nos. 98-99 (2)	13.55	15.75
Nos. 52-53 (2)	55.55	50.45
Nos. 148-149 (2)	45.25	40.30
Nos. 210-211 (2)	18.35	13.55
Nos. 39-40 (2)	52.80	55.25
Nos. 147-148 (2)	42.85	47.75
Nos. 133-134 (2)	47.75	55.25
Nos. 244-245 (2)	24.25	28.45
Nos. 129-130 (2)	25.25	53.20
Nos. 116-117 (2)	25.25	33.50
Nos. 158-159 (2)	58.50	78.05
Nos. 114-115 (2)	25.25	32.75
Nos. 99-100 (2)	112.10	76.10
Nos. 1L11-1L12 (2)	4.25	6.00
Nos. 139-140 (2)	18.20	11.50
Nos. 146-147 (2)	21.25	21.25
Nos. 121-122 (2)	61.00	78.00
Nos. 54-55 (2)	14.25	26.25
Nos. 142-143 (2)	35.25	48.20
Nos. 145-146 (2)	21.75	21.75
Nos. 178-179 (2)	283.50	96.50
Nos. 138-139 (2)	27.85	60.25
Nos. 92-93 (2)	50.25	67.75
Nos. 118-119 (2)	7.00	8.25
Nos. 128-129 (2)	29.25	53.25
Nos. 55-56 (2)	35.25	50.25
Nos. 44-45 (2)	35.75	62.75
Nos. 1-2 (2)	35.40	49.75
Nos. 36-37 (2)	28.10	38.20
Nos. 44-45 (2)	28.00	38.05
Nos. 1-2 (2)	40.50	37.80

Nos. 99-100 (2)	27.80	37.75
Nos. 1-2 (2)	33.50	58.00
Nos. 74-75 (2)	30.25	25.30
Nos. 47-48 (2)	32.75	61.75
Nos. 223-224 (2)	40.55	45.25
Nos. 229-230 (2)	17.75	45.25
Nos. 106-107 (2)	8.75	17.25
Nos. 73-74 (2)	17.85	22.80
Nos. 238-239 (2)	35.30	45.75
Nos. 48-49 (2)	100.30	90.25
Nos. 85-86 (2)	18.25	30.25
Nos. 11-12 (2)	44.75	48.50
Nos. 130-131 (2)	32.80	42.80
Nos. 93-94 (2)	11.25	10.50
Nos. 129-130 (2)	22.25	45.25
Nos. 154-155 (2)	27.75	30.25
Nos. 174-175 (2)	50.40	52.90
Nos. 151-152 (2)	16.25	48.25
Nos. 188-189 (2)	25.25	29.75
Nos. 21-22 (2)	116.00	45.40
Nos. 82-83 (2)	13.40	13.40
Nos. 110-111 (2)	8.40	8.75
Nos. 48-49 (2)	40.30	47.75
Nos. 64-65 (2)	32.75	38.25
Nos. 92-93 (2)	11.25	16.25
Nos. 90-91 (2)	16.25	22.25
Nos. 224-225 (2)	29.60	38.00
Nos. 267-268 (2)	30.40	25.25
Nos. 93-94 (2)	20.10	25.35
Nos. 525-526 (2)	23.10	29.25
Nos. 62-63 (2)	38.50	57.75
Nos. 82-83 (2)	45.50	45.50
Nos. 25-26 (2)	41.00	42.50
No. 106 (1)	.80	1.00
No. 159 (1)	1.10	.35
Set total (136) Stamps	2,468.	2,686.

U.P.U.

Mercury and Symbols of
Communications — CD306

Plane, Ship and
Hemispheres — CD307

Mercury
Scattering
Letters over
Globe
CD308

U.P.U.
Monument,
Bern
CD309

Universal Postal Union, 75th anniversary.

1949

Aden	32-35
Kathiri State of Seiyun	16-19
Qu'aiti State of Shihr and Mukalla	
	16-19
Antigua	100-103
Ascension	57-60
Bahamas	150-153
Barbados	212-215
Basutoland	41-44
Bechuanaland Protectorate	149-152
Bermuda	138-141
British Guiana	246-249
British Honduras	137-140
Brunei	79-82
Cayman Islands	118-121
Cyprus	160-163
Dominica	116-119
Falkland Islands	103-106
Falkland Islands Dep.	1L14-1L17
Fiji	141-144
Gambia	148-151
Gibraltar	123-126

Gilbert & Ellice Islands	56-59
Gold Coast	144-147
Grenada	147-150
Hong Kong	180-183
Jamaica	142-145
Kenya, Uganda, Tanzania	94-97
Leeward Islands	126-129
Malaya	
Johore	151-154
Kedah	57-60
Kelantan	46-49
Malacca	18-21
Negri Sembilan	59-62
Pahang	46-49
Penang	23-26
Perak	101-104
Perlis	3-6
Selangor	76-79
Trengganu	49-52
Malta	225-228
Mauritius	231-234
Montserrat	108-111
New Hebrides, British	62-65
New Hebrides, French	79-82
Nigeria	75-78
North Borneo	240-243
Northern Rhodesia	50-53
Nyasaland Protectorate	87-90
Pitcairn Islands	13-16
St. Helena	132-135
St. Kitts-Nevis	95-98
St. Lucia	131-134
St. Vincent	170-173
Sarawak	176-179
Seychelles	153-156
Sierra Leone	190-193
Singapore	23-26
Solomon Islands	84-87
Somaliland Protectorate	112-115
Southern Rhodesia	71-72
Swaziland	50-53
Tonga	87-90
Trinidad & Tobago	66-69
Turks & Caicos Islands	101-104
Virgin Islands	92-95
Zanzibar	226-229

The following have different designs but are included in the omnibus set:

Great Britain	276-279
Offices in Morocco (Tangier)	546-549
Australia	223
Bahrain	68-71
Burma	116-121
Ceylon	304-306
Egypt	281-283
India	223-226
Kuwait	89-92
Oman	31-34
Pakistan-Bahawalpur	26-29, O25-O28
South Africa	109-111
South-West Africa	160-162

Nos. 32-35 (4)	5.85	8.45
Nos. 16-19 (4)	2.75	8.00
Nos. 16-19 (4)	2.60	8.00
Nos. 100-103 (4)	3.60	7.70
Nos. 57-60 (4)	11.10	9.00
Nos. 150-153 (4)	5.35	9.30
Nos. 212-215 (4)	4.40	14.85
Nos. 41-44 (4)	4.75	10.00
Nos. 149-152 (4)	3.35	7.25
Nos. 138-141 (4)	4.75	6.15
Nos. 246-249 (4)	2.75	4.20
Nos. 137-140 (4)	3.30	6.35
Nos. 79-82 (4)	9.50	8.45
Nos. 118-121 (4)	3.60	7.25
Nos. 160-163 (4)	4.60	10.70
Nos. 116-119 (4)	2.30	5.65
Nos. 103-106 (4)	14.00	17.10
Nos. 1L14-1L17 (4)	14.60	14.50
Nos. 141-144 (4)	3.35	15.75
Nos. 148-151 (4)	3.10	7.10
Nos. 123-126 (4)	5.90	8.75
Nos. 56-59 (4)	4.30	13.00
Nos. 144-147 (4)	2.55	10.35
Nos. 147-150 (4)	2.15	3.55
Nos. 180-183 (4)	57.25	18.25
Nos. 142-145 (4)	2.25	2.45
Nos. 94-97 (4)	2.90	3.40
Nos. 126-129 (4)	3.05	9.60
Nos. 151-154 (4)	4.70	8.90
Nos. 57-60 (4)	4.80	12.00
Nos. 46-49 (4)	4.25	12.65
Nos. 18-21 (4)	4.25	17.30
Nos. 59-62 (4)	3.50	10.75
Nos. 46-49 (4)	3.00	7.25
Nos. 23-26 (4)	5.10	11.75
Nos. 101-104 (4)	3.65	10.75
Nos. 3-6 (4)	3.95	14.25
Nos. 76-79 (4)	4.90	12.30
Nos. 49-52 (4)	5.55	12.25
Nos. 225-228 (4)	4.50	4.85
Nos. 231-234 (4)	4.35	6.70
Nos. 108-111 (4)	3.30	4.35
Nos. 62-65 (4)	1.60	4.25
Nos. 79-82 (4)	24.25	24.25

Nos. 75-78 (4)	2.80	9.25
Nos. 240-243 (4)	7.15	6.50
Nos. 50-53 (4)	5.00	6.50
Nos. 87-90 (4)	4.05	4.05
Nos. 13-16 (4)	18.50	16.50
Nos. 132-135 (4)	4.85	7.10
Nos. 95-98 (4)	3.35	5.55
Nos. 131-134 (4)	2.55	3.85
Nos. 170-173 (4)	2.20	5.05
Nos. 176-179 (4)	8.15	10.85
Nos. 153-156 (4)	3.00	5.15
Nos. 190-193 (4)	2.90	9.15
Nos. 23-26 (4)	19.00	13.70
Nos. 84-87 (4)	4.05	4.90
Nos. 112-115 (4)	3.95	8.70
Nos. 71-72 (2)	1.95	2.25
Nos. 50-53 (4)	2.80	4.65
Nos. 87-90 (4)	3.00	5.25
Nos. 66-69 (4)	3.15	3.15
Nos. 101-104 (4)	2.70	4.10
Nos. 92-95 (4)	2.60	5.90
Nos. 226-229 (4)	5.45	13.50
Nos. 276-279 (4)	1.35	1.00
Nos. 546-549 (4)	3.20	10.15
No. 223 (1)	.40	.40
Nos. 68-71 (4)	4.75	16.50
Nos. 116-121 (6)	7.30	5.35
Nos. 304-306 (3)	3.35	4.25
Nos. 281-283 (3)	5.75	2.70
Nos. 223-226 (4)	27.25	10.50
Nos. 89-92 (4)	6.10	10.25
Nos. 31-34 (4)	8.00	15.75
Nos. 26-29, O25-O28 (8)	2.00	42.00
Nos. 109-111 (3)	2.00	2.70
Nos. 160-162 (3)	3.00	5.50
Set total (313) Stamps	463.20	712.30

University

Arms of
University
College
CD310

Alice, Princess
of Athlone
CD311

1948 opening of University College of the West Indies at Jamaica.

1951

Antigua	104-105
Barbados	228-229
British Guiana	250-251
British Honduras	141-142
Dominica	120-121
Grenada	164-165
Jamaica	146-147
Leeward Islands	130-131
Montserrat	112-113
St. Kitts-Nevis	105-106
St. Lucia	149-150
St. Vincent	174-175
Trinidad & Tobago	70-71
Virgin Islands	96-97

Nos. 104-105 (2)	1.35	3.75
Nos. 228-229 (2)	1.75	2.65
Nos. 250-251 (2)	1.10	1.25
Nos. 141-142 (2)	1.40	2.20
Nos. 120-121 (2)	1.40	1.75
Nos. 164-165 (2)	1.20	1.60
Nos. 146-147 (2)	.90	.70
Nos. 130-131 (2)	1.35	4.00
Nos. 112-113 (2)	.85	2.00
Nos. 105-106 (2)	.90	2.25
Nos. 149-150 (2)	1.40	1.50
Nos. 174-175 (2)	1.00	2.15
Nos. 70-71 (2)	.75	.75
Nos. 96-97 (2)	1.50	3.75
Set total (28) Stamps	16.85	30.30

Coronation

Queen Elizabeth
II — CD312

1953

Aden	47
Kathiri State of Seiyun	28

Qu'aiti State of Shihr and Mukalla	
	28
Antigua	106
Ascension	61
Bahamas	157
Barbados	234
Basutoland	45
Bechuanaland Protectorate	153
Bermuda	142
British Guiana	252
British Honduras	143
Cayman Islands	150
Cyprus	167
Dominica	141
Falkland Islands	121
Falkland Islands Dependencies	1L18
Fiji	145
Gambia	152
Gibraltar	131
Gilbert & Ellice Islands	60
Gold Coast	160
Grenada	170
Hong Kong	184
Jamaica	153
Kenya, Uganda, Tanzania	101
Leeward Islands	132
Malaya	
Johore	155
Kedah	82
Kelantan	71
Malacca	27
Negri Sembilan	63
Pahang	71
Penang	27
Perak	126
Perlis	28
Selangor	101
Trengganu	74
Malta	241
Mauritius	250
Montserrat	127
New Hebrides, British	77
Nigeria	79
North Borneo	260
Northern Rhodesia	60
Nyasaland Protectorate	96
Pitcairn Islands	19
St. Helena	139
St. Kitts-Nevis	119
St. Lucia	156
St. Vincent	185
Sarawak	196
Seychelles	172
Sierra Leone	194
Singapore	27
Solomon Islands	88
Somaliland Protectorate	127
Swaziland	54
Trinidad & Tobago	84
Tristan da Cunha	13
Turks & Caicos Islands	118
Virgin Islands	114

The following have different designs but are included in the omnibus set:

Great Britain	313-316
Offices in Morocco (Tangier)	579-582
Australia	259-261
Bahrain	92-95
Canada	330
Ceylon	317
Cook Islands	145-146
Kuwait	113-116
New Zealand	280-284
Niue	104-105
Oman	52-55
Samoa	214-215
South Africa	192
Southern Rhodesia	80
South-West Africa	244-248
Tokelau Islands	4

No. 47 (1)	1.25	1.25
No. 28 (1)	.75	1.50
No. 28 (1)	1.10	.60
No. 106 (1)	.40	.60
No. 61 (1)	1.25	2.75
No. 157 (1)	1.40	.75
No. 234 (1)	1.00	.25
No. 45 (1)	.50	.60
No. 153 (1)	.75	.35
No. 142 (1)	.85	.50
No. 252 (1)	.45	.25
No. 143 (1)	.60	.40
No. 150 (1)	.40	1.75
No. 167 (1)	1.60	.75
No. 141 (1)	.40	.40
No. 121 (1)	.90	1.50
No. 1L18 (1)	1.80	1.40
No. 145 (1)	1.00	.60
No. 152 (1)	.50	.50
No. 131 (1)	.50	.50
No. 60 (1)	.65	2.25
No. 160 (1)	1.00	.25

No. 170 (1)	.30	.25
No. 184 (1)	6.00	.35
No. 153 (1)	.70	.25
No. 101 (1)	.40	.25
No. 132 (1)	1.00	2.25
No. 155 (1)	1.40	.30
No. 82 (1)	2.25	.60
No. 71 (1)	1.60	1.60
No. 27 (1)	1.10	1.50
No. 63 (1)	1.40	.65
No. 71 (1)	2.25	.25
No. 27 (1)	1.75	.30
No. 126 (1)	1.60	.25
No. 28 (1)	1.75	4.00
No. 101 (1)	1.75	.25
No. 74 (1)	1.50	1.00
No. 241 (1)	.50	.25
No. 250 (1)	1.00	.25
No. 127 (1)	.60	.45
No. 77 (1)	.75	.60
No. 79 (1)	.45	.25
No. 260 (1)	1.75	1.00
No. 60 (1)	.70	.25
No. 96 (1)	.75	.75
No. 19 (1)	2.25	2.25
No. 139 (1)	1.25	1.25
No. 119 (1)	.35	.25
No. 156 (1)	.70	.35
No. 185 (1)	.50	.30
No. 196 (1)	2.00	1.75
No. 172 (1)	.80	.80
No. 194 (1)	.40	.40
No. 27 (1)	2.50	.40
No. 88 (1)	1.00	1.00
No. 127 (1)	.40	.25
No. 54 (1)	.30	.25
No. 84 (1)	.25	.25
No. 13 (1)	1.00	1.75
No. 118 (1)	.40	1.10
No. 114 (1)	.40	1.00
Nos. 313-316 (4)	16.35	5.95
Nos. 579-582 (4)	7.40	5.20
Nos. 259-261 (3)	3.60	2.75
Nos. 92-95 (4)	15.25	12.75
No. 330 (1)	.25	.25
No. 317 (1)	1.40	.25
Nos. 145-146 (2)	2.65	2.65
Nos. 113-116 (4)	16.00	8.50
Nos. 280-284 (5)	3.30	4.55
Nos. 104-105 (2)	1.60	1.60
Nos. 52-55 (4)	11.25	6.50
Nos. 214-215 (2)	2.50	.80
No. 192 (1)	.45	.30
No. 80 (1)	7.25	7.25
Nos. 244-248 (5)	3.00	2.35
No. 4 (1)	2.75	2.75
Set total (106) Stamps	164.80	115.45

Separate designs for each country for the visit of Queen Elizabeth II and the Duke of Edinburgh.

Royal Visit 1953

1953

Aden	62
Australia	267-269
Bermuda	163
Ceylon	318
Fiji	146
Gibraltar	146
Jamaica	154
Kenya, Uganda, Tanzania	102
Malta	242
New Zealand	286-287

No. 62 (1)	.65	4.00
Nos. 267-269 (3)	2.75	2.05
No. 163 (1)	.50	.25
No. 318 (1)	1.00	.25
No. 146 (1)	.65	.35
No. 146 (1)	.50	.30
No. 154 (1)	.50	.25
No. 102 (1)	.50	.25
No. 242 (1)	.35	.25
Nos. 286-287 (2)	.50	.50
Set total (13) Stamps	7.90	8.45

West Indies Federation

Map of the Caribbean
CD313

Federation of the West Indies, April 22, 1958.

1958

Antigua	122-124
Barbados	248-250
Dominica	161-163
Grenada	184-186
Jamaica	175-177
Montserrat	143-145
St. Kitts-Nevis	136-138
St. Lucia	170-172

St. Vincent	198-200
Trinidad & Tobago	86-88

Nos. 122-124 (3)	5.80	3.80
Nos. 248-250 (3)	1.60	2.90
Nos 161-163 (3)	1.95	1.85
Nos. 184-186 (3)	1.50	1.20
Nos. 175-177 (3)	2.65	3.45
Nos. 143-145 (3)	2.35	1.35
Nos. 136-138 (3)	3.00	3.10
Nos. 170-172 (3)	2.05	2.80
Nos. 198-200 (3)	1.50	1.75
Nos. 86-88 (3)	.75	.90
Set total (30) Stamps	23.15	23.10

Freedom from Hunger

Protein Food
CD314

U.N. Food and Agricultural Organization's "Freedom from Hunger" campaign.

1963

Aden	65
Antigua	133
Ascension	89
Bahamas	180
Basutoland	83
Bechuanaland Protectorate	194
Bermuda	192
British Guiana	271
British Honduras	179
Brunei	100
Cayman Islands	168
Dominica	181
Falkland Islands	146
Fiji	198
Gambia	172
Gibraltar	101
Gilbert & Ellice Islands	76
Grenada	190
Hong Kong	218
Malta	291
Mauritius	270
Montserrat	150
New Hebrides, British	93
North Borneo	296
Pitcairn Islands	35
St. Helena	173
St. Lucia	179
St. Vincent	201
Sarawak	212
Seychelles	213
Solomon Islands	109
Swaziland	108
Tonga	127
Tristan da Cunha	68
Turks & Caicos Islands	138
Virgin Islands	140
Zanzibar	280

No. 65 (1)	1.50	1.75
No. 133 (1)	.35	.35
No. 89 (1)	1.00	.50
No. 180 (1)	.65	.65
No. 83 (1)	.50	.25
No. 194 (1)	.50	.50
No. 192 (1)	1.00	.50
No. 271 (1)	.45	.25
No. 179 (1)	.60	.25
No. 100 (1)	3.25	2.25
No. 168 (1)	.55	.30
No. 181 (1)	.30	.30
No. 146 (1)	10.50	2.50
No. 198 (1)	3.50	2.25
No. 172 (1)	.50	.25
No. 161 (1)	4.00	2.25
No. 76 (1)	1.40	.40
No. 190 (1)	.30	.25
No. 218 (1)	47.50	7.50
No. 291 (1)	2.00	2.00
No. 270 (1)	.50	.50
No. 150 (1)	.55	.35
No. 93 (1)	.60	.25
No. 296 (1)	1.90	.75
No. 35 (1)	10.00	4.50
No. 173 (1)	2.25	1.10
No. 179 (1)	.40	.40
No. 201 (1)	.90	.50
No. 212 (1)	1.60	1.75
No. 213 (1)	.85	.35
No. 109 (1)	3.00	.85
No. 108 (1)	.50	.50
No. 127 (1)	.60	.35
No. 68 (1)	.75	.35
No. 138 (1)	.50	.25
No. 140 (1)	.50	.50
No. 280 (1)	1.50	.80
Set total (37) Stamps	107.25	39.30

Red Cross Centenary

Red Cross and Elizabeth II
CD315

1963

Antigua	134-135
Ascension	90-91
Bahamas	183-184
Basutoland	84-85
Bechuanaland Protectorate	195-196
Bermuda	193-194
British Guiana	272-273
British Honduras	180-181
Cayman Islands	169-170
Dominica	182-183
Falkland Islands	147-148
Fiji	203-204
Gambia	173-174
Gibraltar	162-163
Gilbert & Ellice Islands	77-78
Grenada	191-192
Hong Kong	219-220
Jamaica	203-204
Malta	292-293
Mauritius	271-272
Montserrat	151-152
New Hebrides, British	94-95
Pitcairn Islands	36-37
St. Helena	174-175
St. Kitts-Nevis	143-144
St. Lucia	180-181
St. Vincent	202-203
Seychelles	214-215
Solomon Islands	110-111
South Arabia	1-2
Swaziland	109-110
Tonga	134-135
Tristan da Cunha	69-70
Turks & Caicos Islands	139-140
Virgin Islands	141-142

Nos. 134-135 (2)	1.00	2.00
Nos. 90-91 (2)	6.75	3.35
Nos. 183-184 (2)	2.30	2.80
Nos. 84-85 (2)	1.20	.90
Nos. 195-196 (2)	.95	.85
Nos. 193-194 (2)	3.00	2.80
Nos. 272-273 (2)	1.05	.80
Nos. 180-181 (2)	1.00	2.50
Nos. 169-170 (2)	1.10	3.00
Nos. 182-183 (2)	.70	1.05
Nos. 147-148 (2)	18.00	5.50
Nos. 203-204 (2)	3.25	2.80
Nos. 173-174 (2)	.75	1.00
Nos. 162-163 (2)	6.25	5.40
Nos. 77-78 (2)	2.00	3.50
Nos. 191-192 (2)	.80	.50
Nos. 219-220 (2)	35.00	7.35
Nos. 203-204 (2)	.75	1.65
Nos. 292-293 (2)	2.50	4.75
Nos. 271-272 (2)	.90	.90
Nos. 151-152 (2)	1.00	.75
Nos. 94-95 (2)	1.00	.50
Nos. 36-37 (2)	6.50	5.50
Nos. 174-175 (2)	1.70	2.30
Nos. 143-144 (2)	.90	.90
Nos. 180-181 (2)	1.25	1.25
Nos. 202-203 (2)	.90	.90
Nos. 214-215 (2)	1.00	1.50
Nos. 110-111 (2)	1.25	1.15
Nos. 1-2 (2)	1.25	1.25
Nos. 109-110 (2)	1.10	1.10
Nos. 134-135 (2)	1.00	1.25
Nos. 69-70 (2)	1.15	.80
Nos. 139-140 (2)	.85	.75
Nos. 141-142 (2)	.80	1.25
Set total (70) Stamps	110.90	74.55

Shakespeare

Shakespeare Memorial Theatre, Stratford-on-Avon — CD316

400th anniversary of the birth of William Shakespeare.

1964

Antigua	151
Bahamas	201
Bechuanaland Protectorate	197
Cayman Islands	171

Dominica	184
Falkland Islands	149
Gambia	192
Gibraltar	164
Montserrat	153
St. Lucia	196
Turks & Caicos Islands	141
Virgin Islands	143

No. 151 (1)	.35	.25
No. 201 (1)	.60	.35
No. 197 (1)	.35	.35
No. 171 (1)	.35	.30
No. 184 (1)	.35	.35
No. 149 (1)	1.60	.50
No. 192 (1)	.35	.25
No. 164 (1)	.65	.55
No. 153 (1)	.35	.25
No. 196 (1)	.45	.25
No. 141 (1)	.40	.25
No. 143 (1)	.45	.45
Set total (12) Stamps	6.25	4.10

ITU

ITU Emblem
CD317

Intl. Telecommunication Union, cent.

1965

Antigua	153-154
Ascension	92-93
Bahamas	219-220
Barbados	265-266
Basutoland	101-102
Bechuanaland Protectorate	202-203
Bermuda	196-197
British Guiana	293-294
British Honduras	187-188
Brunei	116-117
Cayman Islands	172-173
Dominica	185-186
Falkland Islands	154-155
Fiji	211-212
Gibraltar	167-168
Gilbert & Ellice Islands	87-88
Grenada	205-206
Hong Kong	221-222
Mauritius	291-292
Montserrat	157-158
New Hebrides, British	108-109
Pitcairn Islands	52-53
St. Helena	180-181
St. Kitts-Nevis	163-164
St. Lucia	197-198
St. Vincent	224-225
Seychelles	218-219
Solomon Islands	126-127
Swaziland	115-116
Tristan da Cunha	85-86
Turks & Caicos Islands	142-143
Virgin Islands	159-160

Nos. 153-154 (2)	1.45	1.35
Nos. 92-93 (2)	1.90	1.30
Nos. 219-220 (2)	1.35	1.50
Nos. 265-266 (2)	1.50	1.25
Nos. 101-102 (2)	.85	.65
Nos. 202-203 (2)	1.10	.75
Nos. 196-197 (2)	2.15	2.25
Nos. 293-294 (2)	.60	.55
Nos. 187-188 (2)	.75	.75
Nos. 116-117 (2)	1.75	1.75
Nos. 172-173 (2)	1.00	.85
Nos. 185-186 (2)	.55	.55
Nos. 154-155 (2)	6.75	3.15
Nos. 211-212 (2)	2.00	1.05
Nos. 167-168 (2)	9.00	5.95
Nos. 87-88 (2)	.85	.60
Nos. 205-206 (2)	.50	.50
Nos. 221-222 (2)	24.50	3.80
Nos. 291-292 (2)	1.20	.65
Nos. 157-158 (2)	1.05	1.15
Nos. 108-109 (2)	.65	.50
Nos. 52-53 (2)	6.25	4.30
Nos. 180-181 (2)	.80	.60
Nos. 163-164 (2)	.60	.60
Nos. 197-198 (2)	1.25	1.25
Nos. 224-225 (2)	.80	.90
Nos. 218-219 (2)	.75	.60
Nos. 126-127 (2)	.70	.55
Nos. 115-116 (2)	.70	.70
Nos. 85-86 (2)	1.00	.65
Nos. 142-143 (2)	.75	.50
Nos. 159-160 (2)	.85	.85
Set total (64) Stamps	75.90	42.35

Intl. Cooperation Year

ICY Emblem CD318

1965

Antigua	155-156	
Ascension	94-95	
Bahamas	222-223	
Basutoland	103-104	
Bechuanaland Protectorate	204-205	
Bermuda	199-200	
British Guiana	295-296	
British Honduras	189-190	
Brunei	118-119	
Cayman Islands	174-175	
Dominica	187-188	
Falkland Islands	156-157	
Fiji	213-214	
Gibraltar	169-170	
Gilbert & Ellice Islands	104-105	
Grenada	207-208	
Hong Kong	223-224	
Mauritius	293-294	
Montserrat	176-177	
New Hebrides, British	110-111	
New Hebrides, French	126-127	
Pitcairn Islands	54-55	
St. Helena	182-183	
St. Kitts-Nevis	165-166	
St. Lucia	199-200	
Seychelles	220-221	
Solomon Islands	143-144	
South Arabia	17-18	
Swaziland	117-118	
Tristan da Cunha	87-88	
Turks & Caicos Islands	144-145	
Virgin Islands	161-162	

Nos. 155-156 (2)	.55	.50
Nos. 94-95 (2)	1.30	1.40
Nos. 222-223 (2)	.65	1.90
Nos. 103-104 (2)	.75	.85
Nos. 204-205 (2)	.85	1.00
Nos. 199-200 (2)	2.05	1.25
Nos. 295-296 (2)	.65	.60
Nos. 189-190 (2)	.60	.55
Nos. 118-119 (2)	.85	.85
Nos. 174-175 (2)	1.00	.75
Nos. 187-188 (2)	.55	.55
Nos. 156-157 (2)	6.00	1.65
Nos. 213-214 (2)	1.95	1.25
Nos. 169-170 (2)	1.25	2.75
Nos. 104-105 (2)	.85	.60
Nos. 207-208 (2)	.50	.50
Nos. 223-224 (2)	22.00	3.10
Nos. 293-294 (2)	.70	.70
Nos. 176-177 (2)	.80	.65
Nos. 110-111 (2)	.50	.50
Nos. 126-127 (2)	12.00	12.00
Nos. 54-55 (2)	6.35	4.50
Nos. 182-183 (2)	.95	.50
Nos. 165-166 (2)	.80	.60
Nos. 199-200 (2)	.55	.55
Nos. 220-221 (2)	.80	.60
Nos. 143-144 (2)	.70	.60
Nos. 17-18 (2)	1.20	.50
Nos. 117-118 (2)	.75	.75
Nos. 87-88 (2)	1.05	.65
Nos. 144-145 (2)	.65	.50
Nos. 161-162 (2)	.65	.50
Set total (64) Stamps	70.80	44.15

Churchill Memorial

Winston Churchill and St. Paul's, London, During Air Attack CD319

1966

Antigua	157-160	
Ascension	96-99	
Bahamas	224-227	
Barbados	281-284	
Basutoland	105-108	
Bechuanaland Protectorate	206-209	
Bermuda	201-204	
British Antarctic Territory	16-19	
British Honduras	191-194	
Brunei	120-123	
Cayman Islands	176-179	
Dominica	189-192	
Falkland Islands	158-161	
Fiji	215-218	

Gibraltar	171-174	
Gilbert & Ellice Islands	106-109	
Grenada	209-212	
Hong Kong	225-228	
Mauritius	295-298	
Montserrat	178-181	
New Hebrides, British	112-115	
New Hebrides, French	128-131	
Pitcairn Islands	56-59	
St. Helena	184-187	
St. Kitts-Nevis	167-170	
St. Lucia	201-204	
St. Vincent	241-244	
Seychelles	222-225	
Solomon Islands	145-148	
South Arabia	19-22	
Swaziland	119-122	
Tristan da Cunha	89-92	
Turks & Caicos Islands	146-149	
Virgin Islands	163-166	

Nos. 157-160 (4)	3.05	3.05
Nos. 96-99 (4)	10.00	6.40
Nos. 224-227 (4)	2.30	3.20
Nos. 281-284 (4)	3.00	4.95
Nos. 105-108 (4)	2.80	3.25
Nos. 206-209 (4)	2.50	2.50
Nos. 201-204 (4)	4.00	4.75
Nos. 16-19 (4)	41.20	18.00
Nos. 191-194 (4)	2.45	1.30
Nos. 120-123 (4)	7.65	6.55
Nos. 176-179 (4)	3.10	3.65
Nos. 189-192 (4)	1.15	1.15
Nos. 158-161 (4)	12.75	9.55
Nos. 215-218 (4)	4.40	3.00
Nos. 171-174 (4)	3.05	5.30
Nos. 106-109 (4)	1.50	1.30
Nos. 209-212 (4)	1.10	1.10
Nos. 225-228 (4)	52.50	11.40
Nos. 295-298 (4)	4.05	4.05
Nos. 178-181 (4)	1.60	1.55
Nos. 112-115 (4)	2.30	1.00
Nos. 128-131 (4)	10.25	10.25
Nos. 56-59 (4)	11.00	6.75
Nos. 184-187 (4)	1.85	1.95
Nos. 167-170 (4)	1.50	1.70
Nos. 201-204 (4)	1.50	1.50
Nos. 241-244 (4)	1.50	1.75
Nos. 222-225 (4)	3.20	4.35
Nos. 145-148 (4)	1.50	1.60
Nos. 19-22 (4)	2.95	2.20
Nos. 119-122 (4)	1.70	2.55
Nos. 89-92 (4)	5.95	2.70
Nos. 146-149 (4)	1.60	1.75
Nos. 163-166 (4)	1.90	1.90
Set total (136) Stamps	212.85	137.95

Royal Visit, 1966

Queen Elizabeth II and Prince Philip CD320

Caribbean visit, Feb. 4 - Mar. 6, 1966.

1966

Antigua	161-162	
Bahamas	228-229	
Barbados	285-286	
British Guiana	299-300	
Cayman Islands	180-181	
Dominica	193-194	
Grenada	213-214	
Montserrat	182-183	
St. Kitts-Nevis	171-172	
St. Lucia	205-206	
St. Vincent	245-246	
Turks & Caicos Islands	150-151	
Virgin Islands	167-168	

Nos. 161-162 (2)	3.50	2.60
Nos. 228-229 (2)	3.05	3.05
Nos. 285-286 (2)	3.00	2.00
Nos. 299-300 (2)	3.35	1.60
Nos. 180-181 (2)	3.45	1.80
Nos. 193-194 (2)	3.00	.60
Nos. 213-214 (2)	.80	.50
Nos. 182-183 (2)	2.00	1.00
Nos. 171-172 (2)	.90	.75
Nos. 205-206 (2)	1.50	1.35
Nos. 245-246 (2)	2.75	1.35
Nos. 150-151 (2)	1.20	.55
Nos. 167-168 (2)	1.75	1.75
Set total (26) Stamps	30.25	18.90

World Cup Soccer

Soccer Player and Jules Rimet Cup CD321

World Cup Soccer Championship, Wembley, England, July 11-30.

1966

Antigua	163-164	
Ascension	100-101	
Bahamas	245-246	
Bermuda	205-206	
Brunei	124-125	
Cayman Islands	182-183	
Dominica	195-196	
Fiji	219-220	
Gibraltar	175-176	
Gilbert & Ellice Islands	125-126	
Grenada	230-231	
New Hebrides, British	116-117	
New Hebrides, French	132-133	
Pitcairn Islands	60-61	
St. Helena	188-189	
St. Kitts-Nevis	173-174	
St. Lucia	207-208	
Seychelles	226-227	
Solomon Islands	167-168	
South Arabia	23-24	
Tristan da Cunha	93-94	

Nos. 163-164 (2)	.80	.85
Nos. 100-101 (2)	2.50	2.00
Nos. 245-246 (2)	.65	.65
Nos. 205-206 (2)	1.75	1.75
Nos. 124-125 (2)	1.30	1.25
Nos. 182-183 (2)	.75	.65
Nos. 195-196 (2)	1.20	.75
Nos. 219-220 (2)	1.70	.60
Nos. 175-176 (2)	1.85	1.75
Nos. 125-126 (2)	.70	.60
Nos. 230-231 (2)	.65	.95
Nos. 116-117 (2)	1.00	1.00
Nos. 132-133 (2)	7.00	7.00
Nos. 60-61 (2)	5.50	5.00
Nos. 188-189 (2)	1.25	.60
Nos. 173-174 (2)	.85	.80
Nos. 207-208 (2)	1.15	.90
Nos. 226-227 (2)	.85	.75
Nos. 167-168 (2)	1.10	1.10
Nos. 23-24 (2)	1.90	.55
Nos. 93-94 (2)	1.25	.80
Set total (42) Stamps	35.70	30.30

WHO Headquarters

World Health Organization Headquarters, Geneva — CD322

1966

Antigua	165-166	
Ascension	102-103	
Bahamas	247-248	
Brunei	126-127	
Cayman Islands	184-185	
Dominica	197-198	
Fiji	224-225	
Gibraltar	180-181	
Gilbert & Ellice Islands	127-128	
Grenada	232-233	
Hong Kong	229-230	
Montserrat	184-185	
New Hebrides, British	118-119	
New Hebrides, French	134-135	
Pitcairn Islands	62-63	
St. Helena	190-191	
St. Kitts-Nevis	177-178	
St. Lucia	209-210	
St. Vincent	247-248	
Seychelles	228-229	
Solomon Islands	169-170	
South Arabia	25-26	
Tristan da Cunha	99-100	

Nos. 165-166 (2)	1.15	.55
Nos. 102-103 (2)	6.60	3.35
Nos. 247-248 (2)	.80	.80
Nos. 126-127 (2)	1.35	1.35
Nos. 184-185 (2)	2.25	1.20
Nos. 197-198 (2)	.75	.75
Nos. 224-225 (2)	4.70	3.30
Nos. 180-181 (2)	6.50	4.50
Nos. 127-128 (2)	.80	.70
Nos. 232-233 (2)	.80	.50
Nos. 229-230 (2)	11.25	2.30
Nos. 184-185 (2)	1.00	1.00
Nos. 118-119 (2)	.75	.50
Nos. 134-135 (2)	8.75	8.75
Nos. 62-63 (2)	7.25	6.50
Nos. 190-191 (2)	3.50	1.50
Nos. 177-178 (2)	.60	.60
Nos. 209-210 (2)	.80	.80
Nos. 247-248 (2)	1.15	1.05
Nos. 228-229 (2)	1.25	.65
Nos. 169-170 (2)	.95	.80

Nos. 25-26 (2)	2.10	.70
Nos. 99-100 (2)	1.90	1.25
Set total (46) Stamps	66.95	43.40

UNESCO Anniversary

"Education" — CD323

"Science" (Wheat ears & flask enclosing globe). "Culture" (lyre & columns). 20th anniversary of the UNESCO.

1966-67

Antigua	183-185	
Ascension	108-110	
Bahamas	249-251	
Barbados	287-289	
Bermuda	207-209	
Brunei	128-130	
Cayman Islands	186-188	
Dominica	199-201	
Gibraltar	183-185	
Gilbert & Ellice Islands	129-131	
Grenada	234-236	
Hong Kong	231-233	
Mauritius	299-301	
Montserrat	186-188	
New Hebrides, British	120-122	
New Hebrides, French	136-138	
Pitcairn Islands	64-66	
St. Helena	192-194	
St. Kitts-Nevis	179-181	
St. Lucia	211-213	
St. Vincent	249-251	
Seychelles	230-232	
Solomon Islands	171-173	
South Arabia	27-29	
Swaziland	123-125	
Tristan da Cunha	101-103	
Turks & Caicos Islands	155-157	
Virgin Islands	176-178	

Nos. 183-185 (3)	1.90	2.50
Nos. 108-110 (3)	11.00	5.80
Nos. 249-251 (3)	2.35	2.35
Nos. 287-289 (3)	2.35	2.15
Nos. 207-209 (3)	3.80	3.90
Nos. 128-130 (3)	4.65	5.40
Nos. 186-188 (3)	2.50	1.50
Nos. 199-201 (3)	1.60	.75
Nos. 183-185 (3)	6.50	3.25
Nos. 129-131 (3)	2.50	2.45
Nos. 234-236 (3)	1.10	1.20
Nos. 231-233 (3)	69.50	17.50
Nos. 299-301 (3)	2.10	1.50
Nos. 186-188 (3)	2.40	2.40
Nos. 120-122 (3)	1.90	1.90
Nos. 136-138 (3)	7.75	7.75
Nos. 64-66 (3)	7.10	4.75
Nos. 192-194 (3)	5.25	3.65
Nos. 179-181 (3)	.90	.90
Nos. 211-213 (3)	1.15	1.15
Nos. 249-251 (3)	2.30	1.35
Nos. 230-232 (3)	2.40	2.40
Nos. 171-173 (3)	2.00	1.50
Nos. 27-29 (3)	5.50	5.50
Nos. 123-125 (3)	1.40	1.40
Nos. 101-103 (3)	2.00	1.40
Nos. 155-157 (3)	1.05	.90
Nos. 176-178 (3)	1.40	1.30
Set total (84) Stamps	156.35	88.50

Silver Wedding, 1972

Queen Elizabeth II and Prince Philip — CD324

Designs: borders differ for each country.

1972

Anguilla	161-162	
Antigua	295-296	
Ascension	164-165	
Bahamas	344-345	
Bermuda	296-297	
British Antarctic Territory	43-44	
British Honduras	306-307	
British Indian Ocean Territory	48-49	

Brunei	186-187
Cayman Islands	304-305
Dominica	352-353
Falkland Islands	223-224
Fiji	328-329
Gibraltar	292-293
Gilbert & Ellice Islands	206-207
Grenada	466-467
Hong Kong	271-272
Montserrat	286-287
New Hebrides, British	169-170
New Hebrides, French	188-189
Pitcairn Islands	127-128
St. Helena	271-272
St. Kitts-Nevis	257-258
St. Lucia	328-329
St. Vincent	344-345
Seychelles	309-310
South Georgia	35-36
Tristan da Cunha	178-179
Turks & Caicos Islands	257-258
Virgin Islands	241-242

Nos. 161-162 (2)	1.10	1.50
Nos. 295-296 (2)	.50	.50
Nos. 164-165 (2)	.70	.70
Nos. 344-345 (2)	.60	.60
Nos. 296-297 (2)	.50	.65
Nos. 43-44 (2)	6.50	5.65
Nos. 306-307 (2)	.80	.80
Nos. 48-49 (2)	2.00	1.00
Nos. 186-187 (2)	.70	.70
Nos. 304-305 (2)	.75	.75
Nos. 352-353 (2)	.65	.65
Nos. 223-224 (2)	1.00	1.15
Nos. 328-329 (2)	.70	.70
Nos. 292-293 (2)	.50	.50
Nos. 206-207 (2)	.50	.50
Nos. 466-467 (2)	.70	.70
Nos. 271-272 (2)	1.70	1.50
Nos. 286-287 (2)	.50	.50
Nos. 169-170 (2)	.50	.50
Nos. 188-189 (2)	1.05	1.05
Nos. 127-128 (2)	.90	.85
Nos. 271-272 (2)	.70	1.20
Nos. 257-258 (2)	.65	.50
Nos. 328-329 (2)	.75	.75
Nos. 344-345 (2)	.55	.55
Nos. 309-310 (2)	.90	.90
Nos. 248-249 (2)	.50	.50
Nos. 35-36 (2)	1.40	1.40
Nos. 178-179 (2)	.70	.70
Nos. 257-258 (2)	.50	.50
Nos. 241-242 (2)	.50	.50
Set total (62) Stamps	30.00	28.95

Princess Anne's Wedding

Wedding of H.R.H. The Princess Anne SEYCHELLES

Princess Anne and Mark Phillips — CD325

Wedding of Princess Anne and Mark Phillips, Nov. 14, 1973.

1973

Anguilla	179-180
Ascension	177-178
Belize	325-326
Bermuda	302-303
British Antarctic Territory	60-61
Cayman Islands	320-321
Falkland Islands	225-226
Gibraltar	305-306
Gilbert & Ellice Islands	216-217
Hong Kong	289-290
Montserrat	300-301
Pitcairn Islands	135-136
St. Helena	277-278
St. Kitts-Nevis	274-275
St. Lucia	349-350
St. Vincent	358-359
St. Vincent Grenadines	1-2
Seychelles	311-312
Solomon Islands	259-260
South Georgia	37-38
Tristan da Cunha	189-190
Turks & Caicos Islands	286-287
Virgin Islands	260-261

Nos. 179-180 (2)	.55	.55
Nos. 177-178 (2)	.60	.60
Nos. 325-326 (2)	.50	.50
Nos. 302-303 (2)	.50	.50
Nos. 60-61 (2)	1.10	1.10
Nos. 320-321 (2)	.50	.50

Nos. 225-226 (2)	.70	.60
Nos. 305-306 (2)	.55	.55
Nos. 216-217 (2)	.50	.50
Nos. 289-290 (2)	2.65	2.00
Nos. 300-301 (2)	.55	.55
Nos. 135-136 (2)	.70	.60
Nos. 277-278 (2)	.50	.50
Nos. 274-275 (2)	.50	.50
Nos. 349-350 (2)	.50	.50
Nos. 358-359 (2)	.50	.50
Nos. 1-2 (2)	.50	.50
Nos. 311-312 (2)	.65	.65
Nos. 259-260 (2)	.70	.70
Nos. 37-38 (2)	.75	.75
Nos. 189-190 (2)	.50	.50
Nos. 286-287 (2)	.50	.50
Nos. 260-261 (2)	.50	.50
Set total (46) Stamps	15.50	14.65

Elizabeth II Coronation Anniv.

BARBADOS 50c CD326

50c 50c BARBADOS Coronation 1953 CD327

BARBADOS 50c CD328

Designs: Royal and local beasts in heraldic form and simulated stonework. Portrait of Elizabeth II by Peter Grugeon. 25th anniversary of coronation of Queen Elizabeth II.

1978

Ascension	229
Barbados	474
Belize	397
British Antarctic Territory	71
Cayman Islands	404
Christmas Island	87
Falkland Islands	275
Fiji	384
Gambia	380
Gilbert Islands	312
Mauritius	464
New Hebrides, British	258
New Hebrides, French	278
St. Helena	317
St. Kitts-Nevis	354
Samoa	472
Solomon Islands	368
South Georgia	51
Swaziland	302
Tristan da Cunha	238
Virgin Islands	337

No. 229 (1)	2.00	2.00
No. 474 (1)	1.35	1.35
No. 397 (1)	1.40	1.75
No. 71 (1)	6.00	6.00
No. 404 (1)	2.00	2.00
No. 87 (1)	3.50	4.00
No. 275 (1)	4.00	5.50
No. 384 (1)	1.75	1.75
No. 380 (1)	1.50	1.50
No. 312 (1)	1.25	1.25
No. 464 (1)	2.75	2.75
No. 258 (1)	1.75	1.75
No. 278 (1)	3.50	3.50
No. 317 (1)	1.75	1.75
No. 354 (1)	1.00	1.00
No. 472 (1)	2.10	2.10
No. 368 (1)	2.50	2.50
No. 51 (1)	3.00	3.00
No. 302 (1)	1.60	1.60
No. 238 (1)	1.50	1.50
No. 337 (1)	1.80	1.80
Set total (21) Stamps	48.00	50.35

Queen Mother Elizabeth's 80th Birthday

80TH BIRTHDAY OF H.M. Queen Elizabeth The Queen Mother 4th AUGUST 1980 $1.30 HONG KONG 香港 CD330

Designs: Photographs of Queen Mother Elizabeth. Falkland Islands issued in sheets of 50; others in sheets of 9.

1980

Ascension	261
Bermuda	401
Cayman Islands	443
Falkland Islands	305
Gambia	412
Gibraltar	393
Hong Kong	364
Pitcairn Islands	193
St. Helena	341
Samoa	532
Solomon Islands	426
Tristan da Cunha	277

No. 261 (1)	.40	.40
No. 401 (1)	.45	.75
No. 443 (1)	.40	.40
No. 305 (1)	.40	.40
No. 412 (1)	.40	.50
No. 393 (1)	.35	.35
No. 364 (1)	1.10	1.25
No. 193 (1)	.60	.60
No. 341 (1)	.50	.50
No. 532 (1)	.55	.55
No. 426 (1)	.50	.50
No. 277 (1)	.45	.45
Set total (12) Stamps	6.10	6.65

Royal Wedding, 1981

Royal Wedding · 29th July 1981 $5.00 香港 HONG KONG

Prince Charles and Lady Diana — CD331

25c 25c HRH Prince Charles & Lady Diana Antigua CD331a

Wedding of Charles, Prince of Wales, and Lady Diana Spencer, St. Paul's Cathedral, London, July 29, 1981.

1981

Antigua	623-627
Ascension	294-296
Barbados	547-549
Barbuda	497-501
Bermuda	412-414
Brunei	268-270
Cayman Islands	471-473
Dominica	701-705
Falkland Islands	324-326
Falkland Islands Dep.	1L59-1L61
Fiji	442-444
Gambia	426-428
Ghana	759-764
Grenada	1051-1055
Grenada Grenadines	440-443
Hong Kong	373-375
Jamaica	500-503
Lesotho	335-337
Maldive Islands	906-909
Mauritius	520-522
Norfolk Island	280-282
Pitcairn Islands	206-208
St. Helena	353-355
St. Lucia	543-549
Samoa	558-560
Sierra Leone	509-518
Solomon Islands	450-452
Swaziland	382-384
Tristan da Cunha	294-296
Turks & Caicos Islands	486-489
Caicos Island	8-11
Uganda	314-317
Vanuatu	308-310
Virgin Islands	406-408

Nos. 623-627 (5)	6.55	2.55
Nos. 294-296 (3)	1.00	1.00

Nos. 547-549 (3)	.90	.90
Nos. 497-501 (5)	10.95	10.95
Nos. 412-414 (3)	2.00	2.00
Nos. 268-270 (3)	2.15	4.50
Nos. 471-473 (3)	1.20	1.30
Nos. 701-705 (5)	8.35	2.35
Nos. 324-326 (3)	1.65	1.70
Nos. 1L59-1L61 (3)	1.45	1.45
Nos. 442-444 (3)	1.35	1.35
Nos. 426-428 (3)	.80	.80
Nos. 759-764 (9)	6.20	6.20
Nos. 1051-1055 (5)	9.85	1.85
Nos. 440-443 (4)	2.35	2.35
Nos. 373-375 (3)	3.05	2.85
Nos. 500-503 (4)	1.45	1.35
Nos. 335-337 (3)	.90	.90
Nos. 906-909 (4)	1.55	1.55
Nos. 520-522 (3)	2.75	2.75
Nos. 280-282 (3)	1.35	1.35
Nos. 206-208 (3)	1.10	1.10
Nos. 353-355 (3)	.85	.85
Nos. 543-549 (5)	8.50	8.50
Nos. 558-560 (3)	.85	.85
Nos. 509-518 (10)	15.50	15.50
Nos. 450-452 (3)	1.25	1.25
Nos. 382-384 (3)	1.30	1.25
Nos. 294-296 (3)	.90	.90
Nos. 486-489 (4)	2.20	2.20
Nos. 8-11 (4)	5.00	5.00
Nos. 314-317 (4)	3.30	3.00
Nos. 308-310 (3)	1.15	1.15
Nos. 406-408 (3)	1.10	1.10
Set total (131) Stamps	110.80	94.65

Princess Diana

Buckingham Palace 45c Commonwealth of DOMINICA CD002

BAHAMAS $1 CD333

Designs: Photographs and portrait of Princess Diana, wedding or honeymoon photographs, royal residences, arms of issuing country. Portrait photograph by Clive Friend. Souvenir sheet margins show family tree, various people related to the princess. 21st birthday of Princess Diana of Wales, July 1.

1982

Antigua	663-666
Ascension	313-316
Bahamas	510-513
Barbados	585-588
Barbuda	544-547
British Antarctic Territory	92-95
Cayman Islands	486-489
Dominica	773-776
Falkland Islands	348-351
Falkland Islands Dep.	1L72-1L75
Fiji	470-473
Gambia	447-450
Grenada	1101A-1105
Grenada Grenadines	485-491
Lesotho	372-375
Maldive Islands	952-955
Mauritius	548-551
Pitcairn Islands	213-216
St. Helena	372-375
St. Lucia	591-594
Sierra Leone	531-534
Solomon Islands	471-474
Swaziland	406-409
Tristan da Cunha	310-313
Turks and Caicos Islands	531-534
Virgin Islands	430-433

Nos. 663-666 (4)	8.25	7.35
Nos. 313-316 (4)	3.50	3.50
Nos. 510-513 (4)	6.00	3.85
Nos. 585-588 (4)	3.40	3.25
Nos. 544-547 (4)	9.75	7.70
Nos. 92-95 (4)	4.25	3.45
Nos. 486-489 (4)	4.75	2.70
Nos. 773-776 (4)	7.05	7.05
Nos. 348-351 (4)	2.95	2.95
Nos. 1L72-1L75 (4)	2.50	2.60
Nos. 470-473 (4)	3.25	2.95
Nos. 447-450 (4)	2.85	2.85
Nos. 1101A-1105 (7)	16.05	15.55

Nos. 485-491 (7)	17.65	17.65
Nos. 372-375 (4)	4.00	4.00
Nos. 952-955 (4)	5.50	3.90
Nos. 548-551 (4)	5.50	5.50
Nos. 213-216 (4)	2.15	2.15
Nos. 372-375 (4)	2.95	2.95
Nos. 591-594 (4)	9.90	9.90
Nos. 531-534 (4)	7.20	7.20
Nos. 471-474 (4)	2.90	2.90
Nos. 406-409 (4)	3.85	2.25
Nos. 310-313 (4)	3.65	1.45
Nos. 486-489 (4)	2.20	2.20
Nos. 430-433 (4)	3.00	3.00
Set total (110) Stamps	145.00	130.80

250th anniv. of first edition of Lloyd's List (shipping news publication) & of Lloyd's marine insurance.

CD335

Designs: First page of early edition of the list; historical ships, modern transportation or harbor scenes.

1984

Ascension	351-354
Bahamas	555-558
Barbados	627-630
Cayes of Belize	10-13
Cayman Islands	522-526
Falkland Islands	404-407
Fiji	509-512
Gambia	519-522
Mauritius	587-590
Nauru	280-283
St. Helena	412-415
Samoa	624-627
Seychelles	538-541
Solomon Islands	521-524
Vanuatu	368-371
Virgin Islands	466-469

Nos. 351-354 (4)	2.90	2.55
Nos. 555-558 (4)	4.15	2.95
Nos. 627-630 (4)	6.10	5.15
Nos. 10-13 (4)	2.65	2.65
Nos. 522-526 (5)	9.30	8.45
Nos. 404-407 (4)	3.50	3.65
Nos. 509-512 (4)	5.30	4.90
Nos. 519-522 (4)	4.20	4.30
Nos. 587-590 (4)	8.95	8.95
Nos. 280-283 (4)	2.40	2.35
Nos. 412-415 (4)	2.40	2.40
Nos. 624-627 (4)	2.55	2.35
Nos. 538-541 (4)	5.00	5.00
Nos. 521-524 (4)	4.65	3.95
Nos. 368-371 (4)	2.40	2.40
Nos. 466-469 (4)	4.25	4.25
Set total (65) Stamps	70.70	66.25

Queen Mother 85th Birthday

CD336

Designs: Photographs tracing the life of the Queen Mother, Elizabeth. The high value in each set pictures the same photograph taken of the Queen Mother holding the infant Prince Henry.

1985

Ascension	372-376
Bahamas	580-584
Barbados	660-664
Bermuda	469-473
Falkland Islands	420-424
Falkland Islands Dep	1L92-1L96
Fiji	531-535
Hong Kong	447-450
Jamaica	599-603
Mauritius	604-608
Norfolk Island	364-368
Pitcairn Islands	253-257
St. Helena	428-432
Samoa	649-653

Seychelles	567-571
Zil Elwannyen Sesel	101-105
Solomon Islands	543-547
Swaziland	476-480
Tristan da Cunha	372-376
Vanuatu	392-396

Nos. 372-376 (5)	4.65	4.65
Nos. 580-584 (5)	7.70	6.45
Nos. 660-664 (5)	8.00	6.70
Nos. 469-473 (5)	9.40	9.40
Nos. 420-424 (5)	7.35	6.65
Nos. 1L92-1L96 (5)	8.00	8.00
Nos. 531-535 (5)	6.15	6.15
Nos. 447-450 (4)	9.50	8.50
Nos. 599-603 (5)	6.15	7.00
Nos. 604-608 (5)	11.80	11.80
Nos. 364-368 (5)	5.05	5.05
Nos. 253-257 (5)	5.25	5.95
Nos. 428-432 (5)	5.25	5.25
Nos. 649-653 (5)	8.40	7.55
Nos. 567-571 (5)	8.70	8.70
Nos. 101-105 (5)	6.60	6.60
Nos. 543-547 (5)	3.95	3.95
Nos. 476-480 (5)	7.75	7.25
Nos. 372-376 (5)	5.40	5.40
Nos. 392-396 (5)	5.25	5.25
Set total (99) Stamps	140.30	136.25

Queen Elizabeth II, 60th Birthday

CD337

1986, April 21

Ascension	389-393
Bahamas	592-596
Barbados	675-679
Bermuda	499-503
Cayman Islands	555-559
Falkland Islands	441-445
Fiji	544-548
Hong Kong	465-469
Jamaica	620-624
Kiribati	470-474
Mauritius	629-633
Papua New Guinea	640-644
Pitcairn Islands	270-274
St. Helena	451-455
Samoa	670-674
Seychelles	592-596
Zil Elwannyen Sesel	114-118
Solomon Islands	562-566
South Georgia	101-105
Swaziland	490-494
Tristan da Cunha	388-392
Vanuatu	414-418
Zambia	343-347

Nos. 389-393 (5)	2.80	3.30
Nos. 592-596 (5)	2.75	3.70
Nos. 675-679 (5)	3.25	3.10
Nos. 499-503 (5)	4.65	5.15
Nos. 555-559 (5)	4.55	5.60
Nos. 441-445 (5)	3.95	4.95
Nos. 544-548 (5)	3.00	3.00
Nos. 465-469 (5)	8.75	6.75
Nos. 620-624 (5)	2.75	2.70
Nos. 470-474 (5)	2.10	2.10
Nos. 629-633 (5)	3.70	3.70
Nos. 640-644 (5)	4.10	4.10
Nos. 270-274 (5)	2.70	2.70
Nos. 451-455 (5)	3.05	3.05
Nos. 670-674 (5)	2.55	2.55
Nos. 592-596 (5)	2.70	2.70
Nos. 114-118 (5)	2.15	2.15
Nos. 562-566 (5)	2.90	2.90
Nos. 101-105 (5)	3.30	3.65
Nos. 490-494 (5)	2.15	2.15
Nos. 388-392 (5)	3.00	3.00
Nos. 414-418 (5)	3.10	3.10
Nos. 343-347 (5)	1.75	1.75
Set total (115) Stamps	75.70	77.85

Royal Wedding

Marriage of Prince Andrew and Sarah Ferguson
CD338

1986, July 23

Ascension	399-400
Bahamas	602-603
Barbados	687-688

Cayman Islands	560-561
Jamaica	629-630
Pitcairn Islands	275-276
St. Helena	460-461
St. Kitts	181-182
Seychelles	602-603
Zil Elwannyen Sesel	119-120
Solomon Islands	567-568
Tristan da Cunha	397-398
Zambia	348-349

Nos. 399-400 (2)	1.60	1.60
Nos. 602-603 (2)	2.75	2.75
Nos. 687-688 (2)	2.00	1.25
Nos. 560-561 (2)	1.70	2.35
Nos. 629-630 (2)	1.35	1.35
Nos. 275-276 (2)	2.40	2.40
Nos. 460-461 (2)	1.05	1.05
Nos. 181-182 (2)	1.50	2.25
Nos. 602-603 (2)	2.50	2.50
Nos. 119-120 (2)	2.30	2.30
Nos. 567-568 (2)	1.00	1.00
Nos. 397-398 (2)	1.40	1.40
Nos. 348-349 (2)	1.10	1.30
Set total (26) Stamps	22.65	23.50

Queen Elizabeth II, 60th Birthday

Queen Elizabeth II & Prince Philip, 1947 Wedding Portrait — CD339

Designs: Photographs tracing the life of Queen Elizabeth II.

1986

Anguilla	674-677
Antigua	925-928
Barbuda	783-786
Dominica	950-953
Gambia	611-614
Grenada	1371-1374
Grenada Grenadines	749-752
Lesotho	531-534
Maldive Islands	1172-1175
Sierra Leone	760-763
Uganda	495-498

Nos. 674-677 (4)	8.00	8.00
Nos. 925-928 (4)	5.50	6.20
Nos. 783-786 (4)	23.15	23.15
Nos. 950-953 (4)	7.25	7.25
Nos. 611-614 (4)	8.25	7.90
Nos. 1371-1374 (4)	6.80	6.80
Nos. 749-752 (4)	6.75	6.75
Nos. 531-534 (4)	5.25	5.25
Nos. 1172-1175 (4)	6.25	6.25
Nos. 760-763 (4)	5.25	5.25
Nos. 495-498 (4)	8.50	8.50
Set total (44) Stamps	90.95	91.30

Royal Wedding, 1986

CD340

Designs: Photographs of Prince Andrew and Sarah Ferguson during courtship, engagement and marriage.

1986

Antigua	939-942
Barbuda	809-812
Dominica	970-973
Gambia	635-638
Grenada	1385-1388
Grenada Grenadines	758-761
Lesotho	545-548
Maldive Islands	1181-1184
Sierra Leone	769-772
Uganda	510-513

Nos. 939-942 (4)	7.00	8.75
Nos. 809-812 (4)	14.55	14.55
Nos. 970-973 (4)	7.25	7.25
Nos. 635-638 (4)	8.55	8.55
Nos. 1385-1388 (4)	8.30	8.30
Nos. 758-761 (4)	9.00	9.00

Nos. 545-548 (4)	7.45	7.45
Nos. 1181-1184 (4)	8.45	8.45
Nos. 769-772 (4)	5.35	5.35
Nos. 510-513 (4)	9.25	10.00
Set total (40) Stamps	85.15	87.65

Lloyds of London, 300th Anniv.

CD341

Designs: 17th century aspects of Lloyds, representations of each country's individual connections with Lloyds and publicized disasters insured by the organization.

1986

Ascension	454-457
Bahamas	655-658
Barbados	731-734
Bermuda	541-544
Falkland Islands	481-484
Liberia	1101-1104
Malawi	534-537
Nevis	571-574
St. Helena	501-504
St. Lucia	923-926
Seychelles	649-652
Zil Elwannyen Sesel	146-149
Solomon Islands	627-630
South Georgia	131-134
Trinidad & Tobago	484-487
Tristan da Cunha	439-442
Vanuatu	485-488

Nos. 454-457 (4)	5.00	5.00
Nos. 655-658 (4)	8.90	4.95
Nos. 731-734 (4)	12.50	8.35
Nos. 541-544 (4)	8.00	6.60
Nos. 481-484 (4)	5.45	3.85
Nos. 1101-1104 (4)	4.25	4.25
Nos. 534-537 (4)	11.00	7.85
Nos. 571-574 (4)	8.35	8.35
Nos. 501-504 (4)	8.70	7.15
Nos. 923-926 (4)	9.40	9.40
Nos. 649-652 (4)	12.85	12.85
Nos. 146-149 (4)	11.25	11.25
Nos. 627-630 (4)	7.00	4.45
Nos. 131-134 (4)	6.30	3.70
Nos. 484-487 (4)	10.25	6.35
Nos. 439-442 (4)	7.60	7.60
Nos. 485-488 (4)	5.90	5.90
Set total (68) Stamps	142.70	117.85

Moon Landing, 20th Anniv.

CD342

Designs: Equipment, crew photographs, spacecraft, official emblems and report profiles created for the Apollo Missions. Two stamps in each set are square in format rather than like the stamp shown; see individual country listings for more information.

1989

Ascension	468-472
Bahamas	674-678
Belize	916-920
Kiribati	517-521
Liberia	1125-1129
Nevis	586-590
St. Kitts	248-252
Samoa	760-764
Seychelles	676-680
Zil Elwannyen Sesel	154-158
Solomon Islands	643-647
Vanuatu	507-511

Nos. 468-472 (5)	9.40	8.60
Nos. 674-678 (5)	23.00	19.70
Nos. 916-920 (5)	22.85	18.10
Nos. 517-521 (5)	12.50	12.50
Nos. 1125-1129 (5)	8.50	8.50
Nos. 586-590 (5)	7.50	7.50

Nos. 248-252 (5)	8.00	8.25
Nos. 760-764 (5)	9.85	9.30
Nos. 676-680 (5)	16.05	16.05
Nos. 154-158 (5)	26.85	26.85
Nos. 643-647 (5)	9.00	6.75
Nos. 507-511 (5)	9.00	9.90
Set total (60) Stamps	163.40	152.00

Queen Mother, 90th Birthday

CD343 CD344

Designs: Portraits of Queen Elizabeth, the Queen Mother. See individual country listings for more information.

1990

Ascension	491-492
Bahamas	698-699
Barbados	782-783
British Antarctic Territory	170-171
British Indian Ocean Territory	106-107
Cayman Islands	622-623
Falkland Islands	524-525
Kenya	527-528
Kiribati	555-556
Liberia	1145-1146
Pitcairn Islands	336-337
St. Helena	532-533
St. Lucia	969-970
Seychelles	710-711
Zil Elwannyen Sesel	171-172
Solomon Islands	671-672
South Georgia	143-144
Swaziland	565-566
Tristan da Cunha	480-481

Nos. 491-492 (2)	4.75	4.75
Nos. 698-699 (2)	5.25	5.25
Nos. 782-783 (2)	4.00	3.70
Nos. 170-171 (2)	6.00	6.00
Nos. 106-107 (2)	18.00	18.50
Nos. 622-623 (2)	4.00	5.50
Nos. 524-525 (2)	4.75	4.75
Nos. 527-528 (2)	7.00	7.00
Nos. 555-556 (2)	4.75	4.75
Nos. 1145-1146 (2)	3.25	3.25
Nos. 336-337 (2)	4.25	4.25
Nos. 532-533 (2)	5.25	5.25
Nos. 069-970 (2)	5.25	5.25
Nos. 710-711 (2)	6.60	6.60
Nos. 171-172 (2)	8.25	8.25
Nos. 671-672 (2)	5.00	5.30
Nos. 143-144 (2)	5.50	6.50
Nos. 565-566 (2)	4.10	4.10
Nos. 480-481 (2)	5.60	5.60
Set total (38) Stamps	111.55	114.55

Queen Elizabeth II, 65th Birthday, and Prince Philip, 70th Birthday

CD345

CD346

Designs: Portraits of Queen Elizabeth II and Prince Philip differ for each country. Printed in sheets of 10 + 5 labels (3 different) between. Stamps alternate, producing 5 different triptychs.

1991

Ascension	506a
Bahamas	731a

Belize	970a
Bermuda	618a
Kiribati	572a
Mauritius	734a
Pitcairn Islands	349a
St. Helena	555a
St. Kitts	319a
Samoa	791a
Seychelles	724a
Zil Elwannyen Sesel	178a
Solomon Islands	689a
South Georgia	150a
Swaziland	587a
Vanuatu	541a

No. 506a (1)	3.50	3.75
No. 731a (1)	4.00	4.00
No. 970a (1)	3.75	3.75
No. 618a (1)	3.50	4.00
No. 572a (1)	4.00	4.00
No. 734a (1)	3.75	3.75
No. 349a (1)	3.25	3.25
No. 555a (1)	2.75	2.75
No. 319a (1)	3.00	3.00
No. 791a (1)	3.75	3.75
No. 724a (1)	5.00	5.00
No. 178a (1)	6.25	6.25
No. 689a (1)	3.75	3.75
No. 150a (1)	4.75	7.00
No. 587a (1)	4.00	4.00
No. 541a (1)	2.50	2.50
Set total (16) Stamps	61.50	64.50

Royal Family Birthday, Anniversary

CD347

Queen Elizabeth II, 65th birthday, Charles and Diana, 10th wedding anniversary: Various photographs of Queen Elizabeth II, Prince Philip, Prince Charles, Princess Diana and their sons William and Henry.

1991

Antigua	1446-1455
Barbuda	1229-1238
Dominica	1328-1337
Gambia	1080-1089
Grenada	2006-2015
Grenada Grenadines	1331-1340
Guyana	2440-2451
Lesotho	871-875
Maldive Islands	1533-1542
Nevis	666-675
St. Vincent	1485-1494
St. Vincent Grenadines	769-778
Sierra Leone	1387-1396
Turks & Caicos Islands	913-922
Uganda	918-927

Nos. 1446-1455 (10)	21.70	20.05
Nos. 1229-1238 (10)	125.00	119.50
Nos. 1328-1337 (10)	30.20	30.20
Nos. 1080-1089 (10)	24.65	24.40
Nos. 2006-2015 (10)	25.45	22.10
Nos. 1331-1340 (10)	23.85	23.35
Nos. 2440-2451 (12)	21.40	21.15
Nos. 871-875 (5)	13.55	13.55
Nos. 1533-1542 (10)	28.10	28.10
Nos. 666-675 (10)	23.65	23.65
Nos. 1485-1494 (10)	26.75	25.90
Nos. 769-778 (10)	25.40	25.40
Nos. 1387-1396 (10)	26.35	26.35
Nos. 913-922 (10)	27.50	25.30
Nos. 918-927 (10)	26.60	26.60
Set total (147) Stamps	470.15	455.60

Queen Elizabeth II's Accession to the Throne, 40th Anniv.

CD348

Various photographs of Queen Elizabeth II with local Scenes.

1992

Antigua	1513-1518
Barbuda	1306-1311
Dominica	1414-1419
Gambia	1172-1177
Grenada	2047-2052
Grenada Grenadines	1368-1373
Lesotho	881-885

Maldive Islands	1637-1642
Nevis	702-707
St. Vincent	1582-1587
St. Vincent Grenadines	829-834
Sierra Leone	1482-1487
Turks and Caicos Islands	978-987
Uganda	990-995
Virgin Islands	742-746

Nos. 1513-1518 (6)	15.00	15.10
Nos. 1306-1311 (6)	125.25	83.65
Nos. 1414-1419 (6)	12.50	12.50
Nos. 1172-1177 (6)	16.60	16.35
Nos. 2047-2052 (6)	15.95	15.95
Nos. 1368-1373 (6)	17.00	15.35
Nos. 881-885 (5)	11.90	11.90
Nos. 1637-1642 (6)	17.55	17.55
Nos. 702-707 (6)	13.55	13.55
Nos. 1582-1587 (6)	14.40	14.40
Nos. 829-834 (6)	19.65	19.65
Nos. 1482-1487 (6)	22.50	22.50
Nos. 913-922 (10)	27.50	25.30
Nos. 990-995 (6)	19.50	19.50
Nos. 742-746 (5)	15.50	15.50
Set total (92) Stamps	364.35	318.75

CD349

1992

Ascension	531-535
Bahamas	744-748
Bermuda	623-627
British Indian Ocean Territory	119-123
Cayman Islands	648-652
Falkland Islands	549-553
Gibraltar	605-609
Hong Kong	619-623
Kenya	563-567
Kiribati	582-586
Pitcairn Islands	362-366
St. Helena	570-574
St. Kitts	332-336
Samoa	805-809
Seychelles	734-738
Zil Elwannyen Sesel	183-187
Solomon Islands	708-712
South Georgia	157-161
Tristan da Cunha	508-512
Vanuatu	555-559
Zambia	561-565

Nos. 531-535 (5)	6.10	6.10
Nos. 744-748 (5)	4.90	4.70
Nos. 623-627 (5)	7.40	7.55
Nos. 119-123 (5)	22.75	19.25
Nos. 648-652 (5)	7.60	6.60
Nos. 549-553 (5)	6.05	5.90
Nos. 605-609 (5)	5.15	5.50
Nos. 619-623 (5)	5.10	5.25
Nos. 563-567 (5)	9.10	9.10
Nos. 582-586 (5)	3.85	3.85
Nos. 362-366 (5)	5.35	5.35
Nos. 570-574 (5)	5.70	5.70
Nos. 332-336 (5)	6.60	5.50
Nos. 805-809 (5)	7.85	5.90
Nos. 734-738 (5)	10.55	10.55
Nos. 183-187 (5)	9.40	9.40
Nos. 708-712 (5)	5.00	5.30
Nos. 157-161 (5)	5.60	5.90
Nos. 508-512 (5)	8.75	8.30
Nos. 555-559 (5)	3.65	3.65
Nos. 561-565 (5)	5.60	5.60
Set total (105) Stamps	153.95	144.95

Royal Air Force, 75th Anniversary

CD350

1993

Ascension	557-561
Bahamas	771-775
Barbados	842-846
Belize	1003-1008
Bermuda	648-651
British Indian Ocean Territory	136-140
Falkland Is.	573-577
Fiji	687-691
Montserrat	830-834

St. Kitts	351-355

Nos. 557-561 (5)	15.60	14.60
Nos. 771-775 (5)	24.65	21.45
Nos. 842-846 (5)	14.15	12.85
Nos. 1003-1008 (6)	16.55	16.50
Nos. 648-651 (4)	9.65	10.45
Nos. 136-140 (5)	16.10	16.10
Nos. 573-577 (5)	10.85	10.85
Nos. 687-691 (5)	17.75	17.40
Nos. 830-834 (5)	14.10	14.10
Nos. 351-355 (5)	22.80	23.55
Set total (50) Stamps	162.20	157.85

Royal Air Force, 80th Anniv.

Design CD350 Re-inscribed

1998

Ascension	697-701
Bahamas	907-911
British Indian Ocean Terr	198-202
Cayman Islands	754-758
Fiji	814-818
Gibraltar	755-759
Samoa	957-961
Turks & Caicos Islands	1258-1265
Tuvalu	763-767
Virgin Islands	879-883

Nos. 697-701 (5)	16.10	16.10
Nos. 907-911 (5)	13.60	12.65
Nos. 136-140 (5)	16.10	16.10
Nos. 754-758 (5)	15.25	15.25
Nos. 814-818 (5)	14.00	10.75
Nos. 755-759 (5)	9.70	9.70
Nos. 957-961 (5)	15.70	14.90
Nos. 1258-1265 (2)	27.50	27.50
Nos. 763-767 (5)	9.75	9.75
Nos. 879-883 (5)	15.00	15.00
Set total (47) Stamps	152.70	149.70

End of World War II, 50th Anniv.

CD351

CD352

1995

Ascension	613-617
Bahamas	824-828
Barbados	891-895
Belize	1047-1050
British Indian Ocean Territory	163-167
Cayman Islands	704-708
Falkland Islands	634-638
Fiji	720-724
Kiribati	662-668
Liberia	1175-1179
Mauritius	803-805
St. Helena	646-654
St. Kitts	389-393
St. Lucia	1018-1022
Samoa	890-894
Solomon Islands	799-803
South Georgia	198-200
Tristan da Cunha	562-566

Nos. 613-617 (5)	21.50	21.50

Nos. 824-828 (5)	22.00	18.70
Nos. 891-895 (5)	14.20	11.90
Nos. 1047-1050 (4)	6.05	5.90
Nos. 163-167 (5)	16.25	16.25
Nos. 704-708 (5)	17.65	13.95
Nos. 634-638 (5)	18.65	17.15
Nos. 720-724 (5)	17.50	14.50
Nos. 662-668 (7)	16.30	16.30
Nos. 1175-1179 (5)	15.25	11.15
Nos. 803-805 (3)	7.50	7.50
Nos. 646-654 (9)	26.10	26.10
Nos. 389-393 (5)	16.40	16.40
Nos. 1018-1022 (5)	14.25	11.15
Nos. 890-894 (5)	15.25	14.50
Nos. 799-803 (5)	14.75	14.75
Nos. 198-200 (3)	14.50	15.50
Nos. 562-566 (5)	20.10	20.10
Set total (91) Stamps	294.20	273.30

UN, 50th Anniv.

CD353

1995

Bahamas		839-842
Barbados		901-904
Belize		1055-1058
Jamaica		847-851
Liberia		1187-1190
Mauritius		813-816
Pitcairn Islands		436-439
St. Kitts		398-401
St. Lucia		1023-1026
Samoa		900-903
Tristan da Cunha		568-571
Virgin Islands		807-810

Nos. 839-842 (4)	7.15	6.40
Nos. 901-904 (4)	7.00	5.75
Nos. 1055-1058 (4)	4.70	4.70
Nos. 847-851 (5)	5.40	5.45
Nos. 1187-1190 (4)	9.65	9.65
Nos. 813-816 (4)	3.90	3.90
Nos. 436-439 (4)	8.15	8.15
Nos. 398-401 (4)	6.15	7.15
Nos. 1023-1026 (4)	7.50	7.25
Nos. 900-903 (4)	9.35	8.20
Nos. 568-571 (4)	13.50	13.50
Nos. 807-810 (4)	7.45	7.45
Set total (49) Stamps	89.90	87.55

Queen Elizabeth, 70th Birthday

CD354

1996

Ascension		632-635
British Antarctic Territory		240-243
British Indian Ocean Territory		176-180
Falkland Islands		653-657
Pitcairn Islands		446-449
St. Helena		672-676
Samoa		912-916
Tokelau		223-227
Tristan da Cunha		576-579
Virgin Islands		824-828

Nos. 632-635 (4)	5.30	5.30
Nos. 240-243 (4)	9.45	8.15
Nos. 176-180 (5)	11.50	11.50
Nos. 653-657 (5)	13.55	11.20
Nos. 446-449 (4)	8.60	8.60
Nos. 672-676 (5)	12.70	12.70
Nos. 912-916 (5)	10.50	10.50
Nos. 223-227 (5)	10.50	10.50
Nos. 576-579 (4)	8.35	8.35
Nos. 824-828 (5)	11.30	11.30
Set total (46) Stamps	101.75	98.10

Diana, Princess of Wales (1961-97)

CD355

1998

Ascension		696
Bahamas		901A-902
Barbados		950
Belize		1091
Bermuda		753
Botswana		659-663
British Antarctic Territory		258
British Indian Ocean Terr.		197
Cayman Islands		752A-753
Falkland Islands		694
Fiji		819-820
Gibraltar		754
Kiribati		719A-720
Namibia		909
Niue		706
Norfolk Island		644-645
Papua New Guinea		937
Pitcairn Islands		487
St. Helena		711
St. Kitts		437A-438
Samoa		955A-956
Seychelles		802
Solomon Islands		866-867
South Georgia		220
Tokelau		252B-253
Tonga		980
Niuafo'ou		201
Tristan da Cunha		618
Tuvalu		762
Vanuatu		718A-719
Virgin Islands		878

No. 696 (1)	5.25	5.25
Nos. 901A-902 (2)	5.30	5.30
No. 950 (1)	6.25	6.25
No. 1091 (1)	5.00	5.00
No. 753 (1)	5.00	5.00
Nos. 659-663 (5)	8.25	8.80
No. 258 (1)	5.50	5.50
No. 197 (1)	5.50	5.50
Nos. 752A-753 (3)	7.40	7.40
No. 694 (1)	5.00	5.00
Nos. 819-820 (2)	5.25	5.25
No. 754 (1)	4.75	4.75
Nos. 719A-720 (2)	4.85	4.85
No. 909 (1)	1.75	1.75
No. 706 (1)	5.50	5.50
Nos. 644-645 (2)	5.25	5.25
No. 937 (1)	6.25	6.25
No. 487 (1)	4.75	4.75
No. 711 (1)	4.25	4.25
Nos. 437A-438 (2)	5.15	5.15
Nos. 955A-956 (2)	7.00	7.00
No. 802 (1)	6.25	6.25
Nos. 866-867 (2)	5.40	5.40
No. 220 (1)	4.50	5.00
Nos. 252B-253 (2)	6.00	6.00
No. 980 (1)	5.75	5.75
No. 201 (1)	6.50	6.50
No. 618 (1)	5.00	5.00
No. 762 (1)	4.00	4.00
Nos. 718A-719 (2)	8.00	8.00
No. 878 (1)	4.50	4.50
Set total (46) Stamps	169.10	170.15

Wedding of Prince Edward and Sophie Rhys-Jones

CD356

1999

Ascension		729-730
Cayman Islands		775-776
Falkland Islands		729-730
Pitcairn Islands		505-506
St. Helena		733-734
Samoa		971-972
Tristan da Cunha		636-637

Virgin Islands		908-909

Nos. 729-730 (2)	4.50	4.50
Nos. 775-776 (2)	4.95	4.95
Nos. 729-730 (2)	14.00	14.00
Nos. 505-506 (2)	7.00	7.00
Nos. 733-734 (2)	5.00	5.00
Nos. 971-972 (2)	5.00	5.00
Nos. 636-637 (2)	7.50	7.50
Nos. 908-909 (2)	7.50	7.50
Set total (16) Stamps	55.45	55.45

1st Manned Moon Landing, 30th Anniv.

CD357

1999

Ascension		731-735
Bahamas		942-946
Barbados		967-971
Bermuda		778
Cayman Islands		777-781
Fiji		853-857
Jamaica		889-893
Kiribati		746-750
Nauru		465-469
St. Kitts		460-464
Samoa		973-977
Solomon Islands		875-879
Tuvalu		800-804
Virgin Islands		910-914

Nos. 731-735 (5)	12.80	12.80
Nos. 942-946 (5)	14.10	14.10
Nos. 967-971 (5)	9.45	8.25
No. 778 (1)	9.00	9.00
Nos. 777-781 (5)	9.25	9.25
Nos. 853-857 (5)	9.25	8.45
Nos. 889-893 (5)	8.30	7.18
Nos. 746-750 (5)	8.85	8.85
Nos. 465-469 (5)	9.25	8.00
Nos. 460-464 (5)	11.35	11.65
Nos. 973-977 (5)	12.60	12.45
Nos. 875-879 (5)	7.50	7.50
Nos. 800-804 (5)	7.45	7.45
Nos. 910-914 (5)	11.75	11.75
Set total (66) Stamps	140.90	136.68

Queen Mother's Century

CD358

1999

Ascension		736-740
Bahamas		951-955
Cayman Islands		782-786
Falkland Islands		734-738
Fiji		858-862
Norfolk Island		688-692
St. Helena		740-744
Samoa		978-982
Solomon Islands		880-884
South Georgia		231-235
Tristan da Cunha		638-642
Tuvalu		805-809

Nos. 736-740 (5)	15.50	15.50
Nos. 951-955 (5)	13.75	12.65
Nos. 782-786 (5)	8.35	8.35
Nos. 734-738 (5)	30.00	28.25
Nos. 858-862 (5)	12.80	13.25
Nos. 688-692 (5)	10.30	10.30
Nos. 740-744 (5)	16.15	16.15
Nos. 978-982 (5)	12.50	12.10
Nos. 880-884 (5)	7.50	7.00
Nos. 231-235 (5)	29.75	30.00
Nos. 638-642 (5)	18.00	18.00
Nos. 805-809 (5)	8.65	8.65
Set total (60) Stamps	183.25	180.20

Prince William, 18th Birthday

CD359

2000

Ascension		755-759
Cayman Islands		797-801
Falkland Islands		762-766
Fiji		889-893
South Georgia		257-261
Tristan da Cunha		664-668
Virgin Islands		925-929

Nos. 755-759 (5)	15.50	15.50
Nos. 797-801 (5)	11.15	10.90
Nos. 762-766 (5)	24.60	22.50
Nos. 889-893 (5)	12.90	12.90
Nos. 257-261 (5)	29.00	28.75
Nos. 664-668 (5)	21.50	21.50
Nos. 925-929 (5)	14.50	14.50
Set total (35) Stamps	129.15	126.55

Reign of Queen Elizabeth II, 50th Anniv.

CD360

2002

Ascension		790-794
Bahamas		1033-1037
Barbados		1019-1023
Belize		1152-1156
Bermuda		822-826
British Antarctic Territory		307-311
British Indian Ocean Territory		239-243
Cayman Islands		844-848
Falkland Islands		804-808
Gibraltar		896-900
Jamaica		952-956
Nauru		491-495
Norfolk Island		758-762
Papua New Guinea		1019-1023
Pitcairn Islands		552
St. Helena		788-792
St. Lucia		1146-1150
Solomon Islands		931-935
South Georgia		274-278
Swaziland		706-710
Tokelau		302-306
Tonga		1059
Niuafo'ou		239
Tristan da Cunha		706-710
Virgin Islands		967-971

Nos. 790-794 (5)	14.10	14.10
Nos. 1033-1037 (5)	15.25	15.25
Nos. 1019-1023 (5)	12.90	12.90
Nos. 1152-1156 (5)	12.65	12.25
Nos. 822-826 (5)	18.00	18.00
Nos. 307-311 (5)	23.00	23.00
Nos. 239-243 (5)	19.40	19.40
Nos. 844-848 (5)	13.25	13.25
Nos. 804-808 (5)	23.00	22.00
Nos. 896-900 (5)	6.65	6.65
Nos. 952-956 (5)	16.65	16.65
Nos. 491-495 (5)	17.75	17.75
Nos. 758-762 (5)	19.50	19.50
Nos. 1019-1023 (5)	14.50	14.50
No. 552 (1)	9.25	9.25
Nos. 788-792 (5)	19.75	19.75
Nos. 1146-1150 (5)	12.25	12.25
Nos. 931-935 (5)	12.40	12.40
Nos. 274-278 (5)	28.00	28.50
Nos. 706-710 (5)	12.50	12.50
Nos. 302-306 (5)	14.50	14.50
No. 1059 (1)	8.50	8.50
No. 239 (1)	8.75	8.75
Nos. 706-710 (5)	18.50	18.50
Nos. 967-971 (5)	16.50	16.50
Set total (113) Stamps	387.50	386.60

Queen Mother Elizabeth (1900-2002)

CD361

2002

Ascension		799-801
Bahamas		1044-1046
Bermuda		834-836
British Antarctic Territory		312-314
British Indian Ocean Territory		245-247
Cayman Islands		857-861
Falkland Islands		812-816
Nauru		499-501
Pitcairn Islands		561-565
St. Helena		808-812
St. Lucia		1155-1159
Seychelles		830
Solomon Islands		945-947
South Georgia		281-285
Tokelau		312-314
Tristan da Cunha		715-717
Virgin Islands		979-983

Nos. 799-801 (3)	8.85	8.85
Nos. 1044-1046 (3)	9.10	9.10
Nos. 834-836 (3)	12.25	12.25
Nos. 312-314 (3)	18.75	18.75
Nos. 245-247 (3)	17.35	17.35
Nos. 857-861 (5)	15.00	15.00
Nos. 812-816 (5)	28.50	28.50
Nos. 499-501 (3)	14.00	14.00
Nos. 561-565 (5)	15.25	15.25
Nos. 808-812 (5)	12.00	12.00
Nos. 1155-1159 (5)	10.00	13.00
No. 830 (1)	6.50	6.50
Nos. 945-947 (3)	9.25	9.25
Nos. 281-285 (5)	19.50	19.50
Nos. 312-314 (3)	11.85	11.85
Nos. 715-717 (3)	16.25	16.25
Nos. 979-983 (5)	23.50	23.50
Set total (63) Stamps	250.90	250.90

Head of Queen Elizabeth II

CD362

2003

Ascension		822
Bermuda		865
British Antarctic Territory		322
British Indian Ocean Territory		261
Cayman Islands		878
Falkland Islands		828
St. Helena		820
South Georgia		294
Tristan da Cunha		731
Virgin Islands		1003

No. 822 (1)	12.50	12.50
No. 865 (1)	50.00	50.00
No. 322 (1)	9.50	9.50
No. 261 (1)	11.00	11.00
No. 878 (1)	14.00	14.00
No. 828 (1)	9.00	9.00
No. 820 (1)	9.00	9.00
No. 294 (1)	8.50	8.50
No. 731 (1)	10.00	10.00
No. 1003 (1)	10.00	10.00
Set total (10) Stamps	143.50	143.50

Coronation of Queen Elizabeth II, 50th Anniv.

CD363

2003

Ascension		823-825

Bahamas		1073-1075
Bermuda		866-868
British Antarctic Territory		323-325
British Indian Ocean Territory		262-264
Cayman Islands		879-881
Jamaica		970-972
Kiribati		825-827
Pitcairn Islands		577-581
St. Helena		821-823
St. Lucia		1171-1173
Tokelau		320-322
Tristan da Cunha		732-734
Virgin Islands		1004-1006

Nos. 823-825 (3)	12.50	12.50
Nos. 1073-1075 (3)	13.00	13.00
Nos. 866-868 (2)	14.25	14.25
Nos. 323-325 (3)	23.00	23.00
Nos. 262-264 (3)	28.00	28.00
Nos. 879-881 (3)	19.25	19.25
Nos. 970-972 (3)	10.00	10.00
Nos. 825-827 (3)	13.50	13.50
Nos. 577-581 (5)	14.40	14.40
Nos. 821-823 (3)	7.25	7.25
Nos. 1171-1173 (3)	8.75	8.75
Nos. 320-322 (3)	17.25	17.25
Nos. 732-734 (3)	16.75	16.75
Nos. 1004-1006 (3)	25.00	25.00
Set total (43) Stamps	222.90	222.90

Prince William, 21st Birthday

CD364

2003

Ascension		826
British Indian Ocean Territory		265
Cayman Islands		882-884
Falkland Islands		829
South Georgia		295
Tokelau		323
Tristan da Cunha		735
Virgin Islands		1007-1009

No. 826 (1)	7.25	7.25
No. 265 (1)	8.00	8.00
Nos. 882-884 (3)	6.95	6.95
No. 829 (1)	13.50	13.50
No. 295 (1)	8.50	8.50
No. 323 (1)	7.25	7.25
No. 735 (1)	6.00	6.00
Nos. 1007-1009 (3)	10.00	10.00
Set total (12) Stamps	67.45	67.45

2018 Scott Specialty Series Supplement Releases

Start collecting a new country today! Take a look at any of the newly released 2018 Scott Specialty Series and the many different countries that are available. Make sure you don't forget to pick up a classic, durable 3-ring or 2-post binder and slipcase to house your collection.

ASIA

Item#	Country	Retail	AA	Release
275HK18	Hong Kong	$22.99	$19.99	June
618S018	India	$22.99	$19.99	July
510S018	Japan	$45.99	$39.99	July
520S018	People's Republic of China	$22.99	$19.99	July
530S018	Republic of China Taiwan	$22.99	$19.99	July
275SG18	Singapore	$22.99	$19.99	September
622S018	Sri Lanka	$19.99	$16.99	July
540S018	Thailand	$22.99	$19.99	July

NORTH AMERICA

Item#	Country	Retail	AA	Release
170S018	American	$34.99	$29.99	March
240S018	Canada	$25.99	$21.99	May
245S018	Master Canada	$28.99	$24.99	May
430S018	Mexico	$19.99	$16.99	September

EASTERN EUROPE

Item#	Country	Retail	AA	Release
361S018	Baltic States	$19.99	$16.99	August
307S018	Czech Republic & Slovakia	$22.99	$19.99	August
323S018	Hungary	$22.99	$19.99	August
338S018	Poland	$19.99	$16.99	August
360S018	Russia	$34.99	$29.99	September
362UK18	Ukraine	$19.99	$16.99	September

WESTERN EUROPE

Item#	Country	Retail	AA	Release
300S018	Austria	$19.99	$16.99	May
303S018	Belgium	$22.99	$19.99	August
203CY18	Cyprus	$11.99	$9.99	May
345DM18	Denmark	$16.99	$13.99	June
345FI18	Faroe Islands	$11.99	$9.99	June
345FN18	Finland/Aland	$22.99	$19.99	June
310S018	France	$34.99	$29.99	May
626S018	French Southern & Antarctic Territory	$16.99	$13.99	August
315S318	Germany	$16.99	$13.99	May
320S018	Greece	$22.99	$19.99	June
345GR18	Greenland	$16.99	$13.99	June
345IC18	Iceland	$11.99	$9.99	June
201S018	Ireland	$16.99	$13.99	June
325S018	Italy	$22.99	$19.99	September
367S018	Liechtenstein	$11.99	$9.99	June
330S018	Luxembourg	$11.99	$9.99	August
203ML18	Malta	$16.99	$13.99	May
333S018	Monaco & French Andorra	$19.99	$16.99	May
335S018	Netherlands	$40.99	$34.99	August
345NR18	Norway	$11.99	$9.99	June
340S018	Portugal/Azores/Maderia	$22.99	$19.99	September

WESTERN EUROPE

Item#	Country	Retail	AA	Release
328S018	San Marino	$11.99	$9.99	July
355S018	Spain & Spanish Andorra	$22.99	$19.99	July
345SW18	Sweden	$16.99	$13.99	September
365S018	Switzerland	$16.99	$13.99	June
375S018	Vatican City	$11.99	$9.99	July

OCEANIA

Item#	Country	Retail	AA	Release
210S018	Australia	$22.99	$19.99	September
211S018	Dependencies of Australia	$22.99	$19.99	September
221S018	Dependencies of New Zealand	$34.99	$29.99	September
625S018	French Polynesia	$11.99	$9.99	August
220S018	New Zealand	$22.99	$19.99	September

UNITED KINGDOM

Item#	Country	Retail	AA	Release
203GB18	Gibraltar	$16.99	$13.99	May
200S018	Great Britain	$22.99	$19.99	May
202GN18	Guernsey & Alderney	$22.99	$19.99	May
202IM18	Isle of Man	$22.99	$19.99	May
202JR18	Jersey	$22.99	$19.99	May
200M018	Great Britain Machins	$9.99	$8.49	July

SOUTH AMERICA

Item#	Country	Retail	AA	Release
642S018	Argentina	$19.99	$16.99	September
644S018	Brazil	$19.99	$16.99	May

CARRIBEAN

Item#	Country	Retail	AA	Release
648S018	Dominican Republic	$16.99	$13.99	September

MIDDLE EAST

Item#	Country	Retail	AA	Release
500S018	Israel Singles	$13.99	$11.89	August
501S018	Israel Tab Singles	$13.99	$11.89	August
505S018	Turkey	$22.99	$19.99	August

SCOTT BINDERS & SLIPCASES

Item#		Retail	AA
ACBR03SET	Large Green 3-Ring, Metal-Hinged, Binder & Slipcase	$79.49	$55.78
ACBR01SET	Small Green 3-Ring, Metal-Hinged, Binder & Slipcase	$79.49	$55.78
ACBS03SET	Large Green Square 2-Post Binder & Slipcase	$92.49	$66.58
ACBUSET	Green Universal Binder & Slipcase (Fit any Scott Album)	$77.49	$53.98

See the Full List of 2018 Scott Supplements at
www.AmosAdvantage.com
or Call 800-572-6885
Outside U.S. & Canada call (937) 498-0800

Ordering Information: *AA prices apply to paid subscribers of Amos Media titles, or for orders placed online. Prices, terms and product availability subject to change. Shipping & Handling: U.S.: Orders total $0-$10.00 charged $3.99 shipping. U.S. Order total $10.01-$79.99 charged $7.99 shipping. U.S. Order total $80.00 or more charged 10% of order total for shipping. Taxes will apply in CA, OH, & IL. Canada: 20% of order total. Minimum charge $19.99 Maximum charge $200.00. Foreign orders are shipped via FedEx Intl. or USPS and billed actual freight.

British Commonwealth of Nations

Dominions, Colonies, Territories, Offices and Independent Members

Comprising stamps of the British Commonwealth and associated nations.

A strict observance of technicalities would bar some or all of the stamps listed under Burma, Ireland, Kuwait, Nepal, New Republic, Orange Free State, Samoa, South Africa, South-West Africa, Stellaland, Sudan, Swaziland, the two Transvaal Republics and others but these are included for the convenience of collectors.

1. Great Britain

Great Britain: Including England, Scotland, Wales and Northern Ireland.

2. The Dominions, Present and Past

AUSTRALIA

The Commonwealth of Australia was proclaimed on January 1, 1901. It consists of six former colonies as follows:

New South Wales	Victoria
Queensland	Tasmania
South Australia	Western Australia

The following islands and territories are, or have been, administered by Australia: Australian Antarctic Territory, Christmas Island, Cocos (Keeling) Islands, Nauru, New Guinea, Norfolk Island, Papua.

CANADA

The Dominion of Canada was created by the British North America Act in 1867. The following provinces were former sepa- rate colonies and issued postage stamps:

British Columbia and	Newfoundland
Vancouver Island	Nova Scotia
New Brunswick	Prince Edward Island

FIJI

The colony of Fiji became an independent nation with dominion status on Oct. 10, 1970.

GHANA

This state came into existence Mar. 6, 1957, with dominion status. It consists of the former colony of the Gold Coast and the Trusteeship Territory of Togoland. Ghana became a republic July 1, 1960.

INDIA

The Republic of India was inaugurated on January 26, 1950. It succeeded the Dominion of India which was proclaimed August 15, 1947, when the former Empire of India was divided into Pakistan and the Union of India. The Republic is composed of about 40 predominantly Hindu states of three classes: governor's provinces, chief commissioner's provinces and princely states. India also has various territories, such as the Andaman and Nicobar Islands.

The old Empire of India was a federation of British India and the native states. The more important princely states were autonomous. Of the more than 700 Indian states, these 43 are familiar names to philatelists because of their postage stamps.

CONVENTION STATES

Chamba	Jhind
Faridkot	Nabha
Gwalior	Patiala

FEUDATORY STATES

Alwar	Jammu and Kashmir
Bahawalpur	Jasdan
Bamra	Jhalawar
Barwani	Jhind (1875-76)
Bhopal	Kashmir
Bhor	Kishangarh
Bijawar	Kotah
Bundi	Las Bela
Bussahir	Morvi
Charkhari	Nandgaon
Cochin	Nowanuggur
Dhar	Orchha
Dungarpur	Poonch
Duttia	Rajasthan
Faridkot (1879-85)	Rajpeepla
Hyderabad	Sirmur
Idar	Soruth
Indore	Tonk
Jaipur	Travancore
Jammu	Wadhwan

NEW ZEALAND

Became a dominion on September 26, 1907. The following islands and territories are, or have been, administered by New Zealand:

Aitutaki	Ross Dependency
Cook Islands (Rarotonga)	Samoa (Western Samoa)
Niue	Tokelau Islands
Penrhyn	

PAKISTAN

The Republic of Pakistan was proclaimed March 23, 1956. It succeeded the Dominion which was proclaimed August 15, 1947. It is made up of all or part of several Moslem provinces and various districts of the former Empire of India, including Bahawalpur and Las Bela. Pakistan withdrew from the Commonwealth in 1972.

SOUTH AFRICA

Under the terms of the South African Act (1909) the self-governing colonies of Cape of Good Hope, Natal, Orange River Colony and Transvaal united on May 31, 1910, to form the Union of South Africa. It became an independent republic May 3, 1961.

Under the terms of the Treaty of Versailles, South-West Africa, formerly German South-West Africa, was mandated to the Union of South Africa.

SRI LANKA (CEYLON)

The Dominion of Ceylon was proclaimed February 4, 1948. The island had been a Crown Colony from 1802 until then. On May 22, 1972, Ceylon became the Republic of Sri Lanka.

3. Colonies, Past and Present; Controlled Territory and Independent Members of the Commonwealth

Aden	Bechuanaland
Aitutaki	Bechuanaland Prot.
Anguilla	Belize
Antigua	Bermuda
Ascension	Botswana
Bahamas	British Antarctic Territory
Bahrain	British Central Africa
Bangladesh	British Columbia and
Barbados	Vancouver Island
Barbuda	British East Africa
Basutoland	British Guiana
Batum	

British Honduras
British Indian Ocean Territory
British New Guinea
British Solomon Islands
British Somaliland
Brunei
Burma
Bushire
Cameroons
Cape of Good Hope
Cayman Islands
Christmas Island
Cocos (Keeling) Islands
Cook Islands
Crete,
  British Administration
Cyprus
Dominica
East Africa & Uganda
  Protectorates
Egypt
Falkland Islands
Fiji
Gambia
German East Africa
Gibraltar
Gilbert Islands
Gilbert & Ellice Islands
Gold Coast
Grenada
Griqualand West
Guernsey
Guyana
Heligoland
Hong Kong
Indian Native States
  (see India)
Ionian Islands
Jamaica
Jersey

Kenya
Kenya, Uganda & Tanzania
Kuwait
Labuan
Lagos
Leeward Islands
Lesotho
Madagascar
Malawi
Malaya
  Federated Malay States
  Johore
  Kedah
  Kelantan
  Malacca
  Negri Sembilan
  Pahang
  Penang
  Perak
  Perlis
  Selangor
  Singapore
  Sungei Ujong
  Trengganu
Malaysia
Maldive Islands
Malta
Man, Isle of
Mauritius
Mesopotamia
Montserrat
Muscat
Namibia
Natal
Nauru
Nevis
New Britain
New Brunswick
Newfoundland
New Guinea

New Hebrides
New Republic
New South Wales
Niger Coast Protectorate
Nigeria
Niue
Norfolk Island
North Borneo
Northern Nigeria
Northern Rhodesia
North West Pacific Islands
Nova Scotia
Nyasaland Protectorate
Oman
Orange River Colony
Palestine
Papua New Guinea
Penrhyn Island
Pitcairn Islands
Prince Edward Island
Queensland
Rhodesia
Rhodesia & Nyasaland
Ross Dependency
Sabah
St. Christopher
St. Helena
St. Kitts
St. Kitts-Nevis-Anguilla
St. Lucia
St. Vincent
Samoa
Sarawak
Seychelles
Sierra Leone
Solomon Islands
Somaliland Protectorate
South Arabia
South Australia
South Georgia

Southern Nigeria
Southern Rhodesia
South-West Africa
Stellaland
Straits Settlements
Sudan
Swaziland
Tanganyika
Tanzania
Tasmania
Tobago
Togo
Tokelau Islands
Tonga
Transvaal
Trinidad
Trinidad and Tobago
Tristan da Cunha
Trucial States
Turks and Caicos
Turks Islands
Tuvalu
Uganda
United Arab Emirates
Victoria
Virgin Islands
Western Australia
Zambia
Zanzibar
Zululand

**POST OFFICES IN
FOREIGN COUNTRIES**
Africa
  East Africa Forces
  Middle East Forces
Bangkok
China
Morocco
Turkish Empire

Colonies, Former Colonies, Offices, Territories Controlled by Parent States

Belgium
Belgian Congo
Ruanda-Urundi

Denmark
Danish West Indies
Faroe Islands
Greenland
Iceland

Finland
Aland Islands

France

COLONIES PAST AND PRESENT, CONTROLLED TERRITORIES
Afars & Issas, Territory of
Alaouites
Alexandretta
Algeria
Alsace & Lorraine
Anjouan
Annam & Tonkin
Benin
Cambodia (Khmer)
Cameroun
Castellorizo
Chad
Cilicia
Cochin China
Comoro Islands
Dahomey
Diego Suarez
Djibouti (Somali Coast)
Fezzan
French Congo
French Equatorial Africa
French Guiana
French Guinea
French India
French Morocco
French Polynesia (Oceania)
French Southern & Antarctic Territories
French Sudan
French West Africa
Gabon
Germany
Ghadames
Grand Comoro
Guadeloupe
Indo-China
Inini
Ivory Coast
Laos
Latakia
Lebanon
Madagascar
Martinique
Mauritania
Mayotte
Memel
Middle Congo
Moheli
New Caledonia
New Hebrides
Niger Territory

Nossi-Be
Obock
Reunion
Rouad, Ile
Ste.-Marie de Madagascar
St. Pierre & Miquelon
Senegal
Senegambia & Niger
Somali Coast
Syria
Tahiti
Togo
Tunisia
Ubangi-Shari
Upper Senegal & Niger
Upper Volta
Viet Nam
Wallis & Futuna Islands

POST OFFICES IN FOREIGN COUNTRIES
China
Crete
Egypt
Turkish Empire
Zanzibar

Germany

EARLY STATES
Baden
Bavaria
Bergedorf
Bremen
Brunswick
Hamburg
Hanover
Lubeck
Mecklenburg-Schwerin
Mecklenburg-Strelitz
Oldenburg
Prussia
Saxony
Schleswig-Holstein
Wurttemberg

FORMER COLONIES
Cameroun (Kamerun)
Caroline Islands
German East Africa
German New Guinea
German South-West Africa
Kiauchau
Mariana Islands
Marshall Islands
Samoa
Togo

Italy

EARLY STATES
Modena
Parma
Romagna
Roman States
Sardinia
Tuscany
Two Sicilies
   Naples
   Neapolitan Provinces
   Sicily

FORMER COLONIES, CONTROLLED TERRITORIES, OCCUPATION AREAS
Aegean Islands
   Calimno (Calino)
   Caso
   Cos (Coo)
   Karki (Carchi)
   Leros (Lero)
   Lipso
   Nisiros (Nisiro)
   Patmos (Patmo)
   Piscopi
   Rodi (Rhodes)
   Scarpanto
   Simi
   Stampalia
Castellorizo
Corfu
Cyrenaica
Eritrea
Ethiopia (Abyssinia)
Fiume
Ionian Islands
   Cephalonia
   Ithaca
   Paxos
Italian East Africa
Libya
Oltre Giuba
Saseno
Somalia (Italian Somaliland)
Tripolitania

POST OFFICES IN FOREIGN COUNTRIES
"ESTERO"*
Austria
China
   Peking
   Tientsin
Crete
Tripoli
Turkish Empire
   Constantinople
   Durazzo
   Janina
Jerusalem
Salonika
Scutari
Smyrna
Valona
*Stamps overprinted "ESTERO" were used in various parts of the world.

Netherlands
Aruba
Caribbean Netherlands
Curacao
Netherlands Antilles (Curacao)
Netherlands Indies
Netherlands New Guinea
St. Martin
Surinam (Dutch Guiana)

Portugal

COLONIES PAST AND PRESENT, CONTROLLED TERRITORIES
Angola
Angra
Azores

Cape Verde
Funchal
Horta
Inhambane
Kionga
Lourenco Marques
Macao
Madeira
Mozambique
Mozambique Co.
Nyassa
Ponta Delgada
Portuguese Africa
Portuguese Congo
Portuguese Guinea
Portuguese India
Quelimane
St. Thomas & Prince Islands
Tete
Timor
Zambezia

Russia

ALLIED TERRITORIES AND REPUBLICS, OCCUPATION AREAS
Armenia
Aunus (Olonets)
Azerbaijan
Batum
Estonia
Far Eastern Republic
Georgia
Karelia
Latvia
Lithuania
North Ingermanland
Ostland
Russian Turkestan
Siberia
South Russia
Tannu Tuva
Transcaucasian Fed. Republics
Ukraine
Wenden (Livonia)
Western Ukraine

Spain

COLONIES PAST AND PRESENT, CONTROLLED TERRITORIES
Aguera, La
Cape Juby
Cuba
Elobey, Annobon & Corisco
Fernando Po
Ifni
Mariana Islands
Philippines
Puerto Rico
Rio de Oro
Rio Muni
Spanish Guinea
Spanish Morocco
Spanish Sahara
Spanish West Africa

POST OFFICES IN FOREIGN COUNTRIES
Morocco
Tangier
Tetuan

Dies of British Colonial Stamps

DIE A:

1. The lines in the groundwork vary in thickness and are not uniformly straight.

2. The seventh and eighth lines from the top, in the groundwork, converge where they meet the head.

3. There is a small dash in the upper part of the second jewel in the band of the crown.

4. The vertical color line in front of the throat stops at the sixth line of shading on the neck.

DIE B:

1. The lines in the groundwork are all thin and straight.

2. All the lines of the background are parallel.

3. There is no dash in the upper part of the second jewel in the band of the crown.

4. The vertical color line in front of the throat stops at the eighth line of shading on the neck.

DIE I:

1. The base of the crown is well below the level of the inner white line around the vignette.

2. The labels inscribed "POSTAGE" and "REVENUE" are cut square at the top.

3. There is a white "bud" on the outer side of the main stem of the curved ornaments in each lower corner.

4. The second (thick) line below the country name has the ends next to the crown cut diagonally.

DIE Ia.
1 as die II.
2 and 3 as die I.

DIE Ib.
1 and 3 as die II.
2 as die I.

DIE II:

1. The base of the crown is aligned with the underside of the white line around the vignette.

2. The labels curve inward at the top inner corners.

3. The "bud" has been removed from the outer curve of the ornaments in each corner.

4. The second line below the country name has the ends next to the crown cut vertically.

Wmk. 1
Crown and C C

Wmk. 2
Crown and C A

Wmk. 3
Multiple Crown
and C A

Wmk. 4
Multiple Crown
and Script C A

Wmk. 4a

Wmk. 46

Wmk. 314
St. Edward's Crown
and C A Multiple

Wmk. 373

Wmk. 384

Wmk. 406

British Colonial and Crown Agents Watermarks

Watermarks 1 to 4, 314, 373, 384 and 406, common to many British territories, are illustrated here to avoid duplication.

The letters "CC" of Wmk. 1 identify the paper as having been made for the use of the Crown Colonies, while the letters "CA" of the others stand for "Crown Agents." Both Wmks. 1 and 2 were used on stamps printed by De La Rue & Co.

Wmk. 3 was adopted in 1904; Wmk. 4 in 1921; Wmk. 46 in 1879; Wmk. 314 in 1957; Wmk. 373 in 1974; Wmk. 384 in 1985; Wmk 406 in 2008.

In Wmk. 4a, a non-matching crown of the general St. Edwards type (bulging on both sides at top) was substituted for one of the Wmk. 4 crowns which fell off the dandy roll. The non-matching crown occurs in 1950-52 printings in a horizontal row of crowns on certain regular stamps of Johore and Seychelles, and on various postage due stamps of Barbados, Basutoland, British Guiana, Gold Coast, Grenada, Northern Rhodesia, St. Lucia, Swaziland and Trinidad and Tobago. A variation of Wmk. 4a, with the non-matching crown in a horizontal row of crown-CA-crown, occurs on regular stamps of Bahamas, St. Kitts-Nevis and Singapore.

Wmk. 314 was intentionally used sideways, starting in 1966. When a stamp was issued with Wmk. 314 both upright and sideways, the sideways varieties usually are listed also – with minor numbers. In many of the later issues, Wmk. 314 is slightly visible.

Wmk. 373 is usually only faintly visible.

THAILAND

'tī-,land

(Siam)

LOCATION — Western part of the Malay peninsula in southeastern Asia
GOVT. — Republic
AREA — 198,250 sq. mi.
POP. — 60,609,046 (1999 est.)
CAPITAL — Bangkok

32 Solot = 16 Atts = 8 Sio =
4 Sik = 2 Fuang = 1 Salung
4 Salungs = 1 Tical
100 Satangs (1909) = 1 Tical
= 1 Baht (1912)

Catalogue values for unused stamps in this country are for Never Hinged items, beginning with Scott 264 in the regular postage section, Scott B34 in the semi-postal section, Scott C20 in the airpost section, and Scott O1 in the official section.

Watermarks

Wmk. 176 — Chakra

Wmk. 233 — Harrison & Sons, London in Script Letters

Wmk. 299 — Thai Characters and Wavy Lines

Wmk. 329 — Zigzag Lines

Wmk. 334 — Rectangles

Wmk. 340 — Alternating Interlaced Wavy Lines

Wmk. 356 — POSTAGE

Wmk. 368 — JEZ Multiple

Wmk. 371 — Wavy Lines

Wmk. 374 — Circles and Crosses

Wmk. 375 — Letters

Wmk. 377 — Interlocking Circles

Wmk. 385 — CARTOR

Wmk. 387 — Squares and Rectangles

King Chulalongkorn
A1   A2

A4

Perf. 14½, 15

		1883, Aug. 4	**Unwmk.**		**Engr.**
1	A1	1sol dark blue		15.00	13.00
b.		Imperf., pair			4,000.
2	A1	1att carmine		16.50	15.00
3	A1	1sio vermilion		32.50	30.00
4	A2	1sik yellow		16.50	15.00
5	A4	1sa orange		45.00	45.00
a.		1sa ocher		52.50	52.50
		Nos. 1-5 (5)		125.50	118.00

There are three types of No. 1, differing mainly in the background of the small oval at the top.

A 1 fuang red, of similar design to the foregoing, was prepared but not placed in use. Value, $2,000.

For surcharges see Nos. 6-8, 19.

No. 1 Handstamp Surcharged in Red

a

b

c

1 Tical   1 Tical

d   e

1885, July 1

6	A1	(a) 1t on 1sol blue	4,800.	3,600.
7	A1	(b) 1t on 1sol blue	450.	350.
c.		"1" inverted	4,000.	4,000.
8	A1	(c) 1t on 1sol blue	3,000.	2,750.

Surcharges of Nos. 6-8 have been counterfeited.

Types "d" and "e" are typeset official reprints.

As is usual with handstamps, double impressions, etc., exist.

King Chulalongkorn — A7

1887-91 Typo. Wmk. 176 Perf. 14

11	A7	1a green ('91)	6.50	2.00
12	A7	2a green & car	6.50	2.00
13	A7	3a grn & blue	12.00	4.00
14	A7	4a grn & org brn	12.00	4.75
15	A7	8a green & yel	12.00	7.00
16	A7	12a lilac & car	17.50	3.50
17	A7	24a lilac & blue	24.00	4.00
18	A7	64a lil & org brn	87.50	29.00
		Nos. 11-18 (8)	178.00	56.25

Nos. 11-18 were printed with fugitive ink. Immersion in water will discolor the stamps.

The design of No. 11 has been redrawn and differs in many minor details from Nos. 12-18.

Issue dates: Nos. 12-18, Apr. 1; No. 11, Feb.

For surcharges see Nos. 20-69, 109, 111, 126.

No. 3 Handstamp Surcharged

1889, Aug. Unwmk. Perf. 15

19	A1	1a on 1sio	21.00	21.00

Three different handstamps were used. Doubles, etc. exist.

Nos. 12 and 13 Handstamp Surcharged

1889-90 Wmk. 176 Perf. 14

20	A7	1a on 2a	10.00	0.00
a.		"1" omitted	450.00	450.00
c.		1st Siamese character invtd	950.00	950.00
d.		First Siamese character omitted	950.00	950.00
e.		Double surcharge	240.00	240.00
f.		Inverted surcharge	1,900.	1,900.
g.		Double surcharge, one inverted	3,500.	
21	A7	1a on 3a ('90)	9.00	9.00
a.		Inverted "1"	150.00	150.00

For surcharge see No. 29.

22	A7	1a on 2a grn & car	475.00	475.00

24	A7	1a on 2a grn & car	350.00	350.00

2 THAILAND

25 A7 1a on 2a grn & car 2,000. 1,000.

26 A7 1a on 3a grn & bl

Some authorities consider No. 26 a forgery. Doubles, etc., exist in this issue. Issue dates: Nov. 1889. Sept. 1890.

No. 13 Handstamp Surcharged

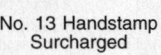

1891

27 A7 2a on 3a grn & bl 95.00 65.00

28 A7 2a on 3a grn & bl 55.00 55.00
a. Double surcharge 250.00 250.00
b. "2" omitted 250.00

No. 21 with Additional 2 Att Surcharge

29 A7 2a on 1a on 3a grn & bl 2,000. 1,800.

On No. 29 the 2a surcharge consists of Siamese numeral like No. 27 and English numeral like No. 28.

Most examples of No. 29 show attempts to remove the "1" of the first surcharge.

Typeset Surcharge

30 A7 2a on 3a grn & bl 60.00 45.00

There are 7 types of this surcharge in the setting.
Issued: #27-28, Jan.; #29, Feb.; #30, Mar.

No. 17 Handstamp Surcharged

f g

1892, Oct.

33 A7 (f) 4a on 24a lil & bl 60.00 50.00
34 A7 (g) 4a on 24a lil & bl 55.00 35.00

Surcharges exist double on Nos. 33-34 and inverted on No. 33.

Nos. 33-34 Handstamp Surcharged in English

1892, Nov.

35 A7 4a on 24a lil & bl 12.00 9.00
c. Inverted "s" 75.00 60.00

36 A7 4a on 24a lil & bl 20.00 10.00
a. Inverted "s" 90.00 90.00

37 A7 4a on 24a lil & bl 15.00 12.50

38 A7 4a on 24a lil & bl 20.00 15.00

Numerous inverts., doubles, etc., exist.
Nos. 35 and 37 are surcharged examples of No. 33. Nos. 36 and 38 are surcharged examples of No. 34. The "4 atts" surcharge is small on Nos. 35 and 36, and large on Nos. 37 and 38.

Nos. 18 and 17 Typeset Srchd. in English (Shown) and Siamese

1894

39 A7 1a on 64a lil & org brn 3.50 3.50
a. Inverted "s" 70.00 60.00
b. Inverted surcharge 900.00 900.00
d. Italic "s" 200.00 200.00
e. Italic "1" 350.00 300.00

40 A7 1a on 64a lil & org brn 2.00 1.50
a. Inverted capital "S" added to the surcharge 75.00 60.00

h i

j k

l m

41 A7 (h) 2a on 64a 20.00 15.00
a. Inverted "s" 90.00 60.00
b. Double surcharge 100.00 100.00
42 A7 (i) 2a on 64a 2,000. 2,000.
43 A7 (j) 2a on 64a 80.00 70.00
44 A7 (k) 2a on 64a 40.00 30.00
45 A7 (l) 2a on 64a 65.00 45.00
46 A7 (m) 2a on 64a 6.00 3.00
a. "Att.s" 60.00 60.00

Nos. 41-46 were in one plate of 120 subjects. The quantities were: h, 38; i, 1; j, 8; k, 18; l, 11 and m, 44.

1894, Oct. 12

47 A7 1a on 64a 5.00 3.00
a. Surcharged on face and back 150.00
b. As "a," surcharge on back inverted 200.00
c. Double surcharge 475.00
d. Inverted surcharge 600.00
e. Siamese surcharge omitted 300.00

See No. 67.

48 A7 2a on 64a 4.00 3.00
a. "Att" 75.00 45.00
b. Inverted surcharge 750.00 650.00
c. Surch. on face and back 200.00 200.00
d. Surcharge on back inverted 210.00 210.00
e. Double surcharge 150.00 150.00
f. Double surch., one inverted 900.00 800.00
g. Inverted "s" 35.00 30.00

1895, July 23

49 A7 10a on 24a lil & bl 9.00 2.00
a. Inverted "s" 60.00 30.00
b. Surch. on face and back 240.00 200.00
c. Surcharge on back inverted 240.00 240.00

No. 16 Surcharged in English (Shown) and Siamese

1896

50 A7 4a on 12a lil & car 25.00 8.00
a. Inverted "s" 90.00 60.00
b. Surcharged on face and back 225.00 200.00
c. Double surcharge on back 175.00 175.00

Two types of surcharge.

Nos. 16-18 Surcharged in English (Shown) and Siamese Antique Surcharges

a b

c d

e f

Atts.
Antique Letters

Atts.
Roman Letters

1898-99

51 A7 (a) 1a on 12a 450.00 400.00
52 A7 (b) 1a on 12a 20.00 7.00
53 A7 (c) 2a on 64a ('99) 35.00 9.00
54 A7 (d) 3a on 12a 12.00 4.00
a. Double surcharge 500.00 450.00
55 A7 (e) 4a on 12a 15.00 5.00
a. Double surcharge 400.00 375.00
56 A7 (e) 4a on 24a ('99) 45.00 14.00
57 A7 (f) 10a on 24a ('99) 825.00 825.00
Nos. 51-57 (7) 1,402. 1,264.

Roman Surcharges

h i

j k

l

1 Atts.
g

58 A7 (g) 1a on 12a 450.00 450.00
59 A7 (h) 1a on 12a 45.00 20.00
60 A7 (i) 2a on 64a ('99) 35.00 10.00
61 A7 (j) 3a on 12a 85.00 19.00
62 A7 (k) 4a on 12a 40.00 14.00
a. Double surcharge 175.00 175.00
b. No period after "Atts." 35.00 35.00
63 A7 (k) 4a on 24a ('99) 60.00 29.00
64 A7 (l) 10a on 24a ('99) 750.00 750.00
Nos. 58-64 (7) 1,465. 1,292.

In making the settings to surcharge Nos. 51 to 64 two fonts were mixed.

Antique and Roman letters are frequently found on the same stamp. Such stamps sell for more.

Issue dates: Nos. 54-55, 61-62, Feb. 22. Nos. 51-52, 58-59, June 4. Nos. 56-57, 63-64, Oct. 3.

Nos. 16 and 18 Surcharged in English (Shown) and Siamese Surcharged

m

n

o

p

r

1894-99
65	A7 (m)	1a on 12a	20.00	6.00
66	A7 (n)	1a on 12a	20.00	6.00
a.	Inverted "1"		300.00	200.00
b.	Inverted 1st "t"		200.00	175.00
67	A7 (o)	1a on 64a	5.00	5.00
68	A7 (p)	2a on 64a	35.00	8.00
a.	"1 Atts."		500.00	500.00
69	A7 (r)	2a on 64a	24.00	8.00
	Nos. 65-69 (5)		104.00	33.00

Issued: No. 67, 10/12/94; others, 2/14/99. See No. 47.

A13

1899, Oct.   Typo.   Unwmk.
70	A13	1a dull green	450.	85.
71	A13	2a dl grn & rose	550.	150.
72	A13	3a car & blue	800.	200.
73	A13	4a black & grn	3,000.	600.
74	A13	10a car & grn	3,000.	600.
	Nos. 70-74 (5)		7,800.	1,635.

The King rejected Nos. 70-74 in 1897, but some were released by mistake to three post offices in Oct. 1899. Used values are for stamps canceled to order at Korat in Dec. 1899. Values for postally used stamps are listed in the Scott Classic Specialized catalog.

A14

1899-1904
75	A14	1a gray green	5.00	.75
76	A14	2a yellow green	3.50	.75
77	A14	2a scarlet & bl	6.00	1.25
78	A14	3a red & blue	8.50	2.00
79	A14	3a green	20.00	12.00
80	A14	4a dark rose	5.50	1.25
81	A14	4a vio brn & rose	12.00	1.75
82	A14	6a dk rose	35.00	14.00
83	A14	8a dk grn & org	10.00	2.00
84	A14	10a ultra	10.50	2.50
85	A14	12a brn vio & rose	40.00	2.00
86	A14	14a ultra	23.00	18.00
87	A14	24a brn vio & bl	300.00	25.00
88	A14	28a vio brn & bl	25.00	25.00
89	A14	64a brn vio & org brn	70.00	11.00
	Nos. 75-89 (15)		574.00	119.25

Two types of 1a differ in size and shape of Thai "1" are in drawing of spandrel ornaments. Issue dates: 6a, 14a, 28a, Nos. 77, 79, 81, Jan. 1, 1904; others, Sept. 1899.
For surcharges see Nos. 90-91, 112, 125, 127.

Nos. 78 and 85 With Typewritten Srch. of 6 or 7 Siamese Characters (1 line) in Violet

1902
78a	A14	2a on 3a	5,000.	5,250.
85a	A14	10a on 12a	5,000.	5,250.

Nos. 78a and 85a were authorized provisionals, surcharged and issued by the Battambang postmaster.

Nos. 86 and 88 Surcharged in Black

1905, Feb.
90	A14	1a on 14a	10.00	10.00
a.	No period after "Att"		60.00	60.00
b.	Double surcharge		175.00	175.00
91	A14	2a on 28a	12.00	10.00
a.	Double surcharge		150.00	150.00
b.	No period after "Att"		60.00	60.00

King Chulalongkorn — A15

1905-08   Engr.
92	A15	1a orange & green	3.50	1.25
93	A15	2a violet & slate	3.50	1.25
94	A15	2a green ('08)	12.50	5.50
95	A15	3a green	7.50	2.00
96	A15	3a vio & sl ('08)	15.00	9.00
97	A15	4a gray & red	10.00	1.25
98	A15	4a car & rose ('08)	12.00	2.50
99	A15	5a carmine & rose	12.00	3.00
100	A15	8a blk & ol bis	13.00	1.50
101	A15	9a blue ('08)	30.00	9.00
102	A15	12a blue	18.00	4.00
103	A15	18a red brn ('08)	80.00	27.50
104	A15	24a red brown	35.00	8.00
105	A15	1t dp bl & brn org	47.50	8.00
	Nos. 92-105 (14)		299.50	83.75

Issue dates: Dec. 1905, Apr. 1, 1908.
For surcharges and overprints see Nos. 110, 113-117, 128-138, 161 162, D15, B21.

Siam.
Postage
40
Ticals.
King Chulalongkorn — A16

No. 106

Nos. 78 and 85 — (middle column continued)

No. 107

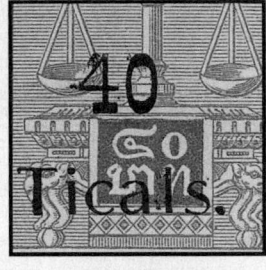
No. 108

1907, Apr. 24   Black Surcharge
106	A16	10t gray green	750.00	100.00
107	A16	20t gray green	6,750.	350.00
108	A16	40t gray green	5,100.	600.00
	Nos. 106-108 (3)		12,600.	1,050.

Counterfeits of Nos. 106-108 exist. In the genuine, the surcharged figures correspond to the Siamese value inscriptions on the basic revenue stamps.

No. 17 Surcharged

1907, Dec. 16
109	A7	1a on 24a lil & bl	5.50	1.50
a.	Double surcharge		450.00	

No. 99 Surcharged

1908, Sept.
110	A15	4a on 5a car & rose	12.00	4.00

The No. 110 surcharge is found in two spacings of the numerals: normally 15mm apart, and a narrow, scarcer spacing of 13½mm.

Nos. 17 and 84 Surcharged in Black

111	A7	2a on 24a lil & bl	4.50	1.20
a.	Inverted surcharge		350.00	350.00
112	A14	9a on 10a ultra	16.00	5.00
a.	Inverted surcharge		450.00	450.00

Jubilee Issue

Nos. 92, 95, 110, 100 and 103 Overprinted in Black or Red

1908, Nov. 11
113	A15	1a	4.50	1.25
a.	Siamese date "137" instead of "127"		1,050.	1,050.
b.	Pair, one without ovpt.		1,500.	1,500.
114	A15	3a	7.50	3.25
115	A15	4a on 5a	9.00	4.50
a.	Pair, imperf on 3 sides		2,400.	

116	A15	8a (R)	24.00	24.00
117	A15	18a	32.50	21.00
	Nos. 113-117 (5)		77.50	54.00

40th year of the reign of King Chulalongkorn. Nos. 113 to 117 exist with a small "i" in "Jubilee."

Statue of King Chulalongkorn A19

1908, Nov. 11   Engr.   Perf. 13½
118	A19	1t green & vio	60.00	9.00
119	A19	2t red vio & org	120.00	20.00
120	A19	3t pale ol & bl	175.00	21.00
121	A19	5t dl vio & dk grn	240.00	42.50
122	A19	10t bister & car	1,050.	125.00
123	A19	20t gray & red brn	700.00	125.00
124	A19	40t sl bl & blk brn	950.00	400.00
	Nos. 118-124 (7)		3,295.	742.50

The inscription at the foot of the stamps reads: "Coronation Commemoration-Forty-first year of the reign-1908."

Stamps of 1887-1904 Surcharged

1909   Perf. 14
125	A14	6s on 6a dk rose	3.00	1.50
126	A7	14s on 12a lil & car	135.00	65.00
127	A14	14s on 14a ultra	27.50	22.50
	Nos. 125-127 (3)		165.50	144.00

Nos. 92-102 Surcharged with Bar and

1909, Aug. 15
128	A15	2s on 1a #92	3.00	1.20
129	A15	2s on 2a #93	60.00	60.00
130	A15	2s on 2a #94	3.00	1.20
a.	"2" omitted		600.00	600.00
131	A15	3s on 3a #95	15.00	12.00
132	A15	3o on 3a #96	6.00	1.25
133	A15	6s on 4a #97	45.00	35.00
134	A15	6s on 4a #98	9.00	2.00
135	A15	6s on 5a #99	13.00	8.75
136	A15	12s on 8a #100	9.00	1.50
137	A15	14s on 9a #101	11.00	1.75
138	A15	14s on 12a #102	27.00	21.00
	Nos. 128-138 (11)		201.00	145.65

King Chulalongkorn — A20

1910   Engr.   Perf. 14x14½
139	A20	2s org & green	3.00	1.50
140	A20	3s green	4.50	1.50
141	A20	6s carmine	7.50	2.50
142	A20	12s blk & ol brn	16.00	2.50
143	A20	14s blue	25.00	3.50
144	A20	28s red brown	47.50	10.00
	Nos. 139-144 (6)		103.50	21.50

Issue dates: 12s, June 5. Others, May 5.
For surcharges see Nos. 163, 223-224.

A21

King
Vajiravudh — A22

Printed at the Imperial Printing Works, Vienna

1912   **Perf. 14½**

145	A21	2s brn org	1.75	.60
a.		Vert. pair, imperf. btwn.	600.00	600.00
b.		Horiz. pair, imperf. btwn.	600.00	600.00
146	A21	3s yellow green	1.75	.60
a.		Horiz. pair, imperf. btwn.	600.00	600.00
b.		Vert. pair, imperf. btwn.	600.00	600.00
147	A21	6s car rose	3.00	1.00
148	A21	12s gray blk & brn	3.50	1.00
149	A21	14s ultramarine	5.50	1.50
150	A21	28s chocolate	20.00	10.00
151	A22	1b blue & blk	30.00	2.40
a.		Vert. pair, imperf. btwn.	1,800.	1,800.
b.		Horiz. pair, imperf. btwn.	1,800.	1,800.
152	A22	2b car rose & ol brn	35.00	3.00
153	A22	3b yel grn & bl blk	42.50	4.50
154	A22	5b vio & blk	65.00	7.50
155	A22	10b ol grn & vio brn	325.00	60.00
156	A22	20b sl bl & red brn	500.00	65.00
		Nos. 145-156 (12)	1,033.	157.10

See Nos. 164-175.
For surcharges and overprints see Nos. 157-160, 176-186, 206, B1-B14, B16-B20, B22, B31-B33.

Nos. 147-150
Surcharged in Red or Blue

1914-15

157	A21	2s on 14s (R) ('15)	3.00	.70
a.		Vert. pair, imperf. btwn.	600.00	600.00
b.		Double surcharge	450.00	450.00
158	A21	5s on 6s (Bl)	5.50	.50
a.		Horiz. pair, imperf. btwn.	600.00	600.00
b.		Double surcharge	300.00	300.00
159	A21	10s on 12s (R)	5.50	.75
a.		Double surcharge	300.00	300.00
160	A21	15s on 28s (Bl)	10.00	1.25
		Nos. 157-160 (4)	24.00	3.20

The several settings of the surcharges on Nos. 157-160 show variations in the figures and letters.

Nos. 92-93
Surcharged

1915, Apr. 3

161	A15	2s on 1a org & grn	8.00	4.00
a.		Pair, one without surcharge	600.00	600.00
162	A15	2s on 2a vio & slate	8.25	4.00

No. 143 Surcharged in Red

1916, Oct.

163	A20	2s on 14s blue	6.00	2.00

Types of 1912 Re-engraved
Printed by Waterlow & Sons, London

1917, Jan. 1   **Perf. 14**

164	A21	2s orange brown	1.50	.30
165	A21	3s emerald	2.50	.60
166	A21	5s rose red	4.00	.30
167	A21	10s black & olive	3.50	.30
168	A21	15s blue	6.00	1.00
170	A22	1b bl & gray blk	28.00	4.00
171	A22	2b car rose & brn	100.00	42.50
172	A22	3b yellow grn & blk	450.00	275.00
173	A22	5b dp violet & blk	350.00	190.00
174	A22	10b ol gray & vio	525.00	25.00
a.		Perf. 12½	600.00	37.50
175	A22	20b sea grn & brn	700.00	70.00
a.		Perf. 12½	750.00	75.00
		Nos. 164-175 (11)	2,171.	609.00

The re-engraved design of the satang stamps varies in numerous minute details from the 1912 issue. Four lines of the background appear between the vertical strokes of the "M" of "SIAM" in the 1912 issue and only three lines in the 1917 stamps.

The 1912 stamps with value in bahts are 37½mm high; those of 1917 are 39mm. In the latter design the king's features, especially the eyes and mouth, are more distinct and the uniform and decorations are more sharply defined.

The 1912 stamps have seven pearls between the earpieces of the crown. The "A" and "M" of "SIAM" are connected. On the 1917 stamps there are nine pearls in the same place. The "A" and "M" of "SIAM" are not connected. Nos. 174 and 175 exist imperforate.

Nos. 164-173
Overprinted in Red

1918, Dec. 2

176	A21	2s orange brown	2.00	.50
a.		Double overprint	175.00	175.00
177	A21	3s emerald	2.50	1.00
a.		Double overprint	175.00	175.00
178	A21	5s rose red	2.50	1.50
a.		Double overprint	240.00	240.00
179	A21	10s black & olive	4.50	3.00
180	A21	15s blue	8.00	6.00
181	A22	1b bl & gray blk	35.00	24.00
182	A22	2b car rose & brn	65.00	47.50
183	A22	3b yel grn & blk	175.00	125.00
184	A22	5b dp vio & blk	475.00	325.00
		Nos. 176-184 (9)	769.50	533.50

Counterfeits of this overprint exist.

Nos. 147-148 Surcharged in Green or Red

1919-20

185	A21	5s on 6s (G)	2.75	.50
186	A21	10s on 12s (R) ('20)	4.50	.60

Issue dates: 5s, Nov. 11. 10s, Jan. 1.

King Vajiravudh — A23

Perf. 14-15, 12½ (#192)

1920-26   **Engr.**

187	A23	2s brn, yel ('21)	2.00	.50
188	A23	3s grn, grn ('21)	3.50	.60
189	A23	3s chocolate ('24)	1.75	.60
190	A23	5s rose, pale rose	3.00	.50
191	A23	5s green ('22)	30.00	4.00
192	A23	5s dk vio, lil ('26)	8.00	.50
193	A23	10s black & org ('21)	6.00	.50
194	A23	15s bl, bluish ('21)	9.50	.60
a.		Perf. 12½ ('25)	500.00	4.25
195	A23	15s carmine ('21)	42.50	6.00
196	A23	25s chocolate ('21)	24.00	3.00
197	A23	25s dk blue ('22)	35.00	1.40

198	A23	50s ocher & blk ('21)	45.00	2.00
a.		Perf. 12½ ('25)	170.00	2.90
		Nos. 187-198 (12)	210.25	20.10

For overprints see Nos. 205, B23-B30.

Throne
Room — A24

1926, Mar. 5   **Perf. 12½**

199	A24	1t gray vio & grn	16.00	3.50
200	A24	2t car & org red	35.00	6.00
201	A24	3t ol grn & bl	67.50	25.00
202	A24	5t dl vio & ol grn	110.00	25.00
203	A24	10t red & ol bis	400.00	32.50
204	A24	20t gray bl & brn	450.00	100.00
		Nos. 199-204 (6)	1,079.	192.00

This issue was intended to commemorate the fifteenth year of the reign of King Vajiravudh. Because of the King's death the stamps were issued as ordinary postage stamps.

Nos. 195 and 150 with Surcharge similar to 1914-15 Issue in Black or Red

1928, Jan.

205	A23	5s on 15s car	5.50	2.75
206	A21	10s on 28s choc (R)	12.00	1.00

King Prajadhipok
A25   A26

1928   **Engr.**   **Perf. 12½**

207	A25	2s dp red brn	1.00	.30
208	A25	3s deep green	1.50	.50
209	A25	5s dark violet	1.00	.30
210	A25	10s deep rose	1.20	.30
211	A25	15s dark blue	2.40	.45
212	A25	25s black & org	4.50	.60
213	A25	50s brn org & blk	7.50	.90
214	A25	80s blue & black	7.50	.90
216	A26	1b dk blue & blk	14.00	1.25
217	A26	2b car rose & blk brn	21.00	2.50
218	A26	3b yellow grn & blk	22.50	4.00
219	A26	5b dp vio & gray blk	30.00	6.00
220	A26	10b ol grn & red vio	65.00	10.00
221	A26	20b Prus grn & brn	120.00	20.00
222	A26	40b dk grn & ol brn	210.00	90.00
		Nos. 207-222 (15)	509.10	138.00
		Set, never hinged	650.00	

On the single colored stamps, type A25, the lines in the background are uniform; those of the bicolored values are shaded and do not extend to the frame.

Issue dates: 5s, 10s, 2b-40b, Apr. 15; 2s, 3s, 15s, 25s, 50s, May 1; 1b, June 1; 80s, Nov. 15.

For overprints & surcharge see Nos. 300-301, B34.

Nos. 142, 144
Surcharged in Red or Blue

1930   **Perf. 14**

223	A20	10s on 12s blk & ol brn	8.75	1.50
224	A20	25s on 28s red brn (Bl)	30.00	2.25
		Set, never hinged	50.00	

King Prajadhipok and Chao P'ya Chakri
A27   A28

Statue of Chao P'ya Chakri — A29

1932, Apr. 1   **Engr.**   **Perf. 12½**

225	A27	2s dark brown	2.00	.40
226	A27	3s deep green	3.50	1.00
227	A27	5s dull violet	2.00	.40
228	A28	10s red brn & blk	2.00	.25
229	A28	15s dull blue & blk	11.00	1.50
230	A28	25s violet & black	18.00	2.00
231	A28	50s claret & black	62.50	3.00
232	A29	1b blue black	100.00	16.00
		Nos. 225-232 (8)	201.00	24.55
		Set, never hinged	275.00	

150th anniv. of the Chakri dynasty, the founding of Bangkok in 1782, and the opening of the memorial bridge across the Chao Phraya River.

Assembly Hall, Bangkok
A30

1939, June 24   **Litho.**   **Perf. 11, 12**

233	A30	2s dull red brown	4.50	1.50
234	A30	3s green	12.00	3.50
235	A30	5s dark violet	6.50	.60
236	A30	10s carmine	16.00	.60
237	A30	15s dark blue	35.00	1.50
		Nos. 233-237 (5)	74.00	7.70
		Set, never hinged	95.00	

7th anniv. of the Siamese Constitution.

Chakri Palace, Bangkok — A31

1940   **Typo.**   **Perf. 12½**

238	A31	2s dull brown	6.50	1.00
239	A31	3s dp yellow grn	11.00	3.50
a.		Cliché of 5s in plate of 3s	900.00	725.00
240	A31	5s dark violet	8.00	.50
241	A31	10s carmine	20.00	.50
242	A31	15s dark blue	40.00	1.50
		Nos. 238-242 (5)	85.50	7.00
		Set, never hinged	135.00	

Issued: 2s, 3s, 5/13; 5s, 5/24; 15s, 5/28; 10s, 5/30.

King Ananda Mahidol — A32   Plowing Rice Field — A33

Royal Pavilion at Bang-pa-in — A34

1941, Apr. 17   **Engr.**

243	A32	2s brown	2.50	.55
244	A32	3s deep green	3.25	1.00
245	A32	5s violet	2.00	.55
246	A32	10s dark red	2.00	.55

247	A33	15s dp bl & gray blk	4.00	1.00
248	A33	25s slate & org	5.50	1.25
249	A33	50s red org & gray	5.00	1.50
250	A34	1b brt ultra & gray	22.50	5.00
251	A34	2b dk car rose & gray	14.00	2.50
252	A34	3b dp grn & gray	55.00	7.00
253	A34	5b blk & rose red	90.00	27.50
a.	Horiz. pair, imperf. btwn.			
254	A34	10b ol blk & yel	140.00	80.00

Nos. 243-254 (12) 345.75 128.40
Set, never hinged 450.00

King Ananda
Mahidol — A35

1943, May 1   Unwmk.   Perf. 11
255	A35	1b dark blue	30.00	3.00
a.	Horiz. pair, imperf. btwn.		140.00	140.00
b.	Vert. pair, imperf. btwn.		140.00	140.00
c.	Imperf. pair		140.00	140.00

See No. 274.

Indo-China War
Monument — A36

1943   Engr.   Perf. 11, 12½
256	A36	3s dark green	25.00	21.00

Litho.
Perf. 12½x11
257	A36	3s dull green	6.50	3.00

Issue dates: #256, June 1. #257, Nov. 2.

Bangkhaen
Monument — A37

Two types of 10s:
I — Size 19½x24mm.
II — Size 20¾x25¼mm.

1943, Nov. 25   Perf. 12½, 12½x11
258	A37	2s brown orange	2.50	3.25
259	A37	10s car rose (I)	10.00	6.00
a.	Type II		5.50	1.75

10th anniv. of the quelling of a counter-revolution led by a member of the royal family on Oct. 11, 1933.

Stamps of similar design, but with values in "cents," are listed under Malaya, Occupation Stamps. See Nos. 2N1-2N6.

King Bhumibol
Adulyadej — A38

1947, Dec. 5   Pin-perf. 12½x11
260	A38	5s orange	6.50	4.50
261	A38	10s olive ('48)	7.50	4.50
a.	10s light brown		90.00	85.00
262	A38	20s blue	12.00	4.50
263	A38	50s blue green	18.00	7.50

Nos. 260-263 (4) 44.00 21.00

Coming of age of King Bhumibol Adulyadej. Issued with and without gum.

> Catalogue values for unused stamps in this section, from this point to the end of the section, are for Never Hinged items.

King Bhumibol
Adulyadej — A39

1947-49   Unwmk.   Engr.   Perf. 12½
Size: 20x25mm.
264	A39	5s violet	3.00	.45
265	A39	10s red	3.25	.45
266	A39	20s chocolate	3.50	.45
267	A39	50s olive	6.50	.60

Size: 22x27mm.
268	A39	1b vio & dp bl	22.50	.70
269	A39	2b ultra & green	80.00	2.25
270	A39	3b brn red & blk	100.00	4.50
271	A39	5b bl grn & brn red	120.00	8.50
272	A39	10b dk brn & pur	325.00	3.00
273	A39	20b blk & rose brn	450.00	10.00

Nos. 264-273 (10) 1,114. 30.90

Issued: 5s, 20s, 11/15/47; 10s, 50s, 1/3/49; 1b-20b, 11/1/48.

For surcharges see Nos. 302-303.

Type of 1943
Perf. 11½, 12½x11½
1948, Jan.   Litho.
274	A35	1b chalky blue	80.00	12.00
a.	Horiz. pair, imperf. btwn.		175.00	175.00
b.	Vert. pair, imperf. btwn.		175.00	175.00
c.	Imperf. pair		175.00	175.00

King Bhumibol
Adulyadej and
Palace — A40

Perf. 12½
1950, May 5   Unwmk.   Engr.
275	A40	5s red violet	4.00	.40
276	A40	10s red	4.00	.40
277	A40	15s purple	16.00	7.50
278	A40	20s chocolate	4.00	.30
279	A40	80s green	45.00	7.50
280	A40	1b deep blue	10.00	.60
281	A40	2b orange yellow	45.00	2.50
282	A40	3b gray	120.00	12.00

Nos. 275-282 (8) 248.00 31.20

Coronation of Bhumibol Adulyadej as Rama IX, May 5, 1950.

King Bhumibol
Adulyadej — A41

1951-60   Perf. 12½
283	A41	5s rose lilac	3.50	.25
a.	Perf. 13x12½		8.50	1.10
284	A41	10s deep green	3.50	.25
b.	Perf. 13x12½		8.50	.85
285	A41	15s red brown	4.50	.30
b.	Perf. 13x12½		22.00	4.25
285A	A41	20s chocolate	6.00	.30
c.	Perf. 13x12½		27.50	1.60
286	A41	25s carmine	2.40	.25
a.	Perf. 13x12½		8.50	.50
287	A41	50s gray olive	6.00	.30
a.	Perf. 13x12½		14.00	1.60
288	A41	1b deep blue	12.00	.40
a.	Perf. 13x12½		22.00	2.75
289	A41	1.15b deep blue	2.40	.30
290	A41	1.25b orange brn	13.00	.75
291	A41	2b dull blue grn	27.50	.75
a.	Perf. 13x12½		50.00	3.75
292	A41	3b gray	35.00	.90
a.	Perf. 13x12½		60.00	2.75
293	A41	5b aqua & red	90.00	1.50
a.	Perf. 13x12½		150.00	6.00
294	A41	10b black brn & vio	325.00	6.00
295	A41	20b gray & olive	350.00	21.00

Nos. 283-295 (14) 880.80 33.25

Issued: 25s, 2/15; 5s, 10s, 1b, 6/4; 2b, 3b, 12/1; 15s, 2/15/52; 1.15b, 9/1/53; 1.25b, 10/1/54; 5b, 10b, 20b, 2/1/55; 50s, 10/15/56; 20s, 1960.

United Nations
Day — A42

1951, Oct. 24
296	A42	25s ultramarine	5.00	4.75

Overprinted in
Carmine

1952, Oct.
297	A42	25s ultramarine	4.50	2.75

Overprinted in
Carmine

1953, Oct.
298	A42	25s ultramarine	2.75	2.00

Overprinted in
Carmine

1954, Oct. 24
299	A42	25s ultramarine	6.00	4.00

Nos. 296-299 (4) 18.25 13.50

For more overprints see Nos. 315, 320.

Nos. 209 and 210
Overprinted in Black

1955, Jan. 4   Perf. 12½
300	A25	5s dark violet	12.00	12.00
301	A25	10s deep rose	12.00	12.00

No. 266 Surcharged with New Value
in Black or Carmine
302	A39	5s on 20s choc	3.50	1.00
303	A39	10s on 20s choc (C)	5.50	1.00

Nos. 300-303 (4) 33.00 26.00

King Naresuan
(1555-1605), on War
Elephant — A43

Perf. 13½
1955, Feb. 15   Unwmk.   Engr.
304	A43	25s brt carmine	2.75	.45
305	A43	80s rose violet	25.00	3.00
306	A43	1.25b dark olive grn	70.00	3.00
307	A43	2b deep blue	15.00	2.00
308	A43	3b henna brown	60.00	3.00

Nos. 304-308 (5) 172.75 13.45

Tao Suranari — A44

1955, Apr. 15   Perf. 12x13½
309	A44	10s purple	4.50	.60
310	A44	25s emerald	4.50	.60
311	A44	1b brown	40.00	3.00

Nos. 309-311 (3) 49.00 4.20

Lady Mo, called Tao Suranari (Brave Woman) for her role in stopping an 1826 rebellion.

King Taksin Statue at
Thonburi — A45

1955, May 1   Perf. 12½x12
312	A45	5s violet blue	4.50	.60
313	A45	25s Prus green	11.00	.30
314	A45	1.25b red	45.00	3.00

Nos. 312-314 (3) 60.50 3.90

King Somdech P'ya Chao Taksin (1734-1782).

No. 296 Overprinted
in Red

1955, Oct. 24   Perf. 12½
315	A42	25s ultramarine	5.50	4.00

United Nations Day, Oct. 24, 1955.

Don Jedi
Monument — A46

1956, Feb. 1   Perf. 13½x13
316	A46	10s emerald	4.75	3.00
317	A46	50s reddish brown	27.50	2.00
318	A46	75s violet	8.00	1.50
319	A46	1.50b brown orange	25.00	1.50

Nos. 316-319 (4) 65.25 8.00

No. 296 Overprinted
in Red Violet

1956, Oct. 24
320	A42	25s ultramarine	6.00	4.50

United Nations Day, Oct. 24, 1956.

Dharmachakra and
Deer — A47

20s, 25s, 50s, Hand of peace and Dharmachakra. 1b, 1.25b, 2b, Pagoda of Nakon Phatom.

Wmk. 329

1957, May 13		**Photo.**		**Perf. 13½**
321	A47	5s dark brown	1.50	.65
322	A47	10s rose lake	1.50	.65
323	A47	15s brt green	3.25	1.75
324	A47	20s orange	3.25	2.00
325	A47	25s reddish brown	1.10	.65
326	A47	50s magenta	2.50	.70
327	A47	1b olive brown	2.90	.85
328	A47	1.25b slate blue	35.00	6.00
329	A47	2b deep claret	8.00	1.25
		Nos. 321-329 (9)	59.00	14.50

2500th anniversary of birth of Buddha.

UN Day — A48

1957, Oct. 24			**Perf. 13½**
330	A48	25s olive	1.60	.80
331	A48	25s bright ocher ('58)	1.60	.80
332	A48	25s indigo ('59)	2.40	.80
		Nos. 330-332 (3)	5.60	2.40

Issued: Oct. 24.

Thai Archway — A49

Designs (inscribed "SEAP Games 1959"): 25s, Royal tiered umbrellas. 1.25b, Thai archer, ancient costume. 2b, Wat Arun pagoda and prow of royal barge.

1959, Oct. 15		**Photo.**		**Perf. 13½**
333	A49	10s orange	1.10	.25
334	A49	25s dk carmine rose	1.40	.25
335	A49	1.25b bright green	5.50	1.50
336	A49	2b light blue	4.75	.85
		Nos. 333-336 (4)	12.75	2.85

Issued to publicize the South-East Asia Peninsula Games, Bangkok, Dec. 12-17.

Wat Arun, WRY Emblem — A50

1960, Apr. 7			
337	A50	50s chocolate	1.00	.40
338	A50	2b yellow green	2.10	1.20

WRY, July 1, 1959-June 30, 1960.

Wat Arun, Bangkok — A51

1960, Aug.		**Wmk. 329**		**Perf. 13½**
339	A51	50s carmine rose	1.20	.25
340	A51	2b ultramarine	4.75	1.00

Anti-leprosy campaign.

Elephants in Teak Forest — A52

1960, Aug. 29		**Photo.**	**Perf. 13½**
341	A52	25s emerald	1.25	.25

5th World Forestry Cong., Seattle, WA, Aug. 29-Sept. 10.

Globe and SEATO Emblem — A53

1960, Sept. 8			
342	A53	50s chocolate	1.25	.25

SEATO Day, Sept. 8.

Siamese Child — A54

1960, Oct. 3			**Wmk. 329**
343	A54	50s magenta	1.75	.25
344	A54	1b orange	6.00	.95

Children's Day, 1960.

Hand with Pen and Globe — A55

1960, Oct. 3			
345	A55	50s carmine rose	1.50	.25
346	A55	2b blue	6.00	1.25

Intl. Letter Writing Week, Oct. 3-9.

UN Emblem and Globe — A56

1960, Oct. 24			**Perf. 13½**
347	A56	50s purple	1.60	.40

15th anniversary of the United Nations. See Nos. 369, 390.

King Bhumibol Adulyadej — A57

		Perf. 13½x13		
1961-68		**Engr.**		**Wmk. 334**
348	A57	5s rose cl ('62)	.80	.25
349	A57	10s green ('62)	.80	.25
350	A57	15s red brn ('62)	.80	.25
351	A57	20s brown ('62)	.80	.25
352	A57	25s carmine ('63)	.80	.25
353	A57	50s olive ('62)	.80	.25
354	A57	80s orange ('62)	5.00	2.00
355	A57	1b vio bl & brn	5.00	.30
355A	A57	1.25b red & citron ('65)	8.50	2.00
356	A57	1.50b dk vio & yel green	2.50	.45
357	A57	2b red & violet	2.50	.25

358	A57	3b brn & bl	13.00	.45
358A	A57	4b olive bis & blk ('68)	15.00	2.50
359	A57	5b blue & green	32.50	.60
360	A57	10b red org & blk	90.00	1.00
361	A57	20b emer & ultra	100.00	3.50
362	A57	25b green & blue	45.00	2.00
362A	A57	40b yellow & blk ('65)	110.00	4.50
		Nos. 348-362A (18)	433.80	21.05

For overprint see No. 588.

Children in Garden — A58

		Wmk. 329		
1961, Oct. 2		**Photo.**		**Perf. 13½**
363	A58	20s indigo	1.50	.30
364	A58	2b purple	6.25	1.10

Issued for Children's Day.

Pen and Envelope with Map — A59

1b, 2b, Pen and letters circling globe.

1961, Oct. 9			
365	A59	25s gray green	1.20	.25
366	A59	50s rose lilac	1.00	.25
367	A59	1b bright rose	2.75	.60
368	A59	2b ultramarine	3.25	.75
		Nos. 365-368 (4)	8.20	1.85

Intl. Letter Writing Week, Oct. 2-8.

UN Type of 1960

1961, Oct. 24	**Wmk. 329**		**Perf. 13½**
369	A56	50s maroon	1.25	.45

Issued for United Nations Day, Oct. 24.

Scout Emblem — A60　　Scouts Saluting and Tents — A61

Design: 2b, King Vajiravudh and Scouts.

1961, Nov. 1			**Photo.**	
370	A60	50s carmine rose	.90	.25
371	A61	1b bright green	2.25	.65
372	A61	2b bright blue	2.75	.90
		Nos. 370-372 (3)	5.90	1.80

Thai Boy Scouts, 50th anniversary.

Malaria Eradication Emblem and Siamese Designs
A62　　　　　A63

1962, Apr. 7		**Wmk. 329**		**Perf. 13**
373	A62	5s orange brown	.30	.25
374	A62	10s sepia	.30	.25
375	A62	20s blue	1.10	.25
376	A62	50s carmine rose	.30	.25
377	A63	1b green	1.50	.25
378	A63	1.50b dk car rose	3.50	.65
379	A63	2d dark blue	2.00	.35
380	A63	3b violet	5.50	2.50
		Nos. 373-380 (8)	14.50	4.75

WHO drive to eradicate malaria.

View of Bangkok and Seattle Fair Emblem A64

1962, Apr. 21	**Wmk. 329**		**Perf. 13**
381	A64	50s red lilac	1.50	.25
382	A64	2b deep blue	7.50	.95

"Century 21" Intl. Expo., Seattle, WA, Apr. 21-Oct. 12.

Mother and Child — A65

		Wmk. 329	
1962, Oct. 1		**Photo.**	**Perf. 13**
383	A65	25s lt blue green	1.25	.50
384	A65	50s bister brown	1.50	.25
385	A65	2b bright pink	6.75	1.00
		Nos. 383-385 (3)	9.50	1.75

Issued for Children's Day.

Globe, Letters, Carrier Pigeons — A66

Design: 1b, 2b, Quill pen and scroll.

1962, Oct. 8			
386	A66	25s violet	.70	.30
387	A66	50s red	.50	.25
388	A66	1b lemon	3.50	.60
389	A66	2b lt bluish green	7.00	.70
		Nos. 386-389 (4)	11.70	1.85

Intl. Letter Writing Week, Oct. 7-13.

UN Type of 1960

1962, Oct. 24			**Perf. 13½**
390	A56	50s carmine rose	1.25	.45

United Nations Day, Oct. 24.

Exhibition Emblem — A67

1962, Nov. 1			**Unwmk.**
391	A67	50s olive bister	1.40	.25

Students' Exhibition, Bangkok.

Woman Harvesting Rice — A68

		Wmk. 334		
1963, Mar. 21		**Engr.**		**Perf. 14**
392	A68	20s green	2.00	.65
393	A68	50s ocher	1.50	.25

FAO "Freedom from Hunger" campaign.

Temple Lion — A69

1963, Apr. 1   Wmk. 329   Perf. 13½
394 A69 50s green & bister   1.25   .25

1st anniv. of the formation of the Asian-Oceanic Postal Union, AOPU.

New and Old Post and Telegraph Buildings — A70

Wmk. 334
1963, Aug. 4   Engr.   Perf. 14
395 A70 50s org, bluish blk & grn 1.75   .30
396 A70 3b grn, dk red & brn   7.50 1.75

80th anniv. of the Post and Telegraph Dept.

King Bhumibol Adulyadej — A71

Perf. 13x13½
1963-71   Wmk. 329   Photo.
397   A71 5s dk car rose   .25   .25
398   A71 10s dark green   .25   .25
399   A71 15s red brown   .25   .25
400   A71 20s black brown   .25   .25
401   A71 25s carmine   .25   .25
402   A71 50s olive gray   .25   .25
402A A71 75s brt vio ('71)   1.25   .25
403   A71 80s dull orange   6.50   1.00
404   A71 1b dk bl & dk brn   6.00   .60
404A A71 1.25b org brn & ol ('65) 16.00 1.75
405   A71 1.50b vio bl & grn   5.00   .90
406   A71 2b dk red & vio   3.00   .25
407   A71 3b brn & dk bl   6.50   .45
407A A71 4b dp bis & blk ('68)   10.00   .60
408   A71 5b blue & green   17.50   .45
409   A71 10b orange & blk   30.00   .75
410   A71 20b brt grn & ind   125.00   4.50
411   A71 25b dk grn & bl   30.00   2.75
411A A71 40b yel & blk ('65)   150.00   6.50
    Nos. 397-411A (19)   408.25 22.25

Nos. 397-403 were issued in 1963; Nos. 404, 405-407, 408-411 in 1964.
For overprint see No. 589.

Child with Dolls — A72

1963, Oct. 7   Litho.   Perf. 13½
412 A72 50s rose red   1.75   .25
413 A72 2b dull blue   7.75   .95

Issued for Children's Day.

Garuda Carrying Letter — A73

Design: 2b, 3b, Thai women writing letters.

1963, Oct. 7   Wmk. 329
414 A73 50s lt blue & claret   2.75   .30
415 A73 1b lt grn & vio brn   4.75   1.50
416 A73 2b yel brn & turq bl   34.00   1.75
417 A73 3b org brn & yel grn   18.00   3.00
    Nos. 414-417 (4)   59.50   6.55

Intl. Letter Writing Week, Oct. 6-12.

UN Emblem — A74

1963, Oct. 24   Wmk. 329   Perf. 13½
418 A74 50s bright blue   1.25   .25

United Nations Day, Oct. 24.

King Bhumibol Adulyadej — A75

1963, Dec. 5   Photo.   Perf. 13½
419 A75 1.50b blue, org & ind   9.00   1.10
420 A75 5b brt lil rose, org & blk 24.00 4.00

King Bhumibol's 36th birthday.

UNICEF Emblem — A76

1964, Jan. 13   Litho.
421 A76 50s blue   1.50   .25
422 A76 2b olive green   5.50   1.00

17th anniv. of UNICEF.

Hand (flags), Pigeon and Globe — A77

Designs: 1b, Girls and world map. 2b, Pen, pencil and unfolded world map. 3b, Globe and hand holding quill.

1964, Oct. 5   Wmk. 329   Perf. 13½
423 A77 50s lilac & lt grn   2.40   .40
424 A77 1b red brown & grn   6.00   1.50
425 A77 2b yellow & vio bl   14.50   1.50
426 A77 3b blue & dk brown   9.50   3.25
    Nos. 423-426 (4)   32.40   6.65

Intl. Letter Writing Week, Oct. 5-11.

UN Emblem and Globe — A78

1964, Oct. 24   Photo.   Perf. 13½
427 A78 50s gray   1.25   .25

United Nations Day, Oct. 24.

King and Queen — A79

1965, Apr. 28   Wmk. 329   Perf. 13½
428 A79 2b brown & multi   17.50   .60
429 A79 5b violet & multi   30.00   3.00

15th wedding anniversary of King Bhumibol Adulyadej and Queen Sirikit.

ITU Emblem, Old and New Communications Equipment — A80

1965, May 17   Photo.
430 A80 1b bright green   7.00   .45

Cent. of the ITU.

World Map, Letters and Goddess — A81

2b, 3b, World map, letters and handshake.

1965, Oct. 3   Wmk. 329   Perf. 13½
431 A81 50s dp plum, gray & sal 1.75   .30
432 A81 1b dk vio bl, lt vio & yel 5.00   .45
433 A81 2b dk gray, bis & dp org 14.00   .90
434 A81 3b multicolored   17.50   2.50
    Nos. 431-434 (4)   38.25   4.15

Intl. Letter Writing Week, Oct. 3-9.

A82

Gates of Royal Chapel of Emerald Buddha.

Engr. & Litho.
Perf. 13½x14
1965, Oct. 24   Wmk. 356
435 A82 50s slate grn, bl & ocher 1.50 .25

International Cooperation Year, 1965.

A83

Map of Thailand and UPU monument, Bern.

Wmk. 329
1965, Nov. 1   Litho.   Perf. 13½
436 A83 20s dk blue & lilac   1.00   .30
437 A83 50s gray & blue   2.25   .45
438 A83 1b orange brn & vio bl 7.00   .90
439 A83 3b green & bister   14.00   2.50
    Nos. 436-439 (4)   24.25   4.15

80th anniv. of Thailand's admission to the UPU.

Lotus Blossom and Child — A84

Design: 1b, Boy with book walking up steps.

1966, Jan. 8   Wmk. 334   Perf. 13½
440 A84 50s henna brn & blk   1.50   .25
441 A84 1b green & black   4.50   1.00

Issued for Children's Day, 1966.

Bicycling — A85

1966, Aug. 4   Photo.   Wmk. 329
442 A85 20s shown   1.00   .30
443 A85 25s Tennis   1.40   .60
444 A85 50s Running   1.00   .25
445 A85 1b Weight lifting   4.50   1.50
446 A85 1.25b Boxing   6.50   3.50
447 A85 2b Swimming   9.50   1.40
448 A85 3b Netball   19.00   4.50
449 A85 5b Soccer   52.50 14.00
    Nos. 442-449 (8)   95.40 26.05

5th Asian Games, Bangkok.

Trade Fair Emblem and Temple of Dawn — A86

1966, Sept. 1   Litho.   Perf. 13½
450 A86 50s lilac   1.75   .60
451 A86 1b brown red   4.50   1.25

1st Intl. Asian Trade Fair, Bangkok.

Letter Writer A87

Design: 50s, 1b, Letters, maps and pen.

1966, Oct. 3   Photo.   Wmk. 329
452 A87 50s scarlet   1.50   .30
453 A87 1b orange brown   4.50   .90
454 A87 2b brt violet   12.00   1.20
455 A87 3b brt blue grn   12.00   2.40
    Nos. 452-455 (4)   30.00   4.80

Intl. Letter Writing Week, Oct. 6-12.

UN Emblem — A88

Wmk. 334
1966, Oct. 24   Litho.   Perf. 13½
456 A88 50s ultramarine   1.25   .25

United Nations Day, Oct. 24.

Rice Field A89

1966, Nov. 1   Engr.   Wmk. 329
457 A89 50s dp bl & grnsh bl   4.50   .90
458 A89 3b plum & pink   16.00   5.50
Intl. Rice Year under sponsorship of the FAO.

Pra Buddha Bata Monastery, UNESCO Emblem — A90

1966, Nov. 4   Photo.   Wmk. 329
459 A90 50s black & yel grn   1.10   .25
20th anniv. of UNESCO.

Thai Boxing A91

Designs: 1b, Takraw (three men playing ball). 2b, Kite fighting. 3b, Cudgel play.

1966, Dec. 9   Wmk. 329   Perf. 13½
460 A91 50s black, brn & red   1.75   .30
461 A91 1b black, brn & red   9.00   1.50
462 A91 2b black, brn & red   22.50   4.25
463 A91 3b black, brn & red   21.00   9.00
    Nos. 460-463 (4)   54.25   15.05
5th Asian Games.

Snakehead — A92

Pigmy Mackerel — A93

Fish: 3b, Barb. 5b, Siamese fighting fish.

1967, Jan. 1   Photo.
464 A92 1b brt blue & multi   7.00   1.50
465 A93 2b multicolored   27.50   3.00
466 A93 3b yel grn & multi   15.00   7.00
467 A92 5b pale grn & multi   20.00   8.00
    Nos. 464-467 (4)   69.50   19.50

Dharmachakra, Globe and Temples — A94

Wmk. 329
1967, Jan. 15   Litho.   Perf. 13½
468 A94 2b black & yellow   6.50   .75
Establishment of the headquarters of the World Fellowship of Buddhists in Thailand.

Great Hornbill — A95

Birds: 25s, Hill myna. 50s, White-rumped shama. 1b, Diard's fireback pheasant. 1.50b, Spotted dove. 2b, Sarus crane. 3b, White-breasted kingfisher. 5b, Asiatic open-bill (stork).

1967, Feb. 1   Photo.
469 A95 20s tan & multi   1.60   .75
470 A95 25s lt gray & multi   3.25   1.50
471 A95 50s yel grn & multi   2.60   .65
472 A95 1b olive & multi   7.25   1.50
473 A95 1.50b dull yel & multi   7.75   2.00
474 A95 2b pale sal & multi   24.00   3.25
475 A95 3b gray & multi   15.00   7.75
476 A95 5b multicolored   24.00   8.00
    Nos. 469-476 (8)   85.45   25.40

Ascocentrum Curvifolium — A96

Orchids: 20s, Vandopsis parishii. 80s, Rhynchostylis retusa. 1b, Rhynchostylus gigantea. 1.50b, Dendrobium falconerii. 2b, Paphiopedilum callosum. 3b, Dendrobium formosum. 5b, Dendrobium primulinum.

1967, Apr. 1   Wmk. 329   Perf. 13½
477 A96 20s black & multi   1.40   .60
478 A96 50s brt blue & multi   2.40   .30
479 A96 80s black & multi   3.50   1.50
480 A96 1b blue & multi   6.50   1.25
481 A96 1.50b black & multi   6.50   1.25
482 A96 2b ver & multi   19.00   3.25
483 A96 3b brown & multi   14.00   7.75
484 A96 5b multicolored   19.00   6.50
    Nos. 477-484 (8)   72.30   22.40

Thai Architecture — A97

1967, Apr. 6   Engr.
485 A97 50s Mansion   1.75   .60
486 A97 1.50b Pagodas   7.25   3.00
487 A97 2b Bell tower   20.00   3.00
488 A97 3b Temple   17.00   8.50
    Nos. 485-488 (4)   46.00   15.10

Grand Palace and Royal Barge on Chao Phraya River — A98

1967, Sept. 15   Wmk. 329   Perf. 13½
489 A98 2b ultra & sepia   10.00   1.25
International Tourist Year, 1967.

Globe, Dove, People and Letters A99

2b, 3b, Clasped hands, globe and doves.

1967, Oct. 8   Photo.
490 A99 50s dk blue & multi   1.50   .25
491 A99 1b multicolored   3.00   .65
492 A99 2b brt yel grn & blk   9.00   .90
493 A99 3b brown & blk   12.00   3.00
    Nos. 490-493 (4)   25.50   4.80
Intl. Letter Writing Week, Oct. 6-12.

UN Emblem — A100

1967, Oct. 24   Wmk. 329   Perf. 13½
494 A100 50s multicolored   1.40   .25
Issued for United Nations Day, Oct. 24.

Flag and Map of Thailand — A101

1967, Dec. 5   Photo.   Perf. 13½
495 A101 50s greenish blue, red & vio bl   2.40   .25
496 A101 2b ol gray, red & vio bl   9.00   1.25
50th anniversary of the flag.

Elephant Carrying Teakwood — A102

1968, Mar. 1   Engr.   Wmk. 329
497 A102 2b rose claret & gray ol   6.50   .60
See Nos. 537, 566.

Syncom Satellite over Thai Tracking Station — A103

1968, Apr. 1   Photo.   Perf. 13
498 A103 50s multicolored   .90   .25
499 A103 3b multicolored   5.25   1.60

Earth Goddess — A104

1968, May 1   Wmk. 329   Perf. 13
500 A104 50s blk, gold, red & bl grn   2.40   .40
Hydrological Decade (UNESCO), 1965-74.

Snake-skinned Gourami — A105

Fish: 20s, Red-tailed black "shark." 25s, Tor tambroides. 50s, Pangasius sanitwongsei. 80s, Bagrid catfish. 1.25b, Vaimosa rambaiae. 1.50b, Catlocarpio siamensis. 4b, Featherback.

1968, June 1   Photo.   Perf. 13
501 A105 10s multicolored   .70   .25
502 A105 20s multicolored   1.00   .30
503 A105 25s multicolored   1.40   .30
504 A105 50s multicolored   1.75   .30
505 A105 80s multicolored   5.50   2.75
506 A105 1.25b multicolored   10.00   5.00
507 A105 1.50b multicolored   24.00   4.50
508 A105 4b multicolored   45.00   17.50
    Nos. 501-508 (8)   89.35   30.90

Arcturus Butterfly — A106

Various butterflies.

1968, July 1   Wmk. 329   Perf. 13
509 A106 50s lt blue & multi   3.00   .45
510 A106 1b multicolored   9.00   2.00
511 A106 3b multicolored   21.00   8.00
512 A106 4b buff & multi   27.00   9.00
    Nos. 509-512 (4)   60.00   19.45

Queen Sirikit — A107

Designs: Various portraits of Queen Sirikit.

Photogravure and Engraved
Perf. 13½x14
1968, Aug. 12   Wmk. 334
513 A107 50s gold & multi   1.20   .30
514 A107 2b gold & multi   4.75   1.75
515 A107 3b gold & multi   7.50   3.00
516 A107 5b gold & multi   13.50   4.00
    Nos. 513-516 (4)   26.95   9.05
Queen Sirikit's 36th birthday, or third 12-year "cycle."

WHO Emblem and Medical Apparatus — A108

1968, Sept. 1   Photo.   Perf. 12½
517 A108 50s olive, blk & gray   1.10   .25
20th anniv. of the WHO.

Globe, Pen and Envelope — A109

1b, 3b, Pen nib, envelope and globe.

1968, Oct. 6   Wmk. 329   Perf. 13½
518 A109 50s brown & multi   .90   .25
519 A109 1b pale brown &
                multi   2.10   .40
520 A109 2b multicolored   3.50   .60
521 A109 3b violet & multi   6.00 2.00
      Nos. 518-521 (4)   12.50 3.25

Intl. Letter Writing Week, Oct. 7-13.

UN Emblem and
Flags — A110

1968, Oct. 24
522 A110 50s multicolored   1.20   .25

Issued for United Nations Day.

Human Rights Flame and Bas-
relief — A111

1968, Dec. 10   Photo.   Perf. 13½
523 A111 50s sl grn, red & vio   1.25   .25

International Human Rights Year.

King Rama II — A112

1968, Dec. 30   Engr.   Wmk. 329
524 A112 50c ocpia & bister   1.40   .25

Rama II (1768-1824), who reigned 1809-24.

National Assembly Building — A113

Photogravure and Engraved
1969, Feb. 10   Wmk. 329   Perf. 13½
525 A113 50s multicolored   1.20   .25
526 A113 2b multicolored   5.50 1.10

First constitutional election day.

ILO Emblem and Cogwheels — A114

1969, May 1   Photo.   Perf. 13½
527 A114 50s rose vio & dk bl   .85   .25

50th anniv. of the ILO.

Ramwong Dance — A115

Designs: 1b, Candle dance. 2b, Krathop Mai
dance. 3b, Nohra dance.

1969, July 15   Wmk. 329   Perf. 13
528 A115 50s multicolored   .60   .25
529 A115 1b multicolored   1.75   .65
530 A115 2b multicolored   3.50   .65
531 A115 3b multicolored   5.75 2.00
      Nos. 528-531 (4)   11.60 3.55

Posting and Receiving Letters — A116

Design: 2b, 3b, Writing and posting letters.

1969, Oct. 5   Photo.   Wmk. 334
532 A116 50s multicolored   .90   .25
533 A116 1b multicolored   1.75   .50
534 A116 2b multicolored   2.40   .75
535 A116 3b multicolored   3.50 1.10
      Nos. 532-535 (4)   8.55 2.60

International Letter Writing Week.

Hand Holding
Globe — A117

1969, Oct. 24   Wmk. 329   Perf. 13
536 A117 50s multicolored   1.10   .25

Issued for United Nations Day.

Teakwood Type of 1968
1969, Nov. 18   Engr.   Perf. 13½
537 A102 2b Tin mine   4.25   .30

Issued to publicize tin export, and the 2nd
Technical Conf. of the Intl. Tin Council,
Bangkok.

Loy Krathong Festival — A118

Designs: 1b, Marriage ceremony. 2b,
Khwan ceremony. 5b, Songkran festival.

1969, Nov. 23   Photo.   Wmk. 329
538 A118 50s gray & multi   .60   .25
539 A118 1b multicolored   2.00   .65
540 A118 2b multicolored   2.50   .55
541 A118 5b multicolored   4.75 1.50
      Nos. 538-541 (4)   9.85 2.95

Biplane, Mailmen and Map of First
Thai Airmail Flight, 1919 — A119

1969, Dec. 10   Engr.   Perf. 13½
542 A119 1b multicolored   1.75   .30

50th anniversary of Thai airmail service.

Shadow Play — A120

Photogravure and Engraved
1969, Dec. 18   Wmk. 329
543 A120 50s Phra Rama   .60   .25
544 A120 2b Ramasura   3.75   .35
545 A120 3b Mekhala   3.25 1.10
546 A120 5b Ongkhot   3.75 1.40
      Nos. 543-546 (4)   11.35 3.10

Symbols of Agriculture, Industry and
Shipping — A121

1970, Jan. 1   Photo.
547 A121 50s multicolored   .90   .25

Productivity Year 1970.

World Map, Thai Temples and
Emblem — A122

1970, Jan. 31   Litho.
548 A122 50s brt blue & blk   1.25   .30

19th triennial meeting of the Intl. Council of
Women, Bangkok.

Earth Station Radar
and Satellite — A123

Perf. 14½x15
1970, Apr. 1   Litho.   Wmk. 356
549 A123 50s multicolored   .90   .25

Communication by satellite.

Household and Population
Statistics — A124

Perf. 13x13½
1970, Apr. 1   Photo.   Wmk. 329
550 A124 1b multicolored   1.10   .25

Issued to publicize the 1970 census.

Inauguration of New UPU
Headquarters, Bern — A125

Lithographed and Engraved
1970, June 15   Wmk. 334   Perf. 13½
551 A125 50s lt bl, lt grn & grn   .95   .25

Khun Ram Kamhang Teaching
(Mural) — A126

1970, July 1   Litho.
552 A126 50s black & multi   1.00   .25

Issued for International Education Year.

Swimming Stadium — A127

1.50b, Velodrome. 3b, Subhajalasaya Stadium. 5b, Kittikachorn Indoor Stadium.

Lithographed and Engraved
1970, Sept. 1   Wmk. 329   Perf. 13½
553 A127 50s yellow, red &
                pur   .90   .25
554 A127 1.50b ultra, grn & dk
                red   1.75   .65
555 A127 3b gold, black &
                dk red   2.10   .90
556 A127 5b brt grn, ultra &
                dk red   3.50 1.10
      Nos. 553-556 (4)   8.25 2.90

6th Asian Games, Bangkok.

Children Writing Letters — A128

Designs: 1b, Woman writing letter. 2b, Two
women reading letters. 3b, Man reading letter.

1970, Oct. 4   Photo.   Perf. 13½
557 A128 50s black & multi   .90   .25
558 A128 1b black & multi   1.75   .55
559 A128 2b black & multi   2.75   .60
560 A128 3b black & multi   3.00 1.25
      Nos. 557-560 (4)   8.40 2.65

Intl. Letter Writing Week, Oct. 6-12.

Royal Palace, Bangkok, and UN Emblem — A129

1970, Oct. 24   Photo.   Perf. 13½
561 A129 50s multicolored   1.25   .25
25th anniversary of the United Nations.

Heroes of Bangrachan — A130

1b, Monument to Thao Thepkrasattri & Thao Sri Sunthon. 2b, Queen Suriyothai riding elephant. 3b, Phraya Phichaidaphak and battle scene.

1970, Oct. 25   Engr.   Perf. 13½
562 A130 50s pink & violet   .90   .30
563 A130 1b violet & maroon   1.50   .90
564 A130 2b rose & brown   3.50   .90
565 A130 3b blue & green   3.00   .90
     Nos. 562-565 (4)   8.90 3.00
Heroes from Thai history.

Teakwood Type of 1968
1970, Nov. 1   Engr.
566 A102 2b Rubber plantation   3.25   .70
Issued to publicize rubber export.

King Bhumibol Lighting Flame — A131

1970, Dec. 9   Photo.   Wmk. 329
567 A131 1b multicolored   1.75   .25
Opening of 6th Asian Games, Bangkok.

Woman Playing So Sam Sai — A132

Women Playing Classical Thai Musical Instruments: 2b, Khlui Phiang-O. 3b, Krachappi. 5b, Thon Rammana.

1970, Dec. 20
568 A132 50s multicolored   .90   .25
569 A132 2b multicolored   2.00   .65
570 A132 3b multicolored   3.25   .95
571 A132 5b multicolored   5.25 1.25
     Nos. 568-571 (4)   11.40 3.10

Chocolate Point Siamese Cats — A133

Siamese Cats: 1b, Blue point. 2b, Seal point. 3b, Pure white cat and kittens.

Perf. 13½x14
1971, Mar. 15   Litho.   Wmk. 356
572 A133 50s multicolored   .65   .45
573 A133 1b multicolored   4.50 1.00
574 A133 2b multicolored   6.00 1.10
575 A133 3b multicolored   8.50 2.75
     Nos. 572-575 (4)   19.65 5.30

Muang Nakhon Temple — A134

Temples: 1b, Phanom. 3b, Pathom Chedi. 4b, Doi Suthep.

Lithographed and Engraved
1971, Mar. 30   Wmk. 329   Perf. 13½
576 A134 50s rose, black & brn   .90   .25
577 A134 1b emerald, bis &
                pur   1.75   .40
578 A134 3b org, brn & dk brn   2.75   .65
579 A134 4b ultra, ocher & brn   4.50 2.50
     Nos. 576-579 (4)   9.90 3.80

Corn and Tractor in Field A135

1971, Apr. 20   Engr.   Wmk. 329
580 A135 2b multicolored   2.40   .30
Export promotion.

Buddha's Birthplace, Lumbini, Nepal — A136

Buddha's: 1b, Place of Enlightenment, Bihar. 2b, Place of first sermon, Benares. 3b, Place of death, Kusinara.

1971, May 9   Engr.   Perf. 13½
581 A136 50s violet blue & blk   .75   .25
582 A136 1b green & black   1.60   .55
583 A136 2b dull yellow & blk   2.75   .75
584 A136 3b red & black   3.25 1.25
     Nos. 581-584 (4)   8.35 2.80
20th anniv. of World Fellowship of Buddhists.

King Bhumibol and Subjects — A137

Perf. 13½
1971, June 9   Unwmk.   Litho.
585 A137 50s silver & multi   1.40   .25
King Bhumibol's Silver Jubilee.

Floating Market — A138

1971, June 20   Photo.   Wmk. 329
586 A138 4b gold & multi   2.50   .45
Visit Asia Year.

Boy Scouts Saluting — A139

1971, July 1   Litho.
587 A139 50s orange & multi   1.25   .25
60th anniversary of Thai Boy Scouts.

Blocks of four of Nos. 354 and 403 Overprinted in Dark Blue

a

b

Perf. 13½x13
1971, Aug.   Wmk. 334   Engr.
588 A57 (a)   Block of 4   8.00 8.00
 a.   80s orange, single stamp   2.00 2.00

Perf. 13x13½
**   Photo.   Wmk. 329**
589 A71 (b)   Block of 4   8.00 8.00
 a.   80s dull orange, single stamp 2.00 2.00
THAILANDPEX '71, Philatelic Exhib., Aug. 4-8.

Woman Writing Letter — A140

Designs: 1b, Women reading mail. 2b, Woman sitting on porch. 3b, Man handing letter to woman.

Wmk. 334
1971, Oct. 3   Litho.   Perf. 13½
590 A140 50s gray & multi   .60   .25
591 A140 1b red brown & multi 1.40   .35
592 A140 2b ultra & multi   2.25   .50
593 A140 3b lt gray & multi   4.00 1.10
     Nos. 590-593 (4)   8.25 2.20
Intl. Letter Writing Week, Oct. 6-12.

Wat Benchamabopit (Marble Temple), Bangkok — A141

Perf. 13½x14
1971, Oct. 24   Litho.   Unwmk.
594 A141 50s multicolored   1.25   .25
United Nations Day, Oct. 24.

Duck Raising — A142

Rural occupations: 1b, Raising tobacco. 2b, Fishermen. 3b, Rice winnowing.

Wmk. 329
1971, Nov. 15   Photo.   Perf. 12½
595 A142 50s lt blue & multi   .65   .25
596 A142 1b multicolored   1.50   .65
597 A142 2b blue & multi   2.40   .60
598 A142 3b buff & multi   3.50   .90
     Nos. 595-598 (4)   8.05 2.40

UNICEF Emblem, Mother and Child — A143

1971, Dec. 11   Wmk. 334   Perf. 13½
599 A143 50s blue & multi   .75   .25
25th anniv. of UNICEF.

Thai Costumes, 17th Century — A144

Thai Costumes: 1b, 13th-14th cent. 1.50b, 14th-17th cent. 2b, 18th-19th cent.

Perf. 13½x14
1972, Jan. 12 Litho. Unwmk.
600	A144	50s multicolored	.80	.30
601	A144	1b multicolored	1.75	.50
602	A144	1.50b multicolored	3.00	.95
603	A144	2b blue & multi	4.50	.95
		Nos. 600-603 (4)	10.05	2.70

Globe
A145

Perf. 13x13½
1972, Apr. 1 Photo. Wmk. 334
604	A145	75s violet blue	.90	.25

Asian-Oceanic Postal Union, 10th anniv.

King Bhumibol
Adulyadej — A146

Perf. 13½x13
1972-77 Litho. Wmk. 329
Size: 21x26mm
605	A146	10s yellow green	.30	.25
606	A146	20s blue	.45	.25
607	A146	25s rose red	.45	.25
608	A146	75s lilac	.60	.25

Engr.
609	A146	1.25b yel grn & pink	1.25	.30
610	A146	2.75b red brn & blue grn	1.50	.65
611	A146	3b brn & dk blue ('74)	7.00	.65
612	A146	4b blue & org red ('73)	2.10	.30
613	A146	5b dk vio & red brown	2.10	.25
614	A146	6b green & vio	6.50	.60
615	A146	10b ver & black	3.25	.25
616	A146	20b org & yel grn	9.25	.60
617	A146	40b dp bis & lilac ('74)	36.00	7.50
618	A146	50b pur & brt grn ('77)	45.00	1.75
619	A146	100b dp org & dk bl ('77)	77.50	3.00
		Nos. 605-619 (15)	193.05	16.85

See Nos. 835-838, 907-908.
For surcharges, see Nos. 2248, 2281-2282.

Iko Women — A147

Hill Tribes: 2b, Musoe musician. 4b, Yao weaver. 5b, Maeo farm woman.

Wmk. 334
1972, May 11 Photo. Perf. 13½
620	A147	50s multicolored	.65	.25
621	A147	2b dark gray & multi	2.60	.60
622	A147	4b multicolored	7.00	4.00
623	A147	5b multicolored	8.00	1.10
		Nos. 620-623 (4)	18.25	5.95

Ruby
A148

Precious Stones: 2b, Yellow sapphire. 4b, Zircon. 6b, Star sapphire.

1972, June 7 Litho.
624	A148	75s gray & multi	1.20	.40
625	A148	2b multicolored	8.00	1.50
626	A148	4b multicolored	13.00	4.50
627	A148	6b crimson & multi	12.00	4.50
		Nos. 624-627 (4)	34.20	10.90

Prince
Vajiralongkorn
A149

Perf. 13½x13
1972, July 28 Photo. Wmk. 329
628	A149	75s tan & multi	1.25	.25

20th birthday of Prince Vajiralongkorn, heir apparent.

Thai Costume
A150

Designs: Costumes of Thai women.

Perf. 14x13½
1972, Aug. 12 Litho. Wmk. 356
629	A150	75s tan & multi	.60	.25
630	A150	2b multicolored	2.00	.70
631	A150	4b yellow & multi	4.00	3.00
632	A150	5b gray & multi	4.75	.90
a.		Souvenir sheet of 4, #629-632	40.00	27.00
		Nos. 629-632 (4)	11.35	4.85

Rambutan — A151

Fruits: 1b, Mangosteen. 3b, Durian. 5b, Mango.

1972, Sept. 7 Wmk. 334 Perf. 13½
633	A151	75s multicolored	.90	.25
634	A151	1b multicolored	2.40	.95
635	A151	3b pink & multi	4.75	1.40
636	A151	5b lt ultra & multi	12.00	2.25
		Nos. 633-636 (4)	20.05	4.85

Lod Cave, Phangnga — A152

1.25b, Kang Krachan Reservoir. 2.75b, Erawan Waterfalls, Kanchanaburi. 3b, Nok-Kaw Cliff, Loei.

1972, Nov. 15 Litho. Wmk. 334
637	A152	75s multicolored	.90	.25
638	A152	1.25b multicolored	1.60	1.00
639	A152	2.75b multicolored	5.50	.45
640	A152	3b multicolored	4.50	1.10
		Nos. 637-640 (4)	12.40	2.80

Intl. Letter Writing Week, Oct. 9-15.

Princess Mother Visiting Old People — A153

1972, Oct. 21 Photo. Wmk. 329
641	A153	75s dk green & ocher	4.50	.50

Princess Mother Sisangwan, 72nd birthday.

UN Emblem and
Globe — A154

Wmk. 334
1972, Nov. 15 Litho. Perf. 14
642	A154	75s blue & multi	.75	.25

25th anniversary of the Economic Commission for Asia and the Far East (ECAFE).

Educational Center and Book Year Emblem — A155

1972, Dec. 8 Perf. 13½
643	A155	75s multicolored	.75	.25

International Book Year 1972.

Crown Prince
Vajiralongkorn
A156

1972, Dec. 28 Photo. Wmk. 329
644	A156	2b brt blue & multi	1.75	.30

Investiture of Prince Vajiralongkorn Salayacheevin as Crown Prince.

Flag, Soldiers and Civilians — A157

1973, Feb. 3 Wmk. 334 Perf. 13½
645	A157	75s multicolored	.90	.25

25th anniversary of Veterans Day.

Savings Bank,
Emblem and
Coin — A158

1973, Apr. 1 Wmk. 329
646	A158	75s emerald & multi	.90	.25

60th anniv. of Government Savings Bank.

WHO Emblem and Deity — A159

1973, Apr. 1 Wmk. 329
647	A159	75s brt green & multi	.90	.25

25th World Health Organization Day.

Water
Lily
A160

Designs: Various water lilies (Thai lotus).

Perf. 11x13
1973, May 15 Litho. Wmk. 356
648	A160	75s violet & multi	1.00	.25
649	A160	1.50b brown & multi	2.00	.35
650	A160	2b dull grn & multi	3.50	.75
651	A160	4b black & multi	9.00	3.50
		Nos. 648-651 (4)	15.50	4.85

King Bhumibol
Adulyadej — A161

Perf. 14x13½
1973-81 Photo. Wmk. 334
652	A161	5s purple	5.50	.30
653	A161	20s blue	2.40	.25
a.		Perf. 14½, wmk. 233	1.00	.25
654	A161	25s rose carmine	2.75	.25

Wmk. 233 Perf. 14½
655	A161	25s brown red ('81)	.90	.25
656	A161	50s dk olive grn ('79)	2.75	.25
657	A161	75s violet	3.60	.25
a.		Perf. 14x13½, wmk. 334	1.40	.25

Wmk. 334
Engr. Perf. 13
658	A161	5b vio & brn	18.00	1.40
659	A161	6b grn & vio	12.00	1.40
660	A161	10b red & black	29.00	1.40
661	A161	20b org & yel grn ('75)	140.00	8.00
		Nos. 652-661 (10)	216.90	13.75

For surcharges see Nos. 1168A, 1548, 2249.

Silversmiths — A162

1973, June 15 Litho. Perf. 13½
662	A162	75s shown	.65	.25
663	A162	2.75b Lacquerware	2.25	.55
664	A162	4b Pottery	5.50	3.00
665	A162	5b Paper umbrellas	5.75	1.00
		Nos. 662-665 (4)	14.15	4.80

Thai handicrafts.

Fresco from Temple of the Emerald
Buddha — A163

Designs: Frescoes illustrating Ramayana in
Temple of the Emerald Buddha.

1973, July 17   Photo.   Wmk. 329

666	A163	25s multicolored	.90	.25
667	A163	75s multicolored	.60	.25
668	A163	1.50b multicolored	2.75	1.60
669	A163	2b multicolored	4.00	1.60
670	A163	2.75b multicolored	3.00	.90
671	A163	3b multicolored	9.00	3.00
672	A163	5b multicolored	14.50	7.00
673	A163	6b multicolored	4.50	2.10
		Nos. 666-673 (8)	39.25	16.70

Development of Postal
Service — A164

2b, Telecommunications development.

1973, Aug. 4   Perf. 13½

674	A164	75s multicolored	.75	.30
675	A164	2b multicolored	2.25	.75

90th anniv. of Post and Telegraph Dept.

No. 1 and Other Stamps — A165

Various Stamps and: 1.25b, No. 147. 1.50b,
No. 209. 2b, No. 244.

1973, Aug. 4   Photo. & Engr.

676	A165	75s dp rose & dk bl	.65	.25
677	A165	1.25b blue & dp rose	1.75	.50
678	A165	1.50b olive & vio blk	5.50	1.60
679	A165	2b org & sl grn	4.00	.65
a.		Souvenir sheet of 4	20.00	12.00
		Nos. 676-679 (4)	11.90	3.00

2nd Natl. Phil. Exhib., THAIPEX '73, Aug. 4-
8. No. 679a contains 4 stamps with simulated
perforations similar to Nos. 676-679.

INTERPOL Emblem — A166

1973, Sept. 3   Photo.

680	A166	75s gray & multi	1.00	.25

Intl. Criminal Police Organization, 50th anniv.

"Lilid Pralaw" — A167

Designs: Scenes from Thai literature.

Perf. 11x13
1973, Oct. 7   Litho.   Wmk. 368

681	A167	75s green & multi	.90	.30
682	A167	1.50b blue & multi	2.10	1.10
683	A167	2b multicolored	3.50	1.40
684	A167	5b blue & multi	6.50	1.75
a.		Souvenir sheet of 4, #681- 684, perf. 13x14	35.00	25.00
		Nos. 681-684 (4)	13.00	4.55

Intl. Letter Writing Week, Oct. 7-13.

Wat Suan Dok,
Chiangmai; UN
Emblem — A168

1973, Oct. 24   Perf. 13x11

685	A168	75s blue & multi	1.20	.25

United Nations Day.

Schomburgk's Deer — A169

25s, Kouprey. 75s, Gorals. 1.25b, Water
buffalos. 1.50b, Javan rhinoceros. 2b, Eld's
deer. 2.75b, Asiatic 2-horned rhinoceros. 4b,
Serows.

Wmk. 329
1973, Nov. 14   Photo.   Perf. 13½

686	A169	20s shown	.90	.30
687	A169	25s multicolored	.90	.30
688	A169	75s multicolored	1.20	.30
689	A169	1.25b multicolored	3.00	1.50
690	A169	1.50b multicolored	5.50	3.00
691	A169	2b multicolored	11.00	3.00
692	A169	2.75b multicolored	6.00	1.25
693	A169	4b multicolored	7.25	7.00
		Nos. 686-693 (8)	35.75	16.65

Protected animals.

Human Rights Flame — A170

Wmk. 371
1973, Dec. 10   Litho.   Perf. 12½

694	A170	75s multicolored	1.25	.25

25th anniversary of the Universal Declaration of Human Rights.

Children and
Flowers — A171

1974, Jan. 12   Litho.   Perf. 13

695	A171	75s multicolored	1.50	.25

Children's Day.

Siriraj Hospital and Statue of Prince
Nakarin — A172

Perf. 13x13½
1974, Mar. 17   Photo.   Wmk. 368

696	A172	75s multicolored	1.10	.25

84th anniversary of Siriraj Hospital, oldest
medical school in Thailand.

Phala Piang
Lai — A173

Classical Thai Dances: 2.75b, Phra Lux
Phlaeng Rit. 4b, Chin Sao Sai. 5b, Charot
Phra Sumen.

Wmk. 334
1974, June 25   Litho.   Perf. 14

697	A173	75s pink & multi	.90	.30
698	A173	2.75b gray bl & multi	2.50	.75
699	A173	4b gray & multi	5.00	2.75
700	A173	5b yellow & multi	5.00	1.75
		Nos. 697-700 (4)	13.40	5.55

Large Teak Tree in Uttaradit
Province — A174

1974, July 5   Wmk. 329   Perf. 12½

701	A174	75s multicolored	.90	.25

15th Arbor Day.

People and WPY Emblem — A175

Perf. 10½x13
1974, Aug. 19   Litho.   Wmk. 368

702	A175	75s multicolored	.90	.25

World Population Year, 1974.

Ban Chiang Painted Vase — A176

75s, Royal chariot. 2.75b, Avalokitesavara
Bodhisattva. 3b, King Mongkut, Rama IV.

1974, Sept. 19   Wmk. 262   Perf. 12½

703	A176	75s blue & multi	.75	.30
704	A176	2b black, brn & bis	2.25	.85
705	A176	2.75b black, brn & tan	3.00	.60
706	A176	3b black & multi	3.00	.90
		Nos. 703-706 (4)	9.00	2.65

Centenary of National Museum. Inscribed
"BATH" in error.

Purging Cassia — A177

1974, Oct. 6   Wmk. 368   Perf. 11x13

707	A177	75s shown	.60	.25
708	A177	2.75b Butea	2.10	.30
709	A177	3b Jasmine	4.25	.90
710	A177	4b Lagerstroemia	2.75	1.40
a.		Souvenir sheet of 4, #707- 710, perf. 13¼x14	35.00	25.00
		Nos. 707-710 (4)	9.70	2.85

Intl. Letter Writing Week, Oct. 6-12.

"UPU" and UPU Emblem — A178

1974, Oct. 9   Wmk. 371   Perf. 12½

711	A178	75s dk green & multi	.90	.25

Centenary of Universal Postal Union.

Wat Suthat Thepvararam — A179

Wmk. 329
1974, Oct. 24   Photo.   Perf. 13

712	A179	75s multicolored	1.25	.25

United Nations Day.

Elephant Roundup — A180

Wmk. 371
1974, Nov. 16   Engr.   Perf. 12½

713	A180	4b multicolored	1.00	2.00

Tourist publicity.

Vanda Coerulea — A181

Orchids: 2.75b, Dendrobium aggregatum.
3b, Dendrobium scabrilingue. 4b, Aerides
falcata.

Perf. 11x13
1974, Dec. 5   Photo.   Wmk. 368

714	A181	75s red & multi	.95	.30
715	A181	2.75b multicolored	2.25	.60
716	A181	3b olive & multi	4.00	.90

717 A181 4b green & multi 3.00 1.25
a. Souvenir sheet of 4, #714-
717, perf. 13½x14 45.00 45.00
Nos. 714-717 (4) 10.20 3.05
See Nos. 745-748.

Boy — A182

Perf. 14x13½
1975, Jan. 11 Litho. Wmk. 374
718 A182 75s vermilion & multi 1.50 .25

Children's Day.

Democracy Monument — A183

Designs: 2b, Mother with children and animals, bas-relief from Democracy Monument. 2.75b, Workers, bas-relief from Democracy Monument. 5b, Top of Democracy Monument and quotation from speech of King Rama VII.

Perf. 14x14½
1975, Jan. 26 Wmk. 233
719 A183 75s dull grn & multi .95 .30
720 A183 2b multicolored 2.10 .60
721 A183 2.75b blue & multi 3.00 .45
722 A183 5b multicolored 4.00 1.10
Nos. 719-722 (4) 10.05 2.45

Movement of Oct. 14, 1973, to re-establish democratic institutions.

Marbled Tiger Cat — A184

1975, Mar. 5 Wmk. 334 Perf. 13½
723 A184 20s shown 1.50 .30
724 A184 75s Gaurs 3.50 .60
725 A184 2.75b Asiatic elephant 5.00 .45
726 A184 9b Clouded leop-
ard 6.50 1.10
Nos. 723-726 (4) 16.50 2.45

Protected animals.

White-eyed River
Martin — A185

Birds: 2b, Paradise flycatchers. 2.75b, Long-tailed broadbills. 5b, Sultan tit.

Wmk. 371
1975, Apr. 2 Litho. Perf. 12½
727 A185 75s ocher & multi 1.60 .30
728 A185 2b lt blue & multi 3.75 1.10
729 A185 2.75b lt violet & multi 4.00 .60
730 A185 5b rose & multi 8.00 1.75
Nos. 727-730 (4) 17.35 3.75

King Bhumibol Adulyadej and Queen
Sirikit — A186

3b, King, Queen, different background design.

Perf. 10½x13
1975, Apr. 28 Photo. Wmk. 368
731 A186 75s violet bl & multi 1.60 .35
732 A186 3b multicolored 4.00 .60

25th wedding anniversary of King Bhumibol Adulyadej and Queen Sirikit.

Round-house Kick — A187

Thai Boxing: 2.75b, Reverse elbow. 3b, Flying knee. 5b, Ritual homage.

Wmk. 371
1975, May 20 Litho. Perf. 12½
733 A187 75s green & multi 1.10 .35
734 A187 2.75b blue & multi 4.50 1.00
735 A187 3b orange & multi 4.00 1.75
736 A187 5b orange & multi 9.50 2.50
Nos. 733-736 (4) 19.10 5.60

Tosakanth
Mask — A188

Masks: 2b, Kumbhakarn. 3b, Rama. 4b, Hanuman.

1975, June 10 Litho. Wmk. 371
737 A188 75s dark gray & multi 1.75 .30
738 A188 2b dull vio & multi 4.75 1.20
739 A188 3b purple & multi 5.50 1.75
740 A188 4b multicolored 13.00 3.50
Nos. 737-740 (4) 25.00 6.75

Thai art and literature.

THAIPEX 75 Emblem — A189

THAIPEX 75 Emblem and: 2.75b, Stamp designer. 4b, Stamp printing plant. 5b, Stamp collector.

1975, Aug. 4 Wmk. 371 Perf. 12½
741 A189 75s yellow & multi .65 .25
742 A189 2.75b orange & multi 1.75 .35
743 A189 4b lt blue & multi 2.75 1.40
744 A189 5b carmine & multi 3.25 .75
Nos. 741-744 (4) 8.40 2.75

THAIPEX 75, Third National Philatelic Exhibition, Aug. 4-10.

Orchid Type of 1974

Orchids: 75s, Dendrobium cruentum. 2b, Dendrobium parishii. 2.75b, Vanda teres. 5b, Vanda denisoniana.

Perf. 11x13
1975, Aug. 12 Photo. Wmk. 368
745 A181 75s olive & multi .90 .30
746 A181 2b multicolored 1.75 .60
747 A181 2.75b scarlet & multi 2.75 .60
748 A181 5b ultra & multi 4.50 1.25
a. Souv. sheet, #745-748, perf
13½ 50.00 35.00
Nos. 745-748 (4) 9.90 2.75

Mytilus Smaragdinus — A190

Sea Shells: 1b, Turbo marmoratus. 2.75b, Oliva mustelina. 5b, Cypraea moneta.

Perf. 14x14½
1975, Sept. 5 Litho. Wmk. 375
749 A190 75s yellow & multi 2.00 1.25
750 A190 1b ver & multi 1.75 .30
751 A190 2.75b blue & multi 5.50 1.10
752 A190 5b green & multi 11.00 2.90
Nos. 749-752 (4) 20.25 5.55

Yachting and Games Emblem — A191

Designs: 1.25b, Badminton. 1.50b, Volleyball. 2b, Target shooting.

Perf. 11x13
1975, Sept. 20 Litho. Wmk. 368
753 A191 75s ultra & black 1.00 .25
754 A191 1.25b brt rose & blk 1.40 .85
755 A191 1.50b red & black 2.50 1.75
756 A191 2b apple grn &
blk 3.50 1.50
a. Souv. sheet, #753-756, perf
13½ 30.00 20.00
Nos. 753-756 (4) 8.40 4.35

8th SEAP Games, Bangkok, Sept. 1975.

Pataya
Beach
A192

Views: 2b, Samila Beach. 3b, Prachuap Bay. 5b, Laem Singha Bay.

1975, Oct. 5 Wmk. 371 Perf. 12½
757 A192 75s orange & multi .90 .25
758 A192 2b orange & multi 2.40 1.50
759 A192 3b orange & multi 4.00 .85
760 A192 5b orange & multi 4.50 2.00
Nos. 757-760 (4) 11.80 4.60

Intl. Letter Writing Week, Oct. 6-12.

"u n," UN Emblem, Food and
Education for Children — A193

1975, Oct. 24 Litho. Wmk. 371
761 A193 75s ultra & multi 1.40 .25

United Nations Day.

Morse Telegraph — A194

Design: 2.75b, Teleprinter and radar.

Perf. 14x14½
1975, Nov. 4 Litho. Wmk. 334
762 A194 75s multicolored 1.00 .40
763 A194 2.75b blue & multi 1.50 .45

Centenary of telegraph system.

Sukhrip Khrong Mueang
Barge — A195

Thai ceremonial barges: 1b, Royal escort barge Anekchat Phuchong. 2b, Royal barge Anantanakarat. 2.75b, Krabi Ran Ron Rap barge. 3b, Asura Wayuphak barge. 4b, Asura paksi barge. 5b, Royal barge Sri Suphanahong. 6b, Phali Rang Thawip barge.

Wmk. 371
1975, Nov. 18 Litho Perf. 13½
764 A195 75s multicolored 1.50 .30
765 A195 1b multicolored 3.00 .90
766 A195 2b lilac & multi 4.50 1.25
767 A195 2.75b multicolored 5.00 1.00
768 A195 3b yellow & multi 7.00 1.75
769 A195 4b multicolored 6.00 3.50
770 A195 5b gray & multi 11.00 5.75
771 A195 6b blue & multi 7.50 3.50
Nos. 764-771 (8) 45.50 17.95

Thai Flag, Arms
of Chakri Royal
Family — A196

King Bhumibol
Adulyadej — A197

Perf. 15x14
1975, Dec. 5 Litho. Wmk. 375
772 A196 75s multicolored 1.75 .45
773 A197 5b multicolored 5.00 1.10

King Bhumibol's 48th birthday.

Shot Put and SEAP Emblem — A198

2b, Table tennis. 3b, Bicycling. 4b, Relay race.

1975, Dec. 9 Wmk. 368 *Perf. 11x13*

774	A198	1b orange & black	.70	.25
775	A198	2b brt green & blk	2.00	1.10
776	A198	3b ocher & blk	3.00	1.25
777	A198	4b violet & blk	3.50	2.00
a.		Souvenir sheet of 4, #774-777, perf. 13½	30.00	20.00
		Nos. 774-777 (4)	9.20	4.60

8th SEAP Games, Bangkok, Dec. 9-20.

IWY Emblem and Globe — A199

Perf. 14x14½
1975, Dec. 20 Wmk. 375
778 A199 75s blk, org & vio bl 1.10 .30

International Women's Year.

Children Writing on Slate — A200

Perf. 13x14
1976, Jan. 10 Litho. Wmk. 368
779 A200 75s lt green & multi 1.75 .40

Children's Day.

Macrobrachium Rosenbergii — A201

Designs: 2b, Penaeus merguiensis. 2.75b, Panulirus ornatus. 5b, Penaeus monodon.

1976, Feb. 18 *Perf. 11x13*

780	A201	75s multicolored	2.50	.30
781	A201	2b multicolored	4.00	1.75
782	A201	2.75b multicolored	4.00	1.25
783	A201	5b multicolored	9.50	3.25
		Nos. 780-783 (4)	20.00	6.55

Shrimp and lobster exports.

Golden-backed Three-toed Woodpecker A202

Birds: 1.50b, Greater green-billed malcoha. 3b, Pomatorhinus hypoleucos. 4b, Green magpie.

Wmk. 371
1976, Apr. 2 Litho. *Perf. 12½*

784	A202	1b multicolored	.60	.25
785	A202	1.50b multicolored	1.25	.65
786	A202	3b yellow & multi	4.00	1.20
787	A202	4b rose & multi	3.25	.95
		Nos. 784-787 (4)	9.10	3.05

Ban Chiang Vase — A203

Designs: Ban Chiang painted pottery, various vessels, Bronze Age.

Perf. 14½x14
1976, May 5 Litho. Wmk. 375

788	A203	1b olive & multi	.90	.25
789	A203	2b dp blue & multi	5.25	.90
790	A203	3b green & multi	3.75	.65
791	A203	4b org red & multi	4.00	2.50
		Nos. 788-791 (4)	13.90	4.30

Mailman, 1883 — A204

Designs: 3b, Mailman, 1935. 4b, Mailman, 1950. 5b, Mailman, 1974.

Wmk. 377
1976, Aug. 4 Litho. *Perf. 12½*

792	A204	1b multicolored	.95	.30
793	A204	3b multicolored	2.75	.75
794	A204	4b multicolored	4.25	2.40
795	A204	5b multicolored	6.00	1.10
		Nos. 792-795 (4)	13.95	4.55

Development of mailmen's uniforms.

Kinnari — A205

Thai Mythology: 2b, Suphan-mat-cha. 4b, Garuda. 5b, Naga.

1976, Oct. 3 Wmk. 368 *Perf. 11x13*

796	A205	1b green & multi	6.00	1.40
797	A205	2b ultra & multi	1.60	.30
798	A205	4b gray & multi	2.40	.30
799	A205	5b slate & multi	3.50	.45
		Nos. 796-799 (4)	13.50	2.45

International Letter Writing Week.

UN Emblem, Drug Addicts, Alcohol, Cigarettes, Drugs — A206

Wmk. 329
1976, Oct. 24 Photo. *Perf. 13½*
800 A206 1b ultra & multi 1.00 .25

United Nations Day.

Old and New Telephones — A207

Perf. 14x14½
1976, Nov. 10 Litho. Wmk. 375
801 A207 1b multicolored 1.00 .25

Centenary of first telephone call by Alexander Graham Bell, Mar. 10, 1876.

Sivalaya-Mahaprasad Hall — A208

Royal Houses: 2b, Cakri-Mahaprasad. 4b, Mahisra-Prasad. 5b, Dusit-Mahaprasad.

Perf. 14x15
1976, Dec. 5 Wmk. 375 Litho.

802	A208	1b multicolored	.95	.25
803	A208	2b multicolored	7.00	1.00
804	A208	4b multicolored	4.00	2.10
805	A208	5b multicolored	4.25	1.25
		Nos. 802-805 (4)	16.20	4.60

Banteng — A209

Protected animals: 2b, Tapir and young. 4b, Sambar deer and fawn. 5b, Hog deer family.

Wmk. 334
1976, Dec. 26 Litho. *Perf. 11*
806 A209 1b multicolored 4.75 1.25
807 A209 2b multicolored 5.50 1.50

Wmk. 368
808 A209 4b multicolored 2.25 .45
809 A209 5b multicolored 3.00 .45
Nos. 806-809 (4) 15.50 3.65

Child Casting Shadow of Man — A210

Wmk. 329
1977, Jan. 8 Photo. *Perf. 13½*
810 A210 1b multicolored 1.40 .25

National Children's Day.

Alsthom's Electric Engine — A211

Locomotives: 2b, Davenport's electric engine. 4b, Pacific's steam engine. 5b, George Egestoff's steam engine.

Perf. 11x13
1977, Mar. 26 Litho. Wmk. 368

811	A211	1b multicolored	2.00	.35
812	A211	2b multicolored	5.50	.65
813	A211	4b multicolored	12.50	4.50
814	A211	5b multicolored	20.00	3.50
		Nos. 811-814 (4)	40.00	9.00

80th anniv. of State Railroad of Thailand.

Chulalongkorn University Auditorium — A212

1977, Mar. 26 Photo.
815 A212 1b multicolored 1.40 .25

Chulalongkorn University, 60th anniversary.

Flags of AOPU Members — A213

Wmk. 371
1977, Apr. 1 Litho. *Perf. 12½*
816 A213 1b multicolored 1.40 .25

Asian-Oceanic Postal Union (AOPU), 15th anniv.

Invalid in Wheelchair and Soldiers — A214

Wmk. 329
1977, Apr. 2 Photo. *Perf. 13½*
817 A214 5b multicolored 1.75 .30

Sai-Jai-Thai Day, to publicize Sai-Jai-Thai Foundation which helps wounded soldiers.

Phra Aphai Mani and Phisua Samut A215

Puppets: 3b, Rusi and Sutsakhon. 4b, Nang Vali and Usren. 5b, Phra Aphai Mani and Nang Laweng's portrait.

Perf. 11x13
1977, June 16 Wmk. 368

818	A215	2b multicolored	.90	.25
819	A215	3b multicolored	1.75	.30
820	A215	4b multicolored	1.50	.30
821	A215	5b multicolored	1.75	.45
		Nos. 818-821 (4)	5.90	1.30

Thai plays and literature.

Drum Dance — A216

Designs: 3b, Dance of dip nets. 4b, Harvest dance. 5b, Kan dance.

1977, July 14   Photo.   Perf. 13x11
822	A216	2b rose & multi	.75	.25
823	A216	3b lt green & multi	2.10	.40
824	A216	4b yellow & multi	1.10	.30
825	A216	5b lt violet & multi	1.60	.30
	Nos. 822-825 (4)		5.55	1.25

Thailand No. 609, Various Stamps and Thaipex Emblem — A217

Wmk. 377
1977, Aug. 4   Litho.   Perf. 12½
826	A217	75s multicolored	1.60	.25

THAIPEX 77, 4th National Philatelic Exhibition, Aug. 4-12.

Scenes from Thai Literature — A218

Perf. 11x13
1977, Oct. 5   Photo.   Wmk. 368
827	A218	75s multicolored	1.25	.25
828	A218	2b multi, diff.	2.50	1.00
829	A218	5b multi, diff.	3.00	.30
830	A218	6b multi, diff.	3.50	.65
	Nos. 827-830 (4)		10.25	2.20

Intl. Letter Writing Week, Oct. 6-12.

Old and New Buildings, UN Emblem — A219

1977, Oct. 5   Litho.   Perf. 11x13
831	A219	75s multicolored	1.40	.25

United Nations Day.

King Bhumibol as Scout Leader, Camp and Emblem — A220

1977, Nov. 21   Photo.   Wmk. 368
832	A220	75s multicolored	2.25	.25

9th National Jamboree, Nov. 21-27.

Diseased Hand and Elbow — A221

1977, Dec. 20   Perf. 11x13
833	A221	75s multicolored	1.10	.25

World Rheumatism Year.

Map of South East Asia and ASEAN Emblem — A222

Wmk. 377
1977, Dec. 1   Litho.   Perf. 12½
834	A222	5b multicolored	2.00	.30

ASEAN, 10th anniv.

King Type of 1972-74 Redrawn
1976   Perf. 12½x13
Size: 21x27mm
835	A146	20s blue	4.50	.30
836	A146	75s lilac	4.50	.30

Engr.
837	A146	10b vermilion & blk	45.00	2.00
838	A146	40b bister & lilac	12.00	1.60
	Nos. 835-838 (4)		66.00	4.20

Numerals are taller and thinner and leaves in background have been redrawn.

Children Carrying Flag of Thailand — A223

Wmk. 329
1978, Jan. 9   Photo.   Perf. 13½
839	A223	75s multicolored	1.75	.25

Children's Day.

Dendrobium Heterocarpum — A224

Orchids: 1b, Dendrobium pulchellum. 1.50b, Doritis pulcherrima. 2b, Dendrobium hercoglossum. 2.75b, Aerides odorata. 3b, Trichoglottis fasciata. 5b, Dendrobium wardianum. 6b, Dendrobium senile.

Perf. 11x14
1978, Jan. 18   Wmk. 368
840	A224	75s multicolored	1.25	.75
841	A224	1b multicolored	2.00	1.00
842	A224	1.50b multicolored	4.00	2.00
843	A224	2b multicolored	.95	.25
844	A224	2.75b multicolored	5.00	.45
845	A224	3b multicolored	.95	.60
846	A224	5b multicolored	1.25	.60
847	A224	6b multicolored	1.25	.60
	Nos. 840-847 (8)		16.65	6.25

9th World Orchid Conference.

Census Chart, Symbols of Agriculture — A225

Wmk. 377
1978, Mar. 1   Litho.   Perf. 12½
848	A225	75s multicolored	.65	.25

Agricultural census, Apr. 1978.

Anabas Testudineus — A226

Fish: 2b, Datnioides microlepis. 3b, Kryptopterus apogon. 4b, Probarbus Jullieni.

Perf. 11x13
1978, Apr. 13   Photo.   Wmk. 368
849	A226	1b multicolored	2.40	.90
850	A226	2b multicolored	.90	.30
851	A226	3b multicolored	.90	.30
852	A226	4b multicolored	1.75	.60
	Nos. 849-852 (4)		5.95	2.10

Birth of Prince Siddhartha — A227

Murals: 3b, Prince Siddhartha cuts his hair. 5b, Buddha descending from Tavatimsa Heaven. 6b, Buddha entering Nirvana.

Wmk. 329
1978, June 15   Photo.   Perf. 13½
853	A227	2b multicolored	1.40	.70
854	A227	3b multicolored	2.40	1.00
855	A227	5b mulitcolored	9.00	2.40
856	A227	6b multicolored	4.50	2.40
	Nos. 853-856 (4)		17.30	6.50

Story of Gautama Buddha, murals in Puthi Savan Hall, National Museum, Bangkok.

Bhumibol Dam — A228

Dams and Reservoirs: 2b, Sirikit dam. 2.75b, Vajiralongkorn dam. 6b, Ubol Ratana dam.

Perf. 14x14½
1978, July 28   Litho.   Wmk. 233
857	A228	75s multicolored	1.50	.45
858	A228	2b multicolored	1.50	.60
859	A228	2.75b multicolored	2.75	.60
860	A228	6b multicolored	3.75	2.00
	Nos. 857-860 (4)		9.50	3.65

Idea Lynceus — A229

Butterflies: 3b, Sephisa chandra. 5b, Charaxes durnfordi. 6b, Cethosia penthesilea methypsia.

Perf. 11x13
1978, Aug. 25   Litho.   Wmk. 368
861	A229	2b lilac, blk & red	2.00	.75
862	A229	3b multicolored	2.25	.75
863	A229	5b multicolored	6.00	1.40
864	A229	6b multicolored	4.00	2.25
	Nos. 861-864 (4)		14.25	5.15

Chedi Chai Mongkhon Temple — A230

Temples: 2b, That Hariphunchai. 2.75b, Borom That Chaiya. 5b, That Choeng Chum.

1978, Oct. 8   Perf. 13x11
865	A230	75s multicolored	1.10	.30
866	A230	2b multicolored	1.40	.45
867	A230	2.75b multicolored	4.50	.45
868	A230	5b multicolored	2.75	1.10
	Nos. 865-868 (4)		9.75	2.30

Intl. Letter Writing Week, Oct. 6-12.

Mother and Children, UN Emblem — A231

Perf. 14½x14
1978, Oct. 24   Litho.   Wmk. 375
869	A231	75s multicolored	.95	.25

United Nations Day.

Boxing, Soccer, Pole Vault — A232

Designs: 2b, Javelin, weight lifting, running. 3b, Ball games and sailing. 5b, Basketball, hockey stick and boxing gloves.

Perf. 14x14½
1978, Oct.   Wmk. 233   Litho.
870	A232	75s multicolored	.60	.25
871	A232	2b multicolored	.90	.25
872	A232	3b multicolored	1.75	.45
873	A232	5b multicolored	3.25	.90
	Nos. 870-873 (4)		6.50	1.85

8th Asian Games, Bangkok.

Five Races and World Map A233

1978, Nov.
874	A233	75s multicolored	.85	.25

Anti-Apartheid Year.

Children Painting Thai Flag — A234

Children and Children's SOS Village, Tambol Bangpu — A235

1979, Jan. 17   *Perf. 14x14½*
875 A234 75s multicolored .65 .25
876 A235 75s multicolored 1.40 .35
    International Year of the Child.

Matuta Lunaris — A236

Crabs: 2.75b, Matuta planipes fabricius. 3b, Portunus pelagicus. 5b, Scylla serrata.

Wmk. 377
1979, Mar. 22   Litho.   *Perf. 12½*
877 A236 2b multicolored 1.90 .60
878 A236 2.75b multicolored 4.50 .60
879 A236 3b multicolored 2.50 .90
880 A236 5b multicolored 5.75 1.50
    Nos. 877-880 (4) 14.65 3.60

A237

1979, June 25
881 A237 1b Sweetsop 1.50 .45
882 A237 2b Pineapple 1.50 .45
883 A237 5b Bananas 3.50 1.40
884 A237 6b Longans (litchi) 3.25 1.60
    Nos. 881-884 (4) 9.75 3.90
    See Nos. 1145-1148.

Arbor Day, 20th Anniv. — A238

Young man and woman planting tree.

Perf. 13x11
1979, July 10   Litho.   **Wmk. 368**
885 A238 75s multicolored .80 .25

Pencil, Pen, Thaipex '79 Emblem — A239

Thaipex '79 Emblem and: 2b, Envelopes. 2.75b, Stamp album. 5b, Magnifying glass and tongs.

1979, Aug. 4   *Perf. 11x13*
886 A239 75s multicolored .60 .25
887 A239 2b multicolored .90 .30
888 A239 2.75b multicolored 1.50 .40
889 A239 5b multicolored 3.00 .90
    Nos. 886-889 (4) 6.00 1.85
    Thaipex '79, 5th National Philatelic Exhibition, Bangkok, Aug. 4-12.

Floral Arrangement A240

Designs: Decorative arrangements.

Perf. 14½x14
1979, Oct. 7   Litho.   **Wmk. 233**
890 A240 75s multicolored .60 .25
891 A240 2b multicolored .90 .30
892 A240 2.75b multicolored 2.25 .40
893 A240 5b multicolored 2.25 .90
    Nos. 890-893 (4) 6.00 1.85
    Intl. Letter Writing Week, Oct. 8-14.

UN Day — A241

1979, Oct. 24   Litho.   *Perf. 14½x14*
894 A241 75s multicolored .85 .25

Frigate Makut Rajakumarn — A242

Thai Naval Ships: 3b, Frigate Tapi. 5b, Fast strike craft, Prabparapak. 6b, Patrol boat T-91.

Wmk. 329
1979, Nov. 20   Photo.   *Perf. 13½*
895 A242 2b multicolored 1.60 .90
896 A242 3b multicolored 2.60 .90
897 A242 5b multicolored 5.50 1.75
898 A242 6b multicolored 6.00 2.50
    Nos. 895-898 (4) 15.70 6.05

Thai Royal Orders (Medallions and Ribbons) — A243

Designs: #900a, Rajamitrabhorn Order. #902a, House of Chakri. #904a, The nine gems. #906a, Chula Chom Klao. Pairs have continuous design.

Perf. 13x11
1979, Dec. 5   Litho.   **Wmk. 368**
899 1b multicolored 1.40 .40
900 1b multicolored 1.40 .40
  a. A243 Pair, #899-900 3.00 3.00
901 2b multicolored 1.40 .40
902 2b multicolored 1.40 .40
  a. A243 Pair, #901-902 3.00 3.00
903 5b multicolored 2.50 .70
904 5b multicolored 2.50 .70
  a. A243 Pair, #903-904 5.50 5.50
905 6b multicolored 3.00 1.10
906 6b multicolored 3.00 1.10
  a. A243 Pair, #905-906 7.00 7.00
    Nos. 899-906 (8) 16.60 5.20
    See Nos. 1278-1285.

King Type of 1972-77
Perf. 13½x13
1979, Dec. 23   Litho.   **Wmk. 329**
Size: 21x26mm
907 A146 50s olive green .60 .25
Engr.
908 A146 2b org red & lilac 1.25 .25

Rice Planting — A245

Children's Day: No. 910, Family in rice field.

Perf. 13x11
1980, Jan. 12   Litho.   **Wmk. 368**
909 A245 75s multicolored .85 .25
910 A245 75s multicolored .85 .25

Family, House, Map of Thailand — A246

Perf. 15x14
1980, Feb. 1   Litho.   **Wmk. 233**
911 A246 75s multicolored .70 .30
    Natl. Population & Housing Census, Apr.

Gold-fronted Leafbird — A247

2b, Yellow-cheeked tit. 3b, Chestnut-tailed siva. 5b, Scarlet minivet.

Perf. 13x11
1980, Feb. 26   **Wmk. 368**
912 A247 75s shown .80 .25
913 A247 2b multicolored 1.20 .45
914 A247 3b multicolored 2.25 .60
915 A247 5b multicolored 3.00 1.25
    Nos. 912-915 (4) 7.25 2.55
    Intl. Commission for Bird Preservation, 9th Conf. of Asian Section, Chieng-mai, 2/26-29.

Smokers and Lungs, WHO Emblem — A248

1980, Apr. 7   **Wmk. 329**   *Perf. 13½*
916 A248 75s multicolored .70 .25
    World Health Day; fight against cigarette smoking.

Garuda and Rotary Emblem — A249

1980, May 6   **Wmk. 368**   *Perf. 13x11*
917 A249 5b multicolored 1.75 .45
    Rotary International, 75th anniversary.

Sai Yok Falls, Kanchanaburi — A250

2b, Punyaban Falls, Ranong. 5b, Heo Suwat Falls, Nakhon Ratchasima. 6b, Siriphum Falls, Chiang Mai.

Perf. 14x15
1980, July 1   Litho.   **Wmk. 233**
918 A250 1b shown .65 .25
919 A250 2b multicolored .80 .25
920 A250 5b multicolored 2.40 .75
921 A250 6b multicolored 2.10 .90
    Nos. 918-921 (4) 5.95 2.15

Queen
Sirikit — A251

Family with Cattle, Ceres Medal
(Reverse) — A252

No. 924, Ceres medal (obverse), potters.

Perf. 13½, 11x13 (5b)
Wmk. 329, 368 (5b)

1980, Aug. 12			Litho.	
922	A251	75s multicolored	.90	.25
	Complete booklet, 10 #922		17.50	
923	A252	5b multicolored	1.75	.80
924	A252	5b multicolored	1.75	.80
	Nos. 922-924 (3)		4.40	1.85

Queen Sirikit's 48th birthday.

Khao Phanomrung Temple, Buri
Ram — A253

Intl. Letter Writing Week, Oct. 6-12 (Temples): 2b, Prang Ku, Chailyaphum. 2.75b, Phimai, Nakhon Ratchasima. 5b, Sikhoraphum, Surin.

Perf. 11x13

1980, Oct. 5			Litho.	Wmk. 368
925	A253	75s multicolored	.80	.25
	Complete booklet, 10 #925		14.00	
926	A253	2b multicolored	.80	.25
927	A253	2.75b multicolored	1.20	.30
928	A253	5b multicolored	2.00	1.00
	Nos. 925-928 (4)		4.80	1.80

Princess
Mother — A254

Perf. 15x14

1980, Oct. 21			Litho.	Wmk. 233
929	A254	75s multicolored	2.75	.45
	Complete booklet, 10 #929		40.00	

Princess Mother, 80th birthday.

Golden Mount,
Bangkok — A255

1980, Oct. 24

930	A255	75s multicolored	.75	.30
	Complete booklet, 10 #930		14.00	

United Nations Day.

King Bhumibol
Adulyadej — A256

Type I   Type II Redrawn

Two types of Nos. 936-938: Type I, asymmetrical shape to mouth and small eye pupils. Type II, symmetrical mouth and large eye pupils.

Perf. 11x13

1980-86(?)			Litho.	Wmk. 368
932	A256	25s salmon	1.10	.25
933	A256	50s olive green	5.50	.25
b.	Wmk. 233, perf. 14x15		4.00	.25
c.	Wmk. 387, perf. 11x13		1.00	.25
934	A256	75s lilac	.50	.25
	Complete booklet, 10 #934		11.00	
935	A256	1.25b yellow green	.50	.25
a.	Wmk. 387, perf. 11x13		1.25	.25
b.	Wmk. 233, perf. 14x15		4.00	.25

Perf. 13½x13

		Engr.		Wmk. 329
936	A256	3b brn & dk bl (II)	.90	.25
a.	Type I		15.00	
937	A256	5b pur & brn (II)	1.25	.30
a.	Type I		17.00	.65
938	A256	6b dk grn & pur (II)	1.40	.25
a.	Type I		15.00	.65
939	A256	8.50b grn & brn org	1.50	.30
940	A256	9.50b olive & dk grn	1.50	.55
	Nos. 932-940 (9)		14.15	2.65

Issued: 25s, 75s, 12/5/80; Nos. 933, 935, 9/7/81; #933b, 12/5/81; Nos. 933b, 935b, 6/8/83; Nos. 936a, 937a, 938a, 8.50b, 9.50b, 12/5/83. Nos. 933c, 935a, 1984. Nos. 936-938, 1985-86.
See Nos. 1080-1093. For surcharges see Nos. 1226-1226A, 2250.

King Rama VII
Monument
Inauguration
A257

Perf. 15x14

1980, Dec. 10				Wmk. 233
946	A257	75s multicolored	.75	.25

Bencharongware Bowl — A258

Perf. 11x13

1980, Dec. 15				Wmk. 368
947	A258	2b shown	.95	.30
948	A258	2.75b Covered bowls	.95	.30
949	A258	3b Covered jar	1.50	.45
950	A258	5b Stem plates	1.50	.75
	Nos. 947-950 (4)		4.90	1.80

King Vajiravudh
Birth Centenary
A259

1981, Jan. 1	Wmk. 233	**Perf. 15x14**	
951	A259	75s multicolored	1.40	.25
	Complete booklet, 10 #951		22.50	

Children's
Day — A260

Perf. 13x11

1981, Jan. 16				Wmk. 368
952	A260	75s multicolored	.60	.25
	Complete booklet, 10 #952		16.00	

Hegira, 1500th Anniv. — A261

Wmk. 377

1981, Jan. 18	Litho.	**Perf. 12½**	
953	A261	5b multicolored	2.75	.60

Dolls in Native Costumes — A262

Wmk. 368

1981, Feb. 6	Litho.	**Perf. 13½**	
954	A262	75s Palm-leaf fish mobile	.45	.25
	Complete booklet, 10 #954		12.50	
955	A262	75s Teak elephants	.45	.25
	Complete booklet, 10 #955		12.50	
956	A262	2.75b shown	1.25	.60
957	A262	2.75b Baskets	1.25	.60
	Nos. 954-957 (4)		3.40	1.70

CONEX '81 International Crafts Exhibition.

Scout Leader and
Boy on
Crutches — A263

1981, Feb. 28		**Perf. 13x11**	
958	A263	75s shown	.30	.25
	Complete booklet, 10 #958		14.00	
959	A263	5b Diamond cutter in wheelchair	1.60	.50

International Year of the Disabled.

Dindaeng-Tarua Expressway
Opening — A264

1981, Oct. 29		**Perf. 13½**	
960	A264	1b Klongtoey	.65	.25
961	A264	5b Vipavadee Rangsit Highway	2.25	.65

Ongkhot, Khon
Mask — A265

Designs: Various Khon masks.

1981, July 1	Litho.	**Perf. 13x11**	
962	A265	75s shown	.45	.25
963	A265	2b Maiyarab	1.00	.25
964	A265	3b Sukrip	1.60	.50
965	A265	5b Indrajit	2.00	1.25
	Nos. 962-965 (4)		5.05	2.25

Exhibition Emblem, No. 83 — A266

Wmk. 370

1981, Aug. 4	Litho.	**Perf. 12**	
966	A266	75s shown	.45	.25
967	A266	75s No. 144	.45	.25
968	A266	2.75b No. 198	1.25	.60
969	A266	2.75b No. 226	1.25	.60
	Nos. 966-969 (4)		3.40	1.70

A267

Perf. 15x14

1981, Aug. 26				Wmk. 233
970	A267	1.25b multicolored	.85	.25
	Complete booklet, 10 #970		13.00	

Luang Praditphairo, court Musician, birth centenary. THAIPEX '81 Intl. Stamp Exhibition.

A268

Designs: Dwarfed trees.

1981, Oct. 4 — Wmk. 329
971	A268	75s Mai hok-hian	.50	.25
972	A268	2b Mai kam-ma-lo	.85	.30
973	A268	2.75b Mai khen	1.40	.25
974	A268	5b Mai khabuan	2.40	.90
		Nos. 971-974 (4)	5.15	1.70

25th Intl. Letter Writing Week, Oct. 6-12.

World Food Day A269

Wmk. 370
1981, Oct. 16   Litho.   Perf. 12
975	A269	75s multicolored	.65	.25

United Nations Day — A270

1981, Oct. 24   Wmk. 368   Perf. 13½
976	A270	1.25b Samran Mukha-mat Pavilion	.65	.25
	Complete booklet, 10 #976		14.00	

King Cobra A271

1981, Dec. 1   Wmk. 329   Perf. 13½
977	A271	75s shown	.65	.25
978	A271	2b Banded krait	1.40	.65
979	A271	2.75b Thai cobra	1.60	.45
980	A271	5b Malayan pit viper	2.00	1.00
		Nos. 977-980 (4)	5.65	2.35

Children's Day — A272

1982, Jan. 9   Wmk. 370   Perf. 12
981	A272	1.25b multicolored	.75	.25
	Complete booklet, strip of 4 #981		12.50	

Scouting Year — A273

1982, Feb. 22
982	A273	1.25b multicolored	.70	.25
	Complete booklet, strip of 4 #982		5.00	

Bicentenary of Bangkok (Thai Capital) A274

Chakri Dynasty kings. (Rama I-Rama IX) — 1b, Buddha Yod-Fa (1736-1809). 2b, Buddha Lert La Naphalai (1767-1824). 3b, Nang Klao (1787-1851). 4b, Mongkut (1804-1868). 5b, Chulalongkorn (1853-1910). 6b, Vajiravudh (1880-1925). 7b, Prachathipok (1893-1941). 8b, Ananda Mahidol (1925-1946). 9b, Bhumibol Adulyadej (b. 1927).

1982, Apr. 4   Litho.   Perf. 12
983	A274	1b multicolored	.60	.30
984	A274	1.25b shown	.60	.30
	Complete booklet, strip of 4 #984		6.50	
985	A274	2b multicolored	.90	.30
986	A274	3b multicolored	2.00	.45
987	A274	4b multicolored	1.50	.60
988	A274	5b multicolored	2.75	.85
989	A274	6b multicolored	2.75	.85
990	A274	7b multicolored	3.00	1.60
991	A274	8b multicolored	2.00	.90
992	A274	9b multicolored	2.40	1.25
a.	Souv. sheet of 10, 205x142mm		45.00	30.00
b.	Souv. sheet of 10, 195x180mm		45.00	30.00
	Nos. 983-992 (10)		18.50	7.40

Nos. 992a-992b each contain Nos. 983-992. No. 992a sold for 60b, No. 992b for 70b. Values for #992a-992b include folder.

TB Bacillus Centenary — A275

Wmk. 368
1982, Apr. 7   Litho.   Perf. 13½
993	A275	1.25b multicolored	.95	.25
	Complete booklet, strip of 4 #993		6.00	

Local Flowers — A276

1.25b, Quisqualis indica. 1.50b, Murraya aniculata. 6.50b, Mesua ferrea. 7b, Desmos chinensis.

Perf. 14x14½
1982, June 30   Wmk. 233
994	A276	1.25b multicolored	.35	.25
	Complete booklet, strip of 4 #994		2.00	
995	A276	1.50b multicolored	.55	.25
996	A276	6.50b multicolored	2.00	.60
997	A276	7b multicolored	1.60	.60
	Nos. 994-997 (4)		4.50	1.70

Buddhist Temples in Bangkok — A277

4.25b, Wat Pho. 6.50b, Mahathat Yuwarat Rangsarit. 7b, Phra Sri Rattana Satsadaram.

1982, Aug. 4   Wmk. 368   Perf. 13½
998	A277	1.25b shown	.45	.25
	Complete booklet, strip of 4 #998		3.00	

999	A277	4.25b multicolored	.75	.30
1000	A277	6.50b multicolored	1.40	.60
1001	A277	7b multicolored	1.60	.45
a.	Souv. sheet of 4, #998-1001, perf. 12½		80.00	45.00
	Nos. 998-1001 (4)		4.20	1.60

BANGKOK '83 Intl. Stamp Exhibition, Aug. 4-13, 1983. No. 1001a sold for 30b. See Nos. 1025-1026.

A278

Design: LANDSAT Satellite.

1982, Aug. 9   Wmk. 370   Perf. 12
1002	A278	1.25b multicolored	.60	.25
	Complete booklet, strip of 4 #1002		6.00	

2nd UN Conference on Peaceful Uses of Outer Space, Vienna, Aug. 9-21.

A279

Prince Purachatra of Kambaengbejra (1882-1936).

1982, Sept. 14   Wmk. 233   Perf. 14
1003	A279	1.25b multicolored	.75	.25
	Complete booklet, strip of 4 #1003		8.00	

26th Intl. Letter Writing Week, Oct. 6-12 — A280

Sangalok Pottery — 1.25b, Covered glazed jar. 3b, Painted jar. 4.25b, Glazed plate. 7b, Painted plate.

1982, Oct. 3   Wmk. 329   Perf. 13½
1004	A280	1.25b multicolored	.45	.25
	Complete booklet, strip of 4 #1004		2.00	
1005	A280	3b multicolored	1.25	.30
1006	A280	4.25b multicolored	.90	.45
1007	A280	7b multicolored	1.60	.60
	Nos. 1004-1007 (4)		4.20	1.60

UN Day — A281

Design: Loha Prasat Tower.

1982, Oct. 24
1008	A281	1.25b multicolored	.60	.25
	Complete booklet, strip of 4 #1008		6.00	

Musical Instruments — A282

50s, Chap, ching. 1b, Pi nai, pi nok. 1.25b, Klong that, taphon. 1.50b, Khong mong, krap. 6b, Khong wong yai. 7b, Khong wong lek. 8b, Ranat ek. 9b, Ranat thum.

1982, Nov. 30   Wmk. 370   Perf. 12
1009	A282	50s multicolored	.35	.25
1010	A282	1b multicolored	.85	.25
1011	A282	1.25b multicolored	.50	.25
	Complete booklet, strip of 4 #1011		2.00	
1012	A282	1.50b multicolored	.85	.30
1013	A282	6b multicolored	3.50	1.10
1014	A282	7b multicolored	1.75	.50
1015	A282	8b multicolored	1.60	.50
1016	A282	9b multicolored	1.75	.50
	Nos. 1009-1016 (8)		11.15	3.65

Pileated Gibbon — A283

3b, Pig-tailed macaque. 5b, Slow loris. 7b, Silvered leaf monkey.

1982, Dec. 26
1017	A283	1.25b shown	.45	.25
	Complete booklet, strip of 4 #1017		5.25	
1018	A283	3b multicolored	1.75	.30
1019	A283	5b multicolored	1.50	.55
1020	A283	7b multicolored	1.60	.75
	Nos. 1017-1020 (4)		5.30	1.85

ASEAN Members' Flags — A284

1982, Dec. 26   Wmk. 233
1021	A284	6.50b multicolored	1.60	.30

15th Anniv. of Assoc. of Southeast Asian Nations.

Children's Day — A285

Perf. 14½x14
1983, Jan. 8   Litho.   Wmk. 233
1022	A285	1.25b multicolored	.75	.25
	Complete booklet, strip of 4 #1022		5.00	

First Anniv of Postal Code A286

1983, Feb. 25   Wmk. 329   Perf. 13½
1023 A286 1.25b Codes .60 .25
　Complete booklet, strip of 4
　　#1023 6.00
1024 A286 1.25b Code on envelope .60 .25
　Complete booklet, strip of 4
　　#1024 6.00

BANGKOK '83 Type of 1982

Design: Old General Post Office.

1983, Feb. 25   Wmk. 368   Photo.
1025 A277 7b multicolored 1.50 .25
1026 A277 10b multicolored 2.10 .35
　a.　Souv. sheet of 2, #1025-
　　1026, perf. 12½ 25.00 14.00

25th Anniv. of Intl. Maritime Org. — A287

Perf. 14x14½
1983, Mar. 17   Litho.   Wmk. 233
1029 A287 1.25b Chinese junks .60 .25
　Complete booklet, strip of 4
　　#1029 5.00

Civil Servants' Day — A288

1983, Apr. 1   Wmk. 370   Perf. 12
1030 A288 1.25b multicolored .60 .25
　Complete booklet, strip of 4
　　#1030 5.00

Prince Sithiporn Kridakara (1883-1971) A289

Perf. 14½x14
1983, Apr. 11   Wmk. 233
1031 A289 1.25b multicolored .60 .25
　Complete booklet, strip of 4
　　#1031 5.00

Domestic Satellite Communications System Inauguration — A290

Design: Map; dish antenna, satellite.

Wmk. 368
1983, Aug. 4   Litho.   Perf. 13½
1032 A290 2b multicolored .95 .25

BANGKOK '83 Intl. Stamp Show, Aug. 4-13 — A291

1.25b, Mail collection. 7.50b, Posting letters. 8.50b, Mail transport. 9.50b, Mail delivery.

1983, Aug. 4   Wmk. 370   Perf. 12
1033 A291 1.25b multicolored .30 .25
　Complete booklet, strip of 4
　　#1033 1.50
1034 A291 7.50b multicolored 1.25 .35
1035 A291 8.50b multicolored 1.00 .45
1036 A291 9.50b multicolored 1.00 .45
　a.　Souv. sheet of 4, #1033-
　　1036 25.00 15.00
　Nos. 1033-1036 (4) 3.55 1.50

No. 1036a exist imperf, sold for 50b. Values: unused $150; used $110.

A292

Prince Bhanurangsi memorial statue.

Perf. 15x14
1983, Aug. 4   Litho.   Wmk. 233
1037 A292 1.25b multicolored .80 .25
　Complete booklet, strip of 4
　　#1037 6.00

A293

Wmk. 370
1983, Sept. 27   Litho.   Perf. 12
1038 A293 1.25b multicolored .30 .25
　Complete booklet, strip of 4
　　#1038 1.75
1039 A293 7b multicolored 1.10 .45
Malaysia/ Thailand/ Singapore submarine cable inauguration.

Intl. Letter Writing Week — A294

1983, Oct. 6   Wmk. 329   Perf. 13½
1040 A294 2b Acropora asper .70 .25
1041 A294 3b Platygyra lamellina 1.60 .25
1042 A294 4b Fungia 1.00 .45
1043 A294 7b Pectinia lactuca 2.00 .75
　Nos. 1040-1043 (4) 5.30 1.70

Prince Mahidol of Songkhla — A295

Wmk. 370
1983, Oct. 10   Litho.   Perf. 12
1044 A295 9.50b multicolored 1.50 .60
Siriraj Hospital Faculty of Medicine and Rockefeller Foundation, 60th Anniv. of cooperation.

World Communications Year — A296

3b, Telecommunications equipment, diff.

Perf. 14x14½
1983, Oct. 24   Litho.   Wmk. 233
1045 A296 2b multicolored .60 .25
1046 A296 3b multicolored .60 .25

United Nations Day — A297

1983, Oct. 24
1047 A297 1.25b multicolored .50 .25
　Complete booklet, strip of 4
　　#1047 4.50

Thai Alphabet, 700th Anniv. — A298

Designs: 3b, Painted pottery, Sukothai period. 7b, Thai characters, reign of King Ramkhamhaeng. 8b, Buddha, Sukothai period. 9b, Mahathat Temple, Sukothai province.

1983, Nov. 17   Wmk. 370   Perf. 12
1048 A298 3b multicolored .90 .25
1049 A298 7b multicolored 1.50 .30
1050 A298 8b multi, vert. 1.10 .35
1051 A298 9b multi, vert. 1.10 .35
　Nos. 1048-1051 (4) 4.60 1.25

National Development Program — A299

#1052, King and Queen initiating Royal Projects. #1053, Technical aid. #1054, Terrace farming, Irrigation dam. #1055, Gathering grain. #1056, Receiving the peoples' gratitude.

1984, May 5
1052 A299 1.25b multicolored .65 .25
1053 A299 1.25b multicolored .65 .25
1054 A299 1.25b multicolored .65 .25
1055 A299 1.25b multicolored .65 .25
1056 A299 1.25b multicolored .65 .25
　a.　Strip of 5, #1052-1056 3.25 3.25

Children's Day — A300

1984, Jan. 14   Wmk. 329   Perf. 13½
1057 A300 1.25b multicolored .65 .25
　Complete booklet, strip of 4
　　#1057 5.00

17th Natl. Games, Jan. 22-28 — A301

1984, Jan. 22
1058 A301 1.25b Running .65 .25
　Complete booklet, strip of 4
　　#1058 3.50
1059 A301 3b Soccer .65 .25

5th Rheumatology Congress, Jan. 22-27 — A302

Design: Rheumatic joints.

Perf. 14x15
1984, Jan. 22   Wmk. 233
1060 A302 1.25b multicolored .60 .25
　Complete booklet, strip of 4
　　#1060 5.00

Armed Forces Day — A303

Design: King Naresuan, tanks, jet, ship.

1984, Jan. 25   Perf. 15x14
1061 A303 1.25b multicolored .60 .25
　Complete booklet, strip of 4
　　#1061 6.00

50th Anniv. of Royal Institute — A304

1984, Mar. 31
1062 A304 1.25b multicolored .60 .25
　Complete booklet, strip of 4
　　#1062 5.00

Thammasat University, 50th
Anniv. — A305

1984, June 27   *Perf. 14x15*
1063 A305 1.25b Dome Building   .60   .25
Complete booklet, strip of 4
#1063   5.00

Asia-Pacific Broadcasting Union, 20th
Anniv. — A306

1984, July 1   **Wmk. 387**   *Perf. 12*
1064 A306 4b Map, emblem   1.00   .25

Seated Buddha,
Chiang Saen
Style — A307

Seated Buddhas in various styles.

                              Perf. 14½x14
1984, July 12   **Wmk. 233**
1065 A307 1.25b shown   1.10   .25
1066 A307 7b Sukhothai   1.40   .60
1067 A307 8.50b U-Thong   1.10   .60
1068 A307 9.50b Ayutthaya   .75   .60
    Nos. 1065-1068 (4)   4.35   2.05

Intl. Letter Writing
Week — A308

Medicinal Succulents: 1.50b, Alocasia
indica. 2b, Aloe barbadensis. 4b, Gynura
pseudochina DC. 10b, Rhoeo spathacea.

                    Wmk. 385
1984, Oct. 7   **Litho.**   *Perf. 13½*
1069 A308 1.50b multicolored   .50   .25
1070 A308 2b multicolored   .85   .35
1071 A308 4b multicolored   1.10   .45
1072 A308 10b multicolored   2.60   1.25
    Nos. 1069-1072 (4)   5.05   2.30

Princess Mother
(b. 1900) — A309

                    Perf. 15x14
1984, Oct. 21   **Wmk. 233**
1073 A309 1.50b Portrait   .70   .25

UN Day — A310

Design: Woman threshing rice.

1984, Oct. 24   **Wmk. 233**
1074 A310 1.50b multicolored   .35   .25

Local Butterflies — A311

2b, Bhutanitis lidderdalei. 3b,
Stichophthalma louisa. 5b, Parthenos sylvia.
7b, Stichophthalma godfreyi.

                    Wmk. 329
1984, Nov. 27   **Photo.**   *Perf. 13½*
1075 A311 2b multicolored   .50   .25
1076 A311 3b multicolored   .70   .25
1077 A311 5b multicolored   1.00   .60
1078 A311 7b multicolored   1.60   .60
    Nos. 1075-1078 (4)   3.80   1.70

King Type of 1980
Perf. 13½x13, 14x15 (1.50b, 2b)
Wmk. 329, 233 (1.50b, 2b)
1984-87   **Litho.**
1080 A256 1b Prus blue   .45   .25
1081 A256 1.50b brt yel org
                      ('85)   2.50   1.50
1082 A256 2b dk car ('85)   1.75   .25
  a.   Wmk. 387, perf. 11x13½
            ('86?)   2.50   .25
  b.   Wmk. 387, perf. 14½x14
            ('87)   1.10   .25

                    Engr.
1083 A256 2b hn brn &
                  gray vio   12.00   .30
1084 A256 4b turq bl & hn
                  brn   1.00   .25
1085 A256 6.50b dk yel grn &
                  ol brn   1.25   .50
1086 A256 7b dl red brn &
                  sep   1.25   .30
1087 A256 7.50b dk org &
                  saph ('85)   1.20   .50
1088 A256 8b brn vio & ol
                  grn ('85)   1.40   .35
1089 A256 9b int bl & dk ol
                  bis ('85)   1.25   .40
1090 A256 10b hn brn & sl
                  grn   2.25   .35
1091 A256 20b dk org & grn   2.75   .40
1092 A256 50b dp vit & grn   12.00   1.20
1093 A256 100b dp org & dk
                  bl   20.00   1.75
    Nos. 1080-1093 (14)   61.05   8.30

For surcharges see Nos. 1212, 2251.
Issued: 1b, 1/25/84; No. 1083, 4b, 6.50b,
7b, 10b, 50b, 100b, 12/5/84; 7.50b, 8b, 9b,
1/25/85; 1.50b, 4/6/85; No. 1082, 8/4/85; No.
1082a, 3/3/86; No. 1082b, 6/19/87.

Children's Day — A313

Children's drawings — No. 1101, Pedestri-
ans, overpass. No. 1102, Climbing overpass,
vert.

                    Wmk. 385
1985, Jan. 12   **Litho.**   *Perf. 13½*
1101 A313 1.50b multicolored   .35   .25
1102 A313 1.50b multicolored   .35   .25

Bangkok Mail Center Opening — A314

1985, Feb. 25
1103 A314 1.50b multicolored   .35   .25

Phuket Province
Heroes
Bicent. — A315

                    Perf. 15x14
1985, Mar. 13   **Litho.**   **Wmk. 233**
1104 A315 2b multicolored   .60   .25

Tao-Thep-Krasattri,   Tao-Sri-Sundhorn
Monument.

Government Savings Bank, 72nd
Anniv. — A316

Design: King Rama VI, headquarters.

1985, Apr. 1   *Perf. 14x15*
1105 A316 1.50b multicolored   .40   .25

Intl. Telecommunications Satellite Org.,
20th Anniv. — A317

1985, Apr. 6   **Wmk. 387**   *Perf. 12*
1106 A317 2b multicolored   .60   .25

Thai Airways Intl., 25th Anniv. — A318

                    Wmk. 385
1985, May 1   **Litho.**   *Perf. 13*
1107 A318 2b DC-6   .40   .25
1108 A318 7.50b DC-10   1.60   .45
1109 A318 8.50b Airbus A-300   2.00   .60
1110 A318 9.50b Boeing 747   2.40   .60
    Nos. 1107-1110 (4)   6.40   1.90

Natl. Flag and
UPU
Emblem — A319

10b, Flag and ITU emblem.

1985, July 1   **Wmk. 387**   *Perf. 12*
1111 A319 2b shown   .35   .25
                    Perf. 13½
                    Wmk. 385
1112 A319 10b multicolored   1.60   .60

Thai membership to UPU and Intl. Telecommunications Union, cent.

Natl. Communications Day, Aug.
5 — A320

1985, Aug. 4   **Wmk. 329**   *Perf. 13½*
1113 A320 2b multicolored   .60   .25

THAIPEX '85, Aug. 4-13 — A321

2b, Aisvarya Pavilion, vert. 3b, Varopas
Piman Pavilion. 7b, Vehas Camrun Pavilion.
10b, Vitoon Tassana Tower, vert.

1985, Aug. 4   **Wmk. 385**
1114 A321 2b multicolored   .65   .25
1115 A321 3b multicolored   .90   .25
1116 A321 7b multicolored   1.60   .65
1117 A321 10b multicolored   1.75   .95
  a.   Souv. sheet of 4, #1114-
          1117   50.00 35.00
    Nos. 1114-1117 (4)   4.90   2.10

No. 1117a exists imperf, sold for 40b. Value,
$600.

Natl. Science Day, Aug. 18 — A322

Design: King Rama IV, solar eclipse.

1985, Aug. 18   **Wmk. 387**   *Perf. 12*
1118 A322 2b multicolored   .90   .25

1885 Seal, Modern Map and
Crest — A323

                    Perf. 14½x15
1985, Sept. 3   **Wmk. 233**
1119 A323 2b multicolored   .60   .25

Royal Thai Survey Department, Cent.

13th SEA Games, Bangkok, Dec. 8-17 — A324

Designs: a, Boxing. b, Shot put. c, Badminton. d, Javelin. e, Weight lifting.

1985, Oct. 1   Wmk. 387   Perf. 12
1120	Strip of 5	4.50	2.50
a.-e.	A324 2b, any single	.65	.25
f.	Souv. sheet of 5, #a.-e. + label	35.00	35.00

No. 1120f sold for 20b.

Climbing Plants — A325

2b, Allemanda cathartica. 3b, Jasminum auriculatum. 7b, Passiflora laurifolia. 10b, Antigonon leptopus.

1985, Oct. 6   Wmk. 385   Perf. 13½
1121	A325	2b multicolored	.65	.25
1122	A325	3b multicolored	.90	.25
1123	A325	7b multicolored	1.60	.60
1124	A325	10b multicolored	2.00	.85
	Nos. 1121-1124 (4)		5.15	1.95

International Letter Writing Week.

UN Child Survival Campaign A326

1985, Oct. 24
| 1125 | A326 | 2b multicolored | .60 | .25 |

UN Day.

Prince Kromamun Bidyalabh Bridhyakorn (1885-1974), Govt. Minister — A327

1985, Nov. 7
1126	A327	2b multi	5.25	.25
1126A	A327	2b multi, diff.	.70	.25
b.	Pair, #1126-1126A		30.00	22.50

No. 1126A has flower design framing portrait reversed.

Rangsit (1885-1951), Prince of Jainad — A328

Perf. 15x14½
1985, Nov. 12   Wmk. 233
| 1127 | A328 1.50b multicolored | .60 | .25 |

Asian-Pacific Postal Union, 5th Congress, Nov. 25-Dec. 4 — A329

1985, Nov. 25   Wmk. 385   Perf. 13½
| 1128 | A329 | 2b multicolored | .40 | .25 |
| 1129 | A329 | 10b multicolored | 2.00 | .50 |

Intl. Youth Year A330

Perf. 14x15
1985, Nov. 26   Wmk. 233
| 1130 | A330 | 2b multicolored | .70 | .25 |

12th Asian-Pacific Dental Congress, Bangkok, Dec. 5-10 — A331

1985, Dec. 5
| 1131 | A331 | 2b multicolored | .70 | .25 |

13th SEA Games — A332

1985, Dec. 8   Wmk. 387   Perf. 12
1132	A332	1b Volleyball	.25	.25
1133	A332	2b Sepak-takraw	.50	.25
1134	A332	3b Women's gymnastics	.80	.25
1135	A332	4b Bowling	1.00	.30
a.	Souv. sheet, #1132-1135 + label		25.00	20.00
	Nos. 1132-1135 (4)		2.55	1.05

No. 1135a sold for 20b.

French Envoys — A333

1985, Dec. 12   Wmk. 385   Perf. 13½
| 1136 | A333 | 2b shown | .45 | .25 |
| 1137 | A333 | 8.50b Thai envoys | 1.40 | .70 |

Diplomatic relations with France, 300th anniv.

Domestic Express Mail Service Inauguration — A334

1986, Jan. 1
| 1138 | A334 2b multicolored | .60 | .25 |
| | Complete booklet, strip of 5 #1138 | 7.00 | |

Intl. Express Mail Service, EMS, 3rd anniv.

Wildlife Conservation — A335

Marine turtles — 1.50b, Chelonia mydas. 3b, Eretmochelys imbricata. 5b, Dermochelys coriacca. 10b, Lepidochelys olivacea.

1986, Jan. 8   Wmk. 329
1139	A335	1.50b multicolored	.55	.25
1140	A335	3b multicolored	1.00	.25
1141	A335	5b multicolored	2.60	.45
1142	A335	10b multicolored	2.60	.65
	Nos. 1139-1142 (4)		6.75	1.60

Natl. Children's Day — A336

Design: Children picking lotus, by Areeya Makarabhundhu, age 12.

1986, Jan. 11   Wmk. 385
| 1143 | A336 2b multicolored | .60 | .25 |
| | Complete booklet, strip of 5 #1143 | 6.00 | |

Statue of Sunthon Phu, Poet — A337

1986, June 26
| 1144 | A337 2b multicolored | .60 | .25 |
| | Complete booklet, strip of 5 #1144 | 6.00 | |

Fruit Type of 1979
1986, June 26   Wmk. 385
1145	A237	2b Watermelon	1.25	.25
	Complete booklet, strip of 5 #1145		12.50	
1146	A237	2b Malay apple	1.25	.25
	Complete booklet, strip of 5 #1146		12.50	
1147	A237	6b Pomelo	1.50	.65
1148	A237	6b Papaya	1.50	.65
	Nos. 1145-1148 (4)		5.50	1.80

Nos. 1145-1148 horiz.

Natl. Year of the Trees A338

1986, July 21
| 1149 | A338 2b multicolored | .60 | .25 |
| | Complete booklet, strip of 5 #1149 | 6.00 | |

Communications Day — A339

1986, Aug. 4
| 1150 | A339 2b multicolored | .60 | .25 |
| | Complete booklet, strip of 5 #1150 | 6.00 | |

Bamboo Baskets — A340

1986, Oct. 5
1151	A340	2b Chalom	.50	.25
	Complete booklet, strip of 5 #1151		4.50	
1152	A340	2b Krabung	.50	.25
	Complete booklet, strip of 5 #1152		4.50	
1153	A340	6b Kratib	1.00	.30
1154	A340	6b Kaleb	1.00	.30
	Nos. 1151-1154 (4)		3.00	1.10

Intl. Letter Writing Week.

Intl. Peace Year A341

1986, Oct. 24
| 1155 | A341 2b multicolored | .60 | .25 |
| | Complete booklet, strip of 5 #1155 | 6.50 | |

Productivity Year — A342

1986, Oct. 24   **Wmk. 329**
1156 A342 2b multicolored   .60   .25
    Complete booklet, strip of 5
    #1156   6.00

6th ASEAN Orchid Congress — A343

2b, Vanda varavuth, vert. 3b, Ascocenda emma, vert. 4b, Dendrobium sri-siam. 5b, Dendrobium ekapol panda.

1986, Nov. 7   **Wmk. 385**
1157 A343 2b multicolored   .60   .25
    Complete booklet, strip of
    5 #1157   6.00
1158 A343 3b multicolored   .75   .25
1159 A343 4b multicolored   1.25   .75
1160 A343 5b multicolored   1.40   .75
  a. Souv. sheet of 4, #1157-
    1160   90.00 80.00
    Nos. 1157-1160 (4)   4.00   2.00

No. 1160a sold for 25b.

Fungi A344

No. 1161, Volvariella volvacea. No. 1162, Pleurotus ostreatus. No. 1163, Auricularia polytricha. No. 1164, Pleurotus cystidiosus.

Perf. 13x13½
1986, Nov. 26   Wmk. 329   Photo.
1161 A344 2b multicolored   .65   .25
    Complete booklet, strip of 5
    #1161   6.50
1162 A344 2b multicolored   .65   .25
    Complete booklet, strip of 5
    #1162   6.50
1163 A344 6b multicolored   1.60   .40
1164 A344 6b multicolored   1.60   .40
    Nos. 1161-1164 (4)   4.50   1.30

Fisheries Dept., 60th Anniv. — A345

No. 1165, Morulius chrysophekadion. No. 1166, Notopterus blanci. No. 1167, Scleropages formosus. No. 1168, Pangasianodon gigas.

Wmk. 385
1986, Dec. 16   Litho.   Perf. 13½
1165 A345 2b multicolored   .60   .25
    Complete booklet, strip of 5
    #1165   5.00
1166 A345 2b multicolored   .60   .25
    Complete booklet, strip of 5
    #1166   5.00
1167 A345 7b multicolored   1.25   .65
1168 A345 7b multicolored   1.25   .65
    Nos. 1165-1168 (4)   3.70   1.80

No. 653 Surcharged in Dark Olive Green

Perf. 14x13½
1986, Dec.   Photo.   Wmk. 233
1168A A161 1b on 20s blue   .50   .25

Children's Day — A346

Child's drawing.

Perf. 14½x15
1987, Jan. 10   Litho.   Wmk. 387
1169 2b School, playground   .60   .25
1170 2b Pool   .60   .25
  a. A346 Pair, #1169-1170   1.60   1.25

No. 1170a has continuous design.

F-16 & F-5 Fighter Planes, Pilot — A347

1987, Mar. 27   Wmk. 385   Perf. 13½
1171 A347 2b multicolored   .70   .25
    Complete booklet, strip of 5
    #1171   9.00

Royal Thai Air Force, 72nd anniv.

King Rama III (Nang Klao, 1787-1851) — A348

Perf. 15x14½
1987, Mar. 31   Wmk. 387
1172 A348 2b multicolored   .60   .25
    Complete booklet, strip of 5
    #1172   9.00

Ministry of Communications, 75th Anniv. — A349

1987, Apr. 1
1173 A349 2b multicolored   .50   .25
    Complete booklet, strip of 5
    #1173   6.00

Forestry Year — A350

1987, July 11   Wmk. 385   Perf. 13½
1174 A350 2b multicolored   .50   .25
    Complete booklet, strip of 5
    #1174   6.00

THAIPEX '87 — A351

Gold artifacts — No. 1175, Peacock, vert. No. 1176, Hand mirrors, vert. No. 1177, Water urn, finger bowls. No. 1178, Dragon vase.

1987, Aug. 4   Wmk. 385
1175 A351 2b multicolored   .40   .25
    Complete booklet, strip of 5
    #1175   3.75
1176 A351 2b multicolored   .40   .25
    Complete booklet, strip of 5
    #1176   3.75
1177 A351 6b multicolored   1.10   .35
1178 A351 6b multicolored   1.10   .35
  a. Souv. sheet of 4, #1175-
    1178   45.00 30.00
    Nos. 1175-1178 (4)   3.00   1.20

No. 1178a exists imperf. Value, $325.

ASEAN, 20th Anniv. — A352

1987, Aug. 20
1179 A352 2b multicolored   .25   .25
    Complete booklet, strip of 5
    #1179   3.75
1180 A352 3b multicolored   .45   .25
1181 A352 4b multicolored   .55   .35
1182 A352 5b multicolored   .80   .45
    Nos. 1179-1182 (4)   2.05   1.30

Natl. Communications Day — A353

1987, Aug. 4
1183 A353 2b multicolored   .60   .25
    Complete booklet, strip of 5
    #1183   7.00

Chulachamklao Royal Military Academy, Cent. — A354

Design: School crest, King Rama V, and King Rama IX conferring sword on graduating officer.

1987, Aug. 5
1184 A354 2b multicolored   1.75   .30
    Complete booklet, strip of 5
    #1184   15.00

Intl. Literacy Day — A355

1987, Sept. 8
1185 A355 2b multicolored   .60   .25
    Complete booklet, strip of 5
    #1185   6.00

Tourism Year — A356

2b, Flower-offering ceremony, Saraburi province. 3b, Duan Sib Festival, Nakhon Si Thammarat province. 5b, Bang Fai Festival, Yasothon province. 7b, Loi Krathong Festival, Sukhothai province.

1987, Sept. 18
1186 A356 2b multicolored   .30   .25
    Complete booklet, strip of 5
    #1186   3.00
1187 A356 3b multicolored   .60   .25
1188 A356 5b multicolored   .90   .30
1189 A356 7b multicolored   1.25   .40
    Nos. 1186-1189 (4)   3.05   1.20

Auditor General's Office, 72nd Anniv. — A357

1987, Sept. 18
1190 A357 2b multicolored   .60   .25
    Complete booklet, strip of 5
    #1190   6.00

Diplomatic Relations Between Thailand and Japan, Cent. — A358

1987, Sept. 26   Wmk. 329
1191 A358 2b multicolored   .70   .25
    Complete booklet, strip of 5
    #1191   7.50

Intl. Letter Writing Week — A359

Floral garlands.

1987, Oct. 4   Wmk. 385
1192 A359 2b Floral tassel   .25   .25
    Complete booklet, strip of 5
    #1192   2.25
1193 A359 3b Tasselled garland   .50   .25
1194 A359 5b Wrist garland   .75   .25
1195 A359 7b Double-ended gar-
    land   1.00   .50
    Nos. 1192-1195 (4)   2.50   1.25

Thai Pavilion — A360

1987, Oct. 9   **Wmk. 387**   **Perf. 15**
1196 A360 2b multicolored   .60 .25
   Complete booklet, strip of 5
   #1196   8.00

Social Education and Cultural Center Inauguration.

A361

A362

King Bhumibol Adulyadej, 60th Birthday — A363

Royal ciphers and: #1197, Adulyadej as a child. #1198, King and Queen, wedding portrait, 1950. #1199, King taking the Oath of Accession, 1950. #1200, King dressed as a monk, collecting alms. #1201, Greeting 100 year-old woman. #1202, In military uniform holding pen and with hill tribes. #1203, Royal couple visiting wounded servicemen. #1204, Visiting farm. #1205, Royal family. #1206, King, Queen Sirikit. #1207, Princess Mother Somdej Phra Sri Nakarindra Boromrajjonnani, emblem of Medical Volunteer Assoc. #1208, Crown Prince Maha Vajiralongkorn, crown prince's royal standard. #1209, Princess Maha Chakri Sirindhorn, emblem of Sai Jai Thai Foundation. #1210, Princess Chulabhorn, Albert Einstein gold medal awarded by UNESCO.

Wmk. 329
1987, Dec. 5   **Photo.**   **Perf. 13½**
1197 A361 2b shown   .50 .25
   Complete booklet, strip of 5
   #1197   6.00
1190 A361 2b multicolored   .50 .25
1199 A361 2b multicolored   .50 .25
1200 A361 2b multicolored   .50 .25
1201 A361 2b multicolored   .50 .25
1202 A361 2b multicolored   .50 .25
1203 A361 2b multicolored   .50 .25
1204 A361 2b multicolored   .50 .25
   a. Souv. sheet, #1197-1204   37.50 37.50

Litho.
Wmk. 385
1205 A362 2b multicolored   1.00 .25
1206 A362 2b multicolored   1.00 .25
1207 A362 2b multicolored   1.00 .25
1208 A362 2b multicolored   1.00 .25
1209 A362 2b multicolored   1.00 .25
1210 A362 2b multicolored   1.00 .25

Litho. & Embossed
1211 A363 100b vio blue & gold   55.00 45.00
   Nos. 1197-1211 (15)   65.00 48.50

Size of Nos. 1206-1210: 45x27mm. No. 1211 printed in sheets of 10. Value, $750. No. 1204a sold for 40b.

No. 1081 Surcharged

1987   **Litho.**   **Wmk. 233**   **Perf. 14x15**
1212 A256 2b on 1.50b brt yel org   .60 .25

Children's Day — A364

Perf. 14x14½
1988, Jan. 9   **Litho.**   **Wmk. 387**
1213 A364 2b multicolored   .60 .25
   Complete booklet, strip of 5
   #1213   6.00

Thai Agricultural Cooperatives, 72nd Anniv. — A365

Design: Prince Bridhyalongkorn, founder.

1988, Feb. 26   **Wmk. 387**
1214 A365 2b multicolored   .60 .25
   Complete booklet, strip of 5
   #1214   5.25

Royal Siam Soc., 84th Anniv. A366

1988, Mar. 10   **Perf. 14½x14**
1215 A366 2b multicolored   .50 .25
   Complete booklet, strip of 5
   #1215   5.25

Cultural Heritage Preservation — A367

Ruins in Sukhothai Historic Park — 2b, Wat Phra Phai Luang. 3b, Wat Traphang Thonglang. 4b, Wat Maha That. 6b, Thewalai Maha Kaset.

1988, Apr. 2   **Perf. 14½x14**
1216 A367 2b multicolored   .30 .25
   Complete booklet, strip of 5
   #1216   4.00
1217 A367 3b multicolored   .60 .25
1218 A367 4b multicolored   .90 .35
1219 A367 6b multicolored   1.25 .40
   Nos. 1216-1219 (4)   3.05 1.25

Red Cross Fair A368

Design: Prevention of rabies.

1988, Apr.   **Wmk. 387**   **Perf. 14**
1220 A368 2b multicolored   .50 .25
   Complete booklet, strip of 5
   #1220   6.00

King Rama V, Founder — A369

Perf. 14x14½
1988, Apr. 26   **Wmk. 387**
1221 A369 5b multicolored   2.25 .60

Siriraj Hospital, cent.

Pheasants — A370

Wmk. 329
1988, June 15   **Photo.**   **Perf. 13½**
1222 A370 2b Crested fireback   .30 .25
   Complete booklet, strip of 5
   #1222   2.75
1223 A370 3b Kalij   .60 .25
1224 A370 6b Silver pheasant   1.25 .30
1225 A370 7b Hume's pheasant   1.50 .40
   Nos. 1222-1225 (4)   3.65 1.20

Nos. 035a, 005 Ourcharged

   a   b

Perf. 11x13
1988-92   **Litho.**   **Wmk. 387**
1226 A256(a) 1b on 1.25b   .60 .25
1226A A256(b) 1b on 1.25b   .60 .25
   b.   Wmk. 368   1.40 .25

Issued: #1226, 1988; #1226A, Dec. 5, 1992.

Intl. Council of Women, Cent. — A371

1988, June 26   **Wmk. 385**   **Perf. 13½**
1227 A371 2b multicolored   .60 .25
   Complete booklet, strip of 5
   #1227   5.25

King Bhumibol Adulyadej
A372   A372a

Perf. 13½x13
1988-95   **Litho.**   **Wmk. 387**
1228 A372 25s brown   .40 .25
   a.   Wmk. 329, perf. 13½x13   .65 .25

Perf. 14x14½
1229 A372 50s olive   .55 .25
   a.   Wmk. 329, perf. 13½x13   .65 .25
1230 A372 1b brt blue   .55 .25
   Complete booklet, 5 #1230   4.25
   a.   Photo, wmk. 233   .80 .25

   b.   Photo., wmk. 340, perf. 13½x13¾   .55 .25
1233 A372 2b scarlet   .70 .25
   Complete booklet, 5 #1233   5.00
   a.   Wmk. 029   .55 .25
   b.   Photo., wmk. 340, perf. 13½x13¾   .70 .25
   Complete booklet, 5 #1233b   6.00

Photo.
Wmk. 233
Perf. 14½
1236 A372 1b bright blue   .80 .25
   Nos. 1228-1236 (5)   3.00 1.25

No. 1236 has blue background without halo effect around head. See #1230.
Issued: 25s, 8/12/92; 1b-2b, 7/2/88; 50s, 7/28/93; #1230a, 1236, 1990; #1233a, 1992; #1230b, 1233b, 12/5/94; #1229a, 1995.

Perf. 13½x13
1988-90   **Engr.**   **Wmk. 329**
1241 A372a 3b brn & bluish gray   .80 .25
1242 A372a 4b brt bl & red brn   .95 .30
1243 A372a 5b violet & brn   1.10 .30
1244 A372a 6b green & vio   1.10 .35
1245 A372a 7b red brn & dk brn   .80 .25
1246 A372a 8b red brn & gray ol   1.10 .40
1247 A372a 9b dk blue & brn   1.75 .40
1248 A372a 10b hen brn & blk   1.60 .25
1249 A372a 20b brn org & sage grn   2.40 1.75
1250 A372a 25b ol grn & dk bl   4.50 .90
1251 A372a 50b violet & grn   8.00 1.00
1252 A372a 100b brn org & bluish blk   13.00 2.25
   Nos. 1241-1252 (12)   37.10 8.40

Issued:3b, 10b, 50b, 100b, 12/5; 5b, 6b, 8b, 9b, 7/1/89; 4b, 7b, 20b, 12/5/89; 25b, 1/9/90.

A373

A374

King Bhumibol's Reign (since 1950) — A375

Designs: No. 1253, King Bhumibol.
Regalia: No. 1254, Great Crown of Victory. No. 1255, Sword of Victory and matching scabbard. No. 1256, Scepter. No. 1257, Fan and feather fly swatter. No. 1258, Royal slippers.
Canopied thrones in the Grand Palace: No. 1259, Queen's round ottoman on 1-tier dais in front of decorative screen. No. 1260, King's throne on 1-tier dais in front of decorative screen. No. 1261, 3-Tier throne with 3 gilded trees. No. 1262, 3-Canopy throne on high gold dais. No. 1263, 3-Tier throne with 4 gilded trees, altar in background. No. 1264, 3-Canopy throne on 5-stair dais, in front of arch flanked by columns.

Wmk. 385

1988, July 2		**Litho.**	**Perf. 13½**	
1253	A373	2b shown	2.50	.40

Complete booklet, strip of 5
#1253 .... 27.50

Photo.
Wmk. 329

1254	A374	2b multi, vert.	.65	.25
1255	A374	2b multicolored	.65	.25
1256	A374	2b multicolored	.65	.25
1257	A374	2b multicolored	.65	.25
1258	A374	2b multicolored	.65	.25

Litho.
Perf. 14x14½
Wmk. 387

1259	A375	2b multicolored	.80	.30
1260	A375	2b multicolored	.80	.30
1261	A375	2b multicolored	.80	.30
1262	A375	2b multicolored	.80	.30
1263	A375	2b multicolored	.80	.30
1264	A375	2b multicolored	.80	.30
a.		Souv. sheet of 6, #1259-1264	60.00	60.00
		Nos. 1253-1264 (12)	10.55	3.45

No. 1264a sold for 25b.

Arbor Year A376

Perf. 14½x14

1988, July 29		**Litho.**	**Wmk. 387**	
1265	A376	2b multicolored	.65	.25

Complete booklet, strip of 5
#1265 .... 5.25

Natl. Communications Day — A377

Wmk. Alternating Interlaced Wavy Lines (340)

1988, Aug. 4			**Perf. 13½**	
1266	A377	2b multicolored	.85	.25

Complete booklet, strip of 5
#1266 .... 7.50

Intl. Letter Writing Week — A378

Designs: Coconut leaf sculptures.

Perf. 14½x14

1988, Oct. 9			**Wmk. 387**	
1267	A378	2b Grasshopper	.30	.25

Complete booklet, strip of 5
#1267 .... 3.00

1268	A378	2b Fish	.30	.25

Complete booklet, strip of 5
#1268 .... 3.00

1269	A378	6b Bird	.90	.50
1270	A378	6b Takro (box)	.90	.50
		Nos. 1267-1270 (4)	2.40	1.50

Housing Development — A379

Wmk. 233

1988, Oct. 24		**Litho.**	**Perf. 14**	
1271	A379	2b multicolored	.65	.25

Complete booklet, strip of 5
#1271 .... 5.25

Traffic Safety — A380

1988, Nov. 11		**Wmk. 329**	**Perf. 13½**	
1272	A380	2b multicolored	.65	.25

Complete booklet, strip of 5
#1272 .... 5.50

King's Bodyguard, 120th Anniv. — A381

1988, Nov. 11			**Wmk. 385**	
1273	A381	2b Chulalongkorn	3.25	.45

Complete booklet, strip of 5
#1273 .... 32.50

New Year — A382

Flowers — No. 1274, Crotalaria sessiliflora. No. 1275, Uvaria grandiflora. No. 1276, Reinwardtia trigyna. No. 1277, Impatiens griffithii.

1988, Dec. 1			**Wmk. 387**	
1274	A382	1b multicolored	.55	.25
1275	A382	1b multicolored	.55	.25
1276	A382	1b multicolored	.55	.25
1277	A382	1b multicolored	.55	.25
		Nos. 1274-1277 (4)	2.20	1.00

Thai Royal Orders Type of 1979

Floral background: Nos. 1278-1279, Knight Grand Commander, Order of Rama, 1918. Nos. 1280-1281, Knight Grand Cordon, Order of the White Elephant, 1861. Nos. 1282-1283, Knight Grand Cordon, Order of the Crown of Thailand, 1869. Nos. 1284-1285, Ratana Varabhorn Order of Merit, 1911. Pairs have continuous designs.

1988, Dec. 5			**Wmk. 385**	
1278	A243	2b multicolored	.30	.25
1279	A244	2b multicolored	.30	.25
a.		Pair, #1278-1279	.80	.40
1280	A243	3b multicolored	.65	.25
1281	A244	3b multicolored	.65	.25
a.		Pair, #1280-1281	1.75	.90
1282	A243	5b multicolored	1.00	.40
1283	A244	5b multicolored	1.00	.40
a.		Pair, #1282-1283	2.75	1.40
1284	A243	7b multicolored	1.20	.55
1285	A244	7b multicolored	1.20	.55
a.		Pair, #1284-1285	4.00	2.00
		Nos. 1278-1285 (8)	6.30	2.90

A383

Buddha Monthon Celebrations, Tambol Salaya — A384

2b, Birthplace. 3b, Enlightenment place. 4b, Location of 1st sermon. 5b, Place Buddha achieved nirvana. 6b, Statue.

Perf. 14x15, 15x14

1988, Dec. 5			**Wmk. 233**	
1286	A383	2b multicolored	.35	.25

Complete booklet, strip of 5
#1286 .... 2.75

1287	A383	3b multicolored	.45	.25
1288	A383	4b multicolored	.65	.45
1289	A383	5b multicolored	.85	.40
1290	A384	6b multicolored	1.00	.50
		Nos. 1286-1290 (5)	3.30	1.85

Souvenir Sheet
Perf. 14½x14

1291	A384	6b like No. 1290	27.50	27.50

No. 1291 sold for 15b.

Children's Day — A385

"Touch" paintings by blind youth: No. 1292, Floating Market, by Thongbai Siyam. No. 1293, Flying Bird, by Kwanchai Kerd-Daeng. No. 1294, Little Mermaid, by Chalermpol Jiengmai. No. 1295, Golden Fish, by Natetip Korsantirak.

Wmk. 387

1989, Jan. 14		**Litho.**	**Perf. 13½**	
1292	A385	2b multicolored	.45	.25

Complete booklet, strip of 5
#1292 .... 3.50

1293	A385	2b multicolored	.45	.25

Complete booklet, strip of 5
#1293 .... 3.50

1294	A385	2b multicolored	.45	.25

Complete booklet, strip of 5
#1294 .... 3.50

1295	A385	2b multicolored	.45	.25

Complete booklet, strip of 5
#1295 .... 3.50

		Nos. 1292-1295 (4)	1.80	1.00

Communications Authority of Thailand, 12th Anniv. — A386

1989, Feb. 25			**Perf. 14½x14**	
1296	A386	2b multicolored	.60	.25

Complete booklet, strip of 5
#1296 .... 5.25

Chulalongkorn University, 72nd Anniv. — A387

Design: 2b, Statue of Chulalongkorn and King Vajiravudh in front of university auditorium.

1989, Mar. 26				
1297	A387	2b multicolored	.60	.25

Complete booklet, strip of 5
#1297 .... 7.00

A388

Perf. 15x14

1989, Mar. 31		**Litho.**	**Wmk. 233**	
1298	A388	2b shown	.60	.30

Complete booklet, strip of 5
#1298 .... 5.25

Wmk. 387
Perf. 13½

1299	A388	10b Emblem	1.25	.35

Thai Red Cross Society, 96th anniv. (2b); Intl. Red Cross and Red Crescent organizations, 125th annivs. (10b).

A389

Phra Nakhon Khiri Historical Park: 2b, Wat Phra Kaeo. 3b, Chatchawan Wiangchai Observatory. 5b, Phra That Chom Phet Stupa. 6b, Wetchayan Wichian Phrasat Throne Hall.

Perf. 14x14½

1989, Apr. 2			**Wmk. 387**	
1300	A389	2b multicolored	.55	.25

Complete booklet, strip of 5
#1300 .... 4.50

1301	A389	3b multicolored	.90	.45
1302	A389	5b multicolored	1.40	.95
1303	A389	6b multicolored	1.60	1.10
		Nos. 1300-1303 (4)	4.45	2.75

Natl. Lottery Office, 50th Anniv. — A390

1989, Apr. 5			**Perf. 13½**	
1304	A390	2b multicolored	.60	.25

Complete booklet, strip of 5
#1304 .... 5.25

Seashells — A391

2b, Conus thailandis. 3b, Spondylus princeps. 6b, Cyprea guttata. 10b, Nautilus pompilius.

1989, June 28		**Wmk. 329**	**Perf. 13½**	
1305	A391	2b multicolored	.30	.25

Complete booklet, strip of 5
#1305 .... 2.75

1306	A391	3b multicolored	.55	.25
1307	A391	6b multicolored	.85	.65
1308	A391	10b multicolored	3.00	1.60
		Nos. 1305-1308 (4)	4.70	2.75

Arts and Crafts Year A392

No. 1309, Gold niello figurines, vert. No. 1310, Ceramic ginger jar, chicken, vert. No. 1311, Textiles. No. 1312, Gemstone flower ornament.

Wmk. 387

1989, June 28	**Litho.**		**Perf. 13½**	
1309	A392	2b multicolored	.30	.25
	Complete booklet, strip of 5 #1309		2.75	
1310	A392	2b multicolored	.30	.25
	Complete booklet, strip of 5 #1310		2.75	
1311	A392	6b multicolored	.95	.50
1312	A392	6b multicolored	.95	.50
	Nos. 1309-1312 (4)		2.50	1.50

Asia-Pacific Telecommunications Organization, 10th Anniv. — A393

APT emblem, map of submarine cable network and satellites of member nations.

1989, July 1	**Wmk. 329**		**Perf. 13½**	
1313	A393	9b multicolored	.60	.25

Phya Anuman Rajadhon (1888-1969), Ethnologist A394

1989, July 1	**Wmk. 387**		**Perf. 13½**	
1314	A394	2b multicolored	.60	.25
	Complete booklet, strip of 5 #1314		5.25	

9th Natl. Phil. Exhib., Aug. 4-13 — A395

Various mailboxes.

1989, Aug. 4	**Wmk. 233**		**Perf. 15x14**	
1315	A395	2b multicolored	.25	.25
	Complete booklet, strip of 5 #1315		2.75	
1316	A395	3b multi, diff.	.40	.25
1317	A395	4b multi, diff.	.40	.30
1318	A395	5b multi, diff.	.65	.30
1319	A395	6b multi, diff.	.85	.40
a.	Souv. sheet, #1315-1319, perf 14		35.00	35.00
	Nos. 1315-1319 (5)		2.55	1.50

No. 1319 sold for 30b. No. 1319a exists imperf. Value, $125.

A396

	Wmk. 387			
1989, June 26	**Litho.**		**Perf. 13½**	
1320	A396	2b multicolored	.50	.25
	Complete booklet, strip of 5 #1320		5.25	

Intl. Anti-drug Day.

A397

1989, Aug. 4	**Wmk. 233**		**Perf. 14x15**	
1321	A397	2b multicolored	.50	.25
	Complete booklet, strip of 5 #1321		5.25	

Post and Telecommunications School, cent.

A398

1989, Aug. 4	**Wmk. 387**		**Perf. 13½**	
1322	A398	2b multicolored	.55	.25
	Complete booklet, strip of 5 #1322		5.25	

Natl. Communications Day.

Dragonflies — A399

	Wmk. 329			
1989, Oct. 8	**Photo.**		**Perf. 13½**	
1323	A399	2b shown	.35	.25
	Complete booklet, strip of 5 #1323		5.25	
1324	A399	5b multi, diff.	.75	.30
1325	A399	6b multi, diff.	1.10	.35
1326	A399	10b Damselfly	1.40	1.00
a.	Souv. sheet of 4, #1323-1326		30.00	30.00
	Nos. 1323-1326 (4)		3.60	1.90

Intl. Letter Writing Week. #1326a sold for 40b.

Transport and Communications Decade for Asia and the Pacific — A400

	Perf. 14½x14			
1989, Oct. 24	**Litho.**		**Wmk. 387**	
1327	A400	2b multicolored	.55	.25
	Complete booklet, strip of 5 #1327		5.25	

Mental Health Care, Cent. — A401

1989, Nov. 1	**Wmk. 233**		**Perf. 15x14**	
1328	A401	2b multicolored	.55	.25
	Complete booklet, strip of 5 #1328		5.25	

New Year 1990 — A402

Flowering plants.

	Perf. 14x14½			
1989, Nov. 15			**Wmk. 387**	
1329	A402	1b Hypericum uralum	.30	.30
1330	A402	1b Uraria rufescens	.30	.30
1331	A402	1b Manglietia garrettii	.30	.30
1332	A402	1b Aeschynanthus macranthus	.30	.30
a.	Souv. sheet of 4, #1329-1332		7.50	7.50
	Nos. 1329-1332 (4)		1.20	1.20

No. 1332a sold for 14b.

Insects — A403

2b, Catacanthus incarnatus. 3b, Aristobia approximator. 6b, Chrysochroa chinensis. 10b, Enoplotrupes sharpi.

	Wmk. 329			
1989, Nov. 15	**Photo.**		**Perf. 13½**	
1333	A403	2b multicolored	.30	.25
	Complete booklet, strip of 5 #1333		2.75	
1334	A403	3b multicolored	.60	.30
1335	A403	6b multicolored	.80	.40
1336	A403	10b multicolored	1.40	.85
	Nos. 1333-1336 (4)		3.10	1.80

Children's Day — A405

	Perf. 15x14			
1990, Jan. 13			**Wmk. 233**	
1338	A405	2b Jumping rope, horiz.	.55	.25
	Complete booklet, strip of 5 #1338		4.00	
1339	A405	2b Sports	.55	.25
	Complete booklet, strip of 5 #1339		4.00	

Emblems — A406

1990, Mar. 29	**Wmk. 387**		**Perf. 13½**	
1340	A406	2b multicolored	.55	.25
	Complete booklet, strip of 5 #1340		5.00	

WHO Fight AIDS Worldwide campaign and the Natl. Red Cross Soc.

Thai Heritage Conservation Day — A407

Prize-winning inlaid mother-of-pearl containers: No. 1341, Tiap (footed bowl with lid), vert. No. 1342, Phan waenfa (two-tiered vessel), vert. No. 1343, Lung (lidded bowl). No. 1344, Chiat klom (spade-shaped lidded container signifying noble rank).

1990, Apr. 2	**Photo.**		**Wmk. 329**	
1341	A407	2b multicolored	.25	.25
1342	A407	2b multicolored	.25	.25
1343	A407	8b multicolored	.80	.45
1344	A407	8b multicolored	.80	.45
	Nos. 1341-1344 (4)		2.10	1.40

Population and Housing Census of 1990 — A404

	Wmk. 387			
1990, Jan. 1	**Litho.**		**Perf. 13½**	
1337	A404	2b multicolored	.60	.25
	Complete booklet, strip of 5 #1337		5.75	

A408

Minerals.

	Perf. 14x14½			
1990, June 29	**Litho.**		**Wmk. 387**	
1345	A408	2b Tin	.45	.25
1346	A408	3b Zinc	.70	.40
1347	A408	5b Lead	.85	.60
1348	A408	6b Fluorite	1.00	.80
a.	Souv. sheet of 4, #1345-1348		4.50	4.50
	Nos. 1345-1348 (4)		3.00	2.05

No. 1348a sold for 30b. Exists imperf, value same as perf.

A409

1990, May 16
1349 A409 2b multicolored   .50   .25
Faculty of Dentistry, Chulalongkorn Univ., 50th anniv.

Communications Day — A410

1990, Aug. 4   Perf. 14½x14
1350 A410 2b multicolored   .65   .25
Complete booklet, strip of 5
#1350   5.75

Asian-Pacific Postal Training Center, 20th Anniv. — A411

1990, Sept. 10
1351 A411 2b multicolored   .35   .25
Complete booklet, strip of 5
#1351   2.25
1352 A411 8b multicolored   1.00   .60

Rotary Intl. in Thailand, 60th Anniv. — A412

1990, Sept. 16   Perf. 13½
1353 A412 2b Health care   .35   .25
Complete booklet, strip of 5
#1353   4.00
1354 A412 3b Immunizations   .55   .30
1355 A412 6b Literacy project   .70   .25
1356 A412 8b Thai museum pro-
        ject   .85   .45
        Nos. 1353-1356 (4)   2.45 1.35

Intl. Letter Writing Week, 1990 — A413

1990, Oct. 7   Perf. 14
1357 A413 2b multicolored   .35   .25
1358 A413 3b multi, diff.   .50   .25
1359 A413 5b multi, diff.   .75   .25
1360 A413 6b multi, diff.   .90   .25
   a.   Souv. sheet of 4, #1357-1360 4.50 4.50
        Nos. 1357-1360 (4)   2.50 1.00
No. 1360a sold for 30b. Exists imperf, value same as perf.

Dept. of Comptroller-General, Cent. — A414

1990, Oct. 7   Perf. 14½x14
1361 A414 2b multicolored   .70   .25
Complete booklet, strip of 5
#1361   5.00

A415

1990, Oct. 21   Perf. 14x14½
1362 A415 2b multicolored   3.00   .50
Complete booklet, strip of 5
#1362   30.00
Princess Mother, 90th birthday.

A416

Flowers: No. 1363, Cyrtandromoea grandiflora. No. 1364, Rhododendron arboreum. No. 1365, Merremia vitifolia. No. 1366, Afgekia mahidolae.

1990, Nov. 15   Wmk. 233   Perf. 14½
1363 A416 1b multicolored   .35   .25
1364 A416 1b multicolored   .35   .25
1365 A416 1b multicolored   .35   .25
1366 A416 1b multicolored   .35   .25
   a.   Sheet of 4, #1363-1366   3.00 3.00
        Nos. 1363-1366 (4)   1.40 1.00
New Year 1991. No. 1366a sold for 10b. Exists imperf, value same as perf. See Nos. 1417-1420.

Wiman Mek Royal Hall — A417

Royal Throne Rooms in the Dusit Palace: 3b, Ratcharit Rungrot Royal House. 4b, Aphisek Dusit Royal Hall. 5b, Amphon Sathan Palace. 6b, Udon Phak Royal Hall. 8b, Anantasamakhom Throne Hall.

Wmk. 329
1990, Dec. 5   Photo.   Perf. 13½
1367 A417 2b multicolored   .30   .25
Complete booklet, strip of 5
#1367   3.25
1368 A417 3b multicolored   .40   .25
1369 A417 4b multicolored   .50   .25
1370 A417 5b multicolored   .50   .25
1371 A417 6b multicolored   .70   .45
1372 A417 8b multicolored   1.00   .65
        Nos. 1367-1372 (6)   3.40 2.10

Somdet Phra Maha Samanachao Kromphra Paramanuchitchinorot (1790-1853), Supreme Patriarch — A418

1990, Dec. 11   Wmk. 387   Perf. 13½
1373 A418 2b multicolored   .70   .25
Complete booklet, strip of 5
#1373   6.25

Petroleum Authority, 12th Anniv. — A419

1990, Dec. 29   Litho.   Wmk. 387
Perf. 14½x14
1374 A419 2b multicolored   .55   .25
Complete booklet, strip of 5
#1374   5.25

Locomotives — A420

Designs: 2b, No. 6, Krauss & Co., Germany, 1908. 3b, No. 32, Kyosan Kogyo, Japan, 1949. 5b, No. 715, C56, Japan, 1946. 6b, No. 953, Mikado, Japan, 1949-1951.

Perf. 14½x14
1990, Dec. 29   Litho.   Wmk. 387
1375 A420 2b multicolored   .90   .25
1376 A420 3b multicolored   1.20   .25
1377 A420 5b multicolored   1.50 1.40
1378 A420 6b multicolored   1.75 1.40
   a.   Souv. sheet of 4, #1375-1378 4.50 4.50
        Nos. 1375-1378 (4)   5.35 3.30
No. 1378a sold for 25b. Exists imperf, value same as perf.

Children's Day — A421

Children's games: 2b, Tops. 3b, Blindfolded child breaking pot with stick. 5b, Race. 6b, Blind-man's buff.

1991, Jan. 12
1379 A421 2b multicolored   .30   .25
Complete booklet, strip of 5
#1379   3.50
1380 A421 3b multicolored   .45   .25
1381 A421 5b multicolored   .55   .30
1382 A421 6b multicolored   .80   .35
        Nos. 1379-1382 (4)   2.10 1.15

A422

1991, Feb. 17   Perf. 14x14½
1383 A422 2b multicolored   .55   .25
Complete booklet, strip of 5
#1383   5.50
Land titling project.

A423

Perf. 14x14½
1991, Mar. 30   Litho.   Wmk. 387
1384 A423 2b Princess Maha   2.50   .25
Complete booklet, strip of 5
#1384   20.00
   a.   Souvenir sheet of 1   4.50 4.50
Red Cross. No. 1384a sold for 8b. Exists imperf, value same as perf.

Cultural Heritage A424

Floral decorations: 2b, Indra's heavenly abode. 3b, Celestial couch. 4b, Crystal ladder. 5b, Crocodile.

Wmk. 329
1991, Apr. 2   Photo.   Perf. 13½
1385 A424 2b multicolored   .30   .25
1386 A424 3b multicolored   .45   .25
1387 A424 4b multicolored   .55   .25
1388 A424 5b multicolored   .70   .30
   a.   Souv. sheet of 4, #1385-1388 4.00 3.00
        Nos. 1385-1388 (4)   2.00 1.05
No. 1388a sold for 30b. Exists imperf, value same as perf.

Songkran Day — A425

Perf. 14x14½
1991, Apr. 13   Wmk. 387   Litho.
1389 A425 2b Demon on
        sheep   3.00   .75
Complete booklet, strip of 5
#1389   22.50
   a.   Souvenir sheet of 1   15.00 15.00
No. 1389a sold for 8b. Exists imperf, value same as perf.
See #1467, 1530, 1566, 1606, 1662, 1724, 1801, 1869, 1940, 1970, 2017.

Prince Narisranuvattivongs (1863-1947) — A426

1991, Apr. 28   Perf. 14½x14
1390 A426 2b brown & yellow   .50   .25
Complete booklet, strip of 5
#1390   5.00

Mosaics — A427

Various lotus flowers.

1991, May 28			Perf. 13½	
1391	A427	2b multi, vert.	.30	.25
	Complete booklet, strip of 5 #1391		4.00	
1392	A427	3b multi, vert.	.40	.25
1393	A427	5b multi	.60	.30
1394	A427	6b multi	.75	.35
	Nos. 1391-1394 (4)		2.05	1.15

Natl. Communications Day — A428

		Wmk. 387		
1991, Aug. 4		Litho.	Perf. 13½	
1395	A428	2b multicolored	.60	.25
	Complete booklet, strip of 5 #1395		7.25	

Thaipex '91, Natl. Philatelic Exhibition A429

Various fabric designs.

1991, Aug. 4			Perf. 14x14½	
1396	A429	2b multicolored	.25	.25
1397	A429	4b multicolored	.40	.25
1398	A429	6b multicolored	.65	.30
1399	A429	8b multicolored	.80	.45
a.	Souv. sheet of 4, #1396-1399		2.10	1.25
	Nos. 1396-1399 (4)		2.10	1.25

No. 1399a sold for 30b. Exists imperf, value $25. No. 1399a overprinted with Philanippon emblem in lower left corner of margin sold for 200b. Value, $190.

Intl. Productivity Congress — A430

			Perf. 14½x14	
1991, Sept. 3		Litho.	Wmk. 387	
1400	A430	2b multicolored	.50	.25
	Complete booklet, strip of 5 #1400		4.25	

26th Intl. Council of Women Triennial — A431

		Wmk. 387		
1991, Sept. 23		Litho.	Perf. 13½	
1401	A431	2b multicolored	.50	.25
	Complete booklet, strip of 5 #1401		4.25	

Bantam Chickens — A432

		Wmk. 329		
1991, Oct. 6		Photo.	Perf. 13½	
1402	A432	2b Black bantams	.40	.25
1403	A432	3b Black-tailed buff bantams	.70	.25
1404	A432	6b Fancy bantams	1.00	.25
1405	A432	8b White bantams	1.50	.65
a.	Souv. sheet of 4, #1402-1405		5.50	5.50
	Nos. 1402-1405 (4)		3.60	1.40

No. 1405a sold for 35b. Exists imperf, value same as perf.
Intl. Letter Writing Week.

World Bank/Intl. Monetary Fund Annual Meetings — A433

Temples, meeting emblem and: 2b, Silver coin of King Rama IV. 4b, Pod Duang money. 8b, Chieng and Hoi money. 10b, Funan, Dvaravati and Srivijaya money.

			Perf. 14½x14	
1991, Oct. 15		Litho.	Wmk. 387	
1406	A433	2b multicolored	.25	.25
	Complete booklet, strip of 5 #1406		3.25	
1407	A433	4b multicolored	.45	.30
1408	A433	8b multicolored	.90	.60
1409	A433	10b multicolored	1.10	.75
a.	Souv. sheet of 4, #1406-1409		4.00	4.00
	Nos. 1406-1409 (4)		2.70	1.90

No. 1409a sold for 35b. Exists imperf, value same as perf.

1993 World Philatelic Exhibition, Bangkok — A434

1991, Oct. 23			Perf. 14x14½	
1410	A434	2b No. 118	.25	.25
	Complete booklet, strip of 5 #1410		4.25	
1411	A434	3b No. 119	.25	.25
1412	A434	4b No. 120	.30	.25
1413	A434	5b No. 121	.45	.30
1414	A434	6b No. 122	.55	.30
1415	A434	7b No. 123	.60	.35
1416	A434	8b No. 124	.75	.45
a.	Souvenir sheet of 7		4.00	4.00
	Nos. 1410-1416 (7)		3.15	2.15

No. 1416a sold for 15b. Exists imperf, value same as perf.

Flower Type of 1990

1991, Nov. 5			Perf. 13½	
1417	A416	1b Dillenia obovata	.25	.25
1418	A416	1b Melastoma sanguineum	.25	.25
1419	A416	1b Commelina diffusa	.25	.25
1420	A416	1b Plumbago indica	.25	.25
a.	Souv. sheet of 4, #1417-1420		2.00	2.00
	Nos. 1417-1420 (4)		1.00	1.00

No. 1420a sold for 10b. Exists imperf, value same as perf.

Asian Elephants — A435

		Wmk. 329		
1991, Nov. 5		Photo.	Perf. 13½	
1421	A435	2b shown	.40	.25
	Complete booklet, strip of 5 #1421		4.25	
1422	A435	4b Pulling logs	.75	.25
1423	A435	6b Lying down	.90	.40
1424	A435	8b In river	1.60	.75
a.	Souvenir sheet of 1, litho.		5.50	5.50
	Nos. 1421-1424 (4)		3.65	1.65

No. 1424a sold for 22b and stamp does not have border. No. 1424a exists imperf, value same as perf.

Wild Animals — A436

		Perf. 14½x14		
1991, Dec. 26		Wmk. 387	Litho.	
1425	A436	2b Viverra zibetha	.45	.25
	Complete booklet, strip of 5 #1425		2.75	
1426	A436	3b Prionodon linsang	.60	.25
1427	A436	6b Felis temmincki	.85	.30
1428	A436	8b Ratufa bicolor	1.25	.45
a.	Sheet of 4, #1425-1428		4.50	4.50
	Nos. 1425-1428 (4)		3.15	1.25

No. 1428a sold for 30b. Exists imperf, value same as perf.

Prince Mahidol of Songkla (1891-1929), Medical Pioneer — A437

1992, Jan. 1			Perf. 14x14½	
1429	A437	2b multicolored	.90	.25
	Complete booklet, strip of 5 #1429		7.25	

Department of Mineral Resources, Cent. — A438

No. 1430, Locating fossils. No. 1431, Mining excavation. No. 1432, Drilling for natural gas and petroleum. No. 1433, Digging artesian wells.

		Perf. 14½x14		
1992, Jan. 1		Litho.	Wmk. 387	
1430	A438	2b multicolored	.90	.25
	Complete booklet, strip of 5 #1430		4.50	
1431	A438	2b multicolored	.90	.25
	Complete booklet, strip of 5 #1431		4.50	
1432	A438	2b multicolored	.90	.25
	Complete booklet, strip of 5 #1432		4.50	
1433	A438	2b multicolored	.90	.25
	Complete booklet, strip of 5 #1433		4.50	
	Nos. 1430-1433 (4)		3.60	1.00

Children's Day — A439

Children's drawings on "World Under the Sea": 2b, Divers, fish. 3b, Fish, sea grass. 5b, Mermaid.

1992, Jan. 11		Wmk. 329	Perf. 13½	
1434	A439	2b multicolored	.35	.25
	Complete booklet, strip of 5 #1434		3.00	
1435	A439	3b multicolored	.35	.25
1436	A439	5b multicolored, vert.	.75	.30
	Nos. 1434-1436 (3)		1.45	.80

Duel on Elephants, 400th Anniv. — A440

		Perf. 14½x14		
1992, Jan. 18		Litho.	Wmk. 387	
1437	A440	2b multicolored	.75	.25
	Complete booklet, strip of 5 #1437		6.00	

Orchids (Paphiopedilum) — A441

1992, Jan. 20				
1438	A441	2b Bellatulum	.25	.25
1439	A441	2b Exul	.25	.25
1440	A441	3b Concolor	.30	.25
1441	A441	3b Godefroyae	.30	.25
1442	A441	6b Niveum	.60	.25
1443	A441	6b Villosum	.60	.30
1444	A441	10b Parishii	1.00	.60
a.	Souv. sheet of 4, #1438, 1440, 1442, 1444		5.00	5.00
1445	A441	10b Sukhakulii	1.00	.60
a.	Souv. sheet of 4, #1439, 1441, 1443, 1445		5.00	5.00
	Nos. 1438-1445 (8)		4.30	2.80

Fourth Asia Pacific Orchid Conference. Nos. 1444a-1445a each sold for 30b. Each exists imperf, value same as perf.

21st Intl. Society of Sugar Cane Technologists Conf. — A442

1992, Mar. 5			Perf. 14x14½	
1446	A442	2b multicolored	.60	.25
	Complete booklet, strip of 5 #1446		6.00	

Intl. Red Cross A443

Perf. 14½x14

1992, Mar.   Litho.   Wmk. 387
1447 A443 2b multicolored   .45   .25
    Complete booklet, strip of 5
    #1447   4.00

Ministry of
Justice,
Cent. — A444

Designs: 3b, Prince Rabi Badhanasakdi of
Ratchaburi, founder of Thailand's School of
Law. 5b, King Rama V, reformer of court
system.

1992, Mar. 25   Perf. 13½
1448 A444 3b multicolored   .65   .25
1449 A444 5b multicolored   1.25   .30

Ministry of Agriculture and
Cooperatives, Cent. — A445

1992, Apr. 1   Perf. 14½x14
1450 A445 2b gray & multi   .35   .25
    Complete booklet, strip of 5
    #1450   3.25
1451 A445 3b lil & multi   .45   .25
1452 A445 4b pink & multi   .60   .30
1453 A445 5b gray bl & multi   .75   .35
    Nos. 1450-1453 (4)   2.15   1.15

A446

Ministry of Interior, Cent.: No. 1454, Prince
Damrong Rajanubharb, first Minister of the
Interior. No. 1455, People voting. No. 1456,
Police and fire protection. No. 1457, Water and
electricity provided to remote areas.

1992, Apr. 1   Perf. 14x14½
1454 A446 2b multicolored   .35   .25
    Complete booklet, strip of 5
    #1454   4.00
1455 A446 2b multicolored   .35   .25
    Complete booklet, strip of 5
    #1455   4.00
1456 A446 2b multicolored   .35   .25
    Complete booklet, strip of 5
    #1456   4.00
1457 A446 2b multicolored   .35   .25
    Complete booklet, strip of 5
    #1457   4.00
    Nos. 1454-1457 (4)   1.40   1.00

A447

1992, Apr. 1
1458 A447 2b Ships, truck   .25   .25
    Complete booklet, strip of 5
    #1458   3.25

1459 A447 3b Truck, bus, train   .35   .25
1460 A447 5b Airplanes   .55   .30
1461 A447 6b Truck, satellites   .65   .40
    Nos. 1458-1461 (4)   1.80   1.20
    Ministry of Transport and Communications,
80th anniv.

Ministry of
Education,
Cent. — A448

Perf. 14x14½
1992, Apr. 1   Litho.   Wmk. 387
1462 A448 2b multicolored   .35   .25
    Complete booklet, strip of 5
    #1462   4.00

Carts
A449

1992, Apr. 2   Perf. 14½x14
1463 A449 2b West   .25   .25
    Complete booklet, strip of 5
    #1463   3.25
1464 A449 3b North   .35   .25
1465 A449 5b Northeast   .50   .35
1466 A449 10b East   1.00   .65
  a. Souv. sheet of 4, #1463-1466   4.00
    Nos. 1463-1466 (4)   2.10   1.50

Heritage Conservation Day. No. 1466a sold
for 30b. Exists imperf without sheet price in
margin, value same as perf.

Songkran Day Type of 1991

1992, Apr. 13   Perf. 14x14½
1467 A425 2b Demon on mon-
              key, zodiac   1.10   .25
    Complete booklet, strip of 5
    #1467   5.50
  a. Souvenir sheet of 1   4.00   4.00

No. 1467a sold for 8b. Exists imperf with
sale price in different colors, value same as
perf.

Department of Livestock Development,
50th Anniv. — A451

Perf. 14½x14
1992, May 5   Litho.   Wmk. 387
1468 A451 2b multicolored   .50   .25
    Complete booklet, strip of 5
    #1468   4.00

Wisakhabucha Day — A452

Scenes from Buddha's life: 2b, Birth. 3b,
Enlightenment. 5b, Death.

Wmk. 387
1992, May 16   Litho.   Perf. 14½
1469 A452 2b multicolored   .35   .25
1470 A452 3b multicolored   .70   .30
1471 A452 5b multicolored   1.00   .65
    Nos. 1469-1471 (3)   2.05   1.20

Meteorological
Department, 50th
Anniv. — A453

1992, June 23   Perf. 14x14½
1472 A453 2b multicolored   .50   .25
    Complete booklet, strip of 5
    #1472   4.00

1993 World
Philatelic
Exhibition,
Bangkok — A454

Perf. 14x14½
1992, July 1   Litho.   Wmk. 387
1473 A454 2b No. 18   .25   .25
    Complete booklet, strip of 5
    #1473   3.25
1474 A454 3b No. 156   .35   .25
1475 A454 5b No. 222   .50   .30
1476 A454 7b No. 255   .60   .40
1477 A454 8b No. 273   .80   .50
  a. Souv. sheet of 5, #1473-1477
       + label   6.00   6.00
    Nos. 1473-1477 (5)   2.50   1.70

No. 1477a sold for 35b. Exists imperf. with
sheet price in blue, value same as #1477a.

Visit ASEAN
Year — A455

Designs: 2b, Bua Tong field, Mae Hong Son
Province. 3b, Klong Larn Waterfall,
Kamphaeng Phet Province. 4b, Coral,
Chumphon Province. 5b, Khao Ta-Poo,
Phangnga Province.

1992, July 1
1478 A455 2b multicolored   .30   .25
    Complete booklet, strip of 5
    #1478   3.25
1479 A455 3b multicolored   .40   .25
1480 A455 4b multicolored   .50   .35
1481 A455 5b multicolored   .60   .40
    Nos. 1478-1481 (4)   1.80   1.25

Prince Chudadhuj
Dharadilok of
Bejraburna
(1892-1923)
A456

Wmk. 368
1992, July 5   Litho.   Perf. 13½
1482 A456 2b multicolored   .50   .25
    Complete booklet, strip of 5
    #1482   4.50

Natl. Communications Day — A457

Perf. 14½x14
1992, Aug. 4   Litho.   Wmk. 387
1483 A457 2b multicolored   .50   .25
    Complete booklet, strip of 5
    #1483   4.00

ASEAN, 25th
Anniv. — A458

Flags and: 2b, Cultures and sports. 3b,
Tourist attractions. 5b, Transportation, communications. 7b, Agriculture.

1992, Aug. 8   Wmk. 368   Perf. 13½
1484 A458 2b multicolored   .25   .25
    Complete booklet, strip of 5
    #1484   3.25
1485 A458 3b multicolored   .35   .25
1486 A458 5b multicolored   .55   .40
1487 A458 7b multicolored   .85   .55
    Nos. 1484-1487 (4)   2.00   1.45

Queen Sirikit, 60th Birthday — A459

#1488, Wedding, with King, Queen being
anointed. #1489, Coronation, King and Queen
on throne. #1490, Being crowned, Queen with
crown, being anointed. #1491, Formal portrait,
Queen seated. #1492, Visiting wounded.
#1493, Visiting public.

Wmk. 329
1992, Aug. 12   Photo.   Perf. 13½
1488 A459 2b multicolored   .60   .25
    Complete booklet, strip of 5
    #1488   5.00
1489 A459 2b multicolored   .60   .25
    Complete booklet, strip of 5
    #1489   5.00
1490 A459 2b multicolored   .60   .25
    Complete booklet, strip of 5
    #1490   5.00
1491 A459 2b multicolored   .60   .25
    Complete booklet, strip of 5
    #1491   5.00
1492 A459 2b multicolored   .60   .25
    Complete booklet, strip of 5
    #1492   5.00
1493 A459 2b multicolored   .60   .25
    Complete booklet, strip of 5
    #1493   5.00
  a. Souv. sheet of 6, #1488-1493   5.00   5.00
    Nos. 1488-1493 (6)   3.60   1.50

No. 1493a sold for 30b. Exists imperf with
sale price in different colors, value same as
perf.

Royal Regalia of Queen Sirikit — A460

No. 1494, Tray. No. 1495, Kettle. No. 1496, Bowl. No. 1497, Box. No. 1498, Covered dish.

1992, Aug. 12   Background Colors
1494 A460 2b dark blue .45 .25
1495 A460 2b violet .45 .25
1496 A460 2b yellow green .45 .25
1497 A460 2b Prussian blue .45 .25
1498 A460 2b dark green .45 .25
    Nos. 1494-1498 (5) 2.25 1.25

Opening of Sirikit Medical Center — A461

Perf. 14½x14
1992, Aug. 12   Litho.   Wmk. 387
1499 A461 2b multicolored .45 .25
    Complete booklet, strip of 5
    #1499 4.00

Queen Sirikit, 60th Birthday — A462

Litho. & Embossed
1992, Aug. 12   Perf. 13½
1500 A462 100b blue & gold 20.00 20.00

No. 1500 was printed in sheets of 10. Value, $210.

A463

Wmk. 387
1992, Aug. 25   Litho.   Perf. 13½
1501 A463 2b multicolored .60 .25
    Complete booklet, strip of 5
    #1501 4.25

Prince Wan Waithayakon Krommun Naradhip Bongsprabandh (1891-1976).

A464

1992, Sept. 15   Perf. 14x14½
1502 A464 2b multicolored .60 .25
    Complete booklet, strip of 5
    #1502 4.25

Professor Silpa Bhirasri, Sculptor, cent. of birth.

Coral A465

2b, Catalaphyllia jardinei. 3b, Porites lutea. 6b, Tubastraea coccinea. 8b, Favia pallida.

Perf. 14½x14
1992, Oct. 4   Litho.   Wmk. 387
1503 A465 2b multicolored .45 .25
    Complete booklet, strip of 5
    #1503 2.75
1504 A465 3b multicolored .75 .25
1505 A465 6b multicolored .85 .30
1506 A465 8b multicolored 1.25 .45
    a.   Souv. sheet of 4, #1503-1506 5.25
    Nos. 1503-1506 (4) 3.30 1.25

Intl. Letter Writing Week. No. 1506a sold for for 30b.

New Year 1993 — A466

Flowers: No. 1507, Rhododendron simsii. No. 1508, Cynoglossum lanceolatum. No. 1509, Tithonia diversifolia. No. 1510, Agapetes parishii.

Perf. 14x13½
1992, Nov. 15   Wmk. 368   Litho.
1507 A466 1b multicolored .30 .25
1508 A466 1b multicolored .30 .25
1509 A466 1b multicolored .30 .25
1510 A466 1b multicolored .30 .25
    a.   Souv. sheet of 4, #1507-1510 3.00 2.00
    Nos. 1507-1510 (4) 1.20 1.00

Nos. 1510a sold for 10b. Exists imperf with sheet price in green, value same as perf.

1st Asian Congress of Allergies and Immunology A467

1992, Nov. 22   Perf. 13½
1511 A467 2b black, red & yellow .50 .25
    Complete booklet, strip of 5
    #1511 5.00

Natl. Assembly, 60th Anniv. — A468

Wmk. 387
1992, Dec. 10   Litho.   Perf. 13½
1512 A468 2b multicolored .60 .25
    Complete booklet, strip of 5
    #1512 4.25

Bank of Thailand, 50th Anniv. — A469

1992, Dec. 10   Perf. 14½x14
1513 A469 2b multicolored .60 .25
    Complete booklet, strip of 5
    #1513 4.25

Children's Day — A470

Children's drawings: No. 1514, River scene. No. 1515, Wild animals, forest. No. 1516, Trains, planes, monorail.

1993, Jan. 9   Wmk. 368   Perf. 13½
1514 A470 2b multicolored .35 .25
    Complete booklet, strip of 5
    #1514 3.50
1515 A470 2b multicolored .35 .25
    Complete booklet, strip of 5
    #1515 3.50
1516 A470 2b multicolored .35 .25
    Complete booklet, strip of 5
    #1516 3.50
    Nos. 1514-1516 (3) 1.05 .75

Pottery — A471

Designs: 3b, Jug with bird's neck spout, two bottles. 6b, Pear-shaped vase, two jars. 7b, Three bowls. 8b, Three jars.

1993, Jan. 9   Photo.   Wmk. 329
1517 A471 3b multicolored .35 .25
1518 A471 6b multicolored .70 .50
1519 A471 7b multicolored .80 .55
1520 A471 8b multicolored .95 .70
    a.   Souv. sheet of 4, #1517-1520 4.25 3.50
    Nos. 1517-1520 (4) 2.80 2.00

1993 World Philatelic Exhibition, Bangkok. No. 1520a sold for 35b.

Thai Teachers' Training Institute, Cent. — A472

Perf. 13½x14
1993, Jan. 16   Litho.   Wmk. 368
1521 A472 2b multicolored .45 .25
    Complete booklet, strip of 5
    #1521 5.00

Kasetsart University, 50th Anniv. — A473

1993, Feb. 2   Wmk. 329   Perf. 13½
1522 A473 2b multicolored .60 .25
    Complete booklet, strip of 5
    #1522 5.00

Maghapuja Day — A474

Wmk. 387
1993, Mar. 7   Litho.   Perf. 14½
1523 A474 2b multicolored .70 .25

Queen Sri Bajarindra A475

1993, Mar. 27   Perf. 14x14½
1524 A475 2b multicolored .70 .25
    Complete booklet, strip of 5
    #1524 6.00

Thai Red Cross, cent.

Office of Attorney General, Cent. — A476

1993, Apr. 1   Wmk. 368   Perf. 12½
1525 A476 2b multicolored .60 .25
    Complete booklet, strip of 5
    #1525 5.00

Heritage Conservation Day — A477

Historical landmarks, Si Satchanalai Park: 3b, Wat Chedi Chet Thaeo. 4b, Wat Chang Lom. 6b, Wat Phra Si Rattanamahathat (Chaliang). 7b, Wat Suan Kaeo Utthayan Noi.

Wmk. 368
1993, Apr. 2   Litho.   Perf. 13½
1526 A477 3b multicolored .35 .25
1527 A477 4b multicolored .45 .30
1528 A477 6b multicolored .70 .50
1529 A477 7b multicolored .80 .55
    a.   Souv. sheet of 4, #1526-1529 3.50 2.75
    Nos. 1526-1529 (4) 2.30 1.60

No. 1529a sold for 25b.
See Nos. 1561-1564, 1650-1653, 1797-1800.

Songkran Day Type of 1991
Design: Demon on rooster's back, zodiac.

Perf. 14x14½
1993   Litho.   Wmk. 387
1530 A425 2b multicolored .40 .25
    Complete booklet, strip of 5
    #1530 2.50
    a.   Souvenir sheet of 1 2.50 1.00
    b.   As "a," ovptd. in gold 15.00 15.00

No. 1530b overprinted on sheet margin in both Thai and Chinese for Chinpex '93.
Nos. 1530a-1530b sold for 8b and exist imperf. with sale price in different colors. Values same as for perf.
Issued: Nos. 1530, 1530a, 4/13.

Mushrooms — A478

Wmk. 368

1993, July 1   Litho.   Perf. 13½
1531 A478 2b Marasmius   .25   .25
　　Complete booklet, strip of 5
　　　#1531   3.50
1532 A478 4b Coprinus   .50   .30
1533 A478 6b Mycena   .70   .45
1534 A478 8b Cyathus   1.00   .60
　a.　Souv. sheet of 4, #1531-1534   3.75   3.75
　　Nos. 1531-1534 (4)   2.45   1.60

No. 1534a sold for 30b.

Natl. Communications Day — A479

1993, Aug. 4   Wmk. 387   Perf. 13½
1535 A479 2b multicolored   .45   .25
　　Complete booklet, strip of 5
　　　#1535   4.00

Post and Telegraph Department, 110th
Anniv. — A480

Wmk. 387
1993, Aug. 4   Litho.   Perf. 13½
1536 A480 2b multicolored   1.00   .25
　　Complete booklet, strip of 5
　　　#1536   9.00

Queen Suriyothai's Monument — A481

1993, Aug. 12
1537 A481 2b multicolored   .60   .25
　　Complete booklet, strip of 5
　　　#1537   5.00

Fruit — A482

Wmk. 368
1993, Oct. 1   Photo.   Perf. 13½
1538 A482 2b Citrus reticulata   .25   .25
　　Complete booklet, strip of 5
　　　#1538   3.50
1539 A482 3b Musa sp.   .40   .25
1540 A482 6b Phyllanthus dis-
　　　tichus   .75   .45
1541 A482 8b Bouea burmanica   1.00   .60
　　Nos. 1538-1541 (4)   2.40   1.55

Thai Ridgeback Dogs — A483

Various dogs.

1993, Oct. 1
1542 A483 2b multicolored   .45   .25
　　Complete booklet, strip of 5
　　　#1542   2.75
1543 A483 3b multicolored   .45   .25
1544 A483 5b multicolored   .65   .30
1545 A483 10b multicolored   1.75   .65
　a.　Souv. sheet of 4, #1542-1545   3.75   3.50
　　Nos. 1542-1545 (4)   3.30   1.45

Intl. Letter Writing Week. No. 1545a sold for
30b.

5th Conference & Exhibition of ASEAN
Council on Petroleum
(ASCOPE) — A484

Wmk. 387
1993, Nov. 2   Litho.   Perf. 13½
1546 A484 2b multicolored   .60   .25
　　Complete booklet, strip of 5
　　　#1546   5.00

King Rama VII
(1893-1941)
A485

1993, Nov. 8   Perf. 14x14½
1547 A485 2b multicolored   1.00   .25
　　Complete booklet, strip of 5
　　　#1547   7.50

No. 655 Surcharged

1993 Photo. Wmk. 233 Perf. 14½
1548 A161 1b on 25s brown red   .70   .25

Bencharong and
Lai Nam Thong
Wares — A486

Designs: 3b, Bencharong cosmetic jar,
divinity design. 5b, Bencharong cosmetic jar,
gold knob. 6b, Lai Nam Thong cosmetic jar,
floral design. 7b, Lai Nam Thong cosmetic jar,
floral design, diff.

Wmk. 368
1993, Oct. 1   Photo.   Perf. 13½
1549 A486 3b multicolored   .40   .25
1550 A486 5b multicolored   .60   .30
1551 A486 6b multicolored   .70   .45

1552 A486 7b multicolored   .90   .50
　a.　Souv. sheet of 4, #1549-1552   3.00   3.00
　　Nos. 1549-1552 (4)   2.60   1.50

Bangkok '93. No. 1552a sold for 30b.
No. 1552a exists imperf. Value, $16.

New Year
1994 — A487

Perf. 14½x14
1993, Nov. 15   Litho.   Wmk. 387
1553 A487 1b Ipomoea cairica   .25   .25
1554 A487 1b Decaschistia
　　　parviflora   .25   .25
1555 A487 1b Hibiscus tiliaceus   .25   .25
1556 A487 1b Passiflora foetida   .25   .25
　a.　Souv. sheet of 4, #1553-1556   2.50   1.75
　　Nos. 1553-1556 (4)   1.00   1.00

No. 1556a sold for 10b.

THAICOM, Natl.
Satellite
Project — A488

1993, Dec. 1   Perf. 14x14½
1557 A488 2b multicolored   .50   .25
　　Complete booklet, strip of 5
　　　#1557   4.50

Children's Day — A489

1994, Jan. 8   Perf. 14½x14
1558 A489 2b Play land   .45   .25
　　Complete booklet, strip of 5
　　　#1558   4.00

Administrative Building, Chulalongkorn
Hospital, 80th Anniv. — A490

Perf. 14½x14
1994, Mar. 30   Litho.   Wmk. 387
1559 A490 2b multicolored   .45   .25
　　Complete booklet, strip of 5
　　　#1559   4.00

Thai Red Cross.

Royal Institute,
60th
Anniv. — A491

1994, Mar. 31   Perf. 14x14½
1560 A491 2b multicolored   .40   .25
　　Complete booklet, strip of 5
　　　#1560   3.50

**Heritage Conservation Day Type of
1993**

Historical landmarks, Phra Nakhon Si
Ayutthaya Park: 2b, Wat Ratchaburana. 3b,
Wat Maha That. 6b, Wat Maheyong. 9b, Wat
Phra Si Samphet.

1994, Apr. 2   Perf. 14½x14
1561 A477 2b multicolored   .30   .25
　　Complete booklet, strip of 5
　　　#1561   2.50
1562 A477 3b multicolored   .35   .25
1563 A477 6b multicolored   .75   .45
1564 A477 9b multicolored   1.00   .70
　a.　Souv. sheet of 4, #1561-1564   3.00   3.00
　　Nos. 1561-1564 (4)   2.40   1.65

No. 1564a sold for 25b.

Opening of Friendship Bridge,
Thailand-Laos — A492

1994, Apr. 8
1565 A492 9b multicolored   1.60   .35

Songkran Day Type of 1991

Design: Demon on dog's back, zodiac.

1994, Apr. 13   Litho.
1566 A425 2b multicolored   .35   .25
　　Complete booklet, strip of 5
　　　#1566   3.00
　a.　Souvenir sheet of 1   2.00   1.75
　b.　As "a," inscribed in margin   4.50   4.50

No. 1566a sold for 8b and exists imperf with
frame around stamp and sale price in different
color. Value same as perf.
　Sheet margin of No. 1566b has no value
inscription and is overprinted in violet with Thai
and Chinese inscriptions for Beijing Stamp
Exhibition. Issued: May 1994. No. 1566b also
exists imperf. Value same as perf.

Intl. Olympic Committee,
Cent. — A493

Wmk. 387
1994, June 23   Litho.   Perf. 14
1567 A493 2b Soccer   .25   .25
　　Complete booklet, strip of 5
　　　#1567   1.75
1568 A493 3b Running   .35   .25
1569 A493 5b Swimming   .60   .45
1570 A493 6b Weight lifting   .80   .55
1571 A493 9b Boxing   1.10   .80
　　Nos. 1567-1571 (5)   3.10   2.30

Thammasat University, 60th
Anniv. — A494

Wmk. 387
1994, June 27   Litho.   Perf. 14
1572 A494 2b multicolored   1.00   .35
　　Complete booklet, strip of 5
　　　#1572   6.00

Asalhapuja Day — A495

1994, July 22   Wmk. 329   Perf. 13½
1573 A495 2b multicolored   .45   .25

Natl. Communications Day — A496

1994, Aug. 4   Wmk. 368
1574 A496 2b multicolored   .45   .25
  Complete booklet, strip of 5
  #1574   4.00

Crabs
A497

3b, Phricotelphusa limula. 5b, Thaipotamon chulabhorn. 6b, Phricotelphusa sirindhorn. 10b, Thaiphusa sirikit.

Wmk. 340 (340)
1994, Aug. 12   Photo.   Perf. 13½x13
1575 A497 3b multicolored   .50   .25
1576 A497 5b multicolored   .75   .35
1577 A497 6b multicolored   .75   .45
1578 A497 10b multicolored   1.50   .75
  a.   Souv. sheet of 4, #1575-1578   4.00   4.00
  b.   As "a," inscribed in margin   6.50   6.00
  Nos. 1575-1578 (4)   3.50   1.80

No. 1578b has PHILAKOREA '94 Exhibition emblem added to sheet margin.

Intl. Letter Writing Week — A498

Winning paintings in design contest: 2b, Gold niello bowls, octagonal footed tray. 6b, Pumpkin shaped bowls. 8b, Silver niello betelnut set. 9b, Covered square bowl with gold finial, small lotus-shaped footed tray.

Wmk. 368
1994, Oct. 9   Photo.   Perf. 13½
1579 A498 2b multicolored   .25   .25
  Complete booklet, 5 #1579   3.50
1580 A498 6b multicolored   .80   .55
1581 A498 8b multicolored   1.00   .70
1582 A498 9b multicolored   1.10   .80
  a.   Souv. sheet of 4, #1579-1582   3.50   3.50
  Nos. 1579-1582 (4)   3.15   2.30

No. 1582a sold for 30b.

ILO, 75th Anniv. A499

Perf. 15x14
1994, Oct. 29   Litho.   Wmk. 387
1583 A499 2b multicolored   .40   .25
  Complete booklet, 5 #1583   3.50

New Year 1995 — A500

Herbs: No. 1584, Utricularia delphinioides. No. 1585, Utricularia minutissima. No. 1586, Eriocaulon odoratum. No. 1587, Utricularia bifida.

1994, Nov. 15   Perf. 14x14½
1584 A500 1b multicolored   .30   .25
1585 A500 1b multicolored   .30   .25
1586 A500 1b multicolored   .30   .25
1587 A500 1b multicolored   .30   .25
  a.   Souv. sheet of 4, #1584-1587   1.75   1.50
  Nos. 1584-1587 (4)   1.20   1.00

No. 1587a sold for 10b.

Suan Dusit Teachers College, 60th Anniv. — A501

Perf. 14½x14
1994, Dec. 4   Litho.   Wmk. 387
1588 A501 2b multicolored   .60   .25
  Complete booklet, 5 #1588   5.00

Council of State, 120th Anniv. — A502

1994, Dec. 5   Wmk. 368   Perf. 13½
1589 A502 2b multicolored   1.00   .25
  Complete booklet, 5 #1589   12.50

ICAO, 50th Anniv. A503

Perf. 14½x14
1994, Dec. 7   Wmk. 387
1590 A503 2b multicolored   .35   .25
  Complete booklet, 5 #1590   4.25

Pharmacy in Thailand, 80th Anniv. — A504

Grinding stones: 2b, Dvaravati, 7th-11th cent. 6b, Lopburi Period, 11th-13th cent. 9b, Bangkok Period, 18th-20th cent.

1994, Dec. 13
1591 A504 2b multicolored   .30   .25
  Complete booklet, 5 #1591   3.00
1592 A504 6b multicolored   .80   .50
1593 A504 9b multicolored   1.10   .80
  Nos. 1591-1593 (3)   2.20   1.55

Bar Assoc., 80th Anniv. — A505

Design: 2b, First Bar Assoc. headquarters, King Vajiravudh, King Bhumibol.

1995, Jan. 1   Wmk. 368   Perf. 13½
1594 A505 2b multicolored   .60   .25
  Complete booklet, 5 #1594   5.00

A506

Children's drawings: No. 1595, Kites Decorate the Summer Sky. No. 1596, Trees and Streams, horiz. No. 1597, Youths and Religion, horiz.

1995, Jan. 14   Wmk. 387   Perf. 14
1595 A506 2b multicolored   .55   .25
  Complete booklet, 5 #1595   3.00
1596 A506 2b multicolored   .55   .25
  Complete booklet, 5 #1596   3.00
1597 A506 2b multicolored   .55   .25
  Complete booklet, 5 #1597   3.00
  Nos. 1595-1597 (3)   1.65   .75

Children's Day.

A507

1995, Mar. 4
1598 A507 2b multicolored   .40   .25
  Complete booklet, 5 #1598   4.25

First Thai newspaper, Bangkok Recorder, 150th anniv.

Royal Thai Air Force, 80th Anniv. A508

1995, Mar. 27   Wmk. 368   Perf. 13½
1599 A508 2b multicolored   .35   .25
  Complete booklet, 5 #1599   5.00

Red Cross Floating Clinic, Wetchapha — A509

1995, Mar. 30
1600 A509 2b multicolored   .35   .25
  Complete booklet, 5 #1600   5.00

Phimai Historical Park — A510

Paintings: 3b, Naga Bridge. 5b, Brahmin Hall. 6b, Gateway of the Inner Wall. 9b, Main Pagoda.

Perf. 14½x14
1995, Apr. 2   Wmk. 387
1601 A510 3b multicolored   .35   .25
1602 A510 5b multicolored   .60   .35
1603 A510 6b multicolored   .80   .50
1604 A510 9b multicolored   1.10   .80
  a.   Souv. sheet of 4, #1601-1604   4.00   4.00
  Nos. 1601-1604 (4)   2.85   1.90

Heritage Conservation Day.
No. 1604a sold for 30b.

Ministry of Defense, 108th Anniv. — A511

Design: 2b, Admin. building, King Rama V.

1995, Apr. 8   Wmk. 387   Perf. 14
1605 A511 2b multicolored   .60   .25
  Complete booklet, 5 #1605   5.00

Songkran Day Type of 1991

Design: Demon on boar's back, zodiac.

1995, Apr. 13   Perf. 11x13
1606 A425 2b multicolored   .30   .25
  a.   Souvenir sheet of 1   1.75   1.00
  Complete booklet, 5 #1606   4.25

No. 1606a sold for 8b and exists imperf with sale price in different color. Value same as perf. No. 1606a and the similar imperf sheet exist with a red marginal inscription in Thai and Chinese (without sale price). Value, each $5.50.

Ministry of Foreign Affairs, 120th Anniv. — A512

2b, Saranrom Palace, King Rama V.

1995, Apr. 14   Perf. 14
1607 A512 2b multicolored   .70   .25
  Complete booklet, 5 #1607   5.00

Visakhapuja Day — A513

Sculptures of Buddha: 2b, Emerald Buddha, temple of Wat Phra Si Rattana Satsadaram, Bangkok. 6b, Phra Phuttha Chinnarat, Wat Phra Si Rattana Maha That, Phitsanulok Province. 8b, Phra Phuttha Sihing, Wat Phra Sing, Chiang Mai Province. 9b, Phra Sukhothai Traimit, Wat Traimit Witthayaram, Bangkok.

Wmk. 340
1995, May 13   Photo.   Perf. 13½
1608 A513 2b multicolored   .30   .25
1609 A513 6b multicolored   .90   .40
1610 A513 8b multicolored   1.20   .60

1611 A513 9b multicolored 1.25 .70
a. Souv. sheet of 4, #1608-1611 4.50 4.50
Nos. 1608-1611 (4) 3.65 1.95
No. 1611a sold for 35b.

ASEAN
Environment
Year — A514

1995, June 5 Litho. Wmk. 368
1612 A514 2b multicolored .40 .25
Complete booklet, 5 #1612 3.50

Information Technology Year — A515

1995, June 9 Wmk. 340
1613 A515 2b multicolored .40 .25
Complete booklet, 5 #1613 3.50

Thailand-People's Republic of China
Diplomatic Relations, 20th
Anniv. — A516

#1614, Elephants walking right into water.
#1615, Elephants walking left into water.

Wmk. 340
1995, July 1 Photo. Perf. 13½
1614 A516 2b multicolored .50 .25
1615 A516 2b multicolored .50 .25
a. Pair, Nos. 1614-1615 1.75 1.75
b. Souv. sheet, #1614-1615 3.50
c. As "b," diff. inscriptions in
sheet margin 18.00

No. 1615c contains Jakarta '95 exhibition
emblem and does not have sheet value in
margin.
#1615b sold for 8b. #1615c sold for 28b.
No. 1615b exists with serial number in sheet
margin, The same number is on China (PRC)
No. 2462a. These two souvenir sheets were
sold as a set. Value, set $26.50. .
See People's Republic of China Nos. 2579-
2580.

Natl. Communications Day — A517

1995, Aug. 4 Litho. Perf. 14½x14
1616 A517 2b multicolored .45 .25
Complete booklet, 5 #1616 3.50

A518

Domestic cats: 3b, Khoa Manee. 6b, Korat
or Si-Sawat. 7b, Seal point Siamese. 9b,
Burmese.

1995, Aug. 4 Photo. Perf. 13½
1617 A518 3b multicolored .50 .25
1618 A518 6b multicolored .75 .45
1619 A518 7b multicolored .95 .50
1620 A518 9b multicolored 1.50 .70
a. Souv. sheet, Nos. 1617-
1620 5.00 5.00
b. As "a," diff. inscriptions in
margin 35.00 35.00
Nos. 1617-1620 (4) 3.70 1.90
Thaipex '95.
No. 1620b contains Singapore '95 exhibition
emblem added to sheet margin and does not
have value inscription.
No. 1620a sold for 35b. No. 1620b sold for
46b.
No. 1620a exists imperf. Value $21.00.

Revenue
Department, 80th
Anniv. — A519

1995, Sept. 2 Litho. Perf. 14x14½
1621 A519 2b multicolored .40 .25
Complete booklet, 5 #1621 3.50

Natl. Auditing & Office of Auditor
General, 120th Anniv. — A520

1995, Sept. 18 Perf. 14½x14
1622 A520 2b multicolored .40 .25
Complete booklet, 5 #1622 3.50

Intl. Letter Writing
Week — A521

Wicker: No. 1623, Vase with handles, legs.
No. 1624, Oval-shaped container. No. 1625,
Lamp shade. No. 1626, Vase.

Wmk. 340
1995, Oct. 8 Photo. Perf. 13½
1623 A521 2b multicolored .25 .25
Complete booklet, 5 #1623 2.25
1624 A521 2b multicolored .25 .25
Complete booklet, 5 #1624 2.25
1625 A521 9b multicolored 1.10 .80
1626 A521 9b multicolored 1.10 .80
a. Souv. sheet, #1623-1626 4.50 4.50
Nos. 1623-1626 (4) 2.70 2.10

FAO,
50th
Anniv.
A522

1995, Oct. 16 Litho. Perf. 14½x14
1627 A522 2b multicolored .35 .25
Complete booklet, 5 #1627 3.00

Total Solar Eclipse in Thailand — A523

1995, Oct. 24 Perf. 13½
1628 A523 2b multicolored .45 .25
Complete booklet, 5 #1628 2.50

UN,
50th
Anniv.
A524

Perf. 13½x14
1995, Oct. 24 Wmk. 387
1629 A524 2b multicolored .35 .25
Complete booklet, 5 #1629 2.50

World Agricultural and Industrial
Exhibition, Nkhon Ratchasima
Province — A525

2b, Worldtech '95 Thailand Symbol Tower,
vert. 5b, Farming equipment, food products,
vert. 6b, Computers, equipment. 9b, Factory,
beach.

Perf. 14x14½, 14½x14
1995, Nov. 4 Wmk. 340
1630 A525 2b multicolored .25 .25
Complete booklet, 5 #1630 2.50
1631 A525 5b multicolored .60 .40
1632 A525 6b multicolored .80 .50
1633 A525 9b multicolored 1.10 .80
Nos. 1630-1633 (4) 2.75 1.95

New Year
1996 — A526

#1634, Adenium obesum. #1635, Bauhinia
acuminata. #1636, Cananga odorata. #1637,
Thumbergia erecta.

1995, Dec. 9 Perf. 13½
1634 A526 2b multicolored .25 .25
1635 A526 2b multicolored .25 .25
a. Souvenir sheet, #1634-1635 4.50
1636 A526 2b multicolored .25 .25
1637 A526 2b multicolored .25 .25
a. Souvenir sheet, #1634-1637 2.75 2.25
b. As "a," inscribed in margin 12.00 8.00
c. Souvenir sheet, #1636-1637 8.00 7.00
Nos. 1634-1637 (4) 1.00 1.00
No. 1637a sold for 15b.
Nos. 1635a, 1637c have "CHINA '96"
emblem inscribed in sheet margin and sold for
22b each. No. 1637b is inscribed in sheet margin with "Indonesia '96" emblem and has the
gold 15b value removed. No. 1637b sold for
14b.
Issued: #1635a, 1637b-1637c, 5/18/96.

Veterinary Science in Thailand, 60th
Anniv. — A527

1995, Dec. 9 Perf. 14½x14
1638 A527 2b multicolored .50 .25
Complete booklet, 5 #1638 4.00

A528

Perf. 14x14½
1996, Jan. 12 Litho. Wmk. 340
1639 A528 2b multicolored .50 .25
Complete booklet, 5 #1639 4.00
Siriraj School of Nursing and Midwifery, cent.

A529

Paintings of Buddha instructing people with:
No. 1640, Bright light, deer. No. 1641, Chil-
dren, animal, person reclined, horiz. No. 1642,
Followers, large tree, river.

1996, Jan. 13 Wmk. 387 Perf. 13½
1640 A529 2b multicolored .40 .25
Complete booklet, 5 #1640 2.50
1641 A529 2b multicolored .40 .25
Complete booklet, 5 #1641 2.50
1642 A529 2b multicolored .40 .25
Complete booklet, 5 #1642 2.50
Nos. 1640-1642 (3) 1.20 .75
Natl. Children's Day.

Natl. Aviation Day — A530

Perf. 14½x14
1996, Jan. 13 Wmk. 340
1643 A530 2b multicolored .40 .25
Complete booklet, 5 #1643 3.50

Asia-Europe
Economic
Meeting — A531

Perf. 14x14½
1996, Mar. 1   Litho.   Wmk. 340
1644 A531 2b multicolored .40 .25
Complete booklet, 5 #1644 3.50

Maghapuja Day — A532

Scenes from the Ten Jataka stories: 2b, Man on knee, another holding chariot. 6b, Two people flying over sea. 8b, Archer approaching man with arrow in side. 9b, Charioteer pointing.

Wmk. 340
1996, Mar. 3   Photo.   Perf. 13½
1645 A532 2b multicolored .25 .25
1646 A532 6b multicolored .75 .45
1647 A532 8b multicolored 1.00 .60
1648 A532 9b multicolored 1.10 .75
  a. Souvenir Sheet #1645-1548 4.50 3.50
  Nos. 1645-1648 (4) 3.10 2.05

No. 1648a sold for 36b.

Cremation of Princess Mother Somdej Phra Sri Nakharindra Barommarajjonnani — A533

Litho. & Embossed
Perf. 14½x14
1996, Mar. 10   Wmk. 340
1649 A533 2b gold & multi .80 .25
Complete booklet, 5 #1649 5.00

Heritage Conservation Day Type of 1993

Historical landmarks, Kamphaeng Phet Park: 2b, Wat Phra Kaeo. 3b, Wat Phra Non. 6b, Wat Chang Rop. 9b, Wat Phra Si Iriyabot.

Wmk. 387
1996, Apr. 2   Litho.   Perf. 13½
1650 A477 2b multicolored .25 .25
Complete booklet, 5 #1650 2.75
1651 A477 3b multicolored .45 .25
1652 A477 6b multicolored .80 .50
1653 A477 9b multicolored 1.10 .80
  a. Souvenir sheet, #1650-1653 3.50 3.50
  Nos. 1650-1653 (4) 2.60 1.80

No. 1653a sold for 28b.

Chiang Mai, 700th Anniv. — A534

Anniv. logo of Chiang Mai and: 2b, Buddhist Pagoda of Wat Chiang Man. 6b, Sculpted angel on wall, Wat Chet Yot's Pagoda. 8b, Insignia of Wat Phan Tao's Vihara. 9b, Sattaphanta.

Wmk. 340
1996, Apr. 12   Photo.   Perf. 13½
1654 A534 2b multicolored .25 .25
Complete booklet, 5 #1654 2.75
1655 A534 6b multicolored .70 .45
1656 A534 8b multicolored .90 .60
1657 A534 9b multicolored 1.00 .70
  a. Souvenir sheet, #1654-1657 4.00 4.00
  Nos. 1654-1657 (4) 2.85 2.00

No. 1657a sold for 37b.

Second Intl. Asian Hornbill Workshop A535

No. 1658, White-crowned. No. 1659, Rufous-necked. No. 1660, Plain-pouched. No. 1661, Rhinoceros.

1996, Apr. 12
1658 A535 3b multicolored .35 .25
1659 A535 3b multicolored .35 .25
1660 A535 9b multicolored 1.10 .80
1661 A535 9b multicolored 1.10 .80
  a. Souvenir sheet, #1658-1661 4.50 4.50
  b. As "a," inscribed in margin 10.00 8.00
  Nos. 1658-1661 (4) 2.90 2.10

No. 1661a sold for 35b. No. 1661b was issued 6/8/96, contains CAPEX '96 exhibition emblem in sheet margin, no value inscription, and sold for 47b.

Songkran Day Type of 1991

Design: Demon on rat's back, zodiac.

Perf. 13½x14
1996, Apr. 13   Litho.   Wmk. 387
1662 A425 2b multicolored .40 .25
Complete booklet, 5 #1662 3.00
  a. Souvenir sheet of 1 3.50 3.50
  b. Souv. sheet, #1389, 1467, 1530, 1565, 1606, 1662 3.50 3.50
  c. As "a," inscribed in margin 5.00 5.00
  d. As "b," inscribed in margin 12.00 12.00

No. 1662c contains CHINA '96 exhibition emblem and "CHINA '96-9th Asian International Philatelic Exhibition" in Chinese and English and no value inscription in sheet margin. No. 1662d contains CHINA '96 and Hong Kong '96 exhibition emblems in margin and no value inscription.

#1662a sold for 8b. #1662b sold for 20b. #1662c, issued 5/15/96, sold for 14b. #1662d, issued 5/10/96, sold for 25b. #1662a-1662d exist imperf.

A536

King Bhumibol Adulyadej, 50th Anniv. of Accession to the Throne A537

Designs: No. 1663, Royal Ablutions Ceremony. No. 1664, Pouring of the Libation. No. 1665, Grand Audience. No. 1666, Royal Progress by Land. No. 1667, Audience from Balcony.

1996, June 9   Photo.   Perf. 11½
Granite Paper
1663 A536 3b multicolored .40 .25
  a. Souvenir sheet 2.00
1664 A536 3b multicolored .40 .25
  a. Souvenir sheet 2.00
1665 A536 3b multicolored .40 .25
  a. Souvenir sheet 2.00
1666 A536 3b multicolored .40 .25
  a. Souvenir sheet 2.00
1667 A536 3b multicolored .40 .25
  a. Souvenir sheet 2.00

Litho. & Typo.
Wmk. 387
Perf. 13½
1668 A537 100b gold & multi 12.00 8.00
  Nos. 1663-1668 (6) 14.00 9.25

Nos. 1663a 1664a, 1665a, 1666a, 1667a have a continuous design and each sold for 8b.

No. 1668 was issued in panes of 10. Value, $150.

Development Programs of King Bhumibol Adulyadej — A538

No. 1669, Using Vetiver grass to prevent soil erosion. No. 1670, Chai pattana aerator to improve water quality. No. 1671, Rain making project to counter droughts. No. 1672, Dam, natural water resource development. No. 1673, Reforestation.

Wmk. 340
1996, June 9   Litho.   Perf. 13½
1669 A538 3b multicolored .40 .25
1670 A538 3b multicolored .40 .25
1671 A538 3b multicolored .40 .25
1672 A538 3b multicolored .40 .25
1673 A538 3b multicolored .40 .25
  a. Souv. sheet, #1669-1673+label 5.00 3.50
  Nos. 1669-1673 (5) 2.00 1.25

No. 1671 has a holographic image. Soaking in water may affect the hologram. No. 1673a sold for 25b.

Royal Utensils — A539

#1674, Gold-enameled cuspidor, golden spittoon. #1675, Royal betel, areca-nut set, vert. #1676, Royal water urn, vert.

Wmk. 329
1996, June 9   Photo.   Perf. 13½
1674 A539 3b green & multi .40 .25
1675 A539 3b blue & multi .40 .25
1676 A539 3b purple & multi .40 .25
  a. Souvenir sheet, #1674-1676 2.50 2.00
  Nos. 1674-1676 (3) 1.20 .75

No. 1676a sold for 17b.

Modern Olympic Games, Cent. — A540

2b, Pierre de Coubertin, grave site. 3b, 1st lighting of Olympic torch, Olympia, Greece. 5b, Olympic Stadium, Athens, Olympic flag. 9b, Discus thrower, medal from 1896 games.

Perf. 14x14½
1996, June 23   Litho.   Wmk. 340
1677 A540 2b multicolored .25 .25
Complete booklet, 5 #1677 3.25
1678 A540 3b multicolored .35 .25
1679 A540 5b multicolored .60 .45
1680 A540 9b multicolored 1.10 .80
  Nos. 1677-1680 (4) 2.30 1.75

Nat. Communications Day — A541

1996, Aug. 4   Wmk. 340
1681 A541 2b King using radio .55 .25
Complete booklet, 5 #1681 3.50

Royal Forest Department, Cent. — A542

Perf. 14½x14
1996, Sept. 18   Litho.   Wmk. 340
Type of Forest
1682 A542 3b Tropical rain .30 .25
1683 A542 6b Hill evergreen .80 .50
1684 A542 7b Swamp .90 .60
1685 A542 9b Mangrove 1.10 .80
  a. Souvenir sheet, #1682-1685 4.50 4.50
  Nos. 1682-1685 (4) 3.10 2.15

No. 1685a sold for 35b.

Intl. Letter Writing Week — A543

Classical Thai novels, characters: No. 1686, "Ramayana," King Rama following deer. No. 1687, "Inao," Inao kidnapping Budsaba, taking her to cave. No. 1688, "Ngao Pa," Lumhap touring forest. No. 1689, "Mathanapatha," Nang Mathana being cursed.

Wmk. 340
1996, Oct. 6   Photo.   Perf. 13½
1686 A543 3b multicolored .35 .25
1687 A543 3b multicolored .35 .25
1688 A543 9b multicolored 1.10 .80
1689 A543 9b multicolored 1.10 .80
  a. Souvenir sheet #1686-1689 4.50 4.50
  Nos. 1686-1689 (4) 2.90 2.10

No. 1689a sold for 36b. For surcharges, see Nos. 2530-2531.

Rotary Intl. 1996 Asia Regional Conference A544

Perf. 14x14½
1996, Oct. 25   Litho.   Wmk. 340
1690 A544 2b multicolored .40 .25
Complete booklet, 5 #1609 2.75

UNESCO, 50th Anniv. — A545

1996, Nov. 4   **Perf. 14½x14**
1691 A545 2b multicolored   .40   .25
   Complete booklet, 5 #1691   2.50

Royal Barge — A546

1996, Nov. 7   Unwmk.   Perf. 11½
Granite Paper
1692 A546 9b multicolored   1.40 1.10
a.   Souvenir sheet of 1   2.75   2.25
   No. 1692a sold for 16b.

New Year
1997 — A547

Designs: No. 1693, Limnocharis flava. No. 1694, Crinum thaianum, vert. No. 1695, Monochoria hastata, vert. No. 1696, Nymphoides indicum.

Perf. 14x14½, 14½x14
1996, Nov. 15   Litho.   Wmk. 387
1693 A547 2b multicolored   .25   .25
1694 A547 2b multicolored   .25   .25
1695 A547 2b multicolored   .25   .25
1696 A547 2b multicolored   .25   .25
a.   Souvenir sheet, #1693-1696   2.25   2.25
b.   As "a," inscribed in margin   6.00   6.00
   Nos. 1693-1696 (4)   1.00   1.00
No. 1696a sold for 15b. No. 1696b inscribed in sheet margin with Hong Kong '97 emblem and vertical Chinese inscription.
No. 1696b issued 2/12/97.

Ducks
A548

No. 1697, Sarkidiornis melanotos. No. 1698, Dendrocygna javanica, vert. No. 1699, Cairina scutulata, vert. No. 1700, Nettapus coromandelianus.

Wmk. 340
1996, Dec. 1   Photo.   Perf. 13½
1697 A548 3b multicolored   .35   .25
1698 A548 3b multicolored   .35   .25
1699 A548 7b multicolored   .90   .60
1700 A548 7b multicolored   .90   .60
a.   Souvenir sheet, #1697-1700   4.50   4.50
   Nos. 1697-1700 (4)   2.50   1.70
No. 1700a sold for 33b.

UNICEF, 50th Anniv. — A549

Perf. 14½x14
1996, Dec. 11   Litho.   Wmk. 340
1701 A549 2b multicolored   .35   .25
   Complete booklet, 5 #1701   2.50

King Bhumibol
Adulyadej — A550

Perf. 14x14½
1996, Dec. 5   Litho.   Wmk. 340
1702 A550 2b carmine   .35   .25
   Complete booklet, 5 #1702   4.50
a.   Unwmkd., granite paper   .50   .25
   No. 1702a issued 9/1/98.
See Nos. 1725-1729, 1743-1745, 1756-1757, 1794-1795, 1819-1820, 1876-1879, 2067, 2212-2213, 2435, 2465A.

Thailand's 1st Olympic Gold Medal,
1996 — A552

Litho. & Embossed
Perf. 14½x14
1996, Dec. 16   Wmk. 340
1704 A552 6b multicolored   .80   .50

Mahavajiravudh
School,
Songkhla,
Cent. — A553

Perf. 14x14½
1997, Jan. 1   Wmk. 387
1705 A553 2b multicolored   .35   .25
   Complete booklet, 5 #1705   2.50

Children's
Day — A554

Children' paintings: No. 1706, Children processing fish. No. 1707, Monument, children in praise.

1997, Jan. 11   Wmk. 340
1706 A554 2b multicolored   .30   .25
   Complete booklet, 5 #1706   1.75
1707 A554 2b multicolored   .30   .25
   Complete booklet, 5 #1707   1.75

Communications Authority of Thailand,
20th Anniv. — A555

Perf. 14½x14
1997, Feb. 25   Litho.   Wmk. 340
1708 A555 2b multicolored   .35   .25
   Complete booklet, 5 #1708   2.50

Statue of Prince
Bhanurangsi
A556

1997, Feb. 25   Perf. 14x14½
1709 A556 2b multicolored   .35   .25
   Complete booklet, 5 #1709   2.50

Laksi
Mail
Center
A557

No. 1710, Outside view of building. No. 1711, Computerized mail sorting machine.

1997, Feb. 25   Perf. 14½x14
1710 A557 2b multicolored   .45   .25
1711 A557 2b multicolored   .45   .25
a.   Pair, #1710-1711   1.00   .50

State Railway, Cent. — A558

3b, 0-6-0 Type. 4b, Garratt. 6b, Sulzer diesel. 7b, Hitachi diesel leaving tunnel.

Wmk. 387
1997, Mar. 26   Litho.   Perf. 13
1712 A558 3b multicolored   .35   .25
a.   Souvenir sheet of 1   2.75   2.75
1713 A558 4b multicolored   .50   .35
1714 A558 6b multicolored   .80   .50
1715 A558 7b multicolored   1.00   .60
a.   Souv. sheet of 4, #1712-1715 5.50   5.50
   Nos. 1712-1715 (4)   2.65   1.70
No. 1712a sold for 20b, No. 1715a sold for 30b.

Chulalongkorn University, 80th
Anniv. — A559

Designs: No. 1716, Palace of Prince Maha Vajirunhis. No. 1717, Faculty of Arts building.

Perf. 14½x14
1997, Mar. 26   Wmk. 340
1716 A559 2b yellow & multi   .35   .25
   Complete booklet, 5 #1716   2.00
1717 A559 2b rose & multi   .35   .25
   Complete booklet, 5 #1717   2.00

Thai
Red
Cross
A560

1997, Mar. 28
1718 A560 3b Rajakarun building   .35   .25

Govt. Savings Bank, 84th
Anniv. — A561

1997, Apr. 1
1719 A561 2b multicolored   .35   .25
   Complete booklet, 5 #1719   2.25

Heritage Conservation Day — A562

Phanomrung historical Park: No. 1720, Outer stairway. No. 1721, Pavilion. No. 1722, Passage, stairway to sanctuary. No. 1723, Naga balustrade, Central Gate of Eastern Gallery.

1997, Apr. 2
1720 A562 3b multicolored   .35   .25
1721 A562 3b multicolored   .35   .25
1722 A562 7b multicolored   .90   .60
1723 A562 7b multicolored   .90   .60
a.   Souvenir sheet, #1720-1723   4.00   4.00
   Nos. 1720-1723 (4)   2.50   1.70
   No. 1723a sold for 30b.

Songkran Day Type of 1991

Design: Demon on ox's back, zodiac.

1997-2002   Wmk. 340   Perf. 14x14½
1724 A425 2b multicolored   .40   .25
   Complete booklet, 5 #1724   3.50
a.   Souvenir sheet of 1   1.75   1.40
b.   Unwmkd., granite paper   .25   .25
   Issued: Nos. 1724, 1724a, 4/13/97; No. 1724b, 4/13/02. No. 1724b issued only in No. 2017b.
No. 1724a sold for 8b and exists imperf. Values same.

King Bhumibol Adulyadej Type of 1996
Litho, Litho & Engraved (#1728-1729)
Perf. 14x14½
1997, May 5   Wmk. 340
1725 A550 4b blue & red brown   1.25   .25
a.   Perf. 13¼, unwmkd.   1.00   .25
b.   Unwmkd., granite paper   1.00   .25
1726 A550 5b pur & org brn   1.25   .30
a.   Perf. 13½, unwmk. & granite paper   1.75   .30
b.   Unwmkd., granite paper   1.25   .25
1727 A550 7b pink & green   1.40   1.40

Wmk. 329
Perf. 13½x13
1728 A550 10b org & dk brn   2.25   .90
1729 A550 20b violet & maroon   3.75   1.75
   Nos. 1725-1729 (5)   9.90   4.60
   Issued: No. 1726a, 12/28/98; No. 1725a, 10/8/99. 1725b, 1726b, 12/1/00.

Waterfowl — A563

Designs: No. 1730, Pheasant-tailed jacana. No. 1731, Bronze-winged jacana. No. 1732, Painted stork. No. 1733, Black-winged stilt.

Perf. 11½x12
1997, May 15   Photo.   Unwmk.
Granite Paper
1730 A563 3b multicolored   .55   .55
1731 A563 3b multicolored   .55   .55
1732 A563 7b multicolored   1.25   1.25

1733	A563	7b multicolored	1.25	1.25
a.		Souvenir sheet, #1730-1733	5.50	5.50
b.		As "a," with added inscription	10.00	10.00
		Nos. 1730-1733 (4)	3.60	3.60

No. 1733a sold for 30b. No. 1733b has PACIFIC 97 emblem in sheet margin, while sales price has been removed from sheet margin. No. 1728b sold for 42b.

King Bhumibol Adulyadej, National Telecommunications — A564

2b, King using hand-held radio, "Suthee" aerial. 3b, King using hand-held radio for communication in local areas. 6b, King using computer. 9b, King, classroom using satellite information.

Perf. 14½x14
1997, June 9   Litho.   Wmk. 340

1734	A564	2b multicolored	.35	.35
		Complete booklet, 5 #1734	2.50	
1735	A564	3b multicolored	.50	.50
1736	A564	6b multicolored	1.00	1.00
1737	A564	9b multicolored	1.50	1.50
a.		Souvenir sheet, #1734-1737	6.00	6.00
		Nos. 1734-1737 (4)	3.35	3.35

No. 1737a sold for 30b. For surcharges, see Nos. 2407-2408, 2532, 2586.

Motion Pictures in Thailand, Cent. — A565

Designs: No. 1738, King Rama VII filming movie, film showing King Chulalongkorn's state visit to Europe. No. 1739, Early motion picture equipment, advertisement, Prince Sanbassatra, founder of Thai motion picures. No. 1740, Poster from "Double Luck," band playing in front of movie theater. No. 1741, Open air theater, poster from "Going Astray."

1997, June 10

1738	A565	3b multicolored	.55	.55
1739	A565	3b multicolored	.55	.55
1740	A565	7b multicolored	1.25	1.25
1741	A565	7b multicolored	1.25	1.25
		Nos. 1738-1741 (4)	3.60	3.60

Faculty of Medicine, Chulalongkorn University, 50th Anniv. — A566

King Rama VIII, building, operating room.

1997, June 11

1742	A566	2b multicolored	.45	.25
		Complete booklet, 5 #1742	2.50	

King Bhumibol Adulyadej Type of 1996
Perf. 14x14½
1997, July 19   Litho.   Wmk. 340

1743	A550	6b grn & gray vio	1.50	.30
1744	A550	9b dk bl & brn org	1.25	.40

Litho. & Engr.
Wmk. 329
Perf. 13½x13

1745	A550	100b lem & dk bl grn	15.00	4.75
		Nos. 1743-1745 (3)	17.75	5.45

Thai-Russian Diplomatic Relations, Cent. — A567

Design: Peterhof Palace, King Chulalongkorn (King Rama V).

1997, July 3   Litho.   Perf. 14½x14

1746	A567	2b multicolored	.35	.25
		Complete booklet, 5 #1746	3.00	

Asalhapuja Day — A568

3b, Mahosathajataka (scene with man on elephant). 4b, Bhuridattajataka (scene with two men, large snake). 6b, Candakumarajataka (scene with pot of fire, three men on knees, man in sky, Buddha). 7b, Naradajataka (scene with people praising human figure with four arms hovering above roof).

Perf. 11½ Syncopated
1997, July 19   Photo.   Unwmk.
Granite Paper

1747	A568	3b multicolored	.55	.55
a.		Souvenir sheet of 1	1.75	.90
b.		As "a," inscribed in margin	3.25	3.25
1748	A568	4b multicolored	.70	.70
a.		Souvenir sheet of 1	1.75	.90
b.		As "a," inscribed in margin	3.25	3.25
1749	A568	6b multicolored	1.10	1.10
a.		Souvenir sheet of 1	1.75	.90
b.		As "a," inscribed in margin	3.25	3.25
1750	A568	7b multicolored	1.25	1.25
a.		Souvenir sheet of 1	2.75	1.75
b.		Souvenir sheet, #1747-1750	6.00	4.50
c.		As "a," inscribed in margin	27.50	27.50
		Nos. 1747-1750 (4)	3.60	3.60

No. 1747a sold for 6b; No. 1748a for 8b; No. 1749a for 10b; No. 1750a for 12b; No. 1750b for 30b.

Sheet margins of lack value inscriptions, but contain Shanghai '97 exhibition emblem (#1747b, 1748b), Chinese insription (#1749b, 1750c); Bangkok '97 exhibition emblem (#1749b, 1750c).

No. 1750b exists imperf. It was issued for sale only at overseas stamp exhibitions.

For surcharges see Nos. 2380, 2382.

1997 Thailand Philatelic Exhibition — A569

Houses from: 2b, Northern region. 5b, Central region. 6b, Northeastern region. 9b, Southern region.

Wmk. 329
1997, Aug. 2   Litho.   Perf. 13½

1751	A569	2b multicolored	.30	.25
		Complete booklet, 5 #1751	1.75	
1752	A569	5b multicolored	.80	.70
1753	A569	6b multicolored	.90	.80
1754	A569	9b multicolored	1.40	1.25
a.		Souvenir sheet, #1751-1754	17.50	17.50
		Nos. 1751-1754 (4)	3.40	3.00

No. 1754a sold for 32b.
No. 1754a exists imperf, sold with an exhibition book. Value, $15.

Natl. Communications Day — A570

Perf. 14x14½
1997, Aug. 4   Wmk. 340

1755	A570	2b multicolored	.35	.25
		Complete booklet, 5 #1755	2.00	

Greeting Stamps — A570a

Lotus flowers: No. 1755A, Nymphaea capensis. No. 1755B, Nymphaea stellata.

Perf. 14x14½
1997, Aug. 4   Litho.   Wmk. 387
Booklet Stamps

1755A	A570a	(2b) multi	1.50	1.50
1755B	A570a	(2b) multi	1.50	1.50
c.		Bklt. pane, 5 ea #1755A-1755B + 4 labels	30.00	
		Complete bklt., #1755Bc	35.00	

Nos. 1755A-1755B were sold only at 7-11 stores, not at post offices or philatelic agencies.

King Bhumibol Adulyadej Type of 1996
Litho. & Engr.
Perf. 13½x13
1997, Aug. 8   Wmk. 329

1756	A550	25b bl grn & ol blk	8.00	3.25
1757	A550	200b lil rose & vio blk	17.50	9.00

ASEAN, 30th Anniv. — A571

Designs: No. 1758, Thi Lo Su Falls, Tak. No. 1759, Luang Chiang Dao Mountain, Chiang Mai. No. 1760, Phromthep Cape, Phuket. No. 1761, Thalu Island, Chumphon.

Perf. 14½x14
1997, Aug. 8   Wmk. 340

1758	A571	2b multicolored	.25	.25
		Complete booklet, 5 #1758	1.75	
1759	A571	2b multicolored	.25	.25
		Complete booklet, 5 #1759	1.75	
1760	A571	9b multicolored	1.25	1.25
1761	A571	9b multicolored	1.25	1.25
		Nos. 1758-1761 (4)	3.00	3.00

Dinosaurs — A572

Designs: 2b, Phuwiangosaurus sirindhornae. 3b, Siamotyrannus isanensis. 6b, Siamosaurus suteethorni. 9b, Psittacosaurus sattayaraki.

Perf. 13½x13 Syncopated
1997, Aug. 28   Photo.   Unwmk.

1762	A572	2b multicolored	.25	.25
		Complete booklet, 5 #1762	1.75	
1763	A572	3b multicolored	.35	.25
1764	A572	6b multicolored	.50	.35

1765	A572	9b multicolored	1.00	.60
a.		Souvenir sheet, #1762-1765	3.25	2.00
		Nos. 1762-1765 (4)	2.10	1.45

No. 1765a sold for 30b.
For surcharge see No. 2355.

King Chulalongkorn's Visit to Switzerland, Cent. — A573

Perf. 14x14½
1997, Sept. 12   Litho.   Wmk. 340

1766	A573	2b multicolored	.45	.25
		Complete booklet, 5 #1766	5.50	

Intl. Letter Writing Week — A574

Winning drawings: No. 1767, Tricycle, combining rickshaw and tricycle. No. 1768, Tricycle with side seat. No. 1769, Motor tricycle. No. 1770. Motor tricycle with light on roof.

Perf. 11½x12
1997, Oct. 5   Photo.   Unwmk.
Granite Paper

1767	A574	3b multicolored	.25	.25
1768	A574	3b multicolored	.25	.25
1769	A574	9b multicolored	.90	.50
1770	A574	9b multicolored	.90	.50
a.		Souvenir sheet, #1767-1770	2.50	2.00
		Nos. 1767-1770 (4)	2.30	1.50

No. 1770a sold for 30b.

Shells of Thailand and Singapore A575

Designs: No. 1771, Drupa morum. No. 1772, Nerita chamaelon. No. 1773, Littoraria melanostoma. No. 1774, Cryptospira elgans.

1997, Oct. 9   Litho.   Perf. 11½
Granite Paper

1771	A575	2b multicolored	.25	.25
		Complete booklet, 5 #1771	1.75	
1772	A575	2b multicolored	.25	.25
		Complete booklet, 5 #1772	1.75	
1773	A575	9b multicolored	.90	.45
1774	A575	9b multicolored	.90	.45
a.		Souvenir sheet, #1771-1774	2.50	2.50
		Nos. 1771-1774 (4)	2.30	1.40

No. 1774a sold for 30b. See Singapore Nos. 825-828A.

Chalerm Prakiat Energy Conserving Building — A576

Perf. 14½x14
1997, Nov. 10   Litho.   Wmk. 340

1775	A576	2b multicolored	.35	.25
		Complete booklet, 5 #1775	2.50	

Christening of Suphannahong Royal Barge, 86th Anniv. — A577

Perf. 11½

1997, Nov. 13   Photo.   Unwmk.
Granite Paper

1776 A577 9b multicolored   .80   .50
  a.   Souvenir sheet of 1   1.75   1.50
  b.   As "a", ovptd. in margin   4.50   3.00
  c.   As "a", ovptd. in margin   7.25   7.25

#1776a, 1776b, 1776c sold for 20b.
The sheet margin of #1776b is ovptd in gold with Thai and Chinese inscriptions for Bangkok/China 98. Issued 10/16/98.
No. 1776c overprinted in margin with World Stamp Expo 2000 emblem in gold. Issued 7/7/00.
For surcharge, see No. 2512.

New Year 1998 — A578

Flowers: No. 1777, Cassia alata. No. 1778, Strophanthus caudatus. No. 1779, Clinacanthus nutans. No. 1780, Acanthus ilicifolius.

1997, Nov. 15   Litho.   Perf. 13½x13
Granite Paper

1777 A578 2b multicolored   .25   .25
1778 A578 2b multicolored   .25   .25
1779 A578 2b multicolored   .25   .25
1780 A578 2b multicolored   .25   .25
  a.   Souvenir sheet, #1777-1780   1.50   .90
  b.   As "a", with added inscription   3.50   2.75
      Nos. 1777-1780 (4)   1.00   1.00

No. 1780a sold for 15b. No. 1780b contains Indepex '97 exhibition emblem, but no value inscription in sheet margin.

King Bhumibol Adulyadej's 70th Birthday — A579

#1781, Playing saxophone. #1782, Painting picture. #1783, Building sailboat. #1784, Wearing gold medal, sailboats. 6b, Taking photograph. 7b, Writing book. 9b, Working at computer.

1997, Dec. 5   Photo.   Perf. 11½
Granite Paper

1781 A579 2b multicolored   .25   .25
1782 A579 2b multicolored   .25   .25
1783 A579 2b multicolored   .25   .25
1784 A579 2b multicolored   .25   .25
1785 A579 6b multicolored   .45   .30
1786 A579 7b multicolored   .55   .40
1787 A579 9b multicolored   .75   .40
      Nos. 1781-1787 (7)   2.75   2.10

For surcharge see No. 2381.

A580

Winners in Yuvabadhana Foundation, "Sports Develop Mind and Body" drawing competition: No. 1788, Children in wheelchair race. No. 1789, Flying kites. No. 1790, Gymnastics. No. 1791, Windsurfing.

Perf. 14x14½

1998, Jan. 10   Litho.   Wmk. 340

1788 A580 2b multicolored   .25   .25
      Complete booklet, 5 #1788   3.25
1789 A580 2b multicolored   .25   .25
      Complete booklet, 5 #1789   3.25
1790 A580 2b multicolored   .25   .25
      Complete booklet, 5 #1790   3.25
1791 A580 2b multicolored   .25   .25
  a.   Complete booklet, 5 #1791   3.25
      Nos. 1788-1791 (4)   1.00   1.00

Natl. Childrens' Day.

A581

1998, Jan. 17   Unwmk.
Granite Paper

1792 A581 2b multicolored   .40   .25
      Complete booklet, 5 #1792   3.50

20th Asia Pacific Dental Congress.

A582

1998, Feb. 3   Wmk. 340

1793 A582 2b multicolored   .25   .25
      Complete booklet, 5 #1793   3.25

Veteran's Day, 50th anniv.

King Bhumibol Adulyadej Type of 1996

1998, Feb. 25   Photo.   Perf. 11½x12
Granite Paper

1794 A550 50s dk ol & lt ol   .35   .25

Litho. & Engr.
Perf. 13½x13
Wmk. 329

1795 A550 50b dp vio & dk grn   6.00   2.25

A583

Perf. 14x14½

1998, Mar. 27   Litho.   Wmk. 340

1796 A583 2b Queen Sirikit   .35   .25
      Complete booklet, 5 #1796   5.00

1998 Thai Red Cross Fair.

Heritage Conservation Day Type of 1993

Paintings of Phanomrung Historical Park: 3b, Main Tower. 4b, Minor Tower. 6b, Scripture Repository. 7b, Lintel depicting Vishnu sleeping in ocean, doorway of Main Tower.

Perf. 14½x14

1998, Apr. 2   Litho.   Wmk. 340

1797 A477 3b multicolored   .30   .25
1798 A477 4b multicolored   .35   .25
1799 A477 6b multicolored   .45   .45
1800 A477 7b multicolored   .55   .50
  a.   Souvenir sheet, #1797-1800   2.75   2.75

No. 1800a sold for 27b.

Songkran Day Type of 1991

Design: Demon on tiger's back, zodiac.

1998-2002   Perf. 14x14½

1801 A425 2b multicolored   .35   .25
      Complete booklet, 5 #1801   3.25
  a.   Souvenir sheet of 1   1.50   1.00
  b.   As "a", inscribed in margin   3.50   2.25
  c.   Unwmkd., granite paper   .25   .25

Issued: Nos. 1801-1801b, 4/13/98. No. 1801c, 4/13/02. No. 1801c issued only in No. 2017b.
No. 1801a sold for 8b and exists imperf. Values same.
Sheet margin of No. 1801b contains flags of Thailand and China (PRC), Thai and Chinese inscriptions, no value inscription, and exists imperf.
No. 1801b sold for 8b and was issued 10/16/98.

Wild Cats A584

Paintings: 2b, Felis viverrina. 4b, Panthera tigris. 6b, Panthera pardus. 8b, Felis chaus.

1998, Apr. 13   Perf. 14½x14

1802 A584 2b multicolored   .35   .25
      Complete booklet, 5 #1802   3.50
1803 A584 4b multicolored   .50   .25
1804 A584 6b multicolored   .50   .45
1805 A584 8b multicolored   .70   .50
  a.   Souvenir sheet, #1802-1805   2.75   2.25
      Nos. 1802-1805 (4)   2.05   1.45

No. 1805a sold for 30b.

AEROTHAI (Aeronautical Radio of Thailand, Ltd.), 50th Anniv. — A585

1998, Apr. 15

1806 A585 2b multicolored   .40   .25
      Complete booklet, 5 #1806   3.00

Visakhapuja Day — A586

Paintings of the "Ten Jataka Stories:" 3b, Riding horse above buildings, Vidhurajataka. 4b, In chariot, Vessantarajataka. 6b, Two figures seated before larger figure, Vessantarajataka. 7b, Figures in front of building, Vessantarajataka.

1998, May 10   Perf. 13½

1807 A586 3b multicolored   .25   .25
1808 A586 4b multicolored   .35   .25
1809 A586 6b multicolored   .55   .35
1810 A586 7b multicolored   .65   .45
  a.   Souvenir sheet, #1807-1810   2.50   1.75
      Nos. 1807-1810 (4)   1.80   1.30

No. 1810a sold for 30b.

Adm. Abhakara Kiartiwongse (1880-1923), Father of Royal Thai Navy — A587

1998, May 19   Perf. 14½x14

1811 A587 2b multicolored   .35   .25
      Complete booklet, 5 #1811   5.00

Educational Development — A588

Perf. 14½x14

1998, June 15   Litho.   Wmk. 340

1812 A588 2b multicolored   .25   .25
      Complete booklet, 5 #1812   4.00

King Chulalongkorn's 1st State Visit to Europe, Cent. — A589

Unwmk.

1998, July 1   Litho.   Perf. 13
Granite Paper

1813 A589 6b multicolored   .70   .45

Litho. & Embossed

1814 A589 20b multicolored   1.60   1.10

Intl. Year of the Ocean A590

2b, Orchaella brevirostris. 3b, Tursiops truncatus. 6b, Physeter catodon. 9b, Dugong dugon.

1998, July 19   Litho.   Perf. 14½x14
Granite Paper

1815 A590 2b multicolored   .35   .25
      Complete booklet, 5 #1815   2.75
1816 A590 3b multicolored   .35   .25
1817 A590 6b multicolored   .50   .40
1818 A590 9b multicolored   .80   .50
  a.   Souvenir sheet, #1815-1818   2.75   2.75
      Nos. 1815-1818 (4)   2.00   1.40

No. 1818a sold for 30b.
For surcharges see Nos. 2356-2357.

King Bhumibol Adulyadej Type of 1996

1998   Photo.   Unwmk.   Perf. 11½x12
Granite Paper

1819 A550 2b carmine   .50   .25
1820 A550 9b violet & brn org   1.25   .45

For surcharges, see Nos. 2335, 2585.

Irrigation Engineering in Thailand, 60th Anniv. — A591

Perf. 14½x14
1998, Aug. 1   Litho.   Unwmk.
Granite Paper
1821 A601 2b multicolored .40 .25
   Complete booklet, 5 #1821 3.00

Natl. Communications Day — A592

1998, Aug. 4   Granite Paper
1822 A592 2b multicolored .40 .25
   Complete booklet, 5 #1822 3.00

School of Political Science, Chulalongkorn University, 50th Anniv. — A593

1998, Aug. 19   Granite Paper
1823 A593 2b multicolored .40 .25
   Complete booklet, 5 #1823 3.00

Sukhothai Thammathirat Open University, Award for Excellence — A594

1998, Sept. 5   Litho.   Perf. 14½x14
Granite Paper
1824 A594 2b multicolored .40 .25
   Complete booklet, 5 #1824 3.00

Amazing Thailand, 1998-99, Thai Arts and Culture A595

1998, Sept. 15   Perf. 13½
Granite Paper
1825 A595 3b With bow & arrow .25 .25
1826 A595 3b Combat .25 .25
1827 A595 7b Seizing opponent .70 .50
1828 A595 7b Sky hovering .70 .50
   Nos. 1825-1828 (4) 1.90 1.50

Chinese Stone Statues — A596

Warriors holding: No. 1829, Staff with loop. No. 1830, Spear with slightly curved blade. No. 1831, Mace. No. 1832, Spear with jagged blade.

1998, Sept. 15   Perf. 14x14½
Granite Paper
1829 A596 2b multicolored .25 .25
   Complete booklet, 5 #1829 2.50
1830 A596 2b multicolored .25 .25
   Complete booklet, 5 #1830 3.25
1831 A596 10b multicolored .75 .50
1832 A596 10b multicolored .75 .50
   a. Souvenir sheet, #1829-1832, perf 13¼ 2.75 2.00
   b. As "a," with added marginal inscription 20.00 16.00
   Nos. 1829-1832 (4) 2.00 1.50

China 1999 World Philatelic Exhibition (#1832b). #1832a-1832b sold for 35b. #1832 is perf 13¼ and was issued 8/21/99.

Intl. Letter Writing Week — A597

Himavanta mythical animals created by ancient Thai artists: No. 1836, Kraisara Rajasiha, 3 king lions, white body, golden collars. No. 1837, Gajasiha, 2 tusked lions. No. 1838, Kesara Singha, 2 hoofed lions. No. 1839, Singha, 3 gray lions.

Perf. 11½
1998, Oct. 3   Photo.   Unwmk.
Granite Paper
1836 A597 2b multicolored .25 .25
   Complete booklet, 5 #1836 3.00
1837 A597 2b multicolored .25 .25
   Complete booklet, 5 #1837 3.25
1838 A597 12b multicolored .80 .60
1839 A597 12b multicolored .80 .60
   a. Souvenir sheet, #1836-1839 3.00 2.50
   Nos. 1000 1000 (4) £.10 1.70

No. 1839a sold for 40b.

Thai Presidency of the Intl. Assoc. of Lions Clubs — A598

1998, Oct. 8   Litho.   Perf. 14½x14
Granite Paper
1840 A598 2b multicolored .40 .25
   Complete booklet, 5 #1840 4.00

New Year 1999 — A599

Flowers: No. 1841, Barleria lupulina. No. 1842, Gloriosa superba. No. 1843, Asclepias curassavica. No. 1844, Sesamum indicum.

Perf. 14½x14
1998, Nov. 15   Photo.   Unwmk.
Granite Paper
1841 A599 2b multicolored .25 .25
1842 A599 2b multicolored .25 .25
1843 A599 2b multicolored .25 .25
1844 A599 2b multicolored .25 .25
   a. Souvenir sheet, #1841-1844 1.50 1.25
   Nos. 1841-1844 (4) 1.00 1.00

No. 1844a sold for 15b.

Knight Grand Cross, Most Admirable Order of the Direkgunabhorn — A600

Perf. 14x14½
1998, Dec. 5   Litho.   Unwmk.
Granite Paper
1845 15b shown 1.00 .45
1846 15b Decoration 1.00 .45
   a. A600 Pair, #1845-1846 2.50 .90

Children's Day — A601

Paintings from competition, "Sports develop body and mind:" No. 1847, Sepak Takraw (game of kicking ball over net). No. 1848, Swimming. No. 1849, Volleyball. No. 1850, Equestrian sports.

Perf. 14½x14
1999, Jan. 9   Litho.   Unwmk.
Granite Paper
1847 A601 2b multicolored .25 .25
   Complete booklet, 5 #1847 3.00
1848 A601 2b multicolored .25 .25
   Complete booklet, 5 #1848 3.00
1849 A601 2b multicolored .25 .25
   Complete booklet, 5 #1849 3.00
1850 A601 2b multicolored .25 .25
   Complete booklet, 5 #1850 3.00
   Nos. 1847-1850 (4) 1.00 1.00

Asian and Pacific Decade of Disabled Persons — A602

1999, Jan. 10   Granite Paper
1851 A602 2b multicolored .45 .25
   a. Complete booklet, 5 #1851 3.25

Thai Rice Production — A603

#1852, Planting rice. #1853, Harvesting rice by hand. #1854, Harvesting rice with machinery. #1855, Rice in field, bowl of rice.

1999, Feb. 25   Litho.   Perf. 14½x14
Granite Paper
1852 A603 6b multicolored .55 .40
1853 A603 6b multicolored .55 .40
1854 A603 12b multicolored .95 .75
1855 A603 12b multicolored .95 .75
   a. Souvenir sheet, #1852-1855 3.25 3.25
   Nos. 1852-1855 (4) 3.00 2.30

No. 1855a sold for 45b.

Maghapuja Day (Buddhist Holiday) — A604

Designs: 3b, Birth of Mahajanaka. 6b, Mani Mekkhala carrying Mahajanaka to Mithila City. 9b, Two mango trees. 15b, Mahajanaka founding an educational institution.

1999, Mar. 1   Litho.   Perf. 13½
Granite Paper
1856 A604 3b multicolored .30 .25
1857 A604 6b multicolored .60 .45
1858 A604 9b multicolored .80 .60
1859 A604 15b multicolored 1.25 1.00
   a. Souvenir sheet, #1856-1859 4.00 3.00
   Nos. 1856-1859 (4) 2.95 2.30

No. 1859a sold for 45b.

Somdetch Phra Sri Savarindira Baromma Raja Devi Phra Phan Vassa Ayika Chao, Queen Grandmother A605

Perf. 14x14½
1999, Mar. 30   Litho.   Wmk. 340
1860 A605 2b multicolored .35 .25
   Complete booklet, 5 #1860 5.00

1999 Red Cross Fair.

Bangkok 2000 World Youth Stamp Expo, 13th Asian Intl. Stamp Expo — A606

Thai children's games: No. 1861, Kite flying. No. 1862, Wheel rolling. No. 1863, Catching last one in line (children going under arms). No. 1864, Snatching baby from mother snake.

Perf. 14½x14
1999, Mar. 30   Unwmk.
Granite Paper
1861 A606 2b multicolored .35 .25
1862 A606 2b multicolored .35 .25
1863 A606 15b multicolored 1.10 1.00
1864 A606 15b multicolored 1.10 1.00
   a. Souvenir sheet, #1861-1864, perf. 13½ 3.50 3.00
   Nos. 1861-1864 (4) 2.90 2.50

No. 1864a sold for 45b.

Heritage Conservation Day — A607

Various Thai silk designs for "Mudmee" textiles.

1999, Apr. 2   Perf. 14x14½
Granite Paper
1865	A607	2b bl grn & multi	.25	.25
		Complete booklet, 5 #1865	3.00	
1866	A607	4b red & multi	.45	.25
1867	A607	12b vermilion & multi	1.00	.90
1868	A607	15b black & multi	1.40	1.10
a.		Souvenir sheet, #1865-1868	3.00	
		Nos. 1865-1868 (4)	3.10	2.50

No. 1868a sold for 45b.

Songkran Day Type of 1991
Design: Woman on rabbit's back, zodiac.

1999, Apr. 13   Granite Paper
1869	A425	2b multicolored	.35	.25
		Complete booklet, 5 #1869	3.25	
a.		Souvenir sheet of 1	1.40	1.40
b.		As "a," with added marginal inscription	5.00	5.00

China 1999 World Philatelic Exhibition (#1869b). #1869a-1869b sold for 8b and exist imperf. Values same.
Issued: #1869b, 8/21.

Consumer Protection Years, 1998-99 — A608

1999, Apr. 30   Perf. 14½x14
Granite Paper
1870	A608	2b multicolored	.35	.25
		Complete booklet, 5 #1870	3.50	

King Bhumibol Adulyadej's 72nd Birthday — A609

Royal palaces: No. 1871, Chitralada Villa, Dusit Palace, Bangkok, tree branch at UL. No. 1872, Phu Phing Ratchaniwet Palace, circular drive, white fence. No. 1873, Phu Phan Ratchaniwet Palace, adjoining buildings, light posts. No. 1874, Thaksin Ratchaniwet Palace, four trees reaching to second story windows.

1999, May 5   Photo.   Perf. 11½
Granite Paper
1871	A609	6b multicolored	.65	.45
1872	A609	6b multicolored	.65	.45
1873	A609	6b multicolored	.65	.45
1874	A609	6b multicolored	.65	.45
a.		Souvenir sheet, #1871-1874	3.75	3.00
		Nos. 1871-1874 (4)	2.60	1.80

No. 1874a sold for 40b.

Political Science Dept., Thammasat University, 50th Anniv. — A610

1999, June 14   Litho.   Perf. 14x14½
1875	A610	3b multicolored	.35	.25

King Bhumibol Adulyadej Type of 1996
Litho. & Engr.
1999		Wmk. 329		Perf. 13
1876	A550	12b bl grn & bl	1.25	.80
1877	A550	15b yel brn & grn	2.00	.45
1878	A550	30b pink & brown	2.90	.45

Size: 25x30mm
Perf. 12¾x13¼
1879	A550	500b org & claret	35.00	19.00
		Nos. 1876-1879 (4)	41.15	22.25

Issued: 12b, 15b, 30b, 7/1; 500b, 9/10.

UPU, 125th Anniv. A611

Designs: 2b, Floating Vessel of Light Festival. 15b, Buddhist Candle Festival, Ubon Ratchathani.

1999, July 1   Litho.   Perf. 14½x14
Granite Paper
1880	A611	2b multicolored	.35	.25
		Complete booklet, 5 #1880	2.90	
1881	A611	15b multicolored	1.10	1.00

Customs Dept., 125th Anniv. — A612

1999, July 3
1882	A612	6b multicolored	.60	.45

Natl. Communications Day — A613

1999, Aug. 4   Litho.   Perf. 14½x14
Granite Paper
1883	A613	4b multicolored	.35	.25

Thaipex '99 — A614

1999, Aug. 4   Granite Paper
Color of Rabbits
1884	A614	6b black & white	.55	.40
1885	A614	6b gldn brn, brn	.55	.40
1886	A614	12b white	.95	.70
1887	A614	12b gray	.95	.70
a.		Souvenir sheet, #1884-1887, perf. 13½	4.25	4.25
		Nos. 1884-1887 (4)	3.00	2.20

No. 1887a sold for 50b and exists imperf. Value, $15.

Bangkok 2000 Stamp Exhibition — A615

Scenes from Thai folk tales and literature: No. 1888, Boy on dragon-like horse. No. 1889, Rishi transforming tiger cub and calf into humans. No. 1890, Boy exiting conch shell. No. 1891, Children playing with kitchenware.

1999, Aug. 4   Perf. 14½x14
Granite Paper
1888	A615	2b multicolored	.35	.25
1889	A615	2b multicolored	.35	.25
1890	A615	15b multicolored	1.10	1.00
1891	A615	15b multicolored	1.10	1.00
a.		Souvenir sheet, #1888-1891, perf. 13½	3.75	3.00
		Nos. 1888-1891 (4)	2.90	2.50

No. 1891a sold for 45b.

King Bhumibol Adulyadej's 72nd Birthday A616

King: No. 1892, On father's knee. No. 1893, With mother, sister and brother. No. 1894, With brother, in suits. No. 1895, With brother, in military uniforms. No. 1896, With wife on wedding day. No. 1897, At coronation ceremony. No. 1898, As Buddhist monk. No. 1899, With Queen, Prince and Princesses. No. 1900, Wearing royal robe.

1999, Sept. 10   Photo.   Perf. 11¾
Granite Paper
1892	A616	3b multicolored	.35	.25
1893	A616	3b multicolored	.35	.25
1894	A616	3b multicolored	.35	.25
1895	A616	6b multicolored	.60	.35
1896	A616	6b multicolored	.60	.35
1897	A616	6b multicolored	.60	.35
1898	A616	12b multicolored	1.25	.80
1899	A616	12b multicolored	1.25	.80
1900	A616	12b multicolored	1.25	.80
a.		Souvenir sheet, #1892-1900	10.50	9.00
		Nos. 1892-1900 (9)	6.60	4.20

No. 1900a sold for 90b.

Intl. Year of Older Persons — A617

1999, Oct. 1   Litho.   Perf. 14½x14
Granite Paper
1901	A617	2b multi	.35	.25
		Complete booklet, 5 #1901	3.50	

Bauhinia Variegata — A618

Intl. Letter Writing Week: No. 1903, Bombax ceiba. No. 1904, Radermachera ignea (orange flowers). No. 1905, Bretschneidera sinensis (pink flowers).

1999, Oct. 2   Perf. 14x14½
Granite Paper
1902	A618	2b shown	.35	.25
		Complete booklet, 5 #1902	2.40	
1903	A618	2b multi	.35	.25
		Complete booklet, 5 #1903	3.25	
1904	A618	12b multi	1.10	.80
1905	A618	12b multi	1.10	.80
a.		Souvenir sheet, #1902-1905, perf. 13¼	3.50	2.75
		Nos. 1902-1905 (4)	2.90	2.10

No. 1905a sold for 35b.

King Bhumibol Adulyadej's 72nd Birthday — A619

King: #1906, And vehicle. #1907, And Buddhist monks. #1908, And Queen. #1909, And soldiers. #1910, And crowd. #1911, And disabled boy. #1912, Wearing green army uniform. #1913, In white suit with camera. #1914, With crowd waving flags.

1999, Oct. 21   Photo.   Perf. 14½
Granite Paper
1906	A619	3b multi	.25	.25
1907	A619	3b multi	.25	.25
1908	A619	3b multi	.25	.25
1909	A619	6b multi	.50	.35
1910	A619	6b multi	.50	.35
1911	A619	6b multi	.50	.35
1912	A619	12b multi	1.10	.80
1913	A619	12b multi	1.10	.80
1914	A619	12b multi	1.10	.80
a.		Souvenir sheet, #1906-1914	7.25	6.25
		Nos. 1906-1914 (9)	5.55	4.20

No. 1914a sold for 90b. Numbers have been reserved for additional stamps in this set.

Design A39 — A620

Litho. & Embossed with Foil Application
1999, Dec. 5		Wmk. 387		Perf. 13¼
1915	A620	100b blue & bronze	7.50	7.50
1916	A620	100b blue & silver	7.50	7.50
1917	A620	100b blue & gold	7.50	7.50
a.		Souvenir sheet, #1915-1917	25.00	20.00
		Nos. 1915-1917 (3)	22.50	22.50

King Bhumibol Adulyadej's 72nd birthday. No. 1917a sold for 350b.

New Year 2000 — A621

Medicinal plants: No. 1918, Thunbergia laurifolia. No. 1919, Gmelina arborea. No. 1920, Prunus cerasoides. No. 1921, Fagraea fragrans.

Perf. 14½x14¼
1999, Nov. 15				Litho.
Granite Paper
1918	A621	2b multi	.25	.25
1919	A621	2b multi	.25	.25
1920	A621	2b multi	.25	.25
a.		Souv. sheet, 5 ea #1918-1920 + 10 labels	30.00	
1921	A621	2b multi	.35	.25
a.		Souvenir sheet, #1918-1921	2.25	1.75
		Nos. 1918-1921 (4)	1.10	1.00

No. 1921a sold for 15b. No. 1920a was issued 3/25/00 and sold for 60b. For an additional fee the blank labels could be personalized with photos taken at a booth not operated by the Thailand postal authorities at the Bangkok 2000 Stamp Exhibition.

Investiture of Crown Prince Vajiralongkorn, 27th Anniv. — A622

1999, Dec. 28   *Perf. 14x14½*
Granite Paper
1922 A622 3b multi   .60 .25

Lake of Lilies, Thale Noi — A623

Kulap Khao Flowers, Doi Chang Dao — A624

Krachieo Flowers, Pa Hin Ngam — A625

Bua Tong Flowers, Doi Mae Ukor — A626

Perf. 14½x14¼

2000		**Litho.**		**Unwmk.**

Granite Paper

1923	A623	Sheet of 12, #a-l		
			8.00	5.50
a.-l.		3b Any single	.55	.35
1924	A624	Sheet of 12, #a-l		
			8.00	5.50
a.-l.		3b Any single	.55	.35
1925	A625	Sheet of 12, #a-l		
			8.00	5.50
a.-l.		3b Any single	.55	.35
1926	A626	Sheet of 12, #a-l		
			8.00	5.50
a.-l.		3b Any single	.55	.35
		Nos. 1923-1926 (4)	32.00	22.00

Issued: #1923, 1/1; #1924, 2/25; #1925, 7/16. #1926, 11/15.

Bees — A627

#1927, Apis andreniformis. #1928, Apis florea. #1929, Apis cerana. #1930, Apis dorsata.

2000, Mar. 19   **Photo.**   *Perf. 11¾*
Granite Paper
1927-1930 A627 3b Set of 4   1.75 1.40
Souvenir Sheets of 1
1927a-1930a   Set of 4   4.50 3.00

Nos. 1927a-1930a do not have white margin on stamps and sold for 8b each.

Bangkok 2000 Stamp Exhibition — A628

Ceremonies: #1931, 2b, 1st month blessing (family & baby). #1932, 2b, Tonsure. #1933, 15b, Teacher respect (teacher, 3 children). #1934, 15b, Novice ordination.

2000, Mar. 25   **Litho.**   *Perf. 14½x14*
Granite Paper
1931-1934 A628 Set of 4   4.00 3.25
1934a   Souvenir sheet, #1931-1934, perf. 13½x14   5.50 4.50

No. 1934a sold for 45b. No 1934a exists imperf. Value, $20.

Thai Red Cross Fair A629

2000, Mar. 30   *Perf. 14½x14*
Granite Paper
1935 A629 3b multi   .35 .35

Thai Heritage Conservation — A630

Chok cloths from: 3b, Hat Seio. 6b, Mae Chaem. 8b, Ban Rai. 12b, Khu Bua.

2000, Apr. 2   **Wmk. 387**   *Perf. 13¼*
1936-1939 A630 Set of 4   4.75 3.75
1939a   Souvenir sheet, #1936-1939   5.50 4.50

No. 1939a sold for 40b.

Songkran Day Type of 1991
Perf. 14x14½
2000, Apr. 13   **Litho.**   **Unwmk.**
Granite Paper
1940 A425 2b Angel on serpent   .35 .25
   Booklet, 5 #1940   3.75
a.   Souvenir sheet of 1   1.60 .75

No. 1940a sold for 8b and exists imperf.

50th Wedding Anniv. of King and Queen — A631

No. 1941 — King Bhumibol Adulyadej and Queen Sirikit: a, Sitting on grass. b, Standing. c, Sitting on thrones. d, With family. e, Standing, wearing regalia.

2000, Apr. 28   **Photo.**   *Perf. 11¾*
Granite Paper
1941   Vert. strip of 5   6.50 5.00
a.-e.   A631 10b Any single   1.25 1.00

Asalhapuja Day — A632

2000, July 16   **Litho.**   *Perf. 14x14½*
Granite Paper
1942 A632 3b multi   .65 .35

Crown Prince Maha Vajiralongkorn, 48th Birthday — A633

2000, July 28   *Perf. 14½x14*
Granite Paper
1943 A633 2b multi   .45 .25
   Booklet, 5 #1943   5.00
a.   Souvenir sheet of 1, perf. 13¼   1.60 .80

No. 1943a sold for 8b.

Natl. Communications Day — A634

2000, Aug. 4   **Granite Paper**
1944 A634 3b multi   .35 .25

A635

Intl. Letter Writing Week — A636

Various tea sets.

Perf. 14½x14
2000, Oct. 7   **Litho.**   **Unwmk.**
Granite Paper

1945	A635	6b shown	.65	.55
1946	A635	6b multi, diff.	.65	.55
1947	A636	12b shown	1.25	1.10
1948	A636	12b multi, diff.	1.25	1.10
a.		Souvenir sheet, #1945-1948, perf. 13¼	5.00	4.50
		Nos. 1945-1948 (4)	3.80	3.30

No. 1948a sold for 45b.

Princess Srinagarindra, Birth Cent. — A637

2000, Oct. 21   **Granite Paper**
1949 A637 2b multi   .45 .25
   Booklet, 5 #1949   3.75
a.   Souvenir sheet of 1, perf. 13¼   1.60 .80

No. 1949a sold for 8b.

Royal Barge Anantanakkharat — A638

Perf. 13¼x14
2000, Nov. 15   **Photo.**   **Wmk. 340**
1950 A638 9b multi   1.00 .75
a.   Souvenir sheet of 1   2.25 1.60

No. 1950a sold for 15b.

New Year 2001 — A639

Flowers: No. 1951, 2b, Clerodendrum philippinum. No. 1952, 2b, Capparis micracantha. No. 1953, 2b, Belamcanda chinensis. No. 1954, 2b, Memecylon caeruleum.

Perf. 14½x14¼
2000, Nov. 15   **Litho.**   **Unwmk.**
Granite Paper
1951-1954 A639 Set of 4   1.25 .85
1954a   Souvenir sheet, #1951-1954   2.25 1.00

No. 1954a sold for 15b.

Parrots — A640

Designs: 2b, Psittacula alexandri. 5b, Psittacula eupatria. 8b, Psittinus cyanurus. 10b, Psittacula roseata.

2001, Jan. 13   *Perf. 14x14½*
Granite Paper
1955-1958 A640 Set of 4   3.50 2.25
   Booklet, 5 #1955   3.75
a.   Souvenir sheet, #1955-1958, perf. 13¼   4.50 3.25
b.   As "a," without price and with show emblem in margin   20.00 15.00

No. 1955a sold for 35b. No. 1955b, Hong Kong 2001 Stamp Exhibition, sold for 50b.

King Chulalongkorn and Land Deed — A641

2001, Feb. 17   **Granite Paper**
1959 A641 5b multi   .55 .45

Dept. of Lands, cent.

Marine Life — A642

Designs: a, Ray. b, Turtle. c, Jellyfish, fish. d, Lionfish. e, Black, yellow fish, coral. f, Eel. g, School of striped fish, angelfish, coral, vert. h, Pufferfish, blue fish, vert. i, Shark, fish.
Stamp sizes: Nos. 1960a-1960f, 29x24mm, Nos. 1960g-1960h, 29x48mm. No. 1960i, 58x42mm.

Perf. 13¾x14¼
2001, Mar. 15   **Photo.**
Granite Paper

1960	A642	Sheet of 9	6.50	5.50
a.-f.		3b Any single	.55	.35
g.-i.		6b Any single	.75	.55

For surcharge, see No. 2511.

Gems A643

Designs: 3b, Diamond. 4b, Green sapphire. 6b, Pearl. 12b, Blue sapphire.

2001   **Litho.**   **Perf. 14½x14**
Granite Paper

1961-1964	A643	Set of 4	2.25	2.25
a.		Souvenir sheet, #1961-1964, perf. 13½x14	4.50	3.25
b.		As "a," ovptd. in margin in gold	13.00	11.00

Issued, Nos. 1961-1964a, 3/30; No. 1964b, 6/9.
No. 1964a sold for 35b.
No. 1964b has Belgica 2001 emblem overprint.

Red Cross A644

Perf. 14½x14
2001, Apr. 1   **Litho.**   **Unwmk.**
Granite Paper

1965	A644	4b multi		.60	.25

Ancient Brocades From Nakhon Si Thammarat National Museum — A645

Colors of brocade: 2b, Orange red, lilac, and gold. 3b, Green and gold. No. 1968, 10b, Orange and gold. No. 1969, 10b, Bright pink and gold.

2001, Apr. 2   **Perf. 14x14½**
Granite Paper

1966-1969	A645	Set of 4	3.00	2.25
		Booklet, 5 #1966	3.00	
a.		Souvenir sheet, #1966-1969, perf. 13¼	4.50	3.25

Heritage Conservation Day.
No. 1969a sold for 35b.

Songkran Day Type of 1991
2b, Man on snake, zodiac.

Perf. 13½x13¾
2001-2002   **Wmk. 387**

1970	A425	2b multicolored	.60	.25
		Booklet, 5 #1970	3.75	
a.		Souvenir sheet of 1	1.60	1.10
b.		Unwmkd., granite paper, perf. 14x14½	3.00	3.00

Issued: Nos. 1970-1970a, 4/13/01. No. 1970b, 4/13/02. No. 1970b issued only in No. 2017b.
No. 1970a sold for 8b and exists imperf.

Visakhapuja Day — A646

2001, May 7   **Unwmk.**   **Perf. 14x14½**
Granite Paper

1971	A646	3b multi		.55	.35

Demon Statues — A647

Designs: 2b, Maiyarap. 5b, Wirunchambang. 10b, Thotsakan. 12b, Sahatsadecha.

Perf. 14x14½
2001, June 13   **Litho.**   **Unwmk.**
Granite Paper

1972-1975	A647	Set of 4	3.50	2.60
		Booklet, 5 #1972	4.00	
1975a		Souvenir sheet, #1972-1975, perf. 13½	4.50	3.25

No. 1975a sold for 33b.

Prince Purachartra Jayakara and Rotary Intl. Emblem — A648

2001, July 1   **Granite Paper**

1976	A648	3b multi		.50	.25

Rotary Intl. in Thailand, 66th anniv.

Mushrooms — A649

Designs: 2b, Schizophyllum commune. 3b, Lentinus giganteus. 5b, Pleurotus citrinopileatus. 10b, Pleurotus flabellatus.

2001, July 4   **Photo.**   **Perf. 13¾x14**
Granite Paper

1977-1980	A649	Set of 4	2.75	2.00
		Booklet, 5 # 1977	3.75	
1980a		Souvenir sheet, #1977-1980, perf. 13½	4.50	3.25

No. 1980 sold for 26b.

Insects A650

Designs: 2b, Cheirotonus parryi. 5b, Mouhotia batesi. 6b, Cladognathus giraffa. 12b, Mormolyce phyllodes.

2001, July 4   **Wmk. 329**   **Perf. 13½**

1981-1984	A650	Set of 4	2.90	2.25
		Booklet, 5 #1981	3.75	
a.		Souvenir sheet, #1981-1984	5.50	4.50
b.		As "a," with Phila Nippon '01 emblem in margin	13.00	12.00

No. 1984a sold for 34b.
No. 1984b sold for 34b, and was issued 8/1.

Natl. Communications Day — A651

Perf. 14½x14
2001, Aug. 4   **Litho.**   **Unwmk.**
Granite Paper

1985	A651	4b multi		.50	.45

Thaipex '01 — A652

Various domesticated fowl: 3b, 4b, 6b, 12b.

2001, Aug. 4   **Photo.**   **Perf. 13¼**
Granite Paper

1986-1989	A652	Set of 4	3.00	2.25
1989a		Souvenir sheet, #1986-1989	4.50	3.25

No. 1989a sold for 33b. No. 1989a also exists imperf. Value, $17.50.

Queen Suriyothai, Heroine of Thailand — A653

2001, Aug. 12   **Litho.**   **Perf. 14x14¾**
Granite Paper

1990	A653	3b multi		.55	.45
a.		Souvenir sheet of 1, perf. 13¼	2.75	1.25

No. 1990a sold for 10b.

Queen Sirikit's Visit to the People's Republic of China — A654

2001, Aug. 12   **Perf. 14¾x14**
Granite Paper

1991	A654	5b multi		.75	.45

Butterflies — A655

Designs: 2b, Pachliopta aristolochiae goniopeltis. 4b, Rhinopalpa polynice. 10b, Poritia erycinoides. 12b, Spindasis lohita.

Perf. 13½ Syncopated
2001, Sept. 10   **Photo.**

1992-1995	A655	Set of 4	4.00	2.75
		Booklet, 5 #1992	3.00	
1995a		Souvenir sheet, #1992-1995	5.50	4.50
1995b		As "a," with Hafnia '01 emblem in margin	16.00	16.00

No. 1995a sold for 40b.
No. 1995b issued 11/16. No. 1995b sold for 43b.

Intl. Letter Writing Week — A656

Medicinal herbs: 2b, Piper nigrum. 3b, Solanum trilobatum. 5b, Boesenbergia rotunda. 10b, Ocimum tenuiflorum.

Perf. 14x14½
2001, Oct. 6   **Litho.**   **Unwmk.**
Granite Paper

1996-1999	A656	Set of 4	2.75	1.90
		Booklet, 5 #1996	3.75	
1999a		Souvenir sheet, #1996-1999, perf. 13½x13¼	3.75	3.25

No. 1999a sold for 25b.

Police Cadet Academy, Cent. — A657

2001, Oct. 13   **Litho.**   **Perf. 14½x14**
Granite Paper

2000	A657	5b multi		.75	.55

Royal Barge Anekkachat Puchong — A658

2001, Nov. 15   **Photo.**   **Perf. 14¼**
Granite Paper

2001	A658	9b multi		1.00	.90
a.		Souvenir sheet of 1	3.25	2.25

No. 2001a sold for 17b.

New Year 2002 — A659

Flowers: No. 2002, 2b, Pedicularis siamensis. No. 2003, 2b, Schoutenia glomerata. No. 2004, 2b, Gentiana crassa. No. 2005, 2b, Colquhounia coccinea.

2001, Nov. 15 Litho. *Perf. 14x14½*
Granite Paper

2002-2005	A659	Set of 4	1.10	1.00
2005a		Souvenir sheet, #2002-2005	2.25	1.75

No. 2005a sold for 11b.

Laying of Foundation Stone for Suvarnabhumi Airport Passenger Terminal — A660

2002, Jan. 19 Litho. *Perf. 14½x14*
Granite Paper

2006	A660	3b multi	.50	.35

Rose — A661

2002, Feb. 1 *Perf. 13¾*
Granite Paper

2007	A661	4b multi	3.75	1.50

12th World Congress of Gastroenterology A662

2002, Feb. 24 *Perf. 14x14½*
Granite Paper

2008	A662	3b multi	.50	.30

Communications Authority of Thailand, 25th Anniv. — A663

No. 2009: a, Satellite dish, CAT Telecom Co. emblem. b, Envelope, mailbox, Thailand Post emblem.

2002, Feb. 25 *Perf. 14½x14*
Granite Paper

2009	A663	3b Horiz. pair, #a-b	1.10	.75
c.		Souvenir sheet, #2009, perf. 13¼x13½	1.60	1.10

No. 2009c sold for 10b.

Maghapuja Day — A664

2002, Feb. 26 *Perf. 14½x14*
Granite Paper

2010	A664	3b multi	1.60	1.10

2002 Red Cross Fair A665

2002, Mar. 30 Granite Paper

2011	A665	4b multi	.50	.40

Ministry of Transport and Communications, 90th Anniv. — A666

2002, Apr. 1 Litho. *Perf. 14½x14*
Granite Paper

2012	A666	3b multi	.50	.30

Heritage Conservation Day — A667

String puppets: No. 2013, 3b, Man. No. 2014, 3b, Woman. 4d, Demon. 15b, Monkey.

2002, Apr. 2 *Perf. 14x14½*
Granite Paper

2013-2016	A667	Set of 4	2.50	2.50
2016a		Souvenir sheet, #2013-2016, perf. 13¼	4.50	3.50

No. 2016a sold for 30b.

Songkran Day Type of 1991

Design: Angel on horse, zodiac.

2002, Apr. 13 *Perf. 14x14½*
Granite Paper

2017	A425	2b multicolored	.60	.25
a.		Souvenir sheet of 1	2.00	2.00
b.		Souvenir sheet, #1724b, 1801c, 1869, 1940, 1970b, 2017	3.00	3.00
c.		As "b," with Beijing 2002 emblem in margin and selling price removed	17.50	17.50

Nos. 2017a and 2017b sold for 8b and 14b respectively. Both exist imperf.
Issued: No. 2017c, 9/29. No. 2017c sold for 30b.

Fighting Fish A668

Designs: No. 2018, 3b, Betta imbellis. No. 2019, 3b, Betta splendens. 4b, Betta splendens, diff. 15b, Betta splendens, diff.

2002, May 15 Litho. *Perf. 14½x14*
Granite Paper

2018-2021	A668	Set of 4	3.00	2.50
2021a		Souvenir sheet, #2018-2021, perf. 13½	4.50	4.00
2021b		As "a," with Amphilex 2002 emblem and selling price removed	15.00	15.00

Issued: No. 2021b, 8/30. No. 2021a sold for 30b; No. 2021b sold for 31b.

Temples — A669

Designs: No. 2022, 3b, Wat Phra Si Rattanasatsadaram. No. 2023, 3b, Wat Phra Chetuphon Wimon Mangkhalaram. 4b, Wat Arun Ratchawararam. 12b, Wat Benchamabophit Dusit Wanaram.

2002, June 17 *Perf. 14½x14*
Granite Paper

2022-2025	A669	Set of 4	3.00	2.25
2025a		Souvenir sheet, #2022-2025, perf. 13½	3.25	2.75
2025b		As "a," with Philakorea 2002 emblem and selling price removed	15.00	15.00

Issued: No. 2025b, 8/2. Nos. 2025a and 2025b each sold for 27b.

Crown Prince Maha Vajiralongkorn, 50th Birthday — A670

2002, July 28 *Perf. 14x14½*
Granite Paper

2026	A670	3b multi	.55	.30

Natl. Communications Day — A671

2002, Aug. 4 Granite Paper

2027	A671	4b multi	.50	.40

Thailand — Australia Diplomatic Relations, 50th Anniv. — A672

Designs: No. 2028, 3b, Nelumbo nucifera (pink flower). No. 2029, 3b, Nymphaea immutabilis (purple flower).

2002, Aug. 6 *Perf. 14½x14*
Granite Paper

2028-2029	A672	Set of 2	1.10	.75
2029a		Souvenir sheet, #2028-2029, perf. 13½	1.60	1.50

See Australia Nos. 2072-2073. No. 2029a sold for 9b.

Queen Sirikit, 70th Birthday — A673

Designs: No. 2030, 3b, Queen and roses. No. 2031, 3b, Queen Sirikit rose. 4b, Queen Sirikit orchid. 15b, Queen Sirikit dona shrub.

2002, Aug. 12 *Perf. 14½x14*
Granite Paper

2030-2033	A673	Set of 4	2.25	2.25
2033a		Souvenir sheet, #2030-2033, perf. 13½	3.75	3.50

No. 2033a sold for 31b.

National Archives, 50th Anniv. — A674

2002, Aug. 18 *Perf. 14½x14*

2034	A674	3b multi	.50	.30

Thai Bank Notes, Cent. A675

2002, Sept. 7 Engr. *Perf. 13½*
Granite Paper

2035	A675	5b org & brown	.75	.50
a.		Souvenir sheet of 1	3.75	3.25

No. 2035a sold for 11b.

Vimanmek Mansion Art Objects — A676

Designs: No. 2036, 3b, Round, lidded betel nut box. No. 2037, 3b, Bowl. 4b, Bowl, diff. 12b, Rectangular betel nut box.

2002, Sept. 7 Litho. *Perf. 14½x14*
Granite Paper

2036-2039	A676	Set of 4	2.75	2.00
2039a		Souvenir sheet, #2036-2039, perf. 13½	3.25	3.25

No. 2039a sold for 26b.

Royal Palaces A677

Designs: No. 2040, 4b, Thailand. No. 2041, 4b, Sweden.

Perf. 12½x13½ Syncopated

2002, Oct. 5 Litho. & Engr.

2040-2041	A677	Set of 2	1.10	.75

See Sweden No. 2445.

Intl. Letter Writing Day A678

Designs: No. 2042, 3b, Animal-shaped coconut grater. No. 2043, 3b, Strainer. 4b, Coconut shell ladle. 15b, Earthenware stove and pot.

2002, Oct. 5 Litho. *Perf. 14½x14*
Granite Paper

2042-2045	A678	Set of 4	2.25	2.00
2045a		Souvenir sheet, #2042-2045, perf. 13½	4.50	3.25

No. 2045a sold for 31b.

Bangkok 2003 World Philatelic Exhibition — A679

Foods from: No. 2046, 3b, Central Thailand (red tablecloth). No. 2047, 3b, Southern Thailand (brown and yellow tablecloth). 4b, Northeastern Thailand. 15b, Northern Thailand.

2002, Oct. 5   *Perf. 14½x14*
2046-2049	A679	Set of 4	2.90 2.25
2049a		Souvenir sheet, #2046-2049, perf. 13½	4.50 3.50

No. 2049a sold for 30b.

New Year 2003 — A680

Flowers: No. 2050, 3b, Guaiacum officinale. No. 2051, 3b, Nyctanthes arbor-tristis. No. 2052, 3b, Barleria cristata. No. 2053, 3b, Thevetia peruviana.

Perf. 14½x14¼
2002, Nov. 15   **Litho.**
Granite Paper
2050-2053	A680	Set of 4	1.50 1.10
2053a		Souvenir sheet, #2050-2053	2.75 2.25

No. 2053a sold for 16b.

20th World Scout Jamboree — A681

Designs: 3b, Scouts. 12b, Jamboree site.

2002, Dec. 28   *Perf. 14½x14*
Granite Paper
2054-2055	A681	Set of 2	1.90 1.25

New Year 2003 (Year of the Goat) — A682

2003, Jan. 1   *Perf. 13*
Granite Paper
2056	A682	3b multi	.50 .25

See Nos. 2108, 2161, 2341a.

National Children's Day — A683

Pangpond and his: a, Dog, Big (blue background). b, Friend, Hanuman (orange background). c, Girlfriend, Namo (green background). d, Teacher (red background).

2003, Jan. 11   *Perf. 14½x14*
Granite Paper
2057	A683	3b Block of 4, #a-d	1.25 1.00

Rose — A684

2003, Feb. 1   *Perf. 13*
Granite Paper
2058	A684	4b multi	.75 .30

No. 2058 is impregnated with rose scent. Compare with Type A716.

Blue Green, by Fua Haribhitak A685

Portrait of Chira Chongkon, by Chamras Kietkong A686

Moonlight, by Prasong Padmanuja A687

Lotus Flowers, by Thawee Nandakwang — A688

2003, Feb. 24   *Perf. 13¼*
Granite Paper
2059	A685	3b multi	.35 .25
2060	A686	3b multi	.35 .25
2061	A687	3b multi	.35 .25
2062	A688	15b multi	1.40 1.25
		Nos. 2059-2062 (4)	2.45 2.00

Bangkok 2003 World Philatelic Exhibition — A689

Tourist attractions: No. 2063, 3b, Doi Inthanon Temple, Chiang Mai. No. 2064, 3b, River Kwai Bridge, Kanchanaburi. No. 2065, 3b, Phu Kradung (cliff), Loei. 15b, Maya Bay, Krabi.

2003, Mar. 3   *Perf. 14½x14*
Granite Paper
2063-2066	A689	Set of 4	2.60 2.10
2066a		Souvenir sheet, #2063-2066, perf. 13¼	4.50 3.25

No. 2066a sold for 29b.

King Bhumibol Adulyadej Type of 1996
Perf. 14x14½
2003, Mar. 14   **Litho.**   **Unwmk.**
Granite Paper
2067	A550	1b blue	.45 .25

2003 Red Cross Fair — A690

2003, Mar. 28   *Perf. 14x14½*
Granite Paper
2068	A690	3b multi	.50 .30

Kick Boxing — A691

Designs: No. 2069, 3b, Boxers punching. No. 2070, 3b, Boxer in black trunks with knee raised. No. 2071, 3b, Boxer in red trunks kicking. 15b, Boxer in red trunks kicking, diff.

2003, Apr. 2   **Litho.**   *Perf. 13¼*
Granite Paper
2069-2072	A691	Set of 4	3.00 2.10
2072a		Souvenir sheet, #2069-2072	4.50 3.50
2072b		As "a," with China 2003 Philatelic Exhibition emblem in margin	13.00 11.00

No. 2072a sold for 29b.
Issued: No. 2072b, 11/20. No. 2072b sold for 29b.

Princess Maha Chakri Sirindhorn, 48th Birthday — A692

2003, Apr. 2   *Perf. 14x14½*
Granite Paper
2073	A692	3b multi	.50 .25

Princess Galyani Vadhana, 80th Birthday — A693

2003, May 6   **Granite Paper**
2074	A693	3b multi	1.00 .50

Kings Chulalongkorn and Vajiravudh A694

2003, May 6   **Granite Paper**
2075	A694	3b multi	.55 .30

Inspector General Dept., cent.

King Prajadhipok Day — A695

2003, May 30   *Perf. 14½x14*
Granite Paper
2076	A695	3b multi	.55 .30

Bantam Chickens — A696

Designs: No. 2077, 3b, White ears jungle fowl. No. 2078, 3b, Sugarcane husk colored. No. 2079, 3b, Black-tailed white. 15b, Dark gray.

2003   **Litho.**   *Perf. 13*
Granite Paper
2077-2080	A696	Set of 4	3.00 2.10
2080a		Souvenir sheet, #2077-2080	4.50 3.25
2080b		As "a," with Lanka Philex 2003 emblem in margin	20.00 16.00

Issued: Nos. 2077-2080, 2080a, 6/10; No. 2080b, 7/31. Nos. 2080a and 2080b each sold for 29b.

Asalhapuja Day — A697

2003, July 13   *Perf. 14x14½*
Granite Paper
2081	A697	3b multi	1.40 .40

National Communications Day — A698

2003, Aug. 4   *Perf. 14½x14*
Granite Paper
2082	A698	3b multi	.50 .25

Communications Organization
Emblems — A699

No. 2083: a, Thailand Post Company Limited. b, Communications Authority of Thailand (23x27mm). c, CAT Telecom Public Company Limited.

Perf. 14¼x14½
2003, Aug. 14   Litho.   Wmk. 340
2083 A699 3b Horiz. strip of 3,
#a-c   1.25   .90

King
Chulalongkorn
(1853-1910)
A700

Litho. & Embossed
2003, Sept. 20   Unwmk.   Perf. 13¼
2084 A700 100b gold & multi   8.25   6.50
a.   Souvenir sheet of 4   35.00 35.00

No. 2084a issued 9/30.
No. 2084a exists imperf. with Bangkok 2003 emblem at lower left. Value, $50.

Government Housing Bank, 50th
Anniv. — A701

2003, Sept. 24   Litho.   Perf. 14½x14
Granite Paper
2085 A701 3b multi   .50   .25

Bangkok 2003 World Philatelic
Exhibition — A702

Handicrafts: No. 2086, 3b, Basketry. No. 2087, 3b, Pottery. No. 2088, 3b, Leatherwork. 15b, Wood carving.

2003, Oct. 4   Granite Paper
2086-2089 A702   Set of 4   2.60   2.10
2089a   Souvenir sheet, #2086-
        2089, perf. 13¼   3.75   3.25

A varnish with a rough surface was applied to portions of the designs.
No. 2089a sold for 29b. No 2089a exists imperf. Value, $16.

Trees of Thailand and Canada — A703

No. 2090: a, Cassia fistula (Thailand). b, Maple leaves (Canada).

2003, Oct. 4   Perf. 14x14½
Granite Paper
2090 A703 3b Horiz. pair, #a-b   1.25   1.10
c.   Souvenir sheet, #2090, perf.
     13¼   2.50   2.50

No. 2090c sold for 9b.

Lychees — A704

Rose
Apples — A705

Fruit: No. 2093, Coconuts. 15b, Jackfruit.

2003, Oct. 4   Granite Paper
2091 A704 3b shown   .45   .25
2092 A705 3b shown   .45   .25
2093 A704 3b multi   .45   .25
2094 A704 15b multi   1.60   1.25
a.   Souvenir sheet, #2091-2094,
     perf. 13¼   4.50   3.25
Nos. 2091-2094 (4)   2.95   2.00

International Letter Writing Week. No. 2094a sold for 29b.

Oct. 14, 1973 Student Uprisings, 30th
Anniv. — A706

2003, Oct. 14   Perf. 14½x14
Granite Paper
2095 A706 3b multi   .50   .25

Asia-Pacific Economic Cooperation
Meeting — A707

2003, Oct. 20   Granite Paper
2096 A707 3b multi   .50   .25

New Year
2004 — A708

Flowers: No. 2097, 3b, Bougainvillea spectabilis. No. 2098, 3b, Eucrosia bicolor. No. 2099, 3b, Canna x generalis. No. 2100, 3b, Zinnia violacea.

2003, Nov. 15   Perf. 14½x14¼
Granite Paper
2097-2100 A708   Set of 4   1.25   1.10
2100a   Souvenir sheet, #2097-
        2100   2.25   1.75
2100b   As "a," with 2004 Hong
        Kong Stamp Expo em-
        blem in margin   7.00   6.50

No. 2100a sold for 16b.

Issued: No. 2100b, 1/30/04. No. 2100b sold for 16b.

Thailand Flag
A709

Thai Pavilion
A710

Elephants
A711

Cassia Fistula
A712

2003, Dec. 1   Perf. 14¼x14½
Granite Paper
2101 A709 3b multi   .45   .25
2102 A710 3b multi   .45   .25
2103 A711 3b multi   .45   .25
2104 A712 3b multi   .45   .25
Nos. 2101-2104 (4)   1.80   1.00
Compare with types A865a-A865d.

Elephants — A713

No. 2105: a, Asian elephant. b, African elephants.

2003, Dec. 9   Perf. 14½x14
Granite Paper
2105 A713 3b Horiz. pair, #a-b   1.00   .75
c.   Souvenir sheet, #2105a, perf.
     13¼   2.75   2.25

No. 2105c sold for 9b.
Thailand-South Africa diplomatic relations, 10th anniv. See South Africa No. 1330.

King Bhumibol Adulyadej Type of 1996
2003, Dec. 3   Litho.   Perf. 14x14½
Granite Paper
2106 A550 50s olive brown   .75   .25
2107 A550 1b blue   .75   .25

Issued: 50s, 12/3, 1b, 1/22/04.

Zodiac Animal Type of 2003
2004, Jan. 1   Litho.   Perf. 13
Granite Paper
2108 A682 3b Monkey   .50   .25

See No. 2341b.

Children's Day — A714

2004, Jan. 10   Perf. 14½x14
Granite Paper
2109 A714 3b multi   .50   .25

Paintings of
Hem Vejakorn
A715

Designs: No. 2110, 3b, A Scene in Thai History (dancers). No. 2111, 3b, Maha Bharatayudh (charioteer). No. 2112, 3b, Khun Chang — Khun Phaen (women with horse). No. 2113, 3b, Phra Lor (woman and rooster).

2004, Jan. 17   Perf. 13¼
Granite Paper
2110-2113 A715   Set of 4   1.40   1.10
2113a   Souvenir sheet, #2110-
        2113   3.25   2.25

No. 2113a sold for 16b.

Rose — A716

2004, Feb. 1   Perf. 13
Granite Paper
2114 A716 4b multi   .65   .30
Compare with type A684. No. 2114 is impregnated with rose scent.

Turtles — A717

Designs: No. 2115, 3b, Cuora amboinensis. No. 2116, 3b, Platysternon megacephalum. No. 2117, 3b, Indotestudo elongata. No. 2118, 3b, Heosemys spinosa.

2004, Mar. 1   Perf. 14½x14
Granite Paper
2115-2118 A717   Set of 4   1.75   1.25
2118a   Souvenir sheet, #2115-
        2118, perf. 13¼   3.25   3.00
2118b   Similar to "a," with 2004
        Singapore World Stamp
        Championship emblem in
        margin   8.75   7.50

Issued: No. 2118b, 8/28.
Nos. 2118a and 2118b sold for 16b.

Siam Society, Cent. — A718

2004, Mar. 10   Perf. 14½x14
2119 A718 3b multi   .50   .25

2004 Red Cross
Fair — A719

2004, Mar. 29   **Perf. 14x14½**
Granite Paper
2120 A719 3b multi   .50   .25

Heritage
Conservation
Day — A720

Fringe colors of hand woven clothes: No.
2121, 3b, Rose red. No. 2122, 3b, Blue. No.
2123, 3b, Green. No. 2124, 3b, Orange red.
Denomination is at LL on Nos. 2122, 2124.

2004, Apr. 2   **Litho.**   **Perf. 14x14½**
Granite Paper
2121-2124 A720   Set of 4   1.60 1.25
2124a   Souvenir sheet, #2121-
     2124, perf. 13¼   3.25 2.75
2124b   As "a," with España 2004
     emblem in margin, perf.
     13¼   10.00 9.00
    Issued: No. 2124b, 5/22. No. 2124a sold for
16b; No. 2124b for 18b.

Architecture in Thailand and
Italy — A721

No. 2125: a, Golden Mountain Temple,
Bangkok. b, Colosseum, Rome.

2004, Apr. 21   **Perf. 14½x14**
Granite Paper
2125 A721 3b Horiz. pair, #a-b   2.75 2.50
2125c   Souvenir sheet, #2125,
     perf. 13¼   24.00 20.00
    No. 2125c sold for 10b.
    See Italy No. 2602.

Sculpture
A722

Designs: No. 2126, 3b, One-sided Drum, by
Chit Rienpracha (yellow green background).
No. 2127, 3b, Dance Drama, by Sitthidet
Saenghiran (rose red background). No. 2128,
3b, Heavenly Flute, by Khien Yimsiri (Prussian
blue background). No. 2129, 3b, The Calf, by
Paitun Muangsomboom, horiz.

2004, May 3   **Perf. 13¼**
2126-2129 A722   Set of 4   1.40   .95

Unseen Tourist Attractions — A723

No. 2130: a, Non Ngai Buddha, Suphan
Buri. b, Khao Laem Dam, Kanchanaburi. c,
Mural, Temple fo the Emerald Buddha, Bang-
kok. d, Ko Li-Pe, Satun. e, Buddha, Wat Phra
Thong, Phuket. f, Khao Luang National Park,
Nakhon Si Thammarat. g, Miracle Beach, Ko
Damikhwan, Krabi. h, Hornbill, Hala-Bala For-
est, Narathiwat. i, Long Ru Waterfall, Ubon
Ratchathani. j, Prasat Hin Phanom Rung, Buri
Ram. k, Red maple leaves, Phu Kradueng
National Park, Loei. l, Phukhao Ya, Ranong.
m, Ko Kradat, Trat. n, Op Luang National Park,
Chiang Mai. o, Dusky leaf monkey, Phetch-
aburi. p, Lalu, Sra Kaeo. q, Pu Kai, Mu Ko
Similan, Phang-Nga. r, Tha Le Noi Waterfowl
Park. Phatthalung. s, Phu Pha Thoep,
Mukdahan National Park. t, Phi Maen Cave,
Mae Hong Son.

2004, May 31   **Perf. 13**
Granite Paper
2130 A723 3b Sheet of 20, #a-t   10.00 8.00
    See Nos. 2137, 2147, 2158.

Buddha
Sculptures
A724

No. 2131: a, Phra Nangpaya. b, Phra
Kampaeng Soumkhor. c, Phra Somdej Wat
Rakangkhositaram. d, Phar Rod. e, Phra
Phongsuphan.

Litho. & Embossed
2004, June 1   **Perf. 13¼**
Granite Paper
2131   Horiz. strip of 5   12.00 9.50
a.-e.   A724 9b Any single   2.40 1.75
f.   Souvenir sheet, #2131a-
     2131e   20.00 20.00
    No. 2131f sold for 53b.

Visakhapuja
Day — A725

2004, June 2   **Litho.**   **Perf. 14x14½**
Granite Paper
2132 A725 3b multi   .50   .25

Bridges — A726

Designs: No. 2133, 5b, Phra Buddha Yodfa
Bridge. No. 2134, 5b, Rama VI Bridge. No.

2135, 5b, Rama VIII Bridge. No. 2136, 5b,
Rama IX Bridge.

2004, July 1   **Litho.**   **Perf. 14¼x14½**
Granite Paper
2133-2136 A726   Set of 4   2.25 1.25
    On Nos. 2135 and 2136 portions of the
design were produced by a thermographic
process which produces a shiny, raised effect.

**Unseen Tourist Attractions Type of
2004**

No. 2137: a, Wat Pho Prathap Chang,
Phichit. b, Phra Prathan Chaturathit, Wat
Phumin, Nan. c, Thalenai, Angthong Archipel-
ago, Surat Thani. d, Wat Na Phra Men, Phra
Nakhon Si Ayutthaya. e, Sanam Chan Palace,
Nakhon Pathom. f, Piyamitr Tunnel, Yala. g,
Ban Khamchanot, Udon Thani. h, Rail line
along Pasak Cholasit Dam, Lop Buri. i, Khlong
Lan Waterfall, Khlong Lan National Park,
Kamphaeng Phet. j, Mo-I-Daeng Cliff, Khao
Phra Wihan National Park, Si Sa Ket. k,
Changkra Wild Orchid Park, Khon Kaen. l,
Canoeists at Ti Lo Re, Tak. m, Khao Ta Mong
Lai, Prachuap Khiri Khan. n, Suriya Patithin
solar calendar, Prasat Phu Phek, Sakon
Nakhon. o, Traditional boat racing, Chumphon.
p, Mokochu Range Mae Wong National Park,
Nakhon Sawan. q, Ordination by elephant in
the sixth month, Surin. r, Rock climbing, Tan
Rattana Waterfall, Khao Yai National Park,
Prachin Buri. s, Monks collecting alms on
horseback, Chiang Rai. t, Cycling in Thung
Salaeng Luang, Phitsanulok.

2004, July 28   **Perf. 13**
Granite Paper
2137 A723 3b Sheet of 20, #a-t   10.00 8.00

Jasmine
Flower — A727

Litho. & Embossed
2004, Aug. 2   **Perf. 13**
Granite Paper
2138 A727 5b multi   .55   .30
    No. 2138 is impregnated with a jasmine
scent.

Princess Maha
Chakri Sirindhorn
Information
Technology
Program — A728

2004, Aug. 4   **Litho.**   **Perf. 14x14½**
Granite Paper
2139 A728 3b multi   .50   .25

National Communications Day — A729

2004, Aug. 4   **Perf. 14½x14**
Granite Paper
2140 A729 3b multi   .50   .25

Opening of First Subway Line — A730

2004, Aug. 12   **Litho.**   **Perf. 14½x14**
Granite Paper
2141 A730 3b multi   .50   .25

Queen Sirikit,
72nd
Birthday
A731

Litho. & Embossed
2004, Aug. 12   **Perf. 13¼**
2142 A731 100b multi   7.00 4.50

Boats
A732

Designs: No. 2143, 3b, Thai junk. No. 2144,
3b, Sampan boat. No. 2145, 3b, Krachaeng
boat. 15b, Packet boat.

2004-05   **Litho.**   **Perf. 14½x14**
Granite Paper
2143-2146 A732   Set of 4   2.00 1.40
2146a   Souvenir sheet, #2143-
     2146, perf. 13¼   3.25 3.00
  b.   As "a," with Pacific Explorer
     2005 emblem in margin   9.00 8.00
    No. 2146a sold for 29b. No. 2146b sold for
30b.
    Issued: Nos. 2143-2146a, 9/1/04; No.
2146b, 4/21/05.

**Unseen Tourist Attractions Type of
2004**

No. 2147: a, Phra Nang Din, Phayad. b,
Phra That Kong Khao Noi, Yasothon. c, Phra
Atchana, Wat Sri Chum, Sukothai. d, Wat
Bang Kung, Samut Songkhram. e, Ku Kut, Wat
Phrathat Chamthewi, Lamphun. f, Dolphin
watching, Chachoengsao. g, Tak Bat Dok Mai
tradition, Saraburi. h, Hat Chao Lao,
Chanthaburi. i, Phu Kum Khao dinosaur fos-
sils, Kalasin. j, Reversed stupa, Wat Phra That
Lampang Luang, Lampang. k, Khu Khut
Waterfowl Park, Songkhla. l, Plant Market
Khlong 15, Nakhon Nayok. m, Huppatad,
Uthai Thani. n, Thai Muang Beach, Nakhon
Phanom. o, Wild gaur, Khao Yai National Park,
Nakhon Ratchasima. p, Canoeing, Le Khao
Kop Cave, Trang. q, Sea of flowers, Pru Soi
Dao, Uttaradit. r, Kolae boat, Ban Paseyawo,
Pattani. s, Sea of Mist, Thap Boek, Phu Hin
Rongkla National Park, Phetchabun. t, Bats,
Khao Chung Phran, Ratchaburi.

2004, Sept. 28   **Perf. 13**
Granite Paper
2147 A723 3b Sheet of 20, #a-t   10.00 8.00

Intl. Letter
Writing
Week — A733

Kites: No. 2148, 3b, Snake. No. 2149, 3b, Star-shaped. No. 2150, 3b, Diamond-shaped with tail. 15b, Buffalo.

2004, Oct. 9   Litho.   Perf. 14x14½
Granite Paper
2148-2151 A733   Set of 4   2.00 1.40
2151a   Souvenir sheet, #2148-
             2151, perf. 13¼   3.25 3.00
2151b   Similar to "a," with Beijing
             2004 emblem in margin   9.00 8.00

Issued: No. 2151b, 10/28. No. 2151a sold for 29b; No. 2151b for 30b.

King Mongkut
(1804-68)
A734

2004, Oct. 18   Perf. 14x14½
Granite Paper
2152 A734 4b multi   .50 .25

E-customs System — A735

2004, Nov. 15   Perf. 14½x14
Granite Paper
2153 A735 3b multi   .50 .25

New Year
2005 — A736

Flowers: No. 2154, 3b, Wrightia sirikitiae. No. 2155, 3b, Eria amica. No. 2156, 3b, Burmannia coelestris. No. 2157, 3b, Utricularia bifida.

2004, Nov. 15   Perf. 14¼x14½
Granite Paper
2154-2157 A736   Set of 4   3.00 2.00
2157a   Souvenir sheet, #2154-
             2157, perf. 14¼x14½   5.00 5.00

No. 2157a sold for 16b.

Unseen Tourist Attractions Type of 2004

No. 2158: a, Phra That Cho Hae, Phrae. b, Wat Karuna, Chai Nat. c, Wat Nang Sao, Samut Sakhon. d, Phra Mutao Pagoda, Nonthaburi. e, Phu Kao Phu Phan Kham National Park, Nong Bua Lam Phu. f, Airvata (three-headed elephant), Erawan Museum, Samut Prakan. g, Wat Chedi Hoi, Pathum Thani. h, White krajiaw field, Chaiyaphum. i, Chet Si Waterfall, Nong Khai. j, Summer Palace, Ko Si Chang, Choi Buri. k, Traditional Drum-making village (Ban Bang Phae), Ang Thong. l, Ko Thalu, Rayong. m, Kosamphi Forest Park, Maha Sarakham. n, Cannonball tree, Wat Phra Non Chaksi, Sing Buri. o, Tung Kula Rong Hai, Roi Et. p, Phu Sra Dok Bua, Amnat Charoen.

2004, Nov. 26   Perf. 13
Granite Paper
2158 A723 3b Sheet of 16, #a-p,
           + 4 labels   9.00 8.00

Bangkok Fashion City
Initiative — A737

No. 2159: a, 3b, Man and woman. b, 3b, Woman in pink dress. c, 3b, Woman with green shirt. d, 15b, Woman with brown eyeshade.

2004, Dec. 5   Perf. 14x14½
Granite Paper
2159 A737 Horiz. strip of 4, #a-
           d   2.25 2.25
e.   Souvenir sheet, #2159a-2159d,
           perf. 13½   3.25 2.75

No. 2159e sold for 30b.

Queen Rambhai
Bharni (1904-84)
A738

2004, Dec. 20   Perf. 14x14½
Granite Paper
2160 A738 3b multi   .50 .25

Zodiac Animal Type of 2003
2005, Jan. 1   Perf. 13
Granite Paper
2161 A682 3b Cock   .50 .30
           See No. 2341c.

Children's Day — A739

2005, Jan. 8   Perf. 14½x14
Granite Paper
2162 A739 3b multi   .50 .25

Thailand - Argentina Diplomatic
Relations, 50th Anniv. — A740

No. 2163: a, Tango dancers, Argentina. b, Tom-tom dancers, Thailand.

2005, Feb. 2   Perf. 13¼
Granite Paper
2163 A740 3b Horiz. pair, #a-b   1.10 1.00
           See Argentina Nos. 2312-2313.

Rose — A741

2005, Feb. 10   Perf. 12½
Flocked Paper
2164 A741 10b multi   1.10 .80

No. 2164 is impregnated with rose scent.

Maghapuja
Day — A742

2005, Feb. 23   Perf. 14x14½
Granite Paper
2165 A742 3b multi   .50 .25

Rotary International, Cent. — A743

2005, Feb. 23   Perf. 14½x14
Granite Paper
2166 A743 3b multi   .50 .25

Red
Cross
A744

2005, Mar. 30   Litho.
Granite Paper
2167 A744 3b multi   .50 .25

Princess
Maha Chakri
Sirindhorn,
50th Birthday
— A774a

2005, Apr. 2   Litho.   Perf. 13¼
Granite Paper
2167A A774a 3b multi   .50 .25

A745

Hanging
Art — A746

2005, Apr. 2   Litho.   Perf. 13¼
Granite Paper
2168 A745 3b shown   .35 .25
2169 A746 3b shown   .35 .25
2170 A746 3b multi, diff.   .35 .25
2171 A745 15b multi, diff.   1.40 .55
a.   Souvenir sheet, #2168-2171   3.25 2.75
           Nos. 2168-2171 (4)   2.45 1.30

Heritage Conservation Day. No. 2171 sold for 30b.

Authors Born in 1905 — A747

Designs: No. 2172, 3b, Dokmaisod (olive green background). No. 2173, 3b, Sri Burapha (Prussian blue background). No. 2174, 3b, Maimuangderm (dark blue background). No. 2175, 3b, Arkatdumkeung Rabibhadana (rose pink background).

2005, May 5   Perf. 14½x14
Granite Paper
2172-2175 A747   Set of 4   2.25 2.10
2175a   Souvenir sheet, #2172-
             2175, perf. 13¼   5.00 4.50

No. 2175a sold for 17b.

Insects — A748

No. 2176: a, Coccinella transversalis. b, Chrysochroa buqueti rugicollis (47x28mm). c, Sagra femorata. d, Chrysochroa maruyamai (47x28mm).

Litho. & Embossed
2005, May 31   Perf. 14¼x14½
Granite Paper
2176   Horiz. strip or block of
           4   2.25 1.60
a.-d.   A748 5b Any single   .55 .40
e.   Sheet, 2 each #2176a-2176d   3.00 3.00

Embossed portions of stamps are covered with a glossy varnish.

No. 2176e issued May 2006, Washington 2006 World Philatelic Exhibition. No. 2176e sold for 54b.

Heart Balloons and Mail Truck — A749

Balloons — A749a

2005 **Litho.** *Perf. 13*
Granite Paper
2177 A749 3b multi .75 .50
2177A A749a 3b multi .75 .50

Issued: No. 2177, June; No. 2177A, 7/15. Nos. 2177 and 2177A were issued in sheets of 12 + 12 personalizable labels the same size as the stamp.

Buddha Amulets A750

No. 2178: a, Phra Ruang Lang Rang Puen. b, Phra Hu Yan. c, Phra Chinnarat Bai Sema. d, Phra Mahesuan. e, Phra Tha Kradan.

Litho. & Embossed
2005, June 19 *Perf. 13¼*
Granite Paper
2178 Horiz. strip of 5 4.50 4.50
a.-e. A750 9b Any single .90 .90
f. Souvenir sheet, #2178a-
2178e 12.00 12.00
g. As "f," with Taipei 2005 emblem in margin 12.00 12.00

No. 2178f sold for 55b.
No. 2178g issued 8/19/05. No. 2178g sold for 85b.

Thailand - People's Republic of China Diplomatic Relations, 30th Anniv. — A751

Panda: a, Showing tongue. b, Feeding on bamboo.

2005, July 1 **Litho.** *Perf.*
Granite Paper
2179 A751 Horiz. pair 1.10 .90
a.-b. 3b Either single .45 .30
c. Souvenir sheet, #2179a-2179b 3.25 2.75

No. 2179 has perf. 13¼ line of perforations between the two stamps, and the surrounding selvage is rouletted 11¾. No. 2179c, which sold for 15b, lacks the perforations between the stamps and has no rouletting.

Thaipex 2005 — A752

Dancers in play "Chuck Nark": No. 2180, 3b, Pra Rama and Princess Srida. No. 2181, 3b, Hanuman (white mask). No. 2182, 3b, Thotsakan (green mask). 15b, Pra Rama and Thotsakan.

Litho. with Foil Application
2005, Aug. 3 *Perf. 13¼*
Granite Paper
2180-2183 A752 Set of 4 2.60 2.00
2183a Souvenir sheet, #2180-
2183 4.50 3.25

No. 2183a sold for 30b. No. 2183a exists imperf. Value $25.

Natl. Communications Day — A753

2005, Aug. 4 **Litho.** *Perf. 14½x14*
Granite Paper
2184 A753 3b multi .50 .25

Building Gables — A754

No. 2185: a, Prasat Phanom Rung. b, Phra Prang at Wat Phra Phai Luang. c, Uposatha Hall at Wat Khao Bandai It. d, Scripture Library at Wat Phra Sing Woramahawihan.

Perf. 13¼x13½
2005, Aug. 4 **Photo.** **Wmk. 340**
2185 Horiz. strip of 4 + central label 2.75 2.25
a.-d. A754 5b Any single .55 .40

Orchids — A755

Designs: No. 2189, 3b, Rhynchostylis gigantea Alba (white flowers). No. 2190, 3b, Rhynchostylis gigantea (pink and red flowers). No. 2191, 3b, Dendrobium gratiosissimum. 15b, Dendrobium thyrsiflorum.

Perf. 14½
2005, Sept. 1 **Litho.** **Unwmk.**
Granite Paper
2189-2192 A755 Set of 4 2.50 2.50
2192a Souvenir sheet, #2189-
2192, perf. 13¼ 3.50 3.50

No. 2192a sold for 30b.

Intl. Day of Peace — A756

2005, Sept. 21 *Perf. 13*
Granite Paper
2193 A756 3b multi .50 .25

Intl. Letter Writing Week — A757

Water buffalo: No. 2194, 3b, Head. No. 2195, 3b, Standing in field. No. 2196, 3b, In mud. 15b, Attached to plow.

Perf. 14½x14
2005, Oct. 8 **Litho.** **Unwmk.**
Granite Paper
2194-2197 A757 Set of 4 2.50 2.50
2197a Souvenir sheet, #2194-
2197, perf. 13¼ 4.50 3.25

National Library, Cent. — A758

2005, Oct. 12 *Perf. 14½x14*
Granite Paper
2198 A758 3b multi .50 .25

Abolition of Slavery, Cent. — A759

2005, Oct. 23 **Litho.**
Granite Paper
2199 A759 3b multi .50 .30

New Year 2006 — A760

Flowers: No. 2200, 3b, Beaumontia murtonii. No. 2201, 3b, Hibiscus mutabilis. No. 2202, 3b, Hibiscus rosa-sinensis. No. 2203, 3b, Cochlospermum religiosum.

2005, Nov. 15 *Perf. 14x14½*
Granite Paper
2200-2203 A760 Set of 4 1.25 1.25
2203a Souvenir sheet, #2200-
2203 2.25 2.00

No. 2203a sold for 17b.

Princess Bejaratana, 80th Birthday — A761

2005, Nov. 24 *Perf. 14x14½*
Granite Paper
2204 A761 3b multi .50 .30

Siamese Roosters — A762

Designs: No. 2205, 3b, Golden Rooster, by Pichai Nirand (olive green panel). No. 2206, 3b, Rooster at Dawn, by Prayat Pongdam (black panel). No. 2207, 3b, Legendary Rooster, by Chakrabhand Posayakrit (dancing woman, brown panel). No. 2208, 3b, Divine Rooster, by Chalermchai Kositpipat (blue panel), horiz.

Perf. 14x14½, 14½x14
2005, Nov. 24
2205-2208 A762 Set of 4 1.25 1.25

King Bhumibol Adulyadej's "New Theory" Agriculture — A763

No. 2209: a, King, easel, farmers, animals. b, King and farmers.

2005, Dec. 5 *Perf. 14¼x14½*
Granite Paper
2209 Horiz. pair, #a-b, +
central label .85 .85
a.-b. A763 3b Either single .35 .30

Buddhist Monks A764

No. 2210: a, Somdet Phra Phutthachan (1788-1872). b, Phra Ratchamuni Samiram Khunupamachan (1582-1682). c, Phra Achan Man Bhuridatto (1870-1949). d, Khruba Si wichai (1877-1938).

Litho. & Engr.
2005, Dec. 5 *Perf. 13½*
Granite Paper
2210 Horiz. strip of 4 2.25 2.25
a.-d. A764 5b Any single .55 .50
e. Souvenir sheet, #2210a-2210d 3.50 3.50

No. 2210e sold for 30b.

Dec. 26, 2004 Tsunami, 1st Anniv. — A765

No. 2211: a, Wave. b, Undivided Kindness of Thai People, by Chanipa Temprom.

2005, Dec. 26 Litho. Perf. 14½x14
Granite Paper
2211 A765 3b Horiz. pair, #a-b 2.50 1.75

King Bhumibol Adulyadej Type of 1996

2006 Litho. Perf. 14x14½
Granite Paper
2212 A550 10b orange & brown 2.00 1.00
2213 A550 15b yel brn & green 3.00 1.50

New Year 2006 (Year of the Dog) — A766

2006, Jan. 1 Litho. Perf. 13
Granite Paper
2214 A766 3b multi .50 .30

Prince Chaturantarasml Krom Phra Chakrabardibongse (1856-1900), Finance Minister — A767

2006, Jan. 13 Perf. 14x14½
Granite Paper
2215 A767 3b multi .50 .30

Natl. Children's Day — A768

Winning designs in children's stamp design competition with panel colors of: No. 2216, 3b, Orange brown. No. 2217, 3b, Blue. No. 2218, 3b, Red violet. No. 2219, 3b, Green.

2006, Jan. 14 Perf. 14½x14
Granite Paper
2216-2219 A768 Set of 4 1.25 1.25

Rose — A769

Litho. & Embossed
2006, Feb. 7 Perf. 13
Granite Paper
2220 A769 5b multi .75 .50

Diplomatic Relations Between Thailand and Iran, 50th Anniv. — A770

2006, Feb. 11 Litho. Perf. 14½x14
Granite Paper
2221 A770 3b multi .50 .30

Queen Sirikit Center for Breast Cancer — A771

2006, Mar. 29 Perf. 14½x14
Granite Paper
2222 A771 3b multi .50 .25

Heritage Conservation Day — A772

Sites in Phu Phrabat Historical Park: No. 2223, 3b, Buddha's Footprint (monument). No. 2224, 3b, Upright rocks and trees, horiz. No. 2225, 3b, Thao Barot horse stable (rock overhang), horiz. 15b, Nang Usa rock pillar.

2006, Apr. 2 Perf. 14x14½, 14½x14
Granite Paper
2223-2226 A772 Set of 4 2.50 2.50
2226a Souvenir sheet, #2223- 2226, perf. 13¼ 4.50 3.25

No. 2226a sold for 36b.

Thon Buri Palace — A773

No. 2227: a, Throne Hall. b, King Taksin's Shrine. c, Two Chinese-style residences. d, King Pinklao's residence.

2006, Apr. 2 Perf. 14½x14
Granite Paper
2227 A773 3b Block of 4, #a-d 1.40 1.40
e. Souvenir sheet, #2227, perf. 13¼ 2.75 2.25

No. 2227e sold for 17b.

A774

King Bhumibol Adulyadej, 60th Anniv. of Accession A775

King Bhumibol Adulyadej: No. 2228, 3b, Wearing tie, red brown background (shown). No. 2229, 3b, Wearing tie, blue background. No. 2230, 3b, Wearing tie, olive brown background. No. 2231, 3b, Without tie, blue violet background. No. 2232, 3b, Without tie, green background. No. 2233, 3b, Without tie, brown background.

2006 Photo. Perf. 13¼
Granite Paper
2228-2233 A774 Set of 6 8.00 7.00
2233a Miniature sheet, #2228- 2233 16.00 16.00
Litho. & Embossed With Foil Application
2234 A775 100b gold & multi 9.00 9.00

Issued: Nos. 2228-2233, 2233a, 5/5; No. 2234, 6/9. No. 2233a sold for 30b.

Visakhapuja Day — A776

2006, May 12 Litho. Perf. 14x14½
Granite Paper
2235 A776 3b multi .50 .30

Buddhadasa Bhikkhu (1906-93), Buddhist Philosopher A777

No. 2236: a, Buddhadasa seated between trees. b, Profile of Buddhadasa. c, Gathering of monks. d, Stone fence.

2006, May 27 Perf. 13
Granite Paper
2236 Horiz. strip of 4 1.60 1.60
a.-d. A777 3b Any single .30 .30
e. Miniature sheet, #2236a-2236d 2.00 2.00

No. 2236e sold for 17b.

Anemonefish — A778

Designs: No. 2237, 3b, Amphiprion clarkii. No. 2238, 3b, Amphiprion perideraion. No. 2239, 3b, Amphiprion ocellaris. No. 2240, 3b, Amphiprion polymnus.

2006, June 24 Perf. 14½x14
Granite Paper
2237-2240 A778 Set of 4 1.40 1.40
2240a Miniature sheet, #2237- 2240, perf. 13½ 2.75 2.25
2240b As "a," with Belgica '06 emblem in margin 11.00 11.00

Issued: Nos. 2237-2240, 2240a, 6/24; No. 2240b, Dec. No. 2240a sold for 20b; No. 2240b, for 30b.

Natl. Communications Day — A779

2006, Aug. 4 Litho.
Granite Paper
2241 A779 3b multi .50 .30

Mitrephora Sirikitiae — A780

Litho. & Embossed
2006, Aug. 12 Perf. 13
Granite Paper
2242 A780 5b multi .55 .40

Royal Dog Tongdaeng A781

Dog: No. 2243, 3b, Sitting. No. 2244, 3b, Standing. No. 2245, 3b, Laying down. No. 2246, 3b, With puppies.

2006 Litho. Perf. 13½
Granite Paper
2243-2246 A781 Set of 4 1.40 1.10
2246a Miniature sheet, #2243- 2246 2.25 2.25
2246b As "a," with MonacoPhil 2006 emblem in margin 10.00 10.00

Issued: Nos. 2243-2246, 2246a, 9/1; No. 2246b, Dec. No. 2246a sold for 17b; No. 2246b, for 26b.

Suvarnabhumi Airport — A782

2006, Sept. 28 Perf. 14½x14
Granite Paper
2247 A782 3b multi .50 .30

Nos, 606, 653a, 934
and 1081
Surcharged

Methods, Perfs and Watermarks As Before

2006, Sept. 15
2248 A146 2b on 20s #606   16.00 16.00
2249 A161 2b on 20s #653a   1.10 .35
  a.   2b on 20s #653   75.00 75.00
2250 A256 2b on 75s #934   2.75 2.75
2251 A256 2b on 1.50b #1081   2.75 2.75
  Nos. 2248-2251 (4)   22.60 21.85
Location and size of surcharges differs.

Fireworks — A783

2006, Apr. 20   Litho.   Perf. 13
Granite Paper
2252 A783 3b multi + label   2.75 2.75
Printed in sheets of 10 stamps + 10 labels that could be personalized. Sheets sold for 100b. Value, $32.50.

Intl. Letter Writing Week — A784

Carnivorous plants: No. 2253, 3b, Nepenthes mirabilis. No. 2254, 3b, Rafflesia kerrii. No. 2255, 3b, Sapria poilanei. 15b, Drosera burmannii.

2006 Litho. Unwmk.   Perf. 14½x14
Granite Paper
2253-2256 A784 Set of 4   2.50 1.60
2256a   Miniature sheet, #2253-2256, perf. 13½   3.25 2.75
2256b   As "a," with Beijing 2006 emblem in margin   10.00 10.00
Issued: Nos. 2253-2256, 2256a, 10/9; No. 2256b, Dec. No. 2256a sold for 29b; No. 2256b, for 44b.

New Year 2007 — A785

Flowers: No. 2257, 3b, Hypoxis aurea. No. 2258, 3b, Murdannia gigantea. No. 2259, 3b, Impatiens phuluangensis. No. 2260, 3b, Caulokaempferia alba.

2006, Nov. 15   Perf. 14½x14
Granite Paper
2257-2260 A785 Set of 4   1.25 .90
2260a   Miniature sheet, #2257-2260   2.50 2.25
No. 2260a sold for 16b.

Royal Thai Naval Academy, Cent. — A786

2006, Nov. 20   Granite Paper
2261 A786 3b multi   .50 .30

King Bhumibol Adulyadej, 60th Anniv. of Accession A787

King Bhumibol Adulyadej: No. 2262, 5b, Standing in forest. No. 2263, 5b, Seated on walkway, taking notes. No. 2264, 5b, Standing on wooden plank over water. No. 2265, 5b, Pointing to ground. No. 2266, 5b, Riding cow. No. 2267, 5b, Walking up hill.

2006, Dec. 5   Photo.   Perf. 13½
Granite Paper
2262-2267 A787 Set of 6   3.75 2.50
2267a   Miniature sheet, #2262-2267   5.50 5.50
No. 2267a sold for 44b. No. 2267a exists imperf. Value, $275.

Opening of Second Thai-Lao Friendship Bridge — A788

No. 2268 — Bridge and flag of: a, Thailand (denomination at LL). b, Laos (denomination at LR).

2006, Dec. 20   Litho.   Perf. 14½x14
Granite Paper
2268 A788 3b Horiz. pair, #a-b   1.10 1.10

New Year 2007 (Year of the Pig) — A789

2007, Jan. 1   Granite Paper   Perf. 13
2269 A789 3b multi   .50 .30
See No. 2341d.

Natl. Children's Day — A790

No. 2270 — Children's drawings: a, Rainbow, birds and butterflies. b, Cat with green face and butterflies. c, Spotted animals. d, Birds, cloud, sun and girl riding horse.

2007, Jan. 13   Perf. 14½x14
Granite Paper
2270 A790 3b Block of 4, #a-d   2.25 1.25

Siam Commercial Bank Public Company, Cent. — A791

2007, Jan. 30   Perf. 14x14½
Granite Paper
2271 A791 3b multi   .50 .30

Bangkok 2007 Intl. Stamp Exhibition — A792

Various carved wooden dolls depicting Thai children with background colors of: No. 2272, 5b, Blue. No. 2273, 5b, Olive green. No. 2274, 5b, Brown olive. No. 2275, 5b, Rose.

Litho. With Foil Application
2007, Feb. 1   Perf. 13
Granite Paper
2272-2275 A792 Set of 4   2.25 1.75
2275a   Miniature sheet, #2272-2275   3.75 3.25
No. 2275a sold for 33b.

Yellow Rose — A793

2007, Feb. 7   Litho.   Perf. 13
Granite Paper
2276 A793 5b multi   .55 .40
No. 2276 is impregnated with a rose scent.

A794

A795

A796

Carved Fruits and Vegetables — A797

2007, Mar. 1   Litho.   Perf. 14½x14
Granite Paper
2277 A794 5b multi   .55 .40
2278 A795 5b multi   .55 .40
2279 A796 5b multi   .55 .40
2280 A797 5b multi   .55 .40
  a.   Souvenir sheet, #2277-2280, perf. 13¼   3.50 3.25
  Nos. 2277-2280 (4)   2.20 1.60
No. 2280a sold for 26b.

No. 617 Surcharged in Bronze and Black

Methods, Perfs and Watermarks As Before
2007, Mar. 29
2281 A146 50b on 40b #617   6.50 6.50
2282 A146 100b on 40b #617   10.00 10.00

Postman on Scooter — A798

Unwmk.
2007, Mar. 29   Litho.   Perf. 13
Granite Paper
2283 A798 3b multi   .35 .30
No. 2283 was printed in sheets of 10 and in sheets of 10 + 10 labels that could be personalized.

Thailand Red Cross Tuberculosis Laboratory — A799

2007, Mar. 29   Litho.   Perf. 14½x14
2285 A799 3b multi   .35 .30

A800

A801

A802

Buddhist Ecclesiastical Ceremonial Fans of King Chulalongkorn Era — A803

Litho. With Foil Application
2007, Apr. 2   *Perf. 13¼*
Granite Paper

2286	A800 5b multi	.55	.40
2287	A801 5b multi	.55	.40
2288	A802 5b multi	.55	.40
2289	A803 5b multi	.55	.40
a.	Souvenir sheet, #2286-2289	3.75	3.25
	Nos. 2286-2289 (4)	2.20	1.60

No. 2289a sold for 27b.

Flowers — A804

No. 2290: a, Lotus flower at UR, sunflowers in center and LR. b, Sunflower at UR, two lotus flowers. c, Rose, sunflower and lotus flowers. d, Three roses.

2007, Apr. 23   **Litho.**   *Perf. 13*
Granite Paper

2290	Vert. strip of 4	1.60	1.60
a.-d.	A804 3b Any single	.35	.30

King Bhumibol Adulyadej, 80th Birthday — A805

Litho. & Embossed With Foil Application
2007, May 5   *Perf. 13¼*
Granite Paper

2291	A805 9b multi	1.40	1.40

Princess Galyani Vadhana, 84th Birthday — A806

2007, May 6   **Litho.**   *Perf. 14x14½*

2292	A806 3b multi	.65	.50

Visakhapuja Day — A807

2007, May 31   *Perf. 14¼x14½*
Granite Paper

2293	A807 3b multi	.45	.40

Seaside Tourist Areas — A808

No. 2294: a, Mu Ko Similan National Park. b, Ko Khai. c, Ko Chang. d, Khao Tapu. e, Hat Cha-am. f, Ao Maya. g, Ko Panyi. h, Hat Chao Mai. i, Thale Waek. j, Hat Pattaya.

2007, June 1   *Perf. 14½x14*
Granite Paper

2294	A808 Sheet of 10	11.00	11.00
a.-j.	15b Any single	1.10	1.10

The original printing of No. 2294 has the bar code in the bottom margin. A later printing with a smaller margin has the bar code at the right side.

Waterfalls — A809

Waterfall at: No. 2295, 3b, Doi Inthanon National Park. No. 2296, 3b, Thung Salaeng Luang National Park. No. 2297, 3b, Khuean Srinagarindra National Park. No. 2298, 3b, Phu Hin Rong Kla National Park.

2007, June 1   *Perf. 14½x14*
Granite Paper

2295-2298	A809 Set of 4	1.40	1.40
2298a	Souvenir sheet, #2295-2298, perf. 13½	2.90	2.25

No. 2298a sold for 16b.

Phi Takhon Masks — A810

No. 2299 — Masks with rice steamer hat in: a, White, black background. b, Black, white

---

background. c, Red, black background. d, White, white background.
10b, Two people wearing masks.

2007, June 23   *Perf. 13¼*
Granite Paper

2299	A810 3b Horiz. strip of 4, #a-d	1.60	1.60

Souvenir Sheet
Perf. 14x14½

2300	A810 10b multi	2.00	2.00

No. 2300 contains one 60x48mm stamp.

A811

A812

A813

Rock Formations in Pa Hin Ngam National Park — A814

2007, July 2   **Litho.**   *Perf. 13¼x12¾*

2301	A811 5b multi	.55	.40
2302	A812 5b multi	.55	.40
2303	A813 5b multi	.55	.40
2304	A814 5b multi	.55	.40
a.	Souvenir sheet, #2301-2304	4.75	3.75
	Nos. 2301-2304 (4)	2.20	1.60

No. 2304a sold for 39b. Portions of the designs of Nos. 2301-2304 and 2304a were printed with a thermographic process producing a shiny, raised effect. A gritty substance was added to these areas to produce a rough texture.

Temples — A815

Designs: No. 2305, 5b, Wat Rajaorasaram. No. 2306, 5b, Wat Rajapradit Sathitmahasimaram. No. 2307, 5b, Wat Rajabopit Sathitmahasimaram. No. 2308, 5b, Wat Suthatthepwararam.

2007, July 2   **Litho.**   *Perf. 14½x14*
Granite Paper

2305-2308	A815 Set of 4	2.25	1.75
2308a	Souvenir sheet, #2305-2308, perf. 13¼	3.50	3.25

No. 2308a sold for 27b.

Bird Figurines A816

Bird figurines covered with beetle wing: No. 2309, 5b, Duck with wings spread. No. 2310, 5b, Bird on rock. No. 2311, 5b, Bird with long tail feathers. No. 2312, 5b, Rooster.

Litho. With Foil Application
2007, Aug. 3   *Perf. 14x14½*
Granite Paper

2309-2312	A816 Set of 4	2.60	1.75
2312a	Souvenir sheet, #2309-2312	3.75	3.25

No. 2312a sold for 33b. Bangkok 2007 Intl. Stamp Exhibition.

Natl. Communications Day — A817

2007, Aug. 4   **Litho.**   *Perf. 14½x14*
Granite Paper

2313	A817 3b multi	.30	.30

24th Summer Universiade, Bangkok — A818

2007, Aug. 8   *Perf. 13¼*
Granite Paper

2314	A010 3b multi	.30	.30

Miniature Sheet

Association of South East Asian Nations (ASEAN), 40th Anniv. — A819

No. 2315: a, Secretariat Building, Bandar Seri Begawan, Brunei. b, National Museum of Cambodia. c, Fatahillah Museum, Jakarta, Indonesia. d, Typical house, Laos. e, Malayan Railway Headquarters Building, Kuala Lumpur, Malaysia. f, Yangon Post Office, Myanmar (Burma). g, Malacañang Palace,

Philippines. h, National Museum of Singapore. i, Vimanmek Mansion, Bangkok. j, Presidential Palace, Hanoi, Viet Nam.

2007, Aug. 8   **Perf. 13¼**
Granite Paper
2315 A819 3b Sheet of 10, #a-j   5.50 4.50

See Brunei No. 607, Burma No. 370, Cambodia No. 2339, Indonesia Nos. 2120-2121, Laos Nos. 1717-1718, Malaysia No. 1170, Philippines Nos. 3103-3105, Singapore No. 1265, and Viet Nam Nos. 3302-3311.

Miniature Sheet

Diplomatic Relations Between Thailand and Japan, 120th Anniv. — A820

No. 2316: a, Buddhist statue. b, Pagoda. c, Elephant. d, Dragon. e, Pink and white orchids. f, White flowers. g, Thai dancer. h, Japanese dancer.

2007, Sept. 26   **Litho.**   **Perf. 13¼**
Granite Paper
2316 A820   3b Sheet of 8, #a-h 4.50 3.25
See Japan No. 2998.

Intl. Letter Writing Week — A821

Utensils: No. 2317, 3b, Betel nut scissors. No. 2318, 3b, Betel nut masher. No. 2319, 3b, Cylinder-and-piston igniter. No. 2320, 3b, Earthenware oil lamp or incense dish.

2007, Oct. 8   **Litho.**   **Perf. 14½x14**
Granite Paper
2317-2320 A821   Set of 4   1.75 1.10
2320a   Miniature sheet, #2317-2320, perf. 13¼   3.00 2.75
No. 2320a sold for 18b.

Miniature Sheets

Provincial Seals — A822

No. 2321, 3b — Seals of: a, Bangkok. b, Krabi. c, Kanchanaburi. d, Kalasin. e, Kamphaeng Phet. f, Khon Kaen. g, Chanthaburi. h, Chachoengsao. i, Chon Buri. j, Chai Nat.

No. 2322, 3b — Seals of: a, Chaiyaphum. b, Chumphon. c, Chiang Rai. d, Chiang Mai. e, Trang. f, Trat. g, Tak. h, Nakhon Nayok. i, Nakhon Pathom. j, Nakhon Phanom.

Litho. & Embossed With Foil Application
2007, Oct. 11   **Perf. 13½**
Granite Paper
Sheets of 10, #a-j
2321-2322 A822   Set of 2   5.50 5.50

Miniature Sheet

People at Work — A823

No. 2323: a, People in palm tree. b, Cook feeding people on wooden walkway. c, People near elephant carving. d, Buddhist monk in canoe. e, People under lanterns. f, Artisan with hammer. g, Woman with flowers. h, Man weaving fishing basket. i, People in boats filled with fruits and vegetables. j, People logging with elephants.

2007, Oct. 26   **Litho.**   **Perf. 13**
Granite Paper
2323 A823 3b Sheet of 10, #a-j   5.50 5.50
   k.   Sheet of 5, #2323b, 2323c, 2323e, 2323f, 2323j   1.25 1.25
   l.   Sheet of 5, #2323c, 2323d, 2323g, 2323i, 2323j   1.25 1.25
Nos. 2323k and 2323l each sold for 20b at Thailand 7-11 stores. No. 2323k exists with three different sheet margins.

Ministry of Defense, 120th Anniv. — A824

2007, Nov. 11   **Perf. 14x14½**
Granite Paper
2324 A824 3b multi   .35 .30

New Year 2008 — A825

Designs: No. 2325, 3b, Pink Plumeria rubra, denomination in red. No. 2326, 3b, Plumeria obtusa. No. 2327, 3b, White and yellow Plumeria rubra, denomination in pink. No. 2328, 3b, Red Plumeria rubra, denomination in red.

2007, Nov. 15   **Perf. 14x14½**
Granite Paper
2325-2328 A825   Set of 4   1.25 1.25
2328a   Souvenir sheet, #2325-2328   2.90 2.90
No. 2328a sold for 18b.

Patrol Boat — A826

Perf. 14½x14¼
2007, Nov. 20   **Litho.**
Granite Paper
2329 A826 3b multi   .55 .30

White Elephant of King Bhumibol Adulyadej — A827

Designs: No. 2330, 5b, King touching elephant's trunk. No. 2331, 5b, Elephant on lawn. No. 2332, 5b, Elephant on lawn with handlers, vert. No. 2333, 5b, King touching elephant's head, vert.

Perf. 14¾x14, 14x14¾
2007, Dec. 5   **Litho.**
Granite Paper
2330-2333 A827   Set of 4   1.75 1.75
2333a   Souvenir sheet, #2333, perf. 13½   2.75 2.25
No. 2333a sold for 10b.

Miniature Sheet

King Bhumibol Adulyadej, 80th Birthday — A828

No. 2334 — King: a, 5b, As small boy. b, 5b, As boy, sitting in wagon. c, 5b, As student, reading book. d, 5b, Wearing suit, sepia photograph. e, 5b, Wearing cap. f, 5b, Wearing red uniform. g, 5b, Wearing suit and red tie. h, 5b, Wearing gold robe. i, 80b, Wearing Buddhist robe.

Litho., Litho. & Embossed With Hologram Affixed (80b)
2007, Dec. 5   **Perf. 13¼x13½**
2334 A828   Sheet of 9, #a-i   16.00 12.00

No. 1820 Surcharged in Gold

Methods and Perfs As Before
2007, Dec. 18   **Granite Paper**
2335 A550 15b on 9b #1820   2.00 .75

Busabok Mala A829

Litho. & Embossed With Foil Application
2007, Dec. 18   **Perf. 13¼x13½**
2336 A829 20b multi   3.00 3.00
   a.   Souvenir sheet of 1   6.00 6.00

Queen's Collection — A830

No. 2337: a, Miniature model of royal barge Anantanakharai. b, Miniature model of royal barge Suphannahongse. c, Sappagab Phragajatarn. d, Sappagab Khram. e, Water jars. f, Miniature vanity set. g, Yan Lipao basketry. h, Evening bag.

Granite Paper
Perf. 13
2337 A830 5b Sheet of 8, #a-h 4.50 3.75
No. 2336a sold for 40b.

Nos. B78-B79 Surcharged in Black

Methods, Perfs and Watermarks As Before
2007, Jan. 16
2338   Horiz. strip of 4 (#B78)   —   —
  a.-d.   SP13 5b on 2b+1b #B78a-B78d, Any single   —   —
2339   Horiz. strip of 4 (#B79)   —   —
  a.-d.   SP13 5b on 2b+1b #B79a-B79d, Any single   —   —

New Year Types of 2003-2007 and

New Year 2008 (Year of the Rat) — A831

Unwmk.
2008, Jan. 1   **Litho.**   **Perf. 13**
Granite Paper
2340 A831 3b multi   .35 .30
2341   Sheet of 6, #2214, 2340, 2341a-2341d   3.50 3.25
   a.   A682 3b As #2056, with gold rings with colored centers   .30 .30
   b.   A682 3b As #2108, with gold rings with colored centers   —   —
   c.   A682 3b As #2161, with gold rings with colored centers   .30 .30
   d.   A789 3b As #2269, with gold rings and dots   .30 .30
   e.   As #2341, with Taipei 2008 emblem in margin   10.00 10.00
No. 2341 sold for 30b. On Nos. 2056, 2108 and 2161, gold rings have white centers. No. 2269 has gold dots only.

A832

A833

A834

A835

Children's Art — A836

No. 2342: a, Stilt walkers, by Kemtis Kumsrijan. b, Flying kites, by Natapol Saelim. c, Puppet show, by Sirada Chokeyangkul. d, Thien Phansa, by Salinthip Narongpun. e, People thanking rice plants, by Amornthep Jitnak.

2008, Jan. 12   Litho.   Perf. 14½x14
Granite Paper

2342	Horiz. strip of 5	2.00	2.00
a.	A832 3b multi	.35	.30
b.	A833 3b multi	.35	.30
c.	A834 3b multi	.35	.30
d.	A835 3b multi	.35	.30
e.	A836 3b multi	.35	.30

Children's Day.

Chinese New Year — A837

No. 2343: a, Mask, black denomination at UR (29x48mm). b, Mask, black denomination at LL (29x48mm). c, Masks, green denomination at UL (29x24mm). d, People celebrating, green denomination at LL (29x24mm).

2008, Feb. 1   Litho.   Perf. 14½x14¼
Granite Paper

2343	A837 5b Block of 4, #a-d	2.25	2.25
e.	Souvenir sheet, #2343a-2343b	2.50	2.50

No. 2343e sold for 20b. For surcharges, see No. 2358.

Pink Rose — A838

2008, Feb. 7   Litho.   Perf. 13
Granite Paper

2344	A838 5b multi	.45	.40

No. 2344 is impregnated with a rose scent.

Postman in Boat — A839

2008, Mar. 3   Perf. 14¼
Granite Paper

2345	A839 3b multi	.25	.25

Stylized People Holding Heart — A840

2008, Mar. 17   Granite Paper

2346	A840 3b multi	.35	.30

Printed in sheets of 10 and in sheets of 10 + 10 labels that could be personalized.

Nos. B78-B79 Surcharged in Gold and Black

Methods, Perfs and Watermarks As Before

2008, Mar. 26

2347	Horiz. strip of 4 (#B78)	4.00	3.00
a.-d.	SP13 15b on 2b+1b #B78a-B78d, Any single	1.00	.75
2348	Horiz. strip of 4 (#B79)	4.00	3.00
a.-d.	SP13 15b on 2b+1b #B79a-B79d, Any single	1.00	.75

Miniature Sheet

Chatukham Rammathep — A841

No. 2349: a, Statue, maroon panels, "Chatukham" above denomination. b, Gold amulet, light gray background. c, Statue, maroon panels, "Rammathep" above denomination. d, Statue, yellow panels, "Chatukham" above denomination. e, Gold amulet with inner ring, dark gray background. f, Statue, yellow panels, "Rammathep" above denomination. g, Silver and brown amulet, bister background. h, Silver amulet, blue background. i, Silver and red amulet, orange brown background. j, Silver and red amulet, olive green background. k, Black amulet, pale blue green background. l, Red brown amulet, pink background.

Litho. & Embossed
Perf. 13½x13¼

2008, Mar. 29   Unwmk.

2310	A841 9b Sheet of 12, #a-l	10.00	10.00

No. 2349 was printed in sheets of 12 with and without a row of perforations through the center of the sheet. For surcharges, see No. 2588.

A842

A843

A844

Angels and Demons — A845

2008, Apr. 2   Litho.   Perf. 14x14½
Granite Paper

2350	A842 3b multi	.35	.30
2351	A843 3b multi	.35	.30
2352	A844 3b multi	.35	.30
2353	A845 3b multi	.35	.30
a.	Miniature sheet, #2350-2353, perf. 13¼	3.00	3.00
	Nos. 2350-2353 (4)	1.40	1.20

No. 2353a sold for 20b.

Miniature Sheet

Provincial Seals — A846

No. 2354 — Seals of: a, Nakhon Ratchasima. b, Nakhon Si Thammarat. c, Nakhon Sawan. d, Nonthaburi. e, Narathiwat. f, Nan. g, Buri Ram. h, Pathum Thani. i, Prachuap Khiri Khan. j, Prachin Buri.

Litho. & Embossed With Foil Application

2008, Apr. 2   Perf. 13
Granite Paper

2354	A846 3b Sheet of 10, #a-j	5.50	5.50

Nos. 1764, 1817-1818 Surcharged in Gold and Black

c

Methods and Perfs As Before
2008

2355	A572(c) 15b on 6b #1764	.95	.95

Granite Paper

2356	A590(c) 15b on 6b #1817	.95	.95
2357	A590(c) 15b on 9b #1818	.95	.95
	Nos. 2355-2357 (3)	2.85	2.85

Nos. 2343a, 2343c, 2343d, and Items Similar to Nos. 2343b and 2343e Surcharged in Gold and Black — d

Methods and Perfs As Before
2008, Apr. 25   Granite Paper

2358	Block of 4 (#2343)	4.50	4.50
a.	A837(d) 15b on 5b #2343a	1.10	1.10
b.	A837(d) 15b on 5b stamp similar to #2343a	1.10	1.10
c.-d.	A837(c) 15b on 5b Either single, #2343c-2343d	1.10	1.10
e.	A837(d) 15b on 5b sheet similar to #2343e	4.50	3.75

No. 2358b is a surcharge on an unissued stamp similar to No. 2343b that was printed with the incorrectly-spelled inscription "Chinese Neww Year." The extra "w" is obliterated by a gold circle in the surcharge on No. 2358b found in in the block of four or in the souvenir sheet, No. 2358e.

Diplomatic Relations Between Thailand and Turkey, 50th Anniv. — A847

No. 2359: a, Flag of Thailand, Wat Rajannada, Bangkok. b, Flag of Turkey, Blue Mosque, Istanbul.

2008, May 12   Litho.   Perf. 13¼
Granite Paper

2359	A847 3b Horiz. pair, #a-b	.55	.55

See Turkey Nos. 3108-3109.

Sunflowers A848

2008, May 16   Perf. 13
Granite Paper

2360	A848 3b multi	.25	.25

Visakhapuja Day — A849

2008, May 19   *Perf. 14¼x14½*
Granite Paper
2361 A849 3b multi   .35 .30

A850

A851

A852

World
Environment
Day — A853

2008, June 5   *Perf. 13½*
Granite Paper
2362 A850 3b multi   .25 .25
2363 A851 3b multi   .25 .25
2364 A852 3b multi   .25 .25
2365 A853 3b multi   .25 .25
    Nos. 2362-2365 (4)   1.00 1.00

Miniature Sheet

Orchids — A854

No. 2366: a, Brassocattleya Ploenpit Star. b,
Aerides falcata. c, Arachnis Hookeriana x
Vanda Doctor Anek. d, Phalaenopsis Little

Mary. e, Dendrobium sutiknoi. f, Paphiopedilum callosum. g, Grammatophyllum
speciosum. h, Vascostylis Prapawan. i, Vanda
Robert's Delight.

2008, June 13   **Litho.**   *Perf. 14x14½*
Granite Paper
2366 A854 3b Sheet of 9, #a-i   3.25 3.25

A855

A856

A857

A858

A859

A860

A861

A862

A863

Bangkok
Attractions
A864

2008, July 11   *Perf. 13¼x13½*
Granite Paper
2367   Sheet of 10   4.50 4.50
  a. A855 3b multi   .35 .25
  b. A856 3b multi   .35 .25
  c. A857 3b multi   .35 .25
  d. A858 3b multi   .35 .25
  e. A859 3b multi   .35 .25
  f. A860 3b multi   .35 .25
  g. A861 3b multi   .35 .25
  h. A862 3b multi   .35 .25
  i. A863 3b multi   .35 .25
  j. A864 3b multi   .35 .25

Miniature Sheet

Mountain Region Attractions — A865

No. 2368: a, Phu Chi Fa. b, Phu Pha Thoep.
c, Heo Narok Waterfall. d, Phang-Ung. e, Sun
Crack. f, Phu Khao Hin Pakarang. g, Phae
Mueang Phi Earth Pillar. h, Phu Kradueng. i,
Phu Soi Dao. j, Khun Mae Ya.

2008, July 11   **Litho.**
Granite Paper
2368 A865 15b Sheet of 10,
    #a-j   11.00 11.00
  o.   Sheet of 3, #2368a, 2368b,
    2368g   3.75 3.75

No. 2368o sold for 60b at Thailand 7-11
stores. No. 2368o exists with two different
sheet margins.

Thailand Flag
— A865a

Thai Pavilion —
A865b

Elephants —
A865c

Cassia Fistula
— A865d

2008, July 25   **Litho.**   *Perf. 14¼x14½*
2368K A865a 3b multi   .45 .25
2368L A865b 3b multi   .45 .25
2368M A865c 3b multi   .45 .25
2368N A865d 3b multi   .45 .25
    Nos. 2368K-2368N (4)   1.80 1.00

Nos. 2368K-2368N were printed by a different printer than Nos. 2101-2104.
No. 2368K has a taller, rounder "3" than No.
2101.
No. 2368L has a black line under the building railing at bottom. On No. 2102, the railing
touches the white frame of the stamp.
On No. 2368M, the country name, having
small dots of color in the lettering, appears
pale gray, and the entire vignette has a fuzzy
appearance. On No. 2103, the country name
is all white and the vignette is sharper.
On No. 2368N, the area without flowers has
a blue appearance, and the flowers have a
greener appearance. On No. 2104, the area
without flowers has a purple appearance, and
the flowers appear browner. The screens used
on these stamps differ, with No. 2368N having
coarser dots than No. 2104. Under magnification the bottom edge of the vignette has more
of a saw-tooth appearance on No. 2368N than
on No. 2104.

Postman, Tree
and
Dove — A866

2008, Aug. 1   *Perf. 14¼*
Granite Paper
2369 A866 3b multi   .35 .30
  a.   Perf. 13   4.50 4.50

A867

Thailand Postal Service, 125th
Anniv. — A868

Designs: No. 2370, 3b, Unissued 1-fuang
stamp of 1883 and various modern Thailand
stamps. No. 2371, 3b, Old and modern post
offices. No. 2372, 3b, Old and modern post
office counters. No. 2373, 3b, Old and modern
postal delivery men. No. 2374, 3b, Old and
modern postal trucks.
No. 2375: a, 5b, Thailand #2 in black and
Post Office. b, 5b, Thailand #3. c, 5b, Thailand
#4. d, 10b, Thailand #5a. e, 25b, Hologram of
Thailand #1 with added Thai words.

**Litho., Litho. With Hologram Affixed
(#2375e)**
2008, Aug. 4   *Perf. 14½x14*
Granite Paper
2370-2374 A867   Set of 5   1.60 1.10
    Perf. 13¼x13½
2375 A868   Sheet of 5 #a-e   4.50 4.50

Communications
Day — A869

2008, Aug. 4   **Litho.**   *Perf. 14x14½*
Granite Paper
2376 A869 3b multi   .35 .30
End of telegraph message service in
Thailand.

Painting of Flowers by Princess Maha Chakri Sirindhorn A870

2008, Aug. 4   Perf. 13½x13¼
Granite Paper
2377 A870 5b multi   .45 .40

Peacocks A871

Designs: No. 2378, 10b, Peacock on branch. No. 2379, 10b, Peacock with tail feathers raised.

Litho. & Embossed With Hologram Affixed
2008, Aug. 9   Perf. 13¼
Granite Paper
2378-2379 A871 Set of 2   2.00 1.60
2379a   Souvenir sheet, #2378-2379   3.75 3.25
No. 2379a sold for 30b.

Nos. 1749-1750, 1785 Surcharged in Black

Methods and Perfs As Before
2008, Oct. 1   **Granite Paper**
2380 A568 10b on 6b #1749   3.25 3.25
2381 A579 10b on 6b #1785   3.25 3.25
2382 A568 50b on 7b #1750   7.50 7.50
    Nos. 2380-2382 (3)   14.00 14.00

Diplomatic Relations Between Thailand and Republic of Korea, 50th Anniv. — A872

No. 2383: a, Chakri Maha Prasat Throne Hall, Thailand (denomination at L). b, Juhamnu Mansion, Changdeok Palace, Korea (denomination at R).

2008, Oct. 1   Litho.   Perf. 14½x14
Granite Paper
2383 A872 3b Horiz. pair, #a-b   .55 .55
See South Korea No. 2295.

Intl. Letter Writing Week — A873

Shadow puppets: No. 2384, 3b, Rishi. No. 2385, 3b, Shiva. No. 2386, 3b, Shadow play preluder. No. 2387, 3b, Theng the Jester.

2008, Oct. 4   Perf. 14x14½
Granite Paper
2384-2387 A873 Set of 4   .90 .90
2387a   Souvenir sheet, #2384-2387, perf. 13½   2.40 2.40
No. 2387a sold for 18b.

Miniature Sheet

Provincial Seals — A874

No. 2388 — Seal of: a, Pattani. b, Phra Nakhon Si Ayutthaya. c, Phang-Nga. d, Phatthalung. e, Phayao. f, Phichit. g, Phitsanulok. h, Phetchaburi. i, Phetchabun. j, Phrae.

Litho. & Embossed With Foil Application
2008, Oct. 10   Perf. 13¾
Granite Paper
2388 A874 3b Sheet of 10, #a-j   4.50 4.50

Thailand No. 119 — A875

2008, Oct. 23   Litho.   Perf. 13½x13¼
Granite Paper
2389 A875 5b multi   .45 .40
Equestrian statue of King Chulalongkorn, cent.

New Year 2009 — A876

Water lilies: No. 2390, 3b, Nymphaea "Suwanna." No. 2391, 3b, Nymphaea "Tankhwan." No. 2392, 3b, Nymphaea "Tanpong." No. 2393, 3b, Nymphaea "Mangala-Ubol."

2008, Nov. 15   Litho.   Perf. 14x14½
Granite Paper
2390-2393 A876 Set of 4   .70 .55
2393a   Souvenir sheet of 4, #2390-2393   .95 .75
No. 2393a sold for 17b. A sheet similar to No. 2393a, with the China 2009 World Stamp Exhibition emblem in the sheet margin, sold for 30b.

Miniature Sheet

Cremation of Princess Galyani Vadhana (1933-2008) — A877

No. 2394 — Princess: a, As child. b, Wearing sash. c, Wearing cap. d, Wearing red dress.

2008, Nov. 11   Perf. 14x14¾
Granite Paper
2394 A877 5b Sheet of 4, #a-d   3.00 1.75
No. 2394 exists imperf. Value, $160.

King Bhumibol Adulyadej, 81st Birthday A070

2008, Dec. 3   Perf. 13¼
Granite Paper
2395 A878 3b multi   .25 .25

Somdet Chao Phraya Borom Maha Sisuriyawong (1808-83), Regent of King Chulalongkorn A879

2008, Dec. 23   Perf. 14x14¼
Granite Paper
2396 A879 3b multi   .35 .30

New Year 2009 (Year of the Ox) — A880

2009, Jan. 2   Litho.   Perf. 14¼
Granite Paper
2397 A880 3b multi   .35 .30
a.   Perf. 13 (#2796a)   .30 .25
Issued: No. 2397a, 1/1/14.

Miniature Sheet

Children's Day — A881

No. 2398 — Characters from "Phra Abhai Manee," poem by Phra Sunthorn Voharn: a, Sri Suvan with pole. b, Phra Abhai Manee with flute. c, Mermaid and fish. d, Giant woman in water. e, Sud Sakhon falling. f, Old man with tiger skin clothes. g, Naked man with stick. h, King's daughter.

2009   Perf. 14¾x14
Granite Paper
2398 A881 3b Sheet of 8, #a-h   6.50 6.50
i.   Souvenir sheet, #2398a-2398d, perf. 13¼   9.00 9.00
Issued: No. 2398, 1/10; No. 2398i, May. Honk Kong 2009 Intl. Philatelic Exhibition (No. 2398i).

A882

A883

A884

Prince Bhanurangsi (1860-1928), Founder of Thai Postal Service — A885

2009, Jan. 11   *Perf. 14x14¾*
Granite Paper

2399	A882 3b multi	.35	.30
2400	A883 3b multi	.35	.30
2401	A884 3b multi	.35	.30
2402	A885 3b multi	.35	.30
a.	Souvenir sheet of 4, #2399-2402, perf. 13½	2.25	2.25
	Nos. 2399-2402 (4)	1.40	1.20

No. 2402a sold for 20b. No. 2402a exists imperf. Value, $27.50.

White Rose — A886

Litho. & Embossed
2009, Feb. 6   *Perf. 13*
Granite Paper

2403	A886 5b multi	.45	.40

School of Postal Services — A887

2009, Feb. 22   **Litho.**   *Perf. 14¾x14*
Granite Paper

2404	A887 3b multi	.35	.30

Red Cross — A888

2009, Mar. 30   **Granite Paper**

2405	A888 3b multi	.35	.30

Prince Krom Luang Wongsa Dhiraj Snid (1808-71), Physician — A889

2009, Mar. 30   *Perf. 14x14¾*
Granite Paper

2406	A889 3b multi	.35	.30

Nos. 1736-1737 Surcharged in Gold

Methods, Perfs and Watermarks As Before
2009, Apr. 1

2407	A564 30b on 6b #1736	22.50	11.00
2408	A564 46b on 9b #1737	37.50	16.00

Prasat Ta Muean, Surin Province — A890

Prasat Ta Muean Thom, Surin Province — A891

Prasat Ta Muean Tot, Surin Province — A892

Prasat Sadok Kok Thom, Sa Kaeo Province — A893

Perf. 14¾x14
2009, Apr. 2   **Litho.**   **Unwmk.**
Granite Paper

2409	A890 3b multi	.35	.30
2410	A891 3b multi	.35	.30
2411	A892 3b multi	.35	.30
2412	A893 3b multi	.35	.30
a.	Souvenir sheet of 4, #2409-2412, perf. 13½	2.00	2.00
	Nos. 2409-2412 (4)	1.40	1.20

Royal Headgear — A894

Designs: No. 2413, 5b, Gold brocade hat. No. 2414, 5b, Felt hat. No. 2415, 5b, Battle helmet. No. 2416, 5b, Grand diamond hat.

2009, Apr. 6   *Perf. 13*
Granite Paper

2413-2416	A894 Set of 4	1.75	1.75
2416a	Souvenir sheet of 4, #2413-2416	2.40	2.40

No. 2416a sold for 25b.

Visakhapuja Day — A895

2009, May 8   *Perf. 14¼x14½*
Granite Paper

2417	A895 3b multi	.35	.30

Statues of Hindu Gods — A896

Designs: No. 2418, 5b, Ganesa. No. 2419, 5b, Brahma. No. 2420, 5b, Narayana. No. 2421, 5b, Siva.

Litho. & Embossed
2009, June 2   *Perf. 13¼*
Granite Paper

2418-2421	A896 Set of 4	1.75	1.75
2421a	Souvenir sheet of 4, #2418-2421	2.40	2.40

No. 2421a sold for 25b. No. 2421a exists imperf. Value, $125.

Orchids — A897

Designs: No. 2422, 3b, Cattleya Queen Sirikhit. No. 2423, 3b, Paphiopedilum Princess Sangwan. No. 2424, 3b, Sirindhornia pulchella. No. 2425, 3b, Phalaenopsis Princess Chulabhorn. No. 2426, 3b, Dendrobium "Pink Nagarindra." No. 2427, 3b, Ascocenda Sukontharat. No. 2428, 3b, Dendrobium "Soamsawali."

2009, June 5   **Litho.**   *Perf. 14½x14*
Granite Paper

2422-2428	A897 Set of 7	1.25	.95
2428a	Sheet of 7, #2422-2428, perf. 13¼	1.75	1.40

No. 2428a sold for 30b.

Diplomatic Relations Between Thailand and the Philippines, 60th Anniv. — A898

No. 2429 — Stick dancers with denomination in: a, Pale yellow. b, Light blue.

2009, June 14   **Granite Paper**

2429	A898 3b Horiz. pair, #a-b	.35	.30

Thammasat University, 75th Anniv. — A899

2009, June 27   *Perf. 14x14½*

2430	A899 3b multi	.35	.30

A900

A901

A902

Candle Procession Festival — A903

2009, July 6   *Perf. 14x14½*

2431	A900 3b multi	.55	.50
2432	A901 3b multi	.55	.50
2433	A902 3b multi	.55	.50
2434	A903 3b multi	.55	.50
a.	Souvenir sheet of 4, #2431-2434, perf. 13¼	3.00	3.00
	Nos. 2431-2434 (4)	2.20	2.00

No. 2434a sold for 20b.

King Bhumibol Adulyadej Type of 1996
Die Cut Perf. 13¼x13¾
2009, Aug. 4   **Litho.**
Self-Adhesive

2435	A550 3b bister brn & bl	.35	.30

Natl. Communications Day — A904

2009, Aug. 4   *Perf. 14½x14*
Granite Paper

2436	A904 3b multi	.35	.30

Hun Lakorn Lek Puppetry — A905

Puppets and puppeteers with: No. 2437, 25b, Orange panel at right. No. 2438, 25b, Orange panel at left.
No. 2439, 25b, No orange panel.

Litho. With Three-Dimensional Plastic Affixed
2009, Aug. 4   *Perf. 17*
Self-Adhesive
2437-2438 A905 Set of 2   5.50 5.50
Souvenir Sheet
Perf. 12¼x12
2439 A905 25b multi   5.50 5.50

Miniature Sheet

Provincial Seals — A906

No. 2440 — Seals of: a, Phuket. b, Maha Sarakham. c, Mukdahan. d, Mae Hong Son. e, Yasothon. f, Yala. g, Roi Et. h, Nanong. I, Rayong. j, Ratchaburi.

Litho. & Embossed With Foil Application
2009, Sept. 7   *Perf. 13*
Granite Paper
2440 A906 3b Sheet of 10, #a-j   3.25 3.25

Guan Yin Bodhisat A907

2009, Sept. 9 Litho.   *Perf. 14½x14¼*
Granite Paper
2441 A907 9b multi   1.00 1.00
  a.   Souvenir sheet of 1   1.60 1.60
No. 2441a sold for 15b. No. 2441a exists imperf. without gum. Value, $160.

Natl. Telecommunications Commission — A908

2009, Oct. 1   *Perf. 14x14½*
Granite Paper
2442 A908 3b multi   .35 .30

Royal Carriages A909

Designs: No. 2443, 3b, Four-wheeled dog cart. No. 2444, 3b, Postillion landau. No. 2445, 3b, C-spring phaeton. No. 2446, 3b, Glass state coach.

2009, Oct. 7   *Perf. 13¼x13½*
Granite Paper
2443-2446 A909 Set of 4   1.25 1.25
2446a   Souvenir sheet of 4,
  #2443-2446   2.25 2.25
No. 2446a sold for 20b.

A910

A911

A912

Intl. Letter Writing Week — A913

2009, Oct. 9   *Perf. 14x14½*
Granite Paper
2447 A910 3b multi   .35 .30
2448 A911 3b multi   .35 .30
2449 A912 3b multi   .35 .30
2450 A913 3b multi   .35 .30
  a.   Souvenir sheet of 4, #2447-2450, perf. 13½   2.25 2.25
  Nos. 2447-2450 (4)   1.40 1.20
No. 2450a sold for 20b.

New Year 2010 — A914

Flowers: No. 2451, 3b, Drosera peltata. No. 2452, 3b, Sonerila griffithii. No. 2453, 3b, Cyanotis arachnoidea. No. 2454, 3b, Caulokaempferia saxicola.

2009, Nov. 15   *Perf. 14½x14*
Granite Paper
2451-2454 A914 Set of 4   1.25 1.25
2454a   Souvenir sheet of 4,
  #2451-2454   1.60 1.60
No. 2454a sold for 15b.

Princess Bejaratana Ratsuda, 84th Birthday — A915

2009, Nov. 24   *Perf. 13¼*
Granite Paper
2455 A915 3b multi   .45 .40

Royal Thai Army Medical Department, 110th Anniv. — A916

Designs: No. 2456, 3b, Building, medic treating soldier. No. 2457, 3b, Soldier with rifle, knapsack and medical bag, soldiers carrying litter to medical helicopter. No. 2458, 3b, Medic treating soldier, doctors in surgery. No. 2459, 3b, Hospital, soldier saluting.

2009, Nov. 25   *Perf. 14½x14*
Granite Paper
2456-2459 A916 Set of 4   1.25 1.25
2459a   Souvenir sheet of 4,
  #2456-2459   16.00 —

King Bhumibol Adulyadej, 82nd Birthday — A917

2009, Dec. 5   *Perf. 14½x14*
Granite Paper
2460 A917 9b multi   1.00 1.00

Thailand Earth Observation Satellite — A918

2009, Dec. 5   *Litho.*
Granite Paper
2461 A918 3b multi   .35 .30
A gritty substance has been applied to portions of the design.

Education for the Blind — A919

2009, Dec. 12   **Litho. & Embossed**
Granite Paper
2462 A919 3b multi   .35 .30

New Year 2010 (Year of the Tiger) — A920

2010, Jan. 1   **Litho.**   *Perf. 13*
Granite Paper
2463 A920 3b multi   .25 .25

2010 Population and Housing Census — A921

2010, Jan. 5   **Litho.**   *Perf. 13½*
Granite Paper
2465 A921 3b multi   .25 .25

King Bhumibol Adulyadej Type of 1996
2010, Jan. 8   *Perf. 14x14½*
Granite Paper
2465A A550 3b bister brn & bl   .25 .25

Young Phra Sang A922

Chao Ngo and Nang Rotchana — A923

Phra Sang A924

Phra Sang Playing Polo — A925

2010, Jan. 9   *Perf. 14½x14*
Granite Paper

2466	A922	3b multi	.25	.25
2467	A923	3b multi	.25	.25
2468	A924	3b multi	.25	.25
2469	A925	3b multi	.25	.25
	Nos. 2466-2469 (4)		1.00	1.00

Characters from Sang Thong. National Children's Day.

Euah Suntornsanan (1910-81), Composer and Musician — A926

2010, Jan. 21   *Perf. 14x14½*
Granite Paper

| 2470 | A926 | 3b multi | .25 | .25 |

Child Praying
A927

Birthday Cake
A928

Flowers
A929

Heart
A930

Moon and Stars
A931

Balloons
A932

2010, Jan. 28   Litho.   *Perf. 14x14½*
Granite Paper (#2471-2476)

2471	A927	3b multi	.25	.25
2472	A928	3b multi	.25	.25
2473	A929	3b multi	.25	.25
2474	A930	3b multi	.25	.25
2475	A931	3b multi	.25	.25
2476	A932	3b multi	.25	.25
	Nos. 2471-2476 (6)		1.50	1.50

Litho. With Holographic Film
Self-Adhesive
Die Cut Perf. 13½x13¾

2477	A927	3b multi	.25	.25
2478	A928	3b multi	.25	.25
2479	A929	3b multi	.25	.25
2480	A930	3b multi	.25	.25
2481	A931	3b multi	.25	.25
2482	A932	3b multi	.25	.25
a.	Sheet of 6, #2477-2482		1.50	
	Nos. 2477-2482 (6)		1.50	1.50

No. 2482a sold for 25b.

Red Rose — A933

Litho. & Embossed
2010, Feb. 5   *Perf. 13*
Granite Paper

| 2483 | A933 | 5b multi | .30 | .25 |

A rose-scented scratch-and-sniff panel was applied over a rose leaf. A souvenir sheet containing one No. 2483 sold for 14b.

A934

A935

Chinese Deities — A936

2010, Feb. 8   Litho.   *Perf. 14x14½*
Granite Paper

2484	A934	5b multi	.30	.25
2485	A935	5b multi	.30	.25
2486	A936	5b multi	.30	.25
a.	Souvenir sheet of 3, #2484-2486, perf. 13½x13¼		1.50	1.10
	Nos. 2484-2486 (3)		.90	.75

No. 2486a sold for 24b.

A937

A938

A939

Fantasy World Painting Competition — A940

2010, Feb. 25   Litho.   *Perf. 13½*
Granite Paper

2487	A937	5b multi	.30	.25
2488	A938	5b multi	.30	.25
2489	A939	5b multi	.30	.25
2490	A940	5b multi	.30	.25
a.	Souvenir sheet of 4, #2487-2490		1.75	1.40
	Nos. 2487-2490 (4)		1.20	1.00

Bangkok 2010 Intl. Stamp Exhibition. No. 2490a sold for 28b.

Red Cross — A941

2010, Mar. 30   *Perf. 13½*
Granite Paper

| 2491 | A941 | 3b multi | .25 | .25 |

Postman Carrying Parcel — A942

2010, Mar. 30   *Perf. 13*
Granite Paper

| 2492 | A942 | 3b multi | .25 | .25 |

Heritage Conservation Day — A943

Designs: No. 2493, 3b, Jalimangalasana Residence, Sanam Chandra Palace. No. 2494, 3b, Phiman Chakri Hall, Phyathai Palace. No. 2495, 3b, Phra Ram Ratchaniwet Palace. No. 2496, 3b, Main Building, Srapathum Palace.

2010, Apr. 2   *Perf. 14½x14*
Granite Paper

| 2493-2496 | A943 | Set of 4 | .75 | .55 |
| 2496a | | Souvenir sheet of 4, #2493-2496, perf. 13½ | 1.25 | .95 |

No. 2496a sold for 19b.

King Chao Phraya Chakkri (Rama I) (1736-1809) A944

2010, Apr. 6   *Perf. 13¼*
Granite Paper

| 2497 | A944 | 3b multi | .25 | .25 |

Wedding of King Bhumibol Adulyadej and Queen Sirikit, 60th Anniv. — A945

King and Queen: No. 2498, 15b, As young couple. No. 2499, 15b, As older couple.

Litho. & Embossed With Foil
Application
2010, Apr. 28   *Perf. 13¼*

| 2498-2499 | A945 | Set of 2 | 1.90 | 1.40 |
| 2499a | | Souvenir sheet of 2, #2498-2499 | 3.75 | 3.00 |

Values for Nos. 2498-2499 are for stamps with surrounding selvage. No. 2499a sold for 60b.

Thai Airways International, 50th Anniv. — A946

Airplanes: No. 2500, 3b, DC-6. No. 2501, 3b, DC-10. No. 2502, 3b, Boeing 747-400. No. 2503, 3b, Airbus A340-600.

Litho. & Embossed
2010, May 1   *Perf. 14¼x14½*
Granite Paper

| 2500-2503 | A946 | Set of 4 | .75 | .55 |
| 2503a | | Souvenir sheet of 4, #2500-2503 | 1.40 | 1.10 |

No. 2503a sold for 22b.

Coronation of King Bhumibol Adulyadej, 60th Anniv. A947

2010, May 5   Litho.   *Perf. 13¼*
Granite Paper

| 2504 | A947 | 9b multi | .55 | .40 |

Visakhapuja Day — A948

2010, May 28   *Perf. 14¼x14½*
Granite Paper
2505 A948 3b multi   .25 .25
a.   Souvenir sheet of 4, #2293,
        2361, 2417, 2505   1.25 .95
        No. 2505a sold for 20b.

Tourism Authority of Thailand, 50th Anniv. — A949

Designs: No. 2506, 3b, Wat Arun, Bangkok. No. 2507, 3b, Royal barge. No. 2508, 3b, Canoeists near shore. No. 2509, 3b, Tourists on elephants fording river.

2010, June 1   **Litho.**
Granite Paper
2506-2509 A949 Set of 4   .75 .55

Election Commission, 12th Anniv. — A950

2010, June 9   *Perf. 13½*
Granite Paper
2510 A950 3b multi   .25 .25

No. 1960 Surcharged in Silver
Miniature Sheet

Designs as before.

Method and Perf. As Before
2010, June 16   **Granite Paper**
2511 A642   Sheet of 9   55.00 42.50
a.-f. 100b on 3b Any single   6.00 4.50
g.-i. 100b on 6b Any single   6.00 4.50

No. 1776 Surcharged in Gold

Method and Perf. As Before
2010, June 16   **Granite Paper**
2512 A577 200b on 9b #1776   12.50 9.50

Bangkok General Post Office Building, 70th Anniv. — A951

Designs: No. 2513, 3b, Sculptures of Type A15 stamp, Garuda. No. 2514, 3b, Sculptures of Type A29 stamp, man at table. 5b, General Post Office Building, horiz. (57x23mm).

Perf. 14x14½, 14½x14
2010, June 24   **Litho.**
Granite Paper
2513-2515 A951 Set of 3   .70 .55

King Nang Khlao Chao Youhua (Rama III) (1787-1851) A952

2010, July 21   *Perf. 13¼*
Granite Paper
2516 A952 3b multi   .25 .25

Miniature Sheet

Provincial Seals — A953

No. 2517 — Seals of: a, Lop Buri. b, Lampang. c, Lamphun. d, Loei. e, Si Sa Ket. f, Sakon Nakhon. g, Songkhla. h, Satun. i, Samut Prakan. j, Samut Songkhram.

Litho. With Foil Application
2010, July 23   *Perf. 13*
Granite Paper
2517 A953 Sheet of 10, #a-j   1.90 1.40

National Communications Day — A954

2010, Aug. 4   Litho.   *Perf. 14½x14*
Granite Paper
2518 A954 3b multi   .25 .25

Peacock A955

Inscriptions: No. 2519, 15b, Thai Silk. No. 2520, 15b, Thai Silk Blend. No. 2521, 25b, Classic Thai Silk. No. 2522, 25b, Royal Thai Silk.

Litho. With Foil Application on
Affixed Silk Oval
2010, Aug. 4   *Perf. 13¼*
2519-2522 A955 Set of 4   5.00 3.75

Bangkok 2010 Intl. Stamp Exhibition. A souvenir sheet containing one No. 2522 sold for 60b.

Orchids — A956

Rhynchostylis gigantea varieties: No. 2523, 3b, Speckle. No. 2524, 3b, Kultana strain. No. 2525, 3b, Alba. No. 2526, 3b, Rubrum.

2010, Aug. 5   Litho.   *Perf. 14x14½*
Granite Paper
2523-2526 A956 Set of 4   .75 .55
2526a   Souvenir sheet of 4,
           #2523-2526, perf. 13½ 1.25 .95

No. 2526a sold for 20b. A sheet similar to No. 2526a with the emblem of the 4th Siam Paragon Bangkok Royal Orchid Paradise sold for 80b.

Thai Literature Heritage — A957

2010, Aug. 7   *Perf. 14½x14*
Granite Paper
2527 A957 3b multi   .25 .25

Flag of Thailand — A958   Cassia Flowers — A959

2010, Aug. 12   *Perf. 14¼x14½*
Granite Paper
2528 A958 3b multi   .25 .25
2529 A959 3b multi   .25 .25

Nos. 1687 and 1689 Surcharged

Methods, Perfs. and Watermarks As
Before
2010, Aug. 27
2530 A543 10b on 9b #1688   .65 .50
2531 A543 10b on 9b #1689   .65 .50

No. 1736 Surcharged in Gold

Method, Perf. and Watermark As
Before
2010, Sept. 1
2532 A564 10b on 6b #1736   .65 .50

Miniature Sheet

Queen Savang Vadhana (1862-1955) — A960

No. 2533: a, Queen Savang Vadhana. b, Prince Mahidol and his wife, Princess Srinagarindra. c, King Bhumibol Adulyadej and women (denomination in yellow), horiz. d, King Bhumibol Adulyadej and Queen Sirikit (denomination in dark blue), horiz.

Perf. 13¼ (#2533a),
13¼x13¼x14½x13¼ (#2533b),
14½x14
2010, Sept. 10   Litho.   Unwmk.
Granite Paper
2533 A960 3b Sheet of 4, #a-d   .80 .60

Royal Thai Mint, 150th Anniv. — A961

No. 2534: a, Coin, old Mint building, denomination at LR. b, Coin, new Mint building, denomination at LL.

Litho. & Embossed
2010, Sept. 17   *Perf. 13¼*
Granite Paper
2534 A961   Horiz. pair   .70 .55
a.-b. 5b Either single   .35 .25
c.   Souvenir sheet of 2, #2534a-
         2534b   1.40 1.10
         No. 2534c sold for 20b.

National Youth Day — A962

2010, Sept. 20   Litho.   *Perf. 14½x14*
Granite Paper
2535 A962 3b multi   .25 .25

Tin Toys — A963

Designs: No. 2536, 3b, Wind-up rabbit and chicken. No. 2537, 3b, Chinese rattle drums. No. 2538, 3b, Pop gun. No. 2539, 3b, Boats. No. 2540, 3b, Boy on tricycle. No. 2541, 3b, Tops.

2010, Oct. 5   **Perf. 13**
Granite Paper
2536-2541 A963 Set of 6   1.25 .95

A souvenir sheet containing Nos. 2536-2538 and a souvenir sheet containing Nos. 2539-2541 exist. Each sold for 20b.

Curves — A964

2010, Oct. 5   **Perf. 13¼**
Granite Paper
2542 A964 3b green   .25 .25
2543 A964 3b lemon   .25 .25
2544 A964 3b blue   .25 .25
    Nos. 2542-2544 (3)   .75 .75

Department of Comptroller General, 120th Anniv. — A965

2010, Oct. 7   **Perf. 14½x14**
Granite Paper
2545 A965 3b multi   .25 .25

Goddess Guan Yin — A966

2010, Oct. 10   **Perf. 14½x14¼**
Granite Paper
2546 A966 9b multi   .60 .45
a.   Souvenir sheet of 1   1.10 .85
    No. 2546a sold for 15b.

King Bhumibol Adulyadej — A967

2010   **Litho.**   **Perf. 13½x13¼**
Granite Paper
2547 A967 1b blue   .25 .25
2548 A967 2b lake   .25 .25
2549 A967 3b green   .25 .25
2550 A967 5b fawn   .35 .30
2551 A967 6b violet   .40 .30
2552 A967 7b lilac rose   .50 .35
2553 A967 9b yel bister   .60 .45
2554 A967 10b brown & blk   .70 .55
2555 A967 12b bl grn & gray   .80 .60
2556 A967 15b bis & dk grn   1.00 .75
a.   Souvenir sheet of 10, #2547-2556   5.25 4.25

Litho. & Engr.
2557 A967 50b pur & bl grn   3.50 2.60
2558 A967 100b apple grn & grn   6.75 5.25
2559 A967 200b rose & brn   13.50 10.00

Size:24x29mm
2560 A967 500b org brn & brn   34.00 26.00
a.   Souvenir sheet of 4, #2557-2560   60.00 45.00
    Nos. 2547-2560 (14)   62.85 47.90

Issued: Nos. 2547-2556, 2556a, 10/10; Nos. 2557-2560, 2560a, 11/11.

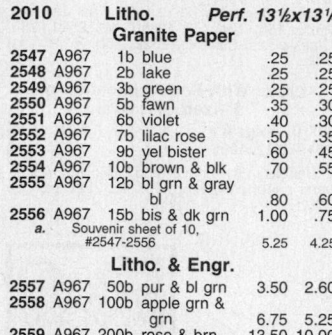

King Chulalongkorn (Rama V) (1853-1910) A968

2010, Oct. 15   **Litho.**   **Perf. 13¼**
Granite Paper
2561 A968 9b multi   .60 .45

Vajiravudh College, Cent. — A969

2010, Nov. 11   **Perf. 13½**
Granite Paper
2562 A969 3b multi   .25 .25

A970

A971

A972

Fireworks A973

2010, Nov. 15   **Perf. 13½**
Granite Paper
2563 A970 3b multi   .25 .25
2564 A971 3b multi   .25 .25
2565 A972 3b multi   .25 .25
2566 A973 3b multi   .25 .25
a.   Souvenir sheet of 4, #2563-2566   1.40 1.10
    Nos. 2563-2566 (4)   1.00 1.00

No. 2566a sold for 20b.

King Bhumibol Adulyadej, 83rd Birthday A974

Litho. With Rice Grain Affixed
2010, Dec. 5   **Perf. 13¼**
Granite Paper
2567 A974 9b multi   .60 .45

New Year 2011 (Year of the Rabbit) — A975

2011, Jan. 1   **Litho.**   **Perf. 13**
Granite Paper
2568 A975 3b multi   .25 .25

Khun Chang — A976

Khun Phaen — A977

Kumanthong — A978

Pimpiralai — A979

2011, Jan. 8   **Perf. 13¼**
Granite Paper
2569 A976 3b multi   .25 .25
2570 A977 3b multi   .25 .25
2571 A978 3b multi   .25 .25
2572 A979 3b multi   .25 .25
    Nos. 2569-2572 (4)   1.00 1.00

Khun Chang Khun Phaen, epic poem.

Fruits and Vegetables A980

Designs: No. 2573, 3b, Bottle gourd. No. 2574, 3b, Lime. No. 2575, 3b, Tomato. No. 2576, 3b, Pumpkin.

2011, Jan. 15   **Perf. 13½**
Granite Paper
2573-2576 A980 Set of 4   .80 .60

Li Tie Guai — A981

Han Zhong Li — A982

Lu Dong Bin — A983

Zhang Guo Lao — A984

Lan Cai
He — A985

He Xian
Gu — A986

Han Xiang
Zi — A987

Cao Guo
Jiu — A988

**2011, Feb. 1   Litho. & Embossed
Granite Paper**

2577	A981	3b multi	.25 .25
2578	A982	3b multi	.25 .25
2579	A983	3b multi	.25 .25
2580	A984	3b multi	.25 .25
2581	A985	3b multi	.25 .25
2582	A986	3b multi	.25 .25
2583	A987	3b multi	.25 .25
2584	A988	3b multi	.25 .25
a.		Souvenir sheet of 8, #2577-2584	2.60 2.00
		Nos. 2577-2584 (8)	2.00 2.00

Eight Chinese Immortals.

No. 1820
Surcharged in Gold

No. 1737 Surcharged in Gold

No. 2349
Surcharged

Methods, Perfs and Papers As Before

2011

2585	A550	12b on 9b #1820	.80 .60
2586	A564	50b on 9b #1737	3.25 2.50
2588	A841	Sheet of 12	39.00 39.00
a.-l.		50b on 9b Any single, #2349a-2349l	3.25 2.50

Issued: Nos. 2585, 2586, 2588, 2/2.

Charoen Krung
Road, 150th
Anniv. — A989

**2011, Feb. 5   Litho.   Perf. 14½x14¼
Granite Paper**

2589 A989 3b multi   .25 .25

Love — A990

No. 2590   Heart of: a, Roses. b, Concentric lines.

**2011, Feb. 7   Perf. 13
Granite Paper**

2590 A990 5b Horiz. pair, #a-b   .65 .50

Suankularb Long Building, Bangkok,
Cent. — A991

**2011, Mar. 8   Perf. 14½x14
Granite Paper**

2591 A991 3b multi   .25 .25

Fine Arts
Department,
Cent. — A992

**2011, Mar. 27   Perf. 14x14½
Granite Paper**

2592 A992 3b multi   .25 .25

Princess Maha
Chakri Sirindhorn
Wearing Red
Cross
Uniform — A993

**2011, Mar. 30   Perf. 13¼
Granite Paper**

2593 A993 3b multi   .25 .25

A994

A995

A996

Muang Tam Religious Sanctuary,
Prakhon Chai — A997

**2011, Apr. 2   Perf. 14½x14
Granite Paper**

2594	A994	3b multi	.25 .25
2595	A995	3b multi	.25 .25
2596	A996	3b multi	.25 .25
2597	A997	3b multi	.25 .25
a.		Souvenir sheet of 4, #2594-2597	1.40 1.10
		Nos. 2594-2597 (4)	1.00 1.00

Thai Heritage Conservation Day. No. 2597a sold for 20b.

Momrajawongse
Kukrit Pramoj
(1911-95), Prime
Minister — A998

Kukrit Pramoj: No. 2598, 3b, Wearing uniform with sash, yellow orange panel at right. No. 2599, 3b, Wearing traditional costume, olive green panel at right. No. 2600, 3b, With dogs, brown panel at right, horiz. No. 2601, 3b, With Mao Zedong, gray panel at right, horiz.

**2011, Apr. 20   Perf. 13¼
Granite Paper**

2598-2601 A998 Set of 4   .80 .60

Diplomatic Relations Between
Thailand and Laos, 60th
Anniv. — A999

No. 2602: a, Woman, denomination at LR. b, Woman, denomination at LL. c, Cassia fistula flowers, denomination at LR. d, Plumeria flowers, denomination at LL.

**2011, Apr. 22   Perf. 14x14½
Granite Paper**

2602 A999 3b Block of 4, #a-d   .80 .60
See Laos Nos. 1836-1839.

Postman With
Fork, Spoon and
Foods — A1000

**2011, May 10   Litho.   Perf. 13
Granite Paper**

2603 A1000 3b multi   .25 .25

**Self-Adhesive
Serpentine Die Cut 12**

2604 A1000 3b multi   .25 .25

Pridi Banomyong (1900-83), Prime
Minister — A1001

No. 2605 — Banomyong: a, In suit and tie. b, Wearing uniform and sash.

**2011, May 11   Perf. 13¼
Granite Paper**

2605 A1001 3b Horiz. pair, #a-b   .40 .30

Panyananda Bhikkhu (1911-2007), Buddhist Monk — A1002

Bhikkhu and: No. 2606, 3b, Thai text. No. 2607, 3b, Buddhist temple. No. 2608, 3b, Sculpture. No. 2609, 3b, Shell-shaped award.

2011, May 11   *Perf. 13¼*
Granite Paper
2606-2609 A1002 Set of 4   .80   .60

Visakhapuja Day — A1003

2011, May 17   *Perf. 14½x14¼*
Granite Paper
2610 A1003 3b multi   .25   .25

A souvenir sheet containing one example of No. 2610 sold for 10b.

Orchid Varieties A1004

Designs: No. 2611, 3b, Dendrobium "Cherluk Red." No. 2612, 3b, Dendrobium "Lai Sirin." No. 2613, 3b, Dendrobium "Suree Peach." No. 2614, 3b, Dendrobium "Cheetah."

2011, June 2   *Perf. 14x14½*
Granite Paper
2611-2614 A1004 Set of 4   .80   .60
2614a   Souvenir sheet of 4,
          #2611-2614, perf. 13½   1.40 1.10

No. 2614a sold for 20b. A sheet similar to No. 2614a, but with the emblem of the 5th Siam Paragon Bangkok Royal Orchid Paradise and the date of the show, sold for 100b.

Department of Science Service, 120th Anniv. — A1005

2011, June 23   *Perf. 14½x14*
Granite Paper
2615 A1005 3b multi   .25   .25

No. 2615 was printed in sheets of 20 with stamps from the right column having purple engine turning lines in the background.

Scouting in Thailand, Cent. — A1006

2011, July 1   *Perf. 13¼*
Granite Paper
2616 A1006 3b multi   .25   .25

A1007

Diplomatic Relations Between Thailand and Portugal, 500th Anniv. — A1008

No. 2617: a, Portuguese caravel, rowboats, Thai buildings and temples. b, Elephant and riders at dockside.
No. 2618: a, Portuguese caravel, Thai buildings. b, Thai boats and buildings.

2011, July 20   *Perf. 13½*
Granite Paper
2617 A1007 3b Horiz. pair, #a-b   .40   .30
2618 A1008 3b Horiz. pair, #a-b   .40   .30

See Portugal Nos. 3334-3335.

Miniature Sheet

Provincial Seals — A1009

No. 2619 — Seals of: a, Samut Sakhon. b, Sa Kaeo. c, Saraburi. d, Sing Buri. e, Sukhothai. f, Suphan Buri. g, Surat Thani. h, Surin. i, Nong Khai. j, Nong Bua Lam Phu.

Litho. & Embossed With Foil Application
2011, July 20   *Perf. 13½*
Granite Paper
2619 A1009 3b Sheet of 10, #a-j   2.00 1.50

Sheets of ten identical stamps were available, but these appear to have been sold locally and not through the philatelic bureau.

Thai Alphabet A1010

No. 2620 — Various characters of Thai alphabet that are the first consonants of the word for: a, Chicken. b, Eggs. c, Bottles. d, Water buffalo. e, Person wearing red shirt. f, Bell. g, Snake. h, Plates. i, Cymbals on string. j, Elephant. k, Chain on stump. l, Trees. m, Woman weaing pink blouse. n, Headdress. o, Javelin. p, Pedestal. q, Mandodari (girl wearing headdress). r, Old man. s, Child wearing Buddhist monk's robe. t, Child in overalls. u, Turtle. v, Bags. w, Soldier. x, Flag.
No. 2621 — Various characters of Thai alphabet that are the first consonants of the word for: a, Mouse. b, Leaves. c, Fish. d, Bee on flowers. e, Lids of pots. f, Bowl. g, Teeth. h, Sailboat. i, Horse. j, Yaksha (Buddhist giant). k, Boat. l, Monkey. m, Ring. n, Pavilion. o,

Hermit in cave. p, Tiger. q, Chest. r, Kite. s, Basin with flower. t, Owl.

2011, July 29   **Litho.**   *Perf. 14¼*
Granite Paper
2620   Sheet of 24   6.00 6.00
a.-x. A1010 1b Any single   .25   .25
2621   Sheet of 20 + 4 labels 5.00 5.00
a.-t. A1010 1b Any single   .25   .25

Communications Day — A1011

2011, Aug. 4   *Perf. 14x14½*
Granite Paper
2622 A1011 3b multi   .25   .25

A1012

A1013

A1014

Likay Performers A1015

Litho. With Glitter Affixed
2011, Aug. 4   *Perf. 14x14½*
Granite Paper
2623 A1012 5b multi   .35   .30
2624 A1013 5b multi   .35   .30
2625 A1014 5b multi   .35   .30
2626 A1015 5b multi   .35   .30
a.   Souvenir sheet of 4, #2623-
       2626, perf. 13½   2.00 1.50
       Nos. 2623-2626 (4)   1.40 1.20

Thaipex 2011 Intl. Philatelic Exhibition, Bangkok. No. 2626a sold for 30b.

Philatelists Association of Thailand — A1016

2011, Aug. 9   **Litho.**   *Perf. 13¼*
Granite Paper
2627 A1016 3b multi   .25   .25

Miniature Sheet

Queen Savang Vadhana (1862-1955) — A1017

No. 2628 — Queen Savang Vadhana: a, As child, with King Chulalongkorn (pink background). b, With Crown Prince Maha Vajirunhis (olive green background). c, With Prince Mahitala Dhibesra Adulyadej Vikrom and Princess Valaya Alongkorn (blue violet background), horiz. d, With King Ananda Mahidol, King Bhumibol Adulyadej, Princess Galyani Vadhana, and Prince Rangsit Prayurasakdi (blue green background), horiz.

2011, Sept. 10   *Perf. 13¼*
Granite Paper
2628 A1017 3b Sheet of 4, #a-d   .80   .60

Worldwide Fund for Nature (WWF) — A1018

Cats: No. 2629, 3b, Marbled cat. No. 2630, 3b, Asiatic golden cat. No. 2631, 3b, Leopard cat. No. 2632, 3b, Flat-headed cat.

2011, Sept. 26   *Perf. 13*
Granite Paper
2629-2632 A1018 Set of 4   .80   .60
2632a   Souvenir sheet of 4, #2629-
          2632, + label   1.40 1.10

No. 2632a sold for 20b.

International Letter Writing Week — A1019

Designs: No. 2633, 3b, Girl and boy writing letters. No. 2634, 3b, Girl bringing letter to mail box. No. 2635, 3b, Postman delivering letter to girl. No. 2636, 3b, Boy and girl reading letters.

2011, Oct. 4   **Granite Paper**
2633-2636   A1019   Set of 4   .80   .60
2636a   Souvenir sheet of 4,
       #2633-2636   1.40   1.10
    No. 2636a sold for 20b.

King Bhumibol Adulyadej in Carpentry
Shop — A1020

2011, Oct. 21   **Perf. 13¼**
        Granite Paper
2637   A1020   3b multi   .25   .25
    Cabinet declaration of King Bhumibol Adulyadej as "Father of the Thai Workmanship Standard."

Princess Mother
Srinigarindra
(1900-95)
A1021

2011, Oct. 21   **Litho.**
        Granite Paper
2638   A1021   3b multi   .25   .25

Children's
Projects of
Princess
Maha Chakri
Sirindhorn,
30th Anniv.
A1022

2011, Oct. 21   **Perf. 13¼**
        Granite Paper
2639   A1022   3b multi   .25   .25

Lotus
Flower — A1023

2011, Nov. 7   **Perf. 13**
        Granite Paper
2640   A1023   3b multi   .25   .25

Festivals — A1024

Designs: No. 2641, 3b, Loy Krathong and Candle Festival, Sukhothai. No. 2642, 3b, Festival of Illuminated Boat Procession, Nakhon

Phanom. No. 2643, 3b, Yi-Peng Festival, Chiang Mai. No. 2644, 3b, Loi Krathong Sai Festival, Tak.

2011, Nov. 10   **Perf. 13¼**
        Granite Paper
2641-2644   A1024   Set of 4   .80   .60
2644a   Souvenir sheet of 4,
       #2641-2644   1.50   1.10
    No. 2644a sold for 22b.

Medallions of
Monks — A1025

    Designs: No. 2645, 9b, Luang Pho Klan, Wat Phrayathkaram. No. 2646, 9b, Luang Pu Iam, Wat Nang Ratchaworawihan. No. 2647, 9b, Luang Pu Suk, Wat Pak Khlong Makham Thao. No. 2648, 9b, Luang Pho Khong, Wat Bang Kaphom. No. 2649, 9b, Luang Pho Chui, Wat Khongkharam.

       Litho. & Embossed
2011, Nov. 11   **Perf. 13¼**
        Granite Paper
2645-2649   A1025   Set of 5   3.00   2.25
2649a   Souvenir sheet of 5,
       #2645-2649   4.00   3.00
    No. 2649a sold for 60b.

A1026

A1027

A1028

Fireworks
A1029

     Stamps With White Frames
    Litho. With Glitter Affixed
2011, Nov. 15   **Granite Paper**
2650   A1026   3b multi   .25   .25
2651   A1027   3b multi   .25   .25
2652   A1028   3b multi   .25   .25
2653   A1029   3b multi   .25   .25
     Nos. 2650-2653 (4)   1.00   1.00
        Souvenir Sheet
   Stamps Without White Frames
2654   Sheet of 4   1.50   1.10
   a.   A1026 3b multi   .35   .25
   b.   A1027 3b multi   .35   .25
   c.   A1028 3b multi   .35   .25
   d.   A1029 3b multi   .35   .25
    No. 2654 sold for 22b.

A1030

A1031

A1032

A1033

A1034

A1035

A1036

Coins Depicting King Bhumibol
Adulyadej — A1037

Awards of King Bhumibol
Adulyadej — A1038

    No. 2663: a, Agricola Medal inscribed: "Golden Jubilee of His Majesty's Reign". b, World Health Organization Award (plate on stand). c, Human Development Lifetime Achievement Award (silver bowl on stand). d, International Rice Award (medallion dated 1996). e, Award inscribed "Glory to the Greatest Inventor." f, WIPO Global Leader Award. g, Brussels Eureka medal.

   Litho. & Embossed With Foil
        Application
2011, Dec. 5   **Perf. 12¼**
        Granite Paper
2655   A1030   5b multi   .35   .25
2656   A1031   5b multi, inscribed
             "7 Cycle"   .35   .25
   a.   Inscribed "7th Cycle"   .65   .50
2657   A1032   5b multi   .35   .25
2658   A1033   5b multi   .35   .25
2659   A1034   5b multi   .35   .25
2660   A1035   5b multi   .35   .25
2661   A1036   5b multi   .35   .25
   a.   Sheet of 7, #2655, 2656a,
       2657-2661   4.75   3.50
2662   A1037   100b multi   6.50   5.00
     Nos. 2655-2662 (8)   8.95   6.75
        Miniature Sheet
2663   A1038   5b Sheet of 7, #a-
           g   2.40   1.75
    King Bhumibol Adulyadej, 84th birthday. No. 2661a sold for 70b.

Diplomatic Relations Between Thailand and Pakistan, 60th Anniv. A1039

2011, Dec. 13   Litho.   *Perf. 13¼*
Granite Paper
2664 A1039 3b multi   .25 .25

New Year 2012 (Year of the Dragon) A1040

2012, Jan. 1   *Perf. 13*
Granite Paper
2665 A1040 3b multi   .25 .25

Prince Mahidol Adulyadej (1892-1929), Father of King Bhumibol Adulyadej A1041

2012, Jan. 1   *Perf. 13¼*
Granite Paper
2666 A1041 3b multi   .25 .25

A1042

A1043

A1044

Children's Day — A1045

2012, Jan. 14   *Perf. 14½x14*
Granite Paper
2667 A1042 3b multi   .25 .25
2668 A1043 3b multi   .25 .25
2669 A1044 3b multi   .25 .25
2670 A1045 3b multi   .25 .25
Nos. 2667-2670 (4)   1.00 1.00

King Bhumibol Adulyadej and Map — A1046

2012, Jan. 16   *Perf. 13¼*
Granite Paper
2671 A1046 3b multi   .25 .25

Caishenye, God of Wealth — A1047

Various depictions with background color of: No. 2672, 3b, Red. No. 2673, 3b, Olive green.

2012, Jan. 23   Litho.
Granite Paper
2672-2673 A1047 Set of 2   .40 .30
A souvenir sheet containing Nos. 2672-2673 sold for 15b.

Chiang Rai, 750th Anniv. — A1048

2012, Jan. 26   *Perf. 14x14½*
Granite Paper
2674 A1048 3b multi   .25 .25

Love — A1049

No. 2675, 5b: a, Heart as padlock. b, Heart on key.
No. 2676, 5b: a, Teddy bear with padlock heart. b, Teddy bear with key.

2012, Feb. 7   *Perf. 13*
Granite Paper
Horiz. Pairs, #a-b
2675-2676 A1049 Set of 2   1.40 1.10

Excise Department, 80th Anniv. — A1050

2012, Feb. 17   *Perf. 13¼*
Granite Paper
2677 A1050 3b multi   .25 .25

Red Cross — A1051

2012, Mar. 30   *Perf. 14x14½*
Granite Paper
2678 A1051 3b multi   .25 .25

Asian-Pacific Postal Union, 50th Anniv. — A1052

2012, Apr. 1   *Perf. 14½x14*
Granite Paper
2679 A1052 3b multi   .25 .25

King Vajiravudh (1881-1925) and Bank Building — A1053

King Prajadhipok (1893-1941) and Bank Building — A1054

King Ananda Mahidol (1925-46) and Bank Building — A1055

King Bhumibol Adulyadej and Bank Building — A1056

2012, Apr. 1   *Perf. 14x14½*
Granite Paper
2680 A1053 3b multi   .25 .25
2681 A1054 3b multi   .25 .25
2682 A1055 3b multi   .25 .25
2683 A1056 3b multi   .25 .25
Nos. 2680-2683 (4)   1.00 1.00
Government Savings Bank, 99th anniv.

Ministry of Transport, Cent. — A1057

Designs: No. 2684, 3b, Aerial view of highway. No. 2685, 3b, Bridge and train. No. 2686, 3b, Ship. No. 2687, 3b, Airplane and airport.

2012, Apr. 1   Litho.
Granite Paper
2684-2687 A1057 Set of 4   .80 .60
2687a   Sheet of 4, #2684-2687   .80 .80

Cultural Preservation — A1058

No. 2688, 3b: a, Monument No. 1, Muang Sing Historical Park. b, Radiating Bodhisattva Avalokitesavara, Muang Sing Historical Park.
No. 2689, 3b: a, Prang Si Thep, Si Thep Historical Park. b, Stone Dharmachakra, Si Thep Historical Park.

2012, Apr. 2   *Perf. 13¼*
Granite Paper
Horiz. Pairs, #a-b
2688-2689 A1058 Set of 2   .80 .60
2689c   Souvenir sheet of 4, #2688a-2688b, 2689a-2689b   1.40 1.10
No. 2689c sold for 20b.

Miniature Sheets

Royal Thai Air Force, Cent. — A1059

No. 2690, 3b: a, Nieuport IIN. b, Breguet III. c, Biplane (Thai inscriptions). d, Ki-30. e, F8F-1. f, F-84G. g, F-86F. h, F-5A.
No. 2691, 3b: a, F-5B. b, F-5E. c, F-16 ADF. d, Gripen C. e, Avro. f, Boeing 737-800. g, Bell 412EP helicopter. h, S-92A helicopter.

2012 Sheets of 8, #a-h Litho.
Granite Paper

2690-2691 A1059 Set of 2 3.00 2.25

Issued: No. 2690, 4/9; No. 2691, 7/2.
Four sheets, containing Nos. 2690a-2690d, 2690e-2690h, 2691a-2691d and 2691e-2691h, respectively, sold for 35b each.

Buddha Statues A1060

Designs: No. 2692, 5b, Phra Phutthasothon, Wat Sothonwararam Worawihan (olive brown inscriptions). No. 2693, 5b, Luang Pho To, Wat Bang Phli Yai Nai (dark blue inscriptions). No. 2694, 5b, Luang Pho Wat Rai Khing, Wat Rai Khing (red brown inscriptions). No. 2695, 5b, Luang Pho Wat Ban Laem, Wat Phetchasamut Worawihan (green inscriptions). No. 2696, 5b, Luang Pho Wat Khao Ta-Khrao, Wat Khao Ta-Khrao (purple inscriptions).

2012, May 5 Perf. 13¼
Granite Paper

2692-2696 A1060 Set of 5 1.60 1.25
2696a Souvenir sheet of 5, #2692-2696 2.60 2.00

No. 2696a sold for 40b.

2012 Rotary International Convention, Bangkok A1061

2012, May 6 Perf. 14x14½
Granite Paper

2697 A1061 3b multi .25 .25

Vesak Day — A1062

2012, June 2 Perf. 13¼
Granite Paper

2698 A1062 3b multi .25 .25

Miniature Sheet

Provincial Seals — A1063

No. 2699 — Seals of: a, Ang Thong. b, Udon Thani. c, Uttaradit. d, Uthai Thani. e, Ubon Ratchathani. f, Amnat Charoen. g, Chang Thai. h, Ratchaphruek. i, Sala Thai. j, Bueng Kan.

Litho. & Embossed With Foil Application
2012, June 28 Granite Paper

2699 A1063 3b Sheet of 10, #a-j 1.90 1.40

Sheets of ten identical stamps were available, but these appear to have been sold locally and not through the philatelic bureau.

Office of the Prime Minister, 80th Anniv. — A1064

2012, June 28 Litho. Perf. 14½x14
Granite Paper

2700 A1064 3b multi .25 .25

Miniature Sheet

Coastlines — A1065

No. 2701: a, Phromthep Cape, Phuket, denomination at LR. b, Phromthep Cape, denomination at UR. c, Muko Ang Thong National Park, Surat Thani, denomination at LR. d, Muko Ang Thong National Park, denomination at UR. e, Rai Le Bay, Krabi, denomination at LR. f, Rai Le Bay, denomination at UR. g, Hong Island, Krabi, denomination at UR. h, Hong Island, denomination at UR. i, Panyi Island, Phang-nga, denomination at LR. j, Panyi Island, denomination at UR.

2012, July 5 Perf. 14¼x14½
Granite Paper

2701 A1065 15b Sheet of 10, #a-j 9.50 7.25

Ranong, 150th Anniv. — A1066

2012, July 21 Perf. 14½x14
Granite Paper

2702 A1066 3b multi .25 .25

Prince Maha Vajiralongkorn, 60th Birthday — A1067

Litho. With Foil Application
2012, July 28 Perf. 13¼
Granite Paper

2703 A1067 9b multi .60 .45

National Communications Day — A1068

2012, Aug. 4 Litho. Perf. 14½x14
Granite Paper

2704 A1068 3b multi .25 .25

Miniature Sheet

Queen Sirikit, 80th Birthday — A1069

No. 2705 — Queen Sirikit: a, 5b, As child, with ribbon in hair. b, 5b, As young girl, wearing white dress and necklace. c, 5b, As young woman, with necklace. d, 5b, As young woman, with hair decoration. e, 5b, With bare shoulder showing, color photograph. f, 5b, With bird decoration on shoulder. g, 5b, Wearing red dress. h, 5b, Wearing blue earring. i, 40b, Profile.

Litho., Litho. & Embossed With Foil Application (#2705i)
2012, Aug. 12 Perf. 13
Granite Paper

2705 A1069 Sheet of 9, #a-i 5.25 4.00
j. Souvenir sheet of 4, #2705a-2705d 2.10 1.60
k. Souvenir sheet of 4, #2705e-2705h 2.10 1.60

Nos. 2705j and 2705k each sold for 33b.

Miniature Sheet

Queen Savang Vadhana (1862-1955) — A1070

No. 2706 — Queen Savang Vadhana: a, As child (brown background). b, As young woman (green background). c, As woman (gray background). d, As older woman (blue background).

2012, Sept. 10 Litho. Perf. 13¼
Granite Paper

2706 A1070 3b Sheet of 4, #a-d .80 .60

Thailand 2013 World Stamp Exhibition — A1071

No. 2707: a, Lanna-style lantern. b, Paper umbrellas. c, Bung Fai rocket. d, Reed mouth organ, circular panpipes. e, Courtier dolls. f, Pottery. g, Kolek boat. h, Wooden bird cage.

2012, Oct. 3 Granite Paper

2707 A1071 Block of 8 2.80 2.00
a.-h. 5b Any single .35 .25
i. Souvenir sheet of 2, #2702a-2702b 1.00 .75
j. Souvenir sheet of 2, #2702c-2702d 1.00 .75
k. Souvenir sheet of 2, #2702e-2702f 1.00 .75
l. Souvenir sheet of 2, #2702g-2702h 1.00 .75

Nos. 2707i-2707l each sold for 15b.

Somdet Phra Nyanasamvara, Supreme Buddhist Patriarch of Thailand, 99th Birthday — A1072

2012, Oct. 3 Perf. 13¼
Granite Paper

2708 A1072 5b multi .35 .25

A souvenir sheet containing one of No. 2708 sold for 15b.

International Letter Writing Week — A1073

Designs: No. 2709, 3b, Girl bowing to grandparents, girl writing letter (denomination in red at LL). No. 2710, 3b, Girl and mother on parke bench, girl writing letter (denomination in dark blue at LR). No. 2711, 3b, Girl and boy, girl writing letter (denomination in red at LR). No. 2712, 3b, Classmates, girl writing letter (denomination in blue at LL).

2012, Oct. 8 Litho.
Granite Paper

2709-2712 A1073 Set of 4 .80 .60
2712a Souvenir sheet of 4, #2709-2712 1.40 1.10

No. 2712a sold for 20b.

Prince Nares Varariddhi (1855-1925) — A1074

2012, Oct. 14   Perf. 13¼
Granite Paper
2713 A1074 3b multi   .25   .25

Souvenir Sheet

Visit of King Chulalongkorn to Austria, 115th Anniv. — A1075

No. 2714: a, 5b, King Chulalongkorn. b, 15b, Emperor Franz Josef of Austria.

2012, Nov. 10   Litho.
Granite Paper
2714 A1075   Sheet of 2, #a-b   1.40 1.10
See Austria No. 2409.

Fireworks
A1076

Various fireworks with background color of: No. 2715, 3b, Violet blue. No. 2716, 3b, Green. No. 2717, 3b, Red. No. 2718, 3b, Light blue.

Litho. With Glitter Affixed
2012, Nov. 15   Granite Paper
2715-2718 A1076   Set of 4   .80   .60
2718a   Souvenir sheet of 4,
                  #2715-2718   1.60 1.25
No. 2718a sold for 24r.

Princess Chulabhorn A1077

Litho. With Foil Application
2012, Dec. 1   Granite Paper
2719 A1077 5b multi   .35   .25

Prince Damrong Rajanubhab (1862-1943) and Military Parade — A1078

Prince Damrong Rajanubhab and Luk Khun Hall — A1079

Prince Damrong Rajanubhab and Books Written by Him — A1080

Prince Damrong Rajanubhab and Woradis Palace — A1081

2012, Dec. 1   Litho.
Granite Paper
2720 A1078 3b multi   .25   .25
2721 A1079 3b multi   .25   .25
2722 A1080 3b multi   .25   .25
2723 A1081 3b multi   .25   .25
 a.   Souvenir sheet of 4, #2720-
         2723   1.40 1.10
  Nos. 2720-2723 (4)   1.00 1.00

King Bhumibol Adulyadej, 85th Birthday A1082

Litho. with Foil Application
2012, Dec. 5   Granite Paper
2724 A1082 9b multi   .60   .45

Princess Bajrakitiyabha, Chairperson of the United Nations Commission on Crime Prevention and Criminal Justice — A1083

2012, Dec. 7   Perf. 13¼
Granite Paper
2725 A1083 5b multi   .35   .25

New Year 2013 (Year of the Snake) — A1084

2013, Jan. 1   Litho.   Perf. 13
Granite Paper
2726 A1084 3b multi   .25   .25

Children's Day — A1085

2013, Jan. 12   Perf. 13
Granite Paper
2727 A1085 5b multi   .35   .25

Tai Sui God — A1086

Tai Sui God with background color of: No. 2728, 5b, Red. No. 2729, 5b, Blue. No. 2730, 5b, Green.

Litho. With Foil Application
2013, Feb. 7   Granite Paper
2728-2730 A1086   Set of 3   1.00   .75
2730a   Souvenir sheet of 3,
                  #2728-2730   2.00 1.50
No. 2730a sold for 30b.

Love — A1087

No. 2731: a, Flag of Thailand. b, Pink rose.

2013, Feb. 7   Litho.
2731 A1087 5b Horiz. pair, #a-b   .70   .55

Miniature Sheet

Thailand 2013 World Stamp Exhibition, Bangkok — A1088

No. 2732: a, Gilded black lacquer cabinet (lai rot nam technique). b, Plaster dragon. c, Khon mask. d, Vessel with mother-of-pearl inlay. e, Figurine of elephant (metal beating). f, Molded sculpture of mythical being. g, Carved wood Buddha. h, Figurine with mirrored-glass inlay.

2013, Mar. 22   Litho.   Perf. 13
Granite Paper
2732 A1088 5b Sheet of 8, #a-h   2.75 2.10
 i.   Souvenir sheet of 2, #2732a-
         2732b   1.25   .95
 j.   Souvenir sheet of 2, #2732c-
         2732d   1.25   .95
 k.   Souvenir sheet of 2, #2732e-
         2732f   1.25   .95
 l.   Souvenir sheet of 2, #2732g-
         2732h   1.25   .95
Nos. 2732i-2732l each sold for 18b.

King Chulalongkorn and Queen Srisavarindira A1089

2013, Mar. 29   Litho.   Perf. 13¼
Granite Paper
2733 A1089 3b multi   .25   .25
Thai Red Cross, 120th anniv.

First Government Savings Bank, 1913 — A1090

Government Savings Bank, 1934 — A1091

Government Savings Bank, 1950 — A1092

Government Savings Bank, 1966 — A1093

2013, Apr. 1   Perf. 14¾x14
Granite Paper
2734 A1090 3b multi   .25   .25
2735 A1091 3b multi   .25   .25
2736 A1092 3b multi   .25   .25
2737 A1093 3b multi   .25   .25
  Nos. 2734-2737 (4)   1.00 1.00
Government Savings Bank, cent.

Heritage Conservation Day — A1094

No. 2738 — Theatrical masks: a, Phra Shiva. b, Phra Vishnu. c, Phra Brahma. d, Phra Parakontap. e, Phra Panjasikorn. f, Phra kanes. g, Phra Vishnukam. h, Phra Indra.

2013, Apr. 2   *Perf. 13¼*
Granite Paper
2738 A1094 3b Block of 8, #a-h   1.75   1.40
A souvenir sheet containing Nos. 2738a-2738c sold for 20b.

Bangkok, 2013 World Book Capital — A1095

2013, Apr. 23   *Perf. 14x13¼*
2739 A1095 5b multi   .35   .25
A souvenir sheet containing No. 2739 sold for 20b.

Vesak Day — A1096

2013, May 24   **Litho.**   *Perf. 14¼x14½*
Granite Paper
2740 A1096 3b multi   .25   .25

Thai Engineering, Cent. — A1097

Designs: No. 2741, 5b, Electrical engineering (workers and generators, gear at left). No. 2742, 5b, Civil engineering (workers and bridge, gear at left). No. 2743, 5b, Mechanical engineering (workers and machine, gear at right).

Litho. & Embossed
2013, June 1   *Perf. 13½x13¾*
2741-2743 A1097 Set of 3   1.00   .75

Royal Irrigation Department, 111th Anniv. — A1098

2013, June 13   **Litho.**   *Perf. 13¼*
Granite Paper
2744 A1098 3b multi   .25   .25

Owls — A1099

Designs: No. 2745, 5b, Bubo sumatranus. No. 2746, 5b, Tyto alba. No. 2747, 5b, Otus lettia. No. 2748, 5b, Glaucidium brodiei.

2013, July 29   **Litho.**   *Perf. 14x14½*
Granite Paper
2745-2748 A1099 Set of 4   1.25   .95
2748a   Souvenir sheet of 4,
    #2745-2748, perf. 13¼   2.25   1.75
No. 2748a sold for 35b.

Phra Si Sakkaya Thotsaphonlayan Phrathan Phutthamonthon Suthat Statue, by Silpa Bhirasri — A1100

Fishing Village, by Damrong Wong-Uparas — A1101

Lord Buddha's Footprint, by Pichai Nirand A1102

Leela, by Sawat Tantisuk — A1103

Phra Mahathat Chalermaj Sattha, by Wanida Phuensuntom A1104

Full Moon, by Manit Poo-aree — A1105

White Ubosot of Wat Rong Khun, by Chalermchai Kositpipat A1106

Bull, by Thawan Duchanee — A1107

2013, Aug. 2   **Litho.**   *Perf. 13¼*
Granite Paper
2749   Sheet of 8 + 4 labels   2.80   2.00
a.   A1100 5b multi   .35   .25
b.   A1101 5b multi   .35   .25
c.   A1102 5b multi   .35   .25
d.   A1103 5b multi   .35   .25
e.   A1104 5b multi   .35   .25
f.   A1105 5b multi   .35   .25
g.   A1106 5b multi   .35   .25
h.   A1107 5b multi   .35   .25
i.   Souvenir sheet of 2, #2749a-2749b   1.40   1.40
j.   Souvenir sheet of 2, #2749c-2749d   1.40   1.40
k.   Souvenir sheet of 2, #2749e-2749f   1.40   1.40
l.   Souvenir sheet of 2, #2749g-2749h   1.40   1.40
Thailand 2013 World Stamp Exhibition, Bangkok. Nos. 2749i-2749l each sold for 20b.

National Communications Day — A1108

Die Cut Perf. 11x10
2013, Aug. 4   **Litho.**
Self-Adhesive
2750 A1108 9b multi   .60   .45
A lottery code number appears under the scratch-off panel on the stamp. Values for unused stamps are for stamps with unscratched panel.

Thailand No. 1 Under Magnifying Glass A1109

2013, Aug. 4   **Litho.**   *Perf. 13¼*
Granite Paper
2751 A1109 5b multi   .35   .25
Thai postal services, 130th anniv.

Bangkok General Post Office Building — A1110

Designs: No. 2753, Plaster renditions of Thailand Nos. 1 and 75. No. 2754, Garuda emblem from Post Office door.

2013, Aug. 4   **Litho.**   *Perf. 14½x14*
Granite Paper
2752 A1110 5b shown   .35   .25
Litho. & Embossed
2753 A1110 5b multi   .35   .25
Litho. & Embossed With Foil Application
2754 A1110 5b multi   .35   .25
   Nos. 2752-2754 (3)   1.05   .75
A souvenir sheet with one perf. 13¼ example of No. 2754 sold for 16b.

A1111

A1112

A1113

A1114

Queen
Sirikit — A1116

A1115

2013, Aug. 12   Litho.   Perf. 14x14½
Granite Paper

2755		Miniature sheet of 6	1.50	1.10
a.	A1111	3b multi	.25	.25
b.	A1112	3b multi	.25	.25
c.	A1113	3b multi	.25	.25
d.	A1114	3b multi	.25	.25
e.	A1115	3b multi	.25	.25
f.	A1116	3b multi	.25	.25

Designation of Queen Sirikit as "Pre-eminent Protector of Arts and Crafts."

Paknam
Incident, 120th
Anniv.
A1117

2013, Aug. 13   Litho.   Perf. 13x13¼
Granite Paper

2756	A1117	5b multi	.35	.25

A souvenir sheet of one sold for 16b.

Thailand Post as Public Company,
10th Anniv. — A1118

2013, Aug. 14   Litho.   Perf. 14¼
Granite Paper

2757	A1118	10b multi	.65	.50

A1119

A1120

A1121

A1122

A1123

A1124

A1125

A1126   A1127

A1128   A1129

A1130   A1131

A1132   A1133

A1134

2013, Sept. 4   Litho.   Perf. 13¼x14¼
Granite Paper

2758	A1119	3b multi	.25	.25
2759	A1120	3b multi	.25	.25
2760	A1121	3b multi	.25	.25
2761	A1122	3b multi	.25	.25
2762	A1123	3b multi	.25	.25
2763	A1124	3b multi	.25	.25
2764	A1125	3b multi	.25	.25
2765	A1126	3b multi	.25	.25

Perf. 14¼x13¼

2766	A1127	3b multi	.25	.25
2767	A1128	3b multi	.25	.25
2768	A1129	3b multi	.25	.25
2769	A1130	3b multi	.25	.25
2770	A1131	3b multi	.25	.25
2771	A1132	3b multi	.25	.25
2772	A1133	3b multi	.25	.25
2773	A1134	3b multi	.25	.25
		Nos. 2758-2773 (16)	4.00	4.00

Flag of Thailand — A1135

2013, Sept. 12   Litho.   Perf. 13¼

2774	A1135	3b multi	.25	.25

Granite Paper
Perf. 14¼x13¼

2775	A1135	15b multi	.95	.70

Government
Housing Bank,
60th
Anniv. — A1136

2013, Sept. 24   Litho.   Perf. 14x14½
Granite Paper

2776	A1136	3b multi	.25	.25

Somdet Phra Nyanasamvara (1913-2013), Supreme Patriarch of
Thailand — A1137

Somdet Phra Nyanasamvara: No. 2777, 5b, As young monk. No. 2778, 5b, As older monk. No. 2779, 5b, Holding bowl for food offerings. No. 2780, 5b, Seated, giving donations to students.

2013, Oct. 3   Litho.   Perf. 13¼
Granite Paper

2777-2780	A1137	Set of 4	1.40	1.10
2780a		Souvenir sheet of 4, #2777-2780	1.90	1.90

No. 2780a sold for 30b.

A1138

A1139

A1140

Intl. Letter Writing Week — A1141

2013, Oct. 7   Litho.   Perf. 13¼
Granite Paper

2781	A1138	3b multi	.25	.25
2782	A1139	3b multi	.25	.25
2783	A1140	3b multi	.25	.25
2784	A1141	3b multi	.25	
a.		Souvenir sheet of 4, #2781-2784	1.50	1.50

No. 2784a sold for 23b.

		Nos. 2781-2784 (4)	1.00	.75

Silpakorn
University,
70th Anniv.
A1142

Depictions of Ganesh with denomination in:
No. 2785, 3b, Silver. No. 2786, 3b, Black.

2013, Oct. 12   Litho.   Perf. 13¼
Granite Paper

2785-2786	A1142	Set of 2	.40	.30

Use of Family
Names in
Thailand,
Cent. — A1143

2013, Oct. 14   Litho.   Perf. 13
Granite Paper

2787	A1143	3b multi	.25	.25

Democracy Day — A1144

2013, Oct. 14   Litho.   Perf. 13¼
Granite Paper

2788	A1144	5b multi	.35	.25

King
Prajadhipok
(1893-1941)
A1145

2013, Nov. 8 Litho. Perf. 13¼
Granite Paper
2789 A1145 3b multi 25 25

Prince Narisaranuvattiwongse (1863-1947) and Wat Rajathiwas Rajaworavihara — A1146

2013, Nov. 11 Litho. Perf. 14½x14
Granite Paper
2790 A1146 3b multi .25 .25

Miniature Sheet

Flags and National Flowers of ASEAN Countries — A1147

Designs: a, Dillenia suffruticosa, flag of Brunei. b, Mitrella mesnyi, flag of Cambodia. c, Phalaenopsis amabilis, flag of Indonesia. d, Plumeria alba, flag of Laos. e, Hibiscus rosa-sinensis, flag of Malaysia. f, Pterocarpus macrocarpus, flag of Myanmar. g, Jasminum sambac, flag of Philippines. h, Vanda "Miss Joaquim" orchid, flag of Singapore. i, Cassia fistula, flag of Thailand. j, Nelumbo nucifera, flag of Viet Nam.

Perf. 14¼x14½
2013, Nov. 15 Litho.
Granite Paper
2791 A1147 3b Sheet of 10, #a-j 1.90 1.90

King Bhumibol Adulyadej and Humanitarian Soil Scientist Medal — A1148

Litho. With Foil Application
2013, Dec. 5 Perf. 13¼x13
Granite Paper
2792 A1148 9b multi .60 .45
86th birthday of King Bhumibol Adulyadej.

Jasminum Bhumibolianum A1149

2013, Dec. 5 Litho. Perf. 13
Granite Paper
2793 A1149 3b multi .25 .25

Siam Cement Factory, Cent. — A1150

2013, Dec. 8 Litho. Perf. 14½x14
Granite Paper
2794 A1150 3b multi 25 25

Map of Thailand and Digital Television Mascot — A1151

2013, Dec. 11 Litho. Perf. 13¼
Granite Paper
2795 A1151 3b multi .25 .25

New Year 2014 (Year of the Horse) — A1152

2014, Jan. 1 Litho. Perf. 13
Granite Paper
2796 A1152 3b multi .25 .25
a. Souvenir sheet of 6, #2397a, 2463, 2568, 2665, 2726, 2796 1.90 1.90
No. 2796a sold for 30b. A sheet containing twelve 3b stamps similar to the 2003-14 New Year stamps but with reflective gold animals sold for 99b.

Chiang Mai University, 50th Anniv. — A1153

2014, Jan. 1 Litho. Perf. 14½x14
Granite Paper
2797 A1153 3b multi .25 .25

National Children's Day — A1154

Children in national costume, greetings, and flags from: a, Thailand and Viet Nam. b, Philippines and Singapore. c, Malaysia and Myanmar. d, Indonesia and Laos. e, Brunei and Cambodia

2014, Jan. 11 Litho. Perf. 14½x14
Granite Paper
2798 Vert. strip of 5 .95 .70
a.-e. 3b Any single .25 .25
No. 2798 was printed in sheets containing two vertical strips.

Thammasat University, 80th Anniv. — A1155

2014, Jan. 15 Litho. Perf. 14½x14
Granite Paper
2799 A1155 3b multi .25 .25

Laughing Buddha — A1156

Litho. With Foil Application
2014, Jan. 24 Perf. 13¼
Granite Paper
2800 A1156 5b multi .30 .25
Chinese New Year.

Khon Kaen University, 50th Anniv. — A1157

2014, Jan. 25 Litho. Perf. 13¼
Granite Paper
2801 A1157 3b multi .25 .25

Love — A1158

Cut-out in center of stamp: a, Hand signing "I love you." b, Heart.

2014, Feb. 7 Litho. Perf. 13¾
2802 A1158 5b Horiz. pair, #a-b .65 .50
No. 2802 is impregnated with a rose scent.

Zoological Park Organization, 60th Anniv. — A1159

2014, Feb. 15 Litho. Perf. 14x14½
Granite Paper
2803 A1159 3b multi .25 .25

Postal School, 125th Anniv. — A1160

2014, Feb. 22 Litho. Perf. 14½x14
Granite Paper
2804 A1160 3b multi .25 .25

Queen Saovabha Phongsri (1861-1919) A1161

2014, Apr. 1 Litho. Perf. 13¼
Granite Paper
2805 A1161 3b multi .25 .25

Thai Heritage Conservation Day — A1162

Masks: a, Tosakanth. b, Kumbhakarn. c, Pipek. d, Thut. e, Khorn. f, Trisian. g, Samanakkha. h, Indrajit.

2014, Apr. 2 Litho. Perf. 13¼
Granite Paper
2806 A1162 3b Block of 8, #a-h 1.50 1.10
A souvenir sheet of 1 containing No. 2806a sold for 13b.

First Thailand-Laos Friendship Bridge, 20th Anniv. — A1163

Bridge and: a, Sai Buddha Image Procession Festival, Nong Khai, Thailand. b, Pho Chai Temple, Nong Khai, and On Thu Temple, Vientiane, Laos.

2014, Apr. 5 Litho. Perf. 14½x14
Granite Paper
2807 A1163 3b Horiz. pair, #a-b .40 .30
See Laos No. 1881.

Thailand Tobacco Monopoly, 75th Anniv. — A1164

2014, Apr. 19 Litho. Perf. 13¼
Granite Paper
2808 A1164 3b multi .25 .25

Vesak Day — A1165

2014, May 13 Litho. Perf. 13
Granite Paper
2809 A1165 3b multi .25 .25

Kings Chulalongkorn and Vajiravudh, King Chulalongkorn Memorial Hospital — A1166

2014, May 30   Litho.   Perf. 14x14½
Granite Paper
2810 A1166 3b multi   .25   .25
King Chulalongkorn Memorial Hospital, cent.

Pomegranates, Mangosteens, Flags of Israel and Thailand — A1167

2014, June 5   Litho.   Perf. 13¼
Granite Paper
2811 A1167 3b multi   .25   .25
Diplomatic relations between Thailand and Israel, 60th anniv. See Israel No. 2020.

Don Mueang International Airport, Bangkok, Cent. — A1168

Centenary emblem and: No. 2812, 3b, Breguet 14 B mail plane. No. 2813, 3b, Terminal, 1973. No. 2814, 3b, Terminal and movable boarding platform, 2014. No. 2815, 3b, Prince Chakrabongse Bhuvanath (1883-1920), commander of Royal Aeronautical Service, vert.

Perf. 14½x14, 14x14½
2014, July 1   Granite Paper   Litho.
2812-2815 A1168   Set of 4   .75   .55
2815a   Perf. 13¼x14x13¼x13¼   .25   .25
2815b   Sheet of 4, #2812-2814,
           2815a   .75   .75

Amphibians — A1169

Designs: No. 2816, 5b, Ingerophrynus macrotis. No. 2817, 5b, Rhacophorus kio. No. 2818, 5b, Megophrys nasuta. No. 2819, 5b, Hylarana erythraea.

2014, July 10   Litho.   Perf. 14½x14
Granite Paper
2816-2819 A1169   Set of 4   1.25   .95
2819a   Souvenir sheet of 4,
           #2816-2819, perf. 13¼   2.25   2.25
           No. 2819a sold for 35b.

Communications Day — A1170

2014, Aug. 4   Litho.   Perf. 14½x14
Granite Paper
2820 A1170 3b multi   .25   .25

Thailand Waterworks, Cent. — A1171

2014, Aug. 15   Litho.   Perf. 13¼
Granite Paper
2821 A1171 3b multi   .25   .25

Synod of Ayutthaya, 350th Anniv. A1172

2014, Aug. 15   Litho.   Perf. 13¼
Granite Paper
2822 A1172 5b multi   .35   .25
           See Vatican City No. 1573.

World Post Day — A1173

2014, Oct. 9   Litho.   Perf. 14¼
Granite Paper
2823 A1173 3b multi   .25   .25

Sports Authority of Thailand, 50th Anniv. — A1174

2014, Oct. 17   Litho.   Perf. 14½x14
Granite Paper
2824 A1174 3b multi   .25   .25

General Post Offices — A1175

No. 2825 — General Post Office in: a, Bangkok, Thailand. b, Macao.

2014, Nov. 1   Litho.   Perf. 13x13¼
Granite Paper
2825 A1175 3b Pair, #a-b   .40   .30
           See Macao No. 1426.

A1176

A1177

A1178

A1179

A1180

A1181

A1182

New Year 2015 — A1183

2014, Nov. 14   Litho.   Perf. 13¼
Granite Paper
2826 A1176   3b multi   .25   .25
2827 A1177   3b multi   .25   .25
2828 A1178   3b multi   .25   .25
2829 A1179   3b multi   .25   .25
2830 A1180   3b multi   .25   .25
2831 A1181 15b multi   .90   .70
2832 A1182 15b multi   .90   .70
2833 A1183 15b multi   .90   .70
      Nos. 2826-2833 (8)   3.95   3.35

Naval Vessels — A1184

Designs: No. 2834, 5b, HTMS Pinklao. No. 2835, 5b, HTMS Phutthayodfachulalok. No. 2836, 5b, HTMS Phutthaloetlanaphalai. No. 2837, 5b, HTMS Chakri Naruebet (81x30mm).

Perf. 14½x14, 13¼ (#2837)
2014, Nov. 20   Litho.
Granite Paper
2834-2837 A1184   Set of 4   1.25   .95
   A souvenir sheet containing one No. 2837 sold for 15b.

Chiang Mai Rajabhat University, 90th Anniv. — A1185

2014, Dec. 1   Litho.   Perf. 14x14½
Granite Paper
2838 A1185 3b multi   .25   .25

King Bhumibol Adulyadej, 87th Birthday — A1186

2014, Dec. 5   Litho.   Perf. 13¼
Granite Paper
2839 A1186 5b multi   .30   .25

Luang Pu Thuat High-Relief Amulet — A1187

Litho. & Embossed
2014, Dec. 15   Perf. 14x14½
Granite Paper
2840 A1187 9b multi   .55   .40
a.   Souvenir sheet of 1, perf. 13¼   .95   .95
           No. 2840a sold for 15b.

New Year 2015 (Year of the Goat) — A1188

2015, Jan. 1   Litho.   Perf. 13¼
Granite Paper
2841 A1188 3b multi   .25   .25

National Children's Day — A1189

No. 2842 — Children, various forms of transportation and flags of: a, Thailand and Viet Nam. b, Philippines and Singapore. c, Malaysia and Myanmar. d, Indonesia and Laos. e, Brunei and Cambodia.

2015, Jan. 10   Litho.   Perf. 14½x14
Granite Paper
2842   Vert. strip of 5   1.25   1.25
a.-e. A1189 3b Any single   .25   .25

Kasetsart University, 72nd
Anniv. — A1190

2015, Feb. 2   Litho.   Perf. 13¼
Granite Paper
2843 A1190 3b multi   .25 .25

Princess Maha
Chakri
Sirindihorn
Rose — A1191

2015, Feb. 9   Litho.   Perf. 13
Granite Paper
2844 A1191 5b multi   — —

No. 2844 has a rose-scented scratch-and-
sniff coating.

Chinese New
Year — A1192

No. 2845: a, Oranges. b, Red envelope and
banknotes.

Litho. With Foil Application
2015, Feb. 9   Perf. 13¼
Granite Paper
2845 A1192 5b Pair, #a-b   .65 .50

60th Birthday of
Princess Maha
Chakri Sirindhorn,
Director of Thai
Red Cross
Society — A1193

2015, Mar. 30   Litho.   Perf. 13¼
Granite Paper
2846 A1193 3b multi   .25 .25

Princess Maha
Chakri
Sirindhorn, 60th
Birthday
A1194

Litho. With Foil Application
Perf. 14½x14¼
2015, Apr. 2   Granite Paper
2847 A1194 5b multi   .30 .25

A souvenir sheet containing one example of
No. 2847 sold for 15b.

Thai Heritage Conservation
Day — A1195

No. 2848 — Masks: a, Hanuman. b, Nilapat.
c, Nilanon. d, Asuraphat. e, Praya
Mahachompu. f, Pali. g, Sukrip. h, Ongot.

2015, Apr. 2   Litho.   Perf. 14x14½
Granite Paper
2848 A1195 3b Block of 8, #a-h   1.50 1.10

A souvenir sheet containing one perf. 13¼
example of No. 2848a sold for 13b.

Pathum Thani, 200th Anniv. — A1196

2015, Apr. 3   Litho.   Perf. 13¼
Granite Paper
2849 A1196 3b multi   .25 .25

Songkran Festival — A1197

Inscriptions: No. 2850, 3b, Purifying the
Buddha statue. No. 2851, 3b, Pouring scented
water on the elders. No. 2852, 3b, Building the
sand pagoda. No. 2853, 3b, Splashing water.

2015, Apr. 7   Litho.   Perf. 14½x14
Granite Paper
2850-2853 A1197 Set of 4   .75 .60
2853a   Souvenir sheet of 4, #2850-
           2853, perf. 13¼   1.40 1.40
2853b   As No. 2853a with Taipei
           2015 emblem in sheet mar-
           gin   .75 .75

No. 2853a sold for 23b.

Diplomatic Relations Between
Thailand and Korea, People's
Democratic Republic, 40th
Anniv. — A1198

No. 2845: a, Siamese fireback (denomination at LL). b, Northern goshawk (denomination at LR).

2015, May 8   Litho.   Perf. 13¼
Granite Paper
2854 A1198 3b Pair, #a-b   .35 .25
See North Korea No.

International Telecommunication
Union, 150th Anniv. — A1199

2015, May 17   Litho.   Perf. 14½x14
Granite Paper
2855 A1199 3b multi   .25 .25

Princess Prem
Purachatra, 100th
Birthday — A1200

2015, June 7   Litho.   Perf. 13¼
Granite Paper
2856 A1200 3b multi   .25 .25

Marine
Life — A1201

Designs: No. 2857, 3b, Hymenocera picta.
No. 2858, 3b, Trapezia areolata. No. 2859, 3b,
Hypselodoris bullockii. No. 2860, 3b, Phyl-
lorhiza punctata.

2015, June 8   Litho.   Perf. 13¼
Granite Paper
2857-2860 A1201 Set of 4   .75 .60
2860a   Souvenir sheet of 4,
           #2857-2860   1.40 1.40

See Malaysia Nos. 1550-1553.

Vesak
Day — A1202

Emerald Buddha in: No. 2861, 5b, Summer
season attire. No. 2862, 5b, Rainy season
attire. No. 2863, 5b, Winter season attire.

Litho. With Foil Application
2015, June 15   Perf. 13¼
Granite Paper
2861-2863 A1202 Set of 3   .90 .70
2863a   Souvenir sheet of 3, #2861-
           2863   1.60 1.60
2863b   As No. 2863a, with Singapore
           2015 emblem in sheet mar-
           gin   .90 .90

No. 2863a sold for 26b.

Ratsadkom Pipat Hall Revenue
Department Building — A1203

Krom Phra Kampaengpet Palace
Revenue Department
Building — A1204

Jakrapong
Revenue
Department
Building — A1205

Soi Arisamphan
Revenue
Department
Building — A1206

2015, July 2   Litho.   Perf. 14½x14
Granite Paper
2864 A1203 3b multi   .25 .25
2865 A1204 3b multi   .25 .25
Perf. 14x14½
2866 A1205 3b multi   .25 .25
2867 A1206 3b multi   .25 .25
       Nos. 2864-2867 (4)   1.00 1.00

Revenue Department, Cent.

Miniature Sheet

Thai Numerals — A1207

No. 2868 — Thai numeral and correspond-
ing number of fruit: a, 0. b, 1. c, 2. d, 3. e, 4. f,
5. g, 6. h, 7. i, 8. j, 9.

2015, July 29   Litho.   Perf. 13
Granite Paper
2868 A1207 3b Sheet of 10, #a-j 1.75 1.75

Musical Instruments — A1208

Designs: No. 2869, 3b, Ranat ayk. No. 2870, 3b, Saw sam sai, vert. No. 2871, 3b, Saw duang, vert. No. 2872, 3b, Jakhay.

Perf. 14½x14, 14x14½
2015, Aug. 3   Litho.
Granite Paper
2869-2872 A1208   Set of 4   .70   .55
2872a   Souvenir sheet of 4,
             #2869-2872 + label, dif-
             ferent perforations   1.40 1.40
  Thaipex 2015 Philatelic Exhibition, Bangkok. No. 2872a sold for 23b and each stamp has at least one side that is perf. 13¼.

National Communications
Day — A1209

2015, Aug. 4   Litho.   Perf. 13¼
Granite Paper
2873 A1209 3b multi   .25   .25

Army Training Command, 120th
Anniv. — A1210

2015, Aug. 6   Litho.   Perf. 13¼
Granite Paper
2874 A1210 3b multi   .25   .25

Flags and
Emblem of
Association of
Southeast Asian
Nations — A1211

2015, Aug. 8   Litho.   Perf. 14¼
Granite Paper
2875 A1211 15b multi   .85   .65
  a.   Souvenir sheet of 1   1.50 1.50
  No. 2875a sold for 26b.
  See Brunei No. 656, Burma Nos. 417-418, Cambodia No. , Indonesia No. 2428, Laos No. , Malaysia No. 1562, Philippines No. 3619, Singapore No. , Viet Nam No. 3529.

Diplomatic Relations Between
Thailand and Singapore, 50th
Anniv. — A1212

No. 2876: a, Khao Niew Manuang (sticky rice with mango). b, Ice cream sandwiches.

2015, Sept. 18   Litho.   Perf. 13¼
Granite Paper
2876 A1212 3b Horiz. pair, #a-b   .35   .25
  See Singapore Nos. 1746-1747.

World Dental Congress,
Bangkok — A1213

2015, Sept. 22   Litho.   Perf. 14½x14
Granite Paper
2877 A1213 3b multi   .25   .25

World Post
Day — A1214

2015, Oct. 9   Litho.   Perf. 13
Granite Paper
2878 A1214 3b multi   .25   .25

Former Bangkok Remand
Prison — A1215

Department of Corrections
Administration Building — A1216

Prison Security Control
Room — A1217

Corrections Officers Training and in
Riot Gear — A1218

2015, Oct. 13   Litho.   Perf. 14½x14
Granite Paper
2879 A1215 3b multi   .25   .25
2880 A1216 3b multi   .25   .25
2881 A1217 3b multi   .25   .25
2882 A1218 3b multi   .25   .25
  a.   Souvenir sheet of 4, #2879-
        2882, perf. 13¼   1.00 1.00
  Nos. 2879-2882 (4)   1.00 1.00
  100th Anniv. of the Department of Corrections.

Diplomatic Relations Between
Thailand and Sri Lanka, 60th
Anniv. — A1219

No. 2883: a, Phrapathomchedi Pagoda, flag of Thailand. b, Jethavana Stupa, flag of Sri Lanka.

2015, Nov. 2   Litho.   Perf. 13¼
Granite Paper
2883 A1219 3b Horiz. pair, #a-b   .35   .25
  A souvenir sheet containing Nos. 2883a and 2883b sold for 16b. See Sri Lanka Nos. 1988-1989.

Exacum Affine — A1220

No. 2884: a, Flowers in vase. b, Painting of flowers by Princess Maha Chakri Sirindhorn.

2015, Nov. 16   Litho.   Perf. 14¼
Granite Paper
2884 A1220 15b Horiz. pair, #a-b 1.75 1.40

Miniature Sheet

New Year 2016 — A1221

No. 2885: a, Boesenbergia alba. b, Etlingera araneosa. c, Alpinia malaccensis. d, Zingiber sirindhorniae. e, Curcuma supraneeana. f, Hedychium flavescens. g, Monolophus appendiculatus. h, Alpinia conchigera. i, Etlingera hemisphaerica. j, Curcuma alismatifolia. k, Zingiber spectabile. l, Rhynchanthus longiflorus.

2015, Nov. 23   Litho.   Perf. 14x14½
Granite Paper
2885 A1221 3b Sheet of 12, #a-l   2.00 2.00

Luang Phor Ngern
Amulet — A1222

Litho. & Embossed
2015, Dec. 1   Perf. 14x14½
Granite Paper
2886 A1222 9b multi   .50   .40
  A souvenir sheet containing a perf. 13¼ example of No. 2886 sold for 20b.

King Bhumibol Adulyadej, 88th
Birthday — A1223

King Bhumibol Adulyadej and: No. 2887, 5b, Farm, cattle, flame. No. 2888, 5b, Village, high tension wires, light bulb. No. 2889, 5b, Classroom, graduate, satellite dish, wind generators. No. 2890, 5b, Man at computer, solar panels, city skyline.

2015, Dec. 5   Litho.   Perf. 13¼
Granite Paper
2887-2890 A1223   Set of 4   1.10   .85
2890a   Souvenir sheet of 4,
             #2887-2890   1.75 1.75
  No. 2890a sold for 32b.

New Year 2016
(Year of the
Monkey) — A1224

2016, Jan. 1   Litho.   Perf. 13¼
Granite Paper
2891 A1224 3b multi   .25   .25

Miniature Sheet

Mailboxes of Members of Association
of South East Asian Nations — A1225

No. 2892 — Mailbox from: a, Brunei. b, Cambodia. c, Indonesia. d, Laos. e, Malaysia. f, Myanmar. g, Philippines. h, Singapore. i, Thailand. j, Viet Nam.

2016, Jan. 9   Litho.   Perf. 14½x14
Granite Paper
2892 A1225 3b Sheet of 10, #a-j 1.75 1.75
  National Children's Day.

National Institute of Development
Administration, 50th Anniv. — A1226

2016, Feb. 1   Litho.   Perf. 13¼
2893 A1226 3b multi   .25   .25
  No. 2893 has 50th anniversary emblem printed on back of stamp.

Chinese New Year — A1227

2016, Feb. 4   Litho.   Perf. 13
Granite Paper
2894 A1227 5b multi   .30   .25

Queen Sirikit Rose — A1228

2016, Feb. 8   Litho.   Perf. 13
Granite Paper
2895 A1228 5b multi   .30   .25

No. 2895 has a rose-scented scratch-and-sniff coating.

Office of the Auditor General, Cent. — A1229

2016, Feb. 18   Litho.   Perf. 13¼
Granite Paper
2896 A1229 3b multi   .25   .25

Prince Bidyalongkorn (1876-1945) — A1230

2016, Feb. 26   Litho.   Perf. 13¼
Granite Paper
2897 A1230 3b multi   .25   .25

Thai Cooperatives, cent.

Burapha University, 60th Anniv. (in 2015) — A1231

2016, Mar. 1   Litho.   Perf. 14½x14
Granite Paper
2898 A1231 3b multi   .25   .25

Princess Valaya Alongkorn (1884-1938) A1232

2016, Mar. 8   Litho.   Perf. 13¼
Granite Paper
2899 A1232 3b multi   .25   .25

Petchburiwittayalongkorn Teacher's Training School, 84th anniv.

A1233

A1234

A1235

Puey Ungphakorn (1916-99), Economist A1236

2016, Mar. 9   Litho.   Perf. 13¼
Granite Paper
2900 A1233 3b multi   .25   .25
2901 A1234 3b multi   .25   .25
2902 A1235 3b multi   .25   .25
2903 A1236 3b multi   .25   .25
         Nos. 2900-2903 (4)   1.00 1.00

Ananta Samagom Throne Hall, Cent. — A1237

2016, Mar. 14   Litho.   Perf. 13¼
Granite Paper
2904 A1237 5b multi   .30   .25

Chulalongkorn University, Cent. — A1238

2016, Mar. 26   Litho.   Perf. 13¼
Granite Paper
2905 A1238 3b multi   .25   .25

Queen Sirikit, 84th Birthday — A1239

2016, Mar. 30   Litho.   Perf. 13¼
2906 A1239 3b multi   .25   .25

Red Cross. No. 2906 has QR code and building printed in blue on back.

A1240

A1241

A1242

Women's Clothing — A1243

2016, Apr. 2   Litho.   Perf. 14x14½
Granite Paper
2907 A1240 3b multi   .25   .25
2908 A1241 3b multi   .25   .25
2909 A1242 3b multi   .25   .25
2910 A1243 3b multi   .25   .25
         Nos. 2907-2910 (4)   1.00 1.00

Thai Heritage Conservation. A souvenir sheet of four stamps containing perf. 13¼ examples of Nos. 2907-2910 sold for 25b.

Chiang Mai, 720th Anniv. — A1244

2016, Apr. 7   Litho.   Perf. 13¼
Granite Paper
2911 A1244 3b multi   .25   .25

Miniature Sheet

Songkran Festival — A1245

No. 2912: a, Tao Kabilaprom and his seven daughters. b, Tung-sa Dhevi and Garuda. c, Ko-ra-ka Dhevi and tiger. d, Rak-sad Dhevi and pig. e, Mon-ta Dhevi and donkey. f, Kiri-nee Dhevi and elephant. g, Kimi-ta Dhevi and water buffalo. h, Maho-torn Dhevi and peacock.

2016, Apr. 7   Litho.   Perf. 14½x14
Granite Paper
2912 A1245 5b Sheet of 8, #a-h   2.40 2.40

Princess Maha Chakri Sirindhorn and World Intellectual Property Organization Award for Creative Excellence — A1246

2016, May 3   Litho.   Perf. 13¼
Granite Paper
2913 A1246 5b multi   .30   .25

Diplomatic Relations Between Thailand and Indonesia — A1247

No. 2914 — Scenes from the epic poem *Ramayana*: a, Characters kneeling. b, Four characters and tree.

2016, May 5   **Litho.**   *Perf. 13¼*
Granite Paper
2914 A1247 3b Horiz. pair, #a-b   .35   .30
See Indonesia Nos. 2446-2447.

Vesak Day A1248

Inscription: No. 2915, 3b, Conquer anger by love. No. 2916, 3b, Conquer evil by good. No. 2917, 3b, Conquer the miser by liberality. No. 2918, 3b, Conquer the liar by truth.

2016, May 20   **Litho.**   *Perf. 13¼*
Granite Paper
2915-2918 A1248   Set of 4   .70   .55
A souvenir sheet containing Nos. 2915-2918 sold for 25b.

UEFA European Soccer Champions — A1249

No. 2919 — Inscriptions: a, Soviet Union, 1960. b, Spain, 1964. c, Italy, 1968. d, West Germany, 1972. e, Czechoslovakia, 1976. f, West Germany, 1980. g, France, 1984. h, Netherlands, 1988. i, Denmark, 1992. j, Germany, 1996. k, France, 2000. l, Greece, 2004. m, Spain, 2008. n, Spain, 2012. o, 2016 @France.

Die Cut Perf. 6¾x7
2016, June 10   **Litho.**
Self-Adhesive
2919 A1249   Booklet pane of 15   2.60
a.-o.   3b Any single   .25   .25

Bangkok Railway Station, Cent. — A1250

Various images of Bangkok Railway Station with denomination at: No. 2920, 3b, LL. No. 2921, 3b, LR. No. 2922, 3b, UL. No. 2923, 3b, UR.

2016, June 25   **Litho.**   *Perf. 14½x14*
Granite Paper
2920-2923 A1250   Set of 4   .70   .55
A souvenir sheet containing perf. 13¼ examples of Nos. 2920-2923 sold for 25b.

A1251

Crown Prince Maha Vajiralongkorn, 64th Birthday — A1252

No. 2924: a, Monument and statue, drawing of finish line of "Bike for Dad" bicycle race. b, Drawing of family on tandem bicycle and cart. No. 2925: a, Crown Prince riding bicycle with both hands on handlebars. b, Crown Prince riding bicycle and waving.

2016, July 28   **Litho.**   *Perf. 14½x14*
Granite Paper
2924 A1251 5b Horiz. pair, #a-b   .60   .45
Perf. 14x14½
2925 A1252 5b Vert. pair, #a-b   .60   .45
c.   Souvenir sheet of 4, #2924a, 2924b, 2925a, 2925b, perf. 13¼   2.00   2.00
No. 2925c sold for 35b.

National Communications Day — A1253

2016, Aug. 4   **Litho.**   *Perf. 13¼*
Granite Paper
2926 A1253 3b multi   .25   .25

Diplomatic Relations Between Thailand and Viet Nam, 40th Anniv. — A1254

No. 2927: a, Three Thai figurines in boat. b, Four Vietnamese figurines in boat.

2016, Aug. 5   **Litho.**   *Perf. 13¼*
Granite Paper
2927 A1254 3b Horiz. pair, #a-b   .35   .25
See Viet Nam Nos. 3551-3552.

Nymphaea "Queen Sirikit" — A1255

2016, Aug. 10   **Litho.**   *Perf. 13¼*
Granite Paper
2928 A1255 5b multi   .30   .25
Thailand 2016 International Stamp Exhibition, Bangkok.

Queen Sirikit, 84th Birthday — A1256

Litho. & Embossed With Foil Application
2016, Aug. 12   *Perf. 12*
Granite Paper
2929 A1256 100b gold & multi   5.75   4.50
Values are for stamps with surrounding selvage.

King Bhumibol Adulyadej and Queen Sirikit A1257

2016, Aug. 16   **Litho.**   *Perf. 13¼*
Granite Paper
2930 A1257 3b multi   .25   .25
Thai rice research, cent.

World Post Day — A1258

No. 2931 — Various people and postal workers with denomination in: a, Red at LR. b, Dark blue at LL.

2016, Oct. 3   **Litho.**   *Perf. 13*
Granite Paper
2931 A1258 3b Horiz. pair, #a-b   .35   .25

A1259   A1260

A1261   A1262

Canna Lilies
A1263   A1264

2016, Nov. 15   **Litho.**   *Perf. 13¼x13*
Granite Paper
2932 A1259 3b multi   .25   .25
2933 A1260 3b multi   .25   .25
2934 A1261 3b multi   .25   .25
2935 A1262 3b multi   .25   .25
2936 A1263 15b multi   .85   .65
2937 A1264 15b multi   .85   .65
  Nos. 2932-2937 (6)   2.70   2.30

Phra Kring Chinabanchorn Amulet, by Luang Pu Tim Wat Lahanrai — A1265

Litho. & Embossed
2016, Dec. 1   *Perf. 14x14½*
Granite Paper
2938 A1265 9b multi   .50   .40
A souvenir sheet containing one perf. 13¼ example of No. 2938 sold for 20b.

New Year 2017 (Year of the Rooster) — A1266

2017, Jan. 1   **Litho.**   *Perf. 13¼*
Granite Paper
2939 A1266 3b multi   .25   .25

National Children's Day — A1267

2017, Jan. 14   **Litho.**   *Perf. 14½x14*
Granite Paper
2940 A1267 3b multi   .25   .25

Stylized Rose — A1268

Litho. & Silk-Screened
2017, Feb. 7   *Perf. 13¼x13*
Granite Paper
2941 A1268 5b multi   .30   .25

State Railway of Thailand, 120th Anniv. — A1269

Various locomotives with identification number of: No. 2942, 3b, #4004. No. 2943, 3b, #3118. No. 2944, 3b, #4552. No. 2945, 3b, #5102.

2017, Mar. 26   Litho.   Perf. 13
Granite Paper

2942-2945 A1269   Set of 4   .70 .55

Values are for stamps with surrounding selvage. A souvenir sheet containing perf. 13½x13 examples of Nos, 2942-2945 sold for 28b.

Accession to the Throne of King Bhumibol Adulyadej (1927-2016), 70th Anniv. (in 2016) — A1270

2017, Apr. 1   Litho.   Perf. 13½
Granite Paper

2946 A1270 9b multi   .55 .40

No. 2946 is shown sideways.

A1271

A1272

A1273

Lanna-Style Murals — A1274

2017, Apr. 2   Litho.   Perf. 14½x14
Granite Paper

2947 A1271 3b multi   .25 .25
2948 A1272 3b multi   .25 .25

Perf. 14x14½

2949 A1273 3b multi   .25 .25
2950 A1274 3b multi   .25 .25
   Nos. 2947-2950 (4)   1.00 1.00

Thai Heritage Conservation Day. A souvenir sheet containing a perf. 13¼ example of No. 2950 sold for 15b.

A1275

A1276

A1277

Long Boat Racing — A1278

2017, Apr. 7   Litho.   Perf. 14½x14
Granite Paper

2951 A1275 3b multi   .25 .25
2952 A1276 3b multi   .25 .25
2953 A1277 3b multi   .25 .25
2954 A1278 3b multi   .25 .25
   Nos. 2951-2954 (4)   1.00 1.00

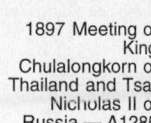

Vesak Day A1279

Statues of Buddha and text from the Dhammapada: No. 2955, 3b "Happy is virtue until old age." No. 2956, 3b, "Happy is faith that firmly stands." No. 2957, 3b, "Happy is it to gain insight." No. 2958, 3b, "Happy is it to commit no sin."

2017, May 3   Litho.   Perf. 13¼
Granite Paper

2955-2958 A1279   Set of 4   .70 .55

A souvenir sheet containing Nos. 2955-2958 sold for 25b.

Suan Sunandha University, 80th Anniv., Bangkok, 80th Anniv. — A1280

2017, May 17   Litho.   Perf. 14½x14
Granite Paper

2959 A1280 3b multi   .25 .25

A1281

A1282

A1283

Chao Phraya River — A1284

2017, June 5   Litho.   Perf. 14x14¼
Granite Paper

2960 A1281 3b multi   .25 .25
2961 A1282 3b multi   .25 .25
2962 A1283 3b multi   .25 .25
2963 A1284 3b multi   .25 .25
   Nos. 2960-2963 (4)   1.00 1.00

1897 Meeting of King Chulalongkorn of Thailand and Tsar Nicholas II of Russia — A1285

2017, July 3   Litho.   Perf. 13¼
Granite Paper

2964 A1285 3b multi   .25 .25

Diplomatic relations between Thailand and Russia, 120th anniv. See Russia No. 7834.

Princess Chulabhorn, 60th Birthday A1286

2017, July 4   Litho.   Perf. 13¼
Granite Paper

2965 A1286 5b multi   .30 .25

King Maha Vajiralongkorn, 65th Birthday — A1287

Litho. With Foil Application
2017, July 28   Perf. 13¼
Granite Paper

2966 A1287 10b gold & multi   .60 .45

Cassia Fistula — A1288

2017, Aug. 8   Litho.   Perf. 13¼
Granite Paper

2967 A1288 3b multi   .25 .25

Association of Southeast Asian Nations, 50th anniv.

Thai Pavilion — A1289

2017, Aug. 14   Litho.   Perf. 14x14½
Granite Paper

2968 A1289 1b deep blue   .25 .25
2969 A1289 2b red   .25 .25
2970 A1289 3b green   .25 .25
2971 A1289 6b deep mauve   .40 .30
2972 A1289 7b magenta   .45 .35
2973 A1289 7b yellow & ocher   .55 .40
2974 A1289 10b peach & black   .60 .45
2975 A1289 50b lilac & blue   3.00 2.25
2976 A1289 100b ol yel & dk grn   6.00 4.50
   Nos. 2968-2976 (9)   11.75 9.00

Flag of Thailand, Cent. — A1290

2017, Sept. 28 Litho. Perf. 14½x14
Granite Paper
2977 A1290 3b multi .25 .25

World Post Day — A1291

2017, Oct. 5 Litho. Perf. 14x14½
Granite Paper
2978 A1291 3b multi .25 .25

King Bhumibol Adulyadej (1927-2016) — A1292

Items Used at Cremation of King Bhumibol Adulyadej — A1293

Royal Crematorium — A1294

No. 2979 — King Bhumibol Adulyadej: a, Wearing gray suit and tie. b, Gesturing with hands. c, Wearing blue suit and tie, d, With camera strap around neck. e, Wearing military uniform and cap. f, Wearing blue jacket and striped shirt. g, Wearing tan shirt. h, Wearing blue plaid suit. i, Wearing brown striped shirt.
No. 2980: a, Honor guard around urn. b, Palanquin, horiz. c, Chariot.

2017, Oct. 25 Litho. Perf. 13¼
Granite Paper (#2979, 2981)
2979 A1292 9b Sheet of 9, #a-i 5.00 3.75
Souvenir Sheets
Litho., Sheet Margin Litho. With Foil Application
2980 A1293 3b Sheet of 3, #a-c .55 .45

Litho. With Foil Application
Perf. 14x14½
2981 A1294 9b gold & multi .55 .45

King Taksin the Great Monument, Talat — A1295

2017, Nov. 6 Litho. Perf. 13¼
Granite Paper
2982 A1295 3b multi .25 .25
King Taksin the Great (1734-82).

A1296

A1297

A1298

A1299

A1300

A1301

New Year 2018
A1300   A1301

2017, Nov. 15 Litho. Perf. 14x14½
Granite Paper
2983 A1296 3b multi .25 .25
2984 A1297 3b multi .25 .25
2985 A1298 3b multi .25 .25
2986 A1299 3b multi .25 .25
2987 A1300 15b multi .95 .75
2988 A1301 15b multi .95 .75
Nos. 2983-2988 (6) 2.90 2.50

Khruba Siwichai Amulet — A1302

Litho. & Embossed
2017, Dec. 1 Perf. 14x14½
Granite Paper
2989 A1302 9b multi .55 .45
A souvenir sheet containing one example of No. 2989 sold for 20b.

National Day — A1303

Litho. With Foil Application
2017, Dec. 5 Perf. 13¼
Granite Paper
2990 A1303 5b gold & multi .30 .25

New Year 2018 (Year of the Dog) — A1304

2018, Jan. 1 Litho. Perf. 13¼
Granite Paper
2991 A1304 3b multi .25 .25

A1305

A1306

A1307

Children's Day — A1308

2018, Jan. 13 Litho. Perf. 13¼
2992 A1305 3b multi .25 .25
2993 A1306 3b multi .25 .25
2994 A1307 3b multi .25 .25
2995 A1308 3b multi .25 .25
Nos. 2992-2995 (4) 1.00 1.00

Knitted Heart — A1309

Litho. & Embossed
2018, Feb. 7 Perf. 13
Granite Paper
2996 A1309 5b multi .35 .25

A1310

A1311

A1312

Murals — A1313

2018, Apr. 2 Litho. Perf. 14½x14
Granite Paper
2997 A1310 3b multi .25 .25
2998 A1311 3b multi .25 .25
Perf. 14x14½
2999 A1312 3b multi .25 .25
3000 A1313 3b multi .25 .25
Nos. 2997-3000 (4) 1.00 1.00
Thai heritage conservation. A souvenir sheet containing a perf. 13½ example of No. 3000 sold for 15b.

A1314

A1315

A1316

Skyrocket Festival — A1317

2018, Apr. 4   Litho.   Perf. 13¼
3001 A1314 3b multi   .25   .25
3002 A1315 3b multi   .25   .25
3003 A1316 3b multi   .25   .25
3004 A1317 3b multi   .25   .25
     Nos. 3001-3004 (4)   1.00 1.00

Diplomatic Relations Between
Thailand and Turkey, 60th
Anniv. — A1318

No. 3005. a, Thai kick boxers. b, Turkish
wrestlers.

2018, May 12   Litho.   Perf. 13¼
Granite Paper
3005 A1318 3b Horiz. pair, #a-b   .40   .30
     See Turkey No. 3610.

Vesak
Day — A1319

Designs: No. 3006, 3b, Phra That Gate
Kaew Chulamanee, Chiang Mai. No. 3007, 3b,
Phra That Doi Tung, Chiang Rai. No. 3008, 3b,
Phra That Sri Jomthong, Chiang Mai. No.
3009, 3b, Phra That Lampang Luang,
Lampang.

2018, May 22   Litho.   Perf. 14x14½
Granite Paper
3006-3009 A1319 Set of 4   .75   .60

A souvenir sheet containing perf. 13½
examples of Nos. 3006-3009 sold for 25b.

Diplomatic Relations Between
Thailand and Romania, 45th
Anniv. — A1320

No. 3010: a, Flag, man and woman from
Thailand. b, Flag, man and woman from
Romania.

2018, May 31   Litho.   Perf. 13¼
Granite Paper
3010 A1320 3b Horiz. pair, #a-b   .40   .30
     See Romania No. 6110.

King Maha Vajiralongkorn, 66th
Birthday — A1324

Litho. With Foil Application
2018, July 28   Perf. 13¼
Granite Paper
3025 A1324 10b gold & multi   .60   .45

Metropolitan Electricity Authority, 60th
Anniv. — A1325

2018, Aug. 1   Litho.   Perf. 13¼
Granite Paper
3026 A1325 3b multi   .25   .25

A1326

A1327

A1328

Thai Postal Services, 135th
Anniv. — A1329

2018, Aug. 4   Litho.   Perf. 13¼
Granite Paper
3027 A1326 3b multi   .25   .25
3028 A1327 3b multi   .25   .25
3029 A1328 3b multi   .25   .25
3030 A1329 3b multi   .25   .25
     Nos. 3027-3030 (4)   1.00 1.00

Queen Sirikit,
86th Birthday
A1330

Litho. With Foil Application
2018, Aug. 31   Perf. 13¼
Granite Paper
3031 A1330 9b gold & multi   .55   .40

SEMI-POSTAL STAMPS

Nos. 164-175
Overprinted in Red

1918, Jan. 11   Unwmk.   Perf. 14
B1   A21   2s orange
                brown   1.75   1.00
B2   A21   3s emerald   1.75   1.00
B3   A21   5s rose red   6.00   4.25
B4   A21 10s black & olive   16.00   6.00
B5   A21 15s blue   10.00   6.00
B6   A22   1b blue & gray
                blk   45.00 24.00
B7   A22   2b car rose &
                brn   60.00 30.00
B8   A22   3b yel grn & blk   120.00 50.00
B9   A22   5b dp vio & blk   350.00 175.00
 a.   Double overprint   775.00 400.00
B10 A22 10b ol grn & vio
                brn   575.00 300.00
B11 A22 20b sea grn &
                brn   2,100. 1,500.
     Nos. B1-B11 (11)   3,286. 2,097.

Excellent counterfeit overprints are known.
These stamps were sold at an advance over
face value, the excess being given to the Siamese Red Cross Society.

Stamps of 1905-19
Handstamp
Overprinted

1920, Feb.
On Nos. 164, 146, 168
B12 A21   2s (+ 3s) org
                brn   42.50 28.00
B13 A21   3s (+ 2s) green   42.50 28.00
B14 A21 15s (+ 5s) blue   120.00 85.00
On No. 105
B15 A15   1t (+ 25s)   340.00 340.00
On Nos. 185-186
B16 A21   5s on 6s (+ 5s)   57.50 42.50
 a.   Overprint inverted
B17 A21 10s on 12s (+
                5s)   57.50 42.50
     Nos. B12-B17 (6)   660.00 566.00
     Set, never hinged   1,150.

Sold at an advance over face value, the
excess being for the benefit of the Wild Tiger
Corps. Counterfeits exist.

Stamps of 1905-20
Handstamp
Overprinted

On Nos. 164, 146, 168
B18 A21   2s (+ 3s) org brn   32.50 24.00
B19 A21   3s (+ 2s) green   32.50 24.00
 a.   Pair, one without ovpt.

B20 A21 15s (+ 5s) blue   60.00 50.00
On No. 105
B21 A15   1t (+ 25s)   275.00 250.00
On No. 186
B22 A21 10s on 12s (+ 5s)   60.00 42.50
On No. 190
B23 A23   5s (+ 5s)   65.00 47.50
     Nos. B18-B23 (6)   525.00 438.00
     Set, never hinged   850.00

Sold at an advance over face value, the
excess being for the benefit of the Wild Tiger
Corps. Counterfeits exist.
No. B23 was issued in late April or May
1920.

Nos. 187-188, 190,
193-194, 196, 198
Overprinted in Blue or
Red

1920, Dec. 17
B24 A23   2s brown, yel   13.50 13.50
B25 A23   3s grn, grn (R)   13.50 13.50
B26 A23   5s rose, pale rose 13.50 13.50
B27 A23 10s blk & org (R)   13.50 13.50
B28 A23 15s bl, bluish (R) 26.00 26.00
B29 A23 25s chocolate   90.00 90.00
B30 A23 50s ocher & blk (R) 210.00 210.00
     Nos. B24-B30 (7)   380.00 380.00
     Set, never hinged   575.00

Nos. B12-B30 were sold at an advance over
face value, the excess being for the benefit of
the Wild Tiger Corps. Counterfeits exist.

Nos. 170-172
Surcharged in Red

1939, Apr. 6   Unwmk.   Perf. 14
B31 A22   5s + 5s on 1b   20.00 16.00
B32 A22 10s + 5s on 2b   25.00 24.00
B33 A22 15s + 5s on 2b   25.00 24.00
     Nos. B31-B33 (3)   70.00 64.00
     Set, never hinged   120.00

Founding of the Intl. Red Cross Soc., 75th
anniv.
Bottom line of overprint is different on Nos.
B32-B33.

**Catalogue values for unused
stamps in this section, from this
point to the end of the section, are
for Never Hinged items.**

No. 214 Surcharged
in Carmine

1952   Unwmk.   Perf. 12½
B34 A25 80s + 20s blue & blk 20.00 15.00
     New constitution.

Red Cross and
Dancer — SP1

Lithographed, Cross Typographed
1953, Apr. 6   Wmk. 299   Perf. 11
Cross in Red, Dancer Dark Blue

B35	SP1	25s + 25s yellow grn	5.00	4.50
B36	SP1	50s + 50s brt rose	16.00	8.00
B37	SP1	1b + 1b lt blue	19.00	12.50
		Nos. B35-B37 (3)	40.00	25.00

60th anniv. of the founding of the Siamese Red Cross Society.

Nos. B35-B37
Overprinted in
Black

1955, Apr. 3
Cross in Red, Dancer Dark Blue

B38	SP1	25s + 25s yel grn	30.00	16.00
B39	SP1	50s + 50s brt rose	120.00	100.00
B40	SP1	1b + 1b lt blue	175.00	150.00
		Nos. B38-B40 (3)	325.00	266.00

Counterfeits exist.

Red Cross Cent. Emblem — SP2

1963   Wmk. 334   Litho.   Perf. 13½

B41	50s + 10s cross at right		.80	.40
B42	50s + 10s cross at left		.80	.40
a.	SP2 Pair, #B41-B42		2.40	1.60

Cent. of the Intl. Red Cross.

Nos. B41-B42
Surcharged

1973, Feb. 15

B43	SP2	75s + 25s on 50s + 10s	1.40	1.20
B44	SP3	75s + 25s on 50s + 10s	1.40	1.20
a.	Pair, #B43-B44		3.00	2.40

Red Cross Fair, Feb. 15-19.

Nos. B41-B42
Surcharged

1974, Feb. 2

B45	SP2	75s + 25s on 50s + 10s	1.40	1.40
B46	SP3	75s + 25s on 50s + 10s	1.40	1.40
a.	Pair, #B45-B46		2.90	2.90

Red Cross Fair, Feb. 1974. Position of surcharge reversed on No. B46.

1975, Feb 11 52

B47	SP2	75s + 25s on 50s + 10s	1.40	1.40
B48	SP3	75s + 25s on 50s + 10s	1.40	1.40
a.	Pair, #B47-B48		2.90	2.90

Red Cross Fair, Feb. 1975. Position of surcharge reversed on No. B48.

Nos. B41-B42
Surcharged

1976, Feb. 26

B49	SP2	75s + 25s on 50s + 10s	1.40	1.40
B50	SP3	75s + 25s on 50s + 10s	1.40	1.40
a.	Pair, #B49-B50		2.90	2.90

Red Cross Fair, Feb. 16-Mar. 1. Position of surcharge reversed on #B50.

Nos. B41-B42
Surcharged

1977, Apr. 6   Wmk. 334   Perf. 13½

B51	SP2	75s + 25s on 50s + 10s	1.40	.65
B52	SP3	75s + 25s on 50s + 10s	1.40	.65
a.	Pair, #B51-B52		2.90	2.90

Red Cross Fair 1977.

Red Cross Blood
Collection — SP4

Wmk. 329
1978, Apr. 6   Photo.   Perf. 13

B53	SP4	2.75b + 25s multi	2.25	2.00

"Give blood, save life."
For surcharge see No. B58.

Eye and Blind
People — SP5

Perf. 14x13½
1979, Apr. 6   Litho.   Wmk. 368

B54	SP5	75s + 25s multi	.85	.50

"Give an eye, save new life." Red Cross Fair. Surtax was for Thai Red Cross.
For surcharge see No. B59.

Extracting Snake Venom, Red
Cross — SP6

1980, Apr.   Perf. 11x13

B55	SP6	75s + 25s multi	1.10	.95
	Complete booklet, 10 #B55		20.00	

Red Cross Fair. Surtax was for Thai Red Cross.
For surcharge see No. B60.

Nurse Helping Victim — SP7

1981, Apr. 6   Wmk. 377   Perf. 12½

B56	SP7	75 + 25s red & gray grn	1.50	1.40

Red Cross Fair (canceled). Surtax was for Thai Red Cross.
For surcharge see No. B65.

Red
Cross
Fair
SP8

Perf. 13x13½
1983, Apr. 6   Litho.   Wmk. 329

B57	SP8	1.25b + 25s multi	1.20	1.00

Surtax was for Thai Red Cross.

No. B53 Surcharged

1984, Apr. 6   Photo.   Perf. 13

B58	SP4	3.25b + 25s on 2.75b + 25s	2.25	4.50

Red Cross Fair. Surtax was for Thai Red Cross. Overprint translates: Red Cross Donation.

No. B54
Surcharged

Wmk. 368
1985, Mar. 30   Litho.   Perf. 13

B59	SP5	2b + 25c on 75s + 25s	1.90	1.90

Surtax for the Thai Red Cross.

**No. B55 Overprinted and
Surcharged**

1986, Apr. 6   Wmk. 368   Perf. 11x13

B60	SP6	2b + 25s on 75s + 25s	2.00	2.00

Natl. Children's Day. Surtax for Natl. Red Cross Society. Overprint translates "Red Cross Donation."

Natl. Scouting Movement, 75th Anniv.,
15th Asia-Pacific Conference,
Thailand — SP9

#B61, Scouts, saluting, community service. #B62, Scout activities. #B63, King & queen at ceremony. #B64, 15th Asia-Pacific conf.

1986, Nov. 7   Wmk. 385   Perf. 13½

B61	SP9	2b + 50s multi	.50	.25
B62	SP9	2b + 50s multi	.50	.25
B63	SP9	2b + 50s multi	.50	.25
B64	SP9	2b + 50s multi	.50	.25
		Nos. B61-B64 (4)	2.00	1.00

Surtax for the Natl. Scouting Fund.

No. B56 Surcharged
1987, Apr.   Wmk. 377   Perf. 12½

B65	SP7	2b + 50s on 75s + 25s	2.00	1.60

Sports — SP10

Designs: No. B66, Hurdles, medal winners. No. B67, Race, nurse treating injured cyclist. No. B68, Boxers training. No. B69, Soccer.

1989, Dec. 16   Wmk. 387   Perf. 13½

B66	SP10	2b +1b multi	.40	.30
B67	SP10	2b +1b multi	.40	.30
B68	SP10	2b +1b multi	.40	.30
B69	SP10	2b +1b multi	.40	.30
		Nos. B66-B69 (4)	1.60	1.20

Surtax for sports welfare organizations.

Sports — SP11

1990, Dec. 16

B70	SP11	2b +1b Judo	.50	.30
B71	SP11	2b +1b Archery	.50	.30
B72	SP11	2b +1b High jump	.50	.30
B73	SP11	2b +1b Windsurfing	.50	.30
		Nos. B70-B73 (4)	2.00	1.20

Surtax for sports welfare organization.

Sports — SP12

Wmk. 387
1991, Dec. 16   Litho.   Perf. 13½

B74	SP12	2b +1b Jogging	.40	.30
B75	SP12	2b +1b Cycling	.40	.30
B76	SP12	2b +1b Soccer, jump-ing rope	.40	.30
B77	SP12	2b +1b Swimming	.40	.30
		Nos. B74-B77 (4)	1.60	1.20

Surtax for sports welfare organizations.

18th South East Asian Games, Chiang
Mai — SP13

No. B78: a, Water polo. b, Tennis. c, Hurdles. d, Gymnastics.
No. B79: a, Fencing. b, Pool. c, Diving. d, Pole vault.

1994, Dec. 16   Wmk. 340

B78	SP13	2b +1b Strip of 4, #a.-d.	2.25	1.75
e.	Souvenir sheet, #B78		2.25	2.25

Wmk. 387

B79	SP13	2b +1b Strip of 4, #a.-d.	1.60	1.40
e.	Souvenir sheet, #B79		2.40	2.40

Nos. B78e, B79e sold for 15b.
Issued: #B78, 12/16/94; #B79, 12/9/95.
For surcharges see Nos. 2338-2339, 2347-2348.

13th Asian Games, Bangkok — SP14

1998, Mar. 27   **Perf. 14½x14**

B80	SP14	2b +1b Shooting	.25 .25
B81	SP14	3b +1b Rhythmic	
		gymnastics	.35 .25
B82	SP14	4b +1b Swimming	.45 .35
B83	SP14	7b +1b Wind-surfing	.70 .55
		Nos. B80-B83 (4)	1.75 1.40

13th Asian Games, Bangkok — SP15

Perf. 14½x14

1998, Dec. 6   **Litho.**   **Unwmk.**

Granite Paper

B84	SP15	2b +1b Field hockey	.35 .25
B85	SP15	3b +1b Wrestling	.40 .25
B86	SP15	4b +1b Rowing	.50 .30
B87	SP15	7b +1b Equestrian	.80 .45
		Nos. B84-B87 (4)	2.05 1.25

AIR POST STAMPS

Garuda — AP1

1925 Unwmk. Engr.   **Perf. 14, 14½**

C1	AP1	2s brown, yel	2.25 .50
C2	AP1	3s dark brown	2.25 .50
C3	AP1	5s green	11.00 .55
C4	AP1	10s black & org	20.00 .60
C5	AP1	15s carmine	18.50 1.00
C6	AP1	25s dark blue	12.50 1.20
C7	AP1	50s brown org &	
		blk	40.00 7.50
C8	AP1	1b blue & brown	40.00 9.00
		Nos. C1-C8 (8)	146.50 20.85
		Set, never hinged	200.00

Issue dates: 2s, 50s, Apr. 21; others, Jan. 3.

Nos. C1-C8 received this overprint ("Government Museum 2468") in 1925, but were never issued. The death of King Vajiravudh caused cancellation of the fair at which this set was to have been released.

They were used during 1928 only in the interdepartmental service for accounting purposes of the money-order sections of various Bangkok post offices, and were never sold to the public. Values for set: unused, $1,400; used, $40.

1930-37   **Perf. 12½**

C9	AP1	2s brown, yel	7.50 .60
C10	AP1	5s green	1.75 .30
C11	AP1	10s black & org	6.00 .30
C12	AP1	15s carmine	24.00 6.00
C13	AP1	25s dark blue ('37)	3.00 .90
a.		Vert. pair, imperf. btwn.	600.00
C14	AP1	50s brn org & blk	
		('37)	3.00 2.00
		Nos. C9-C14 (6)	45.25 10.10
		Set, never hinged	70.00

Monument of Democracy, Bangkok AP2

1942-43   **Engr.**   **Perf. 11**

C15	AP2	2s dk org brn	
		('43)	3.25 2.40
C16	AP2	3s dk grn ('43)	32.50 24.00
a.		Vert. pair, imperf. btwn.	275.00 275.00
C17	AP2	5s deep claret	3.25 1.20
a.		Horiz. pair, imperf. btwn.	150.00 150.00
b.		Vert. pair, imperf. btwn.	150.00 150.00
C18	AP2	10s carmine ('43)	15.00 1.20
a.		Vert. pair, imperf. btwn.	150.00 150.00
C19	AP2	15s dark blue	5.25 2.00
a.		Vert. pair, imperf. btwn.	175.00 175.00
		Nos. C15-C19 (5)	59.25 30.80
		Set, never hinged	90.00

> **Catalogue values for unused stamps in this section, from this point to the end of the section, are for Never Hinged items.**

Garuda and Bangkok Skyline — AP3

1952-53   **Perf. 13x12½**

C20	AP3	1.50b red violet ('53)	4.75 1.00
C21	AP3	2b dark blue	13.00 2.00
C22	AP3	3b gray ('53)	17.50 1.25
		Nos. C20-C22 (3)	35.25 4.25

Issue dates: June 15, 1952. Sept. 15, 1953.

OFFICIAL STAMPS

> **Catalogue values for unused stamps in this section are for Never Hinged items.**

O1   O2

Perf. 10½ Rough

1963, Oct. 1   **Typo.**   **Unwmk.**

Without Gum

O1	O1	10s pink & dp car	.25 .25
O2	O1	20s brt grn & car rose	.25 .25
O3	O1	25s blue & dp car	.30 .35
O4	O1	50s deep carmine	1.10 2.00
O5	O2	1b silver & car rose	1.25 3.00
O6	O2	2b bronze & car rose	2.25 2.25
		Nos. O1-O6 (6)	5.40 8.10

Issued as an official test from Oct. 1, 1963, to Jan. 31, 1964, to determine the amount of mail sent out by various government departments.

Nos. O5, O9, O10 exist with oval frame of type O1.

1964   **Without Gum**

O7	O1	20s green	.50 .50
O8	O1	25s blue	.50 .50
O9	O2	1b silver	1.00 1.00
O10	O2	2b bister	2.50 2.50
		Nos. O7-O10 (4)	4.50 4.50

Others values exist printed in one color.

THRACE

'thrās

LOCATION — In southeastern Europe between the Black and Aegean Seas **GOVT.** — Former Turkish Province **AREA** — 89,361 sq. mi. (approx.)

Thrace underwent many political changes during the Balkan Wars and

---

World War I. It was finally divided among Turkey, Greece and Bulgaria.

100 Lepta = 1 Drachma
40 Paras = 1 Piaster
100 Stotinki = 1 Leva (1919)

> A large number of minor overprint errors exist on most issues of Thrace. See the *Scott Classic Specialized Catalogue of Stamps and Covers 1840-1940* for much more specialized listings.

Giumulzina District Issue

Turkish Stamps of 1909 Surcharged in Blue or Red

1913   **Unwmk.**   **Perf. 12, 13½**

1	A21	10 l on 20pa rose (Bl)	45.00 50.00
a.		Inverted overprint	170.00
b.		Double overprint	170.00
2	A21	25 l on 10pa bl grn	67.50 75.00
a.		Inverted overprint	175.00
b.		Double overprint	175.00
3	A21	25 l on 20pa rose (Bl)	67.50 75.00
a.		Inverted overprint	170.00
b.		Double overprint	170.00
c.		Béhié ovpt. (#162)	200.00
4	A21	25 l on 1pi ultra	110.00 125.00
a.		Inverted overprint	220.00
b.		Double overprint	220.00
		Nos. 1-4 (4)	290.00 325.00

Counterfeits exist of Nos. 1-4.

Eight other values exist, bearing surcharges differing in color or denomination from Nos. 1-4. These stamps were not issued. Values, each: unused $175; never hinged $350.

Turkish Inscriptions
A1   A2

Type 1

Type 2

1913   **Litho.**   **Imperf.**

Laid Paper

Control Mark in Rose

Without Gum

5	A1	1pi blue, type 1	17.50 17.50
a.		Double print	250.00
b.		Type 2	85.00 75.00
6	A1	2pi violet	17.50 17.50
a.		Double print	500.00 200.00
b.		Type 2	200.00

Wove Paper

7	A2	10pa vermilion	35.00 30.00
8	A2	20pa blue	35.00 30.00
9	A2	1pi violet	37.50 30.00
		Nos. 5-9 (5)	142.50 125.00

Turkish Stamps of 1913 Surcharged in Red or Black

1913   **Perf. 12**

10	A22	1pi on 2pa ol grn	30.00 27.50
10A	A22	1pi on 2pa ol grn (R)	30.00 27.50
11	A22	1pi on 5pa ocher	30.00 27.50
11A	A22	1pi on 5pa ocher (R)	30.00 27.50
12	A22	1pi on 20pa rose	35.00 35.00
13	A22	1pi on 5pi dk vio	70.00 70.00
13A	A22	1pi on 5pi dk vio (R)	70.00 70.00
14	A22	1pi on 10pi dl red	125.00 125.00
15	A22	1pi on 25pi dk grn	500.00 500.00
		Nos. 10-15 (9)	920.00 910.00

On Nos. 13-15 the surcharge is vertical, reading up. No. 15 exists with double surcharge, one black, one red.

Nos. 10-15 exist with forged surcharges.

Bulgarian Stamps of 1911 Handstamped Surcharged in Red or Blue

1913

16	A20	10pa on 1s myr grn (R)	25.00 25.00
a.		Top ovpt. inverted	100.00
b.		Top ovpt. double	100.00
c.		Top ovpt. omitted	150.00
d.		Bottom ovpt. omitted	150.00
e.		Bottom ovpt. inverted	100.00
17	A21	20pa on 2s car & blk	25.00 25.00
a.		Inverted overprint	60.00
18	A23	1pi on 5s grn & blk (R)	25.00 25.00
a.		Inverted overprint	125.00 125.00
c.		Double ovpt., one at top, one at bottom	
19	A22	2pi on 3s lake & blk	28.00 28.00
a.		Inverted overprint & surcharge	80.00 80.00
20	A24	2½pi on 10s dp red & blk	40.00 40.00
b.		2½pi on 2s	265.00
21	A25	5pi on 15s brn bis	70.00 70.00
a.		Inverted overprint & surcharge	260.00
		Nos. 16-21 (6)	213.00 213.00

Same Surcharges on Greek Stamps

On Issue of 1911

1913   **Serrate Roulette 13½**

22	A24	10pa on 1 l grn (R)	25.00 25.00
23	A24	10pa on 1 l grn	25.00 25.00
24	A26	10pa on 5 l grn	125.00 125.00
25	A25	10pa on 25 l ultra (R)	35.00 35.00
26	A25	20pa on 2 l car rose	25.00 25.00
27	A24	1pi on 3 l ver	25.00 25.00
a.		Value omitted	65.00 65.00
b.		Red overprint	25.00 25.00
27C	A24	1pi on 10 l car rose	550.00
28	A26	2pi on 5 l grn	65.00 65.00
29	A24	2½pi on 10 l car rose	65.00 65.00
30	A25	5pi on 40 l dp bl (R)	125.00 125.00
		Nos. 22-30 (9)	515.00 455.60

On Occupation Stamps of 1912

31	O1	10pa on 1 l brn	25.00 20.00
a.		Value omitted	125.00
b.		Value srch. inverted	65.00
32	O1	10pa on 1 l brn	25.00 20.00
33	O1	20pa on 1 l brn	25.00 20.00
		Nos. 31-33 (3)	75.00 60.00

These surcharges were made with handstamps, two of which were required for each surcharge. The upper handstamp, reads "Administration of Autonomous Western Thrace" in old Turkish. The lower handstamp expresses the new value. On horizontal designs, the text appears on the right, and the value appears on the left. On inverted overprints on horizontal stamps, this is reversed. One or both parts may be found inverted or omitted.

Nos. 16-33 exist with forged surcharges.

OCCUPATION STAMPS

Issued under Allied Occupation

Bulgarian Stamps
of 1915-19
Handstamped in
Violet Blue

Perf. 11½, 11½x12, 14

1919			Unwmk.	
N1b	A43	1s black	2.50	2.00
N2	A43	2s olive green	2.50	2.00
N3	A44	5s green	.85	.85
N4	A44	10s rose	.85	.85
N5	A44	15s violet	.85	.85
N6	A26	25s indigo & black	.85	.85

The overprint on Nos. N1-N6 exists applied both ascending and descending, as well as inverted in both positions. On the 1s value, the usual position of the overprint is upright, reading from lower left to upper right; on the rest of the set, the overprint is usually inverted, reading from lower right to upper left. See the *Scott Classic Specialized Catalogue of Stamps and Covers* for detailed listings.

Bulgarian Stamps
of 1911-19
Overprinted in Red
or Black

1919				
N7	A43	1s black (R)	.25	.25
N8	A43	2s olive green	.25	.25
c.		Inverted ovpt.	40.00	—
d.		Pair, one without ovpt.	—	
N9	A44	5s green	.25	.25
c.		Inverted ovpt.	—	
d.		Pair, one without ovpt.	—	
e.		Double ovpt.	50.00	
N10	A44	10s rose	.25	.25
d.		Pair, one without ovpt.	—	
e.		Double ovpt.	35.00	
f.		Imperf., pair	—	
N11	A44	15s violet	.25	.25
c.		Imperf., pair	—	
N12	A26	25s indigo & black	.25	.25
N13	A29	1 l chocolate	5.00	5.00
N14	A37a	2 l brown orange	9.00	9.00
N15	A38	3 l claret	12.50	12.50
		Nos. N7-N15 (9)	28.00	28.00

Overprint is vertical, reading up, on Nos. N9-N13.

The following varieties are found in the setting of "INTERALLIEE": Inverted "V" for "A," second "L" inverted, "F" instead of final "E."

Bulgarian Stamps of
1919 Overprinted

1920				
N16	A44	5s green	.25	.25
d.		Imperf, pair	75.00	
N17	A44	10s rose	.25	.25
N18	A44	15s violet	.25	.25
N19	A44	50s yel brn, ovpt. reading up	1.50	1.50
d.		Ovpt. reading down	25.00	30.00
h.		As "d," imperf, pair	140.00	
		Nos. N16-N19 (4)	2.25	2.25

Various typographical errors in the overprint are found on all values.

Bulgarian Stamps of
1919 Overprinted

1920			*Perf.* 12x11½	
N20	A44	5s green	.25	.25
a.		Inverted overprint	35.00	50.00
b.		Pair, one without ovpt.	42.50	65.00
c.		Imperf, pair	45.00	65.00
d.		As "c," inverted overprint	55.00	75.00
N21	A44	10s rose	.25	.25
a.		Inverted overprint	30.00	40.00
b.		Double ovpt., one on gum side	45.00	65.00
c.		Imperf, pair	45.00	65.00
d.		As "c," inverted overprint	55.00	75.00

N22	A44	15s violet	.25	.25
a.		Inverted overprint	30.00	40.00
b.		Imperf, pair	45.00	65.00
c.		As "b," inverted overprint	55.00	75.00
N23	A44	25s deep blue	.25	.25
a.		Inverted overprint	30.00	40.00
b.		Imperf, pair	45.00	65.00
c.		As "b," inverted overprint	55.00	75.00
d.		Double ovpt., one on gummed side	45.00	
N24	A44	50s ocher	.25	.25
a.		Inverted overprint	35.00	50.00
b.		Imperf, pair	45.00	65.00
c.		As "b," inverted ovpt.	55.00	80.00

Imperf

N25	A44	30s chocolate	1.50	1.50
a.		Inverted overprint	35.00	55.00
b.		Perforated	22.50	
		Nos. N20-N25 (6)	2.75	2.75

No. N25 is not known without overprint.

ISSUED UNDER GREEK OCCUPATION

Counterfeits exist of Nos. N26-N84.

For Use in Western Thrace

Greek Stamps of
1911-19 Overprinted
"Administration
Western Thrace" in
Greek

Serrate Roulette 13½

1920			Litho.	Unwmk.
N26	A24	1 l green	.25	.25
a.		Inverted overprint	20.00	
b.		Double overprint	20.00	
c.		Double overprint, one inverted	75.00	
N27	A25	2 l rose	.25	.25
N28	A24	3 l vermilion	.25	.25
a.		Inverted overprint	32.50	
N29	A26	5 l green	.25	.25
a.		Inverted overprint	25.00	
b.		Double overprint	25.00	
N30	A24	10 l rose	.40	.85
N31	A25	15 l dull blue	.40	.75
a.		Inverted overprint	20.00	
b.		Double overprint	20.00	
c.		Dbl. ovpt., one inverted	30.00	
N32	A25	25 l blue	.40	.85
N34	A25	40 l indigo	2.00	4.00
N35	A26	50 l violet brn	2.50	6.50
N36	A27	1d ultra	9.00	15.00
N37	A27	2d vermilion	30.00	35.00
a.		Double overprint	75.00	
		Nos. N26-N37 (11)	45.70	63.95

The 20 l value with this overprint was not issued. Values: unused $25; never hinged $65.

Engr.

N38	A25	2 l car rose	1.25	1.00
N39	A24	3 l vermilion	1.25	1.00
N39A	A25	20 l slate	32.50	
N39B	A25	25 l blue	35.00	
N39C	A25	30 l rose	45.00	
N40	A27	1d ultra	30.00	25.00
N41	A27	2d vermilion	45.00	35.00
N42	A27	3d car rose	62.50	80.00
N43	A27	5d ultra	25.00	30.00
N44	A27	10d deep blue	25.00	30.00
		Nos. N38-N44 (10)	302.50	

Nos. N38-N44 were not issued. Values for used examples of Nos. N38-N39 and N40-N44 are for cancelled-to-order stamps.

Nos. N42-N44 are overprinted on the reissues of Greece Nos. 210-212. See footnote below Greece No. 213.

Overprinted

N45	A28	25d deep blue	62.50	35.00

This overprint reads: "Administration Western Thrace."

With Additional
Overprint

			Litho.	
N46	A24	1 l green	5.00	3.50
N47	A25	2 l rose	.25	.50
a.		Inverted overprint	65.00	
N47B	A26	5 l green	27.50	
N48	A24	10 l rose	.65	.85
a.		Inverted overprint	19.00	
N49	A25	20 l slate	.65	.85
a.		Inverted overprint	19.00	
N49B	A25	25 l blue	45.00	
N50	A26	30 l rose (#240)	.65	1.25

Engr.

N50A	A26	30 l rose (#244)	75.00	
N51	A27	2d vermilion	35.00	30.00
N52	A27	3d car rose	47.50	35.00
N53	A27	5d ultra	42.50	32.50
N54	A27	10d deep blue	35.00	22.50
		Nos. N46-N54 (12)	314.70	126.95

Nos. N46, N47B, N49B, N50A, N51, N53 and N54 were not issued. Used values for Nos. N46, N51, N53 and N54 are for canceled-to-order stamps.

For Use in Eastern and Western Thrace

Greek Stamps of
1911-19 Overprinted
"Administration Thrace"
in Greek

1920			Litho.	
N55	A24	1 l green	.25	1.00
a.		Inverted overprint	15.00	
b.		Double overprint	15.00	
N56	A25	2 l rose	.25	.50
a.		Inverted overprint	12.50	
b.		Double overprint	15.00	
c.		Triple overprint	25.00	
N57	A24	3 l vermilion	.25	.50
a.		Inverted overprint	12.50	
b.		Double overprint	15.00	
c.		Double overprint, one inverted	17.50	
N58	A26	5 l green	.25	.50
a.		Inverted overprint	20.00	
b.		Double overprint	35.00	
N59	A24	10 l rose	.50	.75
a.		Inverted overprint	85.00	
N59B	A25	15 l dull blue	60.00	
a.		Inverted overprint	62.50	
N60	A25	20 l slate	.65	1.50
a.		Inverted overprint	17.50	
b.		Double overprint	15.00	
N61	A25	25 l blue	1.75	2.50
N62	A25	40 l indigo	2.50	7.00
N63	A26	50 l violet brn	3.00	6.50
N64	A27	1d ultra	15.00	30.00
N65	A27	2d vermilion	32.50	45.00

Engr.

N65A	A25	2 l rose	2.50	4.00
N66	A24	3 l vermilion	3.00	4.00
N67	A25	20 l gray lilac	8.50	22.50
N68	A28	25d deep blue	75.00	100.00
		Nos. N55-N68 (16)	205.90	226.25

Nos. N59B and N65A-N68 were not issued. Used values for Nos. N65A-N68 are for canceled-to-order stamps.

With Additional
Overprint

			Litho.	
N68A	A24	1 l green	12.50	6.00
N69	A25	2 l car rose	.25	.50
a.		Inverted overprint	35.00	
b.		Double overprint	30.00	
N70	A26	5 l green	7.50	8.00
N71	A25	20 l slate	.25	.50
a.		Double overprint	350.00	325.00
N72	A26	30 l rose	.25	.50

Engr.

N73	A27	3d car rose	17.50	25.00
a.		Inverted overprint	—	
N74	A27	5d ultra	27.50	45.00
N75	A27	10d deep blue	45.00	60.00
a.		Double overprint	125.00	
		Nos. N68A-N75 (8)	110.75	145.50

Nos. N68A, N70 and N74-N75 were not issued. Used values are for canceled-to-order stamps.

Turkish
Stamps of
1916-20
Srchd. in
Blue, Black
or Red

1920			*Perf.* 11½, 12½	
N76	A43	1 l on 5pa org (Bl)	.40	.50
a.		Inverted overprint	35.00	35.00
b.		Double overprint	30.00	30.00
c.		Double overprint, one inverted	50.00	50.00
d.		Double overprint, one on gummed side	35.00	
N77	A32	5 l on 3pi blue	.40	.50
a.		Inverted overprint	100.00	100.00
b.		Double overprint	70.00	70.00
N78	A30	20 l on 1pi bl grn	.65	.75
a.		Inverted overprint	27.50	27.50
b.		Double overprint	27.50	27.50
c.		Double overprint, one inverted	40.00	40.00
d.		Double overprint, one on gummed side	37.50	
N79	A53	25 l on 5pi on 2pa Prus bl (R)	.85	1.00
a.		Inverted overprint	50.00	50.00
b.		Double overprint	50.00	50.00
N80	A49	50 l on 5pi bl & blk (R)	6.50	7.50
N81	A45	1d on 20pa dp rose (Bl)	1.75	1.75
a.		Double overprint	40.00	40.00
N82	A22	2d on 10pa on 2pa ol grn (R)	2.50	3.00
a.		Double overprint	60.00	60.00
N83	A57	3d on 1pi dp bl (R)	12.50	12.50
a.		Inverted overprint	60.00	60.00
b.		Double overprint	65.00	65.00
N84	A23	5d on 20pa rose	12.50	12.50
a.		Inverted overprint	75.00	75.00
b.		Double overprint, one inverted	75.00	75.00
		Nos. N76-N84 (9)	38.05	40.00

On Nos. N83 and N84, the normal overprint is reading down. On the inverted overprints, it is reading up.

Nos. N77, N78 and N84 are on the 1920 issue with designs modified. Nos. N81, N82 and N83 are on stamps with the 1919 overprints.

POSTAGE DUE STAMPS

Issued under Allied Occupation

1919 Bulgarian
Postage Due Stamps
Overprinted, Reading
Vertically Up

1919		Unwmk.	*Perf.* 12x11½	
NJ1	D6	5s emerald	.50	.50
c.		Imperf. pair		
NJ2	D6	10s purple	1.00	1.25
c.		Imperf. pair		
NJ3	D6	50s blue	2.75	3.50
c.		Imperf. pair		
		Nos. NJ1-NJ3 (3)	4.25	5.25

Type of Bulgarian
Postage Due Stamps of
1919-22 Overprinted

1920			*Imperf.*	
NJ4	D6	5s emerald	.25	.50
a.		Inverted overprint	40.00	
NJ5	D6	10s deep violet	2.00	2.00
a.		Inverted overprint	40.00	
NJ6	D6	20s salmon	1.00	1.00
NJ7	D6	50s blue	1.50	1.50

			Perf. 12x11½	
NJ8	D6	10s deep violet	1.25	1.25
		Nos. NJ4-NJ8 (5)	6.00	6.25

No. NJ6 issued without gum.

TIBET
tə-'bet

LOCATION — A high tableland in Central Asia

GOVT. — A semi independent state, nominally under control of China (under Communist China since 1950-51). In 1965 Tibet became a nominally autonomous region of the People's Republic of China.

AREA — 463,200 sq. mi.

POP. — 1,500,000 (approx.)

CAPITAL — Lhasa

Tibet's postage stamps were valid only within its borders.

6 ⅔ Trangka = 1 Sang

"Stamps" produced by the "Tibetan Government in Exile" have no postal value. These include four-value sets for Himalayan animals and the UPU that were put on sale in the early 1970s.

Excellent counterfeits of Nos. 1-18 exist. Numerous shades of all values. All stamps issued without gum.

Small bits of foreign matter (inclusions) are to be expected in Native Paper. These do not reduce the value of the stamp unless they have caused serious damage to the design or paper.

A1

1912-50   Unwmk.   Typo.   Imperf.
Native Paper

1	A1	⅛t green	40.00	45.00
2	A1	⅛t blue	40.00	55.00
a.		⅛t ultramarine	50.00	60.00
3	A1	½t violet	40.00	55.00
4	A1	⅔t carmine	50.00	60.00
a.		"POTSAGE"	150.00	175.00
5	A1	1t vermilion	55.00	75.00
6	A1	1s sage green ('50)	100.00	110.00
		Nos. 1-6 (6)	325.00	400.00

The "POTSAGE" error is found on all shades of the ⅔t (positions 6 and 7).
Pin-perf. examples of Nos. 1 and 3 exist.
Issued in sheets of 12.
Beware of private reproductions of #1-5 that were printed in the US around 1986. Sheets of 12 bear "J. Crow Co." imprint. The set of 5 sheets was sold for $5.

Printed Using Shiny Enamel Paint

1920

1a	A1	⅛t green	60.00	40.00
2b	A1	⅛t blue	500.00	500.00
3d	A1	½t purple	100.00	110.00
4h	A1	⅔t carmine	100.00	110.00
i.		"POTSAGE"	225.00	250.00
5c	A1	1t carmine	350.00	400.00

In some 1920-30 printings, European enamel paint was used instead of ink. It has a glossy surface.

Lion — A2

1914

7	A2	4t milky blue	750.	850.
a.		4t dark blue	1,100.	1,100.
8	A2	8t carmine rose	165.	175.
a.		8t carmine	1,100.	1,100.

Issued in sheets of 6.

Printed Using Shiny Enamel Paint

1920

7b	A2	4t blue	1,350.	1,500.
8b	A2	8t carmine	1,350.	1,500.

See note following No. 5c.

A3

Thin White Native Paper

1933   Pin-perf.

9	A3	½t orange	95.00	100.00
10	A3	⅔t dark blue	95.00	120.00
11	A3	1t rose carmine	95.00	120.00
12	A3	2t scarlet	95.00	120.00
13	A3	4t emerald	95.00	120.00
		Nos. 9-13 (5)	475.00	580.00

Issued in sheets of 12.
Exist imperf.

Heavy Toned Native Paper

1934   Imperf.

14	A3	½t yellow	16.00	18.00
15	A3	⅔t blue	14.00	15.00
16	A3	1t orange ver	14.00	15.00
a.		1t carmine	16.00	18.00
17	A3	2t red	14.00	15.00
a.		2t orange vermilion	14.00	15.00
18	A3	4t green	14.00	15.00
a.		25x25mm instead of 24x24mm	55.00	65.00
		Nos. 14-18 (5)	72.00	78.00

Nos. 14-18 are also known with a private pin-perf.
The ½t and 1t exist printed on both sides.
Issued in sheets of 12.

OFFICIAL STAMPS

O1

O2

Sizes: No. O1, 32½x32½mm. No. O2, 38x28½mm. No. O3, 34x33mm. No. O4, 44x44mm. No. O5, 66x66mm.

Various Designs and Sizes Inscribed "STAMP"

1945   Unwmk.   Typo.   Imperf.
Native Paper

O1	O1	½t bronze green	
O2	O2	½t slate black	
O3	O1	⅔t reddish brown	
O4	O1	1 ½t olive green	
O5	O1	1s dark gray blue	

The status of Nos. O1-O5 is in question. Other values exist.

TIMOR
'tē-ˌmor

LOCATION — The eastern part of Timor island, Malay archipelago

GOVT. — Former Portuguese Overseas Territory

AREA — 7,330 sq. mi.

POP. — 660,000 (est. 1974)

CAPITAL — Dili

The Portuguese territory of Timor was annexed by Indonesia May 3, 1976. Timor-Leste achieved independent statehood status on May 20, 2002.

1000 Reis = 1 Milreis
78 Avos = 1 Rupee (1895)
100 Avos = 1 Pataca
100 Centavos = 1 Escudo (1960)
100 Cents = 1 Dollar (2000)

> **Catalogue values for unused stamps in this country are for Never Hinged items, beginning with Scott 256 in the regular postage section, Scott J31 in the postage due section, and Scott RA11 in the postal tax section.**

Watermark

Wmk. 232 — Maltese Cross

Stamps of Macao Overprinted in Black or Carmine

1885   Unwmk.   Perf. 12½, 13½

1	A1	5r black (C)	5.75	2.50
a.		Double overprint	85.00	85.00
b.		Triple overprint	200.00	
2	A1	10r green	9.25	5.75
a.		Overprint on Mozambique stamp	25.00	
b.		Overprinted on Portuguese India stamp	300.00	
3	A1	20r rose, perf. 13½	13.00	9.25
a.		Double overprint	35.00	
b.		Perf. 12½	26.00	9.25
4	A1	25r violet	4.00	1.75
a.		Perf. 13½	45.00	22.50
5	A1	40r yellow	7.00	5.00
a.		Double overprint	25.00	
b.		Inverted overprint	42.50	27.50
c.		Perf. 13½	28.00	19.00
6	A1	50r blue	8.25	3.25
a.		Perf. 13½	28.00	19.00
7	A1	80r slate	15.00	6.50
8	A1	100r lilac	8.00	3.25
a.		Double overprint	30.00	
b.		Perf. 13½	17.50	7.75
9	A1	200r org, perf. 13½	12.50	7.00
a.		Perf. 12½	25.00	8.50
10	A1	300r brown	11.50	7.75
		Nos. 1-10 (10)	94.25	52.00

The 20r bister, 25r rose and 50r green were prepared for use but not issued.
The reprints are printed on a smooth white chalky paper, ungummed, with rough perforation 13½, and on thin white paper with shiny white gum and clean-cut perforation 13½.

King Luiz — A2

1887   Embossed   Perf. 12½

11	A2	5r black	4.25	2.25
12	A2	10r green	5.00	3.25
13	A2	20r bright rose	7.50	3.25
14	A2	25r violet	9.25	4.00
15	A2	40r chocolate	15.50	5.25
16	A2	50r blue	15.50	6.00
17	A2	80r gray	17.00	8.00
18	A2	100r yellow brown	25.00	10.50
19	A2	200r gray lilac	40.00	17.50
20	A2	300r orange	45.00	21.00
		Nos. 11-20 (10)	184.00	81.00

Reprints of Nos. 11, 16, 18 and 19 have clean-cut perforation 13½.
For surcharges see Nos. 34-43, 83-91.

Macao No. 44
Surcharged in Black

1892   Without Gum   Perf. 12½, 13

21	A7	30r on 300r orange	12.00	6.75

For surcharge see No. 44.

King Carlos — A3

1894   Typo.   Perf. 11½

22	A3	5r yellow	3.00	1.40
23	A3	10r red violet	3.00	1.40
24	A3	15r chocolate	4.00	1.40
25	A3	20r lavender	4.00	1.40
26	A3	25r green	4.50	2.50
27	A3	50r light blue	6.50	4.75
a.		Perf. 13½	575.00	425.00
28	A3	75r rose	9.25	6.00
29	A3	80r light green	9.25	6.00
30	A3	100r brown, buff	7.00	5.25
31	A3	150r car, rose	29.00	13.00
32	A3	200r dk bl, lt bl	29.00	14.00
33	A3	300r dk bl, salmon	34.00	15.50
		Nos. 22-33 (12)	142.50	72.60

For surcharges and overprints see Nos. 92-102, 120-122, 124-128, 131-133, 183-193, 199.

Stamps of 1887
Surcharged in Red, Green or Black

1895   Without Gum   Perf. 12½

34	A2	1a on 5r black (R)	4.00	1.75
35	A2	2a on 10r green	4.00	2.25
a.		Double surcharge	25.00	
36	A2	3a on 20r brt rose (G)	6.00	2.25
37	A2	4a on 25r violet	0.00	2.25
38	A2	6a on 40r choc	8.00	3.25
39	A2	8a on 50r blue (R)	9.25	5.00
40	A2	13a on 80r gray	17.50	15.00
41	A2	16a on 100r yellow brn	20.00	15.00
42	A2	31a on 200r gray lilac	45.00	33.00
43	A2	47a on 300r org (G)	52.50	37.50
		Nos. 34-43 (10)	172.25	117.25

No. 21 Surcharged

1895   Without Gum   Perf. 12½, 13

44	A7	5a on 30r on 300r org	18.50	7.50

> Common Design Types pictured following the introduction.

Vasco da Gama Issue
Common Design Types

1898   Engr.   Perf. 14 to 15

45	CD20	½a blue green	3.00	2.00
46	CD21	1a red	3.00	2.00
47	CD22	2a red violet	3.00	2.00
48	CD23	4a yellow green	3.00	2.00
49	CD24	8a dark blue	4.75	3.25
50	CD25	12a violet brown	6.00	4.00
51	CD26	16a bister brown	7.00	5.00
52	CD27	24a bister	10.00	7.00
		Nos. 45-52 (8)	39.75	27.25

400th anniversary of Vasco da Gama's discovery of the route to India.
For overprints and surcharge see Nos. 148-155.

King Carlos — A5

1898-1903   Typo.   Perf. 11½
Name & Value in Black Except #79

53	A5	½a gray	.85	.70
a.		Perf. 12½	5.75	3.50
54	A5	1a orange	.85	.70
a.		Perf. 12½	5.75	3.50
55	A5	2a light green	.95	.70
56	A5	2½a brown	2.50	1.50
57	A5	3a gray violet	2.50	1.50
58	A5	3a gray green ('03)	3.50	1.90
59	A5	4a sea green	2.50	1.50
60	A5	5a rose ('03)	3.25	1.90
61	A5	6a pale yel brn ('03)	3.25	1.90
62	A5	8a blue	2.50	1.50
63	A5	9a red brown ('03)	3.25	1.90
64	A5	10a slate blue ('00)	2.50	1.50
65	A5	10a gray brown ('03)	3.25	1.90
66	A5	12a rose	6.00	5.00
67	A5	12a dull blue ('03)	22.50	12.00
68	A5	13a violet	6.00	5.00
69	A5	13a red lilac ('03)	4.25	2.50
70	A5	15a gray lilac ('03)	7.00	4.00
71	A5	16a dark bl, *bl*	6.00	5.00
72	A5	20a brn, *yelsh* ('00)	8.00	5.00
73	A5	22a brn org, *pink* ('03)	8.00	4.75
74	A5	24a brown, *buff*	7.00	5.00
75	A5	31a red lil, *pinkish*	7.00	5.00
76	A5	31a brn, *straw* ('03)	10.00	4.75
77	A5	47a dk blue, *rose*	12.00	8.50
78	A5	47a red vio, *pink* ('03)	10.00	4.75
79	A5	78a blk & red, *bl* ('00)	17.50	10.50
80	A5	78a dl bl, *straw* ('03)	20.00	10.25
		Nos. 53-80 (28)	182.90	111.10

Most of Nos. 53-80 were issued without gum.
For surcharges & overprints see #81-82,
104-119, 129-130, 134-147, 195-196.

King Carlos — A6

1899   Black Surcharge

81	A6	10a on 16a dk bl, *bl*	8.25	6.50
82	A6	20a on 31a red lil, *pnksh*	8.25	6.50

Surcharged in Black

1902   On Issue of 1887

83	A2	5a on 25r violet	5.00	2.25
84	A2	5a on 200r gray lil	7.75	4.00
85	A2	6a on 10r blue grn	290.00	210.00
86	A2	6a on 300r orange	7.00	5.75
87	A2	9a on 40r choc	7.75	5.75
88	A2	9a on 100r yel brn	7.75	5.75
89	A2	15a on 20r rose	7.75	5.75
90	A2	15a on 50r blue	290.00	210.00
91	A2	22a on 80r gray	16.50	12.00
		Nos. 83-91 (9)	639.50	461.25

Reprints of Nos. 83-88, 90-91, 104A have
clean-cut perf. 13½.

On Issue of 1894

92	A3	5a on 5r yellow	3.00	1.75
a.		Inverted surcharge	42.50	35.00
93	A3	5a on 25r green	3.00	1.00
94	A3	5a on 50r lt blue	3.00	1.75
95	A3	6a on 20r lavender	3.00	2.25
96	A3	9a on 15r choc	3.00	2.25
97	A3	9a on 75r rose	3.00	2.25
98	A3	15a on 10r red vio	5.00	3.25
99	A3	15a on 100r brn, *buff*	5.00	3.25
100	A3	15a on 300r bl, *sal*	5.00	3.25
101	A3	22a on 80r lt green	7.75	6.00
102	A3	22a on 200r bl, *blue*	8.00	6.00

On Newspaper Stamp of 1893

103	N2	6a on 2½r brn	2.10	1.40
a.		Inverted surcharge	42.50	35.00
		Nos. 92-103 (12)	50.85	34.40

Nos. 93-97, 99-102 issued without gum.

Stamps of 1898
Overprinted in Black

104	A5	3a gray violet	4.00	2.40
104A	A5	12a rose	9.25	6.25

Reprint noted after No. 91.

No. 67 Surcharged in
Black

1905

105	A5	10a on 12a dull blue	8.25	4.25

Stamps of 1898-1903
Overprinted in
Carmine or Green

1911

106	A5	½a gray	1.00	.60
a.		Inverted overprint	20.00	20.00
107	A5	1a orange	1.00	.60
a.		Perf. 12½	9.25	7.00
108	A5	2a light green	1.00	.60
109	A5	3a gray green	1.00	.60
110	A5	5a rose (G)	1.40	.80
111	A5	6a yel brown	1.40	.80
112	A5	9a red brown	2.00	.80
113	A5	10a gray brown	2.00	1.75
114	A5	13a red lilac	2.00	1.75
115	A5	15a gray lilac	3.00	2.00
116	A5	22a brn org, *pink*	3.00	2.00
117	A5	31a brown, *straw*	3.00	2.00
118	A5	47a red vio, *pink*	5.75	4.00
119	A5	78a dl bl, *straw*	7.00	4.75
		Nos. 106-119 (14)	34.55	23.05

Preceding Issues
Overprinted in Red

1913   Without Gum
On Provisional Issue of 1902

120	A3	5a on 5r yellow	5.75	4.50
121	A3	5a on 25r green	5.75	4.00
122	A3	5a on 50r lt bl	9.00	7.00
123	N2	6a on 2½r brn	9.00	7.00
124	A3	6a on 20r lavender	7.00	4.00
125	A3	9a on 15r choc	7.00	4.00
126	A3	15a on 100r brn, *buff*	9.00	5.50
127	A3	22a on 80r lt grn	10.00	8.00
128	A3	22a on 200r bl, *bl*	10.00	7.50

On Issue of 1903

129	A5	3a gray green	9.25	7.50

On Issue of 1905

130	A5	10a on 12a dull bl	7.00	4.00
		Nos. 120-130 (11)	88.75	62.50

Overprinted in Green
or Red

On Provisional Issue of 1902

1913

131	A3	9a on 75r rose (G)	8.00	6.00
132	A3	15a on 10r red vio (G)	7.00	6.00
a.		Inverted overprint	35.00	35.00
133	A3	15a on 300r bl, *sal* (R)	11.00	8.00
a.		"REUBPLICA"	40.00	35.00
b.		"REPBLICAU"	40.00	35.00

On Issue of 1903

134	A5	5a rose (G)	14.00	10.50
		Nos. 131-134 (4)	40.00	29.50

Stamps of 1898-1903
Overprinted in Red

1913

135	A5	6a yellow brown	6.00	3.25
136	A5	9a red brown	6.00	3.25
137	A5	10a gray brown	6.00	3.25
138	A5	13a violet	7.00	3.25
a.		Inverted overprint	40.00	40.00
139	A5	13a red lilac	7.00	3.25
140	A5	15a gray lilac	57.50	42.50
141	A5	22a brn org, *pnksh*	10.00	6.00
142	A5	31a red lil, *pnksh*	10.00	7.00
143	A5	31a brown, *straw*	12.00	7.75
144	A5	47a blue, *pink*	20.00	13.00
145	A5	47a red vio, *pink*	20.00	13.00
146	A5	78a dl bl, *straw*	25.00	17.00

No. 79 Overprinted in
Red

147	A5	78a blk & red, *bl*	27.00	14.00
		Nos. 135-147 (13)	213.50	136.50

Vasco da Gama Issue of 1898
Overprinted or Surcharged in Black

1913

148	CD20	½a blue green	1.00	.70
149	CD21	1a red	1.00	.70
150	CD22	2a red violet	1.00	.70
151	CD23	4a yellow green	1.00	.70
152	CD24	8a dark blue	2.00	1.40
153	CD25	10a on 12a vio brn	4.00	3.00
154	CD26	16a bister brown	3.00	2.10
155	CD27	24a bister	4.25	3.50
		Nos. 148-155 (8)	17.25	12.80

Ceres — A7

Name and Value in Black
Chalky Paper

1914   Typo.   Perf. 15x14

156	A7	½a olive brown	.85	.60
157	A7	1a black	.85	.60
158	A7	2a blue green	.85	.60
159	A7	3a lilac brown	1.90	1.00
160	A7	4a carmine	1.90	1.00
161	A7	6a light violet	2.50	1.00
162	A7	10a deep blue	2.50	1.00
163	A7	12a yellow brown	3.50	2.10
164	A7	16a slate	3.50	3.50
165	A7	20a org brown	25.00	8.50
166	A7	40a plum	14.00	7.00
167	A7	58a brown, *grn*	14.00	7.50
168	A7	76a brown, *rose*	15.00	9.50
169	A7	1p org, *salmon*	25.00	16.50
170	A7	3p green, *blue*	57.50	31.00
		Nos. 156-170 (15)	168.85	91.40

For surcharges see Nos. 200-201, MR1.

1920   Ordinary Paper

171	A7	1a black	2.10	1.40
172	A7	2a blue green	2.10	1.40

1922-26			*Perf. 12x11½*	
173	A7	½a olive brown	2.10	1.40
174	A7	1a black	2.10	1.40
175	A7	1½a yel grn ('23)	1.40	*1.15*
176	A7	2a blue green	2.10	1.40
177	A7	4a carmine	4.00	3.00
178	A7	7a lt green ('23)	2.10	*1.75*
179	A7	7½a ultra ('23)	3.25	*2.10*
180	A7	9a blue ('23)	3.50	*2.10*
181	A7	11a gray ('23)	4.00	*4.25*
182	A7	12a yellow brown	4.00	3.00
182A	A7	15a lilac ('23)	10.50	*8.00*
182B	A7	18a dp blue ('23)	11.00	7.00
182C	A7	19a gray grn ('23)	11.00	6.00
182D	A7	36a turq blue ('23)	10.50	5.25
182E	A7	54a choc ('23)	11.00	8.00
182F	A7	72a brt rose ('23)	21.00	17.50

Glazed Paper

182G	A7	5p car rose ('23)	92.50	57.50
		Nos. 173-182G (17)	196.05	130.80

Preceding Issues
Overprinted in
Carmine

1915			*Perf. 11½*	
		On Provisional Issue of 1902		
183	A3	5a on 5r yellow	1.75	1.20
184	A3	5a on 25r green	1.75	1.20
185	A3	5a on 50r lt blue	1.75	1.20
186	A3	6a on 20r lavender	1.75	1.20
187	A3	9a on 15r chocolate	1.75	1.20
188	A3	9a on 75r rose	2.10	1.20
189	A3	15a on 10r red vio	2.50	1.50
190	A3	15a on 100r brn, *buff*	4.00	2.10
191	A3	15a on 300r bl, *sal*	4.00	3.00
192	A3	22a on 80r lt grn	6.50	4.25
193	A3	22a on 200r bl, *bl*	10.50	7.00

On No. 103

194	N2	6a on 2½r, perf. 13½	1.75	1.40
a.		Perf. 12½	3.50	3.00
b.		Perf. 11½	7.00	3.50

On No. 104

195	A5	3a gray violet	2.10	1.40

On No. 105

196	A5	10a on 12a dull bl	2.10	1.40
		Nos. 183-196 (14)	44.30	29.25

Type of 1915 with
Additional Surcharge
in Black

Perf. 11½

199	A3	½a on 5a on 50r lt bl	47.50	35.00
a.		Perf. 13½	75.00	57.50

Nos. 178 and 169
Surcharged

1932   Perf. 12x11½

200	A7	6a on 72a brt rose	2.10	1.50
201	A7	12a on 15a lilac	2.10	1.50

"Portugal" and Vasco
da Gama's Flagship
"San Gabriel" — A8

Perf. 11½x12

1935		Typo.	Wmk. 232	
202	A8	½a bister	.65	.30
203	A8	1a olive brown	.65	.30
204	A8	2a blue green	.65	.30
205	A8	3a red violet	.65	.50
206	A8	4a black	1.00	.50
207	A8	5a gray	1.00	.65
208	A8	6a brown	1.00	.60
209	A8	7a bright rose	1.00	.85
210	A8	8a bright blue	1.40	1.10

211	A8	10a red orange	1.60	1.15
212	A8	12a dark blue	2.25	1.15
213	A8	14a olive green	2.25	1.15
214	A8	15a maroon	2.25	1.15
215	A8	20a orange	3.00	1.15
216	A8	30a apple green	3.00	1.40
217	A8	40a violet	9.00	3.75
218	A8	50a olive bister	9.25	3.75
219	A8	1p light blue	22.00	11.50
220	A8	2p brn orange	50.00	16.50
221	A8	3p emerald	67.50	24.00
222	A8	5p dark violet	100.00	50.00
		Nos. 202-222 (21)	280.10	121.75

Common Design Types
1938 Unwmk. Engr. Perf. 13½x13
Name and Value in Black

223	CD34	1a gray green	.65	.45
224	CD34	2a orange brown	.65	.45
225	CD34	3a dk violet brn	.65	.45
226	CD34	4a brt green	.65	.65
227	CD35	5a dk carmine	.85	.45
228	CD35	6a slate	.85	.45
229	CD35	8a rose violet	.85	.70
230	CD37	10a brt red violet	.85	.70
231	CD37	12a red	1.15	1.15
232	CD37	15a orange	1.75	1.90
233	CD36	20a blue	1.75	1.15
234	CD36	40a gray black	3.75	1.50
235	CD36	50a brown	4.00	2.25
236	CD38	1p brown carmine	10.00	6.00
237	CD38	2p olive green	27.50	7.75
238	CD38	3p blue violet	31.00	15.00
239	CD38	5p red brown	65.00	28.00
		Nos. 223-239 (17)	151.90	69.25

For overprints see Nos. 245A-245K.

Mozambique Nos. 273, 276, 278, 280, 282 and 283 Surcharged in Black

1946 **Perf. 13½x13**

240	CD34	1a on 15c dk vio brn	9.00	5.50
241	CD35	4a on 35c brt grn	9.00	5.50
242	CD35	8a on 50c brt red vio	9.00	5.50
243	CD36	10a on 70c brn vio	9.00	5.50
244	CD36	12a on 1e red	9.00	5.50
245	CD37	20a on 1.75e blue	9.00	5.50
		Nos. 240-245 (6)	54.00	33.00

Nos. 223-227 and 229-234 Overprinted "Libertacao"
1947

245A	CD34	1a gray green	22.00	15.00
245B	CD34	2a org brown	47.50	24.00
245C	CD34	3a dk vio brn	21.00	8.50
245D	CD34	4a brt green	21.00	10.00
245E	CD35	5a dark car	9.25	3.50
245F	CD35	8a rose viol	3.50	2.00
245G	CD37	10a brt red vio	10.00	5.00
245H	CD37	12a red	12.50	5.75
245I	CD37	15a orange	9.25	3.50
245J	CD36	20a blue	102.50	60.00
	m.	Inverted overprint	270.00	225.00
245K	CD36	40a gray black	25.00	15.00
		Nos. 245A-245K (11)	283.50	152.25

Timor Woman — A9

Designs: 3a, Gong ringer. 4a, Girl with basket. 8a, Aleixo de Ainaro. 10a, 1p, 3p, Heads of various chieftains. 20a, Warrior and horse.

1948 **Litho.** **Perf. 14**

246	A9	1a aqua & dk brn	1.50	.60
247	A9	3a gray & dk brn	3.00	1.00
248	A9	4a pink & dk grn	4.25	2.25
249	A9	8a red & blue blk	2.40	.70
250	A9	10a blue grn & org	2.40	.60
251	A9	20a ultra, aqua & bl	1.40	.70
252	A9	1p org, bl & ultra	40.00	8.50
253	A9	3p vio & dk brn	45.00	15.00
	a.	Sheet of 8, #240-253	105.00	105.00
		Nos. 246-253 (8)	99.95	29.35

No. 253a sold for 5p.

Lady of Fatima Issue
Common Design Type
1948, Oct.

254	CD40	8a slate gray	6.00	6.00

UPU Issue

UPU Symbols — A10

1949 **Unwmk.** **Perf. 14.**

255	A10	16a brown & buff	29.00	17.50

UPU, 75th anniversary.

> Catalogue values for unused stamps in this section, from this point to the end of the section, are for Never Hinged items.

Craftsman A11 / Timor Woman A12

1950 **Perf. 14½**

256	A11	20a dull vio blue	2.50	1.25
257	A12	50a dull brown	9.00	1.90

Holy Year Issue
Common Design Types
1950, May **Perf. 13x13½**

258	CD41	40a green	3.00	1.50
259	CD42	70a black brown	5.00	2.50

Blackberry Lily — A13

Designs: Various flowers.

1950 **Unwmk.** **Litho.** **Perf. 14½**

260	A13	1a multicolored	1.20	.35
261	A13	3a multicolored	3.50	1.45
262	A13	10a multicolored	4.00	1.60
263	A13	16a multicolored	8.00	2.25
264	A13	20a multicolored	3.50	1.45
265	A13	30a multicolored	4.00	1.60
266	A13	70a multicolored	5.25	1.75
267	A13	1p multicolored	8.75	3.25
268	A13	2p multicolored	12.50	6.00
269	A13	5p multicolored	20.50	10.50
		Nos. 260-269 (10)	71.20	30.20

Holy Year Extension Issue
Common Design Type
1951 **Perf. 14**

270	CD43	86a bl & pale bl + label	5.75	2.40

Stamp without label attached sells for much less.

Medical Congress Issue
Common Design Type

Design: Weighing baby.

1952 **Litho.** **Perf. 13½**

271	CD44	10a ol blk & brn	2.50	1.30

St. Francis Xavier Issue

Statue of St. Francis Xavier — A14

Designs: 16a, Miraculous Arm of St. Francis. 1p, Tomb of St. Francis.

1952, Oct. 25 **Perf. 14**

272	A14	1a black	.50	.25
273	A14	16a blk brn & brn	2.60	.80
274	A14	1p dk car & gray	7.75	2.60
		Nos. 272-274 (3)	10.85	3.65

400th death anniv. of St. Francis Xavier.

Madonna and Child — A15

1953 **Perf. 13x13½**

275	A15	3a dk brn & dull gray	.25	.25
276	A15	16a dk brown & cream	1.00	.60
277	A15	50a dk bl & dull gray	3.00	1.40
		Nos. 275-277 (3)	4.25	2.25

Exhibition of Sacred Missionary Art, Lisbon, 1951.

Stamp Centenary Issue

Stamp of Portugal and Arms of Colonies — A16

1953 **Photo.** **Perf. 13**

278	A16	10a multicolored	3.00	1.15

Sao Paulo Issue
Common Design Type

1954 **Litho.** **Perf. 13½**

279	CD46	16a dk brn red, bl & blk	3.00	1.25

Map of Timor — A17

1956 **Unwmk.** **Perf. 14x12½**
Inscription and design in brown, red, green, ultramarine & yellow

280	A17	1a pale salmon	.40	.25
281	A17	3a pale gray blue	.40	.25
282	A17	8a buff	.60	.45
283	A17	24a pale green	.65	.45
284	A17	32a lemon	.85	.45
285	A17	40a pale gray	1.05	.60
286	A17	1p yellow	3.00	1.10
287	A17	3p pale blue	8.25	4.00
		Nos. 280-287 (8)	15.20	7.55

For surcharges see Nos. 291-300.

Brussels Fair Issue

Exhibition Emblems and View — A18

1958 **Perf. 14½**

288	A18	40a multicolored	1.50	.75

Tropical Medicine Congress Issue
Common Design Type

Design: Calophyllum inophyllum.

1958 **Perf. 13½**

289	CD47	32a multicolored	3.50	2.75

Symbolical Globe — A19

1960 **Unwmk.** **Litho.** **Perf. 13½**

290	A19	4.50e multicolored	1.25	.75

500th death anniv. of Prince Henry the Navigator.

Nos. 280-287 Surcharged with New Value and Bars
Inscription and design in brown, red, green, ultramarine & yellow

1960 **Unwmk.** **Perf. 14x12½**

291	A17	5c on 1a pale salmon	.45	.25
292	A17	10c on 3a pale gray bl	.45	.25
293	A17	20c on 8a buff	.45	.25
294	A17	30c on 24a pale grn	.45	.25
295	A17	50c on 32a lemon	.45	.25
296	A17	1e on 40a pale gray	.50	.35
297	A17	2e on 40a pale gray	.85	.35
298	A17	5e on 1p yellow	1.50	1.00
299	A17	10e on 3p pale blue	5.00	2.50
300	A17	15e on 3p pale blue	5.75	2.50
		Nos. 291-300 (10)	15.85	7.95

Carved Elephant Jar — A20

Native Art: 10c, House on stilts. 20c, Madonna and Child. 30c, Silver rosary. 50c, Two men in boat, horiz. 1e, Silver box in shape of temple. 2.50e, Archer. 4.50e, Elephant. 5e, Man climbing tree. 10e, Woman carrying pot on head. 20e, Cockfight. 50e, House on stilts and animals.

Multicolored Designs

1961 **Litho.** **Perf. 11½x12**

301	A20	5c pale violet	.25	.25
302	A20	10c pale green	.25	.25
	a.	Value & legend inverted	57.50	57.50
303	A20	20c pale blue	.25	.25
304	A20	30c rose	.50	.40
305	A20	50c pale grnsh bl	.50	.35
306	A20	1e bister	1.00	.35
307	A20	2.50e pale ol bis	1.00	.35
308	A20	4.50e lt salmon	1.00	.35
309	A20	5e lt gray	1.00	.35
310	A20	10e gray	1.75	.60
311	A20	20e yellow	5.00	1.50
312	A20	50e lt bluish gray	14.00	4.75
		Nos. 301-312 (12)	26.50	9.75

Sports Issue
Common Design Type

Sports: 50c, Duck hunting. 1e, Horseback riding. 1.50e, Swimming. 2e, Gymnastics. 2.50e, Soccer. 15e, Big game hunting.

1962, Mar. 22 **Unwmk.** **Perf. 13½**
Multicolored Designs

313	CD48	50c gray & bis	.25	.25
314	CD48	1e olive bister	1.25	.45
315	CD48	1.50e gray & bl grn	1.00	.60
316	CD48	2e buff	1.00	.65

317	CD48	2.50e gray	1.40	1.00
318	CD48	15e salmon	4.25	2.10
		Nos. 313-318 (6)	9.15	5.05

Anti-Malaria Issue
Common Design Type

Design: Anopheles sundaicus.

1962		**Litho.**	**Perf. 13½**	
319	CD49	2.50e multicolored	1.50	1.00

National Overseas Bank Issue
Common Design Type

Design: 2.50e, Manuel Pinheiro Chagas.

1964, May 16		**Unwmk.**	**Perf. 13½**	
320	CD51	2.50e grn, gray, yel, lt bl & blk	1.50	.85

ITU Issue
Common Design Type

1965, May 17		**Litho.**	**Perf. 14½**	
321	CD52	1.50e multicolored	1.50	.90

National Revolution Issue
Common Design Type

Design: 4.50e, Dr. Vieira Machado Academy and Dili Health Center.

1966, May 28		**Litho.**	**Perf. 11½**	
322	CD53	4.50e multicolored	1.75	.95

Navy Club Issue
Common Design Type

10c, Capt. Gago Coutinho and gunboat Patria. 4.50e, Capt. Sacadura Cabral and seaplane Lusitania.

1967, Jan. 31		**Litho.**	**Perf. 13**	
323	CD54	10c multicolored	1.15	.50
324	CD54	4.50e multicolored	3.50	1.40

Sepoy Officer, 1792 — A21

Designs: 1e, Officer, 1815. 1.50e, Infantry soldier, 1879. 2e, Infantry soldier, 1890. 2.50e, Infantry officer, 1903. 3e, Sapper, 1918. 4.50e, Special forces soldier, 1964. 10e, Paratrooper, 1964.

1967, Feb. 12		**Photo.**	**Perf. 13½**	
325	A21	35c multicolored	.40	.30
326	A21	1e multicolored	2.00	1.00
327	A21	1.50e multicolored	.70	.40
328	A21	2e multicolored	.70	.40
329	A21	2.50e multicolored	1.00	.40
330	A21	3e multicolored	1.50	.60
331	A21	4.50e multicolored	2.00	.70
332	A21	10e multicolored	3.00	1.75
		Nos. 325-332 (8)	11.30	5.55

Our Lady of Fatima — A22

1967, May 13		**Litho.**	**Perf. 12½x13**	
333	A22	3e multicolored	.95	.30

Apparition of the Virgin Mary to three shepherd children at Fatima, Portugal, 50th anniv.

Cabral Issue

Map of Brazil, by Lopo Homem-Reinéis, 1519 — A23

1968, Apr. 22		**Litho.**	**Perf. 14**	
334	A23	4.50e multicolored	2.00	.80

See note after Macao No. 416.

Admiral Coutinho Issue
Common Design Type

Design: 4.50e, Adm. Coutinho and frigate Adm. Gago Coutinho.

1969, Feb. 17		**Litho.**	**Perf. 14**	
335	CD55	4.50e multicolored	2.50	1.05

View of Dili, 1834 — A24

1969, July 25		**Litho.**	**Perf. 14**	
336	A24	1e multicolored	.75	.40

Bicentenary of Dili as capital of Timor.

Vasco da Gama Issue

da Gama Medal in St. Jerome's Convent — A25

1969, Aug. 29		**Litho.**	**Perf. 14**	
337	A25	5e multicolored	1.00	.50

Vasco da Gama (1469-1524), navigator.

Administration Reform Issue
Common Design Type

1969, Sept. 25		**Litho.**	**Perf. 14**	
338	CD56	5e multicolored	1.25	.50

King Manuel I Issue

Emblem of King Manuel, St. Jerome's Convent — A26

1969, Dec. 1		**Litho.**	**Perf. 14**	
339	A26	4e multicolored	1.25	.50

King Manuel I, 500th birth anniv.

Capt. Ross Smith, Arms of Great Britain, Portugal and Australia, and Map of Timor
A27

1969, Dec. 9				
340	A27	2e multicolored	1.25	.60

50th anniv. of the first England to Australia flight of Capt. Ross Smith and Lt. Keith Smith.

Marshal Carmona Issue
Common Design Type

Antonio Oscar Carmona in civilian clothes.

1970, Nov. 15		**Litho.**	**Perf. 14**	
341	CD57	1.50e multicolored	1.00	.35

Lusiads Issue

Sailing Ship and Monks Preaching to Islanders — A28

1972, May 25		**Litho.**	**Perf. 13**	
342	A28	1e brown & multi	1.00	.50

4th centenary of publication of The Lusiads by Luiz Camoens.

Olympic Games Issue
Common Design Type

Design: 4.50e, Soccer, Olympic emblem.

1972, June 20			**Perf. 14x13½**	
343	CD59	4.50e multicolored	1.60	.80

Lisbon-Rio de Janeiro Flight Issue
Common Design Type

Design: 1e, Sacadura Cabral and Gago Coutinho in cockpit of "Lusitania."

1972, Sept. 20		**Litho.**	**Perf. 13½**	
344	CD60	1e multicolored	1.40	.60

WMO Centenary Issue
Common Design Type

1973, Dec. 15		**Litho.**	**Perf. 13**	
345	CD61	20e multicolored	4.25	2.50

United Nations Transitional Authority in East Timor

A30

2000, Apr. 29		**Litho.**	**Perf. 12x11¾**	
350	A30	Dom. red & multi	37.50	115.00
351	A30	Int. blue & multi	52.50	125.00

No. 350 sold for 10c and No. 351 sold for 50c on day of issue.

INDEPENDENT STATE OF TIMOR-LESTE

Independence — A31

Designs: 25c, Crocodile. 50c, Palm fronds. $1, Coffee beans and picker. $2, Flag.

2002, May 20		**Litho.**	**Perf. 14½x14**	
352-355	A31	Set of 4	17.50	35.00

A32

Flag and: 10c, Pres. Xanana Gusmao. 50c, Map of country.

2002		**Litho.**	**Perf. 13x13¼**	
356-357	A32	Set of 2	19.00	25.00

A33

Independence From Portugal, 30th Anniv. — A34

Designs: 15c, Timorese flag, old man. 25c, Timorese flag, child. 50c, Timorese coin, rooster. 75c, Timorese flag, Pres. Nicolau Lobato.

2005, Nov. 28		**Litho.**	**Perf. 12x12½**	
358	A33	15c multi	2.00	3.00
359	A33	25c multi	4.00	3.00
360	A33	50c multi	4.00	4.00
361	A34	75c multi	9.00	8.00
		Nos. 358-361 (4)	19.00	18.00

AIR POST STAMPS

Common Design Type

1938	**Unwmk.**	**Engr.**	**Perf. 13½x13**	
Name and Value in Black				
C1	CD39	1a scarlet	.85	.45
C2	CD39	2a purple	.90	.55
C3	CD39	3a orange	.90	.60
C4	CD39	5a ultra	1.00	.65
C5	CD39	10a lilac brown	2.00	1.50
C6	CD39	20a dark green	3.50	1.75
C7	CD39	50a red brown	6.00	4.00
C8	CD39	70a rose carmine	9.00	7.50
C9	CD39	1p magenta	17.50	8.25
		Nos. C1-C9 (9)	41.65	25.25

No. C7 exists with overprint "Exposicao Internacional de Nova York, 1939-1940" and Trylon and Perisphere. Counterfeits exist. For overprints see Nos. C15-C23.

Mozambique Nos. C3, C4, C6, C7 and C9 Surcharged in Black

1946		**Unwmk.**	**Perf. 13½x13**	
C10	CD39	8a on 50c orange	9.00	5.00
C11	CD39	12a on 1e ultra	9.00	5.00
C12	CD39	40a on 3e dk green	9.00	5.00
C13	CD39	50a on 5e red brn	9.00	5.00
C14	CD39	1p on 10e mag	9.00	5.00
		Nos. C10-C14 (5)	45.00	25.00

Nos. C1-C9 Overprinted "Libertacao"

1947				
C15	CD39	1a scarlet	25.00	19.00
C16	CD39	2a purple	25.00	19.00
C17	CD39	3a orange	26.50	20.00
C18	CD39	5a ultra	25.00	19.00
C19	CD39	10a lilac brown	8.00	4.75
C20	CD39	20a dark green	8.75	5.50
C21	CD39	50a red brown	8.00	4.50
C22	CD39	70a rose carmine	40.00	20.00
C23	CD39	1p magenta	17.50	10.00
		Nos. C15-C23 (9)	183.75	121.75

POSTAGE DUE STAMPS

D1

1904 Unwmk. Typo. *Perf. 12*
Without Gum
Name and Value in Black

J1	D1	1a yellow green	.75	.50
J2	D1	2a slate	.75	.50
J3	D1	5a yellow brown	2.50	1.50
J4	D1	6a red orange	2.75	2.25
J5	D1	10a gray brown	3.00	2.00
J6	D1	15a red brown	4.75	3.25
J7	D1	24a dull blue	7.50	6.00
J8	D1	40a carmine	9.00	6.75
J9	D1	50a orange	14.00	8.00
J10	D1	1p dull violet	22.50	15.00
		Nos. J1-J10 (10)	67.50	45.75

Overprinted in
Carmine or Green

1911 Without Gum

J11	D1	1a yellow green	.25	.25
J12	D1	2a slate	.30	.25
a.		Inverted overprint		
J13	D1	5a yellow brown	.60	.40
J14	D1	6a deep orange	.80	.50
J15	D1	10a gray brown	1.50	.70
J16	D1	15a brown	1.75	1.10
J17	D1	24a dull blue	2.50	2.00
J18	D1	40a carmine (G)	3.25	2.50
J19	D1	50a orange	3.75	2.50
J20	D1	1p dull violet	7.50	7.00
		Nos. J11-J20 (10)	22.20	17.20

Nos. J1-J10
Overprinted in Red
or Green

1913 Without Gum

J21	D1	1a yellow green	10.00	9.00
J22	D1	2a slate	10.00	9.00
J23	D1	5a yellow brown	8.00	6.00
J24	D1	6a deep orange	8.00	6.00
a.		Inverted surcharge	45.00	
J25	D1	10a gray brown	8.00	6.00
J26	D1	15a red brown	8.00	6.00
J27	D1	24a dull blue	9.00	7.00
J28	D1	40a carmine (G)	9.00	7.00
J29	D1	50a orange	12.00	12.00
J30	D1	1p gray violet	15.00	12.00
		Nos. J21-J30 (10)	97.00	80.00

Catalogue values for unused stamps in this section, from this point to the end of the section, are for Never Hinged items.

Common Design Type
1952 Photo. & Typo. *Perf. 14*
Numeral in Red, Frame Multicolored

J31	CD45	1a chocolate	.80	.40
J32	CD45	3a brown	.80	.40
J33	CD45	5a dark green	.80	.40
J34	CD45	10a green	.80	.40
J35	CD45	30a purple	1.00	.65
J36	CD45	1p brown carmine	2.00	1.25
		Nos. J31-J36 (6)	6.20	3.50

WAR TAX STAMP

Regular Issue of 1914
Surcharged in Red

1919 Unwmk. *Perf. 15x14*
Without Gum

MR1	A7	2a on ½a ol brn	30.00	22.50
a.		Inverted surcharge	150.00	100.00

See note after Macao No. MR2.

NEWSPAPER STAMPS

Macao Nos. 37, 39, 41
Surcharged in Black

1892 Unwmk. *Perf. 12½*
Without Gum

P1	A7	2½r on 20r rose	2.00	.75
a.		"TIMOR" inverted		
P2	A7	2½r on 40r chocolate	2.00	.75
a.		"TIMOR" inverted		
b.		Perf. 13½	8.00	3.50
c.		As "a," perf. 13½		
P3	A7	2½r on 80r gray	2.00	.75
a.		"TIMOR" inverted		
b.		Perf. 13½	25.00	15.00
		Nos. P1-P3 (3)	6.00	2.25

 N2

No. P4 Surcharged

1893-95 Typo. *Perf. 11½, 13½*

P4	N2	2½r brown	.40	.35
a.		Perf. 12½	2.00	1.50
P5	N2	½a on 2½r brn ('95)	.45	.30

For surcharges see Nos. 103, 123, 194.

POSTAL TAX STAMPS

Pombal Issue
Common Design Types
1925 Unwmk. *Perf. 12½*

RA1	CD28	2a lake & black	.30	.30
RA2	CD29	2a lake & black	.30	.30
RA3	CD30	2a lake & black	.30	.30
		Nos. RA1-RA3 (3)	.90	.90

Type of War Tax Stamp of Portuguese India Overprinted in Red

1934-35 *Perf. 12*

RA4	WT1	2a green & blk	6.50	8.00
RA5	WT1	5a green & blk	8.00	8.00

Surcharged in Black

RA6	WT1	7a on ½a rose & blk ('35)	12.00	10.00
		Nos. RA4-RA6 (3)	26.50	26.00

The tax was for local education.

Type of War Tax Stamp of Portuguese India Overprinted in Black

1936 *Perf. 12x11½*

RA7	WT1	10a rose & black	7.00	9.00

1937 *Perf. 11½*

RA8	WT1	10a green & blk	5.50	8.25

 PT1

1948 Unwmk. Typo. *Perf. 11½*
Without Gum

RA9	PT1	10a dark blue	3.00	2.00
RA10	PT1	20a green	3.50	3.00

The 20a bears a different emblem.

Catalogue values for unused stamps in this section, from this point to the end of the section, are for Never Hinged items.

PT2

1960 Without Gum *Perf. 11½*

RA11	PT2	70c dark blue	1.50	1.25
RA12	PT2	1.30e green	2.25	2.25

See Nos. RA13-RA16. For surcharges see Nos. RA20-RA25.

Type of 1960 Redrawn
1967 Typo. *Perf. 10½*
Without Gum

RA13	PT2	70c deep blue	15.00	20.00
RA14	PT2	1.30e emerald	20.00	20.00

The denominations of Nos. RA13-RA14 are 2mm high. They are 2½mm high on Nos. RA11-RA12. Other differences exist. The printed area of No. RA13 measures 18x31mm; "Republica" 16mm.

Type of 1960
1967 Serif Type Face

RA14A	PT2	70c deep blue	12.00	10.00

Type of 1960, 2nd Redrawing
1967-68 Typo. *Perf. 10½*
Without Gum

RA15	PT2	70c violet blue	.60	.60
RA16	PT2	1.30e bluish grn ('68)	1.25	1.25

The printed area measures 13x30mm on Nos. RA15-RA16; "Republica" measures 10½mm.

Woman and
Star — PT3

1969-70 Litho. *Perf. 13½*

RA17	PT3	30c vio bl & lt bl ('70)	.25	.25
RA18	PT3	50c dl org & maroon	.25	.25
RA19	PT3	1e yellow & brown	.25	.25
		Nos. RA17-RA19 (3)	.75	.75

The 2.50e and 10e in design PT3 were revenue stamps. Value $1.50 each.

Nos. RA15-RA16
Surcharged in Red or
Carmine

1970 Typo. *Perf. 10½*
Without Gum

RA20	PT2	30c on 70c	7.00	6.00
RA21	PT2	30c on 1.30e	6.00	6.00
RA22	PT2	50c on 70c	275.00	200.00
RA23	PT2	50c on 1.30e	7.25	7.25
RA24	PT2	1e on 70c (C)	400.00	300.00
RA25	PT2	1e on 1.30e	10.00	10.00
		Nos. RA20-RA25 (6)	705.25	529.25

POSTAL TAX DUE STAMPS

Pombal Issue
Common Design Types
1925 Unwmk. *Perf. 12½*

RAJ1	CD28	4a lake & black	.40	1.00
RAJ2	CD29	4a lake & black	.40	1.00
RAJ3	CD30	4a lake & black	.40	1.00
		Nos. RAJ1-RAJ3 (3)	1.20	3.00

TOBAGO

tə-'bā-ˌgō

LOCATION — An island in the West Indies lying off the Venezuelan coast north of Trinidad
GOVT. — British Colony
AREA — 116 sq. mi.
POP. — 25,358
CAPITAL — Scarborough (Port Louis)

In 1889 Tobago, then an independent colony, was united with Trinidad under the name of Colony of Trinidad and Tobago. It became a ward of that colony January 1, 1899.

12 Pence = 1 Shilling
20 Shillings = 1 Pound

Queen Victoria — A1

Wmk. Crown and C C (1)

		1879	Typo.	Perf. 14	
1	A1	1p rose		145.00	110.00
2	A1	3p blue		145.00	87.50
3	A1	6p orange		67.50	82.50
4	A1	1sh green		425.00	82.50
a.	Half used as 6p on cover				
5	A1	5sh slate		925.00	825.00
6	A1	£1 violet			4,500.

Stamps of the above set with revenue cancellations sell for a small fraction of the price of postally used examples.
Stamps of Type A1, watermarked Crown and C A, are revenue stamps.

1880　Manuscript Surcharge

7	A1	1p on half of 6p org	6,250.	875.

Queen Victoria — A2

1880

8	A2	½p brown violet	77.50	115.00
9	A2	1p red brown	145.00	72.50
a.	Half used as ½p on cover			2,250.
10	A2	4p yellow green	325.00	40.00
a.	Half used as 2p on cover			2,250.
11	A2	6p bister brown	425.00	125.00
12	A2	1sh bister	115.00	145.00
a.	Imperf.			
	Nos. 8-12 (5)		1,088.	497.50

No. 11 Surcharged in Black

1883

13	A2	2½p on 6p bister brn	110.00	110.00
a.	Double surcharge		4,000.	2,250.

1882-96　Wmk. Crown and C A (2)

14	A2	½p brown vio ('82)	3.50	21.00
15	A2	½p dull green ('86)	6.00	2.25
16	A2	1p red brown ('82)	14.50	3.75
a.	Diagonal half used as ½p on cover			—
17	A2	1p rose ('89)	9.50	2.50
18	A2	2½p ultra ('83)	16.50	1.60
a.	2½p dull blue ('83)	67.50	3.75
b.	2½p bright blue	17.50	1.60
19	A2	4p yel grn ('82)	230.00	100.00
20	A2	4p gray ('85)	9.50	4.25
a.	Imperf., pair		2,250.	
21	A2	6p bis brn ('84)	625.00	550.00
a.	Imperf.			
22	A2	6p brn org ('86)	2.75	9.50
23	A2	1sh olive bis ('94)	5.00	32.50
24	A2	1sh brn org ('96)	29.00	145.00

Stamps of 1882-96 Surcharged in Black

Nos. 25-29　　　　　　　No. 30

1886-92

25	A2	½p on 2½p ultra	12.00	27.50
a.	Inverted surcharge		16,000.	
b.	Pair, one without surcharge			
c.	Space between "½" and "PENNY" 3mm		42.50	82.50
d.	Double surcharge		2,800.	2,600.
26	A2	½p on 4p gray	32.50	87.50
a.	Space between "½" and "PENNY" 3mm		75.00	
b.	Double surcharge		3,500.	
27	A2	½p on 6p bis brn	4.25	29.00
a.	Inverted surcharge		3,250.	
b.	Space between "½" and "PENNY" 3mm		30.00	125.00
c.	Double surcharge		3,750.	
28	A2	½p on 6p brn org	160.00	210.00
a.	Space between "½" and "PENNY" 3mm		375.00	450.00
b.	Double surcharge			2,750.
29	A2	1p on 2½ ultra	110.00	25.00
a.	Space between "1" and "PENNY" 4mm		300.00	90.00
b.	Half used as ½p on cover			1,650.
30	A2	2½p on 4p gray	25.00	11.00
a.	Double surcharge		3,500.	3,500.
	Nos. 25-30 (6)		343.75	390.00

Revenue Stamp Type A1 Surcharged in Black

1896

31	A1	½p on 4p lilac & rose	110.00	57.50
a.	Space between "½" and "d"			
	1½ to 2½mm		150.00	82.50

Tobago stamps were replaced by those of Trinidad or Trinidad and Tobago.

TOGO

'tō-ˌgō

LOCATION — Western Africa, bordering on the Gulf of Guinea
GOVT. — Republic
AREA — 20,400 sq. mi.
POP. — 4,320,000 (1997 est.)
CAPITAL — Lome

The German Protectorate of Togo was occupied by Great Britain and France in World War I, and later mandated to them. The British area became part of Ghana. The French area was granted internal autonomy in 1956 and achieved independence in 1958.

100 Pfennig = 1 Mark
12 Pence = 1 Shilling
100 Centimes = 1 Franc

Catalogue values for unused stamps in this country are for Never Hinged items, beginning with Scott 309 in the regular postage section, Scott B11 in the semipostal section, Scott C14 in the airpost section, Scott J32 in the postage due section, and Scott O1 in the official section.

Watermark

Wmk. 125 —
Lozenges

German Protectorate

AREA — 34,934 sq. mi.
POP. — 1,000,368 (1913)

Stamps of Germany
Overprinted in Black

1897   Unwmk.   Perf. 13½x14½

1	A9	3pf dark brown	5.25	6.00
a.		3pf yellow brown	9.25	25.00
b.		3pf reddish brown	47.50	120.00
c.		3pf pale gray brown	1,600.	1,200.
2	A9	5pf green	4.75	2.75
3	A10	10pf carmine	5.50	3.00
4	A10	20pf ultra	5.50	12.50
5	A10	25pf orange	35.00	55.00
6	A10	50pf red brown	35.00	55.00
		Nos. 1-6 (6)	91.00	134.25

A3

Kaiser's Yacht, the
"Hohenzollern" — A4

1900   Typo.   Perf. 14

7	A3	3pf brown	1.00	1.25
8	A3	5pf green	11.00	2.00
9	A3	10pf carmine	20.00	1.60
10	A3	20pf ultra	1.00	1.50
11	A3	25pf org & blk, yel	1.00	9.50
12	A3	30pf org & blk, sal	1.25	9.50
13	A3	40pf lake & blk	1.00	9.50
14	A3	50pf pur & blk, sal	1.25	7.25
15	A3	80pf lake & blk, rose	2.40	16.00

Engr.
Perf. 14½x14

16	A4	1m carmine	3.25	52.50
17	A4	2m blue	5.25	80.00
18	A4	3m black vio	6.75	140.00
19	A4	5m slate & car	120.00	475.00
		Nos. 7-19 (13)	175.15	805.60

Counterfeit cancellations are found on Nos. 10-19 and 22.

1909-19   Wmk. 125   Typo.   Perf. 14

20	A3	3pf brown ('19)	.80	
21	A3	5pf green	1.25	2.00
22	A3	10pf carmine ('14)	1.60	110.00

Engr.
Perf. 14½x14

23	A4	5m slate & carmine ('19)		22.50
		Nos. 20-23 (4)		26.15

Nos. 20 and 23 were never placed in use.

British Protectorate

Nos. 7, 10-19, 21-22
Overprinted or
Surcharged

First (Wide) Setting
3mm between Lines
2mm between "Anglo" & "French"
Wmk. 125 (5pf, 10pf); Unwmkd.

1914, Oct. 1   Perf. 14, 14½

33	A3	½p on 3pf brn	160.00	140.00
a.		Thin "y" in "penny"	400.00	350.00
34	A3	1p on 5pf grn	160.00	140.00
a.		Thin "y" in "penny"	400.00	350.00
35	A3	3pf brown	130.00	100.00
36	A3	5pf green	130.00	100.00
37	A3	10pf carmine	130.00	100.00
a.		Inverted overprint	10,000.	3,000.
b.		Unwmk.		5,500.
38	A3	20pf ultra	42.50	50.00
39	A3	25pf org & blk, yel	40.00	47.50
40	A3	30pf org & blk, sal	47.50	60.00
41	A3	40pf lake & blk	225.00	250.00
42	A3	50pf pur & blk, sal	12,000.	10,000.
43	A3	80pf lake & blk, rose	275.00	275.00
44	A4	1m carmine	5,000.	2,750.
45	A4	2m blue	13,500.	15,000.
a.		Inverted overprint	16,000.	
b.		"Occupation" double	24,500.	16,000.

On Nos. 33-34, the surcharge line ("Half penny" or "One penny") was printed separately and its position varies in relation to the 3-line overprint. On Nos. 46-47, the surcharge and overprint lines were printed simultaneously.

Second (Narrow) Setting
2mm between Lines
2mm between "Anglo" & "French"

1914, Oct.

46	A3	½p on 3pf brown	47.50	26.00
a.		Thin "y" in "penny"	75.00	60.00
b.		"TOG"	425.00	300.00
47	A3	1p on 5pf green	8.00	4.25
a.		Thin "y" in "penny"	12.00	15.00
b.		"TOG"	130.00	110.00
48	A3	3pf brown	6,500.	1,100.
a.		"Occupation" omitted		
49	A3	5pf green	1,500.	750.00
50	A3	10pf carmine		3,000.
51	A3	20pf ultra	30.00	12.00
a.		"TOG"	3,500.	2,500.
b.		Vert. pair, #51 & #38	9,000.	
52	A3	25pf org & blk, yel	40.00	32.50
a.		"TOG"	12,000.	
53	A3	30pf org & blk, sal	20.00	29.00
54	A3	40pf lake & blk	6,000.	1,600.
55	A3	50pf pur & blk, sal		9,000.
56	A3	80pf lake & blk, rose	3,250.	2,250.
57	A4	1m carmine	8,000.	4,250.
58	A4	2m blue		14,500.
59	A4	3m black violet		110,000.
60	A4	5m slate & car		110,000.

Third Setting
1¼mm btwn. "Anglo" & "French"
2mm between Lines
"Anglo-French" 15mm Wide

1915, Jan. 7

61	A3	3pf brown	9,000.	2,500.
62	A3	5pf green	225.	130.
63	A3	10pf carmine	200.	130.
64	A3	20pf ultra	1,400.	400.
64A	A3	40pf lake & blk		9,000.
65	A3	50pf pur & blk, sal	16,000.	11,000.

Stamps of Gold Coast
Overprinted Locally

"OCCUPATION" 14½-14¾mm Long

1915, May   Wmk. 3   Perf. 14

66	A7	½p green	.35	3.75
a.		Double overprint		
67	A8	1p scarlet	.35	.60
a.		Double ovpt.	350.00	475.00
b.		Inverted ovpt.	175.00	250.00
c.		As "b," "Togo" omitted	8,000.	
68	A7	2p gray	.35	1.50
69	A7	2½p ultra	4.00	7.00

Chalky Paper

70	A7	3p violet, yel	3.50	6.00
71	A7	6p dl vio & red vio	2.75	2.00
72	A7	1sh black, grn	2.50	11.00
a.		Double overprint	1,500.	
73	A7	2sh vio & bl, bl	15.00	22.50
74	A7	2sh6p blk & red, bl	5.50	30.00
75	A7	10sh grn & red, grn	50.00	60.00
76	A7	20sh vio & blk, red	150.00	160.00

Surfaced-Colored Paper

77	A7	3p violet, yel	4.00	24.00
78	A7	5sh grn & red, yel	9.50	15.00
		Nos. 66-78 (13)	247.80	343.35

Nos. 66-78 exist with small "F" in "French" and thin "G" in "Togo." Value, set $450.
Eight denominations are known without the hyphen between "Anglo-French." Value, set of eight $1,500. All denominations but No. 77 without the first "O" in "Occupation."

Stamps of Gold Coast
Overprinted in London

"OCCUPATION" 15mm Long

1916, Apr.   Ordinary Paper

80	A7	½p green	.35	2.75
81	A8	1p scarlet	.35	.85
a.		Inverted overprint		
82	A7	2p gray	.60	3.00
83	A7	2½p ultra	.70	1.50

Chalky Paper

84	A7	3p violet, yel	6.00	1.25
85	A7	6p dl vio & red vio	2.50	2.00
86	A7	1sh black, grn	8.00	13.00
a.		1sh black, emerald	400.00	850.00
b.		1sh black, bl grn, ol back	12.00	18.00
87	A7	2sh vio & ultra, bl	4.50	8.50
88	A7	2sh6p blk & red, bl	4.50	7.00
89	A7	5sh grn & red, yel	37.50	27.50
90	A7	10sh grn & red, bl grn, ol back ('20)	21.00	75.00
a.		10sh green & red, grn	27.50	65.00
91	A7	20sh vio & blk, red	160.00	190.00
		Nos. 80-91 (12)	246.00	332.35

The overprint on Nos. 80-91 is in heavier letters than on Nos. 66-78 and the 2nd and 3rd lines are each ½mm longer. The letter "O" on Nos. 80-91 is narrower and more oval.

Issued under French Occupation
Stamps of German Togo Surcharged

c

d   e

f   g

h   i

Wmk. Lozenges (5pf and 10pf) (125), Unwmk. (other values)

1914   Perf. 14, 14½

151	A3(c+d)	5c on 3pf brn	70.00	70.00
152	A3(c+e)	5c on 3pf brn	67.50	67.50
153	A3(c+f)	5c on 3pf brn	77.50	77.50
154	A3(c+g)	10c on 3pf grn	25.00	25.00
a.		Double surcharge	1,200.	1,200.
155	A3(c+h)	10c on 5pf grn	25.00	25.00
156	A3(c+i)	10c on 5pf grn	50.00	50.00
158	A3(c)	20pf ultra	55.00	55.00
a.		3½mm between "TOGO" and "Occupation"	875.00	875.00
159	A3(c)	25pf org & blk, yel	80.00	80.00
160	A3(c)	30pf org & blk, sal	100.00	100.00
161	A3(c)	40pf lake & black	600.00	625.00
162	A3(c)	80pf lake & blk, rose	600.00	625.00
		Nos. 151-162 (11)	1,750.	1,800.

Surcharged or Overprinted in Sans-Serif Type

1915

164	A3	5c on 3pf brown	21,000.	4,500.
165	A3	5pf green	1,050.	450.
166	A3	10pf carmine	1,150.	450.
a.		Inverted overprint	27,000.	16,500.
167	A3	20pf ultra	1,400.	1,050.
168	A3	25pf org & blk, yel	15,000.	7,000.
169	A3	30pf org & blk, sal	15,000.	7,000.
170	A3	40pf lake & blk	15,000.	7,000.
171	A3	50pf pur & blk, sal	21,000.	12,500.
171A	A3	80pf red & blk, rose	—	—
172	A4	1m carmine	—	—
173	A4	2m blue	—	—
174	A4	3m black vio	—	—
175	A4	5m slate & car	—	—

Stamps of Dahomey, 1913-17, Overprinted

1916-17		Unwmk.	Perf. 13½x14	
176	A5	1c violet & blk	.35	.50
177	A5	2c choc & rose	.35	.50
178	A5	4c black & brn	.35	.80
a.		Double overprint	500.00	500.00
179	A5	5c yel grn & bl grn	.70	.70
180	A5	10c org red & rose	.70	.70
181	A5	15c org red & dk vio ('17)	1.75	1.75
182	A5	20c gray & choc	.70	1.10
183	A5	25c ultra & dp bl	1.10	1.10
184	A5	30c choc & vio	1.10	1.40
185	A5	35c brown & blk	1.75	2.10
186	A5	40c blk & red org	1.40	1.75
187	A5	45c gray & ultra	1.75	2.10
188	A5	50c choc & brn	1.75	2.10
189	A5	75c blue & vio	7.00	8.00
190	A5	1fr bl grn & blk	8.50	10.50
191	A5	2fr buff & choc	12.00	14.00
192	A5	5fr brn org & do bl	14.00	16.00
		Nos. 176-192 (17)	55.25	65.10

All values of the 1916-17 issue exist on chalky paper and all but the 15c, 25c and 35c on ordinary paper. See the *Scott Classic Specialized Catalogue of Stamps & Covers* for detailed listings.

French Mandate

AREA — 21,893 sq. mi.
POP. — 780,497 (1938)

Type of Dahomey, 1913-39, Overprinted

1921				
193	A5	1c gray & yel grn	.35	.35
a.		Overprint omitted	125.00	125.00
194	A5	2c blue & org	.35	.35
195	A5	4c ol grn & org	.35	.35
196	A5	5c dull red & blk	.35	.35
a.		Overprint omitted	410.00	425.00
197	A5	10c bl grn & yel grn	.35	.70
198	A5	15c brown & car	.70	.70
199	A5	20c bl grn & org	1.10	1.10
200	A5	25c slate & org	1.10	1.10
201	A5	30c dp rose & ver	1.40	1.75
202	A5	35c red brn & yel grn	1.10	1.40
203	A5	40c bl grn & do bl	2.10	1.75
204	A5	45c red brn & ol	2.10	2.10
205	A5	50c deep blue	2.10	1.40
206	A5	75c dl red & ultra	2.10	2.10
207	A5	1fr gray & ultra	2.10	2.10
208	A5	2fr ol grn & rose	7.00	7.00
209	A5	5fr orange & blk	10.50	10.50
		Nos. 193-209 (17)	35.15	35.10

Stamps and Type of 1921 Surcharged

No. 210

No. 213

1922-25				
210	A5	25c on 15c ol brn & rose red	.35	.55
211	A5	25c on 2fr ol grn & rose	.70	.80
212	A5	25c on 5fr org & blk	.70	.80
a.		"TOGO" omitted	275.00	275.00
213	A5	60c on 75c vio, pnksh	1.10	1.40
a.		"60" omitted	200.00	210.00
214	A5	65c on 45c red brn & ol	1.40	1.75
a.		"TOGO" omitted	190.00	200.00

215	A5	85c on 75c dull red & ultra	2.10	2.75
		Nos. 210-215 (6)	6.35	8.05

Issue years: #213, 1922; #211-212, 1924; others, 1925.

Coconut Grove A6

Cacao Trees — A7

Oil Palms A8

1924-38			Typo.	
216	A6	1c yellow & blk	.25	.35
217	A6	2c dp rose & blk	.25	.35
218	A6	4c dk blue & blk	.25	.35
219	A6	5c dp org & blk	.25	.35
220	A6	10c red vio & blk	.25	.35
221	A6	15c green & blk	.25	.35
222	A7	20c gray & blk	.30	.50
223	A7	25c grn & blk, yel	.70	.70
224	A7	30c gray grn & blk	.35	.35
225	A7	30c dl grn & lt grn ('27)	.70	.70
226	A7	35c lt brown & blk	.70	.70
227	A7	35c dp bl grn & grn ('38)	.70	.70
228	A7	40c red org & blk	.35	.35
229	A7	45c carmine & blk	.35	.35
230	A7	50c ocher & blk, bluish	.35	.70
231	A7	55c vio bl & car rose ('38)	1.10	1.10
232	A7	60c vio brn & blk, pnksh	.35	.35
233	A7	60c dp red ('26)	.35	.70
234	A7	65c gray lil & brn	.70	.70
235	A7	75c blue & black	.70	.70
236	A7	80c ind & dl vio ('38)	1.75	1.75
237	A7	85c brn org & brn	1.10	1.10
238	A7	90c brn red & cer ('27)	1.10	1.10
239	A8	1fr red brn & blk, bluish	1.10	1.10
240	A8	1fr blue ('26)	.70	.70
241	A8	1fr gray lil & grn ('28)	2.75	2.75
242	A8	1fr dk red & red org ('38)	1.10	1.10
243	A8	1.10fr vio & dk brn ('28)	4.25	5.50
244	A8	1.25fr mag & rose ('33)	1.40	1.75
245	A8	1.50fr bl & lt bl ('27)	.70	1.10
246	A8	1.75fr bis & pink ('33)	8.50	5.25
247	A8	1.75fr vio bl & ultra ('38)	1.40	1.40
248	A8	2fr bl blk & blk, bluish	1.10	1.40
249	A8	3fr bl grn & red org ('27)	1.40	1.75
250	A8	5fr red org & blk, bluish	2.10	3.50
251	A8	10fr ol brn & rose ('26)	2.50	2.75
252	A8	20fr brn red & blk, yel ('26)	3.50	3.50
		Nos. 216-252 (37)	45.65	48.20

For surcharges see Nos. 253, 301-302, B8-B9.

No. 240 Surcharged with New Value and Bars in Red

1926				
253	A8	1.25fr on 1fr lt bl	.70	.70

> Common Design Types pictured following the introduction.

Colonial Exposition Issue
Common Design Types
Engr., "TOGO" Typo. in Black

1931, Apr. 13			Perf. 12½	
254	CD70	40c deep green	5.50	5.50
255	CD71	50c violet	5.50	5.50
256	CD72	90c red orange	5.50	5.50
257	CD73	1.50fr dull blue	5.50	5.50
		Nos. 254-257 (4)	22.00	22.00
		Set, never hinged	42.00	

Paris International Exposition Issue
Common Design Types

1937			Perf. 13	
258	CD74	20c deep violet	1.60	1.60
259	CD75	30c dark green	1.60	1.60
260	CD76	40c car rose	1.60	1.60
261	CD77	50c dark brown	1.60	1.60
262	CD78	90c red	1.75	1.75
263	CD79	1.50fr ultra	1.75	1.75
		Nos. 258-263 (6)	9.90	9.90
		Set, never hinged	17.50	

Colonial Arts Exhibition Issue
Souvenir Sheet
Common Design Type

1937			Imperf.	
264	CD77	3fr Prus bl & blk	10.50	10.50
		Never hinged	14.00	

Caillié Issue
Common Design Type

1939, Apr. 5			Perf. 12½x12	
265	CD81	90c org brn & org	.35	1.10
266	CD81	2fr brt violet	.35	1.10
267	CD81	2.25fr ultra & dk bl	.35	1.10
		Nos. 265-267 (3)	1.05	3.30
		Set, never hinged	2.10	

New York World's Fair Issue
Common Design Type

1939, May 10				
268	CD82	1.25fr carmine lake	.70	1.40
		Never hinged	1.10	
269	CD82	2.25fr ultra	.70	1.40
		Never hinged	1.10	

Togolese Women A9   A12

Mono River Bank A10

Hunters A11

1941		Engr.	Perf. 12½	
270	A9	2c brown vio	.25	.30
271	A9	3c yellow grn	.35	.35
272	A9	4c brown blk	.25	.30
273	A9	5c lilac rose	.25	.30
274	A9	10c light blue	.25	.30
275	A9	15c chestnut	.25	.25
276	A10	20c plum	.25	.25
277	A10	25c violet blue	.25	.25
278	A10	30c brown blk	.25	.25
279	A10	40c dk carmine	.35	.35
280	A10	45c dk green	.35	.35
281	A10	50c chestnut	.35	.35
282	A10	60c red violet	.35	.70
283	A11	70c black	.70	1.10
284	A11	90c lt violet	1.40	1.40
285	A11	1fr yellow grn	.35	.70
286	A11	1.25fr cerise	1.10	1.40
287	A11	1.40fr orange brn	.70	.70
288	A11	1.60fr orange	.70	1.10
289	A11	2fr lt ultra	.70	.70
290	A12	2.25fr ultra	1.40	2.10
291	A12	2.50fr lilac rose	1.10	1.10
292	A12	3fr brown vio	1.10	1.10
293	A12	5fr vermilion	1.10	1.10

294	A12	10fr rose violet	1.75	1.75
295	A12	20fr brown blk	2.50	2.50
		Nos. 270-295 (26)	18.35	21.05
		Set, never hinged	26.00	

For surcharges see Nos. 303-308, B7, B10.

Mono River Bank and Marshal Pétain A12a

1941		Engr.	Perf. 12½x12	
296	A12a	1fr green		.35
297	A12a	2.50fr blue		.35
		Set, never hinged	1.40	

Nos. 296-297 were issued by the Vichy government in France, but were not placed on sale in Togo.
For surcharges, see Nos. B10D-B10E.

Types of 1941 Without "RF"

1942-44			Perf. 12½	
298	A9	10c blue green		.35
299	A9	15c yel brn & black		.70
300	A10	20c lil brn & blk		.70
300A	A11	1fr yellow grn		1.10
300B	A11	1.50fr lilac & green		.70
300C	A12	3fr brown violet		1.10
300D	A12	5fr red brown		1.10
300E	A12	10fr rose violet		1.40
300F	A12	20fr black		1.40
		Nos. 298-300F (9)		8.55
		Set, never hinged		12.00

Nos. 298-300F were issued by the Vichy government in France, but were not placed on sale in Togo.

Nos. 231, 238, 284 Surcharged in Various Colors

a

b

1943-44		Perf. 14x13½, 12½	Unwmk.	
301	A7(a)	1.50fr on 55c (Bk)	1.10	1.10
302	A7(a)	1.50fr on 90c (Bk)	1.10	1.10
303	A11(b)	3.50fr on 90c (Bk)	.70	.70
304	A11(b)	4fr on 90c (R)	1.40	1.40
305	A11(b)	5fr on 90c (Bl)	2.10	2.10
306	A11(b)	5.50fr on 90c (Br)	2.10	2.10
307	A11(b)	10fr on 90c (G) ('44)	2.10	2.10
308	A11(b)	20fr on 90c (R)	3.50	3.50
		Nos. 301-308 (8)	14.10	14.10
		Set, never hinged	17.50	

> Catalogue values for unused stamps in this section, from this point to the end of the section, are for Never Hinged items.

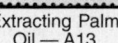

Extracting Palm Oil — A13

Hunter — A14

Cotton
Spinners — A15

Village of
Atakpamé
A16

Red-fronted Gazelles — A17

Houses of
the Cabrais
A18

1947, Oct. 6   Engr.   Perf. 12½
309	A13	10c dark red	.70	.35
310	A13	30c brt ultra	.70	.35
311	A13	50c bluish green	.70	.35
312	A14	60c lilac rose	.70	.35
313	A14	1fr chocolate	.70	.35
314	A14	1.20fr yellow grn	1.10	.70
315	A14	1.50fr brown org	1.10	.70
316	A15	2fr olive	1.10	.70
317	A15	2.50fr gray blk	1.75	1.40
318	A16	3fr slate	1.10	.70
319	A16	3.60fr rose car	1.10	1.10
320	A16	4fr Prus green	1.10	.35
321	A17	5fr black brn	2.10	.70
322	A17	6fr ultra	2.10	1.40
323	A17	10fr orange red	2.75	.70
324	A18	15fr dp yel grn	2.75	.70
325	A18	20fr grnsh black	2.10	.70
326	A18	25fr lilac rose	2.75	1.10
		Nos. 309-326 (18)	26.40	12.70

Military Medal Issue
Common Design Type
Engr. & Typo.
1952, Dec. 1   Perf. 13
327	CD101	15fr multicolored	5.50	4.75

Gathering
Palm Nuts
A19

1954, Nov. 29   Engr.
328	A19	8fr vio & vio brn	1.40	.70
329	A19	15fr indigo & dk brn	1.75	.70

Goliath
Beetle — A20

1955, May 2
330	A20	8fr black & green	3.25	1.40

Intl. Exhibition for Wildlife Protection, Paris,
May 1955.

FIDES Issue
Common Design Type
Design: 15fr, Teacher and children planting
tree.
1956   Unwmk.   Perf. 13x12½
331	CD103	15fr dk vio brn & org brn	4.25	2.10

Republic

Woman
Holding
Flag — A21

1957, June 8   Engr.   Perf. 13
332	A21	15fr dk bl grn, sepia & red	.70	.25

Konkomba
Helmet — A22

Teak Forest
A23

Design; 4fr, 5fr, 6fr, 8fr, 10fr, Buffon's kob.

1957, Oct.   Unwmk.
333	A22	30c violet & claret	.25	.25
334	A22	50c indigo & blue	.25	.25
335	A22	1fr pur & lil rose	.25	.25
336	A22	2fr dk brn & olive	.25	.25
337	A22	3fr black & green	.25	.25
338	A22	4fr blue & gray	.60	.25
339	A22	5fr bluish gray & mag	.60	.25
340	A22	6fr crim rose & bl gray	.75	.25
341	A22	8fr bluish gray & vio	.75	.25
342	A22	10fr grn & red brn	.75	.25
343	A23	15fr multicolored	.50	.25
344	A23	20fr violet, mar & org	.60	.25
345	A23	25fr indigo & bis brn	.75	.25
346	A23	40fr dk brn, ol & dk grn	1.10	.35
		Nos. 333-346 (14)	7.65	3.60

See Nos. 350-363.

Flags, Dove and UN
Emblem — A24

1958, Dec. 10   Engr.   Perf. 13
347	A24	20fr dk grn & rose red	.65	.25

Universal Declaration of Human Rights,
10th anniversary.

Flower Issue
Common Design Type
Designs: 5fr, Flower of Bombax tree
(kapok). 20fr, Tectona grandis (teakwood)
flower, horiz.
Perf. 12x12½, 12½x12
1959, Jan. 15   Photo.   Unwmk.
348	CD104	5fr dp bl, rose & grn	.55	.25
349	CD104	20fr black, yel & grn	.55	.25

Types of 1957
Inscribed:"Republique du Togo"
1959, Jan. 15   Engr.   Perf. 13
Designs as Before
350	A22	30c ultra & gray	.45	.25
351	A22	50c org & brt grn	.45	.25
352	A22	1fr red lil & ol grn	.45	.25
353	A22	2fr olive & bl grn	.45	.25
354	A22	3fr vio & rose car	.45	.25

355	A22	4fr lil rose & pale pur	.45	.25
356	A22	5fr green & brown	.45	.25
357	A22	6fr ultra & gray bl	.45	.25
358	A22	8fr sl grn & bis	.45	.25
359	A22	10fr vio & lt brn	.45	.25
360	A23	15fr dk brn, bis & cl	.45	.25
361	A23	20fr blk, bl grn & brn	.45	.25
362	A23	25fr sep, red brn, ol & vio	.60	.25
363	A23	40fr dk grn, org brn & bl	.60	.25
		Nos. 350-363 (14)	6.60	3.50

"Five Continents,"
Ceiling Painting,
Palais des
Nations,
Geneva — A25

1959, Oct. 24   Engr.   Perf. 12½
Centers in Dark Ultramarine
364	A25	15fr brown	.35	.25
365	A25	20fr purple	.35	.25
366	A25	25fr dark orange	.35	.25
367	A25	40fr dark green	.55	.25
368	A25	60fr carmine rose	.60	.30
		Nos. 364-368 (5)	2.20	1.30

Issued for United Nations Day, Oct. 24.

Skier
A26

Bicyclist
A27

Sports: 50c, Ice Hockey. 1fr, Tobogganing.
15fr, Discus thrower, vert. 20fr, Boxing, vert.
25fr, Runner.

1960   Unwmk.   Perf. 13
369	A26	30c sl grn, car & bl grn	.45	.25
370	A26	50c red & black	.45	.25
371	A26	1fr red, blk & emer	.45	.25
372	A27	10fr brown, ultra & sl	.45	.25
373	A27	15fr dk red brn & grn	.45	.25
374	A27	20fr dk grn, gldn brn & brn	.55	.25
375	A27	25fr orange, mag & brn	.65	.25
		Nos. 369-375 (7)	3.45	1.75

8th Winter Olympic Games, Squaw Valley,
Calif. (Nos. 369-371); 17th Olympic Games,
Rome (Nos. 372-375).

Prime Minister
Sylvanus Olympio
and Togo
Flag — A28

1960, Apr. 27   Litho.
**Center in Green, Red, Yellow &
Brown**
376	A28	30c black & buff	.25	.25
377	A28	50c brown & buff	.25	.25
378	A28	1fr lilac & buff	.25	.25
379	A28	10fr blue & buff	.25	.25
380	A28	20fr red & buff	.25	.25
381	A28	25fr green & buff	.25	.25
		Nos. 376-381 (6)	1.50	1.50

Proclamation of Togo's full independence,
Apr. 27, 1960.
See Nos. C31-C33.

Flags of
"Big Four,"
and British
Flag — A29

1960, May 21   Perf. 14x14½
382	A29	50c shown	.35	.25
383	A29	1fr USSR	.35	.25
384	A29	20fr France	.35	.25
385	A29	25fr US	.35	.25
		Nos. 382-385 (4)	1.40	1.00

Summit Conference of France, Great Britain, United States and USSR, Paris, May 16.

Flag of
Togo and
UN
Emblem
A30

1961, Jan. 6   Perf. 14½x15
Flag in red, olive green & yellow
386	A30	30c red	.30	.25
387	A30	50c brown	.30	.25
388	A30	1fr ultramarine	.30	.25
389	A30	10fr maroon	.30	.25
390	A30	25fr black	.30	.25
391	A30	30fr violet	.30	.25
		Nos. 386-391 (6)	1.80	1.50

Togo's admission to United Nations.

Crowned Cranes
over Map — A31

1961, Apr. 1   Perf. 14½x15
392	A31	1fr multicolored	.40	.25
393	A31	10fr multicolored	.40	.25
394	A31	25fr multicolored	.50	.25
395	A31	30fr multicolored	.70	.25
		Nos. 392-395 (4)	2.00	1.00

Augustino de
Souza — A32

1961, Apr. 27   Litho.   Perf. 15
396	A32	50c yellow, red & blk	.35	.25
397	A32	1fr emerald, brn & blk	.35	.25
398	A32	10fr grnsh bl, vio & blk	.35	.25
399	A32	25fr salmon, grn & blk	.35	.25
400	A32	30fr rose lil, bl & blk	.35	.25
		Nos. 396-400 (5)	1.75	1.25

1st anniv. of independence; "Papa" Augustino de Souza, leader of the independence
movement.

Daniel
C.
Beard
A33

Designs: 1fr, Lord Baden-Powell. 10fr,
Togolese Scout and emblems. 25fr, Togolese
Scout and flag, vert. 30fr, Symbolic tents and
fire, vert. 100fr, Three hands of different races
giving Scout sign.

1961, Oct. 7   Photo.   Perf. 13
401	A33	50c brt rose & grn	.45	.25
402	A33	1fr dp violet & car	.45	.25
403	A33	10fr dk gray & brn	.45	.25
404	A33	25fr multicolored	.45	.25
405	A33	30fr grn, red & org brn	.55	.25
406	A33	100fr rose car & bl	1.25	.25
		Nos. 401-406 (6)	3.60	1.50

Togolese Boy Scouts; 20th anniv. of the
deaths of Daniel C. Beard and Lord Baden-
Powell.

Four imperf. souvenir sheets each contain
the six stamps, Nos. 401-406. Two sheets
have a solid background of bright yellow, two a
background of pale grayish brown. One yellow

and one brown sheet have simulated perforations around the stamps. Size: 120x145mm. "REPUBLIQUE DU TOGO" is inscribed in white on bottom sheet margin. Value, each $4.

Plane, Ship and Part of Map of Africa — A34

Part of Map of Africa and: 25fr, Electric train and power mast. 30fr, Tractor and oil derricks. 85fr, Microscope and atomic symbol.

1961, Oct. 24   **Litho.**
Black Inscriptions; Map in Ocher

407	A34 20fr vio bl, org & yel	.50	.25
408	A34 25fr gray, org & yel	.50	.25
409	A34 30fr dk red, yel & org	.60	.25
410	A34 85fr blue, yel & org	1.10	.25
a.	Souvenir sheet of 4	4.00	2.75
	Nos. 407-410 (4)	2.70	1.00

UN Economic Commission for Africa. No. 410a contains one each of Nos. 407-410, imperf., printed without separating margin between the individual stamps to show a complete map of Africa.

Children Dancing around Globe — A35

UNICEF Emblem, children and globe.

1961, Dec. 9   **Unwmk.**   **Perf. 13½**
Black Inscription; Multicolored Design

411	A35 1fr ultra	.40	.25
412	A35 10fr red brown	.40	.25
413	A35 20fr lilac	.40	.25
414	A35 25fr gray	.40	.25
415	A35 30fr bright blue	.45	.25
416	A35 85fr deep lilac	.85	.25
a.	Souvenir sheet of 6	5.00	3.50
	Nos. 411-416 (6)	2.90	1.50

UNICEF, 15th anniv. Nos. 411-416a assembled in two rows show the globe and children of various races dancing around it.

Cmdr. Alan B. Shepard — A36

Designs: 1fr, 30fr, Yuri A. Gagarin. 25fr, Shepherd.

1962, Feb. 24   **Perf. 15x14**

417	A36 50c green	.25	.25
418	A36 1fr carmine rose	.25	.25
419	A36 25fr blue	.30	.25
420	A36 30fr purple	.45	.25
	Nos. 417-420 (4)	1.25	1.00

Astronauts of 1961. Issued in sheets of 50 and in miniature sheets of 12 stamps plus four central labels showing photographs of Alan B. Shepard (US), Virgil I. Grissom (US), Yuri A. Gagarin (USSR), Gherman S. Titov (USSR).

No. 417 Surcharged in Black

1962, Apr. 7

421	A36 100fr on 50c green	2.00	.50
a.	Carmine surcharge	2.00	.50

Orbital flight of Lt. Col. John H. Glenn, Jr., US, Feb. 20, 1962.

Independence Monument, Lomé — A37

Woman Carrying Fruit Basket — A38

1962, Apr. 27   **Litho.**   **Perf. 13½x14**

422	A37 50c multicolored	.25	.25
423	A38 1fr green & pink	.25	.25
424	A37 5fr multicolored	.25	.25
425	A37 20fr purple & yel	.35	.25
426	A37 25fr multicolored	.40	.25
427	A38 30fr red & yellow	.40	.25
a.	Souv. sheet of 3, #424-425, 427, imperf.	2.40	1.75
	Nos. 422-427 (6)	1.90	1.50

2nd anniversary of Togo's independence.

Malaria Eradication Emblem A39

1962, June 2   **Perf. 13½x13**
Multicolored Design

428	A39 10fr yellow green	.35	.25
429	A39 25fr pale lilac	.50	.25
430	A39 30fr ocher	.55	.25
431	A39 85fr light blue	1.10	.25
	Nos. 428-431 (4)	2.50	1.00

WHO drive to eradicate malaria.

Capitol, Pres. John F. Kennedy and Pres. Sylvanus Olympio — A40

1962, July 4   **Unwmk.**   **Perf. 13**
Inscription and Portraits in Slate Green

432	A40 50c yellow	.25	.25
433	A40 1fr blue	.25	.25
434	A40 2fr vermilion	.25	.25
435	A40 5fr lilac	.25	.25
436	A40 25fr pale violet	.45	.25
437	A40 100fr brt green	1.75	.80
a.	Souvenir sheet, imperf.	5.50	5.75
	Nos. 432-437 (6)	3.20	2.05

Visit of Pres. Sylvanus Olympio of Togo to the US, Mar. 1962.

Mail Coach and Stamps of 1897 — A41

50c, Mail ship, stamps of 1900. 1fr, Mail train, stamps of 1915. 10fr, Motorcycle truck, stamp of 1924. 25fr, Mail truck, stamp of 1941. 30fr, DC-3, stamp of 1947.

1963, Jan. 12   **Photo.**   **Perf. 13**

438	A41 30c multicolored	.25	.25
439	A41 50c multicolored	.25	.25
440	A41 1fr multicolored	.35	.25
441	A41 10fr vio, dp org & blk	.40	.25
442	A41 25fr dk red brn, blk & yel grn	.75	.25
443	A41 30fr ol brn & lil rose	.75	.25
	Nos. 438-443, C34 (7)	4.35	1.95

65th anniv. of Togolese mail service. For souvenir sheet see No. C34a.

Hands Reaching for FAO Emblem A42

1963, Mar. 21   **Perf. 14**

444	A42 50c bl, org & dk brn	.25	.25
445	A42 1fr ol grn, org & dk brn	.25	.25
446	A42 25fr brn, dk brn & org	.75	.25
447	A42 30fr vio, dk brn & org	1.10	.25
	Nos. 444-447 (4)	2.35	1.00

FAO "Freedom from Hunger" campaign.

Togolese Flag and Lomé Harbor — A43

1963, Apr. 27   **Litho.**   **Perf. 13x12½**
Flag in Red, Green and Yellow

448	A43 50c red brn & blk	.25	.25
449	A43 1fr dk car rose & blk	.25	.25
450	A43 25fr dull bl & blk	.35	.25
451	A43 50fr bister & blk	.40	.25
	Nos. 448-451 (4)	1.25	1.00

3rd anniversary of independence.

Centenary Emblem — A44

1963, June 1   **Photo.**   **Perf. 14**
Flag in Red, Olive Green, Yellow

452	A44 25fr blue, blk & red	1.00	.25
453	A44 30fr dull grn, blk & red	1.20	.25

International Red Cross centenary.

Lincoln, Broken Fetters, Maps of Africa and US. — A45

1963, Oct.   **Unwmk.**   **Perf. 13x14**

454	A45 50c multicolored	.25	.25
455	A45 1fr multicolored	.25	.25
456	A45 25fr multicolored	.35	.25
	Nos. 454-456, C35 (4)	2.35	1.20

Centenary of the emancipation of the American slaves. See souvenir sheet No. C35a. For overprints see Nos. 473-475, C41.

UN Emblem and "15" — A46

1963, Dec. 10   **Photo.**   **Perf. 14x13**

457	A46 50c ultra, dk bl & rose red	.25	.25
458	A46 1fr yel grn, dk bl & rose red	.25	.25
459	A46 25fr lil, dk bl & rose red	.50	.25
460	A46 85fr gold, dk bl & rose red	1.10	.30
	Nos. 457-460 (4)	2.10	1.05

15th anniv. of the Universal Declaration of Human Rights.

Hibiscus — A47

Designs: 50c, Orchid. 2fr, Butterfly. 5fr, Hinged tortoise. 8fr, Ball python. 10fr, Bunea alcinoe (moth). 20fr, Octopus. 25fr, John Dory (fish). 30fr, French angelfish. 40fr, Hippopotamus. 60fr, Bohor reedbuck. 85fr, Anubius baboon.

1964   **Size: 22½x31mm**   **Perf. 14**

461	A47 50c multicolored	.25	.25
462	A47 1fr yellow, car & grn	.25	.25
463	A47 2fr lilac, yel & blk	.35	.25
464	A47 5fr gray & multi	.25	.25
465	A47 8fr cit, red brn & blk	.45	.25
466	A47 10fr multicolored	1.20	.25
467	A47 20fr dl bl, yel & brn	1.40	.25
468	A47 25fr dl bl, grn & yel	1.40	.25
469	A47 30fr multicolored	1.55	.25
470	A47 40fr grn, red brn & blk	2.10	.25
471	A47 60fr grnsh bl & red brn	4.50	.25
472	A47 85fr lt grn, brn & org	5.50	.25
	Nos. 461-472 (12)	19.20	3.00

See Nos. 511-515, C36-C40, J56-J63.

Nos. 454-456 Overprinted Diagonally

1964, Mar. 7   **Perf. 13x14**

473	A45 50c multicolored	.25	.25
474	A45 1fr multicolored	.25	.25
475	A45 25fr multicolored	.50	.25
	Nos. 473-475 (3)	1.00	.75

Issued in memory of John F. Kennedy. See No. C41 and note on souvenir sheets following it.

Isis of Kalabsha A48

Designs: 25fr, Head of Ramses II. 30fr, Colonnade of Birth House at Philae.

1964, Mar. 8   **Litho.**   **Perf. 14**

476	A48 20fr blk, pale grn & red	.35	.25
477	A48 25fr black & lil rose	.45	.25
478	A48 30fr black & citron	.70	.25
a.	Souvenir sheet of 3	2.75	2.50
	Nos. 476-478 (3)	1.50	.75

UNESCO world campaign to save historic monuments in Nubia. No. 478a contains three imperf. stamps similar to Nos. 476-478 with simulated perforations.

Phosphate
Mine,
Kpeme
A49

25fr, Phosphate plant, Kpeme. 60fr,
Phosphate train. 85fr, Loading ship with
phosphate.

1964, Apr. 27   Unwmk.   Perf. 14
479 A49 5fr brown & bis brn   .30 .25
480 A49 25fr dk pur & brn car   .30 .25
481 A49 60fr dk green & olive   .70 .25
482 A49 85fr vio blk & Prus bl   1.00 .25
    Nos. 479-482 (4)   2.30 1.00
Fourth anniversary of independence.

African Breaking
Slavery Chain, and
Map — A50

1964, May 25   Photo.   Perf. 14x13
483 A50 5fr dp orange & brn   .25 .25
484 A50 25fr olive grn & brn   .40 .25
485 A50 85fr rose car & brn   1.00 .25
    Nos. 483-485,C42 (4)   3.15 1.05
1st anniv. of the meeting of African heads of
state at Addis Ababa.

Pres.
Nicolas
Grunitzky
and
Butterfly
A51

1964, Aug. 18   Litho.   Perf. 14
486 A51 1fr shown   .55 .25
487 A51 5fr Dove   .55 .25
488 A51 25fr Flower   .55 .25
489 A51 45fr as 1fr   .90 .25
490 A51 85fr Flower   1.75 .25
    Nos. 486-490 (5)   4.30 1.25
National Union and Reconciliation.

Soccer
A52

1964, Oct.   Photo.   Perf. 14
491 A52 1fr shown   .25 .25
492 A52 5fr Runner   .30 .25
493 A52 25fr Discus   .50 .25
494 A52 45fr as 1fr   .65 .25
    Nos. 491-494,C43 (5)   2.95 1.30
18th Olympic Games, Tokyo, Oct. 10-25.
For souvenir sheet see No. C43a.

Cooperation Issue
Common Design Type
1964, Nov. 7   Engr.   Perf. 13
495 CD119 25fr mag, dk brn & ol
                    bis   .70 .25

Dirigible and Balloons — A53

25fr, 45fr, Otto Lilienthal's glider, 1894;
Wright Brothers' plane, 1903; Boeing 707.

1964, Dec. 5   Photo.   Perf. 14x13
496 A53 5fr org lil & grn   .25 .25
497 A53 10fr brt grn, dl bl & dk
                     red   .30 .25
498 A53 25fr bl, vio bl & org   .50 .25
499 A53 45fr brt pink, vio bl &
                     grn   1.10 .25
  a. Souv. sheet of 4   8.75 7.25
    Nos. 496-499,C44 (5)   3.65 1.50
Inauguration of the national airline, Air Togo.
#499a contains 4 imperf. stamps similar to
#497-499 and #C44 with simulated perfs.

Orbiting Geophysical Observatory and
Mariner — A54

Space Satellites: 15fr, 25fr, Tiros, Telstar
and Orbiting Solar Observatory. 20fr, 50fr,
Nimbus, Syncom and Relay.

1964, Dec. 12   Litho.   Perf. 14
500 A54 10fr dp rose, bl & yel   .40 .25
501 A54 15fr multi   .40 .25
502 A54 20fr yel, grn & vio   .40 .25
503 A54 25fr multi   .40 .25
504 A54 45fr brt grn, dk bl & yel .55 .25
505 A54 50fr yel, grn & org   .75 .25
  a. Souv. sheet, #502-505, imperf. 3.00 2.50
    Nos. 500-505 (6)   2.90 1.50
Intl. Quiet Sun Year.

Togo Olympic
Stamps Printed in
Israel — A55

Arms of Israel and Togo — A56

Pres. Nicolas Grunitzky of Togo and: 20fr,
Church of the Mount of Beatitudes. 45fr, Ruins
of Synagogue at Capernaum.

Perf. 13½x14½, 14x13½
1964, Dec. 26   Photo.
506 A55 5fr rose violet   .40 .25
507 A56 20fr grnsh bl, grn & dl
                    pur   .40 .25
508 A56 25fr red & bluish grn   .40 .25
509 A56 45fr dl yel, ol & dl pur .85 .25
510 A56 85fr mag & bluish grn   1.75 .25
  a. Souv. sheet of 4, imperf. 4.60 3.50
    Nos. 506-510 (5)   2.70 1.25
Israel-Togo friendship.

Type of Regular Issue, 1964
Designs: 3fr, Morpho aega butterfly. 4fr,
Scorpion. 6fr, Bird-of-paradise flower. 15fr,
Flap-necked chameleon. 45fr, Ring-tailed
palm civet.

1965, June   Unwmk.   Perf. 14
         Size: 23x31mm
511 A47 3fr bister & multi   1.20 .25
512 A47 4fr org & bluish blk   .30 .25
513 A47 6fr multi   .45 .25
514 A47 15fr brt pink, yel & brn 1.75 .25
515 A47 45fr dl grn, org & brn   3.50 .25
    Nos. 511-515 (5)   7.20 1.25

Syncom Satellite, Radar Station and
ITU Emblem — A57

1965, June   Perf. 13x14
516 A57 10fr Prus blue   .45 .25
517 A57 20fr olive bister   .45 .25
518 A57 15fr bright blue   .45 .25
519 A57 45fr crimson   .65 .25
520 A57 50fr green   .75 .25
    Nos. 516-520 (5)   2.75 1.25
ITU, centenary.

Abraham
Lincoln — A58

1965, June 26 Photo. Perf. 13x14
521 A58 1fr magenta   .25 .25
522 A58 5fr dull green   .25 .25
523 A58 20fr brown   .40 .25
524 A58 25fr slate   .40 .25
    Nos. 521-524,C45 (5)   3.30 1.35
Death cent. of Abraham Lincoln. For souvenir sheet see No. C45a.

Discus Thrower,
Flags of Togo and
Congo — A59

Flags and: 10fr, Javelin thrower. 15fr, Handball player. 25fr, Runner.

1965, July   Unwmk.   Perf. 14x13
Flags in Red, Yellow and Green
525 A59 5fr deep magenta   .25 .25
526 A59 10fr dark blue   .25 .25
527 A59 15fr brown   .35 .25
528 A59 25fr dark purple   .90 .25
    Nos. 525-528,C46 (5)   3.50 1.35
1st African Games, Brazzaville, July 18-25.

Winston Churchill
and "V" — A60

Stalin, Roosevelt and Churchill at
Yalta — A61

Perf. 13½x14, 14x13½
1965, Aug. 7   Photo.
529 A60 5fr dull green   .25 .25
530 A61 10fr brt vio & gray   .25 .25
531 A60 20fr brown   .50 .25
532 A61 45fr Prus bl & gray   .85 .25
    Nos. 529-532,C47 (5)   3.35 1.40
Sir Winston Spencer Churchill (1874-1965),
British statesman and World War II leader.

Unisphere and New York
Skyline — A62

10fr, Togolese dancers & drummer, Unisphere. 50fr, Michelangelo's Pieta &
Unisphere.

1965, Aug. 28   Photo.   Perf. 14
533 A62 5fr grnsh bl & vio blk .35 .25
534 A62 10fr yel grn & dk brn   .35 .25
535 A62 25fr brn org & dk grn   .35 .25
536 A62 50fr vio & sl grn   .50 .25
537 A62 85fr rose red & brn   1.10 .30
  a. Souvenir sheet of 2   2.75 1.75
    Nos. 533-537 (5)   2.65 1.30
New York World's Fair, 1964-65. No. 537a
contains two imperf. stamps similar to Nos.
536-537 with simulated perforations.

"Constructive Cooperation" and Olive
Branch — A63

Designs: 25fr, 40fr, Hands of various races
holding globe and olive branch. 85fr, Handclasp, olive branch and globe.

1965, Sept. 25   Unwmk.   Perf. 14
538 A63 5fr violet, lt bl & org .35 .25
539 A63 15fr brn, org & gray   .35 .25
540 A63 25fr blue & orange   .35 .25
541 A63 40fr dp car, gray & org .55 .25
542 A63 85fr green & org   1.00 .30
    Nos. 538-542 (5)   2.60 1.30
International Cooperation Year.

Major White and Gemini 4 — A64

25fr, Lt. Col. Alexei Leonov and Voskhod 2.

1965, Nov. 25   Photo.   Perf. 13½x14
543 A64 25fr dp bl & brt car rose   .60   .25
544 A64 50fr green & brown   1.00   .25

"Walks in Space" of Lt. Col. Alexei Leonov (USSR), and Major Edward H. White (US). Printed in sheets of 12 with ornamental borders.

For overprints and surcharges see Nos. 563-566.

Adlai E. Stevenson and UN Headquarters — A65

5fr, "ONU" and doves. 10fr, UN emblem and headquarters. 20fr, "ONU" and orchids.

1965, Dec. 15   Perf. 14x13½
545 A65 5fr dk brn, yel & lt bl   .40   .25
546 A65 10fr org, dk bl & grn   .40   .25
547 A65 20fr dk grn, yel grn &
            org brn   .40   .25
548 A65 25fr brt yel, dk bl & blu-
            ish grn   .40   .25
     Nos. 545-548,C48 (5)   3.35   1.40

UN, 20th anniv.; Adlai E. Stevenson (1900-1965), US ambassador to the UN.

Pope Paul VI, Plane and UN Emblem — A66

15fr, 30fr, Pope addressing UN General Assembly & UN emblem, vert. 20fr, Pope, NYC skyline with UN Headquarters.

1966, Mar. 5   Litho.   Perf. 12
549 A66 5fr blue & multi   .25   .25
550 A66 15fr lt violet & multi   .25   .25
551 A66 20fr bister & multi   .35   .25
552 A66 30fr lt ultra & multi   .50   .25
     Nos. 549-552,C49-C50 (6)   3.90   1.50

Visit of Pope Paul VI to the UN, New York City, Oct. 4, 1965.

Surgical Operation and Togolese Flag — A67

Togolese Flag and: 10fr, 30fr, Blood transfusion. 45fr, Profiles of African man and woman.

1966, May 7   Litho.   Perf. 12
553 A67 5fr multicolored   .40   .25
554 A67 10fr multicolored   .40   .25
555 A67 15fr multicolored   .40   .25
556 A67 30fr multicolored   .40   .25
557 A67 45fr multicolored   .60   .25
     Nos. 553-557,C51 (6)   4.45   1.60

Togolese Red Cross, 7th anniversary.

Talisman Roses and WHO Headquarters, Geneva — A68

Various flowers & WHO Headquarters.

1966, May   Litho.   Perf. 12
558 A68 5fr lt yel grn & multi   .25   .25
559 A68 10fr pale pink & multi   .35   .25
560 A68 15fr dull yel & multi   .45   .25
561 A68 20fr pale gray & multi   .55   .25
562 A68 30fr tan & multi   .75   .25
     Nos. 558-562,C52-C53 (7)   4.70   1.75

Inauguration of WHO Headquarters, Geneva.

Nos. 543-544 Overprinted or Surcharged in Red

No. 563, Envolée Surveyor 1. No. 564, Envolée Gemini 9. No. 565, Envolée Luna 9. No. 566, Envolée Venus 3.

1966, July 11   Photo.   Perf. 13½x14
563 A64 50fr multi   .70   .25
564 A64 50fr multi   .70   .25
  a.   Pair, #563-564   1.50   .60
565 A64 100fr on 25fr multi   1.60   .25
566 A64 100fr on 25fr multi   1.60   .25
  a.   Pair, #565-566   3.50   .90
     Nos. 563-566 (4)   4.60   1.00

US and USSR achievements in Space.

Wood Carver — A69

Arts and Crafts: 10fr, Basket maker. 15fr, Woman weaver. 30fr, Woman potter.

1966, Sept.   Photo.   Perf. 13x14
567 A69 5fr blue, yel & dk brn   .25   .25
568 A69 10fr emer, org & dk brn   .25   .25
569 A69 15fr ver, yel & dk brn   .30   .25
570 A69 30fr lilac, dk brn & yel   .40   .25
     Nos. 567-570,C55-C56 (6)   4.00   1.50

Togolese Dancer — A70

Designs: 5fr, Togolese man. 20fr, Woman dancer from North Togo holding branches. 25fr, Male dancer. 30fr, Male dancer from North Togo with horned helmet. 45fr, Drummer.

1966, Nov.   Photo.   Perf. 13x14
571 A70 5fr emerald & multi   .25   .25
572 A70 10fr dl yel & multi   .25   .25
573 A70 20fr lt ultra & multi   .40   .25
574 A70 25fr dp orange & multi   .50   .25
575 A70 30fr red violet & multi   .55   .25
576 A70 45fr blue & multi   .95   .25
     Nos. 571-576,C57-C58 (8)   5.10   2.00

Soccer Players and Jules Rimet Cup — A71

Various Soccer Scenes.

1966, Dec. 14   Photo.   Perf. 14x13
577 A71 5fr blue, brn & red   .25   .25
578 A71 10fr brick red & multi   .30   .25
579 A71 20fr ol, brn & dk grn   .40   .25
580 A71 25fr vio, brn & org   .40   .25
581 A71 30fr ocher & multi   .50   .25
582 A71 45fr emerald, brn & mag   .85   .25
     Nos. 577-582,C59-C60 (8)   4.95   2.00

England's victory in the World Soccer Cup Championship, Wembley, July 30. For souvenir sheet see No. C60a.

African Mouthbreeder and Sailboat — A72

Designs: 10fr, Yellow jack and trawler. 15fr, Banded distichodus and seiner. 25fr, Jewelfish and galley. 30fr, like 5fr.

1967, Jan. 14   Photo.   Perf. 14
Fish in Natural Colors
583 A72 5fr lt ultra & blk   .25   .25
584 A72 10fr brn org & brn   .40   .25
585 A72 15fr brt rose & dk bl   .45   .25
586 A72 25fr olive & blk   .70   .25
587 A72 30fr grnsh bl & blk   .85   .25
     Nos. 583-587,C61-C62 (7)   5.90   1.85

African Boy and Greyhound — A73

UNICEF Emblem and: 10fr, Boy and Irish setter. 20fr, Girl and doberman.

1967, Feb. 11   Photo.   Perf. 14x13½
588 A73 5fr orange, plum & blk   .25   .25
589 A73 10fr yel grn, red brn &
            dk grn   .35   .25
590 A73 15fr brt rose, brn & blk   .50   .25
591 A73 20fr bl, vio bl & blk   .60   .25
592 A73 30fr ol, sl grn & blk   1.10   .25
     Nos. 588-592,C63-C64 (7)   5.95   1.85

UNICEF, 20th anniv. (in 1966).

French A-1 Satellite — A74

5fr, Diamant rocket, vert. 15fr, Fr-1 satellite, vert. 20fr, 40fr, D-1 satellite. 25fr, A-1 satellite.

Perf. 14x13½, 13½x14
1967, Mar. 18   Photo.
593 A74 5fr multi   .25   .25
594 A74 10fr multi   .25   .25
595 A74 15fr multi   .35   .25
596 A74 20fr multi   .40   .25
597 A74 25fr multi   .55   .25
598 A74 40fr multi   .75   .25
     Nos. 593-598,C65-C66 (8)   5.30   2.05

French achievements in space.

Johann Sebastian Bach and Organ — A75

UNESCO Emblem and: 10fr, Ludwig van Beethoven, violin and oboe. 15f, Duke Ellington, saxophone, trumpet, drums. 20fr, Claude A. Debussy, piano and harp. 30fr, like 15fr.

1967, Apr. 15   Photo.   Perf. 14x13½
599 A75 5fr org & multi   .25   .25
600 A75 10fr multi   .50   .25
601 A75 15fr multi   .70   .25
602 A75 20fr lt bl & multi   1.10   .25
603 A75 30fr lil & multi   1.50   .25
     Nos. 599-603,C67-C68 (7)   6.05   1.75

20th anniv. (in 1966) of UNESCO.

EXPO Emblem, British Pavilion and Day Lilies — A76

10fr, French pavilion, roses. 30fr, African village, bird-of-paradise flower.

1967, May 30   Photo.   Perf. 14
604 A76 5fr brt pink & multi   .25   .25
605 A76 10fr dull org & multi   .25   .25
606 A76 30fr blue & multi   .55   .25
     Nos. 604-606,C69-C72 (7)   5.65   2.05

EXPO '67 Intl. Exhibition, Montreal, Apr. 28-Oct. 27.

For overprints see Nos. 628-630, C86-C89.

Lions Emblem — A77

20fr, 45fr, Lions emblem and flowers.

1967, July 29   Photo.   Perf. 13x14
607 A77 10fr yellow & multi   .45   .25
608 A77 20fr multicolored   .45   .25
609 A77 30fr green & multi   .55   .25
610 A77 45fr blue & multi   .80   .25
     Nos. 607-610 (4)   2.25   1.00

50th anniversary of Lions International.

Montagu's Harriers — A78

5fr, Bohor reedbucks. 15fr, Zebras. 20fr, 30fr, Marsh harriers. 25fr, Leopard.

1967, Aug. 19   Photo.   Perf. 14x13½
611	A78	5fr lilac & org brn	.55	.25
612	A70	10fr dk red, yel & dl bl	.55	.25
613	A78	15fr grn, blk & lil	.55	.25
614	A78	20fr dk brn, yel & dl bl	.55	.25
615	A78	25fr brn, ol & yel	.55	.25
616	A78	30fr vio, yel & dl bl	.65	.25
		Nos. 611-616,C79-C80 (8)	6.10	2.00

Stamp Auction and Togo Nos. 16 and C42 — A79

10fr, 45fr, Exhibition, #67 (British) & 520. 15fr, 30fr, Stamp store, #230. 20fr, Stamp packet vending machine, #545.

Stamps on Stamps in Original Colors

1967, Oct. 14   Photo.   Perf. 14x13
617	A79	5fr purple	.30	.25
618	A79	10fr dk brown	.30	.25
619	A79	15fr deep blue	.30	.25
620	A79	20fr slate green	.35	.25
621	A79	30fr red brown	.50	.25
622	A79	45fr Prus blue	.80	.25
		Nos. 617-622,C82-C83 (8)	5.80	2.15

70th anniv. of the 1st Togolese stamps. For souvenir sheet see No. C82a.
See Nos. 853-855, C205.

Monetary Union Issue
Common Design Type

1967, Nov. 4   Engr.   Perf. 13
| 623 | CD125 | 30fr dk bl, vio bl & brt grn | .60 | .25 |

Broad Jump, Summer Olympics Emblem and View of Mexico City — A80

15fr, Ski jump, Winter Olympics emblem, ski lift. 30fr, Runners, Summer Olympics emblem, view of Mexico City. 45fr, Bobsledding, Winter Olympics emblem, ski lift.

1967, Dec. 2   Photo.   Perf. 13x14
624	A80	5fr orange & multi	.50	.25
625	A80	15fr multicolored	.50	.25
626	A80	30fr multicolored	.50	.25
627	A80	45fr multicolored	.05	.25
		Nos. 624-627,C84-C85 (6)	5.15	1.95

1968 Olympic Games. For souvenir sheet see No. C85a.

**Nos. 604-606 Overprinted:
"JOURNÉE NATIONALE / DU TOGO / 29 SEPTEMBRE 1967"**

1967, Dec.   Perf. 14
628	A76	5fr multicolored	.30	.25
629	A76	10fr multicolored	.30	.25
630	A76	30fr blue & multi	.40	.25
		Nos. 628-630,C86-C89 (7)	5.40	1.85

National Day, Sept. 29, 1967.

The Gleaners, by François Millet and Phosphate Works, Benin — A81

Industrialization of Togo: 20fr, 45fr, 90fr, The Weaver at the Loom, by Vincent van Gogh, and textile plant, Dadia.

1968, Jan.   Photo.   Perf. 14
631	A81	10fr olive & multi	.45	.25
632	A81	20fr multicolored	.45	.25
633	A81	30fr brown & multi	.55	.25
634	A81	45fr multicolored	.65	.25

635	A81	60fr dk blue & multi	.95	.25
636	A81	90fr multicolored	1.60	.25
		Nos. 631-636 (6)	4.65	1.50

Togolese Women Brewing Beer — A82

The Beer Drinkers, by Edouard Manet — A83

Design: 45fr, Modern beer bottling plant.

1968, Mar. 26   Litho.   Perf. 14
637	A82	20fr emerald & multi	.55	.25
638	A83	30fr dk car & multi	.70	.25
639	A82	45fr orange & multi	.85	.25
		Nos. 637-639 (3)	2.10	.75

Publicity for local beer industry.

Symbolic Water Cycle, Flower and Cogwheels A84

1968, Apr. 6
| 640 | A84 | 30fr multicolored | .65 | .25 |

Hydrological Decade (UNESCO), 1965-74. See No. C90.

Viking Ship and Portuguese Brigantine — A85

10fr, Fulton's steamship and modern steamship. 20fr, Harbor activities and map of Africa.

1968, Apr. 26   Photo.   Perf. 14x13½
641	A85	5fr brt green & multi	.25	.25
642	A85	10fr dp orange & multi	.25	.25
643	A85	20fr green & multi	.40	.25
644	A85	30fr yel grn & multi	.85	.25
		Nos. 641-644,C91-C92 (6)	4.85	1.50

Inauguration of Lomé Harbor. See Nos. C91-C92.

Adenauer and 1968 Europa Emblem — A86

1968, May 25   Photo.   Perf. 14
| 645 | A86 | 90fr olive grn & brn org | 1.90 | .25 |

Konrad Adenauer (1876-1967), chancellor of West Germany (1949-63).

Adam and Eve Expelled from Paradise, by Michelangelo — A87

Paintings: 20fr, The Anatomy Lesson of Dr. Tulp, by Rembrandt. 30fr, The Anatomy Lesson, by Rembrandt (detail). 45fr, Jesus Healing the Sick, by Raphael.

1968, June 22   Photo.   Perf. 14
646	A87	15fr crimson & multi	.35	.25
647	A87	20fr multicolored	.40	.25
648	A87	30fr green & multi	.70	.25
649	A87	45fr multicolored	1.00	.25
		Nos. 646-649,C93-C94 (6)	4.70	1.50

WHO, 20th anniv.

Olympic Monument, San Salvador Island, Bahamas — A88

1968, July 27   Perf. 14x13½
650	A88	15fr Wrestling	.25	.25
651	A88	20fr Boxing	.40	.25
652	A88	30fr Judo	.60	.25
653	A88	45fr Running	.75	.25
		Nos. 650-653,C95-C96 (6)	4.10	1.50

19th Olympic Games, Mexico City, 10/12-27.

Chick Holding Lottery Ticket — A89

45fr, Lottery ticket, horseshoe & 4-leaf clover.

1968, Oct. 5   Litho.   Perf. 14
| 654 | A89 | 30fr dk green & multi | .65 | .25 |
| 655 | A89 | 45fr multicolored | .75 | .25 |

2nd anniversary of National Lottery.

Scout Before Tent — A90

10fr, 45fr, Scout leader training cub scouts, horiz. 20fr, First aid practice, horiz. 30fr, Scout game.

1968, Nov. 23
656	A90	5fr dp org & multi	.25	.25
657	A90	10fr emerald & multi	.25	.25
658	A90	20fr multicolored	.40	.25
659	A90	30fr multicolored	.50	.25
660	A90	45fr blue & multi	.70	.25
		Nos. 656-660,C97-C98 (7)	4.50	1.85

Issued to honor the Togolese Boy Scouts.

Adoration of the Shepherds, by Giorgione — A91

Paintings: 20f, Adoration of the Magi, by Pieter Brueghel. 30fr, Adoration of the Magi, by Botticelli. 45fr, Adoration of the Magi, by Durer.

1968, Dec. 28   Litho.   Perf. 14
661	A91	15fr green & multi	.35	.25
662	A91	20fr multicolored	.40	.25
663	A91	30fr multicolored	.55	.25
664	A91	45fr multicolored	.90	.25
		Nos. 661-664,C100-C101 (6)	4.80	1.60

Christmas.

Martin Luther King, Jr. — A92

Portraits and Human Rights Flame: 20fr, Professor René Cassin (author of Declaration of Human Rights). 45fr, Pope John XXIII.

1969, Feb. 1   Photo.   Perf. 13½x14
665	A92	15fr brn org & sl grn	.25	.25
666	A92	20fr grnsh bl & vio	.40	.25
667	A92	30fr ver & slate bl	.60	.25
668	A92	45fr olive & car rose	1.25	.25
		Nos. 665-668,C102-C103 (6)	4.90	1.65

International Human Rights Year.
For overprints see Nos. 683-686, C110-C111.

Omnisport Stadium and Soccer — A93

Stadium and: 15fr, Handball. 20fr, Volleyball. 30fr, Basketball. 45fr, Tennis.

1969, Apr. 26   Photo.   Perf. 14x13½
669	A93	10fr emer, dp car & dk brn	.25	.25
670	A93	15fr org, ultra & dk brn	.35	.25
671	A93	20fr yel, ol & dk brn	.40	.25
672	A93	30fr dl grn, bl & dk brn	.55	.25
673	A93	45fr org, lil & dk brn	.70	.25
		Nos. 669-673,C105-C106 (7)	4.60	1.80

Opening of Omnisport Stadium, Lomé.

Astronaut and Eagle on Moon, Earth and Stars in Sky — A94

Designs: 1f, 30f, Lunar Module Eagle Landing on Moon. 45fr, Astronaut and Eagle on moon, earth and stars in sky.

1969, July 21   Litho.   Perf. 14
674 A94 1fr green & multi   .25   .25
675 A94 20fr brown & multi   .25   .25
676 A94 30fr scarlet & multi   .40   .25
677 A94 45fr ultra & multi   .70   .25
  Nos. 674-677,C107-C108 (6)   4.00 1.75

Man's 1st landing on the moon, 7/20/69. US astronauts Neil A. Armstrong & Col. Edwin E. Aldrin, Jr., with Lieut. Col. Michael Collins piloting Apollo 11.
For overprints see #710-712, C120-C121.

Christ at Emmaus, by Velazquez A95

Paintings: 5fr, The Last Supper, by Tintoretto. 20fr, Pentecost, by El Greco. 30fr, The Annunciation, by Botticelli. 45fr, Like 10fr.

1969, Aug. 16   Litho.   Perf. 14
678 A95 5fr red, gold & multi   .25   .25
679 A95 10fr multicolored   .35   .25
680 A95 30fr grn & multi   .55   .25
681 A95 30fr multicolored   .75   .25
682 A95 45fr pur, gold & multi   1.25 .25
  Nos. 678-682,C109 (6)   5.25 1.75

Nos. 665-668 Overprinted

1969, Sept. 1   Photo.   Perf. 13½x14
683 A92 15fr brn org & sl grn   .30   .25
684 A92 20fr grnsh bl & vio   .50   .25
685 A92 30fr ver & slate bl   .55   .25
686 A92 45fr olive & car rose   1.00 .25
  Nos. 683-686,C110-C111 (6)   4.50 1.55

Gen. Dwight D. Eisenhower (1890-1969), 34th President of the US.

African Development Bank and Emblem — A96

Designs: 45fr, Bank emblem and hand holding railroad bridge and engine.

1969, Sept. 10   Photo.   Perf. 13x14
687 A96 30fr ultra, blk gold & grn .65 .25
688 A96 45fr grn, dk bl, gold &
              dk red   2.00 .35

5th anniv. of the African Development Bank. See No. C112.

Louis Pasteur and Help for 1968 Flood Victims — A97

Designs: 15fr, Henri Dunant and Red Cross workers meeting Biafra refugees at airport. 30fr, Alexander Fleming and help for flood victims. 45fr, Wilhelm C. Roentgen and Red Cross workers with children in front of Headquarters.

1969, Sept. 27   Litho.   Perf. 14
689 A97 15fr red & multi   .35   .25
690 A97 20fr emerald & multi   .40   .25
691 A97 30fr purple & multi   .75   .25
692 A97 45fr brt blue & multi   .90   .25
  Nos. 689-692,C113-C114 (6)   4.50 1.70

League of Red Cross Societies, 50th anniv.

Glidji Agricultural Center A98

Designs (Emblem of Young Pioneer and Agricultural Organization and): 1fr, Corn harvest. 3fr, Founding meeting of Agricultural Pioneer Youths, Mar. 7, 1967. 4fr, Class at Glidji Agricultural School. 5fr, Boys forming human pyramid. 7fr, Farm students threshing. 8fr, Instruction in gardening. 10fr, 50fr, Cooperative village. 15fr, Gardening School. 20fr, Cattle breeding. 25fr, Chicken farm. 30fr, Independence parade. 40fr, Boys riding high wire. 45fr, Tractor and trailer. 60fr, Instruction in tractor driving.

1969-70   Litho.   Perf. 14
693 A98 1fr multi ('70)   .25   .25
694 A98 2fr multi   .25   .25
695 A98 3fr multi ('70)   .25   .25
696 A98 4fr multi ('70)   .25   .25
697 A98 5fr ultra & multi   .25   .25
698 A98 7fr multi ('70)   .25   .25
699 A98 8fr red & multi   .25   .25
700 A98 10fr bl & multi ('70)   .25   .25
701 A98 15fr red & multi ('70)   .30   .25
702 A98 20fr lilac & multi   .35   .25
703 A98 25fr multi ('70)   .50   .25
704 A98 30fr brt bl & multi   .50   .25
705 A98 40fr brt yel & multi   .70   .25
706 A98 45fr rose lil & multi   .75   .25
707 A98 50fr blue & multi   .85   .25
708 A98 60fr orange & multi   .85   .25
  Nos. 693-708,C115-C119 (21)   25.40 6.55

Books and Map of Africa A99

1969, Nov. 27   Litho.   Perf. 14
709 A99 30fr lt blue & multi   .60   .25

12th anniv. of the Intl. Assoc. for the Development of Libraries in Africa.

Christmas Issue
Nos. 674-675, 677 Overprinted "JOYEUX NOEL"

1969, Dec.   Litho.   Perf. 14
710 A94 1fr green & multi   .60   .25
711 A94 20fr brown & multi   1.90 .35
712 A94 45fr ultra & multi   2.60 .65
  Nos. 710-712,C120-C121 (5)   13.85 2.35

George Washington — A100

Portraits: 20fr, Albert Luthuli. 30fr, Mahatma Gandhi. 45fr, Simon Bolivar.

1969, Dec. 27   Photo.   Perf. 14x13½
713 A100 15fr dk brn, emer &
               buff   .35   .25
714 A100 20fr dk brn, org & buff   .35   .25
715 A100 30fr dk brn, grnsh bl &
               ocher   .60   .25
716 A100 45fr dk brn, sl grn & dl
               yel   1.00 .25
  Nos. 713-716,C122-C123 (6)   4.70 1.60

Issued to honor leaders for world peace.

For overprint & surcharges see #764-766, C143.

Plower, by M.K. Klodt and ILO Emblem A101

Paintings and ILO Emblem: 10fr, Gardening, by Camille Pissarro. 20fr, Fruit Harvest, by Diego Rivera. 30fr, Spring Sowing, by Vincent van Gogh. 45fr, Workers, by Rivera.

1970, Jan. 24   Litho.   Perf. 12½x13
717 A101 5fr gold & multi   .25   .25
718 A101 10fr gold & multi   .35   .25
719 A101 20fr gold & multi   .60   .25
720 A101 30fr gold & multi   1.40 .25
721 A101 45fr gold & multi   1.40 .25
  Nos. 717-721,C124-C125 (7)   8.50 1.75

ILO, 50th anniversary.

Togolese Hair Styles — A102

Various hair styles. 20fr, 30fr, vertical.

1970, Feb. 21   Perf. 13x12½, 12½x13
722 A102 5fr multicolored   .25   .25
723 A102 10fr ver & multi   .35   .25
724 A102 20fr purple & multi   .50   .25
725 A102 30fr yellow grn & multi 1.25 .25
  Nos. 722-725,C126-C127 (6)   5.00 1.65

Togo No. C127 and Independence Monument, Lomé — A103

30fr, Pres. Etienne G. Eyadéma, Presidential Palace and Independence Monument. 50fr, Map of Togo, dove and Independence Monument, vert.

Perf. 13x12½, 12½x13
1970, Apr. 27   Litho.
726 A103 20fr multicolored   .50   .25
727 A103 30fr multicolored   .70   .25
728 A103 50fr multicolored   1.20 .25
  Nos. 726-728,C128 (4)   3.25 1.00

10th anniv. of independence.

Inauguration of UPU Headquarters, Bern — A104

1970, May 30   Photo.   Perf. 14x13½
729 A104 30fr orange & pur   1.20 .25
  See No. C129.

Soccer, Jules Rimet Cup and Flags of Italy and Uruguay — A105

Designs (Various Scenes from Soccer, Rimet Cup and Flags of): 10fr, Great Britain and Brazil. 15fr, USSR and Mexico. 20fr, Germany and Morocco. 30fr, Romania and Czechoslovakia.

1970, June 27   Litho.   Perf. 13x14
730 A105 5fr olive & multi   .25   .25
731 A105 10fr pink & multi   .30   .25
732 A105 15fr yellow & multi   .50   .25
733 A105 20fr multicolored   .60   .25
734 A105 30fr emerald   1.20 .25
  Nos. 730-734,C130-C132 (8)   6.40 2.10

Soccer Championships for the Jules Rimet Cup, Mexico City, May 30-June 21, 1970.

Lenin and UNESCO Emblem A106

1970, July 25   Litho.   Perf. 12½
735 A106 30fr fawn & multi   1.75 .25

Lenin (1870-1924), Russian communist leader. See No. C133.
For surcharge see No. C179.

EXPO '70 Emblem and View of US Pavilion — A107

Designs: 2fr, Paper carp flying over Sanyo pavilion. 30fr, Russian pavilion. 50fr, Tower of the Sun pavilion. 60fr, French and Japanese pavilions.

1970, Aug. 8   Litho.   Perf. 13
Size: 56½x35mm
736 A107 2fr gray & multi   .25   .25
Size: 50x33mm
737 A107 20fr blue & multi   .30   .25
738 A107 30fr blue & multi   .50   .25
739 A107 50fr blue & multi   1.00 .25
740 A107 60fr blue & multi   1.25 .25
  a.   Strip of 4, #737-740   3.50 1.90
  Nos. 736-740 (5)   3.30 1.25

EXPO '70 Intl. Exhibition, Osaka, Japan, Mar. 15-Sept. 13. No. 740a has continuous view of EXPO. See No. C134.

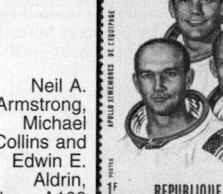

Neil A. Armstrong, Michael Collins and Edwin E. Aldrin, Jr. — A108

Designs: 2fr, US flag, moon rocks and Apollo 11 emblem. 20fr, Astronaut checking Surveyor 3 on moon, and Apollo 12 emblem. 30fr, Charles Conrad, Jr., Richard F. Gordon, Jr., Alan L. Bean and Apollo 12 emblem. 50fr, US flag, moon rocks and Apollo 12 emblem.

1970, Sept. 26
741	A108	1fr multi	.25 .25
742	A108	2fr multi	.25 .25
743	A108	20fr multi	.40 .25
744	A108	30fr multi	.75 .25
745	A108	50fr multi	1.20 .25
	Nos. 741-745,C135 (6)		5.75 2.00

Moon landings of Apollo 11 and 12.
For overprints see Nos. 746-750, C136.

Nos. 741-745 Inscribed: "FELICITATIONS / BON RETOUR APOLLO XIII"

1970, Sept. 26
746	A108	1fr multi	.25 .25
747	A108	2fr multi	.25 .25
748	A108	20fr multi	.40 .25
749	A108	30fr multi	.75 .25
750	A108	50fr multi	1.20 .25
	Nos. 746-750,C136 (6)		5.60 1.85

Safe return of the crew of Apollo 13.

Forge of Vulcan, by Velazquez, and ILO Emblem — A109

Paintings and Emblems of UN Agencies: 15fr, Still Life, by Delacroix, and FAO emblem. 20fr, Portrait of Nicholas Kratzer, by Holbein, and UNESCO emblem. 30fr, UN Headquarters, New York, and UN emblem. 50fr, Portrait of a Little Girl, by Renoir, and UNICEF emblem.

1970, Oct. 24   Litho.   Perf. 13x12½
751	A109	1fr car, gold & dk brn	.65 .25
752	A109	15fr ultra, gold & blk	.65 .25
753	A109	20fr grnsh bl, gold & dk grn	.65 .25
754	A109	30fr lil & multi	.80 .25
755	A109	50fr org brn, gold & sepia	1.25 .25
	Nos. 751-755,C137-C138 (7)		6.85 1.80

United Nations, 25th anniversary.

Euchloron Megaera — A110

Butterflies and Moths: 2fr, Cymothoe chrysippus. 30fr, Danaus chrysippus. 50fr, Morpho.

1970, Nov. 21   Litho.   Perf. 13x14
756	A110	1fr yellow & multi	2.00 .25
757	A110	2fr lt vio & multi	2.00 .25
758	A110	30fr multicolored	2.00 .25
759	A110	50fr orange & multi	3.75 .25
	Nos. 756-759,C139-C140 (6)		20.25 1.50

For surcharge see No. 859.

Nativity, by Botticelli — A111

Paintings: 20fr, Adoration of the Shepherds, by Veronese. 30fr, Adoration of the Shepherds, by El Greco. 50fr, Adoration of the Kings, by Fra Angelico.

1970, Dec. 26   Litho.   Perf. 12½x13
760	A111	15fr gold & multi	.65 .25
761	A111	20fr gold & multi	.65 .25
762	A111	30fr gold & multi	.65 .25
763	A111	50fr gold & multi	1.10 .25
	Nos. 760-763,C141-C142 (6)		6.80 1.55

Christmas.

No. 715 Overprinted

No. C123 Surcharged

No. 714 Surcharged

1971, Jan. 9   Photo.   Perf. 14x13½
Nos. 764-766 in memory of Gandhi:
764	A100	30fr multicolored	2.00 .25
765	A100	30fr on 90fr multi	2.00 .25
766	A100	150fr on 20fr multi	8.50 .35
	Nos. 764-766,C143 (4)		24.00 1.45

"Aerienne" obliterated with heavy bar on No. 765.

De Gaulle and Churchill A112

De Gaulle and: 30fr, Dwight D. Eisenhower. 40fr, John F. Kennedy. 50fr, Konrad Adenauer.

1971, Feb. 20   Photo.   Perf. 13x14
767	A112	20fr blk & brt blue	.90 .25
768	A112	30fr blk & crimson	.90 .25
769	A112	40fr blk & dp green	1.40 .25
770	A112	50fr blk & brown	1.60 .25
	Nos. 767-770,C144-C145 (6)		10.00 1.50

Nos. 764-770 issued in memory of Charles de Gaulle (1890-1970), President of France.

Resurrection, by Raphael — A113

Easter: 30fr, Resurrection, by Master of Trebon. 40fr, like 1fr.

1971, Apr. 10   Litho.   Perf. 10½x11½
771	A113	1fr gold & multi	.50 .25
772	A113	30fr gold & multi	.50 .25
773	A113	40fr gold & multi	.50 .25
	Nos. 771-773,C146-C148 (6)		5.20 1.55

Cmdr. Alan B. Shepard, Jr. — A114

Designs: 10fr, Edgar D. Mitchell and astronaut on moon. 30fr, Stuart A. Roosa, module on moon. 40fr, Take-off from moon, and spaceship.

1971, May   Litho.   Perf. 12½
774	A114	1fr blue & multi	.40 .25
775	A114	10fr green & multi	.40 .25
776	A114	30fr dull red & multi	.40 .25
777	A114	40fr dk green & multi	.45 .25
	Nos. 774-777,C149-C151 (7)		5.90 2.55

Apollo 14 moon landing, Jan. 31-Feb. 9.
For overprints see Nos. 788, C162-C164.

Cacao Tree and Pods — A115

Designs: 40fr, Sorting and separating beans and pods. 50fr, Drying cacao beans.

1971, June 6   Litho.   Perf. 14
778	A115	30fr multicolored	.40 .25
779	A115	40fr ultra & multi	.60 .25
780	A115	50fr multicolored	.75 .25
	Nos. 778-780,C152-C154 (6)		4.85 1.85

International Cacao Day, June 6.

Napoleon, Death Sesquicentennial — A115a

Die Cut Perf. 12

1971, June 11   Embossed
780A	A115a	1000fr gold	37.50 37.50
b.		Sheet of 1, imperf.	27.50 27.50

No. 780Ab contains one 48x69mm stamp.

Control Tower and Plane — A116

1971, June 26   Litho.   Perf. 14
781	A116	30fr multicolored	1.00 .25

10th anniv. of the Agency for the Security of Aerial Navigation in Africa and Madagascar (ASECNA). See No. C155.

Great Market, Lomé — A117

Tourist publicity: 30fr, Bird-of-paradise flower and sculpture of a man. 40fr, Aledjo Gorge and anubius baboon.

1971, July 17
782	A117	20fr multicolored	.35 .25
783	A117	30fr multicolored	.55 .25
784	A117	40fr multicolored	.85 .25
	Nos. 782-784,C156-C158 (6)		4.05 1.65

For surcharge and overprint see Nos. 804, C172.

Great Fetish of Gbatchoume — A118

Religions of Togo: 30fr, Chief Priest in front of Atta Sakuma Temple. 40fr, Annual ceremony of the sacred stone.

1971, July 31   Litho.   Perf. 14½
785	A118	20fr multicolored	.30 .25
786	A118	30fr multicolored	.40 .25
787	A118	40fr multicolored	.70 .25
	Nos. 785-787,C159-C161 (6)		3.65 1.50

No. 777 Overprinted in Silver "EN MEMOIRE / DOBROVOLSKY — VOLKOV — PATSAYEV / SOYUZ 11"

1971, Aug.   Perf. 12½
788	A114	40fr multicolored	1.10 .25
	Nos. 788,C162-C164 (4)		5.40 1.65

Russian astronauts Lt. Col. Georgi T. Dobrovolsky, Vladislav N. Volkov and Victor I. Patsayev, who died during the Soyuz 11 space mission, June 6-30, 1971.

Sapporo '72 Emblem and Speed Skating — A119

Sapporo '72 Emblem and: 10fr, Slalom skiing. 20fr, Figure skating, pairs. 30fr, Bobsledding. 50fr, Ice hockey.

1971, Oct. 30   Perf. 14
789	A119	1fr multicolored	.25 .25
790	A119	10fr multicolored	.25 .25
791	A119	20fr multicolored	.35 .25
792	A119	30fr multicolored	.50 .25
793	A119	50fr multicolored	1.00 .25
	Nos. 789-793,C165 (6)		4.45 1.75

11th Winter Olympic Games, Sapporo, Japan, Feb. 3-13, 1972.

Toy Crocodile and UNICEF
Emblem — A120

Toys and UNICEF Emblem: 30fr, Fawn and
butterfly. 40fr, Monkey. 50fr, Elephants.

1971, Nov. 27
794 A120 20fr multicolored .35 .25
795 A120 30fr violet & multi .35 .25
796 A120 40fr green & multi .45 .25
797 A120 50fr bister & multi .65 .25
　Nos. 794-797,C167-C168 (6) 3.20 1.50
　　UNICEF, 25th anniv.
For overprints see Nos. 918, C263-C264.

Virgin and
Child, by
Botticelli
A121

Virgin and Child by: 30fr, Master of the Life
of Mary. 40fr, Dürer. 50fr, Veronese.

1971, Dec. 24　　　Perf. 14x13
798 A121 10fr purple & multi .25 .25
799 A121 30fr green & multi .40 .25
800 A121 40fr brown & multi .85 .25
801 A121 50fr dk blue & multi .95 .25
　Nos. 798-801,C169-C170 (6) 5.20 1.80
　　Christmas.

St. Mark's Basilica — A122

Design: 40fr, Rialto Bridge.

1972, Feb. 26　Litho.　　Perf. 14
802 A122 30fr multicolored .90 .25
803 A122 40fr multicolored 1.40 .25
　Nos. 802-803,C171 (3) 4.05 1.05
　　UNESCO campaign to save Venice.

No. 784 Surcharged

1972, Mar.　Litho.　　Perf. 14
804 A117 300fr on 40fr multi 3.25 1.60
　Visit of Pres. Richard M. Nixon to the People's Republic of China, Feb. 20-27.
See No. C172.

Easter
A123

Paintings: 25s, Crucifixion, by Master MS.
30fr, Pietà, by Botticelli. 40fr, Like 25fr.

1972, Mar. 31
805 A123 25fr gold & multi .60 .25
806 A123 30fr gold & multi .95 .25
807 A123 40fr gold & multi 1.20 .25
　Nos. 805-807,C173-C174 (5) 5.95 1.25

Heart, Smith, WHO
Emblem — A124

Heart, WHO Emblem and: 40fr, Typist. 60fr,
Athlete with javelin.

1972, Apr. 4
808 A124 30fr multicolored .50 .25
809 A124 40fr multicolored .55 .25
810 A124 60fr multicolored .90 .25
　Nos. 808-810,C175 (4) 3.20 1.20
　"Your heart is your health," World Health
Day.

Org. of African and Malagasy Union
Conf. — A124a

Die Cut Perf. 12x12½
1972, Apr. 24　Litho. & Embossed
Self-adhesive
810A A124a 1000fr gold, red &
　　grn 9.00 9.00
On No. 810A embossing may cut through
stamp and embossed backing paper may not
adhere well to the unused stamps.
　For overprint see No. 893A.

Video
Telephone — A125

1972, June 24　Litho.　　Perf. 14
811 A125 40fr violet & multi 1.00 .25
　4th World Telecommunications Day. See
No. C176.
For overprints see Nos. 880, C229.

Cassava Production — A126

25fr, Cassava collection by truck, horiz. 40fr,
Grating Cassava.

1972, June 30
812 A126 25fr yellow & multi .45 .25
813 A126 40fr multicolored .60 .25
　Nos. 812-813,C177-C178 (4) 3.40 1.00
For overprint & surcharge see #866-867.

Basketball
A127

1972, Aug. 26　Litho.　　Perf. 14
814 A127 30fr shown .40 .25
815 A127 40fr Running .65 .25
816 A127 50fr Discus .85 .25
　Nos. 814-816,C180-C181 (5) 4.30 1.90
　20th Olympic Games, Munich, 8/26-9/11.
See Nos. C180-C181. For overprints see
Nos. C234-C235.

Pin-tailed
Whydah — A128

Birds: 30fr, Broad-tailed widowbird. 40fr,
Yellow-shouldered widowbird. 60fr, Yellow-
tailed widowbird.

1972, Sept. 9
817 A128 25fr citron & multi .55 .25
818 A128 30fr lt blue & multi .75 .25
819 A128 40fr multicolored 1.10 .25
820 A128 60fr lt green & multi 2.10 .25
　Nos. 817-820,C182 (5) 7.25 1.45

Paul P. Harris,
Rotary
Emblem — A129

50fr, Flags of Togo and Rotary Club.

1972, Oct. 7　Litho.　　Perf. 14
821 A129 40fr green & multi .40 .25
822 A129 50fr multicolored .45 .25
　a.　Souvenir sheet of 2 2.10 1.25
　Nos. 821-822,C183-C185 (5) 3.65 1.60
　Rotary International, Lomé. No. 822a contains 2 stamps with simulated perforations
similar to Nos. 821-822.
　For overprints see Nos. 862, 898, C212-
C213, C244-C235.

Mona Lisa,
by
Leonardo
da Vinci
A130

40fr, Virgin and Child, by Giovanni Bellini.

1972, Oct. 21
823 A130 25fr gold & multi 1.50 .25
824 A130 40fr gold & multi 1.60 .25
　Nos. 823-824,C186-C188 (5) 8.50 1.50

West African Monetary Union Issue
Common Design Type

Design: 40fr, African couple, city, village
and commemorative coin.

1972, Nov. 2　Engr.　　Perf. 13
825 CD136 40fr red brn, rose red
　　& gray .60 .25

Presidents Pompidou and Eyadema,
Party Headquarters — A131

1972, Nov. 23　Litho.　　Perf. 14
826 A131 40fr purple & multi 1.60 .25
　Visit of Pres. Georges Pompidou of France
to Togo, Nov. 1972. See No. C189.

Christmas
A132

Paintings: 25fr, Anunciation, Painter
Unknown. 30fr, Nativity, Master of
Vyshchibrod. 40fr, Like 25fr.

1972, Dec. 23
827 A132 25fr gold & multi .40 .25
828 A132 30fr gold & multi .65 .25
829 A132 40fr gold & multi 1.00 .25
　Nos. 827-829,C191-C193 (6) 5.65 1.80

Raoul Folureau and Lepers — A133

1973, Jan. 23　Photo.　　Perf. 14x13½
830 A133 40fr violet & green 1.75 .25
　World Leprosy Day and 20th anniv. of the
Raoul Folureau Foundation. See No. C194.

WHO
Emblem — A134

1973, Apr. 7   Photo.   Perf. 14x13
831 A134 30fr blue & multi   .50 .25
832 A134 40fr dp yellow & multi   .65 .25
WHO, 25th anniv.

Christ on the
Cross — A135

1973, Apr. 21   Litho.   Perf. 14
833 A135 25fr shown   .50 .25
834 A135 30fr Pietá   .50 .25
835 A135 40fr Ascension   .60 .25
    Nos. 833-835,C195 (4)   3.00 1.15
Easter.

Eugene Cernan, Ronald Evans,
Harrison Schmitt, Apollo 17
Badge — A136

Design: 40fr, Lunar rover on moon.

1973, June 2   Litho.   Perf. 14
836 A136 30fr multicolored   .50 .25
837 A136 40fr multicolored   .60 .25
    Nos. 836-837,C196-C197 (4)   5.95 1.60
Apollo 17 moon mission, Dec. 7-19, 1972.

Scouts Pitching
Tent — A137

20fr, Campfire, horiz. 30fr, Rope climbing.

1973, June 30
838 A137 10fr multicolored   .25 .25
839 A137 20fr multicolored   .40 .25
840 A137 30fr violet & multi   .65 .25
841 A137 40fr ocher & multi   .90 .25
    Nos. 838-841,C198-C199 (6)   5.95 2.15
24th Boy Scout World Conference (1st in
Africa), Nairobi, Kenya, July 16-21.
For overprints see Nos. C265-C266.

Nicolaus
Copernicus, 500th
Anniv.
Birth — A138

Designs: 10fr, Heliocentric system. 20fr,
Nicolaus Copernicus. 30fr, Seated figure of
Astronomy and spacecrafts around earth and
moon. 40fr, Astrolabe.

1973, July 18
842 A138 10fr multicolored   .25 .25
843 A138 20fr multicolored   .40 .25
844 A138 30fr multicolored   .85 .25
845 A138 40fr lilac & multi   1.10 .25
    Nos. 842-845,C200-C201 (6)   6.10 1.80

Red Cross
Ambulance
Crew — A139

1973, Aug. 4
846 A139 40fr multicolored   1.40 .25
Togolese Red Cross. See No. C202.
For overprints see Nos. 942, C294.

Teacher and Students — A140

40fr, Hut and man reading under tree, vert.

1973, Aug. 18   Litho.   Perf. 14
847 A140 30fr multicolored   .50 .25
848 A140 40fr multicolored   .65 .25
    Nos. 847-848,C203 (3)   2.65 .85
Literacy campaign.

African Postal Union Issue
Common Design Type

1973, Sept. 12   Engr.   Perf. 13
849 CD137 100fr yel, red & claret 1.00 .35

INTERPOL
Emblem and
Headquarters
A141

1973, Sept. 29   Photo.   Perf. 13½x14
850 A141 30fr yel, brn & gray grn   .55 .25
851 A141 40fr yel grn, bl & mag   .65 .25
50th anniv. of Intl. Criminal Police Org.

Weather Vane and
WMO
Emblem — A142

1973, Oct. 4   Perf. 14x13
852 A142 40fr yel, dp brn & grn   1.00 .25
Intl. meteorological cooperation, cent. See
No. C204.

Type of 1967

Designs: 25fr, Old and new locomotives,
No. 795. 30fr, Mail coach and bus, No. 613.
90fr, Mail boat and ship, Nos. C61 and 469.

1973, Oct. 20   Photo.   Perf. 14x13
853 A79 25fr multicolored   .60 .25
854 A79 30fr purple & green   .80 .25
855 A79 90fr dk blue & multi   2.10 .35
    Nos. 853-855,C205 (4)   6.00 1.20
Togolese postal service, 75th anniv.

John F. Kennedy
and Adolf
Schaerf — A143

Designs: 30fr, Kennedy and Harold MacMil-
lan. 40fr, Kennedy and Konrad Adenauer.

1973, Nov. 22   Litho.   Perf. 14
856 A143 20fr blk, gray & vio   .55 .25
857 A143 30fr blk, rose & brn   .55 .25
858 A143 40fr blk, lt grn & grn   .65 .25
    Nos. 856-858,C206-C208 (6)   9.10 2.55
John F. Kennedy (1917-1963).

**No. 758 Surcharged with New Value,
2 Bars and Overprinted in
Ultramarine: "SECHERESSE
SOLIDARITE AFRICAINE"**

1973, Dec.   Photo.   Perf. 13x14
859 A110 100fr on 30fr multi   1.40 .50
African solidarity in drought emergency.

Virgin and Child,
Italy, 15th
Century — A144

30fr, Adoration of the Kings, Italy, 15th cent.

1973, Dec. 22   Litho.   Perf. 14
860 A144 25fr gold & multi   .60 .25
861 A144 30fr gold & multi   .70 .25
    Nos. 860-861,C210-C211 (4)   3.90 1.30
Christmas.

**No. 821 Overprinted: "PREMIERE
CONVENTION / 210eme DISTRICT /
FEVRIER 1974 / LOME"**

1974, Feb. 21   Litho.   Perf. 14
862 A129 40fr green & multi   .40 .25
    Nos. 862,C212-C213 (3)   2.05 .85
First convention of Rotary Intl., District 210,
Lomé, Feb. 22-24.

Soccer and
Games'
Cup
A145

Various soccer scenes and games' cup.

1974, Mar. 2   Litho.   Perf. 14
863 A145 20fr lt blue & multi   .35 .25
864 A145 30fr yellow & multi   .50 .25
865 A145 40fr lilac & multi   .55 .25
    Nos. 863-865,C214-C216 (6)   5.30 2.65
World Soccer Championships, Munich, Germany, June 13-July 7.

**Nos. 812-813 Overprinted and
Surcharged: "10e ANNIVERSAIRE
DU P.A.M."**

1974, Mar. 25   Litho.   Perf. 14
866 A126 40fr multicolored   .65 .25
867 A126 100fr on 25fr multi   1.40 .50
10th anniv. of World Food Program. Overprint on No. 866 is in one line; 2 lines on No.
867 and 2 bars through old denomination.

Girl Before Mirror,
by
Picasso — A146

Paintings by Picasso: 30fr, The Turkish
Shawl. 40fr, Mandolin and Guitar.

1974, Apr. 6
868 A146 20fr vio blue & multi   .40 .25
869 A146 30fr maroon & multi   .65 .25
870 A146 40fr multicolored   .85 .25
    Nos. 868-870,C217-C219 (6)   9.50 2.45
Pablo Picasso (1881-1973), Spanish painter.

Kpeme
Village and
Wharf
A147

Design: 40fr, Tropicana tourist village.

1974, Apr. 20
871 A147 30fr multicolored   .45 .25
872 A147 40fr multicolored   .45 .25
    Nos. 871-872,C220-C221 (4)   3.25 1.10

Mailman, UPU
Emblem — A148

Design: 40fr, Mailman, different uniform.

1974, May 10   Litho.   Perf. 14
873 A148 30fr salmon & multi   .45 .25
874 A148 40fr multicolored   .50 .25
    Nos. 873-874,C222-C223 (4)   2.90 1.10
UPU, centenary.

Map and Flags of Members — A148a

1974, May 29   Litho.   Perf. 13x12½
875   A148a 40fr blue & multi   .60 .25
15th anniversary of the Council of Accord.

Fisherman with Net A149

40fr, Fisherman casting net from canoe.

1974, June 22   Litho.   Perf. 14
876   A149 30fr multicolored   .55 .25
877   A149 40fr multicolored   .65 .25
   Nos. 876-877,C224-C226 (5)   5.70 1.65
Lagoon fishing.

Pioneer Communicating with Earth — A150

30fr, Radar station and satellite, vert.

1974, July 6   Perf. 14
878   A150 30fr multicolored   .35 .25
879   A150 40fr multicolored   .40 .25
   Nos. 878-879,C227-C228 (4)   3.65 1.50
US Jupiter space probe.

**No. 811 Overprinted with
INTERNABA Emblem in Silver
Similar to No. C229**

1974, July
880   A125 40fr multicolored   3.00 .55
   INTERNABA 1974 Intl. Philatelic Exhibition,
Basel, June 7-16. See No. C229.
   No. 880 exists overprint in black. Value,
unused $10.

Tympanotomus Radula — A151

Designs: Seashells.

1974, July 13   Litho.   Perf. 14
881   A151 10fr shown   .85 .25
882   A151 20fr Tonna galea   .85 .25
883   A151 30fr Conus mercator   1.00 .25
884   A151 40fr Cardium cos-
              tatum   1.40 .25
   Nos. 881-884,C230-C231 (6)   8.10 1.70

Groom with Horses A152

Design: 40fr, Trotting horses.

1974, Aug. 3   Litho.   Perf. 14
885   A152 30fr multicolored   .90 .25
886   A152 40fr multicolored   1.10 .25
   Nos. 885-886,C232-C233 (4)   6.50 1.20
Horse racing.

Leopard A153

1974, Sept. 7   Litho.   Perf. 14
887   A153 20fr shown   .70 .25
888   A153 30fr Giraffes   .70 .25
889   A153 40fr Elephants   .95 .25
   Nos. 887-889,C236-C237 (5)   6.70 1.50
Wild animals of West Africa.

1974, Oct. 14
890   A153 30fr Herding cattle   .40 .25
891   A153 40fr Milking cow   .55 .25
   Nos. 890-891,C238-C239 (4)   3.30 1.10
Domestic animals.

Churchill and Frigate F390 A154

Design: 40fr, Churchill and fighter planes.

1974, Nov. 1   Photo.   Perf. 13x13½
892   A154 30fr multicolored   .55 .25
893   A154 40fr multicolored   .70 .25
   Nos. 892-893,C240-C241 (4)   5.25 1.55
Winston Churchill (1874-1965).

**No. 810A Ovptd. "Inauguration de
l'hotel de la Paix 9-1-75"
Litho. & Embossed**

1975, Jan. 9   Perf. 12½
Self-adhesive
893A A124a 1000fr gold, red &
             grn   10.00 10.00
   On No. 893A embossing may cut through
stamp and embossed backing paper may not
adhere well to the unused stamps.

Chlamydocarya Macrocarpa — A155

Flowers of Togo: 25fr, Strelitzia reginae,
vert. 30fr, Storphanthus sarmentosus, vert.
60fr, Clerodendrum scandens.

1975, Feb. 15   Litho.   Perf. 14
894   A155 25fr multicolored   .35 .25
895   A155 30fr multicolored   .50 .25
896   A155 40fr multicolored   .80 .25
897   A155 60fr multicolored   1.10 .25
   Nos. 894-897,C242-C243 (6)   7.25 1.80

**No. 821 Overprinted: "70e
ANNIVERSAIRE / 23 FEVRIER 1975"**

1975, Feb. 23   Litho.   Perf. 14
898   A129 40fr green & multi   .55 .25
   Nos. 898,C244-C245 (3)   2.45 .85
Rotary Intl., 70th anniv.

Radio Station, Kamina A156

30fr, Benedictine Monastery, Zogbegan.
40fr, Causeway, Atchinedji. 60fr, Ayome
Waterfalls.

1975, Mar. 1   Photo.   Perf. 13x14
899   A156 25fr multicolored   .35 .25
900   A156 30fr multicolored   .35 .25
901   A156 40fr multicolored   .45 .25
902   A156 60fr multicolored   .65 .25
   Nos. 899-902 (4)   1.80 1.00

Jesus Mocked, by El Greco — A157

Paintings: 30fr, Crucifixion, by Master
Janoslet. 40fr, Descent from the Cross, by
Bellini. 90fr, Pietà, painter unknown.

1975, Apr. 19   Litho.   Perf. 14
903   A157 25fr black & multi   .35 .25
904   A157 30fr black & multi   .45 .25
905   A157 40fr black & multi   .55 .25
906   A157 90fr black & multi   1.10 .30
   Nos. 903-906,C246-C247 (6)   5.45 1.85
Easter.

Stilt Walking, Togolese Flag A158

Design: 30fr, Flag and dancers.

1975, Apr. 26   Litho.   Perf. 14
907   A158 25fr multicolored   .40 .25
908   A158 30fr multicolored   .40 .25
   Nos. 907-908,C248-C249 (4)   2.00 1.00
15th anniv. of independence.

Rabbit Hunter with Club A159

40fr, Beaver hunter with bow and arrow.

1975, May 24   Photo.   Perf. 13x13½
909   A159 30fr multicolored   .75 .25
910   A159 40fr multicolored   .95 .25
   Nos. 909-910,C250-C251 (4)   5.55 1.10

Pounding Palm Nuts A160

Design: 40fr, Man extracting palm oil, vert.

1975, June 28   Litho.   Perf. 14
911   A160 30fr multicolored   .95 .25
912   A160 40fr multicolored   .95 .25
   Nos. 911-912,C252-C253 (4)   5.65 1.50
Palm oil production.

Apollo-Soyuz Link-up — A161

1975, July 15
913   A161 30fr multicolored   .40 .25
   Nos. 913,C254-C258 (6)   5.80 1.85
Apollo Soyuz space test project (Russo-
American cooperation), launching July 15;
link-up July 17.

Women's Heads, IWY Emblem — A162

1975, July 26   Litho.   Perf. 12½
914   A162 30fr blue & multi   .50 .25
915   A162 40fr multicolored   .60 .25
International Women's Year.

Dr. Schweitzer and Children — A163

1975, Aug. 23   Litho.   Perf. 14x13½
916   A163 40fr multicolored   .75 .25
   Nos. 916,C259-C261 (4)   4.50 1.30
Dr. Albert Schweitzer (1875-1965), medical
missionary and musician.

Merchant Writing Letter, by Vittore Carpaccio A164

1975, Oct. 9   Litho.   Perf. 14
917   A164 40fr multicolored   .60 .25
Intl. Letter Writing Week. See No. C262.

**No. 797 Overprinted: "30ème
Anniversaire / des Nations-Unies"**

1975, Oct. 24   Litho.   Perf. 14
918   A120 50fr multi   .50 .25
   Nos. 918,C263-C264 (3)   1.85 .75
UN, 30th anniv.

Virgin and Child, by Mantegna A165

Paintings of the Virgin and Child: 30fr, El
Greco. 40fr, Barend van Orley.

1975, Dec. 20   Litho.   Perf. 14
919   A165 20fr red & multi   .35 .25
920   A165 30fr bl & multi   .40 .25
921   A165 40fr red & multi   .50 .25
   Nos. 919-921,C267-C269 (6)   4.70 1.75
Christmas.

Crashed Plane and Pres. Eyadema A166

1976, Jan. 24   Photo.   *Perf. 13*
922 A166 50fr multi   11.00 .45
923 A166 60fr multi   26.00 .50

Airplane crash at Sara-kawa, Jan. 24, 1974, in which Pres. Eyadema escaped injury.

1976 Summer Olympics, Montreal — A166a

Litho. & Embossed
1976, Feb. 24   *Perf. 11*
923A A166a 1000fr Diving   15.00 —
923B A166a 1000fr Track   15.00 —
923C A166a 1000fr Pole vault 15.00 —
923D A166a 1000fr Equestrian 15.00 —
923E A166a 1000fr Cycling   15.00 —
    Nos. 923A-923E (5)   75.00

Exist imperf.

Frigates on the Hudson — A167

American Bicentennial: 50fr, George Washington, by Gilbert Stuart, and Bicentennial emblem, vert.

1976, Mar. 3   Litho.   *Perf. 14*
924 A167 35fr multicolored   .45 .25
925 A167 50fr multicolored   .65 .25
    Nos. 924-925,C270-C273 (6) 5.50 1.80

For overprints see Nos. C280-C283.

ACP and CEE Emblems A168

50fr, Map of Africa, Europe and Asia.

1976, Apr. 24   Photo.   *Perf. 13x14*
926 A168 10fr orange & multi   .30 .25
927 A168 50fr pink & multi   .50 .30
    Nos. 926-927,C274-C275 (4) 2.00 1.05

First anniv. of signing of treaty between Togo and European Common Market, Lomé, Feb. 28, 1975.

Cable-laying Ship — A169

30fr, Telephone, tape recorder, speaker.

1976, Mar. 10   Photo.   *Perf. 13x14*
928 A169 25fr ultra & multi   .25 .25
929 A169 30fr pink & multi   .35 .25
    Nos. 928-929,C276-C277 (4) 1.70 1.15

Centenary of first telephone call by Alexander Graham Bell, Mar. 10, 1876.

Blind Man and Insect — A170

1976, Apr. 8   *Perf. 14x13*
930 A170 50fr brt grn & multi   .75 .25

World Health Day: "Foresight prevents blindness." See No. C278.

Air Post Type, 1976, and

Marine Exhibition Hall — A171

10fr, Pylon, flags of Ghana, Togo and Dahomey.

1976   Litho.   *Perf. 14*
931 A171   5fr multicolored   .25 .25
932 AP19 10fr multicolored   .50 .25
933 A171 50fr multicolored   .70 .45
    Nos. 931-933,C279 (4)   2.45 1.20

Marine Exhibition, 10th anniv. (5fr, 50fr). Ghana-Togo-Dahomey electric power grid, 1st anniversary (10fr).
Issue dates: 50fr, May 8; 5fr, 10fr, August.

Running — A172

Montreal Olympic Emblem and: 30fr, Kayak. 50fr, High jump.

1976, June 15   Photo.   *Perf. 14x13*
934 A1/2 25fr multicolored   .30 .25
935 A172 30fr multicolored   .30 .25
936 A172 50fr multicolored   .45 .25
    Nos. 934-936,C284-C286 (6) 4.10 2.05

21st Olympic Games, Montreal, Canada, July 17-Aug. 1.
For overprints see Nos. 947, C298-C299.

Titan 3 and Viking Emblem — A173

50fr, Viking trajectory, Earth to Mars.

1976, July 15   Litho.   *Perf. 14*
937 A173 30fr blue & multi   .35 .25
938 A173 50fr rose & multi   .50 .25
    Nos. 937-938,C287-C290 (6) 4.70 2.00

US Viking Mars missions.

Young Routy at Celeyran, by Toulouse-Lautrec A174

Paintings by Toulouse-Lautrec: 20fr, Model in Studio. 35fr, Louis Pascal, portrait.

1976, Aug. 7   Litho.   *Perf. 14*
939 A174 10fr black & multi   .25 .25
940 A174 20fr black & multi   .50 .25
941 A174 35fr black & multi   .65 .25
    Nos. 939-941,C291-C293 (6) 5.80 1.80

Henri Toulouse-Lautrec (1864-1901), French painter, 75th death anniversary.

No. 846 Overprinted: "Journée / Internationale / de l'Enfance"
1976, Nov. 27   Litho.   *Perf. 14*
942 A139 40fr multi   .40 .25

Intl. Children's Day. See No. C294.

Adoration of the Shepherds, by Pontormo — A175

Paintings: 30fr, Nativity, by Carlo Crivelli. 50fr, Virgin and Child, by Jacopo da Pontormo.

1976, Dec. 18
943 A175 25fr multi   .35 .25
944 A175 30fr multi   .50 .25
945 A175 50fr multi   .85 .25
    Nos. 943-945,C295-C297 (6) 5.10 2.35

Christmas.

Mohammed Ali Jinnah, Flags of Togo and Pakistan — A176

1976, Dec. 24   Litho.   *Perf. 13*
946 A176 50fr multi   .60 .25

Jinnah (1876-1948), first Governor General of Pakistan.

No. 936 Overprinted: "CHAMPIONS OLYMPIQUES / SAUT EN HAUTEUR / POLOGNE"
1976, Dec.   Photo.   *Perf. 14x13*
947 A172 50fr multi   .55 .25
    Nos. 947,C298-C299 (3) 2.95 1.15

Olympic winners.

Queen Elizabeth II, Silver Jubilee — A176a

Designs: No. 947A, Portrait. No. 947B, Wearing coronation regalia.

Litho. & Embossed
1977, Jan. 10   *Perf. 11*
947A A176a 1000fr silver & multi   7.00
Souvenir Sheet
947B A176a 1000fr silver & multi   8.50

Exist imperf.

Kpeme Phosphate Mine, Sara-kawa Crash A177

1977, Jan. 13   Photo.   *Perf. 13x14*
948 A177 50fr multi   .55 .25
    Nos. 948,C300-C301 (3) 1.95 .85

Presidency of Etienne Eyadema, 10th anniv.

Musical Instruments A178

1977, Feb. 7   Litho.   *Perf. 14*
949 A178   5fr Gongophone   .25 .25
950 A178 10fr Tamtam, vert.   .25 .25
951 A178 25fr Dondon   .60 .25
    Nos. 949-951,C302-C304 (6) 4.40 1.55

Victor Hugo and his Home A179

1977, Feb. 26   *Perf. 13x14*
952 A179 50fr multi   .65 .25

Victor Hugo (1802-1885), French writer, 175th birth anniversary. See No. C305.
For overprints see Nos. 959, C316.

Beethoven and Birthplace, Bonn A180

50fr, Bronze bust, 1812, & Heiligenstadt home.

1977, Mar. 7   *Perf. 14*
953 A180 30fr multi   .50 .25
954 A180 50fr multi   .75 .25
    Nos. 953-954,C306-C307 (4) 4.60 1.45

Benz, 1894, Germany — A181

Early Automobiles: 50fr, De Dion Bouton, 1903, France.

1977, Apr. 11   Litho.   *Perf. 14*
955 A181 35fr multi   .65 .25
956 A181 50fr multi   .90 .25
    Nos. 955-956,C308-C311 (6) 6.05 2.10

Lindbergh, Ground Crew and Spirit of
St. Louis — A182

50fr, Lindbergh and Spirit of St. Louis.

1977, May 9
957 A182 25fr multi   .35 .25
958 A182 50fr multi   .70 .25
Nos. 957-958,C312-C315 (6)   4.15 1.55
Charles A. Lindbergh's solo transatlantic
flight from New York to Paris, 50th anniv.

**No. 952 Overprinted: "10ème
ANNIVERSAIRE DU / CONSEIL
INTERNATIONAL / DE LA LANGUE
FRANCAISE"**

1977, May 17   Litho.   Perf. 14
959 A179 50fr multi   .70 .25
Intl. French Language Council, 10th anniv.
See No. C316.

African Slender-snouted
Crocodile — A183

Endangered wildlife: 15fr, Nile crocodile.

1977, June 13
960 A183 5fr multi   .35 .25
961 A183 15fr multi   .35 .25
Nos. 960-961,C317-C320 (6)   5.90 1.60

Agriculture
School,
Tove
A184

1977, July 11   Litho.   Perf. 14
962 A184 50fr multi   .50 .25
Nos. 962,C321-C323 (4)   3.60 1.20
Agricultural development.

Landscape with Cart, by Peter Paul
Rubens (1577-1640) — A185

Rubens Painting: 35fr, Exchange of the
Princesses at Hendaye, 1623.

1977, Aug. 8
963 A185 15fr multi   .45 .25
964 A185 35fr multi   .60 .25
Nos. 963-964,C324-C325 (4)   3.35 1.00

Orbiter 101 on Ground — A186

Designs: 30fr, Launching of Orbiter, vert.
50fr, Ejection of propellant tanks at take-off.

1977, Oct. 4   Litho.   Perf. 14
965 A186 20fr multi   .30 .25
966 A186 30fr multi   .40 .25
967 A186 50fr multi   .50 .25
Nos. 965-967,C326-C328 (6)   4.50 1.60
Space shuttle trials in the US.

Lafayette
Arriving in
Montpelier,
Vt. — A187

Design: 25fr, Lafayette, age 19, vert.

1977, Nov. 7   Perf. 14x13, 13x14
968 A187 25fr multi   .35 .25
969 A187 50fr multi   .60 .25
Nos. 968-969,C329-C330 (4)   2.70 1.00
Arrival of the Marquis de Lafayette in North
America, 200th anniv.

Lenin,
Cruiser
Aurora,
Red Flag
A188

1977, Nov. 7   Litho.   Perf. 12
970 A188 50fr multi   1.20 .25
Russian October Revolution, 60th anniv.

Virgin and Child,
by Lorenzo
Lotto — A189

Virgin and Child by: 30fr, Carlo Crivelli. 50fr,
Cosimo Tura.

1977, Dec. 19   Perf. 14
971 A189 20fr multi   .25 .25
972 A189 30fr multi   .35 .25
973 A189 50fr multi   .50 .25
Nos. 971-973,C331-C333 (6)   4.20 1.65
Christmas.

Edward
Jenner — A190

Design: 20fr, Vaccination clinic, horiz.

Perf. 14x13, 13x14
1978, Jan. 9   Litho.
974 A190 5fr multi   .25 .25
975 A190 20fr multi   .25 .25
Nos. 974-975,C334-C335 (4)   1.25 1.00
Worldwide eradication of smallpox.

Orville and Wilbur Wright — A191

Design: 50fr, Wilbur Wright flying at Kill
Devil Hill, 1902.

1978, Feb. 6   Litho.   Perf. 14
976 A191 35fr multi   .40 .25
977 A191 50fr multi   .55 .25
Nos. 976-977,C336-C339 (6)   6.55 1.95
75th anniversary of first motorized flight.

Anniversaries and Events — A192

Designs: No. 978, High jump. No. 979,
Westminster Abbey. No. 980, Soccer players,
World Cup. No. 981, Apollo 8. No. 982, Duke
of Wellington, by Goya. No. 983, Hurdles. No.
984, Coronation coach. No. 985, Soccer players. No. 986, Apollo launch. No. 987, Dona
Isabel Cobos de Porcel, by Goya.

1978, Mar. 13   Litho.   Perf. 11
978 A192 1000fr gold & multi   9.00
979 A192 1000fr gold & multi   9.00
980 A192 1000fr gold & multi   9.00
981 A192 1000fr gold & multi   9.00
982 A192 1000fr gold & multi   9.00
Souvenir Sheets
983 A192 1000fr gold & multi   12.00
984 A192 1000fr gold & multi   12.00
985 A192 1000fr gold & multi   12.00
986 A192 1000fr gold & multi   12.00
987 A192 1000fr gold & multi   12.00
Nos. 978, 983, 1980 Summer Olympics,
Moscow. Nos. 979, 984, Coronation of Queen
Elizabeth II, 25th anniv. Nos. 980, 985, 1978
World Cup Soccer Championships, Argentina.
Nos. 981, 986, 1st manned lunar orbit, 10th
anniv. Nos. 982, 987, Death sesquicent. of
Francisco Goya.
For overprints see Nos. 1056A-1056B,
1094A-1094B.
Exist imperf.

John, the Evangelist
and Eagle — A197

Evangelists: 10fr, Luke and ox. 25fr, Mark
and lion. 30fr, Matthew and angel.

1978, Mar. 20   Litho.   Perf. 13½x14
988 A197 5fr multi   .25 .25
989 A197 10fr multi   .25 .25
990 A197 25fr multi   .25 .25
991 A197 30fr multi   .35 .25
a.   Souvenir sheet of 4   1.25 .60
Nos. 988-991 (4)   1.10 1.00
No. 991a contains one each of Nos. 988-
991 with simulated perforations.

Anchor,
Fishing
Harbor,
Lomé
A199

1978, Apr. 26   Photo.   Perf. 13
997 A199 25fr multi   .25 .25
Nos. 997,C340-C342 (4)   3.05 1.15

Venera I,
USSR — A200

Designs: 30fr, Pioneer, US, horiz. 50fr,
Venera, fuel base and antenna.

1978, May 8   Litho.   Perf. 14
998 A200 20fr multi   .25 .25
999 A200 30fr multi   .30 .25
1000 A200 40fr multi   .40 .25
Nos. 998-1000,C343-C345 (6)   3.90 1.60
US Pioneer and USSR Venera space
missions.

Soccer — A201

50fr, Soccer players and Argentina '78
emblem.

1978, June 5   Perf. 14
1001 A201 30fr multi   .30 .25
1002 A201 50fr multi   .45 .25
Nos. 1001-1002,C346-C349 (6)   5.40 1.95
11th World Cup Soccer Championship,
Argentina, June 1-25.

Celerifère,
1818
A202

History of the Bicycle: 50fr, First bicycle
sidecar, c. 1870, vert.

Perf. 13x14, 14x13
1978, July 10   Photo.
1003 A202 25fr multi   .35 .25
1004 A202 50fr multi   .75 .25
Nos. 1003-1004,C350-C353 (6)   4.25 1.70

Thomas A. Edison,
Sound
Waves — A203

Design: 50fr, Victor's His Master's Voice
phonograph, 1905, and dancing couple.

1978, July 8   Photo.   Perf. 14x13
1005 A203 30fr multicolored   .30 .25
1006 A203 50fr multicolored   .40 .25
Nos. 1005-1006,C354-C357 (6)   5.35 1.85
Centenary of the phonograph, invented by
Thomas Alva Edison.

Dunant's Birthplace, Geneva — A204

Designs: 10fr, Henri Dunant and red cross. 25fr, Help on battlefield, 1864, and red cross.

1978, Sept. 4   Photo.   Perf. 14x13
1007	A204	5fr Prus bl & red	.25 .25
1008	A204	10fr red brn & red	.25 .25
1009	A204	25fr grn & red	.25 .25

Nos. 1007-1009,C358 (4)   1.20 1.00

Dunant (1828-1910), founder of Red Cross.

Threshing, by Raoul Dufy — A205

50fr, Horsemen on Seashore, by Paul Gauguin.

1978, Nov. 6   Litho.   Perf. 14
1010	A205	25fr multi	.30 .25
1011	A205	50fr multi	.50 .25

Nos. 1010-1011,C359-C362 (6)   4.70 2.15

Eiffel Tower, Paris — A206

1978, Nov. 27   Photo.   Perf. 14x13
1012	A206	50fr multi	.60 .25

Nos. 1012,C365-C367 (4)   3.45 1.70

Centenary of the Congress of Paris.

Virgin and Child, by Antonello da Messina — A207

Paintings (Virgin and Child): 30fr, by Carlo Crivelli. 50fr, by Francesco del Cossa.

1978, Dec. 18   Litho.   Perf. 14
1013	A207	20fr multi	.30 .25
1014	A207	30fr multi	.40 .25
1015	A207	50fr multi	.50 .25

Nos. 1013-1015,C368-C370 (6)   4.65 2.20

Christmas.

Capt. Cook's Ship off New Zealand — A208

Design: 50fr, Endeavour in drydock, N.E. Coast of Australia, horiz.

1979, Feb. 12   Litho.   Perf. 14
1016	A208	25fr multi	.25 .25
1017	A208	50fr multi	.45 .25

Nos. 1016-1017,C371-C374 (6)   4.25 2.55

200th death anniv. of Capt. James Cook.

Entry into Jerusalem A209

Easter: 40fr, The Last Supper, horiz. 50fr, Descent from the Cross, horiz.

1979, Apr. 9
1018	A209	30fr multi	.30 .25
1019	A209	40fr multi	.35 .25
1020	A209	50fr multi	.40 .25

Nos. 1018-1020,C375-C377 (6)   3.70 2.10

Einstein Observatory, Potsdam — A210

Design: 50fr, Einstein and James Ramsay MacDonald, Berlin, 1931.

1979, July 2   Photo.   Perf. 14x13
1021	A210	35fr multi	.30 .25
1022	A210	50fr multi	.45 .25

Nos. 1021-1022,C380-C383 (6)   4.65 2.45

Albert Einstein (1879-1955), theoretical physicist.

Children and Children's Village Emblem — A211

IYC: 10fr, Mother and children. 15fr, Map of Africa, Children's Village emblem, horiz. 20fr, Woman and children walking to Children's Village, horiz. 25fr, Children sitting under African fan palm. 30fr, Map of Togo with location of Children's Villages.

1979, July 30   Photo.   Perf. 14x13
1023	A211	5fr multi	.25 .25
1024	A211	10fr multi	.25 .25
1025	A211	15fr multi	.25 .25
1026	A211	20fr multi	.25 .25
1027	A211	25fr multi	.25 .25
1028	A211	30fr multi	.25 .25
a.		Souv. sheet of 2, #1027-1028	.75 .45

Nos. 1023-1028 (6)   1.50 1.50

Man Planting Tree — A212

1979, Aug. 13   Perf. 14x13
1029	A212	50fr lilac & green	.60 .25

Second Arbor Day. See No. C384.

Sir Rowland Hill (1795-1879), Originator of Penny Postage — A213

30fr, French mail-sorting office, 18th cent., horiz. 50fr, Mailbox, Paris, 1850.

1979, Aug. 27
1030	A213	20fr multi	.25 .25
1031	A213	30fr multi	.30 .25
1032	A213	50fr multi	.40 .25

Nos. 1030-1032,C385-C387 (6)   3.80 2.05

Norris Locomotive, 1843 — A214

35fr, Stephenson's "Rocket," 1829, vert.

1979, Oct. 1   Litho.   Perf. 14
1033	A214	35fr multi	.50 .25
1034	A214	50fr multi	.55 .25

Nos. 1033-1034,C388-C391 (6)   4.90 2.60

Olympic Flame, Lake Placid 80 Emblem, Slalom — A215

1980 Olympic Emblems, Olympic Flame and: 30fr, Yachting 50fr, Discus.

1979, Oct. 18   Litho.   Perf. 13½
1035	A215	20fr multi	.25 .25
1036	A215	30fr multi	.25 .25
1037	A215	50fr multi	.55 .25

Nos. 1035-1037,C392-C394 (6)   3.90 2.05

13th Winter Olympic Games, Lake Placid, NY, 2/12-24/80 (90fr); 22nd Summer Olympic Games, Moscow, 7/19-8/3/80.

Catholic Priests A216

Design: 30fr, Native praying, vert.

1979, Oct. 29   Perf. 13x14
1038	A216	30fr multi	.25 .25
1039	A216	50fr multi	.40 .25

Nos. 1038 1039,C396-C397 (4)   1.70 1.05

Religions in Togo.

Astronaut Walking on Moon — A217

Design: 50fr, Space capsule orbiting moon.

1979, Nov. 5
1040	A217	35fr multi	.30 .25
1041	A217	50fr multi	.40 .25

Nos. 1040-1041,C398-C401 (6)   5.25 2.65

Apollo 11 moon landing, 10th anniversary.

Telecom 79 — A218

1979, Nov. 26   Photo.   Perf. 13x14
1042	A218	50fr multi	.35 .25

3rd World Telecommunications Exhibition, Geneva, Sept. 20-26. See No. C402.

Holy Family — A219

Christmas: 30fr, Virgin and Child. 50fr, Adoration of the Kings.

1979, Dec. 17   Litho.   Perf. 14
1043	A219	20fr multi	.25 .25
1044	A219	30fr multi	.30 .25
1045	A219	50fr multi	.50 .25

Nos. 1043-1045,C403-C405 (6)   4.15 2.20

Rotary Emblem — A220

Rotary Emblem and: 30fr, Anniversary emblem. 40fr, Paul P. Harris, Rotary founder.

1980, Jan. 14
1046	A220	25fr multi	.25 .25
1047	A220	30fr multi	.35 .25
1048	A220	40fr multi	.40 .25

Nos. 1046-1048,C406-C408 (6)   4.25 2.45

Rotary International, 75th anniversary.

Biathlon, Lake Placid '80 Emblem — A221

1980, Jan. 31　Litho.　Perf. 13½
1049　A221　50fr multi　.40　.25
　Nos. 1049,C409-C411 (4)　3.00　1.50
13th Winter Olympic Games, Lake Placid, NY, Feb. 12-24. See No. C412.

1980 Winter Olympics, Lake Placid — A221a

Gold medalist: No. 1049F, Hanni Wenzel, Liechtenstein, women's slalom. No. 1049G, Eric Heiden, US, men's speed skating. No. 1049H, Jouko Tormanen, Finland, 90-meter ski jumping. No. 1049I, Erich Schaerer, Josef Benz, Switzerland, 2-man bobsled. No. 1049J, US, ice hockey.

1980　Litho.　Perf. 11
1049A　A221a　1000fr multi　20.00　4.50
1049B　A221a　1000fr multi　20.00　4.50
1049C　A221a　1000fr multi　20.00　4.50
1049D　A221a　1000fr multi　20.00　4.50
1049E　A221a　1000fr multi　20.00　4.50
　Nos. 1049A-1049E (5)　100.00　22.50

Souvenir Sheets
1049F　A221a　1000fr gold & multi　—
1049G　A221a　1000fr gold & multi　—
1049H　A221a　1000fr gold & multi　—
1049I　A221a　1000fr gold & multi　—
1049J　A221a　1000fr gold & multi　—
Exist imperf.

Swimming, Moscow '80 Emblem — A222

1980, Feb. 29　Litho.　Perf. 13½
1050　A222　20fr shown　.25　.25
1051　A222　30fr Gymnastics　.30　.25
1052　A222　50fr Running　.50　.25
　Nos. 1050-1052,C413-C415 (6)　5.20　3.25
22nd Summer Olympic Games, Moscow, July 19-Aug. 3.

Christ and the Angels, by Andrea Mantegna A223

Easter 1980 (Paintings by): 40fr, Carlo Crivelli. 50fr, Jacopo Pontormo.

1980, Mar. 31　Perf. 14
1053　A223　30fr multi　.30　.25
1054　A223　40fr multi　.55　.25
1055　A223　50fr multi　.55　.25
　Nos. 1053-1055,C416-C418 (6)　4.05　2.00

Jet over Map of Africa A224

1980, Mar. 24　Litho.　Perf. 12½
1056　A224　50fr multi　.60　.25
ASECNA (Air Safety Board), 20th anniv. See No. C419.

Nos. 979, 984 Ovptd. "Londres / 1980"
Litho. & Embossed
1980, May 6　Perf. 11
1056A　A192　1000fr gold & multi　6.50　—
Souvenir Sheet
1056B　A192　1000fr gold & multi　7.25　—

12th World Telecommunications Day — A225

1980, May 17　Photo.　Perf. 14x13½
1057　A225　50fr multi　.50　.25
See No. C420.

Red Cross over Globe Showing Lomé, Togo — A226

1980, June 16　Photo.　Perf. 14x13
1058　A226　50fr multi　.60　.25
Togolese Red Cross. See No. C421.

Jules Verne (1828-1905), French Science Fiction Writer — A227

50fr, Shark (20,000 Leagues Under the Sea).

1980, July 14　Litho.　Perf. 14
1059　A227　30fr multi　.30　.25
1060　A227　50fr multi　.55　.25
　Nos. 1059-1060,C422-C425 (6)　4.05　2.00

Baroness James de Rothschild, by Ingres — A228

Paintings by Jean Auguste Dominique Ingres (1780-1867): 30fr, Napoleon I on Imperial Throne. 40fr, Don Pedro of Toledo and Henri IV.

1980, Aug. 29　Litho.　Perf. 14
1061　A228　25fr multi　.25　.25
1062　A228　30fr multi　.35　.25
1063　A228　40fr multi　.40　.25
　Nos. 1061-1063,C426-C428 (6)　4.25　2.05

Minnie Holding Mirror for Leopard A229

Disney Characters and Animals from Fazao Reserve: 2fr, Goofy (Dingo) cleaning teeth of hippopotamus. 3fr, Donald holding snout of crocodile. 4fr, Donald dangling over cliff from horn of rhinoceros. 5fr, Goofy riding water buffalo. 10fr, Monkey taking picture of Mickey. 100fr, Mickey as doctor examining giraffe with sore throat. 200fr, Pluto in party hat. No. 1071, Elephant giving shower to Goofy. No. 1072, Lion carrying Goofy by seat of his pants. No. 1072A, Pluto.

1980, Sept. 15　Perf. 11
1064　A229　1fr multi　.25　.25
1065　A229　2fr multi　.25　.25
1066　A229　3fr multi　.25　.25
1067　A229　4fr multi　.25　.25
1068　A229　5fr multi　.25　.25
1069　A229　10fr multi　.25　.25
1070　A229　100fr multi　.75　.35
1070A　A229　200fr multi　1.50　.75
1071　A229　300fr multi　2.25　1.10
　Nos. 1064-1071 (9)　6.00　3.70
Souvenir Sheets
1072　A229　300fr multi　8.00　3.00
1072A　A229　300fr multi　4.00　1.50
50th anniv. of the Disney character Pluto.

Market Activities, Women Preparing Meat A230

1fr, Grinding savo. 3fr, Truck going to market. 4fr, Unloading produce. 5fr, Sugar cane vendor. 6fr, Barber curling child's hair, vert. 7fr, Vegetable vendor. 8fr, Sampling mangos, vert. 9fr, Grain vendor. 10fr, Spiced fish vendor. 15fr, Clay pot vendor. 20fr, Straw baskets. 25fr, Selling lemons and onions, vert. 30fr, Straw baskets, diff. 40fr, Shore market. 45fr, Vegatable stall. 50fr, Women carrying produce, vert. 60fr, Rice wine.

1980-81　Perf. 14
1073　A230　1fr multicolored　.25　.25
1074　A230　2fr shown　.25　.25
1075　A230　3fr multicolored　.25　.25
1076　A230　4fr multicolored　.25　.25
1077　A230　5fr multicolored　.25　.25
1078　A230　6fr multicolored　.25　.25
1079　A230　7fr multicolored　.25　.25
1080　A230　8fr multicolored　.25　.25
1081　A230　9fr multicolored　.25　.25
1082　A230　10fr multicolored　.25　.25
1083　A230　15fr multicolored　.25　.25
1084　A230　20fr multicolored　.25　.25
1085　A230　25fr multicolored　.25　.25
1086　A230　30fr multicolored　.25　.25
1087　A230　40fr multicolored　.30　.25
1087A　A230　45fr multicolored　.30　.25
1088　A230　50fr multicolored　.40　.25
1088A　A230　60fr multicolored　.40　.25
　Nos. 1073-1088A (18)　4.90　4.50
Issued: 45fr, 60fr, 3/8/81; others, 3/17/80. Nos. 1087A, 1088A dated 1980.
See Nos. C440-C445, J68-J71. For overprints see Nos. C486-C487.

Commemorative Wreath — A231

Famous Men of the Decade: 40fr, Mao Tse-tung, vert.

1980, Feb. 11　Perf. 14x13
1089　A231　25fr multi　.40　.25
1090　A231　40fr emer grn & dk grn　.60　.25
　Nos. 1089-1090,C429-C431 (5)　5.10　1.80

World Tourism Conference, Manila, Sept. 27 — A232

1980, Sept. 15　Litho.　Perf. 14
1091　A232　50fr Hotel tourism emblem, vert.　.35　.25
1092　A232　150fr shown　1.10　.75

Map of Australia and Human Rights Flame A233

1980, Oct. 13　Photo.　Perf. 13x14
1093　A233　30fr shown　.30　.25
1094　A233　50fr Europe and Asia map　.50　.25
　Nos. 1093-1094,C432-C433 (4)　2.20　1.25
Declaration of Human Rights, 30th anniv.

Nos. 980, 985 Ovptd. in Gold & Black

Litho. & Embossed
1980, Nov. 24　Perf. 11
1094A　A192　1000fr gold & multi　8.50　—
Souvenir Sheet
1094B　A192　1000fr gold & multi　7.00　—
No. 1094B ovptd. with additional text and black bars in sheet margin.

Melk Monastery, Austria, 18th Century
A234

30fr, Tarragon Cathedral, Spain, 12th cent. 50fr, St. John the Baptist, Florence, 1964.

Perf. 14½x13½

			Litho.	
1980, Dec. 22				
1095	A234	20fr shown	.25	.25
1096	A234	30fr multicolored	.35	.25
1097	A234	50fr multicolored	.55	.25
Nos. 1095-1097,C435-C437 (6)			4.35	2.25

Christmas.

African Postal Union, 5th Anniversary
A235

1980, Dec. 24		Photo.	Perf. 13½	
1098	A235	100fr multi	.75	.35

February 2nd Hotel Opening
A236

1981, Feb. 2		Litho.	Perf. 12½x13	
1099	A236	50fr multi	.60	.25

See No. C437B.

A236a

1981, Dec. 21		Litho.	Perf. 12½	
1100	A236a	70fr lt grn & multi	.70	.35

West African Rice Development Assoc.
See No. C461.

A237

Easter (Rembrandt Paintings): 30fr, Rembrandt's Father. 40fr, Self-portrait. 50fr, Artist's father as an old man. 60fr, Rider on Horseback.

1981, Apr. 13			Perf. 14½x13½	
1101	A237	30fr multi	.35	.25
1102	A237	40fr multi	.40	.25
1103	A237	50fr multi	.50	.25
1104	A237	60fr multi	.60	.30
Nos. 1101-1104,C438-C439 (6)			4.50	2.15

Wedding of Prince Charles and Lady Diana Spencer — A237a — 1105

1981, July 29		Litho.	Perf. 11	
1105	A237a	1000fr gold & multi	4.00	2.50

Souvenir Sheet
Litho. & Embossed

1106	A237a	1000fr Charles & Diana, diff.	5.00	3.00

No. 1105 printed with embossed se-tenant label.
For overprints see Nos. 1143A-1143B.

Red-headed Rock Fowl — A238

40fr, Splendid sunbird. 60fr, Violet-backed starling. 90fr, Red-collared widowbird.

1981, Aug. 10			Perf. 13½x14½	
1107	A238	30fr shown	.45	.25
1108	A238	40fr multicolored	.55	.25
1109	A238	60fr multicolored	.90	.25
1110	A238	90fr multicolored	1.40	.30
Nos. 1107-1110,C446-C447 (6)			5.60	1.65

1982 World Soccer Championships, Spain — A238a

Flags (Nos. 1110A-1110E) or Players (Nos. 1110F-1110J) and stadiums; 1000fr: Nos. 1110A, 1110F, Athletico de Madrid. Nos. 1110B, 1110G, Real Madrid C.F. Nos. 1110C, 1110H, R.C.D. Espanol. Nos. 1110D, 1110I, Real Zaragoza. Nos. 1110E, 1110J, Valencia.

Litho. & Embossed

1981, Aug. 17		Perf. 11	
1110A-1110E	A238a	Set of 5	40.00 10.00

Souvenir Sheets

| 1110F-1110J | A238a | Set of 2 | 35.00 10.00 |

African Postal Union Ministers, 6th Council Meeting, July 28-20
A239

1981, Aug. 31		Litho.	Perf. 12½	
1111	A239	70fr Dish antenna	.50	.25
1112	A239	90fr Computer operator, vert.	.70	.35
1113	A239	105fr Map	.80	.40
Nos. 1111-1113 (3)			2.00	1.00

Intl. Year of the Disabled
A240

1981, Aug. 31			Perf. 14	
1114	A240	70fr Blind man	.85	.45
Nos. 1114,C448-C449 (3)			3.25	1.70

See No. C449A.

Woman with Hat, by Picasso, 1961 — A241

Picasso Birth Centenary: Sculptures.

1981, Sept. 14			Perf. 14½x13½	
1116	A241	25fr shown	.30	.25
1117	A241	50fr She-goat	.50	.25
1118	A241	60fr Violin, 1915	.55	.25
Nos. 1116-1118,C450-C452 (6)			5.75	2.55

Aix-la-Chapelle Cathedral, Germany — A242

World Heritage Year: 40fr, Geyser, Yellowstone Natl. Park. 50fr, Nahanni Natl. Park, Canada. 60fr, Stone churches, Ethiopia.

1981, Sept. 28			Perf. 13½x14½	
1119	A242	30fr multi	.25	.25
1120	A242	40fr multi	.30	.25
1121	A242	50fr multi	.40	.25
1122	A242	60fr multi	.50	.35
Nos. 1119-1122,C453-C454 (6)			4.00	2.35

Yuri Gagarin's Vostok I, 20th. — A243

Space Anniversaries: 50fr, 20th Anniv. of Alan Shepard's Flight. 60fr, Lunar Orbiter I, 15th.

1981, Nov.			Perf. 14	
1123	A243	25fr multi	.25	.25
1124	A243	50fr multi	.45	.25
1125	A243	60fr multi	.55	.25
Nos. 1123-1125,C455-C456 (5)			2.60	1.25

Christmas
A244

Rubens Paintings: 20fr, Adoration of the Kings. 30fr, Adoration of the Shepherds. 50fr, St. Catherine.

Perf. 14½x13½

			Litho.	
1981, Dec. 10				
1126	A244	20fr multi	.25	.25
1127	A244	30fr multi	.25	.25
1128	A244	50fr multi	.40	.25
Nos. 1126-1128,C457-C459 (6)			5.20	2.75

15th Anniv. of Natl. Liberation — A245

1982, Jan. 13		Litho.	Perf. 12½	
1129	A245	70fr Dove, flag	.70	.35
1130	A245	90fr Citizens, Pres. Eyadema, vert.	.90	.45
Nos. 1129-1130,C462-C463 (4)			3.20	1.55

Scouting Year
A246

1982, Feb. 25		Litho.	Perf. 14	
1131	A240	70fr Pitching tent	.55	.25
Nos. 1131,C464-C467 (5)			4.50	1.80

Easter — A247

Designs: The Ten Commandments.

1982, Mar. 15			Perf. 14x14½	
1132	A247	10fr multi	.25	.25
1133	A247	25fr multi	.25	.25
1134	A247	30fr multi	.25	.25
1135	A247	45fr multi	.30	.25
1136	A247	50fr multi	.35	.25
1137	A247	70fr multi	.45	.25
1138	A247	90fr multi	.60	.30
Nos. 1132-1138,C469-C470 (9)			3.95	2.55

Papilio Dardanus
A248

1982, July 15   Litho.   Perf. 14½x14
1139 A248 15fr shown   .35 .25
1140 A248 20fr Belenois calypso   .55 .25
1141 A248 25fr Palla decius   .55 .25
Nos. 1139-1141,C474-C475 (5)   4.80 1.60

1982 World
Cup — A249

Designs: Various soccer players.

1982, July 26   Perf. 14x14½
1142 A249 25fr multi   .25 .25
1143 A249 45fr multi   .35 .25
Nos. 1142-1143,C477-C479 (5)   4.90 2.50

For overprints see Nos. 1150-1155.

**Nos. 1105-1106 Overprinted on one
or two lines**

1982, Oct. 28   Litho.   Perf. 11
1143A A237a 1000fr gold & multi   8.00 4.00
Souvenir Sheet
Litho. & Embossed
1143B A237a 1000fr gold & multi   9.25 3.50

Christmas
A250

Madonna of Baldacchino, by Raphael.
#1144-1148 show details; #1149 entire
painting.

1982, Dec. 24   Litho.   Perf. 14½x14
1144 A250 45fr multi   .45 .25
1145 A250 70fr multi   .65 .25
1146 A250 105fr multi   .85 .25
1147 A250 130fr multi   1.20 .25
1148 A250 150fr multi   1.40 .35
Nos. 1144-1148 (5)   4.55 1.40
Souvenir Sheet
Perf. 14x14½
1149 A250 500fr multi, vert.   3.75 1.75

**Nos. 1142-1143, C477-C480
Overprinted: VAINQUER / COUPE
DU MONDE / FOOTBALL 82 /
"ITALIE"**

1983, Jan. 31   Litho.   Perf. 14x14½
1150 A249 25fr multi   .25 .25
1151 A249 45fr multi   .35 .25
1152 A249 105fr multi   .75 .35
1153 A249 200fr multi   1.40 .50
1154 A249 300fr multi   2.10 .85
Nos. 1150-1154 (5)   4.85 2.25
Souvenir Sheet
1155 A249 500fr multi   4.25 2.50

Italy's victory in 1982 World Cup. Nos.
1152-1155 airmail.

20th Anniv. of West
African Monetary
Union
(1982) — A251

1983, May   Litho.   Perf. 12½x12
1156 A251 70fr Map   .60 .25
1157 A251 90fr Emblem   .80 .30

Visit of Pres. Mitterand of France, Jan.
13-15 — A252

35fr, Sokode Regional Hospital. 45fr, Citi-
zens joining hands. 70fr, Soldiers, vert. 90fr,
Pres. Mitterand, vert. 105fr, Pres. Eyadema,
Mitterand, vert. 130fr, Greeting crowd.

1983, Jan. 13   Litho.   Perf. 13
1158 A252 35fr multicolored   .25 .25
  a.   Souvenir sheet, imperf.   1.00 .55
1159 A252 45fr multicolored   .40 .25
  a.   Souvenir sheet, imperf.   1.00 .55
1160 A252 70fr multicolored   .60 .25
  a.   Souvenir sheet, imperf.   1.00 .55
1161 A252 90fr multicolored   .70 .30
  a.   Souvenir sheet, imperf.   1.00 .55
1162 A252 105fr multicolored   .90 .35
  a.   Souvenir sheet, imperf.   1.00 .55
1163 A252 130fr multicolored   1.25 .45
  a.   Souvenir sheet, imperf.   1.00 .55
Nos. 1158-1163 (6)   4.10 1.85

Nos. 1161-1163 airmail.

Easter — A253

Paintings: 35fr, Mourners at the Death of
Christ, by Bellini. 70fr, Crucifixion, by Raphael.
90fr, Descent from the Cross, by Carracci.
500fr Christ, by Reni.

1983   Litho.   Perf. 13½x14½
1164 A253 35fr multi   .35 .25
1165 A253 70fr multi, vert.   .55 .25
1166 A253 90fr multi   .85 .25
Nos. 1164-1166 (3)   1.75 .75
Souvenir Sheet
Perf. 14½x13½
1167 A253 500fr multi   3.75 1.75

90fr, 500fr airmail.

Folkdances — A254

1983, Dec. 1   Perf. 14½x14
1168 A254 70fr Kondona   .55 .25
1169 A254 90fr Kondona, diff.   .65 .25
1170 A254 105fr Toubole   .85 .30
1171 A254 130fr Adjogbo   1.00 .25
Nos. 1168-1171 (4)   3.05 1.05

90fr, 105fr, 130fr airmail.

World
Communications
Year — A255

1983, June 20   Litho.   Perf. 14x14½
1172 A255 70fr Drummer   .60 .25
1173 A255 90fr Modern commu-
                  nication   .70 .25

90fr airmail.

Christmas — A256

70fr, Catholic Church, Kante. 90fr, Altar,
Dapaong Cathedral. 105fr, Protestant Church,
Dapaong.
500fr, Ecumenical Church, Pya.

1983, Dec.   Perf. 13½x14½
1174 A256 70fr multicolored   .55 .25
1175 A256 90fr multicolored   .65 .25
1176 A256 105fr multicolored   .80 .25
Nos. 1174-1176 (3)   2.00 .75
Souvenir Sheet
1177 A256 500fr multi   4.50 1.75

90fr, 105fr, 500fr airmail.

Sarakawa Presidential Assassination
Attempt, 10th Anniv. — A257

70fr, Wrecked plane. 90fr, Plane, diff. 120fr,
Memorial Hall. 270fr, Pres. Eyadema statue,
vert.

1984, Jan. 24   Litho.   Perf. 13
1178 A257 70fr multicolored   .60 .25
1179 A257 90fr multicolored   .70 .25
1180 A257 105fr multicolored   1.00 .25
1181 A257 270fr multicolored   2.25 .45
Nos. 1178-1181 (4)   4.55 1.20

120fr, 270fr airmail.

20th Anniv.
of World
Food
Program
(1983)
A258

1984, May 2   Litho.   Perf. 13
1182 A258 35fr Orchard   .25 .25
1183 A258 70fr Fruit tree   .50 .25
1184 A258 90fr Rice paddy   .65 .25
Nos. 1182-1184 (3)   1.40 .75
Souvenir Sheet
1185 A258 300fr Village, horiz.   3.00 1.90

25th Anniv. of
Council of
Unity — A259

1984, May 29   Perf. 12
1186 A259 70fr multi   .55 .25
1187 A259 90fr multi   .70 .25

Easter
1984 — A260

Various stained-glass windows.

1984   Litho.   Perf. 14x14½
1188 A260 70fr multi   .55 .25
1189 A260 90fr multi   .65 .25
1190 A260 120fr multi   .85 .25
1191 A260 270fr multi   1.90 .50
1192 A260 300fr multi   2.10 .55
Nos. 1188-1192 (5)   6.05 1.80
Souvenir Sheet
1193 A260 500fr multi   4.50 3.50

Nos. 1189-1193 airmail.

Centenary of German-Togolese
Friendship — A261

#1194, Degbenou Catholic Mission, 1893.
#1195, Kara Bridge, 1911. #1196, Treaty Site,
Baguida, 1884. #1197, Degbenou Students,
1893. #1198, Sansane Administrative Post,
1908. #1199, Adjido Official School.
    #1200, Sokode Cotton Market, 1910.
#1201, William Fountain, Atakpame, 1906.
#1202, Lome Main Street, 1895, No. 19.
#1203, Police, 1905. #1204, Lome Railroad
Construction, 1905. #1205, Governor's Palace,
Lome, 1905. #1206, No. 9, Commerce Street,
Lome.
    #1207, Nos. 10, 17. #1208, Lome Wharf,
1903. #1209, G. Nachtigal. #1210, Wilhelm II.
#1211, O.F. de Bismark. #1212, J. de
Puttkamer. #1213, A. Koehler. #1214, W.
Horn. #1215, J.G. de Zech. #1216, E. Bruck-
ner. #1217, A.F. de Mecklenburg. #1218, H.G.
de Doering. #1219, Land Development, 1908.
    #1220, Postal Courier, No. 8. #1221, Treaty
Signers, 1885. 150fr, German & Togolese
Children, Flags. #1223, Aneho Line Locomo-
tive, 1905. #1224, Mallet Locomotive, 1907.
#1225, German Ship "Mowe," 1884. #1226,
"La Sophie," 1884. 300fr, Pres. Eyadema,
Helmut Kohl.

1984, July 5   Litho.   Perf. 13
1194 A261 35fr multi   .50 .25
1195 A261 35fr multi   .50 .25
1196 A261 35fr multi, vert.   .50 .25
1197 A261 35fr multi   .50 .25
1198 A261 35fr multi   .50 .25
1199 A261 35fr multi   .50 .25
1200 A261 35fr multi   .50 .25
1201 A261 45fr multi   .50 .25
1202 A261 45fr multi   .50 .25
1203 A261 45fr multi   .50 .25
1204 A261 45fr multi   .50 .25
1205 A261 45fr multi   .50 .25
1206 A261 45fr multi   .50 .25
1207 A261 70fr multi   .60 .25
1208 A261 70fr multi   .60 .25
1209 A261 90fr multi, vert.   .75 .25
1210 A261 90fr multi, vert.   .75 .25
1211 A261 90fr multi, vert.   .75 .25

1212	A261	90fr multi, vert.	.75	.25
1213	A261	90fr multi, vert.	.75	.25
1214	A261	90fr multi, vert.	.75	.25
1215	A261	90fr multi, vert.	.75	.25
1216	A261	90fr multi, vert.	.75	.25
1217	A261	90fr multi, vert.	75	.25
1218	A261	90fr multi, vert.	.75	.25
1219	A261	90fr multi, vert.	.75	.25
1220	A261	120fr multi, vert.	1.00	.25
1221	A261	120fr multi, vert.	1.00	.25
1222	A261	150fr multi, vert.	1.25	.25
1223	A261	270fr multi	2.25	.45
1224	A261	270fr multi	2.25	.45
1225	A261	270fr multi	2.25	.45
1226	A261	270fr multi	2.25	.45
1227	A261	300fr multi	2.40	.50
		Nos. 1194-1227 (34)	30.60	9.55

Souvenir sheets of one exist for each design. Stamp size: 65x80mm. Value, set of 34, $35.

Donald Duck, 50th Anniv. A262

1fr, Donald, Chip. 2fr, Donald, Chip and Dale. 3fr, Louie, Chip and Dale. 5fr, Donald, Chip. 10fr, Daisy Duck, Donald. 15fr, Goofy, Donald. 105fr, Huey, Dewey and Louie. 500fr, Nephews, Donald. No. 1238, 1000fr, Nephews, Donald.
No. 1239, Surprised Donald. No. 1240, Perplexed Donald.

1984, Sept. 21   Litho.   Perf. 11

1230	A262	1fr multi	.55	.25
1231	A262	2fr multi	.55	.25
1232	A262	3fr multi	.55	.25
1233	A262	5fr multi	.55	.25
1234	A262	10fr multi	.55	.25
1235	A262	15fr multi	.55	.25
1236	A262	105fr multi	.80	.25
1237	A262	500fr multi	3.75	.70
1238	A262	1000fr multi	8.25	1.40
		Nos. 1230-1238 (9)	16.10	3.85

Souvenir Sheets
Perf. 14

1239	A262	1000fr multi	7.50	7.50
1240	A262	1000fr multi	7.50	7.50

Nos. 1236-1240 airmail.
For overprints see Nos. C551-C554.

Endangered Mammals — A263

45fr, Manatee swimming. 70fr, Manatee eating. 90fr, Manatees floating. 105fr, Young manatee, mother.
No. 1245, Olive Colobus monkey, vert. No. 1246, Galago (Bushbaby)

1984, Oct. 1   Litho.   Perf. 15x14½

1241	A263	45fr multi	1.60	.50
1242	A263	70fr multi	2.25	1.00
1243	A263	90fr multi	2.25	1.00
1244	A263	105fr multi	2.75	1.00
		Nos. 1241-1244 (4)	8.85	3.00

Souvenir Sheets
Perf. 14x15, 15x14

1245	A263	1000fr multi	10.00	6.00
1246	A263	1000fr multi	10.00	6.00

Nos. 1243-1246 airmail. See #1444-1447.

Birth Centenary of Eleanor Roosevelt A264

90fr, Mrs. Roosevelt, Statue of Liberty.

1984, Oct. 10   Litho.   Perf. 13½

1247	A264	70fr shown	.55	.25
1248	A264	90fr multicolored	.70	.25

No. 1248 airmail.

Classic Automobiles — A265

1984, Nov. 15   Litho.   Perf. 15

1249	A265	1fr 1947 Bristol	.25	.25
1250	A265	2fr 1925 Frazer Nash	.25	.25
1251	A265	3fr 1950 Healey	.25	.25
1252	A265	4fr 1925 Kissell	.25	.25
1253	A265	50fr 1927 La Salle	.80	.25
1254	A265	90fr 1921 Minerva	.65	.25
1255	A265	500fr 1950 Morgan	4.00	.70
1256	A265	1000fr 1921 Napier	8.00	1.40
		Nos. 1249-1256 (8)	14.45	3.60

Souvenir Sheets

1257	A265	1000fr 1941 Nash	8.00	2.00
1258	A265	1000fr 1903 Peugeot	8.00	2.00

Nos. 1254-1258 airmail.
For overprints see Nos. 1328-1331, C542-C544, C564-C565.

Christmas A266

70fr, Connestable Madonna. 290fr, Cowper Madonna. 300fr, Alba Madonna. 500fr, Madonna of the Curtain. 1000fr, Madonna with Child.

Perf. 14½x13½

1984, Nov. 23   Litho.

1259	A266	70fr multi	.50	.25
1260	A266	290fr multi	2.00	.50
1261	A266	300fr multi	2.10	.55
1262	A266	500fr multi	3.50	.85
		Nos. 1259-1262 (4)	8.10	2.15

Souvenir Sheet

1263	A266	1000fr multi	7.00	6.75

Nos. 1260-1263 airmail.

African Locomotives — A267

1fr, Decapod, Madeira. 2fr, 2-6-0, Egypt. 3fr, 4-8-2+2-8-4, Algeria. 4fr, Congo-Ocean diesel. 50fr, 0-4-0+0-4-0, Libya. 90fr, #49, Malawi. 105fr, 1907 Mallet, Togo. 500fr, 4-8-2, Rhodesia. 1000fr, Beyer-Garratt, East Africa.
No. 1273, 2-8-2, Ghana. No. 1274, Locomotive, Senegal.

1984, Nov. 30   Litho.   Perf. 15

1264	A267	1fr multi	.25	.25
1265	A267	2fr multi	.25	.25
1266	A267	3fr multi	.25	.25
1267	A267	4fr multi	.25	.25
1268	A267	50fr multi	.25	.25
1269	A267	90fr multi	.75	.25
1270	A267	105fr multi	.90	.25
1271	A267	500fr multi	3.75	.80
1272	A267	1000fr multi	6.50	1.60
		Nos. 1264-1272 (9)	10.15	4.15

Souvenir Sheets

1273	A267	1000fr multi	9.00	6.00
1274	A267	1000fr multi	9.00	6.00

Nos. 1269-1274 airmail.
For overprints see Nos. 1343-1346, 1356-1360, C541, C566.

Economic Convention, Lome — A268

100fr, Map of the Americas. 130fr, Map of Eurasia, Africa. 270fr, Map of Asia, Australia. 500fr, President Eyadema.

1984, Dec. 8   Litho.   Perf. 12½

1275	A268	100fr multicolored	.70	.25
1276	A268	130fr multicolored	1.00	.25
1277	A268	270fr multicolored	1.90	.50
a.	A268	Strip of 3, #1275-1277	3.75	3.75

Souvenir Sheet

1278	A268	500fr multicolored	3.75	3.25

No. 1277a has continuous design.

Intl. Civil Aviation Org., 40th Anniv. A269

Map of Togo, ICAO emblem and: 70fr, Lockheed Constellation, 1944. 105fr, Boeing 707, 1954. 200fr, Doublas DC-8-61, 1966. 500fr, Bac/Sud Concorde, 1966. 1000fr, Icarus, by Hans Erni.

1984, Oct. 15   Litho.   Perf. 15x14

1279	A269	70fr multi	.65	.25
1280	A269	105fr multi	.85	.25
1281	A269	200fr multi	1.40	.25
1282	A269	500fr multi	3.75	.75
		Nos. 1279-1282 (4)	6.65	1.50

Souvenir Sheet

1283	A269	1000fr multi	6.50	6.00

Nos. 1280-1283 airmail.

Mosaic of the 12 Apostles, Baptistry of the Aryans, Ravenna, Italy, — A270

Designs: 1fr, St. Paul. 2fr, St. Thomas. 3fr, St. Matthew. 4fr, St. James the Younger. 5fr, St. Simon. 70fr, St. Thaddeaus Judas. 90fr, St. Bartholomew. 105fr, St. Philip. 200fr, St. John. 270fr, St. James the Greater. 400fr, St. Andrew. 500fr, St. Peter. No. 1296, The Last Supper, by Andrea del Castagno, c. 1421-1457, horiz. No, 1297, Coronation of the Virgin, by Raphael, 1483-1520, horiz.

1984, Dec. 14   Perf. 15

1284	A270	1fr multi	.25	.25
1285	A270	2fr multi	.25	.25
1286	A270	3fr multi	.25	.25
1287	A270	4fr multi	.25	.25
1288	A270	5fr multi	.25	.25
1289	A270	70fr multi	1.20	.25
1290	A270	90fr multi	.80	.25
1291	A270	105fr multi	.95	.25
1292	A270	200fr multi	1.75	.25
1293	A270	270fr multi	2.25	.35
1294	A270	400fr multi	3.50	.45
1295	A270	500fr multi	4.75	.55
		Nos. 1284-1295 (12)	16.45	3.60

Souvenir Sheets

1296-1297	A270	1000fr each	10.00	4.50

Nos. 1290-1297 airmail.
For overprints see Nos. C545-C547.

Race Horses A271

1fr, Allez France. 2fr, Arkle, vert. 3fr, Tingle Creek, vert. 4fr, Interco. 50fr, Dawn Run. 90fr, Seattle Slew, vert. 500fr, Nijinsky. No. 1305, 1000fr, Politician.
No. 1306, Shergar. No. 1307, Red Rum.

1985, Jan. 10

1298	A271	1fr multi	.25	.25
1299	A271	2fr multi	.25	.25
1300	A271	3fr multi	.25	.25
1301	A271	4fr multi	.25	.25
1302	A271	50fr multi	.75	.25
1303	A271	90fr multi	.75	.25
1304	A271	500fr multi	3.75	.60
1305	A271	1000fr multi	6.00	1.25
		Nos. 1298-1305 (8)	12.25	3.35

Souvenir Sheets

1306	A271	1000fr multi	7.00	5.50
1307	A271	1000fr multi	7.00	5.50

Nos. 1303-1307 airmail.
For overprints see Nos. 1353-1355A.

Easter — A272

Paintings by Raphael (1483-1520) — 70fr, Christ and His Flock. 90fr, Christ and the Fishermen. 135fr, The Blessed Christ, vert. 150fr, The Entombment, vert. 250fr, The Resurrection, vert. 1000fr, The Transfiguration.

Perf. 13½x14½, 14½x13½

1985, Mar 7

1308	A272	70fr multi	.65	.25
1309	A272	90fr multi	.70	.25
1310	A272	135fr multi	1.20	.25
1311	A272	150fr multi	1.25	.25
1312	A272	250fr multi	2.10	.35
		Nos. 1308-1312 (5)	5.90	1.35

Souvenir Sheet

1313	A272	1000fr multi	8.50	6.50

Nos. 1309-1313 airmail.

Technical & Cultural Cooperation Agency, 15th Anniv. — A273

1985, Mar. 20   Perf. 12½

1314	A273	70fr multi	.60	.25
1315	A273	90fr multi	.60	.25

Philexafrica '85, Lome — A274

No. 1316, Woman carrying fruit basket. No. 1317, Man plowing field.

1985, May 9   Perf. 13

1316	A274	200fr multi	1.75	.25
1317	A274	200fr multi	1.75	.25
a.		Pair, #1316-1317 + label	4.00	4.00

Scarification Ritual — A275

25fr, Kabye (Pya). 70fr, Mollah (Kotokoli). 90fr, Maba (Dapaong). 105fr, Kabye (Pagouda). 270fr, Peda.

1985, May 14			Perf. 14x15	
1318	A275	25fr multi	.60	.25
1319	A275	70fr multi	.60	.25
1320	A275	90fr multi	.60	.25
1321	A275	105fr multi	.75	.25
1322	A275	270fr multi	1.75	.30
	Nos. 1318-1322 (5)		4.30	1.30

Nos. 1320-1322 airmail.

Seashells A276

70fr, Clavatula muricata. 90fr, Marginella desjardini. 120fr, Clavatula nifat. 135fr, Cypraea stercoraria. 270fr, Conus genuanus. 1000fr, Dancers wearing traditional shell decorations.

1985, June 1			Perf. 15x14	
1323	A276	70fr multi	.85	.25
1324	A276	90fr multi	.90	.25
1325	A276	120fr multi	1.10	.25
1326	A276	135fr multi	1.40	.25
1327	A276	270fr multi	2.75	.35
	Nos. 1323-1327 (5)		7.00	1.35
Souvenir Sheet				
1327A	A276	1000fr multi	8.50	6.00

Nos. 1324-1327A airmail.

Nos. 1253, 1256-1258 Overprinted "Exposition Mondiale 1985 / Tsukuba, Japon"

1985, June			Perf. 15	
1328	A265	50fr #1253	1.50	.25
1329	A265	1000fr #1256	11.50	3.50
Souvenir Sheets				
1330	A265	1000fr #1257	9.75	3.75
1331	A265	1000fr #1258	9.75	3.75

EXPO '85.

Audubon Birth Bicent. — A277

Illustrations by artist-naturalist J.J. Audubon (1785-1851) — 90fr, Larus bonapartii. 120fr, Pelecanus occidentalis. 135fr, Cassidix mexicanus. 270fr, Aquila chrysaetos. 500fr, Picus erythrocephalus.
1000fr, Dendroica petechia.

1985, Aug. 13			Perf. 13	
1332	A277	90fr multi	.95	.25
1333	A277	120fr multi	1.25	.25
1334	A277	135fr multi	1.25	.25
1335	A277	270fr multi	2.50	.35
1336	A277	500fr multi	4.50	.60
	Nos. 1332-1336 (5)		10.45	1.70
Souvenir Sheet				
1337	A277	1000fr multi	9.50	7.50

Nos. 1332, 1334 and 1336-1337 airmail.

Dove, UN Emblem — A278

Kara Port Construction — A279

Designs: 115fr, Hands, UN emblem. 250fr, Millet crop, Atalote Research Facility. 500fr, UN, Togo flags, statesmen.

1985, Oct. 24			Litho.	Perf. 13	
1338	A278	90fr multi		.70	.25
1339	A278	115fr multi		.95	.25
1340	A279	150fr multi		1.25	.25
1341	A279	250fr multi		1.60	.35
1342	A279	500fr multi		3.50	.65
	Nos. 1338-1342 (5)			8.00	1.75

UN, 40th anniv. Nos. 1340-1342 are airmail.

Nos. 1267, 1270, 1272, 1273 Ovptd. with Rotary Emblem and "80e ANNIVERSAIRE DU / ROTARY INTERNATIONAL"

1985			Litho.	Perf. 15	
1343	A267	4fr multi		.60	.40
1344	A267	105fr multi		1.10	1.00
1345	A267	1000fr multi		11.00	5.00
	Nos. 1343-1345 (3)			12.70	6.40
Souvenir Sheet					
1346	A267	1000fr multi		12.50	6.50

Nos. 1344-1346 are airmail.

Christmas A280

Religious paintings and statuary: 90fr, The Garden of Roses Madonna. 115fr, Madonna and Child, Byzantine, 11th cent. 150fr, Rest During the Flight to Egypt, by Gerard David (1450-1523). 160fr, African Madonna, 16th cent. 250fr, African Madonna, c. 1900. 500fr, Mystic Madonna, by Sandro Botticelli (1444-1510).

			Perf. 14½x13½	
1985, Dec. 10				Litho.
1347	A280	90fr multi	.70	.25
1348	A280	115fr multi	.90	.25
1349	A280	150fr multi	1.10	.25
1350	A280	160fr multi	1.10	.25
1351	A280	250fr multi	2.00	.40
	Nos. 1347-1351 (5)		5.80	1.40
Souvenir Sheet				
1352	A280	500fr multi	4.50	3.50

Nos. 1348-1352 air airmail. No. 1352 contains one stamp 36x51mm.

Nos. 1302, 1305-1307 Ovptd. "75e Anniversaire / du Scoutisme Feminin"

1986, Jan.			Perf. 15	
1353	A271	50fr multi	1.60	.30
1354	A271	1000fr multi	15.00	3.50

Souvenir Sheet

1355	A271	1000fr multi	9.50	7.50
1355A	A271	1000fr multi	9.50	7.50

Nos. 1354-1355A airmail.

Nos. 1268-1269, 1271, 1273-1274 Ovptd. "150e ANNIVERSAIRE / DE CHEMIN FER 'LUDWIG'"

1985, Dec. 27			Litho.	Perf. 15	
1356	A267	50fr multi		1.25	.35
1357	A267	90fr multi		1.25	.60
1358	A267	500fr multi		8.00	3.50
	Nos. 1356-1358 (3)			10.50	4.45
Souvenir Sheets					
1359	A267	1000fr No. 1273		9.00	6.50
1360	A267	1000fr No. 1274		9.00	6.50

Halley's Comet A281

Designs: 70fr, Suisei space probe, comets. 90fr, Vega-1 probe. 150fr, Space telescope. 200fr, Giotto probe, comet over Togo. 1000fr, Edmond Halley, Sir Isaac Newton.

1986, Mar. 27			Perf. 13	
1361	A281	70fr multi	.70	.25
1362	A281	90fr multi	.70	.30
1363	A281	150fr multi	1.20	.45
1364	A281	200fr multi	1.75	.60
	Nos. 1361-1364 (4)		4.35	1.60
Souvenir Sheet				
1365	A281	1000fr multi	7.00	6.50

Nos. 1362-1365 are airmail.
For overprints see Nos. 1405-1409.

Flowering and Fruit-bearing Plants A282

70fr, Anacardium occidentale. 90fr, Ananas comosus. 120fr, Persea americana. 135fr, Carica papaya. 290fr, Mangifera indica, vert.

1986, June			Perf. 14	
1366	A282	70fr multi	.55	.25
1367	A282	90fr multi	.80	.30
1368	A282	120fr multi	.90	.40
1369	A282	135fr multi	1.10	.45
1370	A282	290fr multi	2.25	.90
	Nos. 1366-1370 (5)		5.60	2.30

Nos. 1368-1370 airmail.

1986 World Cup Soccer Championships, Mexico — A283

Various soccer plays.

1986, May 5			Litho.	Perf. 15x14	
1371	A283	70fr multi		.55	.25
1372	A283	90fr multi		.55	.30
1373	A283	130fr multi		.85	.40
1374	A283	300fr multi		2.00	.90
	Nos. 1371-1374 (4)			3.95	1.85
Souvenir Sheet					
1375	A283	1000fr multi		7.00	5.50

Nos. 1372-1375 are airmail.
For overprints see Nos. 1394-1397.

Mushrooms — A284

70fr, Ramaria moelleriana. 90fr, Hygrocybe firma. 150fr, Kalchbrennera corallocephala. 200fr, Cookeina tricholoma.

1986, June 9			Perf. 13x12½	
1376	A284	70fr multi	1.10	.25
1377	A284	90fr multi	1.40	.30
1378	A284	150fr multi	2.25	.45
1379	A284	200fr multi	3.00	.60
	Nos. 1376-1379 (4)		7.75	1.60

Intl. Youth Year — A285

1986, June			Perf. 13½x14½	
1380	A285	25fr shown	.80	.25
1381	A285	90fr Youths, doves	2.10	.30

Dated 1985.

Wrestling — A286

15fr, Single-leg takedown move. 20fr, Completing takedown. 70fr, Pinning combination. 90fr, Riding.

1986, July 16			Perf. 14x15, 15x14	
1382	A286	15fr multicolored	.40	.25
1383	A286	20fr multicolored	.40	.25
1384	A286	70fr multicolored	.65	.25
1385	A286	90fr multicolored	.95	.35
	Nos. 1382-1385 (4)		2.40	1.10

Nos. 1384-1385 horiz. No. 1385 is airmail.

Wedding of Prince Andrew and Sarah Ferguson — A287

No. 1386, Sarah Ferguson. No. 1387, Prince Andrew. No. 1388, Couple.

1986, July 23			Perf. 14	
1386	A287	10fr multi	.50	.25
1387	A287	1000fr multi	6.50	2.75
Souvenir Sheet				
1388	A287	1000fr multi	7.50	6.00

Nos. 1387-1388 are airmail.

Easter A288

Paintings (details): 25fr, 1000fr, The Resurrection, by Andrea Mantegna (1431-1506), vert. 70fr, The Calvary, by Paolo Veronese (1528-1588), vert. 90fr, The Last Supper, by Jacopo Tintoretto (1518-1594). 200fr, Christ at the Tomb, by Alonso Berruguette (1400-1561).

Perf. 14x15, 15x14
1986, Mar. 24   Litho.

1389	A288	25fr multi	.25	.25
1390	A288	70fr multi	.50	.25
1391	A288	90fr multi	.75	.30
1392	A288	200fr multi	1.60	.60
		Nos. 1389-1392 (4)	3.10	1.40

Souvenir Sheet

1393	A288	1000fr multi	7.50	5.00

Nos. 1391-1393 are airmail.

Nos. 1371-1374 Overprinted

No. 1394

No. 1395

No. 1396

No. 1397

1986, Aug. 4   Litho.   Perf. 15x14

1394	A283	70fr multi	.60	.25
1395	A283	90fr multi	.75	.30
1396	A283	130fr multi	1.00	.40
1397	A283	300fr multi	2.40	.90
		Nos. 1394-1397 (4)	4.75	1.85

Nos. 1395-1397 are airmail.

Hotels — A289

1986, Aug. 18   Perf. 12½

1398	A289	70fr Fazao	.55	.25
1399	A289	90fr Sarakawa	.60	.35
1400	A289	120fr Le Lac	1.00	.40
		Nos. 1398-1400 (3)	2.15	1.00

Nos. 1399-1400 are airmail.

Keran Natl. Park A290

1986, Sept. 15   Litho.   Perf. 14½

1401	A290	70fr Wild ducks	.95	.25
1402	A290	90fr Antelope	1.10	.25
1403	A290	100fr Elephant	1.25	.30
1404	A290	130fr Waterbuck	1.75	.05
		Nos. 1401-1404 (4)	5.05	1.15

Nos. 1402-1404 are airmail.

Nos. 1361-1365 Ovptd. with Halley's Comet Emblem in Silver

1986, Oct. 9   Perf. 13

1405	A281	70fr multi	1.60	.25
1406	A281	90fr multi	1.90	.30
1407	A281	150fr multi	3.25	.50
1408	A281	200fr multi	4.25	.65
		Nos. 1405-1408 (4)	11.00	1.70

Souvenir Sheet

1409	A281	1000fr multi	21.00	7.25

Nos. 1406-1409 are airmail.

Frescoes from Togoville Church — A291

Togoville Church — A292

45fr, Annunciation. 120fr, Nativity. 130fr, Adoration of the Magi. 200fr, Flight into Egypt.

1986, Dec. 22   Litho.   Perf. 14½x15

1410	A291	45fr multicolored	.40	.25
1411	A291	120fr multicolored	.90	.30
1412	A291	130fr multicolored	1.10	.35
1413	A291	200fr multicolored	1.50	.55
		Nos. 1410-1413 (4)	3.90	1.45

Souvenir Sheet

1414	A292	1000fr multicolored	7.00	5.50

Christmas. Nos. 1411-1414 are airmail.

Phosphate Mining — A293

Natl. Liberation, 20th Anniv. — A294

50fr, Sugar refinery, Anie. 70fr, Nangbeto Dam. 90fr, Hotel, post office in Lome. 100fr, Post office, Kara. 120fr, Peace monument. 130fr, Youth vaccination campaign.

1987, Jan. 13   Litho.   Perf. 12½

1415	A293	35fr shown	.30	.25
1416	A293	50fr multicolored	.40	.25
1417	A293	70fr multicolored	.50	.25
1418	A293	90fr multicolored	.70	.40
1419	A293	100fr multicolored	.80	.40
1420	A293	120fr multicolored	.90	.45
1421	A293	130fr multicolored	1.00	.60
		Nos. 1415-1421 (7)	4.60	2.60

Souvenir Sheet
Perf. 13

1422	A294	500fr shown	3.50	3.25

Nos. 1419-1422 are airmail.

Easter — A295

Paintings in Nadoba Church, Keran: 90fr, The Last Supper. 130fr, Christ on the Cross. 300fr, The Resurrection. 500fr, Evangelization in Tamberma, fresco, horiz.

1987, Apr. 13   Litho.   Perf. 14½x15

1423	A295	90fr multi	.65	.35
1424	A295	130fr multi	.95	.45
1425	A295	300fr multi	2.10	1.00
		Nos. 1423-1425 (3)	3.70	1.80

Souvenir Sheet
Perf. 15x14½

1426	A295	500fr multi	4.00	3.75

Nos. 1424-1426 are airmail.

World Rugby Cup A296

70fr, Dive. 130fr, Running with the ball. 300fr, Scrimmage. 1000fr, Stands, goal, vert.

1987, May 11   Perf. 15x14½

1427	A296	70fr multicolored	.75	.25
1428	A296	130fr multicolored	1.50	.45
1429	A296	300fr multicolored	3.00	1.10
		Nos. 1427-1429 (3)	5.25	1.80

Souvenir Sheet
Perf. 14½x15

1430	A296	1000fr multicolored	9.50	9.50

Nos. 1427-1429 are horiz. Nos. 1428-1430 are airmail.

Indigenous Flowers A297

70fr, Adenium obesum. 90fr, Amorphophallus abyssinicus, vert. 100fr, Ipomoea mauritana. 120fr, Salacia togoica, vert.

1987, June 22   Litho.   Perf. 13

1431	A297	70fr multi	.70	.25
1432	A297	90fr multi	.85	.25
1433	A297	100fr multi	.95	.30
1434	A297	120fr multi	1.25	.35
		Nos. 1431-1434 (4)	3.75	1.15

Nos. 1432-1434 are airmail.

Fish A298

70fr, Chaetodon hoefleri. 90fr, Tetraodon lineatus. 120fr, Chaetodipterus goreensis. 130fr, Labeo parvus.

1987, Sept. 8   Litho.   Perf. 13

1435	A298	70fr multi	.75	.30
1436	A298	90fr multi	.85	.35
1437	A298	120fr multi	1.10	.50
1438	A298	130fr multi	1.25	.55
		Nos. 1435-1438 (4)	3.95	1.70

1988 Summer Olympics, Seoul — A299

Buddha and athletes

1987, Sept. 14   Perf. 12½

1439	A299	70fr Long jump	.60	.30
1440	A299	90fr Relay	.75	.35
1441	A299	200fr Cycling	1.75	.80
1442	A299	250fr Javelin	2.25	.85
		Nos. 1439-1442 (4)	5.35	2.30

Souvenir Sheet

1443	A299	1000fr Tennis	7.50	5.50

Nos. 1440-1443 are airmail.

World Wildlife Fund Type of 1984
1987, Dec. 15   Litho.   Perf. 14
Size: 32x24mm

1444	A263	60fr like 45fr	1.10	.30
1445	A263	75fr like 70fr	1.25	.30
1446	A263	80fr like 90fr	1.75	.30
1447	A263	100fr like 105fr	2.75	.50
		Nos. 1444-1447 (4)	6.85	1.40

No. 1447 is airmail.

Christmas A300

Paintings: 40fr, Springtime in Paradise, horiz. 45fr, Creation of Man, Sistine Chapel, by Michelangelo, horiz. 105fr, Presentation in the Temple. 270fr, Original Sin. 500fr, Nativity, horiz.

Perf. 15x14, 14x15
1987, Dec. 15   Litho.

1448	A300	40fr multi	.40	.25
1449	A300	45fr multi	.45	.25
1450	A300	105fr multi	1.10	.45
1451	A300	270fr multi	2.75	1.00
		Nos. 1448-1451 (4)	4.70	1.95

Souvenir Sheet

1452	A300	500fr multi	4.50	4.00

Nos. 1450-1452 are airmail.

Eradication of Tuberculosis A301

80fr, Inoculation, horiz. 90fr, Family under umbrella. 115fr, Hospital, horiz.

1987, Dec. 28   Perf. 12½x13, 13x12½

1453	A301	80fr multicolored	.55	.30
1454	A301	90fr multicolored	.65	.30
1455	A301	115fr multicolored	.80	.40
		Nos. 1453-1455 (3)	2.00	1.00

Health for all by the year 2000. Nos. 1454-1455 are airmail.

Intl. Fund for Agricultural Development (IFAD), 10th Anniv. — A302

1988, Feb. 25   Litho.   Perf. 13½
1456 A302 90fr multi   .75 .30

Easter 1988 — A303

Stained-glass windows: 70fr, Jesus and the Disciples at Emmaus. 90fr, Mary at the Foot of the Cross. 120fr, The Crucifixion. 200fr, St. Thomas Touching the Resurrected Christ. 500fr, The Agony of Jesus on the Mount of Olives.

1988, June 6   Litho.   Perf. 14x15
1457 A303 70fr multi   .55 .25
1458 A303 90fr multi   .85 .35
1459 A303 120fr multi   .85 .50
1460 A303 200fr multi   1.60 .85
    Nos. 1457-1460 (4)   3.85 1.95
Souvenir Sheet
1461 A303 500fr multi   3.50 2.75
    Nos. 1459-1461 are airmail.

Paintings by Picasso (1881-1973) — A304

Designs: 45fr, The Dance. 160fr, Portrait of a Young Girl. No. 1464, Gueridon. No. 1465, Mandolin and Guitar.

1988, Apr. 25   Litho.   Perf. 12½x13
1462 A304 45fr multi   .50 .25
1463 A304 160fr multi   1.60 .75
1464 A304 300fr multi   3.00 1.50
    Nos. 1462-1464 (3)   5.10 2.50
Souvenir Sheet
1465 A304 300fr multi   2.75 2.00
    Nos. 1464-1465 are airmail.

1988 Summer Olympics, Seoul — A305

1988, Aug. 30   Perf. 14x15
1466 A305 70fr Basketball   .55 .30
1467 A305 90fr Tennis   .70 .35
1468 A305 120fr Archery   .90 .50
1469 A305 200fr Discus   1.75 .80
    Nos. 1466-1469 (4)   3.90 1.95
Souvenir Sheet
1470 A305 500fr Marathon   3.50 2.75
    Nos. 1468-1470 are airmail.

WHO, 40th Anniv. — A306

1988, Oct. 28   Litho.   Perf. 13
1471 A306 80fr shown   .65 .35
1472 A306 125fr Emblems   .95 .45

Traditional Costumes A307

1988, July 25   Litho.   Perf. 13½
1473 A307 80fr Watchi chief   .55 .25
1474 A307 125fr Watchi woman   .85 .40
1475 A307 165fr Kotokoli   1.25 .60
1476 A307 175fr Ewe   1.25 .60
    Nos. 1473-1476 (4)   3.90 1.85
Souvenir Sheet
1477 A307 500fr Moba   3.50 2.75

PHILTOGO 3, Aug. 11-12 — A308

Children's drawings by: 10fr, B. Gossner. 35fr, K. Ekoue-Kouvahey. 70fr, A. Abbey. 90fr, T.D. Lawson. 120fr, A. Tazzar.

1988, Dec. 3
1478 A308 10fr multi   .25 .25
1479 A308 35fr multi   .25 .25
1480 A308 70fr multi   .75 .30
1481 A308 90fr multi   .90 .35
1482 A308 120fr multi   1.10 .50
    Nos. 1478-1482 (5)   3.25 1.65

Christmas — A309

Paintings: 80fr, Adoration of the Magi, by Brueghel. 150fr, The Virgin, Infant Jesus, Sts. Jerome and Dominic, by Lippi. 175fr, Madonna, Infant Jesus, St. Joseph and Infant John the Baptist, by Barocci. 195fr, Virgin and Child, by Bellini. 750fr, The Holy Family and a Shepherd, by Titian.

1988, Dec. 15   Perf. 14½x15
1483 A309 80fr multi   .55 .35
1484 A309 150fr multi   1.25 .60
1485 A309 175fr multi   1.40 .70
1486 A309 195fr multi   1.75 .80
    Nos. 1483-1486 (4)   4.95 2.45
Souvenir Sheet
1487 A309 750fr multi   5.25 4.25
    Nos. 1484-1487 are airmail.

Natl. Industries A310

1988, May 28   Litho.   Perf. 13
1488 A310 125fr Cement factory   .80 .40
1489 A310 165fr Bottling plant   1.20 .60
1490 A310 195fr Phosphate mine   1.40 .70
1491 A310 200fr Plastics factory   1.40 .70
1492 A310 300fr Manufacturing
                   plant   2.10 1.10
    Nos. 1488-1492 (5)   6.90 3.50

John F. Kennedy A311

Designs: 125fr, Arrival in Paris, 1961. 155fr, At Hotel de Ville, vert. 165fr, With De Gaulle at Elysee Palace, vert. 180fr, Boarding Air Force One with Jackie at Orly, France. 750fr, Kennedy and De Gaulle, natl. colors, vert.

1988, July 30   Litho.   Perf. 14
1493 A311 125fr multi   1.90 .40
1494 A311 155fr multi   1.25 .55
1495 A311 165fr multi   1.40 .60
1496 A311 180fr multi   1.50 .65
    Nos. 1493-1496 (4)   6.05 2.20
Souvenir Sheet
Perf. 13½x13
1497 A311 750fr multi   5.25 4.25

Hairstyles A312

1988, Nov. 20   Perf. 13
1498 A312 80fr shown   .45 .25
1499 A312 125fr multi, diff.   .85 .40
1500 A312 170fr multi   1.25 .55
1501 A312 180fr multi, diff., vert.   1.40 .60
    Nos. 1498-1501 (4)   3.95 1.80
Souvenir Sheet
Perf. 14
1502 A312 500fr multi, diff.   3.50 2.75

Sarakawa Plane Crash, 15th Anniv. A313

Portrait and various views of the wreckage.

1989, Jan. 24   Perf. 13½
1503 A313 10fr multi   .25 .25
1504 A313 80fr multi, vert.   .70 .35
1505 A313 125fr multi   1.10 .55
    Nos. 1503-1505 (3)   2.05 1.15

1990 World Cup Soccer Championships, Italy — A314

ITALIA '90 emblem, flag of Togo, athletes and architecture: 80fr, Cathedral of St. Januarius, Naples. 125fr, Milan Cathedral. 165fr, Bevilacqua Palace, Verona. 175fr, Baptistery of San Giovanni, Florence. 380fr, Madama Palace, Turin. 425fr, Cathedral of

San Lorenzo, Genoa. 650fr, The Colosseum, Rome.

1989, Jan. 10   Litho.   Perf. 13½
1506 A314 80fr multi   .55 .30
1507 A314 125fr multi   .90 .45
1508 A314 165fr multi   1.25 .60
1509 A314 175fr multi   1.25 .65
1510 A314 380fr multi   2.75 1.50
1511 A314 425fr multi   3.00 1.50
    Nos. 1506-1511 (6)   9.70 5.00
Souvenir Sheet
1512 A314 650fr multi   5.25 5.25
    Nos. 1510-1512 are airmail.

A316

Prince Emanuel of Liechtenstein Foundation — A316a

1988 Summer Olympics, Seoul: Flags of Liechtenstein, Togo, athletes, Pres. Eyadema. No. 1522A, Olympic rings. No. 1522B, Tennis players Miroslav Mecir, Steffi Graf, vert.

1989, May 25   Litho.   Perf. 13½
1520 A316 80fr Boxing   1.10 .30
1521 A316 125fr Long jump   1.25 .45
1522 A316 165fr Running   2.10 .55
    Nos. 1520-1522 (3)   4.45 1.30
Litho. & Embossed
1522A A316a 1500fr gold &
                     multi   10.00
1522B A316a 1500fr gold &
                     multi   10.00
    Nos. 1522A-1522B are airmail and exist imperf. and in souvenir sheets of 1 both perf. and imperf.

Federal Republic of Germany, 40th Anniv. A317

1989, June 1
1523 A317 90fr Palace   .65 .30
1524 A317 125fr Statesmen, vert.   1.00 .40
1525 A317 180fr Natl. flag, crest   1.50 .60
    Nos. 1523-1525 (3)   3.15 1.30

Council for Rural Development, 30th Anniv. — A318

75fr, Flags, well, tractor, field.

1989, June 19   Perf. 15x14
1526 A318 75fr multicolored   .70 .35
    See Ivory Coast No. 874.

Intl. Red Cross, 125th Anniv. A319

1989, June 30   **Perf. 13½**
1527 A319   90fr shown   .70   .35
1528 A319   125fr Geneva Convention, 1864   .90   .50

French Revolution, Bicent. A320

Designs: 90fr, Storming of the Bastille, vert. 125fr, Tennis Court Oath. 180fr, Abolition of privileges. 1000fr, Declaration of Human Rights and Citizenship, vert.

1989, July 15
1529 A320   90fr multi   .70   .30
1530 A320   125fr multi   1.10   .45
1531 A320   180fr multi   1.40   .65
    Nos. 1529-1531 (3)   3.20   1.40

Souvenir Sheet
1532 A320   1000fr multi   8.50   2.75

Electric Corp. of Benin, 20th Anniv. A321

1989, July 15
1533 A321   80fr multi   .65   .30
1534 A321   125fr multi   1.10   .45

A322

PHILEXFRANCE '89, French Revolution, Bicent. — A322a

Figures and scenes from the revolution: 90fr, Jacques Necker (1732-1804), financier, statesman, and The Three Estates. 190fr, Guy Le Chapelier (1754-1794), politician, and abolition of feudalism (seigniorial privileges), Aug. 4, 1789. 425fr, Talleyrand-Perigord (1754-1838), statesman, and Lafayette's Oath at the Festival of Federation, July 14, 1790. 480fr, Paul Barras (1755-1829), revolutionary, and overthrowing of Robespierre during the Revolution of 9th Thermidor, July 27, 1794. 750fr, Georges Jacques Danton (1759-1794), revolutionary leader, and arrest of Louis XVI at Varennes, June 21, 1791, horiz. Nos. 1537-1539 are airmail.
No. 1539A, Assassination of Jean-Paul Marat (1743-93). No. 1539B, Fabré d'Eglantine (1750-94), making of the calendar of the republic.

1989   **Litho.**   **Perf. 13½**
1535 A322   90fr multi   .70   .25
1536 A322   190fr multi   1.40   .40
1537 A322   425fr multi   3.25   .60
1538 A322   480fr multi   3.75   .60
    Nos. 1535-1538 (4)   9.10   1.85

Souvenir Sheet
1539 A322   750fr multi   8.00   2.00
Litho. & Embossed
1539A A322a   1500fr gold & multi   10.00   2.00
Souvenir Sheet
1539B A322a   1500fr gold & multi   8.00

#1539A-1539B are airmail and exist imperf. Nos. 1535-1538 exist in souvenir sheets of 1, No. 1539A in souvenir sheets of 1, perf. and imperf.
Issued: 90fr-750fr, 6/12; 1500fr, 7/15.

Gen. Kpalime's Role in Natl. Unity and Peace Struggle, 20th Anniv. A323

1989, Aug. 21
1540 A323   90fr shown   .70   .30
1541 A323   125fr Giving speech   1.00   .40

A324

Butterflies — 5fr, Danaus chrysippus. 10fr, Morpho aega. 15fr, Papilio demodocus. 90fr, Papilio dardanus.
500fr, Papilio zalmoxis.

1990, Apr. 30   **Litho.**   **Perf. 13½**
1542 A324   5fr multicolored   .60   .25
1543 A324   10fr multicolored   .60   .25
1544 A324   15fr multicolored   .60   .25
1545 A324   90fr multicolored   2.10   .60
    Nos. 1542-1545 (4)   3.90   1.35

Souvenir Sheet
1545A A324   500fr multicolored   5.50   2.75

No. 1545A is airmail.

A325

1989, Dec. 1   **Litho.**   **Perf. 13½**
1546 A325   40fr Apollo 11 liftoff   .25   .25
1547 A325   90fr Module transposition   .55   .30
1548 A325   150fr Eagle   1.25   .45
1549 A325   250fr Splashdown   1.90   .80
    Nos. 1546-1549 (4)   3.95   1.80

Souvenir Sheet
1550 A325   500fr Astronaut on Moon   3.50   2.75

1st Moon Landing, 20th anniv.

Lome IV Conference, Dec. 1989 — A326

1989, Dec. 15   **Litho.**   **Perf. 13**
1551 A326   100fr "Dec. 89"   .70   .30
1552 A326   100fr "15 Dec. 89"   .70   .30

A327

Boy Scouts, Flora and Fauna A327a

80fr, Myrina silenus. 90fr, Phlebobus silvaticus. 125fr, Volvariella esculenta. 165fr, Hypolicaena antifaunus. 380fr, Termitomyces striatus. 425fr, Axiocerces harpax.
750fr, Cupidopsis jobates. No. 1559A, Kalchbrennera corallocephala. No. 1559B, Spindasis mozambica.

1990, Jan. 8   **Litho.**   **Perf. 13½**
1553 A327   80fr multicolored   .65   .25
1554 A327   90fr multicolored   .65   .25
1555 A327   125fr multicolored   .90   .25
1556 A327   165fr multicolored   1.10   .35
1557 A327   380fr multicolored   2.50   .50
1558 A327   425fr multicolored   3.25   .50
    Nos. 1553-1558 (6)   9.05   2.10

Souvenir Sheet
1559 A327   750fr multicolored   6.00   1.10
Litho. & Embossed
1559A A327a   1500fr gold & multi   12.00
Souvenir Sheet
1559B A327a   1500fr gold & multi   6.50

Nos. 1557-1559B are airmail. Nos. 1559A-1559B exist imperf. No. 1559A exists in souvenir sheet of 1 both perf. and imperf.

People's Republic of Togo, 20th Anniv. — A328

45fr, Government House, Kara. 90fr, Pres. Eyadema, House.

1990, Jan. 8
1560 A328   45fr multicolored   .45   .25
1561 A328   90fr multicolored   .80   .40

Pan-African Postal Union, 10th Anniv. — A329

1990, Jan. 1   **Perf. 13½**
1562 A329   125fr bronze, blk & bl   1.10   .30

Ninth Convention of Lions Club International Multidistrict 403, Lome — A329a

Frame color: 90fr, Blue. 125fr, Rose. 165fr, Yellow.

1990, May 5   **Litho.**   **Perf. 13½**
1562A-1562C   A329a   Set of 3   3.00   1.50

US-Togo Relations A330

180fr, Pres. Bush, Pres. Eyadema, horiz.

1990, July 20   **Litho.**   **Perf. 13½**
1563 A330   125fr multicolored   .85   .40
1564 A330   180fr multicolored   1.20   .40
    Size: 90 x 75mm
1565 A330   125fr multicolored   .85   .50
1566 A330   180fr multicolored   1.10   .70
    Nos. 1563-1566 (4)   4.00   2.00

Nos. 1565-1566 printed in sheets of 1.

Reptiles A331

1fr, Varanus niloticus. 25fr, Vipera bitis arietans. 60fr, Naja melaneuloca. 90fr, Python de sebae.

1990, May 22
1567 A331   1fr multicolored   .25   .25
1568 A331   25fr multicolored   .25   .25
1569 A331   60fr multicolored   .65   .25
1570 A331   90fr multicolored   .70   .30
    Nos. 1567-1570 (4)   1.85   1.05

Cowrie Shell Ornaments A332

1990, July, 20   **Litho.**   **Perf. 13½**
1571 A332   90fr shown   .65   .35
1572 A332   125fr Shell necklace   1.10   .45
1573 A332   180fr Shells on horned helmet   1.40   .60
    Nos. 1571-1573 (3)   3.15   1.40

Stamp Day A333

1990, Aug. 23
1574 A333   90fr multicolored   .70   .40

Traditional Homes A334

1990, Sept. 9
1575	A334	90fr shown	.65	.35
1576	A334	125fr multi, diff.	.90	.45
1577	A334	190fr multi, diff.	1.40	.70
		Nos. 1575-1577 (3)	2.95	1.50

Charles de Gaulle (1890-1970), Speech at Brazzaville, 1944 — A335

1990, Aug. 30   Litho.   *Perf. 14*
1578	A335	125fr multicolored	1.10	.45

New Lome Airport A336

1990, Sept. 17   *Perf. 13½*
1579	A336	90fr multicolored	.70	.30

Children's Art — A337

1990, Sept. 28   Litho.   *Perf. 13½*
1580	A337	90fr multicolored	.70	.40

Forest Wildlife — A342

1991, June 5   Litho.   *Perf. 13½x14*
1593	A342	90fr Chimpanzee	.55	.35
1594	A342	170fr Green parrot	1.25	.60
1595	A342	185fr White parrot	1.40	.80
		Nos. 1593-1595 (3)	3.20	1.75

Python Regius A343

Various snakes emerging from eggs.

1992, Aug. 24   Litho.   *Perf. 13½*
1596	A343	90fr multicolored	.65	.30
1597	A343	125fr multicolored	.85	.30
1598	A343	190fr multicolored	1.25	.60
1599	A343	300fr multicolored	1.90	.80
		Nos. 1596-1599 (4)	4.65	2.00

Dated 1991.

Voodoo Dances A344

Various women dancing.

1992, Aug. 24
1600	A344	90fr multicolored	.70	.30
1601	A344	125fr multicolored	.90	.45
1602	A344	190fr multicolored	1.40	.65
		Nos. 1600-1602 (3)	3.00	1.40

Dated 1991.

A345

1994 World Cup Soccer Championships, US — A346

Various soccer players in action: 5fr, 10fr, 25fr, 60fr, 90fr, 100fr, 200fr, 1000fr.
1500fr, Player in white & green uniform. 3000fr, Two players in air, horiz.

1994, Nov. 15   Litho.   *Perf. 14*
1603-1610	A345	Set of 8	6.75	3.50

Souvenir Sheets
1611	A346	1500fr multicolored	7.50	3.50
1612	A346	3000fr multicolored	12.50	6.25

UPU, 120th Anniv. — A347

1994, July 29   *Perf. 13½*
1613	A347	180fr multicolored	.70	.35

A miniature sheet may exist.

Stamp Day — A348

1994, Oct. 9
1614	A348	90fr pale bl & multi	.60	.25
1615	A348	125fr pale yel & multi	.75	.40

Intl. Olympic Committee, Cent. — A348a

Designs, each 300fr: b, Pierre de Coubertin, Olympic Hymn. c, Original members of IOC. d, Olympic flame.
900fr, Pierre de Coubertin holding document.

1994, Oct.   Litho.   *Perf. 13½*
1615A	A348a	Strip of 3, #b.-d.	4.25	4.25

Souvenir Sheet
1615E	A348a	900fr multicolored	4.25	2.10

Nos. 1615A, 1615E exist imperf. No. 1615c is 60x51mm. No. 1615E is airmail and contains one 36x51mm stamp.

Birds A349

Designs: #1616, 5fr, Secretary bird, vert. #1617, 10fr, Paradise flycather, vert. #1618, 25fr, African spoonbill. #1619, 60fr, Cordon bleu waxbill. #1620, 90fr, Orange-breasted sunbird, vert. #1621, 100fr, Yellow-billed hornbill, vert. #1621A, 180fr, Barn owl. #1622, 200fr, African hoopoe. #1622A, 300fr, Firecrowned bishop, vert. #1623, 1000fr, Redthroated bee eater, vert.

1995   Litho.   *Perf. 14*
1616-1623	A349	Set of 10	7.75	3.75

Souvenir Sheet
1624	A349	1500fr Vulture	7.50	3.50

Issued: 180fr, 300fr, 8/7; others, 1/23.

A350

Motion Picture, Alien: a, Alien creature. b, Humans in combat with creature. c, Sigourney Weaver.

1994   Litho.   *Perf. 13½*
1625	A350	600fr Strip of 3, #a.-c.	7.50	3.75

No. 1625b is 60x48mm. No. 1625 is a continuous design and exists in souvenir sheets of 1.

First Manned Moon Landing, 25th Anniv. — A351

No. 1626, each 600fr: a, Edwin "Buzz" Aldrin. b, Eagle, olive branch, Neil Armstrong. c, Michael Collins.
No. 1627, each 600fr: a, Apollo emblem, footprint. b, Crew of Apollo 11. c, Moon rock, NASA emblem.

1994   Strips of 3, #a.-c.
1626-1627	A351	Set of 2	15.00	7.50

Nos. 1626b, 1627b are each 60x47mm. Nos. 1626-1627 are continuous designs and exist in souvenir sheets of 1.

Dinosaurs — A352

125fr, Polacanthus. 180fr, Pachycephalosaurus. 425fr, Coelophysis. 480fr, Brachiosaurus. 500fr, Dilophosaurus. 1500fr, Scutellosaurus.

No. 1634, Velociraptor, vert.

1994
1628-1633	A352	Set of 6	13.00	6.50

Souvenir Sheet
1634	A352	1500fr multicolored	6.25	3.00

No. 1634 is airmail.

Flowers — A353

Designs: 15fr, Belvache de Madagascar. 90fr, Oeuillets. 125fr, Agave, horiz.

1995, May 12
1635-1637	A353	Set of 3	1.10	.55

Easter — A354

Details or entire paintings: 90fr, The Resurrection, by A. Mantegna. 180fr, Calvary, by Veronese. 190fr, The Last Supper, by Tintoretto, horiz.

1995, May 12
1638-1640	A354	Set of 3	2.10	1.10

Fish A355

10fr, Pike. 90fr, Capitaine. 180fr, Carp.

1995, May 12
1641-1643	A355	Set of 3	2.10	1.10

Miniature Sheets of 6 and 8

VJ Day, 50th Anniv. — A356

Japanese leaders: No. 1644a, Adm. Isoroko Yamamoto. b, Gen. Hideki Tojo. c, Vice Adm. Shigeru Fukudome. d, Adm. Shigetaro Shimada. e, Contre-Adm. Chuichi Nagumo. f, Gen. Shizu Ichi Tanaka.
VE Day: No. 1645a, 200fr, German fighter planes making final attacks. b, 200fr, Allies win Battle of the Atlantic. c, 200fr, Ludendorf Bridge at Remagen is taken intact. d, 200fr, Russian rockets fired at Berlin. e, 45fr, Hostilities suspended in Italy. f, 90fr, Russians capture devastated Warsaw. g, 125fr, Russian tanks enter Berlin. h, 500fr, UN flag.
No. 1646, Japanese signing peace agreement. No. 1647, German U-236 surrenders.

1995, July 20   Litho.   *Perf. 14*
1644	A356	200fr #a.-f.	4.75	2.50
1645	A356	#a.-h.	6.25	3.25

Souvenir Sheets

1646	A356	1500fr multicolored	6.00	3.00
1647	A356	1500fr multicolored	10.00	5.00

UN, 50th Anniv. — A357

No. 1648: a, 25fr, Doves, earth from space. b, 90fr, Doves, UN headquarters. c, 400fr, Doves, earth from space. 1000fr, Earth, dove.

1995, June 26

1648	A357	Strip of 3, #a.-c.	2.40	1.25

Souvenir Sheet

1649	A357	1000fr multicolored	6.25	3.00

1995 Boy Scout Jamboree, Holland — A358

Designs: 90fr, Nat. flag. 190fr, Scout oath. 300fr, Lord Baden-Powell. 1500fr, Scout salute.

1995, July 20

1650-1652	A358	Set of 3	2.75	1.40

Souvenir Sheet

1653	A358	1500fr multicolored	6.00	3.00

Queen Mother, 95th Birthday — A359

No. 1654: a, Formal portrait. b, Cutting cake. c, As younger woman wearing jewels, waving. d, Drawing.

No. 1654E, Holding umbrella. No. 1654F, Formal portrait as young woman.

No. 1655, Royal attire, pearls.

No. 1655A, Early picture of King George VI, Queen Mother.

1995, July 20   Perf. 13½x14

1654	A359	250fr Strip of 4, #a.-d.	5.00	2.50
1654E	A359	250fr multicolored	1.25	.65
1654F	A359	250fr multicolored	1.25	.65
g.		Block or strip of 4, #1654a, 1654d, 1654E, 1654F	5.00	2.50
		Nos. 1654-1654F (3)	7.50	3.80

Souvenir Sheets

1655	A359	1000fr multicolored	4.00	2.00
1655A	A359	1000fr multicolored	4.00	2.00

Nos. 1654, 1654Fg were issued in sheets of 8 stamps.

Issued: #1654, 1655, 7/20; # 1654E, 1654F, 1655A, 11/22.

FAO, 50th Anniv. — A360

No. 1656: a, 45fr, Cattle. b, 125fr, Water buffalo. c, 200fr, Boy, man with water buffaloes. 1000fr, Woman milking cow.

1995, Mar. 3   Litho.   Perf. 14

1656	A360	Strip of 3, #a.-c.	2.25	1.10

Souvenir Sheet

1657	A360	1000fr multicolored	4.50	2.10

No. 1656 is a continuous design.

Nobel Prize Winners — A361

No. 1658, each 200fr: a, Elihu Root, peace, 1912. b, Alfred Fried, peace, 1911. c, Henri Moissan, chemistry, 1906. d, Charles Barkla, physics, 1917. e, Rudolf Eucken, literature, 1908. f, Carl von Ossietzky, peace, 1935. g, Sir Edward Appleton, physics. 1947. h, Camillo Golgi, physiology, 1906. i, Wilhelm Roentgen, physics, 1901.

No. 1659, each 200fr: a, Manfred Eigen, chemistry, 1967. b, Donald J. Cram, chemistry, 1987. c, Paul J. Flory, chemistry, 1974. d, Johann Deisenhofer, chemistry, 1988. e, P.W. Bridgman, physics, 1946. f, Otto Stern, physics, 1943. g, Arne Tiselius, chemistry, 1948. h, J. Georg Bednorz, physics, 1987. i, Albert Claude, medicine, 1974.

Each 1500fr: No. 1660, Albert Einstein, physics, 1921. No. 1661, Woodrow Wilson, peace, 1919.

1995, Aug. 21

Miniature Sheets of 9, a-i

1658-1659	A361	Set of 2	25.00	12.00

Souvenir Sheets

1660-1661	A361	Set of 2	12.50	6.50

Rotary Intl., 90th Anniv. — A362

No. 1663, Natl. flag, Rotary emblem.

1995, July 20

1662	A362	1000fr shown	4.25	2.00

Souvenir Sheet

1663	A362	1000fr multi	4.25	2.00

Miniature Sheets

Fauna A363

Primates, each 200fr, vert: No. 1664a, Black-faced monkey in tree. b, Brown monkey in tree. c, Black monkey. d, Baboon.

Wild animals, each 200fr: No. 1665a, Hyena. b, Hyrax. c, Mongoose. d, Elephant. e, Mandrill. f, Okapi. g, Hippopotamus. h, Flamingo. i, Wild boar. 1500fr, Potto.

1995, Oct. 2   Litho.   Perf. 14

1664	A363	Sheet of 4, #a.-d.	3.25	1.60
1665	A363	Sheet of 9, #a.-i.	7.25	3.50

Souvenir Sheet

1666	A363	1500fr multicolored	6.00	3.00

FAO, 50th Anniv. A364

1995, Mar. 3   Litho.   Perf. 14

1667	A364	125fr shown	.50	.25

Souvenir Sheet

1668	A364	300fr like No. 1667	1.50	.75

Sir Rowland Hill (1795-1879) A365

1995, June 3   Perf. 13½

1669	A365	125fr multicolored	.75	.40

UN, 50th Anniv. — A366

1995, June 26

1670	A366	180fr multicolored	.90	.50

Mushrooms A367

No. 1671: a, Cortinarius violaceus. b, Hygrocybe flavescens. c, Mycena haematopus. d, Coprinus micaceus. e, Helvella lacunosa. f, Flammulina velutipes. g, Aleuria aurantia. h, Geastrum triplex.

No. 1672: a, Russula laurocerasi. b, Phyllotopsis nidulans. c, Xeromphalina campanella. d, Psathyrella hydrophila. e, Entoloma murraii. f, Hygrophorus speciosus. g, Mycena leaiana. h, Cystoderma amianthinum.

No. 1673, each 200fr: a, Amanita muscaria. b, Amanita virosa. c, Galerina autumnalis. d, Omphalotus illudens. e, Naematoloma fasciculare. f, Paxillus involutus. g, Russula emetica. h, Scleroderma citrinum.

No. 1674, each 200fr: a, Armillaria ponderosa. b, Agaricus augustus. c, Gomphidius subroseus. d, Morchella esculenta. e, Stropharia rugoso. f, Boletus edulis. g, Clitocybe nuda. h, Lactarius deliciosus.

Each 1500fr: No. 1675, Trametes versicolor. No. 1676, Collybia iocephala.

1995, Nov. 1   Perf. 14

1671	A367	180fr Sheet of 8, #a.-h.	9.00	4.50
1672	A367	195fr Sheet of 8, #a.-h.	10.00	4.75
1673-1674	A367	Set of 2 Sheets, #a.-h.	21.00	10.50

Souvenir Sheets

1675-1676	A367	Set of 2	20.00	10.00

Miniature Sheets

History of Transportation — A368

Steam locomotives: No. 1677, each 200fr: a, SNCF Class 231 D Le Havre-Paris Express. b, Princess Royal Class Pacific, England. c, Class 52 2-10-0, German Railroad. d, Class "15A" 4-6-4+4-6-4 Beyer-Garratt, Rhodesia. e, Japanese 2-8-0. f, Class 940, 2-8-2 engine, Italy.

Various vehicles: No. 1678, each 200fr: a, Semi truck. b, Roman chariot. c, Motorcycle. d, Hummer 4-wheel drive. e, Bicycle. f, London autobus. g, Lunar rover. h, 1954 Jaguar XK 140. i, Ski-doo.

No. 1679, First land vehicle to break sound barrier.

1995, Dec. 1   Litho.   Perf. 14

1677	A368	Sheet of 6, #a.-f.	5.50	2.75
1678	A368	Sheet of 9, #a.-i.	8.00	3.75

Souvenir Sheet

1679	A368	1500fr multicolored	6.50	3.50

No. 1679 contains one 85x28mm stamp.

World Post Day A369

Designs: 220fr, Selling stamps. 315fr, Sorting stamps. 335fr, Post office workers handling large sacks of mail.

1995   Litho.   Perf. 13½

1680-1682	A369	Set of 3	4.50	2.25

Christmas A370

Paintings: 90fr, Nativity scene, vert. 325fr, Adoration of the Magi, vert. 340fr, 500fr, Adoration of the shepherds.

1995, Sept. 13   Litho.   Perf. 13½

1683-1685	A370	Set of 3	4.00	2.00

Souvenir Sheet

Perf. 12½

1686	A370	500fr multi, vert.	3.75	1.90

Sheets of 6

Wildlife of Africa — A371

No. 1687: a, Gorilla. b, Uroota suraka. c, Pan troglodytes. d, Panthera pardus. e, Crocodylus niloticus. f, Leptailurus serval.

No. 1688a, Papilio tynderaeus. b, Bongo taurotragus. c, Epiphora aldiha. d, Cephalophus zebra. e, Cercopithecus cephus. f, Arctocebus calabarensis.

1996, May 10   Litho.   Perf. 14

1687	A371	150fr #a.-f.	3.75	1.90
1688	A371	180fr #a.-f.	4.75	2.50

China '96, 9th Asian Intl. Philatelic Exhibition.

A372

Designs: 50fr, Olympic Stadium, Mexico, 1968, horiz. 90fr, Yevgeny Petrov, skeet shooter, Mexico, 1968, horiz. 220fr, Lia Manoliu, women's discus, Mexico, 1968, horiz. 325fr, Dumb-bell lifting, discontinued sport.

Medal winners from past games: No. 1693, each 200fr: a, China, Women's Volleyball, 1984. b, Wayne Wells, wrestling, 1972. c, Bob Beamon, long jump, 1968. d, Victor Kurentsov, weight lifting, 1968. e, Shirley Strong, 100m hurdles, 1984. f, Nadia Comaneci, balance beam, 1976. g, Giovanni Parisi, boxing, 1988. h, Emil Zatopek, 10,000m, 1948. i, USSR, Brazil, Germany, soccer, 1988. 1000fr, Helen Mayer, fencing, 1936.

1996, July 8   Litho.   Perf. 14

1689-1692	A372	Set of 4	2.75	1.40

1693 A372   Sheet of 9, #a.-i.   7.25 3.50
Souvenir Sheet
1694 A372 1000fr multicolored   4.00 2.00

1996 Summer
Olympics,
Atlanta — A373

100fr, Women's gymnastics. 150fr,
Women's tennis. 200fr, Javelin. 300fr, Men's
field hockey. 400fr, Weight lifting. 500fr, Men's
soccer.
1000fr, Synchronized swimming.

1996, Mar. 25   **Perf. 12½**
1695-1700 A373 Set of 6   7.50 3.75
Souvenir Sheet
1701 A373 1000fr multicolored   5.50 2.75

Butterflies
A374

Designs: 40fr, Euphaedra eleus, vert. 90fr,
Papilio dardanus, vert. 220fr, Iolaus timon.
315fr, Charaxes cynthia.

1996, June 17   **Litho.**   **Perf. 13**
1702-1705 A374 Set of 4   2.75 1.50

Beetles — A375

Designs: 100fr, Purpuricenus kaehleri.
150fr, Carabus auronitens. 200fr, Semanotus
rassicus. 300fr, Rosalia alpina. 400fr, Mylabris
variabilis. 500fr, Odontolabis cuvera.
1000fr, Psalidognathus atys.

1996, May 5
1706-1711 A375 Set of 6   7.75 3.75
Souvenir Sheet
Perf. 12½
1712 A375 1000fr multicolored   5.50 2.75
No. 1712 contains one 40x32mm stamp.

1998 World Cup
Soccer
Championships,
France — A376

French flag, various action scenes: 100fr,
150fr, 200fr, 300fr, 400fr, 500fr.

1996, Apr. 10   **Perf. 12½**
1713-1718 A376 Set of 6   7.75 3.75
Souvenir Sheet
1719 A376 1000fr multicolored   5.50 2.75

World Wildlife Fund — A377

Designs: a, 325fr, Cephalophus drosalis. b,
220fr, Cephalophus maxwelli. c, 180fr,
Cephalophus rufilatus. d, 370fr, Cephalophus
syvicultor.
1500fr, Cephalophus dorsalis, diff.

1996, July 30   **Perf. 14**
1720 A377 Block of 4, #a.-d.   7.00 3.00
Souvenir Sheet
1721 A377 1500fr multicolored   8.25 4.00
No. 1720 was issued in sheets of 16 stamps.

Endangered Species — A378

Designs, vert: 220fr, Zebra. 315fr, Cheetah.
325fr, Antelope. 335fr, Madoqua Kirki.
No. 1726, each 200fr: a, African elephants.
b, Toucan (c, d, e, f.). c, Mamba (f). d, Lion-
esses. e, Impala. f, Nyala. g, Hippoppotamus.
h, Crocodile. i, Kingfisher.
Each 1500 fr: No. 1727, Buphagus
erythrorhynchus, vert. No. 1728, Leopard,
vert.

1996, July 30
1722-1725 A378 Set of 4   8.50 4.00
1726 A378 Sheet of 9, #a.-i.   9.50 4.75
Souvenir Sheets
1727-1728 A378 Set of 2   17.00 9.25

Endangered
Species
A379

75fr, Elephant. 90fr, Crocodile. 315fr, Deer.

1996, July 30   **Litho.**   **Perf. 13**
1729-1731 A379 Set of 3   5.50 3.00

Traditional
Musical
Instruments
A380

90fr, Gongs. 220fr, Cymbals (balafon).
325fr, String instrument. 500fr, Drums.

1996, July 15
1732-1735 A380 Set of 4   5.00 2.50

Traditional
Dances
A381

Designs: 10fr, Kamou dance, Kabyes. 90fr,
Kondona dance, Kabyes. 220fr, Bassar. 315fr,
Kloto. 335fr, Voudoussis.

1996, June 30
1736-1740 A381 Set of 5   8.00 4.00

New Year 1997 (Year of the
Ox) — A382

Paintings, by Ren Bonian (1840-95): No.
1741: a, Herdboy on Buffalo. b, Return from
the Pasture. c, Grazing by the Pond.
500fr, Reading Beside an Ox.

1997, Jan. 2   **Litho.**   **Perf. 14**
1741 A382 180fr Strip of 3, #a.-c. 2.50 2.50
  d. Souvenir sheet of 6, 2x #a-c   5.00 5.00
Souvenir Sheet
Perf. 13½x14
1742 A382 500fr multicolored   2.75 2.75
No. 1741 was issued in sheets of 6 stamps.
No. 1742 contains one 34x46mm stamp.

Fruits
A383

100fr, Mango. 150fr, Bananas. 200fr,
Peaches. 300fr, Papaya. 400fr, Lemon. 500fr,
Coconuts.
1000fr, Various fruits.

1996, June 2   **Litho.**   **Perf. 12½**
1743-1748 A383 Set of 6   7.25 7.25
Souvenir Sheet
Perf. 13
1749 A383 1000fr multicolored   5.25 5.25
No. 1749 contains one 40x32mm stamp.

Souvenir Sheet

Chinese Stone Carving — A384

1996, May 10   **Litho.**   **Perf. 12**
1750 A384 370fr multicolored   1.50 1.50
China '96. No. 1750 was not available until
March 1997.

Jaffar Ballogou,
Boxer — A384a

1996   **Litho.**   **Perf. 13**
1750A A384a 90fr red & multi   —
1750B A384a 220fr blk & multi   —
1750C A384a 315fr red & multi   —
World Telecommunications Day.

UNESCO,
50th Anniv.
A385

World Heritage Sites: No. 1751, each 235fr:
a, Axum archaeological site, Ethiopia. b, Victo-
ria Falls, Zambia. c, Archaeological site,
Zimbabwe. d, Nature reserve, Niger. e, Arguin
Natl. Park, Mauritania. f, Goree Island, Sene-
gal. g, Timgad Ruins, Algeria. h, Ait Ben-Had-
dou, Morocco.
No. 1752, each 235fr: a, Kyoto, Japan. b,
Waterfalls, Colombia. c, Necropolis, Egypt. d,
Old Rama Church, Finland. e, Palladian villa,
Vicenza, Italy. f, Church, Ouro Preto, Brazil. g,
Church, Ouro Preto, Brazil. h, Rhodes,
Greece.
No. 1753, each 235fr: a, Exterior of Cister-
cian Abbey, Fontenay, France. b, Dubrovnik,
Croatia. c, Interior of Cistercian Abbey,
Fontenay. d, e, Quedlinberg, Germany. f, Iron-
bridge Gorge, England. g, Grand Canyon, US.
h, Village, Ironbridge Gorge, England.
Each 1000fr: No. 1754, Kyoto, Japan, horiz.
No. 1755, Mt. Huangshan, China, horiz. No.
1756, Village, Ironbridge, England, horiz.

1997, Mar. 24   **Litho.**   **Perf. 14**
Sheets of 8, a-h, + Label
1751-1753 A385 Set of 3   25.00 25.00
Souvenir Sheets
1754-1756 A385 Set of 3   12.50 12.50

Cats
A386

150fr, American shorthair. 200fr, Siamese,
vert. 300fr, Java. 400fr, "Ocicat," vert. 500fr,
Scottish fold. f, 1762, Persian, vert.
No. 1763, Colorpoint shorthair, vert.

1997   **Litho.**   **Perf. 12½**
1757-1762 A386 Set of 6   12.00 12.00
Souvenir Sheet
1763 A386 1000fr multicolored   4.50 4.50
No. 1763 contains one 32x40mm stamp.

Military
Uniforms — A387

Designs: 150fr, Officer of cuirassiers. 200fr,
Norman regiment officer. 300fr, Volunteer bat-
talion foot soldier. 400fr, Berlin Campaign Mili-
tiaman. 500fr, Foot soldier. No. 1769, 1000fr,
Musketeer.
No. 1770, Belling Regiment Hussar.

1997   **Perf. 13x12½**
1764-1769 A387 Set of 6   12.00 12.00
Souvenir Sheet
1770 A387 1000fr multicolored   4.50 4.50
No. 1770 contains one 40x32mm stamp.

Return of Hong Kong to China — A388

Deng Xiaoping (1904-97) — A388a

Views of city: 220fr, Chinese flag as inscription, skyscraper. 315fr, Chinese flag as inscription, night scene. 325fr, Circular stair railing, skyscraper at night. 340fr, Chinese flag, view of city through inscription. 370fr, Deng Xiaoping (1904-97), fireworks over city. #1775A: a, shown. b, Looking left.

1997, June 2   **Perf. 14**
1771-1775 A388 Set of 5   7.50 7.50
Sheet of 2
Perf. 13½
1775A A388a 500fr #a.-b.   4.50 4.50
Nos. 1771-1773 are 28x44mm and were each issued in sheets of 4. Nos. 1774-1775 were each issued in sheets of 3.

Queen Elizabeth II and Prince Philip, 50th Wedding Anniv. A389

No. 1776: a, Queen. b, Royal arms. c, Queen in yellow hat, Prince in military uniform. d, Queen in white hat, Prince. e, Windsor Castle. f, Prince.
1000fr, Portrait of Queen, Prince.

1997, June 25
1776 A389 315fr Sheet of 6, #a.-f.   7.50 7.50
Souvenir Sheet
1777 A389 1000fr multicolored   4.50 4.50

Locomotives — A390

150fr, Light locomotive, Adams Bridges. 200fr, Norris Type, England 1866. 300fr, Jones and Ports locomotive with long boiler, 1848. 400fr, Cargo and passenger locomotive, Ansaldo, 1850. 500fr, Birkenhead, Italy, 1863. #1783, 1000fr, Quarter locomotive, New York, 1890.
#1783A, Six-wheeled locomotive, Robert Stephenson, 1830, vert.

1996, Dec. 5 Litho. Perf. 12½x12
1778-1783 A390 Set of 6   12.00 12.00
Souvenir Sheet
Perf. 12½
1783A A390 1000fr multi   4.50 4.50

Birds — A391

150fr, Poephila guttata. 200fr, Lonchura malacca. 300fr, Acanthis cannabina. 400fr, Fringilla coelebs. 500fr, Emblema guttata. #1789, 1000fr, Passerina amoena. #1789A, Chloebia gouldiae.

1996, Nov. 27   **Perf. 13**
1784-1789 A391 Set of 6   11.00 11.00
Souvenir Sheet
1789A A391 1000fr multi   4.50 4.50
Nos. 1784-1789 are dated 1996.
No. 1789A contains one 32x40mm stamp.

Turtles A392

Designs: 150fr, Asterochelys yniphora. 200fr, Staurotypus triporcatus. 300fr, Puxidea mouhoti. 400fr, Geomyda spengleri. 500fr, Cuora galbinifrons. #1795, 1000fr, Malaclemys terrapin.
#1795A, Asterochelys radiata.

1996, Nov. 30
1790-1795 A392 Set of 6   11.00 11.00
Souvenir Sheet
1795A A392 1000fr multi   4.50 4.50
Nos. 1790-1795 are dated 1996.
No. 1795A contains one 40x32mm stamp.

Natl. Liberation, 30th Anniv. — A393

1997 Litho. Perf. 13½
1796 A393 90fr yellow & multi   .30 .30
1797 A393 220fr green & multi   .75 .75

Diana, Princess of Wales (1961-97) A394

Nos. 1798a-1798i: Various portraits of Princess Diana in designer gowns, each 180fr.
Views up close, each 180fr: No. 1799, like #1798a. No. 1799A, Like #1798b. No. 1800, like #1798c. No. 1801, like #1798d. No. 1802, like #1798e. No. 1802A, Like #1798f. No. 1802B, Like #1798g. No. 1803, like #1798h. No. 1804, like #1798i.

1997
1798 A394 Sheet of 9, #a.-i.   7.50 7.50
Souvenir Sheets
1799-1804 A394 Set of 9   50.00 50.00

Diana, Princess of Wales (1961-97) — A395

Nos. 1805-1807, Various pictures of Diana during her lifetime as Princess of Wales.
Each 1000fr: Pictures of Diana with (in margin): No. 1808, French Pres. Giscard d'Estaing. No. 1809, Mother Teresa. No. 1810, US First Lady Hillary Clinton.

1998, Jan. 2 Sheets of 6 Perf. 14
1805 A395 240fr #a.-f.   5.00 5.00
1806 A395 315fr #a.-f.   6.50 6.50
1807 A395 340fr #a.-f.   7.25 7.25
Souvenir Sheets
1808-1810 A395 Set of 3   10.50 10.50

Souvenir Sheet

Marilyn Monroe (1926-62) — A396

1997 Litho. Perf. 13½
1811 A396 2000fr multicolored   8.50 8.50

New Year 1998 (Year of the Tiger) — A397

Various paintings of tigers, by Liu Jiyou (1918-83): No. 1812: a, 180fr. b, 200fr. No. 1813: a, 90fr. b, 100fr. c, 180fr. d, 200fr.

1998, Jan. 5 Litho. Perf. 14
1812 A397 Sheet of 2, #a.-b.   1.25 1.25
1813 A397 Sheet of 4, #a.-d.   2.00 2.00
No. 1812 contains two 26x65mm stamps.

Hiroshige (1797-1858), Painter — A398

Paintings: No. 1814: a, Sixty-Nine Stations of the Kisokaido Road: Mochizuki. b, Eight Views of Lake Biwa Evening Snow at Mt. Hira. c, Kinkizan Temple on Enoshima Island, Sagami Provence. d, Cherry Blossoms. e, Evening Snow at Asakusa. f, Miyanokoshi.
No. 1815: a, Two Terrapins (Fan print). b, Swimming Carp. c, Takanawa by Moonlight. d, Night Rain at Karasaki. e, Chiryu: The Summer Horse Fair. f, Shower over the Nihonbashi.
No. 1816, vert: a, Takata Riding Grounds. b, Sugatami & Omokage Bridges & Jariba at Takata. c, Dam on the Otonashi River at Oji. d, Basho's Hermitage and Camellia Hill. e, Fudo Falls, Oji. f, Takinogawa Oji.

Each 1000fr: No. 1817, Bird in a Tree. No. 1818, Title Page for Hiroshige's One Hundred Views of Edo, by Baisotei. No. 1819, Memorial Portrait of Hiroshige, by Utagawa. No. 1820, Street Stalls and Tradesmen in Jouricho. No. 1821, Cherry Blossom, Morning Glory, Cranes and Rabbits. No. 1822, Three Wild Geese Flying Across the Moon. No. 1823, Suwa Bluff, Nippori. Nos. 1817-1823 are vert.

Perf. 14x13½, 13½x14
1998, Mar. 2 Sheets of 6 Litho.
1814 A398 220fr #a.-f.   5.50 5.50
1815 A398 315fr #a.-f.   7.50 7.50
1816 A398 370fr #a.-f.   8.50 8.50
Souvenir Sheets
Perf. 13½x14
1817-1823 A398 Set of 7   30.00 30.00
Nos. 1817-1823 each contain one 26x72mm stamp.

Fauna, Flora, Minerals — A399

Dolphins and whales: No. 1824: a, Souffleur nesarnack. b, Lagenorhynque. c, Sotalie du cameroun. d, Petit rorqual. e, Rorqual commun. f, Faux orque.
Insects and spiders: No. 1825: a, Lasius niger. b, Sceliphron spirifex. c, Peucetia. d, Mygale. e, Theraphoside. f, Dynaste hercule.
Precious stones, minerals: No. 1826: a, Ruby. b, Diamond in kimberlite. c, Cut diamond. d, Rock salt. e, Tiger's eye. f, Uraninite.
Moths and butterflies: No. 1827: a, Pirate. b, Euchromie des liserons. c, Asterope. d, Psalis de kiriakoff. e, Sphinx de fabricius. f, Pensee bleue.
Mushrooms: No. 1828: a, Lepiote. b, Hypholome. c, Lactaire. d, Russule fetide. e, Russule doree. f, Strophaire.
Each 2000fr: No. 1829, Tricholome a odeur de savon. No. 1830, Potto.

1998(?) Litho. Perf. 13½
Sheets of 6
1824 A399 180fr #a.-f.   4.00 4.00
1825 A399 250fr #a.-f.   5.75 5.75
1826 A399 300fr #a.-f.   6.75 6.75
1827 A399 400fr #a.-f.   9.00 9.00
1828 A399 460fr #a.-f.   10.25 10.25
Souvenir Sheets
1829-1830 A399 Set of 2   15.50 15.50
Intl. Scouting, 90th Anniv. (#1825, 1827-1830). Nos. 1829-1830 each contain one 41x60mm stamp.

Jerry Garcia (1942-95) — A400

Various portraits.

1998 Litho. Perf. 13½
1831 A400 250fr Sheet of 9, #a.-i.   7.75 7.75
Souvenir Sheet
1832 A400 2000fr multicolored   7.00 7.00
No. 1832 contains one 42x51mm stamp.

Dinosaurs — A401

Various unidentified dinosaurs.

1998
1833   A401   290fr   Sheet of 9,
                    #a.-i.   10.00 10.00
Souvenir Sheet
1834   A401   2000fr multicolored   7.50 7.50
No. 1834 contains one 42x51mm stamp.

1998 Winter Olympic Games,
Nagano — A402

No. 1835: a, Hockey. b, Speed skating. c,
Pairs figure skating. d, Luge. e, Curling. f,
Bobsledding.
No. 1836: a, Downhill skiing. b, Freestyle ski
jumping (blue skis). c, Ski jumping. d, Downhill
skiier in tuck. e, Snow boarding. f, Freestyle
skiing (red skis).

1998   **Sheets of 6**
1835   A402   250fr   #a.-f.   5.75 5.75
1836   A402   300fr   #a.-f.   6.75 6.75
Nos. 1835-1836 each have 3 labels.

1998 World Cup Soccer
Championships, France — A403

Player, country, vert: No. 1837, Kluivert,
Netherlands. No. 1838, Asprilla, Colombia.
No. 1839, Bergkamp, Netherlands. No. 1840,
Gascoigne, England. No. 1841, Ravanelli,
Italy. No. 1842, Sheringham, England.
No. 1843: a, Paul Gascoigne, England, diff.
b, Ryan Giggs, Wales. c, Roy Keane, Ireland.
d, Stuart Pearce, England. e, Tony Adams,
England. f, Teddy Sheringham, England, diff.
g, Paul Ince, England. h, Steve McManaman,
England.
No. 1844: a, Rossi, Italy. b, Lineker,
England. c, Lato, Poland. d, Futre, Poland. e,
Klinsmann, Germany. f, Hurst, England. g,
Kempes, Argentina. h, McCoist, Scotland.
World Cup Champions, year, vert. — #1845:
a, Argentina, 1978. b, Italy, 1982. c, England,
1966. d, Uruguay, 1930. e, Germany, 1954. f,
Argentina, 1986. g, Brazil, 1994.
Each 1500fr: No. 1846, Ronaldo, Brazil,
vert. No. 1847, Gary Lineker, England, vert.
No. 1848, Shearer, England, vert.

Perf. 13½x14, 14x13½
1998, July 10   **Litho.**
1837-1842 A403 370fr Set of 6 10.00 10.00

Sheets of 8 + Label
1843   A403   220fr   #a.-h.   6.50 7.75
1844   A403   315fr   #a.-h.   11.00 11.00
Sheet of 7 + 2 Labels
1845   A403   325fr   #a.-g.   10.00 10.00
Souvenir Sheets
1846-1848 A403 Set of 3   18.00 18.00

Bella Bellow (d. 1973),
Singer — A403a

1998-2004   **Litho.**   **Perf. 13½**
1848A   A403a   5fr   yel orange
1848B   A403a   10fr   ol grn
1848C   A403a   25fr   emerald
1848D   A403a   40fr   violet
1848E   A403a   50fr   grnsh blk
        s.   gray green, dated "2002"   —
1848F   A403a   75fr   yel orange   —   —
        t.   Dated "2002"   —   —
1848G   A403a 100fr   orange
1848H   A403a 125fr   blue
        v.   Dated "2002"   —   —
1848I   A403a 200fr   brt purple
        x.   Dated "2002"   —   —
1848J   A403a 240fr   red violet
1848K   A403a 280fr   green
1848L   A403a 300fr   Prus blue
        y.   Dated "2002"   —   —
1848M   A403a 320fr   red org
1848N   A403a 340fr   car lake
1848O   A403a 390fr   car rose
1848P   A403a 450fr   brt blue
                       ('02)   —   —
1848Q   A403a 470fr   rose
1848R   A403a 500fr   gray ol
                       ('02)   —   —
1848T   A403a 1000fr   gray   —   —
1848W   A403a 5000fr   vio, dated
                       "2004"   —   —
   Nso. 1848E-1848F, 1848H are dated
"1998." Two additional stamps were issued in
this set. The editors would like to examine any
examples.
   See Nos. 1990A-1990O.

Star Wars Movies — A404

   Return of the Jedi — #1849: a, Princess
Leia. b, Darth Vader. c, Han Solo. d, R2-D2,
C-3PO. e, Emperor Palpatine. f, Chewbacca.
g, Leia on speeder. h, Luke Skywalker. i,
Storm trooper on speeder.
   Empire Strikes Back — #1850: a, Lando
Calrissian. b, Yoda. c, Chewbacca. d, C-3PO,
R2-D2. e, Luke Skywalker. f, Darth Vader. g,
Battle on snow planet. h, Leia. i, Rider on
snow planet.
   2000fr, Han Solo, Luke Skywalker, Princess
Leia, R2-D2.

1997   **Litho.**   **Perf. 13½**
                        Sheets of 9
1849   A404   190fr   #a.-i.   6.50 6.50
1850   A404   350fr   #a.-i.   11.50 11.50
Souvenir Sheet
1851   A404   2000fr multicolored   8.00 8.00
No. 1851 contains one 42x60mm.

Jacqueline Kennedy Onassis (1929-
94) — A405

No. 1852: Various portraits.
No. 1853: Various portraits of John F. Kennedy (1917-63).

1997   **Sheets of 9**
1852   A405   250fr   #a.-i.   10.00 10.00
1853   A405   400fr   #a.-i.   12.00 12.00

Diana, Princess of Wales (1961-
97) — A406

No. 1854: Various portraits.
2000fr, Diana in black (Mother Teresa in
sheet margin).

1997   **Sheet of 8 + Label**
1854   A406   500fr   #a.-h.   16.00 16.00
Souvenir Sheet
1854I A406   2000fr multicolored 10.00 10.00

Marilyn Monroe (1926-62) — A407

Various portraits, each 300fr.

1997   **Litho.**   **Perf. 13½**
1855   A407   Sheet of 9, #a.-i.   11.00 11.00

Minerals
A408

Designs: 100fr, Calcite. 150fr, Turquoise,
vert. 200fr, Pyrite, vert. 300fr, Tourmaline,
vert. 400fr, Pyrargirite, vert. 500fr, Malachite.
1000fr, Beryl, vert.

1999   **Litho.**   **Perf. 12¾**
1856-1861 A408 Set of 6   6.00 6.00
Souvenir Sheet
            Perf. 13
1861A A408 1000fr multicolored   4.00 4.00
No. 1861A contains one 32x40mm stamp.

Butterflies — A408a

Designs: 100fr, Quercusia quercus. 150fr,
Pseudacraea boisduvali. 200fr, Argynnis
paphia. 300fr, Erebia pandrose. 400fr,
Euphydryas maturna. 500fr, Pyronia tithonus.
1000fr, Charaxes pollux.

1999, June 7 **Litho.**   **Perf. 12¾**
1861B-1861G A408a Set of 6   5.75 5.75
Souvenir Sheet
            Perf. 13
1861H A408a 1000fr multi   3.75 3.75
No. 1861H contains one 40x32mm stamp.

Flowers — A409

Designs: No. 1862, Caralluma burchardii.
No. 1863, Dimorphotheca barberiae. No.
1864, Hoya carnosa. No. 1865, Amaryllis belladonna. No. 1866, Watsonia beatricis. No.
1867, Anthurium schezerianum. No. 1868,
Thumbergia alata. No. 1869, Arctotis brevis-
capa. No. 1870, Glaucium flavum. No. 1871,
Impatiens petersiana. No. 1872, Chrysanthemum segetum. No. 1873, Zantedeschia aethi-
opica, horiz.

1999   **Perf. 12¼**
1862   A409   100fr   brown   .30   .30
1863   A409   100fr   violet   .30   .30
1864   A409   100fr   pale red   .30   .30
1865   A409   150fr   dark grn bl   .55   .55
1866   A409   150fr   red brown   .55   .55
1867   A409   150fr   violet blue   .55   .55
1868   A409   200fr   orange   .75   .75
1869   A409   200fr   bright grn bl   .75   .75
1870   A409   300fr   olive   1.10 1.10
1871   A409   300fr   blue   1.10 1.10
1872   A409   500fr   brown   1.75 1.75
1873   A409   1000fr bright pink   3.75 3.75
       Nos. 1862-1873 (12)   11.75 11.75

1998 World Cup Soccer Championship, France — A410

Predominant colors of player's shirts. No. 1874: a, Yellow. b, White. c, Blue. d, Red.
No. 1875: a, White. b, Blue. c, Red. d, Green.
No. 1876: a, White, with black shorts. b, Yellow, with blue shorts. c, Yellow, with yellow shorts. d, White, with white shorts.
No. 1877: a, Red. b, Green. c, White. d, Red & white striped.
No. 1878: a, Blue. b, Yellow. c, Red. d, White.
No. 1879: a, Orange. b, White. c, Red. d, Multicolored diamonds.
No. 1880: a, White, with black shorts. b, White, with blue and red chest stripes. c, White, with green trim. d, White, with red and blue arm stripes.
No. 1881: a, Blue & white stripes. b, Red & white checks. c, Yellow & green, d, Blue.
2000fr, Player, map of France.

1998	Litho.		Perf. 13¼
	Sheets of 4		
1874	A410	180fr #a.-d.	3.25	3.25
1875	A410	200fr #a.-d.	3.50	3.50
1876	A410	250fr #a.-d.	4.25	4.25
1877	A410	290fr #a.-d.	5.00	5.00
1878	A410	300fr #a.-d.	5.25	5.25
1879	A410	350fr #a.-d.	6.25	6.25
1880	A410	400fr #a.-d.	6.75	6.75
1881	A410	425fr #a.-d.	7.25	7.25
	Nos. 1874-1881 (8)		41.50	41.50
	Souvenir Sheet		
1882	A410	2000fr multicolored	7.50	7.50

Birds 1882A

Designs: 100fr, Luscinia svecica. 150fr, Oriolus oriolus. 200fr, Carduelis carduelis. 300fr, Parus caeruleus. 400fr, Fringilla coelebs. 500fr, Parus montanus.
1000fr, Regulus ignicapillus.

1999	Litho.		Perf. 12¾
1882A-1882F	A410a	Set of 6	6.00	6.00
	Souvenir Sheet		
	Perf. 13x13¼		
1882G	A410a	1000fr multi	4.00	4.00

No. 1882G contains one 40x32mm stamp.

Antique Automobiles — A410b

Designs: 100fr, 1913 Peugeot Bebe. 150fr, 1950 Rolls-Royce. 200fr, 1921 Stutz Bearcat. 300fr, 1923 Ford Model T. 400fr, 1907 Packard. 500fr, 1950 Citroen II Legere sedan.
1000fr, 1929 Ford Model A Tudor sedan.

1999			Perf. 12¾
1882H-1882M	A410b	Set of 6	6.00	6.00
	Perf. 13		
1882N	A410b	1000fr multi	4.00	4.00

No. 1882N contains one 40x32mm stamp.

Mushrooms — A410c

Designs: 100fr, Ganoderma lucidum. 150fr, Cantharellus lutescens. 200fr, Lactarius deliciosus. 300fr, Amanita caesarea. 400fr, Cortinarius violaceus. 500fr, Amanita rubescens.
1000fr, Clitopilus prunulus.

1999, Feb. 23	Litho.		Perf. 12¾
1882O-1882T	A410c	Set of 6	—	—
	Souvenir Sheet		
	Perf. 13¼		
1882U	A410c	1000fr multi	—	—

Cats — A411

No. 1883: a, 100fr, Colorpoint. b, 150fr, British shorthair.
No. 1884: a, 200fr, Ocicat. b, 300fr, Ragdoll.
No. 1885: a, 400fr, Ballnese. b, 500fr, California Spangled.
1000fr, Somali.

1999	Litho.		Perf. 12½
1883	A411	Pair, #a.-b.	.85	.85
1884	A411	Pair, #a.-b.	1.00	1.00
1885	A411	Pair, #a.-b.	3.50	3.50
	Nos. 1883-1885 (3)		6.25	6.25
	Souvenir Sheet		
1886	A411	1000fr multicolored	4.00	4.00

Millennium A412

No. 1886A, Invention of Paper by Chinese (with millennium emblem).
No. 1887 — Chinese Science & Technology: a, Lacquerware. b, Counting rods. c, Sericulture. d, Acupuncture. e, "Tuned chime bell." f, Piston bellows. g, Compass. h, Manufacture of steel. i, Crossbow. j, Spinning wheel. k, Water conservancy. l, Pulse taking. m, Multi-tube seed drill. n, Rotary winnowing fan. o, Like #1886A (no millennium emblem). p, Silk loom (60x40mm). q, Wheelbarrow.
No. 1888 — Highlights of the 11th Century: a, Chinese invent gunpowder. b, Islamic bronze griffin. c, Battle of Clontarf. d, William becomes Duke of Normandy. e, Norman knight. f, Spinning wheels in use in China. g, Yaroslav becomes Grand Prince of Kiev. h, Polyphonic singing introduced. i, Macbeth becomes King of Scotland. j, Edward the Confessor becomes King of England. k, Astrolabe. l, Harp introduced in Europe. m, Trier Cathedral. n, Mandingo Empire founded in Africa. o, Toltecs invade Yucatan. p, Vikings reach North

Americam (60x40mm). q, Movable type used in China.
No. 1889 — Western Paintings of the 20th century by: a, Henri Matisse. b, Pablo Picasso. c, Marc Chagall. d, Wassily Kandinsky. e, Fernand Léger. f, Piet Mondrian. g, George Bellows. h, Georgia O'Keeffe. i, Salvador Dali. j, Francis Bacon. k, Edward Hopper. l, Andy Warhol. m, Helen Frankenthaler. n, Richard Anuszkiewicz. o, Audrey Flack. p, Jackson Pollack, Lee Krasner (60x40mm). q, Jean-Michel Basquiat.

1999	Litho.		Perf. 13¼x13
1886A	A412	120fr multi	.70	.70
	Sheets of 17		
	Perf. 12½		
1887	A412	120fr #a.-q. + label	9.00	9.00
1888	A412	130fr #a.-q. + label	9.00	9.00
1889	A412	140fr #a.-q. + label	11.00	11.00

Inscriptions on Nos. 1887b, 1887e, 1888i, and perhaps others, are incorrect or misspelled.
Issued: 130fr, 7/20.

US Civil War Photographs A413

Various Civil War photographs making up a photomosaic of Abraham Lincoln, each 300fr.

1999, July 20	Litho.		Perf. 13½
1890	A413	Sheet of 8, #a.-h.	10.00	10.00
	See Nos. 1939-1940.		

Free Trade Zone, 10th Anniv. — A414

Symbol and: 125fr, Map. 240fr, Clouds. 340fr, Wall.

1999	Litho.		Perf. 12¾
1891	A414	125fr multi	.45	.45
1892	A414	240fr multi	.85	.85
1893	A414	340fr multi	1.25	1.25
	Nos. 1891-1893 (3)		2.55	2.55

Rural Development Council, 40th Anniv. — A414a

1999	Litho.		Perf. 13x13¼
1893A	A414a	100fr grn & multi	—
1893B	A414a	125fr blue & multi	—
1893C	A414a	240fr red & multi	—
1893D	A414a	380fr vio & multi	—
1893E	A414a	390fr blk & multi	—

Other stamps for this subject may exist. The editors would like to examine any examples. Numbers may change.

Goldfish A415

Various depictions of Carassius auratus auratus: 100fr, 150fr, 200fr, 300fr, 400fr, 500fr.

1999			
1894-1899	A415	Set of 6	6.00	6.00
	Souvenir Sheet		
	Perf. 13		
1899A	A415	1000fr multi	4.00	4.00

No. 1899A contains one 40x31mm stamp.

SOS Children's Villages, 50th Anniv. — A416

1999	Litho.		Perf. 13¼x13
1900	A416	125fr multi ('01)	.70	.70
1901	A416	240fr multi	
1902	A416	340fr multi	

Additional stamps may have been issued in this set. The editors would like to examine any examples.

Sailing Vessels — A417

Designs: 100fr, Phoenician boat. 150fr, Roman cargo boat. 200fr, New Guinea fishing boat. 300fr, Caravel, vert. 400fr, 16th cent. English ship, vert. 500fr, 17th cent. English ship, vert.
1000fr, Steamship with sails.

1999	Litho.		Perf. 12½
1905-1910	A417	Set of 6	6.00	6.00
	Souvenir Sheet		
	Perf. 12¼x12		
1911	A417	1000fr multi	4.00	4.00

No. 1911 contains one 42x30mm stamp.

Dogs — A417a

Designs: 100fr, St. Bernard. 150fr, Teckel. 200fr, German shepherd. 300fr, Italian hound. 400fr, Yorkshire terrier. 500fr, Schnauzer.
1000fr, Afghan hound.

1999	Litho.		Perf. 12¾
1911A-1911F	A417a	Set of 6	6.00	6.00
	Souvenir Sheet		
	Perf. 12½		
1911G	A417a	1000fr multi	4.00	4.00

No. 1911G contains one 40x31mm stamp.

Trains
A417b

Designs: 100fr, Baldwin 0-4-0. 150fr, Baldwin 2-6-2. 200fr, Baldwin gasoline locomotive. 300fr, H.K. Porter 0-4-0. 400fr, H.K. Porter 2-6-2. 500fr, Vulcan 0-4-0.
1000fr, Jordanian locomotive.

1999 **Litho.** **Perf. 12¾**
1911H-1911M A417b Set of 6 6.00 6.00
Souvenir Sheet
1911N A417b 1000fr multi 4.00 4.00
No. 1911N contains one 40x31mm stamp.

Orchids
A417c

Designs: 100fr, Gramangis ellisii. 150fr, Habenaria columbae. 200fr, Epidendrum atroporpureum. 300fr, Odontoglossum majale. 400fr, Oncidium splendidum. 500fr, Zygopetalum mackai.
1000fr, Paphiopedilum pairieanum.

1999, Nov. 8 **Litho.** **Perf. 12x12¼**
1911O-1911T A417c Set of 6 7.25 7.25
Souvenir Sheet
Perf. 12½
1911U A417c 1000fr multi 4.00 4.00
No. 1911U contains one 31x39mm stamp.

New Year 2000 (Year of the Dragon) — A418

Various views of dragon: 100fr, 150fr, 200fr, 300fr, 500fr.
1000fr, Head of dragon, horiz.

2000 **Perf. 12¾x12**
1912-1917 A418 Set of 6 6.25 6.25
Souvenir Sheet
Perf. 13¼
1918 A418 1000fr multi 3.50 3.50
No. 1918 contains one 40x32mm stamp.

Wild Cats
A419

Designs: 100fr, Panthera tigris. 150fr, Acinonyx jubatus. 200fr, Felis concolor. 300fr, Panthera leo, female. 400fr, Felis pardalis. 500fr, Panthera leo, male.
1000fr, Panthera tigris, diff.

2000 **Perf. 13**
1919-1924 A419 Set of 6 6.25 6.25
Souvenir Sheet
1925 A419 1000fr multi 3.50 3.50
No. 1925 contains one 40x32mm stamp.

Flowers — A420

No. 1926, 290fr: a, Cyrtanthus contractus. b, Sandersonia aurantiaca. c, Anomateca grandiflora. d, Helichrysum ecklonis. e, Striga elegans. f, Nymphaea odorata.
No. 1927, 290fr: a, Leomotis leonii. b, Strelitzia reginae. c, Freesia refracta. d, Garzania nivea. e, Dimophotheca sinuata. f, Pelargonium domesticum.
No. 1928, 290fr: a, Gloriosa rothchiliana. b, Clematis vitalba. c, Rochea falcato. d, Plumbago capensis. e, Thunbergia alata. f, Lampranthus coccineus.
No. 1929, 1500fr, Epiphyllum hybrid. No. 1930, 1500fr, Agapanthus africanus.
Illustration reduced.

2000, July 28 **Litho.** **Perf. 14**
Sheets of 6, #a-f
1926-1928 A420 Set of 3 24.00 24.00
Souvenir Sheets
1929-1930 A420 Set of 2 13.50 13.50

Wildlife
A421

Designs: 200fr, Thompson's gazelle. 300fr, Felis margarita. 400fr, Blesbok. 500fr, Kob.
No. 1935, 290fr, vert.: a, Hoopoe. b, Harpactira spider. c, Marabou. d, Bee-eater. e, Oryx. f, Okapi. g, Wart hog. h, Baboon.
No. 1936, 290fr, vert.: a, Hornbill. b, Pygmy kingfisher. c, Vulture. d, Bateleur eagle. e, Kudu. f, Hyena. g, Gorilla. h, Lizard.
No. 1937, 1500fr, Eland, vert. No. 1938, 1500fr, Mongoose, vert.

2000, July 28
1931-1934 A421 Set of 4 6.75 6.75
Sheets of 8, #a-h
1935-1936 A421 Set of 2 22.50 22.50
Souvenir Sheets
1937-1938 A421 Set of 2 13.50 13.50

Mushrooms
A421a

Designs: 100fr, Hebeloma crustuliniforme. 150fr, Polyporellus squamosus, horiz. 200fr, Morchella deliciosa. 300fr, Disciotis venosa, horiz. 400fr, Cantharellus tubiformis. 500fr, Otidea onotica, horiz.
1000fr, Ixocomus granulatus, horiz.

2000, July 30 **Litho.** **Perf. 12¾**
1938A-1938F A421a Set of 6 6.25 6.25
Souvenir Sheet
Perf. 13
1938G A421a 1000fr multi 3.50 3.50
No. 1938G contains one 39x31mm stamp.

Civil War Photographs Type of 1999

No. 1939, 290fr: Various photographs with a science theme making up a photomosaic of Albert Einstein.
No. 1940, 290fr: Various photographs with an Oriental theme making up a photomosaic of Mao Zedong.

2000, Sept. 5 **Perf. 13¾**
Sheets of 8, #a-h
1939-1940 A413 Set of 2 24.00 24.00

Queen Mother, 100th Birthday — A422

No. 1941: a, With Princesses Elizabeth and Margaret, 1931. b, With daughter, 1940. c, Black and white photo. d, In 1990.
1500fr, With Princess Margaret, 1939.

2000, Sept. 5 **Perf. 14**
1941 A422 650fr Sheet of 4, #a-d, + label 12.50 12.50
Souvenir Sheet
Perf. 13¾
1942 A422 1500fr multi 7.25 7.25
No. 1942 contains one 38x51mm stamp.

Popes — A423

No. 1943, 400fr: a, Anastasius I, 399-401. b, Boniface I, 418-22. c, Gaius, 283-96. d, Hilarius, 461-68. e, Hyginus, 136-40. f, Innocent I, 402-17.
No. 1944, 400fr: a, Martin I, 649-55. b, Nicholas I, 858-67. c, Paschal I, 817-24. d, Paul I, 757-67. e, Pelagius, 556-61. f, Pelagius II, 579-90.
No. 1945, 400fr: a, Sergius, 687-701. b, Sergius II, 844-47. c, Severinus, 640. d, Sisinnius, 708. e, Stephen II, 752-57. f, Stephen IV, 816-17.
No. 1946, 1500fr, Pontian, 230-35. No. 1947, 1500fr, Pelagius II, diff. No. 1948, 1500fr, Stephen V, 885-91.
Illustration reduced.

2000, Sept. 5 **Perf. 12x12¼**
Sheets of 6, #a-f
1943-1945 A423 Set of 3 32.50 32.50
Souvenir Sheets
1946-1948 A423 Set of 3 20.00 20.00

British Monarchs — A424

No. 1949, 400fr: a, Charles II, 1660-85. b, Anne, 1702-14. c, George I, 1714-27. d, George IV, 1820-30. e, James II, 1685-88. f, George II, 1727-60.
No. 1950, 400fr: a, Elizabeth II, 1952-present. b, Edward VIII, 1936. c, George VI, 1936-52. d, George V, 1910-36. e, Edward VII, 1901-10. f, William IV, 1830-37.
No. 1951, 1500fr, William III and Mary, 1689-1702. No. 1952, 1500fr, Victoria, 1837-1901.

2000, Sept. 5 **Sheets of 6, #a-f**
1949-1950 A424 Set of 2 22.50 22.50
Souvenir Sheets
1951-1952 A424 Set of 2 13.50 13.50

Millennium Type of 1999

Highlights of 1950-59: a, US sends troops to defend South Korea. b, Rock and roll hits the air waves. c, Death of Eva Peron. d, Structure of DNA revealed by Watson and Crick. e, Sir Edmund Hillary and Tenzing Norgay reach peak of Mt. Everest. f, John F. Kennedy marries Jacqueline Bouvier. g, Coronation of Queen Elizabeth II. h, Millionth Volkswagen produced. i, German soccer team wins World Cup. j, Roger Bannister runs 1st 4-minute mile. k, Dr. Jonas Salk develops polio vaccine. l, 1st McDonald's franchise. m, New phone lines cross Atlantic. n, Soviet Union launches Sputnik. o, Jack Kerouac writes "On the Road." p, China begins "Great Leap Forward." q, Communist revolution in Cuba. r, Computer chip patented.

2000 **Perf. 12¾x12½**
1953 A412 200fr Sheet of 18, #a-r, + label 17.50 17.50

36th Organization of African Unity Summit, Lomé — A425

OAU emblem, map of Africa, doves and panel color of: 10fr, Bright yellow. 25fr, Green. 100fr, Dull yellow. 125fr, Blue violet. 250fr, Red violet. 375fr, Red. 400fr, Brown. 425fr, Orange.
No. 1954: a, Peace dove statue. b, Hotel du 2 Février. c, Congress building, Lomé. d, Alédjo Fault. e, Temberma hut. f, Cacao plantation.
No. 1955: a, Pres. Gnassingbé Eyadema, map of Europe and Africa, handshakes. b, Algerian Pres. Abdelazir Bouteflika, Pres. Eyadema, and map of Africa. c, Pres. Eyadema and OAU emblem. d, Map of Africa, doves, OAU emblem.
Illustration reduced.

2000 **Litho.** **Perf. 14x13¾**
1953S-1953Z A425 Set of 8 7.25 7.25
Sheets of 6 and 4
1954 A425 350fr #a-f 7.50 7.50
1955 A425 550fr #a-d 7.75 7.75

Trains — A426

No. 1956, 425fr: a, Richard Trevethick's engine. b, Stephenson's Adler. c, Crampton Continent. d, Atlantic Coastlines 4-4-2. e, Great Northern Railway Ivatt Atlantic. f, Great Western Railway City of Truro 4-4-0.

No. 1957, 425fr: a, Paris-Lyon-Mediterranean Railway, compound 4-8-2. b, Canadian Pacific Railway Royal Hudson 4-6-4. c, London-Midland Railway Duchess. d, New York Central Twentieth Century Limited. e, New Zealand Government Railway J class 4-8-4. f, British Railways Evening Star 5-10-0.

No. 1958, 1800fr, Eurostar. No. 1959, 1800fr, TGV Atlantique.

2000, Sept. 8   Litho.   Perf. 14
Sheets of 6, #a-f
1956-1957 A426   Set of 2   22.50 22.50
Souvenir Sheets
1958-1959 A426   Set of 2   16.00 16.00

Ships — A427

No. 1960, 425fr: a, Norse knaar. b, Hanseatic cog. c, Iberian caravel. d, Henri Grace à Dieu. e, Ark Royal. f, Dutch Hooker.

No. 1961, 425fr: a, HMS Victory. b, HMS Warrior. c, Cutty Sark. d, USS Olympia. e, Empress of Canada. f, James Clark Ross.

No. 1962, 1800fr, Discovery. No. 1963, 1800fr, Sea Cat ferry.

2000, Sept. 8   Litho.   Perf. 14
Sheets of 6, #a-f
1960-1961 A427   Set of 2   22.50 22.50
Souvenir Sheets
1962-1963 A427   Set of 2   16.00 16.00

Dogs and Cats — A428

Designs: 275fr, Bloodhound. 300fr, Sphinx cat. 325fr, Basset hound. 350fr, Cocker spaniel. No. 1968, 375fr, American curl cat. 400fr, Scottish fold cat.

No. 1970, 375fr, horiz. — Dogs: a, Bearded collie. b, Chow chow. c, Boxer. d, Irish setter. e, Bracco Italiano. f, Pointer.

No. 1971, 375fr, horiz. — Cats: a, Devon Rex. b, Cornish Rex. c, Siamese. d, Balinese. e, Birman. f, Korat.

No. 1972, 1500fr, Yorkshire terrier. No. 1973, 1500fr, Chinchilla cat.

Perf. 13½x13¼, 13¼x13½
2001, Dec. 17   Litho.
1964-1969 A428   Set of 6   10.00 10.00
Sheets of 6, #a-f
1970-1971 A428   Set of 2   22.50 22.50
Souvenir Sheets
1972-1973 A428   Set of 2   15.00 15.00

Marine Life — A429

No. 1974, 200fr (31x31mm): a, Priacanthus arenatus. b, Diplodus annularis. c, Lithognathus mormyrus. d, Selene vomer. e, Penaeus duorarum. f, Arbacia lixula. g, Serranus scriba. h, Trachurus trachurus. i, Lepas anatifera. j, Octopus vulgaris. k, Scorpaena scrofa. l, Dardanus arrosor.

No. 1975, 250fr (31x31mm): a, Porcupine fish. b, Blue shark. c, Sting ray. d, Physalia physalis. e, Turtles. f, Coryphaena hippurus. g, Caranx hippos. h, Sawfish. i, Todaropsis eblanae. j, Pompano. k, Diplodus cervinus. l, Barracuda.

No. 1976, 1500fr, Octopus vulgaris, diff. No. 1977, 1500fr, Blue shark, diff.

2001, Dec. 17   Perf. 12½
Sheets of 12, #a-l
1974-1975 A429   Set of 2   26.00 26.00
Souvenir Sheets
Perf. 13¼x13½
1976-1977 A429   Set of 2   15.00 15.00

African Wildlife A430

Designs: 150fr, Okapia johnstoni, vert. 200fr, Sagittarius serpentarius. 250fr, Lemur catta, vert. 300fr, Gorilla gorilla. 350fr, Genetta genetta, vert. 400fr, Fennecus zerda.

No. 1984, 380fr: a, Papio hamadryas. b, Felis serval. c, Suricata suricatta. d, Orycteropus afer. e, Connochataetes taurinus. f, Tragelaphus strepsiceros.

No. 1985, 380fr: a, Panthera pardus. b, Loxodonta africana. c, Cercopithecus hamlyni. d, Ephippiorhynchuus senegalensis. e, Hippopotamus amphibius. f, Hippotragus niger.

No. 1986, 415fr: a, Equus burchelli boehmi. b, Ceratotherium simum. c, Achionyx jubatus. d, Gazella dama. e, Crocuta crocuta. f, Lyacon pictus.

No. 1987, 1500fr, Crocodylus niloticus. No. 1988, 1500fr, Panthera leo, vert. No. 1989, 1500fr, Giraffa camelopardalis.

Perf. 13½x13¼, 13¼x13½
2001, Dec. 17
1978-1983 A430   Set of 6   8.00 8.00
Sheets of 6, #a-f
1984-1986 A430   Set of 3   35.00 35.00
Souvenir Sheets
1987-1989 A430   Set of 3   22.50 22.50

United We Stand A431

2002, Mar. 18   Litho.   Perf. 14
1990 A431   400fr multi   2.00 2.00

Bella Bellow Type of 1998-2004
2002-04   Litho.   Perf. 13½
1990A A403a   20fr yel green   — —
1990B A403a   30fr brown   — —
1990C A403a   110fr blue green   — —
1990D A403a   150fr aquamarine   — —
1990E A403a   175fr brt pur ('04)   — —
1990F A403a   275fr red   — —
1990G A403a   350fr lilac ('04)   — —
1990H A403a   400fr yellow green   — —
1990I A403a   550fr pale orange   — —
1990J A403a   600fr brown ('04)   — —
1990K A403a   650fr black   — —
1990L A403a   750fr brt blue ('04)   — —
1990M A403a   1000fr rose   — —

1990N A403a   2000fr dull brn ('04)   — —
1990O A403a   3000fr light blue   — —

The editors suspect that additional stamps were issued in this set and would like to examine any examples. Numbers may change.

2004 Summer Olympics, Athens — A432

Designs: 150fr, Chariot rider and horses. 300fr, Pin from 1960 Rome Olympics, vert. 450fr, Emblem of 1960 Squaw Valley Winter Olympics, vert. 500fr, Diver, vert.

2004, Aug. 25   Litho.   Perf. 13¼
1991-1994 A432   Set of 4   6.50 6.50

Pres. Gnassingbé Eyadema (1935-2005) A433

2004   Perf. 13½x13¼
Panel Color
1995 A433   25fr dark blue   .25 .25
1996 A433   50fr yel green   .25 .25
1997 A433   150fr olive green   .60 .60
1998 A433   400fr dull brown   1.60 1.60
1999 A433   550fr green   2.25 2.25
2000 A433   650fr brt blue   2.75 2.75
2001 A433   1000fr lilac   4.25 4.25
2002 A433   2000fr salmon pink   8.25 8.25
2003 A433   3000fr blue green   12.50 12.50
Nos. 1995-2003 (9)   32.70 32.70

Cooperation Between Togo and People's Republic of China, 30th Anniv. (in 2002) — A434

2004, Mar. 1   Perf. 12
Frame Color
2003A A434   150fr org yellow   —
2004 A434   300fr gray   —

Two additional stamps exist in this set. The editors would like to examine any examples.

Pope John Paul II (1920-2005) A435

2006, Jan. 24   Perf. 13½
2007 A435   550fr multi   2.50 2.50
Printed in sheets of 4.

Jules Verne (1828-1905), Writer — A436

No. 2008: a, Home of Verne from 1882-1900. b, Monument to Verne, Amiens, France. c, Sculpture of Verne, Amiens. d, Mysterious Island.

2006, Jan. 24   Litho.   Perf. 13½
2008 A436   550fr Sheet of 4, #a-d   10.00 10.00

Rotary International, Cent. (in 2005) — A437

No. 2009 — Children and denomination in: a, Yellow in upper right. b, Red. c, Yellow in upper left. 1000fr, Child.

2006, Jan. 24
2009 A437   700fr Sheet of 3, #a-c   10.00 10.00
Souvenir Sheet
2010 A437   1000fr multi   4.50 4.50

Friedrich von Schiller (1759-1805), Writer — A438

No. 2011, vert. — Schiller: a, Monument. b, Bust. c, Portrait. 1000fr, Birthplace of Schiller.

2006, Jan. 24
2011 A438   700fr Sheet of 3, #a-c   10.00 10.00
Souvenir Sheet
2012 A438   1000fr multi   4.50 4.50

World Cup Soccer Championships, 75th Anniv. (in 2005) — A439

No. 2013: a, David Beckham. b, Ronaldo Nazario. c, Fernando Hierro. 1000fr, Eusebio.

2006, Jan. 24
2013 A439 700fr Sheet of 3, #a-c   10.00 10.00
Souvenir Sheet
2014 A439 1000fr multi   4.50 4.50

V-E Day, 50th Anniv. (in 2005) — A440

No. 2015, vert.: a, Monument to victory. b, New York Times front page with war reports. c, Soldiers at Battle of the Bulge, 1944. d, Airplanes. e, Sculpture of Holocaust victim. 1000fr, DUKW.

2006, Jan. 24   Litho.   Perf. 13¼
2015 A440 400fr Sheet of 5, #a-e   7.50 7.50
Souvenir Sheet
2016 A440 1000fr multi   3.75 3.75

V-J Day, 50th Anniv. (in 2005) — A441

No. 2017: a, USS Charles Carroll. b, BB-35. c, LCT-515. d, LST-388. e, Destroyer Thompson DD-627. f, USS Thomas Jefferson. 1000fr, Battle of Iwo Jima.

2006, Jan. 24
2017 A441 350fr Sheet of 6, #a-f   7.75 7.75
Souvenir Sheet
2018 A441 1000fr multi   3.75 3.75

Railroads, Bicent. — A442

No. 2019: a, DX5287. b, W192. c, Central Pacific Jupiter. d, LWDHAM.
No. 2020, 1000fr, Rovos Ralf Class 25NC. No. 2021, 1000fr, Class 242 streamlined tank locomotive.

2006, Jan. 24
2019 A442 550fr Sheet of 4, #a-d   8.25 8.25
Souvenir Sheets
2020-2021 A442 Set of 2   7.50 7.50

Léopold Sédar Senghor Year — A443

2006, July 28
2022 A443 150fr multi   .60   .60
2023 A443 550fr multi   2.25   2.25
2024 A443 650fr multi   2.60   2.60
2025 A443 1000fr multi   4.00   4.00
2026 A443 2000fr multi, horiz.   8.00   8.00
2027 A443 3000fr multi, horiz. 12.00 12.00
2028 A443 5000fr multi, horiz. 20.00 20.00
2029 A443 10,000fr multi, horiz. 40.00 40.00
      Nos. 2022-2029 (8)   89.45 89.45
Souvenir Sheet

Wolfgang Amadeus Mozart (1756-91), Composer — A444

2006, Dec. 21   Perf. 14
2030 A444 1500fr multi   6.00 6.00

Space Achievements — A445

Designs: 150fr, Luna 9. 300fr, Hayabusa probe. 450fr, Venus Express. 500fr, Space Shuttle Discovery, vert.
No. 2035: a, Intl. Space Station. b, Deep Impact probe. c, Muse Asteroid. d, Artist's view of L1 spacecraft. e, Odyssey. f, Calipso.
No. 2036: a, Viking 1 in oribit around Mars. b, Viking 1. c, Phobos. d, Viking Lander 1.
No. 2037, 1500fr, Mars Reconnaissance Orbiter. No. 2038, 1500fr, Apollo 11, vert.

2006, Dec. 21   Perf. 13¼
2031-2034 A445 Set of 4   5.75   5.75
2035 A445 400fr Sheet of 6, #a-f   9.50   9.50
2036 A445 550fr Sheet of 4, #a-d   8.75   8.75
Souvenir Sheets
2037-2038 A445 Set of 2   12.00 12.00

Worldwide Fund for Nature (WWF) — A446

No. 2039 — Cyclanorbis senegalensis: a, On sand, facing left. b, With foliage, facing left. c, Head. d, With foliage, facing right.

2006, Dec. 28
2039 A446 350fr Block or strip of 4, #a-d   5.75 5.75
  e.   Minature sheet, 2 each #a-d   11.50 11.50

Birds — A447

No. 2040: a, Platnea alba. b, Ceryle rudis. c, Ardea alba. d, Ephipphorhynchus senegalensis. 1500fr, Ephipphorhynchus senegalensis, diff.

2006, Dec. 28   Perf. 14
2040 A447 450fr Sheet of 4, #a-d   7.25 7.25
Souvenir Sheet
2041 A447 1500fr multi   6.00 6.00

Mushrooms — A448

No. 2042: a, Coprinus micaceus. b, Cookeina sulcipes. c, Hygrocybe firma. d, Chlorophyllum molybdites. 1500fr, Volvariella esculenta.

2006, Dec. 28
2042 A448 450fr Sheet of 4, #a-d   7.25 7.25
Souvenir Sheet
2043 A448 1500fr multi   6.00 6.00

Butterflies — A449

No. 2044, horiz.: a, Papilio nobilis. b, Colotis celimene. c, Salamis anacardii. d, Eronia cleodora. 1500fr, Colotis regina.

2006, Dec. 28   Perf. 14
2044 A449 450fr Sheet of 4, #a-d   7.25 7.25
Souvenir Sheet
2045 A449 1500fr multi   6.00 6.00

Orchids — A450

No. 2046, vert.: a, Triphora trianthophora. b, Amerorchis rotundifolia. c, Cypripedium x andrewsii. d, Pogonia ophioglossoides. 1500fr, Platanthera x keenanii.

2006, Dec. 28   Perf. 14
2046 A450 450fr Sheet of 4, #a-d   7.25 7.25
Souvenir Sheet
2047 A450 1500fr multi   6.00 6.00

Rembrandt (1606-69), Painter A451

Designs: 50fr, Three Oriental Figures (Jacob and Laban). 100fr, The Pancake Woman. 150fr, The Goldsmith. 250fr, The Golf Player. 325fr, The Persian. 350fr, Jacob and Rachel Listening to an Account of Joseph's Dreams.
1250fr, The Conspiracy of Julius Civilis, horiz.

2006   **Perf. 14¼**
2048-2053 A451   Set of 6   5.00 5.00
                 Imperf
                 Size: 106x76mm
2054 A451 1250fr multi   5.00 5.00

Souvenir Sheets

A452

Elvis Presley (1935-77) — A453

No. 2055 — Country name in: a, Pale blue.
b, Pale yellow. c, Pink. d, Pale green.
No. 2056 — Country name in: a, Pale blue.
b, Pale yellow. c, Pink. d, Pale green.

2006, Dec. 21   Litho.   Perf. 14
2055 A452 550fr Sheet of 4, #a-d   8.75 8.75
2056 A453 550fr Sheet of 4, #a-d   8.75 8.75

New Year
2007
(Year of
the Pig)
A454

2008, Jan. 21   Litho.   Perf. 13½
2057 A454 275fr multi   1.25 1.25
Printed in sheets of 4.

Pope Benedict
XVI — A455

2008, Jan. 21   Perf. 12½x12¾
2058 A455 300fr multi   1.40 1.40
Printed in sheets of 8.

Miniature Sheet

Inauguration of Pres. John F.
Kennedy, 47th Anniv. — A456

No. 2059: a, Band passing reviewing stand.
b, Kennedy taking oath of office. c, Capitol. d,
Kennedy giving inaugural address.

2008, Jan. 21   Perf. 13¼
2059 A456 450fr Sheet of 4, #a-d 8.00 8.00

Wedding of Queen Elizabeth II and
Prince Philip, 60th Anniv. — A457

No. 2060: a, Couple, white frame. b, Queen,
pink frame. c, Couple, light blue frame. d,
Queen, light blue frame. e, Couple, pink frame.
f, Queen, white frame.
1250fr, Couple, diff., green frame.

2008, Jan. 21   Perf. 12¾
2060 A457 400fr Sheet of 6,
          #a-f   11.00 11.00
Souvenir Sheet
2061 A457 1250fr multi   5.75 5.75

Princess Diana (1961-97) — A458

No. 2062, vert.: a, Wearing double-stranded
pearl necklace, large photo. b, Wearing white
hat, cropped photo. c, Wearing black and
white houndstooth dress, large photo. d,
Wearing double stranded pearl necklace,
cropped photo. e, Wearing white hat, large
photo. f, Wearing black and white houndstooth
dress, cropped photo.
1500fr, Wearing black jacket.

2008, Jan. 21
2062 A458 400fr Sheet of 6,
          #a-f   11.00 11.00
Souvenir Sheet
2063 A458 1500fr multi   6.75 6.75

Campaign to
Prevent
AIDS — A459

Red AIDS ribbon and: 200fr, Colored
squares. 350fr, Hand, horiz. 650fr, Man and
woman carrying Togo flags, horiz.

2008, Feb. 8   Perf. 11½
2064-2066 A459   Set of 3   5.75 5.75
Dated 2007.

Miniature Sheet

2008 Summer Olympics,
Beijing — A460

No. 2067: a, Swimming. b, Running. c, Soccer. d, Sailing.

2008, Aug. 18   Litho.   Perf. 12
2067 A460 240fr Sheet of 4, #a-d 4.50 4.50

Peony
A461

2009, Apr. 10   Litho.   Perf. 13¼
2068 A461 200fr multi   .80 .80
Printed in sheets of 8.

Miniature Sheet

Pope Benedict XVI — A462

No. 2069 — Pope Benedict XVI: a, Seated,
with hands in prayer. b, With covered chalices.
c, Wearing miter. d, Wearing red vestments
and red and gold stole. e, Wearing white vestments, hand raised. f, Seated with hands
crossed.

2010, Feb. 11   Perf. 11½
2069 A462 350fr Sheet of 6, #a-f 8.75 8.75

Miniature Sheet

U.S. Pres. Barack Obama — A463

No. 2070 — Pres. Obama: a, With people in
background. b, With blue sky in background. c,
On telehone. d, Wearing suit, with hand
raised.

2010, Feb. 11   Perf. 12x11½
2070 A463 450fr Sheet of 4,
          #a-d   7.50 7.50

A464

A465

Michael Jackson (1958-2009),
Singer — A466

No. 2071 — Jackson with microphone: a,
Near mouth, gray area at top. b, Near eyes,
black area behind head. c, Near eyes, tan area
behind head. d, Near mouth, black area
behind head.
No. 2072 — Jackson wearing: a, White costume with pearls. b, Black costume with
sequins. c, Sunglasses, with hands together.
d, Sunglasses, hands not visible.

2010, Feb. 11   Perf. 11½x12
2071 A464 450fr Sheet of 4, #a-
          d   7.50 7.50
                 Perf. 11½
2072 A465 450fr Sheet of 4, #a-
          d   7.50 7.50
Souvenir Sheet
2073 A466 1000fr black & gray 4.25 4.25

A467

A468

A469

Phataginus
Tricuspis
A470

2010, Mar. 6 — Perf. 13x13¼

2074	Horiz. strip of 4	9.00	9.00
a.	A467 550fr multi	2.25	2.25
b.	A468 550fr multi	2.25	2.25
c.	A469 550fr multi	2.25	2.25
d.	A470 550fr multi	2.25	2.25
e.	Sheet of 8, 2 each #2074a-2074d, + 2 labels	18.00	18.00

Pan-African Postal Union, 30th Anniv. A471

Pan-African Postal Union emblem and various Tamberma dwellings.

2010 — Litho. — Perf. 13x13½

2075	A471 50fr multi	—	—
2076	A471 200fr multi	—	—
2077	A471 500fr multi	—	—

Independence, 50th Anniv. — A472

2010 — Litho. — Perf. 13

2079	A472 550fr yel & multi	—	—

Two additional items were issued in this set. The editors would like to examine any examples.

Granary — A472b

2011 — Litho. — Perf. 13

2081	A472b 200fr red & multi	—	—
2082	A472b 550fr brt blue & multi	—	—

Lomé Cathedral — A472c

2011 — Litho. — Perf. 13

2083	A472c 550fr multi	—	—

King Mensah, Musician, 15th Anniv. of Performing — A472d

2011 — Litho. — Perf. 13

2084	A472d 550fr multi	—	—

Post Bus — A473

2011 — Litho. — Perf. 13

2085	A473 200fr yel grn & multi	—	—

An additional stamp was issued in this set. The editors would like to examine any example.

SEMI-POSTAL STAMPS

Curie Issue
Common Design Type

1938 — Unwmk. — Engr. — Perf. 13

B1	CD80 1.75fr + 50c brt ultra	20.00	20.00
	Never hinged	32.50	

French Revolution Issue
Common Design Type
Photo., Name and Value Typo. in Black

1939

B2	CD83 45c + 25c green	8.50	8.50
B3	CD83 70c + 30c brown	8.50	8.50
B4	CD83 90c + 35c red org	8.50	8.50
B5	CD83 1.25fr + 1fr rose pink	8.50	8.50
B6	CD83 2.25fr + 2fr blue	8.50	8.50
	Nos. B2-B6 (5)	42.50	42.50
	Set, never hinged	70.00	

French Revolution, 150th anniv. Surtax for defense of the colonies.

Nos. 281, 236, 245, 289 Srchd. in Red or Black

1941 — Perf. 14 x 13½, 12½

B7	A10 50c + 1fr	3.50	3.50
B8	A7 80c + 2fr	7.00	7.00
B9	A8 1.50fr + 2fr	7.00	7.00
B10	A11 2fr + 3fr (R)	7.00	7.00
	Nos. B7-B10 (4)	24.50	24.50
	Set, never hinged	50.00	

> Catalogue values for unused stamps in this section, from this point to the end of the section, are for Never Hinged items.

Common Design Type and

Togolese Militiaman SP1

Military Infirmary SP2

1941 — Photo. — Perf. 13½

B10A	SP1 1fr + 1fr red	1.10	
B10B	CD86 1.50fr + 3fr maroon	1.10	
B10C	SP2 2.50fr + 1fr blue	1.10	
	Nos. B10A-B10C (3)	3.30	

Nos. B10A-B10C were issued by the Vichy government in France, but were not placed on sale in Togo.

Nos. 296-297 Surcharged in Black or Red

1944 — Engr. — Perf. 12x12½

B10D	50c + 1.50fr on 2.50fr deep blue (R)	.70	
B10E	+ 2.50fr on 1fr green	.70	

Colonial Development Fund.
Nos. B10D-B10E were issued by the Vichy government in France, but were not placed on sale in Togo.

Tropical Medicine Issue
Common Design Type

1950 — Engr. — Perf. 13

B11	CD100 10fr + 2fr indigo & dk bl	5.00	3.50

The surtax was for charitable work.

Republic

Patient on Stretcher — SP3

Designs: 30fr+5fr, Feeding infant. 50fr+10fr, Blood transfusion.

1959 — Engr. — Perf. 13

B12	SP3 20fr + 5fr multicolored	.75	.75
a.	Souvenir sheet of 4	5.00	5.00
B13	SP3 30fr + 5fr bl, car & brn	.75	.75
a.	Souvenir sheet of 4	5.00	5.00
B14	SP3 50fr + 10fr emer, brn & car	.75	.75
a.	Souvenir sheet of 4	5.00	5.00
	Nos. B12-B14 (3)	2.25	2.25

Issued for the Red Cross.
Nos. B12a, B13a, B14a exist imperf.; same values.

Uprooted Oak Emblem — SP4

No. B16 similar to No. B15, with emblem on top.

1960 — Unwmk. — Perf. 13

B15	SP4 25fr + 5fr dk bl, brn & yel grn	.45	.45
B16	SP4 45fr + 5fr dk bl, brn & ol	.80	.80

World Refugee Year, July 1, 1959-June 30, 1960. The surtax was for aid to refugees.

AIR POST STAMPS

Common Design Type

1940 — Unwmk. — Engr. — Perf. 12½x12

C1	CD85 1.90fr ultra	.35	.35
C2	CD85 2.90fr dark red	.35	.35
C3	CD85 4.50fr dk gray grn	.35	.35
C4	CD85 4.90fr yellow bister	.70	.70
C5	CD85 6.90fr deep orange	1.40	1.40
	Nos. C1-C5 (5)	3.15	3.15
	Set, never hinged	5.00	

Common Design Type
Inscribed "Togo" across top

1942

C6	CD88 50c car & bl	.25	
C7	CD88 1fr brn & blk	.35	
C8	CD88 2fr grn & red brn	.50	
C9	CD88 3fr dk bl & scar	.65	
C10	CD88 5fr vio & brn red	.70	

Frame Engraved, Center Typographed

C11	CD89 10fr ultra, ind & org	1.10	
C12	CD89 20fr rose car, mag & gray blk	1.10	
C13	CD89 50fr yel grn, dl grn & lt vio	2.10	—
	Nos. C6-C13 (8)	6.75	
	Set, never hinged	10.50	

There is doubt whether Nos. C6-C12 were officially placed in use.

> Catalogue values for unused stamps in this section, from this point to the end of the section, are for Never Hinged items.

Elephants — AP1

Plane — AP2

Plane — AP3

Post Runner and Plane — AP4

1947, Oct. 6 — Engr. — Perf. 12½

C14	AP1 40fr blue	8.50	3.50
C15	AP2 50fr lt ultra, & red vio	4.25	1.40
C16	AP3 100fr emer & dk brn	8.50	2.10
C17	AP4 200fr lilac rose	13.00	3.50
	Nos. C14-C17 (4)	34.25	10.50

UPU Issue
Common Design Type

1949, July 4 — Perf. 13

C18	CD99 25fr multi	8.50	7.00

Liberation Issue
Common Design Type

1954, June 6

C19	CD102 15fr indigo & pur	7.00	5.50

Freight
Highway — AP5

1954, Nov. 29
C20 AP5 500fr indigo & dk grn 52.50 42.50

Republic

Independence Allegory — AP6

Unwmk.
1957, Oct. 29   Engr.   Perf. 13
C21 AP6 25fr bl, brn & ver   .60 .30

1st anniv. of Togo's autonomy.

Flag and Torch — AP7

Great White Egret — AP8

1957, Oct. 29
C22 AP7 50fr multi   .65 .35
C23 AP7 100fr multi   1.10 .60
C24 AP7 200fr multi   2.25 1.00
C25 AP8 500fr ind, lt bl & grn 18.00 6.75
  Nos. C22-C25 (4)   22.00 8.70

Types of 1957 Inscribed
"Republique du Togo" and

Flag, Plane and
Map — AP9

1959, Jan. 15   Engr.   Perf. 13
C26 AP9 25fr ultra, emer & vio
        brn   .40 .25
C27 AP7 50fr dk bl, dl grn &
        red   .60 .35
C28 AP7 100fr multi   1.40 .60
C29 AP7 200fr dk grn, red & ul-
        tra   3.50 1.25
C30 AP8 500fr blk brn, rose lil &
        grn   14.00 3.50
  Nos. C26-C30 (5)   19.90 5.95

Hotel Le
Benin
AP10

Eagle and Map of
Togo — AP11

Perf. 14½x15, 15x14½
1960, Apr. 27   Litho.   Unwmk.
C31 AP10 100fr crim, emer &
         yel   1.75 .25
C32 AP10 200fr multi   4.00 .40
C33 AP11 500fr grn & gldn brn 8.50 1.00
  Nos. C31-C33 (3)   14.25 1.65

Proclamation of Togo's full independence,
Apr. 27, 1960.

Mail Service Type
100fr, Boeing 707 and stamps of 1960.

1963, Jan. 12   Photo.   Perf. 13
C34 A41 100fr multi   1.60 .45
  a. Souvenir sheet of 4 4.50 3.50

No. C34a contains 4 stamps similar to Nos.
441-443 and C34, with simulated perforations.

Emancipation Type
1963, Oct.   Unwmk.   Perf. 13x14
C35 A45 100fr multi   1.50 .45
  a. Souv. sheet of 4, #454-456, C35,
      imperf.   2.50 2.00

For overprint see No. C41.

Type of 1964 Regular Issue
50fr, Pirenestes ostrinus. 100fr, Spermestes
bicolor. 200fr, Agapornis pullaria. 250fr, Psittacus erithacus. 500fr, Trachyphonus
margaritaceus.

1964-65   Photo.   Perf. 14
Size: 22½x31mm
Birds in Natural Colors
C36 A47 50fr yel grn   3.00 .30
C37 A47 100fr ocher   6.00 .35
C38 A47 200fr dl bl grn 11.50 .90
C39 A47 250fr dl rose ('65) 15.50 1.10
C40 A47 500fr violet   30.00 1.60
  Nos. C36-C40 (5)   66.00 4.25

No. C35
Ovptd.
Diagonally

1964, Feb.   Perf. 13x14
C41 A45 100fr multi   1.75 .30

Issued in memory of John F. Kennedy.
Same overprint was applied to stamps of
No. C35a, with black border and commemorative inscription added. Two sheets exist: with
and without gray silhouetted head of Kennedy
covering all four stamps. Value: without silhouette, $15; with silhouette, $25.

Liberation Type
1964, May 25   Perf. 14x13
C42 A50 100fr dl bl grn & dk brn 1.50 .30

Olympic Games Type
1964, Oct.   Photo.   Perf. 14
C43 A52 100fr Tennis   1.25 .30
  a. Souv. sheet of 3, #493-494, C43,
      imperf.   2.50 2.00

Flag of Togo and Jet — AP12

1964, Dec. 5   Unwmk.   Perf. 14x13
C44 AP12 100fr multi   1.50 .50

Inauguration of the national airline "Air
Togo." For souvenir sheet see No. 499a.

Lincoln Type
1965, June   Photo.   Perf. 13½x14
C45 A58 100fr ol gray   2.00 .35
  a. Souv. sheet, #545, C45, imperf. 3.00 2.25

Sports Type
100fr, Soccer player, flags of Togo and
Congo.

1965, July   Unwmk.   Perf. 14x13
C46 A59 100fr multi   1.75 .35

Churchill Type
1965, Aug. 7   Photo.   Perf. 13½x14
C47 A60 85fr car rose   1.50 .40
  a. Souv. sheet, #532, C47, imperf. 2.50 2.00

UN Type
100fr, Apple, grapes, wheat and "ONU."

1965, Dec. 15   Perf. 14x13½
C48 A65 100fr dk bl & bis 1.75 .40
  a. Souvenir sheet of 2 2.40 1.75

No. C48a contains two imperf. stamps similar to Nos. 548 and C48 with simulated
perforations.

Pope Type
Designs: 45fr, Pope speaking at UN ros-
trum, world map and UN emblem. 90fr, Pope,
plane and UN emblem.

1966, Mar. 5   Litho.   Perf. 12
C49 A66 45fr emer & multi .80 .25
C50 A66 90fr gray & multi 1.75 .25
  a. Souvenir sheet of 2, #C49-C50 3.00 2.00

Red Cross Type
Jean Henri Dunant and Togolese Flag.

1966, May 7   Litho.   Perf. 12
C51 A67 100fr multi   2.25 .35

WHO Type
Flowers: 50fr, Daisies and WHO Headquar-
ters. 90fr, Talisman roses and WHO
Headquarters.

1966, May   Litho.   Perf. 12
C52 A68 50fr lt bl & multi .90 .25
C53 A68 90fr gray & multi 1.50 .25
  a. Souvenir sheet of 2, #C52-C53 3.00 2.00

Air Afrique Issue
Common Design Type
1966, Aug. 31   Photo.   Perf. 13
C54 CD123 30fr brt grn, blk & lem .80 .25

Arts and Crafts Type
60fr, Basket maker. 90fr, Wood carver.

1966, Sept.   Perf. 13x14
C55 A69 60fr ultra, org & blk 1.40 .25
C56 A69 90fr brt rose, yel & blk 1.40 .25

Dancer Type
50fr, Woman from North Togo holding
branches. 60fr, Man from North Togo with
horned helmet.

1966, Nov.   Photo.   Perf. 13x14
C57 A70 50fr multi   .95 .25
C58 A70 60fr olive & multi 1.25 .25

Soccer Type
Designs: Different Soccer Scenes.

1966, Dec. 14   Photo.   Perf. 14x13
C59 A71 50fr org, brn & pur .85 .25
C60 A71 60fr ultra, brn & org 1.40 .25
  a. Souv. sheet of 3, #582, C59-
      C60, imperf.   3.25 2.40

Fish Type
Designs: 45fr, Yellow jack and trawler. 90fr,
Banded distichodus and seiner.

1967, Jan. 14   Photo.   Perf. 14
Fish in Natural Colors
C61 A72 45fr org & brn   1.25 .25
C62 A72 90fr emer & dk bl 2.00 .35

UNICEF Type
UNICEF Emblem and: 45fr, Girl and miniature poodle. 90fr, African boy and greyhound.

1967, Feb. 11   Photo.   Perf. 14x13½
C63 A73 45fr yel, red brn & blk 1.25 .25
C64 A73 90fr multi, dk grn & blk 1.90 .35
  a. Souvenir sheet of 2 4.00 2.25

No. C64a contains 2 imperf., lithographed
stamps with simulated perforations similar to
Nos. C63-C64.

Satellite Type
50fr, Diamant rocket. 90fr, Fr-1 satellite.

1967, Mar. 18   Photo.   Perf. 13½x14
C65 A74 50fr multi, vert. 1.00 .25
C66 A74 90fr multi, vert. 1.75 .30
  a. Souvenir sheet of 2 3.00 1.75

No. C66a contains 2 imperf. stamps similar
to Nos. C65-C66 with simulated perforations.

Musician Type
UNESCO Emblem and: 45fr, Johann
Sebastian Bach and organ. 90fr, Ludwig van
Beethoven, violin and oboe.

1967, Apr. 15   Photo.   Perf. 14x13½
C67 A75 45fr multi   .75 .25
C68 A75 90fr pink & multi 1.25 .25
  a. Souvenir sheet of 2 3.50 1.40

No. C68a contains 2 imperf. stamps similar
to Nos. C67-C68 with simulated perforations.

EXPO '67 Type
EXPO '67 Emblem and: 45fr, French pavil-
ion, roses. 60fr, British pavilion, day lilies. 90fr,
African village, bird-of-paradise flower. 105fr,
US pavilion, daisies.

1967, May 30   Photo.   Perf. 14
C69 A76 45fr multi   .75 .25
C70 A76 60fr multi   .85 .25
C71 A76 90fr yel & multi 1.25 .30
  a. Souv. sheet, #C69-C71, imperf. 3.50 1.50
C72 A76 105fr multi   1.75 .50
  Nos. C69-C72 (4)   4.60 1.30

For overprints see Nos. C86-C89.

Mural by José Vela Zanetti — AP13

The designs are from a mural in the lobby of
the UN Conf. Building, NYC. The mural
depicting mankind's struggle for a lasting
peace is shown across 3 stamps twice in the
set: on the 5fr, 15fr, 30fr and 45fr, 60fr, 90fr.

1967, July 15   Litho.   Perf. 14
C73 AP13 5fr multi   .40 .25
C74 AP13 15fr org & multi .40 .25
C75 AP13 30fr multi   .45 .25
C76 AP13 45fr multi   .70 .25
C77 AP13 60fr car & multi 1.10 .25
C78 AP13 90fr ind & multi 1.75 .30
  a. Souvenir sheet of 3, #C76-C78 3.50 2.50
  Nos. C73-C78 (6)   4.80 1.55

Issued to publicize general disarmament.

Animal Type
1967, Aug. 19   Photo.   Perf. 14x13½
C79 A78 45fr Lion   1.10 .25
C80 A78 60fr Elephant   1.60 .25

African Postal Union Issue, 1967
Common Design Type
1967, Sept. 9   Engr.   Perf. 13
C81 CD124 100fr bl, brt grn & ol
         brn   1.90 .30

Stamp Anniversary Type

Designs: 90fr, Stamp auction and Togo Nos. 16 and C42. 105fr, Father and son with stamp album and No. 474.

1967, Oct. 14   Photo.   Perf. 14x13

Stamps on Stamps in Original Colors

C82	A79	90fr olive	1.25 .25
a.		Souvenir sheet of 3	3.00 2.50
C83	A79	105fr dk car rose	2.00 .40

No. C82a contains 3 imperf. stamps similar to Nos. 621-622 and C82 with simulated perforations.

Pre-Olympics Type

View of Mexico City, Summer Olympics emblem and: 60fr, Runners. 90fr, Broad jump.

1967, Dec. 2   Perf. 13x14

C84	A80	60fr pink & multi	1.50 .45
C85	A80	90fr multi	1.50 .50
a.		Souv. sheet of 3, #627, C84-C85, imperf.	5.00 3.00

Nos. C69-C72 Overprinted

1967, Dec.   Photo.   Perf. 14

C86	A76	45fr multi	.60 .25
C87	A76	60fr multi	.90 .25
C88	A76	90fr yel & multi	1.40 .25
C89	A76	105fr multi	1.50 .35
		Nos. C86-C89 (4)	4.40 1.10

Issued for National Day, Sept. 29, 1967.

Hydrological Decade Type

1968, Apr. 6   Litho.   Perf. 14

C90	A84	60fr multi	1.75 .25

Ship Type

Designs: 45fr, Fulton's and modern steamships. 90fr, US atomic ship Savannah and atom symbol.

1968, Apr. 26   Photo.   Perf. 14x14½

C91	A85	45fr yel & multi	1.10 .25
C92	A85	90fr bl & multi	2.00 .25
a.		Souvenir sheet of 2	3.75 1.75

No. C92a contains 2 imperf. stamps similar to Nos. C91-C92 with simulated perforations.

WHO Type

Paintings: 60fr, The Anatomy Lesson, by Rembrandt (detail). 90fr, Jesus Healing the Sick, by Raphael.

1968, June 22   Photo.   Perf. 14

C93	A87	60fr multi	1.00 .25
C94	A87	90fr pur & multi	1.25 .25
a.		Souvenir sheet of 2	3.50 2.50

No. C94a contains 2 imperf. stamps similar to Nos. C93-C94 with simulated perforations.

Olympic Games Type

1968, July 27   Perf. 14x13½

C95	A88	60fr Wrestling	.85 .25
C96	A88	90fr Running	1.25 .25
a.		Souvenir sheet of 2	2.50 2.10

No. C96a contains 2 imperf. stamps similar to Nos. C95-C96 with simulated perforations.

Boy Scout Type

60fr, First aid practice, horiz. 90fr, Scout game.

1968, Nov. 23   Litho.   Perf. 14

C97	A90	60fr ol & multi	1.00 .25
C98	A90	90fr org & multi	1.40 .35
a.		Souvenir sheet of 2	3.00 1.75

No. C98a contains 2 imperf. stamps with simulated perforations similar to Nos. C97-C98.

PHILEXAFRIQUE Issue

The Letter, by Jean Auguste Franquelin AP14

1968, Nov. 9   Photo.   Perf. 12½x12

C99	AP14	100fr multi	2.75 1.75

PHILEXAFRIQUE Philatelic Exhibition in Abidjan, Feb. 14-23. Printed with alternating light ultramarine label.

Christmas Type

Paintings: 60fr, Adoration of the Magi, by Pieter Brueghel. 90fr, Adoration of the Magi, by Dürer.

1968, Dec. 28   Litho.   Perf. 14

C100	A91	60fr red & multi	1.10 .25
C101	A91	90fr multi	1.50 .35
a.		Souvenir sheet	3.75 1.75

No. C101a contains 2 imperf. stamps similar to Nos. C100-C101 with simulated perforations.

Human Rights Type

Human Rights Flame and: 60fr, Robert F. Kennedy. 90fr, Martin Luther King, Jr.

1969, Feb. 1   Photo.   Perf. 13½x14

C102	A92	60fr brt rose lil & vio bl	1.00 .25
C103	A92	90fr emer & brn	1.40 .40
a.		Souvenir sheet	2.50 1.75

No. C103a contains 2 imperf. stamps similar to Nos. C102-C103 with simulated perforations.

For overprints see Nos. C110-C111.

2nd PHILEXAFRIQUE Issue
Common Design Type

Design: 50fr, Togo #16 and Aledjo Fault.

1969, Feb. 14   Engr.   Perf. 13

C104	CD128	50fr red brn, grn & car rose	2.25 .45

Sports Type

Stadium and: 60fr, Boxing. 90fr, Bicycling.

1969, Apr. 26   Photo.   Perf. 14x13½

C105	A93	60fr bl, red & dk brn	.95 .25
C106	A93	90fr ultra, brt pink & dk brn	1.40 .30
a.		Souvenir sheet	2.50 1.75

No. C106a contains 2 imperf. stamps similar to Nos. C105-C106 with simulated perforations.

Lunar Type

Designs: 60fr, Astronaut exploring moon surface. 100fr, Astronaut gathering rocks.

1969, July 21   Litho.   Perf. 14

C107	A94	60fr dk bl & multi	.90 .25
C108	A94	100fr multi	1.50 .50
a.		Souvenir sheet	14.00 5.00

No. C108a contains 4 imperf. stamps with simulated perforations similar to Nos. 676-677 and C107-C108, magenta margin. No. C108a also exists with colors of 30fr and 100fr stamps changed, and margin in orange. Value, unused $6, used $2.

For overprints see Nos. C120-C121.

Painting Type

Painting: 90fr, Pentecost, by El Greco.

1969, Aug. 16   Litho.   Perf. 14

C109	A95	90fr multi	2.10 .50
a.		Souvenir sheet	2.75 1.50

No. C109a contains two imperf. stamps with simulated perforations similar to Nos. 682 and C109.

Nos. C102-C103 Overprinted Like Nos. 683-686

1969, Sept. 1   Photo.   Perf. 13½x14

C110	A92	60fr brt rose lil & vio bl	.90 .25
C111	A92	90fr emer & brn	1.25 .30
a.		Souv. sheet of 2	3.00 2.00

#C111a is #C103a with Eisenhower overprint.

Bank Type

Design: 100fr, Bank emblem and hand holding cattle and farmer.

1969, Sept. 10   Photo.   Perf. 13x14

C112	A96	100fr multi	1.10 .40

Red Cross Type

60fr, Wilhelm C. Roentgen & Red Cross workers with children in front of Togo Headquarters. 90fr, Henri Dunant & Red Cross workers meeting Biafra refugees at airport.

1969, Sept. 27   Litho.   Perf. 14

C113	A97	60fr brn & multi	.85 .30
C114	A97	90fr ol & multi	1.25 .40
a.		Souvenir sheet of 2	2.75 2.10

No. C114a contains 2 imperf. stamps with simulated perforations similar to Nos. C113-C114.

Agricultural Center Type

Emblem of Young Pioneer and Agricultural Organization and: 90fr, Manioc harvest. 100fr, Instruction in gardening. 200fr, Corn harvest. 250fr, Marching drum corps. 500fr, Parade of Young Pioneers.

1969-70   Litho.   Perf. 14

C115	A98	90fr multi	1.20 .25
C116	A98	100fr org & multi	1.40 .30
C117	A98	200fr multi ('70)	2.75 .40
C118	A98	250fr ol & multi	4.25 .70
C119	A98	500fr multi ('70)	9.00 .90
		Nos. C115-C119 (5)	18.60 2.55

Christmas Issue
Nos. C107-C108, C108a Overprinted: "JOYEUX NOEL"

1969, Dec.   Litho.   Perf. 14

C120	A94	60fr multi	3.50 .45
C121	A94	100fr multi	5.25 .65
a.		Souvenir sheet of 4	60.00 60.00

Peace Leaders Type

60fr, Friedrich Ebert. 90fr, Mahatma Gandhi.

1969, Dec. 27   Litho.   Perf. 14x13½

C122	A100	60fr dk brn, dk red & yel	1.00 .25
C123	A100	90fr dk brn, vio bl & ocher	1.40 .35

For surcharges see Nos. 765, C143.

ILO Type

Paintings and ILO Emblem: 60fr, Spring Sowing, by Vincent van Gogh. 90fr, Workers, by Diego de Rivera.

1970, Jan. 24   Litho.   Perf. 12½x13

C124	A101	60fr gold & multi	1.75 .25
C125	A101	90fr gold & multi	2.75 .25
a.		Souvenir sheet of 2	3.50 1.40

No. C125a contains two stamps similar to Nos. C124-C125, with simulated perforations.

Hair Styles Type

Various hair styles. 45fr, vert. 90fr, horiz.

1970, Feb. 21   Perf. 12½x13, 13x12½

C126	A102	45fr car & multi	.90 .25
C127	A102	90fr multi	1.75 .40

Independence Type

Design: 60fr, Togo No. C33 and Independence Monument, Lomé.

1970, Apr. 27   Litho.   Perf. 13x12½

C128	A103	60fr yel & multi	.85 .25

UPU Type

1970, May 30   Photo.   Perf. 14x13½

C129	A104	50fr grnsh bl & dk car	.90 .25

Soccer Type

Various Scenes from Soccer, Rimet Cup and Flags of: 50fr, Sweden and Israel. 60fr, Bulgaria and Peru. 90fr, Belgium and Salvador.

1970, June 27   Litho.   Perf. 13x14

C130	A105	50fr multi	.75 .25
C131	A105	60fr lil & multi	.90 .25
C132	A105	90fr multi	1.90 .35
a.		Souvenir sheet of 4	4.00 4.00
		Nos. C130-C132 (3)	3.55 .85

No. C132a contains 4 stamps similar to Nos. 734, C130-C132, but imperf. with simulated perforations.

Lenin Type

Design: 50fr, Lenin Meeting Peasant Delegation, by V. A. Serov, and UNESCO emblem.

1970, July 25   Litho.   Perf. 12½

C133	A106	50fr multi	1.95 .25

For overprint see No. C179.

EXPO '70 Type
Souvenir Sheet

150fr, Mitsubishi pavilion, EXPO '70 emblem.

1970, Aug. 8   Litho.   Perf. 13

C134	A107	150fr yel & multi	5.00 3.50
a.		Inscribed "AERINNE"	

No. C134 contains one stamp 86x33mm.

Astronaut Type

Design: 200fr, James A. Lovell, Fred W. Haise, Jr. and Tom Mattingly (replaced by John L. Swigert, Jr.) and Apollo 13 emblem.

1970, Sept. 26

C135	A108	200fr multi	2.90 .75
a.		Souvenir sheet of 3	3.75 2.50

Space flight of Apollo 13. No. C135a contains 3 stamps similar to Nos. 741, 744 and C135, with simulated perforations. For overprint see No. C136.

Nos. C135, C135a Inscribed: "FELICITATIONS / BON RETOUR APOLLO XIII"

1970, Sept. 26

C136	A108	200fr multi	2.75 .60
a.		Souvenir sheet of 3	3.75 2.50

Safe return of the crew of Apollo 13.

UN Type

Paintings and Emblems of UN Agencies: 60fr, The Mailman Roulin, by van Gogh, and UPU emblem. 90fr, The Birth of the Virgin, by Vittore Carpaccio, and WHO emblem.

1970, Oct. 24   Litho.   Perf. 13x12½

C137	A109	60fr grn, gold & blk	1.10 .25
C138	A109	90fr red org, gold & brn	1.75 .30
a.		Souvenir sheet of 4	3.50 2.50

No. C138a contains one each of Nos. 754-755 and C137-C138 with simulated perforations.

Moth Type

Moths: 60fr, Euchloron megaera. 90fr, Pseudacraea boisduvali.

1970, Nov. 21   Photo.   Perf. 13x14

C139	A110	60fr multi	5.25 .25
C140	A110	90fr multi	5.25 .25

Christmas Type

Paintings: 60fr, Adoration of the Magi, by Botticelli. 90fr, Adoration of the Kings, by Tiepolo.

1970, Dec. 26   Litho.   Perf. 12½x13

C141	A111	60fr gold & multi	1.50 .25
C142	A111	90fr gold & multi	2.25 .30
a.		Souv. sheet of 2, #C141-C142	3.50 1.75

No. C122 Surcharged and Overprinted

1971, Jan. 9   Photo.   Perf. 14x13½

C143	A100	200fr on 60fr	11.50 .60

De Gaulle Type

Designs: 60fr, De Gaulle and Pope Paul VI. 90fr, De Gaulle and satellite.

1971, Feb. 20   **Photo.**   *Perf. 13x14*
C144 A112 60fr blk & dp vio   2.20   .25
C145 A112 90fr blk & bl grn   3.00   .25
  a.   Souvenir sheet of 4   8.50   3.00

Nos. C143-C145 issued in memory of Charles De Gaulle (1890-1970), President of France. No. C145a contains 4 imperf. stamps similar to Nos. 769-770, C144-C145.

Easter Type

Paintings: 50fr, Resurrection, by Matthias Grunewald. 60fr, Resurrection, by Master of Trebon. 90fr, Resurrection, by El Greco.

1971, Apr. 10   **Litho.**   *Perf. 10½x11½*
C146 A113 50fr gold & multi   .85   .25
C147 A113 60fr gold & multi   1.25   .25
C148 A113 90fr gold & multi   1.60   .30
  a.   Souvenir sheet of 4, #773,   C146-C148   4.50   .50
    Nos. C146-C148 (3)   3.70   .80

Apollo 14 Type

Designs: 50fr, 200fr, Apollo 14 badge. 100fr, Take-off from moon, and spaceship.

1971, May   **Litho.**   *Perf. 12½*
C149 A114 50fr grn & multi   .65   .25
C150 A114 100fr multi   1.10   .45
C151 A114 200fr org & multi   2.50   .85
  a.   Souv. sheet of 4   3.75   3.90
    Nos. C149-C151 (3)   4.25   1.55

No. C151a contains 4 stamps similar to Nos. 777 and C149-C151 with simulated perforations.
For surcharge and overprints see Nos. C162-C164.

Cacao Type

60fr, Ministry of Agriculture. 90fr, Cacao tree and & pods. 100fr, Sorting & separating beans from pods.

1971, June 6   **Litho.**   *Perf. 14*
C152 A115 60fr multi   .75   .25
C153 A115 90fr multi   1.10   .40
C154 A115 100fr multi   1.25   .45
    Nos. C152-C154 (3)   3.10   1.10

ASECNA Type

1971, June 26
C155 A116 100fr multi   1.60   .35

Tourist Type

Designs: 50fr, Château Viale and antelope. 60fr, Lake Togo and crocodile. 100fr, Old lime furnace, Tokpli, and hippopotamus.

1971, July 17
C156 A117 50fr multi   .55   .25
C157 A117 60fr multi   .75   .25
C158 A117 100fr multi   1.00   .40
    Nos. C156-C158 (3)   2.30   .90

For overprint see No. C172.

Religions Type

Designs: 50fr, Mohammedans praying in front of Lomé Mosque. 60fr, Protestant service. 90fr, Catholic bishop and priests.

1971, July 31   **Litho.**   *Perf. 14½*
C159 A118 50fr multi   .55   .25
C160 A118 60fr multi   .75   .25
C161 A118 90fr multi   .95   .25
  a.   Souvenir sheet of 4, #787,   C159-C161   4.25   2.50
    Nos. C159-C161 (3)   2.25   .75

Nos. C149-C151 Overprinted and Surcharged in Black or Silver: "EN MEMOIRE / DOBROVOLSKY — VOLKOV — PATSAYEV / SOYUZ 11"

1971, Aug.   *Perf. 12½*
C162 A114 90fr on 50fr multi   1.00   .35
C163 A114 100fr multi (S)   1.20   .25
C164 A114 200fr multi   2.10   .65
  a.   Souvenir sheet of 4, #788,   C162-C164   7.00   7.00
    Nos. C162-C164 (3)   4.30   1.40

See note after No. 788.

Olympic Type

200fr, Sapporo '72 emblem and Ski jump

1971, Oct. 30   **Litho.**   *Perf. 14*
C165 A119 200fr multi   2.10   .50
  a.   Souvenir sheet of 4   4.25   3.50

No. C165 contains 4 stamps with simulated perforations similar to Nos. 791-793 and C165 printed on glazed paper.

African Postal Union Issue
Common Design Type

Design: 100fr, Adjogbo dancers and UAMPT Building, Brazzaville, Congo.

1971, Nov. 13   **Photo.**   *Perf. 13x13½*
C166 CD135 100fr bl & multi   1.25   .40

Intl. Organization for the Protection of Children (U.I.P.E.) — AP14a

Die Cut Perf. 10½

1971, Nov. 13   **Embossed**
C166A AP14a 1500fr gold   20.00

UNICEF Type

Toys: 60fr, Turtle. 90fr, Parrot.

1971, Nov. 27   **Litho.**   *Perf. 14*
C167 A120 60fr lt bl & multi   .55   .25
C168 A120 90fr multi   .85   .25
  a.   Souvenir sheet of 4   2.75   2.50

No. C168a contains 4 stamps with simulated perforations similar to Nos. 796-797 and C167-C168.
For overprints see Nos. C263-C264.

Christmas Type

Virgin and Child by: 60fr, Giorgione. 100fr, Raphael.

1971, Dec. 24   *Perf. 14x13*
C169 A121 60fr olive & multi   1.00   .30
C170 A121 100fr multi   1.75   .50
  a.   Souvenir sheet of 4   5.25   2.25

No. C170a contains 4 stamps with simulated perforations similar to Nos. 800-801, C169-C170.

Venice Type

Design: 100fr, Ca' d'Oro, Venice.

1972, Feb. 26   **Litho.**   *Perf. 14*
C171 A122 100fr multi   1.75   .55
  a.   Souvenir sheet of 3   5.75   2.50

No. C171a contains 3 stamps similar to Nos. 802-803, C171 with simulated perforations.

No. C156 Overprinted

1972, Mar.   **Litho.**   *Perf. 14*
C172 A117 50fr multi   .90   .25

Visit of Pres. Richard M. Nixon to the People's Republic of China, Feb. 20-27.

Easter Type

Paintings: 50fr, Resurrection, by Thomas de Coloswa. 100fr, Ascension by Andrea Mantegna.

1972, Mar. 31
C173 A123 50fr gold & multi   1.10   .25
C174 A123 100fr gold & multi   2.10   .25
  a.   Souvenir sheet of 4   3.00   1.50

No. C174a contains 4 stamps similar to Nos. 806-807, C173-C174 with simulated perforations.

Heart Type

100fr, Heart, WHO emblem and smith.

1972, Apr. 4
C175 A124 100fr multi   1.25   .45
  a.   Souvenir sheet of 2   3.25   1.40

No. C175a contains 2 stamps similar to Nos. 810 and C175 with simulated perforations.

Telecommunications Type

Design: 100fr, Intelsat 4 over Africa.

1972, June 24   *Perf. 14*
C176 A125 100fr multi   1.60   .30

For overprint see No. C229.

Cassava Type

60fr, Truck and cassava processing factory, horiz. 80fr, Children, mother holding tapioca cake.
Stamps inscribed "POSTE AERIENNE".

1972, June 30
C177 A126 60fr multi   1.10   .25
C178 A126 80fr multi   1.25   .25

No. C133 Srchd. in Deep Carmine

1972, July 15   **Litho.**   *Perf. 12½*
C179 A106 300fr on 50fr multi   4.75   1.40

President Nixon's visit to the USSR, May 1972. Old denomination obliterated with 6x5mm rectangle.

Olympic Type

1972, Aug. 26   **Litho.**   *Perf. 14*
C180 A127 90fr Gymnastics   .65   .40
  a.   Souv. sheet of 2   3.25   1.60
C181 A127 200fr Basketball   1.75   .75

No. C180a contains 2 stamps with simulated perforations similar to Nos. 816 and C180.
For overprints see Nos. C234-C235.

Bird Type

Bird: 90fr, Rose-ringed parakeet.

1972, Sept. 9
C182 A128 90fr multi   2.75   .45
  a.   Souvenir sheet of 4   13.00   2.60

No. C182a contains 4 stamps similar to Nos. 818-820, C182 with simulated perforations.

Rotary Type

Rotary Emblem and: 60fr, Map of Togo, olive branch. 90fr, Flags of Togo and Rotary Club. 100fr, Paul P. Harris.

1972, Oct. 7   **Litho.**   *Perf. 14*
C183 A129 60fr brn & multi   .65   .25
C184 A129 90fr multi   .90   .40
C185 A129 100fr multi   1.25   .45
    Nos. C183-C185 (3)   2.80   1.10

For overprints see Nos. C212-C213, C244-C245.

Type of 1972 Painting

Designs: 60fr, Mystical Marriage of St. Catherine, by Assistant to the P. M. Master. 80fr, Self-portrait, by Leonardo da Vinci. 100fr, Sts. Mary and Agnes by Botticelli.

1972, Oct. 21
C186 A130 60fr gold & multi   1.40   .25
C187 A130 80fr gold & multi   1.75   .30
C188 A130 100fr gold & multi   2.25   .45
  a.   Souvenir sheet of 4   4.50   2.00
    Nos. C186-C188 (3)   5.40   1.00

No. C188a contains 4 stamps with simulated perforations similar to Nos. 824, C186-188.

Presidential Visit Type

Design: 100fr, Pres. Pompidou and Col. Etienne Eyadema, front view of party headquarters

1972, Nov. 23   **Litho.**   *Perf. 14*
C189 A131 100fr multi   2.40   .40

Johann Wolfgang von Goethe (1749-1832), German Poet and Dramatist AP15

1972, Dec. 2   **Photo.**   *Perf. 13x14*
C190 AP15 100fr grn & multi   1.40   .40

Christmas Type

Paintings: 60fr, Nativity, by Master Vyshchibrod. 80fr, Adoration of the Kings, anonymous. 100fr, Flight into Egypt, by Giotto.

1972, Dec. 23   **Litho.**   *Perf. 14*
C191 A132 60fr gold & multi   1.00   .25
C192 A132 80fr gold & multi   1.20   .35
C193 A132 100fr gold & multi   1.40   .45
  a.   Souvenir sheet of 4   5.00   2.75
    Nos. C191-C193 (3)   3.60   1.05

No. C193a contains 4 stamps with simulated perforations similar to Nos. 829, C191-C193.

Leprosy Day Type

Design: 100fr, Dr. Armauer G. Hansen, apparatus, microscope and Petri dish.

1973, Jan. 23   **Photo.**   *Perf. 14x13½*
C194 A133 100fr rose car & bl   2.75   .40

World Leprosy Day and centenary of the discovery of the Hansen bacillus, the cause of leprosy.

Miniature Sheets

1972 Summer Olympics, Munich — AP15a

Medalists, each 1500fr: #C194A, Mark Spitz, US, swimming. #C194B, L. Linsenhoff, West Germany, equestrian. #C194C, D. Morelon, France, cycling.

Litho. & Embossed

1973, Jan.   *Perf. 13½*
C194A-C194C AP15a   Set of 3   375.00

Exist imperf.

Miniature Sheet

Apollo 17 Moon Landing — AP15b

1973, Jan.
C194D AP15b 1500fr gold &
                          multi   55.00
           Exists imperf.

Easter Type
1973, Apr. 21   Litho.   Perf. 14
C195 A135 90fr Christ in Glory   1.40   .40
 a.   Souvenir sheet of 2   2.75   1.75
 No. C195a contains one each of Nos. 835
and C195 with simulated perforations.

Apollo 17 Type
Designs: 100fr, Astronauts on moon and
orange rock. 200fr, Rocket lift-off at Cape
Kennedy and John F. Kennedy.

1973, June 2   Litho.   Perf. 14
C196 A136 100fr multi   1.60   .45
C197 A136 200fr multi   3.25   .65
 a.   Souvenir sheet of 2   4.25   3.00
 No. C197a contains 2 stamps similar to
Nos. C196-C197 with simulated perforations.

Boy Scout Type
100fr, Canoeing, horiz. 200fr, Campfire,
horiz.

1973, June 30   Litho.   Perf. 14
C198 A137 100fr bl & multi   1.25   .45
C199 A137 200fr bl & multi   2.50   .70
 a.   Souvenir sheet of 2   3.50   2.10
 No. C199a contains 2 stamps similar to
Nos. C198-C199 with simulated perforations.
For overprints see Nos. C265-C266.

Copernicus Type
Designs: 90fr, Heliocentric system. 100fr,
Nicolaus Copernicus.

1973, July 18
C200 A138 90fr multi   1.60   .35
C201 A138 100fr bis & multi   1.90   .45
 a.   Souv. sheet of 2, #C200-C201 3.00 1.60

Red Cross Type
Design: 100fr, Dove carrying Red Cross
letter, sun, map of Togo.

1973, Aug. 4
C202 A139 100fr multi   3.00   .35
 For overprint see No. C294.

Literacy Type
Design: 90fr, Woman teacher in classroom.

1973, Aug. 18   Litho.   Perf. 14
C203 A140 90fr multi   1.50   .35

WMO Type
1973, Oct. 4   Photo.   Perf. 14x13
C204 A142 200fr dl bl, pur & brn 2.00 .60

Type 1967
Early & contemporary planes, #758, C36.

1973, Oct. 20   Photo.   Perf. 14x13
C205 A79 100fr multi   2.50   .35
 a.   Souvenir sheet of 2   3.00   1.75
 75th anniversary of Togolese postal service.
No. C205a contains 2 stamps similar to Nos.
855 and C205 with simulated perforations.

Kennedy Type
Designs: 90fr, Kennedy and Charles De
Gaulle. 100fr, Kennedy and Nikita Krushchev.
200fr, Kennedy and model of Apollo
spacecraft.

1973, Nov. 22   Litho.   Perf. 14
C206 A143 90fr blk & pink   1.60   .45
C207 A143 100fr blk, lt bl & bl 1.75   .60
C208 A143 200fr blk, buff & brn 4.00   .75
 a.   Souvenir sheet of 3   4.00   2.00
        Nos. C206-C208 (3)   7.35   1.80
 No. C208a contains 2 stamps similar to
Nos. C207-208 with simulated perforations.

Human Rights
Flame and
People — AP16

1973, Dec. 8   Photo.   Perf. 13x14
C209 AP16 250fr lt bl & multi   2.75   .80
 25th anniversary of the Universal Declaration of Human Rights.

Christmas Type
Paintings: 90fr, Virgin and Child. 100fr,
Adoration of the Kings. Both after 15th cen-
tury Italian paintings.

1973, Dec. 22   Litho.   Perf. 14
C210 A144 90fr gold & multi   1.10   .35
C211 A144 100fr gold & multi   1.50   .45
 a.   Souvenir sheet of 2   2.75   1.50
 No. C211a contains 2 stamps with simu-
lated perforations similar to Nos. C210-C211.

Nos. C183 and C185 Overprinted: "PREMIERE CONVENTION / 210eme DISTRICT / FEVRIER 1974 / LOME"
1974, Feb. 21   Litho.   Perf. 14
C212 A129 90fr brn & multi   .65   .25
C213 A129 100fr multi   1.00   .35
 First convention of Rotary International, Dis-
trict 210, Lomé, Feb. 22-24.

Soccer Type
Various soccer scenes and games' cup.

1974, Mar. 2   Litho.   Perf. 14
C214 A145 90fr multi   .90   .45
C215 A145 100fr multi   1.00   .50
C216 A145 200fr multi   2.00   .95
 a.   Souvenir sheet of 2   3.75   2.10
        Nos. C214-C216 (3)   3.90   1.90
 No. C216a contains 2 stamps with simu-
lated perforations similar to Nos. C215-C216.

Picasso Type
Paintings: 90fr, The Muse. 100fr, Les Dem-
oiselles d'Avignon. 200fr, Sitting Nude.

1974, Apr. 6   Litho.   Perf. 14
C217 A146 90fr brn & multi   1.60   .40
C218 A146 100fr pur & multi   2.00   .45
C219 A146 200fr multi   4.00   .85
 a.   Souvenir sheet of 3   7.00   4.00
        Nos. C217-C219 (3)   7.60   1.70
 No. C219a contains 3 stamps similar to
Nos. C217-C219 with simulated perforations.

Coastal Views Type
Designs: 90fr, Fishermen on Lake Togo.
100fr, Mouth of Anecho River.

1974, Apr. 20
C220 A147 90fr multi   1.10   .25
C221 A147 100fr multi   1.25   .35
 a.   Souvenir sheet of 2   2.50   1.25
 No. C221a contains 2 stamps similar to
Nos. C220-C221 with simulated perforations.

UPU Type
Designs: Old mailmen's uniforms.

1974, May 10   Litho.   Perf. 14
C222 A148 50fr multi   .70   .25
C223 A148 100fr multi   1.25   .35
 a.   Souvenir sheet of 2   40.00 17.00
 No. C223a contains 2 stamps similar to
Nos. C222-C223, rouletted.

Fishing Type
Designs: 90fr, Fishermen bringing in net
with catch. 100fr, Fishing with rod and line.
200fr, Fishing with basket, vert.

1974, June 22   Litho.   Perf. 14
C224 A149 90fr multi   1.00   .25
C225 A149 100fr multi   1.10   .25
C226 A149 200fr multi   2.40   .65
 a.   Souvenir sheet of 3   5.25   2.50
        Nos. C224-C226 (3)   4.50   1.15
 No. C226a contains 3 stamps with simu-
lated perforations similar to Nos. C224-C226.

Jupiter Probe Type
Designs: 100fr, Rocket take-off, vert. 200fr,
Satellite in space.

1974, July 6   Perf. 14
C227 A150 100fr multi   .90   .35
C228 A150 200fr multi   2.00   .65
 a.   Souvenir sheet of 2   5.50   4.00
 No. C228a contains 2 stamps similar to
Nos. C227-C228 with simulated perforations;
imperf. or rouletted.

No. C176
Overprinted in Black

1974, July   Perf. 14
C229 A125 100fr multi   3.50   1.20
 INTERNABA 1974 Intl. Philatelic Exhibition,
Basel, June 7-16.
 No. C229 exists overprinted in silver. Value,
unused $11.

Seashell Type
1974, July 13   Litho.   Perf. 14
C230 A151 90fr Alcithoe pon-
                      sonbyi   1.75   .30
C231 A151 100fr Casmaria
                      iredalei   2.25   .40
 a.   Souvenir sheet of 2   4.50   1.40
 No. C231a contains 2 stamps similar to
Nos. C230-C231 with simulated perforations.

Horse Racing Type
90fr, Steeplechase. 100fr, Galloping horses.

1974, Aug. 3   Litho.   Perf. 14
C232 A152 90fr multi   2.10   .30
C233 A152 100fr multi   2.40   .40
 a.   Souvenir sheet of 2   6.50   2.25
 No. C233a contains one each of Nos. C232-
C233 with simulated perforations.

Nos. C180,
C180a and C181
Overprinted

1974, Aug. 19
C234 A127 90fr multi   .75   .25
 a.   Souvenir sheet of 2   18.00   —
C235 A127 200fr multi   1.50   .65
 World Cup Soccer Championship, Munich,
1974, victory of German Federal Republic. For
description of No. C234a see note after No.
C181.

Animal Type
1974, Sept. 7   Litho.   Perf. 14
C236 A153 90fr Lions   2.10   .35
C237 A153 100fr Rhinoceroses   2.25   .40
 a.   Souvenir sheet of 3   3.75   1.90
 Wild animals of West Africa. No. C237a
contains 3 stamps similar to Nos. 889, C236-
C237 with simulated perforations.

1974, Oct. 14
C238 A153 90fr Herd at
                      waterhole 1.10   .25
C239 A153 100fr Village and
                      cows   1.25   .35
 a.   Souvenir sheet of 2   2.50   1.25
 Domestic animals. No. C239a contains 2
stamps with simulated perforations similar to
Nos. C238-C239.

Churchill Type
Designs: 100fr, Churchill and frigate. 200fr,
Churchill and fighter planes.

Jupiter Probe Type

1974, Nov. 1   Photo.   Perf. 13x13½
C240 A154 100fr multi   1.25   .35
C241 A154 200fr org & multi   2.75   .70
 a.   Souvenir sheet of 2   4.50   2.10
 No. C241a contains 2 stamps similar to
Nos. C240-C241; perf. or imperf.

Flower Type
Flowers of Togo: 100fr, Clerodendrum
thosonae. 200fr, Gloriosa superba.

1975, Feb. 15   Litho.   Perf. 14
C242 A155 100fr multi   1.75   .30
C243 A155 200fr multi   2.75   .50
 a.   Souvenir sheet of 2   7.00   1.90
 No. C243a contains one each of Nos. C242-
C243, perf. 13x14 or imperf.

Nos. C184-C185 Overprinted: "70e ANNIVERSAIRE / 23 FEVRIER 1975"
1975, Feb. 23   Litho.   Perf. 14
C244 A129 90fr multi   .90   .25
C245 A129 100fr multi   1.00   .35
 Rotary International, 70th anniversary.

Easter Type
Paintings: 100fr, Christ Rising from the
Tomb, by Master MS. 200fr, Holy Trinity
(detail), by Dürer.

1975, Apr. 19   Litho.   Perf. 14
C246 A157 100fr multi   1.00   .25
C247 A157 200fr multi   2.00   .55
 a.   Souvenir sheet of 2   3.50   2.00
 No. C247a contains 2 stamps similar to
Nos. C246-C247 with simulated perforations.

Independence Type
50fr, National Day parade, flag and map of
Togo. 60fr, Warriors' dance and flag of Togo.

1975, Apr. 26   Litho.   Perf. 14
C248 A158 50fr multi, vert.   .50   .25
C249 A158 60fr multi   .70   .25
 a.   Souvenir sheet of 2   1.50   .75
 No. C249a contains 2 stamps similar to
Nos. C248-C249 with simulated perforations.

Hunt Type
Designs: 90fr, Running deer. 100fr, Wild
boar hunter with shotgun.

1975, May 24   Photo.   Perf. 13x13½
C250 A159 90fr multi   1.75   .30
C251 A159 100fr multi   2.10   .30

Palm Oil Type
Designs: 85fr, Selling palm oil in market,
vert. 100fr, Oil processing plant, Alokoegbe.

1975, June 28   Litho.   Perf. 14
C252 A160 85fr multi   1.75   .50
C253 A160 100fr multi   2.00   .50

Apollo-Soyuz Type and

Soyuz Spacecraft
AP17

Designs: 60fr, Donald K. Slayton, Vance D.
Brand and Thomas P. Stafford. 90fr, Aleksei
A. Leonov and Valery N. Kubasov. 100fr,
Apollo-Soyuz link-up, American and Russian
flags. 200fr, Apollo-Soyuz emblem and globe.

1975, July 15
C254 AP17 50fr yel & multi   .50   .25
C255 A161 60fr lil & multi   .70   .25
C256 A161 90fr bl & multi   .85   .25
C257 A161 100fr grn & multi   1.25   .40
C258 A161 200fr yel & multi   2.10   .45
 a.   Souv. sheet of 4, #C255-C258 6.00 3.50
        Nos. C254-C258 (5)   5.40   1.60
 See note after No. 913.

Schweitzer Type
Dr. Schweitzer: 80fr, playing organ, vert.
90fr, with pelican, vert. 100fr, and Lambarene
Hospital.

1975, Aug. 23   Litho.   Perf. 14x13½

C259	A163	80fr multi	1.10	.30
C260	A163	90fr multi	1.25	.35
C261	A163	100fr multi	1.40	.40
		Nos. C259-C261 (3)	3.75	1.05

Letter Writing Type

80fr, Erasmus Writing Letter, by Hans Holbein.

1975, Oct. 9   Litho.   Perf. 14

C262	A164	80fr multi	1.00	.25

Nos. C167-C168a Overprinted: "30ème Anniversaire / des Nations-Unies"

1975, Oct. 24   Litho.   Perf. 14

C263	A120	60fr multi	.60	.25
C264	A120	90fr multi	.75	.25
a.		Souvenir sheet of 4	3.00	1.00

UN, 30th anniv. #C264a contains Nos. 796 (with overprint), 918, C263-C264.

Nos. C198-C199 Overprinted: "14ème JAMBOREE / MONDIAL / DES ÉCLAIREURS"

1975, Nov. 7

C265	A137	100fr multi	.90	.25
C266	A137	200fr multi	1.75	.50
a.		Souvenir sheet of 2	3.25	2.00

14th World Boy Scout Jamboree, Lillehammer, Norway, July 29-Aug. 7. No. C266a contains one each of Nos. C265-C266 with simulated perforations.

Christmas Type

Paintings of the Virgin and Child: 90fr, Nativity, by Federico Barocci. 100fr, Bellini. 200fr, Correggio.

1975, Dec. 20   Litho.   Perf. 14

C267	A165	90fr bl & multi	.80	.25
C268	A165	100fr red & multi	.90	.25
C269	A165	200fr bl & multi	1.75	.50
a.		Souv. sheet of 2, #C268-C269	3.50	2.00
		Nos. C267-C269 (3)	3.45	1.00

Bicentennial Type

Paintings (and Bicentennial Emblem): 60fr, Surrender of Gen. Burgoyne, by John Trumbull. 70fr, Surrender at Trenton, by Trumbull, vert. 100fr, Signing of Declaration of Independence, by Trumbull. 200fr, Washington Crossing the Delaware, by Emanuel Leutze.

1976, Mar. 3   Litho.   Perf. 14

C270	A167	60fr multi	.65	.25
C271	A167	70fr multi	.75	.25
C272	A167	100fr multi	1.00	.25
C273	A167	200fr multi	2.00	.55
a.		Souv. sheet of 2, #C272-C273	4.00	2.00
		Nos. C270-C273 (4)	4.40	1.30

No. C273a also exists imperf. Value $22.50.
For overprints see Nos. C280-C283.

Common Market Type

Designs: 60fr, ACP and CEE emblems. 70fr, Map of Africa, Europe and Asia.

1976, Apr. 24   Photo.   Perf. 13x14

C274	A168	60fr lt bl & multi	.55	.25
C275	A168	70fr yel & multi	.65	.25

Telephone Type

Designs: 70fr, Thomas A. Edison, old and new communications equipment. 105fr, Alexander Graham Bell, old and new telephones.

1976, Mar. 10   Photo.   Perf. 13x14

C276	A169	70fr multi	.50	.25
C277	A169	105fr multi	.60	.40
a.		Souv. sheet of 2, #C276-C277	2.25	1.40

No. C277a exists imperf. Value $10.00.

Eye Examination
AP18

1976, Apr. 8   Perf. 14x13

C278	AP18	60fr dk red & multi	.60	.25

World Health Day: "Foresight prevents blindness."

Pylon, Flags of Ghana, Togo, Dahomey — AP19

1976, May 8   Litho.   Perf. 14

C279	AP19	60fr multi	1.00	.25

Ghana-Togo-Dahomey electric power grid, 1st anniv. See No. 932.

Nos. C270-C273, C273a, Overprinted: "INTERPHIL / MAI 29-JUIN 6, 1976"

1976, May 29

C280	A167	60fr multi	.50	.25
C281	A167	70fr multi	.55	.25
C282	A167	100fr multi	.80	.25
C283	A167	200fr multi	1.60	.55
a.		Souvenir sheet of 2	3.00	3.00
		Nos. C280-C283 (4)	3.45	1.30

Interphil 76 Intl. Philatelic Exhibition, Philadelphia, Pa., May 29-June 6. Overprint on No. C281 in 3 lines; overprint on No. C283a applied to each stamp.

Olympic Games Type

Montreal Olympic Emblem and: 70fr, Yachting. 105fr, Motorcycling. 200fr, Fencing.

1976, June 15   Photo.   Perf. 14x13

C284	A172	60fr multi	.60	.25
C285	A172	105fr multi	.85	.40
C286	A172	200fr multi	1.60	.65
a.		Souvenir sheet of 2, #C285-C286, perf. 14	3.00	2.25
		Nos. C284-C286 (3)	3.05	1.30

For overprints see Nos. C298-C299.

Viking Type

60fr, Viking landing on Mars. 70fr, Nodus Gordii (view on Mars). 105fr, Lander over Mare Tyrrhenum. 200fr, Landing on Mars.

1976, July 15   Litho.   Perf. 14

C287	A173	60fr bis & multi	.55	.25
C288	A173	70fr multi	.65	.25
C289	A173	105fr bl & multi	.90	.40
C290	A173	200fr multi	1.75	.60
a.		Souv. sheet of 2, #C289-C290, perf. 14x13½	3.50	2.25
		Nos. C287-C290 (4)	3.85	1.50

Toulouse-Lautrec Type, 1976

Paintings: 60fr, Carmen, portrait. 70fr, Maurice at the Somme. 200fr, "Messalina."

1976, Aug. 7   Litho.   Perf. 14

C291	A174	60fr blk & multi	1.00	.25
C292	A174	70fr blk & multi	1.00	.25
C293	A174	200fr blk & multi	2.40	.55
a.		Souv. sheet of 2, #C292-C293, perf. 13½x14	5.00	2.25
		Nos. C291-C293 (3)	4.40	1.05

No. C202 Overprinted: "Journée / Internationale / de l'Enfance"

1976, Nov. 27   Litho.   Perf. 14

C294	A139	100fr multi	.55	.35

International Children's Day.

Christmas Type

Paintings: 70fr, Holy Family, by Lorenzo Lotto. 105fr, Virgin and Child with Saints, by Jacopo da Pontormo. 200fr, Virgin and Child with Saints, by Lotto.

1976, Dec. 18

C295	A175	70fr multi	.55	.25
C296	A175	105fr multi	1.10	.45
C297	A175	200fr multi	1.75	.90
a.		Souv. sheet of 2, #C296-C297	1.75	2.00
		Nos. C295-C297 (3)	3.40	1.60

No. C284 Overprinted

No. C286 Overprinted

1976, Dec.   Photo.   Perf. 14x13

C298	A172	70fr multi	.65	.25
C299	A172	100fr multi	1.75	.65
a.		Souvenir sheet of 2	3.50	2.50

Olympic winners. No. C299a (on No. C286a) contains Nos. C285 and C299.

Eyadema Anniversary Type

60fr, National Assembly Building. 100fr, Pres. Eyadema greeting people at Aug. 30th meeting.

1977, Jan. 13   Photo.   Perf. 13x14

C300	A177	60fr multi	.55	.25
C301	A177	100fr multi	.85	.35
a.		Souv. sheet of 2, #C300-C301	1.75	1.10

Musical Instrument Type

Musical Instruments: 60fr, Atopani. 80fr, African violin, vert. 105fr, African flutes, vert.

1977, Feb. 7   Litho.   Perf. 14

C302	A178	60fr multi	.80	.25
C303	A178	80fr multi	1.00	.25
C304	A178	105fr multi	1.50	.30
a.		Souv. sheet of 2, #C303-C304	2.75	1.50
		Nos. C302-C304 (3)	3.30	.80

Victor Hugo Type

Victor Hugo in exile on Guernsey Island.

1977, Feb. 26   Perf. 13x14

C305	A179	60fr multi	.70	.25
a.		Souvenir sheet of 2, #952, C305	1.25	.75

For overprint see No. C316.

Beethoven Type

Designs: 100fr, Beethoven's piano and 1818 portrait. 200fr, Beethoven on his deathbed and Holy Trinity Church, Vienna.

1977, Mar. 7   Perf. 14

C306	A180	100fr multi	1.25	.25
C307	A180	200fr multi	2.10	.60
a.		Souv. sheet of 2, #C306-C307	3.25	1.50

Automobile Type

Early Automobiles: 60fr, Cannstatt-Daimler, 1899, Germany. 70fr, Sunbeam, 1904, England. 100fr, Renault, 1908, France. 200fr, Rolls Royce, 1909, England.

1977, Apr. 11   Litho.   Perf. 14

C308	A181	60fr multi	.80	.25
C309	A181	70fr multi	.85	.25
C310	A181	100fr multi	1.10	.35
C311	A181	200fr multi	1.75	.75
a.		Souv. sheet of 2, #C310-C311	5.00	1.75
		Nos. C308-C311 (4)	4.50	1.60

Lindbergh Type

Designs: 60fr, Lindbergh and son Jon, birds in flight. 85fr, Lindbergh home in Kent, England. 90fr, Spirit of St. Louis over Atlantic Ocean. 100fr, Concorde over NYC.

1977, May 9

C312	A182	60fr multi	.50	.25
C313	A182	85fr multi	.75	.25
C314	A182	90fr multi	.75	.25
C315	A182	100fr multi	1.10	.30
a.		Souv. sheet of 2, #C314-C315	2.40	1.20
		Nos. C312-C315 (4)	3.10	1.05

No. C305 Overprinted: "10ème ANNIVERSAIRE DU / CONSEIL INTERNATIONAL / DE LA LANGUE FRANÇAISE"

1977, May 17   Litho.   Perf. 14

C316	A179	60fr multi	.70	.25

10th anniv. of the French Language Council.

Wildlife Type

60fr, Colobus monkeys. 90fr, Chimpanzee, vert. 100fr, Leopard. 200fr, West African manatee.

1977, June 13

C317	A183	60fr multi	.70	.25
C318	A183	90fr multi	1.00	.25
C319	A183	100fr multi	1.10	.25

C320	A183	200fr multi	2.40	.35
a.		Souv. sheet of 2, #C319-C320	4.00	1.75
		Nos. C317-C320 (4)	5.20	1.10

Agriculture Type

Designs: 60fr, Corn silo. 100fr, Hoeing and planting by hand. 200fr, Tractor on field.

1977, July 11   Litho.   Perf. 14

C321	A184	60fr multi	.50	.25
C322	A184	100fr multi	.85	.25
C323	A184	200fr multi	1.75	.45
a.		Souv. sheet of 2, #C322-C323, perf. 13x14	3.40	1.60
		Nos. C321-C323 (3)	3.10	.95

Rubens Type

Paintings: 60fr, Heads of Black Men, 1620. 100fr, Anne of Austria, 1624.

1977, Aug. 8

C324	A185	90fr multi	.90	.25
C325	A185	100fr multi	1.40	.25
a.		Souv. sheet of 2, #C324-C325, perf. 14x13	2.10	1.25

Orbiter Type

90fr, Retrieval of unmanned satellite in space. 100fr, Satellite's return to space after repairs. 200fr, Manned landing of Orbiter.

1977, Oct. 4   Litho.   Perf. 14

C326	A186	90fr multi, vert.	.75	.25
C327	A186	100fr multi	.80	.25
C328	A186	200fr multi	1.75	.35
a.		Souv. sheet of 2, #C327-C328	3.00	1.50
		Nos. C326-C328 (3)	3.30	.85

Lafayette Type

60fr, Lafayette landing in New York, 1824. 105fr, Lafayette and Washington at Valley Forge.

1977, Nov. 7   Perf. 13x14

C329	A187	60fr multi	.65	.25
C330	A187	105fr multi	1.10	.25
a.		Souv. sheet of 2, #C329-C330	1.75	1.00

Christmas Type

Virgin & Child by: 90fr, 200fr, Carlo Crivelli, diff. 100fr, Bellini.

1977, Dec. 19   Perf. 14

C331	A189	90fr multi	.70	.25
C332	A189	100fr multi	.90	.25
C333	A189	200fr multi	1.50	.40
a.		Souv. sheet of 2, #C332-C333	3.25	1.75
		Nos. C331-C333 (3)	3.10	.90

Jenner Type

Designs: 50fr, Edward Jenner. 60fr, Smallpox vaccination clinic, horiz.

1978, Jan. 9   Perf. 14x13, 13x14

C334	A190	50fr multi	.35	.25
C335	A190	60fr multi	.40	.25
a.		Souvenir sheet of 2	1.40	.65

No. C335a contains 2 stamps with simulated perforations similar to Nos. C334-C335.

Wright Brothers Type

Designs: 60fr, Orville Wright's 7½-minute flight. 70fr, Orville Wright injured in first aircraft accident, 1908. 200fr, Wrights' bicycle shop, Dearborn, Mich. 300fr, First flight, 1903.

1978, Feb. 6   Litho.   Perf. 14

C336	A191	60fr multi	1.00	.25
C337	A191	70fr multi	1.10	.25
C338	A191	200fr multi	1.40	.35
C339	A191	300fr multi	2.10	.60
a.		Souvenir sheet of 2	9.25	5.25
		Nos. C336-C339 (4)	5.60	1.45

No. C339a contains one each of Nos. C338-C339 with simulated perforations.

Port of Lomé Type, 1978

Anchor and: 60fr, Industrial harbor. 100fr, Merchant marine harbor. 200fr, Bird's-eye view of entire harbor.

1978, Apr. 26   Photo.   Perf. 13

C340	A199	60fr multi	.45	.25
C341	A199	100fr multi	.75	.25
C342	A199	200fr multi	1.60	.40
a.		Souv. sheet of 2, #C341-C342	3.00	1.50
		Nos. C340-C342 (3)	2.80	.90

Space Type

Designs: 90fr, Module camera, horiz. 100fr, Module antenna. 200fr, Pioneer, US, in orbit.

1978, May 8   Litho.   Perf. 14

C343	A200	90fr multi	.70	.25
C344	A200	100fr multi	.75	.25
C345	A200	200fr multi	1.50	.35
a.		Souv. sheet of 2, #C344-C345, perf. 13½x14	2.50	1.50
		Nos. C343-C345 (3)	2.95	.85

Soccer Type

Various soccer scenes & Argentina '78 emblem.

1978, June 5   *Perf. 14*
C346 A201 60fr multi   .50 .25
C347 A201 80fr multi   .65 .25
C348 A201 200fr multi   1.40 .40
C349 A201 300fr multi   2.10 .55
  a. Souvenir sheet of 2, #C348-
    C349, perf. 13½x14   3.25 1.90
    Nos. C346-C349 (4)   4.65 1.45

Bicycle Type

History of Bicycle: 60fr, Bantam, 1896, vert. 85fr, Fold-up bicycle for military use, 1897. 90fr, Draisienne, 1816, vert. 100fr, Penny-farthing, 1884, vert.

Perf. 14x13, 13x14
1978, July 10   Photo.
C350 A202 60fr multi   .50 .25
C351 A202 85fr multi   .70 .25
C352 A202 90fr multi   .85 .35
C353 A202 100fr multi   1.10 .35
  a. Souv. sheet of 2, #C352-C353 2.75 1.10
    Nos. C350-C353 (4)   3.15 1.20

Phonograph Type

60fr, Edison's original phonograph, horiz. 80fr, Emile Berliner's phonograph, 1888. 200fr, Berliner's improved phonograph, 1894, horiz. 300fr, His Master's Voice phonograph, 1900, horiz.

Perf. 13x14, 14x13
1978, July 8   Photo.
C354 A203 60fr multi   .45 .25
C355 A203 80fr multi   .60 .25
C356 A203 200fr multi   1.40 .35
C357 A203 300fr multi   2.20 .50
  a. Souv. sheet of 2, #C356-C357 3.50 2.00
    Nos. C354-C357 (4)   4.65 1.35

Red Cross Type

Design: 60fr, Red Cross and other pavilions at Paris Exhibition, 1867.

1978, Sept. 4   Photo.   *Perf. 14x13*
C358 A204 60fr pur & red   .45 .25
  a. Souv. sheet, #1009, C358   1.10 .55

Paintings Type

60fr, Langlois Bridge, by Vincent van Gogh. 70fr, Witches' Sabbath, by Francisco Goya. 90fr, Jesus among the Doctors, by Albrecht Dürer. 200fr, View of Arco, by Dürer.

1978, Nov. 6   Litho.   *Perf. 14*
C359 A205 60fr multi   .60 .25
C360 A205 70fr multi   .65 .30
C361 A205 90fr multi   .90 .40
C362 A205 200fr multi   1.75 .70
  a. Souv. sheet of 2, #C361-C362 3.25 1.40
    Nos. C359-C362 (4)   3.90 1.65

Birth and death anniversaries of famous painters.

Philexafrique II — Essen Issue

Common Design Types

#C363, Warthog and Togo No. C36. #C364, Firecrest and Thurn and Taxis No. 1.

1978, Nov. 1   Litho.   *Perf. 13x12½*
C363 CD138 100fr multi   1.40 .50
C364 CD139 100fr multi   1.40 1.00
  a. Pair, #C363-C364 + label   3.00 1.50

Congress of Paris Type

60fr, Mail ship "Slieve Roe" 1877, post horn. 105fr, Congress of Paris medal. 200fr, Locomotive, 1870. All horizontal.

1978, Nov. 27   Photo.   *Perf. 14x13*
C365 A206 60fr multi   .55 .25
C366 A206 105fr multi   .90 .45
C367 A206 200fr multi   1.40 .75
  a. Souv. sheet of 2, #C366-C367 2.50 1.20
    Nos. C365-C367 (3)   2.85 1.45

Christmas Type

Paintings (Virgin and Child): 90fr, 200fr, by Carlo Crivelli, diff. 100fr, by Cosimo Tura.

1978, Dec. 18
C368 A207 90fr multi   .75 .35
C369 A207 100fr multi   .95 .40
C370 A207 200fr multi   1.75 .70
  a. Souv. sheet of 2, #C369-C370 3.25 1.40
    Nos. C368-C370 (3)   3.45 1.45

Capt. Cook Type

Designs: 60fr, "Freelove," Whitby Harbor, horiz. 70fr, Trip to Antarctica, 1773, horiz. 90fr, Capt. Cook. 200fr, Sails of Endeavour.

1979, Feb. 12   Litho.   *Perf. 14*
C371 A208 60fr multi   .50 .25
C372 A208 70fr multi   .55 .25
C373 A208 90fr multi   .75 .30
C374 A208 200fr multi   1.75 1.25
  a. Souv. sheet, #C373-C374   3.00 1.75
    Nos. C371-C374 (4)   3.55 2.05

Easter Type

60fr, Resurrection. 100fr, Ascension. 200fr, Jesus appearing to Mary Magdalene.

1979, Apr. 9
C375 A209 60fr multi   .45 .25
C376 A209 100fr multi   .70 .40
C377 A209 200fr multi   1.50 .70
  a. Souv. sheet of 2, #C376-C377 2.75 1.40
    Nos. C375-C377 (3)   2.65 1.35

UPU Emblem, Drummer — AP20

Design: 100fr, UPU emblem, hands passing letter, satellites.

1979, June 8   Engr.   *Perf. 13*
C378 AP20 60fr multi   1.40 .50
C379 AP20 100fr multi   1.20 1.00

Philexafrique II, Libreville, Gabon, June 8-17.

Einstein Type

Designs: 60fr, Sights and actuality diagram. 85fr, Einstein playing violin, vert. 100fr, Atom symbol and formula of relativity, vert. 200fr, Einstein portrait, vert.

Perf. 14x13, 13x14
1979, July 2   Photo.
C380 A210 60fr multi   .50 .25
C381 A210 85fr multi   .80 .40
C382 A210 100fr multi   .85 .45
C383 A210 200fr multi   1.75 .85
  a. Souv. sheet of 2, #C382-C383 3.00 1.50
    Nos. C380-C383 (4)   3.90 1.95

Tree Type

Design: 60fr, Man watering tree.

1979, Aug. 13   *Perf. 14x13*
C384 A212 60fr blk & brn   .40 .25

Rowland Hill Type

Designs: 90fr, Bellman, England, 1820. 100fr, "Centercycles" used for parcel delivery, 1883, horiz. 200fr, French P.O. railroad car, 1848, horiz.

1979, Aug. 27   Photo.
C385 A213 90fr multi   .65 .30
C386 A213 100fr multi   .70 .35
C387 A213 200fr multi   1.50 .65
  a. Souv. sheet of 2, #C386-C387 2.50 1.25
    Nos. C385-C387 (3)   2.85 1.30

Train Type

Historic Locomotives: 60fr, "Le General," 1862. 85fr, Stephenson's, 1843. 100fr, "De Witt Clinton," 1831. 200fr, Joy's "Jenny Lind," 1847.

1979, Oct. 1   Litho.   *Perf. 14*
C388 A214 60fr multi   .55 .25
C389 A214 85fr multi   .70 .45
C390 A214 100fr multi   .85 .50
C391 A214 200fr multi   1.75 .85
  a. Souv. sheet of 2, #C390-C391 6.00 3.00
    Nos. C388-C391 (4)   3.85 2.10

Olympic Type

1980 Olympic Emblems and: 90fr, Ski jump. No. C393, Doubles canoeing, Olympic flame. No. C394, Rings. No. C395a, Bobsledding, horiz. No. C395b, Gymnast, horiz.

1979, Oct. 18   Litho.   *Perf. 13½*
C392 A215 90fr multi   .70 .30
C393 A215 100fr multi   .75 .35
C394 A215 200fr multi   1.40 .65
    Nos. C392-C394 (3)   2.85 1.30

Souvenir Sheet

C395   Sheet of 2   2.50 1.25
  a. A215 100fr multi   .65 .35
  b. A215 200fr multi   1.40 .65

Religion Type

Designs: 60fr, Moslems praying. 70fr, Protestant ministers.

1979, Oct. 29   *Perf. 13x14*
C396 A216 60fr multi   .50 .25
C397 A216 70fr multi   .55 .30
  a. Souv. sheet, #C396-C397   1.40 .50

Apollo 11 Type

60fr, Astronaut leaving Apollo 11. 70fr, US flag. 200fr, Sun shield. 300fr, Lunar take-off.

1979, Nov. 5
C398 A217 60fr multi   .45 .25
C399 A217 70fr multi   .50 .25
C400 A217 200fr multi   1.50 .65
C401 A217 300fr multi   2.10 1.00
  a. Souv. sheet of 2, #C400-C401 4.00 1.75
    Nos. C398-C401 (4)   4.55 2.15

Telecom Type

Design: 60fr, Telecom 79, dish antenna.

1979, Nov. 26   Photo.   *Perf. 14x13*
C402 A218 60fr multi   .55 .25

Miniature Sheets

President Eyadema, 10th Anniv. of the People's Republic — AP21

Litho. & Embossed
1979, Nov. 30   *Perf. 13½*
C402A AP21 1000fr In uniform   6.00 —

Imperf
C402B AP21 1000fr In suit, vert.   6.00 —
    Exist imperf.

Christmas Type

90fr, Adoration of the Kings. 100fr, Presentation of Infant Jesus. 200fr, Flight into Egypt.

1979, Dec. 17   Litho.   *Perf. 14*
C403 A219 90fr multi   .55 .35
C404 A219 100fr multi   .80 .40
C405 A219 200fr multi   1.75 .70
  a. Souv. sheet of 2, #C404-C405 3.10 1.45
    Nos. C403-C405 (3)   3.10 1.45

Rotary Type

3-H Emblem and: 90fr, Man reaching for sun. 100fr, Fish, grain. 200fr, Family, globe.

1980, Jan. 14
C406 A220 90fr multi   .80 .40
C407 A220 100fr multi   .85 .45
C408 A220 200fr multi   1.60 .85
  a. Souv. sheet of 2, C407-C408 3.25 1.60
    Nos. C406-C408 (3)   3.25 1.70

Rotary Intl., 75th anniv.; 3-H program (health, hunger, humanity).

Winter Olympic Type, 1980

1980, Jan. 31   *Perf. 13½*
C409 A221 60fr Downhill skiing   .45 .25
C410 A221 100fr Speed skating   .75 .35
C411 A221 200fr Cross-country
    skiing   1.40 .65
    Nos. C409-C411 (3)   2.60 1.25

Souvenir Sheet

C412   Sheet of 2   2.50 1.25
  a. A221 100fr Ski jump, horiz.   .65 .35
  b. A221 200fr Hockey, horiz.   1.25 .65

Olympic Type

1980, Feb. 29   Litho.   *Perf. 13½*
C413 A222 100fr Fencing   .65 .45
C414 A222 200fr Pole vault   1.40 .80
C415 A222 300fr Hurdles   2.10 1.25
  a. Souv. sheet of 2, #C414-C415 3.75 1.75
    Nos. C413-C415 (3)   4.15 2.50

Easter Type

Easter 1980 (Paintings by): 60fr, Lorenzo Lotto. 100fr, El Greco. 200fr, Carlo Crivelli.

1980, Mar. 31   *Perf. 14*
C416 A223 60fr multi   .50 .25
C417 A223 100fr multi   .75 .35
C418 A223 200fr multi   1.40 .65
  a. Souv. sheet of 2, #C417-C418 2.50 1.25
    Nos. C416-C418 (3)   2.65 1.25

ASECNA Type

1980, Mar. 24   Litho.   *Perf. 12½*
C419 A224 60fr multi   .60 .25

Telecommunications Type

1980, May 17   Photo.   *Perf. 13½x14*
C420 A225 60fr "17 MAI", vert.   .60 .25

Red Cross Type

1980, June 16   Photo.   *Perf. 14x13*
C421 A226 60fr Nurses, patient   .60 .25

Jules Verne Type

Designs: 60fr, Rocket (From Earth to Moon). 80fr, Around the World in 80 Days. 100fr, Rocket and moon (From Earth to Moon). 200fr, Octopus (20,000 Leagues Under the Sea).

1980, July 14   Litho.   *Perf. 14*
C422 A227 60fr multi   .45 .25
C423 A227 80fr multi   .55 .25
C424 A227 100fr multi   .80 .35
C425 A227 200fr multi   1.40 .65
  a. Souv. sheet of 2, #C424-C425,
    perf. 13½x14   2.50 1.25
    Nos. C422-C425 (4)   3.20 1.50

Ingres Type

Ingres Paintings: 90fr, Jupiter and Thetis. 100fr, Countess d'Haussonville. 200fr, "Tu Marcellus Eris."

1980, Aug. 29   Litho.   *Perf. 14*
C426 A228 90fr multi   .80 .30
C427 A228 100fr multi   .85 .35
C428 A228 200fr multi   1.60 .65
  a. Souv. sheet of 2, #C427-C428 3.00 1.25
    Nos. C426-C428 (3)   3.25 1.30

Famous Men Type

90fr, Salvador Allende, vert. 100fr, Pope Paul VI, vert. 200fr, Jomo Kenyatta, vert.

1980, Feb. 11   Litho.   *Perf. 14x13*
C429 A231 90fr ultra & lt bl grn   1.00 .30
C430 A231 100fr pur & pink   1.10 .35
C431 A231 200fr brn & yel bis   2.00 .65
  a. Souv. sheet of 2, #C430-C431 2.50 1.25
    Nos. C429-C431 (3)   4.10 1.30

Human Rights Type

1980, Oct. 13   *Perf. 13x14*
C432 A233 60fr Map of Ameri-
    cas   .40 .25
C433 A233 150fr Map of Africa   1.00 .50
  a. Souv. sheet of 2, #C432-C433 1.75 1.25

American Order of Rosicrucians Emblem — AP22

1980, Nov. 17   Litho.   *Perf. 13*
C434 AP22 60fr multi   .60 .25

General Conclave of the American Order of Rosicrucians, meeting of French-speaking countries, Lome, Aug.

Christmas Type

Designs: 100fr, Cologne Cathedral, Germany, 13th cent. 150fr, Notre Dame, Paris, 12th cent. 200fr, Canterbury Cathedral, England, 11th cent.

1980, Dec. 22   *Perf. 14½x13½*
C435 A234 70fr multi   .70 .35
C436 A234 150fr multi   1.10 .50
C437 A234 200fr multi   1.40 .65
  a. Souv. sheet of 2, #C436-C437 3.00 1.40
    Nos. C435-C437 (3)   3.20 1.50

Hotel Type of 1981

1981, Feb. 2   Litho.   *Perf. 12½x13*
C437B A236 60fr multi   .60 .25

Easter Type of 1981

Rembrandt Paintings: 100fr, Artist's Mother. 200fr, Man in a Ruff.

1981, Apr. 13   Litho.   Perf. 14½x13½

C438	A237	100fr multi	.90	.40
C439	A237	200fr multi	1.75	.70
a.		Souv. sheet of 2, #C438-C439	3.50	1.50

Market Type

1981, Mar. 8   Litho.   Perf. 14

C440	A230	90fr Fabric dealer	.60	.30
C441	A230	100fr Bananas	.65	.35
C442	A230	200fr Clay pottery	1.40	.65
C443	A230	250fr Setting up	1.60	.80
C444	A230	500fr Selling	3.50	1.50
C445	A230	1000fr Measuring grain	6.50	3.50
		Nos. C440-C445 (6)	14.25	7.20

For overprints see Nos. C486-C487.

Bird Type

50fr, Violet-backed sunbird. 100fr, Red bishop.

Perf. 13½x14½

1981, Aug. 10   Litho.

C446	A238	50fr multi	.80	.25
C447	A238	100fr multi	1.50	.35
a.		Souv. sheet, #1110, C447	5.50	2.50

IYD Type

90fr, Carpenter. 200fr, Basketball players. 300fr, Weaver.

1981, Aug. 31   Perf. 14

C448	A240	90fr multi	.80	.40
C449	A240	200fr multi	1.60	.85

Souvenir Sheet

C449A	A240	300fr multi	2.75	1.60

Picasso Type

90fr, Violin and Bottle on Table, 1916. 100fr, Baboon and Young. 200fr, Mandolin and Clarinet, 1914.

1981, Sept. 14   Perf. 14½x13½

C450	A241	90fr multi	.90	.40
C451	A241	100fr multi	1.10	.50
C452	A241	200fr multi	2.40	.90
a.		Souv. sheet of 2, #C451-C452	3.50	1.40
		Nos. C450-C452 (3)	4.40	1.80

World Heritage Year Type

100fr, Cracow Museum, Poland. 200fr, Goree Isld., Senegal.

1981, Sept. 28   Perf. 13½x14½

C453	A242	100fr multi	.80	.40
C454	A242	200fr multi	1.75	.85
a.		Souv. sheet of 2, #C453-C454	2.75	1.25

Space Type

1981, Nov.   Perf. 14

C455	A243	90fr multi	.65	.25
C456	A243	100fr multi	.70	.25

Souvenir Sheet

Perf. 13x14

C456A	A243	300fr multi, vert.	2.25	1.25

10th anniv. of Soyuz 10 (90fr) and Apollo 14 (100fr).

Christmas Type

Rubens Paintings: 100fr, Adoration of the Kings. 200fr, Virgin and Child. 300fr, Virgin giving Chasuble to St. Idefonse.

Perf. 14½x13½

1981, Dec. 10   Litho.

C457	A244	100fr multi	.70	.35
C458	A244	200fr multi	1.50	.65
C459	A244	300fr multi	2.10	1.00
a.		Souv. sheet of 2, #C458-C459	4.00	1.90
		Nos. C457-C459 (3)	4.30	2.00

West African Rice Development Assoc. Type

1981, Dec. 21   Litho.   Perf. 12½

C461	A236a	105fr yel & multi	.70	.35

Liberation Type

Designs: 105fr, Citizens holding hands, Pres. Eyadema, vert. 130fr, Hotel.

1982, Jan. 13   Litho.   Perf. 12½

C462	A245	105fr multi	.70	.35
C463	A245	130fr multi	.90	.40

Scouting Year Type

1982, Feb. 25   Litho.   Perf. 14

C464	A246	90fr Semaphore	.75	.30
C465	A246	120fr Tower	1.00	.40
C466	A246	130fr Scouts, canoe	1.10	.40
C467	A246	135fr Scouts, tent	1.10	.45
		Nos. C464-C467 (4)	3.95	1.55

Souvenir Sheet

Perf. 13x14

C468	A246	500fr Baden-Powell	4.25	1.60

Easter Type

1982, Apr.   Perf. 14x14½

C469	A247	105fr multi	.70	.35
C470	A247	120fr multi	.80	.40

Souvenir Sheet

C471	A247	500fr multi	4.00	1.60

PHILEXFRANCE '82 Intl. Stamp Exhibition, Paris, June 11-21 — AP23

1982   Litho.   Perf. 13

C472	AP23	90fr shown	.70	.30
C473	AP23	105fr ROMOLYMPHIL '82, vert.	.90	.35

Issue dates: 90fr, June 11; 105fr, May 19.

Butterfly Type

90fr, Euxanthe eurionome. 105fr, Mylothris rhodope. 500fr, Papilio zalmoxis.

1982, July 15   Perf. 14½x14

C474	A248	90fr multi	1.60	.40
C475	A248	105fr multi	1.75	.45

Souvenir Sheet

C476	A248	500fr multi	4.25	1.60

World Cup Type

1982, July 26   Perf. 14x14½

C477	A249	105fr multi	.80	.35
C478	A249	200fr multi	1.40	.65
C479	A249	300fr multi	2.10	1.00
		Nos. C477-C479 (3)	4.30	2.00

Souvenir Sheet

C480	A249	500fr multi	3.75	1.65

For overprints see Nos. 1152-1155.

Pre-Olympics, 1984 Los Angeles — AP24

1983, Oct. 3   Photo.   Perf. 12½

C481	AP24	70fr Boxing	.55	.25
C482	AP24	90fr Hurdles	.70	.25
C483	AP24	105fr Pole vault	.80	.25
C484	AP24	130fr Runner	.90	.25
		Nos. C481-C484 (4)	2.95	1.00

Souvenir Sheet

C485	AP24	500fr Runner, diff.	4.00	1.50

Nos. C443-C444 Overprinted: "19E CONGRES UPU HAMBOURG 1984"

1984, June   Perf. 14

C486	A230	250fr multi	1.75	1.00
C487	A230	500fr multi	3.75	2.00

1984 Summer Olympics — AP25

1984, July 27   Perf. 13

C488	AP25	70fr Pole vault	.45	.25
C489	AP25	90fr Bicycling	.45	.25
C490	AP25	120fr Soccer	.75	.25
C491	AP25	250fr Boxing	1.50	.40
C492	AP25	400fr Running	2.25	.65
		Nos. C488-C492 (5)	5.40	1.80

Souvenir Sheet

C493	AP25	1000fr like 120fr, without flag	7.50	6.50

Nos. C488-C490, C493 vert.

Olympic Champions AP26

No. C494, Jim Thorpe, US. No. C495, Jesse Owens, US. No. C496, Muhammad Ali, US. No. C497, Bob Beamon, US. No. C498, Bill Steinkraus, US. No. C499, New Zealand rowing team. No. C500, Pakistani hockey team. No. C501, Yukio Endo, Japan.

1984, Nov. 15   Litho.   Perf. 15

C494	AP26	500fr multi	7.25	3.25
C495	AP26	500fr multi	7.25	3.25
C496	AP26	500fr multi	40.00	3.25
C497	AP26	500fr multi	7.25	3.25
		Nos. C494-C497 (4)	61.75	13.00

Souvenir Sheets

C498	AP26	500fr multi	7.25	3.25
C499	AP26	500fr multi	7.25	3.25
C500	AP26	500fr multi	7.25	3.25
C501	AP26	500fr multi	7.25	3.25

West German Olympians

No. C502, Dietmar Mogenburg. No. C503, Fredy Schmidtke. No. C504, Matthias Behr. No. C505, Sabine Everts. No. C506, Karl-Heinz Radschinsky. No. C507, Pasquale Passarelli. No. C508, Michale Gross. No. C509, Jurgen Hingsen.

1984, Nov. 15

C502	AP26	500fr multi	7.25	3.25
C503	AP26	500fr multi	7.25	3.25
C504	AP26	500fr multi	7.25	3.25
C505	AP26	500fr multi	7.25	3.25
		Nos. C502-C505 (4)	29.00	13.00

Souvenir Sheets

C506	AP26	500fr multi	7.25	3.25
C507	AP26	500fr multi	7.25	3.25
C508	AP26	500fr multi	7.25	3.25
C509	AP26	500fr multi	7.25	3.25

For overprints see Nos. C521-C536, C563.

Peace and Human Rights — AP28

230fr, Map of Togo, globe, doves. 270fr, Palm tree, emblem. 500fr, Opencast mining operation. 1000fr, Human Rights Monument, UN, NYC.

1985, Jan. 14   Litho.   Perf. 13½x14

C510	AP28	230fr multi	1.50	.25
C511	AP28	270fr multi	1.90	.30
C512	AP28	500fr multi	3.50	.50
C513	AP28	1000fr multi	7.00	1.00
		Nos. C510-C513 (4)	13.90	2.05

Tribal Dances AP29

120fr, Adifo, Adangbe. 135fr, Fouet (whip), Kente. 290fr, Idjombi, Pagouda. 500fr, Moba, Dapaong.

1985, July   Perf. 15x14

C514	AP29	120fr multicolored	.85	.25
C515	AP29	135fr multicolored	.85	.25
C516	AP29	290fr multicolored	2.00	.30
C517	AP29	500fr multicolored	3.50	.50
		Nos. C514-C517 (4)	7.20	1.30

Visit of Pope John Paul II — AP30

90fr, The Pope outside Lome Cathedral. 130fr, Blessing crowd in St. Peter's Square. 500fr, Greeting Pres. Eyadema.

1985, Aug. 9   Perf. 13

C518	AP30	90fr multi	.75	.25
C519	AP30	130fr multi, vert.	1.25	.25
C520	AP30	500fr multi	3.50	.50
		Nos. C518-C520 (3)	5.50	1.00

Nos. C495, C497, C499, C502, C505-508 Overprinted with Winners Names, Country and Type of Olympic Medal

No. C521, Kirk Baptiste, US. No. C522, Carl Lewis, US. No. C523, Patrik Sjoberg, Sweden. No. C524, Glynis Nunn, Australia. No. C525, Rowing eights, Canada. No. C526, Rolf Milser, W. Germany. No. C527, Takashi Irie, Japan. No. C528, Frederic Delcourt, France.

1985, Aug.   Perf. 15

C521	AP26	500fr multicolored	6.50	1.50
C522	AP26	500fr multicolored	6.50	1.50
C523	AP26	500fr multicolored	6.50	1.50
C524	AP26	500fr multicolored	6.50	1.50
		Nos. C521-C524 (4)	26.00	6.00

Souvenir Sheets

C525	AP26	500fr multicolored	3.50	3.00
C526	AP26	500fr multicolored	3.50	3.00
C527	AP26	500fr multicolored	3.50	3.00
C528	AP26	500fr multicolored	3.50	3.00

Nos. C494, C496, C503-C504, C498, C500, C501, C509 Ovptd. with Winners Names, Country and Type of Olympic Medal

No. C529, Italy. No. C530, Kevin Barry. No. C531, Rolf Golz. No. C532, Philippe Boisse. No. C533, Karen Stives. No. C534, R.F.A. (West Germany). No. C535, Koji Gushiken. No. C536, Daley Thompson.

1985, Sept. 19   Litho.   Perf. 15

C529	AP26	500fr multicolored	6.50	1.50
C530	AP26	500fr multicolored	6.50	1.50
C531	AP26	500fr multicolored	6.50	1.50
C532	AP26	500fr multicolored	6.50	1.50
		Nos. C529-C532 (4)	26.00	6.00

Souvenir Sheets

C533	AP26	500fr multicolored	3.50	3.00
C534	AP26	500fr multicolored	3.50	3.00
C535	AP26	500fr multicolored	3.50	3.00
C536	AP26	500fr multicolored	3.50	3.00

Traditional Instruments — AP31

Youth and Development — AP32

Designs: No. C537, Xylophone, Kante horn, tambour. No. C538, Bongo drums, castanets, bassar horn. No. C539, Communications. No. C540, Agriculture and industry.

1985	Litho.	Perf. 13	
C537	AP31 100fr multi	.90	.60
C538	AP31 100fr multi	.90	.60
a.	Pair, #C537-C538	3.00	3.00
C539	AP32 200fr multi	1.75	1.25
C540	AP32 200fr multi	1.75	1.25
a.	Pair, #C539-C540	7.50	7.50
	Nos. C537-C540 (4)	5.30	3.70

PHILEXAFRICA '85, Lome, Togo, 11/16-24. Issued: 100fr, Nov. 4; 200fr, Nov. 16.

No. 1274 Ovptd. with Organization Emblem and "80e Anniversaire du Rotary International."

1985, Nov. 15	Litho.	Perf. 15	
	Souvenir Sheet		
C541	A267 1000fr multi	20.00	6.50

Nos. 1254-1255, 1258 Ovptd. "10e ANNIVERSAIRE DE APOLLO-SOYUZ" in 1 or 2 lines

1985, Dec. 27	Litho.	Perf. 15	
C542	A265 90fr multi	1.25	.40
C543	A265 500fr multi	6.75	2.00
	Souvenir Sheet		
C544	A265 1000fr multi	8.50	2.90

Nos. 1294-1295, 1297 Ovptd. "75e ANNIVERSAIRE DE LA MORT DE HENRI DUNANT FONDATEUR DE LA CROIX ROUGE" in 2 or 4 lines

1985, Dec. 27			
C545	A270 400fr multi	4.75	1.50
C546	A270 500fr multi	6.25	2.00
	Souvenir Sheet		
C547	A270 1000fr multi	7.50	6.00

Statue of Liberty, Cent. — AP33

70fr, Eiffel Tower. 90fr, Statue of Liberty. 500fr, Empire State Building.

1986, Apr. 10		Perf. 13	
C548	AP33 70fr multicolored	.55	.25
C549	AP33 90fr multicolored	.65	.25
C550	AP33 500fr multicolored	3.75	1.40
	Nos. C548-C550 (3)	4.95	1.90

Nos. 1237-1240 Ovptd. with AMERIPEX '86 Emblem

1986, May 22		Perf. 11	
C551	A262 500fr multi	6.50	1.40
C552	A262 1000fr multi	12.50	2.75
	Souvenir Sheets		
	Perf. 14		
C553	A262 1000fr No. 1239	8.50	3.50
C554	A262 1000fr No. 1240	8.50	3.50

Air Africa, 25th Anniv. AP34

1986, Dec. 29	Litho.	Perf. 12½x13	
C555	AP34 90fr multi		.75 .25

Konrad Adenauer (1876-1967) West German Chancellor — AP35

120fr, At podium. No. C557, 500fr, With Pres. Kennedy, 1962. No. C558, 500fr, Portrait, vert.

1987, July 15	Litho.	Perf. 12½x13	
C556	AP35 120fr multi	.90	.60
C557	AP35 500fr multi	3.50	3.00
	Souvenir Sheet		
	Perf. 13x12½		
C558	AP35 500fr multi	3.50	3.00

Berlin, 750th Anniv. AP36

Designs: 90fr, Wilhelm I (1781-1864) coin, Victory statue. 150fr, Frederick III (1831-1888) coin, Brandenburg Gate. 300fr, Wilhelm II (1882-1951) coin, Reichstag building. 750fr, Otto Leopold von Bismarck (1815-1898), first chancellor of the German empire, and Charlottenburg Palace.

1987, Aug. 31	Litho.	Perf. 13½	
C559	AP36 90fr multi	.60	.30
C560	AP36 150fr multi	1.00	.50
C561	AP36 300fr multi	2.00	1.00
	Nos. C559-C561 (3)	3.60	1.80
	Souvenir Sheet		
C562	AP36 750fr multi	5.50	4.25

Nos. C506, 1258, 1273 and 1274 Overprinted in Black for Philatelic Exhibitions

a

b

c

d

1988, Apr. 25	Litho.	Perf. 15	
	Souvenir Sheets		
C563	AP26 (a) 500fr #C506	9.50	3.00
C564	A265 (b) 1000fr #1258	10.00	5.50
C565	A265 (c) 1000fr #1273	10.00	5.50
C566	A267 (d) 1000fr #1274	10.00	5.50
	Nos. C563-C566 (4)	39.50	19.50

Additional overprints appear on souvenir sheets away from stamps.

AIR POST SEMI-POSTAL STAMPS

Nursery — SPAP1

		Perf. 13½x12½	
1942, June 22		Unwmk.	Photo.
CB1	SPAP1 1.50fr + 3.50fr green	.55	5.50
CB2	SPAP1 2fr + 6fr brown	.55	5.50
	Set, never hinged	1.40	

Native children's welfare fund. Nos. CB1-CB2 were issued by the Vichy government in France, but were not placed on sale in Togo.

Colonial Education Fund
Common Design Type

1942, June 22			Engr.
CB3	CD86a 1.20fr + 1.80fr blue & red	.35	5.50
	Set, never hinged	.70	

No. CB3 was issued by the Vichy government in France, but was not placed on sale in Togo.

POSTAGE DUE STAMPS

Postage Due Stamps of Dahomey, 1914 Overprinted

1921		Unwmk.	Perf. 14x13½
J1	D2 5c green	.65	.85
J2	D2 10c rose	.65	.90
J3	D2 15c gray	1.25	1.75
J4	D2 20c brown	2.50	2.50
J5	D2 30c blue	2.50	2.50
J6	D2 50c black	2.10	2.50
J7	D2 60c orange	2.10	2.50
J8	D2 1fr violet	3.75	4.50
	Nos. J1-J8 (8)	15.50	18.25

Cotton Field — D3

1925		Typo.	Unwmk.
J9	D3 2c blue & blk	.25	.35
J10	D3 4c dl red & blk	.25	.35
J11	D3 5c ol grn & blk	.25	.35
J12	D3 10c cerise & blk	.35	.45
J13	D3 15c orange & blk	.70	.85
J14	D3 20c red vio & blk	.35	.55
J15	D3 25c gray & blk	1.10	1.10
J16	D3 30c ocher & blk	.35	.55
J17	D3 50c brown & blk	1.10	1.10
J18	D3 60c green & blk	1.10	1.10
J19	D3 1fr dk vio & blk	1.10	1.10
	Nos. J9-J19 (11)	6.90	7.85

Type of 1925 Issue Surcharged

1927			
J20	D3 2fr on 1fr rose red & vio	7.00	7.00
J21	D3 3fr on 1fr org brn, blk & ultra	7.00	7.00

Mask — D4

1941		Engr.	Perf. 13
J22	D4 5c brown black	.25	.30
J23	D4 10c yellow green	.25	.30
J24	D4 15c carmine	.25	.30
J25	D4 20c ultra	.30	.35
J26	D4 30c chestnut	.55	.65
J27	D4 50c olive green	1.40	1.75
J28	D4 60c violet	.70	.85
J29	D4 1fr light blue	.90	1.00
J30	D4 2fr orange vermilion	.85	.90
J31	D4 3fr rose violet	.85	1.10
	Nos. J22-J31 (10)	6.30	7.50
	Set, never hinged	8.00	

For type D4 without "RF," see Nos. J31A-J31F.

Type of 1941 Without "RF"

1942-44			
J31A	D4 5c brown black		.25
J31B	D4 10c green & violet		.30
J31C	D4 15c car rose & brn		.35
J31D	D4 30c brown & black		.55
J31E	D4 2fr brn org & brn vio		.70
J31F	D4 3fr violet & green		.70
	Nos. J31A-J31F (6)		2.85
	Set, never hinged		3.50

Nos. J31A-J31F were issued by the Vichy government in France, but were not placed on sale in Togo.

Catalogue values for unused stamps in this section, from this point to the end of the section, are for Never Hinged items.

Carved Figures — D5

1947			
J32	D5 10c brt ultra	.30	.30
J33	D5 30c red	.30	.30
J34	D5 50c dp yellow grn	.30	.30
J35	D5 1fr chocolate	.50	.50
J36	D5 2fr carmine	.50	.50
J37	D5 3fr gray blk	.50	.50
J38	D5 4fr ultra	.80	.80
J39	D5 5fr sepia	1.10	.90
J40	D5 10fr dp orange	1.10	1.00
J41	D5 20fr dk blue vio	1.50	1.40
	Nos. J32-J41 (10)	6.90	6.50

Republic

Konkomba Helmet — D6

1957		Engr.	Perf. 14x13
J42	D6 1fr brt violet	.25	.25
J43	D6 2fr brt orange	.25	.25
J44	D6 3fr dk gray	.25	.25
J45	D6 4fr brt red	.25	.25
J46	D6 5fr ultra	.25	.25
J47	D6 10fr dp green	.35	.35
J48	D6 20fr dp claret	.50	.50
	Nos. J42-J48 (7)	2.10	2.10

Konkomba Helmet — D7

1959   Perf. 14x13

J49	D7	1fr orange brn	.25	.35
J50	D7	2fr lt blue grn	.25	.35
J51	D7	3fr orange	.25	.35
J52	D7	4fr blue	.25	.45
J53	D7	5fr lilac rose	.25	.45
J54	D7	10fr violet blue	.45	.65
J55	D7	20fr black	.80	.85
		Nos. J49-J55 (7)	2.50	3.45

Type of Regular Issue

Shells: 1fr, Conus papilionaceus. 2fr, Marginella faba. 3fr, Cypraea stercoraria. 4fr, Strombus latus. 5fr, Costate cockle (sea shell). 10fr, Cancellaria cancellata. 15fr, Cymbium pepo. 20fr, Tympanotomus radula.

1964-65   Unwmk.   Photo.   Perf. 14
Size: 20x25½mm

J56	A47	1fr gray grn & red brn ('65)	.25	.25
J57	A47	2fr tan & ol grn ('65)	.25	.25
J58	A47	3fr gray, brn & yel ('65)	.25	.25
J59	A47	4fr tan & multi ('65)	.30	.25
J60	A47	5fr sep, org & grn	.70	.30
J61	A47	10fr sl bl, brn & bis	.95	.40
J62	A47	15fr grn & brn	2.75	1.00
J63	A47	20fr sl, dk brn & yel	3.25	1.25
		Nos. J56-J63 (8)	8.70	3.95

Tomatoes — D8

1969-70   Litho.   Perf. 14

J64	D8	5fr yellow & multi	.25	.25
J65	D8	10fr blue & multi	.45	.25
J66	D8	15fr multi ('70)	.70	.30
J67	D8	20fr multi ('70)	1.00	.40
		Nos. J64-J67 (4)	2.40	1.20

Market Type

1981, Mar. 8   Litho.   Perf. 14
Size: 23x32mm, 32x23mm

J68	A230	5fr Millet, vert.	.25	.25
J69	A230	10fr Packaged goods	.25	.25
J70	A230	25fr Chickens	.25	.25
J71	A230	50fr Ivory vendor	.50	.25
		Nos. J68-J71 (4)	1.25	1.00

OFFICIAL STAMPS

Catalogue values for unused stamps in this section are for never hinged items.

RÉPUBLIQUE TOGOLAISE —OFFICIEL—   O1

1991?   Litho.   Perf. 13½

O1	O1	15fr multicolored	—	—
O2	O1	100fr multicolored	—	—
O3	O1	125fr multicolored	—	—
O4	O1	500fr multicolored	—	—

1991?

O5	O1	10fr multicolored	—	—
O6	O1	90fr yellow & multi	—	—

1991?

O7	O1	180fr ap grn & multi	—	—

1991

O8	O1	50fr yellow & multi	—	—
O9	O1	90fr ap grn & multi	—	—

The editors would like information on dates of issue and stamps of other denominations. The catalogue numbers will change.

TOKELAU
'tō-kə-‚lau

(Union Islands)

LOCATION — Pacific Ocean 300 miles north of Apia, Western Samoa
GOVT. — A dependency of New Zealand
AREA — 4 sq. mi.
POP. — 1,487 (1996)

The Tokelau islands consist of three atolls: Atafu, Nukunono and Fakaofo, which span 100 miles of ocean.

12 Pence = 1 Shilling
100 Cents = 1 Dollar (1967)

Catalogue values for all unused stamps in this country are for Never Hinged items.

Map and Scene on Atafu — A1

Nukunono Dwelling and Map — A2

Fakaofo Shore Line and Map — A3

Perf. 13½x13
1948, June 22   Wmk. 253   Engr.

1	A1	½p red brown & rose lilac	.25	.45
2	A2	1p dp green & orange brn	.25	.50
3	A3	2p deep ultra & green	.25	.50
		Nos. 1-3 (3)	.75	1.45

For surcharges see Nos. 5, 9-11.

Coronation Issue

Queen Elizabeth II — A3a

1953, May 25   Photo.   Perf. 14x14½

4	A3a	3p brown	2.75	2.75

No. 1 Srchd. in Black

Perf. 13½x13
1956, Mar. 27   Engr.   Wmk. 253

5	A1	1sh on ½p	1.30	3.25

Postal-Fiscal Type of New Zealand, 1950, Surcharged

Wmk. 253
1966, Nov.   Typo.   Perf. 14

6	A109	0p light blue	.50	1.00
7	A109	8p light green	.50	1.00
8	A109	2sh pink	.75	1.25
		Nos. 6-8 (3)	1.75	3.25

Nos. 1-3 Surcharged with New Value and Dots Obliterating Old Denomination

1967, July 10   Engr.   Perf. 13½x13

9	A2	1c on 1p	.45	.45
10	A3	2c on 2p	.85	.85
11	A1	10c on ½p	2.25	2.25
		Nos. 9-11 (3)	3.55	3.55

The 1c and 2c surcharges include two dots, the 10c surcharge has only one.

Postal Fiscal Type of New Zealand, 1950, Surcharged

1967, July 10   Typo.   Perf. 14

12	A109	3c light lilac	.25	.25
13	A109	5c light blue	.40	.40
14	A109	7c light green	.40	.40
15	A109	20c pink	.75	.75
		Nos. 12-15 (4)	1.80	1.80

1877, British Protectorate — A4

History of Tokelau: 10c, 1916, part of Gilbert and Ellice Islands Colony. 15c, 1925, administration transferred to New Zealand. 20c, 1948, New Zealand Territory.

Perf. 13x12½
1969, Aug. 8   Litho.   Wmk. 253

16	A4	5c ultra, yellow & blk	.75	.45
17	A4	10c rose red, yel & blk	.85	.75
18	A4	15c dull grn, yel & blk	1.00	.90
19	A4	20c brown, yel & blk	1.25	1.75
		Nos. 16-19 (4)	3.85	3.85

Nativity, by Federico Fiori — A4a

1969, Oct. 1   Photo.   Perf. 13½x14

20	A4a	2c multicolored	.30	.30

Christmas.

Adoration, by Correggio — A4b

Perf. 12½
1970, Oct. 1   Unwmk.   Litho.

21	A4b	2c multicolored	.30	.30

Christmas.

"Dolphin," 1765, Map of Atafu — A5

Designs: 10c, "Pandora," 1791, and map of Nukunono. 25c, "General Jackson," 1835, and map of Fakaofo, horiz.

1970, Dec. 9   Unwmk.   Perf. 13½

22	A5	5c yellow & multi	.75	.50
23	A5	10c multicolored	1.75	1.00
24	A5	25c pink & multi	3.50	2.50
		Nos. 22-24 (3)	6.00	4.00

Discovery of Tokelau Islands.

Fan — A6

Native Handicrafts: 2c, Round vessel. 3c, Hexagonal box. 5c, Shoulder bag. 10c, Handbag. 15c, Jewelry box with beads. 20c, Outrigger canoe model. 25c, Fish hooks.

1971, Oct. 20   Litho.   Perf. 14

25	A6	1c olive & multi	.25	.25
26	A6	2c red & multi	.25	.30
27	A6	3c dk violet & multi	.35	.45
28	A6	5c dull blue & multi	.40	.50
29	A6	10c dp orange & multi	.50	.60
30	A6	15c emerald & multi	.70	.90
31	A6	20c multicolored	.90	1.00
32	A6	25c violet blue & multi	1.00	1.00
		Nos. 25-32 (8)	4.35	5.00

Windmill Pump, Map of Atafu — A7

South Pacific Commission Emblem and: 10c, Community well, map of Fakaofo. 15c, Eradication of rhinoceros beetle, map of Nukunono. 20c, members.

1972, Sept. 6   Litho.   Perf. 14x13½

33	A7	5c lt blue grn & multi	.75	.70
34	A7	10c grnsh blue & multi	.85	.85
35	A7	15c lilac & multi	1.00	1.00
36	A7	20c violet bl & multi	1.50	1.40
		Nos. 33-36 (4)	4.10	3.95

South Pacific Commission, 25th anniversary. On 15c, "PACIFIC" reads "PACFIC."

Horny Coral — A8

1973, Sept. 12   Litho.   Perf. 13x13½

37	A8	3c shown	1.00	.75
38	A8	5c Soft coral	1.00	.75
39	A8	15c Mushroom coral	1.60	1.15
40	A8	25c Staghorn coral	2.00	1.35
		Nos. 37-40 (4)	5.60	4.00

Cowrie (Cypraea Mauritiana) A9

Cowrie shells: 5c, Cypraea tigris. 15c, Cypraea talpa. 25c, Cypraea argus.

1974, Nov. 13　　Litho.　　Perf. 14
41	A9	3c apple grn & multi	1.05	.75
42	A9	5c dk blue & multi	1.40	1.00
43	A9	15c blue & multi	1.90	1.35
44	A9	25c green & multi	2.10	1.50
		Nos. 41-44 (4)	6.45	4.60

Moorish Idol — A10

Fish: 10c, Long-nosed butterflyfish. 15c, Lined butterflyfish. 25c, Red firefish.

1975, Nov. 19　　Litho.　　Perf. 14
45	A10	5c blue & multi	.50	.50
46	A10	10c brown & multi	.90	.90
47	A10	15c lilac & multi	1.35	1.35
48	A10	25c multicolored	2.25	2.25
		Nos. 45-48 (4)	5.00	5.00

Canoe Making A11

Designs: 2c, Reef fishing. 3c, Woman preparing pandanus leaves for weaving. 5c, Communal kitchen (umu). 9c, Wood carving. 20c, Husking coconuts. 50c, Wash day. $1, Meal time. 9c, 20c, 50c, $1, vertical.

1976, Oct. 27　　Litho.　　Perf. 14
49	A11	1c pink & multi	.55	.55
50	A11	2c multicolored	.40	1.40
51	A11	3c lt blue & multi	.35	.50
52	A11	5c yellow & multi	.40	.50
53	A11	9c bister & multi	.25	.50
54	A11	20c multicolored	.25	.50
55	A11	50c tan & multi	.35	.70
56	A11	$1 multicolored	.70	1.00
		Nos. 49-56 (8)	3.25	5.65

1981, July 17　　　　　　Perf. 15
49a	A11	1c	.50	.40
51a	A11	3c	.50	.40
52a	A11	5c	.50	.40
53a	A11	9c	.90	.75
54a	A11	20c	.90	.75
55a	A11	50c	1.75	1.00
56a	A11	$1	3.00	3.00
		Nos. 49a-56a (7)	8.05	6.70

White Tern — A12

Birds of Tokelau: 10c, Turnstone. 15c, White-capped noddy. 30c, Brown noddy.

1977, Nov. 16　　Litho.　　Perf. 14½x15
57	A12	8c multicolored	.45	.35
58	A12	10c multicolored	.60	.40
59	A12	15c multicolored	.70	.65
60	A12	30c multicolored	1.50	1.40
		Nos. 57-60 (4)	3.25	2.80

Westminster Abbey — A13

10c, King Edward's Chair. 15c, Scepter, Crown, Orb, Bible and Staff of State. 30c, Elizabeth II.

1978, June 28　　Litho.　　Perf. 14
61	A13	8c multicolored	.25	.25
62	A13	10c multicolored	.30	.25
63	A13	15c multicolored	.45	.45
64	A13	30c multicolored	.80	.80
		Nos. 61-64 (4)	1.80	1.75

25th anniv. of coronation of Elizabeth II.

Canoe Racing A14

Designs: Various canoe races.

1978, Nov. 8　　Litho.　　Perf. 13½x14
65	A14	8c multicolored	.30	.35
66	A14	12c multicolored	.45	.50
67	A14	15c multicolored	.50	.60
68	A14	30c multicolored	.85	.90
		Nos. 65-68 (4)	2.10	2.35

1979, Nov. 7　　Photo.　　Perf. 14
69	A14	10c Rugby	.35	.35
70	A14	15c Cricket	.70	.70
71	A14	20c Rugby, diff.	.70	.70
72	A14	30c Cricket, diff.	.75	.75
		Nos. 69-72 (4)	2.50	2.50

1980, Nov. 5　　Litho.　　Perf. 13½
73	A14	10c Surfing	.25	.25
74	A14	20c Surfing, diff.	.25	.25
75	A14	30c Swimming	.35	.40
76	A14	50c Swimming, diff.	.50	.55
		Nos. 73-76 (4)	1.35	1.45

1981, Nov. 4　　Photo.　　Perf. 14
77	A14	10c Pole vaulting, vert.	.25	.25
78	A14	20c Volleyball, vert.	.30	.25
79	A14	30c Running, vert.	.40	.35
80	A14	50c Volleyball, vert., diff.	.50	.55
		Nos. 77-80 (4)	1.45	1.40

Wood Carving — A15

1982, May 5　　Litho.　　Perf. 13½x13
81	A15	10s shown	.30	.30
82	A15	22s Bow-drilling sea shells	.30	.30
83	A15	34s Bowl finishing	.40	.40
84	A15	60s Basket weaving	.80	.80
		Nos. 81-84 (4)	1.80	1.80

Octopus Lure Fishing — A16

Designs: Fishing Methods.

1982, Nov. 3　　Litho.　　Perf. 14
85	A16	5s shown	.25	.25
86	A16	18s Multiple-hook	.25	.25
87	A16	23s Ruvettus	.25	.25
88	A16	34s Netting flying fish	.30	.30
89	A16	63s Noose	.50	.50
90	A16	75s Bonito	.65	.65
		Nos. 85-90 (6)	2.20	2.20

Outrigger Canoe A17

1983, May 4　　Litho.　　Perf. 13½x14
91	A17	5s shown	.25	.25
92	A17	18s Whale boat	.25	.25
93	A17	23s Aluminium whale boat	.25	.25
94	A17	34s Alia fishing boat	.25	.25
95	A17	63s Cargo ship	.45	.45
96	A17	75s Seaplane	.75	.75
		Nos. 91-96 (6)	2.20	2.20

Traditional Games A18

1983, Nov. 2　　Litho.　　Perf. 14
97	A18	5s Javelin throwing	.25	.25
98	A18	18s Tifaga string game	.25	.25
99	A18	23s Fire making	.25	.25
100	A18	34s Shell throwing	.25	.25
101	A18	63s Handball	.30	.30
102	A18	75s Mass wrestling	.50	.50
		Nos. 97-102 (6)	1.80	1.80

Planting, Harvesting Copra — A19

Copra Industry: b, Husking, splitting. c, Drying, cutting. d, Bagging, weighing. e, Shipping. Continuous design.

1984, May 2　　Litho.　　Perf. 13½x13
103		Strip of 5	2.50	2.50
a.-e.	A19	48s any single	.45	.45

Local Fish — A20

1984, Dec. 5　　Litho.　　Perf. 14½x14
104	A20	1c Manini	.25	.25
105	A20	2c Hahave	.25	.25
106	A20	5c Uloulo	.25	.25
107	A20	9c Ume Ihu	.25	.25
108	A20	23c Lifilafi	.25	.25
109	A20	34c Fagamea	.30	.30
110	A20	50c Kakahi	.40	.40
111	A20	75c Palu Po	.80	.80
112	A20	$1 Mokoha	1.00	1.00
113	A20	$2 Hakula	1.75	1.75
		Nos. 104-113 (10)	5.50	5.50

No. 110 exists overprinted "STAMPEX 86 / 4-10 AUGUST / 1986." These overprinted stamps were not available at post offices in Tokelau. Used examples were sent to the islands for cancellation.

Trees, Fruits and Herbs — A21

1985, June 26　　Litho.　　Perf. 13½
114	A21	5c Mati	.25	.25
115	A21	18c Nonu	.25	.25
116	A21	32c Ulu	.30	.30
117	A21	48c Fala	.35	.35
118	A21	60c Kanava	.50	.50
119	A21	75c Niu	.75	.75
		Nos. 114-119 (6)	2.40	2.40

Public Buildings and Churches A22

Designs: 5c, Administration Center, Atafu. 18c, Administration Center, Nukunonu. 32c, Administration Center, Fakaofo. 48c, Congregational Church, Atafu. 60c, Catholic Church, Nukunonu. 75c, Congregational Church, Fakaofo.

1985, Dec. 4
120	A22	5c multicolored	.25	.25
121	A22	18c multicolored	.25	.25
122	A22	32c multicolored	.30	.30
123	A22	48c multicolored	.35	.35
124	A22	60c multicolored	.50	.50
125	A22	75c multicolored	.75	.75
		Nos. 120-125 (6)	2.40	2.40

Hospitals and Schools A23

Designs: 5c, Atafu Hospital. 18c, St. Joseph's Hospital, Nukunonu. 32c, Fenuafala Hospital, Fakaofo. 48c, Matauala School, Atafu. 60c, Matiti School, Nukunonu. 75c, Fenuafala School, Fakaofo.

1986, May 7　　　　　　Perf. 13½
126	A23	5c multicolored	.25	.25
127	A23	18c multicolored	.25	.25
128	A23	32c multicolored	.30	.30
129	A23	48c multicolored	.35	.35
130	A23	60c multicolored	.50	.50
131	A23	75c multicolored	.75	.75
		Nos. 126-131 (6)	2.40	2.40

Fauna A24

1986, Dec. 3　　Litho.　　Perf. 14
132	A24	5c Coconut crab	.25	.25
133	A24	18c Pigs	.25	.25
134	A24	32c Chickens	.40	.40
135	A24	48c Turtles	.65	.65
136	A24	60c Goats	.80	.80
137	A24	75c Ducks	.95	.95
		Nos. 132-137 (6)	3.30	3.30

Flora A25

1987, May 6
138	A25	5c Gahu	.40	.50
139	A25	18c Puka	.60	.75
140	A25	32c Higano	.75	.95
141	A25	48c Tialetiale	1.00	1.30
142	A25	60c Gagie	1.25	1.50
143	A25	75c Puapua	1.50	1.60
		Nos. 138-143 (6)	5.50	6.60

Olympic Sports A26

1987, Dec. 2　　Litho.　　Perf. 14x14½
144	A26	5c Javelin	.25	.35
145	A26	18c Shot put	.50	.60
146	A26	32c Long jump	.65	.75
147	A26	48c Hurdles	.75	.85
148	A26	60c Running	1.00	1.05
149	A26	75c Wrestling	1.35	1.45
		Nos. 144-149 (6)	4.50	5.05

Australia Bicentennial, SYDPEX '88 — A27

Re-enactment of the arrival of the First Fleet in Sydney Harbor, Jan. 26, 1988 (in a continuous design): a, Ships in harbor, building (LL). b, Ships in harbor, tall ship (LR). c, Ships in harbor, Sydney Opera House. d, Bridge. e, North Sydney.

1988, July 30   Litho.   Perf. 13½x13
| 150 | | Strip of 5 | 10.00 | 10.00 |
| a.-e. | A27 | 50c any single | 1.90 | 1.90 |

Political Development A28

Designs: 5c, Transfer of administration from the New Zealand Department of Maori and Island Affairs to the Ministry of Foreign Affairs, 1975. 18c, The General Fono empowered as the decision-making body of Tokelau, 1977. 32c, 1st Visit of New Zealand's prime minister, 1985. 48c, 1st Visit of UN representatives, 1976. 60c, 1st Tokelau delegation to go to the UN, 1987. 75c, 1st Tokelau appointed to the office of Official Secretary, 1987.

1988, Aug. 10   Perf. 11¼
151	A28	5c multicolored	.25	.25
152	A28	18c multicolored	.25	.25
153	A28	32c multicolored	.65	.65
154	A28	48c multicolored	1.00	1.00
155	A28	60c multicolored	1.10	1.10
156	A28	75c multicolored	1.60	1.60
		Nos. 151-156 (6)	4.85	4.85

Island Christmas A29

Designs: 5c, Three Wise Men (Na Makoi). 20c, Holy family (He Tala). 40c, Escape into Egypt (Fakagagalo ki Aikupito). 60c, Christmas presents (Meaalofa Kilihimahi). 70c, Christ child (Pepe ko Iesu). $1, Christmas parade (Holo Tamilo).

1988, Dec. 7   Litho.   Perf. 13½
157	A29	5c multicolored	.25	.25
158	A29	20c multicolored	.25	.25
159	A29	40c multicolored	.50	.50
160	A29	60c multicolored	.80	.80
161	A29	70c multicolored	.90	.90
162	A29	$1 multicolored	1.25	1.25
		Nos. 157-162 (6)	3.95	3.95

Food Gathering — A30

Fishing and gathering coconuts. Printed setenant in continuous designs.
No. 163: a, Launching outrigger canoe. b, Outrigger canoe and sailboat starboard side. c, Outrigger canoe and sailboat stern.
No. 164: a, Outrigger and sailboat port side. b, Islander carrying baskets of coconuts. c, Gathering coconuts from palm trees.

1989, June 28   Litho.   Perf. 14x14½
163	A30	Strip of 3	4.00	4.25
a.-c.		50c any single	1.30	1.30
164	A30	Strip of 3	4.00	4.25
a.-c.		50c any single	1.30	1.30

Women's Work and Leisure — A31

1990, May 2   Litho.   Perf. 14½
165	A31	5c Weavers	.50	.50
166	A31	20c Washing clothes	.75	75
167	A31	40c Resting among palm trees	1.25	1.25
168	A31	60c Weaving mat	1.60	1.60
169	A31	80c Weaving, diff.	2.50	2.50
170	A31	$1 Basket weaver	2.75	2.75
		Nos. 165-170 (6)	9.35	9.35

Souvenir Sheet

Penny Black, 150th Anniv. — A32

1990, May 3   Litho.   Perf. 11½
| 171 | A32 | $3 multicolored | 15.00 | 15.00 |

Men's Handicrafts — A33

1990, Aug. 1   Photo.   Perf. 13
172	A33	50c shown	1.30	1.10
173	A33	50c Carving pots	1.30	1.10
174	A33	50c Tying rope on pot	1.30	1.10
a.		Strip of 3, #172-174	5.00	5.00
175	A33	50c Finishing pots	1.30	1.10
176	A33	50c Shaping a canoe	1.30	1.10
177	A33	50c Three men working	1.30	1.10
a.		Strip of 3, #175-177	5.00	5.00

1992 Summer Olympics, Barcelona — A34

1992, July 8   Litho.   Perf. 13½
178	A34	40c Swimming	.50	.50
179	A34	60c Long jump	1.75	75
180	A34	$1 Volleyball	2.25	2.25
181	A34	$1.80 Running	3.00	3.00
		Nos. 178-181 (4)	7.50	6.50

Discovery of America, 500th Anniv. A35

1992, Dec. 18
182	A35	40c Santa Maria	.50	.50
183	A35	60c Columbus	.75	.75
184	A35	$1.20 Columbus' fleet	2.25	2.25
185	A35	$1.80 Landfall	3.50	3.50
		Nos. 182-185 (4)	7.00	7.00

Coronation of Queen Elizabeth II, 40th Anniv. A36

25c, Queen, early portrait. 40c, Prince Philip. $1, Queen, recent portrait. $2, Queen & Prince Philip.

1993, July 8   Litho.   Perf. 13½
186	A36	25c multicolored	.55	.55
187	A36	40c multicolored	1.00	1.00
188	A36	$1 multicolored	1.75	1.75
189	A36	$2 multicolored	3.00	3.00
		Nos. 186-189 (4)	6.30	6.30

Birds A37

25c, Numenius tahitiensis. 40c, Phaethon rubricauda. $1, Egretta sacra. $2, Pluvialis fulva.

1993-94   Litho.   Perf. 13½
190	A37	25c multicolored	.75	.75
191	A37	40c multicolored	1.00	1.00
192	A37	$1 multicolored	2.00	2.00
193	A37	$2 multicolored	2.75	2.75
a.		Souvenir sheet of 4, #190-193, perf. 14x14½	8.00	8.00
		Nos. 190-193 (4)	6.50	6.50

No. 193a contains Hong Kong '94 emblem, inscription in Chinese and English in sheet margin and sold for $20 HK at the show.
Issued: #190-193, 12/15/93; #193a, 2/1/94.

PHILAKOREA '94 — A38

1994, Aug. 16   Litho.   Perf. 12
| 194 | A38 | $2 White heron | 3.25 | 3.25 |
| a. | | Souvenir sheet of 1 | 4.75 | 4.75 |

No. 194a has a continuous design.

Handicrafts A39

1995   Litho.   Perf. 13½
195	A39	5c Outrigger canoe	.25	.25
196	A39	30c Plaited fan	.30	.30
197	A39	40c Plaited baskets	.45	.45
198	A39	50c Fishing box	.60	.60
199	A39	80c Water bottle	.85	.85
200	A39	$1 Fishing hook	1.00	1.00
201	A39	$2 Coconut gourds	2.00	2.00
202	A39	$5 Shell necklace	4.50	4.50
		Nos. 195-202 (8)	9.95	9.95

Souvenir Sheet

New Year 1995 (Year of the Boar) — A40

1995, Feb. 3   Litho.   Perf. 14
203	A40	$5 multicolored	7.50	7.50
a.		Ovptd. in sheet margin	14.00	14.00
b.		Ovptd. in sheet margin	9.00	9.00

No. 203a ovptd. in red in sheet margin "POST'X 95 / 3-0 February / 1995 / AUCKLAND" surrounded by simulated perforations.
No. 203b ovptd. in red in sheet margin with Singapore '95 exhibition emblem.

Pacific Imperial Pigeon A41

1995, Apr. 27   Litho.   Perf. 13½
204	A41	25c shown	.50	.50
205	A41	40c Full view	1.00	1.00
206	A41	$1 In tree, red berries	1.75	1.75
207	A41	$2 Nesting	3.25	3.25
		Nos. 204-207 (4)	6.50	6.50

World Wildlife Fund.

Reef Fish — A42

Designs: 25c, Long nosed butterfly fish. 40c, Emperor angelfish. $1, Moorish idol. $2, Lined butterfly fish.
$3, Red fire fish.

1995, Sept. 1   Litho.   Perf. 12
208	A42	25c multicolored	.30	.30
209	A42	40c multicolored	.50	.50
210	A42	$1 multicolored	1.45	1.45
211	A42	$2 multicolored	3.25	3.25
		Nos. 208-211 (4)	5.50	5.50

Souvenir Sheet
| 212 | A42 | $3 multicolored | 4.25 | 4.25 |

No. 212 contains one 40x35mm stamp and is inscribed in sheet margin for Singapore '95.

Butterflies A43

Designs: 25c, Danaus plexippus. 40c, Precis villida samoensis. $1, Hypolimnas bolina. $2, Euploea lewenii.

1995, Oct. 16   Litho.   Perf. 12
213	A43	25c multicolored	.50	.50
214	A43	40c multicolored	.75	.75
215	A43	$1 multicolored	2.25	2.25
216	A43	$2 multicolored	3.00	3.00
		Nos. 213-216 (4)	6.50	6.50

Sea Turtles A44

1995, Nov. 27   Litho.   Perf. 12
217	A44	25c Hawksbill	.50	.50
218	A44	40c Leatherback	.75	.75
219	A44	$1 Green	2.25	2.25
220	A44	$2 Loggerhead	3.25	3.25
		Nos. 217-220 (4)	6.75	6.75

Souvenir Sheet
| 221 | A44 | $3 like #220 | 4.75 | 4.75 |

No. 221 contains one 50x40mm stamp and is a continuous design.

Souvenir Sheet

New Year 1996 (Year of the Rat) — A45

1996, Feb. 19	Litho.	Perf. 12	
222 A45 $3 Pacific rat		4.25	4.25
a. Ovptd. in sheet margin		4.25	4.25
b. Ovptd. in sheet margin		4.25	4.25

Overprinted in sheet margin with red exhibition emblem: No. 222a, CHINA '96; No. 222b, TAIPEI '96.

Common Design Types pictured following the introduction.

Queen Elizabeth II, 70th Birthday
Common Design Type

Various portraits of Queen, scenes of Tokelau: 40c, Nukunonu. $1, Atafu, silhouette of island, boat. $1.25, Atafu, building on island, boat. $2, Atafu, huts.
$3, Queen wearing tiara, formal dress.

1996, Apr. 22	Litho.	Perf. 13½	
223 CD354 40c multicolored		.50	.50
224 CD354 $1 multicolored		1.50	1.50
225 CD354 $1.25 multicolored		1.75	1.75
226 CD354 $2 multicolored		2.50	2.50
Nos. 223-226 (4)		6.25	6.25

Souvenir Sheet

| 227 CD354 $3 multicolored | | 4.25 | 4.25 |

Dolphins — A46

1996, July 15	Litho.	Perf. 14	
228 A46 40c Fraser's		1.00	1.00
229 A46 $1 Common		2.25	2.25
230 A46 $1.25 Striped		2.50	2.50
231 A46 $2 Spotted		3.50	3.50
Nos. 228-231 (4)		9.25	9.25

Shells A47

Designs: 40c, Cypraea talpa. $1, Cypraea mauritiana. $1.25, Cypraea argus. $2, Cypraea tigris.
$3, Cypraea mauritana, diff.

1996, Oct. 16	Litho.	Perf. 12	
232 A47 40c multicolored		.50	.50
233 A47 $1 multicolored		1.25	1.25
234 A47 $1.25 multicolored		1.75	1.75
235 A47 $2 multicolored		2.75	2.75
Nos. 232-235 (4)		6.25	6.25

Souvenir Sheet

| 236 A47 $3 multicolored | | 4.25 | 4.25 |

No. 236 contains one 50x40mm stamp with a continuous design.

Souvenir Sheet

New Year 1997 (Year of the Ox) — A48

1997, Feb. 12	Litho.	Perf. 15x14	
237 A48 $2 multicolored		3.50	3.50
a. Overprinted in gold		4.00	4.00
b. Overprinted in red		6.00	6.00

No. 237a ovptd. in sheet margin HONG KONG '97 / STAMP EXHIBITION" in English and Chinese.
No. 237b overprinted in sheet margin with Pacific 97 emblem. Issued 5/29.

Humpback Whale A49

Designs: 40c, With school of fish. $1, Calf, adult, young adult. $1.25, With mouth open, school of fish. $2, Adult, calf.
$3, Mouth, head of whale.

1997, May 29	Litho.	Perf. 12	
238 A49 40c multicolored		.50	.50
239 A49 $1 multicolored		1.25	1.25
240 A49 $1.25 multicolored		2.00	2.00
241 A49 $2 multicolored		2.75	2.75
Nos. 238-241 (4)		6.50	6.50

Souvenir Sheet

| 242 A49 $3 multicolored | | 4.25 | 4.25 |
| a. Ovptd. in sheet margin | | 4.50 | 4.50 |

No. 242a ovptd. in sheet margin, "AUPEX '97 / 13-16 NOVEMBER / NZ NATIONAL / STAMP EXHIBITION." Issued: 11/13.

South Pacific Commission, 50th Anniv. — A50

1997, Sept. 17	Litho.	Perf. 14	
243 A50 40c Church, waterfront		.50	.50
244 A50 $1 Beach, child		1.25	1.25
245 A50 $1.25 Island		1.75	1.75
246 A50 $2 Atoll		3.75	3.75
Nos. 243-246 (4)		7.25	7.25

Year of the Coral Reef — A51

Designs: No. 247, Gorgonian coral, emperor angelfish. No. 248, Soft coral. No. 249, Mushroom coral. No. 250, Staghorn coral. No. 251, Staghorn coral, Moorish idol.

1997, Oct. 20	Litho.	Perf. 13½	
247 A51 $1 multicolored		1.20	1.20
248 A51 $1 multicolored		1.20	1.20
249 A51 $1 multicolored		1.20	1.20
250 A51 $1 multicolored		1.20	1.20
251 A51 $1 multicolored		1.20	1.20
a. Strip of 5, #247-251		6.00	6.00

Souvenir Sheet

New Year 1998 (Year of the Tiger) — A52

1998, Jan. 28	Litho.	Perf. 14x14½	
252 A52 $2 multicolored		2.75	2.75
a. Ovptd. in sheet margin		4.00	4.00

No. 252a overprinted in sheet margin with emblem of Singpex '98 Stamp Exhibition, Singapore.

Diana, Princess of Wales (1961-97)
Common Design Type

Designs: No. 252B, Holding yellow flowers. No. 253: a, Wearing high-collared ruffled blouse. b, Wearing red beret. c, Wearing pink and yellow jacket.

1998, May 15	Litho.	Perf. 14½x14	
252B CD355 $1 multi		1.75	1.75

Souvenir Sheet

| 253 CD355 $1 Sheet of 4, #252B, 253a-253c | | 4.25 | 4.25 |

No. 253 sold for $4 + 50c, with surtax from international sales being donated to the Princess Diana Memorial Fund and surtax from national sales being donated to designated local charity.

Souvenir Sheet

First Stamps of Tokelau, 50th Anniv. — A53

Designs: a, #3. b. #1. c, #2.

1998, June 22	Litho.	Perf. 14½	
254 A53 $1 Sheet of 3, #a.-c.		4.00	4.00

Beetles A54

Designs: 40c, Oryctes rhinoceros. $1, Tribolium castaneum. $1.25, Coccinella repanda. $2, Amarygmus hyorophiloides.
$3, Coccinella repanda, diff.

1998, Aug. 24	Litho.	Perf. 14	
255 A54 40c multicolored		.50	.50
256 A54 $1 multicolored		1.50	1.50
257 A54 $1.25 multicolored		1.75	1.75
258 A54 $2 multicolored		2.50	2.50
Nos. 255-258 (4)		6.25	6.25

Souvenir Sheet

| 259 A54 $3 multicolored | | 3.75 | 3.75 |

Tropical Flowers A55

40c, Ipomoea pes-caprae. $1, Ipomoea littoralis. $1.25, Scaevola taccada. $2, Thespesia populnea.

1998, Nov. 19	Litho.	Perf. 14	
260 A55 40c multicolored		.55	.55
261 A55 $1 multicolored		1.20	1.20
262 A55 $1.25 multicolored		1.60	1.60
263 A55 $2 multicolored		2.40	2.40
Nos. 260-263 (4)		5.75	5.75

Souvenir Sheet

New Year 1999 (Year of the Rabbit) — A56

1999, Feb. 16	Litho.	Perf. 14	
264 A56 $3 multicolored		4.00	4.00
a. Ovptd. in sheet margin		4.00	4.00

No. 264a overprinted in sheet margin with emblem of IBRA '99 Intl. Stamp Exhibtion, Nuremburg. Issued: 4/27.

Souvenir Sheet

Australia '99, World Stamp Exhibition — A57

1999, Mar. 19			
265 A57 $3 HMS Pandora		4.50	4.50

First Manned Moon Landing, 30th Anniv. — A58

Designs: 25c, Lift-off. 50c, Separation of stages. 75c, Aldrin deploying instruments on moon. $1, Planting flag. $1.25, Returning to Earth. $2, Splashdown.
$3, Apollo 11, Moon, Earth.

Perf. 13½x13¼			
1999, Aug. 31		Litho.	
266 A58 25c multicolored		.25	.25
267 A58 50c multicolored		.50	.50
268 A58 75c multicolored		.75	.75
269 A58 $1 multicolored		1.10	1.10
270 A58 $1.25 multicolored		1.50	1.50
271 A58 $2 multicolored		2.25	2.25
Nos. 266-271 (6)		6.35	6.35

Souvenir Sheet

| 272 A58 $3 multicolored | | 3.50 | 3.50 |
| a. Ovptd. in silver "World Stamp Expo 2000 7-16 July Anaheim - U.S.A." on sheet margin | | 7.50 | 7.50 |

Crabs A59

1999   Litho.   Perf. 14¼x14½
273	A59	40c Coconut	.50	.50
274	A59	$1 Ghost	1.25	1.25
275	A59	$1.25 Land hermit	1.50	1.50
276	A59	$2 Purple hermit	2.50	2.50
		Nos. 273-276 (4)	5.75	5.75

Souvenir Sheet
| 277 | A59 | $3 Ghost, diff. | 3.50 | 3.50 |

Black-naped
Tern — A60

Designs: 40c, Chick and egg. $1, On nest.
$1.25, Pair near water. $2, Pair in flight.

Perf. 13½x14
1999, Dec. 31   Litho.   Unwmk.
| 278-281 | A60 | Set of 4 | 5.25 | 5.25 |

Souvenir Sheet

New Year 2000 (Year of the
Dragon) — A61

2000   Litho.   Perf. 14x14¼
| 282 | A61 | $3 multi | 4.50 | 4.50 |
| a. | | Overprinted in sheet margin | 4.50 | 4.50 |

No. 282a overprinted in sheet margin with
emblem "Bangkok 2000," "World Youth Stamp
Exhibition" and Thai text.

Souvenir Sheet

The Stamp Show 2000,
London — A62

Unwmk.
2000, May 22   Litho.   Perf. 14
| 283 | A62 | $6 multi | 6.25 | 6.25 |

Queen Mother,
100th
Birthday — A63

Various photos. Denominations 40c, $1.20,
$1.80, $3.

Perf. 14½x14¼
2000, Aug. 4   Wmk. 373
| 284-287 | A63 | Set of 4 | 6.75 | 6.75 |

Lizards
A64

Designs: 40c, Gehyra oceanica. $1,
Lepidodactylus lugubris. $1.25, Gehyra muti-
lata. $2, Emoia cyanura.

2001, Feb. 1   Litho.   Perf. 14
| 288-291 | A64 | Set of 4 | 7.25 | 7.25 |

Souvenir Sheet

New Year 2001 (Year of the
Snake) — A65

2001, Feb. 1
| 292 | A65 | $3 multi | 4.75 | 4.75 |
| a. | | With gold ovpt. in margin | 5.00 | 5.00 |

Overprint in margin on No. 292a is for Hong
Kong 2001 Stamp Exhibition.

Hippocampus
Histrix — A66

Various views of seahorses. Denominations.
40c, $1, $1.25, $2.

2001, Aug. 23   Litho.   Perf. 14
| 293-296 | A66 | Set of 4 | 5.50 | 5.50 |

Souvenir Sheet
| 297 | A66 | $3 multi | 4.00 | 4.00 |

Island
Scenery
A67

Designs: 40c, Sky over Atafu. $1, Waters of
Fakaofo. $2, Sunrise over Nukunonu village.
$2.50, Ocean, Nukunonu.

Unwmk.
2001, Dec. 17   Litho.   Perf. 14
| 298-301 | A67 | Set of 4 | 7.50 | 7.50 |
| a. | | Souvenir sheet, #298-301 | 13.00 | 13.00 |

Issued: No. 301a issued 5/27/06 for Washington 2006 World Philatelic Exhibition.

Reign Of Queen Elizabeth II, 50th Anniv. Issue
Common Design Type

Designs: Nos. 302, 306a, 40c, Princess
Elizabeth, Prince Philip on honeymoon, 1947.
Nos. 303, 306b, $1, Wearing purple hat. Nos.
304, 306c, $1.25, Holding Prince Charles,
1948. Nos. 305, 306d, $2, In 1996. No. 306e,
$3, 1955 portrait by Annigoni (38x50mm).

Perf. 14¼x14½, 13¾ (#306e)
2002, Feb. 6   Litho.   Wmk. 373
With Gold Frames
302	CD360	40c multicolored	.50	.50
303	CD360	$1 multicolored	1.25	1.25
304	CD360	$1.25 multicolored	1.50	1.50
305	CD360	$2 multicolored	2.25	2.25
		Nos. 302-305 (4)	5.50	5.50

Souvenir Sheet
Without Gold Frames
| 306 | CD360 | Sheet of 5, #a-e | 9.00 | 9.00 |

Souvenir Sheet

New Year 2002 (Year of the
Horse) — A68

2002, Feb. 12   Litho.   Perf. 14
| 307 | A68 | $4 multi | 5.25 | 5.25 |
| a. | | As #307, with gold ovpt. in margin | 5.75 | 5.75 |

No. 307a was issued 2/22 and has overprint
reading "STAMPEX 2002 / HONG KONG / 22-
24 FEBRUARY 2002."

Worldwide Fund for Nature
(WWF) — A69

Various views of Pelagic thresher shark:
40c, $1, $2, $2.50.

2002, July 2   Litho.   Perf. 14¼
| 308-311 | A69 | Set of 4 | 7.25 | 7.25 |

Queen Mother Elizabeth (1900-2002)
Common Design Type

Designs: 40c, Wearing broad-brimmed hat
(black and white photograph). $2, Wearing
blue hat.
No. 314: a, $2.50, Wearing hat (black and
white photograph). b, $4, Wearing purple hat.

Wmk. 373
2002, Aug. 5   Litho.   Perf. 14¼
With Purple Frames
| 312 | CD361 | 40c multicolored | .60 | .60 |
| 313 | CD361 | $2 multicolored | 3.25 | 3.25 |

Souvenir Sheet
Without Purple Frames
Perf. 14½x14¼
| 314 | CD361 | Sheet of 2, #a-b | 8.00 | 8.00 |

New
Zealand
Navy Ships
That Have
Stopped at
Tokelau
A70

Designs: 40c, HMNZS Kaniere. $1, HMNZS
Endeavour. $2, HMNZS Wellington. $2.50,
HMNZS Monowai.

2002, Dec.   Litho.   Unwmk.   Perf. 14
| 315-318 | A70 | Set of 4 | 8.50 | 8.50 |

Souvenir Sheet

New Year 2003 (Year of the
Ram) — A71

2003, Feb. 3
| 319 | A71 | $4 multi | 5.50 | 5.50 |
| a. | | With Bangkok 2003 overprint in gold in margin | 5.50 | 5.50 |

Issued: No. 319a, 10/13.

Coronation of Queen Elizabeth II, 50th Anniv.
Common Design Type

Designs: Nos. 320, 322a, $2.50, Queen with
maids of honor. Nos. 321, 322b, $4, Queen
with Prince Philip.

Perf. 14¼x14½
2003, June 2   Litho.   Wmk. 373
Vignettes Framed, Red Background
| 320 | CD363 | $2.50 multicolored | 3.25 | 3.25 |
| 321 | CD363 | $4 multicolored | 5.25 | 5.25 |

Souvenir Sheet
Vignettes Without Frame, Purple Panel
| 322 | CD363 | Sheet of 2, #a-b | 8.75 | 8.75 |

Prince William, 21st Birthday
Common Design Type

No. 323: a, Color photograph at right. b,
Color photograph at left.

Wmk. 373
2003, June 21   Litho.   Perf. 14¼
323		Horiz. pair	7.25	7.25
a.		CD364 $1.50 multi	2.25	2.25
b.		CD364 $3 multi	5.00	5.00

Souvenir Sheet

Welpex 2003 Stamp Show, Wellington,
New Zealand — A72

Unwmk.
2003, Nov. 7   Litho.   Perf. 14
| 324 | A72 | $4 multi | 6.00 | 6.00 |

Souvenir Sheet

New Year 2004 (Year of the
Monkey) — A73

2004   Litho. with Foil Application
| 325 | A73 | $4 multi | 5.50 | 5.50 |
| a. | | With 2004 Hong Kong Stamp Expo emblem in gold in margin | 5.50 | 5.50 |

Issued: No. 325, 1/22; No. 325a, 1/28.

Island
Scenes
A74

Designs: 40c, Atafu dawn. $1, Return of the
fishermen, Nukunonu. $2, A Fakaofo calm
evening glow. $2.50, Solitude in Atafu.

2004, June 30   Litho.   Perf. 14¼x14
| 326-329 | A74 | Set of 4 | 7.75 | 7.75 |

No. 324 Overprinted in Silver

2004, Aug. 8   **Litho.**   **Perf. 14**
330 A72 $4 multi   6.50 6.50

Fregata
Ariel
A75

Designs: 40c, Bird on nest. $1, Birds in flight. $2, Birds on nest and in flight. $2.50, Bird on nest, diff.

2004, Dec. 20   **Litho.**   **Perf. 14**
331-334 A75 Set of 4   9.25 9.25

Souvenir Sheet

New Year 2005 (Year of the
Rooster) — A76

2005, Feb. 9
335 A76 $4 multi   7.25 7.25
  a. Ovptd. in gold in margin with Pa-
      cific Explorer 2005 emblem   7.25 7.25

  No. 335a issued 4/21/05.

Pope John Paul II
(1920-2005)
A77

2005, Aug. 18   **Litho.**   **Perf. 14**
336 A77 $1 multi   1.80 1.80

Visit of
HMNZS Te
Kaha
A78

Various views of ship: 40c, $1, $2, $2.50.

2005, Dec. 15   **Litho.**   **Perf. 14**
337-340 A78 Set of 4   10.00 10.00

Souvenir Sheet

New Year 2006 (Year of the
Dog) — A79

2006, Jan. 29
341 A79 $4 multi   7.25 7.25

Queen
Elizabeth
II, 80th
Birthday
A80

Queen: 40c, With head on hands. $1, In wedding gown. No. 344, $2, Wearing tiara. No. 345, $2.50, Wearing blue hat.
  No. 346: a, $2, Like $1. b, $2.50, Like #344.
  No. 347: a, #346a overprinted "KIWIPEX." b, #346b overprinted "2006"

2006   **Litho.**   **Perf. 14**
With White Frames
342-345 A80 Set of 4   9.00 9.00
Souvenir Sheets
Without White Frames
346 A80 Sheet of 2, #a-b   7.00 7.00
Overprinted in Metallic Blue
347 A80 Sheet of 2, #a-b   7.75 7.75

  Issued: Nos. 342-346, 4/21; No. 347, 11/2. No. 347 is also overprinted in sheet margin "National Stamp Exhibition, Christchurch, New Zealand."

Souvenir Sheet

New Year 2007 (Year of the
Pig) — A81

2007, Feb. 18   **Litho.**   **Perf. 14**
348 A81 $4 multi   8.00 8.00

Worldwide
Fund for
Nature
(WWF)
A82

Pacific golden plover: 40c, Flock of birds. $1, Head. $2, Bird standing on one leg. $2.50, Birds and driftwood.

2007, Oct. 19   **Litho.**   **Perf. 14**
349-352 A82 Set of 4   8.00 8.00
352a   Miniature sheet of 16, 4
       each #349-352   40.00 40.00

Marine
Life — A83

Designs: 10c, Bicolor angelfish. 20c, Staghorn coral. 40c, Black-tipped reef sharks. 50c, Sea star. $1, Porcupine fish. $1.50, Thorny seahorses. $2, Spotted eagle rays. $2.50, Small giant clams. $5, Green turtles. $10, Slate pencil urchin.

2007, Dec. 19   **Perf. 14½x14¼**
353 A83 10c multi   .25   .25
354 A83 20c multi   .30   .30
355 A83 40c multi   .65   .65
356 A83 50c multi   .80   .80
357 A83 $1 multi   1.60 1.60
358 A83 $1.50 multi   2.40 2.40
359 A83 $2 multi   3.25 3.25
360 A83 $2.50 multi   4.00 4.00
361 A83 $5 multi   7.75 7.75
362 A83 $10 multi   15.50 15.50
  a. Miniature sheet, #353-362 42.50 42.50
      Nos. 353-362 (10)   36.50 36.50

Souvenir Sheet

New Year 2008 (Year of the
Rat) — A84

2008, Feb. 7   **Perf. 14**
363 A84 $4 multi   8.00 8.00

Sir Edmund Hillary
(1919-2008),
Mountaineer
A85

Hillary: 50c, As young man. $1, Wearing plaid shirt. $2, Wearing hat and glasses. $2.50, Wearing blue jacket.
  $5, On mountain, horiz.

2008, Nov. 5   **Litho.**   **Perf. 14¼**
364-367 A85 Set of 4   10.00 10.00
Souvenir Sheet
Perf. 13¾x13¼
368 A85 $5 multi   8.50 8.50

Local
Scenes
A86

Designs: 50c, Buildings near seashore. $1, Boats on beach. $2, Trees. $2.50, Boat anchored near buildings.
  $5, Islets.

2008, Nov. 7   **Perf. 14¼**
369-372 A86 Set of 4   10.00 10.00
Souvenir Sheet
Perf. 13¾x13¼
373 A86 $5 multi   7.50 7.50

  Tarapex National Exhibition, New Plymouth, New Zealand (#373).

Souvenir Sheet

New Year 2009 (Year of the
Ox) — A87

2009, Jan. 26   **Litho.**   **Perf. 14**
374 A87 $4 multi   7.25 7.25

Coins of the
Pacific
Area — A88

Obverse and reverse of: 50c, Chile 1875 one-peso. $1, Great Britain 1911 one-sover-eign. $2, New Zealand 1950 half-crown. $2.50, Tokelau 1997 ten-dollar.

2009, Dec. 22   **Litho.**   **Perf. 14x14¼**
375-378 A88 Set of 4   9.00 9.00
378a   Souvenir sheet of 4, #375-
          378   9.00 9.00

  For overprint, see No. 380.

Souvenir Sheet

New Year 2010 (Year of the
Tiger) — A89

2010, Feb. 12   **Perf. 13¼x13½**
379 A89 $4 multi   6.50 6.50

No. 378a Overprinted in Gold

Designs as before.

Method and Perf. As Before
2010, May 8
380 A88 Sheet of 4, #a-d   10.00 10.00

  London 2010 Festival of Stamps.

2009
Tokelauan
Bible
Translation
A90

Open Bible and: 50c, Atafu Church. $1, Fakaofo Church. $2, Nukunonu Church. $2.50, Closed Tokelauan Bibles.

Perf. 13½x13¼
2010, Sept. 21   **Litho.**
381-384 A90 Set of 4   9.00 9.00

Souvenir Sheet

New Year 2011 (Year of the
Rabbit) — A91

Perf. 13¼x13¾

2011, Feb. 3   **Unwmk.**
385   A91 $5 multi   7.75   7.75

Worldwide Fund for Nature (WWF) A92

Yellow-bellied sea snake: 50c, On rocks. $1, On beach. $2, In sea. $2.50, Three in sea.

2011, Mar. 25   **Unwmk.**   **Perf. 13½**
386-389   A92   Set of 4   9.50   9.50
389a   Miniature sheet of 16, 4   40.00   40.00
     each #386-389

Souvenir Sheet

Wedding of Prince William and Catherine Middleton — A93

Perf. 14¾x14¼

2011, Apr. 29   **Wmk. 406**
390   A93 $6 multi   9.50   9.50

Christmas — A94

Designs: 40c, Christmas tree. 45c, Ornament. $1.40, Stocking. $2, Angel.

2011, Nov. 16   **Unwmk.**   **Perf. 13½**
391-394   A94   Set of 4   6.75   6.75

Island Scenes A95

Designs: 10c, Man in coconut palm. 20c, Clouds over island. 25c, Small inhabited island. 40c, Snorkelers. 45c, Sailboat. 50c, House and boats. $1, Beach and trees. $1.40, Fisherman. $2, Beach and trees, diff.

2012, Apr. 11   **Perf. 13½x13¼**
395   A95   10c multi   .25   .25
396   A95   20c multi   .35   .35
397   A95   25c multi   .40   .40
398   A95   40c multi   .65   .65
399   A95   45c multi   .75   .75
400   A95   50c multi   .80   .80
401   A95 $1 multi   1.60   1.60
402   A95 $1.40 multi   2.25   2.25
403   A95 $2 multi   3.25   3.25
    Nos. 395-403 (9)   10.30   10.30

Reign of Queen Elizabeth II, 60th Anniv. A96

Photograph of Queen Elizabeth II from: $2, 1963. $3, 2012.

2012, May 23
404-405   A96   Set of 2   7.75   7.75
405a   Souvenir sheet of 2, #404-   7.75   7.75
     405

Fish A97

Designs: 40c, Yellowfin tuna. 45c, Ruby snapper. $1.40, Wahoo. $2, Common dolphinfish.

2012, Oct. 3
406-409   A97   Set of 4   7.00   7.00
409a   Souvenir sheet of 4, #406-   7.00   7.00
     409

Christmas — A98

Designs: 45c, Santa Claus, sleigh, reindeer over Atafu. $2, Reindeer over Nukunonu. $3, Reindeer over Fakaofo.

2012, Nov. 21   **Perf. 13¼x13½**
410-412   A98   Set of 3   9.25   9.25
412a   Horiz. strip of 3, #410-412   9.25   9.25
412b   Souvenir sheet of 3, #410-   9.25   9.25
     41?

Coronation of Queen Elizabeth II, 60th Anniv. A99

Designs: $2, Queen Elizabeth II and Prince Philip waving from Buckingham Palace balcony. $3, Queen Elizabeth II and family.

2013, May 8   **Perf. 13½x13¼**
413-414   A99   Set of 2   8.00   8.00
414a   Souvenir sheet of 2, #413-   8.00   8.00
     414

Butterflies A100

Designs: 45c, Female Blue moon butterfly. $1, Male Blue moon butterfly. $1.40, Common crow butterfly. $3, Meadow argus butterfly.

2013, Aug. 7   **Perf. 13½**
415-418   A100   Set of 4   9.50   9.50
418a   Souvenir sheet of 4, #415-   9.50   9.50
     418

Christmas — A101

Designs: 45c, Journey to Bethlehem. $1.40, Nativity. $2, Shepherds. $3, Magi.

Perf. 13¼x13½

2013, Nov. 20   **Litho.**
419-422   A101   Set of 4   10.00   10.00
422a   Souvenir sheet of 4, #419-   10.00   10.00
     422

Woven Items A102

Designs: 45c, Taulima (bracelets). $1.40, Pupu (water containers). $2, Tapili (fan). $3, Ato (basket).

2014, Apr. 23   **Litho.**   **Perf. 13½x13¼**
423-426   A102   Set of 4   10.00   10.00
426a   Souvenir sheet of 4,   10.00   10.00
     #423-426

Vakas — A103

Designs: 45c, Vakas in water. $1.40, Men building vaka. $2, Men rowing vaka. $3, Men bringing vaka ashore.

Perf. 13¼x13½

2014, June 14   **Litho.**
427-430   A103   Set of 4   10.00   10.00
430a   Souvenir sheet of 4,   10.00   10.00
     #427-430

Tokelau Language Week A104

Stylized people and speech balloons with English and Tokelauan words for: 45c, "Hello." $1.40, "How are you?" $2, "What is your name?" $3, "Farewell then."

2014, Oct. 15   **Litho.**   **Perf. 13½x13¼**
431-434   A104   Set of 4   10.00   10.00
434a   Souvenir sheet of 4,   10.00   10.00
     #431-434

Christmas A105

Designs: 45c, Shepherds. $2, Holy Family. $3, Magi.

Perf. 13¼x13½

2014, Dec. 10   **Litho.**
435-437   A105   Set of 3   8.50   8.50
437a   Souvenir sheet of 3, #435-   8.50   8.50
     437

Fishing A106

Fishing gear and: 45c, Atu (skipjack tuna). $1.40, Manini (convict tang). $2, Laulaufau (Moorish idols). $3, Pala (wahoos).

2015, Apr. 7   **Litho.**   **Perf. 13½x13¼**
438-441   A106   Set of 4   9.00   9.00
441a   Souvenir sheet of 4,   9.00   9.00
     #438-441

Crabs A107

Designs: 45c, Birgus latro. $1.40, Cardisoma sp. $2, Ocypode sp. $3, Grapsus sp.

2015, June 3   **Litho.**   **Perf. 13½x13¼**
442-445   A107   Set of 4   9.25   9.25
445a   Souvenir sheet of 4, #442-   9.25   9.25
     445

Miniature Sheets

Tokelau Language Week — A108

No. 446: a, One pandanus tree. b, Two tackle boxes. c, Three atolls. d, Four wickets. e, Five crabs.
No. 447: a, Six butterflies. b, Seven fish. c, Eight fans. d, Nine canoes. e, Ten fish hooks.

2015, Oct. 13   **Litho.**   **Perf. 13¼x13½**
446   A108   45c Sheet of 5, #a-e   3.25   3.25
447   A108 $1.40 Sheet of 5, #a-e   9.50   9.50

Christmas A109

Designs: 45c, Tropical snowman. $1.40, Palm tree decorated as Christmas tree. $2, Reindeer making sand angels. $3, Santa Claus on beach.

Perf. 13¼x13½

2015, Nov. 25   **Litho.**
448-451   A109   Set of 4   9.25   9.25
451a   Souvenir sheet of 4, #448-   9.25   9.25
     451

Miniature Sheet

Keyhole Gardening — A110

No. 452 — Construction of a keyhole garden with inscriptions of: a, 45c, Step one. b, $1, Step two. c, $1.40, Step three. d, $2, Step four. e, $3, Step five.

2016, Apr. 6   **Litho.**   **Perf. 13¼x13½**
452   A110   Sheet of 5, #a-e   11.00   11.00
  f.   Like #452, 180x48mm sheet   11.00   11.00
     size

Queen Elizabeth II, 90th Birthday — A111

Queen Elizabeth II: 45c, As child, with mother. $1.40, With Princes Philip and Charles. $2, With Prince Philip. $3, Wearing yellow dress.

2016, May 4   **Litho.**   **Perf. 13¼x13½**
453-456   A111   Set of 4   9.50   9.50

MV Matliki — A112

Designs: 45c, Deck, flags and anchor. $1.40, Ship and dinghy. $2, Two ships. $3, Ship and passengers on barge.

2016, Aug. 3   Litho.   Perf. 14x14¼
457-460 A112   Set of 4   10.00 10.00
460a   Souvenir sheet of 4,
         #457-460   10.00 10.00

Tokelau Language Week A113

English and Tokelauan words for foods: 45c, Coconut. $1.40, Coconut crab. $2, Fish. $3, Breadfruit.

2016, Oct. 5   Litho.   Perf. 13½x13¼
461-464 A113   Set of 4   10.00 10.00
464a   Souvenir sheet of 4,
         #461-464   10.00 10.00

Christmas — A114

Designs: 45c, Shepherd. $1.40, Holy Family. $2, Magi. $3, Angel.

2016, Dec. 7   Litho.   Perf. 13¼x13½
465-468 A114   Set of 4   9.50 9.50
468a   Souvenir sheet of 4, #465-
         468   9.50 9.50

Birds — A115

Designs: 45c, Bristle-thighed curlew. $1.40, Black noddy. $2, Great frigatebird. $3, Brown booby.

2017, Mar. 1   Litho.   Perf. 14x14¼
469-472 A115   Set of 4   9.75 9.75
472a   Souvenir sheet of 4, #469-
         472   9.75 9.75

Worldwide Fund for Nature (WWF) A116

Corals: 45c, Common mushroom coral, open. $1.40, Common mushroom coral, closed. $2, Brain coral, up close view. $3, Brain coral, not up close.

2017, Aug. 2   Litho.   Perf. 13½x13¼
473-476 A116   Set of 4   10.00 10.00
476a   Souvenir sheet of 4, #473-
         476   10.00 10.00

Reptiles A117

Designs: 45c, Moth skink. $1.40, Pelagic gecko. $2, Copper-tailed skink. $3, Black skink.

Perf. 13½x13¼
2017, Sept. 20   Litho.
477-480 A117   Set of 4   10.00 10.00
480a   Souvenir sheet of 4, #477-
         480   10.00 10.00

70th Wedding Anniversary of Queen Elizabeth II and Prince Philip — A118

Designs: 45c, Engagement photograph, 1947. $1.40, Family photograph, 1972. $2, Queen and Prince Philip on tour of Pacific, 1977. $3, Queen Elizabeth II, Princes Philip, Charles and William, 2003.

Perf. 13¼x13½
2017, Nov. 20   Litho.
481-484 A118   Set of 4   9.50 9.50
484a   Souvenir sheet of 4, #481-484   9.50 9.50

Christmas A119

Designs: 45c, Angel. $1.40, Madonna and Child. $2, Adoration of the Magi. $3, Infant Jesus in manger.

2017, Dec. 6   Litho.   Perf. 13¼x13½
485-488 A119   Set of 4   9.75 9.75
488a   Souvenir sheet of 4, #485-488   9.75 9.75

Sea Walls A120

Various buildings near sea walls: 45c, $1.40, $2, $3.

2018, May 2   Litho.   Perf. 13½x13¼
489-492 A120   Set of 4   9.75 9.75
492a   Souvenir sheet of 4, #489-492   9.75 9.75

Wedding of Prince Harry and Meghan Markle — A121

Various photographs of the couple: 45c, $1.40, $2, $3.

2018, May 21   Litho.   Perf. 13¼x13½
493-496 A121   Set of 4   9.75 9.75
496a   Souvenir sheet of 4, #493-496   9.75 9.75

Aerial Photographs — A122

Photographs of: 45c, Atafu Atoll. $1.40, Fakaofo Atoll. $2, Atafu Atoll, diff. $3, Nukunonu Atoll.

2018, Sept. 5   Litho.   Perf. 13½x13¼
497-500 A122   Set of 4   9.25 9.25
500a   Souvenir sheet of 4, #497-500   9.25 9.25

TONGA

ˈtäŋ-gə

LOCATION — A group of islands in the south Pacific Ocean, south of Samoa
GOVT. — Kingdom in British Commonwealth
AREA — 289 sq. mi.
POP. — 109,082 (1999 est.)
CAPITAL — Nuku'alofa

This group, also known as the Friendly Islands, became a British Protectorate in 1900 under the Anglo-German Agreement of 1899. On June 4, 1970, the United Kingdom ceased to have any responsibility for the external relations of Tonga.

12 Pence = 1 Shilling
20 Shillings = 1 Pound
100 Seniti = 1 Pa'anga (1967)

> **Catalogue values for unused stamps in this country are for Never Hinged items, beginning with Scott 87 in the regular postage section, Scott B1 in the semipostal section, Scott C1 in the air post section Scott CE1 in the air post special delivery section, Scott CO1 in the air post official section, and Scott O11 in the officials section.**

Watermarks

Wmk. 62 — NZ and Small Star Wide Apart

Wmk. 79 — Turtles

King George I — A1

Perf. 12x11½
			Wmk. 62
1886-92		**Typo.**	
1	A1	1p car rose ('87)	11.50 4.00
a.		Perf. 12½	450.00 7.00
b.		Perf. 12½x10	
2	A1	2p violet ('87)	45.00 3.50
a.		Perf. 12½	57.50 14.00
3	A1	6p ultra ('88)	57.50 2.75
a.		Perf. 12½	67.50 4.00

4	A1	6p org yel ('92)	18.00	*40.00*
5	A1	1sh blue grn ('88)	62.50	*7.25*
a.		Perf. 12½	110.00	*4.50*
b.		Half used as 6p on cover		*4.50*
		Nos. 1-5 (5)	194.50	*57.50*

Stamps with Perf. 11½ to 12 on 4 sides are made on the same machine as the Perf. 12x11½.
For surcharges and overprints see #6-9, 24.

Nos. 1 and 2 Surcharged in Black

a

1891, Nov. 10   Perf. 12x11½
6 A1(a) 4p on 1p car rose   3.50 *15.00*
a.   No period after "PENCE"   57.50 *135.00*
7 A1(a) 8p on 2p violet   45.00 *110.00*

Nos. 1 and 2 Overprinted in Black

b

Type I   Type II

Two types of overprint:
I — Solid stars, rays pointed and short.
II — Open-center stars, rays blunt and long.

1891, Nov. 23   Perf. 12½
8 A1(b) 1p car rose (I)   50.00 *70.00*
a.   Overprinted with 3 stars (I)   400.00
b.   Overprinted with 4 stars (I)   550.00
c.   Overprinted with 5 stars (I)   800.00
d.   Type II   50.00 *70.00*
e.   Perf. 12x11½ (I or II)   350.00
9 A1(b) 2p violet (I)   80.00 *42.50*
a.   Type II   80.00 *42.50*
b.   Perf. 12x11½ (I or II)   425.00

Coat of Arms A4   George I A5

1892, Nov. 10   Typo.   Perf. 12x11½
10 A4 1p rose   18.00 *35.00*
a.   Diagonal half used as ½p on cover   975.00
11 A5 2p olive gray   40.00 *18.00*
12 A4 4p red brown   55.00 *80.00*
13 A5 8p violet   70.00 *200.00*
14 A5 1sh brown   90.00 *140.00*
         Nos. 10-14 (5)   273.00 *473.00*

For surcharges and overprints see Nos. 15-23, 25-28, 36-37, O1-O10.

Types A4 and A5 Surcharged in Carmine or Black

c   d

e   f

1893

15	A4(c)	½p on 1p ultra (C)	26.00	30.00
a.		Surcharge omitted		
16	A4(c)	½p on 1p ultra	50.00	55.00
17	A5(d)	2½p on 2p blue grn (C)	27.50	13.50
18	A5(r)	2½p on 2p blue grn	19.00	19.00
a.		Double surcharge	3,000.	2,000.
19	A4(e)	5p on 4p org yel (C)	4.50	8.50
20	A5(f)	7½p on 8p rose (C)	32.50	85.00
		Nos. 15-20 (6)	159.50	211.00

Stamps of 1886-92 Surcharged in Blue or Black

g   h

1894

21	A4	½p on 4p red brn (Bl)	2.25	8.00
a.		"SURCHARGE"	10.00	22.50
b.		Pair, one without surcharge		
c.		"HALF PENNY" omitted		
22	A5	½p on 1sh brn (Bk)	2.75	12.50
a.		Double surcharge	310.00	
b.		"SURCHARGE"	11.50	45.00
c.		As "b," double surcharge	1,000.	
23	A5	2½p on 8p vio (Bk)	15.00	9.25
a.		No period after "SURCHARGE"	55.00	62.50
24	A1	2½p on 1sh blue grn (Bk), perf. 12½	65.00	30.00
a.		No period after "SURCHARGE"	200.00	
b.		Perf. 12x11½	17.50	50.00
		Nos. 21-24 (4)	85.00	59.75

Type A5 with Same Surcharges in Carmine

1895			**Unwmk.**	
25	A5(g)	1p on 2p lt blue	50.00	45.00
26	A5(h)	1½p on 2p lt bl, perf. 12x11	55.00	55.00
a.		Perf. 12	70.00	55.00
27	A5(h)	2½p on 2p lt blue	45.00	50.00
b.		Without period	250.00	250.00
28	A5(h)	7½p on 2p lt bl, perf. 12x11	70.00	50.00
a.		Perf. 12	550.00	
		Nos. 25-28 (4)	220.00	200.00

King George II — A13

1895, Aug. 16			**Perf. 12**	
29	A13	1p gray green	35.00	30.00
a.		Diagonal half used as ½p on cover		850.00
b.		Pair, imperf. btwn.		7,500.
30	A13	2½p dull rose	32.50	15.00
31	A13	5p brt blue, perf. 12x11	26.00	70.00
a.		Perf. 12	45.00	75.00
b.		Perf. 11	400.00	
32	A13	7½p yellow	50.00	55.00
		Nos. 29-32 (4)	143.50	170.00

Type A13 Redrawn and Surcharged "g" or "h" in Black

33	A13(g)	1p on 2½p red	55.00	37.50
a.		"SURCHARGE"	100.00	75.00
b.		Period after "Postage"	115.00	75.00
34	A13(g)	1p on 2½p red	115.00	50.00
a.		Period after "Postage"	170.00	110.00
35	A13(h)	7½p on 2½p red	62.50	75.00
a.		Period after "Postage"	110.00	120.00
		Nos. 33-35 (3)	232.50	162.50

Nos. 26 and 28 with Additional Surcharge in Violet and Black

1896, May			**Perf. 12x11**	
36	A5	½p on 1½p on 2p	500.00	
a.		Tongan surch. reading up	475.00	475.00
b.		Perf. 12	475.00	475.00
c.		As "a," perf. 12	500.00	500.00
d.		As "a," "Haalt"	3,500.	
e.		Halef	7250.	
37	A5	½p on 7½p on 2p	97.50	125.00
a.		"Half penny" inverted	3,250.	
b.		"Half penny" double		
c.		Tongan surch. reading up	97.50	125.00
d.		Tongan surcharge as "c" and double		

---

e.		"Half Penny"	2,500.	2,750.
f.		"Half" only	5,500.	
g.		"Hwlf"		
h.		Periods instead of hyphens after words	1,100.	
j.		Perf. 12	925.00	

Coat of Arms — A17 Ovava Tree — A18

George II — A19

Prehistoric Trilithon, Tongatabu — A20

Breadfruit A21 Coral Formations A22

View of Haabai A23

Red-breasted Musk Parrot — A24

View of Vavau — A25

Type I   Type II

Two types of 2p:
I — Top of sword hilt shows above "2."
II — No hilt shows.

1897-1934		**Engr. Wmk. 79**	**Perf. 14**	
38	A17	½p dark blue	.70	3.00
39	A17	½p green ('34)	1.10	1.40
40	A18	1p dp red & blk	.90	.90
41	A19	2p bis & sep (I)	20.00	7.00
a.		bister & gray, type II	35.00	3.75
42	A19	2½p lt blue & blk	8.00	1.60
a.		"½" without fraction bar	110.00	75.00
43	A20	3p ol grn & blk	4.00	9.75
44	A21	4p dull vio & grn	4.25	4.50
45	A19	5p orange & blk	35.00	16.00

46	A22	6p red	9.00	7.00
47	A19	7½p green & blk	20.00	26.00
a.		Center inverted	6,500.	
48	A19	10p carmine & blk	50.00	55.00
49	A19	1sh red brn & blk	16.00	9.00
a.		"SILENI-E-TAHA" missing second hyphen	350.00	
50	A23	2sh dk ultra & blk	30.00	32.50
51	A24	2sh6p dk violet	65.00	50.00
52	A25	5sh dull red & blk	26.00	32.50
		Nos. 38-52 (15)	289.95	256.15

See Nos. 73-74, 77-78, 80-81. For surcharges see Nos. 63-69.

Stamp of 1897 Overprinted in Black

1899, June 1				
53	A18	1p red & black	45.00	72.50
a.		"1889" instead of "1899"	250.00	400.00
b.		Comma omitted after June		
c.		Double overprint		

Marriage of George II to Lavinia, June 1, 1899. The letters "T L" are the initials of Taufa'ahau, the King's family name, and Lavinia.

No. 53 exists with serifed "T" and "L". Some specialists consider it to be an essay or proof.

Queen Salote — A26

Die I

Die II

Dies of 2p:
Die I — Ball of "2" smaller.
Die II — Ball of "2" larger. "U" has spur at left.

1920-35		**Engr.**	**Wmk. 79**	
54	A26	1½p gray blk ('35)	.55	3.50
55	A26	2p violet & sepia	12.00	15.00
56	A26	2p dl vio & blk (I) ('24)	15.00	2.75
a.		Die II	6.00	9.50
57	A26	2½p blue & black	9.00	45.00
58	A26	2½p ultra ('34)	5.00	1.10
59	A26	5p red org & blk	3.75	5.50
60	A26	7½p green & blk	2.00	2.00
61	A26	10p carmine & blk	2.90	5.50
62	A26	1sh red brown & blk	1.40	2.90
		Nos. 54-62 (9)	51.60	83.25

See Nos. 75-76, 79.

Stamps of 1897 Srchd. in Dark Blue or Red

1923				
63	A19	2p on 5p org & blk	1.10	1.00
64	A19	2p on 7½p grn & blk	37.50	45.00
65	A19	2p on 10p car & blk	25.00	65.00

66	A19	2p on 1sh red brn & blk	75.00	25.00
a.		"SILENI-E-TAHA" missing second hyphen	600.00	
67	A23	2p on 2sh ultra & blk (R)	12.00	12.00
68	A24	2p on 2sh6p dk vio (R)	35.00	7.50
69	A25	2p on 5sh dull red & blk (R)	3.50	2.50
		Nos. 63-69 (7)	189.10	158.00

Queen Salote — A27

Inscribed "1918-1938"

1938, Oct. 12			**Perf. 14**	
70	A27	1p carmine & blk	.65	4.00
71	A27	2p violet & blk	8.00	3.00
72	A27	2½p ultra & blk	8.00	3.75
		Nos. 70-72 (3)	16.65	10.75
		Set, never hinged	32.00	

Accession of Queen Salote Tupou, 20th anniv.
See Nos. 82-86.

Types of 1897-1920

Die III of 2p:
Foot of "2" longer than in Die II, extending beyond curve of loop.

1942		**Engr.**	**Wmk. 4**	
73	A17	½p green	.00	2.75
74	A18	1p scarlet & blk	1.75	2.75
75	A26	2p dull vio & blk (II)	4.50	3.00
a.		Die III	5.50	10.00
76	A26	2½p ultra	1.10	2.00
77	A20	3p green & black	.40	4.25
78	A22	6p orange red	2.00	2.25
79	A26	1sh red brown & gray blk	3.00	3.50
80	A24	2sh6p dk violet	25.00	30.00
81	A25	5sh dull red & brn blk	12.00	60.00
		Nos. 73-81 (9)	50.05	110.50
		Set, never hinged	70.00	

Type of 1938, Inscribed "1918-1943"

1944, Jan. 25				
82	A27	1p rose car & blk	.25	1.10
83	A27	2p purple & blk	.25	1.10
84	A27	3p dk yel grn & blk	.25	1.10
85	A27	6p red orange & blk	.40	2.00
86	A27	1sh dk red brn & blk	.25	2.00
		Nos. 82-86 (5)	1.40	7.30
		Set, never hinged	2.00	

25th anniv. of the accession of Queen Salote.

> **Catalogue values for unused stamps in this section, from this point to the end of the section, are for Never Hinged items.**

UPU Issue
Common Design Types
Engr.; Name Typo. on 3p, 6p
Perf. 13½, 11x11½

1949, Oct. 10			**Wmk. 4**	
87	CD306	2½p ultra	.25	.90
88	CD307	3p deep olive	2.00	3.25
89	CD308	6p deep carmine	.30	.55
90	CD309	1sh red brown	.45	.55
		Nos. 87-90 (4)	3.00	5.25

Common Design Types pictured following the introduction.

A28

A29

Queen Salote — A30

1950, Nov. 1   Photo.   Perf. 12½
91 A28 1p cerise   1.20 3.00
92 A29 5p green   1.20 2.75
93 A30 1sh violet   1.20 3.00
Nos. 91-93 (3)   3.60 8.75

50th anniv. of the birth of Queen Salote.

Map and Island Scene — A31

Badges and Royal Palace A32

2½p, Queen Salote & coastal scene. 3p, Queen Salote & ship "Bellona." 5p, Flag of Tonga, island view. 1sh, Arms of Tonga & Great Britain.

Perf. 13x13½ (1p), 13½x13, 12½ (3p)
1951, July 2   Engr.   Wmk. 4
94 A31 ½p deep green   .30 3.25
95 A32 1p carmine & black .30 3.25
96 A32 2½p choc & dp grn   .60 3.25
97 A31 3p ultra & org yel 1.80 3.25
98 A32 5p dp green & car   2.25 1.50
99 A32 1sh purple & orange 2.25 1.50
Nos. 94-99 (6)   7.50 16.00

50th anniv. of the treaty of friendship between Tonga and Great Britain.

Royal Palace, Nukualofa A33

Fisherman — A33a

Canoe and Schooners — A33b

Swallows' Cave, Vavau — A34

Map of Tongatabu — A34a

Vavau Harbor — A34b

Post Office, Nukualofa — A34c

Fuaamotu Airport — A34d

Wharf, Nukualofa — A34e

Map of Tonga Islands — A34f

Beach at Lifuka, Haapai — A34g

Mutiny on the Bounty — A34h

Queen Salote — A34i   Arms of Tonga — A34j

Perf. 11½x11, 11x11½
1953, July 1   Wmk. 79
100 A33   1p chocolate & blk   .25   .25
101 A33a 1½p emerald & ultra   .25   .25
102 A33b 2p black & aqua   1.00   .25
103 A34   3p dk grn & ultra   2.00   .25
104 A34a 3½p carmine & yel   1.40   .60
105 A34b 4p rose car & yel   2.00   .25
106 A34c 5p choc & ultra   .80   .25
107 A34d 6p black & dp ultra   1.25   .25
108 A34e 8p purple & pale grn   1.25 1.75
109 A34f 1sh black & ultra   1.80   .25
110 A34g 2sh choc & ol grn   8.00   .80
111 A34h 5sh dp vio & yel   18.00 7.75

112 A34i 10sh black & yellow   11.00 7.75
113 A34j £1 ultra, car & yel   11.00 5.00
Nos. 100-113 (14)   60.00 25.65

For surcharges and overprints see Nos. 119-126, 158-174, 182-202, 210-215, 218-221, 237, 269-273, C34-C39, C47-C54, C87-C91, CO4-CO6, CO11-CO20, CO27-CO43.

Whaling Ship and Longboat A35

1p, Stamp of 1886. 4p, Post Office, Customs & Treasury Building & Queen Salote. 5p, Diesel-driven ship Aoniu. 1sh, Plane over Tongatabu.

1961, Dec. 1   Photo.   Perf. 14½x13½
114 A35 1p brn org & car rose   .30 .25
115 A35 2p ultra   .90 .30
116 A35 4p bright green   .30 .30
117 A35 5p purple   .90 .30
118 A35 1sh red brown   1.00 .60
Nos. 114-118 (5)   3.40 1.75

75th anniversary of postal service.
For surcharges & overprints see #146-151, 216-221, C16-C21, C55-C57, CO1-CO3, CO9-CO10.

Stamps of 1953 & 1961 Overprinted in Red

No. 119

No. 125

Perf. 11½x11, 11x11½, 14½x13
Engr.; Photo. (4p)
1962, Feb. 7   Wmk. 79
119 A33   1p choc & blk   .25   .60
120 A35   4p brt green   .25   .65
121 A34c 5p choc & ultra   .25   .65
122 A34d 6p black & dp ultra   .25 1.10
123 A34e 8p purple & emer   .50 1.60
124 A34f 1sh black & ultra   .35   .80
125 A34   2sh on 3p dk grn & ultra .60 3.75
126 A34h 5sh purple & yellow   6.25 3.75
Nos. 119-126 (8)   8.70 12.90

Cent. of emancipation. See Nos. CO1-CO6.
Nos. 119-126 were overprinted locally. Nos. 124-125 exist with inverted overprint. No. 125 exists surcharged "2/" instead of "2/-".

Freedom from Hunger Issue
Common Design Type with Portrait of Queen Salote
Perf. 14x14½
1963, June 4   Wmk. 79   Photo.
127 CD314 11p ultra   .60 .35

Coat of Arms, ¼ Koula Coin, Reverse A36

Designs: 2p, 9p, 2sh, Queen Salote (head), ¼-koula coin, obverse.

Litho.; Embossed on Gilt Foil
1963, July 15   Unwmk.   Die Cut
Diameter: 40mm
128 A36 1p dp carmine   .50 .40
129 A36 2p violet blue   .50 .40
130 A36 6p dp green   .50 .40
131 A36 9p magenta   .50 .40
132 A36 1sh6p violet   .70 .70
133 A36 2sh emerald   .75 .75
Nos. 128-133,C1-C6,CO7 (13) 16.10 15.70

1st gold coinage of Polynesia. Backed with paper inscribed in salmon-colored alternating rows: "TONGA" and "THE FRIENDLY ISLANDS" in multiple.
For surcharges see #140-145, C11-C15, CO8.

Red Cross Centenary Issue
Common Design Type with Portrait of Queen Salote
Wmk. 79
1963, Sept. 2   Litho.   Perf. 13
134 CD315 2p black & red   .25   .25
135 CD315 11p ultra & red   .75 1.00

Queen Salote on ¼-Koula Coin A37

Litho.; Embossed on Gilt Foil
1964, Oct. 19   Unwmk.   Die Cut
136 A37 3p pink   .50 .40
137 A37 9p light blue   .50 .40
138 A37 2sh yellow green .50 .50
139 A37 5sh pale lilac   1.50 1.50
Nos. 136-139,C7-C10 (8)   6.45 6.25

Pan-Pacific and Southeast Asia Women's Association Conf., Nukualofa, Aug. 1964. See note on paper backing after No. 133.
For surcharges & overprints see #152-157, 263-268.

Nos. 128-133 Surcharged in Red, White or Black

1965, Mar. 18
140 A36 1sh3p on 1sh6p (R)   1.00   .50
141 A36 1sh9p on 9p (W)   1.00   .50
142 A36 2sh6p on 6p (R)   1.50   .75
143 A36 5sh on 1p   29.00 29.00
144 A36 5sh on 2p   5.00 5.00
145 A36 5sh on 2sh   2.50 2.00
Nos. 140-145,C11-C15,CO8 (12) 110.75 106.00

Nos. 114-115 Overprinted and Surcharged in Purple or Red

Perf. 14½x13½
1966, June 18   Photo.   Wmk. 79
146 A35 1p (P)   .25 .25
147 A35 3p on 1p (P)   .25 .25
148 A35 6p on 2p (R)   .25 .25
149 A35 1sh2p on 2p (R) .30 .25

150	A35	2sh on 2p (R)	.40	.25
151	A35	3sh on 2p (R)	.40	.30

Nos. 146-151,C16-C21,CO9-CO10 (14) 6.60 4.45

Centenary of Tupou College and of secondary eucation.

Nos. 136-137 Ovptd. and Srchd. in Silver on Black or Ultramarine

Litho.; Embossed on Gilt Foil

1966, Dec. 16		Unwmk.	Die Cut	
152	A37	3p pink (U)	.50	.40
153	A37	5p on 9p lt blue	.50	.40
154	A37	9p lt bl	.50	.40
155	A37	1sh7p on 3p pink (U)	1.25	.65
156	A37	3sh6p on 9p lt blue	1.50	1.00
157	A37	6sh6p on 3p pink (U)	2.00	1.25

Nos. 152-157,C22-C26 (11) 12.25 9.90

Nos. 100-110, 147 and 151 Srchd. in Black or Red

No. 158-165 Surcharged

Nos. 166-167 Surcharged

No. 168 Surcharged

No. 169 Surcharged

Nos. 170-171, 173 Surcharged

Nos. 172, 174 Surcharged

Perf. 11½x11, 11x11½, 14½x13½

1967, Mar. 25			Wmk. 79	
158	A33	1s on 1p	.25	.25
159	A34b	2s on 4p	.25	.25
160	A34a	3s on 5p	.25	.25
161	A34c	4s on 5p	.25	.25
162	A34a	5s on 3½p	.25	.25
163	A34e	6s on 8p	.25	.25
164	A33a	7s on 1½p	.25	.25
165	A34d	8s on 6p	.25	.25

166	A34	9s on 3p	.25	.25
167	A34f	10s on 1sh	.30	.30
168	A35	11s on 3p on 1p	.40	.40
169	A35	21s on 3sh on 2p	.60	.60
170	A33	23s on 1p	.65	.65
171	A34g	30s on 2sh (R) (1-line surcharge)	1.40	1.40
172	A34g	30s on 2sh (R) (3-line surcharge)	1.50	1.50
173	A34d	50s on 6p (R)	1.75	1.75
174	A33b	60s on 2p (R)	2.25	2.25

Nos. 158-174 (17) 11.10 11.10

The size, typeface and arrangement of surcharge vary on the different denominations.

King Taufa'ahau IV — A38

Designs: 1s, 4s, 28s, 1pa, Coat of Arms, reverse of new palladium coins. Diameter: 1s, 44mm; 2s, 50s, 52mm; 4s, 59mm; 15s, 68mm; 28s, 40mm; 1pa, 74mm.

Litho.; Embossed on Palladium Foil

1967, July 4		Unwmk.	Die Cut	
175	A38	1s orange & brt bl	.50	.40
176	A38	2s brt bl & dp mag	.50	.40
177	A38	4s emerald & mag	.50	.40
178	A38	15s blue grn & vio	.50	.40
179	A38	28s blk & brt red lil	.60	.60
180	A38	50s red & vio bl	1.10	1.10
181	A38	1pa ultra & brt rose	2.75	2.75

Nos. 175-181,C27-C33 (14) 14.80 14.10

Coronation of King Taufa'ahau IV, July 4, 1967. Backed with paper inscribed in yellow alternating rows: "Tonga The Friendly Islands" and "Historically The First Palladium Coinage." For surcharges and overprints see Nos. 203-209, C40-C46, CO21-CO24,

Types of Regular Issue, 1953, Surcharged

1967, Dec. 15		Wmk. 79 Engr.	Die Cut	
182	A33	1s on 1p yellow & blk	.25	.25
183	A33b	2s on 2p car & ultra	.25	.25
184	A34	3s on 3p brn org & yel	.25	.25
185	A34b	4s on 4p purple & yel	.25	.25
186	A34c	5s on 5p green & yel	.25	.25
187	A34f	10s on 1sh rose red & yel	.25	.25
188	A34g	20s on 2sh car & ultra	.35	.35
189	A34h	50s on 5sh sepia & yel	3.00	3.00
190	A34i	1pa on 10sh org yel	1.00	.75

Nos. 182-190,C34-C36,CO12-CO14 (15) 9.95 9.60

Arrival of US Peace Corps.

Nos. 100-111 Surcharged in Red, Black or Ultra

No. 191

No. 193

Perf. 11½x11, 11x11½

1968, Apr. 6		Engr.	Wmk. 79	
191	A33	1s on 1p (R)	.25	.25
192	A34b	2s on 4p	.25	.25
193	A34	3s on 3p (U)	.25	.25
194	A34c	4s on 5p (R)	.25	.25
195	A33b	5s on 2p (R)	.25	.25
196	A34d	6s on 6p (R)	.25	.25
197	A33a	7s on 1½p (R)	.25	.25
198	A34e	8s on 8p (R)	.25	.25
199	A34a	9s on 3½p	.30	.30
200	A34f	10s on 1sh (R)	.30	.30
201	A34h	20s on 5sh (R)	2.00	2.00
202	A34g	2pa on 2sh (R)	3.00	3.00

Nos. 191-202,C37-C39,CO15-CO18 (19) 15.75 13.90

Surcharge on 3s and 10s is vertical.

Nos. 175-181 Overprinted: "H.M'S BIRTHDAY / 4 July 1968" in Gold on Red Panel on 1s, 4s, 28s and 1pa. "HIS MAJESTY'S 50th BIRTHDAY" in Silver on Blue Panel on 2s, 15s and 50s

Litho.; Embossed on Palladium Foil

1968, July 4		Unwmk.	Die Cut	
203	A38	1s orange & brt bl	.25	.25
204	A38	2s brt bl & dp mag	.25	.25
205	A38	4s emerald & mag	.25	.25
206	A38	15s blue grn & vio	.55	.55
207	A38	28s blk & brt red lil	1.10	1.10
208	A38	50s red & vio bl	1.90	1.90
209	A38	1pa ultra & brt rose	4.00	4.00

Nos. 203-209,C40-C46,CO21-CO24 (18) 33.20 29.15

Types of 1953 Surcharged in Red, Black or Green

No. 210

No. 211

No. 212

No. 213

No. 214

Designs as before.

1968, Dec. 19		Wmk. 79 Engr.	Die Cut	
210	A34c	5s on 5p grn & yel (R)	.25	.25
211	A34f	10s on 1sh cer & buff	.25	.25
212	A34g	15s on 2sh rose car & bl	.25	.25
213	A33b	25s on 2p rose car & bl	.55	.55
214	A33	50s on 1p yel & blk	.75	.75
215	A34i	75s on 10sh org (G)	1.10	1.10

Nos. 210-215,C47-C54,CO19-CO20 (16) 9.30 7.30

Issued to publicize the field and track trials for the third South Pacific Games, Port Moresby, 1969. The overprint is in 5 lines on the horizontal stamps, in 7 lines on vertical stamps. On the vertical stamps "Trial" is

printed on the line ahead of "Field & Track." On #215 the denomination is spelled out.

Nos. 149-150 and Types of 1953 Surcharged

Nos. 216-217 Surcharged

Nos. 218, 221 Surcharged

No. 219 Surcharged

No. 220 Surcharged

Perf. 14½x13½

1968		Photo	Wmk. 79	
216	A33	1s on 1sh2p on 2p	1.60	1.60
217	A35	1s on 2sh on 2p	1.60	1.60

		Engr.	Die Cut	
218	A34d	1s on 6p yel & blk	.90	.90
219	A34a	2s on 3½p dk blue	1.00	1.00
220	A33a	3s on 1½p lt green	1.00	1.00
221	A34e	4s on 8p blk & pale grn	1.10	1.10

Nos. 216-221,C55-C57 (9) 12.00 10.20

Banana — A39

Unwmk.

1969, Apr. 21		Typo.	Die Cut	
Self-adhesive				
222	A39	1s yellow, black & red	1.00	.85
223	A39	2s yel, black & emer	1.10	1.00
224	A39	3s yellow, black & lil	1.25	1.10
225	A39	4s yellow, black & ultra	1.40	1.10
226	A39	5s yel, blk & ol grn	1.75	1.75

Nos. 222-226 (5) 6.50 5.80

Packed in boxes of 200. See Nos. 248-252, 297-301, O11-O15, design A75.

Peelable Backing Inscribed
Starting in 1969, self-adhesive stamps are attached to peelable paper backing printed with "TONGA where time begins" in multiple rows and various colors, unless otherwise stated.

Shot-putter — A40

1969, Aug. 13		Litho.	Die Cut	
Self-adhesive				
227	A40	1s bister, red & blk	.25	.25
228	A40	3s bis, red & emer	.25	.25
229	A40	6s bister, red & bl	.25	.25

| 230 | A40 | 10s bister, red & pur | .25 | .25 |
| 231 | A40 | 30s bister, red & bl | .40 | .40 |

Nos. 227-231,C58-C62,CO25-CO26 (12)   8.95 8.95

3rd Pacific Games, Port Moresby, Papua and New Guinea, Aug. 13-23.

Oil Derrick and Map of Tonga Islands — A41

1969, Dec. 23   Litho.   Die Cut
Self-adhesive

232	A41	3s brown & multi	.50	.50
233	A41	7s brt blue & multi	.60	.60
234	A41	20s multicolored	1.00	1.00
235	A41	25s orange & multi	1.10	1.10
236	A41	35s henna brn & multi	1.50	1.50

Type of 1953 Regular Issue Surcharged in Red

Wmk. 79   Die Cut

| 237 | A34j | 1.10pa on £1 grn & multi | 4.50 | 4.50 |

Nos. 232-237,C63-C67,CO27 (12)   18.40 18.40

First scientific search for oil in Tonga.

British and Tongan Royal Families — A42

Litho.; Gold Embossed
1970, Mar. 7   Self-adhesive   Die Cut

238	A42	3s multicolored	.25	.25
239	A42	5s multicolored	.25	.25
240	A42	10s multicolored	.55	.40
241	A42	25s multicolored	1.25	.90
242	A42	50s multicolored	2.75	2.00

Nos. 238-242,C68-C72,CO28-CO30 (13)   27.55 16.60

Visit of Elizabeth II, Prince Philip and Princess Anne, Mar. 1970.

Open Book, George Tupou I and II, Salote Tupou III, Taufa'ahau Tupou IV and Tonga Flag — A43

Litho.; Gold Embossed
1970, June 4   Die Cut
Self-adhesive

243	A43	3s multicolored	.50	.50
244	A43	7s multicolored	.65	.65
245	A43	15s multicolored	1.00	1.00
246	A43	25s multicolored	1.25	1.25
247	A43	50s multicolored	2.00	2.00

Nos. 243-247,C73-C77,CO31-CO33 (13)   24.60 24.60

Tonga's independence and entry into the British Commonwealth of Nations.
For surcharges see Nos. CO49-CO51, CO71.

Banana Type of 1969 redrawn and

Coconut — A44

1970, June 9   Typo.
Self-adhesive

248	A39	1s yellow, blk & mag	.40	.40
249	A39	2s yellow, blk & bl	.50	.50
250	A39	3s yellow, blk & brn	.50	.50
251	A39	4s yellow, blk & grn	.50	.50
252	A39	5s yellow, blk & org	.55	.55

Typo.; Embossed on Gilt Foil
Coconut Brown

253	A44	6s blue, grn & mag	.65	.65
254	A44	7s purple & green	.70	.70
255	A44	8s gold, grn & vio bl	.75	.75
256	A44	9s carmine & green	.85	.85
257	A44	10s gold, grn & org	.85	.85

Nos. 248-257,O11-O20 (20)   16.00 16.00

Nos. 248-252 have no white shading in upper part of the banana, Nos. 222-226 have white shading. Nos. 253-256 have self-adhesive control numbers in lower left corner of paper backing. Paper backing is green on Nos. 253-257.
See Nos. 302-306, O26-O30.

Red Cross and Arms of Tonga A45

1970, Oct. 17   Litho.   Die Cut
Self-adhesive

258	A45	3s red, black & grn	.25	.25
259	A45	7s red, blk & vio bl	.25	.25
260	A45	15s red, blk & red lil	.55	.55
261	A45	25s red, black & brt grn	.90	.90
262	A45	75s red, black & brn	4.50	4.50

Nos. 258-262,C78-C82,CO34-CO36 (13)   29.35 29.35

Centenary of the British Red Cross.
See Nos. C78-C82.

Nos. 153, 152 Surcharged

Litho.; Embossed on Gilt Foil
1971, Jan. 31   Die Cut

263	A37	2s on 9p lt blue	.25	.25
264	A37	3s on 9p lt blue	.25	.25
265	A37	5s on 3p pink	.35	.25
266	A37	15s on 9p lt blue	1.10	.65
267	A37	25s on 3p pink	1.50	1.00
268	A37	50s on 3p pink	3.50	2.10

Nos. 263-268,C83-C86,CO37-CO40 (14)   35.10 24.55

In memory of Queen Salote (1900-65). The "In Memoriam" inscription is in silver on black panel on the 2s, 3s and 15s; in silver on ultramarine panel on the 5s, 25s and 50s. The dates and denominations are all on black panels in silver and metallic red, green, bronze, magenta or gold respectively.

Type of Regular Issue, 1953,
Surcharged in Red and Black

No. 269

Nos. 270-272

1971   Engr.   Wmk. 79   Imperf

269	A34e	3s on 8p blk & pale grn	.25	.25
270	A34b	7s on 4p pur & yel	.25	.25
271	A33	25s on 1p yel & blk	.55	.40
272	A34g	75s on 2sh rose car & blue	3.25	2.10

Nos. 269-272,C87-C89,CO41-CO43 (10)   14.05 9.40

Philatokyo 71, Philatelic Exposition, Tokyo, Apr. 19-29.

Type of Regular Issue, 1971, Surcharged

1971

| 273 | A34f | 15s on 1sh car & buff | .50 | .50 |

Nos. 273,C90-C91 (3)   4.00 4.00

Centenary of Japanese postal service.

Self-adhesive & Die Cut
Starting with Nos. 274-278, all issues are self-adhesive and die cut, unless otherwise stated.

Pole Vault — A46

1971, July Litho. Unwmk. Die Cut

274	A46	3s green, blk & brn	.25	.25
275	A46	7s red, blk & brn	.25	.25
276	A46	15s green, blk & brn	.35	.35
277	A46	25s rose lil, blk & brn	.50	.50
278	A46	50s dk bl, blk & brn	1.00	1.00

Nos. 274-278,C92-C96,CO44-CO46 (13)   14.80 14.80

4th South Pacific Games, Papeete, French Polynesia, Sept. 8-19.
For surcharges see Nos. 332, C140.

Gold Medal of Merit — A47

24s, Silver Medal of Merit. 38s, Bronze Medal of Merit, obverse (King Taufa'ahau IV).

Litho; Embossed
1971, Oct. 30   Imperf.

279	A47	3s gold & multi	.25	.25
280	A47	24s silver & multi	.45	.45
281	A47	38s bronze & multi	.85	.85

Nos. 279-281,C99-C101,CO49-CO51 (9)   10.65 10.65

First investiture of Tongan Medal of Merit.
For surcharges see Nos. 333-336.

Juggler, UNICEF Emblem A48

1971, Dec.   Litho.   Die Cut

282	A48	2s violet & multi	.25	.25
283	A48	4s multicolored	.25	.25
284	A48	8s blue & multi	.25	.25
285	A48	16s emerald & multi	.35	.35
286	A48	30s lil rose & multi	.70	.70

Nos. 282-286,C102-C106,CO52-CO54 (13)   15.40 15.40

25th anniv. of UNICEF.

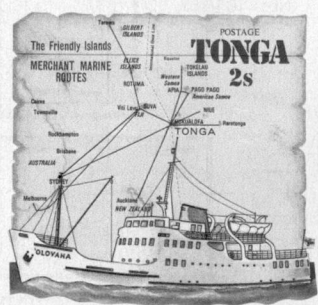

Merchant Marine Routes from Tonga and "Olovaha" — A49

1972, Apr. 14

287	A49	2s blue & multi	.35	.35
288	A49	10s magenta & multi	.85	.35
289	A49	17s brown & multi	1.25	.35
290	A49	21s dk green & multi	1.40	.50
291	A49	60s multicolored	6.50	4.00

Nos. 287-291,C107-C111,CO55-CO57 (13)   41.95 28.75

Togan Merchant Marine publicity
For surcharges see Nos. C124, CO66-CO69.

King Taufa'ahau IV Coronation Coin, ¼ Hau — A50

Litho.; Embossed on Metallic Foil
1972, July 15
292	A50	5s silver & multi	.25	.25
293	A50	7s silver & multi	.25	.25
294	A50	10s silver & multi	.25	.25
295	A50	17s silver & multi	.40	.40
296	A50	60s silver & multi	1.40	1.40

Nos. 292-296, C112
C116, CO58-CO60 (13) 15.45 15.45

Coronation of King Taufa'ahau IV, 5th anniv.

Coconut Type of 1970 and

Banana
A51

Watermelon — A52

1972, Sept. 30 Typo.
297	A51	1s brt yel, red & blk	.35	.25
298	A51	2s brt yel, bl & blk	.40	.25
299	A51	3s brt yel, emer & blk	.45	.25
300	A51	4s brt yel & blk	.45	.25
301	A51	5s brt yel & brn blk	.45	.25
302	A44	6s brn, org & grn	.50	.25
303	A44	7s brn, ultra & grn	.55	.30
304	A44	8s brn, mag & grn	.55	.30
305	A44	9s brn, red & grn	.55	.30
306	A44	10s brn, bl & grn	.65	.35
307	A52	15s green, org brn & ultra	1.40	.50
308	A52	20s grn, bl & red	1.50	.70
309	A52	25s grn, red & brn	1.75	.80
310	A52	40s grn, bl & org	3.00	1.75
311	A52	50s grn, dk bl & yel	3.00	2.00

Nos. 297-311, O21-O35 (30) 28.85 17.35

Paper backing is brown on Nos. 302-311. Nos. 302-306 have self-adhesive control number in lower left corner of paper backing.

Flag Raising, Minerva Reef — A53

1972, Dec. 9 Litho.
312	A53	5s black & multi	.25	.25
313	A53	7s green & multi	.25	.25
314	A53	10s purple & multi	.25	.25
315	A53	15s orange & multi	.40	.40
316	A53	40s ultra & multi	1.50	1.50

Nos. 312-316, C119-
C123, CO63-CO65 (13) 13.75 13.75

Tonga's proclamation of sovereignty over the Minerva Reefs, June 1972.

Tongan Coins and Bank Building — A54

1973, Mar. 30 Litho.
317	A54	5s silver & multi	.25	.25
318	A54	7s silver & multi	.25	.25
319	A54	10s silver & multi	.25	.25
320	A54	20s silver & multi	.45	.25
321	A54	30s silver & multi	.60	.35

Nos. 317-321, C125-
C129, CO66-CO68 (13) 17.95 17.10

Establishment of Bank of Tonga.

Handshake, Outrigger Canoe — A55

1973, June 29
322	A55	5s silver & multi	.30	.25
323	A55	7s silver & multi	.45	.25
324	A55	15s silver & multi	1.40	.55
325	A55	21s silver & multi	1.90	.70
326	A55	50s silver & multi	6.75	3.25

Nos. 322-326, C130-
C134, CO69-CO71 (13) 135.00 70.10

Tongan Boy Scout Movement, 25th anniv.

Capt. Cook's Report and Tongan Rulers — A56

Litho.; Embossed on Gilt Foil
1973, Oct. 2
327	A56	6s multicolored	.50	.45
328	A56	8s multicolored	.50	.45
329	A56	11s multicolored	.70	.55
330	A56	35s multicolored	4.75	1.90
331	A56	40s multicolored	4.75	2.25

Nos. 327-331, C135-
C139, CO72-CO74 (13) 60.00 31.45

Bicentenary of Capt. Cook's arrival. Design is from the manuscript in British Museum.

Nos. 278, 281, C100-C101 and 280 Srchd. & Ovptd. in Silver or Gold on Red (12s, 14s) or Black Panels (5s, 20s, 50s): "Commonwealth Games Christchurch 1974"
1973, Dec. 19 Litho.
332	A46	5s on 50s (G)	.25	.25

Litho.; Embossed
333	A47	12s on 38s (S)	.50	.50
334	A47	14s on 75s (G)	.50	.50
335	A47	20s on 1pa (G)	.85	.85
336	A47	50s on 24s (S)	1.60	1.60

Nos. 332-336, C140-
C144, CO75-CO77 (13) 17.10 16.45

10th British Commonwealth Games, Christchurch, N.Z., Jan. 24-Feb. 2, 1974.

Letter Addressed to Tonga, Names of UPU Members — A57

1974, June 20 Typo.
337	A57	5s tan & multi	.25	.25
338	A57	10s tan & multi	.25	.25
339	A57	15s tan & multi	.45	.45
340	A57	20s tan & multi	.50	.50
341	A57	50s tan & multi	1.60	1.60

Nos. 337-341, C154-
C158, CO87-CO89 (13) 14.55 14.55

Centenary of Universal Postal Union.

Girl Guide Badges — A58

1974, Sept. 11 Litho.
342	A58	5s multicolored	.45	.30
343	A58	10s multicolored	.85	.50
344	A58	20s multicolored	2.00	1.25
345	A58	40s multicolored	4.00	2.40
346	A58	60s multicolored	5.50	3.25

Nos. 342-346, C159-
C163, CO90-CO92 (13) 49.00 29.20

Girl Guides of Tonga.
For surcharges see Nos. C189, C192.

Sailing Ship and Anchors A59

1974, Dec. 11
347	A59	5s blue & multi	.40	.35
348	A59	10s blue & multi	.90	.45
349	A59	25s blue & multi	2.00	.80
350	A59	50s blue & multi	4.00	2.75
351	A59	75s blue & multi	6.00	4.50

Nos. 347-351, C164-
C168, CO93-CO95 (13) 47.00 27.00

Establishment of Royal Marine Institute.

Dateline Hotel, Nukualofa — A60

1975, Mar. 11
352	A60	5s blue & multi	.25	.25
353	A60	10s green & multi	.25	.25
354	A60	15s scarlet & multi	.35	.35
355	A60	30s purple & multi	.75	.75
356	A60	1pa orange & multi	2.75	2.75

Nos. 352-356, C169-
C173, CO96-CO98 (13) 15.15 15.15

First meeting of South Pacific area Prime Ministers. See note after No. 226.

Boxing and Games' Emblem — A61

1975, June 11 Litho.
357	A61	5s black & multi	.25	.25
358	A61	10s green & multi	.35	.35
359	A61	20s brown & multi	.55	.55
360	A61	25s orange & multi	.65	.65
361	A61	65s violet & multi	1.40	1.40

Nos. 357-361, C174-
C178, CO99-CO101 (13) 13.35 13.35

5th South Pacific Games, Guam, Aug. 1-10.
See note after No. 226.
For surcharges see Nos. 412, 482.

King Taufa'ahau IV Coin — A62

Designs (FAO Coins): 5s, Chicken. 20s, like 1pa, (small coin, 27mm). 50s, School of fish. 2pa, Animals and plants on reverse, King on obverse (large coin, 42mm).

1975, Sept. 3
362	A62	5s red, sil & blk	.25	.25
363	A62	20s ultra, grn, sil & blk	.55	.55
364	A62	50s blue, sil & blk	1.10	1.10
365	A62	1pa silver & black	2.25	2.25
366	A62	2pa silver & black	3.75	3.75

Nos. 362-366, C179-C183 (10) 13.25 13.25

Coinage issued for the benefit of the FAO. Size of paper backing of 2pa: 82x50mm; others 45x45mm. See note after No. 226.
For surcharge see Nos. 413.

Coat of Arms, 5pa Coin, Reverse — A63

George Tupou I Coin, Reverse and Obverse — A64

Coins: 20s, King Taufa'ahau IV. 50s, King George Tupou II, 50pa obverse and reverse. 75s, 20pa reverse.

Litho.; Embossed on Gilt Foil
1975, Nov. 4 Pink Background
367	A63	5s black, sil & vio bl	.30	.30
368	A64	10s gold, blk & red	.40	.40
369	A63	20s black, sil & grn	.75	.75
370	A64	50s gold, blk & vio	1.75	1.75
371	A63	75s black, sil & red lil	2.75	2.75

Nos. 367-371, C184-
C188, CO102-CO104 (13) 18.10 18.10

Centenary of Constitution of Tonga. Size of paper backing of Nos. 367 and 369: 65x60mm; of No. 371, 87x78mm. See note after No. 226.
For surcharges see Nos. C232, C296.

Montreal Olympic Games
Emblem — A65

1976, Feb. 24		Litho.	
372 A65	5s red, ultra & blk	.40	.35
373 A65	10s red, green & blk	.60	.35
374 A65	25s red, lt brown & blk	1.40	.80
375 A65	35s red, lilac & blk	1.75	1.10
376 A65	70s red, bister & blk	3.50	2.75
Nos. 372-376,C189-C193,CO105-CO107 (13)		31.00	20.05

21st Olympic Games, Montreal, Canada, July 17-Aug. 1. See note after No. 226.
For surcharges see Nos. 414, 478.

William Hooper, William Floyd, John Penn, Francis Lightfoot Lee — A66

Signers of Declaration of Independence, Flags of US and Tonga: 10s, Benjamin Franklin, Thomas Nelson, Jr., Benjamin Harrison, William Ellery. 15s, Oliver Wolcott, Lyman Hall, William Whipple, Carter Braxton. 25s, George Taylor, Thomas Stone, Arthur Middleton, Richard Stockton. 75s, Stephen Hopkins, Elbridge Gerry, James Wilson, Francis Hopkinson.

1976, May 26		Litho.	
377 A66	9s buff & multi	.45	.25
378 A66	10s buff & multi	.45	.25
379 A66	15s buff & multi	.65	.50
380 A66	25s buff & multi	1.00	1.00
381 A66	75s buff & multi	5.75	4.50
Nos. 377-381,C194-C198,CO108-CO110 (13)		34.50	21.45

American Bicentennial. Printed on peelable buff paper backing, inscribed in carmine with facsimile of Declaration of Independence.
For surcharges see #481, C233, C236-C237, C297.

Nathaniel Turner and John Thomas — A67

1976, Aug. 25			
382 A67	5s yellow & multi	.25	.25
383 A67	10s multicolored	.40	.25
384 A67	20s multicolored	.90	.50
385 A67	25s multicolored	1.00	.55
386 A67	85s multicolored	2.75	2.75
Nos. 382-386,C199-C203,CO111-CO113 (13)		18.75	16.65

Sesquicentennial of the arrival of Methodist missionaries and establishment of Christianity in Tonga. Printed on peelable paper backing inscribed in manuscript with segments of John Thomas's Tonga diary.

For surcharges see Nos. 415-416, 479-480.

Wilhelm I and George Tupou I — A68

1976, Nov. 1			
387 A68	9s yellow & multi	.35	.35
388 A68	15s yellow & multi	.55	.50
389 A68	22s yellow & multi	.85	.85
390 A68	50s yellow & multi	1.50	1.50
391 A68	73s yellow & multi	2.00	2.00
Nos. 387-391,C204-C208,CO114-CO116 (13)		17.50	17.45

Tonga-Germany Friendship Treaty, centenary. Printed on peelable paper backing showing reproduction of original treaty.

Queen Salote in Coronation Procession, 1953 — A69

1977, Feb. 7		Litho.	
392 A69	11s blue & multi	.40	.40
393 A69	20s green & multi	.50	.50
394 A69	30s vio blue & multi	.30	.30
395 A69	50s lt green & multi	.45	.45
396 A69	75s violet & multi	.80	.80
Nos. 392-396,C209-C213,CO117-CO119 (13)		45.80	23.55

25th anniv. of the reign of Elizabeth II. Printed on peelable paper backing showing replica of handwritten Proclamation of Accession.
For surcharge see No. 417.

Various Coins — A70

1977, July 4			
397 A70	10s multicolored	.25	.25
398 A70	15s multicolored	.30	.30
399 A70	22s multicolored	.40	.40
400 A70	50s multicolored	.85	.85
401 A70	75s multicolored	1.50	1.50
Nos. 397-401,C214-C218,CO120-CO122 (13)		13.50	13.50

10th anniversary of coronation of King Taufa'ahau IV. Printed on peelable paper backing showing multicolored replicas of Tongan stamps.

Capt. Cook's Resolution — A71

1977, Sept. 27		Litho.	
402 A71	10s multicolored	1.00	.75
403 A71	17s multicolored	2.25	1.25
404 A71	25s multicolored	2.50	2.50
405 A71	30s multicolored	3.50	3.00
406 A71	40s multicolored	3.50	3.00
Nos. 402-406,C219-C223,CO123-CO125 (13)		81.95	61.90

Bicentenary of Capt. Cook's farewell voyage.

Humpback Whale — A72

1977, Dec. 16			
407 A72	15s ultra & black	4.25	.85
408 A72	22s green & black	4.50	1.50
409 A72	31s orange & black	5.25	2.00
410 A72	38s lilac & black	5.50	5.25
411 A72	64s red & black	9.25	5.50
Nos. 407-411,C224-C228,CO126-CO128 (13)		87.25	38.15

Whale protection.

Stamps of 1975-77 Surcharged in Black, Green, Brown or Black on Silver

1978, Feb. 17			
412 A61	15s on 20s (#359;B)	2.00	1.75
413 A62	15s on 5s (#362;B)	2.00	1.75
414 A65	15s on 10s (#373;G)	2.00	1.75
415 A67	15s on 5s (#382;Br)	2.00	1.75
416 A67	15s on 10s (#383;B)	2.00	1.75
417 A69	15s on 11s (#392;B on S)	2.00	3.00
418 OA11	15s on 38s (#CO99;B)	2.00	1.75
Nos. 412-418,C229-C238 (17)		79.75	70.50

The surcharge on No. 413 is only the "1," and on No. 418 includes "postage."

Flags of Canada and Tonga A73

1978, May 5		Litho.	
419 A73	10s red & multi	.25	.25
420 A73	15s red & multi	.35	.35
421 A73	20s red & multi	.45	.45

422 A73	25s red & multi	.60	.60
423 A73	45s red & multi	2.00	2.00
Nos. 419-423,C239-C243,CO129-CO131 (13)		14.05	14.05

11th Commonwealth Games, Edmonton, Canada, Aug. 3-12. See note after No. 226.

King Taufa'ahau IV — A74

1978, July 4			
424 A74	2s multicolored	.25	.25
425 A74	5s multicolored	.25	.25
426 A74	10s multicolored	.25	.25
427 A74	25s multicolored	.65	.65
428 A74	75s multicolored	2.00	2.00
Nos. 424-428,C244-C248,CO132-CO134 (13)		13.10	13.10

60th birthday of King Taufa'ahau IV. See note after No. 226.

Two Bananas
A75

Coconut — A76

Designs: 1s to 5s, Bananas. 6s to 10s, Coconuts. 15s to 1pa, Pineapples.

1978, Sept. 29		Typo.	
429 A75	1s yellow & black	.30	.30
430 A75	2s yellow & dk blue	.30	.30
431 A75	3s multicolored	.40	.40
432 A75	4s multicolored	.40	.40
433 A75	5s multicolored	.40	.40
434 A76	6s multicolored	.60	.60
435 A76	7s multicolored	.60	.60
436 A76	8s multicolored	.60	.60
437 A76	9s multicolored	.60	.60
438 A76	10s brown & green	.60	.60
439 A76	15s green & lt brown	1.75	1.75
440 A76	20s multicolored	2.00	2.00
441 A76	30s multicolored	2.25	2.25
442 A76	50s multicolored	2.75	2.75
443 A76	1pa multicolored	3.25	3.25
Nos. 429-443,O36-O50 (30)		31.95	31.95

Nos. 429-443 issued in coils; self-adhesive control numbers on paper backing, except on 1s and 5s. See note after No. 226.
See No. 529.

Whale — A77

1978, Dec. 15   Litho. & Typo.
444 A77	15s shown	4.00	2.00
445 A77	18s Bat	4.00	2.00
446 A77	25s Turtle	4.00	2.00
447 A77	28s Parrot	6.50	3.00
448 A77	60s like 15s	10.50	6.00

Nos. 444-448,C249-
C253,CO150-CO152 (13)   85.75 45.50

Wildlife conservation. See note after No. 226.

Introduction of Metric System — A78

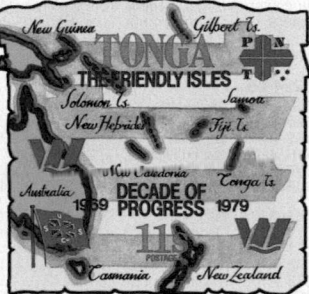

Shipping Routes, South Pacific
Map — A79

Peace
Corps — A80

22s, New church buildings. 50s, Air routes to Auckland, Suva, Apia & Pago Pago.

1979, Feb. 16   Litho.
449 A78	5s multicolored	.25	.25
450 A79	11s multicolored	.60	.60
451 A80	18s multicolored	.60	.60
452 A79	22s multicolored	.60	.60
453 A79	50s multicolored	2.25	2.25

Nos. 449-453,C254-
C258,CO153-CO155 (13)   19.30 16.30

Decade of Progress. Paper backing shows map of Tonga.

Tongan First Day Covers — A81

1979, June 1   Litho.
454 A81	5s multicolored	.30	.25
455 A81	10s multicolored	.40	.30
456 A81	25s multicolored	.70	.60

457 A81	50s multicolored	1.25	1.25
458 A81	1pa multicolored	1.75	1.75

Nos. 454-458,C259-
C263,CO156-CO158 (13)   14.15 12.65

10th anniversary of introduction of self-adhesive stamps and for Bernard Mechanick, inventor of self-adhesive, free-form stamps; death centenary of Sir Rowland Hill.

Printed on peelable paper backing showing advertisement.

For surcharges and overprints see Nos. 469-473.

Eua Island through Camera
Lens — A82

1979, Nov. 23   Litho.
459 A82	10s multicolored	.40	.40
460 A82	18s multicolored	.45	.45
461 A82	31s multicolored	.80	.80
462 A82	50s multicolored	1.25	1.25
463 A82	60s multicolored	1.40	1.40

Nos. 459-463,C275-
C279,CO170-CO172 (13)   13.35 13.35

Printed on peelable paper backing showing film and camera.

King George Tupou I, Admiral du
Bouzet, Map of Tonga — A83

1980, Jan. 9   Litho.
464 A83	7s multicolored	.30	.30
465 A83	10s multicolored	.40	.40
466 A83	14s multicolored	.50	.50
467 A83	50s multicolored	1.50	1.50
468 A83	75s multicolored	2.00	2.00

Nos. 464-468,C280-
C284,CO173-CO175 (13)   14.85 14.85

Tongan-French Friendship Treaty, 125th anniversary. Printed on peelable paper; multicolored backing shows map of Tonga.

Nos. 454-458 Surcharged and Overprinted in Black on Silver: "1980 OLYMPIC GAMES," Moscow '80 and Bear Emblems

1980, Apr. 30   Litho.
469 A81	13s on 5s multi	.50	.50
470 A81	20s on 10s multi	.75	.75
471 A81	25s multicolored	.90	.90
472 A81	33s on 50s multi	1.10	1.10
473 A81	1pa multicolored	3.50	3.50

Nos. 469-473,C285-
C289,CO176-CO178 (13)   18.15 18.15

Boy Scout Cooking over
Campfire — A84

1980, Sept. 30   Litho.
474 A84	9s multicolored	.25	.25
475 A84	13s multicolored	.40	.40
476 A84	15s multicolored	.45	.45
477 A84	30s multicolored	.90	.90

Nos. 474-477,C290-
C293,CO179-CO180 (10)   17.00 17.00

Boy Scout Jamboree; Rotary Intl., 75th anniv. Peelable backing shows map of Tonga.

Nos. 361, 375, 380, 384-385 Surcharged

1980, Dec. 3   Litho.
478 A65	9s on 35s multi	.50	.50
479 A67	13s on 20s multi	.75	.75
480 A67	13s on 25s multi	.75	.75
481 A66	19s on 35s multi	1.10	1.10
482 A61	1pa on 65s multi	6.25	6.25

Nos. 478-482,C294-
C299,CO181 (12)   27.85 27.85

Intl. Year of the Disabled — A85

1981, Sept. 9   Litho.
483 A85	2pa multicolored	3.25	3.25
484 A85	3pa multicolored	5.00	5.00

Nos. 483-484,C300-C302 (5)   10.45 10.45

Prince
Charles and
Lady
Diana — A86

Designs: 13s, Charles, King Taufa'ahau. 47s, 1.50pa, Couple, diff.

1981, Oct. 21   Litho.
485 A86	13s multicolored	.75	.50
486 A86	47s multicolored	1.00	.50
487 A86	1.50pa multicolored	1.50	1.75
488 A86	3pa multicolored	2.00	3.25

Nos. 485-488 (4)   5.25 6.00

Royal Wedding and Gt. Britain-Tonga Friendship Treaty centenary. Issued in sheets of 20 (2x10) and 5 labels in vert. center row. For surcharge see No. B1.

Bicentenary
of Discovery
of Vavau by
Francisco
Maurelle
A87

18th century Spanish engravings and maps.

1981, Nov. 25   Litho.
489 A87	9s multicolored	.60	.50
490 A87	13s multicolored	.90	.60
491 A87	47s multicolored	2.75	1.40
492 A87	1pa multicolored	3.75	3.75
a.	Souvenir sheet, imperf.	9.00	9.00

Nos. 489-492 (4)   8.00 6.25

No. 492a contains one No. 492 (32x25mm).

Bible Class, 1830 Print — A88

1981, Nov. 25
493 A88	9s Open book	.25	.25
494 A88	13s Book, diff.	.50	.40
495 A88	32s Type	.90	.90
496 A88	47s shown	1.60	1.60

Nos. 493-496 (4)   3.25 3.15

Christmas 1981 and sesquicentennial of books printed in Tonga.

175th Anniv. of Capture of The Port-au-Prince — A89

1981, Dec. 16   Litho.
497 A89	29s Battle	1.00	.75
498 A89	32s Battle, diff.	1.25	.90
499 A89	47s Map	1.00	1.50
500 A89	47s Sinking ship	1.60	1.50
a.	Pair, #499-500	3.25	
501 A89	1pa Ship	3.50	3.50

Nos. 497-501 (5)   8.95 8.15

Nos. CO179-CO180 Surcharged

1982, Jan. 4   Litho.
502 OA19	5pa on 25s multi	17.50	17.50
503 OA19	5pa on 2pa multi	17.50	17.50

Scouting
Year — A90

29s, Brownsea Isld. Camp, 1907. 32s, Baden-Powell, horse. 47s, Imperial Jamboree, 1924. 1.50pa, "Scouting for Boys". 2.50pa, Mafeking stamp.

1982, Feb. 22   Litho.
504 A90	29s multicolored	1.00	.60
505 A90	32s multicolored	1.00	.65
506 A90	47s multicolored	1.50	1.00
507 A90	1.50pa multicolored	4.00	4.00
508 A90	2.50pa multicolored	5.50	6.00

Nos. 504-508 (5)   13.00 12.25

1982 World
Cup — A91

Designs: Various soccer players, map showing match sites.

1982, July 7 — Litho.
509	A91	32s multicolored	.85	.60
510	A91	47s multicolored	1.25	.85
511	A91	75s multicolored	1.40	1.40
512	A91	1.50pa multicolored	3.00	2.50
		Nos. 509-512 (4)	6.50	5.35

Inter-island Transport A92

9s, 13s, Ferry Olovaha. 47s, 1pa SPIA Twin Otter (Niuatoputapu Airport opening).

1982, Aug. 11
513	A92	9s multicolored	.50	.25
514	A92	13s multicolored	.60	.30
515	A92	47s multicolored	2.00	1.00
516	A92	1pa multicolored	3.25	2.75
		Nos. 513-516 (4)	6.35	4.30

Tin Can Mail Centenary A93

13s, 32s, 47s, Collecting mail. 2pa, Map. Nos. 517-519 form continuous design.

1982, Sept. 29 — Litho.
517	A93	13s multicolored	.25	.25
518	A93	32s multicolored	.55	.55
519	A93	47s multicolored	.90	.90
a.		Souv. sheet of 3 (13s, 32s, 47s)	2.00	2.00
520	A93	2pa multicolored	2.00	2.00
a.		Souvenir sheet of 1	3.00	3.00
		Nos. 517-520 (4)	3.70	3.70

No. 520 comes with different labels. For surcharges see Nos. 526-528.

Tonga College Centenary — A94

1982, Oct. 25   Size: 42x30mm (5s)
521	A94	5s Students	.35	.35
522	A94	29s King George Tupou I	2.25	2.25
523	A94	29s Monument	2.25	2.25
a.		Pair, #522-523	5.00	
		Nos. 521-523 (3)	4.85	4.85

Nos. 521-523 inscribed in English or Tongan.

12th Commonwealth Games, Brisbane, Australia, Sept. 30-Oct. 9 — A95

1982, Oct. 25
524	A95	32s Decathlon, vert.	1.00	.75
525	A95	1.50pa Opening ceremony	8.00	8.00

Nos. 517-519 Overprinted in Red or Silver in 1 or 2 Lines: "Christmas / Greetings / 1982"

1982, Nov. 17
526	A93	13s multicolored	.30	.30
527	A93	32s multicolored	.70	.70
528	A93	47s multicolored	1.00	1.00
		Nos. 526-528 (3)	2.00	2.00

Pineapple Type of 1978 and

Fruit — A96

1982, Nov. 17
529	A76	13s multicolored	5.50	5.50
530	A96	2pa multicolored	12.00	12.00
531	A96	3pa multicolored	15.00	15.00
		Nos. 529-531 (3)	32.50	32.50

Capt. Cook's Resolution, 1777 and Canberra, 1983 — A96a

32s, like 29s. 47s, 1.50pa, Montgolfier Bros. balloon, 1783, Concorde. 2.50pa, Concorde, Canberra. 29s se-tenant with label showing Resolution.

1983, Feb. 22 — Litho.
532	A96a	29s multicolored	2.25	1.50
533	A96a	32s multicolored	3.00	1.50
534	A96a	47s multicolored	4.25	2.50
535	A96a	1.50pa multicolored	11.00	11.00
		Nos. 532-535 (4)	20.50	16.50

Souvenir Sheet
536	A96a	2.50pa multicolored	6.50	6.50

Pacific Forum of Sea and Air Transport (29s, 32s, 2.50pa); manned flight bicentenary (47s, 1.50pa).
For overprints see Nos. O68-O70.

A96b

29s, Map. 32s, Dancers. 47s, Fishermen. 1.50pa, King Taufa'ahau IV, flag.

1983, Mar. 14
537	A96b	29s multi	1.00	1.00
538	A96b	32s multi	5.00	5.00
539	A96b	47s multi	2.00	2.00
540	A96b	1.50pa multi	2.00	2.00
		Nos. 537-540 (4)	10.00	10.00

Commonwealth Day.

Niuafo'ou Airport Opening A97

1983, May 11 — Litho.
541	A97	32s De Havilland Otter	.90	.50
542	A97	47s like 32s	1.25	.50
543	A97	1pa Boeing 707	2.10	1.40
544	A97	1.50pa like 1pa	3.25	1.70
		Nos. 541-544 (4)	7.50	4.50

World Communications Year — A98

1983, June 22 — Litho.
545	A98	29s Intelsat IV	.50	.50
546	A98	32s Intelsat IV-A	.60	.60
547	A98	75s Intelsat V	1.40	1.40

Size: 45x32mm
548	A98	2pa Apollo 15 Moon post cover	3.00	3.00
		Nos. 545-548 (4)	5.50	5.50

10th Anniv. of Bank of Tonga A99

Various banknotes.

1983, Aug. 3 — Litho.
549	A99	1pa multicolored	2.25	2.25
550	A99	2pa multicolored	3.75	3.75

Printing Press, 1830 — A100

1983, Sept. 22 — Litho.
551	A100	13s shown	.30	.30
552	A100	32s Woon's arrival, 1831	.75	.75
553	A100	1pa Print	1.75	1.75
554	A100	2pa Tonga Chronicle	2.40	2.40
		Nos. 551-554 (4)	5.20	5.20

Sesquicentennial of printing in Tonga (by missionary William Woon).

Christmas 1983 A101

Designs: Various sailboats off Vava'u.

1983, Nov. 17 — Litho.
555	A101	29s multicolored	.50	.40
556	A101	32s multicolored	.60	.50
557	A101	1.50pa multicolored	2.40	2.40
558	A101	2.50pa multicolored	4.00	4.00
		Nos. 555-558 (4)	7.50	7.30

Abel Tasman, Discoverer of Tonga, and his Zeehan — A102

Navigators and Explorers of the Pacific and their Ships — 47s, Samuel Wallis, Dolphin. 90s, William Bligh, Bounty. 1.50pa, James Cook, Resolution.

1984, Mar. 12 — Litho.
559	A102	32s shown	2.00	2.00
560	A102	47s multi	2.75	2.75
561	A102	90s multi	5.00	5.00
562	A102	1.50pa multi	7.00	7.00
		Nos. 559-562 (4)	16.75	16.75

See Nos. 593-596.

Swainsonia Casta — A103

Shells, fish — 2s, Porites (coral). 3s, Holocentrus ruber. 5s, Cypraea mappa viridis. 6s, Dardanus megistos (crab). 9s, Stegostoma fasciatum. 10s, Conus bullatus. 13s, Pterois volitans. 15s, Conus textile. 20s, Dascyllus aruanus. 29s, Conus aulicus. 32s, Acanthurus leucosternon. 47s, Lambis truncata. 1pa, Millepora dichotama (coral). 2pa, Birgus latro (crab). 3pa, Chicoreus palma-rosae. 5pa, Thunnus albacares.

1984-85 — Litho.
563	A103	1s shown	.50	*1.90*
564	A103	2s multi	1.25	*1.90*
565	A103	3s multi	1.60	*2.25*
566	A103	5s multi	.60	*1.90*
567	A103	6s multi	1.60	*2.25*
568	A103	9s multi	1.60	.90
a.		Perf. 14½ ('85)	1.60	.90
569	A103	10s multi	1.25	.95
570	A103	13s multi	1.90	.95
571	A103	15s multi	1.25	*2.25*
572	A103	20s multi	2.75	2.75
573	A103	32s multi	2.25	1.25
574	A103	32s multi	4.00	1.25
575	A103	47s multi	4.00	2.00

Size: 39x25mm
576	A103	1pa multi	12.00	12.00
577	A103	2pa multi	17.50	*19.00*
578	A103	3pa multi	11.00	*19.00*
579	A103	5pa multi	13.50	*22.50*
		Nos. 563-579 (17)	78.55	95.00

See Nos. 682-692, 701-709, 756-759. For surcharges and overprints see Nos. 618-625, 808-810, O52-O67, O71-O77.

Tonga Chronicle, 20th Anniv. — A104

1984, June 26
580	A104	3s multicolored	.25	.25
a.		Sheet of 12	.75	
581	A104	32s multicolored	.60	.60
a.		Sheet of 12	7.00	

Nos. 580-581 issued in sheets of 12; sheet backgrounds show pages of Chronicle, giving each stamp different background.

1984 Summer Olympics A105

1984, July 23
582	A105	29s Running	.40	.40
583	A105	47s Javelin	.65	.65
584	A105	1.50pa Shot put	1.75	1.75
585	A105	3pa Torch	2.25	2.25
		Nos. 582-585 (4)	5.05	5.05

Intl. Dateline Centenary — A106

47s, George Airy, Greenwich Meridian pioneer. 2pa, Sandford Fleming, time zone pioneer.

1984, Aug. 20

586	A106	47s multicolored	2.00	1.50
587	A106	2pa multicolored	7.00	5.50

Ausipex '84 — A107

1984, Sept. 17

588	A107	32s Australia #18	1.25	.85
589	A107	1.50pa Tonga #51	4.50	3.75

Souvenir Sheet

589A	Sheet of 2, #588-589	4.75	4.75

Nos. 588-589 each printed se-tenant with label showing exhibition emblem.

No. 589A contains two imperf. stamps similar to Nos. 588-589, but with denomination replacing logo. No. 589A without denominations was not valid for postage.

Christmas 1984 — A108

Christmas Carols in local settings.

1984, Nov. 12   Litho.

590	A108	32s Silent Night	.90	.50
591	A108	47s Away in a Manger	1.35	.80
592	A108	1pa I Saw Three Ships	2.50	2.50
		Nos. 590-592 (3)	4.75	3.80

Explorers Type of 1984

Designs: 32s, Willem Schouten (c. 1580-1625), The Eendracht, 1616. 47s, Jakob Le Maire (1585-1616), The Hoorn, 1615. 90s, Lt. Fletcher Christian, The Bounty, 1789. 1.50pa, Francisco Maurelle, La Princessa, 1781.

1985, Feb. 27   Litho.   Die Cut

593	A102	32s multicolored	2.50	1.50
a.		Perf. 14	35.00	35.00
594	A102	47s multicolored	3.75	1.75
595	A102	90s multicolored	6.75	5.00
596	A102	1.50pa multicolored	10.00	7.75
		Nos. 593-596 (4)	23.00	16.00

Nos. 593-596 each printed se-tenant with self-adhesive label picturing anchor.

Geological Survey of Tonga Trench for Oil — A110

Designs: 29s, Tonga Trench and islands. 32s, Marine exploration, seismic surveying. 47s, Search for oil off Tongatapu, vert. No. 600, Exploration of sea bed, vert. No. 601, Angler fish.

1985, Apr. 10

597	A110	29s multicolored	1.50	1.10
598	A110	32s multicolored	1.60	1.10
599	A110	47s multicolored	2.50	1.60
600	A110	1.50pa multicolored	8.25	8.25
		Nos. 597-600 (4)	13.85	12.05

Souvenir Sheet

601	A110	1.50pa multicolored	13.00	7.75
a.		Perf. 14	13.00	7.75

Nos. 597-600 printed in sheets of 40, 2 panes of 20 separated by labels inscribed "Proof 1," etc.

Adventures of Will Mariner — A111

29s, Readying Port au Prince for sail, Gravesend, 1805. 32s, Captured & set afire, 1806. 47s, Mariner taken prisoner by Chief Finow, Tonga. 1.50pa, Passage to China aboard brig Favourite. 2.50pa, Returning to England aboard East Indiaman Cuffnells, 1810.

1985, June 18   Die Cut

602	A111	29s multicolored	.60	.50
a.		Perf. 14	.60	.50
603	A111	32s multicolored	.65	.55
a.		Perf. 14	.65	.55
604	A111	47s multicolored	1.00	.80
a.		Perf. 14	1.00	.80
605	A111	1.50pa multicolored	3.75	3.75
a.		Perf. 14	3.75	3.75
606	A111	2.50pa multicolored	6.00	6.00
a.		Perf. 14	6.00	6.00
		Nos. 602-606 (5)	12.00	11.60
		Nos. 602a-606a (5)	12.00	11.60

Mutiny on the Bounty, Film 50th Anniv. A112

Designs: a, Byron Russell (Quintal), Stanley Fields (Muspratt) and Charles Laughton (Capt. Bligh). b, Laughton, Donald Crisp (Burkitt), Eddie Quillon (Ellison) and David Thursby (Maxwell). c, Clark Gable (Fletcher Christian). d, Russell, Alec Craig (McCoy), Laughton and Fields. e, Laughton and Franchot Tone (Roger Byam).

1985, July 16   Perf. 14

607	Strip of 5	57.50	57.50
a.-e.	A112 47s, any single	10.00	5.00

Sheets consist of four strips of 5 and a central strip of labels showing film credits.

Queen Mother, 85th Birthday A113

Designs: 32s, Age 10. 47s, At Hadfield Girl Guides rally, 1931. 1.50pa, In Guide uniform. 2.50pa, Portrait by Norman Parkinson, 1985.

1985, Aug. 20   Imperf.

608	A113	32s multicolored	1.25	.90
a.		Perf. 14	2.00	1.50
609	A113	47s multicolored	2.00	1.50
a.		Perf. 14	3.25	2.40
610	A113	1.50pa multicolored	6.00	6.00
a.		Perf. 14	9.25	9.25
611	A113	2.50pa multicolored	9.75	9.75
a.		Perf. 14	15.00	15.00
		Nos. 608-611 (4)	19.00	18.15
		Nos. 608a-611a (4)	29.50	28.15

Girl Guides movement, 75th anniv.

Christmas — A114

32s, No room at the inn. 42s, Shepherds follow star. 1.50pa, The three kings. 2.50pa, Holy family.

1985, Nov. 12

612	A114	32s multicolored	.50	.35
613	A114	42s multicolored	.75	.50
614	A114	1.50pa multicolored	2.50	2.50
615	A114	2.50pa multicolored	3.50	3.50
		Nos. 612-615 (4)	7.25	6.85

Self-adhesive Discontinued
In 1986, die cut self-adhesive stamps attached to peelable paper backing were no longer issued, unless otherwise stated.

Halley's Comet A115

Designs: Nos. 616a, 617a, Comet. Nos. 616b, 617b, Edmond Halley. Nos. 616c, 617c, Solar system. Nos. 616d, 617d, Telescope. Nos. 616e, 617e, Giotto space probe.

1986, Mar. 26   Perf. 14

616	Strip of 5	19.00	19.00
a.-e.	A115 42s, any single	3.00	3.00
617	Strip of 5	19.00	19.00
a.-e.	A115 57s, any single	3.00	3.00

Nos. 564, 570, 565, 568, 567, 572, 577 and 579 Surcharged

1986, Apr. 16   Litho.   Die Cut

Self-adhesive

618	A103	4s on 2s, #564	1.10	2.25
619	A103	4s on 13s, #570	1.10	2.25
620	A103	42s on 3s, #565	2.90	1.75
621	A103	42s on 9s, #568	2.90	1.75
622	A103	57s on 6s, #567	3.50	2.50
623	A103	57s on 20s, #572	3.50	2.50
624	A103	2.50pa on 2pa, #577	11.00	11.00
625	A103	2.50pa on 5pa, #579	11.00	11.00
		Nos. 618-625 (8)	37.00	35.00

For overprints see Nos. O71-O77.

Royal Links with the United Kingdom — A116

1986, May 22   Perf. 14

626	A116	57s Taufa'ahau IV	1.50	1.50
627	A116	57s Elizabeth II	1.50	1.50
a.		A116 Pair, #626-627	3.50	3.50

Size: 40x40mm

628	A116	2.50pa King and queen	6.00	6.00
		Nos. 626-628 (3)	9.00	9.00

Queen Elizabeth II, 60th birthday. No. 628 printed in sheets of 5 + one label.

AMERIPEX '86, Chicago, May 22-June 1 — A117

Peace Corps activities: No. 629, Health care. No. 630, Education.

1986, May 22

629	A117	57s multicolored	1.10	1.10
630	A117	1.50pa multicolored	2.75	2.75
a.		Souv. sheet, #629, 630, imperf	4.50	4.50
b.		Pair, #629-630	5.75	5.75

Peace Corps in Tonga, 20th anniv.

Intl. Sporting Events — A118

Designs: 42s, 1986 Field Hockey World Cup, London. 57s, Women's basketball, 13th Commonwealth Games, Scotland. 1pa, Boxing, Commonwealth Games. 2.50pa, 1986 World Cup Soccer Championships, Mexico.

1986, July 23   Litho.   Perf. 14

631	A118	42s multicolored	1.25	1.25
632	A118	57s multicolored	2.00	2.00
633	A118	1pa multicolored	3.25	3.25
634	A118	2.50pa multicolored	6.00	6.00
		Nos. 631-634 (4)	12.50	12.50

Postage Stamp Cent. A119

Stamps on stamps: No. 635, #1. No. 636, #47a. No. 637, #91. No. 638, #628. No. 639a, #40, UL portion of #C29. No. 639b, UR portion of #C29, left side #245. No. 639c, Center of #245, Type AP10. No. 639d, Left side #245, #C148. No. 639e, LL portion of #C29, #429, #440. No. 639f, LR portion of #C29, #C135. No. 639g, #507. No. 639h, #514. Nos. 639a-639h, vert.

1986, Aug. 27

635	A119	32s multi	2.50	1.75
636	A119	42s multi	2.75	2.00
637	A119	57s multi	3.00	2.00
638	A119	2.50pa multi	5.00	5.75
		Nos. 635-638 (4)	13.25	11.50

Souvenir Sheet

639	Sheet of 8	13.50	13.50
a.-h.	A119 50s, any single	1.50	1.50

Christmas — A120

Designs: 32s, Girls wearing shell jewelry. 42s, Boy, totem poles, vert. 57s, Folk dancers, vert. 2pa, outrigger canoe.

1986, Nov. 12   Litho.   Perf. 14

640	A120	32s multicolored	2.50	.75
641	A120	42s multicolored	2.75	1.00
642	A120	57s multicolored	3.00	1.50
643	A120	2pa multicolored	7.50	7.50
		Nos. 640-643 (4)	15.75	10.75

Nos. 641-642 Ovptd. with Jamboree Emblem and "BOY SCOUT / JAMBOREE / 5th-10th DEC '86" in Silver

1986, Dec. 2   Litho.   Perf. 14

644	A120	42s multicolored	3.50	3.50
645	A120	57s multicolored	3.75	3.75

Dumont d'Urville's Second Voyage A121

Designs: 32s, D'Urville and ship Astrolabe. 42s, Four Tongan girls, detail from D'Urville's engraving, Voyage au Pole et dans l'Oceanie. 1pa, Map of voyage. 2.50pa, Wreck of the Astrolabe.

1987, Feb. 24

646	A121	32s multicolored	4.25	2.00
647	A121	42s multicolored	4.25	2.00
648	A121	1pa multicolored	10.00	6.00
649	A121	2.50pa multicolored	16.00	16.00
		Nos. 646-649 (4)	34.50	26.00

Dumont d'Urville (1790-1842), explorer and admiral.

Wildlife Conservation — A122

Fauna: a, Noah's Ark. b, Eagles. c, Giraffes, birds. d, Seagulls. e, Elephants, ostriches. f, Elephant. g, Lions, zebras, antelopes. h, Chimpanzees. i, Antelope, frogs. j, Tigers, lizard. k, Tiger, snake. l, Butterfly.

1987, May 6   **Perf. 13½**

650	A122	Sheet of 12	57.50	57.50
a.-l.		42s any single	4.25	4.25

1st Inter-island Canoe Race, Tonga to Samoa — A123

1987, July 1   **Perf. 14**

651	A123	32s Two paddlers	.55	.45
652	A123	42s Five paddlers	.85	.70
653	A123	57s Three paddlers	1.10	.90
654	A123	1.50pa Two, diff.	2.50	2.50
a.		Souvenir sheet of 4, #651-654	7.75	7.75
		Nos. 651-654 (4)	5.00	4.55

Coronation of King Taufa'ahau IV, 20th Anniv. — A124

Booklet Stamps

1987-88   Self-Adhesive   Imperf.

655	A124	1s green & yel grn	.35	.85
655A	A124	2s blk & pale yel org	4.00	4.00
656	A124	5s black & brt pink	.35	.85
a.		Bklt. pane of 12 (6 5s plus 1 5s, 2 10s, 3 15s with gutter between)	5.00	
657	A124	10s black & bluish lil	.45	.95
658	A124	15s brn blk & org ver	.60	.95
a.		Bklt. pane of 12 (1s, 2 2s, 3 10s, plus 2 5s, 10s, 3 15s with gutter between) ('88)	14.00	
659	A124	32s Prus bl & aqua	.70	1.00
a.		Bklt. pane, 4 32s, 2 15s + 4 10s, 2 1s with gutter between)	7.00	
b.		Bklt. pane, 6 32s + 2 2s, 4 1s with gutter btwn. ('88)	14.00	
		Nos. 655-659 (6)	6.45	8.60

Issued: 2s, 7/4/88; others, 7/1/87.

Parliament, 125th Anniv. — A125

1987, Sept. 2   Litho.   Perf. 14½

660	A125	32s multicolored	.50	.50
661	A125	42s multicolored	.75	.75
662	A125	75s multicolored	1.25	1.25
663	A125	2pa multicolored	2.75	2.75
		Nos. 660-663 (4)	5.25	5.25

Christmas 1987 — A126

Cartoons featuring Octopus as Santa Claus and mouse as his helper: 42s, Sack of gifts. 57s, Delivering them by canoe. 1pa, By automobile. 3pa, Sipping tropical drinks.

1987, Nov. 18   Litho.   Perf. 14

664	A126	42s multicolored	1.25	.80
665	A126	57s multicolored	1.50	1.50
666	A126	1pa multicolored	3.00	3.00
667	A126	3pa multicolored	6.50	6.50
		Nos. 664-667 (4)	12.25	11.80

King Taufa'ahau Tupou IV, 70th Birthday — A127

Portrait and: 32s, M.V. Olovaha inter-island ship, athlete pole vaulting and offshore oil derrick. 42s, Banknote and coins, Ha'Amonga Trilithon and traditional craftsman. 57s, Rowing, Red Cross nurse and communications satellite. 2.50pa, Tonga Scouts emblem, No. 506 and Friendly Islands Airways passenger plane.

1988, July 4   Litho.   Perf. 11½

668	A127	32s multicolored	2.25	1.00
669	A127	42s multicolored	1.60	1.10
670	A127	57s multicolored	1.75	1.10
671	A127	2.50pa multicolored	8.00	8.00
		Nos. 668-671 (4)	13.60	11.20

See Nos. 744-747 for stamps inscribed for the silver jubilee.

Souvenir Sheet

Australia Bicentennial — A128

Designs: a, Cook and his journal. b, List of stores shipped aboard the Lady Juliana, the ship, Arthur Philip, 1st gov. of New South Wales, 1788, and left half of the list of sentences of all the prisoners tried at Glo'ster Assizes. c, Right half of list of sentences, Australia Type A59 redrawn and aerial view of an early settlement. d, Robert O'Hara Burke (1820-61) and W.J. Wills (1834-61), the 1st explorers to cross Australia from south to north. e, Emu pictured on a Player's cigarette card, U.R. Stuart's (gold) prospecting license and opals. f, Australian Commonwealth Military Forces emblem, WW I recruit on cigarette card, and war poster. g, Souv. card commemorating 1st overland mail delivery by transcontinental railway, and Australia Type A4 on cover. h, Hand-canceled cover commemorating the 1st England-Australia transcontinental airmail flight, Nov. 12-Dec.10, 1919, aviator Capt. Ross Smith (1892-1922) and Great Britain #588. i, Don Bradman and Harold

---

Larwood, cricket champions of the 1930s, on cigarette cards, and era newspaper frontispiece. j, Frontispiece of Hulton's natl. weekly Picture Post Victory Special issue, and WW II campaign medals. k, Australia #676 and a sheep station. l, Sydney Harbor Bridge, Opera House and theater tickets to The Bartered Bride.

1988, July 11   Litho.   Perf. 13½

672	A128	Sheet of 12	45.00	45.00
a.-l.		42s any single	3.00	3.00

1988 Summer Olympics, Seoul — A129

57s, Running. 75s, Yachting. 2pa, Cycling. 3pa, Women's tennis.

1988, Aug. 11   Perf. 14

673	A129	57s multicolored	.90	.90
674	A129	75s multicolored	1.10	1.10
675	A129	2pa multicolored	7.00	7.00
676	A129	3pa multicolored	6.50	6.50
		Nos. 673-676 (4)	15.50	15.50

Music of Tonga A130

42s, Choir. 57s, Tonga Police Band. 2.50pa, The Jets.

No. 681b, Olympic eternal flame.

1988, Sept. 9   Litho.   Perf. 14

677	A130	32s shown	.40	.40
678	A130	42s multi	.50	.50
679	A130	57s multi	1.25	1.00
680	A130	2.50pa multi	3.00	3.00
		Nos. 677-680 (4)	5.15	4.90

Souvenir Sheet

681		Sheet of 2	4.50	4.50
a.		A130 57s like 2.50pa	1.40	1.40
b.		A130 57s multicolored	1.40	1.40

SPORT AID '88.

Marine Type of 1984

Two types of background shading on No. 690:
Type I: Shading at top and sides extends to vert. & horiz. edges of design.
Type II: Shading is oval shaped.

1988   Litho.   Perf. 14½
Size: 27x34mm

682	A103	1s like No. 563	.30	.30
683	A103	2s like No. 564	.40	.40
684	A103	5s like No. 566	.55	.55
685	A103	6s like No. 567	1.10	1.10
686	A103	10s like No. 569	.65	.65
687	A103	15s like No. 571	.65	.65
688	A103	20s like No. 572	.95	.95
689	A103	32s like No. 574	1.10	1.10
690	A103	42s Fregata ariel, type I	4.00	.95
a.		Type II	35.00	
691	A103	57s Sula leucogaster	4.75	1.25

Size: 41x27mm
Perf. 14

692	A103	3pa Like No. 578	3.00	9.00
		Nos. 682-692 (11)	17.45	16.90

Issued: 1s, 5s, 10s, 20s, 32s, Oct. 4; 2s, 6s, 15s, 42s, 57s, 3pa, Oct. 18.
Nos. 683-684, 686, 689 exist inscribed "1990."
See #701-709. For surcharge see #808.

Tonga-US Treaty, Cent. A131

42s, Resolution. 57s, Santa Maria. 2pa, Capt. Cook, Columbus.

1988, Oct. 20   Perf. 14

693	A131	42s multicolored	1.00	.75
694	A131	57s multicolored	1.50	1.10
695	A131	2pa multicolored	4.50	4.50
a.		Souvenir sheet of 3, #693-695	6.50	6.50
		Nos. 693-695 (3)	7.00	6.35

Christmas — A132

Designs (a, Intl. Red Cross, b, Natl. Red Cross): 15s, Girl, teddy bear. 32s, Nurse reading to child. 42s, Checking pulse. 57s, Tucking child into bed. 1.50pa, Boy in wheelchair.

1988, Nov. 17   Litho.   Perf. 14½

696	A132	15s Pair, #a.-b.	.50	.50
697	A132	32s Pair, #a.-b.	1.00	1.00
698	A132	42s Pair, #a.-b.	1.10	1.10
699	A132	57s Pair, #a.-b.	1.90	1.90
700	A132	1.50pa Pair, #a.-b.	3.75	3.75
		Nos. 696-700 (5)	8.25	8.25

Intl. Red Cross 125th anniv. and 25th anniv. of the natl. Red Cross.

Marine Type of 1984

7s, Diomedea exulans. 35s, Hippocampus. 1pa, Chelonia mydas. 1.50pa, Megaptera novaeangliae.

1989, Mar. 2   Litho.
Size: 27x34mm

701	A103	4s like No. 570	1.90	1.90
702	A103	7s multicolored	4.50	3.00
703	A103	35s multicolored	4.00	3.25
704	A103	50s like No. 573	4.50	2.40

Size: 41x27mm
Perf. 14

705	A103	1pa multicolored	7.25	5.50
706	A103	1.50pa multicolored	14.50	9.00
707	A103	2pa like No. 577	10.50	10.50
709	A103	5pa like No. 579	17.00	20.00
		Nos. 701-709 (8)	64.15	55.55

Mutiny on the Bounty, Bicent. — A133

32s, Map of Tofua & Kao Isls., breadfruit. 42s, Bounty, chronometer. 57s, William Bligh & castaways in longboat. 2pa, Mutineers on the Bounty, vert. 3pa, Castaways.

Perf. 13½x14, 14x13½

1989, Apr. 28   Photo.

710	A133	32s multicolored	4.50	2.50
711	A133	42s multicolored	6.50	3.25
712	A133	57s multicolored	8.00	4.75
		Nos. 710-712 (3)	19.00	10.50

Souvenir Sheet

713		Sheet of 2	15.00	15.00
a.		A133 2pa multicolored	5.00	5.00
b.		A133 3pa multicolored	7.50	7.50

Butterflies A134

42s, Hypolimnas bolina. 57s, Jamides bochus. 1.20pa, Melanitis leda solandra. 2.50pa, Danaus plexippus.

1989, May 15   Litho.   Perf. 14½

714	A134	42s multi	1.25	.85
715	A134	57s multi	1.50	1.10
716	A134	1.20pa multi	3.75	2.75
717	A134	2.50pa multi	5.50	5.50
		Nos. 714-717 (4)	12.00	10.20

A135

Rugby (No. 718): a, Rugby Public School, 1870. b, Dave Gallaher and the Springboks vs. East Midlands, 1906. c, King George V inspecting Cambridge team of 1922 and Wavell Wakefield, captain of England. d, Ernie Crawford, captain of Ireland, Danie Craven demonstrating the dive pass and cigarette cards from the 1930's. e, Sioni Mafi, captain of Tonga, and match scene.

Tennis (No. 719): a, Royal tennis, 1659. b, Walter Clopton Wingfield and game of lawn tennis, 1873. c, Oxford and Cambridge teams of 1884. d, Bunny Ryan in 1910 and cigarette cards. e, Tennis players, 1980's.

Cricket (No. 720): a, Match in 1743 and bronze memorial to Fuller Pilch. b, W.G. Grace, 19th cent. c, *The Boys Own Paper*, 1909. d, Australian team of 1909 and cigarette cards. e, The Ashes trophy and modern match scene.

1989, Aug. 22   Litho.   Perf. 14
718		Strip of 5	6.25	6.25
a.-e.		A135 32s any single	1.00	1.00
719		Strip of 5	9.50	9.50
a.-e.		A135 42s any single	1.50	1.50
720		Strip of 5	14.50	14.50
a.-e.		A135 57s any single	2.50	2.50
		Nos. 718-720 (3)	30.25	30.25

Opening of the Natl. Sports Stadium and the South Pacific Mini Games, Aug. 22.
Printed in sheets of 10 containing descriptions and emblem.

Natl. Aviation History — A136

Designs: 42s, Short S30. 57s, Vought F4U Corsair. 90s, Boeing 737. 3pa, Montgolfier brothers' hot-air balloon, the Wright Flyer, Concorde jet and space shuttle.

1989, Oct. 23   Litho.   Perf. 14½x14
721	A136	42s multicolored	3.25	1.60
722	A136	57s multicolored	3.75	2.00
723	A136	90s multicolored	6.50	6.00

Size: 97x126½mm
724	A136	3pa multicolored	16.00	16.00
		Nos. 721-724 (4)	29.50	25.60

1st Flight to Tonga, 1939 (42s); military base on the island, 1943 (57s); civil aviation, Fua'amotu Airport (90s); aviation through the ages (3pa).

Flying Home for Christmas A137

32s, Aircraft landing. 42s, Islanders waving, aircraft. 57s, Tongan in outrigger canoe, aircraft. 3pa, Islanders waving, aircraft, diff.

1989, Nov. 9   Perf. 14x13½
725	A137	32s multi	2.40	1.10
726	A137	42s multi	2.75	1.10
727	A137	57s multi	3.00	1.50
728	A137	3pa multi	8.00	8.00
		Nos. 725-728 (4)	16.15	11.70

World Stamp Expo '89 A138

20th UPU Congress, Washington, DC — A139

Postal history and communications (No. 730): a, Sir Rowland Hill, penny blacks on Mulready envelope. b, Clipper ship, early train. c, Pony Express advertisement, stagecoach, post rider. d, Hot-air balloon and flight cover. e, Samuel Morse, miniature, telegraph key. f, Early Royal Mail truck, mailbox. g, Biplane and early aviators. h, Zeppelin flight cover, HMS *Queen Mary*. i, Helicopter, truck. j, Computer operator, facsimile machine. k, Apollo 11 mission emblem, flight cover, planetary bodies. l, American space shuttle, UPU monument.

1989, Nov. 17   Litho.   Perf. 14
729	A138	57s #730k-730l	3.50	3.50

Souvenir Sheet
Perf. 13½
730	A139		Sheet of 12	47.50	47.50
a.-l.		A139 57s any single	2.75	2.75

A140

1990, Feb. 14   Litho.   Perf. 14
731	A140	42s Boxing	1.25	.75
732	A140	57s Archery	2.25	1.50
733	A140	1pa Bowls	2.50	2.50
734	A140	2pa Swimming	4.50	4.50
		Nos. 731-734 (4)	10.50	9.25

1990 Commonwealth Games.

Protect the Environment A141

32s, Wave power, ocean pollution. 57s, Wind power, acid rain. $1.20, Solar power, ozone layer. $2.50, Green earth, rain forests.

1990, Apr. 11   Litho.   Perf. 14
735	A141	32s multicolored	2.00	.90
736	A141	57s multicolored	3.00	1.50
737	A141	1.20pa multicolored	6.00	6.00
		Nos. 735-737 (3)	11.00	8.40

Souvenir Sheet
738	A141	2.50pa multicolored	11.00	11.00

First Postage Stamps, 150th Anniv. A142

1990   Litho.   Perf. 14
739	A142	42s G. B. #1	2.10	1.50
740	A142	42s G. B. #2	2.10	1.50
a.		Pair, #739-740	3.75	3.75
741	A142	57s Tonga #1	2.50	1.50
742	A142	1.50pa Tonga #CO180	5.00	5.00
743	A142	2.50pa Tonga #736	7.00	7.00
		Nos. 739-743 (5)	18.70	16.50

King's Birthday Type of 1988
Inscribed "Silver Jubilee of His Majesty King Taufa'ahau Tupou IV 1965-1990"

1990, July 4   Litho.   Perf. 11½
744	A127	32s like No. 668	1.50	1.00
745	A127	42s like No. 669	1.50	1.00
746	A127	57s like No. 670	2.25	1.25
747	A127	2.50pa like No. 671	7.75	7.75
		Nos. 744-747 (4)	13.00	11.00

Native Catamaran — A143

1990, June 6   Perf. 14½
748	A143	32s buff & green	1.60	.75
749	A143	42s buff & bl, diff.	1.60	.85
750	A143	1.20pa buff & brn, diff.	3.75	3.75
751	A143	3pa buff & vio, diff.	7.00	7.00
		Nos. 748-751 (4)	13.95	12.35

Randed Iguana A144

1990, Sept. 12   Litho.   Perf. 14
752	A144	32s multicolored	2.00	1.25
753	A144	42s buff & bl. diff.	2.50	1.75
754	A144	57s multi, diff.	3.25	2.25
755	A144	1.20pa multi, diff.	6.25	4.75
		Nos. 752-755 (4)	14.00	10.00

Marine Type of 1984

1990, July 6   Litho.   Perf. 14
Size: 20x22mm
756	A103	2s like No. 564	1.25	.85
a.		Booklet pane of 10	12.50	12.50
757	A103	5s like No. 566	1.25	.85
a.		Booklet pane of 10	12.50	12.50
758	A103	10s like No. 569	1.25	.85
a.		Booklet pane of 10	12.50	12.50
759	A103	32s like No. 574	2.25	2.25
a.		Booklet pane of 10	22.50	22.50
		Nos. 756-759 (4)	6.00	4.80

Nos. 756-758 exist inscribed "1992."
For surcharges see Nos. 809-810.
Issue date: #756a-759a, Sept. 4.

UN Development Program, 40th Anniv. — A145

No. 760, Tourism. No. 761, Agriculture, fisheries. No. 762, Education. No. 763, Healthcare.

1990, Oct. 25   Litho.   Perf. 14
760	A145	57s multicolored	2.00	2.00
761	A145	57s multicolored	2.00	2.00
a.		Pair, #760-761	4.50	4.50
762	A145	3pa multicolored	8.00	8.00
763	A145	3pa multicolored	8.00	8.00
a.		Pair, #762-763	18.50	18.50
		Nos. 760-763 (4)	20.00	20.00

Rotary Intl. — A146

1990, Nov. 28
764	A146	32s shown	1.00	.55
765	A146	42s Two boys	1.50	.80
766	A146	2pa Three children	4.00	4.00
767	A146	3pa Two girls	5.50	5.50
		Nos. 764-767 (4)	12.00	10.85

Accident Prevention — A147

No. 768: a, d, Care at work; hard hats save lives. b, c, Keep matches and medicines out of children's reach. e, as "d," corrected inscription

No. 769: a, d, Don't drink and drive. b, c, Crash helmets save lives; mind cyclists and children.

No. 770: a, d, Listen to forecasts; learn to swim. b, c, Swim from safe beaches; beware of broken glass.

"a" and "b" have English inscriptions, denominations at top; "c" and "d" have Tongan inscriptions, denominations at bottom.

Strips of 4 + Label

1991, Apr. 10   Litho.   Perf. 14½
768	A147	32s #a.-d.	4.50	4.50
f.		Strip of 4, #a.-c., e.	35.00	
769	A147	42s #a.-d.	7.50	7.50
770	A147	57s #a.-d.	8.50	8.50
		Nos. 768-770 (3)	20.50	20.50

Center label is a progressive proof.
No. 768d was incorrectly inscribed, "Ngauo tokanga." No. 768e was issued 8/11/91 with correct inscription, "Ngaue tokanga."
For surcharges see No. 811, 1124.

Heilala Week — A148

1991, July 2   Litho.   Perf. 14½
771	A148	42s Fish	.80	.70
772	A148	57s Island, boat	.95	.85
773	A148	2pa Fruit, island	3.50	3.50
774	A148	3pa Turtle, beach	6.25	6.25
		Nos. 771-774 (4)	11.50	11.30

Around the World Yacht Race — A149

Racing yachts: a, Red spinnaker. b, Yellow spinnaker. c, Green striped spinnaker. d, Yacht at sunset. e, Yacht, moon.

Miniature Sheet of 5 + Label

1991, July 2
775	A149	1pa #775a-775e	11.00	11.00

Church of Jesus
Christ of Latter
Day Saints in
Tonga,
Cent. — A150

1991, Aug. 19
776 A150 42s Tonga Temple   1.75 1.75
777 A150 57s Temple at night   2.75 2.75

Rowing
Festival
A151

42s, Women's coxed eight. 57s, Men's longboat. 1pa, Outrigger. No. 781, Bow of large
canoe. No. 782, Stern of large canoe.

1991, Oct. 29   Litho.   Perf. 14
778 A151 42s multicolored   1.00 1.00
779 A151 57s multicolored   1.50 1.50
780 A151 1pa multicolored   2.75 2.75
781 A151 2pa multicolored   4.50 4.50
782 A151 2pa multicolored   4.50 4.50
  a. Pair, #781-782   9.00 9.00
     Nos. 778-782 (5)   14.25 14.25

For surcharges see Nos. 898-899C.

Telecommunications — A152

No. 783: a, Recording television program. b,
Communications Satellite. c, Watching television program.
No. 784: a, Man on telephone, woman at
computer. b, Communications satellite, diff. c,
Man in city on telephone.
No. 785: a, Seaman on sinking ship broadcasting SOS. b, Man on telephone, satellite
relay station. c, Rescue missions.
No. 786: a, Weather satelite. b, Men at computers. c, Television weather report, storm.

1991, Oct. 15   Litho.   Perf. 14½
783 A152 15s Strip of 3, #a.-c.   1.50 1.50
784 A152 32s Strip of 3, #a.-c.   3.00 3.00
785 A152 42s Strip of 3, #a.-c.   4.25 4.25
786 A152 57s Strip of 3, #a.-c.   6.00 6.00
     Nos. 783-786 (4)   14.75 14.75

For surcharges, see 1095-1098.

Christmas — A153

Designs: 32s, Turtles pulling Santa's sleigh.
42s, Santa on roof. 57s, Family with presents.
3.50pa, Waving goodbye to Santa.

1991, Nov. 11   Perf. 14
787 A153 32s multicolored   1.00   .70
788 A153 42s multicolored   1.25   .90
789 A153 57s multicolored   1.75 1.75
790 A153 3.50pa multicolored 8.25 8.25
     Nos. 787-790 (4)   12.25 11.60

For surcharges, see 1120-1122.

Armed Forces — A154

1991, Dec. 15
791 42s Royal Tonga Marine   1.00 1.00
792 42s Patrol boat Pangai   1.00 1.00
  a. A154 Pair, #791-792   2.50 2.50
793 57s Patrol boat Neiafu   1.50 1.50
794 57s Tonga Royal Guards   1.50 1.50
  a. A154 Pair, #793-794   3.50 3.50
795 2pa King Tupou IV, mili-
       tary parade   5.25 5.25
796 2pa Patrol boat Savea   5.25 5.25
  a. A154 Pair, #795-796   11.00 11.00
     Nos. 791-796 (6)   15.50 15.50

Miniature Sheet

Discovery of America, 500th
Anniv. — A155

Designs: a, Columbus. b, Monastery of
Santa Maria de la Chevas. c, Obverse and
reverse of coin of Ferdinand and Isabella. d,
Spain #C48, #426. e, Compass, astrolabe. f,
Santa Maria. g, Map, Columbus' signature. h,
Columbus arriving in New World. i, Lucayan
artifacts, parrot. j, Pineapple, artifacts. k,
Columbus announcing his discovery. l, Medal
of Columbus, signature.

1992, Apr. 28   Litho.   Perf. 13½
797 A155 57s Sheet of 12,
       #a.-l.   42.50 42.50

Marine Type of 1984 and

A155a

1s, Swainsonia casta. 3s, Holocentrus
ruber. 5s, Cypraea mappa viridis. 10s, Conus
bullatus. 20s, Dascyllus aruanus. 45s, Lambis
truncata. 60s, Conus aulicus. 80s, Pterois
volitans.

Perf. 13x13½, 14 (15s, 20s, 10pa)
1992-93   Litho.
798 A155a 1s multicolored   .25   .25
799 A155a 3s multicolored   .25   .25
800 A155a 5s multicolored   .25   .25
801 A155a 10s multicolored   .25   .25
802 A103   15s like #567   .30   .30
803 A155a 20s multicolored   .35   .35
804 A155a 45s multicolored   .75   .75
805 A155a 60s multicolored   1.00 1.00
806 A155a 80s multicolored   1.40 1.40

Size: 27x41mm
807 A103 10pa like #568   20.00 20.00
     Nos. 798-807 (10)   24.80 24.80

Issued: 1s, 3s, 5s, 10s, 20s, 45s, 60s, 80s,
May 12, 1993. 15s, 10pa, May 5, 1992.
See Nos. 874-884. Area covered by back-
ground colors on Nos. 874, 876-879 has been
reduced in size. See Nos. 920-924.
For inscribed stamps see Nos. O78-O87.

Surcharges

On #688

On #756 in
Blue

On #759

On #769 in Red
and Black

1992-93   Litho.   Perf. 14½, 14
808 A103   1s on 20s #688   .25   .25
809 A103 10s on 2s #756   65.00 65.00
810 A103 45s on 32s #759   4.00 4.00
811 A147 60s on 42s Strip of
       4, #a.-d. + la-
       bel   16.00 16.00

Issued: 1s, 5/19; 45s, 60s, 8/11; 10s,
3/29/93.

Miniature Sheet

World
War II in
Pacific,
50th
Anniv.
A156

Designs: a, Newspaper headline, Japanese
attack on Pearl Harbor. b, Map of Bataan, Cor-
regidor, and Manila, pilot's wings, airplanes. c,
Newspaper headline, troops landing in Gilbert
Islands, Marine Corps emblem, dogtags. d,
Uniform patch, B-29 "Enola Gay," troops land-
ing on Iwo Jima. e, Map of Battle of Midway,
Admiral Nimitz. f, Southwest Pacific campaign
map, Gen. MacArthur. g, Map of Saipan and
Tinian, Lt. Gen. Holland Smith. h, Map outling
bombing of Japan, Maj. Gen. Curtis Lemay. i,
Mitsubishi A6M Zero. j, Douglas SBD Daunt-
less. k, Grumman F4F Wildcat. l, Supermarine
Seafire.

1992, May 26   Litho.   Perf. 14
814 A156 42s Sheet of 12,
       #a.-l.   30.00 30.00

1992 Summer
Olympics,
Barcelona — A157

1992, June 16
815 A157 42s Boxing   1.25   .85
816 A157 57s Diving   1.75 1.10
817 A157 1.50pa Tennis   4.50 4.50
818 A157 3pa Cycling   9.50 9.50
     Nos. 815-818 (4)   17.00 15.95

For surcharges, see 1123, 1125.

King
Taufa'ahau
IV, 25th
Anniv. of
Coronation
A158

Designs: 45s, 2pa, King, Queen Halaevalu.
No. 820a, King, crown. b, Extract from investiture ceremony. c, King, #C33.

1992, July 4   Perf. 13½x13
819 A158 45s multicolored   1.25   .90
           Size: 51x38mm
           Perf. 12½x12
820 A158 80s Strip of 3, #a.-
       c.   6.00 6.00
821 A158 2pa multicolored   5.00 5.00
     Nos. 819-821 (3)   12.25 11.90

Sacred Bats of Kolovai — A159

Designs: No. 822a, Bats in flight. b, Close-
up of flying bat. c, Flying bats, tree. d, Bats
hanging in tree. e, Bat hanging from tree limb.
Origin of sacred bats: No. 823a, 45s, Kula
leaving for Upolu to be tattooed as Tongan
chief. b, 45s, Kula looking through path of
fires. c, 2pa, Kula walking down path, Hina. d,
2pa, Hina waving, Kula leaving with pet fruit
bats.
Nos. 823a-823d are horiz.

1992, Oct. 20   Litho.   Perf. 14
822 A159 60s Strip of 5, #a.-e. 12.00 12.00
           Souvenir Sheet
           Perf. 14½
823 A159 Sheet of 4, #a.-d.   13.00 13.00

Christmas
A160

1992, Nov. 10   Perf. 14
824 A160 60s Pearls   1.25 1.10
825 A160 80s Reef fish   1.50 1.40
826 A160 2pa Pacific orchids 4.75 4.75
827 A160 3pa Eua parrots   6.50 6.50
     Nos. 824-827 (4)   14.00 13.75

For surcharges, see Nos. 894-897.

Anniversaries and Events — A161

Designs: 60s, Tonga flag, Rotary emblem.
80sh, John F. Kennedy, Peace Corps emblem.
1.50pa, FAO, WHO emblems. 3.50pa, Globe,
Rotary Foundation emblem.

1992, Dec. 15   Perf. 14½
828 A161 60s multicolored   1.40 1.00
829 A161 80s multicolored   1.90 1.40
830 A161 1.50pa multicolored 3.50 3.50
831 A161 3.50pa multicolored 6.50 6.50
     Nos. 828-831 (4)   13.30 12.40

Rotary Intl. in Tonga, 25th anniv. (#828).
Peace Corps in Tonga, 25th anniv. (#829). Intl.
Conference of FAO and WHO (#830). Rotary
Foundation of Rotary Intl., 75th anniv. (#831).
For overprint see No. 869.

Family Planning — A163

Outdoor silhouette scenes: No. 832, Mother,
girl, butterflies. No. 833, Child on tricycle pulling kite. No. 834, Girl, kittens. No. 835, Adult,
child playing chess.

1993, Jan. 26   *Perf. 14x13½*

832	A163	15s Pair, #a.-b.	2.50	2.50
833	A163	45s Pair, #a.-b.	3.50	3.50
834	A163	60s Pair, #a.-b.	5.00	5.00
835	A163	2pa Pair, #a.-b.	15.00	15.00
		Nos. 832-835 (4)	26.00	26.00

Nos. 832a-835a have Tongan inscriptions. Nos. 832b-835b have English inscriptions and are mirror images of Nos. 832a-835a.

Health and Fitness — A164

Designs: 60s, Fresh fruit, fish, anti-smoking and anti-drug symbols. 80s, Anti-smoking symbol, weight training. 1.50pa, Anti-drug symbol, water sports. 2.50pa, Fresh fruit, fish, cyclist, jogger.

1993, Mar. 16   *Litho.*   *Perf. 14*

836	A164	60s multicolored	2.00	2.00
837	A164	80s multicolored	2.75	2.75
838	A164	1.50pa multicolored	3.50	3.50
839	A164	2.50pa multicolored	6.50	6.50
		Nos. 836-839 (4)	14.75	14.75

Tonga Fire Service, 25th Anniv. — A165

No. 840, Fireman's badge. No. 841, Police van, badge. No. 842, Police band. No. 843, Putting out fire. No. 844, Fire truck at station No. 845, Policeman, police dog.

1993, May 18   *Litho.*   *Perf. 14*

840		45s multi	2.00	2.00
841		45s multi	2.00	2.00
a.		A165 Pair, #840-841	4.50	3.50
842		60s multi	2.50	2.50
843		60s multi	2.50	2.50
a.		A165 Pair, #842-843	5.50	4.50
844		2pa multi	7.00	7.00
845		2pa multi	7.00	7.00
a.		A165 Pair, #844-845	16.00	14.00
		Nos. 840-845 (6)	23.00	23.00

Tonga Police Training College, 25th anniv. (#841-842, 845),
For surcharges see Nos. 943-948.

A166

Abel Tasman's Voyage to Eua, 350th Anniv.: 30s, Map of islands. 60s, Sailing ships, Heemskirk and Zeehaen. 80s, Sailing ships, natives in canoes. 3.50pa, Landing on Eua.

1993, June 21

846	A166	30s multicolored	.80	.50
847	A166	60s multicolored	1.75	1.10
848	A166	80s multicolored	2.00	2.00
849	A166	3.50pa multicolored	8.25	8.25
		Nos. 846-849 (4)	12.80	11.85

A167

King Taufa'ahau IV, 75th Birthday: 45s, 2pa, Musical instruments.
No. 851a, Sporting events. b, Ancient landmarks. c, Royal Palace.

1993, July 1   *Litho.*   *Perf. 13x13½*

850	A167	45s multicolored	.65	.65

      Perf. 12x12½
      Size: 37x48mm

851	A167	80s Strip of 3, #a.-c.	4.50	4.50
852	A167	2pa multicolored	3.00	3.00
		Nos. 850-852 (3)	8.15	8.15

A168

Children's Stamp Designs: Nos. 853a, 854a, Beach scene. Nos. 853b, 854b, "Maui-The Fisher of the Islands." Nos. 853c, 854c, Raft on ocean. Nos. 853d, 854d, Woman with hands in mixing bowl. Nos. 853e, 854e, "Maui and his Hook." Nos. 853f, 854f, "Communication in the South Pacific."

1993, Dec. 1   *Litho.*   *Perf. 14*

853	A168	10s Strip of 6, #a.-f.	3.00	3.00
854	A168	80s Strip of 6, #a.-f.	14.00	14.00

A168a

Christmas traditions: 60s, Festive dinner. 80s, Shooting cannon. 1.50pa, Musicians. 3pa, Going to church.

1993, Nov. 10   *Litho.*   *Perf. 14*

855	A168a	60s multicolored	1.50	1.25
856	A168a	80s multicolored	2.00	1.50
857	A168a	1.50pa multicolored	3.25	3.25
858	A168a	3pa multicolored	6.00	6.00
		Nos. 855-858 (4)	12.75	12.00

      Miniature Sheet

Kindness to Animals — A169

Designs: a, 80s, Boy holding puppy. b, 80s, Girl holding kitten. c, 60s, Boy holding rooster (b). d, 60s, Girl with butterfly. e, 60s, Three dogs. f, 60s, Boy, puppy.

1994, Jan. 14   *Perf. 14½*

859	A169	Sheet of 6, #a.-f.	15.00	15.00

For overprint see No. 868.

Game Fishing — A170

60s, Tiger shark. 80s, Dolphin fish. 1.50pa, Yellow fin tuna. 2.50pa, Pacific blue marlin.

1994, Feb. 28   *Litho.*   *Perf. 12*

860	A170	60s multicolored	1.50	1.00
861	A170	80s multicolored	2.00	1.40
862	A170	1.50pa multicolored	3.50	3.50
863	A170	2.50pa multicolored	5.00	5.00
		Nos. 860-863 (4)	12.00	10.90

1994 World Cup Soccer Championships, US — A171

Designs: No. 864a, Player's legs. No. 864b, World Cup trophy. No. 865a, American player in red, white, & blue. No. 865b, German player in black shorts, white shirt.

1994, June 1   *Perf. 14x14½*

864	A171	80s Pair, #a.-b.	4.00	4.00
865	A171	2pa Pair, #a.-b.	8.00	8.00

Pan Pacific & South East Asia Women's Assoc. Conference — A172

Career women: No. 866a, Lawyer. No. 866b, Policewoman. No. 867a, Doctor. No. 867b, Nurse.

1994, Aug. 18   *Litho.*   *Perf. 14*

866	A172	45s Pair, #a.-b.	3.50	3.50
867	A172	2.50pa Pair, #a.-b.	9.00	9.00

      No. 859 Overprinted

1994, Nov. 10   *Litho.*   *Perf. 14½*

868	A169	Sheet of 6, #a.-f.	10.00	10.00

No. 831 Ovptd. in Dark Blue

1994, Nov. 17   *Litho.*   *Perf. 14½*

869	A161	60s on 3.50pa multi	3.00	3.00

      Types of 1969-85 and

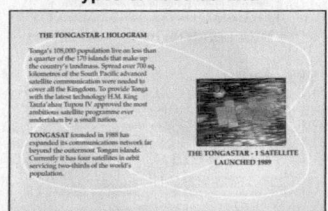

Tongastar 1 Satellite — A173

Design: a, 10s, Type A39 banana, size 22x11mm. b, 25s, Type AP12. c, Booklet pane, 12 #870a, 3 #870b. d, 45s, like #608 e, 45s, like #609. f, 45s, like #610. g, 45s, like #611. h, Booklet pane of 3 each #870d-870e, 2 #870f, 1 #870g. i, 60s, Type A72. j, 60s, Type OA19. k, 80s, Type OA17. l, Booklet pane, #870l-870k. m, 2pa, Tongastar 1. n, Booklet pane of 1 #870m.

      Unwmk.
1994, Dec. 14   *Litho.*   *Die Cut*
      Self-adhesive

870	A173	Souvenir booklet	27.50

First full-scale production of self-adhesive stamps by Tonga, 25th anniv. (#870). Satellite communications network for Tongan Islands (#870m).
No. 870b is airmail. Nos. 870j-870k are air post official stamps.
No. 870m contains a holographic image. Soaking in water may affect the hologram.

      Marine Type of 1992-93 Redrawn
1994-95   *Litho.*   *Perf. 14*

874	A155a	10s like #801	.25	.25
876	A155a	20s like #803	.35	.35
877	A155a	45s like #804	.80	.80
878	A155a	60s like #805	1.10	1.10
879	A155a	80s like #806	1.75	1.75

      Size: 41x27mm, 27x41mm

880	A155a	1pa like #705, horiz.	3.00	3.00
881	A155a	2pa like #577, horiz.	5.00	5.00
882	A155a	3pa like #578, horiz.	7.00	7.00
883	A155a	5pa like #706	10.00	10.00
884	A155a	10pa like #568	22.00	22.00
		Nos. 874-884 (10)	51.25	51.25

Area covered by background colors on Nos. 874, 876-879 has been reduced in size.
Issued: 1pa, 2pa, 3pa, 6/21/94; 5pa, 9/21/94; 10pa, 1/18/95; 10s, 20s, 45s, 60s, 80s, 9/25/95.
For overprints, see Nos. O78-O87.

FAO, 50th Anniv. A174

1995, May 16   *Litho.*   *Perf. 14*

886	A174	5pa multicolored	15.00	15.00

Tonga's Entry into British Commonwealth, 25th Anniv. — A175

Children with bicycles from parts of Commonwealth.

1995, June 6

887	A175	45s Polynesia	1.10	.90
888	A175	60s Asia	1.50	1.25
889	A175	80s Africa	1.75	1.75
890	A175	2pa India	3.75	3.75
891	A175	2.50pa Europe	4.75	4.75
		Nos. 887-891 (5)	12.85	12.40

1995 Rugby World Cup, South Africa — A176

Designs: No. 892a, Player running right with ball, two others. b, Two players. No. 893a, Three players. b, Player ready to catch ball.

1995, June 20   *Perf. 14½*

892	A176	80s Pair, #a.-b.	6.00	6.00
893	A176	2pa Pair, #a.-b.	13.50	13.50

Nos. 892-893 were each issued in sheets of 4 stamps.
For surcharges see Nos. 954A, 956A.

Nos. 824-827 Surcharged

i

j

1995, June 30   Litho.   Perf. 14

894	60s Pair	4.50	4.50
a.	A160(i) on #824	2.00	2.00
b.	A160(j) on #824	2.00	2.00
895	60s Pair	4.50	4.50
a.	A160(i) on 80s #825	2.00	2.00
b.	A160(j) on 80s #825	2.00	2.00
896	60s Pair	4.50	4.50
a.	A160(i) on 2pa #826	2.00	2.00
b.	A160(j) on 2pa #826	2.00	2.00
897	60s Pair	4.50	4.50
a.	A160(i) on 3pa #827	2.00	2.00
b.	A160(j) on 3pa #827	2.00	2.00
	Nos. 894-897 (4)	18.00	18.00

Nos. 779-782 Surcharged

1995, June 30   Litho.   Perf. 14

898	A151	60s on 57s #779	1.50	1.50
899	A151	80s on 2pa #781	1.75	1.75
899A	A151	80s on 2pa #782	1.75	1.75
b.		Pair, #899-899A	4.00	4.00
899C	A151	1pa on #780	2.00	2.00
	Nos. 898-899C (4)		7.00	7.00

Victory in the Pacific, 50th Anniv. — A177

Nos. 900, 901: a, Soldier climbing from rope ladder. b, Ship, soldiers. c, Ship, landing craft with troops, soldiers up close. d, Ship, landing craft with troops. e, Map.

1995, Aug. 1   Litho.   Perf. 14x14½

900	A177	60s Strip of 5, #a.-e.	10.00	10.00
901	A177	80s Strip of 5, #a.-e.	10.00	10.00

Nos. 900-901 are continuous designs and were issued together in sheet containing ten stamps.

Singapore '95 — A178

Designs: No. 902a, 45s, #887. b, 60s, #888. 2pa, Boy cycling in Singapore.

1995, Sept. 1   Litho.   Perf. 12

902	A178	Pair, #a.-b.	3.25	3.25

Souvenir Sheet

903	A178	2pa multicolored	4.50	4.50

Souvenir Sheet

Beijing Intl. Coin & Stamp Show '95 — A179

Design: 1.40pa, Mount Song, Henan Province, China.

1995, Sept. 14   Perf. 14½

904	A179	1.40pa multicolored	4.25	4.25

End of World War II, UN, 50th Anniv. — A180

No. 905a, Holocaust survivors. b, UN emblem, "50." c, Children of Holocaust survivors in celebration.
No. 906a, Mushroom cloud from atom bomb explosion. b, Like #905b. c, Space shuttle.

1995, Oct. 20   Litho.   Perf. 13

905	A180	60s Strip of 3, #a.-c.	4.00	4.00
906	A180	80s Strip of 3, #a.-c.	6.00	6.00

Nos. 905b, 906b are 23x31mm.

Christmas and New Year — A181

Orchids: 20s, Calanthe triplicata. Nos. 908, Spathoglottis plicata, inscribed "MERRY CHRISTMAS." No. 909, like #908, inscribed "A HAPPY 1996." No. 910, Dendrobium platygastrium, inscribed "MERRY CHRISTMAS". No. 911, like #910, inscribed "A HAPPY 1996." 80s, Goodyera rubicunda. 2pa, Dendrobium toki. 2.50pa, Phaius tankervilliae.

1995, Nov. 15   Litho.   Perf. 14x14½

907	A181	20s multicolored	.75	.75
908	A181	45s multicolored	1.00	1.00
909	A181	45s multicolored	1.00	1.00
910	A181	60s multicolored	1.25	1.25
911	A181	60s multicolored	1.25	1.25
912	A181	80s multicolored	1.75	1.75
913	A181	2pa multicolored	4.00	4.00
914	A181	2.50pa multicolored	5.00	5.00
	Nos. 907-914 (8)		16.00	16.00

Humpback Whale — A182

1996, Jan. 7   Perf. 14

915	A182	45s In water	2.00	2.00
916	A182	60s With calf	3.00	3.00
917	A182	1.50pa Sounding	4.50	4.50
918	A182	2.50pa Breaching	7.00	7.00
	Nos. 915-918 (4)		16.50	16.50

World Wildlife Fund.

Miniature Sheet

New Year 1996 (Year of the Rat) — A183

Denomination: a, UR. b, UL. c, LR. d, LL.

1996, Feb. 23

919	A183	60s Sheet of 4,		
		#a.-d.	7.50	7.50

No. 919 is a continuous design.
See Nos. 930-932, 932E, 942, 986.

Marine Type of 1992-93 Redrawn

1996, May 31   Litho.   Perf. 14
Size: 40x26mm

920	A155a	1pa like #880	3.00	3.00
921	A155a	2pa like #881	5.50	5.50
922	A155a	3pa like #882	8.00	8.00
923	A155a	5pa like #883	15.00	15.00
924	A155a	10pa like #884	27.50	27.50
	Nos. 920-924 (5)		59.00	59.00

Size of "TONGA" on Nos. 920-923 is smaller than on Nos. 880-883. Name of species appears at top instead of bottom on Nos. 920-924. Background colors vary. Inscribed "1996."

1996 Summer Olympic Games, Atlanta — A184

Statues of classical Greek figures, modern athletes: 45s, Zeus, runner. 80s, The Discus Thrower. 2pa, The Javelin Thrower. 3pa, The Horseman, dressage competitor.

1996, July 2   Litho.   Perf. 14

925	A184	45s multicolored	1.25	.80
926	A184	80s multicolored	2.00	1.90
927	A184	2pa multicolored	5.00	5.00
928	A184	3pa multicolored	6.00	6.00
	Nos. 925-928 (4)		14.25	13.70

For surcharges & overprint see Nos. 949-952.

13th Congress of Intl. Union of Preshistoric and Protohistoric Sciences — A185

a, Prehistoric man using fire, knife, bow & arrow, animals. b, Ancient Egyptians, Greeks, Romans.

1996, Sept. 5   Litho.   Perf. 12

929	A185	1pa Pair, #a.-b.	5.00	5.00

No. 929 was issued in sheets of 6 stamps.

New Year 1996 (Year of the Rat) Type

Denomination: a, UR. b, UL. c, LR. d, LL.

1996, June 27   Litho.   Perf. 14
Sheets of 4

930	A183	10s #a.-d.	1.40	1.40
931	A183	20s #a.-d.	2.75	2.75
932	A183	45s #a.-d.	6.75	6.75
932E	A183	60s #a.-d.	10.00	10.00

The denominations are larger on No. 932E than those on No. 919.

Christmas A186

Paintings: 20s, Virgin and Child, by Sassoferrato. 60s, Adoration of the Shepherds, by Murillo. 80s, Virgin and Child, by Delaroche. 1pa, Adoration of the Shepherds, by Champaigne.

1996, Oct. 29   Litho.   Perf. 14

933	A186	20s multicolored	.75	.75
934	A186	60s multicolored	2.00	1.50
935	A186	80s multicolored	2.50	2.50
936	A186	1pa multicolored	7.50	7.50
	Nos. 933-936 (4)		12.75	12.00

UNICEF, 50th Anniv. — A187

Children in sports activities: a, Running, playing rugby. b, Tennis. c, Cycling.

1996, Oct. 29

937	A187	80s Strip of 3, #a.-c.	8.00	8.00

No. 937 is a continuous design.

Queen Halaevalu Mata'aho, 70th Birthday — A188

Designs: 60s, Queen, natl. flag. No. 939a, Queen, coin with portrait. No. 939b, Coin with natl. arms, Queen.

1996, Nov. 27   Litho.   Perf. 12

938	A188	60s multicolored	2.50	2.50
939	A188	2pa Pair, #a.-b.	9.50	9.50

Towards the Year 2000 — A189

Year "2000" rising out of Pacific, Tonga landmarks: Nos. 940a, 941a, The Ha'amonga stone monument, globe, Kao Island. Nos. 940b, 941b, Mount Talau overlooking Port of Reguge, Royal Palance, Tongatapu, communication satellite.

1996, Dec. 9

940	A189	80s Pair, #a.-b.	4.00	4.00
941	A189	2pa Pair, #a.-b.	8.00	8.00

New Year Type of 1996 Redrawn with Ox

Denomination located: a, 60s, UR. b, 60s, UL. c, 80s, LR. d, 2pa, LL.

1997, Jan. 24   Litho.   Perf. 14

942	A183	Sheet of 4, #a.-d.	9.50	9.50

New Year 1997 (Year of the Ox).

Nos. 840-845 Surcharged

1997, Mar. 3   Litho.   *Perf. 14*

943	A165	10s on 45s #840	3.50	3.25
944	A165	10s on 45s #841	3.50	3.25
a.		Pair, #943-944	7.00	6.50
945	A165	10s on 60s #842	3.50	3.25
946	A165	10s on 60s #843	3.50	3.25
a.		Pair, #945-946	7.00	6.50
947	A165	20s on 2pa #844	4.00	3.75
948	A165	20s on 2pa #845	4.00	3.75
a.		Pair, #947-948	8.00	7.50
		Nos. 943-948 (6)	22.00	20.50

Nos. 925-928
Surcharged &
Overprinted.

1997, Mar. 24   Litho.   *Perf. 14*

949	A184	10s on 45s #925	.90	.90
950	A184	10s on 80s #926	.90	.90
951	A184	10s on 2pa #927	.90	.90
952	A184	3pa on #928	9.25	9.25
		Nos. 949-952 (4)	11.95	11.95

Size and location of surcharge varies.

Nos. 892-893 Surcharged

a   b

1997, Mar. 24   *Perf. 14½*

Sheets of 4

954A	A176	10s on 80s	2.00	2.00
956A	A176	1pa on 2pa	14.00	14.00

#954A contains #892a (a), #892a (a), #892b (b), #892a (b). #956A contains #893a (a), #893b (a), #893b (b), #893a (b).

Christianity in Tonga, Birth of King
George Tupou I, Bicent. — A190

#957, 961a, 962a, Arrival of missionary ship, Duff, Captain James Wilson. #958, King George Tupou I, village. #959, 961b, 962b, People in water, rowboats coming ashore from Duff. #960, 961c, 962c, Natives, missionaries, Duff.

1997, Apr. 28   *Perf. 14*

957	A190	10s multicolored	2.00	2.00
958	A190	10s multicolored	.65	.65
959	A190	10s multicolored	2.00	2.00
960	A190	10s multicolored	2.00	2.00
a.		Sheet of 6, #957, 959-960, 3 #958	7.50	7.50
961	A190	60s Strip of 3, #a.-c.	6.00	6.00
962	A190	80s Strip of 3, #a.-c.	7.00	7.00

Nos. 961-962 were each issued in sheets of 9 stamps.
See Nos. 972-975.

Souvenir Sheet

Pacific Swallow, Golden Gate
Bridge — A191

1997, May 30

963	A191	2pa multicolored	6.50	6.50
		Pacific '97.		

Tonga
High
School,
50th
Anniv.
A192

Designs: 20s, Students in uniforms outside of school. 60s, Dressed for sports. 80s, Brass band. 3.50pa, Running competition.

1997, June 4

964	A192	20s multicolored	.75	.40
965	A192	60s multicolored	1.75	1.10
966	A192	80s multicolored	2.00	1.50
967	A192	3.50pa multicolored	6.00	6.00
		Nos. 964-967 (4)	10.50	9.00

A193

Nos. 968, 970: a, Queen, King with bowed heads, royal escorts. b, Coronation ceremony. c, Queen, King. 45s, 2pa, King's crown.

1997, June 30   Litho.   *Perf. 13x13½*

968	A193	10s Strip of 3, #a.-		
		c.	4.00	4.00
969	A193	45s multicolored	1.75	1.75
		Size: 34x47mm		
		Perf. 12		
970	A193	60s Strip of 3, #a.-		
		c.	6.00	6.00
971	A193	2pa multicolored	4.75	4.75

King Taufa'ahau IV, Queen Halaevalu Mata'aho, 50th wedding anniv., coronation, 30th anniv.

Christianity in Tonga Type of 1997

1997, Aug. 27   *Perf. 14*

Size: 27x18mm

972	A190	10s like #957	.25	.25
973	A190	10s like #958	.25	.25
974	A190	10s like #959	.25	.25
975	A190	10s like #960	.25	.25
a.		Sheet of 12, 6 #973, 2 each #972, #974-975	5.50	5.50

A194

Mushrooms: Nos. 976a, 977a, Lenzites elegans. Nos. 976b, 977b, Marasmiellus semiustus. No. 976c, 978a, Aseroe rubra. Nos. 976d, 978b, Podoscypha involuta. Nos. 976e, 979a, Microporus xanthopus. Nos. 976f, 979b, Lentinus tuberregium.

1997, Oct. 1   Litho.   *Perf. 14*

976	A194	10s Strip of 6, #a.-f.	13.50	13.50
		Size: 26x40mm		
977	A194	20s Pair, #a.-b.	5.00	5.00
978	A194	60s Pair, #a.-b.	6.00	6.00
979	A194	2pa Pair, #a.-b.	8.00	8.00
c.		Sheet of 6, #977-979	35.00	35.00

No. 976 is a continuous design.

Diana, Princess of Wales (1961-97)
Common Design Type

Various portraits: a, 10s. b, 80s, c, 1pa. d, 2.50pa.

Perf. 13½x14

1998, May 29   Litho.   Unwmk.

980	CD355	Sheet of 4, #a.-d	5.75	5.75

No. 980 sold for 4.40pa + 50s with surtax from international sales going to the Princess Diana Memorial Fund and surtax from local sales going to designated local charity.
For surcharge, see No. 1192.

Flying Home for
Christmas
A195

Designs: 60s, Airplane on ground, people waving, 80s, People waving, house, plane overhead. 1.50pa, Man in outrigger canoe waving to airplane. 3.50pa, Man, woman, people in boat on lake waving, airplane overhead.

1997, Oct. 20   Litho.   *Perf. 14x13½*

981	A195	60s bister & red	.90	.90
982	A195	80s bister & red	1.20	1.20
983	A195	1.50pa bister & red	2.20	2.20
984	A195	3.50pa bister & red	5.20	5.20
		Nos. 981-984 (4)	9.50	9.50

King Taufa'ahau
Tupou IV, 80th
Birthday — A196

1998, July 4   Litho.   *Perf. 14*

985	A196	2.70pa multicolored	6.50	6.50
a.		Souv. sheet, #985, Niuafo'ou #207	9.00	9.00

New Year 1998 (Year of the Tiger)

Tiger: a, 55s, Leaping down. b, 80s, Lying down. c, 1pa, Leaping upward. d, 1pa, Stalking.

1998, July 23

986	A183	Sheet of 4, #a.-d.	6.00	6.00

No. 986 is a continuous design. Singpex '98.
For surcharges, see No. 1098.

Birds
A197

5s, Fairy tern, vert. 10s, Tongan whistler, vert. 15s, Common barn owl, vert. 20s, Purple swamp hen, vert. 30s, Red footed booby, vert. 40s, Banded rail. 50s, Swamp harrier. 55s, Blue-crowned lorikeet, vert. 60s, Great frigate bird, vert. 70s, Friendly ground dove. 80s, Red-tailed tropic bird, vert. 1pa, Red shining parrot, vert. 2pa, Pacific pigeon, vert. 3pa, Pacific golden plover. 5pa, Tongan megapode.

Perf. 14x14½, 14½x14

1998, Aug. 26   Litho.

992	A197	5s multicolored	.25	.25
993	A197	10s multicolored	.25	.25
994	A197	15s multicolored	.25	.25
995	A197	20s multicolored	.30	.30
996	A197	30s multicolored	.50	.50
997	A197	40s multicolored	.65	.65
998	A197	50s multicolored	.75	.75
999	A197	55s multicolored	.90	.90
1000	A197	60s multicolored	.95	.95
1001	A197	70s multicolored	1.10	1.10
1002	A197	80s multicolored	1.25	1.25
1003	A197	1pa multicolored	1.60	1.60
1004	A197	2pa multicolored	3.00	3.00
1005	A197	3pa multicolored	4.75	4.75
1006	A197	5pa multicolored	8.00	8.00
		Nos. 992-1006 (15)	24.50	24.50

For surcharges, see Nos. 1077A, 1077B, 1099-1114, 1126, 1147.

Fish
A198

Designs: a, 10s, Chaetodon pelewensis. b, 55s, Chaetodon lunula. c, 1pa, Chaetodon ephippium.

1998, Sept. 23   Litho.   *Perf. 14*

1008	A198	Strip of 3, #a.-c.	4.50	4.50

Intl. Year of the Ocean. No. 1008 was issued in sheets of 9 stamps.

Christmas
A199

Designs: 10s, Angel, "Kilisimasi Fiefia." 80s, Angel, "Merry Christmas." 1pa, Children, candle, "Ta'u Fo'ou Monu'ia." 1.60pa, Children, candle, "Happy New Year."

1998, Nov. 12   Litho.   *Perf. 14x14½*

1009	A199	10s multicolored	.60	.40
1010	A199	80s multicolored	2.25	1.00
1011	A199	1pa multicolored	2.50	2.00
1012	A199	1.60pa multicolored	3.50	3.50
		Nos. 1009-1012 (4)	8.85	6.90

New Year 1999 (Year of the
Rabbit) — A200

a, 10s, Three rabbits. b, 55s, Rabbit eating. c, 80s, Rabbit looking upward. d, 1pa, Rabbit hopping.

1999, Feb. 16   **Perf. 14**
1013 A200 Sheet of 4, #a.-d.   4.00   4.00

Explorers — A201

Explorer, ship: 55s, Tasman, Heemskerck, 1643. 80s, La Perouse, Astrolabe, 1788. 1pa, William Bligh, Bounty, 1789. 2.50pa, James Cook, Resolution, 1777.

1999, Mar. 19   **Litho.**   **Perf. 14**
1014	A201	55s multicolored	1.75	.65
1015	A201	80s multicolored	2.25	1.00
1016	A201	1pa multicolored	3.25	2.50
1017	A201	2.50pa multicolored	5.00	5.50
a.		Souvenir sheet of 1	6.50	6.50
		Nos. 1014-1017 (4)	12.25	9.65

Australia '99 World Stamp Expo (#1017a).

Scenic Views, Vava'u — A202

Designs: 10s, Neiafu. 55s, Boats on water, Port of Refuge. 80s, Aerial view, Port of Refuge. 1pa, Sunset, Neiafu. 2.50pa, Mounu Island.

1999, May 19   **Perf. 14½**
1018	A202	10s multicolored	.75	.40
1019	A202	55s multicolored	1.00	.60
1020	A202	80s multicolored	1.75	.80
1021	A202	1pa multicolored	2.00	2.00
1022	A202	2.50pa multicolored	3.50	3.50
		Nos. 1018-1022 (5)	9.00	7.30

For surcharge see No. 1148.

Flowers — A203

Designs: 10s, Fagraea berteroana. 80s, Garcinia pseudoguttfera. 1pa, Phlaeria disperma, vert. 2.50pa, Gardenia taitensis, vert.

Perf. 13¼x13, 13x13¼
1999, Sept. 29   **Litho.**
1023	A203	10s multicolored	.30	.30
1024	A203	80s multicolored	1.40	1.40
1025	A203	1pa multicolored	1.75	1.75
1026	A203	2.50pa multicolored	2.80	2.80
		Nos. 1023-1026 (4)	6.25	6.25

Millennium — A204

Designs: a, 55s, Ha'amonga monument, people, clocks at 11:15 to 11:25. b, 80s, Monument, people, clocks at 11:30 to 11:40. c, 1pa, People, clocks at 11:45 to 11:55. d, 2.50pa, King Taufa'ahau IV, clocks at 12:00, 12:05.

1999, Dec. 1
1027 A204 Strip of 4, #a.-d.   6.50   6.50

Millennium — A205

Clock, dove and: 10s, Flowers. 1pa, Ha'amonga Monument. 2.50pa, Native boat. 2.70pa, Crown.

Litho. & Embossed
2000, Jan. 1   **Perf. and Die Cut**
1028	A205	10s multi	.25	.25
1029	A205	1pa multi	1.50	1.50
1030	A205	2.50pa multi	3.50	3.50
1031	A205	2.70pa multi	3.75	3.75
a.		Souv. sheet, #1030-1031	7.50	7.50
		Nos. 1028-1031 (4)	9.00	9.00

Values are for stamps with attached selvage.

Souvenir Sheet

New Year 2000 (Year of the Dragon) — A206

Various dragons; a, 10s. b, 55s, c, 80s. d, 1pa.

Litho. with Foil Application
2000, Feb. 4   **Perf. 14½**
1032 A206 Sheet of 4, #a.-d.   4.50   4.50

Souvenir Sheet

The Stamp Show 2000, London — A207

Litho. with Foil Application
2000, May 22   **Perf. 13x13¼**
1033	A207	Sheet of 2	5.00	5.00
a.		1pa Queen Mother	1.50	1.50
b.		2.50pa Queen Salote Tupou III	3.50	3.50

Geostationary Orbital Slot Program — A208

Designs: 10s, Proton RU500 lauch vehicle, vert. 1pa, LM3 launch vehicle. 2.50pa, Apstar 1. 2.70pa, Gorizont.

Litho. with Foil Application
2000, July 5   **Perf. 14½x15, 15x14½**
1034-1037	A208	Set of 4	8.50	8.50
1037a		Souvenir sheet, #1036-1037	7.50	7.50

World Stamp Expo 2000, Anaheim.

2000 Summer Olympics, Sydney — A209

No. 1038: a, Runner, koalas, sailboats. b, Boxers, kangaroos, Ayers Rock. c, Torchbearers, Ayers Rock, Sydney Opera House (60x45mm). d, Discus thrower, Sydney Harbour Bridge, flower. e, Weight lifter, kookaburra, fish.

2000, Sept. 15   **Litho.**   **Perf. 14**
1038	A209	Horiz. strip of 5	5.50	5.50
a.-e.		80s Any single	1.00	1.00

Commonwealth Membership, 30th Anniv. — A210

Designs: 10s, Education. 55s, Arts. 80s, Health. 2.70pa, Agriculture.

2000, Oct. 25
1039-1042 A210 Set of 4   5.50   5.50
For surcharge see No. 1149.

Souvenir Sheet

New Year 2001 (Year of the Snake) — A211

No. 1043 — Various snakes: a, 10s. b, 55s, c, 80s, d, 1pa.

Litho. with Foil Application
2001, Feb. 1   **Perf. 14¼**
1043 A211 Sheet of 4, #a-d   4.50   4.50
Hong Kong 2001 Stamp Exhibition.

Dance — A212

Designs: 10s, Ma'ulu'ulu. 55s, Me'etupaki. 80s, Tau'olunga. 2.70pa, Faha'iula.

2001, Apr. 4   **Litho.**   **Perf. 13¼**
1044-1047 A212 Set of 4   5.25   5.25
For surcharge see No. 1151.

Year of the Mangrove — A213

Designs: 10s, Fiddler crab. 55s, Black duck, gray mullet, vert. 80s, Red mangrove, emperor fish, vert. 1pa, Reef heron, mangrove. 2.70pa, Mangrove crab.

2001, May 5   **Litho.**   **Perf. 13¾**
1048-1052	A213	Set of 5	6.00	6.00
1052a		Souvenir sheet, #1048-1052, perf. 13½	6.50	6.50

For surcharge see No. 1150.

Sport Fishing — A214

2001, July 31   **Perf. 14¾x14**
1053	A214	Horiz. strip of 4 with central label	8.25	8.25
a.		45s Sailfish	.50	.50
b.		80s Blue marlin	1.00	1.00
c.		2.40pa Wahoo	3.00	3.00
d.		2.60pa Dorado	3.25	3.25

Fruit — A215

2001, Sept. 19   *Serpentine Die Cut*
Self-Adhesive
1054		Horiz. strip of 5	6.75	6.75
a.	A215	10s Banana	.50	.50
b.	A215	45s Coconut	.90	.90
c.	A215	60s Pineapple	1.00	1.00
d.	A215	80s Watermelon	1.10	1.10
e.	A215	2.40pa Passion fruit	2.40	2.40

Shells — A216

Designs: 10s, Haliotis ovina. 80s, Turbo petholatus. 1pa, Trochus niloticus. 2.70pa, Turbo marmoratus.

Perf. 12¾
2001, Dec. 13   **Litho.**   **Unwmk.**
1055-1058 A216 Set of 4   6.50   6.50
Values are for stamps with surrounding selvage.

Reign Of Queen Elizabeth II, 50th Anniv. Issue
Common Design Type
Souvenir Sheet

No. 1059: a, 15s, Princess Elizabeth as child. b, 90s, Wearing yellow hat. c, 1.20pa, With Princess Anne and Prince Charles. d, 1.40pa, Wearing crown. e, 2.25pa, 1955 portrait by Annigoni (38x50mm).

Perf. 14¼x14½, 13¾ (2.25pa)
2002, Feb. 6   **Litho.**   **Wmk. 373**
1059 CD360 Sheet of 5, #a-e   8.50   8.50

Souvenir Sheet

New Year 2002 (Year of the Horse) — A217

Various horses: a, 65s. b, 80s. c, 1pa. d, 2.50pa.

Litho. With Foil Application
2002, Feb. 12 Unwmk. *Perf. 14*
1060 A217 Sheet of 4, #a-d 7.75 7.75

Intl. Year of Ecotourism — A218

Designs: 5s, Whale, surfer. 15s, Woman, shoreline. 70s, Beach, fish. 1.40pa, Arch, man. 2.25pa, Boats, man.

2002, Apr. 9 Litho. *Perf. 13¼x13¾*
1061-1065 A218 Set of 5 6.75 6.75

Pearls
A219

Pearls and: 90s, Workers preparing oysters for pearl cultivation. 1pa, Diver checking strung oysters. 1.20pa, Woman, pearl on necklace. 2.50pa, Islands.

2002, June 12 Litho. *Perf. 13½*
1066-1069 A219 Set of 4 8.00 8.00
1069a Souvenir sheet, #1068-
       1069 6.75 6.75

Values are for stamps with surrounding selvage.

Participation of Tongan Team in Rugby
Sevens Tournament — A220

Designs: 15s, Player leaping for ball. 30s, Players ready for scrum. 90s, Player attempting tackle. 4pa, Players on ground.

2002, July 27
1070-1073 A220 Set of 4 11.00 11.00

Values are for stamps with surrounding selvage.

Weaving — A221

Designs: 30s, Woman and young girl. 90s, Woman with work hanging on line, boy with baskets. 1.40pa, Women weaving baskets. 2.50pa, Woman weaving basket lid.

2002, Sept. 17 *Perf. 12¼*
1074-1077 A221 Set of 4 7.00 7.00

No. 999 Surcharged

Type 1 — Slash
Over First "5"

No. 1003
Surcharged

Methods and Perfs As Before
2002, Sept.
1077A A197 5s on 55s #999,
                Type 1 65.00 —
1077B A197 15(s) on 1pa
                #1003 75.00 —

See Nos. 1099-1114 for additional surcharges on No. 999.

'Eua National Park,
10th Anniv. — A222

Various depictions of red shining parrots 45s, 1pa, 1.50pa, 2.50pa.

2002, Nov. 27 Litho. *Perf. 12¼*
1078-1081 A222 Set of 4 8.00 8.00

New Year 2003 (Year of the
Ram) — A223

No. 1082: a, 65s, One ram. 80s, Three sheep. 1pa, Three sheep, diff. 2.50pa, Two sheep.

2003, Apr. 14 Litho. *Perf. 13¼*
1082 A223 Sheet of 4, #a-d 7.50 7.50

Coronation of Queen Elizabeth II, 50th
Anniv. — A224

Designs: 90s, Queen Elizabeth II in coach. 1.20pa, Queen Salote of Tonga. 1.40pa, Queen Salote in coach. 2.50pa, Queen Elizabeth II.

Litho. With Foil Application
2003, June 2
1083-1086 A224 Set of 4 8.50 8.50

Boats of Abel
Tasman — A225

Various boats: 15s, 75s, 90s, 2.50pa.

2003, Aug. 7 Litho. *Perf. 13¼*
1087-1090 A225 Set of 4 11.00 11.00
1090a Souvenir sheet, #1087-
       1090 11.00 11.00

Beaches — A226

Flower and: 15s, Euakafa Beach. 90s, Pangaimotu Beach. 1.40pa, Fafa Beach. 2.25pa, Nuku Beach.

2003, Sept. 11
1091-1094 A226 Set of 4 8.50 8.50

Nos. 784, 785a, 785b, 785c, 786
Surcharged

Methods and Perfs As Before
2003, Sept.
1095 A152 10s on 32s Horiz.
             strip of 3,
             #784a-784c 150.00 —
1096 A152 10s on 42s
             #/85a —
1097 A152 10s on 42s
             #785b —
1097A A152 10s on 42s #785c —
1098 A152 10s on 57s Horiz.
             strip of 3,
             #786a-786c 150.00 —

No. 999 Surcharged

Type 2 — Small numerals and cent
sign

Type 3 — Small numerals and "s"

Type 4 — Thin numerals and "s"

Type 5 — Large numerals and "s"

Type 6 — Medium-sized numerals and
"s"

Type 7 — Very large, bold numerals
and "c"

Methods and Perfs As Before
2003-04
1099 A197 05s on 55s, Type 3 150.00 —
   a.   Obliterators 2x1 ½mm
1100 A197 05s on 55s, Type 4 350.00 —
1101 A197 5s on 55s, Type 5 20.00 —
1102 A197 5c on 55s, Type 7 10.00 —
1103 A197 10s on 55s, Type 4 50.00 —
1104 A197 10s on 55s, Type 5 45.00 —
1105 A197 10c on 55s, Type 7 25.00 —
1106 A197 15c on 55s, Type 2 75.00 —
1107 A197 15s on 55s, Type 4 350.00 —
1108 A197 15s on 55s, Type 5 20.00 —
1109 A197 15c on 55s, Type 7 25.00 —
1110 A197 20s on 55s, Type 2 65.00 —
1111 A197 20s on 55s, Type 4 25.00 —
1112 A197 20s on 55s, Type 5 50.00 —
1113 A197 45c on 55s, Type 2 50.00 —
1114 A197 45s on 55s, Type 6 75.00 —

Earliest known uses: Nos. 1099, 1106, 1110, 10/03; Nos. 1100, 1103, 1107, 1111, 12/03; Nos. 1101, 1108, 2/04; Nos. 1113, 4/04; Nos. 1104, 1112, 1114, 6/04; Nos. 1105, 1109, 8/04; No. 1102, 9/04;

Churches
A227

Designs: 15s, Catholic Church, Neiafu, Vava'u. 90s, Wesleyan Church, Uiha, Ha'apai.

1.40pa, Cathedral of the Immaculate Conception of Mary. 2.25pa, Free Wesleyan Church, Nuku'alofa.

2003, Nov. 10
1115-1118 A227   Set of 4   8.25   8.25
Christmas.

Year of the Monkey 2004

New Year 2004 (Year of the Monkey) — A228

No. 1119: a, 60s, Spider monkey. b, 80s, Ring-tailed lemur. c, 1pa, Cotton-top tamarin. d, 2.50pa, White-cheeked gibbon.

2004, Feb. 12   Litho.   Perf. 13¼
1119 A228   Sheet of 4, #a-d   7.00   7.00

Nos. 770, 787, 788, 815, 816, 1001, Niuafo'ou Nos. 140, 141 and 145 Surcharged

Type 1 — Small denomination and obliterator

Type 2 — Large denomination and obliterator

Methods and Perfs As Before
2004
1120 A153   10s on 32s #787   50.00   —
1121 A153   10s on 42s #788,   —   —
           Type 1
1122 A153   10s on 42s #788,   150.00   —
           Type 2
1123 A157   10s on 42s #815   350.00   —
1124 A147   10s on 57s Horiz.
           strip of 4, +
           central label,
           #770a-770d   350.00   —
1125 A157   10s on 57s #816   90.00   —
1126 A197   60s on 70s #1001   30.00   —

On Stamps of Niuafo'ou
1127 A25   10s on 42s #140   350.00   —
1128 A26   10s on 42s #145   110.00   —
1129 A25   10s on 57s #141   350.00   —

Size and location of obliterators and new denominations varies. Earliest known use: No. 1126, 3/04; Nos. 1120, 1121, 4/04; Nos. 1122, 1123, 1124, 1125, 1127, 1128, 1129, 6/04. The surcharged Niuafo'ou stamps were not necessarily sent only to Niuafo'ou for sale there.

Fruit
Plants — A229

Designs: 45s, Mango. 60s, Pineapple. 80s, Coconut. 1.80pa, Banana.

2004, Sept. 21   Litho.   Perf. 14¼x14
1130-1133 A229   Set of 4   6.00   6.00

Christmas
A230

Designs: 65s, Madonna and Child. 80s, Journey to Bethlehem. 1.20pa, Annunciation to the Shepherds. 2.50pa, Magi.

2004, Dec.   Perf. 14
1134-1137 A230   Set of 4   8.25   8.25

Royalty — A231

Designs: 65s, King George Tupou I. 90s, King George Tupou II. 1.40pa, Queen Salote Tupou III. 3.05pa, King Taufa'ahau Tupou IV.

2004, July 7   Litho.   Perf. 14
1138-1141 A231   6.75   6.75
1141a   Souvenir sheet of 4, #1138-1141
                   6.75   6.75

Souvenir Sheet

Year of the Rooster 2005
Sheet Value $4.95

New Year 2005 (Year of the Rooster) — A232

No. 1142 — Various roosters with panel color of: a, 65s, Yellow orange. b, 80s, Light green. c, 1pa, Tan. d, 2.50pa, Gray blue.

2005, Feb. 12
1142 A232   Sheet of 4, #a-d   8.50   8.50

Souvenir Sheet

Whales — A233

No. 1143 — Various whales with denominations in: a, 65s, Purple. b, 80s, Yellow. c, 1pa, Green. d, 2.50pa, Pink.

2005, May 4   Perf. 13¼
1143 A233   Sheet of 4, #a-d   8.25   8.25

Coronation of
King Siaosi Tupou
V — A234

King Siaosi Tupou V wearing: 30s, Uniform and sash. 1pa, Tuxedo and sash. 5pa, Robe and crown.

Litho. With Foil Application
2008, Aug. 1   Perf. 14
1144-1145 A234   Set of 2   1.50   1.50

Souvenir Sheet
1146 A234   5pa multi   5.50   5.50
No. 1146 contains one 30x60mm stamp.

Tonga Nos. 999, 1019, 1040, 1045, 1049, and Niuafo'ou Nos. 203, 211, 225 and 235 Surcharged

Type 1 — Serifed
Surcharge

Type 2 — Unserifed Surcharge

Methods and Perfs As Before
2008-10   On Stamps of Tonga
1147 A197   30s on 55s
           #999, type
           1   —   —
1148 A202   30s on 55s
           #1019, type
           1   60.00   —
   a.   Surcharge double   120.00
1149 A210   30s on 55s
           #1040, type
           2   40.00   900.00
1150 A213   30s on 55s
           #1049, type
           2   40.00   —
1151 A212   70s on 55s
           #1045, type
           1   50.00   —

On Stamps of Niuafo'ou
1152 A41   30s on 55s
           #203, type
           2   —   —
1153 A44   30s on 55s
           #211, type
           2   —   —
1154 A52   30s on 55s
           #225, type
           2   —   —
1155 A41   70s on 55s
           #203, type
           2   90.00   —
1156 A56   70s on 55s
           #235, type
           2   —   —

Size, location and obliterators of surcharges vary. Surcharged Niuafo'ou stamps were used in Tonga.
Issued: No. 1147, Nov. 2009; No. 1148, Nov. 2008; Nos. 1149, 1153, July 2008; No. 1150, Feb. 2010; No. 1151, June 2010; Nos. 1152, 1154, 2008; Nos. 1155, 1156, May 2010.
No. 1149 used is valued on cover.

Christmas — A235

No. 1157: a, 3pa, Lighthouse ornament on Christmas tree. b, 5pa, Christmas lights and Free Church of Tonga Cathedral.

2011, Dec. 24   Litho.   Perf. 14
1157 A235   Horiz. pair, #a-b   9.25   9.25

Birds
A236

Designs: 60s, Prosopeia tabuensis. 2.25pa, Anas superciliosa. 2.40pa, Halcyon chloris. 2.50pa, Egretta novaehollandiae. 2.70pa, Aplonis tabuensis. 3pa, Megapodius pritchardii. 3.40pa, Megapodius pritchardii, diff. 4pa, Lalage maculosa. 5pa, Tyto alba. 6.60pa, Halcyon chloris, diff. 7.30pa, Prosopeia tabuensis, diff. 10pa, Swamp harrier.

2012, Feb. 6   Perf. 14
Stamps With White Frames
1158 A236   60s multi   .75   .75
1159 A236   2.25pa multi   2.75   2.75
1160 A236   2.40pa multi   3.00   3.00
1161 A236   2.50pa multi   3.00   3.00
1162 A236   2.70pa multi   3.25   3.25
1163 A236   3pa multi   3.75   3.75
1164 A236   3.40pa multi   4.00   4.00
1165 A236   4pa multi   4.75   4.75
1166 A236   5pa multi   6.00   6.00
1167 A236   6.60pa multi   8.00   8.00
1168 A236   7.30pa multi   8.75   8.75
1169 A236   10pa multi   12.00   12.00
   Nos. 1158-1169 (12)   60.00   60.00

Stamps Without White Frames
1170   Sheet of 12   60.00   60.00
  a.   A236 60s multi   .75   .75
  b.   A236 2.25pa multi   2.75   2.75
  c.   A236 2.40pa multi   3.00   3.00
  d.   A236 2.50pa multi   3.00   3.00
  e.   A236 2.70pa multi   3.25   3.25
  f.   A236 3pa multi   3.75   3.75
  g.   A236 3.40pa multi   4.00   4.00
  h.   A236 4pa multi   4.75   4.75
  i.   A236 5pa multi   6.00   6.00
  j.   A236 6.60pa multi   8.00   8.00
  k.   A236 7.30pa multi   8.75   8.75
  l.   A236 10pa multi   12.00   12.00

Reign of Queen
Elizabeth II, 60th
Anniv. — A237

2012, Mar. 6   Perf. 14¾x14
1171 A237   3.40pa multi   4.00   4.00

Souvenir Sheet
1172 A237   10pa multi   12.00   12.00

Worldwide Fund for Nature
(WWF) — A238

Various depictions of Thorny seahorse: 45s, 2pa, 2.40pa, 3.40pa.

2012, Mar. 12   Perf. 14¼x14
1173-1176 A238   Set of 4   9.75   9.75
1176a   Sheet of 16, 4 each
      #1173-1176   39.00   39.00

For surcharges, see Nos. 1262-1265.

Miniature Sheet

Reconstruction and Development
Porjects — A239

No. 1177: a, 45s, Nuku'alofa construction. b,
85s, Vuna Wharf. c, 2.70pa, Vaiola Hospital. d,
5pa, New construction. e, 8pa, New Vuna
Wharf. f, 10pa, Nuku'alofa sidewalks.

2012, May 30			Perf. 12½	
1177	A239	Sheet of 6, #a-f	30.00	30.00

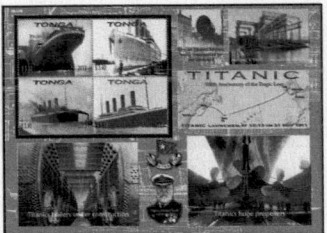

Sinking of the Titanic, Cent. — A240

No. 1178: a, Titanic under construction with
ship under gantries. b, Titanic at dock, ropes
at right. c, Titanic and tuboat. d, Titanic at sea.
No. 1179a, Like #1178a.

2012, June 6			Perf. 12½	
1178	A240	3.40pa Sheet of 4, #a-d	16.00	16.00
Souvenir Sheet				
1179	A240	Sheet of 2, #1178c, 1179a	4.50	4.50
a.		45s multi	.50	.50

ANZAC
Day — A241

Designs: 45s, Council of the South Pacific
Scout Association emblem. 1pa, Flag of
Tonga. 2.40pa, Tonga Girl Guides Emblem.
3.40pa, Rotary International emblem.
No. 1184: a, 3.40pa, Scouts and leaders. b,
5pa, Scouts and leaders, diff.

2012, June 25			Perf. 13½	
1180-1183	A241	Set of 4	8.25	8.25
Souvenir Sheet				
1184	A241	Sheet of 2, #a-b	9.50	9.50

2012 Summer
Olympics,
London — A242

Designs: 45s, Boxing. 1.40pa, Track.
3.40pa, Swimming.

2012, June 25			Perf. 13¾	
1185-1187	A242	Set of 3	6.00	6.00
1187a		Souvenir sheet of 3, #1185-1187	6.00	6.00
1187b		Souvenir sheet of 6, 2 each #1185-1187	12.00	12.00

Personalizable
Stamp
A243

2012, Aug. 8			Perf. 13¼	
1188	A243	3pa multi	3.50	3.50

Tongan Monarchs — A244

2012, Aug. 20			Imperf.	
1189	A244	20pa multi	23.00	23.00

Miniature Sheets

43rd Pacific Islands Forum — A245

No. 1190 — Flags of: a, Canada. b, People's Republic of China. c, European Union. d,
France. e, India. f, Indonesia. g, Italy. h,
Japan. i, Republic of Korea. j, Malaysia. k,
Philippines. l, Thailand. m, United Kingdom. n,
United States.
No. 1191 — Flags of: a, Australia. b, Cook
Islands. c, Fiji. d, Kiribati. e, Micronesia. f,
Nauru. g, New Zealand. h, Niue. i, Palau. j,
Papua New Guinea. k, Marshall Islands. l,
Samoa. m, Solomon Islands. n, Tonga. o,
Tuvalu. p, Vanuatu.

2012, Aug. 31			Perf. 14	
1190	A245	2pa Sheet of 14, #a-n	32.50	32.50
1191	A245	2pa Sheet of 16, #a-p	37.50	37.50

No. 980 Surcharged in Gold and Black

No. 1192: a, 5pa on 10s. b, 5pa on 80s. c,
5pa on 1pa. d, 5pa on 2.50pa.

2012, Sept. 4			Litho.	
1192	CD355	Sheet of 4, #a-d	23.00	23.00

Overprint is printed across the four stamps
of the sheet. It reads "In Loving Memory of
Diana, Princess of Wales / 31 August 1997 /
Her Legacy will live on forever. / William and
Kate, Duke and Duchess of Cambridge / 1st
Anniversary of their Royal Wedding 2011".

Miniature Sheet

Christmas — A246

No. 1193 — Mystical Nativity, by Sandro
Botticelli: a, Angel in red robe at left, angels
with white and brown robes at center. b, White
angel's robe at UL, angels in brown and red
robes at center. c, Parts of five angels, with
angel with red robe at right. d, Angels and
manger roof. e, Virgin Mary, heads of cow and
donkey. f, Angel with green robe to left of manger post. g, Infant Jesus. h, Angels to right of
manger post. i, Angel in green robe embracing
man. j, Angel in white robe embracing man. k,
Angel in red robe embracing man.

2012, Nov. 21			Perf. 14¾x14¼	
1193	A246	1pa Sheet of 11, #a-k, + 2 labels	13.00	13.00

Wedding of Crown Prince Tupouto'a
'Ulukulala and Sinaitakala
Fakafanua — A247

Designs: No. 1194, Photograph of bride,
groom and families.
No. 1195: a, King Tupou VI and Queen
Nanasipau'u (36x36mm). b, Like No. 1194,
without top panel. c, Procession of dignitaries
(36x36mm). d, Bride and groom in robes
(36x36mm). e, Limousine (36x36mm).

2012, Dec. 14			Perf. 13¼	
1194	A247	3pa multi	3.50	3.50
1195	A247	3pa Sheet of 5, #a-e	17.50	17.50

Miniature Sheet

New Year 2013 (Year of the
Snake) — A248

No. 1196: a, Olive green snake with yellow
green underside. b, Red brown snake with
green underside. c, Yellow green snake with
orange red underside. d, Purple snake with
yellow green underside.

2013, Feb. 20			Perf. 14¾x14¼	
1196	A248	2.45pa Sheet of 4, #a-d	11.50	11.50

A249

A250

A251

A252

A253

A254

A255

Turtles
A256

2013, Feb. 21			Perf. 14	
Stamps With White Backgrounds				
1197		Horiz. strip of 4	19.00	19.00
a.	A249	4pa multi	4.75	4.75
b.	A250	4pa multi	4.75	4.75
c.	A251	4pa multi	4.75	4.75
d.	A252	4pa multi	4.75	4.75
1198		Horiz. strip of 4	23.00	23.00
a.	A253	5pa multi	5.75	5.75
b.	A254	5pa multi	5.75	5.75
c.	A255	5pa multi	5.75	5.75
d.	A256	5pa multi	5.75	5.75
Miniature Sheets				
Stamps With Colored Backgrounds				
1199		Sheet of 4	19.00	19.00
a.	A249	4pa multi	4.75	4.75
b.	A250	4pa multi	4.75	4.75
c.	A251	4pa multi	4.75	4.75
d.	A252	4pa multi	4.75	4.75
1200		Sheet of 4	23.00	23.00
a.	A253	5pa multi	5.75	5.75
b.	A254	5pa multi	5.75	5.75
c.	A255	5pa multi	5.75	5.75
d.	A256	5pa multi	5.75	5.75

Souvenir Sheet

Australia 2013 World Stamp Expo, Melbourne — A257

No. 1201: a, Koala. b, Royal Exhibition Building, Melbourne. c, Red kangaroo.

2013, May 10   *Perf. 13¼*
1201	A257	3pa Sheet of 3, #a-c	10.00	10.00

Miniature Sheet

Blow Holes and Fish — A258

No. 1202 — Fish: a, 3pa, Chaetodon flavirostris, Pseudanthias pleurotaenia. b, 3pa, Pygoplites diacanthus, Amblyglyphidodon melanopterus. c, 4pa, Acanthurus guttatus, Myripristis hexagona. d, 4pa, Pseudanthias pleurotaenia, Zanclus comutus. e, 5pa, Zanclus comutus, Pygoplites diacanthus. f, 5pa, Amblyglyphidodon melanopterus, Myripristis hexagona.

2013, June 4   *Perf. 13¾*
1202	A258	Sheet of 6, #a-f	27.00	27.00

Birds and Flora A259

Designs: 10s, Halcyon chloris, Adenanthera pavonina. 20s, Aplonis tabuensis, Myristica hypagyraea. 30s, Vini australis, Artocarpus altilis. 40s, Fregata minor, Hibiscus tiliaceus. 50s, Sula sula, Terminalia catappa. 80s, Phaeton rubricauda, Cocos nucifera. 90s, Anous minutus, Elattostachys falcata. 1.10pa, Lalage maculosa, Tarenina sambucina. 1.20pa, Porzana tabuensis, Mimosa pigra. 2pa, Foulehaio carunculatus, Solanum mauritianum. 12.50pa, Prosopeia tabuensis, Adenanthera pavonina. 20pa, Ptilinopus perousil, Psidium guajava.

2013, June 6   *Perf. 14*
Stamps With White Frames
1203	A259	10s multi	.25	.25
1204	A259	20s multi	.25	.25
1205	A259	30s multi	.35	.35
1206	A259	40s multi	.45	.45
1207	A259	50s multi	.55	.55
1208	A259	80s multi	.90	.90
1209	A259	90s multi	1.00	1.00
1210	A259	1.10pa multi	1.25	1.25
1211	A259	1.20pa multi	1.40	1.40
1212	A259	2pa multi	2.25	2.25
1213	A259	12.50pa multi	14.00	14.00
1214	A259	20pa multi	22.50	22.50
		Nos. 1203-1214 (12)	45.15	45.15

Miniature Sheet
Stamps Without White Frames
1215		Sheet of 12	46.00	46.00
a.	A259	10s multi	.25	.25
b.	A259	20s multi	.25	.25
c.	A259	30s multi	.35	.35
d.	A259	40s multi	.45	.45
e.	A259	50s multi	.55	.55
f.	A259	80s multi	.90	.90
g.	A259	90s multi	1.00	1.00
h.	A259	1.10pa multi	1.25	1.25
i.	A259	1.20pa multi	1.40	1.40
j.	A259	2pa multi	2.25	2.25
k.	A259	12.50pa multi	14.00	14.00
l.	A259	20pa multi	22.50	22.50

Fire Dancers, Hana's Cave, Oholei Beach Resort A260

Designs: 15s, Girl clapping. 1.75pa, Dancers. 4.70pa, Dancers with three torches.
No. 1219, vert.: a, 5.25pa, Dancer with torch burining on both ends. b, 7.85pa, Dancer holding torch well above head. c, 8.65pa, Dancer holding torch close to mouth.

2013, Aug. 14   *Litho.*   *Perf. 13¾*
1216-1218	A260	Set of 3	7.25	7.25

Souvenir Sheet
Perf. 13¾x13½
1219	A260	Sheet of 3, #a-c	23.50	23.50

Birth of Prince George of Cambridge A261

Designs: 1.75pa, Baby's feet on adult's hands. 2.40pa, Adult's hands touching baby's feet. 2.60pa, Baby's hand holding adult's finger. 3.40pa, Baby's hand holding adult's finger, diff.
11.30pa, Baby's hand in adult's hand.

2013, Aug. 30   *Litho.*   *Perf. 13¾*
1220-1223	A261	Set of 4	11.00	11.00

Souvenir Sheet
1224	A261	11.30pa multi	12.50	12.50

Miniature Sheet

Giant Pandas — A262

No. 1225 — Panda: a, Sitting under tree. b, In snow. c, Chewing on long stick. d, Face. e, Eating bamboo leaves.

2013, Sept. 26   *Litho.*   *Perf. 12*
1225	A262	2.50pa Sheet of 5, #a-e	14.00	14.00

Souvenir Sheet

China International Collection Expo 2013, Beijing — A263

No. 1226: a, Painting by Paul Gauguin. b, Beijing Exhibition Center.

2013, Sept. 26   *Litho.*   *Perf. 12*
1226	A263	2pa multi	4.50	4.50

Watercraft and Tin Can Island Mail Cans — A264

Design: 2.25pa, Ship and mail can at sea. 5.40pa, Canoe, mail can on shore.

2013, Sept. 27   *Litho.*   *Perf. 14¼*
1227	A264	2.25pa multi	2.50	2.50

Souvenir Sheet
1228	A264	5.40pa multi	6.00	6.00

Dragon A265

2013, Oct. 15   *Litho.*   *Perf. 12*
1229	A265	8pa multi	8.75	8.75

No. 1229 was printed in sheets of 2.

Souvenir Sheets

A266

Diplomatic Relations Between Tonga and People's Republic of China, 15th Anniv. — A267

No. 1230: a, Vaipua Bridge, Tonga. b, MA60 airplane.
No. 1231: a, Great Wall of China. b, Haamonga Trilithon, Tonga.

2013, Nov. 2   *Litho.*   *Perf. 13½x13¾*
1230	A266	3pa Sheet of 2, #a-b	6.75	6.75

Perf. 13x13¼
1231	A267	3pa Sheet of 2, #a-b	6.75	6.75

King Tupou VI — A268

2013, Nov. 12   *Litho.*   *Perf. 14¼*
Panel Color
1232	A268	45s blue gray	.50	.50
1233	A268	50s dull org	.55	.55
1234	A268	75s yel bister	.80	.80
1235	A268	1.05pa dull yel grn	1.10	1.10
1236	A268	2.40pa brown	2.60	2.60
1237	A268	2.60pa dull yel org	2.75	2.75
1238	A268	3.40pa dull brn	3.75	3.75
		Nos. 1232-1238 (7)	12.05	12.05

Christmas A269

Paintings by: 1.75pa, Simon Vouet. 2.35pa, Giotto di Bondone. 2.60pa, Jan van Eyck.

2013, Nov. 13   *Litho.*   *Perf. 13½*
1239-1241	A269	Set of 3	7.25	7.25

Miniature Sheets

Cruise Ships and Wharves — A270

No. 1242: a, 1.75pa, Ocean Princess at New Vuna Wharf. b, 1.75pa, MS Amadea. c, 1.75pa, Seabourne Quest. d, 2.40pa, MS Columbus. e, 2.40pa, MS Europa. f, 2.40pa, New Vuna Wharf.
No. 1243: a, 2.60pa, Pacific Jewel. b, 2.60pa, MS Dawn Princess. c, 2.60pa, MS Artania. d, 3.40pa, Sea Princess. e, 3.40pa, MS Regatta. f, 3.40pa, New Vuna Wharf, diff.

2013, Dec. 11   *Litho.*   *Perf. 14*
1242	A270	Sheet of 6, #a-f	13.50	13.50
1243	A270	Sheet of 6, #a-f	19.50	19.50

Souvenir Sheet

Christening of Prince George of Cambridge — A271

2014, Jan. 3   *Litho.*   *Perf. 13¼*
1244	A271	10pa multi	11.00	11.00

Miniature Sheet

New Year 2014 (Year of the Horse) — A272

No. 1245: a, Horse's head. b, Horse facing left, leaping. c, Horse facing right, walking. d, Horse facing right, leaping.

2014, Jan. 6   *Litho.*   *Perf. 13¾*
1245	A272	2.45pa Sheet of 4, #a-d	10.50	10.50

Chinese Space Program A273

Spacecraft and: 1.75pa, Astronaut Liu Yang. 2.40pa, Map of People's Republic of China. 2.60pa, Astronaut Jing Haipeng. 3.40pa, Jing Haipeng, diff.

2014, Feb. 3   Litho.   Perf. 14¾x14¼
1246-1249 A273   Set of 4   11.00 11.00

Miniature Sheet

Easter — A274

No. 1250 — Various paintings of the resurrected Christ by Tiziano Vecellio (Titian): a, 2.35pa. b, 3pa. c, 4.60pa. d, 6.95pa.

2014, Apr. 7   Litho.   Perf. 13¼
1250 A274   Sheet of 4, #a-d   18.50 18.50

Bactrian Camels, by Wu Zuoren (1908-97) — A275

2014, Apr. 9   Litho.   Perf. 14¾x14¼
1251 A275   5pa multi   5.50 5.50
No. 1251 was printed in sheets of 4.

Souvenir Sheet

Nelson Mandela (1918-2013), President of South Africa — A276

No. 1252 — Mandela: a, Carrying book and papers. b, Wearing necklace.

2014, May 13   Litho.   Perf. 14¾x14¼
1252 A276   5pa Sheet of 2, #a-b   11.00 11.00

Pacific Small Island Developing States — A277

No. 1253: a, Rising sea levels. b, Tropical Cyclone Ian. c, Emblem of Pacific Small Island Developing States. d, Map of Tonga and Fiji. e, Island Voices Global Choices emblem. f, Sailboat. g, Cruise ship. h, USS Cleveland. i, Fishing boat. j, Landing Craft Utility 1665. k, Tubastraea micranthus. l, Pseudanthias squaminnis. m, Amphiprion ocellaris. n, Rhincodon typus. o, Laticauda colubrina. p, Flag of Tonga.
No. 1254: a, Like #1253a. b, Like #1253p. c, Like #1253b. d, Like #1253c. e, Like #1253d. f, Like #1253e.
No. 1255: a, Like #1253f. b, Like #1253p. c, Like #1253g. d, Like #1253h. e, Like #1253i. f, Like #1253j.
No. 1256: a, Like #1253k. b, Like #1253p. c, Like #1253l. d, Like #1253m. e, Like #1253n. f, Like #1253o.

2014, May 20   Litho.   Perf. 13¼
1253   Block of 18, #1253a-   9.00 9.00
    1253o, 3 #1253p
a.-p. A277 45s Any single   .50 .50

Miniature Sheets
1254   Sheet of 6   11.50 11.50
a.-f. A277 1.75pa Any single   1.90 1.90
1255   Sheet of 6   15.00 15.00
a.-f. A277 2.35pa Any single   2.50 2.50
1256   Sheet of 6   15.00 15.00
a.-f. A277 2.60pa Any single   2.75 2.75
    Nos. 1254-1256 (3)   41.50 41.50

No. 1253 was printed in sheets containing 3 blocks of 18. The frame on each stamp in the sheet, depicting a map of the Pacific Ocean, differs.

Birds — A278

No. 1257: a, 11.30pa, Barn owl. b, 16.90pa, Blue-crowned lorikeet. c, 28pa, Buff-banded rail.

2014, Sept. 15   Litho.   Perf. 13¼
1257 A278   Horiz. strip of 3,   57.50 57.50
    #a-c, + 3 labels

Miniature Sheet

Tongan Participation in the Commonwealth Games, 40th Anniv. — A279

No. 1258: a, 1.75pa, Boxing. b, 2.35pa, Pole vault. c, 2.40pa, Rugby sevens. d, 2.60pa, Judo. e, 3.40pa, Weight lifting.

2014, Sept. 17   Litho.   Perf. 14
1258 A279   Sheet of 5, #a-e,   13.00 13.00
    + label

Miniature Sheet

Christmas — A280

Bells and: a, Musical score with five staffs, denomination in white. b, Musical score with five staffs, denomination in black. c, Musical score with three staffs, denomination in black. d, Curving staff with G clef and notes, denomination in white.

2014, Dec. 15   Litho.   Perf. 13¾
1259 A280   2.25pa Sheet of 4,   9.25 9.25
    #a-d

A281

New Year 2015 (Year of the Sheep) — A282

No. 1261 — Sheep with background colors of: a, 11.30pa, Yellow green and green. b, 16.90pa, Yellow brown and brown.

2015, Jan. 5   Litho.   Perf. 13¼
1260 A281   8pa multi   7.75 7.75

Souvenir Sheet
Self-Adhesive
Die Cut Perf. 13½
1261 A282   Sheet of 2, #a-b   27.00 27.00
No. 1261 has rouletting in sheet margin allowing the entire sheet to be folded into a hangable lantern.

Nos. 1173-1176 Surcharged

Methods and Perfs. As Before
2015, Apr. 1
1262 A238   90s on 2.40pa   .90 .90
    #1175
1263 A238   1pa on 3.40pa   1.00 1.00
    #1176
1264 A238   1.10pa on 45s #1173   1.10 1.10
1265 A238   1.20pa on 2pa #1174   1.25 1.25
    Nos. 1262-1265 (4)   4.25 4.25

Appointment of Soane Patita Paini Mafi as Cardinal of Tonga — A283

Cardina Mafi: 2.25pa, Holding scroll. 2.70pa, Smiling. 5pa, Pope Francis. 8.50pa, Cardinal Mafi and Pope Francis.

2015, Apr. 1   Litho.   Perf. 13¼
1266-1268 A283   Set of 3   10.00 10.00
Souvenir Sheet
1269 A283   8.50pa multi   8.50 8.50

Miniature Sheet

Easter — A284

No. 1270 — Details of painting by Rembrandt: a, Christ and another man on cross. b, Another man on cross. c, People at base of Christ's cross. d, Foliage and mourning women.

2015, Apr. 3   Litho.   Perf. 14¼
1270 A284   2.25pa Sheet of 4,   9.00 9.00
    #a-d

Souvenir Sheet

Birth of Princess Charlotte of Cambridge — A285

No. 1271: a, Duchess of Cambridge holding Princess Charlotte. b, Duke of Cambridge holding Prince George.

2015, June 30   Litho.   Perf. 14¾x14
1271 A285   5pa Sheet of 2, #a-b   9.75 9.75

Coronation of
King Tupou
VI — A286

Designs: No. 1272, 2.25pa, King Tupou VI.
$5, King Tupou VI and Queen Nanasipau'u.
No. 1274, 2.25pa: a, Throne (30x30mm). b,
King Tupou VI and Queen Nanasipau'u, diff.
(40x30mm). c, Crown (40x30mm).

2015, July 4   Litho.   Perf. 14¼x14¾
1272-1273 A286   Set of 2   7.00 7.00
Souvenir Sheet
Perf. 14¾ (#1274a), 14¾x14¼
1274 A286 2.25pa Sheet of 3,
    #a-c   6.50 6.50

Magna
Carta,
800th
Anniv.
A287

Designs: 2pa, Medallion depicting King
John. 2.25pa, Statue of Justice. 2.70pa, King
John. 5pa, Arms of England and Tonga.

2015, July 20   Litho.   Perf. 14x14¾
1275-1278 A287   Set of 4   11.50 11.50

New Year
2016 (Year
of the Monkey)
A288

Designs: 8pa, Monkey with peach. 11.70pa,
Monkey.
No. 1281: a, 11.30pa, Monkey with peach,
diff. b, 16.90pa, Monkey, diff.

2015, Sept. 25   Litho.   Perf. 13¼
1279-1280 A288   Set of 2   18.00 18.00
Souvenir Sheet
Self-Adhesive
Die Cut Perf. 11
1281 A288   Sheet of 2, #a-b 26.00 26.00

No. 1281 has rouletting in the sheet margin
allowing the entire sheet to be folded into a
lantern and contains two 51x51 diamond-
shaped stamps.

Miniature Sheet

Queen Elizabeth II, Longest-Reigning
British Monarch — A289

No, 1282 — Queen Elizabeth II in Tonga: a,
Laying wreath at War Memorial. b, Approaching feast house. c, Holding plate at feast

house. d, With Tongan Queen Salote Tupou III
and Prince Philip.

2015, Nov. 23   Litho.   Perf. 14
1282 A289 2pa Sheet of 4, #a-d 7.00 7.00

Miniature Sheet

Christmas — A290

No. 1283 — Religious paintings by: a, Pietro
Perugino. b, Sandro Botticelli. c, Martin
Schongauer. d, Fra Diamante.

2015, Dec. 7   Litho.   Perf. 13¾
1283 A290 1.50pa Sheet of 4,
    #a-d   5.25 5.25

Second Summit of the Forum for
India-Pacific Islands Cooperation,
Jaipur, India — A291

Mohandas K. Gandhi, Garcinia sessilis,
lotus flower and: 2.25pa, Red pandas. 4.20pa,
Bengal tigers. 5pa, Indian cobras. 6.50pa,
Indian leopards.

2016, Jan. 14   Litho.   Perf. 13¼
1284-1287 A291   Set of 4   15.50 15.50
1287a   Souvenir sheet of 4,
    #1284-1287   15.50 15.50

Miniature Sheets

World War I, Cent. — A292

World War II, 75th Anniv. — A293

No. 1288: a, Inscription on Tonga World War
I Memorial. b, View of World War I Memorial
from side. c, View of World War I Memorial
from front. d, Inscription of war casualties.

No. 1289 — Inscription: a, Aircraft front. b,
Bayonet drill. c, Carrier platoon. d, Governor
General inspecting Guard of Honor.

2016, Feb. 2   Litho.   Perf. 14¼
1288 A292   2pa Sheet of 4,
    #a-d   7.00 7.00
1289 A293 2.25pa Sheet of 4,
    #a-d   7.75 7.75

Worldwide
Fund for
Nature
(WWF)
A294

Banded iguana: Nos. 1290, 1294a, 1.20pa,
On rock with head raised. Nos. 1291, 1294b,
2pa, On rock. Nos. 1292, 1294c, 2.25pa, On
heliconia flower. Nos. 1293, 1294d, 2.70pa,
On branch.

2016, Mar. 14   Litho.   Perf. 14¾x14
Stamps With White Frames
1290-1293 A294   Set of 4   7.50 7.50
Stamps Without White Frames
1294   Strip of 4   7.50 7.50
  a. A294 1.20pa multi   1.10 1.10
  b. A294 2pa multi   1.75 1.75
  c. A294 2.25pa multi   2.10 2.10
  d. A294 2.70pa multi   2.50 2.50

Miniature Sheet

Landing of Dutch Explorers in Tonga,
400th Anniv. — A295

No. 1295: a, 1.20pa, Willem Schouten,
ships Eendracht and Hoorn. b, 2.25pa, Schouten and Jacob Le Maire, astrolabe. c, 2.70pa,
Le Maire and Eendracht. d, 5pa, Le Maire,
Schouten and compass.

2016, Apr. 25   Litho.   Perf. 14
1295 A295   Sheet of 4, #a-d 10.00 10.00

Souvenir Sheet

Queen Elizabeth II, 90th
Birthday — A296

No. 1296 — Queen Elizabeth II: a, Wearing
military cap. b, Holding baby.

2016, May 3   Litho.   Perf. 13
1296 A296 2pa Sheet of 2, #a-b 3.50 3.50

Souvenir Sheet

Tupou College, Toloa, 150th
Anniv. — A297

No. 1297: a, 2.25pa, Students. b, 5pa, University building.

2016, June 10   Litho.   Perf. 13
1297 A297   Sheet of 2, #a-b 6.75 6.75

2016 Summer
Olympics, Rio de
Janeiro — A298

Nos. 1298 and 1299: a, Swimming. b, Athletics. c, Archery. d, Taekwondo.

2016, Sept. 5   Litho.   Perf. 13¼
1298   Horiz. strip of 4   7.00 7.00
  a.-d. A298 2pa Any single   1.75 1.75
1299   Horiz. strip of 4   8.00 8.00
  a.-d. A298 2.25pa Any single 2.00 2.00

Marine Life and
Birds — A299

Designs: 90s, Stony coral. 1pa, Black
noddy. 1.10pa, Brown booby. 1.20pa, Bryde's
whale. 2pa, Yellowfin goatfish. 2.25pa, Short-
beaked common dolphin. 2.70pa, Fairy terns.
4.20pa, Whale shark. 5pa, Blue-footed booby.
6.70pa, Freckled hawkfish. 9.20pa, Spinner
dolphin. 11.70pa, Tiger shark.

2016, Mar. 2   Perf. 14x14¾
1300 A299   90s multi   .80   .80
1301 A299   1pa multi   .90   .90
1302 A299 1.10pa multi   1.00   1.00
1303 A299 1.20pa multi   1.10   1.10
1304 A299   2pa multi   1.75   1.75
1305 A299 2.25pa multi   2.00   2.00
1306 A299 2.70pa multi   2.40   2.40
1307 A299 4.20pa multi   3.75   3.75
1308 A299   5pa multi   4.50   4.50
1309 A299 6.70pa multi   6.00   6.00
1310 A299 9.20pa multi   8.25   8.25
1311 A299 11.70pa multi   10.50 10.50
    Nos. 1300-1311 (12)   42.95 42.95

New Year
2017 (Year of
the Rooster)
A300

Designs: No. 1312, 5pa, No. 1314a, 15pa,
One rooster. No. 1313, 5.50pa, No. 1314b,
16.90pa, Two roosters.

2016, Aug. 10   Litho.   Perf. 13½
1312-1313 A300   Set of 2   9.75 9.75
Souvenir Sheet
Self-Adhesive
Die Cut Perf. 11
1314 A300   Sheet of 2, #a-b 29.50 29.50

No. 1314 contains two 50x50mm diamond-
shaped stamps, and sheet could be folded into
a lantern.

Miniature Sheet

Queen Mother Halaevalu Mata'aho,
90th Birthday — A301

No. 1315 — Queen Mother and: a, Girls at
play, "Education" at right. b, Girls and infant,
"Empowerment of women" at left. c, Woman
with fishing net, "Empowerment of women" at
right. d, Girl and boy, "Education" at left.

2016, Dec. 2   Litho.   *Perf. 13¾*
1315 A301 2.25pa Sheet of 4,
       #a-d   8.25 8.25

Christmas — A302

No. 1316 — Various churches with "Christmas" at: a, 2pa, Left. b, 2pa, Right. c, 2.70pa,
Left. d, 2.70pa, Right.

2016, Dec. 19   Litho.   *Perf. 13¼*
1316 A302   Block of 4, #a-d   8.25 8.25

Miniature Sheet

Easter — A303

No. 1317 — Paintings depicting the resurrection of Christ by: a, Jean François de Troy.
b, Carl Bloch. c, Benjamin West. d, Rembrandt
van Rijn.

2017, Apr. 10   Litho.   *Perf. 12¾*
1317 A303 2.25pa Sheet of 4,
       #a-d   8.00 8.00

Miniature Sheet

Reign of Queen Elizabeth II, 65th
Anniv. — A304

No. 1318 — Queen Elizabeth II wearing: a,
Blue jacket and hat. b, Red jacket and hat. c,
Pink and white dress and pink hat. d, Bright
yellow green jacket and hat.

2017, June 7   Litho.   *Perf. 12¾*
1318 A304 3pa Sheet of 4, #a-
       d   11.00 11.00

Miniature Sheet

Pres. John F. Kennedy (1917-
63) — A305

No. 1319 — Pres. Kennedy: a, 2.50pa,
Signing Peace Corps Act. b, 2.50pa, Signing
Cuba quarantine order. c, 2.75pa, Meeting first
Peace Corps volunteers. d, 2.75pa, With
Peace Corps director Sargent Shriver.

2017, June 21   Litho.   *Perf. 12¾*
1319 A305   Sheet of 4, #a-d   9.75 9.75

'Eua National Park — A306

No. 1320: a, Red shining parrot facing left.
b, 'Eua National Park lookout. c, Coastline as
seen from overlook. d, Red shining parrot facing right.
7.50pa, Red shining parrot, horiz.

2017, July 10   Litho.   *Perf. 13x13¼*
1320 A306   5pa Block of 4,
       #a-d   19.00 19.00

Souvenir Sheet
Perf. 13¼x13
1321 A306   7.50pa multi   7.00 7.00

Halley's Comet — A307

No. 1322: a, People viewing comet. b,
Comet and squares. c, Comet appearance on
Bayeux Tapestry. d, Man holding string of
comet model.
5pa, Cross-sections of meteorites.

2017, July 12   Litho.   *Perf. 13¼x13*
1322 A307 2.25pa Block of 4, #a-
       d   8.50 8.50

Souvenir Sheet
1323 A307   5pa multi   4.75 4.75

Miniature Sheet

Cheongsams With Seasonal
Designs — A308

No. 1324 — Background color of cheong-
sam: a, 5pa, Apple green. b, 6.50pa, Light
blue. c, 9pa, Light brown. d, 11.50pa, Salmon
pink.

2017, July 14   Litho.   *Die Cut*
Self-Adhesive
1324 A308   Sheet of 4, #a-d   30.00 30.00
   e.   Souvenir sheet of 4,
      #1324a-1324d,
      269x163mm sheet   30.00 30.00
Nos. 1324a-1324d have simulated
perforations.

Miniature Sheet

International Year of Sustainable
Tourism for Development — A309

No. 1325: a, Kayaker near Vava'u Islands. b,
Bananas, papayas and breadfruit. c, Wait-
resses at Friends Café. d, Tourists viewing
Mounu Island from boat. e, Woman holding
decanter. f, Members of Church of Tonga.

2017, July 18   Litho.   *Perf. 12¾*
1325 A309 2.25pa Sheet of 6,
       #a-f   13.00 13.00

Peace Corps in
Tonga, 50th
Anniv. — A310

Designs: No. 1326, 2.25pa, Scarlet dove in
white emblem. No. 1327, 6.50pa, Scarlet dove
in black emblem. No. 1328, 6.50pa, White
dove in black emblem. No. 1329, 8pa, White
dove in scarlet emblem.

2017, Aug. 31   Litho.   *Perf. 13*
1326-1329 A310 Set of 4   21.50 21.50

Elimination
of
Lymphatic
Filariasis
in Tonga
— A311

2017, Sept. 9   Litho.   *Perf. 13*
1330 A311 10pa multi   9.00 9.00

New Year
2018 (Year of
the
Dog) — A312

Designs; 6.50pa, One dog. 6.70pa, Two stylized dogs.

2017, Nov. 1   Litho.   *Perf. 13¼*
1331-1332 A312 Set of 2   12.00 12.00
1332a   Souvenir sheet of 2,
      #1331-1332   12.00 12.00

Christmas — A313

No. 1333: a, Shell. b, Birds, palm trees and
Christmas ornament. c, Bat. d, Whale.

2017, Dec. 4   Litho.   *Perf. 12½*
1333 A313 2.25pa Block of 4, #a-
       d   8.25 8.25

Miniature Sheet

Easter — A314

No. 1334: a, Purple flowers and butterfly. b,
Church and palm trees. c, Flowers, shells and
Easter eggs. d, Palm fronds.

2018, Mar. 15   Litho.   *Perf. 12¾*
1334 A314 2.25pa Sheet of 4,
       #a-d   8.25 8.25

Birdpex 2018, Mondorf-les-Bains,
Luxembourg — A315

No. 1335 — Orange-footed scrubfowl facing: a, Left. b, Right.

2018, May 3   Litho.   *Perf. 13¼*
1335 A315 5pa Horiz. pair, #a-b   9.00 9.00

Souvenir Sheet

Birth of Prince Louis of Cambridge — A316

No. 1336: a, Duke and Duchess of Cambridge with Prince Louis. b, Public birth announcement. c, Duke of Cambridge with Prince George and Princess Charlotte.

2018, May 25   Litho.   *Perf. 13*
1336 A316 2.50pa Sheet of 3, #a-c   6.75   6.75

Wedding of Prince Harry and Meghan Markle — A317

No. 1337: a, Bride and page boys. b, Couple kissing.
9.20pa, Couple in coach, waving.

2018, July 27   Litho.   *Perf. 13*
1337 A317   5pa Sheet of 2, #a-b   8.75   8.75

Souvenir Sheet
1338 A317 9.20pa multi   8.25   8.25

Animals of the World — A318

No. 1339, 2.50pa: a, Mini lop-eared rabbit. b, Fennec fox.
No. 1340, 5pa: a, Derbyana flower beetle. b, Big-eyed tree frog.
10pa, Tiger swallowtail butterfly.

2018-19   Litho.   *Perf. 13*
Horiz. Pairs, #a-b
1339-1340 A318 Set of 2   13.50   13.50
Souvenir Sheet
1341 A318 10pa multi   9.00   9.00
Issued: Nos. 1339-1340, 2/8/19; No. 1341, 9/10.

New Year 2019 (Year of the Pig) — A319

Designs: 6.50pa, Two pigs. 6.70pa, Two pigs, diff.

2018, Dec. 10   Litho.   *Perf. 13¼*
1342-1343 A319 Set of 2   11.50   11.50

Miniature Sheets

A320

Christmas — A321

No. 1344 — Madonna and Child paintings by: a, Hugo van der Goes. b, Sandro Botticelli (hands of Jesus on Mary's breasts). c, Hans Memling. d, Peter Paul Rubens. e, Botticelli (hand of Jesus on book). f, Master of the Legend of St. Catherine.
No. 1345 — Madonna and Child paintings by: a, Raphael (two angels in foreground). b, Rubens (Jesus held by Mary and Joseph). c, Giovanni Battista Tiepolo. d, Rubens (Jesus in swaddling cloth). e, Rubens (Jesus held by Mary). f, Raphael (halo above Mary).

2018, Dec. 17   Litho.   *Perf. 13*
1344 A320   50s Sheet of 6, #a-f   2.75   2.75
1345 A321 2.30pa Sheet of 6, #a-f   12.00   12.00

Birds of Prey — A322

Designs: 5s, Bat hawk. 10s, White-tailed kite. 1.40pa, Black-winged kite. 2.30pa, Madagascan fish eagle. 2.50pa, Gray-headed kite. 2.80pa, Lesser fish eagle. 4.30pa, Besra. 5.20pa, Jerdon's baza. 6.90pa, Black baza. 9.30pa, African cuckoo-hawk. 9.50pa, Dark chanting goshawk. 11.50pa, Scissor-tailed kite.

2018, Dec. 18   Litho.   *Perf. 13*
Stamps With White Frames
1346	A322	5s multi	.25	.25
1347	A322	10s multi	.25	.25
1348	A322	1.40pa multi	1.25	1.25
1349	A322	2.30pa multi	2.00	2.00
1350	A322	2.50pa multi	2.25	2.25
1351	A322	2.80pa multi	2.50	2.50
a.		Souvenir sheet of 6, #1346-1351	8.50	8.50
1352	A322	4.30pa multi	3.75	3.75
1353	A322	5.20pa multi	4.75	4.75
1354	A322	6.90pa multi	6.00	6.00
1355	A322	9.30pa multi	8.25	8.25
1356	A322	9.50pa multi	8.50	8.50
1357	A322	11.50pa multi	10.00	10.00
a.		Souvenir sheet of 6, #1352-1357	41.50	41.50
		Nos. 1346-1357 (12)	49.75	49.75

Miniature Sheet
Stamps Without White Frame
1358	Sheet of 12	50.00	50.00
a.	A322 5s multi	.25	.25
b.	A322 10s multi	.25	.25
c.	A322 1.40pa multi	1.25	1.25
d.	A322 2.30pa multi	2.00	2.00
e.	A322 2.50pa multi	2.25	2.25
f.	A322 2.80pa multi	2.50	2.50
g.	A322 4.30pa multi	3.75	3.75
h.	A322 5.20pa multi	4.75	4.75
i.	A322 6.90pa multi	6.00	6.00
j.	A322 9.30pa multi	8.25	8.25
k.	A322 9.50pa multi	8.50	8.50
l.	A322 11.50pa multi	10.00	10.00

Stamps on Nos. 1351a and 1357a have white frames on one or two sides.

SEMI-POSTAL STAMP

Catalogue values for unused stamps in this section are for Never Hinged items.

No. 488 Surcharged in Silver

1982, Apr. 14   Litho.
B1 A86 1pa +50s on 3pa multi   4.50   4.50

AIR POST STAMPS

Catalogue values for unused stamps in this section are for Never Hinged items.

Type of Regular Gold Coin Issue

Designs: 10p, 1sh1p, Queen Salote standing, ½-koula coin, obverse. 11p, Coat of arms, ½-koula coin, reverse. 2sh1p, 2sh9p, Queen Salote standing, 1-koula coin, obverse. 2sh4p, Coat of arms, 1-koula coin, reverse.

Litho.; Embossed on Gilt Foil
1963, July 15   Unwmk.   *Die Cut*
Diameter: 54mm
C1	A36	10p dp carmine	.50	.50
C2	A36	11p green	.70	.70
C3	A36	1sh1p violet blue	.70	.70

Diameter: 80mm
C4	A36	2sh1p magenta	1.25	1.25
C5	A36	2sh4p emerald	1.25	1.25
C6	A36	2sh9p violet	2.00	2.00
		Nos. C1-C6 (6)	6.40	6.40

See note after No. 133.

Map of Tongatabu and ¼-Koula Coin — AP1

Litho.; Embossed on Gilt Foil
1964, Oct. 19
C7	AP1	10p deep green	.30	.30
C8	AP1	1sh2p black	.45	.45
C9	AP1	3sh6p carmine	.95	.95
C10	AP1	6sh6p purple	1.75	1.75
		Nos. C7-C10 (4)	3.45	3.45

Pan-Pacific and Southeast Asia Women's Association Conf., Nukualofa, Aug. 1964. See note after No. 133.
For overprints and surcharges see Nos. C22-C26, C83-C86.

Nos. C1-C2, C4-C6 Srchd. like Regular Issue, 1965, in Black, White or Red

1965, Mar. 18
C11	A36	2sh3p on 10p (B)	2.00	1.00
C12	A36	2sh9p on 11p (W)	3.50	2.00
C13	A36	4sh6p on 2sh1p	22.50	22.50
C14	A36	4sh6p on 2sh4p	22.50	22.50
C15	A36	4sh6p on 2sh9p	13.50	13.50
		Nos. C11-C15 (5)	54.25	54.25

Nos. 114-115, 117-118 Ovptd. or Srchd.

Perf. 14½x13½
1966, June 18   Wmk. 79
C16	A35	5p purple	.25	.25
C17	A35	10p on 1p brn org & car rose	.25	.25
C18	A35	1sh red brown	.40	.25
C19	A35	2sh9p on 2p ultra	.50	.25
C20	A35	3sh6p on 5p purple	.50	.25
C21	A35	4sh6p on 1sh red brn	.75	.30
		Nos. C16-C21 (6)	2.25	1.20

Centenary of Tupou College and secondary education. The overprint or surcharge is spaced differently on other values.
For Surcharges see Nos. C55-C57.

Nos. C7-C8 Ovptd. and Srchd. in Silver or Gold on Black, or in Black on Gold

Litho.; Embossed on Gilt Foil
1966, Dec. 16   Unwmk.   *Die Cut*
C22	AP1	10p (S on B)	.50	.40
C23	AP1	1sh2p (B on G)	.50	.40
C24	AP1	4sh on 10p (S on B)	1.00	1.00
C25	AP1	5sh6p on 1sh2p (B on G)	1.50	1.50
C26	AP1	10sh6p on 1sh2p (G on B)	2.50	2.50
		Nos. C22-C26 (5)	5.40	5.40

In memory of Queen Salote (1900-65). See Nos. C83-C86.

King Taufa'ahau Type of Regular Issue, 1967

Designs: 7s, 11s, 23s, 2pa, Taufa'ahau IV, obverse of new palladium coins. 9s, 21s, 29s, Coat of Arms, reverse.

Litho.; Embossed on Palladium Foil
1967, July 4
Diameter: 7s, 44mm; 9s, 29s, 52mm; 11s, 59mm; 21s, 68mm; 23s, 40mm; 2pa, 74mm.
C27	A38	7s red & black	.50	.40
C28	A38	9s maroon & emer	.50	.40
C29	A38	11s brt blue & org	.50	.40
C30	A38	21s black & emer	.55	.55
C31	A38	23s magenta & emer	.60	.60

C32 A38 29s vio blue & erner .70 .70
C33 A38 2pa magenta & orange 5.00 5.00
Nos. C27-C33 (7) 7.60 7.60

See note after No. 181.

Regular
Issues of
1953 Srchd.
in Red or
Black

Wmk. 79

1967, Dec. 15 Engr. *Die Cut*
C34 A34a 11s on 3½p ultra (R) .30 .30
C35 A33a 21s on 1½p emerald .40 .35
C36 A34a 23s on 3½p ultra (R) .40 .35
Nos. C34-C36 (3) 1.00 1.00

Arrival of the United States Peace Corps.

No. 112 Surcharged
in Red

1968, Apr. 6 Engr. *Perf. 11x11½*
C37 A34i 11s on 10sh blk & yel .50 .50
C38 A34i 21s on 10sh blk & yel .65 .65
C39 A34i 23s on 10sh blk & yel .65 .65
Nos. C37-C39 (3) 1.65 1.65

Nos. C27-C33 Overprinted "HIS
MAJESTY'S 50th BIRTHDAY" in
Silver on Blue Panel on 7s, 11s, 23s
and 2pa. "H.M.'s BIRTHDAY / 4.
JULY. 1968" in Gold on Red Panel
on 9s, 21s and 29s

Litho.; Embossed on Palladium Foil
1968, July 4 Unwmk. *Die Cut*
C40 A38 7s red & black .25 .25
C41 A38 9s maroon & emer .25 .25
C42 A38 11s brt blue & org .25 .25
C43 A38 21s black & emerald .75 .35
C44 A38 23s mag & emerald .75 .35
C45 A38 29s vio blue & emer 1.00 .40
C46 A38 2pa magenta & org 6.75 6.00
Nos. C40-C46 (7) 9.90 7.70

50th birthday of King Taufa'ahau IV.

Types of 1953 Surcharged

No. C47

No. C48

Nos. C49-
C50, C52-
C53

No. C51   No. C54

Designs as before.

1968, Dec. 19 Engr. Wmk. 79
C47 A34d 6s on 6p yel & blk .25 .25
C48 A34b 7s on 4p purple & yel .25 .25
C49 A34e 8s on 8p blk & lt grn .25 .25
C50 A33a 9s on 1½p emerald .25 .25
C51 A34 11s on 3p brn org & yel .25 .25
C52 A34a 21s on 3½p dk blue .30 .30
C53 A34h 38s on 5sh sepia & yel 2.10 .50
C54 A34i 1pa on 10sh orange yel 1.00 .60
Nos. C47-C54 (8) 4.40 2.40

Issued to publicize the field and track trials
for the third South Pacific Games, Port
Moresby, 1969. The overprint is in 5 lines on
the horizontal stamps, in 7 lines on the vertical
stamps. On the vertical stamps "Trial" is
printed on the line ahead of "Field & Track." On
No. C54 the denomination is spelled out.

Nos. C19-
C21 Srchd.

Perf. 14½x13½
1968 Photo. Wmk. 79
C55 A35 1s on 2sh9p on 2p ultra 1.60 1.00
C56 A35 1s on 3sh6p on 5p pur 1.60 1.00
C57 A35 1s on 4sh6p on 1sh red brown 1.60 1.00
Nos. C55-C57 (3) 4.80 3.00

Pacific Games Type of Regular Issue

Design: Boxer.

1969, Aug. 13 Litho. *Die Cut*
Self-adhesive
C58 A40 9s orange, blk & pur .35 .35
C59 A40 11s orange, blk & dk bl .35 .35
C60 A40 20s org, blk & yel grn .55 .55
C61 A40 60s orange, blk & scar 1.40 1.40
C62 A40 1pa orange, blk & grn 1.90 1.90
Nos. C58-C62 (5) 4.10 4.10

See note after No. 231.

Oil Derrick on
Map of
Tongatabu and
King Taufa'ahau
IV — AP2

Litho.; Gold Embossed
1969, Dec. 23 Self-adhesive
C63 AP2 9s multicolored .55 .55
C64 AP2 10s multicolored .55 .55
C65 AP2 24s multicolored 1.00 1.00
C66 AP2 29s multicolored 1.10 1.10
C67 AP2 38s multicolored 1.50 1.50
Nos. C63-C67 (5) 3.90 3.90

1st scientific search for oil in Tonga.

King Taufa'ahau IV and Queen
Elizabeth II — AP3

Litho.; Gold Embossed
1970, Mar. 7 Self-adhesive
C68 AP3 7s multicolored .40 .30
C69 AP3 9s multicolored .50 .35
C70 AP3 24s multicolored 1.25 .65

C71 AP3 29s multicolored 1.50 .75
C72 AP3 38s multicolored 2.10 1.00
Nos. C68-C72 (5) 5.75 3.05

See note after No. 242.

King Taufa'ahau Tupou IV
Medal — AP4

Litho.; Gold Embossed
1970, June 4 Self-adhesive
C73 AP4 9s grnsh bl, ver & gold .35 .35
C74 AP4 10s lilac, bl & gold .35 .35
C75 AP4 24s yel, grn & gold .80 .80
C76 AP4 29s ultra, org & gold 1.10 1.10
C77 AP4 38s ocher, emer & gold 1.60 1.60
Nos. C73-C77 (5) 4.05 4.05

See note after No. 247.

Centenary
of the British
Red Cross
— AP4a

1970, Oct. 17 Litho. *Die Cut*
Self-adhesive
C78 AP4a 9s red & silver .25 .25
C79 AP4a 10s red & magenta .35 .35
C80 AP4a 18s red & brt green .75 .75
C81 AP4a 38s red & blue 2.75 2.75
C82 AP4a 1pa red & turq blue 6.00 6.00
Nos. C78-C82 (5) 10.00 10.00

See Nos. 258-262.

Nos. C22-C24 Surcharged

Lithographed; Embossed on Gilt Foil
1971, Jan. 31 *Die Cut*
C83 AP1 9s on #C22 (S on B) .70 .25
C84 AP1 24s on #C24 (G on B) 1.50 1.00
C85 AP1 29s on #C23 (R on B) 2.10 1.25
C86 AP1 38s on #C23 (G on B) 3.25 1.60
Nos. C83-C86 (4) 7.55 4.05

In memory of Queen Salote (1900-1965).

Regular
Issues of
1953, Srchd.
in Red and
Black

1971 Engr. Wmk. 79 *Imperf*
C87 A33a 9s on 1½p green .25 .25
C88 A34b 10s on 4p purple & yol .25 .25
C89 A33 38s on 1p yellow & blk 1.10 .60
Nos. C87-C89 (3) 1.60 1.00

See note after No. 272.

**Types of Regular Issue Srchd. in
Purple or Black "AIRMAIL," New
Denomination and "HONOURING
JAPANESE POSTAL CENTENARY
1871-1971"**

1971
C90 A34f 18s on 1sh car & buff (P) .50 .50
C91 A34g 1pa on 2sh car & ultra 3.00 3.00

Surcharge on #C90 in 6 lines, on #C91 in 4.

Self-adhesive & Die Cut
Starting with Nos. C92-C96, all airmail issues are self-adhesive and die
cut, unless otherwise stated.

High
Jump
AP5

1971, July Litho. Unwmk.
C92 AP5 9s brown, mag & blk .25 .25
C93 AP5 10s brown, blue & blk .25 .25
C94 AP5 24s brn, dk grn & blk .45 .45
C95 AP5 29s brown, vio & blk .75 .75
C96 AP5 38s brown, red & blk 1.00 1.00
Nos. C92-C96 (5) 2.60 2.60

4th South Pacific Games, Papeete, French
Polynesia, Sept. 8-19.
For surcharges see Nos. C141-C142.

Prehistoric
Trilithon,
King's Watch
and Portrait
AP6

Litho. and Embossed
1971, July 20
C97 AP6 14s dk brown & multi .75 .75
C98 AP6 21s ocher & multi 1.10 1.10

2nd anniversary of man's first landing on the
moon and the placement of a Bulova Accutron
there. See Nos. C117-118, CO47-CO48,
CO61-CO62. Advertisement on peelable
paper backing.

Medal Type of Regular Issue

Designs: 10s, Gold Medal of Merit, obverse
(King Taufa'ahau IV). 75s, Silver Medal of
Merit, obverse (King Taufa'ahau IV). 1pa,
Bronze Medal of Merit, reverse.

1971, Oct. 30 Litho. & Embossed
C99 A47 10s gold & multi .25 .25
C100 A47 75s silver & multi 1.60 1.60
C101 A47 1pa bronze & multi 1.75 1.75
Nos. C99-C101 (3) 3.60 3.60

Girl with Blocks
and UNICEF
Emblem — AP7

1971, Dec. Litho.
C102 AP7 10s multicolored .30 .30
C103 AP7 15s multicolored .40 .40
C104 AP7 25s multicolored .65 .65
C105 AP7 50s multicolored 1.50 1.50
C106 AP7 1pa multicolored 2.75 2.75
Nos. C102-C106 (5) 5.40 5.40

25th anniversary of UNICEF.

Ship Type of Regular Issue

Design: Map of Merchant Marine routes from Tonga and cargo ship "Niuvakai."

1972, Apr. 14
C107	A49	9s ver & multi	.85	.35
C108	A49	12s multicolored	1.10	.35
C109	A49	14s dk pur & multi	1.25	.35
C110	A49	75s olive & multi	6.75	5.00
C111	A49	90s black & multi	7.00	6.50
		Nos. C107-C111 (5)	16.95	12.55

For surcharge and overprint see No. C124.

Coin Type of Regular Issue

Design: Coins on top; panel at bottom inscribed "5th anniversary world's first palladium coinage."

Litho.; Embossed on Metallic Foil
1972, July 15
C112	A50	9s silver & multi	.30	.30
C113	A50	12s silver & multi	.35	.35
C114	A50	14s silver & multi	.50	.50
C115	A50	21s silver & multi	.75	.75
C116	A50	75s silver & multi	2.25	2.25
		Nos. C112-C116 (5)	4.15	4.15

Watch Type of 1971
Litho. and Embossed
1972, July 20
C117	AP6	17s multicolored	.85	.85
C118	AP6	38s multicolored	1.75	1.75

Advertisement on peelable paper backing.

Proclamation of Sovereignty — AP8

1972, Dec. 9   **Litho.**
C119	AP8	9s ultra & multi	.25	.25
C120	AP8	12s red brown & multi	.25	.25
C121	AP8	14s magenta & multi	.40	.40
C122	AP8	38s brn org & multi	1.10	1.10
C123	AP8	1pa olive & multi	3.00	3.00
		Nos. C119-C123 (5)	4.55	4.55

Tonga's proclamation of sovereignty over the Minerva Reefs, June 1972.

No. C107 Surcharged

1972, Nov.   **Litho.**
C124	A49	7s on 9s multicolored	3.00	3.00

Inauguration of internal airmail service Nukualofa-Vavau, Nov. 1972.

Tongan Bank Notes and Bank Building — AP9

1973, Mar. 30   **Litho.**
C125	AP9	9s multicolored	.25	.25
C126	AP9	12s ultra & multi	.25	.25
C127	AP9	17s dp car & multi	.40	.25
C128	AP9	50s lt blue & multi	1.50	1.25
C129	AP9	90s multicolored	2.75	2.75
		Nos. C125-C129 (5)	5.15	4.60

Establishment of Bank of Tonga.

Boy Scout Emblem — AP10

1973, June 29   **Litho.**
C130	AP10	9s silver & multi	.70	.35
C131	AP10	12s silver & multi	.85	.45
C132	AP10	14s silver & multi	1.25	.70
C133	AP10	17s silver & multi	1.40	.85
C134	AP10	1pa silver & multi	15.00	9.25
		Nos. C130-C134 (5)	19.20	11.60

See note after No. 326.
For surcharges see Nos. C143-C144.

"Resolution" — AP11

1973, Oct. 2   **Litho.**
C135	AP11	9s multicolored	.80	.40
C136	AP11	14s multicolored	1.50	.60
C137	AP11	29s multicolored	4.50	2.75
C138	AP11	38s multicolored	5.50	3.00
C139	AP11	75s multicolored	10.50	4.25
		Nos. C135-C139 (5)	22.80	11.00

Bicentenary of Capt. Cook's arrival.

Nos. 277, C96, C94, C130 and C132 Surcharged in Silver, Violet or Black: "Commonwealth Games Christchurch 1974"

1973, Dec. 19
C140	A46	7s on 25s multi (S)	.25	.25
C141	AP5	9s on 38s multi (V)	.30	.25
C142	AP5	24s multicolored (B)	1.00	.65
C143	AP10	29s on 9s multi (V)	1.25	1.10
C144	AP10	40s on 14s multi (B)	1.60	1.50
		Nos. C140-C144 (5)	4.10	2.35

10th British Commonwealth Games, Christchurch, New Zealand, Jan. 24-Feb. 2, 1974. No. C140 is overprinted "AIRMAIL" in black; the silver surcharge and overprint are on black panels.

Parrot of Eua — AP12

1974, Mar. 20   **Litho.**
C145	AP12	7s multicolored	.50	.25
C146	AP12	9s multicolored	.60	.30
C147	AP12	12s multicolored	.60	.30
C148	AP12	14s multicolored	.90	.45
C149	AP12	17s multicolored	1.00	.50
C150	AP12	29s multicolored	1.75	.90
C151	AP12	38s multicolored	2.50	1.25
C152	AP12	50s multicolored	3.00	1.50
C153	AP12	75s multicolored	4.50	2.25
		Nos. C145-C153 (9)	15.35	7.70

Printed in rolls of 500. Self-adhesive rose red control number in upper left corner.

Carrier Pigeon Scattering Letters over Tonga — AP13

1974, June 20   **Typo.**
C154	AP13	14s lt blue & multi	.45	.45
C155	AP13	21s lt blue & multi	.55	.55
C156	AP13	60s lt blue & multi	1.75	1.75
C157	AP13	75s lt blue & multi	1.90	1.90
C158	AP13	1pa lt blue & multi	2.50	2.50
		Nos. C154-C158 (5)	7.15	7.15

Centenary of Universal Postal Union.

Girl Guide Leaders — AP14

1974, Sept. 11   **Litho.**
C159	AP14	14s blue & multi	.80	.50
C160	AP14	16s blue & multi	1.40	.80
C161	AP14	29s blue & multi	2.75	1.60
C162	AP14	31s blue & multi	3.50	2.10
C163	AP14	75s blue & multi	7.50	4.50
		Nos. C159-C163 (5)	15.95	9.50

Girl Guides of Tonga.
For surcharges and overprints see Nos. C190-C191, C193.

Freighter "James Cook" and List of Tongan Merchantmen — AP15

1974, Dec. 11
C164	AP15	9s blue & multi	.80	.30
C165	AP15	14s blue & multi	1.40	.55
C166	AP15	17s blue & multi	1.50	.60
C167	AP15	60s blue & multi	5.50	3.75
C168	AP15	90s blue & multi	8.75	4.75
		Nos. C164-C168 (5)	17.95	9.95

Establishment of Royal Marine Institute.

Beach AP16

Designs: 12s, 14s, like 9s. 17s, 38s, Surf.

1975, Mar. 11   **Litho.**
C169	AP16	9s gold & multi	.25	.25
C170	AP16	12s gold & multi	.25	.25
C171	AP16	14s gold & multi	.30	.30
C172	AP16	17s gold & multi	.30	.30
C173	AP16	38s gold & multi	.95	.95
		Nos. C169-C173 (5)	2.00	2.00

First meeting of South Pacific area Prime Ministers. See note after No. 226.
For surcharges see Nos. C229, C298.

Women's Discus and Games' Emblem — AP17

1975, June 11
C174	AP17	9s multicolored	.35	.35
C175	AP17	12s multicolored	.45	.45
C176	AP17	14s multicolored	.45	.45
C177	AP17	17s black & multi	.60	.60
C178	AP17	90s olive & multi	2.40	2.40
		Nos. C174-C178 (5)	4.25	4.25

5th South Pacific Games, Guam, Aug. 1-10. See note after No. 226.
For surcharges see Nos. C230-C231.

FAO Type of 1975

Designs (FAO Coins): 12s, Coins showing cattle, corn and pig. 14s, Cornucopias; coins showing king, family planning emblem and melons. 25s, Bananas and treasure chest. 50o, King Taufa'ahau. 1pa, Palms.

1975, Sept. 3
C179	A62	12s multicolored	.45 .45
C180	A62	14s blue & multi	.45 .45
C181	A62	25s silver, blk & org	.70 .70
C182	A62	50s car, sil & blk	1.25 1.25
C183	A62	1pa silver & black	2.50 2.50
		Nos. C179-C183 (5)	5.35 5.35

Size of paper backing of 14s: 82x50mm; others 45x45mm. See note after No. 226.

Coin Type of 1975

Coins: 9s, King Taufa'ahau IV, obverse. 12s, Queen Salote III, 75pa reverse and obverse. 14s, 10pa reverse. 38s, King Taufa'ahau IV, 10pa reverse and observe. 1pa, Heads of four constitutional monarchs.

1975, Nov. 4   Lt. Blue Background
C184	A63	9s black, sil & red	.40 .40
C185	A63	12s gold, blk & grn	.50 .50
C186	A63	14s black, sil & ol	.50 .50
C187	A63	38s gold, blk & org	1.25 1.25
C188	A63	1pa black, sil & blue	3.00 3.00
		Nos. C184-C188 (5)	4.85 4.00

Size of paper backing of 1pa: 87x78mm, others 65x60mm. See note after No. 226.

Nos. 344-345, C160, C163 Srchd. and Ovptd. in Carmine on Silver, Green or Gold

a

b

1976, Feb. 24   Litho.
C189	A58 (a)	12s on 20s (S)	.80 .50
C190	AP14 (b)	14s on 16s (Gr)	.80 .50
C191	AP14 (b)	16s (G)	1.00 .50
C192	A58 (a)	38s on 40s (G)	2.50 .70
C193	AP14 (b)	75s (G)	4.50 2.75
		Nos. C189-C193 (5)	9.60 4.95

21st Olympic Games, Montreal, Canada, July 17-Aug. 1. See note after No. 226.

Bicentennial Type of 1976

Signers of Declaration of Independence, Flags of US and Tonga: 12s, Abraham Clark, George Ross, Thomas Lynch, Jr., Charles Carroll, Roger Sherman (no flags). 14s, Robert Treat Paine, Thomas Jefferson, Thomas McKean, John Adams. 17s, Button Gwinnett, Lewis Morris, Caesar Rodney, Richard Henry Lee. 38s, John Hart, Samuel Huntington, Philip Livingston, John Morton. 1pa, John Hancock, Joseph Hewes, Josiah Bartlett, John Witherspoon.

1976, May 26
C194	A66	12s buff & multi	.65 .25
C195	A66	14s buff & multi	.75 .25
C196	A66	17s buff & multi	.80 .45
C197	A66	38s buff & multi	3.50 1.00
C198	A66	1pa buff & multi	6.75 4.25
		Nos. C194-C198 (5)	12.45 6.10

See note after No. 381.

Missionary Ship "Triton" — AP18

1976, Aug. 25   Litho.
C199	AP18	9s pink & multi	.35 .30
C200	AP18	12s multicolored	.55 .40
C201	AP18	14s multicolored	.60 .45
C202	AP18	17s buff & multi	.80 .55
C203	AP18	38s multicolored	1.40 .90
		Nos. C199-C203 (5)	3.70 2.60

See note after No. 386.
For surcharges see Nos. C234, C294, C299.

Treaty Signing Ceremony, Nukualofa — AP19

1976, Nov. 1
C204	AP19	11s multicolored	.45 .45
C205	AP19	17s multicolored	.60 .60
C206	AP19	18s multicolored	.65 .65
C207	AP19	31s multicolored	1.25 1.25
C208	AP19	39s multicolored	1.40 1.40
		Nos. C204-C208 (5)	4.20 3.80

See note after No. 391.
For surcharges see Nos. C235, C295.

Elizabeth II and Taufa'ahau IV — AP20

1977, Feb. 7
C209	AP20	15s gray & multi	1.60 .55
C210	AP20	17s gray & multi	2.25 .80
C211	AP20	22s gray & multi	22.50 10.00
C212	AP20	31s gray & multi	3.00 1.75
C213	AP20	39s gray & multi	6.00 3.00
		Nos. C209-C213 (5)	35.35 16.10

See note after No. 396.

Coronation Coin — AP21

1977, July 4   Litho.
C214	AP21	11s multicolored	.40 .40
C215	AP21	17s multicolored	.50 .50
C216	AP21	18s multicolored	.50 .50
C217	AP21	39s multicolored	.80 .80
C218	AP21	1pa multicolored	2.75 2.75
		Nos. C214-C218 (5)	4.95 4.95

See note after No. 401.
See Nos. CO120-CO122.

Capt. Cook Medal and Journal Quotation — AP22

1977, Sept. 27
C219	AP22	15s multicolored	.90 .75
C220	AP22	22s multicolored	1.40 1.25
C221	AP22	31s multicolored	3.50 3.00
C222	AP22	50s multicolored	10.00 5.00
C223	AP22	1pa multicolored	21.00 9.00
		Nos. C219-C223 (5)	36.80 19.00

Bicentenary of Capt. Cook's farewell voyage. See Nos. CO123-CO125.

Sei and Fin Whales — AP23

1977, Dec. 16
C224	AP23	11s blk, vio & bl	4.25 .80
C225	AP23	17s blk, red & bl	4.75 .90
C226	AP23	18s blk, grn & bl	4.75 1.10
C227	AP23	39s blk, brn & bl	5.75 2.25
C228	AP23	50s blk, mag & bl	7.25 3.50
		Nos. C224-C228 (5)	26.75 8.55

Whale protection.
See Nos. CO126-CO128.

Stamps of 1975-77 Surcharged in Various Colors

1978
C229	AP16	17s on 38s (#C173;Gr)	2.25 1.50
C230	AP17	17s on 9s (#C174;B)	2.25 1.50
C231	AP17	17s on 12s (#C175;DBl)	2.25 1.50
C232	A63	17s on 38s (#C187;B)	2.25 1.50
C233	A66	17s on 12s (#C194; R on G)	2.25 1.50
C234	AP18	17s on 9s (#C199; B)	2.25 1.50
C235	AP19	17s on 18s (#C206; G on Brn)	2.25 1.50
C236	A66	1pa on 75s (#381; Gr on S)	11.75 9.50
C237	A66	1pa on 38s (#C197; DBl on G)	11.75 9.50

C238	OA15	1pa on 1.10pa, S (#CO119; S on DBl)	26.50 27.50

Edmonton Games Type of 1978

Canadian Maple leaf and Tongan coat of arms.

1978, May 5   Litho.
C239	A73	17s red & multi	.45 .45
C240	A73	35s red & multi	.90 .90
C241	A73	38s red & multi	.95 .95
C242	A73	40s red & multi	2.00 2.00
C243	A73	65s red & multi	1.50 1.50
		Nos. C239-C243 (5)	5.80 5.80

See note after No. 423.

King Type of 1978

Design: Head of King Taufa'ahau IV within 6-pointed star.

1978, July 4
C244	A74	11s multicolored	.25 .25
C245	A74	15s multicolored	.35 .35
C246	A74	17s multicolored	.45 .45
C247	A74	39s multicolored	1.00 1.00
C248	A74	1pa multicolored	2.50 2.50
		Nos. C244-C248 (5)	4.55 4.55

See note after No. 226.

Wildlife Type of 1978

1978, Dec. 15   Litho. & Typo.
C249	A77	17s Whale	4.00 2.00
C250	A77	22s Bat	4.00 2.00
C251	A77	31s Turtle	4.00 2.00
C252	A77	39s Parrot	8.50 3.50
C253	A77	45s like 17s	8.75 4.00
		Nos. C249-C253 (5)	29.25 13.50

Wildlife conservation. See note after No. 226.

Types of 1979

Designs: 15s, like No. 453. 17s, like No. 450. 31s, Rotary emblem. 39s, Ministry and tourism buildings, Bank of Tonga, GPO. 1pa, Dish antenna and map of Tonga.

1979, Feb. 16   Litho.
C254	A79	15s multicolored	1.25 .50
C255	A79	17s multicolored	1.25 .50
C256	A78	31s vio blue & gold	1.25 .75
C257	A79	39s multicolored	1.25 .75
C258	A79	1pa multicolored	3.50 3.50
		Nos. C254-C258 (5)	5.50 3.35

Decade of Progress. Paper backing shows map of Tonga.

Type of 1979

Tongan self-adhesive, free-form stamps.

1979, June 1
C259	A81	15s multicolored	.45 .35
C260	A81	17s multicolored	.55 .45
C261	A81	18s multicolored	.65 .60
C262	A81	31s multicolored	.85 .85
C263	A81	39s multicolored	1.00 1.00
		Nos. C259-C263 (5)	3.15 3.15

See note after No. 458.

Jet — AP24

1979, Aug. 17
C264	AP24	5s multicolored	.60 .60
C265	AP24	11s multicolored	.65 .65
C266	AP24	14s multicolored	.65 .65
C267	AP24	15s multicolored	.70 .70
C268	AP24	17s multicolored	.70 .70
C269	AP24	18s multicolored	.75 .75
C270	AP24	22s multicolored	.90 .90
C271	AP24	31s multicolored	1.25 1.25
C272	AP24	39s multicolored	1.50 1.50
C273	AP24	75s multicolored	2.50 1.75
C274	AP24	1pa multicolored	3.50 2.50
		Nos. C264-C274 (11)	13.70 11.95

Nos. C264-C274 issued in coils; self-adhesive control number in lower left corner of paper backing except on 14s, 18s, 22s, 75s. See note after No. 226.
See Nos. C303-C305.

View Type of 1979

Design: Kao Island. See note after No. 463.

1979, Nov. 23
C275	A82	5s multicolored	.30 .30
C276	A82	15s multicolored	.50 .50
C277	A82	17s multicolored	.50 .50

C278	A82	39s multicolored	1.25	1.25
C279	A82	75s multicolored	1.75	1.75
		Nos. C275-C279 (5)	3.85	3.85

Friendship Treaty Type of 1980

George Tupou I, Napoleon III, Adventure. See notes over #464 & after #468.

1980, Jan. 9   **Litho.**

C280	A83	15s multicolored	.50	.50
C281	A83	17s multicolored	.60	.60
C282	A83	22s multicolored	.65	.65
C283	A83	31s multicolored	.90	.90
C284	A83	39s multicolored	1.00	1.00
		Nos. C280-C284 (5)	3.45	3.45

Nos. C259-C263 Surcharged and Overprinted in Black on Silver "1980 OLYMPIC GAMES," Moscow '80 and Bear Emblems

1980, Apr. 30   **Litho.**

C285	A81	9s on 15s multi	.30	.30
C286	A81	16s on 17s multi	.65	.65
C287	A81	29s on 18s multi	1.00	1.00
C288	A81	32s on 31s multi	1.10	1.10
C289	A81	47s on 39s multi	1.75	1.75
		Nos. C285-C289 (5)	4.80	4.80

22nd Summer Olympic Games, Moscow, July 19-Aug. 3.

Scouting Activities in Rotary Emblem — AP25

1980, Sept. 30   **Litho.**

C290	AP25	29s multicolored	1.00	1.00
C291	AP25	32s multicolored	1.00	1.00
C292	AP25	47s multicolored	1.50	1.50
C293	AP25	1pa multicolored	3.00	3.00
		Nos. C290-C293 (4)	6.50	6.50

Boy Scout Jamboree; Rotary International, 75th anniversary. Peelable backing shows map of Tonga.

Nos. C170, C185, C195, C200-C201, C208 Surcharged

1980, Dec. 3   **Litho.**

C294	AP18	29s on 14s multi	1.75	1.75
C295	AP19	29s on 39s multi	1.75	1.75
C296	A63	32s on 12s multi	2.00	2.00
C297	A66	32s on 14s multi	2.00	2.00
C298	AP16	47s on 12s multi	2.75	2.75
C299	AP18	47s on 12s multi	2.75	2.75
		Nos. C294-C299 (6)	13.00	13.00

IYD Type of 1981

1981, Sept. 9   **Litho.**

Size: 25x32mm

C300	A85	29s multicolored	.50	.50
C301	A85	32s multicolored	.60	.60
C302	A85	47s multicolored	1.10	1.10
		Nos. C300-C302 (3)	2.20	2.20

Jet Type of 1979

1982, Nov. 17   **Litho.**

C303	AP24	29s pink & black	12.00	5.00
C304	AP24	32s pale yel & blk	12.00	5.00
C305	AP24	47s lt brown & blk	12.00	5.00
		Nos. C303-C305 (3)	36.00	15.00

AIR POST SPECIAL DELIVERY STAMP

> Catalogue values for unused stamps in this section are for Never Hinged items.

Owl — APSD1

1990, Feb. 21   **Litho.**   **Perf. 11½**

CE1	APSD1	10pa multi	12.50	12.50

APSD2

APSD3

APSD4

Short-eared Owl — APSD5

2012, Aug. 30   **Perf. 14¼**

Stamps With White Frame All Around

CE2	APSD2	25pa multi	25.00	25.00
CE3	APSD3	25pa multi	25.00	25.00
CE4	APSD4	25pa multi	25.00	25.00
CE5	APSD5	25pa multi	25.00	25.00
		Nos. CE2-CE5 (4)	100.00	100.00

Stamps With White Frame on Two Sides

CE6		Sheet of 4	100.00	100.00
a.		APSD2 25pa multi	25.00	25.00
b.		APSD3 25pa multi	25.00	25.00
c.		APSD4 25pa multi	25.00	25.00
d.		APSD5 25pa multi	25.00	25.00

A sheet of 16 ontaining four of each of types APSD2-APSD5 without white frames on the stamps was produced in a limited printing.

Butterflies — APSD6

Designs: 15pa, Scarlet Mormon butterfly. 50pa, Eggfly butterfly. 53pa, Great Mormon butterfly. 71pa, Dark cerulean butterfly. 83pa, Common lime butterfly. 89pa, Old world swallowtail butterfly.

2015-16   **Litho.**   **Perf. 14¼**

Stamps With White Frames

CE7	APSD6	15pa multi	14.00	14.00
CE8	APSD6	50pa multi	47.00	47.00
CE9	APSD6	53pa multi	49.00	49.00
CE10	APSD6	71pa multi	65.00	65.00
a.		Souvenir sheet of 4, #CE7-CE10	175.00	175.00
CE11	APSD6	83pa multi	72.50	72.50
CE12	APSD6	89pa multi	77.50	77.50
a.		Souvenir sheet of 2, #CE11-CE12	150.00	150.00
		Nos. CE7-CE12 (6)	325.00	325.00

Souvenir Sheets
Stamps Without White Frame

CE13	APSD6	15pa multi	14.00	14.00
CE14	APSD6	50pa multi	47.00	47.00
CE15	APSD6	53pa multi	49.00	49.00
CE16	APSD6	71pa multi	65.00	65.00
CE17	APSD6	83pa multi	72.50	72.50
CE18	APSD6	89pa multi	77.50	77.50
		Nos. CE13-CE18 (6)	325.00	325.00

Issued: 15pa, 50pa, 9/1; 53pa, 71pa, No. CE10a, 11/2; 83pa, 89pa, No. CE12a, 1/4/16. Stamps on No. CE10a have white frames on 2 sides. Stamps on No. CE12a have white frames on 3 sides.

AIR POST OFFICIAL STAMPS

> Catalogue values for unused stamps in this section are for Never Hinged items.

Nos. 115, 117-118, 111-113 Overprinted in Red

Engr.; Photo. (A35)

1962, Feb. 7   **Wmk. 79**

CO1	A35	2p ultra	16.00	7.50
CO2	A35	5p purple	16.00	8.00
CO3	A35	1sh red brown	9.00	4.00
CO4	A34h	5sh pur & yel	90.00	55.00
CO5	A34i	10sh black & yel	42.50	22.50
CO6	A34j	£1 ultra, car & yel	75.00	37.50
		Nos. CO1-CO6 (6)	248.50	134.50

Centenary of emancipation. Nos. CO1-CO6 were overprinted locally. Overprint varieties of nos. CO1-CO6 exist with "OFFICIAI" instead of "OFFICIAL" and "MAII" instead of "MAIL".

Type of Regular Gold Coin Issue

Design: 15sh, Queen Salote standing, 1-koula coin, obverse.

Litho.; Embossed on Gilt Foil
1963, July 15   **Unwmk.**   **Die Cut**
Diameter: 80mm

CO7	A36	15sh black	6.25	6.25

Note after No. 133 also applies to No. CO7.

No. CO7 Surcharged like Regular Issue of 1965 in Black

1965, Mar. 18

CO8	A36	30sh on 15sh black	6.75	6.75

No. 116 Surcharged in Italic Letters Similarly to Nos. C16-C21

Perf. 14½x13½

1966, June 18   **Wmk. 79**

CO9	A35	10sh on 4p brt green	1.00	.60
CO10	A35	20sh on 4p brt green	1.10	.75

Centenary of Tupou College and secondary education.

No. 111 Srchd. in Red

1967, Mar. 25   **Engr.**   **Perf. 11½x11**

CO11	A34h	1p on 5sh pur & yel	3.00	3.00

Type of Regular Issue Surcharged

1967, Dec. 15   **Wmk. 79**   **Die Cut**

CO12	A34j	30s on £1 multi	.60	.60
CO13	A34j	70s on £1 multi	.90	.90
CO14	A34j	1.50pa on £1 multi	1.50	1.50
		Nos. CO12-CO14 (3)	2.60	2.60

Arrival of US Peace Corps.

No. 113 Surcharged

Nos. CO15-CO16   Nos. CO17-CO18

1968, Apr. 6   **Engr.**   **Perf. 11x11½**

CO15	A34j	40s on £1 multi	.85	.50
CO16	A34j	60s on £1 multi	1.25	.75
CO17	A34j	1pa on £1 multi	1.75	1.25
CO18	A34j	2pa on £1 multi	2.50	2.00
		Nos. CO15-CO18 (4)	6.35	4.50

Type of 1953 Surcharged: "Friendly Islands / Trials / Field & Track / South Pacific / Games / Port Moresby / 1969 / OFFICIAL AIRMAIL"
Wmk. 79

1968, Dec. 19   Engr.

CO19	A34j	20s on £1 grn & multi	.40 .40
CO20	A34j	1pa on £1 grn & multi	1.10 1.10

No. 176 Overprinted and Surcharged in Gold on Colored Panels (Green, Emerald, Violet or Lilac) like Nos. 203-209

Litho.; Embossed on Palladium Foil

1968   Unwmk.

CO21	A38	40s on 2s (G)	1.90 .90
CO22	A38	60s on 2s (E)	2.50 1.60
CO23	A38	1pa on 2s (V)	3.75 3.75
CO24	A38	2pa on 2s (L)	6.75 6.75
		Nos. CO21-CO24 (4)	14.90 13.00

50th birthday of King Taufa'ahau IV.

Pacific Games Type of Regular Issue

Design: Boxer.

1969, Aug. 13   Litho.   Die Cut
Self-adhesive

CO25	A40	70s gray, red & grn	1.40 1.40
CO26	A40	80s gray, red & org	1.60 1.60

See note after No. 231.

Type of 1953 Regular Issue Surcharged

1969, Dec. 23   Die Cut Wmk. 79

CO27	A34j	90s on £1 grn & multi	4.50 4.50

First scientific search for oil in Tonga.

Type of 1953 Regular Issue Surcharged in Black, Violet Blue or Emerald

1970, Mar. 7   Engr.   Wmk. 79

CO28	A34f	75s on 1sh red & yel	4.25 2.25
CO29	A34f	1pa on 1sh (VBl)	5.50 3.25
CO30	A34f	1.25pa on 1sh (E)	7.00 4.25
		Nos. CO28-CO30 (3)	16.75 9.75

See note after No. 242.

Regular Issue Srchd. in Black, Red or Emerald

1970, June 4   Wmk. 79   Die Cut

CO31	A34h	50s on 5sh (B)	4.00 4.00
CO32	A34h	90s on 5sh (R)	5.00 5.00
CO33	A34h	1.50pa on 5sh (E)	6.00 6.00
		Nos. CO31-CO33 (3)	15.00 15.00

See note after No. 247.

Regular Issue of 1953, Srchd. in Red and Purple or Black

1970, Oct. 17   Engr.   Die Cut

CO34	A33a	30s on 1½p (B & R)	1.90 1.90
CO35	A34h	80s on 5sh (P & P)	5.00 5.00
CO36	A34h	90s on 5sh (P & R)	6.00 6.00
		Nos. CO34-CO36 (3)	12.90 12.90

Centenary of the British Red Cross.

Type of Regular Issue, 1953, Surcharged in Black, Purple, Blue or Green

1971, Jan. 31   Engr.   Die Cut

CO37	A34i	20s on 10sh (Bk)	1.25 .85
CO38	A34i	80s on 10sh (P)	2.10 1.25
CO39	A34i	50s on 10sh (Bl)	3.50 2.10
CO40	A34i	2pa on 10sh (G)	13.75 11.75
		Nos. CO37-CO40 (4)	20.60 15.95

In memory of Queen Salote (1900-1965).

Type of Regular Issue, 1953, Surcharged in Red and Blue, Black or Purple

1971   Engr.   Wmk. 79   Imperf
Colors: Green & Yellow

CO41	A34c	30s on 5p (R & Bl)	1.40 .80
CO42	A34c	80s on 5p (R & Bk)	3.25 2.10
CO43	A34c	90s on 5p (R & P)	3.50 2.40
		Nos. CO41-CO43 (3)	8.15 5.30

See note after No. 272.

Self-adhesive & Die Cut
Starting with Nos. CO44-CO46, all airmail official issues are self-adhesive and die cut, unless otherwise stated.

Soccer Ball — OA1

1971, July   Litho.   Unwmk.

CO44	OA1	50s multi	1.75 1.75
CO45	OA1	90s multi	2.75 2.75
CO46	OA1	1.50pa multi	5.25 5.25
		Nos. CO44-CO46 (3)	4.85 4.85

4th South Pacific Games, Papeete, French Polynesia, Sept. 8-19.
For overprints see Nos. CO75-CO77.

Watch Type of Air Post Issues Litho. and Embossed

1971, July 20

CO47	AP6	14s brown & multi	1.25 1.25
CO48	AP6	21s brn red & multi	1.75 1.75

Advertisement on peelable paper backing.

Nos. 243-244, 246 Surcharged

Litho.; Gold Embossed

1971, Oct. 30

CO49	A43	60s on 3s multi	1.50 1.50
CO50	A43	80s on 25o multi	1.75 1.75
CO51	A43	1.10pa on 7s multi	2.25 2.25
		Nos. CO49-CO51 (3)	4.50 4.50

First investure of Tongan Medal of Honor.

"UNICEF" — OA2

1971, Dec.   Litho.

CO52	OA2	70s black & multi	2.25 2.25
CO53	OA2	80s multicolored	2.75 2.75
CO54	OA2	90s multicolored	3.00 3.00
		Nos. CO52-CO54 (3)	7.00 7.00

25th anniversary of UNICEF.
For overprint see No. CO70.

Ship Type of Regular Issue

Design: Map of Merchant Marine routes from Tonga and tanker "Aoniu."

1972, Apr. 14

CO55	A49	20s multi	1.90 .90
CO56	A49	50s multi	4.00 2.75
CO57	A49	1.20pa multi	8.75 7.00
		Nos. CO55-CO57 (3)	14.65 10.65

Coin Type of Regular Issue

Design: Coins in center, inscription panel above, date below coins.

Litho.; Embossed on Metallic Foil

1972, July 15

CO58	A50	50s silver & multi	1.75 1.75
CO59	A50	70s silver & multi	2.50 2.50
CO60	A50	1.50pa silver & multi	4.50 4.50
		Nos. CO58-CO60 (3)	8.75 8.75

Watch Type of Air Post Issue

1972, July 20   Litho.; Embossed

CO61	AP6	17s multicolored	1.25 1.25
CO62	AP6	38s ocher & multi	2.50 2.50

Advertisement on peelable paper backing.

Flags and Map of Tonga Islands — OA3

1972, Dec. 9   Litho.

CO63	OA3	25s black & multi	.60 .60
CO64	OA3	75s multicolored	1.75 1.75
CO65	OA3	1.50pa multicolored	3.75 3.75
		Nos. CO63-CO65 (3)	5.65 2.15

Tonga's proclamation of sovereignty over the Minerva Reefs, June 1972.

No. 290 Surcharged in Black, Ultramarine or Green

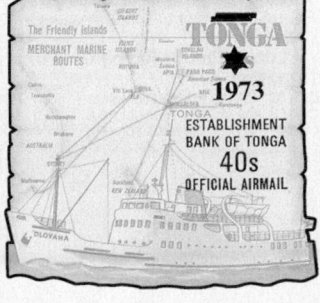

1973, Mar. 30   Litho.

CO66	A49	40s on 21s (B)	2.00 2.00
CO67	A49	85s on 21s (U)	4.00 4.00
CO68	A49	1.25pa on 21s (G)	5.00 5.00
		Nos. CO66-CO68 (3)	11.00 11.00

Establishment of Bank of Tonga.

Nos. CO55 Ovptd. & Srchd. in Silver

No. CO53 Ovptd. in Silver

No. 247 Srchd. & Ovptd. in Silver on Dark Blue Panels

1973, June 29

CO69	A49	30s on 20s	15.00 4.00
CO70	OA2	80s multi	37.50 14.50
CO71	A43	1.40pa on 50s	52.50 35.00
		Nos. CO69-CO71 (3)	105.00 53.50

25th anniv. of Tongan Boy Scout movement.

Tanker James Cook and Cook Medal — OA4

1973, Oct. 2   Litho.

CO72	OA4	25s multi	4.00 1.60
CO73	OA4	80s multi	10.00 5.00
CO74	OA4	1.30pa multi	12.00 8.25
		Nos. CO72-CO74 (3)	26.00 14.85

Bicentenary of Capt. Cook's arrival.

Nos. CO44-CO46 Ovptd. in Dark Blue, Black or Green

1973, Dec. 19

CO75	OA1	50s multi (DBl)	1.75 1.75
CO76	OA1	90s multi (B)	3.00 3.00
CO77	OA1	1.50pa multi (G)	4.25 4.25
		Nos. CO75-CO77 (3)	7.25 6.50

10th British Commonwealth Games, Christchurch, N.Z., Jan. 24-Feb. 2, 1974.

Peace
Dove
OA5

1974, Mar. 20 Litho.
CO78	OA5	7s multicolored	.50	.25
CO79	OA5	9s multicolored	.65	.35
CO80	OA5	12s multicolored	.65	.35
CO81	OA5	14s multicolored	.90	.50
CO82	OA5	17s multicolored	1.00	.65
CO83	OA5	29s multicolored	1.75	1.10
CO84	OA5	38s multicolored	2.50	1.40
CO85	OA5	50s multicolored	3.00	3.00
CO86	OA5	75s multicolored	4.25	4.25
	Nos. CO78-CO86 (9)		15.20	11.85

Printed in rolls of 500. Self-adhesive lilac control number in upper left corner.

"UPU Centenary" — OA6

1974, June 20 Typo.
CO87	OA6	25s red, green & blk	1.00	1.00
CO88	OA6	35s yel, red lil & blk	1.10	1.10
CO89	OA6	70s dp org, bl & blk	2.25	2.25
	Nos. CO87-CO89 (3)		4.35	4.35

Centenary of Universal Postal Union.

Lady Baden-
Powell
OA7

1974, Sept. 11 Litho.
CO90	OA7	45s emer & multi	4.50	2.75
CO91	OA7	55s emer & multi	6.50	3.75
CO92	OA7	1pa emer & multi	9.25	5.50
	Nos. CO90-CO92 (3)		20.25	12.00

Girl Guides of Tonga.
For overprints see Nos. CO105-CO107.

Handshake and Institute's
Emblem — OA8

Institute's Emblem and
Banknotes — OA9

1974, Dec. 11
CO93	OA8	30s multicolored	3.25	1.60
CO94	OA8	35s multicolored	3.75	2.10
CO95	OA9	80s red & multi	8.75	4.50
	Nos. CO93-CO95 (3)		15.75	8.20

Establishment of Royal Marine Institute.

Arch
and
Palms
OA10

Designs: 75s, 1.25pa, Dawn over lagoon.

1975, Mar. 11 Litho.
CO96	OA10	50s multi	1.75	1.75
CO97	OA10	75s multi	3.00	3.00
CO98	OA10	1.25pa multi	4.00	4.00
	Nos. CO96-CO98 (3)		8.75	8.75

First meeting of South Pacific area Prime Ministers. See note after No. 226.

Track and Games' Emblem — OA11

1975, June 11
CO99	OA11	38s multi	1.00	1.00
CO100	OA11	75s multi	1.90	1.90
CO101	OA11	1.20pa multi	3.00	3.00
	Nos. CO99-CO101 (3)		5.90	5.90

5th South Pacific Games, Guam, Aug. 1-10.
See note after No. 226.
For surcharge see No. 418.

Four Constitutional Monarchs — OA12

Litho.; Embossed on Gilt Foil
1975, Nov. 4
CO102	OA12	17s multicolored	1.00	1.00
CO103	OA12	60s multicolored	2.50	2.50
CO104	OA12	90s multicolored	3.00	3.00
	Nos. CO102-CO104 (3)		5.40	5.00

**No. CO90-CO92 Ovptd. in Carmine
on Blue, Silver or Gold**

1976, Feb. 24 Litho.
CO105	OA7	45s multi (B)	3.50	1.40
CO106	OA7	55s multi (S)	3.50	1.60
CO107	OA7	1pa multi (G)	6.75	6.75
	Nos. CO105-CO107 (3)		13.75	9.75

21st Olympic Games, Montreal, Canada, July 17-Aug. 1. See note after No. 226.

Bicentennial Type of 1976

Signers of Declaration of Independence: 20s, William Paca, Francis Lewis, George Read, Edward Rutledge, Thomas Heyward, Jr. 50s, George Walton, Matthew Thornton, Robert Morris, William Williams, James Smith. 1.15pa, Benjamin Rush, Samuel Adams, Samuel Chase, George Wythe, George Clymer.

1976, May 26
CO108	A66	20s buff & multi	1.25	1.00
CO109	A66	50s buff & multi	4.00	2.50
CO110	A66	1.15pa buff & multi	8.50	5.25
	Nos. CO108-CO110 (3)		13.75	8.75

See note after No. 381.

Inside View of Lifuka Chapel — OA13

1976, Aug. 25 Litho.
CO111	OA13	65s multi	2.75	2.75
CO112	OA13	85s multi	3.00	3.00
CO113	OA13	1.15pa multi	4.00	4.00
	Nos. CO111-CO113 (3)		9.75	9.75

See note after No. 386.
For surcharge see No. CO181.

OA14

1976, Nov. 1
CO114	OA14	30s silver & multi	.90	.90
CO115	OA14	60s silver & multi	2.25	2.25
CO116	OA14	1.25pa silver & multi	4.75	4.75
	Nos. CO114-CO116 (3)		7.35	7.35

See note after No. 391.

Flags of Great Britain and
Tonga — OA15

1977, Feb. 7 Litho.
CO117	OA15	35s multi	5.00	3.25
CO118	OA15	45s multi	1.00	.50
CO119	OA15	1.10pa multi	2.00	1.25
	Nos. CO117-CO119 (3)		8.00	5.00

See note after No. 396.
For surcharge see No. C238.

Coin Type of Air Post Stamps 1977

Design: Coronation coin, inscriptions in round upper panel.

1977, July 4
CO120	AP21	20s multicolored	.75	.75
CO121	AP21	40s multicolored	1.50	1.50
CO122	AP21	80s multicolored	3.00	3.00
	Nos. CO120-CO122 (3)		5.25	5.25

See note after No. 401.

**Capt. Cook Type of Air Post Stamps
1977**

Design: Inscription and flying dove.

1977, Sept. 27
CO123	AP22	20s gold & multi	1.40	1.40
CO124	AP22	55s on 20s multi	10.00	10.00
CO125	AP22	85s on 20s multi	21.00	21.00
	Nos. CO123-CO125 (3)		32.40	32.40

Printed on peelable paper backing showing dark brown replica of entry in Capt. Cook's diary.

**Whale Type of Air Post Stamps
1977**

Design: Blue whale.

1977, Dec. 16
CO126	AP23	45s multicolored	7.75	3.50
CO127	AP23	65s multicolored	11.00	5.00
CO128	AP23	85s multicolored	13.00	6.00
	Nos. CO126-CO128 (3)		31.75	14.50

Whale protection.

Games'
Emblem and
Athletes
OA16

1978, May 5 Litho.
CO129	OA16	30s red & multi	.70	.70
CO130	OA16	60s red & multi	1.40	1.40
CO131	OA16	1pa red & multi	2.50	2.50
	Nos. CO129-CO131 (3)		4.60	4.60

See note after No. 423.

King Type of 1978

Head of King Taufa'ahau IV on medal.

1978, July 4
CO132	A74	26s multicolored	.65	.65
CO133	A74	85s multicolored	2.00	2.00
CO134	A74	90s multicolored	2.50	2.50
	Nos. CO132-CO134 (3)		5.15	5.15

See note after No. 226.

Wildlife Type of 1978

1978, Dec. 15   Litho. & Typo.
CO150 A77   40s Whale   8.25   4.00
CO151 A77   50s Bat   8.25   4.00
CO152 A77   1.10pa Turtle   11.00   9.00
 Nos. CO150-CO152 (3)   27.50 17.00

Wildlife conservation. See note after No. 226.

Types of 1979

Designs: 38s, Red Cross and star. 74s, like
No. 451. 80s, like No. 450.

1979, Feb. 16   Litho.
CO153 A78   38s multicolored   1.50   1.00
CO154 A80   74s multicolored   2.00   2.00
CO155 A79   80s multicolored   3.00   3.00
 Nos. CO153-CO155 (3)   5.60   3.70

Decade of Progress. Paper backing shows
map of Tonga.

Hands Peeling off No. CO118 — OA17

1979, June 1   Litho.
CO156 OA17   45s multicolored   1.50   1.25
CO157 OA17   65s multicolored   2.00   1.75
CO158 OA17   80s multicolored   2.75   2.25
 Nos. CO156-CO158 (3)   5.25   5.25

See note after No. 458.
For surcharges see Nos. CO176-CO178.

Parrot — OA18

1979, Aug. 1
CO159 OA18   5s multicolored   .60   .60
CO160 OA18   11s multicolored   .65   .65
CO161 OA18   14s multicolored   .65   .65
CO162 OA18   15s multicolored   .70   .70
CO163 OA18   17s multicolored   .70   .70
CO164 OA18   18s multicolored   .70   .70
CO165 OA18   22s multicolored   .80   .80
CO166 OA18   31s multicolored   1.10   1.10
CO167 OA18   39s multicolored   1.50   1.50
CO168 OA18   75s multicolored   2.25   2.25
CO169 OA18   1pa multicolored   2.75   2.75
 Nos. CO159-CO169 (11)   12.40 12.40

Nos. CO159-CO169 issued in coils. See
note after No. 226.
 The 5s exists with denomination in magenta
and the leaves behind the bird missing. This
seems to be a special printing that was not
available for postal purposes.

View Type of 1979

Design: Niuatoputapu and Tafahi Islands.
See note after No. 463.

1979, Nov. 23   Litho.
CO170 A82   35s multicolored   1.00   1.00
CO171 A82   55s multicolored   1.25   1.25
CO172 A82   1pa multicolored   2.50   2.50
 Nos. CO170-CO172 (3)   4.20   4.20

Friendship Treaty Type of 1980

Design: Church. See note after No. 468.

1980, Jan. 9   Litho.
CO173 A83   40s multicolored   1.25   1.25
CO174 A83   55s multicolored   1.75   1.75
CO175 A83   1.25pa multicolored 3.50   3.50
 Nos. CO173-CO175 (3)   5.75   5.75

Nos. CO156-CO158 Srchd. & Ovptd. in Black on Silver "1980 OLYMPIC GAMES," Moscow '80 and Bear Emblems

1980, Apr. 30   Litho.
CO176 OA17   26s on 45s   1.00   1.00
CO177 OA17   40s on 65s   1.60   1.60
CO178 OA17   1.10pa on 80s   4.00   4.00
 Nos. CO176-CO178 (3)   6.60   6.60

22nd Summer Olympic Games, Moscow,
July 19-Aug. 3.

Tents and Rotary Emblem — OA19

1980, Sept. 30   Litho.
CO179 OA19   25s multicolored   1.75   1.75
CO180 OA19   2pa multicolored   6.75   6.75

Boy Scout Jamboree; Rotary Intl., 75th
anniv. Peelable backing shows map of Tonga.
For surcharges see Nos. 502-503.

No. CO111 Surcharged

1980, Dec. 3   Litho.
CO181 OA13   2pa on 65s multi   5.50   5.50

REGISTRATION STAMPS

Souvenir Sheets

Common Eggfly Butterfly — R1

Inscriptions: No. F1, Domestic Registered
Mail. No. F2, International Registered Mail.

2018, Sept. 6   Litho.   Perf. 13
F1 R1   8s multi   7.00   7.00
F2 R1   20.60pa multi   18.50 18.50

OFFICIAL STAMPS

Types of Postage Issue
of 1892 Overprinted in
Carmine

Perf. 12x11½
1893, Feb. 13   Wmk. 62
O1 A4   1p ultra   11.50 55.00
 a. Half used as ½p on cover

O2 A5   2p ultra   30.00   62.50
O3 A4   4p ultra   55.00 110.00
O4 A5   8p ultra   100.00 200.00
O5 A5   1sh ultra   110.00 210.00
 Nos. O1-O5 (5)   306.50 637.50

Values are for stamps of good color. Faded
and discolored stamps sell for much less.
 The overprinted initials stand for "Gaue
Faka Buleaga" (On Government Service).

Nos. O1-O5 with
Additional Surcharge
Handstamped in Black

1893
O6 A4   ½p on 1p ultra   20.00   57.50
O7 A5   2½p on 2p ultra   27.50   50.00
O8 A4   5p on 4p ultra   27.50   50.00
O9 A5   7½p on 8p ultra   27.50   92.50
O10 A5 10p on 1sh ultra 32.50   95.00
 Nos. O6-O10 (5)   135.00 345.00

> Catalogue values for unused
> stamps in this section, from this
> point to the end of the section, are
> for Never Hinged items.

Redrawn Banana and Coconut Types of Regular Issue, 1970, Inscribed "Official Post"

1970, June 9   Typo.   Die Cut
Self-adhesive
O11 A39   1s yel, blk & dp car   .55   .55
O12 A39   2s yel, blk & blue   .70   .70
O13 A39   3s yel, blk & brn   .70   .70
O14 A39   4s yel, blk & emer   .70   .70
O15 A39   5s yel, blk & org   .80   .80
Litho., Embossed on Gift Foil
O16 A44   6s brown & multi   .95   .95
O17 A44   7s brown & multi   1.00   1.00
O18 A44   8s brown & multi   1.10   1.10
O19 A44   9s brown & multi   1.50   1.50
O20 A44 10s brown & multi   1.75   1.75
 Nos. O11-O20 (10)   9.75   9.75

Nos. O13, O17-O18 and O20 have self-
adhesive control numbers in lower left corner
of paper backing.

Types of Regular Issue 1970-72

1972, Sept. 30   Typo.   Die Cut
Self-adhesive
O21 A51   1s yel, red & brn   .25   .25
O22 A51   2s yel, grn & brn   .30   .25
O23 A51   3s yel, emer & brn   .35   .25
O24 A51   4s yel, blk & brn   .35   .25
O25 A51   5s yellow & brn   .35   .25
O26 A44   6s brown & green   .45   .25
O27 A44   7s brown & green   .50   .30
O28 A44   8s brown & green   .50   .30
O29 A44   9s brown & green   .50   .30
O30 A44 10s brown & green   .60   .35
O31 A52 15s green & ultra   1.00   .70
O32 A52 20s green & ver   1.25   .70
O33 A52 25s green & dk brn   1.40   .90
O34 A52 40s green & org   2.50   1.75
O35 A52 50s green & vio bl   3.00   2.25
 Nos. O21-O35 (15)   13.30   8.70

Paper backing is brown on Nos. O26-O35.
Nos. O30-O35 have self-adhesive control
number in lower left corner, Nos. O21-O29
lower right corner.

Types of Regular Issue 1978

Designs: 1s-5s, Bananas (similar to type
A75). 6s-10s, Coconuts. 15s-1pa, Pineapples.

1978, Sept. 29   Typo.   Die Cut
Self-Adhesive
O36 A75   1s yellow & lilac   .30   .30
O37 A75   2s yellow & brown   .30   .30
O38 A75   3s multicolored   .40   .40
O39 A75   4s multicolored   .40   .40
O40 A75   5s multicolored   .40   .40
O41 A76   6s multicolored   .60   .60
O42 A76   7s multicolored   .60   .60
O43 A76   8s multicolored   .60   .60
O44 A76   9s multicolored   .60   .60
O45 A76 10s multicolored   .60   .60
O46 A76 15s multicolored   1.50   1.50
O47 A76 20s multicolored   1.60   1.60
O48 A76 30s multicolored   1.75   1.75
O49 A76 50s multicolored   2.25   2.25
O50 A76   1pa multicolored   3.25   3.25
 Nos. O36-O50 (15)   15.15 15.15

Nos. O36-O50 issued in coils; self-adhesive
control numbers on paper backing except on
1s. See note after No. 226.

Nos. 563-577,
579 Ovptd.

1984-85   Litho.   Die Cut
Self-Adhesive
O52 A103   1s multicolored   .50   .50
O53 A103   2s multicolored   .50   .50
O54 A103   3s multicolored   .50   .50
O55 A103   5s multicolored   .50   .50
O56 A103   6s multicolored   .50   .50
O57 A103   9s multicolored   .75   .75
 a. Perf. 14½ ('85)   .75   .75
O58 A103 10s multicolored   .75   .75
O59 A103 13s multicolored   1.25   1.25
O60 A103 15s multicolored   1.25   1.25
O61 A103 20s multicolored   1.50   1.50
O62 A103 29s multicolored   1.75   1.75
O63 A103 32s multicolored   1.75   1.75
O64 A103 47s multicolored   2.00   2.00
O65 A103   1pa multicolored   4.00   4.00
O66 A103   2pa multicolored   7.00   7.00
O67 A103   5pa multicolored
           ('85)   12.00 12.00
 Nos. O52-O67 (16)   36.50 36.50

Nos. 532-534 Overprinted

1983, Feb. 22   Litho.   Die Cut
Self-Adhesive
O68 A96a 29s multicolored   4.75   4.75
O69 A96a 32s multicolored   4.75   4.75
O70 A96a 47s multicolored   10.00 10.00
 Nos. O68-O70 (3)   19.50 19.50

O68-O70 handstamped.

Nos. 618-624
Overprinted

1986, Apr. 16   Litho.   Die Cut
Self-adhesive
O71 A103   4s on 2s, #618   1.00   1.00
O72 A103   4s on 13s,
           #619   1.00   1.00
O73 A103 42s on 3s, #620   3.25   3.25
O74 A103 42s on 9s, #621   3.25   3.25
O75 A103 57s on 6s, #622   3.50   3.50
O76 A103 57s on 20s,
           #623   3.50   3.50
O77 A103 2.50pa on 2pa,
           #624   12.00 12.00
 Nos. O71-O77 (7)   27.50 27.50

Marine Type Inscribed "POSTAGE & REVENUE" and "OFFICIAL"

1995-96   Litho.   Perf. 14
O78 A155a 10s multicolored   .60   .60
O79 A155a 20s multicolored   .90   .40
O80 A155a 45s multicolored   1.10   .95
O81 A155a 60s multicolored   1.40   .95
O82 A155a 80s multicolored   1.75   1.75
O83 A155a   1pa multicolored   2.25   1.75
O84 A155a   2pa multicolored   4.00   4.00
O85 A155a   3pa multicolored   5.00   5.00
O86 A155a   5pa multicolored   9.75   9.75
O87 A155a 10pa multicolored   14.00 14.00
 Nos. O78-O87 (10)   40.75 38.40

Issued: 10s-80s, 9/25/95; 1pa-10pa, 5/31/96.

Nos. 1158-1169 Overprinted

2014, May 9   Litho.   Perf. 14
Stamps With White Frames

O88	A236	60s multi	.65	.65
O89	A236	2.25pa multi	2.40	2.40
O90	A236	2.40pa multi	2.60	2.60
O91	A236	2.50pa multi	2.75	2.75
O92	A236	2.70pa multi	3.00	3.00
O93	A236	3pa multi	3.25	3.25
O94	A236	3.40pa multi	3.75	3.75
O95	A236	4pa multi	4.25	4.25
O96	A236	5pa multi	5.50	5.50
O97	A236	6.60pa multi	7.00	7.00
O98	A236	7.30pa multi	7.75	7.75
O99	A236	10pa multi	11.00	11.00
		Nos. O88-O99 (12)	53.90	53.90

Nos. 1203-1214 Overprinted

2014, May 9   Litho.   Perf. 14
Stamps With White Frames

O100	A259	10s multi	.25	.25
O101	A259	20s multi	.25	.25
O102	A259	30s multi	.35	.35
O103	A259	40s multi	.45	.45
O104	A259	50s multi	.55	.55
O105	A259	80s multi	.85	.85
O106	A259	90s multi	.95	.95
O107	A259	1.10pa multi	1.25	1.25
O108	A259	1.20pa multi	1.40	1.40
O109	A259	2pa multi	2.25	2.25
O110	A259	12.50pa multi	13.50	13.50
O111	A259	20pa multi	21.50	21.50
		Nos. O100-O111 (12)	43.55	43.55

NIUAFO'OU

Tin Can Island

> Catalogue values for all unused stamps in this country are for Never Hinged items.

Nos. 1-63 are die cut self-adhesive stamps on peelable inscribed backing paper.

Niuafo'ou Airport Type of Tonga
1983, May 11   Litho.   Die Cut

1	A97	29s multicolored	1.75	1.75
2	A97	1pa multicolored	3.75	3.75

Map of Niuafo'ou — A1

1983, May 11

3	A1	1s buff, blk & red	.45	.45
4	A1	2s buff, blk & brt green	.45	.45
5	A1	3s buff, blk & brt blue	.45	.45
6	A1	3s buff, blk & brn org	.45	.45
7	A1	5s buff, blk & deep rose lil	.45	.45
8	A1	6s buff, blk & grnsh blue	.45	.45
9	A1	9s buff, blk & lt ol grn	.45	.45
10	A1	10s buff, blk & brt bl	.45	.45
11	A1	13s buff, blk & brt grn	.50	.50
12	A1	15s buff, blk & brn org	.60	.60
13	A1	20s buff, blk & grnsh blue	.75	.75
14	A1	29s buff, blk & deep rose lil	1.25	1.25
15	A1	32s buff, blk & lt ol grn	1.40	1.40
16	A1	47s buff, blk & red	1.90	1.90
		Nos. 3-16 (14)	10.00	10.00

See Nos. 19-22.

Tonga No. 520 Surcharged or Ovptd. in Purple or Gold "NIUAFO'OU / Kingdom of Tonga"
1983, May 11

17	A93	1pa on 2pa multi (P)	3.25	3.25
18	A93	2pa multicolored (G)	4.50	4.50

Nos. 17-18 each exist se-tenant with label.

Map Type of 1983
Value Typo. in Violet Blue
1983, May 30

19	A1	3s buff & black	.25	.25
20	A1	5s buff & black	.25	.25
21	A1	32s buff & black	1.50	1.50
22	A1	2pa buff & black	8.00	8.00
		Nos. 19-22 (4)	10.00	10.00

The denomination on Nos. 19-22 added like a surcharge and is larger than on Nos. 5-7, 15, covering part of the design.
Nos. 19-22 each exist se-tenant with label.

Eruption of Niuafo'ou, Sept. 9, 1946 — A2

29s, Lava flow. 32s, Moving to high ground. 1.50pa, Evacuation to Eua.

1983, Sept. 29

23	A2	5s shown	.75	.70
24	A2	29s multicolored	1.50	1.25
25	A2	32s multicolored	1.75	1.25
26	A2	1.50pa multicolored	5.00	6.00
		Nos. 23-26 (4)	9.00	9.20

Birds — A3

1s, Purple swamphen. 2s, White-collared kingfisher. 3s, Red-headed parrotfinch. 5s, Banded rail. 6s, Niuafo'ou megapode. 9s, Giant forest honeyeater. 10s, Purple swamphen, drinking. 13s, Banded rail, diff. 15s, Niuafo'ou megapode, diff. 29s, Red-headed parrotfinch, diff. 32s, White-collared kingfisher, diff.

1983, Nov. 15

27	A3	1s multicolored	1.00	1.00
28	A3	2s multicolored	1.00	1.00
29	A3	3s multicolored	1.00	1.00
30	A3	5s multicolored	1.25	1.25
31	A3	6s multicolored	1.60	1.60
32	A3	9s multicolored	2.50	2.50
33	A3	10s multicolored	2.50	2.50
34	A3	13s multicolored	2.75	2.75
35	A3	15s multicolored	2.75	2.75

Size: 25x39mm

36	A3	20s like #34	3.25	3.25
37	A3	29s multicolored	3.50	3.50
38	A3	32s multicolored	3.50	3.50
39	A3	47s like #35	4.25	4.25

Size: 32x42mm

40	A3	1pa like #33	8.00	9.75
41	A3	2pa like #35	11.00	14.00
		Nos. 27-41 (15)	49.85	54.60

Nos. 34-36, 39 and 41 horiz.
For surcharges see Nos. 66-73.

Wildlife — A4

29s, Green turtle. 32s, Flying fox, vert. 47s, Humpback whale. 1.50pa, Niuafo'ou megapode, vert.

1984, Mar. 7

42	A4	29s multicolored	.75	.75
43	A4	32s multicolored	.75	.75
44	A4	47s multicolored	3.00	2.10
45	A4	1.50pa multicolored	5.50	8.25
		Nos. 42-45 (4)	10.00	11.85

Map — A5

47s, Intl. Date Line, Cent.

1984, Aug. 20

46	A5	47s multicolored	1.00	1.00
47	A5	2pa shown	3.50	3.50

AUSIPEX '84 — A6

1984, Sept. 17

48	A6	32s Australia No. 15	.90	.90
49	A6	1.50pa No. 10	3.75	3.75

Souvenir Sheet

50		Sheet of 2	4.75	4.75

No. 50 contains two imperf. stamps similar to Nos. 48-49, but with denomination replacing logo. No. 50 without denominations was not valid for postage.

A7

Jacob Le Maire, 400th Birth Anniv.: 13s, Dutch band entertaining natives. 32s, Natives preparing kava. 47s, Native outrigger canoes. 1.50pa, Le Maire's ship at anchor.

1985, Feb. 20

51	A7	13s multicolored	.40	.40
52	A7	32s multicolored	.85	.85
53	A7	47s multicolored	1.15	1.15
54	A7	1.50pa multicolor	3.50	3.50
		Nos. 51-54 (4)	5.90	5.90

Souvenir Sheet

55	A7	1.50pa multicolored	3.50	3.50

Mail Ships — A8

1985, May 22   Die Cut

56	A8	9s Ysabel, 1902	.75	.75
a.		Perf. 14	.90	.90
57	A8	13s Tofua I, 1908	.85	.85
a.		Perf. 14	1.25	1.25
58	A8	47s Mariposa, 1934	1.75	1.75
a.		Perf. 14	2.00	2.00
59	A8	1.50pa Matua, 1936	3.50	3.50
a.		Perf. 14	4.50	6.50
		Nos. 56-59 (4)	6.85	6.85
		Nos. 56a-59a (4)	8.65	10.65

Rocket Mail — A9

Designs: 32s, Preparing to fire rocket. 42s, Rocket airborne. 57s, Captain watching rocket's progress. 1.50pa, Islanders reading mail.

1985, Nov. 5

60	A9	32s multicolored	1.50	.90
61	A9	42s multicolored	1.75	1.10
62	A9	57s multicolored	2.00	1.60
63	A9	1.50pa multicolored	4.25	6.25
		Nos. 60-63 (4)	9.50	9.85

Self-adhesive stamps discontinued.

Halley's Comet — A10

Nos. 64, 65: a, Drawing of Comet in 684. b, Comet shown in Bayeux Tapestry, 1066. c, Edmond Halley. d, Comet, 1910. e, Infrared photography, 1986.

1986, Mar. 26   Perf. 14

64	A10	42s Strip of #a.-e.	30.00	20.00
65	A10	57s Strip of #a.-e.	30.00	20.00

Nos. 32-39 Surcharged in Blue

1986, Apr. 16   Die Cut
Self-Adhesive

66	A3	4s on 9s #32	1.00	2.75
67	A3	4s on 10s #33	1.00	2.75
68	A3	42s on 13s #34	3.25	2.75
69	A3	42s on 15s #35	3.25	2.75
70	A3	57s on 29s #37	4.25	3.25
71	A3	57s on 32s #38	4.25	3.25
72	A3	2.50pa on 20s #36	12.50	14.00
73	A3	2.50pa on 47s #39	12.50	14.00
		Nos. 66-73 (8)	42.00	45.50

Placement of surcharge varies.

AMERIPEX '86 Type of Tonga
1986, May 22   Perf. 14

74	A117	57s Surveying	2.25	2.25
75	A117	1.50pa Agriculture	4.00	4.00
a.		Souv. sheet of 2, #74-75, imperf.	7.00	7.00

Peace Corps in Tonga, 25th anniv.

First Tongan Postage Stamps, Cent. — A11

42s, Swimmers with mail. 57s, Loading tin can mail into canoe. 1pa, Rocket mail. 2.50pa, Outrigger canoe.
No. 80, Outrigger canoe, diff.

1986, Aug. 27

76	A11	42s multicolored	1.25	1.25
77	A11	57s multicolored	1.50	1.50
78	A11	1pa multicolored	3.25	3.25
79	A11	2.50pa multicolored	4.25	4.25
		Nos. 76-79 (4)	10.25	10.25

Souvenir Sheet

80	A11	2.50pa multicolored	9.50	9.50

Red Cross — A12

15s, Balanced diet. 42s, Post-natal care. 1pa, Insects spread disease. 2.50pa, Fight against drugs, alcohol, smoking.

1987, Mar. 11   Perf. 14x14½
81	A12	15s multicolored	1.00	1.00
82	A12	42s multicolored	2.00	2.00
83	A12	57s multicolored	3.75	3.75
84	A12	2.50pa multicolored	6.25	6.25
		Nos. 81-84 (4)	13.00	13.00

Sharks
A13

1987, Apr. 29   Perf. 14
85	A13	29s Hammerhead	2.50	2.25
86	A13	32s Tiger	2.50	2.25
87	A13	47s Gray nurse	3.00	2.75
88	A13	1pa Great white	5.25	7.00
		Nos. 85-88 (4)	13.25	14.25

Souvenir Sheet
89	A13	2pa Shark attack	15.50	15.50

Aviators and Aircraft A14

Designs: 42s, Capt. E. C. Musick and Sikorsky S-42. 57s, Capt. J.W. Burgess and Shorts S-30. 1.50pa, Sir Charles Kingsford Smith and Fokker F.VIIb-3m. 2pa, Amelia Earhart and Lockheed Electra 10A.

1987, Sept. 2
90	A14	42s multicolored	2.50	1.75
91	A14	57s multicolored	3.00	2.00
92	A14	1.50pa multicolored	5.00	5.00
93	A14	2pa multicolored	5.25	5.25
		Nos. 90-93 (4)	15.75	14.00

First Niuafo'ou Postage Stamps, 5th Anniv. A15

Designs: 42s, 57s, Niuafo'ou megapode, No. 15. 1pa, 2pa, Concorde, No. 1.

1988, May 18
94	A15	42s multicolored	1.00	.75
95	A15	57s multicolored	1.00	.95
96	A15	1pa multicolored	5.00	3.25
97	A15	2pa multicolored	6.00	4.50
		Nos. 94-97 (4)	13.00	9.45

#96-97, Niuafo'ou Airport Inauguration, 5th anniv.

Settlement of Australia, Bicent.
Type of Tonga
Miniature Sheet

Designs: a, Arrival of First Fleet, Sydney Cove, Jan. 1788. b, Aborigines. c, Early settlement. d, Soldier on guard. e, Herd of sheep. f, Horseman. g, Locomotive, kangaroos. h, Train, kangaroos. i, Flying doctor service. j, Cricket players. k, Stadium, batsman guarding wicket. l, Sydney Harbor Bridge, Opera House.

1988, July 11   Perf. 13½
98	A128	42s Sheet of 12,		
		#98a-98 l	45.00	45.00

Polynesian Islands — A16

Birds and landmarks: 42s, Audubon's shearwater, blowholes at Houma, Tonga. 57s, Kiwi, Akaroa Harbor, New Zealand. 90s, Red-tailed tropicbird, Rainmaker Mountain, Samoa.

2.50pa, Laysan albatross, Kapoho Volcano, Hawaii.

1988, Aug. 18   Perf. 14
99	A16	42s multicolored	1.50	1.00
100	A16	57s multicolored	2.25	1.40
101	A16	90s multicolored	2.50	2.50
102	A16	2.50pa multicolored	4.75	4.75
		Nos. 99-102 (4)	11.00	9.65

Miniature Sheet

Mutiny on the Bounty, Bicent. — A17

Designs: a, Sextant. b, William Bligh. c, Royal Navy lieutenant. d, Midshipman. e, Contemporary newspaper, Tahitian girl. f, Breadfruit. g, *Mutiny on the Bounty* excerpt, pistol grip. h, Pistol barrel, illustration of Bounty castaways. i, Tahitian girl, newsprint. j, Bligh's and Fletcher Christian's signatures. k, Christian, Pitcairn Island. l, Tombstone of John Adams.

1989, Apr. 28   Perf. 13½
103	A17	42s Sheet of 12, #a.-l.	25.00	25.00

Marine Conservation — A18

1989, June 2   Perf. 14
104	A18	32s Hatchet fish	1.40	1.40
105	A18	42s Snipe eel	1.60	1.60
106	A18	57s Viper fish	2.00	2.00
107	A18	1.50pa Angler fish	5.00	5.00
		Nos. 104-107 (4)	10.00	10.00

Evolution of the Earth — A19

Designs: 1s, Formation of the crust. 2s, Cross-section of crust. 5s, Volcanism. 10s, Surface cools. 13s, Gem stones. 15s, Oceans form. 20s, Mountains develop. 32s, River valley. 42s, Silurian Era plant life. 45s, Early marine life. 50s, Trilobites, Cambrian Era marine life. 57s, Carboniferous Era forest, coal seams. 60s, Dinosaurs feeding. 80s, Dinosaurs fighting. 1pa, Carboniferous Era insect, amphibians. 1.50pa, Stegosaurus, Jurassic Era. 2pa, Birds and mammals, Jurassic Era. 5pa, Hominid family, Pleistocene Era. 10pa, Mammoth, saber tooth tiger.

1989-93   Perf. 14½
108	A19	1s multicolored	.70	.70
109	A19	2s multicolored	.70	.70
110	A19	5s multicolored	.90	.90
111	A19	10s multicolored	.90	.90
111A	A19	13s multicolored	1.10	1.10
112	A19	15s multicolored	.90	.90
113	A19	20s multicolored	.90	.90
114	A19	32s multicolored	1.10	1.10
115	A19	42s multicolored	1.50	1.50
115A	A19	45s multicolored	1.50	1.50
116	A19	50s multicolored	1.60	1.60
117	A19	57s multicolored	1.60	1.00
117A	A19	60s multicolored	1.75	1.75
117B	A19	80s multicolored	2.10	2.10

Size: 26x40mm
Perf. 14
118	A19	1pa multicolored	3.00	3.00
119	A19	1.50pa multicolored	4.75	4.75
120	A19	2pa multicolored	4.75	4.75
121	A19	5pa multicolored	9.25	9.25

Perf. 14
121A	A19	10pa multicolored	16.00	16.00
		Nos. 108-121A (19)	55.00	55.00

Issued: 1o 10o, 15s-42s, 50s-57s, 6/6/89; 13s, 45s, 60s, 80s, 5/3/93; 10pa, 9/14/93; others, 8/1/89.

A20

1989, Nov. 17   Perf. 14
122	A20	57s multicolored	1.90	1.90

Miniature Sheet

Nos. 108-121 with UPU emblem: Nos. 123a-123e, #108-112, Nos. 123f-123j, #113-117, Nos. 123k-123n, #118-121.

123		Sheet of 15, #a.-n.,		
		122	27.50	27.50
a.-e.		A19 32s any single, perf. 14½	1.00	1.00
f.-j.		A19 42s any single, perf. 14½	1.60	1.50
k.-n.		A19 57s any single, perf. 14	2.00	2.00

Miniature Sheet

Lake Vai Lahi, Niuafo'ou — A21

a, d, Left part of lake. b, e, Small islands in center of lake. c, f, Small islet in right side of lake.

1990, Apr. 4   Perf. 14
124	A21	Sheet of 6	8.75	8.75
a.-c.		A19 42s any single	.75	.75
d.-f.		A19 1pa any single	2.00	2.00

Nos. 124a-124c and 124d-124f printed in continuous designs.

Penny Black, 150th Anniv. A22

Tin Can Mail and: 42s, Penny Black. 57s, US #2. 75s, Western Australia #1. 2.50pa, Cape of Good Hope #178.

1990, May 1
125	A22	42s multicolored	1.50	1.00
126	A22	57s multicolored	1.75	1.25
127	A22	75s multicolored	2.00	2.00
128	A22	2.50pa multicolored	5.25	5.50
		Nos. 125-128 (4)	10.50	9.75

Polynesian Whaling — A23

Designs: 15s, Whale surfacing. 42s, Whale diving beneath outrigger canoe. 57s, Tail flukes. 1pa, 2pa, Old man, two whales.

1990   Perf. 11½
129	A23	15s multicolored	2.25	2.25
130	A23	42s multicolored	3.25	3.25
131	A23	57s multicolored	3.50	0.50
132	A23	2pa multicolored	9.50	9.50
		Nos. 129-132 (4)	18.50	18.50

Souvenir Sheet
Perf. 14x14½
133	A23	1pa multicolored	19.00	19.00

Issue dates: #133, Sept. 4, others, June 6.
The entire souvenir sheet, No. 133, shows a modified No. 132. The 37½x30½mm stamp shows the two whales.
For surcharges see Nos. 139, 174-178.

UN Development Program, 40th Anniv. — A24

Designs: No. 134a, Agriculture and fisheries. No. 134b, Education. No. 135a, Health care. No. 135b, Communications.

1990, Oct. 25   Perf. 14
134	A24	57s Pair, #a.-b.	2.75	2.75
135	A24	2.50pa Pair, #a.-b.	11.50	11.50

Charting of Niuafo'ou, Bicent. — A24a

Designs: No. 136a, 32s, The Bounty. b, 42s, Chart showing location of Niuafo'ou and Tonga. c, 57s, The Pandora. No. 137a, 2pa, Capt. Edwards of the Pandora. b, 3pa, Capt. Bligh of the Bounty.

1991, July 25   Litho.   Perf. 14½
136	A24a	Strip of 3, #a.-c.	5.25	5.25

Souvenir Sheet
137	A24a	Sheet of 2, #a.-b.	15.50	15.50

No. 133 Surcharged in Dark Blue Violet

1991, July 31   Litho.   Perf. 14x14½
139	A23	1pa on 1pa #133	13.00	13.00

"1991 Ornithological and Scientic Expedition" overprint appears on souvenir sheet at top center.

Ceresium Unicolor — A25

42s, Larva stage. 57s, Mature beetle. 1.50pa, Larva stage, diff. 2.50pa, Mature beetle on tree limb.

1991, Sept. 11   Perf. 14½x14
140	A25	42s multicolored	1.25	1.25
141	A25	57s multicolored	1.50	1.50
142	A25	1.50pa multicolored	3.25	3.25
143	A25	2.50pa multicolored	6.00	6.00
		Nos. 140-143 (4)	12.00	12.00

For surcharges, see Tonga Nos. 1127, 1129.

Christmas
A26

Legend of the origin of the coconut tree: 15s, No. 146a, Heina bathing in lake being watched by eel. 42s, No. 146b, Heina weeping over plant growing from eel's grave. No. 146c, 1.50pa, Heina's boy climbing coconut tree. No. 146d, 3pa, "Eel's face" on coconut.

1991, Nov. 12   Litho.   Perf. 14½
144 A26 15s multicolored   .75   .75
145 A26 42s multicolored   2.00   2.00
146 A26   Sheet of 4, #a.-d. 14.00 14.00
         Nos. 144-146 (3)   16.75 16.75

For surcharge, see Tonga No. 1128.

Nos. 144-145 inscribed "Christmas Greetings 1991." No. 146 contains Nos. 144-145, 146a-146d inscribed "A Love Story."

Miniature Sheet

Discovery of America, 500th
Anniv. — A27

Designs: a, Columbus. b, Queen Isabella, King Ferdinand. c, Columbus being blessed by Abbot of Palos. d, Men in boat, 15th century compass. e, Wooden traverse, wind rose, Nina. f, Bow of Santa Maria. g, Stern of Santa Maria. h, Australian mortar crew, Kokoda Trail. i, Pinta. i, Two men raising cross. j, Explorers, natives. k, Columbus kneeling before King and Queen. l, Columbus' second coat of arms.

1992, Apr. 28   Litho.   Perf. 13½
147 A27 57s Sheet of 12, #a.-l. 30.00 30.00

Miniature Sheet

World War II in Pacific, 50th
Anniv. — A28

Newspaper headline and: a, Battleship ablaze at Pearl Harbor. b, Destroyed aircraft. c, Japanese A6M Zero fighter. d, Declaration of war, Pres. Franklin D. Roosevelt. e, Japanese T95 tank, Gen. MacArthur, Japanese naval ensign. f, Douglas SBD Dauntless dive bomber, Admiral Nimitz. g, Bren gun, Gen. Sir Thomas Blamey. h, Australian mortar crew, Kokoda Trail. i, US battleship, Maj. Gen. Julian C. Smith. j, Aircraft carrier USS Enterprise. k, American soldier, flag, Maj. Gen. Curtis Lemay. l, B-29 bomber, surrender ceremony on USS Missouri in Tokyo bay.

1992, May 12   Litho.   Perf. 14
148 A28 42s Sheet of 12, #a.-l. 25.00 25.00

King
Taufa'ahau
IV, 25th
Anniv. of
Coronation
A29

45s, 2pa, King, Queen Halaevalu during coronation. No. 150a, King, Tongan national anthem. b, Extract from investiture ceremony. c, Tongan national anthem, singers.

1992, July 4   Perf. 13½x13
149 A29 45s multicolored   1.10   1.10
         Size: 51x38mm
         Perf. 12½x12
150 A29 80s Strip of 3, #a.-c.   5.00   5.00
151 A29 2pa multicolored   4.00   4.00
         Nos. 149-151 (3)   10.10 10.10

Megapodius Pritchardii — A30

1992, Sept. 15   Litho.   Perf. 14
152 A30 45s Female & male   1.50   1.75
153 A30 60s Female with egg   2.00   2.10
154 A30 80s Chick   2.75   3.00
155 A30 1.50pa Head of male   5.00   6.00
         Nos. 152-155 (4)   11.25 12.85

World Wildlife Fund.

First
Niuafo'ou
Postage
Stamps,
10th Anniv.
A31

1993, May 3   Litho.   Perf. 14x14½
156 A31 60s Nos. 4, 117A   1.90   1.90
157 A31 80s Nos. 7, 117B   2.10   2.10

Aviation in
Niuafo'ou,
10th
Anniv. — A32

Airplanes of: 1pa, South Pacific Island Airways. 2.50pa, Friendly Islands Airways.

1993, May 3
158 A32 1pa multicolored   2.50   2.50
159 A32 2.50pa multicolored   5.50   5.50

King's 75th Birthday Type of Tonga

King and: 45s, 2pa, Patrol boat Pangai. No. 161a, Sporting events. b, Aircraft and communications. c, Musical instruments.

1993, July 1   Perf. 13x13½
160 A167 45s multicolored   1.00   1.00
         Perf. 12x12½
         Size: 37x48mm
161 A167 80s Strip of 3, #a.-
            c.   5.00   5.00
162 A167 2pa multicolored   3.75   3.75
         Nos. 160-162 (3)   9.75   9.75

Wildlife — A33

Designs: a, Two parrots. b, Bird with fish. c, Butterfly, beetle. d, Birds, dragonfly, butterfly. e, Bird in flight, two on ground.

1993, Aug. 10   Litho.   Perf. 14
163 A33 60s Strip of 5, #a.-e. 6.50   6.50

No. 163 is a continuous design.

Winners of Children's Painting
Competition — A34

Designs: Nos. 164a, 165a, Ofato Beetle Grubbs of Niuafo'ou, by Peni Finau. Nos. 164b, 165b, Crater Lake Megapode, Volcano, by Paea Puletau.

1993, Dec. 1   Litho.   Perf. 14
164 A34 10s Pair, #a.-b.   .75   .75
165 A34 1pa Pair, #a.-b.   6.75   6.75

Beetles
A35

1994, Mar. 15   Litho.   Perf. 14
168 A35 60s Scarabaeidea   1.25   1.25
169 A35 80s Coccinellidea   1.75   1.75
170 A35 1.50pa Cerambycidea   3.00   3.00
171 A35 2.50pa Pentatomidae   5.50   5.50
         Nos. 168-171 (4)   11.50 11.50

A36

Sailing Ships: a, Stern of HMS Bounty. b, Bow of HMS Bounty. c, HMS Pandora. d, Whaling ship. e, Trading schooner.

1994, June 21   Litho.   Perf. 14
172 A36 80s Strip of 5, #a.-e. 12.50 12.50

No. 172 is a continuous design.

A37

1946 Volcanic Eruption: a, Blue-crowned lorikeet, lava flow. b, Black Pacific ducks, lava flow. c, Megapodes, palm trees (b). d, White-tailed tropic birds, people evacuating island (c). e, People wading out to sailboats, Pacific reef heron.

1994, Sept. 21   Litho.   Perf. 14½
173 A37 80s Strip of 5, #a.-e. 8.50   8.50

No. 173 is a continuous design.

Nos. 129-133 Surcharged in Blue

1995, June 30   Litho.   Perf. 11½
174 A23 60s on 42s #130   2.25   2.25
175 A23 80s on 15s #129   3.00   3.00
176 A23 80s on 57s #131   4.00   4.00
177 A23 2pa on #132   7.50   7.50
         Nos. 174-177 (4)   16.75 16.75

Souvenir Sheet
178 A23 1.50pa on 1pa #133   8.50   8.50

Size and location of surcharge varies. Surcharge on No. 178 includes "COME WHALE WATCHING / IN THE SOUTH PACIFIC."

Victory in the Pacific Type of Tonga

Nos. 179, 180: a, Soldier holding rifle. b, Soldier aiming rifle, tank. c, Front of tank. d, Troops coming off boat, firing weapons. e, Troops on beach.

1995, Aug. 1   Litho.   Perf. 14x14½
179 A177 60s Strip of 5, #a.-e. 9.50   9.50
180 A177 80s Strip of 5, #a.-e. 12.50 12.50

Nos. 179-180 are continuous designs and were issued together in sheets containing 10 stamps.

Singapore '95 Type of Tonga

Designs, vert: No. 181a, 45s, like #117A. b, 60s, like #117B.
2pa, Plesiosaurus.

1995, Sept. 1   Litho.   Perf. 12
181 A178   Pair, #a.-b.   4.50   4.50

Souvenir Sheet
182 A178 2pa multicolored   5.50   5.50

Beijing Intl. Coin & Stamp Show '95 Type of Tonga

Souvenir Sheet

Design: 1.40pa, The Great Wall of China.

1995, Sept. 14   Perf. 14½
183 A179 1.40pa multicolored   4.00   4.00

End of World War II, UN, 50th Anniv. Type of Tonga

No. 184: a, London blitz. b, UN emblem, "50." c, Concorde.
No. 185: a, Building of Siam-Burma Railway by Allied prisoners of war. b, Like #184b. c, Japanese bullet train.

1995, Oct. 26   Litho.   Perf. 14
184 A180 60s Strip of 3, #a.-
            c.   5.50   5.50
185 A180 80s Strip of 3, #a.-
            c.   6.50   6.50

Nos. 184b, 185b are 23x31mm.

Mailmen
of
Niuafo'ou
A38

Portrait, illustration of postal history: 45s, Charles Stuart Ramsey, companions, floating with poles. 60s, Ramsey with can of mail encountering shark. 1pa, Walter George Quensell, mail being lowered from ship to canoes. 3pa, Quensell, original "tin can" mail cancels.

1996, Aug. 21   Litho.   Perf. 14
186 A38 45s multicolored   .75   .75
187 A38 60s multicolored   1.25   1.25
188 A38 1pa multicolored   2.00   2.00
189 A38 3pa multicolored   8.00   8.00
         Nos. 186-189 (4)   12.00 12.00

Congress of Preshistoric and Protohistoric Sciences Type of Tonga

a, Prehistoric man making drawings, fire, living in huts, animals. b, Ancient Egyptians, Romans.

1996, Sept. 5		Perf. 12	
190	A185 1pa Pair, #a.-b.	6.25	6.25

Evacuation of Niuafo'ou, 50th Anniv. — A39

a, Island, two canoes. b, Volcano, four canoes. c, Edge of island, canoe. d, Canoe. e, People boarding MV Matua.

1996, Dec. 2		Perf. 14	
191	A39 45s Strip of 5, #a.-e.	6.00	6.00
192	A39 60s Strip of 5, #a.-e.	8.00	8.00

Nos. 191-192 are continuous designs and were issued together in sheet containing 10 stamps.

UNICEF, 50th Anniv. Type of Tonga

Children's toys on checkerboard: a, Dolls, truck, balls on pegs. b, Tricycle, car, balls on pegs, teddy bear, train. c, Car, helicopter, roller skates, books, blocks.

1996, Oct. 29		Litho.	Perf. 14	
193	A187 80s Strip of 3, #a.-c.		6.50	6.50

No. 193 is a continuous design.

Ocean Environment — A40

Various zooplankton and phytoplankton.

1997, May 19		Litho.	Perf. 14	
194	A40	60s red & multi	1.50	1.50
195	A40	80s brown & multi	2.00	2.00
196	A40	1.50pa blue & multi	3.00	3.00
197	A40	2.50pa green & multi	4.25	4.25
		Nos. 194-197 (4)	10.75	10.75

Pacific '97 Type of Tonga
Souvenir Sheet

Design: Oakland Bay Bridge, back-naped tern.

1997, May 30			
198	A191 2pa multicolored	5.25	5.25

1997 Wedding Anniv., Coronation Anniv. Type of Tonga

No. 199: a, King Taufa'ahau, Queen Halaevalu Mata'aho on wedding day. b, King in coronation regalia.

5pa, King in coronation procession, horiz.

1997, June 30		Litho.	Perf. 12	
		Size: 34x47mm		
199	A193 80s vert. pair, #a.- b.		4.50	4.50
	Souvenir Sheet			
200	A193 5pa multicolored		10.00	10.00

No. 199 was issued in sheets of 6 stamps.

Diana, Princess of Wales (1961-97)
Common Design Type

Various portraits: a, 10s. b, 80s. c, 1pa. d, 2.50pa.

		Perf. 13½x14		
1998, May 29		Litho.	Unwmk.	
201	CD355 Sheet of 4, #a.-d.		6.50	6.50

No. 201 sold for 4.40pa + 50s with surtax from international sales going to the Princess Diana Memorial Fund and surtax from local sales going to designated local charity.
For surcharge, see No. 291.

Blue Crowned Lorikeet — A41

World Wildlife Fund: 10s, Young birds in nest. 55s, Adult on branch of flower. 80s, Adult on branch of bush. 3pa, Two adults on tree branch.

1998, May 15		Litho.	Perf. 14½x15	
202	A41	10s multicolored	1.00	1.00
203	A41	55s multicolored	2.50	1.00
204	A41	80s multicolored	3.50	2.00
205	A41	3pa multicolored	7.50	7.50
a.		Sheet, 2 each #202-205	32.50	32.50
		Nos. 202-205 (4)	14.50	11.50

For surcharges see Tonga Nos. 1152, 1155.

King Taufa'ahau Tupou IV Type of Tonga

1998, July 4		Litho.	Perf. 14	
207	A196 2.70pa multicolored		4.00	4.00

See Tonga #985a for souvenir sheet containing one #207.

Fish — A43

a, 10s, Amphipiron melanopus. b, 55s, Amphipiron perideraion. c, 80s, Amphipiron chrysopterus.

1998, Sept. 23		Litho.	Perf. 14	
208	A43 Strip of 3, #a.-c.		2.25	2.25

Intl. Year of the Ocean. No. 208 was issued in sheets of 9 stamps.

Year of the Tiger Type of Tonga

Designs: a, 55s, Head of tiger with mouth open. b, 80s, Two tigers standing. c, 1pa, Two tigers lying down. 1pa, Head of tiger.

1998, July 23		Litho.	Perf. 14	
209	A183 Sheet of 4, #a.-d.		5.75	5.75

No. 209 is a continuous design. Singpex '98.

Christmas A44

Designs: 20s, Angel playing mandolin. 55s, Angel playing violin. 1pa, Children singing, bells. 1.60pa, Children singing, candles.

1998, Nov. 12			Perf. 14x14½	
210	A44	20s multicolored	.80	.80
211	A44	55s multicolored	1.35	1.35
212	A44	1pa multicolored	1.75	1.75
213	A44	1.60pa multicolored	2.50	2.50
		Nos. 210-213 (4)	6.40	6.40

For surcharge see Tonga No. 1153.

New Year 1999 (Year of the Rabbit) A45

Stylized rabbits: a, 10s. b, 55s. c, 80s. d, 1pa.

1999, Feb. 16		Perf. 14	
214	A45 Sheet of 4, #a.-d.	4.00	4.00

Jakob le Maire (1585-1616), Explorer — A46

1999, Mar. 19		Litho.	Perf. 14	
215	A46	80s shown	1.80	1.80
216	A46	2.70pa Tongiaki canoe	4.50	4.50
a.		Souvenir sheet, #215-216	7.00	7.00

Australia '99 World Stamp Expo (#216a).

Flowers A47

55s, Cananga odorata. 80s, Gardenia tannaensis, vert. 1pa, Coleus amboinicus, vert. 2.50pa, Hernandia moerenhoutiana.

		Perf. 13x13¼, 13¼x13		
1999, Sept. 29		Litho.		
217	A47	55s multicolored	.75	.75
218	A47	80s multicolored	1.25	1.25
219	A47	1pa multicolored	1.50	1.50
220	A47	2.50pa multicolored	3.00	3.00
		Nos. 217-220 (4)	6.50	6.50

Souvenir Sheet

Millennium — A48

a, 1pa, Dove. b, 2.50pa, Native boat.

2000, Jan. 1		Litho.	Perf. 14½x15	
221	A48 Sheet of 2, #a.-b.		4.50	4.50

Souvenir Sheet

New Year 2000 (Year of the Dragon) — A49

Various dragons: a, 10s. b, 55s, c, 80s. d, 1pa.

Litho. with Foil Application

2000, Feb. 4		Perf. 14½	
222	A49 Sheet of 4, #a.-d.	3.75	3.75

Souvenir Sheet

The Stamp Show 2000, London — A50

Litho. with Foil Application

2000, May 22		Perf. 13x13¼	
223	A50 Sheet of 2	5.00	5.00
a.	$1.50 Queen Mother	2.00	2.00
b.	$2.50 Queen Salote Tupou III	3.00	3.00

Souvenir Sheet

World Stamp Expo 2000, Anaheim — A51

No. 224: a, 10s, Man and woman. b, 2.50pa, Satellite dish. c, 2.70pa, Intelsat.

2000, July 7		Litho.	Perf. 13x13¼	
224	A51 Sheet of 3, #a-c		6.75	6.75

Butterflies — A52

Designs: 55s, Jamides bochus. 80s, Blue moon. 1pa, Eurema hecabe aprica. 2.70pa, Monarch.

2000, Oct. 25		Perf. 14	
225-228	A52 Set of 4	8.25	8.25

For surcharge see Tonga No. 1154.

Souvenir Sheet

New Year 2001 (Year of the Snake) — A53

No. 229 — Various snakes: a, 10s. b, 55s, c, 80s, d, 1pa.

Litho. with Foil Application

2001, Feb. 1		Perf. 14¼	
229	A53 Sheet of 4, #a-d	4.00	4.00

Hong Kong 2001 Stamp Exhibition.

Fish — A54

Designs: 80s, Prognichthys sealei. 1pa, Xiphias gladius. 2.50pa, Katsuwonus pelamis.

2001, June 5   **Litho.**   **Perf. 13¾**
230-232   A54   Set of 3   8.50   8.50
232a   Souvenir sheet, #230-232   9.00   9.00

Souvenir Sheet

Fruit — A55

No. 233: a, 55s, Papaya. b, 80s, Limes. c, 1pa, Mangos. d, 2.50pa, Bananas.

Perf. 14¼x14
2001, Sept. 19   **Litho.**   **Unwmk.**
233   A55   Sheet of 4, #a-d   7.00   7.00

Barn Owl A56

Designs: Nos. 234, 238a, 10s, Owl in flight. Nos. 235, 238b, 55s, Adult feeding young. Nos. 236, 238c, 2.50pa, Four owls. Nos. 237, 238d, 2.70pa, Owl's head.

2001, Nov. 21   **Perf. 12¾x13¼**
Without Vertical Bister Line Separating Panels
234-237   A56   Set of 4   8.50   8.50

Souvenir Sheet
With Vertical Bister Line Separating Panels
238   A56   Sheet of 4, #a-d   8.75   8.75

For surcharge see Tonga No. 1156.

Reign Of Queen Elizabeth II, 50th Anniv. Issue
Common Design Type

No. 239: a, 15s, Princess Elizabeth with Queen Mother. b, 90s, Wearing purple hat. c, 1.20pa, As young woman. d, 1.40pa, Wearing red hat. e, 2.25pa, 1955 portrait by Annigoni (38x50mm).

Perf. 14¼x14½, 13¾ (2.25pa)
2002, Feb. 6   **Litho.**   **Wmk. 373**
239   CD360   Sheet of 5, #a-e   8.75   8.75

Souvenir Sheet

New Year 2002 (Year of the Horse) — A57

Various horses: a, 65s. b, 80s. c, 1pa. d, 2.50pa.

Litho. With Foil Application
2002, Feb. 12   **Unwmk.**   **Perf. 14**
240   A57   Sheet of 4, #a-d   7.25   7.25

Megapodius Pritchardii A58

Designs: 15s, Bird, eggs. 70s, Two birds. 90s, Bird, vert. 2.50pa, Two birds, vert.

Perf. 14x13½, 13½x14
2002, Apr. 9   **Litho.**
241-244   A58   Set of 4   5.75   5.75
244a   Souvenir sheet, #243-244   6.75   6.75

Nos. 243-244 lack white frame around stamp.

Cephalopods A59

Designs: 80s, Octopus vulgaris. 1pa, Sepioteuthis lessoniana. 2.50pa, Nautilus belauensis.

2002, July 25   **Litho.**   **Perf. 13¾**
245-247   A59   Set of 3   7.50   7.50
247a   Souvenir sheet, #245-247   8.50   8.50

Souvenir Sheet

Mail Planes — A60

No. 248: a, 80c, Casa C-212 Aviocar. b, 1.40pa, Britten-Norman Islander. c, 2.50pa, DHC 6-300 Twin Otter.

2002, Nov. 27   **Litho.**   **Perf. 12¾**
248   A60   Sheet of 3, #a-c   7.00   7.00

New Year 2003 (Year of the Ram) Type of Tonga

No. 249: a, 65s, One ram. 80s, Three sheep. 1pa, Three sheep, diff. 2.50pa, Two sheep.

2003, Apr. 14   **Litho.**   **Perf. 13¼**
249   A223   Sheet of 4, #a-d   8.00   8.00

Coronation of Queen Elizabeth II, 50th Anniv. Type of Tonga

Designs: 90s, Queen Elizabeth II. 1.20pa, Queen Elizabeth II seated. 1.40pa, Queen Salote of Tonga in coach. 2.50pa, Queen Salote.

2003, June 2   **Litho.**
250-253   A224   Set of 4   10.00   10.00

New Year (Year of the Monkey) Type of Tonga

No. 254: a, 60s, Spider monkey. b, 80s, Ring-tailed lemur. c, 1pa, Cotton-top tamarin. d, 2.50pa, White-cheeked gibbon.

2004, Feb. 12   **Litho.**   **Perf. 13¼**
254   A228   Sheet of 4, #a-d   6.00   6.00

Trees Type of Tonga

Designs: 45s, Pawpaw (papaya). 60s, Banana. 80s, Coconut. 1.80pa, Lime.

2004   **Litho.**   **Perf. 14¼x14**
255-258   A229   Set of 4   5.50   5.50

Christmas Type of Tonga

Designs: 15s, Madonna and Child. 90s, Journey to Bethlehem. 1.20pa, Annunciation to the Shepherds. 2.60pa, Magi.

2004, Dec.   **Perf. 14**
259-262   A230   Set of 4   5.75   5.75

Royalty Type of Tonga

Designs: 30s, King George Tupou I. 65s, King George Tupou II. 80s, Queen Salote Tupou III. 3.05pa, King Taufa'ahau Tupou IV.

2004, July 7   **Litho.**   **Perf. 14**
263-266   A231   Set of 4   5.25   5.25
266a   Souvenir sheet, #263-266   5.75   5.75

New Year 2005 (Year of the Rooster) Type of Tonga
Souvenir Sheet

No. 267 — Various roosters with panel color of: a, 65s, Gray. b, 80s, Grayish tan. c, 1pa, Gray. d, 2.50pa, Yellow green.

2005, Feb. 12
267   A232   Sheet of 4, #a-d   6.75   6.75

Christmas — A61

No. 268: a, 3.40pa, Palm frond and Christmas lights. b, 5pa, Grass and snowflakes.

2011, Dec. 24
268   A61   Horiz. pair, #a-b   9.00   9.00

Miniature Sheets

Megaptera Novaeangliae — A62

No. 269 — Various depictions of humpback whale: a, 1pa. b, 1.40pa. c, 1.60pa.
No. 270 — Various depictions of humpback whale: a, 2pa. b, 2.25pa. c, 2.40pa.

2012, Jan. 16
269   A62   Sheet of 3, #a-c, + label   4.00   4.00
270   A62   Sheet of 3, #a-c, + label   6.00   6.00

Worldwide Fund for Nature (WWF) — A63

Various depictions of Zebra shark: 45s, 2pa, 2.40pa, 3.40pa.

2012, Mar. 12   **Perf. 14¼x14**
271-274   A63   Set of 4   8.25   8.25
274a   Sheet of 16, 4 each #271-274   35.00   35.00

For surcharges, see Nos. 324-327.

Butterflies — A64

Designs: 45s, Australian meadow-argus. 1.95pa, Crow butterfly. 2pa, Monarch butterfly. 2.40pa, Monarch butterfly, diff. 2.50pa, Blue moon butterfly. 3pa, Australian meadow-argus, diff. 3.40pa, Crow butterfly, diff. 4pa, Blue moon butterfly, diff. 5pa, Monarch butterfly, diff. 6pa, Blue moon butterfly, diff. 7.30pa, Crow butterfly, diff. 8pa, Australian meadow-argus, diff.

2012, Apr. 20   **Perf. 12¾x12½**
Stamps With White Backgrounds
275   A64   45s multi   .55   .55
276   A64   1.95pa multi   2.25   2.25
277   A64   2pa multi   2.40   2.40
278   A64   2.40pa multi   2.75   2.75

---

279   A64   2.50pa multi   3.00   3.00
280   A64   3pa multi   3.50   3.50
281   A64   3.40pa multi   4.00   4.00
282   A64   4pa multi   4.75   4.75
283   A64   5pa multi   6.00   6.00
284   A64   6pa multi   7.00   7.00
285   A64   7.30pa multi   8.50   8.50
286   A64   8pa multi   9.50   9.50
   Nos. 275-286 (12)   54.20   54.20

Stamps With Light Blue Background
287   Sheet of 12   55.00   55.00
a.   A64   45s multi   .55   .55
b.   A64   1.95pa multi   2.25   2.25
c.   A64   2pa multi   2.40   2.40
d.   A64   2.40pa multi   2.75   2.75
e.   A64   2.50pa multi   3.00   3.00
f.   A64   3pa multi   3.50   3.50
g.   A64   3.40pa multi   4.00   4.00
h.   A64   4pa multi   4.75   4.75
i.   A64   5pa multi   6.00   6.00
j.   A64   6pa multi   7.00   7.00
k.   A64   7.30pa multi   8.50   8.50
l.   A64   8pa multi   9.50   9.50

Titanic Type of Tonga

No. 288: a, Titanic facing left at dock. b, Photograph of Titanic facing right. c, Titanic facing left at sea. d, Color painting of Titanic at sea.
No. 289a, Like #288d.

2012, June 6   **Perf. 12½**
288   A240   3.40pa Sheet of 4, #a-d   16.00   16.00

Souvenir Sheet
289   A240   Sheet of 2, #288a, 289a   4.50   4.50
a.   45s multi   .50   .50

Personalizable Stamp — A65

2012, Aug. 8   **Perf. 14x14¾**
290   A65   3pa multi   3.00   3.00

No. 201 Surcharged in Gold and Black

No. 1192: a, 4pa on 10s. b, 4pa on 80s. c, 4pa on 1pa. d, 4pa on 2.50pa.

2012, Sept. 4   **Litho.**
291   CD355   Sheet of 4, #a-d   18.50   18.50

Overprint is printed across the four stamps of the sheet. It reads "In Loving Memory of Diana, Princess of Wales / 31 August 1997 / Her Legacy will live on forever. / William and Kate, Duke and Duchess of Cambridge / 1st Anniversary of their Royal Wedding 2011".

Miniature Sheet

Christmas — A66

No. 292 — Nativity, by Giotto di Bondone: a, Angels, manger roof at LR, denomination at UL. b, Angels, manger roof at LL, denomination at LL. c, Angels in sky, no roof visible. d, Angels, manger post at left. e, Angels, manger post at right. f, Angel and tree. g, Madonna and Child, cow and donkey. h, Two shepherds. i, Joseph. j, Attendant holding infant Jesus. k,

Attendant and sheep. l, Sheep and legs of shepherds.

2012, Nov. 21 *Perf. 14¾x14¼*
292 A66 1pa Sheet of 12, #a-l,
        + 2 labels   12.50 12.50

New Year 2013 (Year of Snake) Type of Tonga

No. 293: a, Red snake with yellow green spots. b, Dark green snake with blue spots. c, Purple snake with green spots. d, Yellow green snake with green spots.

2013, Feb. 20
293 A248 2.45pa Sheet of 4,
        #a-d   10.50 10.50

Tin Can Island Mail Cans — A67

Designs: 2.25pa, Can on beach, ship at sea. 5.40pa, Can on beach, ship at sea, diff.

2013, Aug. 21 *Litho.* *Perf. 14x14¾*
294-295 A67 Set of 2   7.00 7.00

Birth of Prinoo George of Cambridge A68

Designs: 2.15pa, Baby's feet in adult's hand. 3.20pa, Baby's hand and foot. 4.10pa, Baby's hand in adult's hand. 4.70pa, Baby's hand.
16.90pa, Baby's feet in adult's hand, diff.

2013, Aug. 30 *Litho.* *Perf. 13¾*
296-299 A68 Set of 4   13.00 13.00
Souvenir Sheet
300 A68 16.90pa multi   16.00 16.00

Butterflies and Flowers A69

Designs: 20s, Blue moon butterfly, Jasmine. 30s, Monarch butterfly, Hibiscus. 40s, Meadow argus butterfly, Elder. 50s, Crow butterfly, Heilala. 60s, Blue moon butterfly, Blue wild indigo. 80s, Monarch butterfly, Purple coneflowers. 90s, Meadow argus butterfly, Yellow bell. 1.10pa, Crow butterfly, Frangipani. 1.20pa, Blue moon butterfly, Tahitian gardenia. 10pa, Blue moon butterfly, Frangipani. 12.50pa, Monarch butterfly, Hibiscus, diff. 20pa, Meadow argus butterfly, Tahitian vanilla orchid.

2013, Sept. 6 *Litho.* *Perf. 14*
Stamps With White Frames
301 A69 20s multi   .25   .25
302 A69 30s multi   .35   .35
303 A69 40s multi   .45   .45
304 A69 50s multi   .55   .55
305 A69 60s multi   .65   .65
306 A69 80s multi   .90   .90
307 A69 90s multi   1.00   1.00
308 A69 1.10pa multi   1.25   1.25
309 A69 1.20pa multi   1.40   1.40
310 A69 10pa multi   11.00 11.00
311 A69 12.50pa multi   13.50 13.50
312 A69 20pa multi   22.00 22.00
        Nos. 301-312 (12)   53.30 53.30
Miniature Sheet
Stamps With Blue Frames
313   Sheet of 12   54.00 54.00
  a. A69 20s multi   .25   .25
  b. A69 30s multi   .35   .35
  c. A69 40s multi   .45   .45
  d. A69 50s multi   .55   .55
  e. A69 60s multi   .65   .65
  f. A69 80s multi   .90   .90
  g. A69 90s multi   1.00   1.00
  h. A69 1.10pa multi   1.25   1.25
  i. A69 1.20pa multi   1.40   1.40

  j. A69 10pa multi   11.00 11.00
  k. A69 12.50pa multi   13.50 13.50
  l. A69 20pa multi   22.00 22.00

China International Collection Expo Type of Tonga of 2013
Souvenir Sheet

No. 314: a, 2.35pa, Painting by Paul Gauguin. b, 2.60pa, Beijing Exhibition Center.

2013, Sept. 26 *Litho.* *Perf. 12*
314 A263 Sheet of 2, #a-b   5.00 5.00

Christmas Type of Tonga of 2013

Paintings of angels by: 1.75pa, Pietro Perugino. 2.35pa, Melozzo da Forli. 2.60pa, Sandro Botticelli.

2013, Nov. 13 *Litho.* *Perf. 13½*
315-317 A269 Set of 3   6.50 6.50

Miniature Sheet

New Year 2014 (Year of the Horse) — A70

No. 318: a, Brown horse, black denomination at UL. b, White horse, white denomination at UR. c, Two horses. d, White horse, white denomination at UL.

2014, Jan. 6 *Litho.* *Perf. 13¾*
318 A70 $1.50 Sheet of 4, #a-d   5.50 5.50

Miniature Sheet

Easter — A71

No. 319 — Various paintings depicting the resurrected Christ by Pietro Perugino: a, 1.75pa. b, 2.25pa. c, 2.75pa. d, 4.55pa.

2014, Apr. 7 *Litho.* *Perf. 13¼*
319 A71 Sheet of 4, #a-d   12.50 12.50

Nelson Mandela (1918-2013), President of South Africa — A72

No. 320 — Mandela's: a, 2.25pa, Head. b, 5.40pa, Head and hands.

2014, May 13 *Litho.* *Perf. 14¾x14¼*
320 A72 Sheet of 2, #a-b   8.25 8.25

Butterflies — A73

No. 321: a, 11.30pa, Small greasy butterfly. b, 16.90pa, Spotted crow butterfly. c, 28pa, Monarch butterfly.

2014, May 22 *Litho.* *Perf. 13¼*
321 A73 Horiz. strip of 3, #a-
        c, + 3 labels   60.00 60.00

Miniature Sheet

Christmas — A74

Bells and: a, Curved staff and notes in foreground, slanted musical score in background. b, Faint musical score with three staffs in background. c, G clef and musical notes, faint musical score with six staffs. d, Curving staff with G clef and notes, faint musical score with four staffs in background.

2014, Dec. 15 *Litho.* *Perf. 13¾*
322 A74 2.25pa Sheet of 4, #a-d   9.25 9.25

Souvenir Sheet

New Year 2015 (Year of the Sheep) — A75

Sheep with background color of: a, 3.40pa, Blue. b, 4.60pa, Purple.

2015, Jan. 5 *Litho.* *Perf. 13¼*
323 A75 Sheet of 2, #a-b   7.75 7.75

Nos. 271-274 Surcharged

Methods and Perfs. As Before
2015, Apr. 1
324 A63 90s on 2.40pa #273   .90   .90
325 A63 1pa on 3.40pa #274   1.00   1.00
326 A63 1.10pa on 45s #271   1.10   1.10
327 A63 1.20pa on 2pa #272   1.25   1.25
        Nos. 324-327 (4)   4.25   4.25

Miniature Sheet

Easter — A76

No. 328 — Details of painting of the Holy Trinity: a, UL quadrant. b, UR quadrant. c, LL quadrant. d, LR quadrant.

2015, Apr. 3 *Litho.* *Perf. 14¼*
328 A76 2.25pa Sheet of 4, #a-d   9.00 9.00

Birth of Princess Charlotte Type of Tonga of 2015
Souvenir Sheet

No. 329: a, Duke and Duchess of Cambridge with Princess Charlotte. b, Duke of Cambridge holding Prince George.

2015, June 30 *Litho.* *Perf. 14¾x14*
329 A285 5pa Sheet of 2, #a-b   9.75 9.75

Year of the Monkey Type of Tonga of 2015

Designs: 2.25pa, Monkey. 3.60pa, Monkey holding flower.

No. 332: a, 3.40pa, Monkey, diff. b, 4.60pa, Monkey holding flower, diff.

2015, Sept. 25   Litho.   Perf. 13¼

330-331 A288   Set of 2   5.50   5.50

Souvenir Sheet

332   A288   Sheet of 2, #a-b   7.50   7.50

No. 332 contains two 51x51 diamond-shaped stamps.

Queen Elizabeth II Type of Tonga of 2015
Miniature Sheet

No. 333 — Queen Elizabeth II in Tonga: a, With Queen Salote Tupou III and her grand-daughter Mele Siuilikutapu. b, Arriving at Wesleyan Church, Nukulofa. c, On path with Queen Salote Tupou III. d, With Queen Salote Tupou III, wearing flower garland.

2015, Nov. 23   Litho.   Perf. 14

333   A289   2pa Sheet of 4, #a-d   7.00   7.00

Christmas Type of Tonga of 2015
Miniature Sheet

No. 334 — Religious paintings with inscription: a, Altar. b, Ghirlandaio. c, Hey. d, Diamante.

2015, Dec. 9   Litho.   Perf. 13¾

334   A290   1.50pa Sheet of 4, #a-d   5.25   5.25

Second Summit of the Forum for India-Pacific Islands Cooperation Type of Tonga of 2016

Mohandas K. Gandhi, Garcinia sessilis, lotus flower and: 2.25pa, Indian elephants. 4.20pa, Indian rhinoceroses. 5pa, Asiatic lions. 6.50pa, Indian peafowl.

2016, Jan. 14   Litho.   Perf. 13¼

335-338 A291   Set of 4   15.50   15.50
338a   Souvenir sheet of 4, #335-338   15.50   15.50

World Wildlife Fund (WWF) A77

Various depictions of black petrel: 50s, 2pa, 2.25pa. 3.50pa.

2016, Feb. 26   Litho.   Perf. 14¾x14
Stamps With White Frames

339-342 A77   Set of 4   7.25   7.25

Stamps Without White Frames

343   Strip of 4   7.25   7.25
   a.   A77 50s multi   .45   .45
   b.   A77 2pa multi   1.75   1.75
   c.   A77 2.25pa multi   2.00   2.00
   d.   A77 3.50pa multi   3.00   3.00

Landing of Dutch Explorers in Tonga, 400th Anniv. — A78

No. 344: a, 2pa, Jacob Le Maire. b, 2.25pa, Ship Eendracht off Tafahi Island. c, 2.50pa, Birds, Tongan natives in boats. d, 2.70pa, Willem Schouten.

2016, Apr. 25   Litho.   Perf. 14

344   A78   Sheet of 4, #a-d   8.50   8.50

Queen Elizabeth II, 90th Birthday Type of Tonga of 2016
Souvenir Sheet

No. 345 — Queen Elizabeth II: a, Waving. b, Wearing strapless gown and tiara.

2016, May 3   Litho.   Perf. 13

345   A296   2pa Sheet of 2, #a-b   3.50   3.50

Tupou College Type of Tonga of 2016
Souvenir Sheet

No. 346: a, 2.25pa, Building and trees. b, 5pa, Building and students.

2016, June 10   Litho.   Perf. 13

346   A297   Sheet of 2, #a-b   6.75   6.75

Marine Life and Birds Type of Tonga of 2016

Designs: 90s, Masked booby. 1pa, Gray reef shark. 1.10pa, Hard coral. 1.20pa, Bottle-nose dolphins. 2pa, Humpback whale. 2.25pa, Atlantic spotted dolphin. 2.70pa, Red-tailed tropicbird. 4.20pa, Whale shark. 5pa, Tiger shark. 6.70pa, Fairy tern. 9.20pa, Killer whales. 11.70pa, Black noddies.

2016, Mar. 2   Litho.   Perf. 14x14¾

347   A299   90s multi   .80   .80
348   A299   1pa multi   .90   .90
349   A299   1.10pa multi   1.00   1.00
350   A299   1.20pa multi   1.10   1.10
351   A299   2pa multi   1.75   1.75
352   A299   2.25pa multi   2.00   2.00
353   A299   2.70pa multi   2.40   2.40
354   A299   4.20pa multi   3.75   3.75
355   A299   5pa multi   4.50   4.50
356   A299   6.70pa multi   6.00   6.00
357   A299   8.25pa multi   8.25   8.25
358   A299   11.70pa multi   10.50   10.50
   Nos. 347-358 (12)   42.95   42.95

Year of the Rooster Type of Tonga of 2016

Designs: 5pa, Rooster. 5.50pa, Rooster and chicks.

2016, Aug. 10   Litho.   Perf. 13½

359-360 A300   Set of 2   9.75   9.75
360a   Souvenir sheet of 2, #359-360   9.75   9.75

Christmas Type of Tonga of 2016

No. 361, vert.: a, 2pa, Church and railing. b, 2pa, Blue church with white steeple. c, 2.70pa, Church. d, 2.70pa, Church doors.

2016, Dec. 19   Litho.   Perf. 13¼

361   A302   Block of 4, #a-d   8.25   8.25

Easter Type of Tonga of 2017
Miniature Sheet

No. 362 — Paintings depicting the resurrection of Christ by: a, Pietro Perugino. b, Carl Bloch (incorrectly identified as Mantegna). c, Titian. d, Sandro Botticelli.

2017, Apr. 10   Litho.   Perf. 12¾

362   A3032pa Sheet of 4, #a-d   7.00   7.00

Reign of Queen Elizabeth II Type of Tonga of 2017
Miniature Sheet

No. 363 — Queen Elizabeth II wearing: a, Turquoise green jacket and hat. b, White jacket and hat. c, Magenta jacket and hat. d, White and Turquoise blue jacket and hat.

2017, June 7   Litho.   Perf. 12¾

363   A304   3pa Sheet of 4, #a-d   11.00   11.00

Kennedy Type of Tonga of 2017
Miniature Sheet

No. 364: a, 2.50pa, Pres. Kennedy signing Peace Corps Act. b, 2.50pa, Women's Strike for Peace in Cuban Missile Crisis. c, 2.75pa, Pres. Kennedy at desk in White House. d, 2.75pa, Sargent Shriver speaking to Peace Corps volunteers at White House.

2017, June 21   Litho.   Perf. 12¾

364   A305   Sheet of 4, #a-d   9.75   9.75

Halley's Comet Type of Tonga of 2017

No. 365, vert.: a, Director of probe to Halley's Comet wearing Halley's Comet shirt. b, Man holding comet dust collector. c, Material streaming from Halley's Comet. d, Man holding good luck charm from Halley's Comet space mission.
6pa, Spacecraft.

2017, July 12   Litho.   Perf. 13x13¼

365   A307   2.25pa Block of 4, #a-d   8.50   8.50

Souvenir Sheet
Perf. 13¼x13

366   A307   6pa multi   5.75   5.75

Year of the Dog Type of 2017

Designs; 6.50pa, Dog facing right. 6.70pa, Dog facing left.

2017, Nov. 1   Litho.   Perf. 13¼

367-368 A312   Set of 2   12.00   12.00
368a   Souvenir sheet of 2, #367-368   12.00   12.00

Christmas Type of 2017

No. 369: a, Sailboat. b, Parrot. c, Hibiscus flowers. d, Starfish.

2017, Dec. 4   Litho.   Perf. 12½

369   A313   2.25pa Block of 4, #a-d   8.25   8.25

Easter Type of Tonga of 2018
Miniature Sheet

No. 370: a, Jesus. b, Easter eggs, shell and butterflies. c, Church and palmtree. d, Cross and flowers.

2018, Mar. 15   Litho.   Perf. 12¾

370   A314   2.25pa Sheet of 4, #a-d   8.25   8.25

Birdpex Type of Tonga of 2018

No. 371: a, New Zealand dotterel. b, Red-capped plover. c, Antipodes parakeet. d, Shore plover.

2018, May 3   Litho.   Perf. 13¼

371   A315   2.25pa Block of 4, #a-d   8.00   8.00

Wedding of Prince Harry and Meghan Markle Type of Tonga of 2018

No. 372: a, Couple walking down aisle in chapel. b, Couple seated in coach.
9.20pa, Couple and automobile.

2018, July 27   Litho.   Perf. 13

372   A317   5pa Sheet of 2, #a-b   8.75   8.75

Souvenir Sheet

373   A317   9.20pa multi   8.25   8.25

Souvenir Sheets

Shells — A79

No. 374, 5pa: a, Giant spider conch. b, Textile cone shell.
No. 375, 5pa: a, Venus comb murex shell. b, Emperor nautilus shell.

2018, Sept. 7   Litho.   Perf. 13
Sheets of 2, #a-b

374-375 A79   Set of 2   18.00   18.00

Animals of the World Type of Tonga of 2018-19

No. 376, 2.80pa: a, Cobalt blue tarantula. b, Veiled chameleon.
No. 377, 4.30pa: a, Sugar glider. b, Rowley's palm pit viper.
10pa, Jandaya conure.

2018-19   Litho.   Perf. 13
Horiz. Pairs, #a-b

376-377 A318   Set of 2   13.00   13.00

Souvenir Sheet

378   A318   10pa multi   9.00   9.00

Issued: Nos. 376-377, 2/8/19; No. 378, 9/10.

Year of the Pig Type of Tonga of 2018

Designs: 6.50pa, Pig facing right. 6.70pa, Pig facing forward.

2018, Dec. 10   Litho.   Perf. 13¼

379-380 A319   Set of 2   11.50   11.50

Birds of Prey Type of Tonga of 2018

Designs: 5s, Black-and-white owl and Band-bellied owl hybrid. 10s, Powerful owl. 1.40pa, Martial eagle. 2.30pa, Great gray owl. 2.50pa, Crested goshawk. 2.80pa, Jungle owlet. 4.30pa, Short-toed snake eagle. 5.20pa, Minahasa masked owl. 6.90pa, Gray-headed fish eagle. 9.30pa, White-eyed buzzard. 9.50pa, Western marsh harrier. 11.50pa, African hawk eagle.

2018, Dec. 18   Litho.   Perf. 13
Stamps With White Frames

381   A322   5s multi   .25   .25
382   A322   10s multi   .25   .25
383   A322   1.40pa multi   1.25   1.25
384   A322   2.30pa multi   2.00   2.00
385   A322   2.50pa multi   2.25   2.25
386   A322   2.80pa multi   2.50   2.50
   a.   Souvenir sheet of 6, #381-386   8.50   8.50
387   A322   4.30pa multi   3.75   3.75
388   A322   5.20pa multi   4.75   4.75
389   A322   6.90pa multi   6.00   6.00
390   A322   9.30pa multi   8.25   8.25
391   A322   9.50pa multi   8.50   8.50
392   A322   11.50pa multi   10.00   10.00
   a.   Souvenir sheet of 6, #387-392   41.50   41.50
   Nos. 381-392 (12)   49.75   49.75

Miniature Sheet
Stamps Without White Frame

393   Sheet of 12   50.00   50.00
   a.   A322 5s multi   .25   .25
   b.   A322 10s multi   .25   .25
   c.   A322 1.40pa multi   1.25   1.25
   d.   A322 2.30pa multi   2.00   2.00
   e.   A322 2.50pa multi   2.25   2.25
   f.   A322 2.80pa multi   2.50   2.50
   g.   A322 4.30pa multi   3.75   3.75
   h.   A322 5.20pa multi   4.75   4.75
   i.   A322 6.90pa multi   6.00   6.00
   j.   A322 9.30pa multi   8.25   8.25
   k.   A322 9.50pa multi   8.50   8.50
   l.   A322 11.50pa multi   10.00   10.00

Stamps on Nos. 386a and 392a have white frames on one or two sides.

AIR POST SPECIAL DELIVERY STAMPS

APSD1

APSD2

APSD3

Barn Owl — APSD4

2012, Aug. 30   Litho.   Perf. 14¼
Stamps With White Frame All Around

CE1	APSD1	25pa multi	21.00	21.00
CE2	APSD2	25pa multi	21.00	21.00
CE3	APSD3	25pa multi	21.00	21.00
CE4	APSD4	25pa multi	21.00	21.00
	Nos. CE1-CE4 (4)		84.00	84.00

Stamps With White Frame on Two Sides

CE5		Sheet of 4	84.00	84.00
a.	APSD1	25pa multi	21.00	21.00
b.	APSD2	25pa multi	21.00	21.00
c.	APSD3	25pa multi	21.00	21.00
d.	APSD4	25pa multi	21.00	21.00

A sheet of 16 ontaining four of each of types APSD1-APSD4 without white frames on the stamps was produced in a limited printing.

Butterflies — APSD5

Designs: 15pa, Common crow butterfly. 50pa, Peablue butterfly. 53pa, Monarch butterfly. 71pa, Meadow argus butterfly. 83pa, Chinese yellow swallowtail butterfly. 89pa, Clipper butterfly.

2015-16   Litho.   Perf. 14¼
Stamps With White Frames

CE6	APSD5	15pa multi	14.00	14.00
CE7	APSD5	50pa multi	47.00	47.00
CE8	APSD5	53pa multi	49.00	49.00
CE9	APSD5	71pa multi	65.00	65.00
a.	Souvenir sheet of 4, #CE6-CE9		175.00	175.00
CE10	APSD5	83pa multi	72.50	72.50
CE11	APSD5	89pa multi	77.50	77.50
a.	Souvenir sheet of 2, #CE10-CE11		150.00	150.00
	Nos. CE6-CE11 (6)		325.00	325.00

Souvenir Sheets
Stamps Without White Frame

CE12	APSD5	15pa multi	14.00	14.00
CE13	APSD5	50pa multi	47.00	47.00
CE14	APSD5	53pa multi	49.00	49.00
CE15	APSD5	71pa multi	65.00	65.00
CE16	APSD5	83pa multi	72.50	72.50
CE17	APSD5	89pa multi	77.50	77.50
	Nos. CE12-CE17 (6)		325.00	325.00

Issued: 15pa, 50pa, 9/1; 53pa, 71pa, No. CE9a, 11/2; 83pa, 89pa, No. CE11a, 1/4/16. Stamps on No. CE9a have white frames on 2 sides. Stamps on No. CE11a have white frames on 3 sides.

TRANSCAUCASIAN FEDERATED REPUBLIC

ˌtranˌts-ko-ˈkā-zhən ˈfe-də-rāted ri-ˈpə-blik

LOCATION — In southeastern Europe, south of the Caucasus Mountains between the Black and Caspian Seas
GOVT. — Former republic
AREA — 71,255 sq. mi.
POP. — 5,851,000 (approx.)
CAPITAL — Tiflis

The Transcaucasian Federation was made up of the former autonomies of Armenia, Georgia and Azerbaijan. Its stamps were replaced by those of Russia.

100 Kopecks = 1 Ruble

Russian Stamps of 1909-17 Overprinted in Black or Red

1923   Unwmk.   Perf. 14½x15

1	A15	10k dark blue	3.00	5.00
2	A14	10k on 7k lt bl	4.00	5.00
3	A11	25k grn & gray vio	10.00	5.00
4	A11	35k red brn & grn (R)	4.00	5.00
a.		Double overprint	75.00	75.00
5	A8	50k brn red & grn	4.00	5.00
6	A9	1r pale brn, brn & org	12.00	12.00
7	A12	3½r mar & lt grn	50.00	

Imperf

8	A9	1r pale brn, brn & red org	10.00	12.00
	Nos. 1-8 (8)		97.00	
	Nos. 1-6,8 (7)			49.00

No. 7 was prepared but not issued.

Overprinted on Stamps of Armenia Previously Handstamped

a

c

Perf. 14½x15

9	A11(c)	25k grn & gray vio	250.00	250.00
10	A8(c)	50k vio & grn	250.00	150.00

Perf. 13½

11	A0(a)	1r pale brn, brn & org	100.00	50.00
12	A9(c)	1r pale brn, brn & org	150.00	50.00

Imperf

13	A9(c)	1r pale brn, brn & red org	35.00	35.00
	Nos. 9-13 (5)		785.00	535.00

Counterfeit overprints exist.

Oil Fields — A1

Soviet Symbols — A2

1923   Perf. 11½

14	A1	40,000r red violet	3.00	2.25
15	A1	75,000r dark grn	3.00	2.25
16	A1	100,000r blk vio	3.00	2.25
17	A1	150,000r red	3.00	2.25
18	A2	200,000r dull grn	3.00	2.25
19	A2	300,000r blue	3.00	2.25
20	A2	350,000r dark brn	3.00	2.25
21	A2	500,000r rose	3.00	2.25
	Nos. 14-21 (8)		24.00	18.00

Nos. 14-21 exist imperf. but are not known to have been issued in that condition. Values, set $125.

Nos. 14-15 Srchd. in Brown

1923

22	A1	700,000r on 40,000r	2.50	5.00
a.		Imperf., pair	30.00	
23	A1	700,000r on 75,000r	2.50	5.00
a.		Imperf., pair	30.00	

Types of Preceding Issue with Values in Gold Kopecks
1923, Oct. 24

25	A2	1k orange	2.25	1.90
26	A2	2k blue green	2.25	1.90
27	A2	3k rose	2.25	1.90
28	A2	4k gray brown	2.25	1.90
29	A1	5k dark violet	2.25	1.90
30	A1	9k deep blue	2.25	1.90
31	A1	18k slate	2.25	1.90
	Nos. 25-31 (7)		15.75	13.30

Nos. 25-31 exist imperf. but are not known to have been issued in that condition. Values, set $100.

TRANSVAAL

tranˌts-ˈväl

(South African Republic)

LOCATION — Southern Africa
GOVT. — A former British Colony
AREA — 110,450 sq. mi.
POP. — 1,261,736 (1904)
CAPITAL — Pretoria

Transvaal was known as the South African Republic until 1877 when it was occupied by the British. The republic was restored in 1884 and continued until 1900 when it was annexed to Great Britain and named "The Transvaal."

12 Pence = 1 Shilling
20 Shillings = 1 Pound

Most unused stamps between Nos. 1-96, 110-122 and 100-107 were issued with gum, but do not expect gum on scarcer stamps as few examples retain their original gum. In many cases removal of the remaining gum may enhance the preservation of the stamps. Otherwise, values for unused stamps are for examples with original gum as defined in the catalogue introduction.

Very fine imperforate stamps will have adequate to large margins. However, roulleted stamps are valued as partly roulleted, with straight edges, and roulleted just into the design, as the roulleting methods were quite inaccurate.

First Republic

Coat of Arms — A1

A1 has spread wings on eagle.

Mecklenburg Printings
By Adolph Otto, Gustrow
Fine Impressions
Thin Paper

1869   Unwmk.   Imperf.

1	A1	1p brown lake	575.00	
a.		1p red	725.00	725.00
2	A1	6p ultra	325.00	325.00
3	A1	1sh dark green	875.00	875.00
a.		Tete beche pair		

Rouletted 15½, 16

4	A1	1p red	185.00	
5	A1	6p ultra	165.00	160.00
6	A1	1sh blue green	210.00	200.00
a.		1sh yellow green	285.00	250.00
b.		1sh deep green	350.00	375.00

Nos. 1-6 were printed from 2 sets of plates, differing in the spacing between the stamps. The only known example of No. 3a is in a museum.
See Nos. 9-24, 26-33, 35-36, 38-39, 41-42, 43-49, 119, 122. For overprints see Nos. 53-61, 63-66, 68-72, 75-78, 81-83, 86-87, 90-91, 94.

Coat of Arms — A2

1871-74

7	A2	3p lilac	92.50	100.00
a.		3p violet	110.00	125.00
8	A2	6p brt ultra ('74)	87.50	32.50
a.		Half used as 3p on cover		1,850.

Many forgeries exist in colors duller or lighter than the genuine stamps.

In forgeries of type A1, all values, the "D" of "EENDRAGT" is not noticeably larger than the other letters and does not touch the top of the ribbon. In type A1 genuine stamps, the "D" is large and touches the ribbon top. The eagle's eye is a dot and its face white on the genuine stamps; the eye is a loop or blob attached to the beak, and the beak is strongly hooked, on the forgeries. Many forgeries of the 1sh have the top line of the ribbon broken above "EENDRAGT."

Forgeries of type A2 usually can be detected only by color.

A sharply struck cancellation of a numeral in three rings is found on many of these forgeries. The similar genuine cancellation is always roughly or heavily struck.

See Nos. 25, 34, 437, 40, 42B, 120-121. For overprints see Nos. 50-52, 62, 67, 73-74, 79-80, 84-85, 88-89, 92-93, 95-96.

Local Printings
(A) By M. J. Viljoen, Pretoria
Poor Impressions,
Overinked and Spotted

1870   Thin Soft Paper   Imperf.

9	A1	1p pink	125.00	
a.		1p rose red	135.00	
b.		1p carmine	110.00	125.00
10	A1	6p dull ultra	425.00	100.00
a.		Tete beche pair		

The only known examples of No. 10a are in museums.

Rouletted 15½, 16

11	A1	1p carmine	875.00	375.00
a.		Rouletted 6½		1,100.
12	A1	6p dull ultra	325.00	135.00

Hard Paper, Thick to Medium
Imperf

13	A1	1p carmine	115.00	125.00
14	A1	6p ultra	—	
15	A1	1sh gray green	210.00	175.00
a.		1sh dark green	—	
b.		Tete beche pair	29,000.	
c.		Half used as 6p on cover		2,800.

The existence of No. 14 is questionable.

Rouletted 15½, 16

16	A1	1p light carmine	125.00	130.00
a.		1p carmine	87.50	92.50
17	A1	6p ultra	145.00	125.00
a.		Tete beche pair	35,000.	25,000.
18	A1	1sh dark green	260.00	125.00
a.		1sh gray green	850.00	850.00

Examples of Nos. 16-18 are sometimes so heavily inked as to be little more than blots of color.

(B) By J. P. Borrius, Potchefstroom
Clearer Impressions Though Often Overinked

1870   Thick Porous Paper   Imperf.

19	A1	1p black	200.00	175.00
20	A1	6p indigo	—	

Rouletted 15½, 16

21	A1	1p black	32.50	42.50
22	A1	6p gray blue	210.00	87.50
a.		6p indigo	145.00	115.00
b.		6p bright ultra	—	

Thin Transparent Paper

23	A1	1p black	325.00	750.00
24	A1	1p brt carmine	260.00	87.50
a.		1p deep carmine	110.00	67.50
25	A2	3p gray lilac	160.00	72.50
26	A1	6p ultra	110.00	42.50
27	A1	1sh yellow green	135.00	72.50
a.		1sh deep green	135.00	72.50
b.		Half used as 6p on cover	—	2,900.

Thick Soft Paper

28	A1	1p dull rose	525.00	115.00
a.		1p brown rose	675.00	155.00
b.		Printed on both sides	—	
29	A1	6p dull blue	135.00	57.50
a.		6p bright blue	325.00	87.50
b.		6p ultramarine	300.00	87.50
c.		Rouletted 6½	—	
30	A1	1sh yellow green	1,400.	875.00

The paper of Nos. 28 to 30 varies considerably in thickness.

(C) By P. Davis & Son, Natal
Thin to Medium Paper

1874			Perf. 12½	
31	A1	1p red	180.00	60.00
a.		1p brownish red	180.00	60.00
32	A1	6p deep blue	225.00	75.00
a.		6p blue	225.00	75.00
b.		Horiz. pair, imperf. between	—	

(D) By the Stamp Commission, Pretoria
Pelure Paper

1875-76			*Imperf.*	
33	A1	1p pale red	75.00	65.00
a.		1p orange red	75.00	35.00
b.		1p brown red	80.00	42.50
c.		Pin perf.	775.00	475.00
34	A2	3p gray lilac	80.00	55.00
a.		3p dull violet	90.00	55.00
b.		Pin perf.	—	500.00
35	A1	6p blue	80.00	55.00
a.		6p pale blue	80.00	70.00
b.		6p dark blue	85.00	60.00
c.		Tete beche pair, thin opaque paper	21,000.	
d.		Tete beche pair, pelure, transparent paper		
e.		Pin perf.		450.00

The only known examples of No. 35c are in museums.

Rouletted 15½, 16

36	A1	1p orange red	450.00	155.00
a.		Rouletted 6½	1,250.	250.00
37	A2	3p dull violet	500.00	180.00
a.		Rouletted 6½	1,100.	320.00
38	A1	6p blue	250.00	130.00
a.		Rouletted 6½	1,275.	145.00

The paper of this group varies slightly in thickness and is sometimes divided into pelure and semipelure. We believe there was only one lot of the paper and that the separation is not warranted.

Thick Hard Paper
Imperf

39	A1	1p org red ('76)	37.50	30.00
40	A2	3p lilac	475.00	160.00
41	A1	6p deep blue	85.00	27.50
a.		6p blue	140.00	32.50
b.		Tete beche pair	21,500.	

Rouletted 15½, 16

42	A1	1p org red ('76)	550.00	200.00
a.		Rouletted 6½ ('75)	750.00	200.00
42B	A2	3p lilac	500.00	
43	A1	6p deep blue	750.00	350.00
a.		6p blue	950.00	135.00
b.		Rouletted 6½ ('75)	800.00	350.00

Soft Porous Paper
Imperf

44	A1	1p orange red	250.00	75.00
45	A1	6p deep blue	300.00	650.00
a.		6p dull blue	450.00	140.00
46	A1	1sh yellow green	600.00	175.00
a.		Half used as 6p on cover		2,200.

Rouletted 15½, 16

47	A1	1p orange red	—	500.00
a.		Rouletted 6½		550.00
48	A1	6p deep blue	—	250.00
a.		Rouletted 6½		1,275.
49	A1	1sh yellow grn	1,000.	450.00
a.		Rouletted 6½		1,400.
b.		Rouletted 15½-16x16½	1,000.	450.00

First British Occupation

Stamps and Types of 1875 Overprinted

Red Overprint
Pelure Paper

1877		Unwmk.	*Imperf.*	
50	A2	3p lilac	1,675.	275.00
a.		Overprinted on back	4,000.	3,750.
b.		Double ovpt., red and black	7,500.	

Rouletted 15½, 16

51	A2	3p lilac	—	1,850.
a.		Rouletted 6½		2,750.

Thin Hard Paper
Imperf

52	A2	3p lilac	1,650.	400.00

Soft Porous Paper

53	A1	6p blue	2,250.	275.00
a.		6p deep blue		350.00
b.		Inverted overprint		6,000.
c.		Double overprint	5,250.	1,250.
54	A1	1sh yellow grn	900.00	300.00
a.		Inverted overprint		5,250.
b.		Half used as 6p on cover		3,000.

Rouletted 15½, 16

55	A1	6p blue		2,000.
a.		Rouletted 6½		2,750.
56	A1	1sh yellow grn	20,000.	900.00
a.		Rouletted 6½	4,750.	2,750.
b.		As "a.", overprint inverted		7,500.

Black Overprint
Pelure Paper
Imperf

57	A1	1p red	400.00	200.00

Rouletted 15½, 16

58	A1	1p red	—	1,350.

Thick Hard Paper
Imperf

59	A1	1p red	40.00	27.50
a.		Inverted overprint	650.00	575.00

Rouletted 15½, 16

60	A1	1p red	250.00	57.50
a.		Rouletted 6½	800.00	350.00
b.		Inverted overprint		
c.		Double overprint		1,275.

Soft Porous Paper
Imperf

61	A1	1p red	40.00	40.00
a.		Double overprint		1,400.
62	A2	3p lilac	140.00	52.50
a.		3p deep lilac	250.00	125.00
b.		Inverted overprint		
63	A1	6p dull blue	200.00	100.00
a.		6p bright blue	—	575.00
c.		6p dark blue	275.00	250.00
d.		Inverted overprint	1,650.	225.00
e.		Double overprint	4,000.	2,400.
64	A1	6p blue, *rose*	150.00	75.00
a.		Tete beche pair	—	
b.		Inverted overprint	160.00	75.00
c.		Overprint omitted	4,000.	2,900.
d.		Half used as 3p on cover		
65	A1	1sh yellow grn	225.00	85.00
a.		Tete beche pair	27,500.	27,500.
b.		Inverted overprint	1,550.	500.00
c.		Half used as 6p on cover		2,100.

The only known examples of No. 64a are in museums.

Rouletted 15½, 16

66	A1	1p red	125.00	125.00
a.		Rouletted 6½	850.00	200.00
67	A2	3p lilac	340.00	95.00
a.		Rouletted 6½		950.00
68	A1	6p dull blue	400.00	85.00
a.		Inverted overprint	—	875.00
b.		Rouletted 6½	—	1,550.
c.		As "a," rouletted 6½		5,000.
69	A1	6p blue, *rose*	400.00	87.50
a.		Inverted overprint	750.00	87.50
b.		Rouletted 6½		
c.		Tete beche pair		
d.		Overprint omitted		
e.		As "a," rouletted 6½		850.00
f.		As "d," rouletted 6½		
70	A1	1sh yellow grn	400.00	135.00
a.		Inverted overprint	1,600.	625.00
b.		Rouletted 6½	725.00	190.00
c.		As "a," rouletted 6½	2,350.	775.00

In this issue the space between "V. R." and "TRANSVAAL" is normally 8½mm but in position 11 it is 12mm. In this and the following issues there are numerous minor varieties of the overprint, missing periods, etc.

The only known examples of No. 69c are in museums.

Types A1 and A2 Overprinted

1877-79			*Imperf.*	
71	A1	1p red, *blue*	85.00	42.50
a.		"Transvral"	6,500.	2,900.
b.		Inverted overprint	975.00	475.00
c.		Double overprint	4,750.	
d.		Overprint omitted		
72	A1	1p red, *org* ('78)	37.50	30.00
a.		Printed on both sides	—	
b.		Pin perf.	—	
73	A2	3p lilac, *buff*	85.00	50.00
a.		Inverted overprint		875.00
b.		Pin perf.	—	
74	A2	3p lilac, *grn* ('79)	300.00	70.00
a.		Inverted overprint		2,450.
b.		Double overprint	—	
c.		Pin perf.	—	
75	A1	6p blue, *grn*	160.00	50.00
a.		Tete beche pair	22,500.	
b.		Inverted overprint		1,375.
c.		Half used as 3p on cover	—	
d.		Pin perf.	—	
76	A1	6p blue, *bl* ('78)	115.00	40.00
a.		Tete beche pair	—	
b.		Overprint omitted		2,750.
c.		Inverted overprint		1,450.
d.		Half used as 3p on cover		1,150.
e.		Double overprint		3,750.
f.		Pin perf.	—	
		Nos. 71-76 (6)	782.50	282.50

The only known examples of No. 76a are in museums.

Rouletted 15½, 16

77	A1	1p red, *blue*	150.00	50.00
a.		"Transvral"		3,500.
b.		Inverted overprint	—	
c.		Double overprint		
78	A1	1p red, *org* ('78)	55.00	40.00
a.		Horiz. pair, imperf. vert.		
b.		Rouletted 6½	375.00	135.00

79	A2	3p lilac, *buff*	155.00	40.00
a.		Inverted overprint		3,500.
b.		Vert. pair, imperf. horiz.	875.00	
c.		Rouletted 6½		135.00
80	A2	3p lilac, *grn* ('79)	900.00	240.00
a.		Inverted overprint		
b.		Rouletted 6½	900.00	375.00
81	A1	6p blue, *green*	135.00	40.00
a.		Inverted overprint		800.00
b.		Overprint omitted		4,750.
c.		Tete beche pair	—	
d.		Half used at 3p on cover	—	950.00
e.		Rouletted 6½		1,450.
82	A1	6p blue, *bl* ('78)	400.00	75.00
a.		Inverted overprint		1,100.
b.		Overprint omitted		4,000.
c.		Tete beche pair	—	
d.		Horiz. pair, imperf. vert.	—	
e.		Half used as 3p on cover		1,050.
f.		Double overprint	—	
g.		Rouletted 6½		400.00
h.		As "a," rouletted 6½	—	
		Nos. 77-82 (6)	1,795.	485.00

The only known examples of No. 81c are in museums. The existence of No. 82c is questioned.

Types A1 and A2 Overprinted
Imperf

83	A1	1p red, *org* ('78)	95.00	52.50
84	A2	3p lilac, *buff* ('78)	110.00	40.00
a.		Pin perf.	875.00	875.00
85	A2	3p lilac, *grn* ('79)	240.00	40.00
a.		Inverted overprint		2,300.
b.		Overprint omitted	—	
c.		Printed on both sides		1,150.
86	A1	6p blue, *bl* ('78)	240.00	50.00
a.		Tete beche pair	19,500.	
b.		Inverted overprint		800.00
		Nos. 83-86 (4)	685.00	182.50

Rouletted 15½, 16

87	A1	1p red, *org* ('78)	240.00	160.00
a.		Rouletted 6½	—	375.00
88	A2	3p lilac, *buff* ('78)	300.00	150.00
a.		Vert. pair, imperf. horiz.	—	
b.		Rouletted 6½		450.00
89	A2	3p lilac, *grn* ('79)	875.00	240.00
a.		Inverted overprint	—	
b.		Overprint omitted	—	
c.		Rouletted 6½ ('97)	900.00	375.00
90	A1	6p blue, *bl* ('78)	650.00	150.00
a.		Tete beche pair	—	
b.		Inverted overprint	—	1,450.
c.		Rouletted 6½		450.00
d.		As "b," rouletted 6½		

Types A1 and A2 Overprinted

1879			*Imperf.*	
91	A1	1p red, *orange*	75.00	50.00
a.		1p red, *yellow*	75.00	55.00
b.		Small capital "T"	375.00	200.00
92	A2	3p lilac, *green*	65.00	40.00
a.		Small capital "T"	325.00	135.00
93	A2	3p lilac, *blue*	75.00	40.00
a.		Small capital "T"	375.00	135.00
		Nos. 91-93 (3)	215.00	130.00

Rouletted 15½, 16

94	A1	1p red, *yellow*	450.00	300.00
a.		1p red, *orange*	1,000.	450.00
b.		Small capital "T"	1,350.	825.00
c.		Rouletted 6½	900.00	775.00
d.		Pin perf.	—	875.00
95	A2	3p lilac, *green*	925.00	350.00
a.		Small capital "T"		1,050.
b.		Rouletted 6½	1,325.	750.00
96	A2	3p lilac, *blue*	—	275.00
a.		Small capital "T"		850.00
b.		Rouletted 6½		950.00
c.		Pin perf.		1,500.

Queen Victoria — A3

1878-80		Engr.	*Perf. 14, 14½*	
97	A3	½p vermilion ('80)	30.00	100.00
98	A3	1p red brown	22.50	7.00
99	A3	3p claret	42.50	12.00
100	A3	4p olive green	45.00	12.25
101	A3	6p slate	20.00	10.00
a.		Half used as 3p on cover	—	
102	A3	1sh green	180.00	57.50
103	A3	2sh blue	325.00	105.00
		Nos. 97-103 (7)	665.00	303.75

For surcharges see Nos. 104-118, 138-139.

No. 101 Surcharged in Red or Black

(a) Surcharged

Surcharge distinction: "PENNY" in gothic capitals.

1879				
104	A3	1p on 6p slate (R)	200.00	95.00
105	A3	1p on 6p slate (Bk)	67.50	27.50

(b) Surcharged

Surcharge distinction: "1" has heavy serif at base; "P," thin serif at base.

106	A3	1p on 6p slate (R)	800.00	400.00
107	A3	1p on 6p slate (Bk)	310.00	95.00

(c) Surcharged

Surcharge distinction: No serif at base of "1."

108	A3	1p on 6p slate (R)	825.00	425.00
109	A3	1p on 6p slate (Bk)	325.00	95.00

(d) Surcharged

Surcharge distinction: Heavy serifs at base of "1" and "p."

110	A3	1p on 6p slate (R)	425.00	210.00
111	A3	1p on 6p slate (Bk)	140.00	65.00
a.		Pair, one without surcharge	—	

(e) Surcharged

Surcharge distinction: Italics.

112	A3	1p on 6p slate (R)	775.00	375.00
113	A3	1p on 6p slate (Bk)	290.00	87.50

(f) Surcharged

Surcharge distinction: "1" has long, sloping serif at top, thin serif at base.

114	A3	1p on 6p slate (R)	375.00	185.00
115	A3	1p on 6p slate (Bk)	120.00	50.00

(g) Surcharged

1 Penny

Surcharge distinction: Tail of "y" missing.

116	A3	1p on 6p slate (R)	7,000.	1,850.
117	A3	1p on 6p slate (Bk)	775.00	190.00

Second Republic

No. 100 Surcharged

1882   **Unwmk.**   **Perf. 14, 14½**
118	A3	1p on 4p olive grn	25.00	9.00
a.		Inverted surcharge	375.00	250.00

1883   **Perf. 12**
119	A1	1p black	9.50	3.50
a.		Imperf.		
b.		Vert. pair, imperf. horiz.	675.00	500.00
c.		Horiz. pair, imperf. vert.	375.00	
120	A2	3p red	19.00	4.00
a.		Horiz. pair, imperf. vert.	—	1,000.
b.		Half used as 1p on cover		825.00
121	A2	3p red	40.00	9.00
a.		Half used as 1p on cover		825.00
122	A1	1sh green	90.00	9.00
a.		Tete beche pair	1,325.	185.00
b.		Half used as 6p on cover		625.00
		Nos. 119-122 (4)	158.50	25.50

The so-called reprints of this issue are forgeries. They were made from the counterfeit plates described in the note following No. 8, plus a new false plate for the 3p. The false 3p plate has many small flaws and defects.

Forgeries of No. 120 are in dull orange red, clearly printed on whitish paper, and those of No. 121 in brownish or grayish black on bright rose. Genuine examples of No. 120 lack the orange tint and the paper is yellowish; genuine examples of No. 121 are in black without gray or brown shade, on dull lilac rose paper.

A 6p in slate on white, apparently of this issue, is a late print from the counterfeit plate.

A4

Perf. 13½, 11½x12, 12½, 12½x12
1885-93   **Typo.**
123	A4	½p gray	2.50	.25
a.		Imperf. at top and bottom (used strip of 4)		
124	A4	1p rose	10.00	2.00
125	A4	2p brown	3.50	5.00
126	A4	2p olive bis ('87)	3.50	.25
127	A4	2½p purple ('93)	4.50	.65
128	A4	3p violet	5.00	3.25
129	A4	4p bronze green	7.00	2.25
130	A4	6p blue	5.00	4.50
a.		Imperf.		—
131	A4	1sh green	4.75	2.50
132	A4	2sh6p yellow	17.50	4.50
133	A4	5sh steel blue	10.00	7.50
134	A4	10sh pale brown	45.00	17.50
135	A4	£5 dk grn ('92)	4,000.	225.00
		Nos. 123-134 (12)	110.25	50.15

Reprints of Nos. 123-137, 140-163, 166-174 closely resemble the originals. Paper is whiter; perf. 12½, large holes.

Excellent counterfeits of No. 135 exist.

For overprint and surcharges see Nos. 140-147, 163, 213.

Nos. 120, 122 Surcharged

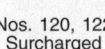

1885   **Perf. 12**
136	A2	½p on 3p red	10.00	15.00
a.		Surcharge reading down	11.00	16.00
137	A1	½p on 1sh green	42.50	70.00
a.		Surcharge reading down	45.00	72.50
b.		Tete beche pair	1,000.	450.00

Almost all examples of No. 137b have telegraph cancellations. Postally used examples are rare.

Nos. 101, 128 Surcharged in Red or Black

Perf. 14
138	A3	½p on 6p slate	85.00	125.00
139	A3	2p on 6p slate	17.50	21.00
a.		Horiz. pair, imperf. vert.		

Perf. 11½x12, 12½x12
140	A4	½p on 3p vio (Bk)	10.00	9.50
a.		"PRNNY"	65.00	85.00
b.		2nd "N" of "PENNY" invtd.	115.00	130.00

No. 128 Surcharged

No. 141   No. 142

1887
141	A4	2p on 3p violet	3.25	6.00
a.		Double surcharge	230.00	225.00
142	A4	2p on 3p violet	15.00	13.25
a.		Double surcharge	—	425.00

Nos. 126, 130, 131 Surcharged

Nos. 143-144   Nos. 145-146

No. 147

1893   **Red Surcharge**
143	A4	½p on 2p olive bis	1.75	3.00
a.		Inverted surcharge	3.75	4.00
b.		Bars 14mm apart	2.50	4.25
c.		As "b," inverted	7.00	13.50

Black Surcharge
144	A4	½p on 2p olive bis	2.00	3.75
a.		Inverted surcharge	5.25	6.00
b.		Bars 14mm apart	2.75	4.50
c.		As "b," inverted	23.00	20.00
145	A4	1p on 6p blue	3.00	2.50
a.		Inverted surcharge	3.25	3.75
b.		Double surcharge	65.00	52.50
c.		Pair, one without surcharge	325.00	
d.		Bars 14mm apart	3.50	3.50
e.		As "d," inverted	7.25	5.75
f.		As "d," double		95.00
146	A4	2½p on 1sh green	3.00	8.00
a.		Inverted surcharge	8.75	9.00
b.		Fraction line misplaced "2/12"	50.00	92.50
c.		As "b," inverted	400.00	350.00
d.		Bars 14mm apart	4.00	10.00
e.		As "d," inverted	11.00	21.00
147	A4	2½p on 1sh green	12.50	10.00
a.		Inverted surcharge	12.50	12.50
b.		Bars 14mm apart	15.00	15.00
c.		As "b," inverted	25.00	25.00
d.		Double surcharge	92.50	105.00
		Nos. 143-147 (5)	22.25	27.25

A13

Wagon with Two Shafts

1894   **Typo.**   **Perf. 12½**
148	A13	½p gray	2.50	1.50
149	A13	1p rose	4.00	.25
150	A13	2p olive bister	4.00	.30
151	A13	6p blue	5.00	1.00
152	A13	1sh yellow grn	22.50	30.00
		Nos. 148-152 (5)	38.00	33.05

Counterfeits of Nos. 148-152 are plentiful.
See note following No. 135 for reprints.

1895-96   **Wagon with Pole**
153	A13	½p gray	2.25	.25
154	A13	1p rose	2.50	.25
155	A13	2p olive bister	2.75	.35
156	A13	3p violet	4.00	1.25
157	A13	4p slate	4.00	1.00
158	A13	6p blue	4.00	1.00
159	A13	1sh green	5.00	1.75
160	A13	5sh slate blue ('96)	25.00	42.50
161	A13	10sh red brown ('96)	25.00	10.00
		Nos. 153-161 (9)	74.50	58.35

Most of the unused examples of Nos. 153-161 now on the market are reprints.

See Nos. 166-174. For surcharge see No. 162.
See note following No. 135 for reprints.

Nos. 159, 127 Surcharged in Red or Green

1895
162	A13	½p on 1sh green (R)	2.50	.25
a.		Inverted surcharge	5.50	5.25
b.		"Pennij" instead of "Penny"	70.00	80.00
c.		Double surcharge	75.00	105.00
163	A4	1p on 2½p pur (G)	.60	.30
a.		Inverted surcharge	25.00	20.00
b.		Surcharge sideways	—	
c.		Surcharge on back	100.00	
d.		Space between "1" and "d"	2.00	1.75

A16

1895   **Perf. 11½**
164	A16	6p rose (G)	3.50	3.00
a.		Vertical pair, imperf. between		

Counterfeits of No. 164 are on the 6p dark red revenue stamp of 1898, and have a shiny green overprint ink for the overprint. The false overprint is also found on other revenue denominations, though only the 6p rose was converted to postal use.

Coat of Arms, Wheat Field and Railroad Train — A17

1895, Sept. 6   **Litho.**
165	A17	1p red	3.00	3.50
a.		Imperf.		
b.		Vertical pair, imperf. between	240.00	260.00

Penny Postage in Transvaal. Horiz. pair, imperf. between also exists.
For overprint see No. 245.

Arms Type of 1894 With Pole

1896   **Typo.**   **Perf. 12½**
166	A13	½p green	1.75	.25
167	A13	1p rose & grn	2.00	.25
168	A13	2p brown & grn	2.00	.25
169	A13	2½p ultra & grn	3.00	.35
170	A13	3p red vio & grn	3.25	3.00
171	A13	4p olive & grn	3.25	4.00
172	A13	6p violet & grn	3.00	3.00
173	A13	1sh bister & grn	2.60	1.50
174	A13	2sh6p hel & grn	4.00	4.50
		Nos. 166-174 (9)	24.85	17.10

See note following No. 135 for reprints.
For overprints and surcharges see Nos. 202-212, 214-235, 237-244, 246-251, Cape of Good Hope Nos. N5-N8.

Pietersburg Issue

Date large; "P" in Postzegel large — A18   Date small; "P" in Postzegel large — A19

Date small; "P" in Postzegel small — A20

1901   **Typeset**   **Imperf.**
Initials in Red
175	A18	½p black, *green*	37.50	
a.		Initials omitted	125.00	
b.		Initials in black	45.00	
176	A19	½p black, *green*	50.00	
a.		Initials omitted	125.00	
b.		Initials in black	52.50	
177	A20	½p black, *green*	50.00	
a.		Initials omitted	125.00	
b.		Initials in black	52.50	

Initials in Black
178	A18	1p black, *rose*	5.00	
179	A19	1p black, *rose*	6.50	
180	A20	1p black, *rose*	8.00	
181	A18	2p black, *orange*	7.50	
182	A19	2p black, *orange*	20.00	
183	A20	2p black, *orange*	25.00	
184	A18	4p black, *dull blue*	12.50	
185	A19	4p black, *dull blue*	15.00	
186	A20	4p black, *dull blue*	40.00	
187	A18	6p black, *green*	17.00	
188	A19	6p black, *green*	20.00	
189	A20	6p black, *green*	55.00	
190	A18	1sh black, *yellow*	12.50	
191	A19	1sh black, *yellow*	20.00	
192	A20	1sh black, *yellow*	30.00	

Perf. 11½
Initials in Red
193	A18	½p black, *green*	6.50	
194	A19	½p black, *green*	20.00	
195	A20	½p black, *green*	15.00	

Initials in Black
196	A18	1p black, *rose*	3.00	
a.		Horiz. pair, imperf. vert.	65.00	
197	A19	1p black, *rose*	3.50	
a.		Horiz. pair, imperf. vert.	100.00	
198	A20	1p black, *rose*	6.50	
a.		Horiz. pair, imperf. vert.	100.00	
199	A18	2p black, *orange*	7.50	
200	A19	2p black, *orange*	9.50	
201	A20	2p black, *orange*	17.00	

Nos. 193-201 inclusive are always imperforate on one side.

The setting consisted of 12 stamps of type A18, 6 of type A19, and 6 of type A20. Numerous type-setting varieties exist. The perforated stamps are from the first printing and were put into use first. Used stamps are not valued because all seem to show evidence of having been canceled to order.

Second British Occupation Issued under Military Authority

Nos. 166-174, 160-161, 135 Overprinted

1900   **Unwmk.**   **Perf. 12½**
202	A13	½p green	.40	1.50
a.		"V.I.R."	850.00	
203	A13	1p rose & grn	.75	1.50
204	A13	2p brown & grn	4.50	4.00
a.		"V.I.R."	900.00	1,000.
205	A13	2½p ultra & grn	1.25	3.50
206	A13	3p red vio & grn	1.50	3.50
207	A13	4p olive & grn	3.75	4.50
a.		"V.I.R."	900.00	
208	A13	6p violet & grn	4.00	3.00
209	A13	1sh bister & grn	4.00	5.00
210	A13	2sh6p hel & grn	5.00	17.50
211	A13	5sh slate blue	10.00	25.00
212	A13	10sh red brown	13.00	27.50
213	A4	£5 dark green	2,500.	925.00
		Nos. 202-212 (11)	48.15	96.50

Nos. 202-213 have been extensively counterfeited. The overprint on the forgeries is clear and clean, with small periods and letters showing completely. In the genuine, letters are worn and lack many or all serifs; the periods are large and oval.

The genuine overprint exists inverted; double; with period missing after "V," after "R," after "I," etc.

Issued in Lydenburg

Nos. 166-169, 171-173
Overprinted in Black

1900

214	A13	½p green	200.00	200.00
215	A13	1p rose & grn	200.00	190.00
216	A13	2p brown & grn	1,500.	1,000.
217	A13	2½p ultra & grn	2,600.	1,150.
218	A13	4p olive & grn	3,750.	1,150.
219	A13	6p violet & grn	4,000.	1,100.
220	A13	1sh bister & grn	5,500.	3,750.

Beware of counterfeits.

No. 167 Surcharged

221	A13	3p on 1p rose & grn	175.00	150.00

Issued in Rustenburg

Nos. 166-170, 172-174
Handstamped in Violet

1900   Perf. 12½

223	A13	½p green	200.00	150.00
224	A13	1p rose & grn	150.00	110.00
225	A13	2p brown & grn	425.00	190.00
226	A13	2½p ultra & grn	275.00	150.00
227	A13	3p red vio & grn	350.00	200.00
229	A13	6p violet & grn	1,475.	600.00
230	A13	1sh bister & grn	2,200.	1,375.
231	A13	2sh6p hel & grn	9,000.	4,400.
a.		Handstamped in black		8,000.

Issued in Schweizer Reneke
Nos. 166-168 and 172 Handstamped "BESIEGED" in Black

1900   Typo.   Perf. 12½

232	A13	½p green		350.00
233	A13	1p rose & green		350.00
234	A13	2p brown & green		475.00
235	A13	6p violet & green		1,275.
		Nos. 232-235 (4)		2,450.

Same Overprint on Cape of Good Hope No. 59 and Type of 1893
Perf. 14

236	A15	½p green	600.00
236A	A15	1p carmine	600.00

In 1902 five revenue stamps overprinted "V.R.I." are said to have been used postally in Volksrust. There seems to be some doubt that this issue was properly authorized for postal use.

Issued in Wolmaransstad

Nos. 166-173
Handstamped in Blue or Red

1900

237	A13	½p green	375.00	500.00
238	A13	1p rose & grn	250.00	400.00
239	A13	2p brown & grn	2,250.	2,250.
240	A13	2½p ultra & grn (R)		2,250.
241	A13	3p red vio & grn	3,500.	3,750.
242	A13	4p olive & grn	5,000.	5,250.
243	A13	6p violet & grn	6,000.	6,400.
244	A13	1sh bister & grn		12,750.

No. 165
Overprinted in Blue

245	A17	1p red	260.00	475.00

Regular Issues
No. 166-168, 170-171, 174 Surcharged or Overprinted

1901-02

246	A13	½p on 2p brn & grn	.80	2.00
247	A13	½p green	.60	3.00
248	A13	1p rose & grn	.60	.25
a.		Overprint "E" omitted	87.50	
249	A13	3p red vio & grn	2.60	4.75
250	A13	4p olive & grn	2.75	11.00
251	A13	2sh6p hel & grn	10.50	40.00
		Nos. 246-251 (6)	17.85	61.00

Excellent counterfeits of Nos. 246-251 are plentiful. See note after No. 213 for the recognition marks of the counterfeits.

Edward VII — A27

Nos. 260, 262 to 267 and 275 to 280 have "POSTAGE" at each side; the other stamps of type A27 have "REVENUE" at the right.

Wmk. Crown and C A (2)
1902-03   Typo.   Perf. 14

252	A27	½p gray grn & blk	3.00	.25
253	A27	1p rose & blk	1.50	.25
254	A27	2p violet & blk	8.50	1.20
255	A27	2½p ultra & blk	16.00	2.25
256	A27	3p ol grn & blk	18.00	2.00
257	A27	4p choc & blk	18.00	3.25
258	A27	6p brn org & blk	5.00	1.50
259	A27	1sh ol grn & blk	21.00	26.00
260	A27	1sh red brn & blk	19.00	6.00
261	A27	2sh brown & blk	75.00	85.00
262	A27	2sh yel & blk	22.50	25.00
263	A27	2sh6p black & vio	18.50	19.00
264	A27	5sh vio & blk, yel	42.50	50.00
265	A27	10sh vio & blk, red	80.00	50.00
266	A27	£1 violet & grn	375.00	225.00
267	A27	£5 violet & grn	2,250.	950.00
		Nos. 252-266 (15)	723.50	496.70

Issue dates: 3p, 4p, Nos. 260, 262, £1, £5, 1903. Others, Apr. 1, 1902.

1904-09   Wmk. 3

268	A27	½p gray grn & blk	13.00	3.50
269	A27	1p rose & blk	12.00	2.00
270	A27	2p violet & blk	27.50	2.40
271	A27	2½p ultra & blk	32.50	14.00
272	A27	3p ol grn & blk	4.50	.60
273	A27	4p choc & blk	6.50	.80
274	A27	6p brn org & blk	19.00	2.40
275	A27	1sh red brn & blk	15.00	.60
276	A27	2sh yellow & blk	35.00	16.00
277	A27	2sh6p blk & red vio	60.00	12.50
278	A27	5sh vio & blk, yel	35.00	1.75
279	A27	10sh vio & blk, red	90.00	5.00
280	A27	£1 violet & grn	425.00	52.50
		Nos. 268-280 (13)	775.00	114.05

The 2p and 3p are on chalky paper, the 2½p, 4p, 6p and £1 on both chalky and ordinary, and the other values on ordinary paper only.

Issue years: ½p, 1p, 5sh, 1904. 2½p, 6p, 1sh, 1905. 2p, 3p, 4p, 2sh, 1906. 10sh, 1907. £1, 1908. 2sh6p, 1909.

1905-10

281	A27	½p green	4.00	.25
a.		Booklet pane of 6	—	
282	A27	1p carmine	1.50	.25
a.		Wmk. 16 (anchor) ('07)	—	375.00
b.		Booklet pane of 6	—	
283	A27	2p dull vio ('10)	4.00	1.50
284	A27	2½p ultra ('10)	30.00	15.00
		Nos. 281-284 (4)	39.50	17.00

Wmk. 16 is illustrated in the Cape of Good Hope.

Some of the above stamps are found with the overprint "C. S. A. R." for use by the Central South African Railway, the control mark being applied after the stamps had left the post office.

POSTAGE DUE STAMPS

D1

Wmk. Multiple Crown and C A (3)
1907   Typo.   Perf. 14

J1	D1	½p green & blk	4.00	1.50
J2	D1	1p carmine & blk	4.75	1.00
J3	D1	2p brown org	5.75	1.50
J4	D1	3p blue & blk	8.75	5.00
J5	D1	5p violet & blk	2.75	14.00
J6	D1	6p red brown & blk	5.00	14.00
J7	D1	1sh black & car	14.00	10.00
		Nos. J1-J7 (7)	45.00	47.00

Most canceled stamps of #J1-J7 were used outside the Transvaal under the Union of South Africa administration in 1910-16.

The stamps of Transvaal were replaced by those of South Africa.

TRINIDAD
'tri-nə-,dad

LOCATION — West Indies, off the Venezuelan coast
GOVT. — British Colony which became part of the Colony of Trinidad and Tobago in 1889
AREA — 1,864 sq. mi.
POP. — 387,000
CAPITAL — Port of Spain

12 Pence = 1 Shilling
20 Shillings = 1 Pound

In 1847 David Bryce, owner of the "Lady McLeod," issued a blue, lithographed, imperf. stamp to prepay his 5-cent rate for carrying letters on his sail-equipped steamer between Port of Spain and San Fernando, another Trinidad port. The stamp pictures the "Lady McLeod" above the monogram "LMcL," expressing no denomination. Value, unused, $50,000, used (pen canceled), $12,500. Used stamps canceled by having a corner skinned off are worth less.

Values for unused stamps are for examples with original gum as defined in the catalogue introduction. However, Nos. 9-12 are seldom found with gum, and these are valued without gum.

Values for Nos. 18-26 are for stamps with pin perforations on two or three sides. Stamps with pin perforations on all four sides are not often seen and command large premiums.

Very fine examples of Nos. 27-47 will have perforations touching the design on one or more sides due to the narrow spacing of the stamps on the plates and imperfect perforating methods. These stamps with perfs clear of the design on all four sides are scarce and command substantially higher prices.

"Britannia" — A1

1851-56   Unwmk.   Engr.   Imperf.
Blued Paper

1	A1	(1p) brick red ('56)	200.00	85.00
a.		(1p) brown red ('53)	360.00	77.50
2	A1	(1p) purple brown	22.50	90.00
3	A1	(1p) blue	24.00	72.50
a.		(1p) deep blue, deeply blued paper	175.00	95.00
4	A1	(1p) gray brn ('53)	57.50	90.00
a.		(1p) gray ('52)	90.00	77.50
		Nos. 1-4 (4)	304.00	337.50

1854-57   White Paper

6	A1	(1p) brown red ('57)	3,250.	77.50
7	A1	(1p) gray	55.00	95.00
8	A1	(1p) black violet	32.50	100.00

See Nos. 14, 18, 22, 27, 33, 39, 43, 45, 48, 58. For surcharges see Nos. 62-64.

"Britannia" — A2

1852   Fine Impressions   Litho.
Yellowish Paper

9	A2	(1p) blue	11,500.	1,950.
a.		(1p) deep blue	11,500.	1,950.
b.		White paper		1,950.

1853   Bluish Paper
10	A2	(1p) blue	10,000.	2,400.

Same, Lines of Background More or Less Worn

1855-60   Thin Paper
11	A2	(1p) slate blue	5,500.	800.00
12	A2	(1p) blue	5,000.	500.00
a.		(1p) greenish blue		800.00
13	A2	(1p) rose	17.50	750.00
a.		(1p) dull red	17.50	725.00

A3

1859   Engr.   Imperf.
White Paper

14	A1	(1p) dull rose	—	—
15	A3	4p gray lilac	125.00	400.00
a.		4p dull lilac		
16	A3	6p green	15,000.	525.00
17	A3	1sh slate blue	125.00	425.00

Pin-perf. 12½

18	A1	(1p) dull rose red	2,000.	70.00
a.		(1p) lake	2,250.	70.00
19	A3	4p brown lilac	—	1,250.
a.		4p dull purple	7,500.	1,250.
20	A3	6p deep green	3,500.	250.00
a.		6p yellow green	3,500.	250.00
21	A3	1sh black violet	9,000.	1,750.

Pin-perf. 14

22	A1	(1p) rose red	275.00	42.50
a.		(1p) carmine	325.00	40.00
23	A3	4p brown lilac	250.00	150.00
a.		4p violet	600.00	160.00
b.		4p dull violet	1,650.	125.00
24	A3	6p deep green	800.00	100.00
25	A3	6p yellow green	200.00	160.00
a.		Vert. pair, imperf. between	8,000.	
26	A3	1sh black violet	9,000.	1,150.

1860   Clean-cut Perf. 14 to 15½
27	A1	(1p) dull rose	190.00	67.50
a.		(1p) lake	100.00	40.00
b.		Horiz. pair, imperf. vert.	3,000.	
29	A3	4p violet brown	210.00	95.00
a.		4p dull violet		375.00
30	A3	6p deep green	300.00	175.00
31	A3	6p yellow green	550.00	115.00
32	A3	1sh black violet		

1861   Rough Perf. 14 to 16½
33	A1	(1p) dull rose	170.00	37.50
34	A3	4p gray lilac	750.00	100.00
35	A3	4p brown lilac	325.00	85.00
a.		4p dull violet	750.00	115.00
36	A3	6p green	475.00	85.00
a.		6p blue green	325.00	95.00
37	A3	1sh indigo	1,000.	350.00
a.		1sh purplish blue	1,675.	550.00

Thick Paper

1863   Perf. 11½ to 12
39	A1	(1p) carmine	160.00	29.00
a.		Perf. 11½-12x11	2,000.	600.00
40	A3	4p dull violet	225.00	72.50
41	A3	6p dp blue green	1,350.	100.00
a.		Perf. 11½-12x11		8,000.
42	A3	1sh indigo	2,750.	110.00

Perf. 12½

43	A1	(1p) lake	62.50	29.00

Perf. 13

45	A1	(1p) lake	52.50	29.00
46	A3	6p emerald	525.00	62.50
47	A3	1sh brt violet	4,500.	300.00

1864-72   Wmk. 1   Perf. 12½
48	A1	(1p) red	65.00	3.50
a.		(1p) lake	65.00	8.25
b.		(1p) rose	65.00	3.00
c.		(1p) carmine	70.00	3.75
d.		Imperf., pair	800.00	800.00
49	A3	4p brt violet	150.00	21.00
a.		4p pale violet	250.00	24.00
b.		Imperf.	600.00	
50	A3	4p lilac	200.00	21.00
a.		4p gray lilac		

51	A3	4p gray ('72)	160.00	8.50
52	A3	6p blue green	190.00	10.00
a.		6p emerald	125.00	19.00
53	A3	6p yellow grn	115.00	8.00
a.		6p dp grn	500.00	10.00
b.		Imperf., pair	800.00	
54	A3	1sh purple	200.00	12.00
a.		1sh lilac	150.00	12.00
b.		1sh violet	150.00	12.00
c.		1sh red lilac	160.00	13.00
d.		Imperf.	750.00	
55	A3	1sh orange yel ('72)	175.00	2.50
		Nos. 48-55 (8)	1,255.	86.50

See Nos. 59-61A, 65. For surcharge see No. 67.

Queen Victoria — A4

1869-94   Typo.   Perf. 12½
56	A4	5sh dull lake	200.00	90.00
a.		Imperf., pair	1,250.	

Perf. 14

57	A4	5sh claret ('94)	67.50	115.00

For overprint see No. O7.

1876   Engr.   Perf. 14
58	A1	(1p) carmine	52.50	3.00
a.		(1p) red	82.50	3.00
b.		(1p) lake	55.00	3.00
c.		Half used as ½p on cover		750.00
59	A3	4p gray	140.00	2.25
60	A3	6p yellow green	120.00	4.00
a.		6p deep green	150.00	3.25
61	A3	1sh orange yellow	165.00	5.00
		Nos. 58-61 (4)	477.50	14.25

Perf. 14x12½

61A	A3	6p yel grn ('80)		6,750.

Value for No. 61A is for stamp with perfs barely touching the design.

Type A1 Surcharged in Black

HALFPENNY

1879   Wmk. 1   Perf. 14
62	A1	½p lilac	22.50	14.00

Same Surcharge

1882   Wmk. Crown and C A (2)
63	A1	½p lilac	250.00	90.00
64	A1	1p carmine	77.50	2.75
a.		Half used as ½p on cover		675.00

Type of 1859

1882   Wmk. 2
65	A3	4p gray	215.00	17.50

No. 60 Surcharged by pen and ink in Black or Red

1882   Wmk. 1
67	A3	1p on 6p green (R)	16.00	10.00
a.		Half used as ½p on cover		400.00
b.		Black surcharge		1,900.

Counterfeits of No. 67b are plentiful. Various handwriting exists on both 60 and 60a.

A7

1883-84   Typo.   Wmk. 2
68	A7	½p green	12.00	1.50
69	A7	1p rose	25.00	.60
a.		Half used as ½p on cover		950.00
70	A7	2½p ultra	29.00	.70
a.		2½p blue	27.50	.75

71	A7	4p slate	5.00	.70
72	A7	6p olive brn ('84)	9.00	7.00
73	A7	1sh orange brn ('84)	16.00	7.00
		Nos. 68-73 (6)	96.00	17.50

For overprints see Nos. O1-O6.

A8   A9

ONE   ONE
Type I   Type II

ONE PENNY:
Type I — Round "O" in "ONE."
Type II — Oval "O" in "ONE."

1896-1904   Perf. 14
74	A8	½p lilac & green	4.00	.35
75	A8	½p gray grn ('02)	1.25	2.40
76	A8	1p lil & car, type I	4.25	.25
77	A8	1p lil & car, type II ('00)	400.00	4.75
78	A8	1p blk, red, type II ('01)	5.50	.25
a.		Value omitted	36,000.	
79	A8	2½p lilac & ultra	7.25	.25
80	A8	2½p vio & bl, bl ('02)	27.50	.75
81	A8	4p lilac & orange	9.00	27.50
82	A8	4p grn & ultra, buff ('02)	4.00	24.00
83	A8	5p lilac & violet	11.00	17.50
84	A8	6p lilac & black	9.00	6.50
85	A8	1sh grn & org brn	8.25	7.75
86	A8	1sh blk & bl, yel ('04)	22.50	6.50

Wmk. C A over Crown (46)

87	A9	5sh green & org	65.00	90.00
88	A9	5sh lil & red vio ('02)	90.00	110.00
89	A9	10sh grn & ultra	350.00	575.00
		Revenue cancel		30.00
90	A9	£1 grn & car	210.00	350.00
		Nos. 74-90 (17)	1,229.	1,224.

No. 82 also exists on chalky paper. Values: unused $3.50, used $14. Nos. 88 and 90 exist on both ordinary and chalky paper.
Circular "Registrar General" cancels are revenue usage and of minimal value.
See Nos. 92-104.

Landing of Columbus — A10

1898   Engr.   Wmk. 1
91	A10	2p gray vio & yel brn	3.25	1.40
		Overprinted "SPECIMEN"	60.00	

400th anniv. of the discovery of the island of Trinidad by Columbus, July 31, 1498.

1904-09   Wmk. 3   Chalky Paper
92	A8	½p gray green	13.00	2.50
a.		Ordinary paper	10.00	1.25
93	A8	1p blk, red, type II	15.00	.25
a.		Ordinary paper	15.00	.25
94	A8	2½p vio & bl, bl	27.50	1.10
95	A8	4p blk & car, yel ('06)	5.00	17.50
96	A8	6p lilac & blk ('05)	24.00	18.00
97	A8	6p vio & dp vio ('06)	12.00	17.50
98	A8	1sh vio & bl, yel	26.00	12.00
99	A8	1sh vio & bl, yel	18.00	28.00
100	A8	1sh blk, grn ('06)	3.00	1.50
101	A9	5sh lil & red vio ('07)	85.00	115.00
102	A9	£1 grn & car ('07)	325.00	400.00
		Nos. 92-102 (11)	553.50	613.35

For overprints see Nos. O8-O9.

1906-07
103	A8	1p carmine ('07)	4.00	.25
104	A8	2½p ultramarine	12.00	.25

A11   A12

1909   Ordinary Paper
105	A11	½p gray green	11.00	.25
106	A12	1p carmine	14.00	.25
107	A11	2½p ultramarine	29.00	4.75
		Nos. 105-107 (3)	54.00	5.25

For overprint see No. O10.

POSTAGE DUE STAMPS

D1

Wmk. Crown and C A (2)

1885, Jan. 1		**Typo.**	**Perf. 14**	
J1	D1	½p black	22.50	55.00
J2	D1	1p black	11.00	.25
J3	D1	2p black	52.50	.25
J4	D1	3p black	62.50	.50
J5	D1	4p black	52.50	7.50
J6	D1	5p black	27.50	.70
J7	D1	6p black	55.00	14.00
J8	D1	8p black	65.00	6.00
J9	D1	1sh black	82.50	9.00
		Nos. J1-J9 (9)	431.00	93.20

1906-07			**Wmk. 3**	
J10	D1	1p black	9.50	.25
J11	D1	2p black	42.50	.25
J12	D1	3p black	15.00	3.75
J13	D1	4p black	15.00	22.50
J14	D1	5p black	21.00	24.00
J15	D1	6p black	7.25	18.00
J16	D1	8p black	21.00	24.00
J17	D1	1sh black	30.00	47.50
		Nos. J10-J17 (8)	161.25	140.25

See Trinidad and Tobago Nos. J1-J16.

OFFICIAL STAMPS

Postage Stamps of 1869-84 Overprinted in Black

1893-94　　Wmk. 2　　Perf. 14

O1	A7	½p green	50.00	65.00
O2	A7	1p rose	52.50	72.50
O3	A7	2½p ultra	57.50	110.00
O4	A7	4p slate	62.50	135.00
O5	A7	6p olive brown	62.50	145.00
O6	A7	1sh orange brown	82.50	200.00

Wmk. Crown and C C (1)

			Perf. 12½	
O7	A4	5sh dull lake	190.00	875.00
		Nos. O1-O7 (7)	557.50	1,603.

Nos. 92 and 103 Overprinted

1909-10		**Wmk. 3**	**Perf. 14**	
O8	A8	½p gray green	3.75	12.00
O9	A8	1p carmine	3.50	13.00
a.		Double overprint		375.00
b.		Inverted overprint	900.00	275.00
c.		Vertical overprint	140.00	160.00

Same Overprint on No. 105

1910				
O10	A11	½p gray green	13.00	17.50

Stamps of Trinidad have been superseded by those inscribed "Trinidad and Tobago."

TRINIDAD & TOBAGO

ˈtri-nə-ˌdad and tə-ˈbā-ˌgō

LOCATION — West Indies off the coast of Venezuela
GOVT. — Republic
AREA — 1,980 sq. mi.
POP. — 1,102,096 (1999 est.)
CAPITAL — Port-of-Spain

The two British colonies of Trinidad and Tobago were united from 1889 until 1899, when Tobago became a ward of the united colony. From 1899 until 1913 postage stamps of Trinidad were used. The two islands became a state in August 1962, and the independent Republic of Trinidad and Tobago on August 1, 1976.

12 Pence = 1 Shilling
20 Shillings = 1 Pound
100 Cents = 1 Dollar (1935)

Catalogue values for unused stamps in this country are for Never Hinged items, beginning with Scott 62 in the regular postage section and Scott J9 in the postage due section.

"Britannia" — A1

1913　　Typo.　　Wmk. 3　　Perf. 14
Ordinary Paper

1	A1	½p green	3.50	.25
2	A1	1p scarlet	1.75	.25
a.		1p carmine	2.75	.25
4	A1	2½p ultra	8.00	.50

Chalky Paper

5	A1	4p scar & blk, yel	.80	7.00
6	A1	6p red vio & dull vio	11.00	8.00
7	A1	1sh black, emerald back	1.75	3.50
a.		1sh black, green	2.00	5.00
b.		1sh black, bl grn, ol back	16.00	10.00
		Nos. 1-2,4-7 (6)	26.80	19.50

"Britannia" — A2

1914
Surface-colored Paper (White Back)

8	A1	4p scar & blk, yel	2.00	11.50
9	A1	1sh black, green	1.60	17.50

Chalky Paper

10	A2	5sh dull vio & red vio	75.00	110.00
11	A2	£1 green & car	260.00	300.00
		Nos. 8-11 (4)	338.60	439.00

1921-22　　Ordinary Paper　　Wmk. 4

12	A1	½p green	3.50	2.75
13	A1	1p scarlet	.75	.40
14	A1	1p brown ('22)	.75	1.90
15	A1	2p gray ('22)	1.25	1.50
16	A1	2½p ultra	1.00	22.50
17	A1	3p ultra ('22)	7.50	4.00

Chalky Paper

18	A1	6p red vio & dull vio	5.00	19.00
19	A2	5sh dull vio & red vio	80.00	170.00
20	A2	£1 green & car	260.00	375.00
		Nos. 12-20 (9)	359.75	597.05

For overprints see #B2-B3, MR1-MR13, O1-O5.

"Britannia" and King George V — A3

1922-28　　　Ordinary Paper

21	A3	½p green	.55	.25
22	A3	1p brown	.55	.25
23	A3	1½p rose red	2.75	.25
24	A3	2p gray	.55	1.40
25	A3	3p ultra	.55	1.40

Chalky Paper

26	A3	4p red & blk, yel ('28)	3.75	3.75
27	A3	6p red vio & dl vio	2.50	29.00
28	A3	6p red & grn, emer ('24)	1.40	.70
29	A3	1sh blk, emer ('25)	6.25	2.00
30	A3	5sh vio & dull vio	32.50	42.50
31	A3	£1 rose & green	150.00	275.00

Wmk. Multiple Crown and C A (3)
Chalky Paper

32	A3	4p red & blk, yel	4.75	20.00
33	A3	1sh blk, emerald	6.00	11.00
		Nos. 21-33 (13)	212.10	387.50

First Boca — A4

Designs: 2c, Agricultural College. 3c, Mt. Irvine Bay, Tobago. 6c, Discovery of Lake Asphalt. 8c, Queen's Park, Savannah. 12c, Town Hall, San Fernando. 24c, Government House. 48c, Memorial Park. 72c, Blue Basin.

1935-37　　Engr.　　Wmk. 4　　Perf. 12

34	A4	1c emer & bl, perf. 12½ ('36)	.40	.25
a.		Perf. 12	.50	1.10
35	A4	2c lt brn & ultra, perf. 12	3.00	1.25
a.		Perf. 12½ ('36)	2.75	.25
36	A4	3c red & blk, perf. 12½ ('36)	3.25	.40
a.		Perf. 12	2.75	.40
37	A4	6c bl & brn, perf. 12	5.00	3.00
a.		Perf. 12½ ('37)	18.00	10.00
38	A4	8c red org & yel grn	4.50	4.25
39	A4	12c dk violet & blk	5.00	2.25
a.		Perf. 12½ ('37)	18.00	12.00
40	A4	24c ol grn & blk	10.00	3.00
a.		Perf. 12½ ('37)	27.50	16.00
41	A4	48c slate green	11.00	19.00
42	A4	72c mag & sl grn	45.00	40.00
		Nos. 34-42 (9)	87.15	73.40

Common Design Types pictured following the introduction.

Silver Jubilee Issue
Common Design Type

1935, May 6			**Perf. 11x12**	
43	CD301	2c black & ultra	.40	1.00
44	CD301	3c car & blue	.40	2.25
45	CD301	6c ultra & brn	2.25	2.50
46	CD301	24c brn vio & blk	11.00	22.00
		Nos. 43-46 (4)	14.05	27.75
		Set, never hinged	26.00	

Coronation Issue
Common Design Type

1937, May 12			**Perf. 13½x14**	
47	CD302	1c deep green	.25	.25
48	CD302	2c yellow brown	.25	.25
49	CD302	8c deep orange	.50	.50
		Nos. 47-49 (3)	1.00	1.00
		Set, never hinged	1.50	

First Boca — A13

George VI — A14

Various Frames and: 2c, Agricultural College. 3c, Mt. Irvine Bay, Tobago. 4c, Memorial Park. 5c, General Post Office and Treasury. 6c, Discovery of Lake Asphalt. 8c, Queen's Park, Savannah. 12c, Town Hall, San Fernando. 24c, Government House. 60c, Blue Basin.

Perf. 11½x11

1938-41		**Wmk. 4**	**Engr.**	
50	A13	1c emer & blue	.60	.25
51	A13	2c lt brn & ultra	.75	.25
52	A13	3c dk car & blk	6.75	1.00
52A	A13	3c vio brn & bl grn ('41)	.25	.25
53	A13	4c brown	19.00	3.25
53A	A13	4c red ('41)	.30	.25
54	A13	5c mag ('41)	.30	.25
55	A13	6c brt bl & sep	1.60	.85
56	A13	8c red org & yel grn	1.75	1.00
57	A13	12c dk vio & blk	3.50	.25
58	A13	24c dk ol grn & blk	5.00	.25
59	A13	60c mag & sl grn	9.00	1.75

Perf. 12

60	A14	$1.20 dk grn ('40)	8.50	2.00
61	A14	$4.80 rose pink ('40)	24.00	60.00
		Nos. 50-61 (14)	81.30	71.60
		Set, never hinged	125.00	

Watermark sideways on Nos. 50-59.

Catalogue values for unused stamps in this section, from this point to the end of the section, are for Never Hinged items.

Peace Issue
Common Design Type
Perf. 13½x14

1946, Oct. 1		**Engr.**	**Wmk. 4**	
62	CD303	3c brown	.25	.25
63	CD303	6c deep blue	.25	.25

Silver Wedding Issue
Common Design Type

1948, Nov. 22		**Photo.**	**Perf. 14x14½**	
64	CD304	3c red brown	.25	.25

Perf. 11½x11
Engr.

65	CD305	$4.80 rose car	32.50	38.00

UPU Issue
Common Design Types
Engr.; Name Typo. on 6c, 12c
Perf. 13½, 11x11½

1949, Oct. 10			**Wmk. 4**	
66	CD306	5c red violet	.35	.35
67	CD307	6c indigo	1.90	1.90
68	CD308	12c rose violet	.45	.45
69	CD309	24c olive	.45	.45
		Nos. 66-69 (4)	3.15	3.15

University Issue
Common Design Types
Inscribed: "Trinidad"

1951, Feb. 16		**Engr.**	**Perf. 14x14½**	
70	CD310	3c choc & grn	.25	.25
71	CD311	12c purple & blk	.50	.50

Types of 1938 with Portrait of Queen Elizabeth II

1953, Apr. 20			**Perf. 11½x11**	
72	A13	1c yel grn & dp blue	.25	.25
73	A13	2c org brn & sl blue	.25	.25
74	A13	3c vio brn & blue grn	.25	.25
75	A13	4c red	.25	.25
76	A13	5c magenta	.25	.25
77	A13	6c blue & brown	.55	.35
78	A13	8c red org & dp grn	2.50	.35
79	A13	12c dk violet & blk	.35	.25
80	A13	24c dk ol grn & blk	2.50	.35
81	A13	60c rose car & grnsh blk	25.00	1.75

Perf. 11½

82	A14	$1.20 dark green	1.40	.65
a.		Perf. 12	2.50	1.00
83	A14	$4.80 rose pink	9.00	19.00
a.		Perf. 12	12.00	17.00
		Nos. 72-83 (12)	42.55	23.95

For surcharge see No. 85.

Coronation Issue
Common Design Type

1953, June 3			**Perf. 13½x13**	
84	CD312	3c dark green & blk	.25	.25

No. 73 Surcharged "ONE CENT"
Perf. 11½x11

1956, Dec. 20			**Wmk. 4**	
85	A13	1c on 2c org brn & sl blue	1.60	1.75

West Indies Federation
Common Design Type
Perf. 11½x11

1958, Apr. 22		**Engr.**	**Wmk. 314**	
86	CD313	5c green	.25	.25
87	CD313	6c blue	.25	.40
88	CD313	12c carmine rose	.25	.25
		Nos. 86-88 (3)	.75	.90

Cipriani Memorial, Port-of-Spain A27

Queen's Hall, Port-of-Spain A28

Crest of Colony — A28a

Copper-rumped Hummingbird and Hibiscus — A28b

Designs: 5c, Whitehall. 6c, Treasury Building. 8c, Governor General's House. 10c, General Hospital, San Fernando. 12c, Oil refinery. 25c, Scarlet ibis. 35c, Lake Asphalt (Pitch). 50c, Jinnah Memorial Mosque. 60c, Anthurium lilies. $4.80, Map.

Perf. 13½x14, 14x13½

1960, Sept. 24   Photo.   Wmk. 314
Sizes: 22¼x26mm, 26x22½mm

89	A27	1c dark gray & buff	1.00	.25
a.		Wmkd. sideways ('66)	.50	.50
90	A28	2c ultra	.25	.25
91	A28	5c dark blue	.25	.25
92	A28	6c lt red brown	.25	.25
93	A28	8c yellow green	.25	.35
94	A28	10c light purple	.25	.25
95	A28	12c bright red	.25	.25
96	A28a	15c orange	3.50	.90
97	A28	25c dk blue & crim	.90	.25
98	A28	35c green & black	4.00	.25
99	A28	50c blue, yel & olive	.40	1.25
100	A27	60c multicolored	.65	.25
a.		Perf. 14 ('65)	185.00	40.00

Size: 48x25mm

101	A28b	$1.20 multicolored	17.50	4.00
102	A28b	$4.80 lt bl & lt yel grn	25.00	20.00
		Nos. 89-102 (14)	54.45	28.75

See #116. For overprints see #123-124, 126.

Scouts and Map of Trinidad and Tobago — A29

1961, Apr. 4   Perf. 13½x14
| 103 | A29 | 8c multicolored | .25 | .25 |
| 104 | A29 | 25c multicolored | .25 | .25 |

2nd Caribbean Scout Jamboree, Valsayn Park, Trinidad, Apr. 4-14.

Independent State

Underwater Scene from Painting by Carlisle Chang — A30

Designs: 8c, Elizabeth II and new Terminal Building, Piarco Airport. 25c, Elizabeth II and Hilton Hotel. 35c, Map and greater bird of paradise. 60c, Map and scarlet ibis.

1962, Aug. 31   Photo.   Perf. 14½
105	A30	5c blue green	.25	.25
106	A30	8c slate	.45	.70
107	A30	25c purple	.30	.25
108	A30	35c emer, yel, brn & blk	2.50	.25
109	A30	60c ultra, black & ver	3.00	3.25
		Nos. 105-109 (5)	6.50	4.70

Issued to mark Trinidad and Tobago's independence, Aug. 31, 1962.

Freedom from Hunger Issue

Protein Food — A31

1963, June 1   Perf. 14x13½
110	A31	5c henna brown	.25	.25
111	A31	8c citron	.25	.25
112	A31	25c violet blue	.40	.40
		Nos. 110-112 (3)	.90	.90

See note in Common Design section.

Girl Guide Emblem A32

Perf. 14½x14
1964, Sept. 15   Wmk. 314
113	A32	6c red, dk blue & yel	.25	.25
114	A32	25c brt blue, dk bl & yel	.25	.25
115	A32	35c lt green, dk bl & yel	.25	.25
		Nos. 113-115 (3)	.75	.75

50th anniv. of the Trinidad and Tobago Girl Guide Association.

Arms of Independent State — A33

1964, Sept. 15   Perf. 14x13½
| 116 | A33 | 15c orange | 4.00 | .30 |

For overprint see No. 125.

ICY Emblem A34

Unwmk.
1965, Nov. 15   Litho.   Perf. 12
Granite Paper
| 117 | A34 | 35c dull yel, red brn & grn | .70 | .70 |

International Cooperation Year, 1965.

Eleanor Roosevelt — A35

Perf. 13½x14
1965, Dec. 10   Wmk. 314
| 118 | A35 | 25c vio blue, red & blk | .35 | .35 |

Issued to honor Eleanor Roosevelt and to publicize the Eleanor Roosevelt Memorial Foundation.

"Redhouse," Parliament Building — A36

8c, Map of Trinidad & Tobago, royal yacht "Britannia," arms of State. 25c, Flag, map. 35c, Flag, Trinity Hills, General Post Office, sugar cane, coconut palms, derricks.

1966, Feb. 8   Photo.   Wmk. 314
119	A36	5c ultra, red, blk & grn	1.00	.25
120	A36	8c ultra, sil, blk & ycl brn	1.90	.75
121	A36	25c red, blk & emerald	1.90	.75
122	A36	35c ultra, red, blk & grn	1.90	.75
		Nos. 119-122 (4)	6.70	2.25

Visit of Elizabeth II and Prince Philip.

Nos. 93-94, 116 Overprinted

No. 100 Overprinted

Perf. 14x13½, 13½x14
1967, Aug. 31   Photo.   Wmk. 314
123	A28	8c yellow green	.25	.25
124	A28	10c lt purple	.25	.25
125	A33	15c orange	.25	.25
126	A27	60c multicolored	.25	.25
		Nos. 123-126 (4)	1.00	1.00

Carnival Symbols A37

Designs: 10c, Calypso King, vert. 15c, Steel band. 25c, Chinese masks. 35c, Carnival King, vert. 60c, Carnival Queen, vert.

Unwmk.
1968, Feb. 16   Litho.   Perf. 12
127	A37	5c pink & multi	.25	.25
128	A37	10c vio blue & multi	.25	.25
129	A37	15c multicolored	.25	.25
130	A37	25c multicolored	.25	.25
131	A37	35c dk purple & multi	.25	.25
132	A37	60c brown ol & multi	.30	.30
		Nos. 127-132 (6)	1.55	1.55

Issued to publicize the Trinidad Carnival.

WHO Emblem and Eye Examination — A38

Wmk. 314
1968, May 7   Photo.   Perf. 14
133	A38	5c rose red, gold & blk	.25	.25
134	A38	25c orange, gold & blk	.25	.25
135	A38	35c brt blue, gold & blk	.30	.30
		Nos. 133-135 (3)	.80	.80

Dancing Children and Human Rights Flame — A39

1968, Aug. 5   Perf. 14
136	A39	5c carmine, yel & blk	.25	.25
137	A39	10c brt blue, yel & blk	.25	.25
138	A39	25c yel grn, yel & blk	.25	.25
		Nos. 136-138 (3)	.75	.75

International Human Rights Year.

Bicycling and Map A40

Designs (Olympic Rings, Map of Trinidad and Tobago and): 15c, Weight lifting. 25c, Relay race. 35c, Running. $1.20, Map of Mexico and flags of Mexico and Trinidad and Tobago.

Photo.; Gold Impressed (except $1.20)
1968, Oct. 12   Perf. 14
139	A40	5c vio, gold & multi	.25	.25
140	A40	15c red, gold & multi	.25	.25
141	A40	25c org, gold & multi	.25	.25
142	A40	35c brt grn, gold & multi	.25	.25
143	A40	$1.20 blue, gold & multi	.95	.50
		Nos. 139-143 (5)	1.95	1.50

19th Olympic Games, Mexico City, 10/12-27.

Cacao A41

Designs: 3c, Sugar refinery. 5c, Redtailed chachalaca. 6c, Oil refinery. 8c, Fertilizer plant. 10c, Green hermit (hummingbird) vert. 12c, Citrus fruit, vert. 15c, Coat of arms, vert. 20c, 25c, Flag and map of islands, vert. 30c, Wild poinsettia, vert. 40c, Scarlet ibis. 50c, Maracas Bay. $1, Blooming tabebuia (tree) vert. $2.50, Fishermen hauling in net. $5, Red House, Port-of-Spain.

Photo.; Silver or Gold Impressed
1969, Apr. 1   Wmk. 314   Perf. 14
144	A41	1c silver & multi	.25	.75
145	A41	3c gold & multi	.25	.25
a.		Wmk. upright ('74)	4.00	9.50
146	A41	5c gold & multi	1.50	.25
a.		Wmk. upright ('73)	8.00	3.50
147	A41	6c gold & multi	.25	.25
a.		Wmk. upright ('74)	3.00	4.00
148	A41	8c silver & multi	3.00	.25
149	A41	10c gold & multi	1.75	.25
b.		Wmk. 373 ('76)	1.50	1.50
150	A41	12c silver & multi	.25	.25
151	A41	15c silver & multi	.25	.25
152	A41	20c gold & multi	.30	.25
153	A41	25c silver & multi	.30	.75
154	A41	30c silver & multi	.35	.25
155	A41	40c gold & multi	4.00	.35
156	A41	50c silver & multi	.35	4.00
157	A41	$1 gold & multi	.60	.25

Perf. 14x14½
158	A41	$2.50 gold & multi	1.00	5.00
159	A41	$5 gold & multi	1.50	5.50
		Nos. 144-159 (16)	15.90	18.85

Nos. 144-157 exists on two paper types. For overprint see No. 187. For surcharges see Nos. 903-904.

Capt. A. A. Cipriani, ILO Emblem and Gate A42

ILO, 50th Anniv.: 15c, Industrial Court's & ILO emblems, & Woodford Square gate.

Unwmk.
1969, May 1   Photo.   Perf. 12
| 160 | A42 | 6c dp car, gold & blk | .25 | .25 |
| 161 | A42 | 15c brt blue, gold & blk | .25 | .25 |

Union Jack and Flags of CARIFTA Members A43

Designs: 6c, Cornucopia, vert. 30c, Map of Caribbean, vert. 40c, Jet plane and "Strength through Unity" emblem.

1969, Aug. 1   Perf. 14x13½, 13½x14
162	A43	6c lilac, gold & multi	.25	.25
163	A43	10c multicolored	.25	.25
164	A43	30c red, emer, blk & gold	.25	.25
165	A43	40c blue, blk, grn & gold	.30	.30
		Nos. 162-165 (4)	1.05	1.05

Caribbean Free Trade Area (CARIFTA).

Moon Landing and Earth — A44

40c, Lunar landing module & astronauts on moon. $1, Astronauts Aldrin at control panel, Armstrong collecting rocks.

1969, Sept. 1   Litho.   Perf. 14
166	A44	6c multi	.25	.25
167	A44	40c multi, vert.	.30	.30
168	A44	$1 multi	.55	.55
		Nos. 166-168 (3)	1.10	1.10

See note after US No. C76.

Maces of Senate and House of Representatives — A45

10c, Chamber of Parliament. 15c, View of Kennedy Complex, University of the West Indies at St. Augustine. 40c, Cannon & view of Scarborough from Fort King George.

Perf. 14x13½
1969, Oct. 23   Photo.   Wmk. 314
169	A45	10c multicolored	.25	.25
170	A45	15c multicolored	.25	.25
171	A45	30c lt blue & multi	.25	.25
172	A45	40c multicolored	.25	.25
		Nos. 169-172 (4)	1.00	1.00

15th Conf. of the Commonwealth Parliamentary Assoc., Port-of-Spain, Oct. 4-19.

Congress Emblem and Landscape — A46

6c, Congress emblem (steel drum and bird). 30c, Palms, landscape and emblem, horiz.

Perf. 14x13½, 13½x14
1969, Nov. 2   Litho.   Unwmk.
173	A46	6c red, black & gold	.25	.25
174	A46	30c lt blue, plum & gold	.25	.25
175	A46	40c ultra, black & gold	.25	.25
		Nos. 173-175 (3)	.75	.75

24th Cong. of the Intl. Junior Chamber of Commerce.

Carnival King as "Man in the Moon" — A47

Designs: 6c, Carnival Queen as "City Beneath the Sea." 15c, Bambara god (antelope) from the Band of the Year. 30c, Pheasant Queen (Chanticleer) of Malaya. 40c, Steel Band of the Year with 1969 Calypso and Road March Kings, horiz.

1970, Feb. 2   Wmk. 314   Perf. 14
176	A47	5c dk brown & multi	.25	.25
177	A47	6c dk blue & multi	.25	.25
178	A47	15c violet bl & multi	.25	.25
179	A47	30c dk green & multi	.25	.25
180	A47	40c green & multi	.25	.25
		Nos. 176-180 (5)	1.25	1.25

Issued to publicize the Trinidad Carnival.

Mahatma Gandhi and Indian Flag — A48

Design: 10c, Gandhi monument, vert.

Unwmk.
1970, Mar. 2   Photo.   Perf. 12
181	A48	10c ultra & multi	.70	.30
182	A48	30c crimson & multi	1.40	.90

Mohandas K. Gandhi (1869-1948), leader in India's fight for independence.

A49

A49a

UN, 25th Anniv. — A49b

Designs: 5c, Culture, Science, Arts and Technology. 10c, Children of various races, map of Trinidad and Tobago and "UNICEF." 20c, Noah's ark, rainbow, dove and UN emblem.

1970, June 26   Photo.   Perf. 13½
183	A49	5c multicolored	.25	.25
184	A49a	10c multicolored	.30	.30
185	A49b	20c multicolored	.45	.45
		Nos. 183-185 (3)	1.00	1.00

UPU Headquarters, Bern — A50

1970, June 26   Unwmk.   Perf. 12
186	A50	30c ultra & multi	.45	.45

Opening of new UPU Headquarters in Bern.

No. 146 Overprinted "NATIONAL / COMMERCIAL / BANK / ESTABLISHED / 1.7.70"
Photo.; Gold Embossed
1970, July 1   Wmk. 314   Perf. 14
187	A41	5c gold & multi	.30	.25

San Fernando Town Hall — A51

Designs: 3c, East Indian Immigrants, 1820, after painting by Cazabon, vert. 40c, Ships in San Fernando Harbor, 1860, after painting by Michel J. Cazabon.

Perf. 14x13½, 13½x14
1970, Nov.   Litho.   Wmk. 314
188	A51	3c bister & multi	.25	.25
189	A51	5c lemon & multi	.25	.25
190	A51	40c lemon & multi	.65	.65
		Nos. 188-190 (3)	1.15	1.15

Municipality of San Fernando, 125th anniv.

Madonna and Child, by Titian — A52

Paintings: 3c, Adoration of the Shepherds, School of Saville. 30c, Adoration of the Shepherds, by Louis Le Nain. 40c, Virgin and Child with St. John and Angel, by Morando. $1, Adoration of the Magi, by Paolo Veronese.

Perf. 13½
1970, Dec. 8   Unwmk.   Litho.
191	A52	3c dull org & multi	.25	.25
a.		Booklet pane of 2	.30	
192	A52	5c brt pink & multi	.25	.25
a.		Booklet pane of 2	.30	
193	A52	30c lt utra & multi	.25	.25
a.		Booklet pane of 2	.60	
194	A52	40c yellow grn & multi	.25	.25
a.		Booklet pane of 2	.75	
b.		Souvenir sheet of 4, #191-194	2.50	2.50
195	A52	$1 pale lilac & multi	.40	1.50
		Nos. 191-195 (5)	1.40	2.50

Brocket Deer — A53

Perf. 14x13½
1971, Aug. 9   Litho.   Wmk. 314
196	A53	3c shown	.35	.25
197	A53	5c Collared peccary	.40	.25
198	A53	6c Paca	.50	.40

199	A53	30c Agouti	1.60	3.00
200	A53	40c Ocelot	1.60	2.25
		Nos. 196-200 (5)	4.45	6.15

Capt. A. A. Cipriani — A54

Design: 30c, Chaconia medal (for distinction in social field).

1971, Aug. 31   Perf. 14
201	A54	5c multicolored	.25	.25
202	A54	30c multicolored	.30	.30

9th anniversary of independence. Capt. Arthur Andrew Cipriani (died 1945) was mayor of Port of Spain and member of First Executive Council.

Virgin and Child with St. John, by Bartolommeo — A55

Christmas: 5c, Local creche. 10c, Virgin and Child with Sts. Jerome and Dominic, by Filippino Lippi. 15c, Virgin and Child with St. Anne, by Gerolamo dai Libri.

1971, Oct. 25   Litho.   Perf. 14x14½
203	A55	3c yellow & multi	.25	.25
204	A55	5c dull blue & multi	.25	.25
205	A55	10c red & multi	.25	.25
206	A55	15c orange & multi	.30	.30
		Nos. 203-206 (4)	1.05	1.05

Satellite Earth Station, Matura A56

Dish Antenna A57

Design: 40c, Satellite over earth (Africa).

1971, Nov. 18   Perf. 14
207	A56	10c ultra & multi	.25	.25
208	A57	30c green & multi	.25	.25
209	A57	40c black & multi	.35	.35
a.		Souvenir sheet of 3	1.90	1.90
		Nos. 207-209 (3)	.85	.85

Opening of Satellite Earth Station at Matura. No. 209a contains 3 imperf. stamps with simulated perforations similar to Nos. 207-209.

Morpho Hybrid A58

Butterflies: 5c, Purple mort bleu. 6c, Jaune d'abricot. 10c, Purple king shoemaker. 20c, Southern white pape. 30c, Little jaune.

1972, Feb. 18   Photo.   Wmk. 314
210	A58	3c olive & multi	.85	.80
211	A58	5c ocher & multi	1.10	.25
212	A58	6c yellow & multi	1.50	1.00
213	A58	10c yel grn & multi	1.75	.30
214	A58	20c lilac & multi	2.25	2.25
215	A58	30c dull grn & multi	3.00	2.75
		Nos. 210-215 (6)	10.45	7.35

S.S. Lady McLeod and Stamp A59

10c, Map of Trinidad and Tobago. 30c, Commemorative inscription.

1972, Apr. 12   Litho.   Perf. 14½x14
216	A59	5c blue & multi	.25	.25
217	A59	15c blue & multi	.25	.25
218	A59	30c blue & multi	.65	.65
a.		Souvenir sheet of 3, #216-218	1.50	1.50
		Nos. 216-218 (3)	1.15	1.15

125th anniv. of the Lady McLeod stamp.

Trinity Cross — A60

Medals: 10c, Chaconia medal. 20c, Hummingbird medal. 30c, Medal of Merit.

1972, Aug. 28   Photo.   Perf. 13½x13
219	A60	5c blue & multi	.25	.25
220	A60	10c multicolored	.25	.25
221	A60	20c yellow grn & multi	.25	.25
222	A60	30c brt rose & multi	.25	.40
a.		Souvenir sheet of 4, #219-222	1.10	1.10
		Nos. 219-222 (4)	1.00	1.20

10th anniversary of independence.
See Nos. 235-238.

Olympic Rings, Relay Race Medal, 1964 A61

Olympic Rings and: 20c, Bronze medal, 200-meters, 1964. 30c, Bronze medals, weight lifting, 1952. 40c, Silver medal, 400-meters, 1964. 50c, Silver medal, weight lifting, 1948.

1972, Sept. 7   Litho.   Perf. 14
223	A61	10c yellow & multi	.25	.25
224	A61	20c multicolored	.25	.25
225	A61	30c lilac & multi	.30	.30
226	A61	40c lt blue & multi	.35	.35
227	A61	50c orange & multi	.45	1.25
a.		Souv. sheet, #223-227 + label	2.00	2.00
		Nos. 223-227 (5)	1.60	2.40

20th Olympic Games, Munich, 8/26-9/11.

Holy Family, by Titian A62

Christmas: 3c, Adoration of the Kings, by Dosso Dossi. 30c, Like 5c.

1972, Nov. 9   Photo.   Wmk. 314
228	A62	3c blue & multi	.25	.25
229	A62	5c rose lilac & multi	.25	.25
230	A62	30c lt green & multi	.50	.50
a.		Souvenir sheet of 3, #228-230	1.75	1.75
		Nos. 228-230 (3)	1.00	1.00

ECLA Headquarters, Santiago, Chile — A63

Designs: 20c, INTERPOL emblem. 30c, WMO emblem. 40c, University of West Indies Administration Building.

1973, Aug. 15   Litho.   Wmk. 314
231	A63	10c orange & multi	.25	.25
232	A63	20c multicolored	.25	.25
233	A63	30c ultra & multi	.35	.35
234	A63	40c lilac & multi	.40	.40
a.		Souvenir sheet of 4, #231-234	1.40	1.40
		Nos. 231-234 (4)	1.25	1.25

Economic Commission for Latin America, 25th anniv. (10c); Intl. Criminal Police Organization, 50th anniv. (20c); Intl. Meteorological cooperation, cent. (30c); Admission of 1st students to the University of West Indies, 25th anniv. (40c).

Medal Type of 1972 Redrawn

Medals: 10c, Trinity Cross. 20c, Medal of Merit. 30c, Chaconia medal. 40c, Hummingbird medal.

1973, Aug. 30   Photo.   Perf. 14½x14
235	A60	10c dark green & multi	.25	.25
236	A60	20c dark brown & multi	.25	.25
237	A60	30c dark blue & multi	.25	.25
238	A60	40c deep violet & multi	.30	.30
a.		Souv. sheet, #235-238, perf. 14	1.10	1.10
		Nos. 235-238 (4)	1.05	1.05

11th anniv. of independence. "Trinidad and Tobago" in one line on #235-238.

General Post Office, Port of Spain A64

40c, Conference Hall & flags, Chagaramas.

1973, Oct. 8   Photo.   Perf. 14
239	A64	30c multicolored	.25	.25
240	A64	40c multicolored	.30	.30
a.		Souvenir sheet of 2, #239-240	1.00	1.00

2nd Commonwealth Conf. of Postal Administrations, Trinidad, Oct. 8-20. On #240a the perforations extend through margin and divide map.

Virgin and Child, by Murillo — A65

1973, Oct. 22   Perf. 14½x14
241	A65	5c pink & multi	.25	.25
242	A65	$1 lt blue & multi	.60	.60
a.		Souv. sheet, #241-242, perf. 14	1.00	1.00

Christmas 1973.

Post Office and UPU Emblem — A66

UPU, Cent.: 50c, Map of Islands, UPU emblem, means of transportation.

1974, Nov. 18   Photo.   Perf. 13½x14
243	A66	40c brt purple & multi	.30	.30
244	A66	50c blue gray & multi	.55	.55
a.		Souvenir sheet of 2, #243-244	16.00	*16.00*

Humming Bird I, Transatlantic Crossing, 1960 — A67

Design: 50c, Globe, Humming Bird II, Harold and Kwailan La Borde.

1974, Dec. 2   Perf. 14½
245	A67	40c multicolored	.60	.60
246	A67	50c multicolored	.75	.75
a.		Souvenir sheet of 2, #245-246	3.00	3.00

First anniversary of the voyage around the world by Harold and Kwailan La Borde aboard Humming Bird II, 1969-1973.

"Equality" and IWY Emblem A68

1975, June 23   Litho.   Wmk. 314
247	A68	15c multicolored	.25	.25
248	A68	30c multicolored	.40	.40

International Women's Year 1975.

Dr. Pawan and Laboratory Equipment — A69

25c, Vampire bat, microscope, syringe, bat's head.

Perf. 14x14½

1975, Sept. 23   Photo.   Wmk. 373
249	A69	25c yellow & multi	.45	.45
250	A69	30c lt blue & multi	.55	.55

Isolation of rabies virus by Dr. Joseph Lennox Pawan (1887-1957).

Boeing 707, BWIA Emblem, Air Routes A70

Designs: 30c, Boeing 707 on ground. 40c, Boeing 707 in the air.

Wmk. 373

1975, Nov. 27   Litho.   Perf. 14½
251	A70	20c dark blue & multi	.45	.45
252	A70	30c deep ultra & multi	.60	.60
253	A70	40c dull green & multi	.75	.75
a.		Souvenir sheet of 3, #251-253	2.25	2.25
		Nos. 251-253 (3)	1.80	1.80

British West Indian Airways, 35th anniv.

Land of the Hummingbird Costume — A71

Carnival 1976: $1, Carib Prince riding pink ibis. Designs show prize-winning costumes from 1974 carnival.

1976, Jan. 12   Photo.   Perf. 14½
254	A71	30c multicolored	.25	.25
255	A71	$1 multicolored	.80	.80
a.		Souvenir sheet of 2, #254-255	1.40	1.40

Angostura Building, Port of Spain A72

Designs (Exposition Medals, obverse and reverse): 35c, New Orleans, 1885-86. 45c, Sydney, 1879. 50c, Brussels, 1897.

1976, July 14   Litho.   Perf. 13
256	A72	5c bister & multi	.25	.25
257	A72	35c yellow grn & multi	.25	.25
258	A72	45c blue & multi	.25	.25
259	A72	50c violet & multi	.25	.25
a.		Souv. sheet, #256-259, perf. 14	1.10	1.10
		Nos. 256-259 (4)	1.00	1.00

Sesquicentennial of the manufacture of Angostura Bitters.

Map of West Indies, Bats, Wicket and Ball A72a

Prudential Cup — A72b

1976, Oct. 4   Unwmk.   Perf. 14
260	A72a	35c lt blue & multi	.40	.40
261	A72b	45c lilac rose & blk	.60	.60
a.		Souvenir sheet of 2, #260-261	2.25	2.25

World Cricket Cup, won by West Indies Team, 1975.

Columbus Sailing through the Bocas, by A. Camps-Campins — A73

Paintings: 10c, View, by Jean Michael Cazabon. 20c, Landscape, by Cazabon. 35c, Los Gallos Point, by Cazabon. 45c, Corbeaux Town, by Cazabon.

1976, Nov. 1   Litho.   Wmk. 373
262	A73	5c ocher & multi	.75	.30
263	A73	10c lilac & multi	.25	.25
264	A73	20c green & multi	.50	.25
265	A73	35c red orange & multi	.60	.25
266	A73	45c blue & multi	.65	.25
a.		Souvenir sheet of 5, #262-266	2.25	2.25
		Nos. 262-266 (5)	2.75	1.30

For overprints see Nos. 325, 327.

Hasely Crawford and Gold Medal A74

1977, Jan. 4   Litho.   Perf. 12½
267	A74	25c multicolored	.35	.35
a.		Souvenir sheet of 1	.70	.70

Hasely Crawford, winner of 100-meter dash at Montreal Olympic Games.

Sikorsky S-38 (Lindbergh's
Plane) — A75

Designs: 35c, Charles Lindbergh delivering
first airmail to Port of Spain, 1927. 45c, Boeing
707, British West Indies Airways. 50c, Boeing
747, British Airways.

1977, Apr.   Wmk. 373   Perf. 13
268 A75 20c lt blue & multi   .35   .25
269 A75 35c lt blue & multi   .50   .35
270 A75 45c lt blue & multi   .60   .60
271 A75 50c lt blue & multi   1.00 2.00
  a. Souv. sheet, #268-271, perf. 14   4.50 4.50
    Nos. 268-271 (4)   2.45 3.20
Airmail to Trinidad & Tobago, 50th anniv.

Trinidad and
Tobago
Flag — A76

35c, Coat of arms. 45c, Government House.

1977, July 26   Litho.   Perf. 13½x13
272 A76 20c yellow & multi   .40   .40
273 A76 35c red & multi   .65   .65
274 A76 45c lt blue & multi   .80   .80
  a. Souv. sheet, #272-274, perf. 14   1.75 1.75
    Nos. 272-274 (3)   1.85 1.85
Inauguration of the Republic, Aug. 1, 1976.

White
Poinsettia — A77

Christmas: 45c, 50c, Red poinsettia.

1977, Oct. 11   Litho.   Perf. 14½
275 A77 10c multicolored   .25   .25
276 A77 35c multicolored   .35   .35
277 A77 45c multicolored   .40   .40
278 A77 50c multicolored   .45   .45
  a. Souvenir sheet of 4, #275-278   1.60 1.60
    Nos. 275-278 (4)   1.45 1.45

Robinson
Crusoe
Hotel,
Tobago
A78

15c, Turtle Beach Hotel, Tobago. 25c,
Mount Irvine Hotel, Tobago. 70c, Mount Irvine
beach, Tobago. $5, Holiday Inn, Trinidad.

1978, Jan. 17   Wmk. 373
         Litho.   Perf. 14
279 A78   6c multicolored   .25 1.75
280 A78 15c multicolored   .40 2.00
281 A78 25c multicolored   .50   .25
282 A78 70c multicolored   .60   .70
283 A78 $5   multicolored   1.75 4.00
  a. Souvenir sheet of 5, #279-283   3.50 3.50
    Nos. 279-283 (5)   3.50 8.70
For overprint see No. 326.

Paphinia
Cristata
A79

Orchids: 30c, Caularthron bicornutum. 40c,
Miltassia. 50c, Oncidium ampliatum. $2.50,
Oncidium papilio.

1978, June 7   Wmk. 373   Perf. 14
284 A79 12c multicolored   1.50 1.75
285 A79 30c multicolored   1.50 1.75
286 A79 40c multicolored   2.00   .25
287 A79 50c multicolored   1.50   .25
288 A79 $2.50 multicolored   2.25 5.50
  a. Souvenir sheet of 5, #284-288   6.00 6.00
    Nos. 284-288 (5)   8.75 9.50

Miss Universe and
Trophy — A80

Designs: 35c, Portrait with crown. 45c, Miss
Universe in evening dress.

1978, Aug. 2   Litho.   Perf. 14½
289 A80 10c multicolored   .35   .35
290 A80 35c multicolored   .60   .60
291 A80 45c multicolored   .75   .75
  a. Souvenir sheet of 3, #289-291   1.50 1.50
    Nos. 289-291 (3)   1.70 1.70
Janelle (Penny) Commissiong, Miss Universe, 1977.

Tayra
A81

1978, Nov. 7   Perf. 13½x14
292 A81 15c shown   .25   .25
293 A81 25c Ocelot   .35   .35
294 A81 40c Porcupine   .55   .55
295 A81 70c Yellow anteater   .75 1.50
  a. Souvenir sheet of 4, #292-295   2.00 2.00
    Nos. 292-295 (4)   1.90 2.65

"Burst of
Beauty" — A82

Costumes: 10c, Rain worshipper. 35c,
Zodiac. 45c, Praying mantis. 50c, Eye of the
hurricane. $1, Steel orchestra.

1979, Feb. 1   Litho.   Perf. 13½
296 A82   5c multicolored   .25   .25
297 A82 10c multicolored   .25   .25
298 A82 35c multicolored   .25   .25
299 A82 45c multicolored   .25   .25
300 A82 50c multicolored   .25   .25
301 A82 $1   multicolored   .25   .25
    Nos. 296-301 (6)   1.50 1.50

Day Care
Center — A83

IYC Emblem and: 10c, School lunch program. 35c, Dental care. 45c, Nursery school.
50c, Free school bus. $1, Medical care.

Unwmk.
1979, June 5   Litho.   Perf. 13
302 A83   5c multicolored   .25   .25
303 A83 10c multicolored   .25   .25
304 A83 35c multicolored   .25   .25
305 A83 45c multicolored   .25   .25
306 A83 50c multicolored   .25   .25
307 A83 $1   multicolored   .45   .45
  a. Souvenir sheet of 6, #302-307   1.50 1.50
    Nos. 302-307 (6)   1.70 1.70
International Year of the Child.

Geothermal
Exploration
A84

Designs: 35c, Hydrogeology. 45c, Petroleum exploration. 70c, Preservation of the
environment.

1979, July 3   Wmk. 373
308 A84 10c multicolored   .25   .25
309 A84 35c multicolored   .35   .35
310 A84 45c multicolored   .40   .40
311 A84 70c multicolored   .55   .55
  a. Souvenir sheet of 4, #308-311   1.90 1.90
    Nos. 308-311 (4)   1.55 1.55
4th Latin American Geological Cong., July
7-15.

Map of Tobago and Tobago No.
1 — A85

15c, Tobago #2, 7. 35c, Tobago #28, 11.
45c, Tobago #25, 4. 70c, Great Britain #28
used in Scarborough and Tobago #5. $1, Gen-
eral Post Office, Scarborough and Tobago #6.

**   Perf. 13½x14**
1979, Aug. 1   Litho.   Wmk. 373
312 A85 10c multicolored   .25   .25
313 A85 15c multicolored   .25   .25
314 A85 35c multicolored   .25   .25
315 A85 45c multicolored   .25   .25
316 A85 70c multicolored   .30 1.00
317 A85 $1   multicolored   .35 1.25
  a. Souvenir sheet of 6, #312-317   1.90 1.90
    Nos. 312-317 (6)   1.65 3.25
Centenary of Tobago's postage stamps.

Rowland Hill, Trinidad and Tobago No.
109 — A86

Hill and: 45c, Trinidad and Tobago #273. $1,
Trinidad #62, Tobago #10.

1979, Oct. 4   Perf. 13
318 A86 25c multicolored   .25   .25
319 A86 45c multicolored   .35   .35
320 A86 $1   multicolored   .55 1.00
  a. Souvenir sheet of 3, #318-320   1.75 1.75
    Nos. 318-320 (3)   1.15 1.60
Sir Rowland Hill (1795-1879), originator of
penny postage.

Poui
Tree
A87

Designs: 10c, Court House. 50c, Royal Train
locomotive. $1.50, Bacchante freighter.

**   Wmk. 373**
1980, Jan. 21   Litho.   Perf. 14½
321 A87   5c multicolored   .25   .25
322 A87 10c multicolored   .25   .25
323 A87 50c multicolored   .40   .40
324 A87 $1.50 multicolored   .95 1.50
  a. Souvenir sheet of 4, #321-324   2.25 2.25
    Nos. 321-324 (4)   1.85 2.40
Princes Town centenary.

**Nos. 262, 279, 263 Overprinted in 3
or 5 Lines "1844-1980 POPULATION
CENSUS 12th MAY 1980"**
1980, Apr. 8   Litho.   Perf. 14
325 A73   5c multicolored   .25   .25
326 A78   6c multicolored   .25   .25
327 A73 10c multicolored   .25   .25
    Nos. 325-327 (3)   .75   .75

Scarlet Ibis Hen
and Nest — A88

Scarlet Ibis: b, Nest and eggs. c, Chick in
nest. d, Male. e, Male and female.

**   Wmk. 373**
1980, May 6   Litho.   Perf. 14½
328   Strip of 5, multi   4.00 6.75
  a.-e. A88 single stamp   .70   .70

Bronze
and Silver
Medals,
1948,
1952
A89

15c, Hasely Crawford, 1976 gold medal.
70c, 1964 silver, bronze medals. $2.50, Mos-
cow '80 emblem, vert.

**   Wmk. 373**
1980, July 22   Litho.   Perf. 14
329 A89 10c shown   .25   .25
330 A89 15c multicolored   .25   .25
331 A89 70c multicolored   .30   .30
    Nos. 329-331 (3)   .80   .80

Souvenir Sheet
332 A89 $2.50 multicolored   2.25 2.25
22nd Summer Olympic Games, Moscow,
July 19-Aug. 3.

Charcoal Production — A90

Wmk. 373
1980, Sept. 8   Litho.   *Perf. 14*
333	A90	10c shown	.25	.25
334	A90	55c Logging	.25	.25
335	A90	70c Teak plantation	.35	.35
336	A90	$2.50 Watershed management	.75	.75
a.		Souvenir sheet of 4, #333-336	2.25	2.25
		Nos. 333-336 (4)	1.60	1.60

11th Commonwealth Forestry Conference.

Elizabeth Bourne, Judiciary and Isabella Tesbier, Government — A91

Decade for Women: No. 338, Beryl McBurnie, dance and culture; Audrey Jeffers, social work. No. 339, Dr. Stella Abidh, public health; Louise Horne, nutrition.

1980, Sept. 29
337	A91	$1 multicolored	.45	.55
338	A91	$1 multicolored	.45	.55
339	A91	$1 multicolored	.45	.55
		Nos. 337-339 (3)	1.35	1.65

Stadium and Netball League Emblem — A92

1980, Oct. 21
340	A92	70c multicolored	.40	.40

1979 World Netball Tournament, Port-of-Spain.

Athlete, Man in Wheelchair, IYD Emblem — A93

Wmk. 373
1981, Apr. 6   Litho.   *Perf. 14½*
341	A93	10c shown	.25	.25
342	A93	70c Amputee with crutch	.30	.50
343	A93	$1.50 Blind people	.55	1.00
344	A93	$2 IYD emblem	.55	1.25
		Nos. 341-344 (4)	1.65	3.00

International Year of the Disabled.

Marine Preservation — A94

1981, July 7   Litho.   *Perf. 13x13½*
345	A94	10c Land	.25	.25
346	A94	55c shown	.40	.40
347	A94	$3 Sky	1.50	1.50
a.		Souvenir sheet of 3, #345-347	4.00	4.00
		Nos. 345-347 (3)	2.15	2.15

World Food Day — A95

1981, Oct. 16   Litho.   *Perf. 14½x14*
348	A95	10c Produce	.25	.25
349	A95	15c Rice threshing, mill	.25	.25
350	A95	45c Bigeye	.30	.30
351	A95	55c Cow, pig, goats	.40	.40
352	A95	$1.50 Poultry	.80	.80
353	A95	$2 Smallmouth grunt	1.25	1.25
a.		Souvenir sheet of 6, #348-353	3.50	3.50
		Nos. 348-353 (6)	3.25	3.25

President Awards — A96

1981, Nov. 30   *Perf. 14*
354	A96	10c First aid	.25	.25
355	A96	70c Motor mechanics	.40	.40
356	A96	$1 Hiking	.60	.60
357	A96	$2 President giving award	1.00	1.50
		Nos. 354-357 (4)	2.25	2.75

Commonwealth Pharmaceutical Conference — A97

1982, Feb. 12   Litho.   *Perf. 14½x14*
358	A97	10c Pharmacist	.50	.50
359	A97	$1 Pluchea symphitfolia	2.00	2.00
360	A97	$2 Nopalea cochenilifera	3.50	3.50
		Nos. 358-360 (3)	6.00	6.00

Scouting Year — A98

1982, June 28   Litho.   *Perf. 14*
361	A98	15c Production	.75	.25
362	A98	55c Tolerance	1.75	.50
363	A98	$5 Discipline	6.25	7.00
		Nos. 361-363 (3)	8.75	7.75

25th Anniv. of Tourist Board — A99

Perf. 13½x14
1982, Oct. 18   Litho.   Wmk. 373
364	A99	55c Charlotteville	.35	.35
365	A99	$1 Boating	.55	.55
366	A99	$3 Fort George	1.60	2.25
		Nos. 364-366 (3)	2.50	3.15

Pa Pa Bois — A100

Designs: Various folklore characters.

1982, Nov. 8
367	A100	10c multicolored	.25	.25
368	A100	15c multicolored	.25	.25
369	A100	65c multicolored	.40	.40
370	A100	$5 multicolored	2.60	2.60
a.		Souvenir sheet of 4, #367-370	6.25	6.25
		Nos. 367-370 (4)	3.50	3.50

Canefarmers' Centenary — A101

1982, Dec. 13   Litho.   *Perf. 14*
371	A101	30c Harvest	.30	.25
372	A101	70c Loading bullock cart	.55	.75
373	A101	$1.50 Field	1.00	2.00
a.		Souvenir sheet of 3, #371-373, perf. 14½	2.25	2.25
		Nos. 371-373 (3)	1.85	3.00

20th Anniv. of Independence — A102

10c, Natl. Stadium. 35c, Caroni Arena Water Treatment Plant. 50c, Mount Hope Maternity Hospital. $2, Natl. Insurance Board Mall, Tobago.

1982, Dec. 28   *Perf. 13½x14*
374	A102	10c multicolored	.55	.55
375	A102	35c multicolored	.70	.70
376	A102	50c multicolored	1.40	1.40
377	A102	$2 multicolored	2.00	2.00
		Nos. 374-377 (4)	4.65	4.65

Commonwealth Day — A103

1983, Mar. 14   *Perf. 14*
378	A103	10c Flags	.25	.25
379	A103	55c Satellite view	.35	.35
380	A103	$1 Oil industry, vert.	.45	.60
381	A103	$2 Maps, vert.	.85	1.10
		Nos. 378-381 (4)	1.90	2.30

10th Anniv. of CARICOM — A104

1983, July 11   Litho.   *Perf. 14*
382	A104	35c Jet, map	2.00	2.00

World Communications Year — A105

15c, Operator. 55c, Scarborough PO, Tobago. $1, Textel Building. $3, Morne Bleu Receiving Station.

1983, Aug. 5   *Perf. 14½*
383	A105	15c multicolored	.25	.25
384	A105	55c multicolored	.40	.30
385	A105	$1 multicolored	.75	.75
386	A105	$3 multicolored	1.90	2.60
		Nos. 383-386 (4)	3.30	3.90

Commonwealth Finance Ministers Conference — A106

Wmk. 373
1983, Sept. 19   Litho.   *Perf. 14*
387	A106	$2 multicolored	.70	.70

World Food Day — A107

1983, Oct. 17   *Perf. 14x13½*
388	A107	10c Kingfish	.35	.35
389	A107	55c Flying fish	1.10	1.10
390	A107	70c Queen conch	1.40	1.40
391	A107	$4 Red shrimp	5.50	5.50
		Nos. 388-391 (4)	8.35	8.35

Flowers — A108

5c, Bois pois. 10c, Maraval Lily. 15c, Star grass. 20c, Bois caco. 25c, Strangling fig. 30c, Cassia moschata. 50c, Chalice flower. 65c, Black stick. 80c, Columnea scandens. 95c, Cats Claws. $1, Bois l'agli. $1.50, Eustoma exeltatum. $2, Chaconia, horiz. $2.50, Chysothemis pulchella, horiz. $5, Centratherum punctatum, horiz. $10, Savanna flower, horiz.

1983, Dec. 14   Wmk. 373   *Perf. 14*
No Year Imprint Below Design
392	A108	5c multicolored	.60	.90
b.		Imprint "1989"	.90	.25
393	A108	10c multicolored	.45	.35
b.		Imprint "1985"	.40	.25
c.		Imprint "1986"	.40	.25
d.		Imprint "1987"	.40	.25
e.		Imprint "1989"	.40	.25
394	A108	15c multicolored	.50	.30
395	A108	20c multicolored	.30	.25
396	A108	25c multicolored	1.00	1.10
397	A108	30c multicolored	.40	.25
398	A108	50c multicolored	.50	.50
399	A108	65c multicolored	.70	.90
400	A108	80c multicolored	.90	1.25
401	A108	95c multicolored	.95	1.25
402	A108	$1 multicolored	1.00	.75
403	A108	$1.50 multicolored	1.50	2.25

Size: 38½x26mm
404	A108	$2 multicolored	2.00	2.50
405	A108	$2.50 multicolored	2.00	3.00
406	A108	$5 multicolored	4.00	7.00
407	A108	$10 multicolored	8.00	9.00
		Nos. 392-407 (16)	24.80	31.55

1984, Oct.
"1984" Imprint Below Design
392a	A108	5c multicolored	3.00	4.00
393a	A108	10c multicolored	1.50	2.00
394a	A108	15c multicolored	2.50	3.00
396a	A108	25c multicolored	4.25	5.00
		Nos. 392a-396a (4)	11.25	14.00

1985-89   Wmk. 384
"1985" Imprint Below Design
392f	A108	5c multicolored	1.50	1.25
401f	A108	95c multicolored	.90	.80
402f	A108	$1 multicolored	.85	.85
406f	A108	$5 multicolored	4.00	3.25
407f	A108	$10 multicolored	9.00	6.50
		Nos. 392f-407f (5)	16.25	12.65

"1986" Imprint Below Design
393g	A108	10c multicolored	.40	.25

"1987" Imprint Below Design
393h	A108	10c multicolored	.40	.25
397h	A108	30c multicolored	.40	.25
399h	A108	65c multicolored	.80	.60
400h	A108	80c multicolored	1.20	.75
401h	A108	95c multicolored	1.50	1.00
402h	A108	$1 multicolored	1.75	.60
403h	A108	$1.50 multicolored	2.75	2.00

404h	A108	$2 multicolored	2.00	2.00
406h	A108	$5 multicolored	8.00	6.00
407h	A108	$10 multicolored	15.00	10.00
		Nos. 393h-407h (10)	33.80	23.45

"1988" Imprint Below Design

393i	A108	10c multicolored	.85	.85
395i	A108	20c multicolored	.40	.25
396i	A108	25c multicolored	.85	.85
397i	A108	30c multicolored	.40	.25
399i	A108	65c multicolored	1.10	.40
400i	A108	80c multicolored	1.60	1.75
401i	A108	95c multicolored	1.75	.95
402i	A108	$1 multicolored	10.00	
406i	A108	$5 multicolored	12.00	5.00
407i	A108	$10 multicolored	20.00	10.00
		Nos. 393i-407i (9)	38.95	19.30

"1989" Imprint Below Design

393j	A108	10c multicolored	.40	.25
395j	A108	20c multicolored	.40	.25
396j	A108	25c multicolored	.85	.85
397j	A108	30c multicolored	.85	.25
399j	A108	65c multicolored	1.60	.40
402j	A108	$1 multicolored	2.25	
403j	A108	$1.50 multicolored	3.50	1.50
404j	A108	$2 multicolored	4.75	1.90
405j	A108	$2.50 multicolored	5.50	2.50
406j	A108	$5 multicolored	12.00	6.50
407j	A108	$10 multicolored	20.00	10.00
		Nos. 393j-407j (11)	52.10	25.00

For surcharges see Nos. 906-907.

Castles on Chess Board — A109

World Chess Federationn, 60th Anniv.: Various chess pieces.

Wmk. 373

1984, Sept. 12		**Litho.**		**Perf. 14**
408	A109	50c multicolored	2.00	.75
409	A109	70c multicolored	2.75	2.75
410	A109	$1.50 multicolored	3.50	3.50
411	A109	$2 multicolored	5.75	5.75
		Nos. 408-411 (4)	14.00	12.75

1984 Summer Olympics — A110

1984, Sept. 21				**Perf. 14x14½**
412	A110	15c Swimming	.30	.30
413	A110	55c Running	.45	.45
414	A110	$1.50 Yachting	1.25	1.25
415	A110	$4 Bicycling	4.50	4.50
a.		Souvenir sheet of 4, #412-415	6.75	6.75
		Nos. 412-415 (4)	6.50	6.50

St. Mary's Children's Home, 125th Anniv. — A111

1984, Nov. 13		**Litho.**		**Perf. 13½**
416	A111	10c Children's band	.25	.25
417	A111	70c St. Mary's Home	.75	.75
418	A111	$3 Group scene	3.00	3.75
		Nos. 416-418 (3)	4.00	4.75

Christmas 1984 A112

10c, Parang Band. 30c, Musical notes, Poinsettia. $1, Bandola, Cuatro, Bandolin. $3, Fiddle, Guitar, Double Bass.

1984, Nov.		**Litho.**		**Perf. 14**
419	A112	10c multicolored		.35 .25
420	A112	30c multicolored		.70 .25
421	A112	$1 multicolored		1.75 1.00
422	A112	$3 multicolored		3.00 5.00
		Nos. 419-422 (4)		5.80 6.50

Emancipation, 150th Anniv. — A113

35c, Slave ship. 55c, Map, Slave Triangle. $1, Book by Eric Williams. $2, Toussaint L'Ouverture.

1984, Oct. 22		**Litho.**		**Perf. 13½x13**
423	A113	35c multicolored	1.00	1.00
424	A113	55c multicolored	1.50	1.50
425	A113	$1 multicolored	2.75	2.75
426	A113	$2 multicolored	3.75	3.75
a.		Souvenir sheet of 4, #423-426	9.50	9.50
		Nos. 423-426 (4)	9.00	9.00

Labor Day — A114

Labor leaders: No. 427, A.A. Cipriani and T.U.B. Butler. No. 428, A. Cola Rienzi and C.T.W.E. Worrell. No. 429, C.P. Alexander and Q. O'Connor.

Wmk. 373

1985, June 17		**Litho.**		**Perf. 14**
427	A114	55c dull rose & blk	1.75	1.75
428	A114	55c brt green & blk	1.75	1.75
429	A114	55c lt orange & blk	1.75	1.75
		Nos. 427-429 (3)	5.25	5.25

Ships A115

Wmk. 373

1985, Aug 20		**Litho.**		**Perf. 14½**
430	A115	30c Lady Nelson	.90	.30
431	A115	95c Lady Drake	1.50	1.50
432	A115	$1.50 Federal Palm	1.60	2.50
433	A115	$2 Federal Maple	3.00	3.25
		Nos. 430-433 (4)	7.00	7.55

UN Decade for Women A116

Women in the arts, public service and education: No. 434, Sybil Atteck, Marjorie Padmore. No. 435, May Cherrie, Evelyn Tracey. No. 436, Jessica Smith-Phillips, Irene Omilta McShine.

1985, Oct. 30		**Wmk. 384**		**Perf. 14**
434	A116	$1.50 multicolored	2.10	2.10
435	A116	$1.50 multicolored	2.10	2.10
436	A116	$1.50 multicolored	2.10	2.10
		Nos. 434-436 (3)	6.30	6.30

Intl. Youth Year — A117

Anniversaries and events: 10c, Natl. Cadet Force, 75th anniv. 65c, Girl Guides, 75th anniv.

1985, Nov. 27			**Perf. 14x14½**
437	A117	10c Cadet emblem	.55	.25
438	A117	65c Badges, anniv. emblem	2.25	2.25
439	A117	95c shown	2.75	2.75
		Nos. 437-439 (3)	5.55	5.25

A118

Sisters of St. Joseph de Cluny in Trinidad, 150th Anniv.: 10c, Sister Anne-Marie Javouhey, founder. 65c, St. Joseph's Convent, Port-of-Spain. 95c, Statue of Sr. Anne-Marie.

			Perf. 14x14½
1986, Mar. 19		**Litho.**		**Wmk. 384**
440	A118	10c multicolored	.25	.25
441	A118	65c multicolored	.50	1.00
442	A118	95c multicolored	.75	1.25
		Nos. 440-442 (3)	1.50	2.50

A119

10c, At the Cenotaph. 15c, Aboard HMY Britannia. 30c, With Pres. Clarke. $5, Receiving bouquet.

Wmk. 384

1986, Apr. 21		**Litho.**		**Perf. 14½**
443	A119	10c multicolored	.35	.25
444	A119	15c multicolored	.75	.30
445	A119	30c multicolored	.50	.30
446	A119	$5 multicolored	3.00	6.00
		Nos. 443-446 (4)	4.60	6.85

Queen Elizabeth II, 60th birthday.

Locomotives, AMERIPEX '86 — A120

65c, Arma tank locomotive. 95c, Canadian-built No. 22. $1.10, Tender engine. $1.50, Saddle tank.

			Perf. 14½x14
1986, May 26			**Wmk. 373**
447	A120	65c multicolored	.30	.30
448	A120	95c multicolored	.45	.45
449	A120	$1.10 multicolored	.55	1.00
450	A120	$1.50 multicolored	.75	1.50
a.		Souvenir sheet of 4, #447-450	3.00	3.00
		Nos. 447-450 (4)	2.05	3.25

Boy Scouts, 75th Anniv. A121

$1.70, Campsite. $2, Uniforms, 1911, 1986.

1986, July 21		**Wmk. 384**		**Perf. 14**
451	A121	$1.70 multicolored	1.25	1.75
452	A121	$2 multicolored	1.75	2.25

Dr. Eric Williams (1911-1981), First Prime Minister — A122

10c, Graduating college, 1935. 30c, Wearing red tie. 95c, Pro-Chancellor of UWI. $5, Williams, prime minister's residence.

Wmk. 373

1986, Sept. 25		**Litho.**		**Perf. 14**
453	A122	10c multicolored	.80	.25
454	A122	30c multicolored	1.25	.30
a.		Black tie	1.40	
455	A122	95c multicolored	2.25	1.00
456	A122	$5 multicolored	4.00	7.00
a.		Souvenir sheet of 4, #453-456	8.50	8.50
		Nos. 453-456 (4)	8.30	8.55
		Nos. 453-454 vert.		

Intl. Peace Year A123

1986, Oct. 30				**Wmk. 384**
457	A123	95c shown	.60	.50
458	A123	$3 Dove	1.50	2.50

Giselle LaRonde, Miss World 1986 — A124

10c, Wearing folk costume. 30c, Bathing suit. 95c, Crown. $1.65, Crown and sash.

Wmk. 384

1987, July 27		**Litho.**		**Perf. 14**
459	A124	10c multi	1.10	.30
460	A124	30c multi	1.75	.50
461	A124	95c multi	3.50	2.00
462	A124	$1.65 multi	4.50	7.00
		Nos. 459-462 (4)	10.85	9.80

Republic Bank, 150th Anniv. A125

Designs: 10c, Colonial Bank, Port of Spain. 65c, Cocoa plantation. 95c, Oil fields. $1.10, Tramcar, Belmont Tramway Co.

Wmk. 373

1987, Dec. 21		**Litho.**		**Perf. 14**
463	A125	10c buff, red brn & blk	.35	.35
464	A125	65c buff, red brn & blk	.70	.70
465	A125	95c buff, red brn & blk	2.50	2.50
466	A125	$1.10 buff, red brn & blk	2.75	2.75
		Nos. 463-466 (4)	6.30	6.30

Defense Force, 25th Anniv. — A126

Various army, coast guard and navy uniforms: 10c, Army. 30c, Army (women). $1.10, Navy, army, coast guard. $1.50, Navy.

Wmk. 384

1988, Feb. 29   Litho.   Perf. 14
467	A126	10c multicolored	1.25	.30
468	A126	30c multicolored	2.75	.50
469	A126	$1.10 multicolored	3.75	3.75
470	A126	$1.50 multicolored	5.00	5.00
		Nos. 467-470 (4)	12.75	9.55

Cricket
A127

Bat, wicket posts, ball, 18th cent. belt buckle and batters: 30c, George John. 65c, Learie Constantine. 95c, Sonny Ramadhin. $1.50, Gerry Gomez. $2.50, Jeffrey Stollmeyer.

Wmk. 373

1988, June 6   Litho.   Perf. 14
471	A127	30c multicolored	2.00	.50
472	A127	65c multicolored	2.75	1.00
473	A127	95c multicolored	3.25	1.75
474	A127	$1.50 multicolored	3.75	3.75
475	A127	$2.50 multicolored	4.75	6.00
		Nos. 471-475 (5)	16.50	13.00

Oilfield Workers' Trade Union, 50th Anniv. — A128

50, Star, oil well and: 10c, Uriah Buzz Butler, labor leader. 30c, Adrian C. Rienzi, pres. from 1937-42. 65c, John Rojas, pres. from 1943-62. $5, George Weekes, pres. from 1962-87.

Wmk. 384

1988, July 11   Litho.   Perf. 14½
476	A128	10c multicolored	.25	.25
477	A128	30c multicolored	.25	.25
478	A128	65c multicolored	.40	.40
479	A128	$5 multicolored	2.60	2.60
		Nos. 476-479 (4)	3.50	3.50

Borough of Arima, Cent.
A129

20c, Mary Werges, Santa Rosa Church. 30c, Gov. W. Robinson, royal charter. $1.10, Mayor C.P. Lopez greeting Gov. Robinson at train station. $1.50, Mayor J.F. Wallen, centennial emblem.

Wmk. 384

1988, Aug. 22   Litho.   Perf. 14½
480	A129	20c multicolored	.35	.35
481	A129	30c multicolored	.35	.35
482	A129	$1.10 multicolored	1.60	1.60
483	A129	$1.50 multicolored	1.60	1.60
		Nos. 480-483 (4)	3.90	3.90

Lloyds of London, 300th Anniv.
Common Design Type

Designs: 30c, Queen Mother at the "Topping Out" ceremony of new Lloyds's building, 1984. $1.10, BWIA Tristar 500, horiz. $1.55, ISCOTT iron and steel mill, horiz. $2, *Atlantic Empress* on fire off Tobago.

1988, Nov. 21   Litho.   Perf. 14
484	CD341	30c multicolored	1.25	.35
485	CD341	$1.10 multicolored	2.75	1.00
486	CD341	$1.55 multicolored	1.75	2.00
487	CD341	$2 multicolored	4.50	3.00
		Nos. 484-487 (4)	10.25	6.35

Unification of the Islands, Cent. — A130

Torch and: 40c, Natl. arms, 1889, and 1p Type A1. $1, Badge from Tobago flag and Tobago No. 31. $1.50, Badge from Trinidad flag and Trinidad No. 71. $2.25, Natl. arms, 1989, and No. 274.

Wmk. 384

1989, Mar. 20   Litho.   Perf. 14½
488	A130	40c multicolored	1.75	.25
489	A130	$1 multicolored	3.00	1.00
490	A130	$1.50 multicolored	3.25	3.50
491	A130	$2.25 multicolored	3.75	7.00
		Nos. 488-491 (4)	11.75	11.75

Rare Species
A131

Designs: a, Pipile pipile. b, Phyllodytes auratus. c, Cebus albifrons trinitatis. d, Tamandua tetradactyla. e, Lutra longicaudis. Printed in a continuous design.

Perf. 14x14½

1989, July 31   Wmk. 373
492		Strip of 5	20.00	20.00
	a.-e.	A131 $1 any single	2.50	2.50

A132

10c, Men using walking sticks. 40c, City Hall. $1, Guides and leader. $2.25, Volunteers, anniv. emblem.

1989, Oct. 2   Perf. 14½
493	A132	10c multi	1.50	.35
494	A132	40c multi	.50	.25
495	A132	$1 multi	0.00	.75
496	A132	$2.25 multi	4.25	3.00
		Nos. 493-496 (4)	9.25	4.35

Blind Welfare, 75th anniv. (10c), Port-of-Spain City Hall, 75th anniv. (40c), Girl Guides, 75th anniv. ($1), and Red Cross, 50th anniv. ($2.25).

A133

Drum instruments played in a steel band.

Perf. 14½x14

1989, Nov. 30   Wmk. 384
497	A133	10c Tenor	.35	.35
498	A133	40c Guitar	.40	.40
499	A133	$1 Cello	.75	.75
500	A133	$2.25 Bass	1.50	1.50
		Nos. 497-500 (4)	3.00	3.00

Mushrooms
A134

10c, Xeromphalina tenuipes. 40c, Dictyophora indusiata. $1, Leucocoprinus birnbaumii. $2.25, Crinipellis perniciosa.

1990, May 3   Perf. 14x13½
501	A134	10c multicolored	.45	.45
502	A134	40c multicolored	.70	.70
503	A134	$1 multicolored	1.50	1.50
504	A134	$2.25 multicolored	3.00	3.00
		Nos. 501-504 (4)	5.65	5.65

Stamp World London '90.

Scarlet Ibis
A135

1990, Sept. 7   Perf. 14
505	A135	40c Immature bird	1.75	1.75
506	A135	80c Mating display	2.00	2.00
507	A135	$1 Adult male	2.50	2.50
508	A135	$2.25 Adult, egg & young	4.25	4.25
		Nos. 505-508 (4)	10.50	10.50

World Wildlife Fund.

Yellow Oriole — A136

No. 510, Green rumped parrotlet. No. 511, Fork-tailed flycatcher. No. 512, Copper rumped hummingbird. No. 513, Bananaquit. No. 514, Semp. No. 515, Channel-billed toucan. No. 516, Bay headed tanager. No. 517, Green honeycreeper. No. 518, Cattle egret. No. 519, Golden olive woodpecker. No. 520, Peregrine falcon.

1990, Dec. 17   Litho.   Wmk. 384
509	A136	20c shown	1.00	.50
510	A136	25c multicolored	1.25	.30
511	A136	40c multicolored	1.40	.25
512	A136	50c multicolored	1.50	.50
513	A136	$1 multicolored	1.60	.50
514	A136	$2 multicolored	2.50	1.50
515	A136	$2.25 multicolored	2.50	2.00
516	A136	$2.50 multicolored	2.00	1.25
517	A136	$5 multicolored	3.50	3.25
518	A136	$10 multicolored	4.25	3.50
519	A136	$20 multicolored	6.00	7.00
520	A136	$50 multicolored	12.00	17.50
		Nos. 509-520 (12)	39.50	38.05

1994-98   Wmk. 373
510a	A136	25c	2.60	.40
512a	A136	50c	.55	.35
513a	A136	$1	3.25	.65
514a	A136	$2	4.00	1.75
516a	A136	$2.50	3.00	2.50
517a	A136	$5	3.75	2.75
	b.	Souvenir sheet of 1, wmk. 373, dated "1997"	4.75	4.75
518a	A136	$10	4.00	5.00
519a	A136	$20	7.00	10.00

Issued: #510a, 8/94; #512a, 4/95; #513a, 514a, 3/3/97; #516a, 518a, 519a, 10/14/98; #517a, 6/1996.
#510a, 512a, 513a, 514a, 516a, 517a, 518a, 519a are dated 1990. No. 517b issued 2/3/97 for Hong Kong '97.
For overprints & surcharges see Nos. 565-568, 597A, 609, 888A, 889, 897, 898, 919, 936, 949.
Two additional items were issued in this set. The editors would like to examine any examples of them.

University of the West Indies
A137

Chancellors and Campus Buildings: 40c, HRH Princess Alice, Administration Building. 80c, Sir Hugh Wooding, Main Library. $1, Sir Allen Lewis, Faculty of Engineering. $2.25, Sir Shridath Ramphal, Faculty of Medical Studies.

Perf. 13½x14

1990, Oct. 15   Litho.   Wmk. 373
521	A137	40c multicolored	.75	.25
522	A137	80c multicolored	1.00	1.00
523	A137	$1 multicolored	1.50	1.25
524	A137	$2.25 multicolored	3.75	4.50
		Nos. 521-524 (4)	7.00	7.00

British West Indies Airways, 50th Anniv.
A138

Airplanes: 40c, Lockheed Lodestar. 80c, Vickers Viking 1A. $1, Vickers Viscount 702. $2.25, Boeing 707. $5, Lockheed TriStar 500.

1990, Nov. 27   Perf. 14
525	A138	40c multicolored	1.75	.50
526	A138	80c multicolored	2.25	1.00
527	A138	$1 multicolored	2.50	1.25
528	A138	$2.25 multicolored	4.25	5.50
		Nos. 525-528 (4)	10.75	8.25

Souvenir Sheet
529	A138	$5 multicolored	7.00	7.00

Ferns
A139

40c, Lygodium volubile. 80c, Blechnum occidentale. $1, Gleichenia bifida. $2.25, Polypodium lycopodiodes.

1991, July 1   Perf. 13½
530	A139	40c multicolored	.50	.50
531	A139	80c multicolored	1.00	1.00
532	A139	$1 multicolored	1.25	1.25
533	A139	$2.25 multicolored	2.75	2.75
		Nos. 530-533 (4)	5.50	5.50

Trinidad & Tobago in World War II — A140

Designs: 40c, Firing practice by Trinidad & Tobago regiment. 80c, Fairey Barracuda surprises U-boat. $1, Avro Lancaster returns from bombing raid. $2.25, River class frigate on convoy duty. No. 538a, Supermarine Spitfire. b, Vickers Wellington.

Perf. 13½x14

1991, Dec. 7   Litho.   Wmk. 384
534	A140	40c multicolored	1.75	.40
535	A140	80c multicolored	2.50	1.10
536	A140	$1 multicolored	3.25	1.25
537	A140	$2.25 multicolored	5.00	6.50
		Nos. 534-537 (4)	12.50	9.25

Souvenir Sheet of 2
538	A140	$2.50 #a.-b.	19.50	19.50

H. E.
Rapsey — A141

Inca Clathrata
Quesneli — A142

Holy Name
Convent — A143

1992, Mar. 30   Wmk. 373   Perf. 14
539	A141	40c multicolored	.50	.25
540	A142	80c multicolored	1.25	1.25
541	A143	$1 multicolored	1.75	1.75
		Nos. 539-541 (3)	3.50	3.25

#539, Building and Loan Assoc., cent. #540, Trinidad & Tobago Field Naturalists' Club. #541, Holy Name Convent, cent.

Religions of
Trinidad and
Tobago — A145

No. 544, Baptist, baptism by immersion. No. 545, Muslim, minaret. No. 546, Hindu, Brahman..the source of all. No. 547, Christianity, cross. No. 548, Baha'i, slogan.

1992, Apr. 21   Litho.   Perf. 14
544	A145	40c multicolored	1.40	1.60
545	A145	40c multicolored	1.40	1.60
546	A145	40c multicolored	1.40	1.60
547	A145	40c multicolored	1.40	1.60
548	A145	40c multicolored	1.40	1.60
		Nos. 544-548 (5)	7.00	8.00

BWIA
Aircraft
A146

Wmk. 373
1992, Aug. 6   Litho.   Perf. 14
549	A146	$2.25 MD83	3.50	3.50
550	A146	$2.25 L1011	3.50	3.50

Natl.
Museum
and Art
Gallery,
Cent.
A147

Wmk. 384
1992, Dec. 7   Litho.   Perf. 14½
551	A147	$1 multicolored	.60	.60

Christmas — A148

1992, Dec. 21
552	A148	40c multicolored	.45	.45

Trinidad Guardian, 75th Anniv. — A149

1992, Dec. 23
553	A149	40c multicolored	.45	.45

Philatelic Society of Trinidad &
Tobago, 50th Anniv.
A150

1992, Dec. 30
554	A150	$2.25 multicolored	1.40	1.40

CARICOM (Caribbean Economic
Community), 20th Anniv. — A151

Map of CARICOM nations, portraits of West Indian men: 50c, $1.50, $2.75, $3, Derek Walcott, Sir Shridath Ramphal, William Demas.
$6, Order of the Caribbean Community.

Perf. 13x13½
1994, Jan. 31   Litho.   Wmk. 373
555	A151	50c pink & multi	.40	.25
556	A151	$1.50 green & multi	.70	.70
557	A151	$2.75 gray & multi	1.10	1.10
558	A151	$3 violet & multi	1.25	1.25
		Nos. 555-558 (4)	3.45	3.30

Souvenir Sheet
Perf. 13½x13
559	A151	$6 multicolored	4.25	4.25

No. 559 contains one 34x56mm stamp.

Drum Instruments Played in a Steel
Band — A152

1994, Feb. 11   Perf. 14x15
560	A152	50c Quadrophonic pan	.45	.30
561	A152	$1 Tenor base pan	.80	.50
562	A152	$2.25 Six pan	1.50	2.00
563	A152	$2.50 Rocket pan	1.75	2.25
		Nos. 560-563 (4)	4.50	5.05

Aldwyn Roberts
Kitchener,
Calypso
Singer — A153

1994, Feb. 11   Perf. 14
564	A153	50c multicolored	2.60	1.00

**Nos. 510-511, 514, 518 Ovptd. with
Hong Kong '94 Exhibition Emblem**
Wmk. 384
1994, Feb. 18   Litho.   Perf. 14
565	A136	25c multicolored	.45	.30
566	A136	40c multicolored	.50	.30
567	A136	$2 multicolored	1.50	1.25
568	A136	$10 multicolored	5.50	6.25
		Nos. 565-568 (4)	7.95	8.10

Hotels &
Lodges
A154

#569, Trinidad Hilton. #570, Sandy Point Village, Tobago. #571, Asa Wright Nature Center and Lodge. #572, ML's Bed and Breakfast.

Wmk. 373
1994, Aug. 10   Litho.   Perf. 14
569	A154	$3 multicolored	1.20	1.40
570	A154	$3 multicolored	1.20	1.40
571	A154	$3 multicolored	1.20	1.40
572	A154	$3 multicolored	1.20	1.40
		Nos. 569-572 (4)	4.80	5.60

Snakes
A155

50c, Boa constrictor. $1.25, Horse whip or vine snake. $2.50, Bushmaster. $3, Large coral snake.

Wmk. 373
1994, Sept. 19   Litho.   Perf. 14
573	A155	50c multicolored	.45	.30
574	A155	$1.25 multicolored	.90	.75
575	A155	$2.50 multicolored	1.60	1.75
576	A155	$3 multicolored	1.75	2.25
		Nos. 573-576 (4)	4.70	5.05

Trinidad Art
Society, 50th
Anniv. — A156

Artworks: No. 577, Copper sculpture, by Ken Morris. No. 578, Fisherman, by Sybil Atteck. No. 579, Snowballman, by Mahmoud P. Alladin.

1995, Mar. 6   Wmk. 384
577	A156	50c multicolored	.70	.90
578	A156	50c multicolored	.70	.90
579	A156	50c multicolored	.70	.90
		Nos. 577-579 (3)	2.10	2.70

Conservation — A157

Designs: $1.25, Leatherback turtle. $2.50, POS Lighthouse, vert. $3, "Knowsley" Ministry of Foreign Affairs.

1995, Aug. 7
580	A157	$1.25 multicolored	.75	.75
581	A157	$2.50 multicolored	1.75	1.75
582	A157	$3 multicolored	1.50	1.50
		Nos. 580-582 (3)	4.00	4.00

Brian Lara, Cricket
Hero — A158

Designs: $1.25, Batting. $2.50, In batting stance. $3, Batting, diff.
No. 587: a, $3.75, With arms raised at crowd. b, $5.01, Down on one knee with bat.

Perf. 13x13½
1996, May 15   Litho.   Wmk. 373
583	A158	50c multicolored	.40	.40
584	A158	$1.25 multicolored	.75	.75
585	A158	$2.50 multicolored	1.40	1.40
586	A158	$3 multicolored	1.75	1.75
		Nos. 583-586 (4)	4.30	4.30

Souvenir Sheet
587	A158	Sheet of 2, #a.-b.	8.75	8.75

Trinidad & Tobago Remembers World
War II — A159

50c, Red Cross Economy Label. $1.25, Battleship USS Missouri. $2.50, US servicemen playing baseball, Queen's Park, Savannah, 1942. $3, Fulmar 1, Royal Naval Air Station.
No. 592: a, Grumman Goose seaplane. b, US Navy Airship.

Wmk. 373
1996, June 7   Litho.   Perf. 14
588	A159	50c multicolored	.60	.30
589	A159	$1.25 multicolored	1.50	.75
590	A159	$2.50 multicolored	1.75	1.75
591	A159	$3 multicolored	2.50	2.50
		Nos. 588-591 (4)	6.35	5.30

Souvenir Sheet of 2
592	A159	$3 #a.-b.	9.25	9.25

A160

Wendy Fitzwilliam, 1998 Miss Universe: $1.25, Lying on beach. $2.50, In traditional costume. $3, Wearing evening gown.
$5, After coronation.

1999, May 3   Litho.   Perf. 14
593	A160	50c multicolored	.75	.75
594	A160	$1.25 multicolored	1.50	1.50
595	A160	$2.50 multicolored	2.25	2.25
596	A160	$3 multicolored	2.75	2.75
		Nos. 593-596 (4)	7.25	7.25

Souvenir Sheet
597	A160	$5 multicolored	7.50	7.50

No. 511
Surcharged

Method and Perf. as Before
1999, May 24
597A A136 75c on 40c multi   *13.00 3.00*

A161

Angostura Bitters, 175th Anniv.: 75c,
Angostura Bitters bottle. $3, Distillery. $4.50,
Bitters bottle, cocktails.

Self-Adhesive
Serpentine Die Cut
2000, Jan. 27   **Litho.**
598 A161   75c multi   .50   .50
599 A161 $3 multi   2.00   2.00
600 A161 $4.50 multi   0.25   2.25
a.   Souvenir sheet, #598-600   5.25   5.25
       Nos. 598-600 (3)   5.75   4.75

Tourism
A162

Shoreline scenes: 75c, Maracas Bay. $1,
Pirates Bay. $3.75, Pigeon Point. $5, Toco,
North Coast.

2000, July 25 Litho. Perf. 14¼x14½
601 A162   75c multi   1.00   .30
602 A162 $1 multi   1.25   .40
603 A162 $3.75 multi   2.50   2.50
604 A162 $5 multi   3.25   3.25
       Nos. 601-604 (4)   8.00   6.45

For surcharge, see No. 890.

Christmas
A163

Design: 75c, Caroni landscape. $3.75, Pas-
telles, sorrel and ginger beer. $4.50, Musi-
cians under palm trees. $5.25, Angels with
steel drums.

Perf. 14¼x14½
2000, Nov. 14   **Litho.**
605 A163   75c multi   .75   .30
606 A163 $3.75 multi   2.25   1.75
607 A163 $4.50 multi   2.50   2.50
608 A163 $5.25 multi   3.25   3.25
       Nos. 605-608 (4)   8.75   7.80

For surcharge, see No. 923.

No. 515
Surcharged

Method and Perf. as Before
2001, Jan. 26
609 A136 75c on $2.25 multi   *13.00 5.00*

National
Mail Center
A164

Designs: $3, Building entrance. $10, Side of
building.

Perf. 14¼x14½
2000, Nov. 20   **Litho.**
610-611 A164   Set of 2   6.75   6.75

Endangered
Fauna
A165

Designs: 25c, Paca, 50c, Prehensile-tailed
porcupine. 75c, Iguana. $1, Leatherback tur-
tle. $2, Golden tegu. $2, Red howler monkey.
$4, Weeping capuchin monkey, vert. $5, River
otter. $10, Ocelot. $20, Trinidad piping guan,
vert.

Perf. 14¼x14½, 14½x14¼
2001, Feb. 6   **Litho.**
612 A165   25c multi   .60   .30
613 A165   50c multi   1.00   .40
614 A165   75c multi   1.25   .45
615 A165 $1 multi   1.50   .50
616 A165 $2 multi   2.00   1.00
617 A165 $3 multi   2.50   1.25
618 A165 $4 multi   2.50   1.50
619 A165 $5 multi   2.75   1.75
620 A165 $10 multi   5.75   5.75
621 A165 $20 multi   15.00 15.00
       Nos. 612-621 (10)   34.85 27.90

For surcharge, see No. 932.

Salvation Army in
Trinidad & Tobago,
Cent. — A166

Designs: 75c, Emblem. $2, William Booth
Memorial Hall.

2001, Aug. 9   Perf. 14½x14¼
622-623 A166   Set of 2   2.50   2.50
623a   Souvenir sheet, #622-623,
         perf. 13¾x14¼   2.50   2.50

For surcharge, see No. 916.

Natl. Library,
150th Anniv.
A167

Designs: 75c, Port of Spain Public Library,
Carnegie Free Library. $3.25, New National
Library building.

2001, Aug. 9   Perf. 14¼x14½
624-625 A167   Set of 2   3.50   3.50
625a   Souvenir sheet #624-625   3.50   3.50

For surcharge, see No. 917.

Under 17 World Soccer
Championships — A168

Designs: $2, Emblem of Soca Warriors.
$3.25, National flag. $4.50, Lion holding flag.
$5.25, Stadiums.

2001, Sept. 6   Perf. 14½x14
626-629 A168   Set of 4   8.25   8.25
629a   Souvenir sheet, #626-629   8.25   8.25

For surcharge, see No. 934.

Flowers — A169

Designs: $1, Pachystachys coccinea. $2.50,
Heliconia psittacorum. $3.25, Brownea
latifolia, horiz. $3.75, Oncidium papilio,

Perf. 14½x14¼, 14¼x14½
2001, Nov. 1
630-633 A169   Set of 4   8.00   8.00

Christmas — A170

People and: $1, Boats, church. $3.75, Flowers. $4.50, House, flowers. $5.25, Church,
post office.

2001, Nov. 15   Perf. 14½x14¼
634-637 A170   Set of 4   8.00   0.00
637a   Souvenir sheet #634-637   8.25   8.25

For surcharge, see No. 924.

Butterflies
A171

Designs: $1, Cracker. $3.75, Tiger. $4.50,
Four continent. $5.25, "89."

2002, June 19 Litho. Perf. 13¼x13
638-641 A171   Set of 4   11.00 11.00

For surcharges, see Nos. 920-922.

Hummingbirds
A172

Designs: $1, Rufous-breasted hermit.
$2.50, Black-throated mango. $3.25, Tufted
coquette. $3.75, White-chested emerald,

2002, Apr. 17   Perf. 13x13¼
642-645 A172   Set of 4   9.00   9.00

For surcharges, see Nos. 918, 928.

Historic
Forts
A173

Designs: $1, Fort Picton. $3.75, Fort
George. $4.50, Fort King George. $5.25, Fort
James.

2002, July 31   Perf. 13¼x13
646-649 A173   Set of 4   10.50 10.50
649a   Souvenir sheet #646-649 10.50 10.50

For surcharges, see Nos. 913-915.

Reign of
Queen
Elizabeth II,
50th Anniv.
A174

Queen: $3.75, At Governor General's
House. $4.50, With Mayor E. Taylor of Port of
Spain. $5.25, At Red House, addressing Par-
liament, #119, and former personal flag of the
Queen.
$10, In limousine, waving to crowd.

2002, Sept. 23 Litho.   Perf. 13¾
650-652 A174   Set of 3   7.50   7.50
Souvenir Sheet
653 A174 $10 multi   10.00 10.00

Independence, 40th Anniv. — A175

2002, Sept. 23
654 A175 $1 multi   1.25   1.25

Christmas
A176

Designs: $1, Child opening gift of steel
drum, vert. $2.50, People, musicians, house.
$3.75, Houses. $5.25, Santa Claus on horse-
drawn cart, vert.

Perf. 14½x14¼, 14¼x14½
2002, Nov. 20   **Litho.**
655-658 A176   Set of 4   8.50   8.50

For surcharges, see Nos. 925-926.

Pan-American Health Organization, Cent. — A177

Designs: $1, Emblem. $2.50, National headquarters, Port of Spain. $3.25, Steel drum with symbols. $4.50, Joseph L. Pawan (1887-1957), discoverer of vampire bat rabies.

2002, Dec. 2   **Perf. 14½x14¼**
659-662 A177   Set of 4   8.00 8.00

Cricket Players — A178

Designs: $1, Ian Raphael Bishop. $2.50, Deryck Lance Murray. $4.50, Augustine Lawrence Logie. $5.25, Ann Browne John.

2003, Feb. 7   **Perf. 13**
663-666 A178   Set of 4   10.00 10.00
For surcharge, see No. 933.

Carnival A179

Various costumed participants: $1, $2.50, $3.75, vert., $4.50, vert., $5.25, vert.

Perf. 14¼x14½, 14½x14¼
2003, Feb. 25   **Litho.**
667-671 A179   Set of 5   8.50 8.50
671a   Souvenir sheet of 1   4.25 4.25
For surcharge, see No. 930.

Inauguration of Intl. Criminal Court — A180

Designs: $1, Trinidad & Tobago Pres. Arthur N. R. Robinson and UN Secretary General Kofi Annan. $2.50, Robinson, Prof. Benjamin Ferencz, Prof. Cherif Bassiouni, Philippe Kirsch, UN Undersecretary for Legal Affairs Hans Corell. $3.75, Robinson and Corell. $4.50, Robinson, Emma Bonino, and Italian Pres. Carlo Ciampi.
$6, Robinson, vert.

Perf. 14¾x14½, 14½x14¾
2003, Feb. 25
672-675 A180   Set of 4   8.00 8.00
Souvenir Sheet
676 A180 $6 multi   4.75 4.75

Rainforest Flora & Fauna — A181

No. 677: a, Mountain immortelle. b, Blue-crowned motmot. c, Red howler monkey. d, Butterfly orchid. e, Channel-billed toucan. f, Ocelot. g, Bromeliads. h, Lineated woodpecker. i, Tamandua. j, Emperor butterfly.

Serpentine Die Cut 12½
2003, Feb. 24   **Litho.**
Self-Adhesive
677   Booklet pane of 10   12.00 —
   a.-j.   A181 $1 Any single   .85 .85

Lighthouses A182

Designs: $1, Port-of-Spain. $3.75, Chacachacare. $4.50, Port-of-Spain, diff. $5.25, Chacacachacare, diff.
No. 681B, Like No. 679, spelled "Chacacharie." No. 681C, Like No. 681, spelled "Chacacharie."

2002-03   **Perf. 14½x14¼**
678-681 A182   Set of 4   11.50 11.50
681a   Souvenir sheet, #678-681   11.50 11.50
681B A182 $3.75 multi
681C A182 $5.25 multi
Nos. 678, 680, 681B and 681C were issued on 11/6/02 and all were withdrawn from sale later that day when the incorrect spelling of the lighthouse was discovered. Nos. 678 and 680 were put back on sale, along with new stamps with the corrected spelling of the lighthouse, Nos. 679 and 681, and the souvenir sheet with the stamps with the corrected spelling, No. 681a, on 5/26/03. The editors would like to examine any examples of the souvenir sheet with stamps with the incorrect spelling.

Scenes of Village Life — A183

Designs: $1, Dancing the cocoa. $2.50, Dirt oven. $3.75, River washing. $4.50, Box cart racing. $5.25, Pitching marbles.

2003, Oct. 28
682-686 A183   Set of 5   8.50 8.50
For surcharge, see No. 931.

Marine Life — A184

Designs: $1, Boulder brain coral. $2.50, Hawksbill turtle. $3.75, Green moray eel. $4.50, Creole wrasse. $5.25, Black-spotted sea goddess.
$10, Queen angelfish.

2003, Oct. 28   **Perf. 14¼x14½**
687-691 A184   Set of 5   10.00 10.00
Souvenir Sheet
692 A184 $10 multi   10.00 10.00

Christmas — A185

Paintings by Jean Michel Cazabon (1813-88): $1, View of Port-of-Spain from Laventille Hill. $2.50, View of Diego Martin from Fort George. $3.75, Corbeaux Town, Trinidad. $4.50, Rain Clouds over Cedros. $5.25, Los Galos, Icacos Bay.
No. 698: a, $5, River at St. Ann's. b, $6.50, House in Trinidad.

2003, Nov. 17   **Perf. 13¾**
693-697 A185   Set of 5   9.50 9.50
698 A185   Sheet of 2, #a-b   9.50 9.50

World AIDS Day — A186

Designs: $1, Unite against AIDS. $2.50, Stigma isolates. $3.75, Care stops AIDS, vert. $4.50, Family protects, vert.
$10, People and AIDS ribbon.

2003, Nov. 21
699-702 A186   Set of 4   7.50 7.50
Souvenir Sheet
703 A186 $10 multi   7.25 7.25

2004 Carnival — A187

Calypso musicians: $1, Aldric Farrel, "The Lord Pretender." $2.50, Roy Lewis, "The Mystic Prowler." $3.75, Lord Kitchener, The Mighty Sparrow and The Roaring Lion. $4.50, McArthur Linda Sandy-Rose, "Calypso Rose." $5.25, Nap Hepburne, Lord Brynner and The Mighty Sparrow.
$10, McArthur Linda Sandy-Rose, diff.

2004, Feb. 18
704-708 A187   Set of 5   7.50 7.50
Souvenir Sheet
709 A187 $10 multi   7.00 7.00

2004 Summer Olympics, Athens — A188

Designs: $1, Track and field. $2.50, Boxing. $3.75, Taekwondo. $4.50, Swimming.

2004, July 19   **Litho.**   **Perf. 13**
710-713 A188   Set of 4   7.00 7.00

Intl. Year Commemorating the Struggle Against Slavery and Its Abolition — A189

Designs: $1, Slave ship. $2.50, Rada community, Belmont. $3.75, Daaga, Prince of Popo. $4.50, Slaves singing freedom songs, horiz. $5.25, Providence Estate Aqueduct, Tobago, horiz.
$15, Sandy's escape, horiz.

2004, Sept. 23   **Litho.**   **Perf. 13**
714-718 A189   Set of 5   8.00 8.00
Souvenir Sheet
719 A189 $15 multi   6.50 6.50

Christmas A190

Paintings by Arthur Aldwin "Boscoe" Holder: $1, Lady with Ginger Lilies. $2.50, View from Maracas Lookout. $3.75, Lady in Peacock Chair. $4.50, Caribbean Beauty in White, horiz. $5.25, Teteron Bay, Chaguaramas, horiz.
$10, Creole Ladies in Straw Hats, horiz.

2004, Nov. 22
720-724 A190   Set of 5   7.75 7.75
Souvenir Sheet
725 A190 $10 multi   5.25 5.25

Fruits — A191

Designs: $1, Mango. $2.50, Lime. $3.75, Pineapple. $4.50, Coconut, horiz. $5.25, Orange, horiz.
$10, Guava, horiz.

2004, June 7
726-730 A191   Set of 5   8.00 8.00
Souvenir Sheet
731 A191 $10 multi   6.50 6.50

Carnival — A192

Designs: $1, Dame Lorraine. $2.50, Jab Jab. $3.25, Burrokeet, horiz. $3.75, Midnight Robber. $4.50, Fancy Indian.
$15, Fancy Sailor.

2005, Jan. 18   **Litho.**   **Perf. 13**
732-736 A192   Set of 5   7.25 7.25
Souvenir Sheet
737 A192 $15 multi   7.50 7.50

Brian Lara, Cricket Player — A193

Various photos of Lara in action: $1, $2.50, $3.75, $4.50, $5.25.
$15, Lara walking under raised cricket bats.

2005, Apr. 12   **Litho.**   **Perf. 13**
738-742 A193   Set of 5   11.00 11.00
Souvenir Sheet
743 A193 $15 multi   11.00 11.00

Tobago Heritage Festival — A194

Designs: $1, Belé. $2.50, Dancing the jig. $3.75, Goat race, horiz. $4.50, Harvest Festival, horiz. $5.25, Drumming Festival, horiz. $15, Traditional Tobago wedding.

Perf. 13½x13¼, 13¼x13½

2005, Aug. 15

744-748 A194   Set of 5   7.50 7.50

Souvenir Sheet

Perf. 13¼

749 A194 $15 multi   7.50 7.50

Medicinal Herbs A195

Designs: 25c, Rachet. 50c, Chandelier. 75c, Worm grass. $1, Black sage. $3, Wonder of the world. $3.25, Vervine. $4, Aloe vera. $5, Senna. $10, Bois bande. $20, Herbal garden.

2005, May 18   **Perf. 13¼x13**

750	A195	25c multi	.40	.25
751	A195	50c multi	.75	.35
752	A195	75c multi	.90	.40
753	A195	$1 multi	1.00	.40
754	A195	$3 multi	1.50	1.25
755	A195	$3.25 multi	2.00	1.50
756	A195	$4 multi	2.25	1.75
757	A195	$5 multi	2.25	2.25
758	A195	$10 multi	3.50	3.50
759	A195	$20 multi	7.00	10.00
	Nos. 750-759 (10)		21.55	21.65

For surcharges see Nos. 905, 935.

Fish and Marine Life — A196

No. 760: a, Foureye butterfly fish. b, Caribbean reef squid. c, Hawksbill turtle. d, Southern sting ray. e, Queen angelfish. f, Giant anemone. g, Peppermint shrimp. h, Rough file clam. i, White-speckled hermit crab. j, Christmas tree worm.

Serpentine Die Cut 12½

2005, May 1   **Self-Adhesive**   **Litho.**

760   Booklet of 10   11.00

a.-j. A196 $1 Any single   .75 .75

Sir Solomon Hochoy (1905-83), First Governor-General — A197

Hochoy and: $1, Prime Minister Dr. Eric E. Williams. $2.50, Haile Selassie. $3.75, His wife, Thelma. $4.50, Queen Elizabeth II. $5.25, Honor Guard. $15, Hochoy in uniform.

2005, Aug. 22   **Perf. 13½x13**

761-765 A197   Set of 5   8.50 8.50

Souvenir Sheet

Perf. 13½x13¼

766 A197 $15 multi   8.50 8.50

For surcharge, see No. 891.

Introduction of Women Police, 50th Anniv. — A198

2005, Sept. 30   **Perf. 12¾**

767 A198 $15 black   8.75 8.75

Souvenir Sheet

Children Against Cancer — A199

2005, Nov. 7   **Perf. 13½x13¼**

768 A199 $15 multi   8.50 8.50

No. 768 sold for $20.

Anansi and the Cricket Match — A200

Anansi: $1, And friends reading cricket brochure. $2.50, And friends hiding in bathroom. $0.75, And friends under umbrella. $4.50, Holding bag, talking to woman. $5.25, Laughing at friends paying woman. $15, Anansi rubbing stomach.

2005, Dec. 12   **Perf. 13½x13**

769-773 A200   Set of 5   7.75 7.75

Souvenir Sheet

774 A200 $15 multi   7.50 7.50

Pope John Paul II (1920-2005) A201

Scenes from Pope's 1985 visit to Trinidad & Tobago: $1, Leaving airplane. $2.50, Kissing ground. $3.75, Shaking hands with priest. $4.50, With bishop, waving. $5.25, Celebrating mass. $15, Waving to crowd from police vehicle.

2006, Apr. 10   **Litho.**   **Perf. 13½x13¼**

775-779 A201   Set of 5   7.25 7.25

Souvenir Sheet

780 A201 $15 multi   6.50 6.50

2006 World Cup Soccer Championships, Germany — A202

Various images of Trinidad & Tobago soccer players in action: $1, $2.50, $3.75, $4.50.

Perf. 13¼x13½

2006, June 28   **Litho.**

781-784 A202   Set of 4   10.00 10.00

Initial reports said this set was available only with the purchase of a first day cover for $50, but the stamps have been made available individually at face value.

CARICOM Single Market and Economy A203

Designs: $1, Cables, palm tree. $2.50, Lighthouse, check. $3.75, Cell phone, diver. $4.50, Sprinter's hands, beach, horiz. $5.25, Hands on computer keyboard, globe, horiz. $15, Map of Caribbean, horiz.

Perf. 13½x13½, 13¼x13½

2006, July 3

785-789 A203   Set of 5   8.25 8.25

Souvenir Sheet

790 A203 $15 multi   7.50 7.50

Souvenir Sheet

Orchid Society, 50th Anniv. — A204

2006, Sept. 5   **Perf. 13½x13¼**

791 A204 $15 multi   8.00 8.00

Arrival of Chinese to Trinidad and Tobago, Bicent. A205

Art: $1, Guayaguayare Beach, by Ou Hing Wan. $2.50, Hosay, by Carlisle Chang. $3.75, Saddle Road, by Amy Leong Pang, vert. $4.50, Mother & Child, sculpture by Patrick Chu Foon, vert. $5.25, Still Life, by Sybil Atteck, vert. $15, Inherent Nobility of Man, by Chang, vert.

Perf. 14¼x14½, 14½x14¼

2006, Oct. 11

792-796 A205   Set of 5   9.50 9.50

Souvenir Sheet

Perf. 13x13¼

797 A205 $15 multi   7.50 7.50

Children's Games — A206

Designs: $1, Rim driving. $2.50, Top spinning. $3.75, Playing 3A. $4.50, Farmer in the Den. $15, Tire swing.

2006, Nov. 29   **Perf. 13¼**

798-801 A206   Set of 4   6.25 6.25

Souvenir Sheet

802 A206 $15 multi   6.25 6.25

2007 Cricket World Cup, West Indies — A207

2007 Cricket World Cup emblem, Cricket World Cup and: $1, Batsman. $2, Bowler. $2.50, Bowler, diff. $3.75, Batsman, diff. $4.50, Wicketkeeper. $15, Cricket World Cup.

2007, Mar. 15   **Litho.**   **Perf. 13**

803-807 A207   Set of 5   5.50 5.50

Souvenir Sheet

Perf. 13½

808 A207 $15 multi   5.50 5.50

No. 808 contains one 27x45mm stamp.

Reopening of Red House, Cent. — A208

Designs: $1, Red House, c. 1907. $2.50, Parliament Chamber. $3.75, Cenotaph and Eternal Flame. $5.25, Rotunda and fountain. $15, Dome.

2007, Sept. 14   **Perf. 13½x13¼**

809-812 A208   Set of 4   4.50 4.50

Souvenir Sheet

813 A208 $15 multi   5.00 5.00

St. Mary's Children's Home, 150th Anniv. — A209

Designs: $1, Main entrance, c. 1930. $2.50, Fountain. $3.75, St. Mary's Anglican Church. $4.50, St. Mary's Children's Home Cub Scout pack.

2007, Sept. 21

814-817 A209   Set of 4   4.00 4.00

Historic Buildings A210

Designs: $1, Roomor. $2, Killarney. $2.50, Queen's Royal College. $3.25, Hayes Court. $3.75, Knowsley. $4.50, Mille Fleurs. $10, Boissiere House. $20, Archbishop's House. $50, White Hall.

2007, Dec. 14   Litho.   Perf. 13

818	A210	$1 multi	.30	.30
819	A210	$2 multi	.90	.65
820	A210	$2.50 multi	1.00	.75
821	A210	$3.25 multi	1.10	1.10
822	A210	$3.75 multi	1.25	1.25
823	A210	$4.50 multi	1.50	1.50
824	A210	$10 multi	3.25	3.25
825	A210	$20 multi	6.50	6.50
826	A210	$50 multi	16.00	16.00
		Nos. 818-826 (9)	31.80	31.30

Souvenir Sheet

Ozone Layer Protection — A211

2008, Jan. 24   Litho.   Perf. 13x13¼
827 A211 $15 multi   5.50 5.50

Miniature Sheet

2008 Summer Olympics, Beijing — A212

No. 828: a, Running. b, Table tennis. c, Cycling. d, Swimming.

2008, June 16   Perf. 12
828 A212 $3.50 Sheet of 4, #a-d   5.25 5.25

Scouting, Cent. (in 2007) A213

Designs: $1, Cub scouts. $2.50, Scouts. $3.75, Venturers. $4.50, Leaders. $15, Lord Robert Baden-Powell, vert.

2008, July 29   Litho.   Perf. 13¼x13½
829-832 A213 Set of 4   4.00 4.00
Souvenir Sheet
Perf. 13½x13¼
833 A213 $15 multi   5.00 5.00

University of the West Indies, 60th Anniv. — A214

Designs: $1, Sir Arthur Lewis, first West Indian principal. $2.50, Princess Alice, Countess of Athlone, first Chancellor. $3.75, Sir Philip Sherlock, first principal of St. Augustine Campus. $4.50, Administration Building, St. Augustine Campus, horiz. $5.25, Samaan tree, St. Augustine Campus, horiz.
$15, Administration Building, St. Augustine Campus, at night.

Perf. 13½x13¼, 13¼x13½
2008, Oct. 3
834-838 A214 Set of 5   5.50 5.50
Souvenir Sheet
839 A214 $15 multi   5.00 5.00
For surcharge, see No. 892.

Souvenir Sheet

Worldwide Fund for Nature (WWF) — A215

No. 840 — Brazilian porcupine: a, Adult on branch (shown). b, Head. c, Adult and juvenile. d, Juvenile on branch.

2008, Nov. 3   Perf. 13½x13¼
840   Strip or block of 4   5.00 5.00
a.-d.   A215 $3.75 Any single   1.25 1.25
e.   Miniature sheet, 2 each
        #840a-840d   10.00 10.00

Commonwealth Heads of Government Meeting, Port of Spain — A216

Designs: $1, International Finance Center, Waterfront Complex, Port of Spain. $2.50, Steel drums. $3.75, Pigeon Point, Tobago. $4.50, Queen Elizabeth II and Commonwealth Secretaries-General chief Emeka Anyaoku, Kamalesh Sharma, Sir Shridath Ramphal, and Sir Donald McKinnon. $5.25, Scarlet ibis.
$15, Emblem of Commonwealth Heads of Government Meeting.

2009, Nov. 16   Perf. 13¼
841-845 A216 Set of 5   5.50 5.50
Souvenir Sheet
Perf. 14x13¾
846 A216 $15 multi   4.75 4.75
a.   As No. 846, with Twelfth Conference of Defense Ministers of the Americas emblem overprinted in sheet margin   4.50 4.50

No. 846 contains one 33x45mm stamp. For surcharges, see Nos. 893, 929.
Issued: No. 846a, 10/10/16.

Souvenir Sheet

Trinidad & Tobago Postal Corporation, 10th Anniv. — A217

No. 847: a, Head office. b, Retail counter.

Litho. & Embossed
2009, Dec. 18   Perf. 13¾x13¼
847 A217 $10 Sheet of 2, #a-b   6.50 6.50

Miniature Sheets

Intl. Year of Biodiversity — A218

No. 848: a, $1, Collared peccary. b, $1, No Man's Land, Bon Accord, Tobago. c, $2.50, Butterfly orchid. d, $2.50, Hot peppers. e, $3.75, Paria Bay, Trinidad. f, $3.75, Ornate hawk eagle. g, $4.50, Trinidad piping-guan. h, $4.50, Royal poinciana tree. i, $5.25, Trinidad select hybrid cocoa pods. j, $5.25, Water buffalos, Aripo Livestock Station.
No. 849: a, $1, Agouti. b, $1, Fishermen at Grafton Beach, Tobago. c, $2.50, Caroni Swamp and Bird Sanctuary, Trinidad. d, $2.50, Red bracket deer. e, $3.75, Turkey vulture. f, $3.75, White-chested emerald hummingbird. g, $4.50, Leatherback turtle. h, $4.50, Nariva Swamp, Trinidad. i, $5.25, Soldado Rock, Gulf of Paria. j, $5.25, Orchid.

2010, May 26   Litho.   Perf. 13¼x12½
Sheets of 10, #a-j
848-849 A218 Set of 2   22.50 22.50
London 2010 Festival of Stamps.

Syrians and Lebanese in Trinidad & Tobago, Cent. — A219

Designs: $1, Rahme Sabga, peddler. $2.50, Kashish, peddler. $3.75, Grand Bazaar Shopping Center. $4.50, Nicholas Tower.
$15, Woman wearing traditional Arab head covering.

2010, July 20   Perf. 13¼x13
850-853 A219 Set of 4   5.50 4.00
Souvenir Sheet
854 A219 $15 multi   6.00 6.00

Trinidad & Tobago Cadet Force, Cent. — A220

Various photographs of cadets: $1, $2.50, $3.75, $4.50, $5.25.
$15, Rifles, Sir George Ruthven Le Hunte, Cadet Force founder, and Pres. George Maxwell Richards.

2010, Dec. 1   Perf. 13x13¼
855-859 A220 Set of 5   6.00 6.00
Souvenir Sheet
860 A220 $15 multi   6.00 6.00

Tobago House of Assembly, 30th Anniv. A221

Designs: $1, Tobago House of Assembly. $2.50, Englishman's Bay. $3.75, St. Patrick's Anglican Church. $4.50, Fort King George. $5.25, Buccoo Goat Race.
$15, Pigeon Point Heritage Park.

2010, Dec. 4   Perf. 13x13¼
861-865 A221 Set of 5   6.00 6.00
Souvenir Sheet
Perf. 13¼
866 A221 $15 multi   6.00 6.00

Festivities A222

Designs: $1, Spiritual Baptist Liberation Day. $2.50, Eid ul-Fitr. $3.75, Christmas. $4.50, Diwali.
$15, Parang.

2010, Dec. 10   Perf. 13¼x13
867-870 A222 Set of 4   5.50 5.50
Souvenir Sheet
Perf. 13¼
871 A222 $15 multi   6.00 6.00

Carnival — A223

Designs: $1, Participant in Sky People costume designed by Peter Minshall. $2.50, Children portraying Pierrot Grenade. $3.75, Junior Carnival Queen on Broadway. $4.50, Children's Carnival on Frederick Street. $5.25, Participant in Black Indian Chief costume designed by Larrie Approo.
$15, Participant in Pan Woman costume designed by Wendy Kallicharan.

2011, Mar. 1   Perf. 12
872-876 A223 Set of 5   6.00 6.00
Souvenir Sheet
877 A223 $15 multi   6.00 6.00

Dr. Eric
Williams (1911-
81), Prime
Minister — A224

Designs: $1, Williams with Sir V. S. Naipaul,
Michael Anthony, and Andre Deutsch. $1.50,
Williams playing cricket with C. L. R. James
and Sir Learie Constantine. $2.50, Williams
and Kwame Nkrumah. $3.75, Painting of Wil-
liams by Georgia M. Cordner. $4.50, Williams
with John Lennon and Ringo Starr. $5.25, Wil-
liams and Jawaharlal Nehru.

$15, Williams with Sir Winston Churchill.

2011, Apr. 5   Litho.   Perf. 13¼x13
878-883 A224   Set of 6   7.00 7.00

Souvenir Sheet
884 A224 $15 multi   6.00 6.00

Independence, 50th Anniv. — A225

Designs: No. 885, $1, Flag of Trinidad &
Tobago. No. 886, $1, Arms of colonial and
independent Trinidad & Tobago. No. 887, $1,
Sir Solomon Hochoy, first Governor-General
and Dr. Eric E. Williams, first Prime Minister.
No. 888, $1, 50th anniversary emblem, vert.

2012, Aug. 8   Perf. 13¼
885-888 A225   Set of 4   1.40 1.40

No. 515 Surcharged

No. 888A

No. 889

**Method, Perf. and Watermark As
Before**
2012 ?
888A A136 $1 on $2.25 #515   —   —
889   A136 $1 on $2.25 #515   3.00 —
  a.   Inverted surcharge   150.00
  b.   Surcharge with decimal
       point omitted   —   —
       Issued: No. 889, 4/2/12.

Nos. 604,
765, 838 &
845 Srchd.
in Blue

Methods and Perfs As Before
2013, July 4
890 A162 $1 on $5 #604   2.00 2.00
891 A197 $1 on $5.25 #765   2.00 2.00
892 A214 $1 on $5.25 #838   2.00 2.00
893 A216 $1 on $5.25 #845   2.00 2.00
       Nos. 890-893 (4)   8.00 8.00

The new denomination on Nos. 890-893
obliterates the old denomination.

A226

World
Food
Day
A227

Designs: $1, Sorrel drink. $2.50, Sorrel
plant. $3.75, Capsular fruit of Hibiscus
sabdariffa. $4.50, Biodiversity of sorrel in Trini-
dad & Tobago. $5.25, Flower of Hibiscus
sabdariffa. $50, Mature Hibiscus sabdariffa
calyces.

2013, Dec. 4   Litho.   Perf. 13¾
894 A226 $1 multi   .40 .40

Self-Adhesive
Serpentine Die Cut
895 A227 $50 multi   14.00 14.00

Miniature Sheet
Serpentine Die Cut 12¼
896   Sheet of 5   8.50
  a.   A226 $1 multi   .50 .50
  b.   A226 $2.50 multi   1.00 1.00
  c.   A226 $3.75 multi   1.40 1.40
  d.   A226 $4.50 multi   1.60 1.60
  e.   A226 $5.25 multi   2.00 2.00

Sorrel seeds were placed under a circle of
plastic affixed to Nos. 895 and 896a-896e.

No. 516
Surcharged
897srch

**Method, Perf. and Watermark As
Before**
2013, July
897 A136 $1 on $2.50 #516   3.50 3.50
  a.   Wmk. 373 (on #516a)

No. 516
Surcharged

Method and Perf. As Before
2014, Dec.   Wmk. 384
898 A136 $1 on $2.50 #516   2.00 5.00
  a.   Wmk. 373 (on #516a)   .90 .90
  b.   As "a," inverted surcharge

No. 516
Surcharged

**Method, Perf. and Watermark As
Before**
2014, July
899 A136 $1 on $2.50 #516   3.50 —
  a.   Wmk. 373 (on #516a)   —   —
  b.   As No. 899a, with two obliter-
       ators   —   —

Diplomatic Relations Between Trinidad
& Tobago and People's Republic of
China, 40th Anniv.
A228

Designs: $1, Chaconia flower. $3, Henan
Luoyang peony. $3.25, Red-crowned crane.
$4, Scarlet ibis.

2014, June 20   Litho.   Perf. 12
901   A228 $1 multi   .30 .30
901A A228 $3 multi   .95 .95
  b.   Souvenir sheet of 2, #901-
       901A   30.00 30.00
902   A228 $3.25 multi   1.00 1.00
902A A228 $4 multi   1.25 1.25
  b.   Souvenir sheet of 2, #902-
       902A   60.00 60.00
       Nos. 901-902A (4)   3.50 3.50

In 2015, Trinidad & Tobago postal
authorities declared as illegal sheets of
6 and 9 stamps depicting Cats, Butterflies and Moths dated 2010 and 2011.

**Nos. 144, 145, 401h, 401i and 750
Surcharged in Black or Red**

No. 903

No. 904

No. 905

Nos. 906-907

**Methods, Perfs and Watermarks As
Before**
2015-16
903 A41 $1 on 1c #144   .35 .35
904 A41 $1 on 3c #145   .65 .65
905 A195 $2 on 25c #750
906 A108 $3.25 on 95c #401h
       (dated 1987)
       (R)   —   —
907 A108 $3.25 on 95c #401i
       (dated 1988)
       (R)   1.00 1.00

Issued: No. 903, 1/7/16; No. 904, 2/25/16.
No. 905, 11/30/15, Nos. 906-907, 9/1/15.

Indigenous
Banking,
Cent. — A229

Emblem of First Citizens Bank and: $1, Trini-
dad Cooperative Bank, 1914. $2, Workers'
Bank and National Commercial Bank, 1970-
71. $2.50, First Citizens Bank, 1993.

No. 911 — Emblem of First Citizens Bank
and: a, $4, People and bank building. b, $6.50,
Men and women on balance. c, $7.50, Auto-
matic teller machine, banking by computer and
smartphone.

Perf. 13x13¼ Syncopated
2015, Sept. 16   Litho.
908-910 A229 Set of 3   1.75 1.75

Souvenir Sheet
911 A229 Sheet of 3, #a-c   50.00 50.00

Souvenir Sheet

United Nations, 70th Anniv. — A230

**Litho, Sheet Margin Litho. With Foil
Application**
2015, Oct. 24   Perf. 13¼
912 A230 $20 gold & multi   6.50 6.50

Nos. 647-649
Surcharged

Methods and Perfs. As Before
2016, Oct. 10

913	A173	$1 on $3.75 #647	.30	.30
a.		Inverted surcharge		
914	A173	$1 on $4.50 #648	.30	.30
a.		Inverted surcharge		
915	A173	$1 on $5.25 #649	.30	.30
		Nos. 913-915 (3)	.90	.90

No. 622
Surcharged

2017 Method and Perf. As Before
916	A166	$1 on 75c #622	.30	.30

No. 624 Surcharged

2017 Method and Perf. As Before
917	A167	$1 on 75c #624	.30	.30

No. 643
Surcharged

Method and Perf. As Before
2017, May 25
918	A172	$1 on $2.50 #643	.30	.30

No. 516a
Surcharged

Method, Perf. and Watermark As Before
2017
919	A136	$3 on $2.50 #516a	.90	.90

No. 639-641 Surcharged in Silver or Black

No. 920

No. 921

No. 922

2017 Method and Perf. As Before
920	A171	$1 on $4.50 #640 (S)	.30	.30
921	A171	$1 on $5.25 #641	.30	.30
922	A171	$2 on $3.75 #639 (S)	.60	.60
		Nos. 920-922 (3)	1.20	1.20

No. 608 Surcharged

2017 Method and Perf. As Before
923	A163	$1 on $5.25 #608	.30	.30

No. 637
Surcharged

2017 Method and Perf. As Before
924	A170	$1 on $5.25 #637	.30	.30

Nos. 656, 658 Surcharged

No. 925

No. 926

2017 Method and Perf. As Before
925	A176	$1 on $2.50 #656	.30	.30
926	A176	$1 on $5.25 #658	.30	.30

Creole
Harvest — A231

No. 927: a, Woman with cocoa knife. b, Mortar and pestle. c, Creole dancers. d, Cocoa house. e, Jar of cocoa. f, Woman carrying cake. g, Creole dancer with dwiyet. h, Man playing bongo drum. i, Man with bamboo kwa-kwa. j, Tapia house.

Serpentine Die Cut 14x13½
2018, Jan. 22 Litho.
Self-Adhesive
927		Booklet pane of 10	3.00
a.-j.		A231 $1 Any single	.30 .30

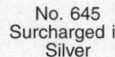

No. 645
Surcharged in
Silver

Method and Perf. As Before
2017, July 28
928	A172	$1 on $3.75 #645	.30	.30

No. 843 Surcharged

Method and Perf. As Before
2018, Aug. 17
929	A216	$1 on $3.75 #843	.30	.30

No. 671
Surcharged

Method and Perf. As Before
2018, Aug. 17
930	A179	$1 on $5.25 #671	.30	.30

Nos. 517a, 614, 629, 664, 683, and 750 Surcharged

No. 931

No. 932

No. 933

No. 934

No. 935

No. 936

Methods, Perfs. and Watermarks As Before
2018
931	A183	50c on $2.50 #683	.25	.25
932	A165	$1 on 75c #614	.30	.30
933	A178	$1 on $2.50 #664	.30	.30
934	A168	$1 on $5.25 #629	.30	.30
935	A195	$2 on 25c #750	.60	.60
936	A136	$3.25 on $5 #517a	1.00	1.00
		Nos. 931-936 (6)	2.75	2.75

Miniature Sheet

Trinidad & Tobago Philatelic Society, 75th Anniv. (in 2017) — A232

No. 937: a, $1, Ambulance bought by Red Cross Fund, Trinidad & Tobago #B1 on cover. b, $2, Trinidad & Tobago #52 with Plymouth cancel, old Plymouth Post Office. c, $3.75, Ships in 1797 Battle of Trinidad, sailor's letter describing battle. d, $4.50, Immigrants from India, Indian postal stationery used in Trinidad & Tobago with additional stamps, Trinidad #75 and 91. e, $5.25, Picture postcard from sailor on USS Missouri franked with trinidad #76, and 1907 picture post depicting sailors visiting Trinidad. f, $6.50, Dornier Do X flying boat, 1931 cover flown on Dornier flight.

Unwmk.
2018, Sept. 27 Litho. Perf. 12
937	A232	Sheet of 6, #a-f	7.00 7.00

Gas Exporting Countries Forum, 10th Anniv. A233

Drilling platform, bird, flower and: $1, Marine production facilities. $2, Natural gas transmission system. $3, Point Lisas Industrial Estate. $3.25, Liquid natural gas production and export. $5.25, Bus at compressed natural gas filling station.

2018, Nov. 13 Litho. Perf. 13x13¼
938-942	A233	Set of 5	4.25 4.25

Royal Botanic Gardens, Trinidad,
200th Anniv. — A234

Flowers: $1, Ixora sp. (59x46mm). $2, Buttercup flower (69x37mm). $3.25, Thunbergia
sp. (36x64mm). $4, Flamboyant (55x52mm).
$6.50, Croton (64x42mm).
$30, Double chaconia.

2018, Dec. 6   Litho.   Die Cut
Self-Adhesive
943-947 A234 Set of 5   5.00 5.00
Souvenir Sheet
948 A234 $30 multi   9.00 9.00
No. 948 contains one 65x42mm stamp.

No. 511
Surcharged

Method, Perf. and Watermark As
Before
2018
949 A136 $1 on 40c #511   .30   .30

SEMI-POSTAL STAMPS

Emblem of
Red Cross
SP1

Perf. 11, 12
1914, Sept. 18   Typo.   Unwmk.
B1 SP1 (½p) red (on cover)   250.00

This stamp was allowed to pay ½p postage
on one day, Sept. 18, 1914, on circulars distributed by the Red Cross. Value on cover is
for proper Red Cross usage. Value unused,
$30.

No. 2 Overprinted in Red (Cross)
and Black (Date)

a   b

1915, Oct. 21   Wmk. 3   Perf. 14
B2 A1 (a) 1p scarlet   3.50 6.00

1916, Oct. 19
B3 A1 (b) 1p scarlet   .80 3.25
  a. Date omitted

POSTAGE DUE STAMPS

D1

1923-45   Typo.   Wmk. 4   Perf. 14
J1 D1 1p black   4.25   4.25
J2 D1 2p black   8.75   1.90
J3 D1 3p black ('25)   13.00   6.50
J4 D1 4p black ('29)   8.75 30.00
J5 D1 5p black ('45)   42.50 140.00
J6 D1 6p black ('45)   77.50 55.00
J7 D1 8p black ('45)   52.50 200.00
J8 D1 1sh black ('45)   90.00 160.00
    Nos. J1-J8 (8)   297.25 597.65

Catalogue values for unused stamps in this section, from this point to the end of the section, are for Never Hinged items.

Denominations in Cents
1947, Sept. 1
J9   D1 2c black   5.50   8.50
J10 D1 4c black   2.75   3.00
J11 D1 6c black   5.00   7.50
J12 D1 8c black   1.25 42.50
J13 D1 10c black   3.25   9.50
J14 D1 12c black   4.00 30.00
J15 D1 16c black   2.00 57.50
J16 D1 24c black   13.00 15.00
    Nos. J9-J16 (8)   36.75 173.50
Nos. J9-J16 also exist on chalky paper.

Wmk. 4a (error)
J9a   D1 2c   60.00
J11a D1 6c   125.00
J14a D1 12c   175.00

D2

1970   Unwmk.   Litho.   Perf. 14x13½
Size: 18x23mm
J17 D2 2c green   .25   2.75
J18 D2 4c carmine rose   .25   8.50
J19 D2 6c brown   .55   5.50
J20 D2 8c lt violet   .75   5.75
J21 D2 10c brick red   1.10   6.25
J22 D2 12c dull orange   1.00   6.25
J23 D2 16c brt yellow grn   1.00   6.75
J24 D2 24c gray   1.00 11.00
J25 D2 50c blue   1.00   5.00
J26 D2 60c olive green   1.00   5.00
    Nos. J17-J26 (10)   7.90 62.75

Perf. 13½x14
1976-77   Litho.   Unwmk.
Size: 17x21mm
J27 D2 2c green   .25   2.00
J28 D2 4c carmine rose   .25   1.50
J29 D2 6c brown   .25   2.40
J30 D2 8c lt violet   .30   2.40
J31 D2 10c brick red   .30   1.75
J32 D2 12c dull orange   .50   2.00
    Nos. J27-J32 (6)   1.85 12.05
Issued: 4c, 12c, 4/1/76; 2c, 6c, 8c, 10, 1977.
The letters in the top label on Nos. J27-J32
are larger with D's and O's more squarish than
the oval letters on Nos. J17-J26. "Postage
Due" is 13mm long and is composed of finer
letters than on Nos. J17-J26, which have a
14mm inscription.

WAR TAX STAMPS

Nos. 1-2 Overprinted

1917   Wmk. 3   Perf. 14
MR1 A1 1p scarlet   4.25   4.25
  a. Invtd. overprint   225.00 300.00

Overprinted

MR2 A1 ½p green   1.50   .40
  a. Overprinted on face and
       back   425.00
  b. Pair, one without over-
       print   1,000. 1,500.
MR3 A1 1p scarlet   4.50   2.25
  a. Pair, one without over-
       print   1,000. 1,500.
  b. Double overprint   175.00

Overprinted

MR4 A1 ½p green   .30 17.50
MR5 A1 1p scarlet   .30   1.00
  a. Pair, one without over-
       print

Overprinted

MR6 A1 ½p green   .30   5.00
MR7 A1 1p scarlet   8.00   1.25

Overprinted

MR8 A1 ½p green   .30   3.25
MR9 A1 1p scarlet   75.00 60.00

Overprinted

MR10 A1 1p scarlet   .80   1.40
  a. Inverted overprint   175.00 175.00

Overprinted

MR11 A1 1p scarlet   2.50   .30
  a. Double overprint   250.00 250.00
  b. Inverted overprint   160.00 175.00

Overprinted

1918
MR12 A1 ½p green   .30   3.50
  a. Pair, one without overprint 1,500.
MR13 A1 1p scarlet   .90   1.75
  a. Double overprint   175.00
  b. Horiz. pair, one without over-
       print   1,700.

The War Tax Stamps show considerable
variations in the colors, thickness of the paper,
distinctness of the watermark, and the gum.
Counterfeits exist of the errors of Nos. MR1-
MR13.

OFFICIAL STAMPS

Regular Issue of 1913
Overprinted

1913   Wmk. 3   Perf. 14
O1 A1 ½p green   2.75 17.50

Same Overprinted

1914
O2 A1 ½p green   4.25 24.50

Same Overprinted

1916
O3 A1 ½p green   5.25   9.50
  a. Double overprint   57.50

Same Overprint without Period
1917
O4 A1 ½p green   .75 10.00

Same Overprinted

1917, Aug. 22
O5 A1 ½p green   4.00 32.50

The official stamps are found in several
shades of green and on paper of varying
thickness.

TRIPOLITANIA

tri-ˌpä-lə-ˈtā-nyə

LOCATION — In northern Africa, bordering on Mediterranean Sea
GOVT. — A former Italian Colony
AREA — 350,000 sq. mi. (approx.)
POP. — 570,716 (1921)
CAPITAL — Tripoli

Formerly a Turkish province, Tripolitania became part of Italian Libya. See Libya.

100 Centesimi = 1 Lira

Used values in italics are for postally used stamps. CTO's or stamps with fake cancels sell for about the same as unused, hinged stamps.

Watermark

Wmk. 140 — Crowns

Propagation of the Faith Issue
Italian Stamps Overprinted

1923, Oct. 24   Wmk. 140   Perf. 14

1	A68	20c ol grn & brn org	9.00	40.00
2	A68	30c claret & brn org	9.00	40.00
a.		Double overprint	2,000.	
b.		Vert. pair, imperf. btwn and at bottom	1,000.	1,400.
3	A68	50c vio & brn org	6.00	45.00
4	A68	1 l blue & brn org	6.00	70.00
		Nos. 1-4 (4)	30.00	195.00
		Set, never hinged	75.00	

Fascisti Issue

Italian Stamps Overprinted in Red or Black

1923, Oct. 29   Unwmk.

5	A69	10c dk green (R)	12.00	15.00
6	A69	30c dk violet (R)	12.00	15.00
7	A69	50c brown car	12.00	15.00
		Wmk. 140		
8	A70	1 l blue	12.00	40.00
9	A70	2 l brown	12.00	50.00
a.		Double overprint	1,350.	
10	A71	5 l blk & bl (R)	12.00	72.50
		Nos. 5-10 (6)	72.00	207.50
		Set, never hinged	180.00	

Manzoni Issue
Stamps of Italy, 1923, Overprinted in Red

1924, Apr. 1   Wmk. 140   Perf. 14

11	A72	10c brown red & blk	9.75	60.00
12	A72	15c blue grn & blk	9.75	60.00
13	A72	30c black & slate	9.75	60.00
14	A72	50c org brn & blk	9.75	60.00
15	A72	1 l blue & blk	60.00	350.00
16	A72	5 l violet & blk	400.00	2,400.
		Nos. 11-16 (6)	499.00	2,990.
		Set, never hinged	1,250.	

On Nos. 15 and 16 the overprint is placed vertically at the left side.

Victor Emmanuel Issue

Italy Nos. 175-177 Overprinted

1925-26   Unwmk.   Perf. 11

17	A78	60c brown car	1.75	11.00
18	A78	1 l dark blue	2.40	11.00
a.		Perf. 13½	8.50	34.00
		Perf. 13½		
19	A78	1.25 l dk bl ('26)	3.00	30.00
a.		Perf. 11	1,600.	2,100.
		Nos. 17-19 (3)	7.15	52.00
		Set, #17-19, 18a, 19a, never hinged	3,200.	

Saint Francis of Assisi Issue
Italy Nos. 178-180 Overprinted

1926, Apr. 12   Wmk. 140   Perf. 14

20	A79	20c gray green	1.75	11.00
a.		Vert. pair, one without ovpt.	4,250.	
21	A80	40c dark violet	1.75	11.00
22	A81	60c red brown	1.75	21.00

Italy No. 182 and Type of A83
Overprinted in Red

Unwmk.

23	A82	1.25 l dark blue	1.75	28.00
24	A83	5 l + 2.50 l ol grn	6.00	55.00
a.		Horiz. pair, imperf. btwn.	1,800.	
		Nos. 20-24 (5)	13.00	126.00
		Set, never hinged	20.00	

Volta Issue

Type of Italy Overprinted

1927, Oct. 10   Wmk. 140   Perf. 14

25	A84	20c purple	3.75	30.00
26	A84	50c deep orange	6.00	21.00
a.		Double overprint	155.00	
27	A84	1.25 l brt blue	11.00	50.00
		Nos. 25-27 (3)	20.75	101.00
		Set, never hinged	50.00	

Monte Cassino Issue
Types of Italy Overprinted in Red or Blue

1929, Oct. 14

28	A96	20c dk green (R)	5.00	17.00
29	A96	25c red org (Bl)	5.00	17.00
30	A98	50c + 10c crim (Bl)	5.00	18.00
31	A98	75c + 15c ol brn (R)	5.00	18.00
32	A96	1.25 l + 25c dk vio (R)	11.00	34.00
33	A98	5 l + 1 l saph (R)	11.00	35.00

Overprinted in Red

Unwmk.

34	A100	10 l + 2 l gray brn	11.00	55.00
		Nos. 28-34 (7)	53.00	194.00
		Set, never hinged	130.00	

Royal Wedding Issue

Type of Italy Overprinted

1930, Mar. 17   Wmk. 140

35	A101	20c yellow green	2.40	7.25
36	A101	50c + 10c dp org	1.75	7.25
37	A101	1.25 l + 25c rose red	1.75	14.50
		Nos. 35-37 (3)	5.90	29.00
		Set, never hinged	15.50	

Ferrucci Issue

Types of Italy Overprinted in Red or Blue

1930, July 26

38	A102	20c violet (R)	5.00	5.00
39	A103	25c dk green (R)	5.00	5.00
40	A103	50c black (R)	5.00	9.00
41	A103	1.25 l dp bl (R)	5.00	17.00
42	A104	5 l + 2 l dp car (Bl)	11.00	35.00
		Nos. 38-42,C1-C3 (8)	60.50	157.00
		Set, never hinged	145.00	

Virgil Issue

Types of Italy Overprinted in Red or Blue

1930, Dec. 4   Photo.

43	A106	15c violet black	.90	9.25
44	A106	20c orange brown	.90	3.75
45	A106	25c dark green	.90	3.75
46	A106	30c lt brown	.90	3.75
47	A106	50c dull violet	.90	3.75
48	A106	75c rose red	.90	7.25
49	A106	1.25 l gray blue	.90	9.25
		Unwmk.		
		Engr.		
50	A106	5 l + 1.50 l dk vio	3.75	35.00
51	A106	10 l + 2.50 l ol brn	3.75	55.00
		Nos. 43-51,C4-C7 (13)	30.80	250.25
		Set, never hinged	72.50	

Saint Anthony of Padua Issue

Types of Italy Overprinted in Blue or Red

1931, May 7   Photo.   Wmk. 140

52	A116	20c brown (Bl)	1.20	17.00
53	A116	25c green (R)	1.20	6.00
54	A118	30c gray brn (Bl)	1.20	6.00
55	A118	50c dull vio (Bl)	1.20	6.00
56	A120	1.25 l slate bl (R)	1.20	30.00

Overprinted in Red or Black

			Unwmk.	**Engr.**
57	A121	75c black (R)	1.20	17.00
58	A122	5 l + 2.50 l dk brn (Bk)	8.50	60.00
		Nos. 52-58 (7)	15.70	142.00
		Set, never hinged	40.00	

Native Village Scene A14

1934, Oct. 16   Wmk. 140

73	A14	5c ol grn & brn	4.25	17.00
74	A14	10c brown & black	4.25	17.00
75	A14	20c scar & indigo	4.25	15.50
76	A14	50c pur & brn	4.25	15.50
77	A14	60c org brn & ind	4.25	21.00
78	A14	1.25 l dk bl & grn	4.25	35.00
		Nos. 73-78,C43-C48 (12)	51.00	242.00
		Set, never hinged	125.00	

2nd Colonial Arts Exhibition, Naples.

SEMI-POSTAL STAMPS

Many issues of Italy and Italian Colonies include one or more semipostal denominations. To avoid splitting sets, these issues are generally listed as regular postage, airmail, etc., unless all values carry a surtax.

Holy Year Issue
Italian Stamps of 1924 Overprinted in Black or Red

1925   Wmk. 140   Perf. 12

B1	SP4	20c+ 10c dk grn & brn	3.00	18.00
B2	SP4	30c+ 15c dk brn & brn	3.00	19.50
B3	SP4	50c+ 25c vio & brn	3.00	18.00
B4	SP4	60c+ 30c dp rose & brn	3.00	24.00
B5	SP8	1 l + 50c dp bl & vio (R)	3.00	30.00
B6	SP8	5 l + 2.50 l org brn & vio (R)	3.00	47.50
		Nos. B1-B6 (6)	18.00	157.00
		Set, never hinged	45.00	

Colonial Institute Issue

Peace Substituting Spade for Sword — SP1

1926, June 1   Typo.   Perf. 14

B7	SP1	5c + 5c brown	.90	7.75
B8	SP1	10c + 5c ol brn	.90	7.75
B9	SP1	20c + 5c bl grn	.90	7.75
B10	SP1	40c + 5c brn red	.90	7.75
B11	SP1	60c + 5c orange	.90	7.75
B12	SP1	1 l + 5c blue	.90	16.00
		Nos. B7-B12 (6)	5.40	54.75
		Set, never hinged	13.50	

The surtax was for the Italian Colonial Institute.

Fiera Campionaria Tripoli
See Libya for stamps with this inscription.

Types of Italian Semi-Postal Stamps of 1926 Overprinted like Nos. 17-19

1927, Apr. 21   Unwmk.   Perf. 11

B19	SP10	40c + 20c dk brn & blk	3.00	32.00
B20	SP10	60c + 30c brn red & ol brn	3.00	32.00
B21	SP10	1.25 l + 60c dp bl & blk	3.00	50.00
B22	SP10	5 l + 2.50 l dk grn & blk	5.00	75.00
		Nos. B19-B22 (4)	14.00	189.00
		Set, never hinged	34.00	

The surtax was for the charitable work of the Voluntary Militia for Italian National Defense.

Allegory of Fascism and Victory — SP2

1928, Oct. 15   Wmk. 140

B29	SP2	20c + 5c bl grn	2.60	11.00
B30	SP2	30c + 5c red	2.60	11.00
B31	SP2	50c + 10c pur	2.60	18.00
B32	SP2	1.25 l + 20c dk bl	3.25	24.00
		Nos. B29-B32 (4)	11.05	64.00
		Set, never hinged	26.00	

46th anniv. of the Societa Africana d'Italia. The surtax aided that society.

Types of Italian Semi-Postal Stamps of 1928 Ovptd.

1929, Mar. 4   Unwmk.   Perf. 11

B33	SP10	30c + 10c red & blk	3.75	21.00
B34	SP10	50c + 20c vio & blk	3.75	22.50
B35	SP10	1.25 l + 50c brn & bl	5.50	40.00
B36	SP10	5 l + 2 l ol grn & blk	5.50	80.00
		Nos. B33-B36 (4)	18.50	163.50
		Set, never hinged	45.00	

The surtax on these stamps was for the charitable work of the Voluntary Militia for Italian National Defense.

Types of Italian Semi-Postal Stamps of 1926, Overprinted in Black or Red Like Nos. B33-B36

1930, Oct. 20

B50	SP10	30c + 10c dp grn & bl grn (Bk)	28.00	42.50
B51	SP10	50c + 10c dk grn & vio (R)	28.00	80.00
B52	SP10	1.25 l + 30c blk brn & red brn (R)	28.00	80.00
B53	SP10	5 l + 1.50 l ind & grn (R)	90.00	210.00
		Nos. B50-B53 (4)	174.00	412.50
		Set, never hinged	425.00	

Ancient Arch — SP3

1930, Nov. 27   Photo.   Wmk. 140

B54	SP3	50c + 20c ol brn	3.00	19.50
B55	SP3	1.25 l + 20c dp bl	3.00	19.50
B56	SP3	1.75 l + 20c green	3.00	26.00
B57	SP3	2.55 l + 50c purple	7.25	35.00
B58	SP3	5 l + 1 l deep car	7.25	75.00
		Nos. B54-B58 (5)	23.50	175.00
		Set, never hinged	60.00	

25th anniv. of the Italian Colonial Agricultural Institute. The surtax was for the benefit of that institution.

AIR POST STAMPS

Ferrucci Issue
Type of Italian Air Post Stamps Overprinted in Blue or Red like #38-42

1030, July 20   Wmk. 140   Perf. 14

C1	AP7	50c brown vio (Bl)	5.00	11.00
C2	AP7	1 l dk blue (R)	5.00	15.00
C3	AP7	5 l + 2 l dp car (Bl)	19.50	60.00
		Nos. C1-C3 (3)	29.50	86.00
		Set, never hinged	72.50	

Virgil Issue
Types of Italian Air Post Stamps Overprinted in Red or Blue like #43-51

1930, Dec. 4   Photo.

C4	AP8	50c deep green	1.75	9.75
C5	AP8	1 l rose red	1.75	9.75

Unwmk.   Engr.

C6	AP8	7.70 l + 1.30 l dk brn	6.75	50.00
C7	AP8	9 l + 2 l gray	6.75	50.00
		Nos. C4-C7 (4)	17.00	119.50
		Set, never hinged	40.00	

Airplane over Columns of the Basilica, Leptis — AP1

Arab Horseman Pointing at Airplane AP2

1931-32   Photo.   Wmk. 140

C8	AP1	50c rose car	.60	.25
C9	AP1	60c red org	1.75	8.50
C10	AP1	75c dp bl ('32)	1.75	7.25
C11	AP1	80c dull violet	9.75	13.50
C12	AP2	1 l deep blue	1.20	.25
C13	AP2	1.20 l dk brown	24.00	18.00
C14	AP2	1.50 l org red	11.00	18.00
C15	AP2	5 l green	28.00	28.00
		Nos. C8-C15 (8)	78.05	93.75
		Set, never hinged	170.00	

For surcharges and overprint see Nos. C29-C32.

Agricultural Institute, 25th Anniv. AP3

1931, Dec. 7

C16	AP3	50c dp blue	2.40	19.50
C17	AP3	80c violet	2.40	19.50
C18	AP3	1 l gray black	2.40	28.00
C19	AP3	2 l deep green	7.25	35.00
C20	AP3	5 l + 2 l rose red	11.00	75.00
		Nos. C16-C20 (5)	25.45	177.00
		Set, never hinged	65.00	

Graf Zeppelin Issue

Mercury, by Giovanni da Bologna, and Zeppelin AP4

Designs: 3 l, 12 l, Mercury. 10 l, 20 l, Guido Reni's "Aurora." 5 l, 15 l, Arch of Marcus Aurelius.

1933, May 5

C21	AP4	3 l dark brown	9.75	97.50
C22	AP4	5 l purple	9.75	97.50
C23	AP4	10 l deep green	9.75	180.00
C24	AP4	12 l deep blue	9.75	190.00
C25	AP4	15 l carmine	9.75	210.00
C26	AP4	20 l gray black	9.75	280.00
		Nos. C21-C26 (6)	58.50	1,055.
		Set, never hinged	145.00	

For overprints and surcharges see Nos. C38-C42.

North Atlantic Flight Issue

Airplane, Lion of St. Mark AP7

1933, June 1

C27	AP7	19.75 l blk & ol brn	16.00	525.00
C28	AP7	44.75 l dk bl & lt grn	16.00	525.00
		Set, never hinged	77.50	

Type of 1931 Ovptd. or Srchd.

1934, Jan. 20

C29	AP2	2 l on 5 l org brn	3.75	72.50
C30	AP2	3 l on 5 l grn	3.75	72.50
C31	AP2	5 l ocher	3.75	85.00
C32	AP2	10 l on 5 l rose	5.00	85.00
		Nos. C29-C32 (4)	16.25	315.00
		Set, never hinged	42.50	

For use on mail to be carried on a special flight from Rome to Buenos Aires.

Types of Libya Airmail Issue Overprinted in Black or Red

1934, May 1   Wmk. 140

C38	AP4	50c rose red	11.00	130.00
C39	AP4	75c lemon	11.00	130.00
C40	AP4	5 l + 1 l brn	11.00	130.00

C41	AP4	10 l + 2 l dk bl	190.00	700.00
C42	AP5	25 l + 3 l pur	190.00	700.00
		Nos. C38-C42,CE1-CE2 (7)	435.00	2,050.
		Set, never hinged	1,050.	

"Circuit of the Oases."

Plane Shadow on Desert AP11

Designs: 25c, 50c, 75c, Plane shadow on desert. 80c, 1 l, 2 l, Camel corps.

1934, Oct. 16   Photo.

C43	AP11	25c sl bl & org red	4.25	17.00
C44	AP11	50c dk grn & ind	4.25	15.50
C45	AP11	75c dk brn & org red	4.25	15.50
C46	AP11	80c org brn & ol grn	4.25	17.00
C47	AP11	1 l scar & ol grn	4.25	21.00
C48	AP11	2 l dk bl & brn	4.25	35.00
		Nos. C43-C48 (6)	25.50	121.00
		Set, never hinged	62.50	

Second Colonial Arts Exhibition, Naples.

AIR POST SEMI-POSTAL STAMPS

King Victor Emmanuel III SPAP1

1934, Nov. 5   Wmk. 140   Perf. 14

CB1	SPAP1	25c + 10c gray grn	7.25	20.00
CB2	SPAP1	50c + 10c brn	7.25	20.00
CB3	SPAP1	75c + 15c rose red	7.25	20.00
CB4	SPAP1	80c + 15c blk brn	7.25	20.00
CB5	SPAP1	1 l + 20c red brn	7.25	20.00
CB6	SPAP1	2 l + 20c brt bl	7.25	20.00
CB7	SPAP1	3 l + 25c pur	20.00	100.00
CB8	SPAP1	5 l + 25c org	20.00	100.00
CB9	SPAP1	10 l + 30c rose vio	20.00	100.00
CB10	SPAP1	25 l + 2 l dp grn	20.00	100.00
		Nos. CB1-CB10 (10)	123.50	520.00
		Set, never hinged	390.00	

65th birthday of King Victor Emmanuel III; non-stop flight from Rome to Mogadiscio. For overprint see No. CBO1.

AIR POST SEMI-POSTAL OFFICIAL STAMP

Type of Air Post Semi-Postal Stamps Ovptd. Crown and "SERVIZIO DI STATO" in Black

1934   Wmk. 140   Perf. 14

CBO1	SPAP1	25 l + 2 l cop red	1,950.	4,800.
		Never hinged	3,900.	

AIR POST SPECIAL DELIVERY STAMPS

Type of Libya Overprinted in Black Like Nos. C38-C42

1934, May 1　Wmk. 140　Perf. 14

CE1	APSD1	2.25 l red orange	11.00	130.00
CE2	APSD1	4.50 l + 1 l dp rose	11.00	130.00
	Set, never hinged		52.00	

AUTHORIZED DELIVERY STAMP

Authorized Delivery Stamp of Italy 1930, Overprinted like Nos. 38-42

1931, Mar.　Wmk. 140　Perf. 14

EY1	AD2	10c reddish brown	15.00	36.00
	Never hinged		36.00	

TRISTAN DA CUNHA

ˌtris-tən-də-'kü-nə

LOCATION — Group of islands in the south Atlantic Ocean midway between the Cape of Good Hope and South America
GOVT. — A dependency of St. Helena
AREA — 40 sq. mi.
POP. — 313 (1988)

12 Pence = 1 Shilling
100 Cents = 1 Rand (1961)
12 Pence = 1 Shilling (1963)
20 Shillings = 1 Pound
100 Pence = 1 Pound (1971)

> Catalogue values for all unused stamps in this country are for Never Hinged items.

Stamps of St. Helena, 1938-49, Overprinted in Black

1952, Jan. 1　Wmk. 4　Perf. 12½

1	A24	½p purple	.25	2.75
2	A24	1p blue grn & blk	1.00	1.50
3	A24	1½p car rose & blk	1.00	1.50
4	A24	2p carmine & blk	1.00	1.50
5	A24	3p gray	1.25	1.50
6	A24	4p ultra	6.50	2.50
7	A24	6p gray blue	6.50	2.50
8	A24	8p olive	6.50	7.50
9	A24	1sh sepia	5.50	2.00
10	A24	2sh6p deep claret	18.00	16.00
11	A24	5sh brown	30.00	20.00
12	A24	10sh violet	45.00	32.50
	Nos. 1-12 (12)		122.50	91.75
	Set, hinged		85.00	

Common Design Types pictured following the introduction.

Coronation Issue
Common Design Type

1953, June 2　Engr.　Perf. 13½x13

13	CD312	3p dk green & black	1.00	1.75

Tristan Crayfish — A1

Carting Flax — A2

Designs: 1½p, Rockhopper penguin. 2p, Factory. 2½p, Mollymauk. 3p, Island boat. 4p, View of Tristan. 5p, Potato patches. 6p, Inaccessible Island. 9p, Nightingale Island. 1sh, St. Mary's Church. 2sh 6p, Elephant seal. 5sh, Flightless rail. 10sh, Island spinning wheel.

1954-58　Perf. 12½

14	A1	½p choc & red	.25	.25
a.	Bklt. pane of 4 ('58)		2.50	
15	A2	1p green & choc	.25	.60
a.	Bklt. pane of 4		4.00	
16	A1	1½p dp plum & blk	2.00	1.40
a.	Bklt. pane of 4		7.00	
17	A2	2p org & vio blue	.35	.25
18	A2	2½p carmine & blk	1.75	.70
19	A1	3p ol grn & ultra	.80	1.40
a.	Bklt. pane of 4 ('58)		10.50	
20	A2	4p dp bl & aqua	.80	.75
a.	Bklt. pane of 4 ('58)		13.00	
21	A2	5p gray & bl grn	.80	.75
22	A2	6p vio & dk ol grn	.80	.75
23	A2	9p henna brn & rose lil	.80	.45
24	A2	1sh choc & ol grn	.80	.45
25	A2	2sh6p blue & choc	17.50	10.00
26	A2	5sh red org & blk	47.50	15.00
27	A2	10sh red vio & org	22.50	14.00
	Nos. 14-27 (14)		96.90	46.75
	Set, hinged		57.50	

Starfish — A3

Fish: 1p, Concha. 1½p, Klipfish. 2p, Heron fish (saury). 2½p, Snipefish ("swordfish"). 3d, Tristan crawfish. 4p, Soldier fish. 5p, Five finger fish. 6p, Mackeral scad. 9p, Stumpnose. 1sh, Bluefish. 2sh6p, Snoek (snake mackerel). 5sh, Shark. 10sh, Atlantic right whale.

Perf. 12½x13

1960, Feb. 1　Engr.　Wmk. 314

28	A3	½p org & blk	.25	.25
a.	Booklet pane of 4		1.50	
29	A3	1p rose lil & blk	.25	.25
a.	Booklet pane of 4		2.50	
30	A3	1½p grnsh bl & blk	.30	.25
a.	Booklet pane of 4		2.60	
31	A3	2p green & black	.40	.35
32	A3	2½p brown & black	.45	.35
33	A3	3p rose red & blk	1.20	1.40
a.	Booklet pane of 4		7.25	
34	A3	4p gray ol & blk	1.10	.65
a.	Booklet pane of 4		6.50	
35	A3	5p org yel & blk	1.40	.70
36	A3	6p blue & black	1.40	.80
37	A3	9p rose car & blk	1.60	.70
38	A3	1sh brn org & blk	2.40	.60
39	A3	2sh6p vio blue & blk	11.00	11.00
40	A3	5sh emerald & blk	12.00	12.00
41	A3	10sh violet & blk	42.50	30.00
	Nos. 28-41 (14)		76.25	59.30

1961, Apr. 15　Perf. 12½x13

42	A3	½c like No. 28	.25	.25
43	A3	1c like No. 29	.25	.25
44	A3	1½c like No. 30	.40	.40
45	A3	2c like No. 32	.75	.75
46	A3	2½c like No. 33	1.00	1.10
47	A3	3c like No. 34	1.00	1.10
48	A3	4c like No. 35	1.25	1.25
49	A3	5c like No. 36	1.25	1.25
50	A3	7½c like No. 37	1.25	1.25
51	A3	10c like No. 38	1.60	1.60
52	A3	25c like No. 39	7.00	7.00
53	A3	50c like No. 40	16.00	17.00
54	A3	1r like No. 41	37.50	35.00
	Nos. 42-54 (13)		69.50	68.20

Nos. 46, 49-51 surcharged for "Tristan Relief" are listed as St. Helena Nos. B1-B4.

Types of St. Helena, 1961 Overprinted

Perf. 11½x12, 12x11½

1963, Apr. 12　Photo.　Wmk. 4

55	A29	1p rose, ultra, yel & grn	.25	1.00
56	A29	1½p bis, sep, yel & grn	.25	.40
57	A29	2p gray & red	.25	1.00
58	A30	3p dk bl, rose & grnsh bl	.30	1.00
a.	Double overprint			
59	A29	4½p slate, brn & grn	.55	.70
60	A29	6p cit, brn & dp car	.80	.40
61	A29	7p vio, blk & red brn	.55	.40
62	A29	10p bl & dp claret	.55	.40
63	A29	1sh red brn, grn & yel	.55	.40
64	A29	1sh6p gray bl & blk	5.00	1.10
65	A29	2sh6p grnsh bl, yel & red	1.25	.75
66	A29	5sh grn, brn & yel	5.00	1.25
67	A29	10sh gray bl, blk & sal	6.00	1.25
	Nos. 55-67 (13)		21.30	10.05

Freedom from Hunger Issue
Common Design Type

Perf. 14x14½

1963, Oct. 2　Photo.　Wmk. 314

68	CD314	1sh6p rose carmine	.75	.35

Red Cross Centenary Issue
Common Design Type

1964, Jan. 2　Litho.　Perf. 13

69	CD315	3p black & red	.40	.30
70	CD315	1sh6p ultra & red	.75	.50

Flagship of Tristáo da Cunha, 1506 — A4

Queen Elizabeth II — A5

½p, Map of South Atlantic Ocean. 1½p, Dutch ship Heemstede, first landing, 1643. 2p, New England whaler. 3p, Confederate ship Shenandoah. 4½p, H.M.S. Galatea, 1867. 6p, H.M.S. Cilicia, 1942. 7p, H.M. Royal Yacht Britannia, 1957. 10p, H.M.S. Leopard, Evacuation, 1961. 1sh, Dutch ship Tjisadane, 1961. 1sh6p, M.V. Tristania. 2sh6p, M.V. Boissevain, returning islanders, 1963. 5sh, M.S. Bornholm, returning islanders, 1963.

Perf. 11x11½

1965, Feb. 17　Engr.　Wmk. 314

71	A4	½p black & dk blue	.25	.25
a.	Booklet pane of 4		.25	
72	A4	1p black & emerald	.85	.25
a.	Booklet pane of 4		4.25	
73	A4	1½p black & ultra	.85	.25
a.	Booklet pane of 4		4.25	
74	A4	2p black & lilac	.85	.25
75	A4	3p blk & grnsh bl	.85	.25
a.	Booklet pane of 4		4.25	
76	A4	4½p black & brown	.85	.25
77	A4	6p black & green	.70	.30
a.	Booklet pane of 4		4.25	
78	A4	7p black & ver	.85	.40
79	A4	10p black & dk brn	.85	.40
80	A4	1sh black & lil rose	.85	.50
81	A4	1sh6p black & olive	7.00	2.75
82	A4	2sh6p black & brn org	9.00	3.00
83	A4	5sh black & violet	9.00	8.00

Perf. 11½x11

84	A5	10sh lil rose & dk bl	1.75	1.50
	Nos. 71-84 (14)		28.50	18.35

See Nos. 113-115. For surcharges see Nos. 108, 141-152. For overprints see No. 132.

ITU Issue
Common Design Type

1965, May 11　Litho.　Perf. 11x11½

85	CD317	3p vermilion & gray	.40	.25
86	CD317	6p purple & orange	.60	.40

Intl. Cooperation Year Issue
Common Design Type

1965, Oct. 25　Wmk. 314　Perf. 14½

87	CD318	1p blue grn & claret	.25	.25
88	CD318	6p lt violet & green	.80	.40

Churchill Memorial Issue
Common Design Type

Wmk. 314

**1966, Jan. 24　Photo.　Perf. 14
Design in Black, Gold and Carmine Rose**

89	CD319	1p bright blue	.25	.25
90	CD319	3p green	.35	.25
91	CD319	6p brown	1.35	.70
92	CD319	1sh6p violet	4.00	1.50
	Nos. 89-92 (4)		5.95	2.70

World Cup Soccer Issue
Common Design Type

1966　Litho.　Perf. 14

93	CD320	3p multicolored	.25	.25
94	CD321	2sh6p multicolored	1.00	.55

Nos. 93-94 were issued Oct. 1 in Tristan da Cunha, but on July 1 in St. Helena.

Light Dragoon of 19th Century and Sailing Ship — A6

Wmk. 314

1966, Aug. 15　Litho.　Perf. 14½

95	A6	3p pale green & multi	.25	.25
96	A6	6p tan & multi	.25	.25
97	A6	1sh6p gray & multi	.40	.30
98	A6	2sh6p multicolored	.55	.45
	Nos. 95-98 (4)		1.45	1.25

150th anniv. of the establishment of a garrison on Tristan da Cunha.

WHO Headquarters Issue
Common Design Type

1966, Oct. 1　Litho.　Perf. 14

99	CD322	6p multicolored	.30	.25
100	CD322	5sh multicolored	1.60	1.00

UNESCO Anniversary Issue
Common Design Type

1966, Dec. 1　Litho.　Perf. 14

101	CD323	10p "Education"	.30	.25
102	CD323	1sh6p "Science"	.60	.40
103	CD323	2sh6p "Culture"	1.10	.75
	Nos. 101-103 (3)		2.00	1.40

Calshot Harbor A7

Perf. 14x14½

1967, Jan. 2　Litho.　Unwmk.

104	A7	6p dull green & multi	.25	.25
105	A7	10p brown & multi	.25	.25
106	A7	1sh6p dull blue & multi	.25	.25
107	A7	2sh6p orange brn & multi	.25	.30
	Nos. 104-107 (4)		1.00	1.05

Opening of the artificial Calshot Harbor.

No. 76 Surcharged with New Value and Three Bars

Perf. 11x11½

1967, May 10　Engr.　Wmk. 314

108	A4	4p on 4½p blk & brn	.45	.30

Tristan da Cunha, Prince Alfred, Queen Elizabeth II and Prince Philip — A8

1967, July 10   Litho.   Perf. 14x14½
109	A8	3p blue grn, dk grn & blk	.25	.25
110	A8	6p dk carmine & blk	.25	.25
111	A8	1sh6p brt grn, gray grn & blk	.25	.25
112	A8	2sh6p dull ultra, sep & blk	.25	.30
		Nos. 109-112 (4)	1.00	1.05

Cent. of the visit of Prince Alfred, First Duke of Edinburgh, to Tristan da Cunha.

Types of 1965

Designs: 4p, H.M.S. Challenger, 1870. 10sh, South African research vessel, R.S.A. £1, Queen Elizabeth II.

Perf. 11x11½
		1967, Sept. 1 Engr. Wmk. 314		
113	A4	4p black & orange	4.00	3.75
114	A4	10sh black & dull grn	14.00	12.00

Perf. 11½x11
115	A5	£1 brn org & dk blue	10.00	12.00
		Nos. 113-115 (3)	28.00	27.75

Wandering Albatross Nest — A9

Birds: 1sh, Big-billed buntings. 1sh6p, Tristan thrushes. 2sh6p, Great shearwaters.

Perf. 14x14½
		1968, May 15 Photo. Wmk. 314		
116	A9	4p multicolored	.25	.25
117	A9	1sh multicolored	.50	.30
118	A9	1sh6p multicolored	.85	.50
119	A9	2sh6p multicolored	1.20	.85
		Nos. 116-119 (4)	2.80	1.90

Union Jack and St. Helena Flag — A10

Design: 9p, 2sh6p, Map showing locations of St. Helena and Tristan da Cunha.

1968, Nov. 1   Wmk. 314
120	A10	6p violet & multi	.25	.25
121	A10	9p brn, bl grn & vio bl	.25	.25
122	A10	1sh6p green & multi	.25	.25
123	A10	2sh6p dp car, bl grn & vio bl	.25	.35
		Nos. 120-123 (4)	1.00	1.10

30th anniv. of Tristan da Cunha as a Dependency of St. Helena.

Frigate A11

Designs: 1sh, Cape Horner. 1sh6p, Barque. 2sh6p, Tea Clipper.

Perf. 11x11½
		1969, June 1 Engr. Wmk. 314		
124	A11	4p brt blue	.25	.25
125	A11	1sh rose carmine	.40	.40
126	A11	1sh6p green	.55	.50
127	A11	2sh6p sepia	.95	.90
		Nos. 124-127 (4)	2.15	2.05

Islanders Going to First Religious Service, 1851 — A12

Designs: 4p, Tristan da Cunha, birds and ship. 1sh6p, Landing at the beach. 2sh6p, St. Mary's Church, 1969, and procession.

Perf. 14½x14
		1969, Nov. 1 Litho. Wmk. 314		
128	A12	4p multicolored	.25	.40
129	A12	9p multicolored	.25	.40
130	A12	1sh6p multicolored	.30	.55
131	A12	2sh6p multicolored	.40	.55
		Nos. 128-131 (4)	1.20	1.90

Issued to honor the work of the United Society for the Propagation of the Faith.

No. 77 Overprinted in Deep Orange: "NATIONAL / SAVINGS"
Perf. 11x11½
		1970, May 15 Engr. Wmk. 314		
132	A4	6p black & green	.45	.25

Issued to promote national savings. No. 132 also used as savings stamp.

In 1971, No. 132 was locally surcharged "2½p" and 3 short bars by means of a rubber handstamp. Value $7.

Globe and Red Cross A13

1sh9p, 2sh6p, British & Red Cross flags, vert.

Perf. 13½x13, 13x13½
		1970, June 1 Litho.		
133	A13	4p emer, red & grnsh bl	.25	.25
134	A13	9p bister, red & grnsh bl	.35	.25
135	A13	1sh9p gray, vio bl & red	.55	.35
136	A13	2sh6p rose cl, vio bl & red	.75	.60
		Nos. 133-136 (4)	1.90	1.45

Centenary of the British Red Cross Society.

Rock Lobster and Lobster Men Placing Trap — A14

10p, 2sh6p, Workers in processing plant and side view of rock lobster (jasus tristani).

Perf. 12½x13
		1970, Nov. 1 Litho. Wmk. 314		
137	A14	4p lilac rose & multi	.25	.30
138	A14	10p dull yel & multi	.25	.35
139	A14	1sh6p brown org & multi	.60	.60
140	A14	2sh6p olive & multi	.90	.75
		Nos. 137-140 (4)	2.00	2.00

Tristan da Cunha rock lobster (crawfish) industry.

Nos. 72-74, 77-83, 113-114
Surcharged with New Value and Three Bars
Perf. 11x11½
		1971, Feb. 15 Engr. Wmk. 314		
141	A4	½p on 1p	.25	.25
142	A4	1p on 2p	.25	.25
143	A4	1½p on 4p	.30	.25
144	A4	2½p on 6p	.30	.25
145	A4	3p on 7p	.30	.25
146	A4	4p on 10p	.30	.25
147	A4	5p on 1sh	.30	.25
148	A4	7½p on 1sh6p	1.90	2.10
149	A4	12½p on 2sh6p	2.50	3.00
150	A4	15p on 1½p	2.50	3.50
151	A4	25p on 5sh	2.50	6.25
152	A4	50p on 10sh	3.75	12.50
		Nos. 141-152 (12)	15.15	29.10

"Quest" — A15

4p, Presentation of Scout Troop flag in front of Tristan school. 7½p, Great Britain #167a with Tristan da Cunha cancellation. 12½p, Sir Ernest Henry Shackleton, boat & expedition cancellations.

Perf. 13½x14
		1971, June 1 Litho. Wmk. 314		
153	A15	1½p lt blue & multi	.95	.25
154	A15	4p buff, yel grn & blk	.95	.45
155	A15	7½p pale grn, rose lil & blk	.95	1.00
156	A15	12½p buff & multi	1.60	2.00
		Nos. 153-156 (4)	4.45	3.70

50th anniversary of the Shackleton-Rowett South Atlantic expedition.

"Victory" at Trafalgar and Thomas Swain Catching Nelson — A16

Ships and Island Families: 2½p, "Emily of Stonington" and inscribed P. W. Green, 1836. 4p, "Italia" and inscribed Gaetano Lavarello, 1892, and Andrea Repetto. 7½p, "Falmouth" and Corp. William Glass, 1816. 12½p, American Whaler and inscribed 1836 Joshua Rogers, 1849, Capt. Andrew Hangan.

1971, Nov. 1
157	A16	1½p bister & multi	.25	.25
158	A16	2½p multicolored	.25	.25
159	A16	4p gray & multi	.40	.55
160	A16	7½p multicolored	.65	.85
161	A16	12½p blue & multi	1.00	1.40
		Nos. 157-161 (5)	2.55	3.30

Cow Pudding — A17

Native Flora: 1p, Peak berry and crater lake. 1½p, Sand flower, horiz. 2½p, New Zealand flax, horiz. 3p, Island tree. 5p, Bog fern and snow-capped mountain. 5p, Dog catcher and albatrosses. 7½p, Celery and terns. 12½p, Pepper tree and waterfall. 25p, Foul berry, horiz. 50p, Tussock and penguins. £1, Tussac and islands, horiz.

Perf. 13½x13, 13x13½
		1972, Feb. 26 Wmk. 314		
162	A17	½p gray & multi	.25	.25
163	A17	1p salmon & multi	.25	.25
164	A17	1½p green & multi	.25	.25
165	A17	2½p multicolored	.25	.25
166	A17	3p multicolored	.25	.25
167	A17	4p lemon & multi	.30	.30
168	A17	5p yol grn & multi	.45	.30
169	A17	7½p dull yel & multi	1.90	1.75
170	A17	12½p multi	1.25	1.00
171	A17	25p gray & multi	2.50	2.40
		Litho. and Engr.		
172	A17	50p multicolored	6.00	4.50
173	A17	£1 lt blue & multi	11.00	4.50
		Nos. 162-173 (12)	24.65	16.00

Coxswain — A18

2½p, Launching longboat. 4p, Men rowing longboat. 12½p, Longboat under sail.

1972, June 1   Litho.   Perf. 14
174	A18	2½p multi, horiz.	.25	.25
175	A18	4p multi, horiz.	.25	.25
176	A18	7½p multi	.50	.40
177	A18	12½p multi	.85	.50
		Nos. 174-177 (4)	1.85	1.40

Silver Wedding Issue, 1972
Common Design Type

Design: Queen Elizabeth II, Prince Philip, thrush and wandering albatrosses.

Perf. 14x14½
		1972, Nov. 20 Photo. Wmk. 314		
178	CD324	2½p multicolored	.25	.25
179	CD324	7½p ultra & multi	.45	.45

Altar, St. Mary's Church — A19

1973, July 8   Litho.   Perf. 13½
180	A19	25p dk blue & multi	1.10	1.10

St. Mary's Church, Tristan da Cunha, 50th anniv.

"Challenger" off Tristan, Steil's Sounding Instrument — A20

Designs: 4p, Challenger's laboratory. 7½p, Challenger off Nightingale Island. 12½p, Map of Challenger's voyage. Each stamp shows an instrument for deep sea soundings.

Perf. 13½x14
		1973, Oct. 15 Wmk. 314		
181	A20	4p multicolored	.25	.25
182	A20	5p multicolored	.25	.25
183	A20	7½p multicolored	.40	.40
184	A20	12½p multicolored	.80	.80
a.		Souv. sheet, #181-184, perf. 13½	2.25	2.25
		Nos. 181-184 (4)	1.70	1.70

Centenary of "Challenger's" visit to Tristan da Cunha during oceanographic exploration world trip, 1872-76.

View of English Port from Shipboard — A21

5p, Inspectors at volcano rim. 7½p, Islanders disembarking from "Bornholm." 12½p, Islanders on board ship approaching Tristan da Cunha.

1973, Nov. 10   *Perf. 14½*
185 A21   4p yellow, blk & gold   .25   .25
186 A21   5p multicolored   .25   .25
187 A21   7½p multicolored   .40   .30
188 A21   12½p multicolored   .50   .40
     Nos. 185-188 (4)   1.40 1.20

10th anniversary of return of islanders to Tristan da Cunha.

Princess Anne's Wedding Issue
Common Design Type

1973, Nov. 14   Wmk. 314   Perf. 14
189 CD325   7½p multicolored   .25   .25
190 CD325   12½p bl grn & multi   .25   .25

Rockhopper Penguin — A22

Designs: Rockhopper penguins.

1974, May 1   Litho.
191 A22   2½p shown   2.60 1.25
192 A22   5p Colony   3.00 1.65
193 A22   7½p Penguins fishing   3.25 2.00
194 A22   25p Penguin and
                 fledgling   6.50 5.00
     Nos. 191-194 (4)   15.35 9.90

Souvenir Sheet

Map of Tristan da Cunha, Penguin and Sea Gull — A23

1974, Oct. 1   Wmk. 314   Perf. 13½
195 A23 35p multicolored   5.25 5.25

Blenheim Palace A24

25p, Churchill and Queen Elizabeth II.

Wmk. 373
1974, Nov. 30   Litho.   Perf. 14
196 A24   7½p black & yellow   .25   .25
197 A24   25p black & brown   .40   .40
a.   Souvenir sheet of 2, #196-197 .90   .90
Sir Winston Churchill (1874-1965).

Plocamium Fuscorubrum — A25

Aquatic Plants: 5p, Ulva lactuca. 10p, Epymenia flabellata. 20p, Macrocystis pyrifera.

Perf. 13x14
1975, Apr. 16   Wmk. 314
198 A25   4p lilac & multi   .25   .25
199 A25   5p ultra & multi   .25   .25
200 A25   10p yellow & multi   .30   .30
201 A25   20p lt green & multi   .65   .65
     Nos. 198-201 (4)   1.45 1.45

Killer Whales — A26

Wmk. 314
1975, Nov. 1   Litho.   Perf. 13½
202 A26   2p shown   .30   .25
203 A26   3p Rough-toothed dol-
                 phins   .55   .25
204 A26   5p Atlantic right whale 1.50   .85
205 A26   20p Finback whales   3.75 1.90
     Nos. 202-205 (4)   6.10 3.25

Tristan da Cunha No. 1 A27

Designs: 9p, Tristan da Cunha #13, vert. 25p, Freighter Tristania II.

Perf. 13½x14, 14x13½
1976, May 6   Litho.   Wmk. 373
206 A27   5p lilac, vio & blk   .25   .25
207 A27   9p bluish gray, grn &
                 blk   .25   .25
208 A27   25p multicolored   .60   .60
a.   Souvenir sheet of 3   3.25 3.25
     Nos. 206-208 (3)   1.10 1.10

Festival of Stamps 1976. #208a contains one each of Ascension #214, St. Helena #297 and Tristan da Cunha #208.

The Patches A28

Views, by Roland Svensson: 3p, Tristan house, vert. 10p, Tristan Settlement and Cliffs. 20p, Huts at Nightingale, vert.

1976, Oct. 4   Litho.   Perf. 14
209 A28   3p multicolored   .25   .25
210 A28   5p multicolored   .25   .25
211 A28   10p multicolored   .30   .30
212 A28   20p multicolored   .45   .45
a.   Souvenir sheet of 4, #209-211 1.60 1.60
     Nos. 209-212 (4)   1.25 1.25

An artist's view of Tristan da Cunha. See Nos. 234-237, 268-271.

Royal Yacht Britannia — A29

15p, Royal standard. 25p, Royal family.

1977, Feb. 7   Wmk. 373   Perf. 13
213 A29   10p multicolored   .25   .25
214 A29   15p multicolored   .25   .25
215 A29   25p multicolored   .25   .25
     Nos. 213-215 (3)   .75   .75

25th anniv. of the reign of Elizabeth II. For surcharges see Nos. 220-221.

H.M.S. Eskimo, Sept. 1970 A30

Royal Naval Ships and Arms: 10p, Naiad, Nov. 1968. 15p, Jaguar, Mar. 1964. 20p, London, Dec. 1964. Dates of visits to island.

1977, Oct. 1   Litho.   Perf. 14½
216 A30   5p multicolored   .25   .25
217 A30   10p multicolored   .25   .25
218 A30   15p multicolored   .25   .25
219 A30   20p multicolored   .30   .30
a.   Souvenir sheet of 4, #216-219 1.75 1.75
     Nos. 216-219 (4)   1.05 1.05

Nos. 214-215 Surcharged with New Value and Bar

1977, Oct. 13   Wmk. 373   Perf. 13
220 A29   4p on 15p multi   2.50 6.50
221 A29   7½p on 25p multi   2.50 6.50

Giant Fulmars — A31

1p, Pterodroma macroptera, horiz. 2p, Fregetta marina, horiz. 3p, Macronectes giganteus. 4p, Pterodroma mollis. 5p, Diomedea exulans. 10p, Pterodroma brevirostris. 15p, Sterna vittata. 20p, Puffinus gravis. 25p, Pachyptila vittata. 50p, Catharacta skua. £1, Pelecanoides urinatrix. £2, Diomedea chlororynchos.

Perf. 13½x14, 14x13½
1977, Dec. 1   Litho.
222 A31   1p multicolored   .25   .45
223 A31   2p multicolored   .25   .75
224 A31   3p multicolored   .25   .75
225 A31   4p multicolored   .25   .85
226 A31   5p multicolored   .25   .85
227 A31   10p multicolored   .30   .85
228 A31   15p multicolored   .50 1.25
229 A31   20p multicolored   .65 1.25
230 A31   25p multicolored   .80 1.25
231 A31   50p multicolored   1.75 1.25
232 A31   £1 multicolored   2.50 2.25
233 A31   £2 multicolored   5.25 3.00
     Nos. 222-233 (12)   13.00 14.75

Nos. 224-233 are vertical. For overprints see Nos. 318-319.

Painting Type of 1976

Views by Roland Svensson: 5p, St. Mary's Church. 10p, Longboats. 15p, A Tristan home. 20p, Harbor, 1970.

Wmk. 373
1978, Mar. 1   Litho.   Perf. 14½
234 A28   5p multicolored   .25   .25
235 A28   10p multicolored   .25   .25
236 A28   15p multicolored   .30   .30
237 A28   20p multicolored   .45   .45
a.   Souvenir sheet of 4, #234-237 1.75 1.75
     Nos. 234-237 (4)   1.25 1.25

An artist's view of Tristan da Cunha.

Elizabeth II Coronation Anniversary
Common Design Types
Souvenir Sheet

1978, Apr. 21   Unwmk.   Perf. 15
238   Sheet of 6   1.50 1.50
a.   CD326 25p King's Bull   .30   .30
b.   CD327 25p Elizabeth II   .30   .30
c.   CD328 25p Tristan crawfish   .30   .30

No. 238 contains 2 se-tenant strips of Nos. 238a-238c, separated by horizontal gutter with commemorative and descriptive inscriptions and showing central part of coronation procession with coach.

Sodalite — A32

Local Minerals: 5p, Aragonite. 10p, Sulphur. 20p, Lava containing pyroxene crystal.

Perf. 13½x14
1978, June 9   Wmk. 373
239 A32   3p multicolored   .40   .40
240 A32   5p multicolored   .45   .45
241 A32   10p multicolored   .70   .70
242 A32   20p multicolored   1.10 1.10
     Nos. 239-242 (4)   2.65 2.65

Fish A33

1978, Sept. 29   Litho.   Perf. 14
243 A33   5p Klipfish   .30   .30
244 A33   10p Fivefinger   .30   .30
245 A33   15p Concha   .35   .35
246 A33   20p Soldier   .40   .40
     Nos. 243-246 (4)   1.35 1.35

Orangeleaf and Navy Flag — A34

Royal Fleet Auxiliary Vessels: 10p, Tarbatness. 20p, Tidereach. 25p, Reliant.

1978, Nov. 24   Litho.   Perf. 12½
247 A34   5p multicolored   .25   .25
248 A34   10p multicolored   .25   .25
249 A34   20p multicolored   .25   .25
250 A34   25p multicolored   .30   .30
a.   Souvenir sheet of 4, #247-250 1.40 2.75
     Nos. 247-250 (4)   1.05 1.05

Fur Seals — A35

Wildlife conservation: 5p, Elephant seal. 15p, Tristan thrush. 20p, Tristan buntings.

Wmk. 373
1979, Jan. 3   Litho.   Perf. 14
251 A35   5p multicolored   .25   .25
252 A35   10p multicolored   .25   .25
253 A35   15p multicolored   .30   .30
254 A35   20p multicolored   .35   .35
     Nos. 251-254 (4)   1.15 1.15

Tristan Longboat — A36

Ships: 10p, Queen Mary. 15p, Queen Elizabeth. 20p, QE II. 25p, QE II, longboat, view of Tristan.

1979, Feb. 8   Perf. 14½
255 A36   5p multicolored   .25   .25
256 A36   10p multicolored   .25   .25
257 A36   15p multicolored   .25   .25
258 A36   20p multicolored   .35   .35
     Nos. 255-258 (4)   1.10 1.10

Souvenir Sheet
259 A36   25p multicolored   1.00 *1.50*

Visit of cruise ship QE II, Feb. 8. No. 259 contains one 132x28mm stamp.

Tristan da Cunha No. 12 A37

Tristan da Cunha Stamps: 10p, No. 26. 25p, No. 58, vert. 50p, 1p-local "potatoe" stamp.

Perf. 14½x14, 14x14½

1979, Aug. 27   Litho.   Wmk. 373

260	A37	5p multicolored	.25 .25
261	A37	10p multicolored	.25 .25
262	A37	25p multicolored	.40 .40
		Nos. 260-262 (3)	.90 .90

Souvenir Sheet

263	A37	50p multicolored	.75 .75

Sir Rowland Hill (1795-1879), originator of penny postage.

The Padre's House, IYC Emblem A38

IYC Emblem, Children's Drawings: 10p, "Houses in the Village." 15p, "St. Mary's Church." 20p, "Rockhopper Penguins."

1979, Nov. 26   Litho.   Perf. 14

264	A38	5p multicolored	.25 .25
265	A38	10p multicolored	.25 .25
266	A38	15p multicolored	.25 .25
267	A38	25p multicolored	.25 .25
		Nos. 264-267 (4)	1.00 1.00

International Year of the Child.

Painting Type of 1976

Views (Sketches by Roland Svensson): 5p, Stoltenhoff Island. 10p, Nightingale from the East. 15p, The Administrator's abode, vert. 20p, "Ridge where the goat jumped off," vert.

1980, Feb.   Litho.   Perf. 14

268	A28	5p multicolored	.25 .25
269	A28	10p multicolored	.25 .25
270	A28	15p multicolored	.25 .25
271	A28	20p multicolored	.25 .25
a.		Souvenir sheet of 4, #268-271	1.00 1.00
		Nos. 268-271 (4)	1.00 1.00

Mail Pickup Boat — A40

1980, May 6   Litho.   Perf. 14

272	A40	5p shown	.25 .25
273	A40	10p Unloading mail	.25 .25
274	A40	15p Truck transport	.25 .25
275	A40	20p Delivery bell	.25 .25
276	A40	25p Distribution	.25 .25
		Nos. 272-276 (5)	1.25 1.25

London 80 Intl. Stamp Exhib., May 6-14.

Queen Mother Elizabeth Birthday
Common Design Type

1980, Aug. 11   Litho.   Perf. 14

277	CD330	14p multicolored	.45 .45

Golden Hinde — A41

1980, Sept. 6   Perf. 14½

278	A41	5p shown	.25 .25
279	A41	10p Drake's route	.25 .25
280	A41	20p Sir Francis Drake	.25 .25
281	A41	25p Queen Elizabeth I	.25 .25
		Nos. 278-281 (4)	1.00 1.00

Sir Francis Drake's circumnavigation, 400th anniversary.

Humpty Dumpty A42

Wmk. 373

1980, Oct. 31   Litho.   Perf. 13½

282		Sheet of 9	1.90 1.90
a.	A42	15p shown	.25 .25
b.	A42	15p Mary had a Little Lamb	.25 .25
c.	A42	15p Little Jack Horner	.25 .25
d.	A42	15p Hey Diddle Diddle	.25 .25
e.	A42	15p London Bridge	.25 .25
f.	A42	15p Old King Cole	.25 .25
g.	A42	15p Sing a Song of Sixpence	.25 .25
h.	A42	15p Tom Tom the Piper's Son	.25 .25
i.	A42	25p Owl and the Pussy Cat	.25 .25

Christmas 1980.

Islands on Mid-Atlantic Ridge, Society Emblem — A43

Royal Geographical Soc., 150th Anniv. (Maps and Expeditions): 10p, Tristan da Cunha, Francis Beaufort, 1806. 15p, Tristan Island, Norwegian expedition, 1937-1938. 20p, Gough Island, scientific survey, 1955-1956.

1980, Dec. 15

283	A43	5p multicolored	.25 .25
284	A43	10p multicolored	.25 .25
285	A43	15p multicolored	.25 .25
286	A43	20p multicolored	.25 .25
		Nos. 283-286 (4)	1.00 1.00

Rev. Edwin Dodgson A44

Wmk. 373

1981, Mar. 23   Litho.   Perf. 14

287	A44	10p portrait, vert.	.25 .25
288	A44	20p shown	.30 .30
289	A44	30p Dodgson preaching, vert.	.40 .40
a.		Souvenir sheet of 3, #287-289	.90 .90
		Nos. 287-289 (3)	.95 .95

Centenary of arrival of Rev. Edwin H. Dodgson, who saved population from starvation.

Map of Tristan da Cunha showing L'heure du Berger Route, 1767 (Dalrymple's Map, 1781) — A45

Early Maps and Charts By: 5p, 21p, Capt. Denham, 1853 (diff.). 35p, Ivan Keulen, 1700.

1981, May 22

290	A45	5p multicolored	.25 .25
291	A45	14p multicolored	.30 .30
292	A45	21p multicolored	.45 .45
		Nos. 290-292 (3)	1.00 1.00

Souvenir Sheet

293	A45	35p multicolored	.65 .85

Royal Wedding Issue
Common Design Type
Wmk. 373

1981, July 22   Litho.   Perf. 14

294	CD331	5p Bouquet	.25 .25
295	CD331	20p Charles	.25 .25
296	CD331	50p Couple	.40 .40
		Nos. 294-296 (3)	.90 .90

Hiking — A46

1981, Sept. 14

297	A46	5p shown	.25 .25
298	A46	10p Camping	.25 .25
299	A46	20p Map reading	.25 .25
300	A46	25p Prince Philip	.25 .25
		Nos. 297-300 (4)	1.00 1.00

Duke of Edinburgh's Awards, 25th anniv.

Inaccessible Island Rail — A47

1981, Nov. 1   Litho.   Perf. 13½x14

301		Strip of 4	1.20 1.20
a.	A47	10p Nest	.30 .30
b.	A47	10p Eggs	.30 .30
c.	A47	10p Chicks	.30 .30
d.	A47	10p Adult rail	.30 .30

Six-gilled Shark A48

1982, Feb. 8   Litho.   Perf. 13½x14

302	A48	5p shown	.25 .25
303	A48	14p Porbeagle shark	.40 .30
304	A48	21p Blue shark	.65 .55
305	A48	35p Hammerhead shark	.90 .85
		Nos. 302-305 (4)	2.20 1.95

Marcella — A49

1982, Apr. 5   Litho.   Perf. 14

306	A49	5p shown	.35 .35
307	A49	15p Eliza Adams	.35 .35
308	A49	30p Corinthian	.50 .50
309	A49	50p Samuel & Thomas	.80 .80
		Nos. 306-309 (4)	2.00 2.00

See Nos. 324-327.

Princess Diana Issue
Common Design Type
Perf. 14½x14

1982, July 1   Litho.   Wmk. 373

310	CD333	5p Arms	.25 .25
311	CD333	15p Diana	.55 .25
312	CD333	30p Wedding	1.10 .35
313	CD333	50p Portrait	1.75 .60
		Nos. 310-313 (4)	3.65 1.45

Scouting Year — A50

5p, Baden-Powell, vert. 20p, Brownsea Isld. camp, 1907, vert. No. 316, 50p, Saluting. No. 317, 50p, Tree illustration, vert.

Perf. 13½x13, 13x13½

1982, Aug. 23   Litho.

314	A50	5p multicolored	.25 .25
315	A50	20p multicolored	.30 .30
316	A50	50p multicolored	.75 .75
		Nos. 314-316 (3)	1.30 1.30

Souvenir Sheet
Perf. 14

317	A50	50p multicolored	1.40 1.25

Nos. 226, 230 Overprinted: "1st PARTICIPATION / COMMONWEALTH / GAMES 1982"
Perf. 13½x14

1982, Sept. 28   Litho.   Wmk. 373

318	A31	5p multicolored	.25 .25
319	A31	25p multicolored	.40 .40

12th Commonwealth Games, Brisbane, Australia, Sept. 30-Oct. 9.

Formation of Volcanic Island A51

1982, Nov. 1   Perf. 14x14½

320	A51	5p shown	.30 .30
321	A51	15p Surface cinder cones	.40 .40
322	A51	25p Eruption	.50 .50
323	A51	35p 1961 eruption	.60 .60
		Nos. 320-323 (4)	1.80 1.80

Ship Type of 1982

1983, Feb. 1   Litho.   Perf. 14

324	A49	5p Islander, vert.	.25 .25
325	A49	20p Roscoe	.40 .40
326	A49	35p Columbia	.75 .60
327	A49	50p Emeline, vert.	1.00 .90
		Nos. 324-327 (4)	2.40 2.15

Tractor Pulling Trailer A52

1983, May 2   Litho.   Perf. 14

328	A52	5p shown	.25 .25
329	A52	15p Pack mules	.25 .25
330	A52	30p Oxen pulling cart	.40 .40
331	A52	50p Jeep	.60 .60
		Nos. 328-331 (4)	1.50 1.50

Map of South Atlantic A53

Island History — 3p, Tristao d'Acunha's flagship. 4p, Landing, 1643. 5p, 17th cent. views. 10p, Landing party, 1815. 15p, Settlement. 18p, Governor Glass's house. 20p, Rev. W.F. Taylor, Peter Green. 25p, Three-master John and Elizabeth. 50p, Dependency declaration of St. Helena, 1938. £1, Commissioning ceremony. £2, Evacuation, 1961.

Wmk. 373

1983, Aug. 1　　Litho.　　Perf. 14

332	A53	1p multicolored	.25	.25
333	A53	3p multicolored	.25	.25
334	A53	4p multicolored	.25	.25
335	A53	5p multicolored	.25	.25
336	A53	10p multicolored	.25	.25
337	A53	15p multicolored	.35	.45
338	A53	18p multicolored	.40	.50
339	A53	20p multicolored	.45	.60
340	A53	25p multicolored	.70	.90
341	A53	50p multicolored	1.25	1.75
342	A53	£1 multicolored	2.50	3.50
343	A53	£2 multicolored	5.25	7.25
		Nos. 332-343 (12)	12.15	16.20

Raphael, 500th Birth Anniv. — A54

1983, Oct. 27　Litho.　　Perf. 14½

344	A54	10p multicolored	.25	.25
345	A54	25p multicolored	.50	.50
346	A54	40p multicolored	.90	.90
		Nos. 344-346 (3)	1.65	1.65

Souvenir Sheet

347	A54	50p multi, horiz.	1.50	1.25

Details from Christ's Charge to St. Peter.

St. Helena Colony Sesquicentenary — A55

1984, Jan. 3　Litho.　　Perf. 14

348	A55	10p No. 7	.25	.25
349	A55	15p No. 9	.25	.25
350	A55	25p No. 10	.40	.40
351	A55	60p No. 12	1.10	1.00
		Nos. 348-351 (4)	2.00	1.90

Local Fungi A56

10p, Agrocybe praecox, vert. 20p, Laccaria tetraspora, vert. 30p, Agrocybe cylindracea. 50p, Sarcoscypha coccinea.

1984, Mar. 26

352	A56	10p multicolored	.50	.75
353	A56	20p multicolored	.85	.85
354	A56	30p multicolored	1.35	1.35
355	A56	50p multicolored	2.10	2.10
		Nos. 352-355 (4)	4.80	5.05

Constellations A57

1984, July 30　　　Perf. 14½

356	A57	10p Orion	.25	.25
357	A57	20p Scorpius	.55	.45
358	A57	25p Canis Major	.60	.55
359	A57	50p Crux	1.20	1.10
		Nos. 356-359 (4)	2.60	2.35

Sheep Shearing — A58

1984, Oct. 1

360	A58	9p shown	.25	.25
361	A58	17p Carding wool	.35	.30
362	A58	29p Spinning	.60	.50
363	A58	45p Knitting	.95	.85
a.		Souvenir sheet of 4, #360-363	2.25	2.25
		Nos. 360-363 (4)	2.15	1.90

Stamps from No. 363a do not have white border around the design.

Christmas 1984 A59

1984, Dec. 3　　　　Perf. 14

364	A59	10p Three angels, Christmas dinner	.25	.25
365	A59	20p Two angels, cart	.40	.35
366	A59	30p Candles, sailboat	.65	.55
367	A59	50p Trees, Nativity	1.00	.85
		Nos. 364-367 (4)	2.30	2.00

Shipwrecks — A60

10p, HMS Julia, 1817, vert. 25p, Bell from Mabel Clark, 1878, vert. 35p, Barque Glenhuntley, 1898.
60p, Map of shipwreck sites.

1985, Feb. 4　Perf. 14x13½, 13½x14

368	A60	10p multicolored	.70	.45
369	A60	25p multicolored	1.10	1.10
370	A60	35p multicolored	1.60	1.50
		Nos. 368-370 (3)	3.40	3.05

Souvenir Sheet

371	A60	60p multicolored	2.25	2.00

No. 371 contains one 48x32mm stamp.
See Nos. 393-396, 412-415.

Queen Mother 85th Birthday
Common Design Type

10p, With Prince Charles, 1954. 20p, With Margaret at Ascot. 30p, Queen Mother. 50p, Holding Prince Henry.
80p, With Anne.

**　　　　　　Perf. 14½x14**

1985, June 7　Litho.　　Wmk. 384

372	CD336	10p multicolored	.25	.25
373	CD336	20p multicolored	.45	.45
374	CD336	30p multicolored	.70	.70
375	CD336	50p multicolored	.85	.85
		Nos. 372-375 (4)	2.25	2.25

Souvenir Sheet

376	CD336	80p multicolored	2.75	2.75

Flags A61

10p, Jonathan Lambert & flag of 1811, Isles of Refreshment. 15p, Cannon & flag of 21st Light Dragoons, 1816-17, Fort Malcolm. 25p, HMS Falmouth, 1816, & flag of HMS Atlantic Isle, HMS JOB 9, 1942-46. 60p, View of Tristan & Union Jack, 1816 to date.

1985, Sept. 30　Wmk. 373　　Perf. 14

377	A61	10p multicolored	.45	.45
378	A61	15p multicolored	.60	.60
379	A61	25p multicolored	1.05	1.05
380	A61	60p multicolored	2.75	2.40
		Nos. 377-380 (4)	4.85	4.50

Nos. 378-380 vert.

Loss of The Lifeboat, Cent. — A62

1985, Nov. 28

381	A62	10p Lifeboat, barque West Riding	.25	.25
382	A62	30p Map	.75	.75
383	A62	50p Death toll	1.25	1.25
		Nos. 381-383 (3)	2.25	2.25

Halley's Comet A63

10p, Bayeux Tapestry, c. 1092. 20p, Trajectory around Earth. 30p, Comet over Inaccessible Is. 50p, Ship Paramour.

1986, Mar. 3　　　　Wmk. 384

384	A63	10p multicolored	.50	.50
385	A63	20p multicolored	.80	.80
386	A63	30p multicolored	1.10	1.10
387	A63	50p multicolored	1.75	1.75
		Nos. 384-387 (4)	4.15	4.15

Queen Elizabeth II 60th Birthday
Common Design Type

Designs: 10p, With Prince Charles, 1950. 15p, Birthday Parade, wearing uniform of Scots Guards, 1976. 25p, At Westminster Abbey, London, 1972, wearing mantle and robes of the Most Noble Order of Bath. 45p, Silver Jubilee Tour, Canada, 1977. 65p, Visiting Crown Agents' offices, 1983.

1986, Apr. 21　　　　Perf. 14½

388	CD337	10p scarlet, blk & sil	.25	.25
389	CD337	15p ultra & multi	.30	.30
390	CD337	25p green & multi	.50	.50
391	CD337	45p violet & multi	.80	.80
392	CD337	65p rose vio & multi	1.15	1.15
		Nos. 388-392 (5)	3.00	3.00

For overprints see Nos. 429-433.

Shipwrecks Type of 1985

9p, SV Allanshaw, 1893. 20p, Church font from Edward Vittery, 1881. 40p, Figurehead, 1940.
65p, Barque Italia, 1892.

1986, June 2　　　　Perf. 13½

393	A60	9p multicolored	.45	.45
394	A60	20p multicolored	.90	.90
395	A60	40p multicolored	1.75	1.75
		Nos. 393-395 (3)	3.10	3.10

Souvenir Sheet
Perf. 13½x13

396	A60	65p multicolored	3.25	3.25

Nos. 394-395 vert.

Royal Wedding Issue, 1986
Common Design Type

Designs: 10p, Informal portrait. 40p, Andrew operating helicopter.

1986, July 23　　　　Perf. 14

397	CD338	10p multicolored	.25	.25
398	CD338	40p multicolored	1.15	1.15

A64

5p, Wandering albatross. 10p, Daisy. 20p, Vanessa butterfly. 25p, Wilkins's bunting. 50p, Ring-eye.

1986, Sept. 30

399	A64	5p multicolored	.25	.25
400	A64	10p multicolored	.50	.50
401	A64	20p multicolored	1.00	1.00
402	A64	25p multicolored	1.25	1.25
403	A64	50p multicolored	2.40	2.40
		Nos. 399-403 (5)	5.40	5.40

Flora & fauna of Inaccessible Island.

A65

Indigenous Flightless Species and Habitats: 10p, Flightless moth, Edinburgh Settlement. 25p, Strap-winged fly, Crater Lake. 35p, Flightless rail, Inaccessible Island. 50p, Gough Island moorhen, Gough Island.

1987, Jan. 23　　　　Perf. 14½

404	A65	10p multicolored	.45	.45
405	A65	25p multicolored	1.10	1.10
406	A65	35p multicolored	1.50	1.50
407	A65	50p multicolored	2.25	2.25
		Nos. 404-407 (4)	5.30	5.30

Rockhopper Penguins A66

1987, June 22

408	A66	10p Swimming	.60	.60
409	A66	20p Nesting	1.30	1.30
410	A66	30p Adult and young	1.90	1.90
411	A66	50p Adult's head	3.50	3.50
		Nos. 408-411 (4)	7.30	7.30

Shipwrecks Type of 1985

Designs: 11p, Castaways attacking sea elephant, vert. 17p, Henry A. Paull, 1879, Sandy Point. 45p, Gustav Stoltenhoff, Stoltenhoff Is., vert. 70p, Map of wrecks off Inaccessible Is.

1987, Apr. 2　　　　Perf. 14

412	A60	11p olive gray & blk	.55	.55
413	A60	17p dark violet & blk	.90	.90
414	A60	45p myrtle green & blk	2.60	2.60
		Nos. 412-414 (3)	4.05	4.05

Souvenir Sheet

415	A60	70p lt bl, royal bl & apple grn	4.50	4.50

Norwegian Scientific Expedition, 50th Anniv. — A67

10p, Microscope and textbooks symbolic of expedition results. 20p, Scientists tagging a mollymawk. 30p, Expedition headquarters on the island. 50p, S.S. Thorshammer.

Wmk. 384

1987, Dec. 7　Litho.　　Perf. 14

416	A67	10p multicolored	.95	.90

417	A67	20p multicolored	1.90	1.50

Wmk. 373

418	A67	30p multicolored	2.75	2.10
419	A67	50p multicolored	4.00	3.50
		Nos. 416-419 (4)	9.60	8.00

Fauna of Nightingale Island — A68

1988, Mar. 21   Wmk. 384   Perf. 14

420	A68	5p Tristan bunting	.30	.30
421	A68	15p Tristan thrush	.55	.55
422	A68	20p Yellow-nosed albatross	.90	.90
423	A68	25p Great shearwater	1.10	1.10
424	A68	50p Elephant seal	2.50	2.50
		Nos. 420-424 (5)	5.35	5.35

Handicrafts A69

1988, May 30   Perf. 14½

425	A69	10p Painted penguin eggs	.35	.35
426	A69	15p Moccasins	.50	.50
427	A69	35p Woolen clothing	1.25	1.25
428	A69	50p Model canvas boats	1.75	1.75
		Nos. 425-428 (4)	3.85	3.85

Nos. 388-392 Ovptd. "40TH WEDDING ANNIVERSARY" In Silver

1988, Mar. 9

429	CD337	10p scar, blk & sil	.25	.25
430	CD337	15p ultra & multi	.35	.35
431	CD337	25p green & multi	.50	.50
432	CD337	45p violet & multi	.90	.90
433	CD337	65p rose vio & multi	1.40	1.40
		Nos. 429-433 (5)	3.40	3.40

19th Cent. Whaling A70

1988, Oct. 6   Perf. 14x14½

434	A70	10p "Trying out" blubber	.70	.70
435	A70	20p Harpoon guns	1.25	1.25
436	A70	30p Scrimshaw	2.10	2.10
437	A70	50p Ships	3.25	3.25
		Nos. 434-437 (4)	7.30	7.30

Souvenir Sheet

438	A70	£1 Right whale	5.00	5.00

Lloyds of London, 300th Anniv.
Common Design Type

10p, Lloyds's new building, 1988. 25p, Cargo ship *Tristania II*, horiz. 35p, Supply ship *St. Helena*, horiz. 50p, Square-rigger *Kobenhavn*, lost at sea.

1988, Nov. 7   Perf. 14

439	CD341	10p multicolored	.60	.60
440	CD341	25p multicolored	1.75	1.75
441	CD341	35p multicolored	2.25	2.25
442	CD341	50p multicolored	3.00	3.00
		Nos. 439-442 (4)	7.60	7.60

Paintings of the Island, 1824, by Augustus Earle (1793-1838) — A71

Designs: 1p, Government House. 3p, Squall off Tristan. 4p, Rafting Blubber. 5p, Tristan.

10p, Man Killing an Albatross. 15p, View on the Summit. 20p, Nightingale Island. 25p, Tristan, diff. 35p, "Solitude," Watching the Horizon. 50p, North Eastern. £1, Tristan, diff. £2, Governor Glass and His Companions.

1988, Dec. 10

443	A71	1p multicolored	.25	.25
444	A71	3p multicolored	.25	.25
445	A71	4p multicolored	.25	.25
446	A71	5p multicolored	.25	.25
447	A71	10p multicolored	.35	.35
448	A71	15p multicolored	.45	.60
449	A71	20p multicolored	.60	1.10
450	A71	25p multicolored	.80	1.25
451	A71	35p multicolored	1.10	2.00
452	A71	50p multicolored	1.40	2.75
453	A71	£1 multicolored	3.00	5.50
454	A71	£2 multicolored	6.00	10.50
		Nos. 443-454 (12)	14.70	25.05

Gough Is. Fauna — A72

1989, Feb. 6   Litho.   Wmk. 384

455	A72	5p Giant petrel	.45	.45
456	A72	10p Gough moorhen	.80	.90
457	A72	20p Gough bunting	1.50	1.50
458	A72	25p Sooty albatross	1.75	1.75
459	A72	50p Amsterdam fur seal	3.50	3.50
		Nos. 455-459 (5)	8.00	8.00

Ferns — A73

10p, Eriosorus cheilanthoides. 25p, Asplenium alvarezense. 35p, Elaphoglossum hybridum. 50p, Ophioglossum opacum.

1989, May 22   Wmk. 373   Perf. 14

460	A73	10p multicolored	.55	.55
461	A73	25p multicolored	1.40	1.40
462	A73	35p multicolored	2.10	2.10
463	A73	50p multicolored	2.60	2.60
		Nos. 460-463 (4)	6.65	6.65

A74

1989, Nov. 20   Wmk. 384

464	A74	10p Cattle egret	1.30	1.10
465	A74	25p Spotted sandpiper	2.75	2.50
466	A74	35p Purple gallinule	4.00	3.50
467	A74	50p Barn swallow	5.25	4.75
		Nos. 464-467 (4)	13.30	11.85

Artifacts on Exhibit in the Nautical Museum A75

10p, Surgeon's mortar. 20p, Parts of a harpoon. 30p, Compass with binnacle hood. 60p, Rope-twisting device.

1989, Sept. 25

468	A75	10p multicolored	.55	.55
469	A75	20p multicolored	1.10	1.10
470	A75	30p multicolored	1.75	1.75
471	A75	60p multicolored	3.50	3.50
		Nos. 468-471 (4)	6.90	6.90

Moths A76

10p, Peridroma saucia. 15p, Ascalapha odorata. 35p, Agrius cingulata. 60p, Eumorpha labruscae.

1990, Feb. 1   Perf. 14

472	A76	10p multicolored	.70	.70
473	A76	15p multicolored	1.10	1.10
474	A76	35p multicolored	2.75	2.75
475	A76	60p multicolored	5.00	5.00
		Nos. 472-475 (4)	9.55	9.55

Starfish (Echinoderms) A77

1990, June 12   Perf. 14x13½

476	A77	10p shown	.80	.80
477	A77	20p multi, diff.	1.10	1.50
478	A77	30p multi, diff.	2.00	2.25
479	A77	60p multi, diff.	4.50	4.50
		Nos. 476-479 (4)	9.00	9.05

Queen Mother, 90th Birthday
Common Design Types

25p, Queen Mother at the Coliseum. £1, Broadcasting to women of the empire, 1939.

1990, Aug. 4   Wmk. 384   Perf. 14x15

480	CD343	25p multicolored	1.10	1.10

Perf. 14½

481	CD344	£1 multicolored	4.50	4.50

Dunnottar Castle, 1942 — A78

Designs: 15p, RMS St. Helena, 1977-1990. 35p, Launching new RMS St. Helena, 1989. 60p, Duke of York launching new RMS St. Helena. £1, New RMS St. Helena.

1990, Sept. 13   Wmk. 373   Perf. 14½

482	A78	10p multicolored	.95	.95
483	A78	15p multicolored	1.50	1.50
484	A78	35p multicolored	4.00	3.25
485	A78	60p multicolored	6.25	5.50
		Nos. 482-485 (4)	12.70	11.20

Souvenir Sheet

486	A78	£1 multicolored	8.75	8.75

See Ascension Nos. 493-497, St. Helena Nos. 535-539.

Royal Navy Warships A79

Perf. 14½x14

1990, Nov. 30   Litho.   Wmk. 373

487	A79	10p Pyramus, 1829	1.25	1.25
488	A79	25p Penguin, 1815	3.00	3.00
489	A79	35p Thalia, 1886	4.25	4.25
490	A79	50p Sidon, 1858	6.00	6.00
		Nos. 487-490 (4)	14.50	14.50

See Nos. 547-550.

1991, Feb. 4

491	A79	10p Milford, 1938	2.10	1.60
492	A79	25p Dublin, 1923	3.25	2.75
493	A79	35p Yarmouth, 1919	4.50	4.00
494	A79	50p Carlisle, 1938	5.00	6.00
		Nos. 491-494 (4)	14.85	14.35

Souvenir Sheet

Royal Viking Sun — A80

Wmk. 384

1991, Apr. 1   Litho.   Perf. 14

495	A80	£1 multicolored	10.00	10.00

Prince Philip, 70th Birthday A81

Designs: 10p, HMS Galatea, Prince Alfred. 25p, Royal Visit, 1957. 30p, HMY Britannia, Prince Philip. 50p, Settlement of Edinburgh, Prince Philip.

1991, June 10   Wmk. 373

496	A81	10p multicolored	1.50	1.25
497	A81	25p multicolored	3.25	3.00
498	A81	30p multicolored	4.00	3.50
499	A81	50p multicolored	6.25	6.00
		Nos. 496-499 (4)	15.00	13.75

Birds A82

8p, Gough moorhens. 10p, Gough bunting. 12p, Gough moorhen in nest. 15p, Gough bunting with chicks.

1991, Oct. 1

500	A82	8p multicolored	2.50	1.60
501	A82	10p multicolored	2.50	1.90
502	A82	12p multicolored	2.75	1.90
503	A82	15p multicolored	3.00	2.25
		Nos. 500-503 (4)	10.75	7.65

World Wildlife Fund.

Discovery of America, 500th Anniv. — A83

10p, STV Eye of the Wind. 15p, STV Soren Larsen. 35p, STV Pinta, Nina, Santa Maria. 60p, Columbus, Santa Maria.

1992, Jan. 23

504	A83	10p multicolored	.95	.75
505	A83	15p multicolored	1.25	1.10
506	A83	35p multicolored	3.00	2.75
507	A83	60p multicolored	5.50	4.75
		Nos. 504-507 (4)	10.70	9.35

World Columbian Stamp Expo '92, Chicago and Genoa '92 Intl. Philatelic Exhibitions.

Queen Elizabeth II's Accession to the Throne, 40th Anniv.
Common Design Type
1992, Feb. 6

508	CD349	10p multicolored	.55	.55
509	CD349	20p multicolored	1.15	1.10
510	CD349	25p multicolored	1.40	1.25
511	CD349	35p multicolored	1.90	1.90
512	CD349	65p multicolored	3.75	3.50
		Nos. 508-512 (5)	8.75	8.30

Fish — A84

Designs: 10p, Caesioperca coatsii. 15p, Mendosoma lineatum. 35p, Physiculus karrerae. 60p, Decapterus longimanus.

1992, June 1

513	A84	10p multicolored	.80	.55
514	A84	15p multicolored	1.50	1.10
515	A84	35p multicolored	2.75	2.40
516	A84	60p multicolored	5.00	4.25
		Nos. 513-516 (4)	10.05	8.30

Wreck of the Italia, Cent. — A85

Designs: 10p, Italia leaving Greenock. 45p, In mid-Atlantic. 65p, Driving ashore on Stony Beach. £1, Italia in peaceful waters.

1992, Sept. 18   Perf. 13½x14

517	A85	10p multicolored	.85	.80
518	A85	45p multicolored	3.50	3.50
519	A85	65p multicolored	5.25	5.25
		Nos. 517-519 (3)	9.60	9.55

Souvenir Sheet

520	A85	£1 multicolored	9.75	9.75

Genoa '92 Intl. Philatelic Exhibition (#520).

Insects — A86

15p, Stenoscelis hylastoides. 45p, Trogloscaptomyza brevilamellata. 60p, Senilites tristanicola.

Perf. 14x13½
1993, Feb. 2   Litho.   Wmk. 384

521	A86	15p multicolored	1.25	1.25
522	A86	45p multicolored	3.50	3.50
523	A86	60p multicolored	4.00	4.00
		Nos. 521-523 (3)	8.75	8.75

Coronation of Queen Elizabeth II, 40th Anniv. — A87

Designs: 10p, Ampulla, spoon. 15p, Orb. 35p, Imperial State Crown. 60p, St. Edward's Crown.

1993, June 14   Perf. 14½

524	A87	10p green & black	.70	.70
525	A87	15p red vio & black	1.10	1.10
526	A87	35p purple & black	2.40	2.40
527	A87	60p blue & black	4.25	4.25
		Nos. 524-527 (4)	8.45	8.45

Resettlement to Tristan, 30th Anniv. — A88

Ships: No. 528, Tristania, Frances Repetto. No. 529, Boissevain. 50p, Bornholm.

1993, Nov. 10   Perf. 13½x14

528	A88	35p multicolored	2.75	2.50
529	A88	35p multicolored	2.75	2.50
a.		Pair, #528-529	6.50	6.00
530	A88	50p multicolored	4.50	4.25
		Nos. 528-530 (3)	10.00	9.25

Christmas — A89

Entire paintings or details: 5p, Madonna with Child, School of Botticelli. 15p, The Holy Family, by Daniel Gran. 35p, The Holy Virgin and Child, by Rubens. 65p, The Mystical Marriage of St. Catherine with the Holy Child, by Jan Van Balen.

1993, Nov. 30   Wmk. 373   Perf. 13

531	A89	5p multicolored	.60	.60
532	A89	15p multicolored	1.75	1.25
533	A89	35p multicolored	3.75	2.75
534	A89	65p multicolored	6.00	5.25
		Nos. 531-534 (4)	12.10	9.85

Ships A90

Designs: 1p, Duchess of Atholl, 1929. 3p, Empress of Australia, 1935. 5p, Anatolia, 1937. 8p, Viceroy of India, 1939. 10p, Rangitata, 1943. 15p, Caronia, 1950. 20p, Rotterdam, 1960. 25p, Leonardo da Vinci, 1972. 35p, Vistafjord, 1974. £1, World Discoverer, 1984. £2, Astor, 1984. £5, RMS St. Helena, 1992.

1994, Feb. 3   Wmk. 384   Perf. 14

535	A90	1p multicolored	.30	.35
536	A90	3p multicolored	.30	.35
537	A90	5p multicolored	.30	.35
538	A90	8p multicolored	.30	.35
539	A90	10p multicolored	.40	.50
540	A90	15p multicolored	.60	.70
541	A90	20p multicolored	.80	.90
542	A90	25p multicolored	1.00	1.10
543	A90	35p multicolored	1.50	1.75
544	A90	£1 multicolored	3.75	4.50
545	A90	£2 multicolored	7.75	9.00
546	A90	£5 multicolored	20.00	17.00
		Nos. 535-546 (12)	37.00	36.85

Royal Navy Warships Type of 1990

10p, HMS Nigeria, 1948. 25p, HMS Phoebe, 1949. 35p, HMS Liverpool, 1949. 50p, HMS Magpie, 1955.

1994, May 2   Wmk. 373

547	A79	10p multicolored	1.00	1.00
548	A79	25p multicolored	2.50	2.50
549	A79	35p multicolored	3.25	3.25
550	A79	50p multicolored	5.25	5.25
		Nos. 547-550 (4)	12.00	12.00

Sharks A91

1994, Aug.   Wmk. 384

551	A91	10p Blue shark	.95	.95
552	A91	45p Seven-gill shark	3.75	3.75
553	A91	65p Mako shark	5.25	5.25
		Nos. 551-553 (3)	9.95	9.95

Farm Animals — A92

1994, Nov.   Wmk. 373

554	A92	10p Donkeys	.75	.75
555	A92	20p Cattle	1.75	1.75
556	A92	35p Ducks, geese	3.25	3.25
557	A92	60p Girl feeding lamb	5.75	5.75
		Nos. 554-557 (4)	11.50	11.50

See Nos. 601-604.

Local Transport A93

Designs: 15p, Pick-up truck. 20p, Leyland Daf Sherpa van. 45p, Yamaha motorcycle, scooter. 60p, Administrator's Landrover.

Wmk. 384
1995, Feb. 27   Litho.   Perf. 14

558	A93	15p multicolored	1.15	1.15
559	A93	20p multicolored	1.35	1.35
560	A93	45p multicolored	3.25	3.25
561	A93	60p multicolored	4.50	4.50
		Nos. 558-561 (4)	10.25	10.25

End of World War II, 50th Anniv.
Common Design Types

Designs: 15p, Lewis gun instruction, 1943. 20p, Tristan defense volunteers, 1943-46. 45p, Radio, weather stations. 60p, HNS Birmingham, 1942. £1, Reverse of War Medal, 1939-45.

Perf. 13x13½
1995, June 19   Litho.   Wmk. 373

562	CD351	15p multicolored	1.50	1.50
563	CD351	20p multicolored	2.10	2.10
564	CD351	45p multicolored	4.00	4.00
565	CD351	60p multicolored	5.75	5.75
		Nos. 562-565 (4)	13.35	13.35

Souvenir Sheet
Perf. 14

566	CD352	£1 multicolored	6.75	6.75

Souvenir Sheet

Queen Mother, 95th Birthday — A94

1995, Aug. 4   Litho.   Perf. 14½x14

567	A94	£1.50 multicolored	9.00	9.00

UN, 50th Anniv.
Common Design Type

20p, Bedford 4-ton truck. 30p, Saxon armored personnel carrier. 45p, Mi26 heavy lift helicopter. 50p, RFA Sir Tristram transporting UN vehicles.

1995, Oct. 24   Perf. 13½x13

568	CD353	20p multicolored	1.75	1.75
569	CD353	30p multicolored	3.00	3.00
570	CD353	45p multicolored	4.00	4.00
571	CD353	50p multicolored	4.75	4.75
		Nos. 568-571 (4)	13.50	13.50

Seals A95

Sub Antarctic fur seal: 10p, On rock. 35p, Coming out of water with young.

Southern elephant seal: 45p, On beach with young. 50p, In water.

1995, Nov. 3   Perf. 13½

572	A95	10p multicolored	.70	.70
573	A95	35p multicolored	2.75	2.75
574	A95	45p multicolored	4.00	4.00
575	A95	50p multicolored	4.25	4.25
		Nos. 572-575 (4)	11.70	11.70

Queen Elizabeth II, 70th Birthday
Common Design Type

Various portraits of Queen, island scenes: 15p, Tristan from sea. 20p, Traditional cottage. 45p, The Residency. 60p, With Prince Philip.

1996, Apr. 22   Litho.   Perf. 13½

576	CD354	15p multicolored	.90	.90
577	CD354	20p multicolored	1.20	1.20
578	CD354	45p multicolored	2.75	2.75
579	CD354	60p multicolored	3.50	3.50
		Nos. 576-579 (4)	8.35	8.35

New Harbor — A96

15p, View of Old Harbor. 20p, Earthmoving, New Harbor construction. 45p, Crane, new construction. 60p, View of New Harbor. Nos. 581-582 are 45x28mm.

1996, July 5   Wmk. 373   Perf. 13

580	A96	15p multicolored	1.75	1.75
581	A96	20p multicolored	2.75	2.75
582	A96	45p multicolored	3.50	3.50
583	A96	60p multicolored	4.50	4.50
		Nos. 580-583 (4)	12.50	12.50

Nos. 581-582 are 45x28mm.

A97

Gough Island Birds: 15p, Gough moorhen. 20p, Wandering albatross. 45p, Sooty albatross. 60p, Gough bunting.

1996, Oct. 1   **Perf. 14**
584 A97 15p multicolored .90 .90
585 A97 20p multicolored 1.35 1.35
586 A97 45p multicolored 3.25 3.25
587 A97 60p multicolored 4.50 4.50
    a.   Souvenir sheet of 1   5.00 5.00
        Nos. 584-587 (4)   10.00 10.00

No. 587a for return of Hong Kong to China, July 1, 1997. Issued 6/20/97.

A98

Presentation of Portrait of Queen Victoria, Cent.: 20p, 19th cent. map of Trista da Cunha. 30p, HMS Magpie. 45p, Peter Green, former governor. 50p, Detail of portrait of Queen Victoria, by Heinrich Von Angell.

1996, Dec. 18   **Perf. 13½**
588 A98 20p multicolored 1.40 1.40
589 A98 30p multicolored 2.25 2.25
590 A98 45p multicolored 3.25 3.25
591 A98 50p multicolored 3.50 3.50
        Nos. 588-591 (4)   10.40 10.40

Atlantic Marine Fauna of the Cretaceous — A99

Designs: a, Archelon. b, Trinacromerum. c, Platecarpus. d, Clidastes.

1997, Feb. 10 **Wmk. 384**   **Perf. 14**
592 A99 35p Sheet of 4, #a.-d. 10.50 10.50
        See No. 619.

Visual Communications — A100

Designs: No. 593, Smoke signals. No. 594, HMS Eurydice. No. 595, HMS Challenger. No. 596, Flag hoists. No. 597, Semaphore. No. 598, HMS Carlisle. No. 599, Light signals. No. 600, HMS Cilicia.

1997 **Litho.** **Wmk. 384**   **Perf. 14½**
593 10p multicolored .65 .65
594 10p multicolored .65 .65
    a.   A100 Pair, #593-594   1.50 1.50
595 15p multicolored .90 .90
596 15p multicolored .90 .90
    a.   A100 Pair, #595-596   2.40 2.40
597 20p multicolored 1.10 1.10
598 20p multicolored 1.10 1.10
    a.   A100 Pair, #597-598   3.00 3.00
599 35p multicolored 1.90 1.90
600 35p multicolored 1.90 1.90
    a.   A100 Pair, #599-600   5.00 5.00
        Nos. 593-600 (8)   9.10 9.10

Farm Animals Type of 1994

1997, Aug. 26 **Litho.**   **Perf. 14**
601 A92 20p Chickens 1.30 1.30
602 A92 30p Cattle 2.25 2.25
603 A92 45p Sheep 3.25 3.25
604 A92 50p Dogs 3.25 3.25
        Nos. 601-604 (4)   10.05 10.05

Queen Elizabeth II and Prince Philip, 50th Wedding Anniv. — A101

Designs: No. 605, Queen up close. No. 606, Prince riding polo pony. No. 607, Queen with horse. No. 608, Prince up close. No. 609, Prince in military attire, Queen in green coat. No. 610, Princess Anne riding horse.
£1.50, Queen, Prince riding in open carriage, horiz.

1997, Nov. 20 **Wmk. 373**   **Perf. 14**
605 15p multicolored .90 .90
606 15p multicolored .90 .90
    a.   A101 Pair, #605-606   2.40 2.40
607 20p multicolored 1.30 1.30
608 20p multicolored 1.30 1.30
    a.   A101 Pair, #607-608   4.25 4.25
609 45p multicolored 2.75 2.75
610 45p multicolored 2.75 2.75
    a.   A101 Pair, #609-610   8.75 8.75
        Nos. 605-610 (6)   9.90 9.90

Souvenir Sheet

611 A101 £1.50 multicolored 12.50 12.50

First Lobster Survey, 50th Anniv. — A102

Ships: 15p, Hilary, Melodie. 20p, Tristania II, Hekla. 30p, Pequena, Frances Repetto. 45p, Tristania, Gillian Gaggins. 50p, MFV. Kelso, MV. Edinburgh.
£1.20, Fr. C.P. Lawrence, lobster.

1998, Feb. 6   **Perf. 14½**
612 A102 15p multicolored .75 .75
613 A102 20p multicolored 1.10 1.10
614 A102 30p multicolored 1.60 1.60
615 A102 45p multicolored 2.75 2.75
616 A102 50p multicolored 2.75 2.75
        Nos. 612-616 (5)   8.95 8.95

Souvenir Sheet

617 A102 £1.20 multicolored 10.50 10.50

Diana, Princess of Wales (1961-97)
Common Design Type

a, In beige dress. b, In white top with black collar. c, In striped top. d, In lilac & white print dress.

1998, May 15   **Perf. 14½x14**
618 CD355 35p Strip of 4, #a.-d. 5.00 5.00

No. 618 sold for £1.40 + 20p with surtax from international sales going to the Princess Diana Memorial Fund and surtax from local sales going to a designated local charity.

Atlantic Marine Fauna Type of 1997

Fauna of the Miocene Epoch: a, Carcharodon. b, Orycterocetus. c, Eurhinodelphis. d, Hexanchus (six gilled shark), myliobatis.

1998, July 8   **Perf. 14**
619 A99 45p Sheet of 4, #a.-d. 16.00 16.00

Visiting Cruise Ships A103

1998, Sept. 15   **Perf. 14**
620 A103 15p Livonia 1.35 1.35
621 A103 20p Professor
            Molchanov 1.90 1.90
622 A103 45p Explorer 4.25 4.25
623 A103 60p Hanseatic 5.50 5.50
        Nos. 620-623 (4)   13.00 13.00

Sailing Ships A104

15p, H.G. Johnson, 1892. 35p, Theodore, 1893. 45p, Hesperides, 1893. 50p, Bessfield, 1894.

1998, Nov. 23 **Wmk. 373**   **Perf. 14½**
624 A104 15p multicolored 1.40 1.40
625 A104 35p multicolored 3.00 3.00
626 A104 45p multicolored 4.25 4.25
627 A104 50p multicolored 4.50 4.50
        Nos. 624-627 (4)   13.15 13.15

1999, Mar. 19

20p, Derwent, 1895. 30p, Strathgryffe, 1898. 50p, Celestial Empire, 1898. 60p, Lamorna, 1902.

628 A104 20p multicolored 2.00 2.00
629 A104 30p multicolored 2.75 2.75
630 A104 50p multicolored 4.25 4.25
631 A104 60p multicolored 4.50 4.50
        Nos. 628-631 (4)   13.50 13.50

Wandering Albatross — A105

World Wildlife Fund: 5p, Two adults. 8p, Adult, juvenile in nest. 12p, Adult spreading wings. 15p, Two in flight.

1999, Apr. 27 **Wmk. 373**   **Perf. 14**
632 A105 5p multicolored .60 .60
633 A105 8p multicolored .65 .65
634 A105 12p multicolored .70 .70
635 A105 15p multicolored .80 .80
    a.   Strip of 4, #632-635   3.00 3.00
        Nos. 632-635 (4)   2.75 2.75

Issued in sheets of 16.

Wedding of Prince Edward and Sophie Rhys-Jones
Common Design Type
Perf. 13¾x14

1999, June 18 **Litho.** **Wmk. 384**
636 CD356   45c Separate portraits 2.25 2.25
637 CD356 £1.20 Couple 5.25 5.25

Queen Mother's Century
Common Design Type

Queen Mother: 20p, With Princess Elizabeth on her 18th birthday. 30p, With King George VI at Balmoral. 50p, With Royal Family, 94th birthday. 60p, As colonel-in-chief of Black Watch.
£1.50, Age 5 photo, airplanes from Battle of Britain, 1940.

1999, Aug. 18 **Wmk. 384**   **Perf. 13½**
638 CD358 20p multi 1.00 1.00
639 CD358 30p multi 1.75 1.75
640 CD358 50p multi 2.75 2.75
641 CD358 60p multi 3.50 3.50
        Nos. 638-641 (4)   9.00 9.00

Souvenir Sheet

642 CD358 £1.50 black 9.00 9.00

Millennium — A106

Various birds.

2000, Jan. 1 **Wmk. 373**   **Perf. 14**
Color of Queen's Head
643 A106 20p bister 1.25 1.25
644 A106 30p green 2.10 2.10
645 A106 50p blue 4.00 4.00
646 A106 60p brown 4.75 4.75
        Nos. 643-646 (4)   12.10 12.10

Royalty — A107

British monarchs on 8p-£5: 1p, King Manuel I of Portugal. 3p, Frederick Henry, Prince of Orange. 5p, Empress Maria Theresa of Austria. 8p, King George III. 10p, King George IV. 15p, King William IV. 20p, Queen Victoria. 25p, Edward VII. 35p, George V. £1, Edward VIII. £2, George VI. £5, Elizabeth II.

2000, Feb. 1 **Wmk. 384**   **Perf. 14**
647 A107 1p multi .25 .25
648 A107 3p multi .25 .25
649 A107 5p multi .25 .25
650 A107 8p multi .30 .30
651 A107 10p multi .40 .40
652 A107 15p multi .55 .80
653 A107 20p multi .70 1.00
654 A107 25p multi .90 1.10
655 A107 35p multi 1.40 1.90
656 A107 £1 multi 3.50 5.25
657 A107 £2 multi 7.50 10.00
658 A107 £5 multi 18.00 24.50
        Nos. 647-658 (12)   34.00 46.00

The Stamp Show 2000, London A108

Designs: 15p, Longboat under oars. 45p, Longboat under sail. 50p, Cutty Sark, 1876. 60p, Cutty Sark, 2000.
£1.50, Cutty Sark visiting Tristan da Cunha, 1876.

Wmk. 373
2000, May 22 **Litho.**   **Perf. 14**
659 A108 15p multi 1.50 1.50
660 A108 45p multi 3.50 3.50
661 A108 50p multi 4.00 4.00
662 A108 60p multi 4.75 4.75
        Nos. 659-662 (4)   13.75 13.75

Souvenir Sheet

663 A108 £1.50 multi 13.00 13.00

Prince William, 18th Birthday
Common Design Type

William: Nos. 664, 668a, As toddler, with Princes Charles and Harry, vert. Nos. 665, 668b, Holding paper, vert. Nos. 666, 668c, Wearing scarf. Nos. 667, 668d, Wearing suit and wearing sweater. No. 668e, As child, with Shetland pony.

Perf. 13¾x14¼, 14¼x13¾
2000, June 21   Litho.   Wmk. 373
Stamps With White Border
664	CD359	45p multi	2.25	2.25
665	CD359	45p multi	2.25	2.25
666	CD359	45p multi	2.25	2.25
667	CD359	45p multi	2.25	2.25
	Nos. 664-667 (4)		9.00	9.00

Souvenir Sheet
Stamps Without White Border
Perf. 14¼
668	CD359	45p Sheet of 5, #a-e	12.50	12.50

Ships and Helicopters — A109

No. 669, 10p: a, SA Agulhas. b, SA 330J Puma, 1999.
No. 670, 15p: a, HMS London. b, Westland Wessex HAS 1, 1964.
No. 671, 20p: a, HMS Endurance. b, Westland Lynx HAS 3, 1996.
No. 672, 50p: a, USS Spiegel Grove. b, Sikorsky UH-19F, 1963.

Wmk. 373
2000, Sept. 4   Litho.   Perf. 14
Pairs, #a-b
669-672	A109	Set of 4	14.50	14.50

First Election of Winston Churchill to Parliament, Cent. — A110

Designs: 20p, During siege of Sidney Street, 1911. 30p, With Franklin D. Roosevelt, 1941. 50p, VE Day broadcast, 1945. 60p, Greeting Queen Elizabeth, 1955.

Perf. 13¾x14
2000, Oct. 2   Wmk. 373
673-676	A110	Set of 4	10.00	10.00

Souvenir Sheet

New Year 2001 (Year of the Snake) — A111

No. 677: a, 30p, Inaccessible Island rail. b, 45p, Black-faced spoonbill.

Wmk. 373
2001, Feb. 1   Litho.   Perf. 14½
677	A111	Sheet of 2, #a-b	10.00	10.00

Hong Kong 2001 Stamp Exhibition.

Age of Victoria A112

Designs: 15p, Letter, 1846. 20p, Prince Alfred, Duke of Edinburgh, vert. 30p, HMS Galatea. 35p, Queen Victoria, vert. 50p, Charles Dickens, vert. 60p, Resupplying ships. £1.50, Jubilee celebrations.

Wmk. 373
2001, May 24   Litho.   Perf. 14
678-683	A112	Set of 6	10.50	10.50

Souvenir Sheet
684	A112	£1.50 multi	8.00	8.00

Longboats — A113

No. 685: a, Boat with dark and light blue striped sails, island in distance. b, Boat with red and blue striped and white sails, boat with blue, red and yellow striped and blue and white striped sails. c, Prow and sail of boat, two boats in distance. d, Boat with blue red and yellow striped and blue and white striped sails. e, Boat with dark and light blue sails near shore. f, Boat with red and blue striped and white sails. g, Boat with gray, red and white sails. h, Boat with sails down.

2001, July 12
685	A113	30p Sheet of 8, #a-h	12.00	12.00

Nos. 669-672 Overprinted in Blue Violet

Wmk. 373
2001, Sept. 17   Litho.   Perf. 14
686	A109	10p Pair, #a-b	2.00	2.00
687	A109	15p Pair, #a-b	2.75	2.75
688	A109	20p Pair, #a-b	3.50	3.50
689	A109	50p Pair, #a-b	9.00	9.00
	Nos. 686-689 (4)		17.25	17.25

Souvenir Sheet

Birdlife International World Bird Festival — A114

Spectacled petrel: a, Head. b, Diving (island in background). c, In flight with legs extended. d, Diving (sea in background). e, Chick.

Wmk. 373
2001, Oct. 1   Litho.   Perf. 14½
690	A114	35p Sheet of 5, #a-e	14.00	14.00

Royal Navy Ships A115

Designs: No. 691, 20p, HMS Penguin, 1815. No. 692, 20p, HMS Julia, 1817. No. 693, 35p, HMS Beagle, 1901. No. 694, 35p, HMS Puma, 1962. No. 695, 60p, HMS Monmouth, 1997. No. 696, 60p, HMS Somerset, 1999.

Wmk. 373
2001, Oct. 31   Litho.   Perf. 14
691-696	A115	Set of 6	14.00	14.00

Churches A116

Designs: No. 697, 35p, Exterior, St. Joseph's Catholic Church. No. 698, 35p, Exterior, St. Mary's Anglican Church. No. 699, 60p, Stained glass window, St. Joseph's. No. 700, 60p, Altar, St. Mary's.

Perf. 13¼x13½, 13½x13¼
2001, Nov. 27
697-700	A116	Set of 4	13.00	13.00

Christmas, Arrival of first USPG missionary, 150th anniv.

Tristan da Cunha Postage Stamps, 50th Anniv. A117

Designs: Nos. 701, 45p, 705a, 45p, #5, 6, 9, 10 canceled. Nos. 702, 20p, 705, 45p, #7, 8, 11, 12 canceled. Nos. 703, 50p, 705c, 45p, #1-4 canceled. Nos. 704, 60p, 705d, 45p, Men at post office, 1952.

2002, Jan. 1   Perf. 13½
Without "Tristan da Cunha" in Script
701-704	A117	Set of 4	12.00	12.00

Souvenir Sheet
With "Tristan da Cunha" in Script at Top or Bottom of Stamps
705	A117	45p Sheet of 4, #a-d	11.50	11.50

Reign Of Queen Elizabeth II, 50th Anniv. Issue
Common Design Type

Designs: Nos. 706, 710a, 15p, Princess Elizabeth, 1947. Nos. 707, 710b, 30p, Wearing tiara, 1991. Nos. 708, 710c, 45p, Wearing red coat. Nos. 709, 710d, 50p, Wearing purple hat, 1997. No. 710e, 60p, 1955 portrait by Annigoni (38x50mm).

Perf. 14¼x14½, 13¾ (#710e)
2002, Feb. 6   Litho.   Wmk. 373
With Gold Frames
706	CD360	15p multicolored	.95	.95
707	CD360	30p multicolored	1.80	1.80
708	CD360	45p multicolored	2.50	2.50
709	CD360	50p multicolored	2.75	2.75
	Nos. 706-709 (4)		8.00	8.00

Souvenir Sheet
Without Gold Frames
710	CD360	Sheet of 5, #a-e	10.50	10.50

Fishing Industry A118

Designs: 20p, Pelagic armorhead. 35p, Yellowtail. 50p, Splendid alfonsino. 60p, Ship San Liberatore.

Wmk. 373
2002, May   Perf. 14
711-713	A118	Set of 3	6.75	6.75
714		Souvenir sheet, #711-713, 714a	8.50	8.50
	a.	A118 60p multi	1.75	1.75

Queen Mother Elizabeth (1900-2002)
Common Design Type

Designs: 20p, Wearing hat (black and white photograph). £1.50, Wearing blue green hat. No. 717: a, 75p, Holding baby (black and white photograph). b, 75p, Wearing dark blue hat.

Wmk. 373
2002, Aug. 5   Litho.   Perf. 14¼
With Purple Frames
715	CD361	20p multicolored	1.00	1.00
716	CD361	£1.50 multicolored	6.25	6.25

Souvenir Sheet
Without Purple Frames
Perf. 14½x14¼
717	CD361	Sheet of 2, #a-b	9.00	9.00

Marine Mammals — A119

No. 718: a, Gray's beaked whale. b, Dusky dolphin. c, False killer whale. d, Long-finned pilot whale. e, Sperm whale. f, Shepherd's beaked whale. £2, Humpback whale.

Wmk. 373
2002, Sept. 24   Litho.   Perf. 13¼
718	A119	30p Sheet of 6, #a-f	13.50	13.50

Souvenir Sheet
719	A119	£2 multi	16.00	16.00

HMS Herald Survey, 150th Anniv. — A120

Designs: 20p, Captain Denham and officers. 35p, HMS Herald in Bay of Biscay. 50p, Surveying, Oct. 30, 1852. 60p, HMS Herald and Torch at sunset, 1852.

2002, Nov. 11   Perf. 14x14¾
720-723	A120	Set of 4	8.75	8.75

Guinness Book of World Records — A121

No. 724: a, Great Barrier Reef (longest reef). b, Greenland (biggest island). c, Sahara Desert (biggest desert). d, Amazon and Nile Rivers (longest rivers). e, Mt. Everest (biggest mountain). f, Tristan da Cunha (most remote inhabited island). £2, Like No. 724f.

Wmk. 373
2003, Jan. 10   Litho.   Perf. 13¾
724	A121	30p Sheet of 6, #a-f	9.50	9.50

Souvenir Sheet
725	A121	£2 multi	11.00	11.00

Atlantic Yellow-nosed Albatross A122

Designs: Nos. 726, 730a, 15p, Heads of two birds. Nos. 727, 730b, 30p, Bird on nest, vert. Nos. 728, 730c, 45p, Bird in flight, vert. Nos. 729, 730d, Two birds in flight. No. 730e, £1, Two birds in flight, diff.

Perf. 14¼x13¾, 13¾x14¼
2003, May 7   Litho.
Stamps With White Frames
726-729 A122   Set of 4   7.50 7.50

Souvenir Sheet
Stamps Without Frames
Perf. 14¼x14½
730 A122   Sheet of 5, #a-e   11.00 11.00
Birdlife International.

Head of Queen Elizabeth II
Common Design Type
Wmk. 373
2003, June 2   Litho.   Perf. 13¾
731 CD362 £2.80 multi   10.00 10.00

Coronation of Queen Elizabeth II, 50th Anniv.
Common Design Type
Designs: Nos. 732, 20p, 734a, Queen and extended family. Nos. 733, £1.50, 734b, Bishops paying homage to Queen at coronation.

Perf. 14¼x14½
2003, June 2   Litho.   Wmk. 373
Vignettes Framed, Red Background
732 CD363   20p multicolored   1.00 1.00
733 CD363 £1.50 multicolored   7.00 7.00

Souvenir Sheet
Vignettes Without Frame, Purple Panel
734 CD363 75p Sheet of 2, #a-b   8.75 8.75

Prince William, 21st Birthday
Common Design Type
No. 735: a, William in polo uniform at right. b, In sweater at left.

Wmk. 373
2003, June 21   Litho.   Perf. 14¼
735   Horiz. pair   0.00 0.00
a, b. CD364 50p Either single   2.60 2.60

William Glass (1787-1853), Governor — A123

No. 736: a, Arrival of Glass on HMS Falmouth, 1816. b, As corporal, stationed on Tristan da Cunha. c, Glass and family onshore, 1817. d, Glass family with dog. e, Gov. Glass conducting daughter's marriage ceremony, 1833. f, Glass as old man.

Perf. 14¼x14½
2003, Nov. 24   Litho.   Wmk. 373
736 A123 30p Sheet of 6, #a-f, + 6 labels   9.00 9.00

Royal Navy Ships — A124

No. 737, 20p: a, RFA Tideflow. b, RFA Tidespring.
No. 738, 35p: a, RFA Gold Rover. b, RFA Diligence.
No. 739, 60p: a, RFA Wave Chief. b, HMY Britannia,

Wmk. 373
2003, Dec. 8   Litho.   Perf. 14
Horiz. pairs, #a-b
737-739 A124   Set of 3   12.00 12.00

History of Writing Implements — A125

Designs: 15p, Cave paintings and pigment blocks. 20p, Clay tablet. 35p, Egyptian writing palette. 45p, Goose quill pen. 50p, Fountain pen. 60p, Ballpoint pen.
£1.50, Word processing.

2004, Jan. 8   Perf. 13¾
740-745 A125   Set of 6   9.25 9.25

Souvenir Sheet
Litho. with Margin Embossed
746 A125   £1.50 multi   8.00 8.00

Worldwide Fund for Nature (WWF) — A126

Subantarctic fur seal: No. 747, 35p, Underwater. No. 748, 35p, Pair on rocks. No. 749, 35p, Seal on rock. No. 750, 35p, Head.

Wmk. 373
2004, July 12   Litho.   Perf. 14
747-750 A126   Set of 4   6.00 6.00
750a   Sheet, 4 each #747-750   26.00 26.00

New Flag — A127

2004, July 27   Unwmk.   Die Cut
Self-Adhesive
Booklet Stamp
751 A127 30p multi   1.35 1.35
a.   Booklet pane of 6   8.25
    Complete booklet, 2 #751a   16.50

Merchant Ships A128

Designs: No. 752, 20p, RMS Dunnottar Castle. No. 753, 20p, RMS Caronia. No. 754, 35p, SA Agulhas. No. 755, 35p, MV Edinburgh. No. 756, 60p, MV Explorer. No. 757, 60p, MV Hanseatic.

Wmk. 373
2004, Nov. 9   Litho.   Perf. 13¼
752-757 A128   Set of 6   11.00 11.00

Battle of Trafalgar, Bicent. — A129

Designs: 15p, Admiral Horatio Nelson's quadrant. 20p, HMS Royal Sovereign breaks the line, horiz. 25p, Thomas Swain aids the wounded Nelson, horiz. 35p, HMS Victory breaks the line, horiz. 50p, Nelson. 60p, HMS Victory, horiz.
No. 764: a, Capt. Thomas Masterman Hardy. b, HMS Victory.

Perf. 13¼
2005, Jan. 20   Litho.   Unwmk.
758-763 A129   Set of 6   11.50 11.50

Souvenir Sheet
764 A129 75p Sheet of 2, #a-b   9.50 9.50
No. 763 has particles of wood from the HMS Victory embedded in the areas covered by a thermographic process that produces a shiny, raised effect.

Island Flora, Fauna and Scenes A130

No. 765 — Tristan da Cunha: a, Rockhopper penguins. b, Southern elephant seals. c, Tristan rock lobster. d, Crowberry. e, Tristan da Cunha island settlement and volcano.
No. 766 — Gough Island: a, Gough moorhen. b, Subantarctic fur seal. c, Bluefish. d, Gough tree fern. e, South African Weather Station.
No. 767 — Inaccessible Island: a, Inaccessible rail. b, Dusky dolphins. c, Sebastes capensis. d, Pepper tree. e, Inaccessible Island Waterfall.
No. 768 — Nightingale Island: a, Tristan thrush. b, Southern right whale. c, Fivefinger fish. d, Tussock grass. e, Nightingale Island.
No. 769 — Middle Island: a, Broad-billed prion. b, False killer whale. c, Wrecktih. d, Fern. e, Middle Island.
No. 770 — Stoltenhoff Island: a, Brown skua. b, Shepherd's beaked whales. c, Snoeks. d, Sea bind weed. e, Stoltenhoff Island.

2005	Wmk. 373	Perf. 13¾	
765	Horiz. strip of 5	11.00	11.00
a.-e.	A130 50p Any single	2.25	2.25
766	Horiz. strip of 5	11.00	11.00
a.-e.	A130 50p Any single	2.25	2.25
767	Horiz. strip of 5	11.00	11.00
a.-e.	A130 50p Any single	2.25	2.25
768	Horiz. strip of 5	11.00	11.00
a.-e.	A130 50p Any single	2.25	2.25
769	Horiz. strip of 5	11.00	11.00
a.-e.	A130 50p Any single	2.25	2.25
770	Horiz. strip of 5	11.00	11.00
a.-e.	A130 50p Any single	2.25	2.25

Issued: No. 765, 2/21; No. 766, 3/28; No. 767, 4/18; No. 768, 2/7/06; No. 769, 3/30/06; No. 770, 9/27/06.
See No. 796.

Birds A131

Designs: 1p, Kerguelen petrel. 3p, Sooty albatross. 5p, Antarctic tern. 8p, Tristan bunting. 10p, Cape petrel. 15p, Tristan moorhen. 20p, Giant fulmar. 25p, Brown skua. 35p, Great-winged petrel. £1, Broad-billed prion. £2, Soft-plumaged petrel. £5, Rockhopper penguin.

Perf. 14¼x14¾
2005, June 1		Litho.	Wmk. 373	
771	A131	1p multi	.25	.25
772	A131	3p multi	.25	.25
773	A131	5p multi	.25	.25
774	A131	8p multi	.30	.30
775	A131	10p multi	.35	.35
776	A131	15p multi	.55	.55
777	A131	20p multi	.75	.75
778	A131	25p multi	.90	.90
779	A131	35p multi	1.25	1.25
780	A131	£1 multi	4.00	4.00
781	A131	£2 multi	7.25	8.75
782	A131	£5 multi	18.00	21.00
	Nos. 771-782 (12)		34.10	38.60

Pope John Paul II (1920-2005) A132

Wmk. 373
2005, Aug. 18   Litho.   Perf. 14
783 A132 50p multi   3.00 3.00

Battle of Trafalgar, Bicent. — A133

Designs: 20p, HMS Victory. 70p, Ships in battle, horiz. £1, Admiral Horatio Nelson.

Perf. 13¼
2005, Oct. 18   Litho.   Unwmk.
784-786 A133   Set of 3   12.00 12.00

Discovery of Tristan da Cunha, 500th Anniv. — A134

No. 787: a, 30p, Discovery by Tristao d'Acunha, 1506. b, 30p, First survey, 1767. c, 30p, Jonathan Lambert of Salem, 1810. d, 50p, William Glass, 1816. e, 50p, Duke of Gloucester (ship), 1824. f, 80p, Wreck of the Emily, 1836.
No. 788: a, 30p, Thomas Swain (1774-1862). b, 30p, HMS Challenger, 1873. c, 30p, Rev. Edwin Dodgson arrives, 1881. d, 50p, Wreck of the Italia, 1892. e, 50p, HMS Milford, 1938. f, 80p, Norwegian Expedition, 1937-38.
No. 789: a, 30p, World War II TDV training. b, 30p, HMS Atlantic Isle, 1944. c, 30p, Hands holding potatoes, 1946 potato stamp. d, 50p, Tristan da Cunha #5. e, 50p, Volcano eruption and evacuation, 1961. f, 80p, Gough Island Scientific Expedition, 1955.
No. 790: a, 30p, Royal Society Expedition, 1962. b, 30p, Resettlement, 1963. c, 30p, Denstone Expedition to Inaccessible Island, 1982. d, 50p, RMS St. Helena, 1992. e, 50p, New coat of arms, 2002. f, 80p, Hurricane disaster, 2001.

Perf. 14¼x14½
2006	Litho.	Wmk. 373	
787 A134	Sheet of 6, #a-f	15.00	15.00
788 A134	Sheet of 6, #a-f	15.00	15.00

Perf. 14¼x14¾
| 789 A134 | Sheet of 6, #a-f | 16.00 | 16.00 |
| 790 A134 | Sheet of 6, #a-f | 16.00 | 16.00 |

Issued: Nos. 787-788, 2/2; Nos. 789-790, 6/1.

Queen Elizabeth II, 80th Birthday
A135

Queen: No. 791, 60p, As child. No. 792, 60p, Wearing feathered hat. No. 793, 60p, Wearing red hat. No. 794, 60p, Wearing sunglasses.

No. 795: a, 50p, Like No. 792. b, 50p, Like No. 793.

2006, Apr. 21   **Perf. 14**
791-794 A135   Set of 4   12.00 12.00
Souvenir Sheet
795 A135 50p Sheet of 2, #a-b   5.25 5.25

Island Flora, Fauna and Scenes Type of 2005-06
Miniature Sheet

No. 796: a, Map of Tristan da Cunha, flag. b, Map of Inaccessible Island, wandering albatross. c, Map of Nightingale Island, humpback whale. d, Map of Middle Island, traditional longboats. e, Map of Stoltenhoff Island, mackerel. f, Map of Gough Island, sub-antarctic fur seal.

Wmk. 373
2007, Jan. 22   **Litho.**   **Perf. 13¾**
796   Sheet of 6   15.00 15.00
a.-f.   A130 50p Any single   2.40 2.40

Local Vehicles
A136

Designs: 15p, Wave Dancer fishery patrol boat. 20p, Ambulance. 30p, Inshore rescue craft. 45p, Police Land Rover. 50p, Fire engine. 85p, Administrator's Land Rover.

Perf. 12½x13
2007, Apr. 17   **Litho.**   **Unwmk.**
797-802 A136   Set of 6   13.00 13.00

Wedding of Queen Elizabeth II and Prince Philip, 60th Anniv. — A137

Designs: No. 803, 50p, Shown. No. 804, 50p, Queen waving. No. 805, 50p, Queen and Prince (black and white photograph). No. 806, 50p, Queen and Prince (color photograph). £2, Queen in wedding gown.

2007, June 1   **Wmk. 373**   **Perf. 13¾**
803-806 A137   Set of 4   9.50 9.50
Souvenir Sheet
Perf. 14
807 A137 £2 multi   9.50 9.50
No. 807 contains one 42x57mm stamp.

Miniature Sheet

BirdLife International — A138

No. 808 — Great shearwater: a, In flight, facing right. b, In flight, facing left, showing land and sky. c, On ground, showing land and sky. d, In flight facing left, showing land and water. e, On ground, showing land only. f, Chick.

2007, July 1   **Unwmk.**   **Perf. 13¾**
808 A138 50p Sheet of 6, #a-f   16.00 16.00

Scouting, Cent.
A139

Designs: 15p, Scout J. W. S. Marr and his book, *Into the Frozen South,* hands tying knot. 20p, The Quest frozen in, Marr, hands tightening rope. £1.25, Flag raising ceremony, hand with compass. £1.40, Children of Tristan da Cunha, trumpeter.

No. 813, vert.: a, Marr and Questie, the ship's cat. b, Lord Robert Baden-Powell.

2007, July 9   **Wmk. 373**
809-812 A139   Set of 4   15.00 15.00
Souvenir Sheet
813 A139 £1.50 Sheet of 2, #a-b   15.00 15.00

A140

A141

A142

A143

A144

Princess Diana (1961-97)
A145

2007, Nov. 30   **Litho.**   **Unwmk.**
814 A140 50p multi   2.40 2.40
815 A141 50p multi   2.40 2.40
816 A142 50p multi   2.40 2.40
817 A143 50p multi   2.40 2.40
818 A144 50p multi   2.40 2.40
819 A145 50p multi   2.40 2.40
Nos. 814-819 (6)   14.40 14.40

Military Uniforms — A146

Designs: No. 820, 15p, Officer, 21st Light Dragoon. No. 821, 15p, Corporal, Royal Artillery. No. 822, 20p, Privates, Royal Artillery. No. 823, 20p, Lieutenant, Royal Artillery. No. 824, £1, Soldiers from Cape Regiment. No. 825, £1, Soldiers from South Africa Army Engineering Corps.

Unwmk.
2007, Dec. 10   **Litho.**   **Perf. 14**
820-825 A146   Set of 6   15.00 15.00

Marine Invertebrates
A147

Designs: 15p, Tristan rock lobster. 20p, Trumpet anemone. 35p, Starfish. No. 829, 60p, Tristan urchin. No. 830, 60p, Sponge. 85p, Strawberry anemone.

2007, Dec. 10   **Unwmk.**   **Perf. 13¼**
826-831 A147   Set of 6   12.50 12.50

A148

Royal Air Force, 90th Anniv. — A149

Designs: No. 832, 30p, Royal Aircraft Factory S. E. 5a. No. 833, 30p, Hawker Hart. No. 834, 30p, Hawker Typhoon. No. 835, 30p, Avro Vulcan. No. 836, 30p, SEPECAT Jaguar. £1.50, Sir Hugh Trenchard reviewing troops.

Wmk. 373
2008, Apr. 1   **Litho.**   **Perf. 14**
832-836 A148   Set of 5   8.00 8.00
Souvenir Sheet
837 A149 £1.50 black   8.00 8.00
Nos. 832-836 each were printed in sheets of 8 + central label.

Tristan Fisheries, 60th Anniv. — A150

Designs: 15p, Fishing boats in harbor. 20p, Fishing boats. 30p, Offloading and loading fish. 70p, Sorting tails. 80p, Wrapping and packaging of rock lobster tails. £1.25, Shipping for export.

Perf. 13¼x13
2008, July 1   **Litho.**   **Unwmk.**
838-843 A150   Set of 6   15.00 15.00

Allan B. Crawford (1912-2007), Writer — A151

Designs: 15p, Crawford. 20p, Local Tristan da Cunha stamp. 50p, First map of Tristan da Cunha. 60p, Members of 1937-38 Norwegian Scientific Expedition, Crawford's book, *I Went to Tristan,* horiz. 85p, Men at opening of Marion Island Meteorological Office, Crawford's book, *Tristan da Cunha and the Roaring Forties,* horiz. £1.20, Crawford and his book, *Penguins, Potatoes and Postage Stamps,* horiz.

Perf. 13x13¼, 13¼x13
2008, Aug. 1   **Litho.**   **Unwmk.**
844-849 A151   Set of 6   15.00 15.00

End of World War I, 90th Anniv.
A152

Paintings: No. 850, 50p, End of Richthofen, by Charles H. Hubbell. No. 851, 50p, Lion Leads in Jutland, by W. L. Wyllie. No. 852, 50p, Oppy Wod, by John Nash. No. 853, 50p, A Battery Shelled, by Percy Wyndham Lewis. No. 854, 50p, Somme Tank, by Louis Dauphin. No. 855, 50p, The Angels of Mons, by R. Crowhurst, vert. £1, Wreath of Remembrance, vert.

Wmk. 406
2008, Sept. 16   **Litho.**   **Perf. 14**
850-855 A152   Set of 6   12.50 12.50
Souvenir Sheet
856 A152 £1 multi   4.50 4.50

Ships
A153

Tristao da Cunha (1460-1540), Explorer — A154

Designs: No. 857, 50p, Mary Rose. No. 858, 50p, Endurance. No. 859, 50p, Cutty Sark. No. 860, 50p, Suomen Joutsen. No. 861, 50p, RFA Lyme Bay. No. 862, 50p, MS Explorer.

Wmk. 406
2009, Mar. 9   **Litho.**   **Perf. 14**
857-862 A153   Set of 6   11.50 11.50
Souvenir Sheet
863 A154 £1 multi   4.00 4.00

Naval
Aviation,
Cent.
A155

Designs: 25p, Felixstowe F.2A. 35p, Short
S.27. No. 866, 50p, Blackburn Dart. No. 867,
50p, Sikorsky Hoverfly helicopter.
£1.50, Lieutenant Commander C. R. Samson in Short S.27 taking off from HMS Hiber-
nia, 1912.

Wmk. 406
2009, Apr. 17   Litho.   Perf. 14
864-867 A155   Set of 4   9.25 9.25
Souvenir Sheet
868 A155   £1.50 multi   6.50 6.50
Nos. 864-867 each were printed in sheets of
8 + central label.

Space
Exploration
A156

Designs: 25p, Goddard Rocket, 1936. 35p,
X-24B Spaceplane, 1972. 60p, Launch of
Apollo 11, 1969. 90p, Space Shuttle Discovery
ferried by Boeing 747, 2005. £1, X-43C experimental hypersonic aircraft.
£1.50, Astronauts on Moon, painting by
Capt. Alan Bean, vert.

Wmk. 406
2009, July 20   Litho.   Perf. 13¼
869-873 A156   Set of 5   12.50 12.50
Souvenir Sheet
Perf. 13x13½
874 A156   £1.50 multi   6.50 6.50
First man on the Moon, 40th anniv. No. 874
contains one 40x60mm stamp.

Potato Production — A157

No. 875, 25p: a, Preparing seed potatoes. b,
Planting.
No. 876, 35p: a, Digging out. b, Harvesting.
No. 877, £1.10: a, Potato blossoms. b,
Potato fields.

Unwmk.
2009, Aug. 3   Litho.   Perf. 13
Horiz. Pairs, #a-b
875-877 A157   Set of 3   13.50 13.50

Island
Traditions
A158

Designs: 25p, Sheep shearing. 35p, Ratting
Day. 70p, Longboats to Nightingale. £1.60,
Old Year's Night Okalolies.

2009, Sept. 28
878-881 A158   Set of 4   10.50 10.50
See Nos. 927-930.

Mail
Delivery
on Tristan
da Cunha
A159

Designs: 25p, Mail arriving by ship. 35p,
Transporting mail to post office. £1, Hitting the
gong. £1.60, Giving out the mail.

Unwmk.
2009, Nov. 23   Litho.   Perf. 13
882-885 A159   Set of 4   12.50 12.50

British History
A160

Designs: No. 886, 35p, Battle of Hastings.
No. 887, 35p, Peasants' Revolt. No. 888, 35p,
King Henry VIII. No. 889, 35p, English Reformation. No. 890, 35p, Elizabethan era. No.
891, 35p, English Civil War. No. 892, 35p, Scientific innovation. No. 893, 35p, Bonnie Prince
Charlie.

Wmk. 406
2010, Jan. 15   Litho.   Perf. 13¼
886-893 A160   Set of 8   11.00 11.00
See Nos. 902-909, 944-951.

A161

A162

A163

A164

A165

Battle of
Britain,
70th
Anniv.
A166

Design: £1.50, Sir Douglas Bader, vert.

Wmk. 406
2010, Mar. 18   Litho.   Perf. 13
894 A161   25p black & gray   1.05 1.05
895 A162   25p black & gray   1.05 1.05
896 A163   50p black & gray   2.10 2.10
897 A164   50p black & gray   2.10 2.10
898 A165   70p black & gray   2.75 2.75
899 A166   70p black & gray   2.75 2.75
            Nos. 894-899 (6)   11.80 11.80
Souvenir Sheet
900 A166   £1.50 black & gray   5.75 5.75

Souvenir Sheet

Great Britain No. 159 — A167

2010, May 8   Perf. 14x14¼
901 A167   £1.50 multi   5.50 5.50
London 2010 Festival of Stamps.

British History Type of 2010
Designs: No. 902, 35p, Thomas Becket. No.
903, 35p, Battle of Agincourt. No. 904, 35p,
Battle of Trafalgar. No. 905, 35p, Engineering
& transportation. No. 906, 35p, Wireless age.
No. 907, 35p, Votes for women. No. 908, 35p,
The Great Depression. No. 909, 35p, Second
World War.

Wmk. 406
2010, July 16   Litho.   Perf. 13¼
902-909 A160   Set of 8   11.00 11.00

Surnames of
Island Families
A168

Surnames of island families, flags and birds:
No. 910, 50p, Hagan and Rogers, US flag,
bald eagle. No. 911, 50p, Repetto and
Lavaretto, Italian flag, hoopoe. No. 912, 50p,
Glass, Scottish flag, golden eagle. No. 913,
50p, Green, Netherlands flag, oystercatcher,
No. 914, 50p, Swain, English flag, avocet.

Perf. 12½x13
2010, Sept. 6   Unwmk.
910-914 A168   Set of 5   10.50 10.50

Conservation — A169

Designs: 1p, New Conservation R1 boat.
3p, Eradication of New Zealand flax on Nightingale Island. 5p, Banding Tristan albatross.
8p, Hag's Tooth, Gough Island UNESCO
World Heritage Site. 10p, Inaccessible rail.
15p, Inaccessible Island UNESCO World Heritage Site. 25p, Counting seals. 35p, Eradication of Sagina plant on Gough Island. 70p,
Eradication of Loganberry plants at Sandy
Point. £1, Banding Yellow-nosed albatross. £2,
Gough bunting. £5, Counting penguins.

2010, Nov. 1   Litho.   Perf. 13
915 A169   1p multi   .30   .30
916 A169   3p multi   .30   .30
917 A169   5p multi   .30   .30
918 A169   8p multi   .30   .30
919 A169   10p multi   .40   .40
920 A169   15p multi   .55   .55
921 A169   25p multi   .90   .90
922 A169   35p multi   1.30 1.30
923 A169   70p multi   2.60 2.60
924 A169   £1 multi   3.75 3.75
925 A169   £2 multi   7.50 7.50
926 A169   £5 multi   19.00 19.00
            Nos. 915-926 (12)   37.20 37.20

Island Traditions Type of 2009
Designs: 25p, Thatching a roof. 35p, Bullock
cart. 70p, Music. £1.00, Pillow dance.

2010, Nov. 24
927-930 A158   Set of 4   11.00 11.00

Service of Queen Elizabeth II and
Prince Philip — A170

Designs: 25p, Queen Elizabeth II. 35p,
Queen and Prince Philip. No. 933, 50p, Queen
and Prince Philip, diff. No. 934, 50p, Queen
(wearing hat) and Prince Philip. No. 935, 70p,
Queen and Prince Philip, diff. No. 936, 70p,
Queen and Prince Philip.
£1.50, Queen and Prince Philip, diff.

2011, Mar. 14   Perf. 13¼
931-936 A170   Set of 6   11.00 11.00
936a   Souvenir sheet of 6,
          #931-936, + 3 labels 11.00 11.00
Souvenir Sheet
937 A170   £1.50 multi   5.50 5.50

Cruise Ships — A171

Designs: 25p, MV Professor Multanovskiy.
35p, MV Aleksey Maryshev. 70p, MV Professor Molchanov. £1.10, MV Plancius.
£1.50, MV Plancius.

Perf. 14x14¾
2011, Apr. 12   Unwmk.
938-941 A171   Set of 4   8.50 8.50
Souvenir Sheet
942 A171   £1.50 multi   5.50 5.50

Souvenir Sheet

Wedding of Prince William and
Catherine Middleton — A172

Perf. 14¾x14¼
2011, Apr. 29   Wmk. 406
943 A172   £3 multi   11.00 11.00

British History Type of 2010
Designs: No. 944, 35p, Magna Carta. No.
945, 35p, Wars of the Roses. No. 946, 35p,
The Gunpowder Plot. No. 947, 35p, Great Fire
of London. No. 948, 35p, Battle of Waterloo.
No. 949, 35p, Age of Empire. No. 950, 35p,
Industry and Commerce. No. 951, 35p, First
World War.

2011, May 24   Wmk. 406   Perf. 13¼
944-951 A160   Set of 8   9.25 9.25

Photographs of
Wedding of
Prince William
and Catherine
Middleton — A173

Couple: No. 952, 70p, Standing, holding hands. No. 953, 70p, Kissing. No. 954, 70p, In coach, waving, horiz. No. 955. 70p, In car, waving, horiz.

2011, Sept. 1　Unwmk.　Perf. 12½
952-955　A173　Set of 4　　9.00　9.00

Eruption of Queen Mary's Peak, 50th Anniv. A174

Queen Mary's Peak and: No. 956, 25p, Tholoid. No. 957, 35p, October 1961 eruption. No. 958, 95p, Islanders leave aboard the MV Tjisadane. No. 959, £1.10, Islanders arrive in Cape Town. No. 960, MV Tjisadane.

2011, Oct. 10　Unwmk.　Perf. 14
956-959　A174　Set of 4　　8.50　8.50
Souvenir Sheet
960　A174　£2 multi　　6.25　6.25

See Nos. 961-965, 999-1003, 1006-1010.

Volcano Eruption Type of 2011
Queen Mary's Peak and: No. 961, 25p, Returning with the report. No. 962, 35p, Resettlement survey team. No. 963, 95p, HMS Protector Whirlwind helicopter. No. 964, £1.10, Royal Society members. No. 965, £2, Landing party.

2012, Jan. 30　Unwmk.　Perf. 14
961-964　A174　Set of 4　　8.50　8.50
Souvenir Sheet
965　A174　£2 multi　　6.50　6.50

Reign of Queen Elizabeth II, 60th Anniv. — A175

Queen Elizabeth II: 25p, Color photograph. 35p, Color photograph, diff. No. 968, 50p, Black-and-white photograph. No. 969, 50p, Color photograph, diff. No. 970, 70p, Color photograph, diff. No. 971, 70p, Black-and-white photograph, diff. £1.50, Queen Elizabeth II wearing crown.

2012, Feb. 6　Unwmk.　Perf. 13¼
966-971　A175　Set of 6　　9.50　9.50
971a　　　　Sheet of 6, #966-971, + 3 labels　　9.50　9.50
Souvenir Sheet
972　A175　£1.50 multi　　4.75　4.75

Miniature Sheet

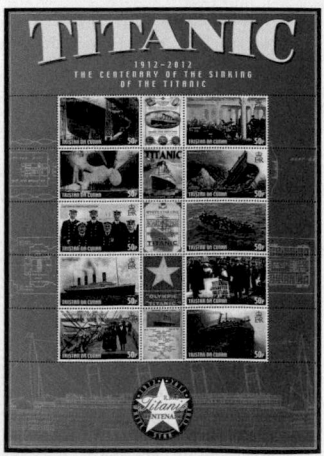

Sinking of the Titanic, Cent. — A176

No. 973: a, Titanic being built in Harland & Wolff Shipyard. b, First class dining room. c, Titanic's propellers. d, Sinking of the ship. e, Captain. E. J. Smith and crew. f, Survivors in lifeboat. g, Titanic setting sail. h, Newspaper reports. i, Passengers strolling on board. j, Discovery of the wreck.

2012, Feb. 27　Unwmk.　Perf. 13¼
973　A176　50p Sheet of 10, #a-j, + 5 labels　　16.00　16.00

Ships A177

Designs: No. 974, 35p, Agulhas I at sea. No. 975, 35p, Agulhas II at sea. 70p, Agulhas I near land. £1.10, Agulhas II near land.

2012, Sept. 17　　　　　Perf. 14
974-977　A177　Set of 4　　8.00　8.00

Miniature Sheet

Royal Navy Ships and Their Crests — A178

No. 978: a, 35p, HMS Portland, 2005. b, 35p, HMS Edinburgh, 2006. c, 70p, HMS Clyde, 2011. d, 70p, HMS Montrose, 2012.

2012, Oct. 15　　　　Perf. 13¼x13½
978　A178　Sheet of 4, #a-d　　6.75　6.75

Members of Shackleton-Rowett Antarctic Expedition — A179

Designs: No. 979, 70p, Frank Wild, Inaccessible Island. No.980, 70p, Hubert Wilkins, Gough Island. No. 981, 70p, James Marr, Tristan da Cunha. No. 982, 70p, Frank Worsley, Nightingale Island.

2012, Nov. 28　　　　　Perf. 14
979-982　A179　Set of 4　　9.00　9.00

Worldwide Fund for Nature (WWF) — A180

Tristan albatross: Nos. 983, 987a, 35p, Bird on nest. Nos. 984, 987b, 45p, Two birds. Nos. 985, 987c, 70p, Two birds, diff. Nos. 986, 987d, £1.10, Bird in flight. £3, Bird landing.

2013, Jan. 28　Litho.　Perf. 13¼x13½
Stamps With White Frames
983-986　A180　Set of 4　　8.25　8.25
Stamps Without White Frames
987　A180　Horiz. strip of 4, #a-d　8.25　8.25
Souvenir Sheet
988　A180　£3 multi　　9.50　9.50

No. 988 contains one 48x30mm stamp.

Tristan Song Project A181

Designs: 35p, Recorder and lyrics of "When Fish Get the Flu." 45p, Violin and lyrics of "Rockhopper Penguins." 70p, Guitar and lyrics of "The Volcano's Black." £1.10, Accordion and lyrics to "The Molly."

2013, Feb. 14　　　　Perf. 13¼x13½
989-992　A181　Set of 4　　8.25　8.25

Items Produced for Coronations — A182

Coronation of Queen Elizabeth II, 60th Anniv. — A183

Items produced for coronation of: 35p, Queen Victoria. 45p, King Edward VII. 70p, King George V. £1.10, King George VI. £1.50, Queen Elizabeth II.

2013, Apr. 15　　　　　Perf. 14
993-997　A182　Set of 5　　13.00　13.00
Souvenir Sheet
Perf. 14¾x14
998　A183　£2 multi　　6.25　6.25

Nos. 993-997 each were printed in sheets of 8 + label.

Volcano Eruption Type of 2011
Queen Mary's Peak and: 25p, Returning islanders sitting near their possessions. 35p, Returning islanders walking toward possessions. 95p, Islanders on shore waiting for ships transporting their possessions. £1.10, Islanders returning to their homes in a tractor-pulled wagon. £2, Islanders pulling longboat over rocks on shore.

2013, Nov. 11　Litho.　Perf. 14
999-1002　A174　Set of 4　　8.50　8.50
Souvenir Sheet
1003　A174　£2 multi　　6.50　6.50

Christmas A184

No. 1004: a, St. Mary's Anglican Church, Tristan da Cunha. b, Canterbury Cathedral, Canterbury, England.
No. 1005: a, St. Joseph's Catholic Church, Tristan da Cunha. b, St. Peter's Basilica, Vatican City.

Perf. 13¼x13½
2013, Nov. 18　　　　　Litho.
1004　Horiz. pair + central label　　5.00　5.00
　a.　A184 35p multi　　1.25　1.25
　b.　A184 £1.10 multi　　3.75　3.75
1005　Horiz. pair + central label　　5.00　5.00
　a.　A184 35p multi　　1.25　1.25
　b.　A184 £1.10 multi　　3.75　3.75

Volcano Eruption Type of 2011
Queen Mary's Peak and: 25p, HMS Puma. 35p, HMS Jaguar. 95p, MV Tristania. £1.10, MV Stirling Castle. £2, MV Bornholm.

2013, Dec. 9　Litho.　Perf. 14
1006-1009　A174　Set of 4　　8.75　8.75
Souvenir Sheet
1010　A174　£2 multi　　6.50　6.50

Polar Explorers and Their Ships A185

Designs: 35p, James Weddell (1787-1834) and Jane. 45p, George Nares (1831-1915) and HMS Challenger. 70p, Carsten Borchgrevink (1864-1934) and SS Antarctic. £1.50, Dr. Alexander Macklin (1889-1967) and Quest.

2014, Apr. 7　Litho.　Perf. 13¼x13½
1011-1014　A185　Set of 4　　10.00　10.00

Royal Christenings A186

Photographs of British royalty with christened infants: 35p, Queen Elizabeth II, 1926. 45p, Prince Charles, 1948. £1.10, Prince William, 1982. £1.50, Prince George, 2013.

2014, May 21　Litho.　Perf. 13¼
1015-1018　A186　Set of 4　　11.50　11.50

Finches A187

Designs: 35p, Gough finch, Gough Island. 45p, Dunn's finch, Inaccessible Island. 50p, Nightingale finch, Nightingale Island Group. £1.50, Wilkin's finch, Nightingale Island. £2, Inaccessible finch, Inaccessible Island.

2014, June 18　Litho.　Perf. 14
1019-1022　A187　Set of 4　　9.75　9.75
Souvenir Sheet
1023　A187　£2 multi　　7.00　7.00

Paintings by Augustus Earle (1793-1838) A188

Designs: No. 1024, 50p, Scudding Before a Heavy Westerly Gale Off the Cape, Latitude 44 Degrees (brown panel). No. 1025, 50p, On Board the Duke of Gloucester, Margate Hoy, Between Rio de Janeiro and Tristan de Acunha (olive green panel). No. 1026, 70p, Tristan da Cunha (blue panel). No. 1027, 70p, Solitude, Watching the Horizon at Sunset, in the Hopes of Seeing a Vessel, Tristan de Acunha in the South Atlantic (brown panel).

2014, July 10　Litho.　Perf. 13¾
1024-1027　A188　Set of 4　　8.25　8.25

World War I, Cent. — A189

Poppies and war posters inscribed: No. 1028, £1, "Rally Round the Flag / We Must Have More Men." No. 1029, £1, "Join the Royal Marines." No. 1030, £1, "The Empire Needs Men." No. 1031, £1, "National Service / Women's Land Army."

2014, Aug. 4   **Litho.**   **Perf. 13¼**
1028-1031   A189   Set of 4   13.50   13.50

Royal Marines, 350th Anniv. A190

Designs: 25p, Battle of Landguard Fort, 1667. 35p, Capture of Gibraltar, 1704. 40p, Zeebrugge Raid, 1918. 60p, Normandy Invasion, 1944. 80p, Falklands Conflict, 1982. £1.10, Marines in Afghanistan, 2013.

2014, Oct. 28   **Litho.**   **Perf. 14**
1032-1037   A190   Set of 6   11.50   11.50

Miniature Sheet

Potato Essays of 1937 and First Tristan da Cunha Postage Stamps — A191

No. 1038: a, Essay for ½p stamp. b, Essay for 1p stamp. c, Essay for 1½p stamp. d, Essay for 2p stamp. e, Essay for 3p stamp. f, Essay for 4p stamp. g, Essay for 6p stamp. h, Essay for 1sh stamp. i, Essay for 2sh6p stamp. j, Tristan da Cunha #1-3.

2015, Apr. 8   **Litho.**   **Perf. 13¼x13½**
1038   A191   50p Sheet of 10,
    #a-j, + 2 labels   15.50   15.50

Last Battle of War of 1812, 200th Anniv. — A192

Designs: No. 1039, £1.10, USS Hornet. No. 1040, £1.10, HMS Penguin. £2.50, Battle between USS Hornet and HMS Penguin off Tristan da Cunha, horiz.

2015, June 1   **Litho.**   **Perf. 13¾**
1039-1040   A192   Set of 2   6.75   6.75
    Souvenir Sheet
    Perf. 14¼x14¾
1041   A193   £2.50 multi   7.75   7.75
No. 1041 contains one 48x33mm stamp.

Magna Carta, 800th Anniv. A193

Designs: 35p, King John, barons with Magna Carta. 80p, Administrator's Residency, Tristan da Cunha. 90p, Administration Building, Tristan da Cunha. £1.50, Arms of Tristan da Cunha, King John.

2015, June 15   **Litho.**   **Perf. 12¾**
1042-1045   A193   Set of 4   11.00   11.00

Queen Elizabeth II, Longest-Reigning British Monarch — A194

Queen Elizabeth II and: 35p, Publications reporting on her coronation, 1953. 45p, Royal yacht Britannia. £1.10, Order of the Garter, Windsor Castle. £2, Trooping of the Color.

2015, Sept. 9   **Litho.**   **Perf. 14**
1046-1049   A194   Set of 4   12.00   12.00

1885 Lifeboat Disaster A195

Designs: 35p, Sighting the SV West Riding. 70p, Launching the lifeboat. 90p, Lifeboat in rough seas. £1.20, SV West Riding.

2015, Nov. 27   **Litho.**   **Perf. 13**
1050-1053   A195   Set of 4   9.50   9.50

Publication of *Alice's Adventures in Wonderland*, by Lewis Carroll, 150th Anniv. A196

Designs: No. 1054, 50p, White Rabbit. No. 1055, 50p, Alice and Caterpillar smoking hookah. No. 1056, 60p, Alice holding pig. No. 1057, 60p, Alice and Cheshire Cat. No. 1058, 70p, Hatter, March Hare and Cheshire Cat. No. 1059, 70p, Queen of Hearts.

2015, Dec. 1   **Litho.**   **Perf. 14**
1054-1059   A196   Set of 6   11.00   11.00
1059a   Souvenir sheet of 6,
    #1054-1059   11.00   11.00

Early Mail Ships A197

Designs: 1p, HMS Odin, 1904. 2p, RMS Asturias, 1927. 5p, SS Empress of France, 1928. 10p, HMS Carlisle, 1932, 1937. 25p, Barque Ponape, 1934. 35p, RMS Atlantis, 1934. 45p, Sailing Ship Cap Pilar, 1937. 60p, RMS Franconia, 1939. £1, HMS Queen of Bermuda, 1940. £1.50, HMS Carnarvon Castle, 1940. £2, RMS Darro, 1945. £5, MV Pequena, 1948-53.

2015, Dec. 8   **Litho.**   **Perf. 14**
1060   A197   1p multi   .25   .25
1061   A197   2p multi   .25   .25
1062   A197   5p multi   .25   .25
1063   A197   10p multi   .30   .30
1064   A197   25p multi   .75   .75

1065	A197	35p multi	1.00	1.00
1066	A197	45p multi	1.40	1.40
1067	A197	60p multi	1.75	1.75
1068	A197	£1 multi	3.00	3.00
1069	A197	£1.50 multi	4.50	4.50
1070	A197	£2 multi	6.00	6.00
1071	A197	£5 multi	15.00	15.00
		Nos. 1060-1071 (12)	34.45	34.45

Queen Elizabeth II, 90th Birthday — A198

Photograph of Queen Elizabeth II from: 35p, 1954. 40p, 1952. 90p, 1979. £1.10, 2011. £3, Queen Elizabeth II, 1962.

2016, Apr. 21   **Litho.**   **Perf. 14**
1072-1075   A198   Set of 4   8.25   8.25
    Souvenir Sheet
1076   A198   £3 multi   9.00   9.00

William Shakespeare (1564-1616), Writer — A199

Characters from Shakespeare plays: 35p, Bottom, Titania and Puck from *A Midsummer Night's Dream*. 50p, Three witches from *Macbeth*. £1, Ophelia from *Hamlet*. £1.20, Falstaff from *The Merry Wives of Windsor*.

2016, July 4   **Litho.**   **Perf. 14**
1077-1080   A199   Set of 4   8.00   8.00

British Garrison on Tristan da Cunha, 200th Anniv. — A200

Designs: 25p, Carronade with Royal Artillery crew. 35p, Thomas Currie and Bastiano Camilla greet Lieutenant David Rice and garrison members. £1, Captain A. Josias Cloete relieves Rice. £2, Arrival of Corporal William Glass and his family.

    Perf. 13½x13¼
2016, Aug. 14   **Litho.**
1081-1084   A200   Set of 4   9.75   9.75

Peter Green (1808-1902), Headman of Tristan da Cunha — A201

Designs: 35p, Green's birthplace, Katwijk aan Zee, Netherlands. 50p, Wreck of the Emily. £1, Green's house, Tristan da Cunha. £1.60, Green.

    Perf. 13¼x13¾
2016, Nov. 10   **Litho.**
1085-1088   A201   Set of 4   8.75   8.75

Biodiversity — A202

Designs: No. 1089, Bog fern. No. 1090, Devil's fingers. No. 1091, Tristan rock lobster. No. 1092, Orange starfish. No. 1093, Klipfish. No. 1094, Gough brass buttons. No. 1095, Antarctic tern. No. 1096, Gough flightless moth. No. 1097, Tristan thrush. No. 1098, Inaccessible rail. No. 1099, Sub-Antarctic fur seal. No. 1100, Spectacled petrel.

2016   **Litho.**   **Perf. 13¼x13¾**
1089   A202   25p multi   .65   .65
1090   A202   25p multi   .65   .65
1091   A202   35p multi   .90   .90
1092   A202   35p multi   .90   .90
1093   A202   45p multi   1.25   1.25
1094   A202   45p multi   1.25   1.25
1095   A202   60p multi   1.50   1.50
1096   A202   60p multi   1.50   1.50
1097   A202   70p multi   1.75   1.75
1098   A202   70p multi   1.75   1.75
1099   A202   £2 multi   5.00   5.00
1100   A202   £2 multi   5.00   5.00
    Nos. 1089-1100 (12)   22.10   22.10

Issued: Nos. 1089, 1091, 1093, 1095, 1097, 1099, 11/30; Nos. 1090, 1092, 1094, 1096, 1098, 1100, 12/7.

Visit of Prince Philip to Tristan da Cunha, 60th Anniv. — A203

No. 1101, 50p: a, Prince Philip with Sidney and Alice Glass and daughters Pamela and Trina. b, Three longboats at sea.
No. 1102, 50p: a, Edinburgh of the Seven Seas in 1957. b, Prince Philip, Dilys Bell and another woman.
No. 1103, 50p: a, Prince Philip with Martha Rogers, Willie Repetto, Pat and Forsyth Thompson. b, Islanders near longboats on shore.

2017, Jan. 24   **Litho.**   **Perf. 13¼x13½**
    Horiz. pairs, #a-b
1101-1103   A203   Set of 3   7.75   7.75
1103c   Souvenir sheet of 6,
    #1101a-1101b, 1102a-
    1102b, 1103a-1103b   7.75   7.75

Subantarctic Fur Seals — A204

Designs: No. 1104, 35p, Mother and pup, resting head on each other. No. 1105, 35p, Pup, with tongue out. No. 1106, 70p, Mother and pup, looking forward. No. 1107, 70p, Adult male, near rocks. No. 1108, £1, Head of adult male. No. 1109, £1, Pup, without tongue out.

2017, Apr. 12   **Litho.**   **Perf. 12¾**
1104-1109   A204   Set of 6   11.00   11.00

Visit of Prince Alfred to Tristan da Cunha, 150th Anniv. — A205

Designs: 40p, Prince Alfred (1844-1900). 80p, HMS Galatea. £1.10, Edinburgh of the Seven Seas, Tristan da Cunha, horiz. £1.50, Tristan da Cunha #110, horiz.

    Perf. 13x12¾, 12¾x13
2017, Aug. 5   **Litho.**
1110-1113   A205   Set of 4   10.00   10.00

Worldwide Fund for Nature (WWF) — A206

Northern rockhopper penguins: 35p, Chicks. 50p, Juveniles. £1.50, Adult. £2, Mother and chick.

2017, Oct. 13   **Litho.**   **Perf. 13x13¼**
1114-1117	A206	Set of 4	10.00	10.00
1117a		Souvenir sheet of 4,		
		#1114-1117	10.00	10.00

70th Wedding Anniversary of Queen Elizabeth II and Prince Philip A207

Photograph of Queen Elizabeth II and Prince Philip from: 25p, 1961. 60p, 1968. £1, 1970s. £2, 2015.

2017, Nov. 20   **Litho.**   **Perf. 13¼x13**
1118-1121	A207	Set of 4	10.50	10.50

Norwegian Scientific Expedition to Tristan da Cunha, 80th Anniv. A208

Designs: 35p, Dr. Sverre Dick Henriksen and Per Oeding in laboratory. 70p, Surveyor Allan Crawford. £1, Dr. Henriksen testing Tristan residents for tuberculosis. £1.50, Expedition members Egil Baardseth, Erling Sivertsen, and Yngvar Hagen on Nightingale Island.

2017, Dec. 7   **Litho.**   **Perf. 13¼x13½**
1122-1125	A208	Set of 4	9.75	9.75

Visiting Royal Navy Ships A209

Designs: 45p, HMS Portland, 2017. 55p, HMS Lancaster, 2015. 80p, HMS Protector, 2017. £1.60, RFA Gold Rover, 2017.

2018, Feb. 20   **Litho.**   **Perf. 13**
1126-1129	A209	Set of 4	9.50	9.50

Tristan Venture, 70th Anniv. A210

Designs: 45p, Captain L. E. Pettit and Reverend C. P. Lawrence. 70p, Tristan da Cunha #1, vert. £1.10, Cover of *The South African Shipping News and Fishing Industry Review*, vert. £1.60, Minesweeper M.V. Pequena.

Perf. 13¼ Syncopated (horiz. stamps), 13½x13¼ Syncopated (vert. stamps)
2018, Mar. 12   **Litho.**
1130-1133	A210	Set of 4	11.00	11.00
1133a		Souvenir sheet of 4,		
		#1130-1133	11.00	11.00

Royal Air Force, Cent. A211

Designs: 45p, Felixstowe F.5. 55p, Supermarine Southampton I. £1.60, Supermarine S.6B. £2, Short Sunderland Mk V.

2018, July 2   **Litho.**   **Perf. 13¼x13½**
1134-1137	A211	Set of 4	12.00	12.00

Wedding of Prince Harry and Meghan Markle A212

Designs: 45p, Engagement photograph. 55p, Couple on trip to Scotland. £1.30, Couple at altar. £2, Couple leaving Windsor Castle. £3, Couple kissing, vert.

2018, Aug. 20   **Perf. 13¼x13½**   **Litho.**
1138-1141	A212	Set of 4	11.00	11.00

Souvenir Sheet
Perf. 13½x13¼
1142	A212	£3 multi	7.75	7.75

Wreck of the Mabel Clark, 140th Anniv. A213

Designs: 45p, Mabel Clark foundering off Molly Gulch. 70p, Arrival of USS Essex to repatriate crew members. £1.15, Gold watch awarded to Tristan da Cunha by Pres. Rutherford B. Hayes. £1.50, HMS Comus delivering messages and gifts of appreciation.

2018, Sept. 3   **Litho.**   **Perf. 13¼x13½**
1143-1146	A213	Set of 4	9.75	9.75

Migratory Birds A214

No. 1147, 85p — Map of migration and Atlantic yellow-nosed albatross: a, In flight. b, On nest.
No. 1148, 95p — Map of migration and Great shearwater: a, In flight. b, On water.

2018, Oct. 18   **Litho.**   **Perf. 13¼x13½**
Vert. Pairs, #a-b
1147-1148	A214	Set of 2	9.00	9.00

Whales A215

Designs: 45c, Shepherd's beaked whale. 70p, Southern right whale. £1, Fin whale. £1.50, Killer whale.

Perf. 13¼x13½
2019, Feb. 11   **Litho.**
1149-1152	A215	Set of 4	9.75	9.75

POSTAGE DUE STAMPS

Type of Barbados 1934-47
Perf. 14
1957, Feb. 1   **Wmk. 4**   **Typo.**
Chalky Paper
J1	D1	1p rose red	3.50	7.00
J2	D1	2p orange yellow	4.25	9.25
J3	D1	3p green	4.50	11.50
J4	D1	4p ultramarine	5.25	13.50
J5	D1	5p deep claret	6.50	16.00
		Nos. J1-J5 (5)	24.00	57.25

Numeral — D2

Perf. 13½x14
1976, Sept. 3   **Litho.**   **Wmk. 373**
J6	D2	1p lilac rose	.25	.70
J7	D2	2p grayish green	.25	1.00
J8	D2	4p violet	.25	1.00
J9	D2	5p light blue	.25	1.00
J10	D2	10p brown	.65	1.50
		Nos. J6-J10 (5)	1.65	5.20

1976, May 31   **Wmk. 314**
J6a	D2	1p lilac rose	.35	.70
J7a	D2	2p grayish green	.35	1.00
J8a	D2	4p violet	.35	1.00
J9a	D2	5p light blue	.35	1.00
J10a	D2	10p brown	.75	1.50
		Nos. J6a-J10a (5)	2.15	5.20

Outline Map of Tristan da Cunha — D3

Perf. 15x14
1986, Nov. 20   **Litho.**   **Wmk. 384**
J11	D3	1p pale yel brn & brn	.25	.45
J12	D3	2p orange & brown	.25	.45
J13	D3	5p crimson rose & brn	.25	.45
J14	D3	7p lt lilac & black	.25	.45
J15	D3	10p pale ultra & blk	.30	.55
J16	D3	25p lt green & blk	.75	1.60
		Nos. J11-J16 (6)	2.05	3.95

TRUCIAL STATES

'trü-shəl 'stāts

LOCATION — Qatar Peninsula, Persian Gulf
GOVT. — Sheikdoms under British Protection
AREA — 32,300 sq. mi.
POP. — 86,000
CAPITAL — Dubai

The Trucial States are: Abu Dhabi, Ajman, Dubai, Fujeira, Ras al Khaima, Sharjah and Kalba, and Umm al Qiwain.
Stamps inscribed "Trucial States" were issued and used only in Dubai. Beginning Aug. 1972 all Trucial States used the stamps of United Arab Emirates.

100 Naye Paise = 1 Rupee

Catalogue values for all unused stamps in this country are for Never Hinged items.

7 Palm Trees — A1

Dhow — A2

Perf. 14½x14
1961, Jan. 7   **Photo.**   Unwmk.
1	A1	5np emerald	1.75	1.40
2	A1	15np red brown	.75	1.10
3	A1	20np ultra	1.60	1.60
4	A1	30np orange	.75	.35
5	A1	40np purple	.75	.40
6	A1	50np brown olive	.75	.60
7	A1	75np gray	.75	1.00
		Engr.	**Perf.**	**13x12½**
8	A2	1r emerald	9.00	4.00
9	A2	2r black	9.00	24.00
10	A2	5r rose red	11.00	26.50
11	A2	10r violet blue	17.50	27.50
		Nos. 1-11 (11)	53.60	88.45

Stamps inscribed "Trucial States" were withdrawn in June, 1963, when the individual states began issuing their own stamps.

TUNISIA

tü-'nē-zhē̱ə̱

LOCATION — Northern Africa, bordering on the Mediterranean Sea
GOVT. — Republic
AREA — 63,362 sq. mi.
POP. — 9,513,603 (1999 est.)
CAPITAL — Tunis

The former French protectorate became a sovereign state in 1956 and a republic in 1957.

100 Centimes = 1 Franc
1000 Millimes = 1 Dinar (1959)

Catalogue values for unused stamps in this country are for Never Hinged items, beginning with Scott 163 in the regular postage section, Scott B78 in the semi-postal section, Scott C13 in the airpost section, Scott CB1 in the airpost semi-postal section, and Scott J33 in the postage due section.

Coat of Arms — A1

Perf. 14x13½
1888-97   **Typo.**   Unwmk.
1	A1	1c black, *blue*	5.50	3.50
2	A1	2c pur brn, *buff*	7.00	3.50
3	A1	5c green, *grnsh*	35.00	17.50
4	A1	15c blue, *grysh*	55.00	27.50
5	A1	25c black, *rose*	110.00	70.00
6	A1	40c red, *straw*	110.00	77.50
7	A1	75c car, *rose*	110.00	85.00
8	A1	5fr gray vio, *grysh*	510.00	275.00
		Nos. 1-8 (8)	942.50	559.50

All values exist imperforate.
Reprints were made in 1893 and some values have been reprinted twice since then. The shades usually differ from those of the originals. Stamps from the 1897 printing are on thicker paper, with white gum instead of grayish, and have a background of horizontal ruled lines.

A2

A3

1888-1902
9	A2	1c blk, *lil bl*	1.75	1.10
10	A2	2c pur brn, *buff*	1.75	1.10
11	A2	5c grn, *grnsh*	7.00	1.10
12	A2	5c yellow grn ('99)	7.00	1.10
13	A2	10c blk, *lav* ('93)	14.00	2.10
14	A2	10c red ('01)	7.00	1.10
15	A2	15c blue, *grysh*	50.00	1.10
16	A2	15c gray ('01)	11.00	2.10
17	A2	20c red, *grn* ('99)	21.00	2.10
18	A2	25c blk, *rose*	25.00	2.10
19	A2	25c blue ('01)	21.00	2.75
20	A2	35c brown ('02)	55.00	3.50
21	A2	40c red, *straw*	21.00	2.10

22	A2	75c car, *rose*	170.00	80.00
23	A2	75c dp vio, *org* ('93)	35.00	11.00
24	A3	1fr olive, *cream*	35.00	9.00
25	A3	2fr dull violet ('02)	175.00	130.00
26	A3	5fr red lil, *lav*	200.00	77.50
		Bar cancellation		1.00

Quadrille Paper

27	A2	15c bl, *grysh* ('93)	50.00	1.40
		Nos. 9-27 (19)	907.50	332.25

For surcharges see Nos. 28, 58-61.

No. 27 Surcharged in Red

1902

28	A2	25c on 15c blue	3.50	3.50

Mosque at Kairouan A4 — Plowing A5

Ruins of Hadrian's Aqueduct A6

Carthaginian Galley — A7

1906-26   Typo.

29	A4	1c blk, *yel*	.25	.25
30	A4	2c red brn, *straw*	.25	.25
31	A4	3c lt red ('19)	.25	.25
32	A4	5c grn, *grnsh*	.35	.25
33	A4	5c orange ('21)	.35	.25
34	A5	10c red	.35	.30
35	A5	10c green ('21)	.35	.35
36	A5	15c vio, *pnksh*	1.40	.30
a.		Imperf., pair	160.00	
37	A5	15c brn, *org* ('23)	.35	.35
38	A5	20c brn, *pnksh*	.35	.30
39	A5	25c deep blue	2.10	.70
a.		Imperf., pair		
40	A5	25c violet ('21)	.35	.35
41	A6	30c red brn & vio ('19)	1.10	.70
42	A6	30c pale red ('21)	1.10	.70
43	A6	35c ol grn & brn	10.50	2.10
44	A6	40c blk brn & red brn	5.50	.70
45	A5	40c blk, *pnksh* ('23)	1.10	.70
46	A5	40c gray grn ('26)	.25	.25
47	A5	50c blue ('21)	1.10	.70
48	A6	60c ol grn & vio ('21)	1.10	1.10
49	A6	60c ver & rose ('25)	.70	.35
50	A6	75c red brn & red	1.10	.70
51	A6	75c ver & dl red ('26)	.50	.50
52	A7	1fr red & dk brn	1.10	.70
53	A7	1fr ind & ultra ('25)	.35	.35
54	A7	2fr brn & ol grn	6.50	2.00
55	A7	2fr grn & red, *pink* ('25)	1.10	.35
56	A7	5fr violet & blue ('25)	12.50	5.50
57	A7	5fr gray vio & grn ('25)	1.10	.70
		Nos. 29-57 (29)	53.40	22.00

For surcharges and overprints see Nos. 62-64, 70-73115-116, B1-B23, B25-B27, B29-B30, B32-B36, C1-C6.

Stamps and Type of 1888-1902 Surcharged

1908, Sept.

58	A2	10c on 15c gray, *lt gray* (R)	2.10	2.10
59	A3	35c on 1fr ol, *ol* (R)	5.50	5.50

60	A3	40c on 2fr dl vio (Bl)	10.50	10.50
61	A3	75c on 5fr red lil, *lav* (Bl)	7.00	7.00
		Nos. 58-61 (4)	25.10	25.10

No. 36 Surcharged

1911

62	A5	10c on 15c vio, *pinkish*	1.75	.70
a.		Inverted surcharge		2,100.

No. 34 Surcharged

1917, Mar. 16

63	A5	15c on 10c red	1.10	.35
a.		"15c" omitted	40.00	
b.		Double surcharge	87.50	

No. 36 Surcharged

1921

64	A5	20c on 15c vio, *pinkish*	1.10	.35
a.		Grayish paper (#36b)	1.40	.45

Arab and Ruins of Dougga — A9

1922-26   Typo.   Perf. 13½x14

65	A9	10c green	.25	.25
66	A9	10c rose ('26)	.30	.30
67	A9	30c rose	1.10	1.10
68	A9	30c lilac ('26)	.45	.45
69	A9	50c blue	.70	.70
		Nos. 65-69 (5)	2.80	2.80

For surcharges see Nos. 117, B24, B28, B31.

Stamps and Type of 1906 Surcharged in Red or Black

a   b

1923-25

70	A4(a)	10c on 5c grn, *grnsh* (R)	.35	.35
a.		Double surcharge	80.00	
b.		Inverted surcharge	115.00	
c.		Double surcharge, one inverted	115.00	
71	A5(b)	20c on 15c vio (Bk)	1.10	.35
a.		Double surcharge	115.00	
72	A5(b)	30c on 20c yel brn (Bk) ('25)	.35	.35
73	A5(b)	50c on 25c blue (R)	1.10	.35
a.		Double surcharge	110.00	
b.		Inverted surcharge	110.00	
		Nos. 70-73 (4)	2.90	1.40

Arab Woman Carrying Water — A10 — Grand Mosque at Tunis — A11

Mosque, Tunis — A12

Roman Amphitheater, El Djem (Thysdrus) — A13

1926-46   Typo.   Perf. 14x13½

74	A10	1c lt red	.25	.25
75	A10	2c olive grn	.25	.25
76	A10	3c slate blue	.25	.25
77	A10	5c yellow grn	.25	.25
78	A10	10c rose	.25	.25
78A	A12	10c brown ('46)	.25	.25
79	A11	15c gray lilac	.25	.25
80	A11	20c deep red	.30	.25
81	A11	25c gray green	.45	.30
82	A11	25c lt violet ('28)	.70	.30
83	A11	30c lt violet	.45	.35
84	A11	30c bl grn ('28)	.35	.30
84A	A12	30c dk ol grn ('46)	.25	.25
85	A11	40c deep brown	.25	.25
85A	A11	40c lil rose ('46)	.30	.30
86	A11	45c emer ('40)	1.10	1.10
87	A12	50c black	.25	.25
88	A12	50c ultra ('34)	.70	.35
88B	A12	50c emer ('40)	.25	.25
88C	A12	50c lt blue ('46)	.30	.30
89	A12	60c red org ('40)	.25	.25
89A	A12	60c ultra ('45)	.25	.25
90	A12	65c ultra ('38)	.70	.35
91	A12	70c dk red ('40)	.25	.25
92	A12	75c vermilion	.35	.70
93	A12	75c lil rose ('28)	1.10	.35
94	A12	80c blue green	1.10	.70
94A	A12	80c blk brn ('40)	.30	.30
94B	A12	80c emer ('45)	.45	.30
95	A12	90c org red ('28)	.35	.35
96	A12	90c ultra ('39)	10.00	10.00
97	A12	1fr brown violet	.70	.70
97A	A12	1fr rose ('40)	.25	.25
98	A13	1.05fr dl bl & mag	.70	.70
98A	A12	1.20fr blk brn ('45)	.35	.30
99	A13	1.25fr gray bl & dk bl	.70	.70
100	A13	1.25fr car rose ('40)	1.10	1.10
100A	A13	1.30fr bl & vio bl ('42)	.35	.30
101	A13	1.40fr brt red vio ('40)	1.20	1.20
102	A13	1.50fr bl & dp bl ('28)	1.40	.50
102A	A13	1.50fr rose red & red org ('42)	.35	.50
102B	A12	1.50fr rose lil ('46)	.25	.25
103	A13	2fr rose & ol brn	1.40	.35
104	A13	2fr red org ('39)	.35	.35
104A	A12	2fr Prus grn ('45)	.35	.25
105	A13	2.25fr ultra ('39)	.70	.90
105A	A13	2.40fr red ('46)	.65	.50
106	A13	2.50fr green ('40)	.80	.80
107	A13	3fr dl bl & org	1.75	.70
108	A13	3fr violet ('39)	.35	.35
108A	A13	3fr blk brn ('46)	.35	.25
108B	A13	4fr ultra ('45)	1.10	.55
109	A13	6fr red & yrn, *grnsh*	2.75	1.40
110	A13	5fr dp red brn ('40)	1.25	1.25
110A	A13	5fr dk grn ('46)	.45	.45
110B	A13	6fr dp ultra ('45)	.70	.45
111	A13	10fr brn red & blk, *bluish*	11.00	3.50
112	A13	10fr rose pink ('40)	.80	.80
112A	A13	10fr ver ('46)	.70	.45
112B	A13	10fr ultra ('46)	.65	.30
112C	A13	15fr rose lil ('45)	.35	.25
113	A13	20fr lil & red, *pnksh* ('28)	2.50	1.10
113A	A13	20fr dk grn ('45)	.70	.45
113B	A13	25fr violet ('45)	.70	.65
113C	A13	50fr carmine ('45)	1.75	.85
113D	A13	100fr car rose ('45)	2.10	1.10
		Nos. 74-113D (66)	64.05	44.65

See Nos. 152A-162, 185-189, 199-206. For surcharges and overprints see Nos. 114, 118-121, 143-152, B74-B77, B87-B88, B91-B95, B98, C7-C12.

No. 99 Surcharged with New Value and Bars in Red

1927, Mar. 24

114	A13	1.50fr on 1.25fr	.80	.30

Stamps of 1921-26 Surcharged

1928, May 1

115	A4	3c on 5c orange	.35	.25
116	A5	10c on 15c brn, *org*	.70	.30
c.		Double surcharge	125.00	
117	A9	25c on 30c lilac	.70	.70
118	A12	40c on 80c bl grn	.70	.45
119	A12	50c on 75c ver	1.10	.50
		Nos. 115-119 (5)	3.55	2.20

No. 83 Surcharged

1929

120	A11	10c on 30c lt violet	1.75	1.10

No. 120 exists precanceled only. The value in first column is for a stamp which has not been through the post and has original gum. The value in the second column is for a postally used, gumless stamp. See No. 199a.

No. 85 Surcharged with New Value and Bars

1930

121	A11	50c on 40c dp brn	5.50	.70

A14 — A15

A16

A17

Perf. 11, 12½, 12½x13

1931-34   Engr.

122	A14	1c deep blue	.25	.25
123	A14	2c yellow brn	.25	.25
124	A14	3c black	.35	.35
125	A14	5c yellow grn	.25	.25
126	A14	10c red	.25	.25
127	A15	15c dull violet	.70	.70
128	A15	20c dull brown	.25	.25
129	A15	25c rose red	.35	.35
130	A15	30c deep green	.35	.35
131	A15	40c red orange	.35	.35
132	A16	50c ultra	.35	.35
133	A16	75c yellow	2.10	2.10
134	A16	90c red	.70	.70
135	A16	1fr olive black	.35	.70
136	A16	1fr dk brn ('34)	.50	.45
137	A17	1.50fr brt ultra	1.00	.70
138	A17	2fr deep brown	.70	1.00
139	A17	3fr blue green	10.50	10.50
140	A17	5fr car rose	28.00	12.00
a.		Perf. 12½	37.50	35.00
141	A17	10fr black	50.00	35.00
142	A17	20fr dark brown	62.50	45.00
		Nos. 122-142 (21)	160.05	121.20

For surcharges see Nos. B54-B73.

Nos. 88, 102 Surcharged in Red or Black

1937   **Perf. 14x13½**
143 A12 65c on 50c (R)   .70   .35
 b.   Double surcharge   105.00 87.50
144 A13 1.75fr on 1.50fr (R)   5.50 1.40
 a.   Double surcharge   95.00 95.00
 b.   In pair with unsurcharged
       stamp   250.00

1938
145 A12 65c on 50c (Bk)   .70   .35
 a.   Double surcharge, one in-
       verted   175.00 175.00
146 A13 1.75fr on 1.50fr (R)   10.50 7.00

Stamps of 1938-39 Surcharged in Red or Carmine

1940
147 A12 25c on 65c ultra (C)   .25   .25
148 A12 1fr on 90c ultra (R)   .50   .50
 a.   Double surcharge   120.00

Stamps of 1938-40 Surcharged in Red or Black

1941
149 A12 25c on 65c ultra (R)   .35   .35
150 A13 1fr on 1.25fr car rose   .70   .35
151 A13 1fr on 1.40fr brt red vio   .70   .70
152 A13 1fr on 2.25fr ultra (R)   .70   .70
      Nos. 149-152 (4)   2.45 2.10

Types of 1926 Without RF

1941-45   Typo.   Perf. 14x13½
152A A11 30c carmine ('45)   .25   .25
152B A12 1.20fr int blue ('45)   .25   .25
153 A13 1.50fr brn red ('42)   .35   .45
154 A13 2.40fr car & brt pink
            ('42)   .45   .45
155 A13 2.50fr dk bl & lt bl   .35   .45
156 A13 3fr l violet ('42)   .30   .30
157 A13 4fr blk & bl vio
            ('42)   .35   .45
158 A13 4.50fr ol grn & brn
            ('42)   .70   .70
159 A13 5fr brown blk
            ('42)   .70   .55
160 A13 10fr lil & dull vio   .35   .50

161 A13 15fr henna brn
            ('42)   5.50 4.50
162 A13 20fr lt vio & car   2.75 1.50
      Nos. 152A-162 (12)   12.30 10.35

> Catalogue values for unused stamps in this section, from this point to the end of the section, are for Never Hinged items.

One Aim Alone - Victory — A18

1943   Litho.   Perf. 12
163 A18 1.50fr rose   .35   .25

Mosque and Olive Tree — A19

1944-45   Unwmk.   Perf. 11½
Size: 15½x19mm
165 A19 30c yellow ('45)   .35   .25
166 A19 40c org brn ('45)   .35   .25
168 A19 60c red org ('45)   .70   .45
169 A19 70c rose pink ('45)   .35   .25
170 A19 80c Prus grn ('45)   .35   .30
171 A19 90c violet ('45)   .35   .30
172 A19 1fr red ('45)   .35   .30
173 A19 1.50fr dp bl ('45)   .35   .30
Size: 21¼x26½mm
175 A19 2.40fr red   .70   .45
176 A19 2.50fr red brn   .70   .45
177 A19 3fr lt vio   1.10 .65
178 A19 4fr brt bl vio   .70   .45
179 A19 4.50fr apple grn   .70   .45
180 A19 5fr gray   1.10 .65
181 A19 6fr choc ('45)   .70   .45
182 A19 10fr brn lake ('45)   1.10 .70
183 A19 15fr copper brn   1.10 .70
184 A19 20fr lilac   1.10 .80
      Nos. 165-184 (18)   12.15 8.15
For surcharge see No. B79.

Types of 1926
1946-47   Typo.   Perf. 14x13½
185 A12 2fr emerald ('47)   .70   .45
186 A12 3fr rose pink   .35   .25
187 A12 4fr violet ('47)   .85   .45
188 A13 4fr violet ('47)   1.10 .50
189 A12 6fr carmine ('47)   .35   .25
      Nos. 185-189 (5)   3.35 1.90

Neptune, Bardo Museum A20

1947-49   Engr.   Perf. 13
190 A20 5fr dk grn & bluish blk   1.10 .90
191 A20 10fr blk brn & bluish blk   .55   .30
192 A20 18fr dk bl gray & Prus bl
            ('48)   1.75 1.00
193 A20 25fr dk bl & bl grn ('49)   2.10 1.10
      Nos. 190-193 (4)   5.50 3.30
For surcharge see No. B108.

Detail from Great Mosque at Kairouan A21

1948-49
194 A21 3fr dk bl grn & bl grn   1.10 .55
195 A21 4fr dk red vio & red
            vio   .70   .45
196 A21 6fr red brn & red   .35   .25
197 A21 8fr purple ('49)   .65   .35
198 A21 12fr henna brn   1.10 .65

198A A21 12fr dk brn & org brn
            ('49)   .90   .55
198B A21 15fr dk red ('49)   .80   .55
      Nos. 194-198B (7)   5.60 3.35
See No. 225. For surcharge see No. B103.

Types of 1926
1947-49   Typo.   Perf. 14x13½
199 A12 2.50fr brown orange   .70   .45
 a.   2.50fr brown   1.50 .80
200 A12 4fr brown org ('49)   1.20 .45
201 A12 4.50fr lt ultra   1.10 .45
202 A12 5fr blue ('48)   .70   .55
203 A12 5fr lt bl grn ('49)   1.20 .45
204 A13 6fr rose red   .35   .25
205 A13 15fr rose red   1.20 .65
206 A13 25fr red orange   2.10 .90
      Nos. 199-206 (8)   8.55 3.95
No. 199a is known only precanceled. See note after No. 120.

Dam on the Oued Mellegue A22

1949, Sept. 1   Engr.   Perf. 13
207 A22 15fr grnsh black   3.50 .70

UPU Symbols and Tunisian Post Rider — A23

1949, Oct. 28   Bluish Paper
208 A23 5fr dark green   1.75 1.40
209 A23 15fr red brown   1.75 1.40
      Nos. 208-209,C13 (3)   6.00 4.55
UPU, 75th anniversary.
Nos. 208-209 exist imperf.

Berber Hermes at Carthage — A24

1950-51
210 A24 15fr red brown   1.10 .70
211 A24 25fr indigo ('51)   1.10 .70
212 A24 50fr dark green ('51)   2.50 .70
      Nos. 210-212 (3)   4.70 2.10

Horse, Carthage Museum — A25

1950, Dec. 26   Typo.   Perf. 13½x14
Size: 21½x17½mm
213 A25 10c aquamarine   .30   .25
214 A25 50c brown   .30   .25
215 A25 1fr rose lilac   .30   .25
216 A25 2fr gray   .35   .30
217 A25 4fr vermilion   .55   .45
218 A25 5fr blue green   .35   .25
219 A25 8fr deep blue   .55   .35
220 A25 12fr red   1.40 .65
221 A25 15fr carmine rose ('50)   .55   .45
      Nos. 213-221 (9)   4.65 3.20
See Nos. 222-224, 226-228.

1951-53   Engr.   Perf. 13x14
Size: 22x18mm
222 A25 15fr carmine rose   1.20 .65
223 A25 15fr ultra ('53)   1.40 .55
224 A25 30fr deep ultra   2.50 .90
      Nos. 222-224 (3)   5.10 1.90

Type of 1948-49
1951, Aug. 1   Perf. 13
225 A21 30fr dark blue   1.40 1.10

Horse Type of 1950
1952   Typo.   Perf. 13½x14
226 A25 3fr brown orange   .70   .45
227 A25 12fr carmine rose   1.40 .45
228 A25 15fr ultra   .70   .25
      Nos. 226-228 (3)   2.80 1.15

Charles Nicolle — A26

1952, Aug. 4   Engr.   Perf. 13
229 A26 15fr black brown   2.10 .90
230 A26 30fr deep blue   2.10 .90
Founding of the Society of Medical Sciences of Tunisia, 50th anniv.

Flags, Pennants and Minaret — A27

1953, Oct. 18
231 A27 8fr black brn & choc   1.40 1.10
232 A27 12fr dk green & emer   1.40 1.10
233 A27 15fr indigo & ultra   1.40 1.10
234 A27 18fr dk pur & pur   1.40 1.10
235 A27 30fr dk car & car   2.10 1.40
      Nos. 231-235 (5)   7.70 5.80
First International Fair of Tunis.

Courtyard at Sousse — A28

Sidi Bou Maklouf Mosque A29

Designs: 1fr, Courtyard at Sousse. 2fr, 4fr, Citadel, Takrouna. 5fr, 8fr, View of Tatahouine. 10fr, 12fr, Oasis of Matmata. 15fr, Street Corner, Sidi Bou Said. 20fr, 25fr, Genoese fort, Tabarka. 30fr, 40fr, Bab-El-Khadra gate. 50fr, 75fr, Four-story building, Medenine.

Perf. 13½x13 (A28), 13
1954, May 29
236 A28 50c emerald   .30   .25
237 A28 1fr carmine rose   .30   .25
238 A28 2fr violet brown   .35   .30
239 A28 4fr turq blue   .55   .25
240 A28 5fr violet   .55   .25
241 A28 8fr black brown   .55   .30
242 A28 10fr dk blue grn   .55   .30
243 A28 12fr rose brown   .55   .30
244 A28 15fr dp ultra   2.25 .35
245 A29 18fr chocolate   2.00 .65
246 A29 20fr dp ultra   1.25 .30
247 A29 25fr indigo   1.25 .30
248 A29 30fr dp claret   1.40 .30
249 A29 40fr dk Prus grn   1.50 .65
250 A29 50fr dk violet   2.50 .30
251 A29 75fr carmine rose   5.50 2.10

Typo.
Perf. 14x13½
252 A28 15fr ultra   .80   .25
      Nos. 236-252 (17)   22.15 7.40
Imperforates exist. Value $50. See Nos. 271-287: For surcharge see No. B125.

Mohammed al-Amin, Bey of Tunis — A30

1954, Oct. | | **Perf. 13**
253 A30 8fr bl & dk bl | 1.10 | .85
254 A30 12fr lil gray & indigo | 1.10 | .85
255 A30 15fr dp car & brn lake | 1.20 | .90
256 A30 18fr red brn & blk brn | 1.20 | .90
257 A30 30fr bl grn & dk bl grn | 1.75 | 1.40
Nos. 253-257 (5) | 6.35 | 4.90

Theater Drapes, Dove and Sun — A31

1955
258 A31 15fr dk red brn, bl & org 1.10 .85
Essor, Tunisian amateur theatrical society.

Rotary Emblem, Map and Symbols of Punic, Roman, Arab and French Civilizations A32

1955, May 14 | | **Unwmk.**
259 A32 12fr vio brn & blk brn | 1.10 | .85
260 A32 15fr vio gray & dk brn | 1.10 | .85
261 A32 18fr rose vio & dk pur | 1.20 | .90
262 A32 25fr blue & dp ultra | 1.20 | .90
263 A32 30fr dk Prus grn & ind | 1.75 | 1.40
Nos. 259-263 (5) | 6.35 | 4.90

Rotary International, 50th anniv.

Bey of Tunis — A33

1955 | **Engr.** | **Perf. 13½x13**
264 A33 15fr dark blue | .70 | .25

Embroiderers — A34

15fr, 18fr, Potters. 20fr, 30fr, Florists.

1955, July 25 | | **Perf. 13**
265 A34 5fr rose brown | 1.10 | .85
266 A34 12fr ultra | 1.10 | .85
267 A34 15fr Prussian green | 1.10 | .90
268 A34 18fr red | 1.10 | .90
269 A34 20fr dark violet | 1.40 | 1.10
270 A34 30fr violet brown | 1.40 | 1.10
Nos. 265-270 (6) | 7.20 | 5.70

For surcharge see No. B126.

Independent Kingdom
Types of 1954 Redrawn with "RF" Omitted

1956, Mar. 1 | **Perf. 13½x13, 13 (A29)**
271 A28 50c emerald | .25 | .25
272 A28 1fr carmine rose | .25 | .25
273 A28 2fr violet brown | .25 | .25
274 A28 4fr turquoise blue | .30 | .25
275 A28 5fr violet | .30 | .25

276 A28 8fr black brown | .30 | .25
277 A28 10fr dk blue grn | .30 | .25
278 A28 12fr rose brown | .30 | .25
279 A28 15fr deep ultra | 1.10 | .25
280 A29 18fr chocolate | .35 | .25
281 A29 20fr deep ultra | .30 | .25
282 A29 25fr indigo | .30 | .25
283 A29 30fr deep claret | 1.10 | .25
284 A29 40fr dk Prus grn | 1.10 | .25
285 A29 50fr dark violet | 1.00 | .25
286 A29 75fr carmine rose | 1.75 | 1.10

Typo.
287 A28 15fr ultra | .70 | .25
Nos. 271-287 (17) | 9.95 | 5.10

Mohammed al-Amin Bey of Tunis — A35

Designs: 12fr, 18fr, 30fr, Woman and Dove. 5fr, 20fr, Bey of Tunis.

1956 | **Unwmk.** | **Engr.** | **Perf. 13**
288 A35 5fr deep blue | .25 | .25
289 A35 12fr brown violet | .30 | .35
290 A35 15fr red | .30 | .35
291 A35 18fr dk blue gray | .45 | .40
292 A35 20fr dark green | .45 | .40
293 A35 30fr copper brown | .85 | .50
Nos. 288-293 (6) | 2.60 | 2.25

Issued to commemorate Tunisian autonomy.

Farhat Hached — A36

1956, May 1
294 A36 15fr rose brown | .30 | .30
295 A36 30fr indigo | .35 | .35
Farhat Hached (1914-1952), nationalist leader.

Grapes — A37

Fruit Market A38

Designs: 15fr, Hand holding olive branch. 18fr, Wheat harvest. 20fr, Man carrying food basket ("Gifts for the wedding").

1956-57 | **Unwmk.** | **Engr.** | **Perf. 13**
296 A37 12fr lil, vio & vio brn | .55 | .25
297 A37 15fr ind, dk ol grn & red brn | .65 | .25
298 A37 18fr brt violet blue | .90 | .40
299 A37 20fr brown orange | .90 | .40
300 A38 25fr chocolate | 1.25 | .80
301 A38 30fr deep ultra | 1.40 | .65
Nos. 296-301 (6) | 5.65 | 2.75

Habib Bourguiba — A39

Farmers and Workers A40

Perf. 14 (A39), 11½x11 (A40)
1957, Mar. 20
302 A39 5fr dark blue | .25 | .25
303 A40 12fr magenta | .25 | .25
304 A39 20fr ultra | .30 | .30
305 A40 25fr green | .35 | .25
306 A40 30fr chocolate | .45 | .35
307 A40 50fr crimson rose | .80 | .55
Nos. 302-307 (6) | 2.40 | 1.95

First anniversary of independence.

Dove and Handclasp A41

Labor Bourse, Tunis — A42

1957, July 5 | **Engr.** | **Perf. 13**
308 A41 18fr dk red violet | .30 | .30
309 A42 20fr crimson | .35 | .35
310 A41 25fr green | .35 | .35
311 A42 30fr dark blue | .45 | .45
Nos. 308-311 (4) | 1.45 | 1.45

5th World Congress of the Intl. Federation of Trade Unions, Tunis, July 5-13.

Republic

Officer and Soldier — A43

1957, Aug. 8 | **Typo.** | **Perf. 11**
312 A43 20fr rose pink | 14.00 | 20.00
313 A43 25fr light violet | 14.00 | 19.00
314 A43 30fr brown orange | 14.00 | 19.00
Nos. 312-314 (3) | 42.00 | 58.00

Proclamation of the Republic.

Bourguiba in Exile, Ile de la Galité A44

1958, Jan. 18 | **Engr.** | **Perf. 13**
315 A44 20fr blue & dk brn | .55 | .40
316 A44 25fr lt blue & vio | .55 | .40

6th anniv. of Bourguiba's deportation.

Map of Tunisia — A45

25fr, Woman & child. 30fr, Hand holding flag.

1958, Mar. 20 | | **Perf. 13**
317 A45 20fr dk brown & emer | .40 | .25
318 A45 25fr blue & sepia | .40 | .25
319 A45 30fr red brown & red | .55 | .25
Nos. 317-319 (3) | 1.35 | .75

2nd anniv. of independence. See No. 321.

Andreas Vesalius and Abderrahman ibn Khaldoun — A46

1958, Apr. 17 | | **Unwmk.**
320 A46 30fr bister & slate grn | .65 | .25

World's Fair, Brussels, Apr. 17-Oct. 19.

Redrawn Type of 1958
1958, June 1 | **Engr.** | **Perf. 13**
321 A45 20fr brt bl & ocher | .65 | .25

Date has been changed to "1 Juin 1955-1958."
3rd anniv. of the return of Pres. Habib Bourguiba.

Gardener — A47

1958, May 1
322 A47 20fr multicolored | .65 | .30

Labor Day, May 1.

A48

1958, July 25 | **Unwmk.** | **Perf. 13**
Blue Paper
323 A48 5fr dk vio brn & ol | .45 | .25
324 A48 10fr dk grn & yel grn | .45 | .25
325 A48 15fr org red & brn lake | .45 | .25
326 A48 20fr vio, ol grn & yel | .45 | .25
327 A48 25fr red lilac | .45 | .25
Nos. 323-327 (5) | 2.25 | 1.25

First anniversary of the Republic.

Pres. Habib
Bourguiba — A49

1958, Aug. 3   Unwmk.   Perf. 13
328 A49 20fr vio & brn lake   .65 .25
Pres. Bourguiba's 55th birthday.

Fishermen Casting
Net — A50

1958, Oct. 18   Engr.   Perf. 13
329 A50 25fr dk brn, grn & red   .65 .30
6th International Fair, Tunis.

UNESCO
Building,
Paris
A51

1958, Nov. 3
330 A51 25fr grnsh black   .65 .30
Opening of UNESCO Headquarters, Nov. 3.

Woman Opening
Veil — A52

1959, Jan. 1   Engr.   Perf. 13
331 A52 20m greenish blue   .65 .25
Emancipation of Tunisian women.

Hand Planting
Symbolic
Tree — A53

Habib
Bourguiba
at Borj le
Boeuf
A54

10m, Shield with flag and people holding
torch. 20m, Habib Bourguiba at Borj le Boeuf,
Sahara.

1959, Mar. 2   Unwmk.   Perf. 13
332 A53 5m vio brn, car & sal   .25 .25
333 A53 10m multicolored   .30 .25
334 A53 20m blue   .40 .25
335 A54 30m grnsh bl, ind & org
            brn   .70 .40
      Nos. 332-335 (4)   1.65 1.15

25th anniv. of the founding of the Neo-
Destour Party at Kasr Helal, Mar. 2, 1934.

"Independence" — A55

1959, Mar. 20
336 A55 50m olive, blk & red   .85 .40
3rd anniversary of independence.

Map of Africa and
Drawings — A56

1959, Apr. 15   Litho.   Perf. 13
337 A56 40m lt bl & red brn   .85 .40
Africa Freedom Day, Apr. 15.

Camel
Camp and
Mosque,
Kairouan
A57

Horseback
Rider — A58

Olive
Picker — A59

Open
Window
A58a

Designs: ½m, Woodcock in Ain-Draham forest. 2m, Camel rider. 3m, Saddler's shop. 4m,
Old houses of Medenine, gazelle and youth.
6m, Weavers. 8m, Woman of Gafsa. 10m,
Unveiled woman holding fruit. 12m, Ivory
craftsman. 15m, Skanes Beach, Monastir, and
mermaid. 16m, Minaret of Ez-Zitouna University, Tunis. 20m, Oasis of Gabès. 25m, Oil,
flowers and fish of Sfax. 30m, Modern and
Roman aqueducts. 40m, Festival at Kairouan
(drummer and camel). 45m, Octagonal minaret, Bizerte (boatman). 50m, Three women of
Djerba island. 60m, Date palms, Djerid. 70m,
Tapestry weaver. 75m, Pottery of Nabeul.
90m, Le Kef (man on horse). 100m, Road to
Sidi-bou-Said. 200m, Old port of Sfax. ½d,
Roman temple, Sbeitla. 1d, Farmer plowing
with oxen, Beja.

1959-61   Unwmk.   Engr.   Perf. 13
338 A58 ½m emer, brn &
            bl grn ('60)   .25 .25
339 A57 1m lt bl & ocher   .25 .25
340 A58 2m multicolored   .25 .25
341 A58 3m slate green   .25 .25
342 A57 4m red brn ('60)   .25 .25
343 A58 5m gray green   .25 .25
344 A58 6m rose violet   .25 .25
345 A58 8m vio brn ('60)   .75 .30
346 A58 10m ol, dk grn &
            car   .25 .25
347 A58 12m vio bl & ol
            bis ('61)   .60 .25
348 A57 15m grnsh blk ('60)   .30 .25
349 A57 16m grnsh blk
            ('60)   .35 .25
350 A58a 20m grnsh blue   1.10 .30
351 A58 20m grnsh blk, ol
            & mar ('60)   2.00 .25
352 A57 25m multi ('60)   .30 .25
353 A58a 30m brn, grnsh bl
            & ol   .45 .25

354 A59 40m dp grn ('60)   1.80 .25
355 A58a 45m brt grn ('60)   .75 .30
356 A58a 50m Prus grn, dk
            bl & rose
            ('60)   1.10 .25
357 A59 60m grn & red
            brn ('60)   1.10 .40
358 A59 70m multi ('60)   1.60 .55
359 A59 75m ol gray ('60)   1.50 .60
360 A58a 90m brt grn, ultra
            & choc ('60)   1.50 .60
361 A59 95m multicolored   2.00 1.10
362 A58a 100m dk bl, ol &
            brn   2.10 1.00
363 A58a 200m brt bl, bis &
            car   5.25 2.40
363A A59 ½d lt brn ('60)   12.00 6.75
363B A58a 1d sl grn & bis
            ('60)   22.50 13.50
      Nos. 338-363B (28)   61.05 31.80

UN Emblem and
Clasped
Hands — A60

1959, Oct. 24
364 A60 80m org brn, brn & ultra   .75 .60
UN Day, Oct. 24.

Dancer and
Coin — A61

1959, Nov. 4
365 A61 50m grnsh bl & blk   .75 .60
Central Bank of Tunisia, first anniversary.

Uprooted Oak
Emblem — A62

Doves and
WRY
Emblem
A63

1960, Apr. 7   Engr.   Perf. 13
366 A62 20m blue black   .60 .35
367 A63 40m red lil & dk grn   .75 .50
World Refugee Year, 7/1/59-6/30/60.

Girl, Boy and Scout
Badge — A64

Designs: 25m, Hand giving Scout sign.
30m, Bugler and tent. 40m, Peacock and
Scout emblem. 60m, Scout and campfire.

1960, Aug. 9
368 A64 10m lt blue green   .30 .30
369 A64 25m green, red & brn   .45 .35
370 A64 30m vio bl, grn & mar   .50 .35
371 A64 40m black, car & bl   .75 .45
372 A64 60m dk brn, vio blk &
            lake   1.10 .60
      Nos. 368-372 (5)   3.10 2.05
4th Arab Boy Scout Jamboree, Tunis, Aug.

Cyclist — A65

Designs: 10m, Olympic rings forming flower.
15m, Girl tennis player and minaret. 25m,
Runner and minaret. 50m, Handball player
and minaret.

1960, Aug. 25
373 A65 5m dk brown & olive   .30 .30
374 A65 10m sl, red vio & emer   .30 .30
375 A65 15m rose red & rose car   .30 .30
376 A65 25m grnsh bl & gray bl   .45 .45
377 A65 50m brt green & ultra   .80 .85
      Nos. 373-377 (5)   2.15 2.20
17th Olympic Games, Rome, 8/25-9/11.

Symbolic Forest
Design — A66

Designs: 15m, Man working in forest. 25m,
Tree superimposed on leaf. 50m, Symbolic
tree and bird.

1960, Aug. 29
378 A66 8m multicolored   .30 .25
379 A66 15m dark green   .45 .25
380 A66 25m dk pur, crim & brt
            grn   .60 .30
381 A66 50m Prus grn, yel grn &
            rose lake   1.10 .55
      Nos. 378-381 (4)   2.45 1.35
5th World Forestry Congress, Seattle,
Wash., Aug. 29-Sept. 10.

National Fair
Emblems — A67

1960, June 1
382 A67 100m black & green   .60 .50
5th Natl. Fair, Sousse, May 27-June 12.

Pres. Bourguiba   Pres. Bourguiba
Signing   A69
Constitution
A68

1960, June 1
383 A68 20m choc, red & emer   .30   .25
384 A69 20m grayish blk   .25   .25
385 A69 30m blue, dl red & blk   .35   .25
386 A69 40m grn, dl red & blk   .50   .25
   Nos. 383-386 (4)   1.40 1.00
Promulgation of the Constitution (No. 383).

UN Emblem and
Arms — A70

1960, Oct. 24   Engr.   Perf. 13
387 A70 40m mag, ultra & gray grn .60 .50
15th anniversary of the United Nations.

Dove and "Liberated
Tunisia" — A71

Design: 75m, Globe and arms.

1961, Mar. 20   Perf. 13
388 A71 20m maroon, bis & bl   .25   .25
389 A71 30m blue, vio & hrn   .35   .25
390 A71 40m yel grn & ultra   .65   .45
391 A71 75m bis, red lil & Prus
        bl   .80   .55
   Nos. 388-391 (4)   2.05 1.50
5th anniversary of independence.

Map of Africa,
Woman and
Animals — A72

Map of Africa: 60m, Negro woman and
Arab. 100m, Arabic inscription and Guinea
masque. 200m, Hands of Negro and Arab.

1961, Apr. 15   Engr.   Unwmk.
392 A72 40m bis brn, red brn &
        dk grn   .30   .25
393 A72 60m sl grn, blk & org
        brn   .35   .30
394 A72 100m sl grn, emer & vio   .75   .45
395 A72 200m dk brn & org brn   1.40 1.10
   Nos. 392-395 (4)   2.80 2.10
Africa Freedom Day, Apr. 15.

Mother and Child
with Flags — A73

Designs: 50m, Tunisians. 95m, Girl with
wings and half-moon.

1961, June 1   Unwmk.   Perf. 13
396 A73 25m pale vio, red & brn   .30   .25
397 A73 50m bl grn, ocp & brn   .45   .25
398 A73 95m pale vio, rose lil &
        ocher   .70   .35
   Nos. 396-398 (3)   1.45   .85
National Feast Day, June 1.

Dag
Hammarskjold — A74

1961, Oct. 24   Photo.   Perf. 14
399 A74 40m ultramarine   .60   .30
UN Day; Dag Hammarskjold (1905-1961),
Secretary General of the UN, 1953-61.

Arms of
Tunisia — A75

1962, Jan. 18   Perf. 11½
Arms in Original Colors
400 A75 1m black & yellow   .25   .25
401 A75 2m black & pink   .25   .25
402 A75 3m black & lt blue   .25   .25
403 A75 6m black & gray   .30   .25
   Nos. 400-403 (4)   1.05 1.00
Tunisia's campaign for independence, 10th
anniv.

Mosquito in Spider
Web and WHO
Emblem — A76

Designs: 30m, Symbolic horseback rider
spearing mosquito. 40m, Hands crushing
mosquito, horiz.

1962, Apr. 7   Engr.   Perf. 13
404 A76 20m chocolate   .50   .30
405 A76 30m red brn & slate grn   .50   .30
406 A76 40m dk brn, mar & grn   .90   .35
   Nos. 404-406 (3)   1.90   .95
WHO drive to eradicate malaria.

Boy and Map of   African Holding
Africa — A77   "Africa" — A78

1962, Apr. 15   Photo.   Perf. 14
407 A77 50m brown & orange   .50   .35
408 A78 100m blue, blk & org   .75   .50
Africa Freedom Day, Apr. 15.

Farm   Industrial
Worker — A79   Worker — A80

1962, May 1   Unwmk.
409 A79 40m multicolored   .50   .25
410 A80 60m dark red brown   .60   .35
       Labor Day.

"Liberated
Tunisia" — A81

1962, June 1   Typo.   Perf. 13½x14
411 A81 20m salmon & blk   .65   .35
National Feast Day, June 1.

Woman of
Gabès — A82

Women in costume of various localities:
10m, 30m, Mahdia. 15m, Kairouan. 20m, 40m,
Hammamet. 25m, Djerba. 55m, Ksar Hellal.
60m, Tunis.

1962-63   Photo.   Perf. 11½
412 A82 5m multi   .65   .25
413 A82 10m multi   .75   .35
414 A82 15m multi ('63)   1.20   .50
415 A82 20m multi   1.20   .65
416 A82 25m multi ('63)   1.20   .65
417 A82 30m multi   1.40   .75
418 A82 40m multi   1.40   .75
419 A82 50m multi   1.40   .85
420 A82 55m multi ('63)   2.10 1.10
421 A82 60m multi ('63)   2.90 1.40
   Nos. 412-421 (10)   14.20 7.25
6 stamps issued July 25, 1962 (July 25) for
the 6th anniv. of Tunisia's independence. 4
issued June 1, 1963 for Natl. Feast Day. See
Nos. 470-471.

UN Emblem, Flag
and Dove — A83

30m, Leaves, globe, horiz. 40m, Dove,
globe.

1962, Oct. 24   Unwmk.
422 A83 20m gray, blk & scar   .30   .25
423 A83 30m multicolored   .45   .25
424 A83 40m claret brn, blk & bl .70   .35
   Nos. 422-424 (3)   1.45   .85
Issued for United Nations Day, Oct. 24.

Aboul-Qasim
Chabbi — A84

1962, Nov. 20   Engr.   Perf. 13
425 A84 15m purple   .65   .25
Aboul-Qasim Chabbi (1904-34), Arab poet.

Pres. Habib
Bourguiba — A85

1962, Dec. 7 Photo. Perf. 12½x13½
426 A85 20m bright blue   .25   .25
427 A85 30m rose claret   .25   .25
428 A85 40m green   .25   .25
   Nos. 426-428 (3)   .75   .75

Hached Telephone
Exchange — A86

Designs: 10m, Carthage Exchange. 15m,
Sfax telecommunications center. 50m, Telephone operators. 100m, Symbol of automati-
zation. 200m, Belvedere Central Exchange.

1962, Dec. 7   Litho.
429 A86 5m multicolored   .30   .25
430 A86 10m multicolored   .35   .25
431 A86 15m multicolored   .50   .35
432 A86 50m multicolored   .80   .50
433 A86 100m multicolored   1.90 1.00
434 A86 200m multicolored   2.75 1.60
   Nos. 429-434 (6)   6.60 3.95
1st Afro-Asian Philatelic Exhibition; automation of the telephone system.

Dove over   "Hunger" — A88
Globe — A87

1963, Mar. 21   Engr.   Perf. 13
435 A87 20m brt bl & brn   .35   .25
436 A88 40m bis brn & dk brn   .65   .25
FAO "Freedom from Hunger" campaign.

Runner and
Walker — A89

1963, Feb. 17   Litho.   Perf. 13
437 A89 30m brn, blk & grn   .45   .50
Army Sports Day; 13th C.I.S.M. cross country championships.

Centenary
Emblem — A90

1963, May 8   Engr.   Perf. 13
438 A90 20m brn, gray & red   1.10   .30
Centenary of International Red Cross.

"Human Rights" — A91

1963, Dec. 10   Unwmk.   Perf. 13
439 A91 30m grn & dk brn   .60   .30
15th anniv. of the Universal Declaration of Human Rights.

Hand Raising Gateway of Great Temple of Philae — A92

1964, Mar. 8   Engr.
440 A92 50m red brn, bis & blu-
              ish blk   .55   .30
UNESCO world campaign to save historic monuments in Nubia.

Sunshine, Rain and Barometer — A93

1964, Mar. 8   Unwmk.   Perf. 13
441 A93 40m brn, red lil & slate .55   .25
4th World Meteorological Day, Mar. 23.

Mohammed Ali — A94

1964, May 15   Engr.
442 A94 50m sepia   .60   .35
Mohammed Ali (1894-1928), labor leader.

Map of Africa and Symbolic Flower — A95

1964, May 25   Photo.   Perf. 13x14
443 A95 60m multicolored   .60   .30
Addis Ababa charter on African Unity, 1st anniv.

Pres. Habib Bourguiba — A96

1964, June 1   Engr.   Perf. 12½x13½
444 A96 20m vio bl   .30   .25
445 A96 30m black   .30   .25

"Ship and Torch" — A97

1964, Oct. 19   Photo.   Perf. 11½x11
446 A97 50m blk & blue grn   .60   .30
Neo-Destour Congress, Bizerte. "Bizerte" in Arabic forms the ship and "Neo-Destour Congress 1964" the torch of the design.

Communication Equipment and ITU Emblem — A98

1965, May 17   Engr.   Perf. 13
447 A98 55m gray & blue   .60   .30
ITU, centenary.

Carthaginian Coin — A99

Perf. 12½x14
1965, July 9   Photo.   Unwmk.
448 A99 5m turq grn & blk brn   .25   .25
449 A99 10m bis & blk brn   .30   .25
450 A99 75m bl & blk brn   .75   .25
    Nos. 448-450 (3)   1.30   .75
Festival of Popular Arts, Carthage.

Girl with Book — A100

1965, Oct. 1   Engr.   Perf. 13
451 A100 25m brt bl, blk & red   .30   .25
452 A100 40m blk, bl & red   .35   .25
453 A100 50m red, bl & blk   .45   .35
    a. Souvenir sheet of 3, #451-453 5.00 5.00
    Nos. 451-453 (3)   1.10   .85
Girl Students' Center; education for women. No. 453a sold for 200m. Issued perf. and imperf.; same value.

Links and ICY Emblem — A101

1965, Oct. 24
454 A101 40m blk, brt bl & rose lil .60 .25
International Cooperation Year.

Man Pouring Water — A102

Symbolic Designs: 10m, Woman and pool. 30m, Woman pouring water. 100m, Mountain and branches.

Inscribed "Eaux Minerales"

1966, Jan. 18   Photo.   Perf. 13x14
455 A102 10m gray, ocher & dk
                red   .30   .25
456 A102 20m multicolored   .45   .35
457 A102 30m yel, bl & red   .45   .35
458 A102 100m ol, bl & yel   1.20   .70
    Nos. 455-458 (4)   2.40 1.65
Mineral waters of Tunisia.

President Bourguiba and Hands A103

"Promotion of Culture" — A104

25m, "Independence" (arms raised), flag and doves. 40m, "Development."

1966, June 1   Engr.   Perf. 13
459 A103 5m dl pur & vio   .25   .25
460 A103 10m gray grn & sl grn   .25   .25
Perf. 11½
Photo.
461 A104 25m multi   .25   .25
462 A104 40m multi, horiz.   .55   .35
463 A104 60m multi   .85   .35
    Nos. 459-463 (5)   2.15 1.35
10th anniversary of independence.

Map of Africa through View Finder, Plane and UN Emblem — A105

1966, Sept. 12   Engr.   Perf. 13
464 A105 15m lilac & multi   .30   .25
465 A105 35m blue & multi   .35   .25
466 A105 40m multicolored   .50   .35
    a. Souvenir sheet, #464-466   10.00 10.00
    Nos. 464-466 (3)   1.15   .85
2nd UN Regional Cartographic Conference for Africa, held in Tunisia, Sept. 12-24. No. 466a sold for 150m. Issued perf. and imperf.; same value.

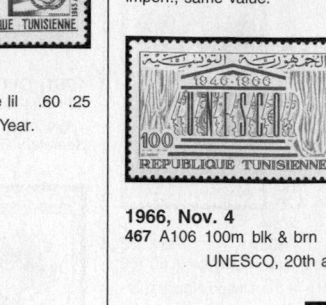

UNESCO Emblem and Nine Muses A106

1966, Nov. 4   Perf. 13
467 A106 100m blk & brn   1.10   .35
UNESCO, 20th anniv.

Runners and Mediterranean Map — A107

1967, Mar. 20   Engr.   Perf. 13
468 A107 20m dk red, brn ol & bl .30   .25
469 A107 30m brt bl & blk   .60   .35
Mediterranean Games, Sept. 8-17.

Types of 1962-63 and 1965-66 with EXPO '67 Emblem, Inscription and

Symbols of Various Activities — A108

Designs: 50m, Woman of Djerba. 75m, Woman of Gabes. 155m, Pink flamingoes.

Photo.; Engr. (A108)
1967, Apr. 28   Perf. 11½, 13 (A108)
470 A82   50m multicolored   .45   .25
471 A82   75m multicolored   .70   .30
472 A108 100m dk grn, sl bl &
                blk   1.10   .30
473 A108 110m dk brn, ultra &
                red   1.40   .55
474 AP6   155m multicolored   2.10   .75
    Nos. 470-474 (5)   5.75 2.15
EXPO '67, Intl. Exhibition, Montreal, Apr. 28-Oct. 27.

Tunisian Pavilion, Pres. Bourguiba and Map of Tunisia — A109

Designs: 105m, 200m, Tunisian Pavilion and bust of Pres. Bourguiba.

1967, June 13   Perf. 13
475 A109 65m red lil & dp org   .45   .35
476 A109 105m multicolored   .50   .35
477 A109 120m brt bl   .65   .40
478 A109 200m red, lil & blk   1.10   .50
    Nos. 475-478 (4)   2.70 1.60
Tunisia Day at EXPO '67.

"Tunisia" Holding 4-leaf Clovers A110

Woman Freeing Doves — A111

1967, July 25   Litho.   Perf. 13½
479 A110 25m multicolored .30 .25
480 A111 40m multicolored .45 .25

10th anniversary of the Republic.

Tennis Courts, Players and Games' Emblem — A112

10m, Games' emblem & sports emblems, vert. 15m, Swimming pool & swimmers. 35m, Sports Palace & athletes. 75m, Stadium & athletes.

1967, Sept. 8   Engr.   Perf. 13
481 A112 5m sl grn & hn brn .25 .25
482 A112 10m brn red & multi .25 .25
483 A112 15m black .30 .25
484 A112 35m dk brn & Prus bl .45 .25
485 A112 75m dk car rose, vio & bl grn .80 .45
Nos. 481-485 (5) 2.05 1.45

Mediterranean Games, Tunis, Sept. 8-17.

Bird, Punic Period — A113

History of Tunisia: 20m, Sea horse, medallion from Kerkouane. 25m, Hannibal, bronze bust, Volubilis. 30m, Stele, Carthage. 40m, Hamilcar, coin. 60m, Mask, funereal pendant.

1967, Dec. 1   Litho.   Perf. 13½
486 A113 15m gray grn, pink & blk .30 .25
487 A113 20m dp bl, red & blk .30 .25
488 A113 25m dk grn & org brn .45 .25
489 A113 30m grnsh gray, pink & blk .45 .25
490 A113 40m red brn, yel & blk .55 .25
491 A113 60m multicolored .65 .35
Nos. 486-491 (6) 2.70 1.60

"Mankind" and Human Rights Flame — A114

1968, Jan. 18   Engr.   Perf. 13
492 A114 25m brick red .55 .35
493 A114 60m deep blue .55 .25

International Human Rights Year.

Computer Fantasy A115

1968, Mar. 20   Engr.   Perf. 13
494 A115 25m mag, bl vio & ol .40 .35
495 A115 40m ol grn, red brn & brn .40 .35
496 A115 60m ultra, slate & brn .50 .40
Nos. 494-496 (3) 1.30 1.10

Introduction of electronic equipment for postal service.

Physician and Patient — A116

1968, Apr. 7   Engr.   Perf. 13
497 A116 25m dp grn & brt grn .45 .35
498 A116 60m magenta & carmine .65 .35

WHO, 20th anniversary.

Arabian Jasmine — A117

Flowers: 5m, Flax. 6m, Canna indica. 10m, Pomegranate. 15m, Rhaponticum acaule. 20m, Geranium. 25m, Madonna lily. 40m, Peach blossoms. 50m, Caper. 60m, Ariana rose. 100m, Jasmine.

Granite Paper
1968-69   Photo.   Perf. 11½
499 A117 5m multicolored .25 .25
500 A117 6m multicolored .26 .25
501 A117 10m multicolored .30 .25
502 A117 12m multicolored .30 .25
503 A117 15m multicolored .35 .25
504 A117 20m multicolored .45 .25
505 A117 25m multicolored .45 .30
506 A117 40m multicolored .65 .30
507 A117 50m multicolored .80 .35
508 A117 60m multicolored 1.20 .60
509 A117 100m multicolored 1.75 .80
Nos. 499-509 (11) 6.75 3.85

Issued: 12, 50, 60, 100m, 4/9/68; others, 3/20/69.

Flower with Red Crescent and Globe — A118

25m, Dove with Red Crescent and globe.

1968, May 8   Engr.   Perf. 13
510 A118 15m Prus bl, grn & red .40 .35
511 A118 25m brt rose lil & red .50 .35

Red Crescent Society.

Flutist — A119

1968, June 1   Litho.   Perf. 13
512 A119 20m vio & multi .50 .25
513 A119 50m multicolored .55 .35

Stamp Day.

Jackal A120

Animals: 8m, Porcupine. 10m, Dromedary. 15m, Dorcas gazelle. 20m, Desert fox (fennec). 25m, Desert hedgehog. 40m, Arabian horse. 60m, Boar.

1968-69   Photo.   Perf. 11½
514 A120 5m dk brn, lt bl & bis .30 .25
515 A120 8m dk vio brn & yel grn .45 .25
516 A120 10m dk brn, lt bl & ocher .65 .25
517 A120 15m dk brn, ocher & yel grn .70 .25
518 A120 20m dl yel & dk brn 1.10 .45
519 A120 25m blk, tan & brt grn 1.40 .60
520 A120 40m blt, lil & pale grn 1.75 .90
521 A120 60m dk brn, buff & yel grn 2.75 1.20
Nos. 514-521 (8) 9.10 4.15

Issued: 5, 8, 20, 60m, 9/15/68; others, 1/18/69.

Worker and ILO Emblem — A121

60m, Young man & woman holding banner.

1969, May 1   Engr.   Perf. 13
522 A121 25m Prus bl, blk & bis .45 .35
523 A121 60m rose car, bl & yel .65 .40

ILO, 50th anniversary.

Veiled Women and Musicians with Flute and Drum A122

1969, June 20   Litho.   Perf. 14x13½
524 A122 100m dp yel grn & multi 1.25 .35

Stamp Day.

Tunisian Coat of Arms — A123

1969, July 25   Photo.   Perf. 11½
525 A123 15m yel & multi .30 .25
526 A123 25m pink & multi .45 .25
527 A123 40m gray & multi .60 .25
528 A123 60m lt bl & multi .75 .25
Nos. 525-528 (4) 2.10 1.00

Symbols of Industry — A124

1969, Sept. 10   Perf. 13x12
529 A124 60m blk, red & yel .60 .30

African Development Bank, 5th anniv.

Lute — A125

Musical Instruments: 50m, Zither, horiz. 70m, Rebab (2-strings). 90m, Drums and flute, horiz.

1970, Mar. 20   Photo.   Perf. 11½
Granite Paper
530 A125 25m multicolored .45 .35
531 A125 50m multicolored .60 .35
532 A125 70m multicolored .80 .35
533 A125 90m multicolored 1.20 .35
Nos. 530-500 (4) 3.05 1.40

Nurse and Maghrib Flags — A126

1970, May 4   Photo.   Perf. 11½
534 A126 25m lilac & multi .60 .25

6th Medical Seminar of Maghrib Countries (Morocco, Algeria, Tunisia and Libya), Tunis, May 4-10.

Common Design Types pictured following the introduction.

UPU Headquarters Issue
Common Design Type
1970, May 20   Engr.   Perf. 13
535 CD133 25m dl red & dk ol bis .60 .25

Mail Service Symbol A127

35m, Mailmen of yesterday and today, vert.

1970, Oct. 15   Litho.   Perf. 12½x13
Size: 37x31½mm
536 A127 25m pink & multi .30 .25
Size: 22x37½mm
Perf. 13x12½
537 A127 35m blk & multi .45 .25

Stamp Day.

Dove, Laurel and UN Emblem A128

1970, Oct. 24　Photo.　Perf. 13x12½
538　A128　40m multicolored　　　.65　.25
United Nations, 25th anniversary.

Jasmine Vendor and Veiled Woman — A129

Scenes from Tunisian Life: 25m, "The 3rd Day of the Wedding." 35m, Perfume vendor. 40m, Fish vendor. 85m, Waiter in coffeehouse.

1970, Nov. 9　Photo.　Perf. 14
539　A129　20m dk grn & multi　　.25　.25
540　A129　25m multicolored　　　.30　.25
541　A129　35m multicolored　　　.45　.35
542　A129　40m dp car & multi　　.50　.35
543　A129　85m brt bl & multi　　.85　.35
　a.　Souvenir sheet of 5, #539-543　7.00　7.00
　　　Nos. 539-543 (5)　　　2.35　1.55
No. 543a sold for 500m. Issued perf. and imperf.; same value.

Lenin, after N.N. Joukov — A130

1970, Dec. 28　Engr.　Perf. 13
544　A130　60m dk car rose　　2.10　.30
Lenin (1870-1924), Russian communist leader.

Radar, Flags and Carrier Pigeon — A131

1971, May 17　Litho.　Perf. 13x12½
545　A131　25m lt bl & multi　　.60　.35
Coordinating Committee for Post and Telecommunications Administrations of Maghrib Countries.

UN Headquarters, Symbolic Flower — A132

1971, May 10　Photo.　Perf. 12½x13
546　A132　80m brt rose lil, blk & yel　.50　.30
Intl. year against racial discrimination.

"Telecommunications" — A133

1971, May 17　Perf. 13x12½
547　A133　70m sil, blk & lt grn　.50　.25
3rd World Telecommunications Day.

Earth, Moon, Satellites A134

Design: 90m, Abstract composition.

1971, June 21　Photo.　Perf. 13x12½
548　A134　15m brt bl & blk　　.40　.25
549　A134　90m scar & blk　　　.75　.30
Conquest of space.

"Pottery Merchant" A135

Life in Tunisia (stylized drawings): 30m, Esparto weaver selling hats and mats. 40m, Poultry man. 50m, Dyer.

1971, July 24　Photo.　Perf. 14x13½
550　A135　25m gold & multi　　.50　.25
551　A135　30m gold & multi　　.60　.25
552　A135　40m gold & multi　　.70　.25
553　A135　50m gold & multi　　.80　.25
　a.　Sheet of 4, #550-553, perf. 13½　7.50　7.50
　　　Nos. 550-553 (4)　　　2.60　1.00
No. 553a sold for 500m. Issued perf. and imperf.; same value.

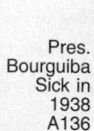

Pres. Bourguiba Sick in 1938 A136

Designs: 25m, Bourguiba and "8," vert. 50m, Bourguiba carried in triumph, vert. 80m, Bourguiba and irrigation dam.

1971, Oct. 11　Perf. 13½x13, 13x13½
554　A136　25m multicolored　　.30　.25
555　A136　30m multicolored　　.35　.25
556　A136　50m multicolored　　.35　.30
557　A136　80m blk, ultra & grn　.50　.30
　　　Nos. 554-557 (4)　　　1.50　1.10
8th Congress of the Neo-Destour Party.

Shah Mohammed Riza Pahlavi and Stone Head 6th Century B.C. — A137

50m, King Bahram-Gur hunting, 4th cent. 100m, Coronation, from Persian miniature, 1614.

1971, Oct. 17　Perf. 11½
Granite Paper
558　A137　25m multicolored　　.30　.30
559　A137　50m multicolored　　.35　.25
560　A137　100m multicolored　.70　.30
　a.　Souvenir sheet of 3, #558-560　4.25　4.25
　　　Nos. 558-560 (3)　　　1.35　.85
2500th anniv. of the founding of the Persian empire by Cyrus the Great. No. 560a sold for 500m. Issued perf. and imperf.; same value.

Pimento and Warrior A138

2m, Mint & farmer. 5m, Pear & 2 men under pear tree. 25m, Oleander & girl. 60m, Pear & sheep. 100m, Grapefruit & fruit vendor.

1971, Nov. 15　Litho.　Perf. 13
561　A138　1m lt bl & multi　　.25　.25
562　A138　2m gray & multi　　.30　.30
563　A138　5m citron & multi　.35　.30
564　A138　25m lilac & multi　.60　.35
565　A138　60m multicolored　1.20　.30
566　A138　100m buff & multi　1.75　.45
　a.　Souvenir sheet of 6, #561-566　7.50　7.50
　　　Nos. 561-566 (6)　　　4.45　1.95
Fruit, flowers and folklore. No. 566a sold for 500m. Exists imperf.; same value.

Dancer and Musician — A139

1971, Nov. 22　Photo.　Perf. 11½
567　A139　50m blue & multi　　.60　.25
Stamp Day.

Map of Africa, Communication Symbols — A139a

Perf. 13½x12½
1971, Nov. 30　　　　　Litho.
568　A139a　95m multicolored　.60　.45
Pan-African telecommunications system.

UNICEF Emblem, Mother and Child — A140

1971, Dec. 6　Photo.　Perf. 11½
569　A140　110m multicolored　　.60　.45
UNICEF, 25th anniv.

Symbolic Olive Tree and Oil Vat — A141

1972, Jan. 9　Litho.　Perf. 13½
570　A141　60m multicolored　　.60　.25
International Olive Year.

Gondolier in Flood Waters — A142

Designs: 30m, Young man and Doge's Palace. 50m, Gondola's prow and flood. 80m, Rialto Bridge and hand holding gondolier's hat, horiz.

1972, Feb. 7　Photo.　Perf. 11½
571　A142　25m lt bl & multi　　.30　.25
572　A142　30m blk & multi　　.50　.25
573　A142　50m yel grn, gray & blk　.50　.40
574　A142　80m bl & multi　　.95　.40
　　　Nos. 571-574 (4)　　　2.25　1.30
UNESCO campaign to save Venice.

Man Reading and Book Year Emblem — A143

1972, Mar. 27　Photo.　Perf. 11½
Granite Paper
575　A143　90m brn & multi　　.60　.45
International Book Year.

"Your Heart is Your Health" — A144

World Health Day: 60m, Smiling man pointing to heart.

1972, Apr. 7　　　　　Perf. 13x13½
576　A144　25m grn & multi　　.50　.25
577　A144　60m red & multi　　.70　.35

"Only One Earth" Environment Emblem — A145

1972, June 5　Engr.　Perf. 13
578　A145　60m lemon & slate green　.75　.25
UN Conference on Human Environment, Stockholm, June 5-16.

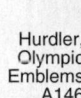

Hurdler, Olympic Emblems A146

1972, Aug. 26   Photo.   Perf. 11½
579	A146	5m Volleyball	.25	.25
580	A146	15m shown	.30	.25
581	A146	20m Athletes	.30	.25
582	A146	25m Soccer	.30	.25
583	A146	60m Swimming, women's	.50	.25
584	A146	80m Running	.65	.30
a.		Souv. sheet of 6	4.50	4.50
		Nos. 579-584 (6)	2.30	1.55

20th Olympic Games, Munich, Aug. 26-Sept. 11. No. 584a contains 6 imperf. stamps similar to Nos. 579-584. Sold for 500m.

Chessboard and Pieces — A147

1972, Sept. 25   Photo.   Perf. 11½
585	A147	60m grn & multi	3.00	1.00

20th Men's Chess Olympiad, Skopje, Yugoslavia, Sept.-Oct.

Fisherman A148

1972, Oct. 23   Litho.   Perf. 13½
586	A148	5m shown	.25	.25
587	A148	10m Basket maker	.25	.25
588	A148	25m Musician	.35	.25
589	A148	50m Married Berber woman	.75	.25
590	A148	60m Flower merchant	1.00	.25
591	A148	80m Festival	1.20	.45
a.		Souvenir sheet of 6, #586-591	4.50	4.50
		Nos. 586-591 (6)	3.80	1.70

Life in Tunisia. No. 591a sold for 500m; exists imperf.

Post Office, Tunis A149

Litho. & Engr.
1972, Dec. 8   Perf. 13
592	A149	25m ver, org & blk	.50	.25

Stamp Day.

Dome of the Rock, Jerusalem A150

1973, Jan. 22   Photo.   Perf. 13½
593	A150	25m multicolored	.60	.35

Globe, Pen and Quill — A151

Design: 60m, Lyre and minaret.

1973, Mar. 19   Photo.   Perf. 14x13½
594	A151	25m gold, brt mag & brn	.30	.25
595	A151	60m bl & multi	.45	.25

9th Congress of Arab Writers.

Family — A152

Family Planning: 25m, profiles and dove.

1973, Apr. 2   Perf. 11½
596	A152	20m grn & multi	.30	.25
597	A152	25m lil & multi	.50	.35

"10" and Bird Feeding Young A153

Design: 60m, "10" made of grain and bread, and hand holding spoon.

1973, Apr. 26   Photo.   Perf. 11½
598	A153	25m multicolored	.60	.25
599	A153	60m multicolored	.60	.25

World Food Program, 10th anniversary.

Roman Head and Ship A154

Drawings of Tools and: 25m, Mosaic with ostriches and camel. 30m, Mosaic with 4 heads and 4 emblems. 40m, Punic stele to the sun, vert. 60m, Outstretched hand & arm of Christian preacher; symbols of 4 Evangelists. 75m, 17th cent. potsherd with Arabic inscription, vert.

1973, May 6
600	A154	5m multicolored	.50	.25
601	A154	25m multicolored	.75	.40
602	A154	30m multicolored	.75	.40
603	A154	40m multicolored	1.10	.40
604	A154	60m multicolored	1.40	.40
605	A154	75m multicolored	1.50	.50
a.		Souvenir sheet of 6	12.00	12.00
		Nos. 600-605 (6)	6.00	2.35

UNESCO campaign to save Carthage. No. 605a contains 6 imperf. stamps similar to Nos. 600-605. Sold for 500m.

Overlapping Circles — A155

Design: 75m, Printed circuit board.

1973, May 17   Photo.   Perf. 14x13½
606	A155	60m yel & multi	.75	.25
607	A155	75m vio & multi	.90	.25

5th Intl. Telecommunications Day.

Map of Africa as Festival Emblem — A156

40m, African heads, festival emblem in eye.

1973, July 15   Photo.   Perf. 13½x13
608	A156	25m multicolored	.40	.35
609	A156	40m multicolored	.50	.35

Pan-African Youth Festival, Tunis.

Scout Emblem and Pennants — A157

1973, July 23   Litho.   Perf. 13½x13
610	A157	25m multicolored	.60	.35

International Boy Scout Organization

Crescent-shaped Racing Cars — A158

1973, July 30   Perf. 13x13½
611	A158	60m multicolored	.05	.40

2nd Pan-Arab auto race.

Highway Cloverleaf A159

Traffic Lights and Signs — A160

Perf. 12½x13, 13x12½
1973, Sept. 28   Litho.
612	A159	25m lt bl & multi	.65	.40
613	A160	30m multicolored	.75	.35

Highway safety campaign.

Stylized Camel — A161

Stamp Day: 10m, Stylized bird and philatelic symbols, horiz.

1973, Oct. 8   Photo.   Perf. 13½
614	A161	10m multicolored	.50	.25
615	A161	65m multicolored	.60	.40

Copernicus — A162

Lithographed and Engraved
1973, Oct. 16   Perf. 13x12½
616	A162	60m blk & multi	2.50	.30

African Unity — A163

1973, Nov. 4   Photo.   Perf. 14x13½
617	A163	25m blk & multi	.65	.25

10th anniv. of the OAU.

Handshake and Emblems A164

1973, Nov. 15   Litho.   Perf. 14½x14
618	A164	65m yel & multi	.65	.40

25th anniv. of Intl. Criminal Police Org.

Globe, Hand Holding Carnation — A165

1973, Dec. 10   Photo.   Perf. 11½
619	A165	60m blk & multi	.75	.35

25th anniv. of Universal Declaration of Human Rights.

National Meteorological Institute and World Meteorological Organization Emblem — A166

Design: 60m, Globe and emblem.

1973, Dec. 24   Litho.   Perf. 14x14½
620 A166 25m multicolored   .55   .25
621 A166 60m multicolored   .75   .30
   Intl. meteorological cooperation, cent.

Bourguiba in the Desert, 1945 — A167

Portraits of Pres. Habib Bourguiba: 25m, Exile transfer from Galite Island to Ile de la Groix, France, 1954. 60m, Addressing crowd, 1974. 75m, In Victory Parade, 1955. 100m, In 1934.

1974, Mar. 2   Photo.   Perf. 11½
622 A167 15m plum & multi   .45   .25
623 A167 25m multicolored   .45   .25
624 A167 60m multicolored   .45   .25
625 A167 75m multicolored   .60   .25
626 A167 100m multicolored   .75   .40
  a. Souvenir sheet of 5, #622-626   3.00 3.00
    Nos. 622-626 (5)   2.70 1.40

40th anniv. of the Neo-Destour Party. No. 626a sold for 500m. Issued perf. and imperf.; same value.

Scientist with Microscope A168

1974, Mar. 21   Perf. 14
627 A168 60m multicolored   1.10   .50
   6th African Congress of Micropaleontology, Mar. 21-Apr. 3.

Woman with Telephones and Globe — A169

60m, Telephone dial, telephones, wires.

1974, July 1   Perf. 11½
628 A169 15m multicolored   .50   .40
629 A169 60m multicolored   .80   .50
  Introduction of international automatic telephone dialing system.

WPY Emblem and Symbolic Design A170

1974, Aug. 19   Photo.   Perf. 11½
630 A170 110m multicolored   .75   .40
   World Population Year.

Pres. Bourguiba and Sun Flower Emblem — A171

60m, Bourguiba and cactus flower, horiz. 200m, Bourguiba and verbena, horiz.

1974, Sept. 12   Photo.   Perf. 11½
631 A171 25m blk, ultra & grnsh
     bl   .35   .25
632 A171 60m red, car & yel   .40   .25
633 A171 200m blk, brt lil & grn   1.50   .60
  a. Souv. sheet, #631-633, imperf. 3.75 3.75
    Nos. 631-633 (3)   2.25 1.10

Congress of the Socialist Destour Party.

Jets Flying over Old World Map A172

1974, Sept. 23   Litho.   Perf. 12½
634 A172 60m brn & multi   .65   .40
   25th anniversary of Tunisian aviation.

Symbolic Carrier Pigeons — A173

Handshake, Letter, UPU Emblem — A174

1974, Oct. 9   Photo.   Perf. 13
635 A173 25m multicolored   .40   .25
636 A174 60m multicolored   .75   .35
   Centenary of Universal Postal Union.

Le Bardo, National Assembly — A175

Pres. Bourguiba Ballot — A176

1974, Nov. 3   Photo.   Perf. 11½
637 A175 25m grn, bl & blk   .40   .30
638 A176 100m org & blk   1.00   .40
  Legislative (25m) and presidential elections (100m), Nov. 1974.

Mailman with Letters and Bird — A177

1974, Dec. 5   Litho.   Perf. 14½x14
639 A177 75m lt vio & multi   .65   .25
   Stamp Day.

Water Carrier — A178

1975, Feb. 17   Photo.   Perf. 13½
640 A178 5m shown   .30   .25
641 A178 15m Perfume vendor   .30   .25
642 A178 25m Laundresses   .30   .25
643 A178 60m Potter   .65   .25
644 A178 110m Fruit vendor   1.40   .65
  a. Souvenir sheet of 5, #640-644   7.00 7.00
    Nos. 640-644 (5)   2.95 1.65

Life in Tunisia. No. 644a sold for 500m. Issued perf. and imperf.; same value.

Steel Tower, Skyscraper — A179

Geometric Designs and Arrow A180

Perf. 14x13½, 13½x14
1975, Mar. 17   Photo.
645 A179 25m yel, org & blk   .30   .25
646 A180 65m ultra & multi   .80   .35
  Union of Arab Engineers, 13th Conference, Tunis, Mar. 17-21.

Brass Coffeepot and Plate — A181

15m, Horse and rider. 25m, Still life. 30m, Bird cage. 40m, Woman with earrings. 60m, Design patterns.

1975, Apr. 14   Perf. 13x14, 14x13
647 A181 10m blk & multi   .25   .25
648 A181 15m blk & multi   .25   .25
649 A181 25m blk & multi   .45   .25
650 A181 30m blk & multi, vert.   .50   .25
651 A181 40m blk & multi, vert.   .50   .25
652 A181 60m blk & multi   .95   .30
    Nos. 647-652 (6)   2.90 1.55

Artisans and their works.

Communications and Weather Symbols — A182

1975, May 17   Photo.   Perf. 11½
653 A182 50m lt bl & multi   .50   .25
  World Telecommunications Day (communications serving meteorology).

Youth and Hope — A183

65m, Bourguiba arriving at La Goulette, Tunis.

1975, June 1   Photo.   Perf. 11½
654 A183 25m multi   .25   .25
655 A183 65m multi, horiz.   .50   .25
  Victory (independence), 20th anniversary.

Tunisian Woman, IWY Emblem — A184

1975, June 19   Litho.   Perf. 14x13½
656 A184 110m multicolored   .75   .35
   International Women's Year.

Children Crossing Street A185

1975, July 5   Photo.   Perf. 13½x14
657 A185 25m multicolored   .60   .25
  Highway safety campaign, July 1-Sept. 30.

Djerbian Minaret, Hotel and Marina, Jerba A186

Old & new Tunisia: 15m, 17th cent. minaret & modern hotel, Tunis. 20m, Fortress, earring & hotel, Monastir. 65m, View of Sousse, hotel & pendant. 500m, Town wall, mosque & palms, Tozeur. 1d, Mosques & Arab ornaments, Kairouan.

1975, July 12   Litho.   Perf. 14x14½
658 A186 10m multicolored   .25   .25
659 A186 15m multicolored   .25   .25
660 A186 20m multicolored   .25   .25
661 A186 65m multicolored   .75   .40
662 A186 500m multicolored   4.75 1.75
663 A186 1d multicolored   7.50 2.50
    Nos. 658-663 (6)   13.75 5.40

Victors — A187

Symbolic
Ship
A188

1975, Aug. 23   Photo.   Perf. 13½
664 A187 25m olive & multi   .25   .25
665 A188 50m blue & multi   .50   .25

7th Mediterranean Games, Algiers, 8/23-9/6.

Flowers in Vase,
Birds Holding
Letters — A189

1975, Sept. 29   Litho.   Perf. 13½x13
666 A189 100m blue & multi   .65   .25

Stamp Day.

Sadiki College, Young
Bourguiba — A190

Engr. & Litho.
1975, Nov. 17   Perf. 13
667 A190 25m sepia, orange &
           olive   .50   .25

Sadiki College, centenary.

Duck — A191

Vergil — A192

Mosaics: 10m, Fish. 25m, Lioness, horiz.
60m, Head of Medusa, horiz. 75m, Circus
spectators.

1976, Feb. 16   Photo   Perf. 13
668 A191   5m multicolored   .30   .25
669 A191 10m multicolored   .45   .25
670 A192 25m multicolored   .75   .50
671 A192 60m multicolored   1.00   .50
672 A192 75m multicolored   1.10   .50

673 A192 100m multicolored   1.40   .50
  a.   Souvenir sheet of 6, #668-673 6.50 6.50
          Nos. 668-673 (6)   5.00 2.50

Tunisian mosaics, 2nd-5th centuries.
No. 673a sold for 500m. Issued perf. and
imperf.; same value.

Telephone
A193

1976, Mar. 10   Litho.   Perf. 14x13½
674 A193 150m blue & multi   .70   .35

Centenary of first telephone call by Alexander Graham Bell, Mar. 10, 1876.

Pres.
Bourguiba
and
"20" — A194

Pres. Bourguiba and: 100m, "20" and symbolic Tunisian flag. 150m, "Tunisia" rising from
darkness, and 20 flowers.

1976, Mar. 20   Photo.   Perf. 11½
675 A194 40m multicolored   .25   .25
676 A194 100m multicolored   .55   .25
677 A194 150m multicolored   .80   .35
           Nos. 675-677 (3)   1.60   .85

Souvenir Sheets
Perf. 11½, Imperf.
678   Sheet of 3   3.50 3.50
  a.   A194 50m like 40m   .50   .50
  b.   A194 200m like 100m   1.00 1.00
  c.   A194 250m like 150m   1.50 1.50

20th anniversary of independence.

Blind Man with
Cane — A195

1976, Apr. 7   Engr.   Perf. 13
679 A195 100m black & red   .60   .25

World Health Day: "Foresight prevents
blindness."

Procession and
Buildings — A196

1976, May 31   Photo.   Perf. 12x11½
680 A196 40m multicolored   .60   .25

Habitat, UN Conf. on Human Settlements,
Vancouver, Canada, May 31-June 11.

Face and Hands
Decorated with
Henna — A197

Old and new Tunisia: 50m, Sponge fishing
at Jerba. 65m, Textile industry. 110m, Pottery
of Guellala.

1976, June 15   Photo.   Perf. 13x13½
681 A197 40m multicolored   .25   .25
682 A197 50m multicolored   .55   .25
683 A197 65m multicolored   .55   .25
684 A197 110m multicolored   .75   .50
           Nos. 681-684 (4)   2.10 1.25

The
Spirit of
'76, by
Archibald
M.
Willard
A198

1976, July 4   Perf. 13x14
685 A198 200m multicolored   1.75   .85

Souvenir Sheets
Perf. 13x14, Imperf.
686 A198 500m multicolored   5.00 5.00

American Bicentennial.

Running
A199

Montreal Olympic Games Emblem and:
75m, Bicycling. 120m, Peace dove.

1976, July 17   Photo.   Perf. 11½
687 A199   50m gray, red & blk   .25   .25
688 A199   75m red, yel & blk   .45   .25
689 A199 120m orange & multi   .70   .35
           Nos. 687-689 (3)   1.40   .85

21st Olympic Games, Montreal, Canada,
July 17-Aug. 1.

Child
Reading — A200

1976, Aug. 23   Litho.   Perf. 13
690 A200 100m brown & multi   .60   .25

Books for children.

Heads and
Bird — A201

1976, Sept. 30   Litho.   Perf. 13
691 A201 150m orange & multi   .75   .25

Non-aligned Countries, 15th anniv. of 1st
Conference.

Mouradite
Mausoleum, 17th
Century — A202

Cultural Heritage: 100m, Minaret, Kairouan
Great Mosque and psalmodist. 150m, Monastir Ribat monastery and Alboracq (sphinx).
200m, Barber's Mosque, Kairouan and man's
bust.

1976, Oct. 25   Photo.   Perf. 14
692 A202   85m multicolored   .40   .25
693 A202 100m multicolored   .50   .25
694 A202 150m multicolored   .75   .25
695 A202 200m multicolored   1.10   .40
           Nos. 692-695 (4)   2.75 1.15

Globe
and
Emblem
A203

1976, Dec. 24   Photo.   Perf. 13x14
696 A203 150m multicolored   .95   .35

25th anniv. of UN Postal Administration.

Electronic Tree
and ITU
Emblem — A204

1977, May 17   Photo.   Perf. 14x13½
697 A204 150m multicolored   1.25   .50

9th World Telecommunications Day.

"Communication," Sassenage Castle,
Grenoble — A205

1977, May 19   Litho.   Perf. 13½x13
698 A205 100m multicolored   1.50   .40

10th anniv. of Intl. French Language Council.

Soccer
A206

1977, June 27   Photo.   Perf. 13½
699 A206 150m multicolored   1.25   .50

Junior World Soccer Tournament, Tunisia,
June 27-July 10.

Gold Coin, 10th
Century — A207

Cultural Heritage: 15m, Stele, Gorjani Cemetery, Tunis, 13th century. 20m, Floral design,
17th century illumination. 30m, Bird and flowers, glass painting, 1922. 40m, Antelope, from

11th century clay pot. 50m, Gate, Sidi Bou Said, 20th century.

1977, July 9   Photo.   *Perf. 13*
700 A207 10m multicolored .25 .25
701 A207 15m multicolored .25 .25
702 A207 20m multicolored .25 .25
703 A207 30m multicolored .40 .25
704 A207 40m multicolored .50 .25
705 A207 50m multicolored .25 .25
a.   Miniature sheet of 6, #700-705 3.75 3.75
Nos. 700-705 (6) 2.15 1.50

"The Young
Republic" and
Bourguiba
A208

Habib Bourguiba and: 100m, "The Confident Republic" and 20 doves. 150m, "The Determined Republic" and 20 roses.

1977, July 25   Photo.   *Perf. 13x13½*
706 A208 40m multicolored .40 .25
707 A208 100m multicolored .50 .25
708 A208 150m multicolored .85 .35
a.   Souvenir sheet of 3, #706-708 2.75 2.75
Nos. 706-708 (3) 1.75 .85

20th anniv. of the Republic. No. 708a sold for 500m. Exists imperf., same value.

Symbolic Cancellation, APU
Emblem — A209

1977, Aug. 16   Litho.   *Perf. 13x12½*
709 A209 40m multicolored .50 .25
Arab Postal Union, 25th anniversary.

Diseased Knee,
Gears and
Globe — A210

1977, Sept. 26   Photo.   *Perf. 14x13½*
710 A210 120m multicolored .95 .35
World Rheumatism Year.

Farmer, Road, Water and
Electricity — A211

1977, Dec. 15   Photo.   *Perf. 13½*
711 A211 40m multicolored .60 .25
Rural development.

Factory
Workers — A212

Designs: 20m, Bus driver and trains, horiz. 40m, Farmer driving tractor, horiz.

1978, Mar. 6   *Perf. 13x14, 14x13*
712 A212 20m rose red & multi .25 .25
713 A212 40m black & green .35 .25
714 A212 100m multicolored .75 .35
Nos. 712-714 (3) 1.35 .85
5th development plan, creation of new jobs.

Pres. Bourguiba,   Bourguiba and
Torch and   "9" — A213a
"9" — A213

1978, Apr. 9   Engr.   *Perf. 13*
715 A213 40m multicolored .30 .25
716 A213a 60m multicolored .30 .25
40th anniv. of 1st fight for independence, 4/9/38.

A214

1978, May 2   Photo.   *Perf. 13x13½*
717 A214 150m Policeman 1.10 .35
6th Regional African Interpol Conference, Tunis, May 2-5.

A215

Designs: 40m, Tunisian Goalkeeper. 150m., Soccer player, maps of South America and Africa, flags.

1978, June 1   Photo.   *Perf. 13x14*
718 A215 40m multicolored .35 .25
719 A215 150m multicolored 1.00 .40
11th World Cup Soccer Championship, Argentina, June 1-25.

Destruction of Apartheid, Map of
South Africa — A216

Fight Against Apartheid: 100m, White and black doves flying in unison.

1978, Aug. 30   Litho.   *Perf. 13½x14*
720 A216 50m multicolored .25 .25
721 A216 100m multicolored .60 .35

"Pollution is a
Plague" — A217

Designs: 50m, "The Sea, mankind's patrimony." 120m, "Greening of the desert."

1978, Sept. 11   Photo.   *Perf. 14x13*
722 A217 10m multicolored .25 .25
723 A217 50m multicolored .60 .25
724 A217 120m multicolored 1.25 .35
Nos. 722-724 (3) 2.10 .85
Protection of the environment.

"Eradication of
Smallpox" — A218

1978, Oct. 16   Litho.   *Perf. 12½*
725 A218 150m multicolored .95 .40
Global eradication of smallpox.

Jerba
Wedding
A219

5m, Horseman from Zlass. 75m, Women potters from the Mogods. 100m, Dove over Marabout Sidi Mahrez cupolas, Tunis. 500m, Plowing in Jenduba. 1d, Spring Festival in Tozeur (man on swing).

1978, Nov. 1   Photo.   *Perf. 13*
726 A219 5m multi, vert. .25 .25
727 A219 60m multi .35 .25
728 A219 75m multi .50 .25
729 A219 100m multi .50 .25
730 A219 500m multi 3.75 1.25
731 A219 1d multi 6.00 2.50
Nos. 726-731 (6) 11.35 4.75
Traditional Arab calligraphy.

Lenin and Red
Banner over
Kremlin — A220

1978, Nov. 7   *Perf. 13½*
732 A220 150m multicolored 1.60 .50
Russian October Revolution, 60th anniv.

Farhat Hached,
Union
Emblem — A221

1978, Dec. 5   Photo.   *Perf. 14*
733 A221 50m multicolored .60 .25
Farhat Hached (1914-1952), founder of General Union of Tunisian Workers.

Family — A222

1978, Dec. 15   Photo.   *Perf. 13½*
734 A222 50m multicolored .60 .25
Tunisian Family Planning Assoc., 10th anniv.

Sun with Man's
Face — A223

1978, Dec. 25   *Perf. 14*
735 A223 100m multicolored .75 .25
Sun as a source of light and energy.

Plane, Weather Map and
Instruments — A224

1978, Dec. 29
736 A224 50m multicolored .60 .25
Tunisian civil aviation and meteorology, 20th anniv.

Habib Bourguiba
and
Constitution — A225

1979, May 31   Photo.   *Perf. 14x13½*
737 A225 50m multicolored .60 .25
20th anniversary of Constitution.

El Kantaoui Port A226

1979, June 3 *Perf. 13½x14*
738 A226 150m multicolored 1.25 .35
Development of El Kantaoui as a resort area.

Landscapes — A227

1979, July 14 *Perf. 12½x13½*
739 A227 50m Korbous .25 .25
740 A227 100m Mides .50 .25

Bow Net Weaving — A228

1979, Aug. 15 Photo. *Perf. 11½*
741 A228 10m shown .30 .25
742 A228 50m Beekeeping .70 .25

Pres. Bourguiba, "10" and Hands — A229

1979, Sept. 5
743 A229 50m multicolored .50 .25
Socialist Destour Party, 10th Congress.

Modes of Communication, ITU Emblem — A230

1979, Sept. 20 Litho. *Perf. 11½*
744 A230 150m multicolored 1.00 .50
3rd World Telecommunications Exhibition, Geneva, Sept. 20-26.

Arab Achievements — A231

1979, Oct. 1 *Perf. 14½*
745 A231 50m multicolored .50 .25

Children Crossing Street, IYC Emblem — A232

1979, Oct. 16 *Perf. 14x13½*
746 A232 50m shown .30 .25
747 A232 100m Child and birds .75 .25
International Year of the Child.

Dove, Olive Tree, Map of Tunisia — A233

1979, Nov. 1 Litho. *Perf. 12*
748 A233 150m multicolored 1.10 .40
2nd International Olive Oil Year.

Woman Wearing Crown — A234

1979, Nov. 3 *Perf. 14½*
749 A234 50m multicolored .50 .25
Central Bank of Tunisia, 20th anniversary.

Children and Jujube Tree — A235

1979, Dec. 25 Litho. *Perf. 15x14½*
750 A235 20m shown .30 .25
751 A235 30m Peacocks .60 .25
752 A235 70m Goats 1.10 .35
753 A235 85m Girl, date palm 1.10 .40
 Nos. 750-753 (4) 3.10 1.25

Postal Code Introduction — A236

1980, Mar. 20 Photo. *Perf. 14*
754 A236 50m multicolored .55 .25

Fight Against Cigarette Smoking A237

1980, Apr. 7
755 A237 150m multicolored .85 .25

Pres. Bourguiba in Flower, Open Book — A238

1980, June 1 Photo. *Perf. 11½*
756 A238 50m shown .25 .25
757 A238 100m Dove, Bourguiba, mosque 1.00 .40
Victory (independence), 25th anniversary.

Butterfly and Gymnast A239

1980, June 3 Photo. *Perf. 12x11½*
 Granite Paper
758 A239 100m multicolored .60 .25
Turin Gymnastic Games, June 1-7.

Artisans
A240 A241

1980, July 21 Photo. *Perf. 13½*
759 A240 30m multicolored .35 .25
760 A241 75m multicolored .75 .25

ibn-Khaldun (1332-1406), Historian — A242

1980, July 28 *Perf. 14*
761 A242 50m multicolored .60 .25

Avicenna (Arab Physician), Birth Millenium — A243

1980, Aug. 18 Engr. *Perf. 12½x13*
762 A243 100m redsh brn & sepia .75 .30

Arab Achievements — A244

1980, Aug. 25 Photo. *Perf. 13½x14*
763 A244 50m multicolored .85 .25

Port Sidi bou Said A245

1980, Sept. 4 *Perf. 14*
764 A245 100m multicolored .50 .30

World Tourism Conference, Manila, Sept. 27 — A246

1980, Sept. 27 Photo. *Perf. 14*
765 A246 150m multicolored .75 .25

Wedding in Jerba, by Yahia (1903-1969) — A247

1980, Oct. 1 *Perf. 12*
766 A247 50m multicolored .75 .40

Tozeur-Nefta International Airport Opening — A248

1980, Oct. 13 Photo. *Perf. 13x13½*
767 A248 85m multicolored .60 .25

Eye and Text A249

1980, Oct. 26 Litho. *Perf. 13½x14*
768 A249 100m multicolored 1.00 .50
7th Afro-Asian Ophthalmologic Congress.

Hegira, 1500th Anniv. A250

1980, Nov. 9
769 A250 50m Spiderweb .25 .25
770 A250 80m City skyline .50 .25

Film Strip and Woman's Head — A251

1980, Nov. 15 **Photo.** *Perf. 14x13½*
771 A251 100m multicolored .75 .35
Carthage Film Festival.

Orchid A252

1980, Nov. 17 *Perf. 13½x14*
772 A252 20m shown .55 .30
773 A252 25m Wild cyclamen .70 .30

Size: 39x27mm

Perf. 14
774 A252 50m Mouflon 1.40 .30
775 A252 100m Golden eagle 3.00 .40
Nos. 772-775 (4) 5.65 1.30

Campaign to Save Kairouan Mosque A253

1980, Dec. 29 **Photo.** *Perf. 12*
Granite Paper
776 A253 85m multicolored .55 .25

Heinrich von Stephan (1831-1897), Founder of UPU — A254

1981, Jan. 7
777 A254 150m multicolored .90 .40

Pres. Bourguiba and Flag — A256

1981, Mar. 20 **Photo.** *Perf. 12x11½*
Granite Paper
779 A256 50m shown .25 .25
780 A256 60m Stork, "25" .50 .25
781 A256 85m Doves .75 .40
782 A256 120m Victory on
winged horse .75 .40
a. Souvenir sheet of 4, #779-782 4.00 4.00
Nos. 779-782 (4) 2.25 1.30

25th anniversary of independence. No. 782 sold for 500m. Exists imperf., same value.

Pres. Bourguiba and Flower A257

1981, Apr. 10 **Photo.** *Perf. 12x11½*
783 A257 50m shown .25 .25
784 A257 75m Bourguiba, flower, diff. .50 .25
Destourien Socialist Party Congress.

Mosque Entrance, Mahdia A258

1981, Apr. 20 *Perf. 13½*
785 A258 50m shown .35 .25
786 A258 85m Tozeur Great Mosque, vert. .50 .35
787 A258 100m Needle Rocks, Tabarka .60 .25
Nos. 785-787 (3) 1.45 .85

A259

1981, May 17 **Litho.** *Perf. 14x15*
788 A259 150m multicolored .95 .35
13th World Telecommunications Day.

Youth Festival — A260

1981, June 2 **Photo.** *Perf. 11½*
Granite Paper
789 A260 100m multicolored .65 .25

A261

1981, June 15 **Photo.** *Perf. 14*
790 A261 150m multicolored .95 .35
Kemal Ataturk (1881-1938), 1st president of Turkey.

A262

1981, July 15 **Photo.** *Perf. 11½x12*
791 A262 150m Skifa, Mahdia .80 .40

Mohammed Tahar Ben Achour (1879-1973), Scholar — A263

1981, Aug. 6 *Perf. 13*
792 A263 200m multicolored 1.50 .50

25th Anniv. of Personal Status Code (Women's Liberation) — A264

1981, Aug. 13
793 A264 50m Woman .25 .25
794 A264 100m shown .75 .35

Intl. Year of the Disabled — A265

1981, Sept. 21 **Photo.** *Perf. 13½*
795 A265 250m multicolored 1.50 .65

Pilgrimage to Mecca — A266

1981, Oct. 7 **Photo.** *Perf. 13½*
796 A266 50m multicolored .60 .25

World Food Day — A267

1981, Oct. 16 **Litho.** *Perf. 12*
Granite Paper
797 A267 200m multicolored 1.50 .65

Traditional Jewelry A268

150m, Mneguech silver earrings. 180m Mahfdha (silver medallion worn by married women). 200m, Essalta gold headdress.

1981, Dec. 7 **Photo.** *Perf. 14*
798 A268 150m multi, vert. .75 .35
799 A268 180m multi .90 .40
800 A268 200m multi, vert. 1.10 .50
Nos. 798-800 (3) 2.75 1.25

Bizerta Bridge A269

1981, Dec. 14 **Litho.** *Perf. 12x11½*
Granite Paper
801 A269 230m multicolored 1.25 .50

A270

Chemist compounding honey mixture, manuscript miniature, 1224.

1982, Apr. 3 **Photo.** *Perf. 13*
802 A270 80m multicolored .95 .35
Arab Chemists' Union, 16th anniv.

A271

1982, May 12 **Photo.** *Perf. 13½*
803 A271 150m multicolored 1.25 .60
Oceanic Enterprise Symposium, Tunis, 5/12-14.

A272

1982, June 26 *Perf. 12½*
Granite Paper
804 A272 80m multicolored .60 .25
The Productive Family Employment campaign.

1981, Mar. 5 **Litho.** *Perf. 14x13½*
778 A255 75m multicolored .90 .50

Blood Donors' Assoc., 20th Anniv. — A255

A273

25th Anniv. of Republic: Pres. Bourguiba and Various Women.

1982, July 25   Litho.   Perf. 14x13½
805 A273 80m multicolored .40 .25
806 A273 100m multicolored .60 .35
807 A273 200m multicolored 1.00 .40
Nos. 805-807 (3) 2.00 1.00

Scouting Year — A274

Perf. 14½x14, 14x14½
1982, Aug. 23
808 A274 80m multicolored .50 .25
809 A274 200m multicolored 1.10 .25
75th anniv. of scouting and 50th anniv. of scouting in Tunisia (80m, horiz.).

Tunisian Fossils — A274a

Designs: 80m, Pseudophillipsia azzouzi, vert. 200m, Mediterraneotrigonia cherahilensis, vert. 280m, Numidiopleura enigmatica. 300m, Micreschara tunisiensis, vert. 500m, Mantelliceras pervinquieri, vert. 1000m, Elephas africanavus.

1982, Sept. 20   Photo.   Perf. 11½x12
809A A274a 80m multi .90 .40
809B A274a 200m multi 1.80 .50
809C A274a 280m multi 2.10 .65
809D A274a 300m multi 2.75 .90
809E A274a 500m multi 5.25 1.40
809F A274a 1000m multi 11.00 2.75
Nos. 809A-809F (6) 23.80 6.60

A275

1982, Sept. 29   Perf. 14x13½
810 A275 80m shown .60 .25
Size: 23x40mm
811 A275 200m Woman, buildings 1.00 .50
30th Anniv. of Arab Postal Union.

A276

1982, Oct. 1   Photo.   Perf. 12
Granite Paper
812 A276 200m multicolored 1.00 .25
ITU Plenipotentiaries Conf., Nairobi.

World Food Day — A277

1982, Oct. 16   Litho.   Perf. 13
813 A277 200m multicolored 1.00 .35

Tahar Haddad (1899-1935), Social Reformer — A278

1982, Oct. 25   Engr.
814 A278 200m brnish black 1.00 .25

TB Bacillus Centenary A279

1982, Nov. 16   Litho.   Perf. 13½
815 A279 100m multicolored 1.25 .25

Folk Songs and Stories — A280

20m, Dancing in the Rain. 30m, Woman Sweeping. 70m, Fisherman and the Child. 80m, Rooster and the Oranges, horiz. 100m, Woman and the Mirror, horiz. 120m, The Two Girls, horiz.

1982, Nov. 22   Photo.   Perf. 14
816 A280 20m multi .30 .25
817 A280 30m multi .30 .25
818 A280 70m multi .30 .25
819 A280 80m multi .40 .25
820 A280 100m multi .60 .25
821 A280 120m multi .85 .30
Nos. 816-821 (6) 2.75 1.55

Intl. Palestinian Solidarity Day — A281

1982, Nov. 30   Litho.   Perf. 13x12
822 A281 80m multicolored .60 .25

Farhat Hached (1914-1952) A282

1982, Dec. 6   Engr.   Perf. 13
823 A282 80m brown red .60 .25

Bourguiba Dam Opening — A283

1982, Dec. 20   Litho.   Perf. 13½
824 A283 80m multicolored .75 .25

Environmental Training College Opening — A284

1982, Dec. 29   Photo.   Perf. 11½
Granite Paper
825 A284 80m multicolored .60 .25

World Communications Year — A285

1983, May 17   Litho.   Perf. 13½x14
826 A285 200m multicolored .80 .35

20th Anniv. of Org. of African Unity — A286

1983, May 25   Photo.   Perf. 12
Granite Paper
827 A286 230m ultra & grnsh bl .90 .50

30th Anniv. of Customs Cooperation Council — A287

1983, May 30   Litho.   Perf. 13½
828 A287 100m multicolored .60 .25

Aly Ben Ayed (1930-1972), Actor — A288

1983, Aug. 15   Engr.   Perf. 13
829 A288 80m dk car, dl red & gray .60 .35

Stone-carved Face, El-Mekta — A289

Pre-historic artifacts: 20m, Neolithic necklace, Kel el-Agab. 30m, Mill and grindstone, Redeyef. 40m, Orynx head rock carving, Gafsa. 80m, Dolmen Mactar. 100m, Acheulian Bi-face flint, El-Mekta.

1983, Aug. 20   Photo.   Perf. 11½x12
830 A289 15m multicolored .25 .25
831 A289 20m multicolored .45 .25
832 A289 30m multicolored .45 .25
833 A289 40m multicolored .45 .25
834 A289 80m multicolored .60 .40
835 A289 100m multicolored .75 .40
Nos. 830-835 (6) 2.95 1.80

Sports for All A290

1983, Sept. 27   Litho.   Perf. 12½
836 A290 40m multicolored .45 .25

World Fishing Day A291

1983, Oct. 17   Perf. 14½
837 A291 200m multicolored 1.25 .25

Evacuation of French Troops, 20th Anniv. — A292

1983, Oct. 17   Litho.   Perf. 14x13½
838 A292 80m multicolored .50 .25

Tapestry Weaver, by Hedi Khayachi (1882-1948) — A293

1983, Nov. 22   Photo.   *Perf. 11½*
Granite Paper
839 A293 80m multicolored   .90   .40

Natl. Allegiance — A294

1983, Nov. 30   Litho.   *Perf. 14½*
840 A294 100m Children, flag   .50   .25

Jet, Woman's Head, Emblem — A295

1983, Dec. 21   *Perf. 13½*
841 A295 150m multicolored   .80   .25

Pres. Bourguiba A296

Destourien Socialist Party, 50th Anniv.: Portraits of Bourguiba. 200m, 230m horiz.

Perf. 12½x12, 12x12½
1984, Mar. 2   Photo.
Granite Paper
842 A296 40m multicolored   .25   .25
843 A296 70m multicolored   .25   .25
844 A296 80m multicolored   .40   .25
  a.   Pair, #843-844   .75   .75
845 A296 150m multicolored   .65   .40
  a.   Pair, #842, 845   1.00   1.00
846 A296 200m multicolored   .85   .40
847 A296 230m multicolored   .90   .60
  a.   Pair, #846-847   2.00   2.00
       Nos. 842-847 (6)   3.30   2.15

Nos. 844a, 845a and 847a were printed checkerwise in sheets of ten.

4th Molecular Biology Symposium A297

1984, Apr. 3   *Perf. 13½x13*
848 A297 100m Map, diagram   .80   .35

Ibn El Jazzar, Physician — A298

1984, May 15   Photo.   *Perf. 14x13*
849 A298 80m multicolored   .70   .40

Economic Development Program, 20th Anniv. — A299

230m, Merchant, worker.

1984, June 15   *Perf. 11½*
Granite Paper
850 A299 230m multicolored   1.25   .40

Coquette, The Sorceress and the Fairy Carabosse A300

80m, Counting with fingers. 100m, Boy riding horse, vert.

Perf. 13½x14, 14x13½
1984, Aug. 27   Photo.
851 A300 20m shown   .30   .25
852 A300 80m multicolored   .50   .25
853 A300 100m mutlicolored   .65   .25
       Nos. 851-853 (3)   1.45   .75

Legends and folk tales.

Family and Education Org., 20th Anniv. — A301

80m, Family looking into future.

1984, Sept. 4   *Perf. 13x14*
854 A301 80m multicolored   .50   .25

Natl. Heritage Protection A302

100m, Medina Mosque Minaret, hand.

1984, Sept. 13   *Perf. 14*
855 A302 100m multicolored   .60   .35

Aboul-Qasim Chabbi, Poet (1909-1934) — A303

1984, Oct. 9   Engr.   *Perf. 12½x13*
856 A303 100m multicolored   —   .25

40th Anniv., ICAO A304

1984, Oct. 25   Photo.   *Perf. 13*
857 A304 200m Aircraft tail, bird 1.00   .60

Sahara Festival A305

1984, Dec. 3   Litho.   *Perf. 14½*
858 A305 20m Musicians   .80   .25

20th Anniv., Intelsat A306

100m, Tunisian Earth Station.

Perf. 13½x14½
1984, Dec. 25   Photo.
859 A306 100m multicolored   .70   .25

Mediterranean Landscape, by Jilani Abdelwaheb (Abdul) — A307

1984, Dec. 31   Photo.   *Perf. 14½*
860 A307 100m multicolored   .80   .40

EXPO '85, Tsukuba, Japan A308

1985, Mar. 20   Photo.   *Perf. 12*
861 A308 200m multicolored   1.00   .50

Civil Protection Week — A309

100m, Hands, water and fire.

1985, May 13   Litho.   *Perf. 14*
862 A309 100m multicolored   .75   .40

Pres. Habib Bourguiba, Crowded Pier — A310

Pres. Bourguiba: 75m, On horseback, vert. 200m, Wearing hat, vert. 230m, Waving to crowd.

1985, June 1   *Perf. 12½*
863 A310 75m multicolored   .50   .50
864 A310 100m multicolored   .80   .80
865 A310 200m multicolored   1.10   1.10
866 A310 230m multicolored   1.40   1.40
       Nos. 863-866 (4)   3.80   3.80

Natl. independence, 30th anniv.

Head of a Statue, Carthage and Pres. Bourguiba A311

1985, June 4   *Perf. 14*
867 A311 250m multicolored   1.00   .65

EXPO '85.

Intl. Amateur Film Festival, Kelibia — A312

1985, July 20   *Perf. 14½x13*
868 A312 250m multicolored   1.40   .65

Natl. Folk Tales — A313

25m, Sun, Sun Shine Again, horiz. 50m, I Met a Man With Seven Wives. 100m, Uncle Shisbene.

1985, July 29   *Perf. 14*
869 A313 25m multi   .25   .25
870 A313 50m multi   .25   .25
871 A313 100m multi   .40   .25
       Nos. 869-871 (3)   .90   .75

Intl. Youth Year — A314

1985, Sept. 30   *Perf. 14½x13½*
872 A314 250m multicolored   1.10   .60

The Perfumers' Courtyard, 1912, by
Hedi Larnaout — A315

1985, Oct. 4   **Perf. 14**
873 A315 100m multicolored   .65 .25

Regional Bridal
Costumes — A316

1985, Oct. 22   **Perf. 12**
874 A316 20m Matmata   .30 .25
875 A316 50m Moknine   .30 .25
876 A316 100m Tunis   .75 .25
     Nos. 874-876 (3)   1.35 .75

UN, 40th
Anniv. — A317

1985, Oct. 24   **Perf. 14x13½**
877 A317 250m multicolored   1.00 .60

Self-Sufficiency in Food
Production — A318

100m, Makhtar stele of feast.

Perf. 13½x14½
1985, Nov. 26   **Photo.**
878 A318 100m multicolored   .60 .25

League of
Arab
States,
40th Anniv.
A319

1985, Nov. 29   **Litho.**   **Perf. 13½x14**
879 A319 100m multicolored   .50 .25

Aziza Othmana (d.
1669) — A320

1985, Dec. 16   **Engr.**   **Perf. 12½x13**
880 A320 100m dk grn, hn brn &
     brn   .75 .25

Land Law,
Cent. — A321

1985, Dec. 25   **Litho.**   **Perf. 13½**
881 A321 100m multicolored   .65 .25

Natl. Independence, 30th
Anniv. — A322

Perf. 13x13½, 13½x13
1986, Mar. 20   **Photo.**
882 A322 100m Dove, vert.   .45 .25
883 A322 120m Rocket   .50 .25
884 A322 280m Horse and rider   1.40 .65
885 A322 300m Balloons, vert.   1.60 .75
   a. Souvenir sheet of 4, #882-885   4.00 4.00
     Nos. 882-885 (4)   3.95 1.90

No. 885a exists imperf. Same value.

A323   A324

1986, Apr. 30   **Litho.**   **Perf. 14x13½**
886 A323 300m multicolored   1.50 .40
887 A324 380m multicolored   2.00 .50

Prof. Hulusi Behcet (1889-1948), discovered virus causing Behcet's Disease affecting
eyes and joints. 3rd Mediterranean Rheumatology Day (#886). Intl. Geographical
Ophtalmological Soc. Cong. (#887).

12th
Destourian
Socialist Party
Congress
A325

1986, June 19   **Photo.**   **Perf. 12**
888 A325 120m shown   .50 .25
889 A325 300m Torchbearer   1.50 .75

A326

Regional bridal costumes.

1986, Aug. 25   **Litho.**   **Perf. 14**
890 A326 40m Homi-Souk   .25 .25
891 A326 280m Mahdia   1.00 .60
892 A326 300m Nabeul   1.40 .65
     Nos. 890-892 (3)   2.65 1.50

A327

1986, Sept. 20   **Engr.**   **Perf. 13**
893 A327 160m dark red   .80 .25

Hassen Husni Abdul-Wahab (1883-1968),
historian, archaeologist

Founding of Carthage, 2800th
Anniv. — A328

1986, Oct. 18   **Engr.**   **Perf. 13**
894 A328 2d dark violet   9.00 3.00

Protohistoric
Artifacts — A329

Design: 10m, Flint arrowhead, El Borma, c.
3000 B.C. 20m, Rock cut-out dwelling,
Sejnane, c. 1000 B.C. 50m, Lintel bas-relief
from a cult site in Tunis, c. 1000 B.C., horiz.
120m, Base of a Neolithic vase, Kesra. 160m,
Phoenician trireme, petroglyph, c. 800 B.C.,
horiz. 250m, Ceramic pot, c. 700 B.C., found
at Sejnane, vert.

1986, Oct. 30   **Litho.**   **Perf. 13½**
895 A329 10m multicolored   .35 .25
896 A329 20m multicolored   .35 .25
897 A329 50m multicolored   .60 .25
898 A329 120m multicolored   .95 .25
899 A329 160m multicolored   1.25 .40
900 A329 250m multicolored   2.40 .60
     Nos. 895-900 (6)   5.90 2.00

Bedouins, by
Ammar
Farhat — A330

1986, Nov. 20   **Photo.**   **Perf. 13½**
901 A330 250m multicolored   1.60 .40

Intl.
Peace
Year
A331

1986, Nov. 24   **Perf. 13½x13**
902 A331 300m multicolored   1.25 .40

FAO, 40th
Anniv. — A332

1986, Nov. 27   **Perf. 13x13½**
903 A332 280m multicolored   1.25 .60

Computer
Education
Inauguration
A333

1986, Dec. 8   **Perf. 13½**
904 A333 2d multicolored   9.50 2.75

Breast-feeding for
Child
Survival — A334

1986, Dec. 22   **Photo.**   **Perf. 14**
905 A334 120m multicolored   .50 .25

Wildlife, Natl.
Parks — A335

Designs: 60m, Mountain gazelle, Chambi
Natl. Park. 120m, Addax, Bou. Hedma.
350m, Seal, Zembretta. 380m, Greylag
goose, Ichkeul.

Granite Paper

1986, Dec. 29   **Perf. 12**
906 A335 60m multicolored   .25 .25
907 A335 120m multicolored   .55 .35
908 A335 350m multicolored   1.60 1.00
909 A335 380m multicolored   1.90 1.10
     Nos. 906-909 (4)   4.30 2.70

City of
Monastir,
Cent. — A336

120m, Pres. Bourguiba, city arms.

1987, Jan. 24   **Litho.**   **Perf. 12x11½**
Granite Paper
910 A336 120m multicolored   .60 .25

Invention of the Telegraph by Samuel
F.B. Morse, 150th Anniv.
A337

1987, June 15   **Litho.**   **Perf. 13½x14**
911 A337 500m multicolored   2.25 1.00

30th Anniv. of the Republic
A338

Pres. Bourguiba and women of various sects.

1987, July 25 **Photo.** **Perf. 13½**
912 A338 150m multi .45 .25
913 A338 250m multi .80 .35
914 A338 350m multi, diff. 1.10 .55
915 A338 500m multi, diff. 1.60 .75
   a. Souvenir sheet of 4, #912-915 5.00 5.00
   Nos. 912-915 (4) 3.95 1.90

No. 915a sold for 1.50d. Exists imperf.

UN Universal Vaccination by 1990 Campaign — A339

1987, Sept. 14 **Perf. 12**
Granite Paper
916 A339 250m multicolored 1.00 .50

The Street, by Azouz ben Raiz (1902-1962) A340

1987, Sept. 22 **Granite Paper**
917 A340 250m multicolored 1.25 .50

Arab Day for Shelter of the Homeless A341

1987, Oct. 5 **Photo.** **Perf. 12x11½**
Granite Paper
918 A341 150m multicolored .65 .25

Advisory Council for Postal Research, 30th Anniv. A342

1987, Oct. 9 **Perf. 14**
919 A342 150m Express mail .65 .25
920 A342 350m Use postal code 1.50 .60

The Arabs, by Ibn-Mandhour (1233-1312), Lexicographer A343

1987, Oct. 26 **Engr.** **Perf. 13**
921 A343 250m plum 1.10 .50

Pasteur Institute, Tunis A344

1987, Nov. 21 **Perf. 13x12½**
922 A344 250m blk, grn & rose lake 2.50 .50

Pasteur Institute, Paris, cent.

Intl. Year of the Vine (Wine) — A345

1987, Nov. 27 **Photo.** **Perf. 14**
923 A345 250m multicolored 1.50 .50

6th Volleyball Championships of African Nations — A346

1987, Dec. 2 **Litho.** **Perf. 14x13½**
924 A346 350m multicolored 1.60 .70

African Basketball Championships A347

1987, Dec. 15
925 A347 350m multicolored 1.60 .70

Folk Costumes — A348

1987, Dec. 25 **Photo.**
926 A348 20m Midoun .25 .25
927 A348 30m Tozeur .25 .25
928 A348 150m Sfax .75 .40
   Nos. 926-928 (3) 1.25 .90

Flowering Plants — A349

30m, Narcissus tazetta. 150m, Gladiolus communis. 400m, Iris xiphium. 500m, Tulipa sylvestris.

1987, Dec. 29 **Perf. 14½**
929 A349 30m multicolored .25 .25
930 A349 150m multicolored .60 .30
931 A349 400m multicolored 1.50 .80
932 A349 500m multicolored 1.90 1.00
   Nos. 929-932 (4) 4.25 2.35

Declaration of Nov. 7, 1987 A350

Cameo portrait of Pres. Zine el Abidine Ben Ali and: 150m, Scales of Justice. 200m, Girl with flowers (party badges) in her hair, vert. 350m, Mermaid, doves, natl. coat of arms. 370m, "CMA," emblem of the Maghreb states (Tunisia, Mauritania, Morocco, Algeria and Libya), vert.

1988, Mar. 21 **Photo.** **Perf. 12**
Granite Paper
933 A350 150m multicolored .60 .25
934 A350 200m multicolored .70 .30
935 A350 350m multicolored 1.25 .55
936 A350 370m multicolored 1.25 .60
   Nos. 933-936 (4) 3.80 1.70

Youth and Change A351

1988, Mar. 22 **Litho.** **Perf. 14x14½**
937 A351 75m shown .25 .25
938 A351 150m Happy family .55 .25

Martyr's Day, 50th Anniv. A352

Perf. 13x13½, 13½x13
1988, Apr. 9 **Photo.**
939 A352 150m shown .65 .25
940 A352 500m Monument, vert. 1.75 .75

Opening Conference of the Constitutional Democratic Assembly — A353

150m, Flag, Pres. Ben Ali.

1988, July 30 **Perf. 12x11½**
Granite Paper
941 A353 150m multicolored .60 .25

1988 Summer Olympics, Seoul A354

430m, Running, boxing, weight lifting, wrestling.

1988, Sept. 20 **Photo.** **Perf. 13½**
942 A354 150m shown .60 .25
943 A354 430m multicolored 1.60 1.00

A355

1988, Sept. 21
944 A355 200m multicolored .75 .35
Restoration of the City of San'a, Yemen.

A356

1988, Nov. 7 **Photo.** **Perf. 14**
945 A356 150m multicolored .50 .30
Appointment of Pres. Zine El Abidine Ben Ali, 1st anniv.

Amilcar Beach, 1942, by A. Debbeche — A357

1988, Nov. 21 **Photo.** **Perf. 13½x13**
946 A357 100m multicolored .75 .25

Tunis Air, 40th Anniv. A358

1988, Nov. 28 **Photo.** **Perf. 12x11½**
Granite Paper
947 A358 500m multicolored 1.60 .80

UN Declaration of Human Rights, 40th Anniv. — A359

1988, Dec. 10 **Perf. 12**
Granite Paper
948 A359 370m black 1.25 .60

Tunisian Postage Stamp Cent. — A360

1988, Dec. 16 **Perf. 12½**
Granite Paper
949 A360 150m multicolored .75 .40

Decorative Doorways — A361

1988, Dec. 26   *Perf. 14x13½*
950 A361 50m multi .30 .25
951 A361 70m multi, diff. .30 .25
952 A361 100m multi, diff. .30 .25
953 A361 150m multi, diff. .50 .25
954 A361 370m multi, diff. 1.00 .40
955 A361 400m multi, diff. 1.25 .40
   Nos. 950-955 (6) 3.65 1.80

Ali Douagi (1909-49) — A362

1989, Mar. 7   Engr.   *Perf. 13½x13*
956 A362 1000m dark blue 3.25 1.60

Natl. Day for the Handicapped A363

1989, May 30   Photo.   *Perf. 13½*
957 A363 150m multicolored .65 .25

Education A364

1989, July 10   *Perf. 14*
958 A364 180m multicolored .65 .25

Family Planning Assoc., 20th Anniv. — A365

1989, Aug. 14   Litho.   *Perf. 14*
959 A365 150m multicolored .65 .25

Family Care A366

1989, Aug. 14   Litho.   *Perf. 14*
960 A366 150m multicolored .65 .25

Fauna A367

1989, Aug. 28   Photo.   *Perf. 13½x14*
961 A367 250m Tortoise 1.10 .50
962 A367 350m Oryx 1.50 .65

Intl. Fair, Tunis — A368

1989, Oct. 16   Photo.   *Perf. 14*
963 A368 150m shown .50 .25
964 A368 370m Pavilion, horiz. 1.25 .60

Mohamed Beyram V (1840-1889) A369

1989, Oct. 28   Engr.   *Perf. 13*
965 A369 150m blk & dp rose lil .65 .25

Theater, Carthage — A370

1989, Nov. 3   Photo.   *Perf. 14*
966 A370 300m multicolored 1.00 .40

Monument — A371

1989, Nov. 7   *Perf. 11½x12*
   Granite Paper
967 A371 150m multicolored .65 .25
   Appointment of Pres. Zine El Abidine Ben Ali, 2nd Anniv.

Nehru — A372

1989, Nov. 29   Engr.   *Perf. 13*
968 A372 300m dark brown 1.25 .35
   Jawaharlal Nehru, 1st prime minister of independent India.

Flags — A373

1990, Jan. 15   Photo.   *Perf. 12x11½*
   Granite Paper
969 A373 200m multicolored .75 .35
   Maghreb Union summit, Tunis.

Museum of Bardo, Cent. A374

1990, Feb. 20   Litho.   *Perf. 13½*
970 A374 300m multicolored 1.00 .50

Pottery A375

1990, Mar. 22   *Perf. 14*
971 A375 75m multicolored .35 .25
972 A375 100m multi, diff. .50 .35

Sheep Museum — A376

1990, Apr. 13   Litho.   *Perf. 13½*
973 A376 400m Sheep 1.25 .75
974 A376 450m Ram's head 1.75 .85
  a.   Souvenir sheet of 2, #973-974 4.50 4.50
   No. 974a sold for 1000m, exists imperf. Nos. 973-974 inscribed 1989.

Tunisian Olympic Movement — A377

1990, May 27
975 A377 150m multicolored .65 .25

Child's Drawing A378

1990, June 5   *Perf. 14*
976 A378 150m multicolored .65 .25

Traditional Costumes A379

1990, July 13   Photo.   *Perf. 14x14½*
977 A379 150m Sbiba .75 .35
978 A379 500m Bou Omrane 2.00 .85

A380

   Relic from Punic city of Dougga.

1990, Aug. 1   Litho.   *Perf. 14*
979 A380 300m multicolored 1.00 .50

Intl. Literacy Year A381

1990, Sept. 8   Photo.   *Perf. 12x11½*
   Granite Paper
980 A381 120m multicolored .65 .25

Water Preservation A382

1990, Oct. 15   *Perf. 11½x12*
   Granite Paper
981 A382 150m multicolored .75 .25

A383

1990, Nov. 7   **Granite Paper**
982 A383 150m shown .50 .25
983 A383 150m Clock tower .50 .25
   Appointment of Pres. Zine El Abidine Ben Ali, 3rd anniv.

A384

1990, Nov. 16　Engr.　Perf. 13½x13
984　A384　150m green　　　　.65　.25
Kheireddine Et-Tounsi (1822-1889), politician.

Fauna and
Flora — A385

150m, Cervus elaphus barbarus. 200m,
Cynara cardenculus. 300m, Bubalus bubalis.
600m, Ophris lutea.

1990, Dec. 17　Photo.　Perf. 13½
985　A385　150m multicolored　　.50　.25
986　A385　200m multicolored　　.80　.35
987　A385　300m multicolored　1.25　.40
988　A385　600m multicolored　2.60　.85
　　Nos. 985-988 (4)　　　　5.15　1.85

Maghreb Arab
Union, 2nd
Anniv. — A386

1991, Jan. 21　Photo.　Perf. 13½
989　A386　180m multicolored　　.75　.25

Harbor of
Tabarka — A387

1991, Mar. 17
990　A387　450m multicolored　1.50　.50

Fish — A388

1991, Sept. 10　Photo.　Perf. 14x13
991　A388　180m Pagre　　　.70　.25
992　A388　350m Rouget de roche　1.40　.40
993　A388　450m Maquereau　1.40　.60
994　A388　550m Pageot commun　2.40　.90
　　Nos. 991-994 (4)　　　5.90　2.15

Child
Welfare — A389

1991, Sept. 29　　　　Perf. 14
995　A389　450m multicolored　2.10　.85

A390

1991, Oct. 9　　　Perf. 13½x14
996　A390　400m multicolored　1.75　.50

Jewelry — A391

120m, Ring, bracelets, horiz. 180m, Necklace. 220m, Earrings. 730m, Belt ring.

Perf. 14x13, 13x14
1991, Oct. 22　　　　Litho.
997　A391　120m multi　　.45　.25
998　A391　180m multi　　.55　.25
999　A391　220m multi　　.70　.35
1000　A391　730m multi　2.75　1.10
　　Nos. 997-1000 (4)　4.45　1.95

A392

1991, Nov. 7　　　　Perf. 11½
1001　A392　180m multicolored　.65　.25
Appointment of Pres. Zine El Abidine Ben
Ali, 4th anniv.

Tunis-Carthage Center — A393

1991, Nov. 22　Engr.　Perf. 13
1002　A393　80m red, blue & grn　1.00　.40

World Day of
Human
Rights — A394

1991, Dec. 12　Photo.　Perf. 14
1003　A394　450m bright blue　1.60　.55

A395

1991, Dec. 26　Engr.　Perf. 12½x13
1004　A395　200m blue　　.65　.35
Mahmoud Bayram Et Tounsi (1893-1960),
poet.

Expo '92,
Seville — A396

1992, Apr. 20　Photo.　Perf. 13½
1005　A396　180m multicolored　.65　.25

A397

General Post
Office, Tunis,
Cent. — A397a

General Post
Office, Tunis,
Cent. — A397a

Perf. 13x12½, 12½x13
1992, June 15　　　　Engr.
1006　A397　180m red brn, horiz.　.60　.25
1007　A397a　450m dark brown　1.60　.45

"When the
Subconscious
Awakes," by
Moncef ben
Amor — A398

1992, July 21　Litho.　Perf. 13½
1008　A398　500m multicolored　1.90　.50

1992
Summer
Olympics,
Barcelona
A399

1992, Aug. 4
1009　A399　180m Running　1.00　.40
1010　A399　450m Judo, vert.　2.25　.65

Birds — A400

100m, Merops apiaster. 180m, Carduelis
carduelis. 200m, Serinus serinus. 500m,
Carduelis chloris.

1992, Sept. 22　Photo.　Perf. 11½
Granite Paper
1011　A400　100m multicolored　.75　.25
1012　A400　180m multicolored　1.25　.40
1013　A400　200m multicolored　1.50　.50
1014　A400　500m multicolored　3.00　1.00
　　Nos. 1011-1014 (4)　6.50　2.15

A401

1992, Oct. 21　　　Perf. 11½x12
Granite Paper
1015　A401　180m multicolored　.85　.40
UN Conference on Rights of the Child.

African Human
Rights Conference,
Tunis — A402

1992, Nov. 2　Photo.　Perf. 11½
Granite Paper
1016　A402　480m multicolored　2.00　.85

A403　　　　A404

1992, Nov. 7　　　Granite Paper
1017　A403　180m multicolored　.95　.40
1018　A404　730m multicolored　3.00　1.10
Appointment of Pres. Zine El Abidine Ben
Ali, 5th anniv.

Arbor Day
A405

1992, Nov. 8   *Perf. 11½x12*
Granite Paper
1019 A405 180m Acacia tortilis   1.00   .50

Intl. Conference on Nutrition,
Rome — A406

1992, Dec. 15   *Litho.*   *Perf. 13½*
1020 A406 450m multicolored   2.00   .65

Traditional
Costumes — A407

1992, Dec. 23
1021 A407 100m Chemesse   .60   .25
1022 A407 350m Hanifites   1.60   .50

Mosaics
A408

1992, Dec. 29
1023 A408 100m Goat   .40   .25
1024 A408 180m Duck   .85   .35
1025 A408 350m Horse   1.40   .50
1026 A408 450m Gazelle   1.50   .90
  Nos. 1023-1026 (4)   4.15 2.00

World Conference on Human Rights,
Vienna — A409

1993, June 8   *Litho.*   *Perf. 13½*
1027 A409 450m multi

Arab-African Fair
of Tunisia — A410

1993, July 10   *Litho.*   *Perf. 13½x14*
1028 A410 450m multicolored   1.75   .50

Relaxation in the
Patio, by Ali
Guermassi
A411

1993, July 20   *Litho.*   *Perf. 13½*
1029 A411 450m multicolored   1.75   .50

Reassembly of the
Democratic
Congress — A412

1993, July 29   *Perf. 13½*
1030 A412 180m multicolored   .65   .25

A413

A414

1993   *Perf. 13*
1031 A413 20m Wolf   1.25   .25
1032 A414 60m Hoya carnosa   .75   .25

Appointment of Pres. Zine El Abidine,
6th Anniv.
A414a   A415

1993, Nov. 7   *Perf. 13½*
1033 A414a 180m multicolored   .75   .25
1034 A415 450m multicolored   1.75   .50

Kairouan
Tapestries — A416

Designs: Various ornate patterns.

1993, Dec. 13   *Perf. 13½*
1035 A416 100m multicolored   .40   .25
1036 A416 120m multicolored   .75   .25
1037 A416 180m multicolored   1.25   .35
1038 A416 350m multicolored   1.40   .75
  Nos. 1035-1038 (4)   3.80 1.60

Pasteur
Institute
of Tunis,
Cent.
A417

Design: 450m, Charles Nicolle (1866-1936), bacteriologist, 1928 Nobel medal.

1993, Oct. 12   *Litho.*   *Perf. 13½*
1039 A417 450m multicolored   2.00   .65

A418

School
Activities
A419

1993, Dec. 30   *Litho.*   *Perf. 13½*
1040 A418 180m Music   .75   .25
1041 A419 180m Art, reading   .75   .25

19th African Cup of Nations Soccer
Tournament — A420

350m, Two players, one in blue, red and gray long sleeve shirt. 450m, Map, player.

1994, Mar. 26
1042 A420 180m shown   1.00   .25
1043 A420 350m multi   2.00   .35
1044 A420 450m multi   2.75   .65
  Nos. 1042-1044 (3)   5.75 1.25

Presidential and
Legislative
Elections — A421

1994, Mar. 20
1045 A421 180m multicolored   .80   .25

Election of
Pres. Zine El
Abidine ben
Ali — A422

1994, May 15   Photo.   *Perf. 11½*
Granite Paper
1046 A422 180m multicolored   .75   .35
1047 A422 350m multicolored   1.25   .75
  a. Souvenir sheet, #1046-1047   3.50 3.50
  No. 1047a exists imperf.

ILO, 75th
Anniv. — A423

1994, May 12   *Perf. 13½x14*
1048 A423 350m multicolored   1.75   .35

Intl. Year of the
Family — A424

1994, May 15   *Litho.*   *Perf. 14x13½*
1049 A424 180m multicolored   .85   .50

Plants — A425

50m, Prunus spinosa. 100m, Xeranthemum inapertum. 200m, Orchis simia. 1d, Scilla peruviana.

1994, June 2
1050 A425 50m multicolored   .35   .25
1051 A425 100m multicolored   .35   .25
1052 A425 200m multicolored   1.00   .30
1053 A425 1d multicolored   4.50 1.50
  Nos. 1050-1053 (4)   6.20 2.30

Organization
of African
Unity Summit
Meeting,
Tunis — A426

1994, June 3   *Perf. 13½*
1054 A426 480m multicolored   2.00   .75

Intl. Olympic
Committee,
Cent.
A427

1994, July 7   *Litho.*   *Perf. 13½*
1055 A427 450m multicolored   1.75   .65

Philakorea
'94 — A428

1994, Aug 18 Litho.   Perf. 13¼x13½
1056 A428 450m multi   3.00   .65

A429

Butterflies: 100m, Colias croceus, horiz.
180m, Vanessa atalanta, horiz. 300m, Papilio
podalirius. 350m, Danaus chrysippus, horiz.
450m, Vanessa cardui. 500m, Papilio
machaon.

Perf. 13½x14, 14x13½

1994, Oct. 13   Litho.
1057 A429 100m multicolored   .45   .25
1058 A429 180m multicolored   .70   .35
1059 A429 300m multicolored   1.00   .50
1060 A429 350m multicolored   1.40   .65
1061 A429 450m multicolored   1.75   .85
1062 A429 500m multicolored   2.10   .90
      Nos. 1057-1062 (6)   7.40 3.50

A430

A430a

350m, Pres. Ali, "7," horiz. 730m, "7,"
Emblem.

1994, Nov. 16   Perf. 13½
1063 A430   350m multi   1.25   .50
1064 A430a 730m multi   2.75 1.00

Pres. Zine El Abidine, 7th anniv. of taking
office.

41st Military
Boxing World
Championships
A431

1994, Nov. 18 Litho.   Perf. 13½x14
1065 A431 450m multicolored   1.75   .70

Intl. Civil Aviation Organization, 50th
Anniv. — A432

1994, Dec. 7 Litho.   Perf. 13¾x14
1066 A432 450m multi   1.25   .50

Wildlife — A433

180m, Anser anser. 350m, Aythya ferina,
Aythya fuligula. 500m, Bubalus bubalis. 1d,
Lutra lutra, horiz.

1994, Dec. 27 Litho.   Perf. 13½
1067 A433 180m multi   .65   .40
1068 A433 350m multi   1.10   .85
1069 A433 500m multi   1.60 1.25
1070 A433 1d multi   3.00 2.75
      Nos. 1067-1070 (4)   6.35 5.25

"Composition," by Ridha
Bettaieb — A434

1994, Dec. 29 Litho.   Perf. 13
1071 A434 500m multicolored   1.50   .85

Arab League, 50th
Anniv. — A435

1995, May 29 Litho.   Perf. 13½
1072 A435 180m multicolored   1.00   .40

Art of Glass
Blowing — A436

1995, June 29
1073 A436 450m Water bottle   1.50   .90
1074 A436 730m Incense burner   2.25 1.50

Aboulkacem Chebbi (1909-34),
Poet — A437

1995, Aug. 12 Litho.   Perf. 13½
1075 A437 180m multicolored   .85   .40

4th World
Conference on
Women,
Beijing
A438

1995. Sept. 6 Litho.   Perf. 13½
1076 A438 180m multicolored   1.40   .40

FAO, 50th
Anniv.
A439

1995, Oct. 2 Litho.   Perf. 13½x13
1077 A439 350m multicolored   1.40   .65

Hannibal (247-
183BC),
Carthaginian
General — A440

1995, Nov. 14 Engr.   Perf. 14x13½
1078 A440 180m maroon   .65   .40
  a.   Souvenir sheet of 1   2.50 2.50

No. 1078a sold for 1d and exists imperf.

United
Nations,
50th
Anniv.
A441

1995, Oct. 24 Litho.   Perf. 14x13½
1079 A441 350m multicolored   1.50   .65

A442   A443

1995, Nov. 7 Litho.   Perf. 13x13½
1080 A442 180m multicolored   .65   .35
1081 A443 350m multicolored   1.25   .65

Appointment of Pres. Zine El Abidine ben
Ali, 8th anniv.

Campaign Against
Desertification — A444

1995, Oct. 31 Litho.   Perf. 13¼
1082 A444 180m multi   .75   .35

Human Rights
Day — A445

1995, Dec. 10 Litho.   Perf. 13x13½
1083 A445 350m multicolored   1.40   .65

Pedestrian
Security
A446

1995, Dec. 19   Perf. 13½x13
1084 A446 350m multicolored   1.10   .65

Flora and
Fauna — A447

Designs: 50m, Ophrys lapethica. 180m,
Gazella dorcas. 300m, Scupellaria cypria.
350m, Chlamydotis undulata.

1995, Dec. 28   Perf. 13½
1085 A447 50m multicolored   .35   .25
1086 A447 180m multicolored   .70   .25
1087 A447 300m multicolored   1.10   .55
1088 A447 350m multicolored   1.25   .75
      Nos. 1085-1088 (4)   3.40 1.80

Traditional
Costumes — A448

170m, Jebra, Khamri. 200m, Kaftan brode,
Hammamet.

1996, Mar.16   Perf. 14x13½
1089 A448 170m multi   .85   .40
1090 A448 200m multi   .85   .40

Independence,
40th
Anniv. — A449

390m, Dove, rainbow, "20, 40."

1996, Mar. 20   **Perf. 13x13½**
1091 A449 200m multicolored   .75   .30
1092 A449 390m multicolored   1.25   .75

Natl. Trade Union,
50th
Anniv. — A450

1996, Jan. 20   **Litho.**   **Perf. 13x13½**
1093 A450 440m multicolored   1.75   .85

Painting, "Hannana," by Noureddine
Khayachi (1917-87) — A451

1996, Apr. 25   **Litho.**   **Perf. 13½**
1094 A451 810m multicolored   2.50   1.60

Environment Day
— A451a

1996, June 5   **Litho.**   **Perf. 13x13½**
1094A A451a 390m multicolored   1.50   .75

CAPEX
'96 — A452

1996, June 8   **Litho.**   **Perf. 13x13½**
1095 A452 200m multicolored   1.10   .35

Insects
A453

200m, Coccinella septempunctata. 810m,
Apis mellifica.

1996, May 23   **Litho.**   **Perf. 14x13½**
1096 A453 200m multicolored   1.00   .40
1097 A453 810m multicolored   5.00   2.00

1996
Summer
Olympic
Games,
Atlanta
A455

Olympic emblem, and: 20m, Flags, Olympic
rings, athletic field. 200m, Torch bearer, fireworks, "100," globe, vert. 390m, Early Olympic
wrestlers.

1996, July 19   **Litho.**   **Perf. 13**
1099 A455   20m multicolored   .40   .25
1100 A455 200m multicolored   .90   .35
1101 A455 390m multicolored   1.75   .85
    Nos. 1099-1101 (3)   3.05   1.45

Code of Personal
Status (Women's
Liberation), 40th
Anniv. — A456

1996, Aug. 13   **Perf. 14**
1102 A456 200m multicolored   .80   .35

Landmarks — A457

Designs: 20m, Ramparts of Sousse, horiz.
200m, Numidian Mausoleum, Dougga. 390m,
Arch of Trajan, Makthar, horiz.

1996, Sept. 16   **Photo.**   **Perf. 11⅙**
    Granite Paper
1103 A457   20m multicolored   .35   .25
1104 A457 200m multicolored   .65   .35
1105 A457 390m multicolored   1.50   .85
    Nos. 1103-1105 (3)   2.50   1.45

Intl. Year to Fight
Poverty — A458

1996, Oct. 17   **Litho.**   **Perf. 13x13½**
1106 A458 390m multicolored   1.50   .65

Appointment of Pres. Zine El Abidine,
9th Anniv.
A459   A460

1996, Nov. 7
1107 A459 200m multicolored   .75   .35
1108 A460 390m multicolored   1.00   .75

National Day of Saharan
Tourism — A461

Designs: No. 1109, Camels, oasis, balloon.
No. 1110, Decorative designs.

1996, Nov. 12   **Litho.**   **Perf. 13¼x13**
1109   200m multi   .85   .35
1110   200m multi   .85   .35
    a. A461 Horiz. pair, #1109-1110   1.75   1.75

Ezzitouna Mosque, 1300th
Anniv. — A462

1996, Nov. 25   **Litho.**   **Perf. 14x13½**
1111 A462 250m multicolored   .85   .40

Natl. Solidarity Day
A463   A464

1996, Dec. 8   **Perf. 13x13½**
1112 A463 500m multicolored   1.50   .95
1113 A464 500m multicolored   1.50   .95

World Human
Rights
Day — A465

1996, Dec. 10
1114 A465 500m multicolored   1.75   .90

UNICEF, 50th
Anniv. — A466

1996, Dec. 11
1115 A466 810m multicolored   2.75   1.50

Musical Instruments — A467

1996, Dec. 26   **Litho.**   **Perf. 13½**
1116 A467 250m Mezoued   .85   .50
1117 A467 300m Gombri   1.00   .60
1118 A467 350m Tabla   1.60   .65
1119 A467 500m Tar Tounsi
       (Riq)   2.50   .90
    Nos. 1116-1119 (4)   5.95   2.65
    Perf. 13½x13¼
    Size: 38x25mm
1119A   Vert. strip of 4   —   —
    b. A467 20m Tabla   —   —
    c. A467 30m Mezoued   —   —
    d. A467 50m Gombri   —   —
    e. A467 100m Tar Tounsi   —   —

World
Book and
Copyright
Day
A468

1997, Apr. 23   **Litho.**   **Perf. 13½**
1120 A468 1d multicolored   3.25   1.75

Marine
Life
A469

Designs: 50m, Mytilus galloprovincialis.
70m, Tapes decussatus. 350m, Octopus vulgaris. 500m, Sepia officinalis.

1997, May 13
1121 A469   50m multicolored   .30   .25
1122 A469   70m multicolored   .30   .25
1123 A469 350m multicolored   1.10   .65
1124 A469 500m multicolored   1.90   1.25
    Nos. 1121-1124 (4)   3.60   2.40

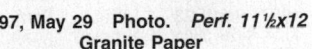

PACIFIC 97, Intl.
Stamp Exhibition,
San
Francisco — A470

1997, May 29   **Photo.**   **Perf. 11½x12**
    Granite Paper
1125 A470 250m multicolored   .85   .40

A471

1997, June 16   **Litho.**   **Perf. 13½**
1126 A471 350m multicolored   1.40   .65
Mediterranean Games, Bari.

A472

1997, July 15
1127 A472 250m multicolored   .85   .40
Tunis, 1997 Cultural Capital.

A473

Republic, 40th Anniv. A474

1997, July 25
1128	A473	130m multicolored	.50	.25
1129	A474	500m multicolored	1.50	1.00

Reptiles A475

100m, Uromastix acanthinurus. 350m, Chamaeleo chamaeleon, vert. 500m, Varanus griseus.

1997, Sept. 9   Litho.   Perf. 13½
1130	A475	100m multicolored	.25	.25
1131	A475	350m multicolored	1.00	.65
1132	A475	500m multicolored	1.25	1.10
		Nos. 1130-1132 (3)	2.50	2.00

Rosa Gallica Flore Pleno — A476

1997, Sept. 23   Litho.   Perf. 13½
1134	A476	350m multicolored	1.40	.85

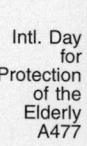

Intl. Day for Protection of the Elderly A477

1997, Oct. 1   Litho.   Perf. 13½
1135	A477	250m multicolored	.85	.40

Tunisian Works of Art — A478

#1136, "L'Automne," by Ammar Farhat. #1137, Sculpture, "Pecheur D'Hommes," by Hedi Selmi. #1138, "Au Cafe-Maure," by Farhat. #1139, "Le Viellard au Kanoun," by Farhat. #1140, "Cafe Des Nattes-Sidi Bou Said," by Hedi Khayachi. #1141, "Le Kouttab," by Yahia Turki. 1000d, "La Fileuse," by Farhat.

1997, Nov. 5
1136	A478	250m multi, vert.	.80	.55
1137	A478	250m multi, vert.	.80	.55
1138	A478	250m multi, vert.	.80	.55
1139	A478	250m multi, vert.	.80	.55
1140	A478	500m multi	1.60	1.10
1141	A478	500m multi	1.60	1.10
1142	A478	250m multi, vert.	3.50	2.25
a.		Sheet of 7, #1136-1142, + 3 labels	10.00	10.00
		Nos. 1136-1142 (7)	9.90	6.65

No. 1142a issued 11/7.

A479

A480

1997, Nov. 7
1143	A479	250m multicolored	.75	.40
1144	A480	500m multicolored	1.75	1.10

Pres. Zine El Abdine, 10th anniv. of taking office.

Desert Rose — A481

1997, Nov. 29
1145	A481	250m multicolored	1.10	.40

Intl. Human Rights Day — A482

1997, Dec. 10   Litho.   Perf. 13½
1146	A482	500m multicolored	1.50	.90

Horses A483

Designs: 50m, Arabian. 70m, Barb. 250m, Arabian barb, vert. 500m, Arabian, vert.

1997, Dec. 18   Perf. 12½x13
1147	A483	50m multicolored	.35	.25
1148	A483	70m multicolored	.35	.25
1149	A483	250m multicolored	1.00	.40
1150	A483	500m multicolored	2.00	.75
		Nos. 1147-1150 (4)	3.70	1.65

Bombing of Sakiet Sidi Yoncef, 40th Anniv. A484

1998, Feb. 8
1151	A484	250m multicolored	.85	.30

School Health Week A485

1998, Feb. 16   Litho.   Perf. 12½x13
1152	A485	250m multicolored	.85	.30

Bar Assoc. of Tunisia, Cent. — A486

1998, Mar. 27   Perf. 13x12½
1153	A486	250m multicolored	.85	.30

Martyr's Day, 60th Anniv.
A487   A488

1998, Apr. 9
1154	A487	250m multicolored	.75	.30
1155	A488	520m multicolored	1.60	.55

Okba Ibn Nafaa Mosque, Kairouan — A489

1998, May 28   Litho.   Perf. 13
1156	A489	500m multicolored	1.75	.60

1998 World Cup Soccer Championships, France — A490

250m, Tunisian team. 500m Player, trophy.

1998, June 10   Litho.   Perf. 13
1157	A490	250m multi	.85	.30
1158	A490	500m multi, vert.	1.90	.60

Crustaceans — A491

1998, July 8   Perf. 12½x13
1159	A491	110m Crab	.30	.25
1160	A491	250m Shrimp	.75	.30
1161	A491	1000m Lobster	3.00	1.10
		Nos. 1159-1161 (3)	4.05	1.65

21st Reassembly of the Democratic Congress (RCD) — A492

#1162, Pres. Zine El Abidine ben Ali, flag, emblems. #1163, People holding torches, flag, dove.

1998, July 30   Perf. 13
1162	A492	250m multi	.85	.30
1163	A492	250m multi, vert.	.85	.30

36th Intl. Congress on the History of Medicine — A493

1998, Sept. 6   Litho.   Perf. 13
1164	A493	500m multicolored	1.75	.60

Paintings — A494

#1165, "The Weaver," by Ali Guermassi (1923-92). #1166, "Woman Musician," by Noureddine Khayachi (1917-87). 500m, Still life by Ali Khouja (1947-91).

1998, Oct. 8
1165	A494	250m multi	.90	.30
1166	A494	250m multi, vert.	.90	.30
1167	A494	500m multi, vert.	1.75	.60
		Nos. 1165-1167 (3)	3.55	1.20

Central Bank of Tunisia, 40th Anniv. A495

1998, Nov. 10   Litho.   Perf. 13
1168	A495	250m multicolored	.85	.30

A496

1998, Nov. 7
1169	A496	250m multicolored	.85	.30

Appointment of Pres. Zine El Abidine ben Ali, 11th anniv.

Universal Declaration of Human Rights, 50th Anniv. A497

1998, Dec. 10 Litho. Perf. 12½x13
1170 A497 250m multicolored .85 .35

Averroes (Ibn Rushd) (1126-1198), Philosopher — A498

1998, Dec. 12
1171 A498 500m multicolored 1.75 .60

Musicians A499

1998, Dec. 21 Perf. 12½x13, 13x12½
1172 A499 250m Kaddour Srarfi .85 .30
1173 A499 250m Saliha, vert. .85 .30
1174 A499 500m Ali Riahi, vert. 1.75 .60
Nos. 1172-1174 (3) 3.45 1.20

Boukornine Natl. Park — A500

1998, Dec. 29 Litho. Perf. 13
1175 A500 70m Gazelles .35 .25
1176 A500 110m Rabbit .35 .25
1177 A500 250m Eagles .85 .30
1178 A500 500m Cyclamens 1.75 .60
Nos. 1175-1178 (4) 3.30 1.40

Fruit Trees A501

1999, Feb. 27 Litho. Perf. 13
1179 A501 250m Orange 1.00 .30
1180 A501 250m Date, vert. 1.00 .30
1181 A501 500m Olive 2.00 .60
Nos. 1179-1181 (3) 4.00 1.20

Archaeological Sites — A502

50m, Gate, Thuburbo Majus. 250m, Thermal baths, Bulla Regia. 500m, Zaghouan Aqueduct.

1999, Mar. 31 Litho. Perf. 13
1182 A502 50m multi, vert. .40 .25
1183 A502 250m multi .95 .30
1184 A502 500m multi 2.10 .60
Nos. 1182-1184 (3) 3.45 1.15

Paintings by Tunisian Artists A503

Designs: No. 1185, "L'Intemporel," by Moncef Ben Amor. No. 1186, "Fiancailles," by Ali Guermassi. No. 1187, "La Poterie," by Ammar Farhat. No. 1188, "Vendeur d'ombrelles et d'eventails," by Yahia Turki.

1999, May 6 Litho. Perf. 13
1185 A503 250m multicolored .85 .30
1186 A503 250m multicolored .85 .30
1187 A503 500m multicolored 1.60 .55
1188 A503 500m multicolored 1.60 .55
Nos. 1185-1188 (4) 4.90 1.70

Constitution, 40th Anniv. — A504

1999, June 1 Litho. Perf. 13
1189 A504 250m multicolored .85 .40

Flowers — A505

70m, Acacia cyanophilla. #1191, Bouganvillea spectabilis. #1192, Papaver rhoeas. 500m, Dianthus caryophylius.

1999, June 25 Litho. Perf. 12¾
1190 A505 70m multicolored .35 .25
1191 A505 250m multicolored .85 .30
1192 A505 250m multicolored .85 .30
1193 A505 500m multicolored 1.90 .70
a. Souvenir sheet, #1190-1193, imperf. 8.25 8.25
Nos. 1190-1193 (4) 3.95 1.55
No. 1193a sold for 1.50d.

Philex France 99 — A506

1999, July 2 Perf. 13x12¾
1194 A506 500m multicolored 2.50 .85

Tahar Haddad (b. 1899), Women's Rights Advocate — A507

1999, Aug. 13 Litho.
1195 A507 500m multicolored 2.50 .85

Marine Life A508

250m, Caretta caretta. 500m, Epinephelus marginatus.

1999, Sept. 22 Perf. 12¾
1196 A508 250m multi .90 .90
1197 A508 500m multi 1.75 1.75

National Organ Donation Day — A509

1999, Oct. 2 Perf. 13x12¾
1198 A509 250m multicolored 1.10 .45

UPU, 125th Anniv. — A510

1999, Oct. 9 Perf. 12¾
1199 A510 500m multicolored 2.00 .75

Elections — A511

1999, Oct. 10 Litho.
1200 A511 500m multicolored 2.25 .85

Tamarisk A512

1999, Oct. 28 Litho. Perf. 12¾x13
1201 A512 250m shown 1.10 .35
1202 A512 500m Dromedary 2.25 .75

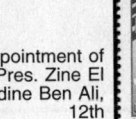

Appointment of Pres. Zine El Abidine Ben Ali, 12th Anniv. — A513

1999, Nov. 7 Perf. 13x12¾
1203 A513 250m multi 1.00 .45

Human Rights Day — A514

1999, Dec. 10 Litho. Perf. 13x12¾
1204 A514 250m multi 1.75 .45

Famous Tunisians — A515

No. 1205, Ahmed Ibn Abi Dhiaf (1802-74), historian. No. 1206, Abdelaziz Thaalbi (1876-1944), anti-colonial leader. 500m, Khemaies Tarnane (1894-1964), musician.

1999, Dec. 28 Perf. 13x12¾, 12¾x13
1205 A515 250m multi .85 .35
1206 A515 250m multi .85 .35
1207 A515 500m multi, horiz. 1.60 .75
Nos. 1205-1207 (3) 3.30 1.45

Millennium — A516

1999, Dec. 31 Perf. 13
1208 A516 250m multi .90 .45

A517

A518

Archaeology
A519

Design: 100m, Methred cup. 110m, Aghla-bide plate. 250m, Zaghouan water temple. 500m, Ulysses and the Sirens mosaic.

2000, Apr. 22   Litho.   Perf. 13x13¼
1209 A517 100m multi   .40   .35
1210 A517 110m multi   .50   .45
            Perf. 13¼
1211 A518 250m multi   1.20 1.00
1212 A519 500m multi   2.40 2.00
      Nos. 1209-1212 (4)   4.50 3.80

Ferry Carthage — A520

2000, Apr. 29   Perf. 13¼x13
1213 A520 500m multi   1.90   .80
  a.   Souvenir sheet, imperf.   6.00 3.00
      No. 1213a sold for 2d.

Expo 2000, Hanover — A521

2000, June 1   Perf. 13¼x13
1214 A521 1d multi   3.50 1.75

Trees
A522

Designs: 50m, Carob. 100m, Apricot. 250m, Avocado, vert. 400m, Apple.

2000, July 5   Litho.   Perf. 12¾
1215-1218 A522 Set of 4   3.00 1.50

2001 Mediterranean Games,
Tunis — A523

2000, Sept. 2   Litho.   Perf. 13
1219 A523 500m multi   1.75   .80
  a.   Souvenir sheet of 1, imperf. 3.75 1.90
      No. 1219a sold for 1500m.

2000 Summer
Olympics,
Sydney — A524

2000, Sept. 22   Perf. 12¾
1220 A524 500m multi   1.75   .80
      Souvenir Sheet
             Imperf
1221 A524 1500m multi   6.00 1.90

Flowers — A525

Designs: 110m, Freesias. 200m, Chrysanthemums. No. 1224, 250m, "Golden Times" roses. No. 1225, 250m, Vase with flowers (33x49mm). 500m, "Calibra" roses.

2000, Oct. 21   Perf. 12¾, 13 (#1225)
1222-1226 A525 Set of 5   4.75 2.40

Appointment
of Pres. Zine
El Abidine
Ben Ali, 13th
Anniv.
A526

2000, Nov. 7   Perf. 13
1227 A526 250m multi   1.00   .50

Art — A527

Designs: 100m, Still Life, by Hédi Khayachi. No. 1229, 250m, Landscape, by Abdelaziz Berraies. No. 1230, 250m, The Knife Sharpener, by Ali Guermassi. 400m, Date and Milk Seller, by Yahia Turki, vert.

2000, Nov. 18
1228-1231 A527 Set of 4   3.50 1.50

Intl. Human
Rights
Day — A528

2000, Dec. 10
1232 A528 500m multi   1.75   .85

Shells — A529

Designs: 50m, Neverita josephinia. No. 1234, 250m, Phyllonotus trunculus. No. 1235, 250m, Columbella rustica. 1d, Arca noe.

2000, Dec. 29   Perf. 13x13¼
1233-1236 A529 Set of 4   8.00 2.50

A530

Famous
Tunisians
A531

Designs: No. 1237, 250m, Imam Sahnoun. No. 1238, 250m, Imam Ibn Arafa. No. 1239, 250m, Ali Belhaouane (1909-58), vert. 1d, Mohamed Jamoussi (1910-82), musician.

2000, Dec. 30   Perf. 12¾
1237 A530 250m shown   .85   .35
1238 A530 250m multi   .85   .35
1239 A531 250m multi   .85   .35
1240 A531 1d shown   3.50 1.50
      Nos. 1237-1240 (4)   6.05 2.55

Tunisian Presidency of UN Security
Council — A532

2001, Feb. 19   Litho.   Perf. 13
1241 A532 250m multi   1.10   .55

World Fund of
Solidarity
A533

2001, Mar. 29
1242 A533 500m multi   1.75   .80

Year of Digital
Culture — A534

2001, May 17   Perf. 12¾
1243 A534 250m multi   1.10   .55

Mohamed Dorra, Child Killed in Israeli-
Palestinian Violence — A535

2001, May 30
1244 A535 600m multi   2.25 1.10

A536   A537

Designs: No. 1245, 19th cent. ceramic tile, Qallaline. No. 1246, Gigthis, horiz. No. 1247, Tunis City Hall, horiz. 500m, Needles of Tabarka.

2001, Aug. 24
1245 A536 250m multi   .60   .25
1246 A537 250m multi   .60   .25
1247 A537 250m multi   .60   .25
1248 A537 500m multi   1.20   .50
      Nos. 1245-1248 (4)   3.00 1.25

2001
Mediterranean
Games,
Tunis — A538

Designs: No. 1249, 250m, No. 1251b, Track, stadium. No. 1250, 500m, No. 1251a, Runners, medal.

2001, Sept. 2   Perf. 12¾
1249-1250 A538 Set of 2   1.75   .75
      Souvenir Sheet
             Imperf
1251 A538 750m Sheet of 2,
            #a-b   3.00 1.50

Paintings — A539

Designs: No. 1252, 250m, Sidi Bou Said, by Pierre Boucherle. No. 1253, 250m, Still Life, by Boucherle. No. 1254, 250m, Dream in Traditional Space, by Aly Ben Salem, vert. 500m, Traditional Open-air Marriage, by Ben Salem.

2001, Sept. 29   Litho.   Perf. 13
1252-1255 A539 Set of 4   3.00 1.40

Year of Dialogue Among Civilizations A540

2001, Oct. 9   **Perf. 12¾x13**
1256 A540 500m multi   2.00 .55

National Employment Fund — A541

2001, Oct. 10
1257 A541 250m multi   .60 .30

Appointment of Pres. Zine El Abidine Ben Ali, 14th Anniv. — A542

2001, Nov. 7   **Perf. 13x12¾**
1258 A542 250m multi   .60 .30

Butterflies — A543

Designs: Nos. 1259, 1263a, 250m, Ariane. No. 1260, 250m, No. 1263c, 500m, Pacha à deux queues. Nos. 1261, 1263b, 250m, Demi-deuil. Nos. 1262, 1263d, 500m, Grand paon de nuit.

2001, Nov. 15   **Perf. 13x13¼**
1259-1262 A543   Set of 4   3.00 1.50
Souvenir Sheet
Imperf
1263 A543   Sheet of 4, #a-d   3.50 1.75

Birds — A544

Designs: No. 1264, 250m, No. 1268a, 300m, Bec-croise des sapins. 500m, Mesange charbonnière. No. 1266, 600m, Cigogne blanche. No. 1267, 600m, Geai des chenes.

2001, Nov. 22   **Perf. 13**
1264-1267 A544   Set of 4   4.50 2.25
Souvenir Sheet
1268 A544   Sheet, #1265-1267, 1268a   5.50 2.50

Intl. Human Rights Day — A545

2001, Dec. 10   **Perf. 13x12¾**
1269 A545 250m multi   .60 .30

Famous Men A546

Designs: No. 1270, 250m, Ibrahim ibn al-Aghlab (757-812), founder of Aghlabid dynasty. No. 1271, 250m, Ibn Rachiq al Kairaouani (1000-71). 350m, Abdelaziz Laroui (1898-1971). 650m, Assad ibn al-Fourat (759-828).

2001, Dec. 29   **Perf. 12¾x13**
1270-1273 A546   Set of 4   3.25 1.60

Arabic Calligraphy A547

Designs: No. 1274, 350m, Shown. No. 1275, 350m, Calligraphy, vert.

2001, Dec. 31   **Perf. 12¾x13, 13x12¾**
1274-1275 A547   Set of 2   2.00 1.10

Archaeology
A548   A549

Designs: 250m, Kef casbah. 390m, Amphitheater, Oudhna, horiz. No. 1278, Baron of Erlanger Palace. No. 1279, Mosaic of Virgil.

Perf. 13x12¾, 12¾x13
2002, Mar. 26   **Litho.**
1276 A548 250m multi   .60 .25
1277 A548 390m multi   .95 .40
1278 A549 600m multi   1.40 .60
1279 A549 600m multi   1.40 .60
   Nos. 1276-1279 (4)   4.35 1.85

Animals of Zembra and Zembretta Natl. Park — A550

Designs: No. 1280, 250m, No. 1284a, 400m, Ovis musimon. No. 1281, 250m, No. 1284b, 400m, Oryctolagus cuniculus. No. 1282, 600m, Falco peregrinus brookei. No. 1283, 600m, Larus audouinii.

2002, Apr. 10   **Perf. 13**
1280-1283 A550   Set of 4   4.50 1.75
Souvenir Sheet
1284 A550   Sheet, #1282-1283, 1284a-1284b   5.50 1.90

Sahara Desert Tourism A551

Designs: No. 1285, 250m, No. 1289a, 400m, Gazella leptoceros. No. 1286, 390m, No. 1289b, 400m, Sahara village. No. 1287, 600m, Horseman. No. 1288, 600m, Tamaghza.

2002, May 22   **Perf. 13¼**
1285-1288 A551   Set of 4   4.00 1.90

Souvenir Sheet
1289 A551   Sheet, #1287-1288, 1289a-1289b, imperf.   5.00 2.00

2002 World Cup Soccer Championships, Japan and Korea — A552

World Cup, Emblem of Tunisia and World Cup tournament and: No. 1290, 390m, No. 1292a, 500m, Player, map of Japan and Korea. No. 1291, 600m, 1292b, 1000m, Ball in goal net.

2002, May 29   **Perf. 13**
1290-1291 A552   Set of 2   2.50 1.00
Souvenir Sheet
1292 A552   Sheet of 2, #a-b   4.00 1.50

Famous Men — A553

Designs: 100m, Sheikh Mohamed Senoussi (1851-1900). No. 1294, 250m, Mosbah Jarbou (1914-58). No. 1295, 250m, Mohamed Daghbaji (1885-1924). 1.10d, Abou al-Hassen al-Housri (1029-95).

2002, July 18   **Perf. 12¾**
1293-1296 A553   Set of 4   4.00 1.75

World Handicapped Games — A554

Tunisian flag and: 100m, Wheelchair racer. 700m, Discus thrower, vert.

2002, July 20   Set of 2   1.75 .85
1297-1298 A554

27th World Veterinary Congress, Tunis A555

2002, Sept. 25   **Litho. Perf. 12¾**
1299 A555 600m multi   1.50 .60

Travel International Club, 20th Anniv. — A556

2002, Oct. 25   **Litho. Perf. 13x13¼**
1300 A556 600m multi   1.50 .60

Appointment of Pres. Zine El Abidine Ben Ali, 15th Anniv. — A557

2002, Nov. 7   **Perf. 13x12¾**
1301 A557 390m multi   .95 .40

Assassination of Farhat Hached (1914-52) — A558

2002, Dec. 3   **Litho. Perf. 13x12¾**
1302 A558 390m multi   .95 .40

Intl. Human Rights Day — A559

2002, Dec. 10
1303 A559 700m multi   1.75 .75

Art Type of 2001

Designs: No. 1304, 250m, Space for Gazelles, by Aly Ben Salem. No. 1305, 250m, Popular Arts, by Ammar Farhat, vert. No. 1306, 250m, Marriage, by Hablb Bouabana, vert. 900m, Still Life, by Pierre Boucherle, vert.

2002, Dec. 28   **Perf. 13**
1304-1307 A539   Set of 4   4.00 1.75

Mosaics A560

Designs: 390m, Spinner. 600m, Africa.

2003, Feb. 28   Set of 2   2.40 1.00
1308-1309 A560

Scouting in Tunisia, 70th Anniv. — A561

"70" and scouts: 250m, Reading map, at computer, planting tree. 600m, Saluting flag, at computer, vert.

2003, Mar. 29   **Litho. Perf. 13**
1310-1311 A561   Set of 2   1.90 .85

National Book
Year — A562

2003, Apr. 23
1312 A562 390m multi   .95 .40

The Washerwoman, by Yahia
Turki — A563

2003, June 13
1313 A563 1d multi   2.40 1.00

National
Tourism
Day — A564

2003, June 28   *Perf. 13¼*
1314 A564 600m multi   1.50 .60

Parks — A565

Designs: 200m, Farhat Hached Park,
Rades. 250m, Friguia Animal Park. 390m, La
Marsa Park. 1d, Ennahli Park.

2003, June 28   *Perf. 13*
1315-1318 A565 Set of 4   4.00 2.00

Congress of
Ambition — A566

2003, July 28 **Litho.** *Perf. 13x12¾*
1319 A566 250m multi   .70 .35

A567

2003, Aug. 3
1320 A567 390m multi   .95 .45
Pres. Habib Bourguiba (1903-2000).

A568

Flora and Fauna — A569

Designs: Nos. 1321a, 50m, 1326, 600m,
Oryx dammah. Nos. 1321b, 50m, 1324, 250m,
Nyctanthes sambac. Nos. 1321c, 100m, 1323,
250m, Aries. Nos. 1321d, 100m, 1327, 1d,
Myrtus communis. Nos. 1321e, 200m, 1325,
390m, Struthio camelus. Nos. 1321f, 200m,
1322, 100m, Rosa canina.

2003, Sept. 25   *Perf. 12¾*
1321   Strip of 6   3.50 .80
 a.-b. A568 50m Either single   .50 .25
 c.-d. A568 100m Either single   .50 .25
 e.-f. A568 200m Either single   .90 .25
1322-1327 A569 Set of 6   5.75 2.75
No. 1321 was issued in a sheet of 6 strips
that sold for 4500m.

Appointment of
Pres. Zine El
Abidine Ben Ali,
16th Anniv. — A570

2003, Nov. 7 **Litho.** *Perf. 13x12¾*
1328 A570 250m multi   .60 .30

First 5+5
Dialogue
Summit,
Tunis — A571

2003, Dec. 5   *Perf. 13¼*
1329 A571 600m multi   1.40 .60

Universal
Declaration of
Human
Rights — A572

2003, Dec. 10   *Perf. 13x12¾*
1330 A572 350m multi   .85 .35

Silver Items
A573

Designs: No. 1331, 600m, Machmoum. No.
1332, 600m, Jewelry.

2003, Dec. 18   *Perf. 12¾x13*
1331-1332 A573 Set of 2   2.75 1.25
 1332a   Souvenir sheet, #1331-
            1332   4.50 2.50
No. 1332a sold for 1.50d.

African Soccer
Championships — A574

Designs: 250m, Stylized soccer players,
African cup, map. 600m, Map of Africa as soccer player.

2004, Jan. 24   *Perf. 13*
1333-1334 A574 Set of 2   1.90 .95
Values are for stamps with surrounding
selvage.

Ksar Helal
Congress, 70th
Anniv. — A575

2004, Mar. 2 **Litho.** *Perf. 13x12¾*
1335 A575 250m multi   .60 .30

Arab League
Conference,
Tunis
A576

2004, May 22   *Perf. 13*
1336 A576 600m multi   2.50 .60

Copper Handicrafts — A577

Designs: 100m, Water jar, 18th cent. 200m,
Ewer, 18th cent. 250m, Bucket, 19th cent.
600m, Brazier, 18th cent. 700m, Amphora,
18th cent. 1000m, Ewer, 19th cent.

2004, June 5   *Perf. 13x13¼*
1337-1342 A577 Set of 6   6.25 3.00
1343   Sheet, 3 each #1337,
              1338, 1343a-1343d 7.50 3.75
 a. A577 50m Like #1340   .25 .25
 b. A577 150m Like #1342   .30 .25
 c. A577 250m Like #1341   .60 .30
 d. A577 300m Like #1339   .70 .35
No. 1343 sold for 3500m.

Coins and
Banknotes
A578

Designs: No. 1344, 250m, Gold coin, 706.
No. 1345, 250m, Gold coin, 1767. No. 1346,
600m, Punic silver coin, 300 B.C. No. 1347,
600m, Punic gold coin, 310-290 B.C. 1000m,
Banknote, 1847 (65x30mm).

2004, July 23   *Perf. 13¼*
1344-1348 A578 Set of 5   5.75 2.75
 1348a   Souvenir sheet, #1344-
            1348 + label   5.75 2.75
No. 1348a sold for 3000m.

African
Development
Bank, 40th
Anniv.
A579

2004, Sept. 10 **Litho.** *Perf. 13*
1349 A579 700m multi   1.50 .75

Children's Art — A580

2004, Oct. 20
1350 A580 250m multi   .60 .30

Presidential
and
Legislative
Elections
A581

2004, Oct. 24
1351 A581 250m multi   .60 .30

Appointment of Pres. Zine El Abidine Ben Ali, 17th Anniv. A582

2004, Nov. 7
1352 A582 250m multi .60 .30

El Abidine Mosque, Carthage — A583

2004, Nov. 11
1353 A583 250m multi .60 .00

Birds — A584

Designs: 100m, Oxyura leucocephala. No. 1355, 600m, Phoenicurus moussieri. No. 1356, 600m, Aythya nyroca. 1000m, Marmaronetta angustirostris.

2004, Nov. 20 **Perf. 13¼**
1354-1357 A584 Set of 4 6.00 2.50

Universal Declaration of Human Rights — A585

2004, Dec. 10 **Perf. 13x12¾**
1358 A585 350m multi .75 .35

Famous People A586

Designs: 250m, Ibn Chabbat (1221-85), writer. 500m, Ibn Charaf (1000-67), writer. No. 1361, 600m, Princess Elyssa. No. 1362, 600m, Hatem El Mekki (1918-2003), stamp designer, and #580, 619. No. 1363, 600m, Dr. Mongi Ben Hmida (1928-2002), neurologist.

2004, Dec. 18 **Perf. 12¾x13**
1359-1363 A586 Set of 5 6.00 2.75

World Handball Championships — A587

2005, Jan. 23 **Perf. 13**
1364 A587 600m multi 1.40 .60

Native Costumes — A588

Designs: 250m, Takhlila, Hammam Sousse. No. 1366, 390m, Tarf-Ras ceremonial costume, Kerkennah. No. 1367, 390m, Karmassoud jebba. 600m, Traditional bridal costume, Matmata.

2005, Mar. 16 **Perf. 13x12¾**
1365-1368 A588 Set of 4 3.75 1.75

World Summit on the Information Society, Tunis A589

2005, Apr. 7 **Litho.** **Perf. 13**
1369 A589 600m multi 1.40 .60

Sculptures of the Punic and Roman Eras — A590

Designs: No. 1370, 250m, Victory, 2nd cent. No. 1371, 250m, Aesculapius, 2nd-3rd cent. 600m, Pottery mask of a woman's face, 4th-5th cent. B.C. 1000m, Baal Ammon, 1st cent.

2005, May 18 **Perf. 13¼**
1370-1373 A590 Set of 4 5.00 2.25

World No Tobacco Day — A591

2005, May 31 **Perf. 13¼x13**
1374 A591 250m multi .60 .30

Rotary International, Cent. — A592

2005, June 22 **Perf. 13x12¾**
1375 A592 600m multi 1.50 .60

Intl. Year of Sport and Physical Education — A593

2005, July 1
1376 A593 600m multi 1.50 .60

World Scout Conference A594

2005, Sept. 5
1377 A594 600m multi 1.50 .60

Intl. Year of Physics A595

2005, Oct. 15 **Litho.** **Perf. 13**
1378 A595 2d multi 5.00 2.00

Appointment of Pres. Zine El Abidine Ben Ali, 18th Anniv. A596

2005, Nov. 8
1379 A596 250m multi .60 .25

World Summit on the Information Society, Tunis — A597

2005, Nov. 12 **Litho.** **Perf. 13¼x13**
1380 A597 600m multi .90 .45

Universal Declaration of the Rights of Man, 57th Anniv. A598

2005, Dec. 10 **Litho.** **Perf. 13**
1381 A598 350m multi 1.10 .55

Medicinal Plants — A599

Designs: 250m, Foeniculum. No. 1383, 600m, Mentha aquatica. No. 1384, 600m, Lavandula angustifloia. 1000m, Origanum majorana.

2005, Dec. 22
1382-1385 A599 Set of 4 5.50 2.50
1386 Booklet pane, 2 each #1383-1384, 1386a, 1386b 9.75 —
a. A599 600m Like #1382 1.40 .60
b. A599 600m Like #1385 1.40 .60
Complete booklet, #1386 11.00

Ibn Khaldun (1332-1406), Philosopher A600

2006, Mar. 15 **Litho.** **Perf. 13x12¾**
1387 A600 390m multi 1.00 .45

A601

Independence, 50th Anniv. — A602

Designs: No. 1390, Stylized map and flag, doctor examining child. No. 1391, Bridge and ship. No. 1392, Stylized woman holding torch.

No. 1393, Woman and book. No. 1394, Computer, man, woman, "@," and stylized dove.

2006, Mar. 18   *Perf. 13x12¾, 12¾x13*
1388	A601	250m shown	.65	.30
1389	A602	250m shown	.65	.30
1390	A601	250m multi	.65	.30
1391	A601	250m multi	.65	.30
1392	A601	390m multi	.85	.40
1393	A601	390m multi	.85	.40
1394	A601	390m multi	.85	.40
a.		Souvenir sheet, #1388-1394, + 2 labels	6.00	6.00
		Nos. 1388-1394 (7)	5.15	2.40

No. 1394a sold for 2.50d.

Dialogue Among Civilizations and Religions A603

2006, Apr. 26   Litho.   *Perf. 13½*
1395   A603   1.35d multi   3.00   1.40

Punic and Roman Era Jewelry A604

Designs: No. 1396, 250m, Gold and garnet vestment clasps. No. 1397, 250m, Gold-plated bronze earrings. No. 1398, 600m, Ring depicting god Baal Hammon. No. 1399, 600m, Gold and amethyst pendants.

2006, May 18   Litho.   *Perf. 13¼*
1396-1399   A604   Set of 4   4.25   1.90

Special Handicapped Employment Program — A605

2006, May 29   *Perf. 13*
1400   A605   2.35d multi   5.50   2.25

National Cleanliness and Environmental Protection Program — A606

2006, June 11
1401   A606   250m multi   .85   .30

2006 World Cup Soccer Championships, Germany — A607

Map, flags of Germany and Tunisia and: 250m, Feet of soccer players. 600m, Soccer player.

2006, June 14
1402-1403   A607   Set of 2   2.10   .95

Tunisian Army, 50th Anniv. A608

2006, June 24
1404   A608   250m multi   .65   .30

Diplomatic Relations Between Tunisia and Japan, 50th Anniv. A609

2006, July 7
1405   A609   700m multi   1.60   .70

Vacation Safety Program — A610

2006, July 31
1406   A610   250m multi   .65   .30

Personal Status Code, 50th Anniv. A611

2006, Aug. 8
1407   A611   2.35d multi   5.25   2.25

Appointment of Pres. Zine El Abidine Ben Ali, 19th Anniv. A612

2006, Nov. 7
1408   A612   250m multi   .75   .30

Universal Declaration of Human Rights — A613

2006, Dec. 10
1409   A613   700m multi   1.60   .70

Traditional Clothing and Textiles A614

Designs: No. 1410, 250m, Jelwa (wedding dress). No. 1411, 250m, Silk jebba. 1.10d, Klim. 1.35d, Woolen blanket from Gafsa.

2007, Mar. 16   Litho.   *Perf. 13*
1410-1413   A614   Set of 4   8.00   3.25

Independence, 51st Anniv. — A615

2007, Mar. 20
1414   A615   250m multi   .75   .30

Youth and Digital Culture A616

2007, Mar. 21
1415   A616   250m multi   1.25   .30

Natl. Energy Conservation Program A617

2007, Apr. 7
1416   A617   1d multi   3.00   1.00

Dialogue Between Cultures, Civilizations and Religions A618

2007, May 7   Litho.   *Perf. 13*
1417   A618   600m multi   1.75   .60

Archaeological Sites — A619

Designs: No. 1418, 250m, Baths of Caracalla, Dougga. No. 1419, 250m, Punic city of Kerkouane. No. 1420, 600m, Baths, Makthar. No. 1421, 600m, Capitol, Sbeitla.

2007, May 18   *Perf. 13½*
1418-1421   A619   Set of 4   4.50   1.90

Carthage Investment Forum — A620

2007, June 21   *Perf. 13*
1422   A620   600m multi   1.60   .60

National Tourism Day — A621

Designs: No. 1423, 250m, Sahara tourism. No. 1424, 250m, Beach tourism. No. 1425, 600m, Tabarka Jazz Festival. No. 1426, 600m, Golf tourism.

2007, June 28
1423-1426   A621   Set of 4   5.00   1.90

A622

Republic of Tunisia, 50th Anniv. A623

2007, July 25 Litho. *Perf. 13*
1427 A622 250m multi .75 .30
1428 A623 250m multi .75 .30

Appointment of Pres. Zine El Abidine Ben Ali, 20th Anniv. A624

2007, Nov. 7 Litho. *Perf. 13*
1429 A624 250m multi .75 .30

Friendship Between Germany and Tunisia, 50th Anniv. A625

2007, Dec. 17
1430 A625 600m multi 1.75 .60

Intl. Human Solidarity Day — A626

2007, Dec. 20
1431 A626 1.35d multi 3.50 1.50

French Air Raid on Sakiet Sidi Youssef, 50th Anniv. A627

2008, Feb. 8 Litho. *Perf. 13*
1432 A627 250m multi .75 .30

Government Accounting Board, 40th Anniv. — A628

2008, Mar. 8 Litho. *Perf. 13*
1433 A628 250m multi .60 .25

Universal Declaration of Human Rights, 60th Anniv. — A629

2008, Mar. 10
1434 A629 600m multi 1.25 .55

World Meteorological Day — A630

2008, Mar. 23
1435 A630 250m multi .75 .25

Terra Cotta Objects — A631

Designs: 250m, Water jug, 19th cent. No. 1437, 600m, Goblet, 3rd cent. B.C. No. 1438, 600m, Plate, 10th cent. B.C. 1.10d, Lamp, 1st cent. B.C.

2008, May 18 *Perf. 13x12¾*
1436-1439 A631 Set of 4 6.00 3.00

National Day of the Disabled A632

2008, May 29 *Perf. 13*
1440 A632 250m multi .65 .25

Fish — A633

Designs: No. 1441, 250m, Mugil cephalus. No. 1442, 250m, Thunnus thynnus. No. 1443, 600m, Sparus aurata. No. 1444, 600m, Dicentrarchus labrax.

2008, June 5 Litho. *Perf. 13x13¼*
1441-1444 A633 Set of 4 4.00 2.00
1444a As #1444, with incomplete frame lines 3.00 .55
1444b Souvenir sheet, #1441-1443, 1444a 5.00 5.00

No. 1444b sold for 1.800d.

Democratic Constitutional Rally — A634

2008, July 30 *Perf. 13*
1445 A634 250m multi .60 .25

Souvenir Sheet

Arab Post Day — A635

No. 1446 — Emblem and: a, World map, pigeon. b, Camel caravan.

2008, Aug. 3 *Perf. 12¾*
1446 A635 600m Sheet of 2, #a-b 3.50 1.00

2008 Summer Olympics, Beijing A636

Olympic rings, star and crescent, emblem of 2008 Summer Olympics, symbols of athletic events and: No. 1447, 250m, Colored dots and ribbons. No. 1448, 600m, Starbursts.

2008, Aug. 8 *Perf. 13½*
1447-1448 A636 Set of 2 2.00 1.00
1448a Souvenir sheet of 2 #1447-1448 2.00 2.00

No. 1448a sold for 900m.

Dialogue With Youth A637

2008, Sept. 20 Litho. *Perf. 13¼*
1449 A637 250m multi .75 .40

Appointment of Pres. Zine El Abidine Ben Ali, 21st Anniv. A638

2008, Nov. 7 *Perf. 13x13¼*
1450 A638 250m multi .60 .30

University of Tunisia, 50th Anniv. — A639

2008, Nov. 11 *Perf. 13¼x13*
1451 A639 250m multi .70 .35

Famous Men A640

Designs: No. 1452, 250m, Ridha El Kalai (1931-2004), musician. No. 1453, 250m, Ammar Farhat (1911-87), painter. No. 1454, 600m, Mahmoud Messadi (1911-2004), writer. No. 1455, 600m, Hedi Jouini (1909-90), musician.

2008, Dec. 20 *Perf. 12¾x13, 13x12¾*
1452-1455 A640 Set of 4 3.50 1.75

Arab Maghreb Union, 20th Anniv. — A641

2009, Feb. 17 Litho. *Perf. 13*
1456 A641 250m multi .50 .25

Aboul Qasem Chebbi (1909-34), Poet — A642

2009, Feb. 24 *Perf. 12¾*
1457 A642 250m multi .50 .25

Kairouan, 2009 Islamic Cultural Capital — A643

Designs: No. 1458, 250m, Mausoleum of Abi Zamaa al-Balawi. No. 1459, 250m, Okba Ibn Nafaa Mosque. 1000m, Emblem.

2009, Mar. 8
1458-1460 A643   Set of 3   3.00 1.50
1460a   Souvenir sheet, #1458-1460   3.00 3.00

Woven Fiber Crafts — A644

Designs: No. 1461, 250m, Esparto basket and jug holder. No. 1462, 250m, Rattan mat. No. 1463, 600m, Palm fiber fan. No. 1464, 600m, Rattan basket.

2009, Mar. 16   **Perf. 13¼**
1461-1464 A644   Set of 4   2.50 1.25

Intl. Society for Military Law and the Law of War, 18th Congress A645

2009, May 5   **Litho.**   **Perf. 13**
1465 A645 700m multi   1.25 .65

Constitution, 50th Anniv. — A646

2009, June 1
1466 A646 250m multi   .90 .45

Fruit — A647

Designs: 250m, Eryobotrica japonica. No. 1468, 600m, Cerasus spp. No. 1469, 600m, Ficus carica. No. 1470, 600m, Prunus persica.

2009, June 5   **Perf. 13¼**
1467-1470 A647   Set of 4   3.50 1.75
1470a   Sheet of 4, #1467-1470   3.50 3.50

No. 1470a sold for 2.10d.

16th Mediterranean Games, Pescara, Italy — A648

2009, June 26   **Litho.**   **Perf. 13**
1471 A648 600m multi   1.00 .50

Presidential and Legislative Elections A649

2009, Oct. 25   **Litho.**   **Perf. 13x13¼**
1472 A649 250m multi   .90 .45

Appointment of Pres. Zine El Abidine Ben Ali, 22nd Anniv. A650

2009, Nov. 7
1473 A650 390m multi   .90 .45

Universal Declaration of Human Rights, 61st Anniv. A651

2009, Dec. 10
1474 A651 1.35d multi   2.50 1.25

Tunisian Cuisine A652

Designs: 250m, Tajine à la viande (meat tagine). 700m, Salade mechouia (grilled vegetable salad). 1000m, Poisson grillé (grilled fish). 1100m, Couscous à la viande (couscous with meat).

2009, Dec. 26   **Perf. 13¼**
1475-1478 A652   Set of 4   6.00 3.00
1478a   Souvenir sheet of 4, #1475-1478   7.00 7.00

Arab Women's Day — A653

2010, Feb. 1   **Perf. 13¼x13**
1479 A653 1350m multi   3.00 1.50

Intl. Year of Rapprochement of Cultures — A654

2010, Feb. 6   **Perf. 13x13¼**
1480 A654 2350m multi   5.00 2.50

Intl. Youth Year — A655

2010, Mar. 21   **Perf. 13¼x13**
1481 A655 390m multi   .90 .45

Expo 2010, Shanghai A656

2010, May 1   **Perf. 13¼**
1482 A656 390m multi   .90 .45

Organic Foods and Food Products A657

Designs: No. 1483, 250m, Cynara scolymus. No. 1484, 250m, Prunus dulcis. No. 1485, 250m, Punica granatum. No. 1486, 600m, Capsicum annuum. No. 1487, 600m, Opuntia ficus-indica. No. 1488, 600m, Solanum lycopersicum. No. 1489, 600m, Olea europaea and picher of olive oil. No. 1490, 600m, Phoenix dactylifera.

2010, May 12
1483-1490 A657   Set of 8   7.00 3.50
1490a   Souvenir sheet, #1483-1490   7.00 7.00

Tunisia, a Technological Pole — A658

2010, May 17   **Perf. 13**
1491 A658 390m multi   .90 .45

Year of Peace and Security in Africa A659

2010, June 25
1492 A659 250m multi   .90 .45

Landmarks in Medina of Tunis — A660

Designs: No. 1493, 250m, Bab El Khadra. No. 1494, 250m, Bab Jedid. No. 1495, 250m, Dar Hsine. No. 1496, 250m, Dar Ben Abdallah. 600m, Bab Bhar. 1000m, Bab Saâdoun.

2010, July 2   **Perf. 12¾**
1493-1498 A660   Set of 6   4.00 2.00

2010 Youth Olympics, Singapore A661

2010, Aug. 4   **Perf. 13**
1499 A661 700m multi   1.10 .55

Famous Men — A662

Designs: 250m, Zoubeir Turki (1924-2009), painter. 600m, Jaâfar Majed (1940-2009), poet. 1000m, Ali Ben Salem (1910-2001), painter. 1100m, Mustapha Khraief (1910-67), poet.

2010, Oct. 10   **Perf. 12¾**
1500-1503 A662   Set of 4   4.50 2.25

Third Congress of Organization of
Arab Women, Tunis — A663

2010, Oct. 28   *Perf. 13*
1504 A663 1350m multi   2.25 1.00

Appointment
of Pres. Zine
El Abidine
Ben Ali, 23rd
Anniv.
A664

2010, Nov. 7
1505 A664 390m multi   .90 .45

National
Year of
Tunisian
Cinema
A665

2010, Nov. 27   *Litho.*
1506 A665 390m multi   .90 .45

Universal
Declaration
of Human
Rights, 62nd
Anniv.
A666

2010, Dec. 10
1507 A666 390m multi   .90 .45

A667

A668

A669

Revolution of
2010-11
A670

2011, Mar. 25   *Litho.*   *Perf. 13*
1508 A667 250m multi   .65 .35
1509 A668 390m multi   .90 .45
1510 A669 600m multi   1.40 .70
1511 A670 1350m multi   3.00 1.50
        Nos. 1508-1511 (4)   5.95 3.00

World Book
and
Copyright
Day — A671

2011, Apr. 23
1512 A671 2350m multi   4.50 2.25

World Press
Freedom
Day — A672

2011, May 3
1513 A672 250m multi   1.25 .40

Children's Art — A673

Designs: 700m, I Love My Country, by
Syrine Zouari. 1350m, Spring, by Mustapha
Gader, vert.

2011, May 20   *Perf. 13*
1514-1515 A673 Set of 2   4.75 2.50

Medicinal
Plants
A674

Designs: No. 1516, 250m, Allium sativum.
No. 1517, 250m, Pimpinella anisum. 600m,
Lippia tryphilla. 1000m, Rosemarinus
officinalis.

2011, June 28   *Perf. 13¼*
1516-1519 A674 Set of 4   5.25 2.75

Phila Nippon
2011 Intl.
Philatelic
Exhibition,
Yokahama,
Japan
A675

2011, July 28
1520 A675 250m multi   .65 .30

Human
Rights
Day — A676

2011, Dec. 10   *Perf. 13*
1521 A676 390m multi   .80 .40

January 14
Revolution,
1st Anniv.
A677

2012, Jan. 14
1522 A677 390m multi   1.60 .80

Pottery
A678

Designs: Nos. 1523, 1527a, 250m, Maajina
plate. Nos. 1524, 1527b, 600m, Borniya jar.
Nos. 1525, 1527c, 900m, Charbiya jug. Nos.
1526, 1527d, 1000m, Quallaline receptacle.

2012, Mar. 23   *Perf. 13¼*
Stamps With White Backgrounds
1523-1526 A678 Set of 4   6.75 3.50
Souvenir Sheet
Stamps With Buff Backgrounds
1527 A678 Sheet of 4, #a-d   6.75 3.50

Organic
Farming
A679

Organic: No. 1528, 250m, Melons. No.
1529, 250m, Strawberries. 600m, Grapes.
1350m, Honey.

2012, May 12   *Litho.*   *Perf. 13¼*
1528-1531 A679 Set of 4   5.50 2.75
1531a   Souvenir sheet of 4,
               #1528-1531   5.50 2.75

National
Army, 56th
Anniv.
A680

2012, June 24   *Perf. 13*
1532 A680 700m multi   1.40 .70

Fish — A681

Designs: No. 1533, 250m, Saupe (Sarpa
salpa). No. 1534, 250m, Marbré (Lithognathus
mormyrus). 600m, Sardine (Sardina
pilchardus). 1100m, Sparaillon (Diplodus
sargus).

2012, Sept. 15   *Perf. 13¼*
1533-1536 A681 Set of 4   5.50 2.75

Arab Post Day — A682

2012, Aug. 3   *Perf. 13*
1537 A682 600m multi   1.40 .70

25th
Universal
Postal
Congress,
Doha,
Qatar
A683

2012, Sept. 24
1538 A683 1000m multi   2.50 1.25
Values are for stamps with surrounding
selvage.

Famous
Tunisians
A684

Designs: No. 1539, 250m, Sheikh Salem
Bouhajeb (1827-1926). No. 1540, 250m,
Hamda Ben Tijani (1901-83), actor. 390m,
Mohamed Bechrouch (1911-44), writer.
600m, Salah Khemissi (1912-58), singer.
900m, Sheikh Mohamed El Fadhel Ben
Achour (1909-70), theologian. 1350m,
Tawhida Ben Cheikh (1909-2010), physician.

2012, Oct. 16   *Perf. 12¾x13*
1539-1544 A684 Set of 6   9.00 4.50

Intl. Anti-Corruption Day — A685

2012, Dec. 9   *Perf. 13*
1545 A685 700m multi   1.60 .80

World Water
Day — A686

2013, Mar. 22   *Perf. 12¾*
1546 A686 2350m multi   4.75 2.50

Train
Station,
Tozeur
A687

Medina,
Tozeur — A688

2013, Apr. 26
1547 A687 250m multi   .50 .25
1548 A688 600m multi   1.20 .60

Kairouani Kufic Calligraphy — A689

2013, May 18   *Perf. 13*
1549 A689 250m multi   .50 .25

African
Union, 50th
Anniv.
A690

2013, May 25   *Perf. 13¼*
1550 A690 1100m multi   2.25 1.10

Handcrafted
Wood
Items — A691

Designs: No. 1551, 250m, Cooking utensils
and spice rack (denomination in green). No.
1552, 250m, Rack (denomination in black).
600m, Mortar and pestle. 900m, Clothing box.

2013, June 28   *Litho.*   *Perf. 13¼*
1551-1554 A691 Set of 4   4.00 2.00

Traffic
Accident
Prevention
A692

2013, Aug. 7   *Litho.*   *Perf. 13*
1555 A692 1350m multi   2.75 1.50

Lighthouses — A693

Designs: 250m, Cani Island Lighthouse.
600m, Galite Island Lighthouse. 700m, Borj
Khadija Lighthouse. 1000m, Borj Jlij
Lighthouse.

2013, Sept. 20 *Litho.*   *Perf. 12¾*
1556-1559 A693 Set of 4   4.75 2.50
                See No. 1598A.

Parental
Love — A694

2013, Oct. 18   *Litho.*   *Perf. 13*
1560 A694 250m multi   .50 .25

Intl. Day Against
Violence Towards
Women — A695

2013, Nov. 25   *Litho.*   *Perf. 12¾*
1561 A695 600m multi   1.10 .55

Universal
Declaration of
Human Rights,
65th
Anniv. — A696

2013, Dec. 10   *Litho.*   *Perf. 12¾*
1562 A696 600m multi   1.10 .55

Famous
People
A697

Designs: No. 1563, 250m, Youssef Rekik
(1940-2012), glass painter and playwright. No.
1564, 250m, Ibrahim Dhahhak (1931-2004),
painter, vert. 600m, Taher Cheriaa (1927-
2010), film maker. 1000m, Zoubeida Bechir
(1938-2011), poet.

2013, Dec. 27   *Litho.*   *Perf. 12¾*
1563-1566 A697 Set of 4   3.50 1.75

Diplomatic
Relations
Between
Tunisia and
People's
Republic of
China, 50th
Anniv.
A698

2014, Jan. 10   *Litho.*   *Perf. 13¼*
1567 A698 700m multi   1.25 .60

Adoption of New Constitution — A699

2014, Feb. 7   *Litho.*   *Perf. 13*
1568 A699 1350m multi   2.25 1.10

Mediterranean Diet — A700

2014, Mar. 25   *Litho.*   *Perf. 13*
1569 A700 2350m multi   4.00 2.00

Cities — A701

Designs: 250m, Sfax. 600m, Djerba.

2014, Apr. 23   *Litho.*   *Perf. 13*
1570-1571 A701 Set of 2   1.50 .75
1571a   Souvenir sheet of 2,
           #1570-1571   1.75 1.75
       No. 1571a sold for 1d.

Labor Day — A702

Designs: 250m, Woman's hand, handicrafts.
390m, Books, chemical flasks and beakers.

2014, May 1   *Litho.*   *Perf. 13*
1572-1573 A702 Set of 2   1.00 .50

A703

National
Cleanliness and
Environmental
Maintenance
Day — A704

2014, June 11   *Litho.*   *Perf. 12¾*
1574 A703 250m multi   .40 .25
1575 A704 1000m multi   1.50 .75

Postal Forum
on Electronic
Commerce,
Hammamet
A705

2014, Sept. 22   Litho.   Perf. 13
1576 A705 600m multi .70 .35
a. Souvenir sheet of 1 1.10 1.10
No. 1576a sold for 1d.

Stamp Day — A706

2014, Oct. 9   Litho.   Perf. 13
1577 A706 250m multi .30 .25

Treaty of Friendship, Commerce and Navigation Between Tunisia and Belgium, 175th Anniv. A707

2014, Oct. 14   Litho.   Perf. 13
1578 A707 1000m multi 1.10 .55

World Rural Women's Day — A708

2014, Oct. 15   Litho.   Perf. 13
1579 A708 2350m multi 2.60 1.40

Lighthouses — A709

Designs: 900m, Taguermess Lighthouse. 1350m, Sidi Bou Said Lighthouse.

2014, Nov. 18   Litho.   Perf. 12¾
1580-1581 A709 Set of 2 2.50 1.25
See No. 1598A.

Butterflies A710

Designs: No. 1582, 250m, Pyronia cecilia. No. 1583, 250m, Zegris eupheme. No. 1584, 250m, Spialia sertorius. 600m. Pieris brassicae.

2014, Dec. 19   Litho.   Perf. 13
1582-1585 A710 Set of 4 1.50 .75
1585a Souvenir sheet of 4, #1582-1585 1.90 1.90
No. 1585a sold for 1750m.

Traditional Pottery — A711

Designs: Nos. 1586, 1590a, 250m, Djerba jar. Nos. 1587, 1590b, 600m, Sejnane couscous pot. Nos. 1588, 1590c, 700m, Jars without decoration. Nos. 1589, 1590d, 1000m, Qalllaline two-handled jar.

2015, Mar. 16   Litho.   Perf. 13x13¼
Stamps With White Frames
1586-1589 A711 Set of 4 2.75 1.40
Souvenir Sheet
Stamps With Colored Frames
Imperf
1590 A711 Sheet of 4, #a-d 3.25 3.25
No. 1590 sold for 3d. Stamps on No. 1590 have simulated perforations.

Room in Palace of the Beyo A712

2015, Apr. 18   Litho.   Perf. 12¾
1591 A712 600m multi .65 .30

A713

Youth Training A714

2015, May 1   Litho.   Perf. 12¾
1592 A713 250m multi .30 .25
1593 A714 250m multi .30 .25

Fauna — A715

Designs: 700m, Houbara bustard. 1000m, Arabian horse, horiz.

2015, June 2   Litho.   Perf. 12¾
1594-1595 A715 Set of 2 1.75 .85

Homage to Tunisian Army Martyrs — A716

2015, June 15   Litho.   Perf. 13
1596 A716 2350m multi 2.40 1.25

Ship — A717

2015, July 9   Litho.   Perf. 13
1597 A717 1350m multi 1.40 .70

Disease Prevention A718

2015, July 28   Litho.   Perf. 13
1598 A718 1100m multi 1.10 .55

Lighthouse Types of 2013-14
Miniature Sheet
2015, Sept. 1   Litho.   Perf. 12¾
1598A Sheet of 5 2.00 1.25
a. A693 390m Like #1557 .40 .25
b. A693 390m Like #1556 .40 .25
c. A693 390m Like #1558 .40 .25
d. A709 390m Like #1580 .40 .25
e. A709 390m Like #1581 .40 .25

Campaign Against Sports Doping A719

2015, Sept. 10   Litho.   Perf. 13
1599 A719 900m multi .95 .45

International Year of Soils — A720

2015, Oct. 16   Litho.   Perf. 13
1600 A720 250m multi .25 .25

United Nations, 70th Anniv. A721

2015, Oct. 24   Litho.   Perf. 13
1601 A721 1000m multi 1.00 .50

Awarding of 2015 Nobel Peace Prize to the Tunisian National Dialogue Quartet A722

2015, Dec. 10   Litho.   Perf. 13
1602 A722 2000m multi 2.00 1.00
a. Souvenir sheet of 1 3.00 3.00
No. 1602a sold for 3d.

Old Trains — A723

Designs: No. 1603, 250m, Dietrich rail cars. No. 1604, 250m, Tunis trams. 390m, Decauville rail cars. 600m, Lezard Rouge train.

2015, Dec. 22   Litho.   Perf. 13
1603-1606 A723 Set of 4 1.50 .75

Tunisian General Labor Union, 70th Anniv. A724

2016, Jan. 20   Litho.   Perf. 13
1607 A724 250m multi .25 .25

World Day of Civil Protection A725

2016, Mar. 1   Litho.   Perf. 13
1608 A725 250m multi .25 .25

Independence, 60th Anniv. — A726

2016, Mar. 20   Litho.   *Perf. 13*
1609 A726 1000m multi   1.00   .50

First Cooperation Agreement Between Tunisia and the European Union, 40th Anniv. A727

2016, Apr. 25   Litho.   *Perf. 13*
1610 A727 2350m multi   2.40 1.25

A728

A729

Sfax, 2016 Capital of Arab Culture A730

2016, May 20   Litho.   *Perf. 12¾*
1611 A728 250m multi   .25   .25
1612 A729 600m multi   .60   .30
1613 A730 1350m multi   1.25   .65
  Nos. 1611-1613 (3)   2.10 1.20

Tunisian Television, 50th Anniv. — A731

2016, May 31   Litho.   *Perf. 13*
1614 A731 250m multi   .25   .25

Tunisian Army, 60th Anniv. A732

2016, June 24   Litho.   *Perf. 13*
1615 A732 250m multi   .25   .25

Diplomatic Relations Between Tunisia and Japan, 60th Anniv. A733

2016, July 7   Litho.   *Perf. 13*
1616 A733 1000m multi   .90   .45

Ministry of Foreign Affairs, 60th Anniv. — A734

2016, Aug. 1   Litho.   *Perf. 13*
1617 A734 900m multi   .85   .40

Arab Postal Day — A735

No. 1618: a, Blue background, denomination at left. b, Green background, denomination at right.

2016, Aug. 3   Litho.   *Perf. 12¾*
1618 A735 600m Horiz. pair, #a-
   b   1.10   .55

National Postal Savings, 60th Anniv. A736

2016, Aug. 28   Litho.   *Perf. 13*
1619 A736 500m multi   .45   .25

Conifers A737

Designs: 50m, Pinus pinea branch, cones and nuts, jar with nuts. 900m, Pinus halepensis tree, branch and cones. 1000d, Pinus halepensis branch, cones, and nuts, bowl. 2000d, Pinus pinea tree and cones.

2016, Sept. 20   Litho.   *Perf. 13¼*
1620-1623 A737 Set of 4   3.75 1.90
1622a Without "Pin d'Alep" inscription   .95   .45
1623a Souvenir sheet of 4, #1620,
   1621, 1622a, 1623   3.75 1.90
  No. 1623a sold for 4d.

National Family Planning Program, 50th Anniv. A738

2016, Oct. 13   Litho.   *Perf. 13*
1624 A738 500m multi   .45   .25

Ahmed Tlili (1916-67), Labor Union Leader — A739

2016, Oct. 16   Litho.   *Perf. 13¼x13*
1625 A739 1200m multi   1.10   .55

World Telecommunication Standardization Assembly, Yasmine Hammamet — A740

2016, Oct. 25   Litho.   *Perf. 13*
1626 A740 2000m multi   1.90   .95

Miniature Sheet

United Nations Sustainable Development Goals — A741

No. 1627: a, Heart and "3." b, Steaming bowl and "2." c, Stylized men, women, children and "1." d, United Nations Headquarters, New York. e, United Nations Headquarters, United Nations emblem and Tunisian flag. f, Arrow on graph and "8." g, Power button in sun and "7." h, Water drop in glass, arrow and "6." i, Combined male and female symbols and "5." j, Book, pencil and "4." k, Globe in eye and "13." l, Arrow in shape of infinity symbol and "12." m, Buildings and "11." n, Equal sign in circle and "10." o, Cubes and "9." p, Sustainable Development Goals emblem and Arabic text. q, Five linked circles and "17." r, Dove on gavel and "16." s, Tree, birds and "15." t, Fish in water and "14."

2016, Nov. 12   Litho.   *Perf. 13¼*
1627 A741 500m Sheet of 20,
   #a-t   8.75 4.50
  Tunisia's admission to United Nations, 60th anniv.

Famous People A742

Designs: 500m, Bchira Ben Mrad (1913-93), founder of Muslim Women's Union of Tunisia. 1000m, Tahar Ben Ammar (1889-1985), Prime Minister.

2016, Dec. 15   Litho.   *Perf. 12¾*
1628-1629 A742 Set of 2   1.50   .75

Tunisian Union of Industry, Commerce and Handicrafts, 70th Anniv. — A743

2017, Jan. 17   Litho.   *Perf. 13*
1630 A743 2000m multi   2.00 1.00

National Internet Freedom Day — A744

Designs: 900m, Zouhair Yahyaoui (1967-2005), convicted cyber-dissident. 1200m, Birds and network.

2017, Mar. 13   Litho.   *Perf. 12¾*
1631-1632 A744 Set of 2   2.10 1.10

Mohamed Sghaier Ouled Ahmed (1955-2016), Poet — A745

2017, Apr. 5   Litho.   Perf. 13
1633 A745 1000m multi   .85   .40

Support for Investment in Tunisia — A746

2017, Apr. 20   Litho.   Perf. 13
1634 A746 2000m multi   1.75   .85

Rouis Primary School, Médenine A747

2017, Apr. 24   Litho.   Perf. 13x13¼
1635 A747 500m multi   .40   .25

Monastir A748

2017, May 24   Litho.   Perf. 12¾
1636 A748 500m multi   .45   .25

Mosques A749

Designs: No. 1637, 500m, Al Baji Mosque, Sidi Bou Said. No. 1638, 500m, Chenini Mosque, Tataouine.

2017, June 15   Litho.   Perf. 13¼
1637-1638 A749 Set of 2   .85   .40

Olive Trees A750

Designs: 900m, Lakarit olive tree, Doiret. 3000m, Zarrazi olive tree.

2017, July 9   Litho.   Perf. 13x13¼
1639-1640 A750 Set of 2   3.25 1.60

53rd Carthage International Festival A751

2017, July 13   Litho.   Perf. 13
1641 A751 1000m multi   .85   .40

Republic of Tunisia, 60th Anniv. A752

2017, July 25   Litho.   Perf. 13
1642 A752 500m multi   .45   .25

Habib Achour (1913-99), Founder of Tunisian General Labor Union — A753

2017, Aug. 5   Litho.   Perf. 12¾
1643 A753 1200m multi   1.00   .50

Victory in 2016 Battle of Ben Guerdane A754

2017, Sept. 11   Litho.   Perf. 12¾
1644 A754 2000m multi   1.60   .80

A755   Transitional Justice Process — A756

Design: 500m, The public open session. 2000m, Logo of the Instance.

2017, Sept. 26   Litho.   Perf. 12¾
1645 A755   500m multi   .40   .25
1646 A756 2000m multi   1.60   .80

Archaeology — A757

Designs: No. 1647, 500m, Amphitheater, Oudhna. No. 1648, 500m, Arches, Great Baths of Makthar. 1000m, Artifact from Chimtou Archaeological Museum. 1200m, Lion mosaic, Salakta.

2017, Oct. 20   Litho.   Perf. 12¾
1647-1650 A757 Set of 4   2.60 1.40
1650a   Souvenir sheet of 4, #1647-1650   2.60 1.40

Taher Cheriaa (1927-2010), Film Critic and Founder of Carthage Film Festival — A757a

National Year of Tunisian Cinema — A757b

2017   Litho.   Perf. 12¾
1650B A757a   1d multi   .80   .40
          Perf. 13
1650C A757b 1.20d multi   1.00   .50

Citrus Fruits — A758

Designs: 50m, Mandarin oranges. No. 1652, 500m, Eureka lemons. No. 1653, 500m, Maltese oranges. 4d, Sweet lemons.

2017, Nov. 22   Litho.   Perf. 13¼
1651-1654 A758 Set of 4   4.25 2.10

National Archives Day A759

2017, Dec. 9   Litho.   Perf. 12¾
1655 A759 2d multi   1.75   .85

Tunisia Post Stamp Printing Plant, 20th Anniv. — A760

2017, Dec. 18   Litho.   Perf. 13
1656 A760 1.20d multi   1.00   .50

Tourism A761

Designs: No. 1657, 1d, Midès Oasis. No. 1658, 1d, Cap Blanc. No. 1659, 1.20d, Jugurtha Tableland. No, 1660, 1.20d, El Haouaria.

2018, Feb. 14   Litho.   Perf. 12¾
1657-1660 A761 Set of 4   3.75 1.90

Holiday Colonies and Patronage National Childhood Organization, 70th Anniv. — A762

2018, Mar. 1   Litho.   Perf. 13x13¼
1661 A762 500m multi   .45   .25

Court of Accounts, 50th Anniv. — A763

2018, Mar. 8   Litho.   Perf. 12¾
1662 A763 500m multi   .45   .25

Handicrafts From Sejnane A764

Designs: 500m. Pottery. 2d, Clay dolls.

2018, Mar. 16   Litho.   Perf. 13½
1663-1664 A764 Set of 2   2.10 1.10
1664a   Souvenir sheet of 2, #1663 1004   2.10 1.10

Amnesty International in Tunisia, 30th Anniv. — A765

2018, Apr. 12   Litho.   Perf. 12¾
1665 A765 110m multi   .25   .25

Taoufik Baccar (1927-2017), Literary Critic — A766

2018, Apr. 24   Litho.   Perf. 13
1666 A766 900m multi   .75   .35

Mohamed Ezzedine Mili (1917-2013),
Secretary General of International
Telecommunication Union — A767

2018, May 10   Litho.   *Perf. 13*
1667 A767 500m multi   .40   .25

Postal
Current
Accounts,
Cent.
A768

2018, May 27   Litho.   *Perf. 13*
1668 A768 4d multi   3.25 1.60

2018 World Cup Soccer
Championships, Russia — A769

2018, June 14   Litho.   *Perf. 13*
1669 A769 500m multi   .40   .25
Values are for stamps with surrounding
selvage.

Houses of the Mediterranean
Area — A770

Various houses with denomination in: No.
1670, 1.20d, Red. No. 1671, 1.20d, Dark
violet.

2018, July 9   Litho.   *Perf. 12¾*
1670-1671 A770 Set of 2   1.90   .95
1671a   Souvenir sheet of 2,
               #1670-1671   1.90   .95

60th International Festival of
Sousse — A771

2018, July 15   Litho.   *Perf. 13*
1672 A771 900m multi   .70   .35

Souvenir Sheet

Nelson Mandela (1918-2013),
President of South Africa — A772

2018, July 18   Litho.   *Perf. 13¼*
1673 A772 500m multi   .40   .25

Habib Bourguiba (1903-2000), First
Minister of Foreign Affairs and First
President — A773

2018, July 31   Litho.   *Perf. 13*
1674 A773 500m multi   .40   .25

National Environmental Protection
Agency, 30th Anniv. — A774

2018, Aug. 2   Litho.   *Perf. 12¾*
1675 A774 2d multi   1.50   .75

National
Real
Estate
Company
of Tunisia
A775

2018, Sept. 2   Litho.   *Perf. 12¾*
1676 A775 500m multi   .40   .25

Hédi Chaker
(1908-53),
Assassinated
Politician
A776

2018, Sept. 13   Litho.   *Perf. 13*
1677 A776 2d multi   1.50   .75

Tunisia No.
1 — A777

2018, Oct. 9   Litho.   *Perf. 13*
1678 A777 2d multi   1.40   .70
Tunisian postage stamps, 130th anniv.

Tunisair, 70th Anniv. — A778

2018, Oct. 21   Litho.   *Perf. 13*
1679 A778 1.20d multi   .85   .40

Mohandas K.
Gandhi (1869-
1948), Indian
Nationalist
Leader — A779

2018, Nov. 5   Litho.   *Perf. 12¾*
1680 A779 1d multi   .70   .35

Calligraphy by Mohamed Salah
Khammassi (1910-92) — A780

2018, Nov. 10   Litho.   *Perf. 13*
1681 A780 2d multi   1.40   .70

Homage to
Killed
Presidential
Security
Team
Members
A781

2018, Nov. 24   Litho.   *Perf. 13*
1682 A781 500m multi   .35   .25

Campaign
Against
Corruption
A782

2018, Dec. 8   Litho.   *Perf. 13*
1683 A782 1d multi   .70   .35

Fauna
A783

Inscriptions: 500m, Orphie (garfish). 900m,
Chacal doré (golden jackal). 1d, Pica pica. 2d,
Cervus elaphus barbarus.

2018, Dec. 18   Litho.   *Perf. 13¼*
1684-1687 A783   Set of 4   3.00 1.50
1687a   Souvenir sheet of 4,
               #1684-1687   3.50 1.75
No. 1687a sold for 5d.

Espérance
Sportive de Tunis
Sports Club,
Cent. — A784

2019, Jan. 15   Litho.   *Perf. 12¾*
1688 A784 500m multi   .35   .25
Size: 40x40mm
Denomination at Upper Left
Perf. 13
1689 A784   2d multi   1.40   .70
Souvenir Sheet
Denomination at Upper Right
1690 A784   5d multi   3.50 1.75
No. 1690 contains one 37x52mm stamp.

SEMI-POSTAL STAMPS

No. 36 Overprinted in
Red

1915, Feb.   Unwmk.   *Perf. 14x13½*
B1 A5 15c vio, *pnksh*   1.40 1.40

No. 32 Overprinted in
Red

1916, Feb. 15
B2 A4 5c grn, *grnsh*   2.10 2.10

Types of Regular
Issue of 1906 in New
Colors and
Surcharged

1916, Aug.

B3	A5	10c on 15c brn vio, bl	1.40	1.10
B4	A5	10c on 20c brn, org	2.10	1.40
B5	A5	10c on 25c bl, grn	3.50	3.50
B6	A6	10c on 35c ol grn & vio	10.50	7.00
B7	A6	10c on 40c bis & blk	7.00	4.50
B8	A6	10c on 75c vio brn & grn	14.00	10.50
B9	A7	10c on 1fr red & grn	7.00	7.00
B10	A7	10c on 2fr bis & bl	110.00	110.00
B11	A7	10c on 5fr vio & red	125.00	125.00
		Nos. B3-B11 (9)	280.50	270.00

Nos. B3-B11 were sold at their face value but had a postal value of 10c only. The excess was applied to the relief of prisoners of war in Germany.

Types of Regular Issue of 1906 in New Colors and Surcharged in Carmine

1918

B12	A5	15c on 20c blk, grn	2.75	2.75
B13	A5	15c on 25c dk bl, buff	2.75	2.75
B14	A6	15c on 35c gray grn & red	3.75	3.75
B15	A6	15c on 40c brn & lt bl	5.00	5.00
B16	A6	15c on 75c red brn & blk	14.00	14.00
B17	A7	15c on 1fr red & vio	32.50	32.50
B18	A7	15c on 2fr bis brn & red	110.00	110.00
B19	A7	15c on 5fr vio & blk	175.00	175.00
		Nos. B12-B19 (8)	345.75	345.75

The different parts of the surcharge are more widely spaced on the stamps of types A6 and A7. These stamps were sold at their face value but had a postal value of 15c only. The excess was intended for the relief of prisoners of war in Germany.

Types of 1906-22 Surcharged

1923

B20	A4	0c on 1c blue	1.10	1.10
B21	A4	0c on 2c ol brn	1.10	1.10
B22	A4	1c on 3c green	1.10	1.10
B23	A4	2c on 5c red vio	1.10	1.10
B24	A9	3c on 10c vio, bluish	1.10	1.10
B25	A5	5c on 15c ol grn	1.10	1.10
B26	A5	5c on 20c bl, pink	2.10	2.10
B27	A5	5c on 25c vio, bluish	2.10	2.10
B28	A9	5c on 30c orange	2.10	2.10
B29	A6	5c on 35c bl & vio	4.25	4.25
B30	A6	5c on 40c bl & brn	4.25	4.25
B31	A9	10c on 50c blk, bluish	7.00	5.50
B32	A6	10c on 60c ol brn & bl	10.50	7.75
B33	A6	10c on 75c vio & lt grn	9.00	8.50
B34	A7	25c on 1fr mar & vio	10.50	8.50
B35	A7	25c on 2fr bl & rose	27.50	26.00
B36	A7	25c on 5fr grn & ol brn	70.00	70.00
		Nos. B20-B36 (17)	155.90	147.65

These stamps were sold at their original values but had postal franking values only to the amounts surcharged on them. The difference was intended to be used for the benefit of wounded soldiers.

This issue was entirely speculative. Before the announced date of sale most of the stamps were taken by postal employees and practically none of them were offered to the public.

Type of 1906 Parcel Post Stamps Surcharged in Black

1925, June 7   Perf. 13½x14

B37	PP1	1c on 5c brn & red, pink	.70	.70
a.		Surcharge omitted	140.00	140.00

B38	PP1	2c on 10c brn & bl, yel	.70	.70
B39	PP1	3c on 20c red vio & rose, lav	1.40	1.40
B40	PP1	5c on 25c sl grn & rose, bluish	1.40	1.40
B41	PP1	5c on 40c rose & grn, yel	1.40	1.40
B42	PP1	10c on 50c vio & bl, lav	2.75	2.75
B43	PP1	10c on 75c grn & ol, grnsh	2.75	2.75
B44	PP1	25c on 1fr bl & grn, bluish	2.75	2.75
B45	PP1	25c on 2fr rose & vio, pnksh	14.00	14.00
B46	PP1	25c on 5fr red & lem	50.00	50.00
		Nos. B37-B46 (10)	77.85	77.85

These stamps were sold at their original values but paid postage only to the amount of the surcharged values. The difference was given to Child Welfare societies.

Tunis-Chad Motor Caravan SP2

1928, Feb.   Engr.   Perf. 13½

B47	SP2	40c + 40c org brn	1.40	1.40
B48	SP2	50c + 50c dp vio	1.75	1.75
B49	SP2	75c + 75c dk bl	1.75	1.75
B50	SP2	1fr + 1fr carmine	1.75	1.75
B51	SP2	1.50fr + 1.50fr brt bl	1.75	1.75
B52	SP2	2fr + 2fr dk grn	2.10	2.10
B53	SP2	5fr + 5fr red brn	2.10	2.10
		Nos. B47-B53 (7)	12.60	12.60

The surtax on these stamps was for the benefit of Child Welfare societies.

Nos. 122-135, 137-142 Surcharged in Black

a

b

1938   Perf. 11, 12½, 12½x13

B54	A14(a)	1c + 1c	2.75	2.75
B55	A14(a)	2c + 2c	2.75	2.75
B56	A14(a)	3c + 3c	2.75	2.75
B57	A14(a)	5c + 5c	2.75	2.75
B58	A14(a)	10c + 10c	2.75	2.75
B59	A15(a)	15c + 15c	2.75	2.75
B60	A15(a)	20c + 20c	2.75	2.75
B61	A15(a)	25c + 25c	2.75	2.75
B62	A15(a)	30c + 30c	2.75	2.75
B63	A15(a)	40c + 40c	2.75	2.75
B64	A16(a)	50c + 50c	2.75	2.75
B65	A16(a)	75c + 75c	2.75	2.75
B66	A16(a)	90c + 90c	2.75	2.75
B67	A16(a)	1fr + 1fr	2.75	2.75
B68	A17(b)	1.50fr + 1fr	2.75	2.75
B69	A17(b)	2fr + 1.50fr	5.00	5.00
B70	A17(b)	3fr + 2fr	5.50	5.50
B71	A17(b)	5fr + 3fr	21.00	21.00
a.		Perf. 12½	110.00	110.00
B72	A17(b)	10fr + 5fr	45.00	45.00
B73	A17(b)	20fr + 10fr	70.00	70.00
		Nos. B54-B73 (20)	187.75	187.75

50th anniversary of the post office.

Nos. 86, 100-101, 105 Surcharged in Black, Blue or Red

1941   Perf. 14x13½

B74	A11	1fr on 45c (Bk)	.55	.55
B75	A13	1.30fr on 1.25fr (Bl)	.55	.55
B76	A13	1.50fr on 1.40fr (Bk)	.55	.55
B77	A13	2fr on 2.25fr (R)	.80	.80
		Nos. B74-B77 (4)	2.45	2.45

The surcharge measures 11x14mm on #B74.

> Catalogue values for unused stamps in this section, from this point to the end of the section, are for Never Hinged items.

British, French and American Soldiers SP3

1943   Litho.   Perf. 12

B78	SP3	1.50fr + 8.50fr crimson	.55	.25

Liberation of Tunisia.

Children — SP3a

1944   Engr.   Perf. 13½

B78A	SP3a	1.20fr + 1.30fr brown	1.10	
B78B	SP3a	1.50fr + 2fr black brown	1.10	
B78C	SP3a	2fr + 3fr dark green	1.10	
B78D	SP3a	3fr + 4fr red orange	1.10	
		Nos. B78A-B78D (4)	4.40	

National welfare fund. Nos. B78A-B78D were issued by the Vichy government in France, but were not issued in Tunisia.

Native Scene — SP4

Surcharged in Black

1944   Perf. 11½

B79	SP4	2fr + 48fr red	1.40	1.10

The surtax was for soldiers.

Sidi Mahrez Mosque — SP5

Ramparts of Sfax — SP6

Fort Saint — SP7

Sidi-bou-Said — SP8

1945   Unwmk.   Litho.   Perf. 11½

B80	SP5	1.50fr + 8.50fr choc & red	1.40	1.10
B81	SP6	3fr + 12fr dk bl grn & red	1.40	1.10
B82	SP7	4fr + 21fr brn org & red	1.40	1.10
B83	SP8	10fr + 40fr red & blk	1.40	1.10
		Nos. B80-B83 (4)	5.60	4.40

The surtax was for soldiers.

France No. B193 Overprinted in Black — c

1945   Perf. 14x13½

B84	SP147	2fr + 1fr red org	.70	.50

The surtax was for the aid of tuberculosis victims.

Same Overprint on Type of France, 1945

1945   Engr.   Perf. 13

B85	SP150	2fr + 3fr dk grn	1.10	.55

Stamp Day.

Same Overprint on France No. B192

1945

B86	SP146	4fr + 6fr dk vio brn	.70	.55

The surtax was for war victims of the P.T.T.

Types of 1926 Surcharged in Carmine

1945   Typo.   Perf. 14x13½

B87	A10	4fr + 6fr on 10c ultra	.70	.35
B88	A12	10fr + 30fr on 80c dk grn	.70	.35

The design of type A12 is redrawn, omitting "RF." The surtax was for war veterans.

Tunisian Soldier — SP9

1946   Unwmk.   Engr.   *Perf. 13*
B89   SP9   20fr + 30fr grn, red & blk   1.75   1.40

The surtax aided Tunisian soldiers in Indo-China.

Type of France Overprinted Type "c" in Carmine

1946
B90   SP160   3fr + 2fr dk bl   1.40   1.10

Stamp Day.

Stamps and Types of 1926-46 Surcharged in Carmine and Black

1946   *Perf. 14x13½*
B91   A12   80c + 50c emerald   1.40   1.10
B92   A12   1.50fr + 1.50fr rose lil   1.40   1.10
B93   A12   2fr + 2fr Prus grn   1.40   1.10
B94   A13   2.40fr + 2fr sal pink   1.40   1.10
B95   A13   4fr + 4fr ultra   2.10   1.40
     Nos. B91-B95 (5)   7.70   5.80

The two parts of the surcharge are more widely spaced on stamps of type A13.

Type of France Overprinted in Carmine

1947   *Perf. 13*
B96   SP172   4.50fr + 5.50fr sepia   1.40   1.10

On Type of France Surcharged in Carmine

B97   SP158   10fr + 15fr on 2fr + 3fr brt ultra   1.40   1.10

Type of 1926 Surcharged in Carmine

1947   Typo.   *Perf. 14x13½*
B98   A13   10fr + 40fr black   1.40   1.10

Feeding Young Bird — SP10

1947   Engr.   *Perf. 13*
B99   SP10   4.50fr + 5.50fr dk bl grn   1.75   1.40
B100   SP10   6fr + 9fr brt ultra   1.75   1.40
B101   SP10   8fr + 17fr dp car   1.75   1.40
B102   SP10   10fr + 40fr dk pur   1.75   1.40
     Nos. B99-B102 (4)   7.00   5.60

The surtax was for child welfare.

Type of Regular Issue of 1948 Surcharged in Blue

1948
B103   A21   4fr + 10fr ol grn & org   1.40   1.10

The surtax was for anti-tuberculosis work.

Arch of Triumph, Sbeitla SP11

1948
B104   SP11   10fr + 40fr ol grn & olive   1.75   1.40
B105   SP11   18fr + 42fr dk bl & indigo   1.75   1.40

Surtax for charitable works of the army.

Arago Type of France Overprinted in Carmine

1948
B106   SP176   6fr + 4fr brt car   1.40   1.10

Stamp Day, Mar. 6-7.

Sleeping Child SP12

1949, June 1
B107   SP12   25fr + 50fr dk grn   2.75   2.10

The surtax was for child welfare.

Neptune Type of 1947 Srchd. in Black

1949, Dec. 8
B108   A20   10fr + 15fr dp ultra & car   1.75   1.40

The surtax was for the Tunisian section of the Association of Free French.

Type of France Overprinted in Carmine — e

1949, Mar. 26
B109   SP180   15fr + 5fr indigo   2.10   1.40

Stamp Days, Mar. 26-27.

Type of France, 1950, Ovptd. Like No. B106 in Ultramarine

1950, Mar. 11   Unwmk.   *Perf. 13*
B110   SP183   12fr + 3fr greenish black   2.75   2.10

Stamp Days, Mar. 11-12.

Tunisian and French Woman Shaking Hands SP13

1950, June 5
B111   SP13   15fr + 35fr red   1.75   1.40
B112   SP13   25fr + 45fr dp ultra   1.75   1.40

The surtax was for Franco-Tunisian Mutual Assistance.

Arab Soldier — SP14

1950, Aug. 21   Engr.
B113   SP14   25fr + 25fr dp bl   2.75   2.10

The surtax was for old soldiers.

Type of France Overprinted Type "c" in Black

1951, Mar. 10
B114   SP186   12fr + 3fr brnsh gray   2.10   1.40

Stamp Days, Mar. 10-11.

Mother Carrying Child SP15

1951, June 19   Engr.   *Perf. 13*
B115   SP15   30fr + 15fr dp ultra   3.50   2.75

The surtax was for child welfare.

National Cemetery of Gammarth SP16

1952, June 15
B116   SP16   30fr + 10fr blue   2.75   2.10

Surtax aided orphans of the military services.

Type of France Overprinted Type "e" in Lilac

1952, Mar. 8   Unwmk.
B117   SP190   12fr + 3fr purple   1.75   1.40

Stamp Day, Mar. 8.

Stucco Work, Bardo — SP17

1952, May 5   Engr.   *Perf. 13*
B118   SP17   15fr + 1fr ultra & indigo   1.40   1.10

Surtax for charitable works of the army.

Boy Campers — SP18

1952, June 15
B119   SP18   30fr + 10fr dk grn   3.50   2.10

The surtax was for the Educational League vacation camps.

Type of France Surcharged Type "c" and Surtax

1952, Oct. 15
B120   A226   15fr + 5fr bl grn   3.50   2.10

Creation of the French Military Medal, cent.

Type of France Overprinted Type "c"

1953, Mar. 14
B121   SP193   12fr + 3fr vermilion   2.10   1.75

"Day of the Stamp."

Type of France Overprinted Type "c"

1954, Mar. 20
B122   SP196   12fr + 3fr indigo   2.10   1.75

Stamp Day.

Balloon Post, 1870 SP19

1955, Mar. 19
B123   SP19   12fr + 3fr red brown   2.10   1.75

Stamp Days, Mar. 19-20.

Independent Kingdom

Franz von Taxis SP20

1956, Mar. 17
B124   SP20   12fr + 3fr dark green   1.25   1.25

Stamp Days, Mar. 17-18

Republic

No. 246 Surcharged in Red

1957, Aug. 8   Engr.
B125   A29   20fr + 10fr dp ultra   .70   .70

15th anniversary of the army.

Florist Type of 1955 with Added Inscriptions, Surcharged in Red

1957, Oct. 19   *Perf. 13*
B126 A34 20fr + 10fr dk vio   .70   .70

No. B126 is inscribed "5e. Foire Internationale" at bottom and lines of Arabic at either side.

Mailman Delivering Mail — SP21

1959, May 1   Engr.   *Perf. 13*
B127 SP21 20fr + 5fr dk brn & org brn   .70   .70

Day of the Stamp. The surtax was for the Post Office Mutual Fund.

Ornamental Cock — SP22

1959, Oct. 24   Litho.   *Perf. 13*
B128 SP22 10m + 5m yel, lt bl & red   .75   .35

Surtax for the Red Crescent Society.

Mailman on Camel Phoning — SP23

1960, Apr. 16   Engr.   *Perf. 13*
B129 SP23 60m + 5m ol, org & ultra   1.25   .75

Day of the Stamp.

Dancer of Kerkennah Holding Stamp — SP24

Stamp Day: 15m+5m, Mail truck, horiz. 20m+6m, Hand holding magnifying glass and stamps. 50m+5m, Running boy, symbols of mail.

1961, May 6   Unwmk.   *Perf. 13*
B130 SP24 12m + 4m multi   .60   .60
B131 SP24 15m + 5m multi   .75   .75
B132 SP24 20m + 6m multi   .85   .85
B133 SP24 50m + 5m multi   .95   .95
    Nos. B130-B133 (4)   3.15   3.15

Nos. B130-D133 Overprinted

1963, Oct. 24
B134 SP24 12m + 4m cl, vio & ol   .35   .35
B135 SP24 15m + 5m ol, cl & vio bl   .40   .40
B136 SP24 20m + 6m multi   .50   .50
B137 SP24 50m + 5m multi   .85   .85
    Nos. B134-B137 (4)   2.10   2.10

United Nations Day.

Old Man, Red Crescent — SP25

Tunisian Red Crescent: 75m+10m, Mother, child and Red Crescent.

1972, May 8   Engr.   *Perf. 13*
B138 SP25 10m + 10m pur & dk red   .50   .35
B139 SP25 75m + 10m bis brn & dl red   .75   .40

SP26

SP26a

Design: 25m+10m, Nurse Holding Bottle of Blood. 60m+10m, Red Crescent and blood donors' arms, horiz.

1973, May 10   Engr.   *Perf. 13*
B140 SP26 25m + 10m multi   .60   .40
B141 SP26a 60m + 10m gray & car   1.00   .40

Red Crescent appeal for blood donors.

Blood Donors — SP27

Red Crescent Society: 75m+10m, Blood transfusion, symbolic design.

1974, May 8   Photo.   *Perf. 14x13*
B142 SP27 25m + 10m multi   .50   .40
B143 SP27 75m + 10m multi   .75   .50

Man Holding Scales with Balanced Diet — SP28

1975, May 8   Photo.   *Perf. 11½*
B144 SP28 50m + 10m multi   .65   .40

Tunisian Red Crescent fighting malnutrition.

Blood Donation, Woman and Man — SP29

1976, May 8   Photo.   *Perf. 11½*
B145 SP29 40m + 10m multi   1.20   .35

Tunisian Red Crescent Society.

Litter Bearers and Red Crescent SP30

1977, May 8   Photo.   *Perf. 13½x14*
B146 SP30 50m + 10m multi   .65   .40

Tunisian Red Crescent Society.

Blood Donors — SP31

1978, May 8   Photo.   *Perf. 13x14*
B147 SP31 50m + 10m multi   .65   .40

Blood drive of Tunisian Red Crescent Society.

Hand and Red Crescent — SP32

1979, May 8   Photo.   *Perf. 13½*
B148 SP32 50m + 10m multi   .65   .40

Tunisian Red Crescent Society.

Red Crescent Society — SP33

1980, May 8   Photo.   *Perf. 13½*
B149 SP33 50m + 10m multi   .65   .40

Red Crescent Society — SP34

1981, May 8   *Perf. 14½x13½*
B150 SP34 50m + 10m multi   .55   .35

Dome of the Rock, Jerusalem SP35

1981, Nov. 29   Photo.   *Perf. 13½*
B151 SP35 50m + 5m multi   .55   .35
B152 SP35 150m + 5m multi   1.00   .60
B153 SP35 200m + 5m multi   1.60   .70
    Nos. B151-B153 (3)   3.15   1.65

Intl. Palestinian Solidarity Day.

Red Crescent Society SP36

1982, May 8   Photo.   *Perf. 13½*
B154 SP36 80m + 10m multi   .65   .40

Red Crescent Society — SP37

1983, May 8   Litho.   *Perf. 14x13½*
B155 SP37 80m + 10m multi   .75   .35

Sabra and Chatilla Massacre — SP38

1983, Sept. 20   Photo.   *Perf. 13*
B156 SP38 80m + 5m multi   .75   .50

Red Crescent Society — SP39

80m + 10m, First aid.

1984, May 8   Litho.   Perf. 12½
B157 SP39 80m + 10m multi   .65 .40

Red Crescent Society — SP40

1985, May 8   Litho.   Perf. 14
B158 SP40 100m + 10m multi   .50 .25

Red Crescent Society — SP41

120m + 10m, Map of Tunisia.

1986, May 9   Litho.   Perf. 14½x13½
B159 SP41 120m + 10m multi   1.10 .40

Red Crescent Society SP42

1987, May 8   Litho.   Perf. 13x13½
B160 SP42 150m + 10m multi   .75 .45

Intl. Red Cross and Red Crescent Organizations, 125th Annivs. — SP43

1988, May 9   Photo.   Perf. 14
B161 SP43 150m + 10m multi   .75 .40

Red Crescent Society SP44

1989, May 8   Photo.   Perf. 11½
Granite Paper
B162 SP44 150m +10m multi   .60 .30

Red Crescent Society — SP45

1990, May 8   Litho.   Perf. 14x13½
B163 SP45 150m +10m multi   .60 .25

Red Crescent Society — SP46

1991, May 8   Litho.   Perf. 13½
B164 SP46 180m +10m multi   .85 .45

Red Crescent Society — SP47

1993, Aug. 17   Litho.   Perf. 14x13½
B165 SP47 120m +30m multi   .85 .30

AIR POST STAMPS

No. 43 Surcharged in Red

1919, Apr.   Unwmk.   Perf. 14x13½
C1   A6   30c on 35c ol grn & brn   1.40 1.40
 a.   Inverted surcharge   160.00
 b.   Double surcharge   160.00
 c.   Double inverted surcharge   190.00
 d.   Double surcharge, one inverted   160.00

Type A6, Overprinted in Rose

1920, Apr.
C2   A6   30c ol grn, bl & rose   1.10 1.10

Nos. 53 and 55 Overprinted in Red

1927, Mar. 24
C3   A7   1fr indigo & ultra   1.10 .70
C4   A7   2fr grn & red, pink   3.50 2.10

Nos. 51 and 57 Srchd. in Black or Red

C5   A6   1.75fr on 75c (Bk)   1.10 .70
C6   A7   1.75fr on 5fr (R)   3.50 2.10

Type A13 Ovptd. like #C3-C4 in Blue
1928, Feb.
C7   A13   1.30fr org & lt vio   3.50 1.40
C8   A13   1.80fr gray grn & red   4.25 1.10
C9   A13   2.55fr lil & ol brn   3.50 1.10
   Nos. C7-C9 (3)   11.25 3.60

Type A13 Surcharged like #C5-C6 in Blue
1930, Aug.
C10   A13   1.50fr on 1.30fr org & lt vio   2.75 .85
C11   A13   1.50fr on 1.80fr gray grn & red   4.25 .70
C12   A13   1.50fr on 2.55fr lil & ol brn   8.50 2.10
   Nos. C10-C12 (3)   15.50 3.65

> **Catalogue values for unused stamps in this section, from this point to the end of the section, are for Never Hinged items.**

UPU Type of Regular Issue
1949, Oct. 28   Engr.   Perf. 13
C13   A23   25fr dk bl, bluish   2.50 1.75
UPU, 75th anniv. Exists imperf.; value $40.

Bird from Antique Mosaic, Museum of Sousse AP2

1949   Unwmk.
C14   AP2   200fr blue & indigo   8.00 2.10

(Arabic on one line) — AP3

1950-51
C15   AP3   100fr bl grn & brn   5.00 1.40
C16   AP3   200fr dk bl & ind ('51)   10.50 3.50

Monastir AP4

Coast at Korbous AP5

Design: 1000fr, Air view of Tozeur mosque.

1953-54
C17   AP4   100fr dk bl, ind & dk grn ('54)   4.50 1.10
C18   AP4   200fr cl, blk brn & red brn ('54)   6.25 1.75
C19   AP5   500fr dk brn & ultra   35.00 12.50
C20   AP5   1000fr dk green   60.00 25.00
   Nos. C17-C20 (4)   105.75 40.35

Imperforates exist.

Independent Kingdom
Types of 1953-54 Redrawn with "RF" Omitted
1956, Mar. 1
C21   AP4   100fr slate bl, indigo & dk grn   1.50 .70
C22   AP4   200fr multi   3.00 1.40
C23   AP5   500fr dk brn & ultra   6.00 6.00
C24   AP5   1000fr dk green   12.00 12.00
   Nos. C21-C24 (4)   22.50 20.10

Republic

Desert Swallows — AP6

Birds: #C26, Butcherbird. #C27, Cream-colored courser. 100m, European chaffinch. 150m, Pink flamingoes. 200m, Barbary partridges. 300m, European roller. 500m, Bustard.

1965-66   Photo.   Perf. 12½
Size: 23x31mm
C25   AP6   25m multi   .75 .30
C26   AP6   55m blk & lt bl   1.10 .75
C27   AP6   55m multi ('66)   .90 .55
Size: 22½x33mm
Perf. 11½
C28   AP6   100m multi   1.50 .90
C29   AP6   150m multi ('66)   4.75 2.25
C30   AP6   200m multi ('66)   5.75 2.40
C31   AP6   300m multi ('66)   7.50 5.00
C32   AP6   500m multi   11.00 6.00
   Nos. C25-C32 (8)   33.25 18.15

See No. 474.

AIR POST SEMI-POSTAL STAMP

> **Catalogue value for the unused stamp in this section is for a Never Hinged item.**

Window, Great Mosque of Kairouan — SPAP1

1952, May 5   Unwmk.   Engr.   Perf. 13
CB1   SPAP1   50fr + 10fr blk & gray grn   4.25 3.25

Surtax for charitable works of the army.

POSTAGE DUE STAMPS

Regular postage stamps perforated with holes in the form of a "T," the holes varying in size and number, were used as postage due stamps from 1888 to 1901.

For listings, see the *Scott Classic Specialized Catalogue of Stamps and Covers.*

D1

Perf. 14x13½
1901-03   Unwmk.   Typo.
J1   D1   1c black   .35 .45
J2   D1   2c orange   .70 .55
J3   D1   5c blue   .70 .45
J4   D1   10c brown   .70 .55

J5	D1	20c blue green		4.25	.85
J6	D1	30c carmine		3.50	.80
J7	D1	50c brown violet		1.75	.85
J8	D1	1fr olive green		1.40	.85
J9	D1	2fr carmine, grn		4.25	1.75
J10	D1	5fr blk, yellow		52.50	35.00
		Nos. J1-J10 (10)		70.10	42.10

No. J10 Surcharged in Blue

1914, Nov.

J11	D1	2fr on 5fr blk, yellow		3.50	3.50

In Jan. 1917 regular 5c postage stamps were overprinted "T" in an inverted triangle and used as postage due stamps.

D2

1922-49

J12	D2	1c black	.35	.30
J13	D2	2c black, yellow	.35	.30
J14	D2	5c violet brown	.70	.30
J15	D2	10c blue	.35	.45
J16	D2	10c yel green ('45)	.25	.25
J17	D2	20c orange, yel	.35	.45
J18	D2	30c brown ('23)	.35	.30
J19	D2	50c rose red	1.05	.50
J20	D2	50c blue vio ('45)	.25	.25
J21	D2	60c violet ('28)	1.05	.50
J22	D2	80c bister ('28)	.70	.35
J23	D2	90c orange red ('28)	1.10	.65
J24	D2	1fr green	.70	.30
J25	D2	2fr olive grn, straw	1.40	.55
J26	D2	2fr oar rose ('45)	.30	.30
J27	D2	3fr vio, pink ('29)	.35	.30
J28	D2	4fr grnsh bl ('45)	.35	.45
J29	D2	5fr violet	.70	.55
J30	D2	10fr cerise ('49)	.35	.35
J31	D2	20fr olive gray ('49)	1.40	1.10
		Nos. J12-J31 (20)	12.40	8.50

Inscribed: "Timbre Taxe"

1950   Unwmk.   Perf. 14x13½

J32	D2	30fr blue	1.75	1.50

> Catalogue values for unused stamps in this section, from this point to the end of the section, are for Never Hinged items.

Independent Kingdom

Grain and Fruit — D3

1957, Apr. 1   Engr.   Perf. 14x13

J33	D3	1fr bright green	.25	.25
J34	D3	2fr orange brown	.25	.25
J35	D3	3fr bluish green	.65	.50
J36	D3	4fr indigo	.65	.50
J37	D3	5fr lilac	.65	.50
J38	D3	10fr carmine	.65	.50
J39	D3	20fr chocolate	2.10	1.60
J40	D3	30fr blue	2.75	2.10
		Nos. J33-J40 (8)	7.95	6.20

Republic

Inscribed "Republique Tunisienne"

1960-77

J41	D3	1m emerald	.50	.25
J42	D3	2m red brown	.50	.25
J43	D3	3m bluish green	.50	.25
J44	D3	4m indigo	.50	.25
J45	D3	5m lilac	.50	.25
J46	D3	10m carmine rose	1.00	.50
J47	D3	20m violet brown	1.50	.75
J48	D3	30m blue	1.75	.90
J49	D3	40m lake ('77)	.50	.25
J50	D3	100m blue green ('77)	1.00	.50
		Nos. J41-J50 (10)	8.25	4.15

PARCEL POST STAMPS

Mail Delivery — PP1

1906   Unwmk.   Typo.   Perf. 13½x14

Q1	PP1	5c grn & vio brn	.70	.55
Q2	PP1	10c org & red	1.10	.70
Q3	PP1	20c dk brn & org	1.75	.70
a.		Center double	450.00	5,000.
Q4	PP1	25c blue & brn	2.50	.70
Q5	PP1	40c gray & rose	2.75	.70
Q6	PP1	50c vio brn & vio	2.75	.70
Q7	PP1	75c bis brn & bl	3.50	.70
Q8	PP1	1fr red brn & red	2.75	.50
Q9	PP1	2fr carmine & bl	8.50	1.10
Q10	PP1	5fr vio & vio brn	23.00	1.40
		Nos. Q1-Q10 (10)	49.30	7.75

For surcharges see Nos. B37-B46.

Gathering Dates — PP2

1926

Q11	PP2	5c pale brn & dk bl	.45	.45
Q12	PP2	10c rose & vio	.55	.45
Q13	PP2	20c yel grn & blk	.55	.45
Q14	PP2	25c org brn & blk	.55	.45
Q15	PP2	40c dp rose & dp grn	2.75	.55
Q16	PP2	50c lt vio & blk	1.75	.80
Q17	PP2	60c ol & brn red	1.75	.70
Q18	PP2	75c gray vio & bl grn	1.75	.70
Q19	PP2	80c ver & ol brn	1.75	.70
Q20	PP2	1fr Prus bl & dp rose	2.10	.70
Q21	PP2	2fr vio & mag	4.25	.70
Q22	PP2	4fr red & blk	4.50	.70
Q23	PP2	5fr red brn & dp vio	7.00	1.10
Q24	PP2	10fr dl red & grn, grnsh	14.00	1.10
Q25	PP2	20fr yel grn & dp vio, lav	27.00	1.75
		Nos. Q11-Q25 (15)	70.70	11.30

Parcel post stamps were discontinued July 1, 1940.

TURKEY
'tər-kē

LOCATION — Southeastern Europe and Asia Minor, between the Mediterranean and Black Seas
GOVT. — Republic
AREA — 300,947 sq. mi.
POP. — 65,599,206 (1999 est.)
CAPITAL — Ankara

The Ottoman Empire ceased to exist in 1922, and the Republic of Turkey was inaugurated in 1923.

40 Paras = 1 Piaster
40 Paras = 1 Ghurush (1926)
40 Paras = 1 Kurush (1926)
100 Kurush = 1 Lira

Catalogue values for unused stamps in this country are for Never Hinged items, beginning with Scott 817 in the regular postage section, Scott B69 in the semipostal section, Scott C1 in the airpost section, Scott J97 in the postage due section, Scott O1 in the official section, Scott P175 in the newspaper section, and Scott RA139 in the postal tax section.

Watermarks

Wmk. 394 — "PTT," Crescent and Star

Wmk. 405

Turkish Numerals

١ ٢ ٣ ٤ ٥
1 2 3 4 5

٦ ٧ ٨ ٩ ٠
6 7 8 9 0

"Tughra," Monogram of Sultan Abdul-Aziz
A1   A2

A3   A4

1863   Unwmk.   Litho.   Imperf.
Red Band: 20pa, 1pi, 2pi
Blue Band: 5pi
Thin Paper

1	A1	20pa blk, *yellow*	75.00	20.00
a.		Tête bêche pair	250.00	250.00
b.		Without band	100.00	
c.		Green band		
2	A2	1pi blk, *dl vio*	125.00	20.00
a.		1pi black, *gray*	125.00	21.50
b.		Tête bêche pair	400.00	300.00
c.		Without band	140.00	
d.		Design reversed		175.00
e.		1pi blk, *yel* (error)	250.00	150.00
4	A3	2pi blk, *grnsh bl*	115.00	20.00
a.		2pi black, *ind*	115.00	21.50
b.		Tête bêche pair	400.00	300.00
c.		Without band	140.00	
5	A4	5pi blk, *rose*	225.00	45.00
a.		Tête bêche pair	500.00	400.00
b.		Without band	250.00	
c.		Green band	275.00	
d.		Red band	275.00	

Thick, Surface Colored Paper

6	A1	20pa blk, *yellow*	250.00	37.50
a.		Tête bêche pair	450.00	450.00
b.		Design reversed	325.00	325.00
c.		Without band	225.00	225.00
d.		Paper colored through	225.00	225.00
7	A2	1pi blk, *gray*	300.00	35.00
a.		Tête bêche pair	900.00	900.00
b.		Design reversed		
c.		Without band		
d.		Paper colored through	350.00	225.00
		Nos. 1-7 (6)	1,090.	177.50

The 2pi and 5pi had two printings. In the common printing, the stamps are more widely spaced and alternate horizontal rows of 12 are inverted. In the first and rare printing, the stamps are more closely spaced and no rows are tête bêche.
See Nos. J1-J4.

Crescent and Star, Symbols of Turkish Caliphate — A5

Surcharged

The bottom characters of this and the following surcharges denote the denomination. The characters at top and sides translate, "Ottoman Empire Posts."

1865   Typo.   Perf. 12½

8	A5	10pa deep green	11.00	35.00
c.		"1" instead of "10" in each corner	300.00	300.00
9	A5	20pa yellow	7.00	6.00
a.		Star without rays	9.00	6.00
10	A5	1pi lilac	12.50	4.00
a.		Star without rays	25.00	10.00
11	A5	2pi blue	6.50	4.00
12	A5	5pi carmine	5.50	4.50
d.		Inverted surcharge		
13	A5	25pi red orange	325.00	250.00

Imperf., Pairs

8b	A5	10pa	125.00	125.00
9b	A5	20pa	125.00	125.00
10b	A5	1pi	100.00	90.00
11a	A5	2pi	100.00	90.00
12b	A5	5pi	150.00	110.00
13a	A5	25pi	900.00	900.00

See Nos. J6-J35. For overprints and surcharges see Nos. 14-52, 64-65, 446-461, 467-468, J71-J77, Eastern Rumelia 1.

Surcharged

1867

14	A5	10pa gray green	9.50	
a.		Imperf., pair	55.00	
15	A5	20pa yellow	15.00	
a.		Imperf., pair	75.00	
16	A5	1pi lilac	20.00	
a.		Imperf., pair	110.00	
b.		Imperf., with surcharge of 5pi	200.00	
17	A5	2pi blue	5.50	45.00
a.		Imperf.	50.00	
18	A5	5pi rose	4.50	45.00
a.		Imperf.	50.00	
19	A5	25pi orange	3,600.	
		Nos. 14-18 (5)	54.50	

Nos. 14, 15, 16 and 19 were never placed in use.

Surcharged

1869   Perf. 13½

20	A5	10pa dull violet	100.00	12.00
a.		Printed on both sides		
b.		Imperf., pair	90.00	80.00
c.		Inverted surcharge		90.00
d.		Double surcharge		
e.		10pa yellow (error)		300.00
21	A5	20pa pale green	400.00	14.00
a.		Printed on both sides	450.00	275.00
22	A5	1pi yellow	10.00	2.50
c.		Inverted surcharge	100.00	
d.		Double surcharge		
e.		Surcharged on both sides		
f.		Printed on both sides		
23	A5	2pi orange red	200.00	10.00
b.		Imperf., pair	125.00	125.00
c.		Printed on both sides		125.00
d.		Inverted surcharge	70.00	70.00
e.		Surcharged on both sides		140.00
24	A5	5pi blue	5.00	10.00
25	A5	5pi gray	30.00	37.50
26	A5	25pi dull rose	37.50	125.00
		Nos. 20-26 (7)	782.50	211.00

Pin-perf., Perf. 5 to 11 and Compound

1870-71

27	A5	10pa lilac	550.00	25.00
28	A5	10pa brown	500.00	15.00
29	A5	20pa gray green	75.00	10.00
a.		Printed on both sides		
30	A5	1pi yellow	550.00	10.00
a.		Inverted surcharge	500.00	80.00
b.		Without surcharge		
31	A5	2pi red	8.00	5.00
a.		Imperf.	20.00	20.00
b.		Printed on both sides		40.00
c.		Surcharged on both sides		
32	A5	5pi blue	5.00	12.50
a.		5pi greenish blue	6.00	8.00
33	A5	5pi slate	40.00	50.00
a.		Printed on both sides		
b.		Surcharged on both sides		80.00
34	A5	25pi dull rose	40.00	75.00
		Nos. 27-34 (8)	1,768.	202.50

1873   Perf. 12, 12½

35	A5	10pa dark lilac	475.00	25.00
a.		Inverted surcharge		90.00
36	A5	10pa olive brown	110.00	17.50
a.		10pa bister	110.00	11.00
37	A5	2pi vermilion	3.50	4.50
a.		Surcharged on both sides	22.50	22.50
		Nos. 35-37 (3)	588.50	47.00

Surcharged

1874-75   Perf. 13½

38	A5	10pa red violet	52.50	7.50
a.		Imperf., pair	210.00	50.00
39	A5	20pa yellow green	15.00	5.00
b.		Inverted surcharge	30.00	13.00
c.		Double surcharge		
40	A5	1pi yellow	210.00	30.00
a.		Imperf., pair	100.00	80.00

Perf. 12, 12½

41	A5	10pa red violet	25.00	10.00
a.		Inverted surcharge	45.00	60.00
		Nos. 38-41 (4)	302.50	52.50

Surcharged

1876, Apr.   Perf. 13½

42	A5	10pa red lilac	2.00	.50
a.		Inverted surcharge	70.00	
b.		Imperf., pair	60.00	60.00
43	A5	20pa pale green	2.00	.50
a.		Inverted surcharge	70.00	
b.		Imperf., pair	60.00	60.00
44	A5	1pi yellow	2.00	.50
a.		Imperf., pair	60.00	60.00
46	A5	5pi gray blue	1,700.	
47	A5	25pi dull rose	1,700.	
		Nos. 42-44 (3)	6.00	

Nos. 46 and 47 were never placed in use.
See Nos. 64-65.

Surcharged

1876, Jan.

48	A5	¼pi on 10pa violet	3.00	2.50
49	A5	½pi on 20pa yel grn	6.25	2.50
50	A5	1¼pi on 50pa rose	2.25	2.50
a.		Imperf., pair	60.00	
51	A5	2pi on 2pi redsh brn	40.00	7.50
52	A5	5pi on 5pi gray blue	10.00	85.00
		Nos. 48-52 (5)	61.50	100.00

The surcharge on Nos. 48-52 restates in French the value originally expressed in Turkish characters.
The vast majority of No. 51 unused are without gum.

A7

1876, Sept.   Typo.   Perf. 13½

53	A7	10pa black & rose lil	2.00	6.25
54	A7	20pa red vio & grn	62.50	5.00
55	A7	50pa blue & yellow	1.50	10.00
56	A7	2pi black & redsh brn	1.60	5.00
57	A7	5pi red & blue	3.00	12.50
b.		Cliché of 25pi in plate of 5pi	400.00	375.00
58	A7	25pi claret & rose	15.00	85.00
a.		Imperf.	160.00	
		Nos. 53-58 (6)	85.60	123.75

Nos. 56-58 exist perf. 11½, but were not regularly issued.
See Nos. 59-63, 66-91, J36-J38. For overprints see Nos. 462-466, 469-476, J78-J79, P10-P14, Eastern Rumelia 2-40.

1880-84   Perf. 13½

59	A7	5pa black & ol ('81)	3.00	6.50
a.		Imperf.	30.00	
60	A7	10pa black & grn ('84)	3.00	3.50
61	A7	20pa black & rose	55.00	2.00
62	A7	1pi blk & bl (*piastres*)	75.00	3.00
a.		1pi black & gray blue	85.00	
b.		Imperf.	60.00	
63	A7	1pi blk & bl (*piastre*) ('81)	110.00	5.00
		Nos. 59-63 (5)	246.00	20.00

A cliché of No. 63 was inserted in a plate of the Eastern Rumelia 1pi (No. 13). This was found in the remainder stock.
Nos. 60-61 and 63 exist perf. 11½, but were not regularly issued.
See Nos. J36-J38.

1881-82

Surcharged like Apr., 1876 Issue

64	A5	20pa gray	4.25	6.25
a.		Inverted surcharge	30.00	
b.		Imperf., pair	40.00	
65	A5	2pi pale salmon	3.00	1.00
a.		Inverted surcharge	30.00	

1884-86   Perf. 11½, 13½

66	A7	5pa lil & pale lil ('86)	200.00	150.00
67	A7	10pa grn & pale grn	1.60	1.25
68	A7	20pa rose & pale rose	2.00	1.25
69	A7	1pi blue & lt blue	2.00	1.25

Perf. 11½

70	A7	2pi ocher & pale ocher	2.25	1.25
71	A7	5pi red brn & pale brn	20.00	25.00
c.		5pi ocher & pale ocher (error)	20.00	30.00

Perf. 11½, 13½

73	A7	25pi blk & pale gray ('86)	300.00	425.00
		Nos. 66-73 (7)	527.85	605.00

Imperf

66a	A7	5pa	60.00	
67a	A7	10pa	40.00	
68b	A7	20pa	40.00	
69b	A7	1pi	40.00	
73a	A7	25pi	150.00	

1886   Perf. 13½

74	A7	5pa black & pale gray	2.00	2.50
75	A7	2pi orange & lt bl	2.00	2.50
76	A7	5pi grn & pale grn	3.00	25.00
77	A7	25pi bis & pale bis	45.00	150.00
		Nos. 74-77 (4)	52.00	179.50

Imperf

74a	A7	5pa		30.00
75b	A7	2pi		40.00
76b	A7	5pi		40.00
77a	A7	25pi		40.00

Stamps of 1884-86, bisected and surcharged as above, 10pa, 20pa, 1pi and 2pi or surcharged "2" in red are stated to have been made privately and without authority. With the aid of employees of the post office, stamps were passed through the mails.

1888 — Perf. 13½

83	A7	5pa green & yellow	2.50	5.00
84	A7	2pi red lilac & bl	1.50	1.50
85	A7	5pi dk brown & gray	5.00	20.00
86	A7	25pi red & yellow	30.00	150.00
		Nos. 83-86 (4)	39.00	176.50

Imperf

83a	A7	5pa	40.00
84a	A7	2pi	40.00
85a	A7	5pi	40.00
86a	A7	25pi	40.00

Nos. 74-86 exist perf. 11½, but were not regularly issued.

1890 — Perf. 11½, 13½

87	A7	10pa green & gray	8.00	1.00
88	A7	20pa rose & gray	1.60	1.00
89	A7	1pi blue & gray	125.00	10.00
90	A7	2pi yellow & gray	2.25	7.50
91	A7	5pi buff & gray	5.00	22.50
		Nos. 87-91 (5)	141.85	33.00

Imperf

87a	A7	10pa	30.00
88a	A7	20pa	30.00
89a	A7	1pi	100.00
90b	A7	2pi	100.00
91a	A7	5pi	35.00

Arms and Tughra of "El Gazi" (The Conqueror) Sultan Abdul Hamid
A10   A11

A12   A13

A14

1892-98 — Typo. — Perf. 13½

95	A10	10pa gray green	2.00	.50
96	A11	20pa violet brn ('98)	1.25	.50
a.		20pa dark pink	7.50	.45
b.		20pa pink	40.00	1.00
97	A12	1pi pale blue	90.00	.50
98	A13	2pi brown org	4.50	.50
a.		Tête bêche pair	120.00	75.00
99	A14	5pi dull violet	2.25	13.00
a.		Turkish numeral in upper right corner reads "50" instead of "5"	50.00	45.00
		Nos. 95-99 (5)	100.00	15.00

See Nos. J39-J42. For surcharges and overprints see Nos. 100, 288-291, 350, 359, 477-478, B38, B41, J80-J82, P25-P34, P36, P121-P122, P134-P137, P153-P154.

No. 95 Surcharged in Red

1897

100	A10	5pa on 10pa gray grn	3.00	1.00
a.		"Cinq" instead of "Cinq"	30.00	25.00

Turkish stamps of types A11, A17-A18, A21-A24, A26, A28-A39, A41 with or without Turkish overprints and English surcharges with "Baghdad" or "Iraq" are listed under Mesopotamia in Vol. 4.

Turkish stamps of types A19 and A21 with Double-headed Eagle and "Shqipenia" handstamp are listed under Albania in Vol. 1.

A16

1901 — Typo. — Perf. 13¼
For Foreign Postage

102	A16	5pa bister	1.25	.60
103	A16	10pa yellow green	1.25	.60
104	A16	20pa magenta	1.25	.60
a.		Perf. 12	2.50	1.00
105	A16	1pi violet blue	1.50	1.00
106	A16	2pi gray blue	2.50	1.00
107	A16	5pi ocher	8.50	3.50
108	A16	25pi dark green	100.00	30.00
109	A16	50pi yellow	250.00	100.00
		Nos. 102-109 (8)	366.25	137.30

A17

For Domestic Postage
Perf. 12, 13¼

110	A17	5pa purple	1.25	.35
111	A17	10pa green	1.25	.35
112	A17	20pa carmine	1.25	.35
113	A17	1pi blue	1.25	.35
a.		Imperf.	20.00	
114	A17	2pi orange	2.00	.35
115	A17	5pi lilac rose	0.00	.35

Perf. 13½

116	A17	25pi brown	12.00	2.25
a.		Perf. 12	25.00	8.50
117	A17	50pi yellow brown	60.00	6.00
a.		Perf. 12	55.00	17.00
		Nos. 110-117 (8)	85.00	10.35

Nos. 110-113 exist perf. 12x13½.
See Nos. J43-J46.
For overprints and surcharges see Nos. 165-180, 292-303, 340-341, 361-377, 479-493, B19-B20, B37, P37-P48, P69-P80, P123-P126, P138-P146, P155-P164.

A18

1905 — Perf. 12, 13½ and Compound

118	A18	5pa ocher	1.00	.35
119	A18	10pa dull green	1.25	.50
a.		Imperf.	30.00	30.00
120	A18	20pa carmine	1.00	.50
a.		Imperf.	30.00	30.00
121	A18	1pi blue	1.00	.50
122	A18	2pi slate	1.50	.90
123	A18	2½pi red violet	1.50	.90
a.		Imperf.	30.00	30.00

124	A18	5pi brown	2.00	.90
125	A18	10pi orange brn	5.00	1.50
126	A18	25pi olive green	15.00	12.00
127	A18	50pi deep violet	50.00	25.00

See Nos. J47-J48. For overprints and surcharges see Nos. 128-131, 181-182, 304-314, 351-354, 378-389, 494-508, B1-B3, B21-B23, B39-B40, P49-P54, P127-P129, P147-P150, P165-P171.

Large "Discount" Overprint in Carmine or Blue

1906

128	A18	10pa dull green (C)	2.50	1.00
129	A18	20pa carmine (Bl)	4.00	1.00
130	A18	1pi blue (C)	4.00	1.00
131	A18	2pi slate (C)	22.50	6.00
		Nos. 128-131 (4)	112.25	52.05

Stamps bearing this overprint were sold to merchants at a discount from face value to encourage the use of Turkish stamps on foreign correspondence, instead of those of the various European powers which maintained post offices in Turkey. The overprint is the Arab "B," for "Béhié," meaning "discount."

Tughra and 'Reshad' of Sultan Abdülhamid — A19

Tughra is upright and there is no space between the script and the frame.

1908

132	A19	5pa ocher	1.25	.50
133	A19	10pa blue green	1.75	.50
134	A19	20pa carmine	45.00	.50
135	A19	1pi bright blue	13.00	.50
a.		1pi ultramarine	50.00	10.00
136	A19	2pi blue black	6.50	1.00
137	A19	2½pi violet brown	2.00	1.00
138	A19	5pi dark violet	140.00	1.50
139	A19	10pi red	35.00	2.00
140	A19	25pi dark green	6.50	5.00
141	A19	50pi red brown	30.00	32.50

See Nos. J49-J50. For overprints and surcharges see Nos. 142-145, 314B-316B, 390-396, 509-516A, B4-B6, B17, B24-B27, P55-P60, P130-P131, P151, P172, Thrace 15.

Small "Discount" Overprint in Carmine or Blue

142	A19	10pa blue green (C)	7.50	1.75
143	A19	20pa carmine (Bl)	7.50	1.75
144	A19	1pi brt blue (C)	19.00	1.75
145	A19	2pi blue black (C)	30.00	8.00
		Nos. 132-145 (14)	345.00	58.25

A20

Perf. 12, 13½ & Compound
1908, Dec. 17

146	A20	5pa ocher	1.00	1.25
147	A20	10pa blue green	1.50	1.25
148	A20	20pa carmine	1.50	1.25
149	A20	1pi ultra	4.50	1.50
150	A20	2pi gray black	20.00	15.00
		Nos. 146-150 (5)	28.50	20.25

Imperf

146a	A20	5pa	15.00	15.00
147a	A20	10pa	15.00	15.00
148a	A20	20pa	15.00	15.00
149a	A20	1pi	30.00	30.00

Granting of a Constitution, the date of which is inscribed on the banderol: "324 Temuz 10" (July 24, 1908).

For overprints see Nos. 397, 517.

Tughra and "Reshad" of Sultan Mohammed V — A21

The Tughra leans slightly to the left, and there is space under the script.

1909, Dec.

151	A21	5pa ocher	1.00	.35
152	A21	10pa blue green	1.00	.35
a.		Imperf.	30.00	30.00
153	A21	20pa carmine rose	1.00	.35
154	A21	1pi ultra	8.00	.50
a.		1pi bright blue	12.50	.50
155	A21	2pi blue black	2.00	.50
156	A21	2½pi dark brown	70.00	14.00
157	A21	5pi dark violet	2.00	1.00
158	A21	10pi dull red	25.00	1.00
159	A21	25pi dark green	325.00	75.00
160	A21	50pi red brown	50.00	75.00

The 2pa olive green, type A21, is a newspaper stamp, No. P68.
Two types exist for the 10pa, 20pa and 1pi. In the second type, the damaged crescent is restored.

See Nos. J51-J52. For overprints and surcharges see Nos. 161-164, 317-327, 342-343, 398-406, 518-528, 567, B7-B14, B18, B28-B32, P61-P68, P81, P132-P133, P152, P173, Turkey in Asia 67, 72, Thrace 1-4, 13, 13A, 14.

Overprinted in Carmine or Blue

161	A21	10pa blue grn (C)	5.00	1.25
a.		Imperf.	30.00	
162	A21	20pa car rose (Bl)	5.00	1.50
a.		Imperf.	30.00	
163	A21	1pi ultra (C)	8.00	2.00
a.		Imperf.	30.00	
b.		1pi bright blue	6.50	3.00
164	A21	2pi blue black (C)	75.00	25.00
a.		Imperf.	50.00	
		Nos. 151-164 (14)	653.00	197.80

Stamps of 1901-05 Overprinted in Carmine or Blue

The overprint was applied to 18 denominations in four settings with change of city name, producing individual sets for each city: "MONASTIR," "PRISTINA," "SALONIQUE" and "USKUB."

1911, June 26 — Perf. 12, 13½

165	A16	5pa bister	4.50	5.00
166	A16	10pa yel grn	4.50	5.00
167	A16	20pa magenta	9.50	10.00
168	A16	1pi violet blue	9.50	10.00
169	A16	2pi gray blue	9.50	10.00
170	A16	5pi ocher	50.00	80.00
171	A16	25pi dark green	70.00	100.00
172	A16	50pi yellow	100.00	150.00
173	A17	5pa purple	5.50	4.50
174	A17	10pa green	6.25	4.50
175	A17	20pa carmine	8.50	9.00
176	A17	1pi blue	8.50	9.00
177	A17	2pi orange	8.50	9.00
178	A17	5pi lilac rose	47.50	70.00
179	A17	25pi chocolate	150.00	200.00
d.		Perf. 12	150.00	200.00
180	A17	50pi yel brn	120.00	145.00
d.		Perf. 12	150.00	200.00
181	A18	2½pi red violet	65.00	110.00
182	A18	10pi org brn	65.00	90.00
		Nos. 165-182 (18)	742.25	1,021.

Sultan's visit to Macedonia. The Arabic overprint reads: "Souvenir of the Sultan's Journey, 1329." See Nos. P69-P81.

General Post Office, Constantinople
A22

1913, Mar. 14   Perf. 12

237	A22	2pa olive green	.65	.50
238	A22	5pa ocher	.65	.50
239	A22	10pa blue green	.80	.50
240	A22	20pa carmine rose	.80	.50
241	A22	1pi ultra	.80	.50
242	A22	2pi indigo	1.50	.50
243	A22	5pi dull violet	12.00	.50
244	A22	10pi dull red	8.00	1.00
245	A22	25pi gray green	22.50	22.50
246	A22	50pi orange brown	85.00	100.00

See Nos. J53-J58. For overprints and surcharges see Nos. 247-250, 328-339, 344, 407-414, 529-538, 568, B14-B16, B33-B36. Mesopotamia Nos. N6, N16-N19, N24-N25. Turkey in Asia 68, Thrace 10, 10A, 11, 11A, 12, N82.

Overprinted in Carmine or Blue

247	A22	10pa blue green (C)	1.50	.50
248	A22	20pa car rose (Bl)	1.75	.50
249	A22	1pi ultra (C)	2.00	.50
250	A22	2pi indigo (C)	25.00	7.50
		Nos. 237-250 (14)	162.95	136.00

Mosque of Selim, Adrianople — A23

1913, Oct. 23   Engr.

251	A23	10pa green	1.50	1.75
252	A23	20pa red	2.50	1.75
253	A23	40pa blue	12.00	2.50
		Nos. 251-253 (3)	16.00	6.00

Recapture of Adrianople (Edirne) by the Turks.

See Nos. 592, J59-J62. For overprints and surcharge see Nos. 415-417, 539-540, J59-J62, J67-J70, J83-J86, Mesopotamia No. N7, Thrace N84.

Obelisk of Theodosius in the Hippodrome A24

Column of Constantine A25

Leander's Tower — A26

One of the Seven Towers — A27

Fener Bahçe (Garden Lighthouse) A28

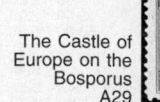

The Castle of Europe on the Bosporus A29

Mosque of Sultan Ahmed — A30

Monument to the Martyrs of Liberty A31

Fountains of Suleiman A32

Cruiser "Hamidie" A33

View of Kandili on the Bosporus A34

War Ministry (Later Istanbul University) — A35

Sweet Waters of Europe Park A36

Mosque of Suleiman A37

The Bosporus A38

Sultan Ahmed's Fountain A39

Sultan Mohammed V — A40

Designs A24-A39: Views of Constantinople.

1914, Jan. 14   Litho.

254	A24	2pa red lilac	1.00	.50
255	A25	4pa dark brown	1.00	.50
256	A26	5pa violet brown	1.00	.50
257	A27	6pa dark blue	1.00	.50

Engr.

258	A28	10pa green	2.25	.50
259	A29	20pa red	2.00	.50
260	A30	1pi blue	1.00	.50
b.		Booklet pane of 2+2 labels		
261	A31	1½pi car & blk	1.25	.50
262	A32	1¾pi sl & red brn	1.50	1.00
263	A33	2pi green & blk	2.00	.50
264	A34	2½pi org & ol grn	2.00	.50
265	A35	5pi dull violet	3.50	.60
266	A36	10pi red brown	5.50	.55
267	A37	25pi olive green	125.00	9.00
268	A38	50pi carmine	5.50	4.50
269	A39	100pi deep blue	75.00	21.00
		Cut cancellation		14.00
270	A40	200pi green & blk	550.00	225.00
		Cut cancellation		50.00
		Nos. 254-270 (17)	780.50	266.65

See Nos. 590-591, 593-598.
For overprints and surcharges see Nos. 271-287, 419, 541, 552-553, 574A, 601, 603-604, P174, Mesopotamia Nos. N1-N5, N28-N41, N50-N53, NO1-NO22, Turkey in Asia 1-3, 5-9, 73-74, Thrace N77, N78.

Nos. 258-260, 262-263, Ovptd. in Red or Blue

271	A28	10pa green (R)	4.00	1.00
272	A29	20pa red (Bl)	8.00	.50
273	A30	1pi blue (R)	2.00	.50
275	A32	1¾pi sl & red brn (Bl)	2.00	1.50
276	A33	2pi green & blk (R)	50.00	5.50
		Nos. 271-276 (5)	66.00	9.00

No. 261 Surcharged

1914, July 23

277	A31	1pi on 1½pi car & blk	7.00	1.50
a.		"1330" omitted	15.00	15.00
b.		Double surcharge		
c.		Triple surcharge	15.00	15.00

7th anniv. of the Constitution. The surcharge reads "10 July, 1330, National fête" and has also the numeral "1" at each side, over the original value of the stamp.

Stamps of 1914 Overprinted in Black or Red

278	A26	5pa violet brn (Bk)	2.00	.60
279	A28	10pa green (R)	5.00	.60
280	A29	20pa red (Bk)	5.00	.60
281	A30	1pi blue (R)	1.00	1.50
282	A33	2pi grn & blk (R)	11.00	1.50
283	A35	5pi dull violet (R)	60.00	3.00
284	A36	10pi red brown (R)	190.00	55.00
		Nos. 278-284 (7)	283.00	62.80

This overprint reads "Abolition of the Capitulations, 1330".

No. 269 Surcharged

1915

286	A39	10pi on 100pi	70.00	20.00
a.		Inverted surcharge	90.00	—

No. 270 Surcharged

287	A40	25pi on 200pi	25.00	8.00

Preceding Issues Overprinted in Carmine or Black

1915   On Stamps of 1892

288	A10	10pa gray green	1.00	.50
a.		Inverted overprint	15.00	15.00
289	A13	2pi brown orange	1.50	.50
a.		Inverted overprint	7.50	7.50
290	A14	5pi dull violet	4.00	.50
a.		On No. 99a	17.00	17.00

On Stamp of 1897

291	A10	5pa on 10pa gray grn	1.00	.50
a.		Inverted overprint	15.00	15.00
b.		On No. 100a	10.00	10.00

On Stamps of 1901

292	A16	5pa bister	1.00	.50
293	A16	1pi violet blue	3.00	.50
294	A16	2pi gray blue	2.50	.50
295	A16	5pi ocher	20.00	.50
296	A16	25pi dark green	50.00	20.00
297	A17	5pa purple	1.00	.50
298	A17	10pa green	1.50	.50
299	A17	20pa carmine	1.50	.50
a.		Inverted overprint	15.00	15.00
300	A17	1pi blue	1.50	.50
a.		Inverted overprint	15.00	15.00
301	A17	2pi orange	2.00	.50
a.		Inverted overprint	7.50	7.50
b.		Double ovpt. (R and Bk)	5.00	5.00
302	A17	5pi lilac rose	2.50	.50
303	A17	25pi brown	12.50	2.00

On Stamps of 1905

304	A18	5pa ocher	1.00	.50
305	A18	10pa dull green	1.00	.50
a.		Inverted overprint	15.00	15.00
306	A18	20pa carmine	1.00	.50
a.		Inverted overprint	15.00	15.00
307	A18	1pi brt blue	1.50	.50
a.		Inverted overprint	15.00	15.00
308	A18	2pi slate	2.50	.50
a.		Inverted overprint	20.00	20.00
309	A18	2½pi red violet	1.50	.50
310	A18	5pi brown	2.00	.50
a.		Inverted overprint	20.00	20.00
311	A18	10pi orange brown	12.50	.50
312	A18	25pi olive green	50.00	8.00

With Additional Overprint On Nos. 313-314

On Stamps of 1906

313	A18	10pa dull green	2.00	.50
314	A18	2pi slate	5.00	.50
a.		Inverted overprint	15.00	15.00

On Stamps of 1908

314B	A19	2pi blue black	225.00	50.00
315	A19	2½pi violet brown	5.00	1.50
315A	A19	5pi dark violet	100.00	35.00

315B	A19	10pi red	15.00	7.50
316	A19	25pi dark green	30.00	5.00
a.		Inverted overprint	50.00	50.00

For surcharges see Mesopotamia Nos. N13-N15.

With Additional Overprint on No. 316B

316B	A19	2pi blue black	15.00	5.00

On Stamps of 1909

317	A21	5pa ocher	1.00	.50
a.		Inverted overprint	15.00	15.00
b.		Double overprint	15.00	15.00
318	A21	20pa car rose	1.25	.75
a.		Inverted overprint	15.00	15.00
319	A21	1pi ultra	2.00	.50
a.		Inverted overprint	15.00	15.00
320	A21	2pi blue blk	2.50	.75
a.		Inverted overprint	15.00	15.00
321	A21	2½pi dark brn	67.50	25.00
322	A21	5pi dark violet	1.00	.50
a.		Inverted overprint	15.00	15.00
323	A21	10pi dull red	10.00	.50
324	A21	25pi dark green	1,750.	1,200.

With Additional Overprint On Nos. 325, 326, and 327

325	A21	20pa carmine rose	2.00	.50
a.		Inverted overprint	20.00	20.00
326	A21	1pi ultra	2.00	.50
327	A21	2pi blue black	3.50	.50

On Stamps of 1913

328	A22	5pa ocher	1.00	.50
a.		Inverted overprint	15.00	14.00
329	A22	10pa blue green	1.00	.50
a.		Inverted overprint	20.00	18.00
330	A22	20pa carmine rose	1.00	.50
a.		Inverted overprint	15.00	14.00
331	A22	1pi ultra	1.50	.50
a.		Inverted overprint	10.00	9.00
332	A22	2pi indigo	2.00	.50
a.		Inverted overprint	10.00	9.00
333	A22	5pi dull violet	3.00	.50
334	A22	10pi dull red	10.00	.50
a.		Inverted overprint	20.00	18.00
335	A22	25pi gray green	30.00	20.00

With Additional Overprint

336	A22	10pa blue green	1.00	.50
337	A22	20pa carmine rose	1.00	.50
338	A22	1pi ultra	2.00	.50
339	A22	2pi indigo	7.50	3.00
a.		Inverted overprint	15.00	15.00

See Nos. P121-P133.

Stamps of 1901-13 Overprinted

1916

340	A17	5pa purple	1.00	.50
a.		5pa purple, #P43	80.00	80.00
341	A17	10pa green	1.50	.50
a.		Double overprint	6.50	6.50
b.		10pa yellow green, #103	80.00	80.00
342	A21	20pa car rose, #153	2.00	.75
a.		20pa carmine rose, #162	110.00	110.00
343	A21	1pi ultra	5.50	1.00
344	A22	5pi dull violet	10.00	3.00
		Nos. 340-344 (5)	20.00	5.75

Occupation of the Sinai Peninsula.

Old General Post Office of Constantinople A41

1916, May 29 Litho. Perf. 12½, 13½

345	A41	5pa green	1.00	.90
346	A41	10pa carmine	1.00	.50
347	A41	20pa ultra	1.00	.50
348	A41	1pi violet & blk	2.00	.50
349	A41	5pi yel brn & blk	30.00	2.50
		Nos. 345-349 (5)	35.00	4.90

Introduction of postage in Turkey, 50th anniv. For overprints see Nos. 418, B42-B45.

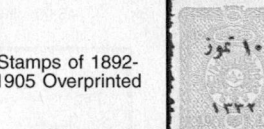

Stamps of 1892-1905 Overprinted

1916

350	A10	10pa gray grn (R)	1.50	1.50
351	A18	20pa carmine (Bl)	2.50	1.50
352	A18	1pi blue (R)	12.00	6.00
353	A18	2pi slate (Bk)	15.00	1.00
354	A18	2½pi red violet (Bk)	25.00	3.00
		Nos. 350-354 (5)	56.00	13.00

National Fête Day. Overprint reads "10 Temuz 1332" (July 23, 1916).

Preceding Issues Overprinted or Surcharged in Red or Black

a   b

1916 **On Stamps of 1892-98**

355	A10(a)	10pa gray green	1.00	.50
355A	A11(a)	20pa vio brn	1.00	.50
b.		Inverted overprint	10.00	10.00
356	A12(a)	1pi gray blue	50.00	50.00
357	A13(a)	2pi brown org	5.00	1.50
358	A14(a)	5pi dull violet	50.00	50.00

On Stamp of 1897

359	A15(b)	5pa on 10pa gray grn	.75	.50

On Stamps of 1901

361	A16(a)	5pa bister	1.00	.75
a.		Double overprint	15.00	7.50
362	A16(a)	10pa yel grn	1.00	.50
363	A16(a)	20pa magenta	.75	.50
364	A16(a)	1pi violet blue	1.00	.50
a.		Inverted overprint	7.50	7.50
365	A16(a)	2pi gray blue	5.00	1.00
366	A16(b)	5pi on 25pi dk grn	55.00	55.00
367	A16(b)	10pi on 25pi dk grn	55.00	55.00
368	A16(a)	25pi dark green	55.00	55.00
369	A17(a)	5pa purple	75.00	50.00
370	A17(a)	10pa green	2.00	1.50
371	A17(a)	20pa carmine	.75	.50
a.		Inverted overprint	15.00	15.00
372	A17(a)	1pi blue	1.00	.50
a.		Inverted overprint	30.00	30.00
373	A17(a)	2pi orange	1.50	.50
374	A17(b)	10pi on 25pi brown	5.00	1.50
375	A17(b)	10pi on 50pi yel brn	7.50	1.50
376	A17(a)	25pi brown	7.50	1.50
377	A17(a)	50pi yel brn	10.00	2.50

On Stamps of 1905

378	A18(a)	5pa ocher	.75	.50
379	A18(a)	20pa carmine	1.00	.50
a.		Inverted overprint	30.00	30.00
380	A18(a)	1pi brt blue	2.00	.50
a.		Inverted overprint	30.00	30.00
381	A18(a)	2pi slate	1.50	1.00
382	A18(a)	2½pi red violet	7.50	1.50
383	A18(b)	10pi on 25pi ol grn	10.00	3.00
384	A18(b)	10pi on 50pi dp vio	10.00	4.00
385	A18(a)	25pi olive green	10.00	5.00
386	A18(a)	50pi deep violet	7.50	5.00

On Stamps of 1906

387	A18(a)	10pa dull green	1.50	.60
388	A18(a)	20pa carmine	1.50	1.00
389	A18(a)	1pi brt blue	1.50	1.00

On Stamps of 1908

390	A19(a)	2½pi violet brown	67.50	67.50
391	A19(b)	10pi on 25pi dk grn	20.00	12.50
392	A19(b)	10pi on 50pi red brn	67.50	67.50
393	A19(b)	25pi on 50pi red brn	67.50	67.50
394	A19(a)	25pi dark green	15.00	5.00
395	A19(a)	50pi red brown	50.00	50.00

With Additional Overprint

396	A19(a)	2pi blue black	67.50	67.50

On Stamps of 1908-09

397	A20(a)	5pa ocher	67.50	67.50
398	A21(a)	5pa ocher	1.00	2.50
399	A21(a)	10pa blue green	50.00	50.00
400	A21(a)	20pa carmine rose	50.00	50.00
401	A21(a)	1pi ultra	2.00	1.00
402	A21(a)	2pi blue black	4.00	2.00
403	A21(a)	2½pi dark brown	50.00	50.00
404	A21(a)	5pi dark violet	50.00	50.00

With Additional Overprint

405	A21(a)	1pi ultra	67.50	67.50
406	A21(a)	2pi blue black	50.00	50.00

On Stamps of 1913

407	A22(a)	5pa ocher	1.00	.75
408	A22(a)	20pa carmine rose	1.50	.50
409	A22(a)	1pi ultra	1.50	.50
410	A22(a)	2pi indigo	3.00	1.00
411	A22(b)	10pi on 50pi org brn	12.50	10.00
412	A22(a)	25pi gray green	7.50	5.00
413	A22(a)	50pi orange brown	15.00	12.50

With Additional Overprint

414	A22(a)	1pi ultra	2.00	1.00

On Commemorative Stamps of 1913

415	A23(a)	10pa green	1.25	.50
416	A23(a)	20pa red	2.00	.75
417	A23(a)	40pa blue	6.00	2.50

On Commemorative Stamp of 1916

418	A41(a)	5pi yel brn & blk	1.00	.50

No. 277 Surcharged in Blue

419	A31	60pa on 1pi on 1½pi	3.25	3.50
a.		"1330" omitted	40.00	40.00

See Nos. P134-P152, J67-J70.

Turkish Artillery A42

Mosque at Orta Köy, Constantinople — A43

Lighthouse on Bosporus — A44

Monument to Martyrs of Liberty — A45

Map of the Dardanelles; Sultan Mohammed V — A46

Map of the Dardanelles A47

Istanbul Across the Golden Horn A48

Pyramids of Egypt A49

Dolma Bahçe Palace and Mohammed V — A50

Sentry and Shell — A51

Sultan Mohammed V — A52

1916-18 Typo. Perf. 11½, 12½

420	A42	2pa violet	1.10	1.10
421	A43	5pa orange	1.00	.50
424	A44	10pa green	1.00	.50

Engr.

425	A45	20pa deep rose	1.00	.50
426	A46	1pi dull violet	2.00	.50

Typo.

428	A47	50pa ultra	1.00	.50
429	A48	2pi org brn & ind	2.00	.50
430	A49	5pi pale blue & blk	25.00	2.25

Engr.

431	A50	10pi dark green	10.00	3.50
432	A50	10pi dark violet	55.00	1.50
433	A50	10pi dark brown	14.00	1.50
434	A51	25pi carmine, *straw*	8.00	3.00
437	A52	50pi carmine	3.50	1.50

438	A52	50pi indigo	3.00	1.50
439	A52	50pi green, *straw*	3.00	10.00

Nos. 420-439 (15)   130.60   28.85

For overprints and surcharges see Nos. 541B-541E, 554-560, 565-566, 569-574, 575, 577-578, 579A-580, Turkey in Asia 4, 10, 64-66, Thrace N76, N80, N81. Compare designs A42-A43 with A53-A54.

Forgeries of Nos. 446-545 abound.

Preceding Issues Overprinted or Surcharged in Red, Black or Blue

    d   e

1917   **On Stamps of 1865**

446	A5(d)	20pa yellow (R)	45.00	67.50
a.		Star without rays (R)	50.00	57.50
447	A5(d)	1pi pearl gray (R)	45.00	67.50
a.		Star without rays (R)	50.00	57.50
448	A5(d)	2pi blue (R)	45.00	67.50
449	A5(d)	5pi car (Bk)	45.00	67.50

On Stamp of 1867

450	A5(d)	5pi rose (Bk)	45.00	67.50

On Stamps of 1870-71

451	A5(d)	2pi red (Bl)	45.00	67.50
452	A5(d)	5pi blue (Bk)	45.00	67.50
453	A5(d)	25pi dl rose (Bl)	45.00	67.50

On Stamp of 1874-75

454	A5(d)	10pa red vio (Bl)	45.00	67.50

On Stamps of April, 1876

455	A5(d)	10pa red lilac (Bl)	45.00	67.50
a.		10pa red violet (Bl)	50.00	67.50
457	A5(d)	20pa pale grn (R)	45.00	67.50
458	A5(d)	1pi yellow (Bl)	45.00	67.50

On Stamps of January, 1876

459	A5(d)	¼pi on 10pa rose lil (Bl)	45.00	67.50
460	A5(d)	½pi on 20pa yel grn (R)	45.00	67.50
461	A5(d)	1¼pi on 50pa rose (Bl)	45.00	67.50

On Stamps of September, 1876

462	A7(d)	50pa blue & yel (R)	45.00	67.50
463	A7(d)	2pi blk & redsh brn (R)	45.00	67.50
464	A7(d)	25pi clar & rose (Bk)	45.00	67.50

On Stamps of 1880-84

465	A7(d)	5pa blk & ol (R)	45.00	67.50
466	A7(d)	10pa blk & grn (R)	45.00	67.50

On Stamps of 1881-82

467	A5(d)	20pa gray (Bl)	45.00	67.50
468	A5(d)	2pi pale sal (Bl)	45.00	67.50

On Stamps of 1884-86

469	A7(d)	10pa grn & pale grn (R)	45.00	67.50
470	A7(d)	20pi ocher & pale ocher (Bk)	45.00	67.50
471	A7(d)	5pi red brn & pale brn (Bk)	45.00	67.50

On Stamps of 1886

472	A7(d)	5pa blk & pale gray (R)	4.00	2.25
a.		Inverted overprint	30.00	30.00
473	A7(d)	2pi org & bl (Bk)	4.50	2.50
a.		Inverted overprint	35.00	35.00
474	A7(d)	5pi grn & pale grn (R)	45.00	67.50
475	A7(d)	25pi bis & pale bis (Bk)	45.00	67.50

On Stamp of 1888

476	A7(d)	5pi dk brn & gray (Bk)	45.00	67.50

On Stamps of 1892-98

477	A11(d)	20pa vio brn (R)	4.00	3.00
478	A13(d)	2pi brn org (R)	4.00	3.50
a.		Tête bêche pair	13.50	13.50

On Stamps of 1901

479	A16(d)	5pa bister (R)	3.00	3.00
a.		Inverted overprint	20.00	20.00
480	A16(d)	20pa mag (Bk)	2.00	1.50
a.		Inverted overprint	25.00	25.00
481	A16(d)	1pi vio bl (R)	3.00	3.00
a.		Inverted overprint	20.00	20.00

482	A16(d)	2pi gray bl (R)	5.00	5.00
483	A16(d)	5pi ocher (R)	32.50	50.00
484	A16(e)	10pi on 50pi yel (R)	32.50	50.00
485	A16(d)	25pi dk grn (R)	100.00	50.00
486	A17(d)	5pa pur (Bk)	32.50	50.00
487	A17(d)	10pa green (R)	5.00	5.00
488	A17(d)	20pa car (Bk)	2.00	1.50
a.		Inverted overprint	20.00	20.00
489	A17(d)	1pi blue (R)	1.00	.90
490	A17(d)	2pi org (Bk)	3.00	3.00
a.		Inverted overprint	20.00	20.00
491	A17(d)	5pi lil rose (R)	32.50	50.00
492	A17(e)	10pi on 50pi yel brn (R)	45.00	50.00
493	A17(d)	25pi brown (R)	25.00	5.00

On Stamps of 1905

494	A18(d)	5pa ocher (R)	1.00	1.00
a.		Inverted overprint	20.00	20.00
495	A18(d)	10pa dl grn (R)	32.50	50.00
496	A18(d)	20pa car (Bk)	1.00	1.00
a.		Double ovpt., one invtd.	35.00	35.00
b.		Inverted overprint	35.00	35.00
497	A18(d)	1pi blue (R)	1.50	1.00
a.		Inverted overprint	35.00	35.00
498	A18(d)	2pi slate (R)	5.00	5.00
499	A18(d)	2½pi red vio (Bk)	5.00	5.00
a.		Inverted overprint	20.00	20.00
500	A18(d)	5pi brown (R)	35.00	45.00
501	A18(d)	10pi org brn (R)	35.00	50.00
502	A18(e)	10pi on 50pi dp vio (R)	35.00	50.00
503	A18(d)	25pi ol grn (R)	35.00	50.00

On Nos. 128-131

504	A18(d)	10pa dl grn (R)	1.50	1.00
a.		Inverted overprint	20.00	20.00
505	A18(d)	20pa car (Bk)	1.00	.75
a.		Double ovpt., one invtd.	20.00	20.00
b.		Inverted overprint	20.00	20.00
506	A18(d)	1pi brt bl (Bk)	1.00	.75
a.		Inverted overprint	20.00	20.00
507	A18(d)	1pi brt bl (R)	1.50	1.25
a.		Inverted overprint	20.00	20.00
508	A18(d)	2pi slate (R)	35.00	50.00

Nos. 494-508 (15)   227.00   311.75

On Stamps of 1908

509	A19(d)	5pa ocher (R)	1.50	1.25
510	A19(d)	10pa bl grn (R)	20.00	20.00
510A	A19(d)	1pi brt blue (R)	125.00	140.00
511	A19(d)	2pi bl blk (R)	35.00	50.00
512	A19(d)	2½pi vio brn (Bk)	35.00	35.00
512A	A19(d)	10pi red (R)	150.00	225.00
513	A19(e)	10pi on 50pi red brn (R)	35.00	50.00
514	A19(d)	25pi dk grn (R)	35.00	50.00

With Additional Overprint

514A	A19(d)	10pa bl grn (Bk)	150.00	225.00
515	A19(d)	1pi brt bl (Bk)	35.00	50.00
516	A19(d)	2pi bl blk (R)	5.00	5.00
516A	A19(d)	2pi bl blk (Bk)	65.00	67.50

On Stamps of 1908-09

517	A20(d)	5pa ocher (R)	3.00	3.00
518	A21(d)	5pa ocher (R)	2.00	1.50
a.		Double overprint	20.00	20.00
b.		Dbl. ovpt., one inverted	20.00	20.00
519	A21(d)	10pa bl grn (R)	2.00	1.50
520	A21(d)	20pa car rose (Bk)	2.00	1.50
a.		Double overprint	35.00	35.00
521	A21(d)	1pi ultra (R)	1.50	1.00
a.		1p bright blue (R)	30.00	30.00
522	A21(d)	2pi bl blk (R)	5.00	5.00
523	A21(d)	2½pi dk brn (Bk)	35.00	50.00
524	A21(d)	5pi dk vio (R)	35.00	50.00
525	A21(d)	10pi dull red (R)	35.00	50.00

With Additional Overprint

525A	A21(d)	10pa bl grn (Bk)	175.00	225.00
526	A21(d)	1pi ultra (Bk)	125.00	190.00
527	A21(d)	1pi ultra (R)	5.00	4.00
a.		1pi bright blue (R)	125.00	140.00
528	A21(d)	2pi bl blk (Bk)	35.00	50.00

On Stamps of 1913

529	A22(d)	5pa ocher (R)	2.50	2.00
530	A22(d)	10pa bl grn (R)	35.00	50.00
531	A22(d)	20pa car rose (Bk)	2.50	2.50
532	A22(d)	1pi ultra (R)	2.50	3.50
533	A22(d)	2pi indigo (R)	3.50	3.50
534	A22(d)	5pi dl vio (R)	35.00	50.00
535	A22(d)	10pi dl red (Bk)	45.00	50.00

With Additional Overprint

536	A22(d)	10pa bl grn (Bk)	1.50	1.50
a.		Inverted overprint	20.00	20.00
537	A22(d)	1pi ultra (Bk)	3.00	3.00
a.		Inverted overprint	20.00	20.00
538	A22(d)	2pi indigo (Bk)	35.00	100.00

On Commemorative Stamps of 1913

539	A23(d)	10pa green (R)	5.00	5.00
a.		Inverted overprint	20.00	20.00
540	A23(d)	40pa blue (R)	7.00	7.00
a.		Inverted overprint	20.00	20.00

On No. 277, with Addition of New Value

541	A31	60pa on 1pi on 1½pi (Bk)	8.00	5.00
a.		"1330" omitted	45.00	45.00

On Stamps of 1916-18

      f   g

541B	A51(f)	25pi car, *straw*	5.00	5.00
541C	A52(g)	50pi carmine	17.50	17.50
541D	A52(g)	50pi indigo	35.00	50.00
541E	A52(g)	50pi grn, *straw*	15.00	27.50

Ovptd. on Eastern Rumelia No. 12

542	A4(d)	20pa blk & rose (Bl)	35.00	35.00

Ovptd. in Black on Eastern Rumelia #15-17

543	A4(d)	5pa lil & pale lil	45.00	45.00
544	A4(d)	10pa grn & pale grn	45.00	45.00
545	A4(d)	20pa car & pale rose	45.00	45.00

Some experts question the status of Nos. 510A, 512A and 525A.
See Nos. J71-J86, P153-P172.

Soldiers in Trench — A52a

1917

545A	A52a	5pa on 1pi red	1.50	.75

It is stated that No. 545A was never issued without surcharge.
See Nos. 548A, 548Af, 602.

Turkish Artillery A53

1917   Typo.   *Perf. 11½, 12½*

546	A53	2pa Prussian blue	125.00

In type A42 the Turkish inscription at the top is in one group, in type A53 it is in two groups. It is stated that No. 546 was never placed in use. Examples were distributed through the Universal Postal Union at Bern.
For surcharges see Nos. 547-548, Turkey in Asia 69-70.

Surcharged

547	A53	5pi on 2pa Prus blue	12.50	.75
a.		Inverted surcharge	35.00	15.00
b.		Turkish "5" omitted at lower left		

Surcharged

1918

548	A53	5pi on 2pa Prus blue	12.50	1.50
g.		Inverted surcharge	35.00	20.00

Top line of surcharge on Nos. 547-548 reads "Ottoman Posts."
For surcharge see Thrace No. N79.

No. 545A Surcharged

1918

548A	A52a	2pa on 5pa on 1pi red	2.50	1.75
b.		Double surcharge	20.00	20.00
c.		Inverted surcharge	30.00	30.00
d.		Double surcharge inverted	30.00	30.00
e.		Dbl. surch., one inverted	30.00	30.00
f.		In pair with No. 545A	30.00	30.00

Enver Pasha and Kaiser Wilhelm II on Battlefield A54

St. Sophia and Obelisk of the Hippodrome A55

1918   Typo.   *Perf. 12, 12½*

549	A54	5pa brown red	125.00
550	A55	10pa gray green	75.00

The stamps, of which very few saw postal use, were converted into paper money by pasting on thick yellow paper and reperforating.
Values are for stamps with original gum. Examples removed from the yellow paper are worth $10 each.

Armistice Issue

Overprinted in Black or Red

1919, Nov. 30

On Stamps of 1913

552	A34	2½pi org & ol grn	125.00	200.00
553	A38	50pi carmine	125.00	200.00

On Stamps of 1916-18

554	A46	1pi dl vio (R)	6.50	11.00
555	A47	50pa ultra (R), perf 11½	1.50	1.00
556	A48	2pi org brn & ind	1.50	1.00
557	A49	5pi pale bl & blk (R), perf 11½	1.50	1.00
558	A50	10pi dk grn (R)	11.00	12.00
559	A51	25pi car, straw	6.25	12.00
560	A52	50pi grn, straw (R)	11.00	12.50

Fountain in Desert near Sinai — A56

Sentry at Beersheba — A57

Turkish Troops at Sinai A58

Typo.

562	A56	20pa claret	1.50	1.10
563	A57	1pi blue (R)	125.00	160.00
564	A58	25pi slate blue (R)	125.00	160.00
		Nos. 552-564 (12)	540.75	771.60

The overprint reads: "Souvenir of the Armistice, 30th October 1334." Nos. 562-564 are not known to have been regularly issued without overprint.

See No. J87. For overprints and surcharges see Nos. 576, 579, 582, 583-584, 586, Turkey in Asia 71, Thrace N83.

Stamps of 1911-19 Overprinted in Turkish

"Accession to the Throne of His Majesty, 3rd July 1334-1918," the Tughra of Sultan Mohammed VI and sometimes Ornaments and New Values

Dome of the Rock, Jerusalem — A59

No. 565

1919

565	A42	2pa violet	1.00	2.00
566	A43	5pa orange	.50	.50
567	A21	5pa on 2pa ol grn	.75	.50
a.		Inverted surcharge	30.00	30.00
568	A22	10pa on 2pa ol grn	.50	.50
569	A44	10pa green	1.50	1.50
a.		Inverted overprint	50.00	—
570	A45	20pa deep rose	1.25	1.00
a.		Inverted overprint	30.00	30.00
571	A46	1pi dull violet	1.25	1.00
572	A47	60pa on 50pa ultra	1.25	1.00
573	A48	60pa on 2pa org brn & ind	.75	.50
574	A48	2pi org brn & ind	.50	1.00
574A	A34	2½pi org & ol grn	35.00	50.00

No. 566

No. 567 No. 568

No. 569 No. 570

No. 571

No. 572

No. 573

No. 574

No. 575

No. 576

575	A49	5pi pale blue & blk	.50	1.00
576	A56	10pi on 20pa clar	.50	1.00
577	A50	10pi dark brown	2.00	2.00
578	A51	25pi car, straw	1.75	1.75
579	A57	35pi on 1pi blue	1.00	2.00
579A	A52	50pi carmine	35.00	50.00
580	A52	50pi grn, straw	4.00	4.00
581	A59	100pi on 10pa grn	4.00	4.00
582	A58	250pi on 25pi sl bl	4.00	4.00
		Nos. 565-582 (20)	97.00	129.25

See note after #586. See #J88-J91.
For overprint and surcharge see Nos. 585, Thrace N82.

Surcharged with Ornaments, New Values

No. 583

No. 584

No. 585

No. 586

Perf. 11½, 12½

583	A56	20pa claret	1.50	8.00
584	A57	1pi deep blue	1.75	13.00
585	A59	60pa on 10pa green	1.00	6.50
586	A58	25pi slate blue	15.00	60.00
a.		Inverted overprint	250.00	
		Nos. 583-586 (4)	19.25	87.50

#576, 579, 581, 582, 583-586 were prepared in anticipation of the invasion and conquest of Egypt by the Turks. They were not issued at that time but subsequently received various overprints in commemoration of Sultan Mehmet Sadi's accession to the throne (#565-582) and of the 1st anniv. of this event (#583-586).

For surcharge see Thrace No. N83.

Designs of 1913 Modified

1920 Litho. Perf. 11, 12

590	A26	5pa brown orange	1.25	.60

Engr.

591	A28	10pa green	1.25	.60
592	A23	20pa rose	1.25	.60
593	A30	1pi blue green	4.75	.60
594	A32	3pi blue	1.25	.60
595	A34	5pi gray	65.00	.60
596	A36	10pi gray violet	8.00	.60
597	A37	25pi dull violet	4.00	2.00
598	A38	50pi brown	4.00	10.00
		Nos. 590-598 (9)	90.75	16.20

On most stamps of this issue the designs have been modified by removing the small Turkish word at right of the tughra of the Sultan. In the 3pi and 5pi the values have been altered, while for the 25pi the color has been changed.

For surcharges see Thrace Nos. N77, N78, N84.

No. B46 Surcharged

No. 258 Surcharged

No. 594 Surcharged

1921-22 **Black Surcharge**

600	SP1	30pa on 10pa red vio	1.50	.50
a.		Double surcharge	37.50	37.50
b.		Imperf.	40.00	40.00
601	A28	60pa on 10pa green	1.50	.50
a.		Double surcharge	22.50	22.50
602	A52a	4½pi on 1pi red	2.50	.50
a.		Inverted surcharge	75.00	—
603	A32	7½pi on 3pi blue	20.00	2.00
604	A32	7½pi on 3pi bl (R) ('22)	25.00	2.00
a.		Double surcharge	35.00	30.00
		Nos. 600-604 (5)	50.50	5.50

Turkish Stamps of 1916-21 with Greek surcharge as above in blue or black are of private origin.

Issues of the Republic

Crescent and Star — A64

TWO PIASTERS:
Type I — "2" measures 3¼x1¾mm
Type II — "2" measures 2¾x1½mm

FIVE PIASTERS:
Type I — "5" measures 3½x2¼mm
Type II — "5" measures 3x1¾mm

Printed by Ahmed Nazmi, Istanbul
Perf. 13¼x12¾-13¼

1923 Litho. Thin Paper

605	A64	10pa gray black	.30	.25
606	A64	20pa olive yel	.30	.25
607	A64	1pi deep violet	.30	.25
a.		Slanting numeral in lower left corner	.50	.25
608	A64	1½pi emerald	.90	.25
609	A64	2pi bluish grn (I)	.90	.25
a.		2pi deep green (II)	.90	.25
610	A64	3pi yel brn	.90	.60
611	A64	3¾pi lilac brown	3.00	3.00

612	A64	4½pi carmine	.90	1.20
613	A64	5pi dp pur (I)	4.50	1.75
a.		5pi purple (II)	21.00	1.25
614	A64	7½pi blue	3.00	.60
615	A64	7½pi slate	12.00	1.25
a.		10pi blue	16.00	1.25
616	A64	11¼pi dull rose	3.00	2.50
617	A64	15pi brown	15.00	1.25
618	A64	18¾pi myr grn	4.25	3.75
619	A64	22½pi orange	12.00	2.50
620	A64	25pi blk brn	50.00	3.00
621	A64	50pi gray	125.00	5.00
622	A64	100pi dark violet	250.00	11.00
623	A64	500pi dp grn	950.00	275.00
		Cut cancellation		15.00
		Nos. 605-623 (19)	1,436.	313.65
		Set, never hinged	4,250.	

Nos. 605-610, 612-617 exist imperf. & part perf.

Printed by Ikdam, Istanbul

		1924	**Thick Paper**	**Perf. 11**
605b	A64	10pa greenish gray	.90	.25
606b	A64	20pa olive yellow	.90	.25
607b	A64	1pi deep violet	1.75	.25
d.		Slanting numeral in lower left corner	2.00	.25
609b	A64	2pi bluish green (I)	6.00	.90
d.		2pi bluish green (II)	175.00	2.00
610b	A64	3pi yellow brown	150.00	7.50
612b	A64	4½pi carmine	1.50	.60
613b	A64	5pi purple (II)	3.50	.25
614b	A64	7½pi blue	3.50	.60
615b	A64	10pi slate	11.00	12.00
617b	A64	15pi yellow brown	11.00	12.00
		Set, never hinged	555.00	

Printed by Ottoman Public Debt Administration, Istanbul

		1924-26	**Thick Paper**	**Perf. 12**
605c	A64	10pa black	.30	.25
606c	A64	20pa olive yellow	.30	.25
607c	A64	1pi violet	.60	.60
609c	A64	2pi green (II)	3.00	.60
610c	A64	3pi yellow brown	3.50	.60
613c	A64	5pi violet	3.50	1.00
615c	A64	10pi dark blue	60.00	12.00
d.		10pi perf. 13¼x12	60.00	12.00
		Set, never hinged	285.00	

Bridge of Sakarya and Mustafa Kemal — A65

		1924, Jan. 1		**Perf. 12**
625	A65	1½pi emerald	1.50	1.00
626	A65	3pi purple	1.50	1.25
627	A65	4½pi pale rose	2.00	2.25
628	A65	5pi yellow brown	2.00	5.00
629	A65	7½pi deep blue	2.00	3.00
630	A65	50pi orange	50.00	40.00
631	A65	100pi brown violet	70.00	50.00
632	A65	200pi olive brown	125.00	75.00
		Nos. 625-632 (8)	254.00	177.50
		Set, never hinged	850.00	

Signing of Treaty of Peace at Lausanne.

The Legendary Blacksmith and his Gray Wolf — A66

 Sakarya Gorge — A67

Fortress of Ankara — A68   Mustafa Kemal Pasha — A69

		1926		**Engr.**
634	A66	10pa slate	.40	.25
635	A66	20pa orange	.40	.25
636	A66	1g brt rose	.40	.25
637	A67	2g green	1.10	.25
638	A67	2½g gray black	1.40	.25
639	A67	3g copper red	1.75	.25
640	A68	5g deep blue	1.75	.40

641	A68	6g red	1.00	.25
642	A68	10g blue	6.00	.40
643	A68	15g deep orange	7.50	.40
644	A69	25g dk grn & blk	12.00	1.10
645	A69	50g car & blk	15.00	1.25
646	A69	100g ol grn & blk	55.00	5.00
647	A69	200g brown & blk	120.00	12.00
		Nos. 634-647 (14)	223.70	22.30
		Set, never hinged	1,300.	

For surcharges see Nos. 648-675.

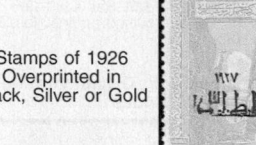

Stamps of 1926 Overprinted in Black, Silver or Gold

		1927, Sept. 9		
648	A66	1g brt rose	.50	.50
649	A67	2g green	.50	1.00
650	A67	2½g gray black	1.25	1.25
651	A67	3g copper red	1.60	1.75
652	A68	5g lilac gray	2.00	2.25
653	A68	6g red	1.25	1.25
654	A68	10g deep blue	2.00	2.50
655	A68	15g deep orange	5.00	3.25
656	A69	25g dk grn & blk		
		(S)	20.00	15.00
657	A69	50g car & blk (S)	60.00	30.00
658	A69	100g ol grn & blk		
		(G)	150.00	65.00
		Nos. 648-658 (11)	244.10	123.75
		Set, never hinged	700.00	

Agricultural and industrial exhibition at Izmir, Sept. 9-20, 1927.
The overprint reads: "1927" and the initials of "Izmir Dokuz Eylul Sergisi" (Izmir Exhibition, September 9).

Second Izmir Exhibition Issue
Nos. 634-647 Overprinted in Red or Black

On A66-A68   On A69

		1928, Sept. 9		
659	A66	10pa slate (R)	.50	.25
660	A66	20pa orange	.50	.25
661	A66	1g brt rose	1.00	.50
662	A67	2g green (R)	1.50	1.10
663	A67	2½g gray blk (R)	1.50	1.10
664	A67	3g copper red	1.50	1.10
665	A68	5g lilac gray (R)	1.60	2.40
666	A68	6g red	2.40	2.40
667	A68	10g deep blue	3.50	2.40
668	A68	15g deep orange	5.00	1.60
669	A69	25g dk grn & blk		
		(R)	12.00	6.00
670	A69	50g car & blk	21.00	20.00
671	A69	100g ol grn & blk		
		(R)	60.00	50.00
672	A69	200g brn & blk (R)	160.00	95.00
		Nos. 659-672 (14)	272.00	184.10
		Set, never hinged	900.00	

The overprint reads "Izmir, September 9, 1928."

No. 636 Surcharged in Black   No. 640 Surcharged in Red

		1929		
673	A66	20pa on 1g brt rose	.50	.25
a.		Inverted surcharge	25.00	12.50
674	A68	2½k on 5g deep blue	1.00	.80
a.		Inverted surcharge	35.00	35.00

No. 642 Surcharged in Red

675	A68	6k on 10g blue	6.00	.75
		Nos. 673-675 (3)	7.50	1.80
		Set, never hinged	40.00	

Railroad Bridge over Kizil Irmak — A70   A71

A72   A73

Latin Inscriptions
Without umlaut over first "U" of "CUMHURIYETI"

		1929		**Engr.**
676	A70	2k gray black	4.50	.80
677	A70	2½k green	2.00	.80
678	A70	3k violet brown	3.25	1.10
679	A71	6k dark violet	22.50	.80
680	A72	12½k deep blue	27.50	3.25
681	A73	50k carmine & blk	90.00	8.75
		Nos. 676-681 (6)	149.75	15.50
		Set, never hinged	500.00	

See Nos. 682-691, 694-695, 697, 699. For surcharges & overprints see #705-714, 716-717, 719, 721, 727, 765-766, 770-771, 777, C2, C7.

Sakarya Gorge — A74   Mustafa Kemal Pasha — A75

With umlaut over first "U" of "CUMHURIYETI"

		1930		
682	A71	10pa green	.30	.25
683	A70	20pa gray violet	.30	.25
684	A70	1k olive green	.50	.50
685	A71	1½k olive black	.50	.50
686	A70	2k dull violet	1.75	.50
687	A70	2½k deep green	1.60	.50
688	A70	3k brown orange	20.00	1.50
689	A71	4k deep rose	11.00	.40
690	A72	5k rose lake	12.50	.40
691	A71	6k indigo	15.00	.25
692	A74	7½k red brown	.25	.35
694	A72	12½k deep ultra	.50	.25
695	A72	15k deep orange	.50	.40
696	A74	17½k dark gray	.40	.40
697	A72	20k black brown	60.00	1.60
698	A74	25k olive brown	2.40	1.00
699	A72	30k yellow brown	1.25	1.00
700	A74	40k red violet	1.10	1.00
701	A75	50k red & black	1.75	1.00
702	A75	100k olive grn & blk	1.75	1.00
703	A75	200k dk green & blk	1.75	1.25
704	A75	500k chocolate & blk	17.50	27.50
		Nos. 682-704 (22)	152.70	41.80
		Set, never hinged	600.00	

For surcharges and overprints see Nos. 715, 718, 720, 722-726, 767-769, 772-773, 775-776, 778-780, 823-828, 848-850, C1, C3-C6, C8-C11.

Nos. 682-704 Surcharged in Red or Black

a   b

---

c

		1930, Aug. 30		
705	A71(a)	10pa on 10pa (R)	1.00	1.25
706	A70(b)	10pa on 20pa	1.00	1.50
707	A70(b)	20pa on 10pa	1.00	1.25
708	A71(a)	1k on 1½k (R)	1.00	1.25
709	A70(b)	1½k on 2k	1.00	1.25
710	A70(b)	2k on 2½k	1.75	1.60
711	A70(b)	2½k on 3k	1.75	1.50
712	A71(a)	3k on 4k	1.75	1.00
713	A72(a)	4k on 5k	1.75	1.00
714	A71(a)	5k on 6k (R)	3.50	3.50
715	A74(a)	6k on 7½k	.75	.50
716	A72(a)	7½k on 12½k (R)	1.25	1.00
717	A72(a)	12½k on 15k	1.25	1.00
718	A74(b)	15k on 17½k (R)	5.00	4.75
719	A72(b)	17½k on 20k (R)	5.00	4.75
720	A74(b)	20k on 25k (R)	5.50	2.25
721	A72(b)	25k on 30k	5.00	2.50
722	A74(b)	30k on 40k	6.50	2.50
723	A75(c)	40k on 50k	12.50	6.25
724	A75(c)	50k on 100k (R)	80.00	17.00
725	A75(c)	100k on 200k (R)	160.00	30.00
726	A75(c)	250k on 500k (R)	95.00	60.00
		Nos. 705-726 (22)	393.25	147.60
		Set, never hinged	1,200.	

Inauguration of the railroad between Ankara and Sivas.

There are numerous varieties in these settings as: "309," "390," "930" inverted, no period after "D," no period after "Y" and raised period before "Y."

No. 685 Surcharged in Red

		1931, Apr. 1		
727	A71	1k on 1½k olive blk	1.75	1.00

Olive Tree with Roots Extending to All Balkan Capitals — A76

		1931, Oct. 20	**Engr.**	**Perf. 12**
728	A76	2½k dark green	.40	.40
729	A76	4k carmine	.40	.40
730	A76	6k steel blue	.40	.40
731	A76	7½k dull red	.40	.40
732	A76	12k deep orange	.50	.40
733	A76	12½k dark blue	.50	.40
734	A76	30k dark violet	1.25	1.25
735	A76	50k dark brown	1.25	1.25
736	A76	100k brown violet	5.50	3.00
		Nos. 728-736 (9)	10.60	7.90
		Set, never hinged	35.00	

Second Balkan Conference.

A77   A78

Mustafa Kemal Pasha (Kemal Atatürk) — A79

1931-42 Typo. Perf. 11½, 12

737	A77	10pa blue green	.50	.25
738	A77	20pa deep orange	.50	.25
739	A77	30pa brt violet ('38)	.50	.25
740	A78	1k dk slate green	.50	.25
740A	A77	1½k magenta ('42)	.65	.25
741	A78	2k dark violet	.50	.25
741A	A78	2k yel grn ('40)	.50	.25
742	A77	2½k green	.50	.25
743	A78	3k brn org ('38)	1.00	.25
744	A78	4k slate	2.00	.25
745	A78	5k rose red	.50	.25
745A	A78	5k brown blk ('40)	2.00	.50
746	A78	6k deep blue	3.00	.25
746A	A78	6k rose ('40)	1.00	.30
747	A77	7½k deep rose ('32)	.75	.25
747A	A78	8k brt blue ('38)	1.50	1.00
b.		8k dark blue ('36)	1.50	1.00
748	A77	10k black brn ('32)	1.00	.25
748A	A77	10k deep blue ('40)	7.00	.60
749	A77	12k bister ('32)	.75	.25
750	A79	12½k indigo ('32)	.75	.25
751	A77	15k org yel ('32)	.75	.25
752	A77	20k olive grn ('32)	.75	.25
753	A77	25k Prus blue ('32)	2.00	.25
754	A77	30k magenta ('32)	8.50	.25
755	A79	100k maroon ('32)	100.00	8.00
756	A79	200k purple ('32)	5.50	2.25
757	A79	250k chocolate ('32)	125.00	20.00
		Nos. 737-757 (27)	267.90	37.65
		Set, never hinged	1,200.	

See Nos. 1015-1033, 1117B-1126. For overprints see Nos. 811-816.

Symbolizing 10th Anniversary of Republic — A80

President Atatürk — A81

1933, Oct. 29 Perf. 10

758	A80	1½k blue green	.50	.65
759	A80	2k olive brown	.50	1.00
760	A81	3k dull red	.65	1.00
761	A81	6k deep blue	.65	1.00
762	A80	12½k dark blue	2.00	2.00
763	A80	25k dark brown	14.00	8.00
764	A81	50k orange brown	15.00	20.00
		Nos. 758-764 (7)	33.30	33.65
		Set, never hinged	80.00	

10th year of the Turkish Republic. The stamps were in use for three days only.

Nos. 682, 685, 692, 694, 696-698, 702 Overprinted or Surcharged in Red

1934, Aug. 26 Perf. 12

765	A71	10pa green	.50	1.00
766	A71	1k on 1½k	1.00	1.00
767	A74	2k on 25k	1.50	1.00
768	A74	5k on 25k	5.00	3.25
769	A74	6k on 17½k	2.00	1.60
770	A72	12½k deep ultra	5.50	5.00
771	A72	15k on 20k	100.00	45.00

772	A74	20k on 25k	40.00	37.50
773	A75	50k on 100k	55.00	37.50
		Nos. 765-773 (9)	210.50	132.35
		Set, never hinged	675.00	

Izmir Fair, 1934.

Nos. 696, 698, 701-704 Surcharged in Black

1936, Oct. 26

775	A74	4k on 17½k	1.00	1.00
776	A74	5k on 25k	1.10	1.00
777	A73	6k on 50k	.50	.50
778	A75	10k on 100k	1.75	2.00
779	A75	20k on 200k	8.50	9.00
780	A75	50k on 500k	10.00	6.00
		Nos. 775-780 (6)	22.85	16.50
		Set, never hinged	90.00	

"1926" in Overprint

775a	A74	4k on 17½k	6.50	3.75
776a	A74	5k on 25k	7.00	3.75
777a	A73	6k on 50k	7.00	3.75
778a	A75	10k on 100k	9.00	4.50
779a	A75	20k on 200k	20.00	10.00
780a	A76	50k on 500k	55.00	27.50
		Nos. 775a-780a (6)	104.50	53.25
		Set, never hinged	250.00	

Re-militarization of the Dardanelles.

Hittite Bronze Stag — A82

Thorak's Bust of Kemal Atatürk — A83

1937, Sept. 20 Litho. Perf. 12

781	A82	3k light violet	1.10	1.10
782	A83	6k blue	1.60	1.60
783	A82	7½k bright pink	2.00	3.25
784	A83	12½k indigo	9.00	8.00
		Nos. 781-784 (4)	13.70	13.95
		Set, never hinged	40.00	

2nd Turkish Historical Congress, Istanbul, Sept. 20-30.

Arms of Turkey, Greece, Romania and Yugoslavia — A84

1937, Oct. 29 Perf. 11½

785	A84	8k carmine	8.00	3.25
786	A84	12½k dark blue	11.00	6.50
		Set, never hinged	60.00	

The Balkan Entente.

Street in Izmir A85

Fig Tree — A87

30pa, View of Fair Buildings. 3k, Tower, Government Square. 5k, Olive branch. 6k, Woman with grapes. 7½k, Woman picking grapes. 8k, Izmir Harbor through arch. 12k, Statue of Pres. Ataturk. 12½k, Pres. Ataturk.

1938, Aug. 20 Photo. Perf. 11½
Inscribed: "Izmir Enternasyonal Fuari 1938"

789	A85	10pa dark brown	.40	.50
790	A85	30pa purple	.60	.40
791	A87	2½k brt green	1.00	.80
792	A87	3k brown orange	1.00	.40
793	A87	5k olive green	1.75	.60
794	A85	6k brown	4.00	.35
795	A87	7½k scarlet	4.00	2.25
796	A87	8k brown lake	2.75	1.25
797	A87	12k rose violet	5.00	2.75
798	A87	12½k deep blue	8.00	7.00
		Nos. 789-798 (10)	28.50	16.30
		Set, never hinged	75.00	

Izmir International Fair.

President Atatürk Teaching Reformed Turkish Alphabet A95

1938, Nov. 2

799	A95	2½k brt green	.65	.55
800	A95	3k orange	.85	.55
801	A95	6k rose violet	1.00	.65
802	A95	7½k deep rose	1.25	1.00
803	A95	8k red brown	1.40	1.10
804	A95	12½k brt ultra	1.75	1.25
		Nos. 799-804 (6)	6.90	5.10
		Set, never hinged	25.00	

Reform of the Turkish alphabet, 10th anniv.

Army and Air Force A96

Atatürk Driving Tractor — A98

3k, View of Kayseri. 7½k, Railway bridge. 8k, Scout buglers. 12½k, President Atatürk.

Inscribed: "Cumhuriyetin 15 inc yil donumu hatirasi"

1938, Oct. 29

805	A96	2½k dark green	.50	.35
806	A96	3k red brown	.50	.35
807	A98	6k bister	.80	.35
808	A96	7½k red	1.75	.90
809	A96	8k rose violet	4.50	2.50
810	A98	12½k deep blue	3.50	1.75
		Nos. 805-810 (6)	11.55	6.20
		Set, never hinged	32.50	

15th anniversary of the Republic.

Stamps of 1931-38 Overprinted in Black

1938, Nov. 21 Perf. 11½x12

811	A78	3k brown orange	.75	.35
812	A78	5k rose red	.75	.35
813	A78	6k deep blue	1.00	.50
814	A77	7½k deep rose	1.25	.55
815	A78	8k dark blue	3.00	.75
a.		8k bright blue	225.00	150.00
816	A79	12½k indigo	3.75	1.75
		Nos. 811-816 (6)	10.50	4.25
		Set, never hinged	35.00	

President Kemal Atatürk (1881-1938). The date is that of his funeral.

Catalogue values for unused stamps in this section, from this point to the end of the section, are for Never Hinged items.

Turkish and American Flags — A102

Presidents İnönü and F. D. Roosevelt and Map of North America A103

Designs: 3k, 8k, Inonu and Roosevelt. 7½k, 12½k, Kemal Ataturk and Washington.

1939, July 15 Photo. Perf. 14

817	A102	2½k ol grn, red & bl	.45	.25
818	A103	3k dk brn & bl grn	.90	.25
819	A102	6k purple, red & bl	.90	.25
820	A103	7½k org ver & bl grn	1.75	.40
821	A103	8k dp cl & bl grn	1.40	.40
822	A103	12½k brt bl & bl grn	3.25	.85
		Nos. 817-822 (6)	8.65	2.40

US constitution, 150th anniversary.

Nos. 698, 702-704 Surcharged in Black

1939, July 23 Unwmk. Perf. 13

823	A74	3k on 25k	.60	.35
824	A75	6k on 200k	.95	.75
825	A74	7½k on 25k	1.10	.75
826	A75	12k on 100k	1.50	.75
827	A75	12k on 200k	3.00	.75
828	A75	17½k on 500k	4.50	1.50
		Nos. 823-828 (6)	11.65	4.85

Annexation of Hatay.

Railroad Bridge A105

Locomotive A106

Track Through Mountain Pass A107

Design: 12½k, Railroad tunnel, Atma Pass.

1939, Oct. 20 Typo. Perf. 11½

829	A105	3k lt orange red	3.50	3.00
830	A106	6k chestnut	4.00	3.50
831	A107	7½k rose pink	6.00	5.50
832	A107	12½k dark blue	9.00	8.00
		Nos. 829-832 (4)	22.50	20.00

Completion of the Sivas to Erzerum link of the Ankara-Erzerum Railroad.

Atatürk Residence in Ankara — A109

Kemal Atatürk — A110

TÜRKİYE POSTALARI

KEMAL ATATÜRK
1880-1938

A111

Designs: 5k, 6k, 7½k, 8k, 12½k, 17½k, Various portraits of Ataturk, "1880-1938."

1939-40   **Photo.**
833	A109	2½k brt green	1.10	.50
834	A110	3k dk blue gray	1.10	.50
835	A110	5k chocolate	1.40	.75
836	A110	6k chestnut	1.40	.75
837	A110	7½k rose red	4.00	1.25
838	A110	8k gray green	1.90	1.25
839	A110	12½k brt blue	2.25	1.60
840	A110	17½k brt rose	7.00	2.25
	Nos. 833-840 (8)		20.15	8.85

Souvenir Sheet
841	A111	100k blue black	75.00	75.00

Death of Kemal Ataturk, first anniversary. Size of No. 841: 90x120mm.
Issued: 2½k, 6k, 12½k, 11/11/39; others, 1/3/40.

Namik Kemal — A118

1940, Jan. 3
842	A118	6k chestnut	2.00	.60
843	A118	8k dk olive grn	3.25	1.50
844	A118	12k brt rose red	4.00	2.00
845	A118	12½k brt blue	8.00	3.00
	Nos. 842-845 (4)		17.25	7.10

Birth cent. of Namik Kemal, poet and patriot.

Arms of Turkey, Greece, Romania and Yugoslavia — A119

Perf. 11½
1940, Jan. 1   **Typo.**   **Unwmk.**
846	A119	8k light blue	4.50	1.00
847	A119	10k deep blue	10.00	2.25

The Balkan Entente.

Nos. 703-704 Surcharged in Red or Black

1940, Aug. 20   **Perf. 12**
848	A75	6k on 200k dk grn & blk (R)	1.00	1.00
849	A75	10k on 200k dk grn & blk	1.50	1.50
850	A75	12k on 500k choc & blk	2.50	2.50
	Nos. 848-850 (3)		5.00	5.00

13th International Izmir Fair.

Map of Turkey and Census Figures A120

1940, Oct. 1   **Typo.**   **Perf. 11½**
851	A120	10pa dark blue green	.50	.25
852	A120	3k orange	1.50	1.25
853	A120	6k carmine rose	2.00	1.50
854	A120	10k dark blue	3.00	2.50
	Nos. 851-854 (4)		7.00	5.50

Census of Oct. 20, 1940.

Runner — A121   Pole Vaulter — A122

Hurdler A123

Discus Thrower — A124

1940, Oct. 5
855	A121	3k olive green	3.00	3.00
856	A122	6k rose	9.00	3.50
857	A123	8k chestnut brown	4.25	4.00
858	A124	10k dark blue	6.50	10.00
	Nos. 855-858 (4)		22.75	20.50

11th Balkan Olympics.

Mail Carriers on Horseback A125

Postman of 1840 and 1940 — A126

Old Sailing Vessel and Modern Mailboat — A127

Design: 12k, Post Office, Istanbul.

1940, Dec. 31   **Typo.**   **Perf. 10**
859	A125	3k gray green	.85	.50
860	A126	6k rose	1.10	.75
861	A127	10k dark blue	1.75	1.00
862	A127	12k olive brown	2.25	1.50
	Nos. 859-862 (4)		5.95	3.75

Centenary of the Turkish post.

Harbor Scene A129

Statue of Atatürk — A132

Designs: 3k, 6k, 17½k, Various Izmir Fair buildings. 12k, Girl picking grapes.

Inscribed: "Izmir Enternasyonal Fuari 1941"

1941, Aug. 20   **Litho.**   **Perf. 11½**
863	A129	30pa dull green	.35	.25
864	A129	3k olive gray	.50	.25
865	A129	6k salmon rose	.75	.25
866	A132	10k blue	.95	.30
867	A129	12k dull brown vio	1.10	.45
868	A129	17½k dull brown	1.75	1.25
	Nos. 863-868 (6)		5.40	2.75

Izmir International Fair, 1941.

Tomb of Barbarossa II — A135

Barbarossa's Fleet in Battle — A136

Barbarossa II (Khair ed-Din) — A137

1941
869	A135	20pa dark violet	.55	.25
870	A136	3k light blue	.85	.75
871	A136	6k rose red	1.40	1.50
872	A136	10k deep ultra	1.60	1.50
873	A136	12k dull brn & bis	1.90	1.75
874	A137	17½k multicolored	3.25	2.25
	Nos. 869-874 (6)		9.55	7.75

400th death anniv. of Barbarossa II.

President İnönü
A138   A138a

1942-45   **Perf. 11½x11, 11**
875	A138	0.25k yellow bis	.25	.25
876	A138	0.50k lt yellow grn	.25	.25
877	A138	1k gray green	.25	.25
877A	A138	1½k brt vio ('45)	.25	.25
878	A138	2k bluish green	.30	.25
879	A138	4k fawn	.30	.30
880	A138	4½k slate	.30	.30
881	A138	5k light blue	.35	.25
882	A138	6k sal rose	.25	.25
883	A138	6¾k ultra	.25	.25
884	A138	9k blue violet	.90	.25
885	A138	10k dark blue	.30	.25
886	A138	13½k brt pink	.30	.25
887	A138	16k Prus green	.60	.25
888	A138	17½k rose lake	.30	.25
889	A138	20k brown violet	.60	.50
890	A138	27½k orange	.60	.50
891	A138	37k buff	.60	.50
892	A138	50k purple	2.25	.25
893	A138	100k olive bister	6.00	3.00
894	A138a	200k brown	19.00	2.50
	Nos. 875-894 (21)		34.25	11.10

Ankara — A139

Antioch — A141

0.50k, Mohair goats. 1½k, Ankara Dam. 2k, Oranges. 4k, Merino sheep. 4½k, Train. 5k, Tile decorating. 6k, Atatürk statue, Ankara. 6¾k, 10k, Pres. Ismet Inonu. 13½k, Grand National Assembly. 16k, Arnavutkoy, Istanbul. 17½k, Republic monument, Istanbul. 20k, Safety monument, Ankara. 27½k, Post Office, Istanbul. 37k, Monument at Afyon. 50k, "People's House," Ankara. 100k, Atatürk & Inonu. 200k, Pres. Inonu.

1943, Apr. 1   **Perf. 11**
896	A139	0.25k citron	.25	.25
897	A139	0.50k brt green	.40	.25
898	A141	1k yellow olive	.25	.25
899	A141	1½k deep violet	.25	.25
900	A139	2k brt blue green	.40	.25
901	A139	4k copper red	4.00	1.00
902	A141	4½k black	6.00	2.00
903	A141	5k sapphire	1.25	.50
904	A139	6k carmine rose	.25	.25
905	A139	6¾k brt ultra	.25	.25
906	A139	10k dark blue	.25	.25
907	A141	13½k brt red violet	.30	.25
908	A141	16k myrtle green	3.50	.25
909	A139	17½k brown orange	2.00	.50
910	A139	20k sepia	2.00	.50
911	A139	27½k dk orange	1.50	1.00
912	A139	37k lt yellow brn	2.50	.50
913	A141	50k purple	10.00	.25
914	A139	100k dk olive grn	12.50	2.50
915	A139	200k dark brown	9.00	2.00
a.		Souvenir sheet	70.00	100.00
	Nos. 896-915 (20)		56.85	13.25

No. 915a contains one stamp similar to No. 915, perf. 13½ and printed in sepia. Issued Apr. 20.
For surcharge see No. 928.

Girl with
Grapes — A158

Entrance
to Izmir
Fair
A159

Fair
Building
A160

1943, Aug. 20   Litho.   Perf. 11½
916 A158 4½k dull olive   .25   .25
917 A159 6k carmine rose   .60   .25
918 A160 6¾k blue   .60   .25
919 A158 10k dark blue   .80   .50
920 A158 13½k sepia   1.25 1.00
921 A160 27½k dull gray   1.75 1.75
  Nos. 916-921 (6)   5.25 4.00
Izmir International Fair.

Soccer
Team on
Parade
A161

Turkish Flag and
Soldier — A162

Designs: 6¾k, Bridge. 10k, Hospital. 13½k,
View of Ankara. 27½k, President Inonu.

**Inscribed: "Cumhuriyetin 20 nci
Yildonomu Hatirasi"**

1943, Oct. 29   Perf. 11x11½, 11½x11
922 A161 4½k lt olive grn   1.50 1.75
923 A162 6k rose red   .75   .25
924 A161 6¾k ultra   .75   .50
925 A161 10k violet blue   .75   .50
926 A161 13½k olive   .75   .25
927 A162 27½k lt brown   .95   .75
  Nos. 922-927 (6)   5.45 4.00
Republic, 20th anniv. Nos. 922-927 exist
imperf. Value, $50.

**No. 905 Surcharged with New Value
in Red**

1945   Perf. 11
928 A139 4½k on 6¾k brt ultra .65 .40

Recording Census
Data — A167

1945, Oct. 21   Litho.   Perf. 11½
929 A167 4½k olive black   .70   .25
930 A167 9k violet   .85   .25
931 A167 10k violet blue   .85   .25
932 A167 18k dark red   1.75   .60
  Nos. 929-932 (4)   4.15 1.35
Souvenir Sheet
Imperf
933 A167 1 l chocolate   65.00 50.00
Census of 1945.

President Ismet
Inönü — A169

Perf. 11½ to 12½
1946, Apr. 1   Unwmk.
934 A169 0.25k brown red   .50   .25
935 A169 1k dk slate grn   .50   .25
936 A169 1½k plum   1.00   .25
937 A169 9k purple   1.75   .25
938 A169 10k deep blue   2.00   .75
939 A169 50k chocolate   8.50   .75
  Nos. 934-939 (6)   14.25 2.50

U.S.S.
Missouri
A170

1946, Apr. 5   Perf. 11½
940 A170 9k dark purple   .50   .30
941 A170 10k dk chalky blue   .65   .40
942 A170 27½k olive green   2.00 2.00
  a. Imperf., pair   50.00
  Nos. 940-942 (3)   3.15 2.70
Visit of the USS Missouri to Istanbul, 4/5.

Sower — A171

1946, June 16   Perf. 11½ to 12½
943 A171 9k violet   .25   .25
944 A171 10k dark blue   .50   .25
945 A171 18k olive green   .75   .75
946 A171 27½k red orange   1.50 1.50
  Nos. 943-946 (4)   3.00 2.75
Passing of legislation to distribute state
lands to poor farmers.

Dove and Flag-
Decorated
Banderol — A172

1947, Aug. 20   Photo.   Perf. 12
947 A172 15k violet & dp violet .40 .25
948 A172 20k blue & dk blue   1.00 .50
949 A172 30k brown & gray blk .40 .25
950 A172 1 l ol grn & dk grn   .50 .50
  Nos. 947-950 (4)   2.30 1.50
Izmir International Fair.

Victory
Monument,
Afyon
Karahisar
A173

Ismet Inönü as
General
A174

Kemal Atatürk as
General — A175

1947, Aug. 30
951 A173 10k dk brn & pale brn .60 .30
952 A174 15k brt violet & gray .50 .30
953 A175 20k dp blue & gray   .60 .25
954 A173 30k grnsh blk & gray 1.25 .70
955 A174 60k ol gray & pale brn 1.75 .90
956 A175 1 l dk green & gray   2.75 1.75
  Nos. 951-956 (6)   7.45 4.20
25th anniv. of the Battle of Dumlupinar, Aug.
30, 1922.

Grapes
and
Istanbul
Skyline
A176

1947, Sept. 22
957 A176 15k rose violet   .40   .25
958 A176 20k deep blue   .80   .40
959 A176 60k dark brown   1.00   .60
  Nos. 957-959 (3)   2.20 1.25
International Vintners' Congress, Istanbul.

Approaching Train,
Istanbul Skyline and
Sirkeci
Terminus — A177

1947, Oct. 9
960 A177 15k reddish violet   .60   .30
961 A177 20k brt blue   1.00   .75
962 A177 60k olive green   2.40 1.90
  Nos. 960-962 (3)   4.00 2.95
International Railroad Congress, Istanbul.

President Ismet Inönü
A178   A179

1948 Unwmk. Engr.   Perf. 12, 14
963 A178 0.25k dark red   .30   .25
964 A178 1k olive black   .30   .25
965 A178 2k brt rose lilac   .30   .25
966 A178 3k red orange   .30   .25
967 A178 4k dark green   .30   .25
968 A178 5k blue   .30   .25
969 A178 10k chocolate   .75   .25
970 A178 12k deep red   1.25   .30
971 A178 15k violet   .75   .25
972 A178 20k deep blue   1.00   .50
973 A178 30k brown   1.50   .30
974 A178 60k black   4.00   .50
975 A179 1 l olive green   8.00   .50
976 A179 2 l dark brown   30.00   .50
977 A179 5 l deep plum   17.50 27.50
  Nos. 963-977 (15)   66.55 36.60
For overprints see Nos. O13-O42.

President Ismet Inönü and Lausanne
Conference — A180

Conference
Building
A180a

1948, July 23   Photo.   Perf. 11½
978 A180 15k rose lilac   .75   .75
979 A180a 20k blue   1.00 1.00
980 A180a 40k gray green   1.25 1.25
981 A180 1 l brown   2.00 2.00
  Nos. 978-981 (4)   5.00 5.00
25th anniversary of Lausanne Treaty.

Statue of Kemal
Atatürk,
Ankara — A181

1948, Oct. 29
982 A181 15k violet   .60   .40
983 A181 20k blue   .75   .50
984 A181 40k gray green   1.50 1.10
985 A181 1 l brown   3.25 3.00
  Nos. 982-985 (4)   6.10 5.00
25th anniv. of the proclamation of the
republic.

A182   A183

A184

Wrestlers
A185

1949, June 3
986 A182 15k rose lilac   2.40   .60
987 A183 20k blue   2.75 1.25
988 A184 30k brown   2.75   .60
989 A185 60k green   4.00 3.50
  Nos. 986-989 (4)   11.90 5.95
5th European Wrestling Championships,
Istanbul, June 3-5, 1949.

Ancient
Galley
A186

Galleon
Mahmudiye
A187

Monument to
Khizr
Barbarossa
A188

Designs: 15k, Cruiser Hamidiye. 20k, Submarine Sakarya. 30k, Cruiser Yavuz.

1949, July 1
990	A186	5k violet	1.00	1.00
991	A186	10k brown	1.00	1.00
992	A186	15k lilac rose	1.00	1.00
993	A186	20k gray blue	2.50	1.00
994	A186	30k gray	2.50	1.00
995	A188	40k olive gray	4.00	1.75
		Nos. 990-995 (6)	12.00	6.75

Fleet Day, July 1, 1949.

A189

UPU
Monument,
Bern
A190

Perf. 11½
1949, Oct. 9   Unwmk.   Photo.
996	A189	15k violet	.55	.30
997	A189	20k blue	.55	.30
998	A190	30k dull rose	.55	.30
999	A190	40k green	1.10	.55
		Nos. 996-999 (4)	2.75	1.45

UPU, 75th anniversary.

Istanbul
Fair
Building
A191

1949, Oct. 1   Litho.   Perf. 10
1000	A191	15k brown	.60	.30
1001	A191	20k blue	.60	.30
1002	A191	30k olive	.80	.60
		Nos. 1000-1002 (3)	2.00	1.20

Istanbul Fair, Oct. 1-31.

Boy and Girl and
Globe — A192

1950, Aug. 13   Perf. 11½
1003	A192	15k purple	.35	.25
1004	A192	20k deep blue	.75	.50

2nd World Youth Council Meeting, 1950. No.
1004 exists imperf. Value $12.

Aged Woman
Casting
Ballot — A193

Kemal
Atatürk
and Map
A194

1950, Aug. 30
1005	A193	15k dark brown	.50	.25
1006	A193	20k dark blue	.50	.25
1007	A194	30k dk blue & gray	1.00	.50
		Nos. 1005-1007 (3)	2.00	1.00

Election of May 14, 1950.

Hazel Nuts — A195

Designs: 12k, Acorns. 15k, Cotton. 20k,
Symbolical of the fair. 30k, Tobacco.

1950, Sept. 9
1008	A195	8k gray grn & buff	.60	.60
1009	A195	12k magenta	1.25	1.25
1010	A195	15k brn blk & lt brn	.60	.60
1011	A195	20k dk blue & aqua	1.75	1.75
1012	A195	30k brn blk & dull org	1.75	1.75
		Nos. 1008-1012 (5)	5.95	5.95

Izmir International Fair, Aug. 20-Sept. 20.

Symbolical of 1950
Census — A196

1950, Oct. 9   Litho.   Perf. 11½
1013	A196	15k dark brown	.40	.25
1014	A196	20k violet blue	1.00	.25

General census of 1950.

Atatürk Types of 1931-42
Perf. 10x11½, 11½x12
1950-51   Typo.
1015	A77	10p dull red brn	.50	.25
1016	A77	10p vermilion ('51)	.60	.50
1017	A77	20p blue green	1.50	.35
1018	A78	1k olive green	.50	.25
1019	A78	2k plum	.50	.25
1020	A78	2k dp yellow ('51)	.90	.30
1021	A78	3k yellow orange	1.25	.45
1022	A78	3k gray ('51)	.90	.25
1023	A78	4k green ('51)	.90	.25
1024	A78	5k blue	1.25	.45
1025	A78	5k plum ('51)	6.50	.45
1026	A77	10k brown orange	2.25	.25
1027	A77	15k purple	2.75	.45
1028	A77	15k brown carmine	18.00	.35
1029	A77	20k dark blue	30.00	.35
1030	A77	30k pink ('51)	25.50	.75
1031	A79	100k red brown ('51)	12.00	1.10
1032	A79	200k dark brown	15.00	1.50
1033	A79	200k rose violet ('51)	20.00	2.25
		Nos. 1015-1033 (19)	140.80	10.75

16th Century Flight
of Hezarfen Ahmet
Celebi — A197

Plane over
Istanbul
A198

40k, Biplane over Taurus Mountains.

1950, Oct. 17   Litho.   Perf. 11
1034	A197	20k dk green & blue	.50	.35
1035	A197	40k dk brown & blue	.75	.75
1036	A198	60k purple & blue	1.25	.90
		Nos. 1034-1036 (3)	2.50	2.00

Regional meeting of the ICAO, Istanbul,
Oct. 17.

Farabi
A199

1950, Dec. 1   Unwmk.   Perf. 11½
Multicolored Center
1037	A199	15k blue	.75	.75
1038	A199	20k blue violet	.75	.75
1039	A199	60k red brown	4.25	4.25
1040	A199	1 l gold & bl vio	4.75	4.25
		Nos. 1037-1040 (4)	10.50	8.50

Death millenary of Farabi, Arab philosopher.

Mithat Pasha and Security Bank
Building — A200

Design: 20k, Agricultural Bank.

1950, Dec. 21   Photo.
1041	A200	15k rose violet	2.00	2.00
1042	A200	20k blue	2.00	2.00

3rd Congress of Turkish Cooperatives,
Istanbul, Dec. 25, 1950.

Floating a
Ship
A201

Lighthouse — A202

1951, July 1
1043	A201	15k shown	.75	.75
1044	A201	20k Steamship	.75	.75
1045	A201	30k Diver rising	1.50	1.50
1046	A202	1 l shown	2.75	2.75
		Nos. 1043-1046 (4)	5.75	5.75

25th anniv. of the recognition of coastal
rights in Turkish waters to ships under the
Turkish flag.

Mosque of
Sultan
Ahmed
A203

Henry Carton de
Wiart — A204

Designs: 20k, Dolma Bahce Palace. 60k,
Rumeli Hisari Fortress.

1951, Aug. 31   Photo.   Perf. 13½
1047	A203	15k dark green	.35	.25
1048	A203	20k deep ultra	.60	.25
1049	A204	30k brown	.75	.35
1050	A203	60k purple brown	1.40	1.40
		Nos. 1047-1050 (4)	3.10	2.25

40th Interparliamentary Conf., Istanbul.

Allegory of
Food and
Agriculture
A205

Designs: 20k, Dam. 30k, United Nations
Building. 60k, University, Ankara.

**Inscribed: "Akdeniz Yetistirme
Merkezi. Ankara 1951."**

1952, Jan. 3   Unwmk.   Perf. 14
1051	A205	15k green	1.00	.65
1052	A205	20k blue violet	1.10	.75
1053	A205	30k blue	2.50	2.00
1054	A205	60k red	3.75	3.25
a.		Souvenir sheet of 4	95.00	85.00
		Nos. 1051-1054 (4)	8.35	6.65

UN Mediterranean Economic Instruction
Center.

No. 1054a contains one each of Nos. 1051-
1054, imperf., with inscriptions in dark blue
gray.

Abdulhak Hamid
Tarhan, Poet,
Birth
Cent. — A206

1952, Feb. 5   Photo.   Perf. 13½
1055	A206	15k dark purple	1.00	1.00
1056	A206	20k dark blue	1.00	1.00
1057	A206	30k brown	1.00	1.00
1058	A206	60k dark olive grn	2.75	1.75
		Nos. 1055-1058 (4)	5.75	4.75

Ruins, Bergama
A207

Pavilion, Istanbul
A208

Designs: 1k, Ruins, Bergama. 2k, Ruins, Milas. 3k, Karatay Gate, Konya. 4k, Kozak plateau. 5k, Urgup. 10k, 12k, 15k, 20k, Kemal Ataturk. 30k, Mosque, Bursa. 40k, Mosque, Istanbul. 50, Tarsus Cataract. 75k, Rocks, Urgup. 1 l, Palace, Istanbul. 5 l, Museum interior, Istanbul.

1952, Mar. 15   **Perf. 13½**

1059	A207	1k brown orange	.25	.25
1060	A207	2k olive green	.25	.25
1061	A207	3k rose brown	.35	.25
1062	A207	4k blue green	.55	.40
1063	A207	5k brown	.35	.25
1064	A207	10k dark brown	.25	.25
1065	A207	12k brt rose car	.75	.50
1066	A207	15k purple	.50	.25
1067	A207	20k chalky blue	.90	.25
1068	A207	30k grnsh gray	.75	.25
1069	A207	40k slate blue	4.50	.75
1070	A208	50k olive	.75	.25
1071	A208	75k slate	.75	.30
1072	A208	1 l deep purple	.55	.25
1073	A208	2 l brt ultra	2.50	1.60
1074	A208	5 l sepia	35.00	9.00
		Nos. 1059-1074 (16)	48.95	13.95

Imperfs, value, set $90.
For surcharge & overprint see #1075, 1255.

No. 1059 Surcharged with New Value in Black

1952, June 1

1075	A207	0.50k on 1k brn org	.30	.25

Technical Faculty Building
A209

1952, Aug. 20   **Perf. 12x12½**

1076	A209	15k violet	.65	.65
1077	A209	20k blue	.95	.95
1078	A209	60k brown	1.60	1.60
		Nos. 1076-1078 (3)	3.20	3.20

8th Intl. Congress of Theoretic and Applied Mechanics.

Turkish Soldier — A210

20k, Soldier with Turkish flag. 30k, Soldier & child with comic book. 60k, Raising Turkish flag.

1952, Sept. 25   **Perf. 14**

1079	A210	15k Prus blue	.40	.40
1080	A210	20k deep blue	.60	.60
1081	A210	30k brown	.85	.85
1082	A210	60k olive blk & car	1.75	1.75
		Nos. 1079-1082 (4)	3.60	3.60

Turkey's participation in the Korean war.

Pigeons Bandaging Wounded Hand — A212

20k, Flag, rainbow and ruined homes.

Dated "1877-1952"

1952, Oct. 29   **Perf. 12½x12**

1085	A212	15k dk green & red	.80	.40
1086	A212	20k blue & red	2.00	.70

Turkish Red Crescent Society, 75th anniv.

Relief From Panel of Aziziye Monument — A213

Aziziye Monument
A214

Design: 40k, View of Erzerum.

1952, Nov. 9   **Perf. 11**

1087	A213	15k purple	.50	.30
1088	A214	20k blue	.60	.50
1089	A214	40k olive gray	1.00	.70
		Nos. 1087-1089 (3)	2.10	1.50

75th anniv. of the Battle of Aziziye at Erzerum.

Humeli Hisari Fortress
A215

Troops Entering Constantinople — A216

Sultan Mohammed II — A217

Designs: 8k, Soldiers moving cannon. 10k, Mohammed II riding into sea, and Turkish armada. 12k, Landing of Turkish army. 15k, Ancient wall, Constantinople. 30k, Mosque of Faith. 40k, Presenting mace to Patriarch Yenadios. 60k, Map of Constantinople, c. 1574. 1 l, Tomb of Mohammed II. 2.50 l, Portrait of Mohammed II.

Inscribed: "Istanbulun Fethi 1453-1953"

1953, May 29   **Photo.**   **Perf. 11½**

1090	A215	5k brt blue	1.25	.60
1091	A215	8k gray	1.90	.60
1092	A215	10k blue	.60	.60
1093	A215	12k rose lilac	1.25	.60
1094	A215	15k brown	.90	.30
1095	A216	20k vermilion	1.25	.30
1096	A216	30k dull green	2.40	1.25
1097	A216	40k violet blue	4.25	1.50
1098	A215	60k chocolate	3.00	1.50
1099	A215	1 l blue green	7.25	2.10

      Perf. 12

1100	A217	2 l multi	15.00	6.00
1101	A217	2.50 l multi	9.00	9.00
a.		Souvenir sheet	125.00	95.00
		Nos. 1090-1101 (12)	48.05	24.35

Conquest of Constantinople by Sultan Mohammed II, 500th anniv.

Ruins of the Odeon, Ephesus
A218

15k, Church of St. John the Apostle. 20k, Shrine of Virgin Mary, Panaya Kapulu. 40k, Ruins of the Double Church. 60k, Shrine of the Seven Sleepers. 1 l, Restored house of the Virgin Mary.

1953, Aug. 16   **Litho.**   **Perf. 13½**
Multicolored Center

1102	A218	12k sage green	.40	.25
1103	A218	15k lilac	.40	.25
1104	A218	20k dk slate blue	.50	.35
1105	A218	40k light green	.75	.60
1106	A218	60k violet blue	1.00	.75
1107	A218	1 l brown red	2.75	2.00
		Nos. 1102-1107 (6)	5.80	4.20

Pres. Celal Bayar, Mithat Pasha. Herman Schulze-Delitzsch and People's Bank — A219

Design: 20k, Pres. Bayar, Mithat Pasha and University of Ankara.

1953, Sept. 2   **Photo.**   **Perf. 10½**

1108	A219	15k orange brown	1.00	.50
1109	A219	20k Prus green	1.00	.50

5th Intl. People's Credit Congress, Istanbul, Sept.

Combined Harvester
A220

Kemal Ataturk — A221

Designs: 15k, Berdan dam. 20k, Military parade. 30k, Diesel train. 35k, Yesilkoy airport.

1953, Oct. 29   **Perf. 14**

1110	A220	10k olive bister	.90	.25
1111	A220	15k dark gray	.90	.25
1112	A220	20k rose red	.90	.25
1113	A220	30k olive green	1.50	1.25
1114	A220	35k dull blue	1.00	.75
1115	A221	55k dull purple	2.25	1.75
		Nos. 1110-1115 (6)	7.45	5.00

Turkish Republic, 30th anniv.

Kemal Ataturk and Mausoleum at Ankara — A222

1953, Nov. 10

1116	A222	15k gray black	.75	.35
1117	A222	20k violet brown	.95	.65

15th death anniv. of Kemal Ataturk.

Type of 1931-42
Without umlaut over first "U" of "CUMHURIYETI"

Perf. 11½x12, 10x11½

1953-56		Typo.	Unwmk.	
1117B	A77	20p yellow	.30	.25
1118	A78	1k brown orange	.30	.25
1119	A78	2k rose pink ('53)	.50	.25
1120	A78	3k yel brn ('53)	.50	.25
1120A	A78	4k slate ('56)	1.50	.40
1121	A78	5k blue	2.00	.25
1121A	A78	8k violet ('56)	.50	.25
1122	A77	10k dark olive ('53)	.50	.25

1123	A77	12k brt car rose ('53)	.50	.25
1124	A77	15k fawn	.60	.25
1125	A77	20k rose lilac	3.50	.40
1126	A77	30k lt blue grn ('54)	1.25	.25
		Nos. 1117B-1126 (12)	11.95	3.30

Compass and Map
A223

Designs: 20k, Globe, crescent and stars. 40k, Tree symbolical of 14 NATO members.

1954, Apr. 4   **Photo.**   **Perf. 14**

1127	A223	15k brown	1.75	1.25
1128	A223	20k violet blue	2.25	1.75
1129	A223	40k dark green	15.50	13.00
		Nos. 1127-1129 (3)	19.50	16.00

NATO, 5th anniv.

Industry, Engineering and Agriculture — A224

Justice and Council of Europe Flag — A225

1954, Aug. 8   **Litho.**   **Perf. 10½**

1130	A224	10k brown	3.25	2.40
1131	A225	15k dark green	3.00	1.25
1132	A225	20k blue	3.25	1.25
1133	A224	30k brt violet	14.50	10.00
		Nos. 1130-1133 (4)	24.00	14.90

Council of Europe, 5th anniv.

Flag Signals to Plane — A226

Amaury de La Grange and Plane
A227

Design: 45k, Kemal Ataturk and air fleet.

1954, Sept. 20   **Perf. 12½**

1134	A226	20k black brown	.55	.25
1135	A227	35k dull violet	.85	.25
1136	A227	45k deep blue	1.25	.30
		Nos. 1134-1136 (3)	2.65	.80

47th Congress of the Intl. Aeronautical Federation, Istanbul, 1954.

Souvenir Sheet

A228

1954, Oct. 18   **Imperf.**
1137 A228 Sheet of 3   16.00 14.00
  a. 20k aquamarine   1.25   .85
  b. 30k violet blue   1.50   .85
  c. 1 l red violet   3.00 1.90

First anniv. of Law of Oct. 17, 1953, reorganizing the Department of Post, Telephone and Telegraph.

Ziya
Gokalp — A229

1954, Oct. 25   **Perf. 11**
1138 A229 15k rose lilac   .50   .50
1139 A229 20k dark green   .60   .60
1140 A229 30k crimson   .90   .90
  Nos. 1138-1140 (3)   2.00 2.00

30th death anniv. of Ziya Gokalp, author and historian.

Kemal Atatürk — A230

1955, Mar. 1   **Perf. 12½**
1141 A230 15k carmine rose   .60   .60
1142 A230 20k blue   .75   .75
1143 A230 40k dark gray   .90   .90
1144 A230 50k blue green   1.25 1.25
1145 A230 75k orange brown   1.50 1.50
  Nos. 1141-1145 (5)   5.00 5.00

Relief Map of Dardanelles — A231

Artillery
Loaders — A232

30k, Minelayer Nusrat. 60k, Col. Kemal Atatürk.

1955, Mar. 18   **Perf. 10½**
1146 A231 15k green   .60   .25
1147 A232 20k orange brown   .60   .25
1148 A231 30k ultra   .90   .45
1149 A232 60k olive gray   1.50   .65
  Nos. 1146-1149 (4)   3.60 1.60

Battle of Gallipoli, 40th anniversary.

Aerial
Map
A233

1955, Apr. 14   **Perf. 11**
1150 A233 15k gray   .35   .25
1151 A233 20k aquamarine   .35   .25
1152 A233 50k brown   .60   .25
1153 A233 1 l purple   1.10   .50
  Nos. 1150-1153 (4)   2.40 1.25

City Planning Congress, Ankara, 1955.

Carnation — A234

1955, May 19   Litho.   **Perf. 10**
1154 A234 10k shown   .55   .55
1155 A234 15k Tulip   .55   .55
1156 A234 20k Rose   .85   .55
1157 A234 50k Lily   2.00 1.10
  Nos. 1154-1157 (4)   3.95 2.75

National Flower Show, Istanbul, May 20-Aug. 20.

Battle First
Aid Station
A235

30k, Gulhane Military Hospital, Ankara.

1955, Aug. 28   Unwmk.   **Perf. 12**
1158 A235 20k red, lake & gray   .75   .50
1159 A235 30k dp grn & yel grn 1.25   .75

XVIII Intl. Congress of Military Medicine, Aug. 8-Sept. 1, Istanbul.

Soccer
Game
A236

Emblem and Soccer
Ball — A237

1 l, Emblem with oak & olive branches.

1955, Aug. 30   **Perf. 10**
1160 A236 15k light ultra   .70   .25
1161 A237 20k crimson rose   .85   .25
1162 A236 1 l light green   1.75 1.10
  Nos. 1160-1162 (3)   3.30 1.60

Intl. Military Soccer Championship games, Istanbul, Aug. 30.

Sureté
Monument,
Ankara
A238

20k, Dolma Bahce Palace. 30k, Police College, Ankara. 45k, Police Martyrs' Monument, Istanbul.

Inscribed: "Enterpol Istanbul 1955"

1955, Sept. 5   **Perf. 10**
1163 A238 15k blue green   .30   .30
1164 A238 20k brt violet   .45   .45
1165 A238 30k gray black   .55   .40
1166 A238 45k lt brown   1.10   .65
  Nos. 1163-1166 (4)   2.40 1.80

24th general assembly of the Intl. Criminal Police, Istanbul, Sept. 5-9.

Early
Telegraph
Transmitter
A239

Modern
Transmitter
A240

Perf. 13½x14, 14x13½

1955, Sept. 10   **Photo.**
1167 A239 15k olive   .40   .25
1168 A240 20k crimson rose   .40   .25
1169 A239 45k fawn   .80   .25
1170 A240 60k ultra   .90   .75
  Nos. 1167-1170 (4)   2.50 1.50

Centenary of telecommunication.

Academy of
Science,
Istanbul
A241

Designs: 20k, University. 60k, Hilton Hotel. 1 l, Kiz Kulesi (Leander's Tower).

1955, Sept. 12   **Perf. 13½x14**
1171 A241 15k yellow orange   .45   .35
1172 A241 20k crimson rose   .45   .35
1173 A241 60k purple   .60   .35
1174 A241 1 l deep blue   .95   .60
  Nos. 1171-1174 (4)   2.45 1.65

10th meeting of the governors of the Intl. Bank of Reconstruction and Development and the Intl. Monetary Fund, Istanbul, Sept. 12-16.

Surlari,
Istanbul
A242

Mosque of Sultan
Ahmed — A243

Designs: 30k, Haghia Sophia. 75k, Map of Constantinople, by Christoforo Buondelmonti, 1422.

1955, Sept. 15   Litho.   **Perf. 11½**
1175 A242 15k grnsh blk & Prus
         grn   .75   .25
1176 A243 20k vermilion & org   .60   .25
1177 A242 30k sepia & vio brn   .60   .25
1178 A243 75k ultramarine   1.60   .75
  Nos. 1175-1178 (4)   3.55 1.50

10th Intl. Congress of Byzantine Research, Istanbul, Sept. 15-21, 1955.

Congress
Emblem — A244

30k, Chalet in Istanbul. 55k, Bridges.

Inscribed: "Beynelmiel X. Vol Kongresi Istanbul 1955"

1955, Sept. 26   **Perf. 10½x11**
1179 A244 20k red violet   .30   .25
1180 A244 30k dk grn & yel grn   .30   .25
1181 A244 55k dp bl & brt bl   1.00   .75
  Nos. 1179-1181 (3)   1.60 1.25

10th International Transportation Congress.

Map of
Turkey,
Showing
Population
Increase
A245

1955, Oct. 22   Unwmk.   **Perf. 10**
Map in Rose
1182 A245 15k lt & dk gray & red .50   .25
1183 A245 20k lt & dk vio & red   .40   .25
1184 A245 30k lt & dk ultra & red .45   .25
1185 A245 60k lt & dk bl grn &
         red   1.00   .30
  Nos. 1182-1185 (4)   2.35 1.05

Census of 1955.

Waterfall,
Antalya — A246

Alanya and
Seljukide
Dockyards
A247

Designs: 30k, Theater at Aspendos. 45k, Ruins at Side. 50k, View of Antalya. 65k, St. Nicholas Church at Myra (Demre) and St. Nicholas.

Perf. 14x13½, 13½x14

1955, Dec. 10   Photo.   Unwmk.
1186 A246 18k bl, ol grn & ultra .50   .25
1187 A247 20k blue, ultra & brn   .50   .25
1188 A247 30k dl grn, ol bis &
         grn   .50   .25
1189 A246 45k yel grn & brn   2.25 1.00
1190 A246 50k Prus grn & ol bis   .60   .30
1191 A247 65k orange ver & blk   .80   .40
  Nos. 1186-1191 (6)   5.15 2.45

Kemal Atatürk — A248

1955-56 Litho. Perf. 12½

1192	A248	0.50k carmine	.60	.25
1193	A248	1k yellow orange	.90	.25
1194	A248	2k brt blue	.60	.25
1195	A248	3k scarlet	.60	.25
1196	A248	5k lt brown	.60	.25
1197	A248	6k lt blue grn	.70	.25
1198	A248	10k blue green	.70	.25
1199	A248	18k rose violet	.80	.25
1200	A248	20k lt violet bl	.95	.25
1201	A248	25k olive green	.95	.45
1202	A248	30k violet	.95	.25
1203	A248	40k fawn	1.00	.40
1204	A248	75k slate blue	3.00	1.25
		Nos. 1192-1204 (13)	12.35	4.60

Issue dates: 3k, 1955. Others, 1956.

Tomb at Nigde — A249

1956, Apr. 12 Perf. 10½

1205	A249	40k violet bl & bl	.35	.25

25th anniv. of the Turkish History Society. The tomb of Hüdavent Hatun, a sultan's daughter, exemplifies Seljukian architecture of the 14th century.

Zubeyde Hanum — A250

1956, May 13 Perf. 11

1206	A250	20k pale brn & dk brn	.65	.50

Imperf

1207	A250	20k lt grn & dk grn	1.00	.60

Mother's Day; Zubeyde Hanum, mother of Kemal Ataturk.

Shah and Queen of Iran A251

1956, May 15 Unwmk. Perf. 11

1208	A251	100k grn & pale grn	1.25	.50

Imperf

1209	A251	100k red & pale grn	6.00	4.50

Visit of the Shah and Queen of Iran to Turkey, May 15.

Erenkoy Sanitarium A252

1956, July 31 Perf. 11

1210	A252	50k dk bl grn & pink	.35	.25

Anti-Tuberculosis work among PTT employees.

Symbol of Izmir Fair — A253

A254

1956, Aug. 20 Perf. 11

1211	A253	45k brt green	.50	.35

Souvenir Sheet
Imperf

1212	A254	Sheet of 2	4.00	3.00
a.		50k rose red	1.25	.45
b.		50k bright ultramarine	1.25	.45

25th Intl. Fair, Izmir, 8/20-9/20. See #C20.

Hands Holding Bottled Serpent — A255

1956, Sept. 10 Litho. Perf. 10½

1213	A255	25k multicolored	.30	.30
a.		Tete beche pair	1.00	1.00

25th Intl. Anti-Alcoholism Congress, Istanbul Sept. 10-15.
Printed both in regular sheets and in sheets with alternate vertical rows inverted.

Medical Center at Kayseri — A256

1956, Nov. 1 Perf. 12½x12

1214	A256	60k violet & yel	.40	.30

750th anniv. of the first medical school and clinic in Anatolia.

Sariyar Dam — A257

1956, Dec. 2 Litho. Perf. 10½

1215	A257	20k vermilion	.50	.30
1216	A257	20k bright blue	.50	.30

Inauguration of Sariyar Dam.

Freestyle Wrestling A258

Design: 65k, Greco-Roman wrestling.

1956, Dec. 8 Unwmk. Perf. 10½

1217	A258	40k brt yel grn & brn	1.00	.40
1218	A258	65k lt bluish gray & dp car	1.25	.40

16th Olympic Games, Melbourne, Nov. 22-Dec. 8, 1956.

Mehmet Akif Ersoy — A259

1956, Dec. 26

1219	A259	20k brn & brt yel grn	.40	.25
1220	A259	20k rose car & lt gray	.40	.25
1221	A259	20k vio bl & brt pink	.40	.25
		Nos. 1219-1221 (3)	1.20	.75

20th death anniv. of Mehmet Akif Ersoy, author of the Turkish National Anthem.
Each value bears a different verse of the anthem.

Theater in Troy — A260

Trojan Vase — A261

Design: 30k, Trojan Horse.

Perf. 13½x14, 14x13½

1956, Dec. 31 Photo. Unwmk.

1222	A260	15k green	1.60	.85
1223	A261	20k red violet	1.60	.85
1224	A260	30k chestnut	2.50	.85
		Nos. 1222-1224 (3)	5.70	2.55

Excavations at Troy.

Mobile Chest X-Ray Unit A262

1957, Jan. 1 Litho. Perf. 12

1225	A262	25k ol brn & red	.35	.25

Fight against tuberculsois.

Kemal Atatürk — A263

1956-57 Perf. 12½

1226	A263	½k blue green	.25	.25
1227	A263	1k yellow orange	.40	.25
1228	A263	3k gray olive	.40	.25
1229	A263	5k violet	.40	.25
1230	A263	6k rose car ('57)	.50	.25
1231	A263	10k rose violet	.50	.25
1232	A263	12k fawn ('57)	.60	.25
1233	A263	15k lt violet bl	.50	.25
1234	A263	18k carmine ('57)	.60	.25
1235	A263	20k lt brown	.50	.25
1236	A263	25k lt blue green	.50	.25
1237	A263	30k slate blue	.50	.25
1238	A263	40k olive ('57)	.75	.25
1239	A263	50k orange	.60	.25
1240	A263	60k brt blue ('57)	.90	.35
1241	A263	70k Prus green ('57)	2.50	1.25
1242	A263	75k brown	1.75	.90
		Nos. 1226-1242 (17)	12.15	6.00

Pres. Heuss of Germany — A264

1957, May 5 Unwmk. Perf. 10½

1243	A264	40k yellow & brown	.25	.25

Visit of Pres. Theodor Heuss of Germany to Turkey, May 5. See No. C29.

View of Bergama and Ruin A265

40k, Dancers in kermis at Bergama.

1957, May 24

1244	A265	30k brown	.30	.25
1245	A265	40k green	.30	.25

20th anniv. of the kermis at Bergama (Pergamus).

Symbols of Industry and Flags A266

1957, July 1 Photo. Perf. 13½x14

1246	A266	25k violet	.40	.40
1247	A266	40k gray blue	.40	.40

Turkish-American collaboration, 10th anniv.

Osman Hamdi Bey A267

Hittite Sun Course from Alaça Höyük — A268

1957, July 6 Perf. 10½

1248	A267	20k beige, pale brn & blk	.35	.25
1249	A268	30k Prussian green	.40	.25

75th anniv. of the Academy of Art. The 20k exists with "cancellation" omitted.

King of Afghanistan — A269

1957, Sept. 1   Litho.   Perf. 10½
1250 A269 45k car lake & pink   .25   .25
Visit of Mohammed Zahir Shah, King of Afghanistan, to Turkey. See No. C30.

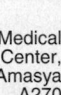

Medical Center, Amasya A270

Design: 65k, Suleiman Medical Center.

1957, Sept. 29   Unwmk.   Perf. 10½
1251 A270 25k vermilion & yellow   .25   .25
1252 A270 65k brt grnsh bl & cit   .30   .25
11th general meeting of the World Medical Assoc.

Mosque of Suleiman A271

Architect Mimar Koca Sinan (1489-1587) A272

1957, Oct. 18   Perf. 11
1253 A271 20k gray green   .25   .25
1254 A272 100k brown   .45   .30
400th anniv. of the opening of the Mosque of Suleiman, Istanbul.

No. 1073 Surcharged with New Value and "ISTANBUL Filatelik n. Sergisi 1957"

1957, Nov. 11   Photo.   Perf. 13½
1255 A208 50k on 2 l brt ultra   .30   .25
1957 Istanbul Philatelic Exhibition.

Forestation Map of Turkey — A273

25k, Forest & hand planting tree, vert.

1957, Nov. 18   Litho.   Perf. 10½
1256 A273 20k green & brown   .25   .25
1257 A273 25k emerald & bl grn   .25   .25
Centenary of forestry in Turkey.
Nos. 1256-1257 each come with two different tabs attached (four tabs in all) bearing various quotations.

A274

1957, Nov. 23
1258 A274 50k pink, vio, red & yel   .40   .25
400th death anniv. of Fuzuli (Mehmet Suleiman Ogiou), poet.

A275

1957, Nov. 28   Photo.   Perf. 14x13½
1259 A275 65k dk Prus blue   .40   .25
1260 A275 65k rose violet   .40   .25
Benjamin Franklin (1706-1790).

Green Dome, Tomb of Mevlana, at Konya — A276

Konya Museum A277

Mevlana — A278

Perf. 11x10½, 10½x11
1957, Dec. 17   Litho.   Unwmk.
1261 A276 50k green, bl & vio   .25   .25
1262 A277 100k dark blue   .50   .25

Miniature Sheet
Imperf
1263 A278 100k multicolored   1.75 1.40
Jalal-udin Mevlana (1207-1273), Persian poet and founder of the Mevlevie dervish order. No. 1263 contains one stamp 32x42mm.

Kemal Atatürk (Double Frame; Serifs) — A279

1957   Unwmk.   Perf. 11½
Size: 18x22mm
1264 A279 ½k lt brown   .60   .25
1265 A279 1k lt violet bl   .50   .25
1266 A279 2k black violet   .50   .25
1267 A279 3k orange   .50   .25
1268 A279 5k blue green   .50   .25
1269 A279 6k dk slate grn   .50   .25
1270 A279 10k violet   .50   .25
1271 A279 12k brt green   .50   .25
1272 A279 15k dk blue grn   .60   .25
1273 A279 18k rose carmine   .60   .25
1274 A279 20k brown   .60   .25
1275 A279 25k brown red   .60   .25
1276 A279 30k brt blue   .60   .25
1277 A279 40k slate blue   .80   .25
1278 A279 50k yellow orange   .80   .25
1279 A279 60k black   .80   .25
1280 A279 70k rose violet   .90   .25
1281 A279 75k gray olive   1.25   .30
Size: 21x29mm
1282 A279 100k carmine   1.50   .40
1283 A279 250k olive   3.50   .90
Nos. 1264-1283 (20)   16.65   5.85

College Emblem — A280

1958, Jan. 16   Litho.   Perf. 10½x11
1288 A280 20k bister, ind & org   .25   .25
1289 A280 25k dk blue, bis & org   .25   .25
"Turkiye" on top of 25k. 75th anniv. of the College of Economics and Commerce, Istanbul.

View of Adana — A281

1958   Photo.   Perf. 11½
Size: 26x20½mm
1290 A281 5k Adana   .25   .25
1291 A281 5k Adapazari   .25   .25
1292 A281 5k Adiyaman   .25   .25
1293 A281 5k Afyon   .25   .25
1294 A281 5k Amasya   .25   .25
1295 A281 5k Ankara   .25   .25
1296 A281 5k Antakya   .25   .25
1297 A281 5k Antalya   .25   .25
1298 A281 5k Artvin   .25   .25
1299 A281 5k Aydin   .25   .25
1300 A281 5k Balikesir   .25   .25
1301 A281 5k Bilecik   .25   .25
1302 A281 5k Bingol   .25   .25
1303 A281 5k Bitlis   .25   .25
1304 A281 5k Bolu   .25   .25
1305 A281 5k Burdur   .25   .25
1306 A281 5k Bursa   .25   .25
1307 A281 5k Canakkale   .25   .25
1308 A281 5k Cankiri   .25   .25
1309 A281 5k Corum   .25   .25
1310 A281 5k Denizli   .25   .25
1311 A281 5k Diyarbakir   .25   .25
Size: 32½x22mm
1312 A281 20k Adana   .25   .25
1313 A281 20k Adapazari   .25   .25
1314 A281 20k Adiyaman   .25   .25
1315 A281 20k Afyon   .25   .25
1316 A281 20k Amasya   .25   .25
1317 A281 20k Ankara   .25   .25
1318 A281 20k Antakya   .25   .25
1319 A281 20k Antalya   .25   .25
1320 A281 20k Artvin   .25   .25
1321 A281 20k Aydin   .25   .25

1322 A281 20k Balikesir   .25   .25
1323 A281 20k Bilecik   .25   .25
1324 A281 20k Bingol   .25   .25
1325 A281 20k Bitlis   .25   .25
1326 A281 20k Bolu   .25   .25
1327 A281 20k Burdur   .25   .25
1328 A281 20k Bursa   .25   .25
1329 A281 20k Canakkale   .25   .25
1330 A281 20k Cankiri   .25   .25
1331 A281 20k Corum   .25   .25
1332 A281 20k Denizli   .25   .25
1333 A281 20k Diyarbakir   .25   .25
Nos. 1290-1333 (44)   11.00 11.00
1959   Size: 26x20½mm
1334 A281 5k Edirne   .25   .25
1335 A281 5k Elazig   .25   .25
1336 A281 5k Erzincan   .25   .25
1337 A281 5k Erzurum   .25   .25
1338 A281 5k Eskisehir   .25   .25
1339 A281 5k Gaziantep   .25   .25
1340 A281 5k Giresun   .25   .25
1341 A281 5k Gumusane   .25   .25
1342 A281 5k Hakkari   .25   .25
1343 A281 5k Isparta   .25   .25
1344 A281 5k Istanbul   .25   .25
1345 A281 5k Izmir   .25   .25
1346 A281 5k Izmit   .25   .25
1347 A281 5k Karakose   .25   .25
1348 A281 5k Kars   .25   .25
1349 A281 5k Kastamonu   .25   .25
1350 A281 5k Kayseri   .25   .25
1351 A281 5k Kirklareli   .25   .25
1352 A281 5k Kirsehir   .25   .25
1353 A281 5k Konya   .25   .25
1354 A281 5k Kutahya   .25   .25
1355 A281 5k Malatya   .25   .25
Size: 32½x22mm
1356 A281 20k Edirne   .25   .25
1357 A281 20k Elazig   .25   .25
1358 A281 20k Erzincan   .25   .25
1359 A281 20k Erzurum   .25   .25
1360 A281 20k Eskisehir   .25   .25
1361 A281 20k Gaziantep   .25   .25
1362 A281 20k Giresun   .25   .25
1363 A281 20k Gumusane   .25   .25
1364 A281 20k Hakkari   .25   .25
1365 A281 20k Isparta   .25   .25
1366 A281 20k Istanbul   .25   .25
1367 A281 20k Izmir   .25   .25
1368 A281 20k Izmit   .25   .25
1369 A281 20k Karakose   .25   .25
1370 A281 20k Kars   .25   .25
1371 A281 20k Kastamonu   .25   .25
1372 A281 20k Kayseri   .25   .25
1373 A281 20k Kirklareli   .25   .25
1374 A281 20k Kirsehir   .25   .25
1375 A281 20k Konya   .25   .25
1376 A281 20k Kutahya   .25   .25
1377 A281 20k Malatya   .25   .25
Nos. 1334-1377 (44)   11.00 11.00
1960   Size: 26x20½mm
1378 A281 5k Manisa   .25   .25
1379 A281 5k Maras   .25   .25
1380 A281 5k Mardin   .25   .25
1381 A281 5k Mersin   .25   .25
1382 A281 5k Mugla   .25   .25
1383 A281 5k Mus   .25   .25
1384 A281 5k Nevsehir   .25   .25
1385 A281 5k Nigde   .25   .25
1386 A281 5k Ordu   .25   .25
1387 A281 5k Rize   .25   .25
1388 A281 5k Samsun   .25   .25
1389 A281 5k Siirt   .25   .25
1390 A281 5k Sinop   .25   .25
1391 A281 5k Sivas   .25   .25
1392 A281 5k Tekirdag   .25   .25
1393 A281 5k Tokat   .25   .25
1394 A281 5k Trabzon   .25   .25
1395 A281 5k Tunceli   .25   .25
1396 A281 5k Urfa   .25   .25
1397 A281 5k Usak   .25   .25
1398 A281 5k Van   .25   .25
1399 A281 5k Yozgat   .25   .25
1400 A281 5k Zonguldak   .25   .25
Size: 32½x22mm
1401 A281 20k Manisa   .25   .25
1402 A281 20k Maras   .25   .25
1403 A281 20k Mardin   .25   .25
1404 A281 20k Mersin   .25   .25
1405 A281 20k Mugla   .25   .25
1406 A281 20k Mus   .25   .25
1407 A281 20k Nevsehir   .25   .25
1408 A281 20k Nigde   .25   .25
1409 A281 20k Ordu   .25   .25
1410 A281 20k Rize   .25   .25
1411 A281 20k Samsun   .25   .25
1412 A281 20k Siirt   .25   .25
1413 A281 20k Sinop   .25   .25
1414 A281 20k Sivas   .25   .25
1415 A281 20k Tekirdag   .25   .25
1416 A281 20k Tokat   .25   .25
1417 A281 20k Trabzon   .25   .25
1418 A281 20k Tunceli   .25   .25
1419 A281 20k Urfa   .25   .25
1420 A281 20k Usak   .25   .25
1421 A281 20k Van   .25   .25
1422 A281 20k Yozgat   .25   .25
1423 A281 20k Zonguldak   .25   .25
Nos. 1378-1423 (46)   11.50 11.50
Nos. 1290-1423 (134)   33.50 33.50

Ruins at Pamukkale
A282

Designs: 25k, Travertines at Pamukkale.

1958, May 18   Litho.   Perf. 12
1424 A282 20k brown   .40 .25
1425 A282 25k blue   .40 .25

"Industry" — A283

1958, Oct. 10   Unwmk.   Perf. 10½
1426 A283 40k slate blue   .40 .25

National Industry Exhibition.

Europa Issue

Symbolizing New
Europe — A284

1958, Oct. 10
1427 A284 25k vio & dull pink   .40 .25
1428 A284 40k brt ultra   .40 .25

Letters
A285

1958, Oct. 5
1429 A285 20k orange & blk   .40 .25

Intl. Letter Writing Week, Oct. 5-11.

Atatürk 20th Anniv. Death — A286

1958, Nov. 10   Perf. 12
1430 25k Flame and mausoleum   .25 .25
1431 75k Atatürk   .25 .25
a. A286 Pair, #1430-1431   .65 .60

20th death anniv. of Kemal Ataturk.

Emblem — A288

1959, Jan. 10   Litho.   Perf. 10
1432 A288 25k dk violet & yel   .40 .25

25th anniv. of the Agricultural Faculty of Ankara University.

Blackboard and School
Emblem — A289

1959, Jan. 15   Perf. 10½
1433 A289 75k black & yellow   .60 .30

75th anniv. of the establishment of a secondary boys' school in Istanbul.

State
Theater,
Ankara
A290

Design: 25k, Portrait of Sinasi.

1959, Mar. 30   Unwmk.   Perf. 10½
1434 A290 20k red brn & emer   .25 .25
1435 A290 25k Prus grn & org   .25 .25
Centenary of the Turkish theater; Sinasi, writer of the first Turkish play in 1859.

Globe and
Stars
A291

1959, Apr. 4   Perf. 10
1436 A291 105k red   .25 .25
1437 A291 195k green   1.00 .50

10th anniversary of NATO.

Aspendos
Theater
A292

1959, May 1   Litho.   Perf. 10½
1438 A292 20k bis brn & vio   .40 .25
1439 A292 20k grn & ol bis   .40 .25

Aspendos (Belkins) Festival.

No. B70 Surcharged in Ultramarine

1959, May 5
1440 SP25 105k on 15k + 5k org   .55 .25

Council of Europe, 10th anniversary.

Basketball — A293

1959, May 21   Perf. 10
1441 A293 25k red org & dk bl   .30 .25

11th European and Mediterranean Basketball Championship.

"Karadeniz"
A294

Telegraph
Mast — A295

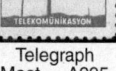

Kemal
Atatürk — A296

Designs: 1k, Turkish Airlines' SEC plane. 10k, Grain elevator, Ankara. 15k, Iron and Steel Works, Karabück. 20k, Euphrates Bridge, Birecik. 25k, Zonguldak Harbor. 30k, Gasoline refinery, Batman. 40k, Rumeli Hisari Fortress. 45k, Sugar factory, Konya. 55k, Coal mine, Zonguldak. 75k, Railway. 90k, Crane loading ships. 100k, Cement factory, Ankara. 120k, Highway. 150k, Harvester. 200k, Electric transformer.

Perf. 10½, 11, 11½, 12½, 13½

		Litho.	Unwmk.
1442	A294	1k indigo	.25 .25
1443	A294	5k brt blue ('59)	.25 .25
1444	A294	10k blue	.25 .25
1445	A294	15k brown	.70 .25
1446	A294	20k slate green	.25 .25
1447	A294	25k violet	.25 .25
1448	A294	30k lilac	.45 .35
1449	A294	40k blue	.70 .25
1450	A294	45k dull violet	.70 .25
1451	A294	55k olive brown	.70 .25
1452	A295	60k green	.95 .25
1453	A295	75k gray olive	3.50 .25
1454	A295	90k dark blue	7.75 .25
1455	A295	100k gray	10.50 .25
1456	A295	120k magenta	3.50 .35
1457	A294	150k orange	3.50 .45
1458	A296	200k yellow green	4.25 .45
1459	A296	250k black brown	4.25 .55
1460	A296	500k dark blue	7.00 .85
		Nos. 1442-1460 (19)	49.70 6.25

Postage Due Stamps of
1936 Surcharged

1959, June 1   Perf. 11½
1461 D6 20k on 20pa brown   .85 .25
1462 D6 20k on 2k lt blue   .35 .25
1463 D6 20k on 3k brt vio   .45 .25
1464 D6 20k on 5k Prus bl   .55 .25
1465 D6 20k on 12k brt rose   .55 .25
Nos. 1461-1465 (5)   2.75 1.25

Anchor
Emblem — A297

Design: 40k, Sea Horse emblem.

1959, July 4   Perf. 11
1466 A297 30k multicolored   .40 .25
1467 A297 40k multicolored   .40 .25

50th anniv. of the Merchant Marine College.

11th
Century
Warrior
A298

1959, Aug. 26   Litho.   Perf. 11
1468 A298 2½ l rose lil & lt bl   .60 .35

Battle of Malazkirt, 888th anniversary.

A299

Ornament — A300

Design: 40k, Mosque.

1959, Oct. 19   Unwmk.   Perf. 12½
1469 A299 30k black & red   .25 .25
1470 A299 40k lt blue, blk & ocher   .25 .25
1471 A300 75k dp blue, yel & red   .50 .25
Nos. 1469-1471 (3)   1.00 .75

Turkish Artists Congress, Ankara.

Kemal
Atatürk — A301

Litho.; Center Embossed

1959, Nov. 10   Perf. 14
1472 A301 500k dark blue   2.50 1.75
a. Min. sheet of 1, red, imperf.   4.00 4.00

School
of
Political
Science,
Ankara
A302

Emblem — A303

1959, Dec. 4   Photo.   Perf. 13½
1473 A302 40k green & brown   .25 .25
1474 A302 40k red brown & bl   .25 .25
1475 A303 l l lt & dk vio & buff   .50 .25
Nos. 1473-1475 (3)   1.00 .75

Political Science School, Ankara, cent.

Crossed Swords Emblem — A304

Design: 40k, Bayonet and flame.

Inscribed: "Kara Harbokulunum 125 Yili"

1960, Feb. 28   Litho.   Perf. 10½
1476 A304 30k vermilion & org   .25 .25
1477 A304 40k brown, car & yel   .25 .25
125th anniv. of the Territorial War College.

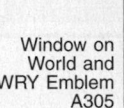

Window on World and WRY Emblem — A305

150k, Symbolic shanties & uprooted oak emblem.

1960, Apr. 7
1478 A305 90k brt grnsh bl & blk   .25 .25
1479 A305 105k yellow & blk   .30 .25
World Refugee Year, 7/1/59-6/30/60.

Spring Flower Festival — A306

1960, June 4   Photo.   Perf. 11½
Granite Paper
1480 A306 30k Carnations   .50 .25
1481 A306 40k Jasmine   .70 .25
1482 A306 75k Rose   1.00 .25
1483 A306 105k Tulip   1.40 .50
     Nos. 1480-1483 (4)   3.60 1.25

Atatürk Square, Nicosia A307

Design: 105k, Map of Cyprus.

1960, Aug. 16   Litho.   Perf. 10½
1484 A307 40k blue & pink   .25 .25
1485 A307 105k blue & yellow   .35 .25
Independence of the Republic of Cyprus.

Women and Nest A308

Design: 30k, Globe and emblem.

1960, Aug. 22   Photo.   Perf. 11½
1486 A308 30k lt vio & yel   .25 .25
1487 A308 75k grnsh bl & gray   .35 .25
16th meeting of the Women's Intl. Council.

Soccer A309

#1489, Basketball. #1490, Wrestling. #1491, Hurdling. #1492, Steeplechase.

1960, Aug. 25
1488 A309 30k yellow green   .55 .45
1489 A309 30k black   .55 .45
1490 A309 30k slate blue   .55 .45
1491 A309 30k purple   .55 .45
1492 A309 30k brown   .55 .45
  a.   Sheet of 25, #1488-1492   20.00 11.50
     Nos. 1488-1492 (5)   2.75 2.25
17th Olympic Games, Rome, 8/25-9/11. Printed in sheets of 25 (5x5) with every horizontal and every vertical row containing one of each design. Also printed in normal sheets of 100.

Common Design Types pictured following the introduction.

Europa Issue
Common Design Type
1960, Sept. 19   Size: 33x22mm
1493 CD3 75k green & bl grn   .85 .50
1494 CD3 105k dp bl & lt bl   1.25 .85

Agah Efendi and Front Page of Turcamani Ahval — A310

1960, Oct. 21   Photo.   Perf. 11½
1495 A310 40k brown blk & sl   .50 .25
1496 A310 60k brn blk & bis brn   .50 .25
Centenary of Turkish journalism.

UN Emblem and Torch — A311

Design: 105k, UN headquarters building and UN emblem forming "15," horiz.

1960, Oct. 24   Unwmk.
1497 A311 90k brt bl & dk bl   .30 .30
1498 A311 105k lt bl grn & brn   .30 .30
15th anniversary of the United Nations.

Army Emblem A312

Tribunal A313

Design: 195k, "Justice," vert.

1960, Oct. 14   Litho.   Perf. 13
1499 A312 40k violet & bister   .25 .25
1500 A313 105k red, gray & brn   .25 .25
1501 A313 195k grn, rose red & brn   .45 .25
     Nos. 1499-1501 (3)   .95 .75
Trial of ex-President Celal Bayar and ex-Premier Adnan Menderes.

Revolutionaries and Statue — A314

Prancing Horse, Broken Chain — A315

Designs: 30k, Ataturk and hand holding torch. 105k, Youth, soldier and broken chain.

1960, Dec. 1   Photo.   Perf. 14½
1502 A314 10k gray & blk   .25 .25
1503 A314 30k purple   .25 .25
1504 A315 40k brt red & blk   .25 .25
1505 A314 105k blue blk & red   .40 .25
     Nos. 1502-1505 (4)   1.15 1.00
Revolution of May 27, 1960.

Faculty Building A316

Sculptured Head of Atatürk — A317

Designs: 40k, Map of Turkey and sun disk.

1961, Jan. 9   Litho.   Perf. 13
1506 A316 30k slate grn & gray   .50 .25
1507 A316 40k brn blk & bis brn   .65 .25
1508 A317 60k dk green & buff   .80 .25
     Nos. 1506-1508 (3)   1.95 .75
25th anniv. of the Faculty of Languages, History and Geography, University of Ankara.

Communication and Transportation — A318

40k, Highway construction, telephone & telegraph. 75k, New parliament building, Ankara.

1961, Apr. 27   Unwmk.   Perf. 13
1509 A318 30k dull vio & blk   .25 .25
1510 A318 40k green & black   .35 .25
1511 A318 75k dull blue & blk   .45 .25
     Nos. 1509-1511 (3)   1.05 .75
9th conference of ministers of the Central Treaty Org. (CENTO), Ankara.

Flag and People — A319

Legendary Wolf and Osman Warriors A320

Design: 60k, "Progress" (Ataturk showing youth the way).

1961, May 27   Litho.
1512 A319 30k multicolored   .30 .25
1513 A320 40k sl grn & yel   .30 .25
1514 A319 60k grn, pink & dk red   .60 .25
     Nos. 1512-1514 (3)   1.20 .75
First anniversary of May 27 revolution.

Rockets A321

Designs: 40k, Crescent and star emblem, "50" and Jet. 75k, Ataturk, eagle and jets, vert.

1961, June 1
1515 A321 30k brn, org yel & blk   .30 .25
1516 A321 40k violet & red   .45 .25
1517 A321 75k slate blk & bis   .60 .25
     Nos. 1515-1517 (3)   1.35 .75
50th anniversary of Turkey's air force.

Europa Issue
Common Design Type
1961, Sept. 18   Perf. 13
Size: 32x22mm
1518 CD4 30k dk violet bl   .35 .25
1519 CD4 40k gray   .45 .30
1520 CD4 75k vermilion   .75 .35
     Nos. 1518-1520 (3)   1.55 .90

Tulip and Cogwheel — A322

Torch, Hand and Cogwheel A323

1961, Oct. 21   Unwmk.   Litho.
1521 A322 30k slate, pink & sil   .25 .25
1522 A323 75k ultra, org & blk   .25 .25
Technical and professional schools, cent.

Open Book and Olive Branch — A324

1961, Oct. 29
1523 A324 30k red, blk & olive   .60 .25
1524 A324 75k brt blue, blk & grn   .85 .25
Inauguration of the new Parliament.

Kemal Atatürk
A325   A326

1961-62   Litho.   Perf. 10x10½
Size: 20x25mm
1525 A325 1k brown org ('62)   .90 .25
1526 A325 5k blue   1.50 .25
1527 A325 10k sepia   2.40 .25
1528 A326 10k car rose   2.40 .25
1529 A325 30k dull grn ('62)   3.50 .30

Size: 21½x31mm

1530 A325 10 l violet ('62)   18.00   1.90
Nos. 1525-1530 (6)   28.70   3.20

NATO Emblem and Dove — A327

Design: 105k, NATO emblem, horiz.

1962, Feb. 18   Unwmk.   Perf. 13
1545 A327 75k dl bl, blk & sil   .25   .25
1546 A327 105k crimson, blk & sil   .60   .25

10th anniv. of Turkey's admission to NATO.

Scouts at Campfire A328

60k, Scouts with flag. 105k, Scouts saluting.

1962, July 22   Litho.
1547 A328 30k lt grn, blk & red   .25   .25
1548 A328 60k gray, blk & red   .60   .25
1549 A328 105k tan, blk & red   .80   .25
Nos. 1547-1549 (3)   1.65   .75

Turkish Boy Scouts, 50th anniversary.

Soldier Statue — A329

Oxcart from Victory Monument, Ankara A330

Design: 75k, Atatürk.

1962, Aug. 30   Unwmk.   Perf. 13
1550 A329 30k slate green   .25   .25
1551 A330 40k gray & sepia   .25   .25
1552 A329 75k gray blk & lt gray   .80   .25
Nos. 1550-1552 (3)   1.30   .75

40th anniv. of Battle of Dumlupinar.

Europa Issue
Common Design Type
1962, Sept. 17   Size: 37x23mm
1553 CD5 75k emerald & blk   .45   .25
1554 CD5 105k red & blk   .60   .40
1555 CD5 195k blue & blk   1.00   .45
Nos. 1553-1555 (3)   2.05   1.10

Brown imprint.

Virgin Mary's House, Ephesus — A331

40k, Inside view after restoration, horiz. 75k, Outside view, horiz. 105k, Statue of Virgin Mary.

1962, Dec. 8   Photo.   Perf. 13½
1556 A331 30k multicolored   .25   .25
1557 A331 40k multicolored   .25   .25
1558 A331 75k multicolored   .35   .25
1559 A001 105k multicolored   .45   .25
Nos. 1556-1559 (4)   1.30   1.00

20pa Stamp of 1863 — A332

Issue of 1863: 30k, 1pi. 40k, 2pi. 75k, 5pi.

1963, Jan. 13   Perf. 13x13½
1560 A332 10k yellow, brn & blk   .25   .25
1561 A332 30k rose, lil & blk   .25   .25
1562 A332 40k lt bl, bluish grn & blk   .25   .25
1563 A332 75k red brn, rose & blk   .45   .25
Nos. 1560-1563 (4)   1.20   1.00

Centenary of Turkish postage stamps. See No. 1601, souvenir sheet.

Starving People A333

Designs: 40k, Sowers. 75k, Hands protecting Wheat Emblem, and globe.

1963, Mar. 21   Unwmk.   Perf. 13
1564 A333 30k dp bl & dk bl   .25   .25
1565 A333 40k brn org & brn   .25   .25
1566 A333 75k grn & dk grn   .55   .25
Nos. 1564-1566 (3)   1.05   .75

FAO "Freedom from Hunger" campaign.

Julian's Column, Ankara — A334

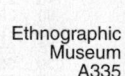

Ethnographic Museum A335

10k, Ankara Citadel. 30k, Gazi Institute of Education. 50k, Atatürk's mausoleum. 60k, President's residence. 100k, Ataturk's home, Cankaya. 150k, Parliament building.

1963   Litho.   Perf. 13
1568 A334 1k sl grn & yel grn   .65   .65
1569 A334 1k purple   .25   .25
1570 A335 5k sepia & buff   .65   .65
1571 A335 10k lil rose & pale bl   .65   .25
1573 A335 30k black & violet   .65   .25
1574 A335 50k blue & yellow   .65   .25
1575 A335 60k dk blue gray   4.00   .65
1576 A335 100k olive brown   2.40   .55
1577 A335 150k dull green   12.00   1.60
Nos. 1568-1577 (9)   21.90   5.10

Map of Turkey and Atom Symbol A336

Designs: 60k, Symbols of medicine, agriculture, industry and atom. 100k, Emblem of Turkish Atomic Energy Commission.

1963, May 27   Unwmk.   Perf. 13
1584 A336 50k red brn & blk   .25   .25
1585 A336 60k grn, dk grn, yel & red   .25   .25
1586 A336 100k violet bl & bl   .55   .30
Nos. 1584-1586 (3)   1.05   .80

Turkish nuclear research center, 1st anniv.

Meric Bridge A337

Sultan Murad I — A338

Designs: 10k, Üçserefeli Mosque. 60k, Summerhouse, Edirne Palace.

1963, June 17
1587 A338 10k dp bl & yel grn   .25   .25
1588 A337 30k red org & ultra   .25   .25
1589 A337 60k dk bl, red & brn   .25   .25
1590 A338 100k multicolored   1.10   .35
Nos. 1587-1590 (4)   1.85   1.10

600th anniv. of the conquest of Edirne (Adrianople).

Soldier and Rising Sun A339

1963, June 28
1591 A339 50k red, blk & gray   .25   .25
1592 A339 100k red, blk & ol   .45   .25

600th anniversary of the Turkish army.

Plowing A340

Mithat Pasha — A341

Design: 50k, Agriculture Bank, Ankara.

Perf. 13x13½, 13½x13
1963, Aug. 27   Photo.   Unwmk.
1593 A340 30k brt yel grn, red brn & grn   .25   .25
1594 A340 50k pale vio & Prus bl   .25   .25
1595 A341 60k gray & green   .30   .25
Nos. 1593-1595 (3)   .80   .75

Centenary of Agriculture Bank, Ankara.

Sports and Exhibition Palace, Istanbul and #5 — A342

Designs: 50k, Sultan Ahmed Mosque & Turkey in Asia #22. 60k, View of Istanbul & Turkey in Asia #83. 100k, Rumeli Hisari Fortress & #679. 130k, Ankara Fortress & #C2.

1963, Sept. 7   Litho.   Perf. 13
1596 A342 10k blk, yel & rose   .25   .25
a.   Rose omitted   37.50   37.50
1597 A342 50k blk, grn & rose lil   .30   .25
1598 A342 60k dk brn, dk bl & blk   .35   .25
1599 A342 100k dk vio & lil rose   .50   .25
1600 A342 130k brn, tan & dp org   .75   .25
Nos. 1596-1600 (5)   2.15   1.25

"Istanbul 63" Intl. Stamp Exhibition.

Type of 1963 Inscribed: "F.I.P. GÜNÜ"
Souvenir Sheet

Issues of 1963: 10k, 20pa. 50k, 1pi. 60k, 2pi. 130k, 5pi.

Unwmk.
1963, Sept. 13   Litho.   Imperf.
1601   Sheet of 4   2.00   1.50
a.   A332 10k yel, brown & blk   .25   .25
b.   A332 50k lilac, pink & blk   .25   .25
c.   A332 60k bluish grn, lt bl & blk   .40   .25
d.   A332 130k red brn, pink & blk   .50   .25

Intl. Philatelic Federation.

Europa Issue
Common Design Type
1963, Sept. 16   Size: 32x24mm
1602 CD6 50k red & black   .50   .25
1603 CD6 130k bl grn, blk & bl   .70   .25

Atatürk and First Parliament Building A343

Atatürk and: 50k, Turkish flag. 60k, New Parliament building.

1963, Oct. 29   Photo.   Perf. 13½
1604 A343 30k blk, gold, yel & mar   .50   .25
1605 A343 50k dk grn, gold, yel & red   .60   .25
1606 A343 60k dk brn, gold & yel   .80   .25
Nos. 1604-1606 (3)   1.90   .75

40th anniversary of Turkish Republic.

Atatürk, 25th Death Anniv. — A344

1963, Nov. 10
1607 A344 50k red, gold, grn & brn   .50   .25
1608 A344 60k red, gold, bl & brn   .75   .25

NATO, 15th Anniv. A346

130k, NATO emblem and olive branch.

1964, Apr. 4   Litho.   Perf. 13
1610 A346 50k grnsh bl, vio bl & red   .45   .25
1611 A346 130k red & black   .75   .70

12 Stars and Europa with Torch A347

Design: 130k, Torch and stars.

1964, May 5   Litho.   Perf. 12
1612	A347	50k red brn, yel & vio bl	.30	.25
1613	A347	130k vio bl, lt bl & org	.50	.35

15th anniversary of Council of Europe.

Hüseyin Rahmi Gürpinar, novelist — A348

Portraits: 1k, Hüseyin Rahmi Gürpinar, novelist. 5k, Ismail Hakki Izmirli, scientist. 10k, Sevket Dag, painter. 50k, Recaizade Mahmut Ekrem, Writer. 60k, Gazi Ahmet Muhtar Pasha, commander. 100k, Ahmet Rasim, writer. 130k, Salih Zeki, mathematician.

1964   Litho.   Perf. 13½x13
1614	A348	1k red & blk	.25	.25
1615	A348	5k dull grn & blk	.25	.25
1616	A348	10k tan & blk	.25	.25
1617	A348	50k ultra & dk bl	1.25	.25
1618	A348	60k gray & blk	1.40	.25
1619	A348	100k grnsh bl & dk bl	1.50	.25
1620	A348	130k brt grn & dk grn	6.50	.65
		Nos. 1614-1620 (7)	11.40	2.15

Mosque of Sultan Ahmed A349

Kiz Kulesi, Mersin — A350

Designs: No. 1622, Zeus Temple, Silifke. No. 1623, View of Amasra. No. 1625, Augustus' Gate and minaret, Ankara.

1964, June 11   Unwmk.   Perf. 13
1621	A349	50k gray ol & yel grn	.25	.25
1622	A349	50k claret & car	.35	.25
1623	A349	50k dk bl & vio bl	.35	.25
1624	A350	60k sl grn & dk gray	.50	.25
1625	A350	60k dk brn & org brn	.60	.25
		Nos. 1621-1625 (5)	2.05	1.25

Kars Castle — A351

Alp Arslan, Conqueror of Kars, 1064 — A352

1964, Aug. 16   Unwmk.   Perf. 13
1626	A351	50k blk & pale vio	.40	.30
1627	A352	130k blk, gold, sal & pale vio	1.10	.50

900th anniversary of conquest of Kars.

Europa Issue
Common Design Type

1964, Sept. 14   Litho.   Perf. 13
Size: 22x33mm
1628	CD7	50k org, ind & sil	.50	.30
1629	CD7	130k lt bl, mag & cit	1.50	.50

Fuat, Resit and Ali Pashas — A353

Design: 60k, Mustafa Resit Pasha, vert.

1964, Nov. 3   Perf. 13
Sizes: 48x33mm (50k, 100k);
22x33mm (60k)
1630	A353	50k multicolored	.50	.25
1631	A353	60k multicolored	.65	.25
1632	A353	100k multicolored	.90	.45
		Nos. 1630-1632 (3)	2.05	.95

125th anniversary of reform decrees.

Parachutist — A354

Designs: 90k, Glider, horiz. 130k, Ataturk watching squadron in flight.

1965, Feb. 16   Litho.   Perf. 13
1633	A354	60k lt bl, blk, red & yel	.25	.25
1634	A354	90k bister & multi	.50	.25
1635	A354	130k lt blue & multi	.80	.25
		Nos. 1633-1635 (3)	1.55	.75

Turkish Aviation League, 40th anniv.

Emblem A355

Designs: 50k, Radio mast and waves, vert. 75k, Hand pressing button.

1965, Feb. 24   Unwmk.   Perf. 13
1636	A355	30k multicolored	.25	.25
1637	A355	50k multicolored	.25	.25
1638	A355	75k multicolored	.55	.25
		Nos. 1636-1638 (3)	1.05	.75

Telecommunications meeting of the Central Treaty Org., CENTO.

Coast of Ordu — A356

50k, Manavgat Waterfall, Antalya. 60k, Sultan Ahmed Mosque, Istanbul. 100k, Hali Rahman Mosque, Urfa. 130k, Red Tower, Alanya.

1965, Apr. 5   Litho.
1639	A356	30k multicolored	.25	.25
1640	A356	50k multicolored	.35	.25
1641	A356	60k multicolored	.35	.25
1642	A356	100k multicolored	.65	.25
1643	A356	130k multicolored	.95	.25
		Nos. 1639-1643 (5)	2.55	1.25

ITU Emblem, Old and New Communication Equipment — A357

1965, May 17   Perf. 13
1644	A357	50k multicolored	.30	.25
1645	A357	130k multicolored	.55	.25

ITU, centenary.

ICY Emblem A358

1965, June 26   Litho.   Unwmk.
1646	A358	100k red org, red brn & brt grn	.40	.25
1647	A358	130k gray, lil & ol grn	.65	.35

International Cooperation Year.

Hands Holding Book A358a

Map and Flags of Turkey, Iran and Pakistan A358b

1965, July 21   Unwmk.   Perf. 13
1648	A358a	50k org brn, yel & dk brn	.30	.25
1649	A358b	75k dl bl, red, grn blk & org	.45	.25

1st anniv. of the signing of the Regional Cooperation Development Pact by Turkey, Iran and Pakistan.

See Iran 1327-1328, Pakistan 217-218.

Kemal Ataturk — A359

1965   Litho.   Perf. 12½
1650	A359	1k brt green	.40	.25
1651	A359	5k violet blue	.80	.25
1652	A359	10k blue	1.25	.25
1653	A359	25k gray	2.75	.25
1654	A359	30k magenta	2.00	.25
1655	A359	50k brown	3.25	.30
1656	A359	150k orange	11.50	.75
		Nos. 1650-1656 (7)	21.95	2.30

Europa Issue
Common Design Type

1965, Sept. 27   Perf. 13
Size: 32x23mm
1665	CD8	50k gray, ultra & grn	.75	.50
1666	CD8	130k tan, blk & grn	1.25	.75

Map of Turkey and People A360

Designs: 50k, "1965." 100k, "1965," symbolic eye and man, vert.

Unwmk.
1965, Oct. 24   Litho.   Perf. 13
1667	A360	10k multicolored	.25	.25
1668	A360	50k grn, blk & lt yel grn	.30	.25
1669	A360	100k orange, sl & blk	.65	.25
		Nos. 1667-1669 (3)	1.20	.75

Issued to publicize the 1965 census.

Plane over Ankara Castle A361

Designs: 30k, Archer and Ankara castle. 50k, Horsemen with spears (ancient game). 100k, Three stamps and medal. 150k, Hands holding book, vert.

1965, Oct. 25
1670	A361	10k brt vio, yel & red	.25	.25
1671	A361	30k multicolored	.25	.25
1672	A361	50k lt gray ol, ind & red	.25	.25
1673	A361	100k gray & multi	.60	.30
		Nos. 1670-1673 (4)	1.35	1.05

Souvenir Sheet
Imperf
1674	A361	150k multicolored	2.50	2.50

1st Natl. Postage Stamp Exhibition "Ankara 65."

Resat Nuri Guntekin, Novelist — A362

Portraits: 5k, Besim Omer Akalin, M.D. 10k, Tevfik Fikret, poet. 25k, Tanburi Cemil, composer. 30k, Ahmet Vefik Pasha, playwright. 50k, Omer Seyfettin, novelist. 60k, Kemalettin Mimaroglu, architect. 150k, Halit Ziya Usakligil, novelist. 220k, Yahya Kemal Beyatli, poet.

1965   Litho.   Perf. 13½x13
Black Portrait and Inscriptions
1675	A362	1k rose	.25	.25
1676	A362	5k blue	.45	.25
1677	A362	10k buff	.45	.25
1678	A362	25k dull red brn	.75	.25
1679	A362	30k gray	.75	.25
1680	A362	50k orange	1.10	.25
1681	A362	60k red lilac	1.25	.25
1682	A362	150k lt green	1.75	.25
1683	A362	220k tan	3.00	.45
		Nos. 1675-1683 (9)	9.75	2.45

Training Ship Savarona A363

Designs: 60k, Submarine "Piri Reis." 100k, Cruiser "Alpaslan." 130k, Destroyer "Gelibolu." 220k, Destroyer "Gemlik."

1965, Dec. 6   Photo.   Perf. 11½
1684	A363	50k blue & brown	.40	.25
1685	A363	60k blue & black	.55	.25
1686	A363	100k blue & black	.90	.25
1687	A363	130k blue & vio blk	1.40	.40
1688	A363	220k blue & indigo	2.10	.65
		Nos. 1684-1688 (5)	5.35	1.80

First Congress of Turkish Naval Society.

Kemal Ataturk — A364

Imprint: "Apa Ofset Basimevi"
Black Portrait and Inscriptions

1965   Litho.   Perf. 13½
1689	A364	1k rose lilac	.90	.25
1690	A364	5k lt green	.90	.25
1691	A364	10k blue gray	1.40	.40
1692	A364	50k olive bister	1.60	.40
1693	A364	150k silver	2.75	.90
		Nos. 1689-1693 (5)	7.55	2.20

See Nos. 1724-1728.

Halide Edip Adivar, Writer — A365

Portraits: 25k, Huseyin Sadettin Arel, writer and composer. 30k, Kamil Akdik, graphic artist. 60k, Abdurrahman Seref, historian. 130k, Naima, historian.

1966		Litho.	Perf. 13½	
1694	A365	25k gray & brn blk	.90	.25
1695	A365	30k rose vio & blk brn	1.10	.25
1696	A365	50k blue & black	1.25	.25
1697	A365	60k lt grn & blk brn	1.40	.25
1698	A365	130k lt vio bl & blk	1.90	.25
		Nos. 1694-1698 (5)	6.55	1.25

Tiles, Green Mausoleum, Bursa — A366

Tiles: 60k, Spring flowers, Hurrem Sultan Mausoleum, Istanbul. 130k, Stylized flowers, 16th century.

1966, May 15		Litho.	Perf. 13½x13	
1699	A366	50k multicolored	.85	.25
1700	A366	60k multicolored	1.40	.50
1701	A366	130k multicolored	2.10	.60
		Nos. 1699-1701 (3)	4.35	1.35

On No. 1700 the black ink was applied by a thermographic process and varnished, producing a shiny, raised effect to imitate the embossed tiles of the design source.

Volleyball — A367

1966, May 20			Perf. 13x13½	
1702	A367	50k tan & multi	.60	.25

4th Intl. Military Volleyball Championship.

View of Bodrum — A368

Views: 30k, Kusadasi. 50k, Anadolu Hisari, Istanbul. 90k, Marmaris. 100k, Izmir.

1966, May 25		Perf. 13x13½, 13½x13		
1703	A368	10k multi	.25	.25
1704	A368	30k multi	.65	.25
1705	A368	50k multi, horiz.	.35	.25
1706	A368	90k multi	.35	.25
1707	A368	100k multi, horiz.	.45	.25
		Nos. 1703-1707 (5)	2.05	1.25

Inauguration of Keban Dam — A369

Design: 60k, View of Keban Dam area.

1966, June 10			Perf. 13½	
1708	A369	50k multicolored	.35	.25
1709	A369	60k multicolored	.65	.40

Visit of King Faisal of Saudi Arabia A370

1966, Aug. 29		Litho.	Perf. 13½x13	
1710	A370	100k car rose & dk car	.90	.30

Symbolic Postmark and Stamp A371

Designs: 60k, Flower made of stamps. 75k, Stamps forming display frames. 100k, Map of Balkan states, magnifying glass and stamp.

1966, Sept. 3			Perf. 13½x13	
1711	A371	50k multicolored	.25	.25
1712	A371	60k multicolored	.25	.25
1713	A371	75k multicolored	.55	.25
		Nos. 1711-1713 (3)	1.05	.75

Souvenir Sheet
Imperf

1714	A371	100k multicolored	2.50	1.50

2nd "Balkanfila" stamp exhibition, Istanbul.

Sultan Suleiman on Horseback A372

90k, Mausoleum, Istanbul. 130k, Suleiman.

1966, Sept. 6			Perf. 13½x13	
1715	A372	60k multicolored	.65	.25
1716	A372	90k multicolored	1.10	.40
1717	A372	130k multicolored	2.25	.65
		Nos. 1715-1717 (3)	4.00	1.30

Sultan Suleiman the Magnificent (1496?-1566). On No. 1717 a gold frame was applied by raised thermographic process.

Europa Issue
Common Design Type

1966, Sept. 26		Litho.	Perf. 13x13½	
		Size: 22x33mm		
1718	CD9	50k lt bl, vio bl & blk	1.10	.65
a.		Black (inscriptions & imprint) omitted	65.00	
1719	CD9	130k lil, dk red lil & blk	2.25	1.10

Symbols of Education, Science and Culture A373

1966, Nov. 4		Litho.	Perf. 13	
1720	A373	130k brn, bis brn & yel	.50	.25

UNESCO, 20th anniversary.

Middle East University of Technology A374

Designs: 100k, Atom symbol. 130k, design symbolizing sciences.

1966, Nov. 15				
1721	A374	50k multicolored	.25	.25
1722	A374	100k multicolored	.55	.25
1723	A374	130k multicolored	.85	.55
		Nos. 1721-1723 (3)	1.65	1.05

10th anniv. of the Middle East University of Technology.

Ataturk Type of 1965
Imprint: "Kiral Matbaasi — Ist"

1966		Litho.	Perf. 12½	
		Black Portrait and Inscriptions		
1724	A364	25k yellow	.35	.25
1725	A364	30k pink	.50	.25
1726	A364	50k rose lilac	1.50	.25
1727	A364	90k pale brown	1.25	.25
1728	A364	100k gray	1.50	.25
		Nos. 1724-1728 (5)	5.10	1.25

Statue of Ataturk, Ankara — A375

Equestrian Statues of Ataturk: No. 1729A, Statue in Izmir. No. 1729B, Statue in Samsun.

Without Imprint

1967		Litho.	Perf. 13x12½	
		Size: 23x16mm		
1729	A375	10k black & yellow	.50	.25

Inscribed "1967"
Imprint: Kiral Matbaasi
Size: 22x15mm

1729A	A375	10k black & salmon	.50	.25
1729B	A375	10k black & lt grn	.50	.25
		Nos. 1729-1729B (3)	1.50	.75

Issued for use on greeting cards. See Nos. 1790-1791A, 1911.

Puppets Karagöz and Hacivat — A376

Intl. Tourist Year Emblem and: 60k, Sword and shield game. 90k, Traditional military band. 100k, raised effect.

		Perf. 13x13½, 13½x13		
1967, Mar. 30			Litho.	
1730	A376	50k multicolored	.90	.25
1731	A376	60k multicolored	1.25	.25
1732	A376	90k multicolored	1.60	.45
1733	A376	100k multicolored	2.50	.65
		Nos. 1730-1733 (4)	6.25	1.60

Intl. Tourist Year. On No. 1733 the black ink was applied by a thermographic process and varnished, producing a shiny, raised effect.

Woman Vaccinating Child, Knife and Lancet — A377

1967, Apr. 1			Perf. 13x13½	
1734	A377	100k multicolored	.50	.25

250th anniv. of smallpox vaccination (variolation) in Turkey. The gold was applied by a thermographic process and varnished, producing a shiny, raised effect.

Fallow Deer — A378

1967, Apr. 23		Litho.	Perf. 13x13½	
1735	A378	50k shown	.50	.25
1736	A378	60k Wild goat	.65	.25
1737	A378	100k Brown bear	.90	.25
1738	A378	130k Wild boar	1.25	.40
		Nos. 1735-1738 (4)	3.30	1.15

Soccer Players and Emblem with Map of Europe A379

130k, Players at left, smaller emblem.

1967, May 1			Perf. 13	
1739	A379	50k multicolored	.75	.25
1740	A379	130k yellow & multi	1.25	.50

20th Intl. Youth Soccer Championships.

Sivas Hospital A380

1967, July 1		Litho.	Perf. 13	
1741	A380	50k multicolored	.40	.25

750th anniversary of Sivas Hospital.

Selim Sirri Tarcan A381

60k, Olympic Rings, Baron Pierre de Coubertin.

1967, July 20				
1742	A381	50k lt blue & multi	.40	.25
1743	A381	60k lilac & multi	.60	.40
a.		Pair, #1742-1743	1.25	1.00

1st Turkish Olympic competitions.

Ahmed Mithat, Writer — A382

Portraits: 5k, Admiral Turgut Reis. 50k, Sokullu Mehmet, statesman. 100k, Nedim, poet. 150k, Osman Hamdi, painter.

1967		Litho.	Perf. 12½	
1744	A382	1k green & blk	.65	.25
1745	A382	5k dp bister & blk	1.00	.25
1746	A382	50k brt violet & blk	1.40	.25
1747	A382	100k citron & blk	2.50	.40
1748	A382	150k yellow & blk	4.00	.40
		Nos. 1744-1748 (5)	9.55	1.55

Ruins of St. John's Church, Ephesus A383

Design: 130k, Inside view of Virgin Mary's House, Ephesus.

1967, July 26   **Perf. 13**
1749 A383 130k multicolored   .40   .25
1750 A383 220k multicolored   .85   .40
Visit of Pope Paul VI to the House of the Virgin Mary in Ephesus, July 26.

Plate on Firing Grid and Ornaments A384

1967, Sept. 1
1751 A384 50k pale lil, blk, ind & bl   .50   .25
5th International Ceramics Exhibition.

View of Istanbul and Emblem A385

1967, Sept. 4   **Litho.**   **Perf. 13**
1752 A385 130k dk blue & gray   .95   .25
9th Congress of the Intl. Commission of Large Dams.

Stamps, Ornament and Map of Turkey A386

Design: 60k, Grapes and stamps.

1967
1753 A386 50k multicolored   .35   .25
1754 A386 60k multicolored   .45   .25
   a.   Souvenir sheet, #1753-1754   2.50   2.50
Intl. Trade Fair, Izmir.

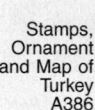

Kemal Ataturk — A387

1967   **Litho.**   **Perf. 11½x12**
Booklet Stamps
1755 A387 10k blk & lt ol grn   3.25   .80
   a.   Booklet pane of 10   100.00
   b.   Booklet pane of 25   250.00
1756 A387 50k blk & pale rose   3.25   .80
   a.   Booklet pane of 2   40.00
   b.   Bklt. pane, 5 #1755, 4 #1756 + label   35.00

Symbolic Water Cycle — A388

1967, Dec. 1   **Litho.**   **Perf. 13**
1757 A388 90k lt grn, blk & org   .60   .25
1758 A388 130k lilac, blk & org   .70   .60
Hydrological Decade (UNESCO), 1965-74.

Child and Angora Cat, Man with Microscope — A389

60k, Horse and man with microscope.

1967, Dec. 23   **Perf. 13**
1759 A389 50k multicolored   .50   .25
1760 A389 60k multicolored   .70   .40
125th anniv. of Turkish veterinary medicine.

Human Rights Flame — A390

1968, Jan. 1   **Perf. 13x13½**
1761 A390 50k rose lil, dk bl & org   .40   .25
1762 A390 130k lt bl, dk bl & red org   .75   .25
International Human Rights Year.

Archer on Horseback — A391

Miniatures, 16th Century: 50k, Investiture. 60k, Sultan Suleiman the Magnificent receiving an ambassador, vert. 100k, Musicians.

Perf. 13x13½, 13½x13
1968, Mar. 1   **Litho.**
1763 A391 50k multicolored   .60   .50
1764 A391 60k multicolored   1.10   .90
1765 A391 90k multicolored   1.50   1.25
1766 A391 100k multicolored   1.75   1.50
     Nos. 1763-1766 (4)   4.95   4.15

Kemal Ataturk — A392

1968   **Litho.**   **Perf. 12½**
1767 A392 1k dk & lt blue   .35   .25
1768 A392 5k dk & lt green   .55   .25
1769 A392 50k org brn & yel   2.10   .25
1770 A392 200k dk brown & pink   6.50   .30
     Nos. 1767-1770 (4)   9.50   1.05

Law Book and Oak Branch A393

Mithat Pasha and Scroll A394

1968, Apr. 1   **Perf. 13**
1771 A393 50k multicolored   .35   .35
1772 A394 60k multicolored   .40   .40
Centenary of the Court of Appeal.

Court Type of 1968

Designs: 50k, Scales of Justice. 60k, Ahmet Cevdet Pasha and scroll.

1968, Apr. 1
1773 A393 50k multicolored   .40   .25
1774 A394 60k multicolored   .60   .25
Centenary of the Supreme Court.

Europa Issue
Common Design Type
1968, May 6   **Litho.**   **Perf. 13**
Size: 31½x23mm
1775 CD11 100k pck bl, yel & red   1.00   .50
1776 CD11 130k green, yel & red   1.50   .75

Yacht Kismet — A395

1968, June 15   **Litho.**   **Perf. 13**
1777 A395 50k lt ultra & multi   .85   .65
Round-the-world trip of the yacht Kismet, Aug. 22, 1965-June 14, 1968.

"Fight Usury" A396

1968, June 19
1778 A396 50k multicolored   .75   .60
Centenary of the Pawn Office, Istanbul.

Sakarya Battle and Independence Medal — A397

130k, Natl. anthem & reverse of medal.

1968, Aug. 30   **Perf. 13x13½**
1779 A397 50k gold & multi   .75   .40
1780 A397 130k gold & multi   1.25   .60
Turkish Independence medal. The gold on Nos. 1779-1780 was applied by a thermographic process and varnished, producing a shiny, raised effect.

Ataturk and Galatasaray High School — A398

50k, "100" and old and new school emblems. 60k, Portraits of Beyazit II and Gulbaba.

1968, Sept. 1   **Litho.**
1781 A398 50k gray & multi   .25   .25
1782 A398 60k tan & multi   .50   .50
1783 A398 100k lt blue & multi   .75   .75
     Nos. 1781-1783 (3)   1.50   1.50
Centenary of Galatasaray High School.

Charles de Gaulle — A399

1968, Oct. 25   **Litho.**   **Perf. 13**
1784 A399 multicolored   1.25   .70
Visit of President Charles de Gaulle of France to Turkey.

Kemal Ataturk — A400

Ataturk and his Speech to Youth — A401

50k, Ataturk's tomb and Citadel of Ankara. 60k, Ataturk looking out a train window. 250k, Framed portrait of Ataturk in military uniform.

1968, Nov. 10
1785 A400 30k orange & blk   .50   .25
1786 A400 50k brt grn & sl grn   .50   .25
1787 A400 60k bl grn & blk   .60   .25
1788 A401 100k blk, gray & brt grn   .90   .25
1789 A401 250k multicolored   1.75   .40
     Nos. 1785-1789 (5)   4.25   1.40
30th death anniv. of Kemal Ataturk.

Ataturk Statue Type of 1967

Equestrian Statues of Ataturk: No. 1790, Statue in Zonguldak. No. 1791, Statue in Antakya. No. 1791A, Statue in Bursa.

Imprint: Kiral Matbaasi 1968
1968-69   **Litho.**   **Perf. 13x12½**
Size: 22x15mm
1790 A375 10k black & lt blue   .75   .25
1791 A375 10k blk & brt rose lil   .75   .25

Perf. 13½
Imprint: Tifdruk Matbaacilik Sanayii A. S. 1969
Size: 21x16½mm
1791A A375 10k dk grn & tan ('69)   .75   .25
     Nos. 1790-1791A (3)   2.25   .75

Ince Minare Mosque, Konya — A402

Historic Buildings: 10k, Doner Kumbet (tomb), Kayseri. 50k, Karatay Medresse (University Gate), Konya. 100k, Ortakoy Mosque, Istanbul. 200k, Ulu Mosque, Divriki.

1968-69   **Photo.**   **Perf. 13x13½**
1792 A402 1k dk brn & buff ('69)   .25   .25
1793 A402 10k plum & dl rose ('69)   .50   .25
1794 A402 50k dk ol grn & gray   .65   .25

1795	A402	100k dk & lt grn ('69)	1.75	.40
1796	A402	200k dp bl & lt bl ('69)	2.75	.55
		Nos. 1792-1796 (5)	5.90	1.70

ILO Emblem
A403

1969, Apr. 15 Litho. Perf. 13
1797 A403 130k dk red & black .80 .25
ILO, 50th anniv.

Sultana
Hafsa,
Medical
Pioneer
A404

1969, Apr. 26 Litho. Perf. 13½x13
1798 A404 60k multicolored 1.25 1.00

Europa Issue
Common Design Type
1969, Apr. 28 Perf. 13
Size: 32x23mm
1799 CD12 100k dull vio & multi 1.00 .65
1800 CD12 130k gray grn & multi 1.50 1.00

Kemal
Ataturk — A405

Ataturk
and S.S.
Dandirma
A406

1969, May 19 Litho. Perf. 13
1801 A405 50k multicolored .60 .25
1802 A406 60k multicolored .90 .35

50th anniv. of the landing of Kemal Ataturk at Samsun.

Map of
Istanbul — A407

1969, May 31
1803 A407 130k vio bl, lt bl, gold & red .60 .25

22nd Congress of the Intl. Chamber of Commerce, Istanbul.

Educational
Progress
A408

Agricultural
Progress
A409

Designs: 90k, Pouring ladle and industrial symbols. 100k, Road sign (highway construction). 180k, Oil industry chart and symbols.

1969 Litho. Perf. 13½x13
1804 A408 1k black & gray .25 .25
1805 A408 1k black & bis brn .25 .25
1806 A408 1k black & lt grn .25 .25
1807 A408 1k black & lt vio .25 .25
1808 A408 1k black & org red .25 .25
1809 A409 50k brown & ocher .65 .25
1810 A409 90k blk & grnsh gray 1.10 .35
1811 A408 100k black & org red 1.50 .25
1812 A408 180k violet & orange 2.50 .25
Nos. 1804-1812 (9) 7.00 2.25

Issued: 1, 100k, 4/8; 50k, 6/11; 90, 180k, 8/15.

Sultan
Suleiman
Receiving
Sheik Abdul
Latif — A410

Designs: 80k, Lady Serving Wine, Safavi miniature, Iran. 130k, Lady on Balcony, Mogul miniature, Pakistan.

1969, July 21 Litho. Perf. 13
1813 A410 50k yellow & multi .45 .25
1814 A410 80k yellow & multi .75 .25
1815 A410 130k yellow & multi 1.25 .50
Nos. 1813-1815 (3) 2.45 1.00

5th anniv. of the signing of the Regional Cooperation for Development Pact by Turkey, Iran and Pakistan.
See Iran 1513-1515, Pakistan 274-276.

Kemal
Ataturk — A411

Design: 60k, Ataturk monument and bas-relief showing congress.

1969, July 23
1816 A411 50k black & gray .90 .25
1817 A411 60k black & grnsh gray 1.75 .50

50th anniversary, Congress of Erzerum.

Sivas
Congress
Delegates
A412

Design: 50k, Congress Hall.

1969, Sept. 4 Litho. Perf. 13
1818 A412 50k dk brn & dp rose .35 .35
1819 A412 60k olive blk & yel .45 .45

50th anniv. of the Congress of Sivas (preparation for the Turkish war of independence).

Bar Dance — A413

Folk Dances: 50k, Candle dance (çaydaçira). 60k, Scarf dance (halay). 100k, Sword dance (kiliç-kalkan). 130k, Two male dancers (zeybek), vert.

1969, Sept. 9
1820 A413 30k brown & multi .40 .25
1821 A413 50k multicolored .50 .25
1822 A413 60k multicolored .80 .25
1823 A413 100k yellow & multi .90 .90
1824 A413 130k multicolored 1.40 .55
Nos. 1820-1824 (5) 4.00 2.20

1914
Airplane
"Prince
Celaleddin"
A414

75k, First Turkish letter carried by air.

1969, Oct. 18 Litho. Perf. 13
1825 A414 60k dk blue & blue .40 .25
1826 A414 75k black & bister .65 .25

55th anniv. of the first Turkish mail transported by air.

"Kutadgu
Bilig"
A415

1969, Nov. 20 Litho. Perf. 13
1827 A415 130k ol bis, brn & gold .55 .25

900th anniv. of "Kutadgu Bilig," a book about the function of the state, compiled by Jusuf of Balasagun in Tashkent, 1069.

Ataturk's Arrival in Ankara, after a
Painting — A416

Design: 60k, Ataturk and his coworkers in automobiles arriving in Ankara, after a photograph.

1969, Dec. 27 Litho. Perf. 13
1828 A416 50k multicolored .75 .25
1829 A416 60k multicolored 1.25 .30

50th anniv. of Kemal Ataturk's arrival in Ankara, Dec. 27, 1919.

Bosporus Bridge, Map of Europe and
Asia — A417

Design: 60k, View of proposed Bosporus Bridge and shore lines.

1970, Feb. 20 Litho. Perf. 13
1830 A417 60k gold & multi .75 .30
1831 A417 130k gold & multi 1.50 .65

Foundation ceremonies for the bridge across the Bosporus linking Europe and Asia.

Kemal Ataturk
and Signature
A418

Kemal Ataturk
A419

1970 Litho. Perf. 13
1832 A418 1k dp orange & brn .25 .25
1833 A419 5k silver & blk .25 .25
1834 A419 30k citron & blk .35 .25
1835 A418 50k lt olive & blk .40 .25
1836 A419 50k pink & blk .70 .25
1837 A419 75k lilac & blk 1.40 .25
1838 A419 100k blue & blk .90 .25
Nos. 1832-1838 (7) 4.25 1.75

For surcharge see No. 2078.

Education Year
Emblem — A420

1970, Mar. 16
1839 A420 130k ultra, pink & rose lil .80 .25

International Education Year.

Turkish EXPO '70
Emblem — A421

100k, EXPO '70 emblem & Turkish pavilion.

1970, Mar. 27
1840 A421 50k gold & multi .25 .25
1841 A421 100k gold & multi .60 .25

EXPO '70 International Exhibition, Osaka, Japan, Mar. 15-Sept. 13.

Opening of
Grand
National
Assembly
A422

Design: 60k, Session of First Grand National Assembly, 1920.

1970, Apr. 23
1842 A422 50k multicolored .35 .25
1843 A422 60k multicolored .55 .25

Turkish Grand National Assembly, 50th anniv.

Emblem of
Cartographic
Service
A423

Map of Turkey and Gen. Mehmet
Sevki Pasha — A424

Designs: 60k, Plane and aerial mapping
survey diagram. 100k, Triangulation point in
mountainous landscape.

Perf. 13½x13 (A423), 13x13½ (A424)
1970, May 2   **Litho.**
1844 A423 50k blue & multi   .40   .25
1845 A424 60k blk, gray grn &
                brick red   .40   .25
1846 A423 100k multicolored   .60   .35
1847 A424 130k multicolored   1.00   .50
       Nos. 1844-1847 (4)   2.40 1.35

Turkish Cartographic Service, 75th anniv.

Europa Issue
Common Design Type
1970, May 4   **Perf. 13**
Size: 37x23mm
1848 CD13 100k ver, blk & org   1.00   .50
1849 CD13 130k dk bl grn, blk &
                org   1.50 1.00

Inauguration of UPU Headquarters,
Bern — A425

1970, May 20
1850 A425 60k blk & dull blue   .40   .25
1851 A425 130k blk & dl ol grn   .75   .35

Lady with
Mimosa, by
Osman Hamdi
(1842-1910)
A426

Paintings: No. 1853, Deer, by Seker Ahmet
(1841-1907). No. 1854, Portrait of Fevzi
Cakmak, by Avni Lifij (d. 1927). No. 1855, Sailboats, by Nazmi Ziya (1881-1937); horiz.

1970   **Litho.**   **Perf. 13**
Size: 29x49mm
1852 A426 250k multicolored   1.00   .35
1853 A426 250k multicolored   1.00   .35
Size: 32x49mm
1854 A426 250k multicolored   1.25   .35
Size: 73½x33mm
1855 A426 250k multicolored   1.25   .35
       Nos. 1852-1855 (4)   4.50 1.40
Issued: #1852-1853, 6/15; #1854-1855,
12/15.

Turkish Folk
Art — A427

1970, June 15
1856 A427 50k multicolored   .60   .25
3rd National Stamp Exhibition, ANKARA 70,
Oct. 28-Nov. 4. Pane of 50, each stamp se-
tenant with label. This 50k, in pane of 50 without labels, was re-issued Oct. 28 with Nos.
1867-1869.

View of
Fethiye
A428

80k, Seeyo-Se-Pol Bridge, Esfahan, Iran.
130k, Saiful Malook Lake, Pakistan.

1970, July 21   **Litho.**   **Perf. 13**
1857 A428 60k multicolored   .35   .25
1858 A428 80k multicolored   .50   .25
1859 A428 130k multicolored   .75   .35
       Nos. 1857-1859 (3)   1.60   .85

6th anniv. of the signing of the Regional
Cooperation for Development Pact by Turkey,
Iran and Pakistan.
See Iran 1558-1560, Pakistan 290-292.

Sultan Balim's
Tomb — A429

Haci Bektas
Veli — A430

30k, Tomb of Haci Bektas Veli, horiz.

1970, Aug. 16   **Litho.**   **Perf. 13**
1860 A429 30k multicolored   .25   .25
1861 A429 100k multicolored   .60   .25
1862 A430 180k multicolored   1.25   .25
       Nos. 1860-1862 (3)   2.10   .75

700th death anniv. of Haci Bektas Veli,
mystic.

Hittite Sun
Disk and
"ISO"
A431

1970, Sept. 15
1863 A431 110k car rose, gold &
                blk   .35   .25
1864 A431 150k ultra, gold & blk   .65   .35
8th General Council Meeting of the Intl.
Standardization Org., Ankara.

UN Emblem, People
and Globe — A432

100k, UN emblem and propeller, horiz.

1970, Oct. 24   **Litho.**   **Perf. 13**
1865 A432 100k gray & multi   .60   .25
1866 A432 220k multicolored   .90   .35
25th anniversary of the United Nations.

Stamp "Flower" and
Book — A433

Designs: 60k, Ataturk monument and
stamps, horiz. 130k, Abstract flower.

1970, Oct. 28
1867 A433 10k multicolored   .50   .25
1868 A433 60k blue & multi   .90   .25
Souvenir Sheet
1869 A433 130k dk green & org   2.50 1.90

3rd National Stamp Exhibition, ANKARA 70,
Oct. 28-Nov. 4. See note below No. 1856.

InönüBattle Scene — A434

Design: No. 1871, Second Battle of Inönü.

1971   **Litho.**   **Perf. 13**
1870 A434 100k multicolored   .80   .25
1871 A434 100k multicolored   .80   .25

1st and 2nd Battles of Inönü, 50th anniv.
Issue dates: #1870, Jan. 10; #1871, Apr. 1.

Village on River Bank, by Ahmet
Sekür — A435

Painting: No. 1872, Landscape, Yildiz Palace Garden, by Ahmet Ragip Bicakcilar.

1971, Mar. 15   **Litho.**   **Perf. 13**
1872 A435 250k multicolored   1.00   .40
1873 A435 250k multicolored   1.00   .40
See #1901-1902, 1909-1910, 1937-1938.

Campaign
Against
Discrimination
A436

1971, Mar. 21   **Litho.**   **Perf. 13**
1874 A436 100k multicolored   .50   .25
1875 A436 250k gray & multi   1.00   .35
Intl. Year against Racial Discrimination.

Europa Issue
Common Design Type
1971, May 3   **Litho.**   **Perf. 13**
Size: 31½x22½mm
1876 CD14 100k lt bl, cl & mag   1.00   .50
1877 CD14 150k dp org, grn &
                red   1.50   .75

Kemal Ataturk
A437   A438

1971
1878 A437 5k gray & ultra   .60   .25
1879 A437 25k gray & dk red   .90   .25
1880 A438 25k brown & pink   .60   .25
1881 A437 100k gray & violet   1.25   .25
1882 A438 100k grn & sal   1.25   .35
1883 A438 250k blue & gray   3.00   .60
1884 A437 400k tan & ol grn   5.00   .70
       Nos. 1878-1884 (7)   12.60 2.65

Pres. Kemal
Gürsel — A439

1971, May 27   **Litho.**   **Perf. 13**
1885 A439 100k multicolored   .75   .25
Revolution of May 27, 1960; Kemal Gürsel
(1895-1966), president.

Mosque of Selim,
Edirne — A440

150k, Religious School, Chaharbagh, Iran.
200k, Badshahi Mosque, Pakistan.

1971, July 21   **Litho.**   **Perf. 13**
1886 A440 100k multi   .40   .25
1887 A440 150k multi   .55   .25
1888 A440 200k multi, horiz.   .80   .25
       Nos. 1886-1888 (3)   1.75   .75

Regional Cooperation by Turkey, Iran and
Pakistan, 7th anniversary.
See Iran 1599-1601, Pakistan 305-307.

Alp Arslan and Battle of
Malazkirt — A441

Design: 250k, Archers on horseback.

1971, Aug. 26 **Litho.** **Perf. 13x13½**
1889 A441 100k multicolored   .65   .25
1890 A441 250k red, org & blk   1.00   .40
900th anniversary of the Battle of Malazkirt,
which established the Seljuk Dynasty in Asia
Minor.

Battle of Sakarya — A442

1971, Sept. 13
1891 A442 100k slate lil & multi 1.00 .45
50th anniversary of the victory of Sakarya.

Turkey-Bulgaria Railroad — A443

Designs: 110k, Ferry and map of Lake Van.
250k, Turkey-Iran railroad.

1971
1892 A443 100k multicolored .60 .25
1893 A443 110k multicolored .60 .25
1894 A443 250k yellow & multi 1.40 .60
Nos. 1892-1894 (3) 2.60 1.10

Turkish railroad connections with Bulgaria
&Iran. Issued: 110, 250k, 9/27; 100k, 10/4.

Soccer and Map of Mediterranean A444

200k, Runner and stadium, vert. 250k, Shot
put and map of Mediterranean, vert.

1971, Oct. 6
1895 A444 100k redsh lil & blk .45 .25
1896 A444 200k brn, blk & emer .80 .35

Souvenir Sheet
Imperf
1897 A444 250k ol bis & slate grn 2.00 1.75
Mediterranean Games, Izmir.

Tomb of Cyrus the Great — A445

Designs: 100k, Harpist, Persian mosaic,
vert. 150k, Ataturk and Riza Shah Pahlavi.

1971, Oct. 13
1898 A445 25k lt blue & multi .30 .25
1899 A445 100k multicolored .70 .25
1900 A445 150k dk brown & buff 1.00 .35
Nos. 1898-1900 (3) 2.00 .85

2500th anniversary of the founding of the
Persian empire by Cyrus the Great.

Painting Type of 1971
No. 1901, Sultan Mohammed I and his Staff.
No. 1902, Palace with tiled walls.

1971, Nov. 15 Litho. Perf. 13
1901 A435 250k multicolored 1.00 .40
1902 A435 250k multicolored 1.00 .40

Yunus Emre — A446

1971, Dec. 27 Litho. Perf. 13
1903 A446 100k brown & multi .60 .25
650th death anniv. of Yunus Emre, Turkish
folk poet.

First Turkish World Map and Book
Year Emblem — A447

1972, Jan. 3 Perf. 13
1904 A447 100k buff & multi .60 .25
International Book Year.

Doves and NATO Emblem — A448

1972, Feb. 18 Litho. Perf. 13
1905 A448 100k dull grn, blk & gray 1.25 .40
1906 A448 250k dull bl, blk & gray 1.50 1.00
Turkey's membership in NATO, 20th anniv.

Europa Issue
Common Design Type
1972, May 2 Perf. 13
Size: 22x33mm
1907 CD15 110k blue & multi 1.50 .75
1908 CD15 250k brown & multi 2.50 1.25

Painting Type of 1971
No. 1909, Forest, Seker Ahmet. No. 1910,
View of Gebze, Anatolia, by Osman Hamdi.

1972, May 15 Litho.
1909 A435 250k multicolored 1.00 .35
1910 A435 250k multicolored 1.00 .35

Ataturk Statue Type of 1967
Imprint: Ajans - Turk/Ankara 1972
Design: 25k, Ataturk Statue in front of Eth-
nographic Museum, Ankara.

Perf. 12½x11½
1972, June 12 Litho.
Size: 22x15½mm
1911 A375 25k black & buff .60 .25

Fisherman, by
Cevat
Dereli — A449

Paintings: 125k, Young Man, by Abdur
Rehman Chughtai (Pakistan). 150k, Persian
Woman, by Behzad,

1972, July 21 Litho. Perf. 13
1912 A449 100k gold & multi .70 .25
1913 A449 125k gold & multi 1.20 .40
1914 A449 150k gold & multi 1.40 .45
Nos. 1912-1914 (3) 3.30 1.10

Regional Cooperation for Development Pact
among Turkey, Iran and Pakistan, 8th anniv.
See Iran 1647-1649, Pakistan 322-324.

Ataturk and Commanders at Mt.
Koca — A450

Designs: No. 1916, Battle of the Com-
mander-in-chief. No. 1917, Turkish army
entering Izmir. 110k, Artillery and cavalry.

1972 Litho. Perf. 13x13½
1915 A450 100k lt ultra & blk 1.00 .25
1916 A450 100k pink & multi 1.00 .25
1917 A450 100k yellow & multi 1.00 .25
1918 A450 110k orange & multi 1.00 .25
Nos. 1915-1918 (4) 4.00 1.00

50th anniv. of fight for establishment of independent Turkish republic. Issued: #1915,
1918, 8/26; #1916, 8/30; #1917, 9/9.

"Cancer is
Curable"
A451

1972, Oct. 10 Litho. Perf. 12½x13
1919 A451 100k blk, brt bl & red .50 .25
Fight against cancer.

International
Railroad Union
Emblem — A452

1972, Dec. 31 Litho. Perf. 13
1920 A452 100k sl grn, ocher & red .60 .25
Intl. Railroad Union, 50th anniv.

Kemal
Ataturk — A453

1972-76 Litho. Perf. 13½x13
Size: 21x26mm
1921 A453 5k gray & blue .45 .25
1922 A453 25k orange ('75) .60 .25
1923 A453 100k buff & red brn ('73) 1.75 .25
1924 A453 100k lt gray & gray ('75) .60 .25
1925 A453 110k lt bl & vio bl 1.25 .35
1926 A453 125k dull grn ('73) 1.60 .25
1927 A453 150k tan & brown 1.75 .25
1928 A453 150k lt grn & grn ('75) .45 .25
1929 A453 175k yel & lil ('73) 2.50 .35
1930 A453 200k buff & red 2.00 .25
1931 A453 250k pink & pur ('75) .60 .25
1931A A453 400k gray & Prus bl ('76) .60 .25
1932 A453 500k pink & violet 3.25 .65
1933 A453 500k gray & ultra ('75) 2.00 .30

Size: 22x33mm
Perf. 13
1934 A453 10 l pink & car rose ('75) 3.25 .30
Nos. 1921-1934 (15) 22.65 4.45
See Nos. 2060-2061. For surcharges see
Nos. 2180-2181.

Europa Issue
Common Design Type
1973, Apr. 4 Litho. Perf. 13
Size: 32x23mm
1935 CD16 110k gray & multi 1.40 .75
1936 CD16 250k multicolored 2.75 1.50

Painting Type of 1971
Paintings: No. 1937, Beyazit Almshouse,
Istanbul, by Ahmet Ziya Akbulut. No. 1938,
Flowers, by Suleyman Seyyit, vert.

1973, June 15 Litho. Perf. 13
1937 A435 250k multicolored 1.25 .50
1938 A435 250k multicolored 1.25 .50

Army Day — A454

Designs: 90k, Helmet, sword and oak
leaves. 100k, Helmet, sword and laurel.

1973, June 28 Perf. 13x12½
1939 A454 90k brn, gray & grn .35 .25
1940 A454 100k brn, lem & grn .35 .25

Mausoleum of
Antiochus I — A455

Designs: 100k, Colossal heads, mausoleum
of Antiochus I (69-34 B.C.), Commagene, Turkey. 150k, Statue, Shahdad Kerman, Persia,
3000 B.C. 200k, Street, Mohenjo-daro,
Pakistan.

1973, July 21 Litho. Perf. 13
1941 A455 100k lt blue & multi .35 .25
1942 A455 150k olive & multi .50 .25
1943 A455 200k brown & multi .75 .95
Nos. 1941-1943 (3) 1.60 1.45

Regional Cooperation for Development Pact
among Turkey, Iran and Pakistan, 9th anniv.
See Iran 1714-1716, Pakistan 343-345.

Minelayer
Nusret
A456

Designs: 25k, Destroyer Istanbul. 100k,
Speedboat Simsek and Naval College. 250k,
Two-masted training ship Nuvid-i Futuh.

1973, Aug. 1 Size: 31½x22mm
1944 A456 5k Prus bl & multi .25 .25
1945 A456 25k Prus bl & multi .25 .25
1946 A456 100k Prus bl & multi 1.10 .25

Size: 48x32mm
1947 A456 250k blue & multi 2.50 .40
Nos. 1944-1947 (4) 4.10 1.15

abu-al-Rayhan al-Biruni — A457

1973, Sept. 4   Litho.   *Perf. 13x12½*
1948 A457 250k multicolored   .60 .40
abu-al-Rayhan al-Biruni (973-1048), philosopher and mathematician.

Emblem of Darussafaka Foundation — A458

1973, Sept. 15   *Perf. 13*
1949 A458 100k silver & multi   .50 .25
Centenary of the educational and philanthropic Darussafaka Foundation.

BALKANFILA IV Emblem — A459

Designs: 110k, Symbolic view and stamps. 250k, "Balkanfila 4."

1973   Litho.   *Perf. 13*
1950 A459 100k gray & multi   .35 .25
1951 A459 110k multicolored   .25 .25
1952 A459 250k multicolored   .45 .25
        Nos. 1950-1952 (3)   1.05 .75
BALKANFILA IV, Philatelic Exhibition of Balkan Countries, Izmir, Oct. 26-Nov. 5. Issued: 100k, Sept. 26; 110k, 250k, Oct. 26.

Sivas Shepherd Dog — A460

1973, Oct. 4
1953 A460 25k shown   .35 .25
1954 A460 100k Angora cat   .90 .25

Kemal Ataturk — A461

1973, Oct. 10   Litho.   *Perf. 13*
1955 A461 100k gold & blk brn   .75 .25
35th death anniv. of Kemal Ataturk.

Flower and "50" — A462

Ataturk — A463

250k, Torch & "50." 475k, Grain & cogwheel.

1973, Oct. 29
1956 A462 100k purple, red & bl   .25 .25
1957 A462 250k multicolored   .70 .25
1958 A462 475k brt blue & org   1.10 .50
        Nos. 1956-1958 (3)   2.05 1.00

Souvenir Sheet
Imperf
1959 A463 500k multicolored   3.00 2.00
50th anniv. of the Turkish Republic. #1959 contains one stamp with simulated perforations.

Bosporus Bridge A464

150k, Istanbul & Bosporus Bridge. 200k, Bosporus Bridge, children & UNICEF emblem, vert.

1973, Oct. 30   *Perf. 13*
1960 A464 100k multicolored   .35 .25
1961 A464 150k multicolored   .55 .35
1962 A464 200k multicolored   .60 .35
        Nos. 1960-1962 (3)   1.50 .95
Inauguration of the Bosporus Bridge from Istanbul to Üsküdar, Oct. 30, 1973; UNICEF; children from East and West brought closer through Bosporus Bridge (No. 1962).

Mevlana's Tomb and Dancers — A465   Jalal-udin Mevlana — A466

1973, Dec. 1   *Perf. 13x12½*
1963 A465 100k blk, lt ultra & grn   .45 .25
1964 A466 250k blue & multi   .65 .35
Jalal-udin Mevlana (1207-1273), poet and founder of the Mevlevie dervish order.

Cotton and Ship — A467

Export Products: 90k, Grapes. 100k, Figs. 250k, Citrus fruits. 325k, Tobacco. 475k, Hazelnuts.

1973, Dec. 10   Litho.   *Perf. 13*
1965 A467   75k black, gray & bl   .25 .25
1966 A467   90k black, olive & bl   .40 .25
1967 A467 100k black, emer & bl   .55 .25
1968 A467 250k blk, brt yel & bl   1.40 .35
1969 A467 325k blk, yel & bl   1.40 .35
1970 A467 475k blk, org brn & bl   2.10 .55
        Nos. 1965-1970 (6)   6.10 2.00

Pres. Inönü — A468

1973, Dec. 25   Litho.   *Perf. 13*
1971 A468 100k sepia & buff   .60 .25
Ismet Inönü, (1884-1973), first Prime Minister and second President of Turkey.

Hittite King, 8th Century B.C. — A469

Europa: 250k, Statuette of a Boy, (2nd millenium B.C.).

1974, Apr. 29   Litho.   *Perf. 13*
1972 A469 110k multicolored   2.50 1.00
1973 A469 250k lt blue & multi   4.00 2.00

Silver and Gold Figure, 3000 B.C. — A470

Archaeological Finds: 175k, Painted jar, 5000 B.C., horiz. 200k, Vessels in bull form, 1700-1600 B.C., horiz. 250k, Pitcher, 700 B.C.

1974, May 24   Litho.   *Perf. 13*
1974 A470 125k multicolored   .30 .25
1975 A470 175k multicolored   .55 .25
1976 A470 200k multicolored   .65 .25
1977 A470 250k multicolored   1.00 .40
        Nos. 1974-1977 (4)   2.50 1.15

Child Care — A471

1974, May 24
1978 A471 110k gray blue & blk   .60 .25
Sisli Children's Hospital, Istanbul, 75th anniv.

Anatolian Rug, 15th Century A472

Designs: 150k, Persian rug, late 16th century. 200k, Kashan rug, Lahore.

1974, July 21   Litho.   *Perf. 12½x13*
1979 A472 100k blue & multi   .90 .25
1980 A472 150k brown & multi   1.40 .25
1981 A472 200k red & multi   2.75 .25
        Nos. 1979-1981 (3)   5.05 .75
10th anniversary of the Regional Cooperation for Development Pact among Turkey, Iran and Pakistan.
See Iran 1806-1808, Pakistan 365-367.

Dove with Turkish Flag over Cyprus A473

1974, Aug. 26   Litho.   *Perf. 13*
1982 A473 250k multicolored   .95 .45
Cyprus Peace Operation.

Wrestling — A474

90k, 250k, various wrestling holds, horiz.

1974, Aug. 29
1983 A474   90k multicolored   .25 .25
1984 A474 100k multicolored   .40 .25
1985 A474 250k multicolored   .70 .25
        Nos. 1983-1985 (3)   1.35 .75
World Freestyle Wrestling Championships.

Arrows Circling Globe — A475

UPU Emblem and: 110k, "UPU" in form of dove. 200k, Dove.

1974, Oct. 9   Litho.   *Perf. 13*
1986 A475 110k bl, gold & dk bl   .25 .25
1987 A475 200k green & brown   .30 .25
1988 A475 250k multicolored   .55 .30
        Nos. 1986-1988 (3)   1.10 .80
Centenary of Universal Postal Union.

"Law Reforms" A476

"National Economy" A477   "Education" A478

1974, Oct. 29
1989 A476   50k blue & black   .30 .25
1990 A477 150k red & multi   .45 .25
1991 A478 400k multicolored   .75 .40
        Nos. 1989-1991 (3)   1.50 .90
Works and reforms of Kemal Ataturk.

Arrows Pointing
Up — A479

Cogwheel
and Map of
Turkey
A480

1974, Nov. 29   Litho.   Perf. 13
1992 A479   25k brown & black   .40   .25
1993 A480 100k brown & gray   .60   .25

3rd 5-year Development Program (#1992),
and industrialization progress (#1993).

Volleyball — A481

1974, Dec. 30
1994 A481 125k shown   .35   .25
1995 A481 175k Basketball   .70   .25
1996 A481 250k Soccer   1.10   .25
     Nos. 1994-1996 (3)   2.15   .75

Automatic
Telex Network
A482

Postal Check
A483

Radio
Transmitter
and Waves
A484

1975, Feb. 5   Litho.   Perf. 13
1997 A482   5k black & yellow   .30   .25
1998 A483 50k ol grn & org   .30   .25
1999 A484 100k blue & black   .40   .25
     Nos. 1997-1999 (3)   1.00   .75

Post and telecommunications.

Child
Entering
Classroom
A485

Children's paintings: 50k, View of village.
100k, Dancing children.

1975, Apr. 23   Litho.   Perf. 13
2000 A485 25k multicolored   .25   .25
2001 A485 50k multicolored   .25   .25
2002 A485 100k multicolored   .30   .25
     Nos. 2000-2002 (3)   .80   .75

Karacaoglan
Monument in Mut,
by Huseyin
Gezer — A486

1975, Apr. 25
2003 A486 110k dk grn, bis &
            red   .75   .30
Karacaoglan (1606-1697), musician.

Orange Harvest in Hatay, by Cemal
Tollu — A487

Europa: 250k, Yoruk Family on Plateau, by
Turgut Zaim.

1975, Apr. 28
2004 A487 110k bister & multi   1.75   .75
2005 A487 250k bister & multi   2.25 1.00

Porcelain
Vase, Turkey
A488

Designs: 200k, Ceramic plate, Iran, horiz.
250k, Camel leather vase, Pakistan.

Perf. 13½x13, 13x13½
1975, July 21   Litho.
2006 A488 110k multicolored   1.25   .35
2007 A488 200k multicolored   1.75   .60
2008 A488 250k ultra & multi   1.75   .95
     Nos. 2006-2008 (3)   4.75 1.90

Regional Cooperation for Development Pact
among Turkey, Iran and Pakistan.
See Iran 1871-1873, Pakistan 383-385.

Horon Folk Dance — A489

Regional Folk Dances: 125k, Kasik. 175k,
Bengi. 250k, Kasap. 325k, Kafkas, vert.

1975, Aug. 30   Litho.   Perf. 13
2009 A489 100k blue & multi   .50   .25
2010 A489 125k green & multi   .70   .25
2011 A489 175k rose & multi   .80   .25
2012 A489 250k multicolored   1.00   .25
2013 A489 325k orange & multi   1.50   .40
     Nos. 2009-2013 (5)   4.50 1.40

Knight Slaying   The Plunder of
Dragon — A490   Salur Kazan's
                      House — A491

Design: 175k, Two Wanderers, horiz.

1975, Oct. 15   Litho.   Perf. 13
2014 A490 90k multicolored   .60   .25
2015 A490 175k multicolored   .60   .30
2016 A491 200k multicolored   .90   .40
     Nos. 2014-2016 (3)   2.10   .95

Illustrations for tales by Dede Korkut.

Common
Carp
A492

1975, Nov. 27   Litho.   Perf. 12½x13
2017 A492 75k Turbot   1.00   .65
2018 A492 90k shown   1.25   .75
2019 A492 175k Trout   2.00 1.00
2020 A492 250k Red mullet   3.75 1.00
2021 A492 475k Red bream   6.00 2.00
     Nos. 2017-2021 (5)   14.00 5.40

Women's
Participation
A493

Insurance
Nationaliza-
tion — A494

Fine
Arts — A495

1975, Dec. 5   Perf. 12½x13, 13x12½
2022 A493 100k bis, blk & red   .25   .25
2023 A494 110k violet & multi   .30   .25
2024 A495 250k multicolored   .40   .25
     Nos. 2022-2024 (3)   .95   .75

Works and reforms of Ataturk.

Ceramic
Plate — A496

Europa: 400k, Decorated pitcher.

1976, May 3   Litho.   Perf. 13
2025 A496 200k purple & multi   3.25 1.50
2026 A496 400k multicolored   6.50 2.50

Sultan Ahmed
Mosque
A497

1976, May 10
2027 A497 500k gray & multi   .95   .45

7th Islamic Conference, Istanbul.

Lunch in
the Field
A498

Children's Drawings: 200k, Boats on the
Bosporus, vert. 400k, Winter landscape.

1976, May 19   Litho.   Perf. 13
2028 A498 50k multicolored   .35   .25
2029 A498 200k multicolored   .35   .25
2030 A498 400k multicolored   .55   .25
     Nos. 2028-2030 (3)   1.25   .75

Samsun 76, First National Junior Philatelic
Exhibition, Samsun.

Storks,
Sultan
Marsh
A499

Conservation Emblem and: 200k, Horses,
Manyas Lake. 250k, Borabay Lake. 400k,
Manavgat Waterfall.

1976, June 5
2031 A499 150k multicolored   2.10   .65
2032 A499 200k multicolored   .75   .25
2033 A499 250k multicolored   1.20   .25
2034 A499 400k multicolored   1.40   .35
     Nos. 2031-2034 (4)   5.45 1.50

European Wetland Conservation Year.

Nasreddin Hodja
Carrying
Liver — A500

Turkish Folklore: 250k, Friend giving recipe
for cooking liver. 600k, Hawk carrying off liver
and Hodja telling hawk he cannot enjoy liver
without recipe.

1976, July 5   Litho.   Perf. 13
2035 A500 150k multicolored   .40   .25
2036 A500 250k multicolored   .60   .25
2037 A500 600k multicolored   1.40   .50
     Nos. 2035-2037 (3)   2.40 1.00

Montreal Olympic
Emblem and
Flame — A501

Designs: 400k, "76," Montreal Olympic
emblem, horiz. 600k, Montreal Olympic
emblem and ribbons.

1976, July 17
2038	A501	100k red & multi	.25	.25
2039	A501	400k red & multi	.75	.40
2040	A501	600k red & multi	1.40	.60
		Nos. 2038-2040 (3)	2.40	1.25

21st Olympic Games, Montreal, Canada, 7/17-8/1.

Kemal Ataturk A502

Designs: 200k, Riza Shah Pahlavi. 250k, Mohammed Ali Jinnah.

1976, July 21   Litho.   Perf. 13½
2041	A502	100k multicolored	.30	.25
2042	A502	200k multicolored	.40	.25
2043	A502	250k multicolored	.70	.35
		Nos. 2041-2043 (3)	1.40	.85

Regional Cooperation for Development Pact among Turkey, Pakistan and Iran, 12th anniversary.
See Iran 1903-1905, Pakistan 412-414.

"Ataturk's Army" A503

Ataturk's Speeches A504

"Peace at Home and in the World" A505

1976, Oct. 29   Litho.   Perf. 13
2044	A503	100k black & red	.25	.25
2045	A504	200k gray grn & multi	.30	.25
2046	A505	400k blue & multi	.70	.30
		Nos. 2044-2046 (3)	1.25	.80

Works and reforms of Ataturk.

Hora A506

1977, Jan. 19   Litho.   Perf. 13
2047	A506	400k multicolored	.95	.30

MTA Sismik 1 "Hora" geophysical exploration ship.

Keyboard and Violin Sound Hole — A507

1977, Feb. 24   Litho.   Perf. 13x13½
2048	A507	200k multicolored	.75	.25

Turkish State Symphony Orchestra, sesquicentennial.

Ataturk and "100" — A508

Design: 400k, Hand holding ballot.

1977, Mar. 21   Litho.   Perf. 13
2049	A508	200k black & red	.50	.25
2050	A508	400k black & brown	.85	.40

Centenary of Turkish Parliament.

Hierapolis (Pamukkale) A509

Europa: 400k, Zelve (mountains and poppies).

1977, May 2   Litho.   Perf. 13½x13
2051	A509	200k multicolored	3.00	1.00
2052	A509	400k multicolored	5.00	1.50

Terra Cotta Pot, Turkey A510

Designs: 225k, Terra cotta jug, Iran. 675k, Terra cotta bullock cart, Pakistan.

1977, July 21   Litho.   Perf. 13
2053	A510	100k multicolored	.35	.25
2054	A510	225k multicolored	1.10	.35
2055	A510	675k multicolored	2.10	.75
a.		Souv. sheet, #2053-2055	8.00	8.00
		Nos. 2053-2055 (3)	3.55	1.35

Regional Cooperation for Development Pact among Turkey, Iran and Pakistan, 13th anniv.
See Iran 1946-1948, Pakistan 431-433.

Finn-class Yacht — A511

200k, Three yachts. 250k, Symbolic yacht.

1977, July 28
2056	A511	150k lt bl, bl & blk	.30	.25
2057	A511	200k ultra & blue	.55	.25
2058	A511	250k ultra & black	.80	.25
		Nos. 2056-2058 (3)	1.60	.75

European Finn Class Sailing Championships, Istanbul, July 28.

Ataturk Type of 1972

1977, June 13   Litho.   Perf. 13½x13
2060	A453	100k olive	.45	.25
2061	A453	200k brown	.65	.25

Kemal Ataturk — A512

Imprint: "GUZEL SANATLAR MATBAASI A.S. 1977"

1977, Sept. 23   Litho.   Perf. 13
Size: 20½x22mm
2062	A512	200k blue	1.25	.25
2063	A512	250k Prussian blue	1.75	.25

Imprint: "TIFDRUK-ISTANBUL 1978"

1978, June 28   Photo.   Perf. 13
Size: 20x25mm
2065	A512	10k brown	.35	.25
2066	A512	50k grnsh gray	.50	.25
2067	A512	1 l fawn	.50	.25
2068	A512	2½ l purple	.65	.25
2069	A512	5 l blue	.80	.25
2072	A512	25 l dl grn & lt bl	2.00	.25
2073	A512	50 l dp org & tan	2.50	.50
		Nos. 2065-2073 (7)	7.30	2.00

No. 1832 Surcharged with New Value and Wavy Lines

1977, Aug. 17
2078	A418	10k on 1k dp org & brn	.30	.25

"Rationalism" A513

"National Sovereignty" A514

"Liberation of Nations" — A515

1977, Oct. 29   Litho.   Perf. 13
2079	A513	100k multicolored	.25	.25
2080	A514	200k multicolored	.25	.25
2081	A515	400k multicolored	.70	.25
		Nos. 2079-2081 (3)	1.20	.75

Works and reforms of Ataturk.

Mohammad Allama Iqbal — A516

1977, Nov. 9   Perf. 13x12½
2082	A516	400k multicolored	.65	.25

Mohammad Allama Iqbal (1877-1938), Pakistani poet and philosopher.

Trees and Burning Match — A517

Design: 250k, Sign showing growing tree.

1977, Dec. 15   Litho.   Perf. 13
2083	A517	50k green, blk & red	.30	.25
2084	A517	250k gray, grn & blk	.60	.25

Forest conservation. See type A542.

Wrecked Car — A518

Passing on Wrong Side — A519

Traffic Sign, "Slow!" — A520

Type I

Type II

Two types of 50k:
I — Number on license plate.
II — No number on plate.

Traffic Safety: 250k, Tractor drawing overloaded farm cart. 800k, Accident caused by incorrect passing. 10 l, "Use striped crossings."

1977-78   Perf. 13½x13, 13x13½
2085	A518	50k ultra, blk & red, II	.60	.55
a.		Type I	.70	.55
2086	A519	150k red, gray & blk	.25	.25
2087	A518	250k ocher, blk & red	.50	.25
2088	A520	500k gray, red & blk	.50	.25
2089	A520	800k multicolored	1.10	.25
2090	A520	10 l dl grn, blk & brn	1.75	.35
		Nos. 2085-2090 (6)	4.70	1.90

Issued: 500k, 1977; others, 1978.
For No. 2089 surcharged, see No. 2182.

Ishak Palace, Dogubeyazit — A521

Europa: 5 l, Anamur Castle.

1978, May 2   Litho.   Perf. 13
2091	A521	2½ l multicolored	4.25	1.50
2092	A521	5 l multicolored	7.50	2.50

Riza Shah
Pahlavi — A522

1978, June 16   Litho.   Perf. 13x13½
2093   A522   5 l   multicolored   .65   .40
Riza Shah Pahlavi (1877-1944) of Iran, birth centenary.

Yellow
Rose,
Turkey
A523

3½ l, Pink roses, Iran. 8 l, Red roses, Pakistan.

1978, July 21   Litho.   Perf. 13
2094   A523   2½ l   multi   .30   .25
2095   A523   3½ l   multi   .60   .25
2096   A523   8 l   multi   1.60   .35
    Nos. 2094-2096 (3)   2.50   .85
Regional Cooperation for Development Pact among Turkey, Iran and Pakistan.
See Iran 1984-1986, Pakistan 449-451.

Anti-Apartheid Emblem — A524

1978, Aug. 14   Litho.   Perf. 13½x13
2097   A524   10 l   multicolored   .85   .25
Anti-Apartheid Year.

View of
Ankara — A525

Design: 5 l, View of Tripoli, horiz.

Perf. 13x12½, 12½x13
1978, Aug. 17
2098   A525   2½ l   multi   .35   .25
2099   A525   5 l   multi   .75   .25
Turkish-Libyan friendship.

Souvenir Sheet

Bridge and Mosque — A526

1978, Oct. 25   Imperf.
2100   A526   15 l   multicolored   1.50   1.00
Edirne '78, 2nd Natl. Phil. Youth Exhib.

Independence
Medal
A527

Latin Alphabet
A529

Speech
Reform
A528

1978, Oct. 29   Perf. 13x13½, 13½x13
2101   A527   2½ l   multi   .25   .25
2102   A528   3½ l   multi   .30   .25
2103   A529   5 l   multi   .45   .25
    Nos. 2101-2103 (3)   1.00   .75
Ataturk's works and reforms.

House on Bosporus, 1600 — A530

Turkish Houses: 2½ l, Izmit, 1774, vert. 3½ l, Kula, 17th cent., vert. 5 l, Milas, 18th-19th cent., vert. 8 l, Safranbolu, 18th-19th cent.

Perf. 13x12½, 12½x13
1978, Nov. 22
2104   A530   1 l   multi   .40   .25
2105   A530   2½ l   multi   .60   .25
2106   A530   3½ l   multi   .60   .40
2107   A530   5 l   multi   .90   .45
2108   A530   8 l   multi   1.50   .45
    Nos. 2104-2108 (5)   4.00   1.75

Carrier
Pigeon,
Plane,
Horseback
Rider,
Train
A531

Europa: 5 l, Morse key, telegraph and Telex machine. 7½ l, Telephone dial and satellite.

1979, Apr. 30   Litho.   Perf. 13
2109   A531   2½ l   multicolored   *1.50   .75*
2110   A531   5 l   org brn & blk   *2.75   .75*
2111   A531   7½ l   brt blue & blk   *3.25   1.00*
    Nos. 2109-2111 (3)   *7.50   2.50*

Plowing,
by Namik
Ismail
A532

Paintings: 7½ l, Potters, by Kamalel Molk, Iran. 10 l, At the Well, by Allah Baksh, Pakistan.

1979, Sept. 5   Litho.   Perf. 13½x13
2112   A532   5 l   multi   .25   .25
2113   A532   7½ l   multi   .50   .25
2114   A532   10 l   multi   .75   .35
    Nos. 2112-2114 (3)   1.50   .85
Regional Cooperation for Development Pact among Turkey, Pakistan and Iran, 15th anniversary.
See Iran 2020-2022, Pakistan 486-488.

A533

1979, Sept. 17   Perf. 13
2115   A533   5 l   Colemanite   .35   .25
2116   A533   7½ l   Chromite   .50   .25
2117   A533   10 l   Antimonite   .80   .25
2118   A533   15 l   Sulphur   1.00   .30
    Nos. 2115-2118 (4)   2.65   1.05
10th World Mining Congress.

A534

8-shaped road, train tunnel, plane and emblem.

1979, Sept. 24
2119   A534   5 l   multicolored   .50   .25
European Ministers of Communications, 8th Symposium.

Youth — A535

Secularization
A536

Design: 5 l, National oath.

1979, Oct. 29   Perf. 13x12½, 12½x13
2120   A535   2½ l   multi   .40   .25
2121   A536   3½ l   multi   .40   .25
2122   A535   5 l   black & orange   .60   .25
    Nos. 2120-2122 (3)   1.40   .75
Ataturk's works and reforms.

Poppies — A537

7½ l, Oleander. 10 l, Late spider orchid. 15 l, Mandrake.

1979, Nov. 26   Litho.   Perf. 13x13½
2123   A537   5 l   shown   .25   .25
2124   A537   7½ l   multicolored   .45   .25
2125   A537   10 l   multicolored   .70   .25
2126   A537   15 l   multicolored   1.10   .25
    Nos. 2123-2126 (4)   2.50   1.00
See Nos. 2154-2157.

Kemal
Ataturk — A538

Perf. 12½x11½, 13x12½(No. 2131)
1979-81   Litho.
2127   A538   50k   olive ('80)   .25   .25
2128   A538   1 l   grn & lt grn   .30   .25
2129   A538   2½ l   purple   .35   .25
2130   A538   2½ l   bl grn & lt bl
          ('80)   .30   .25
2131   A538   2½ l   orange ('81)   .35   .25
2132   A538   5 l   ultra & gray   .55   .25
    a.   Sheet of 8   3.25   3.25
2133   A538   7½ l   brown   .55   .25
2134   A538   7½ l   red ('80)   .75   .25
2135   A538   10 l   rose carmine   1.00   .30
2136   A538   20 l   gray ('80)   1.40   .40
    Nos. 2127-2136 (10)   5.80   2.70
No. 2132a for Ankara '79 Philatelic Exhibition, Oct. 14-20.
For surcharge see No. 2261.

Kemal
Ataturk — A538a

1980-82   Photo.   Perf. 13½
2137   A538a   7½ l   red brown   .45   .25
    c.   Sheet of 4   4.00   2.50
2137A   A538a   10 l   brown   .90   .25
2138   A538a   20 l   lilac   .90   .25
2138A   A538a   30 l   gray   1.10   .30
2139   A538a   50 l   orange red   2.00   .30
2140   A538a   75 l   brt green   2.75   .75
2141   A538a   100 l   blue   3.50   1.00
    Nos. 2137-2141 (7)   11.00   3.10
No. 2137c for ANTALYA '82 4th Natl. Junior Stamp Show. Exists both perf 13½ and imperf. Same value.
    Issued: #2137, 7/15/81; #2137c, 10/3/82; 30 l, 9/23/81; others, 12/10/80.
See Nos. 2164-2169.

Turkish Printing, 250th
Anniversary — A539

1979, Nov. 30   Litho.   Perf. 13
2142   A539   10 l   multicolored   .75   .40

2nd
International
Olive Oil
Year — A540

10 l, Globe, oil drop, vert.

Perf. 12½x13, 13x12½
1979, Dec. 20   Litho.
2143   A540   5 l   shown   .25   .25
2144   A540   10 l   multicolored   .45   .25

Uskudarli Hoca Ali Riza Bey (1857-
1930), Painter — A541

Europa: 15 l, Ali Sami Boyar (1880-1967), painter. 20 l, Dr. Hulusi Behcet (1889-1948), physician, discovered Behcet skin disease.

1980, Apr. 28   Perf. 13
2145   A541   7½ l   multi   1.10   .50
2146   A541   15 l   multi   1.50   .75
2147   A541   20 l   multi   2.00   .75
    Nos. 2145-2147 (3)   4.60   2.00

Forest
Conservation — A542

1980, July 3   *Perf. 13½x13*
2148 A542 50k ol grn & red org   .35   .25
See type A517. For surcharge see No. 2262.

Earthquake
Destruction — A543

1980, Sept. 8   *Perf. 13*
2149 A543 7½ l shown   .30   .25
2150 A543 20 l Seismograph   .70   .50

7th World Conference on Earthquake Engineering, Istanbul.

Games' Emblem,
Sports — A544

20 l, Emblem, sports, diff.

1980, Sept. 26   *Perf. 13x13½*
2151 A544 7½ l shown   .30   .25
2152 A544 20 l multicolored   .70   .25

First Islamic Games, Izmir.

Hegira — A545

1980, Nov. 9
2153 A545 20 l multicolored   .80   .40

Plant Type of 1979

2 ½ l, Manisa tulip. 7 ½ l, Ephesian bellflower. 15 l, Angora crocus. 20 l, Anatolian orchid.

1980, Nov. 26   *Perf. 13*
2154 A537 2½ l multicolored   .25   .25
2155 A537 7½ l multicolored   .50   .25
2156 A537 15 l multicolored   .75   .25
2157 A537 20 l multicolored   1.25   .25
   Nos. 2154-2157 (4)   2.75 1.00

Avicenna
Treating
Patient
A546

Avicenna (Arab Physician), Birth Millenium: 20 l, Portrait, vert.

1980, Dec. 15
2158 A546 7½ l multi   .45   .25
2159 A546 20 l multi   .55   .30

Balkanfila
VIII Stamp
Exhibition,
Ankara
A547

1981, Jan. 1   *Litho.*   *Perf. 13*
2160 A547 10 l red & black   .85   .25

Kemal
Ataturk — A548

1981, Feb. 4   *Perf. 13*
2163 A548 10 l lilac rose   .65   .25

Ataturk Type of 1980

1983-84   *Perf. 13x13½*
2164 A538a 15 l grnsh blue   .35   .25
2165 A538a 20 l orange ('84)   .45   .25
2167 A538a 65 l bluish grn   1.25   .25
2169 A538a 90 l lilac rose   1.60   .25
   Nos. 2164-2169 (4)   3.65 1.00
   Issued: #2164, 2167, 2169, 11/30; #2165, 7/25.

Sultan Mehmet the
Conqueror (1432-
1481) — A549

1981, May 3   *Litho.*   *Perf. 13x12½*
2173 A549 10 l multicolored   .45   .25
2174 A549 20 l multicolored   .95   .50

Gaziantep
(Folk
Dance)
A550

Antalya
A551

1981, May 4   *Litho.*   *Perf. 13*
2175 A550 7½ l shown   .25   .25
2176 A550 10 l Balikesir   .30   .25
2177 A550 15 l Kahramanmaras   1.40   .60
2178 A551 35 l shown   1.50   .50
2179 A551 70 l Burdur   2.00 1.00
   Nos. 2175-2179 (5)   5.45 2.60

Nos. 2178-2179 show CEPT (Europa) emblem.

Nos. C40, 1925, 1931A, 2089
Surcharged in Black with New Value
and Wavy Lines

1981, June 3   *Perf. 13½x13*
2179A AP7 10 l on 60k   .90   .25
2180 A453 10 l on 110k   .90   .25
2181 A453 10 l on 400k   .90   .25
2182 A520 10 l on 800k   .90   .25
   Nos. 2179A-2182 (4)   3.60 1.00

A552

7 ½ l, Rug, Bilecik. 10 l, Embroidery. 15 l, Drum, zurna players. 20 l, Embroidered napkin. 30 l, Yellow, red & black rug.

1981, June 22   *Perf. 13x12½*
2183 A552 7½ l multicolored   .25   .25
2184 A552 10 l multicolored   .30   .25
2185 A552 15 l multicolored   .50   .25
2186 A552 20 l multicolored   .50   .25
2187 A552 30 l multicolored   1.00   .25
   Nos. 2183-2187 (5)   2.55 1.25

22nd Intl. Turkish Folklore Congress.

Kemal Ataturk
A553

1981, May 19   *Litho.*   *Perf. 14x15*
2188 A553 2½ l No. 1801   .25   .25
2189 A553 7½ l No. 1816   .25   .25
2190 A553 10 l No. 1604   .30   .25
2191 A553 20 l No. 804   .60   .25
2192 A553 25 l No. 777   .75   .30
2193 A553 35 l No. 1959   1.00   .40
   Nos. 2188-2193 (6)   3.15 1.70

Souvenir Sheet

2194   Sheet of 6   15.00 12.50
  a.   A553 2½ l like 2½ l   .25   .25
  b.   A553 37½ l like 7½ l   .35   .25
  c.   A553 50 l like 10 l   .50   .25
  d.   A553 100 l like 20 l   1.00   .30
  e.   A553 125 l like 25 l   1.40   .60
  f.   A553 175 l like 35 l   2.00   .70

Souvenir Sheet

Balkanfila VIII Stamp Exhibition,
Ankara — A554

1981, Aug. 8   *Litho.*   *Perf. 13*
2195 A554   Sheet of 2   3.50 3.00
  a.   50 l No. B68   1.00   .60
  b.   50 l No. 733   1.00   .60

5th General Congress of European
Physics Society
A555

1981, Sept. 7   *Perf. 12½x13*
2196 A555 10 l red & multi   .50   .25
2197 A555 30 l blue & multi   1.00   .40

World
Food Day
A556

1981, Oct. 16
2198 A556 10 l multicolored   .45   .25
2199 A556 30 l multicolored   1.00   .25

Constituent Assembly
Inauguration — A557

1981, Oct. 23   *Perf. 13*
2200 A557 10 l multicolored   .40   .25
2201 A557 30 l multicolored   1.10   .25

Ataturk — A558

Portraits of Ataturk.

1981-82   *Perf. 11½x12½, 13 (#2204)*
2202 A558   1 l green   .25   .25
2203 A558 2½ l purple   .25   .25
2204 A558 2½ l gray & org   .50   .25
2205 A558   5 l blue   .25   .25
2206 A558 10 l orange   .25   .25
2207 A558 35 l brown   .70   .25
   Nos. 2202-2207 (6)   2.20 1.50

   Issued: #2204, 12/10/81; others, 1/27/82.

Literacy
Campaign — A559

1981, Dec. 24   *Perf. 13½*
2217 A559 2½ l Procession   .55   .25

Energy
Conservation — A560

1982, Jan. 11   *Perf. 13*
2218 A560 10 l multicolored   .55   .25

Magnolias, by
Ibrahim Calli
(b. 1882) — A561

1982, Mar. 17   *Perf. 13x13½, 13½x13*
2219 A561 10 l shown   .45   .25
2220 A561 20 l Fishermen, horiz.   .90   .25
2221 A561 30 l Sewing Woman   1.10   .25
   Nos. 2219-2221 (3)   2.45   .75

Europa Issue

Sultanhan
Caravanserai
A562

1982, Apr. 26   *Perf. 13x12½*
2222 A562 30 l shown   .50   .25
2223 A562 70 l Silk Route   .75   .35
  a.   Min. sheet, 2 each #2222-2223   3.50 3.50
  b.   Pair, #2222-2223   1.25   .75

1250th Anniv. of
Kul-Tigin
Monument, Kosu
Saydam,
Mongolia — A563

10 l, Monument. 30 l, Kul-Tigin (685-732), Gok-Turkish commander.

1982, June 9   *Perf. 13*
2224 A563 10 l multicolored   .25   .25
2225 A563 30 l multicolored   .60   .25

Pendik
Shipyard
Opening
A564

1982, July 1   *Perf. 12½x13*
2226 A564 30 l Ship, emblem   .65   .25

Mountains
of Anatolia
A565

7½ l, Agri Dagi, vert. 10 l, Buzul Dagi. 15 l,
Demirkazik, vert. 20 l, Erciyes. 30 l, Kackar
Dagi, vert. 35 l, Uludag.

1982, July 17   *Perf. 13*
2227 A565 7½ l multicolored   .30   .25
2228 A565 10 l multicolored   .55   .25
2229 A565 15 l multicolored   .85   .25
2230 A565 20 l multicolored   1.10   .25
2231 A565 30 l multicolored   1.75   .25
2232 A565 35 l multicolored   2.25   .25
   Nos. 2227-2232 (6)   6.80   1.50

Beyazit
State
Library
Centenary
A566

1982, Sept. 27
2233 A566 30 l multicolored   .70   .35

Musical Instruments of
Anatolia — A567

1982, Oct. 13
2234 A567 7½ l Davul   .60   .25
2235 A567 10 l Baglama   .60   .25
2236 A567 15 l shown   .90   .25
2237 A567 20 l Komonce   1.10   .25
2238 A567 30 l Ney   1.50   .25
   Nos. 2234-2238 (5)   4.70   1.25

Roman
Temple
Columns,
Sardis
A568

1982, Nov. 3
2239 A568 30 l multi   1.25   .40

Family Planning and Mother-Child
Health — A569

1983, Jan. 12   *Litho.*   *Perf. 13*
2240 A569 10 l Family on map   .25   .25
2241 A569 35 l Mother and child   .75   .25

30th Anniv. of Customs Cooperation
Council — A570

1983, Jan. 26
2242 A570 45 l multi   1.00   .25

1982 Constitution — A571

1983, Jan. 27
2243 A571 10 l Ballot box   .40   .25
2244 A571 30 l Open book, scale   .60   .25

Manastirli
Bey
A572

1983, Mar. 16   *Litho.*
2245 A572 35 l multi   1.00   .25
Manastirli Hamdi Bey (1890-1945), telegra-
pher of news of Istanbul's occupation to Ataturk, 1920.

Europa Issue

Piri Reis,
Geographer
A573

100 l, Ulugh Beg (1394-1449), astronomer.

1983, May 5   *Litho.*   *Perf. 12½x13*
2246 A573 50 l shown   *6.00*   *1.50*
2247 A573 100 l multi   *15.00*   *5.00*

Youth
Week
A574

1983, May 16
2248 A574 15 l multi   .65   .25

World Communications Year — A575

15 l, Carrier pigeon, vert. 50 l, Phone lines.
70 l, Emblem, vert.

1983, May 16   *Perf. 13*
2249 A575 15 l multicolored   .40   .25
2250 A575 50 l multicolored   .80   .25
2251 A575 70 l multicolored   1.50   .25
   Nos. 2249-2251 (3)   2.70   .75

50th
Anniv. of
State Civil
Aviation
A576

1983, May 20   *Litho.*   *Perf. 13*
2252 A576 50 l Plane, jet   1.10   .25
2253 A576 70 l Airport   1.50   .45

18th
Council of
Europe Art
Exhibition
A577

15 l, Eros, 2nd cent. BC, vert. 35 l, Two-
headed duck, Hittite, 14th cent BC. 50 l, Zinc
jugs, plate, 16th cent., vert. 70 l, Marcus Aurelius and his wife Faustina the Young, 2nd cent.

1983, May 22   *Perf. 13*
2254 A577 15 l multi   .50   .25
2255 A577 35 l multi   1.25   .25
2256 A577 50 l multi   1.25   .25
2257 A577 70 l multi   1.40   .25
   Nos. 2254-2257 (4)   4.40   1.00

Council of Europe's
"The Water's Edge"
Campaign — A578

Coastal Views.

1983, June 1   *Litho.*   *Perf. 13x12½*
2258 A578 10 l Olodeniz   .60   .35
2259 A578 25 l Olympus   .60   .35
2260 A578 35 l Kekova   1.25   .65
   Nos. 2258-2260 (3)   2.45   1.35

Nos. 2127, 2148 Surcharged
Perf. 12½x11½, 13½x13
1983, June 8
2261 A538 5 l on 50k olive   .50   .25
2262 A542 5 l on 50k ol grn &   red org   .50   .25

Kemal Ataturk — A579

1983, June 22   *Perf. 13*
2263 A579 15 l bl grn & bl   .35   .25
   a.   Sheet of 5 + label   2.50   2.00
2264 A579 50 l green & blue   1.40   .25
2265 A579 100 l orange & blue   2.75   .45
   Nos. 2263-2265 (3)   4.50   .95

For surcharge see No. 2432.

Aga Khan
Architecture
Award — A580

1983, Sept. 4   *Photo.*   *Perf. 11½*
2266 A580 50 l View of Istanbul   .95   .25

60th Anniv. of
the Republic
A582

1983, Oct. 29   *Perf. 13½x13*
2268 A582 15 l multi   .30   .25
2269 A582 50 l multi   .95   .25

Columns, Aphrodisias — A583

1983, Nov. 2   *Perf. 13*
2270 A583 50 l multi   1.10   .85

UNESCO Campaign
for Istanbul and
Goreme — A584

25 l, St. Sophia Basilica. 35 l, Goreme. 50 l,
Istanbul.

1984, Feb. 15   *Litho.*   *Perf. 13*
2271 A584 25 l multicolored   .50   .25
2272 A584 35 l multicolored   .75   .25
2273 A584 50 l multicolored   1.00   .25
   Nos. 2271-2273 (3)   2.25   .75

Natl. Police
Org. Emblem
A585

1984, Apr. 10   *Litho.*   *Perf. 13*
2274 A585 15 l multi   .75   .30

Europa (1959-
84)
A586

1984, Apr. 30   *Perf. 13½x13*
2275 A586 50 l blue & multi   6.00   1.00
2276 A586 100 l gray & multi   10.00   2.00

Mete
Khan, Hun
Ruler, 204
BC, Flag
A587

Sixteen States (Hun Rulers and Flags): 20 l,
Panu, Western Hun empire (48-216). 50 l,
Attila, 375-454. 70 l, Aksunvar, Ak Hun
empire, 420-562.

1984, June 20   *Litho.*   *Perf. 13*
2277 A587 10 l multi   .70   .25
2278 A587 20 l multi   .90   .35
2279 A587 50 l multi   1.75   .45
2280 A587 70 l multi   3.00   .45
   Nos. 2277-2280 (4)   6.35   1.50

See Nos. 2315-2318, 2349-2352, 2382-2385.

Occupation of
Cyprus, 10th
Anniv.
A588

70 l, Dove, olive branch.

1984, July 20   *Litho.*   *Perf. 13*
2281 A588 70 l multicolored   1.40   .60

Wild Flowers — A589

10 l, Marshmallow flower. 20 l, Red poppy. 70 l, Sowbread. 200 l, Snowdrop. 300 l, Tulip.

1984, Aug. 1   *Perf. 11½x12½*
2282	A589	10 l	multicolored	.25 .25
2283	A589	20 l	multicolored	.30 .25
2284	A589	70 l	multicolored	.90 .25
2285	A589	200 l	multicolored	2.50 .35
2286	A589	300 l	multicolored	4.00 .45
		Nos. 2282-2286 (5)		7.95 1.55

See Nos. 2301-2308. For surcharges see Nos. 2467, 2479-2480.

Armed Forces Day — A590

20 l, Soldier, dove, flag. 50 l, Sword. 70 l, Arms, soldier, flag. 90 l, Map, soldier.

1984, Aug. 26   *Perf. 13½x13*
2287	A590	20 l	multicolored	.45 .25
2288	A590	50 l	multicolored	.90 .25
2289	A590	70 l	multicolored	1.40 .25
2290	A590	90 l	multicolored	1.75 .25
		Nos. 2287-2290 (4)		4.50 1.00

Trees and Wood Products — A591

Seed, Tree and Product: 10 l, Liquidambar, liquidambar grease. 20 l, Oriental spruce, stringed instrument. 70 l, Oriental beech, chair. 90 l, Cedar of Lebanon, ship.

1984, Sept. 19   **Litho.**   *Perf. 13x12½*
2291	A591	10 l	multi	.55 .25
2292	A591	20 l	multi	.55 .25
2293	A591	70 l	multi	1.40 .25
2294	A591	90 l	multi	2.00 .25
		Nos. 2291-2294 (4)		4.50 1.00

Pres. Ismet Inonu (1884-1973), A592

1984, Sept. 24   *Perf. 13*
2295	A592	20 l	Portrait	1.10 .25

First Intl. Turkish Carpet Congress — A593

70 l, Seljukian carpet, 13th cent.

1984, Oct. 7   *Perf. 13x13½*
2296	A593	70 l	multicolored	1.10 .75

Ruins of Ancient City of Harran A594

1984, Nov. 7   *Perf. 13½x13*
2297	A594	70 l	Columns, arch	1.75 1.25

Turkish Women's Suffrage, 50th Anniv. A595

1984, Dec. 5   **Litho.**   *Perf. 13*
2298	A595	20 l	Women voting	.65 .25

40th Anniv., ICAO — A596

100 l, Icarus, ICAO emblem.

1984, Dec. 7   **Litho.**   *Perf. 13*
2299	A596	100 l	multicolored	1.50 1.25

Souvenir Sheet

No. 1047 — A597

1985, Jan. 13   **Litho.**   *Imperf.*
2300	A597	Sheet of 4, 2 each #a.-b.	3.75 2.50
a.-b.		70 l, any single	.45 .45

Istanbul '87. No. 2300b has denomination in lower right.

Flower Type of 1984

1985   *Perf. 11½x12½*
2301	A589	5 l	Narcissus	.65 .25

    Perf. 12½x13
2308	A589	100 l	Daisy	1.40 .25

Issue dates: #2301, Feb. 6; #2308, July 31. For surcharge see No. 2465.

Turkish Aviation League, 60th Anniv. A598

10 l, Parachutist, glider. 20 l, Hot air balloon, vert.

1985, Feb. 16   *Perf. 13*
2310	A598	10 l	multicolored	.50 .25
2311	A598	20 l	multicolored	1.25 .55

INTELSAT, 20th Anniv. — A599

1985, Apr. 3
2312	A599	100 l	multi	1.50 .75

Europa Issue

Ulvi Cemal Erkin (1906-1972) and Kosekce — A600

Composers and music: 200 l, Mithat Fenmen (1916-1982) and Concertina.

1985, Apr. 29   *Perf. 13½x13*
2313	A600	100 l	multi	10.00 1.50
2314	A600	200 l	multi	15.00 2.50

States Type of 1984

Sixteen States (Kagan rulers and flags): 10 l, Bilge, Gokturk Empire (552-743) and Orhon-Turkish alphabet. 20 l, Bayan, Avar Empire (565-803). 70 l, Hazar, Hazar Empire (651-983). 100 l, Kutlug Kul Bilge, Uygur State (774-1335).

1985, June 20
2315	A587	10 l	multi	.60 .25
2316	A587	20 l	multi	1.25 .25
2317	A587	70 l	multi	2.40 .25
2318	A587	100 l	multi	4.75 .25
		Nos. 2315-2318 (4)		9.00 1.00

Intl. Youth Year A601

1985, Aug. 8
2319	A601	100 l	multi	1.00 .75
2320	A601	120 l	multi	1.50 1.00

Postal Code Inauguration A602

1985, Sept. 4   *Perf. 13*

Background Color
2321	A602	10 l	pale yel brn	.35 .25
2322	A602	20 l	fawn	.55 .25
2323	A602	20 l	gray green	.55 .25
2324	A602	20 l	brt blue	.55 .25
2325	A602	70 l	rose lilac	1.25 .25
2326	A602	100 l	gray	1.75 .45
		Nos. 2321-2326 (6)		5.00 1.70

Symposium of Natl. Palaces — A603

20 l, Aynalikavak, c. 1703. 100 l, Beylerbeyi, 1865.

1985, Sept. 25   *Perf. 13½x13*
2327	A603	20 l	multicolored	.40 .25
2328	A603	100 l	multicolored	1.60 .25

UN, 40th Anniv. A604

1985, Oct. 24
2329	A604	100 l	multi	1.00 .75

Alanya Fortress and City A605

1985, Nov. 7
2330	A605	100 l	multi	1.50 .75

A606

1985, Nov. 12   *Perf. 13x13½*
2331	A606	100 l	multi	1.50 .75

Turkish Meteorological Service, 60th anniv.

Isik Lyceum, Istanbul, Cent. — A607

1985, Dec. 14
2332	A607	20 l	multi	.75 .25

Ataturk — A608

    Perf. 11½x12½

1985, Dec. 18   *Litho.*
2334	A608	10 l	pale bl & ultra	.30 .25
2335	A608	20 l	beige & brn	.40 .25
2336	A608	100 l	lt pink & claret	1.50 .25
		Nos. 2334-2336 (3)		2.20 .75

For surcharges see Nos. 2433-2434, 2449.

7th Intl. Children's Festival, Ankara A609

Various children's drawings.

1986, Apr. 23   **Litho.**   *Perf. 12½x13*
2342	A609	20 l	multi	.40 .30
2343	A609	100 l	multi	1.20 .30
2344	A609	120 l	multi	1.40 1.40
		Nos. 2342-2344 (3)		3.00 2.00

Europa Issue

Pollution A610

200 l, Bandaged leaf.

1986, Apr. 28   *Perf. 13*
2345	A610	100 l	shown	6.50 1.50
2346	A610	200 l	multi	8.50 2.50

1st Ataturk Intl. Peace Prize — A611

1986, May 19   **Litho.**   *Perf. 13*
2347	A611	20 l gold & multi	.55	.55
2348	A611	100 l silver & multi	1.40	.75

States Type of 1984

Sixteen States (Devleti rulers and flags): 10 l, Bilge Kul Kadir Khan, Kara Khanids State (840-1212). 20 l, Alp-Tekin, Ghaznavids State (963-1183). 100 l, Seldjuk Bey, Seldjuks State (1040-1157). 120 l, Muhammed Harezmsah, Khwarizm-Shahs State (1157-1231).

1986, June 20
2349	A587	10 l multi	.45	.25
2350	A587	20 l multi	1.25	.40
2351	A587	100 l multi	1.90	.70
2352	A587	120 l multi	4.50	1.40
		Nos. 2349-2352 (4)	8.10	2.75

1st Turkish Submarine, Cent. — A612

20 l, Torpedo sub Abdulhamid.

1986, June 16   **Litho.**   *Perf. 13*
2353	A612	20 l multi	1.25	.50

Kirkpinar Wrestling Matches, Edirne — A613

1986, June 30
2354	A613	10 l	Oiling bodies	.65	.65
2355	A613	20 l	Five wrestlers	.65	.65
2356	A613	100 l	Two wrestlers	1.90	1.25
			Nos. 2354-2356 (3)	3.20	2.55

Organization for Economic Cooperation and Development, 25th Anniv. — A614

1986, Sept. 30   **Litho.**   *Perf. 13½x13*
2357	A614	100 l multi	1.40	.45

Automobile, Cent. — A615

10 l, Benz Velocipede, 1886. 20 l, Rolls-Royce Silver Ghost, 1906. 100 l, Mercedes Touring Car, 1928. 200 l, Abstract speeding car.

1986, Oct. 15
2358	A615	10 l multi	.75	.50
2359	A615	20 l multi	1.00	.50
2360	A615	100 l multi	2.00	1.00
2361	A615	200 l multi	2.75	1.40
		Nos. 2358-2361 (4)	6.50	3.40

Paintings A616

Designs: 100 l, Bouquet with Tulip, by Feyhaman Duran (1886-1970). 120 l, Landscape with Fountain, by H. Avni Lifij (1886-1927), horiz.

1986, Oct. 22   *Perf. 13½x13, 13x13½*
2362	A616	100 l multi	1.50	.50
2363	A616	120 l multi	3.75	.75

Celal Bayar (1883-1986), 3rd President — A617

1986, Oct. 27   *Perf. 13*
2364	A617	20 l	shown	.60	.25
2365	A617	100 l	Profile	1.00	.25

Kubad-Abad Ruins, Beysehir Lake — A618

1986, Nov. 7   *Perf. 13½x13*
2366	A618	100 l multi	1.40	.50

Mehmet Akif Ersoy (1873-1936), Composer of the Turkish National Anthem — A619

1986, Dec. 27   **Litho.**   *Perf. 13½x13*
2367	A619	20 l multi	.75	.25

Road Safety — A620

10 l, Use seatbelts. 20 l, Don't drink alcohol and drive. 150 l, Observe speed limit.

1987, Feb. 4   **Litho.**   *Perf. 13x13½*
2368	A620	10 l multi	.25	.25
2369	A620	20 l multi	.45	.25
2370	A620	150 l multi	1.60	.25
		Nos. 2368-2370 (3)	2.30	.75

For surcharges see Nos. 2466, 2477-2478.

Butterflies A621

10 l, Celerio euphorbiae. 20 l, Vanessa atalanta. 100 l, Euplagia quadripunctaria. 120 l, Colias crocea.

1987, Feb. 25   *Perf. 13½x13*
2371	A621	10 l multi	.80	.25
2372	A621	20 l multi	1.20	.40
2373	A621	100 l multi	4.00	1.40
2374	A621	120 l multi	5.00	2.00
		Nos. 2371-2374 (4)	11.00	4.05

Intl. Year of Shelter for the Homeless — A622

1987, Mar. 18   **Litho.**   *Perf. 13x13½*
2375	A622	200 l multi	1.25	.75

Karabuk Iron and Steel Works, 50th Anniv. A623

1987, Apr. 3   **Litho.**   *Perf. 13½x13*
2376	A623	50 l	Interior	.55	.25
2377	A623	200 l	Exterior	1.40	.25

Natl. Sovereignty — A624

1987, Apr. 23   *Perf. 13½x13*
2378	A624	50 l multi	.90	.25

Founding of the Turkish state, 67th anniv.

Architecture — A625

Europa: 50 l, Turkish History Institute, 1951-67, designed by Turgut Cansever with Ertur Yener. 200 l, Social Insurance Institute, 1963, designed by Sedad Hakki Eldem.

1987, Apr. 28   *Perf. 13*
2379	A625	50 l multi	5.00	1.00
2380	A625	200 l multi	12.50	2.00

92nd Session, Intl. Olympic Committee, Istanbul, May 9-12 — A626

1987, May 9   **Litho.**   *Perf. 13x13½*
2381	A626	200 l multi	1.75	1.00

States Type of 1984

Sixteen states (Devleti and Imparatorlugu rulers and flags): 10 l, Datu Khan, Golden Horde State (1227-1502). 20 l, Kutlug Timur Khan, Great Timur Empire (1368-1507). 50 l, Babur Shah, Babur Empire (1526-1858). 200 l, Osman Bey Gasi, Ottoman Empire (1299-1923).

1987, June 20   *Perf. 12½x13*
2382	A587	10 l multi	.50	.25
2383	A587	20 l multi	1.00	.30
2384	A587	50 l multi	1.50	.30
2385	A587	200 l multi	3.00	1.00
		Nos. 2382-2385 (4)	6.00	1.85

Album of the Conqueror, Mehmet II, 15th Cent., Topkapi Palace Museum — A627

Untitled paintings by Mehmet Siyah Kalem: 10 l, Two warriors, vert. 20 l, Three men, donkey. 50 l, Blackamoor whipping horse. 200 l, Demon, vert.

Perf. 13½x13, 13x13½

1987, July 1   **Litho.**
2386	A627	10 l multi	.75	.40
2387	A627	20 l multi	1.00	.40
2388	A627	50 l multi	1.25	.40
2389	A627	200 l multi	2.00	1.00
		Nos. 2386-2389 (4)	5.00	2.20

Natl. Palaces A628

50 l, Ihlamur, c. 1850. 200 l, Kucuksu Pavilion, 1857.

1987, Sept. 25   *Perf. 13½x13*
2390	A628	50 l	multicolored	1.00	.60
2391	A628	200 l	multicolored	2.00	.75

See Nos. 2425-2426.

"Tughra," Suleiman's Calligraphic Signature — A629

Designs: 30 l, Portrait, vert. 200 l, Suleiman Receiving a Foreign Minister, contemporary miniature, vert. 270 l, Bust, detail of bas-relief, The Twenty-Three Law-Givers, entrance to the gallery of the US House of Representatives.

Litho., Litho. & Engr. (270 l)
1987, Oct. 1   *Perf. 13½x13, 13x13½*
2392	A629	30 l	multi	.50	.35
2393	A629	50 l	shown	.75	.45
2394	A629	200 l	multi	2.25	.90
2395	A629	270 l	multi	2.75	1.25
			Nos. 2392-2395 (4)	6.25	2.95

Suleiman the Magnificent (1494-1566), sultan of the Turkish Empire (1520-1566). On No. 2395, the gold ink was applied by a thermographic process producing a shiny, raised effect.

A630

Presidents: a, Cemal Gursel (1961-1966). b, Cevdet Sunay (1966-1973). c, Fahri S. Koruturk (1973-1980). d, Kenan Evren (1982-). e, Ismet Inonu (1938-1950). f, Celal Bayar (1950-1960). g, Mustafa Kemal Ataturk (1923-1938).

1987, Oct. 29   Litho.   Imperf.
Souvenir Sheet
2396 A630 Sheet of 7 ... 6.00 6.00
  a.-f. 50 l any single ... .55 .55
  g. 100 l multi, 26x37mm ... .75 .75

A631

200 l, Mosque, architectural elements.

1988, Apr. 9   Litho.   Perf. 13
2397 A631 50 l shown ... .65 .40
2398 A631 200 l multi ... 2.00 .80

Joseph (Mimar) Sinan (1489-1588), architect.

Health — A632

50 l, Immunization, horiz. 200 l, Fight drug abuse. 300 l, Safe work conditions, horiz. 600 l, Organ donation.

1988, May 4
2399 A632 50 l multicolored ... .25 .25
2400 A632 200 l multicolored ... .65 .25
2401 A632 300 l multicolored ... .95 .25
2402 A632 600 l multicolored ... 2.10 .55
  Nos. 2399-2402 (4) ... 3.95 1.30

Europa Issue

Telecommunications — A633

Transport and communication: 200 l, Modes of transportation, vert.

1988, May 2   Litho.   Perf. 13, 12½
2403 A633 200 l multi ... 3.50 1.25
2404 A633 600 l multi ... 11.00 1.50

Steam, Electric and Diesel Locomotives A634

50 l, American Standard steam engine, c. 1850. 100 l, Steam engine produced in Esslingen for Turkish railways, 1913. 200 l, Henschel Krupp steam engine, 1926. 300 l, E 43001 Toshiba electric engine produced in Japan, 1987. 600 l, MTE-Tulomsas #24361 diesel-electric high-speed engine, 1984.

1988, May 24   Perf. 13
2405 A634 50 l buff, brn & blk ... 1.10 .45
2406 A634 100 l buff, brn & blk ... 2.25 .90
2407 A634 200 l buff, brn & blk ... 3.50 1.50
2408 A634 300 l buff, brn & blk ... 4.50 1.75
2409 A634 600 l buff, brn & blk ... 6.25 2.75
  Nos. 2405-2409 (5) ... 17.60 7.35

Court of Cassation (Supreme Court), 120th Anniv. A635

1988, July 1   Litho.   Perf. 13½x13
2410 A635 50 l multi ... .75 .35

Bridge Openings — A636

Designs: 200 l, Fatih Sultan Mehmet Bridge, Kavacik-Hisarustu. 300 l, Seto Ohashi (Friendship) Bridges, the Minami and Kita.

1988, July 3   Litho.   Perf. 13x13½
2411 A636 200 l multi ... 1.90 1.10
2412 A636 300 l multi ... 3.00 1.50

Telephone System A637

1988, Aug. 24   Litho.   Perf. 13½x13
2413 A637 100 l multi ... .65 .25

1988 Summer Olympics, Seoul A638

Perf. 12½x13, 13x12½
1988, Sept. 17   Litho.
2414 A638 100 l Running ... .50 .25
2415 A638 200 l Archery ... .80 .25
2416 A638 400 l Weight lifting ... 1.10 .35
2417 A638 600 l Gymnastics, vert. ... 1.60 .45
  Nos. 2414-2417 (4) ... 4.00 1.30

Naim Suleymanoglu, 1988 Olympic Gold Medalist, Weight Lifting — A639

1988, Oct. 5   Litho.   Perf. 13x12½
2418 A639 1000 l multi ... 7.00 3.50

Aerospace Industries A640

50 l, Gear, aircraft, vert.

1988, Oct. 28   Perf. 13½x13, 13x13½
2419 A640 50 l multicolored ... .35 .25
2420 A640 50 l shown ... .90 .25

Butterflies A641

100 l, Gonepteryx rhamni. 200 l, Chazara briseis. 400 l, Allancastria cerisyi godart. 600 l, Nymphalis antiopa.

1988, Oct. 28   Perf. 13½x13
2421 A641 100 l multi ... 1.25 .65
2422 A641 200 l multi ... 3.00 1.10
2423 A641 400 l multi ... 5.00 1.75
2424 A641 600 l multi ... 6.25 3.00
  a. Souvenir sheet of 4, #2421-2424 ... 20.00 20.00
  Nos. 2421-2424 (4) ... 15.50 6.50

ANTALYA '88.

Natl. Palaces Type of 1987

100 l, Maslak Royal Lodge, c. 1890. 400 l, Yildiz Sale Pavilion, 1889.

1988, Nov. 3   Litho.   Perf. 13
2425 A628 100 l multicolored ... .45 .35
2426 A628 200 l multicolored ... 1.00 .85

Souvenir Sheet

Kemal Ataturk — A642

1988, Nov. 10   Perf. 13x13½
2427 A642 400 l multi ... 1.60 1.60

Medicinal Plants of Anatolia A643

150 l, Tilia rubra. 300 l, Malva silvestris. 600 l, Hyoscyamus niger. 900 l, Atropa belladonna.

1988, Dec. 14   Litho.   Perf. 13
2428 A643 150 l multicolored ... .50 .25
2429 A643 300 l multicolored ... .60 .25
2430 A643 600 l multicolored ... 1.25 .25
2431 A643 900 l multicolored ... 2.50 .45
  Nos. 2428-2431 (4) ... 4.85 1.20

Stamps of 1983-85 Surcharged

Perf. 13, 11½x12½
1989, Feb. 8   Litho.
2432 A579 50 l on 15 l No. 2263 ... .50 .25
2433 A608 75 l on 10 l No. 2334 ... .75 .25
2434 A608 150 l on 20 l No. 2336 ... 1.40 .25
  Nos. 2432-2434 (3) ... 2.65 .75
Surcharge on No. 2432 is slightly different.

Artifacts in the Museum of Anatolian Civilizations, Ankara — A644

Designs: 150 l, Seated Goddess with Child, neolithic bisque figurine, Hacilar, 6th millennium B.C. 300 l, Lead figurine, Alisar Huyuk, Assyrian Trading Colonies Era, c. 19th cent. B.C. 600 l, Human-shaped vase, Kultepe, Assyrian Trading Colonies Era, 18th cent. B.C. 1000 l, Ivory mountain god, Bogazkoy, Hittite Empire, 14th cent. B.C.

1989, Feb. 8   Litho.   Perf. 13½x13
2435 A644 150 l multi ... .75 .25
2436 A644 300 l multi ... 1.10 .70
2437 A644 600 l multi ... 1.75 1.40
2438 A644 1000 l multi ... 3.75 2.00
  Nos. 2435-2438 (4) ... 7.35 4.35

See Nos. 2458-2461, 2495-2498, 2520-2523, 2617-2620.

NATO, 40th Anniv. A645

Wmk. 394
1989, Apr. 4   Litho.   Perf. 13½
2439 A645 600 l multi ... 1.50 .25

Europa Issue

Children's Games — A646

600 l, Leapfrog. 1000 l, Open the door, Headbezirgan.

Perf. 13x12½
1989, Apr. 23   Wmk. 394
2440 A646 600 l multi ... 10.00 1.75
2441 A646 1000 l multi ... 15.00 2.50

Steamships — A647

Perf. 13½x13
1989, July 1   Litho.   Wmk. 394
2442 A647 150 l Sahilbent ... 2.75 1.50
2443 A647 300 l Ragbet ... 4.00 2.10
2444 A647 600 l Tari ... 5.50 2.50
2445 A647 1000 l Guzelhisar ... 8.00 4.00
  Nos. 2442-2445 (4) ... 20.25 10.10

French Revolution, Bicent. — A648

Wmk. 394
1989, July 14   Litho.   Perf. 14
2446 A648 600 l multi ... 1.75 .25

Kemal
Ataturk — A649

1989, Aug. 16   *Perf. 13x13½*
2447 A649 2000 l gray & bluish
           gray   2.50 .50
2448 A649 5000 l gray & deep
           red brn   5.00 1.50
   See Nos. 2485-2486, 2538-2541. For
surcharge see No. 2656.

No. 2336 Surcharged in Bright Blue
       Perf. 11½x12½
1989, Aug. 31   **Litho.**   **Unwmk.**
2449 A608 500 l on 20 l   .80 .25

Photography, 150th Anniv. — A650

1989, Oct. 17   *Perf. 13½x13*
2450 A650 175 l Camera   .40 .25
2451 A650 700 l Shutter   1.40 .25

State
Exhibition
of
Paintings
and
Sculpture
A651

Designs: 200 l, *Manzara*, by Hikmet Onat.
700 l, *Sari Saz*, by Bedri Rahmi Eyuboglu.
1000 l, *Kadin*, by Zuhtu Muridoglu.

       Perf. 13½x13
1989, Oct. 30   **Litho.**   **Wmk. 394**
2452 A651 200 l multicolored   .30 .25
2453 A651 700 l multicolored   1.10 .25
2454 A651 1000 l multicolored   1.40 .35
    Nos. 2452-2454 (3)   2.80 .85

Jawaharlal Nehru,
1st Prime Minister
of Independent
India — A652

1989, Nov. 14   *Perf. 13½x12½*
2455 A652 700 l multicolored   1.65 .25

Sea
Turtles
A653

   700 l, Caretta caretta. 1000 l, Chelonia
mydas.

1989, Nov. 16   *Perf. 13½x13*
2456 A653 700 l multi   3.00 1.00
2457 A653 1000 l multi   6.00 2.00
   a.   Souv. sheet of 2, #2456-
       2457   17.50 17.50

Artifacts Type of 1989

   100 l, Ivory female deity. 200 l, Ceremonial
vessel. 500 l, Seated goddess pendant. 700 l,
Carved lion.

     Perf. 13x12½, 12½x13
1990, Feb. 8   **Litho.**   **Wmk. 394**
2458 A644 100 l multi   .30 .30
2459 A644 200 l multi   .50 .50
2460 A644 500 l multi   1.00 .75
2461 A644 700 l multi   1.75 1.25
    Nos. 2458-2461 (4)   3.55 2.80
    Nos. 2458 and 2460 vert.

Wars of
Dardanelles,
1915 — A654

1990, Mar. 18   *Perf. 13*
2462 A654 1000 l multicolored   1.10 .25

EXPO '90 Intl. Garden and Greenery
Exposition, Osaka — A655

      Perf. 12½x13
1990, Apr. 1   **Litho.**   **Wmk. 394**
2463 A655 1000 l Bridge at left   1.40 .35
2464 A655 1000 l Pavilion at left   1.40 .35
   a.   A655 Pair, #2463-2464   3.00 3.00

**Nos. 2301, 2368 and 2284
Surcharged**
      Perfs. as Before
1990, Apr. 4   **Litho.**
2465 A589 50 l on 5 l #2301   .85 .25
2466 A620 100 l on 10 l #2368   2.25 .25
2467 A589 200 l on 70 l #2284   5.00 .30
    Nos. 2465-2467 (3)   8.10 .80

Grand Natl.
Assembly, 70th
Anniv. — A657

1990, Apr. 23   *Perf. 13*
2468 A657 300 l multicolored   .95 .50

Europa
1990 — A658

   Post offices — 700 l, Ulus, Ankara. 1000 l,
Sirkeci, Istanbul, horiz.

1990, May 2
2469 A658 700 l multicolored   5.00 1.50
2470 A658 1000 l multicolored   0.50 2.00

8th
European
Supreme
Courts
Conf.
A659

1990, May 7   **Litho.**   *Perf. 12½x13*
2471 A659 1000 l multicolored   2.00 .75

Salamandra Salamandra — A660

   World Environment Day: No. 2473, Trituris
vittatus. No. 2474, Bombina bombina. No.
2475, Hyla arborea, vert.

1990, June 5   *Perf. 13½x13*
2472 A660 300 l multicolored   .70 .70
2473 A660 500 l multicolored   .70 .70
2474 A660 1000 l multicolored   1.50 1.50
2475 A660 1500 l multicolored   2.50 2.50
    Nos. 2472-2475 (4)   5.40 5.40

Turkey-Japan Relations, Cent. — A661

1990, June 13   *Perf. 12½x13*
2476 A661 1000 l multicolored   1.75 1.10

**Traffic Types of 1987 and Nos.
2283-2284 Surcharged**
1990, June 20   *Perf. 14*
2477 A620 150 l on 10 l   7.00 1.75
2478 A620 300 l on 10 l   11.00 1.75
       Perf. 11½x12½
2479 A589 300 l on 70 l #2284   3.00 .75
2480 A589 1500 l on 20 l #2283   8.75 .75
    Nos. 2477-2480 (4)   29.75 5.00

Boats in Saintes Marines — A662

   Paintings by Vincent Van Gogh (1853-
1890): 300 l, Self-portrait, vert. 1000 l, Vase
with Sunflowers, vert. 1500 l, Road of Cypress
and Stars.

       Wmk. 394
1990, July 29   **Litho.**   *Perf. 13*
2481 A662 300 l multicolored   2.00 1.40
2482 A662 700 l multicolored   3.50 2.00
2483 A662 1000 l multicolored   4.50 3.00
2484 A662 1500 l multicolored   5.00 4.00
    Nos. 2481-2484 (4)   15.00 10.40

Ataturk Type of 1989
1990, Aug. 1   **Unwmk.**   *Perf. 14*
2485 A649 500 l gray & ol grn   1.40 .25
2486 A649 1000 l gray & rose vio   1.75 .70

Intl. Literacy
Year — A664

      Perf. 13x13½
1990, Aug. 22   **Wmk. 394**
2487 A664 300 l multicolored   .50 .50

A665

   State exhibition of paintings and sculpture
by: 300 l, Nurullah Berk. 700 l, Cevat Dereli.
1000 l, Nijad Sirel.

1990, Oct. 17   **Litho.**   *Perf. 13x13½*
2488 A665 300 l multicolored   .45 .25
2489 A665 700 l multicolored   .90 .35
2490 A665 1000 l multicolored   1.40 .50
    Nos. 2488-2490 (3)   2.75 1.10

PTT, 150th
Anniv.
A666

   Past and present communication methods:
200 l, Post rider, truck, train, airplane, ship.
250 l, Telegraph key, computer terminal. 400 l,
Telephone switchboard, computerized telephone exchange. 1500 l, Power lines, satellite.

1990, Oct. 23   *Perf. 14*
2491 A666 200 l multicolored   .25 .25
2492 A666 250 l multicolored   .25 .25
2493 A666 400 l multicolored   .70 .25
2494 A666 1500 l multicolored   2.75 1.50
   a.   Souv. sheet of 4 #2491-2494   4.00 4.00
    Nos. 2491-2494 (4)   3.95 2.25
   For surcharges see Nos. 2657-2659.

Artifacts Type of 1989

   300 l, Figurine of a woman, c. 5000-4500
BC. 500 l, Sistrum, c. 2100-2000 BC. 1000 l,
Spouted vessel with 3-footed pedestal, c.
2000-1750 BC. 1500 l, Ceremonial vessel,
1900-1700 BC.

1991, Feb. 8   **Litho.**   *Perf. 13x12½*
2495 A644 300 l multi   .35 .25
2496 A644 500 l multi   .70 .40
2497 A644 1000 l multi   1.00 .70
2498 A644 1500 l multi   2.00 1.00
    Nos. 2495-2498 (4)   4.05 2.35
    Nos. 2495-2498 are vert.

Lakes of
Turkey
A667

       Wmk. 394
1991, Apr. 24   *Perf. 13*
2499 A667 250 l Abant   .25 .25
2500 A667 500 l Egridir   .60 .25
2501 A667 1500 l Van   1.75 .90
    Nos. 2499-2501 (3)   2.60 1.40

Europa — A668

       Unwmk.
1991, May 6   **Litho.**   *Perf. 13*
2502 A668 1000 l multicolored   9.00 2.00
2503 A668 1500 l multi, diff.   13.50 3.00

Natl. Statistics Day — A669

1991, May 9   *Perf. 13½x13*
2504 A669 500 l multicolored   .75 .25

Eastern Mediterranean Fiber Optic Cable System — A670

1991, May 13
2505 A670 500 l multicolored   .55 .25

European Conf. of Transportation Ministers — A671

1991, May 22   *Perf. 13*
2506 A671 500 l multicolored   .90 .60

Caricature Art A672

500 l, "Amcabey" by Cemal Nadir Guler. 1000 l, "Abdulcanbaz" by Turhan Selcuk, vert.

Wmk. 394
1991, Sept. 11   Litho.   *Perf. 13*
2507 A672 500 l multicolored   .70 .25
2508 A672 1000 l multicolored   1.10 .60

Ceramics A673

Wall facings: 500 l, 13th cent. Seljuk bird. 1500 l, 16th cent. Ottoman floral pattern.

1991, Sept. 23   *Perf. 13½x13*
2509 A673 500 l multicolored   .40 .25
2510 A673 1500 l multicolored   1.40 .65

Symposium on Intl. Protection of Human Rights, Antalya — A674

1991, Oct. 4   *Perf. 13x12½*
2511 A674 500 l multicolored   .75 .25

Southeastern Anatolia Irrigation and Power Project A675

1991, Oct. 6 Unwmk.   *Perf. 13½x13*
2512 A675 500 l multicolored   .75 .25

Turkish Fairy Tales — A676

Baldboy: 500 l, With genie. 1000 l, At party. 1500 l, Plowing field.

1991, Oct. 9   *Perf. 13x13½*
2513 A676 500 l multicolored   .40 .25
2514 A676 1000 l multicolored   .90 .45
2515 A676 1500 l multicolored   1.40 .65
   Nos. 2513-2515 (3)   2.70 1.35

Snakes A677

250 l, Eryx jaculus. 500 l, Elaphe quatuorlineata. 1000 l, Vipera xanthina. 1500 l, Vipera kaznakovi.

Perf. 12½x13
1991, Oct. 23   **Wmk. 394**
2516 A677 250 l multi   2.40 .60
2517 A677 500 l multi   3.50 1.25
2518 A677 1000 l multi   7.25 2.40
2519 A677 1500 l multi   9.50 4.25
   Nos. 2516-2519 (4)   22.65 8.50

World Environment Day.

Antiquities Type of 1989

300 l, Statuette of Mother Goddess, Neolithic, 6000 B.C., vert. 500 l, Hasanoglan statuette, Early Bronze Age, 3000 B.C., vert. 1000 l, Inandik vase, Old Hittite, 18th cent. B.C., vert. 1500 l, Lion statuette, Urartian, 8th cent. B.C., vert.

Wmk. 394
1992, Feb. 12   Litho.   *Perf. 13*
2520 A644 300 l multicolored   .30 .25
2521 A644 500 l multicolored   .40 .25
2522 A644 1000 l multicolored   .80 .40
2523 A644 1500 l multicolored   1.25 .50
   Nos. 2520-2523 (4)   2.75 1.40

Discovery of America, 500th Anniv. A678

2000 l, Balloons, vert.

Wmk. 394
1992, May 4   Litho.   *Perf. 13*
2524 A678 1500 l shown   *4.50 1.00*
2525 A678 2000 l multicolored   *7.50 1.50*
   Europa.

Settlement of Jews in Turkey, 500th Anniv. A679

1992, May 15   *Perf. 12½x13*
2526 A679 1500 l multicolored   1.00 1.00

A681

Wmk. 394
1992, June 1   Litho.   *Perf. 13*
2529 A681 500 l multicolored   .45 .45
Turkish Court of Accounts, 130th anniv.

Economics Congress, Izmir — A682

1992, June 4
2530 A682 1500 l multicolored   .90 .90

World Environment Day — A683

500 l, Vanellus vanellus. 1000 l, Oriolus oriolus. 1500 l, Tadorna tadorna. 2000 l, Halcyon smyrnensis, vert.

1992, June 5   Litho.   *Perf. 13*
2531 A683 500 l multi   .60 .60
2532 A683 1000 l multi   .90 .60
2533 A683 1500 l multi   1.25 .60
2534 A683 2000 l multi   1.75 1.25
   Nos. 2531-2534 (4)   4.50 3.05

Ataturk Type of 1989 and

Kemal Ataturk — A683a   A683b

10,000 l, Full face. 100,000 l, Facing left.

Perf. 13, 14 (#2539, 2541, 2543-2544)
1992-96   Litho.   Unwmk.
2538 A649 250 l gold, brn & org   1.50 .25
2539 A649 5000 l gold & vio   2.00 .40
2540 A649 10,000 l gold & blue   4.50 1.90
2541 A649 20,000 l gold & lil rose   8.00 1.60
2542 A683a 50,000 l multi   4.50 1.75
2543 A683b 50,000 l lake & pink   3.50 .90
2544 A683b 100,000 l grn bl & yel org   4.50 1.75
   Nos. 2538-2544 (7)   28.50 8.55

Issued: 250 l, 10,000 l, 5/28/92; 5000 l, 20,000 l, 9/29/93; #2542, 11/10/94; #2543, 100,000 l, 6/1/96.
For surcharges see Nos. 2655, 2732.

Black Sea Economic Cooperation Summit — A684

Wmk. 394
1992, June 25   Litho.   *Perf. 13*
2545 A684 1500 l multicolored   1.00 .45

1992 Summer Olympics, Barcelona A685

1992, July 25   **Wmk. 394**
2546 A685 500 l Doves   .45 .25
2547 A685 1000 l Boxing   .60 .35
2548 A685 1500 l Weight lifting   1.10 .45
2549 A685 2000 l Wrestling   2.25 .65
   Nos. 2546-2549 (4)   4.40 1.70

Anatolian Folktales — A686

Scenes: 500 l, Woman carrying milk to soldiers. 1000 l, Pouring milk into trough. 1500 l, Soldiers dipping into trough.

Perf. 13x12½
1992, Sept. 23   Litho.   **Wmk. 394**
2550 A686 500 l multicolored   .25 .25
2551 A686 1000 l multicolored   .60 .25
2552 A686 1500 l multicolored   1.00 .45
   Nos. 2550-2552 (3)   1.85 .95

Turkish Handicrafts — A687

500 l, Embroidered flowers. 1000 l, Dolls in traditional costumes, vert. 3000 l, Saddlebags.

1992, Oct. 21   *Perf. 13½x13, 13x13½*
2553 A687 500 l multicolored   .25 .25
2554 A687 1000 l multicolored   .55 .25
2555 A687 3000 l multicolored   1.50 .80
   Nos. 2553-2555 (3)   2.30 1.30

See Nos. 2585-2588, 2611-2612.

Fruits — A688

Wmk. 394
1992, Nov. 25   Litho.   *Perf. 13*
2556 A688 500 l Cherries   .30 .25
2557 A688 1000 l Peaches   .55 .25
2558 A688 3000 l Grapes   1.10 .50
2559 A688 5000 l Apples   2.50 .80
   Nos. 2556-2559 (4)   4.45 1.80

See Nos. 2565-2568.

Famous Men — A689

Designs: No. 2560, Sait Faik Abasiyanik (1906-54), writer. No. 2561, Fikret Mualla Saygi (1904-67), artist. No. 2562, Cevat Sakir Kabaagacli (1886-1973), author. No. 2563, Muhsin Ertugrul (1892-1979), actor and producer. No. 2564, Asik Veysel Satiroglu (1894-1973), composer.

Perf. 14, 13½x13 (#2561, 2564)

1992, Dec. 30   **Litho.**

2560	A689	T multicolored	1.10 .25
2561	A689	T multicolored	1.10 .25
2562	A689	M multicolored	1.50 .25
2563	A689	M multicolored	1.50 .25
2564	A689	M multicolored	1.50 .25
	Nos. 2560-2564 (5)		6.70 1.25

Value on day of issue: Nos. 2560-2561, 500 l. Nos. 2562-2564, 1000 l.
See Nos. 2577-2581.

Fruit Type of 1992
Wmk. 394

1993, Apr. 28   **Litho.**   **Perf. 13**

2565	A688	500 l	Bananas	.50 .30
2566	A688	1000 l	Oranges	.50 .50
2567	A688	3000 l	Pears	1.00 .75
2568	A688	5000 l	Pomegranates	2.00 1.40
	Nos. 2565-2568 (4)			4.00 2.95

Europa — A690

Sculptures by: 1000 l, Hadi Bara. 3000 l, Zuhtu Muridoglu.

1993, May 3

2569	A690	1000 l multicolored	*1.00 .50*
2570	A690	3000 l multicolored	*2.25 .75*

A691

Wmk. 394

1993, July 6   **Litho.**   **Perf. 13**

2571	A691	2500 l lt bl, dk bl & gold	.90 .60

Economic Cooperation Organization Meeting, Istanbul.

Houses — A692

Various houses from Black Sea region.

1993, July 7

2572	A692	1000 l multicolored	.65 .25
2573	A692	2500 l multi, horiz.	.65 .50
2574	A692	3000 l multicolored	1.25 .80
2575	A692	5000 l multi, horiz.	1.40 1.00
	Nos. 2572-2575 (4)		3.95 2.55

See Nos. 2604-2607, 2631-2634, 2647-2650, 2676-2679.

Hodja Ahmet Yesevi (1093-1166), Poet — A693

1993, July 28

2576	A693	3000 l lt bl, dk bl & gold	.85 .35

Famous Men Type of 1992

Designs: No. 2577, Haci Arif Bey (1831-84), composer. No. 2578, Neyzen Tevfik Kolayli (1878-1953), poet. No. 2579, Munir Nurettin Selcuk (1900-81), composer, musician. No. 2580, Cahit Sitki Taranci (1910-56), poet. No. 2581, Orhan Veli Kanik (1914-50), writer.

Perf. 14, 13½x13 (2578-2580)

1993, Aug. 4   **Litho.**   **Unwmk.**

2577	A689	T brown & red brown	1.10 .25
2578	A689	T brown & red brown	1.10 .25
2579	A689	M brown & red brown	1.50 .25
2580	A689	M brown & red brown	1.50 .25
2581	A689	M brown & red brown	1.50 .25
	Nos. 2577-2581 (5)		6.70 1.25

Value on day of issue: Nos. 2577-2578, 500 l. Nos. 2579-2581, 1000 l.

Istanbul, Proposed Site for 2000 Olympics A694

1993, Aug. 11   **Perf. 12½x13**

2582	A694	2500 l multicolored	.90 .45

Protection of Mediterranean Sea Against Pollution — A695

1000 l, Amphora on sea floor. 3000 l, Dolphin jumping.

Unwmk.

1993, Oct. 12   **Litho.**   **Perf. 13**

2583	A695	1000 l multicolored	.25 .25
2584	A695	3000 l multicolored	1.60 .65

Handicrafts Type of 1992
Perf. 12½x13, 13x12½

1993, Oct. 21   **Wmk. 394**

2585	A687	1000 l	Painted rug	.25 .25
2586	A687	2500 l	Earrings	.75 .25
2587	A687	5000 l	Money purse, vert.	1.60 .75
	Nos. 2585-2587 (3)			2.60 1.25

Republic, 70th Anniv. — A696

1993, Oct. 29   **Wmk. 394**   **Perf. 13**

2588	A696	1000 l multicolored	.50 .35

Civil Defence Organization — A697

Perf. 12½x13

1993, Nov. 25   **Unwmk.**

2589	A697	1000 l multicolored	.50 .35

Turksat Satellite — A698

Designs: 1500 l, Satellite, globe, map of Turkey. 5000 l, Satellite transmissions to areas in Europe and Asia.

Perf. 13x13½

1994, Jan. 21   **Litho.**   **Wmk. 394**

2590	A698	1500 l multicolored	.25 .25
2591	A698	5000 l multicolored	1.10 .25

Natl. Water Project — A699

1994, Feb. 28   **Perf. 13x12½**

2592	A699	1500 l multicolored	.60 .35

Native Cuisine A700

1000 l, Ezogel in corbasi. 1500 l, Mixed dolma. 3500 l, Shish kebabs. 5000 l, Baklava.

Perf. 12½x13

1994, Mar. 23   **Litho.**   **Wmk. 394**

2593	A700	1000 l	multi	.65 .65
2594	A700	1500 l	multi	.65 .65
2595	A700	3500 l	multi	.65 .65
2596	A700	5000 l	multi	1.25 .65
	Nos. 2593-2596 (4)			3.20 2.60

Europa A701

1500 l, Marie Curie (1867-1934), chemist, vert. 5000 l, Albert Einstein (1879-1955), physicist.

Unwmk.

1994, May 2   **Litho.**   **Perf. 13**

2597	A701	1500 l multicolored	*.50 .50*
2598	A701	5000 l multicolored	*1.50 1.50*

World Environment Day — A703

Views of: 6000 l, Antalya. 8500 l, Mugla, vert.

Wmk. 394

1994, June 5   **Litho.**   **Perf. 13**

2602	A703	6000 l multicolored	1.00 .75
2603	A703	8500 l multicolored	1.75 1.10

Houses Type of 1993

2500 l, 2-story housing complex. 3500 l, 3-story home with balconies. 6000 l, Tri-level country home. 8500 l, 2-story home.

1994, July 7

2604	A692	2500 l	multi, horiz.	.60 .60
2605	A692	3500 l	multi, horiz.	.60 .60
2606	A692	6000 l	multi, horiz.	.60 .60
2607	A692	8500 l	multi, horiz.	1.75 .60
	Nos. 2604-2607 (4)			3.55 2.40

Tourism A704

1994, Aug. 3

2608	A704	5000 l	Hiking	.75 .45
2609	A704	10,000 l	Rafting	1.50 .75

Project of the Year 2001 A705

1994, Aug. 27

2610	A705	2500 l multicolored	.65 .50

Handicrafts Type of 1992

Designs: 7500 l, Kusak pattern used on 18th cent. clothing, vert. 12,000 l, Pacalik pattern used on 19th cent. clothing.

1994, Oct. 21

2611	A687	7500 l multicolored	.90 .50
2612	A687	12,500 l multicolored	1.60 1.60

Mushrooms — A706

2500 l, Morchella conica. 5000 l, Agaricus bernardii. 7500 l, Lactarius deliciosus. 12,500 l, Macrolepiota procera.

1994, Nov. 16

2613	A706	2500 l	multi	.50 .50
2614	A706	5000 l	multi	.90 .90
2615	A706	7500 l	multi	1.60 1.60
2616	A706	12,500 l	multi	3.25 3.25
	Nos. 2613-2616 (4)			6.25 6.25

See Nos. 2637-2640.

Antiquities Type of 1989

Lydian Treasures, 6th cent. B.C.: 2500 l, Silver pitcher, vert. 5000 l, Silver incense burner, vert. 7500 l, Gold, glass necklace. 12,500 l, Gold brooch.

1994, Dec. 7

2617	A644	2500 l multicolored	.50 .40
2618	A644	5000 l multicolored	.75 .45
2619	A644	7500 l multicolored	1.10 .85
2620	A644	12,500 l multicolored	2.00 .85
	Nos. 2617-2620 (4)		4.35 2.35

Nevruz, New Day A707

1995, Mar. 21

2621	A707	3500 l multicolored	.65 .45

Europa — A708

1995, May 5
2622 A708 3500 l Flowers 1.00 1.00
2623 A708 15,000 l Olive branch 2.00 2.00

Istanbul '96 World Stamp
Exhibition — A709

a, 7000 l, Buildings. b, 25,000 l, Tower, buildings. c, 7000 l, Mosque, city along harbor. c, 25,000 l, Residential area, mosque, harbor.

1995, May 24
2624 A709 Block of 4, #a.-d. 6.00 4.50
Nos. 2624a-2624b and 2624c-2624d are each continuous designs.

European Nature Conservation
Year — A710

5000 l, Field of poppies. 15,000 l, Trees. 25,000 l, Mountain valley.

1995, June 5
2625 A710 5000 l multi .40 .25
2626 A710 15,000 l multi 1.25 .60
2627 A710 25,000 l multi 2.00 1.00
Nos. 2625-2627 (3) 3.65 1.85

Motion Pictures,
Cent. — A711

1995, Feb. 1
2628 A711 15,000 l red & blue 1.75 1.25

A712

1995, Apr. 23
2629 A712 5000 l multicolored .65 .45
1sh Conference of the Moslem Women Parliamentaries, Pakistan.

Houses Type of 1993

5000 l, 2-story block house. 10,000 l, Tower of part-stone house. 15,000 l, Interior view of 2-story house, horiz. 20,000 l, Three unit-connecting apartment, horiz.

1995, July 7
2631 A692 5000 l multicolored .75 .35
2632 A692 10,000 l multicolored 1.10 .40
2633 A692 15,000 l multicolored 1.25 .55
2634 A692 20,000 l multicolored 1.40 1.10
Nos. 2631-2634 (4) 4.50 2.40

UN, 50th
Anniv. — A713

1995, Oct. 24
2635 A713 15,000 l shown .75 .40
2636 A713 30,000 l UN emblem, "50" 1.50 .80

Mushroom Type of 1994

Designs: 5000 l, Amanita phalloides. 10,000 l, Lepiota helveola. 20,000 l, Gyromitra esculenta. 30,000 l, Amanita gemmata.

1995, Nov. 16
2637 A706 5000 l multicolored .65 .65
2638 A706 10,000 l multicolored 1.10 1.10
2639 A706 20,000 l multicolored 2.25 2.25
2640 A706 30,000 l multicolored 2.50 2.50
Nos. 2637-2640 (4) 6.50 6.50

Children's
Rights
A714

6,000 l, Rainbow, hearts, flower, sun in sky. 10,000 l, Child's hand drawing letter "A."

1996, Mar. 13
2641 A714 6,000 l multicolored .35 .25
2642 A714 10,000 l multicolored .90 .65

Fauna — A715

Designs: a, 5,000 l, Bee. b, 10,000 l, Dog. c, 15,000 l, Rooster. d, 30,000 l, Fish.

1996, Apr. 10 **Unwmk.**
2643 A715 Sheet of 4, #a.-d. 4.50 4.50
ISTANBUL '96.

Famous
Women
A716

10,000 l, Nene Hatun. 40,000 l, Halide Edip Adivar.

Perf. 12½x13
1996, May 5 **Litho.** **Unwmk.**
2644 A716 10,000 l multi 1.25 .75
2645 A716 40,000 l multi 2.00 1.50
Europa.

World Environment Day — A717

Unwmk.
1996, June 3 **Litho.** **Perf. 13**
2646 A717 50,000 l multicolored 1.60 .80

Houses Type of 1993

Designs: 10,000 l, Tri-level block house, horiz. 15,000 l, Two story with bay window, gate at entrance to side courtyard, horiz. 25,000 l, Two story townhouse, double wooden doors at bottom. 50,000 l, Flat-roofed, two-story townhouse.

1996, July 7 **Perf. 13**
2647 A692 10,000 l multicolored .45 .25
2648 A692 15,000 l multicolored .75 .35
2649 A692 25,000 l multicolored 1.00 .55
2650 A692 50,000 l multicolored 2.10 1.10
Nos. 2647-2650 (4) 4.30 2.25

1996 Summer Olympic Games,
Atlanta — A718

a, 10,000 l, Archery. b, 15,000 l, Wrestling. c, 25,000 l, Weight lifting. d, 50,000 l, Hurdles.

1996, July 19
2651 A718 Sheet of 4, #a.-d. 6.00 6.00
ISTANBUL '96.

Turkish
Press,
50th
Anniv.
A719

1996, July 24 **Perf. 12½x13**
2652 A719 15,000 l multicolored .60 .30

Euro '96, European Soccer
Championships, Great Britain — A720

15,000 l, Player, vert. 50,000 l, Soccer ball, flags.

1996, June 8 **Perf. 13**
2653 A720 15,000 l multi 1.10 .45
2654 A720 50,000 l multi 2.50 1.25

Nos. 2447, 2491, 2493-2494, 2538
Surcharged in Orange or Deep
Violet Blue

or

Perfs., Printing Methods as Before
1996, July 22
2655 A649 T on 250 l #2538
(O) 1.25 .25
2656 A649 T on 2000 l #2447 1.25 .25
2657 A666 M on 200 l #2491 2.00 .25
2658 A666 M on 400 l #2493 2.00 .25
2659 A666 M on 1500 l #2494 2.00 .25
Nos. 2655-2659 (5) 8.50 1.25
Nos. 2655-2656 and 2657-2659 had face values of 10,000 l and 15,000 l on day of issue.
See No. 2732.

Methods of Transportation — A721

a, 25,000 l, Airplane (b). b, 50,000 l, Helicopter, ship (d). c, 75,000 l, Train. d, 100,000 l, Bus (c).

Unwmk.
1996, Sept. 27 **Litho.** **Perf. 13**
2660 A721 Sheet of 4, #a.-d. 12.00 12.00
ISTANBUL '96. Exists imperf. Value, $85.

New Year
A722

Unwmk.
1996, Oct. 23 **Litho.** **Perf. 13**
2661 A722 15,000 l multicolored .55 .30

Social and
Cultural
Heritage
A723

10,000 l, Public Library, Bayezit, Amasya. 15,000 l, Mosque and hospital, Divrigi.

1996, Dec. 17 **Litho.** **Perf. 13**
2662 A723 10,000 l multicolored .35 .35
2663 A723 15,000 l multicolored .55 .55

Stories and Legends — A724

Europa: 25,000 l, Little children dressed in flowers and leaves riding a giant peacock. 70,000 l, Genie, man being riding a giant bird.

1997, May 5 **Litho.** **Perf. 13**
2664 A724 25,000 l multicolored 1.25 1.25
2665 A724 70,000 l multicolored 2.50 2.50

White Cat — A725

Designs: a, 25,000 l, Tail, hindquarters. b, 50,000 l, Back legs. c, 75,000 l, Front legs. d, 150,000 l, Face.

1997, Apr. 23
2666 A725 Sheet of 4, #a.-d. 8.00 8.00

Language
Day — A726

1997, May 13 **Litho.** *Perf. 13*
2667 A726 25,000 l multicolored .50 .50

World Environment Day — A727

1997, June 5
2668 A727 35,000 l multicolored 1.00 .90

Orchids — A728

Designs: 25,000 l, Ophrys tenthredinifera. 70,000 l, Ophrys apifera.

1997, May 28
2669 A728 25,000 l multicolored .80 .25
2670 A728 70,000 l multicolored 1.90 .55

25th Intl.
Istanbul
Festival
A729

1997, June 13 *Perf. 13½*
Background Color
2671 A729 15,000 l blue .25 .25
2672 A729 25,000 l pink .55 .45
2673 A729 70,000 l blue green 1.40 1.20
2674 A729 75,000 l purple 1.75 1.50
2675 A729 100,000 l green blue 2.40 2.00
  Nos. 2671-2675 (5) 6.35 5.40

House Type of 1993
Inscribed: 25,000 l, Bir Urfa Evi, vert. 40,000 l, Bir Mardin Evi. 80,000 l, Bir Diyarbakir Evi. 100,000 l, Kemaliye'de Bir Ev, vert.

1997, July 7 **Litho.** *Perf. 13*
2676 A692 25,000 l multicolored .50 .50
2677 A692 40,000 l multicolored .90 .90
2678 A692 80,000 l multicolored 1.75 1.75
2679 A692 100,000 l multicolored 2.25 2.25
  Nos. 2676-2679 (4) 5.40 5.40

A730

Flowers: 40,000 l, Lilium candidum. 100,000 l, Euphorbia pulcherima.

1997, Sept. 8 **Litho.** *Perf. 13*
2680 A730 40,000 l multicolored .75 .25
2681 A730 100,000 l multicolored 2.00 .65

A731

World Air Games: No. 2682, Hang gliding. No. 2683, Sailplane. No. 2684, Man pointing up at biplanes. No. 2685, Hot air balloon.

1997, Sept. 13
2682 A731 40,000 l multi 1.00 .65
2683 A731 40,000 l multi 1.00 .65
2684 A731 100,000 l multi 3.00 2.00
2685 A731 100,000 l multi 4.00 3.00
  Nos. 2682-2685 (4) 9.00 6.30

Forestry
Congress
A732

1997, Oct. 13 **Litho.** *Perf. 13*
2686 A732 50,000 l multicolored 1.00 .80

15th European
Gymnastics
Congress — A733

1997, Oct. 13
2687 A733 100,000 l multicolored 2.25 1.90

Traditional
Women's
Headcovers
A734

1997, Nov. 19 **Litho.** *Perf. 13*
2688 A734 50,000 l Gaziantep 1.40 .70
2689 A734 50,000 l Canakkale 1.40 .70
2690 A734 100,000 l Isparta 2.25 1.25
2691 A734 100,000 l Bursa 2.25 1.25
  Nos. 2688-2691 (4) 7.30 3.90

See Nos. 2711-2714, 2748-2751, 2765-2768, 2790-2793.

1998 Winter Olympic Games,
Nagano — A735

Slalom skiers: No. 2692, #1 on bib. No. 2693, #119 on bib.

1998, Feb. 7 **Litho.** *Perf. 13*
2692 125,000 l multicolored 1.75 1.50
2693 125,000 l multicolored 1.75 1.50
  a. A735 Pair, #2692-2693 4.00 4.00

Intl. Year of the Ocean — A736

Designs: a, 50,000 l, Turtle, jellyfish. b, 75,000 l, Fish, octopus. c, 125,000 l, Coral, crab. d, 125,000 l, Fish, coral, starfish.

1998, Apr. 18 **Litho.** *Perf. 13*
2694 A736 Sheet of 4, #a.-d. 6.00 6.00

Dardenelles
Campaign — A737

Memorial Statues: #2695, "Mother with Children," Natl. War Memorial, Wellington. #2696, "With Great Respect to the Mehmetcik, Gallipoli" (Turkish soldier carrying wounded ANZAC).

1998, Mar. 18 **Litho.** *Perf. 13*
2695 A737 125,000 l multicolored 1.75 1.75
2696 A737 125,000 l multicolored 1.75 1.75

See New Zealand Nos. 1400-1401.

A738

Europa (National Festivals and Holidays): 100,000 l, Kemal Ataturk, natl. flag, people celebrating. 150,000 l, Ataturk, natl. flag, children of different races celebrating together.

1998, May 5
2697 A738 100,000 l multicolored *1.25* *1.25*
2698 A738 150,000 l multicolored *2.25* *2.25*

A739

Tulips: 50,000 l, Sylvestris. 75,000 l, Armena (pink). 100,000 l, Armena (violet). 125,000 l, Saxatilis.

1998, May 1 **Litho.** *Perf. 13*
2699 A739 50,000 l multicolored .75 .75
2700 A739 75,000 l multicolored 1.60 1.60
2701 A739 100,000 l multicolored 1.90 1.90
2702 A739 125,000 l multicolored 3.00 3.00
  Nos. 2699-2702 (4) 7.25 7.25

Souvenir Sheet

World Environment Day — A740

Owls: a, Two on branches. b, One flying, one standing.

1998, June 5 **Litho.** *Perf. 13½*
2703 A740 150,000 l Sheet of 2,
    #a.-b. 6.25 4.00

Contemporary Arts — A741

75,000 l, Couple dancing. 100,000 l, Man playing cello. 150,000 l, Ballerina.

1998, Aug. 14 **Litho.** *Perf. 13*
2704 A741 75,000 l multi 1.00 .50
2705 A741 100,000 l multi, vert. 1.25 .70
2706 A741 150,000 l multi, vert. 1.90 1.10
  Nos. 2704-2706 (3) 4.15 2.30

Kemal
Ataturk — A742

1998, Aug. 20 **Litho.** *Perf. 13*
2707 A742 150,000 l cl & brn 1.60 .65
2708 A742 175,000 l bl & rose
    brn 2.25 .85
2709 A742 250,000 l brn & cl 3.00 1.25
2710 A742 500,000 l brn & dk
    bl 6.50 2.50
  Nos. 2707-2710 (4) 13.35 5.25

Women's Headcovers Type of 1997
1998, Nov. 24 **Litho.** *Perf. 13*
2711 A734 75,000 l Afyon .85 .40
2712 A734 75,000 l Ankara .85 .40
2713 A734 175,000 l Mus 1.90 .95
2714 A734 175,000 l Mugla 1.90 .95
  Nos. 2711-2714 (4) 5.50 2.70

Turkish Republic, 75th Anniv. — A743

275,000 l, Flag, silhouette of Ataturk.

1998, Oct. 29 **Litho.** *Perf. 13*
2715 A743 175,000 l shown 1.75 .90
  a. Souvenir sheet of 1, imperf. 1.75 1.25
2716 A743 275,000 l red & blk 2.75 1.40
  a. Souvenir sheet of 1, imperf. 3.75 2.00

Nos. 2715a, 2716a have simulated perforations.

Famous
People
A744

#2717, Ihap Hulusi Görey (1898-1986). #2718, Bedia Muvahhit (1897-1993). No. 2719, Feza Gürsey (1921-92). #2720, Haldun Taner (1915-86). #2721, Vasfi Riza Zobu (1902-92).

1998, Dec. 31   Photo.   Perf. 13
2717	A744	M gray bl, bl & plum	1.40	.30
2718	A744	M lil, dp lil & plum	1.40	.30
2719	A744	T org, brn & plum	1.75	.50
2720	A744	T gray vio, vio & plum	1.75	.50
2721	A744	T grn, blk & plum	1.75	.50
	Nos. 2717-2721 (5)		8.05	2.10

On day of issue, Nos. 2717-2718 were valued at 50,000 l each, and Nos. 2719-2721 were valued at 75,000 l each.

NATO, 50th Anniv. A745

1999, Apr. 4   Litho.   Perf. 13
2722 A745 200,000 l multicolored 2.00 1.50

Ottoman Empire, 700th Anniv. A746

Designs: No. 2723, Man on horse surrounded by people in buildings. No. 2724, Man on horse, three men in foreground. No. 2725, Men seated.
No. 2726, Man on white horse, castle. No. 2727, Group of women, horiz.

1999, Apr. 12
2723	A746	175,000 l multicolored	1.75	1.25
2724	A746	175,000 l multicolored	1.75	1.25
2725	A746	175,000 l multicolored	1.75	1.25
	Nos. 2723-2725 (3)		5.25	3.75

Size: 79x119mm, 119x79mm
Imperf
2726 A746 200,000 l multicolored 3.00 2.75
2727 A746 200,000 l multicolored 3.00 2.75

Europa A747

Natl. Parks: 175,000 l, Köprülü Canyon, vert. 200,000 l, Kackarlar.

Perf. 13¼x13, 13x13¼
1999, May 5   Litho.
2728 A747 175,000 l multicolored 2.00 2.00
2729 A747 200,000 l multicolored 2.00 2.00

World Environment Day — A748

No. 2730: a, 100,000 l, Tetrax tetrax. 200,000 l, Hoplopterus spinosus.
No. 2731: a, 100,000 l, Marbled duck. b, 200,000 l, Sitta kruperi.

1999, June 3   Litho.   Perf. 13¼
2730 A748 Sheet of 2, #a.-b. 5.00 2.50
2731 A748 Sheet of 2, #a.-b. 5.00 2.50

See Nos. 2763-2764, 2800-2801.

No. 2538 Surcharged in Violet Blue

1999   Litho.   Perf. 13
2732 A649 T on 250 l #2537 .75 .40

No. 2732 sold for 50,000 l on day of issue.

Souvenir Sheet

National Congress During the War for Independence — A749

Designs: a, 100,000 l, Ataturk, two other men, building. b, 100,000 l, Ataturk, two other men seated. c, 200,000 l, Two men standing in front of building. d, 200,000 l, Ataturk standing in front of building.

Perf. 13¼x13
1999, June 22   Litho.   Unwmk.
2733 A749 Sheet of 4, #a.-d. 6.25 6.25

Art — A750

1999, July 8   Litho.   Perf. 13x13¼
2734 A750 250,000 l shown 2.25 1.10
2735 A750 250,000 l multi, diff. 2.25 1.10

Tourism — A751

No. 2736, Temple to Zeus. No. 2737, Antakya Archaelogical Museum, horiz. No. 2738, Golf course, Antalya. No. 2739, Sailboat off Bodrum.

Perf. 13x13¼, 13¼x13
1999, Sept. 19   Litho.
2736	A751	125,000 l multi	1.40	1.40
2737	A751	125,000 l multi	1.40	1.40
2738	A751	225,000 l multi	2.10	2.10
2739	A751	225,000 l multi	2.10	2.10
	Nos. 2736-2739 (4)		7.00	7.00

Dams A752

225,000 l, Cubuk 1. 250,000 l, Ataturk.

1999, Sept. 19   Litho.   Perf. 13¼x13
2740 A752 225,000 l multi 2.25 2.25
2741 A752 250,000 l multi 2.25 2.25

Kemal Atatürk — A753

1999, Sept. 27   Litho.   Perf. 13¾
2742	A753	225,000 l grn & brn	2.50	.55
2743	A753	250,000 l brn & lil	2.50	.65
2744	A753	500,000 l pink & grn	3.75	1.40
2745	A753	1,000,000 l bl & red	9.00	4.00
	Nos. 2742-2745 (4)		17.75	6.60

Thanks for Earthquake Rescue Efforts — A754

Designs: 225,000 l, Hands holding wreckage, flowers, vert. 250,000 l, Rescuers, handclasp.

Perf. 13¼x13, 13x13¼
1999, Oct. 15   Litho.
2746 A754 225,000 l multi 1.25 .65
2747 A754 250,000 l multi 1.50 .75

Women's Headcovers Type of 1997
1999, Nov. 24   Litho.   Perf. 13¼
2748	A734	150,000 l Manisa	1.10	.55
2749	A734	150,000 l Nigde	1.10	.55
2750	A734	250,000 l Antalya	2.00	.90
2751	A734	250,000 l Amasya	2.00	.90
	Nos. 2748-2751 (4)		6.20	2.90

Caravansaries — A755

1999, Dec. 24   Litho.   Perf. 13¼x13
2752 A755 150,000 l Sarapsa .85 .25
2753 A755 250,000 l Obruk 1.75 .45

Millennium A756

Designs: 275,000 l, Earth, brain, satellite. 300,000 l, Monachus monachus.

2000, Feb. 1   Litho.   Perf. 13¼
2754 A756 275,000 l multi 2.00 2.00
2755 A756 300,000 l multi 2.00 2.00

Merchant Ships A757

125,000 l, Bug. 150,000 l, Gülcemal. 275,000 l, Nusret. 300,000 l, Bandirma.

2000, Mar. 16
2756	A757	125,000 l multi	.65	.65
2757	A757	150,000 l multi	.90	.90
2758	A757	275,000 l multi	2.40	2.40
2759	A757	300,000 l multi	2.75	2.75
	Nos. 2756-2759 (4)		6.70	6.70

See Nos. 2813-2816, 2840-2843.

Grand National Assembly, 80th Anniv. — A758

300,000 l, Sprouts, horiz.

Perf. 13x13¼, 13¼x13
2000, Apr. 23   Litho.
2760 A758 275,000 l shown 2.00 1.00
2761 A758 300,000 l multi 2.25 1.10

Europa, 2000
Common Design Type
2000, May 9   Perf. 13x13¼
2762 CD17 300,000 l multi 2.75 2.00

World Environment Day Type of 1999
Souvenir Sheets
No. 2763, 275,000 l: a, Aquila heliaca. b, Picus viridis.
No. 2764, 275,000 l: a, Oxyura leucocephala. b, Recurvirostra avosetta.

2000, June 5   Litho.   Perf. 13¼
Sheets of 2, #a-b
2763-2764 A748 Set of 2 14.00 14.00

Women's Headcover Type of 1997
Designs: No. 2765, 275,000 l, Trabzon. No. 2766, 275,000 l, Tunceli. No. 2767, 275,000 l, Corum. No. 2768, 275,000 l, Izmir.

2000, July 15
2765-2768 A734 Set of 4 6.50 6.50

Souvenir Sheet

Nomadic Life — A759

a, Woman at loom, woman seated. b, Women & containers. c, Women, 2 goats, carpet on tent rope. d, Woman, children, 6 goats, carpet on rope.

2000
2769 A759 Sheet of 4 9.00 9.00
a.-d. 300,000 l Any single 1.60 1.60

Military Leaders — A760

Designs: 100,000 l, Gen. Yakup Sevki Subasi. 200,000 l, Lt. Gen. Musa Kazim Karabekir (c. 1882-1948). 275,000 l, Marshal Mustafa Fevzi Cakmak (1876-1950). 300,000 l, Gen. Cevat Cobanli (1871-1938).

2000
2770-2773 A760 Set of 4 5.50 5.50

2000 Summer Olympics, Sydney A761

Designs: 125,000 l, Rhythmic gymnastics. 150,000 l, Swimming. 275,000 l, High jump. 300,000 l, Archery.

2000
2774-2777 A761 Set of 4 5.50 5.50

Crocuses — A762

Designs: 250,000 l, Crocus chrysanthus. 275,000 l, Crocus olivieri. 300,000 l, Crocus biflorus. 1,250,000 l, Crocus sativus.

2000, Oct. 9 **Litho.** **Perf. 13¾x14**
2778-2781 A762 Set of 4 12.00 5.50

Architecture — A763

Designs: 200,000 l, Arslan Baba. 275,000 l, Karasaç Ana. 300,000 l, Hoca Ahmet Yesevi.

2000, Oct. 19 **Litho.** **Perf. 13¼x13**
2782-2784 A763 Set of 3 8.00 8.00

Turksat 2A — A764

2001, Jan. 25 **Litho.** **Perf. 13x13¾**
2785 A764 200,000 l multi 1.25 1.25

Women's Clothing — A765

Designs: No. 2786, 200,000 l, Afyon. No. 2787, 200,000 l, Balikesir. No. 2788, 325,000 l, Kars. No. 2789, 325,000 l, Tokat.

2001, Mar. 19 Set of 4 6.25 6.25
See Nos. 2822-2825, 2757-2760, 2880-2883.

Women's Headcovers Type of 1997
Designs: 200,000 l, Mersin-Silifke. 250,000 l, Sivas. 425,000 l, Aydin. 450,000 l, Hakkari.

2001, Apr. 16 **Litho.** **Perf. 13¼**
2790-2793 A734 Set of 4 7.25 7.25

Europa — A766

Waterfalls: 450,000 l, Düdenbasi. 500,000 l, Yerköprü.

2001, May 5 **Perf. 13**
2794-2795 A766 Set of 2 4.00 3.00

Aviators A767

Designs: 250,000 l, Capt. Ismail Hakki Bey. 300,000 l, Lieut. Nuri Bey. 450,000 l, Lieut. Sadik Bey. 500,000 l, Capt. Fethi Bey.

2001, May 15 Set of 4 6.00 5.00
2796-2799 A767

World Environment Day Type of 1999
No. 2800, 300,000 l: a, Turdus pilaris. b, Carduelis carduelis.
No. 2801, 450,000 l: a, Merops apiaster. b, Upupa epops.

2001, June 5 **Perf. 13¼**
Sheets of 2, #a-b
2800-2801 A748 Set of 2 7.00 7.00

Kemal Ataturk — A768

Ataturk (1881-1938) and: 300,000 l, Turkish flag. 450,000 l, Birthplace.

2001, May 19 **Litho.** **Perf. 13**
2802-2803 A768 Set of 2 3.25 3.25

Medicinal Plants — A769

Designs: 250,000 l, Myrtus communis. 300,000 l, Achillea millefolium. 450,000 l, Hypericum perforatum. 500,000 l, Rosa moyesii. 1,750,000 l, Crataegus oxyacantha.

2001, June 27 **Perf. 13¾**
2804-2808 A769 Set of 5 11.00 2.50

Horses A770

Designs: 300,000 l, Horse and foal. No. 2810, 450,000 l, Three horses. No. 2811, 450,000 l, Two horses galloping. 500,000 l, Horse, vert.

2001, July 16 **Perf. 13**
2809-2812 A770 Set of 4 5.50 5.50

Merchant Ships Type of 2000
Designs: 250,000 l, Resitpasa. No. 2814, 300,000 l, Mithatpasa. No. 2815, 300,000 l, Gülnihal, 500,000 l, Aydin.

2001, Sept. 3 **Perf. 13¼**
2813-2816 A757 Set of 4 5.00 5.00

Architecture A771

Designs: No. 2817, 300,000 l, Sirvansahlar Palace, Baku, Azerbaijan. No. 2818, 300,000 l, Sultan Tekes Mausoleum, Urgench, Uzbekistan. 450,000 l, Timur Mausoleum, Samarkand, Uzbekistan. 500,000 l, While Tlightning Mausoleum, Bursa.

2001, Oct. 15 Set of 4 6.25 6.25
2817-2820 A771

Sultan Nevruz A772

2002, Mar. 21 **Litho.** **Perf. 13¼**
2821 A772 400,000 l multi 2.25 2.25

Women's Clothing Type of 2001
Designs: 350,000 l, Kastamonu. 400,000 l, Canakkale. 500,000 l, Amasya-Ilisu. 600,000 l, Elazig.

2002, Apr. 16 **Perf. 13x13¼**
2822-2825 A765 Set of 4 7.25 7.25

Europa — A773

2002, May 5 **Litho.** **Perf. 13x13¼**
2826 A773 500,000 l multi 2.50 1.50

2002 World Cup Soccer Championships, Japan and Korea — A774

Designs: 400,000 l, Players, referee. 600,000 l, Crowd, player making scissors kick.

2002, May 31 **Litho.** **Perf. 13¼x13**
2827-2828 A774 Set of 2 4.50 4.50

Famous Men — A775

Designs: 100,000 l, Muzaffer Sarisözen (1898-1963), musician. 400,000 l, Arif Nihat Asya (1904-75), writer. 500,000 l, Vedat Tek (1873-1942), architect. 600,000 l, Hilmi Ziya Ulken (1901-74), philosopher. 2,500,000 l, Ibrahim Calli (1882-1960), painter.

2002, June 3 **Perf. 13¾x14**
2829-2833 A775 Set of 5 16.00 5.50

Souvenir Sheet

Wild Cats — A776

No. 2834: a, Panthera pardus tulliana. b, Lynx lynx. c, Panthera tigris. d, Caracal caracal.

2002, June 20 **Perf. 13¼x13**
2834 A776 400,000 l Sheet of 4, #a-d 9.00 9.00

Souvenir Sheet

Shells — A777

Various shells: a, 400,000 l. b, 500,000 l. c, 600,000 l. d, 750,000 l.

2002, June 25
2835 A777 Sheet of 4, #a-d 9.00 9.00

Third Place Finish of Turkish Team in World Cup Soccer Championships — A778

Designs: 400,000 l, Players in action. 700,000 l, Team photo.

2002, July 29 **Perf. 13x13¼**
2836-2837 A778 Set of 2 4.50 4.50

String Instruments A779

Designs: 450,000 l, Violin. 700,000 l, Bass.

2002, Oct. 10 **Perf. 13¼x13**
2838-2839 A779 Set of 2 4.50 4.50

Merchant Ships Type of 2000
Designs: 450,000 l, Ege. 500,000 l, Ayvalik. No. 2842, 700,000 l, Karadeniz. No. 2843, 700,000 l, Marakaz.

2002, Nov. 4 **Litho.** **Perf. 13**
2840-2843 A757 Set of 4 8.00 8.00

Souvenir Sheet

Turkish and Hungarian Buildings — A780

No. 2844: a, 450,000 l, Gazi Kassim Pasha Mosque, Pécs, Hungary. b, 700,000 l, Rakoczi House, Tekirdag, Turkey.

2002, Dec. 2 **Litho.** **Perf. 13¼**
2844 A780 Sheet of 2, #a-b 4.50 4.50
See Hungary Nos. 3819-3820.

BJK Soccer Team, Cent. — A781

Team emblem and: 500,000 l, Eagle, Turkish and team flags. 700,000 l, Eagle, stadium. 750,000 l, Soccer players. 1,000,000 l, Eagle's head.

2003, Mar. 3 **Perf. 13x13¼**
2845-2848 A781 Set of 4 8.00 8.00

A782

Europa: 500,000 l, Travel poster. 700,000 l, Ankara State Theater poster.

2003, May 9 **Litho.** **Perf. 13**
2849-2850 A782 Set of 2 3.00 3.00

A783

Conquest of Constantinople, 550th Anniv.: No. 2851, 500,000 l, Leaders at table. No. 2852, 500,000 l, Sultan Mehmet II seated. 700,000 l, Robe. 1,500,000 l, Sultan Mehmet II and cartouche.

2003, May 29
2851-2854 A783 Set of 4 7.25 7.25

Souvenir Sheet

World Environment Day — A784

No. 2855: a, Gazella subgutturosa. b, Cervus elaphus. c, Capreolus capreolus. d, Cervus dama.

2003, June 5
2855 A784 500,000 l Sheet of 4,
#a-d 6.25 6.25

Zodiac
A785

2003, June 19 **Perf. 13¼**
2856 A785 500,000 l multi 1.40 1.40

Women's Clothing Type of 2001
Designs: No. 2857, 500,000 l, Sivas. No. 2858, 500,000 l, Gaziantep. No. 2859, 700,000 l, Erzincan. No. 2860, 700,000 l, Ankara-Beypazari.

2003, July 8 **Perf. 13**
2857-2860 A765 Set of 4 7.25 7.25

Fruit Blossoms — A786

Blossoms: 500,000 l, Ayva cicegi (quince). 700,000 l, Erik cicegi (plum). 750,000 l, Kiraz cicegi (cherry). 1,000,000 l, Nar cicegi (pomegranate). 3,000,000 l, Portakal cicegi (orange).

2003, July 25 **Perf. 13¾x14**
2861-2865 A786 Set of 5 13.50 7.25

Brass Instruments A787

Designs: 600,000 l, French horn. 800,000 l, Trumpet.

2003, Sept. 23 **Litho.** **Perf. 13¼x13**
2866-2867 A787 Set of 2 4.50 4.50

Republic of Turkey, 80th Anniv. A788

Kemal Ataturk, flag and: No. 2868, 600,000 l, Cavalry. No. 2869, 600,000 l, Buildings.

2003, Oct. 29 **Litho.** **Perf. 13¼x13**
2868-2869 A788 Set of 2 3.50 3.50

Navy Ships A789

Designs: No. 2870, 600,000 l, Karadeniz. No. 2871, 600,000 l, Gediz. No. 2872, 700,000 l, Salihreis. No. 2873, 700,000 l, Kocatepe.

2003, Nov. 14
2870-2873 A789 Set of 4 9.00 9.00

Agriculture Bank, 140th Anniv. — A790

2003, Nov. 20 **Perf. 13x13¼**
2874 A790 600,000 l multi 1.75 1.75

Buildings Associated with Kemal Ataturk — A791

Designs: 600,000 l, House, Trabzon. 700,000 l, Museum, Sakarya. 800,000 l, House, Selanik. 1,000,000 l, Museum, Ankara.

2003, Dec. 12
2875-2878 A791 Set of 4 7.25 7.25

PTT Bank — A792

2004, Mar. 3 **Perf. 14**
2879 A792 600,000 l multi 1.75 .80

Women's Clothing Type of 2001
Designs: 600,000 l, Edirne. No. 2881, 700,000 l, Tunceli. No. 2882, 700,000 l, Burdur. 800,000 l, Trabzon.

2004, Apr. 30 **Perf. 13x13¼**
2880-2883 A765 Set of 4 7.25 7.25

Europa — A793

Designs: 700,000 l, Skier, windsurfer. 800,000 l, Tourist at archaeological ruins, ships.

2004, May 9
2884-2885 A793 Set of 2 3.00 3.00

Souvenir Sheet

World Environment Day — A794

No. 2886: a, Falco tinnunculus. b, Buteo buteo. c, Aquila chrysaetos. d, Milvus migrans.

2004, June 5 **Perf. 13¼x13**
2886 A794 700,000 l Sheet of 4,
#a-d 7.00 6.25

Caravansaries — A795

Designs: 600,000 l, Mamahatun Caravansary, Erzincan. 700,000 l, Cardak Caravasary, Denizli.

2004, June 7
2887-2888 A795 Set of 2 3.50 3.50

Gendarmerie, 165th Anniv. — A796

2004, June 14 **Perf. 13x13¼**
2889 A796 600,000 l multi 1.40 .70

Birds — A797

Designs: 100,000 l, Regulus regulus. 250,000 l, Sylvia rueppelli. 600,000 l, Hippolais polyglotta. 700,000 l, Passer domesticus. 800,000 l, Emberiza bruniceps. 1,000,000 l, Fringilla coelebs. 1,500,000 l, Phoenicurus phoenicurus. 3,500,000 l, Erithacus rubecula.

2004, July 23 **Perf. 14**
2890 A797 100,000 l multi .25 .25
2891 A797 250,000 l multi .35 .25
2892 A797 600,000 l multi .80 .40
2893 A797 700,000 l multi 1.40 .70
2894 A797 800,000 l multi 1.50 .75
2895 A797 1,000,000 l multi 2.00 1.00
2896 A797 1,500,000 l multi 3.00 1.40
2897 A797 3,500,000 l multi 6.75 3.25
Nos. 2890-2897 (8) 16.05 8.00

2004 Summer Olympics, Athens A798

Designs: 600,000 l, Wrestling. No. 2899, 700,000 l, Weight lifting. No. 2900, 700,000 l, Women's track and field, vert. 800,000 l, Wrestling, diff.

Perf. 13¼x13, 13x13¼
2004, Aug. 13 Set of 4 6.25 6.25
2898-2901 A798

Souvenir Sheet

Navy Submarines — A799

No. 2902: a, 600,000 l, 18 Mart. b, 700,000 l, Preveze. c, 700,000 l, Anafartalar. d, 800,000 l, Atilay.

2004, Sept. 14 **Perf. 13x13¼**
2902 A799 Sheet of 4, #a-d 7.00 6.25

Piri Reis (1465-1554), Admiral and Map Compiler — A800

2004, Sept. 20
2903 A800 600,000 l multi 1.40 1.40

Waterfalls
A801

Designs: 600,000 l, Kapuzbasi Waterfall. 700,000 l, Sudüsen Waterfall, vert.

2004, Oct. 19   Perf. 13x13¼, 13¼x13
2904-2905 A801   Set of 2   3.50 3.50

Buildings Associated With Kemal Ataturk — A802

Designs: 600,000 l, Ataturk Summer House, Bursa. No. 2907, 700,000 l, Ataturk House Museum, Erzurum. No. 2908, 700,000 l, Ataturk House, Havza. 800,000 l, State Railways Director's Building, Ankara.

2004, Nov. 8   Litho.   Perf. 13¼x13
2906-2909 A802   Set of 4   6.25 6.25

Souvenir Sheet

Turkish Stars Aerobatics Team — A803

No. 2910: a, 600,000 l, Two airplanes. b, 700,000 l, Five airplanes. c, 800,000 l, Seven airplanes flying upwards. d, 900,000 l, Seven airplanes flying left.

2004, Dec. 7   Litho.   Perf. 13¼x13
2910 A803   Sheet of 4, #a-d   9.00 9.00

Provinces
A804

2005, Jan. 1   Litho.   Perf. 14
2914 A804   1k Adana   .25   .25
2915 A804   5k Adiyaman   .25   .25
2916 A804   10k Afyon   .25   .25
2917 A804   25k Agri   .35   .25
2918 A804   50k Amasya   .75   .35
2919 A804   60k Ankara   .90   .40
2920 A804   60k Bitlis   .90   .40
2921 A804   70k Antalya   1.10   .50
2922 A804   70k Bolu   1.10   .50
2923 A804   80k Artvin   1.20   .55
2924 A804   80k Burdur   1.20   .55
2925 A804   90k Aydin   1.40   .60
2926 A804   1 l Balikesir 1.60   .75
2927 A804   1.50 l Bilecik 2.50 1.10
2928 A804   3.50 l Bingol 5.50 2.50
2929 A804   3.50 l Bursa 5.50 2.50
       Nos. 2914-2929 (16) 24.75 11.70

A805

Designs: 60k, Batiburnu Lighthouse, Canakkale. 70k, Zonguldak Lighthouse, Zonguldak.

2005, Mar. 18   Litho.   Perf. 13x13¼
2930-2931 A805   Sot of 2   2.75 1.40

A806

Marmaris Intl. Maritime Festival: 70k, Sailboat. 80k, Sailboat, sun on horizon.

2005, Apr. 1
2932-2933 A806   Set of 2   2.75 1.40

A807

2005, Apr. 10
2934 A807   70k multi   1.40   .70

Turkish Police, 100th anniv.

A808

Grand National Assembly, 85th anniv.: 60k, Torch, star and crescent. 70k, Crescent and fireworks over Grand National Assembly.

2005, Apr. 23
2935-2936 A808   Set of 2   2.25 1.10

Europa — A809

2005, May 9
2937 A809   70k multi   1.50   .55

Caftans of Sultans — A810

Caftan of Sultan: No. 2938, 70k, Ahmed I (shown). No. 2939, 70k, Ahmed I, diff. No. 2940, 70k, Murad III. No. 2941, 70k, Selim.

2005, May 20
2938-2941 A810   Set of 4   5.00 2.50

Souvenir Sheet

World Environment Day — A811

No. 2942: a, 60k, Pagellus bogaraveo. b, 70k, Epinephelus guaza. c, 70k, Merlanyus euxinus. d, 80k, Maena smaris.

2005, June 5   Litho.   Perf. 13¼x13
2942 A811   Sheet of 4, #a-d   5.50 2.75

Tapestries & Carpets — A812

Designs: 60k, Carpet from Hereke region, Turkey. 70k, L'humanité Assaillie par les Sept Peches Capitaux tapestry, Belgium.

2005, June 22   Litho.   Perf. 13x13¼
2943-2944 A812   Set of 2   3.00 1.10

See Belgium Nos. 2098-2099.

World Architecture Congress, Istanbul — A813

2005, July 3
2945 A813   70k multi   1.50   .70

Mosaics
A814

Designs: 60k, Akelos. No. 2947, 70k, Oceanos and Tethys. No. 2948, 70k, Achilles. 80k, Menad.

2005, July 5   Perf. 13¼x13
2946-2949 A814   Set of 4   5.50 2.75

Clocks — A815

Designs: 60k, Musical clock, 1770. 70k, Clock, 1867.

2005, July 20   Perf. 13x13¼
2950-2951 A815   Set of 2   2.50 1.25

Turkish Grand Prix, Istanbul — A816

2005, Aug. 19   Litho.   Perf. 13x13¼
2952 A816   70k multi   1.50   .65

Philanthropic Businessmen — A817

Designs: 60k, Sakip Sabanci (1933-2004). 70k, Vehbi Koç (1901-96).

2005, Sept. 21   Litho.   Perf. 13¼x13
2953-2954 A817   Set of 2   2.50 1.25

Provinces
A818

2005, Sept. 28   Perf. 13¾
2955 A818   50k Canakkale   .75   .35
2956 A818   60k Cankiri   1.00   .50
2957 A818   60k Corum   1.00   .50
2958 A818   60k Denizli   1.00   .50
2959 A818   60k Diyarbakir 1.00   .50
2960 A818   60k Edirne   1.00   .50
2961 A818   60k Elazig   1.00   .50
2962 A818   70k Erzincan   1.25   .60
2963 A818   70k Erzurum   1.25   .60
2964 A818   70k Eskisehir   1.25   .60
2965 A818   70k Gaziantep   1.25   .60
2966 A818   70k Giresun   1.25   .60
2967 A818   70k Gumushane   1.25   .60
2968 A818   1 l Hakkari   1.75   .80
2969 A818   1.50 l Hatay   2.50 1.25
2970 A818   2.50 l Isparta 4.25 2.10
       Nos. 2955-2970 (16)   22.75 11.10

Mevlana Jalal ad-Din ar-Rumi (1207-73), Islamic Philosopher
A819

2005, Sept. 30   Perf. 13x13¼
2971 A819   70k multi   1.50   .65
See Afghanistan Nos. 1449-1451, Iran No. 2911 and Syria No. 1574.

Galatasaray Sports Club, Cent. — A820

Club emblem and: No. 2972, 60k, Soccer stadium crowd, lion and "100." No. 2973, 70k, Soccer stadium, trophy.

No. 2974: a, 60k, Man, lion and "100." b, 70k, Club emblem, building. c, 80k, Soccer players. d, 1 l, Soccer players with trophy.

2005, Oct. 11 — Perf. 13x13¼
2972-2973 A820 Set of 2 — 2.25 1.10

Souvenir Sheet
Perf. 13¼x13
2974 A820 Sheet of 4, #a-d — 6.00 3.00

No. 2974 contains four 41x26mm stamps.
Exist imperf. Value, $40.

Start of Negotiations for Turkish
Admission to European Union — A821

2005, Nov. 3 — Perf. 13¼x13
2975 A821 70k multi — 1.40 .65

Vegetables — A824

Designs, 60k, Allium porrum (leeks). 70k,
Allium sativum (garlic). 80k, Allium cepa
(onions).

2005, Nov. 21 Litho. Perf. 13x13¼
2978-2980 A824 Set of 3 — 3.50 1.75

Europa Stamps,
50th Anniv. (in
2006) — A825

Designs: No. 2981, 60k, Vignette of #1907.
No. 2982, 70k, Vignette of #1628. 80k,
Vignette of #B120. 1 l, Vignette of #1719.
No. 2985, horiz.: a, 10k, #1520. b, 25k,
#1800. c, 60k, #1553. d, 70k, #1775.
No. 2986, horiz.: a, 10k, #1493. b, 25k,
#1936. c, 60k, #1602. d, 70k, #1876.

2005, Dec. 15 Litho. Perf. 13x13¼
2981-2984 A825 Set of 4 — 8.00 4.00

Souvenir Sheets
Perf. 13¼x13
2985 A825 Sheet of 4, #a-d — 9.00 4.50

Imperf
2986 A825 Sheet of 4, #a-d — 13.50 6.75

2006
Winter
Olympics,
Turin
A826

Designs: 60k, Speed skating. 70k, Skiing.

2006, Feb. 10 — Perf. 13¼x13
2987-2988 A826 Set of 2 — 2.00 1.00

March 29
Total Solar
Eclipse
A827

2006, Mar. 29 Litho. Perf. 13¼x13
2989 A827 70k multi — 1.10 .55

Support
for
Education
A828

2006, Apr. 10
2990 A828 60k multi — .95 .45

Karaoglan, Cartoon
Hero — A829

Karaoglan: 60k, With bow and arrow. No.
2992, 70k, Attacking swordsman. No. 2993,
70k, On horseback. 80k, On horseback, diff.

2006, Apr. 20 — Perf. 13x13¼
2991-2994 A829 Set of 4 — 4.25 2.10

Izzet Baysal (1907-2000),
Architect — A830

2006, May 11 Litho. Perf. 13¼x13
2995 A830 60k multi — .85 .45

A831

A832

A833

A834

A835

A836

A837

A838

A839

Kemal Ataturk (1881-1938) — A840

2006, May 19
2996 Block of 10 — 8.00 3.75
  a. A831 60k multi — .75 .35
  b. A832 60k multi — .75 .35
  c. A833 60k multi — .75 .35
  d. A834 60k multi — .75 .35
  e. A835 60k multi — .75 .35
  f. A836 60k multi — .75 .35
  g. A837 60k multi — .75 .35
  h. A838 60k multi — .75 .35
  i. A839 60k multi — .75 .35
  j. A840 60k multi — .75 .35

Europa — A841

2006, May 30 — Perf. 13x13¼
2997 A841 70k multi — 1.25 .45

Miniature Sheet

World Environment Day — A842

No. 2998: a, 25k, Parched earth. b, 50k,
Tree. c, 60k, Tree, diff. d, 70k, Forest.

2006, June 5
2998 A842 Sheet of 4, #a-d — 3.50 3.00

Intl. Year of Deserts and Desertification.

2006 World Cup
Soccer
Championships,
Germany — A843

Designs: No. 2999, 70k, Player dribbling
ball. No. 3000, 70k, Player kicking ball, horiz.

2006, June 9 Perf. 13x13¼, 13¼x13
2999-3000 A843 Set of 2 — 2.25 .95

Airplanes
A844

Designs: 60k, Deperdussin monoplane. No.
3002, 70k, Bleriot monoplane. No. 3003, 70k,
R. E. P. monoplane.

2006, June 22 — Perf. 13¼x13
3001-3003 A844 Set of 3 — 3.25 1.40

See Nos. 3034-3036.

Treasures of Karun — A845

Designs: No. 3004, 70k, Bracelet and coins.
No. 3005, 70k, Winged sun disc pectoral and
bracelet. 80k, Lion's head bracelets.

2006, July 10 — Perf. 13¼x13
3004-3006 A845 Set of 3 — 3.25 1.40

Provinces
A846

2006, Sept. 11   **Perf. 13¼x13**

3007	A846	10k Kahramanmaras	.25	.25
3008	A846	10k Manisa	.25	.25
3009	A846	50k Kirsehir	.70	.35
3010	A846	50k Kocaeli	.70	.35
3011	A846	60k Izmir	.80	.40
3012	A846	60k Konya	.80	.40
3013	A846	60k Mardin	.80	.40
3014	A846	60k Mugla	.80	.40
3015	A846	70k Istanbul	.95	.50
3016	A846	70k Mersin	.95	.50
3017	A846	1 l Kastamonu	1.40	.70
3018	A846	1 l Kirklareli	1.40	.70
3019	A846	1.60 l Kayseri	2.25	1.10
3020	A846	2 l Malatya	2.75	1.40
3021	A846	4 l Kars	5.50	2.75
3022	A846	4 l Kutahya	5.50	2.75
		Nos. 3007-3022 (16)	25.80	13.20

See nos. 3055-3062.

Scenes From Movie, "Selvi Boylum Al Yazmalim" — A847

Various scenes: 60k, 70k.

2006, Sept. 16   **Perf. 13x13¼**
3023-3024 A847   Set of 2   1.75   .85

Turkish Railroads, 150th Anniv. A848

Designs: 60k, Steam locomotive. 70k, Electric train.

2006, Sept. 23   **Perf. 13¼x13**
3025-3026 A848   Set of 2   1.75   .85

Central Bank, 75th Anniv. A849

2006, Oct. 3
3027 A849 60k multi   1.00   .40

Intl. Telecommunications Union Conference, Antalya — A850

Conference emblem and: 60k, Globe with spotlight on Turkey. 70k, Map with lines drawn to Turkey.

2006, Nov. 6   **Perf. 13x13¼**
3028-3029 A850   Set of 2   1.90   .95

Middle East Technical University, Ankara, 50th Anniv. — A851

2006, Nov. 15   Litho.   **Perf. 13x13¼**
3030 A851 60k multi   .85   .40

Turkish Atomic Energy Authority, 50th Anniv. A852

2006, Nov. 22   Litho.   **Perf. 13¼x13**
3031 A852 60k multi   .85   .40

Geothermal Resources — A853

Designs: 60k, Four steam clouds. 70k, Steam leaving smokestack.

2006, Dec. 11
3032-3033 A853   Set of 2   1.90   .95

Airplanes Type of 2006

Designs: 60k, Breguet XIV B-2. No. 3035, 70k, Albatros C-XV. No. 3036, 70k, Fiat R2.

2007, Mar. 15   Litho.   **Perf. 13¼x13**
3034-3036 A844   Set of 3   3.00   1.50

A854

A855

A856

Hittite Artifacts A857

2007, Mar. 30

3037	A854	60k multi	1.00	.45
3038	A855	60k multi	1.00	.45
3039	A856	60k multi	1.00	.45
3040	A857	60k multi	1.00	.45
		Nos. 3037-3040 (4)	4.00	1.80

Third Meeting of Economic Cooperation Organization Postal Authorities, Tehran — A858

2007, Apr. 5   **Perf. 13x13¼**
3041 A858 60k multi   1.00   .45

See Iran No. 2917, Kazakhstan No. 526 and Pakistan No. 1101.

Tekirdag as Part of Turkey, 650th Anniv. A859

2007, Apr. 14   **Perf. 13¼x13**
3042 A859 60k multi   1.00   .45

Fenerbahce Sports Club, Cent. — A860

Club emblem and: No. 3043, 60k, Men witnessing signing ceremony. No. 3044, 70k, Quotation and Arabic text.

No. 3045 — Club emblem and: a, 60k, Lighthouse. b, 70k, Three men seated at table. c, 80k, Building, stadium interior. d, 90k, Stadium exterior.

2007, May 3   **Perf. 13x13¼**
3043-3044 A860   Set of 2   2.00   1.00

Souvenir Sheet
Perf. 13¼x13
3045 A860   Sheet of 4, #a-d   4.50   4.50

No. 3045 contains four 38x23mm stamps. No. 3045 exists affixed to a booklet cover which was only sold in a set with an imperforate sheet of eight 41x31mm stamps depicting various athletes, two first day covers, and a folder, for 25 l. Value $15.

Souvenir Sheet

Mevlana Jalal ad-Din ar-Rumi (1207-73), Islamic Philosopher — A861

No. 3046: a, 25k, Portrait. b, 50k, Arabic calligraphy. c, 60k, Dervishes. d, 70k, Mausoleum.

2007, May 8   **Perf. 13x13¼**
3046 A861   Sheet of 4, #a-d   3.50   2.50

Europa A862

Designs: 60k, Turkish Scouting emblem, Scout at campfire. 70k, Scouts saluting.

2007, May 9   **Perf. 13¼**
3047-3048 A862   Set of 2   2.00   1.00

Scouting, cent.

Mehmetcik Foundation, 25th Anniv. — A863

2007, May 17   Litho.   **Perf. 13¼x13**
3049 A863 60k multi   .95   .45

Souvenir Sheet

World Environment Day — A864

No. 3050: a, 25k, Goats. b, 50k, Cattle. c, 60k, Sheep. d, 70k, Chickens.

2007, June 5   Litho.   **Perf. 13¼x13**
3050 A864   Sheet of 4, #a-d   4.50   2.50

Turkish Cuisine — A865

Designs: No. 3051, 1 l, Nohutlu Bulgur Pilavi (chick pea and bulgur pilaf). No. 3052, 1 l, Yüksük Corbasi (soup). 2 l, Asure (vegetables).

2007, June 20   Litho.   Perf. 13x13¼
3051-3053   A865   Set of 3   6.25 3.25

Black Sea Economic Cooperation Organization, 15th Anniversary Summit A866

2007, June 25   Perf. 13¼
3054   A866   60k multi   .95 .95

Provinces Type of 2006
2007, July 10   Perf. 13¼x13
3055   A846   10k Siirt   .25 .25
3056   A846   50k Ordu   .80 .40
3057   A846   60k Rize   .95 .45
3058   A846   1 l Nigde   1.60 .80
3059   A846   2 l Nevsehir   3.25 1.60
3060   A846   2 l Samsun   3.25 1.60
3061   A846   4 l Mus   6.25 3.25
3062   A846   4 l Sakarya   6.25 3.25
   Nos. 3055-3062 (8)   22.60 11.60

Turkish Language Association, 75th Anniv. — A867

2007, July 12   Perf. 13x13¼
3063   A867   70k multi   1.10 .55

Roses A869

Color of rose: No. 3065, 60k, White. No. 3066, 60k, Red. No. 3067, 60k, Yellow.

2007, Aug. 16   Litho.   Perf. 13¼
3065-3067   A869   Set of 3   2.75 1.40

Shadow Play Characters A870

Designs: 60k, Tuzsuz Deli Bekir and Efe. 70k, Hacivat and Karagöz. 80k, Tiryaki and Celebi.

2007, Sept. 13   Litho.   Perf. 13¼x13
3068-3070   A870   Set of 3   3.75 1.90

Miniature Sheet

Balkanfila XIV Intl. Philatelic Exhibition, Istanbul — A871

No. 3071: a, 60k, Blue Mosque, Galata Tower. b, 70k, Hagia Sophia. c, 80k, City walls and painting. d, 1 l, Bosporus Bridge.

2007, Oct. 28
3071   A871   Sheet of 4, #a-d   5.50 3.50

An imperforate sheet containing a 60k dove and flags stamp, a 70k bridge stamp, 80k flags stamp and a 1 l flags and map of Turkey stamp exists. It sold for considerably above face value. Value, $25.

Mimar Sinan (1489-1588), Architect A873

Sinan and: 60k, Büyükcekmece Bridge. No. 3074, 70k, Bath of Roxelana (Haseki Hürrem Sultan Hamami Ayasofya). No. 3075, 70k, Selimye Mosque, Edirne. 80k, Suleiman Mosque, Istanbul.

2007, Nov. 14   Perf. 13¼
3073-3076   A873   Set of 4   4.75 2.40

World Philosophy Day — A874

2007, Nov. 22   Perf. 13x13¼
3077   A874   60k multi   1.00 .50

Cartoon Character "Keloglan" — A875

Designs: 60k, Keloglan in giant's hand. No. 3079, 70k, Keloglan leaving house. No. 3080, 70k, Keloglan on horse. 80k, Keloglan with carpet and birds.

2007, Nov. 28
3078-3081   A875   Set of 4   4.75 2.40

Provinces Type of 2006
2007, Dec. 4   Perf. 13¼x13
3082   A846   5k Tunceli   .25 .25
3083   A846   10k Tokat   .25 .25
3084   A846   65k Sanliurfa   1.10 .55
3085   A846   65k Trabzon   1.10 .55
3086   A846   80k Sivas   1.40 .70
3087   A846   85k Usak   1.50 .75
3088   A846   1 l Tekirdag   1.75 .90
3089   A846   4.50 l Sinop   7.75 4.00
   Nos. 3082-3089 (8)   15.10 7.95

TRT Television, 40th Anniv. A876

Designs: 65k, Emblem. 80k, Emblem and headquarters.

2008, Jan. 31   Litho.   Perf. 12¾x13
3090-3091   A876   Set of 2   2.50 1.25

Nasreddin Hoca Fables, 800th Anniv. — A877

Hoca: 25k, And two men at table. 65k, Sitting backward on horse. 80k, Showing two pots to man. 85k, Spooning water into lake.

2008, Feb. 7   Perf. 13x13¼
3092-3095   A877   Set of 4   4.25 2.10

A878

St. Valentine's Day — A879

2008, Feb. 14   Perf. 13
3096   A878   65k multi   1.10 .55
3097   A879   80k multi   1.40 .70

Miniature Sheet

Amasya Medical Center, 700th Anniv. — A880

No. 3098: a, 50k, Building. b, 65k, Six musicians. c, 80k, Seven people. d, 85k, Four people.

2008, Mar. 13   Perf. 13x13¼
3098   A880   Sheet of 4, #a-d   4.50 2.25

Urartian Cultural Artifacts A881

Designs: No. 3099, 65k, Carved ivory spirit figure (Fildisi Kanati Cin). No. 3100, 65k, Gold earring, bronze pin and necklace (Altin küpe, Tunc igne, Boncuk kolye). No. 3101, 80k, Bronze cauldron (Uc ayak uzerinde tunc

---

kazan). No. 3102, 80k, Harput Castle (Harput Kalesi).

2008, Mar. 27   Perf. 13¼x13
3099-3102   A881   Set of 4   4.50 2.25

Military Aircraft A882

Designs: 65k, Consolidated B24 D. 80k, Curtiss Hawk. 85k, PZL XXIV.

2008, Apr. 25
3103-3105   A882   Set of 3   3.75 1.90
   See Nos. 3148-3150.

Europa A883

Designs: 65k, Letter, fingers making heart. 80k, Pen, inkwell.

2008, May 9   Litho.   Perf. 13¼
3106-3107   A883   Set of 2   2.40 1.25

Diplomatic Relations Between Turkey and Thailand, 50th Anniv. A884

Designs: 65k, Loha Prasat, Bangkok, Thailand. 80k, Sultan Ahmed Mosque, Istanbul.

2008, May 12   Litho.   Perf. 13¼x13
3108-3109   A884   Set of 2   2.40 1.25
   See Thailand No. 2359.

National Olympic Committee, Cent. — A885

Olympic Committee emblem and: 65k, Dove and Olympic flag. 80k, Parading athletes. 85k, Stadium. 1 l, Athlete and Olympic flag.

2008, May 26   Perf. 13x13¼
3110-3113   A885   Set of 4   5.25 2.60

Provinces A886

2008, May 28   Perf. 13¼x13
3114   A886   5k Zonguldak   .25 .25
3115   A886   50k Yozgat   .80 .40
3116   A886   65k Aksaray   1.10 .55
3117   A886   65k Kirikkale   1.10 .55
3118   A886   80k Karaman   1.40 .70
3119   A886   85k Van   1.40 .70

3120	A886	1 l Bayburt	1.60	.80
3121	A886	4.50 l Batman	7.25	3.75
		Nos. 3114-3121 (8)	14.90	7.70

See Nos. 3129-3137.

Miniature Sheet

World Environment Day — A887

No. 3122: a, 25k, Boy and polar bears. b, 65k, Sea ice. c, 80k, Mountains and stream. d, 85k, Girl, flower, parched earth.

2008, June 5　　　**Perf. 13x12¾**
3122	A887	Sheet of 4, #a-d	4.25	2.10

Turkish Diplomats Who Saved Jews During World War II — A888

Birds and: 65k, Selehattin Ulkümen (1914-2003). 80k, Necdet Kent (1911-2002).

2008, July 17　　　**Perf. 12¾x13**
3123-3124	A888	Set of 2	2.50	1.25

2008 Summer Olympics, Beijing — A889

Designs: 25k, Archery. 65k, Taekwondo, vert. No. 3127, 80k, Weight lifting. No. 3128, 80k, Wrestling.

Perf. 13x13¼, 13¼x13
2008, Aug. 8　　　**Litho.**
3125-3128	A889	Set of 4	4.25	2.10

Provinces Type of 2008
Perf. 13¼x13¼, 13x13¼
2008, Aug. 29
3129	A886	50k Kilis	.85	.40
3130	A886	65k Bartin, vert.	1.10	.85
3131	A886	1 l Ardahan	1.75	.85
3132	A886	1 l Igdir	1.75	.85
3133	A886	1.50 l Yalova	2.60	1.25
3134	A886	2 l Karabuk	3.50	1.75
3135	A886	2 l Osmaniye	3.50	1.75
3136	A886	4.50 l Düzce	7.75	3.75
3137	A886	4.50 l Sirnak	7.75	3.75
		Nos. 3129-3137 (9)	30.55	14.90

Glassware — A890

Designs: 65k, Bowl. 80k, Vase.

2008, Sept. 11　　　**Perf. 13x12¾**
3138-3139	A890	Set of 2	2.25	1.10

Battle of Preveza, 470th Anniv. — A891

Designs: 65k, Khair ed-Din (Barbarossa), battle, map. 80k, Kemal Ataturk, ships.

2008, Sept. 27　　　**Perf. 13x13¼**
3140-3141	A891	Set of 2	2.25	1.10

Miniature Sheet

Friendship Between Turkey and Indonesia — A892

No. 3142: a, 80k Blue Mosque, Turkey. b, 65k Istiqlal Mosque, Indonesia. c, 80k Bosporus Bridge, Turkey. d, 65k Darelang Bridge, Indonesia. e, 80k Whirling dervishes. f, 65k Saman dance. g, 80k Turkish tulip (ters lale). h, 65k Flame of Irian (Mucuna bennettii). i, 80k Turkish Van cat. j, 65k Flat-headed cat (Yassibas kedi).

2008, Oct. 24　　　**Perf. 13x13¼**
3142	A892	Sheet of 10, #a-j	9.50	4.75

See Indonesia No. 2167.

Republic of Turkey, 85th Anniv. A893

Kemal Ataturk, Turkish flag and: No. 3143, 80k, Airplane, ship, truck and train. No. 3144, 80k, Computer keyboard, satellite, dish antenna.

2008, Oct. 29　　**Litho.**　　**Perf. 12¾x13**
3143-3144	A893	Set of 2	2.10	1.10

Turkish Maritime Enterprises, 160th Anniv. A894

Designs: 65k, Docked ship. No. 3146, 80k, Emblem. No. 3147, 80k, Ship at sea, horiz.

Perf. 13½x13¼, 13¼x13½
2008, Nov. 29　　　**Litho.**
3145-3147	A894	Set of 3	3.00	1.50

Military Aircraft Type of 2008
Designs: 65k, C-47 Dakota. 80k, F-100 D Super Sabre. 1 l, F-86 E Sabre.

2009, Mar. 12　　**Litho.**　　**Perf. 13¼x13**
3148-3150	A882	Set of 3	3.25	1.60

Miniature Sheet

Fifth World Water Forum, Istanbul — A895

No. 3151 — Emblem and: a, 25k, Head, Earth, water. b, 65k, Bosporus Bridge, water drop. c, 80k, Bosporus Bridge, waterfall. d, 80k, Waterfall, parched land, clay jug pouring water.

2009, Mar. 16　　　**Perf. 13x13¼**
3151	A895	Sheet of 4, #a-d	3.25	1.60

Sultan's Boats — A896

Boats from Istanbul Sea Museum: No. 3152, 80k, Boat with yellow hull and short bowsprit, gray green sky. No. 3153, 80k, Boat with brown hull, long bowsprit, blue gray sky.

2009, Apr. 2
3152-3153	A896	Set of 2	2.10	1.10

Council of Europe, 60th Anniv. A897

European Court for Human Rights, 50th Anniv. A898

2009, May 5　　　**Perf. 13¼x13**
3154	A897	80k multi	1.10	.55
3155	A898	80k multi	1.10	.55

Mother's Day — A899

Designs: 65k, Bird, hatchlings in nest shaped like heart. 80k, Mother's hands holding infant, hearts. No. 3158, 1 l, Mother and child. No. 3159, 1 l, Hands of mother and baby, flower.

2009, May 10　　　**Perf. 13¾**
3156-3159	A899	Set of 4	4.50	2.25

Nos. 3156-3159 each have perforations in a heart shape in the vignette.

Ceramics — A900

Designs: 80k, Ceramic pot, Portugal. 85k, Faience mosque lamp, Turkey.

2009, May 12　　　**Perf. 13x13¼**
3160-3161	A900	Set of 2	2.25	1.10

See Portugal Nos. 3111-3112.

Miniature Sheet

Arrival of Kemal Ataturk at Samsun, 90th Anniv. — A901

No. 3162: a, 25k, Congress Building, Sivas. b, 65k, Congress Building, Erzurum. c, 65k, Government building, Amasya. d, 80k, Statue of Ataturk, Samsun.

2009, May 19　　　**Litho.**
3162	A901	Sheet of 4, #a-d	3.25	1.60

Ministry of Transport and Communication, 70th Anniv. — A902

Designs: 50k, Ship, map. 65k, Bridge, highway interchange, bus. 80k, Earth, satellite, dish antenna, envelopes, computer, cellular phone. No. 3166, 1 l, Map, train. No. 3167, 1 l, Postal worker delivering parcel, envelope, airplane, globe.

2009, May 27　　　**Perf. 13¼x13**
3163-3167	A902	Set of 5	5.25	2.60

Miniature Sheet

World Environment Day — A903

No. 3168 — Butterflies: a, 25k, Aporia crataegi. b, 65k, Lasiommate megera. c, 80k, Plebeius agestis. d, 80k, Gonepteryx rhamni.

2009, June 5　　　**Perf. 13x13¼**
3168	A903	Sheet of 4, #a-d	3.25	1.60

Kemal Ataturk — A904

Various photographs of Ataturk.

2009, June 5　　**Perf. 13½ Syncopated**
3169	A904	5k multi	.25	.25
3170	A904	10k multi	.25	.25
3171	A904	25k multi	.35	.25
3172	A904	50k multi	.65	.35
3173	A904	65k multi	.85	.40
3174	A904	80k multi	1.10	.55
3175	A904	85k multi	1.10	.55
3176	A904	1 l multi	1.40	.70
3177	A904	2 l multi	2.60	1.40
3178	A904	4.50 l multi	6.00	3.00
		Nos. 3169-3178 (10)	14.55	7.70

Europa A905

Designs: 80k, Cacabey Astronomy Madrassa, Kirsehir. 1 l, Ali Kuscu (1403-74), astronomer.

2009, June 16   **Perf. 13¼x13**
3179-3180 A905   Set of 2   2.40 1.25

Items of the Phrygians — A906

Designs: 65k, Pitcher. 80k, Clay ceremonial cup with birds. No. 3183, 1 l, Goose-shaped clay ceremonial cup. No. 3184, 1 l, Cauldron.

2009, June 25   **Perf. 13x13¼**
3181-3184 A906   Set of 4   4.50 2.25

Embroidery — A907

Various embroidered pieces with background color of: 75k, Blue. 90k, Pink.

2009, July 2   **Perf. 13¼x13**
3185-3186 A907   Set of 2   2.25 1.10

Kemal Ataturk — A908

Various photographs of Ataturk.

2009, July 16   **Perf. 13½ Syncopated**
3187 A908 75k multi   1.10 .55
3188 A908 90k multi   1.25 .60
3189 A908 5 l multi   7.00 3.50
    Nos. 3187-3189 (3)   9.35 4.65

Miniature Sheet

Haci Bektas Veli (1209-71), Mystic — A909

No. 3190: a, 75k, Haci Bektas Veli, birds. b, 75k, Birds over town. c, 90k, Dancers. d, 90k, Haci Bektas Veli, deer, lion, birds.

2009, Aug. 12   **Perf. 13x13¼**
3190 A909   Sheet of 4, #a-d   4.50 2.25

Postal Cooperation Between Turkey and Bosnia and Herzegovina — A910

2009, Oct. 9   **Litho.**
3191 A910 90k multi   1.25 .60
    See Bosnia and Herzegovina No. 656.

Namik Kemal Yolga (1914-2001), Diplomat Who Rescued Jews in World War II — A911

2009, Oct. 20   **Perf. 13¼x13**
3192 A911 75k multi   1.00 .50

Castles A912

Designs: 25k, Kolan Castle, Adana. 75k, Afyon Castle. 90k, Amasya Castle. 1 l, Ankara Castle.

2009, Nov. 5
3193-3196 A912   Set of 4   4.00 2.00

Mekteb-i Mülkiye Political Science Faculty, 150th Anniv. A913

Designs: 75k, Political Science Faculty Building, anniversary emblem. 90k, Anniversary emblem.

2009, Dec. 4   **Perf. 13¼x13**
3197-3198 A913   Set of 2   2.25 1.10

Süleyman Celebi (1351-1422), Writer — A914

Cengiz Aytmatov (1928-2008), Writer — A915

2009, Dec. 17
3199 A914 75k multi   1.00 .50
3200 A915 90k multi   1.25 .60

Miniature Sheets

A916

Istanbul, 2010 Capital of European Culture — A917

No. 3201: a, Silhouette of Hagia Sophia, red sky. b, Sculpture. c, Artwork of main dome of Blue Mosque. d, Blue Mosque, blue sky. e, Tower on coastline, blue sky. f, Bread. g, Tram. h, Haydarpasa Station, cloudy sky.

No. 3202: a, Silhouettes of buildings, pink sky. b, Religious painting. c, Fishermen. d, Man in boat, Bosporus Bridge. e, Ship. f, Birds over Bosporus. g, Topkapi Palace. h, Silhouettes of Hagia Sophia and Blue Mosque, orange red sky.

2010, Jan. 7   **Perf. 13x13x¼**
3201 A916 75k Sheet of 8, #a-h   8.00 4.00
    Perf. 13¼x13
3202 A917 90k Sheet of 8, #a-h   8.00 4.00

2010 Winter Olympics, Vancouver A918

Designs: 25k, Slalom skier. 75k, Snowboarder. No. 3205, 90k, Cross-country skier. No. 3206, 90k, Speed skater.

2010, Feb. 12   **Perf. 13¼**
3203-3206 A918   Set of 4   3.75 1.90

Military Aircraft A919

Designs: 75k, F-4. 90k, F-16. 1 l, CN-235.

2010, Mar. 18   **Perf. 13x13¼**
3207-3209 A919   Set of 3   3.50 1.75

Early Bronse Age Items — A920

Designs: 75k, Twinned figures. 90k, Ceremonial symbol. No. 3212, 1 l, Necklace. No. 3213, 1 l, Sculpture of nursing woman, vert.

    Perf. 13¼x13½, 13½x13¼
2010, Mar. 31
3210-3213 A920   Set of 4   5.00 2.50

Anatolian News Agency, 90th Anniv, A921

2010, Apr. 6   **Perf. 13¼x13**
3214 A921 75k multi   1.00 .50

A922

National Assembly, 90th Anniv. — A923

2010, Apr. 23   **Perf. 13x13¼**
3215 A922 75k multi   1.00 .50
3216 A923 90k multi   1.25 .60

Sile Lighthouse, 150th Anniv. — A924

2010, May 1
3217 A924 75k multi   1.00 .50

Labor Day — A925

Designs: No. 3218, 80k, Dove with olive branch. No. 3219, 80k, Hands holding globe. No. 3220, 110k, Dove with banner. No. 3221, 110k, Worker.

2010, May 1   **Perf. 13x12¾**
3218-3221 A925   Set of 4   5.00 2.50

Yunus Emre (c. 1240-c. 1321), Poet A926

Emre and: 75k, Tomb, Eskisehir. 90k, Poem, vert.

2010, May 3   **Perf. 13¼x13, 13x13¼**
3222-3223 A926   Set of 2   2.10 1.10

Europe Day A927

2010, May 9   **Perf. 12¾x13**
3224 A927 75k multi   .95 .45

Europa
A928

Children's stories: 80k, Balik Cobani (The Fish and the Shepherd). 110k, Book of Dede Korkut.

2010, May 9 Perf. 13¼x13
3225-3226 A928 Set of 2 2.40 1.25

RASAT Observational Satellite — A929

2010, May 17 Perf. 13x13¼
3227 A929 75k multi .95 .45

Miniature Sheet

World Environment Day — A930

No. 3228 — Flowers: a, Crocus stevenii. b, Crocus mathewii. c, Astragalus lineatus. d, Erica bocquetii.

2010, June 5
3228 A930 110k Sheet of 4, #a-d 5.75 3.00

Sultan's Boats — A931

Boats from Istanbul Sea Museum: 80k, Boat with red orange and white hull. 110k, Boat with white and gold hull with bird figurehead.

2010, June 14 Perf. 13x13¼
3229-3230 A931 Set of 2 2.50 1.25

Kemal Atatürk — A932

Various portraits.

Perf. 13½ Syncopated
2010, June 24
3231 A932 25k multi .35 .25
3232 A932 80k multi 1.10 .55
3233 A932 110k multi 1.40 .70
3234 A932 355k multi 4.50 2.25
  Nos. 3231-3234 (4) 7.35 3.75

2010 World Men's Basketball Championships, Turkey
A933 A934

2010, Aug. 28 Perf. 13x12¾
Background Color
3235 A933 80k blue 1.10 .55
3236 A934 80k brown 1.10 .55
3237 A933 110k yellow brown 1.50 .75
3238 A934 110k red 1.50 .75
  Nos. 3235-3238 (4) 5.20 2.60

Miniature Sheet

Japan Year in Turkey — A935

No. 3239: a, 80k, Bridge in Ritsurin Garden, Takamatsu, Japan. b, 80k, Traditional Japanese dancer. c, 80k, Japanese dancers with drums. d, 80k, Tokyo skyline. e, 80k, Noh theater. f, 110k, Samurai headgear. g, 110k, Mt. Fuji. h, 110k, Kokeshi dolls. i, 110k, Turkish frigate Ertugrul. j, 110k, Sushi.

2010, Sept. 2 Perf. 13x13¼
3239 A935 Sheet of 10, #a-j 13.00 6.50

Souvenir Sheet

Religious Buildings in Spain and Turkey — A936

No. 3240: a, 80k, Santa María de la Mayor Collegiate Church, Toro, Spain. b, 110k, Ortaköy Mosque, Istanbul.

2010, Oct. 18 Perf. 12¾x13
3240 A936 Sheet of 2, #a-b 2.75 1.40
  See Spain No. 3755.

Miniature Sheet

11th Economic Cooperation Orgaization Summit, Istanbul — A937

No. 3241 — Emblem with background color of: a, 90k, Blue. b, 100k, Lilac. c, 130k, Rose. d, 150k, Green

2010, Dec. 20 Perf. 13x12¾
3241 A937 Sheet of 4, #a-d 6.25 3.00

Miniature Sheet

2011 Winter Universiade, Erzurum — A938

No. 3242 — Emblems and: a, 90k, Twin Minaret Madrasa, Erzurum. b, 90k, Ice hockey player. c, 1.30 l, Mascot. d, 1.30 l, Ski jumper.

2011, Jan. 27 Perf. 13¼x13
3242 A938 Sheet of 4, #a-d 5.75 2.75
A sheet of four imperforate 1.30 l stamps sold for 30 l.

Lilies
A939

Various lilies.

2011, Feb. 4 Perf. 13¾
3243 A939 25k multi .35 .25
3244 A939 1 l multi 1.25 .65
3245 A939 3.65 l multi 4.75 2.40
3246 A939 6 l multi 7.75 3.75
  Nos. 3243-3246 (4) 14.10 7.05

Values are for stamps with surrounding selvage.

Souvenir Sheet

Treaty of Moscow, 90th Anniv. — A940

No. 3247: a, Turkish flag, building. b, Treaty negotiators.

2011, Feb. 4 Perf. 13¼x13
3247 A940 90k Sheet of 2, #a-b 2.40 1.25

Evliya Celebi (1611-82), Travel Writer — A941

Map and: 90k, Celebi writing, silhouette of Celebi on horse. 1.30 l, Celebi on horse.

2011, Mar. 25 Perf. 13x13¼
3248-3249 A941 Set of 2 3.00 1.50

Fish
A942

Designs: No. 3250, 1.30 l, Trigla lucerna. No. 3251, 1.30 l, Diplodus vulgaris. No. 3252, 1.30 l, Xiphias gladius.

2011, Apr. 28 Perf. 13¼x13
3250-3252 A942 Set of 3 5.25 2.60

Organization for Economic Cooperation and Development, 50th Anniv. — A943

2011, May 5 Perf. 13x13¼
3253 A943 1.30 l multi 1.75 .85

Europa
A944

Forest and: 90k, Woodpecker. 1.30 l, Deer.

2011, May 9 Perf. 13¼x13
3254-3255 A944 Set of 2 2.75 1.40
Intl. Year of Forests.

Week of the Disabled
A945

Week of the Disabled emblem, stylized person in wheelchair, Turkish text, and: 90k, Stylized person walking. 1.30 l, Hand with blackboard eraser.

2011, May 10 Litho.
3256-3257 A945 Set of 2 2.75 1.40

Souvenir Sheet

Kemal Atatürk (1881-1938) — A946

2011, May 19 Perf. 13x13¼
3258 A946 90k multi 1.25 .60

Miniature Sheet

Turkish Air Force, Cent. — A947

No. 3259: a, Jet on ground, blue skies. b, Jets over bridge. c, Jet in flight. d, Jet on runway, gray skies.

2011, June 1 Perf. 13¼x13
3259 A947 1.30 l Sheet of 4 #a-d 6.75 3.50
A sheet of four imperforate 1.30 l vertical stamps depicting jets in flight sold for 30 l.

Miniature Sheet

World Environment Day — A948

No. 3260: a, 25k, Anas acuta. b, 90k, Streptopelia turtur. c, 1.30 l, Phasianus colchicus. d, 1.30 l, Alectoris chukar.

2011, June 5   *Perf. 13¾*
3260 A948   Sheet of 4, #a-d   4.75 2.40

Korean War, 60th Anniv. A949

2011, June 25   *Perf. 13¼x13*
3261 A949 1.30 l multi   1.60 .80

Social Services and Child Protection Agency, 90th Anniv. — A950

2011, June 30   *Perf. 13x13¼*
3262 A950 90k multi   1.10 .55

Miniature Sheet

Kirkpinar Oil Wrestling Festival, 650th Anniv. — A951

No. 3263: a, 90k, Two wrestlers, both heads visible. b, 90k, Two wrestlers, heads not visible. c, 1.30 l, Two wrestlers. d, 1.30 l, Two wrestlers and referee.

2011, July 8   *Perf. 13¼x13*
3263 A951   Sheet of 4, #a-d   5.50 2.75

Miniature Sheet

Tourist Attractions of Van — A952

No. 3264: a, 25k, Van Castle. b, 90k, Hüsrev Pasha Mosque. c, 1.30 l, Bridge and fish. d, 1.30 l, Akdamar Church, Van cat.

2011, July 12   *Perf. 13x13¼*
3264 A952   Sheet of 4, #a-d   4.25 2.10

A953

Festival mascot and: 25k, Festival emblem. 90k, Festival emblem, diff. No. 3267, 1.30 l, Festival flag and balloons. No. 3268, 1.30 l, Festival emblem, vert.

2011, July 23   *Perf. 13¼x13, 13x13¼*
3265-3268 A953   Set of 4   4.25 2.10
2011 European Youth Summer Olympic Festival, Trabzon.

Yildiz Technical University, Cent. A954

Centenary emblem and: 90k, University building. 1.30 l, Star, University building.

2011, Aug. 22   *Perf. 13¼x13*
3269-3270 A954   Set of 2   2.50 1.25

Fruit — A955

Designs: 10k, Pyracantha coccinea. 1 l, Prunus persica. 1.30 l, Prunus avium. 3.65 l, Rubus fruticosus.

         Perf. 13½ Syncopated
2011, Aug. 26
3271 A955   10k multi   .25 .25
3272 A955   1 l multi   1.10 .55
3273 A955   1.30 l multi   1.50 .75
3274 A955   3.65 l multi   4.25 2.10
     Nos. 3271-3274 (4)   7.10 3.65

39th Mechanized Infantry Brigade — A956

Designs: 50k, Turkish flag and soldiers carrying flag. 90k, Turkish flag and soldiers. 1.30 l, Soldiers on ship, horiz.

2011, Oct. 6   *Litho.*
3275-3277 A956   Set of 3   3.00 1.50

Sultan's Boats — A957

Designs: 90k, Boat with pointed tip. 1.30 l, Boat with white hull and eagle figurehead.

2011, Nov. 28   *Perf. 13x13¼*
3278-3279 A957   Set of 2   2.40 1.25

Photographs of Turkish People and Agriculture — A958

Designs: No. 3280, 50k, Woman and string of pepers. No. 3281, 50k, Workers in field of protected plants. No. 3282, 1 l, Boy swimming in water with livestock, horiz. No. 3283, 1 l, Farm worker in field of plants under protective tents, horiz.

2011, Dec. 28   *Perf. 13x13¼, 13¼x13*
3280-3283 A958   Set of 4   3.25 1.60

Istanbul, 2012 European Capital of Sports A959

Emblem, Istanbul landmarks and: 50k, Runners, wheelchair racer. No. 3285, 1 l, Sailing. No. 3286, 1 l, Tennis. 2 l, Cycling.

         Perf. 13¾ Syncopated
2012, Feb. 15
3284-3287 A959   Set of 4   5.25 2.60

Stylized Man and Woman Holding Up Globe A960

Woman and Flower A961

2012, Mar. 8   *Perf. 13½*
3288 A960 10k multi + label   .25 .25
3289 A961 1 l multi + label   1.10 .55
3290 A960 2 l multi + label   2.25 1.10
     Nos. 3288-3290 (3)   3.60 1.90
Equality of opportunities for men and women.

Miniature Sheet

2012 World Track and Field Championships, Istanbul — A962

No. 3291 — Bridge and: a, 50k, Female hurdler. b, 1 l, Female long jumper. c, 1 l, Male high jumper. d, 2 l, Male hurdler.

2012, Mar. 9   *Perf. 13¾*
3291 A962   Sheet of 4, #a-d   5.00 2.50

National History Society Building, Cent. — A963

         Perf. 13¾ Syncopated
2012, Mar. 25
3292 A963 1 l multi   1.10 .55

Pertevniyal High School, 140th Anniv. — A964

2012, Apr. 6
3293 A964 1 l multi   1.10 .55

Souvenir Sheet

Morality and Rights — A965

No. 3294: a, Hands and emblem. b, Rose, Arabic inscription.

2012, Apr. 14   *Perf. 14 Syncopated*
3294 A965 1 l Sheet of 2, #a-b   2.25 1.10

Constitutional Court, 50th Anniv. — A966

Designs: 1 l, 50th anniversary emblem. 2 l, Court and 50th anniversary emblem.

2012, Apr. 25   *Perf. 13¾ Syncopated*
3295-3296 A966   Set of 2   3.50 1.75

Tourism — A967

Hands and: No. 3297, 2 l, Aspendos (Amphitheater), Antalya. No. 3298, 2 l, Yat Limani (Harbor), Antalya. No. 3299, 2 l, Kiz Kulesi (Leander's Tower), Istanbul. No. 3300, 2 l, Ortaköy, Istanbul. No. 3301, 2 l, Efes (Ephesus), Izmir. No. 3302, 2 l, Saat Kulesi (Clock tower), Izmir. No. 3303, 2 l, Göreme, Nevsehir. No. 3304, 2 l, Zelve Monastery and balloon, Nevsehir.

2012, Apr. 30   *Perf. 14 Syncopated*
3297-3304 A967   Set of 8   18.50 9.25

Europa
A968

Designs: No. 3305, 2 l, Skier and parachute skier. No. 3306, 2 l, Whirling dervishes, sea turtle, tourist attractions.

2012, May 9   Perf. 13¾ Syncopated
3305-3306 A968 Set of 2   4.50 2.25

Union of Chambers and Commodity Excahnges of Turkey, 60th Anniv.
A969

2012, May 17
3307 A969 1 l multi   1.10 .55

Treasury and Audit Department, 150th Anniv. — A970

Designs: 1 l, Building and 150th anniversary emblem. 2 l, 150th anniversary emblem.

2012, May 29 Set of 2   3.25 1.60
3308-3309 A970

Miniature Sheet

10th Turkish Olympics — A971

No. 3310: a, 50k, "10 Yasinda." b, 1 l, Globe tethered to map of Turkey with crescent and star. c, 1 l, Flags of various nations around flag of Turkey in oval. d, 2 l, Stylized faces of people of various cultures.

2012, May 30   Perf. 13
3310 A971 Sheet of 4, #a-d   5.00 2.50

Miniature Sheet

World Environment Day — A980

No. 3312 — Dinosaurs: a, 50k, Carnotaurus. b, 1 l, Pteranodon. c, 1 l, Tyrannosaurus rex. d, 2 l, Triceratops.

2012, June 5   Litho.   Perf. 13¼x13
3312 A980 Sheet of 4, #a-d   5.00 2.50
   A 46x46mm 3-dimensional 2 l stamp was sold only with a booklet to which the stamp was not attached.

Intl. Year of Cooperatives — A981

Designs: 1 l, Ants carrying Earth. 2 l, Stylized people carrying Turkey.

2012, June 6
3313-3314 A981 Set of 2   3.25 1.60

Istanbul Shopping Festival — A982

Designs: 1 l, Istanbul skyline, woman in red dress. 2 l, Folding fan.

2012, June 9   Perf. 13¾ Syncopated
3315-3316 A982 Set of 2   3.50 1.75

Miniature Sheet

2012 Summer Olympics, London — A983

No. 3317: a, 50k, Volleyball, London Eye. b, 1 l, Hurdles, Tower Bridge. c, 1 l, Wrestling, Regent Street buildings. d, 2 l, Basketball, Buckingham Palace.

2012, July 27   Perf. 13½x14
3317 A983 Sheet of 4, #a-d   5.00 2.50

Souvenir Sheet

European Kick Boxing Championships, Ankara — A984

No. 3318 — Kick boxers and map of: a, Western Europe. b, Central and Eastern Europe.

2012, Oct. 27   Perf. 13¼x13½
3318 A984 1 l Sheet of 2, #a-b   2.25 1.10

Souvenir Sheet

Bridges — A985

No. 3319: a, Bosporus Bridge, Istanbul. b, Yangtze River Bridge, Taizhou, People's Republic of China.

2012, Nov. 26   Perf. 14x13½
3319 A985 1 l Sheet of 2, #a-b   2.25 1.10
   See People's Republic of China Nos. 4056-4057.

Souvenir Sheet

Cultural Heritage of Kütahya — A986

No. 3320: a, 1 l, Shaft of light on altar. b, 2 l, Temple of Zeus.

2012, Nov. 29   Perf. 13¼
3320 A986 Sheet of 2, #a-b   3.50 1.75

Photographs of Everyday Life — A987

Designs: No. 3321, 50k, Fishermen tending nets. No. 3322, 50k, Hands of goat herder and goat. No. 3323, 1 l, Fisherman casting net. No. 3324, 1 l, Sheep grazing in field. No. 3325, 2 l, Woman with harvesting basket. No. 3326, 2 l, Horses in corral.

2012, Dec. 26   Perf. 13½x14
3321-3326 A987 Set of 6   8.00 4.00

A988

Black line and: 20k Flowers. 1.10 l, Tulips. 2.20 l, Flowers, diff. 3.85 l, Decorative circles. 8 l, Flowers, diff.

2013, Jan. 7   Perf. 13x12½
3327 A988 20k multi   .25   .25
3328 A988 1.10 l multi   1.25 .65
3329 A988 2.20 l multi   2.50 1.25
3330 A988 3.85 l multi   4.50 2.25
3331 A988 8 l multi   9.25 4.50
      Nos. 3327-3331 (5)   17.75 8.90

Miniature Sheet

Turkish Postage Stamps, 150th Anniv. — A989

No. 3332: a, Emblem of Turkish PTT. b, Leaves, star and crescent. c, Tughra of Sultan Abdul-Aziz. d, Stamp inscribed "150 Yil."

Litho. & Embossed With Foil Application
2013, Jan. 14   Perf. 14¼
3332 A989 1.10 l Sheet of 4, #a-d, + label   5.00 2.50

Souvenir Sheet

Yildiz Palace, Istanbul — A990

No. 3333: a, Palace and fountain. b, Palace, photograph and tughra of Sultan Abdul Hamid II.

2013, Feb. 27   Perf. 13½x13¼
3333 A990 1.10 l Sheet of 2, #a-b   2.50 1.25

Miniature Sheet

Eskisehir, 2013 UNESCO Intangible Culture Capital — A991

No. 3334: a, 1.10 l, Train. b, 1.10 l, Meerschaum pipe, spa pool. c, 2.20 l, Porsuk River. d, 2.20 l, Houses in Odupazari District.

2013, Mar. 21 Litho. Perf. 13¾x14
3334 A991 Sheet of 4, #a-d   7.50 3.75

Souvenir Sheet

World Down Syndrome Day — A992

No. 3335 — Face of child with Down Syndrome and: a, 50k, Chromosomes, strand of DNA, heart (40x30mm). b, 1.10 l, Heart (40x30mm). c, 2.20 l, Children in field of flowers, hearts (80x30mm).

Perf. 13½x13¼

2013, Mar. 21			**Litho.**
3335	A992	Sheet of 3, #a-c	4.25 2.10

Souvenir Sheet

Expo 2020, Izmir — A993

No. 3336: a, 1.10 l, Izmir tourist attractions, emblem of Expo 2020. b, 1.10 l, Man and woman jogging on waterside path. c, 2.20 l, Emblem of Expo 2020.

2013, Apr. 4		**Litho.**	**Perf. 13½**
3336	A993	Sheet of 3, #a-c	5.00 2.50

Tourist Attractions in Antalya A994

Designs: No. 3337, 2.20 l, Alanya Kalesi (Alanya Castle). No. 3338, 2.20 l, Apollon Tapinagi (Temple of Apollo), Side. No. 3339, 2.20 l, Hadrian Kapisi (Hadrian's Gate). No. 3340, 2.20 l, Kaleiçi (historic city center). No. 3341, 2.20 l, Manavgat Selalesi (Manavgat Waterfalls). No. 3342, 2.20 l, Saat Kulesi ve Yivli Minare (Clock Tower and Yivli Minaret).

Perf. 13¾ Syncopated

2013, Apr. 12			**Litho.**
3337-3342	A994	Set of 6	15.00 7.50

Miniature Sheet

Piri Reis Map, 500th Anniv. — A995

No. 3343 — Part of map with: a, 1.10 l, Ship and compass rose. b, 1.10 l, Ship, birds, monkeys. c, 2.20 l, Ships and compass rose. d, 2.20 l, Text and Piri Reis (c.1464-1553).

2013, Apr. 18		**Litho.**	**Perf. 13½**
3343	A995	Sheet of 4, #a-d, + label	7.50 3.75

Europa — A996

Designs: 1.10 l, Mailbox, envelope, postal vans and motorcycle. 2.20 l, Postrider, sealed

scroll, horse-drawn carrialge, postal trucks, mailbox.

2013, May 9	**Litho.**	**Perf. 13½x13¼**	
3344-3345	A996	Set of 2	3.50 1.75

Miniature Sheet

Istanbul Technical University, 240th Anniv. — A997

No. 3346: a, Building with eight short pillars. b, Doors and windows. c, Building without pillars. d, Building with four tall pillars.

2013, May 24	**Litho.**	**Perf. 13¾x14**	
3346	A997	1.10 l Sheet of 4, #a-d	4.75 2.40

Miniature Sheet

World Environment Day — A998

No. 3347: a, Head and neck with water and dry earth. b, House, stylized globe, flower and trees. c, Farm, tractor, polar bears, map of Northern Africa. d, Family, foxes, rabbit, seal.

2013, June 5	**Litho.**	**Perf. 14x13¾**	
3347	A998	1.10 l Sheet of 4, #a-d	4.75 2.40

Miniature Sheet

17th Mediterranean Games, Mersin — A999

No. 3348: a, Shell, track and field athletes, boxer. b, Boxer, weight lifter, yacht. c, Yacht, archer, gymnast. d, Volleyball player, cyclist.

2013, June 10	**Litho.**	**Perf. 14x13¾**	
3348	A999	1.10 l Sheet of 4, #a-d	4.75 2.40

A 5 l self-adhesive three-dimensional plastic stamp depicting turtles and the turtle mascot of the Mediterranean Games was produced in a limited quantity and sold only in a folder that also contained No. 3348 and a first day cover of No. 3348.

Public Administration Institute for Turkey and the Middle East, 60th Anniv. — A1000

Perf. 13¾ Syncopated

2013, June 28			**Litho.**
3349	A1000	1.10 l multi	1.10 .55

Expo 2016, Antalya — A1001

Designs: No. 3350, 2.20 l, Children, flowers, Yivli Minaret. No. 3351, 2.20 l, Emblem of Expo 2016.

Perf. 13¾ Syncopated

2013, July 25			**Litho.**
3350-3351	A1001	Set of 2	4.75 2.40

Miniature Sheet

Cuisine of Central Anatolia — A1002

No. 3352: a, Tomato, bread, meat dish, bowl of vegetables and sauce. b, Wheat stalk, three plates of food. c, Scallions, radishes, food in clay pots, rolls. d, Grapes, two plates of food.

2013, Aug. 16	**Litho.**	**Perf. 14x13¾**	
3352	A1002	1.10 l Sheet of 4, #a-d	4.50 2.25

Calligraphy A1003

Various depictions of Arabic "w."

Perf. 13¾ Syncopated

2013, Aug. 27				**Litho.**
3353	A1003	10k lilac & blk		.25 .25
3354	A1003	1 l gray & blk		1.00 .50
3355	A1003	1.10 l blue & blk		1.10 .55
3356	A1003	8 l multi		8.00 4.00
	Nos. 3353-3356 (4)			10.35 5.30

Council of State Building A1004

Council of State 145th Anniv. Emblem A1005

2013, Sept. 2	**Litho.**	**Perf. 13¾x14**	
3357	A1004	1.10 l multi	1.10 .55
3358	A1005	1.10 l multi	1.10 .55

11th Transportation, Maritime Affairs and Communication Forum, Istanbul — A1006

Forum emblem and: No. 3359, 1.10 l, Satellite above Earth. No. 3360, 1.10 l, Airplane over new Istanbul Airport. No. 3361, 2.20 l, Train, Marmaray Tunnel, map of Istanbul. No. 3362, 2.20 l, Yavuz Sultan Selim Bridge, Istanbul.

2013, Sept. 5	**Litho.**	**Perf. 13¾**	
3359-3362	A1006	Set of 4	6.50 3.25

A sheet of four 1.10 l stamps depicting parts of the Izmit Bay Bridge was only offered in a presentation folder that sold for 30 l.

13th Istanbul Biennial Contemporary Art Exhibition — A1007

2013, Sept. 14	**Litho.**	**Perf. 13¾**	
3363	A1007	1.10 l black	1.10 .55

Turkish Language Festival A1008

2013, Sept. 26	**Litho.**	**Perf. 13¾**	
3364	A1008	1.10 l multi	1.10 .55

Souvenir Sheet

King Carol I Mosque, Constanta, Romania — A1009

2013, Oct. 10	**Litho.**	**Perf. 13½**	
3365	A1009	3.85 l multi	4.00 2.00

Diplomatic relations between Turkey and Romania, 135th anniv. See Romania No. 5492.

Turkish Postage Stamp Museum A1010

Designs: 1.10 l, Turkey #3094-3095. 2.20 l, Museum displays.

2013, Oct. 22	**Litho.**	**Perf. 13¾**	
3366-3367	A1010	Set of 2	3.25 1.60

Values for Nos. 3366-3367 are for stamps with surrounding selvage. A 8 l souvenir sheet depicting postal workers, buildings and equipment was only offered in a presentation folder that sold for 30 l.

Souvenir Sheet

Republic of Turkey, 90th Anniv. — A1011

No. 3368 — Bridge and; a, Tank, military jet and helicopter, map of Europe. b, Satellite, train, Kemal Ataturk.

2013, Oct. 29 Litho. Perf. 13¼
3368 A1011 1.10 l Sheet of 2,
#a-b 2.25 1.10

Souvenir Sheet

Completion of Marmaray Tunnel Project — A1012

Perf. 13¾ Syncopated
2013, Oct. 29 Litho.
3369 A1012 1.10 l multi 1.10 .55

No. 3369 exists imperforate in a limited printing.

Fifth Izmir Economic Congress A1013

2013, Oct. 30 Litho. Perf. 13¾x14
3370 A1013 1.10 l multi 1.10 .55

Souvenir Sheet

Mosques — A1014

No. 3371: a, 1.10 l, Sultan Ahmed Mosque, Istanbul. b, 2.20 l, Al-Aqsa Mosque, Jerusalem.

Perf. 13½x13¾
2013, Dec. 12 Litho.
3371 A1014 Sheet of 2, #a-b 3.25 1.60
See Palestinian Authority No. 245.

University of Ankara Faculty of Dentistry, 50th Anniv. — A1015

2013, Dec. 14 Litho. Perf. 13½
3372 A1015 1.10 l multi 1.00 .50

Yasar Dogu (1913-61), Wrestler A1016

Perf. 13¾ Syncopated
2013, Dec. 23 Litho.
3373 A1016 50k multi .45 .25

Turkish Republic of Northern Cyprus Postal Service, 50th Anniv. — A1017

Perf. 14x13¾ Syncopated
2014, Jan. 6 Litho.
3374 A1017 1.10 l multi 1.00 .50

Altay Sports Club, Cent. A1018

Designs: No. 3375, 1.10 l, Basketball. No. 3376, 1.10 l, Soccer. No. 3377, 2.20 l, Swimming. No. 3378, 2.20 l, Handball.

2014, Jan. 16 Litho. Perf. 13¾
3375-3378 A1018 Set of 4 0.00 3.00
Values are for stamps with surrounding selvage.

2014 Winter Olympics, Sochi, Russia A1019

Designs: No. 3379, 1.10 l, Ski jumping. No. 3380, 1.10 l, Pairs figure skating. No. 3381, 2.20 l, Alpine skiing. No. 3382, 2.20 l, Speed skating.

2014, Feb. 7 Litho. Perf. 13¾
3379-3382 A1019 Set of 4 6.00 3.00

Turkish Radio and Television, 50th Anniv. A1020

50th anniv. emblem and: 1.10 l, Text. 2.20 l, Building.

2014, Feb. 20 Litho. Perf. 13¾
3383-3384 A1020 Set of 2 3.00 1.50

Souvenir Sheet

Topkapi Palace — A1021

No. 3385: a, Tower of Justice and Gate of Salutation, b, Palace interior, Sultan Mehmed II (1432-81) and his monogram.

Litho. With Foil Application
2014, Feb. 27 Perf. 13½x13¼
3385 A1021 1.10 l Sheet of 2,
#a-b 2.00 1.00

Miniature Sheet

First Deaths of Turkish Military Aviators, Cent. — A1022

No. 3386: a, 50k, Lieutenant Selim Salq Bey and Captain Mehmet Fethi Bey. b, 1.10 l, Fethi Bey and airplane. c, 1.10 l, Memorial, Haon, Israel. d, 2.20 l, Building and Fethi Bey Monument, Istanbul.

Perf. 13½x13¼
2014, Feb. 27 Litho.
3386 A1022 Sheet of 4, #a-d 4.50 2.25

General Directorate of Hydraulic Works, 60th Anniv. A1023

2014, Mar. 22 Litho. Perf. 13¾
3387 A1023 1.10 l multi + label 1.10 .55

Souvenir Sheet

Mother's Day — A1024

2014, Apr. 17 Litho. Perf.
3388 A1024 1.10 l multi + 4 labels 1.10 .55

Tour of Turkey Bicycle Race, 50th Anniv. — A1025

2014, Apr. 27 Litho. Perf. 13½x13¼
3389 A1025 1.10 l multi 1.10 .55

A folder containing No. 3389, a first day cover of No. 3389, and a souvenir sheet containing a 2.20 l stamp was produced in limited quantities.

Europa — A1026

Musical instruments: 1.25 l, Kabak kemane. 2.50 l, Ud.

2014, May 9 Litho. Perf. 13½x13¼
3390-3391 A1026 Set of 2 3.75 1.90

Tourist Attractions — A1027

Attractions in: No. 3392, Erzurum Province. No. 3393, Sanliurfa Province. No. 3394, Izmir Province. No. 3395, Konya Province. No. 3396, Antalya Province. No. 3397, Istanbul Province. 4 l, Trabzon Province. 9 l, Ankara Province.

Perf. 13¾ Syncopated
2014, May 22 Litho.
3392 A1027 35k multi .35 .25
3393 A1027 35k multi .35 .25
3394 A1027 1.25 l multi 1.25 .60
3395 A1027 1.25 l multi 1.25 .60
3396 A1027 2.50 l multi 2.40 1.25
3397 A1027 2.50 l multi 2.40 1.25
3398 A1027 4 l multi 3.75 1.90
3399 A1027 9 l multi 8.50 4.25
Nos. 3392-3399 (8) 20.25 10.35

Souvenir Sheet

World Environment Day — A1028

No. 3400: a, 1.25 l, Bee in flight. b, 1.25 l, Two bees in flight. c, 2.50 l, Bee on flower.

2014, June 5 Litho. Perf. 13½
3400 A1028 Sheet of 3, #a-c 4.75 2.40

Turkish Gendarmerie, 175th Anniv. — A1030

Perf. 13½x13¼
2014, June 14 Litho.
3405 A1030 1.25 l multi 1.25 .60

Souvenir Sheet

Deer and Mushrooms in National Park — A1031

2014, July 9 Litho. **Perf. 13¼**
3406 A1031 2.50 l multi 2.40 1.25

2014 World Cup Soccer Championships, Brazil — A1032

Designs: 1.25 l, World Cup trophy. 2.50 l, Mascot of 2014 World Cup, horiz.

Perf. 14x13¾, 13¾x14
2014, Aug. 6 Litho.
3407-3408 A1032 Set of 2 3.50 1.75

Miniature Sheet

Local Cuisine — A1033

No. 3409: a, 1.25 l, Agzi açik (lamb pies), Sanliurfa Province. b, 1.25 l, Sihlmahsi (stuffed zucchini), Kilis Province. c, 2.50 l, Sogan kebabi (stuffed onions), Mardin Province. d, 2.50 l, Saçma tavasi (stew), Gaziantep Province.

2014, Aug. 15 Litho. **Perf. 14x13¾**
3409 A1033 Sheet of 4, #a-d 7.00 3.50

Ottoman Navy Galleon Mahmudiya — A1034

Various depictions of the Mahmudiya, 1.25 l, 2.50 l.

Litho. With Foil Application
Perf. 13¾ Syncopated
2014, Sept. 10
3410-3411 A1034 Set of 2 3.50 1.75

2014 Women's World Basketball Championships, Istanbul and Ankara — A1035

Design: 1.25 l, Emblem. 2.50 l, Emblem and stylized basketball (38x38mm).

Perf. 13¼x13½, 13¼
2014, Sept. 29 Litho.
3412-3413 A1035 Set of 2 3.50 1.75

Souvenir Sheet

Presidential Palace, Ankara — A1036

Litho., Sheet Margin Litho & Embossed With Foil Application
2014, Oct. 29 **Perf. 13½x13¼**
3414 A1036 1.25 l multi 1.10 .55
Republic of Turkey, 91st anniv. A limited edition packet contained three imperforate souvenir sheets showing different images of the Presidential Palace, with denominations of 1.25 l, 2.50 l, and 4 l, along with first day covers of these items.

Turkish Cinema, Cent. — A1037

Perf. 13½x13¼
2014, Nov. 14 Litho.
3415 A1037 1.25 l multi 1.10 .55
A souvenir sheet of 3 containing two 1.25 l and one 2.50 l stamp was produced in limited quantities and sold for 12.50 l.

Souvenir Sheet

Diplomatic Relations Between Turkey and Poland, 600th Anniv. — A1038

Perf. 13½x13¼
2014, Nov. 28 Litho.
3416 A1038 4 l multi 3.75 1.90
See Poland No. 4155.

Safranbolu Tourist Attractions A1039

Antalya Tourist Attractions A1040

Antalya Tourist Attractions A1041

Izmir Tourist Attractions A1042

Izmir Tourist Attractions A1043

Izmir Tourist Attractions A1044

Perf. 13¾ Syncopated
2014-15 Litho.
3417 A1039 50k multi .40 .25
3418 A1040 2.50 l multi 2.10 1.10
3419 A1041 2.50 l multi 2.00 1.00
3420 A1042 2.50 l multi 2.00 1.00
3421 A1043 2.50 l multi 2.00 1.00
3422 A1044 2.50 l multi 2.00 1.00
Nos. 3417-3422 (6) 10.50 5.35
Issued: No. 3418, 12/10; others, 3/20/15. Compare Nos. 3418-3419 with No. 3396.

Battle of Sarikamish, Cent. — A1045

Perf. 13½x13¼
2014, Dec. 22 Litho.
3423 A1045 1.25 l multi 1.10 .55
A souvenir sheet containing one 2.50 l stamp was printed in limited quantities and sold for 12.50 l.

Campaign to Prevent Waste of Bread A1046

2015, Jan. 19 Litho. **Perf. 13x13¼**
3424 A1046 1.25 l multi + label 1.10 .55

Mosques — A1047

No. 3425: a, Green Mosque, Bursa, Turkey. b, Kabood Mosque, Tabriz, Iran.

Perf. 13½x13¼
2015, Feb. 18 Litho.
3425 Sheet of 2 2.00 1.00
a.-b. A1047 1.25 l Either single 1.00 .50
See Iran No. 3135.

Souvenir Sheet

Dolmabahce Palace, Istanbul — A1048

No. 3426: a, Palace exterior, Gate to the Bosporus. b, Gate of the Treasury, portrait and monogram of Sultan Abdülmecid I.

Litho. With Foil Application
2015, Feb. 27 **Perf. 13½x13¼**
3426 A1048 1.25 l Sheet of 2, #a-b 2.00 1.00

Battle of Gallipoli, Cent. A1049

Designs: 1.10 l, Statue of soldier carrying fallen comrade, Gallipoli. 1.35 l, Soldiers, Turkish flag. 2.50 l, Battle scene.

2015, Mar. 18 Litho. **Perf. 13¼**
3427-3429 A1049 Set of 3 3.75 1.90
A 2.50 l imperforate souvenir sheet and a 4 l perforated souvenir sheet were produced in limited quantities and were sold with a first day cover for 25 l.

Frigate "Ertugrul," 125th Anniv. — A1050

Designs: 1.25 l, Frigate "Ertugrul." 2.50 l, Crew members.

2015, Apr. 1 Litho. **Perf. 13½x13¼**
3430-3431 A1050 Set of 2 3.00 1.50

Court of Military Appeals, Cent. — A1051

2015, Apr. 6 Litho. Perf. 13½x13¼
3432 A1051 1.25 l multi 1.00 .50

Grand National Assembly, 95th Anniv. — A1052

Designs: 1.25 l, Old Assembly Building. 2.50 l, Current Assembly Building, Assembly Room.

2015, Apr. 23 Litho. Perf. 13½x13¼
3433-3434 A1052 Set of 2 2.75 1.40

Peace Summit — A1053

Designs: 1.25 l, Turkish flag, soldiers, women. 2.50 l, Statue of soldier carrying fallen comrade, Gallipoli, soldiers with artillery.

Perf. 13¾ Syncopated
2015, Apr. 23 Litho.
3435-3436 A1053 Set of 2 2.75 1.40

A 2.50 l imperforate souvenir sheet and a 4 l perforated souvenir sheet were produced in limited quantities and were sold with a first day cover for 25 l.

Jewelry A1054

Jewelry made from: 1.25 l, Sepiolite (lüle tasi). 2.50 l, Black amber (oltu tasi).

Litho. & Thermography
2015, Apr. 29 Perf. 13¼
3437-3438 A1054 Set of 2 2.75 1.40

Europa — A1055

Children and: 1.25 l, Doll in cradle. 2.50 l, Pull toy with hammers.

2015, May 9 Litho. Perf. 13½x13¼
3439-3440 A1055 Set of 2 3.00 1.50

Miniature Sheet

Historic Areas of Istanbul UNESCO World Heritage Site — A1056

No. 3441: a, 1.25 l, Sultanahmet Mosque Archaeological Park. b, 1.25 l, Süleymaniye Quarter. c, 2.50 l, Zeyrek Quarter. d, 2.50 l, Walls of Istanbul.

2015, May 21 Litho. Perf. 14x13¾
3441 A1056 Sheet of 4, #a-d 5.75 3.00

Miniature Sheet

World Environment Day — A1057

No. 3442 — Mushrooms: a, 1.25 l, Auricularia auricula-judae. b, 1.25 l, Coprinopsis picacea. c, 2.50 l, Morchella deliciosa. d, 2.50 l, Mucidula mucida.

Perf. 13¾ Syncopated
2015, June 5 Litho.
3442 A1057 Sheet of 4, #a-d 5.75 3.00

2015 Women's World Cup Soccer Championships, Canada — A1058

Designs: No. 3443, 1.25 l, Trophy. No. 3444, 1.25 l, Mascot holding soccer ball. No. 3445, 2.50 l, Mascot preparing to kick soccer ball, horiz. No. 3446, 2.50 l, Emblem, horiz.

Perf. 14x13¾, 13¾x14
2015, June 6 Litho.
3443-3446 A1058 Set of 4 5.75 3.00

Fire Fighting A1059

Designs: 50k, Fire station, fire fighters battling blaze. 1 l, Fire fighters and trucks, vert. 9 l, Rescue crews, fire trucks, vert.

Perf. 13¾ Syncopated
2015, June 26 Litho.
3447-3449 A1059 Set of 3 7.75 4.00

Souvenir Sheet

Kazdagi National Park — A1060

2015, July 9 Litho. Perf. 13¼
3450 A1060 1.25 l multi .90 .45

Tapestries A1061

Tapestries depicting: 30k, Ducks in pond. 1.40 l, Swans and flowers. 2.80 l, Birds, nest, flowers, vert. 4.50 l, House, fence, ducks, vert. 10 l, Chickens, feeder, fence, vert.

Perf. 13¼ Syncopated
2015, Aug. 6 Litho.
3451-3455 A1061 Set of 5 13.00 6.50

Miniature Sheet

Turkish Cuisine — A1062

No. 3456: a, 60k, Börülce. b, 60k, Sevket-i-Bostan. c, 2.80 l, Sinkonta. d, 2.80 l, Cökertme Kebabi.

2015, Aug. 17 Litho. Perf. 14x13¾
3456 A1062 Sheet of 4, #a-d 4.75 2.40

Occupations of the Past — A1063

Designs: No. 3457, 1.40 l, Saddle maker (semerci). No. 3458, 1.40 l, Blacksmith (demirci). No. 3459, 2.80 l, Cobbler (kösker). No. 3460, 2.80 l, Street vendor (macuncu).

2015, Sept. 3 Litho. Perf. 13¼x13½
3457-3460 A1063 Set of 4 5.75 3.00

Souvenir Sheet

Water Conservation — A1064

No. 3461: a, 60k, Dead trees, dry creek bed. b, 1.40 l, Water drop, healthy tree. c, 2.80 l, Trees, bird.

2015, Oct. 7 Litho. Perf. 14x13¾
3461 A1064 Sheet of 3, #a-c 3.50 1.75

Turkish Posts, Telegraph and Telephone, 175th Anniv. — A1065

Designs: No. 3462, 1.40 l, Postal sorting boxes and machinery. No. 3463, 1.40 l, Exteriors of post offices. No. 3464, 1.40 l, Telegraph, computer, dove. 2.80 l, Turkey #2, envelope and "@" symbol.

2015, Oct. 23 Litho. Perf. 13½x13¼
3462-3465 A1065 Set of 4 5.00 2.50

An imperforate 2.80 l souvenir sheet was produced in limited quantities and sold with a first day cover for 25 l.

Postmen A1066

Inscriptions at left: No. 3466, Tatar Agasi. No. 3467, Müjdecibasi. No. 3468, Peyk (sword hilt close to body). No. 3469, Peyk (sword hilt away from body). No. 3470, Posta Tatari. No. 3471, Posta Tatari (coat with red piping). No. 3472, Posta Memuru (Postaci) (wearing red fez). No. 3473, Posta Memuru (wearing cap, holding mail bag). No. 3474, Posta Dagiticisi (wearing red scarves). No. 3475, Posta Dagiticisi (man at right with yellow and black uniform).

Litho. With Foil Application
Perf. 13¾ Syncopated
2015, Oct. 23 Booklet Panes of 1
3466 A1066 60k multi .60 .60
3467 A1066 60k multi .60 .60
3468 A1066 1.40 l multi 1.40 1.40
3469 A1066 1.40 l multi 1.40 1.40
3470 A1066 1.40 l multi 1.40 1.40
3471 A1066 1.40 l multi 1.40 1.40
3472 A1066 2.80 l multi 2.75 2.75
3473 A1066 2.80 l multi 2.75 2.75
3474 A1066 2.80 l multi 2.75 2.75
3475 A1066 2.80 l multi 2.75 2.75
Complete booklet, #3466-3475 18.00
Nos. 3466-3475 (10) 17.80 17.80

Complete booklet sold for 25 l.

Souvenir Sheet

Republic of Turkey, 92nd Anniv. — A1067

Perf. 13¾ Syncopated
2015, Oct. 29   **Litho.**
3476 A1067 1.40 l multi   1.00 .50

G20 Summit, Antalya A1068

2015, Nov. 15   **Litho.**   **Perf. 13¼**
3477 A1068 2.80 l multi   2.00 1.00

Dr. Aziz Sancar, 2015 Nobel Chemistry Laureate — A1069

Perf. 13½x13¼
2015, Dec. 10   **Litho.**
3478 A1069 2.80 l multi   1.90 .95

Souvenir Sheet

Haliç Shipyards — A1070

No. 3479: a, 1.40 l, Buildings, boats and crane. b, 1.40 l, Buildings and boats. c, 2.80 l, Buildings, ships and boats

Perf. 13¾ Syncopated
2015, Dec. 11   **Litho.**
3479 A1070   Sheet of 3, #a-c   4.00 2.00

Animals — A1071

Designs: No. 3480, 1.40 l, Lepus cuniculus angorensis. No. 3481, 1.40 l, Capra hircus angorensis. 2.80 l, Felis catus angolensis.

2015, Dec. 31   **Litho.**   **Perf. 14x13¾**
3480-3482 A1071   Set of 3   4.00 2.00

Post Offices A1072

Buildings: 30k, Meram Post Office. 50k, Kozlu Post Office. 1 l, PTT Museum, Ankara. 1.40 l, Sirkeci Post Office. 4.50 l, Artuklu Post Office. 10 l, Old Parcel Building, Izmir.

Perf. 13¾ Syncopated
2016, Feb. 22   **Litho.**
3483-3488 A1072   Set of 6   12.00 6.00

Souvenir Sheet

Ishak Pasha Palace — A1073

No. 3489 — Palace and: a, Gate at right. b, Minaret at right.

Litho. With Foil Application
2016, Feb. 26   **Perf. 13¾x14**
3489 A1073 1.40 l   Sheet of 2,
       #a-b   1.90 .95

Souvenir Sheets

Grand Bazaar, Istanbul — A1074

Egyptian Bazaar, Istanbul — A1075

No. 3490 — "Kapali Carsi" and: a, 1.40 l, Shoppers, drinking fountain in aisle. b, 2.80 l, Shoppers.
No. 3491 — "Misir Carsisi" and: a, 1.40 l, Building exterior. b, 2.80 l, Building ceiling.

Litho., Sheet Margin Litho. With Foil Application
2016, Mar. 22   **Perf. 13½x13¾**
3490 A1074   Sheet of 2, #a-b   3.00 1.50
3491 A1075   Sheet of 2, #a-b   3.00 1.50

13th Islamic Summit, Istanbul A1076

2016, Apr. 14   **Litho.**   **Perf. 13¼x13½**
3492 A1076 2.80 l multi   2.00 1.00

Horticultural Expo 2016, Antalya — A1077

Emblem and: No. 3493, 1.40 l, Girls, flowers, pillars. No. 3494, 1.40 l, Turkcell Expo Tower, boy and girl. 2.80 l, Paeonia turcia.

2016, Apr. 23   **Litho.**   **Perf. 13¾x14**
3493-3495 A1077   Set of 3   4.00 2.00

A1078

End of Siege of Kut Al Amara, Cent. A1079

2016, Apr. 29   **Litho.**   **Perf. 13¾x14**
3496 A1078 1.40 l multi   1.00 .50
3497 A1079 2.80 l multi   2.00 1.00

World Humanitarian Summit, Istanbul — A1080

2016, May 23   **Litho.**   **Perf. 13¾x14**
3498 A1080 2.80 l multi   1.90 .95

Souvenir Sheet

World Environment Day — A1081

No. 3499: a, 1.40 l, Water molecule. b, 1.40 l, Arms wrapped around Earth. c, 2.80 l, Umbrella over Earth.

2016, June 5   **Litho.**   **Perf. 13¾**
3499 A1081   Sheet of 3, #a-c   4.00 2.00

2016 European Soccer Championships, France — A1082

Emblem and: No. 3500, 1.40 l, Player on knees celebrating goal, orange background. No. 3501, 1.40 l, Player kicking ball, blue background. No. 3502, 2.80 l, Player holding trophy, green background. No. 3503, 2.80 l, Trophy, red background.

2016, June 10   **Litho.**   **Perf. 14x13¾**
3500-3503 A1082   Set of 4   6.00 3.00

UNESCO World Heritage Committee, 40th Meeting, Istanbul — A1083

Perf. 13¾ Syncopated
2016, July 10   **Litho.**
3504 A1083 3.20 l blk & blue   2.25 1.10

A souvenir sheet containing a 3.20 l stamp was printed in limited quantities and sold for 15 l.

Souvenir Sheet

Sarikamis-Allahuekber Mountains National Park — A1084

2016, July 12   **Litho.**   **Perf. 13**
3505 A1084 3.20 l multi   2.25 1.10

Ahmed Yesevi (1083-1166), Poet — A1085

Mausoleum of Ahmed Yesevi, Turkistan, Kazakhstan — A1086

2016, July 26   **Litho.**   **Perf. 13¼**
3506 A1085 1.60 l multi   1.10 .55
3507 A1086 3.20 l multi   2.25 1.10

Tourist Attractions — A1087

Attractions in: 20k, Ordu. 40k, Erzincan. 1.60 l, Denizli, horiz. 3.20 l, Nevsehir, horiz. 5.10 l, Izmir, horiz. 11 l, Kars, horiz.

Perf. 13¾ Syncopated
2016, July 27   **Litho.**
3508 A1087   20k multi   .25 .25
3509 A1087   40k multi   .25 .25
3510 A1087   1.60 l multi   1.10 .55
3511 A1087   3.20 l multi   2.25 1.10
3512 A1087   5.10 l multi   3.50 1.75
3513 A1087   11 l multi   7.50 3.75
     Nos. 3508-3513 (6)   14.85 7.65

A1088

A1089

A1090

Konya, 2016
Islamic
Capital of
Tourism
A1091

2016, Aug. 4   Litho.   Perf. 13
3514 A1088 1.60 l multi   1.10   .55
3515 A1089 1.60 l multi   1.10   .55
3516 A1090 1.60 l multi   1.10   .55
3517 A1091 3.20 l multi   2.25 1.10
      Nos. 3514-3517 (4)   5.55 2.75

Martyr's Day — A1092

2016, Aug. 5   Litho.   Perf. 13¼
3518 A1092 1.60 l multi   1.10   .55

Miniature Sheet

Eastern Anatolian Dishes — A1093

No. 3519: a, 1.60 l, Kete (butter pastry). b, 1.60 l, Kaz eti (goose). c, 1.60 l, Jagli yumurta (scrambled eggs). d, 3.20 l, Kadayif dolmasi (filled pastry).

2016, Aug. 8   Litho.   Perf. 14x13¾
3519 A1093 Sheet of 4, #a-d   5.50 2.75

Justice and Development Party, 15th Anniv. — A1094

2016, Aug. 14   Litho.   Perf. 13¼
3520 A1094 1.60 l multi   1.10   .55

An imperforate 1.60 l stamp with a different design was produced in limited quantities and sold with No. 3520 and a first day cover for 15 l.

Victory Day — A1095

Perf. 13¾ Syncopated
2016, Aug. 30   Litho.
3521 A1095 1.60 l multi   1.10   .55

A 1.60 l souvenir sheet with a different design was produced in limited quantities and sold with No. 3521 and a first day cover for 12.50 l.

Souvenir Sheet

Leaders of the Battle of Szigetvár — A1096

No. 3522: a, Nikola Zrinski (1508-66). b, Suleiman the Magnificent (1495-1566).

2016, Sept. 7   Litho.   Perf. 13¼
3522 A1096 3.20 l Sheet of 2, #a-b   4.25 2.10

See Hungary No. 4403.

26th Universal Postal Union Congress, Istanbul — A1097

Perf. 13¾ Syncopated
2016, Sept. 20   Litho.
3523 A1097 3.20 l multi   2.10 1.10

A miniature sheet containing five 1.60 l stamps with different designs was produced in limited quantities and sold with No. 3523 and a first day cover for 25 l.

23rd World Energy Council Congres, Istanbul A1098

2016, Oct. 9   Litho.   Perf. 13
3524 A1098 3.20 l multi   2.10 1.10

Miniature Sheet

Gaziantep, 2015 UNESCO Creative City of Gastronomy — A1099

No. 3525 — Various foods: a, Three plates. b, Bowl, two plates, tray and spoon. c, Three plates and lid. d, Two plates.

2016, Oct. 12   Litho.   Perf. 13
3525 A1099 1.60 l Sheet of 4, #a-d   4.25 2.10

Turkey to Turkish Republic of Northern Cyprus Water Pipeline Project — A1100

2016, Oct. 17   Litho.   Imperf.
3526 A1100 1.60 l multi   1.10   .55

See Turkish Republic of Northern Cyprus No. 800.

South Eastern Europe Defense Ministerial Process, 20th Anniv. — A1101

2016, Oct. 18   Litho.   Perf. 13¼
3527 A1101 3.20 l multi   2.10 1.10

Republic Day A1102

2016, Oct. 29   Litho.   Perf. 13
3528 A1102 1.60 l multi   1.10   .55

A 3.20 l souvenir sheet with a different design was produced in limited quantities and sold with No. 3528 and a first day cover for 12.50 l.

A1103   A1104

A1105   A1106

Art
A1107   A1108

Perf. 13¾ Syncopated
2016, Nov. 28   Litho.
3529 A1103 10k multi   .25   .25
3530 A1104 20k multi   .25   .25
3531 A1105 1 l multi   .60   .30
3532 A1106 1.60 l multi   .90   .45
3533 A1107 2 l multi   1.25   .60
3534 A1108 11 l multi   6.25 3.25
      Nos. 3529-3534 (6)   9.50 5.10

Women's Right to Vote, 82nd Anniv. A1109

2016, Dec. 5   Litho.   Perf. 13
3535 A1109 1 l multi + label   .55   .30

Souvenir Sheet

Opning of Eurasla Tunnel (in 2016) — A1110

Perf. 13¾x13½ Syncopated
2017, Jan. 30   Litho.
3536 A1110 1.60 l multi   .85   .40

European Youth Olympic Winter Festival, Erzurum — A1111

European Olympic Committees emblem and: No. 3537, 1.60 l, Festival emblem. No. 3538, 1.60 l, Festival mascot. 3.70 l, Skiers and mosques.

2017, Feb. 12   Litho.   Perf. 13
3537-3539 A1111 Set of 3   3.75 1.90

Tombs, Myra — A1112

Temple of Apollo, Side — A1113

Alanya Harbor — A1114

Clock Tower and Yivliminare Mosque
Minaret, Antalya — A1115

Perf. 13¼ Syncopated
2017, Apr. 4 **Litho.**
3540 A1112 3.70 l multi 2.10 1.10
3541 A1113 3.70 l multi 2.10 1.10
3542 A1114 3.70 l multi 2.10 1.10
3543 A1115 3.70 l multi 2.10 1.10
Nos. 3540-3543 (4) 8.40 4.40

Antalya Province tourist attractions.

Souvenir Sheet

Kemeralti Bazaar, Izmir — A1116

Litho. & Silk-Screened
2017, Apr. 4 **Perf. 13½x14**
3544 A1116 1.60 l multi .90 .45

Slogans — A1117

Designs: No. 3545, 3.70 l, Turkish slogan
"Gücü Keşfet." No. 3546, 3.70 l, English slogan "Discover the potential."

Perf. 13¼ Syncopated
2017, Apr. 17 **Litho.**
3545-3546 A1117 Set of 2 4.25 2.10

Souvenir Sheet

Beylerbeyi Palace, Istanbul — A1118

**Litho., Sheet Margin Litho. With Foil
Application**
2017, Apr. 21 **Perf. 13½x14**
3547 A1118 1.60 l multi .90 .45

Europa — A1119

Designs: 1.60 l, Bayburt Castle. 3.70 l, Kars
Castle.

2017, May 9 **Litho.** **Perf. 13½x13¼**
3548-3549 A1119 Set of 2 3.00 1.50

A1120

2017, May 30 **Litho.** **Perf. 13¼**
3550 A1120 3.70 l multi 2.10 1.10

Diplomatic Relations Between Turkey and
Azerbaijan, Belarus, Georgia, Kazakhstan,
Kyrgyzstan, Moldova, Tajikistan, Turkmeni-
stan, Ukraine, and Uzbekistan, 25th Anniv.

World Environment Day — A1121

2017, June 5 **Litho.** **Imperf.**
Self-Adhesive
3551 A1121 1.60 l multi .90 .45

Souvenir Sheet

Ankapark Amusement Park,
Ankara — A1122

No. 3552: a, Dinosaur statue. b, Door in
archway, vert.

Perf. 13¼ (#3552a), 14x13½ (#3552b)
2017, June 15 **Litho.**
3552 A1122 1.60 l Sheet of 2,
#a-b 1.90 .95

Fountain of Sultan Ahmed III,
Istanbul — A1123

2017, June 20 **Litho.** **Perf. 13¼**
3553 A1123 1.60 l multi .90 .45

22nd World Petroleum Congress,
Istanbul — A1124

2017, July 9 **Litho.** **Perf. 13¼**
3554 A1124 1.60 l multi .90 .45

A1125

Democracy and National Unity
Day — A1126

2017, July 15 **Litho.** **Perf. 13¼**
3555 A1125 1.60 l multi .90 .45
3556 A1126 1.60 l multi .90 .45

A souvenir sheet of four 60k stamps was
printed in limited quantities and sold with Nos.
3555-3556 and a first day cover for 17.50 l.

A1127

A1128

A1129

Turkish
Language
Year — A1130

Perf. 13½x13¾ Syncopated
2017, July 31 **Litho.**
3557 A1127 1.50 l multi .85 .45
3558 A1128 1.80 l multi 1.10 .55
3559 A1129 5.80 l multi 3.25 1.60
3560 A1130 12.50 l multi 7.25 3.75
Nos. 3557-3560 (4) 12.45 6.35

Ismir Clock
Tower
A1131

Perf. 13½x13¾ Syncopated
2017, Sept. 9 **Litho.**
3561 A1131 1.80 l multi 1.00 .50

Souvenir Sheet

Spil Dagi National Park — A1132

2017, Sept. 15 **Litho.** **Perf. 13¼**
3562 A1132 3.70 l multi 2.10 1.10

Miniature Sheet

Turkish Cuisine — A1133

No. 3563: a, 75k, Adana kebap and salgam (lamb kebabs and turnip juice). b, 75k, Banak and bicibici, vert. c, 1.80 l, Burdur sis and hibes (shishkebab and garlic dip), vert. d, 3.70 l, Maras dondurmasi, tantuni, and künefe (ice cream, meat wrap, and cheese pastry).

2017, Sept. 29   Litho.   Perf. 13¾
3563 A1133   Sheet of 4, #a-d   4.00 2.00

World Post Day — A1134

Birds, UPU emblem and: 75k, Man making smoke signals. No. 3565, 1.80 l, Man, quill pen. No. 3566, 1.80 l, Postal workers, horse-drawn cart, telephone poles and wires. 3.70 l, Postman on scooter, mail sorting equipment.

2017, Oct. 9   Litho.   Perf. 13¼
3564-3567 A1134   Set of 4   4.25 2.10

A souvenir sheet with a self-adhesive 3.70 l stamp printed on silk and a souvenir sheet of four stamps (1.80 l, 3.70 l and two 75k stamps) were printed in limited quantities and sold together with Nos. 3564-3567 for 40 l.

Republic of Turkey, 94th Anniv. A1135

Inscription: No. 3568, 75k, "Tek Devlet" (one state). No. 3569, 75k, "Tek Vatan" (one homeland). No. 3570, 1.80 l, "Tek Millet" (one nation). No. 3571, 3.70 l, "Tek Bayrak" (one flag).

2017, Oct. 29   Litho.   Perf. 13¼
3568-3571 A1135   Set of 4   3.75 3.75

A souvenir sheet containing one 1.80 l stamp of a different design was printed in limited quantities and was sold with a first day cover for 20 l.

Souvenir Sheet

Baku-Tbilisi-Kars Railway — A1136

2017, Oct. 30   Litho.   Perf. 13¼x13
3572 A1136   3.70 l multi   2.00 1.00
See Azerbaijan No. 1141.

Turkish Animal Breeds A1137

Designs: No. 3573, 75k, Anatolian shepherd. No. 3574, 75k, Van cat, vert. 1.80 l, Turkish horses. 3.70 l, Turkish mastiff.

Perf. 13½x13¾, 13¾x13½
2017, Nov. 7   Litho.
3573-3576 A1137   Set of 4   3.75 1.90

Souvenir Sheet

TÜRKİYE • PAKİSTAN ORTAK PUL
Diplomatic Relations Between Turkey and Pakistan, 70th Anniv. — A1138

No. 3577: a, Mehmet Akif Ersoy (1873-1936), Turkish poet. b, Allama Muhammed Iqbal (1877-1938), Pakistani poet.

2017, Nov. 9   Litho.   Perf. 13¼
3577 A1138 3.70 l Sheet of 2, #a-b   3.75 1.90
See Pakistan No. 1254.

Hieropolis-Pamukkale UNESCO World Heritage Sites, Denizli — A1139

2017, Dec. 8   Litho.   Perf. 13¼
3578 A1139 1.80 l multi   .95 .50

A souvenir sheet of five stamps (3.70 l, two 75k, and two 1.80 l) was printed in limited quantities and sold for 15 l.

Lakes A1140

Designs: No. 3579, 1.80 l, Lake Van. No. 3580, 1.80 l, Flamingo at Lake Tuz.

2017, Dec. 12   Litho.   Perf. 13¼
3579-3580 A1140   Set of 2   1.90 .95

Legumes — A1141

Designs: 20k, Lens culinaris. 2 l, Vigna sinensis. 3 l, Phaseolus vulgaris (fasulye). 4 l, Phaseolus vulgaris (barbunya). 6.50 l, Vicia faba. 14 l, Cicer arietinum.

Perf. 13¾x13½ Syncopated
2018, Jan. 5   Litho.
3581 A1141   20k multi   .25 .25
3582 A1141   2 l multi   1.10 .55
3583 A1141   3 l multi   1.60 .80
3584 A1141   4 l multi   2.10 1.10
3585 A1141   6.50 l multi   3.50 1.75
3586 A1141   14 l multi   7.50 3.75
    Nos. 3581-3586 (6)   16.05 8.20

Sultan Süleyman Fountain, Istanbul — A1142

2018, Jan. 31   Litho.   Perf. 13¼
3587 A1142 2 l multi   1.10 .55

Souvenir Sheet

TÜRKİYE - KATAR ORTAK PULU
DİPLOMATİK İLİŞKİLERİN 45. YILDÖNÜMÜ

Diplomatic Relations Between Turkey and Qatar, 45th Anniv. — A1143

No. 3588: a, 2 l, Rumeli Fortress, Istanbul, Al Zubara Fort, Qatar. b, 4 l, Barzan Towers, Qatar, Ankara Castle, Ankara.

Litho., Sheet Margin Litho. With Foil Application
2018, Feb. 21   Perf. 13¼
3588 A1143   Sheet of 2, #a-b   3.25 1.60
See Qatar No. 1143.

Court of Cassation, 150th Anniv. A1144

Perf. 13½x13¾ Syncopated
2018, Mar. 6   Litho.
3589 A1144 2 l multi   1.00 .50

Liberation of Erzurum, Cent. A1145

Perf. 13½x13¾ Syncopated
2018, Mar. 12   Litho.
3590 A1145 2 l multi   1.00 .50

Flora — A1146

Designs: No. 3591, 2 l, Fritillaria imperialis. No. 3592, 2 l, Olea europaea. No. 3593, 2 l, Tulipa. No. 3594, 2 l, Centaurea tchihatcheffii. No. 3595, 2 l, Rhododendron ponticum. No. 3596, 2 l, Crocus antalyensis subsp. antalyensis. No. 3597, 2 l, Centaurea cyanus.

Perf. 13¾x13½
2018, Mar. 21   Litho.
3591-3597 A1146   Set of 7   7.00 3.50

Liberation of Van, Cent. A1147

2018, Apr. 2   Litho.   Perf. 13½x13¾
3598 A1147 2 l multi   1.00 .50

Dolmabahçe Clock Tower, Istanbul A1148

Perf. 13½x13¾ Syncopated
2018, Apr. 5   Litho.
3599 A1148 2 l multi   1.00 .50

Spices — A1149

Designs: 20k, Mentha. 50k, Piper nigrum. 2.30 l, Capsicum annum. 6.50 l, Cuminum cyminum.

Perf. 13¾x13½ Syncopated
2018, Apr. 18   Litho.
3600-3603 A1149   Set of 4   4.75 2.40

National Sovereignty Day and
Children's Day — A1150

2018, Apr. 23   Litho.   Perf. 13¼
3604   A1150   2 l   multi   1.00   .50

A souvenir sheet containing one 78x36mm
2 l stamp was produced in limited quantities.

Europa — A1151

Designs: 2 l, Twin bridges, Artvin. 4 l, Meriç
Bridge, Edirne.

2018, May 9   Litho.   Perf. 13¼
3605-3606   A1151   Set of 2   2.60   1.40

Universal Postal Union World Chief
Executive Officer Forum,
Istanbul — A1152

Perf. 14 Syncopated
2018, May 9   Litho.
3607   A1152   4 l   multi   1.75   .85

Council of State (Administrative Court),
150th Anniv. — A1153

Designs: 1 l, Modern building. 2 l, Drawing
of old building and street scene.

Perf. 13¾ Syncopated
2018, May 10   Litho.
3608-3609   A1153   Set of 2   1.40   .70

Diplomatic Relations Between Turkey
and Thailand, 60th Anniv. — A1154

No. 3610: a, Wrestlers (denomination at
LL). b, Kick boxers (denomination at LR).

2018, May 12   Litho.   Perf. 13¼x13½
3610   A1154   2 l   Sheet of 2, #a-b   1.75   .85

See Thailand No. 3005.

Perge Archaeological Site, Antalya
Province — A1155

Perf. 13½x13¾ Syncopated
2018, May 22   Litho.
3611   A1155   4 l   multi   1.75   .85

Souvenir Sheet

World Environment Day — A1156

No. 3612 — Wind generator and: a, Tanks
and house. b, Solar panels and domed tanks.

2018, June 5   Litho.   Perf. 13¼
3612   A1156   2 l   Sheet of 2, #a-b   1.75   .85

Camlica Mosque, Istanbul — A1157

2018, June 10   Litho.   Perf. 13¼
3613   A1157   2 l   multi   .90   .45

2018 World Cup
Soccer
Championships,
Russia — A1158

Designs: No. 3614, 2 l, Mascot holding soc-
cer ball. No. 3615, 2 l, Emblerm. No. 3616, 4 l,
Mascot kicking soccer ball. No. 3617, 4 l,
Poster.

2018, June 14   Litho.   Perf. 14x13¾
3614-3617   A1158   Set of 4   5.25   2.60

Houses of the Mediterranean
Area — A1159

Various houses: 2 l, 4 l.

2018, July 9   Litho.   Perf. 13¼
3618-3619   A1159   Set of 2   2.50   1.25

Democracy
and National
Unity
Day — A1160

Perf. 13½x13¾ Syncopated
2018, July 15   Litho.
3620   A1160   2 l   multi   .85   .40

A souvenir sheet containing one 38x38mm
2 l stamp was printed in limited quantities.

Souvenir Sheet

Troy UNESCO World Heritage
Site — A1161

No. 3621: a, Buildings (26x26mm octagonal). b, Trojan Horse (18x24mm). c, Amphitheater (18x24mm octagonal).

2018, Aug. 1   Litho.   Perf. 13¼
3621   A1161   2 l   Sheet of 3, #a-c   2.50   1.25

Mosque, Milodraz, Bosnia and
Herzegovina — A1162

2018, Aug. 10   Litho.   Perf. 13¼
3622   A1162   4 l   multi   1.25   .60

Joint Issue between Turkey and Bosnia and
Herzegovina.
See Bosnia and Herzegovina No.

Miniature Sheet

Cuisine of Marmara Region — A1163

No. 3623: a, 1 l, Edirne Tava Ciger, Boza
(fried livers and fermented bulgur wheat drink).
b, 2 l, Peynir Helvasi, Tekirdag Köftesi (cheese
halvah and meatballs), vert. c, 2 l, Iskender
Kebabi, Mustafakemalpasa Peynir Tatlisi (lamb
kebab and cheese-filled biscuits), vert. d, 4 l,
Kestane Sekeri, Islama Köfte (chestnut candy
and meatballs).

2018, Aug. 16   Litho.   Perf. 13¾
3623   A1163   Sheet of 4, #a-d   2.75   1.40

Victory Day — A1164

Perf. 13¾ Syncopated
2018, Aug. 30   Litho.
3624   A1164   2 l   multi   .60   .30

An imperforate 111x62mm 2 l sheet was
printed in limited quantities.

Souvenir Sheet

Islamic Army of the Caucasus,
Cent. — A1165

2018, Sept. 15   Litho.   Perf. 13¾
3625   A1165   2 l   multi   .70   .35

Souvenir Sheet

Flamingos, Sultan Marshes National
Park — A1166

2018, Sept. 26   Litho.   Perf. 13¼
3626   A1166   2 l   multi   .70   .35

Opening of New Istanbul
Airport — A1167

2018, Oct. 29   Litho.   Perf. 13¼
3627   A1167   2 l   multi   .75   .35

Kastamonu,
2018 Cultural
Capital of the
Turkic World
A1168

Emblem and various tourist attractions: 2 l,
4 l.

2018, Nov. 26   Litho.   Perf. 13¼
3628-3629   A1168   Set of 2   2.25   1.10

An imperforate 75x75mm 2 l stamp was
printed in limited quantities.

World Map by Erzurumlu ibrahim
Hakki's (1705-72) in his Marifetname
Book — A1169

2018, Nov. 27   Litho.   Perf. 13¾
3630   A1169   4 l   multi   1.50   .75

Joint Issue between Turkey and Slovakia.
See Slovakia No. 807.

Houses
Connected to
Kemal
Atatürk — A1170

Designs: 50k, Atatürk's Headquarters for
Battle of Dumlupinar, Dumlupinar. 2 l, Atatürk
Museum, Istanbul, vert. 14 l, Atatürk House
Museum, Kayseri.

Perf. 12¾x13, 13x12¾
2018, Dec. 26   Litho.
3631 A1170 50k multi   .25   .25
3632 A1170 2 l multi   .75   .35
3633 A1170 14 l multi   5.25 2.60
      Nos. 3631-3633 (3)   6.25 3.20

Valuable
Stones
A1171

Designs: 2 l, Striped agate. 4 l, Blue
chalcedony.

Litho. & Silk-Screened
2019, Jan. 9   Perf. 13¼
3634-3635 A1171 Set of 2   2.40 1.25

Souvenir Sheet

Train Stations — A1172

No. 3636: a, 2 l, Main Ankara Station. b, 4 l,
Ankara YHT (high-speed train) Station.

2019, Jan. 24 Litho. Perf. 13½x13¼
3636 A1172 Sheet of 2, #a-b 2.40 1.25

Folk Dances
A1173

Designs: No. 3637, 2 l, Zeybek. No. 3638,
2 l, Segmen.

2019, Feb. 5   Litho.   Perf. 13¼
3637-3638 A1173 Set of 2   1.50   .75

SEMI-POSTAL STAMPS

Regular Issues
Overprinted in
Carmine or Black

Overprint reads: "For War Orphans"

Perf. 12, 13½ and Compound
1915   Unwmk.
On Stamps of 1905
B1 A18 10pa dull grn (#119) 2.00   .75
B2 A18 10pi orange brown   12.50   .80
On Stamp of 1906
B3 A18 10pa dull grn (#128) 40.00 25.00
On Stamps of 1908
B4 A19 10pa blue green   1.50   .75
B5 A19 5pi dark violet   75.00 12.50
    Nos. B1-B5 (5)   131.00 39.80

No. B6 with Additional
"Discount" Overprint on
No. B4

B6 A19 10pa blue green   240.00 175.00
On Stamps of 1909
B7 A21 10pa blue green   2.00   .75
  a. Inverted overprint   30.00 30.00
  b. Double overprint, one invtd. 30.00 30.00
B8 A21 20pa carmine rose   2.00   .75
  a. Inverted overprint   30.00 30.00
B9 A21 1pi ultra   2.00   .75
B10 A21 5pi dark violet   8.75 1.50
    Nos. B7-B10 (4)   14.75 3.75
    See note after No. 131.

Nos. B11-B13 with
Additional Overprint on
Nos. B7-B9

B11 A21 10pa blue green   2.00   .75
  b. Double overprint, one inverted 30.00 30.00
B12 A21 20pa carmine rose   1.50   .75
B13 A21 1pi ultra   2.00   .75
On Stamps of 1913
B14 A22 10pa blue green   2.00   .75
  a. Inverted overprint   35.00 35.00
B15 A22 1pi ultra   2.00   .75
  a. Double overprint   20.00 20.00
    Nos. B11-B15 (5)   9.50 3.75

No. B16 with
Additional
Overprint on No.
B14

B16 A22 10pa blue green   1.75   .75
  a. Inverted overprint   30.00 30.00
On Newspaper Stamp of 1908
B17 A19 10pa blue green   360.00 175.00
On Newspaper Stamp of 1909
B18 A21 10pa blue green   1.75 1.00

Regular Issues
Overprinted in
Carmine or Black

1916   **On Stamps of 1901**
B19 A17 1pi blue   2.00   .50
B20 A17 5pi lilac rose   10.00 1.50
On Stamps of 1905
B21 A18 1pi brt blue   7.50 2.00
B22 A18 5pi brown   7.50 5.00
On Stamp of 1906
B23 A18 1pi brt blue   1.00   .75
On Stamps of 1908
B24 A19 20pa carmine (Bk)   300.00
B25 A19 10pi red   500.00 200.00

Nos. B26-B27 with
Additional Overprints

B26 A19 20pa carmine   8.00 8.00

B27 A19 1pi brt blue (C)   20.00 5.00
On Stamps of 1909
B28 A21 20pa carmine rose   2.00 1.25
B29 A21 1pi ultra   1.50 1.00
B30 A21 10pi dull red   175.00 100.00
No. B26 is No. B24 with an additional over-
print. No. B27 is the design of 1908, with two
overprints. Its was not issued with one.

Nos. B31-B32 with
Additional Overprint on
Nos. B28-B29

B31 A21 20pa carmine rose   1.50   .75
B32 A21 1pi ultra   2.00 1.00
On Stamps of 1913
B33 A22 20pa carmine rose   2.00 1.50
B34 A22 1pi ultra   2.00 1.00
  a. Inverted overprint   30.00 30.00
B35 A22 10pi dull red   22.50 15.00

No. B36 with
Additional Overprint
on No. B33

B36 A22 20pa carmine rose   2.00 1.25
On Newspaper Stamps of 1901
B37 A16 5pi ocher   11.50 6.00
  a. 5pa bister, No. P37 150.00 150.00

Regular Issues
Surcharged in Black

On Stamp of 1898
B38 A11 10pa on 20pa vio brn 2.00 1.50
On Stamp of 1905
B39 A18 10pa on 20pa carmine 2.00 1.50
On Stamp of 1906
B40 A18 10pa on 20pa carmine 1.50 1.25
On Newspaper Stamp of 1893-99
B41 A11 10pa on 20pa violet brn 2.00 1.50
    Nos. B38-B41 (4)   7.50 5.75

Nos. 346-349
Overprinted

B42 A41 10pa carmine   1.50   .75
  a. Inverted overprint   20.00 20.00
B43 A41 20pa ultra   1.50   .75
  a. Inverted overprint   20.00 20.00
B44 A41 1pi violet & blk   1.50   .90
  a. Inverted overprint   20.00 20.00
B45 A41 5pi yel brn & blk   1.50   .75
  a. Inverted overprint   30.00 30.00
    Nos. B42-B45 (4)   6.00 3.15
Nos. B42-B45 formed part of the Postage
Commemoration issue of 1916.

A Soldier's
Farewell — SP1

1917, Feb. 20   Engr.   Perf. 12½
B46 SP1 10pa red violet   1.25   .50
For surcharges see Nos. 600, B47.

Stamp of Same
Design Surcharged

B47 SP1 10pa on 20pa car rose 2.00 .50

Badge of the   School
Society — SP9   Teacher — SP10

Marie   Kemal
Sklodowska   Atatürk — SP23
Curie — SP16

Designs: 2k+2k, Woman farmer. 2½k+2½k,
Typist. 4k+4k, Aviatrix and policewoman.
5k+5k, Women voters. 7½k+7½k, Yildiz Palace, Istanbul. 10k+10k, Carrie Chapman Catt.
12½k+12½k, Jane Addams. 15k+15k, Grazia
Deledda. 20k+20k, Selma Lagerlof. 25k+25k,
Bertha von Suttner. 30k+30k, Sigrid Undset.

1935, Apr. 17   Photo.   Perf. 11½
      Inscribed: "XII Congres
      Suffragiste International"
B54 SP9 20pa + 20pa brn   .50   50
B55 SP10 1k + 1k rose car   .75   .50
B56 SP10 2k + 2k sl bl   1.00   .75
B57 SP10 2½k + 2½k yel grn 1.00   .75
B58 SP10 4k + 4k blue   1.50 1.00
B59 SP10 5k + 5k dl vio   2.50 2.00
B60 SP10 7½k + 7½k org red 2.50 2.00
B61 SP10 10k + 10k org   2.50 2.50
B62 SP16 12½k + 12½k dk bl 2.50 2.50
B63 SP16 15k + 15k violet   5.00 5.00
B64 SP16 20k + 20k red org 7.50 6.25
B65 SP16 25k + 25k grn   15.00 14.00
B66 SP16 30k + 30k ultra   90.00 100.00
B67 SP16 50k + 50k dk sl grn 175.00 150.00
B68 SP23 100k + 100k brn car 125.00 140.00
    Nos. B54-B68 (15)   432.25 427.75
    Set, never hinged   750.00
12th Congress of the Women's Intl. Alliance.

Catalogue values for unused
stamps in this section, from this
point to the end of the section, are
for Never Hinged items.

Katip
Chelebi — SP24

Perf. 10½

1958, Sept. 24   Litho.   Unwmk.
B69 SP24 50k + 10k gray   .50 .25
Mustafa ibn 'Abdallah Katip Chelebi Hajji Khalifa (1608-1657), Turkish author.

Road Building Machine SP25

Kemal Atatürk — SP26

Design: 25k+5k, Tanks and planes.

1958, Oct. 29
B70 SP25 15k + 5k orange   .40 .25
B71 SP26 20k + 5k lt red brn   .40 .25
B72 SP25 25k + 5k brt grn   .40 .25
       Nos. B70-B72 (3)   1.20 .75
The surtax went to the Red Crescent Society and to the Society for the Protection of Children.
For surcharge see No. 1440.

Ruins, Göreme SP27

1959, July 8   Litho.   Perf. 10
B73 SP27 105k + 10k pur & buff   .50 .25
Issued for tourist publicity.

Istanbul SP28

1959, Sept. 11
B74 SP28 105k + 10k lt bl & red   .50 .25
15th International Tuberculosis Congress.

Manisa Asylum SP29

Merkez Muslihiddin SP30

Kermis at Manisa: 90k+5k, Sultan Camil Mosque, Manisa, vert.

1960, Apr. 17   Unwmk.   Perf. 13
B75 SP29 40k + 5k grn & lt bl   .25 .25
B76 SP29 40k + 5k vio & rose lil   .25 .25
B77 SP29 90k + 5k dp cl & car rose   .50 .25
B78 SP30 105k + 10k multi   .65 .25
       Nos. B75-B78 (4)   1.65 1.00

Census Chart SP31

Census Symbol — SP32

1960, Sept. 23   Photo.   Perf. 11½
Granite Paper
B79 SP31 30k + 5k bl & rose pink   .25 .25
B80 SP32 50k + 5k grn, dk bl & ultra   .35 .25
Issued for the 1960 Census.

Old Observatory SP33

Fatin Gökmen — SP34

Designs: 30k+5k, Observatory emblem. 75k+5k, Building housing telescope.

1961, July 1   Litho.   Perf. 13
B81 SP33 10k + 5k grnsh bl & grn   .25 .25
B82 SP33 30k + 5k vio & blk   .60 .60
B83 SP34 40k + 5k brown   .25 .25
B84 SP33 75k + 5k olive grn   .60 .60
       Nos. B81-B84 (4)   1.70 1.70
Kandili Observatory, 50th anniversary.

Anti-Malaria Work — SP35

UNICEF, 10th anniv.: 30k+5k, Mother and infant, horiz. 75k+5k, Woman distributing pasteurized milk.

1961, Dec. 11   Unwmk.   Perf. 13
B85 SP35 10k + 5k Prus green   .25 .25
B86 SP35 30k + 5k dull violet   .30 .25
B87 SP35 75k + 5k dk olive bis   .60 .25
       Nos. B85-B87 (3)   1.15 .75

Malaria Eradication Emblem, Map and Mosquito SP36

1962, Apr. 7   Litho.
B88 SP36 30k + 5k dk & lt brn   .25 .25
B89 SP36 75k + 5k blk & lil   .50 .25
WHO drive to eradicate malaria.

Poinsettia — SP37

Flowers: 40k+10k, Bird of paradise flower. 75k+10k, Water lily.

1962, May 19   Perf. 12½x13½
Flowers in Natural Colors
B90 SP37 30k + 10k lt bl & blk   .25 .25
B91 SP37 40k + 10k lt bl & blk   .45 .25
B92 SP37 75k + 10k lt bl & blk   .95 .40
       Nos. B90-B92 (3)   1.65 .90

Wheat and Census Chart — SP38

Design: 60k+5k, Wheat and chart, horiz.

Inscribed: "Umumi Ziraat Sayimi"

1963, Apr. 14   Photo.   Perf. 11½
B93 SP38 40k + 5k gray grn & yel   .35 .25
B94 SP38 60k + 5k org yel & blk   .35 .25
1961 agricultural census. Two black bars obliterate "Kasim 1960" inscription.

Red Lion and Sun, Red Crescent, Red Cross and Globe SP39

Designs: 60k+10k, Emblems in flowers, vert. 100k+10k, Emblems on flags.

1963, Aug. 1   Perf. 13
B95 SP39 50k + 10k multi   .25 .25
B96 SP39 60k + 10k multi   .40 .25
B97 SP39 100k + 10k multi   .60 .45
       Nos. B95-B97 (3)   1.25 .95
Centenary of International Red Cross.

Angora Goat — SP40

Animals: 10k+5k, Steppe cattle, horiz. 50k+5k, Arabian horses, horiz. 60k+5k, Three Angora goats. 100k+5k, Montofon cattle, horiz.

1964, Oct. 4   Litho.   Perf. 13
B98 SP40 10k + 5k multi   .35 .25
B99 SP40 30k + 5k multi   .35 .25
B100 SP40 50k + 5k multi   .60 .25
B101 SP40 60k + 5k multi   .85 .25
B102 SP40 100k + 5k multi   1.10 .25
       Nos. B98-B102 (5)   3.25 1.25
Issued for Animal Protection Day.

Olympic Torch Bearer — SP41

Designs: 10k+5k, Running, horiz. 60k+5k, Wrestling. 100k+5k, Discus.

1964, Oct. 10   Unwmk.
B103 SP41 10k + 5k org brn, blk & red   .40 .25
B104 SP41 50k + 5k ol, blk & red   .40 .25
B105 SP41 60k + 5k bl, blk & red   1.00 .25
B106 SP41 100k + 5k vio, blk, red & sil   1.40 .40
       Nos. B103-B106 (4)   3.20 1.15
18th Olympic Games, Tokyo, Oct. 10-25.

Map of Dardanelles and Laurel SP42

Designs: 90k+10k, Soldiers and war memorial, Canakkale. 130k+10k, Turkish flag and arch, vert.

1965, Mar. 18   Litho.   Perf. 13
B107 SP42 50k + 10k vio, yel & gold   .25 .25
B108 SP42 90k + 10k vio bl, bl, yel & grn   .60 .25
B109 SP42 130k + 10k dk brn, red & yel   1.10 .90
       Nos. B107-B109 (3)   1.95 1.40
50th anniversary of Battle of Gallipoli.

Tobacco Plant — SP43

50k+5k, Tobacco leaves and Leander's tower, horiz. 100k+5k, Tobacco leaf.

1965, Sept. 16   Unwmk.   Perf. 13
B110 SP43 30k + 5k brn, lt brn & grn   .25 .25
B111 SP43 50k + 5k vio bl, ocher & grn   .60 .25
B112 SP43 100k + 5k blk, ol grn & ocher   1.00 .50
       Nos. B110-B112 (3)   1.85 1.00
Second International Tobacco Congress.

Goddess, Basalt Carving — SP44

Archaeological Museum, Ankara: 30k+5k, Eagle and rabbit, ivory carving, horiz. 60k+5k, Bronze bull. 90k+5k, Gold pitcher.

Perf. 13½x13, 13x13½
1966, June 6   Litho.
B113 SP44 30k + 5k multi   .25 .25
B114 SP44 50k + 5k multi   .55 .25
B115 SP44 60k + 5k multi   .85 .45
B116 SP44 90k + 5k multi   1.10 .60
       Nos. B113-B116 (4)   2.75 1.55

Grand Hotel Ephesus SP45

Designs: 60k+5k, Konak Square, Izmir, vert. 130k+5k, Izmir Fair Grounds.

1966, Oct. 18   Litho.   *Perf. 12*

B117	SP45	50k + 5k multi	.25 .25
B118	SP45	60k + 5k multi	.45 .25
B119	SP45	130k + 5k multi	.95 .55
	Nos. B117-B119 (3)		1.65 1.05

33rd Congress of the Intl. Fair Assoc.

Europa Issue, 1967
Common Design Type

1967, May 2   Litho.   *Perf. 13x13½*
Size: 22x33mm

B120	CD10	100k + 10k multi	.75 .75
B121	CD10	130k + 10k multi	1.75 1.25
	Nos. B120-B121 (2)		2.50 2.00

Cloverleaf Crossing, Map of Turkey SP46

130k+5k, Highway E5 & map of Turkey.

1967, June 30   Litho.   *Perf. 13*

B122	SP46	60k + 5k multi	.60 .25
B123	SP46	130k + 5k multi, vert.	1.00 .60

Inter-European Express Highway, E5.

WHO Emblem SP47

1968, Apr. 7   Litho.   *Perf. 13*

B124	SP47	130k + 10k lt ultra, blk & yel	.80 .25

WHO, 20th anniversary.

Efem Pasha, Dr. Marko Pasha and View of Istanbul — SP48

60k+10k, Omer Pasha, Dr. Abdullah Bey & wounded soldiers. 100k+10k, Ataturk & Dr. Refik Saydam in front of Red Crescent head-quarters, vert.

1968, June 11   Litho.   *Perf. 13*

B125	SP48	50k + 10k multi	.45 .25
B126	SP48	60k + 10k multi	.60 .30
B127	SP48	100k + 10k multi	.95 .45
	Nos. B125-B127 (3)		2.00 1.00

Centenary of Turkish Red Crescent Society.

NATO Emblem and Dove SP49

NATO, 20th anniv.: 130k+10k, NATO emblem and globe surrounded by 15 stars, symbols of the 15 NATO members.

1969, Apr. 4   Litho.   *Perf. 13*

B128	SP49	50k + 10k brt grn, blk & lt bl	.45 .25
B129	SP49	130k + 10k bluish blk, bl & gold	.75 .35

Red Cross, Crescent, Lion and Sun Emblems SP50

Design: 130k+10k, Conference emblem and Istanbul skyline.

1969, Aug. 29   Litho.   *Perf. 13*

B130	SP50	100k + 10k dk & lt bl & red	.50 .25
B131	SP50	130k + 10k red, lt bl & blk	.65 .40

21st Intl. Red Cross Conf., Istanbul.

Erosion Control SP51

60k+10k, Protection of flora (dead tree). 130k+10k, Protection of wildlife (bird of prey).

1970, Feb. 9   Litho.   *Perf. 13*

B132	SP51	50k + 10k multi	.40 .40
B133	SP51	60k + 10k multi	.60 .60
B134	SP51	130k + 10k multi	1.40 1.40
	Nos. B132-B134 (3)		2.40 2.40

1970 European Nature Conservation Year.

Globe and Fencer SP52

Design: 130k+10k, Globe, fencer and folk dancer with sword and shield.

1970, Sept. 13   Litho.   *Perf. 13*

B135	SP52	90k + 10k bl & blk	.50 .25
B136	SP52	130k + 10k ultra, lt bl, blk & org	.70 .25

International Fencing Championships.

"Children's Protection" SP53

Designs: 100k+15k, Hand supporting child, vert. 110k+15k, Mother and child.

1971, June 30   Litho.   *Perf. 13*
Star and Crescent Emblem in Red

B137	SP53	50k + 10k lil rose & blk	.25 .25
B138	SP53	100k + 15k brn, rose & blk	.35 .25
B139	SP53	110k + 15k org brn, bis & blk	.45 .25
	Nos. B137-B139 (3)		1.05 .75

50th anniv. of the Child Protection Assoc.

UNICEF, 25th Anniv. — SP54

1971, Dec. 11

B140	SP54	100k + 10k multi	.35 .25
B141	SP54	250k + 15k multi	.90 .70

"Your Heart is your Health" — SP55

1972, Apr. 7   Litho.   *Perf. 13*

B142	SP55	250k + 25k gray, blk & red	.80 .65

World Health Day,

Olympic Emblems, Runners SP56

100k+15k, Olympic rings & motion emblem. 250k+25k, Olympic rings & symbolic track ('72).

1972, Aug. 26

B143	SP56	100k + 15k multi	.40 .25
B144	SP56	110k + 25k multi	.50 .25
B145	SP56	250k + 25k multi	.70 .45
	Nos. B143-B145 (3)		1.60 .95

20th Olympic Games, Munich, 8/26-9/11.

Emblem of Istanbul Technical University SP57

1973, Apr. 21   Litho.   *Perf. 13*

B146	SP57	100k + 25k multi	.65 .25

Istanbul Technical University, 200th anniv.

Dove and "50" SP58

1973, July 24   Litho.   *Perf. 12½x13*

B147	SP58	100k + 25k multi	.75 .35

Peace Treaty of Lausanne, 50th anniversary.

World Population Year — SP59

1974, June 15   Litho.   *Perf. 13*

B148	SP59	250k + 25k multi	.75 .35

Guglielmo Marconi (1874-1937), Italian Electrical Engineer and Inventor SP60

1974, Nov. 15   Litho.   *Perf. 13½*

B149	SP60	250k + 25k multi	.75 .35

Dr. Albert Schweitzer — SP61

1975, Jan 14   Litho.   *Perf. 13*

B150	SP61	250k + 50k multi	.90 .45

Dr. Albert Schweitzer (1875-1965), medical missionary and music scholar.

Africa with South-West Africa — SP62

1975, Aug. 26   Litho.   *Perf. 13x12½*

B151	SP62	250k + 50k multi	.70 .35

Namibia Day (independence for South-West Africa).

Ziya Gökalp — SP63

1976, Mar. 23   Litho.   *Perf. 13*

B152	SP63	200k + 25k multi	.60 .30

Ziya Gökalp (1876-1924), philosopher.

Spoonbill — SP64

Birds: 150k+25k, European roller. 200k+25k, Flamingo. 400k+25k, Hermit ibis, horiz.

1976, Nov. 19   Litho.   *Perf. 13*

B153	SP64	100k + 25k multi	.65 .25
B154	SP64	150k + 25k multi	.80 .25
B155	SP64	200k + 25k multi	1.25 .35
B156	SP64	400k + 25k multi	2.25 .45
	Nos. B153-B156 (4)		4.95 1.30

Decree by Mehmet Bey, and Ongun Holy Bird — SP65

1977, May 13   Litho.   *Perf. 13*

B157	SP65	200k + 25k grn & blk	.60 .25

700th anniv. of Turkish as official language.

10th World Energy Conference SP66

Design: 600k+50k, Conference emblem and globe with circles.

1977, Sept. 19   Litho.   *Perf. 12½*

B158	SP66	100k + 25k multi	.25 .25
B159	SP66	600k + 50k multi	1.00 .40

Running SP67

Designs: 2½ l+50k, Gymnastics. 5 l+ 50k, Table tennis. 8 l+50k, Swimming.

1978, July 18   Litho.   Perf. 13

B160	SP67	1 l + 50k multi	.25	.25
B161	SP67	2½ l + 50k multi	.30	.25
B162	SP67	5 l + 50k multi	.55	.25
B163	SP67	8 l + 50k multi	1.00	.30
	Nos. B160-B163 (4)		2.10	1.05

GYMNASIADE '78, World School Games, Izmir.

Ribbon and Chain SP68

Design: 5 l+50k, Ribbon and flower, vert.

Perf. 12½x13, 13x12½

1978, Sept. 3   Litho.

B164	SP68	2½ l + 50k multi	.65	.25
B165	SP68	5 l + 50k multi	1.10	.25

European Declaration of Human Rights, 25th anniversary.

Children, Head of Ataturk — SP69

IYC Emblem and: 5 l+50k, Children with globe as balloon. 8 l+50k, Kneeling person and child, globe.

1979, Apr. 23   Litho.   Perf. 13x13½

B166	SP69	2½ l + 50k multi	.35	.25
B167	SP69	5 l + 50k multi	.55	.25
B168	SP69	8 l + 50k multi	.85	.35
	Nos. B166-B168 (3)		1.75	.85

International Year of the Child.

Black Francolin — SP70

No. B170, Great bustard. No. B171, Crane. No. B172, Gazelle. No. B173, Mouflon muffelwild.

1979, Dec. 3   Litho.   Perf. 13x13½

B169	SP70	5 l + 1 l multi	.55	.25
B170	SP70	5 l + 1 l multi	.55	.25
B171	SP70	5 l + 1 l multi	.55	.25
B172	SP70	5 l + 1 l multi	.55	.25
B173	SP70	5 l + 1 l multi	.55	.25
a.	Strip of 5, #B169-B173		3.00	3.00

European Wildlife Conservation Year. No. B173a has continuous design.

Flowers, Trees and Sun — SP71

Environment Protection: 7½ l+ 1 l, Sun, water. 15 l+1 l, Industrial pollution, globe. 20 l+1 l, Flower in oil puddle.

1980, June 4   Litho.   Perf. 13

B174	SP71	2½ l + 1 l multi	.25	.25
B175	SP71	7½ l + 1 l multi	.25	.25
B176	SP71	15 l + 1 l multi	.45	.25
B177	SP71	20 l + 1 l multi	.50	.35
	Nos. B174-B177 (4)		1.45	1.10

Rodolia Cardinalis — SP72

Useful Insects: 7½ l+1 l, Bracon hebetor; 15 l+1 l, Calosoma sycophanta; 20 l+1 l, Deraeocoris rutilus.

1980, Dec. 3   Litho.   Perf. 13

B178	SP72	2½ l + 1 l multi	.25	.25
B179	SP72	7½ l + 1 l multi	.45	.25
B180	SP72	15 l + 1 l multi	.80	.25
B181	SP72	20 l + 1 l multi	1.00	.25
	Nos. B178-B181 (4)		2.50	1.00

Intl. Year of the Disabled — SP73

1981, Mar. 25   Litho.   Perf. 13

B182	SP73	10 l + 2½ l multi	.50	.25
B183	SP73	20 l + 2½ l multi	.75	.25

Insects SP74

Useful Insects: No. B184, Cicindela campestris. No. B185, Syrphus vitripennis. No. B186, Ascalaphus macaronius. No. B187, Empusa fasciata.

1981, Dec. 16   Litho.   Perf. 13

B184	SP74	10 l + 2½ l multi	.50	.25
B185	SP74	20 l + 2½ l multi	.85	.25
B186	SP74	30 l + 2½ l multi	1.40	.45
B187	SP74	40 l + 2½ l multi	1.75	.60
	Nos. B184-B187 (4)		4.50	1.55

See Nos. B190-B194, B196-B200.

TB Bacillus Centenary — SP75

Portraits: #B188, Dr. Tevfik Saglam (1882-1963). #B189, Robert Koch.

1982, Mar. 24   Perf. 13x12½

B188	SP75	10 l + 2½ l multi	.35	.25
B189	SP75	30 l + 2½ l multi	.65	.25

Insect Type of 1981

Useful Insects: 10 l+2½ l, Eurydema spectabile. 15 l+2½ l, Dacus oleae. 20 l+2½ l, Klapperichicen viridissima. 30 l+2½ l, Leptinotarsa decemlineata. 35 l+2½ l, Rhynchites auratus.

1982, Aug. 18   Litho.   Perf. 13

B190	SP74	10 l + 2½ l multi	.55	.25
B191	SP74	15 l + 2½ l multi	.80	.25
B192	SP74	20 l + 2½ l multi	.80	.25
B193	SP74	30 l + 2½ l multi	.90	.25
B194	SP74	35 l + 2½ l multi	1.00	.25
	Nos. B190-B194 (5)		4.05	1.25

Richard Wagner (1813-1883), Composer — SP76

1983, Feb. 13

B195	SP76	30 l + 5 l multi	1.00	.65

Insect Type of 1981

Harmful Insects: 15 l+5 l, Eurygaster Intergriceps Put. 25 l+5 l, Phyllobius nigrofasciatus Pes. 35 l+5 l, Cercopis intermedia Kbm. 50 l+10 l, Graphosoma lineatum (L). 75 l+10 l, Capnodis miliaris (King).

1983, Sept. 14   Litho.   Perf. 13

B196	SP74	15 l + 5 l multi	.40	.25
B197	SP74	25 l + 5 l multi	.55	.25
B198	SP74	35 l + 5 l multi	.65	.25
B199	SP74	50 l + 10 l multi	1.00	.25
B200	SP74	75 l + 10 l multi	1.40	.40
	Nos. B196-B200 (5)		4.00	1.40

Topkapi Museum Artifacts — SP77

1984, May 30   Litho.   Perf. 13

B201	SP77	20 l + 5 l Kaftan, 16th cent.	.50	.25
B202	SP77	70 l + 15 l Ewer	1.60	.75
B203	SP77	90 l + 20 l Swords	2.50	.85
B204	SP77	100 l + 25 l Lock, key	3.00	1.00
	Nos. B201-B204 (4)		7.60	2.85

Surtax was for museum. See Nos. B208-B211, B213-B216, B218-B221.

1984 Summer Olympics — SP78

Designs: 20 l+5 l, Banners, horiz. 70 l+15 l, Medalist. 100 l+20 l, Running, horiz.

1984, July 28

B205	SP78	20 l + 5 l multi	1.25	.70
B206	SP78	70 l + 15 l multi	1.50	1.10
B207	SP78	100 l + 20 l multi	2.25	1.40
	Nos. B205-B207 (3)		5.00	3.20

Artifacts Type of 1984

Ceramicware: 10 l+5 l, Iznik plate. 20 l+10 l, Iznik boza pitcher and mug, 16th cent. 100 l+15 l, Du Paquier ewer and basin, 1730. 120 l+20 l, Ching dynasty plate, 1522-1566.

1985, May 30   Litho.   Perf. 13

B208	SP77	10 l + 5 l multi	.50	.25
B209	SP77	20 l + 10 l multi	.85	.40
B210	SP77	100 l + 15 l multi	1.75	1.10
B211	SP77	120 l + 20 l multi	2.50	1.25
	Nos. B208-B211 (4)		5.60	3.00

Rabies Vaccine, Cent. — SP79

1985, July 16   Perf. 13x13½

B212	SP79	100 l + 15 l Pasteur	1.25	.90

Artifacts Type of 1984

20 l+5 l, Metal and ceramic incense burner, c. 17th cent. 100 l+10 l, Jade lidded mug decorated with precious gems, 16th cent. 120 l+15 l, Dagger designed by Mahmut I, 1714. 200 l+30 l, Willow buckler, defensive shield, undated.

1986, May 30   Litho.   Perf. 13x12½

B213	SP77	20 l + 5 l multi	.70	.45
B214	SP77	100 l + 10 l multi	1.40	.70
B215	SP77	120 l + 15 l multi	1.60	.90
B216	SP77	200 l + 30 l multi	3.25	1.40
	Nos. B213-B216 (4)		6.95	3.45

General Assembly of NATO SP80

1986, Nov. 13   Litho.   Perf. 13½x13

B217	SP80	100 l + 20 l multi	1.50	.85

Artifacts Type of 1984

Designs: 20 l+5 l, Crystal and gold ewer, 16th cent., vert. 50 l+10 l, Emerald and gold pendant, 17th cent. 200 l+15 l, Sherbet jug, 19th cent., vert. 250 l+30 l, Crystal and gold pen box, 16th cent.

1987, May 30   Litho.   Perf. 13

B218	SP77	20 l + 5 l multi	.60	.25
B219	SP77	50 l + 10 l multi	.90	.45
B220	SP77	200 l + 15 l multi	1.10	1.10
B221	SP77	250 l + 30 l multi	1.75	1.40
	Nos. B218-B221 (4)		4.35	3.20

15th Intl. Chemotherapy Congress, Istanbul — SP81

1987, July 19   Litho.   Perf. 13

B222	SP81	200 l + 25 l multi	1.50	.25

Intl. Road Transport Union (IRU) 21st World Congress SP82

1988, June 13   Litho.   Perf. 12½x13

B223	SP82	200 l +25 l multi	.65	.25

European Environmental Campaign Balancing Nature and Development — SP83

Designs: 100 l+25 l, Hands, desert reclamation. 400 l+50 l, Eye, road, planted field.

1988, Oct. 19   Litho.   Perf. 12½x13

B224	SP83	100 l +25 l multi	.35	.25
B225	SP83	400 l +50 l multi	1.40	.40

Silkworm Industry SP84

No. B226, Silkworm. No. B227, Cocoon, strands.

Perf. 13½x13

1989, Apr. 15   Litho.   Wmk. 394

B226	SP84	150 l +50 l multi	.40	.25
B227	SP84	600 l +100 l multi	1.50	.40

Council of Europe, 40th Anniv. SP85

1989, May 5   Litho.   Perf. 13
B228 SP85 600 l +100 l multi   1.50   .45

European Tourism Year SP86

1990, Apr. 26   Wmk. 394
B229 SP86 300 l +50 l Antalya   .50   .25
B230 SP86 1000 l +100 l Istanbul 1.25 .40

Fight Against Addictions — SP87

Fight Against: No. B231, Smoking. No. B232, Drugs, horiz.

1990, June 26   Litho.   Perf. 13
B231 SP87 300 l +50 l multi   .50   .25
B232 SP87 1000 l +100 l multi   1.40   .65

Yunus Emre (died c.1321), Poet
SP88   SP89

1991, June 26   Litho.   Perf. 13
B233 SP88 500 l +100 l multi   .50   .35
B234 SP89 1500 l +100 l multi   1.40   .65

Wolfgang Amadeus Mozart (1756-1791), Composer — SP90

1991, July 24
B235 SP90 1500 l +100 l multi   1.75   .90

Turkish Supreme Court, 30th Anniv. SP91

1992, Apr. 25
B236 SP91 500 l + 100 l multi   .65   .25

Scouts Planting Tree SP92

No. B238 Mountain climber on rope, vert.

1992, Dec. 18
B237 SP92 1000 l +200 l multi   1.00   .60
B238 SP92 3000 l +200 l multi   1.75 1.00

Travertine, Pamukkale — SP93

Different views of rock formations.

1993, June 6
B239 SP93 1000 l +200 l multi   .75   .25
B240 SP93 3000 l +500 l multi   1.50   .55

Intl. Day for Natural Disaster Reduction SP94

1993, Oct. 13   Perf. 12½x13
B241 SP94 3000 l + 500 l multi   1.25   .75

Intl. Olympic Committee, Cent. — SP95

1994, Aug. 17   Perf. 13
B242 SP95 12,500 l +500 l multi 1.75 1.10

Trees SP96

Designs: No. B243, Platanus orientalis. No. B244, Cupressus sempervirens, vert.

1994, Nov. 30
B243 SP96 7500 l +500 l multi   .75   .50
B244 SP96 12,500 l +500 l multi 1.75   .75

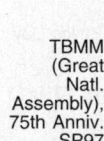

TBMM (Great Natl. Assembly), 75th Anniv. SP97

1995, Apr. 23
B245 SP97 3500 l +500 l multi   .65   .25

The Epic of Manas SP98

Designs: No. B246, Lancers charging. No. B247, Abay Kunanbay (1845-1904), poet, vert.

1995, June 28
B246 SP98 3500 l +500 l multi   .75   .25
B247 SP98 3500 l +500 l multi   .75   .25

For the People of Bosnia-Herzegovina — SP99

1996, Feb. 28
B248 SP99 10,000 l +2500 l multi .65   .65

Ankara University, 50th Anniv. SP100

Unwmk.
1996, Nov. 20   Litho.   Perf. 13
B249 15,000 l +2500 l multi   .65   .30

Fight Against Cancer, 50th Anniv. SP101

1997, Feb. 18   Litho.   Perf. 12½x13
B250 SP101 25,000 l +5000 l
        multi   .65   .30

Pakistan Independence, 50th Anniv. — SP102

Mohammed Ali Jinnah (1876-1948).

1997, Mar. 23   Litho.   Perf. 13
B251 SP102 25,000 l +5000 l
        multi   .65   .30

Universal Declaration of Human Rights SP103

Stylized designs: 75,000 l, Puzzle piece with outlines of people's faces. 175,000 l, Heart-shaped kite with people as tail.

1998, Dec. 10   Litho.   Perf. 13½
B252 SP103 75,000 l +25,000 l   .80   .40
B253 SP103 175,000 l +25,000 l   1.60   .80

GATA (Gulhane Military Medical Academy), Cent. SP104

1998, Dec. 30   Litho.   Perf. 13
B254 SP104 75,000 l +10,000 l
        multi   .80   .40

Kemal Ataturk's Entry Into War College, Cent. — SP105

1999, Mar. 13   Litho.   Perf. 13
B255 SP105 75,000 l +5,000 l
        multi   1.00   .25

Council of Europe, 50th Anniv. SP106

1999, Apr. 30   Litho.   Perf. 13¼
B256 SP106 175,000 l +10,000 l   2.00 1.10

Church, Mosque and Synagogue — SP107

Dancers SP108

2000, May 25   Litho.   Perf. 13¼
B257 SP107 275,000 l +10,000 l   2.00 2.00
B258 SP108 300,000 l +10,000 l   2.00 2.00

Tombs and Mausoleums SP109

150,000 l+25,000 l, Usta Sagirt Kumbeti Ahlat, vert. 200,000 l+25,000 l, Kocbasli Mezar Tasi Tunceli. 275,000 l+25,000 l, Isabey Turbesi, Uskup, vert. 300,000 l+25,000 l, Yusuf bin Kuseyr Turbesi, Nahcivan, vert.

2000
B259-B262 SP109 Set of 4   7.25 7.25

Coins SP110

Various coins with background colors of: No. B263, 300,000 l + 25,000 l, Red. No. B264, 300,000 l + 25,000 l, Blue green. 450,000 l + 25,000 l, Dark carmine. 500,000 l + 25,000 l, Blue violet.

2001, Oct. 1   Litho.   Perf. 13
B263-B266 SP110 Set of 4   7.25 7.25

Caravansaries — SP111

Designs: 300,000 l + 25,000 l, Ashab i Kehf Han, Afsin. 500,000 l + 25,000 l, Horozlu Han, Konya.

2001, Nov. 19　　Litho.　　Perf. 13
B267-B268　SP111　Set of 2　　4.50　4.50

Scouting — SP117

Designs: 600,000 l + 50,000 l, Girl Scout in foreground. 700,000 l + 50,000 l, Boy Scout in foreground.

2004, Sept. 30
B277-B278　SP117　Set of 2　　3.50　3.50

Marbled Art — SP123

Designs: 60k+10k, White flowers. 70k+10k, Red tulips.

2007, Dec. 6　　　　Perf. 13¼x13
B285-B286　SP123　Set of 2　　2.60　2.60

Locomotives — SP128

Various locomotives: 80k+10k, 110k+10k.

2010, Aug. 4　　　　Perf. 12¾x13
B294-B295　SP128　Set of 2　　3.00　3.00

Turkey's Admission to NATO, 50th Anniv. SP112

2002, Feb. 18
B269　SP112　400,000 l + 25,000 l　2.25　1.90

Rotary International, Cent. — SP118

2005, Feb. 23　Litho.　Perf. 13x13¼
B279　SP118　80k +10k multi　　1.50　1.50

Kasgarli Mahmut (1008-1105), Lexicographer — SP124

Kasgarli: 65k+10k, On horseback. 80k+10k, Holding book.

2008, Apr. 10　Litho.　Perf. 13¼x13
B287-B288　SP124　Set of 2　　2.60　2.60

Rugs SP129

Various rugs: 80k+10k, 110k+10k.

2010, Nov. 17
B296-B297　SP129　Set of 2　　3.00　3.00

Trains SP113

Designs: 500,000 l + 25,000 l, Steam locomotive. 700,000 l + 25,000 l, Electric locomotive.

2002, Sept. 16　Litho.　Perf. 13¼x13
B270-B271　SP113　Set of 2　　7.25　5.50

Intl. Year of Physics SP119

2005, Sept. 13　Litho.　Perf. 13¼x13
B280　SP119　70k +10k multi　　1.25　1.25

Railway Terminals in Istanbul — SP125

Designs: 65k+10k, Haydarpasa Terminal. 80k+10k, Sirkeci Terminal.

2008, Oct. 15　Litho.　Perf. 13x13¼
B289-B290　SP125　Set of 2　　2.25　2.25

Hasankeyf — SP130

2011, Sept. 21　　　　Perf. 13x13¼
B298　SP130　130k +10k multi　　1.60　1.60

Trains SP114

Designs: 600,000 l+50,000 l, Trolley. 800,000 l+50,000 l, Subway.

2003, Sept. 9　Litho.　Perf. 13¼x13
B272-B273　SP114　Set of 2　　3.50　3.50

World Forests Day SP120

2006, Mar. 21　Litho.　Perf. 13¼x13
B281　SP120　60k +10k multi　　1.10　1.10

Ethics Day SP126

2009, May 25　　　　Perf. 13¼x13
B291　SP126　65k +10k multi　　1.00　1.00

State Personnel Department, 50th Anniv. SP131

2011, Dec. 17　　　　Perf. 13¼x13
B299　SP131　100k +10k multi　　1.25　1.25

Ibrahim Hakki Erzurumlu (1703-72), Writer — SP115

2003, Dec. 24　Litho.　Perf. 13x13¼
B274　SP115　600,000 l +50,000 l
　　　　　　　　　　multi　　2.00　1.40

Mehmet Akif Ersoy (1873-1936), Poet — SP121

Ersoy at: 60k+10k, Left. 70k+10k, Right.

2006, Oct. 13　Litho.　Perf. 13¼x13
B282-B283　SP121　Set of 2　　2.10　2.10

Katip Celebi (1609-57), Historian SP127

Celebi, book and: 75k+10k, Quill pen. 90k+10k, Ships.

2009, July 16
B292-B293　SP127　Set of 2　　2.60　2.60

Souvenir Sheet

Turkish Cuisine — SP132

No. B300: a, 50k+10k, Tursu Kavurma (roasted pickles). b, 1 l+10k, Kara Lahana Dolmasi (stuffed collard greens). c, 1 l+10k, Mihlama (corn meal and cheese fondue). d, 2 l+10k, Hamsi Tava (fried anchovies).

2012, Aug. 16　　　　Perf. 14¼
B300　SP132　Sheet of 4, #a-d +
　　　　　　　　　label　　5.50　5.50

Lighthouses SP116

Designs: 600,000 l + 50,000 l, Kerempe Lighthouse, Kastamonu. 700,000 l + 50,000 l, Taslikburnu Lighthouse, Antalya.

2004, Apr. 5
B275-B276　SP116　Set of 2　　4.50　4.50

Coast Guard Command, 25th Anniv. — SP122

2007, July 13　Litho.　Perf. 13¼x13
B284　SP122　60k + 10k multi　　1.10　1.10

Karsiyaka Sporting Club, Cent. SP133

Designs: 50k+10k, Bowling, motorcycling, billiards. 1 l+10k, Volleyball, swimming, tennis. 2 l+10k, Basketball, sailing, soccer.

2012, Nov. 1 Litho. Perf. 13¼x13½
B301-B303 SP133 Set of 3 4.25 4.25

Souvenir Sheet

Eurasian Social Business Forum, Erzincan — SP134

No. B304: a, Bridge, roads, wind genera-tors, buildings, power lines. b, Earth in droplet.

Perf. 13¾ Syncopated
2013, May 23 Litho.
B304 SP134 1.10 l +10k Sheet
of 2, #a-b 2.60 2.60

Beypazari District, 130th Anniv. — SP135

Designs: No. B305, 1 l0 l+10k, Plates of food, carrots, bottle and decorative butterflies. No. B306, 1.10 l+10k, House, vert.

Perf. 13½x13¼, 13¼x13½
2013, May 29 Litho.
B305-B306 SP135 Set of 2 2.60 2.60

Historic Bridges — SP136

Designs: No. B307, 1.10 l +10k, Kesik Bridge, Sivas. No. B308, 1.10 l + 10k, Clandiras Bridge, Usak.

2014, Apr. 10 Litho. Perf. 13½x13¼
B307-B308 SP136 Set of 2 2.25 2.25

Souvenir Sheet

Organ Donation — SP137

Hands and: a, Heart at right. b, Heart at left.

2014, Nov. 3 Litho. Perf. 14x13¾
B309 SP137 1.25 l +10k Sheet of 2, #a-b 2.40 2.40

Bridges — SP138

Designs: No. B310, 1.25 l +10k, Malabadi Bridge. No. B311, 1.25 l + 10k, On Gozlu Bridge (Dicle Bridge).

2015, Apr. 10 Litho. Perf. 13½x13¼
D310-B311 SP138 Set of 2 2.00 2.00

Campaign Against Obesity SP139

2015, Nov. 12 Litho. Perf. 13¼x13
B312 SP139 1.40 l +10k multi + label 1.10 1.10

Bridges — SP140

Designs: No. B313, 1.40 l+10k, Varda Rail-road Bridge. No. B314, 1.40 l+10k, Irgandi Bridge.

2016, Mar. 9 Litho. Perf. 13½x13¼
B313-B314 SP140 Set of 2 2.25 2.25

Think Green SP141

Designs: No. B315, 1.40 l+10k, Umbrella over Earth and animals. No. B316, 1.40 l+10k, Tree in head.

2016, May 9 Litho. Perf. 13¼
B315-B316 SP141 Set of 2 2.10 2.10

Bitlis Tourist Attractions SP142

Designs: 75k+10k, Seljuk Cemetery. No. B318, 1.80 l+10k, Narlidere (Kasrik) Bridge, Ihlasiye Madrasa. No. B319, 1.80 l+10k, Tomb of Emir Bayindir.

2017, Aug. 10 Litho. Perf. 13¼
B317-B319 SP142 Set of 3 2.75 2.75

Military Equipment SP143

Designs: No. B320, 75k+10k, Anka drone. No. B321, 75k+10k, ATAK helicopter. No. B322, 1.80 l+10k, Bayraktar TB2 drone. No. B323, 1.80 l+10k, Hürkus airplane. No. B324, 3.70 l+10k, Milgem combat ship. No. B325, 3.70 l+10k, Altay tank.

2017, Nov. 23 Litho. Perf. 13¼
B320-B325 SP143 Set of 6 6.75 6.75

Souvenir Sheet

Safranbolu Bazaar — SP144

No. B326: a, Table and chairs under tree and booths, denomination at LL. b, Bazaar booths, denomination at LR.

Litho., Sheet Margin Litho. With Foil Application
2018, Mar. 30 Perf. 13½x13¾
B326 SP144 2 l + 10k Sheet of 2, #a-b 2.10 1.10

SP145

Health Tourism — SP146

2018, Sept. 12 Litho. Perf. 13¼
B327 SP145 2 l +10k multi .70 .70
B328 SP146 2 l +10k multi .70 .70

AIR POST STAMPS

Catalogue values for unused stamps in this section are for Never Hinged items.

Nos. 692, 695, 698, 700 Overprinted or Surcharged in Brown or Blue

1934, July 15 Unwmk. Perf. 12
C1 A74 7½k (Br) 1.25 .25
C2 A72 12½k on 15k (Br) 1.25 .25
C3 A74 20k on 25k (Br) 1.50 .25
C4 A74 25k (Bl) 1.75 .40
C5 A74 40k (Br) 3.00 1.25
  Nos. C1-C5 (5) 8.75 2.40

Regular Stamps of 1930 Surcharged in Brown

1937
C6 A74 4½k on 7½k red brn 6.00 1.00
C7 A72 9k on 15k dp org 47.50 20.00
C8 A74 35k on 40k red vio 12.00 4.25
  Nos. C6-C8 (3) 65.50 25.25

Nos. 698, 703-704 Surcharged in Black

1941, Dec. 18
C9 A74 4½k on 25k 2.25 1.50
C10 A75 9k on 200k 10.50 8.25
C11 A75 35k on 500k 6.75 5.25
  Nos. C9-C11 (3) 19.50 15.00

Plane over Izmir AP1

Planes over: 5k, 40k, Izmir. 20k, 50k, Ankara. 30k, 1 l, Istanbul.

1949, Jan. 1 Photo. Perf. 11½
C12 AP1 5k gray & vio .40 .25
C13 AP1 20k bl gray & brn .40 .25
C14 AP1 30k bl gray & ol brn 1.50 .25
C15 AP1 40k bl & dp ultra 1.50 1.00
C16 AP1 50k gray vio & red brn 1.50 .25
C17 AP1 1 l gray bl & dk grn 4.25 .65
  Nos. C12-C17 (6) 9.55 2.65

For overprints see Nos. C19-C21.

Plane Over Rumeli Hisari Fortress AP2

1950, May 19   **Unwmk.**
C18 AP2 2½ l gray bl & dk grn   22.50   14.00

Nos. C12, C14 and C16 Overprinted in Red

1951, Apr. 9   **Perf. 11½**
C19 AP1 5k gray & vio   1.50   .50
C20 AP1 30k bl gray & ol brn   2.00   .60
C21 AP1 50k gray vio & red brn   2.50   .70
    Nos. C19-C21 (3)   6.00   1.80

Industrial Congress, Ankara, Apr. 9.

Yesilkoy Airport and Plane AP3

Designs: 20k, 45k, Yesilkoy Airport and plane in flight. 35k, 55k, Ankara Airport and plane. 40k, as No. C22.

1954, Nov. 1   **Perf. 14**
C22 AP3 5k red brn & bl   1.25   .25
C23 AP3 20k brn org & bl   .85   .25
C24 AP3 35k dk grn & bl   .85   .25
C25 AP3 40k dp car & bl   .85   .25
C26 AP3 45k violet & bl   .95   .25
C27 AP3 55k black & bl   1.90   .50
    Nos. C22-C27 (6)   6.65   1.75

Symbol of Izmir Fair — AP4

1956, Aug. 20   **Litho.**   **Perf. 10½**
C28 AP4 25k reddish brown   .75   .30

25th Intl. Fair at Izmir, Aug. 20-Sept. 20.

Heuss Type of Regular Issue, 1957
1957, May 5
C29 A264 40k sal pink & magenta   .75   .30

Zahir Shah Type of Regular Issue, 1957
1957, Sept. 1
C30 A269 25k grn & lt grn   .75   .30

Hawk — AP5

Crane — AP6

Birds: 40k, 125k, Swallows. 65k, Cranes. 85k, 195k, Gulls. 245k, Hawk.

1959, Aug. 13   **Litho.**   **Perf. 10½**
C31 AP5 40k bright lilac   .50   .25
C32 AP5 65k blue green   3.00   .40
C33 AP5 85k bright blue   1.00   .40
C34 AP5 105k yel & sepia   .75   .40
C35 AP6 125k brt violet   1.00   .40
C36 AP6 155k yel green   1.25   .40
C37 AP6 195k violet blue   1.50   .40
C38 AP6 245k brn & brn org   3.50   1.00
    Nos. C31-C38 (8)   12.50   3.65

De Havilland Rapide Biplane AP7

Designs: 60k, Fokker Friendship transport plane. 130k, DC9-30. 220k, DC-3. 270k, Viscount 794.

1967, July 13   **Litho.**   **Perf. 13½x13**
C39 AP7 10k pink & blk   .65   .25
C40 AP7 60k lt grn, red & blk   .95   .25
C41 AP7 130k bl, blk & red   1.15   .25
C42 AP7 220k lt brn, blk & red   1.75   .35
C43 AP7 270k org, blk & red   2.75   .45
    Nos. C39-C43 (5)   7.25   1.55

For surcharge see No. 2179A.

Kestrel — AP8

Birds: 60k, Golden eagle. 130k, Falcon. 220k, Sparrow hawk. 270k, Buzzard.

1967, Oct. 10   **Litho.**   **Perf. 13**
C44 AP8 10k brown & salmon   1.10   .25
C45 AP8 60k brown & yellow   .85   .25
C46 AP8 130k brown & lt bl   2.10   .25
C47 AP8 220k brown & lt grn   3.25   .45
C48 AP8 270k org brn & gray   4.75   .65
    Nos. C44-C48 (5)   12.05   1.85

F-104 Jet Plane — AP9

Turkish Air Force Emblem and Jets AP10

Designs: 200k, Victory monument, Afyon, and Jets. 325k, F-104 jets and pilot. 400k, Bleriot XI plane with Turkish flag. 475k, Flight of Hezarfen Ahmet Celebi from Galata Tower to Uskudar.

1971, June 1   **Litho.**   **Perf. 13**
C49 AP9 110k multi   .90   .25
C50 AP9 200k multi   2.00   .25
C51 AP10 250k multi   2.00   .45
C52 AP9 325k multi   3.10   .45

C53 AP10 400k multi   3.50   .55
C54 AP10 475k multi   4.50   .65
    Nos. C49-C54 (6)   16.00   2.60

The gold ink on No. C51 is applied by a thermographic process which gives a raised and shiny effect.

F-28 Plane — AP11

1973, Dec. 11   **Litho.**   **Perf. 13**
C55 AP11 110k shown   .95   .25
C56 AP11 250k DC-10   1.25   .45

POSTAGE DUE STAMPS

Same Types as Regular Issues of Corresponding Dates
1863   **Unwmk.**   *Imperf.*
Blue Band
J1 A1 20pa blk, *red brn*   100.00   32.50
  a. Tête bêche pair   225.00   225.00
  b. Without band   50.00
  c. Red band   90.00   45.00
J2 A2 1pi blk, *red brn*   150.00   22.50
  a. Tête bêche pair   225.00   225.00
  b. Without band   50.00
J3 A3 2pi blk, *red brn*   500.00   70.00
  a. Tête bêche pair   650.00   450.00
J4 A4 5pi blk, *red brn*   300.00   80.00
  a. Tête bêche pair   425.00   425.00
  b. Without band   100.00
  c. Red band   150.00
    Nos. J1-J4 (4)   1,050.   205.00

1865   **Perf. 12½**
J6 A5 20pa brown   4.00   5.00
J7 A5 1pi brown   4.00   5.00
  b. Half used as 20pa on cover   25.00
  c. Printed on both sides   25.00
J8 A5 2pi brown   12.50   25.00
  a. Half used as 1pi on cover
J9 A5 5pi brown   5.00   30.00
  a. Half used as 2½pi on cover
J10 A5 25pi brown   45.00   100.00
    Nos. J6-J10 (5)   70.50   165.00

Exist imperf. Values, $60 to $100 each.
The 10pa brown is an essay. Value about $2,750.

1867
J11 A5 20pa bister brn   9.00   100.00
J12 A5 1pi bister brn   9.00
  a. With surcharge of 5pi   13.50
  b. Imperf., pair   65.00
J13 A5 2pi fawn   75.00
J14 A5 5pi fawn   17.50
J15 A5 25pi bister brn   21,250.
    Nos. J11-J14 (4)   110.50

Nos. J12-J15 were not placed in use.

1869   *Perf. 13½*
With Yellow-Brown Border
J16 A5 20pa bister brn   10.00   10.00
  a. Without surcharge
J17 A5 1pi bister brn   550.00   20.00
  a. Without surcharge
J18 A5 2pi bister brn   800.00   20.00
J19 A5 5pi bister brn   2.25   12.50
  b. Without border
  c. Printed on both sides   15.00
J20 A5 25pi bister brn
    Nos. J16-J19 (4)   1,362.   62.50

With Brown Border
Color of border ranges from brown to reddish brown and black brown.
J21 A5 20pa bister brn   125.00   20.00
  a. Inverted surcharge
  b. Without surcharge
J22 A5 1pi bister brn   550.00   12.50
  a. Without surcharge
J23 A5 2pi bister brn   450.00   12.50
  b. Inverted surcharge
J24 A5 5pi bister brn   2.50   15.00
  b. Without surcharge
J25 A5 25pi bister brn   37.50   100.00
    Nos. J21-J25 (5)   1,165.   160.00

Pin-perf., Perf. 5 to 11½ and Compound
1871   **With Bright Red Border**
J26 A5 20pa bister brn   1,250.   50.00
J27 A5 1pi bister brn   *5,000.*
J28 A5 2pi bister brn   110.00   140.00
With Orange Brown Border
J29 A5 5pi bister brn   7.50   25.00
With Brown to Deep Brown Border
J31 A5 20pa bister brn   150.00   3.50
  a. Half used as 10pa on cover

  b. Imperf., pair   16.50
  c. Printed on both sides   40.00   40.00
J32 A5 1pi bister brn   225.00   2.50
  a. Half used as 20pa on cover
  c. Inverted surcharge   50.00   35.00
  d. Printed on both sides
J33 A5 2pi bister brn   6.00   6.00
  a. Half used as 1pi on cover
  c. Imperf., pair   16.50
J34 A5 5pi bister brn   2.50   20.00
  a. Half used as 2½pi on cover
  c. Printed on both sides
J35 A5 25pi bister brn   40.00   125.00
    Nos. J31-J35 (5)   423.50   160.00

1888   **Perf. 11½ and 13½**
J36 A7 20pa black   3.00   10.00
J37 A7 1pi black   3.00   10.00
J38 A7 2pi black   3.00   10.00
  b. Diagonal half used as 1pi
    Nos. J36-J38 (3)   9.00   30.00

     Imperf
J36a A7 20pa   17.50
J37a A7 1pi   17.50
J38a A7 2pi   17.50

1892   *Perf. 13½*
J39 A11 20pa black   7.00   12.50
J40 A12 1pi black   25.00   12.50
  a. Printed on both sides
J41 A13 2pi black   17.50   12.50
    Nos. J39-J41 (3)   49.50   37.50

1901
J42 A11 20pa black, *deep rose*   2.50   20.00

1901
J43 A17 10pa black, *deep rose*   4.00   6.00
J44 A17 20pa black, *deep rose*   3.75   8.75
J45 A17 1pi black, *deep rose*   3.00   10.00
J46 A17 2pi black, *deep rose*   2.50   15.00
    Nos. J43-J46 (4)   13.25   39.75

1905   *Perf. 12*
J47 A18 1pi black, *deep rose*   3.00   10.00
J48 A18 2pi black, *deep rose*   4.50   20.00

1908,   *Perf. 12, 13½ and Compound*
J49 A19 1pi black, *deep rose*   80.00   7.50
J50 A19 2pi black, *deep rose*   12.50   45.00

1909
J51 A21 1pi black, *deep rose*   15.00   *50.00*
J52 A21 2pi black, *deep rose*   150.00   175.00
  a. Imperf.   65.00

1913   *Perf. 12*
J53 A22 2pa black, *deep rose*   2.00   .50
J54 A22 5pa black, *deep rose*   2.00   .50
J55 A22 10pa black, *deep rose*   2.00   .50
J56 A22 20pa black, *deep rose*   2.00   .50
J57 A22 1pi black, *deep rose*   6.00   10.00
J58 A22 2pi black, *deep rose*   9.00   17.50
    Nos. J53-J58 (6)   23.00   29.50

Adrianople Issue
Nos. 251-253 Surcharged in Black, Blue or Red

1913
J59 A23 2pa on 10pa green (Bk)   3.25   .35
J60 A23 5pa on 20pa red (Bl)   3.25   .35
J61 A23 10pa on 40pa blue (R)   10.00   .80
J62 A23 20pa on 40pa blue (Bk)   32.50   11.00
    Nos. J59-J62 (4)   49.00   12.50

For surcharges see Nos. J67-J70, J83-J86.

D1   D2

D3

D4

1914   Engr.
J63	D1	5pa claret	2.00	10.00
J64	D2	20pa red	2.00	10.00
J65	D3	1pi dark blue	2.00	10.00
J66	D4	2pi slate	2.00	10.00
		Nos. J63-J66 (4)	8.00	40.00

For surcharges and overprints see Nos. J87-J91.

Nos. J59 to J62 Surcharged in Red or Black

1916
J67	A23	10pa on 2pa on 10pa (R)	55.00	55.00
J68	A23	20pa on 5pa on 20pa	55.00	55.00
J69	A23	40pa on 10pa on 40pa	55.00	55.00
J70	A23	40pa on 20pa on 40pa (R)	55.00	55.00
		Nos. J67-J70 (4)	220.00	220.00

Preceding Issues Overprinted in Red, Black or Blue

1917   On Stamps of 1865
J71	A5	20pa red brn (Bl)	45.00	67.50
J72	A5	1pi red brn (Bl)	45.00	67.50
J73	A5	2pi bis brn (Bl)	45.00	67.50
J74	A5	5pi bis brn (Bl)	45.00	67.50
J75	A5	25pi bis brn (Bl)	45.00	67.50
		Nos. J71-J75 (5)	225.00	337.50

On Stamp of 1869
Red Brown Border
J76	A5	5pi bis brn (R)	45.00	67.50

On Stamp of 1871
Black Brown Border
J77	A5	5pi bis brn	75.00	50.00

On Stamps of 1888
J78	A7	1pi black (R)	45.00	67.50
J79	A7	2pi black (R)	45.00	67.50

On Stamps of 1892
J80	A11	20pa black (R)	2.50	2.50
J81	A12	1pi black (R)	2.50	2.50
J82	A13	2pi black (R)	2.50	2.50
		Nos. J80-J82 (3)	7.50	7.50

Adrianople Issue
On Nos. J59 to J62 with Addition of New Value
J83	A23	10pa on 2pa on 10pa (R)	1.95	1.00
J84	A23	20pa on 5pa on 20pa (Bk)	2.50	1.00
J85	A23	40pa on 10pa on 40pa (Bk)	3.00	1.50
a.		"40pa" double		
J86	A23	40pa on 20pa on 40pa (R)	5.25	3.50
		Nos. J83-J86 (4)	12.70	7.00

Nos. J71-J86 were used as regular postage stamps.

Armistice Issue

No. J65 Overprinted

1919, Nov. 30
J87	D3	1pi dark blue	125.00	150.00

Accession to the Throne Issue
Postage Due Stamps of 1914 Overprinted in Turkish "Accession to the Throne of His Majesty. 3rd July, 1334-1918"

1919
J88	D1	10pa on 5pa claret	25.00	37.50
J89	D2	20pa red	25.00	37.50
J90	D3	1pi dark blue	25.00	37.50
J91	D4	2pi slate	25.00	37.50
		Nos. J88-J91 (4)	100.00	150.00

Railroad Bridge over Kizil Irmak — D5

1926   Engr.
J92	D5	20pa ocher	1.25	2.50
J93	D5	1g red	2.00	5.00
J94	D5	2g blue green	3.00	5.00
J95	D5	3g lilac brown	3.50	12.50
J96	D5	5g lilac	6.00	20.00
		Nos. J92-J96 (5)	15.75	45.00
		Set, never hinged	40.00	

> Catalogue values for unused stamps in this section, from this point to the end of the section, are for Never Hinged items.

Kemal Atatürk — D6

1936   Litho.   Perf. 11½
J97	D6	20pa brown	.40	.25
J98	D6	2k light blue	.40	.25
J99	D6	3k bright violet	.40	.25
J100	D6	5k Prussian blue	.40	.25
J101	D6	12k bright rose	.50	.25
		Nos. J97-J101 (5)	2.10	1.25

For surcharges see Nos. 1461-1465.

LOCAL ISSUES

Type I

Type II

Type III

Type IV

Type V

Type VI

During 1873//1882 Turkish stamps with the above overprints were used for local postage in Constantinople (types 1-5) and Mount Athos (type 6).

MILITARY STAMPS
For the Army in Thessaly

Tughra and Bridge at Larissa — M1

1898, Apr. 21   Unwmk.   Perf. 13
M1	M1	10pa yellow green	10.00	7.50
M2	M1	20pa rose	10.00	7.50
M3	M1	1pi dark blue	10.00	7.50
M4	M1	2pi orange	10.00	7.50
M5	M1	5pi violet	10.00	7.50
		Nos. M1-M5 (5)	50.00	37.50
		Set, never hinged	75.00	

Issued for Turkish occupation forces to use in Thessaly during the Greco-Turkish War of 1897-98.

Forgeries of Nos. M1-M5 are perf. 11½.

OFFICIAL STAMPS

> Catalogue values for unused stamps in this section are for Never Hinged items.

O1

Perf. 10 to 12 and Compound
1948   Typo.   Unwmk.
O1	O1	10pa rose brown	.50	.25
O2	O1	1k gray green	.50	.25
O3	O1	2k rose violet	.50	.25
O4	O1	3k orange	.50	.25
O5	O1	5k blue	25.00	.90
O6	O1	10k brown org	7.50	.25
O7	O1	15k violet	2.50	.25
O8	O1	20k dk blue	3.00	.25
O9	O1	30k olive bister	5.00	.80
O10	O1	50k black	5.00	.80
O11	O1	1 l bluish grn	5.00	.80
O12	O1	2 l lilac rose	10.00	1.00
		Nos. O1-O12 (12)	65.00	6.05

Regular Issue of 1948 Overprinted Type "a" in Black

1951
O13	A178	5k blue	.50	.25
O14	A178	10k chocolate	.60	.25
O15	A178	20k deep blue	.90	.25
O16	A178	30k brown	1.50	.25
		Nos. O13-O16 (4)	3.50	1.00

Overprint "a" is 15½mm wide. Points of crescent do not touch star. The 0.25k (No. 963) exists with overprint "a" but its status is questionable.

b

Overprinted Type "b" in Dark Brown

1953
O17	A178	0.25k dk red	.50	.25
O18	A178	5k blue	.60	.25
O19	A178	10k chocolate	.80	.25
O20	A178	15k violet	1.50	.25
O21	A178	20k deep blue	7.00	1.00

O22	A178	30k brown	2.00	.30
O23	A178	60k black	2.50	.25
		Nos. O17-O23 (7)	14.90	2.55

Overprint "b" is 14mm wide. Lettering thin with sharp, clean corners.

c

Overprinted Type "c" in Black or Green Black

1953-54
O23A	A178	0.25k dk red (G Bk) ('53)	.25	.25
f.		Black overprint	4.00	4.00
g.		Violet overprint ('53)	4.00	4.00
O23B	A178	10k chocolate	12.50	.65
O23C	A178	15k violet	15.00	1.00
O23D	A178	30k brown	6.50	.65
O23E	A178	60k black	8.00	1.00
		Nos. O23A-O23E (5)	42.25	3.55

Lettering of type "c" heavy with rounded corners.

Small Star — d

Overprinted or Surcharged Type "d" in Black

1955
O24	A178	0.25k dark red	.30	.25
O25	A178	1k olive black	.30	.25
O26	A178	2k brt rose lil	.30	.25
O27	A178	3k red orange	.40	.25
O28	A178	4k dk green	.50	.25
O29	A178	5k on 15k vio	.50	.25
O31	A178	10k on 15k vio	.60	.25
O32	A178	15k violet	.70	.25
O33	A178	20k deep blue	.70	.25
O35	A178	40k on 1 l ol grn	.80	.35
O36	A179	75k on 2 l dk brn	1.10	.80
O37	A179	75k on 5 l dp	1.10	.80
		plum	8.00	8.00
		Nos. O24-O37 (12)	14.10	11.40

Type "d" measures 15x16mm. Overprint on Nos. O35-O37 measures 10x22mm. Nos. O29, O31, O35-O37 have two bars and new value added.

Large Star — e

Overprinted or Surcharged Type "e" in Black

1955
O25a	A178	1k olive black	.60	.25
O29a	A178	5k on 15k violet	1.60	.25
O30	A178	5k blue	3.00	.25
O31a	A178	10k on 15k violet	3.00	1.00
c.		"10" without serif	.90	.30
O33a	A178	20k deep blue	1.20	.30
O34	A178	30k brown	.90	.30

Heavy crescent — f

Overprinted or Surcharged Type "f" in Black

1957
O24b	A178	0.25k dark red	.75	.25
O25b	A178	1k olive black	.60	.30
O31b	A178	10k on 15k violet	1.10	.30
O35b	A179	75k on 1 l olive grn	1.90	.50
O38b	A178	½k on 1k ol blk	.85	.25
		Nos. O24b-O38b (5)	5.20	1.60

Type "f" crescent is larger and does not touch wavy line. The surcharged "10" on No. O31b exists only without serifs. The overprint on O35b measures 17x22½mm.

Thin crescent — g

Overprinted or Surcharged Type "g" in Black

1957

O38	A178	½k on 1k ol blk	.90	.30
O39	A178	1k ol blk	.90	.30
O40	A178	2k on 4k dk grn	.90	.30
O41	A178	3k on 4k dk grn	.90	.30
O42	A178	10k on 12k dp red	.90	.30
	Nos. O38-O42 (5)		4.50	1.50

The shape of crescent and star on type "g" varies on each value. Overprint measures 14x18mm. The surcharged stamps have two bars and new value added.

O2

1957 Litho. Perf. 10½

O43	O2	5k blue	.25	.25
O44	O2	10k orange brn	.25	.25
O45	O2	15k lt violet	.25	.25
O46	O2	20k red	.25	.25
O47	O2	30k gray olive	.25	.25
O48	O2	40k brown vio	.25	.25
O49	O2	50k grnsh blk	.25	.25
O50	O2	60k lt yel grn	.30	.25
O51	O2	75k yellow org	.50	.25
O52	O2	100k green	.75	.25
O53	O2	200k deep rose	1.25	.50
	Nos. O43-O53 (11)		4.55	3.00

1959 Unwmk. Perf. 10

O54	O2	5k rose	.25	.25
O55	O2	10k ol grn	.25	.25
O56	O2	15k car rose	.25	.25
O57	O2	20k lilac	.25	.25
O58	O2	40k blue	.25	.25
O59	O2	60k orange	.25	.25
O60	O2	75k gray	.50	.25
O61	O2	100k violet	.65	.25
O62	O2	200k red brn	1.10	.65
	Nos. O54-O62 (9)		3.75	2.65

O3

1960 Litho. Perf. 10½

O63	O3	1k orange	.25	.25
O64	O3	5k vermilion	.25	.25
O65	O3	10k gray grn	.75	.25
O67	O3	30k red brn	.25	.25
O70	O3	60k green	.25	.25
O71	O3	1 l rose lilac	.65	.25
O72	O3	1½ l brt ultra	2.00	.25
O74	O3	2½ l violet	3.00	.35
O75	O3	5 l blue	7.50	.85
	Nos. O63-O75 (9)		14.90	2.95

For surcharge see No. O83.

O4

1962 Typo. Perf. 13

O76	O4	1k olive bister	.30	.25
O77	O4	5k brt green	.30	.25
O78	O4	10k red brown	.30	.25
O79	O4	15k dk blue	.30	.25
O80	O4	25k carmine	.30	.25
O81	O4	30k ultra	.30	.25
	Nos. O76-O81 (6)		1.80	1.50

For surcharge see No. O82.

Nos. O81 and O70 Surcharged

1963

O82	O4	50k on 30k ultra	.35	.25

Perf. 10½
Litho.

O83	O3	100k on 60k green	.50	.25

O5

1963 Litho. Perf. 12½

O84	O5	1k gray	.50	.25
O85	O5	5k salmon	.50	.25
O86	O5	10k green	.50	.25
O87	O5	50k car rose	.50	.25
O88	O5	100k ultra	1.00	.50
	Nos. O84-O88 (5)		3.00	1.50

For surcharge see No. O139.

O6

1964 Unwmk. Perf. 12½

O89	O6	1k gray	.25	.25
O90	O6	5k blue	.25	.25
O91	O6	10k yellow	.25	.25
O92	O6	30k red	.40	.25
O93	O6	50k lt green	.50	.25
O94	O6	60k brown	1.50	.25
O95	O6	80k pale grnsh bl	3.50	.40
O96	O6	130k indigo	3.00	.60
O97	O6	200k lilac	7.50	.80
	Nos. O89-O97 (9)		17.15	3.30

For surcharge see No. O140.

O7

1965 Litho. Perf. 13

O98	O7	1k emerald	.40	.25
O99	O7	10k ultra	.40	.25
O100	O7	50k orange	.50	.25
	Nos. O98-O100 (3)		1.30	.75

For surcharge see No. O141.

Carpet Designs — O8

1k, Usak. 50k, Bergama. 100k, Ladik. 150k, Seljuk. 200k, Nomad. 500k, Anatolia.

1966 Litho. Perf. 13

O101	O8	1k orange	.25	.25
O102	O8	50k green	.25	.25
O103	O8	100k brt pink	.45	.25
O104	O8	150k violet blue	.85	.25
O105	O8	200k olive bister	1.00	.25
O106	O8	500k lilac	4.00	.40
	Nos. O101-O106 (6)		6.80	1.65

For surcharge see No. O142.

Seljuk Tile, 13th Century — O9

1967 Litho. Perf. 11½x12

O107	O9	1k dk bl & lt bl	.50	.25
O108	O9	50k org & dk bl	.50	.25
O109	O9	100k lil & dk bl	.50	.25
	Nos. O107-O109 (3)		1.50	.75

For surcharge see No. O143.

O16

Leaf Design — O10

1968 Litho. Perf. 13

O110	O10	50k brn & lt grn	.35	.25
O111	O10	150k blk & dl yel	1.00	.25
O112	O10	500k red brn & lt bl	3.00	.25
	Nos. O110-O112 (3)		4.35	.75

O11

1969, Aug. 25 Litho. Perf. 13

O113	O11	1k lt grn & red	.30	.25
O114	O11	10k lt grn & bl	.35	.25
O115	O11	50k lt grn & brn	.40	.25
O116	O11	100k lt grn & red vio	1.00	.25
	Nos. O113-O116 (4)		2.05	1.00

O12

1971, Mar. 1 Litho. Perf. 11½x12

O117	O12	5k brown & blue	.25	.25
O118	O12	10k vio bl & ver	.25	.25
O119	O12	30k org & vio bl	.35	.25
O120	O12	50k Prus bl & sepia	.60	.25
O121	O12	75k yellow & green	1.00	.25
	Nos. O117-O121 (5)		2.45	1.25

O13

1971, Nov. 15 Litho. Perf. 11½x12

O122	O13	5k lt bl & gray	.25	.25
O123	O13	25k cit & lt brn	.35	.25
O124	O13	100k org & olive	.45	.25
O125	O13	200k dk brn & bis	1.00	.25
O126	O13	250k rose lil & vio	1.25	.25
O127	O13	500k dk bl & brt bl	2.00	.45
	Nos. O122-O127 (6)		5.30	1.70

O14

1972, Apr. 7 Litho. Perf. 13

O128	O14	5k buff & blue	.45	.25
O129	O14	100k buff & olive	.55	.25
O130	O14	200k buff & carmine	1.25	.25
	Nos. O128-O130 (3)		2.25	.75

O15

1973, Sept 20 Litho. Perf. 13

O131	O15	100k violet & buff	.65	.25

1974, June 17 Litho. Perf. 13½x13

O132	O16	10k sal pink & brn	.25	.25
O133	O16	25k blue & dk brn	.25	.25
O134	O16	50k brt pink & brn	.25	.25
O135	O16	150k lt grn & brn	.50	.25
O136	O16	250k rose & brn	.75	.25
O137	O16	500k yellow & brn	1.50	.25
	Nos. O132-O137 (6)		3.50	1.50

O17

1975, Nov. 5 Litho. Perf. 12½x13

O138	O17	100k lt blue & maroon	.25	.25

Nos. O84, O89, O98, O101, O107 Surcharged in Red or Black
Perf. 12½, 13, 11½x12

1977, Aug. 17 Litho.

O139	O5	5k on 1k gray	.25	.25
O140	O6	5k on 1k gray	.25	.25
O141	O7	5k on 1k emer	.25	.25
O142	O8	5k on 1k org (B)	.25	.25
O143	O9	5k on 1k dk & lt bl	.25	.25
	Nos. O139-O143 (5)		1.25	1.25

O18

1977, Dec. 29 Litho. Perf. 13½x13

O144	O18	250k lt bl & grn	.50	.25

O19

1978 Photo. Perf. 13½

O145	O19	50k pink & rose	.25	.25
O146	O19	2½ l buff & grnsh blk	.25	.25
O147	O19	4½ l lil rose & sl grn	.40	.25
O148	O19	5 l lt blue & pur	.40	.25
O149	O19	10 l lt grn & grn	.85	.25
O150	O19	25 l yellow & red	2.25	.25
	Nos. O145-O150 (6)		4.40	1.50

O20

1979 Litho. Perf. 13½

O151	O20	50k dp org & brn	.25	.25
O152	O20	2½ l bl & dk bl	.25	.25

O21

1979, Dec. 20 Litho. Perf. 13½

O153	O21	50k sal & dk bl	.40	.25
O154	O21	1 l lt grn & red	.40	.25
O155	O21	2½ l lil rose & red	.50	.25
O156	O21	5 l lt bl & mag	.40	.25
O157	O21	7½ l lt lil & dk bl	.40	.25
O158	O21	10 l yel & dk bl	.50	.40
O159	O21	35 l gray & rose ('81)	1.65	.45
O160	O21	50 l pnksh & dk bl ('81)	2.90	.55
	Nos. O153-O160 (8)		7.15	2.65

O22

1981, Oct. 23   Litho.   Perf. 13½
O161	O22	5 l	yel & red	2.75	.25
O162	O22	10 l	salmon & red	3.50	.25
O163	O22	35 l	gray & rose	4.25	.25
O164	O22	50 l	pink & dk bl	5.00	.25
O165	O22	75 l	pale grn & grn	8.50	.25
O166	O22	100 l	lt bl & dk bl	11.00	.45
Nos. O161-O166 (6)				35.00	1.70

O23

1983-84   Litho.   Perf. 12½x13
Background Color
O167	O23	5 l	yellow	1.00	.25
O168	O23	15 l	yellow bister	1.25	.25
O169	O23	20 l	gray ('84)	.50	.25
O170	O23	50 l	sky blue	3.00	.25
O171	O23	65 l	pink	3.75	.25
O172	O23	70 l	pale rose ('84)	.75	.25
O173	O23	90 l	bister brn	5.50	.25
O174	O23	90 l	bl gray ('84)	1.10	.25
O175	O23	100 l	lt green ('84)	1.75	.25
O176	O23	125 l	lt green	6.00	.50
O177	O23	230 l	pale salmon ('84)	3.00	.40
Nos. O167-O177 (11)				27.60	3.15

For surcharges see Nos. O184, O186-O190.

O24

1986-87
O178	O24	5 l	yel & vio	.45	.25
O179	O24	10 l	org & vio	.45	.25
O180	O24	20 l	gray & vio	.45	.25
O180A	O24	50 l	pale blue & dp ultra ('87)	.55	.25
O181	O24	100 l	lt yel grn & vio	2.25	.25
O182	O24	300 l	pale vio & blue ('87)	2.75	.25
Nos. O178-O182 (6)				6.90	1.50

For surcharges see Nos. O183, O185.

Nos. O179, O168, O180, O172, O173, O177 Surcharged in Dark Orange
1989
O183	O24	500 l	on 10 l	2.25	.25
O184	O23	500 l	on 15 l	2.25	.25
O185	O24	500 l	on 20 l	2.25	.25
O186	O23	1000 l	on 70 l	3.25	.25
O187	O23	1000 l	on 90 l	3.25	.25
O188	O23	1250 l	on 230 l	4.50	.50
Nos. O183-O188 (6)				17.75	1.75

Issued: #O183, O185-O188, 8/9; #O184, 6/7.

Nos. O171, O173 & O174 Surcharged in Black

1991, Mar. 27
O189	O23	100 l	on 65 l	1.20	.30
O189A	O23	250 l	on 90l (#O173)	—	
O190	O23	250 l	on 90 l (#O174)	1.90	.30

O25

Perf. 11½x12½
1992, Mar. 24   Litho.
| O191 | O25 | 3000 l | lt brn & dk brn | 2.00 | .30 |
| O192 | O25 | 5000 l | lt grn & dk grn | 6.00 | .50 |

O26

1992, Dec. 2   Litho.   Perf. 12½x13
| O193 | O26 | 1000 l | bl grn & vio bl | .75 | .25 |
| O194 | O26 | 10,000 l | vio bl & bl grn | 6.00 | .50 |

O27

1993, Sept. 27   Litho.   Perf. 12½x13
O195	O27	1000 l	brown & green	1.25	.25
O196	O27	1500 l	brown & green	1.75	.25
O197	O27	5000 l	green & claret	4.50	.40
Nos. O195-O197 (3)				7.50	.90

O28

1994, May 9   Litho.   Perf. 11½x12
| O198 | O28 | 2500 l | pink & violet | 2.00 | .25 |
| O199 | O28 | 25,000 l | yel & brn | 5.00 | .50 |

O29

1995, Jan. 25
| O200 | O29 | 3500 l | violet & lt vio | 1.50 | .25 |
| O201 | O29 | 17,500 l | bl grn & lt grn | 6.00 | .45 |

O30

1995, May 17
| O202 | O30 | 50,000 l | ol & apple grn | 3.50 | 1.60 |

O31

1995, Nov. 8   Litho.   Perf. 12½x13
| O203 | O31 | 5000 l | salmon & org | 1.25 | .25 |

O32   O32a

O32b   O32c

1996, July 10   Litho.   Perf. 11½x12¼
O204	O32	15,000 l	bl & red	1.00	.25
O205	O32a	20,000 l	grn & pur	1.50	.25
O206	O32b	50,000 l	pur & grn	2.00	.40
O207	O32c	100,000 l	red & bl	3.00	.75
Nos. O204-O207 (4)				7.50	1.65

O33

1997, Feb. 5   Litho.   Perf. 12½x13
| O208 | O33 | 25,000 l | red & blue | 1.50 | .30 |

O34   O35

1997, Aug. 4   Litho.   Perf. 12½x13
| O209 | O34 | 40,000 l | multicolored | 1.00 | .30 |
| O210 | O35 | 250,000 l | multicolored | 6.00 | 1.75 |

O36   O37

O38   O39

1998, June 10   Litho.   Perf. 12½x13
O211	O36	40,000 l	dk bl & lt bl	.75	.25
O212	O37	100,000 l	purple	2.00	.50
O213	O38	200,000 l	brn & pale bl grn	3.75	1.00
O214	O39	500,000 l	brn & pale bl grn	9.00	2.50
Nos. O211-O214 (4)				15.50	4.25

O40

1998, July 29   Litho.   Perf. 12½x13
| O215 | O40 | 75,000 l | multicolored | 1.25 | .30 |

O41   O42

1999   Litho.   Perf. 11½x12¼
| O216 | O41 | (R) vio & blue grn | 3.00 | .45 |
| O217 | O42 | (RT) black & pink | 7.00 | .45 |

On day of issue, No. O216 sold for 75,000 l; No. O217, 275,000 l.

O43   O44

O45   O46

2000, Apr. 3   Litho.   Perf. 11½x12¼
O218	O43	50,000 l	blue & pink	.60	.25
O219	O44	75,000 l	brn & gray	.75	.25
O220	O45	500,000 l	red brn & lt bl	4.50	.40
O221	O46	1,250,000 l	dk bl & buff	7.50	1.00
Nos. O218-O221 (4)				13.35	1.90

O46a   O46b

Perf. 11½x12¼
2000, Nov. 20   Litho.
| O221A | O46a | R blue & yel grn | 4.00 | .25 |
| O221B | O46b | RT dk bl & lt bl | 6.00 | .75 |

No. O221A sold for 300,000 l on day of issue. No. O221B sold for 500,000 l on day of issue.

O47

Perf. 11½x12¼
2001, Dec. 13   Litho.
| O222 | O47 | R blue & yel org | 3.00 | .25 |

Sold for 300,000 l on day of issue.

O48   O49

O50   O51

O52

Perf. 11½x12¼

2002, Dec. 10   **Litho.**
O223	O48	50,000 l multi	.35	.25
O224	O49	100,000 l multi	.35	.25
O225	O50	250,000 l multi	.75	.30
O226	O51	500,000 l multi	1.50	.60
O227	O52	1,500,000 l multi	5.50	1.75
	Nos. O223-O227 (5)		8.45	3.15

O53   O54

O55   O56

Perf. 11½x12¼

2003, Aug. 18   **Litho.**
O228	O53	500,000 l bl & red	2.00	.70
O229	O54	750,000 l bl & yel	3.00	.80
O230	O55	1,000,000 l bl & grn	3.00	1.00
O231	O56	3,000,000 l bl & yel	10.00	2.10
	Nos. O228-O231 (4)		18.00	4.60

O57

2003, Oct. 13   Litho.   Perf. 11½x12¼
O232	O57	R pink & purple	1.25	.85

Sold for 600,000 l on day of issue.

Buildings O58

Designs: 100,000 l, Hamidiye Etfal Children's Sanitorium. 500,000 l, Heating Plant, Silahtaraga. 600,000 l, PTT Headquarters, Ankara, vert. 1,000,000 l, Finance Ministry building, Ankara, vert. 3,500,000 l, Old Post and Telegraph Ministry building, Istanbul.

2004, Oct. 15   Perf. 13¼x13, 13x13¼
O233	O58	100,000 l multi	.25	.25
O234	O58	500,000 l multi	.75	.50
O235	O58	600,000 l multi	.80	.60
O236	O58	1,000,000 l multi	1.50	1.00
O237	O58	3,500,000 l multi	5.50	2.00
	Nos. O233-O237 (5)		8.80	4.35

Building Type of 2004

Design: 60k, Prime Minister's Building, Ankara.

2005, Jan. 1   Litho.   Perf. 14
O238	O58	60k multi	.90	.90

Buildings O59

Designs: 10k, Museum of the Republic, Ankara. 25k, Culture and Tourism Ministry, Ankara. 50k, State Guest House, Ankara. 60k, Sculpture Museum, Ankara. 1 l, Ethnographic Museum, Ankara. 3.50 l, National Library, Ankara.

2005, July 4   Litho.   Perf. 13¼x13
Frame Color
O239	O59	10k orange	.25	.25
O240	O59	25k orange	.35	.35
O241	O59	50k yel green	.75	.75
O242	O59	60k blue	.90	.90

O243	O59	1 l yellow	1.50	1.50
O244	O59	3.50 l dull org	5.25	5.25
	Nos. O239-O244 (6)		9.00	9.00

Kemal Ataturk — O60

Various portraits.

2006, Apr. 21   Litho.   Perf. 13x13¼
Background Color
O245	O60	10k blue	.25	.25
O246	O60	50k brown	.75	.75
O247	O60	60k dark red	.95	.95
O248	O60	1 l blue green	1.50	1.50
O249	O60	3.50 l red	5.50	5.50
	Nos. O245-O249 (5)		8.95	8.95

Kemal Ataturk — O61

Various portraits.

Perf. 13x13½

2007, Feb. 26   **Wmk. 405**
O250	O61	10k multi	.25	.25
O251	O61	50k multi	.70	.70
O252	O61	60k multi	.85	.85
O253	O61	1 l multi	1.40	1.40
O254	O61	4 l multi	5.75	5.75
	Nos. O250-O254 (5)		8.95	8.95

Kemal Ataturk — O62

2007, Dec. 4   **Wmk. 405**
O255	O62	65k multi	1.10	1.10

Kemal Ataturk

O63   O64

Various portraits.

Perf. 13x13¼

2008, Feb. 29   **Wmk. 405**
O256	O63	5k multi	.25	.25
O257	O64	65k multi	1.10	1.10
O258	O64	85k multi	1.40	1.40
O259	O64	1 l multi	1.75	1.75
O260	O64	3.35 l multi	5.50	5.50
O261	O64	4.50 l multi	7.50	7.50
	Nos. O256-O261 (6)		17.50	17.50

O65

O66

Kemal Ataturk

O67   O68

Perf. 13x13¼, 13¼x13

2008, Dec. 4   **Wmk. 405**
O262	O65	5k multi	.25	.25
O263	O66	50k multi	.65	.65
O264	O67	65k multi	.85	.85
O265	O68	1 l multi	1.25	1.25
	Nos. O262-O265 (4)		3.00	3.00

Flowers O69

Designs: 5k, Nergis (daffodils). 10k, Nilüfer (water lily). 25k, Papatya (daisies). 50k, Cigdem (crocuses). 65k, Zambak (lilies). 75k, Yildiz (dahlia). 1 l, Kardelen (snowdrops). 3.35 l, Menekse (violet). 4.50 l, Ortanca (hydrangea). 5 l, Sardunya (geraniums).

2009   **Wmk. 405**   **Perf. 13¾**
O266	O69	5k multi	.25	.25
O267	O69	10k multi	.25	.25
O268	O69	25k multi	.35	.35
O269	O69	50k multi	.65	.65
O270	O69	65k multi	.85	.85
O271	O69	75k multi	1.10	1.10
O272	O69	1 l multi	1.25	1.25
O273	O69	3.35 l multi	4.25	4.25
O274	O69	4.50 l multi	5.75	5.75
O275	O69	5 l multi	7.00	7.00
	Nos. O266-O275 (10)		21.70	21.70

Issued: 75k, 5 l, 7/16; others, 3/26.

Flowers — O70

Designs: 5k, Ayçiçegi (sunflowers). 10k, Gelincik (poppies). 25k, Carkifelek (passion flower). 80k, Zinya (zinnia). 1 l Gül (rose).

Perf. 13x13¼

2010, Aug. 26   **Wmk. 405**
O276	O70	5k multi	.25	.25
O277	O70	10k multi	.25	.25
O278	O70	25k multi	.35	.35
O279	O70	80k multi	1.10	1.10
O280	O70	1 l multi	1.40	1.40
	Nos. O276-O280 (5)		3.35	3.35

Stylized Flowers — O71

Various stylized flowers.

2010, Dec. 10   **Wmk. 405**
O281	O71	5k multi	.25	.25
O282	O71	50k multi	.70	.70
O283	O71	80k multi	1.10	1.10
O284	O71	90k multi	1.25	1.25
O285	O71	1 l multi	1.40	1.40
	Nos. O281-O285 (5)		4.70	4.70

Stylized Flowers Type of 2010

Various stylized flowers.

Perf. 13½ Syncopated

2011, Apr. 18   **Wmk. 405**
Inscribed "2011"
O286	O71	10k multi	.25	.25
O287	O71	1 l multi	1.40	1.40
O288	O71	2.80 l multi	3.75	3.75
O289	O71	6 l multi	7.75	7.75
	Nos. O286-O289 (4)		13.15	13.15

Abstract Art — O72

Various abstract designs.

Perf. 13x13¼

2011, Dec. 19   **Wmk. 405**
O290	O72	10k multi	.25	.25
O291	O72	1 l multi	1.10	1.10
O292	O72	2 l multi	2.25	2.25
O293	O72	7 l multi	7.50	7.50
	Nos. O290-O293 (4)		11.10	11.10

Flowers — O73

Various flowers.

2012, May 2   Perf. 13¾ Syncopated
Background Color
O294	O73	25k dull orange	.30	.30
O295	O73	50k buff	.60	.60
O296	O73	1 l pink	1.10	1.10
O297	O73	3.75 l lilac	4.25	4.25
O298	O73	7 l light blue	8.00	8.00
	Nos. O294-O298 (5)		14.25	14.25

Four Seasons — O74

Designs: 10k, Evergreen branch in winter. 25k, Blossoms on tree in spring. 50k, Cherries on branch in summer. 1k, Brown leaves on tree in autumn.

2012, Sept. 11   **Perf. 14x13¾**
O299	O74	10k multi	.25	.25
O300	O74	25k multi	.30	.30
O301	O74	50k multi	.55	.55
O302	O74	1 l multi	1.10	1.10
	Nos. O299-O302 (4)		2.20	2.20

Carpets — O75

Carpet from: 10k, Balikesir. 25k Kayseri. 1.10 l, Aksaray. 3.85 l, Mugla.

Perf. 13x12½
2013, Feb. 14   **Wmk. 405**

O303	O75	10k multi	.25	.25
O304	O75	25k multi	.30	.30
O305	O75	1.10 l multi	1.25	1.25
O306	O75	3.85 l multi	4.25	4.25
Nos. O303-O306 (4)			6.05	6.05

Kemal Ataturk — O76

Various portraits.

Perf. 13¾ Syncopated
2013, Sept. 19   **Litho.**   **Unwmk.**

O307	O76	10k multi	.25	.25
O308	O76	25k multi	.25	.25
O309	O76	1 l multi	1.00	1.00
O310	O76	1.10 l multi	1.10	1.10
O311	O76	8 l multi	8.00	8.00
Nos. O307-O311 (5)			10.60	10.60

Kemal Ataturk — O77

Various portraits.

Perf. 13¾ Syncopated
2014, Apr. 16   **Litho.**   **Unwmk.**

O312	O77	10k multi	.25	.25
O313	O77	1 l multi	.95	.95
O314	O77	1.10 l multi	1.10	1.10
Nos. O312-O314 (3)			2.30	2.30

Carpets — O78

Carpet from: 15k, Manisa Province. 1.25 l, Kocaeli Province. 9 l, Konya Province.

Perf. 13¾ Syncopated
2014, May 7   **Litho.**

O315	O78	15k multi	.25	.25
O316	O78	1.25 l multi	1.25	1.25
O317	O78	9 l multi	8.50	8.50
Nos. O315-O317 (3)			10.00	10.00

Tourist Attractions O79

Various tourist attractions.

Perf. 13¾ Syncopated
2014, June 18   **Litho.**

O318	O79	15k multi	.25	.25
O319	O79	25k multi	.25	.25
O320	O79	1.25 l multi	1.25	1.25
O321	O79	9 l multi	8.50	8.50
Nos. O318-O321 (4)			10.25	10.25

Museum of Anatolian Civilizations, Ankara O80

Atatürk Mausoleum and Museum, Ankara O81

Ethnographic Museum, Ankara O82

Perf. 13¾ Syncopated
2015, Mar. 10   **Litho.**   **Unwmk.**

O322	O80	15k multi	.25	.25
O323	O81	1.25 l multi	1.00	1.00
O324	O82	9 l multi	7.00	7.00
Nos. O322-O324 (3)			8.25	8.25

Painting and Sculpture Museum, Ankara — O83

Perf. 13¾ Syncopated
2015, June 8   **Litho.**   **Wmk. 405**

O325	O83	1 l multi	.75	.75

O84

Zeugma Mosaic Museum, Gaziantep O85

Perf. 13¾ Syncopated
2015, June 19   **Litho.**   **Unwmk.**

O326	O84	25k multi	.25	.25
O327	O85	50k multi	.40	.40

Turkish and Islamic Arts Museum, Istanbul O86

Hagia Sophia Museum, Istanbul O87

Rumeli Hisari Museum, Istanbul O88

Galata Tower Museum, Istanbul — O89

Archaeological Museum, Istanbul — O90

Perf. 13¾ Syncopated
2015, Aug. 7   **Litho.**   **Unwmk.**

O328	O86	15k multi	.25	.25
O329	O87	30k multi	.25	.25
O330	O88	1.40 l multi	.95	.95
O331	O89	4.50 l multi	3.00	3.00
O332	O90	10 l multi	6.75	6.75
Nos. O328-O332 (5)			11.20	11.20

O91

O92

O93

Miniatures by Nusret Colpan (1952-2008) — O94

Perf. 13¾ Syncopated
2015, Dec. 14   **Litho.**   **Unwmk.**

O333	O91	50k multi	.35	.35
O334	O92	1 l multi	.70	.70
O335	O93	4.50 l multi	3.00	3.00
O336	O94	10 l multi	6.75	6.75
Nos. O333-O336 (4)			10.80	10.80

Stylized Flowers — O95

Various flowers.

Perf. 13¾ Syncopated
2016, Jan. 15   **Litho.**   **Unwmk.**

O337	O95	1 l multi	.70	.70
O338	O95	1.40 l multi	.95	.95
O339	O95	10 l multi	6.75	6.75
Nos. O337-O339 (3)			8.40	8.40

Miniature Roses — O96

Various roses with background colors of: 20k, Gray brown. 60k, Light blue. 65k, Dull orange and pink. 1.60 l, Yellow and lavender. 5.10 l, Mauve and pale green. 11 l, Lavender gray and pale green.

Perf. 13¾ Syncopated
2016, July 25   **Litho.**   **Unwmk.**

O340	O96	20k multi	.25	.25
O341	O96	60k multi	.40	.40
O342	O96	65k multi	.45	.45
O343	O96	1.60 l multi	1.10	1.10
O344	O96	5.10 l multi	3.50	3.50
O345	O96	11 l multi	7.50	7.50
Nos. O340-O345 (6)			13.20	13.20

Glazed Pottery Vessels — O97

Various vessels: 10k, Short wide neck, wide opening. 20k, Long skinny neck. 50k, Short wide neck with handles. 60k, Long skinny neck with lid.

Perf. 13¾ Syncopated
2016, Dec. 8   **Litho.**   **Unwmk.**

O346	O97	10k multi	.25	.25
O347	O97	20k multi	.25	.25
O348	O97	50k multi	.30	.30
O349	O97	60k multi	.35	.35
Nos. O346-O349 (4)			1.15	1.15

Flower — O98

Perf. 12½x13
2017, May 23   **Litho.**   **Unwmk.**
Background Color

O350	O98	10k turq blue	.25	.25
O351	O98	20k org yellow	.25	.25
O352	O98	50k red violet	.30	.30
O353	O98	1 l yel grn	.60	.60
O354	O98	5.10 l brt blue	3.00	3.00
Nos. O350-O354 (5)			4.40	4.40

Flowers

O99   O100

Perf. 12½x13
2017, July 31   **Litho.**   **Unwmk.**
Flower Color

O355	O99	10k dk grn	.25	.25
O356	O99	20k orange	.25	.25
O357	O99	50k ultra	.30	.30
O358	O99	75k pink	.30	.30
O359	O100	1 l reddish pur	.60	.60
O360	O100	1.50 l yellow	.85	.85
O361	O100	1.80 l black	1.10	1.10
O362	O100	5.80 l brt grn	3.25	3.25
O363	O100	12.50 l vermilion	7.25	7.25
Nos. O355-O363 (9)			14.15	14.15

O101　　　O102

O103　　　O104

O105　　　O106

O107　　　O108

Anatolian Rug Design
Elements — O109

Perf. 13½x13¾

2017, Dec. 13		Litho.	Unwmk.	
O364	O101	20k multi	.25	.25
O365	O102	70k multi	.40	.40
O366	O103	1 l multi	.55	.55
O367	O104	1.50 l multi	.80	.80
O368	O105	2 l multi	1.10	1.10
O369	O106	2.75 l multi	1.50	1.50
O370	O107	4 l multi	2.10	2.10
O371	O108	6.50 l multi	3.50	3.50
O372	O109	14 l multi	7.50	7.50
		Nos. O364-O372 (9)	17.70	17.70

Kemal
Atatürk — O110

Various portraits.

Perf. 13¾ Syncopated

2018, May 23		Litho.	Unwmk.	
O373	O110	10k multi	.25	.25
O374	O110	20k multi	.25	.25
O375	O110	50k multi	.25	.25
O376	O110	1 l multi	.45	.45
O377	O110	2 l multi	.90	.90
		Nos. O373-O377 (5)	2.10	2.10

Museums — O111

Designs: 50k, National Struggle Museum, Kayseri. 1 l, Liberation Museum, Eskisehir. 2 l, Western Front Headquarters Museum, Akshehir. 4 l, Victory Museum, Afyon.

2018, Dec. 26		Litho.	Perf. 13x12½	
O378	O111	50k multi	.25	.25
O379	O111	1 l multi	.40	.40
O380	O111	2 l multi	.75	.75
O381	O111	4 l multi	1.50	1.50
		Nos. O378-O381 (4)	2.90	2.90

NEWSPAPER STAMPS

N1

Black Overprint

1879		Unwmk.	Perf. 11½ and 13½	
P1	N1	10pa blk & rose lilac	225.00	225.00

Other stamps found with this "IMPRIMES" overprint were prepared on private order and have no official status as newspaper stamps. Counterfeits exist of No. P1.

The 10pa surcharge, on half of 20pa rose and pale rose was made privately. See note after No. 77.

Regular Issue of 1890 Handstamped in Black, Blue or Red

Nos. P10-P29 were overprinted with a single wooden handstamp. Variations in size are due to inking and pressure.

The handstamps on Nos. P10-P29 are found double, inverted and sideways. Counterfeit overprints comprise most of the examples offered for sale in the marketplace.

1891		Perf. 13½, 11½		
P10	A7	10pa grn & gray	40.00	12.50
a.		Imperf.	22.50	12.50
P11	A7	20pa rose & gray	75.00	15.00
P12	A7	1pi blue & gray	210.00	150.00
P13	A7	2pi yel & gray	525.00	400.00
P14	A7	5pi buff & gray	1,050.	750.00
		Nos. P10-P14 (5)	1,900.	1,328.

Blue Handstamp

P10b	A7	10pa green & gray	210.00	125.00
P11a	A7	20pa rose & gray	340.00	250.00
P12a	A7	1pi blue & gray	425.00	375.00
		Nos. P10b-P12a (3)	975.00	750.00

This overprint on 2pi and 5pi in blue is considered bogus.

Red Handstamp

P10c	A7	10pa green & gray	400.00	325.00
P11b	A7	20pa rose & gray	600.00	450.00
P12b	A7	1pi blue & gray	900.00	1,000.
		Nos. P10c-P12b (3)	1,900.	1,775.

This overprint in red on 2pi and 5pi is considered bogus.

Excellent forgeries of Nos. P10-P14 exist. Certification by a competant authority is suggested.

Same Handstamp on Regular Issue of 1892

1892		Perf. 13½		
P25	A10	10pa gray green	500.00	100.00
P26	A11	20pa rose	1,250.	375.00
P27	A12	1pi pale blue	110.00	150.00
P28	A13	2pi brown org	200.00	175.00
P29	A14	5pi pale violet	1,800.	1,250.
a.		On No. 99a	500.00	
		Nos. P25-P29 (5)	3,860.	2,050.

Regular Issues of 1892-98 Overprinted in Black

1893-98				
P30	A10	10pa gray grn	3.75	2.50
P31	A11	20pa vio brn ('98)	3.00	1.50
a.		20pa dark pink	3.50	2.00
b.		20pa pink	325.00	22.50
P32	A12	1pi pale blue	3.75	2.00
P33	A13	2pi brown org	27.50	12.50
a.		Tete beche pair	90.00	22.50
P34	A14	5pi pale violet	85.00	75.00
a.		On No. 99a	140.00	65.00
		Nos. P30-P34 (5)	123.00	93.50

For surcharge and overprints see Nos. B41, P121-P122, P134-P136, P153-P154.

No. 95 Surcharged

1897

P36	A10	5pa on 10pa gray grn	5.00	3.00
a.		"Cniq" instead of "Cinq"	15.00	15.00

For overprint see No. P137.

Nos. 102-107 Overprinted in Black

1901		Perf. 12, 13½ and Compound		
P37	A16	5pa bister	1.75	1.00
a.		Inverted overprint		
P38	A16	10pa yellow grn	6.25	6.25
P39	A16	20pa magenta	32.50	7.50
P40	A16	1pi violet blue	60.00	22.50
P41	A16	2pi gray blue	125.00	37.50
P42	A16	5pi ocher	300.00	90.00
		Nos. P37-P42 (6)	525.50	164.75

For overprints see Nos. B37, P69-P74, P123, P138-P141, P155-P158.

Same Overprint on Nos. 110-115

1901				
P43	A17	5pa purple	8.75	2.00
P44	A17	10pa green	32.50	2.50
P45	A17	20pa carmine	8.75	1.50
a.		Overprinted on back		
P46	A17	1pi blue	25.00	2.00
P47	A17	2pi orange	87.50	4.00
a.		Inverted overprint		
P48	A17	5pi lilac rose	160.00	27.50
		Nos. P43-P48 (6)	322.50	39.50

For overprints see Nos. P75-P80, P124-P126, P142-P146, P159-P164.

Same Overprint on Regular Issue of 1905

1905				
P49	A18	5pa ocher	2.50	1.00
P50	A18	10pa dull green	30.00	1.50
P51	A18	20pa carmine	2.50	1.25
P52	A18	1pi pale blue	2.50	1.25
P53	A18	2pi slate	70.00	10.00
P54	A18	5pi brown	175.00	20.00
		Nos. P49-P54 (6)	282.50	35.00

For overprints see Nos. P127-P129, P147-P150, P165-P171.

Regular Issue of 1908 Overprinted in Carmine or Blue

1908				
P55	A19	5pa ocher (Bl)	10.00	.50
P56	A19	10pa blue grn (C)	17.50	.50
P57	A19	20pa carmine (Bl)	22.50	1.00
P58	A19	1pi brt blue (C)	100.00	2.50
P59	A19	2pi blue blk (C)	150.00	7.50
P60	A19	5pi dk violet (C)	200.00	17.50
		Nos. P55-P60 (6)	500.00	29.50

For overprints see Nos. B17, P130-P131, P151, P172.

Same Overprint on Regular Issue of 1909

1909				
P61	A21	5pa ocher (Bl)	3.50	1.25
a.		Imperf.	30.00	30.00
P62	A21	10pa blue grn (C)	8.75	1.50
P63	A21	20pa car rose (Bl)	60.00	1.75
a.		Imperf.	80.00	80.00
P64	A21	1pi brt blue (C)	100.00	5.00
P65	A21	2pi blue blk (C)	250.00	30.00
P66	A21	5pi dk violet (C)	500.00	65.00
		Nos. P61-P66 (6)	922.25	104.50

For surcharge and overprints see Nos. B18, P67-P68, P81, P132-P133, P152.

No. 151 Surcharged in Blue

1910		Perf. 12, 13½ and Compound		
P67	A21	2pa on 5pa ocher	.75	.75

Type of 1909 Tughra and "Reshad" of Sultan Mohammed V

1911			Perf. 12	
P68	A21	2pa olive green	1.00	.50

For overprints see Nos. 567, P173.

Newspaper Stamps of 1901-11 Overprinted in Carmine or Blue

The overprint was applied to 13 denominations in four settings with change of city name, producing individual sets for each city: "MONASTIR," "PRISTINA," "SALONIQUE" and "USKUB."

1911, June 26		Perf. 12, 13½		
P69	A16	5pa bister	16.50	20.00
P70	A16	10pa yellow grn	16.50	20.00
P71	A16	20pa magenta	16.50	20.00
P72	A16	1pi violet blue	16.50	20.00
P73	A16	2pi gray blue	22.50	30.00
P74	A16	5pi ocher	45.00	60.00
P75	A17	5pa purple	8.75	11.50
P76	A17	10pa green	8.75	11.50
P77	A17	20pa carmine	8.75	11.50
P78	A17	1pi blue	8.75	11.50
P79	A17	2pi orange	11.00	14.50
P80	A17	5pi lilac rose	30.00	32.50
P81	A21	2pa olive green	3.00	3.75
		Nos. P69-P81 (13)	212.50	266.75

Values for each of the 4 city sets of 13 are the same.

The note after No. 182 will also apply to Nos. P69-P81.

Newspaper Stamps of 1901-11 Overprinted in Carmine or Black

1915		On Stamps of 1893-98		
P121	A10	10pa gray green	6.00	20.00
a.		Inverted overprint	20.00	20.00
P122	A13	2pi yellow brn	1.50	1.00
a.		Inverted overprint	20.00	20.00
		On Stamps of 1901		
P123	A16	10pa yellow grn	2.00	.50
P124	A17	5pa purple	2.00	1.00
P125	A17	20pa carmine	2.00	1.00
P126	A17	5pi lilac rose	20.00	20.00
		On Stamps of 1905		
P127	A18	5pa ocher	2.00	1.00
a.		Inverted overprint	20.00	20.00
P128	A18	2pi slate	17.50	5.00
P129	A18	5pi brown	10.00	.60
		On Stamps of 1908		
P130	A19	2pi blue blk	1,375.	550.00

P131	A19	5pi dk violet	10.00	1.25

On Stamps of 1909

P132	A21	5pa ocher	3.00	1.00
P133	A21	5pi dk violet	100.00	35.00

Nos. P121-P129, P131-P133 (12) 176.00 52.85

Preceding
Newspaper Issues
with additional
Overprint in Red or
Black

1916   On Stamps of 1893-98

P134	A10	10pa gray green	2.00	.75
P135	A11	20pa violet brn	2.00	.75
P136	A14	5pi dull violet	50.00	50.00

On Stamp of 1897

P137	A10	5pa on 10pa gray grn	.60	.50

On Stamps of 1901

P138	A16	5pa bister	1.00	.30
P139	A16	10pa yellow grn	1.50	.90
P140	A16	20pa magenta	1.50	.90
a.		Inverted overprint	20.00	20.00
P141	A17	1pi violet blue	1.00	1.00
P142	A17	5pa purple	50.00	50.00
P143	A17	10pa green	50.00	50.00
P144	A17	20pa carmine	1.50	.90
P145	A17	1pi blue	1.50	.90
P146	A17	2pi orange	1.50	.90

On Stamps of 1905

P147	A18	5pa ocher	1.50	.75
P148	A18	10pa dull green	50.00	50.00
P149	A18	20pa carmine	50.00	50.00
P150	A18	1pi pale blue	1.75	1.00

On Stamp of 1908

P151	A19	5pa ocher	62.50	62.50

On Stamp of 1909

P152	A21	5pa ocher	62.50	62.50

Nos. P134-P152 (19) 392.35 384.55

Preceding
Newspaper Issues
with additional
Overprint in Red or
Black

1917   On Stamps of 1893-98

P153	A12	1pi gray (R)	2.50	2.00
P154	A11	20pa vio brn (R)	3.75	3.75

On Stamps of 1901

P155	A16	5pa bister (Bk)	2.00	1.50
a.		Inverted overprint	20.00	20.00
P156	A16	10pa yellow grn (Bk)	1.50	1.25
P157	A16	20pa magenta (Bk)	1.50	1.25
P158	A16	2pi gray blue (R)	40.00	30.00
P159	A17	5pa purple (Bk)	2.25	2.25
a.		Inverted overprint	20.00	20.00
b.		Double overprint	20.00	20.00
c.		Double ovpt., one inverted	25.00	25.00
P160	A17	10pa green (R)	22.50	35.00
P161	A17	20pa carmine (Bk)	1.50	1.25
P162	A17	1pi blue (R)	3.00	3.00
P163	A17	2pi orange (Bk)	2.50	2.50
P164	A17	5pi lilac rose (R)	32.50	50.00

On Stamps of 1905

P165	A18	5pa ocher (R)	2.50	2.00
a.		Inverted overprint	20.00	20.00
P166	A18	5pa ocher (Bk)	3.00	2.50
a.		Inverted overprint	20.00	20.00
P167	A18	10pa dull green (R)	2.50	2.00
P168	A18	20pa carmine (Bk)	2.50	2.00
a.		Double overprint	20.00	20.00
P169	A18	1pi blue (R)	2.50	2.00
a.		Inverted overprint	25.00	25.00
P170	A18	2pi slate (R)	32.50	50.00
P171	A18	5pi brown (R)	32.50	50.00

On Stamp of 1908

P172	A19	5pa ocher (R)	32.50	50.00

Nos. P153-P172 (20) 226.00 294.25

Nos. P153-P172 were used as regular postage stamps.

Type of 1909
Surcharged in Blue
and Overprinted in Red

1919

P173	A21	5pa on 2pa ol grn	1.25	1.00
a.		Red overprint double	20.00	10.00
b.		Blue surcharge double	20.00	10.00

No. 255 Surcharged
in Red

1920

P174	A25	5pa on 4pa brn	1.25	.50

**Catalogue values for unused
stamps in this section, from this
point to the end of the section, are
for Never Hinged items.**

Dove and Citadel of
Ankara — N6

1952-55   Litho.   *Perf. 12½*

P175	N6	0.50k grnsh gray	.25	.25
P176	N6	0.50k violet ('53)	.25	.25

Perf. 10½, 10

P177	N6	0.50k red org ('54)	.25	.25
P178	N6	0.50k brown ('55)	.25	.25

Nos. P175-P178 (4) 1.00 1.00

POSTAL TAX STAMPS

Map of Turkey
and Red
Crescent
PT1

1928   Unwmk.   Typo.   *Perf. 14*
Crescent in Red

RA1	PT1	½pi lt brown	.90	.35
RA2	PT1	1pi red violet	.90	.35
RA3	PT1	2½pi orange	.95	.35

Engr.
Various Frames

RA4	PT1	5pi dk brown	.90	.45
RA5	PT1	10pi yellow green	1.10	.60
RA6	PT1	20pi slate	1.60	.80
RA7	PT1	50pi dark violet	6.25	1.75

Nos. RA1-RA7 (7) 12.60 4.65

Set, never hinged 13.00

The use of these stamps on letters, parcels, etc. in addition to the regular postage, was obligatory on certain days in each year.
For surcharges see Nos. RA16, RA21-RA22.

Cherubs Upholding
Star — PT2

1932

RA8	PT2	1k ol bis & red	1.00	.30
RA9	PT2	2½k dk brn & red	1.25	.30
RA10	PT2	5k green & red	1.50	.30
RA11	PT2	25k black & red	3.00	1.00

Nos. RA8-RA11 (4) 6.75 1.90

Set, never hinged 9.00

For surcharges and overprints see Nos. RA12-RA15, RA28-RA29, RA36-RA38.

No. RA8 Surcharged

RA12	PT2	20pa on 1k	1.00	.50
RA13	PT2	3k on 1k	1.75	.70
a.		3 "kruus"	2.50	2.50

By a law of Parliament the use of these stamps on letters and telegraph forms, in addition to the regular fees, was obligatory from Apr. 20-30 of each year. The inscription in the tablet at the bottom of the design states that the money derived from the sale of the stamps is devoted to child welfare work.

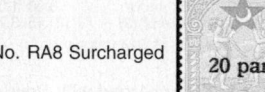

No. RA8 Surcharged

1933

RA14	PT2	20pa on 1k ol bis & red	1.00	.50
RA15	PT2	3k on 1k ol bis & red	1.75	1.00

No. RA5
Surcharged

RA16	PT1	5k on 10pi yel grn & red	1.50	.75

Nos. RA14-RA16 (3) 4.25 2.25

PT3   PT4

1933   *Perf. 11, 11½*

RA17	PT3	20pa gray vio & red	1.00	.50
RA18	PT4	1k violet & red	1.00	.50
RA19	PT4	5k dk brown & red	2.50	.50
RA20	PT3	15k green & red	3.50	.50

Nos. RA17-RA20 (4) 8.00 2.00

Set, never hinged 12.00

Nos. RA17 and RA20 were issued in Ankara; Nos. RA18 and RA19 in Izmir.
For overprint see No. RA27.

Nos. RA3,
RA1
Surcharged in
Black

1933-34

RA21	PT1	1k on 2½pi orange	.75	.30
RA22	PT1	5k on ½pi lt brown	2.25	.50

Map of
Turkey
PT5

1934-35   Crescent in Red   *Perf. 12*

RA23	PT5	½k blue ('35)	.40	.25
RA24	PT5	1k red brown	.40	.25
RA25	PT5	2½k green ('35)	.60	.25
RA26	PT5	5k blue green ('35)	1.50	.25

Nos. RA23-RA26 (4) 2.90 1.00

Set, never hinged 5.00

Frame differs on No. RA26.
See Nos. RA30-RA35B.

Nos. RA17, RA8-
RA9 Overprinted in
Roman Capitals

1936   *Perf. 11, 14*

RA27	PT3	20pa gray vio & red	.75	.25
RA28	PT2	1k ol bis & red	.75	.25
RA29	PT2	3k on 2½k dk brn & red	1.50	.30

Nos. RA27-RA29 (3) 3.00

Set, never hinged 6.00

Type of 1934-35, Inscribed "Türkiye Kizilay Cemiyeti"

1938-46   *Perf. 8½-11½*

Type I — Imprint, "Devlet Basimevi". Crescent red.
Type II — Imprint, "Alaeddin Kiral Basimevi". Crescent carmine.
Type III — Imprint, "Damga Matbaasi". Crescent red.

Crescent in Red or Carmine

RA30	PT5	½k blue (I)	1.25	.50
a.		Type II	4.00	1.00
b.		Type III	1.75	.50
RA31	PT5	1k red vio (I)	.75	.25
a.		Type II	6.50	2.00
b.		Type III	.75	.25
RA32	PT5	2½k orange (I)	.90	.30
a.		Type II	2.00	1.00
RA33	PT5	5k blue grn (I)	.75	.25
RA33A	PT5	5k choc (III) ('42)	1.25	.25
RA34	PT5	10k pale grn (I)	1.50	.30
a.		Type III	2.00	1.00
RA35	PT5	20k black (I)	3.50	1.50
RA35A	PT5	50k pur (III) ('46)	7.50	1.00
RA35B	PT5	1 l blue (III) ('44)	30.00	2.50

Nos. RA30-RA35B (9) 47.40 6.85

Set, never hinged 78.00

For surcharge see No. RA63.

No. RA9 Surcharged
in Black

1938   *Perf. 14*

RA36	PT2	20pa on 2½k	1.00	.50
RA37	PT2	1k on 2½k	1.00	.50

No. RA9 Surcharged
in Black

1938   Unwmk.   *Perf. 14*

RA37A	PT2	20pa on 2½k	1.25	.60
RA37B	PT2	1k on 2½k	1.50	.75

No. RA9 Surcharged "1 Kurus" in Black

1939   Perf. 14
RA38 PT2 1k on 2½k dk brn & red   .90 .90

Child — PT6

Nurse with Child — PT7

1940   Typo.   Perf. 12
Star in Carmine

RA39	PT6	20pa bluish grn	.30	.25
RA40	PT6	1k violet	.30	.25
RA41	PT7	1k lt blue	.30	.25
RA42	PT7	2½k pale red lil	.30	.25
RA43	PT6	3k black	.35	.25
RA44	PT7	5k pale violet	.30	.25
RA45	PT7	10k blue green	1.00	.40
RA46	PT7	15k dark blue	.75	.30
RA47	PT7	25k olive bister	2.50	1.25
RA48	PT7	50k olive gray	6.00	2.50
		Nos. RA39-RA48 (10)	12.10	5.95
		Set, never hinged	30.00	

Soldier and Map of Turkey — PT8

1941-44   Perf. 11½

RA49	PT8	1k purple	.40	.25
RA50	PT8	2k light blue	2.50	.25
RA51	PT8	3k chestnut	2.75	.50
RA51A	PT8	4k mag ('44)	9.50	.35
RA52	PT8	5k brt rose	7.75	2.50
RA53	PT8	10k dk blue	11.00	4.00
		Nos. RA49-RA53 (6)	33.90	7.85
		Set, never hinged	75.00	

The tax was used for national defense.

Baby — PT9

Nurse and Baby — PT13

Nurse and Children PT10

Nurse Feeding Child PT11

Nurse and Child PT12

Nurse and Child — PT14

President Inonu Holding Child — PT15

Children PT16

1942   Unwmk.   Typo.   Perf. 11½
Star in Red

RA54	PT9	20pa brt violet	.75	.25
RA55	PT9	20pa chocolate	.75	.25
RA56	PT10	1k dk slate grn	.75	.25
RA57	PT11	2½k yellow grn	.75	.30
RA58	PT12	3k dark blue	.75	.30
RA59	PT13	5k brt pink	.90	.30
RA60	PT14	10k lt blue	1.20	.40
RA61	PT15	15k dk red brn	1.60	.70
RA62	PT16	25k brown	3.00	1.00
		Nos. RA54-RA62 (9)	10.45	3.75

See Nos. RA175, RA179-RA180.

No. RA32 Surcharged with New Value in Brown

1942   Perf. 10
RA63 PT5 1k on 2½k org & red (I)   .25 .25

Child Eating — PT17

Nurse and Child — PT18

Nurse and Child PT19

Child and Red Star — PT20

President Inönü and Child — PT21

Inscribed: "Sefcat Pullari 23 Nisan 1943 Cocuk Esirgeme Kurumu."

1943   Star in Red   Perf. 11

RA64	PT17	50pa lilac	.65	.25
RA65	PT17	50pa gray green	.65	.25
RA66	PT18	1k lt ultra	.65	.25
RA67	PT19	3k dark red	.65	.25
RA68	PT20	15k cream & blk	2.50	.40
RA69	PT21	100k brt violet blue	3.75	1.60
a.		Souvenir sheet, #RA64-RA69, imperf.	5.50	5.50
		Nos. RA64-RA69 (6)	8.85	3.00

Star and Crescent PT23

Hospital PT24

Nurse and Children PT25

Baby PT26

Nurse Bathing Baby — PT27

Nurse Feeding Child — PT28

Baby with Bottle — PT29

Child — PT30

Hospital — PT31

Perf. 10 to 12 and Compound
1943-44   Star in Red

RA71	PT23	20pa deep blue	.50	.30
RA72	PT24	1k gray green	.50	.25
RA73	PT25	3k pale gray brn	.50	.25
RA74	PT26	5k yellow orange	.90	.30
RA75	PT26	5k violet brn	.50	.25
RA76	PT27	10k red	.50	.30
RA77	PT28	15k red violet	.75	.40
RA78	PT29	25k pale violet	1.10	.50
RA79	PT30	50k lt blue	2.50	1.00
RA80	PT31	100k lt green	6.50	4.00
		Nos. RA71-RA80 (10)	14.25	7.55
		Set, never hinged	27.50	

For surcharge see No. RA156.

Nurse Holding Baby — PT32

Nurse Feeding Child — PT33

Child — PT34

Star and Crescent PT35

1945-47   Unwmk.   Litho.   Perf. 11½
Star in Red

RA81	PT32	1k lilac brn	.40	.25
a.		1k rose violet	.50	.25
RA82	PT33	5k yellow grn	.70	.25
a.		5k green	.70	.25
RA83	PT34	10k red brown	.50	.25
RA84	PT35	250k gray black	9.50	3.50
RA84A	PT35	500k dull vio ('47)	37.50	12.50
		Nos. RA81-RA84A (5)	48.60	16.75
		Set, never hinged	90.00	

Imprint on No. RA82: "Kagit ve Basim isleri A.S. ist." On No. RA82a: "Guzel Sanatlar Matbaasi — Ankara."

Nurse and Wounded Soldier PT36

President Inönü and Victim of Earthquake PT37

Removing Wounded from Hospital Ship — PT38

Nurse and Soldier — PT39

Feeding the Poor — PT40

Wounded Soldiers on Landing Raft — PT41

Symbolical of Red Crescent Relief — PT42

1945   Perf. 12x10, 10x12
Crescent in Red

RA85	PT36	20pa dp bl & brn org	.50	.25
RA86	PT37	1k ol grn & ol bis	.50	.25
RA87	PT38	2½k dp bl & red	1.00	.50
RA88	PT39	5k dp bl & red	2.00	1.00
RA89	PT40	10k dp bl & lt grn	2.00	1.00
RA90	PT41	50k blk & gray grn	4.50	2.00
RA91	PT42	1 l black & yel	15.00	7.50
		Nos. RA85-RA91 (7)	25.50	12.50
		Set, never hinged	45.00	

See Nos. RA181-RA182.

Ankara
Sanatorium
PT43

1946   **Perf. 12**
RA92 PT43 20k red & lt bl   .65 .30
   See No. RA210. For surcharge see No. RA186.

Covering Sleeping
Child — PT44

Designs: 1k, Mother and child. 2½k, Nurse at playground. 5k, Doctor examining infant. 15k, Feeding child. 25k, Bathing child. 50k, Weighing baby. 150k, Feeding baby.

Inscribed: "25ci Yil Hatirasi 1946"
Star in Carmine

1946		Litho.	Perf. 12½
RA93	PT44	20pa brown	.50 .25
RA94	PT44	1k blue	.50 .25
RA95	PT44	2½k carmine	.50 .25
RA96	PT44	5k vio brn	.75 .25
RA97	PT44	15k violet	1.15 .50
RA98	PT44	25k gray grn	1.50 .50
RA99	PT44	50k bl grn	1.75 1.50
RA100	PT44	150k gray brn	4.00 1.75
Nos. RA93-RA100 (8)			*10.65 5.35*
Set, never hinged			20.00

For surcharge see No. RA155.

Hospital
Ship — PT52

Ambulance
Plane — PT53

Hospital
Train — PT54

Ambulance
PT55

Boy Scout and Red
Crescent
Flag — PT56

Stretcher
Bearers and
Wounded
Soldier
PT57

Nurse and
Hospital — PT58

Sanatorium
PT59

1946			Perf. 11½
RA101	PT52	1k multi	1.75 1.75
RA102	PT53	4k multi	1.75 1.75
RA103	PT54	10k multi	6.00 6.00
RA104	PT55	25k multi	6.25 6.25
RA105	PT56	40k multi	9.50 9.50
RA106	PT57	70k multi	8.00 8.00
RA107	PT58	1 l multi	6.50 6.50
RA108	PT59	2½ l multi	14.00 14.00
Nos. RA101-RA108 (8)			*53.75 53.75*

For overprints see Nos. RA139-RA146.

Souvenir Sheet

Pres. Inönü and Child — PT60

1946   **Unwmk.**   **Typo.**   **Imperf.**
Without Gum
RA109 PT60 250k slate blk,
        pink & red 20.00 17.50
   Turkish Society for the Prevention of Cruelty to Children, 25th anniv.

Nurse and
Wounded Soldier
PT61

Pres. Inönü and
Victim of
Earthquake
PT62

Nurse and
Soldier — PT64

Symbolical of
Red Crescent
Relief — PT67

1946-47   **Litho.**   **Perf. 11½**
Crescent in Red
RA113	PT61	20pa dk bl vio & ol	
		('47)	.40 .25
RA114	PT62	1k dk brn & yel	.60 .25
RA115	PT64	5k dp bl & red	.60 .25
RA116	PT67	1 l brn blk & yel	2.25 1.25
Nos. RA113-RA116 (4)			*3.85 2.00*

PT68   Nurse and
            Wounded
            Soldier — PT69

Victory and
Soldier — PT70

1947   **Crescent in Red**
RA117	PT68	250k brn blk &	
		grn	5.25 2.00
RA118	PT69	5 l sl gray &	
		org	0.75 3.50

Booklet Pane of One
Perf. 11½ (top) x Imperf.
RA119 PT70 10 l deep blue 22.50 —
   Black numerals above No. RA119 indicate position in booklet.

President Inönü   Nurse and Child
and Victim of   PT72
Earthquake
PT71

1947   **Perf. 11½**
RA120	PT71	1k dk brn, pale bl	
		& red	.65 .25
RA121	PT72	2½k bl vio & car	.65 .25

See Nos. RA221-RA223. For surcharge see No. RA154.

Nurse Offering   Plant with Broken
Encouragement   Stem
PT73   PT74

Perf. 8½, 11½x10, 11x10½
1948-49		Typo.	Unwmk.
		Crescent in Red	
RA122	PT73	½k ultra ('49)	.75 .25
RA123	PT73	1k indigo	.50 .25
RA124	PT73	2k lilac rose	.50 .25
RA125	PT73	2½k org ('49)	.50 .25
RA126	PT73	3k bl grn	.50 .25
RA127	PT73	4k gray ('49)	.60 .25
RA128	PT73	5k blue	.90 .25
RA129	PT73	10k pink	1.50 .25
RA130	PT73	25k chocolate	1.75 .25
		Perf. 10	
RA130A	PT74	50k ultra & bl	
		gray ('49)	2.25 .75
RA130B	PT74	100k grn & pale	
		grn ('49)	5.25 1.00
Nos. RA122-RA130B (11)			*15.00 4.00*
Set, never hinged			00.00

For surcharges see Nos. RA151-RA153, RA187.

Nurse and
Children — PT75

Various Scenes with Children.

**Inscribed: "1948 Cocuk Yili
Hatirasi"**

1948		Litho.	Perf. 11
		Star in Red	
RA131	PT75	20pa dp ultra	.50 .25
RA132	PT75	20pa rose lilac	.50 .25
RA133	PT75	1k dp Prus bl	.60 .30
RA134	PT75	3k dk brn vio	.90 .50
RA135	PT75	15k slate black	3.25 1.25
RA136	PT75	30k orange	4.00 3.00
RA137	PT75	150k yellow grn	5.25 4.00
RA138	PT75	300k brown red	8.25 6.50
Nos. RA131-RA138 (8)			*23.25 16.05*
Set, never hinged			30.00

No. RA136 is arranged horizontally. For overprints and surcharges see Nos. RA199-RA206.

> Catalogue values for unused stamps in this section, from this point to the end of the section, are for Never Hinged items.

Nos. RA101
to RA108
Overprinted in
Carmine

1949			Perf. 11½
RA139	PT52	1k multi	10.00 10.00
RA140	PT53	4k multi	10.00 10.00
RA141	PT54	10k multi	10.00 10.00
RA142	PT55	25k multi	10.00 10.00
RA143	PT56	40k multi	20.00 20.00
RA144	PT57	70k multi	10.00 10.00
RA145	PT58	1 l multi	10.00 10.00
RA146	PT59	2½ l multi	10.00 10.00
Nos. RA139-RA146 (8)			*90.00 90.00*

Ruins and
Tent — PT76

Booklet Panes of One
1949		Perf. 10 (top) x Imperf.	
RA149	PT76	5k gray, vio gray &	
		red	4.00 3.00
RA150	PT76	10k red vio, sal &	
		red	4.00 3.00

Black numerals above each stamp indicate its position in the booklet.

No. RA124 Surcharged in Black
1950		Unwmk.	Perf. 8½
RA151	PT73	20pa on 2k	1.25 1.00

**Postal Tax Stamps of 1944-48
Surcharged with New Value in Black
or Carmine**
Perf. 8½ to 12½ and Compound
1952			
RA152	PT73	20pa on 3k bl grn	.50 .25
RA153	PT73	20pa on 4k gray	.75 .25
RA154	PT72	1k on 2½k bl vio	
		& car (C)	1.00 1.50
RA155	PT44	1k on 2½k car	2.00 1.00
RA156	PT25	1k on 3k pale	
		gray brn	2.00 1.00
Nos. RA152-RA156 (5)			*6.25 4.00*

"Protection"
PT77

Various Symbolical Designs
Inscribed "75 iNCi" etc.

1952		Typo.		Perf. 10
Crescent in Carmine				

RA157	PT77	5k bl grn & bl	2.00	1.50
RA158	PT77	15k yel grn, bl & cr	2.00	1.50
RA159	PT77	30k bl, grn & brn	2.00	1.50
RA160	PT77	1 l blk, bl & cr	2.00	1.50
a.		Souvenir sheet, #RA157-RA160, imperf.	30.00	30.00
		Nos. RA157-RA160 (4)	8.00	6.00

Printed in sheets of 20 containing one horizontal row of each value.

Nurse and Children PT78

Design: 1k, Nurse and baby.

1954		Litho.		Perf. 10½
Star in Red				

RA161	PT78	20pa aqua	.60	.35
RA162	PT78	20pa yellow	.90	.35
RA163	PT12	1k deep blue	1.50	.80
		Nos. RA161-RA163 (3)	3.00	1.50

Globe and Flag — PT79

Designs: 5k, Winged nurse in clouds. 10k, Protecting arm of Red Crescent.

1954

RA164	PT79	1k multi	.50	.25
RA165	PT79	5k multi	.75	.25
RA166	PT79	10k car, grn & gray	1.25	.25
		Nos. RA164-RA166 (3)	2.50	.75

See Nos. RA208, RA211-RA213. For surcharges see Nos. RA187A-RA187B.

Florence Nightingale — PT80

Selimiye Barracks PT81

30k, Florence Nightingale, full-face.

Crescent in Carmine

1954, Nov. 4

RA167	PT80	20k gray grn & dk brn	.60	.50
RA168	PT80	30k dl brn & blk	.90	.50
RA169	PT81	50k buff & blk	1.40	.50
		Nos. RA167-RA169 (3)	2.90	1.50

Arrival of Florence Nightingale at Scutari, cent.

Type of 1942 and

Children Kissing — PT82

Nurse Holding Baby — PT83

1955, Apr. 23			Star in Red	
RA170	PT82	20pa chalky bl	.25	.25
RA171	PT82	20pa org brn	.25	.25
RA172	PT82	1k lilac	.25	.25
RA173	PT82	3k gray bis	.25	.25
RA174	PT82	5k orange	.25	.25
RA175	PT12	10k green	2.50	.75
RA176	PT83	15k dk blue	.25	.25
RA177	PT83	25k brn car	1.50	1.40
RA178	PT83	50k dk gray grn	2.00	1.50
RA179	PT12	2½ l dull brn	375.00	125.00
RA180	PT12	10 l rose lil	875.00	250.00
		Nos. RA170-RA180 (11)	1,258.	380.15

Types of 1945
Inscribed: "Turkiye Kizilay Dernegi"

1955		Litho.	Perf. 10½x11½, 10½	
Crescent in Red				
RA181	PT36	20pa vio brn & lem	.50	.25
RA182	PT41	1k blk & gray grn	.50	.25

Nurse — PT85

Nurses on Parade PT86

Design: 100k, Two nurses under Red Cross and Red Crescent flags and UN emblem.

Perf. 10½

1955, Sept. 5		Unwmk.	Litho.	
Crescent and Cross in Red				
RA183	PT85	10k blk & pale brn	.75	.35
RA184	PT86	15k dk grn & pale yel grn	.75	.45
RA185	PT85	100k lt ultra	3.50	1.75
		Nos. RA183-RA185 (3)	5.00	2.55

Meeting of the board of directors of the Intl. Council of Nurses, Istanbul, Aug. 29-Sept. 5, 1955.

Nos. RA92 and RA130B Surcharged "20 Para"

1955

RA186	PT43	20p on 20k	.75	.40

Typo.

RA187	PT74	20p on 100k (surch. 11½x2mm)	.90	.40
c.		Surcharge 13½x2½mm	2.00	.75

No. RA164 Surcharged with New Value and Two Bars

1956		Litho.		Perf. 10½
RA187A	PT79	20p on 1k multi	.25	.25
RA187B	PT79	2.50k on 1k multi	.25	.25

Woman and Children — PT87

Designs: 10k, 25k, 50k, Flag and building. 250k, 5 l, 10 l, Mother nursing baby.

1956		Litho.		Perf. 10½
Star in Red				
RA188	PT87	20pa red org	.75	.75
RA189	PT87	20pa gray grn	.75	.75
RA190	PT87	1k purple	.75	.75
RA191	PT87	1k grnsh bl	.75	.75
RA192	PT87	3k lt red brn	1.25	1.25
RA193	PT87	10k rose car	2.25	2.25
RA194	PT87	25k brt grn	5.00	5.00
RA195	PT87	50k brt ultra	6.50	6.50
RA196	PT87	250k red lilac	17.00	17.00
RA197	PT87	5 l sepia	35.00	15.00
RA198	PT87	10 l dk sl grn	57.50	30.00
		Nos. RA188-RA198 (11)	127.50	80.00

Nos. RA131-RA138 Overprinted and Surcharged in Black or Red: "IV. DUNYA Cocuk Gunu 1 Ekim 1956"

1956, Oct. 1		Unwmk.	Perf. 11	
RA199	PT75	20pa (R)	12.00	12.00
RA200	PT75	20pa	12.00	12.00
RA201	PT75	1k (R)	12.00	12.00
RA202	PT75	3k (R)	12.00	12.00
RA203	PT75	15k (R)	12.00	12.00
RA204	PT75	25k on 30k	12.00	12.00
RA205	PT75	100k on 150k (R)	12.00	12.00
RA206	PT75	250k on 300k	18.00	18.00
		Nos. RA199-RA206 (8)	102.00	102.00

The tax was for child welfare.

Type of 1954, Redrawn Type of 1946, and

Flower — PT88

Crescent in Red

1957		Unwmk.		Perf. 10½
RA207	PT88	½k lt ol gray & brn	.50	.25
RA208	PT79	1k ol bis, blk & grn	.50	.25
RA209	PT88	2½k yel grn & bl grn	.50	.25
RA210	PT43	20k red & lt bl	2.75	1.25
RA211	PT79	25k lt gray, blk & grn	2.75	1.25
RA212	PT79	50k bl, dk grn & grn	8.00	1.50
RA213	PT79	100k vio, blk & grn	8.75	3.00
		Nos. RA207-RA213 (7)	23.75	7.75

No. RA210 inscribed "Turkiye Kizilay Cemiyeti." No. RA92 inscribed ". . . . Dernegi."

Children — PT89

1957		Unwmk.		Perf. 10½
RA214	PT89	20pa car & red	.50	.25
RA215	PT89	20pa grn & red	.50	.25
RA216	PT89	1k ultra & car	.50	.25
RA217	PT89	3k red org & car	2.25	1.50
		Nos. RA214-RA217 (4)	3.75	2.25

"Blood Donor and Recipient" — PT90

Designs: 75k, Figure showing blood circulation. 150k, Blood transfusion symbolism.

1957, May 22		Size: 24x40mm		
RA218	PT90	25k gray, blk & red	.25	.25
Size: 22½x37½mm				
RA219	PT90	75k grn, blk & red	.50	.30
RA220	PT90	150k yel grn & red	1.25	.60
		Nos. RA218-RA220 (3)	2.00	1.15

Redrawn Type of 1947
Inscribed: "V Dunya Cocuk Gunu"

1957		Star in Red		Perf. 10½
RA221	PT72	100k blk & bis brn	1.25	.75
RA222	PT72	150k yel grn	1.25	.75
RA223	PT72	250k blk & vio	2.50	1.00
		Nos. RA221-RA223 (3)	5.00	2.50

The tax was for child welfare.

Child and Butterfly — PT91

Various Butterflies. 50k, 75k horiz.

1958		Litho.		Unwmk.
RA224	PT91	20k gray & red	.75	.75
RA225	PT91	25k multi	.75	.75
RA226	PT91	50k multi	1.50	1.50
RA227	PT91	75k grn, yel & blk	2.00	2.00
RA228	PT91	150k multi	2.50	2.50
		Nos. RA224-RA228 (5)	7.50	7.50

Florence Nightingale — PT92

1958			Crescent in Red	
RA229	PT92	1 l bluish green	.75	.25
RA230	PT92	1½ l gray	.90	.50
RA231	PT92	2½ l blue	1.25	.60
		Nos. RA229-RA231 (3)	2.90	1.35

Turkey stopped issuing postal tax stamps in June, 1958. Similar stamps of later date are private charity stamps issued by the Red Crescent Society and the Society for the Protection of Children.

POSTAL TAX AIR POST STAMPS

Air Fund Issues

These stamps were obligatory on all air mail for 21 days a year. Tax for the Turkish Aviation Society: 20pa for a postcard, 1k for a regular letter, 2 1/2k for a registered letter, 3k for a telegram, 5k-50k for a package, higher values for air freight. Postal tax air post stamps were withdrawn Aug. 21, 1934 and remainders destroyed later that year.

Biplane
PTAP1

Type PTAP1

Perf. 11, Pin Perf.

1926	Unwmk.	Litho.

Size: 35x25mm

| RAC1 | 20pa brn & pale grn | 3.00 | .30 |
| RAC2 | 1g blue grn & buff | 2.00 | .30 |

Size: 40x29mm

RAC3	5g vio & pale grn	8.00	1.00
RAC4	5g car lake & pale grn	35.00	15.00
	Nos. RAC1-RAC4 (4)	48.00	16.60
	Set, never hinged	275.00	

PTAP2

PTAP3

1927-29		Type PTAP2
RAC5	20pa dl red & pale grn	1.75	.50
RAC6	1k green & yel	1.50	.50

Type PTAP3

Perf. 11½

RAC7	2k dp cl & yel grn	1.75	.50
RAC8	2½k red & yel grn	11.00	2.50
RAC9	5k dk bl gray & org	2.75	1.00
RAC10	10k dk grn & rose	5.00	1.25
RAC11	15k green & yel	5.00	1.00
RAC12	20k ol brn & yel	7.00	2.00
RAC13	50k dk bl & cob bl	10.00	4.50
RAC14	100k car & lt bl	110.00	80.00
	Nos. RAC5-RAC14 (10)	155.75	93.75
	Set, never hinged	825.00	

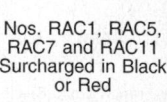

Nos. RAC1, RAC5,
RAC7 and RAC11
Surcharged in Black
or Red

1930-31			
RAC15	1k ("Bir kurus") on RAC1	200.00	125.00
RAC16	1k ("Bir Kurus") on RAC5	1.50	.50
RAC17	100pa ("Yuz Para") on RAC7	2.00	.75
RAC18	5k ("Bes Kurus") on RAC5	8.00	1.50
RAC19	5k ("5 Kurus") on RAC5	3.00	.75
RAC20	10k ("On kurus") on RAC7	4.00	1.25
RAC21	50k ("Elli kurus") on RAC7	12.00	4.00
RAC22	1 l ("Bir lira") on RAC7	37.50	9.00
RAC23	5 l ("Bes lira") on RAC11	2,000.	400.00
	Nos. RAC15-RAC23 (9)	2,268.	542.75
	Set, never hinged	5,000.	

PTAP4

PTAP5

1931-32	Litho.	Perf. 11½
RAC24	PTAP4 20pa black	5.00	1.75

Typo.

RAC25	PTAP5 1k brown car ('32)	2.00	.50
RAC26	PTAP5 5k red ('32)	4.00	.75
RAC27	PTAP5 10k green ('32)	6.00	1.50
	Nos. RAC24-RAC27 (4)	17.00	4.50
	Set, never hinged	65.00	

PTAP6

1933		Type PTAP6
RAC28	10pa ("On Para") grn	3.50	2.00
RAC29	1k ("Bir Kurus") red	8.00	2.75
RAC30	5k ("Bes Kurus") lil	12.00	3.00
	Nos. RAC28-RAC30 (3)	23.50	7.75
	Set, never hinged	70.00	

TURKEY IN ASIA

'tər-kē in 'ā-zhə

(Anatolia)

40 Paras = 1 Piaster

This designation, which includes all of Turkey in Asia Minor, came into existence during the uprising of 1919, led by Mustafa Kemal Pasha. Actually there was no separation of territory, the Sultan's sovereignty being almost immediately reduced to a small area surrounding Constantinople. The formation of the Turkish Republic and the expulsion of the Sultan followed in 1923. Subsequent issues of postage stamps are listed under Turkey (Republic).

Issues of the Nationalist Government

Turkish Stamps of
1913-18 Surcharged
in Black or Red

(The Surcharge reads "Angora 3 Piastres")

1920	Unwmk.	Perf. 12

On Stamps of 1913

1	A24	3pi on 2pa red lilac	4.75	5.25
2	A25	3pi on 4pa dk brn	37.50	37.50
3	A27	3pi on 6pa dk bl	250.00	150.00

On Stamp of 1916-18

| 4 | A42 | 3pi on 2pa vio (Bk) | 35.00 | 20.00 |
| | | Nos. 1-4 (4) | 327.25 | 212.75 |

Turkish
Stamps of
1913-18
Hstmpd. in
Black or Red

(The Srch. reads "Post, Piastre 3")

1921	On Stamps of 1913	Perf. 12
5	A24	3pi on 2pa red lilac	35.00	25.00
a.		On No. 1	47.50	72.50
6	A25	3pi on 4pa dk brown	30.00	30.00
a.		On No. 2	160.00	175.00
7	A25	3pi on 4pa dk brn (R)	150.00	175.00
a.		On No. 2	160.00	175.00
8	A27	3pi on 6pa dk blue	125.00	150.00
a.		On No. 3	300.00	325.00
9	A27	3pi on 6pa bl (R)	62.50	75.00
a.		On No. 3	110.00	140.00

On Stamps of 1916-18

10	A42	3pi on 2pa vio (R)	62.50	75.00
a.		On No. 4	97.50	125.00
		Nos. 5-10 (6)	465.00	530.00

Turkish Revenue Stamps
Handstamped in Turkish "Osmanli
Postalari, 1336" (Ottoman Post,
1920).

Type a

Dash at upper left is set high. Bottom (date)
line is 8½mm long.

عثمانلى بوسته لرى
١٣٣٦

Type b

Dash at upper left is set lower. Bottom
(date) line is 10mm long.

عثمانلى بوسته لرى
١٣٣٦

Type c

Dash at upper left is set lower. Bottom
(date) line is 9mm long.

Religious
Tribunals
Revenue
R1

12	R1	1pi grn (a, b, c)	750.00	300.00
13	R1	5pi ultra (a, b)	16,000.	15,500.
14	R1	50pi gray grn (a, b, c)	25.00	35.00
		Cut cancellation		3.00
15	R1	100pi buff (a)	140.00	97.50
a.		100pi yellow (a)	95.00	72.50
		Cut cancellation		7.50
16	R1	500pi org (a)	225.00	150.00
		Cut cancellation		20.00
17	R1	1000pi brn (a)	3,000.	1,750.
		Cut cancellation		175.00

See Nos. 29-32.

Court Costs
Revenue
R2

Black Overprint

18	R2	10pa grn (b, c)	110.00	100.00
19	R2	1pi ultra (a, c)	—	19,000.
20	R2	5pi rose (c)	17,500.	
21	R2	50pi ocher (a, b, c)	50.00	50.00
a.		50pi yellow (a, b, c)	12.00	17.00
		Cut cancellation, #21, 21a		2.00
22	R2	100pi brown (a)	150.00	100.00
		Cut cancellation		20.00
23	R2	500pi slate (a)	325.00	325.00
		Cut cancellation		20.00

See Nos. 24, 33-39.

Notary Public
Revenue
R3

Design R2 Overprinted "Katibi Adliye Masus dur" in Red

| 24 | R3 | 50pi ocher (a) | 1,250. | 150.00 |
| | | Cut cancellation | | 20.00 |

Laborer's
Passport Tax
Stamp — R4

Notary Public
Revenue — R5

Black Overprint

25	R4	2pi emerald (a, c)	—	22,000.
26	R5	100pi yellow brn (a)	1,250.	150.00
		Cut cancellation		30.00

See Nos. 46-48.

Theater Tax
Stamp — R6

Land Registry
Revenue
R7

| 27 | R6 | 20pa black | 5,000. | 5,000. |
| 28 | R7 | 2pi blue black | 6,250. | 6,250. |

See Nos. 40, 45.

Hejaz Railway Tax
Stamp — R8

Black Overprint

Perf. 11½

28A	R8	2pi dk red & bl (b)	1,750.	1,750.

See Nos. 53-57.

Turkish Revenue Stamps Overprinted in Turkish "Osmanli Postalari, 1337" (Ottoman Post, 1921)

On #29-63

Perf. 12

29	R1	10pa slate	20.00	16.00
a.		Handstamped overprint	100.00	50.00
b.		Double overprint		
30	R1	1pi green	32.50	20.00
a.		Inverted overprint	35.00	22.50
b.		Handstamped overprint	3,500.	3,250.
31	R1	5pi ultra	29.00	14.50
a.		"1337" inverted	100.00	90.00
b.		Half used as 2½pi on cover		
c.		Handstamped overprint	875.00	875.00
		Nos. 29-31 (3)	81.50	50.50

Handstamped Overprint

32	R1	50pi green	7,250.	7,250.

Design R2 Overprinted

33	R2	10pa green	24.50	24.50
a.		Handstamped overprint	3,500.	3,500.
34	R2	1pi ultra	50.00	25.00
a.		Handstamped overprint	875.00	875.00
35	R2	5pi red	24.50	25.00
a.		Inverted overprint		
b.		"1337" inverted	100.00	100.00
c.		Half used as 2½pi on cover		
d.		Handstamped overprint	7,500.	7,500.
36	R2	50pi ocher, handstamped ovpt.	500.00	100.00
		Cut cancellation		20.00
		Nos. 33-36 (4)	599.00	174.50

Design R3 Overprinted
Additional Turkish Overprint in Red or Black

37	R3	10pa green (R)	100.00	60.00
38	R3	1pi ultra (R)	72.50	50.00
39	R3	5pi rose (Bk)	72.50	50.00
a.		"1337" inverted	200.00	200.00
b.		Handstamped overprint	7,000.	7,000.
		Nos. 37-39 (3)	245.00	160.00

Design R7 Overprinted

40	R7	2pi blue black	125.00	110.00
a.		Handstamped overprint	5,500.	5,500.

R12

1921 Overprinted in Black   Perf. 12

41	R12	5pi green	150.00	125.00
		Cut cancellation		17.50
a.		Handstamped overprint	5,500.	5,000.

Museum
Tax Stamp
R13

Overprinted in Black

42	R13	1pi ultra	525.00	425.00
a.		Handstamped overprint	5,500.	5,500.
43	R13	5pi deep green	575.00	475.00
a.		Handstamped overprint	5,500.	5,500.

Handstamped Overprint

44	R13	5pi dark vio	7,000.	7,000.

The overprint variety "337" for "1337" exists on Nos. 42-43.

Design R6
Overprinted

Perf. 12, 12½

45	R6	20pa black	12.50	5.00
a.		Date 4½mm high	15.00	
b.		"337" for "1337"	25.00	

Design R5
Overprinted

46	R5	10pa green	25.00	25.00
a.		Overprint 21mm long		
b.		"131" for "1337"		
47	R5	1pi ultra	37.50	25.00
a.		"13" for "1337"	50.00	50.00
b.		"131" for "1337"	50.00	50.00
c.		Inverted overprint	90.00	90.00
d.		Handstamped overprint	4,500.	4,500.
48	R5	5pi red	62.50	25.00
a.		Inverted overprint	90.00	90.00
b.		"131" for "1337"	85.00	85.00
c.		Handstamped overprint	4,500.	4,400.
		Nos. 46-48 (3)	125.00	75.00

R16

Perf. 11½, 11½x11
Overprinted in Black

49	R16	10pa pink	4.00	1.50
a.		Imperf.		
b.		Date "1237"	5.00	2.00
d.		Inverted overprint	15.00	
e.		Handstamped overprint	1,950.	1,950.
50	R16	1pi yellow	10.00	5.00
a.		Overprint 18mm long	10.00	5.00
b.		Date "1332"	12.00	
c.		Date "1317"		
d.		Inverted overprint	30.00	
e.		Handstamped overprint	1,950.	1,950.
51	R16	2pi yellow grn	12.50	5.00
a.		Date "1237"		
b.		Date "1317"	15.00	
c.		Imperf.		
d.		Inverted overprint	40.00	9.00
e.		Handstamped overprint	1,950.	1,950.
52	R16	5pi red	20.00	1.00
a.		Horiz. pair, imperf. vert.		
b.		Inverted overprint	25.00	7.50
c.		Double overprint	30.00	12.50
d.		Date "1332"	45.00	
e.		Half used as 2½pi on cover		

f.		Overprint 18mm long	20.00	7.50
g.		Handstamped overprint	1,950.	1,950.
		Nos. 49-52 (4)	46.50	12.50

Design R8 Overprinted
Turkish Inscriptions

20 Paras   1 Piaster

2 Piasters   5 Piasters

1921   Dark Red & Blue   Perf. 11½

53	R8	20pa on 1pi	75.00	75.00
54	R8	1pi on 1pi	7.50	4.00
55	R8	2pi on 1pi	7.50	4.00
a.		Inverted surcharge	25.00	
56	R8	5pi on 1pi	12.00	6.00
		Nos. 53-56 (4)	102.00	89.00

See No. 57.

No. 54 Overprinted

57	R8	1pi on 1pi dk red & bl	50.00	50.00

Hejaz Railway Tax
Stamp — R19

Overprinted in Black

58	R19	1pi grn & brn red	6.00	4.00
a.		Double overprint		
b.		Handstamped overprint		

The errors "1307," "1331" and "2337" occur once in each sheet of Nos. 53-58.

Naval League
Labels — R20

Overprinted in Black

1921   Perf. 12x11½

59	R20	1pa orange	11.00	15.00
a.		Date "1327"	45.00	45.00
60	R20	2pa indigo	12.00	15.00
61	R20	5pa green	25.00	20.00
62	R20	10pa brown	30.00	30.00
63	R20	40pa red brown	225.00	190.00
		Nos. 59-63 (5)	303.00	270.00
		Set, never hinged	1,100.	

The error "2337" occurs on all values of this issue.

The Naval League stamps have pictures of three Turkish warships. They were sold for the benefit of sailors of the fleet but did not pay postage until they were overprinted in 1921.

Turkish Stamps of 1915-20 Overprinted

a

b

The overprints on Nos. 64-77 read "Adana December 1st, 1921." This issue commemorated the withdrawal of the French from Cilicia. On No. 71 the lines of the overprint are further apart than on Nos. 68-70 and 73-74.

1921   Perf. 12

64	A44 (a)	10pa grn (424)	10.00	7.00
65	A45 (a)	20pa deep rose (425)	10.00	7.00
a.		Inverted overprint	30.00	
66	A51 (a)	25pi car, straw (434)	20.00	25.00
a.		Double overprint		
b.		Inverted overprint	60.00	37.50
		Nos. 64-66 (3)	40.00	39.00

On Newspaper Stamp of 1915

67	A21 (a)	5pa och (P132)	90.00	150.00

On Stamp of 1915

68	A22 (b)	5pa och (328)	350.00	400.00

On Stamps of 1917-18

69	A53 (b)	5pi on 2pa (547)	15.00	17.50
70	A53 (b)	5pi on 2pa (548)	15.00	17.50

On Stamp of 1919

71	A57 (b)	35pi on 1pi bl (Bk; 579)	42.50	50.00
a.		Inverted surcharge	100.00	

On Newspaper Stamp of 1915

72	A21 (b)	5pa och (P132)	200.00	200.00

On No. 72 the overprint is vertical, half reading up and half reading down.

On Stamps of 1920

73	A32 (b)	3pi blue (594)	15.00	12.50
74	A36 (b)	10pi gray vio (596)	20.00	20.00

On Postage Due Stamps of 1914

75	D1 (a)	5pa claret (J63)	350.00	350.00
76	D2 (a)	20pa red (J64)	350.00	400.00
a.		Inverted overprint	750.00	
77	D3 (b)	1pi dk bl (J65)	350.00	400.00
a.		Inverted overprint	750.00	750.00
		Nos. 75-77 (3)	1,050.	1,150.

Withdrawal of the French from Cilicia. Forged overprints exist.

Pact of Revenge, Burning Village at Top — A21

Izmir Harbor — A22

Mosque of Selim, Adrianople A23

Mosque of Selim, Konya — A24   Soldier — A25

Legendary Gray Wolf — A26

Snake Castle and Seyhan River, Adana — A27

Parliament Building at Sivas — A28

A29

Mosque at Urfa — A30

Map of Anatolia A31

Declaration of Faith from the Koran — A32

1922   **Litho.**   *Perf. 11½*

78	A21	10pa violet brn	1.00	.25
79	A22	20pa blue grn	1.00	.25
80	A23	1pi dp blue	1.50	.35
81	A24	2pi red brown	3.00	.50
82	A25	5pi dk blue	3.00	.50
83	A26	10pi dk brown	12.50	.75
a.	Vert. pair, imperf between		100.00	
b.	Vert. strip of 3, imperf between		300.00	
84	A27	25pi rose	15.00	2.00
85	A28	50pi indigo	1.50	15.00
86	A29	50pi dk gray	1.50	1.25
87	A30	100pi violet	75.00	8.00
	Cut cancellation			2.00
88	A31	200pi slate	200.00	62.50
	Cut cancellation			20.00
89	A32	500pi green	145.00	45.00
	Cut cancellation			30.00
	Nos. 78-89 (12)		460.00	136.35
	Set, never hinged		2,075.	

Imperf

79a	A22	20pa	25.00	30.00
80a	A23	1pi	20.00	20.00
82a	A25	5pi	20.00	20.00
84a	A27	25pi	35.00	30.00
85a	A28	50pi	27.50	30.00

Stamps of Type A23 Overprinted

1922

90	A23	1pi deep blue	7.25	15.00
91	A23	5pi deep blue	7.25	20.00
92	A23	10pi brown	7.25	20.00
93	A23	25pi rose	10.00	25.00
94	A23	50pi slate	12.50	25.00
95	A23	100pi violet	17.50	37.50
96	A23	200pi black vio	17.50	50.00
97	A23	500pi blue green	25.00	75.00
	Nos. 90-97 (8)		104.25	267.50
	Set, never hinged		300.00	

Withdrawal of the French from Cilicia and the return of the Kemalist Natl. army. The overprint reads: "Adana, Jan. 5, 1922."

No. 90-97 without overprint were presented to some high government officials.

First Parliament House, Ankara — A33

1922   **Litho.**

98	A33	5pa violet	.75	2.50
99	A33	10pa green	1.75	2.50
100	A33	20pa pale red	2.50	2.00
101	A33	1pi brown org	12.00	1.50
102	A33	2pi red brown	20.00	4.25
103	A33	3pi rose	6.00	.70
a.	Arabic "13" in right corner		10.00	7.50
b.	Thin grayish paper		55.00	7.50
	Nos. 98-103 (6)		43.00	13.45
	Set, never hinged		140.00	

Nos. 98-100, 103b exist imperf. In 1923 several stamps of Turkey and Turkey in Asia were overprinted in Turkish for advertising purposes. The overprint reads: "Izmir Economic Congress, 17 Feb., 1339."

POSTAGE DUE STAMPS

D1

1922   **Litho.**   *Perf. 11½*

J1	D1	20pa dull green	1.00	5.00
a.	Imperf.			25.00
J2	D1	1pi gray green	1.00	5.00
J3	D1	2pi red brown	2.50	17.50
J4	D1	3pi rose	4.50	25.00
J5	D1	5pi dark blue	6.00	55.00
	Nos. J1-J5 (5)		15.00	
	Set, never hinged		55.00	

TURKISH REPUBLIC OF NORTHERN CYPRUS

ˈtər-kish ri-ˈpə-blik of ˈnor-thərn ˈsī-prəs

LOCATION — Northern 40% of the Island of Cyprus in the Mediterranean Sea off the coast of Turkey.

Established following Turkish invasion of Cyprus in 1974. On Nov. 15, 1983 Turkey declared the Turkish Republic of Northern Cyprus to be independent. No other country has recognized this country.

1000 Milliemes = 1 Pound

100 Kurus = 1 Turkish Lira (1978)

Catalogue values for all unused stamps in this country are for Never Hinged items.

Letters bearing these stamps enter international mail via the Turkish Post Office.

Watermark

Wmk. 390

Republic of Turkey, 50th Anniv.
A1   A2

Designs: 3m, Woman sentry. 5m, Military parade. 10m, Flag bearers. 15m, Anniversary emblem. 20m, Ataturk statue. 50m, Painting "The Fallen." 70m, Turkish flag, map of Cyprus.

Perf. 12x11½, 11½x12

1974, July 27   **Litho.**   **Unwmk.**

1	A1	3m multicolored	45.00	37.50
2	A2	5m multicolored	1.00	.50
3	A1	10m multicolored	2.00	.50
4	A2	15m multicolored	1.50	.90
5	A1	20m multicolored	1.25	.70
6	A1	50m multicolored	4.00	2.75
7	A2	70m multicolored	35.00	15.00
	Nos. 1-7 (7)		89.75	57.85

First day covers are dated 1/29/73.

Nos. 5, 3 Surcharged

1975, Mar. 3   *Perf. 12x11½*

8	A1	30m on 20m, #5	1.50	1.00
9	A1	100m on 10m, #3	3.00	2.25

Surcharge appears in different positions.

Historical Sites and Landmarks A3

Designs: 3m, Namik Kemal's bust, Famagusta. 5m, 30m, Kyrenia Harbor. 10m, Ataturk Statue, Nicosia. 15m, St. Hilarion Castle. 20m, Ataturk Square, Nicosia. 25m, Coastline, Famagusta. 50m, Lala Mustafa Pasha Mosque, Famagusta vert. 100m, Kyrenia Castle. 250m, Kyrenia Castle, exterior walls. 500m, Othello Tower, Famagusta vert.

1975-76   *Perf. 13*

10	A3	3m pink & multi	.40	.30
11	A3	5m bl & multi	.40	.30
12	A3	10m pink & multi	.45	.40
13	A3	15m pink & multi	.50	.40
14	A3	15m bl & multi	.50	.40
15	A3	20m pink & multi	3.00	.40

16	A3	20m bl & multi	.50	.40
17	A3	25m pink & multi	.70	.50
18	A3	30m pink & multi	1.00	.75
19	A3	50m plnk & multi	1.50	1.00
20	A3	100m pink & multi	1.75	1.25
21	A3	250m pink & multi	2.50	1.75
22	A3	500m pink & multi	3.50	3.00
	Nos. 10-22 (13)		16.70	10.85

Issued: #10, 12-13, 15, 17-22, 4/21; #11, 14, 16, 8/2/76. #1, 14, 16 have different inscriptions and "1976."

For surcharges see Nos. 28-29.

Peace in Cyprus — A4

Designs: 50m, Map, olive branch, severed chain. 150m, Map, globe, olive branch, vert.

1975, July 20   *Perf. 13½x13, 13x13½*

23	A4	30m multicolored	.40	.25
24	A4	50m multicolored	.50	.35
25	A4	150m multicolored	1.10	1.00
	Nos. 23-25 (3)		2.00	1.60

Europa — A5

Paintings: 90m, Pomegranates by I.V. Guney. 100m, Harvest Time by F. Direkoglu.

1975, Dec. 29   *Perf. 13*

26	A5	90m multicolored	2.00	1.00
27	A5	100m multicolored	3.00	1.50

Nos. 19, 20 Surcharged

1976, Apr. 28   *Perf. 13*

28	A3	10m on 50m, #19	.75	.50
29	A3	30m on 100m, #20	1.25	1.25

Europa — A6

1976, May 3

30	A6	60m Expectation	1.00	.30
31	A6	120m Man in Meditation	1.25	.65

Fruits — A7

1976, June 28

32	A7	10m Ceratonia siliqua	.35	.25
33	A7	25m Citrus nobilis	.40	.25
34	A7	40m Fragaria vesca	.50	.25
35	A7	60m Citrus sinensis	.60	.30
36	A7	80m Citrus limon	.90	.45
	Nos. 32-36 (5)		2.75	1.50

For surcharges see Nos. 66-69.

Olympic Games,
Montreal — A8

Design: 100m, Olympic rings, doves, horiz.

1976, July 17
37	A8	60m multicolored	.75	.25
38	A8	100m multicolored	1.00	.35

Liberation
Monument — A9

1976, Nov. 1   **Perf. 13x13½**
39	A9	30m multi	.35	.25
40	A9	150m multi, diff.	.75	.45

Europa — A10

1977, May 2   **Perf. 13**
41	A10	80m Salamis Bay	2.00	.75
42	A10	100m Kyrenia Port	3.00	1.25

Handicrafts
A11

1977, June 27
43	A11	15m Pottery	.45	.25
44	A11	30m Gourds, vert.	.65	.25
45	A11	125m Baskets	1.25	.30
		Nos. 43-45 (3)	2.35	.80

Landmarks
A12

Designs: 20m, Arap Ahmet Pasha Mosque, Nicosia, vert. 40m, Paphos Castle. 70m, Bekir Pasha aqueduct, Larnaca. 80m, Sultan Mahmut library, Nicosia.

1977, Dec. 2   **Perf. 13x13½, 13½x13**
46	A12	20m multicolored	.25	.25
47	A12	40m multicolored	.30	.25
48	A12	70m multicolored	.40	.25
49	A12	80m multicolored	.60	.40
		Nos. 46-49 (4)	1.55	1.15

Namik Kemal
(1840-1888),
Writer — A13

1977, Dec. 21   **Perf. 13**
50	A13	30m Bust, home	.45	.25
51	A13	140m Portrait, vert.	1.00	.50

Social
Security — A14

Designs: 275k, Man with sling, crutch. 375k, Woman with children.

1978, Apr. 17   **Perf. 13x13½**
52	A14	150k blk, bl & yel	.30	.25
53	A14	275k blk, grn & red org	.40	.25
54	A14	375k blk, red org & bl	.70	.25
		Nos. 52-54 (3)	1.40	.75

Europa — A15

225k, Oratory in Buyuk Han, Nicosia. 450k, Reservoir, Selimiye Mosque, Nicosia.

1978, May 2   **Perf. 13x13½, 13½x13**
55	A15	225k multi	3.25	1.00
56	A15	450k multi, horiz.	6.50	1.50

Transportation
A16

1978, July 10   **Perf. 13½x13**
57	A16	75k Roadway	.50	.25
58	A16	100k Hydrofoil	.60	.25
59	A16	650k Airplane	.90	.70
		Nos. 57-59 (3)	2.00	1.20

National
Oath — A17

1978, Sept. 13
60	A17	150k Dove, olive branch	.35	.25
61	A17	225k Stylized pen, vert.	.50	.25
62	A17	725k Stylized dove	.90	.65
		Nos. 60-62 (3)	1.75	1.15

Kemal
Ataturk — A18

1978, Nov. 10
63	A18	75k bl grn & lt grn	.50	.25
64	A18	450k brn & buff	.50	.25
65	A18	650k Prus bl & lt bl	.50	.30
		Nos. 63-65 (3)	1.50	.80

Nos. 33-36
Surcharged

1979, June 4
66	A7	50k on 25m	.40	.25
67	A7	1 l on 40m	.50	.25
68	A7	3 l on 60m	.75	.25
69	A7	5 l on 80m	.90	.25
		Nos. 66-69 (4)	2.55	1.00

Souvenir Sheet

Turkish Invasion of Cyprus, 5th
Anniv. — A19

1979, July 2   *Imperf.*
70	A19	15 l multicolored	4.00	3.25

Europa
A20

Communications: 3 l, Stamps, building, map. 8 l, Early and modern telephones, globe, satellite.

1979, Aug. 20   **Litho.**   **Perf. 13**
71	A20	2 l multicolored	1.50	.40
72	A20	3 l multicolored	2.00	.65
73	A20	8 l multicolored	4.25	1.00
		Nos. 71-73 (3)	7.75	2.05

Intl. Consultative
Radio Committee,
50th Anniv. — A21

1979, Sept. 24
74	A21	2 l blue & multi	.25	.25
75	A21	5 l gray & multi	.25	.25
76	A21	6 l green & multi	.35	.30
		Nos. 74-76 (3)	.85	.80

Intl. Year
of the
Child
A22

Childrens' drawings of children.

1979, Oct. 29
77	A22	1½ l multi, vert.	.35	.25
78	A22	4½ l multicolored	.45	.30
79	A22	6 l multi, vert.	.60	.40
		Nos. 77-79 (3)	1.40	.95

Press reports in Jan. 1980 state that the 1979 UPU Congress declared Turkish Cyprus stamps invalid for international mail.

A23

Anniv. and events: 2½ l, Lala Mustafa Pasha Mosque, Famagusta. 10 l, Arap Ahmet Pasha Mosque, Lefkosa. 20 l, Holy Kaaba, Mosque.

1980, Mar. 23
80	A23	2½ l multicolored	.25	.25
81	A23	10 l multicolored	.45	.25
82	A23	20 l multicolored	.70	.70
		Nos. 80-82 (3)	1.40	1.20

1st Islamic Conference in Turkish Cyprus (2½ l). General Assembly of World Islam Congress (10 l). Moslem year 1400 AH (20 l).

Europa — A24

1980, May 23
83	A24	5 l Ebu-Suud Efendi	.75	.40
84	A24	30 l Sultan Selim II	2.50	.80

Historic
Landmarks
A25

Designs: 2½ l, Omer's Shrine, Kyrenia. 3½ l, Entrance gate, Famagusta. 5 l, Funerary monuments, Famagusta. 10 l, Bella Paise Abbey, Kyrenia. 20 l, Selimiye Mosque, Nicosia.

1980, June 25   **Blue Paper**
85	A25	2½ l buff & Prus bl	.30	.25
86	A25	3½ l pale pink & dk grn	.30	.25
87	A25	5 l pale bl grn & dk car	.30	.25
88	A25	10 l lt grn & red lil	.30	.25
89	A25	20 l buff & dk bl	.50	.35
		Nos. 85-89 (5)	1.70	1.35

For overprints and surcharges see Nos. 198-200.

Cyprus
Postage
Stamps,
Cent.
A26

7½ l, No. 5, vert. 15 l, No. 199. 50 l, Social welfare, vert.

1980, Aug. 16
90	A26	7½ l multicolored	.25	.25
91	A26	15 l multicolored	.35	.25
92	A26	50 l multicolored	.90	.80
		Nos. 90-92 (3)	1.50	1.30

Palestinian
Solidarity
A27

15 l, Dome of the Rock, entrance, vert.

1980, Mar. 24
93	A27	15 l multicolored	.50	.25
94	A27	35 l multicolored	1.25	.60

World Muslim
Congress
Statement — A28

1981, Mar. 24
95	A28	1 l In Turkish	.35	.25
96	A28	35 l In English	.90	.65

Ataturk by Feyhaman Duran — A29

1981, May 19
97 A29 20 l multicolored 1.50 .75
Printed with se-tenant label promoting Ataturk Stamp Exhibition.

Europa
A30

Folk dances.

1981, June 29
98 A30 10 l multicolored .90 .40
99 A30 30 l multi, diff. 2.25 1.00

Souvenir Sheet

Ataturk, Birth Cent. — A31

1981, July 23 *Imperf.*
100 A31 150 l multicolored 3.00 1.75
No. 100 has simulated perfs.

Flowers
A32

Designs: 1 l, Convolvulus althaeoides, vert. 5 l, Cyclamen persicum. 10 l, Mandragora officinarum. 25 l, Papaver rhoeas, vert. 30 l, Arum dioscoridis, vert. 50 l, Chrysanthemum segetum. 100 l, Cistus salyiaefolius, vert. 150 l, Ferula communis.

1981-82 *Perf. 13*
101 A32 1 l multicolored .25 .25
102 A32 5 l multicolored .25 .25
103 A32 10 l multicolored .25 .25
104 A32 25 l multicolored .40 .40
105 A32 30 l multicolored .45 .45
106 A32 50 l multicolored .75 .75
107 A32 100 l multicolored 1.50 1.50
108 A32 150 l multicolored 2.25 2.25
Nos. 101-108 (8) 6.10 6.10
Issue dates: 1 l, 10 l, 25 l, 150 l, Sept. 28; 5 l, 30 l, 50 l, 100 l, Jan. 22, 1982.
For surcharge & overprints see #138-141, 201.

Intl. Year for Disabled Persons A33

Fight Against Apartheid — A34

World Food Day — A35

1981, Oct. 16
109 A33 7½ l multicolored .25 .25
110 A34 10 l multicolored .35 .30
111 A35 20 l multicolored .65 .50
Nos. 109-111 (3) 1.25 1.05

Palestinian Solidarity A36

1981, Nov. 29
112 A36 10 l multicolored .35 .25

Royal Wedding of Prince Charles and Lady Diana Spencer — A37

1981, Nov. 30
113 A37 50 l multicolored 1.00 .70

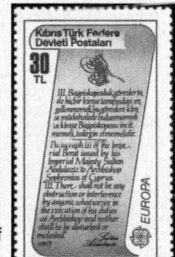

Charter of Cyprus, 1865 — A38

Turkish Forces Landing in Tuzla — A39

1982, July 30
114 Sheet of 4 5.00 5.00
a. A38 30 l multicolored 1.00 1.00
b. A39 70 l multicolored 1.00 1.00
Europa. #114 contains 2 each #114a, 114b.

Buffavento Castle — A40

Windsurfing — A41

Kantara Castle A42

Tourism: 30 l, Shipwreck museum.

Perf. 12½x12, 12x12½
1982, Aug. 20
116 A40 5 l multicolored .25 .25
117 A41 10 l multicolored .30 .25
118 A42 15 l multicolored .35 .30
119 A42 30 l multicolored .60 .40
Nos. 116-119 (4) 1.50 1.20

Art Treasures — A43

Designs: 30 l, The Wedding by Aylin Orek. 50 l, Carob Pickers by Ozden Nazim, vert.

1982, Dec. 3 *Perf. 13x13½, 13½x13*
120 A43 30 l multicolored 1.00 .30
121 A43 50 l multicolored 1.25 .50

Robert Koch, TB Bacillus A44

World Cup Soccer Championships, Spain — A45

Scouting, 75th Anniv. — A46

1982, Dec. 15 *Perf. 12½*
122 A44 10 l multicolored .25 .25
123 A45 30 l multicolored .75 .60
124 A46 70 l multicolored 2.00 1.50
Nos. 122-124 (3) 3.00 2.35

Paintings
A47

30 l, Calloused Hands by Salih Oral. 35 l, Malya-Limassol Bus by Emin Cizenel.

1983, May 16 *Perf. 13½x13*
125 A47 30 l multicolored .90 .75
126 A47 35 l multicolored 1.25 1.00

Miniature Sheet

Europa — A48

a, Map by Piri Reis. b, Cyprus seen from Skylab.

1983, June 30 *Perf. 13*
127 A48 Sheet of 2 60.00 30.00
a.-b. 100 l any single 15.00 15.00

25th Anniv. of Turkish Resistance A49

Designs: 15 l, No. 3. 20 l, Exploitation, Suppression & Resurrection by Aziz Hasan. 25 l, Resistance by Guner Pir.

1983, Aug. 1 *Perf. 13*
129 A49 15 l multi, vert. .30 .30
130 A49 20 l multi .45 .45
131 A49 25 l multi, vert. .50 .50
Nos. 129-131 (3) 1.25 1.25

World Communications Year — A50

1983, Aug. 1
132 A50 30 l shown .90 .60
133 A50 50 l Letters 1.50 1.00

Birds
A51

10 l, Merops apiaster. 15 l, Carduelis carduelis. 50 l, Erithacus rubecula. 65 l, Oriolus oriolus.

1983, Oct. 10
134 A51 10 l multicolored .40 .25
135 A51 15 l multicolored .55 .25
136 A51 50 l multicolored 1.25 .70
137 A51 65 l multicolored 1.50 1.00
a. Block of 4, #134-137 4.25 4.25
Nos. 134-137 (4) 3.70 2.20

Nos. 103, 108
Ovptd.

Nos. 101,
104
Ovptd. or
Srchd.

1983, Dec. 7
138	A32	10 I multicolored	.25	.25
139	A32	15 I on 1 I multi	.25	.25
140	A32	25 I multicolored	.35	.35
141	A32	150 I multicolored	2.00	2.00
		Nos. 138-141 (4)	2.85	2.85

Europa,
25th Anniv.
A52

1984, May 30   *Perf. 12x12½*
142	A52	50 I blk, yel & brn	1.00	.50
143	A52	100 I blk, bl & ultra	2.00	1.00
a.		Pair, #142-143	3.25	2.75

Olympics,
Los
Angeles
A53

   Perf. 12½x12, 12x12½
1984, June 19
144	A53	10 I Olympic flame, vert.	.30	.25
145	A53	20 I Olympic rings	.40	.25
146	A53	70 I Judo	.80	.60
		Nos. 144-146 (3)	1.50	1.10

Ataturk
Cultural
Center
A54

   Perf. 12x12½
1984, July 20   **Wmk. 390**
147	A54	120 I blk, yel & brn	1.00	.90

Turkish
Invasion
of
Cyprus,
10th
Anniv.
A55

70 I, Map, flag, olive branch.

1984, July 20
148	A55	20 I shown	.40	.40
149	A55	70 I multicolored	.70	.70

Forest Conservation — A56

1984, Aug. 20
150	A56	90 I multicolored	1.25	.75

Paintings — A57

20 I, Old Turkish Houses in Nicosia by
Cevdet Cagdas. 70 I, Scenery by Olga Rauf.

1984, Sept. 21   *Perf. 13*
151	A57	20 I multicolored	.40	.40
152	A57	70 I multicolored	1.10	1.10

Proclamation of
Turkish Republic of
Northern
Cyprus — A58

Unanimous Vote by Legislative
Assembly — A59

   Perf. 12½x12, 12x12½
1984, Nov. 15
153	A58	20 I multicolored	.75	.30
154	A59	70 I multicolored	1.40	.70

Independence, 1st Anniv.

European Taekwondo Championship,
Kyrenia — A60

1984, Dec. 10
155	A60	10 I Competitors	.30	.25
156	A60	70 I Flags	.60	.55

Balance of the Spirit — A61

Paintings by Saulo Mercader: 20 I, The
Look, vert. 70 I, L'equilibre De
L'esprit.

1984, Dec. 10   *Perf. 12½x13, 13x12½*
157	A61	20 I multicolored	.25	.25
158	A61	70 I multicolored	.50	.50

Visit by
Nuremburg
Chamber
Orchestra
A62

1984, Dec. 10   *Perf. 12½*
159	A62	70 I multicolored	1.00	.50

Dr. Fazil Kucuk
(1906-1984),
Politician — A63

70 I, Kucuk reading newspaper, c. 1970.

1985, Jan.
160	A63	20 I multicolored	.50	.25
161	A63	70 I multicolored	.70	.50

Domestic
Animals
A64

1985, May 29   *Perf. 12x12½*
162	A64	100 I Capra	.55	.55
163	A64	200 I Bos taurus	1.10	1.10
164	A64	300 I Ovis aries	1.60	1.60
165	A64	500 I Equus asinus	2.75	2.75
		Nos. 162-165 (4)	6.00	6.00

Europa — A65

Composers: No. 166, George Frideric Handel (1685-1759). No. 167, Domenico Scarlatti
(1685-1757). No. 168, Johann Sebastian Bach
(1685-1750). No. 169, Buhurizade Mustafa Itri
(1640-1712).

1985, June 26   *Perf. 12½x12*
166	A65	20 I grn & multi	.30	.25
167	A65	20 I brn lake & multi	.30	.25
168	A65	100 I bl & multi	1.25	.80
169	A65	100 I brn & multi	1.25	.80
a.		Block of 4, #166-169	3.75	3.75

Printed in sheets of 16, containing 4 No.
169a.

Paintings — A66

Paintings: 20 I, Pastoral Life by Ali Atakan.
50 I, Woman Carrying Water by Ismet V.
Guney.

1985, Aug.   *Perf. 12½x13*
170	A66	20 I multicolored	.35	.35
171	A66	50 I multicolored	.55	.55

Intl. Youth
Year
A67

    Wmk. 390
1985, Oct. 29   **Litho.**   *Perf. 12½*
172	A67	20 I shown	.40	.25
173	A67	100 I Globe, dove	.90	.60

Northern Cyprus
Air
League — A68

Development of
Rabies Vaccine,
Cent. — A69

Ismet Inonu (1884-
1973), Turkish
Pres. — A70

UN, 40th
Anniv.
A71

Blood
Donor
Services
A72

1985, Nov. 29
174	A68	20 I multicolored	.25	.25
175	A69	50 I Pasteur	.30	.30
176	A70	100 I brown	.60	.60
177	A71	100 I multicolored	.60	.60
178	A72	100 I multicolored	.60	.60
		Nos. 174-178 (5)	2.35	2.35

Paintings — A73

20 I, House with Arches by Gonen Atakol.
100 I, Ataturk Square by Yalkin Muhtaroglu.

1986, June 20   *Perf. 13*
179	A73	20 I multicolored	.40	.25
180	A73	100 I multicolored	.75	.40

Miniature Sheet

Europa — A74

1986, June 20   *Perf. 12x12½*
181	A74	Sheet of 2	16.00	16.00
a.		100 I Gyps fulvus	4.00	2.00
b.		200 I Roadside litter	8.00	4.00

Karagöz
Puppets — A75

1986, July 25   *Perf. 12½x13*
182 A75 100 l multicolored   .90   .40

Anatolian
Artifacts
A76

Designs: 10 l, Ring-shaped composite pottery, Kernos, Old Bronze Age (2300-1050 B.C.). 20 l, Bird-shaped lidded pot, Skuru Hill tomb, Morphou, late Bronze Age (1600-1500 B.C.), vert. 50 l, Earthenware jug, Vryse, Kyrenia, Neolithic Age (4000 B.C.). 100 l, Terra sigillata statue of Artemis, Sea of Salamis, Roman Period (200 B.C.), vert.

1986, Sept. 15   *Perf. 12½*
183 A76   10 l multicolored   .25   .25
184 A76   20 l multicolored   .25   .25
185 A76   50 l multicolored   .25   .25
186 A76 100 l multicolored   .50   .50
    Nos. 183-186 (4)   1.25   1.25

For surcharge see No. 295A.

Defense Forces,
10th
Anniv. — A77

World Food
Day — A78

World Cup Soccer Championships,
Mexico — A79

Halley's
Comet
A80

1986, Oct. 13
187 A77   20 l multicolored   .25   .25
188 A78   50 l multicolored   .30   .30
189 A79 100 l multicolored   .35   .35
190 A80 100 l multicolored   .40   .40
    Nos. 187-190 (4)   1.30   1.30

Development Projects — A81

1986, Nov. 17
191 A81   20 l Water resources   .25   .25
192 A81   50 l Housing   .25   .25
193 A81 100 l Airport   .45   .45
    Nos. 191-193 (3)   .95   .95

Royal Wedding of
Prince Andrew
and Sarah
Ferguson — A82

Anniv. and events: No. 195, Queen Elizabeth II, 60th birthday.

       Perf. 12½x13
1986, Nov. 20   **Wmk. 390**
194 A82 100 l multicolored   .50   .35
195 A82 100 l multicolored   .50   .35
   a.   Pair, #194-195   1.00   .70

Trakhoni
Station,
1904
A83

100 l, Locomotive #1, 1904.

1986, Dec. 31
196 A83   50 l shown   .40   .25
197 A83 100 l   1.00   .60

Rail transport, 1904-1951.

Nos. 86, 88-89, 105 Overprinted or Surcharged

a

b

1987, May 18   **Unwmk.**   *Perf. 13*
198 A25(a) 10 l on #89   .40   .25
199 A25(a) 15 l on 3½ l, #86   .40   .25
200 A25(a) 20 l on #88   .50   .25
201 A32(b) 30 l on #105   .80   .35
    Nos. 198-201 (4)   2.10   1.10

Paintings — A84

Designs: 50 l, Shepherd by Feridun Isiman. 125 l, Pear Woman by Mehmet Uluhan.

       Perf. 12½x13
1987, May 27   **Wmk. 390**
202 A84   50 l multicolored   .45   .25
203 A84 125 l multicolored   1.10   .40

Europa
A85

Modern architecture: 50 l, Bauhaus-style house, designed by A. Vural Behacddin, 1973. 200 l, House, designed by Necdet Turgay, 1979.

1987, June 30   *Perf. 12½*
204 A85   50 l multicolored   3.00   .40
205 A85 200 l multicolored   6.00   1.75
   a.   Bkt. pane, 2 each #204-205   20.00

No. 205a contains two copies each of Nos. 204-205, printed alternately, with unprinted selvage at each end of the pane, perf between stamps and selvage and imperf on outside edges. Thus, singles from the pane gauge 12½ by imperf.

Folk Dancers — A86

1987, Aug. 20
206 A86   20 l multicolored   .25   .25
207 A86   50 l multi, diff.   .25   .25
208 A86 200 l multi, diff.   .50   .50
209 A86 1000 l multi, diff.   2.50   2.50
    Nos. 206-209 (4)   3.50   3.50

For surcharge see No. 295B.

Infantry
Regiment, 1st
Anniv. — A87

5th Islamic
Summit Conf.,
Kuwait — A88

Pharmaceutical Federation — A89

1987, Sept. 30
210 A87   50 l multicolored   .25   .25
211 A88 200 l multicolored   .50   .50
212 A89 200 l multicolored   .50   .50
    Nos. 210-212 (3)   1.25   1.25

Ahmet Belig
Pasha (1851-
1924), Egyptian
Judge — A90

Mehmet Emin
Pasha (1813-
1871), Turkish
Grand
Vizier — A91

Famous men: 125 l, Mehmet Kamil Pasha (1832-1913), grand vizier.

213 A90   50 l brn & yel   .25   .25
214 A91   50 l multicolored   .25   .25
215 A91 125 l multicolored   .35   .30
    Nos. 213-215 (3)   .85   .80

A92

Design: Pres. Rauf Denktash, Turkish Prime Minister Turgut Ozal.

1987, Nov. 2
216 A92   50 l multi   .45   .25

New
Kyrenia
Harbor
A93

200 l, Eastern Mediterranean University.

       Wmk. 390
1987, Nov. 20   **Litho.**   *Perf. 12½*
217 A93 150 l shown   .40   .40
218 A93 200 l multicolored   .55   .55

Chair Weaver, by Osman
Guvenir — A94

Paintings: 20 l, Woman Making Pastry, by Ayhan Mentes, vert. 150 l, Woman Weaving a Rug, by Zekai Yesiladali, vert.

       Wmk. 390
1988, May 2   **Litho.**   *Perf. 13*
219 A94   20 l multi   .25   .25
220 A94   50 l multi   .45   .25
221 A94 150 l multi   .85   .35
    Nos. 219-221 (3)   1.55   .85

Europa
A95

200 l, Tugboat Piyale Pasha. 500 l, Satellite dish, broadcast tower, vert.

1988, May 31   *Perf. 12½*
222 A95 200 l multicolored   2.75   1.00
223 A95 500 l multicolored   4.00   1.25

Bayrak Radio and Television Corporation, 25th anniv. (500 l).

Tourism
A96

Photographs: 150 l, Nicosia, by Aysel Erduran. 200 l, Famagusta, by Sonia Halliday and Laura Lushington. 300 l, Kyrenia, by Halliday and Lushington.

1988, June 17
224 A96 150 l multi   .25   .25
225 A96 200 l multi   .35   .35
226 A96 300 l multi   .50   .50
    Nos. 224-226 (3)   1.10   1.10

Turkish Prime Ministers — A97

No. 227, Bulent Ecevit, 1970's. No. 228, Bulent Ulusu, Sept. 21, 1980-Dec. 13, 1983. No. 229, Turgut Ozal, from Dec. 13, 1983.

1988, July 20
227	A97	50 l shown	.25	.25
228	A97	50 l multi	.25	.25
229	A97	50 l multi	.25	.25
		Nos. 227-229 (3)	.75	.75

Civil Defense A98

1988, Aug. 8   Perf. 12x12½
230	A98	150 l multicolored	.35	.35

Summer Olympics, Seoul A99

1988, Sept. 17   Perf. 12½
231	A99	200 l shown	.30	.30
232	A99	250 l Women's running	.40	.40
233	A99	400 l Seoul	.65	.65
		Nos. 231-233 (3)	1.35	1.35

Sedat Simavi (1896-1953), Turkish Journalist — A100

Intl. Conferences, Kyrenia — A101

North Cyprus Intl. Industrial Fair — A102

Intl. Red. Cross and Red Crescent Organizations, 125th Anniv. — A103

US-USSR Summit Meeting on Nuclear Arms Reduction A104

WHO, 40th Anniv. — A105

No. 238, Gorbachev and Reagan.

1988, Oct. 17   Perf. 12½x12, 12x12½
234	A100	50 l olive grn	.25	.25
235	A101	100 l multi	.25	.25
236	A102	300 l multi	.55	.55
237	A103	400 l multi	.85	.85
238	A104	400 l multi	.85	.85
239	A105	600 l multi	1.10	1.10
		Nos. 234-239 (6)	3.85	3.85

Miniature Sheet

Portraits and Photographs of Kemal Ataturk — A106

b, Holding canteen. c, In uniform. d, Facing left.

1988, Nov. 10   Perf. 12½
240	A106	Sheet of 4	3.00	3.00
a.-d.		250 l any single	.50	.40

Souvenir Sheet

Turkish Republic of Northern Cyprus, 5th Anniv. — A107

1988, Nov. 15   Imperf.
241	A107	500 l multicolored	3.25	1.75

A108

Designs: 400 l, Gamblers' Inn, 17th cent., Asmaalti Meydani. 600 l, Camii Cedit Mosque, 1902, Paphos, vert.

1989, Apr. 28   Perf. 13
242	A108	150 l shown	.30	.30
243	A108	400 l multi	.80	.80
244	A108	600 l multi	1.25	1.25
		Nos. 242-244 (3)	2.35	2.35

Dervis Pasha Mansion, 19th Cent., Nicosia.

Europa — A109

1989, May 31   Perf. 12½x12
245	A109	600 l Girl, doll	3.00	1.00
246	A109	1000 l Flying kite	4.00	1.25
a.		Bklt. pane, 2 each #245-246, perf. 12½	16.00	

Geneva Peace Summit, Aug. 24, 1988 A110

1989, June 30   Perf. 12½
247	A110	500 l blk & dark red	1.00	1.00

Wildlife A111

100 l, Alectoris chukar. 200 l, Lepus cyprius. 700 l, Francolinus francolinus. 2000 l, Vulpes vulpes.

1989, July 31
248	A111	100 l multicolored	.25	.25
249	A111	200 l multicolored	.40	.40
250	A111	700 l multicolored	1.40	1.40
251	A111	2000 l multicolored	4.00	4.00
		Nos. 248-251 (4)	6.05	6.05

Natl. Development Projects — A112

100 l, Road construction. 150 l, Sanitary water supply. 200 l, Afforestation. 450 l, Telecommunications. 650 l, Power station. 700 l, Irrigation ponds.

Perf. 12½x12, 12x12½
1989, Sept. 29
252	A112	100 l multicolored	.30	.25
253	A112	150 l multicolored	.40	.30
254	A112	200 l multicolored	.45	.40
255	A112	450 l multicolored	1.00	.90
256	A112	650 l multicolored	1.40	1.25
257	A112	700 l multicolored	1.50	1.40
		Nos. 252-257 (6)	5.05	4.50

Nos. 253-256 vert.

Free Port, Famagusta, 15th Anniv. — A113

Turkish Cypriot Post, 25th Anniv. — A114

Saded Newspaper, Cent. — A115

Intl. Marine Organization, 30th Anniv. — A116

Erenkoy Uprising, 25th Anniv. A117

Perf. 12x12½, 12½x13 (450 l)
1989, Nov. 17
258	A113	100 l multicolored	.25	.25
259	A114	450 l multicolored	.90	.90
260	A115	500 l multicolored	1.00	1.00
261	A116	600 l multicolored	1.25	1.25
262	A117	1000 l multicolored	2.00	2.00
		Nos. 258-262 (5)	5.40	5.40

Erdal Inonu — A118

1989, Dec. 15   Perf. 12½x12
263	A118	700 l multicolored	1.60	1.40

Visit of Inonu, Turkish politician, to northern Cyprus.

Agriculture — A119

150 l, Mule drawn. 450 l, Ox drawn. 550 l, Millstone, olive press.

1989, Dec. 25   Perf. 12x12½, 12½x12
264	A119	150 l multicolored	.30	.30
265	A119	450 l multicolored	.90	.90
266	A119	550 l multicolored	1.10	1.10
		Nos. 264-266 (3)	2.30	2.30

Nos. 264-265 horiz.

World Health Day A120

Perf. 12x12½
1990, Apr. 19   Litho.   Wmk. 390
267	A120	200 l shown	.40	.25
268	A120	700 l Cigarette, heart	1.50	.40

Europa
A121

Post offices: 1000 l, Yenierenkoy. 1500 l, Ataturk Meydani.

Perf. 12x12½

1990, May 31		**Litho.**		**Wmk. 390**	
269	A121	1000 l multicolored		3.00	1.50
270	A121	1500 l multicolored		4.50	2.00
a.		Souv. sheet, 2 #269, 2 #270		18.00	16.00

A122

300 l, Turkish Cypriot team. 1000 l, Ball, emblem, globe.

1990, June 8
271	A122	300 l multicolored	.65	.65
272	A122	1000 l multicolored	2.00	2.00

World Cup Soccer Championships, Italy.

A123

World Environment Day: Birds: 150 l, Turdus philomelos. 300 l, Sylvia atricapilla. 900 l, Phoenicurus ochruros. 1000 l, Phyllosopus collybita.

1990, June 5   **Perf. 12**
273	A123	150 l multicolored	4.00	.75
274	A123	300 l multicolored	5.75	1.25
275	A123	900 l multicolored	12.00	2.75
276	A123	1000 l multicolored	15.00	5.00
		Nos. 273-276 (4)	36.75	9.75

World Wildlife Fund. For surcharge see No. 386.

A125

Designs: 300 l, Painting by Filiz Ankac. 1000 l, Sculpture by Sinasi Tekman, vert.

1990, July 31   **Perf. 13x12½, 12½x13**
279	A125	300 l multicolored	.65	.65
280	A125	1000 l multicolored	2.00	2.00

European Tourism
Year — A126

150 l, Amphitheater, Soli. 1000 l, Mosaic, Soli.

Wmk. 390
1990, Aug. 24		**Litho.**	**Perf. 12½**	
281	A126	150 l multicolored	.35	.35
282	A126	1000 l multicolored	2.00	2.00

Visit by
Turkish
President
Kenan
Evren
A127

1990, Sept. 19
283	A127	500 l multicolored	1.00	1.00

Traffic
Safety
A128

150 l, Wear seat belts. 300 l, Obey the speed limit. 1000 l, Obey traffic signals.

1990, Sept. 21
284	A128	150 l multicolored	.35	.35
285	A128	300 l multicolored	.65	.65
286	A128	1000 l multicolored	2.00	2.00
		Nos. 284-286 (3)	3.00	3.00

A129

1990, Oct. 1
287	A129	1000 l multicolored	2.00	2.00

Visit by Turkish Prime Minister Yildirim Akbulut.

Flowers — A130

150 l, Rosularia cypria. 200 l, Silene fraudratrix. 300 l, Scutellaria sibthorpii. 600 l, Sedum lampusae. 1000 l, Onosma caespitosum. 1500 l, Arabis cypria.

Perf. 12½x12
1990, Oct. 31		**Litho.**	**Wmk. 390**	
288	A130	150 l multicolored	.35	.25
289	A130	200 l multicolored	.40	.25
290	A130	300 l multicolored	.65	.25
291	A130	600 l multicolored	1.25	.30
292	A130	1000 l multicolored	2.00	.50
293	A130	1500 l multicolored	3.25	.80
		Nos. 288-293 (6)	7.90	2.35

For surcharges see Nos. 295C, 387.

Intl.
Literacy
Year
A131

300 l, Ataturk as teacher. 750 l, A, b, c, books, map.

1990, Nov. 24   **Perf. 12x12½**
294	A131	300 l multicolored	.65	.25
295	A131	750 l multicolored	1.60	.40

Nos. 183, 206, 288
Surcharged

1991, June 3
Perfs. & Printing Methods as Before
295A	A76	250 l on 10 l #183	.35	.25
295B	A86	250 l on 20 l #206	.35	.25
295C	A130	500 l on 150 l #288	.45	.25
		Nos. 295A-295C (3)	1.15	.75

Shape of obliterator varies.

Orchids — A132

Wmk. 390
1991, July 8		**Litho.**	**Perf. 14**	
296	A132	250 l Ophrys lapethica	.55	.55
297	A132	500 l Ophrys kotschyi	1.60	1.60

See Nos. 303-306.

A133

Europa: a, Hermes space shuttle. b, Ulysses probe.

Perf. 12½x12
1991, July 29		**Litho.**	**Wmk. 390**	
Miniature Sheet				
298	A133	2000 l Sheet of 2, #a.-b.	10.00	8.00

Public
Fountains
A134

250 l, Kuchuk Medrese. 500 l, Djafer Pasha. 1500 l, Sarayonu Square. 5000 l, Arabahmet Mosque.

Wmk. 390
1991, Sept. 9		**Litho.**	**Perf. 12**	
299	A134	250 l multicolored	.25	.25
300	A134	500 l multicolored	.35	.35
301	A134	1500 l multicolored	1.10	1.10
302	A134	5000 l multicolored	3.50	3.50
		Nos. 299-302 (4)	5.20	5.20

Orchid Type of 1991

100 l, Serapias levantina. 500 l, Dactylorhiza romana. 2000 l, Orchis simia. 3000 l, Orchis sancta.

1991, Oct. 10   **Perf. 14**
303	A132	100 l multicolored	.25	.25
304	A132	500 l multicolored	.40	.40
305	A132	2000 l multicolored	1.40	1.40
306	A132	3000 l multicolored	2.00	2.00
		Nos. 303-306 (4)	4.05	4.05

Hindller by Salih M. Cizel — A135

Painting: 500 l, Dusme by Asik Mene.

Wmk. 390
1991, Nov. 5		**Litho.**	**Perf. 13**	
307	A135	250 l multicolored	.25	.25
308	A135	500 l multicolored	.25	.25

See type A143. For surcharge see No. 381.

World Food Day
A136

Basbakan
Mustafa Cagatay
(1937-1989)
A137

Eastern
Mediterranean
University — A138

Wolfgang
Amadeus
Mozart,
Death
Bicent.
A139

1991, Nov. 20   **Perf. 12**
309	A136	250 l multicolored	.25	.25
310	A137	500 l multicolored	.30	.30
311	A138	500 l multicolored	.30	.30
312	A139	1500 l multicolored	.85	.85
		Nos. 309-312 (4)	1.70	1.70

For surcharge see No. 380.

World
AIDS Day
A140

1991, Dec. 13   **Perf. 12**
313	A140	1000 l multicolored	.55	.55

Lighthouses — A141

250 l, Canbulat Burcu, Famagusta. 500 l, Yat Limani, Kyrenia. 1500 l, Turizm Limani, Kyrenia.

1991, Dec. 16   **Perf. 12x12½**
314	A141	250 l multicolored	.25	.25
315	A141	500 l multicolored	.30	.30
316	A141	1500 l multicolored	.85	.85
		Nos. 314-316 (3)	1.40	1.40

Tourism
A142

Designs: 250 l, Elephant and hippopotamus fossils, Kyrenia. 500 l, Roman fish ponds, Lambusa (58 BC-398 AD). 1500 l, Roman tomb and church, Lambusa (58 BC-1192 AD).

1991, Dec. 27
317 A142 250 l multicolored   .25   .25
318 A142 500 l multicolored   .30   .30
319 A142 1500 l multicolored   .85   .85
        Nos. 317-319 (3)   1.40 1.40

Paintings
A143

Designs: 500 l, Ebru, by Arife Kandulu. 3500 l, Nicosia, by Ismet Tartar.

Wmk. 390
1992, Mar. 31   Litho.   Perf. 14
320 A143 500 l multicolored   .25   .25
321 A143 3500 l multicolored   1.75 1.75
            See type A135.

Tourism
A144

No. 322, Ancient building, Famagusta. No. 323, Trap shooting range, Nicosia. 1000 l, Salamis Bay resort, Famagusta. 1500 l, Casino, Kyrenia.

1992, Apr. 21   Perf. 13½x14, 14x13½
322 A144 500 l multicolored   .25   .25
323 A144 500 l multicolored   .25   .25
324 A144 1000 l multicolored   .50   .50
325 A144 1500 l multi, vert.   .75   .75
        Nos. 322-325 (4)   1.75 1.75

Souvenir Sheet

Discovery of America, 500th
Anniv. — A145

Europa: a, 1500 l, Santa Maria, Nina and Pinta. b, 3500 l, Columbus.

1992, May 29   Perf. 13½x14
326 A145 Sheet of 2, #a.-b.   10.00 10.00

Sea
Turtles
A146

Perf. 13½x14
1992, June 30   Litho.   Wmk. 390
327 A146 500 l Green turtle   3.00 3.00
328 A146 1500 l Loggerhead
                    turtle   3.50 3.50
a.   Souv. sheet, 2 ea #327-328   14.00 14.00
        World Wildlife Fund.

1992
Summer
Olympics,
Barcelona
A147

#329: a, Women's gymnastics, vert. b, Tennis, vert. 1000 l, High jump. 1500 l, Cycling.

1992, July 25   Perf. 14x13½
329 A147 500 l Pair, #a-b.   .75   .75
            Perf. 13½x14
330 A147 1000 l multicolored   .50   .50
331 A147 1500 l multicolored   .75   .75
        Nos. 329-331 (3)   2.00 2.00

Electric
Power
Plant,
Kyrenia
A148

Social
Insurance,
15th Anniv.
A149

Intl.
Federation
of Women
Artists
A150

Veterinary
Services
A151

Perf. 13½x14
1992, Sept. 30   Litho.   Wmk. 390
332 A148 500 l multicolored   .25   .25
333 A149 500 l multicolored   .25   .25
334 A150 1500 l multicolored   .75   .75
335 A151 1500 l multicolored   .75   .75
        Nos. 332-335 (4)   2.00 2.00

Civil
Aviation
Office,
17th Anniv.
A152

Meteorology Office, 18th
Anniv. — A153

Mapping,
14th
Anniv.
A154

Perf. 13½x14
1992, Nov. 20   Litho.   Wmk. 390
336 A152 1000 l multicolored   .50   .50
337 A153 1000 l multicolored   .50   .50
338 A154 1200 l multicolored   .60   .60
        Nos. 336-338 (3)   1.60 1.60

Native
Cuisine
A155

Food: 2000 l, Zulbiye (pastry). 2500 l, Cicek Dolmasi (stuffed squash flowers). 3000 l, Tatar Boregi (flaky pastry dish). 4000 l, Seftali kebab (meat dish).

1992, Dec. 14
339 A155 2000 l multicolored   1.00 1.00
340 A155 2500 l multicolored   1.25 1.25
341 A155 3000 l multicolored   1.50 1.50
342 A155 4000 l multicolored   2.00 2.00
        Nos. 339-342 (4)   5.75 5.75

Intl. Conference on Nutrition, Rome.
See Nos. 388-390.

Tourism
A156

Designs: 500 l, Church and Monastery of St. Barnabas. 10,000 l, Bowl.

Perf. 13½x14
1993, Apr. 1   Litho.   Wmk. 390
343 A156 500 l multi   .25   .25
344 A156 10,000 l multi   5.00 5.00

Souvenir Sheet

Europa — A157

Contemporary paintings by: a, 2000 l, Turksal Ince. b, 3000 l, Ilkay Onsoy.

Perf. 14x13½
1993, May 5   Litho.   Wmk. 390
345 A157 Sheet of 2, #a.-b.   3.00 3.00

Trees — A158

500 l, Olea europaea. 1000 l, Eucalyptus camaldulensis. 3000 l, Platanus orientalis. 4000 l, Pinus brutia tenore.

1993, June 11   Perf. 14x13½
346 A158 500 l multicolored   .25   .25
347 A158 1000 l multicolored   .50   .50
348 A158 3000 l multicolored   1.50 1.50
349 A158 4000 l multicolored   2.00 2.00
        Nos. 346-349 (4)   4.25 4.25

Arabahmet Rehabilitation
Project — A159

Perf. 13½x14
1993, Sept. 20   Litho.   Wmk. 390
350 A159 1000 l shown   .25   .25
351 A159 3000 l Homes, diff.   .50   .50

Creation of Turkish Republic of
Northern Cyprus, 10th Anniv.
A160

Designs: No. 353, Flags changing to dove, vert. 1000 l, Dove flying from flag. 5000 l, Flowers forming "10," map.

Perf. 13½x14, 14x13½
1993, Nov. 15   Litho.   Wmk. 390
352 A160 500 l multicolored   .25   .25
353 A160 500 l multicolored   .25   .25
354 A160 1000 l multicolored   .25   .25
355 A160 5000 l multicolored   .80   .80
        Nos. 352-355 (4)   1.55 1.55

Ataturk, 55th Death
Anniv. — A161

State
Theaters,
30th Anniv.
A162

Turkish Resistance Organization, 35th
Anniv. — A163

Turkish
News
Agency,
20th
Anniv.
A164

Tchaikovsky, Death Cent. — A165

Perf. 14x13½, 13½x14
1993, Dec. 27   Litho.   Wmk. 390
356 A161 500 l multicolored   .25   .25
357 A162 500 l multicolored   .25   .25
358 A163 1500 l multicolored   .30   .30
359 A164 2000 l multicolored   .40   .40
360 A165 5000 l multicolored   1.10 1.10
        Nos. 356-360 (5)   2.30 2.30

Soyle Falci, by Goral Özkan
A166

Design: 6500 l, Sculpture, IV Hareket, by Senol Özdevrim.

1994, Mar. 31   *Perf. 14*
361 A166 1000 l multicolored   .25   .25
362 A166 6500 l multicolored   1.40 1.40

Fazil Kucuk (1906-84), Physician and Political Leader — A167

1994, Apr. 1
363 A167 1500 l multicolored   .45   .30

Souvenir Sheet

Archaeological Discoveries — A168

Europa: a, Neolithic village, Ayios Epectitos Vrysi. b, Neolithic man, early tools found in excavation.

1994, May 16   *Perf. 13½*
364 A168 8500 l Sheet of 2, #a.-b.   4.00 4.00

1994 World Cup Soccer Championships, US — A169

1994, June 30
365 A169   2500 l Trophy, vert.   .25   .25
366 A169 10,000 l US map   .80   .80

Turkish Postal Service in Northern Cyprus, 30th Anniv.
A170

1994, June 30
367 A170 50,000 l multicolored   4.00 4.00

A171

A172

Turkish Peace Operation, 20th Anniv.
A173

1994, July 20   *Perf. 14*
368 A171 2500 l shown   .25   .25
369 A172 5000 l Monument   .40   .40
370 A172 7000 l Monument, diff. .50   .50
371 A173 8500 l shown   .65   .65
       Nos. 368-371 (4)   1.80 1.80

First Rural Postal Cancellations, Cent. — A174

Postmarks, stamps: 1500 l, Karpas, Cyprus #131. 2500 l, Gazi Magusa (Famagusta), #71. 5000 l, Bey Keuy, Cyprus #150. 7000 l, Aloa, Cyprus, #179. 8500 l, Pyla, Cyprus #152.

1994, Aug. 15   *Perf. 13½*
372 A174 1500 l multicolored   .25   .25
373 A174 2500 l multicolored   .25   .25
374 A174 5000 l multicolored   .35   .35
375 A174 7000 l multicolored   .55   .55
376 A174 8500 l multicolored   .70   .70
       Nos. 372-376 (5)   2.10 2.10

Sea Shells — A175

No. 377, Charonia tritonis. No. 378, Tonna galea. No. 379, Cypraea talpa.

1994, Nov. 15   *Perf. 14*
377 A175   2500 l multi   .25   .25
378 A175 12,500 l multi   .70   .35
379 A175 12,500 l multi   .70   .35
       Nos. 377-379 (3)   1.65   .95

Nos. 307, 309 Surcharged

1994, Dec. 12   *Perfs., etc. as Before*
380 A136 1500 l on 250 l multi   .25   .25
381 A135 2500 l on 250 l multi   .25   .25

Size and location of surcharge varies.

European Nature Conservation Year — A176

Designs: 2000 l, Donkeys on mountain top. 3500 l, Shoreline. 15,000 l, Donkeys in field.

1995, Feb. 10   **Wmk. 390**   *Perf. 14*
382 A176   2000 l multicolored   .25   .25
383 A176   3500 l multicolored   .25   .25
384 A176 15,000 l multicolored   1.00 1.00
       Nos. 382-384 (3)   1.50 1.50

Souvenir Sheet

Peace and Freedom — A177

Europa: a, Globe, dove. b, Doves over Europe.

1995, Apr. 20   *Perf. 13½x14*
385 A177 15,000 l Sheet of 2, #a.-b.   3.50 3.50

Nos. 275 & 290 Surcharged

1995, Apr. 21   *Perfs., etc. as Before*
386 A123 2000 l on 900 l #275   1.75 1.50
387 A130 3500 l on 300 l #290   3.50 3.50

Size and location of surcharge varies.

Native Cusine Type of 1992

Food: 3500 l, Sini katmeri. 10,000 l, Kolokas musakka, Bullez kizartma. 14,000 l, Enginar dolmasi.

Perf. 13½x14
1995, May 29   **Litho.**   **Wmk. 390**
388 A155   3500 l multicolored   .25   .25
389 A155 10,000 l multicolored   .55   .55
390 A155 14,000 l multicolored   .80   .80
       Nos. 388-390 (3)   1.60 1.60

Butterflies A178

3500 l, Papilio machaon. 4500 l, Charaxes jasius. 15,000 l, Cynthia cardui. 30,000 l, Vanessa atalanta.

1995, June 30
391 A178   3500 l multicolored   .25   .25
392 A178   4500 l multicolored   .25   .25
393 A178 15,000 l multicolored   .70   .70
394 A178 30,000 l multicolored   1.40 1.40
       Nos. 391-394 (4)   2.60 2.60

Visit by Turkish Pres. Suleyman Demirel
A179

1995, Aug. 21   *Perf. 13½*
395 A179 5000 l multicolored   .25   .25

Tourism A180

Designs: 3500 l, Beach scene, Kyrenia. 7500 l, Sailboats. 15,000 l, Ruins, Famagusta, vert. 20,000 l, St. George Cathedral, Famagusta, vert.

1995, Aug. 21
396 A180   3500 l multicolored   .25   .25
397 A180   7500 l multicolored   .40   .40
398 A180 15,000 l multicolored   .80   .80
399 A180 20,000 l multicolored   1.00 1.00
       Nos. 396-399 (4)   2.45 2.45

State Printing Office, 20th Anniv.
A181

Turkish Natl. Assembly, 75th Anniv.
A182

Louis Pasteur (1822-95)
A183

UN, 50th Anniv.
A184

G. Marconi (1874-1937), Radio, Cent. — A185

Motion Pictures, Cent. — A186

Perf. 13½x14, 14x13½
1995, Nov. 7   **Litho.**   **Wmk. 390**
400 A181   3000 l multicolored   .25   .25
401 A182   3000 l multicolored   .25   .25
402 A183   5000 l multicolored   .25   .25
403 A184 22,000 l multicolored   1.25 1.25
404 A185 30,000 l multicolored   1.60 1.60
405 A186 30,000 l multicolored   1.60 1.60
       Nos. 400-405 (6)   5.20 5.20

A187

Tombstone inscriptions, Orhon and Yenisey river region: 5000 l, Kültigin Heykelinin Basi. 10,000 l, Kültigin Yaziti.

1995, Dec. 28   **Perf. 14x13½**
406 A187 5000 l multicolored   .25 .25
407 A187 10,000 l multicolored   .55 .55
Reading of Orhon Epitaphs, cent.

Tribute to Bosnia-Herzegovina
A188

1996, Jan. 31
408 A188 10,000 l multicolored   .55 .55

Fish
A189

Designs: 6,000 l, Mullus surmuletus. 10,000 l, Thalassoma pavo. 28,000 l, Diplodus vulgaris. 40,000 l, Epinephelus guaza.

1996, Mar. 29   **Perf. 14**
409 A189 6,000 l multicolored   .25 .25
410 A189 10,000 l multicolored   .30 .30
411 A189 28,000 l multicolored   .80 .80
412 A189 40,000 l multicolored   1.10 1.10
    Nos. 409-412 (4)   2.45 2.45
For surcharge see no. 506.

Tourism
A190

Designs: 100,000 l, Palm trees, vert. 150,000 l, Pomegranate fruit, vert. 250,000 l, Bellapais Monastery. 500,000 l, Folk dancing.

Perf. 14x13½, 13½x14
1996, Apr. 26   **Litho.**   **Wmk. 390**
413 A190 100,000 l multi   3.00 3.00
414 A190 150,000 l multi   5.00 5.00
415 A190 250,000 l multi   7.00 7.00
416 A190 500,000 l multi   15.00 15.00
    Nos. 413-416 (4)   30.00 30.00

Famous Women
A191

Europa: 15,000 l, Beria Remzi Ozoran. 50,000 l, Kadriye Hulusi Hacibulgur.

1996, May 31   **Perf. 13½x14**
417 A191 15,000 l multicolored   .50 .50
418 A191 50,000 l multicolored   2.00 2.00

World Environment Day — A192

Designs: a, Older, dying trees in mountainous area. b, Newly-planted trees.

1996, June 28   **Perf. 13½**
419 A192 50,000 l Sheet of 2,
    #a.-b.   2.00 2.00

1996 Summer Olympic Games, Atlanta — A193

a, 15,000 l, Basketball. b, 50,000 l, Javelin. c, 15,000 l, Discus. d, 50,000 l, Volleyball.

1996, July 31
420 A193 Sheet of 4, #a.-d.   3.00 3.00

Euro '96, European Soccer Championship, Great Britain — A194

35,000 l, Flags, soccer ball.

1996, Oct. 31   **Perf. 13½x14**
421 A194 15,000 l shown   .40 .40
422 A194 35,000 l multi   1.40 1.40
   a.   Pair, #421-422   2.00 2.00

Civil Defense
A195

Security Forces — A196

Nasreddin Hodja
A197

Children's Rights
A198

Perf. 13½x14, 14x13½
1996, Dec. 23   **Litho.**   **Wmk. 390**
423 A195 10,000 l multicolored   .25 .25
424 A196 20,000 l multicolored   .50 .50
425 A197 50,000 l multicolored   1.25 1.25
426 A198 75,000 l multicolored   1.90 1.90
    Nos. 423-426 (4)   3.90 3.90

Paintings — A199

Designs: 25,000 l, Buildings, people, by Lebibe Sonuc. 70,000 l, Woman seated beside plant, by Ruzen Atakan.

1997, Jan. 31   **Perf. 14**
427 A199 25,000 l multicolored   .65 .65
428 A199 70,000 l multicolored   1.75 1.75

Mushrooms — A200

Designs: 15,000 l, Amanita phallioides. No. 430, Morchella esculenta. No. 431, Pleurotus eryngii. 70,0000 l, Amanita muscaria.

1997, Mar. 31
429 A200 15,000 l multicolored   .45 .45
430 A200 25,000 l multicolored   .65 .65
431 A200 25,000 l multicolored   .65 .65
432 A200 70,000 l multicolored   1.75 1.75
    Nos. 429-432 (4)   3.50 3.50

Natl. Flag on Mountainside
A201

1997, Apr. 23
433 A201 60,000 l multicolored   1.50 1.50

Stories and Legends
A202

Europa: 25,000 l, Woman with broom, children playing, man with donkey. 70,000 l, Well, apple tree, man behind bushes.

1997, May 30   **Perf. 13½x14**
434 A202 25,000 l multicolored   .75 .75
435 A202 70,000 l multicolored   1.75 1.75

Visit by Turkish Leaders
A203

Designs: 15,000 l, Prime Minister Necmeddin Erbakan, vert. 80,000 l, Pres. Süleyman Demirel.

Perf. 14x13½, 13½x14
1997, June 20
436 A203 15,000 l multicolored   .30 .30
437 A203 80,000 l multicolored   1.50 1.50

A204

Raptors: No. 438, Aquila chrysaetos. No. 439, Falco eleanorae. 75,000 l, Falco tinnunculus. 100,000 l, Pernis apivorus.

1997, July 31   **Perf. 14x13½**
438 A204 40,000 l multicolored   .55 .55
439 A204 40,000 l multicolored   .55 .55
440 A204 75,000 l multicolored   1.00 1.00
441 A204 100,000 l multicolored   1.40 1.40
    Nos. 438-441 (4)   3.50 3.50

A205

Old Coins Used in Cyprus: 25,000 l, 1861 Abdül Aziz gold lira. 40,000 l, 1808 Mahmud II gold rumi. 75,000 l, 1566 Selim II gold lira. 100,000 l, 1909 Mehmed V gold besibirlik.

1997, Oct. 28
442 A205 25,000 l multicolored   .35 .35
443 A205 40,000 l multicolored   .55 .55
444 A205 75,000 l multicolored   1.00 1.00
445 A205 100,000 l multicolored   1.40 1.40
    Nos. 442-445 (4)   3.30 3.30

Turk Lisesi, Cent.
A206

Scouting, 90th Anniv.
A207

Fight Against AIDS — A208

Diesel Engine, Cent. A209

Perf. 13½x14, 14x13½
1997, Dec. 22   Litho.   Wmk. 390
446 A206 25,000 l multicolored .30 .30
447 A207 40,000 l multicolored .50 .50
448 A208 100,000 l multicolored 1.25 1.25
449 A209 150,000 l multicolored 1.75 1.75
Nos. 446-449 (4) 3.80 3.80

Ismet Sevki (1884-1957) and Ahmet Sevki (1874-1959), Photographers — A210

105, 000 l, Ahmet Sevki, vert.

1998, Jan. 28   Perf. 13½x14
450 A210 40,000 l brn, *cream* .50 .50
451 A210 105,000 l brn, *cream* 1.25 1.25

Insects A211

Designs: 40,000 l, Agrion splendens. 65,000 l, Ascalaphus macaronius. 125,000 l, Podalonia hirsuta. 150,000 l, Rhyssa persuasoria.

1998, Mar. 30
452 A211 40,000 l multicolored .40 .40
453 A211 65,000 l multicolored .65 .65
454 A211 125,000 l multicolored 1.25 1.25
455 A211 150,000 l multicolored 1.50 1.50
Nos. 452-455 (4) 3.80 3.80

For surcharge, see No. 766.

Doors — A212

1998, Apr. 30   Perf. 14x13½
456 A212 115,000 l shown 1.10 1.10
457 A212 140,000 l Door, steps 1.40 1.40

Natl. Festival A213

Europa: 150,000 l, Globe, map of Cyprus, flags, vert.

1998, May 30   Perf. 13½x14, 14x13½
458 A213 40,000 l multicolored .65 .65
459 A213 150,000 l multicolored 2.10 2.10

Intl. Year of the Ocean A214

Various marine life.

1998, June 30   Perf. 13½x14
460 A214 40,000 l multicolored .30 .30
461 A214 90,000 l multicolored .65 .65

For surcharge, see No. 767.

Visit by Turkish Prime Minister Mesut Yilmaz A215

1998, July 20
462 A215 75,000 l multicolored .55 .55

Turkish Pres. Süleyman Demirel — A216

Design: 175,000 l, Pres. Demirel, Pres. Rauf R. Denktash, view of ocean, horiz.

1998, July 25   Perf. 13½x14, 14x13½
463 A216 75,000 l multicolored .55 .55
464 A216 175,000 l multicolored 1.25 1.25

Establishment of Yaylacik water program.

1998 World Cup Soccer Championships, France — A217

75,000 l, Team coming across field, fans in stadium. 175,000 l, Holding up World Cup trophy.

1998, July 31   Perf. 13½x14, 13x13½
465 A217 75,000 l multi, horiz. .55 .55
466 A217 175,000 l multi 1.25 1.25

Visit of Turkish Deputy Prime Minister Bülent Ecevit — A218

1998, Sept. 5   Perf. 14
467 A218 200,000 l multicolored 1.50 1.50

Traditional Crafts — A219

No. 468, Kalayci, horiz. No. 469, Sepetci. No. 470, Bileyici. No. 471, Oymaci, horiz.

1998, Oct. 26   Perf. 13½x14, 14x13½
468 A219 50,000 l multi .40 .40
469 A219 75,000 l multi .60 .60
470 A219 130,000 l multi 1.00 1.00
471 A219 400,000 l multi 3.00 3.00
Nos. 468-471 (4) 5.00 5.00

Bayrak Radio & Television, 35th Anniv. A220

Turkish Cyprus, 15th Anniv. A221

Turkish Republic, 75th Anniv. A222

Universal Declaration of Human Rights, 50th Anniv. — A223

No. 476a, 75,000 l, Natl. flag, map of Turkish Cyprus.

1998, Nov. 15
472 A220 50,000 l multicolored .40 .40
473 A221 75,000 l multicolored .55 .55
474 A222 75,000 l multicolored .55 .55
475 A223 175,000 l multicolored 1.25 .65
Nos. 472-475 (4) 2.75 2.15
Souvenir Sheet
476 Sheet of 2, #473, #476a 1.10 1.10

A224

1999, Jan. 15   Perf. 14
477 A224 75,000 l multicolored .55 .55

Dr. Fazil Kücük (1906-84), politician.

Scene from "Othello," by Verdi: a, Singers standing. b, Singer on floor.

A225

1999, Jan. 30
478 A225 200,000 l Sheet of 2, #a.-b. 2.00 2.00

Snakes A226

Designs: 50,000 l, Malpolon monspessulanus insignitus. 75,000 l, Hierophis jugularis. 195,000 l, Vipera lebetina. 220,000 l, Natrix natrix.

1999, Mar. 26   Perf. 13½x14
479 A226 50,000 l multicolored .40 .40
480 A226 75,000 l multicolored .60 .60
481 A226 195,000 l multicolored 1.60 1.60
482 A226 220,000 l multicolored 1.75 1.75
Nos. 479-482 (4) 4.35 4.35

Europa A227

No. 483, Sütunlu Cave. No. 484, Incirli Cave, vert.

1999, May 17   Perf. 14
483 A227 75,000 l multi 1.00 1.00
484 A227 200,000 l multi 2.25 2.25

Turkish Peace Operation, 25th Anniv. A228

No. 486, Dove, map, sun.

Wmk. 390
1999, July 20   Litho.   Perf. 13¾
485 A228 150,000 l multi 1.25 1.25
486 A228 250,000 l multi 2.00 2.00

Turkish Postal Administration in Cyprus, 35th Anniv. — A229

1999, Nov. 12   Litho.   Perf. 13¾
487 A229 75,000 l multicolored .50 .50

UPU, 125th Anniv. A230

1999, Nov. 12
488 A230 225,000 l multicolored .80 .80

Total Solar Eclipse, Aug. 11 — A231

1999, Nov. 12
489 A231 250,000 l multicolored .90 .90

Destruction of Turkish Heritage in Southern Cyprus — A232

Photos of: 75,000 l, Building, Limassol. 150,000 l, Mosque, Evdim. 210,000 l, Bayraktar Mosque, Nicosia (Lefkosa). 1,000,000 l, Cami-i Kebir Mosque, Paphos (Baf), vert.

1999, Dec. 3
490	A232	75,000 l multi	.25	.25
491	A232	150,000 l multi	.55	.55
492	A232	210,000 l multi	.75	.75
493	A232	1,000,000 l multi	3.75	3.75
	Nos. 490-493 (4)		5.30	5.30

Millennium
A233

Designs: 75,000 l, Cellular phone. 150,000 l, "Welcome 2000." 275,000 l, Computer. 300,000 l, Satellite.

2000, Mar. 3   Litho.   Perf. 13¾
494	A233	75,000 l multi	.25	.25
495	A233	150,000 l multi	.50	.50
496	A233	275,000 l multi	.95	.95
497	A233	300,000 l multi	1.00	1.00
	Nos. 494-497 (4)		2.70	2.70

Beach Scenes
A234

Designs: 300,000 l, Umbrella, pail, shovel, beach ball, sailboats. 340,000 l, Beach chair.

2000, Apr. 29   Litho.   Perf. 13¾
498	A234	300,000 l multi	1.00	1.00
499	A234	340,000 l multi	1.10	1.10

Europa Issue
Common Design Type and

A235

2000, May 31   Wmk. 390   Perf. 14
500		Sheet of 2	2.50	2.50
a.	CD17	300,000 l multi	1.10	.95
b.	A235	300,000 l multi	1.10	.95

4th Intl. Music Festival, Bellapais Abbey
A236

Designs: 150,000 l, Bellapais Abbey. 350,000 l, Blended colors, vert.

2000, June 21   Perf. 13¾
501	A236	150,000 l multi	.45	.45
502	A236	350,000 l multi	1.10	1.10

Visit of Turkish Pres. Ahmet N. Sezer — A237

2000, June 22
503	A237	150,000 l multi	.45	.45

2000 Summer Olympics, Sydney
A238

125,000 l, Torch and Olympic rings, vert. 200,000 l, Runner.

2000, July 25
504-505	A238	Set of 2	.90	.90

No. 409 Surcharged

Method & Perf. as Before
2000, Sept. 28   Wmk. 390
506	A189	50,000 l on 6000 l	.25	.25

Flora and Fauna — A239

Designs: 125,000 l, Praying mantis on flower. 200,000 l, Butterfly on flower. 275,000 l, Bee on flower. 600,000 l, Snail on flower stem.

Wmk. 390
2000, Oct. 16   Litho.   Perf. 13¾
507-510	A239	Set of 4	3.75	3.75

Kerchief Borders
A240

Background colors: 125,000 l, Yellow. 200,000 l, Lilac. 265,000 l, Green. 350,000 l, Brown.

2000, Nov. 28
511-514	A240	Set of 4	3.00	3.00

Restored Buildings, Nicosia (Lefkosa)
A241

Designs: 125,000 l, Lusignan House. 200,000 l, Eaved House.

Wmk. 390
2001, Mar. 28   Litho.   Perf. 13¾
515-516	A241	Set of 2	.75	.75

Art
A242

Works by: 125,000 l, Inci Kansu. 200,000 l, Emel Samioglu. 350,000 l, Ozden Selenge, vert. 400,000 l, Ayhatun Atesin.

2001, Mar. 30
517-520	A242	Set of 4	2.50	2.50

Europa — A243

Designs: 200,000 l, Degirmenlik Reservoir. 500,000 l, Waterfall, Sinar.

2001, May 31
521-522	A243	Set of 2	1.60	1.60

World Environment Day — A244

Designs: 125,000 l, Atomic model, x-ray images. 450,000 l, X-ray images, radiation symbol.

2001, June 22
523-524	A244	Set of 2	1.10	1.10

Police Uniforms — A245

Uniforms from: 125,000 l, 1885. 200,000 l, 1933. 500,000 l, 1934. 750,000 l, 1983.

2001, Aug. 24
525-528	A245	Set of 4	2.75	2.75

Automobiles — A246

Designs: 175,000 l, 1954 MG TF. 300,000 l, 1948 Vauxhall 14. 475,000 l, 1922 Bentley. 600,000 l, 1955 Jaguar XK 120.

Wmk. 390
2001, Nov. 2   Litho.   Perf. 13¾
529-532	A246	Set of 4	1.90	1.90

Publication of The Genocide Files, by Harry Scott Gibbons — A247

2001, Dec. 24
533	A247	200,000 l multi	.30	.30

July 20th Technical School, Cent.
A248

2001, Dec. 24
534	A248	200,000 l multi	.30	.30

Cartoon Art
A249

Designs: 250,000 l, Chef with grinder and book, by Utku Karsu, vert. 300,000 l, People singing "We Are the World," malnourished Africans, by Musa Kayra. 475,000 l, Can of diet cola airdropped for a malnourished African, by Serhan Gazi, vert. 850,000 l, Child viewing city and painting a country scene, by Mustafa Tozaki, vert.

Wmk. 390
2002, Feb. 28   Litho.   Perf. 13¾
535-538	A249	Set of 4	2.60	2.60

Tourism
A250

Underwater photographs: 250,000 l, Turtle swimming. 300,000 l, Starfish on coral. 500,000 l, Fish. 750,000 l, Shipwreck.

2002, Mar. 27
539-542	A250	Set of 4	2.50	2.50

Souvenir Sheet

Europa — A251

No. 543: a, Man on stilts. b, Tightrope walker.

Wmk. 390
2002, May 27   Litho.   Perf. 13¾
543	A251	600,000 l Sheet of 2, #a-b	1.50	1.50

A252

Designs: 300,000 l, Soccer team. 1,000,000 l, "Lift Embargo on Sports."

2002, June 24
544-545	A252	Set of 2	1.60	1.60

2002 World Cup Soccer Championships, Japan and Korea.

Native Costumes — A253

Designs: 250,000 l, Woman. 300,000 l, Man. 425,000 l, Man, diff. 700,000 l, Woman, diff.

2002, Aug. 8
546-549 A253   Set of 4   2.00 2.00

Children's Art A254

Art by: 300,000 l, M. A. Alpdogan. 600,000 l, S. Avci, vert.

Wmk. 390
2002, Sept. 30   Litho.   Perf. 13¾
550-551 A254   Set of 2   .90   .90

Sports Personalities A255

Designs: 300,000 l, Sureyya Ayhan, winner of women's 1500m race at 2002 European Track and Field Championships. 1,000,000 l, Park Jung-tae (1944-2002), father of modern taekwondo.

2002, Oct. 28
552-553 A255   Set of 2   1.60 1.60

Famous Men — A256

Designs: 100,000 l, Oguz Karayel (1933-96), soccer player. 175,000 l, Mete Adanir (1961-89), soccer player. 300,000 l, M. Necati Ozkan (1899-1970). 575,000 l, Osman Turkay (1927-2001), poet, horiz.

2002, Dec. 3
554-557 A256   Set of 4   1.40 1.40

Art — A257

Paintings by: 250,000 l, S. Bayraktar. 1,000,000 l, F. Sükan.

Wmk. 390
2003, Feb. 21   Litho.   Perf. 13¾
558-559 A257   Set of 2   1.50 1.50

Souvenir Sheet

Europa — A258

Poster art: a, Tree. b, Question mark.

2003, May 8
560 A258 600,000 l Sheet of 2,
       #a-b   1.60 1.60

Birds A259

Designs: 100,000 l, Oenanthe cypriaca. 300,000 l, Sylvia melanothorax. 500,000 l, Phalacrocorax pygmeus, vert. 600,000 l, Phoenicopterus ruber, vert.

2003, June 3
561-564 A259   Set of 4   2.10 2.10

Chests A260

Chest from: 250,000 l, Seher. 300,000 l, Lapta. 525,000 l, Baf. 1,000,000 l, Karpaz ve Akatu.

Perf. 13¾x14
2003, July 25   Litho.   Wmk. 390
565-568 A260   Set of 4   3.00 3.00

Flowers — A261

Designs: 150,000 l, Gladiolus triphyllus. 175,000 l, Tulipa cypria. 500,000 l, Ranunculus asiaticus. 525,000 l, Narcissus tazetta.

2003, Oct. 21   Perf. 14x13¾
569-572 A261   Set of 4   1.75 1.75

National Anniversaries — A262

No. 573 — Kemal Ataturk and flag of: a, Turkey. b, Turkish Republic of Northern Cyprus.

2003, Nov. 14   Perf. 13¾x14
573 A262 3,000,000 l Horiz. pair,
       #a-b   8.50 8.50

Republic of Turkey, 80th anniv. (#573a), Turkish Republic of Northern Cyprus, 20th anniv. (#573b).

Federation of Agricultural Producers, 60th Anniv. A263

2003, Dec. 12
574 A263 300,000 l multi   .45   .45

Lions International in Turkish Republic of Northern Cyprus, 40th Anniv. — A263a

2003, Dec. 12
575 A263a 500,000 l multi   .70   .70

Turkish Postal Service in Northern Cyprus, 40th Anniv. A264

Emblem and: 250,000 l, Mailbox and Nicosia Post Office. 1,500,000 l, Globe, winged envelopes.

Perf. 13¾x14
2004, Apr. 30   Litho.   Wmk. 390
576-577 A264   Set of 2   2.40 2.40

Souvenir Sheet

Europa — A265

No. 578: a, Beach, sailboat. b, Woman holding drink, beach.

2004, May 25
578 A265 600,000 l Sheet of 2,
       #a-b   1.60 1.60
       Exists imperf.

Eurasia Postal Union A266

2004, June 7
579 A266 300,000 l multi   .40   .40

Flowers — A267

Designs: 250,000 l, Salvia veneris. 300,000 l, Phlomis cypria. 500,000 l, Pimpinella cypria. 600,000 l, Rosularia cypria.

2004, July 9   Perf. 14x13¾
580-583 A267   Set of 4   2.40 2.40

Soccer Stadiums A268

Stadium and: 300,000 l, European Soccer Championships emblem. 1,000,000 l, UEFA (European Football Union) 50th anniv. emblem.

2004, Aug. 20   Perf. 13¾x14
584-585 A268   Set of 2   1.75 1.75

2004 Summer Olympics, Athens — A269

No. 586, 300,000 l: a, Sailing, handball. b, Boxing, equestrian.
No. 587, 300,000 l: a, Weight lifting, gymnastics. b, Canoeing, tennis.

2004, Sept. 24   Perf. 14x13¾
Horiz. pairs, #a-b
586-587 A269   Set of 2   2.25 2.25

Eastern Mediterranean University, 25th Anniv. (in 2004) — A270

2005, Feb. 15   Litho.   Perf. 13¾x14
588 A270 15k multi   .25   .25

Cyprus Turkish Philatelic Association, 25th Anniv. (in 2004) — A271

2005, Feb. 15
589 A271 30k multi   .50   .50

Website for Universities in Turkish Republic of Northern Cyprus — A272

2005, Feb. 15
590 A272 50k multi   .80   .80

A273

Tourism
A274

2005, Mar. 9
591 A273 10k multi   .25 .25
592 A274 1 l multi   1.60 1.60

Children's
Drawings — A275

Drawings of men and women by: 25k, E.
Demirci. 50k, E. Oztemiz.

2005, Apr. 22   *Perf. 14x13¾*
593-594 A275 Set of 2   1.10 1.10

Europa — A276

No. 595: a, Woman at left, round table. b,
Oven, square table, woman at right.

2005, May 30   *Perf. 13¾x14*
595 A276 60k Pair, #a-b   1.75 1.75
c.   Souvenir sheet, 2 #595   3.50 3.50

Flowers — A277

Designs: 15k, Fianthus cyprius. 25k, Delphinium caseyi. 30k, Brassica hilarionis. 50k,
Limonium albidum.

2005, July 8   *Perf. 14x13¾*
596-599 A277 Set of 4   1.90 1.90
See Nos. 608-613.

Arts in
Towns
A278

Designs: 10k, Beach, umbrellas, musical
symbols, artist's palette, olive branches,
Kyrenia (Girne). 25k, Musical symbols,
mosque, Famagusta (Gazimagusa). 50k,
Dancers, building, Nicosia (Lefkosa). 1 l, Theater and masks, Kyrenia, Famagusta and
Nicosia.

                            Perf. 13½x13¾
2005, Sept. 9   Litho.   Wmk. 390
600-603 A278 Set of 4   2.75 2.75

Ercan
Airport — A279

2005, Nov. 23   *Perf. 13¾x13½*
604 A279 50k multi   .75 .75

University
of
Northern
Cyprus
A280

2005, Nov. 23   *Perf. 13½x13¾*
605 A280 1 l multi   1.50 1.50

Europa
Stamps,
50th Anniv.
A281

Designs: No. 606, 1.40 l, Map of Cyprus.
No. 607, 1.40 l, Photo of Cyprus from space,
satellite.

2006, Jan. 6   Set of 2   4.25 4.25
606-607 A281
607a   Souvenir sheet, #606-607 4.25 4.25
No. 607a exists imperf.

Flowers Type of 2005

Designs: 15k, Helianthemum obtusifolium.
25k, Iris sisyrhinchium, horiz. 40k, Ranunculus
asiaticus, horiz. 50k, Crocus veneris, horiz.
60k, Anemone coronaria, horiz. 70k, Cyclamen persicum.

2006   Litho.   Wmk. 390
608-613 A277 Set of 6   3.75 3.75

Art — A282

Design: 55k, Sculpture by S. Oztan. 60k,
Painting by M. Hastürk.

                            Perf. 13¾x13½
2006, Apr. 7   Litho.   Wmk. 390
614-615 A282 Set of 2   1.75 1.75

Dr. Fazil Kucuk
(1906-84),
Politician — A283

2006, May 18
616 A283 40k multi   .50 .50

Kemal Ataturk
(1881-1938) — A284

2006, May 18
617 A284 1 l multi   1.25 1.25

Europa — A286

Designs: No. 618, 70k, Birds and stars. No.
619, 70k, Pregnant woman, fetus, flags of
European countries.

2006, May 18
618-619 A286 Set of 2   1.75 1.75
619a   Souvenir sheet, #618-619 1.75 1.75
No. 619a exists imperf.

2006 World Cup Soccer
Championships, Germany — A287

No. 620: a, 50k, World Cup trophy, map of
Germany, mascots, soccer ball and field. b,
1 l, Soccer ball, player, Brandenburg Gate.

2006, July 7   *Perf. 13¾x13½*
620 A287 Pair, #a-b   2.00 2.00

Birds — A288

Designs: 40k, Vanellus vanellus. 50k, Anas
platyrhynchos. 60k, Alcedo atthis. 1 l,
Himantopus himantopus.

2006, Sept. 22
621-624 A288 Set of 4   3.50 3.50

Forest Fire
Prevention — A289

2006, Oct. 10   *Perf. 14x13¾*
625 A289 50k multi   .70 .70

Naci Talat
(1945-91),
Politician
A290

2006, Oct. 10   *Perf. 14*
626 A290 70k multi   .95 .95

Eastern
Mediterranean Intl.
Regatta — A291

2006, Oct. 10   *Perf. 14x13¾*
627 A291 1.50 l multi   2.10 2.10

Environmental
Conference — A292

Designs: 50k, Leaf. 80k, Globe, plant and
drought-stricken ground.

                            Wmk. 390
2007, Feb. 19   Litho.   Perf. 14
628-629 A292 Set of 2   1.90 1.90

Antique
Household
Items
A293

Designs: 70k, Pitcher. 80k, Iron. 1.50 l, Oil
lamp, vert. 2 l, Gas burner and pot, vert.

2007, Apr. 6   Perf. 13¾x14, 14x13¾
630-633 A293 Set of 4   7.50 7.50

Europa — A294

Emblems, tent, campfire, hand giving Scout
sign, dove and: No. 634, 80k, One Scout. No.
635, 80k, Three Scouts playing musical
instruments.

2007, May 4   *Perf. 14x13¾*
634-635 A294 Set of 2   2.40 2.40
635a   Souvenir sheet, #634-635,
           imperf.   2.40 2.40
Scouting, cent.

Painting by O. Keten — A295

Painting by S. Cavusoglu A296

2007, July 12 **Perf. 14x13¾, 13¾x14**
636 A295 50k multi .80 .80
637 A296 70k multi 1.10 1.10

Occupations of the Past — A297

Designs: 40k, Rattan weaver. 65k, Fruit peddler. 70k, Shoemaker. 1 l, Shoeshiner.

2007, Sept. 14 **Perf. 13¾x14**
638-641 A297 Set of 4 4.75 4.75

Methods of Postal Transport — A298

Designs: 50k, Carrier pigeons. 60k, Mounted postman, coach, automobile. 1 l, Postman on bicycle, horiz. 1.25 l, Postman on motor scooter, horiz.

Perf. 14x13¾, 13¾x14
2007, Nov. 16
642-645 A298 Set of 4 5.75 5.75

Flowers — A299

Designs: 25k, Asphodelus aestivus. 50k, Ophrys fusca. 60k, Bellis perennis. 70k, Ophrys sphegodes. 80k, Dianthus strictus. 1.60 l, Ophrys argolica. 2.20 l, Crocus cyprius. 3 l, Limodorum abortivum. 5 l, Carlina pygmaea. 10 l, Ophrys kotschyi.

Wmk. 390
2008, Mar. 20 **Litho.** **Perf. 14**
646 A299 25k multi .40 .40
647 A299 50k multi .80 .80
648 A299 60k multi .95 .95
649 A299 70k multi 1.10 1.10
650 A299 80k multi 1.25 1.25
651 A299 1.60 l multi 2.50 2.50
652 A299 2.20 l multi 3.50 3.50
653 A299 3 l multi 4.75 4.75
654 A299 5 l multi 7.75 7.75
655 A299 10 l multi 15.50 15.50
Nos. 646-655 (10) 38.50 38.50

Europa — A300

Designs: No. 656, 80k, Woman writing letter. No. 657, 80k, Quill pen, world map.

2008, May 8 **Perf. 14x13¾**
656-657 A300 Set of 2 2.60 2.60

Souvenir Sheet

2008 Summer Olympics, Beijing — A301

No. 658: a, Diving. b, Gymnastics.

2008, July 24
658 A001 65k Sheet of 2, #a-b 2.25 2.25
Exists imperf.

Souvenir Sheet

Turkish Resistance Organization, 50th Anniv. — A302

No. 659: a, Emblem and "50." b, Monument, Lefkosa.

2008, Aug. 1 **Imperf.**
659 A302 1 l Sheet of 2, #a-b 3.50 3.50

Nicosia (Lefkosa) Municipal Government, 50th Anniv. A303

Inner Wheel International A304

Cyprus Turkish Airlines Jet A305

Civil Defense Organization A306

Perf. 14x13¾, 13¾x14
2008, Sept. 18
660 A303 55k multi .85 .85
661 A304 80k multi 1.25 1.25
662 A305 1 l multi 1.60 1.60
663 A306 1.50 l multi 2.40 2.40
Nos. 660-663 (4) 6.10 6.10

Turkish Declaration of Independence of Northern Cyprus, 25th Anniv. A307

2008, Nov. 15 **Perf. 14**
664 A307 1 l multi 1.25 1.25

Tradesmen A308

Designs: 60k, Upholsterer. 70k, Miller. 80k, Bicycle mechanic. 2 l, Circumcisor.

2008, Nov. 20 **Perf. 13¾x14**
665-668 A308 Set of 4 5.25 5.25

Archaeology — A309

Items from Soli archaeological site: 60k, Gold ring. 2 l, Gold crown.

Perf. 13¾x14
2009, Mar. 23 **Litho.** **Wmk. 390**
669-670 A309 Set of 2 3.25 3.25

Europa — A310

No. 671: a, Solar system. b, Galaxy and comet.

2009, May 5
671 A310 80k Pair, #a-b 2.10 2.10
Intl. Year of Astronomy.

Medicinal Plants — A311

Designs: 50k, Cistus creticus. 60k, Capparis spinosa. 70k, Pancratium maritimum. 1 l, Passiflora caerulea.

2009, July 9 **Perf. 14x13¾**
672-675 A311 Set of 4 3.75 3.75

Reptiles and Amphibians — A312

Designs: 80k, Agama stellio. 1.50 l, Bufo viridis.

2009, Sept. 14 **Perf. 13¼**
676-677 A312 Set of 2 3.25 3.25

Turkish Cypriot Air Traffic Controllers Association — A313

Turkish Cypriot Chamber of Commerce A314

Ziya Rizki (1919-94), Politician A315

2009, Nov. 12 **Perf. 13¾x14**
678 A313 65k multi .90 .90
Perf. 14x13¾
679 A314 1 l multi 1.40 1.40
680 A315 1.50 l multi 2.00 2.00
Nos. 678-680 (3) 4.30 4.30

Turkish Cypriot Representation at Organization of the Islamic Conference, 34th Anniv. — A316

Emblem and: 70k, Map of Islamic Conference countries, flag, mosque, arch. 1 l, Mosque, flag, arch.

2010, Mar. 17 **Perf. 14x13¾**
681-682 A316 Set of 2 2.25 2.25

Europa
A317

2010, May 28   **Perf. 13¾x14**
683 A317   Pair   2.00 2.00
   a.   80k Two faces   1.00 1.00
   b.   80k Girl reading book   1.00 1.00
   c.   As "a," perf. 13¾ horiz.   1.00 1.00
   d.   As "b," perf. 13¾ horiz.   1.00 1.00
   e.   Vert. pair, #683c-683d   2.00 2.00
   f.   Booklet pane, 2 #683e   4.00 —
     Complete booklet, #683f   4.00 —

Worldwide
Fund for
Nature
(WWF)
A318

Designs: No. 684, 25k, Larus melanocephalus. No. 685, 25k, Larus audouinii. No. 686, 30k, Larus ridibundus. No. 687, 30k, Larus genei.

2010, June 4   **Perf. 14**
684-687 A318   Set of 4   1.40 1.40

2010 World Cup
Soccer
Championships,
South
Africa — A319

2010 World Cup Soccer Championships emblem and: 50k, World Cup trophy, crowd. 2 l, Flag of South Africa, elephants, soccer player, mascot.

2010, July 8   **Perf. 14x13¾**
688-689 A319   Set of 2   3.25 3.25

Foreign Press
Association — A320

Journalists: 60k, Kemal Asik (1925-89). 70k, Abdi Ipekçi (1929-79). 80k, Adem Yavuz (1943-74). 1 l, Sedat Simavi (1896-1953).

2010, Sept. 1   **Perf. 14**
690-693 A320   Set of 4   4.25 4.25

Cruise
Ships and
Tourist
Attractions
A321

Various ships and attractions: 1.50 l, 2 l.

2010, Oct. 20   **Perf. 13¾x14**
694-695 A321   Set of 2   5.00 5.00

Workers for Turkish
Cypriot
Society — A322

Designs: 50k, Ozdemir Sennaroglu (1931-85). 60k, Osman Orek (1925-99). 70k, Salih Miroglu (1953-2005). 80k, Ozker Özgür (1940-2005).

2010, Dec. 24   **Perf. 14x13¾**
696-699 A322   Set of 4   3.50 3.50

American
University,
Girne
(Kyrenia),
25th Anniv.
A323

2010, Dec. 24   **Perf. 13¾x14**
700 A323 1 l multi   1.40 1.40

Politicians — A324

Designs: 80k, Dr. Niyazi Manyera (1911-99), Republic of Cyprus Minister of Health. 1.10 l, Mustafa Fazil Plümer (1914-2001), Republic of Cyprus Agriculture Minister. 2 l, Osman Orek (1925-99), Prime Minister of Turkish Republic of Northern Cyprus. 2.20 l, Dr. Fazil Küçük (1906-84), Vice-president of Republic of Cyprus.

2011, Mar. 9   **Perf. 14x13¾**
701-704 A324   Set of 4   7.75 7.75

Tourism
A325

Designs: 50k, Ayios Philon Church. 80k, Ayios Trias Basilica, vert. 1.10 l, Aphendrika. 2 l, Apostolos Andreas Monastery, vert.

2011, Apr. 18   **Perf. 13¾x14, 14x13¾**
705-708 A325   Set of 4   5.75 5.75

Europa — A326

Designs: No. 709, 1.50 l, Ladybug, forest on hillside. No. 710, 1.50 l, Pinecone, forest.

Perf. 14x13¾
2011, May 16   **Wmk. 390**
709-710 A326   Set of 2   4.00 4.00
709a   Souvenir sheet of 2, #709-710   4.00 4.00

Intl. Year of Forests.

Wedding of Prince
William and
Catherine
Middleton — A327

2011, May 27
711 A327 1 l multi   1.25 1.25

Trees — A328

Designs: 1 l, Quercus infectoria. 2.50 l, Olea europaea.

2011, July 18
712-713 A328   Set of 2   4.00 4.00

Art — A329

Design: 60k, Drawing by Birol Ruhi. 70k, Painting by Kemal Ankaç. 80k, Sculpture by Baki Bogaç. 1 l, Painting by Salih Bayraktar, horiz.

Perf. 14x13¾, 13¾x14
2011, Sept. 14
714-717 A329   Set of 4   3.50 3.50

Flora — A330

Designs: 25k, Ziziphus lotus. 50k, Cynara cardunculus. 60k, Oxalis pes-caprae. 70k, Malva sylvestris. 80k, Rubus sanctus. 1.50 l, Crataegus monogyna.

2011, Nov. 25   **Perf. 13¾**
718-723 A330   Set of 6   4.75 4.75

Miniature Sheet

Rauf Denktash (1924-2012), First
President of Turkish Republic of
Northern Cyprus — A331

No. 724 — Denktash: a, 60k, With dove on arm, flag in background. b, 60k, With flag in background. c, 1 l, At microphone. d, 1 l, Wearing striped tie.

2012, Mar. 16   **Perf. 14**
724 A331   Sheet of 4, #a-d   3.75 3.75

Europa — A332

No. 725 — Birds and various tourist attractions with denomination at: a, Left. b, Right.

2012, May 8   **Litho.**   **Wmk. 390**
725 A332 80k Horiz. pair, #a-b   1.75 1.75

Reign of Queen Elizabeth II, 60th
Anniv. — A333

2012, June 1
726 A333 80k multi   .90 .90

2012 European
Soccer
Championships,
Poland and
Ukraine — A334

Emblem of Euro 2012, legs of soccer players, soccer balls and: 70k, Clock tower. 1 l, Stadium.

2012, June 29   **Perf. 14x13¾**
727-728 A334   Set of 2   1.90 1.90

2012 Summer
Olympics,
London — A335

Sites in London and: 2 l, Track. 2.20 l, Sailing.

2012, July 27   **Perf. 13¾**
729-730 A335   Set of 2   4.75 4.75

Motorcycles and Buses — A336

Designs: 60k, 1952 Triumph Tiger Twin motorcycle. 70k, 1948 Ariel Army W110 motorcycle. 80k, 1963 Bedford bus. 1 l, 1960 Fagor bus.

2012, Nov. 22   Perf. 13¾x14
731-734 A336   Set of 4   3.50 3.50

Politicians — A337

Designs: 60k, Ahmet Mithat Berberoglu (1921-2002). 70k, Faiz Kaymak (1904-82). 80k, Dr. Mehmet Dervis Manizade (1903-2003). 1 l, Mehmet Zeka (1903-84).

2013, Mar. 12   Wmk. 390   Perf. 14
735-738 A337   Set of 4   3.50 3.50

Traffic Safety
A338   A339
2013, Apr. 18   Perf. 14x13¾
739 A338   1 l multi   1.10 1.10
740 A339   2.20 l multi   2.50 2.50

Europa
A340

Postal vehicles: Nos. 741, 743, Bicycle. Nos. 742, 744, Van.

Thick Lettering in Country Name and Bottom Inscriptions

Perf. 13¾x14
2013, May 6   Litho.   Wmk. 390
741 A340   80k multi   .85 .85
742 A340   80k multi   .85 .85

Thin Lettering in Country Name and Bottom Inscriptions

743 A340   80k multi   .85 .85
744 A340   80k multi   .85 .85
      Nos. 741-744 (4)   3.40 3.40

Nos. 741 and 742 were each printed in sheets of 15 stamps + label. Each of the 15 stamps on the sheet of No. 741 and 13 of the 15 stamps on the sheet of No. 742 have a gray background design that reproduces the building shown on the label. Values for Nos. 741 and 742 are for any single stamp from the sheets of 15 + label. Nos. 743 and 744 were each printed in sheets of 40 having no gray background design.

A341

Flora and Fauna A342

Designs: 25k, Polyommatus icarus, Iris oratoria. 50k, Upupa epops. 60k, Teucrinum divaricatum ssp.canescens.

Perf. 13¾x14
2013, July 8   Litho.   Wmk. 390
745 A341   25k multi   .25 .25

Perf. 13½
746 A342   50k multi   .55 .55
747 A342   60k multi   .65 .65
      Nos. 745-747 (3)   1.45 1.45

Islamic Art — A343

Designs: 60k, 18th cent.ceremonial leather shield. 70k, 19th cent. prayer rug. 2 l, 16th cent. candlestick.

Wmk. 390
2013, Sept. 10   Litho.   Perf. 14
748-750 A343   Set of 3   3.25 3.25

Conflict Between Greek and Turkish Cypriots, 50th Anniv. — A344

Turkish Republic of Northern Cyprus, 30th Anniv. — A345

Republic of Turkey, 90th Anniv. A346

Perf. 14x13¾
2013, Nov. 20   Litho.   Wmk. 390
751 A344   60k black & gray   .60 .60
752 A345   70k multi   .70 .70

Perf. 13¾x14
753 A346   80k red & black   .80 .80
      Nos. 751-753 (3)   2.10 2.10

Turkish Cypriot Post, 50th Anniv. A347

Designs: 50k, Cover bearing Cyprus #227. 60k, Cover bearing Cyprus #230. 1 l, Cover bearing Cyprus #223 and three U.S. #1213.

Perf. 13¾x14
2014, Jan. 6   Litho.   Wmk. 390
754-756 A347   Set of 3   1.90 1.90

Turkish Education College, 50th Anniv. — A348

Perf. 14x13¾
2014, Jan. 27   Litho.   Wmk. 390
757 A348   2.20 l multi   2.00 2.00

2014 World Cup Soccer Championships, Brazil — A349

2014 World Cup emblem and various soccer players: 70k, 2 l.

Wmk. 390
2014, Feb. 17   Litho.   Perf. 13¾
758-759 A349   Set of 2   2.50 2.50

Scenes From The Only Witness Was the Fig Tree, Play by Abdullah Oztoprak — A350

Various scenes: 25k, 60k, 70k, 1 l.

Perf. 14x13¾
2014, Mar. 10   Litho.   Wmk. 390
760-763 A350   Set of 4   2.40 2.40

Europa A351

Musicians and instruments: 80k, Tef (tambourine). 1.80 l, Davul and zurna (drum and reed pipe).

2014, May 23   Litho.   Perf. 13¾
764-765 A351   Set of 2   2.50 2.50
765a   Souvenir sheet of 2, #764-765   2.50 2.50

Nos. 452 and 461 Surcharged

Methods, Perfs. And Watermarks As Before

2014, July 4
766 A211   30k on 40,000 l #452   .30 .30
767 A214   40k on 90,000 l #461   .40 .40

Erenköy Uprising, 50th Anniv. — A352

Perf. 14x13¾
2014, Aug. 8   Litho.   Wmk. 390
768 A352   1 l multi   95 95

Fruit Blossoms A353

Designs: 60k, Apple blossom. 70k, Orange blossom. 80k, Pomegranate blossom. 1 l, Peach blossom.

Wmk. 390
2014, Sept. 19   Perf. 13¾
769-772 A353   Set of 4   2.75 2.75

Adjacent stamps in the sheet are rotated 90 degrees.

St. Valentine's Day — A354

Perf. 13¾x14
2015, Feb. 9   Litho.   Wmk. 390
773 A354   2.20 l multi   1.75 1.75

Naval Battle of the Dardanelles, Cent. — A355

Perf. 14x13¾
2015, Mar. 18   Litho.   Wmk. 390
774 A355   2 l multi   1.60 1.60

Road Safety A356

Designs: 1 l, Stylized man. 2.20 l, Motorcyclist and caution sign.

Wmk. 390
2015, May 14   Litho.   Perf. 13¼
775-776 A356   Set of 2   2.40 2.40

Europa — A357

Designs: 70k, Toy cars. 80k, Dolls.

Perf. 14x13¾
2015, June 25   Litho.   Wmk. 390
777-778   A357   Set of 2   1.10 1.10
778a   Souvenir sheet of 2, #777-
     778, imperf.   1.10 1.10

Cats and
Dogs — A358

Designs: No. 779, 60k, Cat. No. 780, 60k,
Dog. No. 781, 70k, Cat, diff. No. 782, 79k,
Dog, diff.

Perf. 14x13¾
2015, Aug. 5   Litho.   Wmk. 390
779-782   A358   Set of 4   1.75 1.75

Archaeological
Artifacts in World
Museums — A359

Designs: 60k, Sculpture from Istanbul
museum. 70k, Coin from New York museum.
80k, Sculpture from Stockholm museum,
horiz. 1 l, Bust from Stockholm museum.

Perf. 14x13¾, 13¾x14
2015, Oct. 12   Litho.   Wmk. 390
783-786   A359   Set of 4   2.25 2.25

Making of
Marzipan
A360

Designs: 50k, Harvesting of almonds. 70k,
Shelling of almonds. 1 l, Drying of almond
paste. 2 l, Cooking equipment and marzipan.

Perf. 13¾x14
2015, Nov. 23   Litho.   Wmk. 390
787-790   A360   Set of 4   3.00 3.00

2016 European
Soccer
Championships,
France — A361

Emblem, soccer player, stadium and: 40k,
French flag, Eiffel Tower. 6 l, Louvre Museum.

Wmk. 390
2016, Feb. 25   Litho.   *Perf. 13¾*
791-792   A361   Set of 2   4.50 4.50

2016
Summer
Olympics,
Rio de
Janeiro
A362

Olympic rings, Rio landmarks and: 1.30 l,
Long jumper. 2.20 l, Gymnast on rings. 3.05 l,
Swimmer.

Perf. 13¾x14
2016, Apr. 28   Litho.   Wmk. 390
793-795   A362   Set of 3   4.75 4.75

Europa
A363

Europa
A364

Perf. 13¾x14
2016, May 12   Litho.   Wmk. 390
796   A363   2.80 l multi   1.90 1.90
797   A364   2.80 l multi   1.90 1.90
     Think Green Issue.

Traditional
Household
Furnishings
A365

Designs: 1.60 l, Kitchen. 2 l, Bedroom.

Wmk. 390
2016, Sept. 22   Litho.   *Perf. 14*
798-799   A365   Set of 2   2.40 2.40

Turkey to Turkish Republic of Northern
Cyprus Water Pipeline Project — A366

Wmk. 390
2016, Oct. 17   Litho.   *Imperf.*
800   A366   4 l multi   2.60 2.60
     See Turkey No. 3526.

Bees — A367

Designs: 1 l, Apis mellifera on purple flower.
1.50 l, Apis mellifera on pink flower. 20 l, Apis
mellifera cypria.

Wmk. 390
2016, Nov. 24   Litho.   *Perf. 13¾*
801-803   A367   Set of 3   13.00 13.00

Delphinus
Delphis
A368

Perf. 13¾x14
2017, Feb. 23   Litho.   Wmk. 390
804   A368   1 l multi   .55 .55

Towns
A369

Cittaslow emblem and: 60k, Grapes, beach,
Mehmetcik (Galateia). 1 l, Ruins, Yenibogaziçi
(Agios Sergios). 2 l, Oranges, arch, Lefke
(Lefka).

Perf. 13¾x14
2017, Mar. 23   Litho.   Wmk. 390
805-807   A369   Set of 3   2.00 2.00

Europa
A370

Designs: 1.50 l, St. Hilarion Castle. 3.30 l,
Kyrenia (Girne) Castle.

Perf. 13¾x14
2017, May 11   Litho.   Wmk. 390
808-809   A370   Set of 2   2.75 2.75

Flowers
A371

Designs: 1 l, Teucrium divaricatum subsp.
canescens. 1.50 l, Dianthus strictus subsp.
troodi. 1.65 l, Teucrium salaminium, vert.
1.80 l, Sideritis cypria, vert.

Perf. 13¾x14, 14x13¾
2017, July 31   Litho.   Wmk. 390
810-813   A371   Set of 4   3.50 3.50

Hakan Asik,
Food Vendor
A372

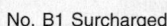

Hasan Eminaga,
Potter — A373

Wmk. 390
2017, Oct. 5   Litho.   *Perf. 14*
814   A372   1 l multi   .55 .55
815   A373   1.50 l multi   .80 .80

No. B1 Surcharged

No. B2 Surcharged

Methods, Perfs., and Watermarks As
Before
2018, Apr. 6
816   SP1   1.50 l on 80k+10k #B1   .75 .75
817   SP2   2 l on 1 l + 10k #B2   1.00 1.00

Europa
A374

Bridge in: 1.50 l, Degirmenlik (Kythrea). 2 l,
Ortaköy.

Perf. 13¾x14
2018, May 18   Litho.   Wmk. 390
818-819   A374   Set of 2   1.60 1.60
   a.   Souvenir sheet of 4, 2 each #818-
     819   3.25 3.25

2018 World Cup Soccer
Championships, Russia — A375

No. 820 — Emblem, mascot, soccer ball,
stadium, nesting doll, with denomination at: a,
LL. b, LR.

Wmk. 390
2018, June 14   Litho.   *Perf. 13¾*
820   A375   1.50 l Horiz. pair, #a-b   1.40 1.40

Reptiles
A376

Designs: 1.50 l, Mauremys rivulata. 1.65 l,
Phoenicolacerta troodica.

Wmk. 390
2018, July 31   Litho.   *Perf. 14*
821-822   A376   Set of 2   1.25 1.25
822a   Souvenir sheet of 4, 2 each
     #821-822   2.50 2.50

Occupational
Health and
Safety — A377

Wmk. 390
2018, Sept. 25   Litho.   *Perf. 14*
823   A377   2 l multi   .70 .70

Outdoor
Activities — A378

Designs: 2.50 l, Kayaking and diving. 4 l, Rock climbing and cycling.

Perf. 14x13½
2018, Dec. 13   Litho.   Wmk. 390
824-825 A378   Set of 2   2.50 2.50

SEMI-POSTAL STAMPS

Campaign Against Cancer
SP1   SP2

Perf. 14x13¾
2015, Apr. 1   Litho.   Wmk. 390
B1 SP1 80k+10k multi   .70 .70
B2 SP2 1 l+10k multi   .85 .85

For surcharges, see Nos. 816-817.

POSTAL TAX STAMP

Trees — PT1

1995, July 24   Litho.   Perf. 14
RA1   PT1 1000 l black & green   9.00 2.00

TURKMENISTAN

ˌtərk-ˌme-nə-ˈstan

LOCATION — Southern Asia, bounded by Kazakhstan, Uzbekistan, Iran and Afghanistan
GOVT. — Independent republic, member of the Commonwealth of Independent States
AREA — 188,417 sq. mi.
POP. — 4,366,383 (1999 est.)
CAPITAL — Ashgabat

With the breakup of the Soviet Union on Dec. 26, 1991, Turkmenistan and ten former Soviet republics established the Commonwealth of Independent States.

100 Kopecks = 1 Ruble
100 Tenge = 1 Manat (1994)

Catalogue values for all unused stamps in this country are for Never Hinged items.

Dagdan
Necklace, 19th
Century — A1

Designs: No. 3, Girl in traditional costume, horiz. No. 4, Akhaltekin horse and rider in native riding dress. No. 5, Mollanepes Theater, horiz. 15r, National arms. No. 7, Pres. Saparmurad Niyazov at left, national flag, horiz. No. 8, Niyazov at right, flag, horiz. No. 9, Map of Turkmenistan.

1992   Litho.   Perf. 12x12½
1 A1 50k multicolored   .35 .35
Perf. 12½
2 A1 10r multicolored   .40 .40
3 A1 10r multicolored   .55 .55
4 A1 10r multicolored   .55 .55
5 A1 10r multicolored   .55 .55
6 A1 15r multicolored   1.10 1.10
7 A1 25r multicolored   1.35 1.35
8 A1 25r multicolored   1.35 1.35
    Nos. 1-8 (8)   6.20 6.20
Size: 112x79mm
Imperf
9 A1 10r multicolored   6.25 6.25

Issued: 50k, 1992; No. 8, 12/8; others, 8/27. Nos. 2-7 exist imperf. Value, set $75.

Nos. 4, 6
Overprinted

1992, Dec. 12   Color of Overprint
10 A1 10r black   4.50 4.50
11 A1 10r brown   4.50 4.50
12 A1 10r red   4.50 4.50
13 A1 10r vermilion   25.00 —
14 A1 10r carmine   4.50 4.50
15 A1 10r green   4.50 4.50
16 A1 15r black   4.50 4.50
17 A1 15r brown   4.50 4.50
18 A1 15r red   4.50 —
19 A1 15r pink   — —
20 A1 15r blue   4.50 4.50
21 A1 15r yellow   6.00 —
    Nos. 10-21 (12)   71.50 40.50

1992 Summer Olympics,
Barcelona — A2

Designs: a, 1r, Weight lifting. b, 3r, Equestrian. c, 5r, Wrestling. d, 10r, Rowing. e, 15r, Emblem of Turkmenistan Olympic Committee. No. 23, Flags, symbols for modern pentathlon, weight lifting, rowing, gymnastics.

1992, Dec. 15   Photo.   Perf. 10½x10
22 A2   Strip of 5, #a.-e.   7.00 7.00
Imperf
Size: 108x82mm
23 A2 15r multicolored   7.50 7.50
For surcharge see No. 33.

Musical Instruments — A3

Photo. & Engr.
1992, Sept. 13   Perf. 12x11½
28 A3 35k buff, red brn, gold & black   .40 .40

Horse
A4

1992, Aug. 9   Photo.   Perf. 12
29 A4 20k shown   .25 .25
30 A4 40k Snake, vert.   .25 .25

A5

1992, Nov. 29   Litho.   Perf. 12x11½
31 A5 1r multicolored   .35 .35

US Pres. Bill Clinton, Pres.
Saparmurad Niyazov — A6

Designs dated: a, 21.30.93. b, 22.03.03. c, 23.03.93. d, 24.03.93. e, 25.03.93.

1993, Mar. 21   Litho.   Perf. 10½
32 A6 100r Strip of 5, #a.-e.   10.00 10.00
Pres. Niyazov's visit to New York City & Washington DC.
Exists imperf. Value, $25.

No. 22 Surcharged

1993, Apr. 1   Photo.   Perf. 10½x10
33 A2   Strip of 5   7.00 7.00
a.   25r on 1r   1.40 1.40
b.   10r on 3r   .65 .65
c.   15r on 5r   .75 .75
d.   15r on 10r   .75 .75
e.   50r on 15r   2.40 2.40
Size of surcharge varies.

Phoca Caspica — A7

World
Wildlife
Fund
A8

Phoca caspica: No. 34a, 25r, Facing right. No. 34b, 500r, Facing left. 15r, Lying in snow. 50r, On rocks. 100r, Mother and young. 150r, Swimming.

1993, Oct. 11   Litho.   Perf. 13½
34 A7   Pair #a.-b.   4.00 4.00
35 A8 15r multicolored   .50 .50
36 A8 50r multicolored   .80 .80
37 A8 100r multicolored   1.05 1.05

---

38 A8 150r multicolored   2.40 2.40
a.   Bklt. pane, 2 ea #34-38   24.00 24.00
    Booklet, #38a   28.00
    Nos. 34-38 (5)   8.75 8.75
Exists imperf. Value, set $350.

Formation of Tovarishch Society for Exploitation of Turkmen Oil Fields, 115th Anniv. — A9

Designs: 1m, Two men viewing oil field. 1.5m, Early tanker Turkmen. 2m, Oil well. 3m, Alfred Nobel, Ludwig Nobel, Robert Nobel, Petr Bilderling, vert. 5m, Early oil field.

1994, June 26   Litho.   Perf. 13
39 A9 1m multicolored   .65 .65
40 A9 1.5m multicolored   1.00 1.00
41 A9 2m multicolored   1.40 1.40
42 A9 3m multicolored   2.10 2.10
a.   Miniature sheet of 8 + label   19.00 19.00
    Nos. 39-42 (4)   5.15 5.15
Souvenir Sheet
43 A9   5m multicolored   4.75 4.75
See Azerbaijan Nos. 415-418a.

Repetek
Natl. Park
A10

Designs: 3m, Repetek Institute. No. 45, Desert, camels. No. 46, Echis carinatus. No. 47, Varanus griseus. 20m, Testudo horsfieldi. No. 49, Haloxylon ammodendron.

1994, Dec. 11   Litho.   Perf. 13
44 A10 3m multicolored   .50 .50
45 A10 5m multicolored   .55 .55
46 A10 5m multicolored   .55 .55
a.   Miniature sheet of 8 + label   10.00 10.00
47 A10 10m multicolored   1.10 1.10
48 A10 20m multicolored   2.00 2.00
    Nos. 44-48 (5)   4.70 4.70
Souvenir Sheet
49 A10 10m multicolored   3.25 3.25

Intl. Olympic Committee, Cent. — A11

1994, Dec. 30   Litho.   Perf. 14
50 A11 11.25m multicolored   2.75 2.75
Souvenir Sheet
51 A11   20m multicolored   5.00 5.00

Miniature Sheet

Save the Aral Sea — A12

Designs: a, Felis caracal. b, Salmo trutta aralensis. c, Hyaena hyaena. d, Pseudoscaphirhynchus kaufmanni. e, Aspiolucius esocinus.

1996, Apr. 29   Litho.   Perf. 14
52 A12 100m Sheet of 5, #a.-e.   7.00 7.00

Independence, 5th Anniv. — A13

No. 53, Map of Turkmenistan on globe, vert.
No. 54, Train pulling into station. No. 55, Natl.
Airport, vert. No. 56, Iranian Pres. Rafsanjani,
Turkmenistan Pres. Saparmurad Niyazov,
Turkish Pres. Demirel. 500m, UN Secretary-
General Boutros Boutros-Gali, Pres. Niyazov,
vert. 1000m, Natl. flag, arms.

1996, Oct. 27	Litho.	Perf. 14		
53	A13	100m multicolored	.40	.40
54	A13	100m multicolored	.50	.50
55	A13	300m multicolored	1.25	1.25
56	A13	300m multicolored	1.60	1.60
57	A13	500m multicolored	1.75	1.75
58	A13	1000m multicolored	3.75	3.75
		Nos. 53-58 (6)	9.25	9.25

1996
Summer
Olympic
Games,
Atlanta
A14

1997, May 5	Litho.	Perf. 14x14½		
59	A14	100m Judo	.70	.70
60	A14	300m Boxing	1.60	1.60
61	A14	300m Track & field	1.60	1.60
62	A14	300m Wrestling	1.60	1.60
63	A14	500m Shooting	3.25	3.25
		Nos. 59-63 (5)	8.75	8.75

Souvenir Sheet

64	A14	1000m Olympic torch	6.25	6.25

Items inscribed "Turkmenistan" that
were not authorized by Turkmenistan
postal officials but which have appeared
on the market include:
Single stamps of 100m depicting
Princess Diana (3 different stamps),
Mother Teresa, Pope John Paul II and
Mother Teresa, 50th Anniv. of India, and
50th Anniv. of Pakistan.
Sheets of 4 stamps with denomina-
tions of 100m depicting JAPEX 98 /
Cats.
Sheets of 9 stamps with denomina-
tions of 100m depicting the Titanic,
Trains, Golfers, Japanese Armor, Japa-
nese Paper Dolls, and Japanese Art.
Sheets of 6 stamps with denomina-
tions of 120m depicting Millennium (8
different sheets).
Sheets of 6 stamps with denomina-
tions of 120m depicting Pokémon, and
Brad Pitt.
Sheets of 4 stamps with denominations of 195m depicting Greenpeace,
Elvis Presley, Birds, Orchids, and Japanese Fashion.
Sheets of 6 stamps with denomina-
tions of 195m depicting Marilyn
Monroe.
Sheets of 9 stamps with denominations of 195m depicting Cacti, and Minerals.
Sheets of 4 stamps with denominations of 250m depicting Akira
Kurosawa.
Sheets of 2 stamps with denominations of 390m depicting Brazilian soccer
players from 1998 World Cup.
Sheets of 9 stamps with denomina-
tions of 1000m depicting IBRA / Mush-
rooms (2 different sheets).
Souvenir sheets of 1 stamp with vari-
ous denominations depicting Hokusai
Artwork (2 different sheets), Pope John
Paul II (2 different sheets), the Titanic (2
different sheets), 1998 Winter Olympics
(2 sheets), Year of the Tiger (2 sheets),
50th Anniv. of Israel, Princess Diana,
Queen Mother, Che Guevara, Frank
Sinatra, Marilyn Monroe, Elvis Presley,
International Year of Older Persons /
Bob Hope, 1998 World Cup Soccer
Championships, Severiano Ballesteros,
Jacques Villeneuve, Leaders of the
World / Automobiles, and Maria de
Medici / Millennium.

Women's
Traditional
Clothing — A15

Various costumes.

1999, July 5	Litho.	Perf. 14		
65	A15	500m multi	.80	.80
66	A15	1000m multi	1.35	1.35
67	A15	1200m multi	1.90	1.90
68	A15	2500m multi	2.50	2.50
69	A15	3000m multi	3.25	3.25
		Nos. 65-69 (5)	9.80	9.80

Falcons — A16

a, 1000m, Falco tinnunculus. b, 1000m,
Falco peregrinus, looking left. c, 1000m, Falco
peregrinus, looking right. d, 2500m, Falco tinnunculus, diff. e, 3000m, Falco peregrinus,
diff.

2000, Mar. 30	Litho.	Perf. 14		
70	A16	Sheet of 5, #a-e	13.00	13.00

Horn — A17

2000, Oct.	Litho.	Imperf.		
Self-Adhesive				
71	A17	A multi	1.50	1.50

Sold for 5000m on day of issue.

UN Resolution on the Permanent
Neutrality of Turkmenistan, 5th
Anniv. — A18

UN emblem, "5," and flags of Turkmenistan
and resolution co-sponsors: a, Afghanistan. b,
Armenia. c, Azerbaijan. d, Bangladesh. e,
Belarus. f, Colombia. g, Czech Republic. h,
Egypt. i, France. j, Georgia. k, India. l, Indone-
sia. m, Iran. n, Kenya. o, Kyrgyzstan. p, Malay-
sia. q, Mauritius. r, Pakistan. s, Moldova. t,
Russia. u, Senegal. v, Tajikistan. w, Turkey. x,
Ukraine.

2000, Dec.	Litho.	Perf. 14		
72		Sheet of 24 + label	65.00	65.00
a.-x.	A18	3000m Any single	2.40	2.40

Trade Center   Flag and Arms
Building   A20
A19

2001, Apr. 24	Litho.	Imperf.		
Self-Adhesive				
73	A19	B multi	.75	.75
74	A20	U multi	1.75	1.75

No. 73 sold for 1,200m, No. 74 sold for
3,000m on day of issue.

Horses — A21

No. 75, horiz.: a, Perenli. b, Garader. c,
Pyyada. d, Tyllanur. e, Arkadas. f, Yanardag.
No. 76, 5000m, Yanardag, diff., horiz.
(denomination at LR). No. 77, 5000m,
Yanardag, diff., horiz. (denomination at UR).
No. 78: a, Bitarap. b, Yanardag, diff.

2001, Aug. 20	Litho.	Perf. 14½x14		
75	A21	3000m Sheet of 6,		
		#a-f	8.75	8.75
		Size: 116x90mm		
		Imperf		
76-77	A21	Set of 2	8.75	8.75
		Souvenir Sheet		
		Perf. 14x14½		
78	A21	5000m Sheet of 2,		
		#a-b	8.75	8.75

Items inscribed "Turkmenistan" that
were not authorized by Turkmenistan
postal officials but which have appeared
on the market include:
Sheets of 9 stamps with denominations of 50m depicting Kim Basinger,
Matt Damon, and Pope John Paul II.
Sheets of 9 stamps with denominations of 100m depicting Leading Per-
sonalities of the 20th Century.
Sheets of 6 stamps with denomina-
tions of 120m depicting Leonardo
DiCaprio, and Princess Diana.
Sheets of 8 stamps with denomina-
tions of 120m and one label depicting
scenes and people from the 20th Cen-
tury (3 different sheets).
Sheets of 9 stamps with denomina-
tions of 120m depicting Princess Diana,
Musical group V.I.P., Television show
"Xena, Warrior Princess," Elizabeth
Taylor, Bruce Lee, Jackie Chan, Tiger
Woods, Muhammad Ali, Monaco Grand
Prix race cars, Auto racer David
Coulthard, Soccer player David Beck-
ham, Euro 2000 European Football
Championships, Rugby players, Tennis
Stars of the Millennium, Sportsmen of
the Millennium, Elephants, Cats, Butter-
flies, and Pokémon.
Sheets of 2 stamps with denomina-
tions of 390m depicting Soccer players
from the 1998 World Cup (2 different
sheets depicting French and Japanese
players).
Souvenir sheets of 1 with denominations of 975m depicting the Mona Lisa,
Marilyn Monroe, and Lucille Ball.

A22

Independence, 10th Anniv. — A23

No. 79 — 500m coins with reverses showing: a, Building with domed roof, coin denomination at right. b, Building with domed roof and tower, coin denomination at left. c, Building with pointed, conical roof. d, Building with archway. e, Building with domed roof on cubic base. f, Statue.

No. 80 — Archaeological sites: a, Soltan Sanjar. b, Nusay. c, Gyz Gala. d, Urgenç. e, Anew. f, Köne Urgenç.

No. 81 — Items in National museum: a, Horn. b, 19th cent. carpet. c, Musical instrument. d, Statue of nude woman. e, Vase. f, 20th cent. decoration.

No. 82, horiz. — Hotels: a, Ahal. b, Gara Altyn. c, Demiryolçy. d, Altyn Suw. e, Köpetdag. f, Aziya.

No. 83 — Buildings: a, Altyn Asyryn Yasayys Jaylary. b, Bitaraplyk Binasy (Arch of Neutrality). c, Türkmendöwletätiyaçlandyrys. d, Random Tower. e, Türkmenbasy Bank. f, Altyn Asyr Söwda Merkezi (Trade Center Building).

No. 84 — Monuments to: a, Oguz Han. b, Seljuk Bay. c, Bayram Han. d, Soltan Sanjar. e, Gorkut Ata. f, Görogly Beg.

No. 85 — Monuments to: a, Sahyrlary Bayram Han. b, Sahyrlary Kemine. c, Sahyrlary Zelili. d, Sahyrlary Seydi. e, Sahyrlary Mollanepes. f, Sahyrlary Mätäji.

2001		**Litho.**		**Imperf.**	
79	A22	500m	Sheet of 6, #a-f	50.00	50.00
80	A23	1000m	Sheet of 6, #a-f	50.00	50.00
81	A23	1200m	Sheet of 6, #a-f	125.00	125.00
82	A23	1250m	Sheet of 6, #a-f	125.00	125.00
83	A23	1250m	Sheet of 6, #a-f	50.00	50.00
84	A23	3000m	Sheet of 6, #a-f	50.00	50.00
85	A23	3000m	Sheet of 6, #a-f	50.00	50.00
		Nos. 79-85 (7)		500.00	500.00

Issued: Nos. 79-80, 10/17; No. 81, 10/19; Nos. 82-83, 10/23; Nos. 84-85, 10/21.

Mohammed Ali Jinnah (1876-1948), First Governor General of Pakistan — A24

2001, Dec. 25		**Litho.**		**Perf. 13**
86	A24	500m multi	1.25	1.25

Birds — A25

No. 87, 3000m: a, Motacilla flava. b, Lanius isabellinus. c, Oenanthe oenanthe. d, Corvus monedula. e, Corvus cornix. f, Upupa pyrrhocorax.

No. 88, 3000m: a, Sylvia communis. b, Cuculus canorus. c, Sylvia curruca. d, Corvus pica. e, Corvus frugilegus. f, Corvus corax.

No. 89, 5000m, Anas crecca. No. 90, 5000m, Riparia riparia.

2002, Dec. 1		**Litho.**		**Perf. 14**
		Sheets of 6, #a-f		
87-88	A25	Set of 2	21.00	21.00
		Souvenir Sheets		
89-90	A25	Set of 2	6.50	6.50

Butterflies — A26

No. 91, 3000m, vert.: a, Vanessa indica. b, Cynthia cardui. c, Pararge aegeria. d, Pieris rapae. e, Lysandra bellargus. f, Anthocharis cardamines.

No. 92, 3000m, vert.: a, Pandoriana pandora. b, Chazara briseis. c, Aphantopus hyperantus. d, Iolana iolas. e, Pararge schakra. f, Maniola jurtina.

No. 93, 5000m, Hamearis lucina. No. 94, 5000m, Quercusia quercus.

2002, Dec. 1		**Sheets of 6, #a-f**		
91-92	A26	Set of 2	21.00	21.00
		Souvenir Sheets		
93-94	A26	Set of 2	6.50	6.50

Mosque — A27

2003, Feb.		**Litho.**		**Imperf.**
		Self-Adhesive		
95	A27	B multi	1.25	1.25

Independence and Peace Monument, Ashkhabad — A28

2003, July 25			**Self-Adhesive**	
96	A28	G multi	1.50	1.50

Building and Flags — A29

2004, Feb. 25			**Self-Adhesive**	
97	A29	B multi	1.25	1.25

Dog — A30

2004, Aug. 13			**Self-Adhesive**	
98	A30	A multi	1.75	1.75

Building — A31

2005		**Self-Adhesive**		**Perf. 11¼**
99	A31	M multi	1.25	1.25

Souvenir Sheet

Permanent Neutrality of Turkmenistan, 10th Anniv. — A32

No. 100: a, UN Secretary General Kofi Annan and Turkmenistan Pres. Saparmurad Niyazov. b, Sculpture on building, UN emblem.

2005, Dec. 1		**Litho.**		**Perf. 11½**
100	A32	5000m	Sheet of 2, #a-b	20.00 20.00

Souvenir Sheets

A33

A34

A35

Akhal-Teke Horses — A36

No. 101: a, Horse's head. b, Horse rearing up.

No. 102: a, Pony nursing. b, Horse walking left.

No. 103: a, Horse facing right. b, Horse facing left.

No. 104: a, Gray horse and mountain. b, Brown horse and mountain.

2005, Dec. 1				
101	A33	2500m	Sheet of 2, #a-b	5.75 5.75
102	A34	2500m	Sheet of 2, #a-b	5.75 5.75
103	A35	2500m	Sheet of 2, #a-b	5.75 5.75
104	A36	2500m	Sheet of 2, #a-b	5.75 5.75
		Nos. 101-104 (4)		23.00 23.00

Miniature Sheet

Ashgabat Architecture — A37

No. 105: a, 3000m, Building with dome, fountain at left. b, 3000m, Rukhiyet Palace (building with three green domes, automobiles). c, 3000m, Building with three golden domes and fountain. d, 3000m, Goktepe Mosque (green domes). e, 3000m, Mosque with golden domes. f, 3000m, Statue of Akhal-Teke horses. g, 3000m, Domed building with fence. h, 3000m, Central Bank and flags. i, 5000m, Neutrality Arch at night, vert. j, 5000m, Oil and Gas Ministry Building with flagpoles at right, vert. k, 5000m, President Hotel with flagpoles at left, vert. l, Independence Monument with statues at left and right, vert. Sizes: Nos. 105a-105h, 40x30mm; Nos. 105i-105l, 40x60mm.

2006		**Litho.**		**Perf. 13x12¾**
105	A37	Sheet of 12, #a-l, + label		21.00 21.00

Independence, 15th Anniv. — A38

2006		**Litho.**		**Imperf.**
		Self-Adhesive		
106	A38	multi	1.00	1.00

Miniature Sheets

Pres. Saparmurat Niyazov (1940-2006) — A39

Nos. 108 and 109 — Pres. Niyazov: a, On reviewing stand, tank in background (34x47mm). b, At airplane's door, waving (34x47mm). c, Walking past women in red costumes (34x24mm). d, Wearing suit, seated in chair (34x24mm). e, Lifting girl, helicopter in background (34x24mm). f, Standing with children in front of helicopter (34x24mm). g, Turning key on box on table (34x24mm). h, Waving at crowd (34x24mm). i, Walking from under canopy (34x47mm). j, Seated in front of microphones (34x24mm). k, Standing in farm field (50x24mm). l, Cutting ribbon (34x24mm). m, Standing on red carpet, holding bowl (34x47mm).

Litho. with Foil Application

2007   *Perf. 11½*
Stamps With Light Blue Panels
107 A39 A Sheet of 13, #a-m   32.50 32.50
Stamps With Green Panels
108 A39 A Sheet of 13, #a-m   32.50 32.50

Leopard — A40

2007   **Litho.**   *Rouletted 8*
Self-Adhesive
109 A40 A multi   2.00 2.00

TURKS & CAICOS ISLANDS

ˈtərks ənˌd ˈ kā-kəs ˈi-ləndz

LOCATION — A group of islands in the West Indies, at the southern extremity of the Bahamas
GOVT. — British colony; a dependency of Jamaica until 1959
AREA — 192 sq. mi.
POP. — 16,863 (1999 est.)
CAPITAL — Grand Turk

12 Pence = 1 Shilling
20 Shillings = 1 Pound
100 Cents = 1 US Dollar (1969)

> **Catalogue values for unused stamps in this country are for Never Hinged items, beginning with Scott 90.**

Dependency's Badge
A6   A7

		1900-04	**Engr.**	**Wmk. 2**	**Perf. 14**	
1	A6	½p green			3.00	4.50
2	A6	1p rose			4.00	.85
3	A6	2p black brown			1.10	1.40
4	A6	2½p gray blue ('04)			2.00	1.10
a.		2½p blue ('00)			11.50	17.50

5	A6	4p orange		4.25	8.00
6	A6	6p violet		2.75	7.50
7	A6	1sh purple brn		3.75	24.00

Wmk. 1

8	A7	2sh violet		50.00	80.00
9	A7	3sh brown lake		80.00	110.00
		Nos. 1-9 (9)		150.85	237.35

1905-08   **Wmk. 3**

10	A6	½p green		6.50	.25
11	A6	1p carmine		20.00	.55
12	A6	3p violet, yel ('08)		2.50	7.00
		Nos. 10-12 (3)		29.00	7.80

King Edward VII — A8

1909, Sept. 2   **Perf. 14**

13	A8	½p yellow green		.85	.45
14	A8	1p carmine		1.40	.45
15	A8	2p gray		6.50	1.60
16	A8	2½p ultra		8.00	4.25
17	A8	3p violet, yel		2.75	2.75
18	A8	4p red, yel		3.75	8.00
19	A8	6p violet		8.00	7.00
20	A8	1sh black, green		8.00	9.50
21	A8	2sh red, grn		45.00	70.00
22	A8	3sh black, red		47.50	45.00
		Nos. 13-22 (10)		131.75	149.00

Turk's-Head Cactus — A9

1910-11   **Wmk. 3**

23	A9	¼p claret		2.00	1.10
24	A9	¼p red ('11)		.70	.50

See Nos. 36, 44.

George V — A10

1913-16

25	A10	½p yellow green		.55	2.00
26	A10	1p carmine		1.10	2.50
27	A10	2p gray		2.50	4.00
28	A10	2½p ultra		2.50	3.50
29	A10	3p violet, yel		2.50	12.50
30	A10	4p scarlet, yel		1.10	11.00
31	A10	5p olive grn ('16)		7.50	25.00
32	A10	6p dull violet		2.75	4.00
33	A10	1sh orange		1.75	5.75
34	A10	2sh red, bl grn		18.00	42.00
a.		2sh red, grnsh white ('19)		30.00	30.00
b.		2sh red, emerald ('21)		55.00	80.00
35	A10	3sh black, red		17.50	30.00
		Nos. 25-35 (11)		57.75	142.25

Issued: 5p, 5/18/16; others, 4/1/13.
For overprints see Nos. MR1-MR13.

1921, Apr. 23   **Wmk. 4**

36	A9	¼p red		4.75	26.00
37	A10	½p green		3.50	6.50
38	A10	1p scarlet		1.10	6.25
39	A10	2p gray		1.10	21.00
40	A10	2½p ultra		2.00	8.50
41	A10	5p olive green		12.00	70.00
42	A10	6p dull violet		7.50	70.00
43	A10	1sh brown orange		13.00	48.00
		Nos. 36-43 (8)		44.95	256.25

A11

1922-26   Inscribed "Postage"

44	A9	¼p gray black ('26)		1.25	1.10
45	A11	½p green		5.50	4.50
46	A11	1p brown		.65	3.75
47	A11	1½p rose red ('25)		9.00	21.00
48	A11	2p gray		.65	7.00
49	A11	2½p violet, yel		.65	2.40
50	A11	3p ultra		.65	7.00
51	A11	4p red, yel		1.60	21.00
52	A11	5p yellow grn		1.25	30.00

53	A11	6p dull violet		.95	13.00
54	A11	1sh orange		1.10	25.00
55	A11	2sh red, green		2.75	12.50

Wmk. 3

56	A11	2sh red, green ('25)		35.00	110.00
57	A11	3sh black, red ('25)		7.00	40.00
		Nos. 44-57 (14)		68.00	298.25

Issued: #47, 56-57, 11/24; #44, 10/11; others, 11/20.

A12

Inscribed "Postage and Revenue"

1928, Mar. 1   **Wmk. 4**

60	A12	½p green		.95	.60
61	A12	1p brown		.95	.90
62	A12	1½p red		.95	4.50
63	A12	2p dk gray		.95	.60
64	A12	2½p vio, yel		.95	6.25
65	A12	3p ultra		.95	11.00
66	A12	6p brown vio		.95	9.25
67	A12	1sh brown org		4.50	9.25
68	A12	2sh red, grn		7.75	45.00
69	A12	5sh green, yel		13.50	45.00
70	A12	10sh violet, bl		62.50	125.00
		Nos. 60-70 (11)		94.90	257.35

Common Design Types pictured following the introduction.

Silver Jubilee Issue
Common Design Type

1935, May 6   **Perf. 11x12**

71	CD301	½p green & blk		.40	1.00
72	CD301	3p ultra & brn		4.00	4.00
73	CD301	6p ol grn & lt bl		2.00	5.50
74	CD301	1sh brn vio & ind		2.00	4.00
		Nos. 71-74 (4)		8.40	14.50
		Set, never hinged		15.00	

Coronation Issue
Common Design Type

1937, May 12   **Perf. 13½x14**

75	CD302	½p deep green		.25	.25
76	CD302	2p gray		.45	.45
77	CD302	3p brt ultra		.60	.45
		Nos. 75-77 (3)		1.30	1.15
		Set, never hinged		1.50	

Raking Salt — A13

Salt Industry — A14

1938-45   **Wmk. 4**   **Perf. 12½**

78	A13	¼p black		.25	.25
79	A13	½p green		2.40	.25
80	A13	1p brown		.45	.25
81	A13	1½p carmine		.45	.25
82	A13	2p gray		.70	.30
83	A13	2½p orange		5.00	1.10
84	A13	3p ultra		.30	.30
85	A13	6p rose violet		6.00	3.25
85A	A13	6p blk brn ('45)		.25	.25
86	A13	1sh bister		2.40	11.00
86A	A13	1sh dk ol grn ('45)		.25	.25
87	A14	2sh rose car		22.00	22.00
88	A14	5sh green		30.00	25.00
89	A14	10sh dp violet		10.00	8.50
		Nos. 78-89 (14)		80.45	72.95
		Set, never hinged		135.00	

> **Catalogue values for unused stamps in this section, from this point to the end of the section, are for Never Hinged items.**

Peace Issue
Common Design Type

1946, Nov. 4   **Engr.**   *Perf. 13½x14*

90	CD303	2p gray black		.25	.25
91	CD303	3p deep blue		.25	.25

Silver Wedding Issue
Common Design Types

1948, Sept. 13 Photo.   *Perf. 14x14½*

| 92 | CD304 | 1p red brown | | .25 | .25 |

Perf. 11½x11

Engr.; Name Typo.

| 93 | CD305 | 10sh purple | | 11.00 | 16.00 |

Dependency's Badge — A17

Flag and Merchant Ship — A18

Map of the Islands A19

Victoria and George VI A20

1948, Dec. 14   **Engr.**   *Perf. 12½*

94	A17	½p green		1.25	.25
95	A17	2p carmine		1.25	.25
96	A18	3p deep blue		1.25	.25
97	A19	6p violet		1.25	.30
98	A20	2sh ultra & blk		1.25	2.00
99	A20	5sh blue grn & blk		1.50	6.00
100	A20	10sh chocolate & blk		4.00	6.00
		Nos. 94-100 (7)		11.75	15.05

Cent. of political separation from the Bahamas.

UPU Issue
Common Design Types
Engr.; Name Typo. on 3p, 6p
Perf. 13½, 11x11½

1949, Oct. 10   **Wmk. 4**

101	CD306	2½p red orange		.25	1.50
102	CD307	3p indigo		1.90	1.25
103	CD308	6p chocolate		.30	1.00
104	CD309	1sh olive		.25	.35
		Nos. 101-104 (4)		2.70	4.10

Loading Bulk Salt — A21

Dependency's Badge — A22

Designs: 1p, Salt Cay. 1½p, Caicos mail. 2p, Grand Turk. 2½p, Sponge diving. 3p, South Creek. 4p, Map. 6p, Grand Turk Light. 1sh, Government House. 1sh6p, Cockburn Harbor. 2sh, Government offices. 5sh, Salt Loading.

1950, Aug. 2   Engr.   Perf. 12½

105	A21	½p deep green	.75	.40
106	A21	1p chocolate	.80	.75
107	A21	1½p carmine	1.00	.55
108	A21	2p red orange	1.00	.40
109	A21	2½p olive green	1.00	.50
110	A21	3p ultra	1.00	.40
111	A21	4p rose car & blk	3.75	.70
112	A21	6p ultra & blk	3.00	.50
113	A21	1sh bl gray & blk	2.50	.40
114	A21	1sh6p red & blk	15.00	3.25
115	A21	2sh ultra & emer	6.50	4.50
116	A21	5sh black & ultra	25.00	8.50
117	A22	10sh purple & blk	27.00	27.00
		Nos. 105-117 (13)	88.30	47.85

Coronation Issue
Common Design Type

1953, June 2   Perf. 13½x13

118	CD312	2p red orange & blk	.40	1.10

M. S. Kirksons A23

Design: 8p, Flamingos in flight.

1955, Feb. 1   Wmk. 4   Perf. 12½

119	A23	5p emerald & blk	1.00	1.00
120	A23	8p yellow brn & blk	3.00	.70

Queen Elizabeth II — A24

Bonefish A25

Pelican and Salinas A26

Designs: 2p, Red grouper. 2½p, Spiny lobster. 3p, Albacore. 4p, Muttonfish snapper. 5p, Permit. 6p, Conch. 8p, Flamingos. 1sh, Spanish mackerel. 1sh6p, Salt Cay. 2sh, Caicos sloop. 5sh, Cable office. 10sh, Dependency's badge.

Perf. 13½x14 (1p), 13½x13

1957-60   Engr.   Wmk. 314

121	A24	1p lil rose & dk bl	.25	.25
122	A25	1½p orange & slate	.25	.25
123	A25	2p ol & brn red	.25	.25
124	A25	2½p brt grn & car	.25	.25
125	A25	3p purple & blue	.25	.25
126	A25	4p blk & dp rose	1.25	.25
127	A25	5p brown & grn	1.25	.40
128	A25	6p ultra & car	1.90	.55
129	A25	8p black & ver	3.25	.25
130	A25	1sh blk & dk blue	1.25	.25
131	A25	1sh6p vio bl & dk brn	15.00	1.75
132	A25	2sh lt brn & vio bl	13.00	3.00
133	A25	5sh brt car & blk	7.00	2.00

Perf. 14

134	A26	10sh purple & blk	17.50	10.00

Perf. 14x14½
Photo.

135	A26	£1 dk red & brn	50.00	20.00
		Nos. 121-135 (15)	112.65	39.70

Issued: £1, 11/1/60; others, 11/25/57.

Map of Islands A27

1959, July 4   Wmk. 4   Photo.
Perf. 13½x14

136	A27	6p ol grn & salmon	.70	.70
137	A27	8p violet & salmon	.80	.40

Granting of a new constitution.

Freedom from Hunger Issue
Common Design Type
Perf. 14x14½

1963, June 4   Wmk. 314

138	CD314	8p carmine rose	.50	.25

Red Cross Centenary Issue
Common Design Type

1963, Sept. 2   Litho.   Perf. 13

139	CD315	2p black & red	.25	.25
140	CD315	8p ultra & red	.60	.50

Shakespeare Issue
Common Design Type

1964, Apr. 23   Photo.   Perf. 14x14½

141	CD316	8p green	.40	.25

ITU Issue
Common Design Type
Perf. 11x11½

1965, May 17   Litho.   Wmk. 314

142	CD317	1p ver & brown	.25	.25
143	CD317	2sh emer & lt blue	.50	.25

Intl. Cooperation Year Issue
Common Design Type

1965, Oct. 25   Wmk. 314   Perf. 14½

144	CD318	1p blue grn & claret	.25	.25
145	CD318	8p lt violet & green	.40	.25

Churchill Memorial Issue
Common Design Type

1966, Jan. 24   Photo.   Perf. 14
Design in Black, Gold and Carmine Rose

146	CD319	1p bright blue	.25	.25
147	CD319	2p green	.25	.25
148	CD319	8p brown	.35	.25
a.		Gold impression double	200.00	
149	CD319	1sh6p violet	.75	1.00
		Nos. 146-149 (4)	1.60	1.75

Royal Visit Issue
Common Design Type

1966, Feb. 4   Litho.   Perf. 11x12
Portraits in Black

150	CD320	8p violet blue	.40	.25
151	CD320	1sh6p dk car rose	.80	.30

Andrew Symmer Landing with Union Jack A28

Designs: 8p, Andrew Symmer, his signature, Royal Warrant and Union Jack. 1sh6p, New coat of arms, Royal Cypher and St. Edward's crown.

Perf. 13½

1966, Oct. 1   Unwmk.   Photo.

152	A28	1p dk blue & dp org	.25	.25
153	A28	8p dk blue, dl yel & car	.25	.25
154	A28	1sh6p multicolored	.25	.25
		Nos. 152-154 (3)	.75	.75

200th anniv. of the landing of Andrew Symmer, British agent, establishing the ties with Great Britain.

UNESCO Anniversary Issue
Common Design Type
Wmk. 314

1966, Dec. 1   Litho.   Perf. 14

155	CD323	1p "Education"	.25	.25
156	CD323	8p "Science"	.30	.25
157	CD323	1sh6p "Culture"	.50	.40
		Nos. 155-157 (3)	1.05	.90

Turk's-head Cactus — A29

Boat Building A30

Designs: 2p, Donkey cart. 3p, Sisal industry. 4p, Conch industry. 6p, Salt industry. 8p, Skin diving. 1sh, Fishing. 1sh6p, Water skiing. 2sh, Crawfish industry. 3sh, Map of Islands. 5sh, Fishing industry. 10sh, Coat of arms. £1, Queen Elizabeth II.

Perf. 14½x14, 14x14½

1967, Feb. 1   Photo.   Wmk. 314

158	A29	1p vio red & yel	.25	.25
159	A30	1½p choc & org yel	1.10	.25
160	A29	2p gray, yel & sl	.25	.25
161	A29	3p green & dk brn	.25	.25
162	A30	4p grnsh bl, blk & pink	2.50	.25
163	A29	6p blue & dk brn	1.75	.25
164	A29	8p aqua, dk bl & yel	.55	.25
165	A30	1sh grnsh bl & red brn	.25	.25
166	A29	1sh6p brt grnsh bl, yel & brn	.40	.40
167	A30	2sh multicolored	1.10	1.75
168	A30	3sh grnsh bl & mar	1.10	.50
169	A30	5sh sky bl, dk bl & yel	1.50	2.50
170	A30	10sh multicolored	2.75	3.50
171	A29	£1 dk car rose, sil & dk bl	4.00	10.00
		Nos. 158-171 (14)	17.75	20.65

See #181, 217-230. For surcharges see #182-195.

Turks Islands No. 1 A31

Designs: 6p, Turks Islands No. 2 and portrait of Queen Elizabeth on simulated stamp. 1sh, Turks Islands No. 3 (like 1p).

1967, May 1   Photo.   Perf. 14½

172	A31	1p lilac rose & blk	.25	.25
173	A31	6p gray & black	.25	.25
174	A31	1sh Prus blue & blk	.40	.25
		Nos. 172-174 (3)	.90	.75

Centenary of Turks Islands stamps.

Human Rights Flame A32

1968, Apr. 1   Perf. 14x14½

175	A32	1p lt green & multi	.25	.25
176	A32	8p lt blue & multi	.25	.25
177	A32	1sh6p multicolored	.25	.25
		Nos. 175-177 (3)	.75	.75

International Human Rights Year.

Martin Luther King, Jr. and Protest March of 1968 A33

1968, Oct. 1   Photo.   Wmk. 314

178	A33	2p dk blue, dk & lt brn	.25	.25
179	A33	8p dk car rose, dk & lt brn	.25	.25
180	A33	1sh6p dp vio, dk & lt brn	.25	.25
		Nos. 178-180 (3)	.75	.75

Martin Luther King, Jr. (1929-68), American civil rights leader.

Nos. 158-171 Surcharged

Designs as before and: ¼c, Coat of arms like 10sh.

Perf. 14x14½, 14½x14

1969, Sept. 8   Photo.   Wmk. 314

181	A30	¼c lt gray & multi	.25	.25
182	A29	1c on 1p multi	.25	.25
183	A29	2c on 2p multi	.25	.25
184	A29	3c on 3p multi	.25	.25
185	A30	4c on 4p multi	.25	.25
186	A29	5c on 6p multi	.25	.25
187	A29	7c on 8p multi	.25	.25
188	A30	8c on 1½p multi	.25	.25
189	A30	10c on 1sh multi	.25	.25
190	A30	15c on 1sh6p multi	.25	.25
191	A30	20c on 2sh multi	.30	.50
192	A30	30c on 3sh multi	.55	.65
193	A30	50c on 5sh multi	1.25	.95
194	A30	$1 on 10sh multi	2.50	2.25
195	A29	$2 on £1 multi	4.00	9.50
		Nos. 181-195 (15)	11.10	16.35

The surcharge is differently arranged on each denomination to fit the design; the old denomination is obliterated with a rectangle on the 8c and 15c.
See Nos. 217-230.

1969   Wmk. 314 Sideways

182a	A29	1c on 1p	.25	.25
183a	A29	2c on 2p	.25	.25
184a	A29	3c on 3p	.25	.50
186a	A29	5c on 6p	.25	.40
187a	A29	7c on 8p	.25	.25
190a	A29	15c on 1sh6p	.25	.30
195a	A29	$2 on £1	2.50	6.00
		Nos. 182a-195a (7)	4.00	7.95

Nativity with John the Baptist — A34

Designs from the Book of Hours of Eleanora, Duchess of Tuscany: 3c, 30c, Flight into Egypt.

Perf. 13x12½

1969, Oct. 20   Litho.   Wmk. 314

196	A34	1c plum & multi	.25	.25
197	A34	3c dk blue & multi	.25	.25
198	A34	15c olive & multi	.25	.25
199	A34	30c yellow brn & multi	.25	.25
		Nos. 196-199 (4)	1.00	1.00

Christmas.

Coat of Arms — A35

1970, Feb. 2　Litho.　Perf. 13x12½
200	A35	7c brown & multi	.25	.25
201	A35	35c violet blue & multi	.55	.40

New Constitution, inaugurated 6/16/69.
See No. 769.

Christ Bearing
the Cross, by
Dürer — A36

Albrecht Dürer Engravings: 7c, Christ on the
Cross. 50c, The Lamentation for Christ.

Perf. 13½x14
1970, Mar. 17　Engr.　Wmk. 314
202	A36	5c dp blue & blk	.25	.25
203	A36	7c vermilion & blk	.25	.25
204	A36	50c dk brown & multi	.50	1.00
		Nos. 202-204 (3)	1.00	1.50

Easter.

Dickens
and
"Oliver
Twist"
Scene
A37

Charles Dickens and Scene from: 3c, "A
Christmas Carol." 15c, "Pickwick Papers." 30c,
"The Old Curiosity Shop."

Litho. & Engr.
1970, June 17　　　Perf. 13½x13
205	A37	1c yel, red brn & blk	.25	.40
206	A37	3c sal pink, sl & blk	.25	.35
207	A37	15c salmon, bl & blk	.30	.25
208	A37	30c lt blue, ol & blk	.60	.40
		Nos. 205-208 (4)	1.40	1.40

Charles Dickens (1812-70), English novelist.

Red Cross Ambulance, 1870 — A38

5c, 30c, Red Cross ambulance, 1970.

1970, Aug. 4　Litho.　Perf. 13½x14
209	A38	1c orange & multi	.25	.25
210	A38	5c ocher & multi	.25	.25
211	A38	15c brt pink & multi	.25	.25
212	A38	30c multicolored	.50	.40
		Nos. 209-212 (4)	1.25	1.15

Centenary of British Red Cross Society.

Gen. George Monck, Duke of
Albemarle, and his Coat of
Arms — A39

Designs: 8c, 35c, Coats of arms of
Charles II and Queen Elizabeth II.

1970, Dec. 1　Litho.　Perf. 12½x13½
213	A39	1c multicolored	.25	.30
214	A39	8c multicolored	.30	.40
215	A39	10c multicolored	.30	.25
216	A39	35c multicolored	.75	.95
		Nos. 213-216 (4)	1.60	1.90

Tercentenary of the issue of Letters Patent
to the Six Lords Proprietors.

Types of 1967
Values in Cents and Dollars

Designs: 1c, Turk's-head cactus. 2c, Donkey cart. 3c, Sisal industry. 4c, Conch industry. 5c, Salt industry. 7c, Skin diving. 8c, Boat
building. 10c, Fishing. 15c, Water skiing. 20c,
Crawfish industry. 30c, Map of Islands. 50c,
Fishing industry. $1, Arms of Colony. $2,
Queen Elizabeth II.

Perf. 14x14½, 14½x14
1971, Feb. 2　Photo.　Wmk. 314
217	A29	1c violet, red & yel	.25	.25
218	A29	2c gray, yel & slate	.25	.25
219	A29	3c green & dk brn	.25	.25
220	A30	4c grnsh bl, blk & pink	1.25	.25
221	A29	5c blue & dk brown	.40	.25
222	A29	7c aqua, dk bl & yel	.30	.25
223	A30	8c choc & org yel	1.25	.25
224	A30	10c grnsh bl & red brn	.75	.25
225	A29	15c brt grnsh bl, yel & brn	1.00	.65
226	A30	20c multicolored	1.50	2.50
227	A30	30c grnsh bl & mar	2.75	1.25
228	A30	50c sky bl, dk bl & yel	3.50	2.00
229	A30	$1 blue & multi	3.00	3.00
230	A29	$2 dk car rose, sil & dk blue	4.00	8.00
		Nos. 217-230 (14)	20.45	19.40

The ¼c, released with this set is a shade of
No. 181, the background being a greenish,
slightly darker gray.

Queen
Conch
and
Emblem
A40

Tourist publicity (Sun, Sea and Sand
Emblem and): 1c, Seahorse, vert. 15c, American oyster catcher. 30c, Blue Marlin.

Perf. 14½x14, 14x14½
1971, May 2　Litho.　Wmk. 314
232	A40	1c multicolored	.35	.25
233	A40	3c multicolored	.35	.25
234	A40	15c multicolored	.55	.30
235	A40	30c multicolored	1.10	.55
		Nos. 232-235 (4)	2.35	1.35

Pirate
Sloop
A41

Designs: 3c, Pirates burying treasure. 15c,
Marooned pirate. 30c, Buccaneers.

1971, July 17　　　Perf. 14½x14
236	A41	2c multicolored	.25	.25
237	A41	3c multicolored	.25	.25
238	A41	15c multicolored	.70	.50
239	A41	30c multicolored	1.40	1.00
		Nos. 236-239 (4)	2.60	2.00

A42

Adoration of the
Virgin and Child,
from Wilton
Diptych, French
School,
c. 1395 — A43

1971, Oct. 12　Litho.　Perf. 14x13½
240	A42	2c dull brn & multi	.25	.25
241	A43	2c dull brn & multi	.25	.25
242	A42	8c green & multi	.25	.25
243	A43	8c green & multi	.25	.25
244	A42	15c dk blue gray & multi	.25	.25
245	A43	15c dk blue gray & multi	.25	.25
		Nos. 240-245 (6)	1.50	1.50

Christmas.

Rocket Launch, Cape
Canaveral — A44

10c, Space capsule in orbit around earth.
15c, Map of Turks & Caicos Islands &
splashdown. 20c, Distinguished Service
Medal, vert.

1972, Feb. 21　　　Perf. 13½
246	A44	5c multicolored	.25	.25
247	A44	10c multicolored	.25	.25
248	A44	15c lt green & multi	.25	.25
249	A44	20c blue & multi	.25	.25
		Nos. 246-249 (4)	1.00	1.00

First orbital flight by US astronaut Lt. Col.
John H. Glenn, Jr., and splashdown off Turks
and Caicos Islands, 10th anniversary.

The Three Crosses, by
Rembrandt — A45

Details from Etchings by Rembrandt: 2c,
Christ Before Pilate, vert. 30c, Descent from
the Cross, vert.

1972, Mar. 17　Perf. 14x13½, 13½x14
250	A45	2c lilac & black	.25	.25
251	A45	15c pink & black	.25	.25
252	A45	30c yellow & black	.30	.25
		Nos. 250-252 (3)	.80	.75

Easter.

Richard Grenville and
"Revenge" — A46

Discoverers and explorers of the Americas:
¼c, Christopher Columbus, Niña, Pinta and
Santa Maria, vert. 10c, Capt. John Smith and
three-master, vert. 30c, Juan Ponce de León
and three-master.

1972, July 4
253	A46	¼c multicolored	.25	.75
254	A46	8c multicolored	1.00	.25
255	A46	10c multicolored	1.00	.25
256	A46	30c multicolored	2.00	.90
		Nos. 253-256 (4)	4.25	2.15

Silver Wedding Issue
Common Design Type

Design: Queen Elizabeth II, Prince Philip,
turk's-head cactus and spiny lobster.

Perf. 14x14½
1972, Nov. 20　Photo.　Wmk. 314
257	CD324	10c ultra & multi	.25	.25
258	CD324	20c multicolored	.25	.25

Treasure Hunting,
c. 1700 — A47

Designs: 5c, Replica of silver bank medallion, 1687, obverse. 10c, Same, reverse. 30c,
Scuba diver, 1973.

Perf. 14x14½
1973, Jan. 18　Litho.　Wmk. 314
259	A47	3c Prus blue & multi	.25	.25
260	A47	5c plum, silver & blk	.25	.25
261	A47	10c brt rose, silver & blk	.25	.25
262	A47	30c violet blue & multi	.50	.50
a.		Souvenir sheet of 4, #259-262	2.00	2.25
		Nos. 259-262 (4)	1.25	1.25

Treasure hunting.

Arms of Jamaica, Turks and Caicos
Islands — A48

1973, Apr. 16　Litho.　Perf. 13½x14
263	A48	15c buff & multi	.30	.25
264	A48	35c lt green & multi	.75	.25

Centenary of annexation to Jamaica.

Sooty Tern — A49

Birds: 1c, Magnificent frigate bird. 2c, Noddy
tern. 3c, Blue gray gnatcatcher. 4c, Little blue
heron. 5c, Catbird. 7c, Black-whiskered vireo.
8c, Osprey. 10c, Flamingo. 15c, Brown pelican. 20c, Parula warbler. 30c, Northern mockingbird. 50c, Ruby-throated hummingbird. $1,
Bahama bananaquit. $2, Cedar waxwing. $5,
Painted bunting.

Wmk. 314 Sideways
1973, Aug. 1　Litho.　Perf. 14
265	A49	¼c yellow & multi	.25	.40
266	A49	1c pink & multi	.25	.60
267	A49	2c orange & multi	.25	.60
268	A49	3c lilac rose & multi	.55	.50
269	A49	4c lt blue & multi	.25	1.50
270	A49	5c lt green & multi	.40	.30
271	A49	7c salmon & multi	5.50	.30
272	A49	8c blue & multi	6.25	3.25
273	A49	10c brt blue & multi	.65	1.25
274	A49	15c tan & multi	3.00	.50
275	A49	20c brt yel & multi	2.00	1.25
276	A49	30c yellow & multi	3.50	1.00
277	A49	50c yellow & multi	3.50	3.75
278	A49	$1 blue & multi	4.00	4.00
279	A49	$2 gray & multi	5.00	7.00
		Nos. 265-279 (15)	35.35	26.20

1974-75　　　Wmk. 314 Upright
266a	A49	1c pink & multi ('75)	.60	2.50
267a	A49	2c orange & multi	1.25	1.60
268a	A49	3c lil rose & multi ('75)	2.00	2.50
275a	A49	20c brt yel & multi ('75)	2.25	4.00
		Nos. 266a-275a (4)	6.10	10.60

1976-77   Wmk. 373

265a	A49	¼c yellow & multi ('77)	.25	.25
266b	A49	1c pink & multi ('77)	.25	.25
267b	A49	2c orange & multi ('77)	.25	.25
268b	A49	3c lilac rose & multi ('77)	.25	.25
269a	A49	4c ol bl & multi ('77)	.25	.25
270a	A49	5c lt grn & multi ('77)	.25	.25
273a	A49	10c brt bl & multi ('77)	.25	.25
274a	A49	15c tan & multi ('77)	.40	.65
275b	A49	20c brt yel & multi ('77)	.50	.80
276a	A49	30c yel & multi ('77)	.75	1.25
277a	A49	50c yel & multi ('77)	1.25	2.00
278a	A40	$1 blue & multi ('77)	2.50	4.00
279b	A40	$2 gray & multi ('77)	5.25	8.00
279A	A49	$5 yel grn & multi	8.50	14.00
		Nos. 265a-279A (14)	20.90	32.45

Bermuda Sloop — A50

Old Sailing Ships: 5c, HMS Blanche. 8c, US privateer Grand Turk and packet Hinchinbrooke. 10c, HMS Endymion. 15c, RMS Medina. 20c, HMS Daring.

1973, July 19   Litho.   Perf. 13½

280	A50	2c multicolored	.25	1.00
281	A50	5c multicolored	.25	.25
282	A50	8c multicolored	.25	.75
283	A50	10c multicolored	.25	.25
284	A50	15c multicolored	.25	.35
285	A50	20c multicolored	.40	1.00
a.		Souvenir sheet of 6, #280-285	2.50	3.75
		Nos. 280-285 (6)	1.65	3.60

Princess Anne's Wedding Issue
Common Design Type

1973, Nov. 14   Wmk. 314   Perf. 14

286	CD325	12c blue grn & multi	.25	.25
287	CD325	18c slate & multi	.25	.25
		Nos. 286-287 (2)	.50	.50

Lucayan Stool A51

Lucayan artifacts: 10c, Broken wood bowl. 12c, Greenstone axe. 18c, Wood bowl. 35c, Animal head, fragment of stool.

1974, July 17   Litho.   Perf. 14½

288	A51	6c brt rose & multi	.25	.25
289	A51	10c ol grn & multi	.25	.25
290	A51	12c brt lil & multi	.25	.25
291	A51	18c turq & multi	.25	.25
292	A51	35c buff & multi	.25	.25
a.		Souvenir sheet of 5, #288-292	1.75	1.75
		Nos. 288-292 (5)	1.25	1.25

Carvings made by Lucayan Indians, first inhabitants of the islands.

Grand Turk G.P.O. A52

UPU Emblem and: 12c, Map of Turks and Caicos Islands and local mail sloop. 18c, "United Service" (globe and "UPU"). 55c, Design symbolic of the Islands joining the UPU in 1881.

1974, Oct. 9   Wmk. 314   Perf. 14

293	A52	4c yellow & multi	.25	.25
294	A52	12c blue & multi	.25	.25
295	A52	18c violet & multi	.25	.25
296	A52	55c lt blue & multi	.35	.35
		Nos. 293-296 (4)	1.10	1.10

Centenary of Universal Postal Union.

"His Finest Hour" A53

12c, Churchill and Franklin D. Roosevelt.

1974, Nov. 30   Wmk. 373

297	A53	12c multicolored	.25	.25
298	A53	18c multicolored	.25	.25
a.		Souvenir sheet of 2, #297-298	.70	.70

Sir Winston Churchill (1874-1965).

Spanish Captain, c. 1492 — A54

Uniforms: 20c, Officer, Royal Artillery, 1783. 25c, Officer, 67th Foot, 1798. 35c, Private, First West India Regiment, 1833.

1975, Mar. 26   Wmk. 314   Perf. 14½

299	A54	5c blue & multi	.25	.25
300	A54	20c blue & multi	.25	.25
301	A54	25c blue & multi	.35	.25
302	A54	35c blue & multi	.50	.50
a.		Souvenir sheet of 4, #299-302	1.50	1.60
		Nos. 299-302 (4)	1.35	1.25

Old Windmill, Salt Cay — A55

Salt industry: 10c, Pink salt pans, horiz. 20c, Salt raking at Salt Cay, horiz. 25c, Unprocessed salt ready for shipment.

1975, Oct. 16   Litho.   Wmk. 373

303	A55	6c violet & multi	.25	.25
304	A55	10c lt brown & multi	.25	.25
305	A55	20c red & multi	.35	.25
306	A55	25c magenta & multi	.45	.35
		Nos. 303-306 (4)	1.30	1.10

Star Coral A56

1975, Dec. 4   Litho.   Wmk. 373

307	A56	6c shown	.25	.25
308	A56	10c Elkhorn coral	.25	.25
309	A56	20c Brain coral	.70	.25
310	A56	25c Staghorn coral	.75	.25
		Nos. 307-310 (4)	1.95	1.00

Schooner A57

American Bicentennial: 20c, Ship of the line. 25c, Frigate Grand Turk. 55c, Ketch.

1976, May 28   Perf. 14x13½

311	A57	6c orange & multi	.25	.25
312	A57	20c violet blue & multi	.35	.25
313	A57	25c brown & multi	.45	.35
314	A57	55c multicolored	.55	.80
a.		Souvenir sheet of 4, #311-314	2.00	4.00
		Nos. 311-314 (4)	1.60	1.65

Turks and Caicos Islands No. 151 A58

25c, Turks and Caicos Islands No. 150.

1976, July 14   Wmk. 373   Perf. 14½

315	A58	20c carmine & multi	.50	.45
316	A58	25c violet blue & multi	.60	.55

Visit of Queen Elizabeth II and Prince Philip to the Caribbean, 10th anniversary.

Virgin and Child, by Carlo Dolci — A59

Christmas: 10c, Virgin and Child with St. John, by Botticelli. 20c, Adoration of the Kings, from Retable by the Master of Paradise. 25c, Adoration of the Kings, illuminated page, French, 15th century.

1976, Nov. 10   Litho.   Perf. 14x13½

317	A59	6c turq grn & multi	.25	.25
318	A59	10c orange & multi	.25	.25
319	A59	20c red lilac & multi	.25	.25
320	A59	25c ol yel & multi	.25	.25
		Nos. 317-320 (4)	1.00	1.00

Queen with Regalia — A60

Designs: 6c, Queen presenting Order of British Empire to E. T. Wood, Grand Turk, 1966. 55c, Royal family on balcony of Buckingham Palace. $5, Portrait of Queen from photograph taken during her 1966 visit to Grand Turk.

1977   Litho.   Perf. 14x13½

321	A60	6c multicolored	.25	.25
322	A60	25c multicolored	.25	.25
323	A60	55c multicolored	.30	.25
		Nos. 321-323 (3)	.80	.75

Souvenir Sheet
Perf. 14

324	A60	$5 multicolored	2.50	2.50

25th anniv. of the reign of Elizabeth II. Nos. 322 and 323 were also issued in booklet panes of 2.
Issued: #321-323, Feb. 7; #324, Dec. 6.

Friendship 7 Capsule — A61

Designs: 3c, Lunar rover, vert. 6c, Tracking Station on Grand Turk. 20c, Moon landing

---

craft, vert. 25c, Col. Glenn's rocket leaving launching pad, vert. 50c, Telstar 1 satellite.

Wmk. 373

1977, June 20   Litho.   Perf. 13½

325	A61	1c multicolored	.25	.25
326	A61	3c multicolored	.25	.25
327	A61	6c multicolored	.25	.25
328	A61	20c multicolored	.25	.25
329	A61	25c multicolored	.25	.25
330	A61	50c multicolored	.50	.50
		Nos. 325-330 (6)	1.75	1.75

US Tracking Station on Grand Turk, 25th anniversary.

Adoration of the Kings, 1634 by Rubens — A63

Rubens Paintings: ¼c, Flight into Egypt. 1c, Adoration of the Kings, 1624. 6c, Madonna with Garland. 20c, $1, Virgin and Child Adored by Angels. $2, Adoration of the Kings, 1618.

1977, Dec. 23

331	A63	¼c multicolored	.25	.25
332	A63	½c multicolored	.25	.25
333	A63	1c multicolored	.25	.25
334	A63	6c multicolored	.25	.25
335	A63	20c multicolored	.25	.25
336	A63	$2 multicolored	1.25	1.25
		Nos. 331-336 (6)	2.50	2.50

Souvenir Sheet

337	A63	$1 multicolored	1.50	1.60

Christmas and 400th anniversary of Peter Paul Rubens (1577-1640).

Map of Turks Island Passage A64

Designs: 20c, Grand Turk lighthouse and sailboat (LUG cargo vessel). 25c, Deepsea fishing yacht. 55c, S.S. Jamaica Planter.

Wmk. 373, Unwmkd.

1978, Feb. 2   Litho.   Perf. 13½

338	A64	6c multicolored	.25	.30
339	A64	20c multicolored	.40	.40
340	A64	25c multicolored	.40	.50
341	A64	55c multicolored	1.25	1.25
a.		Souv. sheet of 4, #338-341, unwmkd.	2.50	2.75
		Nos. 338-341 (4)	2.30	2.45

Turks Island Passage, a major Caribbean shipping route.
No. 341a exists watermarked. Value $50.

Queen Victoria in Coronation Regalia — A65

British Monarchs in Coronation Regalia: 10c, Edward VII. 25c, George V. $2, George VI. $2.50, Elizabeth II.

1978, June 2   Litho.   Perf. 14

342	A65	6c multicolored	.25	.25
343	A65	10c multicolored	.25	.25
344	A65	25c multicolored	.25	.25
345	A65	$2 multicolored	.65	.75
		Nos. 342-345 (4)	1.40	1.50

Souvenir Sheet

346	A65	$2.50 multicolored	1.50	1.50

25th anniversary of coronation of Queen Elizabeth II. Nos. 342-345 also issued in sheets of 3 plus label, perf. 12.

Wilbur Wright and Flyer 3
A66

Aviation Progress: 6c, Cessna 337 and Wright brothers. 10c, Southeast Airlines' Electra and Orville Wright. 15c, C47 cargo plane on South Caicos runway. 35c, Norman-Britten Islander at Grand Turk airport. $1, Orville Wright and Flyer, 1902. $2, Wilbur Wright and Flyer.

1978, June 29   **Litho.**   **Perf. 14½**

347	A66	1c multicolored	.25	.25
348	A66	6c multicolored	.25	.25
349	A66	10c multicolored	.25	.25
350	A66	15c multicolored	.25	.25
351	A66	35c multicolored	.50	.30
352	A66	$2 multicolored	1.60	1.90
		Nos. 347-352 (6)	3.10	3.20

Souvenir Sheet

353	A66	$1 multicolored	1.25	1.60

Coronation of Queen Elizabeth II, 25th Anniv. — A67

Designs: 15c, Ampulla and anointing spoon. 25c, St. Edward's crown. $2 Queen Elizabeth II

Imperf. x Roulette 5

1978, July 24   **Litho.**

Self-adhesive

354	Souvenir booklet		3.75
a.	A67 Bklt. pane of 3, 15c, 25c, $2		2.40
b.	15c value from #354a		.25
c.	25c value from #354a		.25
d.	$2 value from #354a		1.90
e.	A67 Bklt. pane, 3 each, 15c, 25c		1.35

No. 354 contains #354a-354b printed on peelable paper backing with music and text of hymns.

11th Commonwealth Games, Edmonton, Canada, Aug. 3-12 — A68

1978, Aug. 3   **Litho.**   **Perf. 15**

355	A68	6c shown	.25	.25
356	A68	20c Weight lifting	.25	.25
357	A68	55c Boxing	.45	.45
358	A68	$2 Bicycling	.80	1.25
		Nos. 355-358 (4)	1.75	2.20

Souvenir Sheet

359	A68	$1 Sprinting	1.40	1.50

Fish
A69

1c, Indigo hamlet. 2c, Tobacco fish. 3c, Passing Jack. 4c, Porkfish. 5c, Spanish grunt. 7c, Yellowtail snapper. 8c, Foureye butterlyfish. 10c, Yellow fin grouper. 15c, Beau Gregory. 20c, Queen angelfish. 30c, Hogfish. 50c, Fairy Basslet. $1, Clown wrasse. $2, Stoplight parrotfish. $5, Queen triggerfish.

No Year Imprint Below Design

1978-79   **Litho.**   **Perf. 14¼**

360	A69	1c multi	.25	.25
361	A69	2c multi	.60	.80
362	A69	3c multi	.40	.25
363	A69	4c multi	.60	.80
364	A69	5c multi	.40	.30

365	A69	7c multi	.90	1.50
366	A69	8c multi	.90	.25
367	A69	10c multi	.40	.25
368	A69	15c multi	1.00	.30
369	A69	20c multi	.80	1.00
370	A69	30c multi	1.50	.60
371	A69	50c multi	1.00	1.00
372	A69	$1 multi	1.90	1.90
373	A69	$2 multi	2.50	4.25
374	A69	$5 multi	4.50	6.00
		Nos. 360-374 (15)	17.65	19.45

Issue dates: 1c, 3c, 5c, 10c, 15c, 20c, Nov. 17, 1978; others Feb. 6, 1979.

1981, Dec. 15   **Perf. 12½x12**

"1981" Imprint Below Design

360a	A69	1c multicolored	2.00	2.25
364a	A69	5c multicolored	2.25	2.75
367a	A69	10c multicolored	2.25	2.75
369a	A69	20c multicolored	2.25	2.50
371a	A69	50c multicolored	1.25	1.00
372a	A69	$1 multicolored	.80	1.25
373a	A69	$2 multicolored	4.50	5.00
374a	A69	$5 multicolored	8.00	9.00
		Nos. 360a-374a (8)	23.30	26.50

1983, Jan. 25   **Perf. 14¼x12**

"1983" Imprint Below Design

368b	A69	15c multicolored	1.50	1.00
369b	A69	20c multicolored	2.00	1.25
372b	A69	$1 multicolored	3.00	3.00
373b	A69	$2 multicolored	4.25	4.25
374b	A69	$5 multicolored	4.50	9.00
		Nos. 368b-374b (5)	15.25	18.50

Virgin with the Goldfinch, by Dürer — A70

Dürer Paintings: 20c, Virgin and Child with St. Anne. 35c, Nativity, horiz. $1, Adoration of the Kings, horiz. $2, Praying Hands.

1978, Dec. 11   **Litho.**   **Perf. 14**

375	A70	6c multicolored	.25	.25
376	A70	20c multicolored	.25	.25
377	A70	35c multicolored	.35	.25
378	A70	$2 multicolored	1.25	1.75
		Nos. 375-378 (4)	2.10	2.50

Souvenir Sheet

379	A70	$1 multicolored	1.75	2.75

Christmas and 450th death anniversary of Albrecht Dürer (1471-1528), German painter.

Ospreys
A71

Endangered Species: 20c, Green turtle. 25c, Queen conch. 55c, Rough-toothed dolphin. $1, Humpback whale. $2, Iguana.

1979, May 17   **Litho.**   **Perf. 14**

380	A71	6c multicolored	.75	.25
381	A71	20c multicolored	.65	.25
382	A71	25c multicolored	.75	.50
383	A71	55c multicolored	2.00	1.20
384	A71	$1 multicolored	4.00	3.00
		Nos. 380-384 (5)	8.15	5.20

Souvenir Sheet

385	A71	$2 multicolored	4.50	5.50

The Beloved, by Dante Gabriel Rossetti A72

Paintings and IYC Emblem: 25c, Tahitian Girl, by Paul Gauguin. 55c, Calmady Children, by Sir Thomas Lawrence. $1, Mother and Daughter (detail), by Gauguin. $2, Marchesa Elena Grimaldi, by Van Dyck.

1979, July 2   **Litho.**   **Perf. 14**

386	A72	6c multicolored	.25	.25
387	A72	25c multicolored	.25	.25
388	A72	55c multicolored	.35	.35
389	A72	$1 multicolored	.55	.50
		Nos. 386-389 (4)	1.40	1.35

Souvenir Sheet

390	A72	$2 multicolored	.80	1.50

International Year of the Child.

Stampless Cover and "Medina" — A73

Designs: 20c, Map of Islands and Rowland Hill. 45c, Stamped envelope and "Orinoco." 75c, Paddlewheeler "Shannon" and letter. $1, Royal Packet "Trent," map of Islands. $2, New and old seals.

1979, Sep. 10   **Litho.**   **Perf. 14**

391	A73	6c multicolored	.25	.25
392	A73	20c multicolored	.25	.25
393	A73	45c multicolored	.25	.25
394	A73	75c multicolored	.30	.30
395	A73	$1 multicolored	.50	.50

Perf. 12

396	A73	$2 multicolored ('80)	3.25	4.00
a.		Souv. sheet of 1, perf. 14 ('79)	1.00	1.50
		Nos. 391-396 (6)	4.80	5.55

Nos. 391-395 were issued in sheets of 40, and in sheets of 5 stamps plus label, in changed colors, perf. 12.

No. 396 issued May 6, 1980 in sheet of 5 plus label picturing signal flags and map.

No. 396a Overprinted
Souvenir Sheet

1979, Sept. 10   **Litho.**   **Perf. 14**

397	A73	$2 multicolored	1.00	1.50

Brasiliana 79 Intl. Philatelic Exhibition, Rio de Janeiro, Sept. 15-23.

Cuneiform Script — A74

Designs: 5c, Egyptian papyrus; Chinese writing. 15c, Greek runner; Roman post horse; Roman ship. 25c, Pigeon post; railway post; steamship postal packet. 40c, Balloon post; first airmail plane; supersonic airmail jet. $1, Original stamp press (3 designs each of 5c, 15c, 25c, 40c).

Imperf. x Roulette 5, Imperf. ($1)

1979, Sept. 27   **Litho.**

Self-adhesive

398	Souvenir booklet		6.00
a.	A74 Bklt. pane of 1 ($1)		
b.	A74 Bklt. pane, 3 each, 5c, 15c		
c.	A74 Bklt. pane, 3 each 25c, 40c		

Sir Rowland Hill (1795-1879), originator of penny postage. No. 398 contains 3 booklet panes on peelable paper backing with descriptions of stamp designs.

International Year of the Child — A74a

Designs: Aquatic scenes — ¼c, Pluto and starfish. ½c, Minnie Mouse. 1c, Mickey Mouse skin-diving. 2c, Goofy riding turtle. 3c, Donald and dolphin. 4c, Mickey Mouse and fish. 5c, Goofy surfing. 25c, Pluto and lobster. $1, Daisy Duck waterskiing.
$1.50, Goofy.

1979, Nov. 2   **Litho.**   **Perf. 11**

399	A74a	¼c multicolored	.25	.25
400	A74a	½c multicolored	.25	.25
401	A74a	1c multicolored	.25	.25
402	A74a	2c multicolored	.25	.25
403	A74a	3c multicolored	.25	.25
404	A74a	4c multicolored	.25	.25
405	A74a	5c multicolored	.25	.25
406	A74a	25c multicolored	.45	.25
407	A74a	$1 multicolored	1.25	2.50
		Nos. 399-407 (9)	3.45	4.50

Souvenir Sheet

Perf. 13½x14

408	A74a	$1.50 multicolored	1.75	1.80

St. Nicholas, Icon, 17th Century — A75

Icons or Illuminations: 3c, Emperor Otto II, 10th century. 6c, St. John, Book of Lindisfarne. 15c, Christ and angels. 20c, Christ attended by angels, Book of Kells, 9th century. 25c, St. John the Evangelist. 65c, Christ enthroned, 17th century. $1, St. John, 8th century. $2, St. Matthew, Book of Lindisfarne.

1979, Nov. 26

409	A75	1c multicolored	.25	.25
410	A75	3c multicolored	.25	.25
411	A75	6c multicolored	.25	.25
412	A75	15c multicolored	.25	.25
413	A75	20c multicolored	.25	.25
414	A75	25c multicolored	.25	.25
415	A75	65c multicolored	.25	.25
416	A75	$1 multicolored	.25	.25
		Nos. 409-416 (8)	2.00	2.00

Souvenir Sheet

417	A75	$2 multicolored	1.00	1.50

Christina's World, by Andrew Wyeth — A76

Art Treasures: 10c, Ivory leopards, Benin, 19th century. 20c, The Kiss, by Gustav Klimt, vert. 25c, Portrait of a Lady, by Rogier van der Weyden, vert. 80c, Sumerian bull's head harp, 2600 B.C., vert. $1, The Wave, by Hokusai. $2, Holy Family, by Rembrandt, vert.

1979, Dec. 19   **Litho.**   **Perf. 13½**

418	A76	6c multicolored	.25	.25
419	A76	10c multicolored	.25	.25
420	A76	20c multicolored	.25	.25
421	A76	25c multicolored	.25	.25

422	A76	80c multicolored	.25	.30
423	A76	$1 multicolored	.30	.50
		Nos. 418-423 (6)	1.55	1.80

Souvenir Sheet

| 424 | A76 | $2 multicolored | 1.40 | 1.50 |

Pied-billed Grebe — A77

25c, Ovenbirds. 35c, Marsh hawks. 55c, Yellow-bellied sapsucker. $1, Blue-winged teals. $2, Glossy ibis.

1980, Feb. 20   Litho.   Perf. 14

425	A77	20c shown	.75	.55
426	A77	25c multicolored	.90	.55
427	A77	35c multicolored	1.25	.65
428	A77	55c multicolored	1.75	.65
429	A77	$1 multicolored	2.50	3.00
		Nos. 425-429 (5)	7.15	5.40

Souvenir Sheet

| 430 | A77 | $2 multicolored | 3.50 | 3.50 |

Stamp Under Magnifier, Perforation Gauge, London 1980 Emblem A78

40c, Stamp in tongs, gauge. $2, Exhibition Hall.

1980, May 6   Litho.   Perf. 14x14½

| 431 | A78 | 25c shown | .25 | .25 |
| 432 | A78 | 40c multicolored | .25 | .25 |

Souvenir Sheet

| 433 | A78 | $2 multicolored | 1.00 | 1.10 |

London 1980 International Stamp Exhibition, May 6-14.

Trumpet Triton A79

1980, June 26   Litho.   Perf. 14

434	A79	15c shown	.25	.25
435	A79	20c Measled cowry	.25	.25
436	A79	30c True tulip	.25	.40
437	A79	45c Lion's paw	.50	.60
438	A79	55c Sunrise tellin	.60	.75
439	A79	70c Crown cone	.70	1.00
		Nos. 434-439 (6)	2.55	3.25

Queen Mother Elizabeth, 80th Birthday — A80

1980, Aug. 4   Litho.   Perf. 14

| 440 | A80 | 80c multicolored | .60 | 1.40 |

Souvenir Sheet
Perf. 12

| 441 | A80 | $1.50 multicolored | 1.20 | 2.00 |

Pinocchio — A81

Christmas: Scenes from Walt Disney's Pinocchio.

1980, Sept. 25   Perf. 11

442	A81	¼c multicolored	.25	.25
443	A81	½c multicolored	.25	.25
444	A81	1c multicolored	.25	.25
445	A81	2c multicolored	.25	.25
446	A81	3c multicolored	.25	.25
447	A81	4c multicolored	.25	.25
448	A81	5c multicolored	.25	.25
449	A81	75c multicolored	1.00	.90
450	A81	$1 multicolored	1.25	1.00
		Nos. 442-450 (9)	4.00	3.65

Souvenir Sheet

| 451 | A81 | $2 multi, vert. | 3.50 | 3.50 |

Medical Examination, Lions — A82

15c, Scholarships, Kiwanis. 45c, Education, Soroptimists. $1, Lobster boat, Rotary. $2, Funds for schools, Rotary.

1980, Oct. 8   Litho.   Perf. 14

452	A82	10c shown	.25	.25
453	A82	15c multicolored	.25	.25
454	A82	45c multicolored	.45	.35
455	A82	$1 multicolored	.75	.80
		Nos. 452-455 (4)	1.70	1.65

Souvenir Sheet

| 456 | A82 | $2 multicolored | 1.75 | 2.25 |

Lions, Rotary, Kiwanis and Soroptimists service organizations; 75th anniv. of Rotary Intl.

Martin Luther King, Jr. (1929-08) — A83

Human Rights Leaders: 30c, John F. Kennedy. 45c, Roberto Clemente (1934-72), baseball player. 70c, Frank Worrel (1927-67), cricket player. $1, Harriet Tubman (1823-1913), born slave, helped others escape to freedom. $2, Marcus Garvey (1887-1940), Jamaican black nationalist leader.

1980, Dec. 22   Litho.   Perf. 14

457	A83	20c multicolored	.25	.25
458	A83	30c multicolored	.30	.25
459	A83	45c multicolored	.45	.35
460	A83	70c multicolored	1.50	1.40
461	A83	$1 multicolored	1.00	1.25
		Nos. 457-461 (5)	3.50	3.50

Souvenir Sheet

| 462 | A83 | $2 multicolored | 1.60 | 1.75 |

Racing Yachts A84

Designs: Racing yachts.

1981, Jan. 29   Litho.   Perf. 14

463	A84	6c multicolored	.25	.25
464	A84	15c multicolored	.25	.25
465	A84	35c multicolored	.25	.25
466	A84	$1 multicolored	.75	.85
		Nos. 463-466 (4)	1.50	1.60

Souvenir Sheet

| 467 | A84 | $2 multicolored | 1.40 | 1.75 |

South Caicos Regatta. No. 467 contains one 28x42mm stamp.

Pluto Listening to Sea Shell — A85

75c, Pluto on raft, dolphin. $1.50, Pluto.

1981, Feb. 16   Perf. 13½x14

| 468 | A85 | 10c shown | .25 | .25 |
| 469 | A85 | 75c multicolored | 1.50 | 1.60 |

Souvenir Sheet

| 470 | A85 | $1.50 multicolored | 3.00 | 3.00 |

50th anniversary of Walt Disney's Pluto.

Night Queen Cactus — A86

35c, Ripsaw cactus. 55c, Royal strawberry cactus. 80c, Caicos cactus. $2, Turks head cactus.

1981, Feb. 10   Perf. 14

471	A86	25c shown	.25	.25
472	A86	35c multicolored	.30	.35
473	A86	55c multicolored	.50	.60
474	A86	80c multicolored	.85	1.00
		Nos. 471-474 (4)	1.90	2.20

Souvenir Sheet

| 475 | A86 | $2 multicolored | 1.75 | 2.25 |

Donald Duck and Louie with Easter Egg — A87

Easter: Various Disney characters with Easter eggs.

1981, Mar. 20   Litho.   Perf. 11

476	A87	10c multicolored	.60	.60
477	A87	25c multicolored	.75	.75
478	A87	60c multicolored	.90	1.60
479	A87	80c multicolored	1.00	2.00
		Nos. 476-479 (4)	3.25	4.95

Souvenir Sheet

| 480 | A87 | $1 multicolored | 6.00 | 6.50 |

Pablo Picasso (1881-1973) A88

20c, Woman with Fan, 1909. 45c, Woman with Pears, 1909. 80c, The Accordionist, 1911. $1, The Aficionado, 1912. $2, Girl with a Mandolin, 1910.

1981, May 28   Litho.   Perf. 14

481	A88	20c shown	.25	.25
482	A88	45c multicolored	.50	.25
483	A88	80c multicolored	.75	.85
484	A88	$1 multicolored	1.00	1.20
		Nos. 481-484 (4)	2.50	2.55

Souvenir Sheet

| 485 | A88 | $2 multicolored | 2.30 | 2.30 |

Royal Wedding Issue
Common Design Type and

A88a

65c, Kensington Palace. 90c, Charles. No. 489, Glass coach.

1981, June 23   Litho.   Perf. 14

486	CD331a	35c Couple	.25	.25
487	CD331a	65c multi	.30	.30
488	CD331a	90c multi	.40	.40
		Nos. 486-488 (3)	.95	.95

Souvenir Sheet

| 489 | CD331 | $2 multi | 1.25 | 1.25 |

Imperf. x Roulette 5 (20c, $1),
Imperf. ($2)

1981, July 7   Self-adhesive

490		Booklet		4.00
	a.	A88a Pane of 6 (3x20c, Lady Diana, 3x$1, Charles)		2.25
	b.	A88a Pane of 1, $2, Couple		1.75

Nos. 486-488 also printed in sheets of 5 plus label, perf. 12, in changed colors.

Underwater Marine Biology Observation — A89

40c, Underwater photography. 75c, Diving for wreckage. $1, Diver, dolphins. $2, Diving flag.

1981, Aug. 21   Litho.   Perf. 14

491	A89	15c shown	.30	.30
492	A89	40c multicolored	.50	.50
493	A89	75c multicolored	1.00	1.10
494	A89	$1 multicolored	1.25	1.50
		Nos. 491-494 (4)	3.05	3.40

Souvenir Sheet

| 495 | A89 | $2 multicolored | 3.00 | 3.00 |

Br'er Rabbit Barricading his
Door — A90

Christmas: Scenes from Walt Disney's
Uncle Remus.

1981, Nov. 2   Litho.   Perf. 14x13½

496	A90	¼c multicolored	.25	.25
497	A90	½c multicolored	.25	.25
498	A90	1c multicolored	.25	.25
499	A90	2c multicolored	.25	.25
500	A90	3c multicolored	.25	.25
501	A90	4c multicolored	.25	.25
502	A90	5c multicolored	.25	.25
503	A90	75c multicolored	1.00	1.00
504	A90	$1 multicolored	1.50	1.25
		Nos. 496-504 (9)	4.25	4.00

Souvenir Sheet

| 505 | A90 | $2 multicolored | 3.50 | 3.50 |

Flags of
Turks and
Caicos
Islands
A91

Maps of Various Islands: a, Grand Turk. b,
Salt Cay. c, South Caicos. d, East Caicos. e,
Middle Caicos. f, North Caicos. g, Caicos
Cays. h, Providenciales. i, West Caicos.

1981, Dec. 1   Perf. 14

506		Strip of 10	5.75	5.50
a.-j.	A91	20c any single	.55	.55

Caribbean
Buckeyes — A92

35c, Clench's hairstreaks. 65c, Gulf fritil-
larys. $1, Bush sulphurs.
$2, Turk Island leaf butterfly.

1982, Jan. 21   Litho.   Perf. 14

507	A92	20c shown	.40	.40
508	A92	35c multicolored	.75	.75
509	A92	65c multicolored	1.00	1.25
510	A92	$1 multicolored	1.50	2.00
		Nos. 507-510 (4)	3.65	4.40

Souvenir Sheet

| 511 | A92 | $2 multicolored | 4.00 | 5.00 |

Scouting
Year — A93

40c, Flag ceremony. 50c, Building raft. 75c,
Cricket match. $1, Nature study.
$2, Baden-Powell, salute.

1982, Feb. 17   Litho.   Perf. 14

512	A93	40c multicolored	.60	.60
513	A93	50c multicolored	.75	1.00
514	A93	75c multicolored	1.50	1.60
515	A93	$1 multicolored	1.75	2.00
		Nos. 512-515 (4)	4.60	5.20

Souvenir Sheet

| 516 | A93 | $2 multicolored | 3.50 | 4.50 |

1982 World Cup
Soccer — A94

Designs: Various soccer players.

1982, Apr. 30   Litho.   Perf. 14

517	A94	10c multicolored	.25	.25
518	A94	25c multicolored	.35	.25
519	A94	45c multicolored	.60	.45
520	A94	$1 multicolored	1.00	1.25
		Nos. 517-520 (4)	2.20	2.20

Souvenir Sheet

| 521 | A94 | $2 multi, horiz. | 2.00 | 2.25 |

#517-520 issued in sheets of 5 + label.

Phillis Wheatley (1753-1784), Poet,
and Washington Crossing
Delaware — A95

Washington's 250th Birth Anniv. and F.D.
Roosevelt's Birth Centenary: 35c, Washing-
ton, Benjamin Banneker (1731-1806), astrono-
mer and mathematician, map. 65c, FDR,
George Washington Carver (1864-1943). 80c,
FDR with stamp collection. $2, FDR examining
Washington stamp.

1982, May 3   Litho.   Perf. 14

522	A95	20c multicolored	.35	.35
523	A95	35c multicolored	.70	.70
524	A95	65c multicolored	.90	1.25
525	A95	80c multicolored	1.00	1.50
		Nos. 522-525 (4)	2.95	3.80

Souvenir Sheet

| 526 | A95 | $2 multicolored | 2.50 | 3.00 |

Second
Thoughts, by
Norman
Rockwell — A96

1982, June 23   Litho.   Perf. 14x13½

527	A96	8c shown	.30	.30
528	A96	15c The Proper Gratuity	.30	.30
529	A96	20c Before the Shot	.35	.35
530	A96	25c The Three Umpires	.35	.35
		Nos. 527-530 (4)	1.30	1.30

Princess Diana Issue
Common Design Type

1982   Litho.   Perf. 14½x14

530A	CD332	8c Sandringham	.30	.35
530B	CD332	35c Wedding	1.40	1.40
530C	CD332	$1.10 Diana	2.50	2.50
		Nos. 530A-530C (3)	4.20	4.25

1982, July 1   Perf. 14½x14

531	CD332	55c Sandringham	.75	1.00
532	CD332	70c Wedding	1.25	1.00
533	CD332	$1 Diana	2.00	1.75
		Nos. 531-533 (3)	4.00	3.75

Also issued in sheetlets of 5 + label.

Souvenir Sheet

| 534 | CD332 | $2 Diana, diff. | 3.50 | 4.00 |

Skymaster over Caicos Cays — A97

15c, Jetstar, Grand Turk. 65c, Helicopter,
South Caicos. $1.10, Seaplane,
Providenciales.
$2, Boeing 727.

1982, Aug. 26   Litho.   Perf. 14

535	A97	8c shown	.25	.25
536	A97	15c multicolored	.35	.35
537	A97	65c multicolored	.85	1.00
538	A97	$1.10 multicolored	1.50	1.60
		Nos. 535-538 (4)	2.95	3.20

Souvenir Sheet

| 539 | A97 | $2 multicolored | 3.00 | 3.25 |

Christmas — A98

Christmas: Scenes from Walt Disney's
Mickey's Christmas Carol.

1982, Dec. 1   Litho.   Perf. 13½

540	A98	1c multicolored	.25	.25
541	A98	1c multicolored	.25	.25
542	A98	2c multicolored	.25	.25
543	A98	2c multicolored	.25	.25
544	A98	3c multicolored	.25	.25
545	A98	3c multicolored	.25	.25
546	A98	4c multicolored	.25	.25
547	A98	65c multicolored	1.10	1.10
548	A98	$1.10 multicolored	1.50	1.40
		Nos. 540-548 (9)	4.35	4.25

Souvenir Sheet

| 549 | A98 | $2 multicolored | 4.25 | 4.25 |

Trams and Locomotives — A99

15c, West Caicos trolley tram. 55c, West
Caicos steam locomotive. 90c, Mule-drawn
tram, East Caicos. $1.60, Sisal locomotive,
East Caicos.
$2.50, Steam engine.

1983, Jan. 18   Litho.   Perf. 14

550	A99	15c multicolored	.30	.30
551	A99	55c multicolored	1.00	1.10
552	A99	90c multicolored	1.5	1.50
553	A99	$1.60 multicolored	2.25	2.50
		Nos. 550-553 (4)	5.05	5.40

Souvenir Sheet

| 554 | A99 | $2.50 multicolored | 3.75 | 3.75 |

Commonwealth Day — A99a

1c, Woman crossing guard. 8c, Wind and
solar energy sources. 65c, Sailing. $1, Cricket
game.

1983, Mar. 14

555	A99a	1c multicolored	.85	.50
556	A99a	8c multicolored	.35	.25
557	A99a	65c multicolored	1.25	1.25
558	A99a	$1 multicolored	2.50	2.50
a.		Block or strip of 4, #555-558	4.95	4.50

Easter — A100

Crucifixion, by Raphael: 35c, Mary Magdalene, St. John. 50c, Mary. 95c, Angel looking
to heaven. $1.10, Angel looking to earth.
$2.50 shows entire painting.

1983, Apr. 7   Litho.   Perf. 14

559	A100	35c multicolored	.40	.40
560	A100	50c multicolored	.60	.60
561	A100	95c multicolored	.90	.90
562	A100	$1.10 multicolored	1.00	1.00
		Nos. 559-562 (4)	2.90	2.90

Souvenir Sheet

| 563 | A100 | $2.50 multicolored | 3.75 | 3.75 |

Piked
Whale
A101

65c, Right whale. 70c, Killer whale. 95c,
Sperm whale. $1.10, Gooseback whale. $2,
Blue whale. $2.20, Humpback whale. No. 571,
Longfin pilot whale.
No. 572, Fin whale.

1983   Litho.   Perf. 14

564	A101	50c shown	2.25	2.25
565	A101	65c multi	2.50	2.50
566	A101	70c multi	2.75	2.75
567	A101	95c multi	3.00	3.00
568	A101	$1.10 multi	3.25	3.25
569	A101	$2 multi	5.00	5.00
570	A101	$2.20 multi	6.50	6.50
571	A101	$3 multi	7.50	7.50
		Nos. 564-571 (8)	32.75	32.75

Souvenir Sheet

| 572 | A101 | $3 multi | 12.00 | 12.00 |

Issued: 50c, $2.20, #571, 5/16; 70c, 95c,
$2, 6/13; others 7/11. Issued in sheets of 4.
For overprints see Nos. 637-639.

Manned Flight
Bicentenary
A102

25c, 1st hydrogen balloon, 1783. 35c,
Friendship 7, 1962. 70c, Montgolfiere, 1783.
95c, Columbia space shuttle.
$2, Montgolfiere, Columbia.

1983, Aug. 30   Litho.   Perf. 14

573	A102	25c multicolored	.35	.35
574	A102	35c multicolored	.50	.50
575	A102	70c multicolored	.75	.90
576	A102	95c multicolored	1.00	1.25
		Nos. 573-576 (4)	2.60	3.00

Souvenir Sheet

| 577 | A102 | $2 multicolored | 2.50 | 3.00 |

Ships
A103

4c, Dug-out canoe. 5c, Santa Maria. 8c,
Spanish treasure galleons. 10c, Bermuda
sloop. 20c, Privateer Grand Turk. 25c, Nelson's Frigate Boreas. 30c, Warship Endymion.
35c, Bark Caesar. 50c, Schooner Grapeshot.

65c, Invincible. 95c, Magicienne. $1.10, Durban. $2, Sentinel. $3, Minerva. $5, Caicos sloop.

1983   Litho.   **Perf. 12½x12**

578	A103	4c multicolored	2.75	4.00
579	A103	5c multicolored	1.00	3.00
580	A103	8c multicolored	3.75	3.50
581	A103	10c multicolored	2.75	2.00
582	A103	20c multicolored	.50	3.50
583	A103	25c multicolored	.50	3.50
584	A103	30c multicolored	2.75	2.00
585	A103	35c multicolored	.50	3.50
586	A103	50c multicolored	.50	2.00
587	A103	65c multicolored	2.50	4.00
588	A103	95c multicolored	2.50	4.25
589	A103	$1.10 multicolored	11.00	6.00
590	A103	$2 multicolored	2.50	7.00
591	A103	$3 multicolored	8.50	16.00
592	A103	$5 multicolored	17.00	18.00
		Nos. 578-592 (15)	59.00	82.25

Issued: 4c, 8c, 10c, 30c, 65c, $1.10, $5, Mar.; 5c, 20c, 25c, 35c, 50c, 95c, $2, Aug. 12; $3, Dec.

1983-84   **Perf. 14**

578a	A103	4c	1.50	4.00
579a	A103	5c	2.00	4.00
580a	A103	8c	2.50	4.00
581a	A103	10c	2.25	1.50
582a	A103	20c	1.75	2.50
583a	A103	25c	3.50	1.75
584a	A103	30c	3.00	1.50
585a	A103	35c	2.00	3.50
586a	A103	50c	3.50	1.25
587a	A103	65c	4.50	2.50
588a	A103	95c	4.50	2.50
589a	A103	$1.10	6.00	3.75
590a	A103	$2	7.00	4.00
591a	A103	$3	7.50	7.50
592a	A103	$5	8.50	14.00
		Nos. 578a-592a (15)	60.00	58.25

Issued: 10c, 30c, 65c, $1.10-$3, 10/5/83; 8c, 25c, 50c, 95c, 12/16/83; 4c, 5c, 20c, 35c, $5, 1/9/84.
For overprints see Nos. 744-746.

Christmas
A104

Scenes from Walt Disney's *Oh Christmas Tree* — No. 593, Fifer Pig. No. 594, Fiddler Pig. No. 595, Practical Pig. No. 596, Pluto. No. 597, Goofy. No. 598, Mickey Mouse. No. 599, Gyro Gearloose. No. 600, Ludwig Von Drake. No. 601, Huey, Dewey and Louie. No. 602, Around the tree.

1983, Nov.   **Perf. 11**

593	A104	1c multi	.25	.25
594	A104	1c multi	.25	.25
595	A104	2c multi	.25	.25
596	A104	2c multi	.25	.25
597	A104	3c multi	.25	.25
598	A104	3c multi	.25	.25
599	A104	35c multi	.75	.35
600	A104	50c multi	.75	.60
601	A104	$1.10 multi	1.50	1.25
		Nos. 593-601 (9)	4.50	3.70

Souvenir Sheet
Perf. 13½

602	A104	$2.50 multi	5.50	6.00

John F. Kennedy (1917-1963), 20th
Death Anniv. — A105

1983, Dec. 22   Litho.   **Perf. 14**

603	A105	20c multicolored	.35	.25
604	A105	$1 multicolored	1.25	1.50

Classic
Cars
A106

4c, Cadillac V-16, 1933. 8c, Rolls Royce Phantom III, 1937. 10c, Saab 99, 1969. 25c, Maserati Bora, 1973. 40c, Datsun 260Z, 1970. 55c, Porsche 917, 1971. 80c, Lincoln Continental, 1939 . $1, Triumph TR3A, 1957. $2, Daimler, 1886.

1984, Mar. 15   Litho.   **Perf. 14**

605	A106	4c multi + label	.25	.25
606	A106	8c multi + label	.25	.25
607	A106	10c multi + label	.25	.25
608	A106	25c multi + label	.75	.50
609	A106	40c multi + label	1.25	1.00
610	A106	55c multi + label	1.75	1.25
611	A106	80c multi + label	2.25	1.50
612	A106	$1 multi + label	2.50	2.00
		Nos. 605-612 (8)	9.25	7.00

Souvenir Sheet

613	A106	$2 multicolored	3.50	3.75

125th anniv. of first commercially productive oil well, Drake's Rig, Titusville, Pa. Nos. 605-612 se-tenant with labels showing flags and auto museum names. No. 613 for 150th birth anniv. of Gotlieb Daimler, inventor of high-speed internal combustion engine.

Easter — A107

450th death anniv. of Antonio Allegri Correggio (Various cameo portraits of Correggio, paintings): 15c, Rest on the Flight to Egypt with St. Francis. 40c, St. Luke and St. Ambrose. 60c, Diana and her Chariot. 95c, Deposition of Christ. $2, Nativity with St. Elizabeth and the Infant St. John.

1984, Apr. 9

614	A107	15c multicolored	.30	.30
615	A107	40c multicolored	.75	.50
616	A107	60c multicolored	1.00	1.00
617	A107	95c multicolored	1.50	1.50
		Nos. 614-617 (4)	3.55	3.30

Souvenir Sheet

618	A107	$2 multi, horiz.	2.75	2.75

1984 Los Angeles Olympics — A108

Various Disney characters participating in Olympic sports. No. 619, 500-meter. No. 620, Diving. No. 621, Single kayak. No. 622, 1000-meter kayak. No. 623, Highboard diving. No. 624, Kayak slalom. No. 625, Freestyle swimming. No. 626, Water polo. No. 627, Yachting. No. 628, Platform diving.

1984, Feb. 21   Litho.   **Perf. 14**

619	A108	1c multi	.25	.25
620	A108	1c multi	.25	.25
621	A108	2c multi	.25	.25
622	A108	2c multi	.25	.25
623	A108	3c multi	.25	.25
624	A108	3c multi	.25	.25
625	A108	25c multi	.80	.80
626	A108	75c multi	2.25	2.00
627	A108	$1 multi	2.25	2.25
		Nos. 619-627 (9)	6.80	6.55

Souvenir Sheet

628	A108	$2 multi	5.50	5.50

1984, Apr.   **Perf. 12½x12**
Same Designs

619a	A108	1c	.25	.25
620a	A108	1c	.25	.25
621a	A108	2c	.25	.25
622a	A108	2c	.25	.25
623a	A108	3c	.25	.25
624a	A108	3c	.25	.25
625a	A108	25c	.75	.75
626a	A108	75c	2.10	2.10
627a	A108	$1	2.10	2.10
		Nos. 619a-627a (9)	6.45	6.45

Souvenir Sheet

628a	A108	$2	5.50	6.50

Nos. 619a-628a inscribed with Olympic rings emblem. Printed in sheets of 5.

Sir Arthur Conan Doyle (1859-
1930) — A109

Scenes from the Adventures of Sherlock Holmes: 25c, Second Stain. 45c, Final Problem. 70c, Empty House. 85c, Greek Interpreter.
$2, Doyle, vert.

1984, July 16   Litho.   **Perf. 14**

629	A109	25c multi	3.00	2.10
630	A109	45c multi	4.00	3.50
631	A109	70c multi	6.00	5.25
632	A109	85c multi	7.00	6.75
		Nos. 629-632 (4)	20.00	17.60

Souvenir Sheet

633	A109	$2 multi	16.00	16.00

Nos. 567-568, 572 Ovptd. with UPU Emblem and "19TH UPU CONGRESS / HAMBURG, WEST GERMANY./ 1874-1984"

1984   Litho.   **Perf. 14**

637	A101	95c multicolored	3.75	3.00
638	A101	$1.10 multicolored	3.75	3.50

Souvenir Sheet

639	A101	$3 multicolored	7.00	7.00

AUSIPEX '84
A110

Darwin, Ship, Map of Australia, Fauna and: 5c, Clown fish. 35c, Monitor lizard. 50c, Rainbow lorikeets. $1.10, Koalas. $2, Grey kangaroo.

1984, Aug. 22   **Perf. 14x13½**

640	A110	5c multi	1.05	.85
641	A110	35c multi	3.00	3.00
642	A110	50c multi	4.00	4.00
643	A110	$1.10 multi	4.50	5.00
		Nos. 640-643 (4)	12.55	12.85

Souvenir Sheet

644	A110	$2 multi	5.00	5.75

Christmas — A111

Scenes from Walt Disney's The Toy Tinkers.

1984   Litho.   **Perf. 14**

645	A111	20c multicolored	1.00	.60
646	A111	35c multicolored	1.40	.75
647	A111	50c multicolored	1.75	1.25
648	A111	75c multicolored	2.25	1.75
649	A111	$1.10 multicolored	3.00	2.50
		Nos. 645-649 (5)	9.40	6.75

Souvenir Sheet

650	A111	$2 multicolored	4.50	5.00

No. 648 issued in sheets of 8. Issue dates: 75c, Nov. 26, others, Oct. 8.

Audubon Birth
Bicentenary
A112

Cameo portrait of Audubon, signature and illustrations from Birds of North America: 25c, Dendroica magnoliae. 45c, Asio flammeus. 70c, Zenaida macroura. 85c, Progne subis. $2, Haematopus ostralegus.

1985, Jan. 28   Litho.   **Perf. 14**

651	A112	25c multicolored	2.00	1.00
652	A112	45c multicolored	3.00	2.00
653	A112	70c multicolored	3.25	3.25
654	A112	85c multicolored	3.25	3.50
		Nos. 651-654 (4)	11.50	9.75

Souvenir Sheet

655	A112	$2 multicolored	6.00	6.00

Intl. Civil
Aviation
Org.,
40th
Anniv.
A113

Pioneers & inventions: 8c, Leonardo da Vinci, 15th century glider wing. 25c, Sir Alliott Verdon Roe, 1949 C. 102 Jet. 65c, Robert H. Goddard, first liquid fuel rocket launch, 1926. $1, Igor Sikorsky, 1939 Sikorsky VS300. $2, Aviator Amelia Earhart, 1937 Lockheed 10E Electra.

1985, Feb. 21

656	A113	8c multicolored	.75	.45
657	A113	25c multicolored	2.00	.60
658	A113	65c multicolored	3.00	2.25
659	A113	$1 multicolored	6.25	5.25
		Nos. 656-659 (4)	12.00	8.55

Souvenir Sheet

660	A113	$2 multicolored	4.00	4.25

Arrival of
the
Statue of
Liberty in
New
York,
Cent.
A114

Designs: 20c, Flags of US, France, Franklin, Lafayette. 30c, Designer Frederic A. Bartholdi, engineer Gustave Eiffel, Statue, Eiffel Tower. 65c, Isere, arriving in New York with Statue, 1885. $1.10, Fund raisers Louis Agassiz, H. W. Longfellow, Charles Sumner, Joseph Pulitzer. $2, Dedication day, Oct. 28, 1886.

1985, Mar. 28

661	A114	20c multicolored	1.00	.80
662	A114	30c multicolored	1.50	.95
663	A114	65c multicolored	3.00	2.10
664	A114	$1.10 multicolored	3.25	2.50
		Nos. 661-664 (4)	8.75	6.35

Souvenir Sheet

665	A114	$2 multicolored	5.00	5.50

Royal Navy — A115

Designs: 20c, Sir Edward Hawke, Royal George. 30c, Lord Nelson, H.M.S. Victory. 65c, Adm. Sir George Cockburn, H.M.S. Albion. 95c, Adm. Sir David Beatty, H.M.S. Indefatigable. $2, 18th century naval gunner, cannons.

1985, Apr. 17

666	A115	20c multicolored	3.00	2.25
667	A115	30c multicolored	3.50	3.25
668	A115	65c multicolored	4.75	4.25
669	A115	95c multicolored	5.75	5.75
		Nos. 666-669 (4)	17.00	15.50

Souvenir Sheet

670	A115	$2 multicolored	5.50	6.00

Intl. Youth Year A116

Anniversaries: 25c, Return of Halley's Comet, 1986. 35c, Mark Twain (1835-1910), Mississippi river boat. 50c, Jakob Grimm (1785-1863), Hansel & Gretel, vert. 95c, Grimm, Rumpelstiltskin, vert. $2, Twain, Grimm, portraits.

1985, May 17

671	A116	25c multicolored	1.50	.65
672	A116	35c multicolored	2.50	.90
673	A116	50c multicolored	2.50	1.75
674	A116	95c multicolored	3.50	3.25
		Nos. 671-674 (4)	10.00	6.55

Souvenir Sheet

675	A116	$2 multicolored	5.25	6.00

Queen Mother, 85th Birthday — A117

Designs: 30c, Queen Mother outside Clarence House, vert. 50c, Visiting Biggin Hill Airfield by helicopter. $1.10, 80th birthday portrait, vert. $2, With Prince Charles at the 1968 Garter Ceremony, Windsor Castle, vert.

1985, July 15

676	A117	30c multicolored	1.00	.50
677	A117	50c multicolored	2.25	1.00
678	A117	$1.10 multicolored	2.25	2.50
		Nos. 676-678 (3)	5.50	4.00

Souvenir Sheet

679	A117	$2 multicolored	4.25	4.25

George Frideric Handel — A118

Johann Sebastian Bach — A119

Handel or Bach and: 4c, King George II, Zadok the Priest music, 1727. 10c, Queen Caroline, Funeral Anthem, 1737. 15c, Bassoon, Invention No. 3 in D Major. 40c, Natural horn, Invention No. 3. 50c, King George I, Water Music, 1714. 60c, Viola d'amore, Invention No. 3 . . . 95c, Clavichord, Invention No. 3 . . . $1.10, Queen Anne, Or la

Tromba from Rinaldo. No. 688, Handel, portrait. No. 689, Bach, portrait.

1985, July 17 **Perf. 15**

680	A118	4c multicolored	.70	.55
681	A118	10c multicolored	1.25	.55
682	A119	15c multicolored	1.25	.50
683	A119	40c multicolored	2.25	1.00
684	A118	50c multicolored	2.75	2.50
685	A119	60c multicolored	2.50	1.25
686	A119	95c multicolored	2.75	2.50
687	A118	$1.10 multicolored	3.50	5.50
		Nos. 680-687 (8)	16.95	14.35

Souvenir Sheets

688	A118	$2 multicolored	6.00	7.50
689	A119	$2 multicolored	5.00	5.00

Motorcycle Centenary — A120

Flag of US, UK, Fed. Rep. of Germany or Japan and: 8c, 1915 dual cylinder Harley-Davidson. 25c, 1950 Thunderbird Triumph. 55c, 1985 BMW K100RS. $1.20, 1985 Honda 1100 Shadow. $2, 1885 Daimler Single Track, vert.

1985, Sept. 4 **Perf. 14**

690	A120	8c multicolored	1.00	.40
691	A120	25c multicolored	2.10	1.00
692	A120	55c multicolored	3.25	2.25
693	A120	$1.20 multicolored	4.50	7.75
		Nos. 690-693 (4)	10.85	11.40

Souvenir Sheet

694	A120	$2 multicolored	5.50	5.50

Pirates of the Caribbean — A121

Disneyland, 30th Anniv.: No. 695, Fate of Capt. Kidd. No. 696, Pirates imprisoned. No. 697, Bartholomew Roberts, church-going pirate. No. 698, Buccaneers in battle. No. 699, Bride auction. No. 700, Plunder. No. 701, Singing pirates. No. 702, Blackbeard. No. 703, Henry Morgan. No. 704, Mary Read, Anne Bonney.

1985, Oct. 4 **Litho.** **Perf. 14**

695	A121	1c multicolored	.25	.25
696	A121	1c multicolored	.25	.25
697	A121	2c multicolored	.25	.25
698	A121	2c multicolored	.25	.25
699	A121	3c multicolored	.25	.25
700	A121	3c multicolored	.25	.25
701	A121	35c multicolored	1.75	1.00
702	A121	75c multicolored	3.75	4.00
703	A121	$1.10 multicolored	4.50	5.00
		Nos. 695-703 (9)	11.50	11.50

Souvenir Sheet

704	A121	$2.50 multicolored	7.75	7.75

Girl Guides, 75th Anniv. A122

Uniforms of Turks and Caicos and: 10c, Papua New Guinea and China brownies. 40c, Surinam and Korea brownies. 70c, Australia and Canada girl guides. 80c, West Germany and Israel girl guides.

1985, Nov. 4

705	A122	10c multicolored	1.00	.50
706	A122	40c multicolored	2.25	2.00
707	A122	70c multicolored	3.25	3.75
708	A122	80c multicolored	3.50	3.75
		Nos. 705-708 (4)	10.00	10.00

Souvenir Sheet

709	A122	$2 Anniv. emblem	4.25	4.25

Grand Turk Chapter, 35th anniv.

World Wildlife Fund A123

Map of the Islands — A124

Turks & Caicos ground iguanas.

1986, Nov. 20 **Perf. 14**

710	A123	8c multicolored	2.50	1.25
711	A123	10c multicolored	2.50	1.25
712	A123	20c multicolored	3.75	2.50
713	A123	35c multicolored	7.50	5.00
		Nos. 710-713 (4)	16.25	10.00

Souvenir Sheet

714	A124	$2 multicolored	16.00	16.00

A125

Wedding pictures: 35c, Couple. 65c, Sarah in coach. $1.10, Couple, close-up. $2, In Westminster Abbey.

1986, Dec. 19 **Litho.** **Perf. 14**

715	A125	35c multi	1.25	.85
716	A125	65c multi	2.25	1.40
717	A125	$1.10 multi	3.00	2.75
		Nos. 715-717 (3)	6.50	5.00

Souvenir Sheet

718	A125	$2 multi	6.00	6.00

Wedding of Prince Andrew and Sarah Ferguson.

Christmas — A126

Illuminations by miniaturist Giorgio Giulio Clovio (1498-1578) from the Farnese Book of Hours: 35c, Prophecy of the Birth of Christ to King Achaz. 50c, The Annunciation. 65c, The Circumcision. 95c, Adoration of the Kings. $2, The Nativity, from the Townley Lectionary.

1987, Dec. 9 **Litho.** **Perf. 14**

719	A126	35c multicolored	1.50	.85
720	A126	50c multicolored	2.00	2.10
721	A126	65c multicolored	2.50	2.75
722	A126	95c multicolored	3.75	4.50
		Nos. 719-722 (4)	9.75	10.20

Souvenir Sheet

723	A126	$2 multicolored	7.00	8.75

Accession of Queen Victoria to the Throne of England, 150th Anniv. A127

Ships and memorials: 8c, HMS Victoria, Victoria Cross. 35c, SS Victoria, coin. 55c, Victoria & Albert I, Great Britain No. 1. 95c, Victoria & Albert II, Victoria Public Library, Turks & Caicos. $2, Bark Victoria.

1987, Dec. 24

724	A127	8c multicolored	2.00	1.25
725	A127	35c multicolored	3.75	3.25
726	A127	55c multicolored	4.00	4.00
727	A127	95c multicolored	5.25	5.25
		Nos. 724-727 (4)	15.00	13.75

Souvenir Sheet

728	A127	$2 multicolored	9.50	9.50

US Constitution Bicentennial — A128

Designs: 10c, NJ state flag. 35c, Freedom of Worship, vert. 65c, US Supreme Court, vert. 80c, John Adams, vert. $2, George Mason, vert.

1987, Dec. 31

729	A128	10c multicolored	.25	.25
730	A128	35c multicolored	.75	.75
731	A128	65c multicolored	1.75	2.00
732	A128	80c multicolored	2.25	3.00
		Nos. 729-732 (4)	5.00	6.00

Souvenir Sheet

733	A128	$2 multicolored	3.50	4.50

Discovery of America, 500th Anniv. (in 1992) A129

4c, Caravel, first sighting of land, Oct. 12, 1492. 25c, Columbus meets with Indians, Oct. 14. 70c, Fleet anchored in harbor, Oct. 15. $1, Landing, Oct. 16. $2, Nina, Pinta and Santa Maria.

1988, Jan. 20

734	A129	4c multicolored	.60	.40
735	A129	25c multicolored	1.40	.75
736	A129	70c multicolored	3.75	4.00
737	A129	$1 multicolored	3.75	4.00
		Nos. 734-737 (4)	9.50	9.15

Souvenir Sheet

738	A129	$2 multicolored	6.50	6.50

Sea Scouts Salute Jamboree and Australia A130

Australia Bicent.: 8c, Arawak artifact, scouts exploring cave on Middle Caicos, vert. 35c, Santa Maria, scouts rowing to Hawks Nest. 65c, Scouts diving to explore a sunken Spanish galleon, vert. 95c, Plantation worker cutting sisal, scouts exploring plantation ruins. $2, Splashdown of Friendship 7, piloted by John Glenn, Feb. 20, 1962, vert.

1988, Feb. 12 **Litho.** **Perf. 14**

739	A130	8c multicolored	.35	.35
740	A130	35c shown	.80	.80
741	A130	65c multicolored	1.50	1.90
742	A130	95c multicolored	2.00	2.25
		Nos. 739-742 (4)	4.65	5.30

Souvenir Sheet

743	A130	$2 multicolored	4.50	5.75

Nos. 581, 583 and 590 Ovptd. "40th WEDDING ANNIVERSARY / H.M. QUEEN ELIZABETH II / H.R.H. THE DUKE OF EDINBURGH"

1900, Mar. 14	Litho.	Perf. 14	
744	A103	10c multicolored	.75	.50
745	A103	25c multicolored	1.25	.50
746	A103	$2 multicolored	4.00	5.00
	Nos. 744-746 (3)		6.00	6.00

A131

1988, Aug. 29		Litho.		
747	A131	8c Soccer	.60	.25
748	A131	30c Yachting	1.00	.75
749	A131	70c Cycling	5.50	2.50
750	A131	$1 Running	2.25	3.00
	Nos. 747-750 (4)		9.35	6.50

Souvenir Sheet

751	A131	$2 Swimming	4.50	4.50

1988 Summer Olympics, Seoul.

A132

Billfish Tournament: 8c, Passenger jet, fishing boat and fisherman reeling-in giant swordfish. 10c, Photographing prize catch. 70c, Fishing boat, lighthouse. $1, Blue marlin. $2, Sailfish.

1988, Sept. 5		Litho.		
752	A132	8c multicolored	.70	.35
753	A132	10c multicolored	.70	.35
754	A132	70c multicolored	2.75	3.25
755	A132	$1 multicolored	3.50	4.25
	Nos. 752-755 (4)		7.65	8.20

Souvenir Sheet

756	A132	$2 multicolored	5.25	6.00

Christmas
A133

Paintings by Titian: 15c, Madonna and Child with St. Catherine and the Infant John the Baptist, c. 1530. 25c, Madonna with a Rabbit, c. 1526. 35c, Virgin and Child with Sts. Stephen, Jerome and Mauritius, c. 1520. 40c, The Gypsy Madonna, c. 1510. 50c, The Holy Family and a Shepherd, c. 1510. 65c, Madonna and Child, c. 1510. $3, Madonna and Child with St. John the Baptist and St. Catherine, c. 1530. No. 764, Adoration of the Magi, c. 1560. No. 765, The Annunciation, c. 1560.

1988, Oct. 24		Litho.		
757	A133	15c multicolored	.40	.40
758	A133	25c multicolored	.60	.60
759	A133	35c multicolored	.85	.85
760	A133	40c multicolored	.95	.95
761	A133	50c multicolored	1.00	1.00
762	A133	65c multicolored	1.25	1.10
763	A133	$3 multicolored	5.50	7.00
	Nos. 757-763 (7)		10.55	11.90

Souvenir Sheets

764	A133	$2 multicolored	4.25	4.50
765	A133	$2 multicolored	4.25	4.50

Visit of Princess Alexandra, 1st Cousin of Queen Elizabeth II — A134

Various portraits and: 70c, Government House. $1.40, Map. $2, Flora, vert.

1988, Nov. 14		Litho.		Perf. 14
766	A134	70c multicolored	3.25	2.00
767	A134	$1.40 multicolored	9.25	5.75

Souvenir Sheet

768	A134	$2 multicolored	15.00	12.50

Arms Type of 1970 Without Inscription

Perf. 14½x15

1988, Dec. 15		Litho.		Unwmk.
769	A35	$10 multicolored	17.50	18.00

Pre-Columbian Societies and Their Customs — A135

UPAE and discovery of America anniv. emblems and: 10c, Hollowing-out tree to make a canoe, vert. 50c, Body painting and statue. 65c, Three islanders with body paint. $1, Canoeing, vert. $2, Petroglyph.

1989, May 15		Litho.		Perf. 14
770	A135	10c multicolored	.40	.40
771	A135	50c multicolored	1.25	1.25
772	A135	65c multicolored	1.50	1.50
773	A135	$1 multicolored	2.75	2.75
	Nos. 770-773 (4)		5.90	5.90

Souvenir Sheet

774	A135	$2 multicolored	6.50	7.50

Discovery of America 500th anniv. (in 1992).

Souvenir Sheet

Lincoln Memorial, Washington, D.C. — A136

1989, Nov. 17		Litho.		Perf. 14
775	A136	$1.50 multicolored	4.50	5.25

World Stamp Expo '89.

Miniature Sheets

American Presidential Office, 200th Anniv — A137

US presidents, historic events and monuments.
No. 776: a, Jackson, early train. b, Van Buren, origins of baseball and Moses Fleetwood Walker, 1st black to play professional baseball. c, Harrison, Harrison's "Keep the Ball Rollin'" slogan and parade. d, Tyler, annexation of Texas, 1845. e, Polk, 1st US

postage stamps (#2), 1847, and discovery of gold in California, 1849. f, Taylor, Mexican-American War, 1847.
No. 777: a, Hayes, end of Civil War reconstruction. b, Garfield, Garfield leading Union soldiers in the Battle of Shiloh. c, Arthur, opening of the Brooklyn Bridge, 1883. d, Cleveland, Columbian Exposition, 1893 (US #245). e, Benjamin Harrison, Pan-American Union building, map. f, McKinley, Spanish-American War (Rough Riders Monument, by Solon Borglum).
No. 778: a, Hoover, 1933 Olympic Games, Los Angeles and Lake Placid (American sprinter Ralph Metcalf and Norwegian figure skater Sonja Henie). b, Franklin Delano Roosevelt, Roosevelt's support of the March of Dimes (dime, 1946). c, 150th anniv. of inauguration of Washington, New York World's Fair, 1939. d, Truman, founding of the U.N., 1945. e, Eisenhower, invasion of Normandy, 1944. f, Kennedy, Apollo 11 mission, 1969.

1989, Nov. 19			Perf. 14
776		Sheet of 6	13.50	13.50
a.-f.		50c any single	2.25	2.25
777	A137	Sheet of 6	13.50	13.50
a.-f.		50c any single	2.25	2.25
778	A137	Sheet of 6	13.50	13.50
a.-f.		50c any single	2.25	2.25

Fraser is incorrectly spelled "Frazer" on No. 778c.

Christmas — A138

Religious paintings by Giovanni Bellini: 15c, Madonna and Child. 25c, The Madonna of the Shrubs. 35c, The Virgin and Child. 40c, The Virgin and Child with a Greek Inscription. 50c, The Madonna of the Meadow. 65c, The Madonna of the Pear. 70c, The Virgin and Child, diff. $1, Madonna and Child, diff. No. 787, The Madonna with John the Baptist and Another Saint. No. 788, The Virgin and Child Enthroned.

1989, Dec. 18				
779	A138	15c multicolored	.85	.60
780	A138	25c multicolored	1.00	.60
781	A138	35c multicolored	1.25	.75
782	A138	40c multicolored	1.50	.90
783	A138	50c multicolored	1.75	1.00
784	A138	65c multicolored	2.25	2.25
785	A138	70c multicolored	2.50	2.50
786	A138	$1 multicolored	4.25	3.50
	Nos. 779-786 (8)		15.35	12.10

Souvenir Sheets

787	A138	$2 multicolored	7.00	8.00
788	A138	$2 multicolored	7.00	8.00

Souvenir Sheet

1st Moon Landing, 20th Anniv. — A139

Designs: a, Liftoff. b, Eagle lunar module on Moon's surface. c, Aldrin obtaining soil samples. d, Neil Armstrong walking on Moon. e, Columbia and Eagle in space.

1990, Jan. 8				
789	A139	Sheet of 5	7.50	7.50
a.-e.		50c any single	1.50	1.50

Flowers — A140

8c, Zephyranthes rosea. 10c, Sophora tomentosa. 15c, Coccoloba uvifera. 20c, Encyclia gracilis. 25c, Tillandsia streptophylla. 30c, Maurandella antirrhiniflora. 35c, Tillandsia balbisiana. 50c, Encyclia rufa. 65c, Aechmea lingulata. 80c, Asclepias curassavica. $1, Caesalpinia bahamensis. $1.10, Capparis cynophallophora. $1.25, Stachytarpheta jamaicensis. $2, Cassia biflora. $5, Clusia rosea. $10, Opuntia bahamana.

1990, Jan. 11		Litho.		Perf. 14
790	A140	8c multicolored	1.00	.25
791	A140	10c multicolored	1.00	.25
792	A140	15c multicolored	1.25	.25
793	A140	20c multicolored	1.25	.30
794	A140	25c multicolored	1.25	.35
795	A140	30c multicolored	1.50	.70
796	A140	35c multicolored	1.50	.50
797	A140	50c multicolored	2.00	1.25
798	A140	65c multicolored	2.25	1.50
799	A140	80c multicolored	2.50	1.50
800	A140	$1 multicolored	2.75	1.60
801	A140	$1.10 multicolored	3.50	2.75
802	A140	$1.25 multicolored	3.50	3.25
803	A140	$2 multicolored	4.25	4.50
804	A140	$5 multicolored	8.00	11.00
805	A140	$10 multicolored	18.00	20.00
	Nos. 790-805 (16)		55.50	49.95

1994			Perf. 12	
790a	A140	8c	1.00	.25
791a	A140	10c	1.00	.25
792a	A140	15c	1.00	.30
793a	A140	20c	1.00	.30
794a	A140	25c	1.00	.35
795a	A140	30c	1.25	.70
796a	A140	35c	1.25	.50
797a	A140	50c	1.50	1.25
798a	A140	65c	1.75	1.50
799a	A140	80c	2.00	1.75
800a	A140	$1	2.25	1.75
801a	A140	$1.10	3.00	3.25
802a	A140	$1.25	3.25	4.25
803a	A140	$2	4.00	5.50
804a	A140	$5	8.50	13.00
805a	A140	$10 ('95)	21.00	24.00
	Nos. 790a-805a (16)		54.75	58.85

Birds
A141

10c, Yellow-billed cuckoo. 15c, White-tailed tropic bird. 20c, Kirtland's warbler. 30c, Yellow-crowned night heron. 50c, West Indian tree duck. 80c, Yellow-bellied sapsucker. $1, American kestrel. $1.40, Mockingbird.
No. 814, Osprey. No. 815, Yellow warbler.

1990, Feb. 19				
806	A141	10c multicolored	1.40	.80
807	A141	15c multicolored	1.60	.80
808	A141	20c multicolored	2.00	1.10
809	A141	30c multicolored	2.50	1.10
810	A141	50c multicolored	3.50	1.60
811	A141	80c multicolored	4.25	3.50
812	A141	$1 multicolored	5.75	6.50
813	A141	$1.40 multicolored	5.50	4.25
	Nos. 806-813 (8)		26.50	19.65

Souvenir Sheets

814	A141	$2 multicolored	12.50	8.00
815	A141	$2 multicolored	12.50	8.00

Fish
A142

8c, Queen parrotfish. 10c, Queen triggerfish. 25c, Sergeant major. 40c, Spotted goatfish. 50c, Neon goby. 75c, Nassau grouper. 80c, Jawfish. $2, Blue tang.
No. 824, Butter hamlet. No. 825, Queen angelfish.

1990, Feb. 12 — Litho. — Perf. 14

816	A142	8c multicolored	.30	.25
817	A142	10c multicolored	.30	.25
818	A142	25c multicolored	.70	.65
819	A142	40c multicolored	1.00	1.00
820	A142	50c multicolored	1.25	1.25
821	A142	75c multicolored	1.75	1.75
822	A142	80c multicolored	2.25	2.50
823	A142	$1 multicolored	2.25	2.50
		Nos. 816-823 (8)	9.80	10.15

Souvenir Sheets

824	A142	$2 multicolored	8.00	8.50
825	A142	$2 multicolored	8.00	8.50

Butterflies A143

15c, White peacock. 25c, Cloudless sulphur. 35c, Mexican fritillary. 40c, Fiery skipper. 50c, Chamberlain's sulphur. 60c, Pygmy blue. 90c, Dusky swallowtail. $1, Antillean dagger wing. No. 834, Thomas's blue. No. 835, 9 Queen species.

1990, Mar. 19

826	A143	15c multicolored	1.00	.45
827	A143	25c multicolored	1.25	.60
828	A143	35c multicolored	1.40	.75
829	A143	40c multicolored	1.50	.80
830	A143	50c multicolored	1.50	1.00
831	A143	60c multicolored	1.75	1.50
832	A143	90c multicolored	3.00	3.25
833	A143	$1 multicolored	3.00	3.25
		Nos. 826-833 (8)	14.40	11.60

Souvenir Sheets

834	A143	$2 multicolored	8.00	8.00
835	A143	$2 multicolored	8.00	8.00

Nos. 826, 831 and 833 vert.

America Issue A144

Fish, UPAE and discovery of America 500th anniv. emblems: 10c, Rock beauty. 15c, Coney. 25c, Red hind. 50c, Banded butterflyfish. 60c, French angelfish. 75c, Blackbar soldierfish. 90c, Stoplight parrotfish. $1, French grunt. No. 844, Gray angelfish. No. 845, Blue chromis.

1990, Apr. 2

836	A144	10c multicolored	.60	.40
837	A144	15c multicolored	.70	.45
838	A144	25c multicolored	1.00	.60
839	A144	50c multicolored	1.60	1.40
840	A144	60c multicolored	1.90	1.75
841	A144	75c multicolored	2.25	2.25
842	A144	90c multicolored	2.50	2.50
843	A144	$1 multicolored	2.50	2.75
		Nos. 836-843 (8)	13.05	12.10

Souvenir Sheets

844	A144	$2 multicolored	4.50	5.00
845	A144	$2 multicolored	4.50	5.00

Penny Black, 150th Anniv. — A145

British Pillar Boxes — A146

25c, 1p essay in blue, without letters. 35c, Letter Box #1, 1855. 50c, Penfold Box, 1866. 75c, Great Britain #3, essay. $1, 2p blue essay. $1.25, Air mail box, 1935. #852, Great Britain #1. #853, K type box, 1979.

1990, May 3 — Litho. — Perf. 14

846	A145	25c bluish blk	1.25	.60
847	A146	35c gray & pale brn	1.00	1.00
848	A146	50c gray & dk blue	1.25	1.00
849	A145	75c red brown	3.00	2.25
850	A145	$1 dk blue	3.50	3.75
851	A146	$1.25 gray & blue	3.00	4.00
		Nos. 846-851 (6)	13.00	12.60

Souvenir Sheets

852	A145	$2 black	5.75	5.75
853	A146	$2 blk & red brn	6.25	6.25

Stamp World London '90.

Queen Mother, 90th Birthday — A147

1990, Aug. 20 — Litho. — Perf. 14

854	A147	10c multicolored	.50	.25
855	A147	25c multi, diff.	1.00	.65
856	A147	75c multi, diff.	1.75	2.00
857	A147	$1.25 multi, diff.	2.50	3.00
		Nos. 854-857 (4)	5.75	5.90

Souvenir Sheet

858	A147	$2 multi, diff.	6.00	6.50

Birds A148

8c, Stripe-headed tanager, vert. 10c, Black-whiskered vireo. 25c, Blue-grey gnatcatcher. 40c, Lesser scaup. 50c, White-cheeked pintail. 75c, Common stilt. 80c, Common oystercatcher, vert. $1, Tricolored heron. No. 867, Bahama woodstar. No. 868, American coot.

1990, Sept. 24 — Litho. — Perf. 14

859	A148	8c multicolored	1.25	.55
860	A148	10c multicolored	1.25	.55
861	A148	25c multicolored	2.00	.55
862	A148	40c multicolored	2.50	1.25
863	A148	50c multicolored	2.50	1.25
864	A148	75c multicolored	3.00	2.00
865	A148	80c multicolored	3.00	3.25
866	A148	$1 multicolored	3.75	4.25
		Nos. 859-866 (8)	19.25	13.65

Souvenir Sheets

867	A148	$2 multicolored	5.25	5.50
868	A148	$2 multicolored	5.25	5.50

Christmas A149

Different details from paintings by Rubens: 10c, 50c, 75c, No. 876, Triumph of Christ over Sin and Death. 35c, 45c, 65c, $1.25, No. 877, St. Theresa Praying for the Souls in Purgatory. Nos. 876-877 show entire painting.

1990, Dec. 17 — Litho. — Perf. 14

869	A149	10c multicolored	.65	.25
870	A149	35c multicolored	1.40	.65
871	A149	45c multicolored	1.50	.85
872	A149	50c multicolored	1.75	1.00
873	A149	65c multicolored	2.50	1.50
874	A149	75c multicolored	2.75	3.75
875	A149	$1.25 multicolored	3.50	5.25
		Nos. 869-875 (7)	14.05	13.25

Souvenir Sheets

876	A149	$2 multicolored	7.50	8.00
877	A149	$2 multicolored	7.50	8.00

1992 Summer Olympics, Barcelona — A150

1991, Jan. 17

878	A150	10c Kayaking	.45	.25
879	A150	25c Track	.90	.60
880	A150	75c Pole vault	2.00	2.00
881	A150	$1.25 Javelin	2.75	3.75
		Nos. 878-881 (4)	6.10	6.60

Souvenir Sheet

882	A150	$2 Baseball	9.00	10.00

No. 878 inscribed Canoeing.

Voyages of Discovery A151

Designs: 5c, Henry Hudson, 1611. 10c, Roald Amundsen (airship), 1926. 15c, Amundsen (ship), 1906. 50c, USS Nautilus, 1958. 75c, Robert Scott, 1911. $1, Richard Byrd, Floyd Bennett, 1926. $1.25, Lincoln Ellsworth, 1935. $1.50, Cook, 1772-75. No. 891, The Nina. No. 892, The search for land.

1991, Apr. 15 — Litho. — Perf. 14

883	A151	5c multicolored	1.00	.75
884	A151	10c multicolored	1.00	.75
885	A151	15c multicolored	1.25	.90
886	A151	50c multicolored	2.25	1.10
887	A151	75c multicolored	3.50	1.75
888	A151	$1 multicolored	3.75	2.50
889	A151	$1.25 multicolored	4.00	3.75
890	A151	$1.50 multicolored	5.00	5.50
		Nos. 883-890 (8)	21.75	17.00

Souvenir Sheets

891	A151	$2 multicolored	6.50	7.00
892	A151	$2 multicolored	6.50	7.00

Discovery of America, 500th anniv. (in 1992).

Butterflies A152

5c, White peacock. 25c, Orion. 35c, Gulf fritillary. 45c, Caribbean buckeye. 55c, Flambeau. 65c, Malachite. 70c, Florida white. $1, Great southern white. No. 901, Giant hairstreak. No. 902, Orange-barred sulphur.

1991, May 13 — Litho. — Perf. 14

893	A152	5c multicolored	.45	.50
894	A152	25c multicolored	1.05	.65
895	A152	35c multicolored	1.15	.85
896	A152	45c multicolored	1.45	1.15
897	A152	55c multicolored	1.60	1.60
898	A152	65c multicolored	2.10	2.10
899	A152	70c multicolored	2.25	2.25
900	A152	$1 multicolored	2.50	2.60
		Nos. 893-900 (8)	12.55	11.70

Souvenir Sheets

901	A152	$2 multicolored	7.00	7.50
902	A152	$2 multicolored	7.00	7.50

Extinct Animals A153

5c, Protohydrochoerus. 10c, Phororhacos. 15c, Prothylacynus. 50c, Borhyaena. 75c,

Smilodon. $1, Thoatherium. $1.25, Cuvieronius. $1.50, Toxodon. No. 911, Mesosaurus. No. 912, Astrapotherium.

1991, June 3

903	A153	5c multi	.80	.60
904	A153	10c multi	.80	.60
905	A153	15c multi	.95	.60
906	A153	50c multi	2.50	1.10
907	A153	75c multi	3.00	1.75
908	A153	$1 multi	3.25	2.00
909	A153	$1.25 multi	3.25	3.75
910	A153	$1.50 multi	3.25	4.00
		Nos. 903-910 (8)	17.80	14.40

Souvenir Sheets

911	A153	$2 multi	7.75	8.00
912	A153	$2 multi	7.75	8.00

Royal Family Birthday, Anniversary
Common Design Type

No. 921, Elizabeth, Philip. No. 922, Diana, sons, Charles.

1991 — Litho. — Perf. 14

913	CD347	10c multicolored	.80	.30
914	CD347	25c multicolored	.70	.50
915	CD347	35c multicolored	1.00	.75
916	CD347	45c multicolored	2.50	1.00
917	CD347	50c multicolored	3.50	1.50
918	CD347	65c multicolored	1.50	1.50
919	CD347	80c multicolored	1.75	3.00
920	CD347	$1 multicolored	3.25	3.00
		Nos. 913-920 (8)	15.00	11.55

Souvenir Sheets

921	CD347	$2 multicolored	5.00	6.25
922	CD347	$2 multicolored	7.50	7.50

10c, 45c, 50c, $1, No. 922, Charles and Diana, 10th wedding anniv., issued: July 29. Others, Queen Elizabeth II, 65th birthday, issued: June 8. For overprints see Nos. 1020-1022.

Mushrooms — A154

10c, Pluteus chrysophlebius. 15c, Leucopaxillus gracillimus. 20c, Marasmius haematocephalus. 35c, Collybia subpruinosa. 50c, Marasmius atrorubens, vert. 65c, Leucocoprinus birnbaumii, vert. $1.10, Trogia cantharelloides, vert. $1.25, Boletellus cubensis, vert. No. 931, Gerronema citrinum. No. 932, Pyrrhoglossum pyrrhum, vert.

1991, June 24 — Litho. — Perf. 14

923	A154	10c multicolored	.55	.40
924	A154	15c multicolored	.75	.40
925	A154	20c multicolored	.90	.55
926	A154	35c multicolored	1.25	.60
927	A154	50c multicolored	1.75	1.00
928	A154	65c multicolored	2.25	1.75
929	A154	$1.10 multicolored	2.75	3.50
930	A154	$1.25 multicolored	2.75	3.75
		Nos. 923-930 (8)	12.95	11.95

Miniature Sheets

931	A154	$2 multicolored	6.50	7.00
932	A154	$2 multicolored	6.50	7.00

Paintings by Vincent Van Gogh — A155

Paintings: 15c, Weaver Facing Left, with Spinning Wheel. 25c, Head of a Young Peasant with Pipe, vert. 35c, The Old Cemetery Tower at Nuenen, vert. 45c, Cottage at Nightfall. 50c, Still Life with Open Bible. 65c, Lane at the Jardin du Luxembourg. 80c, The Pont du Carrousel and the Louvre. $1, Vase with Poppies, Cornflowers, Peonies and Chrysanthemums, vert. No. 941, Entrance to the Public Park. No. 942, Plowed Field.

1991, Aug. 26 — Perf. 13

933	A155	15c multicolored	1.25	.60
934	A155	25c multicolored	1.50	.60
935	A155	35c multicolored	1.75	.60
936	A155	45c multicolored	1.75	.70

937	A155	50c multicolored	1.75	.75
938	A155	65c multicolored	2.25	1.60
939	A155	80c multicolored	2.75	3.25
940	A155	$1 multicolored	3.00	3.25
		Nos. 933-940 (8)	16.00	11.35

Size: 107x80mm
Imperf

941	A155	$2 multicolored	7.50	7.75
942	A155	$2 multicolored	7.50	7.75

Phila
Nippon
'91
A156

Japanese steam locomotives.

1991, Nov. 4   Litho.   Perf. 14

943	A156	8c Series 8550	.80	.70
944	A156	10c C 57	.80	.60
945	A156	45c Series 4110	1.75	.80
946	A156	50c C 55	1.75	.80
947	A156	65c Series 6250	2.25	1.60
948	A156	80c E 10	2.60	2.60
949	A156	$1 Series 4500	2.60	2.75
950	A156	$1.25 C 11	4.00	6.25
		Nos. 943-950 (8)	16.55	16.10

Souvenir Sheets

951	A156	$2 C 62	6.00	6.00
952	A156	$2 C 58	6.00	6.00

Christmas
A157

Details or entire paintings by Gerard David: 8c, Adoration of the Shepherds. 15c, Virgin and Child Enthroned with Two Angels. 35c, The Annunciation (outside wings). 45c, The Rest on the Flight into Egypt. 50c, The Rest on the Flight into Egypt, diff. 65c, Virgin and Child with Angels. 80c, The Adoration of the Shepherds, diff. $1.25, The Perussis Altarpiece. No. 961, The Adoration of the Kings. No. 962, The Nativity.

1991, Dec. 23   Perf. 12

953	A157	8c multicolored	.75	.25
954	A157	15c multicolored	.95	.25
955	A157	35c multicolored	1.75	.50
956	A157	45c multicolored	1.75	.75
957	A157	50c multicolored	1.75	.90
958	A157	65c multicolored	2.25	1.25
959	A157	80c multicolored	2.75	3.00
960	A157	$1.25 multicolored	3.50	5.50
		Nos. 953-960 (8)	15.45	12.40

Souvenir Sheets
Perf. 14½

961	A157	$2 multicolored	6.50	6.50
962	A157	$2 multicolored	6.50	6.50

Boy
Scouts
A160

No. 968, Member of Boy Scout Service Corps at New York World's Fair, 1964-65. No. 969, Lord Robert Baden-Powell, vert. $2, Silver Buffalo Award.

1992, July 6   Litho.   Perf. 14

968	A160	$1 multicolored	3.75	4.00
969	A160	$1 multicolored	3.75	4.00

Souvenir Sheet

970	A160	$2 multicolored	8.00	9.50

17th World Scout Jamboree, Korea.

Anniversaries and Events — A161

Designs: 25c, Astronaut releasing communications satellite. 50c, Tree with dead side, healthy side. 65c, Emblems, globe, food products. 80c, Fish in polluted, clean water. $1, Runners, Lions Intl. emblem. $1.25, Orbiting quarantine facility modules. No. 977, Planned orbital transfer vehicle for Mars. No. 977A, Industrial pollution, clean beach.

1992-93   Litho.   Perf. 14

971	A161	25c multicolored	2.50	.80
972	A161	50c multicolored	2.75	1.00
973	A161	65c multicolored	2.25	1.75
974	A161	80c multicolored	3.75	3.50
975	A161	$1 multicolored	3.75	3.50
976	A161	$1.25 multicolored	4.00	5.00
		Nos. 971-976 (6)	19.00	15.55

Souvenir Sheets

977	A161	$2 multicolored	8.50	9.00
977A	A161	$2 multicolored	8.50	9.00

Intl. Space Year (#971, 976-977). Earth Summit, Rio de Janeiro (#972, 974, 977A). Intl. Conf. on Nutrition, Rome (#973). Lions Intl., 75th anniv. (#975).
Issued: #972, 974, 977A, 1/93; others, 12/92.

Queen Elizabeth II's Accession to the Throne, 40th Anniv.
Common Design Type

1992, Feb. 6   Litho.   Perf. 14

978	CD348	10c multicolored	.80	.50
979	CD348	20c multicolored	1.25	.70
980	CD348	25c multicolored	1.40	.75
981	CD348	35c multicolored	1.50	.90
982	CD348	50c multicolored	2.00	1.25
983	CD348	65c multicolored	2.25	2.00
984	CD348	80c multicolored	2.50	2.50
985	CD348	$1.10 multicolored	2.75	2.75
		Nos. 978-985 (8)	14.45	11.35

Souvenir Sheets

986	CD348	$2 Queen at left, boat dock	6.50	6.50
987	CD348	$2 Queen at right, shoreline	6.50	6.50

Spanish
Art — A162

Paintings: 8c, St. Monica, by Luis Tristan. 20c, 45c, The Vision of Ezekiel: The Resurrection of the Flesh (different details) by Francisco Collantes. 50c, The Martyrdom of St. Philip, by Jose de Ribera. 65c, St. John the Evangelist, by Juan Ribalta. 80c, Archimedes by Jose de Ribera. $1, St. John the Baptist in the Desert by de Ribera. $1.25, The Martyrdom of St. Philip (detail), by de Ribera. No. 996, The Baptism of Christ by Juan Fernandez Navarrete. No. 997, Battle between Christians and Moors at El Sotillo, by Francisco de Zurbaran.

1992, May 26   Litho.   Perf. 13

988	A162	8c multicolored	.80	.25
989	A162	20c multicolored	1.25	.30
990	A162	45c multicolored	1.75	.65
991	A162	50c multicolored	1.75	.65
992	A162	65c multicolored	2.25	1.25
993	A162	80c multicolored	2.50	2.50
994	A162	$1 multicolored	2.50	2.75
995	A162	$1.25 multicolored	2.75	3.25
		Nos. 988-995 (8)	15.55	11.60

Size: 95x120mm
Imperf

996	A162	$2 multicolored	7.25	7.25
997	A162	$2 multicolored	7.25	7.25

Granada '92.

Discovery of America, 500th Anniv. A163

Commemorative coins, scenes of first voyage: 10c, Nina, ship. 15c, Pinta, ship. 20c, Santa Maria, Columbus' second coat of arms. 25c, Fleet at sea, ships. 30c, Landfall, sailing ship. 35c, Setting sail, Columbus departing. 50c, Columbus sighting New World, Columbus. 65c, Columbus exploring Caribbean, ship. 80c, Claiming land for Spain, Columbus, priest and cross. $1.10, Columbus exchanging gifts with native, Columbus, native.
No. 1008, Coins like #998-1000. No. 1009, Coins like #1004, 1006-1007.

1992, Oct.   Litho.   Perf. 14

998	A163	10c multicolored	1.00	.65
999	A164	15c multicolored	1.10	.65
1000	A164	20c multicolored	1.10	.80
1001	A164	25c multicolored	1.75	.80
1002	A164	30c multicolored	1.75	.80
1003	A164	35c multicolored	1.75	.85
1004	A164	50c multicolored	2.00	1.25
1005	A164	65c multicolored	2.25	1.50
1006	A164	80c multicolored	2.25	2.50
1007	A164	$1.10 multicolored	2.50	3.50
		Nos. 998-1007 (10)	17.45	13.30

Souvenir Sheets

1008	A164	$2 multicolored	7.25	7.25
1009	A164	$2 multicolored	7.25	7.25

Christmas
A164

Details or entire paintings by Simon Bening: 8c, Nativity. 15c, Circumcision. 35c, Flight to Egypt. 50c, Massacre of the Innocents.
By Dirk Bouts: 65c, The Annunciation. 80c, The Visitation. $1.10, The Adoration of the Angels. $1.25, The Adoration of the Wise Men. No. 1018, The Virgin and Child. No. 1019, The Virgin Seated with the Child.

1992, Nov.   Litho.   Perf. 13½x14

1010	A164	8c multicolored	.55	.55
1011	A164	15c multicolored	1.10	1.10
1012	A164	35c multicolored	1.60	1.60
1013	A164	50c multicolored	2.00	2.00
1014	A164	65c multicolored	2.75	2.75
1015	A164	80c multicolored	3.25	3.25
1016	A164	$1.10 multicolored	3.75	3.75
1017	A164	$1.25 multicolored	3.75	3.75
		Nos. 1010-1017 (8)	18.75	18.75

Souvenir Sheets

1018	A164	$2 multicolored	7.25	7.25
1019	A164	$2 multicolored	7.25	7.25

Nos. 915, 918 & 921 Ovptd. in Red or Black

1993, Mar. 20   Litho.   Perf. 14

1020	CD347	35c on #915	3.00	1.50
1021	CD347	65c on #918	4.50	2.50

Souvenir Sheet

1022	CD347	$2 on #921 (Bk)	8.50	8.50

Coronation of Queen Elizabeth II, 40th Anniv. — A165

Designs: a, 15c, Chalice and paten from royal collection. b, 50c, Official coronation photograph. c, $1, Coronation ceremony. d, $1.25, Queen, Prince Philip. $2, New Portrait.

1993, June 2   Litho.   Perf. 13½x14

1023	A165	Sheet, 2 ea #a.-d.	13.50	14.50

Souvenir Sheet
Perf. 14

1024	A165	$2 multicolored	8.00	8.25

No. 1024 contains one 28x42mm stamp.

Christmas
A166

Details or entire woodcut, Mary, Queen of the Angels, by Durer: 8c, 20c, 35c, $1.25.
Details or entire paintings by Raphael: 50c, $1, Virgin and Child with St. John the Baptist. 65c, The Canagiani Holy Family. 80c, The Holy Family with the Lamb.
Each $2: No. 1033, Mary, Queen of the Angels, by Durer. No. 1034, The Canagiani Holy Family, diff., by Raphael.

Perf. 13½x14, 14x13½

1993, Dec.   Litho.

1025-1032	A166	Set of 8	16.00	16.00

Souvenir Sheets

1033-1034	A166	Set of 2	11.00	12.00

Dinosaurs
A167

8c, Omphalosaurus. 15c, Coelophysis. 20c, $2 (#1043), Triceratops. 35c, $2 (#1044), Dilophosaurus. 50c, Pterodactylus. 65c, Elasmosaurus. 80c, Stegosaurus. $1.25, Euoplocephalus.

1993, Nov. 15   Litho.   Perf. 14

1035-1042	A167	Set of 8	8.50	8.50

Souvenir Sheets

1043-1044	A167	Set of 2	14.50	14.50

Birds
A168

Designs: 10c, Killdeer. 15c, Yellow-crowned night heron, vert. 35c, Northern mockingbird. 50c, Eastern kingbird, vert. 65c, Magnolia warbler. 80c, Cedar waxwing, vert. $1.10, Ruby-throated hummingbird. $1.25, Painted bunting, vert. No. 1053, American kestrel. No. 1054, Ruddy duck.

1993, Dec.

1045	A168	10c multicolored	1.40	.80
1046	A168	15c multicolored	1.75	.80
1047	A168	35c multicolored	2.50	.80
1048	A168	50c multicolored	2.75	1.10
1049	A168	65c multicolored	3.00	1.75
1050	A168	80c multicolored	3.25	3.25
1051	A168	$1.10 multicolored	3.50	3.50
1052	A168	$1.25 multicolored	3.50	4.50
	Nos. 1045-1052 (8)		21.65	16.50

Souvenir Sheets

1053	A168	$2 multicolored	7.50	7.50
1054	A168	$2 multicolored	7.50	7.50

Fish
A169

Designs: 10c, Bluehead wrasse. 20c, Honeycomb cowfish. 25c, Glasseye snapper. 35c, Spotted drum. 50c, Jolthead porgy. 65, Smallmouth grunt. 80c, Peppermint bass. $1.10, Indigo hamlet.
Each $2: No. 1063, Bonnethead shark. No. 1064, Sharpnose shark.

1993, Dec. 15

1055-1062	A169	Set of 8	8.50	8.50

Souvenir Sheets

1063-1064	A169	Set of 2	8.75	9.75

1994 World Cup Soccer
Championships, US — A170

Designs: 8c, Segrio Goycochea, Argentina. 10c, Bodo Illgner, Germany. 50c, Nico Claesen, Belgium. 65c, West German team. 80c, Cameroun team. $1, Santin, Francescoli, Uruguay; Cuciuffo, Argentina. $1.10, Sanchez, Mexico.
Each $2: No. 1072, Imre Garaba, Hungary, vert. No. 1073, Pontiac Silverdome.

1994, Sept. 26   Litho.   *Perf. 14*

1065-1071	A170	Set of 7	11.50	10.00

Souvenir Sheets

1072-1073	A170	Set of 2	8.00	8.50

Mushrooms — A171

Designs: 5c, Xerocomus guadelupae, vert. 10c, Volvariella volvacea, vert. 35c, Hygrocybe atrosquamosa. 50c, Pleurotus ostreatus. 65c, Marasmius pallescens. 80c, Coprinus plicatilis, vert. $1.10, Bolbitius vitellinus. $1.50, Pyroglossum lilaceipes, vert.
Each $2: No. 1082, Lentinus edodes. No. 1083, Russula cremeolilacina, vert.

1994, Oct. 10

1074-1081	A171	Set of 8	10.50	10.50

Souvenir Sheets

1082-1083	A171	Set of 2	10.00	10.00

Christmas
A172

Illustrations from French Book of Hours: 25c, The Annunciation. 50c, The Visitation. 65c, Annunciation to the Shepherds. 80c, The Nativity. $1, Flight into Egypt.
$2, The Adoration of the Magi.

1994, Dec. 5   Litho.   *Perf. 14*

1084-1088	A172	Set of 5	11.50	8.75

Souvenir Sheet

1089	A172	$2 multicolored	7.00	7.00

Butterflies
A173

Designs: 15c, Dryas julia. 20c, Urbanus proteus. 25c, Colobura dirce. 50c, Papilio homerus. 65c, Chiodes catillus. 80c, Eurytides zonaria. $1, Hypolymnas misippus. $1.25, Phoebis avellaneda.
Each $2: No. 1098, Eurema adamsi. No. 1099, Morpho peleides.

1994, Dec. 12

1090-1097	A173	Set of 8	11.50	11.50

Souvenir Sheets

1098-1099	A173	Set of 2	8.25	8.75

D-Day, 50th Anniv.
A174

Designs: 10c, Gen. Montgomery, British landing on Juno Beach. 15c, Adm. Sir Bertram Ramsay, British commandos at Sword Beach. 35c, Gun crew aboard HMS Belfast. 50c, Montgomery, Eisenhower, Tedder review battle scene. 65c, Gen. Eisenhower, 101st Airborne Div. paratroopers. 80c, Gen. Omar Bradley, US landings on Omaha Beach. $1.10, Second wave of US troops on D-Day. $1.25, Supreme Commander Eisenhower presents Operation Overload.
Each $2: No. 1108, Eisenhower, Montgomery seated at table. No. 1109, Beachhead secured.

1994, Dec. 19

1100-1107	A174	Set of 8	10.00	10.00

Souvenir Sheets

1108-1109	A174	Set of 2	8.50	8.50

Orchids
A175

Designs: 8c, Cattleya deckeri. 20c, Epidendrum carpophorum. 25c, Epidendrum ciliare. 50c, Encyclia phoenicea. 65c, Bletia patula. 80c, Brassia caudata. $1, Brassavola nodosa. $1.25, Bletia purpurea.
Each $2: No. 1118, Ionopsis utricularioides. No. 1119, Vanilla planifolia.

1995, Jan. 5

1110-1117	A175	Set of 8	10.00	9.50

Souvenir Sheets

1118-1119	A175	Set of 2	9.50	9.50

Miniature Sheet of 12

PHILAKOREA '94 — A176

Jurassic marine reptiles: a, Elasmosaurus. b, Plesiosaurus. c, Ichthyosaurus. d, Arcfielon. e, Askeptosaurus. f, Macroplata. g, Ceresiosaurus. h, Lipoleurodon. i, Henodus. j, Muraenosaurus. k, Placodus. l, Kronosaurus.

1995, Jan. 23

1120	A176	35c #1120a-1120 l	9.50	9.50

First Manned Moon Landing, 25th Anniv.
A177

Designs: 10c, Apollo XI in flight. 20c, Simulated moon landing. 25c, Painting, Astronauts on the Moon, by Kovales. 35c, First foot, footprint on moon. 50c, Aldrin, solar wind experiment. 65c, Armstrong, Aldrin setting up flag on moon. 80c, Command module Columbia in Lunar orbit. $1.10, Recovery of Apollo XI in Pacific.
Each $2: No. 1129, Lift-off at Cape Canaveral, vert. No. 1130, Moon rock on display in Houston.

1995, Jan. 9   Litho.   *Perf. 14*

1121-1128	A177	Set of 8	9.00	9.00

Souvenir Sheets

1129-1130	A177	Set of 2	9.00	9.00

Intl. Olympic Committee, Cent. — A178

Summer, Winter Olympic events: 8c, Fencing. 10c, Speed skating. 15c, Diving. 20c, Cycling. 25c, Ice hockey. 35c, Figure skating. 50c, Soccer. 65c, Bobsled. 80c, Super giant slalom. $1.25, Equestrian.
Each $2: #1141, Gymnastics. #1142, Downhill skiing.

1995, Feb. 6

1131-1140	A178	Set of 10	15.00	11.00

Souvenir Sheets

1141-1142	A178	Set of 2	9.50	9.50

Domestic Cats
A179

Various cats, kittens: 15c, 20c, 35c, 50c, 65c, 80c, $1, $1.25.
Each $2: No. 1151, Two sleeping. No. 1152, Kitten, ladybugs in flowers.

1995, July 3   Litho.   *Perf. 14*

1143-1150	A179	Set of 8	15.00	11.00

Souvenir Sheets

1151-1152	A179	Set of 2	10.00	10.00

Birds — A180

A180a

10c, Belted kingfisher. 15c, Clapper rail. 20c, American redstart. 25c, Roseate tern. 35c, Purple gallinule. 45c, Ruddy turnstone. 50c, Barn owl. 60c, Brown booby. 80c, Great blue heron. $1, Antillean nighthawk. $1.25, Thick-billed vireo. $1.40, American flamingo. $2, Wilson's plover. $5, Blue-winged teal. $10, Reddish egret.

1995, Aug. 2   Litho.   *Perf. 13*

1153	A180	10c multi	1.50	1.00
1154	A180	15c multi	1.50	1.00
1155	A180	20c multi	1.50	1.00
1156	A180	25c multi	1.75	1.00
1157	A180	35c multi	1.75	1.00
1158	A180	45c multi	2.25	1.25
1159	A180	50c multi	3.75	2.25
1160	A180	60c multi	2.50	1.50
1161	A180	80c multi	3.00	1.50
1162	A180	$1 multi	3.75	2.50
1163	A180	$1.25 multi	4.25	2.75
1164	A180	$1.40 multi	4.75	4.00
1165	A180	$2 multi	5.25	6.75
1166	A180	$5 multi	8.00	12.00
1166A	A180a	$10 multi	14.00	20.00
	Nos. 1153-1166A (15)		59.50	59.50

Queen Mother, 95th Birthday
A181

No. 1167: a, Drawing. b, Wearing crown jewels. c, Formal portrait. d, Blue dress with pearls.
$2, Green blue outfit.

1995, Aug. 4   *Perf. 13½x14*

1167	A181	50c Block or strip of 4, #a.-d.	7.75	7.75

Souvenir Sheet

1168	A181	$2 multicolored	7.75	7.75

No. 1167 was issued in sheets of 8 stamps.

VE Day, 50th Anniv.
A182

Designs: 10c, "Big Three" meet at Yalta. 15c, Allied war prisoners released. 20c, American, Soviets meet at Elbe River. 25c, Death of Franklin D. Roosevelt. 60c, US 9th Army confirms cease fire. 80c, New York City celebrates VE Day. $1, Nuremberg War Crimes trials begin.
$2, Big Ben, US Capitol, St. Basil's Cathedral.

1995, Aug. 14   Litho.   *Perf. 14*

1169-1175	A182	Set of 7	9.50	9.50

Souvenir Sheet

1176	A182	$2 multicolored	8.00	8.00

Miniature Sheet of 9

Singapore '95 — A183

Diving equipment, each 60c: No. 1177a, Wm. James, scuba, 1825. b, Rouquayrol apparatus, 1864. c, Fluess oxygen rebreathing apparatus, 1878. d, Armored diving suit, 1900. e, Jim Janett explores sunken Lusitania in Peress armored diving suit, 1935. f, Cousteau-

Gagnan aqualung, 1943. g, Underwater camera, 1955. h, Sylvia Earle dives to 1,520 ft. in Jim suit, 1979. i, Spider propeller-driven rigid suit, 1984.

Each $2: No. 1178, Helmet diver, 1935. No. 1179, Jacques-Yves Cousteau.

1995, Sept. 1   **Perf. 14½**
1177 A183 Sheet of 9, #a.-i.   13.00 13.00

Souvenir Sheets
1178-1179 A183 Set of 2   8.50 8.50

Christmas
A184

Details or entire paintings, by Piero di Cosimo (1462-1521): 20c, Madonna and Child with Young St. John. 25c, Adoration of the Child. 60c, Madonna and Child with Young St. John, St. Margaret, and An Angel. $1, Madonna and Child with An Angel.
$2, Madonna and Child with Angels and Saints.

1995, Dec. 29   **Litho.**   **Perf. 14**
1180-1183 A184 Set of 4   8.00 6.25

Souvenir Sheet
1184 A184 $2 multicolored   9.00 10.00

UN, 50th Anniv. — A185

Designs: 15c, Rights of women and children. 60c, Peace. 80c, Human rights. $1, Education.
Each $2: No. 1180, Flags of nations forming "50." No. 1190, Tractor, portions of UN, FAO emblems.

1996, Feb. 26   **Litho.**   **Perf. 14**
1185-1188 A185 Set of 4   5.50 5.50

Souvenir Sheets
1189-1190 A185 Set of 2   8.75 10.00

Queen Elizabeth II, 70th Birthday
A186

No. 1191: a, Portrait. b, Wearing blue hat. c, In uniform, on horseback.
$2, As younger woman wearing white and yellow hat.

1996, Apr. 21   **Litho.**   **Perf. 13½x14**
1191 A186 80c Strip of 3, #a.-c.   4.75 4.75

Souvenir Sheet
1192 A186 $2 multicolored   4.25 4.75

No. 1191 was issued in sheets of 9 stamps.

History of Underwater Exploration
A187

No. 1193, each 55c: a, Glaucus, God of Divers, 2500BC. b, Alexander the Great descends to ocean bottom, 332BC. c, Salvage diver, 1430. d, Borelli's rebreathing device, 1680. e, Edmond Halley's diving bell, 1690. f, John Lethbridge's diving machine, 1715. g, Klingert's diving apparatus, 1789. h, Drieberg's triton, 1808. i, Seibe's diving helmet, 1819.

No. 1194, each 60c: a, Jim Jarrat in "Iron Man" armored diving suit explores Lusitania, 1935. b, Cousteau, team excavate first shipwreck using scuba gear, 1952. c, Oldest shipwreck ever found, coast of Turkey, 1959. d, Swedish warship Vasa raised, 1961. e, Mel Fisher discovers Spanish galleon Atocha, 1971. f, Whydah, first pirate ship found, is discovered by Barry Clifford, 1984. g, Dr. Robert Ballard, using robot sub Argo finds battleship Bismarck, 1989. h, Radeau "Land Tortoise" scuttled in 1758 during French and Indian War found in Lake George, NY, 1991. i, Deep-diving nuclear submarine recovers ancient Roman shipwreck cargo, 1994.

Each $2: No. 1195, Arab diver Issa, 12th cent. No. 1196, Pearl diver in Caribbean, 1498. No. 1197, Diver in Newtsuit investigates Edmund Fitzgerald. No. 1198, Submarine Alvin explores Titanic, 1985.

1996, May 13   **Litho.**   **Perf. 14**
1193 A187 Sheet of 9, #a.-i.   15.00 15.00
1194 A187 Sheet of 9, #a.-i.   11.00 11.00

Souvenir Sheets
1195-1198 A187 Set of 4   17.75 17.75

CHINA '96 (Nos. 1193, 1195-1196). CAPEX '96 (Nos. 1194, 1197-1198).

1996 Summer Olympics, Atlanta
A188

Olympic gold medals for: No. 1199, Equestrian. No. 1200, Cycling. No. 1201, Fencing. No. 1202, Gymnastics. No. 1203, Hurdles. No. 1204, Pole vault. No. 1205, Sprints. No. 1206, Swimming. No. 1207, Diving. No. 1208, Running.

1996, May 27   **Perf. 13½**
1199-1208 A188 55c Set of 10   10.00 11.00
1208a   Sheet of 10, #1199-1208   10.00

Nos. 1199-1208 issued in sheets as well as in No. 1208a.

A189

James A.G.S. McCartney (1945-80), 1st Chief Minister of Turks & Caicos Islands.

1996, July 8   **Litho.**   **Perf. 14**
1209 A189 60c multicolored   1.00 1.00

Ministerial Government, 20th anniv.
No. 1209 was issued in sheets of 9.

A190

Working Dogs: No. 1210: a, Space research. b, Racing. c, Rescue. d, Military. e, Sporting. f, Companion. g, Hearing ear. h, Sled. i, Police. j, Guarding. k, Watch. l, Security.

Each $2: No. 1211, Guide. No. 1212, Sheep dog.

1996, Sept. 8   **Litho.**   **Perf. 14**
1210 A190 25c Sheet of 12,
    #a.-l.   11.00 11.00

Souvenir Sheets
1211-1212 A190 Set of 2   11.00 11.00

Winnie the Pooh, Christmas
A191

Designs: 15c, Pooh trying to stay awake. 20c, Piglet, star. 35c, Ribbons and bows. 50c, Jingle bells. 60c, "Pooh loves Christmas." 80c, "Big hearts come in bouncy packages." $1, Santa Pooh. $1.25, "My most favorite."
No. 1221, Piglet, cookie. No. 1222, Piglet placing star atop tree.

1996, Nov. 25   **Litho.**   **Perf. 13½x14**
1213-1220 A191 Set of 8   15.00 12.50

Souvenir Sheets
1221 A191 $2 multicolored   7.50 7.50
1222 A191 $2.60 multicolored   7.50 7.50

Flowers — A192

No. 1223: a, Giant milkweed. b, Geiger tree. c, Passion flower. d, Hibiscus.
No. 1224: a, Yellow elder. b, Prickly poppy. c, Frangipani. d, Seaside mahoe.
Each $2: No. 1225, Chain of love. No. 1226, Firecracker.

1997, Feb. 10   **Litho.**   **Perf. 14**
1223 A192 20c Strip or block of
    4, #a.-d.   3.25 3.25
1224 A192 60c Strip or block of
    4, #a.-d.   3.50 3.50

Souvenir Sheets
1225-1226 A192 Set of 2   8.00 8.00

Nos. 1223-1224 were each issued in sheets of 8 stamps.

UNICEF, 50th Anniv. — A193

a, Dove flying right. b, Three children. c, Dove flying left. d, Boy with dog, girl holding cat.

1997, Mar. 24   **Litho.**   **Perf. 14**
1227 A193 60c Sheet of 4, #a.-d.   7.25 8.00

Souvenir Sheets

UNESCO, 50th Anniv. — A194

Canterbury Cathedral: No. 1228, View from rear. No. 1229, Interior view.

1997, Mar. 24   **Litho.**   **Perf. 14**
1228 A194 $2 multicolored   4.25 4.25
1229 A194 $2 multicolored   4.25 4.25

Queen Elizabeth II, Prince Philip, 50th Wedding Anniv.
A195

Designs: a, Queen waving. b, Royal arms. c, Queen, Prince riding in car. d, Prince, Queen seated. e, Windsor Castle. f, Prince Philip.
$2, Wedding portrait.

1997, Apr. 21   **Litho.**   **Perf. 14**
1230 A195 60c Sheet of 6,
    #a.-f.   11.00 10.00

Souvenir Sheet
1231 A195 $2 multicolored   7.50 7.50

Heinrich von Stephan (1831-97), Founder of UPU
A196

Portrait of Von Stephan and: No. 1232: a, British mail coach, 1700's. b, UPU emblem. c, Space shuttle, future transport.
$2, Von Stephan, Hemerodrome, messenger of ancient Greece.

1997, July 1   **Litho.**   **Perf. 14**
1232 A196 50c Sheet of 3, #a.-c.   5.00 5.00

Souvenir Sheet
1233 A196 $2 multicolored   5.00 5.00

PACIFIC 97.

Underwater Exploration
A197

No. 1234: a, Edgerton camera taking photos at 6,000 ft., 1954. b, Conshelf Habitat, 1963. c, Sealab II, 1965. d, Research Habitat, Tektite,

1970. e, Discovery of Galapagos Volcanic Rift, 1974. f, Epaulard, robot survey craft, 1979. g, Sea life discovered thriving in undersea oil field, 1995. h, Deep flight, 1996, one-man research vessel. i, Sea ice is studied from above, under sea, Okhotsk Tower, off Japan, 1996.

Each $2: No. 1235, Coelacanth. No. 1236, John Williamson makes first underwater movies, 1914.

1997, Aug. 21   Litho.   Perf. 14
1234 A197 20c Sheet of 9,
#a.-i.   6.75 7.00
Souvenir Sheets
1235-1236 A197 Set of 2   8.50 9.00
Stampshow 97.

Christmas
A198

Entire paintings or details: 15c, Adoration of an Angel, by Studio of Fra Angelico. 20c, Scenes from the Life of St. John the Baptist, by Master of Saint Severin. 35c, Archangel Gabriel, by Masolino de Panicale. 50c, 60c, Jeremiah with Two Angels, by Gherardo Starnina (diff. angels). 80c, The Annunciation, by Giovanni di Palo di Grazia. $1, The Annunciation, by Carlo di Bracceso. $1.25, The Nativity, by Benvenuto di Giovanni Guasta.

Each $2: No. 1245, The Wilton Diptych (right panel), by unknown English or French artist, c. 1395. No. 1246, Adoring Angels, from The Journey of the Magi, by Benozzo Gozzoli.

1997, Dec. 8   Litho.   Perf. 14
1237-1244 A198 Set of 8   10.00 10.00
Souvenir Sheets
1245-1246 A198 Set of 2   9.00 9.00

World Wildlife Fund — A199

Snapper: a, Blackfin. b, Dog. c, Cubera. d, Mahogany.

1998, Feb. 24   Litho.   Perf. 14
1247 A199 25c Block of 4, #a.-d. 3.25 3.25
No. 1247 was issued in sheets of 16 stamps.
Intl. Year of the Reef.

Marine Life — A200

Underwater photographs: 20c, Spotted flamingo tongue. 50c, Feather duster. 60c, Squirrel fish. 80c, Queen angelfish. $1, Barracuda. $1.25, Fairy basslet.

Each $2: No. 1254, Rough file clam. No. 1255, Spotted cleaning shrimp.

1998, May 1   Litho.   Perf. 14
1248-1253 A200 Set of 6   11.00 11.00
Souvenir Sheets
1254-1255 A200 Set of 2   8.75 8.75

A201

Stylized designs showing symbol for earth, water, and — No. 1256: a, Dove. b, Crab. c, Fish. d, Clover leaf.
$2, Symbol for earth and water.

1998, July 30   Litho.   Perf. 14
1256 A201 50c Sheet of 4, #a.-d. 6.00 6.00
Souvenir Sheet
1257 A201 $2 multicolored   5.50 5.50
Intl. Year of the Ocean.

Royal Air Force, 80th Anniv.
Common Design Type Re-Inscribed

Designs: 20c, SE 5A. 50c, Sopwith Camel. 60c, Supermarine Spitfire. 80c, Avro Lancaster. $1, Panavia Tornado. $1.25, Hawker Hurricane.

Each $2: No. 1264, Hawker Siddeley Harrier. No. 1265, Avro Vulcan.

1998, Aug. 18   Litho.   Perf. 14
1258-1263 CD350 Set of 6   14.00 14.00
Souvenir Sheets
1264-1265 CD350 Set of 2   13.50 13.50

A202

Anniversaries and Events: 20c, University of the West Indies, 50th anniv. 60c, UNESCO, World Summit Program. 80c, Universal Declaration of Human Rights. $1, John Glenn's return to space.
$2, NASA Space Shuttle leaving launching pad.

1998, July 30   Litho.   Perf. 14
1266-1269 A202 Set of 4   5.50 5.50
Souvenir Sheet
1270 A202 $2 multicolored   4.75 4.75

A203

1998, Aug. 31
1271 A203 60c multicolored   2.00 1.75
Diana, Princess of Wales (1961-97). No. 1271 was issued in sheets of 6.

Paintings by Sister Thomasita Fessler — A204

a, Magi's Visit. b, Flight Into Egypt. c, Wedding Feast. d, Maria. e, Annunciation & Visitation. f, Nativity.
$2, Queen of Mothers.

1998, Nov. 30   Litho.   Perf. 14
1272 A204 50c Sheet of 6,
#a.-f.   8.75 8.75
Souvenir Sheet
1273 A204 $2 multicolored   4.75 4.75
Christmas. Nos. 1272e-1272f are each 58x48mm.

Coral
Gardens
A205

No. 1274: a, Flamingos in flight. b, Sailboats. c, Seagulls, lighthouse. d, House along shore, seagulls. e, Pillar coral, yellowtail snapper (f). f, Eliptical star coral. g, Porkfish. h, Spotted eagle ray. i, Large ivory coral. j, Mustard hill coral, shy hamlet. k, Blue crust coral. l, Fused staghorn coral. m, Queen angelfish, massive starlet coral. n, Pinnate spiny sea fan. o, Knobby star coral, squirrelfish. p, Lowridge cactus coral, juvenile porkfish. q, Orange telesto coral. r, Spanish hogfish (q), Knobby ten-ray star coral. s, Boulder brain coral, clown wrasse. t, Rainbow parrotfish, regal sea fan. u, Great star coral, bluestriped grunt. v, Stinging coral, blue tang. w, Lavender thin finger coral. x, Juvenile french grunt (w), brilliant sea fingers.

Each $2: No. 1275, Sea fan. No. 1276, Elkhorn coral.

1999, June 7   Litho.   Perf. 14¼x14½
1274 A205 20c Sheet of 24,
#a.-x.   21.00 21.00
Souvenir Sheets
1275-1276 A205 Set of 2   18.00 18.00

Wedding of Prince Edward and Sophie Rhys-Jones
A206

Portraits — #1277: a, Couple facing forward. b, Edward. c, Sophie. d, Couple walking arm in arm.

Each $2: No. 1278, Couple facing forward. No. 1279, Couple facing each other.

1999, June 19   Litho.   Perf. 14
1277 A206 60c Sheet of 4,
#a.-d.   6.25 6.25
Souvenir Sheets
1278-1279 A206 Set of 2   10.00 10.00

Queen Mother (b. 1900)
A207

Designs: a, At age 7. b, At age 19. c, At wedding. d, With daughters. e, With King George VI during World War II. f, In 1958. g, At age 60. h, In 1970. i, With Princes Charles and William, 1983. j, Current photograph.

1999, Aug. 4   Litho.   Perf. 13½x13¾
1280 A207 50c Sheet of 10,
#a.-j.   17.00 17.00
Stamp inscription on No. 1280f is incorrect.
No. 1280 was reissued in 2002 with added inscription in margin, "Good Health and Happiness to her Majesty The Queen Mother on her 101st Birthday." Value, $19.

2nd World Underwater Photography Competition Winners
A208

No. 1281: a, 10c, Painted tunicates (8th place). b, 20c, Peacock flounder (7th). c, 50c, Squirt anemone shrimps (6th). d, 60c, Juvenile drum (5th). e, 80c, Batwing coral crab (4th). f, $1, Moon jellyfish (3rd).

Each $2: No. 1282, Christmas tree worms (2nd). No. 1283, Longhorn nudibranch (1st).

1999, Oct. 11   Litho.   Perf. 14¼x13¾
1281 A208 Sheet of 6, #a.-f.   9.75 10.00
g.   As No. 1281, with corrected
      pictures   9.75 10.00
Issued: No. 1281g, 11/6/00.
On No. 1281, the illustrations for the 10c and 20c stamps are incorrect, with the 10c stamp inscribed "Painted tunicates," but depicting a peacock flounder, and the 20c stamp inscribed "Peacock flounder," but depicting painted tunicates. The pictures were switched on No. 1281g, making the inscriptions match the pictures.

Souvenir Sheets
Perf. 13¾
1282-1283 A208 Set of 2   14.00 14.00
Nos. 1282-1283 each contain one 50x38mm stamp.

Christmas
A209

Paintings by Anthony Van Dyck: 20c, The Mystic Marriage of Saint Catherine. 50c, Rest on the Flight into Egypt. No. 1286, $2, Holy Family with Saints John and Elizabeth. No. 1287, The Madonna of the Rosary.

1999, Dec. 7   Perf. 13¾
1284-1286 A209 Set of 3   9.00 9.00
Souvenir Sheet
1287 A209 $2 multicolored   8.75 9.00

Millennium
A210

Perf. 14½x14¼
1999, Nov. 15   Litho.
1288 A210 20c silver & multi   .80   .80
1289 A210 $1 gold & multi   3.75 3.75

Millennium — A211

Globe, clock and: No. 1290: a, London. b, Turks & Caicos Islands. c, New York. d, Rome. e, Jerusalem. f, Paris.

Each $2: No. 1291, Flag of Islands. No. 1292, Arms of Islands.

2000, Jan. 18   Litho.   Perf. 14x13¾
1290 A211 50c Sheet of 6,
#a.-f.   12.00 12.00
Souvenir Sheets
1291-1292 A211 Set of 2   17.00 17.00

Mushrooms — A212

No. 1293, vert.: a, Pholiota squarroides. b, Psilocybe squamosa. c, Spathularia velutipes. d, Russula. e, Clitocybe clavipes. f, Boletus frostii.
No. 1294, Strobilurus conigenoides. No. 1295, Stereum ostrea.

2000, July 6   Litho.   Perf. 14
1293 A212 50c Sheet of 6, #a-
       f   9.00 9.00
Souvenir Sheets
1294-1295 A212 $2 Set of 2 11.00 11.00

Souvenir Sheet

2000 Summer Olympics, Sydney — A213

No. 1296: a, Johan Gabriel Oxenstierna. b, Javelin. c, Aztec Stadium, Mexico City and Mexican flag. d, Ancient Greek runners.

2000, Sept. 25
1296 A213 50c Sheet of 4, #a-d 7.00 7.00

Birds
A214

Designs: No. 1297, Chickadee. No. 1298, Scrub turkey. No. 1299, Sickle-bill gull.
No. 1300: a, Egret. b, Tern. c, Osprey. d, Great blue heron. e, Pelican. f, Bahama pintail.
No. 1301, Flamingo, vert. No. 1302, Macaw, vert.

2000, Oct. 2
1297-1299 A214 50c Set of 3 5.25 5.25
1300 A214 60c Sheet of 6, #a-
       f   11.00 11.00
Souvenir Sheets
1301-1302 A214 $2 Set of 2 14.00 14.00

Dogs and Cats — A215

No. 1303, 60c: a, Airedale terrier. b, Beagle. c, Dalmatian. d, Chow chow. e, Chihuahua. f, Pug.
No. 1304, 80c: a, Egyptian mau. b, Manx. c, Burmese. d, Korat. e, Maine coon cat. f, American shorthair.

No. 1305, $2, Collie. No. 1306, $2, Devon rex.

2000, Nov. 13   Litho.   Perf. 14
Sheets of 6, #a-f
1303-1304 A215 Set of 2 22.00 22.00
Souvenir Sheets
1305-1306 A215 Set of 2 11.00 12.00

Battle of Britain, 60th Anniv. A216

Designs: No. 1307, 50c, Douglas Robert Stewart Bader. No. 1308, 50c, Alan Christopher "Al" Deere. No. 1309, 50c, James Edgar "Johnny" Johnson. No. 1310, 50c, Edgar James "Cobber" Kain. No. 1311, 50c, James Harry "Ginger" Lacey. No. 1312, 50c, Air Vice-marshal Trafford Leigh Mallory. No. 1313, 50c, Adolph Gysbert "Sailor" Malan. No. 1314, Air Vice-marshal Keith Park.
No. 1315, each 50c: a, Winston Churchill. b, Barrage balloon. c, Heinkel He-111 Casa 2 111E. d, Soldier's farewell kiss to son. e, Hawker Hurricane. f, Dr, Jocelyn Henry Temple Perkins, clergyman in Home Guard. g, RAF fighter pilots scramble after an alert. h, Civilian volunteers scan the skies.
No. 1316, $2, Churchill, British flag. No. 1317, $2, London children.

2000, Dec. 4   Perf. 14
Stamps + labels
1307-1314 A216 Set of 8 12.00 12.00
1315 A216 Sheet of 8, #a-h 12.00 12.00
Souvenir Sheets
1316-1317 A216 Set of 2 10.00 10.00

Butterflies — A217

No. 1318, 50c: a, Clorinde. b, Blue night. c, Small lace-wing. d, Mosaic. e, Monarch. f, Grecian shoemaker.
No. 1319, 50c: a, Giant swallowtail. b, Common morpho. c, Tiger pierid. d, Banded king shoemaker. e, Figure-of-eight. f, Polydamas swallowtail.
No. 1320, $2, Orange-barred sulphur. No. 1321, $2, White peacock.

2000, Dec. 11   Litho.
Sheets of 6, #a-f
1318-1319 A217 Set of 2 21.00 21.00
Souvenir Sheets
1320-1321 A217 Set of 2 13.00 13.00

Ships
A218

Designs: No. 1322, 60c, Neptune. No. 1323, 60c, Eagle. No. 1324, 60c, Gloria. No. 1325, 60c, Clipper ship, vert.

No. 1326, 60c: a, Viking long ship. b, Henri Grace à Dieu. c, Golden Hind. d, Endeavor. e, Anglo-Norman. f, Libertad.
No. 1327, 60c: a, Northern European cog. b, Carrack. c, Mayflower. d, Queen Anne's Revenge. e, Holkar. f, Amerigo Vespucci.
No. 1328, $2, USS Constitution, vert. No. 1329, $2, Denmark, vert.

2001, May 15   Litho.   Perf. 14
1322-1325 A218 Set of 4 8.75 8.75
Sheets of 6, #a-f
1326-1327 A218 Set of 2 24.00 24.00
Souvenir Sheets
1328-1329 A218 Set of 2 16.00 16.00

Whales
A219

Designs: No. 1330, 50c, Beluga. No. 1331, 50c, Killer. No. 1332, 50c, Dwarf sperm. No. 1333, 50c, Shortfin pilot.
No. 1334, 50c: a, Bowhead. b, Two killer. c, Pygmy sperm. d, Right. e, Sperm. f, California gray.
No. 1335, 50c: a, Narwhal. b, One killer (in air). c, Bryde's. d, Belugas. e, Sperm (and starfish). f, Pilot.
No. 1336, $2, Cuvier's beaked. No. 1337, $2, Humpback (with calf).

2001, May 15
1330-1333 A219 Set of 4 8.25 8.25
Sheets of 6, #a-f
1334-1335 A219 Set of 2 25.00 25.00
Souvenir Sheets
1336-1337 A219 Set of 2 16.00 16.00

UN Women's Human Rights Campaign — A220

Designs: 60c, Woman. 80c, Woman, bird, torch.

2001, June 18   Litho.   Perf. 14
1338-1339 A220 Set of 2 6.00 6.00

Phila Nippon '01 — A221

Designs: No. 1340, 60c, Autumn Moon in Mirror, by Suzuki Harunobu. No. 1341, 60c, Rikaku II as a Fisherman, by Hirosada. No. 1342, 60c, Musical Party, by Hishikawa Moronobu. No. 1343, 60c, Kannon and Four Farmers, by H. Gatto. No. 1344, 60c, Rain in Fifth Month, by Kunisada I. No. 1345, 60c, The Lives of Women, by Kuniyoshi Utagawa.

2001, July 30   Perf. 12x12¼
1340-1345 A221 Set of 6 10.00 10.00

Queen Victoria (1819-1901) — A222

No. 1346, 60c, oval frames: a, Wearing white headcovering. b, Wearing crown as young woman. c, Wearing black hat. d, Wearing crown as old woman.
No. 1347, 60c, rectangular frames: a, Wearing white headcovering. b, Holding flowers. c, Wearing white dress. d, Wearing crown, white dress with blue sash.
No. 1348, $2, Brown orange background. No. 1349, $2, Holding umbrella.

2001, July 2   Perf. 14
Sheets of 4, #a-d
1346-1347 A222 Set of 2 16.00 16.00
Souvenir Sheets
1348-1349 A222 Set of 2 12.00 12.00

Queen Elizabeth II, 75th Birthday — A223

No. 1350: a, In pink hat. b, With crown looking left. c, In green hat. d, With crown looking forward. e, In red orange hat. f, With crown and veil.
$2, Wearing robe.

2001, July 2
1350 A223 60c Sheet of 6, #a-
       f   12.00 12.00
Souvenir Sheet
1351 A223 $2 multi 6.75 6.75

Butterflies — A224

Designs: 10c, Cuban mimic. 15c, Gundlach's swallowtail, vert. 20c, Graphium androcles. 25c, Eastern black swallowtail. 35c, Papilio velvois, vert. 45c, Schaus swallowtail, vert. 50c, Pipevine swallowtail, vert. 60c, Euploea mniszecki, vert. 80c, Poey's black swallowtail, vert. $1, Graphium oncelades, vert. $1.25, Jamaican ringlet. $1.40, Eastern tiger swallowtail. $2, Graphium milon, vert. $5, Palamedes swallowtail. $10, Zebra swallowtail.

Perf. 14x14¾, 14¾x14

2001, Sept. 27

1352	A224	10c multi	.40	.40
1353	A224	15c multi	.50	.50
1354	A224	20c multi	.75	.75
1355	A224	25c multi	2.25	.75
1356	A224	35c multi	2.25	.75
1357	A224	45c multi	1.00	.80
1358	A224	50c multi	1.00	.80
1359	A224	60c multi	1.25	1.00
1360	A224	80c multi	1.50	1.25
1361	A224	$1 multi	2.00	1.75
1362	A224	$1.25 multi	2.50	2.25
1363	A224	$1.40 multi	2.75	3.00
1364	A224	$2 multi	4.50	5.00
1365	A224	$5 multi	10.00	12.00
1366	A224	$10 multi	18.00	20.00
	Nos. 1352-1366 (15)		50.65	51.00

25c, 35c, $5, $10 exist dated "2003." Value, set $32.50.

Reign of Queen Elizabeth II, 50th Anniv. — A225

No. 1367: a, Crossing Place Trail, Middle Caicos. b, Wades Green Plantation, North Caicos. c, Underwater scenery, Grand Turk. d, St. Thomas Anglican Church, Grand Turk. e, Ripsaw band, Grand Turk. f, Basketweaving.

No. 1368: a, Visit of Princess Royal, 1960. b, Visit of Queen Elizabeth II, 1966. c, Visit of Princess Alexandra, 1988. d, Visit of Duke of Edinburgh, 1993. e, Visit of Prince Andrew, 2000.

No. 1369: a, Salt Industry, 1952-62. b, Space splashdown, 1962-72. c, Ministerial government system, 1972-82. d, Quincentennial of Columbus' landfall, 1982-92. e, National Museum, 1992-2002.

2002, June 1   **Litho.**   **Perf. 14¼**

1367	Sheet of 6	3.50	3.50
a.-f.	A225 25c Any single	.60	.60

Perf. 13¾

1368	Sheet of 5	7.50	7.50
a.-e.	A225 60c Any single	1.50	1.50

Perf. 13¾x14¼

1369	Sheet of 5	9.00	9.00
a.-e	A225 80c Any single	1.80	1.80

No. 1368 contains five 31x31mm stamps; No. 1369 contains five 30x34mm stamps.

20th World Scout Jamboree, Thailand — A226

No. 1370: a, Scout with mallet and chisel. b, Scout with rifle. c, Scout hanging on rope above water. d, Scouts and lantern. $2, Handicapped Scouts.

2002, July 15   **Perf. 14**

1370	A226 80c Sheet of 4, #a-d	8.00	8.00

Souvenir Sheet

1371	A226 $2 multi	5.00	5.00

Intl. Year of Ecotourism — A227

No. 1372, vert.: a, Humpback whale. b, Water sports. c, Regattas. d, Queen angelfish. e, Manta ray. f, Turtle.
$2, Jojo dolphin.

2002, July 15

1372	A227 60c Sheet of 6, #a-f	11.00	11.00

Souvenir Sheet

1373	A227 $2 multi	5.25	5.50

No. 1372 contains six 28x42mm stamps.

Intl. Year of Mountains — A228

No. 1374: a, Devil's Peak, South Africa. b, Mt. Drakensburg, South Africa. c, Mt. Blanc, France. d, Roan Mountain, US. e, Mt. Sefton, New Zealand. f, Mt. Cook, New Zealand.
$2, Northwest Highlands, Scotland.

2002, July 22

1374	A228 80c Sheet of 6, #a-f	11.50	11.50

Souvenir Sheet

1375	A228 $2 multi	5.25	5.50

United We Stand — A229

2002, Aug. 5

1376	A229 50c multi	1.50	1.50

Printed in sheets of 4.

Insects and Birds — A230

No. 1377, 60c: a, Hawk moth. b, Burnet moth. c, Mammoth wasp. d, Branch-boring

beetle. e, Flower mantid, Pseudocrebotra species. f, Flower mantid, Creobroter species.
No. 1378, 60c: a, Sooty tern. b, Magnificent frigatebird. c, American white pelican. d, Northern shoveler. e, Baltimore oriole. f, Roseate spoonbill.
No. 1379, $2, Tiphiid wasp. No. 1380, $2, Greater flamingo, vert.

2002, Aug. 12   **Perf. 14**

Sheets of 6, #a-f

1377-1378	A230	Set of 2	22.50	20.00

Souvenir Sheets

1379-1380	A230	Set of 2	10.00	10.00

Queen Mother Elizabeth (1900-2002) — A231

No. 1381: a, Without hat. b, With hat.

2002, Oct. 21

1381	A231 80c Sheet, 2 each #a-b	8.00	8.00

First Nonstop Solo Transatlantic Flight, 75th Anniv. — A232

No. 1382: a, Charles Lindbergh's early exploits as a barnstormer. b, Lindbergh standing in front of Spirit of St. Louis. c, Spirit of St. Louis. d, Take-off from Roosevelt Field. e, Crossing the Atlantic. f, Arrival and welcome in Paris.

2002, Nov. 18   **Litho.**   **Perf. 14**

1382	A232 60c Sheet of 6, #a-f	11.50	10.00

Pres. John F. Kennedy (1917-63) — A233

No. 1383 — Portrait color: a, Orange brown. b, Red violet. c, Greenish gray. d, Blue violet. e, Purple. f, Dull brown.

2002, Nov. 18

1383	A233 60c Sheet of 6, #a.-f.	10.00	10.00

Christmas — A234

Designs: 20c, Madonna and Child, by Giovanni Bellini. 25c, Adoration of the Magi, by Correggio. 60c, Transfiguration of Christ, by Bellini, vert. 80c, Polyptych of St. Vincent Ferrer, by Bellini, vert. $1, Miraculous Mass, by Simone Martini, vert.
$2, Christ in Heaven with Four Saints, by Domenico Ghirlandaio.

2002, Nov. 25

1384-1388	A234 Set of 5	8.00	7.50

Souvenir Sheet

1389	A234 $2 multi	5.50	6.00

Japanese Art — A235

Designs: 25c, Nagata no Taro Nagamune, by Kuniyoshi Utagawa. 35c, Danjuro Ichikawa VII, by Kunisada Utagawa. 60c, Nagata no Taro Nagamune, by Kuniyoshi Utagawa, diff. $1, Nagata no Taro Nagamune, by Kuniyoshi Utagawa, diff.
No. 1394 — Scroll of Actors, by Chikanobu Toyohara and others: a, Smiling man holding fan. b, Man holding sword at mouth. c, Man holding sword vertically. d, Man with tree branch above head.
$2, Two Women by a River, by Chikanobu Hashimoto.

2003, June 17   **Litho.**   **Perf. 14¼**

1390-1393	A235 Set of 4	4.50	4.50
1394	A235 80c Sheet of 4, #a-d	6.50	6.50

Souvenir Sheet

1395	A235 $2 multi	4.00	4.00

Rembrandt Paintings A236

Designs: 25c, Portrait of a Young Man Resting His Chin on His Hand. 50c, A Woman at an Open Door. No. 1398, $1, The Return of the Prodigal Son. $1, Portrait of an Elderly Man.
No. 1400: a, Nicolaas van Bambeeck. b, Agatha Bas, Wife of Nicolaas van Bambeeck. c, Portrait of a Man Holding His Hat. d, Saskia in a Red Hat.
$2, Christ Driving the Money Changers from the Temple.

Perf. 14¼, 13¼ (#1400)

2003, June 17

1396-1399	A236 Set of 4	6.00	6.00
1400	A236 60c Sheet of 4, #a-d	5.00	5.00

Souvenir Sheet

1401	A236 $2 multi	4.50	4.50

Paintings by Joan Miró — A237

Designs: 25c, Portrait of a Young Girl. 50c, Table with Glove. 60c, Self-portrait, 1917. $1, The Farmer's Wife.
No. 1406: a, Portrait of Ramon Sunyer. b, Self-portrait, 1919. c, Portrait of a Spanish Dancer. d, Portrait of Joana Obrador.
No. 1407, Flowers and Butterfly. No. 1408, Still Life of the Coffee Grinder, horiz.

2003, June 17			**Perf. 14¼**	
1402-1405	A237	Set of 4	4.75	4.75
1406	A237	80c Sheet of 4, #a-d	6.50	6.50
		Imperf		
		Size: 104x83mm		
1407	A237	$2 multi	4.25	4.25
		Size: 83x104mm		
1408	A237	$2 multi	4.25	4.25

Caribbean Community, 30th Anniv. — A238

2003, July 4			**Perf. 14**	
1409	A238	60c multi	2.75	1.50

Tanya Streeter, World Champion Freediver — A239

No. 1410: a, Wearing wetsuit in water. b, Diving underwater, portrait. c, Wearing bathing suit at shore. d, Standing in front of map. e, Holding on to diving apparatus.

2003, July 15				
1410	A239	20c Sheet of 5, #a-e	3.25	3.50

Coronation of Queen Elizabeth II, 50th Anniv. — A240

No. 1411: a, Wearing crown and white robe. b, Wearing lilac dress. c, Wearing tiara and red dress. $2, Wearing hat and blue cape. $5, Profile portrait.

2003, Aug. 25				
1411	A240	80c Sheet of 3, #a-c	6.50	6.50
		Souvenir Sheets		
1412-1413	A240	Set of 2	16.00	16.00

Prince William, 21st Birthday — A241

No. 1414: a, Portrait in blue. b, Pink background. c, Purple background. $2, Dark blue background.

2003, Aug. 25				
1414	A241	$1 Sheet of 3, #a-c	7.00	7.50
		Souvenir Sheet		
1415	A241	$2 multi	5.00	5.50

Tour de France Bicycle Race, Cent. — A242

No. 1416: a, Eddy Merckx, 1974. b, Bernard Thévenet, 1975. c, Lucien Van Impe, 1976. d, Thévenet, 1977. $2, Bernard Hinault, 1979.

2003, Aug. 25			**Perf. 13¾x14¼**	
1416	A242	$1 Sheet of 4, #a-d	10.00	11.00
		Souvenir Sheet		
1417	A242	$2 multi	6.50	7.00

100 Years of Aviation

Powered Flight, Cent. — A243

No. 1418: a, Vought F4U Corsair. b, Messerschmidt Me 262. c, A6M. d, Hawker Hurricane. $2, Supermarine Spitfire Mk IX.

2003, Aug. 25			**Perf. 14**	
1418	A243	60c Sheet of 4, #a-d	7.00	7.00
		Souvenir Sheet		
1419	A243	$2 multi	6.00	7.00

German Teddy Bears — A244

No. 1420, vert.: a, Bear with red and yellow uniform. b, Bear with dress. c, Bear with violin case. d, Bear with sword. $2, Bear on beer mug.

2003, Aug. 25			**Perf. 12x12¼**	
1420	A244	50c Sheet of 4, #a-d	5.50	5.50
		Souvenir Sheet		
		Perf. 12¼x12		
1421	A244	$2 multi	5.50	5.50

Butterflies A245

Designs: 50c, Papilio thersites. 60c, Papilio andraemon. 80c, Papilio pelaus. $1, Consul hippona. $2, Papilio pelaus, diff.

2003, Nov. 17			**Perf. 14**	
1422-1425	A245	Set of 4	11.00	9.00
		Souvenir Sheet		
1426	A245	$2 multi	7.00	8.00

Orchids A246

Designs: 50c, Laelia anceps. 60c, Laelia briegeri. 80c, Laelia fidelensis. $1, Laelia cinnabarina. $2, Laelia rubescens.

2003, Nov. 17				
1427-1430	A246	Set of 4	11.00	9.00
		Souvenir Sheet		
1431	A246	$2 multi	7.50	8.50

Dogs A247

Designs: 50c, Beagle. 60c, Sabueso Espanol, vert. 80c, Basset hound, vert. $1, Jack Russell terrier, vert. $2, Dachshund.

2003, Nov. 17				
1432-1435	A247	Set of 4	8.00	8.00
		Souvenir Sheet		
1436	A247	$2 multi	6.00	6.00

Cats A248

Designs: 50c, Persian. 60c, Cymric. 80c, Main Coon, vert. $1, Tiffany. $2, Kurile Island bobtail.

2003, Nov. 17				
1437-1440	A248	Set of 4	8.00	8.00
		Souvenir Sheet		
1441	A248	$2 multi	6.00	6.00

Christmas A249

Paintings: 25c, Madonna of the Harpies, by Andrea del Sarto. 60c, Madonna and Child with St. John, by del Sarto. 80c, Madonna and Child with St. Joseph and St. Peter Martyr, by del Sarto. $1, Madonna and Child with the Angels, by del Sarto. $2, Montefeltro Altarpiece, by Piero della Francesca.

2003, Nov. 24			**Perf. 14¼**	
1442-1445	A249	Set of 4	5.50	5.50
		Souvenir Sheet		
1446	A249	$2 multi	5.00	5.00

Marine Life — A250

Photographs from underwater photography contest: Nos. 1447, 1452a, 25c, Golden Rough Head Blennie, by Rand McMeins. Nos. 1448, 1452b, 50c, Octopus at Night, by Marc Van Driessche. Nos. 1449, 1452c, 60c, Sea Turtle, by Mike Nebel. Nos. 1450, 1452d, 80c, Juvenile Octopus, by Amber Blecker. Nos. 1451, 1452e, $1, School of Horse Eye Jacks, by Blecker. $2, Coral Reef, by Keith Kaplan, vert.

		Perf. 12, 12¾ (#1452)		
2006, June 1			**Litho.**	
		Stamps With Thin "Shadow" Frame		
1447-1451	A250	Set of 5	6.50	6.50

Miniature Sheet
Stamps With Thick "Shadow" Frame

1452 A250   Sheet of 5, #a-e   6.50   6.50

Souvenir Sheet

1453 A250 $2 multi   4.75   5.00

Washington 2006 World Philatelic Exhibition. (Nos. 1452-1453). The perforation tips at the tops of the stamps on Nos. 1452a-1452e are all white, gradiating to blue on the lower halves of the stamps, while the perforation tips on Nos. 1447-1451 show other colors. The shadow frames at the bottom of Nos 1452a-1452e are 1mm thick and about ½mm thick on Nos. 1447-1451. The distances between the bottom of the denomination and the top of the country name differ on Nos. 1452a-1452e from those found on Nos. 1447-1451. No. 1447 has incorrect spelling, "Ruogh," in inscription, while No. 1452a has word correctly spelled as "Rough."

Queen Elizabeth II, 80th Birthday — A251

No. 1454 — Various depictions of Queen Elizabeth II: a, 50c. b, 60c. c, 80c. d, $1. $6, Wearing crown.

2006, Sept. 12   **Litho.**   **Perf. 13½**

1454 A251   Sheet of 4, #a-d   8.25   8.25

Souvenir Sheet

1455 A251 $6 multi   14.00   14.00

Christmas
A252

The Birth of Christ and Adoration of the Shepherds, by Peter Paul Rubens: Nos. 1456, 1460a, 25c, Praying shepherd. Nos. 1457, 1460b, 60c, Infant Jesus. Nos. 1458, 1460c, 80c, Heads of two shepherds. Nos. 1459, 1460d, $1, Virgin Mary.
$6, Our Lady, The Christ Child and Saints, by Rubens, vert.

2006, Dec. 27   **Perf. 13¼x13½**
Stamps With Painting Title

1456-1459 A252   Set of 4   5.50   5.50
Stamps Without Painting Title

1460 A252   Sheet of 4, #a-d   6.50   6.50

Souvenir Sheet
Perf. 13½x13¼

1461 A252 $6 multi   12.00   12.00

Shells — A253

Designs: 10c, Cymatium muricinum. 15c, Tellina radiata. 20c, Tonna maculosa. 25c, Leucozonia nassa. 35c, Trachycardium magnum. 45c, Papyridea soleniformis. 50c, Epitonium lamellosum. 60c, Astraea brevispina. 80c, Bulla striata. $1, Murex margaritensis. $1.25, Chama macerophyla. $1.40, Vasum capitellum. $2, Coralliophila abbreviata. $5, Trachycardium isocardia. $10, Oliva reticularis.

2007, June 11   **Litho.**   **Perf. 12¾**

1462 A253   10c multi   .70   .80
1463 A253   15c multi   1.00   .80
1464 A253   20c multi   1.25   1.00
1465 A253   25c multi   1.25   .50

1466 A253   35c multi   1.50   .70
1467 A253   45c multi   2.00   1.25
1468 A253   50c multi   2.00   1.25
1469 A253   60c multi   2.50   1.50
1470 A253   80c multi   3.00   2.00
1471 A253 $1 multi   3.50   2.75
1472 A253 $1.25 multi   4.00   3.25
1473 A253 $1.40 multi   4.25   4.00
1474 A253 $2 multi   5.00   6.00
1475 A253 $5 multi   9.00   10.00
1476 A253 $10 multi   16.00   20.00
     Nos. 1462-1476 (15)   56.95   55.80

Christmas
A254

Paintings: 25c, The Virgin and Child, by Carlo Maratta. 60c, The Adoration of the Magi, by Vincent Malo, horiz. 80c, The Annunciation, by Robert Campin, horiz. $1, The Adoration of the Magi, by Giovanni di Paolo, horiz. $6, The Adoration of the Magi, by Quentin Massys.

Perf. 14¼x14¾, 14¾x14¼

2007, Dec. 10

1477-1480 A254   Set of 4   7.50   6.50

Souvenir Sheet
Perf. 14

1481 A254 $6 multi   14.00   15.00

No. 1481 contains one 28x42mm stamp.

Worldwide Fund for Nature (WWF)
A255

No. 1482 — Red-tailed hawk: a, Pair on fenceposts. b, Adults and chicks at nest. c, Adults on hill and in flight. d, Head of hawk.

2007, Dec. 24   **Perf. 13¼**

1482   Horiz. strip of 4   5.50   5.50
a.-d   A255 50c Any single   1.35   1.35
e.   Souvenir sheet, 2 each #a-d   13.50   13.50

Wedding of Queen Elizabeth II and Prince Philip, 60th Anniv. — A256

No. 1483, vert.: a, Couple, country name in purple. b, Queen, country name in purple. c, Queen, country name in blue. d, Couple, country name in blue. e, Couple, country name in black. f, Queen, country name in black.
$6, Couple on balcony.

2007, Dec. 28   **Perf. 13¼**

1483 A256 $1 Sheet of 6, #a-f   12.75   12.75

Souvenir Sheet

1484 A256 $6 multi   12.00   12.00

Princess Diana (1961-97) — A257

No. 1485 — Various photographs as shown. $6, Princess Diana wearing hat.

2007, Dec. 28

1485 A257 $1 Sheet of 4, #a-d   8.00   8.00

Souvenir Sheet

1486 A257 $6 multi   12.00   12.00

Pope Benedict XVI — A258

2008, Sept. 15   **Litho.**   **Perf. 13¼**

1487 A258   75c multi   3.00   3.00

Printed in sheets of 8.

Scouting, Cent. (in 2007) — A259

No. 1488, horiz.: a, Fleur-de-lis, silhouette of Lord Robert Baden-Powell and flags of Tanzania, United States and Colombia on top row. b, Dove, silhouette of fleur-de-lis and green, light green and red national Scouting emblem at UL. c, As "b," with orange, brown and dark green national Scouting emblem at UL. d, As "a," with flags of Israel, Canada, Chile and Macedonia on second row. e, As "a," with flags of Taiwan, Luxembourg and Philippines on top row. f, As "b," with Israel Scouting emblem at UL.
$6, Lord Baden-Powell.

2008, Sept. 23

1488 A259   80c Sheet of 6, #a-f   10.00   10.00

Souvenir Sheet

1489 A259 $6 multi   13.75   13.75

Space Exploration, 50th Anniv. (in 2007) — A260

No. 1490 — International Space Station: a, With solar panels under silhouette of Queen. b, With solar panels touching nose of Queen. c, With solar panels spread horizontally. d, With solar panels running to UL from Queen's chest.
$6, International Space Station, diff.

2008, Sept. 23

1490 A260 $1 Sheet of 4, #a-d   10.00   10.00

Souvenir Sheet

1491 A260 $6 multi   17.50   18.50

Marine Life
A261

Photographs from underwater photography contest: 25c, Arrow Crab, by Garin Bescoby. 60c, Trumpet Fish, by Karin Nargis. 80c, Sting

---

Ray, by Barbara Shively. $1, Giant Anemone, by Roddy Mcleod.
$6, Red Banded Lobster, by Jayne Baker.

2008, Nov. 25   **Litho.**   **Perf. 13¼**

1492-1495 A261   Set of 4   5.50   6.00
1495a   Souvenir sheet, #1492-1495   5.50   6.00

Souvenir Sheet

1496 A261 $6 multi   16.00   17.50

Christmas — A262

Paintings: 25c, The Nativity, by Philippe de Champaigne. 60c, Mystic Nativity, by Sandro Botticelli. 80c, The Virgin in a Rose Arbor, by Stefan Lochner. $1, The Adoration of the Shepherds, by Francisco Zurbaran.
$6, The Virgin with Angels, by William Bouguereau.

2008, Nov. 25   **Perf. 14x14¾**

1497-1500 A262   Set of 4   7.25   6.50

Souvenir Sheet

1501 A262 $6 multi   14.00   15.00

Souvenir Sheet

New Year 2012 (Year of the Dragon) — A263

2012, July 12   **Perf.**

1502 A263 $3 multi   6.00   6.00

Charles Dickens (1812-70), Writer — A264

No. 1503: a, Dickens in 1858. b, Illustration from "A Tale of Two Cities." c, Dickens, c. 1860. d, Statue of Dickens in Philadelphia. e, Illustration from "Oliver Twist." f, Illustration from "A Christmas Carol."
$5, Dickens in his study, horiz.

2012, July 12   **Perf. 14**

1503 A264   30c Sheet of 6, #a-f   5.50   5.50

Souvenir Sheet
Perf. 12½

1504 A264 $5 multi   11.00   11.00

No. 1504 contains one 51x38mm stamp.

Flight of John Glenn in Friendship 7, 50th Anniv. — A265

No. 1505: a, Glenn in space helmet. b, Launch of Friendship 7. c, Launch of Space Shuttle (incorrectly identified as launch of Friendship 7). d, Friendship 7 capsule in ocean.
$6, Glenn in space suit, U.S. flags.

2012, July 12   *Perf. 14*
1505 A265 $1.25 Sheet of 4,
   #a-d   10.00 10.00
Souvenir Sheet
Perf. 12
1506 A265 $6 multi   12.00 12.00

Sinking of the Titanic, Cent. — A266

No. 1507: a, Sky, smokestacks of the Titanic. b, Sky, bow of the Titanic. c, Hull of Titanic at top, waves, smokestacks of Titanic at bottom. d, Hull of Titanic, waves, top of iceberg. e, Titanic at top. f, Prow of Titanic, iceberg. g, Passengers on lifeboat. h, Titanic sinking, lifeboat.
No. 1508, Titanic approaching iceberg. No. 1509, Titanic sinking, lifeboat, diff.

2012, July 12   *Perf. 14*
1507 A266 $1 Sheet of 8, #a-h   18.00 18.00
Souvenir Sheets
1508 A266 $5 multi   13.00 13.00
1509 A266 $5 multi   13.00 13.00

Reign of Queen Elizabeth II, 60th Anniv. — A267

Roses and Queen Elizabeth II wearing: $0.50, Crown. $9, Tiara.

2012, Oct. 10   *Perf. 13¾*
1510 A267 $3.50 multi   7.00 7.00
Souvenir Sheet
1511 A267 $9 multi   18.50 18.50
No. 1510 was printed in sheets of 4.

Souvenir Sheet

Replica of Slave Cabin, Cheshire Hall Plantation Ruins — A268

2013, Mar. 7   *Perf. 12½x13¼*
1512 A268 $3.50 multi   7.50 8.00
Turks & Caicos National Trust, 20th anniv.

New Year 2013 (Year of the Snake) — A269

No. 1513: a, Tail of snake. b, Head of snake. $3.50, Entire snake.

2013, July 12   *Perf. 13¾*
1513 A269 $1.25 Horiz. pair, #a-b   5.00 5.00
Souvenir Sheet
1514 A269 $3.50 multi   7.00 7.00
No. 1513 was printed in sheets containing two pairs.

Birth of Prince George of Cambridge — A270

No. 1515 — Illustrations of characters from *Alice's Adventures in Wonderland,* by Lewis Carroll: a, White Rabbit. b, Knave of Hearts carrying crown. c, Alice.
$2.50, Playing Card Gardeners and rose bush.

2013, Oct. 1   Litho.   *Perf. 12¾*
1515 A270 $1 Sheet of 3, #a-c   6.00 6.00
Souvenir Sheet
1516 A270 $2.50 multi   5.00 5.00

A271

Nelson Mandela (1918-2013), President of South Africa — A272

No. 1517: a, Mandela without hat. b, Mandela with hat.
No. 1518: a, Mandela casting ballot. b, Mandela in stadium.
No. 1519, $3.50, Mandela seated, black-and-white photograph. No. 1520, $3.50, Mandela seated, color photograph.

2014, Mar. 3   Litho.   *Perf. 13¾*
1517 A271 $1 Pair, #a-b   4.00 4.00
1518 A272 $1 Pair, #a-b   4.00 4.00
Souvenir Sheets
1519-1520 A272 Set of 2   13.50 13.50
Nos. 1517-1518 each were printed in sheets containing two pairs.

Tang Sancai Glazed Horses — A273

No. 1521: a, Brown horse with blue green saddle. b, Brown horse with white saddle with gray trim and straps, two ornaments on hindquarters. c, Brown horse with white saddle with black trim and straps, three ornaments on hindquarters. d, Light brown horse with red saddle. e, Brown horse with light brown saddle and blue pads. f, Black horse with blue green saddle.
$2.50, Black horse with black saddle, vert.

2014, Mar. 3   Litho.   *Perf. 14*
1521 A273 75c Sheet of 6, #a-f 8.75 8.75
Souvenir Sheet
Perf. 12½
1522 A273 $2.50 multi   4.75 4.75
New Year 2014 (Year of the Horse). No. 1522 contains one 38x51mm stamp.

James Alexander George Smith McCartney (1945-80), First Chief Minister of Turks & Caicos Islands — A274

Frame color: 25c, Purple. $10, Red.

2014, May 1   Litho.   *Perf. 12x12½*
1523 A274 25c multi   .50 .50
Souvenir Sheet
1524 A274 $10 multi   19.00 19.00
No. 1523 was printed in sheets of 4.

Shells — A275

No. 1525: a, Junonia. b, Channeled duck clam. c, Zigzag scallop. d, Scotch bonnet. $4, Queen conch.

2014, Nov. 3   Litho.   *Perf. 14*
1525 A275 $1.20 Sheet of 4, #a-d   9.75 9.75
Souvenir Sheet
Perf. 12¾
1526 A275 $4 multi   8.00 8.00
No. 1526 contains one 51x38mm stamp.

Orchids — A276

No. 1527: a, Oncidium auriferum. b, Oncidium excavatum. c, Oncidium graminifolium. d, Oncidium altissimum.
No. 1528: a, Oncidium citrinum. b, Oncidium wentworthianum.

2014, Nov. 3   Litho.   *Perf. 12¾*
1527 A276 $1.20 Sheet of 4, #a-d   9.75 9.75
Souvenir Sheet
1528 A276 $2 Sheet of 2, #a-b   8.00 8.00

Signs of the Zodiac — A277

No. 1529, $1.20: a, Taurus. b, Scorpio. c, Libra. d, Sagittarius.
No. 1530, $1.20: a, Aquarius. b, Cancer. c, Capricorn. d, Leo.
No. 1531, $2: a, Gemini. b, Aries.
No. 1532, $2: a, Virgo. b, Pisces.

2014, Nov. 3   Litho.   *Perf. 12½*
Sheets of 4, #a-d
1529-1530 A277 Set of 2   19.50 19.50
Souvenir Sheets of 2, #a-b
1531-1532 A277 Set of 2   10.00 10.00

Miniature Sheets

A278

New Year 2015 (Year of the Ram) — A279

No. 1533 — Chinese character for "ram" on ram in: a, Green. b, Red. c, Blue. d, Bister.
No. 1534: a, Chinese character for "happiness." b, "Happy New Year." c, Flower and ram, denomination at right. d, Ram and flower, denomination at left. e, "2015 Year of the Ram." f, Chinese character for "ram."

			2014, Nov. 24	Litho.	Perf. 14	
1533	A278	$1.20 Sheet of 4, #a-d	9.75	9.75

		Perf. 13¾		
1534	A279	$1.20 Sheet of 6, #a-f, + central label	14.50	14.50

Christmas
A280

Paintings by Titian: 34c, Madonna and Child, 1528. 49c, Madonna and Child, 1511. $1.50, Madonna and Child in an Evening Landscape, 1562-65. $3.50, Madonna and Child, 1560-65.

		2015, Dec. 1	Litho.	Perf. 12¾	
1535-1538	A280	Set of 4	12.00	12.00

Miniature Sheet

New Year 2016 (Year of the Monkey) — A281

No. 1539 — Various monkeys with denomination color of: a, Magenta. b, Green. c, Red. d, Blue.

		2015, Dec. 1	Litho.	Perf. 14	
1539	A281	75c Sheet of 4, #a-d	6.00	6.00

Travels of Queen Elizabeth II — A282

No. 1540 — Queen Elizabeth visiting: a, South Africa, 1947. b, Australia, 1954. c, Rome, Italy, 1961. d, India, 1961 (attendant with red coat in background). e, India, 1961 (attendant with white coat in background). f, Pakistan, 1961. g, Nepal, 1961. h, Sri Lanka, 1981. i, New Zealand, 1981. j, United States, 1983 (bearded man in background). k, United States, 1983, (with park ranger). l, Kathmandu, Nepal, 1986. m, Germany, 1992. $4, Queen Elizabeth II and Prince Philip in Ireland, 2011.

		2015, Dec. 7	Litho.	Perf. 12	
1540	A282	50c Sheet of 13, #a-m, + label	13.00	13.00

Souvenir Sheet

1541	A282	$4 multi	8.00	8.00

Queen Elizabeth II, longest-reigning British monarch.

WAR TAX STAMPS

Regular Issue of 1913-16 Overprinted

Black Overprint at Bottom of Stamp

		1917	Wmk. 3	Perf. 14	
MR1	A10	1p carmine	.25	1.75
	a.	Double overprint	200.00	275.00
	b.	"TAX" omitted		
	c.	Pair, one without ovpt.	700.00	
MR2	A10	3p violet, yel	1.40	9.50
	a.	Double overprint	110.00	

Black Overprint at Top or Middle of Stamp

		1917			
MR3	A10	1p carmine	.25	1.40
	a.	Inverted overprint	65.00	
	b.	Double overprint	65.00	77.50
	c.	Pair, one without overprint	650.00	
MR4	A10	3p violet, yel	.70	2.25
	a.	Double overprint	50.00	60.00
	b.	Dbl. ovpt., one inverted	375.00	

Same Overprint in Violet or Red

		1918-19			
MR5	A10	1p car (V) ('19)	1.50	7.00
	a.	Double overprint	24.00	
	b.	"WAR" omitted	200.00	
MR6	A10	3p violet, yel (R)	22.00	60.00
	a.	Double overprint	375.00	

Regular Issue of 1913-16 Overprinted in Black

		1918			
MR7	A10	1p carmine	.25	2.75
MR8	A10	3p violet, yel	6.50	7.00

Same Overprint in Red

		1919			
MR9	A10	3p violet, yel	.25	6.00

Regular Issue of 1913-16 Overprinted in Black

MR10	A10	1p carmine	.25	2.25
	a.	Double overprint	160.00	190.00
MR11	A10	3p violet, yel	.45	3.00

Regular Issue of 1913-16 Overprinted

MR12	A10	1p carmine	.25	4.00
	a.	Double overprint	100.00	
MR13	A10	3p violet, yel	1.75	4.00

The bottom two rows of this setting show the words "War" and "Tax" about 1mm farther apart.

CAICOS

Catalogue values for all unused stamps in this country are for Never Hinged items.

Turks & Caicos Nos. 360, 364, 366, 369, 371-373 Ovptd.

1c, Indigo hamlet. 5c, Spanish grunt. 8c, Foureye butterflyfish. 20c, Queen angelfish. 50c, Fairy basslet. $1, Clown wrasse. $2, Stoplight parrotfish.

Unwmk.

		1981, July 24	Litho.	Perf. 14	
1	A69	1c multi	.25	.25
2	A69	5c multi	.25	.25
3	A69	8c multi	.25	.25
4	A69	20c multi	.40	.40
5	A69	50c multi	.85	.85
6	A69	$1 multi	1.00	1.75
7	A69	$2 multi	2.00	3.25
		Nos. 1-7 (7)	5.00	7.00

Common Design Types pictured following the introduction.

Royal Wedding Issue
Common Design Type

Turks & Caicos Nos. 486-489 Overprinted

35c, Charles & Diana. 65c, Kensington Palace. 90c, Prince Charles. $2, Glass coach.

		1981, July 24			
8	CD331a	35c multicolored	.25	.25
9	CD331a	65c multicolored	.50	.50
10	CD331a	90c multicolored	.75	.75
		Nos. 8-10 (3)	1.50	1.50

Souvenir Sheet

11	CD331	$2 multicolored	3.50	3.50

	Roulette x Imperf. (#12a), Imperf. (#12b)		
1981, Oct. 29		Self-Adhesive
12	Souvenir booklet	13.00
a.	A88a Pane, 3 each 20c, Diana, $1, Charles	4.00
b.	A88a Pane of 1 $2, Couple	5.00

No. 12 is similar to Turks & Caicos No. 490. No. 12 has Caicos Islands instead of Turks & Caicos Islands.

Hawksbill turtle
C1

8c, Diver with lobster and conch shell. 20c, Stone idol, Arawak Indians. 35c, Sloop construction. 50c, Marine biology. 95c, 707 Jetliner. $1.10, 15th cent. Spanish ship. $2, British soldier, Fort St. George. $3, Pirates Anne Bonny, Calico Jack.

		1983-84		Perf. 14	
13	C1	8c multicolored	1.60	.80
14	C1	10c shown	1.80	1.40
15	C1	20c multicolored	1.80	1.40
16	C1	35c multicolored	1.80	1.80
17	C1	50c multicolored	2.60	2.75
18	C1	95c multicolored	4.75	2.75
19	C1	$1.10 multicolored	4.75	2.75
20	C1	$2 multicolored	3.50	4.00
21	C1	$3 multicolored	4.75	4.00
		Nos. 13-21 (9)	27.35	21.65

Issued: Nos. 13-19, 6/6/83; Nos. 20-21, 5/18/84.
For overprints see Nos. 47-49.

Christmas Type of Turks and Caicos

Walt Disney characters in Santa Claus is Coming to Town: No. 22, Chip 'n Dale. No. 23, Goofy & Patch. No. 24, Morty, Ferdie & Pluto. No. 25, Morty. No. 26, Donald, Huey, Dewey & Louie. No. 27, Goofy & Louie. No. 28, Uncle Scrooge. No. 29, Mickey Mouse & Ferdie. No. 30, Pinocchio, Jiminy Cricket and Figaro. No. 31, Morty & Ferdie, fireplace.

		1983, Nov. 7		Perf. 11	
22	A104	1c multicolored	.25	.30
23	A104	1c multicolored	.25	.30
24	A104	2c multicolored	.25	.30
25	A104	2c multicolored	.25	.30
26	A104	3c multicolored	.25	.30
27	A104	3c multicolored	.25	.30
28	A104	50c multicolored	4.00	3.25
29	A104	70c multicolored	4.25	3.75
30	A104	$1.10 multicolored	5.00	4.50
		Nos. 22-30 (9)	14.75	13.30

Souvenir Sheet
Perf. 13½x14

31	A104	$2 multicolored	4.75	4.50

Drawings by Raphael — C2

Designs: 35c, Leda and the Swan. 50c, Study of Apollo for Parnassus. 95c, Study of two figures for The Battle of Ostia. $1.10, Study for the Madonna of the Goldfinch. $2.50, The Garvagh Madonna.

		1983, Dec. 15		Perf. 14	
32	C2	35c multicolored	1.00	.65
33	C2	50c multicolored	1.25	.90
34	C2	95c multicolored	2.50	1.60
35	C2	$1.10 multicolored	2.50	1.90
		Nos. 32-35 (4)	7.25	5.05

Souvenir Sheet

36	C2	$2.50 multicolored	5.75	5.75

500th birth anniv. of Raphael.

1984 Summer Olympics, Los Angeles — C3

4c, High jump. 25c, Archery. 65c, Cycling. $1.10, Soccer. $2, Show jumping, horiz.

1984, Mar. 1

37	C3	4c multicolored	.25	.25
38	C3	25c multicolored	.30	.25
39	C3	65c multicolored	2.25	.75
40	C3	$1.10 multicolored	1.25	.90
		Nos. 37-40 (4)	4.05	2.15

Souvenir Sheet

41	C3	$2 multicolored	4.00	4.00

Easter — C4

Walt Disney characters: 35c, Horace Horsecollar, Clarabelle Cow. 45c, Mickey, Minnie & Chip. 75c, Gyro Gearloose, Chip 'n Dale. 85c, Mickey, Chip 'n Dale. $2.20, Donald sailing with nephews.

1984, Apr. 15   *Perf. 14x13½*

42	C4	35c multicolored	1.40	.75
43	C4	45c multicolored	1.60	1.00
44	C4	75c multicolored	2.50	1.50
45	C4	85c multicolored	2.50	1.75
		Nos. 42-45 (4)	8.00	5.00

Souvenir Sheet

46	C4	$2.20 mulitcolored	5.50	4.00

Nos. 18-19 Ovptd. in Black

1984, June 19   *Perf. 14*

47	C1	95c multicolored	1.50	1.75
48	C1	$1.10 multicolored	1.75	2.00

No. 20 Overprinted

1984, Aug. 22

49	C1	$2 multicolored	3.50	3.75

Columbus' First Landfall — C5

1984, Sept. 21

50	C5	10c Sighting manatees	1.00	.80
51	C5	70c Fleet	3.75	3.25
52	C5	$1 West Indies landing	4.25	3.25
		Nos. 50-52 (3)	9.00	7.30

Souvenir Sheet

53	C5	$2 Fleet, map	3.50	3.75

Columbus' first landing, 492nd anniv.

Christmas — C6

Walt Disney characters: 20c, Santa Claus, Donald and Mickey. 35c, Donald at refrigerator. 50c, Donald, Micky riding toy train. 75c, Donald carrying presents. $1.10, Huey, Louie, Dewey and Donald singing carols. $2, Donald as Christmas tree.

Perf. 13½x14, 12x12½ (75c)

1984, Nov. 26

54	C6	20c multicolored	1.50	.85
55	C6	35c multicolored	1.75	1.00
56	C6	50c multicolored	2.50	2.25
57	C6	75c multicolored	3.00	3.00
58	C6	$1.10 multicolored	3.25	3.25
		Nos. 54-58 (5)	12.00	10.35

Souvenir Sheet
Perf. 13½x14

59	C6	$2 multicolored	3.75	4.00

No. 57 printed in sheets of 8.

Audubon Birth Bicentenary — C7

20c, Thick-billed vireo. 35c, Black-faced grassquit. 50c, Pearly-eyed thrasher. $1, Greater Antillean bullfinch. $2, Stripe-headed tanagers.

1985, Feb. 12   *Perf. 14*

60	C7	20c multicolored	2.25	.65
61	C7	35c multicolored	2.60	1.25
62	C7	50c multicolored	3.00	2.00
63	C7	$1 multicolored	3.50	3.25
		Nos. 60-63 (4)	11.35	7.15

Souvenir Sheet

64	C7	$2 multicolored	4.75	5.25

No. 64 exists imperf.

Intl. Youth Year — C8

1985, May 8

65	C8	16c Education	.25	.30
66	C8	35c Health	.65	.70
67	C8	70c Love	1.25	1.40
68	C8	90c Peace	1.50	1.75
		Nos. 65-68 (4)	3.65	4.15

Souvenir Sheet

69	C8	$2 Peace dove, child	3.50	4.50

UN 40th anniv.

Intl. Civil Aviation Org., 40th Anniv. C9

1985, May 26

70	C9	35c DC-3	3.50	.55
71	C9	75c Convair 440	4.50	1.40
72	C9	90c TCNA Islander	4.50	1.60
		Nos. 70-72 (3)	12.50	3.55

Souvenir Sheet

73	C9	$2.20 Hang glider	3.50	4.50

Queen Mother, 85th Birthday Type of Turks & Caicos

35c, Wearing green hat. 65c, With Princess Anne, horiz. 95c, Wearing white hat. $2, Inspecting guardsmen.

1985, July 7

74	A117	35c sal pink & multi	1.25	.55
75	A117	65c yel & multi	1.75	.95
76	A117	95c lt blue & multi	2.25	1.60
		Nos. 74-76 (3)	5.25	3.10

Souvenir Sheet

77	A117	$2 sage grn & multi	6.00	4.00

Mark Twain, 150th Birth Anniv. — C10

Walt Disney characters in Tom Sawyer, Detective (Intl. Youth Year): 8c, Mickey and Goofy as Tom and Huck reading reward poster. 35c, Meeting Jake Dunlap. 95c, Spying on Jubiter Dunlap. $1.10, With Pluto finding body. No. 86, Unmasking Jubiter Dunlap.
Walt Disney characters portraying Six Soldiers of Fortune (The Brothers Grimm, Bicent.): 16c, Donald receiving his meager pay. 25c, Donald meets Horace Horsecollar as strong man. 65c, Donald meets Mickey the marksman. $1.35, Goofy wins footrace against Princess Daisy. No. 87, Soldiers with sack of gold.

1985, Dec. 5   *Perf. 14x13½*

78	C10	8c multicolored	.30	.30
79	C10	16c multicolored	.45	.45
80	C10	25c multicolored	.70	.70
81	C10	35c multicolored	1.00	1.00
82	C10	65c multicolored	1.75	1.75
83	C10	95c multicolored	2.60	2.60
84	C10	$1.10 multicolored	3.25	3.25
85	C10	$1.35 multicolored	4.00	4.00
		Nos. 78-85 (8)	14.05	14.05

Souvenir Sheet

86	C10	$2 multicolored	6.00	6.00
87	C10	$2 multicolored	6.00	6.00

Stamps are no longer being produced for Caicos.

TURKS ISLANDS

ˈtərks ˈī-ləndz

LOCATION — West Indies, at the southern extremity of the Bahamas
GOVT. — Former dependency of Jamaica
POP. — 2,000 (approx.)
CAPITAL — Grand Turk

In 1848 the Turks Islands together with the Caicos group, lying to the northwest, were made a British colony. In 1873 the Colony became a dependency under the government of Jamaica although separate stamp issues were continued. Postage stamps inscribed Turks and Caicos Islands have been used since 1900.

12 Pence = 1 Shilling

Values for unused stamps are for examples with original gum as defined in the catalogue introduction. Very fine examples of Nos. 1-42 will have generally rough perforations that cut into the design on one or more sides due to the narrow spacing of the stamps on the plates and imperfect perforating methods. Stamps with perfs clear of the design on all four sides are extremely scarce and will command substantially higher prices.

Because of the printing and imperfect perforating methods, stamps are often found scissor separated. Prices will not be adversely affected on those stamps where the scissor cut does not remove the perforations.

Watermark

Wmk. 5 — Small Star

Queen Victoria — A1

Perf. 11½ to 13

			Unwmk.	Engr.
1867				
1	A1	1p rose	67.50	67.50
2	A1	6p gray black	125.00	140.00
3	A1	1sh slate blue	105.00	67.50
		Nos. 1-3 (3)	297.50	275.00

Perf. 11 to 13x14 to 15

				Wmk. 5
1873-79				
4	A1	1p lake	57.50	57.50
5	A1	1p dull red ('79)	62.50	67.50
a.		Horiz. pair, imperf. btwn.	30,000.	
b.		Perf. 11-12	1,100.	
6	A1	1sh violet	5,750.	2,250.

Stamps offered as No. 6 are often examples from which the surcharge has been removed.

Stamps of 1867-79 Surcharged in Black

a   b

c

12 settings of the ½p.

			Unwmk.	Perf. 11 to 13
1881				
7	(a)	½p on 6p gray blk	100.00	170.00
7A	(b)	½p on 6p gray blk	100.00	150.00
8	(b)	½p on 1sh slate bl	140.00	200.00
a.		Double surcharge	8,000.	
8B	(c)	½p on 1sh slate bl	11,000.	
c.		Without fraction bar		
d.		Double surcharge	16,000.	
e.		#8a and #8Bd in pair	27,000.	

d   e

Perf. 11 to 13x14 to 15
Wmk. 5

9	(a)	½p on 1p dull red	150.00	200.00
a.		Double surcharge		

10	(b) ½p on 1p dull red	60.00	150.00
11	(c) ½p on 1p dull red	210.00	275.00
a.	Double surcharge	4,250.	
12	(d) ½p on 1p dull red	260.00	
a.	Without fraction bar	1,150.	
b.	Double surcharge		
13	(e) ½p on 1p dull red	600.00	
14	(a) ½p on 1sh violet	175.00	225.00
a.	Double surcharge	4,000.	
15	(b) ½p on 1sh violet	140.00	225.00
a.	Without fraction bar	625.00	
16	(c) ½p on 1sh violet	105.00	190.00

f

g

h

9 settings of the 2½p.

Perf. 11 to 13
Unwmk.

17	(f) 2½p on 6p gray blk	16,000.	
18	(g) 2½p on 6p gray blk	425.	600.
a.	Horiz. pair, imperf. between	42,500.	
b.	Double surcharge	18,500.	
19	(h) 2½p on 6p gray blk	250.	475.
a.	Double surcharge	17,500.	

i

j

Perf. 11 to 13x14 to 15
Wmk. 5

20	(i) 2½p on 1sh violet	4,000.	
21	(h) 2½p on 1sh violet	625.00	950.00
22	(j) 2½p on 1sh violet	9,500.	

k

l

m

n

Perf. 11 to 13
Unwmk.

24	(k) 2½p on 6p gray blk	9,500.	
25	(k) 2½p on 1sh slate bl	28,000.	
26	(l) 2½p on 1sh slate bl	1,500.	
27	(m) 2½p on 1sh slate bl	2,200.	
a.	Without fraction bar	8,000.	
28	(n) 2½p on 1sh slate bl	6,500.	

o

Perf. 11 to 13x14 to 15
Wmk. 5

29	(l) 2½p on 1p dull red	750.00	
30	(o) 2½p on 1p dull red	1,500.	
31	(l) 2½p on 1sh violet	850.00	
a.	Double surcharge of "½"	4,750.	
32	(o) 2½p on 1sh violet	1,350.	
b.	Double surcharge of "½"	9,000.	

p

q

r

6 settings of the 4p.

Perf. 11 to 13
Unwmk.

33	(p) 4p on 6p gray black	110.00	165.00
34	(q) 4p on 6p gray black	425.00	575.00
35	(r) 4p on 6p gray black	750.00	500.00

Examples of No. 33 with top of "4" painted in are sometimes offered as No. 35.

Perf. 11 to 13x14 to 15
Wmk. 5

36	(r) 4p on 1p dull red	950.00	625.00
a.	Inverted surcharge	3,250.	
37	(p) 4p on 1p dull red	850.00	550.00
a.	Inverted surcharge		
38	(p) 4p on 1sh violet	475.00	750.00
39	(q) 4p on 1sh violet	2,750.	

Wmk. Crown and C C (1)

1881	Engr.		**Perf. 14**
40	A1 1p brown red	87.50	105.00
a.	Diagonal half used as ½p on cover		
41	A1 6p olive brown	165.00	210.00
42	A1 1sh slate green	210.00	155.00
	Nos. 40-42 (3)	462.50	470.00

A2

1881		Typo.	
43	A2 4p ultramarine	170.00	67.50

1882-95	Engr.	**Wmk. 2**	
44	A1 1p orange brn ('83)	100.00	35.00
a.	Half used as ½p on cover		5,000.
45	A1 1p car lake ('89)	3.50	2.25
46	A1 6p yellow brn ('89)	5.50	6.75
47	A1 1sh black brn ('87)	7.25	5.25
a.	1sh deep brown	7.25	5.25

Typo.
Die A

48	A2 ½p dull green ('85)	7.25	6.50
a.	½p blue green ('82)	29.00	29.00
49	A2 2½p red brown ('82)	40.00	16.00
50	A2 4p gray ('84)	38.00	4.00
a.	Half used as 2p on cover		5,000.

Die B

51	A2 ½p gray green ('94)	7.00	4.50
52	A2 2½p ultra ('93)	7.50	5.00
53	A2 4p dk vio & bl ('95)	11.00	15.00

For descriptions of dies A and B see "Dies of British Colonial Stamps" in table of contents.

1887	Engr.	**Perf. 12**	
54	A1 1p carmine lake	14.00	3.25
a.	Horiz. pair, imperf. btwn.	28,000.	

No. 49 Surcharged in Black

1889			
55	A2 1p on 2½p red brn	24.00	21.00
a.	Double surcharge		
b.	Double surcharge, one inverted		
c.	"One" omitted		1,800.
d.	Half used as ½p on cover		5,500.

No. 55c caused by the misplacement of the surcharge. Stamps also exist from the same sheet reading "Penny One."

No. 50 Surcharged in Black

Two types of surcharge:
Type I — Upper bar continuous across sheet.
Type II — Upper bar breaks between stamps.

1893			
56	A2 ½p on 4p gray (I)	225.00	180.00
a.	Type II	3,250.	1,450.

This surcharge exists in five settings.

A3

1894		Typo.	
57	A3 5p olive grn & carmine	12.50	27.50
a.	Diag. half used as 2½p on cover		5,000.

TUVALU

tü-'vä-ֽü

LOCATION — A group of islands in the Pacific Ocean northeast of Australia.
GOVT. — Independent state in the British Commonwealth
AREA — 9½ sq. mi.
POP. — 10,588 (1999 est.)
CAPITAL — Fongafale

Tuvalu, formerly Ellice Islands, consists of nine islands.

Australian dollar

Catalogue values for all unused stamps in this country are for Never Hinged items.

Watermark

Wmk. 380 — "POST OFFICE"

Gilbert and Ellice Islands Types of 1971 Overprinted in Violet Blue or Silver (35c)

No. 1

No. 12

Wmk. 373

1976, Jan. 1	Litho.	**Perf. 14**	
1	A18 1c	1.00	.50
2	A19 2c	1.25	.70
a.	Wmk. 314 sideways	200.00	25.00
b.	Wmk. 314 upright	1,400.	140.00
3	A19 3c Wmk. 314	2.00	1.00
a.	Wmk. 373	.65	.45
4	A19 4c	1.25	.70
5	A19 5c Wmk. 314	1.25	1.00
6	A18 6c	1.25	.70
7	A18 8c Wmk. 314	1.25	1.00
8	A18 10c Wmk. 314	1.25	1.25
9	A18 15c	2.00	.80
10	A19 20c	1.25	1.00
11	A19 25c Wmk. 314	8.00	2.75
a.	Wmk. 373	.70	.60
12	A18 35c	2.00	1.10
13	A18 50c	1.25	1.00
a.	Wmk. 314	47.50	22.50
14	A18 $1	1.25	1.25
a.	Wmk. 314	110.00	70.00
15	A18 $2	1.60	1.25
	Nos. 1-15 (15)	27.85	16.00

Men from Gilbert and Ellice — A1

Designs: 10c, Map of Gilbert and Ellice Islands, vert. 35c, Gilbert and Ellice canoes.

1976, Jan. 1		**Wmk. 373**	
16	A1 4c multicolored	.50	.60
17	A1 10c multicolored	.65	.70
18	A1 35c multicolored	.90	1.00
	Nos. 16-18 (3)	2.05	2.30

Separation of the Gilbert and Ellice Islands.

50c Coin and Octopus — A2

New coinage: 10c, 10c-coin and red-dyed crab. 15c, 20c-coin and flyingfish. 35c, $1-coin and green turtle.

Wmk. 373

1976, Apr. 21	Litho.	**Perf. 14**	
19	A2 5c bister & multi	.25	.25
20	A2 10c ultra & multi	.40	.30
21	A2 15c blue & multi	.60	.40
22	A2 35c lt green & multi	1.10	.70
	Nos. 19-22 (4)	2.35	1.65

Map of Niulakita, Leathery Turtle — A3

2c, Map of Nukulaelae and sleeping mat. 4c, Map of Nui and talo vegetable. 5c, Map of Nanumanga and grass dancing skirt. 6c, Map of Nukufetau and coconut crab. 8c, Map of Funafuti and banana tree. 10c, Map of Tuvalu Islands. 15c, Map of Niutao and flyingfish. 20c, Map of Vaitupu and maneapa (house). 25c, Map of Nanumea and palu fish hook. 35c, Te Ano Game, horiz. 50c, Canoe pole fishing, horiz. $1, Reef fishing by flare, horiz. $2, House, horiz. $5, Colony Ship M.V. Nivanga, horiz.

1976	Wmk. 373	Litho.	**Perf. 13½**	
23-37	A3 Set of 15		30.00	8.50

Issue dates: $5, Sept. 1; others July 1.
See #58-70. For overprints see #85-91.

New Testament
A5

Designs: 20c, Lotolelei Church, Nanumea. 25c, Kelupi Church, Nui. 30c, Mataloa o Tuvalu Church, Vaitupu. 35c, Palataiso o Keliso Church, Nanumanga.

Perf. 14x14½

1976, Oct. 6		Litho.	Wmk. 373	
38-42	A5	Set of 5	6.50	4.00

Christmas 1976. Printed in sheets of 10 stamps and 2 labels.

Prince Philip Carried Ashore at Vaitupu — A6

Designs: 15c, Queen and Prince Philip on Buckingham Palace balcony. 50c, Queen Leaving Buckingham Palace for coronation.

1977, Feb. 9		Litho.	Perf. 13½x14	
43	A6	15c multicolored	1.25	1.05
44	A6	35c multicolored	1.60	1.75
45	A6	50c multicolored	2.50	2.50
a.		Souv. sheet, #43-45, perf. 15	6.50	6.50
		Nos. 43-45 (3)	5.35	5.30

25th anniv. of the reign of Elizabeth II.

Health (Microscope) — A7

20c, Education (blackboard). 30c, Fruit growing (palm). 35c, Map of South Pacific Territory.

1977, May 4		Litho.	Perf. 13½x14	
46	A7	5c lilac & multi	.50	.30
47	A7	20c orange & multi	.50	.30
48	A7	30c yellow grn & multi	.50	.30
49	A7	35c lt blue & multi	.75	.45
		Nos. 46-49 (4)	2.25	1.35

South Pacific Commission, 30th anniv.

Swearing-in Ceremony and Scout Emblem — A8

Designs (Scout Emblem and): 20c, Scouts in outrigger canoe. 30c, Scouts under sun shelter. 35c, Lord Baden-Powell.

Perf. 13½x14

1977, Aug. 10		Litho.	Wmk. 373	
50	A8	5c multicolored	.30	.30
51	A8	20c multicolored	.30	.30
52	A8	30c multicolored	.50	.50
53	A8	35c multicolored	.50	.50
		Nos. 50-53 (4)	1.60	1.60

Scouting in Tuvalu (Ellice Islands), 50th anniv.

Hurricane Beach and Coral — A9

Designs: 20c, Boring apparatus on "Porpoise," vert. 30c, Map of islands showing line of dredgings to prove Darwin's theory, vert. 35c, Charles Darwin and "Beagle."

Perf. 13½

1977, Nov. 2		Unwmk.	Litho.	
54	A9	5c multicolored	.35	.35
55	A9	20c multicolored	.35	.35
56	A9	30c multicolored	.55	.45
57	A9	35c multicolored	.55	.45
		Nos. 54-57 (4)	1.80	1.60

1896-97 Royal Soc. of London Expeditions to explore coral reefs by dredging and boring.

Types of 1976

Designs: 30c, Fatele, local dance. 40c, Screw pine. Others as before.

1977-78		Unwmk.	Perf. 13½	
58	A3	1c multicolored	.25	.25
59	A3	2c multicolored	.25	.25
60	A3	4c multicolored	.25	.25
61	A3	5c multicolored	.25	.25
62	A3	6c multicolored	.25	.25
63	A3	8c multicolored	.25	.25
64	A3	10c multicolored	.25	.25
66	A3	20c multicolored	1.25	.85
67	A3	25c multicolored	.85	.30
68	A3	30c multi, horiz.	.35	.35
69	A3	40c multi, horiz.	.45	.50
70	A3	$5 multi, horiz.	3.50	3.50
		Nos. 58-70 (12)	8.15	7.25

Issued: #58, 61, 63-64, 67, 1977; others, 1978.

Pacific Pigeon — A10

Wild Birds of Tuvalu: 20c, Reef heron. 30c, Fairy tern. 40c, Lesser frigate bird.

Perf. 14x13½

1978, Jan. 25		Litho.	Unwmk.	
73	A10	8c lilac & multi	1.50	.90
74	A10	20c ocher & multi	1.90	1.25
75	A10	30c dull green & multi	2.40	1.75
76	A10	40c brt green & multi	2.40	2.00
		Nos. 73-76 (4)	8.20	5.90

Lawedua — A11

Ships: 20c, Tug Wallacia. 30c, Freighter Cenpac Rounder. 40c, Pacific Explorer.

1978, Apr. 5		Unwmk.	Perf. 13½x14	
77	A11	8c multicolored	.25	.25
78	A11	20c multicolored	.35	.35
79	A11	30c multicolored	.50	.45
80	A11	40c multicolored	.60	.60
		Nos. 77-80 (4)	1.70	1.65

Canterbury Cathedral — A12

Designs: 30c, Salisbury Cathedral. 40c, Wells Cathedral. $1, Hereford Cathedral.

1978, June 2		Litho.	Perf. 13½x14	
81	A12	8c multicolored	.25	.25
82	A12	30c multicolored	.25	.25
83	A12	40c multicolored	.25	.25
84	A12	$1 multicolored	.25	.25
a.		Souv. sheet, #81-84, perf. 15	.60	.60
		Nos. 81-84 (4)	1.00	1.00

25th anniv. of coronation of Elizabeth II. #81-84 were also issued in bklt. panes of 2.

Types of 1976 Overprinted

1978, Oct. 1		Litho.	Perf. 13½	
85	A3	8c multicolored	.25	.25
86	A3	10c multicolored	.25	.25
87	A3	15c multicolored	.25	.25
88	A3	20c multicolored	.25	.25
89	A3	30c multi, horiz.	.25	.25
90	A3	35c multi, horiz.	.25	.25
91	A3	40c multi, horiz.	.25	.25
		Nos. 85-91 (7)	1.75	1.75

Independence, Oct. 1, 1978. Overprint in 3 lines on vert. stamps, 1 line on horiz.

White Frangipani — A13

Wild Flowers: 20c, Zephyrantes rosea. 30c, Gardenia taitensis. 40c, Clerodendron inerme.

1978, Oct. 4		Unwmk.	Perf. 14	
92	A13	8c multicolored	.25	.25
93	A13	20c multicolored	.25	.30
94	A13	30c multicolored	.25	.40
95	A13	40c multicolored	.35	.70
		Nos. 92-95 (4)	1.10	1.65

Squirrelfish — A14

Fish: 2c, Yellow-banded goatfish. 4c, Imperial angelfish. 5c, Rainbow butterfly. 6c, Blue angelfish. 8c, Blue striped snapper. 10c, Orange clownfish. 15c, Chevroned coralfish. 20c, Fairy cod. 25c, Clown triggerfish. 30c, Long-nosed butterfly. 35c, Yellowfin tuna. 40c, Spotted eagle ray. 45c, Black-tipped rock cod. 50c, Hammerhead shark. 70c, Lionfish, vert. $1, White-barred triggerfish, vert. $2, Beaked coralfish, vert. $5, Tiger shark, vert.

1979, Jan. 24		Litho.	Perf. 14	
96	A14	1c multicolored	.25	.25
97	A14	2c multicolored	.25	.25
98	A14	4c multicolored	.25	.25
99	A14	5c multicolored	.25	.25
100	A14	6c multicolored	.25	.25
101	A14	8c multicolored	.25	.25
102	A14	10c multicolored	.25	.25
103	A14	15c multicolored	.25	.25
104	A14	20c multicolored	.25	.25
105	A14	25c multicolored	.25	.25
106	A14	30c multicolored	.25	.25
107	A14	35c multicolored	.25	.25
108	A14	40c multicolored	.30	.30
108A	A14	45c multicolored	1.50	1.00
109	A14	50c multicolored	.45	.45
110	A14	70c multicolored	.50	.50
111	A14	$1 multicolored	.65	.65
112	A14	$2 multicolored	1.50	1.50
113	A14	$5 multicolored	3.50	3.50
		Nos. 96-113 (19)	11.40	10.90

No. 108A issued June 16, 1981. #101, 104, 106, 108 and #102, 105, 107, 108A were also issued in booklet panes of 4.

For surcharge & overprints see #150, O1-O19.

Capt. Cook
A15

Designs: 30c, Flag raising on new island. 40c, Observation of transit of Venus. $1, Death of Capt. Cook.

1979, Feb. 14		Litho.	Perf. 14x14½	
114	A15	8c multicolored	.25	.25
115	A15	30c multicolored	.25	.25
116	A15	40c multicolored	.25	.25
117	A15	$1 multicolored	.30	.30
a.		Strip of 4, #114-117	1.40	1.40

Bicentenary of death of Capt. James Cook (1728-1779). Nos. 114-117 printed se-tenant horizontally in sheets of 12 (4x3) with gutters between horizontal rows.

Grumman Goose over Nukulaelae — A16

Grumman Goose over: 20c, Vaitupu. 30c, Nui. 40c, Funafuti.

1979, May 16		Litho.	Perf. 14x13½	
118	A16	8c multicolored	.25	.25
119	A16	20c multicolored	.25	.25
120	A16	30c multicolored	.25	.30
121	A16	40c multicolored	.30	.30
		Nos. 118-121 (4)	1.05	1.10

Inauguration of internal air service.

Hill, Tuvalu No. 16, Letterbox, London, 1855 — A17

Hill, Stamps of Tuvalu and: 40c, No. 17, Penny Black. $1, No. 18, mail coach.

1979, Aug. 20		Litho.	Perf. 13½x14	
122	A17	30c multicolored	.25	.25
123	A17	40c multicolored	.25	.25
124	A17	$1 multicolored	.35	.35
a.		Souvenir sheet of 3, #122-124	1.00	1.00
		Nos. 122-124 (3)	.85	.85

Sir Rowland Hill (1795-1879), originator of penny postage.

Boy — A18

Designs: Children of Tuvalu.

1979, Oct. 20		Litho.	Perf. 14	
125	A18	8c multicolored	.25	.25
126	A18	20c multicolored	.25	.25
127	A18	30c multicolored	.25	.25
128	A18	40c multicolored	.25	.25
		Nos. 125-128 (4)	1.00	1.00

International Year of the Child.

Cowry Shells A19

1980, Feb.　　Litho.　　Perf. 14
129	A19	8c Cypraea Argus	.25	.25
130	A19	20c Cypraea scurra	.25	.25
131	A19	30c Cypraea carneola	.30	.30
132	A19	40c Cypraea aurantium	.40	.40
		Nos. 129-132 (4)	1.20	1.20

Philatelic Bureau, Funafuti, Tuvalu No. 28, Arms, London 1980 Emblem — A20

Coat of Arms, London 1980 Emblem and: 20c, Gilbert and Ellice #41, Nukulaelae cancel, Tuvalu #24. 30c, US airmail cover. $1, Map of Tuvalu.

1980, Apr. 30　Litho.　Perf. 13½x14
133	A20	10c multicolored	.25	.25
134	A20	20c multicolored	.25	.25
135	A20	30c multicolored	.30	.30
136	A20	$1 multicolored	.75	.75
a.		Souvenir sheet of 4, #133-136	1.75	1.75
		Nos. 133-136 (4)	1.55	1.55

London 80 Intl. Stamp Exhib., May 6-14.

Queen Mother Elizabeth, 80th Birthday — A21

1980, Aug. 14　Litho.　Perf. 14
137	A21	50c multicolored	.40	.40

Issued in sheets of 10 plus 2 labels.

Aethaloessa Calidalis — A22

20c, Parotis suralis. 30c, Dudua aprobola. 40c, Decadarchis simulans.

1980, Aug. 20　Litho.　Perf. 14
138	A22	8c shown	.25	.25
139	A22	20c multicolored	.25	.25
140	A22	30c multicolored	.30	.30
141	A22	40c multicolored	.40	.40
		Nos. 138-141 (4)	1.20	1.20

Air Pacific Heron (First Regular Air Service to Tuvalu, 1964) — A23

Aviation Anniversaries: 20c, Hawker Siddeley 748 (air service to Tuvalu). 30c, Sunderland Flying Boat (War time service to Funafuti, 1945. 40c, Orville Wright and Flyer (Wright brothers' first flight, 1903).

1980, Nov. 5　　Litho.　　Perf. 14
142	A23	8c multicolored	.25	.25
143	A23	20c multicolored	.25	.25
144	A23	30c multicolored	.30	.25
145	A23	40c multicolored	.40	.40
		Nos. 142-145 (4)	1.20	1.15

Hypolimnas Bolina Elliciana — A24

1981, Feb. 3　　Litho.　　Perf. 14½
146	A24	8c shown	.30	.30
147	A24	20c Hypolimnas, diff.	.35	.35
148	A24	30c Hypolimnas, diff.	.40	.40
149	A24	40c Junonia vallida	.65	.65
		Nos. 146-149 (4)	1.70	1.70

No. 109 Surcharged

1981, Feb. 24　Litho.　Perf. 14
150	A14	45c on 50c multicolored	.60	.60

Elizabeth, 1809 A25

25c, Rebecca, 1819. 35c, Independence II, 1821. 40c, Basilisk, 1872. 45c, Royalist, 1890. 50c, Olivebank, 1920.

Wmk. 373

1981, May 13　Litho.　Perf. 14
151	A25	10c shown	.25	.25
152	A25	25c multicolored	.25	.25
153	A25	35c multicolored	.25	.25
154	A25	40c multicolored	.30	.30
155	A25	45c multicolored	.35	.35
156	A25	50c multicolored	.45	.45
		Nos. 151-156 (6)	1.85	1.85

See Nos. 216-221, 353-356, 410-413.

Prince Charles, Lady Diana, Royal Yacht Charlotte A25a

Prince Charles and Lady Diana — A25b

No. 157, Couple, Carolina. No. 158, Couple. No. 159, Victoria and Albert III. No. 161, Britannia.

Wmk. 380

1981, July 10　Litho.　Perf. 14
157	A25a	10c multicolored	.25	.25
a.		Blkt. pane of 4, perf. 12, unwmkd.		.60
158	A25b	10c multicolored	.25	.25
159	A25a	45c multicolored	.25	.25
160	A25b	45c like #158	.25	.25
a.		Blkt. pane of 2, perf. 12, unwmkd.		1.00
161	A25a	$2 multicolored	.50	.50
162	A25b	$2 like #158	1.40	1.40
		Nos. 157-162 (6)	2.90	2.90

Royal wedding. Issued in sheets of 7 (6 design A25a; 1 design A25b). Set of 3 $12. For surcharges see Nos. B1-B2.

Souvenir Sheet

1981, Dec.　Litho.　Perf. 12
163	A25b	$1.50 Couple	1.00	1.00

Admission to UPU — A26

Wmk. Harrison's, London
1981, Nov. 19　Engr.　Perf. 14½x14
164	A26	70c dark blue	.45	.45
165	A26	$1 dark red brown	.65	.65
a.		Souv. sheet of 2, #164-165, unwmkd.	1.75	1.75

Amatuku Maritime School — A27

1982, Feb. 17　Litho.　Perf. 13½x14
166	A27	10c Map	.25	.25
167	A27	25c Motorboat	.25	.25
168	A27	35c School, dock	.35	.35
169	A27	45c Flag, ship	.45	.45
		Nos. 166-169 (4)	1.30	1.30

A27a

Wmk. 380
1982, May 19　Litho.　Perf. 14
170	A27a	10c Caroline of Brandenburg-Ansbach, 1714	.25	.25
171	A27a	45c Brandenburg-Ansbach arms	.25	.25
172	A27a	$1.50 Diana	.50	.50
		Nos. 170-172 (3)	1.00	1.00

21st birthday of Princess Diana, July 1.

Nos. 170-172 Overprinted "ROYAL BABY"

1982, July 14　Litho.　Perf. 14
173	A27a	10c multicolored	.30	.30
174	A27a	45c multicolored	.30	.30
175	A27a	$1.50 multicolored	.40	.40
		Nos. 173-175 (3)	1.00	1.00

Birth of Prince William of Wales, June 21.

Scouting Year — A28

1982, Aug. 18
176	A28	10c Emblems	.25	.25
177	A28	25c Campfire	.30	.30
178	A28	35c Parade	.35	.35
179	A28	45c Scout	.40	.40
		Nos. 176-179 (4)	1.30	1.30

Visit of Queen Elizabeth II and Prince Philip — A29

25c, Arms, Duke of Edinburgh's Personal Standard. 45c, Flags. 50c, Queen Elizabeth II, maps.

1982, Oct. 26　Litho.　Perf. 14
180	A29	25c multicolored	.25	.25
181	A29	45c multicolored	.30	.30
182	A29	50c multicolored	.35	.35
a.		Souvenir sheet of 3, #180-182	1.25	1.25
		Nos. 180-182 (3)	.90	.90

Handicrafts — A30

1c, Fisherman's hat, lures, hooks. 2c, Cowrie shell handbags. 5c, Wedding & baby food baskets. 10c, Canoe model. 15c, Women's sun hats. 20c, Climbing rope. 25c, Pandanus baskets. 30c, Tray, coconut stands. 35c, Pandanus pillows, shell necklaces. 40c, Round baskets, fans. 45c, Reef sandals, fish trap. 50c, Rat trap, vert. 60c, Waterproof boxes, vert. $1, Pump drill, adze, vert. $2, Fisherman's hat, canoe bailers, vert. $5, Fishing rod, lures, scoop nets, vert.

1983-84　　Litho.　　Perf. 14
183	A30	1c multicolored	.30	.25
184	A30	2c multicolored	.30	.25
185	A30	5c multicolored	.30	.25
186	A30	10c multicolored	.30	.25
186A	A30	15c multicolored	2.25	2.50
187	A30	20c multicolored	.30	.25
188	A30	25c multicolored	.30	.25
188A	A30	30c multicolored	2.00	2.00
189	A30	35c multicolored	.40	.30
190	A30	40c multicolored	.30	.45
191	A30	45c multicolored	.35	.55
192	A30	50c multicolored	.40	.60
192A	A30	60c multicolored	2.75	2.00
193	A30	$1 multicolored	.40	.60
194	A30	$2 multicolored	.60	.75
195	A30	$5 multicolored	1.00	1.10
		Nos. 183-195 (16)	12.25	12.35

Issued: 15c, 1984; others, 3/14/83. For surcharges & overprints see #207, 230, O20-O32.

Commonwealth Day — A31

Wmk. 373
1983, Mar. 14　Litho.　Perf. 14
196	A31	20c Fishing industry	.25	.25
197	A31	35c Traditional dancing	.25	.25
198	A31	45c Satellite view	.25	.25
199	A31	50c First container ship	.30	.30
		Nos. 196-199 (4)	1.05	1.05

Dragonflies — A32

10c, Pantala flavescens. 35c, Anax guttatus. 40c, Tholymis tillarga. 50c, Diplacodes bipunctata.

1983, May 25 — Wmk. 380

200	A32	10c multicolored	.25	.25
201	A32	35c multicolored	.50	.50
202	A32	40c multicolored	.60	.60
203	A32	60c multicolored	.65	.65
		Nos. 200-203 (4)	2.00	2.00

Boys Brigade Centenary — A33

1983, Aug. 10 — Wmk. 373

204	A33	10c Running, emblem	.25	.25
205	A33	35c Canoeing	.30	.30
206	A33	$1 Officer, boys	.75	.75
		Nos. 204-206 (3)	1.30	1.30

No. 193 Surcharged in Black

1983, Aug. 26 — Wmk. 380

207	A30	60c on $1 multi	1.00	.60

First Manned Flight
Bicentenary — A34

25c, Montgolfier balloon, vert. 35c, McKinnon Turbo Goose. 45c, Beechcraft Super King Air 200. 50c, Double Eagle II Balloon, vert.

1983, Sept. 21 — Wmk. 373

208	A34	25c multicolored	.30	.30
209	A34	35c multicolored	.40	.40
210	A34	45c multicolored	.45	.45
211	A34	50c multicolored	.55	.55
a.		Souvenir sheet of 4, #208-211	2.50	2.50
		Nos. 208-211 (4)	1.70	1.70

World Communications Year — A35

25c, Conch Shell Trumpet, vert. 35c, Radio Operator, vert. 45c, Teleprinter. 50c, Transmitting station.

1983, Nov. 18 — Wmk. 380

212	A35	25c multicolored	.25	.25
213	A35	35c multicolored	.30	.30
214	A35	45c multicolored	.35	.35
215	A35	50c multicolored	.40	.40
		Nos. 212-215 (4)	1.30	1.30

Ship Type of 1981

1984, Feb. 16 — Wmk. 380

216	A25	10c Titus, 1897	.25	.25
217	A25	20c Malaita, 1905	.25	.25
218	A25	25c Aymeric, 1906	.25	.25
219	A25	35c Anshun, 1965	.35	.35
220	A25	45c Beaverbank, 1970	.40	.40
221	A25	50c Benjamin Bowring, 1981	.55	.55
		Nos. 216-221 (6)	2.05	2.05

Leaders of the World
Large quantities of some Leaders of the World issues were sold at a fraction of face value when the printer was liquidated.

Historic Locomotives — A36

1c, Class GS-4, US, 1941. 15c, AD-60, Australia, 1952. 40c, C38, Australia, 1943. 60c, Achilles England, 1892.

Se-tenant Pairs, #a.-b.
a. — Side and front views.
b. — Action scene.

Perf. 12½x13

1984, Feb. 29 — Unwmk.

222	A36	1c multicolored	.25	.25
223	A36	15c multicolored	.25	.25
224	A36	40c multicolored	.50	.50
225	A36	60c multicolored	.75	.75
		Nos. 222-225 (4)	1.75	1.75

See Nos. 235-246, 291-294, 320-323.

No. 191 Surcharged
Wmk. 380

1984, Feb. 1 — Litho. — Perf. 14

230	A30	30c on 45c multi	.40	.40

For overprint see No. O25.

Beach Flowers A38

25c, Ipomoea pes-caprae. 45c, Ipomoea macrantha. 50c, Triumfetta procumbens. 60c, Portulaca quadrifida.

1984, May 30

231	A38	25c multicolored	.25	.25
232	A38	45c multicolored	.40	.40
233	A38	50c multicolored	.50	.50
234	A38	60c multicolored	.65	.65
		Nos. 231-234 (4)	1.80	1.80

Train Type of 1984

No. 235, Class 9700, Japan, 1897. No. 236, Casey Jones, US, 1896. No. 237, Class 231C/K, France, 1909. No. 238, Triplex, US, 1914. No. 239, Class 370, Gt. Britain, 1981. No. 240, Class 4F, Gt. Britain, 1924. No. 241, Class 640, Italy, 1907. No. 242, Tornado, Gt. Britain, 1888. No. 243, Broadlands, Gt. Britain, 1967. No. 244, Locomotion, Gt. Britain, 1825. No. 245, C57, Japan, 1937. No. 246, Class 4500, France, 1906.

Se-tenant Pairs, #a.-b.
a. — Side and front views.
b. — Action scene.

1984 — Litho. — Perf. 12½x13

235	A36	1c multicolored	.25	.25
236	A36	10c multicolored	.25	.25
237	A36	15c multicolored	.25	.25
238	A36	15c multicolored	.25	.25
239	A36	20c multicolored	.25	.25
240	A36	25c multicolored	.25	.25
241	A36	30c multicolored	.30	.30
242	A36	40c multicolored	.40	.40
243	A36	50c multicolored	.50	.50
244	A36	60c multicolored	.65	.65
245	A36	$1 multicolored	1.00	1.00
246	A36	$1 multicolored	1.00	1.00
		Nos. 235-246 (12)	5.35	5.35

Issued: Nos. 235, 237, 241, 245, 10/4; others, 6/27.

15th South Pacific Forum A38a

1984, Aug. 21 — Litho. — Perf. 14

255	A38a	60c National flag	.55	.55
256	A38a	60c Tuvalu crest	.55	.55

Ausipex '84 A38b

1984, Aug. 21 — Perf. 14

257	A38b	60c Exhib. emblem	.45	.45
258	A38b	60c Royal Exhibi. Building	.45	.45

A. Shrewsbury Playing Cricket — A39

Cricket players in action or portrait

Se-tenant Pairs #a.-b.

1984, Nov. 5 — Litho. — Perf. 12½

259	A39	5c shown	.25	.25
260	A39	30c H. Verity	.50	.50
261	A39	50c E.H. Hendren	.50	.50
262	A39	60c J. Briggs	.60	.60
		Nos. 259-262 (4)	1.85	1.85

Drawings, Christmas 1984 — A40

1984, Nov. 14 — Litho. — Perf. 14½x14

267	A40	15c By Eli Faalata	.25	.25
268	A40	40c By Toakai Niutao	.30	.30
269	A40	50c By Falesa Touila	.40	.40
270	A40	60c By Piuani Talie	.50	.50
		Nos. 267-270 (4)	1.45	1.45

Classic Automobiles — A41

Sketch listed first followed by angled view: 1c, Morris Minor, 1949. 15c, Studebaker Avanti, 1963. 50c, Chevrolet International Six, 1929. $1, Allard J2, 1950.

Se-tenant Pairs, #a.-b.
a. — Side and front views.
b. — Action scene.

1984, Dec. 7 — Litho. — Perf. 12½x13

271	A41	1c multicolored	.30	.30
272	A41	15c multicolored	.30	.30
273	A41	50c multicolored	.60	.60
274	A41	$1 multicolored	1.25	1.25
		Nos. 271-274 (4)	2.45	2.45

See Nos. 299-302, 332-339, 396-396, 414-425.

John J. Audubon — A42

#279a, Common flicker. #279b, Say's phoebe. #280a, Townsend's warbler. #280b, Bohemian waxwing. #281a, Prothonotary warbler. #281b, Worm-eating warbler. #282a, Broad-winged hawk. #282b, Northern harrier.

1985, Feb. 12 — Litho. — Perf. 12½

279	A42	1c Pair, #a.-b.	.30	.30
280	A42	25c Pair, #a.-b.	.70	.70
281	A42	50c Pair, #a.-b.	1.40	1.40
282	A42	70c Pair, #a.-b.	1.75	1.75
		Nos. 279-282 (4)	4.15	4.15

Birds and Eggs A43

15c, Black-naped tern. 40c, Black noddy. 50c, White-tailed tropicbird. 60c, Sooty tern.

1985, Feb. 27 — Perf. 14

287	A43	15c multicolored	.50	.35
288	A43	40c multicolored	1.10	.85
289	A43	50c multicolored	1.40	.95
290	A43	60c multicolored	1.75	1.25
		Nos. 287-290 (4)	4.75	3.40

Train Type of 1984

5c, Churchward, U.K. 10c, Class K.F., China. 30c, Class 99.77, East Germany. $1, Pearson, U.K.

Se-tenant Pairs, #a.-b.
a. — Side and front views.
b. — Action scene.

1985, Mar. 19 — Perf. 12½

291	A36	5c multicolored	.25	.25
292	A36	10c multicolored	.25	.25
293	A36	30c multicolored	.45	.45
294	A36	$1 multicolored	1.50	1.50
		Nos. 291-294 (4)	2.45	2.45

Automobile Type of 1984

1c, Rickenbacker, 1923. 20c, Detroit-Electric, 1914. 50c, Packard Clipper, 1941. 70c, Audi Quattro, 1982.

Se-tenant Pairs, #a.-b.
a. — Side and front views.
b. — Action scene.

1985, Apr. 3

299	A41	1c multicolored	.30	.30
300	A41	20c multicolored	.30	.30
301	A41	50c multicolored	.65	.65
302	A41	70c multicolored	1.00	1.00
		Nos. 299-302 (4)	2.25	2.25

World War II Aircraft A44

15c, Curtiss P-40N. 40c, Consolidated B-24D Liberator. 50c, Lockheed PV-1 Ventura. 60c, Douglas C-54 Skymaster.

1985, May 29 — Litho. — Perf. 14

307	A44	15c multicolored	1.75	1.00
308	A44	40c multicolored	2.00	1.50
309	A44	50c multicolored	2.00	2.25

310	A44	60c multicolored	2.00	2.25
a.		Souvenir sheet of 4, #307-310	5.50	5.50
		Nos. 307-310 (4)	7.75	7.00

Queen Mother, 85th Birthday — A45

Designs: No. 311a, Facing right. No. 311b, Facing left. Nos. 312a, 317a, Facing right, diff. Nos. 312b, 317b, Facing front. Nos. 313a, 316a, Waving to crowd. Nos. 313b, 316b, Facing front, diff. No. 314a, Facing front. No. 314b, Facing left. No. 315a, As a young woman. No. 315b, As Queen Consort.

1985-86 Litho. Perf. 12½

311	A45	5c Pair, #a.-b.	.30	.30
312	A45	30c Pair, #a.-b.	.35	.35
313	A45	60c Pair, #a.-b.	.70	.70
314	A45	$1 Pair, #a.-b.	1.05	1.05
		Nos. 311-314 (4)	2.40	2.40

Souvenir Sheets

315	A45	$1.20 #a.-b.	1.90	1.90
316	A45	$2 #a.-b.	4.50	4.50
317	A45	$3 #a.-b.	6.50	6.50

Issued: #316-317, 6/10/86; others, 7/4/85.

Train Type of 1984

10c, 1936 Green Arrow, U.K. 40c, 1982 G.M. (EMD) SD-50, US. 65c, 1932 DRG Flying Hamburger, Germany. $1, 1908 JNR Class 1070, Japan.

Se-tenant Pairs, #a.-b.
a. — Side and front views.
b. — Action scene.

1985, Sept. 18

320	A36	10c multicolored	.25	.25
321	A36	40c multicolored	.55	.55
322	A36	65c multicolored	.75	.75
323	A36	$1 multicolored	.80	.80
		Nos. 320-323 (4)	2.35	2.35

Girl Guides, 75th Anniv. — A46

1985, Aug. 28 Litho. Perf. 15

328	A46	15c Playing guitar	.25	.25
329	A46	40c Camping	.50	.50
330	A46	50c Flag bearer	.60	.60
331	A46	60c Guides' salute	.70	.70
a.		Souvenir sheet of 4, #328-331	2.00	2.00
		Nos. 328-331 (4)	2.05	2.05

Car Type of 1984

5c, 1929 Cord L-29, US. 10c, 1932 Horch 670 V-12, Germany. 15c, 1901 Lanchester, UK. 35c, 1950 Citroen 2 CV, France. 40c, 1957 MGA, UK. 55c, 1962 Ferrari 250-GTO, Italy. $1, 1932 Ford V-8, US. $1.50, 1977 Aston Martin-Lagonda, UK.

a. — Side and front views.
b. — Action scene.

1985, Oct. 8 Perf. 12½

332-339	A41	Set of 8 pairs	4.75	4.75

Crabs A47

15c, Stalk-eyed ghost. 40c, Red and white painted. 50c, Red-spotted. 60c, Red hermit.

1986, Jan. 7 Perf. 15

348	A47	15c multicolored	.35	.35
349	A47	40c multicolored	.95	.95
350	A47	50c multicolored	1.10	1.10
351	A47	60c multicolored	1.40	1.40
		Nos. 348-351 (4)	3.80	3.80

Souvenir Sheet of 2

Fischer & Karpov, World Chess Champions; Rotary Intl., 80th Anniv. — A48

No. 352a, American and Soviet flags, chess board & knight. No. 352b, Rotary Intl. emblem.

1986, Mar. 19 Perf. 13x12½

352	A48	$3 #a.-b.	6.50	6.50

No. 352 exists with plain or decorated border.

Ship Type of 1981

15c, Messenger of Peace. 40c, John Wesley. 50c, Duff. 60c, Triton.

1986, Apr. 14 Perf. 15

353	A25	15c multicolored	.30	.30
354	A25	40c multicolored	.80	.80
355	A25	50c multicolored	.90	.90
356	A25	60c multicolored	1.00	1.00
		Nos. 353-356 (4)	3.00	3.00

Queen Elizabeth II, 60th Birthday — A49

Various portraits.

1986, Apr. 21 Perf. 12½

357	A49	10c multicolored	.25	.25
358	A49	90c multicolored	.35	.35
359	A49	$1.50 multicolored	.60	.60
360	A49	$3 multi, vert.	1.10	1.10
		Nos. 357-360 (4)	2.30	2.30

Souvenir Sheet

361	A49	$4 multicolored	3.50	3.50

Peace Corps, 25th Anniv. A50

1986, May 22 Perf. 14

362	A50	50c multicolored	.80	.80

For overprint see No. 374.

AMERIPEX '86 — A51

1986, May 22 Perf. 14x13½

363	A51	60c multicolored	.80	.80

A52

Players and teams: 1c, South Korea. 5c, France. 10c, W. Germany, 1974. 40c, Italy. 60c, W. Germany vs. Holland, 1974. $1, Canada. $2, Northern Ireland. $3, England.

1986, June 30 Litho. Perf. 15

364	A52	1c multi	.25	.25
365	A52	5c multi	.25	.25
366	A52	10c multi	.25	.25
367	A52	40c multi	.40	.40

Size: 60x40mm
Perf. 13x12½

368	A52	60c multi	.50	.50
369	A52	$1 multi	.80	.80
370	A52	$2 multi	1.75	1.75
371	A52	$3 multi	2.40	2.40
		Nos. 364-371 (8)	6.60	6.60

Souvenir Sheets

372	A52	$1.50 like #369	1.75	1.75
373	A52	$2.50 like #370	3.00	3.00

1986 World Cup Soccer Championships. Nos. 366 and 368 picture emblem; others picture character trademark.

No. 362 Ovptd. with STAMPEX '86 Emblem

1986, Aug. 4 Litho. Perf. 14

374	A50	50c multicolored	.70	.70

A53

Wedding of Prince Andrew and Sarah Ferguson — A54

#381a, Andrew, vert. #381b, Couple, vert. #382a, Andrew. #382b, Princess Diana, Sarah.

Perf. 12½

1986, July 18 Litho. Unwmk.

381	A53	60c Pair, #a.-b.	.75	.75
382	A53	$1 Pair, #a.-b.	1.25	1.25

Souvenir Sheet
Perf. 13x12½

383	A54	$6 Newlyweds	3.00	3.00

No. 382a pictures Westminster Abbey in LR. For overprints see Nos. 389-390.

Geckos A55

1986, July 30 Litho. Perf. 14

384	A55	15c Mourning gecko	.35	.30
385	A55	40c Oceanic stump-toed	1.15	1.00
386	A55	50c Azure-tailed skink	1.50	1.30
387	A55	60c Moth skink	2.10	1.75
		Nos. 384-387 (4)	5.10	4.35

Souvenir Sheet

South Pacific Forum, 15th Anniv. A56

Flags and maps: a, Australia. b, Cook Islands. c, Micronesia. d, Fiji. e, Kiribati. f, Nauru. g, New Zealand. h, Niue. i, Papua New Guinea. j, Solomon Islands. k, Tonga. l, Tuvalu. m, Vanuatu. n, Western Samoa.

Wmk. 380

1986, Aug. 4 Litho. Perf. 15

388		Sheet of 14 + label	9.00	9.00
a.-n.		A56 40c any single	.60	.60

No. 388 has center label picturing Executive Committee headquarters, Suva, Fiji.

Nos. 381-382 Ovptd. "Congratulations to T.R.H. The Duke & Duchess of York" in Silver

1986 Unwmk. Perf. 12½

389	A53	60c Pair, #a.-b.	1.75	1.75
390	A53	$1 Pair, #a.-b.	2.75	2.75

Exist tete-beche.

Car Type of 1984

15c, 1953 Cooper, UK. 40c, 1964 Rover 2000, UK. 50c, 1930 Ruxton, US. 60c, 1950 Jowett Jupiter, UK. 90c, 1964 Cobra Daytona Coupe, US. $1.50, 1903 Packard Model F "Old Pacific," US.

Se-tenant Pairs, #a.-b.
a. — Side and front views.
b. — Action scene.

1986, Oct.   Litho.   Perf. 12½
391-396 A41 Set of 6 pairs   3.50 3.50

Marine
Life
A57

1986, Nov. 5   Unwmk.   Perf. 14
397 A57 15c Sea star   .95   .95
398 A57 40c Pencil urchin   1.60 1.60
399 A57 50c Fragile coral   1.75 1.75
400 A57 60c Pink coral   2.00 2.00
Nos. 397-400 (4)   6.30 6.30
See Nos. 465-468, 524-527.

Souvenir Sheets

Statue of Liberty, Cent. — A58

Various views of the statue.

1986, Nov. 24
401 A58 $1.25 multicolored   .65   .65
402 A58 $1.50 multicolored   .90   .90
403 A58 $1.80 multicolored   1.15 1.15
404 A58 $2 multicolored   1.25 1.25
405 A58 $2.25 multicolored   1.50 1.50
406 A58 $2.50 multicolored   1.60 1.60
407 A58 $3 multicolored   2.00 2.00
408 A58 $3.25 multicolored   2.10 2.10
409 A58 $3.50 multicolored   2.50 2.50
Nos. 401-409 (9)   13.65 13.65

A perforated set of sixteen 65c stamps commemorating the Statue of Liberty centennial in a different design were printed but never issued. The stamps were sold in the liquidation sale of the printer.

Ships Type of 1981

1987, Feb. 4   Unwmk.   Perf. 14
410 A25 15c Southern Cross IV   .80   .80
411 A25 40c John Williams IV   1.75 1.75
412 A25 50c John Williams IV   2.00 2.00
413 A25 60c M.S. Southern
           Cross   2.00 2.00
Nos. 410-413 (4)   6.55 6.55

Car Type of 1984

1c, 1938 Talbot-Lago, France. 2c, 1930 Dupont Model G, US. 5c, 1950 Riley RM, U.K. 10c, 1915 Chevrolet Baby Grand, US. 20c, 1968 Shelby Mustang GT 500 KR, US. 30c, 1952 Ferrari 212 Export Barchetta, Italy. 40c, 1912 Peerless Model 48-Six, US. 50c, 1954 Sunbeam Alpine, U.K. 60c, 1969 Matra-Ford MS80, France. 70c, 1934 Squire 1-Litre, U.K. 75c, 1931 Talbot 105, U.K. $1, 1928 Plymouth Model Q, US.

Se-tenant Pairs, #a.-b.
a. — Side and front views.
b. — Action scene.

Perf. 12½
1987, May 7   Litho.   Unwmk.
414-425 A41 Set of 12 pairs,
              #a.-b.   6.50 6.50
425c   Souv. sheet of 2 4.00 4.00

Ferns — A59

15c, Nephrolepis saligna. 40c, Asplenium nidus. 50c, Microsorum scolopendria. 60c, Pteris tripartita. $1.50, Psilotum nudum.

1987, July 7   Wmk. 380   Perf. 14
438 A59 15c multicolored   .25   .25
439 A59 40c multicolored   .80   .80
440 A59 50c multicolored   1.00 1.00
441 A59 60c multicolored   1.10 1.10
Nos. 438-441 (4)   3.15 3.15

Souvenir Sheet
442 A59 $1.50 multicolored 3.25 3.25

A60

#443a, 444b, 445a, 456b, Flowers, all diff. #440b, 444a, 445b, 456a, Woman wearing fou, all diff.

1987, Aug. 12   Wmk. 380
443 A60 15c Pair, #a.-b.   .40   .40
444 A60 40c Pair, #a.-b.   1.00 1.00
445 A60 50c Pair, #a.-b.   1.20 1.20
446 A60 60c Pair, #a.-b.   1.60 1.60
Nos. 443-446 (4)   4.20 4.20

Crayfish
and
Coconut
Crabs
A61

Wmk. 380
1987, Nov. 11   Litho.   Perf. 14
451 A61 40c Coconut crabs   1.20   .90
452 A61 50c Painted crayfish 1.50 1.10
453 A61 60c Ocean crayfish 1.75 1.40
Nos. 451-453 (3)   4.45 3.40

Photograph of Queen Victoria, 1897,
by Downey — A62

60c, Elizabeth and Philip on their wedding day, 1947. 80c, Elizabeth, Charles, Philip, c. 1950. $1, Elizabeth, Anne, 1950. $2, Elizabeth, 1970. $3, Elizabeth, children, 1950.

1987, Nov. 20   Unwmk.   Perf. 15
454-458 A62 Set of 5   4.75 4.75

Souvenir Sheet
459 A62 $3 red org & blk   3.00 3.00

Accession of Queen Victoria to the throne of England, sesquicentennial; wedding of Queen Elizabeth II and Prince Philip, 40th anniv.

16th World Scout Jamboree, Australia,
1987-88 — A63

Jamboree and Australia bicentennial emblems plus: 40c, Aborigine, Ayer's Rock. 60c, Capt. Cook, by Dance, and HMS Endeavor. $1, Scout and Scout Park Arch. $1.50, Koala and kangaroo. $2.50, Lord and Lady Baden-Powell.

1987, Dec. 2   Litho.   Perf. 13x12½
460 A63 40c multicolored   .35   .35
461 A63 60c multicolored   .50   .50
462 A63 $1 multicolored   .85   .85
463 A63 $1.50 multicolored 1.15 1.15
Nos. 460-463 (4)   2.85 2.85

Souvenir Sheet
464 A63 $2.50 multicolored 2.50 2.50

Marine Life Type of 1986
Unwmk.
1988, Feb. 29   Litho.   Perf. 15
465 A57 15c Spanish dancer   .55   .35
466 A57 40c Hard corals   1.30   .75
467 A57 50c Feather stars   1.60   .95
468 A57 60c Staghorn corals 1.90 1.10
Nos. 465-468 (4)   5.35 3.15

Birds
A64

5c, Jungle fowl. 10c, White tern. 15c, Brown noddy. 20c, Phoenix petrel. 25c, Pacific golden plover. 30c, Crested tern. 35c, Sooty tern. 40c, Bristle-thighed curlew. 45c, Eastern bar-tailed godwit. 50c, Reef heron. 55c, Greater frigatebird. 60c, Red-footed booby. 70c, Red-necked stint. $1, New Zealand long-tailed cuckoo. $2, Red-tailed tropicbird. $5, Banded rail.

1988, Mar. 2   Perf. 15
469 A64 5c multicolored   .25   .25
470 A64 10c multicolored   .25   .25
471 A64 15c multicolored   .25   .25
472 A64 20c multicolored   .25   .25
473 A64 25c multicolored   .25   .25
474 A64 30c multicolored   .30   .30
475 A64 35c multicolored   .35   .35
476 A64 40c multicolored   .40   .40
477 A64 45c multicolored   .45   .45
478 A64 50c multicolored   .50   .50
479 A64 55c multicolored   .55   .55
480 A64 60c multicolored   .65   .65
481 A64 70c multicolored   .75   .75
482 A64 $1 multicolored   1.25 1.25
483 A64 $2 multicolored   2.25 2.25
484 A64 $5 multicolored   5.50 5.50
Nos. 469-484 (16)   14.20 14.20

For overprints see Nos. 676-679, 796-799, O33-O48.

Intl. Red Cross and Red Crescent
Organizations, 125th Anniv. — A65

15c, Jean-Henri Dunant. 40c, Junior Red Cross. 50c, Care for the handicapped. 60c, First aid training. $1, Lecture.

Perf. 12½
1988, May 9   Litho.   Unwmk.
485 A65 15c multicolored   .25   .25
486 A65 40c multicolored   .25   .25
487 A65 50c multicolored   .25   .25
488 A65 60c multicolored   .30   .30
Nos. 485-488 (4)   1.05 1.05

Souvenir Sheet
489 A65 $1.50 multicolored 2.25 2.25

A66

Voyages of Capt. Cook — A67

Designs: 20c, HMS Endeavour (starboard side). 40c, Endeavour (stern). 50c, Landing, Tahiti, 1769, vert. 60c, Maori chief, vert. 80c, Resolution and native Hawaiian sail ship. $1, Cook, by Sir Nathaniel Dance-Holland (1735-1811), vert. $2.50, Antarctic icebergs surrounding the Resolution.

1988, June 15   Litho.   Perf. 12½
490-495 A66 Set of 6   4.50 4.50

Souvenir Sheet
496   A67 $2.50 shown 10.00 10.00

Fungi — A68

40c, Ganoderma applanatum. 50c, Pseudoepicoccum cocos. 60c, Rigidoporus zonalis. 90c, Rigidoporus microporus.

1988, July 25   Litho.   Perf. 15
497 A68 40c multicolored   1.00 1.00
498 A68 50c multicolored   1.20 1.20
499 A68 60c multicolored   1.40 1.40
500 A68 90c multicolored   2.00 2.00
Nos. 497-500 (4)   5.60 5.60
See Nos. 520-523.

1988 Summer Olympics, Seoul — A69

Perf. 12½
1988, Aug. 19   Litho.   Unwmk.
501 A69 10c Rifles, target   .30   .30
502 A69 20c Judo   .55   .55
503 A69 40c One-man kayak   1.20 1.20
504 A69 60c Swimming   1.75 1.75
505 A69 80c Yachting   2.25 2.25
506 A69 $1 Balance beam   3.25 3.25
Nos. 501-506 (6)   9.30 9.30

Natl. Independence, 10th
Anniv. — A70

60c, Queen Elizabeth in boat. 90c, In sedan
chair. $1.20, Seated at dais.

Wmk. 380

1988, Sept. 28		**Litho.**		**Perf. 14**	
507	A70	60c multi		1.00	1.00
a.		Souvenir sheet of 1		1.00	1.00
508	A70	90c multi		1.50	1.50
a.		Souvenir sheet of 1		1.50	1.50
509	A70	$1 shown		1.75	1.75
a.		Souvenir sheet of 1		1.75	1.75
510	A70	$1.20 multi		2.10	2.10
a.		Souvenir sheet of 1		2.10	2.10
		Nos. 507-510 (4)		6.35	6.35

Nos. 507-508 and 510 vert.

Christmas — A71

Unwmk.

1988, Dec. 5		**Litho.**		**Perf. 14**	
511	A71	15c Mary		.35	.35
512	A71	40c Christ child		.90	.90
513	A71	60c Joseph		1.25	1.25
		Nos. 511-513 (3)		2.50	2.50

Souvenir Sheet

514	A71	$1.50 Heraldic angel	2.50	2.50

Palm-frond or Pandanus-leaf
Skirts — A72

1989, Mar. 31		**Litho.**		**Perf. 14**	
515	A72	40c multi		.80	.80
516	A72	50c multi, diff.		1.00	1.00
517	A72	60c multi, diff.		1.20	1.20
518	A72	90c multi, diff.		1.75	1.75
		Nos. 515-518 (4)		4.75	4.75

Souvenir Sheet

519	A72	$1.50 multi, vert.	3.50	3.50

Fungi Type of 1988

40c, Trametes muelleri. 50c, Pestalotiopsis
palmarum. 60c, Trametes cingulata. 90c,
Schizophyllum commune.

1989, May 24		**Litho.**		**Perf. 14**	
520	A68	40c multicolored		1.00	1.00
521	A68	50c multicolored		2.25	2.25
522	A68	60c multicolored		2.75	2.75
523	A68	90c multicolored		4.00	4.00
		Nos. 520-523 (4)		10.00	10.00

Marine Life Type of 1986

40c, Pennant coralfish. 50c, Anemone fish.
60c, Batfish. 90c, Threadfin coralfish.

1989, July 31		**Litho.**		**Perf. 14**	
524	A57	40c multicolored		1.50	1.50
525	A57	50c multicolored		1.90	1.90
526	A57	60c multicolored		2.25	2.25
527	A57	90c multicolored		4.00	4.00
a.		Miniature sheet of 4, #524-527		9.75	9.75
		Nos. 524-527 (4)		9.65	9.65

Souvenir Sheet

Maiden Voyage of M.V. *Nivaga II*,
1988 — A73

1989, Oct. 9		**Litho.**		**Perf. 14**	
528	A73	$1.50 multicolored		5.75	5.75

Christmas — A74

Unwmk.

1989, Nov. 29		**Litho.**		**Perf. 14**	
529	A74	40c Conch shell		.85	.85
530	A74	50c Flower bouquet		1.20	1.20
531	A74	60c Germinated coconut		1.35	1.35
532	A74	90c Shell jewelry		1.90	1.90
		Nos. 529-532 (4)		5.30	5.30

Tropical
Trees — A75

15c, Cocus nucifera. 30c, Rhizophora
samoensis. 40c, Messerschmidia argentea.
50c, Pandanus tectorius. 60c, Hernandia
nymphaeifolia. 90c, Pisonia grandis.

1990, Feb. 28		**Litho.**		**Perf. 14½**	
533	A75	15c multicolored		.55	.55
534	A75	30c multicolored		1.00	1.00
535	A75	40c multicolored		1.25	1.25
536	A75	50c multicolored		1.50	1.50
537	A75	60c multicolored		1.90	1.90
538	A75	90c multicolored		3.25	3.25
		Nos. 533-538 (6)		9.45	9.45

Penny
Black,
150th
Anniv.
A76

1990, May 3		**Litho.**		**Perf. 14**	
539	A76	15c multicolored		.90	.90
540	A76	40c multicolored		2.40	2.40
541	A76	90c multicolored		5.75	5.75
		Nos. 539-541 (3)		9.05	9.05

Souvenir Sheet

542	A76	$2 multicolored	7.50	7.50

Stamp World London '90.

World
War II
Ships
A77

Designs: 15c, Japanese merchant conversion, 1940. 30c, USS Unimak, seaplane
tender, 1944. 40c, Amagari, Japanese Hubuki
class, 1942. 50c, AO-24 USS Platte, Nov. 1,
1943. 60c, Japanese Shumushu Class (Type
A) escort. 90c, CV-22 USS Independence.

1990

543-548	A77	Set of 6	14.50	14.50

Flowers — A78

1990, Sept. 21		**Litho.**		**Perf. 14½**	
549	A78	15c Erythrina fusca		.30	.30
550	A78	30c Capparis cordifolia		.60	.60
551	A78	40c Portulaca pilosa		.80	.80
552	A78	50c Cordia subcordata		.95	.95
553	A78	60c Scaevola taccada		1.15	1.15
554	A78	90c Suriana maritima		1.75	1.75
		Nos. 549-554 (6)		5.55	5.55

UN Development Program, 40th
Anniv. — A79

40c, Surveyor. 60c, Communications station. $1.20, Fishing boat Te Tautai.

1990, Nov. 20		**Litho.**		**Perf. 14**	
555	A79	40c multicolored		1.40	1.40
556	A79	60c multicolored		1.90	1.90
557	A79	$1.20 multicolored		3.75	3.75
		Nos. 555-557 (3)		7.05	7.05

Christmas
A80

1990, Nov. 20

558	A80	15c Mary and Joseph		.45	.45
559	A80	40c Nativity		1.25	1.25
560	A80	60c Shepherds		1.90	1.90
561	A80	90c Three Kings		2.75	2.75
		Nos. 558-561 (4)		6.35	6.35

Seashells — A81

40c, Murex ramosus. 50c, Conus
marmoreus. 60c, Trochus niloticus. $1.50,
Cypraea mappa.

1991, Jan. 18		**Litho.**		**Perf. 14**	
562	A81	40c multicolored		1.30	1.30
563	A81	50c multicolored		1.75	1.75
564	A81	60c multicolored		1.90	1.90
565	A81	$1.50 multicolored		4.25	4.25
		Nos. 562-565 (4)		9.20	9.20

Insects
A82

40c, Cylas formicarius. 50c, Heliothis armi-
ger. 60c, Spodoptera litura. $1.50, Agrius
convolvuli.

1991, Mar. 22		**Litho.**		**Perf. 14**	
566	A82	40c multicolored		1.50	1.50
567	A82	50c multicolored		2.00	2.00
568	A82	60c multicolored		2.25	2.25
569	A82	$1.50 multicolored		5.50	5.50
		Nos. 566-569 (4)		11.25	11.25

Endangered
Marine Life — A83

40c, Green turtle. 50c, Humpback whale.
60c, Hawksbill turtle. $1.50, Sperm whale.

1991, May 31		**Litho.**		**Perf. 14**	
570	A83	40c multi		1.25	1.25
571	A83	50c multi		1.50	1.50
572	A83	60c multi		2.00	2.00
573	A83	$1.50 multi		4.75	4.75
		Nos. 570-573 (4)		9.50	9.50

A84

1991, July 31		**Litho.**		**Perf. 14**	
574	A84	40c Soccer		1.60	1.60
575	A84	50c Volleyball		2.10	2.10
576	A84	60c Lawn tennis		2.50	2.50
577	A84	$1.50 Cricket		5.75	5.75
		Nos. 574-577 (4)		11.95	11.95

9th South Pacific Games.

World
War II
Ships
A85

40c, USS Tennessee. 50c, IJN Haguro. 60c,
HMS Achilles. $1.50, USS North Carolina.

1991, Oct. 15		**Litho.**		**Perf. 14**	
578	A85	40c multi		3.00	2.25
579	A85	50c multi		3.25	3.00
580	A85	60c multi		4.00	3.25
581	A85	$1.50 multi		8.50	8.50
		Nos. 578-581 (4)		18.75	17.00

Christmas — A86

Various traditional dance costumes.

1991, Dec. 13

582	A86	40c multicolored		1.50	1.50
583	A86	50c multicolored		1.90	1.90
584	A86	60c multicolored		2.25	2.25
585	A86	$1.50 multicolored		5.75	5.75
		Nos. 582-585 (4)		11.40	11.40

A87

Constellations.

1992, Jan. 29   Litho.   Perf. 14
586	A87	40c Southern Fish	1.60	1.60
587	A87	50c Scorpio	2.00	2.00
588	A87	60c Sagittarius	2.50	2.50
589	A87	$1.50 Southern Cross	6.00	6.00
		Nos. 586-589 (4)	12.10	12.10

British Annexation of the Gilbert & Ellice Islands, Cent. — A88

40c, King George VI. 50c, King George V. 60c, King Edward VII. $1.50, Queen Victoria.

1992, Mar. 23   Litho.   Perf. 14
590	A88	40c multi	1.60	1.60
591	A88	50c multi	1.90	1.90
592	A88	60c multi	2.50	2.50
593	A88	$1.50 multi	6.50	6.50
		Nos. 590-593 (4)	12.50	12.50

Discovery of America, 500th Anniv. A89

Columbus and: 40c, Queen Isabella & King Ferdinand of Spain. 50c, Polynesians. 60c, South American Indians. $1.50, North American Indians.

1992, May 22   Litho.   Perf. 14
594	A89	40c black & dk blue	1.10	1.10
595	A89	50c blk & dk plum	1.20	1.20
596	A89	60c blk & dk grn	1.40	1.40
597	A89	$1.50 blk & dk pur	3.25	3.25
		Nos. 594-597 (4)	6.95	6.95

World Columbian Stamp Expo '92, Chicago.

Fish A90

Designs: 15c, Bluespot butterflyfish. 20c, Pink parrotfish. 25c, Stripe surgeonfish. 30c, Moon wrasse. 35c, Harlequin filefish. 40c, Bird wrasse. 45c, Black-finned pigfish. 50c, Blue-green chromis. 60c, Hump-headed Maori wrasse. 70c, Ornate coralfish, vert. 90c, Saddled butterflyfish, vert. $1, Vagabond butterflyfish, vert. $2, Longfin bannerfish, vert. $3, Moorish idol, vert.

1992, July 15
598-611	A90	Set of 14	14.50 14.50

For overprints & surcharge see #629-632, 716.

1992 Summer Olympics, Barcelona — A91

40c, Discus. 50c, Javelin. 60c, Shotput. $1.50, Track & field. $2, Olympic stadium.

1992, July 27   Litho.   Perf. 14
612	A91	40c multi	.90	.90
613	A91	50c multi	1.15	1.15
614	A91	60c multi	1.60	1.60
615	A91	$1.50 multi	4.00	4.00
		Nos. 612-615 (4)	7.65	7.65

Souvenir Sheet
616	A91	$2 multi	5.00	5.00

Blue Coral A92

Various views of blue coral.

1992, Sept. 1
617	A92	10c multicolored	1.25	1.25
618	A92	25c multicolored	2.75	2.75
619	A92	30c multicolored	2.75	2.75
620	A92	35c multicolored	3.25	3.25
		Nos. 617-620 (4)	10.00	10.00

World Wildlife Fund.

Christmas — A93

Designs: 40c, Fishermen seeing angel. 50c, Fishermen sailing canoes toward island. 60c, Adoration of the fishermen. $1.50, Flowers, shell necklaces.

1992, Dec. 25   Litho.   Perf. 14
621	A93	40c multicolored	.70	.70
622	A93	50c multicolored	.85	.85
623	A93	60c multicolored	.95	.95
624	A93	$1.50 multicolored	2.50	2.50
		Nos. 621-624 (4)	5.00	5.00

Wild Flowers — A94

40c, Calophyllum inophyllum. 50c, Hibiscus tiliaceus. 60c, Lantana camara. $1.50, Plumeria rubra.

1993, Feb. 2   Litho.   Perf. 14
625	A94	40c multicolored	.95	.95
626	A94	50c multicolored	1.20	1.20
627	A94	60c multicolored	1.30	1.30
628	A94	$1.50 multicolored	3.00	3.00
		Nos. 625-628 (4)	6.45	6.45

Nos. 601, 603, & 605-606 Ovptd.

1992, Sept. 1   Litho.   Perf. 14
629	A90	30c on #601	1.15	1.15
630	A90	40c on #603	1.40	1.40
631	A90	50c on #605	2.10	2.10
632	A90	60c on #606	2.25	2.25
		Nos. 629-632 (4)	6.90	6.90

World War II in the Pacific, 50th Anniv. A95

40c, Japanese bombers. 50c, Anti-aircraft gun, vert. 60c, Using flame thrower. $1.50, Map of Funafuti Atoll, vert.

1993, Apr. 23   Litho.   Perf. 14
633	A95	40c multicolored	1.60	1.60
634	A95	50c multicolored	1.90	1.90
635	A95	60c multicolored	2.25	2.25
636	A95	$1.50 multicolored	6.25	6.25
		Nos. 633-636 (4)	12.00	12.00

Souvenir Sheet

Indopex '93 — A96

1993, May 29   Perf. 14x14½
637	A96	$1.50 Cepora porimale	5.75 5.75

Marine Life A97

1993, June 29   Litho.   Perf. 14
638	A97	40c Giant clam	.80	.80
639	A97	50c Anemone crab	1.00	1.00
640	A97	60c Octopus	1.25	1.25
641	A97	$1.50 Green turtle	3.00	3.00
		Nos. 638-641 (4)	6.05	6.05

Coronation of Queen Elizabeth II, 40th Anniv. — A98

Queen: 40c, Riding in parade with Prince Phillip. 50c, Drinking coconut milk. 60c, Holding umbrella. $1.50, With natives. $2, Coronation ceremony.

1993, July 5
642	A98	40c multicolored	.70	.70
643	A98	50c multicolored	.90	.90
644	A98	60c multicolored	1.15	1.15
645	A98	$1.50 multicolored	2.75	2.75
		Nos. 642-645 (4)	5.50	5.50

Souvenir Sheet
646	A98	$2 multicolored	7.75	7.75

Souvenir Sheet

Taipei '93 — A99

Litho. & Typo.
1993, Aug. 14   Perf. 14½x14
647	A99	$1.50 Geoffroyi godart	5.25 5.25

Souvenir Sheet

Bangkok '93 — A100

$1.50, Paradisea staudinger.

1993, Oct. 1   Litho.   Perf. 14x14½
648	A100	$1.50 multi	3.50 3.50

Greenhouse Effect — A101

Beach scene with: 40c, Sun at UR. 50c, Sun at UL. 60c, Crab on beach. $1.50, Sea gull in flight.

1993, Nov. 2   Litho.   Perf. 13½
649	A101	40c multicolored	.65	.65
650	A101	50c multicolored	.85	.85
651	A101	60c multicolored	1.10	1.10
652	A101	$1.50 multicolored	2.60	2.60
a.		Souvenir sheet of 4, #649-652, perf. 14½x14	6.50	6.50
		Nos. 649-652 (4)	5.20	5.20

Christmas — A102

50c, Candle, flowers. 60c, Angel, flowers. $1.50, Palm tree, candles.

1993, Dec. 6   **Litho.**   **Perf. 13½**
653	A102	40c shown	.75	.75
654	A102	50c multicolored	.90	.90
655	A102	60c multicolored	1.15	1.15
656	A102	$1.50 multicolored	2.75	2.75
		Nos. 653-656 (4)	5.55	5.55

Souvenir Sheet

Hong Kong '94 — A103

1994, Feb. 18   **Perf. 14½x14**
657	A103	$2 Monarch	5.25	5.25

Scenic Views A104

50c, Beach, trees, diff. 60c, Boats, ocean. $1.50, Boats, beach.

1994, Feb. 18   **Litho.**   **Perf. 14**
658	A104	40c shown	.90	.90
659	A104	50c multi	1.10	1.10
660	A104	60c multi	1.25	1.25
661	A104	$1.50 multi	3.25	3.25
		Nos. 658-661 (4)	6.50	6.50

New Year 1994 (Year of the Dog) — A105

40c, Irish setter. 50c, Golden retriever. 60c, West Highland terrier. $1.50, German shepherd.

1994, Apr. 23   **Litho.**   **Perf. 14**
662	A105	40c multicolored	1.00	1.00
663	A105	50c multicolored	1.10	1.10
664	A105	60c multicolored	1.40	1.40
665	A105	$1.50 multicolored	3.50	3.50
		Nos. 662-665 (4)	7.00	7.00

A106

1994, June 7
666	A106	40c Australia	.60	.60
667	A106	50c England	.80	.80
668	A106	60c Argentina	.90	.90
669	A106	$1.50 Germany	2.40	2.40
		Nos. 666-669 (4)	4.70	4.70

Souvenir Sheet
670	A106	$2 US	6.25	6.25

1994 World Cup Soccer Championships, US.

Seashells — A107

40c, Umbonium giganteum. 50c, Turbo petholatus. 60c, Planaxis savignyi. $1.50, Hydatina physis.

1994, Aug. 16   **Litho.**   **Perf. 14**
671	A107	40c multicolored	.90	.90
672	A107	50c multicolored	1.10	1.10
673	A107	60c multicolored	1.35	1.35
674	A107	$1.50 multicolored	3.25	3.25
		Nos. 671-674 (4)	6.60	6.60

Souvenir Sheet

PHILAKOREA '94 — A108

1994, Aug. 16
675	A108	$1.50 Pekinese dog	4.25	4.25

Nos. 469-470, 476-477 Ovptd.

1994, Aug. 31   **Litho.**   **Perf. 15**
676	A64	5c multicolored	.30	.30
677	A64	10c multicolored	.30	.30
678	A64	40c multicolored	.90	.90
679	A64	45c multicolored	1.00	1.00
		Nos. 676-679 (4)	2.50	2.50

First Manned Moon Landing, 25th Anniv. — A109

a, 40c, Saturn V. b, 50c, Apollo 11. c, 60c, Neil Armstrong. d, $1.50, Splash-down.

1994, Oct. 31   **Perf. 14**
680	A109	Strip of 4, #a.-d.	6.00	6.00

Christmas — A110

40c, Boys playing in water. 50c, Islanders, fish being gathered. 60c, People seated under canopy, food. $1.50, Traditional dancers.

1994, Dec. 15   **Litho.**   **Perf. 14**
681	A110	40c multicolored	.80	.80
682	A110	50c multicolored	.90	.90
683	A110	60c multicolored	1.10	1.10
684	A110	$1.50 multicolored	3.00	3.00
		Nos. 681-684 (4)	5.80	5.80

New Year 1995 (Year of the Boar) A111

40c, One pig. 50c, Pig, piglet. 60c, Three pigs. $1.50, Sow nursing litter.

1995, Jan. 30   **Litho.**   **Perf. 14**
685-688	A111	Set of 4	4.75	4.75

FAO, 50th Anniv. A112

40c, Men with vegetables in wheelbarrow. 50c, Man with sack of vegetables. 60c, Girl cleaning vegetables. $1.50, Girl mixing food.

1995, Mar. 31   **Litho.**   **Perf. 14**
689-692	A112	Set of 4	5.75	5.75

Visit South Pacific Year A113

1995, May 26   **Litho.**   **Perf. 14**
693	A113	40c shown	.65	.65
694	A113	50c Sailboat	.80	.80
695	A113	60c Hut	.95	.95
696	A113	$1.50 Home, beach	2.40	2.40
		Nos. 693-696 (4)	4.80	4.80

Pacific Coastal Orchids A114

40c, Dendrobium comptonii. 50c, Dendrobium aff. involutum. 60c, Dendrobium rarum. $1.50, Grammatophyllum scriptum.

1995, July 28   **Litho.**   **Perf. 14**
697-700	A114	Set of 4	6.25	6.25

Souvenir Sheet

Jakarta '95, Asian World Stamp Exhibition — A116

1995, Aug. 19   **Litho.**   **Perf. 12**
702	A116	$1 Traditional dancer	2.50	2.50

For overprint see No. 715.

Souvenir Sheet

Singapore '95 World Stamp Exhibition — A117

$1, Phalaenopsis amabillis.

1995, Sept. 1
703	A117	$1 multicolored	2.75	2.75

End of World War II, 50th Anniv. A118

40c, Soldier with sub-machine gun, map of Japan, Tuvalu. 50c, Soldier holding rifle, landing exercise on beach. 60c, US Marine, offshore air and sea battle. $1.50, Soldier firing rifle, atomic mushroom cloud.

1995, Aug. 19   **Litho.**   **Perf. 14**
704-707	A118	Set of 4	9.50	9.50

Souvenir Sheet

UN, 50th Anniv. — A119

a, Rowing in outrigger canoes. b, UN New York headquarters.

1995, Oct. 24   **Perf. 14½**
708	A119	$1 Sheet of 2, #a.-b.	4.00	4.00

Christmas — A120

Scores and verses to Christmas carols and: 40c, Map of island, "Silent Night." 50c, Boy carolers, "O Come All Ye Faithful." 60c, Girl carolers, "The First Noel." $1.50, Angel, "Hark the Herald Angels Sing."

1995, Dec. 15   **Litho.**   **Perf. 14**
709-712	A120	Set of 4	5.75	5.75

Miniature Sheet

Independence, First Tuvalu Postage Stamps, 20th Anniv. — A121

a, 40c, #16. b, 60c, #17. c, $1, #18.

1996, Jan. 1   Litho.   Perf. 14
713 A121 Sheet of 3, #a.-c.   5.00 5.00

Miniature Sheet

New Year 1996 (Year of the Rat) — A122

Stylized rats: a, Looking right. b, Facing left, drinking from container.

1996, Feb. 23   Litho.   Perf. 14x14½
714 A122 50c Sheet of 2, #a.-b.   5.00 5.00
c.   Ovptd. in sheet margin   5.00 5.00
d.   With added inscription in sheet margin   5.00 5.00

No. 714c is overprinted in sheet margin with exhibition emblem of Hongpex '96.
No. 714d is inscribed in sheet margin with two exhibition emblems of China '96. Issued: 5/18.

No. 702 Ovptd. in Gold

1996, Mar. 21   Litho.   Perf. 12
715 A116 $1 multicolored   2.40 2.40

No. 604 Surcharged in Black, Red & Blue

1996, Oct. 21   Litho.   Perf. 14
716 A90 $1 on 45c multi   2.10 2.10

1996 Summer Olympic Games, Atlanta
A123

1996, Sept. 11   Litho.   Perf. 14
717 A123 40c Beach volleyball   .55 .55
718 A123 50c Swimming   .70 .70
719 A123 60c Weight lifting   .85 .85
720 A123 $1.50 David Tua, boxer   2.10 2.10
Nos. 717-720 (4)   4.20 4.20

UNICEF, 50th Anniv. A124

1996, Oct. 28
721 A124 40c Immunization   .55 .55
722 A124 50c Education for life   .65 .65
723 A124 60c Water tank project   .80 .80
724 A124 $1.50 Hydroponic farm   2.25 2.25
Nos. 721-724 (4)   4.25 4.25

Christmas A125

Designs: 40c, Magi following star. 50c, Shepherds seeing star. 60c, Adoration of the Magi. $1.50, Nativity scene.

1996, Nov. 25   Perf. 14½
725 A125 40c multicolored   .65 .65
726 A125 50c multicolored   .75 .75
727 A125 60c multicolored   .90 .90
728 A125 $1.50 multicolored   2.25 2.25
Nos. 725-728 (4)   4.55 4.55

Fish A126

25c, Bluetail mullet. 30c, Queen fish leatherskin. 40c, Paddletail. 45c, Long-nose emperor. 50c, Long-snouted unicornfish. 55c, Brigham's snapper. 60c, Red bass. 70c, Red jobfish. 90c, Leopard flounder. $1, Red snapper. $2, Longtail snapper. $3, Black trevally.

1997, Mar. 15   Perf. 14
729 A126 25c multicolored   .35 .35
730 A126 30c multicolored   .40 .40
731 A126 40c multicolored   .55 .55
732 A126 45c multicolored   .65 .70
Complete bklt., 4 ea #729-732   10.00
733 A126 50c multicolored   .70 .70
734 A126 55c multicolored   .75 .75
735 A126 60c multicolored   .85 .85
736 A126 70c multicolored   .90 .90
737 A126 90c multicolored   1.25 1.25
738 A126 $1 multicolored   1.30 1.30
739 A126 $2 multicolored   2.60 2.60
a.   Souv. sheet of 1, wmk. 373   4.00 4.00
740 A126 $3 multicolored   4.00 4.00
Nos. 729-740 (12)   14.30 14.35

No. 739a for return of Hong Kong to China, July 1, 1997.

Souvenir Sheet

New Year 1997 (Year of the Ox) — A127

1997, June 20   Litho.   Perf. 14
741 A127 $2 multicolored   6.00 6.00

Hong Kong '97.

Ducks and Drakes A128

1997, May 29   Litho.   Perf. 14
742 A128 40c White pekin   .60 .60
743 A128 50c Muscovy   .75 .75
744 A128 60c Pacific black   .90 .90
745 A128 $1.50 Mandarin   2.25 2.25
Nos. 742-745 (4)   4.50 4.50

PACIFIC 97.

Domestic Cats — A129

40c, Korat king. 50c, Long-haired ginger kitten. 60c, Shaded cameo. $1.50, American Maine coon.

1997, June 20
746 A129 40c multicolored   .70 .70
747 A129 50c multicolored   .85 .85
748 A129 60c multicolored   1.00 1.00
749 A129 $1.50 multicolored   2.50 2.50
Nos. 746-749 (4)   5.05 5.05

Queen Elizabeth II and Prince Philip, 50th Wedding Anniv. — A130

Designs: No. 750, Queen, Prince standing in open vehicle. No. 751, Queen in yellow hat. No. 752, Queen holding umbrella. No. 753, Queen reading, Prince up close. No. 754, Three pictures of Queen. No. 755, Prince in top hat, Queen.
$2, Queen, Prince riding in open carriage, horiz.

Wmk. 373
1997, Oct. 1   Litho.   Perf. 14½
750   40c multicolored   .50 .50
751   40c multicolored   .50 .50
a.   A130 Pair, #750-751   1.00 1.00
752   50c multicolored   .65 .65
753   50c multicolored   .65 .65
a.   A130 Pair, #752-753   1.30 1.30

---

754   60c multicolored   .75 .75
755   60c multicolored   .75 .75
a.   A130 Pair, #754-755   1.50 1.50
Nos. 750-755 (6)   3.80 3.80

Souvenir Sheet
756 A130 $2 multicolored   3.00 3.00

No. 756 contains one 38x32mm stamp.

Traditional Activities — A131

Christmas: 40c, Turtle hunting. 50c, Pole fishing. 60c, Canoe racing. $1.50, Traditional dance.

Perf. 13½x13
1997, Nov. 25   Litho.   Wmk. 373
757 A131 40c multicolored   .55 .55
758 A131 50c multicolored   .65 .65
759 A131 60c multicolored   .80 .80
760 A131 $1.50 multicolored   2.00 2.00
Nos. 757-760 (4)   4.00 4.00

Souvenir Sheet

New Year 1998 (Year of the Tiger) — A132

1998, Feb. 2   Litho.   Perf. 13
761 A132 $1.40 multicolored   4.00 4.00

Diana, Princess of Wales (1961-97)
Common Design Type

Designs: a, Wearing red evening dress. b, Wearing black evening dress. c, Wearing tiara. d, With collar up on coat.

Perf. 14½x14
1998, Mar. 31   Litho.   Wmk. 373
762 CD355 80c Sheet of 4, #a.-d. 4.00 4.00

No. 762 sold for $3.20 + 20c, with surtax from international sales being donated to the Princess Diana Memorial Fund and surtax from national sales being donated to designated local charity.

Royal Air Force, 80th Anniv.
Common Design Type of 1993 Reinscribed

Designs: 40c, Hawker Woodcock. 50c, Vickers Victoria. 60c, Bristol Brigand $1.50, De Haviland DHC 1 Chipmunk.
No. 767: a, Sopwith Pup. b, Armstrong Whitworth FK8. c, North American Harvard. d, Vultee Vengeance.

Wmk. 384
1998, Apr. 1   Litho.   Perf. 13½
763 CD350 40c multicolored   .70 .70
764 CD350 50c multicolored   .80 .80
765 CD350 60c multicolored   1.00 1.00
766 CD350 $1.50 multicolored   2.25 2.25
Nos. 763-766 (4)   4.75 4.75

Souvenir Sheet
767 CD350 $1 Sheet of 4, #a.-d.   5.00 5.00

Ships A133

Designs: 40c, "Los Reyes," "Santiago," 1567. 50c, "Morning Star," missionary topsail schooner, 1867. 60c, "The Light," brigantine of Church of the Resurrection, 1870. $1.50, New Zealand missionary schooner, 1900.

386 TUVALU

Wmk. 373

1998, May 19   Litho.   Perf. 14
768	A133	40c multicolored	.50	.50
769	A133	50c multicolored	.60	.60
770	A133	60c multicolored	.75	.75
771	A133	$1.50 multicolored	1.60	1.60
		Nos. 768-771 (4)	3.45	3.45

Dolphins and Porpoises — A134

40c, Bottlenose dolphin. 50c, Dall's porpoise. 60c, Harbor porpoise. $1.50, Common dolphin.

Perf. 13½x13
1998, Aug. 21   Litho.   Wmk. 384
772	A134	40c multicolored	.50	.50
773	A134	50c multicolored	.65	.65
774	A134	60c multicolored	.80	.80
775	A134	$1.50 multicolored	2.00	2.00
		Nos. 772-775 (4)	3.95	3.95

Greenpeace, Save Our Seas A135

Marine life: 20c, Bleached platygyra daedalea, psammocora digitata. 30c, Bleached acropora robusta. 50c, Bleached acropora hyacinthus. $1, Bleached acropora danai, montastrea curta. $1.50, Bleached seriatopora, bleached stylophora.

Wmk. 373
1998, Nov. 6   Litho.   Perf. 14½
776	A135	20c multicolored	.30	.30
777	A135	30c multicolored	.50	.50
778	A135	50c multicolored	.85	.85
779	A135	$1 multicolored	1.40	1.40
		Nos. 776-779 (4)	3.05	3.05

Souvenir Sheet
| 780 | A135 | $1.50 multicolored | 2.50 | 2.50 |

Intl. Year of the Ocean (#780).

Christmas — A136

40c, Flight into Egypt. 50c, Angel speaking to shepherds. 60c, Nativity. $1.50, Adoration of the Magi.

1998, Nov. 20   Perf. 14½x14
781	A136	40c multicolored	.55	.55
782	A136	50c multicolored	.70	.70
783	A136	60c multicolored	.80	.80
784	A136	$1.50 multicolored	2.00	2.00
		Nos. 781-784 (4)	4.05	4.05

Independence, 20th Anniv. — A137

Stamps on stamps, Prime Ministers: 40c, #722, Bikenibeu Paeniu. 60c, Kamuta Latasi. 90c, Tomasi Puapua. $1.50, Design like #166, Toaripi Lauti.

Wmk. 384
1998, Oct. 1   Litho.   Perf. 14
785	A137	40c multicolored	.55	.55
786	A137	60c multicolored	.85	.85
787	A137	90c multicolored	1.10	1.10

788	A137	$1.50 multicolored	1.75	1.75
a.	Souvenir sheet, #785-788		4.25	4.25
		Nos. 785-788 (4)	4.25	4.25

Souvenir Sheet

New Year 1999 (Year of the Rabbit) — A138

Perf. 14½x14
1999, Feb. 16   Litho.   Wmk. 373
| 789 | A138 | $2 multicolored | 4.50 | 4.50 |

Australia '99, World Stamp Expo A139

Maritime history: 40c, Heemskerck, 1642. 50c, HMS Endeavour, 1769. 90c, PS Sophie Jane, 1831. $1.50, P&O SS Chusan, 1852. $2, HM Brig "Supply."

1999, Mar. 19   Perf. 14
790	A139	40c multicolored	.60	.60
791	A139	50c multicolored	.70	.70
792	A139	90c multicolored	1.40	1.40
793	A139	$1.50 multicolored	2.10	2.10
		Nos. 790-793 (4)	4.80	4.80

Souvenir Sheet
| 794 | A139 | $2 multicolored | 2.75 | 2.75 |

Nos. 472, 475, 479, 482 Ovptd.

1999, June 11   Litho.   Perf. 15
796	A64	20c on #472	.30	.30
797	A64	35c on #475	.50	.50
798	A64	55c on #479	.80	.80
799	A64	$1 on #482	1.40	1.40
		Nos. 796-799 (4)	3.00	3.00

50% of the sales of Nos. 796-799 will be donated to the Kosovo Relief Fund.

1st Manned Moon Landing, 30th Anniv.
Common Design Type

40c, Lift-off. 60c, Lunar module prepares to touchdown. 90c, Ascent stage approaches Command module. $1.50, Recovery. $2, Looking at earth from moon.

Perf. 14x13¾
1999, July 20   Litho.   Wmk. 384
800	CD357	40c multicolored	.60	.60
801	CD357	60c multicolored	.80	.80
802	CD357	90c multicolored	1.40	1.40
803	CD357	$1.50 multicolored	1.90	1.90
		Nos. 800-803 (4)	4.70	4.70

Souvenir Sheet
Perf. 14
| 804 | CD357 | $2 multicolored | 2.75 | 2.75 |

No. 804 contains one circular stamp 40mm in diameter.

Queen Mother's Century
Common Design Type

Queen Mother: 40c, With King George VI inspecting bomb damage. 60c, With daughters at Balmoral. 90c, With Princes Harry and William, 95th birthday. $1.50, As colonel-in-chief of Queen's Dragoon Guards. $2, Age 6 photo, photo of Yuri Gagarin.

Wmk. 384

1999, Aug. 16   Litho.   Perf. 13½
805	CD358	40c multicolored	.55	.55
806	CD358	60c multicolored	.80	.80
807	CD358	90c multicolored	1.30	1.30
808	CD358	$1.50 multicolored	2.00	2.00
		Nos. 805-808 (4)	4.65	4.65

Souvenir Sheet
| 809 | CD358 | $2 multicolored | 4.00 | 4.00 |

Flowers — A141

No. 810: a, Fetai. b, Ateate. c, Portulacacae lueta. d, Tamoloc. e, Beach pea. f, Pomegranate (red letters).
No. 811: a, Cup of gold. b, Rock rose. c, Bower plant. d, Lavender star. e, Hybrid mandevilla. f, Pomegranate (white letters).
No. 812, Scrambled eggs, vert.

Perf. 13¾
1999, Nov. 22   Litho.   Unwmk.
| 810 | A141 | 90c Sheet of 6, #a.-f. | 7.75 | 7.75 |
| 811 | A141 | 90c Sheet of 6, #a.-f. | 7.75 | 7.75 |

Souvenir Sheet
| 812 | A141 | $3 multi | 5.50 | 5.50 |

A142

No. 813, Lady of peace with frame.
No. 814: a, Like No. 813, no frame. b, Olive branch. c, Dove. d, Lion. e, Lamb. f, War crowning peace.
No. 815: Sun on horizon, clock, computer keyboard.

Perf. 14½x14¼
1999, Dec. 31   Litho.
| 813 | A142 | 90c multi | 1.25 | 1.25 |
| 814 | A142 | 90c Sheet of 6, #a.-f. | 9.00 | 9.00 |

Souvenir Sheet
Perf. 14
| 815 | A143 | $2 multi | 3.00 | 3.00 |

No. 813 printed in sheets of 6.

Millennium — A143

Worldwide Fund for Nature — A144

Sand tiger shark: a, 10c, Close-up of head. b, 30c, Facing left. c, 50c, Swimming above seaweed. d, 60c, Three sharks.

Perf. 13¼x13½
2000, Feb. 7   Litho.   Unwmk.
| 816 | A144 | Strip of 4, #a.-d. | 3.00 | 3.00 |
| e. | Souvenir sheet, 2 #816 | | 9.50 | 9.50 |

Souvenir Sheet
Stamps Without WWF Emblem
| 817 | A144 | Sheet of 4, #a.-d | 2.75 | 2.75 |

Marine Life and Birds — A145

No. 818, each 90c: a, Common tern. b, White-tailed tropicbird. c, Red emperor snapper. d, Clown triggerfish. e, Longfin bannerfish. f, Harlequin tuskfish.
No. 819, each 90c: a, Wilson's storm petrel. b, Common dolphin. c, Spotted seahorse. d, Threeband demoiselle. e, Coral hind. f, Palette surgeonfish.
No. 820, each 90c: a, Great frigatebird. b, Brown booby. c, Dugong. d, Red knot. e, Common starfish. f, Hawksbill turtle.
No. 821, each 90c: a, Manta ray. b, White shark. c, Hammerhead shark. d, Tiger shark. e, Great barracuda. f, Leatherback turtle.
No. 822, each 90c: a, Great frigatebird. b, Bluestreak cleaner wrasse. d, Lemon shark. e, Spotted trunkfish. f, Longnosed butterflyfish.
No. 823, each 90c: a, Chevroned butterflyfish. b, Mandarinfish. c, Bicolor angelfish. d, Copperbanded butterflyfish. e, Clown anemonefish. f, Lemonpeel angelfish.
Each $3: No. 824, Picassofish. No. 825, Pygmy parrotfish. No. 826, Sailfish.

2000, Mar. 8   Perf. 14
Sheets of 6, #a.-f.
| 818-823 | A145 | Set of 6 | 45.00 | 45.00 |

Souvenir Sheets
| 824-826 | A145 | Set of 3 | 13.00 | 13.00 |

Butterflies — A146

No. 827, each 90c: a, Birdwing. b, Tailed emperor. c, Orchid swallowtail. d, Union Jack. e, Long-tailed blue. f, Common Jezabel.
No. 828, each 90c: a, Caper white. b, Common Indian crow. c, Eastern flat. d, Cairns birdwing. e, Monarch. f, Meadow argus.
No. 829, each 90c, horiz.: a, Glasswing. b, Leftwing. c, Moth butterfly. d, Blue triangle. e, Beak. f, Plane.
Each $3: No. 830, Great egg-fly. No. 831, Palmfly, horiz.

2000, May 1   Sheets of 6, #a.-f.
| 827-829 | A146 | Set of 3 | 22.50 | 22.50 |

Souvenir Sheets
| 830-831 | A146 | Set of 2 | 7.50 | 7.50 |

Birds — A147

#832, each 90c: a, Red-billed leiothrix. b, Gray shrike-thrush. c, Great frigatebird. d, Common kingfisher. e, Chestnut-breasted finch. f, White tern.
#833, each 90c: a, White-collared kingfisher. b, Scaled petrel. c, Superb blue wren. d, Osprey. e, Great cormorant. f, Peregrine falcon.
#834, each 90c: a, Rainbow lorikeet. b, White-throated tree creeper. c, White-tailed kingfisher. d, Golden whistler. e, Black-bellied plover. f, Beach thick-knee.
Each $3: #835, Morepork. #836, Broadbilled prion, horiz.
Illustration reduced.

2000, June 1	Litho.	Perf. 14
Sheets of 6, #a-f		
832-834 A147	Set of 3	22.50 22.50
Souvenir Sheets		
835-836 A147	Set of 2	7.50 7.50

Dogs and Cats — A148

No. 837: a, Fox terrier. b, Collie. c, Boston terrier. d, Pembroke Welsh corgi. e, Pointer. f, Dalmatian.
No. 838, vert.: a, Dalmatian. b, Boston terrier. c, Fox terrier. d, Pointer. e, Pembroke Welsh corgi. f, Collie.
No. 839, vert. (denominations in orange): a, Ticked tabby oriental shorthair. b, Balinese. c, Somali. d, Chinchilla Persian. e, Tonkinese. f, Japanese bobtail.
No. 840, vert. (denominations in green): a, Lilac oriental shorthair. b, Balinese. c, Somali. d, Chinchilla Persian. e, Tonkinese. f, Japanese bobtail.
No. 841, Scottish terrier. No. 842, Oriental shorthair, vert.
Illustration reduced.

2000, July 3	Litho.	Perf. 14
Sheets of 6, #a-f		
837-840 A148 90c	Set of 4	22.50 22.50
Souvenir Sheets		
841-842 A148 $3	Set of 2	7.75 7.75

Birds and Animals — A149

No. 843, horiz.: a, Brown noddy. b, Great frigatebird. c, Emperor angelfish. d, Common dolphin. e, Hermit crab. f, Threadfin butterflyfish.
No. 844, horiz.: a, Red-footed booby. b, Red-tailed tropicbird. c, Black-bellied plover. d, Common tern. e, Ruddy turnstone. f, Sanderling.
$3, Great frigatebird.

2000, Aug. 3	Sheets of 6, #a-f
843-844 A149 90c	Set of 2	14.50 14.50
Souvenir Sheet		
845 A149 $3 Great frigatebird		3.75 3.75

New Year 2000 and 2001 (Years of the Dragon and Snake) A150

Designs: 40c, Dragon. 60c, Snake. 90c, Snake, diff. $1.50, Dragon, diff.

| 2001, Jan. 15 | Litho. | Perf. 13½x13¼ |
| 846-849 A150 | Set of 4 | 8.00 8.00 |

Motofoua Secondary School Fire, 1st Anniv. A151

Fire trucks: 60c, Anglo specialist rescue uUnit. 90c, Anglo 4800 water/foam tender. $1.50, Bronto 33-2T1 combined telescopic ladder/hydralulic platform. $2, Anglo 450 LRX water tender. $3, Wormold "Arrestor" ARFFV.

2001, Mar. 9	Litho.	Perf. 13¼
850-853 A151	Set of 4	14.50 14.50
Souvenir Sheet		
854 A151 $3 multi		7.75 7.75

.tv Corporation A152

Palm fronds, satellite dish and: 40c, Woman. 60c, Dancers. 90c, Man. $1.50, Child. $2, Map.

2001, May 30	Litho.	Perf. 14¼x14½
855-858 A152	Set of 4	5.75 5.75
Souvenir Sheet		
859 A152 $2 multi		4.00 4.00

Souvenir Sheet

Phila Nippon '01 — A153

| 2001, Aug. 1 | | Perf. 13 |
| 860 A153 $3 multi | | 4.50 4.50 |

Nos. 806-808 Overprinted in Gold

No. 805 Surcharged in Gold

Wmk. 384

2001, Aug. 4	Litho.	Perf. 13½
860A CD358	60c multi	.75 .75
860B CD358	90c multi	1.10 1.10
860C CD358	$1.50 multi	1.75 1.75
860D CD358	$2 on 40c multi	2.50 2.50
Nos. 860A-860D (4)		6.10 6.10

No. 809 Surcharged in Gold

2001, Aug. 4	Wmk. 384	Perf. 13½
Souvenir Sheet		
861 CD358 $5 on $2 multi		6.00 6.00

Fauna A154

Designs: 25c, Mosquito. 30c, Giant African snail. 40c, Cockroach. 45c, Stick insect. 50c, Green stink bug. 55c, Dragonfly. 60c, Monarch caterpillar. 70c, Coconut beetle. 90c, Honeybee. $1, Monarch butterfly. $2, Common eggfly butterfly. $3, Painted lady butterfly.

Unwmk.

2001, Oct. 31	Litho.	Perf. 13
862 A154 25c multi		.40 .40
863 A154 30c multi		.50 .50
864 A154 40c multi		.65 .65
865 A154 45c multi		.75 .75
866 A154 50c multi		.80 .80
867 A154 55c multi		.90 .90
868 A154 60c multi		1.00 1.00
869 A154 70c multi		1.10 1.10
870 A154 90c multi		1.50 1.50
871 A154 $1 multi		1.60 1.60
872 A154 $2 multi		3.25 3.25
873 A154 $3 multi		5.00 5.00
Nos. 862-873 (12)		17.45 17.45

United We Stand — A155

Statue of Liberty and Tuvalu flag: No. 874, $2, Blue background. No. 875, $2, Yellow background.

| 2002, Jan. 10 | | Perf. 14 |
| 874-875 A155 | Set of 2 | 5.00 5.00 |

Paintings Depicting Chapter Scenes From "The Tale of Genji" — A156

No. 876, 40c — Chapter: a, 1. b, 2. c, 3. d, 4. e, 5. f, 6.
No. 877, 60c — Chapter: a, 8. b, 9. c, 10. d, 11. e, 12. f, 13.
No. 878, 90c — Chapter: a, 15. b, 16. c, 17. d, 18. e, 19. f, 20.
No. 079, $4 — Chapter 7. No. 880, $4, Chapter 14. No. 881, $4, Chapter 21.

2002, Apr. 24	Litho.	Perf. 14¼
Sheets of 6, #a-f		
876-878 A156	Set of 3	15.00 15.00
Imperf		
879-881 A156	Set of 3	16.00 16.00

Nos. 876-878 each contain six 37x50mm stamps.

UN Special Session on Children and Convention on Rights of the Child — A157

Designs: 40c, Boy in wheelchair. 60c, Boy and girl sitting near fence. 90c, Nauti Primary School, Funafuti. $4, Mother and child.
No. 886: a, Taulosa Karl. b, Simalua Jacinta Enele.

2002, May 8	Litho.	Perf. 13¼x13½
882-885 A157	Set of 4	6.50 6.50
Souvenir Sheet		
886 A157 $1 Sheet of 2, #a-b		3.50 3.50

For surcharge, see No. 971A.

Reign of Queen Elizabeth II, 50th Anniv. — A158

No. 887: a, Princes William and Harry. b, Queen in blue green suit. c, Queen and Prince Philip. d, Queen wearing red hat.
$4, Queen on horseback.

2002, June 17   **Perf. 14¼**
887 A158 $1.50 Sheet of 4, #a-d   7.75 7.75
Souvenir Sheet
888 A158 $4 multi   5.50 5.50

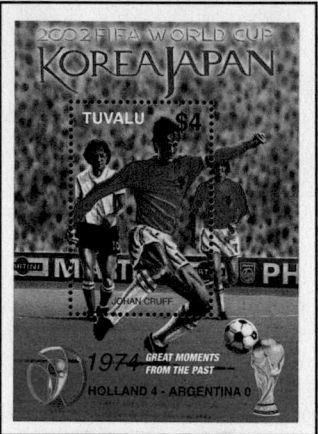

2002 World Cup Soccer Championships, Japan and Korea — A159

No. 889: a, Tom Finney. b, Poster from 1974 World Cup. c, Portuguese player and flag. d, Uruguayan player and flag. e, Suwon World Cup Stadium, Seoul (56x42mm).
$4, Johann Cruyff.

2002, July 15   **Perf. 14**
889 A159 90c Sheet of 5, #a-e   6.00 6.00
Souvenir Sheet
890 A159 $4 multi   5.25 5.25

Queen Mother Elizabeth (1900-2002) — A160

No. 891: a, 60c, Wearing tiara (lilac shading at UL) (26x29mm). b, 60c, Wearing tiara (lilac shading at UR) (26x29mm). c, 90c, In crowd, holding bouquet of flowers (lilac shading at UL) (28x23mm). d, 90c, Receiving flowers from children (lilac shading at UR) (28x23mm). e, 90c, With teddy bear (lilac shading at UL) (28x23mm). f, With man, woman and children (lilac shading at UR) (28x23mm). g, Color photograph (40x29mm).
No. 892, $2, lilac shading at UL: a, As child, with another young girl. b, As older woman.
No. 893, $2, lilac shading at UR: a, Smelling flower. b, Wearing brooch.

Perf. Compound x14¼ (60c), 13¼x10¾ (90c), 13¼x14¼ ($1.50)
2002, Aug. 12
891 A160   Sheet of 7, #a-g   7.00 7.00
Souvenir Sheets
Perf. 14¾
892-893 A160 Set of 2   9.00 9.00

20th World Scout Jamboree, Thailand — A161

No. 894 — Merit badges: a, Citizenship in the World. b, First Aid. c, Personal Fitness. d, Environmental Science.
$5, Lord Robert Baden-Powell.

2002, Oct. 2   **Perf. 14¼**
894 A161 $1.50 Sheet of 4, #a-d   7.00 7.00
Souvenir Sheet
895 A161 $5 multi   6.00 6.00

Intl. Year of Mountains — A162

No. 896, horiz.: a, Mt. Fitzroy, Chile. b, Mt. Foraker, US. c, Mt. Fuji, Japan. d, Mt. Malaku, Nepal and China.
$4, Mt. Godwin Austen, Kashmir.

2002, Oct. 2
896 A162 $1.50 Sheet of 4, #a-d   7.00 7.00
Souvenir Sheet
897 A162 $4 multi   5.00 5.00

Elvis Presley (1935-77) A163

2002, Dec. 27   **Litho.**   **Perf. 14¼**
898 A163 $1 multi   1.75 1.75
No. 898 was printed in sheets of 6. Value, $12.

Princess Diana (1961-97) — A164

No. 899 — Diana wearing: a, Black dress, no necklace. b, Black dress, choker necklace. c, Blue dress. d, Blue green scarf. e, Pink blouse, hand at chin. f, Pink dress.
$4, Black dress, hand on chin.

2002, Dec. 27   **Perf. 14**
899 A164 $1 Sheet of 6, #a-f   7.50 7.50
Souvenir Sheet
900 A164 $4 multi   5.00 5.00

Year of the Horse (in 2002) — A165

Various horses: 40c, 60c, 90c, $2.
No. 905: a, Head of horse, seahorse. b, Heads of horse, three seahorses.

2003, Jan. 23   **Perf. 13¼**
901-904 A165   Set of 4   7.50 7.50
Souvenir Sheet
905 A165 $1.50 Sheet of 2, #a-b   6.50 6.50

New Year 2003 (Year of the Ram) — A166

No. 906: a, Green and black background. b, White background. c, Blue background.

2003, Feb. 1   **Perf. 14x13¾**
906 A166 75c Vert. strip of 3,   #a-c   6.00 6.00
No. 906 printed in sheets containing two strips.

Pres. John F. Kennedy (1917-63) — A167

No. 907: a, In Solomon Islands, 1943. b, On PT 109, 1942. c, Receiving medal for gallantry, 1944. d, Campaigning for Senate, 1952.
$4, With father and brothers.

2003, Mar. 24   **Perf. 14**
907 A167 $1.75 Sheet of 4,   #a-d   10.00 10.00
Souvenir Sheet
908 A167 $4 multi   6.00 6.00

Powered Flight, Cent. — A168

No. 909, $1.75: a, Orville Wright in early plane, 1903. b, Wilbur Wright and King Alfonso XIII of Spain, 1909. c, Wilbur Wright's plane, 1908. d, Gabriel Voisin's plane piloted by Léon Delagrange, 1907.

No. 910, $1.75: a, Voisin's motor boat powered glider, 1905. b, Trajan Vuia's single winged plane, 1906. c, Santos-Dumont's biplane, 1906. d, Orville Wright circles parade ground, 1908.

No. 911, $4, Wright Brothers biplane in flight, 1908. No. 912, $4, Glenn Curtiss pilots June Bug, 1908.

2003, May 19   Litho.   Perf. 14
Sheets of 4, #a-d
909-910 A168   Set of 2   21.00 21.00
Souvenir Sheets
911-912 A168   Set of 2   11.50 11.50

Coronation of Queen Elizabeth II, 50th Anniv. — A169

No. 913: a, Wearing gray dress. b, Wearing tiara. c, Wearing yellow hat.
$4, Wearing hat and pearl necklace.

2003, Aug. 11
913 A169 $2 Sheet of 3, #a-c   9.00 9.00
Souvenir Sheet
914 A169 $4 multi   6.25 6.25

Prince William, 21st Birthday — A170

No. 915: a, Wearing school cap. b, Wearing blue shirt. c, Wearing polo helmet.
$4, Wearing suit and tie.

2003, Aug. 11
915 A170 $1.50 Sheet of 3, #a-c   6.50 6.50
Souvenir Sheet
916 A170 $4 multi   5.75 5.75

General Motors Automobiles — A171

No. 917, $1 — Corvettes: a, Yellow 1979. b, Red 1979. c, Silver 1979. d, 1980.
No. 918, $1.50 — Cadillacs: a, 1931 V-16 Sport Phaeton. b, 1959 Eldorado convertible. c, 1979 Seville Elegante. d, 1983 Seville Elegante.
No. 919, $4, 1990 Corvette. No. 920, $4, 1954 Cadillac Coupe de Ville.

2003, Sept. 8   Perf. 13¾
Sheets of 4, #a-d
917-918 A171   Set of 2   15.00 15.00
Souvenir Sheets
919-920 A171   Set of 2   11.50 11.50
Corvettes, 50th anniv.; Cadillacs, 100th anniv.

Tour de France Bicycle Race, Cent. — A172

No. 921: a, Gastone Nencini, 1960. b, Jacques Anquetil, 1961. c, Anquetil, 1962. d, Anquetil, 1963.
$4, Jan Janssen, 1968.

2003, Oct. 6   Perf. 13¾x13¼
921 A172 $1 Sheet of 4, #a-d   6.50 6.50
Souvenir Sheet
922 A172 $4 multi   6.50 6.50

Butterflies — A173

No. 923, horiz.: a, Malachite. b, White M hairstreak. c, Giant swallowtail. d, Bahamian swallowtail.
$3, Polydamas swallowtail.

2003, Dec. 16   Perf. 14
923 A173 $1.25 Sheet of 4, #a-d   8.25 8.25
Imperf
924 A173 $3 multi   5.00 5.00
No. 923 contains four 42x28mm stamps.

Flowers — A174

No. 925: a, Rhododendron. b, Golden Artist tulip. c, Golden Splendor lily. d, Flamingo flower.
$3, Candy Bianca rose.

2000, Dec. 10   Perf. 14
925 A174 $1.25 Sheet of 4, #a-d   8.25 8.25
Imperf
926 A174 $3 multi   5.00 5.00
No. 925 contains four 28x42mm stamps.

Orchids — A175

No. 927, vert.: a, Dimerandra emarginata. b, Oncidium lanceanum. c, Isochilus linearis. d, Oeceoclades maculata.
$3, Oncidium ampliatum.

2003, Dec. 16   Perf. 14
927 A175 $1.25 Sheet of 4, #a-d   8.25 8.25
Souvenir Sheet
928 A175 $3 multi   5.00 5.00

Birds — A176

No. 929: a, Blue-gray gnatcatcher. b, White-eyed vireo. c, Clapper rail. d, Sandhill crane.
$3, Grasshopper sparrow.

2003, Dec. 16
929 A176 $1.25 Sheet of 4, #a-d   8.50 8.50
Souvenir Sheet
930 A176 $3 multi   5.00 5.00

New Year 2004 (Year of the Monkey) A177

Paintings by Chang Dai-chen: 75c, Monkey and Old Tree. $1.50, Two Monkeys.

2004, Jan. 4   Perf. 13½
931 A177   75c multi   5.00 5.00
Souvenir Sheet
932 A177 $1.50 multi   6.00 6.00
No. 931 printed in sheets of 4.

Paintings by Norman Rockwell — A178

No. 933, vert.: a, 100th Year of Baseball. b, The Locker Room (The Rookie). c, The Dugout. d, Game Called Because of Rain.
$3, New Kids in the Neighborhood.

2004, Jan. 30   Perf. 14¼
933 A178 $1.25 Sheet of 4, #a-d   8.25 8.25
Souvenir Sheet
934 A178 $3 multi   5.50 5.50
2004 AmeriStamp Expo, Norfolk, Va. (#933).

Paintings by Pablo Picasso (1881-1973) — A179

No. 935, vert.: a, Seated Woman. b, Woman in Armchair. c, Bust of Françoise. d, Head of a Woman.
$4, Françoise Gilot with Paloma and Claude.

2004, Mar. 1   Litho.   Perf. 14¼
935 A179 $1.50 Sheet of 4, #a-d   11.50 11.50
Imperf
936 A179 $4 multi   7.00 7.00
No. 935 contains four 37x50mm stamps.

Paintings by Paul Gauguin (1848-1903) A180

Designs: 50c, Les Seins aux Fleurs Rouges. 60c, Famille Tahitienne. No. 939, $1, Tahitiennes sur la Plage. $2, Jeune Fille à L'Eventail.

No. 941, $1: a, Nafea Faa Ipoipo. b, Le Cheval Blanc. c, Pape Moe. d, Contes Barbares. $4, Femmes de Tahiti, horiz.

2004, Mar. 1　　　**Perf. 14¼**
937-940　A180　Set of 4　7.00 7.00
941　A180　$1 Sheet of 4, #a-d　7.00 7.00
　　　　　Imperf
　　　Size: 93x73mm
942　A180　$4 multi　7.00 7.00

Paintings in the Hermitage, St. Petersburg, Russia A181

Designs: 50c, Philadelphia and Elizabeth Wharton, by Anthony Van Dyck. 80c, A Glass of Lemonade, by Gerard Terborch. $1, A Mistress and Her Servant, by Pieter de Hooch. $1.20, Portrait of a Man and His Three Sons, by Bartholomaeus Bruyn the Elder.

$4, The Milkmaid's Family, by Louis le Nain, horiz.

2004, Mar. 1　　　**Perf. 14¼**
943-946　A181　Set of 4　6.25 6.25
　　　　　Imperf
　　　Size: 80x68mm
947　A181　$4 multi　7.00 7.00

Fight Against HIV and AIDS A182

Designs: 60c, Speaker at conference. 90c, Speaker and dais. $1.50, People standing in front of banner. $2, People seated at dais. $3, Conference participants.

2004, May 17　　　**Perf. 13x13½**
948-951　A182　Set of 4　8.00 8.00
　　Souvenir Sheet
952　A182　$3 multi　5.25 5.25

Souvenir Sheet

Inauguration of Republic of China President Chen Shui-bian — A183

No. 953: a, Pres. Chen Shui-bian. b, Saufatu Sopoanga, Prime Minister of Tuvalu.

2004, May 20　　　**Perf. 13½x13¼**
953　A183　$2 Sheet of 2, #a-b　6.50 6.50

Souvenir Sheet

Diplomatic Relations Between Tuvalu and the Republic of China, 25th Anniv. A183a

2004, Sept. 19　Litho.　Perf. 13¼x13
953C　A183a　$5 multi　10.00 10.00

FIFA (Fédération Internationale de Football Association), Cent. — A184

No. 954: a, Sebastiano Rossi. b, Clarence Seedorf. c, Zico. d, Jack Charlton. $3, Geoff Hurst.

Perf. 12¾x12½
2004, Nov. 29　　　**Litho.**
954　A184　$1 Sheet of 4, #a-d　7.25 7.25
　　Souvenir Sheet
955　A184　$3 multi　5.75 5.75

Miniature Sheet

World Peace — A185

No. 956: a, Alfred Nobel. b, Doves. c, Nelson Mandela.

2005, Jan. 14　　　**Perf. 12¾**
956　A185　$1.50 Sheet of 3, #a-c　7.75 7.75

Miniature Sheet

Election of Pope John Paul II, 25th Anniv. (in 2003) — A186

No. 957: a, With papal arms. b, At microphone. c, Wearing miter. d, Placing prayer in Wailing Wall, Jerusalem.

2005, Jan. 14
957　A186　$1.50 Sheet of 4, #a-d　11.00 11.00

D-Day, 60th Anniv. (in 2004) — A187

No. 958: a, Gen. George C. Marshall. b, Adm. Sir Ramsay Bertram Home. c, Gen. Walter Bedell Smith. d, Field Marshal Alan Francis Brooke. $3, Gen. George S. Patton.

2005, Jan. 14
958　A187　$1.50 Sheet of 4,
　　　　　#a-d　10.00 10.00
　　Souvenir Sheet
959　A187　$3 multi　5.25 5.25

Dogs — A188

Designs: 20c, Rat terrier. 75c, Large Spanish hound. $1, Lundehund. $2, Beagle harrier. $3, Old Danish pointer.

2005, Apr. 26　Litho.　Perf. 13¾x13¼
960-963　A188　Set of 4　6.50 6.50
　　Souvenir Sheet
964　A188　$3 multi　5.00 5.00

Marine Life — A189

No. 965: a, Striped-face unicornfish. b, Great barracuda. c, Blue-ringed octopus. d, Giant clam. $3, Humpback whale.

2005, Apr. 26　　　**Perf. 13¼x13¾**
965　A189　$1 Sheet of 4, #a-d　8.00 8.00
　　Souvenir Sheet
966　A189　$3 multi　6.75 6.75

Medicinal Plants — A190

No. 967: a, Common toadflax. b, Pomegranate. c, Black horehound. d, Agnus castus $3, Black henbane.

2005, Apr. 26　　　**Perf. 13¾x13¼**
967　A190　$1 Sheet of 4, #a-d　6.75 6.75
　　Souvenir Sheet
968　A190　$3 multi　5.25 5.25

Insects — A191

No. 969, vert.: a, Louse fly. b, Predacious dung beetle. c, Ladybug. d, Mosquito. $3, House fly.

2005, Apr. 26　　　**Perf. 13¾x13¼**
969　A191　$1 Sheet of 4, #a-d　6.75 6.75
　　Souvenir Sheet
　　Perf. 13¼x13¾
970　A191　$3 multi　5.25 5.25

Pope John Paul II (1920-2005) and Queen Elizabeth II — A192

2005, July 12　　　**Perf. 13½**
971　A192　$4 multi　10.00 10.00

No. 886 Surcharged

Methods and Perfs As Before
2005, July 17
971A　A157　Sheet of 2　7.75 7.75
　b.　$2.50 on $1 #886a　3.75 3.75
　c.　$2.50 on $1 #886b　3.75 3.75

Battle of Trafalgar, Bicent. — A193

No. 972: a, HMS Victory collides with French ship Redoubtable. b, Admiral Horatio Nelson. c, HMS Victory leads the British fleet. d, Nelson breaths his last breath.
$3, Admiral Cuthbert Collingwood.

2005, July 28   *Perf. 12*
972 A193 $1.50 Sheet of 4,
    #a-d   10.00 10.00
    Souvenir Sheet
973 A193 $3 multi   5.25 5.25

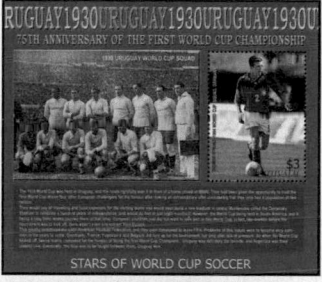

World Cup Soccer Championships, 75th Anniv. — A194

No. 974: a, Thomas Berthold. b, Bobby Charlton. c, Klaus Augenthaler.
$3, Thomas Strunz.

2005, July 28   *Perf. 13¼*
974 A194 $2 Sheet of 3, #a-c   10.00 10.00
    Souvenir Sheet
    Perf. 12
975 A194 $3 multi   5.25 5.25

End of World War II, 60th Anniv. — A195

No. 976, $2: a, Sir Winston Churchill. b, Gen. Charles de Gaulle. c, Newspaper report on death of Adolf Hitler.
No. 977, $2: a, Pres. Harry S. Truman. b, Newspaper report on end of war. c, Gen. Dwight D. Eisenhower.
No. 978, $3, Gen. George S. Patton. No. 979, $3, Brig. Gen. Paul W. Tibbets, Jr. and Enola Gay.

2005, Sept. 21   *Perf. 12¾*
    Sheets of 3, #a-c
976-977 A195   Set of 2   20.00 20.00
    Souvenir Sheets
978-979 A195   Set of 2   10.00 10.00

Albert Einstein (1879-1955), Physicist — A196

No. 981 — Einstein and: a, Hendrik Lorentz. b, Fritz Haber. c, David Ben-Gurion.
$3, Einstein with Thomas Mann.

2005, Sept. 21
980 A196 $2 Sheet of 3, #a-c   10.00 10.00
    Souvenir Sheet
981 A196 $3 multi   5.00 5.00

Rotary International, Cent. — A197

No. 982: a, Child. b, Hand holding pills. c, Children.
$3, Paul P. Harris, founder.

2005, Nov. 28
982 A197 $2 Sheet of 3, #a-c   10.00 10.00
    Souvenir Sheet
983 A197 $3 multi   5.00 5.00

Hans Christian Andersen (1805-75), Author — A198

No. 984: a, Andersen seated. b, Sculpture of Andersen. c, Head of Andersen.
$3, Statue of Andersen.

2005, Nov. 28
984 A198 $2 Sheet of 3, #a-c   10.00 10.00
    Souvenir Sheet
985 A198 $3 multi   5.00 5.00

A199

Elvis Presley (1935-77) — A200

No. 987 — Presley and: a, Gable and top of column of house. b, Roofline of house. c, Bottom of column of house. d, Archway of house.

2006, Jan. 30   *Perf. 13½*
986 A199 $3 multi   4.50 4.50
987 A200 $3 Sheet of 4, #a-d   18.00 18.00
   No. 986 printed in sheets of 4.

National Basketball Association Players and Team Emblems — A201

No. 988, 35c: a, Emblem of Detroit Pistons. b, Chauncey Billups.
No. 989, 35c: a, Emblem of New Jersey Nets. b, Rodney Buford.
No. 990, 35c: a, Emblem of Boston Celtics. b, Ricky Davis.
No. 991, 35c: a, Emblem of Miami Heat. b, Udonis Haslem.
No. 992, 35c: a, Emblem of Indiana Pacers, horiz. b, Stephen Jackson.
No. 993, 35c: a, Emblem of Minnesota Timberwolves. b, Wally Szczerbiak.

2006, Jan. 30   *Perf. 13¼*
  Sheets of 12, 2 #a, 10 #b
988-993 A201   Set of 6   37.50 37.50

    Souvenir Sheet

2006 World Cup Soccer Championships, Germany — A202

No. 994 — Player and uniform for: a, 90c, Spain. b, $1, South Korea. c, $1.50, France. d, $2, United States.

2006, June 9   Litho.   *Perf. 13¼*
994 A202 Sheet of 4, #a-d   8.25 8.25

Corals
A203

Designs: 10c, Montipora aequituberculata. 25c, Montipora capricornis. 30c, Montipora verrucosa. 40c, Acropora caroliniana. 50c, Acropora aculeus. 60c, Acropora anthocercis. 65c, Acropora granulosa. 80c, Acropora rosaria. 90c, Acropora cerealis. $1, Acropora yongei. $2, Acropora echinata. $5, Astreopora myriophthalma.

2006, Oct. 12   *Perf. 12¾*
995 A203 10c multi   .25 .25
996 A203 25c multi   .40 .40
997 A203 30c multi   .45 .45
998 A203 40c multi   .60 .60
999 A203 50c multi   .75 .75
1000 A203 60c multi   .90 .90
1001 A203 65c multi   1.00 1.00
1002 A203 80c multi   1.25 1.25
1003 A203 90c multi   1.40 1.40
1004 A203 $1 multi   1.50 1.50
1005 A203 $2 multi   3.00 3.00
1006 A203 $5 multi   7.50 7.50
  Nos. 995-1006 (12)   19.00 19.00

    Miniature Sheets

Pres. John F. Kennedy (1917-63) — A204

No. 1007, $1.30: a, On PT109, 1942. b, Receiving medal for gallantry, 1944. c, Portrait with brown background. d, In Ensign's uniform, 1941.
No. 1008, $1.30: a, Wearing bow tie. b, Wearing tan suit. c, With Eleanor Roosevelt. d, Portrait and U.S. Capitol.

2006, Sept. 21   Litho.   *Perf. 13½*
    Sheets of 4, #a-d
1007-1008 A204   Set of 2   15.50 15.50

Queen Elizabeth II, 80th Birthday — A205

No. 1009: a, As child holding dog. b, Wearing crown and holding scepter. c, Wearing jacket. d, Wearing sash and tiara.
$3, Wearing crown.

2006, Sept. 21
1009 A205 $1.30 Sheet of 4, #a-
    d   7.75 7.75
Souvenir Sheet
1010 A205 $3 multi   4.50 4.50

Space Achievements — A206

No. 1011 — Space Shuttle Discovery's return to space: a, Nose of Shuttle, open cargo doors, text in white reading down. b, Tail of Shuttle, stars, Earth, text in red reading across. c, Tail and wings of Shuttle, open cargo doors, text in red reading down. d, Astronaut on robotic arm. e, Head-on view of Shuttle nose, text in red reading across. f, Robotic arm, text in red and white.

No. 1012 — International Space Station: a, Top of rocket boosters. b, Space Station, text in white reading across. c, Space Shuttle. d, Space Station, text in white reading up.
$3, Calipso Satellite.

2006
1011 A206 $1 Sheet of 6, #a-f   9.50 9.50
1012 A206 $1.30 Sheet of 4, #a-
    d   7.75 7.75
Souvenir Sheet
1013 A206 $3 multi   4.50 4.50
   Issued: No. 1011, 12/21; Nos. 1012-1013, 9/21.

Miniature Sheet

Wolfgang Amadeus Mozart (1756-91), Composer — A207

No. 1014: a, Mozart gazing out window. b, Mozart family, 1780. c, Mozart in 1763. d, Art deco illustration of the young Mozart.

2006, Oct. 26
1014 A207 $1.30 Sheet of 4, #a-
    d   8.00 8.00

Rembrandt (1606-69), Painter A208

Designs: 10c, Woman in Bed. 20c, The Flight into Egypt. 35c, The Suicide of Lucretia. 95c, Esther Preparing to Intercede with Ahasuerus. $1, Rembrandt's Mother. $2, Child with Dead Peacock.
   $3, The Abduction of Ganymede.

2006, Nov. 9   *Perf. 14¼*
1015-1020 A208   Set of 6   7.25 7.25
         Imperf
    Size: 76x106mm
1021 A208 $3 multi   4.75 4.75

Worldwide Fund for Nature (WWF) — A209

Various Pygmy killer whales.

2006, Nov. 9   *Perf. 13½*
1022   Horiz. strip of 4   11.00 11.00
   a.   A209 40c Four whales   .65   .65
   b.   A209 60c Two whales   .95   .95
   c.   A209 90c Four whales, diff.   1.40 1.40
   d.   A209 $5 Two whales, diff.   8.00 8.00
   e.   Miniature sheet, 2 each
       #1022a-1022d   22.00 22.00

Butterflies — A210

No. 1023: a, Tailed jay. b, Ixias undatus. c, Hebomoia leucippe detanii. d, Rajah Brooke's birdwing.
   $3, Painted lady.

2006, Nov. 23
1023 A210 $1 Sheet of 4, #a-d   7.00 7.00
    Souvenir Sheet
1024 A210 $3 multi   5.00 5.00

Birds — A211

No. 1025: a, Reed warbler. b, Indian pitta. c, Gurney's pitta. d, Northern shrike.
   $3, Black-backed fairy wren.

2006, Nov. 23
1025 A211 $1 Sheet of 4, #a-d   7.00 7.00
    Souvenir Sheet
1026 A211 $3 multi   5.00 5.00

Miniature Sheet

Wedding of Queen Elizabeth II and Prince Philip, 60th Anniv. — A212

No. 1027: a, Photograph, denomination in pink. b, Drawing, denomination in white. c, Photograph, denomination in light green. d, Drawing, denomination in pink. e, Photograph, denomination in white. f, Drawing, denomination in light green.

2007, May 1   **Litho.**   *Perf. 13¼*
1027 A212 $1 Sheet of 6, #a-f   10.00 10.00

Princess Diana (1961-97) — A213

No. 1028: a, Wearing black and white hat, pink frame. b, Wearing beige dress, pink frame. c, Wearing pink hat, pink frame. d, Wearing pink hat, lilac frame. e, Wearing beige dress, no frame. f, Wearing black and white hat, lilac frame.
   $3, Princess Diana in Tomb of King Seti I, Egypt.

2007, May 1
1028 A213 $1 Sheet of 6, #a-f   10.00 10.00
    Souvenir Sheet
1029 A213 $3 multi   5.00 5.00

Global Warming — A214

No. 1030, $1: a, Windmills. b, Smokestacks, graph of atmospheric carbon dioxide. c, Tree seedling. d, Robotic arm lifting logs, thermometer. e, Recycling emblem. f, Thermometer, graph of global temperatures.
No. 1031, $1 — Text: a, Cause: Deforestation. b, Effect: Melting ice cap. c, Cause: Industrialization. d, Effect: Warmer temperature. e, Cause: Traffic. f, Effect: Extreme weather.
No. 1032, $1 — Text: a, Effect: Habitats destroyed. b, Prevention: Use renewable energy. c, Effect: Coral reef bleaching. d, Prevention: Recycle. e, Effect: Erratic weather patterns. f, Prevention: Plant trees.
No. 1033, $3, Earth on fire, smokestacks, automobile getting fuel. No. 1034, $3, Windmills. No. 1035, $3, Plant in parched soil, vert.

2007, July 21   **Litho.**
    Sheets of 6, #a-f
1030-1032 A214   Set of 3   32.50 32.50
    Souvenir Sheets
1033-1035 A214   Set of 3   16.00 16.00

First Helicopter Flight, Cent. — A215

Designs: 20c, BO-105. 75c, NH 90, horiz. $1, S-65/RH-53D, horiz. $2, AH 64 Apache, horiz.
   No. 1040, horiz.: a, BO-105, diff. b, S-65/RH-53D, diff. c, AH 64 Apache, diff. d, NH 90, diff.
   $3, HUP Retriever, horiz.

2007, July 28   *Perf. 13¼*
1036-1039 A215   Set of 4   6.75 6.75
1040 A215 $1.30 Sheet of 4,
      #a-d   9.00 9.00
    Souvenir Sheet
1041 A215 $3 multi   5.25 5.25

Scouting, Cent. A216

Scout: 20c, On bicycle. 75c, At campfire. $1, Playing cricket. $2, Shooting arrow.
   $3, Dove, Scouting flag, vert.

2007, Aug. 15
1042-1045 A216   Set of 4   6.50 6.50
    Souvenir Sheet
1046 A216 $3 multi   5.00 5.00
   No. 1046 contains one 37x51mm stamp.

Paintings by Qi Baishi (1864-1957) — A217

No. 1047: a, A Good Wind for Thousands of Miles, top half. b, As "a," bottom half. c, The Yuxia and Lianhua Mountains, top half. d, As "c," bottom half. e, Autumn Landscape with Cormorants, top half. f, As "e," bottom half.
No. 1048: a, Grasshopper on a Branch. b, Fish and Catfish.
   $3, Ink Landscape.

2007, Sept. 21
1047 A217 $1 Sheet of 6,
      #a-f   11.00 11.00
1048 A217 $2.50 Sheet of 2,
      #a-b   9.00 9.00
    Souvenir Sheet
1049 A217 $3 multi   5.50 5.50

Princess Diana (1961-97) — A218

Litho. & Embossed
2007, Oct. 1   *Serpentine Die Cut*
Without Gum
1050 A218 $9 gold & multi   16.50 16.50

Miniature Sheet

Elvis Presley (1935-77) — A219

No. 1051: a, Holding guitar. b, Wearing white shirt. c, Wearing suit and tie. d, Wearing Hawaiian shirt. e, Wearing blue shirt. f, Wearing Army uniform.

2007, Oct. 1   **Litho.**   **Perf. 13¼**
1051 A219 90c Sheet of 6, #a-f   9.75 9.75

Miniature Sheet

Pres. John F. Kennedy (1917-63) — A220

No. 1052 — Kennedy: a, Pointing, text at left. b, Pointing, text at right. c, Not pointing, text at left. d, Not pointing, text at right.

2007, Oct. 15   **Perf. 12¾**
1052 A220 $1 Sheet of 4, #a-d   7.50 7.50

Miniature Sheet

Marilyn Monroe (1926-62), Actress — A221

No. 1053: a, Wearing white boa. b, Wearing black dress, denomination in white. c, Wearing black and white dress, denomination in purple. d, Wearing beige dress.

2007, Oct. 15
1053 A221 $1 Sheet of 4, #a-d   7.50 7.50

Miniature Sheet

Pope Benedict XVI — A222

No. 1054: a, Photomosaic (Pope's ear). b, Photomosaic (Pope's neck and shoulder). c, Photomosaic (Pope's chest). d, Photograph of Pope.

2007, Nov. 11   **Perf. 12¼x12**
1054 A222 $1.30 Sheet of 4, #a-d   9.25 9.25

Christmas — A223

Paintings: 20c, The Adoration of the Shepherds, by Francisco Zurbaran. 75c, Madonna and Child with Angels, by Hans Memling. $1, The Nativity, by Maestro Esiguo. $2, The Nativity, by Philippe de Champaigne.

2007, Dec. 14   **Perf. 14**
1055-1058 A223 Set of 4   7.00 7.00

Miniature Sheet

2008 Summer Olympics, Beijing — A224

No. 1059: a, Baseball. b, Fencing. c, Field hockey. d, Gymnastics.

2008, Jan. 8   **Litho.**   **Perf. 12¾**
1059 A224 60c Sheet of 4, #a-d   4.25 4.25

Miniature Sheet

New Year 2008 (Year of the Rat) — A225

No. 1060 — Rat and Chinese character with yellow background color at: a, LR. b, LL. c, UR. d, UL.

2008, Feb. 28   **Perf. 12**
1060 A225 $1.30 Sheet of 4, #a-d   9.75 9.75

Taiwan Tourist Attractions — A226

No. 1061, horiz.: a, River and Red Suspension Bridge. b, Chinese New Year dragon. c, National Palace Museum. d, Taipei Main Railroad Station. e, Golden Waterfall, Jin Gua Shi. f, National Concert Hall, Taipei.
$2, Buddhist temple.

2008, Mar. 15   **Perf. 13¼**
1061 A226 50c Sheet of 6, #a-f   5.50 5.50
Souvenir Sheet
1062 A226 $2 multi   3.75 3.75

Flowers of the Holy Land — A227

No. 1063: a, Crocuses. b, Aleppo adonis. c, Wild chamomile. d, Fig buttercup. e, Dwarf chicory. f, Queen mallow.
$2, Yellow crocus.

2008, May 14   **Perf. 11½x11¼**
1063 A227 50c Sheet of 6, #a-f   5.75 5.75
Souvenir Sheet
1064 A227 $2 multi   4.00 4.00
2008 World Stamp Championship, Israel.

Cats — A228

No. 1065: a, Siberian. b, California spangled. c, Siamese. d, Burmilla. e, European shorthair. f, Devon rex.
$3, American wirehair.

2008, May 31   **Perf. 13¼**
1065 A228 $1 Sheet of 6, #a-f   11.50 11.50
Souvenir Sheet
1066 A228 $3 multi   5.75 5.75

Miniature Sheet

Orchids — A229

No. 1067: a, Vuylstekeara cambria. b, Dendrobium nobile (pink petals). c, Phalaenopsis nivacolor. d, Cattleya trianae. e, Dendrobium nobile (purple and green petals). f, Cymbidium alexanderi.

2008, June 15   **Perf. 11½x11¼**
1067 A229 $1 Sheet of 6, #a-f   11.50 11.50

A230

Elvis Presley (1935-77) — A231

No. 1068 — Presley: a, Without microphone. b, Holding microphone in right hand. c, Holding microphone in both hands.
No. 1069 — Presley: a, In white suit, yellow spirals at left and right. b, In leather jacket, yellow spirals at left and right. c, In white suit, yellow spirals at left. d, In white suit, yellow spirals at right. e, In leather jacket, yellow spirals at left. f, In white suit, no yellow spirals.

2008   **Perf. 11½x11¼**
1068   Horiz. strip of 3   5.75 5.75
a.-c. A230 $1 Any single   1.90 1.90
    Perf. 13¼
1069 A231 $1 Sheet of 6, #a-f   9.50 9.50

Issued: No. 1068, 7/14; No. 1069, 9/11. No. 1068 was printed in sheets containing two of each stamp.

Miniature Sheet

Birds — A232

No. 1070: a, Magnificent frigatebird. b, Townsend's warbler. c, Sooty tern. d, Common noddy. e, Masked booby. f, Red-tailed tropicbird.

2008, July 25   **Perf. 13¼**
1070 A232 $1 Sheet of 6, #a-f   11.50 11.50

Visit to Lourdes of Pope Benedict XVI — A233

2008, Aug. 31   **Litho.**
1071 A233 $1.30 multi   2.10 2.10
Printed in sheets of 4.

Miniature Sheets

A234

Space Exploration, 50th Anniv. (in 2007) — A235

No. 1072: a, Saturn V rocket carrying Apollo 11 on launch pad. b, Buzz Aldrin's footprint on Moon. c, Apollo 11 command module. d, Apollo 11 commander Neil A. Armstrong. e, Command module pilot Michael Collins. f, Lunar module pilot Edwin "Buzz" Aldrin.

No. 1073, $1.30 — Chandra X-ray Observatory with: a, Orange nebula at center. b, Stars in background. c, Red background. d, Blue green background.

No. 1074, $1.30 — Sputnik 1: a, Opened up. b, In orbit, satellite above denomination. c, R-7 Senyorka rocket. d, In orbit, with antenna running through denomination.

No. 1075, $1.30 — Cassini-Huygens probe: a, Cassini-Huygens in laboratory. b, Titan IV-B Centaur launch vehicle. c, Cassini-Huygens, Saturn. d, Cassini-Huygens, Saturn and Titan.

No. 1076, $1.30 — Galileo probe: a, Galileo in laboratory. b, Galileo, Europa, Jupiter and Io. c, Galileo probe (orange background). d, Jupiter, Io, Galileo and Ganymede.

2008, Sept. 11		Perf. 13¼	
1072 A234 $1 Sheet of 6, #a-f		9.50	9.50
Sheets of 4, #a-d			
1073-1076 A235	Set of 4	32.50	32.50

Miniature Sheet

Solo Aerial Circumnavigation of Wiley Post, 75th Anniv. — A236

No. 1077: a, Post wearing pressure suit. b, Post and airplane. c, The Winnie Mae. d, Post atop airplane. e, Post and wife, Mae. f, Harold Gatty, navigator.

2008, Oct. 23	Perf. 13¼	
1077 A236 $1.30 Sheet of 6, #a-f	10.50	10.50

Miniature Sheet

Princess Diana (1961-97) — A237

No. 1078 — Princess Diana at: a, Left, denomination on lilac background. b, Right (Princess looking to left). c, Left, denomination on white background. d, Right (Princess looking to right).

2008, Nov. 25		
1078 A237 $1.30 Sheet of 4, #a-d	6.75	6.75

Christmas
A238

Designs: 60c, Holly leaves and berries. 90c, Ornament. $1, Gift. $2.50, Candy cane.

2008, Nov. 25	Perf. 14¼x14¾	
1079-1082 A238 Set of 4	6.50	6.50

Miniature Sheet

New Year 2009 (Year of the Ox) — A239

No. 1083: a, 60c. b, 90c. d, $1.20. e, $2.50.

2009, Jan. 20	Litho.	Perf. 11½	
1083 A239	Sheet of 4, #a-d	7.00	7.00

Miniature Sheet

Inauguration of US President Barack Obama — A240

No. 1084: a, Pres. Abraham Lincoln. b, Emancipation Proclamation. c, Dr. Martin Luther King, Jr. d, King at March on Washington. e, Pres. Barack Obama. f, Obama giving victory speech.

2009, Jan. 20		
1084 A240 $1.30 Sheet of 6, #a-f, + 3 label	10.50	10.50

Miniature Sheet

Elvis Presley (1935-77) — A241

No. 1085 — Presley and: a, Red bird. b, Sun. c, Black bird. d, Flames. e, Sequin eagle. f, Peacock.

2009, Mar. 12		
1085 A241 $1 Sheet of 6, #a-f	8.75	8.75

Miniature Sheet

Visit of Pope Benedict XVI to Israel — A242

No. 1086: a, 60c. b, 90c. c, $1.20. d, $2.50.

2009, Apr. 23		
1086 A242 Sheet of 4, #a-d	7.50	7.50

Miniature Sheets

A243

Michael Jackson (1958-2009), Singer — A244

No. 1087 — Jackson and stage lighting above country name in: a, Blue. b, White. c, Orange. d, Red, with fireworks.

No. 1088 — Jacskon: a, Wearing jacket and hat, tie above "U." b, Holding microphone. c, Wearing sunglasses. d, Wearing jacket and hat, tie above "L."

2009, July 7	Perf. 13¼x13	
1087 A243 $1.30 Sheet of 4, #a-d	8.25	8.25
Perf. 13x13¼		
1088 A244 $1.30 Sheet of 4, #a-d	8.25	8.25

Miniature Sheet

The Obama Family — A245

No. 1089 — a, First Lady Michelle Obama. b, Pres. Barack Obama. c, Barack Obama and dog, Bo. d, Obama family with dog.

2009, July 13	Perf. 13½	
1089 A245 $1.30 Sheet of 4, #a-d	8.75	8.75

Miniature Sheet

The Three Stooges — A246

No. 1090 — The Three Stooges in various scenes with country name in: a, Red brown. b, Blue. c, Yellow brown. d, Green.

2009, July 14	Perf. 11½	
1090 A246 $1.30 Sheet of 4, #a-d	8.75	8.75

Miniature Sheets

First Man on the Moon, 40th Anniv. — A247

No. 1091: a, Golden olive branch left on Moon. b, Apollo 11 Command Module. c, Saturn V rocket. d, Astronaut Neil Armstrong. e, Congressional Space Medal of Honor. f, Apollo 11 Lunar Module.

No. 1092: a, Buzz Aldrin on Moon. b, Saturn V rocket taking off with Apollo 11. c, Apollo 11 Command Module. d, Apollo 11 crewmen awaiting pickup.

2009, July 20	Perf. 13½	
1091 A247 $1 Sheet of 6, #a-f	10.00	10.00
1092 A247 $1.30 Sheet of 4, #a-d	8.75	8.75

Miniature Sheet

Visit of Prince Harry to New York — A248

No. 1093: a, Prince Harry and woman at Harlem Children's Zoo. b, Wreath laid by Prince Harry at World Trade Center site. c, Prince Harry playing polo. d, Prince Harry and soldier at Veterans Affairs Medical Center.

2009, Aug. 25   *Perf. 12x11½*
1093 A248 $1.30 Sheet of 4, #a-
          d   8.75 8.75

Souvenir Sheet

Diplomatic Relations Between Tuvalu and the Republic of China, 30th Anniv. — A249

2009, Sept. 19   *Perf. 13½*
1094 A249 $5 multi   8.75 8.75

Christmas
A250

Designs: 60c, Stuffed reindeer, Santa Claus suit and hat with Tuvalu flag. 90c, Bells, Christmas ornament with Tuvalu flag. $1, Cloth Christmas decorations, Tuvalu arms. $2, Santa Claus on cake, bell with Tuvalu flag.

2009, Nov. 25   *Perf. 13½x13*
1095-1098 A250 Set of 4   8.25 8.25

Miniature Sheet

Pres. John F. Kennedy (1917-63) — A251

No. 1099 — Pres. Kennedy: a, Seated at desk. b, With wife, Jacqueline. c, With son, John, Jr. d, At podium.

2009, Nov. 28   *Perf. 12x11½*
1099 A251 $1.30 Sheet of 4, #a-
          d   9.50 9.50

Butterflies
A252

Designs: 60c, Hyposcada kezia. 90c, Heteronympha mirifica. No. 1102, $1, Libythea geoffroy. $2.50, Protographium leosthenes. No. 1104, $1: a, Horago selina. b, Ornithoptera victoriae. c, Polyura eudamippus. d, Catopsilia scylla. e, Graphium mendana. f, Melanitis amabilis.

2009, Nov. 28   *Perf. 11½*
1100-1103 A252   Set of 4   9.25 9.25
1104 A252 $1 Sheet of 6, #a-f 11.00 11.00

Miniature Sheet

Reign of Pope Benedict XVI, 5th Anniv. — A252a

No. 1104G — Pope Benedict XVI: h, Waving. i, Wearing red vestments, facing left. j, Wearing red vestments, facing right. k, Holding crucifix.

2009, Dec. 10   *Perf. 12x11½*
1104G A252a $1.30 Sheet of 4,
          #h-k   9.50 9.50

Miniature Sheet

Princess Diana (1961-97) — A252b

No. 1104L: m, Holding infant. b, With arms on hips. c, Wearing face shield. d, Talking with child.

2009, Dec. 20
1104L A252b $1.30 Sheet of 4,
          #m-p   9.25 9.25

Miniature Sheet

Elvis Presley (1935-77) — A253

No. 1105 — Presley: a, With hands at bottom of guitar. b, With one hand over guitar strings. c, With hand over guitar strings and hand holding neck of guitar. d, Playing guitar and singing.

2010, Jan. 9   *Perf. 13½*
1105 A253 $1.30 Sheet of 4, #a-
          d   9.25 9.25

Boy Scouts of America, Cent. — A254

No. 1106, $1.30: a, Scout saluting. b, Scout planting tree.
No. 1107, $1.30: a, Scout with backpack and walking stick. b, Scout fishing.

2010, Feb. 1   Pairs, #a-b   Litho.
1106-1107 A254   Set of 2   9.00 9.00
Nos. 1106-1107 were each printed in sheets containing two pairs.

Souvenir Sheet

Elvis Presley (1935-77) — A255

No. 1108: a, Presley facing left. b, Presley and guitar neck.

2010, Jan. 8   *Imperf.*
          Without Gum
1108 A255 $6 Sheet of 2, #a-b 21.50 21.50

Miniature Sheet

Earth Day, 40th Anniv. — A256

No. 1109 — Various drawings by children: a, 50c. b, 60c. c, 90c. d, $1.50.

2010, Apr. 22   *Perf. 13¼*
1109 A256   Sheet of 4, #a-d 6.50 6.50

Miniature Sheets

Battle of Britain, 70th Anniv. — A257

No. 1110, $1.30: a, Winston Churchill (black-and-white photograph) b, Coventry Cathedral in ruins. c, London in ruins (bicyclists at left). d, London in ruins (automobiles and trucks on street).
No. 1111, $1.30: a, Winston Churchill (color photograph). b, Messerschmitt BF 109E. c, Emblems of Luftwaffe and Royal Air Force. d, Supermarine Spitfire.

2010, Apr. 23   Sheets of 4, #a-d
1110-1111 A257 Set of 2   19.50 19.50

Palaces of the World — A258

No. 1112, horiz.: a, Imperial Palace, Tokyo, Japan. b, Dolmabahçe Palace, Istanbul, Turkey. c, Winter Palace, St. Petersburg, Russia. d, Schönbrunn Palace, Vienna, Austria. e, Summer Palace, Beijing, China. f, Buckingham Palace, London, England.
$3, Palace of Versailles, Versailles, France.

2010, July 28   *Perf. 11½*
1112 A258 $1 Sheet of 6, #a-f 11.00 11.00
          Souvenir Sheet
1113 A258 $3 multi   5.50 5.50

Souvenir Sheets

A259

A260

A261

Elvis Presley (1935-77) — A262

2010, July 28   *Perf. 14¼*
1114 A259 $3 multi   5.50   5.50
1115 A260 $3 multi   5.50   5.50
1116 A261 $3 multi   5.50   5.50
1117 A262 $3 multi   5.50   5.50
       Nos. 1114-1117 (4)   22.00   22.00

Girl Guides, Cent. — A263

No. 1118 — Drawings of Girl Guides in sepia and: a, Four Girl Guides in blue uniforms. b, Girl Guide wearing red neckerchief. c, Girl Guide with bongo drum. d, Two Girl Guides wearing red neckerchiefs.
$3, Centenary emblem, six Girl Guides, vert.

2010, Aug. 16   *Perf. 12½x12*
1118 A263 $1.30 Sheet of 4, #a-d
                                   9.50   9.50
       Souvenir Sheet
       Perf. 11¼x11½
1119 A263 $3 multi   5.50   5.50

Miniature Sheets

A264

Pres. Abraham Lincoln (1809-65) — A265

No. 1120 — Lincoln with denomination in: a, Orange. b, Rose. c, Blue. d, Green.
No. 1121: Lincoln with country name in: a, Green. b, Purple. c, Dark red. d, Red brown.

2010, Aug. 21   *Perf. 13¼x13*
1120 A264 $1.30 Sheet of 4, #a-d
                                   9.50   9.50
                  Perf. 12
1121 A265 $1.30 Sheet of 4, #a-d
                                   9.50   9.50

Souvenir Sheets

Popes and their Coats of Arms — A266

No. 1122, $4: a, Pope John Paul II. b, Arms of Pope John Paul II.
No. 1123, $4: a, Pope Benedict XVI. b, Arms of Pope Benedict XVI.

2010, Aug. 30   *Imperf.*
       Sheets of 2, #a-b
       Without Gum
1122-1123 A266 Set of 2   30.00   30.00

Election of Pres. John F. Kennedy, 50th Anniv. — A267

No. 1124, $1.30 — Gray frames and blue panels with Kennedy: a, Talking with Tobacco Association representative at Greenbrier Hotel, 1958. b, Signing Cuban quarantine proclamation, 1962. c, Campaigning, 1960. d, At televised debate, 1960.

No. 1125, $1.30 — Olive green frames and brown panels with Kennedy: a, With wife, Jacqueline, on sailboat. b, Reading newspaper on the Honey Fitz, 1963. c, With wife and children, 1962. d, With wife in limousine, 1961.
No. 1126, $1.30 — Bluish black frames and red panels with Kennedy: a, Kennedy with son, John, Jr. b, Crowd at Grand Rapids, Michigan campaign rally, 1960. c, Kennedy debating Richard M. Nixon, 1960. d, Kennedy at lectern at 1960 campaign rally.

2010, Sept. 12   *Perf. 12*
       Sheets of 4, #a-d
1124-1126 A267 Set of 3   30.00   30.00

Frédéric Chopin (1810-49), Composer — A268

No. 1127: Various portraits of Chopin facing: a, Left. b, Right. c, Left, diff. d, Right diff.
No. 1128, $3, Chopin, black background.
No. 1129, $3, Chopin, brown background.

2010, Sept. 12
1127 A268 $1.30 Sheet of 4, #a-d
                                   10.00   10.00
       Souvenir Sheets
1128-1129 A268 Set of 2   12.00   12.00

Miniature Sheets

A269

Pope Benedict XVI — A270

No. 1130 — Pope Benedict XVI and: a, "XVI" above building at right. b, "I" of "XVI" above building ar right. c, Crowd, window of Vatican City building at UL. d, Crowd, pillars of Vatican City building at UL.
No. 1131 — Pope Benedict XVI and: a, Part of building to left of face. b, No building to left or right of face. c, Purple area to left of face. d, Purple area to left of face with white spot near tip of ear.

2010, Sept. 21   *Perf. 12x12½*
1130 A269 $1.30 Sheet of 4, #a-d
                                   10.00   10.00
1131 A270 $1.30 Sheet of 4, #a-d
                                   10.00   10.00

Miniature Sheets

A271

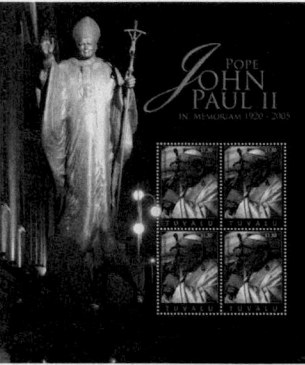

Pope John Paul II (1920-2005) — A272

No. 1132 — Pope John Paul II waving and: a, "T" of "Tuvalu" on pillar, lower part of first "U" in "Tuvalu" above arch. b, "T" of "Tuvalu" on arc, lower part of first "U" in "Tuvalu" above arc. c, Country name over area with darker gray area near "L" in "Tuvalu." d, Darker gray lines to left of first "U," below "V," to right of "A," and to left of second "U" in "Tuvalu."
No. 1133 — Pope John Paul II holding crucifix and: a, Light area in frame next to lower left corner of photo. b, Blackish brown frame.

2010, Oct. 7
1132 A271 $1.30 Sheet of 4, #a-d
                                   10.50   10.50
1133 A272 $1.30 Sheet of 4, #1133a, 3
                                   10.50   10.50
                  #1133b

Princess Diana (1961-97) — A273

No. 1134 — Princess Diana wearing: a, White jacket and dress, tan background. b, Red and black dress. c, White jacket, black background. d, Red and white tress, tiara.
No. 1135, $3, Strapless white dress. No. 1136, $3, Red and white hat.

2010, Oct. 28   *Perf. 12*
1134 A273 $1.30 Sheet of 4, #a-d
                                   10.50   10.50
       Souvenir Sheets
1135-1136 A273 Set of 2   12.50   12.50

Miniature Sheets

A274

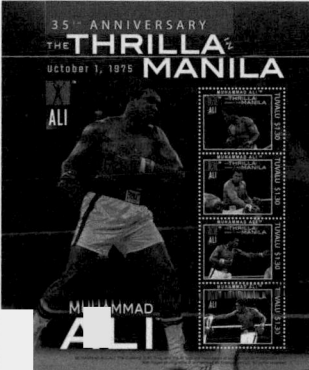

Fight Between Muhammad Ali and Joe
Frazier, Manila, 35th Anniv. — A275

No. 1137: a, Ali wearing robe encircled by
reporters with eight microphones. b, Ali wearing robe, standing. c, Ali, bare-chested, facing
right, talking to reporters. d, Ali, bare-chested,
looking left, talking to reporters.
No. 1138 — Ali in boxing ring: a, White rope
at lower right. b, Frazier at lower left, white and
red ropes at lower right. c, Ali with arm
extended to right, white rope at bottom. d, Ali
with arm extended to left, white and red ropes
at bottom.

2010, Nov. 25		Perf. 11¼x11½		
1137	A274	$1.30 Sheet of 4,		
		#a-d	10.50	10.50
		Perf. 11½x11¼		
1138	A275	$1.30 Sheet of 4,		
		#a-d	10.50	10.50

Christmas
A276

Details of paintings: 60c, Pierre Bladelin
Triptych, by Rogier van der Weyden. 90c,
Annunciation, by Pietro Cavallini. $1, Altar-
piece of the Virgin, by Jacques Daret. $2,
Nativity, by Matthias Grunewald.

2010, Nov. 25		Perf. 12		
1139-1142	A276	Set of 4	9.00	9.00

Nos. 1139-1142 each were printed in sheets
of 4.

2010 World Cup Soccer
Championships, South Africa — A277

No. 1143, $1 — Scenes from June 16, 2010
Spain vs. Switzerland match (Spain in red
shirts): a, Spanish player #15 and Swiss
goalie. b, Spanish player #22 and Swiss player
#17. c, Spanish player #8 and Swiss players
#8 and #6. d, Spanish players #15 and #3 and
Swiss player #16.
No. 1144, $1 — Scenes from June 21, 2010
Spain vs. Honduras match (Spain in red
shirts): a, Spanish players #7 and #8. b, Span-
ish player #10 and Honduran player #11. c,
Spanish player #8 and Honduran player #8. d,
Spanish players #11 and #16 and Honduran
players #11 and #1?
No. 1145, $1 — Scenes from June 25, 2010
Spain vs. Chile match (Spain in black shirts):
a, Spanish players #7 and #10. b, Spanish
player #9 and Chilean player #3. c, Spanish
players #5, #14 and #16 and Chilean player
#10. d, Spanish player #11 and Chilean player
#7.
No. 1146, $1 — Scenes from June 29, 2010
Spain vs. Portugal match (Spain in red shirts):
a, Spanish goalie leaping into arms of Spanish
player #19. b, Spanish player #16 and Portuguese player #20. c, Spanish player #7. d,
Spanish player falling and Portuguese player
#23.
No. 1147, $1 — Scenes from July 3, 2010
Spain vs. Paraguay match (Spain in black
shirts): a, Spanish players #8 and #10 and
Paraguayan player #16. b, Spanish goalie
(player #1). c, Spanish player #16 and
Paraguayan player #3. d, Spanish player #15
and Paraguayan player #21.
No. 1148, $1 — Scenes from July 7, 2010
Spain vs. Germany match (Spain in red
shirts): a, Spanish player #11 and German
player #15 (with hand on Spanish player's
back). b, Spanish player #8 and German
player #7. c, Spanish player #6 and German
player #6. d, Spanish player #11 and German
player #15 (both players with arms extended).
No. 1149, $1 — Scenes from July 11, 2010
Spain vs. Netherlands match (Spain in black
shirts): a, Spanish player #15 and Netherlands
player #4. b, Spanish player #15 on knees and
Netherlands player #10. c, Spanish player #7
and Netherlands player #4. d, Spanish player
#10 and Netherlands player #9.
$3, Spanish team celebrating
championship.

2010, July 11		Sheets of 4, #a-d		
1143-1149	A277	Set of 7	52.50	52.50
		Souvenir Sheet		
1150	A277	$3 multi	5.50	5.50

Nos. 1143-1150 could not have been issued
on the stated day of issue as Nos. 1149 and
1150 depict photographs taken that day.

Miniature Sheet

Expo 2010, Shanghai — A278

No. 1151 — Expo 2010 emblem and various
views of Green Island: a, 60c. b, 90c. c, $1.50.
d, $2.

2010, Aug. 25		Perf. 13¼		
1151	A278	Sheet of 4, #a-d	9.25	9.25

Whales — A279

No. 1152: a, Orca. b, Short-finned pilot
whale. c, Melon-headed whale. d, Pygmy killer
whale. e, False killer whale. f, Sperm whale.
$3, Dwarf sperm whale.

2011, Jan. 30		Perf. 13 Syncopated		
1152	A279	$1 Sheet of 6, #a-f	12.50	12.50
		Souvenir Sheet		
1153	A279	$3 multi	6.25	6.25

Famous Indians — A280

No. 1154: a, Amrita Sher-Gil (1913-41),
painter. b, Subrahmanyan Chandrasekhar
(1910-95), astrophysicist. c, Satyajit Ray
(1921-92), filmmaker. d, Rabindranath Tagore
(1861-1941), writer.
$3, Mohandas K. Gandhi (1869-1948),
nationalist leader.

2011, Feb. 12		Perf. 12¾x12½		
1154	A280	$1.30 Sheet of 4,		
		#a-d	10.50	10.50
		Souvenir Sheet		
		Perf. 13¼		
1155	A280	$3 multi	6.25	6.25

Indipex 2011 Intl. Philatelic Exhibition, New
Delhi. No. 1155 contains one 38x50mm
stamp.

Miniature Sheets

A281

Elvis Presley (1935-77) — A282

No. 1156 — Presley: a, Standing, with arm
extended. b, With both hands near
microphone. c, Holding microphone with arm
at side. d, With bent knees and arm extended.
No. 1157 — Presley: a, Standing in front of
man on stage. b, With guitar, audience in
background. c, Playing guitar. d, Holding
microphone.

2011, Feb. 15		Perf. 13 Syncopated		
1156	A281	$1.30 Sheet of 4,		
		#a-d	10.50	10.50
		Perf. 12		
1157	A282	$1.30 Sheet of 4,		
		#a-d	10.50	10.50

Personalities of the U.S. Civil
War — A283

No. 1158: a, Head of Pres. Abraham Lincoln. b, Lieutenant General Ulysses S. Grant.
c, Major General George G. Meade. d, Lincoln, standing.
No. 1159, horiz.: a, Lincoln, no hands visible. b, Lincoln, with hand on chin.

2011, Feb. 28		Perf. 13 Syncopated		
1158	A283	$1.30 Sheet of 4		
		#a-d	10.50	10.50
		Souvenir Sheet		
		Perf. 12		
1159	A283	$3 Sheet of 2,		
		#a-b	12.50	12.50

A284

Statue of Liberty, 125th Anniv. — A285

No. 1160 — Statue of Liberty and: a, Gray
backround, "86" at left b, Blue background,
denomination at LL. c, Gray and purple background, denomination at UL. d, Gray background, "20" at right.
No. 1161: a, Side view of statue. b, Head of
statue.

2011, Mar. 15		Perf. 13 Syncopated		
1160	A284	$1.30 Sheet of 4,		
		#a-d	11.00	11.00
		Souvenir Sheet		
1161	A285	$1.50 Sheet of 2,		
		#a-b	6.50	6.50

Beatification of Pope John Paul
II — A286

Pope John Paul II: No. 1162, $1, Greeting
crowd. No. 1163, $1, With mass attendants,
reading. $3, Pope John Paul II in crowd, diff.

2011, Apr. 15   Perf. 13 Syncopated
1162-1163 A286   Set of 2   4.25 4.25
Souvenir Sheet
Perf. 12
1164 A286 $3 multi   6.50 6.50
   Nos. 1162 and 1163 were printed in a sheet
of six containing three of each stamp.

Wedding of Prince William and
Catherine Middleton — A287

No. 1165, $1.30: a, Couple, facing forward.
b, Bride.
   No. 1166, $1.30: a, Groom waving. b,
Couple, looking at each other.
$3, Couple, kissing.

2011, Apr. 29   Perf. 12
Pairs, #a-b
1165-1166 A287   Set of 2   11.50 11.50
Souvenir Sheet
Perf. 11¼x11½
1167 A287 $3 multi   6.50 6.50
   Nos. 1165-1166 each were printed in sheets
containing two pairs. No. 1167 contains one
30x79mm stamp. Nos. 1165-1167 could not
have been issued on the stated day of issue
because stamps have photographs taken that
day, which was the day of the wedding.

Parrots — A288

No. 1168: a, Western rosella. b, Australian
ringneck. c, Budgerigar. d, Northern rosella. e,
Red-capped parrot. f, Regent parrot.
$3, Red-winged parrot.

2011, June 6   Perf. 12
1168 A288 $1 Sheet of 6, #a-f 13.00 13.00
Souvenir Sheet
1169 A288 $3 multi   6.50 6.50

Personalizable
Stamp — A289

2011, June 15   Perf. 14¼x14¾
1170 A289 20c multi   .45   .45

A290

Meeting of U.S. Pres. Barack Obama
and Australian Prime Minister Julia
Gillard — A291

No. 1171: a, Prime Minister Gillard and
Pres. Obama, no hands visible. b, Obama. c,
Gillard and Obama shaking hands. d, Gillard.
   No. 1172: a, Gillard. b, Obama.

2011, June 15   Perf. 11½x12
1171 A290 $1.30 Sheet of 4,
                  #a-d   11.50 11.50
Souvenir Sheet
1172 A291 $1.25 Sheet of 2,
                  #a-b   5.50 5.50

First Man in Space, 50th
Anniv. — A292

No. 1173, $1.30, horiz.: a, Sergei Korolev
(1907-66), spacecraft designer, and rocket. b,
Yuri Gagarin, first man in space, with helmet.
c, Erecting rocket from train. d, John Glenn,
U.S. astronaut.
   No. 1174, $1.30, horiz.: a, Vostok capsule.
b, Vostok 1A rocket. c, Vostok Memorial. d,
Virgil Grissom, U.S. astronaut.
   No. 1175, $3, Gagarin wearing brown uni-
form. No. 1176, $3, Gagarin wearing white
uniform and medal.

2011, June 27   Perf. 12½x12
Sheets of 4, #a-d
1173-1174 A292 Set of 2   22.50 22.50
Souvenir Sheets
Perf. 11¼x11½
1175-1176 A292 Set of 2   13.00 13.00

U.S. Pres. Ronald Reagan (1911-
2004) — A293

No. 1177 — Pres. Reagan: a, Wearing red
and blue striped tie. b, Wearing overcoat,
striped shirt and polka dot tie. c, Wearing

black suit. d, With American flag in
background.
   No. 1178 — Pres. Reagan: a, Wearing
maroon patterned tie. b, Wearing striped tie,
American flag in background.

2011, June 30   Litho.   Perf.
1177 A293 $1 Sheet of 4, #a-d 8.50 8.50
Souvenir Sheet
1178 A293 $3 Sheet of 2, #a-b 13.00 13.00

Miniature Sheets

U.S. Civil War, 150th Anniv. — A294

No. 1179, $1.30 — Eagle, shield, Union and
Confederate flags, General Robert E. Lee,
Major General John Pope, and scenes from
Second Battle of Bull Run, Aug. 28-30, 1862:
a, Soldiers carrying Union flag at center. b,
General Sigel's Corps at the battle site. c,
Soldiers marching, green background. d, Bat-
tle scene, horses and building at right.
   No. 1180, $1.30 — Eagle, shield, Union and
Confederate flags, General Braxton Bragg,
Major General William S. Rosecrans, and
scenes from Battle of Stones River, Dec. 31,
1862-Jan. 2, 1863: a, Gen. Rosecrans rallies
troops at Stones River. b, Union Army flees a
Confederate onslaught. c, Confederates fron-
tal attack on the Union. d, General Rosecrans
tries to save his army.
   No. 1181, $1.30 — Eagle, shield, Union and
Confederate flags, General Robert E. Lee,
General Ulysses S. Grant and scenes from the
Battle of the Wilderness, May 5-7, 1864: a,
Battle near Orange Court House Plank Road.
b, The gloom at the outset in dense woods. c,
Army of the Potomac charging the enemy. d,
Carrying a wounded soldier to safety.

2011, July 4   Perf. 12½x12
Sheets of 4, #a-d
1179-1181 A294   Set of 3   34.00 34.00

Miniature Sheets

Mother Teresa (1910-97),
Humanitarian — A295

No. 1182, $1.30 — Mother Teresa: a, Hold-
ing child, children in background. b, With wall
inscribed "Peace" in background. c, With
hands held together. d, Holding Nobel Peace
Prize diploma and medal box.
   No. 1183, $1.30 — Mother Teresa: a, Black-
and-white photograph of head. b, With Pres.
Ronald Reagan and wife, Nancy. c, Holding
baby, door in background. d, Under umbrella.

Perf. 12x12½, 11¼ (#1183)
2011, July 5   Sheets of 4, #a-d
1182-1183 A295   Set of 2   22.50 22.50

Miniature Sheets

Woodblock Prints of Morning
Glories — A296

Woodblock Prints of Mount Fuji, by
Hiroshige — A297

No. 1184: a, Unopened buds on vine. b,
Brownish purple flower with thin, spiked
leaves, three Japanese characters at LL. c,
Red flower on vine. d, Pink flowers on thin vine
running horizontally. e, Pink flower on thick
vine running vertically. f, Dark red and black
flower on thin vine, one Japanese character at
LL.
   No. 1185: a, Mount Fuji above village. b,
Mount Fuji with hill in foreground. c, Reflection
of Mount Fuji in lake. d, Ocean wave and
Mount Fuji.

2011, July 28   Perf. 13 Syncopated
1184 A296 $1 Sheet of 6,
                  #a-f   12.50 12.50
Perf. 12
1185 A297 $1.30 Sheet of 4,
                  #a-d   11.00 11.00
   PhilaNippon '11 Intl. Philatelic Exhibition,
Yokohama.

Princess Diana (1961-97) — A298

No. 1186 — Princess Diana wearing: a, Tiara. b, Dark dress. c, Pearl necklace and hat with striped ribbon. d, Dress with ruffled collar.
$3, Princess Diana wearing pearl necklace and hat with black ribbon.

2011, Aug. 1   **Perf. 12½x12**
1186 A298 $1.30 Sheet of 4,
    #a-d   11.00 11.00

Souvenir Sheet
Perf. 11½
1187 A298 $3 multi   6.25 6.25

Souvenir Sheets

War Horses — A299

Carriage Horses — A300

Race Horses — A301

No. 1188: a, Denomination at LR. b, Denomination at LL.
No. 1189: a, White horse pulling man and woman in carriage. b, Silhouette of horse and carriage.
No. 1190: a, Three horses. b, Four horses.

2011, Aug. 31   **Litho.**   **Perf. 12**
1188 A299 $3 Sheet of 2, #a-b 12.50 12.50
1189 A300 $3 Sheet of 2, #a-b 12.50 12.50
1190 A301 $3 Sheet of 2, #a-h 12.50 12.50
   Nos. 1188-1190 (3)   37.50 37.50

Miniature Sheet

2011 Women's World Cup Soccer Championships, Germany — A302

No. 1191: a, Japanese team captain Homare Sawa. b, Japanese Team. c, U.S. team. d, U.S. team captain Christie Rampone.

2011, Sept. 21   **Perf. 12x12½**
1191 A302 $1.30 Sheet of 4,
    #a-d   10.50 10.50

Marine Fauna — A303

No. 1192: a, Christmas shearwater. b, Flying fish. c, Albacore tuna. d, Pantropical spotted dolphin. e, Pygmy killer whale.
$3, Parrotfish.

2012, Jan. 1   **Perf. 13x13¼**
1192 A303 $1 Sheet of 5, #a-e 10.50 10.50

Souvenir Sheet
Perf. 13¼
1193 A303 $3 multi   6.25 6.25

No. 1192 contains five 40x30mm stamps.

Disappearance of Amelia Earhart, 75th Anniv. — A304

No. 1194 — Earhart: a, Wearing leather pilot's helmet, brick wall in background. b, Without pilot's helmet, airplane fuselage in background. c, Wearing leather pilot's helmet, airplane propeller in background. d, Without pilot's helmet, airplane propeller in background.
$3.50, Earhart on side of airplane.

2012, Feb. 6   **Perf. 13**
1194 A304 $1.25 Sheet of 4,
    #a-d   11.00 11.00

Souvenir Sheet
1195 A304 $3.50 multi   7.75 7.75

Miniature Sheet

Sinking of the Titanic, Cent. — A305

No. 1196: a, Smokestacks. b, Mast and aft deck. c, Flagpole and ship's stern.
$3.50, Flagpole and ship's stern, diff.

2012, Apr. 15   **Perf. 13 Syncopated**
1196 A305 $1.50 Sheet of 3, #a-
    c   9.25 9.25

Souvenir Sheet
1197 A305 $3.50 multi   7.25 7.25

Climate Change Awareness — A306

Inscriptions: No. 1198, $1, Plant a tree to help reduce greenhouse gases. No. 1199, $1, Turning off lights to save energy. No. 1200, $1, Distillation plants turn seas into clean drinking water. No. 1201, $1, Crops that are genetically enhanced to grow near salt water. No. 1202, $1, Mangrove trees encourage new land formation.

2012, May 1   **Perf. 14**
1198-1202 A306   Set of 5   10.50 10.50
   Expo 2012, Yeosu, South Korea.

Souvenir Sheets

Elvis Presley (1935-77) — A307

Designs: No. 1203, $3.50, Red background, Presley on stage. No. 1204, $3.50, Red background, close-up of Presley. No. 1205, $3.50, Red background, two photographs of Presley. No. 1206, $3.50, Light blue background, black-and-white photograph of Presley. No. 1207, $3.50, Light blue background, color photograph of Presley.

2012, May 14   **Perf. 12¾**
1203-1207 A307   Set of 5   35.00 35.00

2012 Summer Olympics, London — A308

No. 1208 — British flag on simulated Olympic medals in: a, Bronze. b, Silver. c, Gold.
$1.50, Olympic rings, colored stripes, London landmarks, vert.

2012, May 30   **Perf.**
1208 A308   50c Sheet of 3, #a-
    c   3.00 3.00

Souvenir Sheet
Perf. 12¼x12
1209 A308 $1.50 multi   3.00 3.00

No. 1209 contains one 30x50mm stamp. Exists Imperf. Value, $25.

A309

A310

A311

Elvis Presley (1935-77) — A312

2012, June 27   **Perf. 13¼**
1210 A309 $3.50 multi   7.25 7.25
1211 A310 $3.50 multi   7.25 7.25
1212 A311 $3.50 multi   7.25 7.25
1213 A312 $3.50 multi   7.25 7.25
   Nos. 1210-1213 (4)   29.00 29.00

Fish — A313

Designs: 10c, Epibulus insidiator. 40c, Zanclus cornutus. 60c, Anampses cuvier. 90c, Rhinecanthus verrucosus. $1, Lactoria fornasini. $1.25, Enchelycore pardalis. $1.50, Diodon liturosus. $1.75, Anampses elegans. $2, Thalassoma trilobatum. $2.75, Pomacanthus imperator. $3.25, Pomacanthus semicirculatus. $5, Cheilinus fasciatus.

2012, July 15   *Perf. 13¾*
1214	A313	10c multi	.25 .25
1215	A313	40c multi	.85 .85
1216	A313	60c multi	1.25 1.25
1217	A313	90c multi	1.90 1.90
1218	A313	$1 multi	2.10 2.10
1219	A313	$1.25 multi	2.75 2.75
1220	A313	$1.50 multi	3.25 3.25
1221	A313	$1.75 multi	3.75 3.75
1222	A313	$2 multi	4.25 4.25
1223	A313	$2.75 multi	6.00 6.00
1224	A313	$3.25 multi	7.00 7.00
1225	A313	$5 multi	10.50 10.50

Nos. 1214-1225 (12)   43.85 43.85

Dogs
A314

No. 1226: a, Duck tolling retriever. b, Berger Picard. c, Chow chow. d, Great Dane. e, Labrador retriever.

2012, July 15   *Perf. 14*
1226		Sheet of 5	10.50 10.50
a.-e.	A314	$1 Any single	2.10 2.10

Exists Imperf.

Miniature Sheet

Cats — A315

No. 1227: a, Siamese. b, Devon Rex. c, American wirehair. d, Cornish Rex. e, Burmese.

2012, Aug. 7
1227 A315 80c Sheet of 5, #a-e   8.50 8.50

Beetles — A316

No. 1228: a, Asian lady beetle. b, Blister beetle. c, Water beetle. d, Clytus arietis. $3, Firefly.

2012, Sept. 5
1228 A316 $1.25 Sheet of 4,
    #a-d   10.50 10.50
     Souvenir Sheet
      Perf. 12
1229 A316 $3 multi   6.25 6.25

Paintings by Raphael — A317

No. 1230: a, St. Margaret. b, Saint Michael Vanquishing Satan. c, Portrait of Elisabetta Gonzaga. d, The Holy Family.
$3, St. Margaret, diff.

2012, Sept. 5   *Perf. 12¾*
1230 A317 $1 Sheet of 4, #a-d   8.50 8.50
     Souvenir Sheet
1231 A317 $3 multi   6.25 6.25

Visit of Duke and Duchess of
Cambridge to Tuvalu — A318

No. 1232: a, Duchess of Cambridge. b, Crest of Tuvalu. c, Duke and Duchess of Cambridge. d, Queen Elizabeth II visiting Tuvalu, 1982. e, Duke of Cambridge.
$3.50, Duke and Duchess of Cambridge, horiz.

2012, Oct. 1   *Perf. 14*
1232 A318 $1.25 Sheet of 5,
    #a-e   13.00 13.00
     Souvenir Sheet
      Perf. 12
1233 A318 $3.50 multi   7.25 7.25

No. 1233 contains one 50x30mm stamp. No. 1232 exists imperf.

Reign of Queen Elizabeth II, 60th
Anniv. — A319

No. 1234 — Queen Elizabeth II and: a, Prince Philip on Great Wall of China, 1986. b, Park ranger with hat at Yosemite National Park, 1983. c, Emperor Haile Selassie at Tissisal Falls, Ethiopia, 1965. d, Prince Philip at Taj Mahal, 1961.
$3.50, Queen Elizabeth II and sailor in Tuvalu, 1982, vert.

2012, Dec. 31   *Perf. 13 Syncopated*
1234 A319 $1.25 Sheet of 4,
    #a-d   10.50 10.50
     Souvenir Sheet
1235 A319 $3.50 multi   7.50 7.50

World Humanitarian Day — A320

No. 1236: a, Earth. b, Dove with olive branch. c, Peace symbol. d, Red cross. $3.50, Heart.

2013, Mar. 21   *Perf. 13¾*
1236 A320 $1.20 Sheet of 4,
    #a-d   10.00 10.00
     Souvenir Sheet
1237 A320 $3.50 multi   7.50 7.50

Mushrooms — A321

No. 1238: a, Devil's bolete. b, Shaggy mane. c, Black trumpet. d, Chanterelle. $3.50, Entoloma clypeatum, vert.

2013, Apr. 29   *Perf. 12*
1238 A321 $1.20 Sheet of 4,
    #a-d   10.00 10.00
     Souvenir Sheet
1239 A321 $3.50 multi   7.25 7.25

A322

Flowers — A323

No. 1240: a, Medinilla magnifica. b, Alpinia purpurata. c, Nymphaea rubra. d, Crotalaria retusa.
No. 1241: a, Hibiscus rosa-sinensis. b, Gardenia taitensis. c, Hibiscus brackenridgei. d, Ranunculus lyallii.
No. 1242, Etlingera elatior. No. 1243, Tecomanthe speciosa, vert.

2013, Apr. 29   *Perf. 14*
1240 A322 $1.20 Sheet of 4,
    #a-d   10.00 10.00
      Perf. 12
1241 A323 $1.20 Sheet of 4,
    #a-d   10.00 10.00
     Souvenir Sheet
1242 A322 $3.50 multi   7.25 7.25
1243 A323 $3.50 multi   7.25 7.25

A324

Election of Pope Francis — A325

No. 1244: a, White smoke rising from chimney of Sistine Chapel. b, Pope Francis waving and holding crucifix. c, Pope Francis in window. d, Head of Pope Francis.
$8, Pope Francis waving.

2013, June 3   *Litho.*   *Perf. 14*
1244 A324 $1.20 Sheet of 4,
    #a-d   9.25 9.25
     Souvenir Sheet
     Without Gum
Litho., Margin Embossed With Foil Application
      Imperf
1245 A325 $8 multi   15.50 15.50

Miniature Sheet

Seashells — A326

No. 1246: a, Depressed cowry. b, Japanese wonder shell. c, Fluted giant clam. d, Chambered nautilus. e, Precious wentletrap.

Perf. 13 Syncopated
2013, June 3   *Litho.*
1246 A326 $1 Sheet of 5, #a-e   9.50 9.50
Tel Aviv 2013 International Stamp Exhibition.

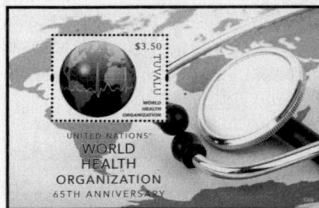

World Health Organization, 65th
Anniv. — A327

No. 1247 — Globe and inscription: a, World Tuberculosis Day. b, World Immunization

Week. c, World Health Day. d, World AIDS Day. e, World No Tobacco Day. f, World Blood Donor Day.

$3.50, Globe and inscription "World Health Organization."

2013, June 25
1247	A327	90c Sheet of 6, #a-f		10.00 10.00

Souvenir Sheet
1248	A327	$3.50 multi	6.50	6.50

Dolphins — A328

No. 1249: a, Short-finned pilot whale. b, Risso's dolphin. c, Pacific white-sided dolphin. d, Northern right whale dolphin.
$3.50, Melon-headed whale.

2013, July 24   *Perf. 12*
1249	A328	$1.25 Sheet of 4, #a-d		9.00 9.00

Souvenir Sheet
1250	A328	$3.50 multi	6.50	6.50

Miniature Sheets

Fish — A329

No. 1251, $1.25: a, Blue-head fairy wrasse. b, Clownfish. c, Clown triggorfish. d, Cupperband butterflyfish.
No. 1252, $1.25: a, Scribbled angelfish. b, Flame angelfish. c, Harlequin tuskfish. d, Flameback angelfish.

2013, July 24   *Perf. 13¾*
Sheets of 4, #a-d
1251-1252	A329	Set of 2	18.00	18.00

Temples of Thailand — A330

No. 1253: a, Wat Pha Sorn Kaew. b, Wat Pho. c, Wat Phra Kaew. d, Wat Phra Singh.
$3.50, Wat Suthat.

2013, July 30   Litho.
1253	A330	$1.20 Sheet of 4, #a-d		8.75 8.75

Souvenir Sheet
1254	A330	$3.50 multi	6.50	6.50

Thailand 2013 World Stamp Exhibition, Bangkok.

Coronation of Queen Elizabeth II, 60th Anniv. — A331

No. 1255 — Queen Elizabeth II: a, Waving. b, Wearing tiara. c, Wearing white hat. d, Watching young Prince Charles at play.
$3.50, Queen Elizabeth II, diff.

2013, Oct. 7   Litho.   *Perf. 13¾*
1255	A331	$1.20 Sheet of 4, #a-d		9.25 9.25

Souvenir Sheet
1256	A331	$3.50 multi	6.75	6.75

Birth of Prince George of Cambridge — A332

No. 1257: a, Duke and Duchess of Cambridge, Prince George. b, Prince Charles, Princess Diana, Prince William. c, Princess Diana holding Prince William. d, Duchess of Cambridge holding Prince George.
$3.50, Duke and Duchess of Cambridge, Prince George, diff.

2013, Oct. 7   Litho.   *Perf. 14*
1257	A332	$1.20 Sheet of 4, #a-d		9.25 9.25

Souvenir Sheet
Perf. 12
1258	A332	$3.50 multi	6.75	6.75

Miniature Sheet

Elvis Presley (1935-77) — A333

No. 1259: a, Album cover for *Elvis' Christmas Album*, Presley to right of text. b, Presley playing guitar. c, Album cover for *Elvis' Christmas Album*, Presley to left of text. d, *Frankie and Johnny* album cover. e, *G.I. Blues* album cover. f, *Girl Happy* album cover.

2013, Dec. 2   Litho.   *Perf. 13¾*
1259	A333	90c Sheet of 6, #a-f		9.75 9.75

Orange Blossom Special — A334

2013, Dec. 9   Litho.   *Perf. 12½*
1260	A334	60c multi	1.10	1.10

Souvenir Sheet
Perf. 13½
1261	A334	$3.50 multi	6.25	6.25

No. 1260 was printed in sheets of 9. No. 1261 contains one 38x51mm stamp.

Meeting of Pres. Barack Obama and Queen Elizabeth II — A335

No. 1262: a, Queen Elizabeth II. b, Pres. Barack Obama. c, Michelle Obama. d, Prince Philip.
No. 1263, horiz.: a, Pres. Obama. b, Michelle Obama.
$3.50, Queen Elizabeth II and Pres. Obama.

Perf. 12½, 13½ (#1263)
2013, Dec. 9   Litho.
1262	A335	$1.20 Sheet of 4, #a-d		8.75 8.75
1263	A335	$1.75 Sheet of 2, #a-b		6.25 6.25

Souvenir Sheet
1264	A335	$3.50 multi	6.25	6.25

No. 1263 contains two 51x38mm stamps.

A336

Nelson Mandela (1918-2013), President of South Africa — A337

No. 1266 — South African flag and Mandela: a, With fist raised, sign at right. b, With fist raised, standing at lectern. c, Wearing suit and tie. d, Standing in crowd with fist raised, man to Mandela's right. e, Waving at crowd, wife, Winnie, to Mandela's right. f, Holding on to railing.

2013, Dec. 15   Litho.   *Perf. 13¾*
1265	A336	$1 multi	1.90	1.90
1266	A337	$1 Sheet of 6, #a-f	11.00	11.00

No. 1265 was printed in sheets of 6.

Pope John Paul II (1920-2005) — A338

No. 1267 — Pope John Paul II with denomination in: a, Black. b, White.
$3.50, Pope John Paul II, horiz.

2013, Dec. 23   Litho.   *Perf. 14*
1267	A338	$1.20 Horiz. pair, #a-b		4.25 4.25

Souvenir Sheet
1268	A338	$3.50 multi	6.25	6.25

No. 1267 was printed in sheets containing two pairs.

World War I, Cent. — A339

No. 1269: a, Army Recruiting Office, Southwark, London, England, 1915. b, U.S. Sergeant Alvin C. York, 1919. c, Victory parade, London, 1919. d, French soldier at Battle of Verdun wearing gas mask, 1916. e, U.S. General John J. Pershing, 1918. f, Women working in ammunition factory, France, 1914.
$4, U.S. Army recruiting poster, vert.

2014, Mar. 5   Litho.   *Perf. 13¾*
1269	A339	$1.20 Sheet of 6, #a-f		13.50 13.50

Souvenir Sheet
Perf. 12½
1270	A339	$4 multi	7.50	7.50

No. 1270 contains one 38x51mm stamp.

Characters From *Downton Abbey* Television Series — A340

No. 1271: a, Sir Richard Carlisle. b, Lady Mary Crawley. c, Matthew Crawley. d, Dr. Richard Clarkson.
$3.50, Matthew Crawley and Lady Mary Crawley, horiz.

2014, Mar. 5   Litho.   *Perf. 14*
1271	A340	$1.20 Sheet of 4, #a-d		9.00 9.00

Souvenir Sheet
1272	A340	$3.50 multi	6.50	6.50

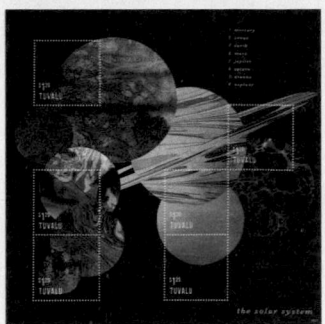

Solar System — A341

No. 1273: a, Jupiter. b, Neptune, rings of Saturn. c, Earth and Venus. d, Saturn and Uranus. e, Venus and Mercury. f, Uranus.
$4.50, Sun.

2014, Mar. 24   Litho.   Perf. 13¾
1273 A341 $1.20 Sheet of 6,
　　#a-f　　　　　13.50 13.50
Souvenir Sheet
1274 A341 $4.50 multi　　8.50 8.50

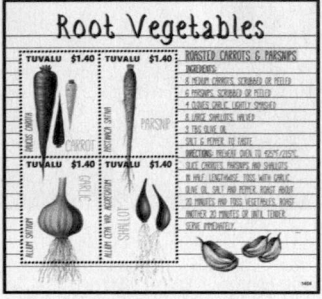

Vegetables — A342

No. 1275, $1.40: a, Carrots. b, Parsnip. c, Garlic. d, Shallots.
No. 1276, $1.40: a, Kohlrabi. b, Turnip. c, Sweet potato. d, Onion.
No. 1277, $2.25, horiz.: a, Radishes. b, Fennel.
No. 1278, $2.25, horiz.: a, Potato. b, Leek.

2014, Apr. 23   Litho.   Perf. 14
Sheets of 4, #a-d
1275-1276 A342　Set of 2　21.00 21.00
Souvenir Sheets of 2, #a-b
1277-1278 A342　Set of 2　17.00 17.00

Giant Pacific Octopus — A343

No. 1279: Various photographs of octopus, as shown.
$4.50, Octopus, vert.

2014, May 8   Litho.   Perf. 13¾
1279 A343　50c Block of 4, #a-d 3.75 3.75
Souvenir Sheet
Perf. 12¾
1280 A343 $4.50 multi　　　8.50 8.50
No. 1280 contains one 38x51mm stamp.

Meeting of Queen Elizabeth II and Pope Francis A344

Designs: No. 1281, Queen Elizabeth II and Pope Francis shaking hands, orange yellow frame.
No. 1282: a, Queen Elizabeth II, Prince Philip and Pope Francis shaking hands, tan frame. b, Queen Elizabeth II and Pope Francis, flowers in background, green frame. c, Queen Elizabeth II and Pope Francis seated, green frame. d, Queen Elizabeth II, Prince Philip, Pope Francis and other men, tan background.
$3.50, Queen Elizabeth II and Pope Francis, vert.

2014, July 21   Litho.   Perf. 14
1281 A344 $1.20 multi　　　2.25 2.25
1282 A344 $1.20 Sheet of 4, #a-
　　d　　　　　　　9.00 9.00
Souvenir Sheet
Perf. 12¾
1283 A344 $3.50 multi　　　6.50 6.50
No. 1281 was printed in sheets of 4. No. 1283 contains one 38x51mm stamp.

A345

A346

A347

Canonization of Pope John Paul II — A348

Various photographs of Pope John Paul II, as shown.

2014, July 21   Litho.   Perf. 14
1284 A345 $1.40 Sheet of 4,
　　#a-d　　　　　10.50 10.50
1285 A346 $1.40 Sheet of 4,
　　#a-d　　　　　10.50 10.50
Souvenir Sheets
1286 A347 $2.25 Sheet of 2,
　　#a-b　　　　　8.50 8.50
1287 A348 $2.25 Sheet of 2,
　　#a-b　　　　　8.50 8.50

Ducks — A349

No. 1288, $1.40: a, Mandarin duck facing right. b, Mandarin duck facing left. c, Mandarin duck with wing extended. d, Mandarin duck in water.
No. 1289, $1.40: a, Female wood duck. b, Mallard. c, Male wood duck. d, Mandarin duck facing left, diff.
No. 1290, $2.25: a, Wood duck, diff. b, Mandarin duck, diff.
No. 1291, $2.25, vert.: a, Mallard. b, Mandarin duck, diff.

2014, July 21   Litho.   Perf. 14
Sheets of 4, #a-d
1288-1289 A349　Set of 2　21.00 21.00
Souvenir Sheets of 2, #a-b
1290-1291 A349　Set of 2　17.00 17.00

Fall of the Berlin Wall, 25th Anniv. — A350

No. 1292 — Berlin Wall graffiti depicting: a, Red bear. b, Animal with boxing gloves, graffiti artist. c, Stylized flower and cartoon balloon. d, Woman wearing cap.
$5, "Change Your Life."

2014, Aug. 14   Litho.   Perf. 14
1292 A350 $1.40 Sheet of 4,
　　#a-d　　　　　10.50 10.50
Souvenir Sheet
Perf. 12¾
1293 A350　$5 multi　　　9.25 9.25
No. 1293 contains one 38x51mm stamp.

A351

Macaws — A352

Nos. 1294 and 1295: a-f, Macaw with different feather lines and colors in background, as shown.
No. 1296, horiz. — Macaw with denomination at: a, Right. b, Left.
$4.50, Macaw, diff.

2014, Aug. 14   Litho.   Perf. 14
1294 A351 $1.40 Sheet of 6,
　　#a-f　　　　　15.50 15.50
1295 A352 $1.40 Sheet of 6,
　　#a-f　　　　　15.50 15.50

Souvenir Sheets
Perf. 12¾
1296 A352 $2.25 Sheet of 2,
　　#a-b　　　　　8.50 8.50
1297 A352 $4.50 multi　　8.50 8.50
No. 1296 contains two 51x38mm stamps.
No. 1297 contains one 38x51mm stamp.

Paintings — A353

No. 1298, $1.50: a, The Large Blue Horses, by Franz Marc. b, The Avenue in the Port at Saint-Cloud, by Henri Rousseau. c, Tulips in a Vase, by Paul Cézanne.
No. 1299, $1.50: a, Woman Reading, by Henri Matisse. b, Pyramid of Skulls, by Cézanne. c, Self-portrait with Pipe, by Vincent van Gogh.
No. 1300, $4.50, Nighthawks, by Edward Hopper. No. 1301, $4.50, Portrait of Père Tanguy, by van Gogh.

2014, Aug. 14   Litho.   Perf. 12¾
Sheets of 3, #a-c
1298-1299 A353　Set of 2　17.00 17.00
Imperf
Size: 100x100mm
1300-1301 A353　Set of 2　17.00 17.00

Sharks — A354

No. 1302, $1.40: a, Whale shark. b, Hammerhead shark. c, Caribbean reef shark. d, Great white shark.
No. 1303, $1.40: a, Whitetip shark. b, Gray reef shark. c, Leopard shark. d, Tiger shark.
No. 1304: a, Whale shark, diff. b, Gray reef shark, diff.
$4.50, Blacktip reef shark.

Perf. 14, 12¾ (#1303, 1305)
2014, Sept. 3   Litho.
Sheets of 4, #a-d
1302-1303 A354　Set of 2　20.00 20.00
Souvenir Sheets
1304 A354 $2.25 Sheet of 2,
　　#a-b　　　　　8.00 8.00
1305 A354 $4.50 multi　　8.00 8.00
No. 1303 contains four 51x38mm stamps.
No. 1305 contains one 51x38mm stamp.

A355

A356

A357

Sea Turtles — A358

Various sea turtles, as shown.

2014, Sept. 3	Litho.		Perf. 12
1306	A355	$1.40 Sheet of 4, #a-d	10.00 10.00
1307	A356	$1.40 Sheet of 4, #a-d	10.00 10.00

Souvenir Sheets
Perf. 12¾

1308	A357	$2.25 Sheet of 2, #a-b	8.00 8.00
1309	A358	$2.25 Sheet of 2, #a-b	8.00 8.00

Christmas
A359

Paintings by Peter Paul Rubens: $1.40, The Adoration of the Magi. $1.50, The Elevation of the Cross. $1.75, Adoration of the Shepherds. $2.25, The Holy Family.

2014, Nov. 24	Litho.	Perf. 13¼
1310-1313	A359 Set of 4	12.00 12.00

Surfing — A360

No. 1314, $1.40 — Various silhouettes of surfers with central background color of: a, Light blue green. b, Blue violet. c, Red. d, Bister.

No. 1315, $1.40, horiz. — Surfboards decorated with: a, Palm tree and sun. b, Flowers and wave. c, Vine and stripes. d, Waves.

No. 1316, $2.25 — Various silhouettes of surfers with central background color of: a, Light blue green (surfer's hands visible). b, Blue (surfer's hands not visible).

No. 1317, $2.25, horiz. — Surfboards decorated with: a, Waves, diff. b, Vine.

Perf. 13¾, 12 (#1315, 1317)
2014, Dec. 16	Litho.

Sheets of 4, #a-d

1314-1315	A360 Set of 2	18.50 18.50

Souvenir Sheets of 2, #a-b

1316-1317	A360 Set of 2	15.00 15.00

Nos. 1316 and 1317 each contain two 50x30mm stamps.

Inaugural Mass of Pope Benedict XVI — A361

No. 1318 — Pope Benedict XVI: a, On steps. b, Wearing zucchetto, waving. c, Swinging censer. d, Wearing miter, waving.
$4.50, Pope Benedict XVI waving, diff.

2014, Dec. 31	Litho.	Perf. 14
1318	A361 $1.40 Sheet of 4, #a-d	9.25 9.25

Souvenir Sheet
Perf. 12

1319	A361 $4.50 multi	7.25 7.25

No. 1319 contains one 30x50mm stamp.

Souvenir Sheet

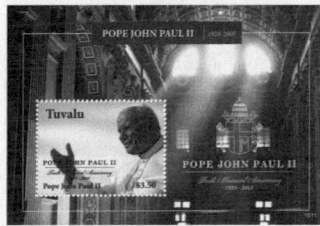

St. John Paul II (1920-2005) — A362

2015, Feb. 2	Litho.	Perf. 14
1320	A362 $3.50 multi	5.50 5.50

Corals — A363

No. 1321: a, Bubble coral. b, Frogspawn coral. c, Mushroom coral. d, Brain coral. $4.50, Coral on giant clam.

2015, Feb. 2	Litho.	Perf. 14
1321	A363 $1.40 Sheet of 4, #a-d	8.75 8.75

Souvenir Sheet
Perf. 12

1322	A363 $4.50 multi	7.00 7.00

Tropical Fish — A364

No. 1323, $1.75: a, Flame angelfish. b, Passer angelfish. c, Palette surgeonfish. d, Scribbled angelfish.

No. 1324, $1.75: a, Clown triggerfish. b, Powder blue surgeonfish. c, Clown anemonefish. d, Emperor angelfish.

No. 1325, $2.25: a, Southern orange-lined cardinalfish. b, Yellow tang.

No. 1326, $2.25: a, Coral grouper. b, Fire clownfish.

2015, Mar. 2	Litho.	Perf. 14

Sheets of 4, #a-d

1323-1324	A364 Set of 2	22.00 22.00

Souvenir Sheets of 2, #a-b
Perf. 12¾

1325-1326	A364 Set of 2	14.00 14.00

Nos. 1325-1326 each contain two 51x38mm stamps.

Trees and Their Fruits — A365

No. 1327: a, Coconut tree. b, Papaya tree. c, Banana tree. d, Coconuts. e, Papaya. f, Bananas.

No. 1328: a, Pandanus tectorius tree. b, Pandanus tectorius fruit.

2015, Mar. 2	Litho.	Perf. 13¾
1327	A365 $1.40 Sheet of 6, #a-f	13.50 13.50

Souvenir Sheet

1328	A365 $2.25 Sheet of 2, #a-b	7.00 7.00

Paintings of World War I Scenes — A366

No. 1329, $1.40 — Details from *Gassed,* by John Singer Sargent: a, Soldiers with bandaged eyes, middle soldier carrying rifle on shoulder. b, Soldiers with bandaged eyes, all wearing helmets. c, Soldiers, man at left holding backpack of another soldier. d, Line of soldiers in distance.

No. 1330, $1.40 — Paintings by Alfred Théodore Joseph Bastien: a, *Cavalry and Tanks at Arras, 1918* (51x38mm). b, *Canadian Sentry, Moonlight, Neuville-Vitasse* (51x76mm). c, *Throwing Grenades* (51x38mm). d, *Canadian Cavalry Ready in a Wood* (51x38mm).

No. 1331, $4.50, *Street in Arras,* by Sargent. No. 1332, $4.50, *Canadian Gunners in the Mud,* by Bastien.

Perf. 13¾ (#1329), 12¾
2015, Mar. 2	Litho.

Sheets of 4, #a-d

1329-1330	A366 Set of 2	17.50 17.50

Souvenir Sheets

1331-1332	A366 Set of 2	14.00 14.00

Nos. 1331-1332 each contain one 51x38mm stamp.

Sites in London — A367

No. 1333: a, Tower Bridge. b, London Eye. c, Westminster Abbey. d, Buckingham Palace. e, Saint Paul's Cathedral. $4.50, Palace of Westminster.

2015, Apr. 13	Litho.	Perf. 14
1333	A367 $1.40 Sheet of 5, #a-e	11.50 11.50

Souvenir Sheet
Perf. 12

1334	A367 $4.50 multi	7.25 7.25

2015 Europhilex Stamp Exhibition, London. No. 1334 contains one 80x30mm stamp.

Pope Francis Presiding Over Feb. 14, 2015 Consistory — A368

No. 1335: a, Pope Francis and Pope Benedict XVI. b, Pope Benedict XVI. c, Pope Francis blessing cardinal. d, Back of Pope Francis, Pope Benedict XVI.
$4.50, Pope Francis at pulpit.

2015, May 4	Litho.	Perf. 14
1335	A368 $1.40 Sheet of 4, #a-d	9.00 9.00

Souvenir Sheet

1336	A368 $4.50 multi	7.25 7.25

Birth of Princess Charlotte of Cambridge — A369

No. 1337: a, Princess Elizabeth and Prince Charles. b, Duke and Duchess of Cambridge with Prince George. c, Princess Charlotte of Cambridge. d, Prince Charles, Princess Diana holding Prince William.
$4.50, Duchess of Cambridge and Princess Charlotte.

2015, May 25   Litho.   Perf. 12
1337 A369 $1.40 Sheet of 4, #a-
          d   8.75 8.75
      Souvenir Sheet
1338 A369 $4.50 multi   7.00 7.00

Long-Reigning British Monarchs — A370

No. 1339: a, Queen Victoria. b, Queen Elizabeth II. c, King George III. d, King George V. e, King George VI. f, King George IV. g, King Edward VII. h, King William IV.
$4.50, Queen Elizabeth II, diff.

2015, May 25   Litho.   Perf. 12¾
1339 A370 $1 Sheet of 8,
          #a-h   12.50 12.50
      Souvenir Sheet
1340 A370 $4.50 multi   7.00 7.00

Italian World War II Aircraft — A371

No. 1341: a, Reggiane Re. 2005 Sagittario. b, CANT Z.501 Gabbiano. c, Macchi C.200 Saetta. d, Savoia-Marchetti SM.81 Pipistrello.
$4.50, CANT Z.1007bis Alcione, vert.

2015, May 25   Litho.   Perf. 12
1341 A371 $1.40 Sheet of 4, #a-
          d   8.75 8.75
      Souvenir Sheet
1342 A371 $4.50 multi   7.00 7.00
No. 1342 contains one 30x40mm stamp.

Lee Kuan Yew (1923-2015), Prime Minister of Singapore — A372

No. 1343 — Lee Kuan Yew: a, With microphone at left. b, In black-and-white photograph. c, Wearing blue and red robe. d, With microphone stand at LR. e, Waring black jacket.
$4.50, Lee Kuan Yew, diff.

2015, May 25   Litho.   Perf. 14
1343 A372 $1.40 Sheet of 5,
          #a-e   11.00 11.00
      Souvenir Sheet
      Perf. 12¾
1344 A372 $4.50 multi   7.00 7.00
No. 1344 contains one 38x51mm stamp.

Birds — A373

No. 1345: a, Red-footed booby. b, Bar-tailed godwit. c, Buff-banded rail. d, Brown noddy. e, Red-tailed tropicbird. f, Greater crested tern.
$4.50, Great frigatebird.

2015, May 25   Litho.   Perf. 12
1345 A373 $1.40 Sheet of 6,
          #a-f   13.00 13.00
      Souvenir Sheet
1346 A373 $4.50 multi   7.00 7.00

Sites in Singapore — A374

No. 1347: a, Chinese Garden. b, Cloud Forest, Gadens by the Bay. c, Pulau Ubin. d, Swan Lake. e, Da Bogong Temple, Kusu Island. f, Super Trees, Gardens by the Bay.
$4.50, Chinese Garden, diff.

2015, Aug. 3   Litho.   Perf. 12
1347 A374 $1.40 Sheet of 6,
          #a-f   12.50 12.50
      Souvenir Sheet
1348 A374 $4.50 multi   6.50 6.50
Singapore 2015 Intl. Stamp Exhibition.

Waterfalls — A375

No. 1349: a, Erawan Falls, Thailand. b, Rio Celeste Waterfall, Costa Rica. c, Krushuna's Waterfalls, Bulgaria. d, Kamienczyk Waterfall, Poland.
$4.50, Air Terjun Tiu Kelep Waterfall, Indonesia.

2015, Sept. 8   Litho.   Perf. 13½
1349 A375 $1.40 Sheet of 4, #a-
          d   8.00 8.00
      Souvenir Sheet
1350 A375 $4.50 multi   6.50 6.50

Humpback Whales — A376

No. 1351 — Various whales, as shown.
$4.50, Two Humpback whales, vert.

2015, Nov. 2   Litho.   Perf. 12
1351 A376 $1.40 Sheet of 6,
          #a-f   12.00 12.00
      Souvenir Sheet
1352 A376 $4.50 multi   6.50 6.50

Gold Medalists in 1896 Olympics — A377

No. 1353: a, William Welles Hoyt (1875-1954), pole vaulter, U.S. b, Launceston Elliot (1874-1930), weight lifter, Great Britain. c, Léon Flameng (1877-1917), cyclist, France. d, Sumner Paine (1868-1904), shooter, U.S.
$4.50, John Boland (1870-1958), tennis player, Great Britain.

2016, Jan. 18   Litho.   Perf. 14
1353 A377 $1.40 Sheet of 4, #a-
          d   8.00 8.00

      Souvenir Sheet
      Perf. 12¾
1354 A377 $4.50 multi   6.50 6.50
No. 1354 contains one 38x51mm stamp.

Pope Francis in Africa — A378

No. 1355 — Pope Francis: a, With curved rail at UR. b, With curved rail and flowers at UR. c, Standing with military officers. d, Holding railing and waving. e, Behind pulpit, waving with both hands. f, Walking with Kenyan Pres. Uhuru Kenyatta and his wife.
$4.50, Pope Francis, diff.

2016, Jan. 28   Litho.   Perf. 14
1355 A378 $1.40 Sheet of 6,
          #a-f   12.00 12.00
      Souvenir Sheet
      Perf.
1356 A378 $4.50 multi   6.50 6.50
No. 1356 contains one 33x43mm oval stamp.

Female Characters in *Star Trek* Television Shows — A379

No. 1357: a, Chief Medical Officer Beverly Crusher. b, Communications Officer Nyota Uhura. c, Captain Kathryn Janeway. d, Communications Officer Hoshi Sato. e, Deep Space 9 First Officer Kira Nerys. f, Science Officer Jadzia Dax.
$4.50, Former Borg Drone Seven of Nine.

2016, Jan. 28   Litho.   Perf. 12
1357 A379 $1.40 Sheet of 6,
          #a-f   12.00 12.00
      Souvenir Sheet
1358 A379 $4.50 multi   6.50 6.50

      Souvenir Sheets

Elvis Presley (1935-77) — A380

Inscriptions: No. 1359, $4.50, Receives five gold records at once. No. 1360, $4.50, Shipping out for Germany.

2016, Jan. 28   Litho.   Perf. 12
1359-1360 A380 Set of 2   13.00 13.00

Muhammad Ali (1942-2016),
Boxer — A381

Various photographs of Ali.

2016, Jan. 28   Litho.   Perf. 12
1361 A381 $1.40 Sheet of 4, #a-
d   8.00 8.00
Souvenir Sheet
1362 A381 $4.50 multi   6.50 6.50
No. 1362 contains one 51x38mm stamp.

A382

A383

A384

Common
Thresher
Shark
A385

2016, Apr. 1   Litho.   Perf. 14
1363   Strip of 4   9.75 9.75
a. A382 $1.50 multi   2.40 2.40
b. A383 $1.50 multi   2.40 2.40
c. A384 $1.50 multi   2.40 2.40
d. A385 $1.50 multi   2.40 2.40
e. Souvenir sheet of 8, 2 each
   #1363a-1363d   19.50 19.50
Worldwide Fund for Nature (WWF).

New York City Landmarks — A386

No. 1364: a, Brooklyn Bridge. b, Grand Central Terminal. c, Gapstow Bridge, Central Park. $7, New York City skyline.

2016, Apr. 29   Litho.   Perf. 12½
1364 A386 $2.50 Sheet of 3,
     #a-c   11.50 11.50

Souvenir Sheet
Perf. 14
1365 A386 $7 multi   11.00 11.00
2016 World Stamp Show, New York. No. 1364 contains one 120x40mm stamp.

A387

Visit of U.S. President Barack Obama
to Cuba — A388

No. 1000. a, Cuban Pres. Raul Castro (40x30mm). b, Pres. Obama (40x30mm). c, Presidents Castro and Obama (40x30mm). d, Pres. Castro, Pres. Obama and wife, Michelle (40x30mm). e, Presidents Obama and Castro, flags of Cuba and U.S. (80x30mm).
No. 1367 — Pres. Obama: a, With microphone at left of tie. b, Waving, no fingers visible. c, With microphone at right of tie. d, Waving, fingers visible.
No. 1368, vert.: a, Pres. Obama. b, Pres. Castro.

2016, Sept. 23   Litho.   Perf. 14
1366 A387 $2 Sheet of 5, #a-e 15.50 15.50
1367 A388 $2 Sheet of 4, #a-d 12.50 12.50
Souvenir Sheet
Perf. 12
1368 A388 $3 Sheet of 2, #a-b 9.25 9.25
No. 1368 contains two 30x50mm stamps.

Purchase of Alaska by the U.S., 150th
Anniv. (in 2017) — A389

No. 1369: a, Tracy Arm Fjord. b, Aurora Borealis. c, Glacier Bay National Park. d, Denali National Park. e, Lake Clark National Park. f, Mendenhall Glacier and fireweed meadow.
$5.50, Denali National Park, vert.

2016, Dec. 30   Litho.   Perf. 14
1369 A389 $1.80 Sheet of 6,
     #a-f   15.50 15.50
Souvenir Sheet
Perf. 12½
1370 A389 $5.50 multi   8.00 8.00
No. 1370 contains one 38x51mm stamp.

Star Trek Television Series, 50th
Anniv. — A390

No. 1371 — Scenes featuring Lieutenant Uhura from episodes: a, Plato's Stepchildren. b, Mirror, Mirror. c, The Trouble with Tribbles. d, The Conscience of the King. $5.50, The Changeling, horiz.

2016, Dec. 30   Litho.   Perf. 14
1371 A390 $2.50 Sheet of 4,
     #a-d   14.50 14.50
Souvenir Sheet
Perf. 12½
1372 A390 $5.50 multi   8.00 8.00
No. 1372 contains one 51x38mm stamp.

Miniature Sheets

Thailand King Bhumibol Adulyadej
(1927-2016) — A391

No. 1373 — Various photographs of King Bhumibol Adulyadej and Queen Sirikit, as shown.
No. 1374 — King Bhumibol Adulyadej with: a, Queen Elizabeth II (black-and-white photograph). b, Queen Elizabeth II (color photograph). c, Pres. George W. Bush. d, Pres. Bill Clinton and wife, Hillary. e, Russian President Vladimir Putin. f, French President Jacques Chirac.

2017, Jan. 11   Litho.   Perf. 14
1373 A391 $2.50 Sheet of 4,
     #a-d   15.00 15.00
1374 A391 $2.50 Sheet of 6,
     #a-f   23.00 23.00

Shimon Peres (1923-2016), President
of Israel — A392

No. 1375: a, Pres. Barack Obama. b, Pres. Peres, U.S. flag in background. c, Peres and Senator Hillary Clinton. d, Peres, soldier in background. e, Obama, soldier in background. f, Benjamin Netanyahu, Prime Minister of Israel.

2017, Feb. 15   Litho.   Perf. 14
1375 A392 $1.80 Sheet of 6,
     #a-f   16.50 16.50

Jellyfish — A393

No. 1376: a, Northern sea nettle. b, Lion's mane jellyfish. c, Mauve stinger. d, Jelly blubber.
No. 1377: a, White-spotted jellyfish. b, Sea wasp.

2017, Feb. 15   Litho.   Perf. 13¾
1376 A393 $2.50 Sheet of 4,
     #a-d   15.50 15.50
Souvenir Sheet
1377 A393 $4.50 Sheet of 2,
     #a-b   14.00 14.00

Miniature Sheet

Environmental Protection — A394

No. 1378: a, Lightbulb. b, Two bottles. c, Recycling bin. d, Water faucet. e, Shopping bag. f, Recycling emblem.

Perf. 13¼x12½
2017, Feb. 28   Litho.
1378 A394 $1.80 Sheet of 6,
     #a-f   16.50 16.50

Miniature Sheets

A395

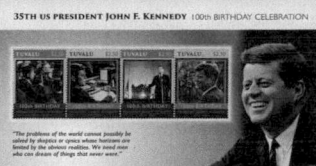

Pres. John F. Kennedy (1917-
63) — A396

No. 1379 — Pres. Kennedy: a, With wife, Jacqueline, at their wedding. b, With wife, and daughter, Caroline (black-and-white photograph). c, With wife and daughter on lawn. d, With wife and daughter, cane chair in background.
No. 1380 — Pres. Kennedy: a, Taking oath of office. b, Sitting at desk, photographer in background. c, Standing behind microphone. d, Standing, photographer in background.

2017, Apr. 14   Litho.   Perf. 14
1379 A395 $2.50 Sheet of 4,
     #a-d   15.00 15.00
1380 A396 $2.50 Sheet of 4,
     #a-d   15.00 15.00

Miniature Sheets

A398

Princess Diana (1961-97) — A399

No. 1383 — Princess Diana wearing: a, Black hat with brim. b, White hat with black ribbon. c. Light blue hat. d, Dark green brimless hat.

No. 1384 — Princess Diana wearing: a, Sailor's cap with crest. b, Black and white hat with wide brim. c, White hat. d, Red Cross uniform.

2017, June 26   Litho.   Perf. 14
1383 A398 $2.50 Sheet of 4,
    #a-d   15.50 15.50
1384 A399 $2.50 Sheet of 4,
    #a-d   15.50 15.50

Octopi — A400

No. 1385: a, Caribbean reef octopus. b, Dumbo octopus. c, Longarm octopus. d, White-spotted octopus.
No. 1386: a, Common octopus. b, Blanket octopus.

Perf. 12½x13¼
2017, Sept. 11   Litho.
1385 A400 $2.50 Sheet of 4,
    #a-d   16.00 16.00
    Souvenir Sheet
1386 A400 $4 Sheet of 2,
    #a-b   12.50 12.50

A401

World War II, 75th Anniv. A402

No. 1387: a, Allied troops in the South Pacific. b, Troops and native carriers on Kokoda Trail.
No. 1388: a, Allied troops in the South Pacific, diff. b, Troops and native carriers.

2017, Oct. 26   Litho.   Perf. 14
1387 A401 $2.50 Pair, #a-b   7.75 7.75
1388 A402 $2.50 Pair, #a-b   7.75 7.75
Nos. 1387-1388 were each printed in sheets containing two pairs.

Hayabusa 2 Space Mission — A403

No. 1389: a, Hayabusa sample collector. b, Hayabusa 2 near 1999 JU3 asteroid, Minerva on asteroid. c, Hayabusa 2 near asteroid. d, Hayabusa 2 returning to Earth.
$5.50, Launch of Hayabusa 2, vert.

2017, Oct. 26   Litho.   Perf. 14
1389 A403 $2.50 Sheet of 4,
    #a-d   15.50 15.50
    Souvenir Sheet
    Perf. 12
1390 A403 $5.50 multi   8.50 8.50

Saltwater Rays — A404

No. 1391: a, Devil ray. b, Reef manta ray. c, Cownose ray. d, Spotted eagle ray. e, Blue-spotted stingray.
$5.50, Giant oceanic manta ray.

2017, Oct. 26   Litho.   Perf.
1391 A404 $2 Sheet of 5,
    #a-e   15.50 15.50
    Souvenir Sheet
    Perf. 12½
1392 A404 $5.50 Sheet of 2,
    #a-b   8.50 8.50
No. 1392 contains one 51x38mm stamp.

Dolphins — A405

No. 1393: a, Three Bottlenose dolphins. b, Head of Bottlenose dolphin. c, Two Bottlenose dolphins. d, Bottlenose dolphin and Atlantic spotted dolphin.
No. 1394, vert.: a, Bottlenose dolphin. b, Bottlenose dolphin and Atlantic spotted dolphin.

2017, Dec. 4   Litho.   Perf. 14
1393 A405 $2.50 Sheet of 4,
    #a-d   16.00 16.00
    Souvenir Sheet
    Perf. 12½
1394 A405 $4 Sheet of 2,
    #a-b   12.50 12.50
No. 1394 contains two 38x51mm stamps.

Butterflies — A406

No. 1395: a, Pearl-bordered fritillary. b, Small tortoiseshell. c, Old world swallowtail. d, American painted lady.
$5.50, Common blue butterfly.

2017, Dec. 4   Litho.   Perf. 13¾
1395 A406 $2.50 Sheet of 4,
    #a-d   16.00 16.00
    Souvenir Sheet
    Perf.
1396 A406 $5.50 multi   8.75 8.75
No. 1396 contains one 38mm diameter stamp.

Underwater Caves — A407

No. 1397: a, Two divers in Chan Hol, Mexico. b, Orda Cave, Russia. c, South China Sea, Malaysia. d, One diver in Chan Hol.
No. 1398: a, Tux Kubaxa, Mexico. b, Cabo de Gata, Spain.

2017, Dec. 4   Litho.   Perf. 14
1397 A407 $2.50 Sheet of 4,
    #a-d   16.00 16.00
    Souvenir Sheet
    Perf. 12½
1398 A407 $4 Sheet of 2,
    #a-b   12.50 12.50
No. 1398 contains two 51x38mm stamps.

A408

Tuvalu Beaches — A409

Various photographs of beaches, as shown.

2017, Dec. 26   Litho.   Perf. 14
1399 A408 $2.50 Sheet of 4,
    #a-d   16.00 16.00
    Souvenir Sheet
    Perf. 12
1400 A409 $2.50 Sheet of 3,
    #a-c   12.00 12.00

Elvis Presley (1935-77) A410

No. 1401 — Presley in movies: a, Stay Away Joe. b, Harum Scarum. c, Roustabout.

2017, Dec. 26   Litho.   Perf. 13¾
1401   Horiz. strip of 3   8.50 8.50
    a. A410 $1.50 multi   2.40 2.40
    b. A410 $1.80 multi   2.75 2.75
    c. A410 $2 multi   3.25 3.25
Printed in sheets containing 2 each Nos. 1401a-1401c.

Miniature Sheet

Wedding of Queen Elizabeth II and Prince Philip, 70th Anniv. — A411

No. 1402: a, Queen Elizabeth II wearing wedding dress. b, Wedding dress and tiara. c, Queen Elizabeth II and Prince Philip on wedding day. d, Engagement ring.

2017, Dec. 26   Litho.   Perf. 12
1402 A411 $2.50 Sheet of 4,
    #a-d   16.00 16.00

Miniature Sheet

Visit to South Korea of Pres. Donald Trump — A412

No. 1403: a, U.S. First Lady Melania Trump. b, Pres. Trump. c, South Korean Pres. Moon Jae-in. c, South Korean First Lady Kim Jung-sook.

2018, Jan. 24   Litho.   Perf. 12
1403 A412 $2.50 Sheet of 4,
#a-d   16.00 16.00

A413

A414

Inauguration of Pres. Donald Trump — A415

No. 1404: a, Melania Trump and Karen Pence. b, Pres. Trump and Vice-President Mike Pence. c, Pres. Barack Obama and Vice-President Joe Biden. d, Michelle Obama and Jill Biden. e, Melania Trump. f, Pres. Trump. g, Pres. Obama. h, Michelle Obama.
No. 1405: a, $2, Ivanka Trump (30x40mm). b, $2, Jared Kushner (30x40mm). c, $3, Melania Trump (30x40mm). d, $4, Pres. Trump (30x40mm). e, $5, Pres. Trump speaking before Congress (60x40mm).
No. 1406: a, $3, Vice-President Pence and his wife, Karen. b, $4, Presidential Seal. c, $5, Pres. Trump and wife, Melania.

2018, Mar. 21   Litho.   Perf. 14
1404 A413 $2 Sheet of 8, #a-h   26.00 26.00
1405 A414   Sheet of 5, #a-e   26.00 26.00
Souvenir Sheet
Perf. 12½
1406 A415   Sheet of 3, #a-c   19.50 19.50

Souvenir Sheet

Engagement of Prince Harry and Meghan Markle — A416

2018, Mar. 21   Litho.   Perf. 12½
1407 A416 $5.50 multi   8.50 8.50

Starfish — A417

No. 1408: a, Knobby star. b, Crown-of-thorns starfish. c, Chocolate chip sea star. d, Red knob sea star.
No. 1409, vert.: a, $3, Red sea star. b, $5, Blue sea star.

2018, Mar. 21   Litho.   Perf. 14
1408 A417 $2.50 Sheet of 4,
#a-d   15.50 15.50
Souvenir Sheet
1409 A417   Sheet of 2, #a-b   12.50 12.50

Miniature Sheet

Rays — A418

No. 1410: a, 50c, Blue-spotted ribbontail ray swimming. b, $1, Cownose ray. c, $1.50, Giant oceanic manta ray. d, $2, Southern stingray. e, $2.50, Leopard whipray. f, $3, Blue-spotted ribbontail ray on ocean floor.

2018, Mar. 21   Litho.   Perf. 14
1410 A418   Sheet of 6, #a-f   16.00 16.00

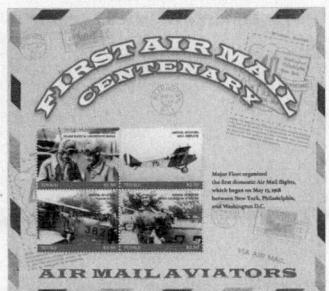

United States Air Mail, Cent. — A419

No. 1411: a, Major Reuben H. Fleet and Lieutenant George Boyle looking at map. b,

DH-4 airplane. c, Major Fleet with arm on airplane. d, Pilot James Edgerton and his sister. $5, United States #C1.

2018, Apr. 3   Litho.   Perf. 14
1411 A419 $2.50 Sheet of 4,
#a-d   15.00 15.00
Souvenir Sheet
Perf. 12½
1412 A419 $5 multi   7.50 7.50
No. 1412 contains one 51x38mm stamp.

Coronation of Queen Elizabeth II, 65th Anniv. — A420

No. 1413: a, $1, Queen Elizabeth II on throne with rod and scepter. b, $2, Procession. c, $3, Queen Elizabeth II and family. d, $4, Queen Elizabeth II on throne, diff.
$5, Queen Elizabeth II and Prince Philip, vert.

2018, May 30   Litho.   Perf. 14
1413 A420   Sheet of 4, #a-d   15.00 15.00
Souvenir Sheet
1414 A420 $5 multi   7.50 7.50

Fruit — A421

No. 1415: a, $2, Papaya (incorrectly identified as "Pomegranate.") b, $2.50, Coconut. c, $3, Cavendish banana.
No. 1416: a, $3.50, Pomegranate. b, $4, Pink grapefruit.

2018, May 30   Litho.   Perf. 13¾
1415 A421   Sheet of 3, #a-c   11.50 11.50
Souvenir Sheet
1416 A421   Sheet of 2, #a-b   11.50 11.50

Shrimp — A422

No. 1417 — $2.50: a, Cleaner shrimp. b, Emperor shrimp. c, Camel shrimp. d, Orange snapping shrimp.
No. 1418 — $3.70: a, Peacock mantis shrimp. b, Modest snapping shrimp.

2018, May 30   Litho.   Perf. 14
1417 A422   Sheet of 4, #a-d   15.00 15.00
Souvenir Sheet
Perf. 12½
1418 A422   Sheet of 2, #a-b   11.50 11.50
No. 1418 contains two 38x51mm stamps.

Coconut Crabs — A423

No. 1419 — Various photographs of coconut crab: a, $1. b, $2. c, $3. d, $4.
No. 1420: a, $3, Crab on leaf. b, $4, Crab on ground.

2018, May 30   Litho.   Perf. 14
1419 A423   Sheet of 4, #a-d   15.00 15.00
Souvenir Sheet
Perf. 12
1420 A423   Sheet of 2, #a-b   10.50 10.50

Orchids — A424

No. 1421: a, $1, Encyclia cordigera. b, $2, Trichocentrum cavendishianum. c, $3, Sobralia macrantha. d, $4, Otoglossum coronarium.
No. 1422: a, $3, Guarianthe aurantiaca. b, $4, Guarlanthe skinneri.

2018, May 30   Litho.   Perf. 14
1421 A424   Sheet of 4, #a-d   15.00 15.00
Souvenir Sheet
Perf. 12½
1422 A424   Sheet of 2, #a-b   10.50 10.50
No. 1422 contains two 38x51mm stamps.

Miniature Sheet

Summit Meeting Between U.S. Pres. Donald Trump and North Korean Chairman Kim Jong Un, Singapore — A425

No. 1423: a, Kim and Trump standing in front of flags. b, Trump and Kim standing in front of building. c, Kim and Trump, sitting and shaking hands. d, Kim and Trump standing and shaking hands.

2018   Litho.   Perf. 14

1423	A425	$2.50 Sheet of 4,			
		a-d		15.00	15.00

No. 1423, which shows photographs taken at the summit, was stated to have been issued on June 12, which was the date of the summit.

Miniature Sheet

Birth of Prince Louis of Cambridge — A426

No. 1424: a, Duke and Duchess of Cambridge. b, Prince George of Cambridge. c, Princess Charlotte of Cambridge. d, Duchess of Cambridge holding Prince Louis.

2018, Sept. 8   Litho.   Perf. 13¾

1424	A426	$2.50 Sheet of 4,			
		#a-d		14.50	14.50

Wedding of Prince Harry and Meghan Markle — A427

No. 1425: a, Bride and groom, Queen Elizabeth II and Princes Philip, Princes Charles and Duchess of Cornwall, Duke and Duchess of Cambridge with their children and Doria Ragland, mother of the bride. b, Queen Elizabeth II and Prince Philip. c, Bride and groom with bridesmaids and page boys. d, Bride and groom with Ragland.

$5, Bride and groom, vert.

2018, Sept. 8   Litho.   Perf. 12

1425	A427	$3 Sheet of 4, #a-d		17.50	17.50

Souvenir Sheet

Perf. 12½

1426	A427	$5 multi		7.25	7.25

No. 1426 contains one 38x51mm stamp.

Miniature Sheet

Nebulae — A428

No. 1427: a, $1, Eight-Burst Nebula (NGC 3132). b, $2, Bug Nebula (NGC 6302). c, $3, Open cluster in Rosette Nebula (NGC 2244). d, $4, Carina Nebula (NGC 3372).

2018, Dec. 5   Litho.   Perf.

1427	A428	Sheet of 4, #a-d		14.00	14.00

Flight of Apollo 11, 50th Anniv. (in 2019) — A429

No. 1428: a, Astronaut on Moon. b, Launch of Apollo 11. c, Equipment and U.S. flag on lunar surface. d, Lunar Module leaving Moon. e, Footprint on lunar surface.

$5, Lunar Module and mission emblem, horiz.

2018, Dec. 5   Litho.   Perf.

1428	A429	$2 Sheet of 5, #a-e	14.00	14.00

Souvenir Sheet

Perf. 12½

1429	A429	$5 multi		7.00	7.00

No. 1429 contains one 51x38mm stamp.

Tawny Nurse Shark — A430

No. 1430: a, $1, Shark's head. b, $2, Shark, mouth not visible. c, $3, Two sharks. d, $4, Shark, mouth visible.

$5, Shark, horiz.

2018, Dec. 5   Litho.   Perf.

1430	A430	Sheet of 4, #a-d	14.00	14.00

Souvenir Sheet

Perf. 14

1431	A430	$5 multi		7.00	7.00

No. 1431 contains one 80x30mm stamp.

Nudibranchs — A431

No. 1432: a, 50c, Variable neon slug. b, $1, Mediterranean violet aeolid. c, $1.50, Spanish shawl. d, $2, Magnificent sea slug. e, $2.50, Willan's chromodoris. f, $3, Hilton's aeolid.

$5, Crested aeolis.

2018, Dec. 5   Litho.   Perf. 14

1432	A431	Sheet of 6, #a-f	15.00	15.00

Souvenir Sheet

1433	A431	$5 multi		7.00	7.00

SEMI-POSTAL STAMPS

Nos. 159-160 Srchd. and Ovptd. "TONGA CYCLONE / RELIEF / 1982" in 1 or 3 Lines Wmk. 380

1982, May 20   Litho.   Perf. 14

B1	A25a	45c + 20c multi	.35	.35
B2	A25b	45c + 20c multi	.35	.35

POSTAGE DUE STAMPS

Arms of Tuvalu — D1

1981, May 13   Litho.   Perf. 14

J1	D1	1c brt rose lil & blk	.25	.25
J2	D1	2c grnsh bl & blk	.25	.25
J3	D1	5c yellow brn & blk	.25	.25
J4	D1	10c blue grn & blk	.25	.25
J5	D1	20c chocolate & blk	.25	.25
J6	D1	30c orange & blk	.25	.25
J7	D1	40c ultra & blk	.25	.25
J8	D1	50c yellow grn & blk	.30	.30
J9	D1	$1 brt lilac & blk	.55	.55
		Nos. J1-J9 (9)	2.60	2.60

1982-83   Perf. 14x15

J1a	D1	1c bright rose lilac & black	.25	.25
J2a	D1	2c greenish blue & black	.25	.25
J3a	D1	5c yellow brown & black	.25	.25
J4a	D1	10c blue green & black	.25	.25
J5a	D1	20c chocolate & black	.25	.25
J6a	D1	30c orange & black	.35	.30
J7a	D1	40c ultra & black	.45	.35
J8a	D1	50c yellow green & black	.55	.45
J9a	D1	$1 bright lilac & black	.90	.65
		Nos. J1a-J9a (9)	3.50	3.00

Issued: 1c-20c, 11/25/82 (inscribed "1982"); 30c-$1, 5/25/83 (inscribed "1983").

OFFICIAL STAMPS

Nos. 96-113 Overprinted "OFFICIAL"

1981   Litho.   Unwmk.   Perf. 14

O1	A14	1c multicolored	.25	.25
O2	A14	2c multicolored	.25	.25
O3	A14	4c multicolored	.25	.25
O4	A14	5c multicolored	.25	.25
O5	A14	6c multicolored	.25	.25
O6	A14	8c multicolored	.25	.25
O7	A14	10c multicolored	.25	.25
O8	A14	15c multicolored	.25	.25
O9	A14	20c multicolored	.25	.25
O10	A14	25c multicolored	.25	.25
O11	A14	30c multicolored	.30	.30
O12	A14	35c multicolored	.35	.35
O13	A14	40c multicolored	.45	.45
O14	A14	45c multicolored	.50	.50
O15	A14	50c multicolored	.55	.55
O16	A14	70c multicolored	.70	.70
O17	A14	$1 multicolored	.90	.90
O18	A14	$2 multicolored	2.00	2.00
O19	A14	$5 multicolored	4.50	4.50
		Nos. O1-O19 (19)	12.75	12.75

No. 207 Srchd. and Ovptd. "OFFICIAL" Wmk. 380

1983, Aug.   Litho.   Perf. 14

O20	A30	60c on $1 multi	.75	.75

Nos. 185-186A, 188, 230, 188A-195 Ovptd. "OFFICIAL"

1984   Litho.   Wmk. 380   Perf. 14

O21	A30	5c multicolored	.25	.35
O22	A30	10c multicolored	.25	.35
O23	A30	15c multicolored	.25	.65
O24	A30	25c multicolored	.30	.55
O25	A30	30c on 45c multi	.65	.65
O25A	A30	30c multicolored	.40	.65
O26	A30	30c multicolored	.50	.70
O27	A30	40c multicolored	.55	.70
O28	A30	45c multicolored	.65	.70
O29	A30	50c multicolored	.65	.65
O29A	A30	60c multicolored	.75	.90
O30	A30	$1 multicolored	.95	.90
O31	A30	$2 multicolored	1.50	1.00
O32	A30	$5 multicolored	3.50	2.25
		Nos. O21-O32 (14)	11.15	11.00

Issued: #O23, O29A, Apr. 30; others Feb. 1.

Nos. 469-484 Overprinted "OFFICIAL"

1989, Feb. 22   Litho.   Perf. 15

O33	A64	5c multicolored	.25	.25
O34	A64	10c multicolored	.25	.25
O35	A64	15c multicolored	.25	.25
O36	A64	20c multicolored	.25	.25
O37	A64	25c multicolored	.30	.30
O38	A64	30c multicolored	.40	.40
O39	A64	35c multicolored	.45	.45
O40	A64	45c multicolored	.50	.50
O41	A64	45c multicolored	.60	.60
O42	A64	50c multicolored	.65	.65
O43	A64	55c multicolored	.70	.70
O44	A64	60c multicolored	.75	.75
O45	A64	70c multicolored	.90	.90
O46	A64	$1 multicolored	1.25	1.25
O47	A64	$2 multicolored	2.50	2.50
O48	A64	$5 multicolored	6.50	6.50
		Nos. O33-O48 (16)	16.50	16.50

For the following islands all are types of Tuvalu unless otherwise specified.

See note following Tuvalu No. 221.

Leaders of the World

Large quantities of some Leaders of the World sets, including unissued stamps, were sold at a fraction of face value when the printer was liquidated.

FUNAFUTI

Catalogue values for all unused stamps in this country are for Never Hinged items.

Locomotive Type of 1984

No. 1, 1919 Class C51, Japan. No. 2, 1935 F.C.C. Andes Class, Peru. No. 3, 1934 Kolhapur Class, UK. No. 4, 1941 V.R. Class H, Australia. No. 5, 1885 S.A.R. Class Y, Australia. No. 6, 1951 Class 4, UK. No. 7, 1928 Class U, UK. No. 8, 1923 Eryri Cog, UK. No. 9, 1927 Royal Scot Class, UK. No. 10, 1828 Lancashire Witch, UK. No. 11, 1906 NY, NH & H RR Class EP-1, US. No. 12, 1942 Springbok Class B1, UK. No. 13, 1827 Royal George, UK. No. 14, 1926 Northern Pacific Class A5, US. No. 15, 1900 Aberdare Class 2600, UK. No. 16, 1829 Sans Pareil, UK. No. 17, 1924 EST Class 241A, France. No. 18, 1911 Class 8K, UK. No. 19, 1913 Sir Gilbert Claughton, UK. No. 20, 1920 Sherlock Holmes, UK. No. 21, 1949 Class K1, UK. No. 22, 1925 Class P1, UK. No. 23, 1940 SNCF Class 232R, France. No. 24, 1904 B&O Class DD-1.

Se-tenant Pairs, #a.-b.
a. — Side and front views.
b. — Action scene.

Perf. 12½x13

			Unwmk.	
1984-86		**Litho.**		
1	A36	5c multicolored	.25	.25
2	A36	5c multicolored	.25	.25
3	A36	15c multicolored	.25	.25
4	A36	15c multicolored	.25	.25
5	A36	15c multicolored	.25	.25
6	A36	20c multicolored	.25	.25
7	A36	20c multicolored	.25	.25
8	A36	25c multicolored	.25	.25
9	A36	30c multicolored	.30	.30
10	A36	35c multicolored	.35	.35
11	A36	35c multicolored	.35	.35
12	A36	40c multicolored	.35	.35
13	A36	40c multicolored	.35	.35
14	A36	40c multicolored	.35	.35
15	A36	40c multicolored	.35	.35
16	A36	50c multicolored	.55	.55
17	A36	55c multicolored	.55	.55
18	A36	55c multicolored	.55	.55
19	A36	60c multicolored	.60	.60
20	A36	60c multicolored	.60	.60
21	A36	60c multicolored	.60	.60
22	A36	$1 multicolored	1.00	1.00
23	A36	$1 multicolored	1.00	1.00
24	A36	$1.50 multicolored	1.50	1.50
		Nos. 1-24 (24)	11.35	11.35

Issued: #3, 6, 9, 12, 16, 19, 4/16/84; 1, 4, 8, 10, 13, 18, 20, 22, 12/24/84; 2, 5, 11, 14, 17, 23, 4/29/85; 7, 15, 21, 24, 12/30/86.

1986 stamps not inscribed "Leaders of the World."

Automobile Type of 1984

No. 25, 1957 Triumph TR3A, UK. No. 26, 1932 Nash Special 8 Convertible, US. No. 27, 1937 Cord 812 Supercharged, US. No. 28, 1925 AC Six, UK. No. 29, 1924 Alfa Romeo P2, Italy. No. 30, 1935 Aston Martin Ulster,

UK. No. 31, 1948 Morgan 4+4, UK. No. 32, 1906 Renault GP, France. No. 33, 1903 Cadillac Model A. No. 34, 1971 Porsche 917K, Germany. No. 35, 1913 Simplex 75HP, US. No. 36, 1939 Delahaye Type 165, France. No. 37, 1938 Opel Admiral, Germany. No 38, 1936 Jaguar SS 100, UK. No. 39, 1965 Aston Martin DB5, UK. No. 40, 1977 Porsche 935.

Se-tenant Pairs, #a.-b.
a. — Side and front views.
b. — Action scene.

1984-87

25	A41	1c multicolored	.25	.25
26	A41	1c multicolored	.25	.25
27	A41	10c multicolored	.25	.25
28	A41	10c multicolored	.25	.25
29	A41	20c multicolored	.25	.25
30	A41	30c multicolored	.30	.30
31	A41	40c multicolored	.40	.40
32	A41	40c multicolored	.40	.40
33	A41	55c multicolored	.55	.55
34	A41	60c multicolored	.60	.60
35	A41	60c multicolored	.60	.60
36	A41	75c multicolored	.75	.75
37	A41	80c multicolored	.80	.80
38	A41	$1 multicolored	1.00	1.00
39	A41	$1 multicolored	1.00	1.00
40	A41	$1.50 multicolored	1.60	1.60
		Nos. 25-40 (16)	9.25	9.25

Issued: #25, 27, 31, 38, 9/13/84; 26, 30, 33, 34, 2/8/85; 28-29, 32, 35-37, 39-40, 8/27/87. 1987 stamps not inscribed "Leaders of the World."

Queen Mother Type of 1985

Hats: #45a, Blue feathered. #45b, White. #46a, 50a, Pink. #46b, 50b, Tiara. #47a, 51a, Blue. #47b, 51b, Blue with veil covering face. #48a, Blue. #48b, Tiara. #49a, Headband. #49b, Hat.

1985-86   *Perf. 13x12½*

45	A45	5c Pair, #a.-b.	.30	.30
46	A45	25c Pair, #a.-b.	.40	.40
47	A45	80c Pair, #a.-b.	1.20	1.20
48	A45	$1.05 Pair, #a.-b.	1.40	1.40
		Nos. 45-48 (4)	3.30	3.30

Souvenir Sheets of 2

49	A45	$1.05 #a.-b.	2.50	2.50
50	A45	$2 #a.-b.	2.75	2.75
51	A45	$3 #a.-b.	4.75	4.75

Issued: #45-49, 8/26; #50-51, 1/3/86.

Elizabeth II 60th Birthday Type

10c, Trooping the colors. 50c, Tiara. $1.50, As young woman, 1952. $3.50, Tiara, diff., vert. $5, Scarf.

1986, Apr. 21   Perf. 13x12½, 12½x13

52	A49	10c multi	.25	.25
53	A49	50c multi	.35	.35
54	A49	$1.50 multi	1.10	1.10
55	A49	$3.50 multi	2.75	2.75
		Nos. 52-55 (4)	4.45	4.45

Souvenir Sheet

56	A49	$5 multi	4.00	4.00

Royal Wedding Type of 1986

#59a, Andrew holding rifle, vert. #59b, Sarah Ferguson, vert. #60a, Couple. #60b, Prince Philip and Andrew.

1986, July 23

59	A53	60c Pair, #a.-b.	1.25	1.25
60	A53	$1 Pair, #a.-b.	2.00	2.00

Souvenir Sheet

61	A56	$4 Newlyweds	4.75	4.75

Nos. 59-60 Ovptd. in Silver "Congratulations to T.R.H. The Duke & Duchess of York"

1986, July 23

62	A53	60c Pair, #a.-b.	2.00	2.00
63	A53	$1 Pair, #a.-b.	3.75	3.75

Royal Anniversaries — A1

1987   *Perf. 15*

66	A1	20c Queen Victoria	.30	.30
67	A1	50c George VI, Family	.65	.65
68	A1	75c Elizabeth	1.05	1.05
69	A1	$1.20 Elizabeth, Philip	1.75	1.76
70	A1	$1.75 Elizabeth, diff.	2.50	2.50
		Nos. 66-70 (5)	6.25	6.25

Souvenir Sheet

71	A1	$3 Elizabeth, Family	5.50	5.50

Elizabeth's 40th wedding anniv., Queen Victoria's accession to the throne, sesquicentennial.

Summer Olympics Type of 1988

1988, Aug. 19   Perf. 13x12½

72	A69	10c Hurdles	.25	.25
73	A69	20c High jump	.25	.25
74	A69	40c Running	.50	.50
75	A69	50c Discus	.60	.60
76	A69	80c Pole vault	1.00	1.00
77	A69	90c Javelin	1.10	1.10
		Nos. 72-77 (6)	3.70	3.70

NANUMAGA

Automobile Type of 1984

No. 1, 1903 De Dion-Bouton Single Cylinder. No. 2, 1955 Ford Thunderbird. No. 3, 1966 Lotus Elan, UK. No. 4, 1915 Stutz Bearcat. No. 5, 1915 Dodge 4-Cylinder Touring Car. No. 6, 1976 Jaguar XJ-S, UK. No. 7, 1920 Morgan Super Sports, UK. No. 8, 1906 Spyker, Holland. No. 9, 1957 Dual-Ghia, US. No. 10, 1966 Lamborghini P400 Miura Coupe, Italy. No. 11, 1947 Kaiser Traveler, US. No. 12, 1951 Lancia Aurelia, Italy. No. 13, 1963 Chevrolet Corvette Coupe. No. 14, 1949 Jaguar XK 120, UK. No. 15, 1930 Renault Reinastella, France. No. 16, 1938 Alvis Speed 25, UK. No. 17, 1956 Studebaker Golden Hawk. No. 18, 1909 Alco, US. No. 19, 1966 Shelby GT-350 Coupe, US. No. 20, 1968 Mercedes 300 SEL, Germany. No. 21, 1953 BRM V 16, UK. No. 22, 1910 Lozier Briarcliff, US.

Se-tenant Pairs, #a.-b.
a. — Side and front views.
b. — Action scene.

Perf. 12½x13

1984-87   Litho.   Unwmk.

1	A41	5c multicolored	.25	.25
2	A41	5c multicolored	.25	.25
3	A41	5c multicolored	.25	.25
4	A41	10c multicolored	.25	.25
5	A41	10c multicolored	.25	.25
6	A41	10c multicolored	.25	.25
7	A41	10c multicolored	.25	.25
8	A41	15c multicolored	.25	.25
9	A41	20c multicolored	.25	.25
10	A41	25c multicolored	.35	.35
11	A41	25c multicolored	.35	.35
12	A41	25c multicolored	.35	.35
13	A41	30c multicolored	.40	.40
14	A41	40c multicolored	.55	.55
15	A41	40c multicolored	.55	.55
16	A41	50c multicolored	.60	.60
17	A41	60c multicolored	.80	.80
18	A41	75c multicolored	1.00	1.00
19	A41	$1 multicolored	1.50	1.50
20	A41	$1 multicolored	1.50	1.50
21	A41	$1 multicolored	1.50	1.50
22	A41	$1 multicolored	1.50	1.50
		Nos. 1-22 (22)	13.20	13.20

Issued: #1, 4, 10, 14, 19, 6/11/84; #2, 5, 16, 20, 12/24/84; #6, 11, 18, 21, 7/23/85; #3, 7-9, 12, 15, 17, 22, 8/6/87. 1987 stamps not inscribed "Leaders of the World."

British Monarchs — A2

Se-tenant Pairs, #a.-b.
a. — Left stamp.
b. — Right stamp.

1984, Nov. 27   Perf. 13x12½

23	A2	10c Richard I	.25	.25
24	A2	20c Richard I, diff.	.25	.25
25	A2	30c Third Crusade	.35	.35
26	A2	40c Alfred the Great	.45	.45
27	A2	50c Alfred, diff.	.55	.55
28	A2	$1 Battle of Edington	1.10	1.10
		Nos. 23-28 (6)	2.95	2.95

Locomotive Type of 1984

10c, 1906 NYC & HR Class S. 25c, 1884 T.R. Class B, Australia. 50c, 1902 Decapod, UK. 60c, 1846 Coppernob, UK.

Se-tenant Pairs, #a.-b.
a. — Side and front views.
b. — Action scene.

1985, Apr. 3   Perf. 12½x13

29	A36	10c multicolored	.25	.25
30	A36	25c multicolored	.50	.50
31	A36	50c multicolored	.90	.90
32	A36	60c multicolored	1.10	1.10
		Nos. 29-32 (4)	2.75	2.75

Flowers — A3

#33a, Tecophilaea cyanocrocus. #33b, Lilium pardalinum. #34a, Canarina abyssinica. #34b, Vanda coerulea. #35a, Lathyrus maritimus. #35b, Narcissus tazetta. #36a, Bauera sessiflora. #36b, Thelymitra venosa.

1985, May 3   Perf. 13x12½

33	A3	25c Pair, #a.-b.	.60	.60
34	A3	30c Pair, #a.-b.	.70	.70
35	A3	40c Pair, #a.-b.	1.00	1.00
36	A3	50c Pair, #a.-b.	1.25	1.25
		Nos. 33-36 (4)	3.55	3.55

Queen Mother Type of 1985

Hats: #45a, White. #45b, Blue feathered. #46a, 50a, Violet blue wide-brimmed. #46b, 50b, Blue green wide-brimmed. #47a, 51a, Tiara. #47b, 51b, Light blue. #48a, Dark blue. #48b, Black.
#49a, As young girl. #49b, As young woman

1985-86

45	A45	15c Pair, #a.-b.	.30	.30
46	A45	55c Pair, #a.-b.	1.00	1.00
47	A45	65c Pair, #a.-b.	1.10	1.10
48	A45	90c Pair, #a.-b.	1.60	1.60
		Nos. 45-48 (4)	4.00	4.00

Souvenir Sheets of 2

49	A45	$1.15 #a.-b.	1.75	1.75
50	A45	$2.10 #a.-b.	2.60	2.60
51	A45	$2.50 #a.-b.	3.00	3.00

Issued: #41-49, 9/5; 50-51, 1/3/86.

Elizabeth II 60th Birthday Type

1986, Apr. 21   Perf. 12½x13, 12½x13

52	A49	5c White hat	.25	.25
53	A49	$1 As young woman	.40	.40
54	A49	$1.75 Tiam	.75	.75
55	A49	$2.50 Tiara, vert.	.95	.95
		Nos. 52-55 (4)	2.35	2.35

Souvenir Sheet

56	A49	$4 Portrait	3.00	3.00

World Cup Soccer Championships, Mexico — A4

Players and teams from participating countries.

Perf. 12½x13, 13x12½

1986, June 30

57	A4	1c Uruguay, vert.	.25	.25
58	A4	5c Morocco, vert.	.25	.25
59	A4	5c Hungary, vert.	.25	.25
60	A4	10c Poland, vert.	.25	.25
61	A4	20c Argentina, vert.	.25	.25
62	A4	30c Bulgaria	.25	.25
63	A4	50c Portugal, vert.	.25	.25
64	A4	60c Belgium	.35	.35
65	A4	75c France	.35	.35
66	A4	$1 Canada, vert.	.55	.55

67	A4	$2 Germany	.85	.85
68	A4	$4 Scotland, vert.	1.75	1.75
		Nos. 57-68 (12)	5.60	5.60

Royal Wedding Type of 1986

#71a, Prince Andrew, vert. #71b, Sarah Ferguson, vert. #72a, Prince Philip, Andrew. #72b, Prince Andrew.

1986, July 23

71	A53	60c Pair, #a.-b.	1.10	1.10
72	A53	$1 Pair, #a.-b.	1.90	1.90

Souvenir Sheet

73	A56	$4 Couple	5.25	5.25

Nos. 71-72 Ovptd. in Silver "Congratulations to T.R.H. The Duke & Duchess of York"

1986, Oct. 26

74	A53	60c Pair, #a.-b.	2.00	2.00
75	A53	$1 Pair, #a.-b.	3.75	3.75

Royal Anniversaries — A5

15c, Queen Victoria. 35c, Princesses Margaret and Elizabeth. 60c, Elizabeth holding Princess Anne. $1.50, Elizabeth, Philip. $1.75, Elizabeth wearing tiara. $3, Elizabeth.

1987, Oct. 15   *Perf. 15*

78	A5	15c multicolored	.25	.25
79	A5	35c multicolored	.40	.40
80	A5	60c multicolored	.65	.65
81	A62	$1.50 multicolored	1.60	1.60
82	A62	$1.75 multicolored	1.75	1.75
		Nos. 78-82 (5)	4.65	4.65

Souvenir Sheet

83	A5	$3 multicolored	3.50	3.50

Elizabeth's 40th wedding anniv.; Victoria's accession to the throne, sesquicentennial.

NANUMEA

Locomotive Type of 1984

No. 1, 1940 Class E94, Germany. No. 2, 1946 Class 2251, UK. No. 3, 1941 Bantam Cock Class V4, UK. No. 4, 1902 Class C1, UK. No. 5, 1952 S.N.C.F. CC 7121, France. No. 6, 1903 La France Frenchmen Class, UK. No. 7, 1929 5700 Class, UK. No. 8, 1954 S.N.C.F. Class BB 1200, France. No. 9, 1881 Fairlight Class G, UK. No. 10, 1928 V.R. Class S, Australia.

Se-tenant Pairs, #a.-b.
a. — Side and front views.
b. — Action scene.

Perf. 12½x13

1984-85   Litho.   Unwmk.

1	A36	1c multicolored	.25	.25
2	A36	15c multicolored	.35	.35
3	A36	20c multicolored	.50	.50
4	A36	30c multicolored	.55	.55
5	A36	35c multicolored	.75	.75
6	A36	40c multicolored	.85	.85
7	A36	50c multicolored	1.00	1.00
8	A36	50c multicolored	1.00	1.00
9	A36	50c multicolored	1.10	1.10
10	A36	60c multicolored	1.10	1.10
		Nos. 1-10 (10)	7.45	7.45

Issued: Nos. 2-4, 6-7, 9, 4/30; others, 2/8/85.

Cricket Players Type of 1984

1c, J.A. Snow. 10c, C.J. Tavare. 40c, G.B. Stevenson. $1, P. Carrick.

Se-tenant Pairs, #a.-b.

1984, Oct. 9   Perf. 13x12½

11	A39	1c multicolored	.30	.30
12	A39	10c multicolored	.30	.30
13	A39	40c multicolored	.80	.80
14	A39	$1 multicolored	1.90	1.90
		Nos. 11-14 (4)	3.30	3.30

Automobile Type of 1984

No. 15, 1965 Humber Supersnipe, UK. No. 16, 1934 Singer 9, UK. No. 17, 1948 Holden

FX 2.1 Liter Sedan, Australia. No. 18, 1953 Buick Skylark. No. 19, 1951 Simca Aronde, France. No. 20, 1967 Toyota 2000 GT, Japan. No. 21, 1960 Elva Courier, UK. No. 22, 1952 Bentley Continental, UK. No. 23, 1938 Hispano-Suiza V12 Saoutchik Cabriolet, Spain/France. No. 24, 1913 Peugeot Bebe, France. No. 25, 1935 Bluebird V (LSR), UK. No. 26, 1978 Mazda RX7, Japan. No. 27, 1970 Lola T70, UK. No. 28, 1908 Locomobile, US.

Se-tenant Pairs, #a.-b.
a. — Side and front views.
b. — Action scene.

1985-86			Perf. 12½x13	
15	A41	5c multicolored	.25	.25
16	A41	10c multicolored	.25	.25
17	A41	15c multicolored	.25	.25
18	A41	20c multicolored	.30	.30
19	A41	20c multicolored	.30	.30
20	A41	35c multicolored	.45	.45
21	A41	40c multicolored	.50	.50
22	A41	50c multicolored	.60	.60
23	A41	50c multicolored	.60	.60
24	A41	50c multicolored	.60	.60
25	A41	60c multicolored	.70	.70
26	A41	60c multicolored	.70	.70
27	A41	75c multicolored	.80	.80
28	A41	$2 multicolored	2.50	2.50
		Nos. 15-28 (14)	8.80	8.80

Issued: Nos. 15, 21-22, 25, 1/14; Nos. 17-18, 23, 26, 2/22; Nos. 16, 19-20, 24, 27-28, 12/30/86.

Cats — A6

#29a, American short-hair. #29b, Turkish Angora. #30a, Korat. #30b, American Maine Coon. #31a, Himalayan. #31b, Shaded Cameo. #32a, Long-haired ginger. #32b, Siamese Seal Point.

1985, May 28			Perf. 13x12½	
29	A6	5c Pair, #a.-b.	.25	.25
30	A6	30c Pair, #a.-b.	.65	.65
31	A6	50c Pair, #a.-b.	1.00	1.00
32	A6	$1 Pair, #a.-b.	2.00	2.00
		Nos. 29-32 (4)	3.90	3.90

Queen Mother Type of 1985

Hats: #41a, 47a, Light gray. #41b, 47b, Light blue. #42a, Lavender. #42b, Blue. #43a, Purple. #43b, Pink. #44a, 46a, Blue. #44b, 46b, Blue flowered. #45a, Feathered. #45b, Veiled.

1985-86				
41	A45	5c Pair, #a.-b.	.25	.25
42	A45	30c Pair, #a.-b.	.45	.45
43	A45	75c Pair, #a.-b.	1.40	1.40
44	A45	$1.05 Pair, #a.-b.	1.75	1.75
		Nos. 41-44 (4)	3.85	3.85

Souvenir Sheets of 2

45	A45	$1.20 #a.-b.	2.25	2.25
46	A45	$1 #a.-b.	1.00	1.00
47	A45	$4 #a.-b.	4.00	4.00

Issued: #41-45, 9/5; 46-47, 1/10/86.

Elizabeth II 60th Birthday Type

1986, Apr. 21			Perf. 13x12½, 12½x13	
48	A49	10c As teenager	.25	.25
49	A49	80c As young woman	.30	.30
50	A49	$1.75 Red hat	.75	.75
51	A49	$3 Tiara, vert.	1.35	1.35
		Nos. 48-51 (4)	2.65	2.65

Souvenir Sheet

52	A49	$4 Green print hat	4.00	4.00

1986 World Cup Soccer Championships, Mexico — A7

1c, Italy, 1934. 2c, Italy, 1938. 5c, Uruguay 1950. 10c, Brazil, 1958. 25c, Argentina vs. Holland, 1978. 40c, Brazil vs. Czechoslovakia, 1962. 50c, Uruguay vs. Argentina, 1930. 75c, West Germany vs. Hungary, 1954. 90c, Brazil, 1970. $1, West Germany, 1974. $2.50, Italy vs. West Germany, 1982. $4, England, 1966.

1986, June 10			Perf. 13x12½	
53	A7	1c multicolored	.25	.25
54	A7	2c multicolored	.25	.25
55	A7	5c multicolored	.25	.25
56	A7	10c multicolored	.25	.25
57	A7	25c multicolored	.25	.25
58	A7	40c multicolored	.25	.25
59	A7	50c multicolored	.30	.30
60	A7	75c multicolored	.40	.40
61	A7	90c multicolored	.50	.50
62	A7	$1 multicolored	.55	.55
63	A7	$2.50 multicolored	1.30	1.30
64	A7	$4 multicolored	1.90	1.90
		Nos. 53-64 (12)	6.45	6.45

Royal Wedding Type of 1986

No. 65, Prince Andrew in jeep, vert. No. 66, Sarah Ferguson, vert. No. 67, Couple. No. 68, Prince Andrew, Princess Anne and parents. No. 69, Newlyweds.

1986, July 23			Perf. 13x12½, 12½x13	
65	A53	60c multicolored	.40	.40
66	A53	60c multicolored	.40	.40
67	A53	$1 multicolored	.65	.65
68	A53	$1 multicolored	.65	.65
		Nos. 65-68 (4)	2.10	2.10

Souvenir Sheet

69	A56	$4 multicolored	3.50	3.50

Nos. 65-68 Ovptd. in Silver "Congratulations to T.R.H. The Duke & Duchess of York"

#70a, Prince Andrew in jeep. #70b, Sarah Ferguson. #71a, Couple. #71b, Prince Andrew, Princess Anne and parents.

1986, Oct. 28				
70	A53	60c Pair, #a.-b.	2.00	2.00
71	A53	$1 Pair, #a.-b.	3.75	3.75

Elizabeth 40th Wedding Anniv. Type

40c, Victoria. 60c, Elizabeth & Philip, wedding portrait. 80c, Elizabeth, Philip & Prince Charles. $1, Elizabeth, Princess Anne. $2, Elizabeth. $3, Royal family, diff.

1987, Oct. 15			Perf. 15	
74	A62	40c multicolored	.40	.40
75	A62	60c multicolored	.65	.65
76	A62	80c multicolored	.85	.85
77	A62	$1 multicolored	1.00	1.00
78	A62	$2 multicolored	2.10	2.10
		Nos. 74-78 (5)	5.00	5.00

Souvenir Sheet

79	A62	$3 multicolored	4.75	4.75

Queen Victoria's accession to the throne, 150th anniv.

NIUTAO

Automobile Type of 1984

No. 1, 1930 Bentley 4½ Liter Supercharged, UK. No. 2, 1935 Wolseley Hornet Special, UK. No. 3, 1920 Crossley 25/30HP, UK. No. 4, 1976 Cadillac Eldorado 7-Liter V-8. No. 5, 1968 Austin Mini Cooper, UK. No. 6, 1958 BMW 507 Cabriolet, W. Germany. No. 7, 1963 Porsche 365C Cabriolet, W. Germany. No. 8, 1971 Tyrrell Ford 001, UK.

Se-tenant Pairs, #a.-b.
a. — Side and front views.
b. — Action scene.

Perf. 12½x13

1984-85			Litho.	Unwmk.
1	A41	15c multicolored	.25	.25
2	A41	20c multicolored	.40	.40
3	A41	25c multicolored	.50	.50
4	A41	30c multicolored	.65	.65
5	A41	40c multicolored	.85	.85
6	A41	40c multicolored	.85	.85
7	A41	50c multicolored	1.05	1.05
8	A41	60c multicolored	1.20	1.20
		Nos. 1-8 (8)	5.75	5.75

Issued: Nos. 1, 4-5, 7, 4/16; Nos. 2-3, 6, 8, 5/2/85.

Locomotive Type of 1984

No. 9, 1830 Planet, UK. No. 10, 1863 Prince, UK. No. 11, 1943 Gordon Austerity Class, UK. No. 12, 1830 Northumbrian, UK. No. 13, 1879 Merddin Emrys, UK. No. 14, 1829 Agenoria, UK. No. 15, 1909 Atchison, Topeka & Santa Fe, 1301. No. 16, 1897 Class 6200, Japan. No. 17, 1938 F.M.S.R. Class O,

---

Malaya. No. 18, 1880 1F, UK. No. 19, 1908 Class E550, Italy. No. 20, 1914 J.N.R. Class 6760, Japan.

Se-tenant Pairs, #a.-b.
a. — Side and front views.
b. — Action scene.

1984-85				
9	A36	5c multicolored	.25	.25
10	A36	10c multicolored	.25	.25
11	A36	10c multicolored	.25	.25
12	A36	20c multicolored	.35	.35
13	A36	30c multicolored	.50	.50
14	A36	40c multicolored	.70	.70
15	A36	45c multicolored	.75	.75
16	A36	50c multicolored	.85	.85
17	A36	60c multicolored	.85	.85
18	A36	75c multicolored	1.20	1.20
19	A36	$1 multicolored	1.75	1.75
20	A36	$1.20 multicolored	2.10	2.10
		Nos. 9-20 (12)	9.80	9.80

Issue dates: Nos. 9-10, 12, 14, 16, 19, Sept. 17; Nos. 11, 13, 15, 18, 20, Aug. 21, 1985.

Cricket Players Type of 1984

1c, S.G. Hinks. 15c, C. Penn. 50c, T.M. Alderman. $1, K.B.S. Jarvis.

Se-tenant Pairs, #a.-b.
a. — Head.
b. — Action scene.

1985, Jan. 7			Perf. 13x12½	
21	A39	1c multicolored	.25	.25
22	A39	15c multicolored	.40	.40
23	A39	50c multicolored	1.60	1.60
24	A39	$1 multicolored	3.00	3.00
		Nos. 21-24 (4)	5.25	5.25

Audubon Bicentennial Type

#25a, Purple finch. #25b, White-throated sparrow. #26a, Anna's hummingbird. #26b, Smith's longspur. #27a, White-tailed kite. #27b, Harris' hawk. #28a, Northern oriole. #28b, Great crested flycatcher.

1985, Apr. 4				
25	A42	5c Pair, #a.-b.	.25	.25
26	A42	15c Pair, #a.-b.	.40	.40
27	A42	25c Pair, #a.-b.	.65	.65
28	A42	$1 Pair, #a.-b.	2.75	2.75
		Nos. 25-28 (4)	4.05	4.05

Queen Mother Type of 1985

Hat: #37a, Light blue. #37b, Yellow. #38a, 43a, Black. #38b, 43b, Blue. #39a, Tiara. #39b, Pink. #40a, 42a, White. #40b, 42b, Blue. #41a, As young woman. #41b, Feathered.

1985-86				
37	A45	15c Pair, #a.-b.	.25	.25
38	A45	35c Pair, #a.-b.	.75	.75
39	A45	70c Pair, #a.-b.	1.60	1.60
40	A45	95c Pair, #a.-b.	2.10	2.10
		Nos. 37-40 (4)	4.70	4.70

Souvenir Sheets

41	A45	$1.05 #a.-b.	1.05	1.05
42	A45	$1.50 #a.-b.	1.50	1.50
43	A45	$4 #a.-b.	3.75	3.75

Issued: #37-41, 9/4; #42-43, 1/10/86.

Elizabeth II 60th Birthday Type

1986, Apr. 21			Perf. 13x12½, 12½x13	
44	A49	5c White & gray hat	.25	.25
45	A49	60c Infant	.30	.30
46	A49	$1.50 Flowered white hat	.75	.75
47	A49	$3.50 Tiara, vert.	1.75	1.75
		Nos. 44-47 (4)	3.05	3.05

Souvenir Sheet

48	A49	$5 With tiara, diff.	4.75	4.75

For overprints see Nos. 58-62.

Royal Wedding Type

#51a, Couple, vert. #51b, Sarah Ferguson, vert. #52a, Prince Andrew. #52b, Sarah in evening gown.

1986, July 23			Perf. 12½x13, 13x12½	
51	A53	60c Pair, #a.-b.	.75	.75
52	A53	$1 Pair, #a.-b.	1.75	1.75

Souvenir Sheet

53	A56	$4 Newlyweds	3.25	3.25

Nos. 51-52 Ovptd. in Silver "Congratulations to T.R.H. The Duke & Duchess of York"

1986, Oct. 28				
54	A53	60c Pair, #a.-b.	2.00	2.00
55	A53	$1 Pair, #a.-b.	3.75	3.75

Nos. 44-48 Ovptd. in Gold "40th WEDDING ANNIVERSARY OF H.M. QUEEN ELIZABETH II"

1987, Mar.			Perf. 13x12½, 12½x13	
58	A49	5c multicolored	.25	.25
59	A49	60c multicolored	.75	.75
60	A49	$1.50 multicolored	1.90	1.90
61	A49	$3.50 multicolored	4.50	4.50
		Nos. 58-61 (4)	7.40	7.40

Souvenir Sheet

62	A49	$5 multicolored	6.00	6.00

NUI

Locomotives Type of 1984

No. 1, 1911 Class 8800, Japan. No. 2, 1932 Soviet Union Railways Class SU. No. 3, 1847 Jenny Lind Type, UK. No. 4, 1907 Victorian Government Railways Class A2, Australia. No. 5, same, 1950 Class R. No. 6, 1913 Class 9600, Japan. No. 7, 1934 LMS Stanier Tilbury Class 4P, UK. No. 8, 1924 Jinty Class 3, UK. No. 9, 1928 Boston & Albany Class D12. No. 10, 1847 Iron Duke Class, UK. No. 11, 1917 Wabash Railroad Class L. No. 12, 1943 South Australian Government Railways 520 Class. No. 13, 1885 Tennant Class 1463, UK. No. 14, 1947 No. 10000, UK. No. 15, 1848 Padarn Railway Fire Queen, UK. No. 16, 1935 Princess Margaret Rose Class 8P, UK. No. 17, 1932 Soviet Union Railways Class IS. No. 18, 1973 D.B. Class ET403, W. Germany. No. 19, 1916 E. Tenn. & W. N. Carolina R.R. No. 10. No. 20, 1973 D.B. Class 151, W. Germany. No. 21, 1909 Tasmanian Goverment Railways Class K Garratt. No. 22, 1927 B&O President Class. No. 23, 1832 Mohawk & Hudson Railroad Experiment. No. 24, 1934 Union Pacific Railroad, M-10000 Streamliner.

Se-tenant Pairs, #a.-b.
a. — Side and front views.
b. — Action scene.

1984-88			Litho.	Perf. 12½x13	
1	A36	5c multicolored	.25	.25
2	A36	5c multicolored	.25	.25
3	A36	10c multicolored	.25	.25
4	A36	10c multicolored	.25	.25
5	A36	15c multicolored	.25	.25
6	A36	15c multicolored	.25	.25
7	A36	20c multicolored	.25	.25
8	A36	25c multicolored	.30	.30
9	A36	25c multicolored	.30	.30
10	A36	25c multicolored	.30	.30
11	A36	25c multicolored	.30	.30
12	A36	30c multicolored	.35	.35
13	A36	35c multicolored	.40	.40
14	A36	40c multicolored	.45	.45
15	A36	40c multicolored	.45	.45
16	A36	50c multicolored	.55	.55
17	A36	50c multicolored	.55	.55
18	A36	60c multicolored	.60	.60
19	A36	60c multicolored	.60	.60
20	A36	75c multicolored	.80	.80
21	A36	75c multicolored	.80	.80
22	A36	$1 multicolored	1.10	1.10
23	A36	$1 multicolored	1.10	1.10
24	A36	$1.25 multicolored	1.40	1.40
		Nos. 1-24 (24)	12.10	12.10

Issued: Nos. 5, 8, 12, 16, 3/19; Nos. 1, 6, 9, 22, 2/22/85; Nos. 3, 10, 13, 14, 18, 20, 23, 24, 8/7/87; Nos. 2, 4, 7, 11, 15, 17, 19, 21, 1/29/88.

1987 and 1988 stamps not inscribed "Leaders of the World."

British Monarchs Type of Nanumaga

1984, July 18			Perf. 13x12½	

Se-tenant Pairs, #a.-b.

25	A2	1c Queen Anne	.25	.25
26	A2	5c Henry V	.25	.25
27	A2	15c Henry V, diff.	.25	.25
28	A2	40c Queen Anne, diff.	.45	.45
29	A2	50c Queen Anne, diff.	.60	.60
30	A2	$1 Henry V, diff.	1.00	1.00
		Nos. 25-30 (6)	2.80	2.80

Automobile Type of 1984

No. 31, 1909 Buick. No. 32, 1966 Oldsmobile Toronado. No. 33, 1947 Railton Mobil Special, UK. No. 34, 1924 Opel Laubfrosch, Germany. No. 35, 1966 Jensen FF, UK. No. 36, 1963 Lotus-Climax GP MK 25, UK. No. 37, 1910 Delaunay Belleville, France. No. 38, 1956 Jensen 541, UK. No. 39, 1924 Hispano-Suiza H6 Boulogne, France. No. 40, 1972 Citroen-Maserati S.M. Coupe, France.

Se-tenant Pairs, #a.-b.
a. — Side and front views.
b. — Action scene.

1985			Perf. 12½x13	
31	A41	5c multicolored	.25	.25
32	A41	15c multicolored	.35	.35
33	A41	25c multicolored	.70	.70
34	A41	30c multicolored	.75	.75

35	A41	40c multicolored	1.00	1.00
36	A41	40c multicolored	1.00	1.00
37	A41	50c multicolored	1.40	1.40
38	A41	60c multicolored	1.50	1.50
39	A41	90c multicolored	2.25	2.25
40	A41	$1.10 multicolored	2.75	2.75
		Nos. 31-40 (10)	11.95	11.95

Issued: #33-35, 37, 4/2; #31-32, 36, 38-40, 10/9.

Cricket Players Type of 1984

1c, S.C. Goldsmith. 40c, S.N.V. Waterton. 60c, A. Sidebottom. 70c, A.A. Metcalfe.

Se-tenant Pairs, #a.-b.

1985, May 27   *Perf. 13x12½*

41	A39	1c multicolored	.25	.25
42	A39	40c multicolored	.65	.65
43	A39	60c multicolored	.95	.95
44	A39	70c multicolored	1.25	1.25
		Nos. 11-44 (4)	3.10	3.10

Queen Mother Type of 1985

#49a, 54a, Purple. #49b, 54b, Tiara. #50a, Light blue. #50b, Lavender. #51a, Violet. #51b, White. #52a, 55a, Light blue. #52b, 55b, Tiara. #53a, White. #53b, Black.

1985-86

49	A45	5c Pair, #a.-b.	.25	.25
50	A45	50c Pair, #a.-b.	.90	.90
51	A45	75c Pair, #a.-b.	1.40	1.40
52	A45	85c Pair, #a.-b.	1.60	1.60
		Nos. 49-52 (4)	4.15	4.15

Souvenir Sheets of 2

53	A45	$1.15 #a.-b.	2.50	2.50
54	A45	$1.50 #a.-b.	2.00	2.00
55	A45	$3.50 #a.-b.	4.50	4.50

Issued: #49-53, 9/4; 54-55, 1/8/86.

Elizabeth II 60th Birthday Type

1986, Apr. 21   *Perf. 13x12½, 12½x13*

56	A49	10c Feathered hat	.25	.25
57	A49	80c As young woman	.55	.55
58	A49	$1.75 Tiara	1.05	1.05
59	A49	$3 Tiara, diff., vert.	1.90	1.90
		Nos. 56-59 (4)	3.75	3.75

Souvenir Sheet

60	A49	$4 Portrait	4.00	4.00

Royal Wedding Type of 1986

#63a, Couple, vert. #63b, Prince Andrew, vert. #64a, Couple, Queen Elizabeth II. #64b, Andrew as young boy.

1986, July 23   *Perf. 12½x13, 13x12½*

63	A53	60c Pair, #a.-b.	.85	.85
64	A53	$1 Pair, #a.-b.	1.15	1.15

Souvenir Sheet

65	A56	$4 Sarah in wedding dress	4.00	4.00

Nos. 63-64 Ovptd. in Silver "Congratulations to T.R.H. The Duke & Duchess of York"

1986, Oct. 28

66	A53	60c Pair, #a.-b.	1.90	1.90
67	A53	$1 Pair, #a.-b.	3.50	3.50

Elizabeth 40th Wedding Anniv. Type of Funafuti

1987, Oct. 15   *Perf. 15*

70	A1	20c Queen Victoria	.25	.25
71	A1	50c George VI, Family	.60	.60
72	A1	75c Elizabeth	.85	.85
73	A1	$1.20 Elizabeth, Philip	1.40	1.40
74	A1	$1.75 Elizabeth, diff.	2.00	2.00
		Nos. 70-74 (5)	5.10	5.10

Souvenir Sheet

75	A1	$3 Elizabeth, Family	4.00	4.00

Queen Victoria's accession to the throne, sesquicentennial.

NUKUFETAU

Automobile Type of 1984

No. 1, 1904 Mercedes 28 PS, Germany. No. 2, 1966 Ford GT40 Mark II. No. 3, 1911 Vauxhall Prince Henry, UK. No. 4, 1956 Lincoln Continental Mark II. No. 5, 1950 Bristol 400, UK. No. 6, 1913 Morris Oxford "Bullnose," UK. No. 7, 1923 Austin Seven Tourer. No. 0, 1921 Bugatti Type 13 "Brescia," France. No. 9, 1967 Monteverdi, Switzerland. No. 10, 1925 Lancia Lambda, Italy. No. 11, 1938 Panhard Dynamic, France. No. 12, 1960 A.C. Ace, UK. No. 13, 1950 Land Rover Model 80, UK.

Se-tenant Pairs, #a.-b.
a. — Side and front views.
b. — Action scene.

Perf. 12½x13

1984-85   Litho.   Unwmk.

1	A41	5c multicolored	.25	.25
2	A41	10c multicolored	.25	.25
3	A41	10c multicolored	.25	.25
4	A41	15c multicolored	.25	.25
5	A41	20c multicolored	.30	.30
6	A41	25c multicolored	.50	.50
7	A41	30c multicolored	.55	.55
8	A41	50c multicolored	1.00	1.00
9	A41	50c multicolored	1.00	1.00
10	A41	60c multicolored	1.00	1.00
11	A41	60c multicolored	1.00	1.00
12	A41	75c multicolored	1.15	1.15
13	A41	$1.50 multicolored	2.75	2.75
		Nos. 1-13 (13)	10.25	10.25

Issued; #2, 6-8, 10, 5/23; others, 6/26/85.

British Monarchs Type of Nanumaga

1984, Nov. 27   *Perf. 13x12½*
Se-tenant Pairs, #a.-b.

14	A2	1c Mary II	.30	.30
15	A2	10c Mary II, diff.	.30	.30
16	A2	30c Mary II, diff.	.50	.50
17	A2	50c Henry IV	.90	.90
18	A2	60c Henry IV, diff.	1.00	1.00
19	A2	$1 Henry IV, diff.	1.60	1.60
		Nos. 14-19 (6)	4.60	4.60

Cricket Players Type of 1984

1985, Jan. 7
Se-tenant Pairs, #a.-b.

20	A39	1c D.G. Aslett	.25	.25
21	A39	10c N.R. Taylor	.25	.25
22	A39	55c S. Oldham	.90	.90
23	A39	$1 C.W.J. Athey	1.90	1.90
		Nos. 20-23 (4)	3.30	3.30

Locomotive Type of 1984

No. 24, 1900 Class XV, Germany. No. 25, 1859 ECR Class Y, UK. No. 26, 1923 Nord Super Pacific, France. No. 27, 1905 LNWR Experiment Class, UK. No. 28, 1941 SR Merchant Navy Class, UK. No. 29, 1830 S. Carolina Railroad Best Friend of Charleston. No. 30, 1941 SR No. 1, UK. No. 31, 1987 Class 89, UK. No. 32, 1923 Southern Pacific Railroad Class 4300, US. No. 33, 1956 New South Wales Government Railways Class 46. No. 34, 1953 D.B. Class V200, Germany. No. 35, 1936 Union Railroad Class S-7, US. No. 36, 1877 Phildelphia & Reading Railroad Camelback. No. 37, 1968 J.N.R. Class 381, Japan. No. 38, 1933 Rio Grande Southern Railroad Galloping Goose Railcar, US. No. 39, 1935 Chicago, Milwaukee, St. Paul & Pacific Class A.

Se-tenant Pairs, #a.-b.
a. — Side and front views.
b. — Action scene.

1985-88

24	A36	1c multicolored	.25	.25
25	A36	5c multicolored	.25	.25
26	A36	10c multicolored	.25	.25
27	A36	10c multicolored	.25	.25
28	A36	15c multicolored	.30	.30
29	A36	20c multicolored	.40	.40
30	A36	25c multicolored	.55	.55
31	A36	30c multicolored	.65	.65
32	A36	40c multicolored	.85	.85
33	A36	50c multicolored	1.10	1.10
34	A36	60c multicolored	1.25	1.25
35	A36	60c multicolored	1.25	1.25
36	A36	60c multicolored	1.25	1.25
37	A36	70c multicolored	1.50	1.50
38	A36	$1 multicolored	2.25	2.25
a.		Souvenir sheet of 2	2.50	2.50
39	A36	$1.50 multicolored	3.25	3.25
		Nos. 24-39 (16)	15.60	15.60

Issued: Nos. 24, 26, 34, 37, 4/2/85; Nos. 29, 32, 35, 39, 3/20/86; Nos. 25, 27-28, 30-31, 33, 36, 38, 38a, 9/10/87.

1986 and 1987 stamps not inscribed "Leaders of the World."

Queen Mother Type of 1985

Hat: #44a, Wide-brimmed blue. #44b, Tiara. #45a, Tiara. #45b, Lavender. #46a, Blue. #46b, White stole. #47a, 50a, White. #47b, 50b, Blue. #48a, 49a, White. #48b, 49b, Wide-brimmed.

1985, Sept. 5   *Perf. 13x12½*

44	A45	10c Pair, #a.-b.	.25	.25
45	A45	45c Pair, #a.-b.	.80	.80
46	A45	65c Pair, #a.-b.	1.10	1.10
47	A45	$1 Pair, #a.-b.	1.75	1.75
		Nos. 44-47 (4)	3.90	3.90

Souvenir Sheets of 2

48	A45	$1.10 #a.-b.	2.00	2.00
49	A45	$1.75 #a.-b.	2.25	2.25
50	A45	$3 #a.-b.	3.25	3.25

Elizabeth II 60th Birthday Type

1986, Apr. 21   *Perf. 13x12½, 12½x13*

51	A49	5c Scarf	.25	.25
52	A49	40c Tiara	.25	.25
53	A49	$2 Bareheaded	.70	.70
54	A49	$4 Tiara, vert.	1.75	1.75
		Nos. 51-54 (4)	2.95	2.95

Souvenir Sheet

55	A49	$5 Blue hat	4.00	4.00

For overprints see Nos. 65-69.

Royal Wedding Type of 1986

#58a, Couple, vert. #58b, Andrew, vert. #59a, Andrew, parents. #59b, Andrew.

1986, July 22

58	A53	60c Pair, #a.-b.	1.00	1.00
59	A53	$1 Pair, #a.-b.	1.50	1.50

Souvenir Sheet

60	A56	$4 Wedding ceremony	4.00	4.00

Nos. 58-59 Ovptd. in Silver "Congratulations to T.R.H. The Duke & Duchess of York"

1986, Oct. 28

61	A53	60c Pair, #a.-b.	2.00	2.00
62	A53	$1 Pair, #a.-b.	3.50	3.50

Nos. 51-55 Ovptd. in Gold "40th WEDDING ANNIVERSARY OF H.M. QUEEN ELIZABETH II"

1987, Oct. 15

65	A49	5c multicolored	.25	.25
66	A49	40c multicolored	.35	.35
67	A49	$2 multicolored	1.75	1.75
68	A49	$4 multicolored	3.50	3.50
		Nos. 65-68 (4)	5.85	5.85

Souvenir Sheet

69	A49	$5 multicolored	5.50	5.50

NUKULAELAE

Locomotive Type of 1984

No. 1, 1891 Calbourne Class 02, UK. No. 2, 1912 K.P.E.V. Class T18, Germany. No. 3, 1942 SNCF Class 141P, France. No. 4, 1962 Class 47, UK. No. 5, 1941 Union Pacific Big Boy, US. No. 6, 1955 DRB 83-10, Germany. No. 7, 1940 S.N.C.F. 160-A-1, France. No. 8, 1901 Class AEG High Speed Railcar, Germany. No. 9, 1839 Albion Railroad Samson, Canada. No. 10, 1907 Saint Class, UK. No. 11, 1900 Nord De Glehn Atlantic, France. No. 12, 1851 Folkstone Class, UK. No. 13, 1914 J.N.R. Class 8620, Japan. No. 14, 1936 Class 8F, UK. No. 15, 1857 Shannon, UK. No. 16, 1948 Class A1, UK. No. 17, 1955 E.A.R. Class 59, Kenya. No. 18, 1897 V.R. Class Na, Australia. No. 19, 1859 Undine Class, UK. No. 20, 1935 Turbomotive, UK.

Se-tenant Pairs, #a.-b.
a. — Side and front views.
b. — Action scene.

Perf. 12½x13

1984-86   Litho.   Unwmk.

1	A36	5c multicolored	.25	.25
2	A36	5c multicolored	.25	.25
3	A36	10c multicolored	.25	.25
4	A36	10c multicolored	.25	.25
5	A36	15c multicolored	.25	.25
6	A36	15c multicolored	.25	.25
7	A36	20c multicolored	.25	.25
8	A36	25c multicolored	.25	.25
9	A36	25c multicolored	.25	.25
10	A36	40c multicolored	.45	.45
11	A36	40c multicolored	.45	.45
12	A36	40c multicolored	.45	.45
13	A36	50c multicolored	.55	.55
14	A36	50c multicolored	.55	.55
15	A36	80c multicolored	.95	.95
16	A36	$1 multicolored	1.20	1.20
17	A36	$1 multicolored	1.20	1.20
18	A36	$1 multicolored	1.20	1.20
19	A36	$1 multicolored	1.20	1.20
20	A36	$1.50 multicolored	1.75	1.75
		Nos. 1-20 (20)	12.20	12.20

Issued: Nos. 5, 10, 16, 5/23; Nos. 2, 7, 11, 17, 12/12; Nos. 3, 8, 13, 18, 3/24/85; Nos. 4, 6, 9, 12, 14, 15, 19-20, 7/11/86.

1986 stamps not inscribed "Leaders of the World."

Cricket Players Type of 1984

1984, Aug. 8   *Perf. 13x12½*
Se-tenant Pairs, #a.-b.

21	A39	5c D.B. Close	.25	.25
22	A39	15c G. Boycott	.25	.25
23	A39	30c D.L. Bairstow	.65	.65
24	A39	$1 T.G. Evans	1.90	1.90
		Nos. 21-24 (4)	3.05	3.05

Automobile Type of 1984

No. 25, 1924 Bugatti Type 35, France. No. 26, 1908 Sizaire-Naudin, France No. 27, 1965 Sunbeam Tiger, UK. No. 28, 1907 Napier 60HP Touring Car, UK. No. 29, 1975 BMW 2002 TII, Germany. No. 30, 1910 Austro-Daimler Prince Henry, Austria. No. 31, 1927 La Salle, US. No. 32, 1901 Oldsmobile Curved Dash Buckboard. No. 33, 1955 Rover 90, UK. No. 34, 1948 Chrysler Town & Country.

Se-tenant Pairs, #a.-b.
a. — Side and front views.
b. — Action scene.

1985   *Perf. 12½x13*

25	A41	5c multicolored	.25	.25
26	A41	10c multicolored	.25	.25
27	A41	25c multicolored	.45	.45
28	A41	35c multicolored	.65	.65
29	A41	35c multicolored	.65	.65
30	A41	50c multicolored	.95	.95
31	A41	50c multicolored	.95	.95
32	A41	70c multicolored	1.25	1.25
33	A41	75c multicolored	1.40	1.40
34	A41	$1 multicolored	1.60	1.60
		Nos. 25-34 (10)	8.40	8.40

Issue dates: Nos. 25, 28, 30, 32, Feb. 8; Nos. 26-27, 29, 31, 33-34, July 23.

Dogs — A8

#35a, Hungarian vizsla. #35b, Bearded collie. #36a, Bernese mountain dog. #36b, Boxer. #37a, Labrador retriever. #37b, Shetland sheepdog. #38a, Welsh springer spaniel. #38b, Scottish terrier.

1985, Apr. 30

35	A8	5c Pair, #a.-b.	.25	.25
36	A8	20c Pair, #a.-b.	.35	.35
37	A8	50c Pair, #a.-b.	.90	.90
38	A8	70c Pair, #a.-b.	1.25	1.25
		Nos. 35-38 (4)	2.75	2.75

Queen Mother Type of 1985

Hat: #47a, Purple. #47b, Blue. #48a, 52a, Tiara. #48b, 52b, Lavender. #49a, 53a, Pink. #49b, 53b, Dark blue. #50a, Light purple. #50b, Light blue. #51a, As young girl. #51b, Lace.

1985-86

47	A45	5c Pair, #a.-b.	.25	.25
48	A45	25c Pair, #a.-b.	.45	.45
49	A45	85c Pair, #a.-b.	1.60	1.60
50	A45	$1 Pair, #a.-b.	2.00	2.00
		Nos. 47-50 (4)	4.30	4.30

Souvenir Sheets of 2

51	A45	$1.20 #a.-b.	1.75	1.75
52	A45	$1.20 #a.-b.	1.50	1.50
53	A45	$3.50 #a.-b.	4.75	4.75

Issued: #46-51, 9/4; #52-53, 1/8/86.

Elizabeth II 60th Birthday Type

1986, Apr. 21   *Perf. 13x12½, 12½x13*

54	A49	10c White hat	.25	.25
55	A49	$1 As young woman	.55	.55
56	A49	$1.50 In orange dress	.85	.85
57	A49	$3 Tiara, vert.	1.50	1.50
		Nos. 54-57 (4)	3.15	3.15

Souvenir Sheet

58	A49	$4 In brown dress	3.00	3.00

Royal Wedding Type of 1986

#61a, Andrew, vert. #61b, Couple, vert. #62a, Sarah Ferguson and Princess Diana. #62b, Andrew.

1986, July 23   *Perf. 12½x13, 13x12½*

61	A53	60c Pair, #a.-b.	1.10	1.10
62	A53	$1 Pair, #a.-b.	1.75	1.75

Souvenir Sheet

63	A56	$4 Sarah in wedding dress	4.50	4.50

Nos. 61-62 Ovptd. in Silver "Congratulations to T.R.H. The Duke & Duchess of York"

1986, Oct. 28

64	A53	60c Pair, #a.-b.	2.00	2.00
65	A53	$1 Pair, #a.-b.	3.25	3.25

Queen Elizabeth II 40th Wedding Anniv. Type of Nanumaga

15c, Queen Victoria. 35c, Princesses Margaret and Elizabeth. 60c, Elizabeth holding Princess Anne. $1.50, Elizabeth, Philip. $1.75, Elizabeth wearing tiara. $3, Elizabeth.

			1987, Oct. 15	**Perf. 15**	
68	A5	15c multicolored	.25	.25
69	A5	35c multicolored	.50	.50
70	A5	60c multicolored	.75	.75
71	A5	$1.50 multicolored	2.10	2.10
72	A5	$1.75 multicolored	2.40	2.40
		Nos. 68-72 (5)	6.00	6.00

Souvenir Sheet

73	A5	$3 multicolored	4.00	4.00

Queen Victoria's accession to the throne, sesquicentennial.

VAITUPU

Automobile Type of 1984

No. 1, 1961 Lotus Elite, UK. No. 2, 1950 MG TD Midget, UK. No. 3, 1932 Hillman Minx, UK. No. 4, 1905 White Model E Steam Car, US. No. 5, 1935 Auburn Supercharged 851, US. No. 6, 1981 Renault RE20, France. No. 7, 1928 Lea-Francis Hyper. No. 8, 1940 Packard Darrin. No. 9, 1938 Graham, US. No. 10, 1968 Chevrolet Camaro. No. 11, 1957 Renault Dauphine-Gordini, France. No. 12, 1930 Packard Eight. No. 13, 1926 Miller Special, US. No. 14, 1950 Healey Silverstone, UK. No. 15, 1970 De Tomaso Pantera, Italy. No. 16, 1927 Bentley 3-Liter, UK.

Se-tenant Pairs, #a.-b.
a. — Side and front views.
b. — Action scene.

Perf. 12½x13

		1984-85	**Litho.**	**Unwmk.**	
1	A41	5c multicolored	.25	.25
2	A41	15c multicolored	.25	.25
3	A41	15c multicolored	.25	.25
4	A41	15c multicolored	.25	.25
5	A41	25c multicolored	.25	.25
6	A41	25c multicolored	.25	.25
7	A41	30c multicolored	.25	.25
8	A41	30c multicolored	.25	.25
9	A41	30c multicolored	.25	.25
10	A41	40c multicolored	.35	.35
11	A41	40c multicolored	.35	.35
12	A41	50c multicolored	.45	.45
13	A41	50c multicolored	.45	.45
14	A41	60c multicolored	.55	.55
15	A41	60c multicolored	.55	.55
16	A41	$1 multicolored	.90	.90
		Nos. 1-16 (16)	5.85	5.85

Issued: Nos. 2, 5, 7, 12, Mar. 19; Nos. 1, 3, 6, 8, 10, 13-14, 16, Dec. 12; Nos. 4, 9, 11, 15, Apr. 4, 1985.

British Monarchs Type of Nanumaga

		1984, July 18	**Perf. 13x12½**	
		Se-tenant Pairs, #a.-b.		
17	A2	1c Richard III	.25	.25
18	A2	5c Charles I	.25	.25
19	A2	15c Charles I, diff.	.25	.25
20	A2	40c Richard III, diff.	.50	.50
21	A2	50c Richard III, diff.	.60	.60
22	A2	$1 Charles I, diff.	1.15	1.15
		Nos. 17-22 (6)	3.00	3.00

Locomotive Type of 1984

No. 23, 1929 D.R.G. V3201, Germany. No. 24, 1841 G.W.R. Leo Class, UK. No. 25, 1937 New York Central Railroad Class J3a. No. 26, 1949 Richmond, Fredericksburg & Potomac Railroad Class E8. No. 27, 1845 Columbine, UK. No. 28, 1954 BR Class 2MT, UK. No. 29, 1980 Amtrak Class AEM-7. No. 30, 1981 Via Rail LRC Class MPA-27a, Canada. No. 31, 1983 British Columbia Railway Class GF6C. No. 32, 1888 D&H Class B, India. No. 33, 1936 D.R. Class 45, Germany. No. 34, 1904 Northern Pacific Railway Class W, US. No. 35, 1855 W. & A. R.R. General, US. No. 36, 1938 Chicago & North Western Railway Class E-4. No. 37, 1911 J.N.R. Class 9020 Mallet, Japan. No. 38, 1977 Chicago Regional Transportation Authority Class F40.

Se-tenant Pairs, #a.-b.
a. — Side and front views.
b. — Action scene.

		1985-87	**Perf. 12½x13**	
23	A36	5c multicolored	.25	.25
24	A36	10c multicolored	.25	.25
25	A36	10c multicolored	.25	.25
26	A36	15c multicolored	.30	.30
27	A36	25c multicolored	.55	.55
28	A36	25c multicolored	.55	.55
29	A36	25c multicolored	.55	.55
30	A36	35c multicolored	.75	.75
31	A36	45c multicolored	.95	.95
32	A36	50c multicolored	1.10	1.10
33	A36	60c multicolored	1.25	1.25
34	A36	65c multicolored	1.40	1.40
35	A36	80c multicolored	1.75	1.75
36	A36	85c multicolored	1.90	1.90
37	A36	$1 multicolored	2.25	2.25
38	A36	$1 multicolored	2.25	2.25
		Nos. 23-38 (16)	16.30	16.30

Issued: Nos. 24, 27, 32-33, 3/7/85; Nos. 23, 28, 35, 37, 1/16/86; Nos. 25-26, 29-31, 34, 36, 38, 9/10/87.

1986 and 1987 stamps not inscribed "Leaders of the World."

A9

Butterfly illustrations by Roger V. Vigurs: #39a, Marpesia petreus. #39b, Pseudolycaena marsyas. #40a, Charaxes jasius. #40b, Junonia coenia. #41a, Palaeochrysophanus hippothoe. #41b, Sticopthalma camadeva. #42a, Phoebis avellaneda. #42b, Apatura iris.

		1985, Mar. 12	**Perf. 13x12½**	
39	A9	5c Pair, #a.-b.	.25	.25
40	A9	15c Pair, #a.-b.	.30	.30
41	A9	50c Pair, #a.-b.	1.00	1.00
42	A9	75c Pair, #a.-b.	1.60	1.60
		Nos. 39-42 (4)	3.15	3.15

Queen Mother Type of 1985

Hat: #51a, 57a, Light blue. #51b, 57b, White. #52a, Tiara. #52b, Lavender. #53a, 56a, Violet. #53b, 56b, Green. #54a, Blue. #54b, Pink. #55a, Looking up. #55b, Looking forward.

		1985-86		
51	A45	15c Pair, #a.-b.	.25	.25
52	A45	40c Pair, #a.-b.	.75	.75
53	A45	65c Pair, #a.-b.	1.10	1.10
54	A45	95c Pair, #a.-b.	1.90	1.90
		Nos. 51-54 (4)	4.00	4.00

Souvenir Sheets of 2

55	A45	$1.10 #a.-b.	2.10	2.10
56	A45	$2 #a.-b.	2.25	2.25
57	A45	$2.50 #a.-b.	3.00	3.00

Issued: #51-55, 8/28; 56-57, 1/8/86.

Elizabeth II 60th Birthday Type

		1986, Apr. 21	**Perf. 13x12½, 12½x13**	
58	A49	5c Green hat	.25	.25
59	A49	60c As young woman	.25	.25
60	A49	$2 Flowered hat	.65	.65
61	A49	$3.50 Tiara, vert.	1.05	1.05
		Nos. 58-61 (4)	2.20	2.20

Souvenir Sheet

62	A49	$5 Straw hat	4.25	4.25

For overprints see Nos. 72-76.

Royal Wedding Type of 1986

#65a, Andrew, vert. #65b, Sarah Ferguson, vert. #66a, Charles, Andrew. #66b, Couple.

		1986, July 18	**Perf. 12½x13, 13x12½**	
65	A53	60c Pair, #a.-b.	1.10	1.10
66	A53	$1 Pair, #a.-b.	1.75	1.75

Souvenir Sheet

67	A56	$4 Newlyweds	4.00	4.00

Nos. 65-66 Ovptd. in Silver "Congratulations to T.R.H. The Duke & Duchess of York"

		1986, Oct. 28		
68	A53	60c Pair, #a.-b.	2.25	2.25
69	A53	$1 Pair, #a.-b.	3.50	3.50

Nos. 58-62 Ovptd. in Gold "40th WEDDING ANNIVERSARY OF H.M. QUEEN ELIZABETH II"

		1987, Oct. 15	**Perf. 13x12½, 12½x13**	
72	A49	5c multicolored	.25	.25
73	A49	60c multicolored	.75	.75
74	A49	$2 multicolored	2.50	2.50
75	A49	$3 multicolored	3.75	3.75
		Nos. 72-75 (4)	7.25	7.25

Souvenir Sheet

76	A49	$5 multicolored	5.75	5.75

UBANGI-SHARI

ü-ˈbaŋ͵gē ˈshär-ē

(Ubangi-Shari-Chad)

LOCATION — In Western Africa, north of the equator
GOVT. — French Colony
AREA — 238,767 sq. mi.
POP. — 833,916
CAPITAL — Bangui

In 1910 French Congo was divided into the three colonies of Gabon, Middle Congo and Ubangi-Shari and officially named "French Equatorial Africa." Under that name in 1934 the group, with the territory of Chad included, became a single administrative unit. See Gabon.

100 Centimes = 1 Franc

Stamps of Middle Congo Ovptd. in Black

		1915-22	**Unwmk.**	**Perf. 14x13½**	
		Chalky Paper			
1	A1	1c ol gray & brn	.35	.70
a.		Double overprint	190.00	
b.		Imperf.	60.00	
2	A1	2c violet & brn	.35	.70
3	A1	4c blue & brn	.70	.70
4	A1	5c dk grn & bl	.70	1.00
5	A1	5c yel & bl ('22)	1.00	1.40
6	A1	10c carmine & bl	1.40	1.00
7	A1	10c dp grn & bl grn ('22)	1.00	1.40
8	A1	15c brn vio & rose	1.75	1.00
9	A1	20c brown & blue	3.50	4.25

No. 8 is on ordinary paper

Overprinted

10	A2	25c blue & grn	2.10	2.10
11	A2	25c bl grn & gray ('22)	1.40	1.40
12	A2	30c scarlet & grn	2.10	2.10
13	A2	30c dp rose & rose ('22)	1.00	1.40
14	A2	35c vio brn & bl	5.50	5.50
15	A2	40c dl grn & brn	5.50	7.00
16	A2	45c vio & red	5.50	7.00
17	A2	50c bl grn & red	7.00	7.00
18	A2	50c blue & grn ('22)	1.00	1.40
19	A2	75c brown & bl	14.00	14.00
20	A3	1fr dp grn & vio	14.00	14.00
21	A3	2fr vio & gray grn	14.00	17.50
22	A3	5fr blue & rose	42.50	42.50
		Nos. 1-22 (22)	126.35	136.15

For surcharges see Nos. B1-B2.

Middle Congo of 1907-22 Ovptd. in Black or Red

		1922		
23	A1	1c violet & grn	.70	1.00
a.		Overprint omitted	170.00	190.00
b.		Imperf.	40.00	
24	A1	2c grn & salmon	.70	1.00
25	A1	4c ol brn & brn	1.00	1.40
a.		Overprint omitted	200.00	225.00
26	A1	5c indigo & rose	1.00	1.40
27	A1	10c dp grn & gray grn	1.75	2.10
28	A1	15c lt red & dl bl	1.75	2.10
29	A1	20c choc & salmon	5.00	5.50

Overprinted

30	A2	25c vio & salmon	7.00	8.50
31	A2	30c rose & pale rose	2.75	3.50
32	A2	35c vio & grn	4.75	5.00
33	A2	40c ind & vio (R)	4.75	5.00
34	A2	45c choc & vio	4.75	5.00
35	A2	50c dk bl & pale bl	2.75	3.50
36	A2	60c on 75c vio, pnksh	3.50	4.25
37	A2	75c choc & sal	5.00	6.25
38	A3	1fr grn & dl bl (R)	10.50	11.00
a.		Overprint omitted	275.00	
39	A3	2fr grn & salmon	14.00	14.00
40	A3	5fr grn & ol brn	21.00	25.00
		Nos. 23-40 (18)	92.65	105.50

Nos. 23-29 with Additional Ovpt. in Black, Blue or Red

		1924-33		
41	A1	1c vio & grn (Bl)	.35	.50
a.		"OUBANGUI CHARI" omitted	140.00	140.00
42	A1	2c grn & sal (Bl)	.35	.55
a.		"OUBANGUI CHARI" omitted	140.00	140.00
b.		Double overprint	150.00	
43	A1	4c ol brn & brn (Bl)	.35	.55
a.		Double overprint (Bl + Bk)	175.00	
b.		"AEF" omitted	160.00	
44	A1	5c ind & rose	.35	.55
a.		"OUBANGUI CHARI" omitted	130.00	
45	A1	10c dp grn & gray grn	.70	.85
46	A1	10c red org & bl ('25)	.70	.70
47	A1	15c sal & dl bl	.80	.85
48	A1	15c sal & dl bl (Bl) ('26)	1.00	1.40
49	A1	20c choc & salmon (Bl)	1.00	1.40

On Nos. 41-49 the color in ( ) refers to the overprint "Afrique Equatoriale Francaise."

Overprinted

50	A2	25c vio & salmon (Bl)	.70	.70
a.		Imperf.		
51	A2	30c rose & pale rose (Bl)	.70	1.00
52	A2	30c choc & red ('25)	.70	1.00
a.		"OUBANGUI CHARI" omitted	140.00	
53	A2	30c dk grn & grn ('27)	1.40	1.75
54	A2	35c vio & grn (Bl)	.70	1.00
a.		"OUBANGUI CHARI" omitted	275.00	
55	A2	40c ind & vio (Bl)	.70	1.00
56	A2	45c choc & vio (Bl)	1.00	1.40
57	A2	50c dk bl & pale bl (R)	.70	.70
58	A2	50c gray & bl vio ('25) (R)	1.40	1.40
59	A2	60c on 75c dk vio, pnksh (R)	.70	.55
60	A2	65c org brn & bl ('28)	1.40	1.75
61	A2	75c choc & sal (Bl)	1.75	2.10
62	A2	75c dp bl & lt bl ('25) (R)	1.40	1.40
a.		"OUBANGUI CHARI" omitted	140.00	
63	A2	75c rose & dk brn ('28)	2.10	2.50
64	A2	90c brn red & pink ('30)	4.25	5.00
65	A3	1fr grn & ind (Bk + Bl) ('25)	.70	1.00
66	A3	1fr grn & ind (R + Bl)	1.40	2.10
67	A3	1.10fr bister & bl ('28)	3.50	3.50
68	A3	1.25fr mag & lt grn ('33)	10.50	10.50
69	A3	1.50fr ultra & bl ('30)	7.00	7.00
70	A3	1.75fr dk brn & dp buff ('33)	10.50	14.00

71	A3	2fr grn & red	1.40	2.10
a.		"OUBANGUI CHARI" omitted	1,250.	1,050.
b.		"OUBANGUI CHARI" double	1,200.	
72	A3	3fr red vio ('30)	5.00	5.50
73	A3	5fr grn & ol brn (Bl)	4.50	5.50
		Nos. 41-73 (33)	69.95	81.80

On Nos. 65, 66 the first overprint color refers to OUBANGUI CHARI.
For surcharges see Nos. 74-81.

Types of 1924 Issue Surcharged with New Values in Black or Red

1925-26

74	A3	65c on 1fr vio & ol	2.10	2.10
a.		"65" omitted	140.00	
75	A3	85c on 1fr vio & ol	2.10	2.10
a.		"AFRIQUE EQUATORIALE FRANCAISE" omitted	140.00	160.00
b.		Double surcharge	160.00	
76	A3	1.25fr on 1fr dk bl & ultra (R) ('26)	1.40	2.25
a.		"1f25" omitted	165.00	

Bars cover old denomination on No. 76.

Types of 1924 Issue Surcharged with New Values and Bars

1927

77	A2	90c on 75c brn red & rose red	2.10	2.75
78	A3	1.50fr on 1fr ultra & bl	2.10	2.75
79	A3	3fr on 5fr org brn & dl red	3.50	3.50
80	A3	10fr on 5fr ver & vio	17.50	19.00
81	A3	20fr on 5fr vio & gray	27.50	29.00
		Nos. 77-81 (5)	52.70	57.00

Common Design Types pictured following the introduction.

Colonial Exposition Issue
Common Design Types

1931   Engr.   Perf. 12½
Name of Country Typo. in Black

82	CD70	40c deep green	5.00	5.00
83	CD71	50c violet	5.00	5.00
84	CD72	90c red orange	5.50	5.50
a.		Imperf.	120.00	
85	CD73l	1.50fr dull blue	5.50	5.50
		Nos. 82-85 (4)	21.00	21.00

SEMI-POSTAL STAMPS

Regular Issue of 1915 Surcharged

1916   Unwmk.   Perf. 14x13½
Chalky Paper

B1	A1	10c + 5c car & blue	2.75	3.25
a.		Inverted surch.		160.00
b.		Double surcharge		160.00
c.		Double surch., one invtd.	125.00	125.00
d.		Vertical surcharge	140.00	140.00
e.		No period under "C"	17.50	17.50

Regular Issue of 1915 Surcharged in Carmine

B2	A1	10c + 5c car & blue	1.75	2.10

POSTAGE DUE STAMPS

Postage Due Stamps of France Overprinted

1928   Unwmk.   Perf. 14x13½

J1	D2	5c light blue	1.40	2.10
J2	D2	10c gray brown	1.75	2.10
J3	D2	20c olive green	1.75	2.10
J4	D2	25c bright rose	1.75	2.10
J5	D2	30c light red	1.75	2.10
J6	D2	45c blue green	1.75	2.10
J7	D2	50c brown violet	2.50	3.50

J8	D2	60c yellow brown	2.75	3.50
J9	D2	1fr red brown	3.50	5.00
J10	D2	2fr orange red	7.00	7.00
J11	D2	3fr bright violet	7.00	7.00
		Nos. J1-J11 (11)	32.90	38.60

Landscape D3

Emile Gentil — D4

1930   Typo.

J12	D3	5c dp bl & olive	.70	1.05
J13	D3	10c dk red & brn	1.05	1.40
J14	D3	20c green & brn	1.05	1.40
J15	D3	25c lt bl & brn	1.40	1.75
J16	D3	30c bis brn & Prus bl	2.50	2.75
J17	D3	45c Prus bl & ol	3.25	3.50
J18	D3	50c red vio & brn	5.25	6.00
J19	D3	60c gray lil & bl blk	5.50	5.50
J20	D4	1fr bis brn & bl blk	5.25	6.00
J21	D4	2fr violet & brown	5.50	7.00
J22	D4	3fr dp red & brn	7.00	8.50
		Nos. J12-J22 (11)	38.45	44.85

Stamps of Ubangi-Shari were replaced in 1936 by those of French Equatorial Africa.

UGANDA
ü-'gan-də

LOCATION — East Africa, at the Equator and separated from the Indian Ocean by Kenya and Tanzania
GOVT. — Independent state
AREA — 91,343 sq. mi.
POP. — 21,619,700 (1999 est.)
CAPITAL — Kampala

Stamps of 1898-1902 were replaced by those issued for Kenya, Tanganyika and Uganda. Uganda became independent October 9, 1962.

Cowries (50 = 4 Pence)
16 Annas = 1 Rupee (1896)
100 Cents = 1 Shilling (1962)

> **Catalogue values for unused stamps in this country are for Never Hinged items, beginning with Scott 79 in the regular postage section and Scott J1 in the postage due section.**

Unused values for Nos. 2-68 are for stamps without gum. Very fine examples will be evenly cut and will show at least two full typewritten framelines.

A1

A2

Nos. 1-53 were produced with a typewriter by Rev. Ernest Millar of the Church Missionary Society. They were 20-26mm wide, with nine stamps in a horizontal row. Later two more were added to each row, and the stamps became narrower, 16-18mm.
Rev. Millar got a new typewriter in 1895, and the stamps he typed on it have a different appearance. A violet ribbon in the machine, inserted late in 1895, resulted in Nos. 35-53.
Nos. 1-53 are on thin, tough, white paper, laid horizontally with traces of a few vertical lines.
Forgeries of Nos. 1-53 are known.

Without Gum
Wide Letters
Typeset on Thin Laid Paper
Stamps 20 to 26mm wide

				Imperf.
1895		**Unwmk.**		**Imperf.**
1	A1	10(c) black	5,750.	3,750.
2	A1	20(c) black	9,600.	2,350.
a.		"U A" instead of "U G"		7,750.
3	A1	30(c) black	2,500.	2,000.
4	A1	40(c) black	7,750.	2,000.
5	A1	50(c) black	1,800.	1,400.
a.		"U A" instead of "U G"		10,000.
6	A1	60(c) black	3,250.	2,850.

Surcharged with New Value in Black, Pen-written

9	A1	10 on 30(c) black		85,000.
10	A1	10 on 50(c) black		85,000.
11	A1	15 on 10(c) black		70,000.
12	A1	15 on 20(c) black		85,000.
13	A1	15 on 40(c) black		85,000.
14	A1	15 on 50(c) black		80,000.
15	A1	25 on 10(c) black		85,000.
16	A1	50 on 60(c) black		85,000.

Stamps 16 to 18mm wide

17	A1	5(c) black	4,000.	1,650.
18	A1	10(c) black	4,000.	2,000.
19	A1	15(c) black	2,500.	1,900.
a.		Vertically laid paper		6,500.
20	A1	20(c) black	4,000.	1,900.
a.		Vertically laid paper		8,250.
21	A1	25(c) black	2,000.	2,000.
22	A1	30(c) black	10,500.	10,000.
23	A1	40(c) black	10,000.	10,000.
24	A1	50(c) black	4,750.	5,750.
25	A1	60(c) black	10,000.	10,000.

Narrow Letters
Stamps 16 to 18mm wide

26	A2	5(c) black	2,000.	
27	A2	10(c) black	2,150.	
28	A2	15(c) black	2,150.	
29	A2	20(c) black	1,800.	
30	A2	25(c) black	2,000.	
31	A2	30(c) black	2,250.	
32	A2	40(c) black	2,000.	

33	A2	50(c) black	2,150.	
34	A2	60(c) black	3,200.	
35	A2	5(c) violet	900.	825.
36	A2	10(c) violet	825.	825.
37	A2	15(c) violet	1,400.	750.
38	A2	20(c) violet	600.	375.
a.		"G A" instead of "U G"		
b.		Vertically laid paper	3,850.	
39	A2	25(c) violet	2,300.	2,000.
40	A2	30(c) violet	2,850.	1,400.
41	A2	40(c) violet	2,800.	1,900.
42	A2	50(c) violet	2,500.	1,900.
43	A2	100(c) violet	3,250.	3,750.

As a favor to a philatelist, 35c and 45c denominations were made in black and violet. They were not intended for postal use and no rate called for those denominations.

A3

1896

44	A3	5(c) violet	950.	1,250.
45	A3	10(c) violet	1,050.	825.
46	A3	15(c) violet	950.	950.
47	A3	20(c) violet	500.	275.
48	A3	25(c) violet	875.	1,150.
49	A3	30(c) violet	950.	1,050.
50	A3	40(c) violet	1,100.	1,150.
51	A3	50(c) violet	950.	1,000.
52	A3	60(c) violet	2,000.	2,500.
53	A3	100(c) violet	1,900.	2,500.

A4

Overprinted "L" in Black

1896	**Typeset**		**White Paper**	
54	A4	1a black (thin "1")	210.	190.
a.		Small "O" in "POSTAGE"	1,550.	1,300.
55	A4	2a black	135.	140.
a.		Small "O" in "POSTAGE"	615.	675.
56	A4	3a black	300.	375.
a.		Small "O" in "POSTAGE"	1,900.	2,250.
57	A4	4a black	135.	180.
a.		Small "O" in "POSTAGE"	625.	

Yellowish Paper

58	A4	8a black	225.	340.
a.		Small "O" in "POSTAGE"	1,675.	2,100.
59	A4	1r black	425.	500.
a.		Small "O" in "POSTAGE"	2,250.	
60	A4	5r black	37,500.	37,500.

A4a

Without Overprint
White Paper

61	A4a	1a black (thin "1")	125.00	110.00
a.		Small "O" in "POSTAGE"	700.00	675.00
62	A4a	1a black (thick "1")	26.00	30.00
a.		Small "O" in "POSTAGE"	95.00	110.00
63	A4a	2a black	32.50	40.00
a.		Small "O" in "POSTAGE"	110.00	140.00
64	A4a	3a black	32.50	50.00
a.		Small "O" in "POSTAGE"	135.00	200.00
65	A4a	4a black	35.00	42.50
a.		Small "O" in "POSTAGE"	125.00	

Yellowish Paper

66	A4a	8a black	42.50	50.00
a.		Small "O" in "POSTAGE"	155.00	200.00
67	A4a	1r black	95.00	110.00
a.		Small "O" in "POSTAGE"	400.00	475.00
68	A4a	5r black	300.00	400.00
a.		Small "O" in "POSTAGE"	1,000.	1,250.

A5

Queen Victoria — A6

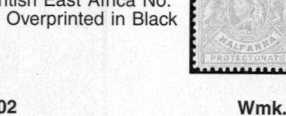

1898-1902 Engr. Wmk. 2 Perf. 14

69	A5	1a red	6.00	4.50
70	A5	1a car rose ('02)	2.50	2.00
71	A5	2a brown	9.25	11.00
72	A5	3a gray	22.50	50.00
73	A5	4a dark green	15.00	16.00
74	A5	8a olive gray	15.00	32.50

Wmk. 1

75	A6	1r ultra	60.00	60.00
76	A6	5r brown	110.00	130.00
		Nos. 69-76 (8)	240.25	306.00

British East Africa No. 72 Overprinted in Black

1902 Wmk. 2

77	A8	½a yellow green	3.25	2.25
a.		Inverted overprint	2,200.	
b.		Double overprint	2,800.	
c.		Pair, one without overprint	2,750.	

British East Africa No. 76 Overprinted in Red

78	A8	2½a dark blue	5.00	3.50
a.		Double overprint	650.00	

> **Catalogue values for unused stamps in this section, from this point to the end of the section, are for Never Hinged items.**

Ripon Falls and Speke Monument A8

Wmk. 314
1962, July 28 Engr. Perf. 14

79	A8	30c vermilion & blk	.30	.30
80	A8	50c violet & blk	.30	.30
81	A8	1.30sh green & blk	.55	.55
82	A8	2.50sh ultra & blk	2.00	2.00
		Nos. 79-82 (4)	3.15	3.15

Cent. of the discovery of the source of the Nile by John Hanning Speke.

Independent State

Murchison Falls — A9

Mulago Hospital, X-Ray Service A10

Designs: 10c, Tobacco growing. 15c, Coffee growing. 20c, Ankole cattle. 30c, Cotton growing. 50c, Mountains of the Moon. 1.30sh, Rubaga and Namirembe Cathedrals and Kibuli Mosque. 2sh, Makerere College and students. 5sh, Copper mining. 10sh, Cement factory. 20sh, Parliament.

Perf. 14½x14, 14x14½
1962, Oct. 9 Photo. Unwmk.

83	A9	5c Prus green	.25	.25
84	A9	10c red brown	.25	.25
85	A9	15c grn, blk & car	.25	.25
86	A9	20c bister & pur	.25	.25
87	A9	30c brt blue	.25	.25
88	A9	50c bluish grn & blk	.25	.25
89	A10	1sh bl grn, sep & red	.75	.65
90	A10	1.30sh pur & ocher	.30	.65
91	A10	2sh grnsh bl, blk & dk car	.50	.80
92	A10	5sh dk grn & red	6.00	1.60

93	A10	10sh red brn & slate	4.00	3.75
94	A10	20sh blue & pale brn	5.50	17.50
		Nos. 83-94 (12)	18.55	26.45

Uganda's independence, Oct. 9, 1962.

Crowned Crane — A11

1965, Feb. 20 Photo. Perf. 14½

95	A11	30c bl grn, blk, yel & red	.30	.25
96	A11	1sh30c ultra, blk, yel & red	.90	.70

Intl. Trade Fair at Lugogo Stadium, Kampala, Feb. 20-28.

Black Bee-eater A12

African Jacana A13

Arms of Uganda and Birds: 15c, Orange weaver. 20c, Narina trogon. 30c, Sacred ibis. 40c, Blue-breasted kingfisher. 50c, Whale-headed stork. 65c, Black-winged red bishop. 1sh, Ruwenzori turaco. 1.30sh, African fish eagle. 2.50sh, Great blue turaco. 5sh, Lilac-breasted roller. 10sh, Black-collared lovebird. 20sh, Crowned crane.

Perf. 14½x14, 14x14½
1965, Oct. 9 Photo. Unwmk.
Birds in Natural Colors
Size: 17x21mm, 21x17mm

97	A12	5c lt vio bl & blk	.30	.40
98	A13	10c dull blue & red	.30	.40
99	A12	15c dk brown & org	.30	.40
100	A12	20c bister & brt grn	.30	.40
101	A13	30c hen brn & blk	2.00	.40
102	A12	40c lt yel grn & red	1.25	.60
103	A12	50c dp pur & gray	.35	.40
104	A13	65c gray & brick red	2.75	2.00

Perf. 14½
Size: 41x25mm, 25x41mm

105	A12	1sh lt blue & blk	.70	.40
106	A12	1.30sh yel & red brn	7.00	.40
107	A13	2.50sh brt yel grn & blk	5.50	.60
108	A12	5sh lil gray & vio bl	8.50	4.00
109	A13	10sh lt brown & blk	13.50	10.50
110	A13	20sh olive grn & blk	25.00	34.00
		Nos. 97-110 (14)	67.75	54.90

Parliament Building — A14

13th Commonwealth Parliamentary Assoc. Conf.: 30c, Animal carvings from entrance hall of Uganda Parliament. 50c, Arms of Uganda. 2.50sh, Parliament Chamber.

1967, Oct. 26 Photo. Perf. 14½

111	A14	30c multicolored	.25	.25
112	A14	50c multicolored	.25	.25
113	A14	1.30sh multicolored	.25	.25
114	A14	2.50sh multicolored	.50	1.25
		Nos. 111-114 (4)	1.25	2.00

Cordia
Abyssinica
A15

Black-galled
Acacia
A16

Flowers: 10c, Grewia similis. 15c, Cassia didymobotrya. 20c, Coleus barbatus. 30c, Ochna ovata. 40c, Ipomoea spathulata (morning glory). 50c, Spathodea nilotica (flame tree). 60c, Oncoba spinosa. 70c, Carissa edulis. 1.50sh, Clerodendrum myricoides (blue butterfly bush). 2.50sh, Acanthus arboreus. 5sh, Kigelia aethiopium (sausage tree). 10sh, Erythrina abyssinica (Uganda coral). 20sh, Monodora myristica.

Perf. 14½x14

			1969, Oct. 9	Photo.	Unwmk.
115	A15	5c multicolored	.25	.25
116	A15	10c multicolored	.25	.25
117	A15	15c multicolored	.25	.25
118	A15	20c multicolored	.25	.25
119	A15	30c multicolored	.25	.25
120	A15	40c gray & multi	.25	.25
121	A15	50c tan & multi	.25	.25
122	A15	60c multicolored	.25	.25
123	A15	70c multicolored	.25	.25

Perf. 14

124	A16	1sh multicolored	.35	.25
125	A16	1.50sh multicolored	.55	.25
126	A16	2.50sh multicolored	.70	.25
127	A16	5sh multicolored	1.25	.25
128	A16	10sh multicolored	3.00	.55
129	A16	20sh multicolored	7.75	1.25
		Nos. 115-129 (15)	15.85	5.05

Values of Nos. 124-129 are for canceled-to-order stamps. Cancellations were printed on Nos. 128-129. Postally used examples sell for higher prices.

Nos. 125-126, 129 Surcharged

			1975, Sept. 29	Photo.	Perf. 14
130	A16	2sh on 1.50sh multi	.90	1.75
131	A16	3sh on 2.50sh multi	17.50	37.50
132	A16	40sh on 20sh multi	7.00	15.00
		Nos. 130-132 (3)	25.40	54.25

Millet — A17

Ugandan Crops: 20c, Sugar cane. 30c, Tobacco. 40c, Onions. 50c, Tomatoes. 70c, Tea. 80c, Bananas. 1sh, Corn. Pineapple. 3sh, Coffee. 5sh, Oranges. 10sh, Peanuts. 20sh, Cotton. 40sh, Beans.

1975, Oct. 9   Photo.   Perf. 14x14½
Size: 21x17mm
Multicolored, Name Panel as follows

133	A17	10c lt brown	.25	.25
134	A17	20c blue	.25	.25
135	A17	30c vermilion	.25	.25
136	A17	40c lilac	.25	.25
137	A17	50c olive	.25	.25
138	A17	70c brt green	.25	.25
139	A17	80c purple	.25	.25

Perf. 14½
Size: 41x25mm

140	A17	1sh ocher	.25	.25
141	A17	2sh slate	.25	.25
142	A17	3sh blue	.30	.40
143	A17	5sh yellow green	.35	.55
144	A17	10sh brown red	.70	1.10
145	A17	20sh rose lilac	1.50	2.25
146	A17	40sh orange	2.75	4.25
		Nos. 133-146 (14)	7.85	10.80

See #195-198. For surcharge & overprints see #175, 203-206, 227-244, 253-257.

Communications Type of Tanzania 1976

Designs: 50c, Microwave tower. 1sh, Cordless switchboard and operators, horiz. 2sh, Telephones of 1880, 1930 and 1976. 3sh, Message switching center, horiz.

1976, Apr. 15   Litho.   Perf. 14½

147	A6a	50c blue & multi	.25	.25
148	A6a	1sh red & multi	.25	.25
149	A6a	2sh yellow & multi	.25	.25
150	A6a	3sh multicolored	.35	.35
a.		Souvenir sheet of 4	1.40	1.40
		Nos. 147-150 (4)	1.10	1.10

Telecommunications development in East Africa. No. 150a contains 4 stamps similar to Nos. 147-150 with simulated perforations.

Olympics Type of Tanzania 1976

Designs: 50c, Akii Bua, Ugandan hurdler. 1sh, Filbert Bayi, Tanzanian runner. 2sh, Steve Muchoki, Kenyan boxer. 3sh, Olympic torch, flags of Kenya, Tanzania and Uganda.

1976, July 5   Litho.   Perf. 14½

151	A6b	50c blue & multi	.25	.25
152	A6b	1sh red & multi	.25	.25
153	A6b	2sh yellow & multi	.30	.30
154	A6b	3sh blue & multi	.50	.40
a.		Souv. sheet of 4, #151-154, perf 13	6.00	5.00
		Nos. 151-154 (4)	1.30	1.20

21st Olympic Games, Montreal, Canada, July 17-Aug. 1.

Railway Type of Tanzania 1976

Designs: 50c, Tanzania-Zambia Railway. 1sh, Nile bridge, Uganda. 2sh, Nakuru Station, Kenya. 3sh, Class A locomotive, 1896.

1976, Oct. 4   Litho.   Perf. 14

155	A6c	50c lilac & multi	.25	.25
156	A6c	1sh emerald & multi	.35	.35
157	A6c	2sh brt rose & multi	.65	.45
158	A6c	3sh yellow & multi	1.00	.65
a.		Souv. sheet of 4, #155-158, perf 13	3.25	3.25
		Nos. 155-158 (4)	2.25	1.60

Rail transport in East Africa.

Fish Type of Tanzania 1977

1977, Jan. 10   Litho.   Perf. 14½

159	A6d	50c Nile perch	.25	.25
160	A6d	1sh Tilapia	.30	.25
161	A6d	3sh Sailfish	.80	.60
162	A6d	5sh Black marlin	1.10	1.00
a.		Souvenir sheet of 4, #159-162	5.50	5.50
		Nos. 159-162 (4)	2.45	2.10

Festival Type of Tanzania 1977

Festival Emblem and: 50c, Masai tribesmen bleeding cow. 1sh, Dancers from Uganda. 2sh, Makonde sculpture, Tanzania. 3sh, Tribesmen skinning hippopotamus.

1977, Jan. 15   Perf. 13½x14

163	A6e	50c multicolored	.25	.25
164	A6e	1sh multicolored	.25	.25
165	A6e	2sh multicolored	.40	.35
166	A6e	3sh multicolored	.60	.60
a.		Souvenir sheet of 4, #163-166	2.25	2.25
		Nos. 163-166 (4)	1.50	1.45

2nd World Black and African Festival, Lagos, Nigeria, Jan. 15-Feb. 12.

Rally Type of Tanzania 1977

Safari Rally Emblem and: 50c, Automobile passing through village. 1sh, Winner at finish line. 2sh, Car passing through washout. 5sh, Car, elephants and Mt. Kenya.

1977, Apr. 5   Litho.   Perf. 14

167	A6f	50c multicolored	.25	.25
168	A6f	1sh multicolored	.25	.25
169	A6f	2sh multicolored	.35	.25
170	A6f	5sh multicolored	.85	.75
a.		Souvenir sheet of 4, #167-170	2.25	2.25
		Nos. 167-170 (4)	1.70	1.50

25th Safari Rally, Apr. 7-11.

Church Type of Tanzania 1977

Designs: 50c, Rev. Canon Apolo Kivebulaya. 1sh, Uganda Cathedral. 2sh, Early grass-topped Cathedral. 5sh, Early tent congregation, Kigezi.

1977, June 30   Litho.   Perf. 14

171	A6g	50c multicolored	.25	.25
172	A6g	1sh multicolored	.25	.25
173	A6g	2sh multicolored	.25	.25
174	A6g	5sh multicolored	.60	.60
a.		Souvenir sheet of 4, #171-174	1.50	1.50
		Nos. 171-174 (4)	1.35	1.35

Church of Uganda, centenary.

Type of 1975 Surcharged with New Value and 2 Bars

1977, Aug. 22   Photo.   Perf. 14x14½

175	A17	80c on 60c bananas	.40	.25

No. 175 was not issued without surcharge.

Wildlife Type of Tanzania 1977

Wildlife Fund Emblem and: 50c, Pancake tortoise. 1sh, Nile crocodile. 2sh, Hunter's hartebeest. 3sh, Red colobus monkey. 5sh, Dugong.

1977, Sept. 26   Litho.   Perf. 14x13½

176	A6h	50c multicolored	.30	.25
177	A6h	1sh multicolored	.50	.40
178	A6h	2sh multicolored	2.25	1.00
179	A6h	3sh multicolored	3.25	1.40
180	A6h	5sh multicolored	3.25	2.50
a.		Souvenir sheet of 4, #177-180	8.50	6.00
		Nos. 176-180 (5)	9.55	5.55

Endangered species.

Soccer Type of Tanzania

Soccer Cup and: 50c, Soccer scene and Joe Kadenge. 1sh, Mohammed Chuma receiving trophy, and his portrait. 2sh, Shot on goal and Omari S. Kidevu. 5sh, Backfield defense and Polly Ouma.

1978, May 3   Litho.   Perf. 14x13½

181	A8a	50c green & multi	.25	.25
182	A8a	1sh lt brown & multi	.25	.25
183	A8a	2sh blue & multi	.30	.30
184	A8a	5sh dk blue & multi	.90	.90
a.		Souvenir sheet of 4, #181-184	2.00	2.00
		Nos. 181-184 (4)	1.70	1.70

World Soccer Cup Championships, Argentina, June 1-25.
See Nos. 203-206.

Crop Type of 1975

Designs as before.

1978, June   Litho.   Perf. 14½
Size: 41x25mm
Multicolored, Name Panel as follows

195	A17	5sh blue	.25	.25
196	A17	10sh rose lilac	.45	.45
197	A17	20sh brown	.90	.90
198	A17	40sh deep orange	1.90	1.90
		Nos. 195-198 (4)	3.50	3.50

For overprint see Nos. 241-244.

Shot Put
A18

1978, July 10   Litho.   Perf. 14

199	A18	50c shown	.25	.25
200	A18	1sh Broad jump	.25	.25
201	A18	2sh Running	.25	.25
202	A18	5sh Boxing	.55	1.00
a.		Souv. sheet of 4, #199-202, perf 12	2.75	2.75
		Nos. 199-202 (4)	1.30	1.75

Commonwealth Games, Edmonton, Canada, Aug. 3-12.
For overprints see Nos. 249-252.

Soccer Type of Tanzania 1978 Inscribed "WORLD CUP 1978"

Designs: 50c, Backfield defense and Polly Ouma. 2sh, Shot on goal and Omari S. Kidevu. 5sh, Soccer scene and Joe Kadenge. 10sh, Mohammed Chuma receiving trophy, and his portrait.

1978, Sept. 11   Perf. 14x13½

203	A8a	50c dk blue & multi	.25	.25
204	A8a	2sh lilac & multi	.30	.25
205	A8a	5sh green & multi	.70	.90
206	A8a	10sh lt brown & multi	1.35	1.75
a.		Souv. sheet of 4, #203-206, perf 12	3.50	3.50
		Nos. 203-206 (4)	2.60	3.15

World Cup Soccer Championship winners.
For overprint see Nos. 253-257.

Blood Pressure Gauge and
Chart — A19

1978, Sept. 25   Litho.   Perf. 14

207	A19	50c shown	.25	.25
208	A19	1sh Heart	.25	.25
209	A19	2sh Retina	.35	.30

210	A19	5sh Kidneys	.80	1.10
a.		Souvenir sheet of 4, #207-210	2.75	2.75
		Nos. 207-210 (4)	1.65	1.90

World Health Day and Hypertension Month.

Cattle
Unloaded
from
Plane
A20

Flyer 1 and: 1.50sh, "Islander" on runway, Kampala. 2.70sh, Coffee loaded on transport jet. 10sh, Concorde.

1978, Dec. 16

211	A20	1sh multicolored	.25	.25
212	A20	1.50sh multicolored	.25	.25
213	A20	2.70sh multicolored	.45	.40
214	A20	10sh multicolored	1.90	1.40
a.		Souvenir sheet of 4, #211-214	3.00	3.00
		Nos. 211-214 (4)	2.85	2.30

75th anniversary of 1st powered flight.
For overprints see Nos. 258-261.

Elizabeth II Leaving Owen Falls
Dam — A21

Designs: 1.50sh, Coronation regalia. 2.70sh, Coronation ceremony. 10sh, Royal family on balcony of Buckingham Palace.

1979, Mar. 1   Litho.   Perf. 12½x12

215	A21	1sh multicolored	.25	.25
216	A21	1.50sh multicolored	.25	.25
217	A21	2.70sh multicolored	.65	1.25
218	A21	10sh multicolored		
a.		Souvenir sheet of 4, #215-218	2.40	2.40
		Nos. 215-218 (4)	1.40	2.00

25th anniv. of coronation of Elizabeth II.
For overprints see Nos. 245-248.

Bishop
Joseph
Kiwanuka
A22

Designs: 1.50sh, Lubaga Cathedral. 2.70sh, Ugandan pilgrims and St. Peter's, Rome. 10sh, Friar Lourdel-Mapeera, missionary.

1979, Feb. 15   Perf. 14

219	A22	1sh multicolored	.25	.25
220	A22	1.50sh multicolored	.25	.25
221	A22	2.70sh multicolored	.25	.25
222	A22	10sh multicolored	.70	.90
a.		Souvenir sheet of 4, #219-222	2.00	2.00
		Nos. 219-222 (4)	1.45	1.65

Ugandan Catholic Church, centenary.
See No. 274. For overprints see Nos. 262-265.

Child Receiving Vaccination — A23

IYC Emblem and: 1.50sh, Handicapped children playing. 2.70sh, Ugandan IYC emblem. 10sh, Teacher and pupils.

1979, July 16   Litho.   Perf. 14

223	A23	1sh multicolored	.25	.25
224	A23	1.50sh multicolored	.25	.25
225	A23	2.70sh multicolored	.25	.30
226	A23	10sh multicolored	.50	.90
a.		Souvenir sheet of 4, #223-226	2.00	2.00
		Nos. 223-226 (4)	1.25	1.70

International Year of the Child.
For overprints see Nos. 266-269.

**Nos. 133-146, 195-198, 215-218
Overprinted "UGANDA / LIBERATED / 1979"**

1979, July 12   Photo.   Perf. 14x14½
Size: 21x17mm

227	A17	10c multicolored	.25	.25
228	A17	20c multicolored	.25	.25
229	A17	30c multicolored	.25	.25
230	A17	40c multicolored	.25	.25
231	A17	50c multicolored	.25	.25
232	A17	70c multicolored	.25	.25
233	A17	80c multicolored	.25	.25

Perf. 14½
Size: 41x25mm

234	A17	1sh multicolored	.25	.25
235	A17	2sh multicolored	.25	.25
236	A17	3sh multicolored	.25	.25
237	A17	5sh multicolored	.35	.35
238	A17	10sh multicolored	.70	.60
239	A17	20sh multicolored	1.50	1.50
240	A17	40sh multicolored	3.00	3.00
		Nos. 227-240 (14)	8.05	7.90

1979   Litho.   Perf. 14½
Multicolored, name panel as follows

241	A17	5sh blue	.45	.35
242	A17	10sh rose lilac	.85	.70
243	A17	20sh brown	1.60	1.40
244	A17	40sh deep orange	3.25	2.75
		Nos. 241-244 (4)	6.15	5.20

1979, July 12   Litho.   Perf. 12½x12

245	A21	1sh multicolored	.25	.25
246	A21	1.50sh multicolored	.25	.25
247	A21	2.70sh multicolored	.25	.25
248	A21	15sh on 10sh multi	1.40	1.10
a.		Souvenir sheet of 4	2.50	
		Nos. 245-248 (4)	2.15	1.85

No. 248a contains Nos. 245-247 and a 15sh in design of No. 218. Issued Aug. 1.

Nos. 199-202, 203-206, 211-214, 219-222, 223-226 Overprinted "UGANDA LIBERATED 1979"

1979, Aug. 1   Litho.   Perf. 14

249	A18	50c multicolored	.25	.25
250	A18	1sh multicolored	.25	.25
251	A18	2sh multicolored	.25	.25
252	A18	5sh multicolored	.40	.35

1979, Aug. 1   Perf. 14x13½

253	A8a	50c multi	.25	.25
255	A8a	2sh multi (#204)	.25	.25
256	A8a	5sh multi	.40	.35
257	A8a	10sh multi	.85	.70

Overprint exists on No. 183.

1979, Aug. 1   Perf. 14

258	A20	1sh multicolored	.25	.25
259	A20	1.50sh multicolored	.25	.25
260	A20	2.70sh multicolored	.30	.25
261	A20	10sh multicolored	1.05	.85

1979, Aug. 1

262	A22	1sh multicolored	.25	.25
263	A22	1.50sh multicolored	.25	.25
264	A22	2.70sh multicolored	.25	.25
265	A22	10sh multicolored	.80	.70

1979, Aug. 16

266	A23	1sh multicolored	.25	.25
267	A23	1.50sh multicolored	.25	.25
268	A23	2.70sh multicolored	.25	.25
269	A23	10sh multicolored	.85	.80
a.		Souvenir sheet of 4, #266-269	2.25	2.25
		Nos. 249-269 (20)	7.90	7.25

ITU Emblem, Radio Waves — A24

1979, Sept. 11

270	A24	1sh lt gray & multi	.25	.25
271	A24	1.50sh orange & multi	.25	.25
272	A24	2.70sh yellow & multi	.35	.35
273	A24	10sh blue & multi	.35	.90
		Nos. 270-273 (4)	1.10	1.65

50th anniv. of Intl. Radio Consultative Committee (CCIR) of the ITU.

No. 222a Redrawn and Inscribed FREEDOM OF WORSHIP DECLARED
Souvenir Sheet

1979, Sept.   Perf. 12

274		Sheet of 4	2.00	2.00
a.		A22 1sh No. 219	.25	.25
b.		A22 1.50sh No. 220	.25	.25
c.		A22 2.70sh No. 221	.25	.25
d.		A22 10sh No. 222	1.25	1.25

In top panel of margin scrolls and coat of arms have been replaced by inscription.

A25

1979, Nov. 12   Litho.   Perf. 14

275	A25	1sh #110	.25	.25
276	A25	1.50sh #112	.25	.25
277	A25	2.70sh #94	.25	.30
278	A25	10sh #69	.40	1.00
a.		Souvenir sheet of 4, #275-278	2.00	2.00
		Nos. 275-278 (4)	1.15	1.80

Sir Rowland Hill (1795-1879), originator of penny postage.
For overprints see Nos. 293-296.

Thomson's Gazelle — A26

Designs: 10c, Impalas. 20c, Large-spotted genet. 50c, Bush babies. 80c, Wild hunting dogs. 1sh, Lions. 1.50sh, Mountain gorillas. 2sh, Zebras. 2.70sh, Leopards. 3.50sh, Black rhinoceroses. 5sh, Defassa waterbucks. 10sh, African black buffaloes. 20sh, Hippopotami. 40sh, African elephants.

1979, Dec. 3   Litho.   Perf. 14
No Date Imprint Below Design
Size: 21x17mm

279	A26	10c multicolored	.25	.25
280	A26	20c multicolored	.25	.25
281	A26	30c multicolored	.25	.25
282	A26	50c multicolored	.25	.25
283	A26	80c multicolored	.25	.25

Size: 39x25mm

284	A26	1sh multicolored	.25	.25
a.		Imprint "1982"	.45	.25
285	A26	1.50sh multicolored	.25	.25
286	A26	2sh multicolored	.25	.25
a.		Imprint "1982"	.60	.30
287	A26	2.70sh multicolored	.25	.25
288	A26	3.50sh multicolored	.30	.25
289	A26	5sh multicolored	.45	.40
a.		Imprint "1982"	.60	.60
290	A26	10sh multicolored	.85	.85
291	A26	20sh multicolored	1.90	1.90
292	A26	40sh multicolored	4.00	4.00
		Nos. 279-292 (14)	9.75	9.65

Nos. 284, 286, 289 reissued inscribed 1982. See Nos. 400-406. For surcharges see Nos. 386-392.

Nos. 275-278a Overprinted: "LONDON 1980"

1980, May 6   Litho.   Perf. 14

293	A25	1sh multicolored	.25	.25
294	A25	1.50sh multicolored	.25	.25
295	A25	2.70sh multicolored	.30	.25
296	A25	10sh multicolored	1.10	1.10
a.		Souvenir sheet of 4, #293-296	2.00	2.00
		Nos. 293-296 (4)	1.90	1.85

London 80 Intl. Stamp Exhib., May 6-14.

Paul Harris Wheeling Rotary Cart — A27

1980, Aug.   Litho.   Perf. 14

297	A27	1sh Rotary emblem, vert.	.25	.25
298	A27	20sh shown	1.60	1.60
a.		Souvenir sheet of 2, #297-298	2.75	2.75

Rotary International, 75th anniversary.

Soccer, Flags of Olympic Participants, Flame — A28

1980, Dec. 29   Litho.   Perf. 14

299	A28	1sh shown	.25	.25
300	A28	2sh Relay race	.25	.25
301	A28	10sh Hurdles	.50	.50
302	A28	20sh Boxing	1.00	1.00
		Nos. 299-302 (4)	2.00	2.00

Souvenir Sheet

303		Sheet of 4	2.50	2.50
a.		A28 2.70sh like #299	.25	.25
b.		A28 3sh like #300	.25	.25
c.		A28 5sh like #301	.35	.30
d.		A28 25sh like #302	1.60	1.40

22nd Summer Olympic Games, Moscow, July 19-Aug. 3.

Nos. 299-303 Overprinted with Sport, Winner and Country

1980, Dec. 29

304	A28	1sh multicolored	.25	.25
305	A28	2sh multicolored	.25	.25
306	A28	10sh multicolored	.50	.50
307	A28	20sh multicolored	1.00	1.00
		Nos. 304-307 (4)	2.00	2.00

Souvenir Sheet

308		Sheet of 4	2.50	2.50
a.		A28 2.70sh like #304	.25	.25
b.		A28 3sh like #305	.25	.25
c.		A28 5sh like #306	.35	.30
d.		A28 25sh like #307	1.60	1.40

Souvenir Sheet

Christ in the Storm on the Sea of Galilee, by Rembrandt — A29

1980, Dec. 31   Imperf.

309	A29	25sh multicolored	6.50	5.50

Christmas 1980.

Heinrich von Stephan and UPU Emblem A30

2sh, UPU headquarters. 2.70sh, Mail plane, 1935. 10sh, Mail train, 1927.

1981, June 2   Litho.   Perf. 14

310	A30	1sh shown	.25	.25
311	A30	2sh multicolored	.35	.25
312	A30	2.70sh multicolored	.45	.35
313	A30	10sh multicolored	1.40	1.25
a.		Souvenir sheet of 4, #310-313	3.75	3.75
		Nos. 310-313 (4)	2.45	2.10

Von Stephan (1831-97), UPU founder.

Common Design Types pictured following the introduction.

Royal Wedding Issue
Common Design Type

10sh, Couple. 50sh, Tower of London. 200sh, Prince Charles. 250sh, Royal mews.

1981   Litho.   Perf. 14

314	CD331a	10sh multi	.25	.25
a.		10sh on 1sh	.25	.25
315	CD331a	50sh multi	.30	.25
a.		50sh on 5sh	.30	

316	CD331a	200sh multi	1.50	1.25
a.		200sh on 20sh	1.50	1.25
		Nos. 314-316 (3)	2.05	1.75
		Nos. 314a-316a (3)	2.05	1.75

Souvenir Sheet

317	CD331	250sh multi	1.25	1.25
a.		250sh on 25sh, light orange	1.25	1.25

Royal wedding. Issue dates: surcharges, July 13; others, July 29. Nos. 314-316 also issued in sheets of 5 plus label, perf. 12, in changed colors.
For overprints see Nos. 342-345.

Sleeping Woman Before Green Shutters, by Picasso — A31

Picasso Birth Centenary: 20sh, Bullfight. 30sh, Nude Asleep on a Landscape. 200sh, Interior with a Girl Drawing. 250sh, Minotaur.

1981, Sept. 21   Litho.   Perf. 14

318	A31	10sh multicolored	.25	.25
319	A31	20sh multicolored	.30	.25
320	A31	30sh multicolored	.40	.30
321	A31	200sh multi	2.00	2.75

Size: 120x146mm
Imperf

322	A31	250sh multicolored	2.50	4.00
		Nos. 318-322 (5)	5.45	7.55

Intl. Year of the Disabled A32

1sh, Sign language. 10sh, Teacher in wheelchair. 50sh, Retarded children. 200sh, Blind man.

1981, Dec.   Perf. 15

323	A32	1sh multicolored	.25	.25
324	A32	10sh multicolored	.25	.25
325	A32	50sh multicolored	.80	.65
326	A32	200sh multicolored	1.75	2.00
a.		Souvenir sheet of 4, #323-326	4.50	4.50
		Nos. 323-326 (4)	3.05	3.15

1982 World Cup Soccer A33

Designs: Various soccer players.

1982, Jan. 11   Litho.   Perf. 14

327	A33	1sh multicolored	.25	.25
328	A33	10sh multicolored	.25	.25
329	A33	50sh multicolored	.75	.75
330	A33	200sh multicolored	2.75	2.25
		Nos. 327-330 (4)	4.00	3.50

Souvenir Sheet

331	A33	250sh World Cup	4.00	4.00

TB Bacillus Centenary — A34

1sh, Dr. Robert Koch. 10sh, Microscope. 50sh, Inoculation. 100sh, Bacteria under microscope. 150sh, Medical School.

1982, June 14 — Litho.

332	A34	1sh multi	.30	.30
333	A34	10sh multi	.50	.35
334	A34	50sh multi	2.25	1.60
335	A04	100sh multi	4.50	3.25
		Nos. 332-335 (4)	7.55	5.50

Souvenir Sheet

336	A34	150sh multi	6.00	3.50

Peaceful Uses of Outer Space
A35

5sh, Mpoma Satellite Earth Station. 10sh, Pioneer II. 50sh, Columbia space shuttle. 100sh, Voyager II, Saturn.
150sh, Columbia shuttle.

1982, May 17 — Litho. — Perf. 15

337	A35	5sh multicolored	.35	.35
338	A35	10sh multicolored	.35	.35
339	A35	50sh multicolored	1.60	1.40
340	A35	100sh multicolored	3.25	2.75
		Nos. 337-340 (4)	5.55	4.85

Souvenir Sheet

341	A35	150sh multicolored	5.25	4.50

Nos. 314-317 Overprinted: "21st BIRTHDAY / HRH Princess of Wales / JULY 1 1982"

1982, July 7 — Perf. 14

342	CD331	10sh multicolored	.25	.25
343	CD331	50sh multicolored	.40	.40
344	CD331	200sh multicolored	1.90	1.50
		Nos. 342-344 (3)	2.55	2.15

Souvenir Sheet

345	CD331	250sh multicolored	3.00	2.50

Also issued in sheets of 5 + label in changed colors, perf. 12x12½.

20th Anniversary of Independence

A 150sh souvenir sheet showing the Coat of Arms was not issued.

Hornbill — A36

20sh, Superb starling. 50sh, Dateleur eagle. 100sh, Saddle-bill stork.
200sh, Laughing dove.

1982, July 12

346	A36	1sh shown	.25	.25
347	A36	20sh multi	.70	.60
348	A36	50sh multi	1.60	1.40
349	A36	100sh multi	3.50	2.90
		Nos. 346-349 (4)	6.05	5.15

Souvenir Sheet

350	A36	200sh multi	11.50	10.00

Scouting Year
A37

5sh, Scouts. 20sh, Trophy presentation. 50sh, Helping disabled. 100sh, First aid instruction.
150sh, Baden-Powell.

1982, Aug. 23

351	A37	5sh multicolored	.30	.30
352	A37	20sh multicolored	.75	.60
353	A37	50sh multicolored	1.90	1.60
354	A37	100sh multicolored	3.75	3.25
		Nos. 351-354 (4)	6.70	5.75

Souvenir Sheet

355	A37	150sh multicolored	4.50	4.00

For overprints see Nos. 376-380.

Franklin D. Roosevelt (1882-1945) — A38

Roosevelt and Washington: 50sh, 200sh, Inaugurations. No. 358, Mount Vernon. No. 359, Hyde Park.

1982, Sept. — Litho.

356	A38	50sh multicolored	.60	.50
357	A38	200sh multicolored	2.50	2.25

Souvenir Sheets

358	A38	150sh multicolored	1.75	1.75
359	A38	150sh multicolored	1.75	1.75

Italy's Victory in 1982 World Cup
A39

1982, Oct. — Litho. — Perf. 14½

359A	A39	10sh Players	.25	.25
359B	A39	200sh Team	2.50	2.50

Souvenir Sheet

359C	A39	250sh Globe	2.50	2.50

A39a

5sh, Dancers. 20sh, Traditional currency. 50sh, Village. 100sh, Drums.

1983, Mar. 14 — Litho. — Perf. 14

360	A39a	5sh multicolored	.25	.25
361	A39a	20ch multicolored	.25	.25
362	A39a	50sh multicolored	.50	.50
363	A39a	100sh multicolored	.70	.70
		Nos. 360-363 (4)	1.70	1.70

Commonwealth Day.

St. George and the Dragon, by Raphael
A40

20sh, St. George and the Dragon, 1505. 50sh, Moses Parts the Red Sea. 200sh, Expulsion of Heliodorus.
250sh, Leo the Great and Attila, 1513.

1983, Apr.

364	A40	5sh multicolored	.25	.25
365	A40	20sh multicolored	.30	.30
366	A40	50sh multicolored	.75	.75
367	A40	200sh multicolored	2.00	2.00
		Nos. 364-367 (4)	3.30	3.30

Souvenir Sheet

368	A40	250sh multicolored	2.75	2.75

A41

7th Non-aligned Summit Conference — A42

1983, Aug. 15 — Litho. — Perf. 14½

369	A41	5sh multicolored	.25	.25
370	A42	200sh multicolored	2.00	2.00

African Elephants and World Wildlife Emblem
A43

5sh, Three adults with elephant bones. 10sh, Three adults walking. 30sh, Elephants standing in water hole. 70sh, Adults with calf.

1983, Aug. 22

371	A43	5sh multicolored	1.10	1.10
372	A43	10sh multicolored	1.75	1.75
373	A43	30sh multicolored	4.25	4.25
374	A43	70sh multicolored	11.00	11.00
		Nos. 371-374 (4)	18.10	18.10

Nos. 371-374 were reprinted in 1990, perf. 14. Value $25.

Souvenir Sheet

375	A43	300sh Zebras, vert.	6.25	5.25

No. 375 does not have the WWF emblem. See Nos. 948-953.

Nos. 351-355 Ovptd. or Srchd. "BOYS BRIGADE CENTENARY 1883-1983"

1983, Sept. 19 — Litho. — Perf. 14

376	A37	5sh multicolored	.25	.25
377	A37	20sh multicolored	.25	.25
378	A37	50sh multicolored	.40	.40
379	A37	400sh on 100sh multi	2.50	2.50
		Nos. 376-379 (4)	3.40	3.40

Souvenir Sheet

380	A37	150sh multicolored	1.75	1.75

World Communications Year — A44

Designs: 20sh, Mpoma Satellite Station. 50sh, Railroad, Computer Operator. 70sh, Filming Lions. 100sh, Pilots, Radio Communications. 300sh, Communications Satellite.

1983, Oct. 3 — Litho. — Perf. 15

381	A44	20sh multicolored	.25	.25
382	A44	50sh multicolored	.65	.65
383	A44	70sh multicolored	.85	.85
384	A44	100sh multicolored	1.25	1.25
		Nos. 381-384 (4)	3.00	3.00

Souvenir Sheet

385	A44	300sh multicolored	2.50	2.50

Nos. 279, 281-285, 289 Surcharged

1983, Nov. 7 — Litho. — Perf. 14

386	A26	100sh on 10c multi	.70	.70
387	A26	135sh on 1sh multi	.85	.85
388	A26	175sh on 30c multi	1.00	1.00
389	A26	200sh on 50c multi	1.40	1.40
390	A26	400sh on 80c multi	3.00	3.00
391	A26	700sh on 100sh multi	4.75	4.75
392	A26	1000sh on 1.50sh	6.50	6.50
		Nos. 386-392 (7)	18.20	18.20

World Food Day
A45

1984, Jan. 12 — Litho. — Perf. 14

393	A45	10sh Plowing	.50	.50
394	A45	300sh Banana crop	3.75	3.75

Christmas — A46

10sh, Nativity. 50sh, Sheperds and Angel. 175sh, Flight into Egypt. 400sh, Angels Blowing Trumpets.
300sh, Three Kings.

1983, Dec. 12 — Litho. — Perf. 14

395	A46	10sh multicolored	.25	.25
396	A46	50sh multicolored	.30	.30
397	A46	175sh multicolored	.70	.70
398	A46	400sh multicolored	1.75	1.75
		Nos. 395-398 (4)	3.00	3.00

Souvenir Sheet

399	A46	300sh multicolored	2.25	2.25

Animal Type of 1979

1983, Dec. 19

400	A26	100sh like No. 284	.70	.70
401	A26	135sh like No. 285	.85	.85
402	A26	175sh like No. 286	1.00	1.00
403	A26	200sh like No. 287	1.40	1.40
404	A26	400sh like No. 288	3.00	3.00
405	A26	700sh like No. 292	4.75	4.75
406	A26	1000sh like No. 291	6.50	6.50
		Nos. 400-406 (7)	18.20	18.20

1984 Summer Olympics
A48

1983 — Perf. 14½

417	A48	5sh Ruth Kyalisiima	.25	.25
418	A48	115sh Javelin	.50	.50
419	A48	155sh Wrestling	.65	.65
420	A48	175sh Rowing	.85	.85
		Nos. 417-420 (4)	2.25	2.25

Souvenir Sheet

421	A48	500sh Akii-Bua	2.10	2.10

For overprints see Nos. 458-462.

Intl. Civil Aviation Org., 40th Anniv.
A49

5sh, Passenger service. 115sh, Cargo service. 155sh, Police airwing. 175sh, Soroti Flying School plane.
250sh, Hot air balloon.

1984, Sept.

422	A49	5sh multi	.45	.45
423	A49	115sh multi	1.75	1.75
424	A49	155sh multi	2.50	2.50
425	A49	175sh multi	3.50	3.50
		Nos. 422-425 (4)	8.20	8.20

Souvenir Sheet

426	A49	250sh multi	4.00	4.00

Butterflies
A50

5sh, Silver-barred Charaxes. 115sh, Western Emperor Swallowtail. 155sh, African Giant Swallowtail. 175sh, Blue Salamis.
250sh, Veinted Yellow.

1984, Oct.   Litho.   Perf. 14½
427 A50   5sh multi   .35   .35
428 A50   115sh multi   2.50 2.50
429 A50   155sh multi   3.50 3.50
430 A50   175sh multi   4.00 4.00
       Nos. 427-430 (4)   10.35 10.35

Souvenir Sheet
431 A50   250sh multi   4.50 4.00

Freshwater Fish — A51

5sh, Nothobranchius taeniopygus. 10sh, Bagrus dogmac. 50sh, Polypterus senegalus. 100sh, Clarias. 135sh, Mormyrus kannume. 175sh, Synodontis victoriae. 205sh, Haplochromis brownae. 400sh, Lates niloticus. 700sh, Protopterus aethiopicus. 1000sh, Barbus radcliffii. 2500sh, Malapterus electricus.

1985   Litho.   Perf. 15
432 A51   5sh multicolored   .55   .55
433 A51   10sh multicolored   .80   .55
434 A51   50sh multicolored   1.50   .45
435 A51   100sh multicolored   1.50   .45
436 A51   135sh multicolored   2.50 1.40
437 A51   175sh multicolored   2.50 2.40
438 A51   205sh multicolored   2.50 2.75
439 A51   400sh multicolored   2.50 3.00
440 A51   700sh multicolored   2.50 3.50
441 A51   1000sh multicolored   2.50 3.50
442 A51   2500sh multicolored   3.00 4.75
       Nos. 432-442 (11)   22.35 23.30

Issued: #432-435, 437-441, 4/1; #436, 442, 6/10.

For overprints see Nos. 490-494.

Easter
A52

5sh, The Last Supper. 115sh, Jesus confronts doubting Thomas. 155sh, Crucifixion. 175sh, Pentecost. 250sh, Last prayer in garden.

1985, May 13   Litho.   Perf. 14
443 A52   5sh multicolored   .50   .50
444 A52   115sh multicolored   1.60 1.60
445 A52   155sh multicolored   1.75 2.50
446 A52   175sh multicolored   2.25 3.25
       Nos. 443-446 (4)   6.10 7.85

Souvenir Sheet
447 A52   250sh multicolored   1.25 1.25

UN Child
Survival
Campaign
A53

5sh, Mother breastfeeding. 115sh, Growth monitorization. 155sh, Immunization. 175sh, Oral rehydration therapy. 500sh, Expectant Mother, food.

1985, July 1
448 A53   5sh multi   .35   .35
449 A53   115sh multi   1.90 1.90
450 A53   155sh multi   2.50 2.50
451 A53   175sh multi   3.00 3.00
       Nos. 448-451 (4)   7.75 7.75

Souvenir Sheet
452 A53   500sh multi   5.25 5.25

Audubon Birth
Bicent. — A54

115sh, Acrocephalus schoenobaenus. 155sh, Ardeola ibis. 175sh, Galerida gristata. 500sh, Aythya fuligula. 1000sh, Strix aluco.

1985, July   Perf. 15
453 A54   115sh multi   1.90 1.75
454 A54   155sh multi   2.25 1.90
455 A54   175sh multi   1.90 2.25
456 A54   500sh multi   3.00 4.75
       Nos. 453-456 (4)   9.05 10.65

Souvenir Sheet
457 A54   1000sh multi   10.00 10.00

See Nos. 469-473.

**Nos. 417-421 Ovptd. or Srchd. with
Winners Names, Medals and
Countries in Gold**

Gold medalists: 5sh, Benita Brown-Fitzgerald, US, 100-meter hurdles. 115sh, Arto Haerkoenen, Finland, javelin. 155sh, Atsuji Miyahara, Japan, 115-pound Greco-Roman wrestling. 100sh, West Germany, quadruple sculls. 1200sh, Edwin Moses, US, 400-meter hurdles.

1985, July   Perf. 15
458 A48   5sh multicolored   .25   .25
459 A48   115sh multicolored   .35   .35
460 A48   155sh multicolored   .50   .50
461 A48   1000sh on 175sh multi 3.00 3.00
       Nos. 458-461 (4)   4.10 4.10

Souvenir Sheet
462 A48   1200sh on 500sh multi 3.50 3.50

UN Decade for
Women — A56

5sh, Natl. Women's Day, Mar. 8. 115sh, Girl Guides 75th anniv., horiz. 155sh, Mother Theresa, 1979 Nobel Peace Prize laureate. 1000sh, Queen Mother. #467, Queen Mother inspecting troops. #468, like 115sh, horiz.

1985   Litho.   Perf. 14
463 A56   5sh multicolored   .25   .25
464 A56   115sh multicolored   1.75 1.60
465 A56   155sh multicolored   2.90 2.50
466 A56   1000sh multicolored   1.40 1.75
       Nos. 463-466 (4)   6.30 6.10

Souvenir Sheets
467 A56   500sh multicolored   3.00 3.00
468 A56   1500sh multicolored   4.50 4.50

Issued: #466-467, Aug. 21; others, Nov. 1.

Audubon Type of 1985

5sh, Rock ptarmigan. 155sh, Sage grouse. 175sh, Lesser yellowlegs. 500sh, Brown-headed cowbird. 1000sh, Whooping crane.

1985, Dec. 23   Perf. 12½x12
469 A54   5sh multi   .50   .40
470 A54   155sh multi   2.00 2.00
471 A54   175sh multi   2.00 2.50
472 A54   500sh multi   3.50 4.50
       Nos. 469-472 (4)   8.00 9.40

**Souvenir Sheet
Perf. 14**
473 A54   1000sh multi   9.50 9.50

UN, 40th
Anniv.
A57

Designs: 10sh, Forest resources, vert. 180sh, UN Peace-keeping Force. 200sh, Emblem, UN Development Project. 250sh, Intl. Peace Year. 2000sh, Natl., UN flags, vert. 2500sh, Flags, UN Building, New York, vert.

1986, Feb.   Perf. 15
474 A57   10sh multicolored   .25   .25
475 A57   180sh multicolored   .35   .35
476 A57   200sh multicolored   .45   .45
477 A57   250sh multicolored   .55   .55
478 A57   2000sh multicolored   4.25 4.25
       Nos. 474-478 (5)   5.85 5.85

Souvenir Sheet
479 A57   2500sh multi   3.25 3.25

1986 World Cup Soccer
Championships, Mexico — A58

Various soccer plays.

1986, Mar.   Perf. 14
480 A58   10sh multicolored   .30   .30
481 A58   180sh multicolored   .90   .60
482 A58   250sh multicolored   1.00   .75
483 A58   2500sh multicolored   5.75 6.50
       Nos. 480-483 (4)   7.95 8.15

Souvenir Sheet
484 A58   3000sh multicolored   5.50 5.50

No. 484 contains vert. stamp.
For overprints see Nos. 514-518.

A59

Halley's Comet — A60

Designs: 50sh, Arecibo radio telescope, Puerto Rico, and Tycho Brahe (1546-1601), Danish astronomer. 100sh, Recovery of Astronaut John Glenn, US space capsule, Caribbean, 1962. 140sh, Adoration of the Magi, 1301, by Giotto (1276-1337). 2500sh, Sighting, 1835, Davy Crockett at The Alamo.

1986, Mar.   Litho.   Perf. 14
485 A59   50sh multicolored   .30   .25
486 A59   100sh multicolored   .40   .25
487 A59   140sh multicolored   .60   .45
488 A59   2500sh multicolored   5.25 6.25
       Nos. 485-488 (4)   6.55 7.20

Souvenir Sheet
489 A60   3000sh multicolored   7.50 7.50

For overprints see Nos. 519-523.

**Nos. 437, 439-442 and 468 Ovptd.
"NRA LIBERATION / 1986" in Silver
or Black**

1986, Apr.   Perf. 15
490   A51   175sh multi   1.25 1.10
490A A51   400sh multi   2.50 2.50
491   A51   700sh multi   3.75 3.75
492   A51   1000sh multi (Bk)   4.00 4.00
493   A51   2500sh multi (Bk)   6.50 7.75
       Nos. 490-493 (5)   18.00 19.10

**Souvenir Sheet
Perf. 14**
494 A56   1500sh multi (Bk)   6.25 4.75

No. 494 ovptd. in one line in margin. A 400sh also exists with silver overprint. All stamps exist with overprint colors transposed.

Queen Elizabeth II, 60th Birthday
Common Design Type

100sh, At London Zoo, c. 1938. 140sh, At the races, 1970. 2500sh, Sandringham, 1982. 3000sh, Engagement, 1947.

1986, Apr. 21   Perf. 14
495 CD339   100sh multi   .25   .25
496 CD339   140sh multi   .25   .25
497 CD339   2500sh multi   3.75 3.75
       Nos. 495-497 (3)   4.25 4.25

Souvenir Sheet
498 CD339   3000sh multi   4.25 4.25

AMERIPEX '86 — A61

50sh, Niagara Falls. 100sh, Jefferson Memorial. 250sh, Liberty Bell. 1000sh, The Alamo. 2500sh, George Washington Bridge. 3000sh, Grand Canyon.

1986, May 22   Perf. 15
499 A61   50sh multicolored   .30   .30
500 A61   100sh multicolored   .30   .30
501 A61   250sh multicolored   .50   .50
502 A61   1000sh multicolored   1.90 1.90
503 A61   2500sh multicolored   4.50 4.50
       Nos. 499-503 (5)   7.50 7.50

Souvenir Sheet
504 A61   3000sh multicolored   3.75 3.75

Statue of Liberty, cent.

A62

Statue of Liberty, Cent. — A63

Tall ships, Operation Sail: 50sh, Gloria, Colombia, vert. 100sh, Mircea, Romania, vert. 140sh, Sagres II, Portugal. 2500sh, Gazela Primero, US.

1986, July   Perf. 14
505 A62   50sh multicolored   .75   .60
506 A62   100sh multicolored   1.00   .60
507 A62   140sh multicolored   1.75 1.75
508 A62   2500sh multicolored   7.75 10.00
       Nos. 505-508 (4)   11.25 12.45

Souvenir Sheet
509 A63   3000sh multicolored   4.50 4.50

Royal Wedding Issue, 1986
Common Design Type

Designs: 50sh, Prince Andrew and Sarah Ferguson. 140sh, Andrew and Princess Anne. 2500sh, At formal affair. 3000sh, Couple diff. Nos. 510-512 horiz.

1986, July 23
510 CD340   50sh multicolored   .25   .25
511 CD340   140sh multicolored   .25   .25
512 CD340   2500sh multicolored 3.75 4.50
       Nos. 510-512 (3)   4.25 5.00

Souvenir Sheet
513 CD340   3000sh multicolored 5.00 5.00

Nos. 480-484 Ovptd. or Surcharged "WINNERS Argentina 3 W. Germany 2" in Gold in 2 or 3 Lines

1986, Sept. 15		**Litho.**	**Perf. 14**
514 A58	50sh on 10sh multi	.25	.25
515 A58	180sh multicolored	.25	.25
516 A58	250sh multicolored	.30	.30
517 A58	2500sh multicolored	3.25	3.75
	Nos. 514-517 (4)	4.05	4.55

Souvenir Sheet

518 A58	3000sh multicolored	6.00	6.00

Nos. 485-489 Ovptd. with Halley's Comet Emblem

1986, Oct. 15		**Litho.**	**Perf. 14**
519 A59	50sh multicolored	.35	.35
520 A59	100sh multicolored	.60	.40
521 A59	140sh multicolored	.80	.70
522 A59	2500sh multicolored	6.75	8.00
	Nos. 519-522 (4)	8.50	9.45

Souvenir Sheet

523 A60	3000sh multicolored	6.50	6.50

Christian Martyrs A64

Designs: 50sh, St. Kizito. 150sh, St. Kizito educating Ganda converts. 200sh, Execution of Bishop James Hannington. 1000sh, Mwanga's execution of converts, cent. 1500sh, King Mwanga sentencing Christians to death.

1986, Oct. 15

524 A64	50sh multicolored	.25	.25
525 A64	150sh multicolored	.25	.25
526 A64	200sh multicolored	.50	.50
527 A64	1000sh multicolored	2.00	3.00
	Nos. 524-527 (4)	3.00	4.00

Souvenir Sheet

528 A64	1500sh multicolored	2.25	2.25

A65

Christmas — A66

Paintings by Albrecht Durer and Titian: 50sh, Madonna of the Cherries. 150sh, Madonna and Child, vert. 200sh, Assumption of the Virgin, vert. 2500sh, Praying Hands, vert. No. 533, Adoration of the Magi. No. 534, Presentation of the Virgin in the Temple.

1986, Nov. 26		**Litho.**	**Perf. 14**
529 A65	50sh multicolored	.25	.25
530 A65	150sh multicolored	.55	.25
531 A65	200sh multicolored	.75	.30
532 A65	2500sh multicolored	5.50	7.00
	Nos. 529-532 (4)	7.05	7.80

Souvenir Sheets

533 A66	3000sh multicolored	5.00	5.00
534 A66	3000sh multicolored	5.00	5.00

Birds and Animals A67

2sh, Red-billed firefinch. 5sh, African pygmy kingfisher. 10sh, Scarlet-chested sunbird. 25sh, White rhinoceros. 35sh, Lion. 45sh, Cheetahs. 50sh, Cordon bleu. 100sh, Giant eland. No. 543, Carmine bee-eaters. No. 544, Cattle egret, zebra.

1987			**Perf. 15**
535 A67	2sh multi	.40	.35
536 A67	5sh multi	.55	.35
537 A67	10sh multi	.80	.35
538 A67	25sh multi	1.25	.95
539 A67	35sh multi	1.25	1.25
540 A67	45sh multi	1.50	1.75
541 A67	50sh multi	1.75	2.10
542 A67	100sh multi	2.75	3.75
	Nos. 535-542 (8)	10.25	10.85

Souvenir Sheets

543 A67	150sh multi	4.50	4.50
544 A67	150sh multi	4.50	4.50

Issue dates: Nos. 535-537, 541, 543, Nov. 2; Nos. 538-540, 542-544, July 22.

Transportation Innovations — A68

2sh, Eagle, 1987. 3sh, Bremen, 1928. 5sh, Winnie Mae, 1933. 10sh, Voyager, 1986. 15sh, Chanute biplane glider, 1896. 25sh, Norge, 1926. 35sh, Curtis biplane, USS Pennsylvania, 1911. 45sh, Freedom 7, 1961. 100sh, Concorde, 1976.

1987, Aug. 14

545 A68	2sh multicolored	.30	.30
546 A68	3sh multicolored	.30	.30
547 A68	5sh multicolored	.35	.35
548 A68	10sh multicolored	.50	.50
549 A68	15sh multicolored	.80	.80
550 A68	25sh multicolored	1.10	1.10
551 A68	35sh multicolored	1.75	1.75
552 A68	45sh multicolored	2.00	2.00
553 A68	100sh multicolored	5.75	6.75
	Nos. 545-553 (9)	12.85	13.85

1988 Summer Olympics, Seoul A69

Flags and athletes.

1987, Oct. 5			**Perf. 14½x14**
554 A69	5sh Torch bearer	.25	.25
555 A69	10sh Swimming	.30	.30
556 A69	50sh Cycling	1.25	1.25
557 A69	100sh Gymnastic rings	2.50	2.50
	Nos. 554-557 (4)	4.30	4.30

Souvenir Sheet

558 A69	150sh Boxing	4.00	4.50

A70

Natl. Independence, 25th Anniv. — A71

10sh, Mulago Hospital. 25sh, Independence Monument. 50sh, High Court.

1987, Oct. 8

559 A70	5sh shown	.25	.25
560 A70	10sh multicolored	.45	.45
561 A70	25sh multicolored	.90	.90
562 A70	50sh multicolored	1.75	1.75
	Nos. 559-562 (4)	3.35	3.35

Souvenir Sheet

563 A71	100sh shown	3.25	3.25

A72

Science and Space — A73

Designs: 5sh, Hippocrates, father of modern medicine, caduceus and surgeons. 25sh, Albert Einstein and Theory of Relativity equation. 35sh, Sir Isaac Newton and Optics Theory. 45sh, Karl Benz (1844-1929), German engineer, automobile pioneer, and the Velocipede, Mercedes-Benz sports coupe and manufacturers' emblems.

1987, Nov. 2			**Perf. 14½x14**
564 A72	5sh multicolored	.60	.60
565 A72	25sh multicolored	2.50	2.50
566 A72	35sh multicolored	3.00	3.00
567 A72	45sh multicolored	3.75	3.75
	Nos. 564-567 (4)	9.85	9.85

Souvenir Sheet

Perf. 14x14½

568 A73	150sh shown	5.75	5.75

Birds — A74

5sh, Golden-backed weaver. 10sh, Hoopoe. 15sh, Red-throated bee-eater. 25sh, Lilac-breasted roller. 35sh, Pygmy goose. 45sh, Scarlet-chested sunbird. 50sh, Crowned crane. 100sh, Long-tailed fiscal shrike.
No. 577, African barn owl, horiz. No. 578, African fish-eagle, horiz.

1987, Nov. 2		**Litho.**	**Perf. 14**
569 A74	5sh multicolored	.75	.75
570 A74	10sh multicolored	1.60	1.40
571 A74	15sh multicolored	1.75	1.40
572 A74	25sh multicolored	2.25	1.90
573 A74	35sh multicolored	2.50	2.10
574 A74	45sh multicolored	2.75	2.75
575 A74	50sh multicolored	2.75	2.75
576 A74	100sh multicolored	5.00	5.00
	Nos. 569-576 (8)	19.35	18.05

Souvenir Sheets

577 A74	150sh multicolored	4.25	4.25
578 A74	150sh multicolored	4.25	4.25

14th World Boy Scout Jamboree, Australia, 1987-88 — A75

Activities: 5sh, Stamp collecting, Uganda Nos. 84 and 116. 25sh, Planting trees, Natl. flag. 35sh, Canoeing on Lake Victoria. 45sh, Hiking and camping. 150sh, Logo of 1987 jamboree and natl. Boy Scout organization emblem.

1987, Nov. 20

579 A75	5sh multicolored	.30	.30
580 A75	25sh multicolored	1.10	1.10
581 A75	35sh multicolored	1.60	1.60
582 A75	45sh multicolored	1.90	1.90
	Nos. 579-582 (4)	4.90	4.90

Souvenir Sheet

583 A75	150sh multicolored	4.75	4.75

Christmas A76

The life of Christ and the Virgin pictured on bas-reliefs, c. 1250, and a tapestry from France: 5sh, The Annunciation. 10sh, The Nativity. 50sh, Flight into Egypt. 100sh, The Adoration of the Magi. 150sh, The Mystic Wine Tapestry.

1987, Dec. 18

584 A76	5sh multicolored	.25	.25
585 A76	10sh multicolored	.25	.25
586 A76	50sh multicolored	1.40	1.75
587 A76	100sh multicolored	2.60	3.00
	Nos. 584-587 (4)	4.50	5.25

Souvenir Sheet

588 A76	150sh multicolored	4.75	4.75

Locomotives — A77

Designs: 5sh, Class 12 2-6-2T light shunter. 10sh, Class 92 1Co-Co1 diesel electric. 15sh, Class 2-8-2. 25sh, Class 2-6-2T light shunter. 35sh, Class 4-8-0. 45sh, Class 4-8-2. 50sh, Class 4-8-4+4-8-4 Garratt. 100sh, Class 87 1Co-Co1 diesel electric. No. 597, Class 59 4-8-2+2-8-4 Garratt. No. 598, Class 31 2-8-4.

1988, Jan. 18

589 A77	5sh multicolored	.25	.25
590 A77	10sh multicolored	.45	.45
591 A77	15sh multicolored	.70	.65
592 A77	25sh multicolored	1.00	1.00
593 A77	35sh multicolored	1.60	1.25
594 A77	45sh multicolored	2.00	1.75
595 A77	50sh multicolored	2.10	1.90
596 A77	100sh multicolored	4.25	2.75
	Nos. 589-596 (8)	12.35	10.00

Souvenir Sheets

597 A77	150sh multicolored	5.00	5.00
598 A77	150sh multicolored	5.00	5.00

Minerals — A78

1sh, Columbite-tantalite. 2sh, Galena. 5sh, Malachite. 10sh, Cassiterite. 35sh, Ferberite. 50sh, Emerald. 100sh, Monazite. 150sh, Microcline.

1988, Jan. 18

599	A78	1sh multicolored	.25	.25
600	A78	2sh multicolored	.25	.25
601	A78	5sh multicolored	.25	.25
602	A78	10sh multicolored	.35	.35
603	A78	35sh multicolored	1.50	1.50
604	A78	50sh multicolored	2.00	2.00
605	A78	100sh multicolored	3.50	3.50
606	A78	150sh multicolored	5.25	5.25
		Nos. 599-606 (8)	13.35	13.35

1988 Summer Olympics, Seoul A79

5sh, Hurdles. 25sh, High jump. 35sh, Javelin. 45sh, Long jump.
150sh, Medals, five-ring emblem.

1988, May 16   Litho.   Perf. 14

607	A79	5sh multi	.30	.30
608	A79	25sh multi	.55	.75
609	A79	35sh multi	.60	.75
610	A79	45sh multi	.85	1.00
		Nos. 607-610 (4)	2.30	2.80

Souvenir Sheet

611	A79	150sh multi	2.25	2.25

For overprints see Nos. 651-655.

Flowers A80

5sh, Spathodea campanulata. 10sh, Gloriosa simplex. 20sh, Thevetica peruviana, vert. 25sh, Hibiscus schizopetalus. 35sh, Aframomum sceptrum. 45sh, Adenium obesum. 50sh, Kigelia africana, vert. 100sh, Clappertonia ficifolia.
No. 620, Costus spectabiis. No. 621, Canarina abyssinica, vert.

1988, July 28   Litho.   Perf. 15

612	A80	5sh multicolored	.60	.25
613	A80	10sh multicolored	.60	.25
614	A80	20sh multicolored	.80	.60
615	A80	25sh multicolored	.80	.80
616	A80	35sh multicolored	.80	.85
617	A80	45sh multicolored	.80	1.10
618	A80	50sh multicolored	1.00	1.40
619	A80	100sh multicolored	1.50	2.25
		Nos. 612-619 (8)	6.90	7.50

Souvenir Sheets

620	A80	150sh multicolored	3.50	3.50
621	A80	150sh multicolored	3.50	3.50

Intl. Red Cross, 125th Anniv. A81

10sh, "AIDS". 40sh, Immunize children. 70sh, Relief distribution. 90sh, First aid. 150sh, Jean-Henri Dunant, vert.

1988, Oct. 28   Litho.   Perf. 14

622	A81	10sh multicolored	.30	.30
623	A81	40sh multicolored	1.00	1.00
624	A81	70sh multicolored	2.00	2.00
625	A81	90sh multicolored	2.50	2.50
		Nos. 622-625 (4)	5.80	5.80

Souvenir Sheet

626	A81	150sh multicolored	3.00	3.00

Paintings by Titian — A82

Designs: 10sh, Portrait of a Lady, c. 1508. 20sh, Portrait of a Man, 1507. 40sh, Portrait of Isabella d'Este, c. 1534. 50sh, Portrait of Vincenzo Mosti, 1520. 70sh, Pope Paul III Farnese, c. 1545. 90sh, Violante, 1515. 100sh, Lavinia, Titian's Daughter, c. 1565. 250sh, Portrait of Dr. Parma, c. 1515. No. 635, The Speech of Alfonso D'Avalos, c. 1540. No. 636, Cain and Abel.

1988, Oct. 31   Perf. 14

627	A82	10sh multicolored	.25	.25
628	A82	20sh multicolored	.40	.40
629	A82	40sh multicolored	.60	.60
630	A82	50sh multicolored	.75	.75
631	A82	70sh multicolored	.85	.85
632	A82	90sh multicolored	.90	.90
633	A82	100sh multicolored	1.10	1.10
634	A82	250sh multicolored	2.10	2.10
		Nos. 627-634 (8)	6.95	6.95

Souvenir Sheets

635	A82	350sh multicolored	3.50	3.50
636	A82	350sh multicolored	3.50	3.50

Game Preserves — A83

Designs: 10sh, Giraffes, Kidepo Valley Natl. Park. 25sh, Zebras, Lake Mburo Natl. Park. 100sh, African buffalo, Murchison Falls Natl. Park. 250sh, Pelicans, Queen Elizabeth Natl. Park. 350sh, Roan antelopes, Lake Mburo Natl. Park.

1988, Nov. 18   Litho.   Perf. 14

637	A83	10sh multicolored	.45	.25
638	A83	25sh multicolored	1.60	.65
639	A83	100sh multicolored	3.25	3.25
640	A83	250sh multicolored	9.00	9.00
		Nos. 637-640 (4)	14.30	13.15

Souvenir Sheet

641	A83	350sh multicolored	4.25	4.25

WHO 40th Anniv., Alma Ata Declaration 10th Anniv. — A84

10sh, Primary health care. 25sh, Mental health. 45sh, Rural health care. 100sh, Dental care. 200sh, Postnatal care.
350sh, Conference Hall, Alma-Ata, USSR.

1988, Dec. 1

642	A84	10sh multicolored	.25	.25
643	A84	25sh multicolored	.45	.45
644	A84	45sh multicolored	.75	.75
645	A84	100sh multicolored	1.60	1.60
646	A84	200sh multicolored	3.00	3.00
		Nos. 642-646 (5)	6.05	6.05

Souvenir Sheet

647	A84	350sh multicolored	4.25	4.25

Miniature Sheet

Christmas, Mickey Mouse 60th Birthday — A85

Walt Disney characters: No. 648a, Santa Claus. b, Goofy. c, Mickey Mouse. d, Huey at conveyor belt. e, Dewey packing building blocks. f, Donald Duck. g, Chip-n-Dale. h, Louie at conveyor belt controls. No. 649, Preparing reindeer for Christmas eve flight. No. 650, Mickey loading sleigh with toys, horiz.

1988, Dec. 2   Perf. 13½x14, 14x13½

648	A85	Sheet of 8	10.00	10.00
a.-h.		50sh any single	.80	.80

Souvenir Sheets

649	A85	350sh multicolored	5.25	5.25
650	A85	350sh multicolored	5.25	5.25

Nos. 607-611 Ovptd. or Surcharged to Honor Olympic Winners

5sh: "110 M HURDLES / R. KINGDOM / USA"
25sh: "HIGH JUMP / G. AVDEENKO / USSR"
35sh: "JAVELIN / T. KORJUS / FINLAND"
300sh: "LONG JUMP / C. LEWIS / USA"

1989, Jan. 30   Litho.   Perf. 14

651	A79	5sh multicolored	.25	.25
652	A79	25sh multicolored	.30	.30
653	A79	35sh multicolored	.35	.35
654	A79	300sh on 45sh multi	3.25	3.25
		Nos. 651-654 (4)	4.15	4.15

Souvenir Sheet

655	A79	350sh on 150sh multi	5.00	5.00

1990 World Cup Soccer Championships, Italy — A86

Various action scenes.

1989, Apr. 24   Litho.   Perf. 14

656	A86	10sh multi, vert.	.35	.35
657	A86	25sh multicolored	.55	.55
658	A86	75sh multicolored	1.25	1.25
659	A86	200sh multi, vert.	2.25	2.25
		Nos. 656-659 (4)	4.40	4.40

Souvenir Sheet

660	A86	300sh multicolored	3.75	3.75

Mushrooms — A87

10sh, Suillus granulatus. 15sh, Omphalotus olearius. 45sh, Oudemansiella radicata. 50sh, Clitocybe nebularis. 60sh, Macrolepiota rhacodes. 75sh, Lepista nuda. 150sh, Suillus luteus. 200sh, Agaricus campestris.
No. 669, Schizophyllum commune. No. 670, Bolbitius vitellinus.

1989, Aug. 14   Litho.   Perf. 14

661	A87	10sh multicolored	.45	.45
662	A87	15sh multicolored	.55	.55
663	A87	45sh multicolored	1.15	1.15
664	A87	50sh multicolored	1.15	1.15
665	A87	60sh multicolored	1.20	1.20
666	A87	75sh multicolored	1.40	1.40
667	A87	150sh multicolored	2.60	2.60
668	A87	200sh multicolored	2.75	2.75
		Nos. 661-668 (8)	11.25	11.25

Souvenir Sheets

669	A87	350sh multicolored	6.00	6.00
670	A87	350sh multicolored	6.00	6.00

"The Thirty-six Views of Mt. Fuji" — A88

Prints by Hokusai (1760-1849): 10sh, Fuji and the Great Wave off Kanogawa. 15sh, Fuji from Lake Suwa. 20sh, Fuji from Kajikazawa. 60sh, Fuji from Shichirigahama. 90sh, Fuji from Ejiri in Sunshu. 120sh, Fuji Above Lightning. 200sh, Fuji from Lower Meguro in Edo. 250sh, Fuji from Edo. No. 679, The Red Fuji from the Foot. No. 680, Fuji from Umezawa.

1989, May 15   Litho.   Perf. 14x13½

671	A88	10sh multicolored	.35	.35
672	A88	15sh multicolored	.35	.35
673	A88	20sh multicolored	.35	.35
674	A88	60sh multicolored	.90	.90
675	A88	90sh multicolored	1.40	1.40
676	A88	120sh multicolored	2.00	2.00
677	A88	200sh multicolored	2.75	2.75
678	A88	250sh multicolored	3.00	3.00
		Nos. 671-678 (8)	11.10	11.10

Souvenir Sheets

679	A88	500sh multicolored	5.25	5.25
680	A88	500sh multicolored	5.25	5.25

Hirohito (1901-1989), Showa emperor, and Akihito, Heisei emperor of Japan.

PHILEXFRANCE '89 — A89

1989, July 7   Litho.   Perf. 14

681	A89	20sh No. 1	.60	.60
682	A89	70sh No. 10	1.50	1.50
683	A89	100sh No. 48	1.75	1.75
684	A89	250sh No. 67	3.50	3.50
a.		Souvenir sheet of 4, #681-684	10.00	10.00
		Nos. 681-684 (4)	7.35	7.35

No. 684a sold for 500sh.

2nd All African Scout Jamboree, Aug. 3-15 — A90

1989, Aug. 3   Litho.   Perf. 14

685	A90	10sh Fatal child ailments	.35	.35
686	A90	70sh Raising poultry	1.50	1.50
687	A90	90sh Immunization	1.90	1.90
688	A90	100sh Brick-making	1.90	1.90
		Nos. 685-688 (4)	5.65	5.65

Souvenir Sheet

689	A90	500sh Natl. emblem, vert.	5.25	5.25

Scouting, 75th anniv.
For surcharges see Nos. 1301-1304.

Miniature Sheet

Wildlife at Waterhole — A91

Designs: a, Saddle-billed stork. b, White pelican. c, Marabou stork. d, Egyptian vulture, giraffes. e, Bateleur eagle, antelope. f, African elephant. g, Giraffe. h, Goliath heron. i, Black rhinoceros, zebras. j, Zebras, oribi. k, African fish eagle. l, Hippopotamus. m, Black-backed jackal, white pelican. n, Cape buffalo. o, Olive baboon. p, Bohor reedbuck. q, Lesser flamingo, serval. r, Shoebill stork. s, Crowned crane. t, Impala. No. 691, Lion. No. 692, Long-crested eagle.

1989, Sept. 12			**Perf. 14½x14**	
690	A91	Sheet of 20	22.00	22.00
a.-t.		30sh any single	.60	.60

Souvenir Sheets

691	A91	500sh multicolored	5.25	5.25
692	A91	500sh multicolored	5.25	5.25

1st Moon Landing, 20th Anniv. — A92

Quotations and scenes from the Apollo 11 mission: 10sh, Launch vehicle, Moon. 20sh, Eagle lower stage on Moon. 30sh, Columbia. 50sh, Eagle landing. 70sh, Aldrin on Moon. 250sh, Armstrong on ladder. 300sh, Eagle ascending. 350sh, Aldrin, diff. No. 701, Liftoff. No. 702, Parachute landing.

1989, Oct. 20		**Litho.**	**Perf. 14**	
693	A92	10sh multicolored	.35	.35
694	A92	20sh multicolored	.35	.35
695	A92	30sh multicolored	.65	.65
696	A92	50sh multicolored	.90	.90
697	A92	70sh multicolored	1.30	1.30
698	A92	250sh multicolored	4.50	4.50
699	A92	300sh multicolored	5.00	5.00
700	A92	350sh multicolored	6.00	6.00
		Nos. 693-700 (8)	19.05	19.05

Souvenir Sheets

701	A92	500sh multicolored	4.50	4.50
702	A92	500sh multicolored	4.50	4.50

Nos. 693-697 and 699 horiz.

Butterflies — A93

5sh, Ioalus pallene. 10sh, Hewitsonia boisduvali. 20sh, Euxanthe wakefeildi. 30sh, Papilio echerioides. 40sh, Acraea semivitrea. 50sh, Colotis antevippe. 70sh, Acraea perenna. 90sh, Charaxes cynthia. 100sh, Euphaedra neophroa. 150sh, Cymothoe beckeri. 200sh, Vanessula milca. 400sh, Mimacraea marshalli. 500sh, Axiocerses amanga. 1000sh, Precis hierta.

1989, Nov. 13		**"UGANDA" in Black**		
703	A93	5sh multicolored	.65	.65
704	A93	10sh multicolored	.70	.70
705	A93	20sh multicolored	1.10	1.10
706	A93	30sh multicolored	1.25	1.25
707	A93	40sh multicolored	1.40	1.40

708	A93	50sh multicolored	1.40	1.40
709	A93	70sh multicolored	1.75	1.75
710	A93	90sh multicolored	1.75	1.75
711	A93	100sh multicolored	1.75	1.75
712	A93	150sh multicolored	2.25	2.25
713	A93	200sh multicolored	2.25	2.25
714	A93	400sh multicolored	3.25	3.25
715	A93	500sh multicolored	3.50	3.50
716	A93	1000sh multicolored	4.50	4.50
		Nos. 703-716 (14)	27.50	27.50

See Nos. 826-839 for "UGANDA" in blue.

Explorers of Africa A94

Designs: 10sh, John Speke (1827-64), satellite view of Lake Victoria. 25sh, Sir Richard Burton (1821-90), satellite view of Lake Tanganyika. 40sh, Richard Lander (1804-34), bronze ritual figure of the Bakota tribe. 90sh, Rene Caillie (1799-1838), mosque. 125sh, Dorcas gazelle and Sir Samuel Baker (1821-93), discoverer of Lake Albert. 150sh, Phoenician galley and Necho II (d. 595 B.C.), king of Egypt credited by Herodotus with sending an expedition to circumnavigate Africa. 250sh, Vasco da Gama (c. 1460-1524), 1st European to sail around the Cape of Good Hope, and caravel. 300sh, Sir Henry Stanley (1841-1904), discoverer of Lake Edward, and Lady Alice . No. 725, Dr. David Livingstone (1813-73), discoverer of Victoria Falls, and steam launch Ma-Robert. No. 726, Mary Kingsley (1862-1900), ethnologist, and tail-spot climbing perch.

1989, Nov. 15		**Litho.**	**Perf. 14**	
717	A94	10sh multicolored	.30	.30
718	A94	25sh multicolored	.35	.35
719	A94	40sh multicolored	.55	.55
720	A94	90sh multicolored	1.10	1.10
721	A94	125sh multicolored	1.60	1.60
722	A94	150sh multicolored	1.90	1.90
723	A94	250sh multicolored	3.25	3.25
724	A94	300sh multicolored	3.75	3.75
		Nos. 717-724 (8)	12.80	12.80

Souvenir Sheets

725	A94	500sh multicolored	5.25	5.25
726	A94	500sh multicolored	5.25	5.25

Anniversaries and Events — A95

10sh, Bank emblem. 20sh, Satellite dishes, arrows. 75sh, Nehru. 90sh, Pan-American Dixie Clipper. 100sh, Locomotion, Stephenson. 150sh, Concorde cockpit. 250sh, Wapen von Hamburg, Leopoldus Primus. 300sh, Concorde cockpit, crew. No. 735, Storming of the Bastille. No. 736, Emperor Frederick I Barbarossa, charter.

1989, Dec. 12				
727	A95	10sh multicolored	.30	.30
728	A95	20sh multicolored	.30	.30
729	A95	75sh multicolored	2.40	2.40
730	A95	90sh multicolored	2.40	2.40
731	A95	100sh multicolored	2.40	2.40
732	A95	150sh multicolored	3.75	3.50
733	A95	250sh multicolored	3.75	3.50
734	A95	300sh multicolored	4.75	4.75
		Nos. 727-734 (8)	20.05	19.55

Souvenir Sheets

735	A95	500sh multicolored	5.25	5.25
736	A95	500sh multicolored	5.25	5.25

African Development Bank 25th anniv. (10sh); World Telecommunications Day, May 17 (20sh); Birth cent. of Jawaharlal Nehru, 1st prime minister of independent India (75sh); 1st scheduled transatlantic airmail flight, 50th anniv. (90sh); 175th anniv. of the invention of the 1st steam locomotive by George Stephenson and opening of the Stockton & Darlington Railway in 1825 (100sh); 1st test flight of the Concorde, 20th anniv. (150sh, 300sh); Port of Hamburg, 800th anniv. (250sh, No. 736); and French revolution bicent. (No. 735).

Christmas — A96

Religious paintings by Fra Angelico: 10sh, Madonna and Child. 20sh, Adoration of the Magi. 40sh, Virgin and Child Enthroned with Saints. 75sh, The Annunciation. 100sh, St. Peter Martyr triptych center panel. 150sh, Virgin and Child Enthroned with Saints, diff. 250sh, Virgin and Child Enthroned. 350sh, Annalena Altarpiece. No. 745, Bosco ai Frati Altarpiece. No. 746, Madonna and Child with Twelve Angels.

1989, Dec. 18				
737	A96	10sh multicolored	.25	.25
738	A96	20sh multicolored	.25	.25
739	A96	40sh multicolored	.50	.50
740	A96	75sh multicolored	.85	.85
741	A96	100sh multicolored	1.00	1.00
742	A96	150sh multicolored	1.40	1.40
743	A96	250sh multicolored	2.00	2.00
744	A96	350sh multicolored	2.25	2.25
		Nos. 737-744 (8)	8.50	8.50

Souvenir Sheets

745	A96	500sh multicolored	3.00	3.00
746	A96	500sh multicolored	3.00	3.00

Orchids — A97

10sh, Aerangis kotschyana. 15sh, Angraecum infundibulare. 45sh, Cyrtorchis chailluana. 50sh, Aerangis rhodosticta. 100sh, Eulophia speciosa. 200sh, Calanthe sylvatica. 250sh, Vanilla imperialis. 350sh, Polystachya vulcanica. No. 755, Ansellia africana. No. 756, Ancistrochilus rothschildianus.

1989, Dec. 18				
747	A97	10sh multicolored	.30	.30
748	A97	15sh multicolored	.30	.30
749	A97	45sh multicolored	.70	.70
750	A97	50sh multicolored	.75	.75
751	A97	100sh multicolored	1.40	1.40
752	A97	200sh multicolored	3.00	3.00
753	A97	250sh multicolored	3.50	3.50
754	A97	350sh multicolored	5.00	5.00
		Nos. 747-754 (8)	14.95	14.95

Souvenir Sheets

755	A97	500sh multicolored	6.75	6.75
756	A97	500sh multicolored	6.75	6.75

For overprints see Nos. 782-786A.

EXPO '90, Osaka — A98

Flowering trees — 10sh, Thevetia peruviana. 20sh, Acanthus eminens. 90sh, Gnidia glauca. 150sh, Oncoba spinosa. 175sh, Hibiscus rosa-sinensis. 400sh, Jacaranda mimosifolia. 500sh, Erythrina abyssinica. 700sh, Bauhinia purpurea. No. 765, Delonix regia. No. 766, Cassia didymobatrya.

1990, Apr. 17		**Litho.**	**Perf. 14**	
757	A98	10sh multi	.30	.30
758	A98	20sh multi	.30	.30
759	A98	90sh multi	.70	.70
760	A98	150sh multi	1.00	1.00
761	A98	175sh multi	1.10	1.10
762	A98	400sh multi	1.75	1.75

763	A98	500sh multi	2.00	2.00
764	A98	700sh multi	2.25	2.25
		Nos. 757-764 (8)	9.40	9.40

Souvenir Sheets

765	A98	1000sh multi	5.50	5.50
766	A98	1000sh multi	5.50	5.50

World War II Milestones — A99

Designs: 5sh, Allies penetrate west wall, Dec. 3, 1944. 10sh, VE Day, May 8, 1945. 20sh, US forces capture Okinawa, June 22, 1945. 75sh, DeGaulle named commander of all Free French forces, Apr. 4, 1944. 100sh, US troops invade Saipan, June 15, 1944. 150sh, Allied troops launch Operation Market Garden, Sept. 17, 1944. 200sh, Gen. MacArthur returns to Philippines, Oct. 20, 1944. 300sh, US victory at Coral Sea, May 8, 1942. 350sh, First battle of El Alamein, July 1, 1942. 500sh, Naval battle at Guadalcanal, Nov. 12, 1942. 1000sh, Battle of Britain.

1990, June 8		**Litho.**	**Perf. 14**	
767	A99	5sh multicolored	.30	.30
768	A99	10sh multicolored	.30	.30
769	A99	20sh multicolored	.30	.30
770	A99	75sh multicolored	.60	.60
771	A99	100sh multicolored	.80	.80
772	A99	150sh multicolored	1.15	1.15
773	A99	200sh multicolored	1.40	1.40
774	A99	300sh multicolored	2.50	2.50
775	A99	350sh multicolored	3.00	3.00
776	A99	500sh multicolored	4.00	4.00
		Nos. 767-776 (10)	14.35	14.35

Souvenir Sheet

777	A99	1000sh multicolored	7.50	7.50

Queen Mother, 90th Birthday — A100

1990, July 5				
778		250sh Hands clasped	1.00	1.00
779		250sh Facing left	1.00	1.00
780		250sh Holding dog	1.00	1.00
a.	A100	Strip of 3, #778-780	4.25	4.25
		Nos. 778-780 (3)	3.00	3.00

Souvenir Sheet

781	A100	1000sh like No. 778	4.00	4.00

Nos. 747-754 Ovptd. in Silver

Nos. 755-756 Ovptd. in Silver in Sheet Margin

1990		**Litho.**	**Perf. 14**	
782	A97	10sh on No. 747	1.00	1.00
782A	A97	15sh on No. 748	1.00	1.00
782B	A97	45sh on No. 749	1.50	1.50
783	A97	50sh on No. 750	1.50	1.50
783A	A97	100sh on No. 751	1.90	1.90
784	A97	200sh on No. 752	2.50	2.50

785	A97	250sh on No. 753	2.50	2.50
785A	A97	350sh on No. 754	3.00	3.00
		Nos. 782-785A (8)	14.90	14.90

Souvenir Sheet

786	A97	500sh on No. 755	5.00	5.00
786A	A97	500sh on No. 756	5.00	5.00

Issue dates: 15sh, 45sh, 100sh, 350sh, No. 786A, Nov.; others, July 30.

Pan African Postal Union, 10th Anniv. A101

Designs: 750sh, UN Conference on the least developed countries, Paris, Sept. 3-14.

1990, Aug. 3   Litho.   Perf. 14

787	A101	80sh multicolored	1.25	1.25

Souvenir Sheet

788	A101	750sh multicolored	3.75	3.75

Great Britain No. O1 — A102

Designs: 50sh, Canada #12. 100sh, Baden #4b. 150sh, Switzerland #3L1. 200sh, US #C3a. 300sh, Western Australia #1. 500sh, Uganda #29. 600sh, Great Britain #2. No. 797, Uganda #29. No. 798, Sir Rowland Hill.

1990, Aug. 6   Litho.   Perf. 14

789	A102	25sh multicolored	.35	.35
790	A102	50sh multicolored	.65	.65
791	A102	100sh multicolored	1.25	1.25
792	A102	150sh multicolored	1.50	1.50
793	A102	200sh multicolored	1.75	1.75
794	A102	300sh gray & black	2.25	2.25
795	A102	500sh multicolored	2.50	2.50
796	A102	600sh multicolored	2.50	2.50
		Nos. 789-796 (8)	12.75	12.75

Souvenir Sheets
Size: 108x77mm

797	A102	1000sh multicolored	5.75	5.75

Size: 119x85mm

798	A102	1000sh scarlet & blk	5.75	5.75

Penny Black, 150th anniversary. Nos. 797-798, Stamp World London '90.

Birds A103

10sh, African jacana. 15sh, Ground hornbill. 45sh, Kori bustard, vert. 50sh, Secretary bird. 100sh, Egyptian geese. 300sh, Goliath heron, vert. 500sh, Ostrich, vert. 650sh, Saddlebill stork, vert.
No. 807, Volturine guinea fowl, vert. No. 808, Lesser flamingo, vert.

1990, Sept. 3   Litho.   Perf. 14

799	A103	10sh multicolored	.90	.90
800	A103	15sh multicolored	.90	.90
801	A103	45sh multicolored	1.10	1.10
802	A103	50sh multicolored	1.10	1.10
803	A103	100sh multicolored	1.75	1.75
804	A103	300sh multicolored	3.00	3.00
805	A103	500sh multicolored	4.00	4.00
806	A103	650sh multicolored	4.25	4.25
		Nos. 799-806 (8)	17.00	17.00

Souvenir Sheets

807	A103	1000sh multicolored	5.75	5.75
808	A103	1000sh multicolored	5.75	5.75

World Cup Soccer Championships, Italy — A104

Players from various national teams.

1990, Sept. 24

809	A104	50sh Cameroun	.25	.25
810	A104	100sh Egypt	.50	.50
811	A104	250sh Ireland	1.25	1.25
812	A104	600sh West Germany	3.25	3.25
		Nos. 809-812 (4)	5.25	5.25

Souvenir Sheets

813	A104	1000sh Sweden	5.25	5.25
814	A104	1000sh Scotland	5.25	5.25

WHO, Promote Better Health — A105

Walt Disney characters in scenes promoting improved health: 10sh, Mickey, Minnie Mouse having a good breakfast. 20sh, Huey, Dewey and Louie looking before crossing street. 50sh, Mickey, Donald Duck against smoking. 90sh, Mickey saving Donald from choking. 100sh, Mickey, Goofy using seat belts. 250sh, Mickey, Minnie avoiding drugs. 500sh, Donald, Daisy exercising. 600sh, Mickey showing bicycle safety. No. 823, Mickey, friends at doctor's office. No. 824, Mickey, friends walking.

1990, Oct. 19   Litho.   Perf. 13½x13

815	A105	10sh multicolored	.30	.30
816	A105	20sh multicolored	.30	.30
817	A105	50sh multicolored	.45	.45
818	A105	90sh multicolored	.75	.75
819	A105	100sh multicolored	.85	.85
820	A105	250sh multicolored	1.75	1.75
821	A105	500sh multicolored	4.00	4.00
822	A105	600sh multicolored	4.50	4.50
		Nos. 815-822 (8)	12.90	12.90

Souvenir Sheets

823	A105	1000sh multicolored	6.00	6.00
824	A105	1000sh multicolored	6.00	6.00

Butterfly Type of 1989

3000sh, Euphaedra eusemoides. 4000sh, Acraea natalica. 5000sh, Euphaedra themis.

"Uganda" in Blue

1990-92   Litho.   Perf. 14

826	A93	10sh like #704	.65	.65
827	A93	20sh like #705	.75	.75
a.		Imprint "1991"	.85	.75
828	A93	30sh like #706	.75	.75
829	A93	40sh like #707	.75	.75
830	A93	50sh like #708	1.00	1.00
831	A93	70sh like #709	1.00	1.00
832	A93	90sh like #710	1.10	1.10
833	A93	100sh like #711	1.10	1.10
a.		Imprint "1991"	1.20	1.10
834	A93	150sh like #712	1.50	1.50
835	A93	200sh like #713	1.90	1.90
a.		Imprint "1991"	1.90	1.90
836	A93	400sh like #714	2.25	2.25
837	A93	500sh like #715	2.25	2.25
838	A93	1000sh like #716	4.50	4.50
839	A93	2000sh like #716	11.00	11.00
a.		Imprint "1991"	5.50	5.50
840	A93	3000sh multi	13.50	13.50
841	A93	4000sh multi	14.50	14.50
842	A93	5000sh multi	14.50	14.50
		Nos. 826-842 (17)	73.00	73.00

Issue dates: 10sh, 20sh, 30sh, 40sh, 70sh, 90sh, 100sh, 150sh, 200sh, 2000sh, 11/90. 50sh, 400sh, 500sh, 1000sh, 11/4/91. 3000sh, 4000sh, 10/9/92.
Nos. 826-829, 831-835, 839-842 do not have a year date imprint below design. Nos. 830, 836-838 are inscribed "1991" below design.

Christmas A106

Details from paintings by Rubens: 10sh, 500sh, The Baptism of Christ. 20sh, 150sh, 400sh, 600sh, St. Gregory the Great and Other Saints. 100sh, Saints Nereus, Domitilla and Achilleus. 300sh, Saint Augustine. No. 853, Victory of Eucharistic Truth Over Heresy, horiz. No. 854, Triumph of Faith, horiz.

1990, Dec. 17   Litho.   Perf. 14

845	A106	10sh multicolored	.25	.25
846	A106	20sh multicolored	.25	.25
847	A106	100sh multicolored	.80	.80
848	A106	150sh multicolored	1.10	1.10
849	A106	300sh multicolored	1.75	1.75
850	A106	400sh multicolored	1.90	1.90
851	A106	500sh multicolored	2.00	2.00
852	A106	600sh multicolored	2.25	2.25
		Nos. 845-852 (8)	10.30	10.30

Souvenir Sheets

853	A106	1000sh multicolored	5.25	5.25
854	A106	1000sh multicolored	5.25	5.25

Natl. Census A107

Design: 1000sh, Counting on fingers, houses, people.

1990, Dec. 28   Litho.   Perf. 14

855	A107	20sh multicolored	1.00	1.00

Souvenir Sheet

856	A107	1000sh multicolored	5.00	5.00

Wetlands Fauna — A108

No. 857: a, Damselfly. b, Purple gallinule. c, Sitatunga. d, Purple heron. e, Bushpig. f, Vervet monkey. g, Long reed frog. h, Malachite kingfisher. i, Marsh mongoose. j, Painted reed frog. k, Jacana. l, Charaxes butterfly. m, Nile crocodile. n, Herald snake. o, Dragonfly. p, Lungfish.
No. 858, Nile monitor, horiz.

1991, Jan. 1   Litho.   Perf. 14

857	A108	70sh Sheet of 16, #a.-p.	21.00	21.00

Souvenir Sheet

858	A108	1000sh multi	11.50	11.50

Fish A109

Designs: 10sh, Haplochromis limax. 20sh, Notobranchius palmqvisti. 40sh, Distichodus affinis. 90sh, Haplochromis sauvagei. 100sh, Aphyosemion calliurum. 350sh, Haplochromis johnstoni. 600sh, Haplochromis dichrourus. 800sh, Hemichromis bimaculatus. No. 867, Haplochromis sp. No. 868, Aphyosemion striatum.

1991, Jan. 18   Litho.   Perf. 14

859	A109	10sh multicolored	.30	.30
860	A109	20sh multicolored	.30	.30
861	A109	40sh multicolored	.30	.30
862	A109	90sh multicolored	.55	.55
863	A109	100sh multicolored	.65	.65
864	A109	350sh multicolored	1.60	1.60
865	A109	600sh multicolored	3.25	3.25
866	A109	800sh multicolored	4.00	4.00
		Nos. 859-866 (8)	10.95	10.95

Souvenir Sheets

867	A109	1000sh multicolored	6.50	6.50
868	A109	1000sh multicolored	6.50	6.50

1992 Summer Olympics, Barcelona — A110

20sh, Women's hurdles. 40sh, Long jump. 125sh, Table tennis. 250sh, Soccer. 500sh, 800-meter race.
No. 874 Women's 4x100-meter relay, horiz. No. 875, Opening ceremony, horiz.

1991, Feb. 25   Litho.   Perf. 14

869	A110	20sh multicolored	.25	.25
870	A110	40sh multicolored	.25	.25
871	A110	125sh multicolored	.80	.80
872	A110	250sh multicolored	1.75	1.75
873	A110	500sh multicolored	3.25	3.25
		Nos. 869-873 (5)	6.30	6.30

Souvenir Sheets

874	A110	1200sh multicolored	5.00	5.00
875	A110	1200sh multicolored	5.00	5.00

Trains A111

Designs: 10sh, 10th Class, Zimbabwe. 20sh, 12th Class, Zimbabwe. 80sh, Tribal class, Tanzania and Zambia. 200sh, 4-6-0 Type, Egypt. 300sh, Mikado, Sudan. 400sh, Mountain class Garrat, Uganda. 500sh, Mallet Type, Uganda. 1000sh, 5 F 1 Electric locomotive, South Africa. No. 884, 4-8-2 Type, Zimbabwe. No. 885, Atlantic type, Egypt. No. 886, 4-8-2 Type, Angola. No. 887, Mallet Compound Type, Natal.

1991, Apr. 2   Litho.   Perf. 14

876	A111	10sh multicolored	.30	.30
877	A111	20sh multicolored	.30	.30
878	A111	80sh multicolored	.45	.45
879	A111	200sh multicolored	1.30	1.30
880	A111	300sh multicolored	1.75	1.75
881	A111	400sh multicolored	2.40	2.40
882	A111	500sh multicolored	3.00	3.00
883	A111	1000sh multicolored	5.75	5.75
		Nos. 876-883 (8)	15.25	15.25

Souvenir Sheets

884	A111	1200sh multicolored	4.50	4.50
885	A111	1200sh multicolored	4.50	4.50
886	A111	1200sh multicolored	4.50	4.50
887	A111	1200sh multicolored	4.50	4.50

Even though Nos. 886-887 have the same issue date as Nos. 876-885, their dollar value was lower when they were released.

Phila Nippon '91 — A112

Walt Disney characters in Japan: 10sh, Scrooge McDuck celebrating Ga-No-Iwai. 20sh, Mickey removes shoes before entering Minnie's home. 70sh, Cartman Goofy leading horse. 80sh, Daisy, Minnie exchange gifts. 300sh, Minnie kneels at entrance to home. 400sh, Mickey, Donald in volcanic sand bath.

500sh, Clarabelle Cow enjoys incense burning. 1000sh, Mickey, Minnie writing New Year cards. No. 896, Mickey, Donald and Goofy in public bath. No. 897, Mickey and friends playing Japanese music.

1991, May 29 Litho. Perf. 14x13½

888	A112	10sh multicolored	.25	.25
889	A112	25sh multicolored	.25	.25
890	A112	70sh multicolored	.45	.45
891	A112	80sh multicolored	.50	.50
892	A112	300sh multicolored	1.90	1.90
893	A112	400sh multicolored	2.40	2.40
894	A112	500sh multicolored	3.25	3.25
895	A112	1000sh multicolored	6.00	6.00
		Nos. 888-895 (8)	15.00	15.00

Souvenir Sheets

896	A112	1200sh multicolored	7.50	7.50
897	A112	1200sh multicolored	7.50	7.50

17th World Scout Jamboree, Korea — A113

Designs: 20sh, Lord Baden-Powell. 80sh, Scouts collecting stamps. 100sh, Scout encampment, NY World's Fair, 1939. 150sh, Cover of 1st Scout Handbook. 300sh, Cooking over campfire. 400sh, Neil Armstrong, Edwin Aldrin, 1st scouts on moon. 500sh, Hands raised for Scout Pledge. 1000sh, Statue to Unknown Scout, Gilwell Park, England. No. 906, William D. Boyce, Lord Baden-Powell, Rev. L. Hadley. No. 907, 17th Jamboree Emblem.

1991, May 27 Perf. 14

898	A113	20sh multicolored	.00	.00
899	A113	80sh multicolored	.45	.45
900	A113	100sh multicolored	.55	.55
901	A113	150sh grn & blk	.80	.80
902	A113	300sh multicolored	1.50	1.50
903	A113	400sh multicolored	2.10	2.10
904	A113	500sh multicolored	2.50	2.50
905	A113	1000sh multicolored	4.75	4.75
		Nos. 898-905 (8)	12.95	12.95

Souvenir Sheets

906	A113	1200sh multicolored	6.25	6.25
907	A113	1200sh cream & blk	6.25	6.25

For surcharge see No. 1305.

Paintings by Vincent Van Gogh — A114

Paintings: 10sh, Snowy Landscape with Arles in the Background. 20sh, Peasant Woman Binding Sheaves, vert. 60sh, The Drinkers. 80sh, View of Auvers. 200sh, Mourning Man, vert. 400sh, Still Life: Vase with Roses. 800sh, The Raising of Lazarus. 1000sh, The Good Samaritan, vert. No. 916, First Steps. No. 917, Village Street and Steps in Auvers with Figures.

1991, June 26 Litho. Perf. 13½

908	A114	10sh multicolored	.25	.25
909	A114	20sh multicolored	.25	.25
910	A114	60sh multicolored	.30	.30
911	A114	80sh multicolored	.40	.40
912	A114	200sh multicolored	1.00	1.00
913	A114	400sh multicolored	2.00	2.00
914	A114	800sh multicolored	4.00	4.00
915	A114	1000sh multicolored	5.00	5.00
		Nos. 908-915 (8)	13.20	13.20

Size: 102x76mm

Imperf

916	A114	1200sh multicolored	7.00	7.00
917	A114	1200sh multicolored	7.00	7.00

Royal Family Birthday, Anniversary
Common Design Type

No. 926, Elizabeth, Philip. No. 927, Sons, Diana, Charles.

1991, July 5 Litho. Perf. 14

918	CD347	20sh multi	.25	.25
919	CD347	70sh multi	.40	.40
920	CD347	90sh multi	.60	.60
921	CD347	100sh multi	.65	.65
922	CD347	200sh multi	1.20	1.20
923	CD347	500sh multi	2.75	2.75
924	CD347	600sh multi	3.50	3.50
925	CD347	1000sh multi	5.75	5.75
		Nos. 918-925 (8)	15.10	15.10

Souvenir Sheets

926	CD347	1200sh multi	5.00	5.00
927	CD347	1200sh multi	6.50	6.50

20sh, 100sh, 200sh, 1000sh, No. 927, Charles and Diana, 10th wedding anniversary. Others, Queen Elizabeth II, 65th birthday.

Charles de Gaulle, Birth Cent. A115

Designs: 20sh, Portrait, vert. 70sh, Liberation of Paris, 1944, vert. 90sh, With King George VI, 1940, vert. 100sh, Reviewing Free French forces, 1940. 200sh, Making his appeal on BBC, 1940. 500sh, In Normandy, 1944. 600sh, At Albert Hall, 1940. 1000sh, Becoming President of France, 1959, vert. No. 936, Entering Paris, 1944, vert. No. 937, With Eisenhower, 1942.

1991, July 15 Perf. 14

928	A115	20sh multicolored	.25	.25
929	A115	70sh multicolored	.30	.30
930	A115	90sh multicolored	.40	.40
931	A115	100sh multicolored	.45	.45
932	A115	200sh multicolored	.85	.85
933	A115	500sh multicolored	2.10	2.10
934	A115	600sh multicolored	2.50	2.50
935	A115	1000sh multicolored	4.25	4.25
		Nos. 928-935 (8)	11.10	11.10

Souvenir Sheets

936	A115	1200sh multicolored	6.00	6.00
937	A115	1200sh multicolored	6.00	6.00

Mushrooms A116

Designs: 20sh, Volvariella bingensis. 70sh, Agrocybe broadwayi. 90sh, Camarophyllus olidus. 140sh, Marasmius arborescens. 180sh, Marasmiellus subcinereus. 200sh, Agaricus campestris. 500sh, Chlorophyllum molybdites. 1000sh, Agaricus bingensis. No. 946, Leucocoprinus cepaestipes, horiz. No. 947, Laccaria lateritia, horiz.

1991, July 19 Litho. Perf. 14

938	A116	20sh multicolored	.30	.30
939	A116	70sh multicolored	.50	.50
940	A116	90sh multicolored	.65	.65
941	A116	140sh multicolored	1.00	1.00
942	A116	180sh multicolored	1.25	1.25
943	A116	200sh multicolored	1.40	1.40
944	A116	500sh multicolored	4.00	4.00
945	A116	1000sh multicolored	8.00	8.00
		Nos. 938-945 (8)	17.10	17.10

Souvenir Sheets

946	A116	1200sh multicolored	5.50	5.50
947	A116	1200sh multicolored	5.50	5.50

World Wildlife Type of 1983

1991, Aug. 1

948	A43	100sh as No. 371	1.00	1.00
949	A43	140sh as No. 372	1.40	1.40
950	A43	200sh as No. 373	1.90	1.90
951	A43	600sh as No. 374	5.50	5.50
		Nos. 948-951 (4)	9.80	9.80

Souvenir Sheets

Perf. 13x12½

952	A43	1200sh Giraffe	8.00	8.00
953	A43	1200sh Rhinoceros	8.00	8.00

World Wildlife Fund. Nos. 952-953 do not have the WWF emblem.

Flowers in Royal Botanical Gardens, Kew — A118

No. 954: a, Cypripedium calceolus. b, Rhododendron thomsonii. c, Ginkgo biloba. d, Magnolia campbellii. e, Wisteria sinensis. f, Clerodendrum ugandense. g, Eulophia horsfallii. h, Aerangis rhodosticta. i, Abelmoschus moschatus. j, Gloriosa superba. k, Carissa edulis. l, Ochna kirkii. m, Canarina abyssinica. n, Nymphaea caerulea. o, Ceropegia succulenta. p, Strelitzia reginae. q, Strongylodon macrobotrys. r, Victoria amazonica. s, Orchis militaris. t, Sophora microphylla.

No. 955 — Royal Botanic Gardens, Melbourne, Australia: a, Anigozanthos manglesii. b, Banksia grandis. c, Olianthus formosus. d, Gossypium sturtianum. e, Callistemon lanceolatus. f, Saintpaulia ionantha. g, Calodendrum capense. h, Aloe ferox. i, Bolusanthus speciousus. j, Lithops schwantesii k, Protea repens. l, Plumbago capensis. m, Clerodendrum thomsoniae. n, Thunbergia alata. o, Schotia latifolia. p, Epacris impressa. q, Acacia pycnantha. r, Telopea speciosissima. s, Wahlenbergia gloriosa. t, Eucalyptus globulus.

No. 956, The Pagoda, Kew. No. 957, Temple of the Winds, Melbourne.

1991, Nov. 25 Litho. Perf. 14½

954	A118	100sh Sheet of 20, #a.-t.	12.00	12.00
955	A118	90sh Sheet of 20, #a.-t.	8.00	8.00

Souvenir Sheets

956	A118	1400sh multicolored	8.00	8.00
957	A118	1400sh multicolored	5.50	5.50

No. 956 contains one 30x38mm stamp. While Nos. 955 and 957 have the same issue date as Nos. 954 and 956, their dollar value was lower when released.

Christmas A120

Paintings by Piero Della Francesca: 20sh, Madonna with Child and Angels. 50sh, The Baptism of Christ. 80sh, Polyptych of Mercy. 100sh, The Madonna of Mercy. 200sh, The Legend of the True Cross: The Annunciation. 500sh, Pregnant Madonna. 1000sh, Polyptych of St. Anthony: The Annunciation. 1500sh, The Nativity. No. 968, The Brera Altarpiece. No. 969, Polyptych of St. Anthony.

1991, Dec. 18 Litho. Perf. 12

960	A120	20sh multicolored	.25	.25
961	A120	50sh multicolored	.25	.25
962	A120	80sh multicolored	.35	.35
963	A120	100sh multicolored	.45	.45
964	A120	200sh multicolored	.85	.85
965	A120	500sh multicolored	2.10	2.10
966	A120	1000sh multicolored	4.25	4.25
967	A120	1500sh multicolored	6.50	6.50
		Nos. 960-967 (8)	15.00	15.00

Souvenir Sheets

Perf. 14½

968	A120	1800sh multicolored	7.50	7.50
969	A120	1800sh multicolored	7.50	7.50

Boy Scouts A121

Designs: 20sh, Boy Scout Monument, Silver Bay, NY and Ernest Thompson Seton, first chief scout. 50sh, Tree house and Daniel Beard, Boy Scout pioneer, vert. 1500sh, Boy Scout emblem.

1992, Jan. 6 Litho. Perf. 14

970	A121	20sh multicolored	.90	.90
971	A121	50sh multicolored	1.25	1.25

Souvenir Sheet

972	A121	1500sh multicolored	7.00	7.00

YMCA-Boy Scouts partnership, Lord Robert Baden-Powell, 50th death anniv. in 1991 (#970) and 17th World Scout Jamboree, Korea (#971-972).

Balloons — A122

Balloons: a, Modern Hot Air. b, Sport. c, Pro Juventute. d, Blanchard's. e, Nadar's Le Géant. f, First trans-Pacific balloon crossing. g, Montgolfier's. h, Paris, Double Eagle II, used in first trans-Atlantic balloon crossing. i, Tethered.

1992, Jan. 6 Litho. Perf. 14

974	A122	200sh Sheet of 9, #a.-i.	9.50	9.50

Japanese Attack on Pearl Harbor, 50th Anniv. (in 1991) — A123

Designs: a, Japanese bombers attack USS Vestal. b, Japanese Zero fighter. c, Zeros over burning USS Arizona. d, Battleship Row, USS Nevada under attack. e, Japanese Val dive bomber. f, US Dauntless dive bomber attacking Hiryu. g, Japanese planes over Midway Island. h, US Buffalo fighter plane. i, US Wildcat fighters over carrier. j, USS Yorktown and Hammann torpedoed by Japanese submarine.

1992, Jan. 6 Perf. 14½x15

975	A123	200sh Sheet of 10, #a.-j.	12.50	12.50

Battle of Midway, 50th anniv. (#975f-975j). Inscription for No. 975i incorrectly describes fighters as Hellcats.

Anniversaries and Events — A124

Designs: 400sh, Glider No. 8. 500sh, Man breaking pieces from Berlin Wall. 700sh, Portrait of Mozart and scene from "The Magic Flute." 1200sh, Electric locomotive.

1992, Jan. 6   Litho.   Perf. 14
976	A124	400sh multicolored	1.60	1.60
977	A124	500sh multicolored	2.00	2.00
978	A124	700sh multicolored	6.50	6.50
		Nos. 976-978 (3)	10.10	10.10

Souvenir Sheet
979	A124	1200sh multicolored	5.75	5.75

Otto Lillienthal, hang glider, cent. (in 1991) (#976). Brandenburg Gate, Bicent. (#977), Wolfgang Amadeus Mozart, death bicent. (#978), Trans-Siberian Railway, cent. (#979).

Walt Disney Characters on World Tour — A125

Designs: 20sh, Safari surprise in Africa. 50sh, Pluto's tail of India. 80sh, Donald's calypso beat in Caribbean. 200sh, Goofy pulling rickshaw in China. 500sh, Minnie, Mickey on camel in Egypt. 800sh, Wrestling, Japanese style. 1000sh, Goofy bullfighting in Spain. 1500sh, Mickey scoring in soccer game. No. 988, Daisy singing opera in Germany. No. 989, Mickey and Pluto as Cossack dancers in Moscow.

1992, Feb.   Perf. 13
980	A125	20sh multi	.30	.30
981	A125	50sh multi	.30	.30
982	A125	80sh multi	.30	.30
983	A125	200sh multi	.70	.70
984	A125	500sh multi	1.75	1.75
985	A125	800sh multi	3.00	3.00
986	A125	1000sh multi	3.50	3.50
987	A125	1500sh multi	5.25	5.25
		Nos. 980-987 (8)	15.10	15.10

Souvenir Sheets
988	A125	2000sh multi, vert.	7.50	7.50
989	A125	2000sh multi	7.50	7.50

Queen Elizabeth II's Accession to the Throne, 40th Anniv.
Common Design Type

No. 994, Queen, waterfalls. No. 995, Queen, dam.

1992, Feb. 6   Litho.   Perf. 14
990	CD348	100sh multi	.50	.50
991	CD348	200sh multi	.75	.75
992	CD348	500sh multi	2.00	2.00
993	CD348	1000sh multi	4.25	4.25
		Nos. 990-993 (4)	7.50	7.50

Souvenir Sheets
994	CD348	1800sh multi	6.00	6.00
995	CD348	1800sh multi	6.00	6.00

Dinosaurs A126

50sh, Kentrosaurus. 200sh, Iguanodon. 250sh, Hypsilophodon. 300sh, Brachiosaurus. 400sh, Peloneustes. 500sh, Pteranodon. 800sh, Tetra- lophodon. 1000sh, Megalosaurus.

1992, Apr. 8   Litho.   Perf. 14
996	A126	50sh multi	.35	.35
997	A126	200sh multi	.65	.65
998	A126	250sh multi	1.25	1.25
999	A126	300sh multi	1.00	1.00
1000	A126	400sh multi	1.75	1.75
1001	A126	500sh multi	1.60	1.60
1002	A126	800sh multi	2.50	2.50
1003	A126	1000sh multi	4.50	4.50
		Nos. 996-1003 (8)	13.60	13.60

Souvenir Sheets
1004	A126	2000sh like #1003	6.50	6.50
1005	A126	2000sh like #998	6.50	6.50

Nos. 1004-1005 printed in continuous design.
While Nos. 997, 999, 1001-1002, 1005 have the same release date as Nos. 996, 998, 1000, 1003-1004, their value in relation to the dollar was lower when they were released.

Easter A127

Paintings: 50sh, The Entry into Jerusalem (detail), by Giotto. 100sh, Pilate and the Watch from psalter of Robert de Lisle. 200sh, The Kiss of Judas (detail), by Giotto. 250sh, Christ Washing the Feet of the Disciples, illumination from Life of Christ. 300sh, Christ Seized in the Garden from Melissande Psalter. 500sh, Doubting Thomas, illumination from Life of Christ. 1000sh, The Marys at the Tomb (detail), artist unknown. 2000sh, The Ascension, from 14th century Florentine illuminated manuscript.
Limoge enamels: No. 1014, Agony at Gethsemane. No. 1015, The Piercing of Christ's Side.

1992   Litho.   Perf. 13½x14
1006	A127	50sh multi	.25	.25
1007	A127	100sh multi	.30	.30
1008	A127	200sh multi	.70	.70
1009	A127	250sh multi	.75	.75
1010	A127	300sh multi	.90	.90
1011	A127	500sh multi	1.50	1.50
1012	A127	1000sh multi	3.00	3.00
1013	A127	2000sh multi	6.25	6.25
		Nos. 1006-1013 (8)	13.65	13.65

Souvenir Sheets
1014	A127	2500sh multi	7.00	7.00
1015	A127	2500sh multi	7.00	7.00

Musical Instruments A128

1992, July 20   Litho.   Perf. 14
1016	A128	50sh Adungu	.25	.25
1017	A128	100sh Endingidi	.30	.30
1018	A128	200sh Akogo	.65	.65
1019	A128	250sh Nanga	.75	.75
1020	A128	300sh Engoma	.90	.90
1021	A128	400sh Amakondere	1.25	1.25
1022	A128	500sh Akakyenkye	1.50	1.50
1023	A128	1000sh Ennanga	3.00	3.00
		Nos. 1016-1023 (8)	8.60	8.60

Discovery of America, 500th Anniv. A129

Designs: 50sh, World map, 1486. 100sh, Map of Africa, 1508. 150sh, New World, 1500. 200sh, Nina, astrolabe. 600sh, Quadrant, Pinta. 800sh, Hour glass. 900sh, 15th century compass. 2000sh, World map, 1492. No. 1032, 1490 Map by Henricus Martellus, 1490. No. 1033, Sections of 1492 globe.

1992, July 24   Litho.   Perf. 14
1024	A129	50sh multi	.25	.25
1025	A129	100sh multi	.25	.25
1026	A129	150sh multi	.25	.25
1027	A129	200sh multi	.70	.70
1028	A129	600sh multi	2.00	2.00
1029	A129	800sh multi	2.60	2.60
1030	A129	900sh multi	2.75	2.75
1031	A129	2000sh multi	2.25	2.25
		Nos. 1024-1031 (8)	11.05	11.05

Souvenir Sheets
1032	A129	2500sh multi, vert.	6.50	6.50
1033	A129	2500sh multi	4.50	4.50

World Columbian Stamp Expo '92, Chicago.
While Nos. 1024-1026, 1031 and 1033 have the same issue date as Nos. 1027-1030 and 1032, their value in relation to the dollar was lower when they were released.

Hummel Figurines — A130

No. 1034, Little Laundry Girl. No. 1035, Scrub Girl. No. 1036, Sweeper Girl. No. 1037, Little Mother. No. 1038, Little Mountaineer. No. 1039, Little Knitter. No. 1040, Little Cowboy. No. 1041, Little Astronomer.
No. 1042: a, Like #1034. b, Like #1035. c, Like #1036. d, Like #1037.
No. 1043: a, Like #1039. b, Like #1038. c, Like #1040. d, Like #1041.

1992, Aug. 28   Litho.   Perf. 14
1034	A130	50sh multi	.25	.25
1035	A130	200sh multi	.65	.65
1036	A130	250sh multi	.70	.70
1037	A130	300sh multi	.90	.90
1038	A130	600sh multi	1.30	1.30
1039	A130	900sh multi	1.75	1.75
1040	A130	1000sh multi	2.25	2.25
1041	A130	1500sh multi	4.50	4.50
		Nos. 1034-1041 (8)	12.30	12.30

Souvenir Sheets
1042	A130	500sh Sheet of 4, #a.-d.	6.75	6.75
1043	A130	500sh Sheet of 4, #a.-d.	6.75	6.75

While Nos. 1034, 1038-1040, 1043 have the same release date as Nos. 1035-1037, 1041-1042, their value in relation to the dollar was lower when they were released.

1992 Summer Olympics, Barcelona — A131

50sh, Javelin. 100sh, High jump, horiz. 200sh, Pentathlon (Fencing). 250sh, Volleyball. 300sh, Women's platform diving. 500sh, Team cycling. 1000sh, Tennis. 2000sh, Boxing, horiz.
No. 1052, Baseball. No. 1053, Basketball.

1992   Litho.   Perf. 14
1044	A131	50sh multi	.35	.35
1045	A131	100sh multi	.35	.35
1046	A131	200sh multi	.55	.55
1047	A131	250sh multi	.65	.65
1048	A131	300sh multi	.80	.80
1049	A131	500sh multi	1.30	1.30
1050	A131	1000sh multi	2.75	2.75
1051	A131	2000sh multi	5.25	5.25
		Nos. 1044-1051 (8)	12.00	12.00

Souvenir Sheets
1052	A131	2500sh multi	5.75	5.75
1053	A131	2500sh multi	5.75	5.75

Wild Animals A132

50sh, Spotted hyena. 100sh, Impala. 200sh, Giant forest hog. 250sh, Pangolin. 300sh, Golden monkey. 800sh, Serval. 1000sh, Bush genet. 3000sh, Defassa waterbuck.
No. 1062, Mountain gorilla. No. 1063, Hippopotamus.

1992, Sept. 25   Litho.   Perf. 14
1054	A132	50sh multi	.25	.25
1055	A132	100sh multi	.25	.25
1056	A132	200sh multi	.45	.45
1057	A132	250sh multi	.55	.55
1058	A132	300sh multi	.70	.70
1059	A132	800sh multi	1.75	1.75
1060	A132	1000sh multi	2.25	2.25
1061	A132	3000sh multi	6.75	6.75
		Nos. 1054-1061 (8)	12.95	12.95

Souvenir Sheets
1062	A132	2500sh multi	5.50	5.50
1063	A132	2500sh multi	5.50	5.50

Birds — A133

Designs: 20sh, Red necked falcon. 30sh, Yellow-billed hornbill. 50sh, Purple heron. 100sh, Regal sunbird. 150sh, White-brown robin chat. 200sh, Shining-blue kingfisher. 250sh, Great blue turaco. 300sh, Emerald cuckoo. 500sh, Abyssinian roller. 800sh, Crowned crane. 1000sh, Doherty's bush shrike. 2000sh, Splendid glossy starling. 3000sh, Little bee eater. 4000sh, Red-headed lovebird.

1992, Aug.   Litho.   Perf. 15x14
1064	A133	20sh multi	.35	.35
1065	A133	30sh multi	.35	.35
1066	A133	50sh multi	.35	.35
1067	A133	100sh multi	.35	.35
1068	A133	150sh multi	.40	.40
1069	A133	200sh multi	.55	.55
1070	A133	250sh multi	.70	.70
1071	A133	300sh multi	.75	.75
1072	A133	500sh multi	1.40	1.40
1073	A133	800sh multi	2.25	2.25
1074	A133	1000sh multi	2.75	2.75
1075	A133	2000sh multi	5.50	5.50
1076	A133	3000sh multi	8.50	8.50
1076A	A133	4000sh multi	11.00	11.00
		Nos. 1064-1076A (14)	35.20	35.20

Issued: 3000sh, Oct.; others, Aug.?

Walt Disney's Goofy, 60th Anniv. — A134

Scenes from Disney animated films: 50sh, Hawaiian Holiday, 1937, vert. 100sh, The Nifty Nineties, 1941, vert. 200sh, Mickey's Fire Brigade, 1935, vert. 250sh, The Art of Skiing, 1941. 300sh, Mickey's Amateurs, 1937. 1000sh, Boat Builders, 1938. 1500sh, The Olympic Champ, 1942, vert. 2000sh, The Olympic Champ, 1942, vert. No. 1085, Goofy and Wilbur, 1939. No. 1086, Goofy's family tree, vert.

Perf. 13½x14, 14x13½
1992, Nov. 2   Litho.
1077	A134	50sh multi	.25	.25
1078	A134	100sh multi	.25	.25
1079	A134	200sh multi	.50	.50
1080	A134	250sh multi	.65	.65
1081	A134	300sh multi	.80	.80
1082	A134	1000sh multi	2.50	2.50
1083	A134	1500sh multi	4.00	4.00
1084	A134	2000sh multi	5.25	5.25
		Nos. 1077-1084 (8)	14.20	14.20

Souvenir Sheets
1085	A134	3000sh multi	7.50	7.50
1086	A134	3000sh multi	7.50	7.50

Souvenir Sheet

UN Headquarters, New York City — A135

1992, Oct. 28   Litho.   Perf. 14
1087	A135	2500sh multi	7.50	7.50

Postage Stamp Mega Event '92, NYC.

CHRISTMAS 1992

THE ANNUNCIATION – ZURBARAN

UGANDA 200/-

Christmas
A136

Details or entire paintings by Zurbaran: 50sh, The Annunciation (angel at left). 200sh, The Annunciation (angel at right). 250sh, The Virgin of the Immaculate Conception. 300sh, The Virgin of the Immaculate Conception (detail). 800sh, 900sh, The Holy Family with Saints Anne, Joachim and John the Baptist (800sh, entire, 900sh, detail). 1000sh, Adoration of the Magi (entire). 2000sh, Adoration of the Magi. No. 1096, The Virgin of the Immaculate Conception (Virgin with arms outstretched). No. 1097, The Virgin of the Immaculate Conception (Virgin with arms folded).

1992, Nov. 16   Litho.   Perf. 13½x14
1088	A136	50sh multi	.25	.25
1089	A136	200sh multi	.45	.45
1090	A136	250sh multi	.60	.60
1091	A136	300sh multi	.75	.75
1092	A136	800sh multi	2.00	2.00
1093	A136	900sh multi	2.25	2.25
1094	A136	1000sh multi	2.40	2.40
1095	A136	2000sh multi	4.75	4.75
		Nos. 1088-1095 (8)	13.45	13.45

Souvenir Sheets
1096	A136	2500sh multi	7.00	7.00
1097	A136	2500sh multi	7.00	7.00

Granary - 'Improving household food security'

50/-

UGANDA

World Health Organization — A137

UN-ISY 1992

Jupiter Voyager 2

UGANDA 300/-

Anniversaries and Events — A138

Designs: 50sh, Improving household food security. 200sh, Continue to breastfeed. 250sh, At four months old, give breast milk and soft food. No. 1101, Drink water from a safe and protected source. No. 1102, Jupiter, Voyager 2. No. 1103, Mother holding baby. No. 1104, Impala. No. 1105, Zebra. No. 1106, Count Ferdinand von Zeppelin, zeppelin. 2000sh, Neptune, Voyager 2. 3000sh, Count Zeppelin, zeppelin, diff. No. 1109, Voyager 2, Jupiter, diff. No. 1110, Wart hog. No. 1111, Doctor examining child, Lions Intl. emblem. No. 1112, Count Zeppelin, balloon.

1992   Litho.   Perf. 14
1098	A137	50sh multi	.25	.25
1099	A137	200sh multi	.40	.40
1100	A137	250sh multi	.50	.50
1101	A137	300sh multi	.60	.60
1102	A138	300sh multi	1.40	1.40
1103	A137	800sh multi	1.60	1.60
1104	A138	800sh multi	3.25	3.25
1105	A138	1000sh multi	3.75	3.75
1106	A138	1000sh multi	2.00	2.00
1107	A138	2000sh multi	9.75	9.75
1108	A138	3000sh multi	6.00	6.00
		Nos. 1098-1108 (11)	29.50	29.50

Souvenir Sheets
1109	A138	2500sh multi	7.75	7.75
1110	A138	2500sh multi	7.75	7.75
1111	A138	2500sh multi	7.75	7.75
1112	A138	2500sh multi	7.75	7.75

WHO (#1098-1101, 1103). Intl. Space Year (#1102, 1107, 1109). Earth Summit, Rio de Janeiro (#1104 1105, 1110). Count Zeppelin, 75th anniv. of death (#1106, 1108, 1112). Lions Intl., 75th anniv. (#1111).

Issue dates: Nos. 1098-1103, 1106, 1109, 1112, Nov.; others, Dec.

UGANDA 50/-

VISIT OF HIS HOLINESS POPE JOHN PAUL II FEBRUARY 1993

1993 Visit of Pope John Paul II to Uganda
A139

A139a

Designs: 50sh, Cathedral in Kampala, site of Papal Mass, Kampala, hands releasing doves. 200sh, Site of Papal Mass, Pope. 250sh, Ugandan man, Pope. 300sh, Three Ugandan Catholic leaders, Pope. 800sh, Pope waving, Ugandan map and flag. 900sh, Ugandan woman, Pope wearing mitre. 1000sh, Pope, Ugandan flag, site of Papal Mass. 2000sh, Ugandan flag, Pope waving.

No. 1121, Pope at door of airplane, vert. No. 1122, Pope delivering message at podium, vert.

No. 1123, Pope John Paul II. No. 1124, Pope with hands raised.

1993, Feb. 1   Litho.   Perf. 14
1113	A139	50sh multi	.30	.30
1114	A139	200sh multi	.50	.50
1115	A139	250sh multi	.60	.60
1116	A139	300sh multi	.70	.70
1117	A139	800sh multi	1.75	1.75
1118	A139	900sh multi	1.90	1.90
1119	A139	1000sh multi	2.25	2.25
1120	A139	2000sh multi	4.50	4.50
		Nos. 1113-1120 (8)	12.50	12.50

Souvenir Sheets
1121	A139	3000sh multi	6.25	6.25
1122	A139	3000sh multi	6.25	6.25

Embossed
Perf. 12
1123	A139a	5000sh gold	30.00	30.00

Souvenir Sheet
Imperf
1124	A139a	5000sh gold	30.00	30.00

Miniature Sheet

AUTOPORTRAIT AU CHEVALET REMBRANDT

UGANDA 500/-

Louvre Museum, Bicent.
A140

Details or entire paintings by Rembrandt: No. 1125a, Self-Portrait with an Easel. b, Birds of Paradise. c, The Beef Carcass. d, The Supper at Emmaus. e, Hendrickje Stoffels. f, Titus, Son of the Artist. g, The Holy Family (left). h, The Holy Family (right).

2500sh, Philosopher in Meditation, horiz.

1993, Apr. 5   Litho.   Perf. 12
1125	A140	500sh Sheet of 8, #a.-h. + label	10.00	10.00

Souvenir Sheet
Perf. 14½
1126	A140	2500sh multi	6.50	6.50

UGANDA Afghan hound

50/-

Dogs
A141

50sh, Afghan hound. 100sh, Newfoundland. 200sh, Siberian huskies. 250sh, Briard. 300sh, Saluki. 800sh, Labrador retriever, vert. 1000sh, Greyhound. 1500sh, Pointer.

No. 1135, Cape hunting dog. No. 1136, Norwegian elkhound.

1993, May 28   Litho.   Perf. 14
1127	A141	50sh multi	.45	.45
1128	A141	100sh multi	.45	.45
1129	A141	200sh multi	.80	.80
1130	A141	250sh multi	1.00	1.00
1131	A141	300sh multi	1.40	1.40
1132	A141	800sh multi	3.50	3.50
1133	A141	1000sh multi	4.00	4.00
1134	A141	1500sh multi	6.50	6.50
		Nos. 1127-1134 (8)	18.10	18.10

Souvenir Sheets
1135	A141	2500sh multi	11.00	11.00
1136	A141	2500sh multi	11.00	11.00

Miniature Sheet

The 40th Anniversary of the Coronation of HM Queen Elizabeth II

1953 1993

Coronation of Queen Elizabeth II, 40th Anniv. — A142

No. 1137: a, 50sh, Official coronation photograph. b, 200sh, Orb, Rod of Equity & Mercy. c, 500sh, Queen during coronation ceremony. d, 1500sh, Queen Elizabeth II, Princess Margaret.

2500sh, The Crown, by Grace Wheatley, 1959.

1993, June 2   Litho.   Perf. 13½x14
1137	A142	Sheet, 2 each #a.-d.	12.50	12.50

Souvenir Sheet
Perf. 14
1138	A142	2500sh multicolored	7.00	7.00

No. 1138 contains one 28x42mm stamp.

Miniature Sheet

Taipei, Taiwan ROC Aug. 14-19

Tri-Color Pottery

Taipei '93 — A143

Funerary objects: No. 1139a, Tomb guardian god. b, Civil official. c, Tomb guardian god, diff. d, Civil official, diff. e, Chimera. f, Civil official, diff.

2500sh, Statue of Sacred Mother, Ceremonial Hall, Taiyuan, Shanxi.

1993, Sept. 22   Litho.   Perf. 14x13½
1139	A143	600sh Sheet of 6, #a.-f.	7.50	7.50

Souvenir Sheet
1140	A143	2500sh multicolored	7.00	7.00

With Bangkok '93 Emblem

Thai sculpture: No. 1141a, Standing Buddha, 13th-15th cent. b, Crowned Buddha, 13th cent. c, Thepanom, 15th cent. d, Crowned Buddha, 12th cent. e, Four-armed Avalokitesvara, 9th cent. f, Lop Buri standing Buddha, 13th cent.

2500sh, Buddha, interior of Wat Mahathat.

1993, Sept. 22
1141	A143	600sh Sheet of 6, #a.-f.	7.50	7.50

Souvenir Sheet
1142	A143	2500sh multicolored	7.00	7.00

With Indopex '93 Emblem

Japanese Wayang Puppets, Indonesia: No. 1143a, Bupati karma, Prince of Wangga. b, Rahwana. c, Sondjeng Sandjata. d, Raden Damar Wulan. e, Klitik figure. f, Hanaman. 2500sh, Candi Mendut in Kedu Plain, Java, Indonesia.

1993, Sept. 22   Litho.   Perf. 13½x14
1143	A143	600sh Sheet of 6, #a.-f.	7.50	7.50

Souvenir Sheet
1144	A143	2500sh multicolored	7.00	7.00

UGANDA 200/-
Tomas Brolin, SWE

A144

50sh, Gutierrez, Voeller. 200sh, Tomas Brolin. 250sh, Gary Lineker. 300sh, Munoz, Butragueno. 800sh, Carlos Valderrama. 900sh, Diego Maradona. 1000sh, Pedro Troglio. 2000sh, Enzo Scifo.

No. 1153, Brazil coaches. No. 1154, De Napoli, Skuhravy, horiz.

1993, Oct. 1   Litho.   Perf. 14
1145	A144	50sh multi	.35	.35
1146	A144	200sh multi	.60	.60
1147	A144	250sh multi	.75	.75
1148	A144	300sh multi	.85	.85
1149	A144	800sh multi	2.40	2.40
1150	A144	900sh multi	2.55	2.55
1151	A144	1000sh multi	3.00	3.00
1152	A144	2000sh multi	6.00	6.00
		Nos. 1145-1152 (8)	16.50	16.50

Souvenir Sheets
1153	A144	2500sh multi	7.25	7.25
1154	A144	2500sh multi	7.25	7.25

1994 World Cup Soccer Championships, US.

UGANDA

50/-

York Minster • England

A145

Cathedrals of the World: 50sh, York Minster, England. 100sh, Notre Dame, Paris. 200sh, Little Metropolis, Athens. 250sh, St. Patrick's, New York. 300sh, Ulm, Germany. 800sh, St. Basil's, Moscow. 1000sh, Roskilde, Denmark. 2000sh, Seville, Spain. No. 1163, Namirembe, Uganda. No. 1163A, St. Peter's, Vatican City.

1993, Nov. 3   Perf. 14
1155	A145	50sh multi	.35	.35
1156	A145	100sh multi	.35	.35
1157	A145	200sh multi	.65	.65
1158	A145	250sh multi	.70	.70
1159	A145	300sh multi	.95	.95
1160	A145	800sh multi	2.25	2.25
1161	A145	1000sh multi	3.00	3.00
1162	A145	2000sh multi	5.75	5.75
		Nos. 1155-1162 (8)	14.00	14.00

Souvenir Sheets
1163	A145	2500sh multi	7.50	7.50
1163A	A145	2500sh multi	7.50	7.50

Christmas
A146

Details or entire woodcut, The Virgin with Carthusian Monks, by Durer: 50sh, 200sh, 300sh, 2000sh.

Details or entire paintings by Raphael: 100sh, 800sh, Sacred Family. 250sh, The Virgin of the Rose. 1000sh, Holy Family (Virgin with Beardless Joseph).

No. 1172, 2500sh, The Virgin with Carthusian Monks, by Durer. No. 1173, 2500sh, Sacred Family, by Raphael.

1993, Nov. 19   Litho.   Perf. 13½x14
1164-1171 A146 Set of 8   13.50 13.50
Souvenir Sheets
1172-1173 A146 Set of 2   15.00 15.00

Mickey Mouse, Friends with Dinosaurs — A147

Disney characters depicted with: 50sh, Stegosaurus. 100sh, Pterandom. 200sh, Mamenchisaurus. 250sh, Rock painting. 300sh, Dino "sails." 500sh, Diplodocus. 800sh, Mamenchisaurus, diff. 1000sh, Triceratops.

No. 1182, 2500sh, Tyrannosaurus rex, Mickey. No. 1183, 2500sh, Minnie, Mickey, mamenchisaurus, diff.

1993, Dec. 22   Litho.   Perf. 14x13½
1174-1181 A147 Set of 8   13.00 13.00
Souvenir Sheets
1182-1183 A147 Set of 2   13.00 13.00

Rinderpest Campaign — A148

1993, Dec. 29   Perf. 14
1184 A148 200sh multicolored   1.00 1.00

Picasso (1881-1973)
A149

Paintings: 100sh, Woman in Yellow, 1907. 250sh, Gertrude Stein, 1906. 2500sh, Woman by a Window, 1956.

1993, Dec. 29
1185-1186 A149 Set of 2   1.50 1.50
Souvenir Sheet
1187 A149 2500sh multicolored 7.50 7.50

Copernicus (1473-1543) — A150

Telescopes: 500sh, Early. 1000sh, Modern. 2500sh, Copernicus.

1993, Dec. 29
1188-1189 A150 Set of 2   4.50 4.50
Souvenir Sheet
1190 A150 2500sh multicolored 7.50 7.50

Polska '93 — A151

Paintings: 800sh, Creation of the World, by S. I. Witkiewicz par J. Gloqowski, 1921. 1000sh, For the Right to Work, by Andrezej Strumillo, 1952. 2500sh, Temptation of St. Anthony I, by S. I. Witkiewicz (1908-21), horiz.

1993, Dec. 29
1191-1192 A151 Set of 2   5.75 5.75
Souvenir Sheet
1193 A151 2500sh multicolored 7.00 7.00

World Meteorological Day — A152

Designs: 50sh, Weather station, horiz. 200sh, Observatory at Meteorological Training School, Entebbe. 250sh, Satellite receiver at National Meteorological Center, horiz. 300sh, Reading temperatures, National Center, Entebbe, horiz. 400sh, Automatic weather station. 800sh, Destruction by hail storm, horiz. 2500sh, Barograph, horiz.

1993, Dec. 29
1194-1199 A152 Set of 6   10.50 10.50
Souvenir Sheet
1200 A152 2500sh multicolored 8.25 8.25

Fruits and Crops — A153

Designs: 50sh, Passiflora edulis. 100sh, Helianthus annus. 150sh, Musa sapientum. 200sh, Vanilla fragrans. 250sh, Ananas comosus. 300sh, Artocarpus heterophyllus. 500sh, Sorghum bicolor. 800sh, Zea mays.

No. 1209, 2000sh, Sesamum indicum. No. 1210, 2000sh, Coffea canephora.

1993, Dec. 29
1201-1208 A153 Set of 8   7.50 7.50
Souvenir Sheets
1209-1210 A153 Set of 2   10.00 10.00

Automotive Anniversaries — A154

No. 1211: a, 1903 Model A Ford, Henry Ford. b, Model T Snowmobile at 1932 Winter Olympics, Jack Shea. c, Lee Iacocca, Ford Mustang at New York World's Fair. d, Jim Clark, Lotus-Ford winning 1965 Indianapolis 500 race.

No. 1212: a, 1994 Mercedes Benz S600 Coupe. b, 1955 Mercedes Benz W196 Grand Prix Champion car, Juan Manuel Fangio. c, 1938 Mercedes Benz W125 road speed record holder, Rudolph Caracciola. d, Carl Benz, 1893 Benz Viktoria.

No. 1213, Carl Benz, vert. No. 1214, Henry Ford, vert.

1994, Jan. 18   Litho.   Perf. 14
1211 A154 700sh Strip of 4,
                    #a.-d.   5.75 5.75
1212 A154 800sh Strip of 4,
                    #a.-d.   6.75 6.75
Souvenir Sheets
1213 A154 2500sh multicolored 6.00 6.00
1214 A154 2500sh multicolored 6.00 6.00

First Ford motor, cent. (#1211, #1214). First Benz four-wheel car, cent. (#1212, #1213).

A155

Hong Kong '94 — A156

Stamps, religious shrines, Repulse Bay: No. 1215, Hong Kong #531. No. 1216, #1163.

Snuff boxes, Qing Dynasty: No. 1217a, Glass painted enamel with pavilion. b, Porcelain with floral design. c, Porcelain with quail design. d, Porcelain with openwork design. e, Agate with pair of dogs. f, Agate with man on donkey.

1994, Feb. 18   Litho.   Perf. 14
1215 A155 500sh multicolored   .90 .90
1216 A155 500sh multicolored   .90 .90
  a. Pair, #1215-1216   1.75 1.75
Miniature Sheet
1217 A156 200sh Sheet of 6,
                    #a.-f.   3.75 3.75

Nos. 1215-1216 issued in sheets of 5 pairs. No. 1216a is continuous design.

New Year 1994 (Year of the Dog) (#1217e).

Miniature Sheet

1994 World Cup Soccer Championships, US — A157

Designs: No. 1218a, Georges Grun, Belgium. b, Oscar Ruggeri, Argentina. c, Frank Rijkaard, Holand. d, Magid "Tyson" Musisi, Uganda. e, Donald Keeman, Holland. f, Igor Shallmov, Russia.

No. 1219, 2500sh, RFK Stadium, Washington DC. No. 1220, 2500sh, Ruud Gullit, Holland.

1994, June 27   Litho.   Perf. 14
1218 A157 500sh Sheet of 6,
                    #a.-f.   10.50 10.50
Souvenir Sheets
1219-1220 A157 Set of 2   12.00 12.00

Heifer Project Intl., 50th Anniv. A158

1994, June 29   Litho.   Perf. 14
1221 A158 100sh multicolored   2.25 2.25

Moths — A159

Designs: 100sh, Lobobunaea goodii. 200sh, Bunaeopsis hersilia. 300sh, Rufoglanis rosea. 350sh, Acherontia atropos. 400sh, Rohaniella pygmaea. 450sh, Euchloron megaera. 500sh, Epiphora rectifascia. 1000sh, Polyphychus coryndoni.

Lobobunaea goodii: No. 1230, 2500sh, Wings down. No. 1231, 2500sh, Wings extended.

1994, July 13
1222-1229 A159 Set of 8   8.75 8.75
Souvenir Sheets
1230-1231 A159 Set of 2   12.00 12.00

Native Crafts — A160

Designs: 100sh, Wood stool. 200sh, Wood & banana fiber chair. 250sh, Raffia & palm leaves basket. 300sh, Wool tapestry showing tree planting. 450sh, Wool tapestry showing hair grooming. 500sh, Wood sculpture, drummer. 800sh, Decorated gourds. 1000sh, Lady's bag made from bark cloth.

No. 1240, 2500sh, Raffia baskets. No. 1241, 2500sh, Papyrus hats.

1994, July 18
1232-1239 A160 Set of 8   8.25 8.25
Souvenir Sheets
1240-1241 A160 Set of 2   11.00 11.00

Cats — A161

Cat, historic landmark: 50sh, Turkish angora, Blue Mosque, Turkey, horiz. 100sh, Japanese bobtail, Mt. Fuji, Japan, horiz. 200sh, Egyptian mau, pyramids, Egypt. 300sh, Rex, Stonehenge, England. 500sh, Chartreux, Eiffel Tower, France, horiz. 1000sh, Burmese, Shwe Dagon Pagoda, Burma. 1500sh, Maine coon, Pemaquid Point Lighthouse, Maine.

No. 1250, 2500sh, Russian blue, horiz. No. 1251, 2500sh, Manx, horiz.

1994, July 22
1242-1249 A161 Set of 8   14.00 14.00
Souvenir Sheets
1250-1251 A161 Set of 2   15.00 15.00

ILO, 75th
Anniv. — A162

1994, July 29
1252 A162 350sh multicolored   1.25 1.25

PHILAKOREA '94 — A163

Designs: 100sh, Eight story Sari pagoda, Paekyangsa. 350sh, Ch'omsongdae (Natl. treasure). 1000sh, Pulguksa Temple exterior. 2500sh, Bronze mural, Pagoda Park, Seoul.

1994, Aug. 8
1253-1255 A163 Set of 3   2.75 2.75
Souvenir Sheet
1256 A163 2500sh multicolored   4.75 4.75

Intl. Year of the Family A164

1994, Aug. 11
1257 A164 100sh multicolored   1.10 1.10

D-Day, 50th Anniv. A165

Designs: 300sh, Mulberry Harbor pierhead moves into position. 1000sh, Mulberry Harbor floating bridge lands armor. 2500sh, Ships, Mulberry Harbor.

1994, Aug. 11
1258 A165 300sh multicolored   .85 .85
1259 A165 1000sh multicolored   2.75 2.75
Souvenir Sheet
1260 A165 2500sh multicolored   7.50 7.50

Intl. Olympic Committee, Cent. — A167

Designs: 350sh, John Akii-bua, Uganda, 100-meter hurdles, 1972. 900sh, Heike Herkel, Germany, high jump, 1992. 2500sh, Aleksei Urmanov, Russia, figure skating, 1994.

1994, Aug. 11
1261 A166 350sh multicolored   .70 .70
1262 A166 900sh multicolored   1.75 1.75
Souvenir Sheet
1263 A167 2500sh multicolored   5.50 5.50

First Manned Moon Landing, 25th Anniv. — A168

No. 1264 — Project Mercury astronauts: a, 50sh, Alan B. Shepard, Jr., Freedom 7. b, 100sh, M. Scott Carpenter, Aurora 7. c, 200sh, Virgil I. Grissom, Liberty Bell 7. d, 300sh, L. Gordon Cooper, Jr., Faith 7. e, 400sh, Walter M. Schirra, Jr., Sigma 7. f, 500sh, Donald K. Slayton, Apollo-Soyuz, 1975. g, 600sh, John H. Glenn, Jr., Friendship 7. 3000sh, Apollo 11 anniv. emblem.

1994, Aug. 11
1264 A168 Sheet of 7, #a.-g., + 2 labels   10.50 10.50
Souvenir Sheet
1265 A168 3000sh multi   10.50 10.50

A169

Disney's The Lion King — A169a

No. 1266: a, Baby Simba. b, Mufasa, Simba, Sarabi. c, Young Simba, Nala. d, Timon. e, Rafiki. f, Pumbaa. g, Hyenas. h, Scar. i, Zazu.
No. 1267: a, Rafiki, Mufasa. b, Rafiki, Mufasa, Sarabi. c, Rafiki, Simba. d, Scar, Zazu. e, Rafiki seeing vision. f, Simba, Scar. g, Simba, Nala. h, Simba trying on mane. i, Simba, Nala, Zazu.
No. 1268: a, Scar plots evil plan. b, Mufasa rescues Simba. c, Destroying Mufasa. d, Simba escaping hyenas. e, Timon, Pumbaa, Simba. f, Simba, Timon, Pumbaa sing Hakuna Matata. g, Rafiki. h, Simba, Nala. i, Simba seeing reflection.
No. 1269, 2500sh, Simba, Timon. No. 1270, 2500sh, Characters of the Lion King, vert. No. 1271, 2500sh, Simba's colorful animal kingdon.
No. 1271A, Mufasa, Simba. No. 1271B, Mufasa, Simba on back, standing on rock. Illustration A169a reduced.

Perf. 14x13½, 13½x14
1994, Sept. 30
1266 A169 100sh Sheet of 9, #a.-i.   2.75 2.75
1267 A169 200sh Sheet of 9, #a.-i.   5.75 5.75
1268 A169 250sh Sheet of 9, #a.-i.   7.50 7.50
    Nos. 1266-1268 (3)   16.00 16.00

Souvenir Sheets
1269-1271 A169 Set of 3   24.00 24.00
Litho. & Embossed
Perf. 11½
1271A A169a 5000sh gold
1271B A169a 5000sh gold

Sierra Club, Cent. — A170

No. 1272, horiz.: a, 200sh, Cheetahs. b, 250sh, Cheetah kittens. c, 300sh, African wild dog. d, 500sh, African wild dog. e, 600sh, Grevy's zebra. f, 800sh, Chimpanzee. g, 1000sh, Grevy's zebra.
No. 1273: a, 100sh, Chimpanzee. b, 200sh, Chimpanzee. c, 250sh, African wild dog. d, 300sh, Cheetah. e-f, 500sh, 600sh, Gelada baboon. g, 800sh, Grevy's zebra. h, 1000sh, Gelada baboon.

1994, Nov. 9
1272 A170 Sheet of 7, #a.-g. + label   8.50 8.50
1273 A170 Sheet of 8, #a.-h.   8.75 8.75

ICAO, 50th Anniv. A171

Designs: 100sh, Entebbe Intl. Airport terminal building. 250sh, Entebbe control tower.

1994, Nov. 14 Litho. Perf. 14
1274 A171 100sh multicolored   .90 .90
1275 A171 250sh multicolored   1.60 1.60

Environmental Protection — A172

Designs: 100sh, Stop poaching. 250sh, Waste disposals. 350sh, Overfishing is a threat. 500sh, Deforestation.

1994, Nov. 15
1276-1279 A172 Set of 4   4.00 4.00

Christmas A173

Paintings: 100sh, Adoration of the Christ Child, by Fillipino Lippi. 200sh, The Holy Family Rests on the Flight into Egypt, by Annibale Carracci. 300sh, Madonna with Christ Child ant St. John, by Piero di Cosimo. 350sh, The Conestabile Madonna, by Raphael. 450sh, Madonna and Child with Angels, after Antonio Rossellino. 500sh, Madonna and Child with St. John, by Raphael. 900sh, Madonna and Child, by Luca Signorelli. 1000sh, Madonna with the Child Jesus, St. John and an Angel, in style of Pier Francesco Fiorentino.
No. 1288, 2500sh, The Madonna of the Magnificat, by Sandro Botticelli. No. 1289,

2500sh, Adoration of the Magi, by Fra Angelico & Filippo Lippi.

1994, Dec. 5 Litho. Perf. 13½x14
1280-1287 A173 Set of 8   10.00 10.00
Souvenir Sheets
1288-1289 A173 Set of 2   11.00 11.00

Tintoretto (1518-94) A174

Details or entire paintings: 100sh, Self-portrait. 300sh, A Philosopher. 400sh, The Creation of the Animals, horiz. 450sh, The Feast of Belshazzar, horiz. 500sh, The Raising of the Brazen Serpent. 1000sh, Elijah Fed by the Angel.
No. 1296, 2000sh, Finding of Moses. No. 1297, 2000sh, Moses Striking Water from a Rock.

1995, Feb. 7 Litho. Perf. 13½
1290-1295 A174 Set of 6   7.00 7.00
Souvenir Sheets
1296-1297 A174 Set of 2   10.50 10.50

Birds A175

No. 1298: a, White-faced tree duck. b, European shoveler. c, Hartlaub's duck. d, Milky eagle-owl. e, Avocet. f, African fish eagle. g, Spectacled weaver. h, Black-headed gonolek. i, Great crested grebe. j, Red-knobbed coot. k, Woodland kingfisher. l, Pintail. m, Squacco heron. n, Purple gallinule. o, African darter. p, African jacana.
No. 1299, 2500sh, Fulvous tree duck. No. 1300, 2500sh, Pygmy goose.

1995, Apr. 24 Litho. Perf. 14
1298 A175 200sh Sheet of 16, #a.-p.   14.00 14.00
Souvenir Sheets
1299-1300 A175 Set of 2   11.00 11.00

Nos. 685-688, 906 Surcharged

1995, June 1 Litho. Perf. 14
1301 A90 100sh on #688 multi   .25 .25
1302 A90 450sh on 70sh #686   1.25 1.25
1303 A90 800sh on 90sh #687   2.00 2.00
1304 A90 1500sh on 10sh #685   3.75 3.75
    Nos. 1301-1304 (4)   7.25 7.25
Souvenir Sheet
1305 A113 5000sh on 1200sh multi   6.00 6.00

UN, 50th Anniv. — A176

Designs: 1000sh, Hands releasing butterflies, dragonfly, dove.

No. 1308, Infant's hand holding adult's finger.

1995, July 6   **Litho.**   **Perf. 14**
1306 A176 450sh shown   1.00 1.00
1307 A176 1000sh multicolored   2.25 2.25
    Souvenir Sheet
1308 A176 2000sh multicolored   4.00 4.00

FAO, 50th Anniv. — A177

No. 1309 — Corn huskers: a, 350sh, Young woman. b, 500sh, Old woman, girl. c, 1000sh, Woman with baby on back.
2000sh, Boy beside bore well for livestock, irrigation.

1995, July 6
1309 A177 Strip of 3, #a.-c.   3.00 3.00
    Souvenir Sheet
1310 A177 2000sh multicolored   4.00 4.00

A178

End of World War II, 50th Anniv. A179

No. 1311: a, Russian 152mm gun fires into center of Berlin. b, Soviets capture Moltke Bridge. c, Emperor William Memorial Church, now war memorial. d, Brandenburg Gate falls to Russian tanks. e, US B-17's continue to devastate industrial Germany. f, Soviet tanks enter Berlin. g, Hitler's chancellery lies in ruins. h, Reichstag burns.
Flags of countries each forming "VJ:" No. 1312a, Australia. b, Great Britain. c, New Zealand. d, US. e, China. f, Canada.
No. 1313, Waving Soviet flag from atop building in Berlin. No. 1314, US flag, combat soldier.

1995, July 6
1311 A178 500sh Sheet of 8, #a.-h. + label   11.00 11.00
1312 A179 600sh Sheet of 6, #a.-f. + label   8.75 8.75
    Souvenir Sheets
1313 A178 2500sh multi   7.00 7.00
1314 A179 2500sh multi   7.50 7.50

No. 1313 contains one 56x42mm stamp.

Rotary Intl., 90th Anniv. — A180

Rotary emblem and: No. 1315, Paul Harris. No. 1316, Natl. flag.

1995, July 6   **Litho.**   **Perf. 14**
1315 A180 2000sh multicolored   4.00 4.00
    Souvenir Sheet
1316 A180 2000sh multicolored   4.00 4.00

Queen Mother, 95th Anniv. — A181

No. 1317: a, Drawing. b, Waving. c, Formal portrait. d, Green blue outfit.
2500sh, Pale blue outfit.

1995, July 6   **Perf. 13½x14**
1317 A181 500sh Block or strip of 4, #a.-d.   7.50 7.50
    Souvenir Sheet
1318 A181 2500sh multicolored   7.25 7.25

No. 1317 was issued in sheets of 8 stamps. Sheets of Nos. 1317-1318 exist with with black border and text "In Memoriam/1900-2002" in sheet margins.

Dinosaurs A182

Designs: 150sh, Veloceraptor. 200sh, Psittacosaurus. 350sh, Dilophosaurus. 400sh, Kentrosaurus. 500sh, Stegosaurus. 1500sh, Pterodaustro.
No. 1325, vert: a, Archaeopteryx. b, Quetzalcoatlus. c, Pteranodon (b, d). d, Brachiosa (g, h). e, Tsintaosaur. f, Allosaur (g-h). g, Tyranosaur (f, i-k). h, Apatosaur (l). i, Giant dragonfly. j, Dimorphodon. k, Triceratops (l). l, Compsognathus.
No. 1326, 2000sh, Parasaurolophus. No. 1327, 2000sh, Shunosaurus.

1995, July 15   **Perf. 14**
1319-1324 A182 Set of 6   9.00 9.00
1325 A182 300sh Sheet of 12, #a.-l.   11.00 11.00
    Souvenir Sheets
1326-1327 A182 Set of 2   9.50 9.50

Reptiles — A183

50sh, Rough scaled bush viper. 100sh, Pygmy python. 150sh, Three horned chameleon. 200sh, African rock python. 350sh, Nile monitor. 400sh, Savannah monitor. 450sh, Bush viper. 500sh, Nile crocodile. 700sh, Bell's hinged tortoise. 900sh, Rhinoceros viper. 1000sh, Gaboon viper. 2000sh, Spitting cobra. 3000sh, Leopard tortoise. 4000sh, Puff adder. 5000sh, Common house gecko. 6000sh, Dwarf chameleon. 10,000sh, Boomslang.

1995   **Litho.**   **Perf. 14x15**
1328 A183 50sh multi   .25 .25
1329 A183 100sh multi   .25 .25
1330 A183 150sh multi   .30 .30
1331 A183 200sh multi   .40 .40
1332 A183 350sh multi   .70 .70
1333 A183 400sh multi   .85 .85
1334 A183 450sh multi   .95 .95
1335 A183 500sh multi   1.00 1.00
    Size: 38x24mm
    Perf. 14
1336 A183 700sh multi   1.40 1.40
1337 A183 900sh multi   1.90 1.90
1338 A183 1000sh multi   2.00 2.00
1339 A183 2000sh multi   4.00 4.00
1340 A183 3000sh multi   6.25 6.25
1341 A183 4000sh multi   8.25 8.25
1341A A183 5000sh multi   10.00 10.00
1341B A183 6000sh multi   12.00 12.00
1341C A183 10,000sh multi   20.00 20.00
    Nos. 1328-1341C (17)   70.50 70.50

Issued: 5000sh, 6000sh, 10,000sh, 11/20; others, 8/21.
Compare with Nos. 1550-1552.

Nsambya Church A184

Designs: 450sh, Namilyango College. 500sh, Intl. Cooperative Alliance, cent. 1000sh, UN Volunteers, 25th anniv.

1995, Sept. 7   **Litho.**   **Perf. 14**
1342-1345 A184 Set of 4   4.00 4.00

Mill Hill Missionaries in Uganda, cent. (#1342-1343).

Scenic Landscapes & Waterfalls of Uganda — A185

Designs: No. 1346, 50sh, Bwindi Forest. No. 1347, 50sh, Sipi Falls, vert. No. 1348, 100sh, Karamoja. No. 1349, 100sh, Murchison Falls. No. 1350, 450sh, Sunset, Lake Mburo Natl. Park. No. 1351, 450sh, Bujagali Falls. No. 1352, 500sh, Sunset, Gulu District. No. 1353, 500sh, Two Falls, Murchison. No. 1354, 900sh, Kabale District. No. 1355, 900sh, Falls, Rwenzoris, vert. No. 1356, 1000sh, Rwenzori Mountains. No. 1357, 1000sh, Falls, Rwenzoris, diff., vert.

1995, Sept. 14
1346-1357 A185 Set of 12   12.50 12.50

1996 Summer Olympics, Atlanta A186

Athletes: 50sh, Peter Rono, runner. 350sh, Reiner Klimke, dressage. 450sh, German cycling team. 500sh, Grace Birungi, runner. 900sh, Francis Ogola, track. 1000sh, Nyakana Godfrey, welter-weight boxer.
No. 1364, 2500sh, Rolf Dannenberg, discus, vert. No. 1365, 2500sh, Sebastian Coe, runner.

1995, Sept. 21
1358-1363 A186 Set of 6   7.25 7.25
    Souvenir Sheets
1364-1365 A186 Set of 2   9.50 9.50

Domestic Animals A187

No. 1366: a, Peafowl (e). b, Pouter pigeon. c, Rock dove. d, Rouen duck. e, Guinea fowl. f, Donkey. g, Shetland pony. h, Palomino. i, Pigs. j, Border collie. k, Merino sheep. l, Milch goat. m, Black dutch rabbit. n, Lop rabbit. o, Somali cat (p). p, Asian cat.
No. 1367, 2500sh, Saddle bred horses. No. 1368, 2500sh, Oxen.

1995, Oct. 2
1366 A187 200sh Sheet of 16, #a.-p.   12.50 12.50
    Souvenir Sheets
1367-1368 A187 Set of 2   12.00 12.00

Boy Scouts at Immunization Centers — A188

Designs: 150sh, Dressing children for weighing, vert. 350sh, Helping mothers carry children, vert. 450sh, Checking health cards. 800sh, Assisting in immunization. 1000sh, Weighing children, vert.

1995, Oct. 18   **Litho.**   **Perf. 14**
1369-1373 A188 Set of 5   6.00 6.00

Establishment of Nobel Prize Fund, Cent. — A189

No. 1374, 300sh: a, Hideki Yukawa, physics, 1949. b, F.W. DeKlerk, peace, 1993. c, Nelson Mandela, peace, 1993. d, Odysseus Elytis, literature, 1979. e, Ferdinand Buisson, peace, 1927. f, Lev Landau, physics, 1962. g, Halldor Laxness, literature, 1955. h, Wole Soyinka, literature, 1986. i, Desmond Tutu, peace, 1984. j, Susumu Tonegawa, physiology or medicine, 1987. k, Louis de Broglie, physics, 1929. l, George Seferis, literature, 1963.
No. 1375, 300sh: a, Hermann Staudinger, chemistry, 1953. b, Fritz Haber, chemistry, 1918. c, Bert Sakmann, physiology or medicine, 1991. d, Adolf O.R. Windaus, chemistry, 1928. e, Wilhelm Wien, physics, 1911. f, Ernest Hemingway, literature, 1954. g, Richard M. Willstätter, chemistry, 1915. h, Stanley Cohen, physiology or medicine, 1986. i, J. Hans D. Jensen, physics, 1963. j, Otto H. Warburg, physiology or medicine, 1931. k, Heinrich O. Wieland, chemistry, 1927. l, Albrecht Kossel, physiology or medicine, 1910.
No. 1376, 2000sh, Werner Forssmann, physiology or medicine, 1956. No. 1377, 2000sh, Nelly Sachs, literature, 1966.

1995, Oct. 31   **Sheets of 12, #a-l**
1374-1375 A189 Set of 2   20.00 20.00
    Souvenir Sheets
1376-1377 A189 Set of 2   10.50 10.50

Christmas A190

Details or entire paintings of the Madonna and Child, by: 150sh, Hans Holbein the Younger. 350sh, Procaccini. 500sh, Pisanello. 1000sh, Crivelli. 1500sh, Le Nain.
No. 1383, 2500sh, The Holy Family, by Andrea Del Sarto. No. 1384, 2500sh, Madonna and Child, by Bellini.

1995, Nov. 30   **Litho.**   **Perf. 13½x14**
1378-1382 A190 Set of 5   7.50 7.50
    Souvenir Sheets
1383-1384 A190 Set of 2   11.00 11.00

Orchids — A191

Designs: 150sh, Ansellia africana. 450sh, Satyricum crassicaule. 500sh, Polystachya cultriformis. 800sh, Disa erubescens.

No. 1389: a, Aerangis iuteoalba. b, Satyrium sacculatum. c, Bolusiella maudiae. d, Habenaria attenuata. e, Cyrtorchis arcuata. f, Eulophia angolensis. g, Tridactyle bicaudata. h, Eulophia horsfallii. i, Diaphananthe fragrantissima.

No. 1390, 2500sh, Diaphananthe pulchella. No. 1391, 2500sh, Rangaeris amaniensis.

1995, Dec. 8   **Perf. 14**
1385-1388   A191   Set of 4   6.00   6.00
Miniature Sheet
1389   A191   350sh Sheet of 9,
    #a.-i.   14.00   14.00
Souvenir Sheets
1390-1391   A191   Set of 2   12.00   12.00

New Year 1996 (Year of the Rat) A192

Rat eating: a, Purple grapes. b, Radishes. c, Corn. d, Squash.
2000sh, Green grapes.

1996, Jan. 29   **Litho.**   **Perf. 14**
1392   A192   350sh Block of 4,
    #a.-d.   2.50   2.50
  e.   Miniature sheet, No. 1392   2.50   2.50
Souvenir Sheet
1393   A192   2000sh multicolored   3.00   3.00
No. 1392 issued in sheets of 16 stamps.

Miniature Sheet

Wildlife A193

No. 1394: a, 150sh, Wild dogs. b, 200sh, Fish eagle. c, 250sh, Hippopotamus. d, Leopard. e, 400sh, Lion. f, 450sh, Lioness. g, 500sh, Meerkat. h, 550sh, Black rhinoceros. No. 1395: a, 150sh, Gorilla. b, 200sh, Cheetah. c, 250sh, Elephant. d, 350sh, Thomson's gazelle. e, 400sh, Crowned crane. f, 450sh, Sattlebill. g, 500sh, Vulture. h, 550sh, Zebra. No. 1396, 2000sh, Giraffe, vert. No. 1397, 2000sh, Gray heron.

1996, Mar. 27   **Litho.**   **Perf. 14**
1394   A193   Sheet of 8, #a.-h.   6.25   6.25
1395   A193   Sheet of 8, #a.-h.   6.75   6.75
Souvenir Sheets
1396-1397   A193   Set of 2   9.00   9.00

Disney Characters on the Orient Express — A194

Designs: 50sh, From London to Constantinople via Calais. 100sh, From Paris to Athens. 150sh, Ticket for the Pullman. 200sh, Pullman Corridor. 250sh, Dining car. 300sh, Staff beyond reproach. 600sh, Fun in the Pullman. 700sh, 1901 Unstoppable train enters the buffet in Frankfurt station. 800sh, 1929 passage

detained five days by snowstorm. 900sh, Filming "Murder on the Orient Express."
No. 1408, 2500sh, Donald Duck in engine. No. 1409, 2500sh, Mickey, Goofy, Minnie waving from back of train.

1996, Apr. 15   **Perf. 14x13½**
1398-1407   A194   Set of 10   12.50   12.50
Souvenir Sheets
1408-1409   A194   Set of 2   13.00   13.00

Paintings by Qi Baishi (1864-1957) — A195

No. 1410: a, 50sh, Autumn Pond. b, 100sh, Partridge and Smartweed. c, 150sh, Begonias and Mynah. d, 200sh, Chrysanthemums, Cocks and Hens. e, 250sh, Crabs. f, 300sh, Wisterias and Bee. g, 350sh, Smartweed and Ink-drawn Butterflies. h, 400sh, Lotus and Mandarin Ducks. i, 450sh, Lichees and Locust. j, 500sh, Millet and Preying Mantis.
No. 1411: a, Locust, flowers. b, Crustaceans.

1996, May 8   **Litho.**   **Perf. 15x14**
1410   A195   Sheet of 10, #a.-j.   8.00   8.00
Souvenir Sheet
    Perf. 14
1411   A195   800sh Sheet of 2,
    #a.-b.   7.50   7.50
No. 1411 contains two 48x34mm stamps. The captions on Nos. 1410c and 1410d are transposed.
CHINA '96, 9th Asian Intl. Philatelic Exhibition.
See Nos. 1475-1476.

Queen Elizabeth II, 70th Birthday — A196

No. 1412: a, Portrait. b, As young woman, wearing crown jewels. c, Wearing red hat, coat.
2000sh, Portrait, diff.

1996, July 10   **Perf. 13½x14**
1412   A196   500sh Strip of 3,
    #a.-c.   4.00   4.00
Souvenir Sheet
1413   A196   2000sh multicolored   4.00   4.00
No. 1412 was issued in sheets of 9 stamps.

Jerusalem, 3000th Anniv. — A197

No. 1414: a, 300sh, Knesset Menorah. b, 500sh, Jerusalem Theater. c, 1000sh, Israel Museum.
2000sh, Grotto of the Nativity.

1996, July 10   **Perf. 14**
1414   A197   Sheet of 3, #a.-c.   4.75   4.75
Souvenir Sheet
1415   A197   2000sh multicolored   4.75   4.75
For overprint see Nos. 1556-1557.

Radio, Cent. A198

Entertainers: 200sh, Ella Fitzgerald. 300sh, Bob Hope. 500sh, Nat "King" Cole. 800sh, Burns & Allen.
2000sh, Jimmy Durante.

1996, July 10   **Perf. 13½x14**
1416-1419   A198   Set of 4   3.75   3.75
Souvenir Sheet
1420   A198   2000sh multicolored   4.00   4.00

Mushrooms — A199

No. 1421: a, 150sh, Coprinus disseminatus. b, 300sh, Caprinus radians. c, 350sh, Hygrophorus coccineus. d, 400sh, Marasmius siccus. e, 450sh, Cortinarius collinitus. f, 500sh, Cortinarius cinnabarinus. g, 550sh, Coltricia cinnamomea. h, 1000sh, Mutinus elegans.
No. 1422, 2500sh, Inocybe soroia. No. 1423, 2500sh, Flammulina velutipes.

1996, June 24   **Perf. 14**
1421   A199   Sheet of 8, #a.-h.   6.50   6.50
Souvenir Sheets
1422-1423   A199   Set of 2   9.00   9.00

Butterflies — A200

No. 1424: a, 50sh, Catopsilia philea. b, 100sh, Dione vanillae. c, 150sh, Metemorpha dido. d, 200sh, Papilio sesotris. e, 250sh, Papilio neophilus. f, 300sh, Papilio thoas. g, 350sh, Diorina periander. h, 400sh, Morpho cipris. i, 450sh, Catonephele numilia. j, 500sh, Heliconius doris. k, 550sh, Prepona antimache. l, 600sh, Eunica alcmena.
No. 1425, 2500sh, Caligo martia. No. 1426, 2500sh, Heliconius doris.

1996, June 26
1424   A200   Sheet of 12, #a.-l.   9.00   9.00
Souvenir Sheets
1425-1426   A200   Set of 2   10.00   10.00

UNICEF, 50th Anniv. A201

Designs: 450sh, Two children. 500sh, Two children wearing hats. 550sh, Boy in classroom.
2000sh, Mother and child, vert.

1996, July 10   **Litho.**   **Perf. 14**
1427-1429   A201   Set of 3   4.00   4.00
Souvenir Sheet
1430   A201   2000sh multicolored   4.00   4.00

UNESCO, 50th Anniv. — A202

Natl. Parks: 450sh, Darien, Panama. 500sh, Los Glaciares, Argentina. 550sh, Tubbatha Reef Marine Park, Philippines.
2500sh, Rwenzori Mountains, Uganda.

1996, July 10
1431-1433   A202   Set of 3   4.75   4.75
Souvenir Sheet
1434   A202   2500sh multicolored   6.25   6.25

Trains — A203

No. 1435: a, Loco Type B.B.B., Japan, 1968. b, Stephenson's "Rocket," 1829. c, "Austria," 1843. d, 19th cent. type. e, Loco Anglo-Indian, India, 1947. f, Type CoCo DB, Germany.
No. 1436: a, "Lady of Lynn," Great Western, England. b, Chinese type, 1000. c, Meyer Nitson, Chile. d, Union Pacific "Centennial," US. e, "581" Japanese Natl. Railway, Japan, 1968. f, Co.Co. Series "120" DB, Germany.
No. 1437, 2500sh, Mallard, Great Britain. No. 1438, 2500sh, "99" Type 1-5-0, Germany.

1996, July 25
1435   A203   450sh Sheet of 6,
    #a.-f.   5.50   5.50
1436   A203   550sh Sheet of 6,
    #a.-f.   6.50   6.50
Souvenir Sheets
1437-1438   A203   Set of 2   10.00   10.00

Uganda Post Office, Cent. A204

Designs: 150sh, Emblem. 450sh, Post bus service. 500sh, Modern mail transportation means. 550sh, "100", #48, #59.

1996, Aug. 30   **Litho.**   **Perf. 14**
1439-1442   A204   Set of 4   6.00   6.00

Fruits A205

Designs: 150sh, Mango, vert. 350sh,
Orange, vert. 450sh, Paw paw, vert. 500sh,
Avocado, vert. 550sh, Watermelon.

1996, Oct. 8   Litho.   *Perf. 14*
1443-1447 A205 Set of 5   6.00 6.00

Christmas
A206

Details or entire paintings: 150sh, Annunciation, by Lorenzo Di Credi. 350sh, Madonna of
the Loggia (detail), by Botticelli. 400sh, Virgin
in Glory with Child and Angels, by Lorenzetti
P. 450sh, Adoration of the Child, by Filippino
Lippi. 500sh, Madonna of the Loggia, by Botticelli. 550sh, The Strength, by Botticelli.
No. 1454, 2500sh, Holy Allegory, by Giovanni Bellini, horiz. No. 1455, 2500sh, The Virgin on the Throne with Child and Saints, by
Ghirlandaio, horiz.

1996, Nov. 18   *Perf. 13½x14*
1448-1453 A206 Set of 6   5.75 5.75
Souvenir Sheets
Perf. 14x13½
1454-1455 A206 Set of 2   10.00 10.00

Sylvester
Stallone in
Movie, "Rocky
III" — A207

1996, Nov. 21   Litho.   *Perf. 14*
1456 A207 800sh Sheet of 3   5.50 5.50

1996
Summer
Olympic
Games,
Atlanta
A208

Scenes from first Olympic Games in US, St.
Louis, 1904: 350sh, Steamboat race, stadium.
450sh, Boxer George Finnegan. 500sh, Quad-
riga race (ancient games). 800sh, John Flana-
gan, hammer throw, vert.

1996, Dec. 8
1457-1460 A208 Set of 4   4.75 4.75

Traditional Attire — A209

Designs: 150sh, Western region, vert.
350sh, Karimo Jong women, vert. 450sh,
Ganda. 500sh, Acholi.
No. 1465, vert. — Headdresses: a, Acholi.
b, Alur. c, Bwola dance. d, Madi. e,
Karimojong. f, Karimojong with feathers.

1997, Jan. 2
1461-1464 A209 Set of 4   4.00 4.00
1465 A209 300sh Sheet of 6,
                       #a.-f.   5.00 5.00

New Year
1997
(Year of
the Ox)
A210

Paintings of oxen: Nos. 1466a, 1467b, Walking left. Nos. 1466b, 1467b, Calf nursing. Nos.
1466c, 1467d, Calf lying down, adult. Nos.
1466d, 1467c, Adult lying down.
1500sh, Calf, vert.

1997, Jan. 24   Litho.   *Perf. 14*
1466 A210 350sh Strip of 4,
                       #a.-d.   4.25 4.25
1467 A210 350sh Sheet of 4,
                       #a.-d.   4.25 4.25
Souvenir Sheet
1468 A210 1500sh multicolored   4.25 4.25
No. 1466 was issued in sheets of 4 vert.
strips.

World Wildlife Fund — A211

No. 1469 — Rothschild's giraffe: a, Running. b, One bending neck across another's
back. c, Head up close. d, Young giraffe, adult
facing opposite directions.
2500sh, like #1469d, horiz.

1997, Feb. 12
1469 A211 300sh Strip of 4,
                       #a.-d.   4.00 4.00
Souvenir Sheet
1470 A211 2500sh multicolored   6.50 6.50
No. 1469 was issued in sheets of 4 strips
with each strip in a different order.
No. 1470 does not have the WWF emblem.

Souvenir Sheet

Mural from Tomb in Xian — A212

1996, May 8   Litho.   *Perf. 14*
1471 A212 500sh multicolored   3.00 3.00
China '96. No. 1471 was not available until
March 1997.

Promulgation of the Constitution, Oct.
8, 1995 — A213

Designs: 150sh, shown. 350sh, Scroll.
550sh, Closed book, vert.

1997, Feb. 25   *Perf. 14x13½*
1472-1474 A213 Set of 3   3.25 3.25

Paintings Type of 1996

No. 1475 — Paintings by Wu Changshuo
(1844-1927): a, 50sh, Red Plum Blossom and
Daffodil. b, 100sh, Peony. c, 150sh,
Rosaceae. d, 200sh, Pomegranate. e, 250sh,
Peach, Peony, and Plum Blossom. f, 300sh,
Calyx canthus. g, 350sh, Chrysanthemum. h,
400sh, Calabash. i, 450sh, Chrysanthemum,
diff. j, 500sh, Cypress tree.
No. 1476: a, 550sh, Litchi. b, 1000sh, Water
lily.

1997, Mar. 5   *Perf. 14x15*
1475 A195 Sheet of 10, #a.-j.   6.50 6.50
Souvenir Sheet
Perf. 14
1476 A195 Sheet of 2, #a.-b.   3.50 3.50
Hong Kong '97. No. 1476 contains two
51x38mm stamps.

Summer Olympic
Winners — A214

No. 1477: a, 150sh, Sohn Kee-chung, marathon, 1936. b, 200sh, Walter Davis, high jump,
1952. c, 250sh, Roland Matthes, swimming,
1968. d, 300sh, Akii Bua, 400m hurdles, 1972.
e, 350sh, Wolfgang Nordwig, pole vault, 1972.
f, 400sh, Wilma Rudolph, 4x100m relay, 1960.
g, 450sh, Abebe Bikila, marathon, 1964. h,
500sh, Edwin Moses, 400m hurdles, 1984. i,
550sh, Randy Williams, long jump, 1972.
No. 1478: a, 150sh, Bob Hayes, 100m,
1964. b, 200sh, Rod Milburn, 110m hurdles,
1972. c, 250sh, Filbert Bayi, running, 1976. d,
300sh, H. Kipchoge Keino, steeple chase,
1972. e, 350sh, Ron Ray, running, 1976. f,
400sh, Joe Frazier, boxing, 1976. g, 450sh,
Carl Lewis, 100m race, 1984. h, 500sh, Gisela
Mauermayer, discus, 1936. i, 550sh, Dietmar
Mogenburg, high jump, 1984.

1997, Mar. 3   Litho.   *Perf. 14*
Sheets of 9, #a-i
1477-1478 A214 Set of 2   15.00 15.00
No. 1478h is inscribed shot put in error.

Disney's "Toy Story" — A215

No. 1479, vert.: a, Woody. b, Buzz Lightyear. c, Bo Peep. d, Hamm. e, Slinky. f, Rex.
No. 1480: a, Woody on Andy's bed. b, "Get
this wagon train a-movin." c, Bo Peep, blocks.
d, Buzz Lightyear. e, Slinky, Rex. f, Woody
hides. g, Buzz, Woody. h, Rex, Slinky, Buzz. i,
Buzz, Woody on bed.
No. 1481: a, Woody telling Buzz he's sheriff.
b, Green Army on alert. c, Woody, Buzz com-
pete. d, Woody sights alien. e, Buzz ponders
fate. f, "The Cla-a-a-a-a-a-w." g, Intergalactic
emergency. h, Buzz, Woody argue at gas station. i, Buzz, Woody give chase.

No. 1482, 2000sh, Woody spots an intruder,
vert. No. 1483, 2000sh, Andy's toys, vert. No.
1484, 2000sh, Buzz Lightyear in space, vert.

1997, Apr. 2   *Perf. 14x13½, 13½x14*
1479 A215 100sh Sheet of 6,
                       #a.-f.   2.75 2.75
1480 A215 150sh Sheet of 9,
                       #a.-i.   6.00 6.00
1481 A215 200sh Sheet of 9,
                       #a.-i.   7.25 7.25
Souvenir Sheets
1482-1484 A215 Set of 3   21.00 21.00

Man in Space
A216

No. 1484A: b, Pioneer 10. c, Voyager 1. d,
Viking Orbiter. e, Pioneer, Venus 1. f, Mariner
9. g, Galileo Entry Probe. h, Mariner 10. i,
Voyager 2.
No. 1485: a, Sputnik 1. b, Apollo. c, Soyuz.
d, Intelsat 1. e, Manned maneuvering unit. f,
Skylab. g, Telstar 1. h, Hubble telescope.
No. 1486, Space shuttle Challenger. No.
1486A, Mars Viking Lander Robot.

1997, Apr. 16   Litho.   *Perf. 14*
1484A A216 250sh Sheet of 8,
                        #b.-i.   5.00 5.00
1485   A216 300sh Sheet of 8,
                        #a.-h.   5.50 5.50
Souvenir Sheet
1486   A216 2000sh multicolored   4.75 4.75
1486A A216 2000sh multicolored   5.00 5.00
No. 1486 contains one 34x61mm stamp,
No. 1486A one 61x35mm stamp.

Deng Xiaoping (1904-97), Chinese
Leader — A217

Designs: a, 500sh. b, 550sh. c, 1000sh.
2000sh, Portrait, diff.

1997, May 9
1487 A217 Sheet of 3, #a.-c.   5.50 5.50
Souvenir Sheet
1488 A217 2000sh multicolored   4.75 4.75

Environmental
Protection — A218

No. 1489: a-d, Various water hyacinths.
No. 1490: a, Buffalo. b, Uganda kob. c,
Guinea fowl. d, Malibu stork.
2500sh, Gorilla.

1997, May 14
1489 A218 500sh Sheet of 4,
                       #a.-d.   3.75 3.75
1490 A218 550sh Sheet of 4,
                       #a.-d.   4.25 4.25
Souvenir Sheet
1491 A218 2500sh multicolored   5.25 5.25

Queen
Elizabeth
II, Prince
Philip,
50th
Wedding
Anniv.
A219

No. 1492: a, Queen. b, Royal arms. c, Queen in purple outfit, Prince. d, Prince, Queen in white hat. e, Buckingham Palace. f, Prince Philip. 2000sh, Queen in wedding dress.

1997, June 2   Litho.   Perf. 14
1492 A219 200sh Sheet of 6,
                #a.-f.   7.00 7.00

Souvenir Sheet
1493 A219 2000sh multicolored   4.75 4.75

Paul E. Harris (1868-1947), Founder of Rotary, Intl. — A220

Designs: 1000sh, Combating hunger, Harris. 2500sh, First Rotarians, Gustavus H. Loehr, Sylvester Schiele, Hiram E. Shorey, Paul E. Harris.

1997, June 2
1494 A220 1000sh multicolored   3.00 3.00

Souvenir Sheet
1495 A220 2500sh multicolored   4.50 4.50

Heinrich von Stephan (1831-97) A221

No. 1496 — Portrait of Von Stephan and: a, Chinese post boat. b, UPU emblem. c, Russian special post. 2500sh, Von Stephan, French postman on stilts.

1997, June 2
1496 A221 800sh Sheet of 3,
                #a.-c.   4.50 4.50

Souvenir Sheet
1497 A221 2500sh multicolored   4.50 4.50
              PACIFIC 97.

Chernobyl Disaster, 10th Anniv. A222

Designs: 500sh, UNESCO. 700sh, Chabad's Children of Chernobyl.

1997, May 21   Litho.   Perf. 14x13½
1498 A222 500sh multicolored   1.50 1.50
1499 A222 700sh multicolored   2.00 2.00

1998 Winter Olympic Games, Nagano A223

Designs: 350sh, Men's slalom, vert. 450sh, Two-man bobsled, vert 800sh, Women's slalom. 2000sh, Men's speed skating.
No. 1504: a, Ski jumping. b, Giant slalom. c, Cross-country skiing. d, Ice hockey. e, Man, pairs figure skating. f, Woman, pairs figure skating.
No. 1505, 2500sh, Downhill skiing. No. 1506, 2500sh, Women's figure skating.

1997, June 23   Litho.   Perf. 14
1500-1503 A223 Set of 4   7.25 7.25

1504 A223 500sh Sheet of 6,
                #a.-f.   6.25 6.25

Souvenir Sheets
1505-1506 A223 Set of 2   9.00 9.00

Makerere University, 75th Anniv. — A224

Designs: 150sh, Main building, administration block. 450sh, East African School of Librarianship, vert. 500sh, Buyana stock farm. 550sh, Ceramic dish, School of Architectural and Fine Arts.

1997, July 31   Perf. 14x13½, 13½x14
1507-1510 A224 Set of 4   3.50 3.50

Mahatma Gandhi (1869-1948) A225

Various portraits.

1997, Oct. 5   Litho.   Perf. 14
1511 A225 600sh multicolored   2.50 2.50
1512 A225 700sh multicolored   2.75 2.75

Souvenir Sheet
1513 A225 1000sh multicolored   4.50 4.50

1998 World Cup Soccer Championships, France — A226

No. 1514, vert: a, 200sh, Fritz Walter, Germany. b, 300sh, Daniel Passarella, Argentina. c, 450sh, Dino Zoff, Italy. d, 500sh, Bobby Moore, England. e, 600sh, Diego Maradona, Argentina. f, 550sh, Franz Beckenbauer, West Germany.
No. 1515 — Argentina vs. West Germany, Mexico City, 1986: a, d, e, f, h, Action scenes. b, Azteca Stadium. c, Argentine player holding World Cup. g, Argentina team picture.
No. 1516 — Top tournament scorers: a, Paulo Rossi. b, Mario Kempes. c, Gerd Muller. d, Grzegorz Lato. e, Ademir. f, Eusebio Ferreica da Silva. g, Salvatore (Toto) Schillaci. h, Leonidas da Silva. i, Gary Lineker.
No. 1517, 2000sh, England, 1966. No. 1518, 2000sh, W. Germany, 1990.

1997, Oct. 3   Litho.   Perf. 14
1514 A226 Sheet of 6, #a.-f.   5.50 5.50
1515 A226 250sh Sheet of 8,
                #a.-h.   5.00 5.00
1516 A226 250sh Sheet of 9,
                #a.-i. + label   5.00 5.00

Souvenir Sheets
1517-1518 A226 Set of 2   8.50 8.50

Diana, Princess of Wales (1961-97) A227

1997, Dec. 1
1519 A227 60sh multicolored   2.00 2.00
No. 1519 was issued in sheets of 6.

Christmas A228

Sculpture, entire paintings or details: 200sh, Putto and Dolphin, by Andrea del Verrocchio. 300sh, The Fall of the Rebel Angels, by Pieter Bruegel the Elder. 400sh, The Immaculate Conception, by Murillo. 500sh, Music-making Angel, by Rosso Fiorentino. 600sh, Cupid and Psyche, by Adolphe-William Bouguereau. 700sh, Cupid and Psyche, by Antonio Canova.
No. 1526, 2500sh, Virgin, Angels from The Assumption of the Virgin, by El Greco. No. 1527, 2500sh, Angel from The Assumption of the Virgin, by El Greco.

1997, Dec. 1
1520-1525 A228 Set of 6   5.75 5.75

Souvenir Sheets
1526-1527 A228 Set of 2   8.50 8.50

New Year 1998 (Year of the Tiger) A229

Various paintings of tigers: No. 1528: a, Looking backward. b, Jumping. c, Lying, looking forward. d, Lying, mouth open. 1500sh, On cliff.

1998, Jan. 16   Litho.   Perf. 13½
1528 A229 350sh Sheet of 4,
                #a.-d.   3.25 3.25

Souvenir Sheet
1529 A229 1500sh multicolored   3.00 3.00

Tourist Attractions — A230

Designs: 300sh, Namugongo Martyrs Shrine, vert. 400sh, Kasubi Tombs. 500sh, Tourist boat, Kazinga Channel. 600sh, Elephant. 700sh, Dujagali Falls, Jinja.

1998, Feb. 6   Litho.   Perf. 14
1530-1534 A230 Set of 5   6.25 6.25

Mother Teresa (1910-97) — A231

No. 1535: a-h, Various portraits. 2000sh, With Diana, Princess of Wales (1961-97).

1998, Feb. 9   Litho.   Perf. 14
1535 A231 300sh Sheet of 8,
                #a.-h.   7.00 7.00

Souvenir Sheet
1536 A231 2000sh multicolored   6.50 6.50

Nos. 1535a, 1535d-1535e, 1535h are each 22x36mm.

UNICEF in Uganda, 30th Anniv. A232

Designs: 300sh, "Support for children with disabilities." 400sh, "Safeguard children against polio." 600sh, "Sanitation... responsibility for all." 700sh, "Children's right to basic education."

1998, Mar. 6   Perf. 13½x14
1537-1540 A232 Set of 4   6.00 6.00

Dinosaurs — A233

Designs, horiz: 300sh, Pteranodon. 400sh, Diplodocus. 500sh, Lambeosaurus. 600sh, Centrosaurus. 700sh, Parasaurolophus.
No. 1546: a, Cetiosaurus. b, Brontosaurus. c, Brachiosaurus. d, Deinonychus. e, Dimetrodon. f, Megalosaurus.
No. 1547, 2500sh, Tyrannosaurus. No. 1548, 2500sh, Iguanodon.

1998, Mar. 24   Litho.   Perf. 14
1541-1545 A233 Set of 5   5.50 5.50
1546 A233 600sh Sheet of 6,
                #a.-f.   8.00 8.00

Souvenir Sheets
1547-1548 A233 Set of 2   12.00 12.00

Nos. 1547-1548 each contain one 43x57mm stamp.

Writers — A234

No. 1549: a, Rita Dove. b, Mari Evans. c, Sterling A. Brown. d, June Jordan. e, Stephen Henderson. f, Zora Neale Hurston.

1998, Apr. 6
1549 A234 300sh Sheet of 6,
　　　#a.-f.　　　　　4.25　4.25

Reptiles — A235

Designs: 300sh, Armadillo girdled lizard.
600sh, Spotted sandveld lizard. 700sh, Bell's
ringed tortoise.

1998, Apr. 21　　　　　**Perf. 13½**
1550 A235 300sh multicolored　　.75　.75
1551 A235 600sh multicolored　　1.50　1.50
1552 A235 700sh multicolored　　1.75　1.75
　　　Nos. 1550-1552 (3)　　　4.00　4.00

Compare with Nos. 1328-1335.

Mickey Mouse, 70th Birthday — A236

No. 1553 — Scenes from cartoon, "Run-
away Brain:" a, Mickey afraid of shadow. b,
Mickey petting Pluto, newspaper. c, Mickey
playing computer game, Pluto. d, Mickey, Minnie running. e, Mickey as target of experiment.
f, Minnie being held captive by Pete on top of
skyscraper. g, Mickey throwing lasso. h,
Mickey surrounding Pete with rope. i, Mickey,
Minnie holding onto rope above skyscrapers.
No. 1554, 3000sh, Mickey, Minnie embracing on top of skyscraper. No. 1555, 3000sh,
Mickey, Minnie kissing on raft, vert.

1998, May 4　　Litho.　　Perf. 14x13½
1553 A236 400sh Sheet of 9,
　　　#a.-i.　　　　　9.75　9.75
Souvenir Sheets
1554-1555 A236　Set of 2　13.50　13.50

Nos. 1414-1415
Ovptd.

1998, May 13　　Litho.　　Perf. 14
1556 A197　Sheet of 3, #a.-c.
　　　　(#1414)　　　　3.75　3.75
Souvenir Sheet
1557 A197 2000sh multi (#1415)　4.00　4.00
Sheet margins of Nos. 1556-1557 each contain additional overprint, "ISRAEL 98 —
WORLD STAMP EXHIBITION/TEL-AVIV 13-
21 MAY 1998."

Sailing
Ships
A237

No. 1558, 1000sh: a, Fishing schooner. b,
Chesapeake oyster boat. c, Java Sea
schooner.
No. 1559, 1000sh: a, Santa Maria, 15th
cent. galleon. b, Mayflower, 15th cent. galleon.
c, Bark.
No. 1560, 3000sh, Boat with lateen sails.
No. 1561, 3000sh, Thames River barge, vert.

1998, June 2　Litho.　Perf. 13x13½
Sheets of 3, #a-c + Label
1558-1559 A237　Set of 2　12.00　12.00
Souvenir Sheets
1560-1561 A237　Set of 2　12.00　12.00
Nos. 1560-1561 are continuous designs.

Aircraft — A238

No. 1562: a, US F4F Wildcat. b, Japanese
Zero. c, British Spitfire. d, British Harrier. e,
S3A Viking. f, US Corsair.
No. 1563: a, Dornier Do-X transatlantic
flyer, 1929. b, German Zucker mail rocket,
1930. c, X-15 Rocket Plane, 1955. d, Goddard's Rocket, 1930's. e, Wright brothers'
flight, 1903. f, 160R Sikorsky helicopter, 1939.
No. 1564, 2500sh, P40 Tomahawk. No.
1565, 2500sh, SH346 Seabat.

1998, July 24　　Litho.　　Perf. 14
1562 A238 500sh Sheet of 6,
　　　#a.-f.　　　　　7.00　7.00
1563 A238 600sh Sheet of 6,
　　　#a.-f.　　　　　8.25　8.25
Souvenir Sheets
1564-1565 A238　Set of 2　11.00　11.00

Flowers of the Mediterranean — A239

No. 1566, vert: a, Onosma. b, Rhododendron luteum. c, Paeonia mascula. d, Geranium
macrorrhizum. e, Cyclamen graecum. f, Lilium
rhodopaedum. g, Narcissus pseudonarcissus.
h, Paeonia rhodia. i, Aquilegia amaliae.
No. 1567: a, Paeonia peregrina. b, Muscari
comutatum. c, Sternbergia. d, Dianthus. e,
Verbascum. f, Aubrieta gracilis. g, Galanthus
nivalis. h, Campanula incurva. i, Crocus
sieberi.
No. 1568, 2000sh, Paeonia parnassica,
vert. No. 1569, 2000sh, Pancratium maritimum, vert.

1998, Sept. 23　　Litho.　　Perf. 14
1566 A239 300sh Sheet of 9,
　　　#a.-i.　　　　　5.00　5.00
1567 A239 600sh Sheet of 9,
　　　#a.-i.　　　　　9.00　9.00
Souvenir Sheets
1568-1569 A239　Set of 2　10.00　10.00

Christmas
A240

Birds: 300sh, Bohemian waxwing. 400sh,
House sparrow. 500sh, Black-capped chickadee. 600sh, Eurasian bullfinch. 700sh, Painted
bunting. 1000sh, Northern cardinal.
No. 1576, 2500sh, Winter wren, vert. No.
1577, 2500sh, Red-winged blackbird, vert.

1998, Dec. 3　　Litho.　　Perf. 14
1570-1575 A240　Set of 6　7.00　7.00
Souvenir Sheets
1576-1577 A240　Set of 2　11.00　11.00

Diana, Princess
of Wales (1961-
97)
A241

1998, Dec. 28　　Litho.　　Perf. 14½
1578 A241 700sh multicolored　2.00　2.00

Picasso
A242

Paintings: 500sh, Woman Reading, 1935,
vert. 600sh, Portrait of Dora Maar, 1937, vert.
700sh, Des Moiselles D'Avignon, 1907.
2500sh, Night Fishing at Antibes, 1939,
vert.

1998, Dec. 28　Perf. 14½x13, 13x14½
1579-1581 A242　Set of 3　4.00　4.00
Souvenir Sheet
1582 A242 2500sh multicolored　4.75　4.75

Gandhi — A243

1998, Dec. 28　　　　　Perf. 14
1583 A243　600sh Portrait　5.50　5.50
Souvenir Sheet
1584 A243 2500sh Family por-
　　　　trait, horiz.　　7.00　7.00
No. 1583 was issued in sheets of 4.

1998 World Scouting Jamboree,
Chile — A244

No. 1585: a, Cub Scouts greet Pres. Eisenhower, Georgia, 1956. b, Uncle Dan Beard at
90th birthday party, 1990. c, Future Vice President Hubert Humphrey leads South Dakota
troop, 1934.
2000sh, Young scout, tamed beaver, vert.

1998, Dec. 28
1585 A244 700sh Sheet of 3,
　　　#a.-c.　　　　　6.00　6.00
Souvenir Sheet
1586 A244 2000sh multicolored　4.00　4.00

New Year
1999 (Year of
the
Rabbit)
A245

No. 1587 — Rabbits: a, White. b, With car-
rot. c, Brown & white. e, Black & white.

1999, Jan. 4
1587 A245　350sh Sheet of 4,
　　　#a.-d.　　　　　4.00　4.00
Souvenir Sheet
1588 A245 1500sh Rabbit, diff.　4.00　4.00

Uganda
Post
Office
A246

1999, Jan. 18
1589 A246 300sh multicolored　1.75　1.75

Traditional
Hairstyles — A247

Hairstyle, region: 300sh, Iru, Bairu. 500sh,
Enshunju, Bahima. 550sh, Elemungole,
Karamojong. 600sh, Longo, Langi. 700sh,
Ekikuura, Bahima.

1999, Feb. 1
1590-1594 A247　Set of 5　6.25　6.25

Marine
Life
A248

No. 1595: a, Wolffish. b, Equal sea star. c,
Purple sea urchin. d, Mountain crab.
No. 1596: a, Blue marlin. b, Arctic tern. c,
Common dolphin. d, Blacktip shark. e, Manta
ray. f, Blackedge moray. g, Loggerhead turtle.
h, Sailfin tang. i, Two-spotted octopus.
No. 1597, 2500sh, Sea nettle jellyfish. No.
1598, 2500sh, Decatopecten striatus.

1999, Mar. 15　　Litho.　　Perf. 14
1595 A248 500sh Sheet of 4,
　　　#a.-d.　　　　　3.50　3.50
1596 A248 500sh Sheet of 9,
　　　#a.-i.　　　　　9.00　9.00
Souvenir Sheets
1597-1598 A248　each　9.50　9.50
Intl. Year of the Ocean.

Intl. Year of
the Elderly
A249

Designs: 300sh, Income generating activity.
500sh, Learning from each other. 600sh, Leisure time for the aged. 700sh, Distributing
food to the aged.

1999, July 19　Litho.　Perf. 13x13½
1599-1602 A249　Set of 4　5.50　5.50

First Manned
Moon Landing,
30th
Anniv. — A250

No. 1603: a, Apollo 11 launch. b, Apollo 11
command and service modules. c, Edwin E.
Aldrin, Jr. on lunar module ladder. d, Saturn V
ready to launch. e, Lunar module descending.
f, Aldrin on moon.
No. 1604: a, Freedom 7. b, Gemini 4. c,
Apollo 11 command and service modules, diff.

d, Vostok 1. e, Saturn V. f, Lunar module on moon.
No. 1605, 3000sh, Aldrin with scientific experiment No. 1606, 3000sh, Command module re-entry.

1999, Nov. 24   Litho.   Perf. 13¾
1603 A250 600sh Sheet of 6,
    #a.-f.   7.00 7.00
1604 A250 700sh Sheet of 6,
    #a.-f.   8.00 8.00
Souvenir Sheets
1605-1606 A250 Set of 2   14.00 14.00

Queen Mother (b. 1900) — A251

No. 1607: a, With stole. b, At wedding. c, With tiara (black and white photo). d, With tiara (color photo).
3000sh, Visiting Cambridge, 1961.

1999, Nov. 24   Perf. 14
1607 A251 1200sh Sheet of 4,
    #a.-d.   10.00 10.00
Souvenir Sheet
Perf. 13¾
1608 A251 3000sh multi   8.00 8.00
No. 1608 contains one 38x51mm stamp.

Hokusai Paintings A252

No. 1609: a, Dragon Flying Over Mount Fuji (dragon). b, Famous Poses From the Kabuki Theater (one figure). c, Kitsune No Yomeiri. d, Dragon Flying Over Mount Fuji (Mount Fuji). e, Famous Poses From the Kabuki Theater (two figures). f, Girl Holding Cloth.
3000sh, Japanese Spaniel.

1999, Nov. 24   Litho.   Perf. 13¾
1609 A252 700sh Sheet of 6,
    #a.-f.   8.00 8.00
Souvenir Sheet
1610 A252 3000sh multicolored   6.25 6.25

Birds — A253

Designs: 300sh, African penduline tit. 1000sh, Yellow-fronted tinkerbird. 1200sh, Zebra waxbill. 1800sh, Sooty anteater chat.
No. 1615: a, Gray-headed kingfisher. b, Green-headed sunbird. c, Speckled pigeon. d, Gray parrot. e, Barn owl. f, Gray crowned crane. g, Shoebill. h, Black heron.
No. 1616: a, Scarlet-chested sunbird. b, Lesser honeyguide. c, African palm swift. d, Swamp flycatcher. e, Lizard buzzard. f, Osprey. g, Cardinal woodpecker. h, Pearl-spotted owlet.
No. 1617: a, Fox's weaver. b, Chin-spot flycatcher. c, Blue swallow. d, Purple-breasted sunbird. e, Knob-billed duck. f, Red-collared widowbird. g, Ruwenzori turaco. h, African cuckoo hawk.
No. 1618, 3000sh, Four-banded sandgrouse. No. 1619, 3000sh, Paradise whydah.

1999, Dec. 6   Perf. 14
1611-1614 A253 Set of 4   9.75 9.75
1615 A253 500sh Sheet of 8,
    #a.-h.   9.00 9.00
1616 A253 600sh Sheet of 8,
    #a.-h.   10.50 10.50
1617 A253 700sh Sheet of 8,
    #a.-h.   12.50 12.50
Souvenir Sheets
1618-1619 A253 Set of 2   14.50 14.50

Primates — A254

Designs: 300sh, L'hoesti monkey. 400sh, Blue monkey. 500sh, Patas monkey. 600sh, Red-tailed monkey. 700sh, Black and white colobus. 1000sh, Mountain gorilla.
2500sh, Olive baboon.

1999, Nov. 19   Litho.   Perf. 13½x14
1620-1625 A254 Set of 6   7.00 7.00
Souvenir Sheet
1626 A254 2500sh multicolored   5.50 5.50

Butterflies A255

Designs: 300sh, Epiphora bauhiniae, vert. 400sh, Phylloxiphia formosa. 500sh, Bunaea alcinoe, vert. 600sh, Euchloron megaera. 700sh, Argema mimosae, vert. 1800sh, Denephila nerii.
3000sh, Lobobunaea angasana.

Perf. 13½x13¼, 13¼x13½
2000, Jan. 19   Litho.
1627-1632 A255 Set of 6   9.25 9.25
Souvenir Sheet
1633 A255 3000sh multi   7.75 7.75

A256

UPU, 125th anniv. (in 1999): 600sh, Postman, two women, girl. 700sh, Woman, girl, mail box. 1200sh, Postman in horse-drawn wagon.

2000, Jan. 28   Litho.   Perf. 14
1634-1636 A256 Set of 3   5.50 5.50

A257

No. 1637, 600sh — Orchids: a, Angraecum eichcerianum. b, Angraecum leonis. c, Arpophyllum giganteum. d, Bulbophyllum barbigerum. e, Angraecum ciryamae. f, Aerangis ellisii. g, Disa umiflora. h, Eulophia alta. i, Ancistrochilius stylosa.
No. 1638, 600sh: a, Eulophia paivenna. b, Ansellia gigantea. c, Anglaecopsis gracillima. d, Bonatea steudneri. e, Bulbophyllum falcatum. f, Aerangis citrata. g, Eulophiella

elisabethae. h, Aerangis rhodosticta. i, Angraecum scottianum.
No. 1639, 700sh: a, Grammangis ellisii. b, Eulophia stenophylia. c, Oeoniella polystachys. d, Cymbidiella humblotti. e, Polystachya bella. f, Vanilla polycepis. g, Eulophileea roemplerana. h, Habenaria englerana. i, Ansellia frallana.
No. 1640, 700sh: a, Eulophia orthoplectra. b, Cirrhopetalum umbellatum. c, Eulophiella rolfei. d, Eulophia porphyroglossa. e, Eulopia petersii. f, Cyrtorchis arcuata. g, Eurychone rothschildiana. h, Eulophia quartiniana. i, Eulophia stenophylia (one flower).
No. 1641, 3000sh, Polystachya tayloriana, horiz. No. 1642, 3000sh, Ancistrochilus rothschildianus, horiz. No. 1643, 3000sh, Calanthe corymbosa, horiz. No. 1644, 3000sh, Cymbidiella rhodochila, horiz.

2000, Feb. 18   Sheets of 9, #a.-i.
1637-1638 A257 Set of 2   20.00 20.00
1639-1640 A257 Set of 2   25.00 25.00
Souvenir Sheets
1641-1644 A257 Set of 4   21.00 21.00

Butterflies — A258

Designs: 300sh, Short-tailed admiral. 400sh, Guineafowl. 1200sh, Club-tailed charaxes. 1800sh, Cymothoe egesta.
No. 1649: a, Charaxes anrticlea. b, Epitola posthumus. c, Beautiful monarch. d, Blue-banded nymph. e, Euxanthe crossleyi. f, African map. g, Western blue charaxes. h, Noble.
No. 1650: a, Green-veined charaxes. b, Ansorge's leaf butterfly. c, Crawshay's sapphire blue. d, Palla ussheri. e, Friar. f, Blood-red cymothoe. g, Mocker. h, Charaxes eupale.
No. 1651: a, Aeraea pseudolycia. b, Veined yellow. c, Buxton's hairstreak. d, Iolaus isomenias. e, Veined swallowtail. f, Figtree blue. g, Scarlet tip. h, Precis octavia.
No. 1652, 3000sh, African monarch. No. 1653, 3000sh, Kigezi swordtail.

2000, May 24   Litho.   Perf. 14
1645-1648 A258 Set of 4   7.75 7.75
1649 A258 500sh Sheet of 8,
    #a-h   8.00 8.00
1650 A258 600sh Sheet of 8,
    #a-h   8.00 8.00
1651 A258 700sh Sheet of 8,
    #a-h   9.00 9.00
Souvenir Sheets
1652-1653 A258 Set of 2   11.00 11.00
The Stamp Show 2000, London (Nos. 1649-1653).

Popes — A259

No. 1654: a, Agapetus II (946-55). b, Alexander II (1061-73). c, Anastasius IV (1153-54). d, Benedict VIII (1012-24). e, Benedict VII (974-83). f, Calixtus II (1119-24).
No. 1655, Celestine III (1191-90).

2000, June 28   Perf. 13¾
1654 A259 900sh Sheet of 6,
    #a-f   14.00 14.00
Souvenir Sheet
1655 A259 3000sh multi   7.00 7.00

Monarchs — A260

No. 1655A: b, Philip II of France (1180-1223). c, Richard I of England (1189-99). d, William I of England (1066-87).
No. 1656: a, Boris III of Bulgaria (1918-43). b, Holy Roman Emperor Charles V (1519-58). c, Pedro II of Brazil (1831-89). d, Empress Elizabeth of Austria (1854-98). e, Francis Joseph of Austria (1848-1916). f, Frederick I of Bohemia (1619-20).
No. 1657, Mutesa I of Buganda (1191-98).
No. 1657A, Cwa II Kabalooga.

2000, June 28   Perf. 13¾
1655A A260 900sh Sheet of 3,
    #b-d   5.00 5.00
1656 A260 900sh Sheet of 6,
    #a-f   9.00 9.00
Souvenir Sheets
1657 A260 3000sh multi   5.50 5.50
1657A A260 3000sh multi   5.50 5.50

Millennium — A261

No. 1658 — Highlights of 1850-1900: a, Opening of Japan. b, First safe elevator. c, Bessemer process of steel production. d, Florence Nightingale establishes nursing as a professsion. e, Louis Pasteur proposes germ theory of disease. f, First oil well drilled. g, Charles Darwin publishes *The Origin of Species*. h, Gregor Mendel discovers laws of heredity. i, Alfred Nobel invents dynamite. j, Suez Canal opens. k, Invention of the telephone. l, Invention of the electric light. m, World's time zones established. n, Invention of the electric motor. o, Motion pictures appear. p, US Civil War (57x37mm). q, Restoration of the Olympic Games.
Illustration reduced.

2000, June 28   Perf. 12¾x12½
1658 A261 300sh Sheet of 17,
    #a-q + label   8.00 8.00

Millennium — A262

Designs: 300sh, Education for all. 600sh, Nile River. 700sh, Non-traditional exports. 1800sh, Tourism.

2000, July 24   *Perf. 14½*
1659-1662 A262   Set of 4   6.00 6.00

Common Market for Eastern and Southern Africa A263

Designs: 500sh, Border checkpoint before and after COMESA treaty. 1400sh, Open border checkpoint.

2000, July 24
1663-1664 A263   Set of 2   2.50 2.50

Modern British Commonwealth, 50th Anniv. — A264

Designs: 600sh, Flags. 1200sh, Map.

2000, July 24
1665-1666 A264   Set of 2   2.25 2.25

Trains A265

Designs: 300sh, Kenya Railways A 60 Class 4-8-2+2-8-4. 400sh, Mozambique Railways Baldwin 2-8-0. 600sh, Uganda Railways 73 Class German locomotive. 700sh, South Africa Railways Baby Garratt. 1200sh, Uganda Railways 82 Class French locomotive. 1400sh, East Africa Railway Beyer Garratt 4-8-2+2-8-4. 1800sh, Rhodesian Railways 2-8-2+2-8-2 Beyer Garratt. 2000sh, East African Railways Garratt.
No. 1675, 700sh: a, Uganda Railways 36 Class German locomotive. b, South African Railways Class 19D 4-8-2. c, Algeria Railways Garratt 4-8-2+2-8-4. d, Cameroon Railways French locomotive. e, South Africa railways electric freight locomotive. f, Rhodesia Railways 14A Class 2-8-2. g, British-built Egyptian railways locomotive. h, Uganda Railways 73 Class German locomotive, diff.
No. 1676, 700sh: a, 36 Class German locomotive (no country specified). b, Rhodesian Railways 12th Class locomotive. c, Rhodesian Railways Garratt. d, 62 Class German locomotive. e, South Africa Railways Beyer Garratt. f, Sudan Railways locomotive. g, Nigerian Railways locomotive. h, 4-8-0 South Africa Railways.
No. 1677, 3500sh, East African Railways locomotive. No. 1678, 3500sh, Rhodesian Railways Alco 2-8-0. No. 1679, 3500sh, Egyptian State Railways 4-8-2.

2000, Aug. 14   *Perf. 14*
1667-1674 A265   Set of 8   11.00 11.00
Sheets of 8, #a-h
1675-1676 A265   Set of 2   14.00 14.00
Souvenir Sheets
1677-1679 A265   Set of 3   13.50 13.50
    Nos. 1677-1679 each contain one 56x42mm stamp.

Christmas — A266

Artwork by: 300sh, Drateru Fortunate Oliver, vert. 400sh, Brenda Tumwebaze. 500sh, Joseph Mukiibi, vert. 600sh, Paul Serunjogi.

700sh, Edward Maswere. 1200sh, Ndeba Harriet. 1800sh, Jude Kasagga, vert.
No. 1687, 3000sh, Nicole Kwiringira, vert. No. 1688, 3000sh, Michael Tinkamanyire, vert.

2000, Dec. 14   *Litho.*   *Perf. 14*
1680-1686 A266   Set of 7   7.00 7.00
Souvenir Sheets
1687-1688 A266   Set of 2   7.50 7.50

New Year 2001 (Year of the Snake) — A267

No. 1689: a, Snake with tongue out. b, Snake wrapped around person. c, Snake with open mouth. d, Snake hanging from branch.

2001, Jan. 5
1689 A267   600sh Sheet of 4,
             #a-d   3.00 3.00
Souvenir Sheet
1690 A267   2500sh shown   3.25 3.25

Wildlife — A268

No. 1691: a, Bongo, horiz. b, Black rhinoceros, horiz. c, Leopard.
No. 1692, 3000sh, Parrot. No. 1693, 3000sh, Mountain gorillas, horiz.

                 Perf. 13⅓x13¾, 13¾x13¼
2001, Feb. 5
1691 A268   600sh Strip of 3, #a-c 2.25 2.25
Souvenir Sheets
1692-1693 A268   Set of 2   7.50 7.50

Holy Year 2000 — A269

Designs: 300sh, Holy Family. 700sh, Madonna and Child. 1200sh, Nativity, horiz.

2001, Apr. 4   *Litho.*   *Perf. 13¼*
1694-1696 A269   Set of 3   2.75 2.75

East African School of Library and Information Science, Makerere University, Kampala — A270

Nairobi University, Kenya — A271

Universities and Flags on Map — A272

Design: 1200sh, Nkrumah Hall, University of Dar es Salaam, Tanzania.

2001, Apr. 23
1697 A270   300sh multi   .40 .40
1698 A271   400sh multi   .50 .50
1699 A270   1200sh multi   1.50 1.50
1700 A272   1800sh multi   2.25 2.25
    Nos. 1697-1700 (4)   4.65 4.65

World Meteorological Organization, 50th Anniv. (in 2000) — A273

Designs: 300sh, Anemometer, vert. 2000sh, Tropical sun recorder.

2001, May 28
1701-1702 A273   Set of 2   3.00 3.00

UN High Commissioner for Refugees — A274

Designs: 300sh, Ensure crop production. 600sh, Ensure community participation. 700sh, Ensure improved skills. 1800sh, Ensure improved health and water services.

2001, June 15
1703-1706 A274   Set of 4   4.25 4.25

Phila Nippon '01, Japan — A275

Designs: 600sh, Kikunojo Segawa I and Danjuro Ichikawa as Samurai, by Kiyonobu II. 700sh, Kamezo Tchimura as a Warrior, by Kiyohiro. 1000sh, Danjuro Ichikawa as Shirobei, by Kiyomitsu. 1200sh, Actor Sangoro

---

Arashi, by Shunsho. 1400sh, Koshiro Matsumoto IV as Sukenari Juro, by Kiyonaga. 2000sh, Pheasant on Pine Branch, by Kiyomasu II.
3500sh, Tale of Ise, by Eishi.

2001, Aug. 1   *Litho.*   *Perf. 14*
1707-1712 A275   Set of 6   8.75 8.75
Souvenir Sheet
1713 A275   3500sh multi   4.50 4.50

Cats and Dogs — A276

Designs: 400sh, Tabby British shorthair. 900sh, Turkish cat.
No. 1716, 600sh, horiz.: a, Blue and cream shorthair. b, Manx. c, Angora. d, Red and white British shorthair. e, Turkish cat, diff. f, Egyptian mau.
No. 1717, 1400sh, horiz.: a, Red tabby shorthair. b, Japanese bobtail. c, Siamese. d, Tabby Persian. e, Black and white Persian. f, Blue Russian.
No. 1718, 3500sh, Blue-eyed British shorthair. No. 1719, 3500sh, Calico American shorthair.

2001, Aug. 23
1714-1715 A276   Set of 2   1.60 1.60
Sheets of 6, #a-f
1716-1717 A276   Set of 2   15.00 15.00
Souvenir Sheets
1718-1719 A276   Set of 2   9.00 9.00

2001, Aug. 23

Designs: 1100sh, German shepherd. 1200sh, Irish setter.
No. 1722, 700sh, horiz.: a, Rottweiler. b, Flat-coated retriever. c, Samoyed. d, Poodle. e, Maltese. f, Irish terrier.
No. 1723, 1300sh, horiz.: a, English sheepdog. b, German shepherd, diff. c, Great Dane. d, Boston terrier. e, Bull terrier. f, Australian terrier.
No. 1724, 3500sh, Bloodhound. No. 1725, 3500sh, Pointer, horiz.

1720-1721 A276   Set of 2   3.00 3.00
Sheets of 6, #a-f
1722-1723 A276   Set of 2   15.00 15.00
Souvenir Sheets
1724-1725 A276   Set of 2   9.00 9.00
    APS Stampshow, Chicago (#1723).

Royal Navy Submarines, Cent. — A277

No. 1726, vert.: a, HMS Tribune. b, HMS Royal Oak. c, HMS Invincible. d, HMS Dreadnought. e, HMS Ark Royal. f, HMS Cardiff.

2001, Aug. 27
1726 A277   1000sh Sheet of 6,
             #a-f   7.50 7.50
Souvenir Sheet
1727 A277   3500sh HMS Triad   4.50 4.50

Queen Victoria (1819-1901) — A278

No. 1728: a, Wearing tiara. b, Wearing white head covering, looking right. c, Wearing black hat. d, Wearing red dress with blue sash. e, Wearing white head covering, looking left. f, With hand on chin.
3500sh, Wearing black, hat, diff.

2001, Aug. 27
1728 A278 1000sh Sheet of 6,
　　 #a-f　　　　　　　7.50 7.50
Souvenir Sheet
1729 A278 3500sh multi　　4.50 4.50

Queen Elizabeth II, 75th Birthday — A279

No. 1730: a, In 1926. b, In 1931. c, In 1939. d, In 1955. e, In 1963. f, In 1999.
3500sh, Wearing cap.

2001, Aug. 27
1730 A279 1000sh Sheet of 6,
　　 #a-f　　　　　　　7.50 7.50
Souvenir Sheet
1731 A279 3500sh multi　　4.50 4.50

Toulouse-Lautrec Paintings — A280

No. 1732: a, Woman Combing Her Hair. b, The Toilette. c, The English Girl at the Star in Le Havre.
3500sh, Ambassadeurs: Aristide Bruant.

2001, Aug. 27　Litho.　Perf. 13¾
1732 A280 1500sh Sheet of 3,
　　 #a-c　　　　　　　5.75 5.75
Souvenir Sheet
1733 A280 3500sh multi　　4.50 4.50

Monet Paintings — A281

No. 1734, horiz.: a, Storm, Belle-Ile Coast. b, The Manneporte, Etretat. c, The Rocks at Pourville, Low Tide. d, The Wild Sea.
3500sh, Sunflowers.

2001, Aug. 27
1734 A281 1200sh Sheet of 4,
　　 #a-d　　　　　　　6.00 6.00
Souvenir Sheet
1735 A281 3500sh multi　　4.50 4.50

Year of Dialogue Among Civilizations A282

Perf. 13¾x13¼
2001, Nov. 16　　　　　Litho.
1736 A282 3000sh multi　　3.75 3.75

Intl. Volunteers Year A283

Designs: 300sh, Ebola outbreak. 700sh, Save life, donate blood. 2000sh, Collective effort for clean water.

2001, Nov. 16　　Perf. 13¼x13¾
1737-1739 A283　Set of 3　3.75 3.75

Mushrooms — A284

Designs: 300sh, Amanita excelsa. 500sh, Coprinus cinereus. 600sh, Scleroderma aurantium. 700sh, Armillaria mellea. 1200sh, Leopiota procera. 2000sh, Flammulina velutipes.
3000sh, Amanita phalloides.

2001, Nov. 26　　　　Perf. 14½
1740-1745 A284　　Set of 6　6.75 6.75
Souvenir Sheets
1746　A284 3000sh multi　　3.75 3.75
1746A A284 3000sh multi　　3.75 3.75

Christmas — A285

Musical instruments: 400sh, Single skin long drum. 800sh, Animal horn trumpet, horiz. 1000sh, Bugisu clay drum. 1200sh, Musical bow. 1400sh, Pan pipes. 2000sh, Log xylophones, horiz.

No. 1753, 3500sh, Eight-stringed giant bow harp. No. 1754, Nativity scene, horiz.

2001　　Perf. 13¾x13¼, 13¼x13¾
1747-1752 A285　Set of 6　8.50 8.50
Souvenir Sheets
1753-1754 A285　Set of 2　9.00 9.00

New Year 2002 (Year of the Horse) — A286

No. 1755: a, White horse facing left. b, Dark brown and gray brown horse facing right with all feet on ground. c, Tan and brown horse facing right, with two feet raised.
3000r, Rearing horse.

2002, May 8　Litho.　Perf. 14x14¼
1755 A286 1200sh Sheet of 3,
　　 #a-c　　　　　　　4.50 4.50
Souvenir Sheet
1756 A286 3000sh multi　　3.75 3.75

Historic Sites of East Africa A287

Designs: 400sh, Namugongo Shrine Church, Uganda. 800sh, Maruhubi Palace Ruins, Zanzibar, Tanzania. 1200sh, Kings' Burial Grounds, Mparo, Uganda. 1400sh, Old Law Courts, Mombasa, Kenya, vert.

2002, May 8　　　　　Perf. 14½
1757-1760 A287　Set of 4　4.75 4.75

Reign of Queen Elizabeth II, 50th Anniv. — A288

No. 1761: a, Wearing blue dress. b, Wearing blue and red hat. c, Without hat. d, Wearing blue hat.
3500sh, Wearing brown hat.

2002, June 17　　　　Perf. 14¼
1761 A288 1500sh Sheet of 4,
　　 #a-d　　　　　　　7.50 7.50
Souvenir Sheet
1762 A288 3500sh multi　　4.50 4.50

8th Intl. Interdisciplinary Congress on Women, Kampala — A289

Designs: 400sh, Women, building. 1200sh, Makerere University arms, vert.

Perf. 13¼x13¾, 13¾x13¼
2002, July 8
1763-1764 A289　Set of 2　2.00 2.00

United We Stand — A290

2002, July 15　　　Perf. 13¾x13¼
1765 A290 1500sh multi　　1.90 1.90

Printed in sheets of 4

Intl. Year of Mountains — A291

No. 1766: a, Tateyama, Japan. b, Mt. Nikko, Japan. c, Mt. Hodaka, Japan.
3500sh, Mt. Fuji, Japan.

2002, July 15　　　Perf. 13¼x13¾
1766 A291 2000sh Sheet of 3,
　　 #a-c　　　　　　　7.50 7.50
Souvenir Sheet
1767 A291 3500sh multi　　4.50 4.50

2002 Winter Olympics, Salt Lake City — A292

Designs: No. 1768, 1200sh, Cross-country skiing. No. 1769, 1200sh, Ski jumping.

2002, July 15　　　Perf. 13¾x13¼
1768-1769 A292　Set of 2　3.00 3.00
1769a　　　 Souvenir sheet, #1768-
　　　　　　 1769　　　　　　3.00 3.00

20th World Scout Jamboree, Thailand — A293

No. 1770: a, Scout in forest, 1930s. b, Scout saluting. c, Scouts hiking. d, Scout badge.
3500sh, Lord Robert Baden-Powell.

2002   **Perf. 13¼x13¾**
1770 A293 1400sh Sheet of 4,
   #a-d   7.00 7.00
Souvenir Sheet
Perf. 13¾x13¼
1771 A293 3500sh multi   4.50 4.50

Mammals, Insects, Flowers and Mushrooms — A294

Designs: 400sh, Ceratotherium simum. 800sh, Macrotermes subhyalinus. No. 1774, 1200sh, Gloriosa superba. 1400sh, Cyptotrama asprata.

No. 1776, 1000sh, horiz. — Insects: a, Nudaurelia cytherea. b, Locusta migratoria. c, Anacridium aegyptium. d, Sternotomis bohemanni. e, Papilio dardanus. f, Mantis polyspilota.

No. 1777, 1000sh, horiz. — Mushrooms: a, Termitomyces microcarpus. b, Agaricus trisulphuratus. c, Macrolepiota zeyheri. d, Lentinus stupeus. e, Lentinus sajor-caju. f, Lentinus velutinus.

No. 1778, 1200sh, horiz. — Flowers: a, Canarina eminii. b, Vigna unguiculata. c, Gardenia ternifolia. d, Canavalia rosea. e, Hibiscus calyphyllus. f, Nymphaea lotus.

No. 1779, 1200sh, horiz. — Mammals: a, Kobus kob. b, Alcelaphus buselaphus. c, Damaliiscus lunatus. d, Papio anubis. e, Panthera leo. f, Phacochoerus africanus.

No. 1780, 4000sh, Glossina austeni, horiz. No. 1781, 4000sh, Podoscypha parvula, horiz. No. 1782, 4000sh, Abutilon grandiflorum, horiz. No. 1783, 4000sh, Kobus ellipsiprymnus.

2002, Nov. 6   **Litho.**   **Perf. 14**
1772-1775 A294   Set of 4   4.75 4.75
Sheets of 6, #a-f
1776-1779 A294   Set of 4   35.00 35.00
Souvenir Sheets
1780-1783 A294   Set of 4   20.00 20.00

A295

Pres. John F. Kennedy (1917-63) — A296

Various photos.

2002, Dec. 30
1784 A295 1200sh Sheet of 4,
   #a-d   6.00 6.00
1785 A296 1400sh Sheet of 4,
   #a-d   7.00 7.00

A297

Pres. Ronald Reagan — A298

Various photos.

2002, Dec. 30
1786 A297 1200sh Sheet of 4,
   #a-d   6.00 6.00
1787 A298 1400sh Sheet of 4,
   #a-d   7.00 7.00

A299

Princess Diana (1961-97) — A300

2002, Dec. 30
1788 A299 1200sh Sheet of 4,
   #a-d   6.00 6.00
1789 A300 2000sh Sheet of 4,
   #a-d   10.00 10.00

New Year 2003 (Year of the Ram) — A301

No. 1790: a, Ram on stage. b, Ram on hill. c, Ram on hill, six ram's heads. d, Six rams. e, Ram in field. f, Ram on mountainside.

2003, Feb. 1   **Perf. 14¼x14**
1790 A301 1000sh Sheet of 6,
   #a-f   7.50 7.50

Japanese Art — A302

Designs: 400sh, Beauty Arranging Her Hair, by Eisen Keisai. 1000sh, Geishas, by Tsukimaro Kitagawa. 1200sh, Woman Behind a Screen, by Chikanobu Toyohara. 1400sh, Geishas, by Kitagawa, diff.

No. 1795: a, Scene in a Villa (basin in foreground), by Kinichika Toyohara. b, Scene in a Villa (screen at left), by Kunichika Toyohara. c, Visiting a Flower Garden (two people), by Kunisada Utagawa. d, Visiting a Flower Garden (one person), by Utagawa.

5000sh, Woman and Children, by Chikakazu.

2003, May 26   **Litho.**   **Perf. 14¼**
1791-1794 A302   Set of 4   5.00 5.00
1795 A302 1200sh Sheet of 4,
   #a-d   6.00 6.00
Souvenir Sheet
1796 A302 5000sh multi   6.25 6.25

Rembrandt Paintings A303

Designs: 400sh, Jacob Blessing the Sons of Joseph. 1000sh, A Young Woman in Profile With Fan. 1200sh, The Apostle Peter Kneeling. 1400sh, The Painter Hendrick Martensz Sorgh.

No. 1801: a, Portrait of Margaretha de Geer. b, Portrait of a White Haired Man. c, Portrait of Nicolaes Ruts. d, Portrait of Catrina Hooghsaet.

5000sh, Joseph Accused by Potiphar's Wife.

2003, May 26
1797-1800 A303   Set of 4   5.00 5.00
1801 A303 1400sh Sheet of 4,
   #a-d   7.00 7.00
Souvenir Sheet
1802 A303 5000sh multi   6.25 6.25

Paintings of Joan Miró — A304

Designs: 400sh, Group of Personages in the Forest. 800sh, Nocturne. 1200sh, The Smile of a Tear. 1400sh, Personage Before the Sun.

No. 1807, vert: a, Man's Head III. b, Catalan Peasant by Moonlight. c, Woman in the Night. d, Seated Woman.

No. 1808, 3500sh, Self-portrait II. No. 1809, 3500sh, Woman with Three Hairs, Birds and Constellations.

2003, May 26   **Perf. 14¼**
1803-1806 A304   Set of 4   4.75 4.75
1807 A304 1400sh Sheet of 4,
   #a-d   7.00 7.00
Imperf
Size: 103x82mm
1808-1809 A304   Set of 2   8.75 8.75

Buganda Princess Katrina-Sarah Ssangalyambogo, 2nd Birthday — A305

Princess and: 400sh, Bulange (government office building). 1200sh, Twekobe (palace), vert. 1400sh, Drummer, vert.

Perf. 13x13¼, 13¼x13
2003, June 16
1810-1812 A305   Set of 3   3.75 3.75

Coronation of Queen Elizabeth II, 50th Anniv. — A306

No. 1813: a, As toddler. b, As young woman, wearing flowered hat. c, Wearing robe and feathered hat.
3500sh, Wearing crown.

2003, July 15   *Perf. 14*
1813 A306 2000sh Sheet of 3,
    #a-c   7.50 7.50

Souvenir Sheet

1814 A306 3500sh multi   4.50 4.50

Prince William, 21st Birthday — A307

No. 1815: a, Wearing cap. b, Wearing blue striped shirt. c, Wearing white shirt.
5000sh, With hand on chin.

2003, July 15
1815 A307 2000sh Sheet of 3,
    #a-c   7.50 7.50

Souvenir Sheet

1816 A307 5000sh multi   6.25 6.25

General Motors Automobiles — A308

No. 1817, 1200sh — Cadillacs: a, 1979 Seville Elegante. b, 1998 Eldorado Touring Coupe. c, 2002 Escalade. d, 1983 Seville Elegante.
No. 1818, 1400sh — Corvettes: a, 1970. b, 1972. c, 1982 Collector Edition. d, 1977.
No. 1819, 3500sh, Cadillac Eldorado convertible, 1950s. No. 1820, 3500sh, 1982 Collector Edition Corvette, diff.

2003, July 15   *Perf. 14¼*
    Sheets of 4, #a-d
1817-1818 A308 Set of 2   13.00 13.00

Souvenir Sheets

1819-1820 A308 Set of 2   8.75 8.75

Millennium Development
Goals — A309

Designs: No. 1821, 400sh, Promote gender equity and empower women. No. 1822, 400sh, Improve maternal health. 600sh, Ensure environmental sustainability. 1000sh, Reduce child mortality. No. 1825, 1200sh, Eradicate extreme poverty and hunger. No. 1826, 1200sh, Combat HIV, AIDS, malaria and other diseases. 1400sh, Achieve universal primary education. 2000sh, Develop a global partnership for development.

2003, Oct. 24   *Perf. 14½*
1821-1828 A309 Set of 8   10.50 10.50

Dances and
Costumes — A310

Dances: 400sh, Entogoro. 800sh, Karimojong. 1400sh, Teso.
No. 1832 — Costumes: a, Kiga. b, Acholi. c, Karimojong. d, Ganda.

2003, Nov. 10   *Perf. 14*
1829-1831 A310 Set of 3   3.25 3.25
1832 A310 1200sh Sheet of 4,
    #a-d   6.00 6.00

Christmas — A311

Dances: 300sh, Journey to Bethlehem. 400sh, Shepherds and angels. 1200sh, Nativity. 1400sh, Adoration of the Magi.
3000sh, Holy Family.

2003, Nov. 10
1833-1836 A311 Set of 4   4.25 4.25

Souvenir Sheet

1837 A311 3000sh multi   3.75 3.75

All-Africa Conference on Assuring
Food and Nutrition Security in Africa
by 2020, Kampala — A312

Map of Africa, food basket, Intl. Food Policy Research Institute emblem and: 400sh, Boy. 1400sh, Boy, diff.

2004, Aug. 31   *Litho.*   *Perf. 14¼*
1838-1839 A312 Set of 2   2.25 2.25

Straight Talk Foundation — A313

Child and: 400sh, "Pioneers in Adolescent Health Communication." 1200sh, "Communication for Better Adolescent Health," vert.

2004, Sept. 22
1840-1841 A313 Set of 2   2.00 2.00

Campaign Against Child
Labor — A314

Inscriptions: 400sh, "Stop Child Domestic Labor." 2000sh, "Keep the Community Informed."

2004, Sept. 22
1842-1843 A314 Set of 2   3.00 3.00

Rotary International, Cent. (in
2005) — A315

Rotary emblem and: 400sh, "Celebrate Rotary." 1200sh, "A Century of Service / A New Century of Success," vert.

2004, Sept. 22
1844-1845 A315 Set of 2   2.00 2.00

New Year 2005 (Year of the
Rooster) — A316

No. 1846 — Rooster shades: a, Blue. b, Orange. c, Purple. d, Red.
5000sh, Yellow.

2005, Apr. 4   *Litho.*   *Perf. 14*
1846 A316 1200sh Sheet of 4,
    #a-d   6.00 6.00

Souvenir Sheet

1847 A316 5000sh multi   6.25 6.25

Fight Against
Tuberculosis,
HIV and
Leprosy — A317

WHO emblem and: No. 1848, 400sh, Ill man in blanket. No. 1849, 400sh, Doctor holding arm of ill man. No. 1850, 400sh, Mother and infant. No. 1851, 400sh, Infant in blanket. No. 1852, 400sh, Leper with artificial leg. No. 1853, 400sh, Leper wearing crucifix.

2005, May 31   *Perf. 13x12¾*
1848-1853 A317 Set of 6   3.00 3.00

Flowering
Plants — A318

Designs: 100sh, Clerodendrum sp. 400sh, Calliandra haematocephala. 600sh, Asteraceae compositae. 850sh, Angraecum sp. 900sh, Delonix regia. 1100sh, Bidens grantii. 1200sh, Musa sapientum. 1400sh, Begonia coccinea. 1600sh, Impatiens walleriana. 2000sh, Strelitzia reginae. 5000sh, Tecomaria capensis. 6000sh, Ixora hybrida. 10,000sh, Datura suaveolens. 20,000sh, Cucurbita pepo.

    Perf. 12¾x13½
2005, June 22   *Litho.*
1854 A318 100sh multi   .25 .25
1855 A318 400sh multi   .45 .45
1856 A318 600sh multi   .70 .70

1857	A318	850sh multi	1.00	1.00
1858	A318	900sh multi	1.10	1.10
1859	A318	1100sh multi	1.25	1.25
1860	A318	1200sh multi	1.40	1.40
1861	A318	1400sh multi	1.60	1.60
1862	A318	1600sh multi	1.90	1.90
1863	A318	2000sh multi	2.40	2.40
1864	A318	5000sh multi	5.75	5.75
1865	A318	6000sh multi	7.00	7.00
1866	A318	10,000sh multi	11.50	11.50
1867	A318	20,000sh multi	23.00	23.00
	Nos. 1854-1867 (14)		59.30	59.30

Fish
A319

Designs: 400sh, Synodontis afrofischeri. 600sh, Protopterus aethiopicus. 1100sh, Clarias gariepinus. 1200sh, Rastrineobola agentea. 1600sh, Bagrus docmac. 2000sh, Schilbe mystus.
No. 1874: a, Mormyrus kannume. b, Barbus jacksonni. c, Bagrus docmac, diff. d, Labeo victorianus.

2005, Oct. 6   *Litho.*   *Perf. 13¼*
1868-1873 A319 Set of 6   8.75 8.75

Souvenir Sheet

1874 A319 1000sh Sheet of 4,
    #a-d   5.00 5.00

Western Union in Africa, 10th
Anniv. — A320

Designs: 400sh, Map of Africa, olive branches. 1600sh, Globe. 2000sh, Globe and flags, vert.

2006, July 20   *Litho.*   *Perf. 14¼*
1875-1877 A320 Set of 3   5.00 5.00

Bank of Uganda,
40th
Anniv. — A321

Designs: 400sh, Bank emblem. 600sh, Bank emblem, building, wildlife. 1600sh, Bank emblem, Tilapia nilotica. 2000sh, Bank emblem, mountain gorilla.

2006, Oct. 3   *Perf. 13¼*
1878-1881 A321 Set of 4   5.75 5.75

Wetlands
A322

Designs: 400sh, Cattle and herdsman at water, Ramsar Convention emblem. 1600sh, People and birds near stream. 2000sh, Fishermen at Lake George.

2006   *Perf. 13x13½*
1882-1884 A322 Set of 3   5.00 5.00

2007 Commonwealth Heads of Government Meeting, Kampala — A323

Flag of Uganda and: 400sh, Commonwealth Heads of Government Meeting emblem. 1600sh, Boniface Kiprop, runner. 2000sh, Dorcas Inzikuru, runner. 5000sh, Arms of Uganda, vert.

2007, Nov. 27　Litho.　Perf. 13x13½
1885-1888　A323　Set of 4　　10.50　10.50

24th UPU Congress, Geneva — A324

People in native costumes: No. 1889, Karimojong man.
No. 1890: a, Omwenda women. b, Ebibaraho man. c, Kikoyi women. d, Kanzu men. e, Gomesi women.

2007, Dec. 7　Litho.　Perf. 13¼x13
1889　A324　1600sh multi　　　1.90　1.90
1890　A324　1600sh Horiz. strip of
　　　　　5, #a-e　　　　　9.50　9.50

The UPU Congress was moved from Nairobi, Kenya, to Geneva because of political unrest.

Miniature Sheet

2008 Summer Olympics, Beijing — A325

No. 1891: a, Javelin. b, Running. c, Boxing. d, Swimming.

2008, June 18　　　　　Perf. 12
1891　A325　1000sh Sheet of 4,
　　　　　#a-d　　　　　5.00　5.00

Worldwide Fund for Nature (WWF) — A326

No. 1892 — Spotted hyena: a, Running. b, With pack, devouring prey. c, Adult and juveniles. d, Two juveniles.

2008, June 18　　　　　Perf. 13¼
1892　　　Strip of 4　　　　5.00　5.00
　a.-d.　A326 1000sh Any single　1.25　1.25
　e.　　Sheet of 8, 2 each #1892a-
　　　　1892d　　　　　10.00　10.00

Reign of Aga Khan, 50th Anniv. (in 2007) A327

Designs: No. 1893, 400sh, Diamond Trust Building. No. 1894, 400sh, Kampala Serena Hotel. No. 1895, 400sh, Jubilee Insurance Company Building.
No. 1896: a, School children (madrasa program). b, Ismaili Jamatkhana, Kampala. c, Aga Khan High School (educational services). d, Air Uganda airplane. e, Dam (Bujagali hydropower project).

2008, Sept. 30　Litho.　Perf. 14½
1893-1895　A327　Set of 3　　1.50　1.50
1896　A327　1100sh Horiz. strip of
　　　　　5, #a-e　　　　6.50　6.50

Peony A328

2009, Apr. 10　Litho.　Perf. 13¼
1897　A328　1600sh multi　　1.50　1.50
　　Printed in sheets of 8 + central label.

Miniature Sheet

China 2009 World Stamp Exhibition, Luoyang — A329

No. 1898 — Tourist attractions in China: a, Longmen Grottoes, Luoyang. b, Bridge over Pearl River, Guangzhou. c, Twin Temples on Fir Lake, Guilin. d, Yu Yuan Garden, Shanghai.

2009, Apr. 10　　　　　Perf. 12
1898　A329　1000sh Sheet of 4,
　　　　　#a-d　　　　　3.75　3.75

Miniature Sheet

Pres. Abraham Lincoln (1809-65) — A330

No. 1899 — Photographs of Lincoln taken in: a, 1857 (wearing vest). b, 1864. c, 1863. d, 1857 (without vest).

2009, Apr. 10　　　　　Perf. 13¼
1899　A330　2000sh Sheet of 4,
　　　　　#a-d　　　　　7.50　7.50

Miniature Sheet

Inauguration of US Pres. Barack Obama — A331

No. 1900: a, Pres. Obama and wife, Michelle, balustrade over heads. b, Pres. Obama with blue striped tie, window at left. c, Pres. Obama with red and gold tie, balustrade above head. d, As "b," window above head. e, As "c," White House portico lamp above head. f, As "a," windows over heads.

2009, Apr. 10　　　Perf. 11½x11¼
1900　A331　2000sh Sheet of 6,
　　　　　#a-f　　　　11.00　11.00

Miniature Sheets

A332

Michael Jackson (1958-2009), Singer — A333

No. 1901: a, Wearing tan jacket, no microphone shown. b, Wearing blue and white shirt, no microphone shown. c, Wearing blue jacket, with microphone. d, Wearing tan jacket, with microphone.
No. 1902: a, Facing right, microphone at mouth. b, Holding microphone on stand. c, Behind microphone on stand. d, Facing left, microphone at mouth.

2009　　　　　Perf. 13¼x13
1901　A332　2000sh Sheet of 4,
　　　　　#a-d　　　　　8.50　8.50
1902　A333　2000sh Sheet of 4,
　　　　　#a-d　　　　　8.50　8.50

The printer of Nos. 1901-1902 claims the stamps were issued June 25, the day Michael Jackson died. The editors doubt this claim.

Chinese Aviation, Cent. — A334

No. 1903: a, Q-5. b, Q-5C. c, JH-7A. d, JH-7 on ground. 4000sh, JH-7 in flight.

2009, Nov. 12　　　　　Perf. 14¼
1903　A334　2000sh Sheet of 4,
　　　　　#a-d　　　　　8.50　8.50
Souvenir Sheet
1904　A334　4000sh multi　　4.25　4.25
Aeropex 2009, Beijing. No. 1903 contains four 42x33mm stamps.

Miniature Sheet

Princess Diana (1961-97) — A335

No. 1905 — Princess Diana: a, Wearing black and white hat. b, Wearing pink hat. c, Wearing white blouse. d, Holding flowers.

2010, Feb. 15　　　　　Perf. 11½
1905　A335　2000sh Sheet of 4,
　　　　　#a-d　　　　　8.00　8.00

Miniature Sheet

Pope John Paul II (1920-2005) — A336

No. 1906 — Pope John Paul II: a, 400sh, Greeting crowd. b, 1600sh, With arms raised. c, 2000sh, Standing in front of painting. d, 4000sh, With hand on chest.

2010, June 24
1906　A336　　Sheet of 4, #a-d　7.25　7.25

Souvenir Sheet

Boy Scouts of America, Cent. — A337

No. 1907 — Emblem of: a, National Scout Jamboree. b, Philmont Scout Ranch, Cimarron, New Mexico. c, Florida High Adventure Sea Base.

2010, Oct. 14　　　　　Perf. 13½
1907　A337　3000sh Sheet of 3,
　　　　　#a-c　　　　　8.00　8.00

Miniature Sheets

A338

Pope Benedict XVI — A339

No. 1908 — Various photographs of Pope Benedict XVI with denomination at upper right: a, 400sh. b, 1600sh. c, 2000sh. d, 4000sh.
No. 1909 — Various photographs of Pope Benedict XVI with denomination at upper left: a, 400sh. b, 1600sh. c, 2000sh. d, 4000sh.

2011, Feb. 25   **Perf. 12**
1908   A338   Sheet of 4, #a-d   6.75   6.75
1909   A339   Sheet of 4, #a-d   6.75   6.75

Miniature Sheets

2010 World Cup Soccer Championships, South Africa — A340

No. 1910 — Team from: a, 400sh, Algeria. b, 400sh, South Africa. c, 1600sh, Ghana. d, 1600sh, Nigeria. e, 3000sh, Ivory Coast. f, 3000sh, Cameroun.
No. 1911 — Team from: a, 900sh, Italy. b, 900sh, Brazil. c, 1100sh, Japan. d, 1100sh, New Zealand. e, 4000sh, Australia. f, 4000sh, United States.

2011, Feb. 25   **Litho.**   **Perf. 12**
Sheets of 6, #a-f
1910-1911   A340   Set of 2   18.50   18.50

Disease Prevention A341

Inscriptions: 400sh, Treat livestock against nagana. 900sh, Treat humans against sleeping sickness, horiz. 1600sh, War against tsetse flies in Uganda, horiz. 3000sh, Empower communities against trypanosomiasis, horiz.

2011, Jan. 18   **Perf. 13x13½, 13½x13**
1912-1915   A341   Set of 4   5.25   5.25

Souvenir Sheet

New Year 2011 (Year of the Rabbit) — A342

No. 1916: a, Rabbit standing on hind legs. b, Rabbit leaping.

2011, Feb. 1   **Perf. 12**
1916   A342   2000sh   Sheet of 2, #a-b   3.50   3.50

Wedding of Prince William and Catherine Middleton — A343

No. 1917 — Stamps with blue panels: a, 600sh, Bride standing. b, 2500sh, Couple.
No. 1918 — Stamps with red panels: a, 600sh, Bride in coach. b, 2500sh, Couple waving.

2011, Apr. 29   **Perf. 13¼x13**
Pairs, #a-b
1917-1918   A343   Set of 2   5.25   5.25

Nos. 1917-1918 each were printed in sheets containing two pairs. Nos. 1917-1918 could not have been issued on the stated day of issue, as the stamps show photographs of the wedding that day.

A344

A345

A346

A347

A348

A349

A350

A351

A352

A353

A354

A355

A356

A357

A358

A359

A360

A361

A362

Gorillas A363

2011, June 18   **Perf. 14½**
1919   Block of 10   3.00   3.00
  a.   A344 400sh multi   .30   .30
  b.   A345 400sh multi   .30   .30
  c.   A346 400sh multi   .30   .30
  d.   A347 400sh multi   .30   .30
  e.   A348 400sh multi   .30   .30
  f.   A349 400sh multi   .30   .30
  g.   A350 400sh multi   .30   .30
  h.   A351 400sh multi   .30   .30
  i.   A352 400sh multi   .30   .30
  j.   A352 400sh multi   .30   .30
1920   Vert. strip of 5   4.00   4.00
  a.   A354 1000sh multi   .80   .80
  b.   A355 1000sh multi   .80   .80
  c.   A356 1000sh multi   .80   .80
  d.   A357 1000sh multi   .80   .80
  e.   A358 1000sh multi   .80   .80
1921   Vert. strip of 5   6.25   6.25
  a.   A359 1600sh multi   1.25   1.25
  b.   A360 1600sh multi   1.25   1.25
  c.   A361 1600sh multi   1.25   1.25
  d.   A362 1600sh multi   1.25   1.25
  e.   A363 1600sh multi   1.25   1.25
   Nos. 1919-1921 (3)   13.25   13.25

Pan-African Postal Union, 30th anniv. (in 2010).

AIDS Prevention
A364

Emblems and: 700sh, Philly Bongoley Lutaaya (1951-89), musician. 1500sh, Man and woman receiving information about AIDS at clinic, horiz. 1800sh, Medical workers in laboratory, horiz. 1900sh, People holding candles, horiz. 2700sh, AIDS ribbon within frame with simulated perforations and cancel. 3400sh, Family at home, horiz.

Perf. 13¼x13, 13x13¼

2012, Mar. 29   **Litho.**
1922-1927 A364   Set of 6   9.75   9.75
Discovery of human immunodeficiency virus, 30th anniv.

Wildlife — A365

No. 1928 — Primates: a, 3400sh, De Brazza's monkey. b, 3400sh, Brown greater galago. c, 4100sh, Patas monkey. d, 4100sh, L'Hoest's monkey.
No. 1929 — Wildcats: a, 3400sh, Cheetah chasing Thomson's gazelle. b, 3400sh, Lions. c, 4100sh, Leopards. d, 4100sh, Caracals.
No. 1930 — Two African bush elephants: a, 3400sh, Elephant at right facing left. b, 3400sh, Elephant at right facing forward. c, 4100sh, Elephant at right facing left. d, 4100sh, Elephant at right facing forward.
No. 1931 — Owls: a, 3400sh, Pel's fishing owls. b, 3400sh, African wood owls. c, 4100sh, Spotted eagle-owls. d, 4100sh, Cape eagle-owls.
No. 1932 — Kingfishers: a, 3400sh, Pied kingfisher. b, 3400sh, Gray-headed kingfishers. c, 4100sh, Malachite kingfishers. d, 4100sh, Malachite kingfisher, Pied kingfisher.
No. 1933 — Birds of prey: a, 3400sh, Tawny eagle. b, 3400sh, Bateleurs. c, 4100sh, Osprey. d, 4100sh, Rüppell's vulture.
No. 1934 — Butterflies: a, 3400sh, Silverbarred charaxes. b, 3400sh, Green-banded swallowtail. c, 4100sh, Crossley's forest queen. d, 4100sh, Acraea swordtail.
No. 1935 — Fish: a, 3400sh, Haplochromis katonga. b, 3400sh, Haplochromis nyererei. c, 4100sh, Lates niloticus. d, 4100sh, Mormyrus macrocephalus.
No. 1936 — Reptiles: a, 3400sh, Graceful chameleon. b, 3400sh, Leopard tortoise. c, 4100sh, Gaboon viper. d, 4100sh, Nile crocodile.
No. 1937 — Endangered species: a, 3400sh, Beaudoin's snake eagles. b, 3400sh, African golden cats. c, 4100sh, Cheetahs. d, 4100sh, Checkered elephant shrews.
No. 1938, 8300sh, Blue monkeys. No. 1939, 8300sh, Leopards, diff. No. 1940, 8300sh, Two African bush elephants, diff. No. 1941, 8300sh, Verreaux's eagle-owl. No. 1942, 8300sh, Gray-headed kingfishers, diff. No. 1943, 8300sh, Western marsh harriers. No. 1944, 8300sh, Two Precis octavia. No. 1945, 8300sh, Haplochromis petronius. No. 1946, 8300sh, Gaboon viper, diff. No. 1947, 8300sh, Black-crowned crane.

2012, Mar. 30   **Litho.**   **Perf. 13¼**
Sheets of 4, #a-d
1928-1937 A365   Set of 10   120.00 120.00
Souvenir Sheets
1938-1947 A365   Set of 10   62.50 62.50

Miniature Sheets

A366

Chimpanzees — A367

Various photographs of chimpanzees, as shown.

2012, Apr. 11   **Litho.**   **Perf. 12**
1948 A366 3500sh Sheet of 4,
      #a-d   11.50 11.50
1949 A367 3500sh Sheet of 4,
      #a-d   11.50 11.50

Orchids — A368

No. 1950: a, Aerangis arachnopus. b, Angraecum leonis. c, Bulbophyllum calyptratum. d, Brachycorythis macrantha.
10,000sh, Bulbophyllum sandersonii, vert.

2012, Apr. 11   **Litho.**   **Perf. 12**
1950 A368 3500sh Sheet of
     4, #a-d   11.50 11.50
Souvenir Sheet
Perf. 12½
1951 A368 10,000sh multi   8.25 8.25
No. 1951 contains one 38x51mm stamp.

Endangered Animals — A369

No. 1952: a, Addax. b, Cheetah. c, Western lowland gorilla. d, Mountain zebra. e, Dama gazelle.
10,000sh, Ostrich.

2012, Apr. 11   **Litho.**   **Perf. 14**
1952 A369 3000sh Sheet of
     5, #a-e   12.50 12.50
Souvenir Sheet
Perf. 12½
1953 A369 10,000sh multi   8.25 8.25
No. 1953 contains one 51x38mm stamp.

Mushrooms — A370

No. 1954: a, Panther cap. b, Death cap. c, Blusher. d, Penny bun. e, Saffron milk cap. f, Yellow morel.
No. 1955: a, Amethyst deceiver. b, Mica cap.

Perf. 13 Syncopated
2012, Apr. 11   **Litho.**
1954 A370 3000sh Sheet of 6,
      #a-f   15.00 15.00
Souvenir Sheet
1955 A370 5000sh Sheet of 2,
      #a-b   8.25 8.25

Sinking of the Titanic, Cent. — A371

No. 1956: a, Titanic under construction. b, Stern of Titanic. c, Table and chairs. d, Deck. e, Bow of Titanic. f, Lifeboats.
10,000d, Titanic, diff.

Perf. 13 Syncopated
2012, Apr. 11   **Litho.**
1956 A371 3000sh Sheet of
     6, #a-f   15.00 15.00
Souvenir Sheet
1957 A371 10,000sh multi   8.25 8.25

American Civil War, 150th Anniv. — A372

No. 1958 — Abraham Lincoln and detail from Battle of Chattanooga print published by Kurz and Allison: a, Red panel at top. b, White panel at top, no flag. c, Blue panel at top. d, White panel at top, flag visible.
10,000sh, Lincoln, Battle of Spotsylvania print by Kurz and Allison.

Perf. 13 Syncopated
2012, Apr. 11   **Litho.**
1958 A372 3500sh Sheet of
     4, #a-d   11.50 11.50
Souvenir Sheet
1959 A372 10,000sh multi   8.25 8.25

Inauguration of Pres. John F. Kennedy, 50th Anniv. (in 2011) — A373

No. 1960 Pres. Kennedy: a, With Vice President Lyndon B. Johnson. b, With wife, Jacqueline. c, Taking oath of office. d, Delivering inaugural speech.
10,000sh, Pres. Kennedy speaking, vert.

2012, Apr. 11   **Litho.**   **Perf. 12**
1960 A373 3500sh Sheet of
     4, #a-d   11.50 11.50
Souvenir Sheet
1961 A373 10,000sh multi   8.25 8.25

Princess Diana (1961-97) — A374

No. 1962 — Princess Diana: a, Holding flowers. b, Wearing hat. c, Without hat.
10,000sh, Princess Diana wearing hat, diff.

Perf. 13 Syncopated
2012, Apr. 11   **Litho.**
1962 A374 3500sh Sheet of 3,
      #a-c   8.50 8.50
Souvenir Sheet
Perf. 12
1963 A374 10,000sh multi   8.25 8.25
No. 1963 contains one 30x50mm stamp.

Paintings by Peter Paul Rubens (1577-1640) — A375

No. 1964: a, 3400sh, The Deposition. b, 3400sh, The Martyrdom of St. Stephen. c, 4100sh, The Last Judgment. d, 4100sh, Christ and Mary Magdalene.
8300sh, Christ at Simon the Pharisee, horiz.

2012, July 26   **Litho.**   **Perf. 13¼**
1964 A375   Sheet of 4, #a-d   12.00 12.00
     Souvenir Sheet
1965 A375 8300sh multi   6.75 6.75

Yuri Gagarin (1934-68), First Man in Space — A376

No. 1966: a, 3400sh, Gagarin, Vostok 1 in orbit. b, 3400sh, Gagarin, MiG-15. c, 4100sh, Monuments to Gagarin. d, 4100sh, Gagarin in helmet, launch of Vostok 1.
8300sh, Gagarin, launch of Vostok 1, diff.

2012, July 26   **Litho.**   **Perf. 13¼**
1966 A376   Sheet of 4, #a-d   12.00 12.00
     Souvenir Sheet
1967 A376 8300sh multi   6.75 6.75

Chess Match Between Deep Blue Computer and Garry Kasparov, 15th Anniv. — A377

No. 1968: a, 3400sh, Kasparov standing at right, television screens at left. b, 3400sh, Kasparov and flags. c, 4100sh, Kasparov seated, computer display of chess board. d, 4100sh, Kasparov seated, television screens at left.
8300sh, Kasparov, chess board, arm of human and mechanical arm wrestling.

2012, July 26   **Litho.**   **Perf. 13¼**
1968 A377   Sheet of 4, #a-d   12.00 12.00
     Souvenir Sheet
1969 A377 8300sh multi   6.75 6.75

Whitney Houston (1963-2012), Singer — A378

No. 1970 — Two images of Houston with larger image of Houston (without microphone) with: a, 3400sh, Hand on cheek. b, 3400sh, Eyes shut. c, 4100sh, Strapless gown. d, 4100sh, Dress with zipper, with hand touching side of head.
8300sh, Houston, diff.

2012, July 26   **Litho.**   **Perf. 13¼**
1970 A378   Sheet of 4, #a-d   12.00 12.00
     Souvenir Sheet
1971 A378 8300sh multi   6.75 6.75

Elvis Presley (1935-77) — A379

No. 1972 — Presley with: a, 3400sh, Wife, Priscilla, and Tom Jones. b, 3400sh, Ann-Margret. c, 4100sh, Sophia Loren. d, 4100sh, Lou Costello and Jane Russell.
8300sh, Presley with Muhammad Ali.

2012, July 26   **Litho.**   **Perf. 13¼**
1972 A379   Sheet of 4, #a-d   12.00 12.00
     Souvenir Sheet
1973 A379 8300sh multi   6.75 6.75

Elvis Presley (1935-77) — A380

No. 1974 — Presley with guitar, with frame color of: a, Dark blue green. b, Light blue green. c, Blue green.
10,000sh, Presley holding microphone.

2012, July 26   **Litho.**   **Perf. 12**
1974 A380   3500sh Sheet of 4, #1974a, 1974b, 2 #1974c   11.50 11.50
     Souvenir Sheet
1975 A380 10,000sh multi   8.00 8.00

Olympic Rings and Stylized Torch — A381

Stadia for the 2012 Summer Olympics, London A382

No. 1977: a, Olympic Stadium. b, Wembley Stadium. c, Old Trafford Stadium.

2012, Aug. 3   **Litho.**   **Perf. 13¼x13**
1976 A381 1500sh multi   1.25 1.25
     Perf. 13¼
1977   Vert. strip of 3   2.60 2.60
   a.-c. A382 1050sh Any single   .85 .85

Independence, 50th Anniv. — A383

Designs: 700sh, 50th anniv. emblem. 1800sh, Independence Monument. 2700sh, Flag of Uganda.

2012, Oct. 9   **Litho.**   **Perf. 14**
1978-1980 A383   Set of 3   4.00 4.00

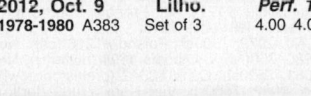

Transportation — A385

No. 1983 — Sailboats, with inscriptions: a, 3400sh, "2010 Extreme Sailing Series, skipper of The Wave, Muscat." b, 3400sh, "McDougall at PUMA Moth Worlds, 2010." c, 4100sh, "Tom Slingsby, ISAF World Sailor of the Year, 2010." d, 4100sh, "Bahrain Pindar Team, Langenargen, World Match Racing Tour 2009."
No. 1984 — Steam trains: a, 3400sh, Tornado 60163. b, 3400sh, Furness Railway No. 20. c, 4100sh, Terrier 32662. d, 4100sh, Brighton Works DS 377.
No. 1985 — High-speed trains: a, 3400sh, Transrapid TR-09, "2012" at LL. b, 3400sh, Transrapid TR-09, "2012" at UR. c, 4100sh, CR380A, black denomination at LL. d, 4100sh, CR380A, white denomination at UR.
No. 1986 — Airplanes: a, 3400sh, Airbus A380. b, 3400sh, Boeing 747-8. c, 4100sh, Aerospatiale BAC Concorde. d, 4100sh, Boeing 777-300.
No. 1987 — Airships: a, 3400sh, LZ-127. b, 3400sh, Hindenburg (LZ-129). c, 4100sh, USS Macon (ZRS-5). d, 4100sh, LZ-17 Sachsen.
No. 1988 — Formula 1 race cars and drivers: a, 3400sh, McLaren-Mercedes car, Lewis Hamilton. b, 3400sh, Lotus-Renault car, Kimi Räikkönen. c, 4100sh, Mercedes car, Michael Schumacher. d, 4100sh, Red Bull Racing-Renault car, Sebastian Vettel.
No. 1989 — Motorcycles: a, 3400sh, Kawasaki VERSYS 650. b, 3400sh, Ferrari V4 Superbike Concept. c, 4100sh, Honda V4 Concept. d, 4100sh, Yamaha YZF R1 1000.
No. 1990 — Unmotorized vehicles: a, 3400sh, Horse and cart. b, 3400sh, Paddleboat. c, 4100sh, Velomobile. d, 4100sh, Skateboard.
No. 1991 — Special transport vehicles: a, 3400sh, 1964 Ford F-600 Young fire truck. b, 3400sh, 1975 Plymouth Grand Fury and 1999 Ford Crown Victoria police cars, 1970 Harley-Davidson FLH police motorcycle. c, 4100sh, 1968 Citroen DS and 2008 Ford E450 Horton Type III ambulances. d, 4100sh, 2010 Ford F550 Gurkha MAPV police vehicle, 1970 Harley-Davidson FLH police motorcycle.
No. 1992 — Futuristic concept cars: a, 3400sh, Audi A9 concept car. b, 3400sh, Pougeot Touch concept car. c, 4100sh, Lotus Esquive concept car. d, 4100sh, Honda 3R-C concept car.
No. 1993, 8300sh, Extreme Sailing Series, Boston, 2011. No. 1994, 8300sh, Brighton Blue Bell steam train, clock. No. 1995, 8300sh, Bombardier Zefiro 380. No. 1996, 8300sh, Boeing 747-8, diff. No. 1997, 8300sh, Hindenburg (LZ-129), diff. No. 1008, 8300sh, Ferrari car, Fernando Alonso. No. 1999, 8300sh, Suzuki Biplane concept motorcycle. No. 2000, 8300sh, Hang glider. No. 2001, 8300sh, 1949 Mack L Model fire trucks. No. 2002, 8300sh, Lotus Hot Wheels concept car.

2012, Oct. 22   **Litho.**   **Perf. 13¼**
     Sheets of 4, #a-d
1983-1992 A385   Set of 10   120.00 120.00
     Souvenir Sheets
1993-2002 A385   Set of 10   65.00 65.00

Endangered Animals — A386

No. 2003 — Chimpanzees: a, 3400sh, Adult and juvenile. b, 3400sh, Adult. c, 4100sh, Adult, diff. d, 4100sh, Adult on tree branch.
No. 2004 — Gorillas: a, 3400sh, Two adult Gorilla gorilla facing right, denomination at top center. b, 3400sh, Gorilla gorilla and Gorilla beringei facing left, denomination at UL. c, 4100sh, Gorilla gorilla and Gorilla beringei. d, 4100sh, Two adult Gorilla beringei beringei and juvenile.
No. 2005 — Lions: a, 3400sh, Female on rock. b, 3400sh, Male and female, animal name at UR. c, 4100sh, Female stalking. d, 4100sh, Male.
No. 2006 — Lions: a, 3400sh, Head of male, female looking left, animal name at top center. b, 3400sh, Two males and one female. c, 4100sh, Female and cub. d, 4100sh, Female and head of cub.
No. 2007 — Cheetahs: a, 3400sh, Running left. b, 3400sh, Standing. c, 4100sh, Walking right. d, 4100sh, Resting.
No. 2008 — Elephants: a, 3400sh, Two animals, animal name above country name. b, 3400sh, Two animals, front animal facing left, animal name at UL. c, 4100sh, Four animals, animal name at UL. d, 4100sh, Two animals, animal name above country name.
No. 2009 — Elephants: a, 3400sh, One animal. b, 3400sh, Two animals walking side-by-side, animal name at UL. c, 4100sh, Adult and juvenile. d, 4100sh, One animal.
No. 2010 — Birds of prey: a, 3400sh, Neophron percnopterus in flight. b, 3400sh, Gyps rueppellii on branch. c, 4100sh, Gyps rueppellii facing right. d, 4100sh, Neophron percnopterus on rock.
No. 2011 — Secretary bird: a, 3400sh, Facing right, in flight. b, 3400sh, Facing left, in flight. c, 4100sh, Head of bird facing right and bird facing left. d, 4100sh, Two birds facing left.
No. 2012, 8300sh, Pan troglodytes (chimpanzee). No. 2013, 8300sh, Gorilla beringei beringei (gorilla). No. 2014, 8300sh, Male and female Panthera leo (lions). No. 2015, 8300sh, Male Panthera leo (lion). No. 2016, 8300sh, Acinonyx jubatus (cheetah). No. 2017, 8300sh, One Loxodonta africana (elephant). No. 2018, 8300sh, Three Loxodonta africana (elephants). No. 2019, 8300sh, Gyps rueppelli (bird of prey), diff. No. 2020, 8300sh, Two Sagittarius serpentarius facing left (secretrary bird).

2012, Nov. 8   **Litho.**   **Perf. 13¼**
     Sheets of 4, #a-d
2003-2011 A386   Set of 9   100.00 100.00
     Souvenir Sheets
2012-2020 A386   Set of 9   55.00 55.00
Compare No. 2020 with No. 2022.

A387

A388

A389

Worldwide Fund for Nature (WWF) A390

Secretary Bird — A391

2012, Nov. 8   Litho.   Perf. 13x13¼

2021		Horiz. strip of 4	12.00	12.00
a.	A387	4100sh multi	3.00	3.00
b.	A388	4100sh multi	3.00	3.00
c.	A389	4100sh multi	3.00	3.00
d.	A390	4100sh multi	3.00	3.00
e.		Souvenir sheet of 4, #2021a-2021d	12.00	12.00
f.		Souvenir sheet of 8, 2 each #2021a-2021d	24.00	24.00

Souvenir Sheet
Perf. 12¾x13¼

2022	A391	8300sh multi	6.25	6.25

Compare No. 2022 with No. 2020.

Endangered Animals — A392

No. 2023 — Birds and their eggs: a, 1000sh, Rynchops flavirostris. b, 4000sh, Neophron percnopterus. c, 7500sh, Haematopus moquini. d, 7500sh, Psittacus erithacus.

No. 2024 — Turtles: a, 1000sh, Aldabrachelys gigantea. b, 4000sh, Kinixys homeana. c, 7500sh, Testudo kleinmanni. d, 7500sh, Malacochersus tornieri.

No. 2025 — Dolphins: a, 1800sh, Orcaella brevirostris. b, 1800sh, Sousa chinensis. c, 7500sh, Lipotes vexillifer. d, 7500sh, Tursiops truncatus ponticus.

No. 2026 — Fish: a, 1800sh, Thunnus maccoyii. b, 1800sh, Schilbe mystus. c, 7500sh, Cheilinus undulatus. d, 7500sh, Oxynotus centrina.

No. 2027 — Butterflies: a, 1800sh, Apodemia mormo langei. b, 1800sh, Heraclides aristodemus ponceanus. c, 7500sh, Lycaeides melissa samuelis. d, 7500sh, Speyeria zerene behrensii.

No. 2028 — Reptiles: a, 1800sh, Osteolaemus tetraspis. b, 1800sh, Cordylus cataphractus. c, 7500sh, Crocodylus cataphractus. d, 7500sh, Acanthodactylus pardalis.

No. 2029, 4000sh — Hippopotami: a, Adult and juvenile Choeropsis liberiensis. b, Hippopotamus amphibius on land. c, Hippopotamus amphibius in water. d, Adult Choeropsis liberiensis with open mouth.

No. 2030, 4000sh — Wildcats: a, Prionailurus rubiginosus. b, Uncia uncia. c, Oreailurus jacobitus. d, Prionailurus viverrinus.

No. 2031, 4000sh — Lycaon pictus: a, Head of dog and two dogs standing. b, Dog and tree. c, Two dogs standing. d, Two dogs resting.

No. 2032, 4000sh — Predators: a, Gymnogyps californianus. b, Canis simensis. c, Alligator sinensis. d, Panthera pardus orientalis.

No. 2033, 7500sh, Struthio camelus and egg. No. 2034, 7500sh, Pyxis arachnoides. No. 2035, 7500sh, Platanista gangetica. No. 2036, 7500sh, Squatina squatina. No. 2037, 7500sh, Icaricia icarioides missionensis. No. 2038, 7500sh, Furcifer labordi. No. 2039, 7500sh, Hippopotamus amphibius on land, diff. No. 2040, 7500sh, Panthera tigris. No. 2041, 7500sh, Lycaon pictus, diff. No. 2042, 7500sh, Cuon alpinus.

2013, July 8   Litho.   Perf. 13¼
Sheets of 4, #a-d

2023-2032	A392	Set of 10	140.00	140.00

Souvenir Sheets

2033-2042	A392	Set of 10	60.00	60.00

Famous People of African Heritage — A393

No. 2043 — Civil rights leaders and activists: a, 1000sh, Malcolm X and Dr. Martin Luther King, Jr. b, 4000sh, Asa Philip Randolph. c, 7500sh, Nelson Mandela and Bill Sutherland. d, 7500sh, Sojourner Truth with Abraham Lincoln.

No. 2044 — Nobel laureates: a, 1000sh, Kofi Annan, 2001 Peace laureate. b, 4000sh, Desmond Tutu, 1984 Peace laureate. c, 7500sh, Wole Soyinka, 1986 Literature laureate, and short-eared owl. d, 7500sh, Wangari Maathai, 2004 Peace laureate.

No. 2045 — Olympic champions: a, 1000sh, Jesse Owens. b, 4000sh, Abebe Bikila. c, 7500sh, Maria Mutola. d, 7500sh, Derartu Tulu.

No. 2046 — Boxing champions: a, 1000sh, Joe Frazier and Muhammad Ali. b, 4000sh, Joe Louis. c, 7500sh, George Foreman and Shannon Briggs. d, 7500sh, Mike Tyson and Evander Holyfield.

No. 2047 — Tennis players: a, 1000sh, Serena Williams. b, 4000sh, Venus Williams. c, 7500sh, Venus Williams and trophy. d, 7500sh, Serena Williams and trophy.

No. 2048 — Baseball players: a, 1800sh, Willie Mays. b, 1800sh, Dan Bankhead. c, 7500sh, Satchel Paige. d, 7500sh, Larry Doby.

No. 2049 — Basketball players: a, 1800sh, Scottie Pippen and Michael Jordan. b, 1800sh, Earvin "Magic" Johnson. c, 7500sh, Charles Barkley. d, 7500sh, Karl Malone.

No. 2050 — Soccer players: a, 1800sh, Roger Milla. b, 1800sh, Nwankwo Kanu. c, 7500sh, Abedi Pele. d, 7500sh, Samuel Eto'o.

No. 2051 — Entertainers: a, 1800sh, Morgan Freeman. b, 1800sh, Denzel Washington. c, 7500sh, Eddie Murphy. d, 7500sh, Oprah Winfrey with Pres. Barack Obama and wife, Michelle.

No. 2052 — Paintings of Henry Ossawa Tanner (1859-1937): a, 1800sh, The Annunciation. b, 1800sh, Mary. c, 7500sh, The Banjo Lesson. d, 7500sh, Spinning by Firelight.

No. 2053, 7500sh, Dr. Martin Luther King, Jr. No. 2054, 7500sh, Pres. Barack Obama. No. 2055, 7500sh, Stephen Kiprotich. No. 2056, 7500sh, Floyd Patterson and Muhammad Ali. No. 2057, 7500sh, Serena and Venus Williams. No. 2058, 7500sh, Jackie Robinson. No. 2059, 7500sh, Michael Jordan. No. 2060, 7500sh, Didier Drogba. No. 2061, 7500sh, Will Smith. No. 2062, 7500sh, Portrait of the Artist's Wife, by Tanner.

2013, July 8   Litho.   Perf. 13¼
Sheets of 4, #a-d

2043-2052	A393	Set of 10	150.00	150.00

Souvenir Sheets

2053-2062	A393	Set of 10	60.00	60.00

Dogs — A394

No. 2063, 3000sh: a, Coton de Tulear. b, Rhodesian ridgeback. c, Catahoula cur. d, Walker coonhound.

No. 2064, 3000sh: a, English mastiff. b, Basenji. c, Boerboel. d, Boxer.

No. 2065, 8800sh, Afghan hound, vert. No. 2066, 8800sh, German shepherd, vert.

2013, Sept. 7   Litho.   Perf. 13¾
Sheets of 4, #a-d

2063-2064	A394	Set of 2	19.00	19.00

Souvenir Sheets
Perf. 12½

2065-2066	A394	Set of 2	14.00	14.00

Nos. 2065-2066 each contain one 38x51mm stamp.

Stephen Kiprotich, 2012 Olympic Gold Medalist in Marathon — A395

Kiprotich: 700sh, Running. 1900sh, Holding Ugandan flag approaching finish line. 2700sh, Holding Ugandan flag, horiz. 3400sh, On knees, horiz.

2013, Nov. 25   Litho.   Perf. 13

2067-2070	A395	Set of 4	7.00	7.00

Stamps on Stamps — A396

No. 2071, 2500sh — Stamps depicting cats: a, Azerbaijan #533. b, Czech Republic #3078. c, People's Republic of China #1853. d, France #3203.

No. 2072, 2500sh — Stamps depicting butterflies: a, Viet Nam #1310. b, Laos #692. c, Hungary #2314. d, Nicaragua #1570.

No. 2073, 2500sh — Stamps depicting owls: a, Hungary #C228. b, France #1338. c, Republic of China #4053. d, Zimbabwe #544.

No. 2074, 2500sh — Stamps depicting turtles: a, New Zealand #1698. b, Unauthorized Benin sticker. c, Tanzania #1128. d, Viet Nam #1968.

No. 2075, 2500sh — Stamps depicting dinosaurs: a, Tanzania #1220. b, Australia #1344. c, Marshall Islands #925i. d, New Zealand #1183.

No. 2076, 2500sh — Stamps depicting Worldwide Fund for Nature emblem: a, Central Africa #325. b, Algeria #875. c, Aruba #104. d, Indonesia #1383.

No. 2077, 2500sh — Stamps depicting orchids: a, Cuba #2328. b, Cambodia #1893. c, Virgin Islands #704. d, Liechtenstein #467.

No. 2078, 2500sh — Stamps depicting minerals: a, Azerbaijan #420. b, Togo #1857. c, Cambodia #1777. d, French Southern & Antarctic Territories #315.

No. 2079, 7500sh, Poland #1216 (cat). No. 2080, 7500sh, Cambodia #694 (butterfly). No. 2081, 7500sh, Cuba #2542 (prehistoric owl). No. 2082, 7500sh, Viet Nam #1969 (turtle). No. 2083, 7500sh, Mali #505 (dinosaur). No. 2084, 7500sh, Viet Nam #2281 (Worldwide Fund for Nature). No. 2085, 7500sh, Equatorial Guinea sticker (orchid). No. 2086, 7500sh, North Korea #3455 (minerals).

2013, Nov. 25   Litho.   Perf. 13¼
Sheets of 4, #a-d

2071-2078	A396	Set of 8	65.00	65.00

Souvenir Sheets

2079-2086	A396	Set of 8	50.00	50.00

Miniature Sheet

Brazilian Animals — A397

No. 2087: a, Tufted capuchin monkey. b, Tayra eira barara. c, Brazilian tapir. d, Jaguar.

2013, Dec. 31   Litho.   Perf. 14

2087	A397	3000sh Sheet of 4, #a-d	9.50	9.50

Brasiliana 2013 World Philatelic Exhibition, Rio de Janeiro.

Miniature Sheet

Mao Zedong (1893-1976), Chinese Communist Leader — A398

No. 2088 — Photographs of: a, Mao, 1938. b, Mao, 1948. c, Mao, 1954. d, Mao, 1961. e, Mao, undated. f, Great Wall of China.

2013, Dec. 31   Litho.   Perf. 14

2088	A398	500sh Sheet of 6, #a-f	2.40	2.40

Birth of Prince George of Cambridge — A399

No. 2089: a, Duchess of Cambridge. b, Duke and Duchess of Cambridge, Prince George. c, Prince George. d, Duke of Cambridge.

8800sh, Duke and Duchess of Cambridge, Prince George, vert.

2013, Dec. 31   Litho.   Perf. 14

2089	A399	3000sh Sheet of 4, #a-d	9.50	9.50

Souvenir Sheet
Perf. 12½

2090 A399 8800sh multi   7.00 7.00

No. 2090 contains one 38x51mm stamp.

Awarding of Nobel Peace Prize to
Nelson Mandela, 20th Anniv. — A400

No. 2091 — Color of image of Mandela at
left: a, Olive brown. b, Red brown. c, Green. d,
Blue.
8800sh, Mandela at awards ceremony.

2013, Dec. 31   Litho.   *Perf. 14*
2091 A400 3000sh Sheet of 4,
     #a-d   9.50 9.50

Souvenir Sheet
2092 A400 8800sh multi   7.00 7.00

Miniature Sheets

A401

Nelson Mandela (1918-2013),
President of South Africa — A402

No. 2093: a, Color photograph of Mandela
waving. b, Color photograph of Mandela's
face. c, Mandela behind microphones. d, Per-
son holding newspaper with story on
Mandela's release from prison.
No. 2094: a, Black-and-white photograph of
Mandela waving. b, Color photograph of
Mandela waving, diff. c, Black-and-white pho-
tograph of Mandela and other people. d,
Mandela holding candle.

2013, Dec. 31   Litho.   *Perf. 13¾*
2093 A401 4400sh Sheet of 4,
     #a-d   14.00 14.00
2094 A402 4400sh Sheet of 4,
     #a-d   14.00 14.00

Sikhs in Uganda, Cent. — A403

Designs: 700sh, Khanda (Sikh symbol).
1100sh, Nishan Sahib (Sikh flag). 2700sh,
Golden Temple, Amritsar, India. 3400sh, Sikh
Temple, Kampala.

2014, Jan. 17   Litho.   *Perf. 12¾*
2095-2098 A403   Set of 4   6.50 6.50

A404

A405

New Year 2014 (Year of the
Horse) — A406

No. 2101 — Horse and Chinese character
for "horse" with background color of: a, Dull
yellow green ("Year of the Horse" at LL). b,
Orange. c, Pink. d, Red brown. e, Lilac. f, Dull
green ("Year of the Horse" at UR).
8800sh, Horse, vert.

2014, Apr. 1   Litho.   *Perf. 13¾*
2099 A404 1300sh multi   1.00 1.00
2100 A405 1300sh multi   1.00 1.00

Miniature Sheet
Perf. 14
2101 A406 2250sh Sheet of 6,
     #a-f   10.50 10.50

Souvenir Sheet
Perf. 12½
2102 A406 8800sh multi   7.00 7.00

No. 2102 contains one 38x51mm stamp.

Pope Francis — A407

No. 2103 — Pope Francis: a, Holding Bible.
b, Looking down, facing right. c, Facing left,
with hand lifted. d, Holding crucifix.
8800sh, Pope Francis, diff.

2014, Apr. 1   Litho.   *Perf. 14*
2103 A407 3000sh Sheet of 4,
     #a-d   9.50 9.50

Souvenir Sheet
2104 A407 8800sh multi   7.00 7.00

African Animals — A408

No. 2105: a, Debrazza's monkey. b, Aardvark. c, African wild dog. d, Okapi.
8800sh, Antelope.

2014, Apr. 1   Litho.   *Perf. 14*
2105 A408 3000sh Sheet of 4,
     #a-d   9.50 9.50

Souvenir Sheet
Perf. 12
2106 A408 8800sh multi   7.00 7.00

Cats — A409

No. 2107: a, Bobcat. b, Caracal. c, Turkish
Van. d, Gray tabby cat.
8800sh, Calico cat, vert.

2014, Apr. 1   Litho.   *Perf. 12*
2107 A409 3000sh Sheet of 4,
     #a-d   9.50 9.50

Souvenir Sheet
Perf. 14
2108 A409 8800sh multi   7.00 7.00

Reptiles — A410

No. 2109: a, Red-headed rock agama. b,
Nile crocodile. c, African spurred tortoise. d,
Eastern green mamba.
8800sh, Cape cobra, vert.

2014, Apr. 1   Litho.   *Perf. 12*
2109 A410 3000sh Sheet of 4,
     #a-d   9.50 9.50

Souvenir Sheet
2110 A410 8800sh multi   7.00 7.00

Bird Watching — A411

No. 2111, 2500sh — Balearica regulorum:
a, Crane near water, Latin name in white at
right. b, Crane near water, Latin name in black
at left. c, Crane in nest, Latin name in white at
LL. d, Head of crane, Latin name in black at
LL.
No. 2112, 2500sh — Flamingos: a, Phoenicopterus andinus. b, Phoenicopterus roseus.
c, Phoenicopterus chilensis. d, Phoenicopterus ruber.
No. 2113, 2500sh — Falcons: a, Falco
rupicoloides. b, Falco biarmicus. c, Falco peregrinus. d, Falco naumanni.

No. 2114, 2500sh — Parrots: a, Ara
chloroptera. b, Probosciger aterrimus. c,
Cacatua galerita. d, Ara ambiguus.
No. 2115, 2500sh — Water birds: a, Larus
argentatus. b, Eudocimus ruber. c, Alcedo
atthis. d, Ardea alba.
No. 2116, 2500sh — Vultures: a, Vultur
gryphus. b, Gyps fulvus. c, Gyps coprotheres.
d, Trigonoceps occipitalis.
No. 2117, 2500sh — Hornbills: a,
Rhyticeros undulatus. b, Bucorvus
leadbeateri. c, Tropicranus albocristatus. d,
Tockus erythrorhynchus.
No. 2118, 2500sh — Eagles: a, Aquila
chrysaetos. b, Terathopius ecaudatus. c,
Haliaeetus leucocephalus. d, Harpia harpyja.
No. 2119, 2500sh — Hummingbirds: a,
Colibri thalassinus. b, Hylocharis chrysura. c,
Coeligena lutetiae. d, Colibri thalassinus in
flight.
No. 2120, 2500sh — Bee-eaters: a, Two
Merops philippinus. b, Merops apiaster. c, One
Merops philippinus. d, Merops bullockoides.
No. 2121, 7500sh, Blaearica regulorum, diff.
No. 2122, 7500sh, Phoenicopterus minor. No.
2123, 7500sh, Falco tinnunculus. No. 2124,
7500sh, Ara ararauna. No. 2125, 7500sh,
Diomedea epomophora. No. 2126, 7500sh,
Gypaetus barbatus. No. 2127, 7500sh, Tockus
leucomelas. No. 2128, 7500sh, Haliaeetus
albicilla. No. 2129, 7500sh, Archilochus alex-
andri. No. 2130, 7500sh, Merops viridis.

2014, Apr. 1   Litho.   *Perf. 13¼*
Sheets of 4, #a-d
2111-2120 A411   Set of 10   80.00 80.00
Souvenir Sheets
2121-2130 A411   Set of 10   60.00 60.00

Nos. 2121-2130 each contain one
36x51mm stamp.

Domestic Animals — A412

No. 2131, 2500sh — Apis mellifera: a, On
yellow flower, Latin name in black. b, On white
flower, Latin name in black. c, Flying below
pink flower, Latin name in white. d, On red
flower, latin name in white.
No. 2132, 2500sh — Betta splendens: a,
One fish with yellow fins. b, One fish with red
fins, facing forward, Latin name at UL. c, Two
fish. d, One fish with red fins, facing back-
wards, Latin name at UR.
No. 2133, 2500sh — Carassius auratus
auratus: a, Fish, aquarium gravel in foreground, Latin name at UL in one line. b, Fish,
Latin name at UL in two lines. c, Fish and
aquarium grass, Latin name at LL. d, Two fish,
Latin name at UR.
No. 2134, 2500sh — Cats: a, Persian. b,
Abyssinian. c, Bengal. d, Russian Blue.
No. 2135, 2500sh — Dogs: a, Papillon. b,
Yorkshire terrier. c, Jack Russell terrier. d,
Chihuahua.
No. 2136, 2500sh — Dogs: a, Elo. b, French
bulldog. c, Beagle. d, Doberman pinscher.
No. 2137, 2500sh — Equus ferus caballus:
a, White and brown horses running b, Adult
and foal running. c, Gray horse. d, Two horses
standing in field.
No. 2138, 2500sh — Canaries: a, Serinus
mozambicus, Latin name in black. b, Serinus
canaria. c, Serinus canaria domestica. d, Serinus mozambicus, Latin name in white.
No. 2139, 2500sh — Farm animals: a,
Anser anser domesticus. b, Ovis aries. c,
Oryctolagus cuniculus. d, Gallus gallus
domesticus.
No. 2140, 2500sh — Capra aegagrus
hircus: a, Goat, Latin name in black at UR on
one line. b, Goats, Latin name at UR on three
lines. c, Adult and juvenile goats, Latin name
at UL on two lines. d, Goat, Latin name at LL.
No. 2141, 7500sh, Apis mellifera and honeycomb. No. 2142, 7500sh, Betta splendens,
diff. No. 2143, 7500sh, Carassius auratus
auratus, diff. No. 2144, 7500sh, Egyptian Mau
cats. No. 2145, 7500sh, Bichon Frise. No.
2146, 7500sh, American cocker spaniel. No.
2147, 7500sh, Equus ferus caballus, diff. No.
2148, 7500sh, Serinus canaria, diff. No. 2149,
7500sh, Bos taurus. No. 2150, 7500sh, Capra
aegagrus hircus, diff.

2014, Apr. 1   Litho.   *Perf. 13¼*

Sheets of 4, #a-d

2131-2140   A412   Set of 10   80.00   80.00

Souvenir Sheets

2141-2150   A412   Set of 10   60.00   60.00

Nos. 2141-2150 each contain one 36x51mm stamp.

Hibiscus Flowers — A413

No. 2151: a, Pink Hibiscus rosa-sinensis. b, Red Hibiscus rosa-sinensis. c, Hibiscus arnottianus. d, Hibiscus clayi. e, Hibiscus kokio. f, Hibiscus splendens.

10,000sh, Hibiscus mutabilis.

2014, Dec. 1   Litho.   *Perf. 12½*

2151   A413   3200sh Sheet of 6, #a-f   14.00   14.00

Souvenir Sheet

2152   A413   10,000sh multi   7.25   7.25

Canoninzation of Ugandan Martyrs, 50th Anniv. (in 2014) — A414

Designs: 700sh, Uganda Martyrs with Bishop Leon Livinhac, 1885. 900sh, 2012 Uganda Martyrs' Day celebration. 1000sh, Uganda Martyrs' Basilica, Namugongo. 1800sh, 2010 Uganda Martyrs' Day celebration. 2000sh, St. Achilles Kiwanuka, vert. 2700sh, St. Kizito. 3200sh, Kasubi Nabulagala, 1881. 3400sh, Map of Uganda, Pope Francis, Ugandan Martyrs, Uganda Martyr's Basilica, flags of Vatican City and Uganda, vert.

No. 2161, 10,000sh, Relics of the Uganda Martyrs. No. 2162, 10,000sh, Uganda Martyrs' Shrine, Namugongo, 2014.

Perf. 13½x13, 13x13½

2015, Nov. 27   Litho.

2153-2160   A414   Set of 8   —   —

Souvenir Sheets

2161-2162   A414   Set of 2   —   —

Visit of Pope Francis to Uganda A415

Designs: 500sh, Pope Francis, Martyrs' Museum, Namugongo. 700sh, Pope Francis waving. 1000sh, Pope Francis seated, no glasses, vert. 1100sh, Pope Francis wearing miter, vert. 1800sh, Pope Francis wearing zucchetto, no glasses, vert. 1900sh, Pope Francis wearing zucchetto, wearing glasses, vert. 2700sh, Pope Francis seated, wearing glasses. 3400sh, Pope Francis waving, wearing zucchetto, vert.

No. 2171, 10,000sh, Pope Francis, Munyonyo Martyrs' Shrine. No. 2172, 10,000sh, Pope Francis, Uganda Martyrs' Shrine, Namugongo.

Perf. 13½x13, 13x13½

2015, Nov. 27   Litho.

2163-2170   A415   Set of 8   —   —

Souvenir Sheets

2171-2172   A415   Set of 2   —   —

Primates A416

Designs: 100sh, Bush baby. 500sh, Chimpanzees. 700sh, Black and white colobus. 800sh, Olive baboon. 900sh, De Brazza's monkey, vert. 1000sh, L'Hoest's monkey, vert. 1100sh, Baby mountain gorilla. 1800sh, Vervet monkey. 1900sh, Adult mountain gorilla. 2000sh, Blue monkey, vert. 2700sh, Olive baboons. 3000sh, Golden monkey. 3400sh, Chimpanzee, vert.

Perf. 13½x13, 13x13½

2017, May 5   Litho.

2173-2185   A416   Set of 13   —   —

SEMI-POSTAL STAMPS

Catalogue values for all unused stamps in this section are for never Hinged items.

PAPU (Pan African Postal Union), 18th Anniv. — SP1

No. B1, Mountain gorilla.

1998, Jan. 18   Litho.   *Perf. 14*

B1   SP1   300sh +150sh multi   1.10   1.10

POSTAGE DUE STAMPS

Catalogue values for unused stamps in this section are for Never Hinged items.

Type of Kenya, 1967

Perf. 14x13½

				Unwmk.	
1967, Jan. 3		Litho.			
J1	D1	5c red		.25	4.25
J2	D1	10c green		.25	4.25
J3	D1	20c dark blue		.25	5.50
J4	D1	30c reddish brown		.40	7.25
J5	D1	40c red lilac		.60	8.00
J6	D1	1sh orange		1.75	20.00
		Nos. J1-J6 (6)		3.50	49.25

			Perf. 14x15	
1970, Mar. 31				
J1a	D1	5c red	.25	1.25
J2a	D1	10c green	.25	1.25
J3a	D1	20c dark blue	.30	4.25
J4a	D1	30c reddish brown	.40	5.25
J5a	D1	40c red lilac	.60	6.25
		Nos. J1a-J5a (5)	1.80	18.25

			Perf. 15	
1973				
J1b	D1	5c red	.25	2.25
J2b	D1	10c green	.25	2.25
J3b	D1	20c dark blue	.70	6.00
J4b	D1	30c reddish brown	.95	9.00
J5b	D1	40c red lilac	1.60	13.50
J6b	D1	1sh orange	4.00	24.00
		Nos. J1b-J6b (6)	7.75	57.00

Nos. J1-J6 Overprinted in Black "LIBERATED / 1979"

			Litho.	Perf. 14	
1979, Dec.					
J7	D1	5c red		.25	.70
J8	D1	10c green		.25	.70
J9	D1	20c violet blue		.25	.70
J10	D1	30c reddish brown		.25	1.00
J11	D1	40c red lilac		.25	1.00
J12	D1	1sh orange		.60	1.25
		Nos. J7-J12 (6)		1.85	5.35

Wildlife — D2

Primates A416

			Litho.	Perf. 15x14	
1985, Mar. 11					
J13	D2	5sh Lion		.25	.95
J14	D2	10sh African buffalo		.25	.95
J15	D2	20sh Kob antelope		.60	1.40
J16	D2	40sh Elephant		1.25	2.10
J17	D2	50sh Zebra		1.25	2.10
J18	D2	100sh Rhinoceros		1.75	3.50
		Nos. J13-J18 (6)		5.35	11.00

UKRAINE

yü-'krān

LOCATION — In southeastern Europe, bordering on the Black Sea

GOVT. — Republic

AREA — 231,900 sq. mi.

POP. — 48,760,474 (2001)

CAPITAL — Kyiv

Following the collapse of the Russian Empire, a national assembly met at Kyiv and declared the Ukrainian National Republic on Jan. 22, 1918. During three years of civil war, the Ukrainian army, as well as Bolshevik, White Russian, Allied and Polish armies, fought back and forth across the country. By November, 1920, Ukraine was finally occupied by Soviet forces, and Soviet stamps were used from that time, until the recreation of the independent Ukraine on Aug. 24, 1991.

  200 Shahiv = 100 Kopiyok (Kopecks) = 1 Karbovanets (Ruble)

  100 Shahiv = 1 Hryvnia

  100 Kopiyok = 1 Karbovanets (1992)

  100 Kopiyok = 1 Hryvnia (1996)

Catalogue values for unused stamps in this country are for Never Hinged items, beginning with Scott 100 in the regular postage section, Scott B9 in the semipostal section, and Scott F1 in the registration section.

Watermarks

Wmk. 116 — Crosses and Circles

Wmk. 399

Republic's Trident Emblem — A1   Ukrainian Peasant — A2

Allegorical Ukraine — A3

Trident — A4

Inscription of Value — A5

			Typo.	Imperf.	
1918, July					
			Thin Paper		
1	A1	10sh buff		.35	1.10
2	A2	20sh brown		.35	1.10
3	A3	30sh ultra		.35	1.10
a.		30sh blue		2.75	6.50
4	A4	40sh green		.35	1.10
5	A5	50sh red		.35	1.10
		Nos. 1-5 (5)		1.75	5.50

The stamps of this issue exist perforated or pin-perforated unofficially.

Forgeries of this set exist on a very thin, glossy paper.

These designs were earlier (April, 1918) utilized for money tokens, printed on thin cardboard, perforated 11½, and bearing an inscription on the reverse "Circulates on par with coins" in Ukrainian. These tokens exist favor canceled but were not postage stamps. Value uncanceled, $6 each.

Stamps of Russia Overprinted in Violet, Black, Blue, Red, Brown or Green

This trident-shaped emblem was taken from the arms of the Grand Prince Volodymyr and adopted as the device of the Ukrainian Republic.

In the early months of independence, Russian stamps were commonly used, but the influx of large quantities of stamps from Russia made it necessary to take measures to protect postal revenue. In August, 1918, local post offices were ordered to send their existing stocks of Russian stamps to regional centers, where they were overprinted with the trident arms. Unoverprinted Russian stamps were declared invalid after October 1, although they were often accepted for use.

This overprint was handstamped, typographed or lithographed. It was applied in various cities in the Ukraine and there are numerous types.

Nos. 6-47 represent the basic Russian stamps that received these overprints. Values are for the most common overprint variety.

For a detailed listing of these overprints, see the *Scott Classic Specialized Catalogue of Stamps and Covers 1840-1940*.

The basic Russian stamps to which Trident overprints were applied

A8

A9

A11   A12

A13 A14

A15

On Stamps of 1902-03

1918	**Wmk. 168**		**Perf. 13½**
6	A12	3½r black & gray	100.00 75.00
7	A12	7r black & yellow	100.00 75.00

On Stamps of 1909-18
Lozenges of Varnish on Face
Perf. 14, 14½x15
Unwmk.

8	A14	1k orange	.25 .35
9	A14	2k green	.25 .35
10	A14	3k red	.25 .35
11	A15	4k carmine	.25 .35
12	A14	5k claret	.25 .35
13	A14	7k light blue	.25 .35
14	A15	10k dark blue	.25 .35
15	A11	14k blue & rose	.25 .35
16	A11	15k red brn & bl	.25 .35
17	A8	20k blue & car	.25 .35
18	A11	25k grn & gray vio	.40 .50
19	A11	35k red brn & grn	.25 .35
20	A8	50k violet & grn	.25 .35
21	A11	70k brown & org	.25 .35

Perf. 13½

22	A9	1r lt brn, brn & org	.55 .75
23	A12	3½r mar & lt grn	1.25 2.50
24	A13	5r dk bl, grn & pale bl	7.50 11.00
25	A12	7r dk grn & pink	9.00 12.00
26	A13	10r scar, yel & gray	13.00 18.00
		Nos. 6-26 (21)	234.95 199.30

On Stamps of 1917
Perf. 14, 14½x15

27	A14	10k on 7k light blue	.75 1.00
28	A11	20k on 14k bl & rose	.75 1.00

On Stamps of 1917-18
Imperf

29	A14	1k orange	.25 .35
30	A14	2k gray green	.25 .35
31	A14	3k red	.25 .35
32	A15	4k carmine	.25 .35
33	A14	5k claret	.90 1.50
34	A11	15k red brn & bl	.25 .35
35	A8	20k bl & car	.75 1.50
36	A11	25k grn & gray vio	60.00
37	A11	35k red brn & grn	.25 .35
38	A8	50k violet & grn	.30 .35
39	A11	70k brown & org	.25 .35
40	A9	1r pale brn, brn & red org	.25 .60
41	A12	3½r mar & lt grn	1.00 2.50
42	A13	5r dk bl, grn & pale bl	1.50 3.00
43	A12	7r dk grn & pink	2.50 4.00
44	A13	10r scar, yel & gray	70.00 85.00
		Nos. 29-44 (16)	138.95 100.90

PF1

Russian Stamps AR1-AR3.

	Wmk. 171		**Litho.**
	Perf. 14, 14½x14¾		
45	PF1	1k red, buff	5.00 25.00
46	PF1	5k green, buff	20.00 120.00
47	PF1	10k brown, buff	35.00 350.00
		Nos. 45-47 (3)	60.00 495.00

Nos. 45-47 were used and accepted as postage stamps during stamp shortages.

The trident overprint was applied by favor to Russia Nos. 88-104, 110-111, the Romanov issue.

For surcharges see Russian Offices in the Turkish Empire Nos. 320-339.

A6

1919, Jan. **Litho.**
48 A6 20h red & green 10.00 25.00

Because of its high face value, No. 48 was used primarily on money transfer forms or parcel receipts. Used value is for a postally used example.

Nos. 1 and 5 Surcharged

1919, Feb. **Unwmk.** **Imperf.**

49	A1	35k on 10sh buff	9.00 20.00
50	A5	70k on 50sh red	70.00 50.00
a.		Surcharge inverted	60.00

Nos. 49 and 50 were originally believed to have been created by the Soviets in the Ukraine in April, 1919, but more recent research seems to indicate that they were created by the White (Don) Army operating in eastern Ukraine at the request of the Ukrainian government. Correctly franked covers have been recorded from the February-June 1919 period.

Excellent forged surcharges exist.

Ukrainian Soviet Socialist Republic

During 1920/1921, hyperinflation of the ruble created a desperate need for stamps to pay ever-rising postal rates. Many Russian cities and districts surcharged existing stocks of Russian stamps in needed denominations for provisional use.

In June 1920 the national government of the Soviet Ukrainian Republic authorized the Kharkiv post office to create such surcharges for use in the Kharkiv region and in adjacent oblasts. Both unoverprinted Russian stamps and stamps bearing the regional trident overprints of Katerynoslav, Kharkiv and Kyiv were surcharged to raise their face value 100-fold. They were sold at 236 post offices in the Ukraine from June 1920 through Feb. 1921.

In Feb. 1922 three Russian postal savings stamps were surcharged for provisional use by the Kyiv post office, at the direction of the central government. As with the Kharkiv surcharges, these stamps were distributed over a wide area within the country.

KHARKIV ISSUE
Ukrainian and Russian Stamps Handstamp Surcharged

Ukrainian trident overprinted issues and unoverprinted Russian stamps revalued 100-fold by changing denominations from kopecks to rubles.

Two types of overprint: type I, Cyrillic RUB (not including periods) 9.5mmx6.5mm; type II, 8.5mmx6.5mm.

Number of basic Ukrainian or Russian stamp shown in parentheses.

On Katerynoslav Trident Ovpt. Issue of 1918
Type I Reading Upward

1920, June
51 A11 15k red brown & blue (#16a) 75.00 75.00

Kharkiv Trident Ovpt.
Issue of 1918

52	A14	1k orange (#8b)	100.00 60.00
a.		Surcharge reading downward	150.00 150.00
53	A14	2k green (#9b)	100.00 65.00
54	A14	3k red (#10b)	80.00 40.00

55	A11	15k red brn & blue (#16b)	40.00 35.00
56	A8	20k blue & car (#17b)	200.00 175.00
a.		Surcharge reading downward	300.00 300.00
57	A11	20k on 14k blue & rose (#28b)	170.00 190.00
		Imperf	
58	A14	1k orange (#29b)	75.00 75.00
a.		Surcharge reading downward	120.00 120.00
59	A14	2k green (#30b)	250.00 250.00
60	A14	3k red (#31b)	40.00 40.00

On Kyiv Trident Ovpt. Issue of 1918

No. 61   No. 63

On Kyiv II Overprint
61 A14 1k orange (#8f) 40.00 40.00

Imperf
62 A14 1k orange (#29f) 40.00 50.00
a. Surcharge reading downward — 50.00

On Kyiv III Overprint
63 A14 3k red (#31g) 15.00 20.00

On Russian Arms Issue of 1909-18

No. 64

64	A14	1k orange (#73)	50.00 50.00
65	A14	2k green (#74)	10.00 15.00
a.		Surcharge reading downward	15.00 20.00
66	A14	3k red (#75)	10.00 15.00
a.		Surcharge reading downward	25.00 20.00
67	A15	4k red (#76)	325.00
68	A14	5k claret (#77)	7.00 6.00
a.		Surcharge reading downward	20.00 20.00
69	A15	10k dk blue (#79)	15.00 15.00
a.		Surcharge reading downward	90.00 100.00
70	A11	15k red brn & blue (#81)	7.00 6.00
a.		Surcharge reading downward	10.00 10.00
71	A8	20k blue & car (#82)	10.00 6.00
a.		Surcharge reading downward	15.00 12.00
		Imperf	
72	A14	1k orange (#119)	50.00 36.00
a.		Surcharge reading downward	100.00 100.00
73	A14	2k green (#120)	45.00 55.00
74	A14	3k red (#121)	30.00 36.00
75	A14	5k claret (#123)	9.00 7.00
a.		Surcharge reading downward	25.00 25.00
76	A11	15k red brn & blue (#125)	120.00 130.00
a.		Surcharge reading downward		

Type II Reading Upward
On Kharkiv Trident Ovpt. Issue of 1918

No. 79a

77 A14 3k red (#31b) 35.00 40.00

On Kyiv Trident Ovpt. Issue of 1918
78 A14 1k orange (#29f) 20.00 25.00

On Russian Arms Issue of 1919-18
Perf. 14x14½

79	A14	2k green (#74)	8.00 7.00
a.		Surcharge reading downward	12.00 12.00
80	A14	5k claret (#77)	8.00 7.00
a.		Surcharge reading downward	15.00 12.00
81	A15	10k dk blue (#79)	18.00 18.00
a.		Surcharge reading downward	100.00 115.00
82	A11	15k red brn & blue (#81)	8.00 7.00
a.		Surcharge reading downward	12.00 10.00

83	A8	20k blue & car (#82)	8.00 7.00
		Imperf	
84	A14	2k green (#120)	50.00 60.00

KYIV ISSUE

Russian Postal Savings Stamps Handstamp Surcharged

1922, Feb.		**Wmk. 171**
85	7500 (r) on 5k, green, buff	50.00 50.00
a.	Surcharge reading downward	60.00 55.00
86	8000 (r) on 5k, green, buff	150.00 90.00
a.	Surcharge reading downward	180.00 150.00
87	15000 (r) on 10k, brown, buff	300.00 150.00
a.	Surcharge reading downward	450.00 250.00

Nos. 85-87 are normally found on stamps watermarked with a vertical diamond pattern (Wmk. 171) but also exist on paper watermarked sideways, with both upward and downward-reading surcharges. These are rare and are worth approximately 8 times the values shown.

Nos. 1-5 surcharged in grivni (hryven) with the Polish eagle were sold as Polish occupation issues. They are of private origin.

Nos. 1-3 and 5 overprinted diagonally as above ("South Russia") are believed to be of private origin.

A lithographed set of 14 stamps (1h-200h) of these types, perf. 11½, was prepared in 1920, but never placed in use. Value, set $5.

All values exist Imperf., some with inverted centers. Trial printings exist on various papers, including inverted, multiple, omitted and misaligned center vignettes. These are from the printer's waste.

This set handstamped "VILNA UKRAINA / 1921" and 6 values additionally overprinted "DOPLATA" are of private origin.

In 1923 the Ukrainian government-in-exile in Warsaw prepared an 11-value set, consisting of the 10h, 20h and 40h denominations of the unissued 1920 set surcharged and overprinted with the Cyrillic "UPP," supposedly intended as a Field Post issue for a planned invasion of the Ukraine. The invasion never occurred, and the stamps were never issued. Value $15.

For German stamps overprinted "Ukraine" see Russia Nos. N29-N48.

Catalogue values for unused stamps in this section, from this point to the end of the section, are for Never Hinged items.

Cossacks in Ukraine, 500th Anniv. — A20

Design: No. 101, Ukrainian emigrants to Canada.

1992, Mar. 1   Litho.   Perf. 12
100 A20 15k multicolored   .45 .45
101 A20 15k multicolored   .45 .45

Ukrainian emigration to Canada, centennial (No. 101). Dated 1991.

Mykola V. Lysenko (1842-1912), Composer — A21

1992, Mar. 22   Perf. 13
102 A21 100k multicolored   .65 .65

Numerous trident overprints on Soviet stamps exist. Many of them are legitimate local issues and were in official use. Locally produced stamps also exist.

Ukrainian Girl — A22

1992   Litho.   Perf. 12x12½
118 A22 50k bright blue   .25 .25
119 A22 70k bister   .25 .25
121 A22 1kb yellow green   .25 .25
122 A22 2kb purple   .25 .25
124 A22 5kb blue   .25 .25
126 A22 10kb red   .40 .40
128 A22 20kb green   1.60 1.60
130 A22 50kb brown   2.40 2.40
      Nos. 118-130 (8)   5.65 5.65

Issued: Nos. 124, 126, 128, 130, 5/16; 118-119, 121-122, 6/17.

Mykola I. Kostomarov (1817-1885), Writer — A23

1992, May 16   Photo.   Perf. 12x11½
133 A23 20k olive green   .65 .65

1992 Summer Olympics, Barcelona
A24   A25

1992, July 25   Litho.   Perf. 13
134 A24 3kb yel green & multi   .40 .40
135 A25 4kb multicolored   .50 .50
136 A24 5kb buff & multi   .70 .70
      Nos. 134-136 (3)   1.60 1.60

World Forum of Ukrainians, Kyiv — A26

1992, Aug. 19   Litho.   Perf. 13
137 A26 2kb multicolored   .70 .70

Declaration of Independence from the Soviet Union — A27

1992, Aug. 19   Perf. 13½x13
138 A27 2kb multicolored   .70 .70

Souvenir Sheet

Union of Ukrainian Philatelists, 25th Anniv. — A28

1992, Aug. 19   Perf. 12
139 A28 2kb multicolored   1.10 1.10

Intl. Letter Writing Week A29

1992, Oct. 4   Perf. 13x13½
140 A29 5kb multicolored   .55 .55

World Congress of Ukrainian Lawyers, Kyiv — A30

1992, Oct. 18   Litho.   Perf. 13
141 A30 15kb multicolored   .90 .90

Ukrainian Diaspora in Austria A31

Perf. 13½x14½
1992, Nov. 27   Litho.
142 A31 5kb multicolored   .55 .55

Embroidery A32

1992, Nov. 16   Litho.   Perf. 11½x12
143 A32 50k black & orange   .65 .65

Mohyla Academy, Kyiv, 360th Anniv. A33

1992, Nov. 27   Litho.   Perf. 12x12½
144 A33 1.50kb multicolored   .70 .70

Souvenir Sheet

Ukrainian Medal Winners, 1992 Summer Olympics, Barcelona — A34

1992, Dec. 14   Litho.   Perf. 14
145 A34 10kb multicolored   2.50 2.50

Coats of Arms — A35

1993, Feb. 15   Litho.   Perf. 14x13½
148 A35 3kb Lviv   .65 .65
150 A35 5kb Kyiv   1.10 1.10
      See No. 292.

Cardinal Joseph Slipyj (1892-1984) A36

1993, Feb. 17   Litho.   Perf. 14x13½
166 A36 15kb multicolored   1.25 1.25

1st Vienna-Cracow-Lviv-Kyiv Air Mail Flight, 75th Anniv. — A37

1993, Mar. 31   Perf. 13½x14
167 A37 35kb Biplane   .75 .75
168 A37 50kb Jet   1.00 1.00

Easter A39

1993, Apr. 18   Litho.   Perf. 13½
169 A39 15kb multicolored   .95 .95

UN Declaration of Human Rights, 45th Anniv. — A40

Design: 5kb, Country Wedding in Lower Austria, by Ferdinand Georg Waldmuller.

Perf. 14½x13½
1993, June 11   Litho.
170 A40 5kb multicolored   1.60 1.60

A41   A41a

A41b   A41c

A41d   A41e

A41f   A41g

A41h

Villagers at Work: 50kb, No. 177, Reaper with scythe. 100kb, No. 183, Ox carts. No. 173, 200kb, 500kb, Reapers with sickles. No. 174, Farmer with oxen. 150kb, 300kb, No. 181, Shepherd. No. 180, Bee keeper. No. 182, Fisherman. No. 185, Potter. (Illustrations A41a-A41h help identify the Cyrillic characters, not the designs.)

Perf. 12x12½, 14 (#174, 180, 182, 184)

1993-98				Litho.
171	A41	50kb green	.40	.40
172	A41	100kb blue	.40	.40
173	A41c	(100kb) brown	.50	.50
174	A41e	(100kb) magenta	.60	.60
175	A41	150kb red	.40	.40
176	A41	200kb orange	.50	.50
177	A41d	(250kb) green	.50	.50
178	A41	300kb violet	.50	.50
179	A41	500kb brown	.50	.50
180	A41f	(1800kb) org brn	.50	.50
181	A41a	(5000kb) red	1.50	1.50
182	A41g	(5300kb) blue	1.00	1.00
183	A41b	(10,000kb) blue	.80	.80
a.		Perf. 14	6.75	6.75
184	A41h	(17,000kb) red brn	1.75	1.75
		Nos. 171-184 (14)	9.85	9.85

Nos. 174, 181 issued for domestic letter rate; Nos. 177, 180 for letters within the Commonwealth of Independent States; Nos. 183-184 for mail abroad, surface and airmail. Actual amounts sold for varied with inflation. No. 183a sold for 30k on date of issue and was used for the domestic rate.

Issued: 50, 100, 150, 200, 300, 500kb, 12/18/93; No. 181, 183a, 5/28/94; No. 173, 177, 7/2/94; No. 174, 182, 10/15/94; No. 180, 184, 11/12/94; No. 183, 12/30/98.

Famine Deaths, 60th Anniv. — A42

1993, Sept. 12   Litho.   *Perf. 12*
188   A42   75kb brown   .70   .70

First Ukrainian Postage Stamp, 75th Anniv. A43

1993, Oct. 9
189   A43   100kb blue & brown   .70   .70

Stamp Day.

Liberation of Kyiv, 50th Anniv. A44

1993, Nov. 6   Litho.   *Perf. 12*
190   A44   75kb multicolored   .70   .70

A45

1994, Jan. 15   Litho.   *Perf. 12*
191   A45   200kb black & red   1.25   1.25

Agapit, Kyivan Rus physician, Middle Ages.

A46

Endangered species: No. 192, Erythronium dens, canis. No. 193, Cypripedium calceolus.

1994, Feb. 19   *Perf. 12x12½*
192   A46   200kb multicolored   .60   .60
193   A46   200kb multicolored   .60   .60

Independence Day — A47

1994, Sept. 3   Litho.   *Imperf.*
194   A47   5000kb multicolored   1.50   1.50

No. 194 has simulated perforations.

Kyiv University A47a

Litho. & Engr.
1994, Sept. 24   *Perf. 13x13½*
194A   A47a   10,000kb multi   .85   .85

Souvenir Sheet
**   *Perf. 12½x13***
194B   A47a   25,000kb multi   2.25   2.25

No. 194B contains one 40x27mm stamp.

Liberation of Soviet Areas, 50th Anniv. — A48

Battle maps and: a, Katyusha rockets, liberation of Russia. b, Fighter planes, liberation of Ukraine. c, Combined offensive, liberation of Belarus.

1994, Oct. 8   Litho.   *Perf. 12½x12*
195   A48   500kb Block of 3, #a.-c.,
             + label   1.25   1.25

See Russia No. 6213, Belarus No. 78.

Excavation of Trypillia culture, Cent. — A49

1994, Dec. 17   Litho.   *Perf. 12x12½*
196   A49   4000kb multicolored   .45   .45

1st Books Printed in Ukrainian, 500th Anniv. — A50

1994, Dec. 17   *Perf. 13½*
197   A50   4000kb multicolored   .45   .45

Sofiyivka Natural Park, Bicent. A51

1994, Dec. 17   *Perf. 12½x12*
198   A51   5000kb multicolored   .65   .65

Ilya Y. Repin (1844-1930), Painter — A52

1994, Dec. 17   *Perf. 12x12½*
199   A52   4000kb multicolored   .45   .45

City of Uzhhorod, 1100th Anniv. — A53

1995, Jan. 28   Litho.   *Perf. 12*
200   A53   5000kb multicolored   .50   .50

Ivan Franko (1856-1916), Writer — A54

Ivan Puliuj (1845-1918), Physicist — A55

No. 203, Lesia Ukrainka (1871-1913), poet.

1995, Feb. 2   *Perf. 13½*
201   A54   3000kb multicolored   .30   .30
202   A55   3000kb multicolored   .40   .40
203   A54   3000kb multicolored   .30   .30
        Nos. 201-203 (3)   1.00   1.00

Falco Peregrinus — A56

1995, Apr. 15   Litho.   *Perf. 12*
204   A56   5000kb multicolored   .40   .40
205   A56   10,000kb Grus grus   .80   .80

Maksym T. Rylskyi (1895-1964), Writer — A57

1995, Apr. 15   *Perf. 13½x14*
206   A57   50,000kb multicolored   1.25   1.25

End of World War II, 50th Anniv. — A58

1995, May 9   Litho.   *Perf. 13½*
207   A58   100,000kb multicolored   1.75   1.75

Artek, Intl. Children's Camp A59

1995, June 16　　Litho.　　Perf. 13½
208　A59　5000kb multicolored　　　　.55　.55

Famous Writers A60

Design: 1000kb, Ivan Kotliarevskyi (1769-1838), depiction of his poem, "Eneida." 3000kb, Taras Shevchenko (1814-61), his book, "Kobzar."

1995, July 8
209　A60　1000kb multicolored　　　.40　.40
210　A60　3000kb multicolored　　　.40　.40

Hetman Petro Konashevych-Sahaidachny — A61

1995, July 22　　Litho.　　Perf. 13½
211　A61　30,000kb multicolored　　　.85　.85

Arms of Luhansk — A62

1995　　　Litho.　　　Perf. 13½
212　A62　10,000kb shown　　　　.40　.40
213　A62　10,000kb Chernihiv　　1.00　1.00

Issued: No. 212, 9/15; No. 213, 10/22.

Hetman Bohdan Khmelnytsky (Khmelnytskyi; 1593?-1657) — A63

1995, Sept. 23　Litho.　Perf. 12½x12
214　A63　40,000kb multi　　　　.90　.90

Hetman Ivan Mazepa (1640?-1709) — A64

1995, Oct. 14　　　　Perf. 13½
215　A64　30,000kb multi　　　　.85　.85

European Nature Protection Year — A65

1995, Oct. 14
216　A65　50,000kb multi　　　1.10　1.10

Intl. Children's Day — A66

1995, Oct. 22
217　A66　50,000kb multi　　　1.00　1.00

UN, 50th Anniv. A67

1995, Oct. 24　　　Perf. 12x12½
218　A67　50,000kb multi　　　1.00　1.00

A68

1995, Dec. 9　　　　Perf. 13½
219　A68　50,000kb multi　　　1.00　1.00

Ivan Karpenko-Karyi, playwright, actor.

Mikhailo Hrushevskyi, 1st Ukrainian President — A69

1995, Dec. 9
220　A69　50,000kb multi　　　　.90　.90

P. Safarik (1795-1861), Writer — A70

1995, Dec. 27
221　A70　30,000kb green　　　1.00　1.00

Trolleybus A71

Streetcar A72

City Bus — A73

1995, Dec. 27　　Litho.　　Perf. 14
No Year Date
222　A71　(1000kb) blue violet　　.25　.25
　a.　Imprint "2003"　　　　1.25　1.25
　b.　Imprint "2005"　　　　1.25　1.25
　c.　Imprint "2006"　　　　1.25　1.25
223　A72　(2000kb) green　　　2.75　2.75
224　A73　(3000kb) red　　　1.00　.80
　a.　Imprint "2006"　　　　　.25　.25
　　　Nos. 222-224 (3)　　　4.00　3.80

The postal rate that No. 223 paid was sharply increased greatly affecting the cost of the stamp at the post offices.
Imprinted values issued: No. 222a, 2003; No. 222b, 12/1/05; No. 222c, 2/3/06. No. 224a, 9/28/06.

Taras Shevchenko University Astronomical Observatory, Kyiv, 150th Anniv. — A74

a, 20,000 l, Early astronomical instruments. b, 30,000 l, Telescope. c, 50,000 l, Observatory, sun.

1996, Jan. 13　　　　Perf. 12
225　A74　Strip of 3, #a.-c.　　1.75　1.75

Souvenir Sheet

1994 Winter Olympics, Lillehammer — A75

Medalists: a, 40,000kb, Valentina Tserbe, bronze, biathlon. b, 50,000kb, Oksana Bayul, gold, figure skating.

1996, Jan. 13
226　A75　Sheet of 2, #a.-b.　　1.60　1.60

Ahatanhel Krymskyi (1871-1942), Writer — A76

1996, Jan. 15　　　　Perf. 13½
227　A76　20,000kb bister & brown　.70　.70

Kharkiv Zoo, Cent. — A77

1996, Mar. 23　　　Perf. 12½x12
228　A77　20,000kb multicolored　　.65　.65

Ivan S. Kozlovskyi (1900-93), Opera Singer — A78

1996, Mar. 23　　　Perf. 13½
229　A78　20,000kb multicolored　　.65　.65

Motion Pictures, Cent. A79

Oleksandr Dovzhenko, film maker, house.

1996, Mar. 23　　　Perf. 12½x12
230　A79　4000kb multicolored　　.70　.70

No. 230 was issued se-tenant with two labels showing scenes from films.

Chernobyl Nuclear Disaster, 10th Anniv. — A80

1996, Apr. 26　　Litho.　　Perf. 13½
231　A80　20,000kb multicolored　　.65　.65

Symyrenko Family A81

Vasyl Fedorovych (1835-1915), Volodymyr Levkovych (1891-1938), Levko Platonovych (1855-1920).

1996, May 25
232　A81　20,000kb multicolored　　.65　.65

Vasil Stefanyk (1871-1936), Writer — A82

1996, June 29
233　A82　20,000kb multicolored　　.65　.65

Mykola M. Myklukho-Maklai (1846-88), Explorer, Philologist — A83

Litho. & Engr.

1996, July 17 *Perf. 13½*
234 A83 40,000kb multicolored 1.25 1.25

1996 Summer Olympic Games, Atlanta — A84

Modern Olympic Games, Cent. A85

1996, July 19 Litho. *Perf. 13½*
235 A84 20,000kb Wrestling .40 .40
236 A84 40,000kb Handball .80 .80
237 A85 40,000kb Greek athletes 1.10 1.10
Nos. 235-237 (3) 2.30 2.30

Souvenir Sheet
Perf. 12
238 A84 100,000kb Gymnast 1.75 1.75

Independence, 5th Anniv. — A86

1996, Aug. 24 *Perf. 13½*
239 A86 20,000kb multicolored .70 .70

First Ukrainian Satellite, "Sich-1" — A87

1996, Aug. 31
240 A87 20,000kb multicolored .70 .70

Locomotives — A88

Designs: 20,000kb, Steam, class OD. 40,000kb, Diesel class 2 TE-116.

1996, Aug. 31
241 A88 20,000kb multicolored .65 .65
242 A88 40,000kb multicolored 1.25 1.25
a. Pair, #241-242 2.25 2.25

Airplanes Designed by O.K. Antonov (1906-84) A89

No. 243, Glider A-15, portrait of Antonov. No. 244, AN-2. No. 245, AN-124. No. 246, AN-225.

1996, Sept. 14
243 A89 20,000kb multicolored .55 .55
244 A89 20,000kb multicolored .55 .55
245 A89 40,000kb multicolored .55 .55
246 A89 40,000kb multicolored .55 .55
a. Block of 4, #243-246 2.25 2.25

Ivan Piddubnyi (1871-1949), Wrestler — A90

1996, Nov. 16
247 A90 40k multicolored .85 .85

First Ukrainian Antarctic Expedition A91

1996, Nov. 23
248 A91 20k multicolored 1.50 1.50

A92

Flowers: 20k, Leontopodium alpinum. 40k, Narcissus angustifolius.

1996, Nov. 23
249 A92 20k multicolored .55 .55
250 A92 40k multicolored .80 .80
a. Pair, #249-250 + label 1.50 1.50

A93

1996, Dec. 7 Litho. *Perf. 13½*
251 A93 20k multicolored .60 .60

UNESCO, 50th anniv.

Viktor S. Kosenko, Composer, Birth Cent. A94

1996, Dec. 21 Litho. *Perf. 13½*
252 A94 20k multicolored .65 .65

St. Sophia's Cathedral, Kyiv — A95

Illinska (St. Elijah) Church, Subotiv A96

St. George Church, Drohobych A97

No. 256, Troitska Cathedral, Novomoskovsk.

1996, Dec. 25
253 A95 20k multicolored .40 .40
254 A96 20k multicolored .40 .40
255 A97 20k multicolored .40 .40
256 A97 20k multicolored .40 .40
a. Block of 4, #253-256 2.00 2.00

UNICEF, 50th Anniv. A98

1996, Dec. 31
257 A98 20k multicolored .60 .60

Petro Mohyla (1596-1647), Metropolitan of Kyiv — A99

1996, Dec. 31
258 A99 20k multicolored .60 .60

Wild Animals — A100

1997, Mar. 22 Litho. *Perf. 13½*
259 A100 20k Lynx lynx .90 .90
260 A100 20k Ursos arctos .90 .90
a. Pair, #259-260 + label 2.75 2.75

Cathedral of the Exaltation of the Holy Cross, Poltava, 17th Cent. A101

Designs: No. 262, St. George's Cathedral, Lviv, 18th cent. No. 263, Protection Fortified Church, Sutkivtsi, 14-15th cent.

1997, Apr. 19 Litho. *Perf. 13½*
261 A101 20k multicolored .90 .90
262 A101 20k multicolored .90 .90
263 A101 20k multicolored .90 .90
Nos. 261-263 (3) 2.70 2.70

Legendary Founders of Kyiv — A101a

Europa: a, Kyi (holding staff and shield) and Shchek (holding sword). b, Khoriv (holding sword, leaning on shield) and sister, Lybid.

1997, May 6 Litho. & Engr. *Perf. 13*
264 A101a 40k Sheet of 2,
#a.-b. 9.00 9.00

4th Natl. Philatelic Exhibition, Cherkasy A102

Design: Statue of Taras Shevchenko, stamps, exhibition hall.

1997, May 17 Litho. *Perf. 13½*
265 A102 10k multicolored .65 .65

Yurii V. Kondratiuk (1897-1942), Space Pioneer — A103

1997, June 21 *Perf. 12½x12*
266 A103 20k multicolored .90 .90

Constitution, 1st Anniv. — A104

1997, June 28 *Perf. 13½*
267 A104 20k multicolored .70 .70

Midsummer Festival of Ivan Kupalo — A104a

1997, July 5 Litho. *Perf. 13½*
268 A104a 20k multicolored .70 .70

Princess Olha A105

Sultana Roksoliana A106

1997, July 12 Litho. *Perf. 13½*
269 A105 40k multicolored 1.15 1.00
270 A106 40k multicolored 1.15 1.00

First Ukrainian Emigration to Argentina, Cent. A107

Design: Monument to poet Taras Shevchenko, Buenos Aires.

1997, Aug. 16 Litho. **Perf. 13½**
271 A107 20k multicolored .75 .75

For Exceptional Service — A108

Order of Yaroslav the Wise — A109

Medals for: No. 273, Military Service. 30k, Bravery. 40k, Order of Bohdan Khmelnytsky. No. 276, Honored Service.
No. 277: a, Medal hanging from chain. b, 8-point star.

Litho. & Engr.
1997, Aug. 20 **Perf. 13½**
272 A108 20k multicolored .45 .45
273 A108 20k multicolored .45 .45
274 A108 30k multicolored .70 .70
275 A108 40k multicolored .90 .90
276 A108 60k multicolored 1.25 1.25
a. Strip of 5, #272-276 5.00 5.00

Souvenir Sheet
Perf. 13
277 A109 60k Sheet of 2, #a.-
 b. 5.25 5.25

Nos. 277a-277b are each 35x50mm.

Hetman — A110

No. 278, Dmytro "Baida" Vyshnevetskyj (?-1563), boats, archers. No. 279, Pylyp Orlyk (1672-1742), Stockholm harbor, crowd in Thessaloniki street.

1997, Sept. 13 Litho. **Perf. 12½x12**
278 A110 20k multicolored .95 .95
279 A110 20k multicolored .95 .95

See Nos. 357-358, 376-377, 412-413, 449-451, 510-511.

Solomiia Krushelnytska (Salomea Krusceniski, 1872-1952), Actress, Singer — A111

1997, Sept. 23 Litho. **Perf. 13½**
280 A111 20k multicolored .85 .85

Airplanes A112

Designs: 20k, Antonov An-74 TK-200. 40k, Antonov An-38-100.

1997, Oct. 30
281 A112 20k multicolored .60 .60
282 A112 40k multicolored 1.40 1.40

Ships A113

20k, Zavyietnyj, 1903. 40k, Serhii Korolev, 1970, Academician.

1997, Dec. 6 Litho. **Perf. 13½**
283 A113 20k multicolored .60 .60
284 A113 40k multicolored 1.40 1.40

A114

1997, Dec. 6 Litho. **Perf. 12x12½**
285 A114 40k multi + label 1.75 1.75
Participation of Ukrainian astronaut in US space shuttle mission.

Vasyl Krychevskyi (1872-1952), Painter and Architect. — A115

1997, Dec. 20 **Perf. 13½**
286 A115 10k multicolored .75 .75

Christmas — A116

1997, Dec. 20
287 A116 20k multicolored .85 .85

Traditional Handicrafts A117

Region: #288, Rooster, Dnipropetrovsk. #289, Vest, Chernivtsi. #290, Ram, Poltava. #291, Molded design, Ivano-Frankivsk.

1997, Dec. 20
288 A117 20k multicolored .75 .75
289 A117 20k multicolored .75 .75
290 A117 40k multicolored 1.25 1.25
291 A117 40k multicolored 1.25 1.25
 Nos. 288-291 (4) 4.00 4.00

Perf. 11½
288a 20k .75 .75
289a 20k .75 .75
290a 40k 1.25 1.25
291a 40k 1.25 1.25
b. Sheet, 2 each #288a-291a 8.00 8.00

Nos. 288-291 have colored border. Nos. 288a-291a do not.

Arms Type of 1993
Arms of Transcarpathia (Zakarpattya).

1997, Dec. 30 Litho. **Perf. 13½**
292 A35 20k multicolored .90 .90

A118

Wildlife: a, 20k, Skylark. b, 40k, White-tailed eagle. c, 20k, Black stork. d, 40k, Long-eared hedgehog. e, 20k, Garden dormouse. f, 40k, Wild boar.

1997, Dec. 30 Litho. **Perf. 11½**
293 A118 Sheet of 6, #a.-f. 5.00 5.00

Hryhorii Skovoroda (1722-94), Philosopher A119

Litho. & Engr.
1997, Dec. 27 **Perf. 13½**
294 A119 60k multicolored 1.10 1.10

Volodymyr Sosiura (1898-1965), Poet — A120

1998, Jan. 6 Litho. **Perf. 13½**
295 A120 20k multicolored 1.00 1.00

1998 Winter Olympic Games, Nagano — A121

1998, Feb. 14 Litho. **Perf. 13½**
296 A121 20k Figure skating .65 .65
297 A121 20k Biathlon .65 .65

Bilhorod Dnistrovskyi Fortress, 2500th Anniv. — A122

1998, Apr. 21 Litho. **Perf. 13½**
298 A122 20k multicolored .80 .80

UKRFILEKS 98 Natl. Philatelic Exhibition, Sevastopol — A123

Design: Frigate, "Hetman Sahaidachnyi."

1998, Apr. 28 Litho. **Perf. 13½**
299 A123 30k multi + label .85 .85

European Bank of Reconstruction and Development — A124

Obverse, reverse of Ukrainian coins: a, 1k, Gold, 11th cent. b, 1k, Silver, 11th cent. c, 60k, 500h St. Sophia Cathedral gold coin. d, 60k, 200h Taras Shevchenko gold coin. e, 30k, 1,000,000k Bohdan Khmelnytsky silver coin. f, 30k, 10h Petro Mohyla silver coin.

Litho. & Engr.
1998, May 8 **Perf. 13½**
300 A124 Sheet of 6, #a.-f. 10.00 10.00

Ivan Kupalo Natl. Festival — A125

1998, May 16 Litho. **Perf. 13½**
301 A125 40k multicolored 2.10 2.10
 Europa.

Souvenir Sheet

Askania Nova Nature Preserve, Cent. — A126

a, 40k, Deer. b, 60k, Przewalski horses.

1998, May 16 Litho. **Perf. 11½**
302 A126 Sheet of 2, #a.-b. 3.25 3.25

Paintings from Lviv Picture Gallery — A127

Designs: No. 303, Portrait of Maria Theresa, by J.E. Liotard. No. 304, Man with a Cello, by Gerard von Honthorst. 40k, Madonna and Child, 17th cent. Lviv School.

1.20h, Madonna and Child and Two Saints, by 16th cent. Italian school.

1998, June 20   **Perf. 13½**
303 A127   20k multicolored   .30   .30
304 A127   20k multicolored   .30   .30
305 A127   40k multicolored   .55   .55
  a.   Strip of 3, #303-305   1.40 1.40
        Souvenir Sheet
306 A127 1.20h multicolored   2.25 2.25

Souvenir Sheet

Polytechnical Institute, Kyiv, Cent. — A128

1998, June 27   Litho.   Perf. 11½
307 A128   1h multicolored   4.00 4.00

Askold & Dyr A129

Litho. & Engr.
1998, July 4   **Perf. 13½**
308 A129   3h multi + label   3.25 3.25

Hetman Bohdan Khmelnytsky — A130

Designs: a, 30k, Battle scene, denomination LR. b, 2k, Portrait of Khmelnytsky. c, 30k, Battle scene, denomination LL. d, 40k, denomination LR. e, 60k, Battle scene. f, 40k, Battle scene, denomination LL.

1998, July 25   **Litho. & Engr.**
309 A130   Sheet of 6, #a.-f.   5.50 5.50
   Ukrainian uprising, 350th anniv.

Iown of Halych, 1100th Anniv. A131

1998, Aug. 1   **Litho.**
310 A131   20k multicolored   .70   .70

Queen Anna Yaroslavna (1024?-75) A132

1998, Aug. 8
311 A132   40k multicolored   .85   .85

Yurii Lysianskyi (1773-1837), Explorer — A133

1998, Aug. 13
312 A133   40k multicolored   1.10 1.10

Natalia Uzhvii (1898-1986), Stage Actress — A134

1998, Sept. 8   Litho.   Perf. 13½
313 A134   40k multicolored   1.00 1.00

Polytechnic Institute, Kyiv, Cent. — A135

Designs: 10k, W.L. Kirpichov, first president. No. 315, E.O. Paton, bridge. No. 316, S.P. Timoschenko, mathematical formula. 30k, Igor I. Sikorsky, biplane. 40k, Sergei P. Korolev, rocket, satellite.

1998, Sept. 10   **Perf. 12½x12**
314 A135   10k multicolored   .55   .55
315 A135   20k multicolored   .55   .55
316 A135   20k multicolored   .55   .55
317 A135   30k multicolored   1.00 1.00
318 A135   40k multicolored   1.00 1.00
   a.   Strip of 5, #314-318   4.25 4.25

World Post Day — A136

1998, Sept. 19   Litho.   Perf. 13½
319 A136   10k multicolored   .70   .70

Ukrainian Book, 1000th Anniv. — A137

1998, Sept.19
320 A137   20k multicolored   .65   .65

Church Architecture A138

Designs: No. 321, Church of the Transfiguration, Chernihiv, 11th cent. No. 322, Church of the Holy Protection, Kharkiv, 17th cent.

1998, Sept. 21
321 A138   20k multicolored   .70   .70
322 A138   20k multicolored   .70   .70

World Wildlife Fund — A139

Branta ruficollis: a, f, 20k, Adults. b, g, 30k, Female on nest. c, h, 40k, Female with goslings. d, i, 60k, Adults, goslings.

1998, Oct. 10   Litho.   Perf. 13½
323   A139   Block of 4, #a.-d.   4.00 4.00
   e.   Block of 4, perf. 11½, #f.-i.   4.75 4.75
   j.   Sheet of 2, #323e   9.50 9.50

Antonov Airplanes A140

1998, Nov. 28   Litho.   Perf. 13½
324 A140   20k Antonov 140   .60   .60
325 A140   40k Antonov 70   .80   .80

Hetman Type of 1997
Design: Petro Doroshenko (1627-98).

1998, Nov. 28   Litho.   Perf. 12½x12
326 A141   20k multicolored   .80   .80

Borys D. Hrinchenko (1863-1910), Writer — A142

1998, Dec. 4   Litho.   Perf. 13½
327 A142   20k multicolored   .85   .85

Christmas — A143

1998, Dec. 11
328 A143   30k multicolored   1.00 1.00

Ukrainians in Australia, 50th Anniv. A144

1998, Dec. 20
329 A144   40k multicolored   .85   .85

Illintsi Meteor Impact Area A145

1998, Dec. 25
330 A145   40k multicolored   1.00 1.00

Universal Declaration of Human Rights, 50th Anniv. — A146

Paintings of various flowers by Kateryna Bilokur (1900-61): 30k, 1940. 50k, 1959.

1998, Dec. 25
331 A146   30k multicolored   .60   .60
332 A146   50k multicolored   .95   .95
   a.   Pair, #331-332 +label   1.60 1.60

Serhii Paradzhanov (1924-90), Film Director — A147

1999, Feb. 27   Litho.   Perf. 13½
333 A147   40k multi + label   1.10 1.10

Volodymyr Ivasiuk (1949-79), Composer A148

1999, Mar. 4
334 A148   30k multicolored   .60   .60

Scythian
Gold
A149

1999, Mar. 20
335 A149 20k Clasp .30 .30
336 A149 40k Boar .50 .50
337 A149 50k Young elk .70 .70
338 A149 1h Necklace 1.10 1.10
   a. Block of 4, #335-338 2.75 2.75

Spring Easter
Dance — A150

1999, Apr. 7
339 A150 30k multicolored .50 .50

Europa — A151

Synevyr Natl. Park: a, 50k, Wooden monuments on bank of Tereblyia River. b, 1h, Thymallus thymallus, river scene.

1999, Apr. 24
340 A151 Pair, #a.-b. 2.75 2.75

Panas Myrnyi
(1849-1920),
Writer — A152

1999, May 13
341 A152 40k multicolored .65 .65

Honoré de Balzac (1799-1850),
Writer — A153

1999, May 20
342 A153 40k multicolored .65 .65

Council of
Europe,
50th Anniv.
A154

1999, May 22
343 A154 40k multicolored .65 .65

Aleksandr Pushkin (1799-1837),
Poet — A155

1999, June 6
344 A155 40k multi + label .65 .65

Sailboats — A156

No. 345: a, Bark (Baidak), double sails, one man at tiller. b, Cossack (Chaika), single sail, rowers.

1999, June 26
345 A156 30k Pair, #a.-b. 1.10 1.10

Souvenir Sheet

Yaroslav the Wise — A157

1999, July 2   Litho.   Perf. 11½
346 A157 1.20h multicolored 2.00 2.00

Principality of Halytsko-Volynskyi,
800th Anniv. — A158

1999, July 27   Perf. 13½
347 A158 50k multicolored 1.00 .80

Natl. Museum of
Art, Cent. — A159

Designs: a, 30k, Icon of St. George. b, 60, Girl in a Red Hat, by O.O. Murashko.

1999, July 27
348 A159 Pair, #a.-b. + label 1.50 1.00

Bee Keeping in
Ukraine — A160

1999, Aug. 7
349 A160 30k Bee on flower 1.00 1.00

UPU, 125th
Anniv. — A161

1999, Aug. 14   Litho.   Perf. 13½
350 A161 30k multicolored .60 .60

Poltava, 1100th
Anniv. — A162

1999, Aug. 14
351 A162 30k multicolored .70 .70

Presidential
Medals — A163

Designs: 30k, Order of Princess Olga. No. 353: a, Medal with trident. b, Medal with star.

1999, Aug. 17   Litho. & Engr.
352 A163 30k multicolored .65 .65
Souvenir Sheet of 2
353 A163 2.50h #a.-b. 6.00 6.00
No. 353 contains two 35x50mm stamps.

Polish-Ukrainian Cooperation in Nature
Conservation — A164

a, Cervus elaphus. b, Felis silvestris.

1999, Sept. 22   Litho.   Perf. 13½
354 A164 1.40h Pair, #a.-b. 3.00 2.00
See Poland Nos. 3477-3478.

National
Bank — A165

1999, Sept. 28   Litho. & Engr.
355 A165 3h multicolored 2.75 2.40
Souvenir Sheet
356 A165 5h multicolored 5.00 5.00

Hetman Type of 1997

Designs: No. 357, Ivan Vyhovskyi (d. 1664), cavalry in water. No. 358, Pavlo Polubotok (1660-1724), ships in water.

1999   Litho.   Perf. 12¼x12
357 A110 30k multi .65 .65
358 A110 30k multi .65 .65

Issued: No. 357, 11/20; No. 358, 12/22.

A166

Christmas
A167

1999, Nov. 26   Wmk. 399   Perf. 13½
359 A166 30k multi .40 .40
Unwmk.
360 A167 60k multi .80 .80

Children's Art — A168

a, Spacecraft, alien creatures. b, Elephant in space. c, Rocket and space car on planet.

1999, Nov. 30   Unwmk.   Perf. 11½
361 A168 10k Strip of 3, #a.-c. 2.00 2.00

Fauna
A169

Designs: a, 40k, Desmana moschata. b, 60k, Gyps fulvus. c, 40k, Lucanus cervus.

1999, Dec. 9   Perf. 13½
362 A169 Strip of 3, #a.-c. 1.75 1.75

Church of St. Andrew, Kyiv — A170

1999, Dec. 12
363 A170 60k multi + label 1.25 1.25

Mushrooms
A171

Designs: a, 30k, Armillariella mellea. b, 30k, Paxillus atrotomentosus. c, 30k, Pleurotus ostratus. d, 40k, Cantharellus cibarius. e. 60k, Agaricus campester.

1999, Dec. 15   **Perf. 11½**
364 A171   Sheet of 5, #a.-e., + label   4.00   4.00

New Year 2000 — A172

1999, Dec. 18   **Perf. 13½**
365 A172 50k multi + label   1.50   1.50

Motor Vehicles — A173

a, Kraz-65032 truck. b, Tavriia Nova car.

1999, Dec. 18   **Litho.**
366 A173 30k Pair, #a.-b.   1.00   1.00

Works of Maria Prymachenko — A174

Denomination colors: a, Green. b, Violet.

1999, Dec. 22
367 A174 30k Pair, #a.-b., + central label   1.00   1.00

Halshka Hulovyohivna, Philanthropist A175

1999, Dec. 25   **Perf. 13½**
368 A175 30k multi   .60   .60

Zoogeographic Endowment Fund — A176

Animals from: a, 10k, Carpathian Reserve. b, 30k, Polissia Reserve. c, 40k, Kaniv Reserve. d, 60k, Trakhtemyriv Reserve. e, 1h, Askanlla-Nova Reserve (ram, birds). f, 1h, Kara-Dag Reserve (birds).

1999, Dec. 28   **Perf. 11½**
369 A176   Sheet of 6, #a.-f.   6.00   4.00

Christianity, 2000th Anniv. — A177

Designs: a, Mother of God mosaic, St. Sofia Cathedral, Kyiv, 11th cent. b, Christ Pantocrator fresco, Church of the Savior's Transfiguration, Polotsk, Belarus, 12th cent. c, Volodymyr Madonna, Tretiakov Gallery, Moscow, 12th cent.

2000, Jan. 5   **Litho.**   **Perf. 11½**
370 A177 80k Sheet of 3, #a.-c.   5.00   4.25

Souvenir Sheet

Opera and Ballet Theaters — A178

No. 371: a, National Academic, Kyiv. b, Odessa State, Odessa. c, Kharkov State Academic, Kharkov. d, Ivan Franko State Academic, Lviv.

2000, Jan. 29   **Litho.**   **Perf. 11½**
371 A178 40k Sheet of 4, #a.-d.   5.50   5.50

Kyiv Bridges — A179

No. 372: a, 10k, Moscow Bridge. b, 30k, Y. O. Paton Bridge. c, 40k, Pedestrian park bridge. d, 60k, Subway bridge.

2000, Jan. 29   **Perf. 12¼x12**
372 A179   Block of 4, #a.-d.   2.50   2.50

Souvenir Sheet

Peresopnytsia Gospel — A180

2000, Feb. 8   **Perf. 11½**
373 A180 1.50h multi   3.00   3.00

A181

2000, Feb. 11   **Perf. 13½**
374 A181 30k multi   1.60   .50
Oksana Petrusenko (1900-40), opera singer

Marusia Churai, 17th Cent. Singer — A182

2000, Feb. 18
375 A182 40k multi   .90   .90

Hetman Type of 1997

Designs: No. 376, Danylo Apostol (1654-1734), church, burning castle. No. 377, Ivan Samoylovych (d. 1690), tent, winter scene.

2000   **Perf. 12¼x12**
376 A110 30k multi   .90   .90
377 A110 30k multi   .90   .90
   Issued: No. 376, 2/22; No. 377, 3/3.

World Meteorological Organization, 50th Anniv. — A183

2000, Mar. 10   **Litho.**   **Perf. 13½**
378 A183 30k multi   1.10   1.10

Europa Issue
Common Design Type
2000, Mar. 29   **Litho.**   **Perf. 13½**
379 CD17 3h multi   4.50   3.00

Souvenir Sheets

Easter Eggs — A184

No. 380: a, 30k, Egg with black and red star design, Podillia region. b, 30k, Flower egg, Chernihiv region. c, 30k, Egg with leaf design, Kyiv region. d, 30k, Egg with green, white and yellow geometric design, Odesa region. e, 70k, Egg with reindeer design, Hutsulshchyna region. f, 70k, Egg with cross design, Volyn region.

2000, Apr. 28   **Perf. 11½**
380 A184   Sheet of 6, #a-f   4.25   4.25

Stamp Exhibitions — A185

No. 381: a, Woman in native costume, Austria #2. b, Man in native costume, Great Britain #1.

2000, May 20
381 A185 80k Sheet of 2, #a-b   3.75   3.75
WIPA 2000 Stamp Exhibition, Vienna; The Stamp Show 2000, London.

Donetsk Oblast — A186

City of Kyiv — A187

2000   **Perf. 12¼x12**
382 A186 30k multi   .70   .70
383 A187 30k multi   .70   .70
Regional and administrative areas. Issued: No. 382, 5/26; No. 383, 5/28.

6th Natl. Philatelic Exhibition, Donetsk — A188

2000, May 28   **Litho.**   **Perf. 12¼x12**
384 A188 30k multi   .70   .70

City of Ostroh, 900th Anniv. — A189

2000, June 16   **Litho.**   **Perf. 13½**
385 A189 30k multi   .70   .70

2000 Summer Olympics, Sydney — A190

2000, June 26
386 A190 30k High jump   .50   .50
387 A190 30k Boxing   .50   .50
388 A190 70k Yachting   .85   .85
389 A190 1h Rhythmic gymnastics   1.50   1.50
   Nos. 386 380 (4)   3.35   3.35

Petro Prokopovych (1775-1850),
Apiarist — A191

2000, July 12   Litho.   Perf. 13½
390 A191 30k multi   .80   .80

Shipbuilding — A192

2000, July 14
391 A192 Pair   1.90 1.90
a.   40k Ship St. Paul   .70   .70
b.   70k Ship St. Nicholas   1.10 1.10

Tetiana Pata (1884-1976),
Artist — A193

No. 392: a, Leafy Plants with Flowers,
1950s. b, Viburnum Berries and Bird, 1957.

2000, July 21
392 A193 Horiz. pair, #a-b +
            central label   1.10 1.10
a.-b. 40k Any single   .50   .50

Dubno, 900th
Anniv. — A194

2000, July 28
393 A194 30k multi   .70   .70

Harvest
Festival — A195

2000, Aug. 4
394 A195 30k multi   .70   .70

Souvenir Sheet

Presidential Symbols — A196

Designs: a, Flag. b, Mace. c, Seal. d,
Badge.

2000, Aug. 18   Litho.   Perf. 11½
395 A196 60k Sheet of 4, #a-d   5.00 5.00

Regional and Administrative Areas

Volynska Oblast — A197

Autonomous Republic of
Crimea — A198

2000   Perf. 12¼x12
396 A197 30k multi   .70   .70
397 A198 30k multi   .70   .70
      Issued: No. 396, 8/23; No. 397, 10/20.

Kyiv Post Office, 225th Anniv. — A199

2000, Sept. 3   Perf. 11½
398 A199 30k multi   .70   .70

Endangered Amphibians — A200

No. 399: a, 30k, Triturus vulgaris. b, 70k,
Salamandra salamandra.

2000, Sept. 8   Perf. 13½
399 A200 Pair, #a-b   1.75 1.75

Yurij
Drohobych
(1450-94),
Writer
A201

2000, Sept. 12
400 A201 30k multi   .70   .70

Souvenir Sheet

Carpathian National Park — A202

No. 401: a, Mt. Breskul, 1911 meters. b, Mt.
Hoberla, 2061 meters.

2000, Sept. 15   Perf. 11½
401 A202 80k Sheet of 2, #a-b   5.00 5.00

Flowers — A203

Designs: a, Marigolds. b, Chamomiles. c,
Hollyhocks. d, Poppies. e, Periwinkles. f, Corn-
flowers. g, Morning glories. h, Martagon lilies.
i, Peonies. j, Bluebells.

2000, Oct. 6
402 A203 30k Sheet of 10, #a-j   8.00 8.00

Children's Folk Tales — A204

Designs: a, "Ivasyk and Telesyk," (boy in
boat, witch). b, "The Crooked Duck," (couple
with duck). c, "The Cat and the Rooster."

2000, Nov. 3
403 30k Horiz. strip of 3   2.25 2.25
a.-c. A204 Any single   .55   .55

New
Year
2001
A205

2000, Nov. 24
404 A205 30k multi   .80   .80

St. Onufrius   Church of Christ's
Church,   Birth,
Lviv — A206   Velyke — A207

Design: 70k, Church of the Resurrection,
Sumy.

2000, Dec. 8   Perf. 13½
405 A206 30k multi   .60   .60
406 A207 30k multi   .60   .60
407 A207 70k multi   1.20 1.20
      Nos. 405-407 (3)   2.40 2.40

Souvenir Sheet

St. Vladimir (c. 956-1015), Kyivan
Prince — A208

2000, Dec. 15   Perf. 11½
408 A208 2h multi   4.50 4.50

Dmytro Rostovskyi (1651-1709),
Religious Leader — A209

2001, Jan. 16   Litho.   Perf. 13½
409 A209 75k multi   1.25 1.25

Love — A210

2001, Jan. 26
410 A210 30k multi   .70   .70

Souvenir Sheet

Prince Danylo Romanovych (1201-
64) — A211

2001, Feb. 1   Perf. 11½
411 A211 3h multi   3.50 3.50

Hetman Type of 1997

Designs: 30k, Yuryi Khmelnytski (1641-85),
as monk in Turkish prison, Kamianets-Podilskyi fortifications. 50k, Mykhailo Khanenko
(1620-80), leading troops, relinquishing power.

2001, Feb. 20   Perf. 12¼x12
412-413 A110 Set of 2   1.00 1.00

Invention of the Telephone, 125th Anniv. A212

2001, Mar. 6   **Perf. 13½**
414 A212 70k multi   1.00 1.00

Children's Art — A213

Art by: 10k, Alyna Nochvaj. 30k, Olyia Pynych. 40k, Dasha Chemberzhi.

2001, Mar. 7   **Perf. 11½**
415-417 A213   Set of 3   1.10 1.10

Hollyhocks A214

Marigolds A215

Sunflower A216

Viburnum Opulus Berries A217

Wheat — A218

2001, Apr. 4   **Litho.**   **Perf. 13¾**
418	A214	(10k) multi	.25	.25
419	A215	(30k) multi	.25	.25
420	A216	(71k) multi	.50	.50
b.		Imprint "2003"	3.00	3.00
c.		Imprint "2004"	2.50	2.50
421	A217	(2.66h) multi	1.75	.85
b.		Imprint "2003"	2.50	2.50
c.		Imprint "2005"	2.00	2.00
d.		Imprint "2006"	2.50	2.50
422	A218	(3.65h) multi	2.50	1.00
b.		Imprint "2003"	3.75	3.75
c.		Imprint "2004"	3.75	3.75
d.		Imprint "2005"	2.50	2.50
e.		Imprint "2006"	2.50	2.50
		Nos. 418-422 (5)	5.25	2.85

2006, Oct. 9
Dated 2006   **Perf. 11½**
418a	A214	(10k) multi	1.10	1.10
419a	A215	(30k) multi	1.10	1.10
420a	A216	(71k) multi	1.25	1.25
421a	A217	(2.66h) multi	4.50	4.50
422a	A218	(3.65h) multi	6.00	6.00
		Nos. 418a-422a (5)	13.95	13.95

Nos. 418a-422a were issued only in No. F2b. See Nos. 453-454, 466-468, 515, 572, 606-609.

Folktales — A219

No. 423: a, The Fox and Wolf (fox on sleigh, fish). b, The Mitten (bear, fox, wolf, rabbit mouse, frog). c, Sirko the Dog (wolf with bottle, dog).

2001, Apr. 14   **Perf. 13½**
423 A219 30k Horiz. strip of 3,   1.40 1.40
     #a-c

Ships — A220

No. 424: a, 20k, Twelve Apostles. b, 30k, Three Priests.

2001, Apr. 20
424 A220   Horiz. pair, #a-b   1.25 1.25

Europa — A221

Fish, jellyfish, seaweed: a, 28x40mm. b, 56x40mm.

2001, Apr. 27
425 A221 1h Horiz. pair, #a-b   3.00 3.00

Holy Trinity A222

2001, May 15
426 A222 30k multi   .50 .50

Souvenir Sheet

Apiculture — A223

No. 427: a, Bee on flower. b, Plant cutting, jar of honey, bowl of pollen, jars. c, Worker on honeycomb. d, Queen. e, Hive. f, Drone.

2001, May 22   **Perf. 11½**
427 A223 50k Sheet of 6, #a-f   6.50 6.50

Souvenir Sheet

Kyievo-Pecherska Monastery, 950th Anniv. — A224

2001, May 25
428 A224 1.50h multi   2.00 2.00

Visit of Pope John Paul II, June 23-27 A225

2001, June 15   **Perf. 13½**
429 A225 3h multi   2.50 2.50

Regional and Administrative Areas

Zakarpatska Oblast — A226

Kharkivska Oblast — A227

Chernihivska Oblast — A228

Kirovohradska Oblast — A229

2001   **Litho.**   **Perf. 12¼x12**
430	A226	30k multi	.60	.60
431	A227	30k multi	.60	.60
432	A228	30k multi	.60	.60
433	A229	30k multi	.60	.60
		Nos. 430-433 (4)	2.40	2.40

Issued: No. 430, 6/29; No. 431, 8/18; No. 432, 9/21; No. 433, 9/22.

Souvenir Sheet

Icons From Khanenko Art Museum — A230

No. 434: a, 20k, Virgin and Child, 28x40mm. b, 30k, St. John the Baptist, 28x40mm. c, Saints Serhyi and Bacchus, 56x40mm.

2001, July 12   **Litho.**   **Perf. 11½**
434 A230   Sheet of 3, #a-c   1.25 1.25

Endangered Species A231

No. 435: a, Milvus milvus. b, Scirtopoda telum.

2001, July 24   **Perf. 13**
435 A231 1h Vert. pair, #a-b   1.75 1.75

Dmytro Bortnianskyi (1751-1825), Composer — A232

2001, July 26
436 A232 20k multi   .50 .50

Soccer — A233

2001, Aug. 10
437 A233 50k multi   .70 .70

Souvenir Sheet

Independence, 10th Anniv. — A234

2001, Aug. 15   **Perf. 11½**
438 A234 3h multi   2.75 2.75

7th Natl. Philatelic Exhibition, Dnipropetrovsk — A235

2001, Oct. 7   **Litho.**   **Perf. 12¼x12**
439 A235 30k multi   .55 .55

Year of Dialogue Among Civilizations A236

2001, Oct. 9   **Perf. 13**
440 A236 70k multi   2.00 2.00

Souvenir Sheet

Black Sea Marine Life — A237

No. 441: a, 30k, Seahorses. b, 70k, Dolphins, birds.

2001, Oct. 19   *Perf. 11½*
441   A237   Sheet of 2, #a-b   2.40   2.40

Christmas — A238

2001, Nov. 9   *Perf. 12¼x12*
442   A238   30k multi   .65   .65

St. Nicholas
A239

2001, Nov. 16   *Perf. 13*
443   A239   30k multi   .65   .65

Happy New
Year — A240

2001, Nov. 23
444   A240   30k multi   .65   .65

Poets — A241

No. 445: a, Taras Shevchenko (1814-61), Ukrainian poet. b, Akakii Tsereteli (1840-1915), Georgian poet.

2001, Dec. 19
445   A241   40k Horiz. pair, #a-b   .90   .90
     See Georgia No. 276.

Regional Costumes

Kyivshchyna Region — A242

Chernihivshchyna Region — A243

Poltavshchyna Region — A244

No. 446: a, 20k, Two women. b, 50k, Man and woman.
No. 447: a, 20k, Musicians and girl. b, 50k, Bride and groom, boy.
No. 448: a, 20k, Priest and family. b, 50k, Two women.

2001, Dec. 20   *Perf. 13¼*
446   A242   Horiz. pair, #a-b   .60   .60
447   A243   Horiz. pair, #a-b   .60   .60
448   A244   Horiz. pair, #a-b   .60   .60
  c.   Souvenir sheet, #446-448, perf.
     11½   2.00   2.00
     Nos. 446-448 (3)   1.80   1.80

Hetman Type of 1997

Designs: No. 449, 40k, Pavlo Teteryia (d. 1670) holding scepter, people in town, horsemen and carriage heading for town. No. 450, 40k, Demyian Mnohohrishnyi, receiving scepter, boats in river. No. 451, 40k, Ivan Briukhovetskyi (d. 1668), battle scenes.

2002, Jan. 17   *Perf. 12¼x12*
449-451   A110   Set of 3   1.10   1.10

Scythian Military History — A245

No. 452: a, Archer on horseback. b, Swordsman in battle. c, Commander on horseback, warrior. d, Female warrior.

2002, Jan. 29   *Perf. 13*
452   A245   40k Block of 4, #a-d   1.25   1.25

Flower Type of 2001 and

Periwinkle — A246

2002   **Litho.**   *Perf. 13¾*
       Year imprint
453   A246   5k multi, "2002"   .50   .50
  a.   Perf. 11½, dated "2006"   1.50   1.50
  b.   As #453, dated "2004"   .75   .75
  c.   As #453, dated "2005"   .75   .75
  d.   As #453, dated "2006"   .75   .75
454   A214   10k multi, "2002"   .50   .50
  a.   Perf. 11½, dated "2006"   1.50   1.50
  b.   As #454, dated "2003"   .75   .75
  c.   As #454, dated "2005"   .75   .75
  d.   As #454, dated "2006"   .75   .75

Issued: No. 453, 2/1; No. 453b, 7/19/04; No. 453c, 2005; No. 453d, 12/1/05. No. 454, 2/26; No. 454b, 2003; No. 454c, 2005; No. 454d, 12/1/05. Nos. 453a-454a, 10/9/06. Nos. 453a-454a were issued only in No. F2b.

Sporting Achievements — A247

Designs: No. 455, 40k, Zhanna Pintusevich-Block winning 100-meter dash at 2001 World Track and Field Championships. No. 456, 40k, Swimmer at 2000 Summer Olympics.

2002, Feb. 15   *Perf. 13*
455-456   A247   Set of 2   .80   .80

Regional and Administrative Areas

Kyivska Oblast — A248

2002, Feb. 18   *Perf. 12¼x12*
457   A248   40k multi   .50   .50

Shipbuilding — A249

No. 458: a, Frigate Sizopol and coast. b, Brigantine Perseus.

2002, Feb. 22   *Perf. 13½*
458   A249   40k Horiz. pair, #a-b   .80   .80

Issuance of First Stamp After Independence, 10th Anniv. — A250

2002, Mar. 1
459   A250   40k No. 100   .80   .80

Leonid Hlibov
(1827-93),
Writer — A251

2002, Mar. 4   **Litho.**   *Perf. 13¼*
460   A251   40k multi   .50   .50

Ruslan Ponomariov, Winner of 16th World Chess Championships — A252

2002, Mar. 29   *Perf. 13½*
461   A252   3.50h multi   2.00   2.00

Souvenir Sheet

Europa — A253

No. 462: a, Lion. b, Tiger, horiz.

2002, Apr. 4   *Perf. 11½*
462   A253   1.75h Sheet of 2, #a-b   3.75   3.75

Palm
Sunday — A254

2002, Apr. 19   *Perf. 13½*
463   A254   40k multi   .45   .45

Worldwide Fund for Nature (WWF) — A255

Various views of Elaphe situla: a, 40k. b, 70k. c, 80k. d, 2.50h.

2002, May 25   *Perf. 13½*
464   A255   Block of 4, #a-d   2.50   2.50
  e.   Perf. 11½   3.50   3.50

Souvenir Sheet

Opera and Ballet Theaters — A256

No. 465: a, Donetsk (tree at center). b, Dnipropetrovsk (trees at side).

2002, May 31   *Perf. 11½*
465   A256   1.25h Sheet of 2, #a-b   1.25   1.25

Flower Type of 2001 and

Blue   Lilac
Cornflower   A258
A257

2002   **Litho.**   *Perf. 13¾*
       Year Imprint
466   A215   30k multi, "2002"   .50   .50
  a.   Perf. 11½, dated "2006"   1.75   1.75
  b.   As #466, dated "2003"   .70   .70
  c.   As #466, dated "2004"   .70   .70
  d.   As #466, dated "2005"   .70   .70
  e.   As #466, dated "2006"   .70   .70

467 A257 45k multi, "2002" .50 .50
  a.   Perf. 11½, dated "2006" 1.75 1.75
  b.   As #467, dated "2003" .70 .70
  c.   As #467, dated "2004" .70 .70
  d.   As #467, dated "2005" .70 .70
  e.   As #467, dated "2006" .70 .70
468 A258 (80k) multi, "2002" .80 .80
  a.   Perf. 11½, dated "2006" 2.50 2.50
  b.   As #468, dated "2003" 1.00 1.00
  c.   As #468, dated "2004" 1.00 1.00

Issued: Issued: No. 466, 6/1/02; No. 466b4/17/03; No. 466c, 1/22/04; No. 466d, 2/3/05; No. 466e, 12/1/05. No. 467, 9/19/02; No. 467b, 4/17/03; No. 467c, 2/6/04; No. 467d, 4/29/05; No. 467e, 3/3/06. No. 468, 7/5/02; No. 468b, 2003; No. 468c, 7/19/04.

Nos. 466a-468a issued 10/9/06. Nos. 466a-468a were issued only in No. F2b.

Regional and Administrative Areas

Luhanska Oblast — A259

Chernivetska Oblast — A260

Odeska Oblast — A261

Cherkaska Oblast — A262

Sumska Oblast — A263

2002   **Perf. 12¼x12**
469 A259 40k multi .50 .50
470 A260 40k multi .50 .50
471 A261 45k multi .50 .50
472 A262 45k multi .50 .50
473 A263 45k multi .50 .50
    Nos. 469-473 (5) 2.50 2.50

Issued: No. 469, 6/2; No. 470, 6/27; No. 471, 9/20. No. 472, 10/9; No. 473, 10/21.

Endangered Species A264

No. 474: a, Phalacrocorax aristotelis. b, Phocoena phocoena.

2002, June 14   **Litho.**   **Perf. 13**
474 A264 70k Pair, #a-b 1.50 1.50

Mykola Leontovich (1877-1921), Composer — A265

2002, June 21   **Perf. 13½**
475 A265 40k multi .50 .50

Souvenir Sheet

Black Sea Nature Reserve — A266

No. 476: a, Haematopus ostralegus (40x28mm). b, Larus genei (40x28mm). c, Iris pumila (22x26mm). d, Numenius arquata (26x22mm). e, Charadrius alexandrinus (26x22mm).

2002, July 13   **Perf. 11½**
476 A266 50k Sheet of 5, #a-e 2.50 2.50

Folk Tales — A267

No. 477: a, Fox and Pancake. b, Mr. Cat. c, Speckled Chicken.

2002, July 19   **Perf. 14¼x14**
477 A267 40k Horiz. strip of 3, #a-c .70 .70

Art of Hanna Sobachko-Shostak — A268

No. 478: a, Cage for Starlings, 1963 (peach background). b, Vase with Flowers, 1964 (red background). c, Chamomile Flowers, 1964 (yellow background).

2002, Aug. 9   **Perf. 14x14¼**
478   Horiz. strip of 3 .90 .90
  a.-c.   A268 45k Any single .30 .30

Space Pioneers — A269

Designs: 40k, Yurii V. Kondratiuk (1897-1942). 45k, Mykhailo Yianhel (1911-71). 50k, Mykola Kybalchych (1853-81). 70k, Serhii Korolov (1907-66).

2002, Aug. 23   **Perf. 12¼x12**
479-482 A269 Set of 4 1.60 1.60
    See Nos. 500-503.

Marine Life — A270

No. 483: a, Phoca caspica. b, Huso huso ponticus.

2002, Sept. 6   **Perf. 14x14¼**
483 A270 75k Horiz. pair, #a-b 1.25 1.25
    See Kazakhstan No. 386.

Khotyn, 1000th Anniv. — A271

2002, Sept. 21   **Perf. 12¼x12**
484 A271 40k multi .50 .50

Odesaphil 2002 Stamp Exhibition, Odesa — A272

2002, Oct. 5   **Litho.**   **Perf. 14¼x14**
485 A272 45k multi .50 .50

Paintings of Kyiv by Taras Shevchenko (1814-61) — A273

Designs: 45k, Askold's Tomb. 75k, Dnieper River Shoreline. 80k, St. Alexander's Church.

Perf. 13¾x14½
2002, Nov. 15   **Litho.**
486-488 A273 Set of 3 1.10 1.10
    See Nos. 516-519, 548-551, 590-593.

Happy New Year A274

2002, Nov. 22   **Perf. 14x14¼**
489 A274 45k multi .65 .65

Regional Costumes

Vinychyna Region — A275

Cherkashchyna Region — A276

Ternopilska Region — A277

No. 490: a, Family, rainbow. b, Family, fruit tree.
No. 491: a, Four girls holding hands. b, Couple gathering crops.
No. 492: a, Priest blessing family. b, People with Easter baskets.

2002, Dec. 6   **Perf. 13¼**
490 A275 45k Horiz. pair, #a-b .45 .45
491 A276 45k Horiz. pair, #a-b .45 .45
492 A277 45k Horiz. pair, #a-b .45 .45
  c.   Souvenir sheet, #490-492, perf. 11½ 4.25 4.25
    Nos. 490-492 (3) 1.35 1.35

Folk Tales — A278

No. 493: a, Koza-Dezera (cow on bridge). b, The Straw Bull. c, The Fox and Crane.

2003, Jan. 17   **Litho.**   **Perf. 14¼x14**
493 A278 45k Horiz. strip of 3, #a-c .75 .75

Speed Skating A279

2003, Jan. 24   **Perf. 14x14¼**
494 A279 65k multi .55 .55

Military History — A280

No. 495: a, War with Goths, 4th cent. (soldier with spear and shield) b, Battles with Huns, 5th cent. (archer). c, Balkan campaigns, 6th cent. (soldier with hatchet). d, Battles with the Avars, 6th cent. (soldier with spears).

2003, Feb. 7
495 A280 45k Block of 4, #a-d 1.10 1.10

Shipbuilding — A281

No. 496: a, Steamship Grozny (denomination at left. b, Steamship Odessa (denomination at right).

2003, Feb. 14
496 A281 1h Horiz. pair, #a-b 1.40 1.40

Mikola Arkas (1853-1909),
Composer — A282

2003, Feb. 21
497 A282 45k multi   .45   .45

Souvenir Sheet

Javorivsky National Nature
Park — A283

No. 498: a, 1h, Alcede atthis (32x44mm). b,
1h, Cypripedium calceolus (36x41mm). c,
1.50h, Eudia pavonia, horiz. (44x32mm)

2003, Mar. 3   *Perf. 11½*
498 A283   Sheet of 3, #a-c   2.50 2.50

Europa — A284

Poster by Oleksiy Shtanko: a, Virgin Mary
with dove. b, Guardian angel.

2003, Mar. 21   *Perf. 11½*
499 A284 1.75h Horiz. pair, #a-
     b   3.50 3.50
   c.   Booklet pane, 2 #499 + central
      label   12.50   —
      Complete booklet, #499c   12.50

Space Pioneers Type of 2002

Designs: 45k, Olkeksandr Zasiadko (1779-
1837). 65k, Kostyantin Konstantinov (1817-
71). 70k, Valyntyn Hlushko (1908-89). 80k,
Volodymyr Chelomei (1914-84).

2003, Apr. 11 Litho. *Perf. 13¾x14½*
500-503 A269   Set of 4   1.60 1.60

Ukrainian Red Cross Society, 85th
Anniv. — A285

2003, Apr. 18
504 A285 45k multi   .50   .50

Regional and Administrative Areas

Dnipropetrovska Oblast — A286

Lvivska Oblast — A287

Khmelnytska Oblast — A288

Mykolayivska Oblast — A289

Zaporizhiya Oblast — A290

2003
505 A286 45k multi   .45   .45
506 A287 45k multi   .45   .45
507 A288 45k multi   .45   .45
508 A289 45k multi   .45   .45
509 A290 45k multi   .45   .45
     Nos. 505-509 (5)   2.25 2.25
Issued: No. 505, 4/21; No. 506, 5/8; No.
507, 9/26; No. 508, 10/4; No. 509, 10/11.

Hetman Type of 1997

Designs: No. 510, 45k, Ivan Skoropadskiy
(1646-1722) wearing robe, serfs in field, subjects bowing. No. 511, 45k, Kyrylo Rozumov-
skiy (1728-1803) holding scepter, attack of
palace, palace ruins.

2003, May 22
510-511 A110   Set of 2   .75   .75

Souvenir Sheet

Volodymyr Monomakh (1053-1125),
Grand Prince of Kyiv — A291

2003, May 28   *Perf. 11½*
512 A291 3.50h multi   2.25 2.25

Owls — A292

No. 513: a, Bubo bubo. b, Strix uralensis. c,
Strix aluco. d, Strix nebulosa. e, Glaucidium
passerinum. f, Aegolius funereus. g, Otus
scops. h, Athene noctua. i, Tyto alba. j, Asio
otus. k, Asio flammeus. l, Surnia ulula. Size of
513e-513h: 25x27mm; others: 25x36mm.

2003, June 14
513 A292 45k Sheet of 12, #a-l   6.50 6.50

Oleksandr
Myshuha (1853-
1922), Opera
Singer — A293

2003, June 20   *Perf. 13¼*
514 A293 45k multi   .50   .50

Sweet Pea — A294

2003, July 4   *Perf. 13¾*
Year Imprint
515 A294 65k multi, "2003"   1.25 1.25
   a.   Perf. 11 ½, dated "2006"   2.50 2.50
   b.   As #515, dated "2004"   2.00 2.00
   c.   As #515, dated "2005"   1.25 1.25
Issued: No. 515b, 2/6/04; No. 515c, 2/1/05.
No. 515a issued 10/9/06. No. 515a was
issued only in No. F2b.

Paintings Type of 2002

Paintings of Kyiv: No. 516, 45k, Podil, by
Mykhailo Sazhyn, 1840. No. 517, 45k, Kyiv-
Pecherska Monastery, by Vasyl Timm, 1857.
No. 518, 45k, Ruins of St. Irene Monastery, by
Sazhyn, 1846. No. 519, 45k, View of Old City
from Yaroslav Embankment, by Timm, 1854.

2003, July 18   *Perf. 13¾x14½*
516-519 A273   Set of 4   1.50 1.50

Customs and Traditions — A295

No. 520: a, Celebration of the Harvest
(Church, flowers and insects). b, Ascension
(Church, fruit).

2003, July 25   *Perf. 14¼x14*
520 A295 45k Horiz. pair, #a-b   .50   .50

Borys
Hmyryia
(1903-69),
Composer
A296

2003, Aug. 5   *Perf. 14x14¼*
521 A296 45k multi   .45   .45

Souvenir Sheet

Manyiavskyi Monastery — A297

No. 522: a, Denomination at LL. b, Denomination at LR.

2003, Aug. 15   *Perf. 11x11½*
522 A297 1.25h Sheet of 2, #a-b   1.75 1.75

Yevpatoriya, 2500th Anniv. — A298

2003, Aug. 29   *Perf. 13¾x14½*
523 A298 45k multi   .50   .50

Ancient Trade Routes — A299

No. 524: a, Arrival of Scandinavian seamen
in rowboat, coin of Danish King Svend Estrid-
sen. b, Silver coin of Prince Volodymyr
Sviatoslavovych, Slavic warship with sail.

2003, Sept. 17   *Perf. 11½*
524 A299 80k Vert. pair, #a-b, +
             central label   .90   .90
   c.   Booklet pane, #524   3.75   —
   d.   Booklet pane, #524a   2.50   —
   e.   Booklet pane, #524b   2.50   —
      Complete booklet, #524c, 524d,
      524e   9.00

Hryhoryi Kvitka-Osnovyianenko (1778-
1843), Writer — A300

2003, Nov. 14 Litho. *Perf. 14¼x14*
525 A300 45k multi   .50   .50

Famine of 1932-33 — A301

2003, Nov. 21   *Perf. 13¾x14½*
526 A301 45k multi   .50   .50

Christmas
A302

Litho. with Foil Application
2003, Nov. 25   *Perf. 13¼x13½*
527 A302 45k multi   1.00 1.00

New Year's Greetings A303

2003, Nov. 25   Litho.   *Perf. 13½*
528 A303 45k multi   1.00 1.00

Regional Costumes

Kharkiv Region — A304

Sumy Region — A305

Donetsk Region — A306

No. 529: a, Women, religious icons. b, Family, lute.
No. 530: a, Woman, men. b, Group of women.
No. 531: a, Family, sled. b, Workers in field.

2003, Dec. 19   *Perf. 13¼*
529 A304 45k Horiz. pair, #a-b   .80 .80
530 A305 45k Horiz. pair, #a-b   .80 .80
531 A306 45k Horiz. pair, #a-b   .80 .80
   c.   Souvenir sheet, #529-531, perf. 11½   3.50 3.50

Unification of Ukraine and Western Ukraine, 85th Anniv. — A307

2004, Jan. 22   Litho.   *Perf. 13¾x14½*
532 A307 45k multi   .40 .40

Stanislav Ludkevych (1879-1979), Composer A308

2004, Jan. 24   *Perf. 13¼*
533 A308 45k multi   .40 .40

Possessions of Hetman Bohdan Khmelnytsky — A309

No. 534: a, Flag. b, Mace. c, Cap. d, Chalice decorated with leaves. e, Tankard. f, Sword.

Litho. With Foil Application
2004, Jan. 29   *Perf. 11½*
534 A309 45k Sheet of 6, #a-f   2.00 2.00

Shipbuilding — A310

No. 535: a, 1h, Oil tanker Kriti Amber (55x26mm). b, 2.50h, Anti-submarine ship Mikolayiv (55x29mm). c, 3.50h Aircraft carrier Admiral Kuznetzov (55x40mm).

2004, Feb. 21   Litho.   *Perf. 11½*
535 A310 Sheet of 3, #a-c   4.25 4.25

Regional and Administrative Areas

Ternopilska Oblast — A311

2004, Mar. 3   *Perf. 13¾x14½*
536 A311 45k multi   .50 .50

Membership in UNESCO, 50th Anniv. — A312

2004, Mar. 19   *Perf. 14¼x14*
537 A312 45k multi   .50 .50

Butterflies — A313

No. 538: a, 45k, Endromis versicolora. b, 75k, Smerinthus ocellatus. c, 80k, Catocala fraxini. d, 2.60h, Apatura ilia. e, 3.50h, Papilio machaon.

2004, Mar. 26   *Perf. 8*
538 A313   Sheet of 5, #a-e   4.75 6.00

Famous Ukrainians A314

Designs: No. 539, 45k, Serhyi Lyfar (1904-86), ballet dancer and choreographer. No. 540, 45k, Maria Zankovetska (1854-1934), actress. No. 541, 45k, Mykhaylo Maksymovych (1804-73), historian.

2004   Litho.   *Perf. 14x14¼*
539-541 A314   Set of 3   1.25 1.25
   Issued: No. 630, 4/2, Nos. 540-541, 7/23.
   See Nos. 574-575, 613-614, 641, 655-656, 750-751, 757-758.

Zenit-1 Rocket A315

2004, Apr. 14
542 A315 45k multi   .50 .50

European Weight Lifting Championships, Kyiv — A316

2004, Apr. 20
543 A316 65k multi   .50 .50

Miniature Sheet

Europa — A317

No. 544: a, 45k, Lastivchyne Hnizdo (22x33mm). b, 75k, Carpathian Mountains (22x33mm). c, 2.61h, Khotyn Castle (29x33mm). d, 3.52h, Pecherska Lavra (39x28mm).

2004, Apr. 23   *Perf. 11½*
544 A317   Sheet of 4, #a-d   6.25 6.25

UEFA (European Football Union), 50th Anniv. — A318

2004, May 17   *Perf. 14¼x14*
545 A318 3.52h multi   1.75 1.75

FIFA (Fédération Internationale de Football Association), Cent. — A319

No. 546: a, 45k, Player #11. b, 75k, Player #6. c, 80k, Fan. d, 2.61h, Two women players.

2004, May 17   *Perf. 13¼*
546 A319   Block of 4, #a-d   2.75 2.75

Symon Petlura (1879-1926), Political Leader — A320

2004, May 21
547 A320 45k multi   .50 .50

Painting Type of 2002
Designs: No. 548, 45k, Kiev with St. Andrew's Church, by unknown artist, 1889. No. 549, 45k, Fountain Near the Golden Gate, by Petro Levchenko, 1910. No. 550, 45k, Spring in Kurenivka, by Abram Manevych, 1914-15. No. 551, 45k, St. Michael's Cathedral From the South, by Mykola Burachek, 1919.

2004, June 11   *Perf. 13¾x14½*
548-551 A273   Set of 4   1.25 1.25

Folktales — A321

No. 552: a, The Cat. b, Ivasyk Telesyk. c, The Fat Man.

2004, June 18   *Perf. 14¼x14*
552 A321 45k Horiz. strip of 3, #a-c   .90 .90

2004 Summer Olympics, Athens A322

2004, June 26   *Perf. 14x14¼*
553 A322 2.61h multi   1.40 1.40

Regional and Administrative Areas

Rovenska Oblast — A323

Khersonska Oblast — A324

Poltavska Oblast — A325

2004   *Perf. 13¾x14½*
554 A323 45k multi   .50 .50
555 A324 45k multi   .50 .50
556 A325 45k multi   .50 .50

   Issued: No. 554, 7/16; No. 555, 8/20; No. 556, 9/22.

Balaklava, 2500th Anniv. — A327

Perf. 13¾x14½
2004, Aug. 14   Litho.
557 A327 45k multi   .50 .50

Kharkiv, 350th
Anniv. — A328

2004, Aug. 20   *Perf. 14¼x14*
558 A328 45k multi   .50 .50

Bridges — A329

   No. 559: a, Inhulskyi Bridge (open drawbridge). b, Darnytska Bridge (three arches above roadway). c, B. M. Preobrazhenskoho Bridge (arches below roadway). d, Southern Buh Bridge (swing bridge).

2004, Aug. 25   *Perf. 13¾x14½*
559 A329 45k Block of 4, #a-d   1.25 1.25

No. 194B Surcharged

Litho. & Engr.
2004, Sept. 15   *Perf. 12½x13*
560 A47a 2.61h on 25,000kb
     multi   1.50 1.50

   Taras Shevchenko University, 170th anniv.

Kirovohrad, 250th Anniv. — A330

Perf. 13¾x14¼
2004, Sept. 17   Litho.
561 A330 45k multi   .50 .50

Military History — A331

   No. 562: a, Infantryman of Prince Oleg, 10th cent. b, National militia, 11th-12th cent. c, Archer on horseback, 12th cent. d, Cavalryman for Danylo Halyts, 13th cent.

2004, Oct. 15   *Perf. 14x14¼*
562 A331 45k Block of 4, #a-d   1.40 1.40

Miniature Sheet

Birds of the Danube Nature
Reserve — A332

   No. 563: a, 45k, Cygnus olor. b, 75k, Phalacrocorax pygmaeus. c, 80k, Egretta alba. d, 2.61h, Anser anser. e, 3.52h, Platalea leucordia.

2004, Oct. 26   *Perf. 11½*
563 A332   Sheet of 5, #a-e   4.75 4.75

Khartron
Control
Systems
in Space
A333

1516 Battle Between Cossacks and
Tartars Using Fiery Projectiles
A334

2004, Nov. 12   *Perf. 14x14¼*
564 A333 45k multi   .50 .50
565 A334 45k multi   .50 .50

Christmas
A335

   No. 566: a, Magi facing right ("2" in background). b, Magi facing left ("5" in background). c, Nativity ("0" in background).

Litho. With Foil Application
2004, Nov. 26   *Perf. 13¼*
566   Horiz. strip of 4, #a-b, 2
     #c   1.00 1.00
a.-c.   A335 45k Any single, gold & multi   .25 .25

   Numbers in background of strip of 4 read "2005."

New Year's
Greetings
A336

   No. 567: a, Santa Claus, large trees at left ("2" in background). b, Santa Claus, large trees at right ("5" in background). c, Tree and gifts ("0" in background).

2004, Nov. 26
567   Horiz. strip of 4, #a-b,
     2 #c   1.00 1.00
a.-c.   A336 45k Any single, silver &
     multi   .25 .25

   Numbers in background of strip of 4 read "2005."

Ukrainian and Iranian Aircraft — A337

   No. 568: a, Antonov-140, Ukraine (denomination at left). b, Iran-140, Iran (denomination at right).

2004, Nov. 30   Litho.   *Perf. 11½*
568   Horiz. pair + central label   1.10 1.00
a.-b.   A337 80k Either single   .50 .50

   See Iran No. 2907.

Regional Costumes

Lvivshchyna Region — A338

Ivano-Frankivshchyna Region — A339

Hutsulshchyna Region — A340

   No. 569: a, Family, rooster. b, Family, pitcher.
   No. 570: a, Musicians. b, Dancers at wedding.
   No. 571: a, Men, child, lamb. b, Family, cradle.

2004, Dec. 10   *Perf. 13¼*
569 A338 60k Horiz. pair, #a-b   .70 .70
570 A339 60k Horiz. pair, #a-b   .70 .70
571 A340 60k Horiz. pair, #a-b   .70 .70
c.   Miniature sheet, #569-571, perf.
     11½   2.10 2.10

Poppy — A341

2005, Jan. 14   Litho.   *Perf. 13¾*
Date Imprint
572 A341 1h multi, "2005"   1.10 1.10
a.   Perf. 11½, dated "2006"   2.75 2.75
b.   As #572, dated "2006"   1.10 1.10

   No. 572b issued 5/23/06.
   No. 572a issued 10/9/06. No. 572a was issued only in No. F2b.

November - December 2004 Protests
Against Rigged Elections — A342

2005, Jan. 23   *Perf. 11½*
573 A342 45k multi   .45 .45

   Printed in sheets of 7 + label.

Famous Ukrainians Type of 2004

   Design: No. 574, Pavlo Virskyi (1905-75), choreographer. No. 575, Volodymyr Vynnychenko (1880-1951), writer and statesman.

2005   Litho.   *Perf. 14x14¼*
574 A314 45k multi   .45 .45
575 A314 45k multi   .45 .45

   Issued: No. 574, 2/4; No. 575, 7/15.

Miniature Sheet

Moths — A343

No. 576: a, 45k, Acherontia atropos. b, 75k, Catocala sponsa. c, 80k, Staurophora celsia. d, 2.61h, Marumba quercus. e, 3.52h, Saturnia pyri.

2005, Feb. 11   *Perf. 11½*
576 A343   Sheet of 5, #a-e   5.00 5.00

Regional and Administrative Areas

Vinnytska Oblast — A344

Sevastopol City — A345

Ivano-Frankivska Oblast — A346

Zhitomyrska Oblast — A347

2005   *Perf. 13¾x14½*
577 A344 45k multi   .45 .45
578 A345 45k multi   .45 .45
579 A346 45k multi   .45 .45
580 A347 70k multi   .55 .55
   Nos. 577-580 (4)   1.90 1.90

Issued: No. 577, 2/23; No. 578, 6/11; No. 579, 7/16; 70k, 9/10.

Paintings by Ivan Aivazovskyi — A348

No. 581: a, Sea — Koktebel, 1853. b, Towers on the Rock Near the Bosporus, 1859.

2005, Mar. 4   **Litho.**   *Perf. 14x14¼*
581 A348   Horiz. pair, #a-b, + central label   .90 .90
a.-b.   45k Either single   .45 .45

The Shepherd, by Heorhyi Yakutovych (1930-2000) — A349

Litho. & Engr.
2005, Mar. 26   *Perf. 11½*
582 A349 3.52h silver & gray blue   2.10 2.10

Cosmos-1 Satellite A350

Zenit-2 Rocket A351

Designs: No. 585, Dnepr rocket. No. 586, Cyclone-3 rocket.

2005, Apr. 12   **Litho.**   *Perf. 14x14¼*
583 A350 45k shown   .40 .40
584 A351 45k shown   .40 .40
585 A351 45k multi   .40 .40
586 A351 45k multi   .40 .40
   Nos. 583-586 (4)   1.60 1.60

A352

End of World War II, 60th Anniv. — A353

2005   *Perf. 14x14¼*
587 A352 45k multi   .55 .55

Souvenir Sheet
Perf. 11½
588 A353 80k multi   .80 .80

Issued: 45k, 4/22; 80k, 5/7. No. 587 issued in sheets of 8 + central label.

Ninth Intl. Philatelic Exhibition, Kyiv — A354

2005, May 17   *Perf. 13¾x14½*
589 A354 45k multi   .45 .45

Painting Type of 2002

Paintings of Kyiv: 45k, New Street, by Serhyi Shyshko, 1966. 75k, Park in Winter, by Shyshko, 1960. 80k, Sacred Sophia, by Yuryi Khymych, 1965. 1h, Khreshchatyk Boulevard, by Khymych, 1967, vert.

Perf. 13¾x14½, 14½x13¾
2005, May 18
590-593 A273   Set of 4   2.75 2.75

Ruslana, Winner of 2004 Eurovision Song Contest — A355

Logo for 2005 Eurovision Song Contest — A356

2005, May 19   *Perf. 11½*
594 A355 45k multi   .45 .45
595 A356 2.50h multi   1.50 1.50

Europa — A357

Nos. 596 and 597: a, 2.61h, Bowl of borscht, beets, onions, garlic, tomatoes, pepper, beans, lard, parsley and dill. b, 3.52h, Lidded tureen, cabbage, carrots, onion, garlic, pepper.

2005, May 20   *Perf. 11½*
Stamp Size: 45x32mm
596 A357   Horiz. pair, #a-b   4.25 4.25

Booklet Stamps
Stamp Size: 40x27mm
Perf. 14x14¼
597 A357   Horiz. pair, #a-b   6.00 6.00
c.   Booklet pane, 2 #597   12.00 —
   Complete booklet, #597c   12.00

Complete booklet sold for 19.38h.

Development of the Cyrillic Alphabet — A358

Litho. & Embossed
2005, May 21   *Perf. 14¼x14*
598 A358 45k multi   .50 .50

Souvenir Sheet

Flora and Fauna in Karadazkyi Nature Reserve — A359

No. 599: a, 45k, Falco cherrug (33x40mm). b, 70k, Ascalaphus macaronius (29x35mm). c, 2.50h, Tursiops truncatus ponticus (33x33mm). d, 3.50h, Martes foina (49x33mm).

2005, July 28   **Litho.**   *Perf. 11½*
599 A359   Sheet of 4, #a-d   3.50 3.50

World Summit on the Information Society, Tunis A360

2005, Aug. 12   *Perf. 14x14¼*
600 A360 2.50h multi   1.40 1.40

Series Ov Locomotive — A361

Series C Locomotive — A362

Series Shch Locomotive — A363

Series Ye Locomotive — A364

2005, Aug. 31
601 A361 70k multi   .55 .55
602 A362 70k multi   .55 .55
603 A363 70k multi   .55 .55
604 A364 70k multi   .55 .55
   Nos. 601-604 (4)   2.20 2.20

Nos. 601-604 were each printed in sheets of 11 + label.

Sumy, 350th Anniv. — A365

2005, Sept. 2
605 A365 45k multi   .45 .45

Nasturtium A366

Water Lily A367

Violets — A368

Wild Rose — A369

2005   **Date imprint**   *Perf. 13¾*
606 A366 25k multi   .65 .65
a.   Perf. 11½, dated "2006"   1.10 1.10
b.   As #606, dated "2006"   1.50 1.50
607 A367 70k multi   1.35 1.35
a.   Perf. 11½, dated "2006"   1.50 1.50
b.   As #607, dated "2006"   1.35 1.35
608 A368 (1.53h) multi   1.50 1.50
a.   Perf. 11½, dated "2006"   4.00 4.00
b.   As #608, dated "2006"   1.50 1.50
609 A369 (2.55h) multi   2.50 2.50
a.   Perf. 11½, dated "2006"   5.00 5.00
b.   As #609, dated "2006"   2.50 2.50
   Nos. 606-609 (4)   6.00 6.00

Issued: No. 606, 9/8/05; No. 606b, 2/7/06. No. 607, 9/12/05; No. 607b, 2/7/06. No. 608, 12/16/05; No. 608b, 9/28/06. No. 609, 11/25/05; No. 609a, 6/5/06.
Nos. 606a-609a issued 10/9/06. Nos. 606a-609a were issued only in No. F2b.

Horses — A370

No. 610: a, Novoolexandrivskyi heavy draft horse (brown horse facing left with four-line inscription). b, Orlov-Rostopchin (white horse). c, Ukrainian riding horse (brown horse facing left with three-line inscription). d, Thoroughbred (brown horse facing right).

2005, Sept. 15   *Perf. 11½*
610 A370 70k Block of 4, #a-d   1.60 1.60

"Safety - Green Light" A371

"Give a Helping Hand" A372

"No to Drugs" A373

2005, Oct. 14   *Perf. 14x14¼*
611   Horiz. strip of 3   1.40 1.40
   a. A371 70k multi   .45 .45
   b. A372 70k multi   .45 .45
   c. A373 70k multi   .45 .45

Military History — A374

No. 612: a, Commander Bobrok Volnyets at Battle of Kulikovo, 1380. b, Artillerymen and riflemen, 14th-15th cent. c, Knight Ivanko Sushyk at Grunwald, 1410. d, Prince Konstiantyn Ostrozkyi at Orsha, 1512.

2005, Oct. 22
612 A374 70k Block of 4, #a-d   1.60 1.60

Famous Ukrainians Type of 2004

Designs: No. 613, Dmytro Yiavornytskyi (1855-1940), historian. No. 614, Oleg Antonov (1906-84), aircraft designer.

2005-06   Litho.
613 A314 70k multi   .50 .50
614 A314 70k multi   .50 .50
   Issued: No. 613, 11/7; No. 614, 2/7/06.

Christmas A375

Litho. With Foil Application
2005, Nov. 11   *Perf. 13¼*
615 A375 70k multi   .50 .50

New Year's Day — A376

2005, Nov. 11   Litho.
616 A376 70k multi   .50 .50

St. Barbara's Church, Vienna, Austria — A377

2005, Dec. 9   *Perf. 14¼x14*
617 A377 75k multi + label   .65 .65

Lviv National Museum, Cent. — A378

No. 618: a, Archangel Michael, by unknown artist (denomination at right). b, Dalmatynka, by Teofil Kopystynskyi (denomination at left).

2005, Dec. 13   Litho.
618 A378 70k Horiz. pair, #a-b, +   central label   1.00 1.00

Regional Costumes

Zhytomyrshchyna Region — A379

Rivnenshchyna Region — A380

Volyn Region — A381

No. 619: a, Family and dog, St. Basil's Day. b, Man and woman, St. Zosyma's Day.
No. 620: a, People with animals, St. George's Day. b, Men, women and musician, Sts. Peter and Paul's Day.
No. 621: a, People with buckets, Annunciation Day. b, Family and cat, St. Nicholas's Day.

2005, Dec. 20   *Perf. 13¼*
619 A379 70k Horiz. pair, #a-b   .90 .90
620 A380 70k Horiz. pair, #a-b   .90 .90
621 A381 70k Horiz. pair, #a-b   .90 .90
   c. Miniature sheet, #619-621, perf. 11½   4.00 4.00

Europa Stamps, 50th Anniv. — A382

Designs: Nos. 622a, 623a, 1.30h, 50th anniversary emblem. Nos. 622a, 622b, 2.50h, CEPT emblem.

2006, Jan. 5   Litho.   *Perf. 13¼*
With Names of Designers at Right of Stamps
622 A382   Vert. pair, #a-b   2.25 2.25
Souvenir Sheet
Without Names of Designers at Right of Stamps
       Perf. 11½
623 A382   Sheet of 2, #a-b   2.25 2.25

Art by Hryhoryi Narbut (1886-1920) — A383

Litho. & Engr.
2006, Mar. 10   *Perf. 11½*
624 A383 3.33h multi   2.10 2.10
   Printed in sheets of 11 + label.

Miniature Sheet

Traditional Women's Headdresses — A384

No. 625: a, Drawing of woman wearing fur hat. b, Woman, facing left, wearing black hat with brown ribbon. c, Drawing of woman facing left, wearing undecorated head covering. d, Woman wearing large floral head covering. e, Woman wearing red kerchief. f, Woman wearing small floral head covering. g, Woman wearing white kerchief with red dots. h, Woman wearing brown kerchief with knot in front. i, Drawing of woman, facing right, wearing undecorated head covering. j, Woman wearing floral headcovering with thin black edge. k, Woman wearing kerchief with floral

---

pattern. l, Woman wearing small floral head covering with ribbon.

2006, Mar. 30   Litho.   *Perf. 11½*
625 A384 70k Sheet of 12, #a-l   5.50 5.50

Coronas-1 Satellite A385

Designs: No. 627, Welding in space. No. 628, International observation of Halley's Comet.

2006, Apr. 12   *Perf. 14x14¼*
Color of Panel Denomination Panel
626 A385 85k gray   .70 .70
627 A385 85k red brown   .70 .70
628 A385 85k dull brown   .70 .70
   Nos. 626-628 (3)   2.10 2.10

Europa — A386

Designs: Nos. 629a, 630a, 2.50h, Earth and Saturn. Nos. 629b, 630b, 3.50h, Earth and Jupiter.

2006, Apr. 28   *Perf. 11½*
Top Cyrillic Inscription in Black
629 A386   Horiz. pair, #a-b   4.25 4.25
Top Cyrillic Inscription in Red
630 A386   Booklet pane of 2, #a-b + 2 labels   8.00 8.00
   Complete booklet, #630   8.00

Nos. 630a-630b are 52x26mm. No. 630 sold for 11.52h.

2006 World Cup Soccer Championships, Germany — A387

Designs: 2.50k, Ukrainian soccer players. 3.50k, Soccer ball.

2006, May 4
631-632 A387 Set of 2   4.50 4.50

Georgia, Ukraine, Azerbaijan and Moldova Summit, Kiev A388

2006, May 23   *Perf. 14x14¼*
633 A388 70k multi   .65 .65

Paintings of Kiev — A389

Designs: No. 634, 70k, Zaborovskyi Gate, by Boris Tulin, 1987 (shown). No. 635, 70k, Olha Basystiuk Sings, by Tulin, 1987. No. 636, 70k, Kiev-Peherska Lavra, by Oleksandr Hubarev, 1990. No. 637, 70k, Andrew's Alley, by Hubarev, 1983.

2006, May 24   *Perf. 13¾x14¼*
634-637 A389 Set of 4   2.25 2.25

Souvenir Sheet

Lviv, 750th Anniv. — A390

No. 638 — View of Lviv, 1618 and: a, 70k, Coat of arms (38x31mm). b, 2.50h, Coin (69x31mm).

2006, June 16   *Perf. 11½*
638 A390   Sheet of 2, #a-b   2.10 2.10

Miniature Sheet

Fauna of Shatskyi National Park — A391

No. 639: a, Lanius excubitor (28x40mm). b, Lynx lynx (33x35mm). c, Anguilla anguilla (41x29mm). d, Bufo calamita (28x29mm). e, Mustela erminea (45x29mm).

2006, July 14
639 A301 70k Sheet of 5, #a-e   3.00 3.00

Miniature Sheet

Cossack Leaders — A392

No. 640: a, Ivan Bohun (denomination at UL). b, Ivan Honta (denomination at UR). c, Ivan Pidkova (denomination at LL). d, Ivan Sirko (denomination at LR).

Litho. & Engr. With Foil Application
2006, Aug. 18
640 A392 3.50h Sheet of 4, #a-d   8.50 8.50

Famous Ukrainians Type of 2004
Design: Ivan Franko (1856-1916), writer.

2006, Aug. 27   Litho.   *Perf. 14x14¼*
641 A314 70k multi   .65 .65

Series L Locomotive — A393

Series SO Locomotive — A394

Series YS Locomotive — A395

Series FD Locomotive — A396

2006, Sept. 15
642 A393 70k multi   .60 .60
643 A394 70k multi   .60 .60
644 A395 70k multi   .60 .60
645 A396 70k multi   .60 .60
   Nos. 642-645 (4)   2.40 2.40
Each stamp printed in sheets of 11 + label.

Tenth Natl. Philatelic Exhibition, Lviv — A397

2006, Oct. 6   Litho. & Embossed
646 A397 70k multi   .65 .65

Miltary History — A398

No. 647: a, Cossack-siroma, 16th-17th cent. b, Naval campaigns of 16th-18th cents. c, Khmelnychna national liberation movement (soldiers aiming guns), 17th cent. d, Haidamachnya national liberation movement (soldier with sword), 17th cent.

2006, Nov. 3   Litho.   *Perf. 14x14¼*
647 A398 70k Block of 4, #a-d   2.40 2.40

Horses in Sports — A399

No. 648: a, Dressage. b, Horse racing. c, Harness racing. d, Show jumping.

2006, Nov. 17   *Perf. 11½*
648 A399 70k Block of 4, #a-d   2.60 2.60
Printed in sheets containing two each of Nos. 648a-648d.

St. Nicholas's Day — A400

No. 649: a, Children following angel. b, Angel and St. Nicholas.

Litho. With Foil Application
2006, Nov. 17   *Perf. 13¼*
649 A400 70k Horiz. pair, #a-b   1.00 1.00

Christmas — A401

2006, Nov. 24   *Perf. 14¼x14*
650 A401 70k multi   .65 .65

Lviv, 750th Anniv. A402

Litho. & Engr.
2006, Dec. 1   *Perf. 14x13¾*
651 A402 3.50h multi   2.75 2.75
Printed in sheets of 10 + 5 labels. See Austria No. 2075.

Regional Costumes

Zaporizhzha Region — A403

Khersonshchyna Region — A404

Odeshchyna Region — A405

No. 652: a, People with flags, candle, and swords, St. Michael's Day. b, People and horses, Assumption Day.
No. 653: a, Women and spinning wheel, St. Catherine's Day. b, Men and oxen, St. Elias's Day.
No. 654: a, People and pig, St. Barbara and St. Sava's Day. b, People and fish, St. Boris and St. Hlib's Day.

2006, Dec. 15   Litho.   *Perf. 13¼*
652 A403 70k Horiz. pair, #a-b   .75 .75
653 A404 70k Horiz. pair, #a-b   .75 .75
654 A405 70k Horiz. pair, #a-b   .75 .75
  c.   Miniature sheet, #652-654, perf. 11½   2.25 2.25

Famous Ukrainians Type of 2004
Designs: No. 655, 70k, Metropolitan Ivan Ohienko (1882-1972). No. 656, 70k, Igor Stravinsky (1882-1971), composer.

2007   Litho.   *Perf. 14x14¼*
655-656 A314   Set of 2   1.25 1.25
Issued: No. 655, 1/12; No. 656, 6/8.

Conjoined Pots
A406

Candelabra
A407

Clay Bull
A408

Inkwell
A409

Mug — A410   Rag Doll — A411

Folk decorative art: 3k, Horse figurine. 5k, Whistle. 10k, Jug. 50k, Spinning wheel. 60k, Demijohn. 70k, Circular water container. 85k, Ladle. 1h, Decorated cup with handle. 2h, Pitcher with handle.

2007		**Litho.**	*Perf. 13¾*	
		Date Imprint		
657 A406	1k multi,			
		"2007"	.30	.30
a.	Imprint "2007-II"		.30	.30
658 A406	3k multi,			
		"2007"	.30	.30
a.	Imprint "2007-II"		.30	.30
b.	Imprint "2008"		.50	.50
659 A406	5k multi,			
		"2007"	.30	.30
a.	Imprint "2007-II"		.30	.30
b.	Imprint "2008"		.30	.30
c.	Imprint "2008-II"		.50	.50
d.	Imprint "2008-III"		.50	.50
e.	Imprint "2010"		.40	.40
f.	Imprint "2010-II"		1.75	1.75
g.	Imprint "2011"		1.75	1.75
660 A406	10k multi,			
		"2007"	.30	.30
a.	Imprint "2007-II"		.30	.30
b.	Imprint "2008"		.50	.60
c.	Imprint "2008-II"		.50	.50
d.	Imprint "2008-III"		.50	.50
e.	Imprint "2008-IV"		.50	.50
f.	Imprint "2009"		.30	.30
g.	Imprint "2010"		.60	.60
h.	Imprint "2010-II"		.60	.60
i.	Imprint "2011"		.70	.70
j.	Imprint "2011-II"		.70	.70
661 A406	50k multi,			
		"2007"	.40	.40
a.	Imprint "2007-II"		.40	.40
b.	Imprint "2008"		.50	.50
c.	Dated "2009"		.50	.50
d.	Imprint "2009-II"		.50	.50
e.	Imprint "2010"		.75	.75
f.	Imprint "2010-II"		.75	.75
g.	Imprint "2011"		.50	.50
h.	Imprint "2011-II"		.50	.50
i.	Imprint "2012"		.25	.25
662 A406	60k multi,			
		"2007"	.50	.50
a.	Imprint "2008"		.50	.50
b.	Imprint "2008-II"		.75	.75
663 A406	70k multi,			
		"2007"	.50	.50
a.	Imprint "2007-II"		.50	.50
b.	Imprint "2008"		.75	.75
c.	Imprint "2008-II"		.75	.75
d.	Imprint "2008-III"		.75	.75
664 A406	85k multi,			
		"2007"	.75	.75
a.	Imprint "2007-II"		.75	.75
b.	Imprint "2008"		.90	.90
665 A406	1h multi,			
		"2007"	.75	.75
a.	Imprint "2007-II"		.75	.75
b.	Imprint "2008"		.80	.80
c.	Imprint "2008-II"		.80	.80
d.	Imprint "2009"		.80	.80
e.	Imprint "2009-II"		.80	.80
f.	Imprint "2010"		.85	.85
g.	Imprint "2010-II"		.85	.85
h.	Imprint "2011"		.60	.60
i.	Imprint "2011-II"		.60	.60
666 A407	(1.52h) multi,			
		"2007"	.80	.80
a.	Imprint "2007-II"		.80	.80
b.	Imprint "2008"		1.00	1.00
c.	Imprint "2010"		1.00	1.00
d.	Imprint "2011"		1.00	1.00
667 A406	2h multi,			
		"2007"	1.40	1.40
a.	Imprint "2007-II"		1.40	1.40
b.	Imprint "2008"		1.40	1.40
c.	Imprint "2008-II"		2.00	2.00
d.	Dated "2009"		1.40	1.40
e.	Imprint "2009-II"		1.50	1.50
f.	Imprint "2010"		1.50	1.50
g.	Imprint "2010-II"		1.50	1.50
h.	Imprint "2010-III"		1.50	1.50
i.	Imprint "2011"		1.00	1.00
j.	Imprint "2011-II"		1.00	1.00

k.	Imprint "2011-III"	.60	.60
l.	Imprint "2012"	.60	.60
668	A408 (2.48h) multi,		
	"2007"	1.25	1.25
a.	Imprint "2007-II"	1.25	1.25
b.	Imprint "2008"	1.25	1.25
669	A409 (3.33h) multi,		
	"2007"	1.75	1.75
a.	Imprint "2007-II"	1.75	1.75
b.	Imprint "2008"	1.75	1.75
670	A410 (3.79h) multi,		
	"2007"	2.00	2.00
a.	Imprint "2008"	2.00	2.00
b.	Imprint "2011"	2.00	2.00
671	A411 (10.10h) multi,		
	"2007"	5.25	5.25
a.	Imprint "2007-II"	5.25	5.25
b.	Imprint "2008"	5.25	5.25
c.	Imprint "2011"	5.25	5.25
	Nos. 657-671 (15)	16.55	16.55

Issued: No. 657, 4/14/07. No. 657a, 12/07. No. 658, 4/14/07; No. 658a,9/6/07; No. 658b, 2008. No. 659, 3/16/07; No. 659a, 9/8/07; No. 659b, 2/08; No. 659c, 9/27/08; No. 659d, 10/27/08; No. 659e, 3/24/10; No. 659f, 8/13/10; No. 659g, 6/7/11. No. 660, 4/14/07; No. 660a, 11/16/07; No. 660b, 4/18/08; No. 660c, 5/30/08; No. 660d, 9/5/08; No. 660e, 2008; No. 660f, 9/7/09; No. 660g, 2/8/10; No. 660h, 8/13/10; Nos. 660i-660j, 6/7/11. No. 661, 1/26/07; No. 661a, 5/07; No. 661b, 8/22/08; No. 661c, 6/10/09; No. 661d, 9/7/09; No. 661e, 2/8/10; No. 661f, 8/13/10; Nos. 661g-661h, 6/7/11; No. 661i, 2012. No. 662, 1/26/07; No. 662a, 6/18/08; No. 662b, 8/22/08. No. 663, 1/26/07; No. 663a, 9/6/07; No. 663b, 4/11/08; No. 663c, 5/30/08; No. 663d, 7/28/08. No. 664, 1/26/07; No. 664a, 8/13/07; No. 664b, 8/22/08. No. 665, 4/6/07; No. 665a, 12/07; No. 665b, 7/26/08; No. 665c, 2008; Nos. 665d, 665e, 2009. No. 665f, 2/8/10; No. 665g, 8/13/10; Nos. 665h-665i, 6/7/11. No. 666, 4/6/07; No. 666a, 10/24/07; No. 666b, 10/21/08; No. 666c, 8/13/10; No. 666d, 6/7/11. No. 667, 3/16/07; No. 667a, 10/24/07; Nos. 667b, 667c, 9/27/08; No. 667d, 7/16/09; No. 667e, 9/7/09; No. 667f, 2/8/10; No. 667g, 3/24/10; No. 667h, 2010; Nos. 667i-667k, 6/7/11, No. 667l, 2012. No. 668, 4/6/07; No. 668a, 11/16/07; No. 668b, 10/17/08. No. 669, 4/14/07; No. 669a, 12/07; No. 669b, 11/08. No. 670, 3/16/07; No. 670a, 11/8/08; No. 670b, 6/7/11. NO. 671, 3/16/07; No. 671a, 11/16/07; No. 671b, 11/8/08; No. 671c, 6/7/11. For surcharges, see Nos. 803-804.

See Nos. 720, 764, 817-820.

St. Michael's Cathedral, Adelaide,
Australia — A412

2007, Feb. 9   **Perf. 13¼**
672 A412 3.35k multi + label   1.75 1.75

Souvenir Sheet

Taras Shevchenko (1814-61),
Poet — A413

No. 673: a, 2.50h, Drawing of Shevchenko's house, poem (66x40mm). b, 3.35k, Shevchenko (36x40mm).

Litho. With Foil Application
2007, Feb. 23   **Perf. 11½**
673 A413   Sheet of 2, #a-b   3.25 3.25

Wedding Rings — A414

Flowers — A415

Pechersk Lavra Monastery,
Kiev — A416

Oranta Monument — A417

2007, Mar. 1   **Litho.**   **Perf. 11½**
674 A414 70k multi + label   2.00 2.00
675 A415 70k multi + label   2.00 2.00
676 A416 70k multi + label   2.00 2.00
677 A417 70k multi + label   2.00 2.00
    Nos. 674-677 (4)   8.00 8.00

Nos. 674-676 were printed in sheets of 22 stamps + 22 labels that could be personalized, and sold for 60.60h per sheet. No. 677 was printed in sheets of 18 stamps + 18 labels that could be personalized, and sold for 54.60h per sheet. Labels shown are generic.

Space
Exploration
A418

Designs: No. 678, 70k, Leonid Kadeniuck, first Ukrainian cosmonaut. No. 679, 70k, Sea Launch rocket lifting off.

2007, Apr. 12   **Perf. 14x14¼**
678-679 A418   Set of 2   .80 .80

Europa — A419

Nos. 680 and 681: a, 2.50h, Scout emblem, neckerchief and "100." b, 3.35h, Scouts.

2007, Apr. 28   **Perf. 14x14¼**
   Stamp Size: 40x28mm
680 A419   Horiz. pair, #a-b   3.50 3.50
   Stamp Size: 45x33mm
      Perf. 11½
681 A419   Booklet pane of 2,
      #a-b   7.50 —
   Complete booklet, #681   7.50
Scouting, cent. No. 681 sold for 11.52h.

Paintings of Kiev — A420

Designs: No. 682, 70k, Sunny Day, Yaroslaviv Val, by Vitalii Petrovskyi, 1997. No. 683, 70k, Street of Recollections, by Tetiana Kuhai, 2004 (red panel), vert. No. 684, 70k, Kiev Walk, by Yulia Kuznietsova, 2004 (lilac panel), vert. No. 685, 70k, Snowing, by Maria Lashkevych, 2007.

   Perf. 13¾x14½, 14½x13¾
2007, May 18
682-685 A420   Set of 4   2.25 2.25

Miniature Sheets

Dogs — A421

Cats — A422

No. 686: a, Pug. b, Irish setter. c, Alaskan malamute. d, Basset hound. e, Bull mastiff. f, American cocker spaniel.
No. 687: a, American shorthair. b, Sphynx. c, Scottish fold. d, Snowshoe. e, Russian blue. f, Somali.

2007, June 15   **Perf. 11½**
686 A421 70k Sheet of 6, #a-f   2.75 2.75
687 A422 70k Sheet of 6, #a-f   2.75 2.75

Roman Shukhevych (1907-50), Military
Leader — A423

2007, June 29   **Perf. 14x14¼**
688 A423 70k multi   .55 .55

TE1 Diesel Locomotive — A424

TE2 Diesel Locomotive — A425

TE3 Diesel Locomotive — A426

TE7 Diesel Locomotive — A427

2007, July 13   **Litho.**   **Perf. 14x14¼**
689 A424 70k multi   .60 .60
690 A425 70k multi   .60 .60
691 A426 70k multi   .60 .60
692 A427 70k multi   .60 .60
    Nos. 689-692 (4)   2.40 2.40
Each stamp printed in sheets of 11 + label.

Miniature Sheet

Wedding Headdresses — A428

No. 693: a, Woman facing right wearing floral headdress with gray ribbon behind head. b, Woman facing left wearing gathered fabric headdress with broad red headband. c, Woman facing left wearing floral headdress with broad red ribbon at back. d, Woman facing right wearing ribboned floral headdress. e, Woman facing forward wearing tall red headdress with black and white spots. f, Woman wearing fabric headdress. g, Woman wearing headdress with wide floral ring above smaller floral rings. h, Man wearing hat and jacket with high collar. i, Woman facing left wearing tall floral headdress covering ear. j, Man wearing tall hat and collarless shirt with decorated front. k, Woman wearing headdress with one floral ring above broad red headband. l, Man wearing hat with chinstrap.

2007, Aug 23   **Litho.**   **Perf. 11½**
693 A428 70k Sheet of 12, #a-l   5.75 5.75

Dnieper River Fish
Preservation — A429

No. 694: a, Acipenser gueldenstaedtii. b, Zingel zingel.

2007, Sept. 6
694   Horiz. pair + central label 3.00 3.00
  a.   A429 1.50h multi   1.25 1.25
  b.   A429 2.50h multi   1.75 1.75

   See Moldova No. 569.

Pereyaslav Khmelnytskyi, 1100th
Anniv. — A430

2007, Sept. 16   **Perf. 14x14¼**
695 A430 70k multi   .60 .60

**Worldwide Fund for Nature
(WWF) — A431**

No. 696 — Pelecanus onocrotalus: a, 70k,
In flight. b, 1.50h, In water. c, 2.50h, Two birds.
d, 3.50h, One bird standing.

2007, Sept. 20   Perf. 14x14¼
696 A431 Block of 4, #a-d   4.25 4.25
  e. Miniature sheet, 4 each
       #696a-696d, perf. 11½, + 4
       labels   17.00 17.00

Souvenir Sheet

**Launch of Sputnik 1, 50th
Anniv. — A432**

2007, Oct. 4   Perf. 11½
697 A432 3.33h multi   2.25 2.25

Miniature Sheets

Λ433

Peasant Houses — A434

No. 698 — House from: a, Podillya, with ox
cart in front. b, Kiev, with couple, cat and
pumpkins in front. c, Lemkivschyna, with horse
and ducks in front. d, Hutsulschyna, with horse
in front. e, Volyn, with wheat sheaves in front.
f, Slobozhanschyna, with sunflowers at sides
of house.
No. 699 — House from: a, Polissya, with
basket weavers and horse in front. b, Khorol-
schyna, with children rolling hoop in front. c,
Bukovyna, with couple in doorway. d, Boikiv-
schyna, with dog and people carrying bundles
of sticks in front. e, Poltava, people threshing
grain in front. f, Lower Dnieper area, with man
with fishing net in front.

2007, Oct. 24
698 A433 70k Sheet of 6, #a-f   2.75 2.75
699 A434 70k Sheet of 6, #a-f   2.75 2.75

**Christmas and New Year's
Day — A435**

No. 700: a, Angels in sled. b, Angels with
Christmas tree.

Litho. With Foil Application
2007, Nov. 16   Perf. 13½
700 A435 70k Horiz. pair, #a-b   .80   .80

**Christmas and New Year's
Day — A436**

2007, Nov. 23   Perf. 11½
701 A436 1h multi + label   2.75 2.75
  Printed in sheets of 18 stamps + 18 labels
that could be personalized.

**2012 European Soccer
Championships, Poland and
Ukraine — A437**

2007, Dec. 22
702 A437 3.33h multi   2.10 2.10

Regional Costumes

Khmelnytska Region — A438

Bukovyna Region — A439

Zakarpatyia Region — A440

No. 703: a, Potter and carolers, Christmas.
b, People celebrating St. Simeon's Day,
horses.
No. 704: a, Woman holding cross, man,
woman, fruit basket, St. Ephrosinia's Day. b,
Man holding violin, women and children,
Ascension Day.
No. 705: a, Men and blacksmith holding
mugs, Kuzma and Demyan Day. b, People
near cross and candle, Easter.

2007, Dec. 22   Litho.   Perf. 13¼
703 A438 70k Horiz. pair, #a-b   .75   .75
704 A439 70k Horiz. pair, #a-b   .75   .75
705 A440 70k Horiz. pair, #a-b   .75   .75
  c. Miniature sheet, #703-705, perf.
       11½   2.25 2.25

Aries — A441

Taurus — A442

Gemini — A443

Cancer — A444

Leo — A445

Virgo — A446

Libra — A447

Scorpio — A448

**Sagittarius
A449**

**Capricorn
A450**

Aquarius — A451

Pisces — A452

2008, Jan. 18   Perf. 14¼x14
706 A441 1h multi   .80   .80
707 A442 1h multi   .80   .80
708 A443 1h multi   .80   .80
709 A444 1h multi   .80   .80
710 A445 1h multi   .80   .80
711 A446 1h multi   .80   .80
712 A447 1h multi   .80   .80
713 A448 1h multi   .80   .80
714 A449 1h multi   .80   .80
715 A450 1h multi   .80   .80
716 A451 1h multi   .80   .80
717 A452 1h multi   .80   .80
  Nos. 706-717 (12)   9.60 9.60

**2008 Summer Olympics,
Beijing — A453**

No. 718: a, 1h, Archery. b, 1.30h, Fencing.
c, 2.47h, Cycling. d, 3.33h, Rowing.

Litho. With Foil Application
2008, Jan. 26   Perf. 11½
718 A453 Block of 4, #a-d   4.25 4.25

Roses and Hearts — A454

2008, Feb. 6   Litho.   Perf. 11½
719 A454 1h multi + label   2.00 2.00
  Printed in sheets of 22 stamps + 22 labels
that could be personalized that sold for
69.90h. Label shown is generic.

Folk Decorative Art Type of 2007
Design: Carved pipe.

2008, Feb. 15   Litho.   Perf. 13¾
720 A406 30k multi, "2008"   .50   .50
  a. Imprint "2008-II"   .40   .40
  b. Imprint "2009"   .50   .50
  c. Imprint "2009-II"   .50   .50
  d. Imprint "2010"   .75   .75
  e. Imprint "2010-II"   .90   .90
  f. Imprint "2011"   .75   .75
  g. Imprint "2012"   .75   .75

  Issued: No. 720a, 7/26/08; No. 720b,
7/16/09; No. 720c, 2009; No. 720d, 2/1/10;
No. 720e, 8/13/10. No. 720f, 6/7/11. No. 720g,
2012.

**Paintings by
Taras
Shevchenko
(1814-61)
A455**

Designs: 1h, Gypsy Fortune Teller. 1.52h,
Kateryna. 2.47h, Self-portrait.

Litho. With Foil Application
2008, Feb. 23   Perf. 11½
721-723 A455 Set of 3   3.00 3.00

Europa — A456

No. 724 — Letter writers with: a, 2.47h, Quill
pen. b, 3.33h, Computer.

2008, Mar. 12   Litho.   Perf. 13¼
724 A456 Horiz. pair, #a-b   3.75 3.75
  A booklet containing two 37x30mm perf.
11½ stamps like Nos. 724a-724b sold for
12.84h.

**Nicolay Gogol (1809-52),
Writer — A457**

No. 725: a, 1.52h, Gogol, gun, quill pen and inkwell, pipe. b, 2.47h, Taras Bulba on horseback.

2008, Mar. 21   *Perf. 14x14¼*
725 A457   Pair, #a-b   2.25 2.25

Easter — A458

Litho. With Foil Application
2008, Apr. 11   *Perf. 13¼*
726 A458   1h multi   .75 .75

Miniature Sheet

18th and 19th Century Decorative Clocks — A459

No. 727: a, French mantle clock with clock as chariot wheel, 19th cent. (33x33mm). b, Russian mantle clock with nymphs, 19th cent. (33x33mm). c, French mantle clock with nude woman and nymphs on goats, 19th cent. (33x33mm). d, French clock by Charles Baltazar with blue green frame and nymph on top, 18th cent. (33x45mm). e, French clock with woman with shield on top, 18th cent. (33x45mm). f, German clock with woman trumpeter on top, 18th cent. (33x45mm). g, English clock with landscape above face, 18th cent. (33x45mm). h, Austrian clock with pillars at sides, 19th cent. (33x45mm). i, French mantle clock with birds at top, 19th cent. (33x45mm).

Litho. With Foil Application
2008, Apr. 18   *Perf. 11½*
727 A459   1h Sheet of 9, #a-i   5.25 5.25

Miniature Sheets

Dogs — A460

Cats — A461

No. 728: a, Smooth-haired dachshund. b, American bulldog. c, Rottweiler. d, Chow chow. e, Schnauzer. f, German shepherd.

No. 729: a, Persian. b, Selkirk Rex. c, Exotic shorthair. d, Burmese. e, Siamese. f, Kuril Island bobtail.

2008, May 16   Litho.
728 A460   1r Sheet of 6, #a-f   3.50 3.50
729 A461   1r Sheet of 6, #a-f   3.50 3.50

Miniature Sheet

Crimean Nature Reserve — A462

No. 730: a, Aegypius monachus (31x38mm). b, Cranes and swans (36x31mm). c, Cervus elaphus (47x31mm). d, Silene jailensis and insect (31x31mm).

2008, June 18
730 A462   1h Sheet of 4, #a-d   2.60 2.60

Souvenir Sheets

Ukrainian Postage Stamps, 90th Anniv. — A463

No. 731: a, 2.47h, Ukraine #1. b, 3.33h, Ukraine #2.
No. 732: a, 1h, Ukraine #4. b, 2.47h, Ukraine #5. c, 3.33j, Ukraine #3.

2008, July 4
731 A463   Sheet of 2, #a-b, + 2 labels   3.25 3.25
732 A463   Sheet of 3, #a-c, + label   3.75 3.75

Souvenir Sheet

Myhailivskyi Monastery, 900th Anniv. — A464

2008, July 11
733 A464   3.33h multi   2.00 2.00

TEP10 Diesel Locomotive — A465

2TE10L Diesel Locomotive — A466

M62 Diesel Locomotive — A467

TE109 Diesel Locomotive — A468

2008, Aug. 8   *Perf. 14x14¼*
734 A465   1h multi   .60 .60
735 A466   1h multi   .60 .60
736 A467   1h multi   .60 .60
737 A468   1h multi   .60 .60
    Nos. 734-737 (4)   2.40 2.40
Each stamp printed in sheets of 11 + label.

Christmas Carols — A469

Songs of Spring — A470

Songs of the Cossacks A471

Songs of the Chumaks A472

2008, Sept. 5   *Perf. 13½*
738 A469   1h multi   .60 .60
739 A470   1h multi   .60 .60
740 A471   1h multi   .60 .60
741 A472   1h multi   .60 .60
    Nos. 738-741 (4)   2.40 2.40
Ukrainian musical heritage.

Jewelry — A473

No. 742: a, 2.47h, Earring, 12th-13th cent. b, 3.33h, Pendant, 19th cent.

2008, Sept. 18   *Perf. 11½*
742 A473   Horiz. pair, #a-b, + central label   3.50 3.50
    See Azerbaijan No. 885.

Ukrainian and Swedish Military and Political Alliances of 17th and 18th Centuries A474

Litho. With Foil Application
2008, Oct. 1
743 A474   1h multi   .70 .70

A475

Ninth Natl. Philatelic Exhibition, Chernivtsi — A476

2008, Oct. 3   Litho.   *Perf. 14x14¼*
744 A475   1h multi   .70 .70
               Perf. 11½
745 A476   1h multi + label   4.25 4.25

No. 745 was printed in sheets of 10 stamps + 10 labels that could be personalized that sold for 88.38h. Label shown is generic.

Chernivtsi, 600th Anniv. A477

2008, Oct. 4   *Perf. 14x14¼*
746 A477   1h multi   .70 .70

Sacking of Baturyn, 300th Anniv. — A478

2008, Oct. 24   *Perf. 14¼x14*
747 A478   1h multi   .70 .70

Christmas — A479

New Year's Day — A480

Litho. With Foil Application
2008, Nov. 21 **Perf. 11½**
748 A479 1h multi .70 .70
749 A480 1h multi .70 .70

Famous Ukrainians Type of 2004
Designs: No. 750, 1h, Marko Vovchok (1833-1907), writer. No. 751, 1h, Vyachyslav Chornovil (1937-99), politician.

2008 **Litho.** **Perf. 14x14¼**
750-751 A314 Set of 2 1.40 1.40

Issued: No. 750, 11/28; No. 751, 12/24.

Miniature Sheet

Headdresses — A481

No. 752: a, Woman facing right wearing brown and red headdress and red necklace. b, Woman facing forward wearing white headdress wrapping under chin. c, Woman facing left with headdress with blue-tipped tassels above eyes. d, Woman facing right wearing white headdress. e, Woman facing forward wearing brown, red and green headdress and red necklace. f, Woman facing forward wearing white, red and green headdress, denomination in white. g, Woman wearing headdress and laurel wreath. h, Woman wearing white, gray and red headdress. i, Woman facing left wearing white, red and green headdress with floral pattern over red striped forehead band. j, Man wearing brown hat. k, Woman facing forward wearing headdress with lace trim on forehead. l, Man wearing black and red hat.

2008, Dec. 10 **Perf. 11½**
752 A481 1h Sheet of 12, #a-l 7.25 7.25

Regional Costumes

Crimea Region — A482

Dnipropetrovshchyna Region — A483

Luhanshchyna Region — A484

No. 753: a, People with grapes, Feast of the Transfiguration. b, Baby being christened.
No. 754: a, Bride and groom receiving crowns. b, Three women at Harvest Festival.
No. 755: a, Musicians, Feast of Saints Cyril and Methodius. b, People and church on hill, Feast of the Miracle Worker.

2008, Dec. 25 **Litho.** **Perf. 13¼**
753 A482 1h Horiz. pair, #a-b .75 .75
754 A483 1h Horiz. pair, #a-b .75 .75
755 A484 1h Horiz. pair, #a-b .75 .75
  c. Miniature sheet, #753-755, perf.
       11½ 2.25 2.25
     Nos. 753-755 (3) 2.25 2.25

Stephan Bandera (1909-59), Nationalist Leader — A485

2009, Jan. 1
756 A485 1h multi .60 .60

Famous Ukrainians Type of 2004
Designs: 1h, Stepan Rudanskyi (1834-73), poet. 2.20h, Sholem Aleichem (1850 1010), writer.

2009 **Perf. 14x14¼**
757-758 A314 Set of 2 1.40 1.40
Issued: No. 757, 1/17; No. 758, 2/18.

Souvenir Sheet

Kiev Zoo, Cent. — A486

2009, Feb. 20 **Litho.** **Perf. 11½**
759 A486 3.20h multi 2.00 2.00

Paintings by Taras Shevchenko A487

Designs: No. 760, 1.50h, Portrait of I. I. Lyzohub, 1846-47. No. 761, 1.50h, Portrait of E. V. Keikuatova, 1847. No. 762, 1.50h, Village Family, 1843, horiz.

Litho. With Foil Application
2009, Mar. 9
760-762 A487 Set of 3 1.75 1.75
Nos. 760-762 each were printed in sheets of 11 + label.

Preservation of Polar Regions — A488

No. 763: a, Academician Vernadskiy Antarctic Station. b, Iceberg.

2009, Mar. 18
763 A488 3.30h Pair, #a-b 2.75 2.75
Printed in sheets containing 4 of each stamp and a central label.

Folk Art Type of 2007
Designs: Tile depicting Cossack on horse.

2009, Mar. 25 **Litho.** **Perf. 13¾**
764 A406 1.50h multi .60 .60
  a. Imprint "2009-II" .75 .75
  b. Imprint "2010" .75 .75
  c. Imprint "2010-II" .75 .75
  d. Imprint "2011" .75 .75
  e. Imprint "2011-II" .75 .75
  f. Imprint "2011-III" .75 .75
  g. Imprint "2009-III" .75 .75

Issued: No. 764a, 7/16; Nos. 764b, 764c, 2010. Nos. 764d, 764e, 6/7/11. No. 764f, 6/7/11.

Souvenir Sheet

Nikolai Gogol (1809-52), Writer — A489

No. 765: a, 1.50h, Scene from "Night Before Christmas." b, 2.20h, Gogol.

Litho. With Foil Application
2009, Apr. 1 **Perf. 11½**
765 A489 Sheet of 2, #a-b 2.00 2.00

Europa — A490

No. 766: a, Telescope and star chart. b, Map of solar system, Galileo Galilei and his telescope.

2009, Apr. 17 **Litho.** **Perf. 13¾x14¼**
Size: 52x25mm
766 Horiz. pair 5.00 5.00
  a. A490 3.75h multi 2.00 2.00
  b. A490 5.25h multi 3.00 3.00

Intl. Year of Astronomy. A booklet containing a pane with a pair of 57x28mm perf. 11½ stamps like Nos. 766a-766b sold for 18.42h. Value, $10.

Architecture in China and Ukraine A491

No. 767: a, Stork Tower, Shanghai. b, Golden Gate, Kiev.

2009, Aug. 14 **Perf. 11½**
767 Horiz. pair + central label 4.25 4.25
  a. A491 3.85h multi 1.75 1.75
  b. A491 5.40h multi 2.25 2.25

Miniature Sheet

Gorgany Game Reserve — A492

No. 768: a, Tetrao urogallus (40x37mm). b, Pinus cembra (30x47mm). c, Arnica montana (40x40mm). d, Felis silvestris (57x30mm).

2009, Sept. 29
768 A492 1.50h Sheet of 4, #a-d 3.00 3.00

Electric Locomotive VL26 — A493

Electric Locomotive VL41 — A494

Diesel Locomotive 2TE116 — A495

Diesel Locomotive 2TE121 — A496

2009, Oct. 22 **Perf. 13¾x14¼**
769 A493 1.50h multi 1.10 1.10
770 A494 1.50h multi 1.10 1.10
771 A495 1.50h multi 1.10 1.10
772 A496 1.50h multi 1.10 1.10
  Nos. 769-772 (4) 4.40 4.40

Miniature Sheet

Lighthouses — A497

No. 773: a, Kyz-Aulskyi Lighthouse (blue top). b, Luparivskyi Front Lighthouse (base with vertical red and white stripes). c, Yaltinskyi Lighthouse (white, with hexagonal base). d, Vorontsovskyi Lighthouse (red top). e, Sarych Lighthouse (white, with circular base). f, Berdianskyi Lower Lighthouse (base with horizontal red and white stripes).

2009, Oct. 30 **Perf. 11½**
773 A497 1.50h Sheet of 6, #a-f 4.75 4.75

Ukrainian Supreme Liberation Council, 65th Anniv. — A498

2009, Nov. 27   **Perf. 14¼x14**
774 A498 1.50h multi   .75   .75

A499

A500

A501

Songs — A502

2009, Nov. 27   **Perf. 11½**
775 A499 1.50h multi   .95   .95
776 A500 1.50h multi   .95   .95
777 A501 2h multi   1.15 1.15
778 A502 2h multi   1.15 1.15
      Nos. 775-778 (4)   4.20 4.20

Christmas A503

New Year 2010 — A504

Litho. With Foil Application
2009, Dec. 9   **Perf. 11½**
779 A503 1.50h multi   .65   .65
                Perf. 13¾x14¼
780 A504 1.50h multi   .65   .65

White Sukholimanskiy Grapes and Vineyard — A505

White Muscat Grapes, Sailboat and Vineyard — A506

2009, Dec. 15 **Litho.** **Perf. 11½**
781 A505 1.50h multi   .65   .65
782 A506 1.50h multi   .65   .65

Narodny Rukh (People's Movement) Party, 20th Anniv. — A507

2009, Dec. 19   **Perf. 13¾**
783 A507 1.50h multi   .65   .65

Miniature Sheet

Minerals — A508

No. 784: a, 1.50h, Quartz. b, 1.90h, Native sulphur. c, 2h, Topaz. d, 2.20h, Beryl. e, 3.30h, Tiger's eye. f, 4.85h, Kertschenite.

Litho. & Embossed
2009, Dec. 23   **Perf. 11½**
784 A508 Sheet of 6, #a-h   7.75 7.75

2010 Winter Olympics, Vancouver — A509

No. 785: a, 1.50h, Cross-country skiing. b, 1.50h, Biathlon. c, 2h, Freestyle skiing. d, 2h, Luge.

Litho. With Foil Application
2010, Feb. 5   **Perf. 11½**
785 A509 Horiz. strip of 4, #a-d 3.50 3.50

Souvenir Sheet

Taras Shevchenko (1814-61), Poet — A510

No. 786: a, 1.50h, Woman at butter churn, poem (66x40mm). b, 2h, Self-portrait (36x40mm).

2010, Mar. 9
786 A510 Sheet of 2, #a-b   1.75 1.75

Souvenir Sheet

Constitution of Pylyp Orlik, 300th Anniv. — A511

2010, Mar. 29   **Litho.**
787 A511 1.50h multi   .85   .85

Victory in World War II, 65th Anniv. — A512

2010, Apr. 15   **Perf. 13¼**
788 A512 1.50h multi   .75   .75

Souvenir Sheets

Prepared But Unissued Postage Stamps of Ukrainian National Republic, 90th Anniv. — A513

No. 789: a, 1.50h, Unissued 1h stamp. b, 1.50h, Unissued 10h stamp. c, 2h, Unissued 2h stamp. d, 2h, Unissued 15h stamp.
No. 790: a, 1.50h, Unissued 20h stamp. b, 1.50h, Unissued 40h stamp. c, 2h, Unissued 30h stamp. d, 2h, Unissued 50h stamp.

2010, Apr. 22   **Perf. 11½**
Sheets of 4, #a-d, + Label
789-790 A513 Set of 2   6.50 6.50

Europa — A514

Nos. 791 and 792 — Scenes from children's books: a, 2.20h, Mare's Head. b, 3.30h, Gold Shoe.

Litho. With Foil Application
2010, Apr. 30   **Perf. 13¼**
791 A514 Horiz. pair, #a-b   2.50 2.50
                Perf. 11½
792 A514 Booklet pane of 2,
           #a-b, + central label 5.00   —
           Complete booklet, #792   5.00

Nos. 792a and 792b are 43x41mm. No. 792 sold for 10.50h.

Famous Ukrainians Type of 2004

Designs: 1h, Oleksandr Potebnia (1835-91), linguist. 1.50h, Mykola Pyrohov (1810-81), surgeon.

2010   **Litho.**   **Perf. 14x14¼**
793 A314 1h multi   .55   .55

---

794 A314 1.50h multi   .75   .75
      Issued: No. 793, 9/10; No. 794, 6/2.

Wladimir and Vitali Klitschko, Boxers A515

2010, June 8
795 A515 1.50h multi   .85   .85

Flowers — A516

Litho. With Foil Application
2010, Aug. 11   **Perf. 13¼x13½**
796 A516 (1.50h) multi + label 3.75 3.75

No. 796 was printed in sheets of 10 stamps + 10 labels that could be personalized that sold for 105h. The label shown is generic.

DE1 Electric Locomotive — A517

DC3 Electric Locomotive — A518

TEM103 Diesel Locomotive — A519

TEP150 Diesel Locomotive — A520

2010, Sept. 4 **Litho.** **Perf. 14x14¼**
797 A517 1h multi   .45   .45
798 A518 1.50h multi   .60   .60
799 A519 2h multi   .85   .85
800 A520 2h multi   .85   .85
      Nos. 797-800 (4)   2.75 2.75

Nos. 797-800 each printed in sheets of 11 + label.

Sculptures by Johann Georg Pinsel — A521

No. 801: a, 1.50h, Mother of God. b, 2h, Angel.

2010, Sept. 8   **Perf. 13¼**
801 A521 Horiz. pair, #a-b   1.25 1.25

Miniature Sheet

National Technical University Kharkhiv Polytechnic Institute, 125th Anniv. — A522

No. 802: a, 1.50h, O. M. Beketov (1862-1941), architect. b, 1.50h, P. P. Kopniaev (1867-1932), electrical engineer. c, 1.50h, O. M. Liapunov (1857-1918), mathematician. d, 1.50h, E. I. Orlov (1865-1944), chemical engineer. e, 1.50h, M. D. Pylchykov (1857-1908), physicist. f, 1.50h, V. M. Khrushchov (1882-1941), electrical engineer. g, 2h, V. L. Kyrpychov (1845-1913), mechanical engineer. h, 2h, M. M. Beketov (1827-1911), chemist. i, 2h, L. D. Landau (1908-68), theoretical physicist. j, 2m, P. M. Mukhachov (1861-1935), engineer. k, 2h, V. A. Stieklov (1863-1926), mathematician.

2010, Sept. 16   **Perf. 11½**
802   A522   Sheet of 11, #a-k, + label   7.75   7.75

Nos. 657a, 658a, 658b Surcharged

Methods and Perfs As Before
2010, Oct. 6
803   A406   1.50h on 3k #658a   1.25   1.25
   a.   A406   1.50h on 3k #658b   1.25   1.25
804   A406   2h on 1k #657a   1.75   1.75

Miniature Sheet

Lighthouses — A523

No. 805: a, 1.50h, Tendrivskyi Lighthouse (with two horizontal black bands). b, 1.50h, Pavlovskyi Fort Lighthouse (hexagonal with brown vertical stripe). c, 1.50h, Khersoneskyi Lighthouse (round white lighthouse with ten windows). d, 2h, Sanzhiiskyi Lighthouse (hexagonal white lighthouse with two windows). e, 2h, Tarkhankutskyi Lighthouse (round white lighthouse with four windows). f, 2h, Illichivskyi Lighthouse (with horizontal red bands).

2010, Oct. 8   **Litho.**   **Perf. 11½**
805   A523   Sheet of 6, #a-f   4.50   4.50

Leaders of Cossack Rebellions — A524

No. 806: a, 1.50h, Kryshtof Kosynskyi (1545-93). b, 2h, Bohdan Mykoshynskyi.

2010, Oct. 15   **Perf. 14x14¼**
806   A524   Block of 2, #a-b, + 2 labels   2.50   2.50

Military History — A525

No. 807: a, 1.50h, Danubian Sich (country name in brown). b, 1.50h, Cossack regiments of 1812 (country name in blue). c, 2h, Defense of Sevastopol (country name in blue). d, 2h, Ataman Yakiv Kukharenko on horse (country name in brown).

2010, Oct. 29
807   A525   Block of 4, #a-d   2.75   2.75

Hetman Pavlo Polubotok (1660-1724) — A526

Litho. With Foil Application
2010, Oct. 29
808   A526   1.50h multi   .65   .65

Miniature Sheet

Kiev Metro, 50th Anniv. — A527

No. 809: a, 1.50h, Dorohzhychi Station escalators. b, 1.50h, Train. c, 2h, Lukianivska Station exterior. d, 2h, Tunnel under construction.

2010, Nov. 3   **Litho.**   **Perf. 11½**
809   A527   Sheet of 4, #a-d   2.75   2.75

Cabernet Sauvignon Grapes and Estate — A528

2010, Dec. 17
810   A528   1.50h multi   .65   .65

Miniature Sheet

Fauna of Sviati Hory National Park — A529

No. 811: a, 1h, Zerynthia polyxena (38x30mm). b, 1.50h, Luscinia svecica (38x30mm). c, 1.50h, Lutra lutra (38x37mm). d, 2h, Emys orbicularis (38x37mm).

2010, Dec. 28
811   A529   Sheet of 4, #a-d   2.50   2.50

Signing of the Universal Declaration of Human Rights, 60th Anniv. A530

2010, Dec. 31   **Perf. 14x14¼**
812   A530   1.50h multi   .65   .65

Miniature Sheet

Minerals — A531

No. 813: a, 1.50h, Syngenite (brown mineral). b, 1.50h, Amber. c, 1.50h, Labradorite (black and red mineral). d, 2h, Carpathite (black arnd brown mineral). e, 2h, Agate (mineral with rings). f, 2h, Rhodonite (red and gray mineral).

Litho. & Embossed
2010, Dec. 31   **Perf. 11½**
810   A531   Sheet of 6, #a-f   4.00   4.00

First Man in Space, 50th Anniv. — A532

2011, Apr. 12   **Litho.**   **Perf. 14x14¼**
814   A532   6h multi   2.25   2.25

Georgy Beregovoi (1921-95), Cosmonaut — A533

2011, Apr. 16   **Perf. 14¼x14**
815   A533   2.20h multi   .75   .75

Kazashka Katya, Painting by Taras Shevchenko (1814-61) A534

Litho. With Foil Application
2011, May 21   **Perf. 11½**
816   A534   1.50h multi   .60   .60

Folk Decorative Art Type of 2007
Designs: 1.90h, Tobacco pouch. 2.20h, Powder flask. 6h, Bandura. 7h, Bowl with lid.

2011   **Litho.**   **Perf. 13¾**
817   A406   1.90h multi   .75   .75
   a.   Imprint "2011-II"   .50   .50
818   A406   2.20h multi   .85   .85
   a.   Imprint "2011-II"   .55   .55
819   A406   6h multi   2.40   2.40
820   A406   7h multi   2.75   2.75
   Nos. 817-820 (4)   6.75   6.75

Issued: Nos. 817-820, 6/7. Nos. 817a, 818a, 6/7.

Leaders of Cossack Rebellions — A535

No. 821: a, 1.50h, Hryhorii Loboda. b, 2h, Severyn Nalyvaiko.

2011, June 9   **Perf. 14x14¼**
821   A535   Block of 2, #a-b, + 2 labels   1.40   1.40

Ukrainian Constitution, 15th Anniv. — A536

Litho. & Embossed With Foil Application
2011, June 17   **Perf. 11½**
822   A536   6h multi   2.25   2.25

Miniature Sheet

Farmhouse and Animals — A537

No. 823: a, 1.50h, Cat. b, 1.50h, Birds. c, 1.50h, Pig. d, 2h, Cow. e, 2h, Dog.

2011, June 25   **Litho.**
823   A537   Sheet of 5, #a-e   3.25   3.25

Personalized Stamp — A538

Litho. With Foil Application
2011, June 25   **Perf. 11½**
824   A538   (1.50h) multi + label   2.75   2.75

No. 824 was printed in sheets of 18 + 18 labels that could be personalized. The label shown, depicting the national arms and posthorns, is the generic label image. Compare with type A552.

Trains — A539

Designs: 1.50h, Diesel train DPL1. 1.90h,
Diesel train, DEP 02. 2.20h, Electric train EPL
2T. 6h, Electric train EPL 9T.

2011, July 5   **Litho.**   **Perf. 14x14¼**
825-828   A539   Set of 4   4.25 4.25

First Flight of Dirigible "Kiev,"
Cent. — A540

2011, Aug. 5
829   A540   2.20h multi   .90   .90

Emigration of
Ukrainians to
Brazil, 120th
Anniv. — A541

2011, Aug. 24   **Perf. 14¼x14**
830   A541   2.20h multi   .90   .90

Independence, 20th Anniv. — A542

Litho. With Foil Application
2011, Aug. 24   **Perf. 14x14¼**
831   A542   2.20h multi   .90   .90

"The Snow Queen" Fairy Tale — A543

No. 832: a, 1.50h, Snow Queen in horse-
drawn sleigh flying above town (43x26mm). b,
6h, Crow and girl (26x26mm).

2011, Sept. 1   **Litho.**   **Perf. 11½**
832   A543   Horiz. pair, #a-b   2.75 2.75

12th Natl.
Philatelic
Exhibition,
Odessa
A544

2011, Sept. 9   **Perf. 14x14¼**
833   A544   4.30h multi   1.75 1.75

Miniature Sheet

Prepared but Unissued Ukrainian
National Republic Stamps, 90th
Anniv. — A545

No. 834: a, 1.50h, Unissued 5h stamp. b,
1.50h, Unissued 3h stamp. c, 2h, Unissued
60h stamp. d, 2h, Unissued 80h stamp. e, 6h,
Unissued 100h stamp. f, 7h, Unissued 200h
stamp.

2011, Sept. 12   **Perf. 11½**
834   A545   Sheet of 6, #a-f   7.75 7.75

Tetiana Markus (1921-43), Anti-Nazi
Resistance Fighter — A546

2011, Sept. 21   **Perf. 14x14¼**
835   A546   1.50h multi   .55   .55

Babi Yar
Massacres, 70th
Anniv. — A547

2011, Sept. 29   **Perf. 13¼**
836   A547   2.20h multi   1.25 1.25

Motion Picture *Natalka Poltavka,* 75th
Anniv. — A548

No. 837: a, 1.50h, People. b, 6h, Woman.

Litho. With Foil Application
2011, Sept. 30   **Perf. 14x14¼**
837   A548   Horiz. pair, #a-b   2.75 2.75

Lvov National University, 350th
Anniv. — A549

2011, Oct. 11   **Litho.**   **Perf. 11½**
838   A549   1.50h multi   .55   .55

Regional Communications
Commonwealth, 20th Anniv. — A550

2011, Oct. 14
839   A550   1.90h multi   .75   .75

Mykhailo
Yanhel (1911-
71), Missile
Designer
A551

2011, Oct. 25   **Perf. 13¼**
840   A551   1.50h multi   .80   .80

Personalized
Stamp — A552

Litho. With Foil Application
2011, Nov. 1   **Perf. 11½**
841   A552   (1.80h) multi + label   2.75 2.75

No. 841 was printed in sheets of 12 + 12
labels that could be personalized. The label
shown, depicting the national arms and posthorns, is the generic label image.
Compare with type A538.

St.
Sophia's
Cathedral,
Kyiv,
1000th
Anniv.
A553

No. 842: a, Painting above three arches. b,
Round ceiling painting.

2011, Nov. 18
842   Horiz. pair + central label 3.00 3.00
  a.   A553   1.90h multi   .75   .75
  b.   A553   6h multi   2.25 2.25

Miniature Sheet

Amphibians — A554

No. 843: a, 1.80h, Pelophylax esculentus. b,
1.80h, Hyla arborea. c, 2.20h, Pelophylax les-
sonae. d, 2.20h, Rana dalmatina. e, 4.30h,
Pelophylax ridibundus.

2011, Nov. 22   **Litho.**
843   A554   Sheet of 5, #a-e   4.50 4.50

Miniature Sheet

Spring — A555

No. 844: a, 1.80h, Bird on flower branch
held by woman (30x40mm). b, 1.80h, Bare
trees, white flowers and pond (30x21mm). c,
1.80h, Purple and yellow flowers (24x32mm).
d. 1.90h, Cut flowers held by woman
(30x40mm). e, 2.20h, Purple flowers
(30x40mm). f, 6h, White flowers (30x40mm).

Litho. With Foil Application
2011, Nov. 25
844   A555   Sheet of 6, #a-f   5.50 5.50

Traminer Grapes and
Vineyard — A556

Aligoté Grapes and Vineyard — A557

2011, Nov. 30   **Litho.**
845   A556   1.90h multi   .70   .70
846   A557   4.30h multi   1.60 1.60

Campaign
Against AIDS,
30th
Anniv. — A558

2011, Dec. 1   **Perf. 13¼**
847   A558   1.80h multi   .90   .90

Commonwealth
of Independent
States, 20th
Anniv. — A559

2011, Dec. 8   **Perf. 13½**
848   A559   2.20h multi   .90   .90

Miniature Sheet

Natural Wonders of Ukraine — A560

No. 849: a, Lake Svityaz (dark blue denomination). b, Lake Synevir (light blue denomination). c, Bug River rapids (red denomination). d, Hill near Dniester River (red denomination). e, Deer in Askania-Nova Nature Reserve (white denomination). f, Podilsky Tovtry Park (orange denomination). g, Marble Cave of the Crimea (white denomination).

2011, Dec. 19   *Perf. 11½*
849 A560   2.20h Sheet of 7, #a-g   6.00 6.00

Europa — A561

No. 850: a, 2.20h, Bird-shaped opening in forest canopy. b, 4.30h, Star in opening in snow-covered forest canopy.

2011, Dec. 20   *Perf. 13¼*
850 A561   Horiz. pair, #a-b   2.75 2.75
    Intl. Year of Forests.

Christmas and New Year's Greetings — A562

No. 851: a, Grandfather Frost with bag of toys. b, People outside of church.

2011, Dec. 23   *Perf. 11½*
851 A562 1.80h Horiz. pair, #a-b   1.40 1.40

Miniature Sheet

Water Mills — A563

No. 852 — Various mills: a, 1.80h. b, 2.20h. c, 6.50h. d, 7.70h.

2011, Dec. 28
852 A563   Sheet of 4, #a-d   6.50 6.50

Tree Leaves and Fruit — A564

Designs: 5k, Sorbus aucuparia. 20k, Robinia pseudoacacia. 30k, Fraxinus excelsior. 40k, Juglans regia. 50k, Aesculus hippocastanum. 70k, Betula pendula. 2h, Quercus robur. 2.50h, Acer platanoides. 3h, Tilia cordata. 4h, Fagus sylvatica. 5h, Alnus incana. 8h, Ulmus laevis. 10h, Populus tremula.

2012-16		**Litho.**	*Perf. 13¾*	
853	A564	5k multi	.30	.30
a.	Imprint "2012-II"		.30	.30
b.	Imprint "2012-III"		.30	.30
c.	Imprint "2013"		.30	.30
d.	Imprint "2014"		.30	.30
e.	Imprint "2014-II"		.30	.30
f.	Imprint "2015"		.30	.30
g.	Imprint "2015-II"		.30	.30
h.	Imprint "2016"		.30	.30
i.	Imprint "2016-II"		.30	.30
854	A564	20k multi	.30	.30
a.	Imprint "2012-II"		.30	.30
b.	Imprint "2012-III"		.30	.30
c.	Imprint "2013"		.30	.30
d.	Imprint "2014"		.30	.30
e.	Imprint "2015"		.30	.30
f.	Imprint "2015-II"		.30	.30
g.	Imprint "2016"		.30	.30
h.	Imprint "2016"		.30	.30
855	A564	30k multi	.30	.30
a.	Imprint "2012-II"		.30	.30
b.	Imprint "2012-III"		.30	.30
c.	Imprint "2013"		.30	.30
d.	Imprint "2013-II"		.30	.30
e.	Imprint "2013-III"		.30	.30
f.	Imprint "2014"		.30	.30
g.	Imprint "2016"		.30	.30
856	A564	40k multi	.30	.30
a.	Imprint "2012-II"		.30	.30
b.	Imprint "2012-III"		.30	.30
c.	Imprint "2013"		.30	.30
d.	Imprint "2014"		.30	.30
e.	Imprint "2015"		.30	.30
f.	Imprint "2015-II"		.30	.30
g.	Imprint "2016"		.30	.30
857	A564	50k multi	.30	.00
a.	Imprint "2012-II"		.30	.30
b.	Imprint "2012-III"		.30	.30
c.	Imprint "2013"		.30	.30
d.	Imprint "2013-II"		.30	.30
e.	Imprint "2013-III"		.30	.30
f.	Imprint "2014"		.30	.30
g.	Imprint "2014-II"		.30	.30
h.	Imprint "2015"		.30	.30
i.	Imprint "2015"		.30	.30
j.	Imprint "2016"		.30	.30
858	A564	70k multi	.30	.30
a.	Imprint "2012-II"		.30	.30
b.	Imprint "2013"		.30	.30
c.	Imprint "2014"		.30	.30
d.	Imprint "2016"		.30	.30
859	A564	2h multi	.90	.90
a.	Imprint "2012-II"		.90	.90
b.	Imprint "2012-III"		.90	.90
c.	Imprint "2013"		.90	.90
d.	Imprint "2013-II"		.90	.90
e.	Imprint "2014"		.85	.05
f.	Imprint "2014-III"		.85	.85
g.	Imprint "2014-III"		.85	.85
h.	Imprint "2016"		.50	.50
i.	Imprint "2016-II"		.50	.50
860	A564	2.50h multi	1.00	1.00
a.	Imprint "2012-II"		1.00	1.00
b.	Imprint "2012-III"		1.00	1.00
c.	Imprint "2013"		1.00	1.00
d.	Imprint "2013-II"		1.00	1.00
e.	Imprint "2016"		1.00	1.00
861	A564	3h multi	1.25	1.25
a.	Imprint "2012-II"		1.25	1.25
b.	Imprint "2013"		1.25	1.25
c.	Imprint "2014"		1.00	1.00
d.	Imprint "2015"		.70	.70
e.	Imprint "2015-II"		.70	.70
f.	Imprint "2016"		.70	.70
g.	Imprint "2016-II"		.70	.70
862	A564	4.80h multi	2.00	2.00
a.	Imprint "2012-II"		2.00	2.00
b.	Imprint "2012-III"		2.00	2.00
c.	Imprint "2013"		2.00	2.00
d.	Imprint "2013-II"		2.00	2.00
e.	Imprint "2016"		2.00	2.00
863	A564	5h multi	2.00	2.00
a.	Imprint "2013"		2.00	2.00
b.	Imprint "2014-II"		2.00	2.00
c.	Imprint "2015"		1.25	1.25
d.	Imprint "2016"		1.25	1.25
864	A564	8h multi	3.25	3.25
a.	Imprint "2013"		3.25	3.25
b.	Imprint "2014"		3.00	3.00
c.	Imprint "2016"		3.00	3.00
865	A564	10h multi	4.00	4.00
a.	Imprint "2015"		2.25	2.25
b.	Imprint "2016"		2.25	2.25
c.	Imprint "2016-II"		2.25	2.25
	Nos. 853-865 (13)		16.20	16.20

Issued: 5k, 30k, 50k, 2h, 2/3; 20k, 40k, 70k, 2.50h, 1/14; 3h, 4.80h, 5h, 8h, 10h, 1/24. Nos. 853c, 857c, 1/11/13. Nos. 855g, 858d, 860e, 862e, 864c, 3/17/17.
See Nos. 882-883, 909, 942-943, 996, 1025-1026.

 A565

 A566

 A567

Personalized Stamps — A568

2012, Feb. 20   **Litho.**   *Perf. 11½*
Background Color
Cyrillic Country Name in Yellow
866 A565 (1.80h) violet blue + label   3.50 3.50
867 A566 (1.80h) blue + label   3.50 3.50
Cyrillic Country Name in Blue
868 A567 (1.80h) blue + label   3.50 3.50
Cyrillic Country Name in Pink
869 A568 (1.80h) blue + label   3.50 3.50
   Nos. 866-869 (4)   14.00 14.00

Nos. 866-869 were each printed in sheets of 14 + 14 labels that could be personalized. The labels shown, depicting a soccer ball and various stadiums used for the 2012 European Soccer Championships, are generic.

Paintings by Taras Shevchenko (1814-61) — A569

Designs: 2h, Fortification at Raim, 1848. 2.50h, Moonlit Night on Kos-Aral, 1849 (49x28mm).

Litho. With Foil Application
2012, Mar. 9
870-871 A569   Set of 2   1.75 1.75

Souvenir Sheet

National Arms and Flag, 20th Anniv. — A570

No. 872: a, 2h, Arms. b, 3h, Flag.

2012, Mar. 23   *Perf. 11½*
872 A570   Sheet of 2, #a-b   1.90 1.90

Ivano-Frankivsk, 350th Anniv. — A571

2012, May 7   **Litho.**   *Perf. 13¾x14¼*
873 A571 2h multi   .80 .80

Mykhailo Stelmakh (1912-93), Writer — A572

2012, May 24   *Perf. 13¼*
874 A572 2h multi   .80 .80
   Printed in sheets of 11 + label.

 A573

 A574

 A575

 A576

A577

2012 UEFA European Soccer Championships, Poland and Ukraine — A578

No. 878 — Buildings in: a, Lviv (country name in purple). b, Kyiv (country name in yellow green). c, Kharkiv (country name in yellow). d, Donetsk (country name in red).

No. 879: a, Lviv Stadium (country name in purple). b, Olympic Stadium, Kyiv (country name in yellow green). c, Metalist Stadium, Kharkiv (country name in yellow). d, Donbass Stadium, Donetsk (country name in red).

No. 880: a, Emblem of 2012 tournament. b, Soccer ball, crowd.

	2012		**Perf. 14x14¼**	
875	A573	4.80h multi	1.60	1.60
876	A574	12h multi	4.00	4.00
877	A575	27.60h multi	10.00	10.00
878	A576	4.80h Block of 4, #a-d	6.50	6.50
879	A577	4.80h Block of 4, #a-d	6.50	6.50
	Nos. 875-879 (5)		30.90	30.90

Souvenir Sheet
Perf. 11½

880	A578	27.60h Sheet of 2, #a-b	20.00	20.00

Issued: No. 875, 6/1; No. 876, 6/8; No. 877, 6/8; Nos. 878-879, 5/28; No. 880, 6/11.

The souvenir sheet containing three 13.80h stamps was issued on June 25 and sold for 300h. The souvenir sheet containing one 62.55h stamp was issued on May 11 and sold for 360h.

Europa — A579

No. 881: a, 4h, Musicians in costume. b, 5.60h, Mountain and direction post.

2012, June 13   **Perf. 14x14¼**

881	A579	Horiz. pair, #a-b	3.75	3.75
c.		Booklet pane of 2, #881a-881b, perf. 11½	8.75	—
		Complete booklet, #881c	8.75	

No. 881 was printed in sheets of 5 pairs + 2 labels. Complete booklet sold for 17.10h.

Tree Leaves and Fruit
A580   A581

Designs: (4.30h), Acer pseudoplatanus. (8.10h), Salix alba.

2012, July 25   **Perf. 13¾**

882	A580	(4.30h) multi	1.60	1.60
a.		Imprint "2016"	1.60	1.60
883	A581	(8.10h) multi	3.00	3.00
a.		Imprint "2016"	3.00	3.00

Issued: Nos. 882a, 883a, 3/17/17.

A582

A583

Railway Passenger Cars — A584

2012, July 27   **Perf. 14x14¼**

884	A582	2h multi	.70	.70
885	A583	2h multi	.70	.70
886	A584	2h multi	.70	.70
	Nos. 884-886 (3)		2.25	2.25

Nos. 884-886 each were printed in sheets of 11 + label.

2012 Summer Olympics, London — A585

No. 887: a, 2h, Canoeing. b, 2h, High jump. c, 2.50h, Running. d, 5.30h, Shot put.

Litho. With Foil Application
2012, July 27   **Perf. 11½**

887	A585	Block of 4, #a-d	4.25	4.25

13th National Philatelic Exhibition, Odessa — A586

2012, Aug. 10   **Perf. 13¼**

888	A586	2h multi	.80	.80

Miniature Sheet

Ukrainian Soviet Socialist Republic Semi-Postal Stamps of 1923, 89th Anniv. — A587

No. 889: a, 2h, #B4. b, 2.50h, #B1. c, 4.30h, #B3. d, 4.80h, #B2.

2012, Aug. 13   **Litho.**   **Perf. 11½**

889	A587	Sheet of 4, #a-d, + label	5.25	5.25

Pavel Popovich (1930-2009), Cosmonaut — A588

2012, Aug. 15   **Perf. 14x14¼**

890	A588	2k multi	.75	.75

Miniature Sheet

Farm Animals — A589

No. 891: a, 2h, Horse. b, 2h, Goat. c, 2h, Ducks. d, 2.50h, Chicken. e, 2.50h, Rabbit.

2012, Aug. 18   **Perf. 11½**

891	A589	Sheet of 5, #a-e	4.25	4.25

Personalized Stamp — A590

2012, Aug. 23

892	A590	(2h) multi + label	3.50	3.50

No. 892 was printed in sheets of 18 + 18 labels that could be personalized. The label shown, depicting the national arms and post-thorns, is the generic label image.

Fairy Tale "Zaliznonosa Bosorkania" — A591

No. 893: a, 2h, Man, man with long nose, cat (43x26mm). b, 2.50h, Men on horse (26x26mm).

2012, Sept. 1   **Perf. 11½**

893	A591	Horiz. pair, #a-b	1.75	1.75

Miniature Sheet

Fruits and Flowers — A592

No. 894: a, 2h, Cerasus vulgaris (30x45mm). b, 2h, Tagetes patula (30x50mm). c, 2.50h, Alcea rosea (30x50mm). d, 3.30h, Fragaria vesca (30x50mm).

Litho. With Foil Application
2012, Sept. 1

894	A592	Sheet of 4, #a-d	3.75	3.75

Ginsburg Apartment House, Kyiv, Cent. — A593

2012, Sept. 14   **Litho.**   **Perf. 14x14¼**

895	A593	2h multi	.80	.80

Sudak, 1800th Anniv. — A594

2012, Sept. 20   **Perf. 11½**

896	A594	2h multi	.80	.80

Souvenir Sheet

Donetsk Region, 80th Anniv. — A595

2012, Sept. 25

897	A595	2h multi	.80	.80

Miniature Sheet

Nikita Botanical Gardens, 200th Anniv. — A596

No. 898: a, 2h, Gazebo (38x31mm). b, 2h, Administration Building (45x31mm). c, 2.50h, Arbor and steps (50x33mm). d, 5.30h, Echinocereus (50x33mmm).

Litho. With Foil Application
2012, Oct. 4
898 A596   Sheet of 4, #a-d   4.50 4.50

Sun and Flowers, by Aliona Panasiuk, Winning Design in Children's Stamp Designing Contest — A597

2012, Oct. 9   Litho.   Perf. 13¼
899 A597   2h multi   .80 .80

Chyhyryn, 500th Anniv. — A598

2012, Oct. 14   Perf. 14x14¼
900 A598   2h multi   .80 .80

Battle of Blue Waters, 650th Anniv. — A599

2012, Oct. 24
901 A599   2h multi   .80 .80

Miniature Sheet

Windmills — A600

No. 902: a, 2h, Four-bladed windmill in winter. b, 2.50h, Six-bladed windmill. c, 3.30h, Six-bladed windmill, diff. d, 4.80h, Four-bladed windmill, diff.

2012, Nov. 9   Perf. 11½
902 A600   Sheet of 4, #a-d   4.50 4.50

Andrii Malyshko (1912-70), Poet — A601

2012, Nov. 14   Perf. 13¼
903 A601   2h multi   .80 .80
No. 903 was printed in sheets of 11 + label.

Miniature Sheet

Seven Wonders of Ukraine — A602

No. 904: a, Akkerman Fortress (name in light blue). b, Khotyn Fortress (name in light green). c, Vorontsov Palace (wall in front). d, Lutsk Castle (name in red). e, Mytropolychyi Palace (diamonds on roof). f, Kamianets-Podilskyi Fortress (with curving road). g, Kachanivka Palace (with cupola and pillars).

2012, Nov. 29   Perf. 11½
904 A602   2.50h Sheet of 7, #a-g   6.75 6.75

Christmas and New Year's Day — A603

No. 905: a, Tree, angel, bird, sleigh, candle, house. b, Decoration, grain, bowl and spoon, church and house.

Litho. With Foil Application
2012, Dec. 8
905 A603   2h Horiz. pair, #a-b   1.60 1.60
No. 905 was printed in sheets containing 6 pairs and 3 labels

Miniature Sheet

Frogs and Toads — A604

No. 906: a, 2h, Bufo bufo. b, 2h, Bombina variegata. c, 4.30h, Bufo viridis. d, 5.40h, Pelobates fuscus. e, 5.40h, Rana temporaria.

2012, Dec. 17   Litho.
906 A604   Sheet of 5, #a-e   7.25 7.25

Traditional Women's Costume — A605

2012, Dec. 28   Perf. 13¼
907 A605   2h multi   .80 .80

Film, Man with a Movie Camera, by Dziga Vertov, 83rd Anniv. — A606

No. 908: a, Lens and eye. b, Camera.

2012, Dec. 29
908 A606   2h Horiz. pair, #a-b   1.60 1.60

Morus Alba Leaf and Fruit — A607

2013, Jan. 11   Perf. 13¾
909 A607   (4k) multi   1.75 1.75
  a. Imprint "2013-II"   1.75 1.75
  b. Imprint "2016"   1.75 1.75
    Issued: No. 909b, 3/17/17.

Souvenir Sheet

Charter of Volodymyr II Monomakh, 900th Anniv. — A608

2013, Feb. 22   Perf. 11½
910 A608   6.40h multi   2.50 2.50

Vladimir Vernadsky (1863-1945), Mineralogist A609

2013, Feb. 28   Perf. 13¼
911 A609   2h multi   .80 .80
No. 911 was printed in sheets of 11 + label.

Honta and Zalizniak, by Mykola Storozhenko A610

Fate, by Oleksandr Ivakhnenko A611

Litho. With Foil Application
2013, Mar. 9   Perf. 11½
912 A610   3.30h multi   1.25 1.25
913 A611   4.80h multi   1.75 1.75
Nos. 912-913 each were printed in sheets of 11 + label.

Semen Hulak-Artemovskyi (1813-73), Composer — A612

2013, Mar. 25   Litho.   Perf. 14x14¼
914 A612   2h multi   .80 .80

12-791 Rail Car — A613

15-1547-03 Rail Tanker — A614

19-7017-01 Rail Tanker — A615

20-7032 Rail Car — A616

2013, Mar. 27
915 A613   2h multi   .80 .80
916 A614   2h multi   .80 .80
917 A615   2.50h multi   .95 .95
918 A616   2.50h multi   .95 .95
    Nos. 915-918 (4)   3.50 3.50
Nos. 915-918 each were printed in sheets of 11 + label.

Boryspil International Airport,
Kyiv — A617

2013, Apr. 2
919 A617 2h multi .80 .80

Khan's Palace, Bakhchisaray — A618

Ayu-Dag
Mountain
A619

Crimean Tourist Attractions — A620

No. 922: a, 2h, Valley of Ghosts, near
Alushta (26x40mm). b, 2h, St. John's Cathedral, Kerch (37x26mm). c, 2.50h, Wine barrels
and grapes, Masandra (37x26mm). d, 2.50h,
Urn (26x40mm). e, 4.80h, Southern coast
(56x26mm).

2013, Apr. 24 **Perf. 14x14¼**
920 A618 2h multi .80 .80
921 A619 2.50h multi .95 .95
Miniature Sheet
Perf. 11½
922 A620 Sheet of 5, #a-e 5.00 5.00

Easter
A621

2013, Apr. 30 **Perf. 14x14¼**
923 A621 2h multi .80 .80

Saints Cyril and
Methodius — A622

2013, May 22 **Perf. 14¼x13¾**
924 A622 2.50h multi 1.25 1.25
Slavic writing, 1150th anniv.

Souvenir Sheet

Medals for First All-Russian Olympiad,
Kyiv, Cent. — A623

2013, May 25 **Perf. 11½**
925 A623 4.80h multi 2.25 2.25

Europa — A624

No. 926 — Postal vehicles: a, 4h, 1953
Moskvich 400. b, 5.60h, 2013 MAZ-5440
truck.

2013, May 29 **Perf. 14x14¼**
926 A624 Pair, #a-b 3.75 3.75
 c. Booklet pane of 2, #926a-926b,
 perf. 11½ 7.50 —
 Complete booklet, #926c 7.50
Complete booklet sold for 12.12h.

Children's Day — A625

No. 927: a, Rainbow, boy on one knee giving heart to girl in wheelchair. b, Children and
balloons.

2013, May 31 **Perf. 13¼**
927 A625 2h Pair, #a-b 1.75 1.75

St.
Volodymyr's
Cathedral,
Sevastopol
A626

2013, June 27 **Litho.** **Perf. 14x14¼**
928 A626 3.30h multi 1.75 1.75

Souvenir Sheet

Tale of Bygone Years (History of
Kievan Rus), by Nestor, 900th
Anniv. — A627

Litho. With Foil Application
2013, July 26 **Perf. 11½**
929 A627 5.70h multi 2.50 2.50

Souvenir Sheet

Christianization of Kievan Rus, 1025th
Anniv. — A628

**Litho., Margin Litho. With Foil
Application**
2013, July 28 **Perf. 11½**
930 A628 5.40h multi 2.40 2.40
See Belarus No. 870, Russia No. 7466.

Personalized
Stamp — A629

2013, Aug. 19 **Litho.** **Perf. 11½**
931 A629 (2h) sil & blk + label 3.00 3.00
No. 931 was printed in sheets of 28 stamps
+ 28 labels that could be personalized. The
label shown, deptincting the national arms and
posthorns, is the generic label image.
Compare with types A727 and A765.

Miniature Sheet

Breads — A630

No. 932: a, 2h, Loaf of white bread. b, 2h,
Kolache with hole in middle. c, 2.50h, Loaf of
black bread. d, 2.50h, Three bubliks. e, 4.80h,
Decorated korovai.

2013, Aug. 20 **Litho.** **Perf. 11½**
932 A630 Sheet of 5, #a-e, + 4
 labels 6.50 6.50

Dnepropetrovsk Skyline — A631

2013, Aug. 23 **Litho.** **Perf. 14x14¼**
933 A631 2h multi .95 .95

Miniature Sheet

Dnepropetrovsk Oblast — A632

No. 934: a, 2h, Trinity Cathedral
(35x26mm). b, 2h, Dnepropetrovsk skyline
(35x26mm). c, 2.50h, Zenit-3SLB rocket
(35x26mm). d, 3.30h, Painting of rooster and
flowers from Petrekivka area (43x52mm).

2013, Aug. 23 **Litho.** **Perf. 11½**
934 A632 Sheet of 4, #a-d 4.50 4.50

Pumpkins,
by Evdokim
Voloshinov
(1824-1913)
A633

2013, Aug. 24 **Litho.** **Perf. 14x14¼**
935 A633 2h multi .95 .95

Antonov AN-158 — A634

2013, Aug. 31 **Litho.** **Perf. 14x14¼**
936 A634 2h multi .95 .95

Water Tower,
Vinnitsa — A635

2013, Sept. 5 **Litho.** **Perf. 14¼x14**
937 A635 2h multi .85 .85

Miniature Sheet

Vinnitsa Oblast — A636

No. 938: a, 2h, Dniester River (26x36mm).
b, 2h, Trinity Monastery, Brailov (26x36mm). c,
2.50h, Shcherbatov Palace, Nemyriv
(45x23mm). d, 4.80h, Roshen Fountain, Vinnitsa (56x30mm).

2013, Sept. 9 **Litho.** **Perf. 11½**
938 A636 Sheet of 4, #a-d 4.00 4.00

Souvenir Sheet

Beheading of St. John the Baptist Monastery, Lyadova, 1000th Anniv. — A637

Litho. With Foil Application

2013, Sept. 15			**Perf. 11½**
939	A637	4.30h multi	1.75 1.75

Post Rider — A638

2013, Oct. 9	Litho.		**Perf. 13½**
940	A638	2h multi	.85 .85

Miniature Sheet

Autumn — A639

No. 941: a, 2h, Sorbus aucuparia (30x45mm). b, 2h, Citrullus lanatus (30x50mm). c, 2.50h, Dahlia (30x50mm). d, 3.30h, Boletus edulis (30x50mm).

Litho. With Foil Application

2013, Oct. 14			**Perf. 11½**
941	A639	Sheet of 4, #a-d	3.75 3.75

Hippophae Rhamnoides Leaf and Fruit — A640

Pyris Communis Leaf and Fruit — A641

2013	Litho.		**Perf. 13¾**
942	A640	(5.60h) multi	1.75 1.75
a.		Imprint "2016"	1.75 1.75
943	A641	(6.40h) multi	2.25 2.25
a.		Imprint "2016"	2.25 2.25

Issued: No. 942, 11/5; No. 943, 10/22. Nos. 942a, 943a, 3/17/17.

Vera Kholodnaya (1893-1919), Film Actress — A642

2013, Oct. 31	Litho.		**Perf. 14x14¼**
944	A642	2h multi	.85 .85

Kyiv Is Ours, by Georgy Malakov (1928-79) A643

2013, Nov. 6	Litho.		**Perf. 13¼**
945	A643	2h multi	.85 .85

Liberation of Kyiv, 70th anniv.

Miniature Sheet

Winter on the Farm — A644

No. 946: a, 2h, Squirrel in tree (32x24mm). b, 2h, Birds in tree (32x24mm). c, 2.50h, Children with Christmas decoration (32x48mm). d, 2.50h, Turkey (32x24mm).

2013, Nov. 22	Litho.		**Perf. 11½**
946	A644	Sheet of 4, #a-d	3.50 3.50

Olha Kobylianska (1863-1942), Writer — A645

2013, Nov. 27	Litho.		**Perf. 14x14¼**
947	A645	2h multi	.85 .85

Christmas A646

Litho. With Foil Application

2013, Dec. 6			**Perf. 13½**
948	A646	2h multi	.85 .85

Mykola Amosov (1913-2002), Surgeon — A647

2013, Dec. 6	Litho.		**Perf. 13¼**
949	A647	2h multi	.85 .85

Printed in sheets of 11 + label.

Miniature Sheet

Pectoral, 4th Cent. — A648

No. 950 — Part of pectoral with denomination at: a, 4h, LL (33x29mm). b, 4h, LR (33x29mm). c, 5.60h, UL (40x29mm). d, 5.60h, LL (40x29mm).

Litho. & Embossed With Foil Application

2013, Dec. 12			**Perf. 11½**
950	A648	Sheet of 4, #a-d	8.50 8.50

Ports of Ukraine and Morocco — A649

No. 951: a, 2h, Odessa, Ukraine. b, 3.30h, Tangiers, Morocco.

2013, Dec. 18	Litho.		**Perf. 11½**
951	A649	Horiz. pair, #a-b	3.00 3.00

See Morocco No. 1182.

Churches in Ukraine and Romania — A650

No. 952: a, 2h, Church of the Savior, Berestovo, Ukraine. b, 3.30h, Church of the Sucevita Monastery, Romania.

Litho. With Foil Application

2013, Dec. 21			**Perf. 11½**
952	A650	Horiz pair, #a-b, + central label	3.00 3.00

See Romania Nos. 5509-5510.

Miniature Sheets

A651

Chinese Zodiac Animals — A652

No. 953: a, Rat. b, Ox. c, Tiger. d, Rabbit. e, Dragon. f, Snake.
No. 954: a, Horse. b, Goat. c, Monkey. d, Rooster. e, Dog. f, Pig.

Litho. With Foil Application

2013, Dec. 25			**Perf. 13½**
953	A651	2.50h Sheet of 6, #a-f	6.50 6.50
954	A652	2.50h Sheet of 6, #a-f	6.50 6.50

Bunch of Daisies, by Andrey Guk — A653

2014, Jan. 24	Litho.		**Perf. 13¼**
955	A653	2h multi	.60 .60

Leonid Kravchuk, First President of Ukraine, 80th Birthday A654

2014, Jan. 31	Litho.		**Perf. 14x14¼**
956	A654	2h multi	.60 .60

Ukrainian Women's Biathlon Relay Team for 2014 Winter Olympics A655

2014, Jan. 31	Litho.		**Perf. 14x14¼**
957	A655	3.30h multi	1.90 1.90

No. 957 was printed in sheets of 16 + 4 labels.

On Apr. 15, No. 957 was overprinted in gold Cyrillic text to commemorate the victory of the biathlon team at the Winter Olympics. It was produced in limited quantities. Value, *$17.50.*

Miniature Sheet

Architecture in Kyiv of Wladislaw Horodecki (1863-1930) — A656

No. 958: a, 2h, Sculpture of lion from House of Chimeras (33x30mm). b, 2h, Sculpture of woman and frogs from House of Chimeras (33x30mm). c, 2h, Karaite Kenesa (33x30mm). d, 3.30h, National Art Museum (40x30mm). e, 4.80h, St. Nicholas Cathedral (33x60mm). f, 5.60h, House of Chimeras (40x30mm).

Litho. & Engr.

2014, Feb. 14			**Perf. 11½**
958	A656	Sheet of 10, #958a, 958b, 2 each #958c-958f	15.00 15.00

Icon Depicting Archangel Gabriel — A657

2014, Feb. 18   Litho.   Perf. 13½
959 A657 4.80h multi   1.75 1.75
No. 959 was printed in sheets of 8 + central label.

Art School, Kirovohrad — A658

2014, Feb. 27   Litho.   Perf. 14x14¼
960 A658 2h multi   .75 .75

Miniature Sheet

Kirovohrad Oblast — A659

No. 961: a, 2h, Ascension Cathedral (30x37mm). b, 2h, Scythian stele (30x37mm). c, 2.50h, Kropivnitsky Theater (35x26mm). d, 4.80h, Dancers (52x47mm).

2014, Feb. 27   Litho.   Perf. 11½
961 A659 Sheet of 4, #a-d   3.25 3.25

Ukrposhta (Ukrainian Postal Service), 20th Anniv. — A660

Litho. & Embossed With Foil Application
2014, Mar. 25   Perf. 14¼x14
962 A660 2h multi   .75 .75

Metropolitan Vasily Lipkivski (1864-1937) A661

2014, May 8   Litho.   Perf. 13¼
963 A661 2h multi   .75 .75

Maria Kapnist (1914-93), Actress A662

2014, May 16   Litho.   Perf. 14x14¼
964 A662 2h multi   .75 .75

Children Playing and UNICEF Emblem A663

2014, May 29   Litho.   Perf. 13½
965 A663 2h multi   .75 .75

Still Life with a Chocolate Mill, by Juan de Zurbarán A664

2014, May 29   Litho.   Perf. 14x14¼
966 A664 5.70h multi   1.75 1.75
No. 966 was printed in sheets of 8 + central label.

Sikorsky Ilya Muromets Airplane — A665

2014, June 17   Litho.   Perf. 14x14¼
967 A665 2h multi   .75 .75

Europa — A666

Designs: 4.80h, Painting depicting Cossack Mamay playing kobza. 5.70h, Kobza.

2014, July 25   Litho.   Perf. 11½
968 A666 4.80h multi   1.40 1.40
 a.   Booklet pane of 1   3.00
969 A666 5.70h multi   1.75 1.75
 a.   Booklet pane of 1   4.00   —
      Complete booklet, #968a, 969a 7.00

Reply of the Zaporozhian Cossacks to Sultan Mehmed IV of the Ottoman Empire, by Ilya Y. Repin (1840-1930) — A667

2014, July 29   Litho.   Perf. 11½
970 A667 3.30h multi   1.10 1.10
No. 970 was printed in sheets of 8 + central label.

Cacti — A668

Designs: 2h, Gymnocalycium anisitsii. 2.50h, Opuntia microdasys. 3.30h, Pilosocereus palmeri. 4.80h, Graptopetalum bellum.

Perf. 13½x13¼
2014, Aug. 15   Litho.
971 A668 2h multi   .85 .85
972 A668 2.50h multi   1.10 1.10
Perf. 14¼x14
Size: 25x52mm
973 A668 3.30h multi   1.35 1.35
Size: 28x40mm
974 A668 4.80h multi   2.10 2.10
   Nos. 971-974 (4)   5.40 5.40

2013 Euromaidan Demonstrations — A669

2014, Aug. 22   Litho.   Perf. 11½
975 A669 2h multi   .80 .80

Statue of Sailor's Wife and Child, Odessa A670

2014, Sept. 2   Litho.   Perf. 13½
976 A670 2h multi   .80 .80

Miniature Sheet

Odessa Oblast — A671

No. 977: a, 2h, Akkerman Fortress (53x25mm). b, 2.50h, Port of Odessa (40x30mm). c, 2.50h, St. Nikolai Church, Vilkove (40x30mm). d, 5.70h, Ilyichevsk Lighthouse and ship (58x45mm).

2014, Sept. 2   Litho.   Perf. 11½
977 A671 Sheet of 4, #a-d   4.75 4.75

Monument to Shipbuilders, Mykolaiv — A672

2014, Sept. 13   Litho.   Perf. 13½
978 A672 2h multi   .80 .80

Miniature Sheet

Mykolaiv Oblast — A673

No. 979: a, 2h, Traffic circles and bridges (26x37mm). b, 2.50h, Kasperovskaya Cathedral of Our Lady, Mykolaiv (37x26mm). c, 2.50h, Buzky Gard National Park (37x26mm). d, 5.70h, Ship factory (51x52mm).

2014, Sept. 13   Litho.   Perf. 11½
979 A673 Sheet of 4, #a-d   4.75 4.75

Portrait of V. L. Kochubey, by Taras Shevchenko (1814-61) — A674

Gifts in Chigrin, 1644, Etching by Shevchenko — A675

A676

No. 982: a, 3.30h, Portraits of Lusha Polusmak and Kobza player (56x35mm). b, 5.70h, Self-portrait of Shevchenko (36x35mm).

Litho. With Foil Application
2014, Sept. 26   Perf. 11½
980 A674 2h multi   .80 .80
981 A675 2.50h multi   1.00 1.00
Souvenir Sheet
982 A676 Sheet of 2, #a-b   3.50 3.50
   Nos. 980-981 were each printed in sheets of 11 + label.

A Lady in Black, by Boris Grigoriev (1886-1939) A677

2014, Oct. 6   Litho.   Perf. 13½
983 A677 2h multi   .80 .80
No. 983 was printed in sheets of 8 + central label.

Pigeons A678

Designs: No. 984, 2h, Kryukovsky pigeon (white bird). No. 985, 2h, Odessa Turman pigeon (brown and white bird). 2.50h, Kiev Tumbler pigeon. 3.30h, Micholaivsky Shield Tumbler pigeon.

2014, Oct. 10   Litho.   Perf. 14x14¼
984-987 A678 Set of 4   3.25 3.25

World War II
Liberation of
Ukraine, 70th
Anniv. — A679

Litho. With Foil Application
2014, Oct. 28　　　　Perf. 11½
988 A679 2h multi　　　　.90 .90

Chernivtsi
Post Office,
125th
Anniv.
A680

Perf. 14x14¼ Syncopated
2014, Oct. 31　　　　Litho.
989 A680 2h multi　　　　.80 .80

Self-Adhesive

Tereshchenko Family — A681

No. 990: a, 4.80h, Tereshchenko coat of
arms. b, 5.70h, Artemi Tereshchenko (1794-
1877), industrialist.

Litho. With Foil Application
2014, Nov. 14　　　　Perf. 11½
990 A681　Sheet of 2, #a-b　　3.00 3.00

Christmas and New
Year's Day — A682

Litho. With Foil Application
2014, Nov. 14　　　　Perf. 14¼x14
991 A682 2h multi　　　　.75 .75

Railroad
Station,
Lutsk
A683

2014, Dec. 4　　Litho.　Perf. 14¼x14
992 A683 2h multi　　　　.65 .65

Miniature Sheet

Volyn Oblast — A684

No. 993: a, Statue of Lesya Ukrainka, Lutsk
(27x41mm). b, 2h, Lake, Okonsk (27x28mm).
c, 2.50h, Angel (30x28mm). d, 4.20h, Monastery, Zimne (56x39mm).

2014, Dec. 4　　　　Litho.　Perf. 11½
993 A684　Sheet of 4, #a-d　　3.25 3.25

Army Day
A685

Perf. 14x14¼ Syncopated
2014, Dec. 5　　　　Litho.
994 A685 2h multi　　　　.65 .65

Miniature Sheet

Flora and Fauna in Winter — A686

No. 995: a, 2h, Lepus timidus (30x56mm).
b, 2h, Sciurus vulgaris (30x56mm). c, 3.30h,
Parus major (37x40mm). d, 3.30h, Viburnum
opulus (30x56mm).

Litho. With Foil Application
2014, Dec. 19　　　　Perf. 11½
995 A686　Sheet of 4, #a-d　　3.25 3.25

Tree Leaves and Fruit Type of 2012
Serpentine Die Cut 12¾x12¼
2014, Dec. 22　　　　Litho.
Self-Adhesive
996 A564 2h Quercus robur　　.65 .65

Souvenir Sheet

Archaeological Artifacts — A687

No. 997 — Artifacts from: a, Trypillian culture, Ukraine (6th-3rd millennium B.C.). b,
Mohenjo-Daro, Pakistan.

2014, Dec. 25　Litho.　Perf. 11½
997 A687 4.80h Sheet of 2, #a-b 2.60 2.60
See Pakistan No. 1219.

Vasyl
Symonenko
(1935-63),
Poet
A688

2015, Jan. 8　Litho.　Perf. 14x14¼
998 A688 2h multi　　　　.65 .65

Unity Day — A689

Litho. With Foil Application
Perf. 14¼x14 Syncopated
2015, Jan. 22
999 A689 2h multi　　　　.65 .65

Heroes
Day — A690

2015, Feb. 20　Litho.　Perf. 13½
1000 A690 2h multi　　　　.65 .65

Mykhailo Verbytsky (1815-70),
Composer — A691

2015, Mar. 4　Litho.　Perf. 13¾x14¼
1001 A691 2h multi　　　　.65 .65

Sviatoslav Richter
(1915-97),
Pianist — A692

2015, Mar. 20　Litho.　Perf. 13¼
1002 A692 2h multi　　　　.65 .65

Boris von Loutzky (1865-c. 1943),
Automobile Manufacturer — A693

2015, Apr. 10　Litho.　Perf. 14x14½
1003 A693 2h multi　　　　.65 .65

Memorial
Day — A694

2015, May 8　Litho.　Perf. 11½
1004 A694 2h multi　　　　.65 .65

Crimean
Tatars — A695

Designs: No. 1005, 3h, Tatar building (Ilk
Qirim Hanlarinin Dürbesi). No. 1006, 3h, Cop-
persmith (Bakirci Usta). No. 1007, 3h,
Haytarma dancers (Haytarma Oyuni). No.
1008, 3h, Tatar warrior on horseback
(Qirimtatar Askeri).

2015, May 14　Litho.　Perf. 13½x13¼
1005-1008 A695　Set of 4　　3.00 3.00

2015
European
Games,
Baku
A696

2015, June 5　Litho.　Perf. 14x14½
1009 A696 4.40h multi　　　　.75 .75

Elie Metchnikoff
(1845-1916),
Zoologist and
Bacteriologist
A697

2015, July 21　Litho.　Perf. 13½
1010 A697 4.80h multi　　　　.75 .75

Funicular,
Kyiv
A698

KTV-55-2
Tram, Kyiv
A699

2015, July 24　Litho.　Perf. 14½x14
1011 A698　2h multi　　　　.35 .35
1012 A699 2.40h multi　　　　.40 .40

Souvenir Sheet

Prince Vladimir the Great (c. 958-1015) — A700

Litho. With Foil Application
2015, July 28 **Perf. 11½**
1013 A700 12.90h multi 3.00 3.00

Andrey Sheptytsky (1865-1944), Metropolitan Archbishop of Lviv — A701

2015, July 29 Litho. Perf. 13½
1014 A701 2.40h multi .45 .45

Yuriy Fedkovych National University, Chernivtsi A702

2015, Aug. 7 Litho. Perf. 13½
1015 A702 2.40h multi .45 .45

Miniature Sheet

Chernivtsi Oblast — A703

No. 1016: a, 2.40h, Cinderella Cave (30x28mm). b, 2.40h, Dormition Cathedral (26x40mm). c, 3h, Malanka Festival participants (37x28mm). d, 6h, Khotyn Fortress (56x39mm).

2015, Aug. 7 Litho. Perf. 11½
1016 A703 Sheet of 4, #a-d 2.25 2.25

Europa — A704

Designs: 4.80h, Cart. 5.40h, Girl on swing.

2015, Aug. 11 Litho. Perf. 11½
1017-1018 A704 Set of 2 1.75 1.75

A booklet containing a pane of two 31x44mm stamps like Nos. 1017-1018 sold for 22.50h.

A705

A706

A707

Cattle A708

2015, Aug. 14 Litho. Perf. 14x14½
1019 A705 2.40h multi .40 .40
1020 A706 2.40h multi .40 .40
1021 A707 2.40h multi .40 .40
1022 A708 2.40h multi .40 .40
　　　Nos. 1019-1022 (4) 1.60 1.60

Solomiya Krushelnytska Monument, Ternopil — A709

2015, Aug. 28 Litho. Perf. 14x14½
1023 A709 2.40h multi .45 .45

Miniature Sheet

Ternopil Oblast — A710

No. 1024: a, 2.40h, Zalishchyky (40x23mm). b, 2.40h, Ternopil at night (40x23mm). c, 3h, Berezhany (23x37mm). d, 6h, Sculpture of angel, Assumption Cathedral, Buchach (58x40mm).

2015, Aug. 28 Litho. Perf. 11½
1024 A710 Sheet of 4, #a-d 2.25 2.25

Cornus Mas Leaf and Fruit — A711　　Euonymus Europaeus Leaf and Fruit — A712

2015 Litho. Perf. 13¾
1025 A711 (2.40h) multi .45 .45
a.　Imprint "2016" .45 .45

1026 A712 (5.40h) multi, imprint "2015" 1.10 1.10
a.　Imprint "2016" 1.10 1.10
b.　Imprint "2016-II" 1.10 1.10
c.　Sheet of 20, #853h, 854g, 855g, 856g, 857j, 858d, 859h, 860e, 861f, 862e, 863e, 864c, 865b, 882a, 883a, 909b, 942a, 943a, 1025a, 1026a 25.00 25.00

Self-Adhesive
Serpentine Die Cut 12¼
1027 A712 (5.40h) multi 1.10 1.10
　Issued: No. 1025, 9/15. Nos. 1026, 1027, 11/19/15. No. 1026c, 3/17/17.

Souvenir Sheet

National University of Kyiv-Mohyla Academy, 400th Anniv. — A713

Litho. With Foil Application
2015, Sept. 18 Perf. 11½
1028 A713 7.65h multi 1.40 1.40

Souvenir Sheet

Pochayiv Monastery, 775th Anniv. — A714

2015, Sept. 21 Litho. Perf. 11½
1029 A714 22.10h multi 5.00 5.00

St. Mary's Church, Boryspil — A715

2015, Sept. 30 Litho. Perf. 14x14½
1030 A715 2.40h multi .45 .45

Miniature Sheet

Kyiv Oblast — A716

No. 1031: a, 2.40h, Horse riding, Kievan Rus Park, Kopachiv (35x26mm). b, 2.40h, Binoklevydna vessel, 5th millennium B.C.

(35x26mm). c, 3h, Church of the Protective Veil, Parhomivka (35x26mm). d, 6h, Flowers on the Fence, painting by Kateryna Bilokur (35x33mm).

2015, Sept. 30 Litho. Perf. 11½
1031 A716 Sheet of 4, #a-d 3.00 3.00

Mosaic by Nicholas Roerich (1874-1947) A717

2015, Oct. 7 Litho. Perf. 13½
1032 A717 3h multi .55 .55
　Roerich Pact, 80th anniv. Values are for stamps with surrounding selvage.

Lviv Brewery, 300th Anniv. A718

2015, Oct. 8 Litho. Perf. 13½
1033 A718 2.40h multi .45 .45
　No. 1033 was printed in sheets of 8 + 4 corner labels.

Postcrossing A719

Serpentine Die Cut 12¼
2015, Oct. 9 Litho.
Self-Adhesive
1034 A719 (15.57h) multi 3.00 3.00

Anna and Mariya Muzychuk, Chess Champions — A720

2015, Oct. 10 Litho. Perf. 11½
1035 A720 2.40h multi .45 .45

Ukrainian Defender's Day A721

2015, Oct. 12 Litho. Perf. 13½
1036 A721 2.40h multi .45 .45
　Values are for stamps with surrounding selvage.

1961 LAZ 695 Bus, Kyiv A722

1963 Kyiv-4 Trolley Bus, Kyiv A723

2015 Litho. Perf. 14½x14
1037 A722 2.40h multi .45 .45
1038 A723 2.40h multi .45 .45
Issued: No. 1037, 10/30; No. 1038, 11/6.

Souvenir Sheet

Princely Ostrogski Family — A724

No. 1039: a, 3.45h, Prince Konstanty Wasyl Ostrogski (1526-1608) (30x47mm). b, 5.25h, Princess Elizaveta Ostrogska (1539-82) (32x40mm). c, 7.65h, Hetman Konstanty Ostrogski (1460-1530) (30x54mm).

Litho. With Foil Application
2015, Nov. 3 Perf. 11½
1039 A724 Sheet of 3, #a-c 3.50 3.50

Orchids — A725

Designs: No. 1040, 2.40h, Ophrys taurica. No. 1041, 2.40h, Cephalanthera rubra. No. 1042, 2.40h, Epipactis palustris.

2015, Nov. 19 Litho. Perf. 14¼x14
1040-1042 A725 Set of 3 2.10 2.10
Nos. 1040-1042 were each printed in sheets of 8 + label.

Christmas and New Year's Day A726

Litho. With Foil Application
2015, Dec. 2 Perf. 13½
1043 A726 2.40h multi .75 .75

Personalized Stamp — A727

2015, Dec. 10 Litho. Perf. 11½
1044 A727 (2.40h) multi + label 4.50 4.50
No. 1044 was printed in sheets of 9 stamps + 9 labels that could be personalized. The label shown, depicting the national arms and posthorn, is the generic label image. Compare with Type A629.

St. Paraskevi Church, Kwiaton, Poland and St. George's Church, Drohobych, Ukraine — A728

2015, Dec. 18 Litho. Perf. 11½
1045 A728 5.40h multi 1.50 1.50
Wooden Churches of the Carpathian Region of Poland and Ukraine UNESCO World Heritage Site. See Poland No. 4208.

Hryhoriy Veryovka (1895-1964), Choir Director — A729

Perf. 14x14¼ Syncopated
2015, Dec. 25 Litho.
1046 A729 2.40h multi .70 .70

Gazebo, Khortytsia A730

2016, Jan. 15 Litho. Perf. 14¼x14
1047 A730 2.40h multi .70 .70

Miniature Sheet

Zaporizhia Oblast — A731

No. 1048: a, 2.40h, Buildings, Khortytsia National Reseve (37x28mm). b, 2.40h, Mi-8MSB helicopter (37x28mm). c, 3h, Sculpture of woman (26x45mm). d, 6h, Hydroelectric power station on Dnieper River (56x35mm).

2016, Jan. 15 Litho. Perf. 11½
1048 A731 Sheet of 4, #a-d 3.00 3.00

Uzhhorod Railway Station A732

2016, Mar. 4 Litho. Perf. 14¼x13¾
1049 A732 2.40h multi .70 .70

Miniature Sheet

Zakarpattia Oblast — A733

No. 1050: a, 2.40h, Palanok Castle, Mukachevo (42x42mm). b, 2.40h, Shypit Waterfall (42x42mm). c, 3h, St. Nicholas Church, Svalyava (42x42mm). d, 6h, Ukrainian woman in traditional costume (62x62mm).

2016, Mar. 4 Litho. Perf. 11½
1050 A733 Sheet of 4, #a-d 3.00 3.00

Troop Carrier A734

BM Tank A735

Perf. 14 Syncopated
2016, Mar. 25 Litho.
1051 A734 2.40h multi .45 .45
1052 A735 2.40h multi .45 .45

Illustration by Anatoliy Bazylevich for Poem Aeneid — A736

2016, Apr. 15 Litho. Perf. 13¼
1053 A736 5.25h multi 1.00 1.00

Europa A737

2016, Apr. 15 Litho. Perf. 14x14¼
1054 A737 (15.27h) multi 1.90 1.90
Think Green Issue.

Chernobyl Nuclear Disaster, 30th Anniv. A738

2016, Apr. 26 Litho. Perf. 11½
1055 A738 2.40h multi .45 .45

Tell Me the Truth, Painting by Ivan Marchuk — A739

2016, May 12 Litho. Perf. 13½
1056 A739 2.40h multi .45 .45

Mikhail Bulgakov (1891-1940), Writer — A740

2016, May 13 Litho. Perf. 14x14¼
1057 A740 2.40h multi .45 .45

National Soccer Team — A741

2016, May 22 Litho. Perf. 14x14¼
1058 A741 7.65h multi 1.40 1.40

Miniature Sheet

Kievan Princesses on European Thrones — A742

No. 1059 — Princess: a, Anne (1032-75), Queen consort of French King Henry I. b, Malmfred (c.1095-1137), Queen consort of Norwegian King Sigurd Iand Danish King Eric II. c, Wyszeslawa (1047-89), Queen of Poland. d, Euphemia (1096-1138), Queen consort of Hungarian King Coloman. e, Eupraxia (c. 1071-1100), Consort of Holy Roman Emperor Henry IV. f, Elisaveta (1025-76), Queen consort of Norwegian King Harald III. g, Anastasia (1074-1094), Queen consort of Hungarian King Andrew I. h, Zbyslava (1090-1114), Queen consort of Polish King Wladyslaw II. i, Dobroniga (c. 1012-87), Duchess consort of Polish Duke Casimir I. j, Predslava (c. 1090-1109), wife of Hungarian Prince Almos. k, Eupraxia-Dobrodjeja (1108-72), wife of Byzantine Co-emperor Alexios Komnenos. l, Euphrosyne (1130-93), Queen consort of Hungarian King Géza II.

2016, May 27 Litho. Perf. 11½
1059 A742 2.40h Sheet of 12, #a-l 7.25 7.25

Personalized Stamp — A743

2016, May 27 Litho. Perf. 11½
1060 A743 (2.40h) multi + label 1.00 1.00
No. 1044 was printed in sheets of 28 stamps + 28 labels that could be personalized. The label shown, depicting the national arms and posthorn, is the generic label image.

Ivan Mykolaichuk (1941-87), Movie Actor — A744

2016, June 15 Litho. Perf. 14x14¼
1061 A744 2.40h multi .45 .45

Frigate Hetman Sahaydachniy — A745

Perf. 14x14¼ Syncopated

2016, July 2   **Litho.**
1062   A745   5.40h multi   1.00   1.00

2016 Summer Olympics, Rio de Janeiro — A746

2016, July 23   **Litho.**   **Perf. 11½**
1063   A746   4.40h multi   .75   .75

Souvenir Sheet

Kolomyia, 775th Anniv. — A747

2016, Aug. 19   **Litho.**   **Perf. 11½**
1064   A747   7.65h multi   1.40   1.40

Luhansk Railroad Station A748

2016, Aug. 23   **Litho.**   **Perf. 14¼x14**
1065   A748   2.40h multi   .45   .45

Miniature Sheet

Luhansk Oblast — A749

No. 1066: a, 2.40h, Luhansk University Institute of Culture and Arts (37x25mm). b, 2.40h, Paeonia tenuifolia (37x25mm). c, 3h, St. Alexander Nevsky Church, Seleznivka (37x25mm). d, 6h, Marmota bobak (37x37mm).

2016, Aug. 23   **Litho.**   **Perf. 11½**
1066   A749   Sheet of 4, #a-d   3.00   3.00

Order of Freedom — A750

Litho. With Foil Application
2016, Aug. 24   **Perf. 13¼**
1067   A750   7.65h gold & multi   1.40   1.40

Jewish Culture — A751

Designs: 3h, Freilachs dancers. No. 1069, 4.40h, People at synagogue, Zhovka. No. 1070, 4.40h, Blowing of the shofar on Rosh Hashanah. 5.40h, Tailor.

2016, Aug. 27   **Litho.**   **Perf. 13¼**
1068-1071   A751   Set of 4   3.75   3.75

Vegetables A752

Designs: 2.40h, Solanum lycopersicum. 3h, Cucumis sativus. 4.40h, Solanum melongena. 5.40h, Capsicum annuum.

Die Cut Perf. 14
2016, Sept. 27   **Litho.**
Self-Adhesive
1072-1075   A752   Set of 4   3.25   3.25

Mykhailo Hrushevsky (1866-1934), Historian and Head of Ukrainian Central Council — A753

2016, Sept. 29   **Litho.**   **Perf. 14¼x14**
1076   A753   2.40h multi   .45   .45
   No. 1076 was printed in sheets of 14 + central label.

Babi Yar Massacre, 75th Anniv. A754

2016, Sept. 29   **Litho.**   **Perf. 14¼x14**
1077   A754   2.40h multi   .45   .45

Bohdan Stupka (1941-2012), Movie Actor — A755

2016, Oct. 5   **Litho.**   **Perf. 14x14¼**
1078   A755   2.40h multi   .45   .45

Fire Trucks — A756

Designs: 2.40h, 1948 PMH-3. 3h, 1921 Magirus. 4.40h, 1916 Benz-Gaggenau.

2016, Oct. 12   **Litho.**   **Perf. 14x14¼**
1079-1081   A756   Set of 3   1.75   1.75
   Nos. 1079-1081 were each printed in sheets of 9 + label.

Miniature Sheet

Motocross Racers and Their Motorcycles — A757

No. 1082: a, Leonid Bratkovsky, M-72 motorcycle without number, 1956. b, Igor Grigoriev, CZ motorcycle No. 8, 1963. c, Vadim Horulko, Kovrovets motorcycle No. 233, 1965. d, Alexei Kibirin, CZ motorcycle without number, 1972. e, Leonid Shinkarenko, CZ motorcycle No. 15, 1967. f, Anatoly Ovchinnikov, CZ motorcycle No. 34, 1973. g, Vladimir Kavinov, KTM motorcycle No. 19, 1977. h, Boris Poganovsky, Evgeniy Nechiporenko, Dnepr motorcycle and sidecar, 1975. i, Evgeniy Rybalchenko, CZ motorcycle No. 18, 1975.

2016, Oct. 28   **Litho.**   **Perf. 14x14¼**
1082   A757   3h Sheet of 9, #a-i   5.00   5.00

New Year 2017 (Year of the Rooster) — A758

Litho. With Foil Application
2016, Nov. 11   **Perf. 13½**
1083   A758   4.40h gold & multi   .75   .75

Personalized Stamp — A759

2016, Dec. 1   **Litho.**   **Perf. 11½**
1084   A759   (2.40h) multi + label   2.75   2.75
   No. 1084 was printed in sheets of 9 stamps + 9 labels that could be personalized. The label shown, depicting the national arms and posthorn, is the generic label image.

Worldwide Fund for Nature (WWF) — A760

No. 1085 — Myotis bechsteinii: a, Hanging. b, Crawling (Latin name at top). c, Flying. d, Crawling (Latin name at left).

2016, Dec. 30   **Litho.**   **Perf. 11½**
1085   A760   (16.25h) Block of 4, #a-d   7.50   7.50

Souvenir Sheet

Paleolithic Era — A761

No. 1086: a, Mammoth hunt. b, Shelter, food retrieval and fire starting

2017, Jan. 20   **Litho.**   **Perf. 11½**
1086   A761   7.50h Sheet of 2, #a-b   2.75   2.75

After the Storm, by Arkhip Kuindzhi (c.1842-1910) — A762

2017, Jan. 27   **Litho.**   **Perf. 11½**
1087   A762   4.40h multi   .85   .85

Flax, by Tetyana Yablonska (1917-2005) — A763

2017, Feb. 24   **Litho.**   **Perf. 13¼**
1088   A763   5.40h multi   1.00   1.00
   No. 1088 was printed in sheets of 8 + label.

Ukrainian Revolution, Cent. — A764

2017, Mar. 4   **Litho.**   **Perf. 14x14¼**
1089   A764   3h multi   .55   .55

Personalized
Stamp — A765

2017, Mar. 6 Litho. Perf. 11½
1090 A765 (2.40h) sil & black +
label 3.00 3.00
  a. Dated "2018" 3.00 3.00

No. 1090 was printed in sheets of 8 stamps
+ 8 labels that could be personalized + a large
central label. The label shown, depicting the
national arms and posthorn, is the generic
label image.
Compare with type A629.

Jamala, Winner
of 2016
Eurovision Song
Contest — A766

2017, May 5 Litho. Perf. 13¼
1091 A766 4h multi .75 .75

Diplomatic
Relations Between
Ukraine and the
United States, 25th
Anniv. — A767

2017, May 8 Litho. Perf. 14¼x14
1092 A767 4.40h multi .85 .85

Souvenir Sheet

Holy Roman Empress Maria Theresa
(1717-80) — A768

2017, May 13 Litho. Perf. 11½
1093 A768 (22h) multi 3.25 3.25

See Austria No. 2677, Croatia No. 1038,
Hungary No. 4433, Slovenia No. 1219.

Souvenir Sheet

Black Sea Marine Life — A769

No. 1094: a, (18h), Barnea candida. b,
(22h), Delphinus delphis ponticus.

2017, May 22 Litho. Perf. 11½
1094 A769 Sheet of 2, #a-b 5.50 5.50

See Bulgaria No. 4808.

Miniature Sheet

Characters in Folk Tale *Nikita the
Tanner* — A770

No. 1095: a, 2.40h, Dragon (49x26mm). b,
3h, Grandfather Danilo (26x26mm). c, 3h,
Squirrel Belka Kamikaze (23x25mm). d,
5.40h, Nikita Kozumyaka on snail (42x51mm).

2017, June 1 Litho. Perf. 11½
1095 A770 Sheet of 4, #a-d 2.50 2.50

Europa — A771

Designs: Nos. 1096a, 1097, Medzhybizh
Castle. Nos. 1096b, 1098, Olesko Castle.

2017, June 9 Litho. Perf. 14x14¼
1096 Horiz. pair 1.40 1.40
  a. A771 5h multi .65 .65
  b. A771 5.80h multi .75 .75
**Booklet Stamps
Perf. 11½**
1097 A771 12.80h multi 3.50 3.50
  a. Booklet pane of 1 3.50 3.50
1098 A771 12.80h multi 3.50 3.50
  a. Booklet pane of 1 3.50 3.50
    Complete booklet, #1097a,
    1098a 7.00

Arms of Chop
A772

Arms of
Marinin
A773

Arms of
Yalta — A774

Arms of
Kleslv — A775

Arms of
Yenakiieve
A776

Arms of Nizhyn
A777

Arms of Shatsk
A778

Arms of
Parutyne
A779

2017 Litho. Perf. 13¾
1099 A772 (40k) multi .25 .25
  a. Imprint "2017-II" .25 .25
  b. Imprint "2017-III" .25 .25
  c. Imprint "2018" .25 .25
  d. Dated "2018-II" .25 .25
1100 A773 (50k) multi .25 .25
  a. Imprint "2017-II" .25 .25
  b. Imprint "2017-III" .25 .25
  c. Dated "2018" .25 .25
1101 A774 (4h) multi .55 .55
  a. Imprint "2017-II" .55 .55
  b. Imprint "2017-III" .50 .50
  d. Dated "2018" .55 .55
1102 A775 (5h) multi .65 .65
  a. Imprint "2017-II" .65 .65
  b. Imprint "2017-III" .65 .65
  c. Imprint "2018" .60 .60
  d. Dated "2018-II" .65 .65
1103 A776 (5.20h) multi .70 .70
  a. Imprint "2017-II" .70 .70
  b. Dated "2018" .70 .70
1104 A777 (8h) multi 1.10 1.10
  a. Imprint "2017-II" 1.10 1.10
  b. Imprint "2017-III" 1.10 1.10
  c. Imprint "2018" 1.00 1.00
  d. Dated "2018-II" 1.10 1.10
1105 A778 (10h) multi 1.40 1.40
  a. Imprint "2017-II" 1.40 1.40
  b. Imprint "2018" 1.25 1.25
  c. Dated "2018-II" 1.40 1.40
1106 A779 (53.10h) multi 7.25 7.25
  a. Dated "2018" 7.25 7.25
    Nos. 1099-1106 (8) 12.15 12.15

Issued: Nos. 1099, 1100, 6/13; No. 1101,
6/10; Nos. 1102-1105, 6/20; No. 1106, 9/28.

One Way, by
Roman
Minin — A780

2017, July 2 Litho. Perf. 13¼
1107 A780 4h multi .55 .55

Roald
Hoffmann, 1981
Nobel Laureate
in Chemistry
A781

2017, July 18 Litho. Perf. 13¼
1108 A781 5h gold & multi .65 .65

Paintings by Ivan Aivazovsky (1817-
1900) — A782

Designs: 3h, Yalta, 1864. 8.80h, Evening in
the Crimea, 1848.

2017, July 29 Litho. Perf. 14
1109 A782 3h multi .45 .45
**Souvenir Sheet
Perf. 11½**
1110 A782 8.80h multi 1.25 1.25

No. 1109 was printed in sheets of 8 + label.

Military Transportation — A783

Designs: 3h, BTR-4 armored transport.
5.40h, AN-178 airplane.

Perf. 14x14¼ Syncopated
2017, Aug. 11 Litho.
1111-1112 A783 Set of 2 1.25 1.25

Medicinal
Plants — A784

Designs: No. 1113, 4h, Chelidonium majus.
No. 1114, 4h, Tilia cordata. 5h, Symphytum
officinale. 5.80h, Cichorium intybus.

2017, Aug. 18 Litho. Perf. 14¼x14
1113-1116 A784 Set of 4 2.60 2.60

Ukrainian Fashion
Week — A785

2017, Sept. 3 Litho. Perf. 13¼
1117 A785 8h multi 1.10 1.10

No. 1117 was printed in sheets of 8 + central label.

ECr1
Tarpan
Train
A786

2017, Sept. 22 Litho. Perf. 14¼x14
1118 A786 4h multi .55 .55

Miniature Sheet

Poltava Oblast — A787

No. 1119: a, Costumed participants at
Sorochynska Fair (28x38mm). b, Goat sculpture (52x45mm). c, Vasyl Krychevsky Ethnographic Museum, Poltava (38x28mm). d, Statues and buildings at Mirgorod Resort
(38x28mm).

2017, Sept. 22 Litho. Perf. 11½
1119 A787 4h Sheet of 4, #a-d 2.25 2.25

Khmelnitsky City Hall and Sculpture — A788

2017, Sept. 23   Litho.   Perf. 13¼
1120 A788 4h multi   .55   .55

Miniature Sheet

Khmelnitsky Oblast — A789

No. 1121: a, Intercession Church (37x28mm). b, Cave of Atlantis (37x28mm). c, Riverside cliffs near Subich (37x28mm). d, Kamyanets-Podilsky Fortress (70x70mm diamond).

Perf. 11½, 8¼ (#1121d)
2017, Sept. 23   Litho.
1121 A789 4h Sheet of 4, #a-d   2.25   2.25

International Year of Sustainable Tourism for Development A790

2017, Sept. 29   Litho.   Perf. 14¼x14
1122 A790 3h multi   .40   .40

No. 1122 was printed in sheets of 8 + central label.

Dancers — A791

Farrier — A792

Gypsy Van — A793

Fortune Teller — A794

2017, Sept. 30   Litho.   Perf. 13¼
1123 A791 4h multi   .55   .55
1124 A792 4h multi   .55   .55
1125 A793 5h multi   .70   .70
1126 A794 5h multi   .70   .70
     Nos. 1123-1126 (4)   2.50   2.50
Roma culture in Ukraine.

Artemy Vedel (c. 1767-1808), Composer A795

2017, Oct. 5   Litho.   Perf. 13¼
1127 A795 4h multi   .55   .55

Premiere of Film *Storozhova Zastava* — A796

2017, Oct. 10   Litho.   Perf. 11½
1128 A796 4h multi   .55   .55

No. 1128 was printed in sheets of 8 + central label.

Miniature Sheet

Cossack Seals — A797

No. 1129 — Seal of: a, Zaporozhian Army, 1763. b, Hetman Bohdan Khmelnytsky, 17th cent. c, Kodak Palanka, 18th cent. d, Petro Doroshenko, 1656-59. e, Zaporozhian sergeant, 17th-18th cent. f, Semen Rakovich, 1672-91.

2017, Oct. 14   Litho.   Perf. 11½
1129 A797 5h Sheet of 6, #a-f   4.25   4.25

Fire Fighting — A798

Designs: No. 1130, 4h, KrAZ-63221 fire truck. No. 1131, 4h, GPM-54 fire tank. No. 1132, 5h, An-32P fire plane. No. 1133, 5h, PK-10/130 (UMS 1000) fire boat.

2017, Oct. 17   Litho.   Perf. 13¾x14¼
1130-1133 A798   Set of 4   2.50   2.50

Nos. 1130-1133 were each printed in sheets of 9 + label.

Ukrainian National Republic, Cent. — A799

2017, Nov. 7   Litho.   Perf. 14x14¼
1134 A799 4h gold & multi   .55   .55

Sharpening of Saws, by Oleksandr Bohomazov (1880-1930) A800

2017, Nov. 10   Litho.   Perf. 13½
1135 A800 4h multi   .55   .55

Christmas A801

Litho. With Foil Application
2017, Nov. 30   Perf. 13½
1136 A801 4h sil & multi   .55   .55

Apostles Peter and Paul Beryl Crystal — A802

2017, Dec. 19   Litho.   Perf. 14x14¼
1137 A802 4h multi   .55   .55

Miniature Sheet

Zhytomyr Oblast — A803

No. 1138: a, Doll (35x44mm). b, St. Barbara's Church, Berdychiv (26x37mm). c, Chatsky Head rock formation (26x37mm). d, Radomysl Castle and statue of angel (26x37mm).

2017, Dec. 19   Litho.   Perf. 11½
1138 A803 4h Sheet of 4, #a-d   2.25   2.25

Uman — A804

Sheshory — A805

Taki Odesa — A806

Luhansk Steppe — A807

Serpentine Die Cut 11¾
2017, Dec. 22   Litho.
Self-Adhesive
1139 A804 4h multi   .55   .55
1140 A805 4h multi   .55   .55
1141 A806 4h multi   .55   .55
1142 A807 4h multi   .55   .55
     Nos. 1139-1142 (4)   2.20   2.20

Nos. 1139-1142 were each printed in sheets of 8 + label.

Miniature Sheet

State Seals — A808

No. 1143: a, Seal of Ukrainian Central Rada and Mykhailo Hrushevsky (1866-1934), President of Central Rada. b, Seal of Ukrainian People's Republic and Volodymyr Vynnychenko (1880-1951), Prime Minister. c, Seal of the State Secretariat and Pavlo Skoropadskyi (1873-1945). d, Seal of the Directorate of Ukraine and Symon Petliura (1879-1926), Chairman of Directorate.

Litho. & Embossed
2018, Jan. 22   Perf. 11½
1143 A808 9h Sheet of 4, #a-d   4.75   4.75

Oleksandr Shalimov (1918-2006), Surgeon — A809

2018, Jan. 23   Litho.   Perf. 14x14¼
1144 A809 5h multi   .65   .65

2018 Winter Olympics, PyeongChang, South Korea — A810

2018, Jan. 23   Litho.   *Perf. 13½*
1145 A810 9h multi   1.25 1.25

Values are for stamps with surrounding selvage.

Arms of Lokachi — A811

2018, Mar. 16   Litho.   *Perf. 13¾*
1146 A811 (4h) multi   .55 .55
   a.   Dated "2018-II"   .55 .55

A812

Characters From Animated Film *The Stolen Princess: Ruslan and Ludmila* — A813

Serpentine Die Cut 11¾
2018, Mar. 30   Litho.
Self-Adhesive
1147 A812 5h multi   .70 .70
1148 A813 5h multi   .70 .70

Souvenir Sheet

Trypillian Neolithic Culture — A814

No. 1149: a, 9h, Agriculture. b, 15h, Melting of metal ore.
2018, Apr. 24   Litho.   *Perf. 11½*
1149 A814   Sheet of 2, #a-b   3.25 3.25

Raising of Ukrainian Flag on Black Sea Ships, Cent. — A815

2018, Apr. 27   Litho.   *Perf. 14¼x14*
1150 A815 5h multi   .70 .70

Suprematist Composition 1, by Kazimir Malevich (1879-1935) A816

2018, Apr. 28   Litho.   *Perf. 13¼*
1151 A816 5h sil & multi   .70 .70

No. 1151 was printed in sheets of 8 + label.

2018 UEFA Champions League Final, Kyiv — A817

2018, May 20   Litho.   *Perf. 14¼x14*
1152 A817 9h multi   1.25 1.25

The Girl on a Background of a Persian Carpet, by Mykhailo Vrubel (1856-1910) A818

2018, June 19   Litho.   *Perf. 11½*
1153 A818 5h multi   .70 .70

See No. 1104.

Four Evangelists Bridge, Mukachevo — A819

Plebanivka Viaduct — A820

2018, June 27   Litho.   *Perf. 14¼x14*
1154 A819 (26.24h) multi   3.00 3.00
1155 A820 (39.36h) multi   4.50 4.50

Booklet Panes of 1
Stamp Size:45x30mm
Perf. 11½
1156 A819 (26.24h) multi   5.25 —
1157 A820 (39.36h) multi   7.75 —
     Complete booklet, #1156, 1157   13.00

Europa. Nos. 1154-1155 were each printed in sheets of 9 + 3 labels. Complete booklet sold for 111h.

Miniature Sheet

Insects — A821

No. 1158: a, Mantis religiosa. b, Lyristes plebejus. c, Sympetrum flaveolum. d, Calopteryx virgo. e, Decticus verrucivorus. f, Apatura ilia. g, Bombus hortorum.

Litho. With Foil Application
2018, July 3   *Perf. 11½*
1158 A821 7.50h Sheet of 7, #a-g   6.50 6.50

Flowers — A822

Designs: No. 1159, 5h, Rosa canina. No. 1160, 5h, Pulmonaria obscura. No. 1161, 5h, Hypericum maculatum. No. 1162, 5h, Valeriana officinalis.

2018, July 13   Litho.   *Perf. 13¼*
1159-1162 A822   Set of 4   2.75 2.75
Nos. 1159-1162 were each printed in sheets of 9 + 3 labels.

Selman A. Waksman (1888-1973), 1952 Nobel Laureate in Physiology or Medicine A823

2018, July 22   Litho.   *Perf. 13¼*
1163 A823 7.50h multi   1.00 1.00

Souvenir Sheet

Paintings by Mykhailo Vrubel (1856-1910) — A824

No. 1164: a, 5h, Self-portrait (33x47mm). b, 7.50h, Angel with Censer and Candle (25x47mm). c, 7.50h, Like No. 1153 (30x47mm).

Litho. With Foil Application
2018, July 27   *Perf. 11½*
1164 A824   Sheet of 3, #a-c   2.75 2.75

Paintings A825

Designs: 5h, Bride, by Olesya Hudyma. 7h, Kiss, by Vsevolod Maksymovych (1894-1914). 9h, Mother and Child, by Vera Barinova-Kuleba.

Litho. With Foil Application
2018, Aug. 14   *Perf. 13½*
1165-1167 A825   Set of 3   3.00 3.00
Nos. 1165-1167 were each printed in sheets of 8 + label.

Andrii Kuzmenko (1968-2015), Rock Musician — A826

2018, Aug. 17   Litho.   *Perf. 14*
1168 A826 9h multi   1.25 1.25

Dormition Cathedral, Kharkiv A827

2018, Aug. 23   Litho.   *Perf. 13¼*
1169 A827 5h multi   .70 .70

Miniature Sheet

Kharkiv Oblast — A828

No. 1170: a, Polovtsian statues (26x37mm). b, Our Savior Orthodox Church, Volodymyrivka (37x26mm). c, Fireworks over Freedom Square, Kharkiv (35x45mm). d, Sharivka Palace, Sharivka (37x26mm).

2018, Aug. 23   Litho.   *Perf. 11½*
1170 A828 5h Sheet of 4, #a-d   2.75 2.75

Personalized Stamp — A829

2018, Sept. 10   Litho.   *Perf. 11½*
1171 A829 (8h) multi + label   2.75 2.75

No. 1171 was printed in sheets of 6 stamps + 6 labels that could be personalized. The label shown, depicting the national arms and posthorn, is the generic label image.

Souvenir Sheets

Stamps of Ukraine and Western Ukraine — A830

Coats of Arms — A831

Peasants From 1918 100-Hryvnia
Note — A832

No. 1172: a, Ukraine #4. b, Western Ukraine #3.

No. 1173: a, Arms of Ukrainian People's Republic (denomination at UR). b, Arms of Ukrainian State (denomination at UL).

No. 1174: Peasant with: a, Sickle and sheaf of grain. b, Hammer.

2018 **Litho.** **Perf. 11½**
1172	A830 15h Sheet of 2, #a-b	4.00	4.00
1173	A831 15h Sheet of 2, #a-b	4.00	4.00
1174	A832 15h Sheet of 2, #a-b	4.00	4.00
	Nos. 1172-1174 (3)	12.00	12.00

Issued: No. 1172, 10/9; No. 1173, 10/10; No. 1174, 10/11. Ukrfilexpo 2018, Kyiv. A booklet containing imperforate examples of Nos. 1172-1174 was printed in limited quantities and sold for 255h.

Soldiers
A833

Designs: No. 1175, 7h, Soldier wearing helmet. No. 1176, 7h, Soldier aiming rifle.

2018, Oct. 12 **Litho.** **Perf. 11½**
1175-1176	A833 Set of 2	1.90	1.90

Innovations
A834

Designs: 7h, First electric tram (picture of horse on tracks with electric motors). 10.50h, Piezomotor. 13h, Corneal transplantation.

2018, Nov. 2 **Litho.** **Perf. 13¼**
1177-1179	A834 Set of 3	4.00	4.00

Miniature Sheet

Ukrainian Alphabet — A835

No. 1180 — Cyrillic letter of Ukrainian alphabet, Ukrainian word and picture of: a, Angel. b, Alien in spaceship. c, Squirrel. d, Dragon. e, Bear. f, Crow. g, Pierogies wrapped in ribbons hanging from tree. h, Hare. i, Raccoon. j, Pumpkin. k, Toad.

2018, Nov. 9 **Litho.** **Perf. 11½**
1180	A835 7h Sheet of 11, #a-k	9.00	9.00

Chicken
Kiev
A836

2018, Nov. 12 **Litho.** **Perf. 11½**
1181	A836 7h multi	.95	.95

No. 1181 was printed in sheets of 8 + 3 labels.

100th Birthday of Borys Paton, Chairman of National Academy of Sciences
A837

2018, Nov. 28 **Litho.** **Perf. 13¼**
1182	A837 7h multi	.95	.95

Miniature Sheet

Flora and Fauna of Carpathian
Biosphere Reserve — A838

No. 1183: a, Lucanus cervus (30x33mm). b, Fagus sylvatica (30x33mm). c, Coccothraustes coccothraustes (37x30mm). d, Rhododendron myrtifolia (30x45mm). e, Narcissus angustifolius (30x45mm). f, Ursus arctos (37x33mm).

2018, Nov. 30 **Litho.** **Perf. 11½**
1183	A838 7h Sheet of 6, #a-f	5.50	5.50

2018 Ukrainian Winter Paralympics
Athletes — A839

2018, Dec. 3 **Litho.** **Perf. 14x14¼**
1184	A839 (8h) multi	.95	.95

No. 1184 was printed in sheets of 9 + label.

St.
Catherine's
Church,
Chernihiv
A840

2018, Dec. 7 **Litho.** **Perf. 13¼**
1185	A840 7h multi	.95	.95

Miniature Sheet

Chernihiv Oblast — A841

No. 1186: a, Hetman's Capital, Baturyn (30x31mm). b, Aerial view of Desna River (38x47mm). c, Chernihiv Train Station (37x26mm). d, Kachanivka Palace (30x31mm).

2018, Dec. 7 **Litho.** **Perf. 11½**
1186	A841 7h Sheet of 4, #a-d	3.75	3.75

New Year 2019 (Year of the
Pig) — A842

Litho. With Foil Application
2018, Dec. 14 **Perf. 11½**
1187	A842 (8h) gold & multi	.95	.95

Embroidery From
Vinnytsia — A843

Embroidery From
Lviv — A844

Embroidery From
Kyiv — A845

Embroidery From
Poltava — A846

2018, Dec. 14 **Litho.** **Perf. 11½**
1188	A843	7h multi	.95	.95
1189	A844	7h multi	.95	.95
1190	A845	(27.74h) multi	4.00	4.00
1191	A846	(27.74h) multi	4.00	4.00
	Nos. 1188-1191 (4)		9.90	9.90

Nos. 1188-1191 were each printed in sheets of 8 + central label.

St. Nicholas — A847

2018, Dec. 19 **Litho.** **Perf. 14¼x14**
1192	A847 (8h) multi	.95	.95

Icon of Virgin
Mary and
Crucified Jesus,
Okhtyrka — A848

2018, Dec. 24 **Litho.** **Perf. 13¼**
1193	A848 7h multi	.95	.95

Miniature Sheet

Sumy Oblast — A849

No. 1194: a, Owl in Desna-Starogutsky National Nature Park. b, Holy Resurrection Cathedral, Sumy. c, Round Courtyard, Trostyanets. d, Oleksandr Dovzhenko Hlukhiv National Pedagogical University, Hlukhiv.

2018, Dec. 24 **Litho.** **Perf. 11½**
1194	A849 7h Sheet of 4, #a-d	3.75	3.75

Souvenir Sheet

Church Bells — A850

No. 1195: a, Mazepa Bell, St. Sophia's Cathedral, Kyiv, 1705. b, Bell, Cathedral of the Nativity, Chisinau, Moldova, 1838.

Litho. & Embossed

			2018, Dec. 26	**Perf. 11½**
1195	A850	(27.39h) Sheet of 2, #a-b, + central label	7.50	7.50

See Moldova No. 1011.

Unification of Ukraine and Western Ukraine, Cent. A851

			2019, Jan. 22 Litho.	**Perf. 14x14¼**
1196	A851	8h silver & multi	.85	.85

Souvenir Sheet

Cimmerian Warriors — A852

			2019, Feb. 27 Litho.	**Perf. 11½**
1197	A852	30h multi	3.25	3.25

"Love is to Quench His Thirst" — A853

"Love is to Give Her Flowers" — A854

"Love is to Dedicate a Song to Her" — A855

"Love is to Make Him Pierogis" — A856

Serpentine Die Cut 12

2019, Mar. 6   Litho.

Self-Adhesive

1198		Block or horiz. strip of 4	3.50	
a.	A853	8h multi	.85	.85
b.	A854	8h multi	.85	.85
c.	A855	8h multi	.85	.85
d.	A856	8h multi	.85	.85

SEMI-POSTAL STAMPS

Ukrainian Soviet Socialist Republic

"Famine" — SP1

Taras H. Shevchenko SP2

"Death" Stalking Peasant — SP3

"Ukraine" Distributing Food — SP4

Perf. 14½x13½, 13½x14½

1923, June   Litho.   Unwmk.

B1	SP1	10k + 10k gray bl & blk	1.00	5.50
B2	SP2	20k + 20k vio brn & org brn	1.00	5.50
B3	SP3	90k + 30k db & blk, straw	1.00	6.75
B4	SP4	150k + 50k red brn & blk	1.00	9.50
		Nos. B1-B4 (4)	4.00	27.25

Imperf., Pairs

B1a	SP1	10k + 10k	50.00	120.00
B2a	SP2	20k + 20k	50.00	120.00
B3a	SP3	90k + 30k	50.00	120.00
B4a	SP4	150k + 50k	50.00	120.00

The values of these stamps are in karbovanets, which by 1923 converted to rubles at 100 to 1.

Wmk. 116
Same Colors

B5	SP1	10k + 10k	40.00	70.00
B6	SP2	20k + 20k	40.00	70.00
a.		Imperf., pair	2,500.	
B7	SP3	90k + 30k	40.00	70.00
B8	SP4	150k + 50k	40.00	70.00
		Nos. B5-B8 (4)	160.00	280.00

> Catalogue values for unused stamps in this section, from this point to the end of the section, are for Never Hinged items.

Charity and Health Fund — SP5

1994, Jan. 15   Litho.   Perf. 12

B9	SP5	150kb +20kb multi	1.10	.80

Third Natl. Philatelic Exhibition, Lviv — SP6

1995, Sept. 23   Litho.   Perf. 13½

B10	SP6	50,000kb +5000kb multi	1.20	1.20

Souvenir Sheet

Zymnenska Icon of Madonna and Child — SP7

1999, Sept. 4   Litho.   Perf. 11½

B11	SP7	1.20h +10k multicolored	3.75	3.75

Intl. Year of the Elderly.

REGISTRATION STAMPS

> Catalogue values for unused stamps in this section are for Never Hinged Items.

Trident — R1

2001, Apr. 1   Litho.   Perf. 13¾

F1	R1	(10.84h) multi	8.00	7.25
a.		Imprint "2003"	9.00	7.25
b.		Perf. 11½, dated "2006"	7.25	7.25

Issued: No. F1a, 1/28/03; No. F1b, 10/9/06. No. F1b was issued only in No. F2c.

Trident With Frame — R2

2005-06   Litho.   Perf. 13¾

F2	R2	(10.10h) multi	7.00	7.00
a.		Imprint "2006"	7.00	7.00
b.		Perf. 11½, dated "2006"	7.00	7.00
c.		Sheet of 18, #418a-422a, 453a-454a, 466a-468a, 515a, 572a, 606a-609a, F1b, F2b	25.00	25.00

Issued: No. F2, 10/28/05; No. F2a, 2/7/06; No. F2b, 10/9/06. No. F2b was issued only in No. F2c. No. F2c sold for 35.41h and exists imperf.

MILITARY STAMPS

COURIER FIELD POST ISSUE

Nos. 1-5, 48 Surcharged

1920, Aug. 26

M1	A1	10h on 10sh buff	20.00	—
a.		Inverted surcharge	80.00	
M2	A2	10h on 20sh brown	40.00	—
M3	A3	10h on 30sh ultramarine	50.00	—
M4	A4	10h on 40sh green	55.00	—
a.		Inverted surcharge	215.00	
M5	A5	10h on 50sh red	50.00	—
M6	A1	20h on 10sh buff	55.00	—
M7	A2	20h on 20sh brown	15.00	—
a.		Inverted surcharge	60.00	
M8	A3	20h on 30sh ultramarine	40.00	—
a.		Inverted surcharge	160.00	
M9	A4	20h on 40sh green	40.00	—
M10	A5	20h on 50sh red	40.00	—
a.		Inverted surcharge	160.00	
M11	A1	40h on 10sh buff	200.00	—
M12	A2	40h on 20sh brown	100.00	—
M13	A3	40h on 30sh ultramarine	400.00	—
M14	A4	40h on 40sh green	200.00	—
M15	A5	40h on 50sh red	400.00	—
M16	A6	40h on 20hr red & green	—	—

Nos. M1-M16 were prepared to facilitate communications between the Ukrainian government-in-exile at Tarnow, Poland, and its military units in the field.

Only two examples of No. M16 are known, one unused and one used on cover.

Forged surcharges and cancellations exist.

UMM AL QIWAIN

'um-al-kī-'wīn

LOCATION — Oman Peninsula, Arabia, on Arabian Gulf
GOVT. — Sheikdom under British protection
AREA — 300 sq. mi.
POP. — 5,700

Umm al Qiwain is one of six Persian Gulf sheikdoms to join the United Arab Emirates which proclaimed independence Dec. 2, 1971. See United Arab Emirates.

100 Naye Paise = 1 Rupee
100 Dirham = 1 Riyal (1967)

Catalogue values for all unused stamps in this country are for Never Hinged items.

Sheik Ahmed bin Rashid al Mulla and Gazelles — A1

Photogravure and Lithographed

		1964, June 29 Unwmk. Perf. 14		
		Size: 35x22mm		
1	A1	1np shown	.25	.25
2	A1	2np Snake	.25	.25
3	A1	3np Hyena	.25	.25
4	A1	4np Conspicuous trig- gerfish	.25	.25
5	A1	5np Fish	.25	.25
6	A1	10np Silver angelfish	.30	.25
7	A1	15np Palace	.30	.25
8	A1	20np Umm al Qiwain	.30	.25
9	A1	30np Tower	.35	.30
		Size: 42x26mm		
10	A1	40np as 1np	.35	.30
11	A1	50np as 2np	.45	.35
12	A1	70np as 3np	.75	.40
13	A1	1r as 4np	1.00	.50
14	A1	1.50r as 4np	1.25	.65
15	A1	2r as 10np	1.75	.90
		Size: 52x33mm		
16	A1	3r as 15np	3.00	2.00
17	A1	5r as 20np	5.25	3.25
18	A1	10r as 30np	9.00	6.00
		Nos. 1-18 (18)	25.30	16.65

National Stadium, Tokyo, and Discobolus — A2

Designs: 1r, 2r, National Stadium, Tokyo. 1.50r, Indoor swimming arena. 3r, Komazawa Gymnasium. 4r, Stadium entrance.

		1964, Nov. 25 Photo. Perf. 14		
19	A2	50np multi	.30	.25
20	A2	1r multi	.50	.25
21	A2	1.50r multi	.65	.25
22	A2	2r multi	1.00	.25
23	A2	3r multi	1.25	.45
24	A2	4r multi	2.50	.85
25	A2	5r multi	3.25	1.00
		Nos. 19-25 (7)	9.45	3.30

18th Olympic Games, Tokyo, Oct. 10-25, 1964. Perf. and imperf. souvenir sheets contain 4 stamps similar to #22-25 in changed colors. Size: 145x115mm.

A3

Designs: 10np, Pres. Kennedy's funeral cortege leaving White House. 15np, Mrs. Kennedy with children, and Robert Kennedy following coffin. 50np, Horse-drawn caisson. 1r, Presidents Truman and Eisenhower, and Margaret Truman Daniels. 2r, Pres. Charles de Gaulle, Emperor Haile Selassie, Chancellor Ludwig Erhart, Sir Alec Douglas-Home and King Frederick IX. 3r, Kennedy family on steps of St. Matthew's Cathedral. 5r, Honor guard at tomb. 7.50r, Portrait of Pres. John F. Kennedy.

		Perf. 14½		
		1965, Jan. 20 Unwmk. Photo.		
		Black Design with Gold Inscriptions		
		Size: 29x44mm		
26	A3	10np pale blue	.25	.25
27	A3	15np pale yellow	.25	.25
28	A3	50np pale green	.30	.25
29	A3	1r pale pink	.60	.35
30	A3	2r pale green	1.00	.45
		Size: 33x51mm		
31	A3	3r pale gray	1.75	.65
32	A3	5r pale blue	3.00	.90
33	A3	7.50r pale yellow	4.00	1.50
		Nos. 26-33 (8)	11.15	4.60

Pres. John F. Kennedy. A souvenir sheet contains 2 stamps similar to Nos. 32-33 with pale green (5r) and pale salmon (7.50r) backgrounds, size: 29x44mm. Size of sheet: 114x70mm.

A4

Designs: 10d, Astronaut on Moon. 20d, Landing module approaching moon. 30d, Apollo XII on launching pad. 50d, Commanders Charles Conrad, Jr., Alan L. Bean, Richard F. Gordon, Jr., earth and moon, horiz. 75d, Earth and Apollo XII, horiz. 1r, Sheik Ahmed, rocket and lunar landing module, horiz.

		1969, Nov. 19 Litho. Perf. 14½		
34	A4	10d multi		.25
35	A4	20d multi		.35
36	A4	30d multi		.45
37	A4	50d emerald & multi		.55
38	A4	75d purple & multi		1.00
39	A4	1r dk bl & multi		1.75
		Nos. 34-39 (6)		4.35

US Apollo XII moon landing mission, 11/14-24/69.
Two imperf. souvenir sheets of 3 exist, containing stamps similar to Nos. 34-36 and Nos. 37-39.

A5

		1970, May 29 Litho. Perf. 14		
40	A5	10d James A. Lovell		.25
41	A5	30d Fred W. Haise, Jr.		.40
42	A5	50d John L. Swigert, Jr.		.90
a.		Souv. sheet of 3, #40-42		2.00
		Nos. 40-42 (3)		1.55

Safe return of the crew of Apollo 13.

A6

Designs: 5d, 1.25r, EXPO '70 Emblem. 10d, 20d, Japanese Pavilion.

		1970, Aug. 14 Litho. Perf. 13½x14		
43	A6	5d yellow & multi		.25
44	A6	10d blue & multi		.35
45	A6	20d red & multi		.45
48	A6	1.25r red & multi		.90
		Nos. 43-48 (4)		1.95

EXPO '70 Intl. Exhib., Osaka, Japan, Mar. 15-Sept. 13, 1970.
A 40d and 1r, and a souvenir sheet showing the Emperor and Empress of Japan, and a souvenir sheet containing these and Nos. 43-45, 48 were prepared, but not issued.

A7

Uniforms: 10d, Private, North Lancashire Regiment. 20d, Royal Navy seaman. 30d, Officer, North Lancashire (Loyal) Regiment. 50d, Private, York and Lancaster Regiment. 75d, Royal Navy officer. 1r, Officer, York and Lancaster Regiment.

		1970, Oct. 12 Litho. Perf. 14½x14		
49	A7	10d multi		.25
50	A7	20d multi		.35
51	A7	30d multi		.55
a.		Souv. sheet of 3, #49-51		2.75
52	A7	50d buff & multi		.90
53	A7	75d multi		1.25
54	A7	1r buff & multi		1.75
a.		Souv. sheet of 3, #52-54		4.00
		Nos. 49-54 (6)		5.05

British landings on the Trucial Coast, 150th anniv.
Stamps of Umm al Qiwain were replaced in 1972 by those of United Arab Emirates.

AIR POST STAMPS

Type of Regular Issue, 1964
Photogravure and Lithographed

		1965 Unwmk. Perf. 14		
		Size: 42x26mm		
C1	A1	15np as #1	.25	.25
C2	A1	25np as #2	.25	.25
C3	A1	35np as #3	.25	.25
C4	A1	50np as #4	.60	.25
C5	A1	75np as #5	1.10	.30
C6	A1	1r as #6	1.40	.40
		Size: 52x33mm		
C7	A1	2r as #7	2.25	.55
C8	A1	3r as #8	3.25	.75
C9	A1	5r as #9	4.50	1.25
		Nos. C1-C9 (9)	13.85	4.25

Issued: #C7-C9, Nov. 6; others, Oct. 18.

AIR POST OFFICIAL STAMPS

Type of Regular Issue, 1964
Size: 42x26mm
Photogravure and Lithographed

		1965, Dec. 22 Unwmk. Perf. 14		
CO1	A1	75np as #6	1.00	.30
		Size: 52x33mm		
CO2	A1	2r as #7	2.50	.75
CO3	A1	3r as #8	3.75	1.00
CO4	A1	5r as #9	5.00	1.50
		Nos. CO1-CO4 (4)	12.25	3.55

OFFICIAL STAMPS

Type of Regular Issue, 1964
Size: 42x26mm
Photogravure and Lithographed

		1965, Dec. 22 Unwmk. Perf. 14		
O1	A1	25np as #1	.35	.25
O2	A1	40np as #2	.45	.25
O3	A1	50np as #3	.75	.25
O4	A1	75np as #4	1.00	.30
O5	A1	1r as #5	1.25	.35
		Nos. O1-O5 (5)	3.80	1.40

UNITED ARAB EMIRATES

yu-ˌnī-təd 'ar-əb i-'mi̱ə̱r-əts

(Trucial States)

LOCATION — Arabia, on Arabian Gulf
GOVT. — Federation of sheikdoms
AREA — 32,300 sq. mi.
POP. — 2,377,453 (1995)
CAPITAL — Abu Dhabi

The UAE was formed Dec. 2, 1971, by the union of Abu Dhabi, Ajman, Dubai, Fujeira, Sharjah and Umm al Qiwain. Ras al Khaima joined in Feb. 1972.

1,000 Fils = 1 Dinar
100 Fils = 1 Dirham (1973)

Catalogue values for all unused stamps in this country are for Never Hinged items.

Abu Dhabi Nos. 56-67 Overprinted

1972, Aug. Litho. Unwmk. Perf. 14

1	A10	5f multicolored	3.25	3.25
2	A10	10f multicolored	3.25	3.25
3	A10	25f multicolored	5.00	5.00
4	A10	15f multicolored	6.50	6.50
5	A10	50f multicolored	11.00	11.00
6	A10	60f multicolored	12.00	12.00
7	A10	70f multicolored	16.00	16.00
8	A10	90f multicolored	20.00	20.00
9	A11	125f multicolored	65.00	65.00
10	A11	150f multicolored	90.00	90.00
11	A11	500f multicolored	210.00	210.00
12	A11	1d multicolored	400.00	400.00
		Nos. 1-12 (12)	842.00	842.00

The overprint differs.
#1-12 were used in Abu Dhabi. #2-3 were placed on sale later in Dubai & Sharjah.

Map and Flag of UAE — A1

Almagta Bridge, Abu Dhabi — A2

Designs: 10f, Like 5f. 15f, 35f, Coat of arms of UAE (eagle). 75f, Khor Fakkan, Sharjah. 1d, Steel Clock Tower, Dubai. 1.25d, Buthnah Fort, Fujeira. 2d, Alfalaj Fort, Umm al Qiwain. 3d, Khor Khwair, Ras al Khaima. 5d, Palace of Sheik Rashid bin Humaid al Nuaimi, Ajman. 10d, Sheik Zayed bin Sultan al Nahayan, Abu Dhabi.

1973, Jan. 1 Unwmk. Perf. 14½
Size: 41x25mm

13	A1	5f multicolored	.25	.25
14	A1	10f multicolored	.25	.25
15	A1	15f bluc & multi	.50	.25
16	A1	35f olive & multi	.75	.30

Perf. 14x15
Size: 45x29½mm

17	A2	65f multicolored	1.25	1.25
18	A2	75f multicolored	1.75	1.25
19	A2	1d multicolored	2.00	1.25
20	A2	1.25d multicolored	4.25	2.00
21	A2	2d multicolored	50.00	12.50
22	A2	3d multicolored	10.00	7.25
23	A2	5d multicolored	11.00	7.50
24	A2	10d multicolored	25.00	16.00
		Nos. 13-24 (12)	107.00	50.05

For surcharge see No. 68.

Festival Emblem A3

1973, Mar. 27 Litho. Perf. 13½x14

25	A3	10f shown	7.50	.35
26	A3	1.25d Trophy	18.50	11.00

National Youth Festival, Mar. 27.

Pedestrian Crossing in Dubai — A4

35f, Traffic light school crossing sign, vert. 1.25d, Traffic policemen with car & radio, vert.

1973, Apr. 1 Perf. 13½x14, 14x13½

27	A4	35f green & multi	4.00	1.75
28	A4	75f blue & multi	7.50	3.50
29	A4	1.25d violet & multi	13.00	6.00
		Nos. 27-29 (3)	24.50	11.25

Traffic Week, Apr. 1-7.

Human Rights Flame and People — A5

1973, Dec. 10 Litho. Perf. 14½x14

30	A5	35f blue, blk & org	1.50	.95
31	A5	65f red, blk & org	5.25	2.00
32	A5	1.25d olive, blk & org	9.75	4.00
		Nos. 30-32 (3)	16.50	6.95

25th anniversary of the Universal Declaration of Human Rights.

UPU and Arab Postal Union Emblems — A6

1974, Aug. 5 Litho. Perf. 14x14½

33	A6	25f multicolored	2.00	1.00
34	A6	60f emerald & multi	3.25	1.75
35	A6	1.25d lt brown & multi	6.75	4.50
		Nos. 33-35 (3)	12.00	7.25

Centenary of Universal Postal Union.

Health Care — A7

Education — A8

Designs: 65f, Construction. 1.25d, UAE flag, UN and Arab League emblems.

1974, Dec. 2 Litho. Perf. 13½

36	A7	10f multicolored	1.10	.40
37	A8	35f multicolored	3.00	1.00
38	A8	65f blue & brown	3.25	1.50
39	A8	1.25d multicolored	7.00	3.25
		Nos. 36-39 (4)	14.35	6.15

Third National Day.

Arab Man and Woman Holding Candle over Book — A9

Man and Woman Reading Book — A10

1974, Dec. 27 Perf. 14x14½, 14½x14

40	A9	35f deep ultra & multi	2.75	.60
41	A10	65f orange brn & multi	3.25	1.25
42	A10	1.25d gray & multi	6.75	2.50
		Nos. 40-42 (3)	12.75	4.35

World Literacy Day.

Oil De-gassing Station — A11

50f, Off-shore drilling platform. 100f, Underwater storage tank. 125f, Oil production platform.

1975, Mar. 10 Litho. Perf. 13x13½

43	A11	25f multicolored	1.50	.55
44	A11	50f multicolored	3.25	1.00
45	A11	100f multicolored	8.00	2.50
46	A11	125f multicolored	11.00	3.00
a.		Souvenir sheet of 4, #43-46	40.00	30.00
		Nos. 43-46 (4)	23.75	7.05

9th Arab Petroleum Conference.

Three stamps to commemorate the 2nd Gulf Long Distance Swimming Championship were prepared in June, 1975, but not issued. Value $500.

Jabal Ali Earth Station — A12

Jabal Ali Earth Station: 35f, 65f, Communications satellite over globe.

1975, Nov. 8 Litho. Perf. 13

47	A12	15f multicolored	1.25	.35
48	A12	35f multicolored	3.00	.65
49	A12	65f multicolored	5.00	1.10
50	A12	2d multicolored	11.00	4.00
		Nos. 47-50 (4)	20.25	6.10

Various Scenes — A13

Sheik Hamad, Fujeira Ruler — A14

Supreme Council Members (Sheikdom rulers): 60f, Sheik Rashid bin Humaid al Naimi, Ajman. 80f, Sheik Ahmed bin Rashid al Mulla, Umm al Qiwain. 90f, Sheik Sultan bin Mohammed al Qasimi, Sharjah. 1d, Sheik Saqr bin Mohammed al Qasimi, Ras al Khaima. 140f, Sheik Rashid bin Said al Maktum, Dubai. 5d, Sheik Zayed bin Sultan al Nahayan, Abu Dhabi.

1975, Dec. 2 Litho. Perf. 14

51	A13	10f multicolored	.85	.25
52	A14	35f multicolored	2.25	.90
53	A14	60f multicolored	3.25	1.75
54	A14	80f multicolored	4.50	2.75
55	A14	90f multicolored	5.25	3.00
56	A14	1d multicolored	5.50	3.50
57	A14	140f multicolored	7.75	4.50
58	A14	5d multicolored	32.50	18.00
		Nos. 51-58 (8)	61.85	34.65

Fourth National Day.

Students and Lamp of Learning — A15

Arab Literacy Day: 15f, Lamp of learning.

1976, Feb. 8 Litho. Perf. 14

59	A15	15f orange & multi	.75	.35
60	A15	50f ultra & multi	2.50	1.00
61	A15	3d multicolored	12.00	7.75
		Nos. 59-61 (3)	15.25	9.10

Children Crossing Street — A16

Traffic Week: 15f, Traffic lights and signals, vert. 80f, Road and traffic lights.

Perf. 14½x14, 14x14½

1976, Apr. 1				Litho.
62	A16	15f brt blue & multi	2.50	1.25
63	A16	80f blue & multi	9.25	4.50
64	A16	140f ocher & multi	18.00	10.00
		Nos. 62-64 (3)	29.75	15.75

Waves and Ear Phones, ITU Emblem, Coat of Arms — A17

1976, May 17			Litho.	*Perf. 14*
65	A17	50f gray grn & multi	1.50	.65
66	A17	80f pink & multi	3.00	1.25
67	A17	2d tan & multi	6.50	3.25
		Nos. 65-67 (3)	11.00	5.15

International Telecommunications Day.

No. 18 Surcharged

1976			Litho.	*Perf. 14x15*
68	A2	50f on 75f multi	75.00	24.00

Coat of Arms — A18

1976, Aug. 15			Litho.	*Perf. 11½*
69	A18	5f dull rose	.35	.25
70	A18	10f golden brown	.35	.25
71	A18	15f orange	.50	.40
72	A18	35f dull red brn	.75	.25
73	A18	50f bright lilac	1.00	.50
74	A18	60f bister	1.25	.60
75	A18	80f yellow green	1.50	.70
76	A18	90f ultra	2.00	.80
77	A18	1d blue	2.25	.80
78	A18	140f olive green	3.50	1.50
79	A18	150f rose violet	5.25	2.00
80	A18	2d slate	5.50	2.25
81	A18	5d blue green	13.00	6.25
82	A18	10d lilac rose	24.00	14.00
		Nos. 69-82 (14)	61.20	30.55

See Nos. 91-104.

Sheik Zayed — A19

1976, Dec. 12			Litho.	*Perf. 13*
83	A19	15f rose & multi	6.00	.60
84	A19	140f blue & multi	12.00	5.00

5th National Day.

Symbolic Falcon and Globe — A20

1976, Dec. 15			*Perf. 14x13½*
85	A20	80f yellow & multi	6.00	1.50
86	A20	2d red & multi	11.00	6.00

International Falconry Congress, Abu Dhabi, Dec. 1976.

A21

1976, Dec. 30			Litho.	*Perf. 13*
87	A21	50f multicolored	5.00	1.50
88	A21	80f multicolored	10.00	3.00

Mohammed Ali Jinnah (1876-1948), 1st Governor General of Pakistan.

A22

APU emblem, members' flags.

1977, Apr. 12			Litho.	*Perf. 13½x14*
89	A22	50f multicolored	6.00	1.50
90	A22	80f multicolored	9.00	3.50

Arab Postal Union, 25th anniversary.

Arms Type of 1976

1977, July 25			Litho.	*Perf. 11½*
91	A18	5f dull rose & blk	.40	.35
92	A18	10f gldn brn & blk	.40	.35
93	A18	15f dull org & blk	.55	.45
94	A18	35f lt brown & blk	1.40	.50
95	A18	50f brt lilac & blk	1.60	.55
96	A18	60f bister & blk	1.75	.60
97	A18	80f yel grn & blk	1.75	.60
98	A18	90f ultra & blk	2.75	.95
99	A18	1d blue & blk	4.00	1.40
100	A18	140f ol grn & blk	6.00	1.90
101	A18	150f rose vio & blk	6.50	2.25
102	A18	2d slate & blk	10.00	3.25
103	A18	5d bl grn & blk	22.50	8.25
104	A18	10d lil rose & blk	37.50	24.50
		Nos. 91-104 (14)	97.10	45.90

Man Reading Book, UAE Arms, UN Emblem A23

1977, Sept. 8			Litho.	*Perf. 14x13½*
105	A23	50f green, brn & gold	3.50	.80
106	A23	3d blue & multi	12.50	5.50

International Literacy Day.

A set of three stamps for the 6th Natl. Day was withdrawn from sale on the day of issue, Dec. 2, 1977. Value, $850.

Post Horn and Sails — A24

1979, Apr. 14			Photo.	*Perf. 12x11½*
107	A24	50f multicolored	1.25	1.00
108	A24	5d multicolored	8.50	6.00

Gulf Postal Organization, 2nd Conf., Dubai.

Arab Achievements — A25

1980, Mar. 22			Litho.	*Perf. 14x14½*
109	A25	50f multicolored	.75	.50
110	A25	140f multicolored	2.25	1.25
111	A25	3d multicolored	4.50	2.75
		Nos. 109-111 (3)	7.50	4.50

9th National Day — A26

1980, Dec. 2			Litho.	*Perf. 13½*
112	A26	15f multicolored	.60	.35
113	A26	80f multicolored	2.00	1.00
114	A26	80f multicolored	2.50	1.50
115	A26	150f multicolored	3.75	2.25
		Nos. 112-115 (4)	8.85	5.10

Souvenir Sheet

Perf. 13½x14

116	A26	3d multicolored	15.00	15.00

Family on Graph — A27

1980, Dec. 15				
117	A27	15f shown	.80	.35
118	A27	80f Symbols	2.75	1.25
119	A27	90f like #118	3.50	2.25
120	A27	2d like #117	7.25	5.00
		Nos. 117-120 (4)	14.30	8.85

1980 population census.

Hegira (Pilgrimage Year) — A28

1980, Dec. 18			Perf. 14x13½
121	A28	15f multicolored	.50	.25
122	A28	80f multicolored	2.00	1.25
123	A28	90f multicolored	2.75	1.50
124	A28	140f multicolored	4.25	2.50
		Nos. 121-124 (4)	9.50	5.50

Souvenir Sheet

125	A28	2d multicolored	11.50	11.50

No. 125 contains one 36x57mm stamp.

OPEC Emblem — A29

1980, Dec. 21			*Perf. 14*
126	A29	50f Men holding OPEC emblem, vert.	1.25	.50
127	A29	80f like #126	2.00	1.25
128	A29	90f shown	2.25	1.50
129	A29	140f like #128	4.00	2.25
		Nos. 126-129 (4)	9.50	5.50

Souvenir Sheet

130	A29	3d like #128	18.00	18.00

Traffic Week — A30

15f, 80f, Crossing guard, students, traffic light. 50f, 5d, Crossing guard, traffic light and signs.

1981, Mar. 26			Litho.	*Perf. 14½*
131	A30	15f multicolored	.65	.30
132	A30	50f multicolored	1.25	.75
133	A30	80f multicolored	2.50	1.50
134	A30	5d multicolored	11.00	7.50
		Nos. 131-134 (4)	15.40	10.05

Size of Nos. 131 and 133: 25½x35mm.

10th Natl. Day — A31

1981, Dec. 2			Litho.	*Perf. 15x14*
135	A31	25f Cogwheel	.75	.40
136	A31	150f Soldiers	5.00	2.50
137	A31	2d UN emblem	6.50	3.00
		Nos. 135-137 (3)	12.25	5.90

Intl. Year of the Disabled — A32

Perf. 14½x14, 14x14½

1981, Dec. 26				Litho.
138	A32	25f Couple	.75	.35
139	A32	45f Man in wheelchair, vert.	1.50	1.10
140	A32	150f like #139	5.00	2.50
141	A32	2d like #138	7.50	3.25
		Nos. 138-141 (4)	14.75	7.20

Natl. Arms — A33

1982-86

142	A33	5f multicolored	.25	.25
143	A33	10f multicolored	.25	.25
144	A33	15f multicolored	.25	.25
145	A33	25f multicolored	.25	.25
145A	A33	35f multicolored	.25	.25
146	A33	50f lt. blue & multi	.40	.40
146A	A33	50f dark blue & multi	3.00	1.50
147	A33	75f multicolored	.60	.60
148	A33	100f multicolored	.90	.90
149	A33	110f multicolored	1.00	1.00
150	A33	150f multicolored	1.75	1.25
151	A33	175f multicolored	1.75	1.25
151A	A33	2.00	2.00	1.25

Size: 23x27mm

Perf. 13

152	A33	2d multicolored	2.25	1.60
152A	A33	250f multicolored	2.40	1.40
153	A33	3d multicolored	3.50	1.90
154	A33	5d multicolored	6.00	3.25
155	A33	10d multicolored	13.00	8.25
156	A33	20d multicolored	24.50	13.50
157	A33	50d multicolored	50.00	24.50
		Nos. 142-157 (20)	114.05	63.95

Issued: 35f, 175f, 250f, 12/15/84; 50d, 2/6/86; others, 3/7/82.

6th Arab Gulf Soccer Championships — A34

1982, Apr. 4   Litho.   Perf. 14

167	A34	25f Emblem, flags	1.25	.60
168	A34	75f Eagle, soccer ball, stadium, vert.	3.25	2.40
169	A34	125f Players, vert.	4.25	3.00
170	A34	3d like 75f, vert.	9.25	7.75
		Nos. 167-170 (4)	18.00	13.75

2nd Disarmament Meeting A35

1982, Oct. 24   Litho.   Perf. 13x13½

171	A35	25f multicolored	.65	.30
172	A35	75f multicolored	2.00	2.25
173	A35	125f multicolored	3.50	2.40
174	A35	150f multicolored	4.00	3.00
		Nos. 171-174 (4)	10.15	7.95

11th Natl. Day — A36

Designs: 25f, 150f, Skyscraper, communications tower, natl. crest, castle turret, open book, flag. 75f, 125f, Sun, bird, vert.

1982, Dec. 2   Litho.   Perf. 14½

175	A36	25f multicolored	.60	.40
176	A36	75f multicolored	2.40	1.60
177	A36	125f multicolored	3.25	2.25
178	A36	150f multicolored	3.75	2.75
		Nos. 175-178 (4)	10.00	7.00

A37

1983, Dec. 20   Litho.   Perf. 14x14½

179	A37	25f multicolored	.80	.30
180	A37	150f multicolored	3.50	1.60
181	A37	2d multicolored	5.00	3.00
182	A37	3d multicolored	7.00	3.75
		Nos. 179-182 (4)	16.30	8.65

World Communications Year.

A38

Arab Literacy Day: 25f, 75f, Oil lamp, open Koran. 35f, 3d, Scribe.

1983, Jan. 8   Litho.   Perf. 14½

183	A38	25f multicolored	42.50	60.00
184	A38	35f multicolored	1.50	.80
185	A38	75f multicolored	42.50	55.00
186	A38	3d multicolored	10.00	5.00

Nos. 183 and 185 withdrawn from sale on day of issue because of an error in Koranic inscription.

INTELSAT, 20th Anniv. — A39

1984, Nov. 24   Litho.   Perf 14½

187	A39	2d multicolored	5.50	5.00
188	A39	2.50d multicolored	8.00	7.00

13th Natl. Day A40

Flag, portrait of an Emir and building or view from each capital.

1984, Dec. 2   Perf. 14½x13½

189	A40	1d Building, pavilion	2.50	1.50
190	A40	1d Fortress, cannon	2.50	1.50
191	A40	1d Port, boats	2.50	1.50
192	A40	1d Fortress	2.50	1.50
193	A40	1d Oil refinery	2.50	1.50
194	A40	1d Building, garden	2.50	1.50
195	A40	1d Oil well, palace	2.50	1.50
		Nos. 189-195 (7)	17.50	10.50

Tidy Week — A41

1985, Mar. 15   Perf. 12½

196	A41	5d multicolored	11.50	10.00

A42

1985, Sept. 10   Perf. 13½x14½

197	A42	2d multicolored	7.00	4.50
198	A42	250f multicolored	10.00	6.50

World Junior Chess Championships, Sharjah, Sept. 10-27.

14th Natl. Day — A43

1985, Dec. 2   Perf. 14x13½

199	A43	50f multicolored	.75	.55
200	A43	3d multicolored	7.00	4.50

Population Census — A44

1985, Dec. 16

201	A44	50f multicolored	1.10	.55
202	A44	1d multicolored	3.00	1.40
203	A44	3d multicolored	7.75	3.50
		Nos. 201-203 (3)	11.85	5.45

Intl. Youth Year A45

50f, Silhouettes, sapling, vert. 175f, Globe, open book. 2d, Youth carrying world, vert.

1985, Dec. 23   Perf. 14½

204	A45	50f multicolored	1.00	.65
205	A45	175f multicolored	3.00	1.60
206	A45	2d multicolored	3.75	2.25
		Nos. 204-206 (3)	7.75	4.50

Women and Family Day — A46

1986, Mar. 21   Perf. 13½

207	A46	1d multicolored	1.50	1.00
208	A46	3d multicolored	4.50	3.25

General Postal Authority, 1st Anniv. A47

Designs: 50f, 250f, Posthorn, map, natl. flag, globe. 1d, 2d, Emblem, globe, vert.

1986, Apr. 1

209	A47	50f multicolored	.60	.50
210	A47	1d multicolored	1.25	.80
211	A47	2d multicolored	3.25	2.25
212	A47	250f multicolored	3.50	2.75
		Nos. 209-212 (4)	8.60	6.30

United Arab Shipping Co., 10th Anniv. A48

1986, Aug. 20   Perf. 13x13½

213	A48	2d shown	4.50	2.75
214	A48	3d Ship's bow, vert.	5.50	3.75

A49

1986, Sept. 1   Perf. 13½x13

215	A49	250f multicolored	4.25	1.65
216	A49	3d multicolored	5.25	1.90

Emirates Telecommunications Corp., Ltd., 10th anniv.

Hawk — A50

1986, Sept. 9   Photo.   Perf. 15x14
Booklet Stamps
Background Color

217	A50	50f pale green	.75	.75
218	A50	75f pink	1.25	1.25
219	A50	125f gray	2.00	2.00
a.		Bklt. pane, 75f, 125f, 2 50f	8.00	
		Nos. 217-219 (3)	4.00	4.00

Emirates Airlines, 1st Anniv. — A51

1986, Oct. 25   Perf. 13½

220	A51	50f Jet, camel	1.75	1.25
221	A51	175f Jet	5.50	4.25

State Crests, GCC Emblem A52

1986, Nov. 2   *Perf. 13*
222　A52　50f shown　　.80　.60
222A A52　175f like no. 223　2.75　2.25
223　A52　3d Tree, emblem　4.50　4.25
   Nos. 222-223 (3)　8.05　7.10

Gulf Cooperation Council supreme council 7th session, Abu Dhabi, Nov. 1986. No. 222A incorrectly inscribed "1.75f."

15th Natl. Day — A53

1986, Dec. 2   **Litho.**   *Perf. 13½*
224　A53　50f shown　　1.10　.55
225　A53　1d like 50f　　2.50　1.60
226　A53　175f Flag, emblem　4.50　2.75
227　A53　2d like 175f　　4.50　3.25
   Nos. 224-227 (4)　12.60　8.15

27th Chess Olympiad, Dubai — A54

1986, Nov. 14   *Perf. 12½*
228　A54　50f Skyscraper, vert.　1.40　.80
229　A54　2d shown　　5.50　4.50
230　A54　250f Tapestry, diff.　7.00　5.50
 a.　Souv. sheet, #228-230, perf
    13　　22.50　22.50
   Nos. 228-230 (3)　13.90　10.80

No. 230a exists imperf. Value, $35.

Arab Police Day — A55

1986, Dec. 18   *Perf. 13½*
231　A55　50f multicolored　1.75　1.00
232　A55　1d multicolored　3.00　2.50

A56

1987, Mar. 15
233　A56　50f multicolored　1.75　1.00
234　A56　1d multicolored　3.00　2.50

Municipalities and Environment Week.

A57

1987, Apr. 10
235　A57　200f multicolored　3.50　3.50
236　A57　250f multicolored　4.00　4.00

UAE Flight Information Region, 1st anniv.

Conservation A58

50f, Water. 2d, Solar energy, oil well.

1987, May 25
237　A58　50f multicolored　1.00　1.00
238　A58　2d multicolored　8.50　8.50

A59

1987, June 23
239　A59　1d multicolored　1.75　1.75
240　A59　3d multicolored　4.50　4.50

United Arab Emirates University, 10th anniv.

1st Shipment of Crude Oil from Abu Dhabi, 25th Anniv. — A60

1987, July 4   *Perf. 13*
241　A60　50f Oil rig　　.80　.80
242　A60　1d Drilling well, vert.　1.90　1.90
243　A60　175f Crew, drill　3.00　3.00
244　A60　2d Oil tanker　3.25　3.25
   Nos. 241-244 (4)　8.95　8.95

Arab Palm Tree and Date Day — A61

1987, Sept. 15   **Litho.**   *Perf. 14x15*
245　A61　50f shown　　.90　.90
246　A61　1d Tree, fruit, diff.　1.60　1.60

A62

1987, Nov. 21   **Litho.**   *Perf. 13x13½*
247　A62　2d multicolored　3.00　3.00
248　A62　250f multicolored　3.50　3.50

Intl. Year of Shelter for the Homeless.

A63

1987, Dec. 15   *Perf. 13½*
249　A63　1d multicolored　2.00　2.00
250　A63　2d multicolored　4.50　4.50

Salim Bin Ali Al-Owais (b. 1887), poet.

UN Child Survival Campaign — A64

50f, Growth monitoring. 1d, Immunization. 175f, Oral rehydration therapy. 2d, Breast feeding, horiz.

1987, Oct. 25   **Litho.**   *Perf. 13*
251　A64　50f multicolored　.60　.50
252　A64　1d multicolored　1.25　1.00
253　A64　175f multicolored　2.00　1.75
254　A64　2d multicolored　2.25　1.90
   Nos. 251-254 (4)　6.10　5.15

Abu Dhabi Intl. Airport, 6th Anniv. — A65

1988, Jan. 2
255　A65　50f Control tower　.85　.85
256　A65　50f Terminal interior　.85　.85
257　A65　100f Aircraft over airport　2.00　2.00
258　A65　100f Aircraft at gates　2.00　2.00
   Nos. 255-258 (4)　5.70　5.70

Natl. Arts Festival A66

1988, Mar. 21   **Litho.**   *Perf. 13½*
259　A66　50f multicolored　1.25　1.25
260　A66　250f multicolored　3.75　3.75

Youth Cultural Festival A67

Winning children's drawings of a design contest sponsored by the Ministry of Education and the Sharjah Cultural and Information Department.

Perf. 13x13½, 13½x13 (262)
1988, May 25   **Litho.**
261　A67　50f Net fisherman　.75　.50
262　A67　1d Woman, vert.　1.40　1.25
263　A67　1.75d Youth as flower　2.25　2.00
264　A67　2d Recreation　2.75　2.50
   Nos. 261-264 (4)　7.15　6.25

Palestinian Uprising — A68

1988, June 28   **Litho.**   *Perf. 13½*
265　A68　2d multicolored　2.75　2.25
266　A68　250f multicolored　3.50　2.75

A69

Banks — A70

1988, July 16   **Litho.**   *Perf. 13½*
267　A69　50f multicolored　2.50　2.50
268　A70　50f multicolored　2.50　2.50

Abu Dhabi Natl. Bank, Ltd., 20th anniv. (No. 267); Natl. Bank of Dubai, Ltd., 25th anniv. (No. 268).

Port Rashid, Dubai, 16th Anniv. — A71

1988, Aug. 31   **Litho.**   *Perf. 13½*
269　A71　50f Ground transporta-
    tion　　.60　.60
270　A71　1d Piers　　1.25　1.25
271　A71　175f Ship at dock　2.50　2.50
272　A71　2d Ship, unloading
    cranes　　2.75　2.75
   Nos. 269-272 (4)　7.10　7.10

1988 Summer Olympics, Seoul — A72

1988, Sept. 17   *Perf. 15x14½*
273　　2d Swimming　3.25　3.25
274　　250f Cycling　4.00　4.00
 a.　A72 Pair, #273-274　7.50　7.50

Ras Al Khaima Natl. Museum, 1st Anniv. — A74

1988, Nov. 19   Litho.   Perf. 14
275 A74 50f Vase, vert.   .75 .55
276 A74 3d   Gold crown   3.25 2.25

18th Arab Scout Conference, Nov. 29-
Dec. 3, Abu Dhabi — A75

1988, Nov. 29   Perf. 12½
277 A75 1d   multicolored   1.20 1.20

10th Arbor
Day — A76

Perf. 13½x13, 13x13½
1989, Mar. 6   Litho.
278 A76 50f   Ghaf, vert.   .60   .60
279 A76 100f Palm   1.25 1.25
280 A76 250f Dahlia blossom   2.75 2.75
        Nos. 278-280 (3)   4.60 4.60

Sharjah
Intl. Airport,
10th Anniv.
A77

1989, Apr. 21   Litho.   Perf. 13½
281 A77 50f   multicolored   .90   .90
282 A77 100f multicolored   2.10 2.10

Postal
Service,
80th Anniv.
A78

1989, Aug. 19   Litho.   Perf. 13x13½
283 A78 50f   Seaplane   1.00 1.00
284 A78 3d   Ship   6.50 6.50

Al-Ittihad
Newspaper, 20th
Anniv. — A79

1989, Oct. 20   Litho.   Perf. 13½
285 A79 50f   shown   .75   .75
286 A79 1d   Al Ittihad Press   1.25 1.25

Gulf Investment Corporation, 5th
Anniv. — A80

1989, Nov. 25
287 A80 50f   multicolored   .75   .75
288 A80 2d   multicolored   3.25 3.25

Child on
Crutches,
Hands — A81

Designs: 2d, Crouched youth, cracked
earth, bread in hand, horiz.

1989, Dec. 5   Perf. 15x14, 14x15
289 A81 2d   multicolored   2.75 2.75
290 A81 250f shown   3.25 3.25

Intl. Volunteer's Day, Red Crescent Soc.

Bank
Building — A82

50f, Emblem, architecture.

1989, Dec. 20   Perf. 13½
291 A82 50f   multicolored   .75   .75
292 A82 1d   shown   1.25 1.25

Commercial Bank of Dubai, Ltd., 20th Anniv.

Astrolabe,
Manuscript
Page and
Ship of Bin
Majid, 15th
Cent.
Navigator
and Writer
A83

1989, Dec. 25   Perf. 13x13½, 13½x13
293 A83 1d   shown   1.25 1.25
294 A83 3d   Ship, page, vert.   4.25 4.25

Heritage revival.

3rd Al Ain
Festival — A84

1990, Jan. 17   Perf. 13½
295 A84 50f   multicolored   .75   .75
296 A84 1d   multicolored   1.90 1.90

Falcon — A85

1990, Feb. 17   Litho.   Perf. 11½
Granite Paper
297 A85 5f   multicolored   .25   .25
298 A85 20f   multicolored   .25   .25
299 A85 25f   multicolored   .25   .25
301 A85 50f   multicolored   .45   .40
302 A85 100f multicolored   2.25 1.25
303 A85 150f multicolored   3.75 1.75
304 A85 175f multicolored   4.00 2.00
Size: 21x26mm
Perf. 11½x12
306 A85 2d   multicolored   5.50 3.00
307 A85 250f multicolored   6.00 3.25
309 A85 3d   multicolored   7.75 3.75
310 A85 5d   multicolored   11.00 6.50
311 A85 10d   multicolored   22.50 13.00

312 A85 20d   multicolored   37.50 22.50
313 A85 50d   multicolored   100.00 60.00
        Nos. 297-313 (14)   201.45 118.15
        See also Nos. 726A-726G.

Children's
Cultural
Festival — A86

1990, Mar. 10   Litho.   Perf. 13½
316 A86 50f   multicolored   .60   .60
317 A86 250f multicolored   2.50 2.50

Red Crescent
Society — A87

1990, Aug. 5   Litho.   Perf. 14x15
318 A87 175f shown   1.90 1.90
319 A87 2d   Starving child   2.50 2.50

Dubai
Chamber
of
Commerce
and
Industry,
25th Anniv.
A88

1990, July 1   Perf. 13
320 A88 50f   multicolored   .75   .75
321 A88 1d   multicolored   1.50 1.50

World Cup Soccer Championships,
Italy — A89

UAE emblem, character trademark and: 1d,
Leaning Tower of Pisa, desert, vert. 2d, Soccer ball, vert. 250f, Circle of flags. 3d, Map,
vert.

1990, June 8   Perf. 13½
322 A89 50f   multicolored   .75   .75
323 A89 1d   multicolored   1.50 1.50
324 A89 2d   multicolored   3.00 3.00
325 A89 250f   multicolored   4.00 4.00
        Nos. 322-325 (4)   9.25 9.25
Souvenir Sheet
Perf. 12½
326 A89 3d   multicolored   7.00 7.00

A90

1990, Sept. 22   Litho.   Perf. 13½
327 A90 50f   shown   .75   .75
328 A90 1d   Emblem, 30 years   2.25 2.25
329 A90 175f Emblem, drop of oil 3.50 3.50
        Nos. 327-329 (3)   6.50 6.50

Organization of Petroleum Exporting Countries (OPEC), 30th anniv.

A91

Flowers: No. 330, Argyrolobeum roseum.
No. 331, Lamranthus roseus. No. 332,
Centavrea pseudo sinaica. No. 333, Calotropis procera. No. 334, Nerium oleander. No.
335, Catharanthus roseus. No. 336, Hibiscus
rosa sinensis. No. 337, Bougainvillea glabra.

1990, Aug. 25   Perf. 14x14½
330 A91 50f   multicolored   .90   .90
331 A91 50f   multicolored   .90   .90
332 A91 50f   multicolored   .90   .90
333 A91 50f   multicolored   .90   .90
    a.   Souvenir sheet of 4, #330-333 4.50 4.50
334 A91 50f   multicolored   .90   .90
335 A91 50f   multicolored   .90   .90
336 A91 50f   multicolored   4.00 4.00
337 A91 50f   multicolored   4.00 4.00
    a.   Souvenir sheet of 4, #334-337 17.00 17.00
        Nos. 330-337 (8)   13.40 13.40

Environmental
Pollution — A92

1990, Oct. 8   Litho.   Perf. 13
338 A92 50f   Water pollution   .50   .50
339 A92 3d   Air pollution   3.25 3.25

Central Bank,
10th
Anniv. — A93

1990, Dec. 2   Perf. 13½
340 A93 50f   shown   .50   .50
341 A93 175f Bank building,
                horiz.   3.25 3.25

Intl. Conference
on High Salinity
Tolerant
Plants — A94

1990, Dec. 8   Perf. 13x13½
342 A94 50f   Tree   .50   .50
343 A94 250f Water, trees   2.75 2.75

Grand
Mosque, Abu
Dhabi — A95

2d, Al Jumeirah Mosque, Dubai, vert.

Perf. 13½x13, 13x13½

1990, Nov. 26

| 344 | A95 | 1d multicolored | 1.10 | 1.10 |
| 345 | A95 | 2d multicolored | 4.50 | 4.50 |

Abu Dhabi Intl. Fair — A96

1991, Jan. 16   Litho.   Perf. 13x13½

| 346 | A96 | 50f multicolored | 1.00 | 1.00 |
| 347 | A96 | 2d multicolored | 2.50 | 2.50 |

A97

1991, May 17   Litho.   Perf. 14x13½

| 348 | A97 | 2d multicolored | 3.00 | 3.00 |
| 349 | A97 | 3d multicolored | 4.50 | 4.50 |

World Telecommunications Day.

A98

1991, June 18   Perf. 13½

| 350 | A98 | 1d Sheikh Saqr Mosque | 1.50 | 1.50 |
| 351 | A98 | 2d King Faisal Mosque | 3.25 | 3.25 |

Children's Paintings A99

Designs: 50f, Celebration. 1d, Women waving flags. 175f, Women playing blind-man's buff. 250f, Women dancing for men.

1991, July 15   Litho.   Perf. 14x13½

352	A99	50f multicolored	.60	.45
353	A99	1d multicolored	1.40	1.00
354	A99	175f multicolored	2.50	2.25
355	A99	250f multicolored	3.00	2.50
		Nos. 352-355 (4)	7.50	6.20

Fish A100

1991, Aug. 5   Litho.   Perf. 13½x14

356	A100	50f Yellow marked butterflyfish	.60	.60
357	A100	50f Golden trevally	.60	.60
358	A100	50f Two banded porgy	.60	.60
359	A100	50f Red snapper	.60	.60
360	A100	1d Three banded grunt	1.25	1.25
361	A100	1d Rabbit fish	1.25	1.25
362	A100	1d Black bream	1.25	1.25
363	A100	1d Greasy grouper	1.25	1.25
a.		Min. sheet of 8, #356-363	8.50	8.50
		Nos. 356-363 (8)	7.40	7.40

A101

Intl. Aerospace Exhibition, Dubai: 175f, Jet fighter over Dubai Intl. Airport. 2d, Fighter silhouette over airport.

1991, Nov. 3   Litho.   Perf. 13½

| 364 | A101 | 175f multicolored | 2.25 | 2.25 |
| 365 | A101 | 2d multicolored | 2.50 | 2.50 |

A102

Sheikh Rashid Bin Said Al Maktum (1912-90), Ruler of Dubai and: 50f, Airport, vert. 175f, City skyline, vert. 2d, Waterfront, satellite dish.

1991, Oct. 7   Perf. 13

366	A102	50f multicolored	.50	.50
367	A102	1d multicolored	1.10	1.10
368	A102	175f multicolored	2.00	2.00
369	A102	2d multicolored	2.25	2.25
		Nos. 366-369 (4)	5.85	5.85

Civil Defense Day — A103

1991, Oct. 8   Litho.   Perf. 13½

| 370 | A103 | 50f multicolored | .75 | .75 |
| 371 | A103 | 1d multicolored | 1.75 | 1.75 |

A104

A105

A106

20th Natl. Day — A107

#374, Emir at left, fortress, cannon. #377, Fortress on rocky outcropping. #378, Emir at right, fortress, cannon. 3d, Sheikh Said bin Sultan al Nahayan, Defense Forces.

1991, Dec. 2   Litho.   Perf. 13

372	A104	75f multicolored	1.20	1.20
373	A105	75f multicolored	1.20	1.20
374	A105	75f multicolored	1.20	1.20
375	A106	75f multicolored	1.20	1.20
376	A107	75f multicolored	1.20	1.20
377	A107	75f multicolored	1.20	1.20
378	A107	75f multicolored	1.20	1.20

Imperf

Size: 70x90mm

| 378A | A107 | 3d multicolored | 8.00 | 8.00 |
| | | Nos. 372-378A (8) | 16.40 | 16.40 |

On Nos. 372-378 portions of the design were applied by a thermographic process producing a shiny, raised effect.

A108

1991, Nov. 16   Perf. 13½

| 379 | A108 | 50f lt green & multi | .45 | .45 |
| 380 | A108 | 3d orange & multi | 3.75 | 3.75 |

Gulf Cooperaton Council, 10th anniv.

A109

1992, Jan. 15   Litho.   Perf. 13½

| 381 | A109 | 175f pink & multi | 2.20 | 2.20 |
| 382 | A109 | 250f lt blue & multi | 2.50 | 2.50 |

Abu Dhabi National Oil Co., 20th anniv.

Al-Jahli Castle Al-Ain A110

1992, Apr. 20   Litho.   Perf. 13½

| 383 | A110 | 2d multicolored | 2.00 | 2.00 |
| 384 | A110 | 250f multicolored | 60.00 | 60.00 |

Expo '92, Seville.
No. 384 was withdrawn because of poor rendition of Arabic word for "postage."

A111

Mosques: 50f, Sheikh Rashid bin Humaid al Nuaimi, Ajman. 1d, Sheikh Ahmed Bin Rashid Al Mualla, Umm Al Quwain.

1992, Mar. 26   Perf. 14x13½

| 385 | A111 | 50f multicolored | .80 | .80 |
| 386 | A111 | 1d multicolored | 1.60 | 1.60 |

See Nos. 417-418.

Week of the Deaf Child — A112

1992, Apr. 20   Perf. 13½x13

| 387 | A112 | 1d shown | 1.75 | 1.75 |
| 388 | A112 | 3d Ear with hearing aid | 4.00 | 4.00 |

Zayed Seaport, 20th Anniv. — A113

1992, June 28   Litho.   Perf. 13½

389	A113	50f Aerial view	.50	.50
390	A113	1d Cargo transport	1.25	1.25
391	A113	175f Ship docked	2.25	2.25
392	A113	2d Map	2.50	2.50
		Nos. 389-392 (4)	6.50	6.50

1992 Summer Olympics, Barcelona A114

1992, July 25   Litho.   Perf. 14x13½

393	A114	50f Yachting	.50	.50
394	A114	1d Running	1.00	1.00
395	A114	175f Swimming	2.00	2.00
396	A114	250f Cycling	2.25	2.25
		Nos. 393-396 (4)	5.75	5.75

Souvenir Sheet

| 396A | A114 | 3d Equestrian | 5.75 | 5.75 |

Children's Paintings A115

1992, Aug. 15   Perf. 13½x14

397	A115	50f Playing soccer	.50	.50
398	A115	1d Playing in field	1.00	1.00
399	A115	2d Playground	2.25	2.25
400	A115	250f Children among trees	3.00	3.00
		Nos. 397-400 (4)	6.75	6.75

Intl. Bank of United Arab Emirates, 15th Anniv. — A116

Design: 175f, Bank emblem.

Litho. & Embossed
1992, Sept. 9   *Perf. 11*
401 A116 50f gold & multi   .75 .75
     Size: 35x41mm
        Perf. 11½
402 A116 175f lake, gold & vio   2.25 2.25

Traditional Musical
Instruments — A116a

No. 402A, Tambourah, vert. No. 402B, Oud,
vert. No. 402C, Rababah, vert. No. 402D,
Mizmar, shindo. No. 402E, Tabel, hibban. No.
402F, Marwas, duff.

1992, Oct. 17   **Litho.**   *Perf. 13½*
402A A116a 50f multicolored   .60 .60
402B A116a 50f multicolored   .60 .60
402C A116a 50f multicolored   1.25 1.25
   g.   Sheet, #402A-402C, perf.
       12¾   3.50 3.50
402D A116a 1d multicolored   2.50 2.50
402E A116a 1d multicolored   2.50 2.50
402F A116a 1d multicolored   2.50 2.50
   h.   Sheet, #402D-402F, perf.
       12¾   7.25 7.25
    Nos. 402A-402F (6)   9.95 9.95

Camels
A117

Designs: 50f, Race. 1d, Used for transportation, vert. 175f, Harnessed for obtaining water
from well. 2d, Roaming free, vert.

1992, Dec. 23   **Litho.**   *Perf. 13½*
403 A117 50f multicolored   .50 .30
404 A117 1d multicolored   1.25 .70
405 A117 175f multicolored   2.50 1.50
406 A117 2d multicolored   2.75 1.50
    Nos. 403-406 (4)   7.00 3.75

A118

1992, Dec. 21
407 A118 50f multicolored   1.25 1.25
408 A118 2d yellow & multi   5.50 5.50
Gulf Cooperation Council, 13th session.

A119

1993, Jan. 28   **Litho.**   *Perf. 13½*
409 A119 2d shown   2.50 2.50
410 A119 250f Building, fishing
       boat   4.25 4.25
Dubai Creek Golf and Yacht Club.

Tourism — A120

1993, Jan. 16
411 A120 50f Golf, horiz.   .75 .75
412 A120 1d Fishing   1.50 1.50
413 A120 2d Boating, horiz.   3.00 3.00
414 A120 250f Motor vehicle
       touring, horiz.   3.75 3.75
    Nos. 411-414 (4)   9.00 9.00

Natl. Youth
Festival — A121

1993, Mar. 27   **Litho.**   *Perf. 14x13½*
415 A121 50f violet & multi   1.00 1.00
416 A121 3d red brown & multi   4.00 4.00

Mosque Type of 1992

50f, Thabit bin Khalid Mosque, Fujeira. 1d,
Sharq al Morabbah Mosque, Al Ain.

1993, Feb. 16   *Perf. 13½*
417 A111 50f multicolored   1.25 1.25
418 A111 1d multicolored   2.50 2.50

Shells
A122

25f, Conus textile. 50f, Pinctada radiata.
100f, Murex scolopax. 150f, Natica pulicaris.
175f, Lambis truncata sebae. 200f, Cardita
bicolor. 250f, Cypraea grayana. 300f, Cymatium trilineatum.

1993, Apr. 3   **Litho.**   *Perf. 13*
419 A122 25f multicolored   .35 .35
420 A122 50f multicolored   .50 .50
421 A122 100f multicolored   1.00 1.00
422 A122 150f multicolored   1.50 1.50
423 A122 175f multicolored   2.25 2.25
424 A122 200f multicolored   2.50 2.50
425 A122 250f multicolored   3.00 3.00
426 A122 300f multicolored   4.00 4.00
    Nos. 419-426 (8)   15.10 15.10

Campaign
Against
Drugs
A123

Design: 1d, Skull, drugs, vert.

1993, Aug. 21   **Litho.**   *Perf. 13½*
427 A123 50f multicolored   1.60 1.60
428 A123 1d multicolored   2.25 2.25

A124

Natl. Bank of Abu Dhabi, 25th Anniv.: 50f,
Abu Dhabi skyline, bank emblem. 1d, Bank

---

emblem. 175f, Bank building, emblem. 2d,
Skyline, emblem, diff.

Litho. & Typo.
1993, Sept. 15   *Perf. 11½*
429 A124 50f silver & multi   .55 .55
430 A124 1d silver & multi   1.10 1.10
431 A124 175f silver & multi   2.50 2.50
432 A124 2d silver & multi   2.75 2.75
    Nos. 429-432 (4)   6.90 6.90

A125

Dubai Ports Authority: 50f, Aerial view of
port. 1d, Loading cargo. 2d, Aerial view, diff.
250f, Globe.

1993, Nov. 10   **Litho.**   *Perf. 13½*
433 A125 50f purple & multi   .60 .60
434 A125 1d green & multi   1.50 1.50
435 A125 2d orange & multi   3.00 3.00
436 A125 250f pink & multi   3.75 3.75
    Nos. 433-436 (4)   8.85 8.85

Natl. Day
A126

Children's paintings: 50f, Soldiers saluting
flag. 1d, Two women sitting, one standing,
flag, vert. 175f, Flag, boat. 2d, Flags atop castle tower.

1993, Dec. 2   **Litho.**   *Perf. 13½*
437 A126 50f multicolored   .60 .60
438 A126 1d multicolored   1.50 1.50
439 A126 175f multicolored   2.75 2.75
440 A126 2d multicolored   3.00 3.00
    Nos. 437-440 (4)   7.85 7.85

Archaeological Discoveries — A127

Designs: 50f, Tomb. 1d, Rectangular artifact. 175f, Animal-shaped artifact. 250f, Bowl.

1993, Dec. 15   *Perf. 14x13½*
441 A127 50f multicolored   .60 .60
442 A127 1d multicolored   1.40 1.40
443 A127 175f multicolored   2.50 2.50
444 A127 250f multicolored   3.25 3.25
    Nos. 441-444 (4)   7.75 7.75

10th
Childrens'
Festival,
Sharjah
A128

Children's paintings: 50f, Children with balloons, flags. 1d, Children playing, three trees.
175f, Child with picture, girls with balloons. 2d,
House, children playing outdoors.

1994, Mar. 19   **Litho.**   *Perf. 13x13½*
445 A128 50f green & multi   .60 .60
446 A128 1d blue & multi   1.50 1.50
447 A128 175f red violet & multi   2.50 2.50
448 A128 2d carmine & multi   2.75 2.75
    Nos. 445-448 (4)   7.35 7.35

Arabian
Horses
A129

50f, Brown horse on hind feet, vert. 1d,
White horse. 175f, Head of brown horse, vert.
250f, Head of white and brown horse.

1994, Jan. 25   *Perf. 13x13½, 13½x13*
449 A129 50f multicolored   .60 .60
450 A129 1d multicolored   1.50 1.50
451 A129 175f multicolored   2.50 2.50
452 A129 250f multicolored   3.25 3.25
    Nos. 449-452 (4)   7.85 7.85

10th
Conference
of Arab
Towns,
Dubai
A130

     Perf. 13x13½, 13½x13
1994, May 15   **Litho.**
453 A130 50f Map, city, vert.   .55 .55
454 A130 1d shown   2.25 2.25

Pilgrimage to
Mecca — A131

1994, Apr. 29   **Litho.**   *Perf. 13x13½*
455 A131 50f shown   .75 .75
456 A131 2d Holy Ka'aba   3.00 3.00

Intl. Year of
the Family
A132

Intl.
Olympic
Committee,
Cent.
A133

Arab Housing
Day — A134

Writers Assoc.,
10th
Anniv. — A135

1994, June 15   *Perf. 13x13½*
457 A132 1d multicolored   1.40 1.40
458 A133 1d multicolored   1.40 1.40

Perf. 13½x13
459 A134 1d multicolored 1.40 1.40
460 A135 1d multicolored 1.40 1.40
Nos. 457-460 (4) 5.60 5.60

Archaeological Finds, Al Qusais, Dubai — A136

Designs: 50f, Lidded pitcher, vert. 1d, Pointed-handle pitcher. 175f, Pitcher, arm-shaped handle. 250f, Short round vase.

1994, Aug. 16   Litho.   Perf. 13½
461 A136 50f multicolored .55 .55
462 A136 1d multicolored 1.30 1.30
463 A136 175f multicolored 2.20 2.20
464 A136 250f multicolored 3.00 3.00
Nos. 461-464 (4) 7.05 7.05

Environmental Protection — A137

Designs: 50f, Arabian leopard. 1d, Gordon's wildcat. 2d, Caracal. 250f, Sand cat.

1994, Oct. 10   Litho.   Perf. 13½
465 A137 50f multicolored .60 .60
466 A137 1d multicolored 1.60 1.60
467 A137 2d multicolored 3.50 3.50
468 A137 250f multicolored 4.25 4.25
Nos. 465-468 (4) 9.95 9.95

12th Arab Gulf Soccer Championships, Abu Dhabi — A138

1994, Nov. 3   Litho.   Perf. 13½
469 A138 50f Ball, emblem, vert. .55 .55
470 A138 3d Soccer players 3.75 3.75

Birds
A139

50f, Merops orientalis. 175f, Halcyon chloris. 2d, Dromas ardeola. 250f, Coracias benghalensis. 3d, Phoenicopterus ruber.

1994, Dec. 12
471 A139 50f multicolored .60 .60
472 A139 175f multicolored 3.25 3.25
473 A139 2d multicolored 3.50 3.50
474 A139 250f multicolored 5.50 5.50
Nos. 471-474 (4) 12.85 12.85

Souvenir Sheet
475 A139 3d multi, vert. 8.00 8.00

Archaeological Finds, Mulaiha, Sharjah — A140

Designs: 50f, Front of carved horse, vert. 175f, Ancient coin, vert. 2d, Inscription on metal, vert. 250f, Inscription on stone.

1995, Jan. 25   Litho.   Perf. 13½
476 A140 50f multicolored .55 .55
477 A140 175f multicolored 2.25 2.25
478 A140 2d multicolored 3.00 3.00
479 A140 250f multicolored 3.25 3.25
Nos. 476-479 (4) 9.05 9.05

Natl. Dances
A141

1995, Feb. 14
480 A141 50f Al-Naashat .50 .50
481 A141 175f Al-Ayaalah 2.10 2.10
482 A141 2d Al-Shahhoh 2.40 2.40
Nos. 480-482 (3) 5.00 5.00

A142

1995, Mar. 19   Litho.   Perf. 13½
483 A142 50f Helicopters .50 .50
484 A142 1d Emblem 1.50 1.50
485 A142 175f Warships, horiz. 2.75 2.75
486 A142 2d Artillery, horiz. 3.25 3.25
Nos. 483-486 (4) 8.00 8.00

Intl. Defense Exhibition & Conf., Abu Dhabi.

A143

1d, Arab League emblem. 2d, FAO emblem. 250f, UN emblem.

1995, Mar. 22
487 A143 1d multicolored 1.25 1.25
488 A143 2d multicolored 2.75 2.75
489 A143 250f multicolored 3.50 3.50
Nos. 487-489 (3) 7.50 7.50

50th Anniv. of Arab League, FAO & UN.

General Post Office Authority, 10th Anniv. — A144

1995, Apr. 1
490 A144 50f multicolored .75 .75

First Gulf Cooperation Council Philatelic Exhibition, Abu Dhabi — A145

1995, Apr. 11   Litho.   Perf. 13½
491 A145 50f multicolored .75 .75

Traditional Games, Ajman Museum — A146

50f, Boy with hoop, stick. 175f, Girl on swing. 2d, Boy, girl playing stick game within marked boundary. 250f, Two girls playing game with stones.

1995, Aug. 28   Litho.   Perf. 13½x13
492 A146 50f multicolored .45 .45
493 A146 175f multicolored 1.90 1.90
494 A146 2d multicolored 2.25 2.25
495 A146 250f multicolored 2.50 2.50
Nos. 492-495 (4) 7.10 7.10

A147

Birds: 50f, Falco naumanni. 175f, Phalacrocorax nigrogularis. 2d, Cursorius cursor. 250f, Upupa epops.

1995, Sept. 25
496 A147 50f multicolored .55 .55
497 A147 175f multicolored 2.10 2.10
498 A147 2d multicolored 2.50 2.50
499 A147 250f multicolored 2.75 2.75
Nos. 496-499 (4) 7.90 7.90

See Nos. 528-532.

A148

Natl. Census: 50f, Stylized family, building. 250f, Mosque, skyscrapers, stylized family.

1995, Nov. 20
500 A148 50f multicolored .50 .50
501 A148 250f multicolored 2.50 2.50

National Day
A149

Children's paintings: 50f, People wearing feathered headdresses, palm trees, building. 175f, Girls with flags, balloons, flowers. 2d, Trees, family in front of house holding balloons, flags. 250f, Groups of children along street watching parade of cars.

1995, Dec. 2   Perf. 13x13½
502 A149 50f multicolored .45 .45
503 A149 175f multicolored 1.25 1.25
504 A149 2d multicolored 1.40 1.40
505 A149 250f multicolored 1.75 1.75
Nos. 502-505 (4) 4.85 4.85

Environmental Protection — A150

50f, Dugong dugon. 2d, Delphinus delphis. 3d, Megaptera novaeangliae.

1996, Jan. 25   Litho.   Perf. 13x13½
506 A150 50f multicolored .50 .50
507 A150 2d multicolored 1.50 1.50
508 A150 3d multicolored 2.25 2.25
a.   Souvenir sheet, #506-508 4.75 4.75
Nos. 506-508 (3) 4.25 4.25

A151

1996, Feb. 27   Perf. 13½
509 A151 50f shown .50 .50
510 A151 3d Building, beach 2.75 2.75

Hobie Cat 16 World Sailing Championships.

A152

Archaelogical Finds, Fujeira Museum: 50f, Two-handled pitcher. 175f, Kettle. 250f, Bracelet. 3d, Metal ornament, horiz.

1996, Apr. 15
511 A152 50f multicolored .50 .50
512 A152 175f multicolored 1.25 1.25
513 A152 250f multicolored 2.25 2.25
514 A152 3d multicolored 2.75 2.75
Nos. 511-514 (4) 6.75 6.75

1996 Summer Olympic Games, Atlanta
A153

Perf. 13½x14, 14x 13½
1996, July 19   Litho.
515 A153 50f Shooting .50 .50
516 A153 1d Cycling, vert. .80 .80
517 A153 250f Running, vert. 2.00 2.00
518 A153 350f Swimming 2.50 2.50
Nos. 515-518 (4) 5.80 5.80

Women's Union, 21st Anniv.
A154

Perf. 14x13½, 13½x14
1996, Aug. 15
519 A154 50f Emblem, vert. .50 .50
520 A154 3d shown 2.75 2.75

A155

1996, Sept. 15   **Perf. 14x13½**
521 A155 1d shown   .75   .75
522 A155 250f Soccer player   2.00 2.00
11th Asian Soccer Cup Championship.

A156

UN Campaign Against Illegal Use of Drugs:
50f, World with snake around it. 3d, Half of
man's face, half of skull, hypodermic needle,
pills.

1996, Oct. 15   **Perf. 13½**
523 A156 50f multicolored   .75   .75
524 A156 3d multicolored   2.75 2.75

Sheikh Saeed Al-Maktoum House,
Cent. — A157

Designs: 250f Sheikh Saeed, close-up view
of house. 350f, Overall view of house.

1996, Nov. 12   **Litho.**   **Perf. 13x13½**
525 A157 50f multicolored   .50   .50
526 A157 250f multicolored   1.75 1.75
527 A157 350f multicolored   2.50 2.50
        Nos. 525-527 (3)   4.75 4.75

Bird Type of 1995

Designs: 50f, Pterocles exustus. 150f, Otus
brucei. 250f, Hypocolus ampelinus. 3d, Irania
gutturalis. 350f, Falco concolor.

1996, Nov. 18   **Perf. 14x13½**
528 A147 50f multicolored   .35   .35
529 A147 150f multicolored   1.25 1.25
530 A147 250f multicolored   2.25 2.25
531 A147 3d multicolored   3.00 3.00
532 A147 350f multicolored   3.25 3.25
        Nos. 528-532 (5)   10.10 10.10

Children's
Paintings
A158

50f, Face. 1d, Boats. 250f, Flowers. 350f,
Woman in long dress, palm tree, tent.

Perf. 14x13½, 13½x14
1996, Nov. 19
533 A158 50f multi, vert.   .35   .35
534 A158 1d multi   .80   .80
535 A158 250f multi, vert.   2.25 2.25
536 A158 350f multi, vert.   2.75 2.75
        Nos. 533-536 (4)   6.15 6.15

Sheik
Zayed bin
Sultan al
Nahayan,
Accession
to the
Throne of
Abu
Dhabi,
30th
Anniv. —
A158a

A159

Sheik and: 50f, 250f, Flowers. 1d, 350f,
Date palm.

1996, Dec. 2   **Photo.**   **Perf. 12**
537 A158a 50f red & multi   .40   .40
538 A158a 1d olive & multi   .65   .65
539 A158a 250f purple & multi   1.60 1.60
540 A158a 350f gray & multi   2.25 2.25
        Nos. 537-540 (4)   4.90 4.90

Photo. & Embossed
Imperf
Size: 90x70mm
541 A159 5d On horseback,
                gazelles   5.00 5.00

Anniversaries
A160

Photo. & Embossed
1996, Dec. 2   **Perf. 12**
542 A160 50f red violet & multi   .30   .30
543 A160 1d silver & multi   1.40 1.40
Sheik Zayed bin Sultan al Nahayan's accession to the throne of Abu Dhabi, 30th anniv.,
Creation of United Arab Emirates, 25th anniv.

Natl. Day, 25th
Anniv. — A161

50f, 150f, Seven rulers of United Arab Emirates. 1d, 3d, Heraldic eagle, national flag. 5d,
Score of Natl. Anthem.

1996, Dec. 2   **Granite Paper**
544 A161 50f green & multi   .70   .70
545 A161 1d multicolored   1.25 1.25
546 A161 150f tan & multi   1.60 1.60
547 A161 3d multicolored   3.25 3.25
        Nos. 544-547 (4)   6.80 6.80

Photo. & Embossed
Imperf
Size: 70x90mm
547A A161 5d multicolored   5.50 5.50

Butterflies
A162

1997, Jan. 28   **Litho.**   **Perf. 14x13½**
548 A162 50f Agrodiaetus
                loewii   .60   .60
549 A162 1d Papilio machaon   1.25 1.25
550 A162 150f Orithya   1.90 1.90
551 A162 250f Chrysippus   3.25 3.25
        Nos. 548-551 (4)   7.00 7.00

Dubai
Shopping
Festival
A163

Perf. 13¼x13¾, 13¾x13¼
1997, Feb. 22   **Litho.**
552 A163 50f shown   .50   .50
553 A163 250f Shopping bag,
                vert.   2.50 2.50

Intl. Defense
Exhibition &
Conference
A164

50f, Helicopter airlifting jeep. 1d, Emblem.
250f, Artillery, emblem. 350f, Ships, emblem.

1997, Mar. 16   **Litho.**   **Perf. 13½**
554 A164 50f multicolored   .50   .50
555 A164 1d multicolored   .85   .85
556 A164 250f multicolored   2.25 2.25
557 A164 350f multicolored   3.25 3.25
        Nos. 554-557 (4)   6.85 6.85

Emirates Bank
Group, 20th
Anniv. — A165

Perf. 13¾x13¼
1997, Mar. 23   **Litho.**
568 A165 50f multi   .55   .55
569 A165 1d buff & multi   1.20 1.20
  a.   Souv. sheet, #568-569, imperf. 6.00 6.00
No. 569a sold for 5d.

Technical
Education and
National
Development
Conference
A166

1997, Apr. 6   **Perf. 13¾x13¼**
570 A166 50f shown   .75   .75
571 A166 250f Emblem   2.75 2.75

Sharjah
Heritage
A167

Designs: 50f, Coins. 3d, Museum.

1997, June 17   **Litho.**   **Perf. 13½**
572 A167 50f multicolored   .75   .75
573 A167 3d multicolored   3.25 3.25

Emirates
Philatelic
Association
A168

Perf. 13¾x13¼, 13¼x13¾
1997, June 24   **Litho.**
574 A168 50f shown   .50   .50
575 A168 250f Stamps, horiz.   2.50 2.50

Children's
Paintings
A169

50f, Cats. 1d, Children playing. 250f, Children, moon, vert. 3d, Abstract.

1997, Sept. 15   **Litho.**   **Perf. 13½**
576 A169 50f multicolored   .55   .55
577 A169 1d multicolored   .95   .95
578 A169 250f multicolored   2.25 2.25
579 A169 3d multicolored   3.00 3.00
        Nos. 576-579 (4)   6.75 6.75

Reunion, by
Sheikha Hassan
Maktoum al
Maktoum — A170

Mindscape, by Sarah Majid al Futtaim
A170a

Blue Musings, by Maha Abdulla Al
Mazroui — A170b

The
Pause,
by
Khulood
Mattar
Rashid
A170c

The Seas I, by Sheikha Sawsan Abdulaziz Al Qasimi — A170d

Still Life, by Sheikha Bodour Sultan Al Qasimi A170e

The Opening, by Tina Ahmed and Others — 170f

1997, Oct. 25   Litho.   *Perf. 13¾*

580	A170	50f multi	.65	.65
581	A170a	50f multi	.65	.65
582	A170b	50f multi	.65	.65
583	A170c	50f multi	.65	.65
584	A170d	50f multi	.65	.65
585	A170e	50f multi	.65	.65
		Nos. 580-585 (6)	3.90	3.90

Imperf

586	A170f	5d multi	7.50	7.50

Intl. Aerospace Exhibition, Dubai A171

Perf. 13½x13¾

1997, Nov. 16   Litho.

587	A171	250f Jet fighter	3.00	3.00
588	A171	3d VTOL airplane	3.75	3.75

26th National Day A172

Sheikh Zayed bin Sultan al Nahayan and: 50f, Gardens. 1d, Trees and mountains. 150f, Water, trees and mountains. 250f, Roadway.

1997, Dec. 2   Litho.   *Perf. 13½x13¾*

589	A172	50f multi	.45	.45
590	A172	1d multi	.75	.75
591	A172	150f multi	1.20	1.20
592	A172	250f multi	1.75	1.75
		Nos. 589-592 (4)	4.15	4.15

3rd Afro-Arab Trade Fair A173

Perf. 13x13¼, 13¼x13

1997, Dec. 6   Litho.

593	A173	150f Emblem, vert.	1.25	1.25
594	A173	350f Handshake	2.75	2.75

Arthropods A174

50f, Blepharopsis mendica. 150f, Galeodes sp. 250f, Crocothemis arythraea. 350f, Xylocopa aestuans.

1998, Feb. 25   Litho.   *Perf. 13¼*

595	A174	50f multicolored	.55	.55
596	A174	150f multicolored	1.50	1.50
597	A174	250f multicolored	2.50	2.50
598	A174	350f multicolored	3.25	3.25
		Nos. 595-598 (4)	7.80	7.80

ISAF World Sailing Championship — A175

Various sailboats.

Perf. 13¼x13, 13x13¼

1998, Mar. 2   Litho.   Litho.

599	A175	50f multi, vert.	.45	.45
600	A175	1d multi	1.25	1.25
601	A175	2d multi	2.10	2.10
602	A175	3d multi, vert.	3.00	3.00
		Nos. 599-602 (4)	6.80	6.80

A176

Triple Intl. Defense Exhibition & Conf., Abu Dhabi: 50f, Combat soldiers in protective gear, horiz. 1d, Emblem over world map, skyline of Abu Dhabi. 150f, Electronic gear. 350f, Missile battery, electronic warfare components.

1998, Mar. 15   Litho.   *Perf. 13½*

603	A176	50f multicolored	.45	.45
604	A176	1d multicolored	1.25	1.25
605	A176	150f multicolored	2.10	2.10
606	A176	350f multicolored	3.00	3.00
		Nos. 603-606 (4)	6.80	6.80

A177

1998, Apr. 20   Litho.   *Perf. 13½*

607	A177	50f shown	.50	.50
608	A177	3d Emblem, monument	3.75	3.75

Sharjah, 1998 Arab cultural capital.

World Environment Day — A178

1998, May 17   Litho.   *Perf. 13½*

609	A178	1d Landscape, oryx	1.75	1.75
610	A178	350f multicolored	3.00	3.00

Henna A179

Various designs painted on hands.

1998, Sept. 9   Litho.   *Perf. 13½*

611	A179	50f multicolored	.60	.60
612	A179	1d multicolored	.90	.90
613	A179	150f multicolored	1.40	1.40
614	A179	2d multicolored	1.75	1.75
615	A179	250f multicolored	2.25	2.25
616	A179	3d multicolored	2.75	2.75
		Nos. 611-616 (6)	9.65	9.65

Art — A180

50f, Fish. 250f, Mosque, palm trees, vert. 350f, Door, jar.

1998, Oct. 20   Litho.   *Perf. 13½*

617	A180	50f multicolored	.50	.50
618	A180	1d shown	.95	.95
619	A180	250f multicolored	2.25	2.25
620	A180	350f multicolored	3.25	3.25
		Nos. 617-620 (4)	6.95	6.95

27th National Day A181

1998, Dec. 2   Litho.   *Perf. 13x13¼*

621	A181	50f Mountain road	.45	.45
622	A181	350f Boat, city skyline	4.25	4.25

Flowers — A182

Designs: 25f, Indigofera arabica. 50f, Centaureum pulchellum. 75f, Lavandula citriodora. 1d, Taverniera glabra. 150f, Convolvulus deserti. 2d, Capparis spinosa. 250f, Rumex vesicrius. 3d, Anagallis arvensis. 350f, Tribulus arabicus. 5d, Reichardia tinitana.

1998, Dec. 8   Litho.   *Perf. 13¼x13¾*

623	A182	25f multicolored	.25	.25
624	A182	50f multicolored	.45	.45
625	A182	75f multicolored	.60	.60
626	A182	1d multicolored	.80	.80
627	A182	150f multicolored	1.25	1.25
628	A182	2d multicolored	1.60	1.60
629	A182	250f multicolored	2.10	2.10
630	A182	3d multicolored	2.50	2.50
631	A182	350f multicolored	2.75	2.75
632	A182	5d multicolored	4.00	4.00
		Nos. 623-632 (10)	16.30	16.30

Arthropods A183

50f, Anthia duodecimguttata. 150f, Daphnis nerii. 250f, Acorypha glaucopsis. 350f, Androctonus crassicauda.

1999, Mar. 15   Litho.   *Perf. 13½x14*

633	A183	50f multicolored	.60	.60
634	A183	150f multicolored	1.40	1.40
635	A183	250f multicolored	2.75	2.75
636	A183	350f multicolored	4.25	4.25
		Nos. 633-636 (4)	9.00	9.00

Intl. Day for Monuments and Sites A184

1999, Apr. 18   Litho.   *Perf. 13x13½*

637	A184	150f shown	1.50	1.50
638	A184	250f Fort	2.75	2.75

UPU, 125th Anniv. — A185

1999   Litho.   *Perf. 13½x13*

639	A185	50f shown	1.00	1.00
640	A185	350f Emblem, "125"	2.75	2.75

Imperf

Size: 90x70mm

641	A185	5d Hemispheres	6.00	6.00

Environmental Protection — A186

Marine life: 50f, Lamprometra klunzingeri. 150f, Pelagia noctiluca. 250f, Hexabranchus sanguineus. 3d, Siphonochalina siphonella.

1999, Nov. 3   Litho.   *Perf. 13½x14*

642	A186	50f multi	.60	.60
643	A186	150f multi	2.00	2.00
644	A186	250f multi	3.25	3.25
645	A186	3d multi	3.75	3.75
		Nos. 642-645 (4)	9.60	9.60

Handicrafts A187

Designs: 50f, Lacemaking. 1d, Embroidery. 250f, Woman with wickerwork. 350f, Finished wickerwork.

1999, Nov. 8   *Perf. 14x13½*

646	A187	50f multi	.60	.60
647	A187	1d multi	1.40	1.40
648	A187	250f multi	3.50	3.50
649	A187	350f multi	5.50	5.50
		Nos. 646-649 (4)	11.00	11.00

14th Pro World
Ten-pin Bowling
Championships
A188

Designs: 50f, Emblem. 250f, Bowler, pins,
Abu Dhabi skyline.

1999, Nov. 16   Litho.   Perf. 14x13½
650-651 A188 Set of 2   3.25 3.25

Children's
Art — A189

Art by: 50f, Nooran Khaleefa. 1d, Khawla Al
Hawal. 150f, Khawla Salem. 250f, Fatimah
Ibrahim.

1999, Dec. 15   Perf. 13x13½
652-655 A189 Set of 4   5.75 5.75

Millennium
A190

Falcon and "2000" in: 50f, Gray and silver.
250f, Blue and gold.

1999, Dec. 22   Perf. 13½x13
656-657 A190 Set of 2   2.75 2.75

Dubai Ports
and
Customs,
Cent.
A191

50f, Old building. 3d, Modern building.

2000, Jan. 26   Perf. 13x13½
658-659 A191 Set of 2   3.75 3.75

Intl.
Desertification
Conference,
Dubai — A192

2000, Feb. 12   Perf. 13½x13
660 A192 250f multi   2.50 2.50

Environmental Protection — A193

Designs: 50f, Palm trees, Al Gheel. 250f,
Aggah Beach.

2000, Feb. 29   Litho.   Perf. 13x13½
661 A193 50f multi   .50 .50
662 A193 250f multi   2.25 2.25

2000
Summer
Olympics,
Sydney
A194

Emblem and: 50f, Swimmer. 2d, Runner.
350f, Shooter.

2000, Sept. 16   Litho.   Perf. 13x13½
663-665 A194 Set of 3   4.25 4.25

Dubai Intl. Holy
Koran
Award — A195

50f, Medal on ribbon of flags. 250f, Sheikh
Zayed bin Sultan al Nahayan and UAE flag.

2000, Sept. 23   Perf. 13½x13
666-667 A195 Set of 2   4.25 4.25

World
Meteorological
Organization,
50th
Anniv. — A196

Designs: 50f, Barometer and modern map.
250f, Gauge's pointer and old map.

2000
668-669 A196 Set of 2   4.25 4.25

Expansion
of Dubai
Intl. Airport
A197

Denominations: 50f, 350f.

2000, Nov. 4   Litho.   Perf. 13x13½
670-671 A197 Set of 2   5.75 5.75

Development and
Environment
A198

Designs: 50f, Smile. 250f, Flower. 3d, Heart
as leaf. 350f, Heart as globe.

2001, Mar. 20   Litho.   Perf. 13¼x13
672-675 A198 Set of 4   10.00 10.00

Dubai
Millennium,
Winner of
2000 Dubai
World Cup
A199

Designs: 3d, Horse's head. 350f, Horse at
track.

2001, Mar. 24   Perf. 13x13¼
676-677 A199 Set of 2   9.50 9.50

Sultan Bin Ali Al
Owais (1925-
2000),
Poet — A200

Designs: 50f, Calligraphy. 1d, Portrait.

2001, Apr. 30   Perf. 13¼x13
678-679 A200 Set of 2   3.75 3.75

Arab Bank for
Investment and
Foreign Trade,
25th
Anniv. — A201

Designs: 50f, Emblem. 1d, Emblem, diff.

2001, July 7   Litho.   Perf. 13¼x13
680-681 A201 Set of 2   2.75 2.75

7th GCC Postage
Stamp Exhibition,
Dubai — A202

2001, July 10
682 A202 50f multi   1.75 1.75

Traditional
Boats
A203

Designs: 50f, Shahoof. 250f, Bagarah. 3d,
Sam'aa. 350f, Jalboot.

2001, Aug. 25   Perf. 14x13¼
683-686 A203 Set of 4   10.00 10.00

Year of Dialogue
Among
Civilizations
A204

Designs: 50f, Emblem. 250f, Branch with
multicolored leaves.

2001, Oct. 9   Perf. 13¼x13
687-688 A204 Set of 2   3.75 3.75

Emirates
Post
A205

Falcons and inscription: 50f, Changing.
250f, Growing. 3d, Achieving.

2001, Sept. 15   Perf. 13x13¼
689-691 A205 Set of 3   7.50 7.50

Children's
Art — A206

Designs: 1d, Mosque. 250f, Boatbuilding.
3d, Man pouring coffee, vert. 350f, Falconry.

Perf. 14x13¼, 13¼x14
2001, Nov. 12   Litho.
692-695 A206 Set of 4   10.50 10.50

Unification of
Armed Forces,
25th
Anniv. — A207

2001, Dec. 30   Perf. 13¼x13
696 A207 1d multi   2.75 2.75

Intl. Water
Resources and
Management
Conference,
Dubai — A208

2002, Feb. 2
697 A208 50f multi   2.00 2.00

UAE University,
25th
Anniv. — A209

Background colors: 50f, Blue. 1d, Red.

2002, Mar. 25   Perf. 13¼x14
698-699 A209 Set of 2   2.75 2.75

Arabian
Saluki
A210

Various salukis: 50f, 150f, 250f, 3d.

2002, Apr. 29   Litho.   Perf. 13½x13¼
700-703 A210 Set of 4   14.00 14.00

Emirates Post, 1st
Anniv. — A211

"1" and: 50f, Ring of text. 3d, Emblem.

2002, May 29   **Perf. 13¼x13**
704 A211 50f blue   2.00 2.00

Souvenir Sheet
Perf. 14¼
705 A211 3d multi   11.50 11.50
No. 705 contains one 45x35mm stamp.

Rashid Bin Salim Al-Suwaidi Al-Khadhar (1905-80), Poet A212

Designs: 50f, Text. 250f, Portrait.

2002, July 17 Litho.   Perf. 13½x13¼
706-707 A212 Set of 2   6.50 6.50

Children's Creativity A213

Designs: 50f, Antelope and boat, by Amna al-Bloushi. 1d, Children, by Fahd al-Habsi. 2d, Earth holding flower, by Hana Mohammed. 250f, Fish, by Hatem al-Dhaheri. 3d, Child holding Earth, by Abdulla Ridha. 350f, Stick figures, by Yousef al-Sind. 5d, Emblem of Latifa Bint Mohammed Award for Childhood Creativity (29x39mm).

Perf. 13x13¼, 13¼x13 (5d)
2002, Oct. 9
708-714 A213 Set of 7   17.50 17.50

Sheikh Hamdan Bin Rashid Al-Maktoum Award for Medical Sciences A214

Designs: 50f, Award, emblem, sand dunes. 250f, Caduceus, map.

2002, Oct. 21   **Perf. 13x13¼**
715-716 A214 Set of 2   4.75 4.75

31st National Day — A215

Landmarks in the Emirates: Nos. 717, 724a, 50f, Ajman. Nos. 718, 724b, 50f, Sharjah. Nos. 719, 724c, 50f, Dubai. Nos. 720, 724d, 50f, Abu Dhabi. Nos. 721, 724e, 50f, Ras al Khaima. Nos. 722, 724f, Fujeira. Nos. 723, 724g, Umm al Qiwain.

2002, Dec. 2 Litho.   Perf. 13¼x14
717-723 A215 Set of 7   7.50 7.50
Souvenir Sheet
Litho. & Embossed
Imperf
724   Sheet of 7   7.50 7.50
a.-g.   A215 50f Any single   1.00 1.00
No. 724 sold for 5d.

Thuraya Satellite Communications A216

Denominations: 25f, 250f.

2002   **Litho.**   **Perf. 14**
725-726 A216   Set of 2   2.75 2.75
Issued: 25f, 1/27; 250f, 1/6.

Falcon Type of 1990
2003-04   Litho.   Perf. 11½
Granite Paper
726A A85 125f multi   .90 .90
Size: 21x26mm
Perf. 11½x11¾
726B A85 225f multi   1.50 1.50
726C A85 275f multi   2.00 2.00
726D A85 325f multi   2.75 2.75
726E A85 375f multi   1.90 1.90
726F A85 4d multi   2.25 2.25
726G A85 6d multi   3.00 3.00
Nos. 726A-726G (7)   14.30 14.30
Issued: 125f, 2/23; 225f, 11/24/04; 275f, 325f, 375f, 4/13; 4d, 6d, 9/16.

Items in Al Ain National Museum A217

Designs: 50f, Jar from Hili tombs. 275f, Pottery from Umm an-Nar tombs. 4d, Bronze axe. 6d, Soapstone vessel.

2003, Feb. 25   **Perf. 14x13½**
727-730 A217   Set of 4   11.50 11.50

National Bank of Dubai, 40th Anniv. A218

Panel color: 50f, Blue. 4d, Orange. 6d, Red.

2003, Apr. 15 Litho.   Perf. 14x13¼
731-733 A218 Set of 3   10.50 10.50

Miniature Sheet

Wildlife — A218a

No. 733A: b, Arabian leopard. c, Blanford's fox. d, Caracal. e, Cheetah. f, Gordon's wild cat. g, Striped hyena. h, Jackal. i, White-tailed mongoose. j, Ruppell's fox. k, Sand cat. l, Small spotted genet. m, Arabian wolf.

2003, June 10   Litho.   Perf. 14½
733A A218a 50f Sheet of 12, #b-m   8.00 8.00

Coins A219

Designs: 50f, Dirham of Caliph Al Walid bin Abdul Malik. 125f, Arab Sasanian Dirham of Caliph Abdul Malik Bin Marwan. 275f, Dinar of Al Mustansir Billah Al Fatimi. 375f, Dinar of Caliph Abdul Malik bin Marwan.
5d, Dirham of Caliph Muhammed Al Ameen to mark election of Mousa Al Natiq Bilhaq.

2003, July 20 Litho.   Perf. 13¼x13¾
734-737 A219 Set of 4   7.50 7.50
Size: 106x73mm
Imperf
738 A219 5d multi   20.00 20.00

Sheikh Zayed bin Sultan al Nahayan, 37th Anniv. of Accession as Ruler of Abu Dhabi A220

Sheikh Zayed and: 50f, Camel and sand dune. 175f, Modern buildings.

2003, Aug. 6   Litho.   Perf. 13
739-740 A220 Set of 2   2.75 2.75

World Youth Soccer Championships, United Arab Emirates — A221

2003, Sept. 7   **Perf. 13x13¼**
741 A221 375f multi   3.75 3.75

World Bank Boards of Governors Annual Meetings, Dubai — A222

Emblem and: 50f, Emirates Tower. 175f, Falcon. 275f, Mosque domes, horiz. 375f, Dhow. 5d, English and Arabic text.

Perf. 13¼x13, 13x13¼
2003, Sept. 23   **Litho.**
742-745 A222   Set of 4   8.50 8.50
Imperf
Size: 118x74mm
746 A222 5d multi   6.75 6.75

Peace A223

Dove and: 50f, Zakharafs. 225f, Door and wind tower. 275f, Columns. 325f, Water taxi.

2003, Oct. 1   **Perf. 13x13¼**
747-750 A223 Set of 4   9.50 9.50

Traditional Housing A224

Designs: 50f, Palm frond house. 175f, Mud house. 275f, Stone house. 325f, Tent.

2003, Oct. 20   **Perf. 13½x14**
751-754 A224 Set of 4   10.00 10.00

Falcons — A225

Designs: 50f, Peregrine falcon. 125f, Hybrid gyr-peregrine falcon. 275f, Gyrfalcon. 375f, Saker falcon.

2003, Nov. 17   **Perf. 13¼x14**
755-758 A225 Set of 4   5.75 5.75

Poetry of Saeed Bin Ateej Al Hamli (1875-1919) A226

Poetry: 125f, Four short lines. 175f, Four long lines.

2003, Dec. 29   **Perf. 13x13¼**
759-760 A226 Set of 2   3.25 3.25

Mohammed Bin Saeed Bin Ghubash (1899-1969), Religious Scholar — A227

Designs: 50f, Portrait. 175f, Books.

2004, Apr. 5   Litho.   Perf. 13¼x14
761-762 A227 Set of 2   3.25 3.25

Fourth Family Meeting — A228

Color of hands: 375f, Orange. 4d, Purple.

2004, Apr. 19
763-764 A228   Set of 2   5.25 5.25

FIFA (Fédération Internationale de Football Association), Cent. — A229

2004, May 21 Litho.   Perf. 13x13¼
765 A229 375f multi   2.75 2.75

Handicrafts by Special Needs Persons — A230

Designs: 50f, Handcrafted vase. 125f, Painting. 275f, Framed branch. 5d, Pottery artwork.

2004, June 29   Perf. 13¼x13
766-769 A230   Set of 4   5.25 5.25

2004 Summer Olympics, Athens A231

Olympic rings and: 50f, Track athlete. 125f, Rifle shooter. 275f, Swimmer. 375f, 2004 Athens Olympics emblem, torch bearer.

2004, Aug. 13 Litho.   Perf. 13x13¼
770-773 A231   Set of 4   4.50 4.50

Endangered or Extinct Persian Gulf Marine Life — A232

Designs: 50f, Black finless porpoise. 175f, Serranidae. 275f, Whale shark. 375f, Dugongidae.

2004, Sept. 26   Perf. 14
774-777 A232   Set of 4   4.75 4.75
777a   Booklet pane, 2 each #774-
         777   9.50   —
         Complete booklet, #777a   9.50

Operation Emirates Solidarity for Mine Clearance in South Lebanon — A233

Flags and: 275f, Person clearing mines. 375f, Map, people clearing mines, horiz.

2004, Oct. 25   Perf. 13x12¾, 12¾x13
778-779 A233   Set of 2   3.50 3.50

Sheik Dr. Sultan bin Mohammed al-Qassimi, Ruler of Sharjah — A234

Color of denomination: 50f, Orange brown. 125f, Green. 275f, Red brown. 4d, Blue.

2004, Nov. 30   Perf. 13½x14
780-783 A234   Set of 4   4.75 4.75

Traditional Women's Clothing — A235

Designs: 50f, Drawers. 125f, Robe. 175f, Gown. 225f, Jalabia. 275f, Scarf. 375f, Yashmak.

2004, Dec. 29 Litho.   Perf. 14
784-789 A235   Set of 6   6.75 6.75
789a   Booklet pane, #784-789   6.75 6.75
         Complete booklet, #789a   6.75

Dubai Aluminum, 25th Anniv. A236

Designs: 50f, Smelting complex. 275f, Smelting complex, sheikhs (brown background). 375f, Like 275f, blue background.

2005, Jan. 8   Perf. 13
790-792 A236   Set of 3   4.00 4.00

10th Dubai Shopping Festival — A237

Designs: 50f, Emblem. 125f, Emblem, diff. 275f, Emblem and "10," green background. 375f, Emblem and "10," red background.

2005, Jan. 12   Perf. 13¼x13
793-796 A237   Set of 4   4.50 4.50

2nd Intl. Gathering of Scouting and Belonging, Sharjah — A238

Designs: 50f, Emblem. 375f, Scouts and truck.

2005, Apr. 1   Litho.   Perf. 13¼x14
797-798 A238   Set of 2   2.40 2.40

Shaikha Fatima Bint Mubarak, Women's Rights Activist — A239

2005, Apr. 10   Perf. 14½
799 A239 50f multi   .30   .30

Al Majedi Bin Dhaher, 17th Century Poet A240

Poetry and: 50f, Sand. 175f, Bricks.

2005, May 30 Litho.   Perf. 14½
800-801 A240   Set of 2   1.25 1.25

Reptiles A241

Designs: 50f, Agama. 125f, Desert monitor. 225f, Sand lizard. 275f, Dune sand gecko. 375f, Spiny-tailed lizard. 5d, Sand skink.

2005, Aug. 2   Perf. 13¾
802-807 A241   Set of 6   8.50 8.50
807a   Booklet pane, #802-807   8.50   —
         Complete booklet, #807a   8.50

Accession of Sheik Khalifa Bin Zayed Al Nahyan, 1st Anniv. — A242

Sheik Khalifa: 50f, With a child. 175f, With another sheik. 275f, With another sheik, diff. 375f, Kissing sheik.

2005, Nov. 3   Litho.   Perf. 14x13¼
808-811 A242   Set of 4   4.75 4.75
811a   Sheet of 4, #808-811   5.50 5.50

No. 811a sold for 10d.

2005 Census — A243

Emblem at: 50f, Bottom. 375f, Left, horiz.

Perf. 13¼x13, 13x13¼
2005, Nov. 10
812-813 A243   Set of 2   2.40 2.40

Desert Plants A244

Designs: 50f, Leptadenia pyrotechnica. 125f, Lycium shawii. 225f, Calotropis procera. 275f, Prosopis cineraria. 325f, Zizyphus spina-christi. 375f, Acacia tortilis.

2005, Nov. 27 Litho.   Perf. 13½
814-819 A244   Set of 6   7.50 7.50
819a   Booklet pane, #814-819   7.50
         Complete booklet, #819a   7.50

34th National Day — A245

Children's art: 50f, Flower in Arabic script, by Shaimaa Mohammed Al Halabi. 125f, Ring of children, by Muaz Jamal Ahmed Hassan, horiz. 275f, Hands, by Pithani Crinidhi. 375f, Doves, flag and plants, by Lina Abu Baker Mukhtar, horiz.

2005, Dec. 2   Perf. 14¼
820-823 A245   Set of 4   4.50 4.50

Pearl Diving Tools A246

Designs: 50f, F'ttam (nose clip). 125f, Al Khabet (finger protectors). 175f, Al Dayeen (basket). 275f, Sea rock (diver's weight). 375f, Diver's outfit.

2005, Dec. 21   Perf. 14
824-828 A246   Set of 5   5.50 5.50

A souvenir sheet containing Nos. 824-828 with pearl halves affixed to each stamp sold for 100d.

Gulf Cooperation Council Day for Autistic Children — A247

2006, Apr. 4   Litho.   Perf. 13
829 A247 4d multi   2.25 2.25

Souvenir Sheet

Hamad Bin Khalifa Abu Shehab (1932-2002), Poet — A248

No. 830: a, 1d, Head. b, 2d, Hands, poetry in Arabic text.

2006, Apr. 26   *Perf. 14¼*
830   A248   Sheet of 2, #a-b   1.75 1.75

A249

Gulf Cooperation Council, 25th Anniv. — A250

Litho. with Foil Application
2006, May 25   *Perf. 14*
831   A249   1d multi   .55 .55
Imperf
    Size: 165x105mm
832   A250   5d multi   2.75 2.75
   See Bahrain Nos. 628-629, Kuwait Nos. 1646-1647, Oman Nos. 477-478, Qatar Nos. 1007-1008, and Saudi Arabia No. 1378.

Dubai Police, 50th Anniv. — A251

2006, June 1   *Perf. 13¼x13*
833   A251   1d multi   .55 .55

19th Asian Stamp Exhibition, Dubai A252

Designs: 1d, shown. 4d, Four towers.

Litho. With Foil Application
2006, June 24   *Perf. 13¾*
834-835   A252   Set of 2   2.75 2.75

Dubai Intl. Holy Koran Award, 10th Anniv. A253

2006, July 24   **Litho.**   *Perf. 14x13½*
836   A253   1d multi   .55 .55

Al Raha Beach Developments — A254

Designs: 1d, Khor Al Raha. 2d, Al Lissaily. 350f, Al Wateed (40x40mm). 4d, Al Bandar (40x40mm).

2006, Sept. 18   **Litho.**   *Perf. 13*
837-840   A254   Set of 4   5.75 5.75

UPU Strategy Conference, Dubai — A255

Designs: 1d, Green arrows. 4d, Blue and green arrows.

Litho. & Embossed
2006, Sept. 27   *Perf. 14x13½*
841-842   A255   Set of 2   2.75 2.75

12th Gulf Cooperation Council Postage Stamp Exhibition A256

2006, Nov. 13   **Litho.**   *Perf. 13¼x13*
843   A256   1d multi   .55 .55

35th National Day — A257

2006, Dec. 1
844   A257   1d multi   .55 .55
   A souvenir sheet containing one stamp sold for 10d.

Sheikh Mohammed bin Rashid al Maktoum, Prime Minister — A258

Sheikh Mohammed: 1d, Wearing kaffiyeh. 4d, Wearing polo helmet (44x53mm).

Litho. With 3-Dimensional Plastic Affixed
2006, Dec. 2   *Serpentine Die Cut 9*
    Self-Adhesive
845-846   A258   Set of 2   2.75 2.75

Gazelles A259

Designs: 1d, Tahr. 2d, Sand gazelle. 3d, Mountain gazelle. 350f, Arabian oryx.

2006, Nov. 29   **Litho.**   *Perf. 14*
847-850   A259   Set of 4   5.25 5.25
850a   Souvenir sheet, #847-850   5.25 5.25

Intl. Volunteers Day A260

Man giving items to: 2d, Two children. 4d, Three children.

2006, Dec. 5   *Perf. 13x13¼*
851-852   A260   Set of 2   3.25 3.25

Women's Jewelry A261

Designs: 1d, Mariya um alnairat. 150f, Mortasha. 2d, Shaghab bu shouk. 3d, Shahid ring. 350f, Bushuq. 4d, Tassah.

2006, Dec. 31   *Perf. 13x13¼*
853-858   A261   Set of 6   8.25 8.25
858a   Booklet pane, #853-858   8.25 —
     Complete booklet, #858a   8.25

Falcon — A262

2007, Jan. 31   *Perf. 13¼x13*
    Background Color
859   A262   1d buff   .55 .55
860   A262   150f gray   .85 .85
861   A262   2d lilac   1.10 1.10
862   A262   3d yellow   1.60 1.60
863   A262   350f yel green   1.90 1.90
864   A262   4d pink   2.25 2.25
865   A262   5d blue vio   2.75 2.75
    Nos. 859-865 (7)   11.00 11.00
    Booklet Stamps
    Self-Adhesive
   Serpentine Die Cut 12½
    Background Color
865A   A262   1d buff   .55 .55
865B   A262   150f gray   .85 .85
865C   A262   2d lilac   1.10 1.10
865D   A262   3d yellow   1.60 1.60
865E   A262   350f yel green   1.90 1.90
865F   A262   4d pink   2.25 2.25
865G   A262   5d blue vio   2.75 2.75
   h.   Booklet pane, #865A-865G   11.00
     Complete booklet, #865Gh   11.00
    Nos. 865A-865G (7)   11.00 11.00
   See Nos. 937, 959-965, 1043A, 1043D, 1081-1085.

Dubai Tennis Championships A263

Background colors: 1d, Orange. 3d, Red violet.

2007, Feb. 19   *Perf. 14*
866-867   A263   Set of 2   2.25 2.25

18th Arabian Gulf Soccer Cup Championships, Abu Dhabi — A264

Arabian Gulf Cup with frame in: 1d, Red. 3d, Green.

2007, May 9   **Litho.**   *Perf. 14x13¾*
868-869   A264   Set of 2   2.25 2.25
869a   Souvenir sheet, #868-869   5.50 5.50
   No. 869a sold for 10d.

Etisalat (Telecommunications Company), 30th Anniv. — A265

Denomination color: 1d, Blue. 3d, Orange red. 350f, Purple. 4d, Red.

2007, May 17   *Perf. 13x13¼*
870-873   A265   Set of 4   6.25 6.25
   Each stamp has a die cut opening.

Souvenir Sheet

World Blood Donor Day — A266

No. 874 — World Blood Donor Day emblem and: a, 1d, Heart. b, 3d, Blood drop.

2007, June 14		Perf. 13	
874	A266 Sheet of 2, #a-b	2.25	2.25

Sheikh Ahmed Mohamed Hasher Al Maktoum, UAE's First Olympic Gold Medalist — A267

2007, July 17		Perf. 14x13½	
875	A267 3d multi	1.75	1.75

A268

Emirates Bank, 30th Anniv. A269

Perf. 14x13¾ (A268), 14 (A269)

2007, Aug. 28			
876	A268 1d blue & multi	.55	.55
877	A209 150f blue & multi	.85	.85
878	A268 3d brn & multi	1.75	1.75
879	A269 350f brn & multi	1.90	1.90
a.	Souvenir sheet, #876-879	8.25	8.25
	Nos. 876-879 (4)	5.05	5.05

No. 879a sold for 15d.

Emirates Banks Association, 25th Anniv. — A270

2007, Oct. 4		Perf. 13¾	
880	A270 1d red & bis brn	.55	.55

Abu Dhabi Islamic Bank, 10th Anniv. — A271

Differing backgrounds with denominations of: 1d, 150f, 2d, 3d.

2007, Nov. 8	Litho.	Perf. 14¼	
881-884	A271 Set of 4	4.25	4.25
884a	Souvenir sheet, #881-884	4.25	4.25

Abu Dhabi Police, 50th Anniv. — A272

Litho. With Foil Application

2007, Nov. 14		Perf. 13¼x14	
885	A272 1d multi	.55	.55

Children's Art — A273

Designs: Nos. 886, 892, Woman and two men in prayer. Nos. 887, 893, Woman presenting gift to another woman, vert. Nos. 888, 894, Children facing mosque. Nos. 889, 895, Hands holding child giving item to woman, vert. Nos. 890, 896, Child helping man across street. Nos. 891, 897, Child helping handicapped person, vert.

2007, Nov. 29	Litho.	Perf. 14	
886	A273 1d multi	.55	.55
887	A273 150f multi	.85	.85
888	A273 2d multi	1.10	1.10
889	A273 3d multi	1.75	1.75
890	A273 350f multi	1.90	1.90
891	A273 4d multi	2.25	2.25
	Nos. 886-891 (6)	8.40	8.40

Booklet Stamps
Self-Adhesive
Die Cut Perf. 11¼x12, 12x11¼

892	A273 1d multi	.55	.55
893	A273 150f multi	.85	.85
894	A273 2d multi	1.10	1.10
895	A273 3d multi	1.75	1.75
896	A273 350f multi	1.90	1.90
897	A273 4d multi	2.25	2.25
a.	Complete booklet, #892-897	8.50	
	Nos. 892-897 (6)	8.40	8.40

Complete booklet is stapled in center with one stamp per page and with the center leaf of the booklet having stamps on both sides.

Souvenir Sheet

Sheikh Mohammed Al Khazraji (1919-2006), Chief Justice — A274

No. 898: a, 1d, Facing right. b, 3d, Facing forward.

2007, Dec. 9		Perf. 13½x13¾	
898	A274 Sheet of 2, #a-b	2.25	2.25

Al Abbas Group, 40th Anniv. A275

Denominations: 1d, 150f, 2d, 3d.

2007, Dec. 16		Perf. 14¼	
899-902	A275 Set of 4	4.25	4.25

Al Rostamani Group, 50th Anniv. A276

Background colors: 1d, Gray. 150f, Prussian blue.

2007, Dec. 23		Perf. 13x13¼	
903-904	A276 Set of 2	1.40	1.40

Union Properties, 20th Anniv. A277

Designs: 1d, Emblem. 150f, F1 Theme Park, Dubai, horiz. 2d, Uptown. 3d, Green community, horiz.

Perf. 13¼x13½, 13½x13¼

2007, Dec. 27			
905-908	A277 Set of 4	4.25	4.25
908a	Souvenir sheet, #905-908	8.50	8.50

No. 908a sold for 15d.

Federal National Council, 36th Anniv. A278

2008, Feb. 12		Perf. 13¼	
909	A278 1d multi	.55	.55

National Bank of Abu Dhabi, 40th Anniv. A279

"40" and: 1d, Yellow panel at top. 150f, Yellow panel at top. 225d, White panel at top. 4d, White panel at top.

2008, Feb. 13		Perf. 13	
910-913	A279 Set of 4	4.75	4.75
913a	Souvenir sheet, #910-913	8.25	8.25

No. 913a sold for 15d.

Municipality and Planning Department of Ajman — A280

Emblems of: 1d, Municipality and Planning Department. 150f, Ajman Urban Planning Conference. 2d, E-services. 4d, Geographic Information Systems.

2008, Mar. 24	Litho.	Perf. 13¼	
914-917	A280 Set of 4	4.75	4.75
917a	Souvenir sheet, #914-917, perf. 13¼x14¼	8.25	8.25

No. 917a sold for 15d.

Souvenir Sheet

Hamdan Bin Rashid Al Maktoum Award for Distinguished Academic Performance — A281

No. 918: a, 1d, Emblem and "10." b, 2d, Rashid Al Maktoum, emblem.

2008, Apr. 1		Perf. 13¼	
918	A281 Sheet of 2, #a-b	1.75	1.75

Traditional Souqs — A282

Marketplaces: 1d, Spice Souq, Dubai. 150f, Al Area Souq, Sharjah. 2d, Gold Souq, Dubai. 3d, Old Souq, Abu Dhabi.

Litho. & Embossed

2008, Apr. 20		Perf. 13½x13¼	
919-922	A282 Set of 4	4.25	4.25

Drydocks World, 25th Anniv. — A283

Designs: 1d, Shown. 4d, Emblem, dhow, horiz.

Perf. 13¼x13, 13x13¼

2008, June 4		Litho.	
923-924	A283 Set of 2	2.75	2.75

Sharjah Intl. Airport, 75th
Anniv. — A284

2008, July 7   *Perf. 13½*
925   A284   1d multi   .55   .55

2008
Summer
Olympics,
Beijing
A285

Emblem of Beijing Olympics, emblems of
five sports and: 1d, Yellow orange background.
4d, Olympic torch, vert. 475f Olympic torch,
diff., vert. 550f, Red violet background.
10d, Olympic torch, vignettes of Nos. 926-929.

2008, Aug. 4   *Perf. 14x13¼, 13¼x14*
926-929   A285   Set of 4   8.50   8.50
          Size: 120x120mm
             Imperf
930   A285   10d multi   5.50   5.50

Gulf News, 30th Anniv. — A286

Background color: 1d, Blue. 150f, Maroon.
225f, Orange.

2008, Sept. 30   *Perf. 13½x13¼*
         Granite Paper
931-933   A286   Set of 3   2.60   2.60
  A souvenir sheet containing Nos. 931-933
sold for 15d.

       Souvenir Sheet

Arab Postal Day — A287

No. 934 — Emblem and: a, 1d, World map,
pigeon. b, 225f, Camel caravan.

   Litho. & Silkscreened With Foil
           Application
2008, Oct. 10
934   A287   Sheet of 2, #a-b   1.75   1.75

       Miniature Sheets

Date Varieties — A288

  No. 935: a, Abuman. b, Jash Hamad. c,
Msalli.
  No. 936, vert.: a, Farth. b, Mirzaban. c,
Abukibal. d, Salani.

2008, Oct. 22   Litho.   *Perf. 13x13¼*
935   A288   1d Sheet of 3, #a-c   1.75   1.75
           Perf. 13¼x13
936   A288   1d Sheet of 4, #a-d   2.25   2.25

  Falcon Type of 2007 Inscribed
          "Priority"
     Litho. & Embossed
2008, Dec. 2   *Perf. 13¼x14*
      Background Color
937   A262   2d vermilion   1.10   1.10

Center for Documentaion and
Research, 40th Anniv. — A289

  Designs: 1d, Building. 4d, Sheikhs and
crowd of people. 10d, Sheikhs, vert.

2008, Dec. 2   Litho.   *Perf. 14¼*
939   A289   1d multi   .55   .55
940   A289   4d multi   2.25   2.25
       Miniature Sheet
  Litho With 3-Dimensional Plastic
          Affixed
       Self-Adhesive
    Serpentine Die Cut 9
941   A289   10d multi   5.50   5.50

Eid Al
Adha — A290

  Designs: 1d, Al Eidiya. 3d, Eid prayers.
   Litho. With Foil Application
2008, Dec. 6   *Perf. 13¾*
942-943   A290   Set of 2   2.25   2.25
  943a   Souvenir sheet, #942-943   3.25   3.25
   No. 943a sold for 6d.

Sheikh Hamdan Bin
Rashid Al Maktoum
Award for Medical
Science, 10th
Anniv. — A291

  Designs: 1d, Award. 2d, Special Recognition Award. 3d, Sheikh Hamdan Bin Rashid Al
Maktoum, award. 4d, 10th anniversary
emblem.

2008, Dec. 15   Litho.   *Perf. 13¼*
944-947   A291   Set of 4   5.50   5.50
  947a   Souvenir sheet, #944-947   8.25   8.25
   No. 947a sold for 15d.

Dubai Duty Free, 25th Anniv. — A292

  Designs: 1d, 25th anniversary emblem in
gray. 2d, 25th anniversary emblem in red. 3d,
Dubai Duty Free shop. 4d, Shop, diff.

2008, Dec. 20   Litho.   *Perf. 13¼x13*
948-951   A292   Set of 4   5.50   5.50
  951a   Souvenir sheet, #948-951   5.50   5.50

Universal
Declaration of
Human Rights,
60th
Anniv. — A293

  Color of top panel: 1d, Red brown. 4d,
Orange and yellow.

      Perf. 13¾x13½
2008, Dec. 31   Litho.
952-953   A293   Set of 2   2.75   2.75
  953a   Souvenir sheet, #952-953   3.25   3.25
   No. 953a sold for 6d.

Second Arab
Stamp Exhibition,
Dubai — A294

    Serpentine Die Cut 12½
2009, Mar. 5   **Litho. & Embossed**
      Self-Adhesive
  Printed on Clear Plastic Film
954   A294   1d multi   .55   .55
   No. 954 has white backing paper.

Emirates
Center for
Strategic
Studies and
Research
(ECSSR),
15th Anniv.
A295

  Designs: 1d, Books published by ECSSR.
150f, UAE Federation Library. 2d, Media monitoring room. 4d, ECSSR Building.

2009, Mar. 26   Litho.   *Perf. 13¼*
       Granite Paper
955-958   A295   Set of 4   4.75   4.75
  958a   Souvenir sheet, #955-958   5.50   5.50
   No. 958a sold for 10d.

   Falcon Type of 2007 Redrawn
2009, Apr. 2   Litho.   *Perf. 13¼x13*
      Background Color
959   A262   25f black   .25   .25
960   A262   1d dark buff   .55   .55
961   A262   150f brownish gray   .80   .80
962   A262   2d gray lilac   1.10   1.10
963   A262   10d orange   5.50   5.50
964   A262   20d lt greenish blue   11.00   11.00
965   A262   50d dark green   27.50   27.50
   Nos. 959-965 (7)   46.70   46.70

  Nos. 959-965 are dated 2009 and lack the
buff curved line to the left of the Arabic country
name found on Nos. 859-865. Denominations
for Nos. 960 and 962 use "AED" rather than
the "Dh." or "Dhs." used on Nos. 859 and 861.

Rashid Bin Tannaf (1910-99),
Poet — A296

  Rashid Bin Tannaf: 1d, Wearing kaffiyeh.
4d, Without kaffiyeh.

2009, Apr. 30   *Perf. 13¼*
       Granite Paper
966-967   A296   Set of 2   2.75   2.75
  A souvenir sheet containing Nos. 966-967
sold for 15d.

Discovery
of Umm An
Nar
Culture,
50th Anniv.
A297

  Umm An Nar tomb with background color of:
1d, Red brown. 150f, Brown. 4d, Olive green.

2009, June 28   *Perf. 13x13¼*
968-970   A297   Set of 3   3.75   3.75

Jerusalem,
Capital of Arab
Culture — A298

2009, Aug. 3   *Perf. 13¼x13*
971   A298   2d multi   1.10   1.10

Postal Services in the Emirates,
Cent. — A299

  Covers bearing: 1d, Pakistan Nos. 1, 2, 5
and 12. 150f, Trucial States No. 4, Oman Nos.
21 and 52. 4f, United Arab Emirates No. 3,
Dubai Nos. 80 and 83, and Sharjah stamp. 5d,
Withdrawn United Arab Emirates National Day
stamp of 1977.
10d, Various India stamps.

2009, Aug. 19   *Perf. 13¼*
       Granite Paper
972-975   A299   Set of 4   6.25   6.25
       Souvenir Sheet
976   A299   10d multi   5.50   5.50

38th National Day
A300

2009, Dec. 2 | **Perf. 13**
977 A300 1d multi | .55 | .55

FIFA 2009 Club World Cup Soccer Championships, Abu Dhabi — A301

Designs: 1d, Shown. 10d, Similar to 1d, with United Arab Emirates flag at right.

2009, Dec. 19 | **Perf. 13¾**
978 A301 1d multi | .55 | .55

Souvenir Sheet
Perf. 13
979 A301 10d multi | 5.50 | 5.50

No. 979 contains one 40x40mm stamp.

Securities and Commodities Authority, 10th Anniv. — A302

Emblem and: 1d, Numerals and squares. 2d, Text on computer screen, graphs. 3d, Emirates Securities Market trading board. 5d, Falcon and numerals.

2010, Feb. 1 | **Perf. 13**
Granite Paper
980-983 A302 Set of 4 | 6.00 | 6.00

A souvenir sheet containing No. 983 sold for 15d.

Emirates Aluminum, 3rd Anniv. A303

Designs: 1d, Emblem. 2d, Hand holding frame with picture of smelting complex. 3d, Falcon, horse. 5d, United Arab Emirates flag.

2010, Feb. 24 | **Perf. 13x14¼**
984-987 A303 Set of 4 | 6.00 | 6.00
987a | Souvenir sheet, #984-987, perf. 14¼ | 8.25 | 8.25

No. 987a sold for 15d.

United Arab Emirates Pavilion, Expo 2010, Shanghai A304

Pavilion: 1d, In daylight. 550f, At dusk.

Litho. With Foil Application
2010, May 13 | **Perf. 13¼x13**
988-989 A304 Set of 2 | 3.75 | 3.75

Diplomatic Relations Between United Arab Emirates and Republic of Korea, 30th Anniv. — A305

No. 990: a, 1d, Flag of United Arab Emirates and air-conditioning tower. b, 550f, Flag of South Korea and Mt. Amisan Chimney, Gyeongbokgung Palace.

2010, June 17 | **Litho.** | **Perf. 13x13¼**
990 A305 Horiz. pair, #a-b | 3.75 | 3.75

See South Korea No. 2337.

Jebel Ali Free Zone, 25th Anniv. — A306

Designs: 1d, Zone in 1986. 2d, Zone in 1997. 3d, Zone in 2009. 4d, 25th anniversary emblem.

2010, June 30 | **Perf. 13¼x13½**
991-994 A306 Set of 4 | 5.50 | 5.50
994a | Sheet of 4, #991-994, perf. 14¼x13½ | 8.25 | 8.25

No. 994a sold for 15d.

Souvenir Sheet

2010 Youth Olympics, Singapore — A307

2010, Aug. 19 | **Perf. 13¾**
995 A307 475f multi | 2.60 | 2.60

Sheikh Zayed Grand Mosque — A308

Designs: 1d, Mosque. 5d, Mosque, horiz. 25d, Mosque, diff., horiz.

Perf. 13½x13¼, 13¼x13½
2010, Aug. 29 | **Litho.**
996-997 A308 Set of 2 | 3.25 | 3.25

Litho. & Embossed With Foil Application
Imperf
Size:145x110mm
998 A308 25d gold & multi | 14.00 | 14.00

Old Schools — A309

Designs: 1d, Al Nehyania School, Abu Dhabi. 150f, Al Ahmadiya School, Dubai. 4d, Al Eslah School, Sharjah.

Perf. 13½x13¾
2010, Sept. 19 | **Litho.**
999-1001 A309 Set of 3 | 3.75 | 3.75

A souvenir sheet containing Nos. 999-1001 sold for 15d.

Organization of the Petroleum Exporting Countries, 50th Anniv. — A310

2010, Sept. 27 | **Perf. 13**
1002 A310 1d multi | .55 | .55

World Post Day A311

Designs: 1d, Dove holding envelope. 550f, Universal Postal Union emblem.

2010, Oct. 9 | **Perf. 13¼x13**
1003-1004 A311 Set of 2 | 3.75 | 3.75

Miniature Sheet

Sea Birds — A312

No. 1005: a, 1d, Black-headed gull. b, 150f, Crab plover. c, 2d, Gray heron ardea. d, 3d, Sooty gull. e, 450f, Socotra cormorant. f, 550f, Caspian gull.

2010, Nov. 4 | **Litho.** | **Perf. 13**
Granite Paper
1005 A312 Sheet of 6, #a-f, + label | 9.50 | 9.50

DP World Marine Terminal Operators A313

DP World emblem and various port scenes: 1d, 2d, 3d, 4d.

2010, Nov. 9 | **Perf. 14¼x13¾**
Granite Paper
1006-1009 A313 Set of 4 | 5.50 | 5.50
1009a | Sheet of 4, #1006-1009 | 8.25 | 8.25

No. 1009a sold for 15d.

Yas Marina Racing Circuit, Abu Dhabi — A314

Designs: 1d, Race car on track. 550f, Grandstands.

2010, Nov. 14 | **Perf. 13¼x13**
1010-1011 A314 Set of 2 | 3.75 | 3.75

Watani (National Identity) A315

Designs: 1d, Four stylized fingerprints. 150f, Map of United Arab Emirates composed of fingerprints, vert.

2010, Dec. 2 | **Perf. 13x13½, 13½x13**
1012-1013 A315 Set of 2 | 1.40 | 1.40

39th National Day — A316

Nos. 1014 and 1015 — Winning designs in children's stamp design contest: a, Four automobiles, people waving flags and signs. b, Children with flags around grills. c, Flag of United Arab Emirates, tower. d, Four people, flags, towers. e, Children with balloons. f, Flag and "December 2."

2010, Dec. 2 | **Perf. 13**
1014 A316 1d Sheet of 6, #a-f | 3.25 | 3.25

Stamp Size: 35x26mm
Self-Adhesive
Serpentine Die Cut 12¾
1015 A316 1d Booklet pane of 12, 2 each #a-f | 6.50 | 6.50

Ghaf Tree — A317

2011, Mar. 31   **Perf. 13¼**
1016 A317 1d green   .55 .55

A souvenir sheet containing No. 1016 and a 4d stamp with a ghaf tree seed and a plastic netting affixed to it sold for 40d.

17th Gulf Cooperation Council Postage Stamp Exhibition, Abu Dhabi — A318

2011, Apr. 4   **Perf. 13**
1017 A318 150f multi   .85 .85

Miniature Sheet

31st Session of the Gulf Cooperation Council Supreme Council, Abu Dhabi — A319

No. 1018 — Various buildings and: a, King Abdullah, flag of Saudi Arabia. b, Sheikh Khalifa, flag of United Arab Emirates. c, Sheikh Sabah, flag of Kuwait. d, King Hamad, flag of Bahrain. e, Sheikh Hamad, flag of Qatar. f, Sultan Qaboos, flag of Oman.

2011, Apr. 5   **Perf. 13½x13¾**
1018 A319 150f Sheet of 6, #a-f   5.00 5.00

Fifth Gulf Federation for Cancer Control Conference, Sharjah — A320

2011, May 31   **Litho.**   **Perf. 14x13½**
      Granite Paper
1019 A320 1d multi   .55 .55

Emblem of Sheikha Fatima Bint Mubarak A321

Litho. With Foil Application
2011, July 24   **Perf. 13**
1020 A321 1d multi   .55 .55

Al Bidyah Mosque, Fujeira — A322

Designs: 1d, Archway. 150f, Mosque exterior.
15d, Mosque exerior, wall carving.

2011, Aug. 27   **Litho.**   **Perf. 14x14¼**
1021 A322 1d multi   .55 .55
1022 A322 150f multi   .85 .85

Litho. & Embossed
Imperf
      Size: 130x80mm
1023 A322 15d multi   8.25 8.25

No. 1023 contains one 40x40mm perforated label.

Fauna of Bu Tinah Island — A323

Designs: No. 1024, 1d, Dugong (35x35mm). No. 1025, 1d, One fish (35x35mm). No. 1026, 1d, Three fish (35x35mm). No. 1027, 1d, Crab (35x35mm). No. 1028, 1d, Bird (35x35mm). No. 1029, 1d, Coral (35x35mm). No. 1030, 1d, Coral (48x30mm). No. 1031, 1d, Dolphin (48x30mm). No. 1032, 1d, Flamingos (48x30mm). No. 1033, 1d, Sea turtle (48x30mm).
15d, Sea turtle, dugong, dolphins, coral, crab, birds.

Perf. 13¼, 13¼x13½ (#1030-1033)
2011, Nov. 30   **Litho.**
1024-1033 A323 Set of 10   5.50 5.50
      Size: 120x70mm
Imperf
1034 A323 15d multi   8.25 8.25

40th National Day — A324

2011, Dec. 2   **Perf. 13½x13¾**
      Granite Paper
1035 A324 1d multi   .55 .55

Winter Plants — A325

Designs: No. 1036, 1d, Bladder dock. No. 1037, 1d, Cart-track plant. No. 1038, 1d, Arta. No. 1039, 1d, Hawa. No. 1040, 150f, Rohida tree. No. 1041, 150f, Puncturevine.

2011, Dec. 26   **Perf. 14x13**
1036-1041 A325 Set of 6   4.00 4.00

Camels — A326

Designs: 1d, Four camels. 4d, One camel.

2011, Dec. 29   **Perf. 13¾**
1042-1043 A326 Set of 2   2.75 2.75

A souvenir sheet containing one each of Nos. 1042-1043 sold for 15d.

Falcon Type of 2007 Redrawn With Area Inside Falcon Shaded
2011   **Litho.**   **Perf. 13¼x13**
      Background Color
      Dated "2011"

1043A A262 1d yel ochre   —
1043D A262 5d dull ultra   —

Denominations on Nos. 1043A and 1043D use "AED" instead of "Dh." or "Dhs."
Two additional stamps were issued in this set. The editors would like to examine any examples.

Sultan Bin Ali Al Owais Cultural Foundation, 25th Anniv. — A327

Designs: 1d, Sultan and "25." 15d, Sultan and "25," diff.

Perf. 13¾x13½
2012, Mar. 14   **Litho.**
1044 A327 1d multi   .55 .55

Litho. With Foil Application
      Size: 100x120mm
Imperf
1045 A327 15d multi + label   8.25 8.25

22nd Al Gaffal 60-Foot Traditional Dhow Sailing Race — A328

No. 1046: a, 1d, View of dhow from air. b, 5d, View of dhow from surface of water.
15d, Various dhows.

2012, May 26   **Litho.**   **Perf. 13¼x13½**
1046 A328   Horiz. pair, #a-b   3.25 3.25
      Size: 185x85mm
Imperf
1047 A328 15d multi + 5 labels   8.25 8.25

First Shipment of Crude Oil, 50th Anniv. — A329

Designs: 1d, Abu Dhabi Marine Operating Company Building. 150f, Offshore oil rig and birds. 3d, Oil platforms and dolphins, horiz. 4d, Oil tanker and tanks, horiz.
15d, Emblem of Abu Dhabi Marine Operating Company, vignettes of Nos. 1048-1051.

Litho. With Foil Application
   Perf. 13¼x13½, 13½x13¼
2012, July 4
1048-1051 A329 Set of 4   5.25 5.25
      Size: 120x95mm
Imperf
1052 A329 15d multi + 5 labels   8.25 8.25

Liwa Date Festival — A330

Designs: 1d, Bowl of dates, palm frond. 5d, Dates, palm frond.
15d, Dates, trees, rug, horiz.

2012, July 17   **Perf. 14**
1053-1054 A330 Set of 2   3.25 3.25
      Size: 120x80mm
Imperf
1055 A330 15d multi   8.25 8.25

Arab Post Day A331

Perf. 13½x13¼
2012, Aug. 15   **Litho.**
1056 A331 225f multi   1.25 1.25

World Energy Forum 2012, Dubai A332

Emblems of World Energy Forum and Supreme Council of Energy and: 1d, "E=WEF." 2d, Building in Dubai. 3d, Solar energy collector. 4d, Sheikhs Khalifa Bin Zayed Al Nahyan and Mohammed bin Rashid al Maktoum.

2012, Oct. 22   **Perf. 14**
1057-1060 A332 Set of 4   5.50 5.50
1060a   Souvenir sheet of 4, #1057-1060   8.25 8.25

No. 1060a sold for 15d.

Snakes A333

No. 1061: a, Arabian horned viper. b, Carpet viper. c, Arabian rearfang. d, Sochurek's saw-scaled viper. e, Sand boa.
25d, Snakes depicted on Nos. 1061a-1061e.

2012, Nov. 1   **Perf. 14x13½**
1061   Vert. strip of 5   8.50 8.50
  a. A333 1d multi   .55 .55
  b. A333 150f multi   .85 .85
  c. A333 3d multi   1.75 1.75
  d. A333 4d multi   2.25 2.25
  e. A333 550f multi   3.00 3.00
      Size: 130x100mm
Imperf
1062 A333 25d multi + 5 perf.   14x13½ labels   14.00 14.00

A334

41st National Day — A335

Ruler and scene from: No. 1064, 4d, Abu Dhabi. No. 1065, 4d, Ajman. No. 1066, 4d, Dubai. No. 1067, 4d, Fujeira. No. 1068, 4d, Ras al Khaima. No. 1069, 4d, Sharjah. No. 1070, 4d, Umm al Qiwain.

Litho. & Embossed With Foil Application

2012, Nov. 29				Perf. 14¼
1063	A334	1d multi		.55 .55
Imperf				
1064-1070	A335	Set of 7		15.50 15.50

Al Ahmadiya School, Dubai, Cent. — A336

No. 1071: a, School room, sheikh and student. b, School building.
6d, Sheikh, various pictures of school.

2012, Dec. 12		Litho.	Perf. 13¼
1071		Horiz. pair	1.40 1.40
a.	A336	1d multi	.55 .55
b.	A336	150f multi	.85 .85

Size: 144x94mm

Litho. With Foil Application
Imperf

1072	A336	6d multi		3.25 3.25

United Arab Emirates Soccer Team, Champions of 21st Gulf Cup Tournament — A337

Designs: 2d, Team. 6d, Gulf Cup, vert.

2013, Feb. 10		Litho.	Perf. 13¼
1073	A337	2d multi	1.10 1.10

Souvenir Sheet
Perf. 13¼x12¾

1074	A337	6d multi		3.25 3.25

No. 1074 contains one 30x50mm stamp.

Mother's Day — A338

Litho. With Foil Application

2013, Mar. 21			Perf. 13
1075	A338	3d red vio & gold	1.75 1.75

Postal Services in Abu Dhabi, 50th Anniv. — A339

50th anniv. emblem and: 1d, Abu Dhabi #26, 80 on covers. 150f, Abu Dhabi #62 on cover, block of Abu Dhabi #10. 3d, Abu Dhabi #42 on cover, block of Abu Dhabi #14. 4d, Abu Dhabi #39, 46 on cover, Abu Dhabi #80, pair of Abu Dhabi #18.
10d, Photographs of various post offices in Abu Dhabi from 1963, 1968, 1975 and 1993, various stamps.

2013, Mar. 30		Litho.	Perf. 14xx13¼
1076-1079	A339	Set of 4	5.25 5.25

Imperf

Size: 100x100mm

1080	A339	10d multi		5.50 5.50

No. 1080 contains four labels showing the various post offices.

Falcon Type of 2007 Redrawn With Area Inside Falcon Shaded

2013, Apr. 7			Perf. 14

Dated "2013"
Background Color

1081	A262	1d yellowish buff	.55 .55
1082	A262	150f grayish sepia	.80 .80
1083	A262	3d dull yellow	1.75 1.75
1084	A262	5d violet blue	2.75 2.75
1085	A262	6d white	3.25 3.25
		Nos. 1081-1085 (5)	9.10 9.10

Denominations on Nos. 1081, 1083-1084 use "AED" instead of "Dh." or "Dhs." used on Nos. 859, 862 and 865. Background colors and color of shading within falcon differ on Nos. 860, 961 and 1082.

Yahsat, Communications Satellite of United Arab Emirates — A340

2013, May 13			Perf. 14
1086	A340	4d multi	2.25 2.25

Fazza Heritage Championships — A341

Designs: 1d, Diver in free diving competition. 150f, Yola (traditional dance) competition.

2013, July 28		Litho.	Perf. 13½
1087-1088	A341	Set of 2	1.40 1.40

Oryxes — A342

Designs: 1d, Oryxes standing and on ground. 150f, Oryxes battling. 3d, Four oryxes running.
15d, Oryxes.

2013, Aug. 26		Litho.	Perf. 13
1089-1091	A342	Set of 3	3.00 3.00

Size: 180x100mm
Imperf

1092	A342	15d multi + 3 labels		8.25 8.25

Abu Dhabi International Triathlon — A343

2013, Oct. 31		Litho.	Perf. 12¾x13¼
1093	A343	3d multi	1.75 1.75

Qasr al-Hosn, Oldest Stone Building in Abu Dhabi — A344

Designs: 1d, Aerial view, desert in background. 150f, Man in doorway (40x30mm). 2d, Gate. 3d, Aerial view, skyscrapers in background (40x30mm).
8d, Colorized aerial view denoting additions to building.

Perf. 12¾x13¼, 14 (150f, 3d)
Litho. With Foil Application

2013, Nov. 25		Set of 4	4.25 4.25
1094-1097	A344		

Size: 131x81mm
Imperf

1098	A344	8d multi		4.50 4.50

10th Dubai International Film Festival — A345

No. 1099 — Horse's head and: a, Top of "1" in "10." b, Top of "0" in "10." c, Bottom of "1" in "10." d, Bottom of "0" in "10."

Litho. With Foil Application

2013, Dec. 3			Perf. 13¼x13¾
1099	A345	3d Block of 4, #a-d	6.50 6.50

Emirates National Bank of Dubai, 50th Anniv. A346

Designs: 1d, Orange and white arcs from bank's emblem. 2d, Bank's emblem and 50th anniv. ribbon. 3d, 50th anniv. ribbon. 4d, Arabic text in circle.

2013, Dec. 18		Litho.	Perf. 13
1100-1103	A346	Set of 4	5.50 5.50
1103a		Souvenir sheet of 4, #1100-1103	5.50 5.50

Coffee Tools A347

Designs: 1d, Al Tawa and Al Mehmas (roasting pan and mixer). 150f, Al Menhaz and Al Rashad (mortar and pestle). 3d, Al Dallah (coffee pot). 4d, Al Fenjan (coffee cup).
10d. Man roasting coffee beans, labels without denominations, similar to Nos.1104-1107.

2013, Dec. 24		Litho.	Perf. 13x13¼
1104-1107	A347	Set of 4	5.25 5.25

Souvenir Sheet
Imperf

1108	A347	10d multi + 4 labels		5.50 5.50

Parts of the design of No. 1108 have a scratch-and-sniff sandalwood scent.

Jumeirah Islamic Archaeological Site — A348

Designs: 1d, Walls and pillars. 150f, Walls.

2013, Dec. 30		Litho.	Perf. 14x14¼
1109-1110	A348	Set of 2	1.40 1.40

Emirates Center for Strategic Studies and Research, 20th Anniv. A349

Building, stylized globe emblem and background color of: 1d, Gray. 150f, Purple. 2d, Green. 4d, Brown.
10d, Stylized globe emblem and labels without denominations similar to Nos. 1111-1114.

2014, Jan. 2		Litho.	Perf. 13
1111-1114	A349	Set of 4	4.75 4.75

Souvenir Sheet
Imperf

1115	A349	10d multi + 4 labels		5.50 5.50

Souvenir Sheet

Crown Prince Hamdan, Sixth Anniv. of Accession — A350

Litho. With Foil Application

2014, Feb. 1			Perf. 14½
1116	A350	3d multi	1.75 1.75

Sharjah, 2014
Islamic Cultural
Capital — A351

2014, Apr. 15   Litho.   Perf. 14
1117   A351 3d multi   1.75 1.75

Miniature Sheet

Union Supreme Court, 40th
Anniv. — A352

No. 1118 — Anniversary emblem and background color of: a, Red. b, Green. c, White. d,
Blue.

2014, May 8   Litho.   Perf. 13¼x13½
1118   A352 1d Sheet of 9, 3
                #1118a, 2 each
                #1118b-1118d   5.00 5.00

Zayed
Humanitarian
Day — A353

2014, July 17   Litho.   Perf. 14¼
1119   A353 1d multi   .55 .55

Expo 2020, Dubai — A354

No. 1120: a, Denomination at left. b,
Denomination at right.
10d, Emblem and perforated labels without
denominations similar to Nos. 1120a-1120b.

2014, Sept. 30   Litho.   Perf. 13x13½
1120   A354 3d Horiz. pair, #a-b   3.25 3.25

Size: 160x90mm
Imperf
1121   A354 10d multi + 2 labels   5.50 5.50

Flag Day — A355

Litho. With Foil Application
2014, Nov. 3   Perf. 14
1122   A355 3d multi   1.75 1.75

43rd
National
Day
A356

Litho. & Embossed
2014, Dec. 2   Perf. 14¼
1123   A356 1d multi   .55 .55

History of Civil Aviation in
Dubai — A357

Designs: 1d, Airplane, Sheikh Sa'id bin
Maktum, 1937 agreement to build airport. 3d,
Airport, Sheikh Rashid, text of 1966 decree
creating Department of Civil Aviation. 5d,
Sheikh Mohammed, airplanes and airport.

2014, Dec. 7   Litho.   Perf. 13¼
1124-1126 A357 Set of 3   5.00 5.00

Miniature Sheets

First United Arab Emirates
Currency — A358

No. 1127 — Obverse and reverse of 1973
coins: a, 1-dirham coin depicting pitcher. b,
50-fils coin depicting oil derricks. c, 25-fils
coin depicting gazelle. d, 10-fils coin depicting
dhow. e, 5-fils coin depicting fish. f, 1-fils coin
depicting date palms.
No. 1128 — Fronts and backs of banknotes:
a, 1973 1-dirham note. b, 1973 50-dirham
note. c, 1973 5-dirham note. d, 1973 100-
dirham note. e, 1973 10-dirham note. f, 1976
1000-dirham note.

Litho. & Embossed
2014, Dec. 25   Serpentine Die Cut
                         Self-Adhesive
1127   A358   Sheet of 6   4.25
a.-c.   1d Any single   .55 .55
d.-f.   150f Any single   .85 .85

Litho. & Embossed With Foil
Application
Serpentine Die Cut 13
1128   A358   Sheet of 6   10.50
a.-b.   2d Either single   1.10 1.10
c.-d.   3d Either single   1.75 1.75
e.-f.   4d Either single   2.25 2.25

History of Civil Aviation in Abu
Dhabi — A359

Abu Dhabi Intl. Airport: 1d, Control tower
and airplane in flight. 150f, Interior of terminal.

2014, Dec. 31   Litho.   Perf. 13¼
1129-1130 A359 Set of 2   1.40 1.40

Sharjah, Arab
Tourism
Capital
A360

2015, Mar. 3   Litho.   Perf. 14¼
1131   A360 3d multi   1.75 1.75

A souvenir sheet containing one perf.
13¼x13½ example of No. 1131 sold for 10d.

Oil Production Anniversaries — A361

2015, Apr. 2   Litho.   Perf. 13¼x13½
1132   A361 3d multi   1.75 1.75

First crude oil shipment, 50th anniv.; con-
cession agreement, 75th anniv.

Women's
Museum
A362

No. 1133 — Various photographs of women
with bottom inscription of: a, Women's contri-
bution to economic activity in the 60's. b,
Women's education in UAE in the 70's. c, 1st
batch of female students, 1953-1954. d, Al
Riwah folklore dance. e, The 1st women
museum in the Arab world - Dubai.

Litho. With Foil Application
2015, June 17   Perf. 14¼
1133   Horiz. strip of 5   8.75 8.75
a.-e.   A362 3d Any single   1.75 1.75

Strategic Projects — A363

No. 1134: a, Masdar City. b, Etihad Rail. c,
Khalifa Port. d, Shams I Solar Power Plant.

2015, July 30   Litho.   Perf. 14¼
1134   A363 1d Block of 4, #a-d   2.25 2.25

Enactment
of National
Service
Law
A364

2015, Sept. 17   Litho.   Perf. 13x13½
1135   A364 1d multi   .55 .55

Stylized
Blind Man
A365

2015, Oct. 15   Litho.   Perf. 13x13½
1136   A365 3d black   1.75 1.75
International White Cane Day. No. 1136
was printed in sheets of 2.

Diplomatic Relations Between United
Arab Emirates and
Kazakhstan — A366

No. 1137: a, Sheikh Khalifa, flag of United
Arab Emirates. b, Pres. Nursultan
Nazarbayev, flag of Kazakhstan.

2015, Oct. 28   Litho.   Perf. 14
1137   A366 3d Horiz. pair, #a-b   3.25 3.25
See Kazakhstan No. 758.

QR
Code — A367

2015, Nov. 22   Litho.   Perf. 14¼
1138   A367 3d multi   1.75 1.75

Commemoration
Day — A368

Designs: 3d, Soldiers and flag. 10d,
Soldiers, woman carrying flag, airplanes, skyline and people, horiz.

Litho. With Foil Application
2015, Nov. 30   Perf. 14
1139   A368 3d multi   1.75 1.75

Size: 142x92mm
Imperf
1140   A368 10d multi + label   5.50 5.50

44th National
Day — A369

Litho. With Foil Application
2015, Dec. 2   Perf. 14
1141   A369 1d multi   .55 .55

Automobile and Touring Club of the United Arab Emirates, 50th Anniv. A370

Designs: 1d, Club headquarters. 3d, 50th anniversary emblem.
15d, Car, motorcycle and rider, club headquarters, 50th anniversary emblem.

2015, Dec. 12   Litho.   Perf. 14
1142-1143 A370   Set of 2   2.25 2.25
Souvenir Sheet
Litho. With Foil Application
Imperf
1144 A370 15d multi + 2 labels   8.25 8.25

Dubai Chamber of Commerce, 50th Anniv. — A371

Various depictions of Dubai Chamber of Commerce Building.

Litho. With Foil Application
2015, Dec. 31   Perf. 13¼x13
1145   Horiz. strip of 4   5.50 5.50
a.   A371 1d multi   .55 .55
b.   A371 2d multi   1.10 1.10
c.   A371 3d multi   1.60 1.60
d.   A371 4d multi   2.25 2.25
Souvenir Sheet
Imperf
1146 A371 10d multi + 4 labels   5.50 5.50

Burj Khalifa, 6th Anniv. — A372

2016, Jan. 24   Litho.   Perf. 14¼
1147 A372 3d multi   1.75 1.75

Khalifa International Award for Date Palm and Agricultural Innovation — A373

Perf. 12¾x13¼
2016, Mar. 15   Litho.
1148 A373 3d multi   1.75 1.75

Dubai Tour Bicycle Race A374

Designs: Nos. 1149a, 1151, 1d, Cyclists racing past buildings. Nos. 1149b, 1150, 1d, Boy waving at cyclists.

2016, June 8   Litho.   Perf. 13x13½
1149 A374 1d Vert. pair, #a-b   1.10 1.10
Booklet Stamps
Self-Adhesive
Serpentine Die Cut 8¾x9
1150 A374 1d multi   .55 .55
1151 A374 1d multi   .55 .55
a.   Booklet pane of 8, 4 each #1150-1151   4.50

Arab Postal Day — A375

No. 1152 — Letters circling globe, with background color of: a, 1d, Blue. b, 2d, Green.

Litho. & Silk-Screened
2016, Aug. 21   Perf. 12¾x13½
1152 A375   Horiz. pair, #a-b   1.75 1.75

Al Jahili Fort, Venue of 2016 Aga Khan Award for Architecture Ceremonies A376

Litho. With Foil Application
2016, Nov. 6   Perf. 14
1153 A376 3d gold & multi   1.75 1.75

Pearl of the U.A.E., World's Oldest Natural Pearl A377

Designs: 3d, Pearl in oyster. 10d, Pearl in oyster, horiz.

Litho. & Silk-Screened
2016, Nov. 15   Perf. 14
1154 A377   3d gold & multi   1.75 1.75
Size: 140x90mm
Imperf
1155 A377 10d multi + label   5.50 5.50

45th National Day — A378

Litho. With Foil Application
2016, Dec. 2   Perf. 14
1156 A378 1d gold & multi   .55 .55

A379

Etihad Museum, Dubai A380

2016, Dec. 2   Litho.   Perf. 13¼x13½
1157 A379 3d multi   1.75 1.75
Foil Application on Clear Plastic
Self-Adhesive
Serpentine Die Cut 11
1158 A380 3d gold   1.75 1.75

Government of Abu Dhabi, 50th Anniv. A381

Perf. 13½x13¼
2016, Dec. 20   Litho.
1159 A381 3d brown ochre   1.75 1.75

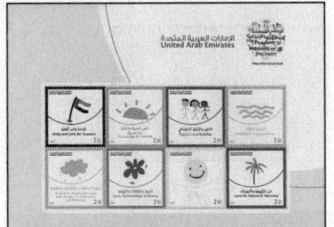

National Program for Happiness and Positivity — A382

No. 1160: a, Flag of United Arab Emirates. b, Sun. c, Three stick-figure people. d, Water. e, Rain cloud. f, Flower g, Happy face. h, Palm tree.
15d, Program emblem, flag, sun, stick-figure people, water, rain cloud, flower, happy face, and palm tree.

Perf. 13, 13x13x14x13 (#1160e-1160h)
2017, Mar. 20   Litho.
1160 A382   2d Sheet of 8, #a-h   8.75 8.75
Souvenir Sheet
Imperf
1161 A382 15d multi + label   8.25 8.25

Hope Probe Mars Mission of United Arab Emirates Space Agency A383

2017, Aug. 16   Litho.   Perf. 14¼
1162 A383 3d multi   1.75 1.75

A384

Year of Giving A385

Serpentine Die Cut12½x12¼
2017, Sept. 5   Litho.
Self-Adhesive
1163 A384 3d multi   1.75 1.75
Serpentine Die Cut 10¾x9½
1164 A385 3d multi   1.75 1.75
Nos. 1164-1165 were printed together on sheets containing 3 of each stamp.

Intl. Year of Sustainable Tourism for Development — A386

Designs: No. 1165, 3d, Burj Khalifa, Dubai. No. 1166, 3d, Al Noor Island, Sharjah. No. 1167, 3d, Fujairah Fort, Fujairah. No. 1168, 3d, Ajman Museum, Ajman. No. 1169, 3d, Al Shohadaa (Martyrs' Memorial) Umm al Qiwain. No. 1170, 3d, Emirates Palace, Abu Dhabi. No. 1171, 3d, Al Jazirah al Hamra ruins, Ras al Khaima.

2017, Nov. 14   Litho.   Perf. 14
1165-1171 A386   Set of 7   11.50 11.50

Abu Dhabi Police, 60th Anniv. — A387

No. 1172: a, Police emblem with eagle. b, 60th anniversary emblem.
15d, Police emblem and non-denominated labels similar to Nos. 1172a-1172b.

Litho. With Foil Application
2017, Nov. 21   Perf. 13
1172 A387   3d Horiz. pair, #a-b   3.25 3.25
Size: 141x91mm
Imperf
1173 A387 15d multi + 2 labels   8.25 8.25

46th National Day — A389

Litho. & Embossed
2017, Dec. 2   Perf. 14
1175 A389 3d multi   1.75 1.75

Dubai Police Emblem — A390

Column 1 (UAE)

No. 1176 — Colors: a, Green and mint green. b, Green and myrtle green.

2018, Jan. 14   Litho.   Perf. 13

1176   A390   3d Horiz. pair, #a-b   3.25   3.25

A souvenir sheet containing No. 1176b sold for 15d.

Abu Dhabi Tour Bicycle Race — A391

Litho. With Foil Application

2018, Feb. 21   Perf. 13

1177   A391   3d multi   1.75   1.75

International Telecommunication Union Plenipotentiaries Conference, Dubai — A395

2018, Oct. 29   Litho.   Perf. 13

1181   A395   3d multi   1.75   1.75

Arab Reading Challenge — A396

No. 1182 — Star medal and: a, Prime Minister Mohammed bin Rashid Al Maktoum. b, Books and lock.

Litho. & Embossed

2018, Oct. 30   Perf. 13x13¼

1182   A396   3d Pair, #a-b   3.25   3.25

47th National Day — A397

2018, Dec. 2   Litho.   Perf. 13¼x13

1183   A397   3d multi   1.75   1.75

Sheikh Zayed bin Sultan Al Nahyan (1918-2004), First President of United Arab Emirates — A398

Designs: 3d, Sheikh Zayed. 100d, Sheikh Zayed at Founder's Memorial, Abu Dhabi.

2018, Dec. 26   Litho.   Perf. 13x13¼

1184   A398   3d multi   1.75   1.75

Size: 178x128mm

Imperf

1185   A398   100d multi   55.00   55.00

UPPER SENEGAL & NIGER

ˈə-pər ˌse-nə-ˈgäl and ˈnī-jər

LOCATION — In Northwest Africa, north of French Guinea and Ivory Coast

GOVT. — A former French Colony

AREA — 617,600 sq. mi.

POP. — 2,474,142

CAPITAL — Bamako

In 1921 the name of this colony was changed to French Sudan and postage stamps so inscribed were placed in use.

100 Centimes = 1 Franc

Gen. Louis Faidherbe — A1

Oil Palms — A2

Dr. N. Eugène Ballay — A3

Perf. 14x13½

1906-07   Unwmk.   Typo.
Name of Colony in Red or Blue

1	A1	1c slate	1.40	1.75
2	A1	2c brown	1.75	2.10
b.		Imperf., pair	120.00	
3	A1	4c brn, *gray bl*	2.50	2.50
4	A1	5c green	5.50	2.75
b.		Imperf., pair	600.00	
5	A1	10c car (B)	6.25	2.75
b.		Imperf., pair	150.00	
6	A1	15c vio ('07)	4.25	5.00
7	A2	20c black & red, *azure*	5.50	5.50
a.		Imperf., pair	150.00	
8	A2	25c bl, *pnksh*	17.50	4.25
9	A2	30c vio brn, *pnksh*	7.00	5.50
10	A2	35c blk, *yellow*	5.50	5.00
11	A2	40c car, *az* (B)	9.00	9.00
12	A2	45c brn, *grnsh*	10.50	11.00
13	A2	50c dp vio	10.50	11.00
14	A2	75c bl, *org*	10.50	12.00
15	A3	1fr blk, *azure*	25.00	27.50
16	A3	2fr bl, *pink*	45.00	52.50
17	A3	5fr car, *straw* (B)	95.00	105.00
		Nos. 1-17 (17)	262.65	265.10

Camel with Rider — A4

1914-17   Perf. 13½x14

18	A4	1c brn vio & vio	.35	.45
19	A4	2c gray & brn vio	.35	.45
20	A4	4c black & blue	.35	.45
21	A4	5c yel grn & bl grn	1.05	.50
b.		Booklet pane of 4		
c.		Complete booklet	2,000.	
22	A4	10c red org & rose	2.50	2.10
23	A4	15c choc & org ('17)	2.10	1.05
b.		Booklet pane of 4	80.00	
c.		Complete booklet	1,400.	
24	A4	20c brn vio & blk	2.10	2.10
25	A4	25c ultra & bl	2.10	1.40
b.		Booklet pane of 4	100.00	
26	A4	30c ol brn & brn	2.10	2.10
27	A4	35c car rose & vio	3.50	2.50
28	A4	40c gray & car rose	2.10	1.40
29	A4	45c bl & ol brn	2.10	2.10

30	A4	50c black & green	2.75	2.75
31	A4	75c org & ol brn	2.75	2.75
32	A4	1fr brown & brn vio	2.75	3.50
33	A4	2fr green & blue	3.50	3.50
34	A4	5fr violet & black	12.50	14.00
		Nos. 18-34 (17)	44.95	43.10

See Burkina Faso for types of this issue that escaped overprinting.

For surcharges see No. B1, French Sudan Nos. 21-49, Niger Nos. 1-28.

SEMI-POSTAL STAMP

Regular Issue of 1914 Surcharged in Red

1915   Unwmk.   Perf. 13½x14

B1   A4   10c + 5c red orange & rose   2.10   2.10

POSTAGE DUE STAMPS

Natives — D1

1906   Unwmk.   Typo.   Perf. 14x13½

J1	D1	5c green, *greenish*	3.50	3.50
J2	D1	10c red brown	7.00	7.00
J3	D1	15c dark blue	10.50	10.50
J4	D1	20c black, *yellow*	14.00	7.00
J5	D1	50c violet	27.50	27.50
J6	D1	60c black, *buff*	21.00	21.00
J7	D1	1fr black, *pinkish*	35.00	37.50
		Nos. J1-J7 (7)	118.50	114.00

D2

1914

J8	D2	5c green	1.10	1.40
a.		Imperf., pair	90.00	
J9	D2	10c rose	1.60	1.75
J10	D2	15c gray	1.60	1.75
J11	D2	20c brown	1.60	1.75
J12	D2	30c blue	2.40	2.60
J13	D2	50c black	2.00	2.25
J14	D2	60c orange	7.25	7.75
J15	D2	1fr violet	7.25	7.75
a.		Imperf., pair	130.00	90.00
		Nos. J8-J15 (8)	24.80	27.00

Stamps of Upper Senegal and Niger were superceded in 1921 by those of French Sudan.

UPPER SILESIA

ˈə-pər sī'lē-zh̵ē-ə

LOCATION — Formerly in eastern Germany and prior to World War I a part of Germany.

A plebiscite held under the terms of the Treaty of Versailles failed to determine the status of the country, the voting resulting about equally in favor of Germany and Poland. Accordingly, the League of Nations divided the territory between Germany and Poland.

100 Pfennig = 1 Mark

100 Fennigi = 1 Marka

Plebiscite Issues

A1

Perf. 14x13½

1920, Feb. 20   Typo.   Unwmk.

1	A1	2½pf slate	.40	.80
2	A1	3pf brown	.40	.85
3	A1	5pf green	.30	.80
4	A1	10pf dull red	.40	.90
5	A1	15pf violet	.25	.80
6	A1	20pf blue	.25	.80
a.		Imperf., pair	275.00	—
7	A1	50pf violet brn	4.75	8.00
8	A1	1m claret	5.00	12.00
9	A1	5m orange	5.00	12.00
		Nos. 1-9 (9)	16.75	36.95
		Set, never hinged	55.00	

Black Surcharge

   I   II   III   IV

10	A1	5pf on 15pf vio (I)	100.00	400.00
		Never hinged	375.00	
a.		Type II	100.00	400.00
b.		Type III	100.00	400.00
c.		Type IV	100.00	400.00
11	A1	5pf on 20pf blue (I)	1.10	3.25
		Never hinged	3.00	
a.		Type II	1.25	3.75
b.		Type III	1.60	4.00
c.		Type IV	2.00	5.00

Red Surcharge

   I   II   III   IV

12	A1	10pf on 20pf bl (I)	1.10	3.25
		Never hinged	3.00	
a.		Type II	1.10	3.25
b.		Type III	1.10	3.25
c.		Type IV	1.10	3.25
d.		Imperf.	60.00	240.00

Black Surcharge

Type I   Type II   Type III   Type IV   Type V

13	A1	50pf on 5m org (I), shiny ovpt.	30.00	52.50
		Never hinged	200.00	
a.		Type II	32.50	55.00
b.		Type III	35.00	87.50
c.		Type IV	35.00	87.50
d.		Type V	42.50	120.00
e.		Type I, matte ovpt.	37.50	87.50

Nos. 10-13 are found with many varieties including surcharges inverted, double and double inverted.

Dove with Olive Branch Flying over Silesian Terrain — A2

A3

1920, Mar. 26   Typo.   Perf. 13½x14

15	A2	2½pf gray	.55	.80
16	A2	3pf red brown	.55	.80
17	A2	5pf green	.55	.80
18	A2	10pf dull red	.55	.80
19	A2	15pf violet	.55	.80
20	A2	20pf blue	.80	2.00
21	A2	25pf dark brown	.55	.80
22	A2	30pf orange	.55	.80
23	A2	40pf olive green	.55	2.00

Perf. 14x13½

24	A3	50pf gray	1.00	.80
25	A3	60pf blue	.55	1.60
26	A3	75pf deep green	1.60	2.00
27	A3	80pf red brown	1.60	1.10
28	A3	1m claret	1.60	.80
29	A3	2m dark brown	1.40	.80
30	A3	3m violet	1.40	.80
31	A3	5m orange	4.00	4.50
		Nos. 15-31 (17)	18.35	22.00
		Set, never hinged	67.50	

Nos. 18-28
Overprinted in Black
or Red

1921, Mar. 20

32	A2	10pf dull red	4.00	10.00
33	A2	15pf violet	4.00	10.00
34	A2	20pf blue	5.50	14.00
35	A2	25pf dk brn (R)	12.00	32.50
36	A2	30pf orange	10.00	20.00
37	A2	40pf olive grn (R)	11.00	20.00

Overprinted

38	A3	50pf gray (R)	11.00	27.50
39	A3	60pf blue	12.00	22.50
40	A3	75pf deep green	12.00	27.50
a.		75pf blue green	1,650.	1,850.
41	A3	80pf red brown	20.00	35.00
42	A3	1m claret	24.00	65.00
		Nos. 32-42 (11)	125.50	284.00
		Set, never hinged	700.00	

Inverted or double overprints exist on Nos. 32-33, 35-40. Counterfeit overprints exist.

Type of
1920 and
Surcharged

1922, Mar.

45	A3	4m on 60pf ol grn	.80	2.00
46	A3	10m on 75pf red	1.25	2.75
47	A3	20m on 80pf orange	6.50	16.00
		Nos. 45-47 (3)	8.55	20.75
		Set, never hinged	32.00	

Stamps of the above design were a private issue not recognized by the Inter-Allied Commission of Government. Value, set of 7, $65 unused, $225 never hinged, $225 used.

OFFICIAL STAMPS

German Stamps of
1905-20 Handstamped
in Blue

1920, Feb. Wmk. 125 Perf. 14, 14½
On Stamps of 1906-19

O1	A22	2pf gray	1.10	1.25
O3	A22	2½pf gray	.55	.65
O4	A16	3pf brown	.55	.65
O5	A16	5pf green	.55	.65
O6	A22	7½pf orange	.55	.65
O7	A16	10pf car rose	.55	.65
O8	A22	15pf dk violet	.55	.65
O9	A16	20pf blue violet	.55	.65
O10	A16	25pf org & blk, yel	8.00	6.50

O11	A16	30pf org & blk, buff	.55	.65
O12	A22	35pf red brown	.55	.65
O13	A16	40pf lake & blk	.55	.65
O14	A16	50pf vio & blk, buff	.55	.65
O15	A16	60pf magenta	.55	.65
O16	A16	75pf green & blk	.55	.65
O17	A16	80pf lake & blk, rose	6.50	8.00
O18	A17	1m car rose	1.10	1.25
O19	A21	2m gray blue	5.25	6.50

On National Assembly Stamps of 1919-20

O25	A23	10pf car rose	.90	1.10
O26	A24	15pf choc & bl	1.60	2.00
O27	A25	25pf green & red	3.25	4.00
O28	A25	30pf red vio & red	2.50	3.00

On Semi-Postal Stamps of 1919

O30	A16	10pf + 5pf carmine	6.50	8.00
O31	A22	15pf + 5pf dk vio	6.50	8.00
		Nos. O1-O31 (24)	50.35	58.05

Red Handstamp

O5a	A16	5pf	10.00	14.00
O8a	A22	15pf	6.50	10.00
O9a	A16	20pf	6.50	10.00
O13a	A16	40pf	20.00	30.00
O16a	A16	75pf	20.00	30.00
O26a	A24	15pf	1.10	1.25
		Nos. O5a-O26a (6)	64.10	95.25

Values of Nos. O1-O31 are for reprints made with a second type of handstamp differing in minor details from the original (example: period after "S" is round instead of the earlier triangular form). Originals are scarce. Counterfeits exist.

Germany No. 66C with this handstamp is considered bogus by experts.

Local Official Stamps
of Germany, 1920,
Overprinted

1920, Apr. Perf. 14

O32	LO2	5pf green	.30	1.50
O33	LO3	10pf carmine	.30	1.50
O34	LO4	15pf violet brn	.30	1.50
O35	LO5	20pf deep ultra	.30	1.50
O36	LO6	30pf orange, buff	.30	1.50
O37	LO7	50pf violet, buff	.80	3.00
O38	LO8	1m red, buff	6.50	15.00
		Nos. O32-O38 (7)	8.80	25.50

Same Overprint on Official Stamps of Germany, 1920-21

1920-21

O39	O1	5pf green	1.00	8.00
O40	O2	10pf carmine	.25	1.50
O41	O3	15pf violet brn	.25	1.50
O42	O4	20pf deep ultra	.25	1.50
O43	O5	30pf orange, buff	.25	1.50
O44	O6	40pf carmine rose	.25	1.50
O45	O7	50pf violet, buff	.25	1.50
O46	O8	60pf red brown	.25	1.50
O47	O9	1m red, buff	.25	1.50
O48	O10	1.25m dk blue, yel	.25	1.50
O49	O11	2m dark blue	7.25	12.00
O50	O12	5m brown, yel	.25	1.50

1922, Feb. Wmk. 126

O51	O11	2m dark blue	.25	1.00
		Nos. O39-O51 (13)	11.00	36.00

This overprint is found both horizontal, reading upright or inverted, and vertical, reading up or down. These variations generally command no premium over the values above.

The overprint also exists on most values double and double, one inverted, in the above formats, as well as at a 45 degree angle, upreading and downreading, either upright or inverted. These varieties generally sell for 25-100 percent over the value of normal examples.

URUGUAY

'yur-ə-ˌgwā

LOCATION — South America, between Brazil and Argentina and bordering on the Atlantic Ocean
GOVT. — Republic
AREA — 68,037 sq. mi.
POP. — 3,137,668 (1996)
CAPITAL — Montevideo

120 Centavos = 1 Real
8 Reales = 1 Peso
100 Centesimos = 1 Peso (1859)
1000 Milesimos = 1 Peso (1898)

Watermarks

Wmk. 90 — Large Sun and RA

Wmk. 187 — R O in Diamond

Wmk. 188 — REPUBLICA O. DEL URUGUAY

Wmk. 189 — Caduceus

Wmk. 227 — Greek Border and REPUBLICA O. DEL URUGUAY in Alternate Curved Lines

---

Wmk. 327 — Coat of Arms

Wmk. 332 — Large Sun and R O U

> Catalogue values for unused stamps in this country are for Never Hinged items, beginning with Scott 534 in the regular postage section, Scott B5 in the semipostal section, Scott C113 in the airpost section, Scott CB1 in the airpost semi-postal section, Scott E9 in the special delivery section, and Scott Q64 in the parcel post section.

CARRIER ISSUES
Issued by Atanasio Lapido, Administrator-General of Posts

A1　　　　　A1a
"El Sol de Mayo"

Unwmk.

1856, Oct. 1		Litho.		Imperf.
1	A1	60c blue	450.	450.
2	A1	80c green	500.	500.
3	A1	1r vermilion	400.	400.

1857, Oct. 1				
3B	A1a	60c blue	2,750.	—

Nos. 1-3B were spaced very closely on the stone. Very fine examples will have clear margins on three sides and touching or slightly cut into the frames on the fourth (consult the grading illustrations in the catalogue introduction). All genuinely used examples are pen canceled. Certification by a recognized authority is recommended.
Stamps with tiny faults, such as small thin spots, sell for about 75% of the values of sound examples.
See Nos. 410-413, 771A.

A2

1858, Mar.				
4	A2	120c blue	575.00	650.00
	c.	Tête bêche pair	—	
5	A2	180c green	150.00	200.00
	c.	Thick paper	500.00	
	d.	Tête bêche pair	—	
6	A2	240c dull ver	150.00	1,200.
	c.	180c in stone of 240c	—	
	d.	Thick paper (dull ver)	—	
	e.	240c setenant with a vacant space	5,000.	
		Nos. 4-6 (3)	875.00	2,050.

Nos. 4-6e have been extensively forged. Certification by a recognized authority is recommended.

GOVERNMENT ISSUES

A3　　　　　　　A4

1859, June 26			**Thin Numerals**	
7	A3	60c lilac	50.00	35.00
	a.	60c gray lilac	45.00	35.00
8	A3	80c orange	450.00	75.00
	a.	80c yellow	300.00	60.00
9	A3	100c brown lake	100.00	70.00
	a.	100c brown rose	120.00	100.00
10	A3	120c blue	55.00	30.00
	a.	120c slate blue	75.00	30.00
11	A3	180c green	22.00	26.00
12	A3	240c vermilion	90.00	90.00
		Nos. 7-12 (6)	767.00	326.00

1860			**Thick Numerals**	
13	A4	60c dull lilac	25.00	12.00
	a.	60c gray lilac	40.00	15.00
	b.	60c brown lilac	30.00	18.00
	c.	60c red lilac	120.00	60.00
	d.	As "a," fine impression (1st printing)	125.00	45.00
14	A4	80c yellow	50.00	25.00
	a.	80c orange	100.00	26.00
15	A4	100c rose	100.00	55.00
	a.	100c carmine	110.00	55.00
16	A4	120c blue	45.00	25.00
17	A4	180c yellow grn	425.00	375.00
	a.	180c deep green	425.00	450.00
		Nos. 13-17 (5)	645.00	492.00

No. 13 was first printed (1860) in sheets of 192 (16x12) containing 24 types. The impressions are very clear; paper is whitish and of better quality than that of the later printings. In the 1861-62 printings, the layout contains 12 types and the subjects are spaced farther apart.

Coat of Arms — A5

1864, Apr. 13				
18	A5	6c rose	12.00	10.00
	a.	6c carmine	40.00	30.00
	b.	6c red	40.00	30.00
	c.	6c brick red	45.00	30.00
20	A5	6c salmon	500.00	500.00
21	A5	8c green	26.00	22.00
	a.	Tête bêche pair	775.00	
22	A5	10c yellow	32.50	25.00
	a.	10c ocher	35.00	25.00
23	A5	12c blue	15.00	12.00
	a.	12c dark blue	25.00	18.00
	b.	12c slate blue	30.00	20.00

No. 20, which is on thicker paper, was never placed in use.

Stamps of 1864 Surcharged in Black

1866, Jan. 1				
24	A5	5c on 12c blue	26.00	55.00
	a.	5c on 12c slate blue	30.00	60.00
	b.	Inverted surcharge	150.00	
	c.	Double surcharge	150.00	
	d.	Pair, one without surcharge		
	e.	Triple surcharge	55.00	
25	A5	10c on 8c brt grn	30.00	55.00
	a.	10c on 8c dl grn	30.00	55.00
	b.	Tête bêche pair	300.00	
	c.	Double surcharge	150.00	
26	A5	15c on 10c ocher	35.00	90.00
	a.	15c on 10c yellow	35.00	90.00
	b.	Inverted surcharge	150.00	
	c.	Double surcharge	150.00	
27	A5	20c on 6c rose	35.00	85.00
	a.	20c on 6c rose red	37.50	75.00
	b.	Inverted surcharge	150.00	
	c.	Double surcharge	150.00	
	d.	Pair, one without surcharge		
28	A5	20c on 6c brick red	400.00	
	a.	Double surcharge	500.00	
		Nos. 24-27 (4)	126.00	285.00

Many counterfeits exist.
No. 28 was not issued.

Coat of Arms and Numeral of Value — A7

A8　　　　　　A8a

A8b　　　　　　A8c

Type I

Type II

ONE CENTESIMO:
Type I — The wavy lines behind "CENTESIMO" are clear and distinct. Stamps 4mm apart.
Type II — The wavy lines are rough and blurred. Stamps 3mm apart.

1866, Jan. 10				Imperf.
29	A7	1c black (type II)	5.00	7.50
	a.	1c black (type I)	5.00	7.50
30	A8	5c blue	13.00	9.00
	a.	5c dull blue	13.00	9.00
	b.	5c ultramarine	32.50	10.00
	c.	Numeral with white flag	25.00	12.00
	d.	"ENTECIMOS"	25.00	12.00
	e.	"CENTECIMO"	25.00	12.00
	f.	"CENTECIMOS" with small "S"	25.00	12.00
	g.	Pelure paper	100.00	100.00
	h.	Thick paper		
31	A8a	10c yellow green	25.00	10.00
	a.	10c blue green	25.00	10.00
	b.	"I" of "CENTECIMOS" omitted	30.00	14.00
	c.	"CENIECIMOS"	30.00	14.00
	d.	"CENTRCIMOS"	30.00	14.00
32	A8b	15c orange yel	30.00	15.00
	a.	15c yellow	30.00	15.00
33	A8c	20c rose	35.00	15.00
	a.	20c lilac rose	35.00	15.00
	b.	Thick paper	37.50	16.00
		Nos. 29-33 (5)	108.00	56.50

See Nos. 34-38. For overprint see No. O11.
Engraved plates were prepared for Nos. 30 to 33 but were not put in use. The stamps were printed from lithographic transfers from the plate. In 1915 a few reprints of the 15c were made from the engraved plate by a California philatelic society, each sheet being numbered and signed by officers of the society; then the plate was defaced.

1866-67			Perf. 8½ to 13½	
34	A7	1c black	6.50	20.00
35	A8	5c blue	5.00	2.50
	a.	5c dark blue	5.00	1.00
	b.	Numeral with white flag	25.00	12.00
	c.	"ENTECIMOS"	25.00	12.00
	d.	"CENTECIMO"	25.00	12.00
	e.	"CENTECIMOS" with small "S"	15.00	8.00
	f.	Pelure paper	90.00	20.00
36	A8a	10c green	12.00	4.00
	a.	10c yellow green	14.00	4.00
	b.	"CENIECIMOS"	35.00	14.00
	c.	"I" of "CENTECIMOS" omitted	35.00	14.00
	d.	"CENTRCIMOS"	35.00	14.00
	e.	Pelure paper	90.00	20.00
37	A8b	15c orange yel	21.00	6.00
	a.	15c yellow	21.00	6.00
	b.	Thin paper	25.00	10.00
38	A8c	20c rose	25.00	10.00
	a.	20c brown rose	25.00	10.00
	b.	Thin paper	30.00	15.00
	c.	Thick paper	30.00	15.00
		Nos. 34-38 (5)	69.50	42.50

A9

A10

A11

A12

1877-79   Engr.   Rouletted 8

39	A9	1c red brown	.80	.50
40	A10	5c green	1.00	.50
a.		Thick paper	5.00	2.50
41	A11	10c vermilion	2.00	.80
42	A11	20c bister	3.50	1.25
43	A11	50c black	12.50	3.50
43A	A12	1p blue ('79)	50.00	22.50
		Nos. 39-43A (6)	69.80	29.05

The first printing of the 1p had the coat of arms smaller with quarterings reversed. These "error" stamps were not issued, and all were ordered burned. One example is known to have been in a celebrated Uruguayan collection and a few others exist.

See No. 44. For overprints and surcharges see Nos. 52-53, O1-O8, O10, O19.

1880, Nov. 10   Engr.   Rouletted 6

44	A9	1c brown	.50	.50
a.		Imperf., pair	10.00	
b.		Rouletted 12½	2.50	

Joaquin Suárez — A13

1881, Aug. 25   Perf. 12½

45	A13	7c blue	2.50	2.50
a.		Imperf., pair	9.00	9.00

For overprint see No. O9.

A14

Devices from Coat of Arms — A14a

1882, May 15

46	A14	1c green	1.50	1.50
a.		1c yellow green	5.00	2.50
b.		Imperf., pair	13.00	
47	A14a	2c rose	1.25	1.00
a.		Imperf., pair	15.00	

These stamps bear numbers from 1 to 100 according to their position on the sheet.

Counterfeits of Nos. 46 and 47 are plentiful. See Nos. 1132-1133. For overprints see Nos. 54, O12-O13, O20.

Coat of Arms

A15   A16

Gen. Máximo Santos — A17   General José Artigas — A18

Perf. 12, 12x12½, 12x13, 13x12

1883, Mar. 1

48	A15	1c green	1.60	1.00
49	A16	2c red	2.50	1.50
50	A17	5c blue	2.75	1.75
51	A18	10c brown	5.00	2.50
		Nos. 48-51 (4)	11.75	6.75

Imperf., Pairs

48a	A15	1c	7.00
49a	A16	2c	7.00
50a	A17	5c	6.50
51a	A18	10c	11.00

For overprints see Nos. O14-O18.

No. 40 Overprinted in Black

1883, Sept. 24   Rouletted 8

52	A10	5c green	1.00	.75
a.		Double overprint	15.00	15.00
b.		Overprint reading down	6.00	6.00
c.		"Provisorio" omitted	7.00	7.00
d.		"1883" omitted	4.50	4.50

No. 52 with overprint in red is a color essay.

No. 41 Surcharged in Black

1884, Jan. 16

53	A11	1c on 10c ver	.50	.50
a.		Small figure "1"	4.25	4.25
b.		Inverted surcharge	4.25	4.25
c.		Double surcharge	8.00	5.00

No. 47 Overprinted in Black

Perf. 12½

54	A14a	2c rose	.75	.75
a.		Double overprint	14.00	
b.		Imperf., pair	40.00	

A22

A23

Thick Paper

1884, Jan. 25   Litho.   Unwmk.

55	A22	5c ultra	2.00	1.00
a.		Imperf., pair	7.50	4.00

Thin Paper

Perf. 12½, 13 and Compound

56	A23	5c blue	1.50	.70
a.		Imperf., pair	14.00	

For overprints see Nos. O21-O22.

A24

A24a

A24b   Artigas — A25

Santos — A26

A27

A28

1884-88   Engr.   Rouletted 8

57	A24	1c gray	.80	.50
58	A24	1c olive	.75	.40
59	A24	1c green	.65	.40
60	A24a	2c vermilion	.40	.25
60A	A24a	2c rose ('88)	.40	.25
61	A24b	5c deep blue	.80	.30
61A	A24b	5c blue, *blue*	2.00	.85
62	A24b	5c violet ('86)	.50	.25
63	A24b	5c lt bl ('88)	.50	.25
64	A25	7c dk brown	2.00	.85
65	A25	7c org ('88)	2.00	.75
66	A26	10c olive brn	.80	.35
67	A27	20c red violet	2.00	1.00
68	A27	20c bis brn ('88)	2.00	1.00
69	A28	25c gray violet	4.00	1.50
70	A28	25c ver ('88)	3.00	1.00
		Nos. 57-70 (16)	22.60	9.90

Water dissolves the blue in the paper of No. 61A.

For overprints see Nos. 73, 98-99, O23-O34, O36-O39, O61.

A29

1887, Oct. 17   Litho.   Rouletted 9

71	A29	10c lilac	2.50	1.25
a.		10c gray lilac	3.00	1.25

For overprint see No. O40.

A30

1888, Jan. 1   Engr.   Rouletted 8

72	A30	10c violet	.60	.25

For overprint see No. O35.

No. 62 Overprinted in Black

1889, Oct. 14

73	A24b	5c violet	.40	.40
a.		Inverted overprint	8.00	6.00
b.		Inverted "A" for "V" in "Provisorio"	4.00	4.00

No. 73 with overprint in red is a color essay.

Coat of Arms — A32

Numeral of Value — A33

A34

A35

A36

A37

Justice A38

Mercury A39

A40

Perf. 12½ to 15½ and Compound

1889-1901   Engr.

74	A32	1c green	.60	.05
a.		Imperf., pair	13.00	
75	A32	1c dull bl ('94)	.50	.25
76	A33	2c rose	.50	.25
77	A33	2c red brn ('94)	.55	.25
78	A33	2c org ('99)	.55	.25
79	A34	5c dp blue	.50	.25
80	A34	5c rose ('94)	.55	.25
81	A35	7c bister brn	1.00	.30
82	A35	7c green ('94)	4.75	2.75
83	A35	7c car ('00)	4.00	1.75
84	A36	10c blue grn	3.50	.85
a.		Printed on both sides	20.00	
85	A36	10c org ('94)	3.25	.60
86	A37	20c orange	2.50	.60
87	A37	20c brown ('94)	4.75	1.75
88	A37	20c lt blue ('00)	2.75	.40
a.		20c greenish blue	3.00	.40
89	A38	25c red brown	3.25	.85
90	A38	25c ver ('94)	6.75	3.50
91	A38	25c bis brn ('01)	3.75	.50
92	A39	50c lt blue	7.50	5.00
93	A39	50c lilac ('94)	11.00	5.50
94	A39	50c car ('01)	6.75	1.00
95	A40	1p lilac	18.00	5.00
96	A40	1p lt blue ('94)	25.00	7.00
97	A40	1p dp grn ('01)	20.00	2.25
a.		Imperf., pair	30.00	
		Nos. 74-97 (24)	132.15	41.35

For surcharges and overprints see Nos. 100-101, 142, 180, 185, C1-C3, O41-O60, O89-O91, O108-O109.

Nos. 59 and 62 Overprinted in Red

a   b

1891-92   Rouletted 8

98	A24 (a)	1c green ('92)	.40	.40
a.		Inverted overprint	6.00	6.00
b.		Double overprint	7.75	7.75
c.		Double ovpt., one invtd.	3.00	2.50
d.		"PREVISORIO"	4.00	4.00
99	A24b (b)	5c violet	.25	.25
a.		"1391"	4.00	2.75
b.		Double overprint	4.00	2.75
c.		Inverted overprint	4.00	2.75
d.		Double ovpt., one invtd.	5.00	3.00

Nos. 86 and 81 Surcharged in Black or Red

c

d

Perf. 12½ to 15½ and Compound
1892

100	A37 (c)	1c on 20c org (Bk)	.40	.40
a.		Inverted surcharge	6.00	6.00
101	A35 (d)	5c on 7c bis brn		
		(R)	.40	.40
a.		Inverted surcharge	1.00	1.00
b.		Double surcharge, one invtd.	3.00	3.00
c.		Double surcharge	3.00	3.00
d.		Vertical surcharge	10.00	
e.		"PREVISORIO"	3.00	3.00
f.		"Cinco" omitted	4.50	

No. 101 with surcharge in green is a color essay.
Several surcharge errors of date and misspelling of "Centésimos" exist. Value $15.

A45

A46

Arms A47

Peace A48

1892   Engr.

102	A45	1c green	.50	.25
103	A46	2c rose	.50	.25
104	A47	5c blue	.50	.25
105	A48	10c orange	2.00	.85
		Nos. 102-105 (4)	3.50	1.60

Issued: 1c, 2c, 3/9; 5c, 4/19; 10c, 12/15.

Liberty A49

Arms A50

1894, June 2

106	A49	2p carmine	30.00	17.50
107	A50	3p dull violet	30.00	17.50

Gaucho A51

Solis Theater A52

Locomotive A53

Bull's Head A54

Ceres — A55

Sailing Ship — A56

Liberty — A57

Mercury — A58

Coat of Arms — A59

Montevideo Fortress — A60

Cathedral in Montevideo A61

Perf. 12 to 15½ and Compound
1895-99

108	A51	1c bister	.50	.25
109	A51	1c slate bl ('97)	.50	.25
a.		Printed on both sides	14.00	
110	A52	2c blue	.50	.25
111	A52	2c claret ('97)	.50	.25
112	A53	5c red	.50	.25
113	A53	5c green ('97)	.65	.25
a.		Imperf., pair	3.50	
114	A53	5c grnsh bl ('99)	1.00	.40
115	A54	7c deep green	7.75	2.50
116	A54	7c orange ('97)	3.50	1.25
117	A55	10c brown	2.00	.50
118	A56	20c green & blk	7.00	.85
119	A56	20c cl & blk ('97)	4.75	.60
120	A57	25c red brn & blk	5.50	1.50
a.		Center inverted		2,000.
121	A57	25c pink & bl ('97)	3.50	.60
122	A58	50c blue & blk	7.00	3.50
123	A58	50c grn & brn ('97)	5.00	1.25
124	A59	1p org brn & blk	14.00	5.50
125	A59	1p yel brn & bl ('97)	9.50	3.50
126	A60	2p violet & grn	32.50	20.00
127	A60	2p bis & car ('97)	9.50	2.00
128	A61	3p carmine & blue	32.50	20.00
129	A61	3p lil & car ('97)	12.50	2.50
		Nos. 108-129 (22)	160.65	67.95

All values of this issue exist imperforate but they were not issued in that form.
For overprints and surcharges see Nos. 138-140, 143, 145, 147, O62-O78.

President Joaquin Suárez
A62   A63

Statue of President Suárez — A64

Perf. 12½ to 15 and Compound
1896, July 18

130	A62	1c brown vio & blk	.25	.25
131	A63	5c pale bl & blk	.25	.25
132	A64	10c lake & blk	1.00	.30
		Nos. 130-132 (3)	1.50	.80

Dedication of Pres. Suárez statue.
For overprints and surcharge see Nos. 133-135, 144, 146, 152, O79-O81.

Same Overprinted in Red

e

f

1897, Mar. 1

133	A62 (e)	1c brn vio & blk	.40	.40
a.		Inverted overprint	6.00	6.00
134	A63 (e)	5c pale blue & blk	.50	.40
a.		Inverted overprint	9.50	6.00
135	A64 (f)	10c lake & blk	1.00	.60
a.		Inverted overprint	12.00	9.50
b.		Double overprint	7.50	
		Nos. 133-135 (3)	1.90	1.40

"Electricity" — A68

1897-99   Engr.

136	A68	10c red	1.75	.40
137	A68	10c red lilac ('99)	.75	.50

For overprints see Nos. 141, O82-O83.

Regular Issues Overprinted in Red or Blue

1897, Sept. 26

138	A51	1c slate bl (R)	.80	.60
a.		Inverted overprint	4.75	4.75
139	A52	2c claret (Bl)	1.25	1.25
a.		Inverted overprint	4.75	4.75
140	A53	5c green (Bl)	1.75	1.60
a.		Inverted overprint	7.75	7.75
b.		Double overprint		
141	A68	10c red (Bl)	2.75	2.75
a.		Inverted overprint	17.00	17.00
		Nos. 138-141 (4)	6.55	6.20

Commemorating the Restoration of Peace at the end of the Civil War.
Issue for use only on the days of the National Fête, Sept. 26-28, 1897.

Regular Issues Surcharged in Black, Blue or Red

1898, July 25

142	A32	½c on 1c bl (Bk)	.40	.40
a.		Inverted surcharge	3.00	3.00
143	A51	½c on 1c bis (Bl)	.40	.40
a.		Inverted surcharge	3.00	
b.		Double surcharge	2.50	
144	A62	½c on 1c brn vio & blk (R)	.40	.40
145	A52	½c on 2c blue (Bk)	.40	.40
146	A63	½c on 5c pale bl & blk (R)	.40	.40
a.		Double surcharge	6.25	
147	A54	½c on 7c dp grn (R)	.40	.40
		Nos. 142-147 (6)	2.40	2.40

The 2c red brown of 1894 (#77) was also surcharged like #142-147 but was not issued. Value $12.

Liberty — A69

1898-99   Litho.   Perf. 11, 11½

148	A69	5m rose	.25	.25
149	A69	5m purple ('99)	.25	.25

Statue of Artigas — A70

1899-1900   Engr.   Perf. 12½, 14, 15

150	A70	5m lt blue	.25	.25
151	A70	5m orange ('00)	.25	.25

No. 135 With Additional Surcharge in Black

1900, Dec. 1

152	A64	5c on 10c lake & blk	.50	.25
a.		Black bar covering "1897" omitted	15.00	

Cattle — A72

Girl's Head — A73

Shepherdess — A74

Perf. 13½ to 16 and Compound
1900-10   Engr.

153	A72	1c yellow green	.40	.25
154	A73	5c dull blue	.80	.25
155	A73	5c slate grn ('10)	.80	.25
156	A74	10c gray violet	1.00	.25
		Nos. 153-156 (4)	3.00	1.00

For surcharges and overprints see Nos. 179, 184, O84, O86, O88, O106-O107.

Eros and Cornucopia A75

Basket of Fruit A76

1901, Feb. 11

157	A75	2c vermilion	.50	.25
158	A76	7c brown orange	1.75	.25

For surcharges and overprints see Nos. 197-198, O85, O87, O105.

General Artigas — A78

Cattle — A79

Eros — A80

Cow — A81

Shepherdess A82

Numeral A83

Justice — A84

1904-05   Litho.   Perf. 11½
160 A78 5m orange   .40   .25
  a.   5m yellow   .40   .25
161 A79 1c green   .50   .25
  a.   Imperf., pair   3.50
162 A80 2c deep orange   .25   .25
  a.   2c orange red   .25   .25
  b.   Imperf., pair   3.00
163 A81 5c blue   .80   .25
  a.   Imperf., pair   3.50
164 A82 10c dk violet ('05)   .50   .25
165 A83 20c gray grn ('05)   2.50   .50
166 A84 25c olive bis ('05)   3.25   .80
      Nos. 160-166 (7)   8.20 2.55
  Design of No. 163 measures 17mm by
23mm. See No. 170.
  For overprints see Nos. 167-169, O92-O98,
O101-O103.

Overprinted Diagonally
in Carmine or Black

1904, Oct. 15
167 A79 1c green (C)   .40   .40
168 A80 2c deep orange (Bk)   .65   .40
169 A81 5c dark blue (C)   1.25   .60
      Nos. 167-169 (3)   2.30 1.40
  End of the Civil War of 1904. In the first
overprinting, "Paz 1904" appears at a 50-
degree angle; in the second, at a 63 degree
angle.

A85

1906, Feb. 23   Litho.   Unwmk.
170 A85 5c dark blue   1.10   .25
  a.   Imperf., pair   6.00
  Design of No. 170 measures 19¼mm by
25½mm. See No. 163.

A86

1906-07
171 A86 5c deep blue   .30   .30
172 A86 7c orange brn ('07)   .70   .50
173 A86 50c rose   5.00 1.25
      Nos. 171-173 (3)   6.00 2.05

Cruiser "Montevideo" — A87

1908, Aug. 23   Typo.   Rouletted 13
174 A87 1c car & dk grn   2.00 1.50
175 A87 2c green & dk grn   2.00 1.50
176 A87 5c org & dk grn   2.00 1.50
      Nos. 174-176 (3)   6.00 4.50

Center Inverted
174a A87 1c   300.00 300.00
175a A87 2c   300.00 300.00
176a A87 5c   300.00 300.00
      Nos. 174a-176a (3)   900.00 900.00

Imperf., Pairs
174b A87 1c   30.00
175b A87 2c   30.00
176b A87 5c   30.00
  Independence of Uruguay, declared Aug.
25, 1825. Counterfeits exist.
  For surcharges and overprints see Nos.
186, O99-O100, O104, O110.

View of the Port of Montevideo — A88

Wmk. 187
1909, Aug. 24   Engr.   Perf. 11½
177 A88 2c lt brown & blk   1.25 1.20
178 A88 5c rose red & blk   1.25 1.20
  Issued to commemorate the opening of the
Port of Montevideo, Aug. 25, 1909.

Nos. 156, 91
Surcharged

Perf. 14 to 16
1909, Sept. 13   Unwmk.
179 A74 8c on 10c dull vio   .75   .25
  a.   "Contesimos"   4.00 2.00
180 A38 23c on 25c bis brn   1.75   .60

Centaur — A89

Wmk. 187
1910, May 22   Engr.   Perf. 11½
182 A89 2c carmine red   .60   .40
183 A89 5c deep blue   .60   .40
  Cent. of Liberation Day, May 25, 1810.
The 2c in deep blue and 5c in carmine red
were prepared for collectors.

Stamps of 1900-06 Surcharged

g

h

i

Perf. 14 to 16, 11½
1910, Oct. 6   Unwmk.
Black Surcharge
184 A72 (g) 5m on 1c yel grn   .25   .25
  a.   Inverted surcharge   4.50 3.75
Dark Blue Surcharge
185 A39 (h) 5c on 50c dull
              red   .40   .25
  a.   Inverted surcharge   4.50 4.50
Blue Surcharge
186 A86 (i) 5c on 50c rose   .80   .45
  a.   Double surcharge   20.00
  b.   Inverted surcharge   10.00 8.75
      Nos. 184-186 (3)   1.45   .95

Artigas
A90

"Commercial
Progress"
A91

1910, Nov. 21   Engr.   Perf. 14, 15
187 A90 5m dk violet   .25   .25
188 A90 1c dp green   .25   .25
189 A90 2c orange red   .25   .25
190 A90 5c dk blue   .25   .25
191 A90 8c gray blk   .40   .25
192 A90 20c brown   .60   .25
193 A91 23c dp ultra   2.75   .40
194 A91 50c orange   4.00 1.25
195 A91 1p scarlet   7.50 1.25
      Nos. 187-195 (9)   16.25 4.40
  See Nos. 199-210. For overprints see Nos.
211-213, O118-O124.

Symbolical of the
Posts — A92

1911, Jan. 6   Wmk. 187   Perf. 11½
196 A92 5c rose car & blk   .80   .60
  1st South American Postal Cong., at Montevideo, Jan. 1911.

No. 158 Surcharged
in Red or Dark Blue

Perf. 14 to 16
1911, May 17   Unwmk.
197 A76 2c on 7c brn org (R)   .40   .40
198 A76 5c on 7c brn org (Bl)   .40   .25
  a.   Inverted surcharge   8.50 8.50
  Centenary of the battle of Las Piedras, won
by the forces under Gen. Jose Gervasio Artigas, May 8, 1811.

Types of 1910
FOUR AND FIVE CENTESIMOS:
Type I — Large numerals about 3mm high.
Type II — Small numerals about 2¼mm
high.

1912-15   Typo.   Perf. 11½
199 A90 5m violet   .25   .25
  a.   5m purple   .25   .25
200 A90 5m magenta   .25   .25
  a.   5m dull rose   .25   .25
201 A90 1c green ('13)   .25   .25
202 A90 2c brown org   .25   .25
203 A90 2c rose red ('13)   .25   .25
  a.   2c deep red ('14)   .25   .25
204 A90 4c org (I) ('14)   .25   .25
  a.   4c orange (II) ('15)   .25   .25
  b.   4c yellow (II) ('13)   .25   .25
205 A90 5c dull bl (I)   .40   .25
  a.   5c blue (II)   .40   .25
206 A90 8c ultra ('13)   .50   .25
207 A90 20c brown ('13)   1.40   .25
  a.   20c chocolate   1.40
208 A91 23c dk blue ('15)   3.50   .60
209 A91 50c orange ('14)   3.50 1.50
210 A91 1p vermilion ('15)   10.50 1.25
      Nos. 199-210 (12)   21.30 5.60

Stamps of 1912-15
Overprinted

1913, Apr. 4
211 A90 2c brown orange   .85   .50
  a.   Inverted overprint   5.00 4.50

212 A90 4c yellow   .85   .50
213 A90 5c blue   .85   .50
      Nos. 211-213 (3)   2.55 1.50
  Cent. of the Buenos Aires Cong. of 1813.

Liberty
Extending
Peace to the
Country — A93

1918, Jan. 3   Litho.
214 A93 2c green & red   .85   .50
215 A93 5c buff & blue   .85   .50
  Promulgation of the Constitution.

Statue of Liberty, New
York Harbor — A94

Perf. 14, 15, 13½
1919, July 15   Engr.
217 A94 2c carmine & brn   .55   .25
218 A94 4c orange & brn   .55   .25
219 A94 5c blue & brn   .80   .40
220 A94 8c org brn & ind   .80   .40
221 A94 20c ol bis & blk   2.00   .80
222 A94 23c green & blk   4.00 1.25
      Nos. 217-222 (6)   8.70 3.35
  Peace at end of World War I.
  Perf 13½ used only on 2c, 20c, 23c.

Harbor of
Montevideo — A95

1919-20   Litho.   Perf. 11½
225 A95 5m violet & blk   .25   .25
226 A95 1c green & blk   .25   .25
227 A95 2c red & blk   .25   .25
228 A95 4c orange & blk   .35   .25
229 A95 5c ultra & slate   .40   .25
230 A95 8c gray bl & lt brn   .50   .25
231 A95 20c brown & blk   1.60   .35
232 A95 23c green & brn   2.75   .65
233 A95 50c brown & blue   5.00 2.00
234 A95 1p dull red & bl   10.00 3.00
      Nos. 225-234 (10)   21.35 7.50
  For overprints see Nos. O125-O131.

José Enrique
Rodó — A96

1920, Feb. 28   Engr.   Perf. 14, 15
235 A96 2c car & blk   .55   .40
236 A96 4c org & bl   .65   .50
237 A96 5c bl & brn   .75   .55
      Nos. 235-237 (3)   1.95 1.45
  Issued to honor José Enrique Rodó, author.
  For surcharges see Nos. P2-P4.

Mercury — A97

1921-22   Litho.   Perf. 11½
238 A97 5m lilac   .25   .25
239 A97 5m gray blk ('22)   .25   .25
240 A97 1c lt grn   .25   .25
241 A97 1c vio ('22)   .25   .25

242	A97	2c fawn	.40	.25
243	A97	2c red ('22)	.40	.25
244	A97	3c bl grn ('22)	.60	.25
245	A97	4c orange	.40	.25
246	A97	5c ultra	.50	.25
247	A97	5c choc ('22)	.60	.25
248	A97	12c ultra ('22)	2.40	.60
249	A97	36c ol grn ('22)	7.75	2.75
		Nos. 238-249 (12)	14.05	5.85

See Nos. 254-260. For overprint and surcharge see Nos. E1, P1.

Dámaso A. Larrañaga (1771-1848), Bishop, Writer, Scientist and Physician — A98

1921, Dec. 10   **Unwmk.**
250	A98	5c slate	1.25	1.00

Mercury Type of 1921-22

1922-23   **Wmk. 188**
254	A97	5m gray blk	.25	.25
255	A97	1c violet ('23)	.25	.25
a.		1c red violet	.25	.25
256	A97	2c pale red	.25	.25
257	A97	2c deep rose ('23)	.30	.25
259	A97	5c yel brn ('23)	.65	.25
260	A97	8c salmon pink ('23)	1.00	.90
		Nos. 254-260 (6)	2.70	2.15

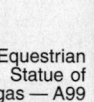

Equestrian Statue of Artigas — A99

Unwmk.
1923, Feb. 26   **Engr.**   **Perf. 14**
264	A99	2c car & sepia	.40	.25
265	A99	5c vio & sepia	.40	.25
266	A99	12c blue & sepia	.40	.25
		Nos. 264-266 (3)	1.20	.75

Southern Lapwing — A100

Perf. 12½, 11½x12½
1923, June 25   **Litho.**   **Wmk. 189**
Size: 18x22½mm
267	A100	5m gray	.25	.25
268	A100	1c org yel	.25	.25
269	A100	2c lt vio	.25	.25
270	A100	3c gray grn	.40	.25
271	A100	5c lt bl	.40	.25
272	A100	8c rose red	.80	.50
273	A100	12c dp bl	.80	.50
274	A100	20c brn org	2.00	.50
275	A100	36c emerald	4.00	1.75
276	A100	50c orange	6.75	2.75
277	A100	1p brt rose	32.50	20.00
278	A100	2p lt grn	47.50	20.00
		Nos. 267-278 (12)	95.90	47.25

See #285-298, 309-314, 317-323, 334-339. For surcharges and overprints see Nos. 345-348, O132-O148, P5-P7.

Battle Monument A101

1923, Oct. 12   **Wmk. 188**   **Perf. 11½**
279	A101	2c dp grn	.55	.40
280	A101	5c scarlet	.55	.40
281	A101	12c dk bl	.55	.40
		Nos. 279-281 (3)	1.65	1.20

Unveiling of the Sarandi Battle Monument by José Luis Zorrilla, Oct. 12, 1923.

"Victory of Samothrace" — A102

Unwmk.
1924, July 29   **Typo.**   **Perf. 11**
282	A102	2c rose	20.00	10.00
283	A102	5c mauve	20.00	10.00
284	A102	12c brt bl	20.00	10.00
		Nos. 282-284 (3)	60.00	30.00

Olympic Games. Sheets of 20 (5x4). Five hundred sets of these stamps were printed on yellow paper for presentation purposes. They were not on sale at post offices. Value for set, $1,500.

Lapwing Type of 1923
First Redrawing
Imprint: "A. BARREIRO Y RAMOS"
1924, July 26   **Litho.**   **Perf. 12½, 11½**
Size: 17¼x21½mm
285	A100	5m gray blk	.25	.25
286	A100	1c fawn	.25	.25
287	A100	2c rose lil	.30	.25
288	A100	3c gray grn	.25	.25
289	A100	5c chalky blue	.25	.25
290	A100	8c pink	.50	.25
291	A100	10c turq blue	.40	.25
292	A100	12c slate blue	.50	.25
293	A100	15c lt vio	.50	.25
294	A100	20c brown	.75	.30
295	A100	36c salmon	3.00	.70
296	A100	50c greenish gray	5.00	2.00
297	A100	1p buff	12.00	4.00
298	A100	2p dl vio	20.00	10.00
		Nos. 285-298 (14)	43.95	19.25

Landing of the 33 "Immortals" Led by Juan Antonio Lavalleja — A103

Perf. 11, 11½
1925, Apr. 19   **Wmk. 188**
300	A103	2c salmon pink & blk	1.40	.80
301	A103	5c lilac & blk	1.40	.80
302	A103	12c blue & blk	1.40	.80
		Nos. 300-302 (3)	4.20	2.40

Cent. of the landing of the 33 Founders of the Uruguayan Republic.

Legislative Palace — A104

Perf. 11½
1925, Aug. 24   **Unwmk.**   **Engr.**
303	A104	5c vio & blk	1.25	.80
304	A104	12c bl & blk	1.25	.80

Dedication of the Legislative Palace.

General Fructuoso Rivera — A105

Wmk. 188
1925, Sept. 24   **Litho.**   **Perf. 11**
305	A105	5c light red	.50	.40

Centenary of Battle of Rincón. See No. C9.

Battle of Sarandí A106

1925, Oct. 12   **Perf. 11½**
306	A106	2c bl grn	1.25	1.00
307	A106	5c dl vio	1.25	1.00
308	A106	12c dp bl	1.25	1.00
		Nos. 306-308 (3)	3.75	3.00

Centenary of the Battle of Sarandí.

Lapwing Type of 1923
Second Redrawing
Imprint: "Imprenta Nacional"
1925-26   **Perf. 11, 11½, 10½**
Size: 17½x21¾mm
309	A100	5m gray blk	1.00	.25
310	A100	1c dl vio	1.25	.25
311	A100	2c brt rose	1.60	.25
312	A100	3c gray grn	1.25	.40
313	A100	5c dl bl ('26)	2.00	.25
314	A100	12c slate blue	4.00	.40
		Nos. 309-314 (6)	11.10	1.80

The design differs in many small details from that of the 1923-24 issues. These stamps may be readily identified by the imprint and perforation.

Lapwing Type of 1923
Third Redrawing
Imprint: "Imp. Nacional" at center
1926-27   **Perf. 11, 11½, 10½**
Size: 17½x21¾mm
317	A100	5m gray	.40	.40
318	A100	1c lt vio ('27)	2.40	.55
319	A100	2c red	1.75	.40
320	A100	3c gray grn	2.40	.65
321	A100	5c lt bl	.75	.40
322	A100	8c pink ('27)	3.50	.80
323	A100	36c rose buff	8.00	4.00
		Nos. 317-323 (7)	19.20	6.90

These stamps may be distinguished from preceding stamps of the same design by the imprint.

Philatelic Exhibition Issue

Post Office at Montevideo A107

Unwmk.
1927, May 25   **Engr.**   *Imperf.*
330	A107	2c green	4.75	3.50
a.		Sheet of 4	20.00	20.00
331	A107	5c dull red	4.75	3.50
a.		Sheet of 4	20.00	20.00
332	A107	8c dark blue	4.75	3.50
a.		Sheet of 4	20.00	20.00
		Nos. 330-332 (3)	14.25	10.50

Printed in sheets of 4 and sold at the Montevideo Exhibition. Lithographed counterfeits exist.

Lapwing Type of 1923
Fourth Redrawing
Imprint: "Imp. Nacional" at right
Perf. 11, 11½
1927, May 6   **Litho.**   **Wmk. 188**
Size: 17¾x21¾mm
334	A100	1c gray vio	.40	.25
335	A100	2c vermilion	.40	.25
336	A100	3c gray grn	.80	.35
337	A100	5c blue	.40	.25
338	A100	8c rose	3.00	.80
339	A100	20c gray brn	4.00	1.60
		Nos. 334-339 (6)	9.00	3.50

The design has been slightly retouched in various places. The imprint is in italic capitals and is placed below the right numeral of value.

No. 292 Surcharged in Red

1928, Jan. 13   **Unwmk.**   **Perf. 11½**
345	A100	2c on 12c slate blue	2.00	2.00
346	A100	5c on 12c slate blue	2.00	2.00
347	A100	10c on 12c slate blue	2.00	2.00
348	A100	15c on 12c slate blue	2.00	2.00
		Nos. 345-348 (4)	8.00	8.00

Issued to celebrate the inauguration of the railroad between San Carlos and Rocha.

General Rivera — A108

1928, Apr. 19   **Engr.**   **Perf. 12**
349	A108	5c car rose	.50	.35

Centenary of the Battle of Las Misiones.

Artigas (7 dots in panels below portrait.) — A109

Imprint: "Waterlow & Sons. Ltd., Londres"

Perf. 11, 12½, 13x13½, 12½x13, 13x12½
1928-43   **Size: 16x19½mm**
350	A109	5m black	.25	.25
350A	A109	5m org ('43)	.25	.25
351	A109	1c dk vio	.25	.25
352	A109	1c brn vio ('34)	.25	.25
352A	A109	1c vio bl ('43)	.25	.25
353	A109	2c dp grn	.25	.25
353A	A109	2c brn red ('43)	.25	.25
354	A109	3c bister	.25	.25
355	A109	3c dp grn ('32)	.25	.25
355A	A109	3c brt grn ('43)	.25	.25
356	A109	5c red	.25	.25
357	A109	5c ol grn ('33)	.25	.25
357A	A109	5c dl pur ('43)	.25	.25
358	A109	7c car ('32)	.25	.25
359	A109	8c dk bl	.25	.25
360	A109	8c brn ('33)	.25	.25
361	A109	10c orange	.25	.25
362	A109	10c red org ('32)	.60	.40
363	A109	12c dp bl ('32)	.40	.25
364	A109	15c dk bl	.40	.25
365	A109	17c dk vio ('32)	.80	.25
366	A109	20c ol brn	.65	.25
367	A109	20c red brn ('33)	1.25	.50
368	A109	24c car rose	.90	.35
369	A109	24c yel ('33)	.80	.40
370	A109	36c ol grn ('33)	1.40	.50
371	A109	50c gray	2.40	1.25
372	A109	50c blk ('33)	3.50	1.60
373	A109	50c blk brn ('33)	3.00	1.25
374	A109	1p yel grn	7.00	4.00
		Nos. 350-374 (30)	27.35	15.50

1929-33   **Perf. 12½**
Size: 22 to 22½x28½ to 29½mm
375	A109	1p ol brn ('33)	6.00	4.00
376	A109	2p dk grn	17.00	9.00
377	A109	2p dl red ('32)	20.00	16.00
378	A109	3p dk bl	25.00	17.00
379	A109	3p blk ('32)	23.00	17.00
380	A109	4p violet	28.00	17.00
381	A109	4p dk ol grn ('32)	23.00	17.00
382	A109	5p car brn	32.50	23.00
383	A109	5p red org ('32)	30.00	20.00
384	A109	10p lake ('33)	92.50	70.00
385	A109	10p dp ultra ('33)	92.50	70.00
		Nos. 375-385 (11)	389.50	286.00

See Nos. 420-423, 462. See type A135.

Equestrian Statue of Artigas — A110

1928, May 1
386 A110 2p Prus bl & choc 16.00 7.75
387 A110 3p dp rose & blk 23.00 12.00

Symbolical of Soccer Victory — A111

1928, July 29
388 A111 2c brn vio 16.00 9.25
389 A111 5c dp red 16.00 9.25
390 A111 8c ultra 16.00 9.25
    Nos. 388-390 (3) 48.00 27.75

Uruguayan soccer victories in the Olympic Games of 1924 and 1928. Printed in sheets of 20, in panes of 10 (5x2).

Gen. Eugenio Garzón — A112

1928, Aug. 25 Imperf.
391 A112 2c red 1.40 1.40
  a. Sheet of 4 6.50 6.50
392 A112 5c yel grn 1.40 1.40
  a. Sheet of 4 6.50 6.50
393 A112 8c dp bl 1.40 1.40
  a. Sheet of 4 6.50 6.50
    Nos. 391-393 (3) 4.20 4.20

Dedication of monument to Garzon. Issued in sheets of 4. Lithographed counterfeits exist.

Black River Bridge A113

Gauchos Breaking a Horse — A114

Peace A115

Montevideo A116

Liberty and Flag of Uruguay A117

Liberty with Torch and Caduceus A118

Statue of Artigas A124

Artigas Dictating Instructions for 1813 Congress A119

Seascape A120

Montevideo Harbor, 1830 — A121

Liberty and Coat of Arms A122

Montevideo Harbor, 1930 — A123

1930, June 16 Perf. 12½, 12
394 A113 5m gray blk .25 .25
395 A114 1c dk brn .25 .25
396 A115 2c brn rose .25 .25
397 A116 3c yel grn .25 .25
398 A117 5c dk bl .25 .25
399 A118 8c dl red .35 .25
400 A119 10c dk vio .50 .35
401 A120 15c bl grn .65 .50
402 A121 20c indigo .80 .65
403 A122 24c red brn 1.10 .80
404 A123 50c org red 3.00 2.00
405 A124 1p black 6.00 3.00
406 A124 2p bl vlo 14.00 8.50
407 A124 3p dk red 20.00 14.00
408 A124 4p red org 23.00 19.00
409 A124 5p lilac 35.00 22.50
    Nos. 394-409 (16) 105.65 72.80

Cent. of natl. independence and the promulgation of the constitution.

Type of 1856 Issue
Values in Centesimos
Wmk. 227
1931, Apr. 11 Litho. Imperf.
410 A1 2c gray blue 3.00 2.00
  a. Sheet of 4 15.00 15.00
411 A1 8c dull red 3.00 2.00
  a. Sheet of 4 15.00 15.00
412 A1 15c blue black 3.00 2.00
  a. Sheet of 4 15.00 15.00
Wmk. 188
413 A1 5c light green 3.00 2.00
  a. Sheet of 4 15.00 15.00
    Nos. 410-413 (4) 12.00 8.00

Sold only at the Philatelic Exhibition, Montevideo, Apr. 11-15, 1931. Issued in sheets of 4.

Juan Zorrilla de San Martin, Uruguayan Poet — A125

1932, June 6 Unwmk. Perf. 12½
414 A125 1½c brown violet .25 .25
415 A125 3c green .25 .25
416 A125 7c dk blue .25 .25
417 A125 12c lt blue .40 .25
418 A125 1p chocolate 20.00 13.00
    Nos. 414-418 (5) 21.15 14.00

Semi-Postal Stamp No. B2 Surcharged

1932, Nov. 1 Perf. 12
419 SP1 1½c on 2c + 2c dp grn .35 .35

Artigas Type of 1928
Imprint: "Imprenta Nacional" at center
1932-35 Litho. Perf. 11, 12½
    Size: 15¾x19¼mm
420 A109 5m lt brown ('35) .25 .25
421 A109 1c pale violet ('35) .25 .25
422 A109 15m black .25 .25
423 A109 5c bluish grn ('35) .50 .25
    Nos. 420-423 (4) 1.25 1.00

Gen. J. A. Lavalleja — A126

1933, July 12 Engr. Perf. 12½
429 A126 15m brown lake .25 .25

Flag of the Race and Globe — A127

Perf. 11, 11½, 11x11½
1933, Aug. 3 Litho.
430 A127 3c blue green .50 .25
431 A127 5c rose .50 .25
432 A127 7c lt blue .50 .25
433 A127 8c dull red 1.00 .55
434 A127 12c deep blue .65 .25
435 A127 17c violet 1.75 .80
436 A127 20c red brown 3.50 1.60
437 A127 24c yellow 3.50 1.75
438 A127 36c orange 5.00 2.40
439 A127 50c olive gray 5.50 3.00
440 A127 1p bister 13.00 6.25
    Nos. 430-440 (11) 35.40 17.35

Raising of the "Flag of the Race" and of the 441st anniv. of the sailing of Columbus from Palos, Spain, on his first voyage to America.

Sower — A128

1933, Aug. 28 Unwmk. Perf. 11½
441 A128 3c blue green .25 .25
442 A128 5c dull violet .40 .25
443 A128 7c lt blue .40 .25
444 A128 8c deep red .80 .50
445 A128 12c ultra 2.00 1.00
    Nos. 441-445 (5) 3.85 2.25

3rd Constituent National Assembly.

Juan Zorrilla de San Martin — A129

1933, Nov. 9 Engr. Perf. 12½
446 A129 7c slate .25 .25

Albatross Flying over Map of the Americas — A130

1933, Dec. 3 Typo. Perf. 11½
447 A130 3c green, blk & brn 2.75 2.00
448 A130 7c turq bl, brn & blk 1.60 .80
449 A130 12c dk bl, gray & ver 2.40 1.60
450 A130 17c ver, gray & vio 5.00 2.75
451 A130 20c yellow, bl & grn 6.00 3.50
452 A130 36c red, blk & yel 7.75 5.50
    Nos. 447-452 (6) 25.50 16.15

7th Pan-American Conf., Montevideo. Issued in sheets of 6. Value $200. For overprints see Nos. C61-C62.

General Rivera — A131

1934, Feb. Engr. Perf. 12½
453 A131 3c green .25 .25

Stars Representing the Three Constitutions — A132

1934, Mar. 23 Typo.
454 A132 3c yellow grn & grn .60 .40
455 A132 7c org red & red .60 .40
456 A132 12c ultra & blue 2.00 .80
Perf. 11½
457 A132 17c brown & rose 2.50 1.25
458 A132 20c yellow & gray 3.50 1.60
459 A132 36c dk vio & bl grn 3.50 1.60
460 A132 50c black & blue 7.00 3.25
461 A132 1p dk car & vio 16.00 6.75
    Nos. 454-461 (8) 35.70 16.05

First Year of Third Republic.

Artigas Type of 1928
Imprint: "Barreiro & Ramos S. A."
1934, Nov. 28 Litho.
462 A109 50c brown black 6.00 2.50

"Uruguay" and "Brazil" Holding Scales of Justice — A133

1935, May 30 Unwmk. Perf. 11
463 A133 5m brown .80 .40
464 A133 15m black .40 .25
465 A133 3c green .40 .25
466 A133 7c orange .40 .25
467 A133 12c ultra .80 .60
468 A133 50c brown 4.00 2.50
    Nos. 463-468 (6) 6.80 4.25

Visit of President Vargas of Brazil.

Florencio Sánchez — A134

1935, Nov. 7
469 A134 3c green .25 .25
470 A134 7c brown .25 .25
471 A134 12c blue .55 .35
 Nos. 469-471 (3) 1.05 .85
 Florencio Sanchez (1875-1910), author.

Artigas (6 dots in panels below portrait) — A135

Imprint: "Imprenta Nacional" at center

1936-44 *Perf. 11, 12½*
474 A135 5m org brn ('37) .25 .25
475 A135 5m lt brown ('39) .25 .25
476 A135 1c lt violet ('37) .25 .25
477 A135 2c brown ('37) .25 .25
478 A135 2c green ('39) .25 .25
479 A135 5c brt blue ('37) .25 .25
480 A135 5c bluish grn ('39) .40 .25
481 A135 12c dull blue ('38) .25 .25
482 A135 20c fawn 1.40 .35
482A A135 20c rose ('44) 1.00 .40
483 A135 50c brown black 3.00 .80

 Size: 21½x28½mm
483A A135 1p brown 8.50 3.00
483B A135 2p blue 14.00 12.00
483C A135 3p gray black 20.00 16.00
 Nos. 474-483C (14) 50.20 34.55
 See Nos. 488, and 576. See type A109.

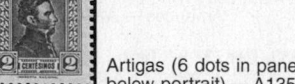

Power Dam on Black River — A136

1937-38
484 A136 1c dull violet .25 .25
485 A136 10c blue .50 .25
486 A136 15c rose 1.25 .60
487 A136 1p choc ('38) 6.25 2.50
 Nos. 484-487 (4) 8.25 3.65

Imprint: "Imprenta Nacional" at right

1938
488 A135 1c bright violet .40 .25

International Law Congress, 1889 — A137

1939, July 16 *Litho.* *Perf. 12½*
489 A137 1c brown orange .25 .25
490 A137 2c dull green .25 .25
491 A137 5c rose ver .25 .25
492 A137 12c dull blue .65 .40
493 A137 50c lt violet 2.50 1.50
 Nos. 489-493 (5) 3.90 2.65
 50th anniversary of the Montevideo Congress of International Law.

Artigas — A138

1939-43 *Litho.* *Unwmk.*
 Size: 15¾x19mm
494 A138 5m dl brn org ('40) .25 .25
495 A138 1c blue .25 .25
496 A138 2c lt violet .25 .25
497 A138 5c violet brn .25 .25
498 A138 8c rose red .25 .25
499 A138 10c green .50 .25
500 A138 15c dull blue 1.25 .60

 Size: 24x29½mm
501 A138 1p dull brn ('41) 2.50 1.00
502 A138 2p dl rose vio ('40) 7.00 3.00
503 A138 4p orange ('43) 9.25 4.00
504 A138 5p ver ('41) 14.00 6.00
 Nos. 494-504 (11) 35.75 16.10
 See No. 578.

Artigas —A138a

Redrawn: Horizontal lines in portrait background

1940-44 *Size: 17x21mm*
505 A138a 5m brn org ('41) .25 .25
506 A138a 1c lt blue .25 .25
507 A138a 2c lt violet ('41) .25 .25
508 A138a 5c violet brn .25 .25
509 A138a 8c sal pink ('44) .25 .25
510 A138a 10c green ('41) .40 .25
511 A138a 50c olive bis ('42) 6.25 1.75
511A A138a 50c yel grn ('44) 4.75 1.75
 Nos. 505-511A (8) 12.65 5.00
 See Nos. 568-575, 577, 601, 632, 660-661.
 For surcharges see Nos. 523, 726.

Juan Manuel Blanes, Artist — A139

1941, Aug. 11 *Engr.* *Perf. 12½*
512 A139 5m ocher .25 .25
513 A139 1c henna brown .25 .25
514 A139 2c green .25 .25
515 A139 5c rose carmine .60 .25
516 A139 12c deep blue 1.25 .60
517 A139 50c dark violet 4.75 3.25
 Nos. 512-517 (6) 7.35 4.85

Francisco Acuna de Figueroa — A140

1942, Mar. 18 *Unwmk.*
518 A140 1c henna brown .25 .25
519 A140 2c deep green .25 .25
520 A140 5c rose carmine .25 .25
521 A140 12c deep blue 1.00 .40
522 A140 50c dark violet 3.25 2.50
 Nos. 518-522 (5) 5.00 3.65
 Issued in honor of Francisco Acuna de Figueroa, author of the National anthem.

No. 506 Surcharged in Red

1943, Jan. 27
523 A138a 5m on 1c lt bl .25 .25

Coat of Arms — A141

1943, Mar. 12 *Litho.*
524 A141 1c on 2c dl vio brn
 (R) .25 .25
525 A141 2c on 2c dl vio brn
 (V) .25 .25
 a. Inverted surcharge 20.00 20.00
 Nos. 524-525 are unissued stamps surcharged. See Nos. 546-555, Q67, Q69, Q74-Q76.

Clio — A142

1943, Aug. 24
526 A142 5m lt violet .25 .25
527 A142 1c lt ultra .25 .25
528 A142 2c brt rose .50 .25
529 A142 5c buff .50 .25
 Nos. 526-529 (4) 1.50 1.00
 100th anniversary of the Historic and Geographic Institute of Uruguay.

Swiss Colony Monument — A143

Overprinted and Surcharged in Various Colors

1944, May 18 *Perf. 11, 12½*
530 A143 1c on 3c dull grn (R) .25 .25
531 A143 5c on 7c brn red (B) .25 .25
532 A143 10c on 12c dk bl (Br) .65 .25
 Nos. 530-532 (3) 1.15 .75
 Founding of the Swiss Colony, 50th anniv. Nos. 530-532 are unissued stamps surcharged.

YMCA Seal — A144

1944, Sept. 8 *Perf. 12½*
533 A144 5c blue .25 .25
 100th anniv. of the YMCA.

> **Catalogue values for unused stamps in this section, from this point to the end of the section, are for Never Hinged items.**

"La Educación del Pueblo" A145

José Pedro Varela A146

Monument A148

A147

Perf. 11½
1945, June 13 *Litho.* *Unwmk.*
534 A145 5m brt green .25 .25
535 A146 1c dp brown .25 .25

 Perf. 12½
536 A147 2c rose red .25 .25
537 A148 5c blue .25 .25
 a. Perf. 11½ .25 .25
 Nos. 534-537 (4) 1.00 1.00
 José Pedro Varela, author, birth cent.

Santiago Vazquez A149

Silvestre Blanco A150

Eduardo Acevedo A151

Bruno Mauricio de Zabala A152

José Pedro Varela — A153

José Ellauri — A154

Gen. Luis de Larrobla — A155

Engraved (5m, 5c, 10c); Lithographed
1945-47 *Perf. 10½, 11, 11½, 12½*
538 A149 5m purple ('46) .25 .25
539 A150 1c yel brn ('46) .25 .25
540 A151 2c brown vio .25 .25
541 A152 3c grn & dp grn ('47) .25 .25
542 A153 5c brt carmine .25 .25
543 A154 10c ultra .40 .25
544 A155 20c dp grn & choc ('47) 1.25 .50
 Nos. 538-544 (7) 2.90 2.00

No. C86A Surcharged in Blue

1946, Jan. 9 *Perf. 12½*
545 AP7 20c on 68c pale vio brn 1.25 .60
 Inauguration of the Black River Power Dam. See No. C120.

Type A141 Overprinted

1946-51 *Unwmk.* *Litho.* *Perf. 12½*
546 A141 5m orange ('49) .35 .25
 a. Inverted overprint
547 A141 2c dl vio brn ('47) .35 .25
548 A141 3c green .35 .25
549 A141 5c ultra ('51) .35 .25
550 A141 10c orange brn .35 .25
551 A141 20c dk green .65 .25
552 A141 50c brown 2.00 1.00
553 A141 3p lilac rose 7.50 4.50
 Nos. 546-553 (8) 11.90 7.00

Type A141 Surcharged

1947-48
554 A141 2c on 5c ultra ('48) .25 .25
555 A141 3c on 5c ultra .25 .25

Statue of
Ariel — A158

Bust of José
Enrique
Rodó — A159

Bas-relief
A160

Bas-relief
A161

Perf. 12½
1948, Jan. 30   Unwmk.   Engr.
Center in Orange Brown

556	A158	1c grnsh gray	.25	.25
557	A159	2c purple	.25	.25
558	A160	3c green	.25	.25
559	A161	5c red violet	.25	.25
560	A160	10c dp orange	.35	.25
561	A161	12c ultra	.40	.25
562	A158	20c rose violet	.80	.25
563	A159	50c dp carmine	2.50	.90
		Nos. 556-563 (8)	5.05	2.65

Dedication of the Rodó monument.

View of the Port,
Paysandú — A162

Arms of
Paysandú
A163

1948, Oct. 9   Litho.

564	A162	3c blue green	.25	.25
565	A163	7c ultra	.40	.25

Exposition of Industry and Agriculture,
Paysandú, October-November 1948.

Santa Lucia
River
Highway
Bridge
A164

1948, Dec. 10

566	A164	10c dark blue	1.00	.25
567	A164	50c green	2.50	1.00

**Redrawn Artigas Types of 1940,
1936, 1939**

1948-51   Litho.   Perf. 12½

568	A138a	5m gray ('49)	.25	.25
569	A138a	1c rose vio ('50)	.25	.25
570	A138a	2c orange	.25	.25
571	A138a	2c choc ('50)	.25	.25
572	A138a	3c blue green	.25	.25
572A	A138a	7c violet blue	.25	.25
573	A138a	8c rose car ('49)	.25	.25
574	A138a	10c orange brn ('51)	.25	.25
575	A138a	12c blue ('51)	.25	.25
576	A135	20c violet	.30	.25
577	A138a	20c rose pink ('51)	.55	.25

Size: 18x21¾mm

578	A138	1p lilac rose ('51)	1.25	.25
		Nos. 568-578 (12)	4.35	3.00

Nos. 571-572A also exist perf. 11.

Plowing
A165

Mounted
Cattle
Herder
A166

1949, Apr. 29   Unwmk.   Perf. 12½

579	A165	3c green	.25	.25
580	A166	7c blue	.40	.25

4th Regional American Conf. of Labor, 1949.

Cannon, Rural
and Urban
Views — A167

1950, Oct. 11   Litho.

581	A167	1c lilac rose	.25	.25
582	A167	3c green	.25	.25
583	A167	7c deep blue	.30	.25
		Nos. 581-583 (3)	.80	.75

200th anniv. of the founding of Cordón, a
district of Montevideo.

Symbolical of
Soccer
Matches — A168

1951, Mar. 20   Perf. 12½, 11

584	A168	3c green	1.00	.25
585	A168	7c violet blue	2.25	.80

4th World Soccer Championship, Rio de
Janeiro.

Gen. José
Artigas — A169

Flight of
the
People
A170

1c, 2c, 5c, Various equestrian portraits of
Artigas. 7c, Dictating instructions. 8c, In congress. 10c, Artigas' flag. 14c, At the citadel.
20c, Arms of Artigas. 50c, In Paraguay. 1p,
Bust.

Engraved and Photogravure

1952, Jan. 7   Unwmk.   Perf. 13½

586	A169	5m slate	.25	.25
587	A169	1c bl & blk	.25	.25
588	A169	2c pur & red brn	.25	.25
589	A170	3c aqua & dk brn	.25	.25
590	A169	5c red org & blk	.25	.25
591	A170	7c ol & blk	.30	.25
592	A170	8c car & blk	.40	.25
593	A170	10c choc, brt ultra & crim	.40	.25
594	A169	14c dp bl	.40	.25
595	A169	20c org yel, dp ultra & car	.90	.25
596	A169	50c org brn & blk	1.75	.40
597	A169	1p bl gray & cit	3.25	1.25
		Nos. 586-597 (12)	8.65	4.15

Centenary (in 1950) of the death of Gen.
José Artigas.

Plane and
Stagecoach
A171

1952, Oct. 9   Photo.   Perf. 13½x13

598	A171	3c bl grn	.25	.25
599	A171	7c blk brn	.25	.25
600	A171	12c ultra	.30	.25
		Nos. 598-600 (3)	.80	.75

75th anniv. (in 1949) of the UPU.

Redrawn Artigas Type of 1940-44
1953, Feb. 23   Litho.   Perf. 11
Size: 24x29½mm

601	A138a	2p fawn	16.00	8.50

Franklin D.
Roosevelt — A172

1953, Apr. 9   Engr.   Perf. 13½

602	A172	3c green	.25	.25
603	A172	7c ultra	.25	.25
604	A172	12c blk brn	.40	.25
		Nos. 602-604 (3)	.90	.75

5th Postal Cong. of the Americas & Spain.

Ceibo, Natl.
Flower — A173

Horse
Breaking — A174

Legislature
Building
A175

"Island of Seals"
(Southern Sea
Lions) — A176

Designs: 2c, 10c, 5p, Ombu tree. 3c, 50c,
Passion Flower. 7c, 3p, Montevideo fortress.
12c, 2p, Outer gate, Montevideo.

**Perf. 13x13½, 13½x13, 12½x13,
13x12½**

Photo. (5m, 3c, 20c, 50c); Engr.

1954, Jan. 14   Unwmk.

605	A173	5m multi	.25	.25
606	A174	1c car & blk	.25	.25
607	A174	2c brn & grn	.25	.25
608	A173	3c multi	.25	.25
609	A175	5c pur & red brn	.25	.25
610	A173	7c brn & grn	.25	.25
611	A176	8c car & ultra	.50	.25
612	A174	10c org & grn	.40	.25
613	A175	12c dp ultra & dk brn	.30	.25
614	A174	14c rose lil & blk	.30	.25
615	A173	20c grn, brn, gray & car	.95	.25
616	A173	50c car & multi	2.40	.25
617	A175	1p car & red brn	2.75	1.00
618	A175	2p car & blk brn	4.75	1.60
619	A173	3p lil & grn	5.50	2.00
620	A176	4p dp brn & dp ultra	16.00	5.00
621	A174	5p vio bl & grn	12.00	4.00
		Nos. 605-621 (17)	47.35	16.60

For surcharges see Nos. 637-639, 750,
C299.

Fair
Entrance — A177

1956, Jan. 19   Litho.   Perf. 11

622	A177	3c pale olive green	.25	.25
623	A177	7c blue	.25	.25
		Nos. 622-623,C166-C168 (5)	2.90	1.60

First Exposition of National Products.

José Batlle y
Ordonez, Birth
Centenary
A178

Design: 7c, Full length portrait.

Perf. 13½
1956, Dec. 15   Wmk. 90   Photo.

624	A178	3c rose red	.25	.25
625	A178	7c sepia	.25	.25
		Nos. 624-025,C169-C172 (6)	2.60	1.90

No. 624
Surcharged

No. 625
Surcharged

1957-58

626	A178	5c on 3c ('58)	.25	.25
627	A178	10c on 7c	.25	.25
a.		Surcharge inverted	25.00	25.00

Diver — A179

Design: 10c, Swimmer at start, horiz.

Perf. 10½, 11½
1958, Feb. 15   Litho.   Unwmk.
628 A179 5c brt bl grn   .25 .25
629 A179 10c brt bl   .50 .25

14th South American swimming meet, Montevideo.

Eduardo Acevedo — A180

1958, Mar. 19   Perf. 11½, 10½
630 A180 5c lt ol grn & blk   .25 .25
631 A180 10c ultra & blk   .25 .25

Eduardo Acevedo (1856-1948), lawyer, legislator, minister of foreign affairs, birth cent.

Redrawn Artigas Type of 1940-44
1958, Sept. 25   Litho.   Perf. 11
632 A138a 5m blue   .25 .25

Baygorria Hydroelectric Works — A181

1958, Oct. 30   Unwmk.   Perf. 11
633 A181 5c yel grn & blk   .25 .25
634 A181 10c brn org & blk   .25 .25
635 A181 1p bl gray & blk   1.25 .25
636 A181 2p rose & blk   2.50 .55
       Nos. 633-636 (4)   4.25 1.30

Nos. 608, 610 and 605 Surcharged Similarly to

Photogravure and Engraved
1958-59   Perf. 13x13½
637 A173 5c on 3c multi ('59)   .30 .25
638 A173 10c on 7c brn & grn   .30 .25
639 A173 20c on 5m multi   .30 .25
       Nos. 637-639 (3)   .90 .75

Gabriela Mistral — A182

Wmk. 327
1959, July 6   Litho.   Perf. 11½
640 A182 5c green   .25 .25
641 A182 10c dark blue   .30 .25
642 A182 20c red   .40 .25
       Nos. 640-642 (3)   .95 .75

Gabriela Mistral, Chilean poet and educator.

Carlos Vaz Ferreira — A183

1959, Sept. 3   Perf. 11
643 A183 5c blk & lt bl   .25 .25
644 A183 10c blk & ocher   .25 .25
645 A183 20c blk & ver   .25 .25
646 A183 50c blk & vio   .35 .25
647 A183 1p blk & grn   .55 .25
       Nos. 643-647 (5)   1.65 1.25

Ferreira (1872-1958), educator and author.

A184

Wmk. 332
1960, May 16   Litho.   Perf. 12
648 A184 3c red lil & blk   .25 .25
649 A184 5c dp vio & blk   .25 .25
650 A184 10c brt bl & blk   .25 .25
651 A184 20c chocolate & blk   .30 .25
652 A184 1p gray & blk   .45 .25
653 A184 2p org & blk   1.10 .25
654 A184 3p olive grn & blk   1.75 .40
655 A184 4p yel brn & blk   2.25 .75
656 A184 5p brt red & blk   2.75 .75
       Nos. 648-656 (9)   9.35 3.40

Dr. Martin C. Martinez (1859-1940), statesman.

A185

1960, June 6   Wmk. 332   Perf. 12
657 A185 10c Uprooted oak emblem   .25 .25

Issued to publicize World Refugee Year, July 1, 1959-June 30, 1960. See No. C207.

Revolutionists and Cabildo, Buenos Aires — A186

1960, Nov. 4   Litho.   Perf. 12
658 A186 5c bl & blk   .25 .25
659 A186 10c bl & ocher   .25 .25
       Nos. 658-659,C208-C210 (5) 1.50 1.25

150th anniv. of the May Revolution of 1810.

Redrawn Artigas Type of 1940-44
1960-61   Wmk. 332   Perf. 11
660 A138a 2c gray   .25 .25
661 A138a 50c brn ('61)   .25 .25

Gen. Manuel Oribe (1796?-1857), Revolutionary Leader, Pres. of Uruguay (1835-38) — A187

1961, Mar. 4   Litho.   Perf. 12
671 A187 10c brt bl & blk   .25 .25
672 A187 20c bis & blk   .30 .25
673 A187 40c grn & blk   .30 .25
       Nos. 671-673 (3)   .85 .75

Cavalry Charge A188

1961, June 12   Wmk. 332   Perf. 12
674 A188 20c bl & blk   .25 .25
675 A188 40c emer & blk   .40 .25

150th anniversary of the revolution.

Welfare, Justice and Education A189

1961, Aug. 14   Wmk. 322   Perf. 12
676 A189 2c bister & lilac   .40 .25
677 A189 5c bister & orange   .40 .25
678 A189 10c bister & scarlet   .40 .25
679 A189 20c bister & yel grn   .40 .25
680 A189 50c bister & light vio .40 .25
681 A189 1p bister & blue   .40 .25
682 A189 2p bister & citron   1.10 .25
683 A189 3p bister & gray   1.50 .65
684 A189 4p bister & light bl   2.50 .80
685 A189 5p bister & chocolate 2.75 1.25
       Nos. 676-685 (10)   10.25 4.45

Inter-American Economic and Social Conference of the Organization of American States, Punta del Este, August, 1961. See Nos. C233-C244.

Gen. José Fructuoso Rivera — A190

Wmk. 332
1962, May 29   Litho.   Perf. 12
686 A190 10c brt red & blk   .25 .25
687 A190 20c bis & blk   .25 .25
688 A190 40c grn & blk   .25 .25
       Nos. 686-688 (3)   .75 .75

Issued to honor Gen. José Fructuoso Rivera (1790-1854), first President of Uruguay.

Spade, Grain, Swiss "Scarf" and Hat — A191

1962, Aug. 1   Wmk. 332   Perf. 12
689 A191 10c bl, blk & car   .25 .25
690 A191 20c lt grn, blk & car .25 .25
       Nos. 689-690,C245-C246 (4) 1.15 1.10

Swiss Settlement in Uruguay, cent.

Bernardo Prudencio Berro — A192

1962, Oct. 22   Litho.   Perf. 12
691 A192 10c grnsh bl & blk   .25 .25
692 A192 20c yel brn & blk   .25 .25

Pres. Bernardo P. Berro (1803-1868).

Damaso Larrañaga A193

1963, Jan. 24   Wmk. 332   Perf. 12
693 A193 20c lt bl grn & dk brn .25 .25
694 A193 40c tan & dk brn   .25 .25

Damaso Antonio Larranaga (1771-1848), teacher, writer and founder of National Library.

Rufous-bellied Thrush — A194

Birds: 50c, Rufous ovenbird. 1p, Chalk-browed mockingbird. 2p, Rufous-collared sparrow.

1963, Apr. 1   Wmk. 332   Perf. 12
695 A194 2c rose, brn & blk   .25 .25
696 A194 50c lt brn & blk   .65 .25
697 A194 1p tan, brn & blk   1.75 .25
698 A194 2p lt brn, blk & gray 3.25 .60
       Nos. 695-698 (4)   5.90 1.35

Thin frame on No. 696, no frame on No. 698.

UPAE Emblem A195

1963, May 31   Litho.
699 A195 20c ultra & blk   .25 .25
       Nos. 699,C252-C253 (3)   .90 .75

50th anniv. of the founding of the Postal Union of the Americas and Spain, UPAE. For surcharge see No. C321.

Wheat Emblem — A196

1963, July 8   Wmk. 332   Perf. 12
700 A196 10c grn & yel   .25 .25
701 A196 20c brn & yel   .25 .25
       Nos. 700-701,C254-C255 (4) 1.25 1.25

FAO "Freedom from Hunger" campaign.

Anchors — A197

1963, Aug. 16
702 A197 10c org & vio .25 .25
703 A197 20c dk red & gray .30 .25
Nos. 702-703,C256-C257 (4) 1.55 1.20

Voyage around the world by the Uruguayan sailing vessel "Alferez Campora," 1960-63.

Large Intestine, Congress Emblem A198

1963, Dec. 9 Litho.
704 A198 10c lt grn, blk & dk car .25 .25
705 A198 20c org, yel, blk & dk car .00 .25

1st Uruguayan Proctology Cong., Montevideo, Dec. 9-15.

Red Cross Centenary Emblem A199

Imprint: "Imp. Nacional"

1964, June 5 Wmk. 332 Perf. 12
706 A199 20c blue & red .25 .25
707 A199 40c gray & red .30 .25

Centenary of International Red Cross. No. 706 exists with imprint missing. Value $4.

Luis Alberto de Herrera A200

1964, July 22 Litho. Unwmk.
708 A200 20c dl grn, bl & blk .25 .25
709 A200 40c lt bl, bl & blk .25 .25
710 A200 80c yel org, bl & blk .25 .25
711 A200 1p lt vio, bl & blk .35 .25
712 A200 2p gray, bl & blk .50 .50
Nos. 708-712 (5) 1.60 1.50

Herrera (1873-1959), leader of Herrerista party and member of National Government Council.

Nile Gods Uniting Upper and Lower Egypt (Abu Simbel) A201

1964, Oct. 30 Wmk. 332 Perf. 12
713 A201 20c multi .25 .25
Nos. 713,C266-C267 (3) 1.50 1.00

UNESCO world campaign to save historic monuments in Nubia. See No. C267a.

Pres. John F. Kennedy A202

1965, Mar. 5 Wmk. 327 Perf. 11½
714 A202 20c gold, emer & blk .25 .25
a. Gold omitted
715 A202 40c gold, redsh brn & blk .30 .25
a. Gold omitted
Nos. 714-715,C269-C270 (4) 1.35 1.30

Tete Beche Pair of 1864, No. 21a A203

1965, Mar. 19 Wmk. 332 Perf. 12
716 A203 40c black & green .25 .25

1st Rio de la Plata Stamp Show, sponsored jointly by the Argentine and Uruguayan philatelic associations, Montevideo, Mar. 19-28. See No. C271. For overprint see No. 736.

Benito Nardone A204

40c, Benito Nardone before microphone.

1965, Mar. 25 Litho.
717 A204 20c blk & emer .30 .25
718 A204 40c blk & emer, vert. .35 .25

1st anniversary of the death of Benito Nardone, president of the Council of Government.

Artigas Quotation — A205

40c, Artigas bust, quotation. 80c, José Artigas.

Perf. 12x11½
1965, May 17 Litho. Wmk. 327
719 A205 20c bl, yel & red .25 .25
720 A205 40c vio bl, cit & blk .25 .25
721 A205 80c brn, yel, red & bl .35 .25
Nos. 719-721,C273-C275 (6) 2.25 1.75

José Artigas (1764-1850), leader of the independence revolt against Spain.

Soccer A206

Designs: 40c, Basketball. 80c, Bicycling. 1p, Woman swimmer.

1965, Aug. 3 Litho. Wmk. 327
722 A206 20c grn, org & blk .25 .25
723 A206 40c hn brn, cit & blk .25 .25
724 A206 80c gray, red & blk .25 .25
725 A206 1p bl, yel grn & blk .25 .25
Nos. 722-725,C276-C281 (10) 4.50 3.45

18th Olympic Games, Tokyo, 10/10-25/64.

No. 572A Surcharged in Red

1965 Unwmk. Perf. 12½
726 A138a 10c on 7c vio bl .25 .25

No. B5 Srchd.

1966, Jan. 25 Wmk. 327 Perf. 11½
727 SP2 4c on 5c + 10c grn & org .25 .25

Association of Uruguayan Architects, 50th anniv.

Winston Churchill A207

Wmk. 332
1966, Apr. 29 Litho. Perf. 12
728 A207 40c car, dp ultra & brn .25 .25

Sir Winston Spencer Churchill, statesman and World War II leader. See No. C284.

Arms of Rio de Janeiro and Sugar Loaf Mountain A208

1966, June 9 Litho. Wmk. 332
729 A208 40c emer & brn .25 .25

400th anniversary of the founding of Rio de Janeiro. See No. C285.

Army Engineer — A209

1966, June 17 Litho.
730 A209 20c blk, red, vio bl & yel .25 .25

50th anniversary of the Army Engineers Corps.

Daniel Fernandez Crespo — A210

Portraits: No. 732, Washington Beltran. No. 733, Luis Batlle Berres.

1966, Sept. 16 Wmk. 332 Perf. 12
731 A210 20c lt bl & blk .25 .25
732 A210 20c lt bl & dk brn .25 .25
733 A210 20c brick red & blk .25 .25
Nos. 731-733 (3) .75 .75

Issued to honor political leaders.

Old Printing Press — A211

1966, Oct. 14 Photo. Perf. 12
734 A211 20c tan, grnsh gray & dk brn .25 .25

50th anniversary of State Printing Office.

Fireman A212

1966, Oct. 21 Litho.
735 A212 20c red & blk .50 .25

Issued to publicize fire prevention. Printed with alternating red and black labels inscribed: "Prevengase del fuego! Del pueblo y para el pueblo." Value, pair with tab $1.

No. 716 Overprinted in Red

1966, Nov. 4
736 A203 40c blk & grn .25 .25

2nd Rio de la Plata Stamp Show, Buenos Aires, Apr. 1966, and cent. of Uruguay's 1st surcharged issue. See No. C298.

General Leandro Gomez — A213

#738, Gen. Juan Antonio Lavalleja. #739, Aparicio Saravia, revolutionary, on horseback.

Wmk. 332
1966, Nov. 24 Litho. Perf. 12
737 A213 20c slate, blk & dp bl .30 .25
738 A213 20c red, blk & bl .30 .25
739 A213 20c blue & blk, horiz. .30 .25
Nos. 737-739 (3) .90 .75

Montevideo Planetarium A214

1967, Jan. 13 Wmk. 332 Perf. 12
740 A214 40c pink & blk .30 .25

10th anniv. of the Montevideo Municipal Planetarium. See No. C301.

Sunflower, Cow and Emblem — A215

1967, Jan. 13   **Litho.**
741   A215   40c dk brn & yel   .30   .25

Young Farmers' Movement, 20th anniv.

Church of San Carlos — A216

1967, Apr. 17   **Wmk. 332**   **Perf. 12**
742   A216   40c lt bl, blk & dk red   .40   .25

Bicentenary of San Carlos.

Eduardo Acevedo A217

1967, Apr. 17
743   A217   20c grn & brn   .25   .25
744   A217   40c org & grn   .30   .25

Issued to honor Eduardo Acevedo, lawyer, legislator and Minister of Foreign Affairs.

Arms of Carmelo — A218

1967, Aug. 11   **Litho.**   **Perf. 12**
745   A218   40c lt & dk bl & ocher   .30   .25

Founding of Carmelo, 150th anniv.

José Enrique Rodó — A219

2p, Portrait of Rodó and sculpture, horiz.

1967, Oct. 6   **Wmk. 332**   **Perf. 12**
746   A219   1p gray, brn & blk   .30   .25
747   A219   2p rose claret, blk &
               tan   .30   .25

50th anniversary of the death of José Enrique Rodó, author.

Senen M. Rodriguez and Locomotive A220

1967, Oct. 26   **Litho.**   **Perf. 12**
748   A220   2p ocher & dk brn   .40   .25

Centenary of the founding of the first national railroad company.

Child and Map of Americas — A221

1967, Nov. 10   **Wmk. 332**   **Perf. 12**
749   A221   1p vio & red   .30   .25

Inter-American Children's Institute, 40th anniv.

No. 610 Surcharged in Red

Perf. 13x13½
1967, Nov. 10   **Engr.**   **Unwmk.**
750   A173   1p on 7c brn & grn   .25   .25

Cocoi Heron — A222

Birds: 1p, Great horned owl. 3p, Brown-headed gull, horiz. No. 754, White-faced tree duck, horiz. No. 754A, Black-tailed stilts. 5p, Wattled jacanas, horiz. 10p, Snowy egret, horiz.

1968-70   **Wmk. 332**   **Litho.**   **Perf. 12**
751   A222   1p dl yel & brn   2.00   .40
752   A222   2p bl grn & blk   2.00   .40
753   A222   3p org, gray & blk
             ('69)   1.50   .35
754   A222   4p brn, tan & blk   3.25   .60
754A   A222   4p ver & blk ('70)   1.50   .35
755   A222   5p lt red brn, blk
              & yel   3.75   .60
756   A222   10p lil & blk   6.75   .80
      Nos. 751-756 (7)   20.75   3.50

Concord Bridge, Presidents of Uruguay, Brazil A223

1968, Apr. 3
757   A223   6p brown   .30   .25

Opening of Concord Bridge across the Uruguay River by Presidents Jorge Pacheco Areco of Uruguay and Arthur Costa e Silva of Brazil.

Soccer Player and Trophy — A224

1968, May 29   **Litho.**
758   A224   1p blk & yel   .30   .25

Victory of the Penarol Athletic Club in the Intercontinental Soccer Championships of 1966.

St. John Bosco, Symbols of Education and Industry A225

1968, July 31   **Wmk. 332**   **Perf. 12**
759   A225   2p brn & blk   .25   .25

75th anniv. of the Don Bosco Workshops of the Salesian Brothers.

Sailors' Monument, Montevideo A226

Designs: 6p, Lighthouse and buoy, vert. 12p, Gunboat "Suarez" (1860).

1968, Nov. 12   **Litho.**   **Perf. 12**
760   A226   2p gray ol & blk   .25   .25
761   A226   6p lt grn & blk   .25   .25
762   A226   12p brt bl & blk   .25   .25
   Nos. 760-762,C340-C343 (7)   2.30   1.75

Sesquicentennial of National Navy.
For surcharge see No. Q101.

Oscar D. Gestido A227

1968, Dec. 6   **Wmk. 332**   **Perf. 12**
763   A227   6p brn, dp car & bl   .25   .25

First anniversary of the death of President Oscar D. Gestido.

Gearwheel, Grain and Two Heads A228

1969, Mar. 17   **Litho.**   **Perf. 12**
764   A228   2p blk & ver   .25   .25

25th anniversary of Labor University.

Bicyclists A229

1969, Mar. 21   **Wmk. 332**
765   A229   6p dk bl, org & emer   .30   .25

1968 World Bicycle Championships. See No. C347.

Gymnasts and Club Emblem A230

1969, May 8   **Wmk. 332**   **Perf. 12**
766   A230   6p blk & ver   .30   .25

75th anniversary of L'Avenir Athletic Club.

Baltasar Brum (1883-1933) A231

Former presidents: No. 768, Tomas Berreta (1875-1947).

1969   **Litho.**   **Perf. 12**
767   A231   6p rose red & blk   .25   .25
768   A231   6p car rose & blk   .25   .25

Fair Emblem — A232

1969, Aug. 15   **Wmk. 332**   **Perf. 12**
769   A232   2p multi   .25   .25

Issued to publicize the 2nd Industrial World's Fair, Montevideo, 1970.

Diesel Locomotive — A233

Design: No. 771, Old steam locomotive and modern railroad cars.

1969, Sept. 19   **Litho.**   **Wmk. 332**
770   6p car, blk & ultra   .40   .25
771   6p car, blk & ultra   .40   .25
  e.   A233 Pair, #770-771   .80   .80

Centenary of Uruguayan railroads. No. 771e has continuous design and label between pairs.
For surcharges see Nos. Q102-Q103.

Souvenir Sheet

Diligencia Issue, 1856 — A233a

1969, Oct. 1   **Imperf.**
771A   A233a   Sheet of 3   8.00   8.00
  b.   60p blue   2.00   2.00
  c.   80p green   2.60   2.60
  d.   100p red   3.00   3.00

Stamp Day 1969. No. 771A contains stamps similar to No. 1-3, with denominations in pesos.
No. 771A was re-issued Apr. 15, 1972, with black overprint for 15th anniv. of 1st Lufthansa flight from Uruguay to Germany and the Munich Olympic Games. Value $30.

"Combat" and Sculptor Belloni — A234

1969, Oct. 22 Wmk. 332 Perf. 12
772 A234 6p olive, slate grn &
　　　　　　　blk .40 .25
　　José L. Belloni (1882-), sculptor.

Reserve
Officers'
Training
Center
Emblem
A235

Design: 2p, Training Center emblem, and officer in uniform and as civilian.

1969, Nov. 5 Litho.
773 A235 1p yel & dk bl .25 .25
774 A235 2p dk brn & lt bl .25 .25
　　Reserve Officers' Training Center, 25th anniv.

Map of Americas
and Sun — A236

1970, Apr. 20 Wmk. 332 Perf. 12
775 A236 10p dp bl & gold .40 .25
　　11th meeting of the governors of the Inter-American Development Bank, Punta del Este.

Stylized
Pine — A237

1970, May 14
776 A237 2p red, blk & brt grn .35 .25
　　2nd National Forestry and Wood Exhibition.

Artigas'
Ancestral
Home in
Sauce
A238

1970, June 18 Wmk. 332 Perf. 12
777 A238 15p ver, ultra & blk .40 .25

Map of
Uruguay,
Sun and
Sea
A239

1970, July 8 Litho.
778 A239 5p greenish blue .35 .25
　　Issued for tourist publicity.

EXPO '70
Emblem, Mt.
Fuji and
Uruguay
Coat of
Arms
A240

EXPO '70 Intl. Exhibition, Osaka, Japan, 3/15-9/13: No. 780, Geisha. No. 781, Sun Tower. No. 782, Youth pole.

1970, Aug. 5 Wmk. 332 Perf. 12
779 A240 25p grn, slate bl & yel .40 .40
780 A240 25p org, slate bl & grn .40 .40
781 A240 25p yel, slate bl & pur .40 .40
782 A240 25p pur, slate bl & org .40 .40
　a.　　Block of 4, #779-782 1.90 1.90

Cobbled Street in
Colonia del
Sacramento
A241

1970, Oct. 21 Litho. Perf. 12
783 A241 5p blk & multi .35 .25
　　290th anniv. of the founding of Colonia del Sacramento, the 1st European settlement in Uruguay.

Mother and Son
by Edmundo Prati
in Salto — A242

1970, Nov. 4 Litho.
784 A242 10p grn & blk .45 .30
　　Issued to honor mothers.

URUEXPO
Emblem
A243

1970, Dec. 9 Wmk. 332 Perf. 12
785 A243 15p bl, brn org & vio .40 .40
　　URUEXPO '70, National Philatelic Exposition, Montevideo, Sept. 26-Oct. 4.

Children Holding Hands, and
UNESCO Emblem — A244

Children's Drawings: No. 786, Two girls holding hands, vert. No. 788, Boy sitting at school desk, vert. No. 789, Astronaut and monster.

1970, Dec. 29 Litho. Perf. 12½
786 A244 10p multi .35 .35
787 A244 10p multi .35 .35
788 A244 10p dp car & multi .35 .35
789 A244 10p bl & multi .35 .35
　a.　　Block of 4, #786-789 + 2 labels 1.60 1.60
　　International Education Year.

Alfonso Espinola
(1845-1905),
Physician,
Professor and
Philanthropist
A245

1971, Jan. 13 Wmk. 332 Perf. 12
790 A245 5p dp org & blk .35 .25

Exposition Poster — A246

1971 Litho. Perf. 12
791 A246 15p multi .35 .25
　　Uruguay Philatelic Exposition, 1971, Montevideo, March 26-Apr. 19.

5c Coin of
1840,
Obverse
A247

Design: #793, 1st coin of Uruguay, reverse.

1971, Apr. 16 Wmk. 332 Perf. 12
792 A247 25p bl, brn & blk .60 .60
793 A247 25p bl, brn & blk .50 .50
　a.　　Pair, #792-793 1.50 1.50
　　Numismatists' Day.

Domingo Arena,
Lawyer and
Journalist — A248

1971, May 3 Wmk. 332 Perf. 12
794 A248 5p dk car .30 .25

National
Anthem
A249

1971, May 19 Litho.
795 A249 15p bl, blk & yel .40 .40

José F. Arias,
Physician — A250

1971, May 25 Wmk. 332 Perf. 12
796 A250 5p sepia .45 .25

Eduardo
Fabini,
Bar from
"Campo"
A251

1971, June 2 Litho.
797 A251 5p dk car rose & blk .60 .30
　　Eduardo Fabini (1882-1950), composer, and 40th anniversary of first radio concert.

José E.
Rodó,
UPAE
Emblem
A252

1971, July 15 Wmk. 332 Perf. 12
798 A252 15p ultra & blk .65 .40
　　José Enrique Rodó (1871-1917), writer, first Uruguayan delegate to Congress of the Postal Union of the Americas and Spain.

Water
Cart and
Faucet
A253

1971, July 17
799 A253 5p ultra & multi .35 .25
　　Centenary of Montevideo's drinking water system.

Sheep
and Cloth
A254

Design: 15p, Sheep, cloth and bale of wool.

1971, Aug. 7
800 A254 5p grn & gray .25 .25
801 A254 15p dk bl, grnsh bl &
　　　　　　　gray .30 .25
　　Wool Promotion.

José
Maria
Elorza
and
Merilin
Sheep
A255

1971, Aug. 10
802 A255 5p lt bl, grn & blk .30 .25
　　José Maria Elorza, developer of the Merilin sheep.

Criollo
Horse
A256

1971, Aug. 11
803 A256 5p blk, gray bl & org .80 .25

Bull and
Ram
A257

1971, Aug. 13
804 A257 20p red, grn, blk & gold .45 .35
Centenary of Rural Association of Uruguay;
19th International Cattle Breeding Exposition,
and 66th National Cattle Championships at
Prado, Aug. 1971.

Symbol of
Liberty
and Order
A258

20p, Policemen, flag of Uruguay and
emblem.

1971
805 A258 10p gray, blk & bl .30 .25
806 A258 20p dk bl, blk, lt bl &
gold .35 .25
To honor policemen killed on duty. Issue
dates: 10p, Sept. 9; 20p, Nov. 4.

10p Banknote of 1896 — A259

Design: No. 808, Reverse of 10p note.

1971, Sept. 23
807 A259 25p dl grn, gold & blk .50 .50
808 A259 25p dl grn, gold & blk .50 .50
a. Pair, #807-808 + label 1.25 1.25
75th anniversary of Bank of the Republic.

Farmer
and Arms
of
Durazno
A260

1971, Oct. 11
809 A260 20p gold, bl & blk .50 .25
Sesquicentennial of the founding of Durazno.

Emblem and Laurel — A261

1971, Oct. 20
810 A261 10p vio bl, gold & red .50 .25
Winners of Liberator's Cup, American Soccer Champions, 1971.
For surcharge see No. 825.

Voter Casting
Ballot — A262

Design: 20p, Citizens voting, horiz.

1971, Nov. 22 Wmk. 332 Perf. 12
811 A262 10p bl & blk .30 .25
812 A262 20p bl & blk .30 .25
Universal, secret and obligatory franchise.

Map of
Uruguay on
Globe
A263

1971, Dec. 23
813 A263 20p lt bl & vio brn .50 .25
7th Littoral Expo., Paysandu, 3/26-4/11.

Juan Lindolfo
Cuestas — A264

No. 815, Julio Herrera y Obes. No. 816,
Claudio Williman. No. 817, José Serrato. No.
818, Andres Martinez Truebá.

1971, Dec. 27
814 A264 10p shown .25 .25
815 A264 10p multicolored .25 .25
816 A264 10p multicolored .25 .25
817 A264 10p multicolored .25 .25
818 A264 10p multicolored .25 .25
a. Horiz. strip of 5, #814-818 1.50 1.50
Presidents of Uruguay.

Souvenir Sheet

Uruguay No. 4, Cathedral of
Montevideo and Plaza de la
Constitucion — A265

1972, Jan. 17 Imperf.
819 A265 120p brn, bl & dp rose 1.25 1.00
Stamp Day 1971 (release date delayed).
See Nos. 834-835, 863.

Bartolomé
Hidalgo — A266

1972, Feb. 28 Perf. 12
820 A266 5p lt brn, blk & red .55 .25
Bartolomé Hidalgo (1788-1822), Uru-
guayan-Argentine poet.

Missa Solemnis, by
Beethoven — A267

1972, Apr. 20 Litho. Wmk. 332
822 A267 20p lil, emer & blk .40 .25
12th Choir Festival of Eastern Uruguay.

Dove and
Wounded
Bird — A268

1972, May 9
823 A268 10p ver & multi .40 .25
To honor Dionision Disz (age 9), who died
saving his sister.

Columbus Arch,
Colon — A269

1972, June 21
824 A269 20p red, bl & blk .40 .25
Centenary of Colon, now suburb of
Montevideo.

No. 810 Surcharged in Silver

(Surcharge 69mm wide)

1972, June 30
825 A261 50p on 10p multi .50 .25
Winners of the 1971 Intl. Soccer Cup.

Tree
Planting — A270

1972, Aug. 5 Wmk. 332 Perf. 12
826 A270 20p grn & blk .35 .25
Afforestation program.

"Collective
Housing" — A271

1972, Sept. 30 Litho.
827 A271· 10p dp bl & multi .35 .25
Publicity for collective housing plan.

Amethyst
A272

Uruguayan Gem Stones: 9p, Agate. 15p,
Chalcedony.

1972, Oct. 7
828 A272 5p gray & multi .50 .25
829 A272 9p gray bl & multi .50 .25
830 A272 15p gray grn & multi .75 .25
Nos. 828-830 (3) 1.75 .75

Uniform of
1830 — A273

Design: 20p, Lancer.

1972, Nov. 21 Litho.
831 A273 10p multi .30 .25
832 A273 20p rose red & multi .35 .25

Red
Cross and
Map of
Uruguay
A274

1972, Dec. 11 Wmk. 332 Perf. 12
833 A274 30p multi .40 .25
75th anniv. of the Uruguayan Red Cross.

Stamp Day Type of 1972
Souvenir Sheets

Designs: 200p, Coat of arms type of 1864
similar to Nos. 18, 20-21, but 60p, 60p and
80p. 220p, Similar to Nos. 22-23, but 100p and
120p.

1972, Dec. 20 Imperf.
834 A265 200p multi 1.25 .60
835 A265 220p multi 1.50 .75
Stamp Day 1972. 1st printed cancellations,
200th anniv., #834; Decree establishing regular postal service, cent., #835.

Scales of
Justice,
Olive
Branch
A275

1972, Dec. 27 Wmk. 332 Perf. 12
836 A275 10p gold, dk & lt bl .30 .25
Civil Rights Law for Women, 25th anniv.

Gen. José
Artigas — A276

1972-74　Wmk. 332　Litho.　Perf. 12

837	A276	5p yel ('74)	.25	.25
838	A276	10p dk bis ('74)	.25	.25
839	A276	15p emer ('74)	.25	.25
040	A276	20p lilac ('73)	.25	.25
841	A276	30p lt bl ('73)	.25	.25
842	A276	40p dp org ('73)	.25	.25
843	A276	50p ver ('73)	.25	.25
844	A276	75p ap grn ('73)	.25	.25
845	A276	100p emerald	.25	.25
846	A276	150p choc ('73)	.25	.25
847	A276	200p dk bl ('73)	.45	.30
848	A276	250p pur ('73)	.50	.35
849	A276	500p gray ('73)	1.25	.60
849A	A276	1000p blue ('73)	2.50	1.25
	Nos. 837-849A (14)		7.20	5.00

For surcharges see Nos. 929-932.

Hand Holding
Cup; Grain, Map
of
Americas — A277

1973, Jan. 9
850　A277　30p rose red, yel & blk　.30　.25
　Intl. Institute for Agricultural Research, 39th anniv.

Elbio Fernandez
and José P.
Varela — A278

1973, Jan. 16
851　A278　10p dl grn, gold & blk　.30　.25
Society of Friends of Public Education, cent.

Map of
Americas,
"1972" and
Columbus
A279

1973, Jan. 30
852　A279　50p purple　.30　.25
　Tourist Year of the Americas 1972.

Carlos
Maria
Ramirez, Scales
and
Books
A280

No. 854, Justino Jimenez de Arechaga. No. 855, Juan Andres Ramirez. No. 856, Justino E. Jimenez de Arechaga.

1973, Feb. 15

853	A280	10p shown	.25	.25
854	A280	10p multicolored	.25	.25
855	A280	10p multicolored	.25	.25
856	A280	10p multicolored	.25	.25
a.	Horiz. strip, #853-856 + label		1.25	1.25

Professorship of Constitutional Rights, cent.

Provincial
Map of
Uruguay
A281

1973, Feb. 27　Litho.　Perf. 12½x12
857　A281　20p bl & multi　.40　.25
　See No. 1167.

Francisco
de los
Santos
A282

1973, May 16　Wmk. 332　Perf. 12
858　A282　20p grn & blk　.35　.25
　Soldiers' Day and Battle of Piedras. Santos was a courier who went through enemy lines.

No. C319 Surcharged in Black

Souvenir Sheet

1973, May 9　Litho.　Imperf.
859　AP57　100p on 5p multi　1.25　1.00
　Founding of Cordoba in Argentina, 400th anniv.

Friar, Indians,
Church — A283

1973, July 25　Perf. 12
860　A283　20p lt ultra, pur & blk　.30　.25
　Villa Santo Domingo Soriano, first Spanish settlement in Uruguay.

Symbolic
Fish
A284

1973, Aug. 15
861　A284　100p bl & multi　.50　.25
　First station of Oceanographic and Fishery Service, Montevideo.

A285

Sun over flower in Italian colors.

1973, Sept.
862　A285　100p multi　.30　.25
　Italian Chamber of Commerce of Uruguay.

Stamp Day Type of 1972
Souvenir Sheet

Design: 240p, Thin numeral sun type of 1859 and street scene.

Wmk. 332

1973, Oct. 1　Litho.　Imperf.
863　A265　240p grn, org & blk　1.50　1.50
　Stamp Day 1973.

Herrera — A286

1973, Nov. 12　Perf. 12
866　A286　50p gray, brn & dk brn　.30　.25
　Centenary of the birth of Luis Alberto de Herrera.

Emblem of
Social
Coordination
Volunteers
A287

Wmk. 352

1973, Nov. 19　Litho.　Perf. 12
867　A287　50p bl & multi　.35　.25
　Festival of Nations, Montevideo.

Arm with
Arteries and
Heart
A288

1973, Nov. 22
868　A288　50p blk, red & pink　.30　.25
　3rd Cong. of the Pan-American Federation of Blood Donors, Montevideo, Nov. 23-25.

Madonna, by
Rafael Perez
Barradas — A289

1973, Dec. 10　Litho.　Wmk. 332
869　A289　50p grn, gray & yel grn　.40　.25
　Christmas 1973.

Nicolaus Copernicus — A290

1973, Dec. 26　Litho.
870　A290　50p grn & multi　.45　.25
　500th anniversary of the birth of Nicolaus Copernicus (1473-1543), Polish astronomer.

Praying Hands
and
Andes — A291

　75p, Statue of Christ on mountain, and flower.

1973, Dec. 26　Litho.
871　A291　50p blk, lt grn & ultra　.25　.25
872　A291　75p bl, blk & org　.30　.25
　Survival and rescue of victims of airplane crash.

OAS
Emblem
and Map
of
Americas
A292

1974, Jan. 14　Wmk. 332　Perf. 12
873　A292　250p gray & multi　.85　.40
　25th anniversary of the Organization of American States (OAS).

Scout
Emblems
and
Flame
A293

1974, Jan. 21
874　A293　250p multi　.85　.40
　1st Intl. Boy Scout Games, Montevideo, 1974.

Hector
Suppici
Sedes and
Car — A294

1974, Jan. 28　Perf. 12
875　A294　50p sep, grn & blk　.50　.25
　70th anniversary of the birth of Hector Suppici Sedes (1903-1948), automobile racer.

Three Gauchos — A295

1974, Mar. 20   Litho.   Wmk. 332
876 A295 50p multi   .60 .25
  Centenary of the publication of "Los Tres Gauchos Orientales" by Antonio D. Lussich.

Rifle, Target and Swiss Flag A296

1974, Apr. 2
877 A296 100p multi   .45 .25
  Centenary of the Swiss Rifle Association.

Map of Uruguay and Compass Rose A297

1974, Apr. 23   Litho.
878 A297 50p multi   .40 .25
  Military Geographical Service.

Montevideo Stadium Tower — A298

  Design: 75p, Soccer player, Games' emblem, horiz. 1000p, similar to 75p.

1974, May 7   Wmk. 332   Perf. 12
879 A298 50p multi   .25 .25
880 A298 75p multi   .25 .25
881 A298 1000p multi   22.50 8.50
  World Cup Soccer Championship, Munich, June 13-July 7.
  No. 881 had limited distribution. A souvenir sheet of one No. 881 was not valid for postage.

Tourism — A299

Wmk. 332
1974, June 6   Litho.   Perf. 12
882 A299 1000p multicolored   35.00 35.00
  No. 882 had limited distribution.

Old and New School and Founders A300

1974, May 21
883 A300 75p black & bister   .40 .25
  Centenary of the Osimani-Llerena Technical School at Salto, founded by Gervasio Osimani and Miguel Llerena.

Gardel and Score — A301

Wmk. 332
1974, June 24   Litho.   Perf. 12
884 A301 100p multi   .50 .25
  Carlos Gardel (1887-1935), singer and motion picture actor. See No. 1173.

Volleyball and Net — A302

1974, July 11   Wmk. 332   Perf. 12
885 A302 200p lil, yel & blk   .50 .25
  First anniversary of Women's Volleyball championships, Montevideo, 1973.

"Protect your Heart" — A303

1974, July 24   Litho.
886 A303 75p ol grn, yel & red   .45 .25
  Heart Foundation publicity.

Portrait and Statue — A304

1974, Aug. 5
887 A304 75p dk & lt bl   .40 .25
  Centenary (in 1973) of the founding of San José de Mayo by Eusebio Vidal.

A305

  Artigas statue, Buenos Aires, flags of Uruguay and Argentina.

1974, Aug. 13   Perf. 12½
888 A305 75p multicolored   .45 .25
  Unveiling of Artigas monument, Buenos Aires.

A306

1974, Sept. 24   Wmk. 332   Perf. 12
889 A306 100p Radio tower and waves   .40 .25
  50th anniv. of Broadcasting in Uruguay.

URUEXPO 74 Emblem — A307

URUEXPO Emblem and Old Map of Montevideo Bay — A308

1974
890 A307 100p blk, dk bl & red   .25 .25
891 A308 300p sepia, red & grn   .60 .60
  URUEXPO 74 Philatelic Exhibition, 10th anniversary of Philatelic Circle of Uruguay (100p) and 250th anniversary of fortification of Montevideo.
  Issue dates: 100p, Oct. 1; 300p, Oct. 19.

Letters and UPU Emblem A309

  UPU Cent.: 200p, UPU emblem, letter, and globe.

1974, Oct. 9
892 A309 100p lt bl & multi   .25 .25
893 A309 200p lil, blk & gold   .35 .25
  Nos. 892-893,C395-C396 (4)   2.60 2.50
  A 1000p souvenir sheet was not valid for postage. Value $45.

Artigas Statue and Map of Lavalleja A310

1974, Oct. 17   Perf. 12
894 A310 100p ultra & multi   .45 .25
  Unveiling of Artigas statue in Minas, Lavalleja.

Ship in Dry Dock, Arsenal's Emblem A312

1974, Nov. 15   Litho.   Wmk. 332
896 A312 200p multi   .45 .30
  Centenary of Naval Arsenal, Montevideo.

Globe Hydrogen Balloon — A313

  No. 898, Farman biplane. No. 899, Castaibert monoplane. No. 900, Bleriot monoplane. No. 901, Military and civilian pilots' emblems. No. 902, Nieuport biplane. No. 903, Breguet-Bidon fighter. No. 904, Caproni bomber.

1974, Nov. 20
897	A313	100p shown	.35	.35
898	A313	100p multicolored	.55	.35
899	A313	100p multicolored	.55	.35
900	A313	100p multicolored	.55	.35
a.		Strip of 4, #897-900	2.25	2.25
901	A313	150p multicolored	.55	.35
902	A313	150p multicolored	.55	.35
903	A313	150p multicolored	.55	.35
904	A313	150p multicolored	.55	.35
a.		Strip of 4, #901-904	2.25	2.25
		Nos. 897-904 (8)	4.40	2.80

Aviation pioneers.

Sugar Loaf Mountain and Summit Cross — A314

1974, Nov. 30
905	A314	150p multicolored	.45	.25

Cent. of the founding of Sugar Loaf City.

Adoration of the Kings — A315

1974   *Perf. 12*
906	A315	100p shown	.30	.25
907	A315	150p Three Kings	.30	.25
		Nos. 906-907,C400 (3)	1.10	.75

Christmas 1974. See No. C401. Issue dates: 100p, Dec. 17; 150p, Dec. 19.

Nike, Fireworks, Rowers and Club Emblem — A316

1975, Jan. 27   Litho.   Wmk. 332
908	A316	150p gray & multi	.45	.25

Centenary of Montevideo Rowing Club.

Treaty Signing, by José Zorilla de San Martin — A317

1975, Feb. 12   *Perf. 12*
909	A317	100p multi	.45	.25

Commercial Treaty between Great Britain and Uruguay, 1817.

Rose — A318

1975, Mar. 18   Litho.   Wmk. 332
910	A318	150p multicolored	.70	.40

Bicentenary of city of Rosario.

"The Oath of the 33," by Juan M. Blanes — A319

1975, Apr. 16   *Perf. 12*
911	A319	150p gold & multi	.45	.25

Sesquicentennial of liberation movement.

Ship, Columbus and Ancient Map — A320

1975, Oct. 9   Litho.   Wmk. 332
912	A320	1p gray & multi	1.40	.80

Hispanic Stamp Day.

Leonardo Olivera and Santa Teresa Fort — A321

Artigas as Young and Old Man A322

1975   Litho.   Wmk. 332   *Perf. 12*
913	A321	10c org & multi	.30	.25
914	A322	50c vio bl & multi	.70	.40

Sesquicentennial of the capture of Fort Santa Teresa (10c) and of Uruguay's declaration of independence (50c).
Issue dates: 10c, Oct. 20; 50c, Oct. 17.

Battle of Rincon, by Diogenes Hequet — A323

#916, Artigas' Home, Ibiray, Paraguay. 25c, Battle of Sarandi, by J. Manuel Blanes.

1975   Litho.
915	A323	15c gold & blk	.30	.25
916	A323	15c gold & multi	.30	.25
917	A323	25c gold & multi	.50	.30
		Nos. 915-917 (3)	1.10	.80

Uruguayan independence. Nos. 915 and 917, 150th anniversary of Battles of Rincon and Sarandi. No. 916, 50th anniversary of school at Artigas mansion.
Issued: #915, 10/23; #916, 11/18; #917, 11/28.

"En Familia," by Sanchez A324

Florencio Sanchez A325

Plays by Sanchez: #919, Barranca Abajo. #920, M'Hijo el Doctor. #921, Canillita.

1975, Oct. 31   Wmk. 332   *Perf. 12*
918	A324	20c gray, red & blk	.35	.25
919	A324	20c bl, grn & blk	.35	.25
920	A324	20c red, bl & blk	.35	.25
921	A324	20c grn, gray & blk	.35	.25
922	A325	20c multi	.35	.25
a.		Block of 5 stamps + 4 labels	2.75	2.75

Florencio Sanchez (1875-1910), dramatist, birth centenary. Nos. 918-922 printed se-tenant in sheets of 30 stamps and 20 labels.

Maria Eugenia Vaz Ferreira A326

Design: No. 924, Julio Herrera y Reissig.

1975
923	A326	15c yel, blk & brn	.35	.25
924	A326	15c org, blk & maroon	.35	.25

Maria Eugenia Vaz Ferreira (1875-1924), poetess, and Julio Herrera y Reissig (1875-1910), poet, birth anniversaries.
Issue dates: #923, Dec. 9; #924, Dec. 29.

A327

Virgin and Child — A328

Fireworks — A329

1975
925	A327	20c bl & multi	.35	.35
926	A328	30c blk & multi	.60	.60
927	A329	60c multi	.75	.75
		Nos. 925-927 (3)	1.70	1.70

Christmas 1975.
Issued: 20c, 12/16; 30c, 12/15; 60c, 12/11.

Col. Lorenzo Latorre (1840-1916), Pres. of Uruguay (1870-80) A330

1975, Dec. 30   *Perf. 12*
928	A330	15c multicolored	.35	.25

Nos. 840, 842-843, 849A Surcharged

1975
929	A276	10c on 20p lilac	.25	.25
930	A276	15c on 40p orange	.25	.25
931	A276	50c on 50p ver	.45	.45
932	A276	1p on 1000p blue	.95	.95
		Nos. 929-932 (4)	1.90	1.90

There are two surcharge types for Nos. 929 and 930. Values are the same.

Ariel, Stars, Book and Youths A331

1976, Jan. 12   Litho.   Wmk. 332
933	A331	15c grn & multi	.35	.25

75th anniversary of publication of "Ariel," by Jose Enrique Rodo (1872-1917), writer.

Water Sports — A332

1976, Mar. 12 Litho. Wmk. 332
934 A332 30c multicolored .45 .25
23rd South American Swimming, Diving and Water Polo Championships.

Telephone A333

1976, Apr. 9 Perf. 12
935 A333 83c multicolored .60 .30
Centenary of first telephone call by Alexander Graham Bell, Mar. 10, 1876.

"Plus Ultra" and Columbus' Ships — A334

Wmk. 332
1976, May 10 Litho. Perf. 12
936 A334 63c gray & multi .50 .30
Flight of Dornier "Plus Ultra" from Spain to South America, 50th anniversary.

A335

Dornier "Wal" and Boeing 727, hourglass.

1976, May 24
937 A335 83c gray & multi .50 .30
Lufthansa German Airline, 50th anniv.

A336

Designs: 10c, Olympics. 15c, Telephone, cent. 25c, UPU, cent., UN #2. 50c, World Cup Soccer Championships, Argentina, 1978.

1976, June 3 Perf. 11½
938 A336 10c shown 1.75 .60
939 A336 15c multicolored 1.75 .60
940 A336 25c multicolored 1.75 .60
941 A336 50c multicolored 1.75 .60
Nos. 938-941 (4) 7.00 2.40

Nos. 938-941 had limited distribution. A souvenir sheet containing one each, Nos. 938-941, was not valid for postage. Value $45.

Louis Braille A340

1976, June 7
942 A340 60c blk & brn .50 .40
Sesquicentennial of the invention of the Braille system of writing for the blind by Louis Braille (1809-1852).

Signing of US Declaration of Independence A341

1976, June 21
943 A341 1.50p multicolored 2.50 2.00
American Bicentennial.

The Candombe, by P. Figari — A342

Wmk. 332
1976, July 29 Litho. Perf. 12
944 A342 30c ultra & multi .45 .25
Abolition of slavery, sesquicentennial.

Gen. Fructuoso Rivera Statue A343

1976, Aug. 2
945 A343 5p on 10p multi 4.00 2.00
No. 945 was not issued without surcharge.

General Accounting Office — A344

Wmk. 332
1976, Aug. 24 Litho. Perf. 12
946 A344 30c bl, blk & brn .35 .25
National General Accounting Office, sesquicentennial.

Old Pump, Emblem and Flame — A345

1976, Sept. 6
947 A345 20c red & blk .85 .25
First official fire fighting service, centenary.

Southern Lapwing A346

Mburucuya Flower A347

Spearhead A348

Figurine A349

La Yerra, by J. M. Blanes A350

The Gaucho, by Blanes A351

Artigas — A352

Designs: 15c, Ceibo flower.

1976-79 Litho. Wmk. 332 Perf. 12
948 A346 1c violet .25 .25
949 A347 5c lt grn .25 .25
950 A347 15c car rose .25 .25
951 A348 20c gray .25 .25
952 A349 30c gray blue .25 .25
953 A352 45c brt bl ('79) .25 .25
954 A350 50c grnsh bl ('77) .25 .25
955 A351 1p dk brn ('77) .50 .25
956 A352 1p brt yel ('79) .25 .25
957 A352 1.75p bl grn ('79) .40 .30
958 A352 1.95p gray ('79) .40 .30
959 A352 2p dl grn ('77) 1.10 .40
960 A352 2p lil rose ('79) .50 .35
961 A352 2.65p vio ('79) .50 .40
962 A352 5p dk bl 3.50 2.00
963 A352 10p brn ('77) 6.75 2.00
Nos. 948-963 (16) 15.65 8.00

"Diligencia" Uruguay No. 1 — A353

Wmk. 332
1976, Sept. 26 Litho. Perf. 12
964 A353 30c bister, red & blue .45 .25
Philatelic Club of Uruguay, 50th anniv.

Games' Emblem — A354

1976, Oct. 26 Litho. Perf. 12
965 A354 83c gray & multi 1.00 .50
5th World University Soccer Championships.

World Cup Soccer Championships, Argentina — A355

Anniversaries and Events: 30c, 1976 Summer Olympics, Montreal. 50c, Viking spacecraft. 80c, Nobel prizes, 75th anniv.

1976, Nov. 12 Perf. 12
966 A355 10c multicolored 1.60 .85
967 A355 30c multicolored 1.60 .85
968 A355 50c multicolored 1.60 .85
969 A355 80c multicolored 1.60 .85
Nos. 966-969 (4) 6.40 3.40

Nos. 966-969 had limited distribution. See Nos. C424-C425.

Eye and Spectrum A356

1976, Nov. 24
970 A356 20c blk & multi .50 .25
Foresight prevents blindness.

Map of Montevideo, 1748 — A357

45c, Montevideo Harbor, 1842. 70c, First settlers, 1726. 80c, Coin with Montevideo arms, vert. 1.15p, Montevideo's first coat of arms, vert.

Wmk. 332
1976, Dec. 30 Litho. Perf. 12
971 A357 30c multi .25 .25
972 A357 45c multi .25 .25
973 A357 70c multi .40 .25
974 A357 80c multi .65 .25
975 A357 1.15p multi 1.00 .45
Nos. 971-975 (5) 2.55 1.45

Founding of Montevideo, 250th anniversary.

Symbolic of Flight A358

1977, May 7 Litho. Perf. 12
976 A358 80c multicolored .75 .50
50th anniversary of Varig airlines.

Artigas Mausoleum — A359

1977, June 17   **Litho.**   *Perf. 12*
977 A359 45c multicolored   .50 .30

A360

1977, July 5   **Wmk. 332**
978 A360 45c Map of Uruguay, arch   .45 .30

Centenary of Salesian Brothers' educational system in Uruguay.

A361

Anniversaries and events: 20c, Werner Heisenberg, Nobel Prize for Physics. 30c, World Cup Soccer Championships, Uruguay Nos. 282, 390. 50c, Lindbergh's trans-Atlantic flight, 50th anniv. 1p, Rubens 400th birth anniv.

1977, July 21
979 A361 20c shown   1.25 .75
980 A361 30c multicolored   1.25 .75
981 A361 50c multicolored   1.25 .75
982 A361 1p multicolored   1.25 .75
   a.   Strip, 2 ea #979-982 + 2 labels   10.00 6.50
   Nos. 979-982 (4)   5.00 3.00

Nos. 979-982 had limited distribution. A souvenir sheet containing Nos. 979-982, imperf., was not valid for postage. It sold for 8p. See Nos. C426-C427.

Children — A362

1977, Aug. 10   **Litho.**   *Perf. 12*
983 A362 45c multi   .50 .30

Interamerican Children's Inst., 50th anniv.

"El Sol de Mayo" A363

1977, Oct. 1   **Litho.**   *Perf. 12*
984 A363 45c multi   .50 .30

Stamp Day 1977.

Windmills — A364

1977, Sept. 29   **Wmk. 332**
985 A364 70c yel, car & blk   .50 .30

Spanish Heritage Day.

Souvenir Sheet

View of Sans (Barcelona), by Barradas — A365

1977, Oct. 7   **Litho.**   *Perf. 12*
986 A365   Sheet of 2   5.00 5.00
   a.-b.   5p, single stamp   2.25 2.25

ESPAMER '77 Philatelic Exhibition, Barcelona, Oct. 7-13.

Planes, UN Emblem, Globe A366

1977, Oct. 17
987 A366 45c multi   .45 .25

30th anniv. of Civil Aviation Organization.

Holy Family — A367

Santa Claus — A368

1977, Dec. 1   **Wmk. 332**
988 A367 45c multi   .25 .25
989 A368 70c blk, yel & red   .25 .25

Christmas 1977.

Map of Rio Negro Province A369

1977, Dec. 16
990 A369 45c multi   .40 .25

Rio Negro Dam; development of argiculture, livestock and beekeeping. See Nos. 1021-1033.

Mail Collection A370

No. 992, Mail truck. No. 993, Post office counter. No. 994, Postal boxes. No. 995, Mail sorting. No. 996, Pigeonhole sorting. No. 997, Route sorting (seated carriers). No. 998, Home delivery. No. 999, Special delivery (motorcyclists). No. 1000, Airport counter.

1977, Dec. 21
991 A370 50c shown   .40 .25
992 A370 50c multicolored   .40 .25
993 A370 50c multicolored   .40 .25
994 A370 50c multicolored   .40 .25
995 A370 50c multicolored   .40 .25
996 A370 50c multicolored   .40 .25
997 A370 50c multicolored   .40 .25
998 A370 50c multicolored   .40 .25
999 A370 50c multicolored   .40 .25
1000 A370 50c multicolored   .40 .25
   a.   Strip of 10, #991-1000   7.50 7.50

Uruguayan postal service, 150th anniv.

Edison's Phonograph, 1877 — A371

1977, Dec. 30
1001 A371 50c vio brn & yel   .40 .25

Centenary of invention of the phonograph.

"R", Rainbow and Emblem A372

1977, Dec. 30   **Wmk. 332**
1002 A372 50c multi   .40 .25

World Rheumatism Year.

Emblem and Diploma A373

1978, Mar. 27   **Litho.**   *Perf. 12*
1003 A373 50c multi   .40 .25

50th anniversary of Military College.

Erhard Schon by Albrecht Durer (1471-1528) — A374

Painting: 50c, Self-Portrait by Peter Paul Rubens (1577-1640).

1978, June 13   *Perf. 12½*
1004 A374 25c blk & brn   1.25 1.00
1005 A374 50c brn & blk   2.00 1.50

Nos. 1004-1005 had limited distribution. See Nos. C430-C432.

Map and Arms of Artigas Department — A375

Wmk. 332
1978, June 16   **Litho.**   *Perf. 12*
1006 A375 45c multi   .45 .25

Souvenir Sheet

Anniversaries — A376

Designs: 2p, Papilio thoas. No. 1007b, "100." No. 1007c, Argentina '78 emblem and globes. 5p, Model T Ford.

Wmk. 332
1978, Aug. 24   **Litho.**   *Perf. 12*
1007 A376   Sheet of 4   14.00 14.00
   a.   2p multi   1.40 1.40
   b.   4p multi   2.75 2.75
   c.   4p multi   2.75 2.75
   d.   5p multi   3.50 3.50

75th anniv. of 1st powered flight; URUEXPO '78 Phil. Exhib.; Parva Domus social club, cent.; 11th World Cup Soccer Championship, Argentina, June 1-25; Ford motor cars, 75th anniv.

Visiting Angels, by Solari — A377

Designs (Details from No. 1008b): No. 1008a, Second angel. No. 1008c, Third angel.

1978, Sept. 13   **Unwmk.**
1008   Strip of 3   2.00   2.00
  a. A377 1.50p, 19x30mm   .40   .25
  b. A377 1.50p, 38x30mm   .40   .25
  c. A377 1.50p, 19x30mm   .40   .25
     Solari, Uruguayan painter.

Bernardo O'Higgins A378

#1010, José de San Martin and monument.

1978   **Wmk. 332**
1009   A378 1p multi   .30   .25
1010   A378 1p multi   .30   .25
    Benardo O'Higgins (1778-1842) and José de San Martin (1778-1850), South American liberators.
    Issued: #1009, Sept. 13; #1010, Oct. 10.

Telephone Dials A379

1978, Sept. 25
1011   A379 50c multi   .30   .25
    Automation of telephone service.

Symbolic Stamps A380

Iberian Tile Pattern — A381

1978, Oct. 31
1012   A380 50c multi   .30   .25
1013   A381 1p multi   .30   .25
    Stamp Day (50c) and Spanish heritage (1p).

Boeing 727 A382

1978, Nov. 27
1014   A382 50c multi   .60   .25
    Inauguration of Boeing 727 flights by PLUNA Uruguayan airlines, Nov. 1978.

Angel Blowing Horn — A383

1978, Dec. 7
1015   A383 50c multi   .25   .25
1016   A383 1p multi   .35   .25
    Christmas 1978.

Flag Flying on Plaza of the Nation — A384

1978, Dec. 15   ***Perf. 12½***
1017   A384 1p multicolored   .40   .25

A385

           Wmk. 332
1978, Dec. 27   Litho.   Perf. 12
1018   A385 1p blk, red & yel   .30   .25
    Horacio Quiroga (1868-1928), short story writer.

Arch, Olympic Rings, Lake Placid and Moscow Emblems A386

7p, Olympic Rings, Lake Placid '80 emblem.

1979, Apr. 28   Litho.   Perf. 12
1019   A386 5p multi   1.75   1.00
1020   A386 7p multi   2.25   1.00
    81st Session of Olympic Organizing Committee, Apr. 3-8 (5p), and 13th Winter Olympic Games, Lake Placid, NY, Feb. 12-24.

         Souvenir Sheets
1021   Sheet of 4   35.00 35.00
  a. A386 3p similar to #1019
  b. A386 5p Olympic rings
  c. A386 7p Rider looking back
  d. A386 10p Rider facing forward
1022   Sheet of 4   35.00 35.00
  a. A386 3p similar to #1020
  b. A386 5p Uruguay '79
  c. A386 7p World Chess Olympics '78
  d. A386 10p Sir Rowland Hill, Great Britain stamp
    No. 1022d shows Great Britain No. 836, but with 11p denomination. No. 1021c-1021d have continuous design.
    Nos. 1021-1022 had limited distribution. Except for No. 1022d, singles were sold for postal use in 1980. Nos. 1021-1022 exist imperf.

Map and Arms of Paysandu A387

Map and Arms of Maldonado A388

1979-81
1023   A387 45c shown   .45   .25
1024   A387 45c Salto   .45   .25
1025   A388 45c shown   .45   .25
1026   A387 45c Cerro Largo   .45   .25
1027   A387 50c Treinta y Tres   .45   .25
1028   A387 50c Durazno ('80)   .45   .25
1029   A388 2p Rocha ('81)   .45   .25
1030   A388 2p Flores   .45   .25
    Nos. 1023-1030 (8)   3.60   2.00
     See No. 990.

Sapper with Pickax, 1837 — A389

    Army Day: No. 1039, Artillery man with cannon, 1830.

1979, May 18   Litho.   Perf. 12
1038   A389 5p multi   1.50   .70
1039   A389 5p multi   1.50   .70

Madonna and Child by Durer A390

    Anniversaries and events: 80c, World Cup Soccer Championships, Spain. 1.30p, Sir Rowland Hill, Greece No. 117.

1979, June 18   ***Perf. 12***
1040   A390   70c brn & gray   6.50   3.25
1041   A390   80c multicolored   5.00   2.75
1042   A390 1.30p multicolored   5.00   2.75
    Nos. 1040-1042 (3)   16.50   8.75
    Nos. 1040-1042 had limited distribution.
    Issued in sheets of 24 containing 6 blocks of 4 with margin around. See #C437-C438.

Salto Dam A391

1979, June 19
1043   A391 2p multi   .75   .30

Crandon Institute Emblem, Grain A392

1979, July 19
1044   A392 1p vio bl & bl   .30   .25
    Crandon Institute (private Methodist school), centenary.

IYC Emblem, Smiling Kites — A393

Cinderella A394

1979
1045   A393 2p multi   .50   .25
1046   A394 2p multi   .50   .25
    International Year of the Child. Issue dates: No. 1045, July 23; No. 1046, Aug. 29.

Uruguay Coat of Arms 150th Anniversary — A395

1979, Sept. 6
1047   A395 8p multi   2.75   1.40

Virgin and Child — A396

           Wmk. 332
1979, Nov. 19   Litho.   Perf. 12
1048   A396 10p multi   2.25   1.25
    Christmas 1979; Intl. Year of the Child.

Symbols, by Torres-Garcia A397

1979, Nov. 12
1049   A397 10p yel & blk   3.00   1.60
    Joaquín Torres-Garcia (1874-1948), painter.

UPU and Brazilian Postal
Emblems — A398

1979, Oct. 11
1050 A398 5p multi   1.25   .80
18th UPU Congress, Rio, Sept.-Oct.

Dish Antenna and Sun — A400

Perf. 12x11½
1979, Nov. 26   Litho.   Wmk. 332
1052 A400 10p multi   3.00 1.25
Telecom '79, 3rd World Telecommunications
Exhibition, Geneva, Sept. 20-26.

Spanish Heritage
Day — A401

1979, Dec. 3   Perf. 12
1053 A401 10p multi   2.00 1.50

Silver
Coin
Centenary
A402

Designs: Obverse and reverse of coins in
denominations matching stamps.

1979, Dec. 26
1054 A402 10c multi   .25   .25
1055 A402 20c multi   .25   .25
1056 A402 50c multi   .25   .25
1057 A402 1p multi   .45   .25
    Nos. 1054-1057 (4)   1.20 1.00

Souvenir Sheet

A403

1980, Jan. 10
1058 A403   Sheet of 4   3.50 3.50
  a.   1p Police emblem   .30   .30
  b.   2p Security Agent   .50   .50
  c.   3p Policeman, 1843   .75   .75
  d.   4p Cadet, 1979   1.00 1.00
Police force sesquicentennial.

Light Bulb, Thomas Edison — A404

1980, Jan. 18
1059 A404 2p multi   .65   .25
Centenary of electric light (1979).

Bass and
Singer — A405

1980, Jan. 30
1060   Sheet of 4   3.00 3.00
  a.   A405 2p Radio waves   .65   .65
  b.   A405 2p shown   .65   .65
  c.   A405 2p Ballerina   .65   .65
  d.   A405 2p Television waves .65   .65
Performing Arts Society, 50th anniversary.

Stamp
Day — A406

1980, Feb.
1061 A406 1p multi   .45   .25

La Leyenda
Patria — A407

1980, Feb. 26
1062 A407 1p multi   .50   .25

Printers'
Association,
50th
Anniversary
A408

1980, Feb.
1063 A408 1p multi   .35   .25

Lufthansa Cargo Container Service
Inauguration — A409

1980, Apr. 12   Unwmk.   Perf. 12½
1064 A409 2p multi   1.00   .25

Conf. Emblem,
Banners — A410

1980, Apr. 28   Wmk. 332   Perf. 12
1065 A410 2p multi   .50   .25
8th World Hereford Conf., Punta del Este
and Livestock Exhib., Prado/Montivideo.

Man, Woman and
Birds — A411

1980   Litho.   Perf. 12
1066 A411 1p multi   .60   .25
International Year of the Child (1979).

Latin-American Lions, 9th
Forum — A412

1980, May 6   Wmk. 332   Perf. 12
1067 A412 1p multi   .60   .25

Souvenir Sheet

Army Day, May 18 — A413

1980, May 16
1068 A413   Sheet of 4   5.00 5.00
  a.   2p Rifleman, 1814   1.00 1.00
  b.   2p Cavalry officer, 1830 1.00 1.00
  c.   2p Private Liberty Dragoons,
       1826   1.00 1.00
  d.   2p, Artigas Militia officer, 1815 1.00 1.00

Arms of
Colonia — A414

Colonia,
1680
A415

1980, June 17   Litho.   Perf. 12
1069 A414 50c multi   1.50   .25
Souvenir Sheet
1070   Sheet of 4   3.00 3.00
  a.   A415 1p shown   .65   .65
  b.   A415 1p 1680, diff.   .65   .65
  c.   A415 1p 1980   .65   .65
  d.   A415 1p 1980, diff.   .65   .65
Colonia, 300th anniversary.

Rotary Emblem
on Globe — A416

1980, July 8
1071 A416 5p multi   1.50   .90
Rotary International, 75th anniversary.

Hand Putting Out
Cigarette — A417

1980, Sept. 8   Photo.
1072 A417 1p multi   .60   .25
World Health Day and anti-smoking
campaign.

Artigas — A418

	Wmk. 332			
1980-85	**Litho.**		**Perf. 12½**	
1073	A418	10c blue ('81)	.40	.25
1074	A418	20c orange	.25	.25
1075	A418	50c red	.25	.25
1076	A418	60c yellow	.25	.25
1077	A418	1p gray	.55	.25
1078	A418	2p brown	.55	.25
1079	A418	3p brt grn	1.00	.35
1080	A418	4p brt bl ('82)	1.25	.45
1081	A418	5p green ('82)	.65	.25
1082	A418	6p brt org ('85)	.25	.25
1083	A418	7p lil rose ('82)	3.00	.75
1084	A418	10p blue ('82)	1.25	.35
1085	A418	12p blk ('85)	.60	.25
1086	A418	15.50p emer ('85)	.80	.30
1087	A418	20p dk vio ('82)	2.75	.75
1088	A418	30p lt brn ('82)	4.00	.75
1089	A418	50p gray bl ('82)	6.00	1.90
		Nos. 1073-1089 (17)	23.80	7.85

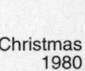

Christmas
1980
A419

1980, Dec. 15   Litho.   Perf. 12
1090 A419 2p multi   .60   .25

Constitution Title Page — A420

1980, Dec. 23   Perf. 12½
1091 A420 4p brt bl & gold   1.00   .55
Sesquicentennial of Constitution.

A421

No. 1092, Montevideo Stadium. No. 1093,
Soccer gold cup. No. 1094, Flags.

1980, Dec. 30   Perf. 12
1092 A421 5p multicolored   2.00   1.00
1093 A421 5p multicolored   2.00   1.00

Size: 25x79mm

1094 A421 10p multicolored   2.00   1.00
   a.   Souv. sheet of 3, #1092-
          1094   12.00 12.00
      Nos. 1092-1094 (3)   6.00   3.00
Soccer Gold Cup Championship,
Montevideo.

A422

1981, Jan. 27
1095 A422 2p multi   .60   .25
Spanish Heritage Day.

Alexander von
Humboldt (1769-
1859), German
Explorer and
Scientist — A424

1981, Feb. 19
1097 A424 2p multi   1.00   .25

Intl. Education Congress and Fair,
Montevideo (1980) — A425

1981, Mar. 31
1098 A425 2p multi   .60   .25

Hand Holding
Gold Cup — A426

1981, Apr. 8
1099 A426 2p multi   .60   .25
1100 A426 5p multi   1.25   .50
1980 victory in Gold Cup Soccer
Championship.

Eighth Notes on
Map of
Americas — A427

1981, Apr. 28
1101 A427 2p multi   .60   .25
Inter-American Institute of Musicology, 40th
anniv.

World Tourism Conference, Manila,
Sept. 27, 1980 — A428

Wmk. 332
1981, June 1   Litho.   Perf. 12
1102 A428 2p multi   .60   .25

Inauguration of PLUNA Flights to
Madrid — A429

Below "1981, Jan. 27" section in column 1:

UPU Membership Centenary — A423

1981, Feb. 6
1096 A423 2p multi   .60   .25

1981, May 12
1103 A429 2p multi   .40   .25
1104 A429 5p multi   .95   .45
1105 A429 10p multi   1.90   .95
   Nos. 1103-1105 (3)   3.25 1.65

Army
Day — A430

No. 1106, Cavalry soldier, 1843. No. 1107,
Infantryman, 1843.

Wmk. 332
1981, May 18   Litho.   Perf. 12
1106 A430 2p multicolored   .60   .25
1107 A430 2p multicolored   .60   .25

Natl. Atomic
Energy
Commission, 25th
Anniv. — A431

1981, July 20
1108 A431 2p multi   .60   .25

Europe-South American Soccer
Cup — A432

1981, Aug. 4
1109 A432 2p multi   .90   .25

Stone Tablets, Salto Grande
Excavation — A433

1981, Sept. 10
1110 A433 2p multi   .75   .25

10th Lavalleja
Week — A434

1981, Oct. 3
1111 A434 4p multi   1.40   .45

Intl. Year
of the
Disabled
A435

Wmk. 332
1981, Oct. 26   Litho.   Perf. 12
1112 A435 2p multi   .60   .25

UN Environmental Law Meeting
Montevideo, Oct. 28-Nov. 6 — A436

1981, Oct. 28
1113 A436 5p multi   1.40   .45

A437

1981, Oct. 13
1114 A437 2p multi   .60   .25
50th anniv. of ANCAP (Natl. Administration
of Combustible Fuels, Alcohol and Cement).

Souvenir Sheets

Uruguay 81 Intl. Philatelic
Exhibition — A438

No. 1114A: b, Copa de Oro trophy. c, Soc-
cer player kicking ball.
No. 1115: a, Chess pieces. b, Prince
Charles and Lady Diana, flags of Uruguay and
Great Britain.

Wmk. 332
1981, Nov. 23   Litho.   Perf. 12
1114A A438 5p Sheet of 2, #b-
              c   23.00 23.00
1115   A438 5p Sheet of 2, #a-
              b   25.00 25.00
   1982 World Cup Soccer Championships,
Spain (No. 1114Ac), World Chess Championships, Atlanta (No. 1115a); Wedding of Prince
Charles and Lady Diana (No. 1115b). Nos.
1114A-1115 exist imperf., which were not valid
for postage.

Topographical Society
Sesequicentennial — A439

1981, Dec. 5   Perf. 12
1116 A439 2p multi   .70   .25
See No. 1407.

Bank of Uruguay, 85th Anniv. — A440

1981, Dec. 17 *Perf. 12½*
1117 A440 2p multi .60 .25

Palmar Dam — A441

1981, Dec. 22 *Perf. 12*
1118 A441 2p multi .70 .25

Christmas 1981 A442

1981, Dec. 23
1119 A442 2p multi .60 .25

Pres. Joaquin Suarez Bicentenary A443

1982, Mar. 15
1120 A443 5p multi 1.00 .50

Artillery Captain, 1872, Army Day — A444

Wmk. 332
1982, May 18 *Litho.* *Perf. 12*
1121 A444 3p shown .85 .25
1122 A444 3p Florida Battalion, 1865 .85 .25
See Nos. 1136-1137.

Cent. (1981) of Pinocchio, by Carlo Collodi — A445

1982, June 17
1123 A445 2p multi .70 .25

2nd UN Conference on Peaceful Uses of Outer Space, Vienna, Aug. 9-21 — A446

1982, June 3
1124 A446 3p multi 1.25 .70

World Food Day A447

1982
1125 A447 2p multi .65 .25

25th Anniv. of Lufthansa's Uruguay Germany Flight — A448

3p, Lockheed L-1049-G Super Constellation. 7p, Boeing 747.

1982, Apr. 14 *Unwmk.* *Perf. 12½*
1126 A448 3p multicolored 1.00 .40
1127 A448 7p multicolored 2.25 .80

American Air Forces Cooperation System — A449

1982, Apr. 14 *Wmk. 332* *Perf. 12*
1128 A449 10p Emblem 2.75 .80

Juan Zorilla de San Martin (1855-1931), Painter — A450

1982, Aug. 18 *Perf. 12½*
1129 A450 3p Self-portrait .80 .40

165th Anniv. of Natl. Navy — A451

1982, Nov. 15 *Perf. 12*
1130 A451 3p Navy vessel Capitan Miranda 1.00 .40

Natl. Literacy Campaign A452

1982, Nov. 30
1131 A452 3p multi .50 .25

Stamp Day — A453

1982, Dec. 23 *Perf. 12½*
1132 A453 3p like #46 .40 .25
1133 A453 3p like #47 .40 .25
a. Pair, #1132-1133 1.40 1.40

These stamps bear numbers from 1 to 100 according to their position on the sheet.

Christmas 1982 — A454

1983, Jan. 4 *Perf. 12*
1134 A454 3p multi .60 .25

Eduardo Fabini (1882-1950), Composer — A455

1983, May 10
1135 A455 3p gold & brn .65 .25

Army Day Type of 1982
1983, May 18
1136 A444 3p Military College cadet, 1885 .70 .25
1137 A444 3p 2nd Cavalry Regiment officer, 1885 .70 .25

Visit of King Juan Carlos and Queen Sofia of Spain, May — A456

1983, May 20 *Unwmk.*
1138 A456 3p Santa Maria, globe .75 .40
1139 A456 7p Profiles, flags 1.75 .80
Size of No. 1138. 29x39mm.

Brasiliana '83 Emblem — A457

80th Anniv. of First Automobile in Uruguay — A458

Opening of UPAE Building, Montevideo A459

Jose Cuneo (1887-1977), Painter — A460

1982
World
Cup
A461

Graf Zeppelin Flight Over Montevideo,
50th Anniv. (1984) — A462

J.W. Goethe (1749-1832), 150th
Death Anniv. — A463

First
Space
Shuttle
Flight
A464

1983   Litho.   Wmk. 332   Perf. 12
1140 A457 3p multi   1.00   1.00
1141 A458 3p multi   1.00   1.00
1142 A459 3p multi   1.00   1.00
1143 A460 3p multi   1.00   1.00
  a.   Souvenir sheet of 4   6.50   6.50
1144 A461 7p multi   1.50   1.50
1145 A462 7p multi   1.50   1.50
1146 A463 7p multi   1.50   1.50
1147 A464 7p multi   1.50   1.50
  a.   Souvenir sheet of 4   11.00 11.00
  Nos. 1140-1147 (8)   10.00 10.00

No. 1143a contains stamps similar to Nos.
1140-1143. No. 1147a stamps similar to Nos.
1144-1147. Nos. 1143a and 1147a for
URUEXPO '83 and World Communications
Year.
  Issued: #1142, 6/8; #1143, 1146, 9/29;
#1143a, 1147a, 6/9; #1140, 7/22; #1144,
12/13; #1146, 9/20; #1145, 12/8.

Bicentenary of
City of
Minas — A465

Wmk. 332
1983, Oct. 17   Litho.   Perf. 12
1148 A465 3p Founder   .75   .25

World Communications Year — A466

1983, Nov. 30
1149 A466 3p multi   .60   .25

Garibaldi
Death
Centenary
A467

1983, Dec. 5
1150 A467 7p multi   .90   .40

Christmas
1983
A468

**Lithographed and Embossed
(Braille)**
1983, Dec. 21   Perf. 12½
1151 A468 4.50p multi   .70   .25

50th Anniv. of Automatic
Telephones — A469

1983, Dec. 27   Perf. 12
1152 A469 4.50p multi   .60   .25

Simon
Bolivar,
Battle
Scene
A470

Wmk. 332
1984, Mar. 28   Litho.   Perf. 12
1153 A470 4.50p brn & gldn brn   1.25   .40

Gen. Leandro
Gomez — A471

1984, Jan. 2
1154 A471 4.50p multi   .60   .25

American
Women's
Day — A472

1984, Feb. 18
1155 A472 4.50p Flags, emblem   .60   .25

Reunion
Emblem
A473

1984, Mar. 23
1156 A473 10p multi   1.25   .45
  Intl. Development Bank Governors, 25th
annual reunion, Punta del Este.

50th
Anniv. of
Radio
Club of
Uruguay
(1983)
A474

1984, Apr. 11
1157 A474 7p multi   .75   .30

A475

1984, Feb. 7   Litho.   Perf. 12
1158 A475 4.50p multi   .60   .25
  Intl. Maritime Org., 25th anniv.

A476

1984, May 2   Litho.   Perf. 12
1159 A476 4.50p multi   .60   .25
  1930 World Soccer Championships,
Montevideo.

Department of San Jose de Mayo,
200th Anniv. — A477

1984, May 9   Litho.   Perf. 12
1160 A477 4.50p multi   .60   .25

Tourism,
50th
Anniv.
A478

1984, May 15   Litho.   Perf. 12
1161 A478 4.50p multi   .60   .25

Military
Uniforms — A479

  No. 1162, Artillery Regiment, 1895. No.
1163, Cazadores, 2nd battalion.

1984, June 19   Litho.   Perf. 12
1162 A479 4.50p multicolored   .60   .25
1163 A479 4.50p multicolored   .60   .25

Artigas on the
Plains — A480

1984, July 2   Litho.   Perf. 12
1164 A480 4.50p bl & blk   .50   .25
1165 A480 8.50p bl & redsh brn .95   .40

A.
Penarol
Soccer
Club
A481

1984, Aug. 21   Litho.   Perf. 12
1166 A481 4.50p Championship
            trophy   .60   .25

Provincial Map Type of 1973
1984, Sept. 21   Litho.   Perf. 12
1167 A281 4.50p multi   .60   .25

Childrens
Council,
50th
Anniv.
A482

1984, Oct. 11   Litho.   Perf. 12
1168 A482 4.50p multi   .50   .25

Christmas A483

1984 **Litho.** **Perf. 12**
1169 A483 6p multi .70 .30

A484

1985, Feb. 13 **Litho.** **Perf. 12**
1170 A484 4.50p multi .60 .25

1st Jr. World Jai Alai Championships.

Don Bruno Mauricio de Zabala, 300th Birth Anniv. — A485

1985, Apr. 16 **Litho.** **Perf. 12**
1171 A485 4.50p multi .60 .25

Intl. Olympic Committee, 90th Anniv. — A486

Design: Olympic rings, Los Angeles and Sarajevo 1984 Games emblems.

1985, May 22 **Perf. 12½**
1172 A486 12p multi 1.00 .50

Carlos Gardel, (1890-1935), Entertainer A487

1985, June 21 **Perf. 12**
1173 A487 6p lt gray, red brn & bl .60 .25

Catholic Circle of Workers, Cent. — A488

Wmk. 332
1985, June 21 **Litho.** **Perf. 12**
1174 A488 6p Cross, clasped hands .30 .25

Icarus, by Hans Erni — A489

1985, July **Photo.** **Wmk. 332**
1175 A489 4.50p multi .60 .25

Intl. Civil Aviation Org., 40th anniv.

American Air Forces Cooperation System, 25th Anniv. — A490

1985, July
1176 A490 12p Emblem, flags .60 .25

FUNSA, Natl. Investment Funds Corp., 50th Anniv. — A491

1985, July 31 **Litho.** **Wmk. 332**
1177 A491 6p multi .60 .25

Intl. Youth Year A492

1985, Aug. 28
1178 A492 12p mar & blk .40 .25

Installation of Democratic Government — A493

1985, Aug. 30
1179 A493 20p brt pur, yel ocher & dk grnsh bl .90 .40

Intl. Book Fair — A494

1985
1180 A494 20p multi .80 .35

Military School, Cent. A495

1985, Nov. 29 **Litho.** **Perf. 12**
1181 A495 10p multi .40 .25

Department of Flores, Cent. — A496

1985, Dec. 9
1182 A496 6p Map, arms .40 .25

Christmas 1985 A497

1985, Dec. 23
1183 A497 10p multi .45 .25
1184 A497 22p multi .65 .30

Day of Hispanic Solidarity — A498

1985, Dec. 27
1185 A498 12p Isabel Monument .50 .25

3rd Inter-American Agricultural Congress — A499

Wmk. 332
1986, Jan. 7 **Photo.** **Perf. 12**
1186 A499 12p blk, dl yel & red .50 .25

UPU Day A500

1986, Jan. 14 **Litho.** **Perf. 12**
1187 A500 15.50p multi .60 .25

1985 Census A501

1986, Jan. 21
1188 A501 10p multi .40 .25

Conaprole, 50th Anniv. — A502

1986, Jan. 25
1189 A502 10p gold, brt ultra & bl .50 .25

UN, 40th Anniv. A503

Wmk. 332
1986, Feb. 26 **Litho.** **Perf. 12**
1190 A503 20p multi .60 .25

Brokers and Auctioneers Assoc., 50th Anniv. — A504

1986, Mar. 19
1191 A504 10p multi .40 .25

Gen. Manuel Ceferino Oribe (1792-1857), President — A505

Portraits: Nos. 1196, 1200, 2p, 7p, 15p, 20p, Oribe. Nos. 1195, 1209, 1211, 3p, Lavalleja. Nos. 1199, 1208, 1210, 30p, 100p, 200p, Artigas. No. 1198, 17p, 22p, 26p, 45p, 75p, Rivera.

1986-89			**Perf. 12½**	
1192	A505	1p dl grn	.25	.25
1193	A505	2p ocarlet	.25	.25
1194	A505	3p ultra	.25	.25
1195	A505	5p dark blue	.25	.25
1196	A505	5p violet blue	.25	.25
1197	A505	7p tan	.25	.25
1198	A505	10p lilac rose	.30	.25
1199	A505	10p brt green	.25	.25
1200	A505	10p bluish grn	.25	.25
1201	A505	15p dull blue	.25	.25
1202	A505	17p deep blue	.30	.25
1203	A505	20p light brown	.25	.25
1204	A505	22p violet	.25	.25
1205	A505	26p olive blk	.35	.25

1206	A505	30p pale org	.35	.25
1207	A505	45p dark red	.35	.25
1208	A505	50p dp bis	.65	.45
1209	A505	50p bright pink	.25	.25
1210	A505	60p dark gray	.90	.45
1211	A505	60p orange	.25	.25
1211A	A505	75p red orange	.35	.25
1211B	A505	100p dl red brn	1.40	.60
1211C	A505	200p brt yel grn	2.00	.75

Nos. 1192-1211C (23) 10.20 7.00

The 22p is airmail.
Issued: 1p, 7p, 4/18; #1195, 30p, 6/16; #1198, 22p, 9/24; #1208, 8/5; 100p, 7/2; 2p, 6/16/87; 3p, #1210, 8/14/87; #1199, 17p, 8/4/87; 26p, 9/2/87; 15p, 9/9/88; 45p, 12/20/88; 200p, 10/19/88; #1211A, 5/19/89; #1211, 7/27/89; #1196, 1203, 8/15/89; #1209, 12/12/89; #1200, 1989.
See Nos. 1321-1329.

Italian Chamber of Commerce in Uruguay — A506

1986, May 5   **Perf. 12**
1212 A506 20p multi   .60   .25

A507

1986, May 28   **Photo.**   **Perf. 12**
1213 A507 20p multi   .60   .30
1986 World Cup Soccer Championships, Mexico.

A508

Wmk. 332
1986, May 19   **Litho.**   **Perf. 12**
1214 A508 10p multi   .60   .30
Genocide of the Armenian people, 71st anniv.

A509

1986, June 16
1215 A509 10p multi   .45   .25
El Dia Newspaper, cent.

Garcia, Peruvian Flag — A510

1986, July 14
1216 A510 20p multi   .40   .25
State visit of Pres. Alan Garcia of Peru.

Simon Bolivar, Gen. Sucre, Map A511

1986, July 24
1217 A511 20p multi   .65   .25
State visit of Pres. Jaime Lusinchi of Venezuela.

State Visit of Pres. Jose Sarney of Brazil — A512

1986, July 31
1218 A512 20p multi   .60   .25

Zelmar Michelini, Assassinated Liberal Senator — A513

1986, Aug. 21
1219 A513 10p vio bl & rose lake   .45   .25

B'nai B'rith of Uruguay, 50th Anniv. A514

1986, Sept. 10
1220 A514 10p red, gold & red brn   .70   .30

General Agreement on Tariffs & Trade (GATT) Committee Meeting, Punta del Este — A515

1986, Sept. 15
1221 A515 10p multi   .50   .25

Scheduled Flights between Uruguay and Spain, 40th Anniv. — A516

1986, Sept. 22
1222 A516 20p multi   .60   .30

Fish Exports A517

1986, Oct. 1
1223 A517 20p multi   .60   .30

Wool Exports A518

1986, Oct. 15
1224 A518 20p multi   .60   .30

Pres. Blanco, Natl. and Dominican Flags A519

1986, Oct. 29
1225 A519 20p multi   .60   .25
State visit of Pres. Salvador Jorge Blanco of the Dominican Republic.

State Visit of Pres. Sandro Pertini of Italy — A520

1986, Oct. 31
1226 A520 20p grn & buff   .60   .25

State Visit of Pres. Raul Alfonsin of Argentina A521

1986, Nov. 10
1227 A521 20p multi   .60   .25

Hispanic Solidarity Day A522

Design: Felipe and Santiago, the patron saints of Montevideo, and cathedral.

Wmk. 332
1987, Jan. 12   **Litho.**   **Perf. 12**
1228 A522 10p rose lake & blk   .60   .30

JUVENTUS, 50th Anniv. (in 1986) — A523

1987, Jan. 28
1229 A523 10p brt yel, blk & ultra   .45   .25
Juventus, a Catholic sports, culture and leisure organization.

Hector Gutierrez Ruiz (1934-1976), Politician — A524

Intl. Symposium on Science and Technology A525

1987, Feb. 23
1230 A524 10p brn & deep mag   .45   .25
1231 A525 20p multi   .60   .25
Ruiz represented Uruguay at an earlier science and technology symposium.

Visit of Pope John Paul II to La Plata Region — A526

1987, Mar. 31
1232 A526 50p blk & deep org   1.00   .50

Dr. Jose F. Arias (1885-1985), Founder of the University of Crafts — A527

1987, Apr. 28
1233 A527 10p multi   .45   .25

Jewish Community in Uruguay, 70th Anniv. — A528

1987, July 8
1234 A528 10p blk, org & brt bl   .60   .30

Pluna Airlines, 50th Anniv. (in 1986) A529

1987, Sept. 16
1235 A529 10p Dragon Fly   .30   .25
1236 A529 20p Douglas DC-3   .40   .25
1237 A529 25p Vickers Viscount   .60   .25
1238 A529 30p Boeing 707   .70   .25
    Nos. 1235-1238 (4)   2.00   1.00

Artigas Antarctic Station A530

1987, Sept. 28
1239 A530 20p multi   1.00   .30

Uruguay Mortgage Bank, 75th Anniv. A531

1987, Oct. 14
1240 A531 26p multi   .60   .25

Exports — A532

1987, Oct. 28
1241 A532 51p Beef   .80   .40
1242 A532 51p Milk products   .80   .40

Christmas 1987 — A533

1987, Dec. 21
1243 A533 17p Nativity, vert.   .45   .25
1244 A533 66p shown   .85   .50

State Visit of Jose Napoleon Duarte, President of El Salvador — A534

1988, Jan. 12
1245 A534 20p brt olive grn & Prus blue   .60   .25

VARIG Airlines, 60th Anniv. (in 1987) — A535

1988, Feb. 9
1246 A535 66p blk, blue & brt yel   1.00   1.00

Post Office Stamp Foundation A536

Wmk. 332
1988, Feb. 9   Litho.   Perf. 12
1247 A536 30p on 10+5p brt blue, blk & yel   1.10   .30

No. 1247 not issued without surcharge.

Intl. Peace Year A537

1988, Feb. 11
1248 A537 10p multi   .40   .25

Euskal Erria, 75th Anniv. (in 1987) — A538

1988, Mar. 9
1249 A538 66p multi   .70   .40

Basque-Uruguayan diplomatic relations.

Air Force, 75th Anniv. A539

1988, Mar. 11
1250 A539 17p multi   .40   .25

Interamerican Children's Institute, 60th Anniv. — A540

Wmk. 332
1988, Mar. 28   Litho.   Perf. 12
1251 A540 30p apple grn, blk & grn   .50   .25

State Hydroelectric Works (UTE), 75th Anniv. — A541

1988, Apr. 20
1252 A541 17p shown   .25   .25
1253 A541 17p Baygorria Dam   .25   .25
1254 A541 51p Gabriel Terra Dam   .70   .30
1255 A541 51p Constitucion Dam   .70   .30
1256 A541 66p Dams on map   1.00   .45
    Nos. 1252-1256 (5)   2.90   1.55

Dated 1987.

Postal Union of America and Spain (UPAE), 75th Anniv. (in 1987) A542

1988, May 10
1257 A542 66p multi   .80   .45

Israel, 40th Anniv. A543

1988, May 17
1258 A543 66p lt ultra & blk   .80   .35

Postal Messenger of Peace — A544

1988, May 24
1259 A544 66p multi   .80   .35

Portrait, La Cumparsita Tango — A545

1988, June 7
1260 A545 17p Parade, horiz.   .45   .25
1261 A545 51p Score   1.40   .55

Gerardo H. Matos Rodrigues, composer.

Firemen, Cent. — A546

17p, Pablo Banales, founder. 26p, Fireman, 1900. 34p, Emblem, horiz. 51p, Merry Weather fire engine, 1907, horiz. 66p, Fire pump, 1888, horiz. 100p, Ladder truck, 1921.

1988, June 21
1262 A546 17p multi   .40   .25
1263 A546 26p multi   .45   .25
1264 A546 34p multi   .60   .30
1265 A546 51p multi   .90   .45
1266 A546 66p multi   1.40   .65

Size: 44x24½mm
1267 A546 100p multi   2.25   1.10
    Nos. 1262-1267 (6)   6.00   3.00

Capitan Miranda Trans-world Voyage, Cent. — A547

1988, July 28
1268 A547 30p multi   .40   .25

Exports A548

1988
1269 A548 30p Citrus fruit   .30   .25
1270 A548 45p Rice   .60   .25
1271 A548 55p Footwear   .70   .25
1272 A548 55p Leather and furs   .70   .35
    Nos. 1269-1272 (4)   2.30   1.10

Issued: 30p, #1272, 9/14; 45p, #1271, 8/23.

Natl. Museum of Natural History, 150th Anniv. — A549

30p, Usnea densirostra fossil. 90p, Toxodon platensis bone, Quaternary period.

1988, Sept. 20
1273 A549 30p blk, yel & red brn   .50   .25
1274 A549 90p blk, ultra & beige   1.20   .65
    a.   Pair, #1273-1274   2.00   2.00

Battle of Carpinteria, 150th Anniv. (in 1986) — A550

1988, Nov. 23
1275 A550 30p multi .40 .25

Horiz. row contains two stamps, label, then two more stamps.

Christmas A551

1988, Dec. 21
1276 A551 115p multi 1.00 1.00

A552

Paintings: a, Manolita Pina, 1920, by J. Torres Garcia. b, 78 Squares and Rectangles, by J.P. Costigliolo. c, Print publicizing an exhibition of works by Pedrero Figari, 1945. d, Self-portrait, 1947, by J. Torres Garcia.

1988, Dec. 27
1277 Block or strip of 4 + label 4.00 4.00
a.-d. A552 115p any single 1.00 .65

No. 1277 can be collected as a vert. or horiz. strip of 4, or block of 4, with label.

Spanish Heritage Day A553

1989, Jan. 9
1278 A553 90p multi .80 .40
1279 A553 115p multi 1.20 .50

Armenian Organization Hnchakian, Cent. — A554

Wmk. 332
1989, June 7 Litho. Perf. 12
1280 A554 210p red, yel & blue 1.75 .70

French Revolution, Bicentennial — A555

No. 1281, Plumb line, frame. No. 1282, Liberty tree. No. 1283, Eye in sunburst. No. 1284, Liberty.

1989, July 3
1281 A555 50p multi .35 .25
1282 A555 50p multi .35 .25
1283 A555 210p multi 1.40 .45
1284 A555 210p multi 1.40 .45
Nos. 1281-1284 (4) 3.50 1.40

Use Postal Codes — A556

50p, Montevideo Dept. map. 210p, National map, vert.

1989, July 25
1285 A556 50p multi .35 .25
1286 A556 210p multi 1.20 .40

3rd Pan American Milk Congress A557

1989, Aug. 24
1287 A557 170p sky blue & ultra 1.20 .45

A558

Wmk. 332
1989, Aug. 29 Photo. Perf. 12
1288 A558 170p multicolored .85 .30

Joaquin Jose da Silva Xavier.

A559

1989, Aug. 31
1289 A559 210p blk, red & bl 1.00 .35

Inter-Parliamentary Union Conf., London.

FAO Emblem, Map, Citrus Slice — A560

1989, Sept. 11
1290 A560 180p multicolored .90 .35

8th Conf., Intergovernmental Group on Citrus Fruits.

UN Decade for the Disabled — A561

1989, Oct. 4
1291 A561 50p shown .35 .25
1292 A561 210p Disabled people .95 .40

America Issue — A562

Nacurutu artifact and UPAE emblem.

1989, Oct. 11 Perf. 12½
1293 A562 60p multicolored 1.00 .40
1294 A562 180p multicolored 3.50 1.10

City of Pando, Bicentennial — A563

1989, Dec. 27 Litho. Perf. 12
1295 A563 60p multicolored .40 .25

Christmas A564

70p, Virgin of Trienta y Tres. 210p, Barradas, horiz.

1989, Dec. 19
1296 A564 70p multi .45 .25
1297 A564 210p multi 1.40 .45

Charity Hospital, Bicent. (in 1988) — A565

1990, Jan. 23 Wmk. 332
1298 A565 60p multicolored .70 .70

Provincial Arms and Maps A566

1990
1299 A566 70p Soriano .40 .40
1300 A566 70p Florida, vert. .45 .45
1301 A566 90p Canelones .50 .50
1302 A566 90p Lavalleja, vert. .50 .50
1303 A566 90p San Jose, vert. .50 .50
1304 A566 90p Rivera .50 .50
Nos. 1299-1304 (6) 2.85 2.85

Dated 1989.

Writers — A567

Designs: a, Luisa Luisi (1883-1940). b, Javier de Viana (1872-1926). c, Delmira Agustini (1886-1914). d, J. Zorrilla de San Martin (1855-1931). e, Alfonsina Storni (1892-1938). f, Julio Casal (1889-1954). g, Juana de Ibarbourou (1895-1979). h, Carlos Roxlo (1861-1926).

1990, Mar. 20
1320 Block of 8 + 2 labels 6.00 6.00
a.-b. A567 60p any single .35 .35
c.-d. A567 75p any single .40 .40
e.-f. A567 170p any single 1.00 1.00
g.-h. A567 210p any single 1.25 1.25

Printed in sheets of 4 blocks of 4 separated by vert. and horiz. rows of 5 labels. Position of denomination varies to form border around each block.
Dated 1989.

Portraits Type of 1986

25p, 30p, Lavalleja. 60p, 90p, Rivera. 100p, 150p, 300p, 500p, 1000p, Artigas.

1990 Litho. Wmk. 332 Perf. 12½
1321 A505 25p orange .30 .25
1322 A505 30p ultra .30 .25
1323 A505 60p purple .30 .25
1324 A505 90p org red .60 .30
1325 A505 100p brown 1.50 .35
1326 A505 150p dk blue green .90 .50
1327 A505 300p blue 1.50 1.00
1328 A505 500p orange red 2.50 1.00
1329 A505 1000p red 5.00 3.00
Nos. 1321-1329 (9) 12.90 6.90

Issued: 30p, 60p, 7/17; 90p, 3/24; 150p, 6/22; 300p, 7/5; 500p, 3/22; 1000p, 7/24.

A568

1990, Apr. 3   *Perf. 12*
1346 A568 70p multicolored   .40 .40
   City of Mercedes, bicent. Dated 1989.

A569

1990, Apr. 24
1347 A569 210p multicolored   1.25 1.25
   Intl. Agricultural Development Fund, 10th anniv. Dated 1989.

Traffic Safety — A570

   Designs: a, Bus, car. b, Don't drink and drive. c, Cross on the green light. d, Obey traffic signs.

1990, May 28
1348 A570 70p Block of 4, #a.-d.   1.15 1.50

General Artigas
A571

1990, June 18
1349 A571 60p red & blue   .45 .45

A572

1990, June 26
1350 A572 70p multicolored   .40 .40
   Intl. Mothers' Day. Dated 1989.

A573

   Treaty of Montevideo, 1889: a, Gonzalo Ramirez. b, Ildefonso Garcia. c, Flags at left. d, Flags at right.

1990, July 10
1351 A573 60p Block of 4, #a.-d.   1.40 1.40
   Nos. 1351c-1351d printed in continuous design. Dated 1989.

Microphone, Tower — A574

   b, Newspaper boy. c, Television camera. d, Books.

1990, Sept. 26
1352 A574 70p Block of 4, #a.-d.   2.00 2.00

Carlos Federico Saez (1878-1901) — A575

   Portraits: b, Pedro Blanes Viale (1879-1926). c, Edmundo Prati (1889-1970). d, Jose L. Zorrilla de San Martin (1891-1075).

1990, Dec. 26
1353   Block of 4   4.00 4.00
a.-b. A575 90p any single   .50 .50
c.-d. A575 210p any single   1.10 1.10

Prevent Forest Fires — A576

1990, Oct. 26   Wmk. 332   Litho.   *Perf. 12*
1354 A576 70np multicolored   2.00 2.00

America Issue — A577

1990, Nov. 6
1355 A577 120p Odocoileus
       bezoarticus   .90 .90
1356 A577 360p Peltophorum
       dubium, vert.   2.50 2.50

Army Corps of Engineers, 75th Anniv. — A578

1991, Jan. 21
1357 A578 170p multicolored   1.00 1.00

The Nativity by Brother Juan B. Maino — A579

1990, Dec. 24
1358 A579 170p bister & multi   1.00 1.00
1359 A579 830p silver & multi   4.75 4.75

Organization of American States, Cent. (in 1989) A580

1991, Mar. 21   Wmk. 332   Litho.   *Perf. 12*
1360 A580 830p bl, blk & yel   4.50 4.50

Prevention of AIDS — A581

1991, Mar. 8
1361 A581 170p bl & multi   1.00 1.00
1362 A581 830p grn & multi   4.75 4.75

Carnival — A582

1991, Feb. 19
1363 A582 170p multicolored   1.00 1.00

Education — A583

   Expanding youth's horizons: a, Stone ax, megalithic monument. b, Wheel, pyramids. c, Printing press, solar system. d, Satellite, diagram.

         Wmk. 332
1991, Apr. 23   Litho.   *Perf. 12*
1364   Block of 4   3.00 3.00
a.-b. A583 120p any single   .40 .40
c.-d. A583 330p any single   1.25 1.25

Natl. Cancer Day — A584

1991, June 17
1365 A584 360p red & black   1.10 1.10

A585

Exports of Uruguay — A586

     Perf. 12½x13, 13x12½
1991   Litho.   Wmk. 332
1366 A585 120p Textiles   .40 .40
1367 A586 120p Clothing   .50 .35
1368 A585 400p Semiprecious
       stones, granite   1.40 1.40
   Nos. 1366-1368 (3)   2.30 2.15
   Issued: #1366, 100p, 4/23, #1367, 6/26.

7th Pan American Maccabiah Games — A587

1991, July 4   *Perf. 12½x13*
1369 A587 1490p multicolored   4.50 4.50

Dornier Wal, Route Map — A588

1991, July 5   *Perf. 12*
1370 A588 1510p multicolored   4.50 4.50
   Espamer '91.

Entrance to Sacramento Colony A589

   Railroads and Trains: 540p, 825p, First locomotive, 1869. 600p, like 360p. 800p, Entrance to Sacramento Colony. 1510p, 2500p, Horse-drawn streetcar.

Wmk. 332

1991-2002		Litho.	Perf. 12	
1378	A589	360p brn & yel	.95	.60
1378A	A589	540p dk bl & gray	1.40	.95
1379	A589	600p brn, yel & blk	.95	.85
1379A	A589	800p grn & yel grn	.95	.95
1379B	A589	825p bl, gray & blk	1.40	1.25
1380	A589	1510p ol bis & emer	4.25	3.00
1382	A589	2500p ol bis, emer & blk	3.50	3.00
	Nos. 1378-1382 (7)		13.40	10.60

Issued: 360p, 540p, 1510p, July 19; 825p, Feb. 11, 1992; 2500p, May 29, 2002; 600p, June 18, 1992; 800p, Feb. 9, 1993.
For surcharges, see Nos. 2011B, 2057-2059.

Sagrada Family College, Cent. — A590

College of the Immaculate Heart of Mary, Cent. — A591

Wmk. 332

1991, June 26		Litho.	Perf. 12	
1383	A590	360p multicolored	.90	.90
1384	A591	1370p multicolored	3.75	3.75

Constitutional Oath — A592

1991, July 17
1385	A592	360p multicolored	.90	.90

Swiss Confederation, 700th Anniv. — A593

1991, Aug. 1   *Perf. 13x12½*
1386	A593	1510p multicolored	5.25	5.25

Souvenir Sheet
Perf. 12
1387	A593	3000p multicolored	11.00	11.00

Photography, 150th Anniv. — A594

Perf. 12½x13
1991, Sept. 12   Litho.   **Wmk. 332**
1388	A594	1370p multi	3.50	3.50

Actors Society of Uruguay, 50th Anniv. — A595

1991, Aug. 24   *Perf. 12*
1389	A595	450p blk & red	1.25	1.25

CREA (Agriculture Association), 25th Anniv. — A596

1991, Sept. 14   *Perf. 12½x13*
1390	A596	450p multicolored	1.25	1.25

Whitbread Around the World Race — A597

1991, Aug. 20   *Perf. 13x12½*
1391	A597	1510p multicolored	4.00	4.00

Amerigo Vespucci (1454-1512) — A598

America Issue: 450p, First landing at River Plate, 1602, vert.

1991, Oct. 11   *Perf. 12*
1392	A598	450p yel & brn	1.25	1.25
1393	A598	1740p ol & brn	3.50	3.50

Automobiles — A599

Designs: 350p, Gladiator, 1902. 1370p, E.M.F., 1909. 1490p, Renault, 1912. 1510p, Clement-Bayard, 1903, vert.

1991, Oct. 18   *Perf. 12½x13, 13x12½*
1394	A599	360p multicolored	.90	.90
1395	A599	1370p multicolored	3.50	3.50
1396	A599	1490p multicolored	3.50	3.50
1397	A599	1510p multicolored	3.50	3.50
	Nos. 1394-1397 (4)		11.40	11.40

Team Nacional Montevideo, Winners of Toyota and Europe-South America Soccer Cups — A600

Wmk. 332
1991, Nov. 8   Litho.   *Perf. 12*
1398	A600	450p shown	1.25	1.25
1399	A600	450p Emblem, trophy, vert.	1.25	1.25

Margarita Xirgu (1888-1969), Actress — A601

1991, Oct. 4
1400	A601	360p yel & brn	1.00	1.00

INTERPOL, 60th Congress A602

1991, Oct. 30
1401	A602	1740p multicolored	3.50	3.50

Maria Auxiliadora Institute, Cent. — A603

1991, Nov. 11
1402	A603	450p multicolored	1.25	1.25

Technological Laboratory, 25th Anniv. — A604

1991, Nov. 11
1403	A604	1570p dk bl & lt bl	2.50	2.50

The Table by Zoma Baitler — A605

1991, Oct. 18
1404	A605	360p multicolored	1.25	1.25

World Food Day A606

1991, Oct. 16   *Perf. 12½x13*
1405	A606	1740p multicolored	4.00	4.00

Ships A607

Designs: a, Steam yacht, Gen. Rivera. b, Coast Guard cutter, Salto. c, Cruiser, Uruguay. d, Tanker, Pte. Oribe.

Wmk. 332
1991, Oct. 4   Litho.   *Perf. 12*
1406		Block of 4	10.00	10.00
a.-b.	A607	450p any single	1.25	1.25
c.-d.	A607	1570p any single	3.50	3.50

Topographical Society Type of 1981
1991, Dec. 3   *Perf. 12½*
1407	A439	550p multi	.85	.85

Topographical Society, 160th anniv.

World AIDS Day — A608

1991, Dec. 1
1408	A608	550p bl, blk & brt yel	.90	.90
1409	A608	2040p lt grn, blk & lil	3.25	3.25

Export Industries A609

Wmk. 332
1991, Mar. 20   Litho.   *Perf. 12½*
1410	A609	120p multicolored	.40	.40

Christmas
A610

1991, Dec. 24   *Perf. 12*
1411 A610 550p Angel   .90   .90
1412 A610 2040p Adoration of
            the Angels   3.00 3.00

Muscians — A611

Designs: a, Juan de Dios Filiberto. b, Pintin Castellanos. c, Francisco Canaro. d, Anibal Troilo.

Wmk. 332
1992, Jan. 20   Photo.   *Perf. 12*
1413 A611 450p Block of 4, #a-d 3.50 3.50

Patricio Aylwin,
Pres. of
Chile — A612

Perf. 11½x12
1992, Mar. 23   Litho.   Unwmk.
1415 A612 550p multicolored   .85   .85

Penarol, Winners
of Liberator's Cup
in Club Soccer —
A612a

Perf. 13x12½
1992, May 29   Litho.   Wmk. 332
1415A A612a 600p yel & blk   1.25 1.25
Souvenir Sheet
Perf. 12
1415B A612a 3000p yel & blk   5.00 5.00

La Paz City,
120th Anniv. —
A612b

1992, May 25   *Perf. 13x12½*
1415C A612b 550p multicolored   .85   .85

World No-
Smoking
Day — A613

Wmk. 332
1992, May 31   Litho.   *Perf. 12*
1416 A613 2500p multicolored   3.75 3.75

United
Nations
World
Health
Day
A614

Wmk. 332
1992, July 28   Litho.   *Perf. 13*
1417 A614 2500p bl, lt bl & red 3.75 3.75

Mercosur
A615

1992, Aug. 5   Photo.   *Perf. 12*
1418 A615 2500p multicolored   3.75 3.75

Olymphilex '92, Barcelona — A616

Wmk. 332
1992, Aug. 8   Photo.   *Perf. 12*
1419 A616 2900p multicolored   4.50 4.50

Discovery of America, 500th
Anniv. — A617

Perf. 11½x12, 12x11½
1992, Oct. 10   Litho.   Unwmk.
1420 A617 700p Ship, masts,
            vert.   1.25 1.25
1421 A617 2900p Globe, ship   4.00 4.00

Jose
Pedro
Varela
Natl.
Teachers
College,
50th
Anniv.
A618

1992, Oct. 22   *Perf. 12x11½*
1422 A618 700p multicolored   .85   .85

22nd Regional FAO
Conference — A619

Designs: 2500p, Emblems. 2900p, Emblems, children with food basket.

1992, Sept. 28
1423 A619 2500p multicolored   3.00 3.00
1424 A619 2900p multicolored   3.75 3.75

Intl. Conf. on Nutrition, Rome, Italy (#1424).

Cesar Vallejo (1892-1938),
Poet — A620

1992, Sept. 30
1425 A620 2500p brn & dk brn   3.25 3.25

1992, Oct. 26   *Perf. 11½x12*
1426 A621 700p gray, red & blk   .85   .85

Assoc. of Wholesalers and Retailers, cent,

A622

Perf. 11½x12
1992, Oct. 10   Litho.   Unwmk.
1427 A622 700p black, blue &
            grn   1.00 1.00

Monument to Columbus, cent.

A623

Ruins and lighthouse, Colonia del Sacramento.

1992, Oct. 10
1428 A623 700p multicolored   1.25 1.25

Discovery of America, 500th anniv.

A624

1992, Oct. 19
1429 A624 700p red lil, rose lil &
            blk   1.25 1.25

Columbus Philanthropic Society, cent.

A625

1992, Oct. 19
1430 A625 2900p multicolored   3.75 3.75

Judaism in the Americas, 500th anniv.

A626

1992, Oct. 30
1431 A626 2900p multicolored   3.75 3.75

Lebanon Society of Uruguay, 50th anniv.

Pan American Health Organization,
90th Anniv. — A627

Perf. 12x11½
1992, Dec. 15   Litho.   Unwmk.
1432 A627 3200p blk, bl & yel   3.75 3.75

22nd Lions Club Forum for Latin
America and the Caribbean — A628

1992, Dec. 2
1433 A628 2700p multicolored   3.00 3.00

Christmas
A629

1992, Dec. 1   *Perf. 11½x12*
1434 A629 800p Nativity scene 1.00 1.00
1435 A629 3200p Star in sky 3.50 3.50

General
Manuel
Oribe,
Birth
Bicent.
A630

Designs: No. 1436, Oribe, Oriental College.
No. 1437, Oribe in military dress uniform, vert.

Perf. 12x11½, 11½x12
1992, Dec. 8   Litho.   Unwmk.
1436 A630 800p multicolored 1.00 1.00
1437 A630 800p multicolored 1.00 1.00

Logosofia, 60th Anniv. — A631

1992, Dec. 29   *Perf. 12x11½*
1438 A631 800p blue & yellow 1.00 1.00

Immigrants'
Day — A632

1992, Dec. 4   *Perf. 11½x12*
1439 A632 800p black & green 1.00 1.00

ANDEBU, 70th Anniv. — A633

Caritas
of
Uruguay,
30th
Anniv.
A634

1992, Dec. 22   Photo.   *Perf. 12x11½*
1440 A633 2700p Satellite 3.00 3.00
1441 A634 3200p Map, huts by
water 3.75 3.75

A635

1992, Dec. 18   *Perf. 11½x12*
1442 A635 800p brown & yellow 1.00 1.00
Jose H. Molaguero S. A., 50th anniv.

A636

Perf. 11½x12
1993, Mar. 1   Litho.   Unwmk.
1443 A636 80c multicolored .90 .90
Wilson Ferreira Aldunate.

Economic Science and Accountancy
College, Cent. — A637

Perf. 12x11½
1993, Apr. 15   Photo.   Unwmk.
1444 A637 1p multicolored 1.10 1.10

Souvenir Sheet

Polska '93, Intl. Philatelic
Exhibition — A638

a, Lech Walesa. b, Pope John Paul II.

1993, May 3   *Perf. 11½x12*
1445 A638 2p Sheet of 2, #a.-b. 6.00 6.00

A639   A639a

A639b

A639c   A639d

A639e   A639f

A639g   A639h

Design A639g shows the Postal Administration Tower.

ONE PESO (Letter Box — A639):
Type I — "Bugon vecinal 1879" 21½mm, letter box 23½mm high.
Type II — "Bugon vecinal 1879" 22mm, letter box 22½mm high.
Type III — "Bugon vecinal 1879" 19½mm, letter box 21mm high.
There are other differences among the three types.

Perf. 12½, 12 (#1449, 1465)
1993-99   Litho.   Wmk. 332
1446 A639 50c gray ol & yel .30 .30
1447 A639 1p lt brn & yel
         (I) .50 .50
  a.   Type II .60 .60
  b.   Type III, unwatermarked .35 .35
  c.   Type III, photo., unwmkd. .35 .35
1448 A639a 1p org yel & bl 1.00 1.00
1449 A639b 1p org & bl .65 .65
1450 A639c (1.20p) blue .70 .70
1451 A639c (1.40p) green .75 .75
1452 A639d 1.40p yel & bl .75 .75
1453 A639c (1.60p) red 1.25 1.25
1454 A639 1.80p bl & yel 1.40 1.40
1455 A639c (1.80p) brown 1.25 1.25
1456 A639c (2p) gray 1.25 1.25
1457 A639c (2.30p) lilac 1.60 1.60
1458 A639 2.60p bl, yel &
     grn 1.60 1.60
1459 A639e (2.60p) grn & yel 1.60 1.60
1460 A639e (2.90p) bl & yel 1.60 1.60
1460A A639e (3p) gray & brt
     yel grn 1.00 1.00
  b.   Unwmkd. 1.00 1.00
1461 A639e (3.10p) red &
     pink 1.10 1.10
1462 A639e (3.20p) rose brn
     & lt brn 5.00 5.00
1462A A639e (3.50p) pur & lt
     bl — —
1462B A639e (3.80p) brt blue 1.60 1.60
1463 A639e (4p) bis & yel,
     litho. 1.25 1.25
1464 A639f 5p bl & yel, perf.
     12½ 3.00 3.00
1465 A639g 6p blue & blk 1.75 1.75
1465A A639f 7p blue & yel 3.75 3.75
1465B A639 7.50p vio & yel 4.00 4.00
1465C A639h 8p bl & yel 4.00 4.00
Nos. 1446-1462,1463-1465C
(24) 41.05 41.05

The design of Nos. 1460A, 1462-1463 does not include "PORTE MINIMO." There are minor design differences between #1464 and 1465A.
Issued: #1448, 4/15/93; #1450, 8/2/93; #1451, 12/1/93; #1452, 1/4/94; #1453, 4/4/94; #1455, 8/1/94; #1454 8/9/94; #1449, 10/3/94; 1456, 12/1/94. #1457, 4/1/95; #1458, (2.60p), 8/10/95; 50c, #1447, 8/27/96; #1460, (3.10p), (3.50p), 4/1/96; 7.50p, 5/21/96; 5p, 1997; (3.80p), 5/9/97; #1463, 8/1/97; 6p, 8/13/97; (3.50p), 7/28/98; (3p), 2/1/99. #1460Ab, 1999.
For surcharges, see Nos. 2056, 2106, 2186, 2269.

Interior Fire
Service, 50th
Anniv. — A640

Perf. 11½x12
1993, May 28   Litho.   Unwmk.
1466 A640 1p multicolored 1.00 1.00

15th Congress of
UPAEP — A641

1993, June 21
1467 A641 3.50p multicolored 3.75 3.75

Uruguayan Navy, 175th Anniv. — A642

Sailing ship, Pedro Campbell, first admiral.

Perf. 12x11½
1993, June 28   Litho.   Wmk. 332
1468 A642 1p multicolored 1.25 1.25

Intl. University Society, 25th
Anniv. — A643

1993, July 2
1469 A643 1p multicolored 1.10 1.10

Automobile Club of Uruguay, 75th
Anniv. — A644

1993, July 19   Photo.   Unwmk.
1470 A644 3.50p 1910
     Hupmobile 3.75 3.75

Uruguay Battalion in UN Peacekeeping
Force, Cambodia — A645

Perf. 12x11½
1993, Aug. 6   Litho.   Unwmk.
1471 A645 1p multicolored 1.25 1.25

Souvenir Sheet

Brasiliana '93 — A646

World Cup Soccer Champions: a, Uruguay, 1930, 1950. b, Brazil, 1958, 1962, 1970.

1993, July 28   **Perf. 11½x12**
1472 A646 2.50p Sheet of 2, #a.-
b.   9.00 9.00

State Television Channel 5, 30th Anniv. — A647

1993, Aug. 19   **Perf. 12x11½**
1473 A647 1.20p multicolored   1.25 1.25

ANDA, 60th Anniv. A648

Perf. 12½
1993, Sept. 24   Litho.   Unwmk.
1474 A648 1.20p multicolored   1.25 1.25

Natl. Police Academy, 50th Anniv. A649

1993, Sept. 24
1475 A649 1.20p multicolored   1.40 1.40

Newspaper Diario El Pais, 75th Anniv. — A650

Perf. 12½
1993, Sept. 30   Litho.   Unwmk.
1476 A650 1.20p multicolored   1.40 1.40

Latin American Conference on Rural Electrification — A651

1993, Oct. 11
1477 A651 3.50p multicolored   3.75 3.75

B'nai B'rith, 150th Anniv. A652

1993, Oct. 13
1478 A652 3.70p multicolored   3.75 3.75

A653   Fauna — A654

1993 Photo. Wmk. 332 Perf. 12½
1482 A653 20c Seriema bird   .55 .25
1484 A653 30c Dragon bird   1.00 .25
1486 A653 50c Anteaters,
horiz.   2.00 .40
1492 A654 1.20p Giant armadillo 2.50 1.25
Nos. 1482-1492 (4)   6.05 2.15
Issued: 1.20p, 8/3/93; 20c, 30c, 50c, 10/22/93.
For surcharges, see Nos. 2011A, 2055, 2150, 2185.

America Issue A655

1.20p, Caiman latirostris. 3.50p, Athene cunicularia, vert.

Perf. 12½
1993, Oct. 6   Litho.   Unwmk.
1504 A655 1.20p multicolored   1.50 1.50
1505 A655 3.50p multicolored   4.25 4.25

Souvenir Sheet

Whitbread Trans-Global Yacht Race — A656

1993, Oct. 22   Perf. 11½x12
1506 A656 5p multicolored   5.00 5.00

Beatification of Mother Francisca Rubatto — A657

1993, Oct. 29   Wmk. 332   Perf. 12
1507 A657 1.20p multicolored   1.25 1.25

Intl. Year of Indigenous People — A658

Perf. 13x12½
1993, Oct. 29   Unwmk.
1508 A658 3.50p multicolored   3.25 3.25

Rotary Club of Montevideo, 75th Anniv. — A658a

Perf. 12½
1993, Nov. 10   Litho.   Unwmk.
1508A A658a 3.50p dk bl & bis   3.25 3.25

Rhea Americana A659

1993, Dec. 20   Litho.   Perf. 12
1509 A659 20c shown   .55 .25
1510 A659 20c With chicks   .55 .25
1511 A659 50c Head   1.25 .40
1512 A659 50c Two walking   1.25 .40
Nos. 1509-1512 (4)   3.60 1.30
World Wildlife Fund.

Children's Rights Day A660

1994, Jan. 4   Perf. 12½
1513 A660 1.40p multicolored   1.25 1.25

Independence of Lebanon, 50th Anniv. — A661

1993, Nov. 22
1514 A661 3.70p multicolored   3.25 3.25

Eduardo Victor Haedo — A662

1993, Nov. 24
1515 A662 1.20p multicolored   1.20 1.20

Christmas A663

1993, Dec. 7
1516 A663 1.40p shown   1.25 1.25
1517 A663 4p Nativity, diff.   3.50 3.50

Intl. AIDS Day — A664

1993, Dec. 1
1518 A664 1.40p multicolored   2.00 2.00

Souvenir Sheets

Anniversaries & Events — A665

Designs: No. 1519a, Switzerland #3L1, 1913 Swiss private air mail stamp. b, Germany #C39, Uruguay #C426c. c, Uruguay #C372, US #C76. d, Uruguay #C282a, U3 #C104.
No. 1520a, Switzerland Types A1, A2. b, Switzerland #B541.

1993, Nov. 18
1519 A665   1p #a.-d.   10.00 10.00
1520 A665 2.50p #a.-b.   10.00 10.00
Swiss postage stamps, 150th anniv. (#1519a, 1520). Dr. Hugo Eckener, 125th anniv. of birth (#1519b). First man on moon, 25th anniv. (#1519c). 1994 World Cup Soccer Championships, US (#1519d).
Nos. 1519-1520 exist imperf. Value $30.

17th Inter-American Naval Conference — A666

1994, Mar. 21   Litho.   Perf. 12½
1521 A666 3.70p multicolored   3.25 3.25

A667

1994, Mar. 11   **Perf. 12½**
1522 A667 4p multicolored   3.75 3.75

5th World Sports Congress, Punta del Este.

A668

Unwmk.
1994, Apr. 4   **Litho.**   **Perf. 12**
1523 A668 3.90p multicolored   2.75 2.75

Latin America Youth Organization, 7th conference.

A669

1994, Apr. 18
1524 A669 4.30p multicolored   3.75 3.75

4th World Congress on Merino Wool.

ILO, 75th Anniv. — A670

1994, Apr. 28   **Perf. 12½**
1525 A670 4.30p multicolored   2.75 2.75

Miniature Sheet

1994 Winter Olympic Medal Winners — A671

Designs: a, Katja Seizinger. b, Markus Wasmeier. c, Vreni Schneider. d, Gustav Weder.

1994, May 6   **Perf. 12**
1526 A671 1.25p Sheet of 4,
   #a.-d.   8.00 8.00

No. 1526 exists demonitized and imperf on paper with watermark 322. This item was sold with No. 1526 and has a matching serial number.

Miniature Sheet

1994 World Cup Soccer Championships, US — A672

a, Soccer ball, flags of Uruguay, Brazil. b, Ball, flags of Italy, Argentina. c, Ball, flags of Germany, Great Britain. d, Olympic Rings.

1994, May 16
1527 A672 1.25p Sheet of 4,
   #a.-d.   8.00 8.00

Uruguay, Olympic soccer gold medalists, 1924-1928 (#1527d).
See note after No. 1526.

Clemente Estable (1894-1976), Biologist — A673

1994, May 23   **Litho.**   **Perf. 12½**
1528 A673 1.60p olive & black   1.25 1.25

Electoral Court, 70th Anniv. — A674

1994, June 7
1529 A674 1.60p multicolored   1.25 1.25

Natl. Commission to Prevent Tapeworms — A675

      Perf. 12½
1994, June 17   **Litho.**   **Unwmk.**
1530 A675 1.60p multicolored   2.00 2.00

Souvenir Sheet

Cesareo L. Berisso, First Aviator to Land at Natl. Airport, Carrasco — A676

1994, June 21   **Perf. 12**
1531 A676 5p multicolored   4.00 4.00

Intl. Cooperatives, 150th Anniv. — A677

1994, July 1   **Perf. 12½**
1532 A677 4.30p multicolored   3.00 3.00

Commission on Integration of Regional Electricity, 30th Anniv. — A678

1994, July 8
1533 A678 1.60p multicolored   1.25 1.25

Abate Pierre A679

      Perf. 12½
1994, Aug. 5   **Litho.**   **Unwmk.**
1534 A679 4.80p multicolored   3.75 3.75

Intl. Year of the Family A680

1994, July 28
1535 A680 4.80p multicolored   3.75 3.75

The Man of Lugano, by Goffredo Sommavilla (1850-1944) — A681

      Perf. 12½
1994, Aug. 15   **Litho.**   **Unwmk.**
1536 A681 4.80p multicolored   2.75 2.75

First Manned Moon Landing, 25th Annvi. A682

1994, July 20
1537 A682 3p multicolored   3.00 3.00

Intl. Olympic Committee, Cent. — A683

1994, Aug. 23
1538 A683 4.80p multicolored   3.75 3.75

Elbio Fernandez School, 125th Anniv. A684

      Perf. 12½
1994, Aug. 29   **Litho.**   **Unwmk.**
1539 A684 1.80p multicolored   1.25 1.25

A685

1994, Sept. 10   **Perf. 12**
1540 A685 1.80p black & blue   1.25 1.25

Gral. Aparicio Saravia, 90th Death Anniv.

A686

1994, Sept. 30   **Perf. 12½**
1541 A686 4.80p multicolored   3.50 3.50

6th Latin American Urban Congress.

General Assoc. of Uruguayan Authors, 65th Anniv. — A687

      Perf. 12½
1994, Sept. 26   **Litho.**   **Unwmk.**
1542 A687 1.80p multicolored   1.25 1.25

America
Issue
A688

1994, Oct. 10
1543 A688 1.80p Stagecoach   1.50 1.50
1544 A688 4.80p Paddle steamer   4.50 4.50

A689

Perf. 12½
1994, Oct. 28   Litho.   Unwmk.
1545 A689 2p multicolored   1.25 1.25
Assoc. of Directors of Marketing, 50th anniv.

A690

1994, Nov. 25
1546 A690 2p multicolored   1.50 1.50
YMCA in Uruguay, 85th anniv.

Lottery,
55th
Anniv.
A691

1994, Nov. 21
1547 A691 2p multicolored   1.75 1.75

First Intl.
Seminar
to
Promote
Roads in
Uruguay,
Punta del
Este
A692

1994, Oct. 14
1548 A692 2p multicolored   1.50 1.50

Uruguayan Press Assoc., 50th
Anniv. — A693

1994, Oct. 24
1549 A693 2p multicolored   1.75 1.75

Miniature Sheet

Natl. Mint, 150th Anniv. — A694

Portions of old coin press and: a, Mint building. b, 1844 Copper coin. c, 1844 Silver coin. d, Montevideo silver peso.

1994, Oct. 17   *Perf. 12*
1550 A694 1.50p Sheet of 4, #a.-
        d.   8.00 8.00

No. 1550 exists demonitized and imperf. on paper with watermark 332. This item was sold with No. 1550 and has matching serial numbers.

Miniature Sheet

Natl. Navy — A695

Ships: a, ROU Uruguay, ROU Artigas. b, ROU Fortuna. c, ROU Uruguay. d, ROU Cte. Pedro Campbell.

1994, Nov. 15
1551 A695 1.50p Sheet of 4, #a.-
        d.   6.00 6.00

Latin American Peace Movement, 25th
Anniv. — A696

1994, Nov. 15   *Perf. 12½*
1552 A696 4.30p multicolored   3.00 3.00

4th Conference of the Latin American and Caribbean Organization of High Fiscal Entities, Montevideo — A697

1994, Dec. 5
1553 A697 5.50p multicolored   4.00 4.00

Christmas
A698

1994, Dec. 2
1554 A698   2p shown   1.00 1.00
1555 A698 5.50p Star, tree,
          house   3.00 3.00

Uruguayan Red Cross & Red Crescent
Societies, 75th Anniv. — A699

Perf. 12½
1994, Dec. 20   Litho.   Unwmk.
1556 A699 5p multicolored   3.25 3.25

City Post
Office — A700

1995-97   Litho.   Wmk. 332   *Perf. 12*
1557 A700 20c yellow green   .50   .50
1565 A700 10p brown   6.75 6.75
1566 A700 10p dark brown   3.75 3.75
        Unwmk.
1566A A700 10p clar & blk   3.75 3.75
   Nos. 1557-1566A (4)   14.75 14.75
Issued: 20c, 1/11/95; 10p, 5/21/96; #1566, 1566A, 1997.
Denomination has no decimal places on Nos. 1566-1566A.

Naval
Aviation,
70th
Anniv.
A704

Perf. 12½
1995, Feb. 7   Litho.   Unwmk.
1567 A704 2p multicolored   1.50 1.50

World Tourism Organization — A705

Designs: No. 1568, Ranch house, sheep herders. No. 1569, Water recreation park. No. 1570, Native wildlife. No. 1571, Beach resort.

1995, Feb. 13
1568 A705 5p multicolored   3.25 3.25
1569 A705 5p multicolored   3.25 3.25
1570 A705 5p multicolored   3.25 3.25
1571 A705 5p multicolored   3.25 3.25
   Nos. 1568-1571 (4)   13.00 13.00

17th World
Conference of
Lifeguard
Services — A706

1995, Feb. 15
1572 A706 5p multicolored   3.25 3.25

Rotary
Intl., 90th
Anniv.
A707

1995, Feb. 22
1573 A707 5p multicolored   3.00 3.00

ICAO,
50th
Anniv.
A708

1995, Mar. 14
1574 A708 5p multicolored   3.25 3.25

Pietro Mascagni (1863-1945),
Composer — A709

Perf. 12½
1995, Mar. 30   Litho.   Unwmk.
1575 A709 5p multicolored   3.50 3.50

Miniature Sheet

Butterflies — A710

Designs: a, Phoebis neocypris. b, Diogas erippus. c, Euryades duponcheli. d, Automeris coresus.

1995, June 15   Litho.   *Perf. 12½*
1576 A710 5p Sheet of 4, #a.-
        d.   12.00 12.00

Wild Dog
A711

1995, May 17   Litho.   *Perf. 12½*
1577 A711 2.30p multicolored   2.00 2.00

America Cup
Soccer
Championships
A712

Game scenes, flags of participating countries, match sites: a, Paysandu. b, Rivera. c, Ball (no site). d, Montevideo. e, Maldonado.

1995, July 4
1578 A712 2.30p Strip of 5, #a.-
    e.   6.50 6.50
No. 1578 is a continuous design.

FAO, 50th
Anniv. — A713

1995, July 7
1579 A713 5.50p multicolored   3.25 3.25

UN Peace-Keeping Missions — A714

1995, July 14   Litho.   Perf. 12½
1580 A714 2.30p multicolored   1.75 1.75

Visit of
Italy's
Pres.
Oscar
Luigi
Scalfaro
A715

1995, July 21
1581 A715 5.50p multicolored   3.00 3.00

A716

1995, July 24
1582 A716 5p multicolored   3.00 3.00
Rotary Intl., 90th anniv.

A717

1995, Sept. 22
1583 A717 2.60p multicolored   1.50 1.50
Jose Pedro Varela, 150th birth anniv.

Miniature Sheet

Shells — A718

a, Zidona dufresnei. b, Boccinanops duartei. c, Dorsanum moniliferum. d, Olivancillaria uretai.

1995, Aug. 4
1584 A718 5p Sheet of 4, #a.-
    d.   20.00 20.00

America
Issue
A719

Designs: 3p, Dicksonia selloviana, vert. 6p, Chrysocyon brachyurus.

Unwmk.
1995, Oct. 10   Litho.   Perf. 12
1585 A719 3p multicolored   1.75 1.75
1586 A719 6p multicolored   3.50 3.50

Carlos
Gardel,
Musician
A720

1995, Sept. 4   Perf. 12½
1587 A720 5.50p blue & black   3.25 3.25

Flowers — A721

Designs: a, Notocactus roseinflorus. b, Verbena chamaedryfolia. c, Bauhinia candicans. d, Tillandsia aeranthos. e, Eichhornia crassipes.

1995, Sept. 12
1588 A721 3p Strip of 5, #a.-e.   10.00 10.00

Miniature Sheet

Uruguay's Artigas Antarctic Scientific
Research Base, 10th Anniv. — A722

Designs: a, 2.50p, Albatross. b, 4p, Fairchild FAU572. c, 4p, ROU Vanguard. d, 2.50p, PTS/M Amphibian transporter.

1995, Oct. 13
1589 A722   Sheet of 4, #a.-d.   12.00 12.00
Uruguayan Antarctic Institute, 20th anniv.
No. 1589 exists demonitized and imperf. on paper with watermark 332. This item was sold with No. 1589 and has matching serial numbers.

Holocaust
Memorial — A723

1995, Sept. 27   Litho.   Perf. 13x12½
1590 A723 6p multicolored   6.00 6.00

UN, 50th
Anniv. — A724

1995, Oct. 24   Litho.   Perf. 12
1591 A724 6p multicolored   3.50 3.50

Early Locomotives — A725

No. 1592, Beyer & Peacock, 1876. No. 1593, Criollo, 1895. No. 1594, Beyer & Peacock, 1910.

1995, Nov. 7
1592 A725 3p multicolored   1.75 1.75
1593 A725 3p multicolored   1.75 1.75
1594 A725 3p multicolored   1.75 1.75
    Nos. 1592-1594 (3)   5.25 5.25

Uruguayan Navy, 178th Anniv. — A726

No. 1595, Sailing ship, Artiguista. No. 1596, ROU Pte. Rivera. No. 1597, ROU Montevideo.

1995, Nov. 15   Perf. 12½
1595 A726 3p multicolored   1.75 1.75
1596 A726 3p multicolored   1.75 1.75
1597 A726 3p multicolored   1.75 1.75
    Nos. 1595-1597 (3)   5.25 5.25

Motion
Pictures,
Cent.
A727

1995, Dec. 13
1598 A727 6p Lumiere Brothers   4.00 4.00

A728

Christmas
A729

1995, Dec. 15
1599 A728 2.90p multicolored   1.50 1.50
1600 A729 6.50p multicolored   3.50 3.50

Modern Olympic Games,
Cent. — A730

Designs: a, Equestrian event, Atlanta 1996. b, Ski jumper, Nagano 1988. c, Torch bearer, Sydney 2000. d, Skier, Salt Lake City 2002.

1996, Jan. 30   Litho.   Perf. 12½
1601 A730 2.50p Sheet of 4, #a.-
    d.   9.50 9.50
Latin America Philatelic Exposition.
No. 1601 exists demonitized and imperf. on paper with watermark 332. This item was sold with No. 1601 and has matching serial numbers.

Carnival
Personalities
A732

1996, Feb. 16   Litho.   Perf. 12½
1603 A732 2.90p Rosa Luna   2.00 2.00
1604 A732 2.90p Pepino   2.00 2.00
1605 A732 2.90p Santiago Luz   2.00 2.00
    Nos. 1603-1605 (3)   6.00 6.00

Golf in
Uruguay
A733

Designs: a, Cantegril Country Club. b, Cerro
Golf Club. c, Fay Crocker. d, Lago Golf Club.
e, Golf Club of Uruguay.

1996, Feb. 27
1606 A733 2.90p Strip of 5,
#a.-e.   8.00 8.00
No. 1606 was issued in sheets of 25 stamps.

Famous People, Events — A734

Designs: a, Statue, Cardinal Barbieri (1892-
1979). b, Yitzhak Rabin (1922-95), Nobel
Peace Prize. c, Soccer players, First World
Cup Soccer Championship, Grand Park Central, July 13, 1930. d, Robert Stolz (1880-
1975), composer.

1996, Mar. 8
1607 A734 2.50p Sheet of 4, #a.-
d.   7.00 7.00
Philatelic Academy of Uruguay. The Stamp
of Today, SODRE TV Chanel 5, 10th anniv.

Montevideo, Capital of Latin American
Culture — A735

1996, Mar. 5
1608 A735 2.90p Solis Theater,
1837   1.75 1.75
  a.   Booklet pane of 3   7.00
         Complete booklet, #1608a   7.00

General
Census
A736

1996, Apr. 29
1609 A736 3.20p multicolored   1.50 1.50

1998 World Cup Soccer
Championships, France — A737

a, Player in early uniform, Olympic champions, 1924-28, world cup champions, 1930-50,
older trophy. b, Trophy, player. d, Two children
playing, UNICEF emblem, soccer emblems. e,
Olympic rings, two players, eliminations for
Atlanta '96.

1996, Apr. 10
1610 A737 2.50p Sheet of 4, #a.-
d.   8.50 8.50
Latin America Philatelic Exposition.
No. 1610 exists demonitized and imperf. on
paper with watermark 332. This item was sold
with No. 1610 and has matching serial
numbers.

Bones from
Indian Burial
Grounds — A738

1996, Apr. 18
1611 A738 3.20p multicolored   1.75 1.75

Alfredo
Zitarrosa
(1936-89),
Guitarist
A739

1996, Mar. 15   *Perf. 12*
1612 A739 3p multicolored   1.75 1.75

Prehistoric Animals — A740

Designs: a, Glyptodon claripes. b,
Macrauchenia patachonica. c, Toxodon
platensis. d, Glossotherium robostum. e,
Titanosaurus.

1996, Apr. 18   *Perf. 12½*
1613 A740 3.20p Strip of 5,
#a.-e.   10.00 10.00
No. 1613 was issued in sheets of 25 stamps.

Taking Care of Planet Earth,
Everyone's Responsibility, by Soraya
Campanella — A741

Unwmk.
1996, June 5 **Litho.** *Perf. 12*
1614 A741 3.20p multicolored   1.75 1.75

Calidris Canutus — A742

1996, May 28   *Perf. 12½*
1615 A742 12p multicolored   11.00 11.00
CAPEX '96.

Early Methods of
Transportation — A743

Designs: a, 1912 Dion-Buton omnibus. b,
1928 Ford Model A. c, 1940 Raleigh bicycle. d,
1926 Magirus firetruck. e, 1917 Hotchkiss
ambulance.

1996, May 21
1616 A743 3.20p Strip of 5,
#a.-e.   10.00 10.00
No. 1616 was issued in sheets of 25 stamps.

Sailing
Ships
A744

Designs: a, Our Lady of Encina, 1726. b,
San Francisco. c, Ships of E. Moreau. d, Bold
Lady. e, Our Lady of the Light.

1996, June 17   **Litho.**   *Perf. 12½*
1617 A744 3.20p Strip of 5, #a.-
e.   7.00 7.00
No. 1617 was issued in sheets of 25 stamps.

Landscape in Las Flores, by Carmelo
de Arzadun — A745

1996, July 15   **Litho.**   *Perf. 12½*
1618 A745 3.50p multicolored   1.50 1.50

Jewish Community in Uruguay, 80th
Anniv. — A746

1996, July 29
1619 A746 7.50p multicolored   4.00 4.00

A747

Scientists
from
Uruguay
A748

No. 1620, Enrique Legrand (1861-1939).
No. 1621, Victor Bertullo (1919-79). No. 1622,
Tomas Beno Hirschfeld (1939-86). No. 1623,
Miguel C. Rubino (1886-1945).

1996, July 30
1620 A747 3.50p multicolored   1.75 1.75
1621 A747 3.50p multicolored   1.75 1.75
1622 A748 3.50p multicolored   1.75 1.75
1623 A748 3.50p multicolored   1.75 1.75
  Nos. 1620-1623 (4)   7.00 7.00

Bank of Uruguay, Cent. — A749

1996, Sept. 9   *Perf. 12*
1624 A749 3.50p 10p note   2.00 2.00
  a.   Booklet pane, #1624   3.00
1625 A749 3.50p 500p note   2.00 2.00
  a.   Booklet pane, #1625   3.00
         Complete bklt., #1624a, 1625a 6.00

Otto Lilienthal (1848-1896) — A750

1996, Aug. 30
1626 A750 12p multicolored   6.00 6.00
AEROFILA '96.

Scientists
A751

No. 1627, Albert Einstein. No. 1628, Aristotle. No. 1629, Isaac Newton.

1996, Sept. 3   *Perf. 12½*
1627 A751 7.50p multicolored   3.50 3.50
1628 A751 7.50p multicolored   3.50 3.50
1629 A751 7.50p multicolored   3.50 3.50
  Nos. 1627-1629 (3)   10.50 10.50

National
Heritage — A752

Designs: No. 1630, Map of Gorriti Island showing locations of Spanish forts, 18th cent. No. 1631, Narbona Church, 18th cent.

Perf. 13x12½

1996, Sept. 12		**Litho.**		**Unwmk.**
1630	A752	3.50p multicolored	1.60	1.60
1631	A752	3.50p multicolored	1.60	1.60

Rural
Assoc.,
125th
Anniv.
A753

1996, Sept. 20			**Perf. 12½x13**	
1632	A753	3.50p multicolored	1.75	1.75

Marine Life — A754

a, Carchardon carcharias. b, Alopias vulpinus. c, Notorynchus cepedianus. d, Squatina dumerili.

1996, Sept. 23				
1633	A754	3.50p Sheet of 4, #a.-d.	8.00	8.00

Istanbul '96.

Sports Champions from
Uruguay — A755

Designs: a, Angel Rodriguez, boxing, 1917. b, Leandro Noli, cycling, 1939. c, Eduardo G. Risso, rowing, 1948. d, Estrella Puente, javelin, 1949. e, Oscar Moglia, basketball, 1956.

1996, Oct. 1				
1634	A755	3.50p Strip of 5, #a.-e.	9.50	9.50

Traditional
Costumes
A756

America issue: 3.50p, Gaucho. 7.50p, Woman of the campana.

1996, Oct. 11			**Perf. 13x12½**	
1635	A756	3.50p multicolored	1.60	1.60
1636	A756	7.50p multicolored	3.50	3.50

3rd Space Conference of the
Americas — A757

1996, Nov. 4		**Wmk. 332**		**Perf. 12**
1637	A757	3.50p multicolored	2.10	2.10

Comic
Strips,
Cent.
A758

"Peloduro," by Julio E. Suarez.

1996, Nov. 7				
1638	A758	4p multicolored	2.40	2.40

Health
Institute,
Cent.
A759

1996, Nov. 20				
1639	A759	4p multicolored	1.75	1.75

Church of the 7th
Day Adventists in
Uruguay,
Cent. — A760

		Wmk. 332		
1996, Nov. 26		**Litho.**		**Perf. 12½**
1640	A760	3.50p multicolored	1.75	1.75

Felix de Azara (1746-1811),
Naturalist — A761

1996, Nov. 20			**Perf. 12**	
1641	A761	4p multicolored	2.00	2.00

Fish
A762

Designs: No. 1642, Cynolebia nigripinnis. No. 1643, Cynolebia viarius.

		Unwmk.		
1997, Feb. 24		**Litho.**		**Die Cut**
		Self-Adhesive		
1642	A762	4p multicolored	2.00	2.00
1643	A762	4p multicolored	2.00	2.00

Popular
Festivals
A763

#1644, Natl. Folklore Festival, Durazno. #1645, Traditional Gaucho Festival, Tacuarembo.

1997		**Wmk. 332**		**Perf. 12½**
1644	A763	4p multi	2.25	2.25
1645	A763	4p multi, vert.	2.25	2.25

Issued: #1644, 1/30; #1645, 3/10.
See Nos. 1653-1656.

Mushrooms — A764

Designs: a, Tricholoma nudum. b, Agaricus xanthodermus. c, Russula sardonia. d, Microsporum canis. e, Polyporus versicolor.

1997, Feb. 7				
1646	A764	4p Strip of 5, #a.-e.	10.00	10.00

No. 1646 was issued in sheets of 25 stamps.

Ports
A765

No. 1647, Colonia. No. 1648, Punta del Este. No. 1649, Santiago Vázquez. No. 1650, Buceo.

1997, Feb. 28		**Litho.**		**Die Cut**
		Self-Adhesive		
1647	A765	4p multicolored	2.00	2.00
1648	A765	4p multicolored	2.00	2.00
1649	A765	4p multicolored	2.00	2.00
1650	A765	4p multicolored	2.00	2.00
		Nos. 1647-1650 (4)	8.00	8.00

Artigas'
Lancers,
Bicent.
A766

1997, Mar. 10		**Wmk. 332**		**Perf. 12½**
1651	A766	4p multicolored	2.00	2.00

Military Academy,
50th
Anniv. — A767

1997, Mar. 13				
1652	A767	4p multicolored	2.00	2.00

Popular Festivals Type of 1997

Coat of arms and: No. 1653, Performers under outdoor pavilion, Beer Week. No. 1654, Ruben Lena, bridge, river, Olimar River Festival, vert. No. 1655, Guitar, man on horse, Festival de Minas Y Abril. No. 1656, Family around person on horseback, Roosevelt Park.

1997			**Litho.**	
1653	A763	5p multicolored	2.50	2.50
1654	A763	5p multicolored	2.50	2.50

1655	A763	5p multicolored	2.50	2.50
		Die Cut		
		Unwmk.		
		Self-Adhesive		
1656	A763	5p multicolored	2.50	2.50
		Nos. 1653-1656 (4)	10.00	10.00

Lions Intl. (#1656). Issued: #1653, 3/23; #1654, 3/24; #1655, 4/26; #1656, 3/21.

United
Mobile
Coronary
Unit
(UCM),
20th
Anniv.
A768

1997, Apr. 4		**Unwmk.**		**Die Cut**
		Self-Adhesive		
1657	A768	5p multicolored	2.50	2.50

UNICEF, 50th
Anniv. — A769

1997, Apr. 8			**Die Cut**	
		Self-Adhesive		
1658	A769	5p multicolored	2.50	2.50

Lighthouses
A770

Various birds and: a, Anchorena Tower, 1920. b, Farallón Lighthouse, 1870. c, José Ignacio Lighthouse, 1877. d, Santa Maria Lighthouse, 1874. e, Vigía Tower, 18th cent.

1997, Apr. 22			**Die Cut**	
		Self-Adhesive		
1659	A770	5p Strip of 5, #a.-e.	12.00	12.00

Prehistoric
Animals
A771

Designs: a, Devincenzia gallinali. b, Smilodon populator. c, Mesosaurus tenuidens. d, Doedicurus clavicaudatus. e, Artigasia magna.

1997, May 5			**Die Cut**	
		Self-Adhesive		
1660	A771	5p Strip of 5, #a.-e.	12.00	12.00

A772

Ecclesiastical Provinces — A772a

#1661, Church, diocese of Salto. #1662, Church, diocese of Melo. #1663, Bishop Jacinto Vera, 1st bishop of Montevideo. #1664, Msgr. Mariano Soler, 1st archbishop of Montevideo.

Wmk. 332

1997, May 9		**Litho.**	*Perf. 12½*	
1661	A772	5p multicolored	2.50	2.50
1662	A772	5p multicolored	2.50	2.50
1663	A772a	5p multicolored	2.50	2.50
1664	A772a	5p multicolored	2.50	2.50
	Nos. 1661-1664 (4)		10.00	10.00

Youth Stamp Collecting A773

Designs: a, 2p, Boy, "Philately?" b, 2p, Boy thinking of stamps. c, 2p, Girl with soccer ball, boy. d, 1p, Boy looking at stamps in album. e, 1p, Boy with tongs and magnifying glass.

1997, May 25			**Unwmk.**
1665	A773	Strip of 5, #a.-e.	4.00 4.00

PACIFIC 97 — A774

1997, May 29			*Perf. 12*
1666	A774	10p Rynchops niger	5.00 5.00

Maccio Theater of San Jose, 85th Anniv. A775

1997, June 5	**Wmk. 332**		*Perf. 12½*
1667	A775	5p multicolored	2.50 2.50

Inter-American Institute of Children, 70th Anniv. — A776

1997, June 9			**Unwmk.**
1668	A776	5p multicolored	2.50 2.50

Colony of Sacramento — A777

1997, July 4			
1669	A777	5p multicolored	2.50 2.50

Punta del Este, 90th Anniv. A778

1997, July 1			
1670	A778	5p multicolored	2.50 2.50

Uruguayan Comics — A779

Scenes from comics by: No. 1671, Julio E. Suarez (Peloduro). No. 1672, Geoffrey Foladori.

		Perf. 12½	
1997, June 30		**Litho.**	**Unwmk.**
1671	A779	5p multicolored	2.00 2.00
1672	A779	5p multicolored	2.00 2.00

Zionism, Cent. A780

Design: Theodor Herzl (1860-1904), founder of Zionist movement

1997, July 17			
1673	A780	5p multicolored	3.00 3.00

Children's Painting A781   Geranoaetus Melanoleucus A782

1997, July 21	**Litho.**		*Die Cut*
	Self-Adhesive		
1674	A781	15p multicolored	*10.00 10.00*
1675	A782	25p multicolored	*16.00 16.00*
a.		Type II ('04)	4.50 4.50

Type I stamps have printer's name at right, designer's name at left, and have an eagle's head that is rounder, with its edge making a sharper angle with the right margin than on type II. Type II stamps have the printer's name at left and the designer's name at right.
No. 1675a issued 2004. No. 1675a also exists dated "2005."
Nos. 1674, 1675 exist dated 1999.
See Nos. 1840, 1850, 1853, 1855.

Isolation of Acetylsalicylic Acid from Willow Trees, Cent. — A783

1997, Aug. 12	**Litho.**		*Perf. 12½*
1676	A783	6p multicolored	2.00 2.00
a.		Booklet pane of 2	6.50
		Complete booklet, #1076a	6.50

Department of Salto — A784

1997, Aug. 26			
1677	A784	6p multicolored	2.00 2.00

Felix Mendelssohn (1809-47) — A785

No. 1679, Johannes Brahms (1833-97).

1997, Sept. 1			
1678	A785	6p multicolored	1.75 1.75
1679	A785	6p multicolored	1.75 1.75
a.		Pair, #1678-1679	4.00 4.00

Natural History Museum of Montevideo, 160th Anniv. — A786

Designs: a, Lucas Kraguevich, paleontologist. b, Jose Arechavaleta, botanist. c, Garibaldi J. Devincenzi, zoologist. d, Antonio Taddei, archaelogist.

1997, Sept. 9			
1680	A786	6p Strip of 4, #a.-d.	6.00 6.00

Mercosur (Common Market of Latin America) A787

1997, Sept. 26			*Perf. 12*
1681	A787	11p multicolored	3.00 3.00

See Argentina, No. 1975; Bolivia No. 1019; Brazil, No. 2646; Paraguay, No. 2564.

Souvenir Sheet

Passiflora Coerulea — A788

1997, Sept. 26			*Perf. 12½*
1682	A788	15p multicolored	4.00 4.00

1st Philatelic Exhibition of Mercosur countries.

Heinrich von Stephan (1831-97) A789

1997, Oct. 9			
1683	A789	11p multicolored	3.25 3.25

Souvenir Sheet

Spanish-Uruguayan Monument — A790

1997, Oct. 9			
1684	A790	15p Monument	4.00 4.00

Philatelic Exhibition, Spain 1997.

America Issue — A791

Designs: 6p, Woman carrying mail. 11p, Man delivering letters.

1997, Oct. 10			
1685	A791	6p multicolored	1.75 1.75
1686	A791	11p multicolored	3.50 3.50

Artigas Scientific Base, Antarctica — A792

1997, Oct. 15			*Perf. 12*
1687	A792	6p Pygoscelis papua	2.00 2.00

Painting, by Domingo Laporte (1855-1928) — A793

1997, Oct. 21			*Perf. 12½*
1688	A793	6p multicolored	1.50 1.50

Galicia House, 80th Anniv. A794

1997, Oct. 24
1689 A794 6p multicolored 1.75 1.75

3rd Intl. Congress of Aeronautical and Space History, Montevideo — A795

1997, Oct. 27 **Litho.** **Unwmk.**
Perf. 12½
1690 A795 6p Arme 2 Biplane 1.75 1.75

1st Biennial Interparliamentary Exhibition of MERCOSUR Paintings, Montevideo — A796

1997, Oct. 28
1691 A796 11p multicolored 3.00 3.00

Souvenir Sheet

Pope John Paul II, Holy Year 2000 — A797

1997, Nov. 7
1692 A797 10p multicolored 6.50 6.50

Third Intl. Assembly Punta del Este, and of arrival of first Polish colonists at River Plate, cent.

Uruguayan Navy, 180th Anniv. — A798

1997, Nov. 14
1693 A798 6p multicolored 1.75 1.75

Shanghai '97 Intl. Stamp and Coin Exhibition — A799

No. 1694: a, 3.50p, Front and back of 1 peso coin. b, 3.50p, Chinese flag, Hong Kong harbor, flower, junk. c, 4p, Michael Schumacher, Formula 1 driving champion, Ferrari. d, 4p, Sojourner on Mars, Pathfinder Mission.
No. 1695: a, 3.50p, Martina Hingis, 1997 Wimbledon Ladies' champion. b, 3.50p, Jan Ullrich, 1997 Tour de France winner. c, 4p, Soccer players, 1998 World Cup Soccer Championship, France. d, 4p, Ski jumper, 1998 Winter Olympic Games, Nagano.

1997, Nov. 19
1694 A799 Sheet of 4, #a.-d. 5.00 5.00
1695 A799 Sheet of 4, #a.-d. 5.00 5.00

Christmas A800

1997, Nov. 20
1696 A800 6p Magi 1.50 1.50
1697 A800 11p Madonna & Child 2.75 2.75

Uruguayan Sportsmen — A801

Designs: a, Adesio Lombardo, Olympic bronze medalist, basketball, Helsinki, 1952. b, Guillermo Douglas, Olympic bronze medalist, single sculls, Rome, 1932. c, Obdulio Varela, soccer player on 1950 World Cup championship team. d, Atilio Francois, silver medalist, 1947 World Cycling Championships, Paris. e, Juan López Testa, South American 100 meters champion, 1947.

1997, Nov. 26
1698 A801 6p Strip of 5, #a.-e. 8.00 8.00

Mevifil '97, 1st Intl. Exhibition of Philatelic Audio-Visual and Computer Systems — A802

1997, Dec. 1 **Perf. 12**
1699 A802 11p multicolored 3.00 3.00

INDEPEX '97 — A803

Early vehicles, inventors: a, 1st Land Rover, 1947. b, Henry Ford (1863-1947), Model A. c, Robert Bosch (1861-1942), inventor of automotive components. d, Rudolf Diesel (1858-1913), patented first diesel engine, 1897.

1997, Dec. 8 **Perf. 12½**
1700 A803 6p Strip of 4, #a.-d. 6.50 6.50

Naval Academy of Uruguay, 90th Anniv. A804

1997, Dec. 12
1701 A804 6p multicolored 1.75 1.75

Supreme Court of Uruguay, 90th Anniv. A805

1997, Dec. 12
1702 A805 6p multicolored 1.75 1.75

Uruguayan Post Office, 170th Anniv. — A806

1997, Dec. 19
1703 A806 6p multicolored 1.60 1.60

MEVIR (Movement for Eradication of Unsanitary Rural Housing), 90th Anniv. — A807

Design: Homes, Dr. A. Gallinal, logo.

1997, Dec. 26
1704 A807 6p multicolored 1.60 1.60

Construction Projects — A808

a, Preparation. b, Planning. c, Execution.

1997, Dec. 29 **Perf. 12**
1705 A808 6p Strip of 3, #a.-c. 5.00 5.00
d. Booklet pane, #1705 6.00 6.00
Complete booklet, #1705d 6.00 6.00

Souvenir Sheet

1897 Revolution, Cent. — A809

Design: Gen. Antonio "Chiquito" Saravia and Col. Diego Lamas.

1997, Dec. 30 **Perf. 12½**
1706 A809 15p multicolored 4.00 4.00

Painting by Héctor Ragni (b. 1898) — A810

1998, Feb. 6
1707 A810 6p multicolored 1.75 1.75

Naval Station, Montevideo — A811

1998, Feb. 13
1708 A811 6p multicolored 1.75 1.75

Native Trees — A812

a, Butia capitata. b, Grove of butia capitata. c, Grove of phytolacca dioica. d, Phytolacca dioica.

1998, Mar. 20 **Perf. 12**
1709 A812 6p Block of 4, #a.-d. 6.50 6.50

Museum of Humor — A813

Cartoons: No. 1710, by Oscar Abín. No. 1711, by Emilio Cortinas.

1998, Mar. 13 **Perf. 12½**
1710 A813 6p multicolored 1.75 1.75
1711 A813 6p multicolored 1.75 1.75
a. Pair, #1710-1711 4.00 4.00

Wilson Ferreira Aldunate (1919-88) A814

1998, Mar. 17   **Perf. 12**
1712 A814 6p multicolored   1.75 1.75

Fossilized Animals — A815

Designs: a, Testudinites sellowi. b, Proborhyaena gigantea. c, Propachyrucos schiaffinos. d, Stegomastodon platensis.

1998, Mar. 26
1713 A815 6p Block of 4, #a.-d.   6.50 6.50

Israel '98, State of Israel, 50th Anniv. — A816

1998, Mar. 31   **Perf. 12**
1714 A816 12p multicolored   3.75 3.75

Birds — A820

a, Plyborus plancus. b, Cygnus melancoryphus. c, Platalea ajaja. d, Theristicus caudatus.

1998, Apr. 30
1718 A820 6p Block of 4, #a.-d.   7.00 7.00

Organization of American States, 50th Anniv. — A821

1998, Apr. 14   **Litho.**   **Perf. 12¾x12½**
1719 A821 12p multi   3.50 3.50

61st World Congress of Sports Journalism A822

1998, Apr. 21   **Litho.**   **Perf. 12**
1720 A822 6p multicolored   1.75 1.75

Land Settlement Institute, 50th Anniv. — A823

1998, Apr. 22   **Litho.**   **Perf. 12¾x12½**
1721 A823 6p multi   2.00 2.00

Souvenir Sheet

Intl. Topical Philatelic Exhibition, Nueva Helvecia — A824

Cross and: a, 3.50p, Switzerland #5, Uruguay #1. b, 3.50p, Obverse and reverse of Euro coin. c, 4p, Olympic rings and mountain. d, 4p, Space station.

1998, May 12   **Perf. 12½x12¾**
1722 A824 Sheet of 4, #a.-d.   6.00 6.00
    Swiss Republic, bicent.

Souvenir Sheet

Whales — A825

a, 3.50p, Balaeneoptera physalus (b). b, 3.50p, Balaeneoptera acutorostrata. c, 4p, Megaptera novaeangliae (d). d, 4p, Eubalaena australis (c).

1998, May 15   **Litho.**   **Perf. 12½**
1723 A825 Sheet of 4, #a.-d.   6.50 6.50
   Ambiente '98, Maia, Portugal; Intl. Year of the Ocean; Expo '98, Lisbon.

1983 Labor Day Democracy Demonstrations — A826

      Perf. 12¼x12¾
1998, May 27   **Litho.**   **Wmk. 332**
1724 A826 6p brn & blk   1.75 1.75
     See Nos. 1740, 1775.

Street Cars — A827

Historic Montevideo trams: a, English "La Comercial," 1906. b, German Transatlantica Co., 1907. c, Transatlantica, 1908. d, Transatlantica double decker, 1916.

1998, May 29   **Litho.**   **Perf. 12**
1725 A827 6p Block of 4, #a.-d.   6.50 6.50

Juvalux '98 — A828

Wildcats: a, Felis colocola. b, Felis pardalis. c, Felis wiedil. d, Panthera onca.

       Unwmk.
1998, June 18   **Litho.**   **Perf. 12**
1726 A828 6p Block of 4, #a.-d.   6.50 6.50

Ships — A829

a, "Sirius." b, Gunboat "18 de Julio." c, Transport, "Maldonado." d, "Instituto de Pesca No. 1."

1998, June 25   **Litho.**   **Perf. 12**
1727 A829 6p Block of 4, #a.-d.   6.50 6.50

Jesuit Mission Church, Calera de las Huérfanas A830

     Perf. 12½x12¾
1998, July 24   **Litho.**   **Unwmk.**
1728 A830 12p multi   3.25 3.25

Monument to the Peace of 1872, San José de Mayo, 125th Anniv. — A831

1998, July 31   **Perf. 12¾x12½**
1729 A831 6p multi   2.00 2.00

155mm Artillery Unit No. 5, Cent. A832

1998, Aug. 7   **Perf. 12½x12¾**
1730 A832 6p multi   1.75 1.75

Butterflies — A833

1998, Aug. 14   **Litho.**   **Perf. 12**
1731 A833 6p Eacles imperialis   2.00 2.00
1732 A833 6p Protoparce luceti-us   2.00 2.00
   a.   Pair, #1731-1732   4.50 4.50

First Monument to José Artigas, San José de Mayo, Cent. — A834

     Perf. 12¾x12½
1998, Aug. 24   **Litho.**
1733 A834 6p multi   1.75 1.75

A835

1998, Aug. 28
1734 A835 6p multi   1.75 1.75

Dr. Mauricio López Lombo (1918-93), zoo founder.

A836

1998, Aug. 31
1735 A836 6p multi   1.75 1.75

Falleri-Balzo Music Conservatory, Montevideo, cent.

José Fernández Vergara (1810-1906), Founder of Pueblo Vergara — A837

1998, Sept. 8
1736 A837 6p multi   1.75 1.75

Souvenir Sheet

El Pais Newspaper, 80th Anniv. — A838

1998, Sept. 14   **Perf. 12½x12¾**
1737 A838 12p multi   3.75 3.75

Collective Medical Assistance Institute, 145th Anniv. — A839

1998, Sept. 24   **Perf. 12¾x12½**
1738 A839 6p multi   1.75 1.75

Postal Link Between Montevideo and Corunna, Spain, 230th Anniv. — A840

1998, Sept. 24
1739 A840 12p multi   3.75 3.75

Espamer '98, Buenos Aires.

Labor Day Type

6p, March of the Social and Cultural Assoc. of Public School Students, 9/25/83.

Perf. 12½x12¾
1998, Sept. 25   **Wmk. 332**
1740 A826 6p brn & blk   1.75 1.75

Iberoamericana '98 Philatelic Exhibition, Maia, Portugal — A841

Airplanes: a, Junkers J52. b, Spad VII. c, Ansaldo SVA-10. d, Neybar.

Unwmk.
1998, Oct. 2   **Litho.**   **Perf. 12**
1741 A841 6p Block of 4, #a.-d.   6.50 6.50

Death of Chilean Pres. Salvador Allende, 25th Anniv. A842

Perf. 12¼x12¾
1998, Oct. 2   **Litho.**   **Unwmk.**
1742 A842 12p multi   3.75 3.75

50th Anniv. of Enrique Rodríguez Fabregat (1885-1976) as UN Commissioner for Palestine — A843

1998, Oct. 5   **Perf. 12¾x12½**
1743 A843 6p multi   2.00 2.00

Radio Carve, 70th Anniv. A844

1998, Oct. 7   **Litho.**   **Perf. 12½x12¾**
1744 A844 6p multi   1.75 1.75

World Post Day A845

1998, Oct. 9   **Litho.**   **Perf. 12½x12¾**
1745 A845 12p multi   3.25 3.25

Ilsapex '98, Johannesburg.

America Issue — A846

Famous women: 6p, Julia Guarino (1897-1985), first woman architect in South America. 12p, Dr. Paulina Luisi (1875-1950).

1998, Oct. 9   **Litho.**   **Perf. 12**
1746 A846 6p multi   1.75 1.75
1747 A846 12p multi   3.50 3.50

Assoc. of Inland Pharmacies, 50th Anniv. — A847

1998, Oct. 10   **Perf. 12½x12¾**
1748 A847 6p multi   1.75 1.75

Postal Services — A847a

Serpentine Die Cut 11¼
1998, Oct. 15   **Litho.**   **Unwmk.**
Self-Adhesive
1748A A847a 25p multi   6.50 6.50

Exists dated 1999.

Classic Vehicles — A848

Designs: a, 1950 Lancia fire engine. b, 1946 Maserati San Remo. c, 1954 Alfa Romeo trolley bus. d, 1936 Fiat Topolino.

1998, Oct. 23   **Litho.**   **Perf. 12**
1749 A848 6p Block of 4, #a.-d.   7.50 7.50

Italia'98.

Artists A849

Designs: No. 1750, Sculpture, "Motherhood," and self-portrait of Nerses Ounanian (1920-57). No. 1751, Illustrations from book "Piquín y Chispita," by Serafín J. Garcia (1905-85), vert. No. 1752, Musical score by Héctor M. Artola (1903-82), vert.

Perf. 12½x12¾, 12¾x12½
1998, Oct. 27   **Litho.**
1750 A849 6p multi   1.75 1.75
1751 A849 6p multi   1.75 1.75
1752 A849 6p multi   1.75 1.75
     Nos. 1750-1752 (3)   5.25 5.25

Juvenalia '98 — A850

1998, Oct. 30   **Litho.**   **Perf. 12¾x12½**
1753 A850 6p multi   1.75 1.75

Souvenir Sheet

Uruguay-Germany Philatelic Exhibition, Montevideo — A851

Designs: a, 3.50p, Zeppelin cover, Zeppelin NT. b, 3.50p, Germany #1592, Germany Berlin #9N584, German Democratic Republic #2791, mail box. c, 4p, Brandenburg Gate, Volkswagen Beetle, Konrad Adenauer. d, 4p, Airplane, German mark note and coin.

1998, Nov. 6   **Litho.**   **Perf. 12½x12¾**
1754 A851 Sheet of 4, #a.-d.   6.50 6.50

IBRA '99, 150th anniv. of German stamps (#1754a, 1754b), 50th anniv. of Federal Republic of Germany (#1754c), 50th anniv. of German mark (#1754d).

16th Congress of Expenditure Control Boards — A852

1998, Nov. 9
1755 A852 12p blue & silver   3.25 3.25

Uruguayan Chamber of Industries, Cent. — A853

1998, Nov. 9
1756 A853 6p multi   1.75 1.75

Flowers
A854

1p, Oxalis pudica. 4p, Oxalis pudica (white). 5p, Oxalis pudica (purple). 6p, Eugenia uniflora. 7p, Eugenia uniflora. 9p, Eugenia uniflora. 10p, Aechmea recurvata. 14p, Acca sellowiana. 50p, Acca sellowiana.

Serpentine Die Cut 11¼

1998-99	Self-Adhesive	Litho.		
1757	A854	1p "98" date	.40	.30
a.		"99" in inscription	.40	.30
b.		"2000" in inscription	.40	.30
c.		"2001" in inscription	.40	.30
d.		"2002" in inscription	.40	.30
1760	A854	4p multi	1.00	1.00
1761	A854	5p multi	.80	.80
1762	A854	6p multi	1.75	1.75
1763	A854	7p multi	1.75	1.75
1765	A854	9p multi	5.50	5.50
1766	A854	10p "98" date	2.75	2.75
a.		"99" in inscription	2.75	2.75
b.		"2002" in inscription	2.75	2.75
1770	A854	14p multi	3.75	3.75
1771	A854	50p multi	9.50	9.50
	Nos. 1757-1771 (9)		27.20	27.10

Issued: 7p, 2/4/99; 4p, 12/23/99; 14p, 8/6/99; 1p, 6p, 10p, 50p, 1998. 9p, 1999. 5p, 2/19/02.
Reprints issued: #1757a, 12/7/99; #1757b, 12/15/00; #1757c, 2/24/01; #1757d, 5/22/02. #1766a, 12/7/99; #1766b, 2/8/02.

Christmas — A855

Designs: 6p, The Virgin's Descent to Reward St. Ildefons' Writings (detail), by El Greco. 12p, St. Peter's Tears (detail), by Bartolomé Esteban Murillo.

1998, Nov. 23		Litho.	Perf. 12	
1772	A855	6p multi	1.50	1.50
1773	A855	12p multi	3.50	3.50

Paso Del Molina Neighborhood of Montevideo, 250th Anniv. — A856

1998, Nov. 26		Perf. 12½x12¾	
1774	A856	6p multi	1.75	1.75

Labor Day Type

6p, Proclamation at the Obelisk, 11/27/83.

		Perf. 12¼x12¾		
1998, Nov. 27		Litho.	Wmk. 332	
1775	A826	6p brn & blk	1.75	1.75

Morosoli Cultural Awards — A857

		Perf. 12¾x12½		
1998, Nov. 27		Litho.	Unwmk.	
1776	A857	6p multi	1.75	1.75

Universal Declaration of Human Rights, 50th Anniv. — A858

1998, Dec. 10		Perf. 12½x12¾	
1777	A858	6p multi	1.75	1.75

Uruguayan Olympic Committee, 75th Anniv. — A859

1998, Dec. 15		Perf. 12	
1778	A859	6p multi	2.00	2.00

Uruguayan Sportsmen A860

Designs: a, Juan Lopez (1907-83), soccer coach. b, Hector Scarone (1899-1967), soccer player. c, Leandro Gomez Harley (1902-79), basketball player, hurdler. d, Liberto Corney (1905-55), boxer.

1998, Dec. 15		Perf. 12¾x12½	
1779	A860	6p Block of 4, #a.-d.	6.50	6.50

Famous Uruguayans — A861

Designs: No. 1780: Dr. Roberto Caldeyro Barcia (1921-96), physiologist. No. 1781, Dr. José Verocay (1876-1923), pathologist. No. 1782, Dr. José L. Duomarco (1905-85), medical researcher.

		Perf. 12¼x12¾		
1998, Dec. 18		Litho.	Unwmk.	
1780	A861	6p multi	1.75	1.75
1781	A861	6p multi	1.75	1.75
1782	A861	6p multi	1.75	1.75
	Nos. 1780-1782 (3)		5.25	5.25

Emile Zola's "J'accuse" Letter, Cent. (in 1998) A862

1999, Jan. 4		Litho.	Perf. 12½x12¾	
1783	A862	14p multicolored	4.00	4.00

Las Cañas Hesort, Fray Bentos A863

1999, Feb. 26			
1784	A863	7p multicolored	2.00	2.00

Rio de la Plata Boundary Treaty, 25th Anniv. A864

1999, Mar. 15			
1785	A864	7p multicolored	2.00	2.00

Famous Uruguayans — A865

Designs: No. 1786, Joaquin Torres Garcia (1874-1949), painter. No. 1787, Luis Ernesto Aroztegui (1930-94), textile artist. No. 1788, Juan José Morosoli (1899-1957), writer.

1999, Mar. 26			
1786	A865	7p multicolored	1.90	1.90
1787	A865	7p multicolored	1.90	1.90
1788	A865	7p multicolored	1.90	1.90
	Nos. 1786-1788 (3)		5.70	5.70

Birds and Flowering Trees A866

a, Psidium cattleianum, Pipraeidea melanonota. b, Tabebuia ipe, Chlorostilbon aureoventris. c, Duranta repens, Tangara preciosa. d, Citharexylum montevidense, Tachuris rubigastra.

1999, Apr. 14		Litho.	Perf. 12¼x12¾	
1789	A866	7p Block of 4, #a.-d.	6.50	6.50

Carriages A867

Designs: a, Break de chasse. b, Mylord. c, Coupé trois quarts. d, Break de champ.

1999, Apr. 29		Litho.	Perf. 12½x12¾	
1790	A867	7p Block of 4, #a.-d.	6.50	6.50

National Soccer Team, Cent. — A868

Designs: a, B. Céspedes, M. Nebel, C. Céspedes, team's first field. b, H. Castro, P. Cea, A. Ciocca, team flag. c, R. Porta, A García, S. Gambetta, team headquarters.

1999, May 5		Litho.	Perf. 12	
1791	A868	7p Strip of 3, #a.-c.	6.00	6.00
	Complete booklet, #1791		7.00	

Children's Millennium Stamp Design Contest Winners A869

Designs: a, By Stefani Andrea Furtado. b, By Pilar Trujillo. c, By Lucia Lavie. d, By Cecilia Chopitea.

1999, May 6		Litho.	Perf. 12½x12¾	
1792	A869	7p Block of 4, #a.-d.	7.50	7.50

Jorge Chebataroff (1909-84), Geographer, Botanist — A870

1999, May 14			
1793	A870	7p multicolored	1.75	1.75

Formation of Infantry Brigade No. 1, 60th Anniv. A871

Paintings: No. 1794, Infantry Battalion No. 2 at Battle of Montecaseros, 1852. No. 1795, Infantry Brigade No. 1 at Battle of Estero Bellaco, 1866. No. 1796, Infantry Battalion No. 1 at Battle of Boquerón, 1866.

1999, May 18			
1794	A871	7p multicolored	1.90	1.90
1795	A871	7p multicolored	1.90	1.90
1796	A871	7p multicolored	1.90	1.90
	Nos. 1794-1796 (3)		5.70	5.70

Villa de la Restauracion, 150th Anniv. — A872

1999, May 24		Perf. 12¾x12½	
1797	A872	7p multicolored	1.75	1.75

Souvenir Sheet

Barcelona, Spain Soccer Team, Cent. — A873

1999, May 28		Litho.	Perf. 12½x12¾	
1798	A873	15p multi	4.25	4.25

1st Festival of Film Critics, Montevideo A874

1999, June 2   *Perf. 12¾x12¼*
Booklet Stamp
1799   A874   7p multi   2.00   2.00
   a.   Booklet pane, 2 #1799   4.00
      Complete booklet, #1799a   4.00

Philex France 99 A875

Horses: a, Arabian. b, Quarter horse. c, Thoroughbred. d, Shetland pony.

        Perf. 12½x12¾
1999, June 10   **Litho.**
1800   A875   7p Block of 4, #a.-d.   6.50   6.50

Publication "Marcha," 60th Anniv. — A876

       Perf. 12¼x12¾
1999, June 23   **Litho.**
1801   A876   7p multi   2.00   2.00

Permanent Home for "Espacio Ciencia" Science Exhibits — A877

1999, July 2   *Perf. 12¾x12¼*
1802   A877   7p multi   2.00   2.00

Artigas Antarctic Scientific Base, 25th Anniv. A878

1999, July 12   *Perf. 12¼x12¾*
1803   A878   7p multi   2.50   2.50

Republic of Uruguay University, 150th Anniv. A879

1999, July 19
1804   A879   7p yel & blk   1.75   1.75

UNESCO Regional Office, 50th Anniv. — A880

1999, July 20   *Perf. 12¾x12¼*
1805   A880   7p multi   1.75   1.75

The Last Charruas — A881

a, One seated, one standing. b, Two seated.

1999, July 22   **Litho.**   *Perf. 12¾x12½*
1806   A881   7p Pair, #a.-b.   4.00   4.00

Souvenir Sheet

Millennium — A882

a, 3.50p, Apollo space program. b, 3.50p, Soccer players, 2000 Olympic Games, Sydney. c, 4p, Centenary of Zeppelins. d, 4p, #C60.

1999, July 30   **Litho.**   *Perf. 12½x12¾*
1807   A882   Sheet of 4, #a.-d.   7.50   7.50

UPU, 125th anniv., Bangkok 2000, Espana 2000, WIPA 2000, Hanover World's Fair.

El Galpón Theater, Montevideo, 50th Anniv. — A883

1999, Aug. 3   *Perf. 12¾x12¼*
1808   A883   7p multi   2.00   2.00

China 1999 World Philatelic Exhibition — A884

Sea planes: a, Piper J-3. b, Short Sunderland.

1999, Aug. 18   *Perf. 12¼x12¾*
1809   A884   7p Pair, #a.-b.   4.00   4.00

Dogs — A885

Designs: a, Cocker spaniel. b, German shepherd. c, Dalmatian. d, Basset hound.

       Perf. 12¾x12½
1999, Aug. 24   **Litho.**
1810   A885   7p Block of 4, #a.-d.   6.50   6.50

Insects & Flowers A886

a, Halictidae, Oxalis sp. b, Apanteles sp., Epidendrum paniculosum. c, Metabolosia univita, Baccharis trimera. d, Compositae, Cantarido.

       Perf. 12½x12¾
1999, Sept. 10   **Litho.**
1811   A886   7p Block of 4, #a.-d.   6.50   6.50

A887

Uruguayan Artists: No. 1812, Orlando Aldama (1904-87), writer. No. 1813, Julio Martínez Oyanguren (1901-73), guitarist.

       Perf. 12¾x12½
1999, Sept. 13   **Litho.**
1812   A887   7p multi   1.90   1.90
1813   A887   7p multi   1.90   1.90

A888

       Perf. 12¾x12¼
1999, Sept. 18   **Litho.**
1814   A888   7p multi   1.90   1.90

Cultural heritage of Mercosur countries.

First Uruguayan Participation in Olympics, Paris, 1924 — A889

Designs: a, Poster, medal. b, Medal, medal-winning soccer team.

1999, Sept. 30   *Perf. 12¼x12¾*
1815   A889   7p Pair, #a.-b.   3.50   3.50

Intl. Year of Older Persons A890

1999, Oct. 1   **Litho.**   *Perf. 12¼x12¾*
1816   A890   7p multi   1.90   1.90

Philatelic Witches Sabbath, by Mariano Barbasán — A891

1999, Oct. 1   *Perf. 12*
1817   A891   7p multi   1.90   1.90

Stamp Day.

America Issue, A New Millennium Without Arms — A892

7p, Arms in trash can. 14p, Earth, satellites.

1999, Oct. 6   *Perf. 13¾x12¼*
1818   A892   7p multi   2.25   2.25
1819   A892   14p multi   3.50   3.00

Inter-American Development Bank, 40th Anniv. — A893

1999, Oct. 6   *Perf. 12¼x12¾*
1820   A893   7p multi   1.90   1.75

Winner of Older Person's Stamp Design Contest A894

1999, Oct. 8
1821   A894   7p multi   1.90   1.75

El Ceibo Society, 50th Anniv. A895

1999, Oct. 8
1822   A895   7p multi   1.90   1.75

Third Intl. Conference of Ministers for Sports, Punta del Este — A896

1999, Oct. 13   *Perf. 12*
1823 A896 7p multi   1.90 1.75

Souvenir Sheets

Official Service of Broadcasting, Television and Entertainment — A897

No. 1824: a, 4p, Television cameraman. b, 4p, Building. c, 3p, Radio studio. d, 3p, Film cameraman.
No. 1825: a, 4p, Symphony orchestra. b, 4p, Chamber music group. c, 3p, Chorus. d, 3p, Ballet dancers.

1999, Oct. 22   *Perf. 12¼x12¾*
1824 A897 Sheet of 4, #a.-d.   4.00 4.00
1825 A897 Sheet of 4, #a.-d.   4.00 4.00

Uruguayan Standards Institute, 60th Anniv. — A898

1999, Nov. 3
1826 A898 7p multi   1.90 1.75

A899

1999, Nov. 3   *Perf. 12¾x12¼*
1827 A899 7p multi   1.90 1.75
Vice-President Hugo Batalla (1926-98).

A900

Cover of 4/29/29 Mundo Uruguayo magazine.

1999, Nov. 12
1828 A900 7p multi   1.90 1.75
Exhibition of art and design from the 1920s, Blanes Museum, Montevideo.

Millennium — A901

No. 1829 — Various buildings and: a, "1999." b, "2000."

1999, Nov. 23   Litho.   *Perf. 12*
1829 A901 3.50p Pair, #a.-b.   2.00 2.00

Celmar Poumé (1924-83), Cartoonist A902

1999, Nov. 26   *Perf. 12¾x12¼*
1830 A902 7p multi   2.00 2.00

Christmas A903

9p, Tree with ornaments. 18p, Carolers.

Perf. 12¼x12¾, 12¾x12¼
1999, Dec. 3
1831 A903 9p multi   2.25 2.25
1832 A903 18p multi, vert.   4.50 4.50

Tannat Wines, 20th Anniv. — A904

1999, Dec. 9   *Perf. 12*
1833 A904 9p shown   2.75 2.75
1834 A904 9p Wine drinker   2.75 2.75

New Maldonado Department Governmental Building — A905

1999, Dec. 11   *Perf. 12¼x12¾*
1835 A905 9p multi   2.75 2.75

Types of 1997 and

Crow's Gorge Nature Reserve A907

Chilean Lapwing — A908

Design: 2p, Penitente Waterfall, vert. 5p, Chilean Lapwing (*Vanellus chilensis*). 10p, Crow's Gorge Nature Reserve. No. 1841, Gruta del Palacio, vert. 100p, Sierra de los Caracoles.

Serpentine Die Cut 11¼, Die Cut
(#1836A, 1840, 1850, 1853)

2000-06	**Self-Adhesive**	**Litho.**
1836 A907	2p multi, "2001"	.30 .30
b.	Dated "2002"	.30 .30
1836A A908	5p multi	.45 .45
1837 A907	10p multi	.85 .85
1838 A907	11p multi	2.00 2.00
1840 A901	20p multi, "2000"	4.50 4.50
a.	Dated "2001"	4.50 4.50
1841 A907	20p multi, "2001"	5.00 5.00
a.	Dated "2006"	5.00 5.00
1850 A782	32p multi	7.25 7.25
1853 A782	80p multi	18.00 18.00
1854 A907	100p multi	14.00 14.00
1855 A782	100p multi	7.50 7.50
1855A A782	100p multi	7.50 7.50
Nos. 1836-1855A (11)		67.35 67.35

Issued: 32p, 1/20. No. 1840, 80p, 12/12, 11p, 3/16/01. No. 1841, 4/20/01. 2p, 8/1/01. No. 1854, 2/13/02. No. 1855, 10/5/04. 5p, 12/1/06; 10p, 10/18/06; No. 1855A, 9/26/06.
No. 1855 has straight numerals in denomination. No. 1855A has slanted numerals.

50th Anniv of Artistic Career of Carlos Páez Vilaró — A916

2000, Jan. 15   Litho.   *Perf. 12*
1856 A916 9p multi   2.75 2.75

Orchids — A917

No. 1857: a, 5p, Laelia purpurata. b, 4p, Cattleya corcovado. c, 4p, Cattleya sp. "hybrid." d, 5p, Laelia tenebrosa.

2000, Mar. 3
1857 A917 Block of 4, #a.-d.   5.50 5.50

Lighthouses — A918

No. 1858: a, 5p, Isla de Flores, 1828. b, 4p, Punta del Este, 1860. c, 4p, Cabo Polonio, 1881. d, 5p, Punta Brava, 1876.

2000, Mar. 14
1858 A918 Block of 4, #a.-d.   6.50 6.50

Carlos Quijano (1900-84), Economics Journalist — A919

2000, Mar. 30   *Perf. 12¼x12¾*
1859 A919 9p multi   2.75 2.75

The Gold Rush, Starring Charlie Chaplin, 75th Anniv. A920

2000, Apr. 7   Litho.   *Perf. 12¼x12¾*
1860 A920 18p multi   5.00 5.00
Lubrapex 2000 Stamp Show, Brazil.

El Cordón Neighborhood of Montevideo, 250th Anniv. — A921

2000, Apr. 10   Litho.   *Perf. 12¼x12¾*
1861 A921 9p multi   2.75 2.75

Mural "Espina de la Cruz," by Children of Mercedes — A922

a, 5p, Branches. b, 4p, Two red flowers.

2000, Apr. 26   *Perf. 12¼x12*
1862 A922 Pair, #a-b   2.75 2.75

Francisco García y Santos (1856-1921), Government Official — A923

2000, May 2   *Perf. 12¾x12¼*
1863 A923 9p multi   2.75 2.75

Uruguayan Notaries Assoc., 125th Anniv. — A924

2000, May 9   **Litho.**   *Perf. 12¾x12¼*
1864 A924 9p multi   2.75 2.75

Intl. Museum Day — A925

2000, May 18   **Litho.**   *Perf. 12¾x12¼*
1865 A925 9p multi   2.75 2.75

Stampin' the Future Children's Stamp Design Contest Winners — A926

Artwork by: a, 5p, Helena Perez. b, 4p, Maria Pia Pereyra. c, 4p, Virginia Regueiro. d, 5p, Blanca E. Lima.

2000, June 2   **Litho.**   *Perf. 12*
1866 A926   Block of 4, #a-d   5.00 5.00

Club Soriano, 90th Anniv. A927

2000, June 9   **Litho.**   *Perf. 12¼x12¾*
1867 A927 9p multi   2.75 2.75

Antonio Rupenian, Founder of Radio Armenia — A928

2000, June 16   *Perf. 12¾x12¼*
1868 A928 18p multi   4.50 4.50

"1900 Generation" Writers, Cent. — A929

2000, June 22   **Litho.**
1869 A929 9p multi   2.75 2.75

Cacti — A930

No. 1870: a, 5p, Notocactus ottonis. b, 4p, Echinopsis multiplex.

2000, July 4   *Perf. 12¼*
1870 A930   Horiz. pair, #a-b   2.75 2.75

Uruguayan Soccer Association, Cent. — A931

No. 1871: a, 5p, Players marching. b, 4p, Team photo. c, 4p, Stadium, World Cup. d, 5p, Players in action, World Cup.

2000, July 14   **Litho.**   *Perf. 12¼x12*
1871 A931   Block of 4, #a-d   6.50 6.50

Opera Anniversaries — A932

No. 1872: a, 9p, Scene from Carmen, composer Georges Bizet. b, 9p, Scene from Tosca, composer Giacomo Puccini.

2000, July 20
1872 A932   Pair, #a-b   5.00 5.00
  Carmen, 125th anniv.; Tosca, cent.

Latin American Integration Association, 20th Anniv. — A933

2000, Aug. 11   *Perf. 12¾x12¼*
1873 A933 18p multi   5.00 5.00

Naval Aviation, 75th Anniv. A934

2000, Aug. 18   *Perf. 12¼x12¾*
1874 A934 9p multi   2.75 2.75

ORT, 120th Anniv. A935

2000, Aug. 28
1875 A935 9p multi   2.75 2.75

Luis de la Robla (1780-1844), First Postmaster General — A936

2000, Aug. 28   *Perf. 12¾x12¼*
1876 A936 9p multi   2.75 2.75

Gonzalo Rodriguez (1971-99), Race Car Driver — A937

a, 9p, Rodriguez, dark blue car. b, 9p, Rodriguez holding trophy, light blue car.

2000, Sept. 11   *Perf. 12x12¼*
1877 A937   Pair, #a-b   5.50 5.50

Gen. José Artigas (1764-1850) A938

2000, Sept. 22   **Litho.**   *Perf. 12¼*
1878 A938 9p multi + label   2.75 2.75

España 2000 Intl. Philatelic Exhibition — A939

Birds: a, 5p, Donacospiza albifrons. b, 4p, Geositta cunicularia. c, 4p, Phacellodomus striaticollis. d, 5p, Cacicus chrysopterus.

2000, Sept. 27   *Perf. 12*
1879 A939   Block of 4, #a-d   6.00 6.00

Soka Gakkai International, 25th Anniv. — A940

2000, Oct. 2   *Perf. 12¼x12¾*
1880 A940 18p multi   6.00 6.00

America Issue, Fight Against AIDS — A941

No. 1881: a, 9p, Tic-tac-toe game with condoms and crosses. b, 18p, Syringe and red ribbon.

2000, Oct. 10   *Perf. 12¼*
1881 A941   Horiz. pair, #a-b   8.00 8.00

Mercosur Cultural Heritage Day — A942

2000, Oct. 14   *Perf. 12¾x12¼*
1882 A942 18p multi   5.50 5.50

Dragon, by Luis Mazzey (1895-1983) — A943

2000, Oct. 19   *Perf. 12¼x12¾*
1883 A943 9p multi   2.75 2.75

Fire Fighters A944

Designs: No. 1884, 9p, At car crash. No. 1885, 9p, Searching for victims, vert.

Perf. 12¼x12¾, 12¾x12¼
2000, Oct. 26
1884-1885 A944   Set of 2   7.00 7.00

Prof. Julio Ricaldoni (1906-93), Structural Engineer A945

2000, Nov. 13   *Perf. 12¼x12¾*
1886 A945 9p multi   2.75 2.75
  29th Conference on Structural Engineering, Punta del Este.

Training Ship "Capitan Miranda," 70th Anniv. A946

2000, Nov. 15
1887 A946 9p multi 2.75 2.75

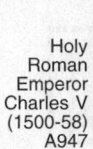

Holy Roman Emperor Charles V (1500-58) A947

2000, Nov. 22 Litho.
1888 A947 22p multi 2.75 2.75

Christmas A948

Designs: 11p, Fireworks. 22p, Holy Family.

2000, Dec. 1
1889-1890 A948 Set of 2 8.00 8.00

Sarandi del Yi, 125th Anniv. — A949

2000, Dec. 14 Perf. 12¾x12¼
1891 A949 11p multi 3.00 3.00

Forest Fire Prevention Service A950

2001, Feb. 9 Litho. Perf. 12½x12¾
1892 A950 11p multi 3.00 3.00

Amphibians and Reptiles — A951

No. 1893: a, Phyllomedusa iheringii. b, Acanthochelys spixii. c, Phrynops hilarii. d, Scinax sqalirostris.

2001, Feb. 15 Perf. 12
1893 A951 11p Block of 4, #a-d 12.00 12.00

Paysandú Rowing Club, Cent. A952

2001, Feb. 28 Perf. 12½x12¾
1894 A952 11p multi 2.75 2.75

17th Congress of Latin American Confederation of Congress Organizers A953

2001, Mar. 2 Perf. 12¾x12½
1895 A953 11p multi 3.00 3.00

City of Belén, Bicent. — A954

2001, Mar. 14
1896 A954 11p multi 2.75 2.75

David, by Michelangelo, 500th Anniv. — A955

2001, Mar. 22
1897 A955 22p multi 6.00 6.00

Uruguayan Society of Performers, 50th Anniv. — A956

2001, Mar. 26 Perf. 12½x12¾
1898 A956 11p multi 3.00 3.00

Casal Catalá, 75th Anniv. — A957

2001, Apr. 20 Perf. 12¾x12½
1899 A957 11p multi 3.00 3.00

Universidad Mayor de la República Engineering Faculty, 85th Anniv. — A958

2001, Apr. 30
1900 A958 11p blue 2.75 2.75

Rodolfo V. Tálice (1899-1999), Biologist — A959

2001, May 2 Perf. 12½x12¾
1901 A959 11p multi 3.00 3.00

Montevideo Lions Club, 50th Anniv. — A960

2001, May 14 Perf. 12¾x12½
1902 A960 11p multi 3.00 3.00

Invention of the Telephone, 125th Anniv. A961

2001, May 22 Perf. 12½x12¾
1903 A961 22p multi 6.00 6.00

Snakes — A962

No. 1904: a, Philodryas olfersii. b, Bothrops alternatus.

2001, May 28 Perf. 12
1904 A962 11p Horiz. pair, #a-b 7.00 7.00

Juan Manuel Blanes (1830-1901), Painter — A963

2001, June 8 Litho. Perf. 12½x12¾
1905 A963 11p multi 2.75 2.75

Start of Pediatrics Teaching by Dr. Luis Morquio, Cent. — A964

2001, June 15 Perf. 12¾x12½
1906 A964 11p multi 2.75 2.75

The Ring of the Nibelung, by Richard Wagner — A965

No. 1907: a, The Rhinegold (El Oro del Rin). b, The Valkyrie (La Walquiria). c, Siegfried (Sigfrido). d, The Twilight of the Gods (El Ocaso de los Dioses).

2001, June 29 Perf. 12
1907 A965 11p Block of 4, #a-d 12.00 12.00

Intl. Organization for Migration, 50th Anniv. — A966

2001, July 5 Perf. 12¾x12½
1908 A966 22p blue & black 5.00 5.00

Thomas Alva Edison (1847-1931) A967

2001, July 12
1909 A967 22p multi 6.00 6.00

Laying of Foundation Stone for Montevideo Port, Cent. — A968

2001, July 18 Perf. 12½x12¾
1910 A968 11p multi 3.50 3.50

Fowl — A969

No. 1911: a, New Hampshire. b, Orpington-Buff. c, Araucanas. d, Leghorn-Light brown.

2001, July 30   *Perf. 12*
1911 A969 11p Block of 4, #a-
d   12.00 12.00

Moby Dick, by Herman Melville, 150th Anniv. — A970

2001, Aug. 2   *Perf. 12¾x12½*
1912 A970 22p multi   6.00 6.00

Bernardo González Pecotche (1901-63), Founder of Logosophy A971

2001, Aug. 7   *Perf. 12*
1913 A971 11p multi   3.00 3.00

First Concorde Flight, 25th Anniv. A972

2001, Aug. 10   *Perf. 12½x12¾*
1914 A972 22p multi   6.00 6.00

Rose Varieties — A973

No. 1915: a, Louis Philippe. b, Souvenir de Mme. Léonie Viennot. c, Kronenbourg. d, Lady Hillingdon.

2001, Aug. 16   *Perf. 12*
1915 A973 11p Block of 4, #a-
d   12.00 12.00

Apiculture — A974

No. 1916: a, Apiculturists. b, Bee on flower.

2001, Sept. 12
1916 A974 12p Horiz. pair, #a-b   7.00 7.00

Town of Dolores, Bicent. — A975

2001, Sept. 21   *Perf. 12¾x12½*
1917 A975 12p multi   3.00 3.00

Uruguay Philatelic Club, 75th Anniv. A976

Sun and inscription: No. 1918, 12p, "75 Años." No. 1919, 12p, "1er Presidente / Dr. Miguel A. Paez Formoso."

2001, Sept. 26   *Perf. 12½x12¾*
1918-1919 A976 Set of 2   6.00 6.00

America Issue - UNESCO World Heritage Sites — A977

Buildings from Historic Quarter of Colonia del Sacramento: a, 12p, Basilica del Santisimo. b, 24p, San Benito de Palermo Chapel.

2001, Sept. 28   *Perf. 12*
1920 A977   Horiz. pair, #a-b   9.50 9.50

Carlos Amoretti, 50th Anniv. as Artist A978

2001, Oct. 2   *Perf. 12½x12¾*
1921 A978 12p multi   3.50 3.50

Town of Sauce, 150th Anniv. — A979

2001, Oct. 12   *Perf. 12¾x12½*
1922 A979 12p multi   3.50 3.50

Uruguay - Japan Diplomatic Relations, 80th Anniv. A980

2001, Sept. 24   Litho.
1923 A980 24p multi   6.00 6.00

Prevention of Illegal Drug Use A981

2001, Oct. 16
1924 A981 12p multi   3.50 3.50

Year of Dialogue Among Civilizations A982

2001, Oct. 23   *Perf. 12¾x12¼*
1925 A982 24p multi   6.00 6.00

Honorary Committee for Fighting Cancer — A983

2001, Oct. 29
1926 A983 12p multi   3.50 3.50

Ultimas Noticias Newspaper, 20th Anniv. — A984

2001, Oct. 31
1927 A984 12p multi   3.50 3.50

Sauce Basketball Club, 50th Anniv. A985

2001, Nov. 9   *Perf. 12¼x12¾*
1928 A985 12p multi   3.50 3.50

Blood Donor's Day — A986

2001, Nov. 12   *Perf. 12¾x12¼*
1929 A986 12p multi   3.50 3.50

Juan Zorrilla de San Martín (1855-1931), Writer — A987

2001, Nov. 13   *Perf. 12¼x12¾*
1930 A987 12p multi   3.50 3.50

Uruguayan Navy's Hydrographic Ship "Oyarvide" — A988

2001, Nov. 14
1931 A988 12p multi   3.50 3.50

Uruguayan Visit of Rotary Intl. President Richard King and Wife Cherie — A989

2001, Nov. 20   *Perf. 12¾x12¼*
1932 A989 24p multi   7.00 7.00

Peñarol Athletic Club, 110th Anniv. — A990

2001, Nov. 22   *Perf. 12*
1933 A990 12p multi   3.50 3.50

Julio Sosa (1926-64), Tango Singer — A991

2001, Nov. 26   *Perf. 12¾x12¼*
1934 A991 12p multi   3.50 3.50

José Nasazzi (1901-68), Soccer Player — A992

2001, Nov. 29
1935 A992 12p multi 3.50 3.50

Christmas — A993

Paintings of Adoration of the Shepherds, by: 12p, José Ribera. 24p, Anton Raphael Mengs.

2001, Dec. 6
1936-1937 A993 Set of 2 10.00 10.00

Church of San Carlos, Bicent. — A994

2001, Dec. 7
1938 A994 12p multi 3.50 3.50

National Museum of Visual Arts, 90th Anniv. — A995

2001, Dec. 12 **Perf. 12**
1939 A995 12p multi 3.50 3.50

State Insurance Bank, 90th Anniv. — A996

2001, Dec. 20 **Perf. 12¾x12¼**
1940 A996 12p multi 3.50 3.50

Guettarda Uruguensis — A997

2001, Dec. 21 **Perf. 12¼x12¾**
1941 A997 24p multi 7.00 7.00

St. Josemaría Escrivá de Balaguer (1902-75) — A998

Balaguer and quotes: a, "El trabajo es. . ." b, "Quieres de verdad. . ." c, "La santidad. . ." d, "Que busques. . ."

2002, Jan. 9 **Perf. 12**
1942 A998 12p Block of 4, #a-d 14.00 14.00

Uruguayan Association of Directors of Carnivals and Folk Festivals, 50th Anniv. — A999

Feet of: a, Ringmaster. b, Clown. c, Acrobat.

2002, Mar. 8 **Litho.** **Perf. 12½**
Self-Adhesive
1943 Booklet pane of 3 6.50 6.50
a.-b. A999 6p Either single 1.50 1.50
c. A999 12p black 3.00 3.00
Booklet, #1943 7.00 7.00

Christianity in Armenia, 1700th Anniv. A1000

2002, Apr. 23 **Perf. 12**
1944 A1000 12p multi 3.00 3.00

New Year 2003 (Year of the Horse) — A1001

2002, May 14 **Perf. 12¾x12¼**
1945 A1001 24p multi 5.50 5.50

2002 World Cup Soccer Championships, Japan and Korea — A1002

No. 1946: a, Flags, soccer ball, and field (38mm diameter). b, Soccer players, years of Uruguayan championships.

2002, May 21 **Perf. 12¾**
1946 A1002 12p Horiz. pair, #a-b 5.50 5.50
See Argentina No. 2184, Brazil No. 2840, France No. 2891, Germany No. 2163 and Italy No. 2526.

Book Day — A1003

2002, May 24 **Perf. 12¾x12¼**
1947 A1003 12p multi 3.00 3.00

Inter-American Children's Institute, 75th Anniv. — A1004

2002, June 10 **Perf. 12¼x12¾**
1948 A1004 12p multi 3.00 3.00

Department of Tacuarembó, 165th Anniv. — A1005

2002, June 14
1949 A1005 12p multi 3.00 3.00

Cerro de Montevideo Lighthouse, Bicent. — A1006

Designs: 12p, Old lighthouse. 24p, New lighthouse, vert.

Perf. 12¼x12¾, 12¾x12¼
1950-1951 A1006 Set of 2 8.50 8.50

Villa Constitución, 150th Anniv. — A1007

2002, July 11 **Perf. 12¼x12¾**
1952 A1007 12p multi 3.00 3.00

"We Are United" A1008

2002, July 17
1953 A1008 6p multi 1.50 1.50
Printed in sheets of 3 + label. Value $5.

Natural Uruguay A1009

2002, July 22 **Litho.**
1954 A1009 24p blue & orange 5.00 5.00

Montevideo Botanical Gardens, Cent. — A1010

No. 1955: a, Botanical Gardens building, Erythrina cristigalli. b, Rhodophiala bifida. c, Prof. Atilio Lombardo and Tillandsia arequitae. d, Heteropterys dumetorum.

2002, July 31 **Perf. 12**
1955 Horiz. strip of 4 12.00 12.00
a.-d. A1010 12p Any single 2.75 2.75

Montevideo Wanderers Soccer Team, Cent. — A1011

2002, Aug. 1 **Perf. 12¾x12¼**
1956 A1011 12p black 3.00 3.00

Sportsmen — A1012

Designs: No. 1957, 12p, Lorenzo Fernández, soccer player. No. 1958, 12p, Josè Leandro Andrade, soccer player. No. 1959, 12p, Alvaro Gestido, soccer player. No. 1960, 12p, César L. Gallardo, fencer. No. 1961, 12p, Pedro Petrone, soccer player.

2002, Aug. 16 **Perf. 12¼x12¾**
1957-1961 A1012 Set of 5 15.00 15.00

Elvis Presley (1935-77) A1013

2002, Aug. 19 **Perf. 12¾x12¼**
1962 A1013 24p multi 5.00 5.00

Agustín Bisio (1894-1952), Poet — A1014

2002, Aug. 30   *Perf. 12¾x12¼*
Self-Adhesive
1963 A1014 12p multi   3.00 3.00

City of Artigas,
150th
Anniv. — A1015

2002, Sept. 12   *Perf. 12¾x12¼*
Self-Adhesive
1964 A1015 12p multi   2.75 2.75

Uruguayan Cooperative Society of Bus
Services, 65th Anniv. — A1016

2002, Sept. 16   *Perf. 12¼x12¾*
1965 A1016 12p multi   3.00 3.00

Psychoanalysis, Cent. — A1017

2002, Sept. 20   *Perf. 12*
1966 A1017 12p multi   2.75 2.75
24th Latin American Psychoanalysis Congress, Montevideo.

Horacio Arredondo (1888-1967),
Historical Preservationist, and San
Miguel Fort — A1018

2002, Sept. 20   *Perf. 12¼x12¾*
1967 A1018 12p multi   2.75 2.75

Paso del Rey Barracks Natl. Historic
Monument — A1019

2002, Sept. 23   *Perf. 12*
1968 A1019 12p multi   2.75 2.75

Intl. Year of Ecotourism — A1020

2002, Sept. 24   *Litho.*
1969 A1020 12p multi   2.75 2.75

Uruguayan Postal
Services, 175th
Anniv. — A1021

Designs: No. 1970, Postal Services headquarters, Montevideo. No. 1971, Letter box.

2002, Oct. 9   *Perf. 12¾x12¼*
1970 A1021 12p multi   2.75 2.75
Souvenir Sheet
Imperf
1971 A1021 12p multi   2.75 2.75

First Equestrian
Statue of Brig.
Gen. Juan Antonio
Lavalleja,
Cent. — A1022

2002, Oct. 11   *Perf. 12¾x12¼*
1972 A1022 12p multi   2.75 2.75

America
Issue —
Youth,
Education
and
Literacy
A1023

"ANALFABETISMO" in: 12p, Word search
puzzle. 24p, Bowl of alphabet soup.

2002, Oct. 16   *Perf. 12¼x12¾*
1973-1974 A1023   Set of 2   7.00 7.00

Christmas
A1024

2002, Nov. 4   *Perf. 12¾x12¼*
1975 A1024 12p multi   2.75 2.75

Association of
Uruguayan
Pharmacies, 65th
Anniv. — A1025

2002, Nov. 8   *Litho.*
1976 A1025 12p multi   2.75 2.75

Tannat
Wine — A1026

2002, Nov. 13
1977 A1026 12p multi   3.50 3.50

Uruguayan
Navy, 185th
Anniv. — A1027

2002, Nov. 13   *Perf. 13½*
1978 A1027 12p multi   2.75 2.75

National
Organ
and
Tissue
Bank,
25th
Anniv.
A1028

2002, Nov. 15
1979 A1028 12p multi   3.00 3.00

Taxis in
Uruguay,
Cent.
A1029

2002, Nov. 25   *Perf. 12¼x12¾*
1980 A1029 12p multi   3.00 3.00

Brig. Gen. Manuel
Oribe (1792-1857)
A1030

2002, Nov. 28   *Perf. 12¾x12¼*
1981 A1030 12p multi   2.75 2.75

George
Harrison (1943-
2001), Rock
Musician
A1031

2002, Nov. 29   *Perf. 13½*
1982 A1031 24p multi   6.00 6.00

Pan-American Health Organization,
Cent. — A1032

2002, Dec. 2
1983 A1032 12p multi   3.00 3.00

Uruguayan Participation in U.N. Peace
Keeping Missions, 50th
Anniv. — A1033

2002, Dec. 6   *Perf. 12¼x12¾*
1984 A1033 12p multi   3.00 3.00

Alfredo Testoni
(1919-2000),
Artist — A1034

2002, Dec. 9   *Perf. 13½*
1985 A1034 12p multi   2.75 2.75

Mercosur
A1035

Designs: 12p, Ship and coastline. 24p,
Beach.

2002, Dec. 12
1986-1987 A1035   Set of 2   7.00 7.00

Battle of
Ituzaingó,
175th
Anniv.
A1036

2002, Dec. 17   *Litho.*
1988 A1036 12p multi   2.75 2.75

Battle of Juncal, 175th Anniv. A1037

2002, Dec. 17
1989 A1037 12p multi   2.75 2.75

Town of Juanicó, 130th Anniv. A1038

2002, Dec. 23   *Perf. 12¼x12¾*
1990 A1038 12p multi   2.75 2.75

Uruguay on World Map A1009

2003, Jan. 17 Litho. *Perf. 12¼x12¾*
1991 A1039 12p multi   2.75 2.75

Busqueda Weekly, 30th Anniv. A1040

2003, Jan. 29
1992 A1040 12p multi   2.75 2.75

Water Goddess Iemanja — A1041

2003, Jan. 29   *Perf. 12¾x12¼*
1993 A1041 12p multi   2.50 2.50

Uruguay - People's Republic of China Diplomatic Relations, 15th Anniv. — A1042

2003, Jan. 31   *Perf. 12*
1994 A1042 12p multi   2.75 2.75

New Year 2003 (Year of the Ram) — A1043

2003, Feb. 7   *Perf. 12¾x12¼*
1995 A1043 5p multi   .85 .85

Explorers A1044

Explorers and maps of their voyages: a, Christopher Columbus, 4th voyage, 1502. b, Juan Díaz de Solís, 1516. c, Sebastian Cabot, 1526-30. d, Hernando Arias de Saavedra, 1597-1618.

2003, Feb. 14   *Perf. 12*
1996   Horiz. strip of 4   7.00 7.00
a.-d.   A1044 12p Any single   1.50 1.50

Communications Services Regulatory Union, 2nd Anniv. — A1045

2003, Feb. 21   *Perf. 12¼x12¾*
1997 A1045 12p multi   1.75 1.75

Intl. Women's Day — A1046

2003, Mar. 7   *Perf. 12¾x12¼*
1998 A1046 12p multi   1.75 1.75

City of Treinta y Tres, 150th Anniv. A1047

2003, Mar. 10   *Perf. 12¼x12¾*
1999 A1047 12p multi   1.75 1.75

Butterflies — A1048

No. 2000: a, Heliconius erato. b, Junonia evarete. c, Dryadula phaetusa. d, Parides perrhebus.

2003, Mar. 18   *Perf. 12*
2000 A1048 12p Block of 4, #a-d 7.00 7.00

First Presidency of José Batlle y Ordóñez, Cent. — A1049

No. 2001 — Batlle y Ordóñez: a, Wearing overcoat. b, Wearing presidential sash. c, With head on hand. d, Wearing white jacket.

2003, Mar. 25   *Perf. 12*
2001   Horiz. strip of 4   5.00 5.00
a.-d.   A1049 12p Any single   1.25 1.25

Rural Women's Crafts A1050

No. 2002: a, Basket weaving. b, Knitting. c, Pottery making. d, Food canning. e, Jewelry making.

2003, Mar. 23 Litho.   *Perf. 12*
2002   Horiz. strip of 5   7.50 7.50
a.-e.   A1050 12p Any single   1.50 1.50

Farruco's Chapel — A1051

2003, Apr. 4 Litho.   *Perf. 12¾x12¼*
2003 A1051 12p multi   2.00 2.00

Natural Foods A1052

2003, Apr. 9   *Perf. 12¼x12¾*
2004 A1052 12p multi   2.00 2.00

Cerros Azules Caiman Farm A1053

Serpentine Die Cut 11¼
2003, Apr. 10
     Self-Adhesive
2005 A1053 12p multi   2.00 2.00

Memorial to 1972 Airplane Crash in the Andes — A1054

2003, Apr. 22   *Perf. 12¾x12¼*
2006 A1054 12p multi   2.00 2.00

Military Center — A1055

2003, May 21
2007 A1055 12p multi   1.90 1.90

May 18, 1811 Military Museum, 150th Anniv. A1056

2003, May 26   *Perf. 12*
2008 A1056 12p multi   1.90 1.90

Casa de Ximénes and Las Bóvedas, Montevideo Historical District — A1057

2003, May 30   *Perf. 12¼*
2009 A1057 14p multi   2.25 2.25

Wilson Ferreira Aldunate (1919-88), Politician — A1058

No. 2010: a, Brown background. b, Green background. c, Dark violet background, text at right. d, Light violet background, text at left.

2003, June 16 Litho.   *Perf. 12*
2010 A1058 14p Block of 4, #a-d 7.00 7.00

Olympic Soccer Gold Medal, 75th Anniv. A1059

2003, June 18
2011 A1059 14p multi   2.25 2.25

Nos. 1382, 1492 Overprinted in Gold

Methods, Perfs and Watermarks as Before
2003, June 18
2011A A654 (14p) on 1.20p
    #1492   1.50 1.50
    Complete booklet of 10   15.00
2011B A589 (36p) on 2500p
    #1382   4.50 4.50
    Complete booklet of 10   45.00
Compare No. 2011A with No. 2055.

Richard Anderson College, 70th Anniv. — A1060

2003, July 15
2012 A1060 14p multi   2.25 2.25

Santa Isabel del Paso de los Toros, Cent. — A1061

2003, July 17
2013 A1061 14p multi   2.25 2.25

National Association of Affiliates, 70th Anniv. — A1062

2003, July 24
2014 A1062 14p multi   2.25 2.25

Jesús María College, Carrasco, 50th Anniv. — A1063

2003, Aug. 4
2015 A1063 14p multi   2.25 2.25

Philatelic Academy of Uruguay, 25th Anniv. A1064

2003, Aug. 5
2016 A1064 14p multi   2.25 2.25

Palacio Heber A1065

2003, Aug. 14
2017 A1065 14p multi   2.25 2.25

Parva Domus Magna Quies, 125th Anniv. — A1066

2003, Aug. 15
2018 A1066 14p multi   2.25 2.25

Security Dept. Commission of Interior Ministry, 4th Anniv. — A1067

2003, Aug. 18
2019 A1067 14p multi   2.25 2.25

First International Victory of Uruguayan Soccer Team, Cent. — A1068

2003, Sept. 12   *Perf. 12½x12¾*
2020 A1068 14p multi   2.25 2.25

Lauro Ayestarán (1913-66), Musicologist — A1069

2003, Sept. 19   *Perf. 12*
2021 A1069 14p multi   2.25 2.25

Asociacion Española Primera de Socorros Mutuos Hospital, 150th Anniv. A1070

2003, Sept. 19   *Perf. 12½x12¾*
2022 A1070 14p multi   2.25 2.25

Dr. Manuel Quintela Clinical Hospital, 50th Anniv. A1071

2003, Sept. 23   *Perf. 12*
2023 A1071 14p multi   2.25 2.25

Society of Friends of Public Education, 135th Anniv. — A1072

2003, Sept. 24
2024 A1072 14p multi   2.25 2.25

Association of Uruguayan Newspaper Reporters, 45th Anniv. — A1073

2003, Sept. 29   *Perf. 12½x12¾*
2025 A1073 14p multi   2.25 2.25

Pres. Fructuoso Rivera (c. 1788-1854) A1074

2003, Oct. 1   *Perf. 12*
2026 A1074 14p multi   2.25 2.25

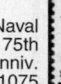

Naval Club, 75th Anniv. A1075

2003, Oct. 1   *Perf. 12½x12¾*
2027 A1075 14p multi   2.25 2.25

Malos Pensamientos Radio Program — A1076

2003, Oct. 3
2028 A1076 14p multi   2.25 2.25

Successes in Intl. Events by Milton Wynants, Cyclist — A1077

2003, Oct. 7   *Perf. 12¾x12½*
2029 A1077 14p multi   2.25 2.25

Ente Nazionale Assistenza Sociale in Uruguay, 50th Anniv. — A1078

2003, Oct. 9   *Perf. 12½x12¾*
2030 A1078 14p multi   2.25 2.25

City of Cardona, Cent. — A1079

2003, Oct. 10   *Perf. 12*
2031 A1079 14p multi   2.25 2.25

Construction League of Uruguay, 84th Anniv. — A1080

2003, Oct. 14   *Perf. 12¾x12½*
2032 A1080 14p multi   2.25 2.25

María Tsakos Foundation, 25th Anniv. — A1081

2003, Oct. 15
2033 A1081 14p multi   2.25 2.25

America Issue — Flora and Fauna A1082

Designs: 14p, Prosopis affinis. 36p, Agouti paca paca.

2003, Oct. 22   Perf. 12½x12¾
2034-2035 A1082   Set of 2   6.00 6.00

Independence of Lebanon, 60th Anniv. — A1083

2003, Oct. 24
2036 A1083 14p olive grn & red   2.25 2.25

Souvenir Sheet

Masons in Uruguay, 147th Anniv. — A1084

2003, Oct. 29   Perf. 12¾x12½
2037 A1084 14p multi   2.25 2.25

Cacho Bochinche Television Show, 30th Anniv. A1085

2003, Oct. 29   Perf. 12½x12¾
2038 A1085 14p multi   2.25 2.25

Morenada, 50th Anniv. — A1086

2003, Oct. 29
2039 A1086 14p multi   2.25 2.25

Brig. Gen. Juan A. Lavalleja (c. 1786-1853) A1087

2003, Oct. 30   Perf. 12
2040 A1087 14p multi   2.25 2.25

Souvenir Sheet

Election of Pope John Paul II, 25th Anniv. — A1088

No. 1089 — Uruguayan flag and: a, Pope John Paul II, Vatican arms. b, Polish eagle, map of Latin America.

2003, Oct. 31
2041 A1088 12p Sheet of 2, #a-b 3.50 3.50
Union of Latin American Polish Societies and Organizations, 10th anniv (#2041b).

Souvenir Sheet

2006 World Cup Soccer Championships, Germany — A1089

No. 2042 — World Cup trophy and: a, Uruguayan flag, J. A. Schiaffino. b, German flag, Fritz Walter.

2003, Oct. 31
2042 A1089 12p Sheet of 2, #a-b 3.50 3.50

Christmas A1090

2003, Nov. 7   Perf. 12¾x12½
2043 A1090 14p multi   2.00 2.00

2003, Nov. 10   Perf. 12½x12¾
2044 A1091 14p multi   2.00 2.00
Italian Chamber of Commerce of Uruguay, 120th Anniv.

Visit of Manuel Fraga Iribarne, President of Spanish Autonomous Community of Galicia — A1092

2003, Nov. 10
2045 A1092 14p multi   2.00 2.00

San Gregorio de Polanco, 150th Anniv. A1093

2003, Nov. 14
2046 A1093 14p multi   2.00 2.00

United Biblical Society, Bicent. A1094

2003, Nov. 24
2047 A1094 14p multi   2.00 2.00

R.O.U. Paysandu A1095

2003, Nov. 25   Perf. 12
2048 A1095 14p multi   2.00 2.00

University Culture Foundation, 35th Anniv. — A1096

2003, Nov. 28
2049 A1096 14p multi   2.00 2.00

Uruguayan Air Force, 50th Anniv. A1097

2003, Dec. 4
2050 A1097 14p multi   2.00 2.00

Visit of Mirko Tremaglia, Italian Minister for Italians Abroad — A1098

2003, Dec. 15
2051 A1098 14p multi   2.00 2.00

Mercosur A1099

Designs: 14p, Horn. 36p, Silver stirrup.

2003, Dec. 16
2052-2053 A1099   Set of 2   6.00 6.00

Powered Flight, Cent. A1100

2003, Dec. 19
2054 A1100 14p multi   2.25 2.25

Nos. 1378, 1382, 1458 and 1492 Surcharged in Black or Blue Violet

j

k

Methods and Perfs. as Before
2004   Wmk. 332
2055 A654(j)   1p on 1.20p
         #1492   .40   .40
2056 A639(j)   2p on 2.60p
         #1458 (BV)   .40   .40
2057 A589(k)   5p on 2500p
         #1382   .80   .50
2058 A589(k) 10p on 360p #1378 1.60 1.20
2059 A589(k) 50p on 825p
         #1379B   6.00 6.00
       Nos. 2055-2059 (5)   9.20 8.50

Issued: Nos. 2055-2056, 1/19; Nos. 2057-2058, 2/16; No. 2059, 3/23. Obliterator on Nos. 2055 and 2056 covers the centesimos portion of the denomination.
Compare No. 2055 with No. 2011A.

Birds — A1101

No. 2060: a, Puffinus gravis. b, Macronectes halli. c, Daption capense. d, Diamedea melanophrys.

Unwmk.
2004, Jan. 22   Litho.   Perf. 12
2060 A1101 14p Block of 4, #a-d   8.25 8.25

Isla de Lobos Lighthouse A1102

No. 2061: a, Isla de Flores Lighthouse. b, Farallon Lighthouse. c, La Panela Lighthouse. d, Banco Ingles Floating Lighthouse.

2004, Feb. 10   Litho.   Perf. 12
2061 A1102 10p Block of 4, #a-d   4.00 4.00
2062 A1102 14p shown   1.50 1.50

Abitab, 10th Anniv. — A1103

Unwmk.
2004, Feb. 12   Litho.   Perf. 12
2063 A1103 14p multi   2.00 2.00

National Naval Prefecture, 175th Anniv. — A1104

2004, Feb. 20   Litho.   Perf. 12
2064 A1104 14p multi   2.25 2.25

Maté Containers — A1105

No. 2065: a, Maté de Cáliz. b, Maté de Plata Colonial. c, Maté de Calabaza.

2004, Mar. 4
2065 A1105 5p Strip of 3, #a-c   2.00 2.00

33 Orientales Mechanized Infantry Battalion No. 10, Cent. — A1106

2004, Mar. 12
2066 A1106 14p multi   2.25 2.25

Intl. Water Day A1107

2004, Mar. 25
2067 A1107 14p multi   2.25 2.25

Regional Energy Integration Commission, 40th Anniv. — A1108

2004, Mar. 25
2068 A1108 14p multi   2.25 2.25

Grenadier Guards, 80th Anniv. — A1109

2004, Apr. 1
2069 A1109 14p multi   2.25 2.25

Expansion of La Teja Refinery — A1110

2004, Apr. 2
2070 A1110 14p multi   2.25 2.25

Florida Infantry Batallion No. 1, 175th Anniv. A1111

2004, Apr. 16
2071 A1111 14p multi   2.25 2.25

Tribute to Servicemen — A1112

2004, May 26
2072 A1112 14p multi   2.25 2.25

Medicinal Plants — A1113

No. 2073: a, Malva sylvestris. b, Achyrocline satureiodes, c, Baccharis trimera. d, Mentha x piperita.

2004, June 3
2073 A1113   Strip of 4   17.00 17.00
a.-d.   36p Any single   4.00 4.00

Map and Arms of Montevideo Department — A1114

2004, June 17
2074 A1114 14p multi   2.25 2.25
a.   Booklet pane of 2   4.50 —
    Complete booklet, #2074a   4.50

No. 2074a sold for 35p.

Carlos Gardel (1890-1935), Singer — A1115

2004, June 24   Litho.   Perf. 12
2075 A1115 14p multi   2.25 2.25

Campaign Against Illegal Drugs — A1116

2004, June 25   Litho.   Perf. 12
2076 A1116 14p multi   2.25 2.25

Renán Rodríguez, Politician — A1117

2004, Aug. 10
2077 A1117 14p multi   2.25 2.25

Maimonides (1135-1204), Philosopher A1118

2004, Aug. 12
2078 A1118 16p multi   2.25 2.25

Galician Center, Montevideo, 125th Anniv. — A1119

2004, Aug. 30
2079 A1119 16p multi   2.25 2.25

1904 Battles of Gen. Aparicio Saravia — A1120

No. 2080 — Battle of: a, Illescas. b, Fray-Marcos. c, Paso del Parque. d, Masoller.

2004, Sept. 8
2080   Block of 4   4.50 4.50
a.-d. A1120 10p Any single   1.10 1.10

Highway Patrol, 50th Anniv. A1121

2004, Sept. 15   Perf. 12½x12¾
2081 A1121 16p multi   2.25 2.25

Joaquín Torres García (1874-1949), Painter — A1122

2004, Sept. 19
2082 A1122 16p multi   2.25 2.25

Magisterial Cooperative, 75th Anniv. — A1123

2004, Sept. 22
2083 A1123 16p multi   2.25 2.25

Army Administrative Corps,
Cent. — A1124

2004, Sept. 22
2084 A1124 16p multi   2.25 2.25

FIFA (Fédération Internationale de
Football Association), Cent. — A1125

2004, Oct. 5   *Perf. 12*
2085 A1125 37p multi   3.75 3.75

Uruguay - Republic of Korea
Diplomatic Relations, 40th
Anniv. — A1126

2004, Oct. 7
2086 A1126 16p multi   2.25 2.25

Montevideo Cathedral,
Bicent. — A1127

2004, Oct. 19   Litho.   *Perf. 12*
2087 A1127 16p multi   2.25 2.25

Montevideo Council Building — A1128

2004, Oct. 22   Litho.   *Perf. 12*
2088 A1128 16p multi   2.25 2.25

Tomás Toribio
House — A1129

2004, Oct. 22
2089 A1129 16p multi   2.25 2.25

America Issue - Environmental
Protection — A1130

Dirty and clean: 16p, Water. 37p, Birds.

2004, Oct. 26
2090-2091 A1130 Set of 2   6.00 6.00

Armored Infantry Batallion No. 13,
Cent. — A1131

2004, Nov. 16
2092 A1131 16p multi   2.25 2.25

Corner
Store,
18th
Cent.
A1132

2004, Nov. 22
2093 A1132 16p multi   1.75 1.75

PriceWaterhouseCoopers in Uruguay,
85th Anniv. — A1133

2004, Dec. 7
2094 A1133 16p multi   2.25 2.25

Review of Court
Clerks,
Cent. — A1134

2004, Dec. 8
2095 A1134 16p multi   2.25 2.25

Christmas
A1135

2004, Dec. 14
2096 A1135 16p multi   2.25 2.25

Water
Conservation
A1136

2004, Dec. 21
2097 A1136 37p multi   5.00 5.00

Souvenir Sheet

Punta del Este — A1137

2004, Dec. 27
2098 A1137 16p multi   3.50 3.50

1912 Orenstein & Kopell
Locomotive — A1138

Serpentine Die Cut 11¼
2004, Dec. 28   Self-Adhesive
2099 A1138 30p multi   5.00 5.00

Rotary
International,
Cent. — A1139

2005, Feb. 23   Litho.   *Perf. 12*
2100 A1139 37p multi   6.00 6.00

Bridges — A1140

No. 2101: a, Chuy del Tacuari Bridge. b,
Barra Bridge, Maldonado. c, Mauá Bridge
Yaguarón River. d, Castells Bridge, Víboras.

2005, Mar. 18
2101 A1140 16p Block of 4, #a-d   9.00 9.00

Ninth Meeting of Latin American
Energy Regulators — A1141

2005, Apr. 5
2102 A1141 16p multi   2.50 2.50

"Liberating Dragoons" Ninth
Mechanized Cavalry Regiment,
Cent. — A1142

2005, Apr. 11
2103 A1142 16p multi   2.50 2.50

Armenian
Genocide, 90th
Anniv. — A1143

2005, Apr. 25
2104 A1143 16p multi   2.25 2.25

Fingerprint Analysis in Uruguay,
Cent. — A1144

2005, Apr. 26
2105 A1144 16p multi   2.50 2.50

No. 1446 Surcharged

Wmk. 332
2005, May 27   Litho.   *Perf. 12½*
2106 A639 2p on 50c #1446   .50 .50

Fountains
A1145

Designs: No. 2107, 10p, Constitution Plaza
Fountain. No. 2108, 10p, Botanical Garden
Fountain. No. 2109, 10p, Athlete's Fountain,
Rodó Park. 37p, Cordier Fountain, Prado,
horiz.

2005, June 8   Litho.   *Perf. 12*
2107-2110 A1145 Set of 4   10.00 10.00

Catholic Circle, 120th Anniv. A1146

2005, June 9
2111 A1146 16p multi 2.50 2.50

SOS Children's Villages, 45th Anniv. A1147

2005, June 23
2112 A1147 16p multi 2.50 2.50

St. John the Baptist College, 75th Anniv. A1148

2005, June 24
2113 A1148 16p multi 2.50 2.50

Souvenir Sheet

Death of Pope John Paul II and Election of Pope Benedict XVI — A1149

No. 2114: a, Cross and statue of Pope John Paul II, Montevideo. b, Pope Benedict XVI.

Perf. 12x11¾
2005, July 15 Litho. Unwmk.
2114 A1149 10p Sheet of 2, #a-b 6.00 4.00

Medical Association Assistance Center, 70th Anniv. — A1150

2005 *Perf. 12*
2115 A1150 16p multi 2.50 2.50
Inscribed "Correos Uruguay" at Right
Perf. 12¾x12½
2116 A1150 16p multi 2.50 2.50
Issued: No. 2115, 7/19; No. 2116, 8/4.

Seminary College, 125th Anniv. A1151

Designs: No. 2117, 16p, St. Ignatius of Loyola, college building. No. 2118, 16p, College building.

2005, July 29 *Perf. 12*
2117-2118 A1151 Set of 2 4.50 4.50

General Liber Seregni (1916-2004) — A1152

No. 2119 — Inscriptions: a, Vocacion. b, Comienzo. c, Liberacion. d, Reconocimiento.

2005
2119 A1152 16p Block of 4, #a-d 9.00 9.00
e. Booklet pane, #2119 9.00
Complete booklet, #2119e 11.00
Issued: No. 2119, 8/1; No. 2119e, 10/11.

Pope John Paul II (1920-2005) A1153

2005, Aug. 11 *Perf. 13½x13¾*
2120 A1153 37p multi 5.50 5.50

Europa Stamps, 50th Anniv. A1154

Designs: 16p, Landscape, by C. De Arzadun, Spain #1263. 37p, The Emus, by De Arzadun, Spain, #1126, vert.

Perf. 13¾x13½, 13½x13¾
2005, Aug. 11 Litho.
2121-2122 A1154 Set of 2 8.00 8.00

Urutem 2005 Philatelic Exhibition A1155

2005, Aug. 15 Litho. *Perf. 12*
2123 A1155 16p multi 2.50 2.50

Legislative Palace, 80th Anniv. A1156

2005, Aug. 24 Litho. Perf. 12
2124 A1156 16p multi 2.50 2.50

Estadio Centenario, 75th Anniv. — A1157

Children's art: No. 2125, $16, Stadium, by Jonatan Belón. No. 2126, 16p, "75" made with flag and soccer field, by Sofia Arca.

2005, Aug. 30
2125-2126 A1157 Set of 2 4.75 4.75

Carlos Solé, Soccer Broadcaster — A1158

2005, Sept. 20
2127 A1158 16p multi 2.50 2.50

World Cup Soccer Championships, 75th Anniv. — A1159

Designs: No. 2128, 16p, Parade of athletes. No. 2129, 16p, Handshake before match. No. 2130, 16p, Awarding of World Cup. 37p, Flags of Germany and Uruguay, emblem of 2006 World Cup Soccer Championships, Germany.

2005, Oct. 3
2128-2131 A1159 Set of 4 12.00 12.00

44th Congress of Intl. Congress and Convention Association, Montevideo — A1160

No. 2132: a, Fish sun and buildings. b, Association emblem.

2005, Nov. 4 Litho. Perf. 12
2132 A1160 8p Horiz. pair, #a-b 2.50 2.50

Uruguay River Fish — A1161

No. 2133: a, Rhamdia sapo. b, Odontesthes bonariensis. c, Hoplias malabaricus. d, Pygocentrus nattereri.

2005, Nov. 22
2133 A1161 16p Block of 4, #a-d 9.00 9.00

El Escolar Magazine, 50th Anniv. — A1162

2005, Nov. 23
2134 A1162 16p multi 3.00 3.00

Customhouse Brokers Association, 70th Anniv. — A1163

2005, Nov. 25
2135 A1163 16p multi 2.50 2.50

Detail From Mural, *Oficios,* by Julio Alpuy — A1164

2005, Dec. 1
2136 A1164 16p multi 2.50 2.50

Writers — A1165

Designs: 16p, Juan Zorilla de San Martin (1855-1931). 37p, Constancio C. Vigil (1876-1954).

2005, Dec. 9
2137-2138 A1165 Set of 2 8.00 8.00

Commercial and Industrial Center of
Salto, Cent. — A1166

2005, Dec. 12
2139 A1166 16p multi   2.50 2.50

Central
Español
Soccer
Team,
Cent.
A1167

2005, Dec. 12
2140 A1167 16p multi   2.50 2.50

Christmas — A1168

2005, Dec. 12
2141 A1168 16p multi   2.50 2.50

Montevideo Atheneum, 137th
Anniv. — A1169

2005, Dec. 14   **Litho.**
2142 A1169 16p multi   2.50 2.50

1924
Paris
Olympics,
80th
Anniv. (in
2004)
A1170

Designs: No. 2143, 16p, Andrés Mazali,
soccer gold medalist. No. 2144, 16p, Juan
Pedro Cea, soccer gold medalist. No. 2145,
16p, Alfredo Ghierra, soccer gold medalist.
37p, Urn showing soccer players, vert.

2005, Dec. 20   **Perf. 12**
2143-2146 A1170 Set of 4   12.00 12.00

America Issue,
Fight Against
Poverty — A1171

Designs: 16p, Children, teacher and school.
37p, Men with shovel.

2005, Dec. 22
2147-2148 A1171 Set of 2   7.50 7.50

Capitán Miranda, 75th Anniv. — A1172

No. 2149: a, Capitán Miranda in 1930. b,
Capitán Miranda in 2005. c, Capt. Francisco P.
Miranda (1869-1925). d, Crests of ships
Capitán Miranda, Cádiz, and Montevideo.

2005, Dec. 28
2149 A1172 16p Block of 4, #a-d   9.00 9.00

No. 1492
Surcharged in
Brown

2005? Photo. Wmk. 332 Perf. 12½
2150 A654 1p on 1.20p #1492   .60 .60
Obliterator on No. 2150 covers the "20" of
original denomination. Compare with Nos.
2055 and 2011A.

Maldonado, 250th Anniv. — A1173

Designs: No. 2151, 16p, San Fernando
Cathedral. No. 2152, 16p, Dragoon Quarters.

2006, Feb. 22   **Litho.**   **Perf. 12**
2151-2152 A1173 Set of 2   5.00 5.00

Alfredo Zitarrosa (1936-80),
Singer — A1174

Zitarrosa and: No. 2153, 16p, Guitar, violin.
No. 2154, 16p, Guitar, violin, vert.

2006, Mar. 10
2153-2154 A1174 Set of 2   4.50 4.50

Solís Theater, 150th Anniv. — A1175

2006, Mar. 28
2155 A1175 16p multi   2.50 2.50

Diario Español
Newspaper,
Cent. — A1176

2006, May 15
2156 A1176 16p multi   2.50 2.50

Public Enterprise Day — A1177

2006, May 19
2157 A1177 16p black   2.50 2.50

Assassinated Politicians — A1178

Designs: No. 2158, 16p, Héctor Gutiérrez
Ruiz (1934-76). No. 2159, 16p, Zelmar Miche-
lini (1924-76). No. 2160, 16p, Michelini and
Gutiérrez Ruiz.

2006, June 1
2158-2160 A1178 Set of 3   7.00 7.00

SODRE Symphonic Orchestra, 75th
Anniv. — A1179

2006, June 20
2161 A1179 16p black   2.25 2.25

Masons in
Uruguay, 150th
Anniv. — A1180

2006, Aug. 15
2162 A1180 16p multi   2.50 2.50

Horse Breeds — A1181

No. 2163: a, Appaloosa. b, Percheron. c,
Belgian Heavy Draft. d, Criollo.

2006, Aug. 18
2163 A1181 16p Block of 4, #a-d   9.50 9.50

First Uruguayan Postage Stamps,
150th Anniv. — A1182

2006, Sept. 29
2164 A1182 16p multi   2.50 2.50

Eladio Dieste (1917-2000),
Architect — A1183

2006, Oct. 3
2165 A1183 16p multi   2.50 2.50

Syndical Unification Congress, 40th
Anniv. — A1184

No. 2166: a, Marchers with banner. b,
Marchers with flag.

2006, Oct. 3
2166 A1184 16p Horiz. pair, #a-b   5.00 5.00

Diplomatic
Relations
Between
Uruguay and
the Sovereign
Military Order
of Malta, 40th
Anniv.
A1185

2006, Oct. 4
2167 A1185 16p multi   2.50 2.50

Paysandú, 250th Anniv. — A1186

2006, Oct. 12
2168 A1186 16p multi   2.50 2.50

Dr. Washington Beltrán (1914-2003), Politician A1187

2006, Oct. 25
2169 A1187 16p multi   2.50 2.50

16th Ibero-American Summit, Montevideo — A1188

2006, Nov. 1   Litho.   Perf. 12
2170 A1188 37p multi   5.00 5.00

Salto, 250th Anniv. A1189

2006, Nov. 7   Litho.   Perf. 12
2171 A1189 16p multi   2.50 2.50

Channel 10, 50th Anniv. — A1190

2006, Nov. 8   Litho.   Perf. 12
2172 A1190 16p multi   2.50 2.50

America Issue, Energy Conservation — A1191

No. 2173: a, 16p, Screw-in fluorescent light bulbs. b, 37p, Solar panels.

2006, Nov. 17   Litho.   Perf. 12
2173 A1191   Horiz. pair, #a-b   7.50 7.50

Sports A1192

Designs: No. 2174, 16p, Indoor soccer. No. 2175, 16p, Handball. No. 2176, 16p, Rugby. No. 2177, 16p, Tennis.

2006, Nov. 30
2174-2177 A1192   Set of 4   9.00 9.00

Christmas A1193

2006, Dec. 7
2178 A1193 37p multi   5.00 5.00

Musical Instruments A1194

Designs: 15p, Guitar. 37p, Drum, horiz.

2006, Dec. 11
2179-2180 A1194   Set of 2   7.50 7.50

Ocean Liners and Ports — A1195

No. 2181: a, Queen Mary 2, Montevideo. b, Costa Fortuna, Montevideo. c, Zuiderman, Montevideo. d, Star Princess, Punta del Este.

2006, Dec. 18
2181 A1195 37p Block of 4,   20.00 20.00
        #a-d

Uruguayan Lottery, 150th Anniv. — A1196

2006, Dec. 22   Litho.   Perf. 12
2182 A1196 15p multi   2.25 2.25

Optimist Class Yacht World Championships — A1197

2006, Dec. 28   Litho.   Perf. 12
2183 A1197 37p multi   5.00 5.00

Uruguay Post Emblem A1198

Serpentine Die Cut 11¼
2006, Dec. 29   Litho.
Self-Adhesive
2184 A1198 15p multi   1.75 1.75

No. 1492 Surcharged in Golden Brown

No. 1454 Surcharged in Black and Silver

Methods, Perfs, and Watermarks As Before
2007, Jan. 24
2185 A654 1p on 1.20p #1492   .60 .60
2186 A639 2p on 1.80p #1454   .60 .60

Compare No. 2185 with Nos. 2011A, 2055 and 2150.

Punta del Este, Cent. — A1199

Unwmk.
2007, Jan. 26   Litho.   Perf. 12
2187 A1199 37p multi   5.00 5.00

José Nasazzi Children's Soccer Cup — A1200

2007, Feb. 5   Litho.   Perf. 12
2188 A1200 15p multi   2.00 2.00

Julia Arévalo (1898-1985), Politician — A1201

2007, Mar. 8   Litho.   Perf. 12
2189 A1201 15p multi   2.25 2.25

Ministry of Transportation and Public Works, Cent. — A1202

No. 2190: a, 5p, Highway construction crew. b, 10p, Airplanes at airport. c, 15p, Bridge.

2007, Mar. 12   Litho.   Perf. 12¼
2190 A1202   Sheet of 3, #a-c   4.50 4.50

Colón Soccer Club, Cent. A1203

2007, Mar. 12   Litho.   Perf. 12
2191 A1203 15p multi   2.25 2.25

Campaign Against Dengue Fever — A1204

Serpentine Die Cut 11¼
2007, Mar. 28   Self-Adhesive
2192 A1204 15p multi   2.25 2.25

National Cadastre, Cent. A1205

2007, Apr. 12   Perf. 12
2193 A1205 15p multi   2.25 2.25

Regional Art Meeting A1206

2007, June 8
2194 A1206 15p multi   2.25 2.25

Shells — A1207

No. 2195: a, 5p, Aequipecten tehuelchus. b, 5p, Trophon pelseneeri. c, 10p, Americominella duartei. d, 10p, Conus clenchi.

2007, June 26
2195 A1207   Block of 4, #a-d   4.00 4.00

Giuseppe Garibaldi (1807-82), Italian Leader — A1208

Designs: 15p, Ship, Garibaldi on horseback. 37p, Garibaldi, ship.

2007, July 4
2196-2197 A1208   Set of 2   7.00 7.00
2197a   Horiz. pair, #2196-2197   7.00 7.00

See Brazil Nos. 3021-3022.

Guichón, Cent. — A1209

2007, July 13
2198 A1209   15p multi   2.25 2.25

Souvenir Sheet

La Estrella del Sur Publication, Bicent. — A1210

2007, July 19   Perf. 12½x12¾
2199 A1210   15p multi   2.50 2.50

Agronomy Faculties, Cent. — A1211

2007, July 30
2200 A1211   15p multi   2.00 2.00

Scouting, Cent. — A1212

Children's drawings: No. 2201, 15p, Scout emblem, by Victoria Ferrer. No. 2202, 15p, Scouts at Flag Ceremony, by Paula Barrios. No. 2203, horiz.: a, Knot, Lord Robert Baden-Powell and Duke of Connaught. b, Knot, International Scout emblem patch.

2007, Aug. 9   Perf. 12
2201-2202 A1212   Set of 2   4.00 4.00
Souvenir Sheet
2203 A1212   25p Sheet of 2, #a-b   7.00 7.00

Three Musicians in Primary Colors, by José Gurvich (1927-74) A1213

2007, Aug. 17
2204 A1213   15p multi   2.00 2.00

Diplomatic Relations Between Uruguay and Guatemala, Cent. — A1214

No. 2205: a, 15p, Santa Catarina Arch, Antigua, Guatemala. b, 37p, City gate, Colonia del Sacramento, Uruguay.

2007, Sept. 3   Litho.   Perf. 12½x12¾
2205 A1214   Horiz. pair, #a-b   7.00 7.00

See Guatemala No. 583.

German College and High School, Montevideo, 150th Anniv. A1215

No. 2206: a, Anniversary emblem. b, Children's drawing of girl and colors of flags of Germany and Uruguay.

2007, Sept. 5   Perf. 12
2206   Horiz. pair + central label   4.00 4.00
a.-b.   A1215 15p Either single   1.75 1.75

Occupations — A1216

Designs: 1p, Peanut vendor. 7p, Knife grinder, vert. 10p, Organ grinder, vert. 25p, Barber, vert. 50p, Druggist, vert.

Serpentine Die Cut 11¼
2007, Oct. 6   **Self-Adhesive**
2207 A1216   1p multi   .30 .30
2208 A1216   7p multi   1.10 1.10
2209 A1216   10p multi   1.10 1.10
2210 A1216   25p multi   3.25 3.25
2211 A1216   50p multi   6.50 6.50
Nos. 2207-2211 (5)   12.25 12.25

See Nos. 2253, 2282, 2290, 2292-2295, B13.

Marine Mammal Conservation — A1217

2007, Oct. 12   **Die Cut**
Self-Adhesive
2212 A1217   37p multi   5.00 5.00

Butterflies — A1218

No. 2213: a, 5p, Eurybia lycisca. b, 10p, Catagramma excelsior pastazza. c, 15p, Agrias claudina. d, 20p, Marpesia marcella.

2007, Oct. 26   Perf. 12½x12¾
2213 A1218   Block of 4, #a-d   0.00 8.00

Torrijos - Carter Panama Canal Treaties, 30th Anniv. A1219

2007, Nov. 5   Perf. 12
2214 A1219   37p multi   5.00 5.00

America Issue, Education For All A1220

Designs: 15p, Rectangles. 37p, Squares and rectangles.

2007, Nov. 22
2215-2216 A1220   Set of 2   7.00 7.00

Naval School, Cent. — A1221

2007, Dec. 5   Perf. 12x11¾
2217 A1221   12p multi   1.75 1.75

Diplomatic Relations Between Uruguay and Russia, 150th Anniv. — A1223

No. 2218: a, 12p, Sacred Heart of Jesus Sanctuary, Uruguay. b, 37p, St. Basil's Cathedral, Russia.

2007, Dec. 21   Litho.   Perf. 12
2218 A1223   Horiz. pair, #a-b + central label   6.00 6.00

Christmas A1224

2007, Dec. 21
2219 A1224   12p multi   1.75 1.75

Architecture A1225

Designs: 12p, House, by Julio Vilamajó. 37p, Joaquín Torres García Building, by Carlos Ott.

2007, Dec. 28
2220-2221 A1225   Set of 2   7.00 7.00

Nelly Goitiño (1924-2007), Actress and Director — A1226

2008, Mar. 24   Litho.   Perf. 12
2222 A1226   12p multi   1.75 1.75

Natl. Association of Milk Producers, 75th Anniv. — A1227

2008, Apr. 23   Litho.   Perf. 12
2223 A1227   12p multi   2.00 2.00

Israel, 60th Anniv. A1228

2008, May 8
2224 A1228 37p multi + label   5.00 5.00

Diplomatic Relations Between Uruguay and the People's Republic of China, 20th Anniv. — A1229

Designs: No. 2225, 12p, Terracotta warriors, China. No. 2226, 12p, The Three Chiripás, painting by J. M. Blaines.

2008, May 19   Litho.   Perf. 12
2225-2226 A1229   Set of 2   3.50 3.50

Dr. Juan J. Crottogini (1908-96), Gynecologist A1230

2008, May 27   Litho.   Perf. 12
2227 A1230 12p multi   2.00 2.00

Souvenir Sheet

Uruguayan Artisans Association, 25th Anniv. — A1231

2008, May 29   Perf. 12½x12¾
2228 A1231 12p multi   2.00 2.00

Discount Bank, 50th Anniv. — A1232

2008, June 4   Perf. 12
Self-Adhesive
2229 A1232 12p multi   2.00 2.00

Intl. Day Against Child Labor — A1233

2008, June 12
2230 A1233 12p multi   2.00 2.00

Birds A1234

Designs: 12p, Piranga flava. 37p, Cyanocorax chrysops, vert.

2008, June 20
2231-2232 A1234   Set of 2   7.00 7.00

Salvador Allende (1908-73), President of Chile — A1235

2008, June 26
2233 A1235 37p multi   5.50 5.50

Francisco Gómez House, 120th Anniv. as Montevideo Government Building A1236

2008, July 11   Perf. 12
2234 A1236 12p multi   2.00 2.00

Hospital Centenaries — A1237

Designs: No. 2235, 12p, Dr. Raul Amorin Cal Hospital, Florida. No. 2236, 12p, Central Hospital of the Armed Forces. No. 2237, 12p, Pereira Rossell Hospital Center.

2008, July 15
2235-2237 A1237   Set of 3   5.50 5.50

2008 Summer Olympics, Beijing — A1238

No. 2238: a, 2p, Pole vault. b, 5p, Cycling. c, 10p, Swimming. d, 20p, Kayaking.

2008, July 22
2238 A1238   Block of 4, #a-d   5.00 5.00

Intl. Swimming Federation (FINA), Cent. A1239

2008, July 22
2239 A1239 37p multi   5.00 5.00

Club Español, Montevideo, 130th Anniv. A1240

2008, Aug. 28   Litho.   Perf. 12
2240 A1240 12p multi   2.00 2.00

Carlos Vaz Ferreira (1872-1958), Philosopher — A1241

2008, Sept. 25   Litho.   Perf. 12
2241 A1241 12p multi   2.00 2.00

Latin American and Caribbean Coalition — A1242

2008, Sept. 25
2242   Horiz. strip of 3   5.50 5.50
  a.   A1242 10p Three people   1.40 1.40
  b.   A1242 12p Three people, diff. 1.75 1.75
  c.   A1242 15p Four people   2.00 2.00

Souvenir Sheet

Intl. Polar Year — A1243

No. 1243: a, Skuas. b, Arctocephalus gazella.

2008, Oct. 7
2243 A1243 20p Sheet of 2, #a-b 6.00 6.00

America Issue, National Festivals A1244

Designs: 12p, Guitarist, dancers. 37p, Dancer, costumed drummers.

Perf. 12¾x12½, 12 (37p)
2008, Oct. 24
2244-2245 A1244   Set of 2   7.00 7.00

Dr. Roberto De Bellis (1938-2007), Hematologist — A1245

2008, Oct. 29   Perf. 12
2246 A1245 12p multi   1.75 1.75

José "Pepe" Sasía, Soccer Player A1246

2008, Nov. 20   Litho.   Perf. 12
2247 A1246 12p multi   2.00 2.00

Flowers A1247

Designs: 1p, Sagittaria montevidensis. 2p, Lantana camara. 10p, Calliandra parvifolia. 17p, Erythrina crista-galli. 25p, Prunus subcoriacea.

2008-09   Litho.   Die Cut
Self-Adhesive
2248 A1247   1p multi   .30   .30
2249 A1247   2p multi   .30   .30
2250 A1247 10p multi   1.40 1.40
  a.   Dated "2009"   1.40 1.40

2251 A1247 17p multi 2.25 2.25
2252 A1247 25p multi 3.50 3.50
Nos. 2248-2252 (5) 7.75 7.75

Issued: 1p, 2p, 3/12/09; 10p, 25p, 11/28; 17p, 12/18.
No. 2250a, 5/15/09.
See Nos. 2265-2266, 2287.

Occupations Type of 2007

2008, Dec. 7 **Die Cut**
Self-Adhesive
2253 A1216 8p Pasta makers 1.25 1.25

Ministry of Foreign Affairs, 180th Anniv. — A1248

2008, Dec. 10 **Litho.** **Perf. 12**
2254 A1248 37p multi 5.50 5.50

Christmas — A1249

2008, Dec. 24
2255 A1249 12p multi 2.00 2.00

National Flag, 180th Anniv. A1250

2008, Dec. 29
2256 A1250 37p multi 5.50 5.50

Pres. Baltasar Brum (1883-1933) — A1251

2009, Mar. 4 **Perf. 12½x12¾**
2257 A1251 12p multi 1.75 1.75

Delmira Agustini (1886-1914), Poet — A1252

2009, Mar. 26
2258 A1252 12p multi 1.75 1.75

Miguelete, Cent. — A1253

2009, Mar. 27 **Perf. 12¾x12½**
2259 A1253 12p multi 1.75 1.75

Fray Bentos, 150th Anniv. — A1254

2009, Apr. 15 **Litho.** **Perf. 12**
2260 A1254 12p multi 1.75 1.75

City of Florida, 200th Anniv. — A1255

2009, Apr. 24 **Perf. 12¾x12½**
2261 A1255 12p multi 1.75 1.75

Carnival Costume Designed by Juan Mascheroni — A1256

2009, May 28 **Die Cut**
Self-Adhesive
2262 A1256 37p multi 5.50 5.50

Souvenir Sheet

Intl. Year of Astronomy — A1257

No. 2263: a, 10p, Intl. Year of Astronomy emblem. b, 12p, Galileo Galilei at Inquisition. c, 25p, Head of Galileo.

2009, June 4 **Perf. 12**
2263 A1257 Sheet of 3, #a-c 6.50 6.50

Juan Carlos Onetti (1909-94), Writer — A1258

2009, July 1 **Perf. 12½x12¾**
2264 A1258 12p multi 1.75 1.75

Flowers Type of 2008-09

Designs: 30p, Tessaria absinthioides. 50p, Eichhornia crassipes.

2009, July 14 **Die Cut**
Self-Adhesive
2265 A1247 30p multi 4.25 4.25
2266 A1247 50p multi 7.00 7.00

Souvenir Sheet

Port of Montevideo, Cent. — A1259

2009, July 21 **Perf. 12**
2267 A1259 37p multi 5.50 5.50

Charles Darwin (1809-82), Naturalist — A1260

No. 2268: a, 12p, Head of Darwin, evolution of humans. b, 37p, HMS Beagle.

2009, Aug. 31
2268 A1260 Horiz. pair, #a-b 7.00 7.00

No. 1454 Surcharged

Method, Perf. and Watermark As Before
2009, Sept. 10
2269 A639 1p on 1.80p #2269 .40 .30
Obliterator covers the centisimos portion of the denomination.

Spiders — A1261

No. 2270: a, Allocosa brasiliensis. b, Argiope argentata.

2009, Sept. 24 **Litho.** **Perf. 12**
2270 A1261 12p Vert. pair, #a-b 3.50 3.50

Acipenser Gueldenstaedtii and Caviar — A1262

Unwmk.
2009, Sept. 30 **Litho.** **Perf. 12**
2271 A1262 37p multi 5.50 5.50

Intl. Labor Organization, 90th Anniv. — A1263

2009, Oct. 7
2272 A1263 37p multi 5.50 5.50

Butterflies and Birds — A1264

No. 2273: a, Hamadryas amphione. b, Anartia amathea. c, Tachuris rubrigasta. d, Colaptes melanochloros.

2009, Oct. 13
2273 A1264 12p Block of 4, #a-d 5.50 5.50

America Issue, Traditional Games A1265

Designs: 12p, Hand holding stone for Taba. 37p, Taba Game, painting by Juan Manuel Blanes.

2009, Oct. 23 **Perf. 12½x12¾**
2274-2275 A1265 Set of 2 5.00 5.00

Government House Museum, 10th Anniv. — A1266

2009, Nov. 6 **Perf. 12**
2276 A1266 12p multi + label 2.00 2.00

Christmas
A1267

2009, Nov. 17   **Perf. 12¾x12½**
2277 A1267 12p multi   1.50 1.50

Exports — A1268

Designs: 10p, Vegetables. 25p, Fruits.

2009, Nov. 19   *Die Cut*
Self-Adhesive
2278 A1268 10p multi   1.25 1.25
2279 A1268 25p multi   3.00 3.00

Inter-American
Development
Bank, 50th
Anniv. — A1269

2009, Nov. 24   **Perf. 12¾x12½**
2280 A1269 37p multi   4.50 4.50

Christian Youth
Association
(YMCA) in
Uruguay,
Cent. — A1270

2009, Nov. 25
2281 A1270 12p multi   1.50 1.50

Occupations Type of 2007
2009, Nov. 27   *Die Cut*
Self-Adhesive
2282 A1216 8p Grocer, vert.   1.25 1.25

Chauffeur's Protection Center,
Montevideo, Cent. — A1271

2009, Dec. 3   **Perf. 12½x12¾**
2283 A1271 12p multi   2.00 2.00

Souvenir Sheet

Battle of the River Plate, 70th
Anniv. — A1272

No. 2284: a, 10p, HMS Ajax. b, 12p,
HMSNZ Achilles. c, 15p, HMS Exeter.

2009, Dec. 16   **Perf. 12**
2284 A1272   Sheet of 3, #a-c   5.50 5.50

Official Service of
Broadcasting,
Television and
Entertainment,
80th
Anniv. — A1273

2009, Dec. 18   **Perf. 12¾x12½**
2285 A1273 37p multi   5.50 5.50

Alba Roballo (1908-96),
Politician — A1274

2010, Mar. 8   **Litho.**   **Perf. 12**
2286 A1274 12p multi   1.50 1.50

Flowers Type of 2008-09
2010, Apr. 12   *Die Cut*
Self-Adhesive
2287 A1247 12p Erithrina crista-
     galli   2.00 2.00

Historic
Hotels — A1275

Designs: No. 2288, 12p, Gran Hotel Concor-
dia, Salto. No. 2289, 12p, Hotel Colón,
Piriápolis.

2010, May 26   **Perf. 12¾x12½**
2288-2289 A1275 Set of 2   3.00 3.00

Occupations Type of 2007
Designs: 5p, Street vendor with basket, vert.
7p, Candy vendor, vert. 10p, Shoemaker, vert.
17p, Cuarteador (man on horseback), vert.
25p, Fish vendor, vert. 30p, Ice cream vendor
with pushcart.

2010   **Litho.**   *Die Cut*
Self-Adhesive
2290 A1216   5p multi   .75 .75
2291 A1216   7p multi   1.00 1.00
2292 A1216   10p multi   1.50 1.50
2293 A1216   17p multi   2.50 2.50
2294 A1216   25p multi   3.75 3.75
2295 A1216   30p multi   4.50 4.50
   Nos. 2290-2295 (6)   14.00 14.00

Issued: 5p, 10p, 5/27; 17p, 30p, 8/10; 25p,
8/19; 7p, 10/20.

First Russians in
Uruguay, 150th
Anniv. — A1276

Perf. 12¾x12½
2010, June 11   **Litho.**
2296 A1276 37p multi   5.50 5.50

Decade of
Peace — A1277

2010, June 30
2297 A1277 12p multi   1.75 1.75

Souvenir Sheet

Frédéric Chopin (1810-49),
Composer — A1278

No. 2298: a, 12p, Chopin. b, 37p, Piano.

2010, July 21   **Perf. 12**
2298 A1278   Sheet of 2, #a-b   7.00 7.00

Diplomatic
Relations
Between
Uruguay and
Romania, 75th
Anniv. — A1279

2010, July 23   **Perf. 12¾x12½**
2299 A1279 37p multi   5.00 5.00

Asturian Center,
Montevideo,
Cent. — A1280

2010, Aug. 28
2300 A1280 37p multi   5.50 5.50

Sporting Club
Uruguay,
Cent.
A1281

2010, Sept. 1   **Litho.**   **Perf. 12**
2301 A1281 12p multi   1.75 1.75

Diplomatic Relations Between Uruguay
and Greece, 135th Anniv. — A1282

2010, Sept. 8   **Litho.**   **Perf. 12**
2302 A1282 37p multi   5.00 5.00

Florencio Sánchez (1875-1910),
Playwright — A1283

2010, Sept. 17   **Perf. 12¼x12¾**
2303 A1283 12p multi   1.75 1.75

Restoration of
Democracy in
Uruguay, 25th
Anniv. — A1284

Perf. 12¾x12½
2010, Sept. 21   **Litho.**
2304 A1284 12p multi   1.75 1.75

Mario Benedetti (1920-2009),
Writer — A1285

No. 2305 — Benedetti at: a, Right. b, Left.

2010, Sept. 25   **Perf. 12½x12¾**
2305 A1285 12p Horiz. pair, #a-b   3.00 3.00
  c.   Booklet pane of 2, #2305a-
       2305b   4.00 —
     Complete booklet, #2305c   4.00

No. 2305c sold for 30p.

Flowers and Birds — A1286

No. 2306: a, Bauhinia forficata var. prui-
nosa. b, Furnarius rufus. c, Guira guira. d,
Passiflora coerulea.

2010, Sept. 30
2306 A1286 12p Block of 4, #a-d 7.00 7.00

Uruguay as Antarctic Treaty
Consultative Member, 25th
Anniv. — A1287

2010, Oct. 8 *Litho.* *Perf. 12½x12¾*
2307 A1287 37p multi 5.50 5.50

Christmas
A1288

2010, Oct. 29 *Perf. 12¾x12½*
2308 A1288 12p multi 1.50 1.50

America Issue — A1289

No. 2309 — Flag of Uruguay and: a, 12p,
National anthem. b, 37p, National coat of
arms.

2010, Nov. 8
2309 A1289 Horiz. pair, #a-b 7.00 7.00

Blue
Uniform
of
Uruguay
Soccer
Team,
Cent.
A1290

No. 2310: a, Team of 1910. b, Team of
2010, emblem of 2010 World Cup Soccer
Tournament, South Africa (84x30mm).

2010, Nov. 15 *Perf. 12½x12¾*
2310 Horiz. pair 3.50 3.50
a.-b. A1290 12p Either single 1.60 1.60

Cruise Ships and Their Ports of
Call — A1291

No. 2311: a, MSC Lirica, Punta del Este. b,
Veendam, Montevideo. c, Silver Whisper,
Punta del Este and Casapueblo. d, Splendour
of the Seas, Punta del Este and Isla de Lobos.

2010, Nov. 19 *Perf. 12*
2311 A1291 37p Block of 4,
#a-d 20.00 20.00

Souvenir Sheet

First Airplane Flights in Uruguay,
Cent. — A1292

No. 2312 — Airplane and: a, Armand
Prevost, pilot of Dec. 7, 1910 flight. b,
Bartolomeo Cattaneo, pilot of Dec. 16, 1910
flight.

2010, Nov. 30 *Perf. 12¾x12½*
2312 A1292 37p Sheet of 2,
#a-b, + cen-
tral label 10.00 10.00

El Telégrafo
Newspaper,
Paysandu,
Cent. — A1293

2010, Dec. 9 *Perf. 12¾x12½*
2313 A1293 12p multi 1.75 1.75

Socialist
Party of
Uruguay,
Cent.
A1294

2010, Dec. 10 *Perf. 12½x12¾*
2314 A1294 12p multi 1.75 1.75

Paintings by Eduardo Vernazza (1910-
91) — A1295

Paintings by Carmelo Arden Quin
(1913-2010) — A1296

No. 2315: a, "Gato con Botas," - Ballet
Ruso. b, Personaje Femenino - Opera China
(Dan).
No. 2316: a, Couronnes I. b, Dualité - Peri-
ode Indienne.

2010, Dec. 22 *Perf. 12¾x12½*
2315 A1295 12p Horiz. pair, #a-b 3.50 3.50
Perf. 12½x12¾
2316 A1296 12p Horiz. pair, #a-b 3.50 3.50

Independence, 200th
Anniv. — A1297

2011, Jan. 3 Self-Adhesive *Die Cut*
2317 A1297 1p multi .30 .30

Artisan
Crafts — A1298

Designs: 2p, Baskets, thistleo and cattails.
No. 2319, Handbag, wool (lana). No. 2320,
Iron toy car (hierro). 12p, Wooden sheep,
wood. 20p, Silver container. 22p, Bamboo
sculpture, bamboo. 37p, Ceramic pot. 44p,
Wire sculpture. 200p, Leather basket, cow.

2011 Self-Adhesive *Die Cut*
2318 A1298 2p multi .40 .40
2319 A1298 10p multi 1.50 1.50
2320 A1298 10p multi 1.50 1.50
2321 A1298 12p multi 1.75 1.75
2322 A1298 20p multi 3.00 3.00
2323 A1298 22p multi 3.25 3.25
2324 A1298 37p multi 5.50 5.50

Size: 27x19mm
2325 A1298 44p multi 6.50 6.50

Size: 42x30mm
2326 A1298 200p multi 30.00 30.00
Nos. 2318-2326 (9) 53.40 53.40

Issed: 2p, 1/31; No. 2319, 37p, 3/23; No.
2320, 22p, 12/15; 12p, 20p, 4/12; 44p, 5/13;
200p, 5/6.

25th Gaucho Culture Festival,
Tacuarembó — A1299

No. 2327: a, Cauldron, meat on grill. b,
Bola, gaucho on horse. c, Spurs, gaucho on
horse.

2011, Feb. 3 *Perf. 12*
2327 Horiz. strip of 3 5.00 5.00
a.-c. A1299 12p Any single 1.60 1.60
Uruguayan Independence, bicent.

Rabindranath
Tagore (1861-
1941),
Poet — A1300

2011, Feb. 16 *Perf. 12¾x12½*
2328 A1300 37p multi 4.75 4.75
Indipex 2011 Intl. Philatelic Exhibition, New
Delhi.

Battle of Las Piedras, by Juan Luis
and Juan Manuel Blanes — A1301

2011, Feb. 25
2329 A1301 12p multi 1.75 1.75
Uruguayan Army, Uruguayan Independence, bicent.

Cry of Asencio, Bicent. — A1302

No. 2330: a, 12p, Hand on sword, hand on
knife, spears. b, 37p, Bearded man with spear,
horse, hand on knife.

2011, Feb. 28
2330 A1302 Horiz. pair, #a-b 7.00 7.00
Uruguayan Independence, bicent.

Gen. Leandro
Gómez (1811-65)
A1303

2011, Mar. 3 *Perf. 12¾x12½*
2331 A1303 12p multi 1.75 1.75

Souvenir Sheet

Las Llamadas, by Carlos Páez
Vilaró — A1304

2011, Mar. 4 *Litho.*
2332 A1304 37p multi 5.00 5.00

Famous Women — A1305

Designs: No. 2333, 12p, Petrona Rosende (1787-1862), writer. No. 2334, 12p, Josefa Oribe (1789-1835), independence supporter.

2011, Mar. 8   *Perf. 12*
2333-2334 A1305   Set of 2   3.00 3.00
Uruguayan Independence, bicent.

Uruguay No. 196 — A1306

2011, Mar. 23   *Perf. 12¾x12½*
2335 A1306 37p multi   5.00 5.00
Postal Union of the Americas, Spain and Portugal (UPAEP), cent.

Planeta Building, Atlántida A1307

2011, Apr. 8   *Perf. 12½x12¾*
2336 A1307 12p multi   1.75 1.75
Atlántida, cent.

Mother's Day — A1308

2011, May 11   *Die Cut*
Self-Adhesive
2337 A1308 12p multi   1.75 1.75

Monte Carlo TV Channel 4, 50th Anniv. A1309

2011, May 11   *Perf. 12½x12¾*
2338 A1309 12p multi   1.75 1.75

Battle of Las Piedras, Bicent. — A1310

2011, May 12   *Perf. 12*
2339 A1310 12p multi   1.75 1.75
Uruguayan Independence, bicent.

2011 Copa América Soccer Tournament, Argentina A1311

2011, June 15   *Perf. 12¾x12½*
2340 A1311 37p multi   5.00 5.00

Aitona, by Ignacio Iturria A1312

2011, June 29   *Perf. 12½x12¾*
2341 A1312 12p multi   1.75 1.75
Basque Center, Montevideo, cent.

Campaign Against Human Immunodeficiency Virus, 30th Anniv. — A1313

2011, June 30   *Perf. 12¾x12½*
2342 A1313 12p multi   1.75 1.75

Natl. Physical Education Commission, Cent. — A1314

2011, July 20   *Perf. 12½x12¾*
2343 A1314 12p multi   1.75 1.75

Uruguay, Champions of 2011 Copa América Soccer Tournament A1315

No. 2344: a, Cristian Rodriguez. b, Alvaro Pereira. c, Abel Hernández. d, Luis Suárez. e, Nicolás Lodeiro. f, Sebastián Abreu. g, Diego Pérez. h, Fernando Muslera. i, Diego Forlán. j, Team manager Washington Tabárez. k, Edinson Cavani. l, Sebastián Eguren. m, Martín Cáceres. n, Diego Godín. o, Egidio Arévalo. p, Alvaro González. q, Maximiliano Pereira. r, Juan Castillo. s, Diego Lugano. t, Walter Gargano. u, Mauricio Victorino. v, Andrés Scotti. w, Martín Silva. x, Sebastián Coates.

2011, Aug. 11   *Perf. 12*
2344   Sheet of 24   20.00 20.00
 a.-x. A1315 6p Any single   .75 .75

Intl. Year of Forests — A1316

2011, Sept. 21   *Litho.*
2345 A1316 12p multi   1.75 1.75

America Issue, Mailboxes A1317

Designs: 12p, Cylindrical mailbox, Avenida 18 de Julio, Montevideo. 37p, Rectangular mailbox, Plaza Independecia, Montevideo.

2011, Sept. 30   *Perf. 12¾x12½*
2346-2347 A1317   Set of 2   7.00 7.00

Diplomatic Relations Between Japan and Uruguay, 90th Anniv. — A1318

2011, Oct. 5   *Perf. 12*
2348 A1318 37p multi + label   5.00 5.00

La Redota (Exodus of Gen. José Artigas and Supporters), Bicent. — A1319

2011, Oct. 13
2349 A1319 12p multi   1.75 1.75
Uruguayan Independece, bicent.

China Zorrilla, Actress — A1320

2011, Oct. 18   *Perf. 12½x12¾*
2350 A1320 37p multi   5.00 5.00

Whale Watching — A1321

No. 2351 — Eubalaena australis: a, 12p, Tail above surface near boat. b, 12p, Tail below water. c, 37p, At water's surface near land. d, 37p, Diving underwater.

2011, Nov. 16   *Litho.*
2351 A1321   Block of 4, #a-d   14.00 14.00

Isla de Flores National Park — A1322

2011, Nov. 16   *Perf. 12*
2352 A1322 12p multi   1.75 1.75

Cruise Ships — A1323

No. 2353: a, Seabourn Sojourn near José Batlle y Ordonez Power Plant. b, Asuka II near Joaquín Torres García Telecommunications Tower. c, Costa Victoria in Port of Montevideo. d, AIDAcara near Cerro de Montevideo.

2011, Nov. 22
2353 A1323 37p Block of 4,
     #a-d   15.00 15.00

PLUNA Airlines, 75th Anniv. — A1324

2011, Nov. 22
2354 A1324 12p multi   1.75 1.75

Tango Musicians A1325

No. 2355: a, César Zagnoli (1911-2002). b, Juan D'Arienzo (1900-76). c, Donato Racciatti (1918-2000).

Perf. 12½x12¾

2011, Nov. 30   Litho.
2355   Horiz. strip of 3   5.00 5.00
   a.-c. A1325 12p Any single   1.60 1.60

Christmas — A1326

2011, Dec. 7   Perf. 12
2356 A1326 12p multi   1.75 1.75

Souvenir Sheet

Intl. Year of Chemistry — A1327

2011, Dec. 9   Perf. 12½x12¾
2357 A1327 37p multi   5.00 5.00

Diplomatic Relations Between Uruguay and the Czech Republic and Slovakia, 90th Anniv. — A1328

2011, Dec. 13   Perf. 12
2358 A1328 37p multi   5.00 5.00

Paintings A1329

Designs: No. 2359, Formas, by María Freire. No. 2360, Composición 17 de Julio - 1968, by Freire, vert.
No. 2361, vert.: a, Crepúsculo, by Vicente Martín. b, Dama con Mandolina, by Martín.

2011, Dec. 19   Perf. 12½x12¾
2359 A1329 12p multi   1.60 1.60
     Perf. 12¾x12½
2360 A1329 12p multi   1.60 1.60
2361   Horiz. pair   3.25 3.25
   a.-b. A1329 12p Either single   1.60 1.60
     Nos. 2359-2361 (3)   6.45 6.45

Intl. Year of People of African Descent A1330

Paintings by Mary Porto Casas: 12p, La Lancera. 37p, Mandela, horiz.

2011, Dec. 27   Perf. 12
2362-2363 A1330   Set of 2   6.50 6.50

State Insurance Bank, Cent. — A1331

2011, Dec. 27
2364 A1331 12p multi   1.75 1.75

Independence, 200th Anniv. — A1332

No. 2365: a, Indigenous man with headband holding stick. b, Man of African descent with hat and gun.

2011, Dec. 28   Litho.
2365 A1332 12p Horiz. pair, #a-b 3.50 3.50

Items Made by Artisans — A1333

No. 2366: a, Cows made of wood and wool, by Carlos Clavelli. b, Woolen garment, by Siv Göransson. c, Leather container and lid, by Albertina Morelli. d, Silver pendant, by Nilda Echenique. e, Wire ball, by Gustavo Genta.

2012, Jan. 31   Die Cut
     Self-Adhesive
2366   Horiz. strip of 5   1.00 1.00
   a.-e. A1333 1p Any single   .25 .25

Written and Sign Language Letters and Their Corresponding International Signal Flags — A1334

Letter: 5p, A. 10p, M. 12p, O. 20p, S. 50p, G. 60p, I.

2012   **Self-Adhesive**   Die Cut
2367 A1334   5p multi   .75 .75
2368 A1334 10p multi   1.50 1.50
2369 A1334 12p multi   1.75 1.75
2370 A1334 20p multi   3.00 3.00
2371 A1334 50p multi   7.50 7.50
     Size: 27x19mm
2372 A1334 60p multi   9.00 9.00
     Nos. 2367-2372 (6)   15.90 15.90

Issued: 5p, 2/9; 10p, 2/28; 12p, 50p, 60p, 4/11; 20p, 5/16.

Intl. Women's Day A1335

2012, Mar. 7   Perf. 12½x12¾
2373 A1335 12p multi   1.75 1.75

Palacio Gandós, Montevideo A1336

2012, Mar. 15   Perf. 12¾x12½
2374 A1336 37p multi   5.00 5.00

Annual Board of Governors Meeting of the Inter-American Development Bank and Inter-American Investment Corporation, Montevideo.

Enrique V. Iglesias, Ex-President of Inter-American Development Bank — A1337

2012, Mar. 20   Litho.
2375 A1337 37p multi   4.50 4.50

2012 Summer Olympics, London — A1338

No. 2376: a, Soccer, ArcelorMittal Orbit. b, Cycling, St. Paul's Cathedral. c, Yachting, Tower Bridge. d, Hurdler, Big Ben and Parliament.

2012, Mar. 30   Perf. 12
2376 A1338 15p Block of 4, #a-d 8.00 8.00

Diplomatic Relations Between Uruguay and Ukraine, 20th Anniv. — A1339

2012, Apr. 25
2377 A1339 37p multi   5.50 5.50

Nueva Helvecia Colony, 150th Anniv. A1340

2012, Apr. 25   Perf. 12½x12¾
2378 A1340 12p multi   1.90 1.90

Euskal Erria Basque Fellowship Center, Montevideo, Cent. — A1341

2012, May 25
2379 A1341 37p multi   5.00 5.00

World Blood Donation Day — A1342

2012, June 14   Die Cut
     Self-Adhesive
2380 A1342 12p multi   2.00 2.00

Intl. Year of Cooperatives — A1343

2012, July 6   Perf. 12½x12¾
2381 A1343 12p multi   2.00 2.00

Uruguay Mortgage Bank, 120th Anniv. — A1344

Perf. 12¾x12½
2012, Aug. 10   Litho.
2382 A1344 12p multi   2.00 2.00

Fauna — A1345

No. 2383: a, Paroaria coronata, Pyrocephalus rubinus. b, Charadrius modestus, Caiman latirostris. c, Pontoporia blainvilleii d, Xylocopa augusti, Rhinella schneideri.

Perf. 12½x12¾
2012, Aug. 31   Litho.
2383 A1345 12p Block of 4, #a-d 6.00 6.00

Intl. Democracy Day — A1346

2012, Sept. 13   *Perf. 12¾x12½*
2384 A1346 37p multi   5.50 5.50

Anibal Barrios Pintos (1918-2011), Writer, and Sculpture of Aboriginal People — A1347

2012, Sept. 27   *Perf. 12½x12¾*
2385 A1347 12p multi   1.75 1.75

America Issue — A1348

Legend of: No. 2386, 12p, The Ceibo Flower. No. 2387, 12p, The Black Shepherd.

2012, Sept. 28   *Perf. 12¾x12½*
2386-2387 A1348   Set of 2   3.25 3.25

Crops Grown for Alternative Energy Sources A1349

Designs: No. 2388, 12p, Saccharum officinarum. No. 2389, 12p, Helianthus annuus.

2012, Oct. 5   *Perf. 12½x12¾*
2388-2389 A1349   Set of 2   3.25 3.25

Souvenir Sheet

25th Universal Postal Union Congress, Doha, Qatar — A1350

2012, Oct. 6   *Perf. 12¾x12½*
2390 A1350 37p multi   5.50 5.50

National Directorate of Mining and Geology, Cent. — A1351

2012, Oct. 22   Litho.
2391 A1351 12p multi   2.00 2.00

Tourist Attractions and Cruise Ships A1352

No. 2392 — Attraction and ship: a, Colonia del Sacramento Lighthouse, National Geographic Explorer. b, Yacht Club Uruguay, Puerto del Buceo, Celebrity Infinity. c, Santa Teresa Fortress, Grand Celebration. d, Argentino Hotel, Piriápolis, MSC Magnifica.

2012, Oct. 22   *Perf. 12*
2392   Horiz. strip of 4   20.00 20.00
a.-d. A1352 37p Any single   5.00 5.00

National Road Safety Union — A1353

Designs: 5p, Stop sign. 10p, Martini glasses. 15p, Passenger with hands over seat belt. 20p, Triangular warning sign with helmeted head of person. 45p, Speed limit sign. 50p, Blue ribbon. 70p. National Road Safety Union emblem. 100p, Road Safety Decade inscription on diamond warning sign.

2012, Oct. 24   *Die Cut*
     Self-Adhesive
2393 A1353   5p multi   1.00 1.00
2394 A1353   10p multi   2.00 2.00
2395 A1353   15p multi   2.50 2.25
2396 A1353   20p multi   3.50 3.00
2397 A1353   45p multi   8.00 6.50
a.   Vert. strip of 5, 2 #2396, 3 #2397   35.00
2398 A1353   50p multi   10.00 7.50
a.   Vert strip of 5, #2393, 2395, 2396, 2 #2398   30.00
2399 A1353   70p multi   12.00 10.00
2400 A1353   100p multi   18.00 15.00
a.   Vert. strip of 5, #2393, 2394, 2395, 2399, 2400   40.00
  Nos. 2393-2400 (8)   57.00 47.25

National Fire Fighting Directorate, 125th Anniv. — A1354

No. 2401 — Fire fighting emblem, fire fighter in protective clothing and: a, Building fire. b, Forest fire. c, Bronto Skylift F68HLA. d, Refinery fire.

2012, Oct. 26   *Perf. 12½x12¾*
2401 A1354 12p Block of 4, #a-d 7.00 7.00

Virginia Brindis de Salas (1908-58), Poet — A1355

2012, Oct. 31   *Perf. 12¾x12½*
2402 A1355 12p multi   2.00 2.00

Paintings A1356

Designs: No. 2403, 12p, Recreo, by Petrona Viera. No. 2404, 12p, Construcción, by Augusto Torres.

2012, Oct. 31   Litho.
2403-2404 A1356   Set of 2   4.00 4.00

National Administration of Electrical Transmission and Usage, Cent. — A1357

No. 2405: a, Rincón de Baygorria Dam, linemen working on wires. b, High tension wire tower, engineer with chart. c, Wind generators. d, Palace of Light, José Battle y Ordoñez Center, worker with hard hat.

2012, Oct. 31   *Perf. 12½x12¾*
2405 A1357 12p Horiz. strip of 4, #a-d, + 4 labels   7.00 7.00

Tango Music A1358

No. 2406: a, Double bass used in tango music. b, Francisco Canaro (1888-1964), tango orchestra leader. c, Edgardo Pedroza (1926-2000), tango orchestra leader.

2012, Nov. 23
2406   Horiz. strip of 3   16.00 16.00
a. A1358 15p multi   2.25 2.25
b.-c. A1358 45p Either single   6.50 6.50

Christmas A1359

2012, Nov. 23   *Perf. 12¾x12½*
2407 A1359 15p multi   2.25 2.25

Club Neptuno, Cent. — A1360

2012, Dec. 3   Litho.
2408 A1360 15p multi   2.25 2.25

Etchepare Colony for Psychiatric Care, Cent. A1361

2012, Dec. 4   *Perf. 12*
2409 A1361 15p multi   2.25 2.25

Independent Party, 10th Anniv. — A1362

2012, Dec. 17   *Perf. 12½x12¾*
2410 A1362 15p multi   2.25 2.25

Souvenir Sheet

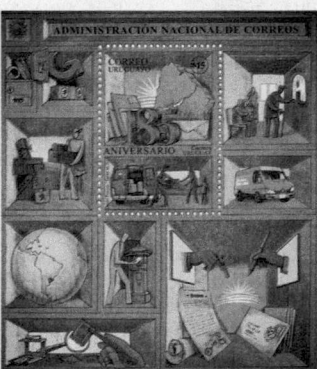

National Postal Administration, 185th Anniv. — A1363

2012, Dec. 21   *Perf. 12¾x12½*
2411 A1363 15p multi   2.25 2.25

Rural Workers A1364

Designs: 1p, Farmer tending to field (agricultor). 5p, Fence builders (alambrador). 10p, Workers tending sheep (esquillador). 15p, Beekeeper and hives (apicultor). 25p, Fruit harvester (recolectora). 30p, Cattle driver (arriero). 45p, Worker processing fish (pesca). 50p, Woman milking cow (tambera). 60p, Woman moving logs (leñadora).

2013   Litho.   *Die Cut*
     Self-Adhesive
2412 A1364   1p multi   .30 .30
2413 A1364   5p multi   .80 .80
2414 A1364   10p multi   1.50 1.50
2415 A1364   15p multi   2.25 2.25
2416 A1364   25p multi   3.75 3.75

2417	A1364	30p multi	4.50	4.50
2418	A1364	45p multi	6.75	6.75
2419	A1364	50p multi	7.50	7.50
2420	A1364	60p multi	9.00	9.00

Nos. 2412-2420 (8)   35.55 35.55

Passage of Law No. 18,441 limiting hours of rural workers.
Issued: 1p, 10p, 2/22; 5p, 7/9; 15p, 60p, 5/17; 25p, 4/18; 30p, 50p, 3/8; 45p, 4/30.

Carnival Costume Designed by Juan Mascheroni A1365

Perf. 12¾x12½

2013, Feb. 28   **Litho.**
2421 A1365 15p multi   2.25 2.25

Souvenir Sheet

Military Aviation in Uruguay, Cont. A1000

2013, Mar. 16   **Perf. 12**
2422 A1366 15p multi   2.75 2.75

Harald Edelstam (1913-89), Swedish Diplomat A1367

2013, Mar. 17   **Perf. 12¾x12½**
2423 A1367 45p multi   7.00 7.00

Edelstam rescued Cuban diplomats, Chilean activists and Uruguayan refugees from persecution during the 1973 Chilean coup.

Defensor Sporting Club, Cent. A1368

2013, Mar. 20   **Perf. 12½x12¾**
2424 A1368 15p multi   2.25 2.25

No. 2424 was printed in sheets of 8 + central label.

Famous Women — A1369

No. 2425: a, María "Tota" Quinteros (1918-2001) holding sign showing kidnapped daughter, Elena (1945-76). b, Jorgelina Martínez (1926-2009), labor leader. c, María Viñas Sendic (1943-2003), labor leader.

2013, Mar. 21   **Perf. 12¾x12½**
2425   Strip of 3   6.50 6.50
a.-c. A1369 15p Any single   2.00 2.00

Nibya Mariño, Pianist A1370

2013, Mar. 22   **Perf. 12½x12¾**
2426 A1370 15p multi   2.25 2.25

No. 2426 was printed in sheets of 8 + central label.

Patient Safety Day — A1371

2013, Apr. 11   **Perf. 12¾x12½**
2427 A1371 15p multi   2.25 2.25

Instructions of the Year XIII, Bicent. A1372

2013, May 3   **Perf. 12**
2428 A1372 15p multi   2.25 2.25

Souvenir Sheet

Red Cross Coach, 1897 — A1373

2013, May 30   **Litho.**
2429 A1373 15p multi   2.25 2.25

Paintings — A1374

No. 2430: a, Zíngaras, by Rafael Barradas (1890-1929). b, Bodegón (Still Life), by Augusto Torres (1913-92).

Perf. 12½x12¾
2013, June 11   **Litho.**
2430 A1374 15p Horiz. pair, #a-b 4.50 4.50

World Day of Autism Awareness A1375

2013, June 12   **Perf. 12¾x12½**
2431 A1375 15p multi   2.25 2.25

City of San Carlos II, by Daniel Arteta A1376

2013, July 8   **Perf. 12½x12¾**
2432 A1376 15p multi   2.25 2.25

San Carlos, 250th Anniv.

Amanda Rorra (1924-2005), Afro-Uruguayan Activist — A1377

2013, July 25 Litho. Perf. 12¾x12½
2433 A1377 15p multi   2.25 2.25

Intl. Year of Quinoa A1378

2013, July 26 Litho. Perf. 12½x12¾
2434 A1378 45p multi   6.50 6.50

Calabrian Association of Uruguay, 50th Anniv. — A1379

2013, Aug. 2 Litho. Perf. 12½x12¾
2435 A1379 45p multi   6.50 6.50

No. 2435 was printed in sheets of 8 + central label.

Tabernacle, Sculpture by Octavio Podestá — A1380

Perf. 12½x12¾
2013, Aug. 22   **Litho.**
2436 A1380 15p multi   2.25 2.25

Insects — A1381

No. 2437: a, Borellia bruneri. b, Diloboderus abderus. c, Sulcophanaeus menelas. d, Apis mellifera.

Perf. 12½x12¾
2013, Aug. 30   **Litho.**
2437 A1381 15p Block of 4, #a-d, + 2 labels   9.50 9.50

International Day of Democracy A1382

Perf. 12¾x12½
2013, Sept. 15   **Litho.**
2438 A1382 45p multi   6.00 6.00

Care Centers for Children and Families, 25th Anniv. — A1383

Perf. 12¾x12½
2013, Sept. 16   **Litho.**
2439 A1383 15p multi   2.25 2.25

Andrés Aguiar (d. 1849), Soldier for Giuseppe Garibaldi in First Italian War of Independence A1384

Perf. 12¾x12½
2013, Sept. 21   **Litho.**
2440 A1384 45p multi   7.00 7.00

Susana Dalmás (1948-2012), Politician A1385

Perf. 12¾x12½
2013, Sept. 26   **Litho.**
2441 A1385 15p multi   2.25 2.25

Tango Heritage A1386

No. 2442: a, Bandoneon. b, Musician playing violin and Romeo Gavioli (1913-57), singer. c, Microphone and Carlos Roldán (1913-73), singer.

Perf. 12½x12¾

2013, Sept. 26		Litho.	
2442	Horiz. strip of 3	24.00	24.00
a.-c.	A1386 45p Any single	8.00	8.00

Association of Chemists and Pharmacists of Uruguay, 125th Anniv. — A1387

Perf. 12¾x12½

2013, Sept. 27		Litho.	
2443	A1387 15p multi	2.25	2.25

Montevideo, 2013 Ibero-American Cultural Capital — A1388

No. 2444: a, Eduardo Galeano, writer. b, Daniel Viglietti, musician. c, Ruben Rada, musician. d, Sara Nieto, ballerina.

2013, Oct. 2	Litho.	**Perf. 12¾x12½**	
2444	Horiz. strip of 4	9.50	9.50
a.-d.	A1388 15p Any single	2.25	2.25
e.	Booklet pane of 4, #2444a-2444d	9.50	—
	Complete booklet, #2444e	9.50	

The Annunciation of Sarah, Painting by José Gurvich — A1389

2013, Oct. 29	Litho.	**Perf. 12½x12¾**	
2445	A1389 45p multi	5.50	5.50

Diplomatic relations between Uruguay and Israel, 65th anniv. See Israel No. 1989.

SODRE Juvenile Orchestra — A1390

No. 2446: a, Child's legs, French horn. b, Violin and bow.

2013, Nov. 4	Litho.	**Perf. 12¾x12½**	
2446	A1390 15p Horiz. pair, #a-b	4.50	4.50

Internet and Integrated Systems A1391

2013, Nov. 7	Litho.	**Perf. 12¾x12½**	
2447	A1391 45p multi	5.50	5.50

Exports — A1392

No. 2448: a, 15p, Wine grapes. b, 15p, Sides of beef. c, 45p, Wine bottle and barrels. d, 45p, Dish of beef and vegetables.

2013, Nov. 8	Litho.	**Perf. 12½x12¾**	
2448	A1392	Block of 4, #a-d	20.00 20.00

Souvenir Sheet

Brasiliana 2013 Intl. Philatelic Exhibition, Rio de Janeiro — A1393

No. 2449 — Brasiliana 2013 emblem and illustrations from song lyrics by Vinicius de Moraes (1913-80): a, 15p, Young man and woman (25x35mm). b, 45p, Woman with head covering (42x31mm).

Perf. 12, 12½x12¾ (45p)

2013, Nov. 20		Litho.	
2449	A1393	Sheet of 2, #a-b	9.50 9.50

Christmas A1394

Perf. 12½x12¾

2013, Nov. 22		Litho.	
2450	A1394 15p multi	2.25	2.25

Wildlife — A1395

No. 2451: a, Calidris canutus rufa. b, Chelonia mydas.

2013, Dec. 4	Litho.	**Perf. 12¾x12½**	
2451	A1395 15p Horiz. pair, #a-b	5.00	5.00

Printed in sheets containing 4 pairs and 5 labels.

High-Speed Ferry Francisco — A1396

2013, Dec. 5	Litho.	**Perf. 12**	
2452	A1396 45p multi	5.50	5.50

Vo Nguyen Giáp (1911-2013), Vietnamese General — A1397

Perf. 12¾x12½

2013, Dec. 10		Litho.	
2453	A1397 45p multi	5.50	5.50

Diplomatic relations between Uruguay and Viet Nam, 20th anniv.

Rampla Juniors Soccer Team, Cent. A1398

Perf. 12½x12¾

2013, Dec. 11		Litho.	
2454	A1398 15p multi	2.25	2.25

Return to Uruguay of Children of Exiles, 30th Anniv. — A1399

2013, Dec. 17	Litho.	**Die Cut**	
	Self-Adhesive		
2455	A1399 20p multi	3.25	3.25

Campaign Against Discrimination A1400

Perf. 12¾x12½

2013, Dec. 19		Litho.	
2456	A1400 45p multi	5.50	5.50

America issue.

New Year 2014 (Year of the Horse) — A1401

2014, Jan. 31	Litho.	**Perf. 12¾x12½**	
2457	A1401 15p multi	2.25	2.25

Carnaval Costume A1402

Perf. 12¾x12½

2014, Feb. 25		Litho.	
2458	A1402 15p multi	2.25	2.25

Hugo Chávez (1954-2013), President of Venezuela — A1403

No. 2459 — Chávez: a, 15p, Waving. b, 45p, Holding map of South America.

2014, Mar. 5	Litho.	**Perf. 12½x12¾**	
2459	A1403	Horiz. pair, #a-b	7.50 7.50

Florida Infantry Battalion No. 1, 185th Anniv. A1404

2014, Mar. 6	Litho.	**Perf. 12½x12¾**	
2460	A1404 15p multi	2.00	2.00

Luisa Cuesta, Leader in Mothers and Relatives of Disappeared Uruguayans Movement — A1405

2014, Mar. 7	Litho.	**Perf. 12½x12¾**	
2461	A1405 15p multi	1.75	1.75

General José Gervasio Artigas (1764-1850) and Quotation A1406

Artigas and quotation starting with: 1p, "Sean los orientales. . ." 10p, "Que los Más infelices. . ." 15p, "La libertad de América. . ." 30p, "La causa. . ." 50p, "Nada podemos esperar. . ." 100p, "Todas las provincias. . ."

2014		Litho.	**Die Cut**	
		Self-Adhesive		
2462	A1406	1p multi	.30	.30
2463	A1406	10p multi	1.50	1.50
2464	A1406	15p multi	2.25	2.25
2465	A1406	30p multi	2.60	2.60
2466	A1406	50p multi	7.50	7.50
2467	A1406	100p multi	15.00	15.00
	Nos. 2462-2467 (6)		29.15	29.15

Issued: 1p, 6/12; 10p, 6/2; 15p, 11/19; 30p, 50p, 3/7; 100p, 4/7. See No. B14.

Uruguayan Transparency Law — A1407

2014, Apr. 10 Litho. Perf. 12¾x12½
2468 A1407 15p multi 2.00 2.00

South American Athletic Institution, Cent. — A1408

2014, Apr. 22 Litho. Perf. 12¾x12½
2469 A1408 15p multi 2.00 2.00
No. 2469 printed in sheets of 8 + central label.

Section 20 of the Communist Party of Uruguay National Historical Monument — A1409

2014, Apr. 23 Litho. Perf. 12½x12¾
2470 A1409 15p multi 2.00 2.00

University Sports League, Cent. A1410

2014, May 5 Litho. Perf. 12½x12¾
2471 A1410 15p multi 2.00 2.00
No. 2471 was printed in sheets of 8 + central label.

Uruguay Society of Architects, Cent. — A1411

2014, May 22 Litho. Perf. 12¾x12½
2472 A1411 15p multi 2.00 2.00

Souvenir Sheet

Alcides Ghiggia, Soccer Player — A1412

No. 2473 — Uruguayan flag and: a, Ghiggia playing soccer. b, Ghiggia in 2014.

2014, May 28 Litho. Perf. 12¾x12½
2473 A1412 15p Sheet of 2, #a-b 4.50 4.50

Souvenir Sheet

Battle of Buceo, 200th Anniv. — A1413

2014, June 4 Litho. Perf. 12½x12¾
2474 A1413 45p multi 5.50 5.50

Mafalda, Comic Strip by Quino, 50th Anniv. — A1414

No. 2475 — Mafalda and: a, 15p, Globe wrapped in bandage. b, 45p, Globe with banners.

2014, June 17 Litho. Perf. 12
2475 A1414 Pair, #a-b 7.50 7.50
No. 2475 was printed in sheets containing three pairs.

Paintings — A1415

No. 2476: a, El Pozo, by Ernesto Laroche (1879-1940). b, Portrait of María de Castro de Figari, by Pedro Blanes Viale (1879-1926).

2014, July 15 Litho. Perf. 12¾x12½
2476 A1415 15p Horiz. pair, #a-b 4.00 4.00

Tranqueras, Cent. — A1416

2014, July 22 Litho. Perf. 12½x12¾
2477 A1416 15p multi 2.00 2.00

Famous People — A1417

Designs: No. 2478, 15p, Federico García Vigil, conductor. No. 2479, 15p, Cristina Morán, actress.

Perf. 12¾x12½
2014, Aug. 13 Litho.
2478-2479 A1417 Set of 2 4.00 4.00

Second Intl. Decade of the World's Indigenous Peoples — A1418

2014, Sept. 2 Litho. Perf. 12¾x12½
2480 A1418 45p multi 5.50 5.50

Miniature Sheet

A1419

No. 2481: a, 15p, La Estanzuela Experimental Station, cent. (scientist and building). b, 15p, Int'l. Day of Biodiversity (zebra and flamingo). c, 15p, World Environment Day (butterfly on flower). d, 45p, Intl. Year of Family Farming.

Perf. 12½x12¾
2014, Sept. 16 Litho.
2481 A1419 Sheet of 4, #a-d 12.00 12.00

People Doing Community Service — A1420

Perf. 12½x12¾
2014, Sept. 22 Litho.
2482 A1420 15p multi 2.00 2.00

Pinnipeds — A1421

No. 2483 — Emblem of Chile Philatelic Society and: a, Arctocephalus australis. b, Otaria flavescens.

Perf. 12½x12¾
2014, Sept. 29 Litho.
2483 A1421 15p Pair, #a-b 3.50 3.50

Diplomatic Relations Between Uruguay and South Korea, 50th Anniv. — A1422

No. 2484 — Dancers and drummers from: a, 15p, Uruguay. b, 45p, South Korea.

2014, Oct. 7 Litho. Perf. 12½x12¾
2484 A1422 Horiz. pair, #a-b 7.00 7.00
See South Korea Nos. 2433-2434.

Visit of Charles de Gaulle to Uruguay, 50th Anniv. — A1423

Uruguayan and French flags, de Gaulle and: 15p, Buildings. 45p, Ship.

2014, Oct. 9 Litho. Perf. 12¾x12½
2485-2486 A1423 Set of 2 7.50 7.50
Nos. 2485-2486 were printed in sheets of 8 containing 4 of each stamp.

Souvenir Sheet

Diplomatic Relations Between Uruguay and Nicaragua — A1424

2014, Oct. 10 Litho. Perf. 12¾x12½
2487 A1424 45p multi 5.50 5.50

Souvenir Sheet

Anniversaries of Parliamentary Organizations — A1425

No. 2488: a, 15p, Interparliamentary Union, 125th anniv. b, 45p, Latin American Parliament, 50th anniv.

2014, Oct. 15 Litho. Perf. 12¾x12½
2488 A1425 Sheet of 2, #a-b 7.50 7.50

General José Gervasio Artigas (1764-1850) and Quotation A1426

Artigas and quotation starting with: C, "Sólo aspiro . . ." S, "Mi autoridad. . ."

2014, Nov. 1   Litho.   Die Cut

Self-Adhesive

2489	A1426	C multi	2.50	2.50
2490	A1426	S multi	7.50	7.50
a.	Dated "2015"		5.00	5.00
b.	Dated "2016"		4.25	4.25

On day of issue, No. 2489 sold for 15p and No. 2490 sold for 60p.
Issued: No. 2490a, 11/23/15.

Fauna — A1427

Designs: No. 2491, 15p, Melanophryniscus sanmartini. No. 2492, 15p, Desmodus rotundus.

2014, Nov. 5   Litho.   Perf. 12¾x12½

2491-2492	A1427	Set of 2	3.50	3.50

Nos. 2491-2492 were printed in sheets of 8 containing 4 of each stamp.

Christmas
A1428

Perf. 12¾x12½

2014, Nov. 12   Litho.

2493	A1428	15p multi	2.00	2.00

Silvio B. Previale Intl. Accordion Festival, Salto — A1429

Perf. 12¾x12½

2014, Nov. 14   Litho.

2494	A1429	15p multi	2.00	2.00

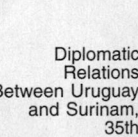

Diplomatic Relations Between Uruguay and Surinam, 35th Anniv. — A1430

2014, Dec. 9   Litho.   Perf. 12¾x12½

2495	A1430	50p multi	6.50	6.50

Campaign Against Discrimination Towards Indigenous People — A1431

2014, Dec. 9   Litho.   Perf. 12

2496	A1431	50p multi	6.50	6.50

Ana Josefa Barbera, 19th Cent. Philanthropist A1432

Perf. 12¾x12½

2014, Dec. 12   Litho.

2497	A1432	15p multi	2.00	2.00

Closure of Auschwitz Concentration Camp, 70th Anniv. — A1433

No. 2498: a, 15p, Ana Benkel de Vinocur (1926-2006), author and survivor of Auschwitz. b, 50p, Tracks leadting to Auschwitz gate, barbed wire.

2015, Jan. 28   Litho.   Perf. 12½x12¾

2498	A1433	Pair, #a-b	10.00	10.00

Battle of Paysandú, 150th Anniv. — A1434

No. 2499: a, 15p, Paysandú Basílica. b, 50p, Corvette Parnahyba.

2015, Feb. 6   Litho.   Perf. 12¾x12½

2499	A1434	Horiz. pair, #a-b	8.50	8.50

URUJAM 2015 Intl. Scout Jamboree, Las Cañas A1435

2015, Feb. 6   Litho.   Perf. 12½x12¾

2500	A1435	50p multi	8.00	8.00

Liverpool Soccer Team of Uruguay, Cent. — A1436

Perf. 12¾x12½

2015, Feb. 10   Litho.

2501	A1436	15p multi	2.00	2.00

Carnaval
A1437

Perf. 12½x12¾

2015, Feb. 11   Litho.

2502	A1437	15p multi	2.00	2.00

New Year 2015 (Year of the Goat) — A1438

Perf. 12¾x12½

2015, Feb. 19   Litho.

2503	A1438	15p multi	2.00	2.00

Prof. Belela Herrera, Vice Chancellor of Uruguay A1439

2015, Mar. 6   Litho.   Perf. 12½x12¾

2504	A1439	15p multi	2.00	2.00

Sport Federation Centenaries — A1440

No. 2505 — Centenary of: a, Uruguayan Volleyball Federation. b, Uruguayan Basketball Federation.

Perf. 12½x12¾

2015, Mar. 18   Litho.

2505	A1440	15p Horiz. pair, #a-b	3.75	3.75

Souvenir Sheet

Armenian Genocide, Cent. — A1441

2015, Apr. 7   Litho.   Perf. 12¾x12½

2506	A1441	50p multi	6.00	6.00

Elevation of Montevideo Archbishop Daniel Sturla to Cardinal — A1442

2015, Apr. 21   Litho.   Perf. 12¾x12½

2507	A1442	50p multi	7.00	7.00
a.	Souvenir sheet of 1		7.00	7.00

No. 2507 was printed in sheets of 5.

General José Gervasio Artigas (1764-1850) A1443

Serpentine Die Cut 9x9¾

2015   Self-Adhesive   Litho.

2508	A1443	3p purple & multi	.25	.25
2509	A1443	5p red org & multi	.35	.35
2510	A1443	10p cerise & multi	.70	.70
2511	A1443	15p blue & multi	1.10	1.10
2512	A1443	20p org red & multi	1.50	1.50
2513	A1443	30p grn & multi	2.25	2.25
	Nos. 2508-2513 (6)		6.15	6.15

Issued: 3p, 5/5; 5p, 7/10; 10p, 9/4; 15p, 8/20; 20p, 5/20; 30p, 5/8.

Miniature Sheet

Wetlands Fauna — A1444

No. 2514: a, Amblyramphus holosericus. b, Rynchops niger intercedens. c, Phoenicopterus chilensis. d, Egretta thula. e, Theristicus caerulescens. f, Hydrochoerus hydrochaeris. g, Xanthopsar flavus. h, Philodryas aestiva. i, Neohelice granulatus. j, Melanophryniscus montevidensis.

2015, June 5   Litho.   Perf. 12½x12¾

2514	A1444	15p Sheet of 10, #a-j, + 3 labels	11.00	11.00

12th Meeting of the Conference of the Parties to the Ramsar Convention on Wetlands, Punta del Este.

José Luis Massera (1915-2002), Mathematician — A1445

2015, June 8   Litho.   Perf. 12½x12¾

2515	A1445	15p multi	1.10	1.10

Miniature Sheet

International Telecommunication
Union, 150th Anniv. — A1446

No. 2516: a, AntelSat, first Uruguayan satellite and ITU 150th anniv. emblem. b, AntelSat
el primer satélite uruguayo.

Perf. 12½x12¾

2015, June 18   Litho.
2516 A1446   Sheet of 8,
                       #2516b, 7
                       #2516a, + cen-
                       tral label   11.50 11.50
a.   15p multi   1.10 1.10
b.   50p multi   3.75 3.75

Technological Laboratory of Uruguay,
50th Anniv. — A1447

2015, July 8   Litho.   **Perf. 12½x12¾**
2517 A1447 15p multi   1.10 1.10

Souvenir Sheet

Diplomatic Relations Between Uruguay
and Egypt, 83rd Anniv. — A1448

No. 2518: a, 15p, Sistrum. b, 50p, Funerary
mask of Eso-Eris mummy.

2015, July 23 Litho. **Perf. 12¾x12½**
2518 A1448 Sheet of 2, #a-b   4.75 4.75

Grand
Orient of
Uruguay,
25th
Anniv.
A1449

Perf. 12½x12¾

2015, Aug. 17   Litho.
2519 A1449 15p multi   1.10 1.10

Paintings — A1450

No. 2520: a, The Red Shawl, by Carlos
Federico Sáez (1878-1901) b, Eros and
Psyche, by Anhelo Hernández (1922-2010).

Perf. 12¾x12½

2015, Aug. 27   Litho.
2520 A1450 15p Horiz. pair, #a-b 2.10 2.10

St. John
Bosco
(1815-88)
A1451

2015, Sept. 8   Litho.   **Perf. 12½x12¾**
2521 A1451 15p multi   1.10 1.10

Democracy in Uruguay, 30th
Anniv. — A1452

Perf. 12½x12¾

2015, Sept. 14   Litho.
2522 A1452 15p multi   1.10 1.10

Galán y
Rocha
Hospital,
Paysandú,
Cent.
A1453

Perf. 12½x12¾

2015, Sept. 24   Litho.
2523 A1453 15p multi   1.10 1.10

Miniature Sheet

Owls — A1454

No. 2524: a, Aegolius harrisii. b, Bubo
virginianus. c, Athene cunicularia. d, Megas-
cops choliba. e, Tyto alba. f, Asio flammeus. g,
Glaucidium brasilianum. h, Asio clamator.

Perf. 12½x12¾

2015, Sept. 30   Litho.
2524 A1454 15p Sheet of 8, #a-h 8.25 8.25

Carrasco International Airport,
Montevideo — A1455

2015, Oct. 2   Litho.   **Perf. 12**
2525 A1455 15p multi   1.10 1.10

Provisional Regulations of the Eastern
Province to Promote the Campaign and
Security of its Landowners — A1456

2015, Oct. 9   Litho.   **Perf. 12**
2526 A1456 15p multi   1.10 1.10

No. 2526 was printed in sheets of 10 + central label.

United Nations, 70th Anniv. — A1457

No. 2527 — Uruguayan United Nations
Peacekeeper with child in: a, 15p, Congo. b,
50p, Haiti.

2015, Oct. 20   Litho.   **Perf. 12**
2527 A1457 Horiz. pair, #a-b   4.50 4.50

Famous
People — A1458

Designs: No. 2528, 15p, Prof. Daniel Vidart,
anthropologist. No. 2529, 15p, Ida Holz, computer engineer.

2015, Oct. 21 Litho. **Perf. 12¾x12½**
2528-2529 A1458 Set of 2   2.10 2.10

Dropping of Atomic Bombs on
Hiroshima and Nagasaki, 70th
Anniv. — A1459

No. 2530: a, Peace Statue, Nagasaki. b,
Atomic Bomb Dome, Hiroshima.

2015, Oct. 23   Litho.   **Perf. 12**
2530 A1459 50p Pair, #a-b   6.75 6.75

Energy
Balance
in
Uruguay,
50th
Anniv.
A1460

No. 2531: a, Water splash, wind generator,
refinery, emblem of Ministry of Industry,
Energy and Mining. b, Solar panels, sunflower,
bar graph.

2015, Nov. 11   Litho.   **Perf. 12**
2531 A1460 20p Vert. pair, #a-b 2.75 2.75

Eight Hour Work Day Law,
Cent. — A1461

2015, Nov. 17   Litho.   **Perf. 12**
2532 A1461 20p multi   1.40 1.40

Maria del Pilar,
Afro-Uruguayan
Woman Freed in
1815 — A1462

2015, Dec. 3   Litho.   **Perf. 12**
2533 A1462 20p multi   1.40 1.40

International Year
of Soils — A1463

2015, Dec. 3   Litho.   **Perf. 12**
2534 A1463 60p multi   4.00 4.00

Cruise Ships and Tourist
Sites — A1464

No. 2535: a, MS Zaandam, Calle de los
Suspiros, Colonia del Sacramento. b, MSC
Splendida, Estadio Centenario, Montevideo. c,
Costa Favolosa, Cabo Polonio Lighthouse. d,
Norwegian Sun, Port of Punta del Este.

2015, Dec. 4   Litho.   **Perf. 12**
2535 A1464 20p Block of 4, #a-d 5.50 5.50

Campaign Against Human Trafficking — A1465

2015, Dec. 7   **Litho.**   *Perf. 12*
2536 A1465 60p multi   4.00 4.00

America Issue.

Tourist Sites in Salto — A1466

Designs: No. 2537, 20p, Hot Springs of Arapey. No. 2538, 20p, Nuestra Señora del Carmen Church, Campanario.

Perf. 12¾x12½
2015, Dec. 14   **Litho.**
2537-2538 A1466   Set of 2   2.75 2.75

Nos. 2537-2538 were printed in sheets of 8 containing four of each stamp + central label.

Christmas A1467

2015, Dec. 15   **Litho.**   *Perf. 12*
2539 A1467 20p multi   1.40 1.40

Souvenir Sheet

Tango Music Personalities — A1468

No. 2540: a, Horacio Ferrer (1933-2014), composer. b, Astor Piazzolla (1921-92), bandoneon player.

Perf. 12½x12¾
2015, Dec. 22   **Litho.**
2540 A1468 60p Sheet of 2, #a-b 8.00 8.00

Souvenir Sheet

International Year of Light — A1469

Perf. 12½x12¾
2015, Dec. 23   **Litho.**
2541 A1469 60p multi   4.00 4.00

New Year 2016 (Year of the Monkey) — A1470

2016, Jan. 28   **Litho.**   *Perf. 12¾x12½*
2542 A1470 20p multi   1.40 1.40

Poster for 1915-16 Summer Festival and Carnival A1471

2016, Feb. 19   **Litho.**   *Perf. 12*
2543 A1471 20p multi   1.25 1.25

No. 2543 was printed in sheets of 5 + label.

Souvenir Sheet

Tacuarembo Gaucho Festival, 30th Anniv. — A1472

2016, Mar. 4   **Litho.**   *Perf. 12¾x12½*
2544 A1472 20p multi   1.25 1.25

Intl. Women's Day — A1473

No. 2545: a, Enriqueta Compte y Riqué (1866-1949), founder of first South American kindergarten. b, Female rider in Lancers of Aparicio. c, State Commitment to End Gender-based Violence.

2016, Mar. 8   **Litho.**   *Perf. 12¾x12½*
2545 A1473 20p Strip of 3, #a-c 3.75 3.75

Police Women — A1474

2016, Mar. 11   **Litho.**   *Perf. 12*
2546 A1474 20p multi   1.25 1.25

Greek Community in Uruguay, Cent. — A1475

Perf. 12½x12¾
2016, Mar. 16   **Litho.**
2547 A1475 20p multi   1.25 1.25

Souvenir Sheet

Eighth Latin American Congress for the Blind, Montevideo — A1476

Litho., Sheet Margin Litho. & Embossed
2016, Apr. 20   *Perf. 12½x12¾*
2548 A1476 20p multi   1.25 1.25

Treaty of Asunción, 25th Anniv. A1477

2016, Apr. 25   **Litho.**   *Perf. 12*
2549 A1477 60p multi   4.00 4.00

No. 2549 was printed in sheets of 24 + label.

Souvenir Sheet

William Shakespeare (1564-1616), Writer — A1478

2016, Apr. 28   **Litho.**   *Perf. 12¾x12½*
2550 A1478 60p multi   4.00 4.00

International Year of Pulses — A1479

2016, May 20   **Litho.**   *Perf. 12¾x12½*
2551 A1479 60p multi   4.00 4.00

Dámaso Antonio Larrañaga (1771-1848), Founder of National Library — A1480

2016, May 26   **Litho.**   *Perf. 12½x12¾*
2552 A1480 20p multi   1.40 1.40

National Library, 200th anniv. No. 2552 was printed in sheets of 8 + central label.

General José Gervasio Artigas (1764-1850) A1481

Serpentine Die Cut 9¾x9
2016   **Self-Adhesive**   **Litho.**
        Portrait Color

2553	A1481	20p green	1.40	1.40
a.		Dated "2017"	1.50	1.50
b.		Dated "2018"	1.40	1.40
2554	A1481	30p blue	2.00	2.00
2555	A1481	50p red	3.25	3.25
a.		Dated "2017"	3.50	3.50
b.		Dated "2018"	3.50	3.50
2556	A1481	60p yellow	4.00	4.00
2557	A1481	200p purple	13.00	13.00
		Nos. 2553-2557 (5)	23.65	23.65

Issued: 20p, 50p, 5/30; 30p, 60p, 6/6; 200p, 6/14; No. 2553a, 1/27/17; No. 2555a, 3/24/17. Nos. 2553b, 2555a, 3/23/18. See Nos. 2586-2588, 2622-2624, 2649-2650.

Souvenir Sheet

Naval Oceanographic, Hydrographic and Meteorological Service, Cent. — A1482

2016, May 31   **Litho.**   *Perf. 12½x12¾*
2558 A1482 20p multi   1.40 1.40

Souvenir Sheet

Uruguayan Mission to Rescue Ernest Shackleton Expedition on Elephant Island, Cent. — A1483

No. 2559: a, Lieutenant Ruperto Elichiribehety (1888-1929), rescue mission leader, and crew. b, Mirounga leonina. c, Fishing boat Instituto No. 1.

Perf. 12½x12¾
2016, June 10   **Litho.**
2559 A1483 20p Sheet of 3, #a-c 4.00 4.00

Symphony
Orchestra of
Official Service of
Broadcasting,
Television and
Entertainment,
85th
Anniv. — A1484

2016, June 20   **Litho.**   **Perf. 12**
2560 A1484 20p multi   1.40 1.40

Copa América Soccer Championships,
Cent. — A1485

No. 2561: a, Héctor Rivadavia Gómez
(1880-1931), director of South American Soccer Federation. b, Players from 1916 Uruguay
championship team.

2016, June 24   **Litho.**   **Perf. 12**
2561 A1485 20p Pair, #a-b   2.75 2.75

Diplomatic
Relations
Between
Uruguay
and
Germany,
Cent.
A1486

No. 2562 — Flags of Uruguay and Germany
and: a, Uruguayan Legislative Palace. b, German Reichstag.

2016, July 14 Litho. Perf. 12½x12¾
2562   Horiz. pair + central la-
         bel   5.50 5.50
  a. A1486 20p multi   1.40 1.40
  b. A1486 60p multi   4.00 4.00
    Printed in sheets containing 3 each Nos.
2562a-2562b and 3 labels.

University of the Republic Engineering
Faculty, Cent. — A1487

2016, July 20   **Litho.**   **Perf. 12**
2563 A1487 20p multi   1.40 1.40

National Ports Administration,
Cent. — A1488

2016, July 21 Litho. Perf. 12½x12¾
2564 A1488 20p multi   1.40 1.40
    No. 2564 was printed in sheets of 8 + central label.

National
Party,
180th
Anniv.
A1489

Perf. 12½x12¾
2016, Aug. 10   **Litho.**
2565 A1489 20p multi   1.40 1.40

2016 Summer Olympics, Rio de
Janeiro — A1490

No. 2566: a, Tennis. b, Rowing. c, Marathon.
d, Equestrian.

2016, Aug. 12   **Litho.**   **Perf. 12**
2566 A1490 20p Block or vert.
         strip of 4, #a-d   5.75 5.75

El Cuello Azul II,
Painting by
Gladys Afamado
A1491

2016, Aug. 31   **Litho.**   **Perf. 12**
2567 A1491 20p multi   1.40 1.40

Trees and Blossoms — A1492

No. 2568: a, Jacaranda mimosifolia. b, Handroanthus impetiginosus. c, Erythrina cristagalli. d, Peltophorum dubium.

2016, Sept. 21   **Litho.**   **Perf. 12**
2568 A1492 20p Block or horiz.
         strip of 4, #a-d   5.75 5.75
    Printed in sheets of 8 (2 each Nos. 2568a-2568d), + 4 labels.

Miniature Sheet

Stained-Glass Windows From José
Pedro Varela, Pedagogical
Museum — A1493

No. 2569: a, Fisica (Physics). b, Pedagogia
(Pedagogy). c, Historia (History). d, Higiene
(Hygiene). e, Astronomia (Astronomy). f,
Quimica (Chemistry).

2016, Sept. 22   **Litho.**   **Perf. 12**
2569 A1493 20p Sheet of 6, #a-f   8.50 8.50
    Heritage Day — Public Education.

Souvenir Sheet

Garcilaso de la Vega (1539-1616),
Historian — A1494

Perf. 12¾x12½
2016, Sept. 28   **Litho.**
2570 A1494 60p multi   4.25 4.25

Butterflies
A1495

No. 2571: a, Junonia genovesa hilaris. b,
Mechanitis lysimnia lysimnia. c, Choricea
licursis.

2016, Oct. 7 Litho. Perf. 12½x12¾
2571   Strip of 3   4.25 4.25
  a.-c. A1495 20p Any single   1.40 1.40
    Printed in sheets of 9 (3 each #2571a-
2571c) + 3 labels.

Souvenir Sheet

Miguel de Cervantes (1547-1616),
Writer — A1496

2016, Oct. 12 Litho. Perf. 12¾x12½
2572 A1496 60p multi   4.25 4.25

Banco
Republica,
120th
Anniv.
A1497

2016, Oct. 21 Litho. Perf. 12½x12¾
2573 A1497 20p multi   1.40 1.40
    No. 2573 was printed in sheets of 6 + central label.

Río Negro Department
Tourism — A1498

Designs: No. 2574, 20p, Cerdocyon thous.
No. 2575, 20p, Machinery in Anglo Meat Packing Plant UNESCO World Heritage Site.

Perf. 12½x12¾
2016, Nov. 16   **Litho.**
2574-2575 A1498   Set of 2   2.75 2.75
    Nos. 2474-2475 were printed together in
sheets containing four of each stamp.

Christmas
A1499

2016, Nov. 28   **Litho.**   **Perf. 12**
2576 A1499 20p multi   1.40 1.40

Tourism — A1500

No. 2577 — Cruise ships and tourist attractions: a, Crystal Serenity and Phleocryptes
melanops. b, Crown Princess and canoe on
lake. c, Fram and blind man with guide dog. d,
Prinsendam and Palacio Salvo, Montevideo.

2016, Dec. 1   **Litho.**   **Perf. 12**
2577 A1500 20p Block or horiz.
         strip of 4, #a-d   5.50 5.50

Antonio Sayago (d. 1902), Afro-Uruguayan Musician — A1501

2016, Dec. 2 Litho. Perf. 12½x12¾
2578 A1501 20p multi 1.40 1.40

Líber Seregni (1916-2004), Military Officer and Politician — A1502

No. 2579: a, Color photograph of Seregni. b, Drawing of Seregni holding loudspeaker. c, Sepia photograph of Seregni.

Perf. 12¾x12½
2016, Dec. 12 Litho.
2579 Booklet pane of 3 5.00 —
a.-c. A1502 20p Any single 1.60 1.60
Complete booklet, #2579 5.00

Complete booklet sold for 70p.

Steam Plant, Aguas Corrientes, Coat of Arms of Canelones Deparatment and Map of Uruguay — A1503

Church, Villa Soriano, Coat of Arms of Soriano Deparatment and Map of Uruguay — A1504

San Carlos Bull Ring, Colonia del Sacramento, Coat of Arms of Colonia Deparatment and Map of Uruguay — A1505

2016 Litho. Perf. 12½x12¾
2580 A1503 20p multi 1.40 1.40
2581 A1504 20p multi 1.40 1.40
2582 A1505 20p multi 1.40 1.40
Nos. 2580-2582 (3) 4.20 4.20
Issued: No. 2580, 12/13; Nos. 2581-2582, 12/15.

Olga Delgrossi, Tango Singer A1506

Perf. 12½x12¾
2016, Dec. 15 Litho.
2583 A1506 20p multi 1.40 1.40

Ida Vitale, Poet — A1507

Perf. 12¾x12½
2016, Dec. 23 Litho.
2584 A1507 20p multi 1.40 1.40

New Year 2017 (Year of the Rooster) A1508

2017, Jan. 22 Litho. Perf. 12½x12¾
2585 A1508 20p multi 1.50 1.50

Artigas Type of 2016
Serpentine Die Cut 9¾x9
2017 Self-Adhesive Litho.
Dated "2017"
Portrait Color
2586 A1481 3p blue .25 .25
2587 A1481 5p orange .35 .35
a. Dated "2018" .35 .35
2588 A1481 10p rose .70 .70
a. Dated "2018" .70 .70
Nos. 2586-2588 (3) 1.30 1.30
Issued: 3p, 5p, 2/2; 10p, 2/14; No. 2587a, 12/3/18; No. 2588a, 4/5/18.

Souvenir Sheet

Diplomatic Relations Between Uruguay and Russia, 160th Anniv. — A1509

No. 2589 — Decorated musical insturments: a, Drums, Uruguay. b, Balalaika, Russia.

Perf. 12¾x12½
2017, Feb. 16 Litho.
2589 A1509 Sheet of 2 6.25 6.25
a. 20p multi 1.50 1.50
b. 65p multi 4.75 4.75

Candombe, Painting by Carlos Páez Vilaró — A1510

Perf. 12½x12¾
2017, Feb. 24 Litho.
2590 A1510 20p multi 1.50 1.50

Friends and Parents of the Disabled of Tacuarembó (APADISTA), 25th Anniv. — A1511

2017, Mar. 8 Litho. Perf. 12
2591 A1511 20p multi 1.40 1.40

Juana de Ibarbourou (1892-1979), Poet — A1512

2017, Mar. 8 Litho. Perf. 12¾x12½
2592 A1512 20p multi 1.40 1.40
No. 2592 was printed in sheets of 8 + central label.

Souvenir Sheet

Asteroids, Comets and Meteors International Conference, Montevideo — A1513

No. 2593: a, Dwarf planet Ceres. b, Comet CG67P. c, Pluto.

2017, Apr. 9 Litho. Perf. 12½x12¾
2593 A1513 20p Sheet of 3, #a-c 4.25 4.25

Club Atlético Progreso Soccer Team, Cent. A1514

2017, Apr. 27 Litho. Perf. 12½x12¾
2594 A1514 20p multi 1.40 1.40
No. 2594 was printed in sheets of 8 + central label.

Lions Clubs International, Cent. — A1515

2017, Apr. 28 Litho. Perf. 12½x12¾
2595 A1515 65p multi 4.75 4.75

José Enrique Rodó (1871-1917), Writer — A1516

2017, May 3 Litho. Perf. 12½x12¾
2596 A1516 20p multi 1.40 1.40
No. 2596 was printed in sheets of 8 + central label.

Premiere of La Cumparsita, Tango Song by Geraldo Matos Rodríguez, Cent. — A1517

2017, May 8 Litho. Perf. 12¾x12½
2597 A1517 65p multi 4.75 4.75
a. Souvenir sheet of 1 4.75 4.75

Commission for the Eradication of Unhealthy Rural Housing (MEVIR), 50th Anniv. — A1518

2017, May 17 Litho. Perf. 12½x12¾
2598 A1518 20p multi 1.40 1.40

Canadian Confederation, 150th Anniv. — A1519

No. 2599: a, Moraine Lake, Alberta. b, Inukshuk.

Perf. 12½x12¾
2017, June 27 Litho.
2599 Horiz. pair + central label 6.25 6.25
a. A1519 20p multi 1.40 1.40
b. A1519 65p multi 4.75 4.75

Souvenir Sheet

Central Bank of Uruguay, 50th Anniv. — A1520

No. 2600 — 2017 Central Bank of Uruguay 2000-peso coin: a, 20p, Obverse. b, 65p, Reverse.

Litho. & Embossed
2017, July 7 Perf. 12¾x12½
2600 A1520 Sheet of 2, #a-b 6.25 6.25

Arrival in Uruguay of Mother Francisca Rubatto (1844-1904), Founder of Capuchin Sisters of Mother Rubatto, 125th Anniv. — A1521

2017, Aug. 8   Litho.   Perf. 12½x12¾
2601 A1521 20p multi   1.40 1.40

Diplomatic Relations Between Uruguay and Belarus, 25th Anniv. — A1522

No. 2602: a, 20p, Solís Theater, Montevideo. b, 65p, Bolshoi Theater of Belarus, Minsk.

2017, Sept. 7   Litho.   Perf. 12¾x12½
2602 A1522   Horiz. pair, #a-b, +
              central label   6.00 6.00
   See Belarus No. 1070.

Banco de Previsión Social (Social Security Institute), 50th Anniv. A1523

Perf. 12½x12¾
2017, Sept. 16   **Litho.**
2603 A1523 20p multi   1.40 1.40

2017 World Chess Youth Championships, Montevideo A1524

Perf. 12¾x12½
2017, Sept. 25   **Litho.**
2604 A1524 65p multi   4.50 4.50

Cooperation and Friendship Between Uruguay and the United States, 150th Anniv. — A1525

2017, Oct. 2   Litho.   Perf. 12½x12¾
2605 A1525 65p multi   4.50 4.50

1910 Beyer Peacock Class N3 2-6-0 Locomotive No. 120 — A1526

2017, Oct. 10   Litho.   Perf. 12½x12¾
2606 A1526 65p multi   4.50 4.50

Obdulio J. Varela (1917-96), Captain of 1950 World Cup Champion Uruguayan Soccer Team — A1527

2017, Oct. 27   Litho.   Perf. 12¾x12½
2607 A1527 20p multi   1.40 1.40

First Year of Uruguay as Associate Observer in Community of Portuguese Language Countries A1528

2017, Oct. 31   Litho.   Perf. 12¾x12½
2608 A1528 65p multi   4.50 4.50

Souvenir Sheet

Uruguayan Navy, 200th Anniv. — A1529

No. 2609: a, MBD Bo105 helicopter. b, Schooner Capitán Miranda. c, Frigate Uruguay.

Perf. 12½x12¾
2017, Nov. 13   **Litho.**
2609 A1529 20p Sheet of 3, #a-c 4.25 4.25

Universal Declaration of Democracy, 20th Anniv. — A1530

Perf. 12¾x12½
2017, Nov. 15   **Litho.**
2610 A1530 65p multi   4.50 4.50

Christmas A1531

Perf. 12¾x12½
2017, Nov. 29   **Litho.**
2611 A1531 20p multi   1.40 1.40

Gregorio, the Town Crier — A1532

2017, Dec. 4   Litho.   Perf. 12¾x12½
2612 A1532 20p multi   1.40 1.40

Forma II, by Guillermo Fernández (1928-2007) A1533

2017, Dec. 8   Litho.   Perf. 12¾x12½
2613 A1533 20p multi   1.40 1.40

Egg of Pachycymbiola Brasiliana on La Paloma Beach, Rocha — A1534

Perf. 12½x12¾
2017, Dec. 14   **Litho.**
2614 A1534 65p multi   4.50 4.50

Colonia Department Tourism — A1535

No. 2615: a, Heterothalamus alienus in Davyt Blancarena Park. b, Sailboat and parasailers near Costa del Immigrante.

Perf. 12¾x12½
2017, Dec. 18   **Litho.**
2615 A1535 20p Horiz. pair, #a-b 2.75 2.75

Uruguayan Postal Service, 190th Anniv. — A1536

No. 2616: a, Francisco de los Santos, last messenger of José Gervasio Artigas. b, Uruguay Post van.

Perf. 12½x12¾
2017, Dec. 21   **Litho.**
2616 A1536 20p Horiz. pair, #a-b 2.75 2.75

Souvenir Sheet

Diplomatic Relations Between Uruguay and People's Republic of China, 30th Anniv. — A1537

No. 2617 — Flags of Uruguay and People's Republic of China and: a, 20p, Tamandua tetradactyla (lesser anteater), Handroanthus impetiginosus. b, 65p, Ailuropoda melanoleuca (giant panda), Bambusa vulgaris.

2018, Jan. 23   Litho.   Perf. 12½x12¾
2617 A1537   Sheet of 2, #a-b   6.00 6.00

New Year 2018 (Year of the Dog) — A1538

Perf. 12¾x12½
2018, Feb. 10   **Litho.**
2618 A1538 65p multi   4.75 4.75

Carnival Costume A1539

Perf. 12¾x12½
2018, Feb. 16   **Litho.**
2619 A1539 20p multi   1.40 1.40

Gen. Victor Licandro (1918-2011) A1540

Perf. 12¾x12½
2018, Feb. 26   **Litho.**
2620 A1540 20p multi   1.40 1.40

International Women's Day — A1541

No. 2621: a, Rural woman, farm field. b, Afro-American woman, building.

2018, Mar. 8   Litho.   Perf. 12½x12¾
2621 A1541 20p Horiz. pair, #a-b 3.00 3.00

Artigas Type of 2016
Serpentine Die Cut 9¾x9
2018   **Self-Adhesive**   Litho.
Dated "2018"
Portrait Color
2622 A1481 1p gray grn .25 .25
2623 A1481 80p ol sepia 5.75 5.75
2624 A1481 100p red lilac 7.00 7.00
Nos. 2622-2624 (3) 13.00 13.00
Issued: 1p, 3/19; 80p, 4/4; 100p, 4/5.

Miniature Sheet

Tall Ships — A1542

No. 2625 — Ship and flag of: a, 20p, Gloria, Colombia. b, 20p, Cisne Branco, Brazil. c, 20p, Juan Sebastián Elcano, Spain. d, 20p, Cuauhtémoc, Mexico. e, 20p, Dr. Bernardo Houssay, Argentina. f, 20p, Libertad, Argentina. g, 20p, Simón Bolívar, Venezuela. h, 20p, Esmerelda, Chile. i, 65p, Capitán Miranda, Uruguay.

2018, Apr. 13 Litho. **Perf. 12½x12¾**
2625 A1542 Sheet of 9, #a-i 16.00 16.00

Oscar W. Tabárez, Soccer Player and Manager A1543

2018, May 4 Litho. **Perf. 12½x12¾**
2626 A1543 20p multi 1.40 1.40

Dr. Martin Luther King (1929-68), Civil Rights Leader — A1544

2018, June 7 Litho. **Perf. 12¾x12½**
2627 A1544 65p multi 4.25 4.25
No. 2627 was printed in sheets of 8 + central label.

Bid by Uruguay, Argentina and Paraguay to Host 2030 World Cup Soccer Championships — A1545

Perf. 12½x12¾
2018, June 14 Litho.
2628 A1545 20p multi 1.40 1.40
No. 2628 was printed in sheets of 5 + 4 labels.

Automobile Club of Uruguay, Cent. — A1546

No. 2629: a, 1904 Clement Bayard. b, 1948 Fordson truck. c, 1900 Delin. d, 1925 Ford Model T.

2018, July 12 Litho. **Perf. 12½x12¾**
2629 A1546 20p Block of 4, #a-d 5.25 5.25

Cry of Asencio of the Blandengues de Artigas Cavalry Regiment, Cent. — A1547

2018, July 20 Litho. **Perf. 12½x12¾**
2630 A1547 20p multi 1.40 1.40

150th Liver Transplant Performed in Uruguay — A1548

2018, July 23 Litho. **Perf. 12¾x12½**
2631 A1548 20p multi 1.40 1.40

Student Martyrs Day, 50th Anniv. A1549

Perf. 12½x12¾
2018, Aug. 14 Litho.
2632 A1549 20p multi 1.25 1.25

Heriberto P. Coates (1866-1940), Founder of Rotary Club of Montevideo, and Hotel Pyramides — A1550

Perf. 12½x12¾
2018, Aug. 17 Litho.
2633 A1550 20p multi 1.25 1.25
Rotary Club of Montevideo, cent.

Items in Uruguayan Museums — A1551

No. 2634: a, 20p, Colonial era vessel, from Antonio Taddei Museum, Canalones. b, 65p, Homage to Gardel, mural by the Gregorio Workshop, from San Gregorio de Polanco Open Air Museum of Art, Tacuarembó.

Perf. 12¾x12½
2018, Aug. 28 Litho.
2634 A1551 Horiz. pair, #a-b 5.25 5.25

San Fructuoso Cathedral, Tacuarembó, Cent. — A1552

2018, Aug. 30 Litho. **Perf. 12**
2635 A1552 20p multi 1.25 1.25

Olimpia Athletic Club, Cent. — A1553

Perf. 12¾x12½
2018, Sept. 10 Litho.
2636 A1553 20p multi 1.25 1.25
No. 2636 was printed in sheets of 8 + central label.

Abel Carlevaro Casal (1916-2001), Guitar Teacher and Composer — A1554

Perf. 12½x12¾
2018, Sept. 18 Litho.
2637 A1554 20p multi 1.25 1.25
No. 2637 was printed in sheets of 8 + central label.

Universal Declaration of Human Rights, 70th Anniv. — A1555

Perf. 12¾x12½
2018, Sept. 28 Litho.
2638 A1555 65p multi 4.00 4.00

Birds — A1556

No. 2639: a, Cathartes aura. b, Ramphastos toco.

2018, Oct. 9 Litho. **Perf. 12¾x12½**
2639 A1556 20p Horiz. pair, #a-b 2.50 2.50
Tourism in Treinta y Tres. No. 2639 was printed in sheets of 4 pairs + central label.

Souvenir Sheet

Untitled Painting by Gabriel Vuljevas — A1557

2018, Oct. 11 Litho. **Perf. 12½**
2640 A1557 65p multi 4.00 4.00
Independence of Lithuania, cent.

Vichadero, Cent. A1558

2018, Oct. 19 Litho. **Perf. 12½x12¾**
2641 A1558 20p multi 1.25 1.25

Ana Gasquen, Slave Ordered to be Freed by Gen. José Artigas in 1818 — A1559

2018, Oct. 24 Litho. **Perf. 12¾x12½**
2642 A1559 20p multi 1.25 1.25

Souvenir Sheet

National Institute of Colonization, 70th Anniv. — A1560

No. 2643: a, Man and woman in farm field. b, Farm worker, tractor, farm house, corn stalks.

2018, Oct. 31 Litho. **Perf. 12½**
2643 A1560 20p Sheet of 2, #a-b 2.50 2.50

Colorín Colorado, by Luis Alberto Solari (1918-93) A1561

2018, Nov. 5   Litho.   Perf. 12½x12¾
2644 A1561 22p multi   1.40   1.40

Miniature Sheet

Ducks — A1562

No. 2645: a, Anas bahamensis. b, Anas georgica. c, Netta peposaca. d, Anas sibilatrix.

2018, Nov. 7   Litho.   Perf. 12½x12¾
2645 A1562 22p Sheet of 4, #a-d 5.50 5.50

Mariano Mores (1918-2016), Tango Composer and Pianist — A1563

2018, Nov. 9   Litho.   Perf. 12½x12¾
2646 A1563 65p multi   4.00   4.00

Javier de Viana (1868-1926), Writer — A1564

Perf. 12¾x12½
2018, Nov. 21   Litho.
2647 A1564 22p multi   1.40   1.40

Artigas Type of 2016
Serpentine Die Cut 9¾x9
2018   Self-Adhesive   Litho.
Portrait Color
2650 A1481 22p lilac   1.40   1.40
    Issued: 22p, 12/3.

Christmas A1566

Perf. 12¾x12½
2018, Dec. 12   Litho.
2653 A1566 22p multi   1.40   1.40

America Issue — A1567

No. 2654 — Domesticated animals: a, 22p, Lamb. b, 65p, Dog.

Perf. 12½x12¾
2018, Dec. 19   Litho.
2654 A1567   Horiz. pair, #a-b   5.50 5.50

End of World War I, Cent. — A1568

Perf. 12¾x12½
2018, Dec. 21   Litho.
2655 A1568 65p multi   4.00   4.00

Souvenir Sheet

Uruguayan Diplomatic Recognition of the Palestinian Authority — A1569

2018, Dec. 31   Litho.   Perf. 12
2656 A1569 65p multi   4.00   4.00

SEMI-POSTAL STAMPS

Indigent Old Man — SP1

Unwmk.
1930, Nov. 13   Engr.   Perf. 12
B1 SP1 1c + 1c dark violet   .30   .30
B2 SP1 2c + 2c deep green   .30   .30
B3 SP1 5c + 5c red   .45   .45
B4 SP1 8c + 8c gray violet   .45   .45
    Nos. B1-B4 (4)   1.50 1.50

The surtax on these stamps was for a fund to assist the aged.
For surcharge see No. 419.

> **Catalogue values for unused stamps in this section, from this point to the end of the section, are for Never Hinged items.**

Dam, Child and Rising Sun — SP2

Wmk. 327
1959, Sept. 29   Litho.   Perf. 11½
B5 SP2 5c + 10c green & org   .25   .25
B6 SP2 10c + 10c dk bl & org   .25   .25
B7 SP2 1p + 10c purple & org   .50   .50
    Nos. B5-B7, CB1-CB2 (5)   1.80 1.80

National recovery. For surcharges see Nos. 727, Q100.

Souvenir Sheet

Taipei '96, Intl. Philatelic Exhibition — SP3

Unwmk.
1996, Oct. 21   Litho.   Perf. 12
B8   SP3 7p +3p multi   5.00 5.00

Gen. Artigas Central Railway Station, Montevideo, Cent. — SP4

a, Baldwin, 1889. b, Hudswell Clarke, 1895. c, Luis Andreoni, engineer & architect. d, Hawthorn Leslie, 1914. e, General Electric, 1954.

Perf. 12½
1997, July 15   Litho.   Unwmk.
B9   SP4 4p +1p, Strip of 5,
        #a.-e.   10.00 10.00

Diana, Princess of Wales (1961-97) — SP5

Designs: No. B10, In protective clothing. No. B11, In blue blouse. No. B12, In white.

1998, Jan. 15   Litho.   Perf. 12½
B10 SP5 2p +1p multi   1.50 1.50
B11 SP5 2p +1p multi   1.50 1.50

Souvenir Sheet
Perf. 12
B12 SP5 12p +3p multi   12.00 12.00

No. B12 contains one 35x50mm stamp.

Occupations Type of 2008
Serpentine Die Cut 11¼
2007, Nov. 18   Litho.
Self-Adhesive
B13 A1216 5p +2p Baker   .90   .90

General José Gervasio Artigas (1764-1850) and Quotation SP6

2014, Apr. 28   Litho.   Die Cut
Self-Adhesive
B14 SP6 15p+2p multi   2.50 2.50

AIR POST STAMPS

No. 91 Overprinted in Dark Blue, Red or Green

1921-22   Unwmk.   Perf. 14
C1 A38 25c bister brn (Bl)   18.00 15.00
  a.   Black overprint   800.00 800.00
C2 A38 25c bister brn (R)   7.00   7.00
  a.   Inverted overprint   100.00 100.00
C3 A38 25c bister brn (G)
       ('22)   7.00   7.00
    Nos. C1-C3 (3)   32.00 29.00

This overprint, on No. C3, also exists in light yellow green. Value, $85 unused and used.
No. C1a was not issued. Some authorities consider it an overprint color trial.

AP2

Wmk. 188
1924, Jan. 2   Litho.   Perf. 11½
C4 AP2 6c dark blue   2.50   2.00
C5 AP2 10c scarlet   3.50   3.00
C6 AP2 20c deep green   5.00   5.00
    Nos. C4-C6 (3)   11.00 10.00

Heron — AP3

1925, Aug. 24   Perf. 12½
Inscribed "MONTEVIDEO"
C7 AP3 14c blue & blk   35.00 25.00
Inscribed "FLORIDA"
C8 AP3 14c blue & blk   35.00 17.50

These stamps were used only on Aug. 25, 1925, the cent. of the Assembly of Florida, on letters intended to be carried by airplane between Montevideo and Florida, a town 60 miles north. The stamps were not delivered to the public but were affixed to the letters and canceled by post office clerks. Later uncanceled stamps came on the market.
One authority believes Nos. C7-C8 served as registration stamps on these two attempted special flights.

Gaucho Cavalryman at Rincón — AP4

1925, Sept. 24   *Perf. 11*
C9 AP4 45c blue green   17.50

Centenary of Battle of Rincon. Used only on Sept. 24. No. C9 was affixed and canceled by post office clerks.

Albatross — AP5

1926, Mar. 3   **Wmk. 188**   *Imperf.*

C10	AP5	6c dark blue	2.00	2.00
C11	AP5	10c vermilion	2.50	2.50
C12	AP5	20c blue green	3.00	3.00
C13	AP5	25c violet	3.50	3.50
		Nos. C10-C13 (4)	11.00	11.00

Excellent counterfeits exist.

1928, June 25   *Perf. 11*

C14	AP5	10c green	3.00	2.00
C15	AP5	20c orange	5.00	3.00
C16	AP5	30c indigo	5.00	3.00
C17	AP5	38c green	8.50	6.00
C18	AP5	40c yellow	8.50	6.00
C19	AP5	50c violet	10.00	7.50
C20	AP5	76c orange	20.00	17.50
C21	AP5	1p red	20.00	15.00
C22	AP5	1.14p indigo	45.00	35.00
C23	AP5	1.52p yellow	75.00	60.00
C24	AP5	1.90p violet	95.00	75.00
C25	AP5	3.80p red	225.00	170.00
		Nos. C14-C25 (12)	520.00	400.00

Counterfeits of No. C25 exist.

1929, Aug. 23   **Unwmk.**
C26 AP5 4c olive brown   3.00   3.00

The design was redrawn for Nos. C14-C26. The numerals are narrower, "CENTS" is 1mm high instead of 2½mm and imprint letters touch the bottom frame line.

Pegasus
AP6

1929-43   **Engr.**   *Perf. 12½*
Size: 34x23mm

C27	AP6	1c red lilac ('30)	.40	.40
C28	AP6	1c dk blue ('32)	.40	.40
C29	AP6	2c yellow ('30)	.40	.40
C30	AP6	2c olive grn ('32)	.40	.40
C31	AP6	4c Prus blue ('30)	.70	.70
C32	AP6	4c car rose ('32)	.70	.70
C33	AP6	6c dull vio ('30)	.70	.70
C34	AP6	6c red brown ('32)	.70	.70
C35	AP6	8c red orange	3.00	2.50
C36	AP6	8c gray ('30)	4.00	3.00
C36A	AP6	8c brt green ('43)	2.50	2.00
C37	AP6	16c indigo	2.00	1.50
C38	AP6	16c rose ('30)	3.25	3.00
C39	AP6	24c claret	3.00	2.50
C40	AP6	24c brt violet ('30)	4.25	3.50
C41	AP6	30c bister	3.00	2.75
C42	AP6	30c dk green ('30)	2.00	1.50
C43	AP6	40c dk brown	5.50	5.00
C44	AP6	40c yel org ('30)	6.00	5.00
C45	AP6	60c blue green	5.00	3.25
C46	AP6	60c emerald ('30)	8.50	7.00
C47	AP6	60c dp orange ('31)	3.00	2.00
C48	AP6	80c dk ultra	8.00	7.00
C49	AP6	80c green ('30)	15.00	12.00
C50	AP6	90c light blue	8.00	6.00

C51	AP6	90c dk olive grn ('30)	15.00	12.00
C52	AP6	1p car rose ('30)	10.00	7.50
C53	AP6	1.20p olive grn	22.00	20.00
C54	AP6	1.20p dp car ('30)	30.00	26.00
C55	AP6	1.50p red brown	25.00	20.00
C56	AP6	1.50p blk brn ('30)	20.00	15.00
C57	AP6	3p deep red	40.00	35.00
C58	AP6	3p ultra ('30)	30.00	25.00
C59	AP6	4.50p black	75.00	55.00
C60	AP6	4.50p violet ('30)	45.00	35.00
C60A	AP6	10p dp ultra ('43)	17.00	12.00
		Nos. C27-C60A (36)	419.40	336.40

See Nos. C63-C82. For surcharges see Nos. C106-C112, C114.

Nos. 450, 452 Overprinted in Red

1934, Jan. 1   *Perf. 11½*

C61	A130	17c ver, gray & vio	20.00	15.00
a.		Sheet of 6	140.00	
b.		Gray omitted	150.00	
c.		Double overprint	150.00	
C62	A130	36c red, blk & yel	20.00	15.00
a.		Sheet of 6	140.00	

7th Pan-American Conference, Montevideo.

Pegasus Type of 1929

1935   **Engr.**   *Perf. 12½*
Size: 31½x21mm

C63	AP6	15c dull yellow	2.50	2.00
C64	AP6	22c brick red	1.50	1.40
C65	AP6	30c brown violet	2.50	2.00
C66	AP6	37c gray lilac	1.40	1.00
C67	AP6	40c rose lake	2.00	1.40
C68	AP6	47c rose	4.00	3.50
C69	AP6	50c Prus blue	1.40	.80
C70	AP6	52c dp ultra	4.00	3.50
C71	AP6	57c grnsh blue	2.00	1.75
C72	AP6	62c olive green	1.75	.80
C73	AP6	87c gray green	5.00	4.00
C74	AP6	1p olive	3.50	2.25
C75	AP6	1.12p brown red	3.50	2.25
C76	AP6	1.20p bister brn	15.00	12.00
C77	AP6	1.27p red brown	15.00	13.00
C78	AP6	1.62p rose	10.00	9.00
C79	AP6	2p brown rose	17.00	14.00
C80	AP6	2.12p dk slate grn	17.00	14.00
C81	AP6	3p dull blue	15.00	13.00
C82	AP6	5p orange	60.00	60.00
		Nos. C63-C82 (20)	184.05	161.65

Counterfeits exist.
For surcharges, see Nos. C106-C112.

Power Dam on Rio Negro — AP7

Imprint: "Imp. Nacional" at center

1937-41   **Litho.**

C83	AP7	20c lt green ('38)	5.50	4.00
C84	AP7	35c red brown	8.00	6.50
C85	AP7	62c blue grn ('38)	.80	.30
C86	AP7	68c yel org ('38)	2.00	1.50
C86A	AP7	68c pale vio brn ('41)	1.75	.70
C87	AP7	75c violet	7.50	5.00
C88	AP7	1p dp pink	2.50	1.75
C89	AP7	1.38p rose ('38)	25.00	20.00
C90	AP7	3p dk blue ('40)	17.00	12.00
		Nos. C83-C90 (9)	70.05	51.75

Imprint at left

C91	AP7	8c pale green ('39)	.60	.50
C92	AP7	20c lt green ('38)	2.00	1.50

For surcharge and overprint see Nos. 545, C120.

Plane over Sculptured Oxcart — AP8

1939-44   *Perf. 12½*

C93	AP8	20c slate	.50	.40
C94	AP8	20c lt violet ('43)	.80	.80
C95	AP8	20c blue ('44)	.60	.40
C96	AP8	35c red	1.00	.80
C97	AP8	50c brown org	1.00	.30
C98	AP8	75c deep pink	1.10	.25
C99	AP8	1p dp blue ('40)	3.25	.60
C100	AP8	1.38p brt vio	5.50	2.25
C101	AP8	1.38p yel org ('44)	5.00	4.00
C102	AP8	2p blue	8.00	1.40
a.		Perf. 11	7.00	1.10
C103	AP8	5p rose lilac	10.00	2.25
C104	AP8	5p blue grn ('44)	15.00	7.00
C105	AP8	10p rose ('40)	100.00	65.00
		Nos. C93-C105 (13)	151.75	85.45

Counterfeits exist. These differ in design detail and are perfed other than 12½. For surcharges see Nos. C116-C119.

Nos. C68, C71, C75, C73, C77-C78, C80 Surcharged in Red or Black

1944, Nov. 22

C106	AP6	40c on 47c	1.00	1.00
C107	AP6	40c on 57c (R)	1.00	1.00
C108	AP6	74c on 1.12p	1.00	1.00
C109	AP6	79c on 87c	2.00	2.00
C110	AP6	79c on 1.27p	3.00	3.00
C111	AP6	1.20p on 1.62p	2.00	2.00
C112	AP6	1.43p on 2.12p (R)	2.00	2.00
		Nos. C106-C112 (7)	12.00	12.00

> **Catalogue values for unused stamps in this section, from this point to the end of the section, are for Never Hinged items.**

Legislature Building AP9

1945, May 11   **Unwmk.**   **Engr.**   *Perf. 11*
C113 AP9 2p ultra   5.00   2.00

Type of 1929, Srchd. in Violet

1945, Aug. 14   *Perf. 12½*
C114 AP6 44c on 75c brown   1.75   .50
a.   Double overprint   45.00

Allied Nations' victory in Europe.

"La Eolo" AP10

1945, Oct. 31   *Perf. 11*
C115 AP10 8c green   4.00   1.00

Nos. C97 and C101 Srchd. in Violet, Black or Blue

1945-46   *Perf. 12½*

C116	AP8	14c on 50c (V) ('46)	1.50	.50
a.		Inverted surcharge	37.50	
C117	AP8	23c on 1.38p	1.50	.50
a.		Inverted surcharge	75.00	
C118	AP8	23c on 50c	1.50	.50
a.		Inverted surcharge	75.00	
C119	AP8	1p on 1.38p (Bl)	1.50	.50
a.		Inverted surcharge	75.00	
		Nos. C116-C119 (4)	6.00	2.00

Victory of the Allied Nations in WWII.

No. C85 Overprinted in Black

1946, Jan. 9
C120 AP7 62c blue green   2.00   1.00

Issued to commemorate the inauguration of the Black River Power Dam.

AP11

1946-49   **Black Overprint**   **Litho.**

C121	AP11	8c car rose	.40	.25
a.		Inverted overprint		
C122	AP11	50c brown	.80	.25
a.		Double overprint	25.00	
C123	AP11	1p lt bl	1.60	.40
C124	AP11	2p ol ('49)	4.00	2.00
C125	AP11	3p lil rose	7.00	3.00
C126	AP11	5p rose car	12.00	6.00
		Nos. C121-C126 (6)	25.80	11.90

Four-Motored Plane — AP12

National Airport AP13

1947-49   *Perf. 11½, 12½*

C129	AP12	3c org brn ('49)	.25	.25
C130	AP12	8c car rose ('49)	.40	.25
C131	AP12	14c ultra	.70	.30
C132	AP12	23c emerald	.55	.25
C133	AP13	1p car & brn ('49)	1.60	.40
C134	AP13	3p ultra & brn ('49)	4.00	1.60
C135	AP13	5p grn & brn ('49)	9.50	4.00
C136	AP13	10p lil rose & brn	15.00	6.00
		Nos. C129-C136 (8)	32.00	13.05

Counterfeits exist, perf 11¼. Design size of genuine stamps is 34½x24mm, while forgeries are 33½x23½mm.
See Nos. C145-C164. For surcharges see Nos. C206, Q94.

AP14

Black Overprint

1948, June 9			Perf. 12½	
C137	AP14	12c blue	.25	.25
C138	AP14	24c Prus grn	.50	.25
C139	AP14	36c slate blue	.55	.35
	Nos. C137-C139 (3)		1.30	.85

School of Architecture, University of Uruguay AP15

Designs: 27c, Medical School. 31c, Engineering School. 36c, University.

1949, Dec. 7				
C141	AP15	15c carmine	.25	.25
C142	AP15	27c chocolate	.25	.25
C143	AP15	31c dp ultra	.50	.25
C144	AP15	36c dull green	.70	.35
	Nos. C141-C144 (4)		1.70	1.10

Founding of the University of Uruguay, cent.

Plane Type of 1947-49

1952-59		Unwmk.	Perf. 11, 12½	
C145	AP12	10c blk ('54)	.25	.25
C146	AP12	10c lt red ('58)	.25	.25
a.	Imperf., pair		30.00	
C147	AP12	15c org brn	.40	.25
a.	Vert. pair, imperf btwn.		42.50	
C148	AP12	20c lil rose		
		('54)	.50	.25
C149	AP12	21c purple	.55	.25
C150	AP12	27c yel grn		
		('57)	.55	.25
C151	AP12	31c chocolate	.70	.25
C152	AP12	36c ultra	.55	.25
C153	AP12	36c blk ('58)	.55	.25
C154	AP12	50c lt bl ('57)	.95	.25
C155	AP12	50c bl blk ('58)	.70	.25
C156	AP12	62c dl sl bl		
		('53)	1.25	.50
C157	AP12	65c rose ('53)	1.25	.50
C158	AP12	84c org ('59)	1.60	.70
C159	AP12	1.08p vio brn	2.40	.00
C160	AP12	2p Prus brn	3.50	1.40
C161	AP12	3p red org	5.00	1.75
C162	AP12	5p dk gray grn	9.50	4.00
C163	AP12	5p gray ('57)	2.00	2.50
C164	AP12	10p dp grn ('55)	24.00	12.50
	Nos. C145-C164 (20)		59.45	27.65

Planes and Show Emblem AP16

1956, Jan. 5		Unwmk. Litho.	Perf. 11	
C166	AP16	20c ultra	.60	.40
C167	AP16	31c olive grn	.70	.30
C168	AP16	36c car rose	1.10	.40
	Nos. C166-C168 (3)		2.40	1.10

First Exposition of National Products.

Type of Regular Issue and

José Batlle y Ordóñez AP17

Designs: 10c, Full-face portrait without hand. 36c, Portrait facing right.

	Perf. 13½			
1956, Dec. 15		Wmk. 90	Photo.	
C169	A178	10c magenta	.40	.25
C170	A178	20c grnsh blk	.40	.25
C171	AP17	31c brown	.50	.40
C172	A178	36c bl grn	.80	.50
	Nos. C169-C172 (4)		2.10	1.40

Stamp of 1856 and Stagecoach — AP18

1956, Dec. 15			Litho.	
C173	AP18	20c grn, bl & pale yel	.40	.30
C174	AP18	31c brn, bl & lt bl	.50	.40
C175	AP18	36c dp claret & bl	.80	.55
	Nos. C173-C175 (3)		1.70	1.25

1st postage stamps of Uruguay, cent.

Organization of American States, 10th Anniv. — AP19

	Perf. 11, 11½ (No. C177)			
1958, June 19		Unwmk.		
C176	AP19	23c blue & blk	.40	.25
C177	AP19	04c green & blk	.55	.25
C178	AP19	44c cerise & blk	.65	.40
	Nos. C176-C178 (3)		1.60	.90

Universal Declaration of Human Rights, 10th Anniv. — AP20

1958, Dec. 10			Perf. 11	
C179	AP20	23c blk & blue	.35	.25
C180	AP20	34c blk & yel grn	.50	.25
C181	AP20	44c blk & org red	.80	.45
	Nos. C179-C181 (3)		1.65	.95

"Flight" from Monument to Fallen Aviators — AP21

1959			Litho.	Perf. 11
	Size: 22x37½mm			
C182	AP21	3c bis brn & blk	.40	.25
C183	AP21	8c brt lil & blk	.40	.25
C184	AP21	38c black	.40	.25
C185	AP21	50c citron & blk	.40	.25
C186	AP21	60c vio & blk	.50	.25
C187	AP21	90c ol grn & blk	.55	.25
C188	AP21	1p blue & blk	.65	.25
C189	AP21	2p ocher & blk	2.00	.55
C190	AP21	3p grn & blk	2.75	.95
C191	AP21	5p vio brn & blk	4.00	1.50
C192	AP21	10p dp rose car & blk	12.00	4.25
	Nos. C182-C192 (11)		24.05	9.00

See Nos. C211-C222. For surcharge see No. Q97.

Alberto Santos Dumont — AP22

1959, Feb. 13		Wmk. 327	Perf. 11½	
C193	AP22	31c multi	.45	.25
C194	AP22	36c multi	.45	.25

Airplane flight of Alberto Santos-Dumont, Brazilian aeronaut, in 1906 in France.

Girl and Waves AP23

Designs: 38c, 60c, 1.05p, Compass and map of Punta del Este.

1959, Mar. 6			Perf. 11½	
C195	AP23	10c ocher & lt bl	.25	.25
C196	AP23	38c grn & bis	.25	.25
C197	AP23	60c lilac & bister	.40	.25
C198	AP23	90c red org & grn	.50	.25
C199	AP23	1.05p blue & bister	.80	.55
	Nos. C195-C199 (5)		2.20	1.55

50th anniv. of Punta del Este, seaside resort.

Torch, YMCA Emblem and Chrismon AP24

1959, Dec. 22		Wmk. 327	Litho.	Perf. 11½
C200	AP24	38c emer, blk & gray	.40	.25
C201	AP24	50c bl, blk & gray	.40	.25
C202	AP24	60c red, blk & gray	.55	.50
	Nos. C200-C202 (3)		1.35	1.00

50th anniv. of the YMCA in Uruguay.

José Artigas and George Washington AP25

1960, Mar. 2			Perf. 11½x12	
C203	AP25	38c red & blk	.30	.25
C204	AP25	50c brt bl & blk	.30	.25
C205	AP25	60c dp grn & blk	.50	.25
	Nos. C203-C205 (3)		1.10	.75

Pres. Eisenhower's visit to Uruguay, Feb. 1960.
No. C204 exists imperforate, but was not regularly issued in this form.

No. C150 Surcharged

1960, Apr. 8		Unwmk.	Perf. 11	
C206	AP12	20c on 27c yel grn	.50	.25
a.	Perf. 12½		.50	.25

Refugees and WRY Emblem — AP26

	Size: 24x35mm			
1960, June 6		Wmk. 332		
C207	AP26	60c brt lil rose & blk	.50	.25

World Refugee Year, 7/1/59-6/30/60.

Type of Regular Issue, 1960
Wmk. 332

1960, Nov. 4			Litho.	Perf. 12
C208	A186	38c bl & ol grn	.25	.25
C209	A186	50c bl & ver	.25	.25
C210	A186	60c bl & pur	.50	.25
	Nos. C208-C210 (3)		1.10	.60

Type of 1959 Redrawn with Silhouette of Airplane Added

1960-61			Litho.	Perf. 12
C211	AP21	3c blk & pale vio	.30	.25
C212	AP21	20c blk & crimson	.30	.25
C213	AP21	38c blk & pale bl	.30	.25
C214	AP21	50c blk & buff	.30	.25
C215	AP21	60c blk & dp grn	.40	.25
C216	AP21	90c blk & rose	.45	.25
C217	AP21	1p blk & gray	.60	.25
C218	AP21	2p blk & yel grn	.85	.25
C219	AP21	3p blk & red lil	1.10	.25
C220	AP21	5p blk & org ver	1.60	.50
C221	AP21	10p blk & yel	3.50	1.60
C222	AP21	20p blk & dk bl ('61)	7.50	3.25
	Nos. C211-C222 (12)		17.20	7.60

Pres. Gronchi and Flag Colors AP27

1961, Apr. 17		Wmk. 332	Perf. 12	
C223	AP27	90c multi	.30	.25
C224	AP27	1.20p multi	.45	.25
C225	AP27	1.40p multi	.50	.40
	Nos. C223-C225 (3)		1.25	.90

Visit of President Giovanni Gronchi of Italy to Uruguay, April, 1961.

Carrasco National Airport AP28

1961, May 16		Wmk. 332	Perf. 12	
	Building in Gray			
C226	AP28	1p lt vio	.30	.25
C227	AP28	2p ol gray	.70	.25
C228	AP28	3p orange	1.25	.40
C229	AP28	4p purple	1.50	.50
C230	AP28	5p aqua	2.00	.70
C231	AP28	10p lt ultra	4.00	1.25
C232	AP28	20p maroon	6.00	2.50
	Nos. C226-C232 (7)		15.75	5.85

Type of Regular "CIES" Issue, 1961

1961, Aug. 3			Wmk. 332	
C233	A189	20c blk & org	.35	.25
C234	A189	45c blk & grn	.35	.25
C235	A189	50c blk & gray	.35	.25
C236	A189	90c blk & plum	.35	.25
C237	A189	1p blk & dp rose	.40	.25
C238	A189	1.40p blk & lt vio	.50	.25
C239	A189	2p blk & bister	.55	.25
C240	A189	3p blk & lt bl	.90	.30
C241	A189	4p blk & yellow	1.40	.55
C242	A189	5p blk & blue	1.60	.85
C243	A189	10p blk & yel grn	2.90	1.50
C244	A189	20p blk & dp pink	6.00	2.75
	Nos. C233-C244 (12)		15.65	7.70

Swiss Flag, Plow, Wheat Sheaf AP29

1962, Aug. 1		Wmk. 332	Perf. 12	
C245	AP29	90c car, org & blk	.25	.25
C246	AP29	1.40p car, bl & blk	.40	.35

Cent. of the Swiss Settlement in Uruguay.

Red-crested
Cardinal — AP30

Birds: 45c, White-capped tanager, horiz.
90c, Vermilion flycatcher. 1.20p, Great kiskadee, horiz. 1.40p, Fork-tailed flycatcher.

1962, Dec. 5 **Litho.** *Perf. 12*
C247 AP30 20c gray, blk & red .25 .25
C248 AP30 45c multi .50 .25
C249 AP30 90c crim rose, blk
  & lt brn 1.25 .25
C250 AP30 1.20p lt bl, blk & yel 1.50 .25
C251 AP30 1.40p blue & sepia 2.00 .30
  Nos. C247-C251 (5) 5.50 1.30

No frame on #C248, thin frame on #C251.
See #C258-C263. For surcharge see #C320.

Type of Regular UPAE Issue, 1963
1963, May 31 **Wmk. 332** *Perf. 12*
C252 A195 45c bluish grn & blk .25 .25
C253 A195 90c magenta & blk .40 .25

**Freedom from Hunger Type of
Regular Issue**
1963, July 9 **Wmk. 332** *Perf. 12*
C254 A196 90c red & yel .25 .25
C255 A196 1.40p violet & yel .50 .50

"Alferez
Campora"
AP31

1963, Aug. 16 **Litho.**
C256 AP31 90c dk grn & org .30 .25
C257 AP31 1.40p ultra & yel .70 .45

Voyage around the world by the Uruguayan
sailing vessel "Alferez Campora," 1960-63.

Bird Type of 1962
Birds: 1p, Glossy cowbird (tordo). 2p, Yellow
cardinal. 3p, Hooded siskin. 5p, Sayaca tanager. 10p, Blue and yellow tanager. 20p, Scar-
let-headed marsh-bird. All horizontal.

1963, Nov. 15 **Wmk. 332** *Perf. 12*
C258 AP30 1p vio bl, blk &
  brn org .65 .25
C259 AP30 2p lt brn, blk &
  yel 1.50 .30
C260 AP30 3p yel, brn & blk 2.00 .50
C261 AP30 5p emer, bl grn &
  blk 3.50 .70
C262 AP30 10p multi 7.25 1.25
C263 AP30 20p gray, org & blk 16.00 7.75
  Nos. C258-C263 (6) 30.90 10.75

Frame on Nos. C260-C263.

Pres.
Charles de
Gaulle
AP32

2.40p, Flags of France and Uruguay.

1964, Oct. 9 **Litho.** *Perf. 12*
C264 AP32 1.50p multi .40 .25
C265 AP32 2.40p multi .95 .35

Charles de Gaulle, Pres. of France, Oct.
1964.

Submerged
Statue of
Ramses
II — AP33

Design: 2p, Head of Ramses II.

1964, Oct. 30 **Litho.** **Wmk. 332**
C266 AP33 1.30p multi .25 .25
C267 AP33 2p bis, red brn &
  brt bl 1.00 .50
  a. Souv. sheet of 3, #713, C266-
    C267, imperf. 2.00 2.00

UNESCO world campaign to save historic
monuments in Nubia.

National
Flag
AP34

1965, Feb. 18 **Wmk. 332** *Perf. 12*
C268 AP34 50p gray, dk bl & yel 8.50 4.00

Kennedy Type of Regular Issue
1965, Mar. 5 **Wmk. 327** *Perf. 11½*
C269 A202 1.50p gold, lil & blk .25 .25
C270 A202 2.40p gold, brt bl &
  blk .55 .55

Issue of
1864, No.
23
AP35

6c, 8c, 10c denominations of 1864 issue.

Wmk. 332
1965, Mar. 19 **Litho.** *Perf. 12*
C271 Sheet of 10 4.50 4.50
"URUGUAY" at bottom
  a. AP35 1p blue & black .35 .35
  b. AP35 1p brick red & black .35 .35
  c. AP35 1p green & black .35 .35
  d. AP35 1p ocher & black .35 .35
  e. AP35 1p carmine & black .35 .35
"URUGUAY" at top
  f. AP35 1p blue & black .35 .35
  g. AP35 1p brick red & black .35 .35
  h. AP35 1p green & black .35 .35
  i. AP35 1p ocher & black .35 .35
  j. AP35 1p carmine & black .35 .35

1st Rio de la Plata Stamp Show, sponsored
jointly by the Argentine and Uruguayan philatelic associations, Montevideo, Mar. 19-28.
No. C271 contains two horizontal rows of
stamps and two rows of labels; Nos. C271a-
C271e are in first row, Nos. C271f-C271j in
second row. Adjacent labels in top and bottom
rows.
For overprint see No. C298.

National
Arms — AP36

1965, Apr. 30 **Wmk. 332** *Perf. 12*
C272 AP36 20p multi 2.00 1.10

Type of Regular Issue and

Artigas
Monument
AP37

Designs: 1.50p, Artigas and wagontrain.
2.40p, Artigas quotation.

Perf. 11½x12, 12x11½
1965, May 17 **Litho.** **Wmk. 327**
C273 AP37 1p multi .25 .25
C274 A205 1.50p multi .40 .25
C275 A205 2.40p multi .75 .50
  Nos. C273-C275 (3) 1.40 1.00

José Artigas (1764-1850), leader of the
independence revolt against Spain.

**Olympic Games Type of Regular
Issue**
Designs: 1p, Boxing. 1.50p, Running. 2p,
Fencing. 2.40p, Sculling. 3p, Pistol shooting.
20p, Olympic rings.

1965, Aug. 3 **Litho.** *Perf. 12x11½*
C276 A206 1p red, gray & blk .25 .25
C277 A206 1.50p emer, bl & blk .25 .25
C278 A206 2p dk car, bl & blk .40 .25
C279 A206 2.40p lt ultra, org &
  blk .55 .35
C280 A206 3p lil, yel & blk .80 .50
C281 A206 20p dk vio bl, pink
  & lt bl 1.25 .85
  Nos. C276-C281 (6) 3.50 2.45

Souvenir Sheet
Designs: 5p, Stamp of 1924, No. 284. 10p,
Stamp of 1928, No. 389.

C282 Sheet of 2 2.50 2.50
  a. 5p buff, blue & black .95 .95
  b. 10p blue, black & rose red 1.40 1.40

18th Olympic Games, Tokyo, 10/10-25/64.

ITU Emblem
and Satellite
AP38

1966, Jan. 25 **Wmk. 332** *Perf. 12*
C283 AP38 1p bl, bluish blk & ver .50 .25
Cent. of the ITU (in 1965).

Winston
Churchill — AP39

1966, Apr. 29 **Wmk. 332** *Perf. 12*
C284 AP39 2p car, brn & gold .50 .25

**Rio de Janeiro Type of Regular
Issue**
1966, June 9 **Wmk. 332** *Perf. 12*
C285 A208 80c dp org & brn .40 .25

International
Cooperation
Year
Emblem
AP40

1966, June 9 **Litho.**
C286 AP40 1p bluish grn & blk .40 .25
UN International Cooperation Year.

President
Zalman
Shazar of
Israel
AP41

1966, June 21 **Wmk. 327**
C287 AP41 7p multi .75 .30
Visit of Pres. Zalman Shazar of Israel.

Crested
Screamer — AP42

1966, July 7 **Wmk. 327** *Perf. 12*
C288 AP42 100p bl, blk, red &
  gray 8.50 2.25

Jules Rimet
Cup, Soccer
Ball and
Globe
AP43

1966, July 11 **Litho.**
C289 AP43 10p dk pur, org & lil .80 .30
World Cup Soccer Championship, Wem-
bley, England, July 11-30.

Bulls
AP44

1966 **Wmk. 327, 332 (10p)**
C290 AP44 4p Hereford .25 .25
C291 AP44 6p Holstein .25 .25
C292 AP44 10p Shorthorn .55 .25
C293 AP44 15p Aberdeen
  Angus 1.00 .35
C294 AP44 20p Norman 2.00 .55
C295 AP44 30p Jersey 2.60 .85
C296 AP44 50p Charolais 4.00 1.50
  Nos. C290-C296 (7) 10.65 4.00

Issued to publicize Uruguayan cattle.
Issued: 4p, 50p, 8/13; 6p, 30p, 8/29; 10p, 15p,
20p, 9/26.

Boiso
Lanza,
Early
Plane and
Space
Capsule
AP45

1966, Oct. 14 **Litho.** *Perf. 12*
C297 AP45 25p ultra, blk & lt bl .95 .50
Issued to honor Capt. Juan Manuel Boiso
Lanza, pioneer of military aviation.

No. C271 Overprinted in Black

1966, Nov. 4   **Wmk. 332**
C298   Sheet of 10   4.50   4.50

"URUGUAY" at bottom
a.-e.   AP35 1p each   .35   .35

"URUGUAY" at top
f.-j.   AP35 1p each   .35   .35

2nd Rio de la Plata Stamp Show, Buenos Aires, Apr. 1966, sponsored by the Argentine and Uruguayan philatelic associations, and for the cent. of Uruguay's 1st surcharged issue. The addition of black numerals makes the designs resemble the surcharged issue of 1866, Nos. 24-28.

Labels in top row are overprinted "SEGUNDA MUESTRA 1966," in bottom row "SEGUNDAS JORNADAS 1966" and "CENTENARIO DEL SELLO / ESCUDITO RESELLADO" in both rows. One label each in top and bottom rows is overprinted "BUENOS AIRES / ABRIL 1966."

No. 613 Surcharged in Dark Blue

     Perf. 12½x13
1966, Dec. 17   **Engr.**   **Unwmk.**
C299   A175   1p on 12c   .50   .25

Philatelic Club of Uruguay, 40th anniv.

Dante Alighieri — AP46

     Wmk. 332
1966, Dec. 27   **Litho.**   ***Perf. 12***
C300   AP46   50c sepia & bister   .55   .25

Dante Alighieri (1265-1321), Italian poet.

Planetarium Projector — AP47

1967, Jan. 13   **Wmk. 332**   ***Perf. 12***
C301   AP47   5p dl bl & blk   .60   .30

Montevideo Municipal Planetarium, 10th anniv.

Archbishop Makarios and Map of Cyprus AP48

1967, Feb. 14   **Wmk. 332**   ***Perf. 12***
C302   AP48   6.60p rose lil & blk   .50   .25

Visit of Archbishop Makarios, president of Cyprus, Oct. 21, 1966.

Dr. Albert Schweitzer Holding Fawn — AP49

1967, Mar. 31   **Litho.**   **Wmk. 332**
C303   AP49   6p grn, blk, brn & sal   .80   .55

Albert Schweitzer (1875-1965), medical missionary.

Corriedale Ram AP50

Various Rams: 4p, Ideal. 5p, Romney Marsh. 10p, Australian Merino.

1967, Apr. 5
C304   AP50   3p red org, blk & gray   1.40   .25
C305   AP50   4p cmel, blk & gray   1.40   .25
C306   AP50   5p ultra, blk & gray   1.40   .25
C307   AP50   10p yel, blk & gray   1.40   .50
    Nos. C304-C307 (4)   5.60   1.25

Uruguayan sheep raising.

Flag of Uruguay and Map of the Americas AP51

1967, Apr. 8
C308   AP51   10p dk gray, bl & gold   .50   .25

Meeting of American Presidents, Punta del Este, Apr. 10-12.

Numeral Stamps of 1866, Nos. 30-31 AP52

Design: 6p, Nos. 32-33; diff. frame.

     Wmk. 332
1967, May 10   **Litho.**   ***Perf. 12***
C309   AP52   3p bl, yel grn & blk   .45   .25
  a.   Souvenir sheet of 4   1.50   1.50
C310   AP52   6p bis, dp rose & blk   .55   .30
  a.   Souvenir sheet of 4   2.50   2.50

Cent. of the 1866 numeral issue. Nos. C309a-C310a each contain 4 stamps similar to Nos. C309 and C310 respectively (the arrangement of colors differs in the souvenir sheets).

Ansina, Portrait by Medardo Latorre — AP53

1967, May 17
C311   AP53   2p gray, dk bl & red   .40   .25

Issued to honor Ansina, servant of Gen. José Artigas.

Plane Landing AP54

1967, May 30
C312   AP54   10p red, bl, blk & yel   .55   .25

30th anniv. (in 1966) of PLUNA Airline.

Shooting for Basket — AP55

Basketball Game — AP56

Basketball Players in Action: No. C314, Driving (ball shoulder high). No. C315, About to pass (ball head high). No. C316, Ready to pass (ball held straight in front). No. C317, Dribbling with right hand.

1967, June 9
C313   AP55   5p multi   .30   .25
C314   AP55   5p multi   .30   .25
C315   AP55   5p multi   .30   .25
C316   AP55   5p multi   .30   .25
C317   AP55   5p multi   .30   .25
  a.   Strip of 5, Nos. C313-C317   1.60   1.60

Souvenir Sheet
C318   AP56   10p org, brt grn & blk   1.75   1.75

5th World Basketball Championships, Montevideo, May 1967.
For overprint see No. C349.

José Artigas, Manuel Belgrano, Flags of Uruguay and Argentina — AP57

     Wmk. 332
1967, June 19   **Litho.**   ***Imperf.***
C319   AP57   5p bl, grn & yel   1.25   1.25

3rd Rio de la Plata Stamp Show, Montevideo, Uruguay, June 18-25.
For surcharge see No. 859.

Nos. C248 and C252 Surcharged in Gold

1967, June 22   ***Perf. 12***
C320   AP30   5.90p on 45c multi   .45   .25
C321   A195   5.90p on 45c multi   .45   .25

Don Quixote and Sancho Panza, Painted by Denry Torres — AP58

1967, July 10
C322   AP58   8p bister brn & brn   .60   .25

Issued in honor of Miguel de Cervantes Saavedra (1547-1616), Spanish novelist.
For surcharge see No. C356.

Stone Axe — AP59

Designs: 15p, Headbreaker stones. 20p, Spearhead. 50p, Birdstone. 75p, Clay pot. 100p, Ornitholite (ritual sculpture). Balizas, horiz. 150p, Lasso weights (boleadores). 200p, Two spearheads.

1967-68   **Wmk. 332**   ***Perf. 12***
O023   AP59   15p gray & blk   .40   .25
C324   AP59   20p gray & blk   .40   .25
C325   AP59   30p gray & blk   .95   .25
C326   AP59   50p gray & blk   1.10   .25
C327   AP59   75p brn & blk   2.00   .35
C328   AP59   100p gray & blk   2.75   .70
C329   AP59   150p gray & blk ('68)   3.25   .70
C330   AP59   200p gray & blk ('68)   5.25   1.50
    Nos. C323-C330 (8)   16.10   4.25

Railroad Crossing AP60

1967, Dec. 4
C331   AP60   4p blk, yel & red   .75   .25

10th Pan-American Highway Congress, Montevideo.

Lions Emblem and Map of South America — AP61

1967, Dec. 29
C332   AP61   5p pur, yel & emer   .70   .25

50th anniversary of Lions International.

Boy Scout AP62

1968, Jan. 24   **Litho.**
C333   AP62   9p sepia & brick red   .75   .30

Issued in memory of Robert Baden-Powell, founder of the Boy Scout organization.

Sun, UN Emblem and Transportation Means — AP63

1968, Feb. 29   Wmk. 332   Perf. 12
C334 AP63 10p gray, yel, lt & dk bl   .50   .25
Issued for International Tourist Year.

Octopus AP64

Marine Fauna: 20p, Silversides. 25p, Characin. 30p, Catfish, vert. 50p, Squid, vert.

1968   Wmk. 332   Perf. 12
C335 AP64 15p lt grn, bl & blk   .75   .25
C336 AP64 20p brn, grn & bl   .75   .25
C337 AP64 25p multi   1.10   .25
C338 AP64 30p bl, grn & blk   1.25   .50
C339 AP64 50p dp org, grn & dk bl   2.00   .65
Nos. C335-C339 (5)   5.85   1.90

Issued: 30p, 50p, 10/10; 15p, 20p, 25p, 11/5.

Navy Type of Regular Issue

Designs: 4p, Naval Air Force. 6p, Naval arms. 10p, Signal flags, vert. 20p, Corsair (chartered by General Artigas).

1968, Nov. 12   Litho.
C340 A226 4p bl, blk & red   .25   .25
C341 A226 6p multi   .25   .25
C342 A226 10p lt ultra, red & yel   .30   .25
C343 A226 20p ultra & blk   .75   .25
Nos. C340-C343 (4)   1.55   1.00

Rowing AP65

1969, Feb. 11   Wmk. 332   Perf. 12
C344 AP65 30p shown   .50   .25
C345 AP65 50p Running   .80   .35
C346 AP65 100p Soccer   1.40   .55
Nos. C344-C346 (3)   2.70   1.15

19th Olympic Games, Mexico City, 10/12-27/68.

Bicycling Type of Regular Issue

Designs: 20p, Bicyclist and globe, vert.

1969, Mar. 21   Wmk. 332   Perf. 12
C347 A229 20p bl, pur & yel   .50   .25

"EFIMEX 68" and Globe AP66

1969, Apr. 10   Wmk. 332   Perf. 12
C348 AP66 20p dk grn, red & bl   .60   .25
EFIMEX '68, International Philatelic Exhibition, Mexico City, Nov. 1-9, 1968.

No. C318 Ovptd. with Names of Participating Countries, Emblem, Bars, etc. and "CAMPEONATO MUNDIAL DE VOLEIBOL"

1969, Apr. 25   Souvenir Sheet
C349 AP56 10p org, brt grn & blk   1.10   1.10
Issued to commemorate the World Volleyball Championships, Montevideo, Apr. 1969.

Book, Quill and Emblem — AP67

1969, Sept. 16   Litho.   Perf. 12
C350 AP67 30p grn, org & blk   .70   .25
10th Congress of Latin American Notaries.

Automobile Club Emblem — AP68

1969, Oct. 7   Wmk. 332   Perf. 12
C351 AP68 10p ultra & red   .50   .25
50th anniv. (in 1968) of the Uruguayan Automobile Club.

ILO Emblem AP69

1969, Oct. 29   Litho.   Perf. 12
C352 AP69 30p dk bl grn & blk   .60   .25
50th anniv. of the ILO.

Exhibition Emblem — AP70

1969, Nov. 15   Wmk. 332   Perf. 12
C353 AP70 20p ultra, yel & grn   .60   .25
ABUEXPO 69 Philatelic Exhibition, San Pablo, Brazil, Nov. 15-23.

Rotary Emblem and Hemispheres AP71

1969, Dec. 6   Perf. 12
C354 AP71 20p ultra, bl & bis   .75   .30
South American Regional Rotary Conference and the 50th anniv. of the Montevideo Rotary Club.

Dr. Luis Morquio — AP72

1969, Dec. 22   Litho.   Wmk. 332
C355 AP72 20p org red & brn   .50   .25
Centenary of the birth of Dr. Luis Morquio, pediatrician.

No. C322 Surcharged "FELIZ AÑO 1970 / 6.00 / PESOS"

1969, Dec. 24
C356 AP58 6p on 8p bis brn & brn   .50   .25
Issued for New Year 1970.

Mahatma Gandhi and UNESCO Emblem AP73

1970, Jan. 26   Wmk. 332   Perf. 12
C357 AP73 100p lt bl & brn   5.00   .90
Mohandas K. Gandhi (1869-1948), leader in India's fight for independence.

Evaristo C. Ciganda — AP74

1970, Mar. 10   Litho.
C358 AP74 6p brt grn & brn   .50   .25
Ciganda, author of the 1st law for teachers' pensions, birth cent.

Giuseppe Garibaldi — AP75

1970, Apr. 7   Unwmk.   Perf. 12
C359 AP75 20p rose car & pink   .60   .25
Centenary of Garibaldi's command of foreign legionnaires in the Uruguayan Civil War.

Fur Seal AP76

Designs: 20p, Rhea, vert. 30p, Common tegu (lizard). 50p, Capybara. 100p, Mulita armadillo. 150p, Puma. 200p, Nutria.

1970-71   Wmk. 332   Perf. 12
C361 AP76 20p pur, emer & blk   .95   .25
C362 AP76 30p emer, yel & blk   1.00   .30
C363 AP76 50p dl yel & brn   2.00   .50
C365 AP76 100p org, sep & blk   2.75   .75
C366 AP76 150p emer & brn   2.00   .85
C367 AP76 200p brt rose, brn & blk ('71)   5.00   2.25
C368 AP76 250p gray, bl & blk   7.00   2.25
Nos. C361-C368 (7)   20.70   7.15

Soccer and Mexican Flag AP77

1970, June 2   Litho.   Perf. 12
C369 AP77 50p multi   .90   .50
9th World Soccer Championships for the Jules Rimet Cup, Mexico City, 5/30-6/21.

"U N" and Laurel — AP78

1970, June 26   Wmk. 332   Perf. 12
C370 AP78 32p dk bl & gold   .60   .25
25th anniversary of the United Nations.

Eisenhower and US Flag — AP79

1970, July 14   Litho.
C371 AP79 30p gray, vio bl & red   .60   .25
Issued in memory of Gen. Dwight David Eisenhower, 34th Pres. of US (1890-1969).

Neil A. Armstrong Stepping onto Moon — AP80

1970, July 21
C372 AP80 200p multi   4.00   1.50
1st anniv. of man's 1st landing on the moon.

Flag of the "Immortals" — AP81

1970, Aug. 24   Wmk. 332   Perf. 12
C373 AP81 500p bl, blk & red   6.00   6.00
The 145th anniversary of the arrival of the 33 "Immortals," the patriots, who started the revolution for independence.

Congress Emblem with Map of South America AP82

1970, Sept. 16   Unwmk.   Perf. 12
C374 AP82 30p bl, dk bl & yel   .60   .25
Issued to publicize the 5th Pan-American Congress of Rheumatology, Punta del Este.

Souvenir Sheet

Types of First Air Post Issue — AP83

1970, Oct. 1   Wmk. 332   Perf. 12½
C375	AP83	Sheet of 3	3.00	3.00
a.		25p brown (Bl)	.90	.90
b.		25p brown (R)	.90	.90
c.		25p brown (G)	.90	.90

Stamp Day. #C375 contains 3 stamps similar to #C1-C3, but with denominations in pesos.

Flags of ALALC Countries — AP84

1970, Nov. 23   Litho.   Perf. 12
C376 AP84 22p multi   .60 .25

For the Latin-American Association for Free Trade (Asociación Latinoamericana de Libre Comercio).

Yellow Fever, by J. M. Blanes AP85

1971, June 8   Wmk. 332   Perf. 12
C377 AP85 50p blk, dk red brn & yel   .80 .35

Juan Manuel Blanes (1830-1901), painter.

Racial Equality, UN Emblem AP86

1971, June 28   Litho.
C378 AP86 27p blk, pink & bis   .60 .25

Intl. Year Against Racial Discrimination.

Congress Emblem with Maps of Americas AP87

1971, July 6   Wmk. 332   Perf. 12
C379 AP87 58p dl grn, blk & org   .70 .40

12th Pan-American Congress of Gastroenterology, Punta del Este, Dec. 5-10, 1971.

 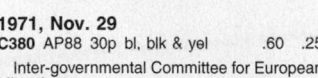

Committee Emblem AP88

1971, Nov. 29
C380 AP88 30p bl, blk & yel   .60 .25

Inter-governmental Committee for European Migration.

Llama and Mountains AP89

1971, Dec. 30
C381 AP89 37p multi   .85 .40

EXFILIMA '71, Third Inter-American Philatelic Exposition, Lima, Peru, Nov. 6-14.

Munich Olympic Games Emblem — AP90

Designs (Munich '72 Emblem and): 100p, Torchbearer. 500p, Discobolus.

1972, Feb. 1   Perf. 11½x12
C382	AP90	50p blk, red & org	.35	.25
C383	AP90	100n multi	.65	.40
C384	AP90	500p multi	3.50	2.00
		Nos. C382-C384 (3)	4.50	2.65

20th Olympic Games, Munich, 8/26-9/11.

Retort and WHO Emblem — AP91

1972, Feb. 22   Perf. 12
C385 AP91 27p multi   .40 .25

50th anniversary of the discovery of insulin by Frederick G. Banting and Charles H. Best.

Ship with Flags Forming Sails — AP92

1972, Mar. 6   Wmk. 332
C386 AP92 37p multi   .60 .25

Stamp Day of the Americas.

1924 and 1928 Gold Medals, Soccer — AP93

Design: 300p, Olympic flag, Motion and Munich emblems, vert.

1972, June 12   Litho.   Perf. 12
C387	AP93	100p bl & multi	.75	.75
C388	AP93	300p multi	2.25	2.25

20th Olympic Games, Munich, 8/26-9/11.

Cross AP94

1972, Aug. 10
C389 AP94 37p vio & gold   .45 .25

Dan A. Mitrione (1920-70), slain US official.

Interlocking Squares and UN Emblem — AP95

1972, Aug. 16
C390 AP95 30p gray & multi   .45 .25

3rd UN Conf. on Trade and Development (UNCTAD III), Santiago, Chile, Apr.-May 1972.

Brazil's "Bull's-eye," 1843 — AP96

Wmk. 332
1972, Aug. 26   Litho.   Perf. 12
C391 AP96 50p grn, yel & bl   .45 .25

4th Inter-American Philatelic Exhibition, EXFILBRA, Rio de Janeiro, Aug. 26-Sept. 2.

Map of South America, Compass Rose — AP97

1972, Sept. 28
C392 AP97 37p multi   .45 .25

Uruguay's support for extending territorial sovereignty 200 miles into the sea.

Adoration of the Kings and Shepherds, by Rafael Perez Barradas — AP98

1972, Oct. 12
C393 AP98 20p lemon & multi + label   .55 .25

Christmas 1972 and first biennial exhibition of Uruguayan painting, 1970.

WPY Emblem AP99

Wmk. 332
1974, Aug. 20   Litho.   Perf. 12
C394 AP99 500p gray & red   1.00 .60

World Population Year 1974.

Soccer, Olympics and UPU Emblems AP100

AP100a

Anniversaries and events: Nos. C396 and C397 are same design as No. C395.
No. C398a, 17th UPU Congress, Lausanne. No. C398b, World Soccer Federation, 1st South American president. No. C398c, 1976 Summer and Winter Olympics, Innsbruck and Montreal.

1974, Aug. 30
C395	AP100	200p grn & multi	1.00	1.00
C396	AP100	300p org & multi	1.00	1.00
C397	AP100	500p lt. bl & multi	9.00	9.00

Souvenir Sheet
With Blue Frame
C398	AP100a	Sheet of 3	70.00	70.00
a.-c.		500p any single	15.00	15.00

Centenary of Universal Postal Union. Nos. C397-C398 had limited distribution.

Mexico No. O1 and Mexican Coat of Arms AP101

Wmk. 332
1974, Oct. 15   Litho.   Perf. 12
C399 AP101 200p multi   .60 .25

EXFILMEX '74 5th Inter-American Philatelic Exhibition, Mexico City, Oct. 26-Nov. 3.

Christmas Type of 1974

240p, Kings following star. 2500p, Virgin & Child.

1974
C400 A315 240p multi   .50 .25
Miniature Sheet
C401 A315 2500p multi   4.50 4.50

Issued: 240p. Dec. 27; 2500p, Dec. 31.

Spain No. 1, Colors of Spain and Uruguay — AP102

1975, Mar. 4
C402 AP102 400p multi .60 .25

Espana 75, International Philatelic Exhibition, Madrid, Apr. 4-13.

Souvenir Sheet

Nos. C253, 893 and C402 — AP103

Wmk. 332
1975, Apr. 4 **Litho.** **Perf. 12**
C403 AP103 Sheet of 3 5.00 5.00
  a. 1000p No. C253 1.50 1.50
  b. 1000p No. 893 1.50 1.50
  c. 1000p No. C402 1.50 1.50

Espana 75 Intl. Phil. Exhib., Madrid, Apr. 4-13.

1976 Summer & Winter Olympics, Innsbruck & Montreal AP104

1975, May 16 **Perf. 12**
C404 AP104 400p shown 1.00 .60
C405 AP104 600p Flags, Olympic rings 1.50 .95

Souvenir Sheets
C406 Sheet of 2 40.00 40.00
  a. AP104 500p Montreal emblem 11.00 11.00
  b. AP104 1000p Innsbruck emblem 24.00 24.00
C407 Sheet of 2 40.00 40.00
  a. AP104 500p Emblems, horiz. 11.00 11.00
  b. AP104 1000p Flags, horiz. 24.00 24.00

Nos. C404-C407 had limited distribution.

Floor Design for Capitol, Rome AP105

1975, Aug. 15
C408 AP105 1p multi 1.25 1.25

500th birth anniversary of Michelangelo Buonarroti (1475-1564), Italian sculptor, painter and architect.

Apollo-Soyuz Space Mission, USA & Uruguay Independence — AP106

Anniversaries and events: 15c, Apollo-Soyuz spacecraft. 20c, Apollo-Soyuz spacecraft. 25c, Artigas monument, vert. 30c, George Washington, Pres. Artigas. No. C412, Early Aircraft, vert. No. C413a, Apollo spacecraft, astronauts. No. C413b, US and Uruguayan Declarations of Independence. No. C413c, Modern aircraft. No. C413d, UN Secretaries General. No. C414c, Boiso Lanza, aviation pioneer. 1p, Flags of UN and Uruguay.

1975, Sept. 29
C409 AP106 10c multicolored 1.10 .85
C410 AP106 15c multicolored 1.60 1.25
C411 AP106 25c multicolored 2.00 1.40
C412 AP106 50c multicolored 2.75 1.75
  Nos. C409-C412 (4) 7.45 5.25
Souvenir Sheets
C413 Sheet of 4 40.00 40.00
  a.-d. AP106 40c any single 8.50 8.50
C414 Sheet of 4 40.00 40.00
  a. AP106 20c multicolored 1.50 1.50
  b. AP106 30c multicolored 3.75 3.75
  c. AP106 50c multicolored 6.00 6.00
  d. AP106 1p multicolored 13.00 13.00

Nos. C409-C414 had limited distribution.

Sun, Uruguay No. C59 and other Stamps — AP108

Wmk. 332
1975, Oct. 13 **Litho.** **Perf. 12**
C415 AP108 1p blk, gray & yel 3.00 1.25

Uruguayan Stamp Day.

Montreal Olympic Emblem and Argentina '78 — AP109

Flags of US and Uruguay — AP110

UPU and UPAE Emblems AP111

Wmk. 332
1975, Oct. 14 **Litho.** **Perf. 11½**
C416 AP109 1p multi 1.75 .70
C417 AP110 1p multi 1.75 .70
C418 AP111 1p multi 1.75 .70
  a. Souvenir sheet of 3 20.00 20.00
  Nos. C416-C418 (3) 5.25 2.10

EXFILMO '75 and ESPAMER '75 Stamp Exhibitions, Montevideo, Oct. 10-19. No. C418a contains 3 stamps similar to Nos. C416-C418, 2p each.

Ocelot AP112

Orchid: #C416, Oncidium bifolium.

1976, Jan. **Litho.** **Perf. 12**
C419 AP112 50c vio bl & multi .80 .35
C420 AP112 50c emer & multi .80 .35

Souvenir Sheets

Olympics, Soccer, Telecommunications and UPU — AP113

1976, June 3 **Perf. 11½**
C422 AP113 Sheet of 3 55.00 55.00
  a. 30c Soccer player 5.50 5.50
  b. 70c Alexander Graham Bell 13.00 13.00
  c. 1p UPU emblem, UN #5 19.00 19.00
C423 Sheet of 3 55.00 55.00
  a. AP113 40c Discus thrower 6.00 6.00
  b. AP113 60c Telephone, cent. 8.50 8.50
  c. AP113 2p UPU emblem, UN #11 24.00 24.00

Nos. C422-C423 had limited distribution.

Anniversaries and Events Type of 1976
Souvenir Sheets

20c, Frederick Passy, Henri Dunant. 35c, Nobel prize, 75th anniv. 40c, Viking spacecraft. 60c, 1976 Summer Olympics, Montreal. 75c, US space missions. 90c, 1976 Summer Olympics, diff. World Cup Soccer Championships, Argentina: 1p, Uruguay, 1930 champions. 1.50p, Uruguay, 1950 champions.

1976, Nov. 12 **Perf. 12**
C424 Sheet of 4 45.00 45.00
  a. A355 20c multicolored 2.50 2.50
  b. A355 40c multicolored 4.75 4.75
  c. A355 60c multicolored 6.50 6.50
  d. A355 1.50p multicolored 16.00 16.00
C425 Sheet of 4 45.00 45.00
  a. A355 35c multicolored 5.00 5.00
  b. A355 75c multicolored 7.00 7.00
  c. A355 90c multicolored 8.00 8.00
  d. A355 1p multicolored 10.00 10.00

Nos. C424-C425 had limited distribution.

Nobel Prize Type of 1977
Souvenir Sheets

Anniversaries and events: 10c, World Cup Soccer Championships. 40c, Victor Hess, Nobel Prize in Physics. 60c, Max Plank, Nobel Prize in Physics. 80c, Graf Zeppelin, Concorde. 90c, Virgin and Child by Rubens. 1.20p, World Cup Soccer Championships, diff. 1.50p, Eduardo Bonilla, Count von Zeppelin. 2p, The Nativity by Rubens.

1977, July 21
C426 Sheet of 4 35.00 35.00
  a. A361 10c multicolored .85 .85
  b. A361 60c multicolored 3.50 3.50
  c. A361 80c multicolored 5.00 5.00
  d. A361 2p multicolored 12.00 12.00
C427 Sheet of 4 35.00 35.00
  a. A361 40c multicolored 2.25 2.25
  b. A361 90c multicolored 5.50 5.50
  c. A361 1.20p multicolored 6.50 6.50
  d. A361 1.50p multicolored 9.50 9.50

Nos. C426-C427 had limited distribution.

Uruguay Natl. Postal System, 150th Anniv. AP114

1977, July 27
C428 AP114 8p multicolored 10.00 10.00
Souvenir Sheet
C429 AP114 10p multicolored 15.00 15.00

No. C428, imperf., was not valid for postage. Souvenir sheets sold in the package with No. C429 not valid for postage.
For overprint see No. C435.

Paintings Type of 1978

Paintings: 1p, St. George Slaying Dragon by Durer. 1.25p, Duke of Lerma by Rubens. No. 432a, Madonna and Child by Durer. No. 432b, Holy Family by Rubens. No. 432c, Flight from Egypt by Francisco de Goya (1746-1828).

1978, June 13 **Perf. 12½**
C430 A374 1p brn & blk 3.50 3.50
C431 A374 1.25p blk & brn 3.75 3.75
Souvenir Sheet
C432 Sheet of 3 22.00 22.00
  a.-c. A374 1p any single 5.50 5.50

Nos. C430-C432 had limited distribution.

Souvenir Sheet

ICAO, 30th Anniv. and 1st Powered Flight, 75th Anniv. — AP115

Designs: a, Concorde, Dornier DO-x. b, Graf Zeppelin, Wright Brothers' Flyer. c, Space shuttle and De Pinedo's plane.

1978, June 13
C433 AP115 Sheet of 3 25.00 25.00
  a.-c. 1p any single 7.00 7.00

No. C433 had limited distribution.

Souvenir Sheet

World Cup Soccer Championships, Argentina — AP116

1978, June 13 **Perf. 12**
C434 AP116 Sheet of 3 50.00 50.00
  a. 50c multicolored 3.50 3.50
  b. 1.50p multicolored 9.00 9.00
  c. 2p multicolored 14.00 14.00

No. C434 had limited distribution.

No. C428 Overprinted in Black

1978, Aug. 28
C435 AP114 8p multicolored   7.50   3.50
   No. C435 had limited distribution.

Madonna and Child Type of 1979

Various Madonna and Child etchings by Albrecht Dürer with Intl. Year of the Child emblem at: a, UL. b, UR.

     Wmk. 332
1979, June 18   **Litho.**   **Perf. 12½**
C436 A390 1.50p Sheet of 2, #a-b   26.00   26.00
   No. C436 had limited distribution.

Boiso Lanza, Wright Brothers AP117

75th anniv. of powered flight.

1979, June 18   **Perf. 12½**
C437 AP117 1.80p multicolored   2.75   1.25
   No. C437 had limited distribution.
   Issued in sheet of 24 containing 6 blocks of 4r with margin around. See Nos. 1040-1042.

Souvenir Sheet

1982 World Cup Soccer Championships, Spain — AP118

1979, June 18   **Perf. 12**
C438 AP118 Sheet of 3   40.00   40.00
   a.   50c Jules Rimet cup   2.50   2.50
   b.   2.50p Uruguay flag   10.00   10.00
   c.   3p Espana '82   14.00   14.00
   No. C438 had limited distribution.

Souvenir Sheet

Rowland Hill Cent. — AP119

1979, June 18
C439 AP119 Sheet of 2   40.00   40.00
   a.   2p Uruguay #1, C1   16.00   16.00
   b.   2p Great Britain #1, 836   16.00   16.00
   No. C439 had limited distribution.

AIR POST SEMI-POSTAL STAMPS

> Catalogue values for unused stamps in this section are for Never Hinged items.

Type of Semi-Postal Stamps, 1959
     Wmk. 327
1959, Dec. 29   **Litho.**   **Perf. 11½**
CB1 SP2 38c + 10c brown & org   .30   .30
CB2 SP2 60c + 10c gray grn & org   .50   .50
   Issued for national recovery.

SPECIAL DELIVERY STAMPS

No. 242 Overprinted

1921, Aug.   **Unwmk.**   **Perf. 11½**
E1 A97 2c fawn   .70   .25
   a.   Double overprint   4.25

Caduceus — SD1

Imprint: "IMP. NACIONAL."

1922, Dec. 2   **Litho.**   **Wmk. 188**
     Size: 21x27mm
E2 SD1 2c light red   .50   .25

1924, Oct. 1
E3 SD1 2c pale ultra   .50   .25

1928   **Unwmk.**   **Perf. 11**
E4 SD1 2c light blue   .50   .25

Imprint: "IMPRA. NACIONAL."

1928-36   **Wmk. 188**
     Size: 16½x19½mm.
E5 SD1 2c black, *green*   .25   .25
     Unwmk.
E6 SD1 2c blue green ('29)   .25   .25

E7 SD1 2c blue ('36)   .25   .25
   Nos. E5-E7 (3)   .75   .75

1944, Oct. 23   **Perf. 12½**
E8 SD1 2c salmon pink   .25   .25

> Catalogue values for unused stamps in this section, from this point to the end of the section, are for Never Hinged items.

1947, Nov. 19
E9 SD1 2c red brown   .25   .25

No. E9 Surcharged in Black

1957, Oct. 30
E10 SD1 5c on 2c red brown   .25   .25

LATE FEE STAMPS

Galleon and Modern Steamship   LF1

     Wmk. Crossed Keys in Sheet
1936, May 18   **Litho.**   **Perf. 11**
I1 LF1 3c green   .25   .25
I2 LF1 5c violet   .25   .25
I3 LF1 6c blue green   .25   .25
I4 LF1 7c brown   .25   .25
I5 LF1 8c carmine   .50   .50
I6 LF1 12c deep blue   .65   .65
   Nos. I1-I6 (6)   2.15   2.15

POSTAGE DUE STAMPS

D1

1902   **Unwmk. Engr.**   **Perf. 14 to 15**
     Size: 21¼x18½mm
J1 D1 1c blue green   .75   .30
J2 D1 2c carmine   .75   .30
J3 D1 4c gray violet   .80   .30
J4 D1 10c dark blue   1.75   .70
J5 D1 20c ocher   2.50   1.25
   Nos. J1-J5 (5)   6.55   2.85

Surcharged in Red

1904
J6 D1 1c on 10c dk bl   1.25   1.25
   a.   Inverted surcharge   12.00   12.00

1913-15   **Litho.**   **Perf. 11½**
     Size: 22½x20mm
J7 D1 1c lt grn   .75   .30
J8 D1 2c rose red   .75   .30
J9 D1 4c dl vio   1.00   .50
J10 D1 6c dp brn   1.00   .50
     Size: 21¼x19mm
J11 D1 10c dl bl   1.50   .60
   Nos. J7-J11 (5)   5.00   2.00

Imprint: "Imprenta Nacional"

1922   **Size: 20x17mm**
J12 D1 1c bl grn   .50   .30
J13 D1 2c red   .50   .30
J14 D1 3c red brn   .70   .50
J15 D1 4c brn vio   .50   .30

J16 D1 5c blue   .80   .50
J17 D1 10c gray grn   1.00   .60
   Nos. J12-J17 (6)   4.00   2.50

1926-27   **Wmk. 188**   **Perf. 11**
     Size: 20x17mm
J18 D1 1c bl grn ('27)   .50   .25
J19 D1 3c red brn ('27)   .50   .25
J20 D1 5c slate blue   .50   .25
J21 D1 6c light brown   .50   .50
   Nos. J18-J21 (4)   2.00   1.25

1929   **Unwmk.**   **Perf. 10½, 11**
J22 D1 1c blue green   .25   .25
J23 D1 10c gray green   .50   .25

Figure of Value Redrawn (Flat on sides)

1932   **Wmk. 188**
J24 D1 6c yel brn   .50   .25

Imprint: "Casa A. Barreiro Ramos S. A."

1935   **Unwmk.**   **Litho.**   **Perf. 12½**
     Size: 20x17mm
J25 D1 4c violet   .50   .25
J26 D1 5c rose   .50   .25

Type of 1935

Imprint: "Imprenta Nacional" at right

1938
J27 D1 1c blue green   .25   .25
J28 D1 2c red brown   .25   .25
J29 D1 3c deep pink   .25   .25
J30 D1 4c light violet   .25   .25
J31 D1 5c blue   .25   .25
J32 D1 8c rose   .25   .25
   Nos. J27-J32 (6)   1.50   1.50

OFFICIAL STAMPS

Regular Issues Handstamped in Black, Red or Blue

Many double and inverted impressions exist of the handstamped overprints on Nos. O1-O83. Prices are the same as for normal stamps or slightly more.

On Stamps of 1877-79

1880-82   **Unwmk.**   **Rouletted 8**
O1 A9 1c red brown   4.00   3.50
O2 A10 5c green   3.00   2.50
O3 A11 20c bister   3.25   3.25
O4 A11 50c black   22.00   22.00
O5 A12 1p blue   22.00   22.00
   Nos. O1-O5 (5)   54.25   53.25

On No. 44
Rouletted 6
O6 A9 1c brown ('81)   6.00   6.00

On Nos. 43-43A
Rouletted 8
O7 A11 50c black (R)   17.00   16.00
O8 A12 1p blue (R)   22.50   20.00

On Nos. 45, 41, 37a
Perf. 12½
O9 A13 7c blue (R) ('81)   4.25   3.25

Rouletted 8
O10 A11 10c ver (Bl)   2.00   2.00

Perf. 13½
O11 A8b 15c yellow (Bl)   5.00   4.50

1883   **On Nos. 46-47**   **Perf. 12½**
O12 A14 1c green   6.50   6.50
O13 A14a 2c rose   9.50   9.50

On Nos. 50-51
Perf. 12½, 12x12½, 13
O14 A17 5c blue (R)   4.00   4.00
   a.   Imperf., pair   4.50
O15 A18 10c brown (Bl)   6.50   6.50
   a.   Imperf., pair   6.00

No. 48 Handstamped

1884 — Perf. 12½
O16 A15 1c green ... 35.00 32.50

Overprinted Type "a" in Black
On Nos. 48-49
1884 — **Perf. 12, 12x12½, 13**
O17	A15	1c green	35.00	32.50
O18	A16	2c red	12.00	9.50

On Nos. 53-56
Rouletted 8
O19	A11	1c on 10c ver	2.00	1.60
a.		Small "1" (No. 53a)	5.00	

Perf. 12½
O20	A14a	2c rose	6.50	6.50
O21	A22	5c ultra	6.50	6.50
O22	A23	5c blue	5.00	2.00
		Nos. O17-O22 (6)	67.00	58.60

On Stamps of 1884-88
1884-89 — **Rouletted 8**
O23	A24	1c gray	12.00	5.50
O24	A24	1c green ('88)	2.50	1.60
O25	A24	1c olive grn	3.25	1.75
O26	A24a	2c vermilion	1.00	.60
O27	A24a	2c rose ('88)	2.25	1.25
O28	A24b	5c slate blue	2.25	1.25
O29	A24b	5c slate bl, bl	6.50	5.00
O30	A24b	5c violet ('88)	6.50	5.00
O31	A24b	5c lt blue ('89)	6.50	5.00
O32	A25	7c dk brown	3.25	1.60
O33	A25	7c orange ('89)	3.25	2.25
O34	A26	10c olive brn	2.00	.90
O35	A30	10c violet ('89)	16.00	9.50
O36	A27	20c red violet	3.00	1.60
O37	A27	20c bister brn ('89)	16.00	7.00
O38	A28	25c gray violet	3.50	2.50
O39	A28	25c vermilion ('89)	16.00	7.00
		Nos. O23-O39 (17)	105.75	59.30

The OFICIAL handstamp, type "a," was also applied to No. 73, the 5c violet with "Provisorio" overprint, but it was not regularly issued.

1887 — On No. 71 — Rouletted 9
O40 A29 10c lilac ... 5.00
No. O40 was not regularly issued.

On Stamps of 1889-1899
Perf. 12½ to 15 and Compound
1890-1900
O41	A32	1c green	.80	.25
O43	A32	1c blue ('95)	2.00	2.00
O44	A33	2c rose	.80	.25
O45	A33	2c red brn ('95)	2.50	2.50
O46	A33	2c orange ('00)	.80	.50
O47	A34	5c deep blue	1.50	1.50
O48	A34	5c rose ('95)	2.00	2.00
O49	A35	7c bister brown	1.25	.80
O50	A35	7c green ('95)	25.00	
O51	A36	10c blue green	1.25	.80
O52	A36	10c orange ('95)	25.00	
O53	A37	20c orange	1.25	.80
O54	A37	20c brown ('95)	25.00	
O55	A38	25c red brown	1.25	.80
O56	A38	25c ver ('95)	55.00	
O57	A39	50c lt blue	4.50	4.50
O58	A39	50c lilac ('95)	5.50	5.50
O59	A40	1p lilac	7.00	5.00
O60	A40	1p lt blue ('95)	40.00	22.50

Nos. O50, O52, O54, O56 and O60 were not regularly issued.

1891 — On No. 99 — Rouletted 8
O61	A24b	5c violet	1.50	1.25
a.		"1391"	9.00	

On Stamps of 1895-99
Perf. 12½ to 15 and Compound
1895-1900
O62	A51	1c bister	.60	.60
O63	A51	1c slate blue ('97)	1.25	.55
O64	A52	2c blue	.25	.25
O65	A52	2c claret ('97)	1.25	.55
O66	A53	5c red	.80	.55
O67	A53	5c green ('97)	1.25	.55
O68	A53	5c grnsh blue ('00)	.95	.75
O69	A54	7c deep green	.50	.50
O70	A55	10c brown	.50	.50
O71	A56	20c green & blk	.80	.80
O72	A56	20c claret & blk ('97)	4.50	2.25
O73	A57	25c red brn & blk	.80	.80
O74	A57	25c pink & bl ('97)	4.50	2.25
O75	A58	50c blue & blk	.95	.95
O76	A58	50c grn & brn ('97)	5.75	2.75
O77	A59	1p org brn & blk	4.75	4.75

O78	A59	1p yel brn & bl ('97)	9.25	5.75
a.		Inverted overprint		
		Nos. O62-O78 (17)	38.65	25.10

1897, Sept. — On Nos. 133-135
O79	A62	1c brown vio & blk	1.25	1.00
O80	A63	5c pale bl & blk	1.75	1.00
O81	A64	10c lake & blk	1.75	1.10
		Nos. O79-O81 (3)	4.75	3.10

Perf. 12½ to 15 and Compound
1897-1900 — On Nos. 136-137
O82	A68	10c red	2.50	1.50
O83	A68	10c red lilac ('00)	1.25	1.25

Regular Issue of 1900-01 Overprinted

1901 — **Perf. 14 to 16**
O84	A72	1c yellow green	.50	.25
O85	A75	2c vermilion	.65	.25
O86	A73	5c dull blue	.65	.25
O87	A76	7c brown orange	.90	.50
O88	A74	10c gray violet	.95	.55
O89	A37	20c lt blue	8.00	4.00
O90	A38	25c bister brown	1.60	.80
O91	A40	1p deep green	10.50	6.00
a.		Inverted overprint	12.50	8.00
		Nos. O84-O91 (8)	23.75	12.60

Most of the used official stamps of 1901-1928 have been punched with holes of various shapes, in addition to the postal cancellations.

Regular Issue of 1904-05 Overprinted

1905 — **Perf. 11½**
O92	A79	1c green	.50	.25
O93	A80	2c orange red	.50	.25
O94	A81	5c deep blue	.50	.25
O95	A82	10c dark violet	1.00	.40
O96	A83	20c gray green	3.25	1.00
a.		Inverted overprint		
O97	A84	25c olive bister	2.25	.80
		Nos. O92-O97 (6)	8.00	2.95

Regular Issues of 1904-07 Overprinted

1907, Mar.
O98	A79	1c green	.25	.25
O99	A86	5c deep blue	.25	.25
O100	A86	7c orange brown	.25	.25
O101	A82	10c dark violet	.25	.25
O102	A83	20c gray green	.40	.35
a.		Inverted overprint	4.00	
O103	A84	25c olive bister	.50	.40
O104	A86	50c rose	.95	.70
		Nos. O98-O104 (7)	2.85	2.45

Regular Issues of 1900-10 Overprinted

1910, July 15 — **Perf. 14½ to 16**
O105	A75	2c vermilion	8.75	4.00
O106	A73	5c slate green	5.25	3.00
O107	A74	10c gray violet	2.75	1.25
O108	A37	20c grnsh blue	2.75	1.25
O109	A38	25c brown bister	4.50	2.40

Perf. 11½
O110	A86	50c rose	6.00	2.50
a.		Inverted overprint	20.00	15.00
		Nos. O105-O110 (6)	30.00	14.40

Peace—O1

1911, Feb. 18 — **Litho.**
O111	O1	2c red brown	.40	.25
O112	O1	5c dark blue	.40	.40
O113	O1	8c slate	.40	.65
O114	O1	20c gray brown	.55	.95
O115	O1	23c claret	.80	.95
O116	O1	50c orange	1.60	1.25
O117	O1	1p red	4.00	1.50
		Nos. O111-O117 (7)	8.15	5.95

Regular Issue of 1912-15 Overprinted

1915, Sept. 16
O118	A90	2c carmine	.55	.40
O119	A90	5c dark blue	.55	.40
O120	A90	8c ultra	.55	.40
O121	A90	20c dark brown	1.25	.50
O122	A91	23c dark blue	4.00	3.50
O123	A91	50c orange	6.00	3.50
O124	A91	1p vermilion	8.00	4.00
		Nos. O118-O124 (7)	20.90	12.70

Regular Issue of 1919 Overprinted

1919, Dec. 25
O125	A95	2c red & black	.80	.40
a.		Inverted overprint	3.50	
O126	A95	5c ultra & blk	.95	.40
O127	A95	8c gray bl & lt brn	.95	.40
a.		Inverted overprint	3.50	
O128	A95	20c brown & blk	2.00	.80
O129	A95	23c green & brn	2.00	.80
O130	A95	50c brown & bl	4.00	2.00
O131	A95	1p dull red & bl	10.00	4.00
a.		Double overprint	15.00	
		Nos. O125-O131 (7)	20.70	8.80

Regular Issue of 1923 Overprinted

1924 — **Wmk. 189** — **Perf. 12½**
O132	A100	2c violet	.25	.25
O133	A100	5c light blue	.25	.25
O134	A100	12c deep blue	.30	.25
O135	A100	20c buff	.40	.25
O136	A100	36c blue green	1.75	1.25
O137	A100	50c orange	3.50	2.50
O138	A100	1p pink	6.25	5.00
O139	A100	2p lt green	12.00	10.00
		Nos. O132-O139 (8)	24.70	19.75

Same Overprint on Regular Issue of 1924
1926-27 — **Unwmk.** — **Imperf.**
O140	A100	2c rose lilac	.40	.25
O141	A100	5c pale blue	.65	.25
O142	A100	8c pink ('27)	.80	.25
O143	A100	12c slate blue	.95	.25
O144	A100	20c brown	2.00	.40
O145	A100	36c dull rose	3.25	.95
		Nos. O140-O145 (6)	8.05	2.35

Regular Issue of 1924 Overprinted

1928 — **Perf. 12½**
O146	A100	2c rose lilac	1.50	.95
O147	A100	8c pink	1.50	.50
O148	A100	10c turq blue	2.00	.50
		Nos. O146-O148 (3)	5.00	1.95

Since 1928, instead of official stamps, Uruguay has used envelopes with "S. O." printed on them, and stamps of many issues which are punched with various designs such as star or crescent.

NEWSPAPER STAMPS

No. 245 Surcharged

1922, June 1 — **Unwmk.** — **Perf. 11½**
P1	A97	3c on 4c orange	.40	.40
a.		Inverted surcharge	9.50	9.50
b.		Double surcharge	2.50	2.50

Nos. 235-237 Surcharged

1924, June 1 — **Perf. 14½**
P2	A96	3c on 2c car & blk	.40	.40
P3	A96	6c on 4c red org & bl	.40	.40
P4	A96	9c on 5c bl & brn	.40	.40
		Nos. P2-P4 (3)	1.20	1.20

Nos. 288, 291, 293 Overprinted or Surcharged in Red

1926 — **Imperf.**
P5	A100	3c gray green	.80	.25
a.		Double overprint	1.00	1.00
P6	A100	9c on 10c turq bl	.95	.40
a.		Double surcharge	1.00	1.00
P7	A100	15c light violet	1.25	.50
		Nos. P5-P7 (3)	3.00	1.15

PARCEL POST STAMPS

Mercury — PP1

Imprint: "IMPRENTA NACIONAL"
Inscribed "Exterior"
Size: 20x29½mm
Perf. 11½
1922, Jan. 15 — **Litho.** — **Unwmk.**
Q1	PP1	5c grn, straw	.25	.25
Q2	PP1	10c grn, bl gray	.40	.25
Q3	PP1	20c grn, rose	2.10	.55
Q4	PP1	30c grn, grn	2.10	.25
Q5	PP1	50c grn, blue	3.50	.40
Q6	PP1	1p grn, org	5.25	1.60
		Nos. Q1-Q6 (6)	13.60	3.30

Inscribed "Interior"
Q7	PP1	5c grn, straw	.25	.25
Q8	PP1	10c grn, bl gray	.25	.25
Q9	PP1	20c grn, rose	1.00	.25
Q10	PP1	30c grn, grn	1.40	.25
Q11	PP1	50c grn, blue	2.25	.35
Q12	PP1	1p grn, org	6.00	1.25
		Nos. Q7-Q12 (6)	11.15	2.60

Imprint: "IMP. NACIONAL"
Inscribed "Exterior"

1926, Jan. 20   **Perf. 11½**
Q13 PP1 20c grn, *rose*   1.75 .50

Inscribed "Interior"
Perf. 11

Q14	PP1	5c grn, *yellow*	.40	.25
Q15	PP1	10c grn, *bl gray*	.50	.25
Q16	PP1	20c grn, *rose*	1.00	.25
Q17	PP1	30c grn, *bl grn*	1.75	.40
	Nos. Q13-Q17 (5)		5.40	1.65

Inscribed "Exterior"
1926   **Perf. 11½**

Q18	PP1	5c blk, *straw*	.40	.25
Q19	PP1	10c blk, *bl gray*	.65	.25
Q20	PP1	20c blk, *rose*	1.75	.25

Inscribed "Interior"

Q21	PP1	5c blk, *straw*	.40	.25
Q22	PP1	10c blk, *bl gray*	.50	.25
Q23	PP1	20c blk, *rose*	1.00	.25
Q24	PP1	30c blk, *bl grn*	1.75	.40
	Nos. Q18-Q24 (7)		6.45	1.90

PP2

Perf. 11, 11½

1927, Feb. 22   **Wmk. 188**

Q25	PP2	1c dp bl	.25	.25
Q26	PP2	2c lt grn	.25	.25
Q27	PP2	4c violet	.25	.25
Q28	PP2	5c red	.25	.25
Q29	PP2	10c dk brn	.40	.25
Q30	PP2	20c orange	.65	.40
	Nos. Q25-Q30 (6)		2.05	1.65

See Nos. Q35-Q38, Q51-Q54.

PP3

Size: 15x20mm

1928, Nov. 20   **Perf. 11**

Q31	PP3	5c blk, *straw*	.25	.25
Q32	PP3	10c blk, *gray blue*	.25	.25
Q33	PP3	20c blk, *rose*	.50	.25
Q34	PP3	30c blk, *green*	.80	.25
	Nos. Q31-Q34 (4)		1.80	1.00

Type of 1927 Issue
1929-30   **Unwmk.**   **Perf. 11, 12½**

Q35	PP2	1c violet	.25	.25
Q36	PP2	1c ultra ('30)	.25	.25
Q37	PP2	2c bl grn ('30)	.25	.25
Q38	PP2	5c red ('30)	.25	.25
	Nos. Q35-Q38 (4)		1.00	1.00

Nos. Q35-Q38, and possibly later issues, occasionally show parts of a papermaker's watermark.

PP4

1929, July 27   **Wmk. 188**   **Perf. 11**

Q39	PP4	10c orange	.50	.50
Q40	PP4	15c slate blue	.50	.50
Q41	PP4	20c ol brn	.50	.50
Q42	PP4	25c rose red	1.00	1.00
Q43	PP4	50c dark gray	2.00	1.00
Q44	PP4	75c violet	8.00	6.00
Q45	PP4	1p gray green	7.50	3.00
	Nos. Q39-Q45 (7)		20.00	12.00

For overprints see Nos. Q57-Q63.

Ship and Train — PP5

1938-39   **Unwmk.**   **Perf. 12½**

Q46	PP5	10c scarlet	.40	.25
Q47	PP5	20c dk bl	.60	.25
Q48	PP5	30c lt vio ('39)	.95	.25
Q49	PP5	50c green	1.75	.25
Q50	PP5	1p brn org	2.50	1.10
	Nos. Q46-Q50 (5)		6.20	2.10

See Nos. Q70-Q73, Q80, Q88-Q90, Q92-Q93, Q95.

Type of 1927 Redrawn
1942-55?   **Litho.**   **Perf. 12½**

Q51	PP2	1c vio ('55)		
Q52	PP2	2c bl grn	.25	.25
Q54	PP2	5c lt red ('44)	.25	.25

The vertical and horizontal lines of the design have been strengthened, the "2" redrawn, etc. No. Q51 has oval "O" in CEN-TESIMO, 2¼mm from frame line at right; No. Q35 has round "O" 1¾mm from frame line.

Numeral of Value — PP6

1943, Apr. 28   **Engr.**

Q55	PP6	1c dk car rose	.25	.25
Q56	PP6	2c grnsh blk	.25	.25

Parcel Post Stamps of 1929 Overprinted in Black

1943, Dec. 15   **Wmk. 188**   **Perf. 11**

Q57	PP4	10c orange	1.00	.50
Q58	PP4	15c slate blue	1.00	.50
Q59	PP4	20c olive brn	1.00	.50
Q60	PP4	25c rose red	1.50	1.00
Q61	PP4	50c dk gray	2.50	2.00
Q62	PP4	75c violet	5.00	4.00
Q63	PP4	1p gray grn	8.00	4.50
	Nos. Q57-Q63 (7)		20.00	13.00

> **Catalogue values for unused stamps in this section, from this point to the end of the section, are for Never Hinged items.**

Bank of the Republic — PP7   University — PP8

Perf. 12½

1945, Sept. 5   **Litho.**   **Unwmk.**

Q64	PP7	1c green	.25	.25
Q65	PP8	2c brt vio	.25	.25

See Nos. Q77-Q79, Q84.

Custom House — PP9

1946, Dec. 11   **Perf. 11½**
Q66 PP9 5c yel brn & bl   .25 .25

Type A141 Overprinted in Red

1946, Dec. 27   **Perf. 12½**
Q67 A141 1p light blue   .95 .25

See Nos. Q69, Q76.

Mail Coach — PP11

1946, Dec. 23
Q68 PP11 5p red & ol brn   12.00 5.00

Type A141 Overprinted in Black

1947
Q69 A141 2c dull violet brn   .25 .25

See Nos. Q74-Q76.

Type of 1938
1947-52   **Unwmk.**   **Perf. 12½**
Size: 16x19.5mm (5c, 30c)

Q70	PP5	5c brown org ('52)	.25	.25

Size: 17x20.5mm

Q71	PP5	10c violet	.25	.25
Q72	PP5	20c vermilion	.40	.25
Q73	PP5	30c blue	.55	.25
	Nos. Q70-Q73 (4)		1.45	1.00

Type of 1947
1948-49   **Black Overprint**

Q74	A141	1c rose lilac ('49)	.25	.25
Q75	A141	5c ultra	.25	.25
Q76	A141	5p rose carmine	4.00	1.75
	Nos. Q74-Q76 (3)		4.50	2.25

Types of 1945
1950

Q77	PP8	1c vermilion	.25	.25
Q78	PP7	2c chalky blue	.25	.25

1952   **Perf. 11**

Q79	PP7	10c blue green	.25	.25

Type of 1938-39
1954   **Perf. 12½**
Q80 PP5 20c carmine   .25 .25

Custom House — PP13

1p, State Railroad Administration Building.

1955   **Unwmk.**   **Litho.**   **Perf. 12½**

Q81	PP13	5c brown	.25	.25
Q82	PP13	1p light ultra	2.10	1.60

See Nos. Q83, Q85-Q86, Q96. For surcharge see No. Q87.

Types of 1945 and 1955
Design: 20c, Solis Theater.

1956-57   **Perf. 11**

Q83	PP13	5c gray ('57)	.30	.25
Q84	PP7	10c lt olive grn	.25	.25
Q85	PP13	20c yellow	.25	.25
Q86	PP13	20c lt red brn ('57)	.25	.25
	Nos. Q83-Q86 (4)		1.05	1.00

No. Q83 Surcharged with New Value in Red
1957
Q87 PP13 30c on 5c gray   .25 .25

Type of 1938-39
1957-60   **Wmk. 327**   **Perf. 11**
Q88 PP5 20c lt blue ('59)   .25 .25

Unwmk.
Q89 PP5 30c red lilac   .25 .25

Perf. 12½
Q90 PP5 1p dk blue ('60)   .50 .50
   Nos. Q88-Q90 (3)   1.00 1.00

Nos. Q88 and Q93 are in slightly larger format-17¼x21mm instead of 16x19½mm.

National Printing Works PP14

1960, Mar. 23   **Wmk. 327**   **Perf. 11**
Q91 PP14 30c yellow green   .25 .25

Type of 1938-39
1962-63   **Wmk. 332**   **Perf. 11**
Q92 PP5 50c slate green   .25 .25

Perf. 10½
Q93 PP5 1p blue grn ('63)   .50 .50

No. C158 Surcharged

1965   **Unwmk.**   **Perf. 11**
Q94 AP12 5p on 84c orange   .35 .25

For use on regular and air post parcels.

Types of 1938-55
1p, State Railroad Administration Building.

1966   **Litho.**   **Perf. 10½**
Q95 PP5 10c blue green   .25 .25

Wmk. 327
Q96 PP13 1p brown   .25 .25

No. C184 Surcharged in Red

1966   **Unwmk.**   **Perf. 11**
Q97 AP21 1p on 38c black   .25 .25

Plane and Bus — PP15

Design: 20p, Plane facing left and bus; "Encomiendas" on top.

1969, July 8   **Wmk. 332**   **Litho.**   **Perf. 12**

Q98	PP15	10p blk, crim & bl grn	.25	.25
Q99	PP15	20p bl, blk & yel	.40	.25

No. B7 Surcharged

1971, Feb. 3   **Wmk. 327**   **Perf. 11½**
Q100 SP2 60c on 1p + 10c   1.25 .60

No. 761 Surcharged in Red

1971, Nov. 12   Wmk. 332   *Perf. 12*
Q101 A226 60c on 6p lt grn & blk   .45   .25

Nos. 770-771 Surcharged

1972, Nov. 6   Litho.   *Perf. 12*
Q102 A233 1p on 6p multi (#770)   1.40   .55
Q103 A233 1p on 6p multi (#771)   1.40   .55
   a.   Pair, #Q102-Q103   3.00   1.10
     See note after No. 771.

Parcels and Arrows PP16

Old Mail Truck PP17

Designs: Early means of mail transport.

1974   Wmk. 332   Litho.   *Perf. 12*
Q104 PP16   75p shown   .25   .25
Q105 PP17   100p shown   .40   .25
Q106 PP17   150p Steam engine   .95   .95
Q107 PP17   300p Side-wheeler   .90   .55
Q108 PP17   500p Plane   1.40   .80
    Nos. Q104-Q108 (5)   3.90   2.80
Issue dates: 75p, Feb. 13; others, Mar. 6.

UZBEKISTAN

„uz-ˌbe-ki-'stan

LOCATION — Central Asia, bounded by Kazakhstan, Turkmenistan, Tajikistan, Afghanistan and Kyrgyzstan
GOVT. — Independent republic, member of the Commonwealth of Independent States
AREA — 172,741 sq. mi.
POP. — 25,155,064 (2001 est.)
CAPITAL — Tashkent (Toshkent)

With the breakup of the Soviet Union on Dec. 26, 1991, Uzbekistan and ten former Soviet republics established the Commonwealth of Independent States.

100 Kopecks = 1 Ruble
100 Tiyin = 1 Sum

Catalogue values for all unused stamps in this country are for Never Hinged items.

Princess Nodira (1792-1842) — A1

Perf. 11½x12
1992, May 7   Unwmk.   Photo.
1   A1   20k multicolored   .45   .45
   For surcharge, see No. 749.

Melitaea Acreina A2

1992, Aug. 31   Litho.   *Perf. 12*
2   A2   1r multicolored   .40   .40
   For surcharge, see No. 752.

Independence from Soviet Union, 1st Anniv. — A3

1992, Sept. 25   Photo.   *Perf. 12*
3   A3   1r multicolored   .40   .40

Khiva Mosque, 19th Cent. — A4

1992, Oct. 20   *Perf. 11½*
4   A4   50k multicolored   .40   .40
   For surcharge, see No. 750.

Samarkand — A5

1992, Oct. 28   Litho.   *Perf. 13x13½*
5   A5   10r multicolored   .60   .60
Winner of 1992 Aga Khan Award for Architecture. For surcharge, see No. 753.

Samovar, 19th Cent. — A6

1992, Nov. 20   *Perf. 12x11½*
6   A6   50k multicolored   .40   .40
   For surcharge, see No. 751.

Fauna A7

Designs: 1r, Teratoscincus scincus. No. 8, Naja oxiana. No. 9, Ondatra zibethica, vert. 3r, Pandion haliaetus, vert. 5r, Remiz pendulinus, vert. 10r, Dryomys nitedula, vert. 15r, Varanus griseus. 20r, Cervus elaphus baktrianus.

1993, Mar. 12   Litho.   *Perf. 12*
7   A7   1r multicolored   .25   .25
8   A7   2r multicolored   .25   .25
9   A7   2r multicolored   .25   .25
10   A7   3r multicolored   .25   .25
11   A7   5r multicolored   .25   .25
12   A7   10r multicolored   .25   .25
13   A7   15r multicolored   .50   .50
    Nos. 7-13 (7)   2.00   2.00
Souvenir Sheet
14   A7   20r multicolored   1.00   1.00
   For surcharges, see Nos. 769-776.

Russia Nos. 4596-4600, 5838, 5841-5843, 5984 Surcharged in Vio Bl, Brt Bl, Bl, Red, Blk and Grn

a

Methods and perfs as before
1993
15   A2765   2r on 1k (#5838, BB)   .60   .60
16   A2138   8r on 4k (#4599, Bl)   .55   .55
17   A2138   15r on 2k (#4597)   4.50   4.50
18   A2765   15r on 2k (#5984)   4.50   4.50
19   A2765   15r on 3k (#5839, R)   4.50   4.50
20   A2765   15r on 4k (#4599, V)   4.50   4.50
21   A2765   15r on 4k (#5840, R)   4.50   4.50
22   A2765   15r on 5k (#5841, R)   4.50   4.50
23   A2139   15r on 6k (#4600, R)   4.50   4.50
24   A2765   15r on 7k (#5985a, R)   4.50   4.50
25   A2765   15r on 10k (#5842)   4.50   4.50
26   A2765   15r on 15k (#5843, R)   4.50   4.50
27   A2138   20r on 4k (#4599, Bk)   .75   .75
28   A2139   30r on 3k (#4598, G)   .75   .75
28A   A2138   100r on 1k (#4596, R)   .90   .90
29   A2138   500r on 1k (#4596, Bl)   5.25   5.25
    Nos. 15-29 (16)   53.80   53.80
   No. 18 exists imperf.

Flag and Coat of Arms — A8

Perf. 12x12½, 11½x12 (#33)
1993, June 10   Litho.
30   A8   8r multicolored   .30   .30
31   A8   15r multicolored   .35   .35
33   A8   50r multicolored   .85   .85
34   A8   100r multicolored   2.00   2.00
    Nos. 30-34 (4)   3.50   3.50
   No. 33 is 19x26½mm.

Flowers — A9

No. 38, Dianthus uzbekistanicus. No. 39, Colchicum kesselringii. No. 40, Crocus alatavicus. No. 41, Salvia bucharica. No. 42, Tulipa kaufmanniana. No. 43, Tulipa greigii. No. 44, Tulip.

1993, Sept. 10   *Perf. 12*
38   A9   20r multicolored   .25   .25
39   A9   20r multicolored   .25   .25
40   A9   25r multicolored   .25   .25
41   A9   25r multicolored   .25   .25
42   A9   30r multicolored   .30   .30
43   A9   30r multicolored   .30   .30
    Nos. 38-43 (6)   1.60   1.60
Souvenir Sheet
44   A9   50r multicolored   1.00   1.00
   For surcharges, see Nos. 777-783.

Coat of Arms — A10

1994-95   Litho.   *Perf. 12*
Denomination Expressed as "1.00"
45   A10   1s green   1.75   1.75
Perf. 11½x12
46   A10   75s claret   .40   .40
   Issued: 1s, 3/20/95; 75s, 7/2.

1995   Litho.   *Perf. 14*
Denominations Expressed With "CYM"
46A   A10   1s green   —   —
47   A10   2s green   2.00   2.00
Size: 20x33mm
48   A10   3s carmine   2.00   2.00
49   A10   6s carmine   3.00   3.00
49A   A10   15s blue   3.00   3.00
Denomination Shown with Decimal
50   A10   3s carmine   .50   .50
51   A10   6s carmine   1.75   1.75
    Nos. 45-51 (8)   14.40   14.40
   Issued: 15s, 12/26; 2s, 3s, 6s, 4/18.
   See Nos. 151A-154, 167-171, 228-237, 405-415.

Arms Type of 1994-95
1997, Dec. 30   Litho.   *Perf. 14*
Size: 14x22mm
51A   A10   6s green   22.50   22.50
   No. 51A is dated 1997.

Statue of Tamerlane, Tashkent — A10a

1994, Sept. 1   Litho.   *Perf. 12½x12*
52   A10a   20t multicolored   .45   .45
   For surcharge, see No. 761.

Bakhouddin, 675th Anniv. — A11

1994, Aug. 1   *Perf. 12½x12*
55   A11   100s multi + label   .50   .50

Souvenir Sheet

President's Cup Intl. Tennis Tournament, Tashkent — A12

1994, June 3   *Perf. 12x12½*
56   A12 500s multicolored   1.25 1.25

Ulugh Beg (1394-1410), Astronomer — A13

30t, Portals of Samarkand. 35t, Portals of Bukhara. 40t, Globe, astrolabe. 45t, Statue. 60t, Portrait.

1994, Sept. 15 Litho.   *Perf. 12x12½*
57   A13 30t multi + label   .30   .30
58   A13 35t multi + label   .30   .30
59   A13 40t multi + label   .30   .30
60   A13 45t multil   .70   .70
     Nos. 57-60 (4)   1.60 1.60

Souvenir Sheet
61   A13 60t multicolored   .75   .75

For surcharges, see Nos. 762-766.

Russia Nos. 4596, 5113, 5839, 5840, 5843, 5984 Surcharged in Red Violet or Red

b

Methods and perfs as before
1995, Jan.
61A A2138(a)   2s on 1k
                (#4596, R)   1.50 1.50
61B A2765(a)   2s on 3k
                (#5839, R)   1.50 1.50
61C A2765(b)   200s on 2k
                (#5984)   1.50 1.50
61D A2765(b)   200s on 4k
                (#5840)   1.50 1.50
61E A2436(b)   200s on 5k
                (#5113)   1.50 1.50
61F A2765(b)   200s on 15k
                (#5843)   1.50 1.50
     Nos. 61A-61F (6)   9.00 9.00

No. 61C exists imperf. Value $7.50.

Souvenir Sheet

End of World War II, 50th Anniv. — A14

1995, May 8   Litho.   *Perf. 12*
62   A14 20s multicolored   3.00 3.00

Souvenir Sheet

UPU — A15

1995, Sept. 21
63   A15 20s multicolored   2.50 2.50

Capra Falconeri A16

1995, Aug. 15   *Perf. 12½*
64   A16 6s shown   .95   .55
65   A16 10s Three on mountain   1.60   .85
66   A16 10s Up close   1.60   .85
67   A16 15s Lying down   2.50 1.40
     Nos. 64-67 (4)   6.65 3.65

World Wildlife Fund.

Intl. Tennis Tournament, Tashkent '95 — A17

1995, Aug. 25   *Perf. 14*
68   A17 10s multicolored   2.25 2.25

Silk Road Architecture A19

Designs: 6s, Mosque, 15th cent. No. 71, Blue-domed mosque, ruins, 15th cent. No. 72, Mosque with 4 minarets, 19th cent. No. 73, Cylindrical-style mosque, 19th cent.
20s, Map of mosque sites, camel, mosque.

1995, Aug. 28 Litho.   *Perf. 12x12½*
70   A19 6s multicolored   1.25 1.25
71   A19 10s multicolored   2.50 2.50
72   A19 10s multicolored   2.50 2.50
73   A19 15s multicolored   3.75 3.75
     Nos. 70-73 (4)   10.00 10.00

Souvenir Sheet
74   A19 20s multicolored   6.00 6.00

Folktales — A20

6s, Man wrestling with creature, woman spilling bowls. No. 76, Man looking at stork, nest of eggs. No. 77, Women watching man cut into watermelon full of gold coins. No. 78, Creature carrying woman. 15s, Man holding beads, parrot.

1995, Aug. 24
75   A20 6s multi + label   2.40 2.40
76   A20 10s multicolored   3.25 3.25
77   A20 10s multicolored   3.25 3.25
78   A20 10s multicolored   3.25 3.25
79   A20 15s multicolored   5.00 5.00
     Nos. 75-79 (5)   17.15 17.15

Moths A21

6s, Karanasa abramovi. No. 81, Colias romanovi. No. 82, Parnassius delphius. No. 83, Neohipparchia fatua. No. 84, Chasara staudingeri. No. 85, Colias wiskotti. 15s, Parnassius tianschanicus.
20s, Colias christophi.

1995, Oct. 10   *Perf. 12½x12*
80   A21 6s multicolored   1.40 1.40
81   A21 10s multicolored   2.25 2.25
82   A21 10s multicolored   2.25 2.25
83   A21 10s multicolored   2.25 2.25
84   A21 10s multicolored   2.25 2.25
85   A21 10s multicolored   2.25 2.25
86   A21 15s multicolored   3.00 3.00
     Nos. 80-86 (7)   15.65 15.65

Souvenir Sheet
87   A21 20s multicolored   3.75 3.75

Aircraft A22

1995, Oct. 10
88   A22 6s JIN-2   1.25 1.25
89   A22 10s IL-76   2.00 2.00
90   A22 10s KA-22   2.00 2.00
91   A22 10s AN-8   2.00 2.00
92   A22 10s AN-22   2.00 2.00
93   A22 10s AN-12   2.00 2.00
94   A22 15s IL-114   3.00 3.00
     Nos. 88-94 (7)   14.25 14.25

Souvenir Sheet
95   A22 20s like No. 94   4.25 4.25

Wildlife from Tashkent Zoo — A23

Designs: 6s, Camelus ferus. No. 97, Aegypius monachus. No. 98, Ursus arctos isabellinus. No. 99, Zebra. No. 100, Macaca mulatta. No. 101, Pelecanus crispus. 15s, Loxodonta africana.
20s, Capra falconeri.

1995, Nov. 30   *Perf. 12x12½*
96   A23 6s multicolored   1.10 1.10
97   A23 10s multicolored   1.75 1.75
98   A23 10s multicolored   1.75 1.75
99   A23 10s multicolored   1.75 1.75
100   A23 10s multicolored   1.75 1.75
101   A23 10s multicolored   1.75 1.75
102   A23 15s multicolored   2.50 2.50
      Nos. 96-102 (7)   12.35 12.35

Souvenir Sheet
103   A23 20s multicolored   3.25 3.25

Wild Animals A24

Designs: 10s, Ovis ammon bocharensis. No. 105, Ovis ammon severtzov. No. 106, Cervus elaphus bactrianus. No. 107, Capra sibirica. No. 108, Ovis ammon karelini. No. 109, Ovis ammon cycloceros. 20s, Saiga tatarica.
25s, Gazella subgutturosa.

1996, Feb. 16   *Perf. 12½x12*
104   A24 10s multicolored   1.25 1.25
105   A24 15s multicolored   1.90 1.90
106   A24 15s multicolored   1.90 1.90
107   A24 15s multicolored   1.90 1.90
108   A24 15s multicolored   1.90 1.90
109   A24 15s multicolored   1.90 1.90
110   A24 20s multicolored   2.75 2.75
      Nos. 104-110 (7)   13.50 13.50

Souvenir Sheet
111   A24 25s multicolored   3.50 3.50

Painting A25

1995, Oct.   Litho.   *Perf. 12x12½*
112   A25 15s multicolored   2.75 2.75

Souvenir Sheet

Save the Aral Sea — A26

a, 15s, Felis caracal. b, 15s, Salmo trutta aralensis. c, 20s, Hyaena hyaena. d, 20t, Pseudoscaphirynchus kaufmanni. e, 25t, Aspiolucius esocinus.

1996, May 15   *Perf. 14*
113   A26   Sheet of 5, #a.-e.   5.00 5.00

See Kazakhstan No. 145, Kyrgyzstan No. 107, Tadjikistan No. 91, Turkmenistan No. 52.

1996 Summer Olympic Games, Atlanta A27

1996, June 23 Litho.   *Perf. 12½x12*
114   A27 6s Soccer   .60   .60
115   A27 10s Equestrian event   1.25 1.25
116   A27 15s Boxing   1.75 1.75
117   A27 20s Cycling   2.50 2.50
      Nos. 114-117 (4)   6.10 6.10

Souvenir Sheet

Tamerlane (1336-1405) — A28

1996, Aug. 31   Litho.   Perf. 14
118 A28 20s multicolored   3.50 3.50
  a. Inscribed "1336-1404," perf
    12x12½   5.00 5.00

  Issued: No. 118a, 8/9/96.

Souvenir Sheet

Independence Day — A29

1996, Aug. 27   Litho.   Perf. 12x12½
119 A29 20s multicolored   2.50 2.50

Tashkent Tennis Cup Championship A30

1996, Sept. 2   Litho.   Perf. 14
121 A30 12s green   11.00 11.00

A31

1996, Sept. 18   Perf. 14
122 A31 15s Faijzulla Khodjaev   6.50 6.50

A32

1996, Oct. 14   Litho.   Perf. 14
123 A32 15s black & buff   6.50 6.50

  Abdurauf Fitrat (1886-1996).

Futuristic Space Travel — A33

  9s, Shuttle-type vehicle. No. 126, Vehicle in front of sun. No. 127, Sun's rays, vehicle traveling left. No. 128, Large vehicle, sun in distance. No. 129, Saucer-shaped vehicle landing on planet. 25s, Two men in cockpit.
  30s, Two different space vehicles.

1997, Mar. 17
124 A33   9s multi, vert.   .90   .90
125 A33 15s shown   1.35 1.35
126 A33 15s multi   1.35 1.35
127 A33 15s multi   1.35 1.35
128 A33 15s multi, vert.   1.35 1.35
129 A33 15s multi, vert.   1.35 1.35
130 A33 25s multi, vert.   2.00 2.00
    Nos. 124-130 (7)   9.65 9.65
Souvenir Sheet
131 A33 30s multi, vert.   5.00 5.00

Fairy Tales A34

  No. 132, Genie. No. 133, Bird. No. 134, Child holding mirror in front of couple. No. 135, Ape. No. 136, Face of creature, horse. No. 137, Large bird attacking deer. 30s, Two people kneeling before throne.
  35s, Man on horse.

1997, Apr. 18
132 A34 15s multicolored   1.10 1.10
133 A34 15s multicolored   1.10 1.10
134 A34 20s multicolored   1.40 1.40
135 A34 20s multicolored   1.40 1.40
136 A34 25s multicolored   1.60 1.60
137 A34 25s multicolored   1.60 1.60
138 A34 30s multicolored   2.25 2.25
    Nos. 132-138 (7)   10.45 10.45
Souvenir Sheet
139 A34 35s multicolored   6.50 6.50

Abdulhamid Sulaymon, Birth Cent. — A35

1997, June 20
140 A35 6s lilac, black & gray   4.75 4.75

Pantera Pardus Tullianus A36

  Designs: No. 142, Yawning. No. 143, Stretching. 25s, Walking on fallen tree. 30s, With mouth open.

1997, May 28
141 A36   9s multicolored   .95   .95
142 A36 15s multicolored   1.75 1.75
143 A36 15s multicolored   1.75 1.75
144 A36 25s multicolored   3.25 3.25
    Nos. 141-144 (4)   7.70 7.70
Souvenir Sheet
145 A36 30s multicolored   3.75 3.75

  No. 145 contains one 30x40mm stamp.

Sites on Silk Road A37

  In Bukhara: No. 146, Ancient citadel. No. 147, Tomb of Ismail Samani, vert. In Khiva: No. 148, Minaret, vert. No. 149, Fortress wall with open door. No. 150, Mosque, Bukhara. No. 151, Minaret, Khiva, diff., vert.

1997   Litho.   Perf. 14
146 A37 15s multicolored   2.50 2.50
147 A37 15s multicolored   2.50 2.50
148 A37 15s multicolored   2.50 2.50
149 A37 15s multicolored   2.50 2.50
    Nos. 146-149 (4)   10.00 10.00
Souvenir Sheets
150 A37 30s multicolored   3.00 3.00
151 A37 30s multicolored   3.00 3.00

  Issued: Nos. 146-147, 150, 10/7; Nos. 148-149, 151, 10/8.

Arms Type of 1994 Redrawn
1998   Litho.   Perf. 14
Size: 14x22mm
151A A10   2s green   .40   .40
152   A10   3s carmine, "1998"   1.25 1.25
   a. Dated "1999"   .50   .50
153   A10   6s green, "1998"   3.00 3.00
   a. Dated "1999"   .70   .70
153A A10 12s green   2.75 2.75
153B A10 15s red   1.75 1.75
154   A10 45s blue   4.25 4.25
    Nos. 151A-154 (6)   13.40 13.40
  Nos. 152-154 have country name "O'ZBEKISTON" at top and "POCHTA 1998" at bottom.
  Issued: 6s, 2/25; 12s, 15s, 45s, 3/25; 2s, 4/16; 3s, 4/17.

Intl. Tennis Tournament, Tashkent A38

  Emblem and: No. 155, President's Cup. No. 156, Tennis player. No. 157, Camel.

1997   Litho.   Perf. 14
155 A38 6s blue & grn   4.00 4.00
156 A38 6s blue & grn   4.00 4.00
157 A38 6s blue & grn   4.00 4.00
    Nos. 155-157 (3)   12.00 12.00

Automobiles — A39

  a, 9s, Tico. b, 12s, Damas. c, 15s, Nexia.

1997, Sept. 19   Litho.   Perf. 14
158 A39 Block of 3, #a.-c. + label   6.00 6.00

Tennis Tournament — A40

1998, Aug. 17   Litho.   Perf. 14
159 A40 15s multicolored   1.25 1.25

Sharq Taronlalari Intl. Music Festival — A41

1998, July 15
160 A41 15s multicolored   1.00 1.00

Berdekh Monument — A42

1998, Aug. 17
161 A42 15s blue & brown   1.00 1.00

Kamal ud-Din Behzad, Painter — A43

1998, Aug. 17
162 A43 15s multicolored   1.40 1.40

Imam al-Buhkari — A44

1998, June 26
163 A44 15s multicolored   1.00 1.00

Ahmad al-Farghani, Astronomer — A45

1998, June 26
164 A45 15s multicolored   1.50 1.50

Folktales — A46

Designs: a, 8s, Woman holding baby. b, 10s, "Alpomish" over rainbow. c, 15s, Three men seated before fire. d, 15s, Man talking to man with sword. e, 18s, Man riding horse. f, 18s, Knight with longbow, squire with arrow. g, 20s, Swordmaker at work. h, 20s, Man fighting lion. i, 25s, Man, woman walking arm in arm.

1998, Nov. 27   Litho.   Perf. 14
165 A46 Sheet of 9, #a.-i.   7.50 7.50
No. 165 is a continuous design.

Arms Type of 1994 Redrawn
1999-2001   Litho.   Perf. 14
Size: 14x23mm
167 A10 5s blue green,
            "2000"   2.00 2.00
   a.   Dated "2004"   2.25 2.25
   b.   Dated "2005"   2.25 2.25
168 A10 6s green   1.00 1.00
168A A10 10s dk green   .50   .50
   d.   10s emerald, dated "2004" 1.50 1.50
168B A10 15s lt blue   .85   .85
168C A10 17s dk blue   .90   .90
169 A10 30s blue   1.00 1.00
170 A10 40s rose, "2000"   1.50 1.50
   b.   Dated "2001"   1.25 1.25
170A A10 45s rose   2.75 2.75
   a.   45s carmine, dated "2001" 3.00 3.00
171 A10 60s rose car   2.75 2.75
         Nos. 167-171 (9)   13.25 13.25

Iooued: 0s, 3/22/99. 15s, 17s, 30s, 45s, 12/5/00. 5s, 60s, 1/17/01; No. 168A, 40s, 2/5/01. No. 168Ad, 6/15/04.
Nos. 167-171 have country name "O'ZBEKISTON" at top and "POCHTA" and year at bottom. Stamps issued in 2001 are inscribed "2000."
No. 168 is inscribed "6 so'm." No. 153 is inscribed "6-00."

Trains — A47

Locomotives: No. 172, OV steam, 1897-1917. No. 173, EA steam, 1931-35. 28s, FD steam, 1931-41. 36s, SO steam, 1934-52. No. 176, VL-22 electric. No. 177, KCh. 69s, TEP-6.

1999, May 11   Litho.   Perf. 14
172 A47 18s multicolored   .70   .70
173 A47 18s multicolored   .70   .70
174 A47 28s multicolored   1.00 1.00
175 A47 36s multicolored   1.10 1.10
176 A47 56s multicolored   2.00 2.00
177 A47 56s multicolored   2.00 2.00
178 A47 69s multicolored   2.25 2.25
         Nos. 172-178 (7)   9.75 9.75

A48

Designs: 18s, Horse rearing.
No. 180, horiz.: a, 36s, Robed rider on horse. b, 28s, White horse. c, 69s, Jockey on race horse.
75s, Black horse, horiz.

1999, May 25
179 A48 18s multicolored   1.75 1.75

180 A48   Vert. strip of 3, #a.-
             c.   4.00 4.00
         Souvenir Sheet
181 A48 75s multicolored   3.25 3.25
No. 180 printed in sheets of 8 stamps containing 2 strips and one each of Nos. 180a and 180c.

A49

No. 182 — Story of Badal Qorachi: a, 18s, Woman, deer. b, 18s, Two archers on horses. c, 28s, Archer on horse. d, 36s, White giant. e, 56s, Black giant. f, 56s, Troll, cat, bones. g, 69s, Man, woman.
75s, Woman on sofa, demon, horiz.

1999, June 8
182 A49 Sheet of 7, #a.-g. + la-
          bel   7.50 7.50
         Souvenir Sheet
183 A49 75s multicolored   3.25 3.25

A50

Reptiles: No. 184, Trapelus sangulnolentus. No. 185, horiz.: a, 18s, Eremias arguta. b, 18s, Vipera ursinii. c, 28s, Phrynocephalus mystaceus. d, 36s, Agkistrodon halys. e, 56s, Eumeces schneideri. f, 69s, Vipera lebetina.
75s, Two lizards, horiz.

1999, June 22
184 A50 56s multicolored   1.25 1.25
185 A50 Sheet of 6, #a.-f. 6.25 6.25
         Souvenir Sheet
186 A50 75s multicolored   3.75 3.75

A51

1999, July 7
187 A51 45s light green & black 1.60 1.60
         UPU, 125th anniv.

A52

1999, July 21
188 A52 30s green & claret   1.25 1.25
Muhammadrizo Erniyozbek ogli-Ogahiy, poet.

A53

Birds of Prey: No. 189, Circaetus qallicus. No. 190, Falco tinnunculus. No. 191, Aquila chrysaetos. No. 192, Gyps fulvus. 36s, Falco cherrug. 56s, Gypaetus barbatus. 60s, Pandion haliaetus.
75s, Bird, hatchlings.

1999, Oct. 22   Litho.   Perf. 14x13¾
189 A53 15s multi   .70   .70
190 A53 15s multi   .70   .70
191 A53 18s multi   .90   .90
192 A53 18s multi   .90   .90
193 A53 36s multi   1.25 1.25
194 A53 56s multi   1.75 1.75
195 A53 60s multi   2.00 2.00
         Nos. 189-195 (7)   8.20 8.20
         Souvenir Sheet
196 A53 75s multi   4.00 4.00

A54

Soccer.

1999, Nov. 8
197 A54 15s Two players   .65   .65
198 A54 18s Two players, diff. .65   .65
199 A54 28s Two players, diff. .85   .85
200 A54 28s Player, goalie .85   .85
201 A54 36s Player, goalie,
          diff.   1.50 1.50
202 A54 56s Two players, diff. 1.75 1.75
203 A54 69s Two players, diff. 2.25 2.25
         Nos. 197-203 (7)   8.50 8.50
         Souvenir Sheet
         Perf. 13¾x14
204 A54 75s Two players,
          horiz.   4.00 4.00

A55

Prehistoric Animals: a, 28s, Meqaneura. b, 28s, Mesosaurus. c, 36s, Rhamphorhynchus. d, 36s, Styracosaurus albertensis. e, 56s, Trachodon annectens. f, 56s, Tarbosaurus bataar. g, 69s, Arsinoitherium. h, 75s, Phororhacos.

1999, Dec. 13   Litho.   Perf. 14x13¾
205 A55 Sheet of 8, #a.-h. 12.00 12.00

Uzbek
National
Circus — A56

28s, Woman and lion. No. 207, 36s, Acrobat with bow and arrow. No. 208, 36s, Acrobat.

No. 209, 56s, Clown on horse. No. 210, 56s, Two riders on horse. 69s, Wire walker. 100s, Woman, camels, llamas, horiz.

2000, Jan. 4   Perf. 14
206 A56 28s multi   .95   .95
207 A56 36s multi   .95   .95
208 A56 56s multi   .95   .95
209 A56 56s multi   1.90 1.90
210 A56 56s multi   1.90 1.90
211 A56 69s multi   2.25 2.25
         Nos. 206-211 (6)   8.90 8.90
         Souvenir Sheet
212 A56 100s multi   3.25 3.25

Horses — A57

Designs: 69s, Horses pulling carriage.
No. 214: a, 36s, Horse in dressage competition. b, 36s, Horse jumping fences. c, 56s, Horses in race. d, 56s, Horse jumping steeplechase fence. e, 75s, Horse with sulky. f, 75s, Race winner.

2000, Feb. 1
213 A57 69s multi   2.00 2.00
214 A57 Sheet of 6, #a.-f. 10.00 10.00

Ajiniyoz Qo'siboy,
Poet — A58

2000, Mar. 31   Litho.   Perf. 14
215 A58 28s multi   1.25 1.25

Famous Islamic Scholars — A59

Designs: No. 216, 60s, Burhan al-Din al-Marghinani. No. 217, 60s, Imam Abu Mansur al-Maturidi, horiz.

2000, Oct. 24   Stamp + label
216-217 A59 Set of 2   3.25 3.25

UN High Commissioner for Refugees,
50th Anniv. — A60

2000, Dec. 11
218 A60 125s multi + label 2.25 2.25

Bats
A61

Designs: 15s, Tadarida teniotis. 30s, Otonycteris hemprichi. 45s, Nyctalus lasiopterus, vert. 50s, Myotis frater, vert. 60s, Rhinolophus hipposideros, vert. 90s, Barbastella leucomelas, vert. 125s, Nyctalus noctula, vert. 160s, Unidentified bat, vert.

2001, Feb. 23　Perf. 13¾x14, 14x13¾
219-225　A61　Set of 7　　6.00 6.00
Souvenir Sheet
226　A61　160s multi　　2.75 2.75

Dated 2000.

Native Costumes — A62

2001, Feb. 26　　Perf. 14x13¾
227　Horiz. strip of 5 + label　7.00 7.00
　a.　A62 45s multi　　　　.60　.60
　b.　A62 50s multi, diff.　　.70　.70
　c.　A62 60s multi, diff.　　.80　.80
　d.　A62 90s multi, diff.　1.15　1.15
　e.　A62 125s multi, diff.　1.75　1.75

Dated 2000.

Arms Type of 1994 Redrawn
2001-05　　Litho.　　Perf. 14
　　　　Size: 14x23mm
228　A10　15s emerald　　.70　.70
229　A10　17s dull green　.70　.70
230　A10　20s dull green　.70　.70
231　A10　25s bright blue　.70　.70
232　A10　30s sky blue　　.70　.70
232A　A10　30s green　　　.90　.90
　a.　Dated "2004"　　　　.90　.90
　b.　light green, dated "2005"　.90　.90
233　A10　33s gray blue　.90　.90
234　A10　45s red　　　1.25　1.25
235　A10　50s rose　　1.40　1.40
236　A10　60s rose pink　1.75　1.75
237　A10　100s rose, "2001"　2.50　2.50
　a.　Dated "2003"　　　1.50　1.50
　　Nos. 228-237 (11)　12.20 12.20

Issued: 15s, 17s, 25s, 33s, 50s, 60s, 100s, 4/3; 20s, 30s, 4/11; 45s, 6/22. No. 232A, 5/26/03; No. 232Aa, 6/15/04; No. 232Ab, 3/25/05. No. 237a, 5/26/03.

Ali Shir Nava'i (1441-1501), Poet — A63

2001, Apr. 11
238　Horiz. strip of 5 + label　8.25 8.25
　a.　A63 60s Hayrat ul-abror　1.00 1.00
　b.　A63 70s Farhod va Shirin　1.00 1.00
　c.　A63 85s Layli va Majnun　1.25 1.25
　d.　A63 90s Sab'ai sayyora　1.25 1.25
　e.　A63 125s Saddi Iskandariy　1.75 1.75

World Environment Day — A64

2001, June 20
239　A64　100s multi　　2.10 2.10

Avesto, 2700th Anniv. — A65

2001, June 20
240　A65　160s multi　　2.50 2.50

Souvenir Sheet

Termiz, 2500th Anniv. — A66

2001, June 20
241　A66　175s multi　　3.75 3.75

Souvenir Sheet

Independence, 10th Anniv. — A67

2001, June 20
242　A67　175s multi　　3.50 3.50

Souvenir Sheet

Regional Communications Cooperation — A68

2001, June 20
243　A68　175s multi　　3.25 3.25

10th Anniv. of Independence Issue

Vertical Label

Horizontal Label

Tourist Hotel — A69

Monuments — A70

Inauguration of Pres. Islam Karimov — A71

Pres. Karimov at United Nations A72

Pres. Karimov at Istanbul Summit A73

Hirmon A74

Silk Cocoons A75

Fergana Refinery A76

Power Station A77

Daewoo Auto Factory A78

Securities Exchange A79

Kamchik Tunnel A80

Pres. Karimov and US Pres. Clinton A81

Pres. Karimov and Russian Pres. Vladimir Putin A82

Pres. Karimov and Japanese Emperor Akihito A83

Pres. Karimov and Chinese Pres. Jiang Zemin A84

Pres. Karimov and German Chancellor Gerhard Schröder A85

Pres. Karimov and French Pres. Jacques Chirac A86

Pres. Karimov and British Prime Minister John Major A87

Pres. Karimov and Iranian Pres. Ali Mohammad Khatami — A88

Pres. Karimov and Egyptian Pres. Hosni Mubarak A89

Pres. Karimov and Italian Pres. Carlos Ciampi A90

Pres. Karimov and Indian Pres. Kocheril Narayanan A91

Pres. Karimov and Pope John Paul II — A92

Textile Workers A93

Shurtan Gas Complex — A94

Muborak Refinery — A95

Solar Collector A97

Soldiers with Flag A98

Missiles A99

Soldiers Training A100

Kurash Sports Complex A101

New Year's Celebration — A102

Mother and Child — A103

Oil Pipeline — A96

Wedding A104

Bukhara Refinery — A105

Nuclear Power Plant — A106

A70 Designs: No. 245, Zahriddin Bobur Monument. No. 246, Amir Temur Monument. No. 247, Al-Motorudi Mausoleum. No. 248, Al-Marginoniy Monument. No. 249, Jaloliddin Manguberdi Monument. No. 250, Al-Bukhoriy Mausoleum. No. 273, Alisher Navoi Monument. No 274, Berdakh Monument. No. 284, Alpomish Monument. No. 288, Al-Fargoni Monument.

2001   Litho.   Perf. 14x13¾, 13¾x14
Stamp + Label with Same
Orientation

244	A69	60s multi	.50	.50
245	A70	60s multi	.50	.50
246	A70	70s multi	.50	.50
247	A70	75s multi	.50	.50
248	A70	75s multi	.50	.50
249	A70	85s multi	.70	.70
250	A70	90s multi	.70	.70
251	A71	90s multi	.70	.70
252	A72	90s multi	.70	.70
253	A73	90s multi	.70	.70
254	A74	90s multi	.70	.70
255	A75	90s multi	.70	.70
256	A76	90s multi	.70	.70
257	A77	90s multi	.70	.70
258	A78	90s multi	.70	.70
259	A79	90s multi	.70	.70
260	A80	90s multi	.70	.70
261	A81	95s multi	.80	.80
262	A82	95s multi	.80	.80
263	A83	95s multi	.80	.80
264	A84	95s multi	.80	.80
265	A85	95s multi	.80	.80
266	A86	95s multi	.80	.80
267	A87	95s multi	.80	.80
268	A88	95s multi	.80	.80
269	A89	95s multi	.80	.80
270	A90	95s multi	.80	.80
271	A91	95s multi	.80	.80
272	A92	95s multi	.80	.80
273	A70	115s multi	1.00	1.00
274	A70	115s multi	1.00	1.00
275	A93	115s multi	1.00	1.00
276	A94	115s multi	1.00	1.00
277	A95	115s multi	1.00	1.00
278	A96	115s multi	1.00	1.00
279	A97	115s multi	1.00	1.00
280	A98	115s multi	1.00	1.00
281	A99	115s multi	1.00	1.00
282	A100	115s multi	1.00	1.00
283	A101	115s multi	1.00	1.00
284	A70	125s multi	1.00	1.00
285	A102	125s multi	1.00	1.00
286	A103	125s multi	1.00	1.00
287	A104	125s multi	1.00	1.00
288	A70	160s multi	1.25	1.25
289	A105	160s multi	1.25	1.25
290	A106	160s multi	1.25	1.25

Nos. 244-290 (47)   39.25 39.25

Nos. 244-290 were each printed in sheets of 2 stamps and 2 labels.
See No. 363.

Uzbekistan Arms — A107

Uzbekistan Flag — A108

Motor Vehicles A109

Central Bank Building — A110

Bank Association Building — A111

Tashkent Khokimiyat Building A112

Central Trade Center Building A113

Shurtan Gas Complex A114

Shurtan Gas Complex A115

Couple with Baby A116

Children A117

Farm Equipment A118

Airplanes
A119

Constitution
A120

Majlis Hall — A121

Gold
Ingots and
Coins
A122

Muruntay
Gold Mine
A123

Independence Day
Celebrations — A124

Independence Day
Celebrations — A125

A109 Designs: No. 292a, Nexia. No. 292b, Damas. No. 293a, Tico. No. 293b, Matiz.

A118 Designs: No. 298a, Case 2022 cotton picker. No. 298b, SHR-100 tractor.

A119 Designs: No. 299a, IL-76 MF cargo plane. No. 299b, IL-114-100 passenger plane.

291	Pair with central label	1.50	1.50
a.	A107 90s multi	.75	.75
b.	A108 90s multi	.75	.75
292	Pair with central label	1.50	1.50
a.-b.	A109 90s Any single	.75	.75
293	Pair with central label	1.50	1.50
a.-b.	A109 90s multi	.75	.75
294	Pair with central label	1.50	1.50
a.	A110 90s multi	.75	.75
b.	A111 90s multi	.75	.75
295	Pair with central label	1.50	1.50
a.	A112 90s multi	.75	.75
b.	A113 90s multi	.75	.75
296	Pair with central label	2.25	2.25
a.	A114 115s multi	1.10	1.10
b.	A115 115s multi	1.10	1.10
297	Pair with central label	2.25	2.25
a.	A116 125s multi	1.10	1.10
b.	A117 125s multi	1.10	1.10
298	Pair with central label	2.50	2.50
a.-b.	A118 160s Any single	1.25	1.25
299	Pair with central label	1.75	1.75
a.	A119 90s multi	.75	.75
b.	A119 115s multi	.95	.95

300	Pair with central label	1.50	1.50
a.	A120 115s multi	.90	.90
b.	A121 60s multi	.50	.50
301	Pair with central label	1.75	1.75
a.	A122 115s multi	.90	.90
b.	A123 90s multi	.60	.60
302	Pair with central label	1.75	1.75
a.	A124 125s multi	.95	.95
b.	A125 90s multi	.70	.70
	Nos. 291-302 (12)	21.25	21.25

Nos. 291-302 printed in sheets of four stamps and two labels (two pairs).
See Nos. 361-362, 364-366, 371.

Theater
A126

Theater
A127

Theater
A128

Medals — A129

Combine
A130

Combine
A131

Pres.
Karimov
and
Farmers
A132

Soldier
Taking
Oath
Before
Flag
A133

Man and
Soldier
Embracing
A134

Frontier
Guards
and Dog
A135

Athletes — A136

Soldiers in
Formation
A137

Diver
Training
A138

Decontamination Training — A139

Modern Architecture — A140

Armed Forces — A141

Archaeology — A142

High School — A143

Uzbekistan on World Map — A144

A129 Designs: No. 304a, Dostelik. No. 304b, I Darajali "Shon-Sharaf." No. 304c, II Darajali "Shon-Sharaf." No. 305a, I Darajali Sog'lom Avlod Uchun. No. 305b, II Darajali Sog'lom Avlod Uchun. No. 305c, Mehnat Shuhrati. No. 306a, Jaloliddin Manguberdi. No. 306b, Buyuk Xizmatlari Uchun. No. 306c, El-Yurt Hurmati. No. 307a, Oltin Yildiz. No. 307b, Mustaqillik. No. 307c, Amir Temur.

A136 Designs: No. 310a, Muhammadqodir Abdullayev. No. 310b, Lina Cheryazova. No. 310c, Artur Grigoryan. No. 312a, 160s, Armen Bagdasarov. No. 312b, 160s, Rustam Qosimjonov. No. 312c, 115s, Otabek Kosimov. No. 312d, 115s, Iroda To'laganova. No. 312e, 100s, Dilshod Muxtorov. No. 312e, 115s, Oksana Chusovitina.

No. 313: a, Temuriylar Tarixi Muzeyi (Amir Temur Museum). b, Oqsaroy. c, Oliy Majlis. d, Motamsaro Ona (Monument to Grieving Mother). e, Shahidlar Xotirasi (Respect Monument). f, Interkontinental mehmonxonasi (Intercontinental Hotel). g, Milliy Bank (National Bank). h, Yunusobod Sport Majmuasi (Yunusobod Sport Complex).

No. 314: a, 60s, Infantrymen, tank. b, 70s, Airplane and crew. c, 80s, Helicopter and crew. d, 90s, Soldier directing tank with flags. e, 90s, Minesweeper. f, 115s, Soldiers in classroom. g, 160s, Tanks. h, 60s, Artillery.

No. 315: a, 75s, Pot. b, 75s, Artifact with arch. c, 75s, Artifact with hole at top and side. d, 80s, Broken pot. e, 80s, Anthropomorphic figure with arms. f, 80s, Buddha. g, 80s, Costumed figure. h, 80s, Disk. i, 80s, Anthropomorphic figure missing arm. j, 80s, Box. k, 80s, Face.

303	Strip of 3 + label	1.90	1.90
a.	A126 90s multi	.60	.60
b.	A127 90s multi	.60	.60
c.	A128 90s multi	.60	.60
304	Strip of 3 + label	3.25	3.25
a.-c.	A129 160s Any single	1.00	1.00
305	Strip of 3 + label	3.25	3.25
a.-c.	A129 160s Any single	1.00	1.00
306	Strip of 3 + label	3.25	3.25
a.-c.	A129 160s Any single	1.00	1.00
307	Strip of 3 + label	3.25	3.25
a.-c.	A129 160s Any single	1.00	1.00
308	Strip of 3 + label	3.25	3.25
a.	A130 160s multi	1.00	1.00
b.	A131 160s multi	1.00	1.00
c.	A132 160s multi	1.00	1.00
309	Strip of 3 + label	2.25	2.25
a.	A133 60s multi	.45	.45
b.	A134 80s multi	.60	.60
c.	A135 90s multi	.70	.70
310	Strip of 3 + label	3.00	3.00
a.	A136 160s multi	1.25	1.25
b.-c	A136 115s Any single	.85	.85
311	Block of 3 + label	2.25	2.25
a.	A137 115s multi	.80	.80
b.	A138 80s multi	.60	.60
c.	A139 70s multi	.50	.50
	Nos. 303-311 (9)	25.65	25.65

Sheets

312	A136	Sheet of 6, #a-f, + 3 labels	6.50	6.50
313	A140	115s Sheet of 8, #a-h, + label	8.50	8.50
314	A141	Sheet of 8, #a-h, + label	6.50	6.50
315	A142	Sheet of 11, #a-k, + label	7.50	7.50

Souvenir Sheets

316	A143	160s multi	2.50	2.50
317	A144	175s multi	2.75	2.75

Labels have same orientation as stamps and are at left side of strips on Nos. 303-310, and at UR on No. 311. No. 312 contains three different labels.
See No. 370.

Commonwealth of Independent States, 10th Anniv. — A145

2001, Nov. 8   **Perf. 13¾x14**
318 A145 60s multi   1.40 1.40

Artwork of Oral Tansiqboyev — A146

No. 319: a, 100s, Mening Qo'shig'im (My Song). b, 125s, Angren-Qo'qon Tog'yo'li (Angren-Kokand Mountain Road).

2001, Nov. 8
319 A146 Pair, #a-b, with central label   4.00 4.00

Flowers — A147

Designs: 45s, Zygophyllum bucharicum. 50s, Viola hissarica. 60s, Bergenia hissarica. 70s, Eremurus hilariae. 85s, Salvia korolkowii. 90s, Lamyropappus schakaptaricus. 145s, Punica granatum. 175s, Undescribed flowers.

2002, May 10   **Litho.**   **Perf. 14x13¾**
320-326 A147   Set of 7   7.00 7.00
Souvenir Sheet
327 A147 175s multi   3.50 3.50

Hominids — A148

No. 328: a, 40s, Dryopithecus maior. b, 45s, Homo erectus modjokertensis. c, 50s, Pithecanthropus erectus. d, 60s, Australopithecus afarensis. e, 70s, Zinjanthropus boisei. f, 85s, Homo sapiens neanderthalensis. g, 90s, Sinanthropus pekinensis. h, 125s, Protanthropus heidelbergensis. i, 160s, Homo sapiens fossilis.

2002, May 10   **Perf. 13¾x14**
328 A148   Sheet of 9, #a-i, + 3 labels   8.50 8.50

Protection of Ozone Layer — A149

2002, June 7   **Litho.**   **Perf. 13¾x14**
329 A149 40s multi   1.40 1.40
Souvenir Sheet

City of Shahrisabz, 2700th Anniv. — A150

2002, June 14   **Perf. 14**
330 A150 30s multi   1.25 1.25

Uzbek Sports A151

Designs: 45s, Chavgon. 50s, Poyga. 60s, Kamondan otish. 70s, Qiz quvmoq. 85s, Ro'molcha olish. 90s, Kurash. 145s, Uloq. 175s, Ro'molcha olish, diff.

2002, July 26   **Perf. 13¾x14**
331-337 A151   Set of 7   6.25 6.25
Souvenir Sheet
338 A151 175s multi   2.75 2.75

Ancient Coins — A152

No. 339: a, 30s, Silver tetradrachm of Eucratides I c. 171-135 BC, obverse. b, 45s, As "a," reverse. c, 60s, Silver coin of Buxoro, obverse. d, 90s, As "c," reverse. e, 125s, Silver miri of Tamerlane, 1370-1405, obverse. f, 160s, As "e," reverse.

2002, Aug. 1
339 A152   Block of 6, #a-f   6.50 6.50
See Nos. 367-369.

City of Nukus, 70th Anniv. — A153

2002, Oct. 2
340 A153 100s multi   1.60 1.60

Iris Varieties — A154

Designs: 15s, Qoraqum. 30s, Solnechniy zaychik. 45s, Simfoniya. 50s, Chimyon. 60s, Ikar. 90s, Babye leto. 125s, Toshkent. 160s, Askiya.

2002, Oct. 2   **Perf. 14x13¾**
341-347 A154   Set of 7   7.00 7.00
Souvenir Sheet
348 A154 160s multi   2.50 2.50

Uzbekistan postal officials have declared the following items as "illegal":
Sheets of eight stamps depicting Trains (4 different sheets with denominations of 56s, 75s, 95s and 125s);
Sheets of six stamps with various denominations depicting Birds (2 different), Animals, Year of the Snake, Chiroptera, Lizards, Chess;
Sheets of one label and five stamps with various denominations depicting Perissodactyla;
Souvenir sheets of one depicting Trains (8 different 36s sheets, 4 different 56s sheets, 2 different 75s sheets).

G'afur G'ulom (1903-66), Poet — A155

2003, May 4   **Litho.**   **Perf. 13¾x14**
349 A155 1000s brown   5.75 5.75

European Bank Annual Meeting Issue

Vertical Label

Horizontal Label

National Bank, Tashkent — A156

Kaltaminor Minaret, Khiva — A157

Aloqabank, Tashkent A158

Pres Karimov and European Bank for Reconstruction and Development Pres. Jean Lemierre — A159

Islamkhodja Minaret, Khiva — A160

East Gates, Khiva — A161

Samanid Museum, Bukhara — A162

Ark, Bukhara — A163

Women's Traditional Dress — A164

Women's
Traditional
Dress — A165

Women's
Traditional
Dress — A166

Women's
Traditional
Dress — A167

Women's
Traditional
Dress — A168

A157 Designs: 630s, Gumbazi Sayyidon Mausoleum, Shahrisabz. 920s, Go'ri Amir Mausoleum, Samarqand. 970s, Chorminor Madrasasi, Bukhara. 1330s, Registon, Samarqand, horiz.

2003, May 4   Perf. 14x13¾, 13¾x14
Stamp + Label with Same
Orientation

350	A156	520s multi	6.25	6.25
351	A157	520s multi	6.25	6.25
352	A157	630s multi	7.25	7.25
353	A157	920s multi	11.00	11.00
354	A157	970s multi	12.00	12.00
355	A158	970s multi	12.00	12.00
356	A157	1330s multi	15.00	15.00
357	A159	1330s multi	15.00	15.00
358	Horiz. pair with central label		14.00	14.00
a.	A160	580s multi	6.25	6.25
b.	A161	520s multi	6.25	6.25
359	Horiz. pair with central label		21.00	21.00
a.	A162	1170s multi	12.50	12.50
b.	A163	630s multi	7.00	7.00
360	Horiz. strip of 5 with flanking label		27.50	27.50
a.	A164	240s multi	2.75	2.75
b.	A165	320s multi	4.00	4.00
c.	A166	520s multi	6.25	6.25
d.	A167	520s multi	6.25	6.25
e.	A168	630s multi	7.25	7.25

Types of 2001-02
Stamp + Label with Same
Orientation

361	A110	520s multi	6.25	6.25
362	A111	580s multi	6.25	6.25
363	Horiz. pair with central label		14.00	14.00
a.	A74	170s multi	2.00	2.00
b.	A93	920s multi	11.00	11.00
364	Horiz. pair with central label		9.75	9.75
a.	A107	240s multi	2.75	2.75
b.	A108	520s multi	6.25	6.25
365	Horiz. pair with central label		10.00	10.00
a.	A114	630s multi	7.25	7.25
b.	A115	240s multi	2.75	2.75
366	Horiz. pair with central label		10.00	10.00
a.	A122	520s multi	6.25	6.25
b.	A123	320s multi	4.00	4.00
367	Horiz. pair with flanking label		14.00	14.00
a.	A152	520s Like #339a	6.25	6.25
b.	A152	520s Like #339b	6.25	6.25

368	Horiz. pair with flanking label		14.00	14.00
a.	A152	580s Like #339c	6.25	6.25
b.	A152	580s Like #339d	6.25	6.25
369	Horiz. pair with flanking label		15.00	15.00
a.	A152	630s Like #339e	7.25	7.25
b.	A152	630s Like #339f	7.25	7.25
370	A140	Sheet of 8 + central label	60.00	60.00
a.	520s Like #313a		6.25	6.25
b.	970s Like #313b		12.00	12.00
c.	580s Like #313c		6.25	6.25
d.	630s Like #313d		7.25	7.25
e.	320s Like #313e		4.00	4.00
f.	630s Like #313f		7.25	7.25
g.	920s Toshkent shahar hokimiyati (mayor's house)		11.00	11.00
h.	240s Like #313h		2.75	2.75

Type of 2001 Redrawn

371	Horiz. pair with central label		19.00	19.00
a.	A109	630s Like #292a	7.25	7.25
b.	A109	970s Like #293b	12.00	12.00
	Nos. 350-371 (22)		325.50	325.50

Famous
Men — A169

Designs: 125s, Komil Yormatov, film director. 500s, Jo'raxon Sultonov, singer.

2003, July 8   Perf. 13¾x14
372-373 A169   Set of 2   5.00 5.00

Birds — A170

Designs: No. 374, 100s, Ciconia ciconia asiatica. No. 375, 100s, Ciconia nigra. No. 376, 125s, Platalea leucorodia. No. 377, 125s, Phoenicopterus ruber.

2003, Sept. 17   Perf. 14x13¾
374-377 A170   Set of 4   5.50 5.50

Caps — A171

Designs: No. 378, 100s, Kula-tung. No. 379, 100s, Erkaklar do'ppisi. No. 380, 100s, Bayram do'ppisi. No. 381, 125s, Ayollar do'ppisi. No. 382, 125s, Ayollar taxya-do'ppisi. No. 383, 155s, Erkaklar do'ppisi, diff. No. 384, 155s, Bolalar bayram do'ppisi.

2003, Oct. 7
378-384 A171   Set of 7   11.00 11.00

Paintings — A172

No. 385: a, Tong. Onalik, by R. Ahmedov. b, Baxt, by S. Ayitbayev.

2003, Nov. 19
385 A172 970s Horiz. pair, #a-b   12.00 12.00
See Kazakhstan No. 434.

Abuxoliq G'ijduvoniy, Bukhara, 900th
Anniv. — A173

2003, Nov. 28   Perf. 13¾x14
386 A173 125s multi + label   1.60 1.60

Souvenir Sheet

2004 Summer Olympics,
Athens — A174

2004, June 15   Litho.   Perf. 14x13¾
387 A174 205s multi   3.00 3.00

Ma'murjon
Uzoqov (1904-
63),
Singer — A175

Abdulla Qodiriy
(1894-1938),
Writer — A176

2004, Oct. 11   Perf. 14
388 A175 100s lt blue & blk   1.50 1.50
389 A176 125s lt blue & blk   1.75 1.75

Grapes — A177

Designs: 60s, Kaltak. No. 391, 100s, Oq husayni. No. 392, 100s, Kattaqo'rg'on. No. 393, 125s, Echkemar. No. 394, 125s, Qizil Xurmoni. 155s, Qora Andijon. 210s, Parkent.

2004, Oct. 11   Perf. 14x13¾
390-396 A177   Set of 7   12.00 12.00

Jewelry of 19th
and 20th
Centuries
A178

Inscriptions: 60s, Tumor, Samarqand. No. 398, 100s, Tumor, Toshkent. No. 399, 100s, Qi'ltiqtumor, Qo'qon. No. 400, 125s, Tumor, Buxoro. No. 401, 125s, Bo'yintumor, Toshkent. 155s, Qo'ltiqtumor, Buxoro. 210s, Tumor, Buxoro, diff.

2004, Oct. 18
397-403 A178   Set of 7   12.00 12.00

Kitab State Geological Reserve, 25th
Anniv. — A179

2004, Dec. 1
404 A179 100s multi + label   2.00 2.00

Arms Type of 1994 Redrawn

2004-06	**Litho.**		**Perf. 14**
	Size: 14x23mm		
405	A10	35s green	.25	.25
406	A10	60s green	.35	.35
a.	light green, dated "2005"		.35	.35
407	A10	65s green	.40	.40
408	A10	125s dark blue	.60	.60
409	A10	200s red	.85	.85
410	A10	250s blue	1.10	1.10
411	A10	290s red	1.25	1.25
412	A10	350s blue	1.50	1.50
413	A10	430s red	1.75	1.75
414	A10	2500s red	10.00	10.00
415	A10	3700s blue	14.00	14.00
	Nos. 405-415 (11)		32.05	32.05

Issued: No. 406, 6/15; Nos. 406a, 408, 4/15/05; others, 1/5/06. Nos. 405, 407, 409-415 are dated "2005," though issued in 2006.

Oybek (1905-68),
Writer — A180

2005, Apr. 25   Litho.   Perf. 14x13¾
416 A180 125s multi   1.60 1.60

Miniature Sheet

End of World War II, 60th
Anniv. — A181

No. 417: a, 60s, Veterans at war memorial. b, 60s, Child with balloon at memorial. c, 100s, Sculptures. d, 100s, Child looking at memorial. e, 125s, Veterans looking at airplane sculpture. f, 125s, Woman passing soldiers. g, 155s, Soldier and floral display. h, 155s, Man looking at scrapbook.

2005, May 6
417 A181   Sheet of 8, #a-h, +
           central label   8.50 8.50

Tashkent University of Information Technologies, 50th Anniv. — A182

2005, May 25   **Perf. 13¾x14**
418 A182 125s multi + label   1.90 1.90

Qarshi, 2700th Anniv. — A183

2005, Aug. 1
419 A183 125s multi   1.25 1.25

Doves   A184

No. 420: a, 85s, Qopqon-chinni. b, 85s, Ruyan. c, 100s, Novvoti. d, 100s, Oq kaptar. e, 125s, Juk. f, 125s, Chelkar. g, 155s, Udi. h, 155s, Gulsor.
   210s, Buxoro kaptari.

2005, Sept. 15
420 A184   Sheet of 8, #a-h   6.75 6.75
           Souvenir Sheet
421 A184 210s multi   2.75 2.75

Miniature Sheet

Toreutic Art — A185

No. 422: a, 60s, Teapot with ribbed ornamentation. b, 60s, Teapot with round ornamentation. c, 100s, Teapot, diff. d, 125s, Teapot, diff. 155s, Teapot-samovar. 340s, Teapot with square lid.

2005, Oct. 25
422 A185   Sheet of 6, #a-f   7.50 7.50

Ma'mun Academy, 1000th Anniv. — A186

2005, Dec. 15   **Perf. 13¾x14**
423 A186 430s multi   3.00 3.00

Paintings A187

Designs: No. 424, 200s, Ko'i, by V. I. Yenin. No. 425, 200s, Osuda Kun, by B. Boboyev, vert. No. 426, 250s, Samarqand, Navro'z, by G. Abdurahmanov, vert. No. 427, 250s, Qo'qondagi Choyxona, by J. Umarbekov, vert. No. 428, 300s, Oqtosh, by R. Ahmedov, vert. No. 429, 300s, Yoz, by Y. P. Melnikov, vert. 350s, Kuz, by N. Qo'ziboyev, vert.

2006, Jan. 3   **Perf. 13¾x14, 14x13¾**
424-430 A187   Set of 7   10.50 10.50
           Dated 2005.

Rustam Qosimjonov, Intl. Chess Federation World Champion — A188

2006, Jan. 5   **Perf. 13¾x14**
431 A188 200s multi   1.75 1.75
           Dated 2005.

Medalists at 2004 Summer Olympics, Athens — A189

Designs: No. 432, 200s, Artur Taymazov, 120kg freestyle wrestling gold medalist. No. 433, 200s, Aleksandr Doxturushvili, 74kg Greco-Roman wrestling gold medalist. 250s, Magomed Ibragimov, 96kg freestyle wrestling silver medalist. 350s, O'tkir Haydarov and Bahodir Sultonov, 81kg and 54kg boxing bronze medalists, horiz.

2006, Jan. 5   **Perf. 14x13¾, 13¾x14**
432-435 A189   Set of 4   6.50 6.50
           Dated 2005.

2006 Winter Olympics, Turin — A190

Designs: 1540s, Skiing. 2155s, Figure skating.

2006, May 19   Litho.   Perf. 14x13¾
436-437 A190   Set of 2   14.00 14.00

Musical Instruments A191

Designs: 200s, Tanbur and Qashqar rubobi. 250s, Surnay and Tor. 290s, Surnay and Doira. 350s, Nay and Dutor. 410s, G'ijjak. 430s, Nog'om. 580s, Tanbur and Chang.

2006, May 19   Set of 7   10.00 10.00
438-444 A191

Dogs A192

Designs: 350s, Labrador retriever. 540s, Cocker spaniel. 600s, German shepherd. 780s, Asian sheepdog.
   1150s, Collie and German shepherd.

2006, May 19   **Perf. 13¾x14**
445-448 A192   Set of 4   9.00 9.00
           Souvenir Sheet
449 A192 1150s multi   4.00 4.00

Souvenir Sheet

2006 World Cup Soccer Championships, Germany — A193

2006, May 19   **Perf. 14x13¾**
450 A193 720s multi   3.50 3.50

Fish — A194

No. 451: a, 45s, Salmo trutta aralensis. b, 90s, Acipenser nudiventris. c, 250s, Pseudoscaphirhynchus kaufmanni. d, 300s, Barbus brachycephalus.
   1010s, Aspiolucius esocinus.

2006, July 10   **Perf. 13¾x14**
451 A194   Sheet of 4, #a-d   3.50 3.50
           Souvenir Sheet
452 A194 1010s multi   4.25 4.25

Bell Tower, Tashkent   Alisher Navoiy Theater
A195   A196

2006, Aug. 10   **Perf. 14x13¾**
453 A195 55s green   .55 .55
           Perf. 13¾x14
454 A196 90s emerald   .75 .75
   See Nos. 543, 545, 548, 597, 599. Compare with Type A249.

Butterflies A197

Designs: 45s, Papilio alexanor. 90s, Parnassius mnemosyne. 200s, Parnassius apollonius. 250s, Parnassius maximinus. 300s, Parnassius honrathi. No. 460, 350s, Hypermnestra helios. No. 461, 350s, Parnassius charltonius.
   1010s, Parnassius actius.

2006, Aug. 10   **Perf. 13¾x14**
455-461 A197   Set of 7   6.75 6.75
           Souvenir Sheet
462 A197 1010s multi   5.00 5.00

15th Anniv. of Independence Issue

Horizontal Label

Vertical Label

Pres. Islam Karimov and Indian Prime Minister Manmohan Singh — A198

School and Children, Kokand — A199

House of Children's Creativity — A200

Senate Chamber — A201

Emblem of 2005 Intl. Cotton Fair, Tashkent, and Cotton Boll — A202

Pres. Karimov and People's Republic of China Chairman Hu Jintao — A203

Pres. Karimov and Latvian Pres. Vaire Vike-Fraiberg — A204

Qungirot Soda Factory — A205

Leaders at Shanghai Cooperation Organization Summit, Tashkent — A206

Cement Factory A207

Railroad Construction — A208

Pres. Karimov and Graduates of Vaseda University — A209

Monument of Independence and Humanism — A210

Mine — A211

Bronze Smelter — A212

Festival — A213

Daewoo Nexia DOHC — A214

Kurash A215

Intl. Kurash Association Medal A216

Pres. Karimov and Cotton Pickers — A217

Pres. Karimov and Cotton Pickers — A218

Pres. Karimov and Farmers — A219

Roads — A220

Textiles — A221

Military — A222

Sports — A223

A198 Designs — Pres. Karimov and: No. 466, Malaysian King Tuanku Syed Sirajuddin. No. 470, Writer Said Akhmad. No. 474, Slovenian Pres. Janez Drnovsek. No. 477, Russian Pres. Vladimir Putin. No. 480, South Korean Pres. Roh Moo-hyun. No. 483, Uzbek labor leader.

A200 Designs: No. 469, Humanism Arch. No. 478, Medical School, Margilan. No. 484, Tashkent Railway Station. No. 486, Senate Building.

A206 Design: No. 482, Leaders at Euro-Asian Economic Union meeting.

A207 Design: No. 481, Angren Coal Mine.

A213 Design: No. 489b, 90s, Festival, diff.

A214 Design: No. 490b, 200s, Daewoo Damas II.

A215 Designs: No. 491b, 90s, Kurash, diff. No. 491c, 100s, Kurash, diff.

A216 Designs: No. 492b, 580s, FILA Wrestling medal. No. 492c, 720s, National Olympic Committee medal.

No. 494: a, 90s, Winding mountain road. b, 180s, Road construction. c, 55s, Highway.

No. 495: a, 410s, Workers and textile mill machinery. b, 580s, Women holding skeins of thread. c, 250s, Textile mill machinery.

No. 496: a, 410s, Soldiers in joint Uzbekistan-Russia anti-terrorism exercises, flags. b, 100s, Graduation of cadets. c, 250s, Soldiers at desks.

No. 497: a, 580s, Pres. Karimov and student athletes. b, 45s Stadium. c, 55s, Swimming meet. d, 90s, Athletes with medals. e, 200s, Karate. f, 250s, Soccer. g, 100s, Synchronized swimming. h, 290s, Equestrian event.

Perf. 13¾x14, 14x13¾
2006, Aug. 25
Stamp + Label With Same Orientation

463	A198	45s multi	.55	.55
464	A199	45s multi	.55	.55
465	A200	45s multi	.55	.55
466	A198	45s multi	.55	.55
467	A201	90s multi	.55	.55
468	A202	90s multi	.55	.55
469	A200	95s multi	.55	.55
470	A198	100s multi	.55	.55
471	A203	200s multi	.90	.90
472	A204	200s multi	.90	.90
473	A205	200s multi	.90	.90
474	A198	250s multi	1.15	1.15
475	A206	250s multi	1.15	1.15
476	A207	250s multi	1.15	1.15
477	A198	290s multi	1.35	1.35
478	A200	290s multi	1.35	1.35
479	A208	290s multi	1.35	1.35
480	A198	350s multi	1.35	1.35
481	A207	350s multi	1.35	1.35
482	A206	410s multi	1.75	1.75
483	A198	430s multi	1.90	1.90
484	A200	430s multi	1.90	1.90
485	A209	580s multi	2.75	2.75

486	A200	720s multi	3.50	3.50
487	A210	1010s multi	4.75	4.75
		Nos. 463-487 (25)	33.85	33.85

Pairs

488		Horiz. pair with central label	1.10	1.10
a.	A211	45s multi	.55	.55
b.	A212	55s multi	.55	.55
489		Horiz. pair with central label	1.10	1.10
a.	A213	55s multi	.55	.55
b.	A213	90s multi	.55	.55
490		Horiz. pair with central label	2.25	2.25
a.	A214	290s multi	1.35	1.35
b.	A214	200s multi	.90	.90
		Nos. 488-490 (3)	4.45	4.45

Strips

491		Strip of 3 + label	3.00	3.00
a.	A215	430s multi	1.90	1.90
b.	A215	90s multi	.55	.55
c.	A215	100s multi	.55	.55
492		Strip of 3 + label	8.00	8.00
a.	A216	410s multi	1.75	1.75
b.	A216	580s multi	2.75	2.75
c.	A216	720s multi	3.50	3.50
493		Strip of 3 + label	2.75	2.75
a.	A217	200s multi	.90	.90
b.	A218	250s multi	1.15	1.15
c.	A219	90s multi	.55	.55
		Nos. 491-493 (3)	13.75	13.75

Sheets

494	A220	Sheet of 3, #a-c, + label	1.45	1.45
495	A221	Sheet of 3, #a-c, + label	5.50	5.50
496	A222	Sheet of 3, #a-c, + label	3.50	3.50
497	A223	Sheet of 8, #a-h, + label	7.50	7.50
		Nos. 494-497 (4)	17.95	17.95

Nos. 463-475, 477-480, 482-486 were printed in sheets of 2 stamps and 2 labels. Nos. 476, 481 and 487 were printed in sheets of 5 stamps and 5 labels. Nos. 488-490 were printed in sheets of 4 stamps and 2 labels (2 pairs).

National Flag, 15th Anniv. — A224

2006, Nov. 1   *Perf. 13¾x14*
498 A224 600s multi + label   2.50 2.50

Miniature Sheet

Intl. Year of Deserts and Desertification — A225

No. 499: a, 45s, Oxyura leucocephala. b, 250s, Haliaeetus albicilla. c, 350s, Phalcrocorax pygmaeus. d, 350s, Marmaronetta angustirostris.

2006, Nov. 1
499 A225 Sheet of 4, #a-d   4.75 4.75

Roses — A226

Designs: 45s, Rosa divina. 90s, Rosa maracandica. 250s, Rosa persica. 350s, Rosa vassilczencoi. 600s, Rosa divina, diff.

2006, Nov. 1   *Perf. 14x13¾*
500-503 A226   Set of 4   3.75 3.75

Souvenir Sheet
504 A226 600s multi   2.00 2.00

Souvenir Sheet

Year of Charity and Medical Workers — A227

2006, Nov. 17   *Perf. 13¾x14*
505 A227 720s multi   2.75 2.75

Souvenir Sheet

Regional Communications Commonwealth, 15th Anniv. — A228

2006, Nov. 17
506 A228 1010s multi   4.50 4.50

2006 Asian Games, Doha, Qatar A229

Designs: 90s, High jump. 250s, Tennis. No. 509, 350s, Basketball. No. 510, 350s, Soccer.

2006, Dec. 27   Litho.   *Perf. 13¾x14*
507-510 A229   Set of 4   4.25 4.25

Diplomatic Relations Between Uzbekistan and People's Republic of China, 15th Anniv. — A230

2006, Dec. 29
511 A230 200s multi   1.25 1.25

Admission to the United Nations, 15th Anniv. — A231

2007, Mar. 1
512 A231 410s multi   1.75 1.75

Souvenir Sheet

Spring Festival — A232

2007, Mar. 1   *Perf. 14x13¾*
513 A232 1440s multi   5.75 5.75

2007 Winter Asian Games, Changchun, People's Republic of China — A233

Designs: 250s, Figure skating. 350s, Skiing.

2007, Mar. 1
514-515 A233   Set of 2   2.75 2.75

Abdulla Qahhor (1907-68), Writer — A234

No. 516: a, 350s, Scene from "Shohi So'zana." b, 420s, Qahhor.

2007, May 31   *Perf. 13¾x14*
516 A234   Horiz. pair, #a-b   3.00 3.00

Souvenir Sheets

A235

A236

A237

Architecture — A238

No. 517: a, 200s, Norbo'tabiy Madrasasi (madrassa). b, 410s, Daxmai Shohon Maqbarasi (mausoleum). c, 430s, Xudoyorxon Saroyi (palace).
No. 518: a, 250s, Modarixon Madrasasi (madrassa). b, 420s, Mir Arab Madrasasi (madrassa). c, 430s, Chor Bakr Me'moriy Majmuasi (mausoleum).
No. 519: a, 90s, Qo'shdarvoza (city gate). b, 250s, Muhammad Rahimxon Madrasasi (madrassa). c, 1010s, Pahlavon Mahmud Maqbarasi (mausoleum).
No. 520: a, 300s, Yunusxon Maqbarasi (mausoleum). b, 350s, Baroqxon Madrasasi (madrassa). c, 750s, Abulqosim Madrasasi (madrassa).

2007, May 31   *Perf. 13¾x14, 14x13¾*
517	A235	Sheet of 3, #a-c, + label	4.00	4.00
518	A236	Sheet of 3, #a-c, + label	4.00	4.00
519	A237	Sheet of 3, #a-c, + label	5.00	5.00
520	A238	Sheet of 3, #a-c, + label	5.00	5.00
		Nos. 517-520 (4)	18.00	18.00

Margilan, 2000th Anniv. — A239

2007, June 30   *Perf. 14x13¾*
521 A239 350s multi   1.40 1.40

Quddus Muhammadiy (1907-99), Poot   A240

2007, July 30   *Perf. 13¾x14*
522 A240 410s light blue & blk   1.60 1.60

Berries
A241

Designs: 100s, Fragaria. 250s, Ribes nigrum. 580s, Rubus idaeus. 720s, Grossularia reclinata.

2007, July 30　　Litho.
523-526　A241　Set of 4　6.50 6.50

Jewelry — A242

Designs: 300s, Yarim tirnoq. 350s, Ko'krak do'zi, horiz. 670s, Shovkala, horiz. 720s, Bodomoy.

2007, July 30　Perf. 14x13¾, 13¾x14
527-530　A242　Set of 4　7.75 7.75

Miniature Sheets

Samarqand, 2750th Anniv. — A243

No. 531: a, 45s, Registon Maydoni, Ulug'bel Madrasasi. b, 55s, Registon Maydoni, Sherdor Madrasasi. c, 100s, Registon Maydoni, Tillakori Madrasasi. d, 180s, Amir Temur Maqbarasi, Umumiy Ko'rinishi. e, 200s, Bibixonim Masjidi. f, 250s, Ruhobod Maqbarasi. g, 490s, Registon Maydoni, Umumiy Ko'rinishi. h, 720s, Shohisinda Majmuasi, Qo'shgumbazli Maqbara.

No. 532, vert.: a, 90s, Imom al-Moturidiy Maqbarasi. b, 100s, Imom Buxoriy Maqbarasi. c, 180s, Amir Temur Maqbarasi Kirish Peshtoqi. d, 200s, Amir Temur Haykali (statue). e, 410s, Bibixonim Maqbarasi. f, 680s, Shohizinda Majmuasi. g, 700s, Bibixonim Masjidi Kirish Peshtoqi. h, 1150s, Shohizinda Majmuasi, Tuman Oqo Maqbarasi.

2007, July 30　　Perf. 13¾x14
531　A243　Sheet of 8, #a-h, +
　　　　central label　7.50 7.50
　　　　Perf. 14x13¾
532　A243　Sheet of 8, #a-h, +
　　　　central label　12.50 12.50

Acinonyx Jubatus
A244

Designs: 90s, Leaping. 490s, Resting. 680s, Walking. 780s, Standing. 1440s, Adult with juvenile, vert.

2007, Oct. 3　　Perf. 13¾x14
533-536　A244　Set of 4　7.25 7.25
　　　Souvenir Sheet
　　　　Perf. 14x13¾
537　A244　1440s multi　5.25 5.25

Souvenir Sheet

Tashkent Subway, 30th Anniv. — A245

No. 538: a, 540s, Train and system map. b, 780s, Subway emblem and station entrance.

2007, Nov. 20　　Perf. 14x13¾
538　A245　Sheet of 2, #a-b　5.00 5.00

Constitution, 15th Anniv. — A246

2007, Dec. 5　　Litho.
539　A246　600s multi　2.25 2.25

Miniature Sheet

Zahiruddin Muhammad Babur (1483-1530), Founder of Mughal Dynasty — A247

No. 540 — Inscriptions: a, 200s, Boburning toj kiyib Farg'ona taxtiga chiqishi (Coronation). b, 250s, Boburning Samarqandliklar tomonidan tantana bilan kutib olinishi (Samarqand people welcome Babur). c, 350s, Bobur Hirotda Sulton Huseyn xonadonida (Babur at Sultan Hussein's house). d, 350s, Bengaliya elchisi Bobur qabulida (Babur receives Bengal ambassador). e, 350s, Babur. f, 410s, Qobul qal'asining qamaldan ozod etilishi (Babur freeing Kabul fortress). g, 490s, Bobur Dehli atrofidagi maqbaralami ziyorat qilmoqda (Babur views Delhi mausoleum). h, 540s, Qobul atrofidagi Xo'ja Seyoron chashmasi (Xo'ja Seyoron Spring near Kabul). i, 680s, Bobur Mon Sing va Bikramojit saroylarini tomosha qilmoqda (Babur views Man Singh and Bikramajit Palaces).

2008, Feb. 13
540　A247　Sheet of 9, #a-i　12.50 12.50

National Academic Drama Theater — A248　Alisher Navoiy Theater — A249

2008, Feb. 28　　Perf. 13¾x14
541　A248　45s blue　.55 .55
542　A249　90s dark green　.55 .55
No. 542 has thicker lettering than No. 454.

Architecture Types of 2006-08
2008　Litho.　Perf. 13¾x14, 14x13¾
543　A195　30s green　.35 .35
544　A249　75s dark green　.35 .35
545　A195　85s dark green　.40 .40
546　A248　100s red　.40 .40
547　A249　150s dark green　.55 .55
548　A195　160s green　.60 .60
549　A248　200s red　.75 .75
550　A249　250s blue　.90 .90
551　A249　310s dark green　1.10 1.10
552　A249　350s blue　1.25 1.25
　　Nos. 543-552 (10)　6.65 6.65

Issued: 75s, 85s, 150s, 310s, 350s, 4/1; 30s, 7/15; 100s, 11/25; 160s, 200s, 250s, 4/1. See Nos. 598, 600-601.

Yahyo Gulomov (1908-77), Archaeologist
A250

2008, June 25　Litho.　Perf. 13¾x14
553　A250　150s multi　.70 .70

2008 Summer Olympics, Beijing
A251

Designs: 150s, Judo. 200s, Boxing. 250s, Running. 310s, Rhythmic gymnastics, vert.

Perf. 13¾x14, 14x13¾
2008, June 25
554-557　A251　Set of 4　5.50 5.50

Flowers — A252

Designs: 150s, Cousinia butkovii. 200s, Cousinia dshisakensis. 250s, Cousinia adenophora. 310s, Cousinia angreni.

2008, June 25　　Perf. 14x13¾
558-561　A252　Set of 4　3.00 3.00

Intl. Swimming Federation (FINA), Cent. — A253

No. 562: a, 310s, Water polo. b, 450s, Synchronized swimming.
No. 563: a, 620s, Diving. b, 750s, Freestyle swimming.

2008, July 24　　Perf. 14x13¾
Horiz. Pairs, #a-b, + Central Label
562-563　A253　Set of 2　8.00 8.00

Souvenir Sheet

Navoi, 50th Anniv. — A254

No. 564: a, 930s, Farkhad monument, Culture Palace. b, 1250s, Gold bars.

2008, Oct. 22　　Perf. 13¾x14
564　A254　Sheet of 2, #a-b, + 2
　　　　labels　7.75 7.75

Writers — A255

Designs: 620s, Maqsud Shayxzoda (1908-67). 750s, Mirzakalon Ismoiliy (1908-86).

2008, Nov. 5
565-566　A255　Set of 2　4.50 4.50

Men's Traditional Costumes
A256

2008, Dec. 31　　Perf. 14x13¾
567　　Horiz. strip of 4 + label　9.50 9.50
a.　A256 310s Joma　1.00 1.00
b.　A256 350s Yaktak　1.10 1.10
c.　A256 750s Erkalar liboslari　2.50 2.50
d.　A256 1250s Joma, diff.　4.50 4.50

Louis Braille (1809-52), Educator of the Blind — A257

2009, Feb. 2　Litho.　Perf. 13¾x14
568　A257　620s multi　2.00 2.00

Intl. Year of Astronomy — A258

No. 569: a, 350s, Observatory of Sultan Ulugh Beg, Samarkand. b, 750s, Statue of Ulugh Beg.

2009, Mar. 22　　Perf. 14x13¾
569　A258　Horiz. pair, #a-b, +
　　　　central label　3.75 3.75

Birds
A259

2009, Apr. 8   *Perf. 13¾x14*
570	Horiz. strip of 4	7.00	7.00
a.	A250 310s Rufibrenta ruticollis	1.05	1.05
b.	A259 350s Cygnus cygnus	1.15	1.15
c.	A259 620s Aythya nyroca	2.00	2.00
d.	A259 750s Anser erythropus	2.60	2.60

A260

A261

A262

A263

A264

Children's
Art — A265

2009, June 1   *Perf. 13¾x14*
571	A260 200s multi	.60	.60
572	A261 200s multi	.60	.60
573	A262 200s multi	.60	.60

Perf. 14x13¾
574	A263 200s multi	.60	.60
575	A264 200s multi	.60	.60
576	A265 200s multi	.60	.60
	Nos. 571-576 (6)	3.60	3.60

2010 Youth
Olympic Games,
Singapore
A266

Designs: 450s, Basketball. 750s, Soccer, horiz.

2009, July 1   *Perf. 14x13¾, 13¾x14*
| 577-578 | A266 | Set of 2 | 3.75 | 3.75 |

Miniature Sheet

Tashkent, 2200th Anniv. — A267

No. 579: a, 310s, Majlis Building (Oliy Majlis binosi). b, 310s, Senate Building (Senat binosi). c, 350s, Intl. Business Center (Xalqaro biznes markazi). d, 350s, Temurids History Museum (Temuriylar tarixi davlat muzeyi). e, 620s, Turkistan Palace (Turkiston saroyi). f, 620s, Madrassa (Hazrat Imom majmuasi Baroqxon madrasasi). g, 750s, Museum of Victims of Oppression. h, 750s, Map of Great Silk Road.

2009, Aug. 17   *Perf. 13¾x14*
| 579 | A267 | Sheet of 8, #a-h | 12.00 | 12.00 |

Cities Along the
Great Silk
Road — A268

Designs: 350s, Khiva. 750s, Madrassa, Tashkent. 1250s, Samarkand Gate, Bukhara.

2009, Oct. 9   *Perf. 14x13¾*
| 580-581 | A268 | Set of 2 | 3.00 | 3.00 |

Souvenir Sheet
| 582 | A268 1250s multi | 3.50 | 3.50 |

Theater Types of 2009
2009, Dec. 1   Litho.   *Perf. 13¾x14*
| 583 | A248 450s red | 1.40 | 1.40 |
| 584 | A249 600s blue | 1.60 | 1.60 |

Circus Performers
A269

Designs: 450s, Two women on horse. 600s, Three women on two horses. 1200s, Three women on horse.

2009, Dec. 28   *Perf. 14x13¾*
| 585-587 | A269 | Set of 3 | 6.50 | 6.50 |

Carpet
Designs
A270

No. 588: a, Samarqand, 19th cent. b, Andijon, 20th cent.
No. 589: a, Bukhara, 19th cent. b, Tashkent, 20th cent.

2009, Dec. 28   *Perf. 13¾x14*
588	Horiz. pair + central label	4.50	4.50
a.	A270 450s multi	1.25	1.25
b.	A270 1200s multi	3.25	3.25
589	Horiz. pair + central label	4.50	4.50
a.	A270 600s multi	1.25	1.25
b.	A270 1000s multi	3.25	3.25

Endangered
Flora — A271

Designs: 450s, Fritillaria eduardii. 1200s, Iridodictyum winklerii.

2010, Jan. 26   *Perf. 14x13¾*
| 590-591 | A271 | Set of 2 | 4.75 | 4.75 |

Tashkent Zoo
Animals — A272

Designs: 450s, Macaca sinica. 800s, Macaca fascicularis. 1000s, Mandrillus sphinx. 1650s, Lemur catta, horiz.

2010, Feb. 12   *Perf. 14x13¾*
| 592-594 | A272 | Set of 3 | 5.50 | 5.50 |

Souvenir Sheet
Perf. 13¾x14
| 595 | A272 1650s multi | 4.50 | 4.50 |

Amir Temur Monument,
Shahrisabz — A273

Qarshi
Railroad
Station
A274

2010, Mar. 29   *Perf. 13¾x14*
596	Horiz. pair + central label	5.25	5.25
a.	A273 800s multi	2.00	2.00
b.	A274 1200s multi	3.25	3.25

Sites in Kashkadarya Vilayet.

Architecture Types of 2006-08
2010, Apr. 1   *Perf. 14x13¾, 13¾x14*
597	A195 25s green	.10	.40
598	A248 100s green	.40	.40
599	A195 110s green	.40	.40
600	A248 125s green	.40	.40
601	A248 200s green	.40	.40
	Nos. 597-601 (5)	2.00	2.00

Endangered
Birds — A275

Designs: 400s, Chettusia gregaria. 800s, Myiophonus caeruleus. 1000s, Tichodroma muraria. 1200s, Grus leucogeranus. 1900s, Cygnus olor.

2010, Apr. 15   *Perf. 14x13¾*
| 602-605 | A275 | Set of 4 | 6.25 | 6.25 |

Souvenir Sheet
| 606 | A275 1900s multi | 4.75 | 4.75 |

No. 606 contains one 37x52mm stamp.

43rd Annual Meeting of the Asian Development Bank Board of Governors Issue

Horizontal
Label

Vertical Label

Combine
A276

Irrigation
Canal
A277

Bukhara
Oil
Refinery
A278

Fergana
Oil
Refinery
A279

Tractor Trailer A280

Train A281

Poytaxt Business Center A282

Uzbekistan Forum — A283

Sitorai Mohi Xosa Palace, Bukhara A284

Hazrati Imam Complex, Tashkent A285

Majlis A286

Conservatory Building — A287

Arch A288

Tashkent Business Center A289

Senate Building A290

White Palace A291 Oqsaroy

Highway Cloverleaf A292

Highway and Bridge A293

Two Highways A294

Bridge Over Highway A295

Seamstresses — A296

Pottery Shop A297

Water Polo A298

Parade of Competitors at Yunusabad Sports Complex — A299

Construction Vehicles — A300

Railway Bridge A301

Daewoo Automobile Plant — A302

Tashkent Tractor Factory A303

Students in Laboratory — A304

Children in Computer Class A305

Flag of Uzbekistan — A306

Coat of Arms A307

Bank Association Building — A308

Central Bank Building — A309 Markaziy bank

Man and Woman in Traditional Clothes — A310

Man, Woman and Child in Traditional Clothes — A311

Infant and Nurse — A312

Surgeons in Operating Room — A313

2010, Apr. 15		Perf. 13¾x14	
607	Horiz. pair + central label	5.50	5.50
a.	A276 800s multi	2.50	2.50
b.	A277 1000s multi	3.00	3.00
608	Horiz. pair + central label	5.50	5.50
a.	A278 800s multi	2.50	2.50
b.	A279 1000s multi	3.00	3.00
609	Horiz. pair + central label	6.25	6.25
a.	A280 800s multi	2.50	2.50
b.	A281 1200s multi	3.75	3.75
610	Horiz. pair + central label	6.25	6.25
a.	A282 800s multi	2.50	2.50
b.	A283 1200s multi	3.75	3.75
611	Horiz. pair + central label	6.25	6.25
a.	A284 800s multi	2.50	2.50
b.	A285 1200s multi	3.75	3.75
612	Horiz. pair + central label	6.25	6.25
a.	A286 800s multi	2.50	2.50
b.	A287 1200s multi	3.75	3.75

613	Horiz. pair + central label	6.25	6.25
a.	A288 800s multi	2.50	2.50
b.	A289 1200s multi	3.75	3.75
614	Horiz. pair + central label	6.25	6.25
a.	A290 800s multi	2.50	2.50
b.	A291 1200s multi	3.75	3.75
615	Horiz. pair + central label	6.25	6.25
a.	A292 900s multi	2.50	2.50
b.	A293 1100s multi	3.75	3.75
616	Horiz. pair + central label	6.25	6.25
a.	A294 900c multi	2.50	2.50
b.	A295 1100s multi	3.75	3.75
617	Horiz. pair + central label	6.50	6.50
a.	A296 900s multi	2.75	2.75
b.	A297 1200s multi	3.75	3.75
618	Horiz. pair + central label	6.50	6.50
a.	A298 900s multi	2.75	2.75
b.	A299 1200s multi	3.75	3.75
619	Horiz. pair + central label	6.75	6.75
a.	A300 1000s multi	3.00	3.00
b.	A301 1200s multi	3.75	3.75
620	Horiz. pair + central label	6.75	6.75
a.	A302 1000s multi	3.00	3.00
b.	A303 1200s multi	3.75	3.75
621	Horiz. pair + central label	6.75	6.75
a.	A304 1000s multi	3.00	3.00
b.	A305 1200s multi	3.75	3.75
622	Horiz. pair + central label	6.75	6.75
a.	A306 1000s multi	3.00	3.00
b.	A307 1200s multi	3.75	3.75

Perf. 14x13¾

623	Horiz. pair + central label	6.25	6.25
a.	A308 800s multi	2.50	2.50
b.	A309 1200s multi	3.75	3.75
624	Horiz. pair + central label	6.50	6.50
a.	A310 900s multi	2.75	2.75
b.	A311 1200s multi	3.75	3.75
625	Horiz. pair + central label	6.50	6.50
a.	A312 900s multi	2.75	2.75
b.	A313 1200s multi	3.75	3.75
	Nos. 607-625 (19)	120.25	120.25

Miniature Sheet

Victory In World War II, 65th Anniv. — A314

No. 626: a, 400s, Young people giving flowers to veterans. b, 800s, Ceremony at Grieving Mother Monument. c, 1000s, Soldier, woman and children. d, 1200s, Celebratory ceremony with soldiers.

2010, May 9   **Perf. 13¾x14**

626 A314	Sheet of 4, #a-d	8.00	8.00

2010 Youth Olympics, Singapore A315

2010, July 12   **Perf. 14x13¾**
627 A315 800s multi		2.00	2.00

Uzbekistan-China Gas Pipeline — A316

2010, July 15   **Litho.**
628 A316 250s multi		.85	.85

Miniature Sheet

19th Century Copperware — A317

No. 629: a, 400s, Bucket, Central Asia. b, 800s, Bowl and pitcher, Khiva. c, 1000s, Pitcher and warming plate, Kokand. d, 1200s, Tray and pitcher, Khiva and Bukhara.

2010, Aug. 25   **Perf. 13¾x14**
629 A317	Sheet of 4, #a-d	8.00	8.00

Tulips — A318

Designs: 400s, Tulipa micheliana. 800s, Tulipa dasystemon. No. 632, 1000s, Tulipa lehmaniana. No. 633, 1200s, Tulipa bifloriformis.

No. 634: a, 1000s, Three Tulipa dasystemon. b, 1900s, One Tulipa dasystemon, rock.

2010, Sept. 27   **Perf. 14x13¾**
630-633 A318	Set of 4	6.25	6.25

Souvenir Sheet
634 A318	Sheet of 2, #a-b	5.75	5.75

Fish A319

Designs: 800s, Pterois volitans. No. 636, 1000s, Trichogaster leeri. 1200s, Carassius auratus.

No. 638: a, 1000s, Pterophyllum scalare. b, 1900s, Trichogaster leeri, diff.

2010, Oct. 9   **Perf. 13¾x14**
635-637 A319	Set of 3	6.00	6.00

Souvenir Sheet
638 A319	Sheet of 2, #a-b	6.00	6.00

16th Asian Games, Guangzhou, China — A320

2010, Oct. 25   **Litho.**
639 A320 800s multi		2.00	2.00

Protection of Polar Regions and Glaciers — A321

2010, Oct. 25   **Perf. 14x13¾**
640 A321 900s multi		2.75	2.75

Bobur Monument, Andijon — A322

Olympic Sports College, Andijon A323

2010, Dec. 30   **Perf. 13¾x14**
641	Horiz. pair + central label	5.25	5.25
a.	A322 900s multi	2.25	2.25
b.	A323 1200s multi	3.00	3.00

Sites in Andijon Vilayet.

Soyib Xo'jayev (1910-82), Actor — A324

2010, Dec. 30   **Perf. 14x13¾**
642 A324 900s multi		2.25	2.25

Seventh Asian Winter Games, Astana and Almaty — A325

Designs: 800s, Figure skater. 900s, Freestyle skier.

2011, Jan. 5
643-644 A325	Set of 2	4.00	4.00

Flowers — A326

Designs: 800s, Lagochilus vevedenskyi. 900s, Echinops babtagensis. No. 647, 1000s, Saxifraga hirculus. 1200s, Nathaliella alaica.

No. 649: a, 1000s, Eremus korolkovii, plant 21mm tall. b, 1900s, Eremus korolkovii, plant 37mm tall.

2011, Mar. 31
645-648 A326	Set of 4	6.75	6.75

Souvenir Sheet
649 A326	Sheet of 2, #a-b	5.25	5.25

Miniature Sheet

Carved Wood Items — A327

No. 650: a, 800s, Table, 1983. b, 900s, Round covered box, 1984. c, 1000s, Lavh, 1990. d, 1200s, Decorative pumpkin, 1985.

2011, Apr. 12   **Perf. 13¾x14**
650 A327	Sheet of 4, #a-d	7.50	7.50

A328

A329

A330

Children's Art — A331

2011, June 1
651 A328 500s multi		.85	.85
652 A329 500s multi		.85	.85
653 A330 500s multi		.85	.85
654 A331 500s multi		.85	.85
	Nos. 651-654 (4)	3.40	3.40

Independence, 20th Anniv. Issue

Vertical Label

Horizontal Label

Navoiyazot Gas Tanks — A332

Maxam-Chirchiq Fertilizer Plant — A333

Wedding Hall, Termez A334

Archaeological Museum, Termez — A335

Plaza, Urgench A336

Al-Xorazmi Monument, Urgench — A337

Theater, Bukhara A338

Monument, Bukhara — A339

Jokorgi Kenes Building, Nukus A340

Berdaq Museum, Nukus A341

Sports Complex, Namangan — A342

Aloqabank Building, Namangan — A343

Daewoo Automotive Plant — A344

Captiva, Epica and Spark Automobiles, Car Dealership — A345

Highway Cloverleaf A346

Highway Overpass A347

Regional Pre-natal Center, Gulistan A348

Denausky Medical Association Hospital — A349

Independence Day Celebrations — A350

Ballet Dancers A351

High Jumper Svetlana Radzivil A352

Judoka Rishat Sabirov and Opponent A353

Zarafshansky Gold Mining Complex — A354

Bekabadsky Metallurgical Complex — A355

Wedding Hall, Samarkand — A356

Concert Hall, Samarkand — A357

Academic Lyceum, State University, Karshi — A358

Fergana Branch of Tashkent University of Information Technology — A359

Youth Center, Andijan A360

College of Light Industry, Andijan A361

Worker at Control Center of MTS-Uzbekistan Company — A362

Uztelecom Control Center — A363

Textile Factory, Bukhara A364

Gulistansky Textile Factory — A365

Talimarzhdansky Power Plant — A366

Sogdiana Substation — A367

Kungradsky Soda Factory — A368

Shurtangas Oil Pumps — A369

Mountains in Winter — A370

Mountains in Spring — A371

Gissar National Park A372

Gissar National Park A373

Uzbekistan Forum, Tashkent — A374

Educational Center, Tashkent — A375

Buildings, Kokand A376

Park Gazebos, Kokand A377

Isuzu Automotive Factory, Samarqand — A378

Isuzu Truck A379

Bodomzor Subway Station — A380

Train on Tashguzar-Baysun-Kumkurgan Bridge — A381

Eski Machit Dancers A382

National Library and Monument to Amir Temur (Tamerlane) — A384

Perf. 14x13¾ (#655, 666), 13¾x14

2011, Aug. 29   Litho.

655		Horiz. pair + central label	3.50 3.50
a.	A332	800s multi	1.40 1.40
b.	A333	1200s multi	2.10 2.10
656		Horiz. pair + central label	3.50 3.50
a.	A334	800s multi	1.40 1.40
b.	A335	1200s multi	2.10 2.10
657		Horiz. pair + central label	3.50 3.50
a.	A336	800s multi	1.40 1.40
b.	A337	1200s multi	2.10 2.10
658		Horiz. pair + central label	3.50 3.50
a.	A338	800s multi	1.40 1.40
b.	A339	1200s multi	2.10 2.10
659		Horiz. pair + central label	3.50 3.50
a.	A340	800s multi	1.40 1.40
b.	A341	1200s multi	2.10 2.10
660		Horiz. pair + central label	3.50 3.50
a.	A342	800s multi	1.40 1.40
b.	A343	1200s multi	2.10 2.10
661		Horiz. pair + central label	3.50 3.50
a.	A344	800s multi	1.40 1.40
b.	A345	1200s multi	2.10 2.10
662		Horiz. pair + central label	3.50 3.50
a.	A346	800s multi	1.40 1.40
b.	A347	1200s multi	2.10 2.10
663		Horiz. pair + central label	3.50 3.50
a.	A348	800s multi	1.40 1.40
b.	A349	1200s multi	2.10 2.10
664		Horiz. pair + central label	3.50 3.50
a.	A350	800s multi	1.40 1.40
b.	A351	1200s multi	2.10 2.10
665		Horiz. pair + central label	3.50 3.50
a.	A352	800s multi	1.40 1.40
b.	A353	1200s multi	2.10 2.10
666		Horiz. pair + central label	3.75 3.75
a.	A354	900s multi	1.60 1.60
b.	A355	1200s multi	2.10 2.10
667		Horiz. pair + central label	3.75 3.75
a.	A356	900s multi	1.60 1.60
b.	A357	1200s multi	2.10 2.10
668		Horiz. pair + central label	3.75 3.75
a.	A358	900s multi	1.60 1.60
b.	A359	1200s multi	2.10 2.10
669		Horiz. pair + central label	3.75 3.75
a.	A360	900s multi	1.60 1.60
b.	A361	1200s multi	2.10 2.10
670		Horiz. pair + central label	3.75 3.75
a.	A362	900s multi	1.60 1.60
b.	A363	1200s multi	2.10 2.10
671		Horiz. pair + central label	3.75 3.75
a.	A364	900s multi	1.60 1.60
b.	A365	1200s multi	2.10 2.10
672		Horiz. pair + central label	3.75 3.75
a.	A366	900s multi	1.60 1.60
b.	A367	1200s multi	2.10 2.10
673		Horiz. pair + central label	3.75 3.75
a.	A368	900s multi	1.60 1.60
b.	A369	1200s multi	2.10 2.10
674		Horiz. pair + central label	3.75 3.75
a.	A370	900s multi	1.60 1.60
b.	A371	1200s multi	2.10 2.10
675		Horiz. pair + central label	3.75 3.75
a.	A372	900s multi	1.60 1.60
b.	A373	1200s multi	2.10 2.10
676		Horiz. pair + central label	4.00 4.00
a.	A374	1000s multi	1.90 1.90
b.	A375	1200s multi	2.10 2.10
677		Horiz. pair + central label	4.00 4.00
a.	A376	1000s multi	1.90 1.90
b.	A377	1200s multi	2.10 2.10
678		Horiz. pair + central label	4.00 4.00
a.	A378	1000s multi	1.90 1.90
b.	A379	1200s multi	2.10 2.10
679		Horiz. pair + central label	4.00 4.00
a.	A380	1000s multi	1.90 1.90
b.	A381	1200s multi	2.10 2.10
680		Horiz. pair + central label	4.00 4.00
a.	A382	1000s multi	1.90 1.90
b.	A383	1200s multi	2.10 2.10

Musicians With Karnays A383

Litho. & Embossed With Foil Application
Perf. 14

681	A384	15,000s multi	26.00	26.00
	Nos. 655-681 (27)		122.00	122.00

Souvenir Sheet

Regional Communications Commonwealth, 20th Anniv. — A385

2011, Nov. 1   Litho.   **Perf. 14x13¾**

682	A385	2000s multi	3.25 3.25

Campaign Against AIDS, 30th Anniv. — A386

2011, Dec. 16

683	A386	900s multi	2.25 2.25

Miniature Sheet

Uzbekistan Armed Forces, 20th Anniv. — A387

No. 684: a, 200s, Soldier with parents. b, 550s, Soldier reading proclamation, honor guard with flag. c, 700s, Soldier with wife and child. d, 900s, Helicopter. e, 1000s, Soldiers in camouflage. f, 1200s, Soldiers taking oath. g, 1900s, Military academy classroom. h, 2150s, Tank.

2012, Jan. 3   **Perf. 13¾x14**

684	A387	Sheet of 8, #a-h, + central label	18.00 18.00

Monuments — A388

Monuments commemorating: 100s, 450s, 600s, Amir Temur (Tamerlane, 1336-1405), conqueror. 150s, 170s, Berdaq (1827-1900), poet. 250s, 300s, Muhammad Al-Khorezmi (c. 780-c.850), mathematician, horiz.

2012   **Perf. 14x13¾, 13¾x14**

685	A388	100s green	.25	.25
686	A388	150s green	.30	.30
687	A388	170s green	.35	.35
688	A388	250s green	.55	.55
689	A388	300s green	.60	.60
690	A388	450s green	.95	.95
691	A388	600s green	1.25	1.25
	Nos. 685-691 (7)		4.25	4.25

Issued: 100s, 5/5; others, 4/5. See Nos. 711-713, 723-725, 736, 754-755, 799.

Paintings
A389

Designs: 800s, Onalik O'ylari, by Rakhim Ahmedov. 900s, Lagan O'yini, by Dzhavlon Umarbekov. 1000s, Bog'da, by Shorasul Shoahmedov. 1200s, Chavgon O'yini, by Shoahmedov.

2012, June 5   *Perf. 14x13¾*
692-695 A389   Set of 4   7.50 7.50

Flowers — A390

Designs: 800s, Hedysarum angrenicum. 900s, Cousinia glabriseta. No. 698, 1000s, Oxytropis pseudoleptophysa. 1200s, Phlomoides tschimganica.
No. 700: a, 1000s, Scorzonera bungei. b, 1900s, Spirostegia bucharica.

2012, June 5
696-699 A390   Set of 4   6.25 6.25
Souvenir Sheet
700 A390   Sheet of 2, #a-b   5.00 5.00

Al-Xakim at-Termizi Mausoleum, Termez — A391

Riders in Game of Ulok-kupkari — A392

2012, June 20   *Perf. 13¾x14*
701   Horiz. pair + central label   4.00 4.00
   a.   A391 900s multi   1.75 1.75
   b.   A392 1200s multi   2.25 2.25

2012 Summer Olympics, London A393

2012, July 27
702 A393 800s multi   1.75 1.75

Endangered Animals — A394

Designs: 400s, Mellivora capensis indica. 800s, Falco pelegrinoides. No. 705, 1000s, Hemiechinus hypomelas. 1200s, Lutra lutra seistanicus.
No. 707, Lynx lynx isabellina.

2012, Aug. 27   *Perf. 14x13¾*
703-706 A394   Set of 4   6.25 6.25
Souvenir Sheet
707 A394 1000s multi   1.75 1.75

Miniature Sheet

Akhal-Teke Horses — A395

No. 708: a, 950s, Amirana. b, 950s, G'ayrat. c, 950s, Asmanbek. d, 1050s, Go'zalli. e, 1050s, Ayg'ir. f, 1050s, Gallas. g, 2200s, Geldi Botir. h, 2200s, Xon. i, 2200s, Potmagul.

2012, Sept. 25   *Perf. 14*
708 A395   Sheet of 9, #a-i   20.00 20.00

Miniature Sheet

Soccer in Uzbekistan, Cent — A396

No. 709 — Various soccer players: a, 600s. b, 650s, c, 950s. d, 1050s. e, 1150s. f, 1300s. g, 2200s. h, 2500s.

2012, Sept. 25   *Perf. 13¾x14*
709 A396   Sheet of 8, #a-h, +   15.00 15.00
     central label

2012 Summer Olympics, London A397

2012, Oct. 25   *Litho.*
710 A397 900s multi   1.75 1.75

Monuments Type of 2012

Monument commemorating: 50s, 200s, Berdaq. 350s, Muhammad Al-Khorezmi, horiz.

2012, Nov. 9   *Perf. 14x13¾, 13¾x14*
711 A388 50s green   .30 .30
712 A388 200s green   .50 .50
713 A388 350s green   .85 .85
    Nos. 711-713 (3)   .85 .85

Tashkent Zoo Animals — A398

Designs: 400s, Threskiornis aethiopicus. 800s, Dolichotis patagonum. 1000s, Struthio camelus.
1200s, Elephas maximus.

2012, Dec. 28   *Perf. 14x13¾*
714-716 A398   Set of 3   4.25 4.25
Souvenir Sheet
717 A398 1200s multi   2.25 2.25

Flora and Fauna of Chatkal National Biosphere Reserve A399

Designs: No. 718, 800s, Trichius fasciatus. No. 719, 900s, Juno tubergeniana. No. 720, 1000s, Bubo bubo. No. 721, 1200s, Ursus arctos isabellinus.
No. 722, vert: a, 1000s, Marmota menzbieri. b, 1900s, Marmota menzbieri, diff.

2012, Dec. 28   *Perf. 13¾x14*
718-721 A399   Set of 4   5.50 5.50
Souvenir Sheet
     Perf. 14x13¾
722 A399   Sheet of 2, #a-b   4.50 4.50

Monuments Type of 2012

Monuments commemorating: 110s, Amir Temur (Tamerlane, 1336-1405), conqueror. 400s, 1500s, Muhammad Al-Khorezmi (c. 780-c. 850), mathematician, horiz.

Perf. 14x13¾, 13¾x14
2013, June 5   *Litho.*
723 A388 110s green   .25 .25
724 A388 400s green   .60 .60
725 A388 1500s green   2.25 2.25
    Nos. 723-725 (3)   3.10 3.10

Architecture of the Great Silk Road — A400

Designs: 1400s, Buildings, Bukhara. 1500s, Kutlug-Murad-inak Madrassa, Khiva.
3200s, Ota Darvoza, Khiva, and map of Great Silk Road.

2013, June 5   *Litho.*   *Perf. 14*
726-727 A400   Set of 2   4.50 4.50
Souvenir Sheet
728 A400 3200s multi   5.00 5.00

Flora — A401

Designs: 1400s, Cousinia platystegia. 1500s, Diospyros lotus.

2013, June 17   *Litho.*   *Perf. 14*
729-730 A401   Set of 2   4.75 4.75

Sports
A402

Designs: No. 731, 1500s, Judo. No. 732, 1500s, Fencing.

2013, June 17   *Litho.*   *Perf. 14*
731-732 A402   Set of 2   5.00 5.00

2013 Summer Universiade, Kazan, Russia (No. 731); 2013 Asian Youth Games, Nanjing, People's Republic of China (No. 732).

Miniature Sheet

Jewelry — A403

No. 733: a, 1400s, Earrings from Bukhara, 19th cent. b, 1400s, Bracelet from Samarkand, 19th cent. c, 1500s, Round cincture from Fergana, 20th cent. d, 1500s, Heart-shaped pendant from Bukhara, 19th cent.

2013, Sept. 25   *Litho.*   *Perf. 14*
733 A403   Sheet of 4, #a-d   10.00 10.00

2014 Winter Olympics, Sochi, Russia — A404

2014, Jan. 31   *Litho.*   *Perf. 14x13¾*
734 A404 1200s multi   2.50 2.50

Yonboshqal'a Fortress — A405

Gas Complex A406

2014, Jan. 31   *Litho.*   *Perf. 13¾x14*
735   Horiz. pair + central label   5.50 5.50
   a.   A405 1500s multi   2.50 2.50
   b.   A406 2000s multi   3.00 3.00

    Sites in Karakalpakstan Region.

Monuments Type of 2012

Design: 1000s, Muhammad Al-Khorezmi (c. 780-c. 850), mathematician, horiz.

2014, Apr. 10   *Litho.*   *Perf. 13¾x14*
736 A388 1000s green   1.50 1.50

Flowers
A407

Designs: 1300s, Delphinium knorringianum.
1500s, Corydalis severzowii.
3200s, Juno magnifica.

2014, Apr. 10　Litho.　Perf. 14
737-738　A407　Set of 2　3.50　3.50
Souvenir Sheet
739　A407　3200s multi　4.00　4.00

A408

A409

Children's
Art
A410

Perf. 13¾x14, 14x13¾
2014, May 30　　　Litho.
740　A408　1200s multi　1.25　1.25
741　A409　1200s multi　1.25　1.25
742　A410　1200s multi　1.25　1.25
Nos. 740-742 (3)　3.75　3.75

Fauna
A411

Designs: 1000s, Chlamydotis undulata.
1300s, Tetrax tetrax.
3200s, Saiga tatarica.

2014, May 30　Litho.　Perf. 14
743-744　A411　Set of 2　3.00　3.00
Souvenir Sheet
745　A411　3200s multi　3.75　3.75

17th
Asian
Games,
Incheon,
South
Korea
A412

2014, July 30　Litho.　Perf. 13¾x14
746　A412　1200s multi　1.90　1.90

Paintings — A413

Designs: 1500s, Ilhom Parisi, by Shorasul
Shoahmedov. 2100s, Teatr, by Muzaffar
Polatov.

2014, Oct. 16　Litho.　Perf. 14x13¾
747-748　A413　Set of 2　4.75　4.75

Nos. 1-2, 4-6
Surcharged

Methods and Perfs. As Before
2014, Nov. 3
749　A1　300s on 20k #1　.55　.55
750　A4　300s on 50k #4　.55　.55
751　A6　300s on 50k #6　.55　.55
752　A2　500s on 1r #2　.85　.85
753　A5　1900s on 10r #5　3.25　3.25
Nos. 749-753 (5)　5.75　5.75

Monuments Type of 2012

Monument commemorating: 290s, Berdaq.
500s, Amir Temur (Tamerlane).

2014, Nov. 6　Litho.　Perf. 14x13¾
754　A388　290s green　.60　.60
755　A388　500s green　1.00　1.00

Bobur Park, Namangan — A414

Mosque, Namangan — A415

2015, Jan. 22　Litho.　Perf. 13¼x14
756　Horiz. pair + central label　2.50　2.50
　a.　A414 1000s multi　1.10　1.10
　b.　A415 1200s multi　1.40　1.40

Tashkent
Zoo
Animals
A416

Designs: 1000s, Phasianus colchicus.
1200s, Anthropoides virgo, Balearica
pavonina. 2100s, Hystrix indica.
2500s, Canis lupus, vert.

2015, Jan. 22　Litho.　Perf. 13¾x14
757-759　A416　Set of 3　4.75　4.75
Souvenir Sheet
Perf. 14x13¾
760　A416　2500s multi　2.75　2.75

No. 52 Surcharged

Methods and Perfs. As Before
2015, Apr. 15
761　A10a 300s on 20t #52　.65　.65

Nos. 57-61 Surcharged

Nos. 762-765 surcharged in black. No. 766
surcharged in blue.

Methods and Perfs. As Before
2015, Apr. 15
762　A13　1000s on 30t + label #57　.85　.85
763　A13　1000s on 35t + label #58　.85　.85
764　A13　1000s on 40t + label #59　.85　.85
765　A13　1900s on 45t #60　1.60　1.60
Nos. 762-765 (4)　4.15　4.15
Souvenir Sheet
766　A13　1900s on 60t #61　4.00　4.00

A417

Victory in
World War
II, 70th
Anniv.
A418

2015, Apr. 15　Litho.　Perf. 14
767　Horiz. pair + central label　3.25　3.25
　a.　A417 1000s multi　1.50　1.50
　b.　A418 1200s multi　1.75　1.75

Miniature Sheet

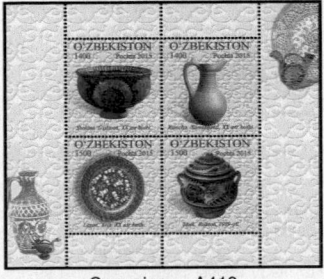

Ceramics — A419

No. 768: a, 1400s, Bowl. b, 1400s, Pitcher.
c, 1500s, Plate. d, 1500s, Bowl with lid.

2015, Apr. 15　Litho.　Perf. 14
768　A419　Sheet of 4, #a-d　5.50　5.50

Nos. 7-14 Surcharged

Nos. 769-775 surcharged in black. No. 776
surcharged in dark blue.
Large Surcharged Numeral: Nos. 769, 774,
776.
Small Surcharged Numeral: Nos. 770-773,
775.

Methods and Perfs. As Before
2015, June 15
769　A7　200s on 2r #8　.30　.30
770　A7　200s on 3r #10　.30　.30
771　A7　500s on 1r #7　.60　.60
772　A7　500s on 2r #9　.60　.60
773　A7　500s on 5r #11　.60　.60
774　A7　500s on 10r #12　.60　.60
775　A7　500s on 15r #13　.60　.60
Nos. 769-775 (7)　3.60　3.60
Souvenir Sheet
776　A7　3900s on 20r #14　4.50　4.50

Nos. 38-44
Surcharged

Nos. 777-782 surcharged in black. No. 783
surcharged in blue.

Methods and Perfs. As Before
2015, June 16
777　A9　400s on 20r #38　.50　.50
778　A9　400s on 20r #39　.50　.50
779　A9　400s on 25r #41　.50　.50
780　A9　400s on 30r #43　.50　.50
781　A9　600s on 25r #40　.65　.65
782　A9　600s on 30r #42　.65　.65
Nos. 777-782 (6)　3.30　3.30
Souvenir Sheet
783　A9　1000s on 50r #44　1.40　1.40

Sports
A420

Designs: 1200s, Gymnastics. 1500s, Pole
vault.

2015, Aug. 20　Litho.　Perf. 14
784-785　A420　Set of 2　3.00　3.00

Flowers
A421

Designs: 1300s, Amygdalus. 1500s, Dip-
sacus laciniatus. 3200s, Thermopsis alterniflora.

2015, Aug. 20　Litho.　Perf. 14
786-787　A421　Set of 2　3.50　3.50
Souvenir Sheet
788　A421　3200s multi　2.75　2.75

Fruit
A422

Designs: 1500s, Cydonia oblonga. 1800s,
Punica granatum.

2015, Oct. 9   Litho.   Perf. 13
789-790 A422   Set of 2   3.75 3.75
Values are for stamps with surrounding
selvage.

Zomin Sanitarium — A423

Aydar
Lake
A424

2015, Dec. 14   Litho.   Perf. 13¾x14
791   Horiz. pair + central label   2.50 2.50
a.   A423 1500s multi   1.25 1.25
b.   A424 1500s multi   1.25 1.25
Sites in Jizzakh Region.

Souvenir Sheet

Ship Hulk and Camel — A425

2016, Jan. 5   Litho.   Perf. 14
792 A425 2200s multi   2.00 2.00
Shrinkage of the Aral Sea.

Souvenir Sheet

International Telecommunication
Union, 150th Anniv. — A426

2016, Jan. 22   Litho.   Perf. 14
793 A426 2500s multi   2.10 2.10

Fauna
A427

Designs: 1000s, Cetonia aurata. 1200s,
Mustela eversmanni.1500s, Salmo trutta oxi-
anus. 1800s, Upupa epops.
2500s, Merops apiaster.

2016, Jan. 22   Litho.   Perf. 14
794-797 A427   Set of 4   4.00 4.00
Souvenir Sheet
798 A427 2500s multi   2.00 2.00

Monuments Type of 2012

Design: 700s, Monument to Berdaq (1827-
1900), poet.

2016, May 23   Litho.   Perf. 14x13¾
799 A388 700s green   .75   .75

2016
Summer
Olympics,
Rio de
Janeiro
A428

Designs: 1900s, Weight lifting. 2100s, Long
jump, vert.

Perf. 13¾x14, 14x13¾
2016, May 23   Litho.
800-801 A428   Set of 2   3.00 3.00

Silk Road Landmarks — A429

Designs: 1500s, Ayoz Fortress. 1700s,
Ko'k-Gumbaz (Blue Dome) mosque, Karshi.
3200s, Ark Fortress, Bukhara.

2016, May 23   Litho.   Perf. 13¾x14
802-803 A429   Set of 2   2.50 2.50
Souvenir Sheet
804 A429 3200s multi   2.50 2.50

Flowers
A430

Designs: 1300s, Capparis spinosa. 1500s,
Datúra métel. 2500s, Paeonia tenuifolia.

2016, May 23   Litho.   Perf. 14
805-806 A430   Set of 2   2.10 2.10
Souvenir Sheet
807 A430 2500s multi   1.90 1.90

Fauna
A431

Designs: 1500s, Latrodectus tredecimgut-
tatus. 1900s, Testudo horsfieldii.
2100s, Coracias garrulus.

2016, May 23   Litho.   Perf. 14
808-809 A431   Set of 2   2.50 2.50
Souvenir Sheet
810 A431 2100s multi   1.75 1.75

Miniature Sheet

Independence, 25th Anniv. — A432

No. 811: a, 1200s, Bunyodkor Stadium,
Tashkent. b, 1200s, Minor Mosque, Tashkent.
c, 1500s, Ustyurt Gas and Chemical Complex.
d, 1500s, Chevrolet automobile dealership. e,
2100s, Afrosiyob high-speed train. f, 2100s,
Graduates. g, 2500s, Soldiers. h, 2500s,
Mother and child.

2016, Aug. 31   Litho.   Perf. 13¾x14
811 A432   Sheet of 8, #a-h, +
            central label   11.50 11.50

Animals at
Tashkent
Zoo — A433

Designs: 1700s, Neofelis nebulosa. 1900s,
Haliaeetus albicilla. 2100s, Ramphastos
vitellinus.
2500s, Eos bornea.

2016, Dec. 30   Litho.   Perf. 14
812-814 A433   Set of 3   4.75 4.75
Souvenir Sheet
815 A433 2500s multi   1.90 1.90

Miniature Sheet

Traditional Costumes — A434

No. 816: a, 1900, Groom, 19th cent. b,
2100s, Bridesmaid, 20th cent. c, 2500s, Costume for boy's circumcision, 19th cent. d,
2500s, Woman, 1930-1940s.

2016, Dec. 30   Litho.   Perf. 14x13¾
816 A434   Sheet of 4, #a-d   7.00 7.00

Syr Darya
River
A435

Sardoba
(Water
Storage
Building)
A436

2017, Feb. 28   Litho.   Perf. 13¾x14
817   Horiz. pair + central label   2.25 2.25
a.   A435 1300s multi   1.00 1.00
b.   A436 1500s multi   1.25 1.25

Birds — A437

Designs: 100s, Grus grus. 200s, Coturnix
coturnix. 250s, Ciconia ciconia. 300s, 600s,
Columba livia. 350s, 700s, Luscinia luscinia.
400s, Pica pica, horiz. 500s, Cygnus olor,
horiz.

Perf. 14x13¾, 13¾x14
2017, Mar. 30   Litho.
818 A437 100s magenta   .25   .25
819 A437 200s blue   .25   .25
820 A437 250s blue   .25   .25
821 A437 300s blue   .25   .25
822 A437 350s blue   .25   .25
823 A437 400s magenta   .30   .30
824 A437 500s magenta   .40   .40
825 A437 600s magenta   .45   .45
826 A437 700s magenta   .55   .55
      Nos. 818-826 (9)   2.95 2.95
See Nos. 834-838, 845-856.

Theater — A438

No. 827: a, Scene from "Sadoqat." b, Alisher
Navoi State Academic Bolshoi Theater, Tashkent. c, Scene from "To'maris."

2017, May 12   Litho.   Perf. 13¾x14
827   Horiz. strip of 3   3.25 3.25
a.   A438 1000s multi   .65   .65
b.   A438 1800s multi   1.10 1.10
c.   A438 2200s multi   1.50 1.50

Flowers
A439

Designs: 1300s, Hibiscus hybridus. 1900s,
Crocus sativus. 2400s, Eremurus lactiflorus.

2017, May 12   Litho.   Perf. 14
828-829 A439   Set of 2   2.10 2.10
Souvenir Sheet
830 A439 2400s multi   1.60 1.60

Fruit
A440

Designs: 1300s, Ficus carica. 1600s, Prunus persica.

2017, June 9 Litho. **Perf. 13**
831-832 A440 Set of 2 1.75 1.75
Values are for stamps with surrounding selvage.

Gold Medalists at 2016 Summer Olympics — A441

No. 833: a, 1800s, Ruslan Nurudinov, weight lifting. b, 1900s, Xasanboy Do'smatov, boxing.

2017, June 9 Litho. **Perf. 14x13¾**
833 A441 Horiz. pair, #a-b, + central label 2.25 2.25

Birds Type of 2017

Designs: 50s, Columba livia. 150s, Cygnus olor, horiz. 450s, Ciconia ciconia. 550s, Pica pica, horiz. 900s. Luscinia luscinia.

Perf. 14x13¾, 13¾x14
2017, July 21 Litho.
834 A437 50s emerald .25 .25
835 A437 150s emerald .25 .25
836 A437 450s emerald .45 .45
837 A437 550s emerald .55 .55
838 A437 900s emerald .85 .85
Nos. 834-838 (5) 2.35 2.35

Souvenir Sheets

Fountain on Khadra Square, Tashkent — A443

Yunus Rajabov Metro Station, Tashkent — A444

2017, Oct. 5 Litho. **Perf. 14x13¾**
840 A443 2700s multi 1.60 1.60
841 A444 4000s multi 2.40 2.40

Souvenir Sheet

Uzbekistan Constitution, 25th Anniv. — A445

2017, Dec. 4 Litho. **Perf. 14x13¾**
842 A445 4000s multi 2.25 2.25

Uzbek Cuisine A446

Designs: 1800s, Palov. 1900s, Somsa.

2018, Jan. 16 Litho. **Perf. 14**
843-844 A446 Set of 2 2.10 2.10

A booklet issued on Jan. 30, 2018 commemorating Pres. Islam Karimov containing a pane of 14 stamps and 32 pairs of stamps with central labels was printed in limited quantities.

Birds Type of 2017

Designs: 650s, Columba livia. 800s, 2500s, Luscinia luscinia. 1000s, 1300s, 1800s, Cygnus olor, horiz. 2600s, Grus grus. 2800s, 4550s, Ciconia ciconia. 3500s, Coturnix coturnix. 7800s, 15,800s, Pica pica, horiz.

2018 Litho. **Perf. 14x13¾, 13¾x14**
845 A437 650s magenta .35 .35
846 A437 800s dull green .45 .45
847 A437 1000s dull green .55 .55
848 A437 1300s blue .75 .75
849 A437 1800s magenta 1.00 .00
850 A437 2500s magenta 1.40 1.40
851 A437 2600s blue 1.50 1.50
852 A437 2800s magenta 1.60 1.60
853 A437 3500s dull green 2.00 2.00
854 A437 4550s blue 2.60 2.60
855 A437 7800s magenta 4.50 4.50
856 A437 15,800s blue 9.00 9.00
Nos. 845-856 (12) 25.70 24.70

Issue date: 845, 848, 3/20; 846, 851, 854-855, 4/10; 847, 850, 852-853, 856, 2/22; 849, 8/17.

Uzbekistan's Membership in UNESCO, 25th Anniv. — A447

2018, July 9 Litho. **Perf. 13¾x14**
857 A447 5800s multi 3.25 3.25

Zangiota Mosque, Tashkent A448

Lake Urungach A449

2018, July 9 Litho. **Perf. 13¾x14**
858 Horiz. pair + central label 3.00 3.00
 a. A448 2700s multi 1.40 1.40
 b. A449 2800s multi 1.60 1.60
Attractions of the Tashkent Region.

18th Asian Games, Jakarta A450

Designs: 2700s, Kurash wrestling. 2800s, Soccer.

2018, Aug. 6 Litho. **Perf. 13¾x14**
859-860 A450 Set of 2 3.00 3.00

Miniature Sheet

Flora and Fauna of Zomin Nature Reserve — A451

No. 861: a, 900s. Corvus corax. b, 1000s, Sus scrofa. c, 1800s, Juniperus. d, 2700s, Vulpes vulpes. e, 2800s, Eremurus. f, 3200s, Alectoris chukar. g, 3400s, Ziziphora. h, 3700s, Noctuidae.

2018, Aug. 6 Litho. **Perf. 13**
861 A451 Sheet of 8, #a-h 11.00 11.00

Miniature Sheet

Railroad Stations — A452

No. 862 — Station at: a, 900s, Samarkand. b, 900s, Jizzakh. c, 1100s, Qarshi. d, 1100s, Andijan. e, 1800s, Bukhara. f, 1800s, Urgench. g, 3700s, South Tashkent. h, 3700s, Nukus. i, 6500s, Tashkent.

2018, Aug. 17 Litho. **Perf. 13¾x14**
862 A452 Sheet of 9, #a-i 25.00 25.00

Diplomatic Relations Between Uzbekistan and Belarus, 25th Anniv. — A453

2018, Nov. 23 Litho. **Perf. 13¾x14**
863 A453 3700s multi 2.10 2.10
See Belarus No.

Fauna — A454

Designs: 900s, Coccinella septempunctata. 1100s, Phrynocephalus interscapularis. 2700s, Carpodacus erythrinus, vert. 2800s, Rhombomys opimus. 3400s, Sciurus vulgaris, vert.

Perf. 13¾x14, 14x13¾
2018, Nov. 23 Litho.
864-867 A454 Set of 4 4.25 4.25
Souvenir Sheet
868 A454 3400s multi 1.90 1.90

Paintings by Pavel Benkov (1879-1949) — A455

Designs: 1100s, Girl with a Dutar. 2800s, Artists in Shahizinde. 3200s, Lyahi hauz Water Carriers.

2018, Dec. 20 Litho. **Perf. 13¾x14**
869-870 A455 Set of 2 2.40 2.40
Souvenir Sheet
871 A455 3200s multi 1.10 1.10

Miniature Sheet

Flowers — A456

No. 872: a, 900s, Adonis vernalis. b, 1000s, Viola tricolor. c, 2700s, Iris hippolyti. d, 2800s, Tagetes.

2019, Jan. 24 Litho. **Perf. 14x13¾**
872 A456 Sheet of 4, #a-d 4.25 4.25

Mausoleum of Abduhalik Gijduvani (1103-79) — A457

Mausoleum of Bahauddin Naqshbandi (1318-89) — A458

2019, Feb. 1 Litho. **Perf. 13¾x14**
873 A457 4000s multi + label 2.25 2.25
874 A458 4200s multi + label 2.25 2.25

Scenes From Uzbek Films — A459

Scene from: 3200s, Tahir and Zuhra, 1945. 3500s, You Are Not an Orphan, 1963. 6200s, The Adventures of Nasreddin, 1947.

2019, Feb. 1   Litho.   Perf. 13¾x14
875-876 A459   Set of 2   3.75 3.75

Souvenir Sheet
877 A459 6200s multi   3.25 3.25

Souvenir Sheet

Alisher Navoi Metro Station, Tashkent — A460

2019, Feb. 1   Litho.   Perf. 13¾x14
878 A460 4200s multi   2.25 2.25

VANUATU

ˌvan-ˌwä-ˈtü

LOCATION — Island group in south Pacific Ocean northeast of New Caledonia
GOVT. — Republic
AREA — 5,700 sq. mi.
POP. — 189,036 (1999 est.)
CAPITAL — Port Vila

The Anglo-French condominium of New Hebrides (Vol. 5) became the independent state of Vanuatu July 30, 1980.

Hebrides franc Vatu (1981)

> **Catalogue values for all unused stamps in this country are for Never Hinged items.**

Watermark

Wmk. 387 — Squares and Rectangles

Erromango Is. and Kaori Tree — A44

Designs: 10fr, Archipelago and man making copra. 15fr, Espiritu Santo Island and cattle. 20fr, Efate Island and Post Office, Vila. 25fr, Malakula Island and headdresses. 30fr, Aoba and Maewo Islands and pig tusks. 35fr, Pentecost Island and land diving. 40fr, Tanna Island and Prophet John Frum's Red Cross. 50fr, Shepherd Island and canoe with sail. 70fr, Banks Island and dancers. 100fr, Ambrym Island and carvings. 200fr, Aneityum Island and decorated baskets. 500fr, Torres Islands and fishing with bow and arrow.

Wmk. 373
1980, July 30   Litho.   Perf. 14
280	A44	5fr multicolored	.25	.25
281	A44	10fr multicolored	.25	.25
282	A44	15fr multicolored	.25	.30
283	A44	20fr multicolored	.30	.40
284	A44	25fr multicolored	.40	.45
285	A44	30fr multicolored	.50	.60
286	A44	35fr multicolored	.55	.65
287	A44	40fr multicolored	.55	.75
288	A44	50fr multicolored	.60	.90
289	A44	70fr multicolored	1.10	1.25
290	A44	100fr multicolored	1.10	1.00
291	A44	200fr multicolored	1.25	1.75
292	A44	500fr multicolored	2.25	3.75
		Nos. 280-292 (13)	9.35	12.30

Inscribed in French
Unwmk.
280a	A44	5fr multicolored	.35	.25
281a	A44	10fr multicolored	.50	.25
282a	A44	15fr multicolored	.55	.45
283a	A44	20fr multicolored	.60	.50
284a	A44	25fr multicolored	.70	.55
285a	A44	30fr multicolored	.70	.65
286a	A44	35fr multicolored	.75	.80
287a	A44	40fr multicolored	1.10	.90
288a	A44	50fr multicolored	1.20	1.10
289a	A44	70fr multicolored	1.75	1.50
290a	A44	100fr multicolored	1.75	1.60
291a	A44	200fr multicolored	2.00	2.75
292a	A44	500fr multicolored	4.75	5.25
		Nos. 280a-292a (13)	16.70	16.55

Rotary Emblem — A52

1980, Sept. 16   Wmk. 373
293 A52 10fr Emblem, horiz.   .25 .25
294 A52 40fr shown   .50 .50

Inscribed in French
Unwmk.
293a A52 10fr multicolored   .25 .25
294a A52 40fr multicolored   .70 .70

75th anniv. of Rotary Intl. and 8th anniv. of Port Vila Rotary Club (40fr).

Kiwanis Emblem — A53

1980, Sept. 16   Wmk. 373
295 A53 10fr shown   .25 .25
296 A53 40fr Emblem, horiz.   .75 .75

Inscribed in French
Unwmk.
295a A53 10fr multicolored   .25 .25
296a A53 40fr multicolored   1.00 1.00

New Zealand District Kiwanis Convention, Port Vila, Sept. 16-18.

Christmas A54

Paintings: 10fr, Virgin and Child, by Michael Pacher. 15fr, Virgin and Child, by Hans Memling. 30fr, Rest on the Flight to Egypt, by Adriaen van der Werff.

1980, Nov. 12   Wmk. 373
297 A54 10fr multicolored   .25 .25
298 A54 15fr multicolored   .25 .25
299 A54 30fr multicolored   .40 .40
   Nos. 297-299 (3)   .90 .90

Erythrura Trichroa — A55

20fr, Chalcophaps indica. 30fr, Pachycephala pectoralis. 40fr, Ptilinopus tannensis.

1981, Feb. 18
300 A55 10fr shown   .60 .30
301 A55 20fr multicolored   1.00 .65
302 A55 30fr multicolored   1.50 1.00
303 A55 40fr multicolored   2.00 1.25
   Nos. 300-303 (4)   5.10 3.20

Duke of Edinburgh's 60th Birthday — A56

1981, June 10   Perf. 14x14½
304 A56 15v Tribesman, portrait   .25 .25
305 A56 25v Portrait   .25 .25
306 A56 35v Family   .35 .35
307 A56 45v shown   .45 .45
   Nos. 304-307 (4)   1.30 1.30

Common Design Types
pictured following the introduction.

Royal Wedding Issue
Common Design Type
1981, July 29
308 CD331 15v Bouquet   .25 .25
309 CD331 45v Charles   .35 .35
310 CD331 75v Couple   .55 .55
   Nos. 308-310 (3)   1.15 1.15

First Anniv. of Independence — A57

1981, July 19
311 A57 15v Map, flag, vert.   .25 .25
312 A57 25v Emblem   .25 .25
313 A57 45v Anthem   .40 .40
314 A57 75v Arms, vert.   .55 .55
   Nos. 311-314 (4)   1.45 1.45

Christmas A58

Children's drawings: 15v, Three kings. 25v, Girl holding lamb, vert. 35v, Butterfly-angel. 45v, Gift bearer, vert.

Wmk. 373
1981, Nov. 11   Litho.   Perf. 14
315 A58 15v multicolored   .25 .25
316 A58 25v multicolored   .25 .25
317 A58 35v multicolored   .40 .40
318 A58 45v multicolored   .60 .60
  a.   Souvenir sheet, #315-318   2.25 2.25
   Nos. 315-318 (4)   1.50 1.50

Broadbills — A59

20v, Rainbow lories. 25v, Buff-bellied flycatchers. 45v, Fantails.

1982, Feb. 8   Perf. 14½x14
319 A59 15v shown   .60 .60
320 A59 20v multicolored   .80 .80
321 A59 25v multicolored   1.00 1.00
322 A59 45v multicolored   1.75 1.75
   Nos. 319-322 (4)   4.15 4.15

Orchids — A60

1v, Flickengeria comata. 2v, Calanthe triplicata. 10v, Dendrobium sladei. 15v, Dendrobium mohlianum. 20v, Dendrobium macrophyllum. 25v, Dendrobium purpureum. 30v, Robiquetia mimus. 35v, Dendrobium mooreanum. 45v, Spathoglottis plicata. 50v, Dendrobium seemannii. 75v, Dendrobium conanthum. 100v, Dendrobium macranthum. 200v, Coelogyne lamellata. 500v, Bulbophyllum longiscapum.

Perf. 14x13½, 13½x14
1982, June 15
323	A60	1v multicolored	.25	.70
324	A60	2v multicolored	.25	.75
325	A60	10v multicolored	.30	.40
326	A60	15v multicolored	.40	.35
327	A60	20v multicolored	.50	.40
328	A60	25v multicolored	.75	.70
329	A60	30v multicolored	.90	1.10
330	A60	35v multicolored	1.00	1.25
331	A60	45v multicolored	1.20	1.40
332	A60	50v multicolored	1.40	1.75
333	A60	75v multicolored	2.25	2.75
334	A60	100v multicolored	2.60	2.75
335	A60	200v multicolored	3.25	4.25
336	A60	500v multicolored	6.25	9.25
		Nos. 323-336 (14)	21.30	27.80

Nos. 330-333 horiz.
For surcharges see Nos. 383, 512, 551-554, 586-589A, B1.

Scouting Year A61

Wmk. 373
1982, Sept. 1   Litho.   Perf. 14
337 A61 15v Around campfire   .35 .35
338 A61 20v First aid   .35 .35
339 A61 25v Signal tower   .45 .45

340	A61	45v Building raft	1.00	1.00
341	A61	75v Scout sign	1.40	1.40
		Nos. 337-341 (5)	3.55	3.55

Christmas — A62

Details from Nativity painting. 35v, 45v horiz.

1982, Nov. 16
342	A62	15v multicolored	.35	.35
343	A62	55v multicolored	.55	.55
344	A62	35v multicolored	.80	.80
345	A62	45v multicolored	1.00	1.00
a.		Souvenir sheet of 4, #342-345	3.25	3.25
		Nos. 342-345 (4)	2.70	2.70

Hypolimnas Octocula A63

1983, Jan. 17   *Perf. 14½*
346		Pair	2.25	1.60
a.	A63	15v shown	1.00	.75
b.	A63	15v Euploea sylvester	1.00	.75
347		Pair	2.60	2.25
a.	A63	20v Polyura sacco	1.20	1.00
b.	A63	20v Papilio canopus	1.20	1.00
348		Pair	3.50	2.40
a.	A63	25v Parantica pumila	1.60	1.20
b.	A63	25v Luthrodes cleotas	1.60	1.20
		Nos. 346-348 (3)	8.35	6.25

A64

1983, Mar. 14   *Perf. 13½x14*
349	A64	15v Pres. Sokomanu	.30	.30
350	A64	20v Fisherman	.30	.30
351	A64	25v Herdsman, cattle	.35	.35
352	A64	75v Flags, map	.75	.75
		Nos. 349-352 (4)	1.70	1.70

Commonwealth Day. 20v, 75v inscribed in French.

Economic Zone — A65

a, Thunnus albacares. b, Map. c, Matthew Isld. d, Hunter Isld. e, Epinephelus morrhua, etelis carbunculus. f, Katsuwonus pelamis.

1983, May 23   *Perf. 14x13½*   **Wmk. 373**   **Litho.**
| 353 | | Sheet of 6 | 4.25 | 4.25 |
| a.-f. | A65 | 25v multicolored | .65 | .65 |

Manned Flight Bicentenary — A66

Balloons or Airships: 15v, Montgolfiere, 1783. 20v, J.A.C. Charles 1st hydrogen balloon, 1783. 25v, Blanchard & Jeffries 1st English Channel crossing, 1785. 35v, H. Giffard's 1st mechanically powered airship, 1852. 40v, Renard and Krebs' airship, 1884. 45v, Graf Zeppelin's 1st transworld flight, 1929.

1983, Aug. 4   **Litho.**   *Perf. 14*
354	A66	15v multi, vert.	.30	.30
355	A66	20v multi, vert.	.35	.35
356	A66	25v multi, vert.	.45	.45
357	A66	35v multi	.60	.60
358	A66	40v multi	.75	.75
359	A66	45v multi	.85	.85
		Nos. 354-359 (6)	3.30	3.30

For overprint see No. 372.

World Communications Year — A67

15v, Mail transport, Bauerfield Airport. 20v, Switchboard operator. 25v, Telex operator. 45v, Satellite earth station.

1983, Oct. 10   **Litho.**   **Wmk. 373**
360	A67	15v multicolored	.25	.25
361	A67	20v multicolored	.40	.40
362	A67	25v multicolored	.55	.55
363	A67	45v multicolored	.95	.95
a.		Souv. sheet of 4, #360-363 + 3 labels	5.50	5.50
		Nos. 360-363 (4)	2.15	2.15

No. 363a issued for WCY and 75th anniv. of New Hebrides stamps.

Local Fungi — A68

15v, Cymatoderma elegans, vert. 25v, Lignosus rhinoceros, vert. 35v, Stereum ostrea. 45v, Ganoderma boninenze, vert.

1984, Jan. 9   **Litho.**   *Perf. 14*
364	A68	15v multicolored	.80	.80
365	A68	25v multicolored	.90	.90
366	A68	35v multicolored	1.50	1.50
367	A68	45v multicolored	1.75	1.75
		Nos. 364-367 (4)	4.05	4.95

Lloyd's List Issue
Common Design Type

1984, Apr. 30   **Litho.**   *Perf. 14½x14*
368	CD335	15v Port Vila	.35	.35
369	CD335	20v Induna	.45	.45
370	CD335	35v Air Vanuatu jet	.60	.60
371	CD335	45v Brahman Express	1.00	1.00
		Nos. 368-371 (4)	2.40	2.40

No. 359 Overprinted "UPU CONGRESS / HAMBURG"

1984, June 11   **Wmk. 373**   *Perf. 14*
| 372 | A66 | 45v multicolored | .85 | .85 |

Cattle A69

1984, July 3   **Litho.**   *Perf. 14*
373	A69	15v Charolais	.30	.30
374	A69	25v Charolais-Afrikaner	.45	.45
375	A69	45v Friesian	.75	.75
376	A69	75v Charolais-Brahman	1.40	1.40
		Nos. 373-376 (4)	2.90	2.90

Ausipex '84 — A70

Ships.

1984, Sept. 7
377	A70	25v Makambo	.70	.50
378	A70	45v Rockton	1.25	1.00
379	A70	100v Waroonga	2.40	4.00
a.		Souvenir sheet of 3, #377-379	5.00	5.25
		Nos. 377-379 (3)	4.35	5.50

Christmas A71

25v, Father Christmas, child in hospital. 45v, Nativity. 75v, Father Christmas, children.

1984, Nov. 19   **Litho.**   **Wmk. 373**
380	A71	25v multicolored	.50	.30
381	A71	45v multicolored	.90	.75
382	A71	75v multicolored	1.50	1.50
		Nos. 380-382 (3)	2.90	2.55

No. 323 Surcharged

1985, Jan. 22   **Litho.**   *Perf. 14x13½*
| 383 | A60 | 5v on 1v multi | 1.50 | 1.00 |

Ceremonial Dance Costumes A71a

1985, Jan. 22   *Perf. 14*
384	A71a	20v Ambrym Island	.35	.35
385	A71a	25v Pentecost Island	.50	.50
386	A71a	45v Women's Grade Ceremony, S.W. Malakula	.80	.80
387	A71a	75v Same, men's	1.25	1.25
		Nos. 384-387 (4)	2.90	2.90

Audubon Birth Bicent. — A72

Peregrine falcons.

Wmk. 373
1985, Mar. 26   **Litho.**   *Perf. 14*
388	A72	20v multicolored	1.00	1.00
389	A72	35v multicolored	1.20	1.20
390	A72	45v multicolored	1.40	1.40
391	A72	100v multicolored	2.40	2.40
		Nos. 388-391 (4)	6.00	6.00

Queen Mother 85th Birthday
Common Design Type

Perf. 14½x14
1985, June 7   **Wmk. 384**
392	CD336	5v Wedding photo	.25	.25
393	CD336	20v 80th birthday celebration	.45	.45
394	CD336	35v At Ancona, Italy	.60	.60
395	CD336	55v Holding Prince Henry	.95	.95
		Nos. 392-395 (4)	2.25	2.25

Souvenir Sheet
| 396 | CD336 | 100v At Covent Garden Opera | 3.00 | 3.00 |

EXPO '85, Tsukuba — A73

35v, Mala naval patrol boat. 45v, Japanese fishing fleet, Port Vila. 55v, Mobile Force Band. 100v, Prime Minister Walter H. Lini.

1985, July 26   **Wmk. 373**   *Perf. 14*
397	A73	35v multicolored	.65	.40
398	A73	45v multicolored	.80	.60
399	A73	55v multicolored	.90	.70
400	A73	100v multicolored	1.00	1.60
a.		Souvenir sheet of 4, #397-400	4.25	4.25
		Nos. 397-400 (4)	3.35	3.30

Natl. independence, 5th anniv.

Intl. Youth Year A74

Children's drawings.

1985, Sept. 16   **Wmk. 373**   *Perf. 14*
401	A74	20v Alain Lagaliu	.55	.55
402	A74	30v Peter Obed	.65	.65
403	A74	50v Mary Estelle	1.00	1.00
404	A74	100v Abel M rani	1.75	1.75
		Nos. 401-404 (4)	3.95	3.95

Natl. and UN Flags, Map A75

1985, Sept. 24   **Litho.**   *Perf. 14*
| 405 | A75 | 45v multicolored | 1.50 | 1.25 |

Admission of Vanuatu to UN, 4th anniv.

Sea Slugs — A76

20v, Chromodoris elisa bethina. 35v, Halgerda aurantiomaculata. 55v, Chromodoris kuniei. 100v, Notodoris minor.

1985, Nov. 11   **Wmk. 373**   *Perf. 14½*
406	A76	20v multicolored	.40	.40
407	A76	35v multicolored	.80	.80
408	A76	55v multicolored	1.10	1.10
409	A76	100v multicolored	2.10	2.10
		Nos. 406-409 (4)	4.40	4.40

Nos. 407-408 horiz. See Nos. 497-500.

Scuba
Diving — A77

1986, Jan. 22   Wmk. 384   *Perf. 14*
410	A77	30v shown	.90	.50
411	A77	35v Volcanic eruption	1.00	.60
412	A77	55v Land diving	1.00	.80
413	A77	100v Wind surfing	1.40	2.00
		Nos. 410-413 (4)	4.30	3.90

See No. 479.

Queen Elizabeth II 60th Birthday
Common Design Type

Designs: 20v, With Prince Charles and Princess Anne, 1951. 35v, At christening of Prince William, the Music Room, Buckhingham Palace, 1982. 45v, State visit, 1985. 55v, State visit to Mexico, 1974. 100v, Visiting Crown Agents' offices, 1983.

1986, Apr. 21   Litho.   *Perf. 14x14½*
414	CD337	20v scar, blk & sil	.25	.25
415	CD337	35v ultra & multi	.45	.45
416	CD337	45v green & multi	.50	.50
417	CD337	55v violet & multi	.65	.65
418	CD337	100v multicolored	1.25	1.25
		Nos. 414-418 (5)	3.10	3.10

For overprints & surcharges see #465-469, B2-B6.

AMERIPEX '86 — A78

45v, SS President Coolidge. 55v, As troop ship, 1942. 135v, Site of sinking, 1942.

1986, May 19   Wmk. 373   *Perf. 14*
419	A78	45v multicolored	1.40	.70
420	A78	55v multicolored	1.60	.90
421	A78	135v multicolored	2.75	2.25
a.		Souvenir sheet of 3, #419-421	6.25	6.25
		Nos. 419-421 (3)	5.75	3.85

Halley's
Comet
A79

30v, Comet, deity statue. 45v, Family sighting comet. 55v, Comet over SW Pacific. 100v, Edmond Halley, manuscript.

1986, June 23   Wmk. 384   *Perf. 14½*
422	A79	30v multicolored	1.20	1.20
423	A79	45v multicolored	1.25	1.25
424	A79	55v multicolored	1.60	1.60
425	A79	100v multicolored	2.10	2.10
		Nos. 422-425 (4)	6.15	6.15

Coral
A80

1986, Oct. 27   Wmk. 373   *Perf. 14*
426	A80	20v Daisy	.70	.70
427	A80	45v Organ pipe	1.50	1.50
428	A80	55v Sea fan	1.75	1.75
429	A80	135v Soft	4.50	4.50
		Nos. 426-429 (4)	8.45	8.45

Intl.
Peace
Year
A81

30v, Children of the world. 45v, Child praying. 55v, UN building, negotiators. 135v, Peoples working in harmony.

1986, Nov. 3   Litho.   *Perf. 14*
430	A81	30v multi	.65	.65
431	A81	45v multi	1.00	1.00
432	A81	55v multi	1.25	1.25
433	A81	135v multi	3.00	3.00
		Nos. 430-433 (4)	5.90	5.90

Automotives
A82

20v, Datsun 240Z, 1969. 45v, Model A Ford, 1927. 55v, Unic, 1924-25. 135v, Citroen DS19, 1975.

1987, Jan. 22   Litho.   *Perf. 14*
434	A82	20v multi	.35	.35
435	A82	45v multi	.65	.65
436	A82	55v multi	.80	.80
437	A82	135v multi	1.90	1.90
		Nos. 434-437 (4)	3.70	3.70

IRHO
Coconut
Research
Station, 25th
Anniv.
A83

35v, Nursery. 45v, Cocos nucifera tree. 100v, Cocos nucifera fruit. 135v, Station.

1987, May 13   *Perf. 14½x14*
438	A83	35v multicolored	.55	.55
439	A83	45v multicolored	.85	.85
440	A83	100v multicolored	1.25	1.25
441	A83	135v multicolored	1.75	1.75
		Nos. 438-441 (4)	4.40	4.40

Fish — A84

1v, Cirrhitichthys aprinus. 5v, Zanclus cornutus. 10v, Canthigaster cinctus. 15v, Amphiprion rubrocinctus. 20v, Acanthurus lineatus. 30v, Thalassoma hardwicki. 35v, Anthias tuka. 40v, Adioryx microstomus. 45v, Balistoides conspicillum. 50v, Xyrichtys taeniouris. 55v, Hemitaurich-thys polyepis. 65v, Pterois volitans. 100v, Paracirrhites forsteri. 300v, Balistapus undulatus. 500v, Chaetodon ephippium.

**   *Perf. 14x14½***
1987, July 15   Wmk. 384
442	A84	1v multicolored	.25	.25
443	A84	5v multicolored	.25	.25
444	A84	10v multicolored	.25	.25
445	A84	15v multicolored	.30	.30
446	A84	20v multicolored	.40	.40
447	A84	30v multicolored	.55	.55
448	A84	35v multicolored	.60	.60
449	A84	40v multicolored	.65	.65
450	A84	45v multicolored	.85	.85
451	A84	50v multicolored	.90	.90
452	A84	55v multicolored	1.00	1.00
453	A84	65v multicolored	1.10	1.10
454	A84	100v multicolored	2.10	2.10
455	A84	300v multicolored	5.50	5.50
456	A84	500v multicolored	7.75	7.75
		Nos. 442-456 (15)	22.45	22.45

Insects
A85

45v, Xylotrupes gideon. 55v, Phyllodes imperialis. 65v, Cyphogaster. 100v, Othreis fullonia.

1987, Sept. 22   Wmk. 373   *Perf. 14*
457	A85	45v multicolored	.90	.90
458	A85	55v multicolored	1.00	1.00
459	A85	65v multicolored	1.40	1.40
460	A85	100v multicolored	2.00	2.00
		Nos. 457-460 (4)	5.30	5.30

Christmas
Carols — A86

1987, Nov. 10   *Perf. 13½x14*
461	A86	20v Away in a Manger	.40	.40
462	A86	45v Once in Royal David's City	.85	.85
463	A86	55v While Shepherds Watched Their Flocks	1.00	1.00
464	A86	65v We Three Kings of Orient Are	1.25	1.25
		Nos. 461-464 (4)	3.50	3.50

Nos. 414-418 Ovptd. in Silver "40TH WEDDING ANNIVERSARY"
**   *Perf. 14x14½***
1987, Dec. 9   Litho.   Wmk. 384
465	CD337	20v scar, blk & sil	.45	.45
466	CD337	35v ultra & multi	.60	.60
467	CD337	45v green & multi	.75	.75
468	CD337	55v violet & multi	.80	.80
469	CD337	100v multicolored	1.50	1.50
		Nos. 465-469 (5)	4.10	4.10

World
Wildlife
Fund — A87

Dugongs.

1988, Feb. 29   *Perf. 13x13½*
470	A87	5v Mother, calf	1.00	.40
471	A87	10v Adult	1.60	.40
472	A87	20v Two adults	2.10	1.10
473	A87	45v Herd	3.75	2.75
		Nos. 470-473 (4)	8.45	4.65

Australia
Bicentennial
A88

Burns Philp emblem, bicent. emblem and steamships.

1988, May 18   Wmk. 373   *Perf. 12*
474	A88	20v S.S. Tambo	.35	.35
475	A88	45v S.S. Induna	.75	.75
476	A88	55v S.S. Morinda	.90	.90
477	A88	65v S.S. Marsina	1.00	1.00
		Nos. 474-477 (4)	3.00	3.00

Capt. James Cook
(1728-1779),
Explorer — A89

Perf. 14 on 2 or 3 Sides
1988, July 29   Wmk. 384
478	A89	45v black & red	.90	.90

SYDPEX '88. No. 478 printed in panes of 10 plus 5 center labels picturing a map of Vanuatu, HMS Resolution, exhibition emblem, HMS Endeavour or a map of Australia.

Tourism Type of 1986
Souvenir Sheet
Wmk. 373

1988, Aug. 24   Litho.   *Perf. 14*
479		Sheet of 2	4.50	4.50
a.		A77 55v like No. 412	1.10	1.10
b.		A77 100v like No. 413	2.25	2.25

EXPO '88. Nos. 479a-479b are dated 1988 and "Vanuatu" is inscribed in violet blue.

1988 Summer
Olympics,
Seoul — A90

1988, Sept. 19   *Perf. 13½x14*
480	A90	20v Boxing	.25	.25
481	A90	45v Track events	.70	.70
482	A90	55v Signing Olympic agreement	.85	.85
483	A90	65v Soccer	1.00	1.00
		Nos. 480-483 (4)	2.80	2.80

Souvenir Sheet
484	A90	150v Tennis	3.50	3.50

Intl. Tennis Federation, 75th anniv. (150v).

Lloyds of London, 300th Anniv.
Common Design Type

Designs: 20v, Lloyds new building, 1988. 55v, Cargo ship Shirrabank, horiz. 65v, Adela, horiz. 145v, Excursion steamer General Slocum on fire in New York Harbor, 1904.

1988, Oct. 25   Wmk. 384   *Perf. 14*
485	CD341	20v multicolored	.45	.45
486	CD341	55v multicolored	1.20	1.20
487	CD341	65v multicolored	1.25	1.25
488	CD341	145v multicolored	3.00	3.00
		Nos. 485-488 (4)	5.90	5.90

FAO — A91

Perf. 14½x14, 14x14½
1988, Nov. 14
489	A91	45v Tending crops	.80	.80
490	A91	55v Fishing, vert.	.90	.90
491	A91	65v Animal husbandry, vert.	.90	.90
492	A91	120v Produce market	1.10	1.10
		Nos. 489-492 (4)	3.70	3.70

Christmas
A92

Carols: 20v, Silent Night, Holy Night. 45v, Angels From the Realms of Glory. 65v, O Come All Ye Faithful. 155v, In That Poor Stable How Charming Jesus Lies.

1988, Dec. 1   Litho.   *Perf. 14½x14*
493	A92	20v multicolored	.40	.40
494	A92	45v multicolored	.65	.65
495	A92	65v multicolored	.75	.75
496	A92	155v multicolored	1.90	1.90
		Nos. 493-496 (4)	3.70	3.70

Marine Life Type of 1985
Shrimp.

1989, Feb. 1   *Perf. 14*
497	A76	20v Periclimenes brevicarpalis	.40	.40
498	A76	45v Lysmata grabhami	1.00	1.00

499	A76	65v Rhynchocinetes	1.40 1.40
500	A76	150v Stenopus hispidus	2.60 2.60
		Nos. 497-500 (4)	5.40 5.40

Economic & Social Commission for Asia and the Pacific (ESCAP) A93

20v, Consolidated Catalina. 45v, Douglas DC-3. 55v, Embraer EMB110 Bandeirante. 200v, Boeing 737-300.

Perf. 12x12½

1989, Apr. 5   Litho.   Wmk. 373

501	A93	20v multicolored	1.00 1.00
502	A93	45v multicolored	1.40 1.40
503	A93	55v multicolored	1.60 1.60
504	A93	200v multicolored	5.00 5.00
		Nos. 501-504 (4)	9.00 9.00

Inauguration of the Sydney-Noumea-Espiritu Santo Service, 1948 (20v).

PHILEXFRANCE '89 — A94

Exhibition emblem and: No. 505a, Porte de Versailles Hall Number 1. No. 505b, Eiffel Tower. No. 506, Revolt of French Troops, Nancy, 1790.

1989, July 5   Wmk. 373   Perf. 12

505	A94	Pair	5.25 5.25
a.-b.		100v any single	2.50 2.50

Souvenir Sheet
Perf. 14
Wmk. 384

506	A94	100v multicolored	2.25 2.25

French revolution, bicent.

Moon Landing, 20th Anniv.
Common Design Type

Apollo 17: 45v, Command module in space. 55v, Harrison Schmitt, Gene Cernan and Ron Evans. 65v, Mission emblem. 120v, Liftoff. 100v, Recovery of Apollo 11 crew after spashdown.

1989, July 20   Wmk. 384   Perf. 14
Size of Nos. 508-509: 29x29mm

507	CD342	45v multicolored	1.40 1.40
508	CD342	55v multicolored	1.40 1.40
509	CD342	65v multicolored	1.60 1.60
510	CD342	120v multicolored	2.75 2.75
		Nos. 507-510 (4)	7.15 7.15

Souvenir Sheet

511	CD342	100v multicolored	2.75 2.75

No. 324 Surcharged

Perf. 14x13½

1989, Oct. 18   Litho.   Wmk. 373

512	A60	100v on 2v multi	5.50 5.50

STAMPSHOW '89, Melbourne.

World Stamp Expo '89 — A95

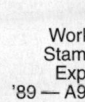

Perf. 14x13½

1989, Nov. 6   Litho.   Wmk. 384

513	A95	65v New Hebrides #256	3.75 3.75

Souvenir Sheet

514		Sheet of 2	9.50 9.50
a.		A95 65v New Hebrides #254	3.00 3.00
b.		A95 100v The White House (detail)	5.00 5.00

Flora — A96

45v, Alocasia macrorrhiza. 55v, Acacia spirorbis. 65v, Metrosideros collina. 145v, Hoya australis.

Perf. 12½x12

1990, Jan. 5   Wmk. 373

515	A96	45v multicolored	.85 .85
516	A96	55v multicolored	1.00 1.00
517	A96	65v multicolored	1.20 1.20
518	A96	145v multicolored	2.75 2.75
		Nos. 515-518 (4)	5.80 5.80

A97

Stamp World London '90 Exhibition emblem and simulated stamps or stamps on stamps: 45v, Kava (simulated stamps). 65v, Luganville P.O. exterior, interior (simulated stamps). 100v, Propeller plane, 19th cent. packet (simulated stamps). 150v, New Hebrides #187-188, first day cancellation. 200v, Great Britain #1, Vanuatu #281.

1990, Apr. 30   Perf. 13x13½

519	A97	45v multicolored	.90 .90
520	A97	65v multicolored	1.40 1.40
521	A97	100v multicolored	2.00 2.00
522	A97	200v multicolored	3.75 3.75
		Nos. 519-522 (4)	8.05 8.05

Souvenir Sheet

523	A97	150v multicolored	7.50 7.50

Penny Black, 150th anniv. No. 523 margin pictures first day cancel and cachet.

Independence, 10th Anniv. — A98

25v, Natl. Council of Women Emblem. 50v, Pres. Frederick Kalomuana Timakata. 55v, Preamble to Constitution. 65v, Vanuaaku Pati flag. 80v, Reserve Bank. 150v, Prime Minister Walter H. Lini.

1990, July 30   Perf. 14

524	A98	25v multicolored	.45 .45
525	A98	50v multicolored	.95 .95
526	A98	55v multicolored	1.10 1.10
527	A98	65v multicolored	1.20 1.20
528	A98	150v multicolored	1.50 1.50
		Nos. 524-528 (5)	5.20 5.20

Souvenir Sheet

529	A98	150v multi	5.75 5.75

Miniature Sheet

Charles De Gaulle (1890-1970) — A99

Wmk. 373

1990, Nov. 22   Litho.   Perf. 14

530	A99	Sheet, 2 ea #530c-530f + 2 labels	22.50 22.50
a.		20v At Bayeux, after D-day landing	4.00 4.00
b.		25v Alsace, 1945	4.00 4.00
c.		30v Portrait	1.60 1.60
d.		45v Spitfire, Biggin Hill, 1942	1.75 1.75
e.		55v Casablanca, 1943	1.90 1.90
f.		65v Day of Glory, Paris, 1944	2.00 2.00

Christmas — A100

1990, Dec. 5   Perf. 13

531		Strip of 5	5.00 5.00
a.	A100	25v Angel facing right	.50 .50
b.	A100	50v Shepherds	.75 .75
c.	A100	65v Nativity	.80 .80
d.	A100	70v The Three Kings	.85 .85
e.	A100	80v Angel facing left	.85 .85

Butterflies A101

25v, Parthenos sylvia. 55v, Euploea leucostictos. 80v, Lampides boeticus. 150v, Danaus plexippus.

Perf. 14x14½

1991, Jan. 9   Wmk. 384

532	A101	25v multicolored	.65 .65
533	A101	55v multicolored	1.25 1.25
534	A101	80v multicolored	1.90 1.90
535	A101	150v multicolored	3.50 3.50
		Nos. 532-535 (4)	7.30 7.30

Art Festival — A102

Wmk. 373

1991, May 2   Litho.   Perf. 13½

536	A102	25v Dance	.45 .45
537	A102	65v Weaving	1.25 1.25
538	A102	80v Carving	1.60 1.60
539	A102	150v Music	3.00 3.00
		Nos. 536-539 (4)	6.30 6.30

Elizabeth & Philip, Birthdays
Common Design Types
Wmk. 384

1991, June 17   Litho.   Perf. 14½

540	CD345	65v multicolored	1.00 1.00
541	CD346	70v multicolored	1.10 1.10
a.		Pair, #540-541 + label	2.50 2.50

Phila Nippon '91 — A103

Birds: 50v, White-collared kingfisher. 55v, Green palm lorikeet. 80v, Scarlet robin. 100v, Pacific swallow. 150v, Reef heron.

Wmk. 373

1991, Nov. 15   Litho.   Perf. 14½

542	A103	50v multicolored	1.00 1.00
543	A103	55v multicolored	1.00 1.00
544	A103	80v multicolored	1.50 1.50
545	A103	100v multicolored	1.75 1.75
		Nos. 542-545 (4)	5.25 5.25

Souvenir Sheet

546	A103	150v multicolored	3.75 3.75

Fight Against AIDS A104

Designs: 25v, Multiple partners, unsafe sex can spread AIDS. 65v, AIDS victim and care giver. 80v, AIDS kills, shark. 150v, Children's playground.

1991, Nov. 29   Wmk. 384   Perf. 14

547	A104	25v multicolored	.65 .65
548	A104	65v multicolored	1.20 1.20
549	A104	80v multicolored	1.50 1.50
550	A104	150v multicolored	2.75 2.75
		Nos. 547-550 (4)	6.10 6.10

Nos. 324-326 & 329 Surcharged

Perf. 14x13½

1991, June 12   Litho.   Wmk. 373

551	A60	20v on 2v #324	.70 .70
552	A60	60v on 10v #325	2.00 2.00
553	A60	70v on 15v #326	2.40 2.40
554	A60	80v on 30v #329	2.60 2.60
		Nos. 551-554 (4)	7.70 7.70

Queen Elizabeth II's Accession to the Throne, 40th Anniv.
Common Design Type

1992, Feb. 6   Wmk. 384   Perf. 14

555	CD349	20v multicolored	.35 .35
556	CD349	25v multicolored	.40 .40
557	CD349	60v multicolored	.90 .90
558	CD349	65v multicolored	1.00 1.00

Wmk. 373

559	CD349	70v multicolored	1.00 1.00
		Nos. 555-559 (5)	3.65 3.65

New Hebrides Participation in World War II — A105

Designs: 50v, Grumman F4F-4 Wildcat. 55v, Douglas SBD-3 Dauntless. 65v, Consolidated PBY-5A Catalina. 80v, USS Hornet. 200v, Vought-Sikorsky OS2U-3.

Perf. 13½x14
1992, May 22   Litho.   Wmk. 373
560	A105	50v multicolored	2.25	2.25
561	A105	55v multicolored	2.25	2.25
562	A105	65v multicolored	2.50	2.50
563	A105	80v multicolored	3.50	3.50
		Nos. 560-563 (4)	10.50	10.50

Souvenir Sheet
564	A105	200v multicolored	12.00	12.00

World Columbian Stamp Expo, Chicago (No. 564).
See Nos. 590-594, 664-667.

Vanuatu's Membership in the World Meteorological Organization, 10th Anniv. — A106

Designs: 25v, Meteorological station, Port Vila. 60v, Cyclone near Vanuatu seen by Japanese satellite GMS 4. 80v, Weather chart showing cyclone. 105v, Cyclone warning broadcast by radio.

1992, June 20   Perf. 14
565	A106	25v multicolored	.50	.50
566	A106	60v multicolored	1.25	1.25
567	A106	80v multicolored	1.60	1.60
568	A106	105v multicolored	1.75	1.75
		Nos. 565-568 (4)	5.10	5.10

1992 Melanesian Cup — A107

1992, July 20   Perf. 13½x14
569	A107	20v Soccer team, trophy	.50	.50
570	A107	65v Soccer players	1.25	1.25
571	A107	70v Men's track	1.50	1.50
572	A107	80v Women's track	1.50	1.50
		Nos. 569-572 (4)	4.75	4.75

1992 Summer Olympics, Barcelona (#571-572).
For surcharges see Nos. 621-622.

World Food Day — A108

Designs: 20v, "Breast is best." 70v, Central Hospital, Port Vila. 80v, "Give your children a healthy future." 150v, Nutritious food.

1992, Oct. 16   Wmk. 384   Perf. 14
573	A108	20v green & brown	.40	.40
574	A108	70v brown & green	1.00	1.00
575	A108	80v green & brown	1.25	1.25
576	A108	150v brown & green	2.25	2.25
		Nos. 573-576 (4)	4.90	4.90

Turtles A109

55v, Leatherback turtle. 65v, Loggerhead turtle. 70v, Hawksbill turtle. 80v, Green turtle. 200v, Green turtle hatchlings.

1992, Dec. 15   Perf. 14x14½
577	A109	55v multicolored	1.60	1.60
578	A109	65v multicolored	1.75	1.75
579	A109	70v multicolored	2.50	2.50
580	A109	80v multicolored	3.25	3.25
		Nos. 577-580 (4)	9.10	9.10

Souvenir Sheet
581	A109	200v multicolored	6.75	6.75

Hibiscus — A110

Designs: 25v, Light pink hibiscus rosa-sinensis. 55v, Hibiscus tiliaceus. 80v, Red hibiscus rosa-sinensis. 150v, Dark pink hibiscus rosa-sinensis.

Wmk. 384
1993, Mar. 3   Litho.   Perf. 14
582	A110	25v multicolored	.45	.45
583	A110	55v multicolored	1.00	1.00
584	A110	80v multicolored	1.25	1.25
585	A110	150v multicolored	2.40	2.40
		Nos. 582-585 (4)	5.10	5.10

Nos. 331, 333-335 Surcharged

Perf. 13½x14, 14x13½
1993, Apr. 21   Litho.   Wmk. 373
586	A60	40v on 45v #331	.85	.85
587	A60	55v on 75v #333	1.10	1.10
588	A60	65v on 100v #334	1.40	1.40
589	A60	150v on 200v #335	3.00	3.00
		Nos. 586-589 (4)	6.35	6.35

Size and location of surcharge varies.

No. 326 Surcharged

1993, June 1
589A	A60	20v on 35v #326	6.75	6.75

World War II Type of 1992

20v, Grumman F6F-3 Hellcat. 55v, Lockheed P-38F Lightning. 65v, Grumman TBF-1 Avenger. 80v, USS Essex. 200v, Douglas C-47 Dakota.

1993, June 30   Perf. 13½
590	A105	20v multicolored	.90	.90
591	A105	55v multicolored	2.50	2.50
592	A105	65v multicolored	3.00	3.00
593	A105	80v multicolored	3.75	3.75
		Nos. 590-593 (4)	10.15	10.15

Souvenir Sheet
594	A105	200v multicolored	9.75	9.75

Island Scenes A111

Designs: 5v, Iririki Island, Port Vila. 10v, Iririki Island, yachts. 15v, Court House, Port Vila. 20v, Two girls, Pentecost Island. 25v, Women dancers, Tanna Island. 30v, Market, Port Vila. 45v, Man with canoe, Erakor Island, vert. 50v, Coconut trees, Champagne Beach. 55v, Coconut trees, North Efate Islands. 60v, Fish (Banks Group). 70v, Sea fan, Tongoa Island, vert. 75v, Espiritu Santo Island. 80v,

---

Sailboat at sunset, Port Vila Bay, vert. 100v, Mele Waterfall, vert. 300v, Yasur Volcano, Tanna Island, vert. 500v, Erakor Island.

1993, July 7   Perf. 14x14½, 14½x14
595	A111	5v multicolored	.25	.25
596	A111	10v multicolored	.25	.25
597	A111	15v multicolored	.30	.30
598	A111	20v multicolored	.40	.40
599	A111	25v multicolored	.45	.45
600	A111	30v multicolored	.55	.50
601	A111	45v multicolored	.80	.80
602	A111	50v multicolored	.90	.90
603	A111	55v multicolored	1.00	1.00
604	A111	60v multicolored	1.10	1.10
605	A111	70v multicolored	1.25	1.25
606	A111	75v multicolored	1.40	1.40
a.		Souvenir sheet, #596, 603, 604, 606 ('94)	4.75	4.75
607	A111	80v multicolored	1.40	1.40
608	A111	100v multicolored	1.75	1.75
609	A111	300v multicolored	5.25	5.25
610	A111	500v multicolored	8.75	8.75
		Nos. 595-610 (16)	25.80	25.75

No. 606a, Philakorea '94 International Stamp Exhibition.
For surcharges see Nos. 619-620, 742-745A, 745D.

Shells — A112

55v, Trochus niloticus. 65v, Lioconcha castrensis. 80v, Turbo petholatus. 150v, Pleuroploca trapezium.

Wmk. 373
1993, Sept. 15   Litho.   Perf. 14½
611	A112	55v multi	1.40	1.40
612	A112	65v multi	1.75	1.75
613	A112	80v multi	2.00	2.00
614	A112	150v multi	4.00	4.00
		Nos. 611-614 (4)	9.15	9.15

See Nos. 632-635, 654-657.

Louvre Museum, Bicent. A113

Paintings by De La Tour: 25v, St. Joseph the Carpenter. 55v, The Newborn. 80v, Adoration of the Shepherds (detail). 150v, Adoration of the Shepherds (entire).

Wmk. 373
1993, Nov. 10   Litho.   Perf. 14
615	A113	25v multicolored	.45	.45
616	A113	55v multicolored	1.00	1.00
617	A113	80v multicolored	1.50	1.50
618	A113	150v multicolored	3.00	3.00
		Nos. 615-618 (4)	5.95	5.95

Nos. 570, 572, 598, 600 Surcharged

1993, Dec. 6   Litho.   Wmk. 373
Perfs. as Before
619	A111	15v on 20v #598	.30	.30
620	A111	25v on 30v #600	.40	.40
621	A107	55v on 65v #570	1.00	1.00
622	A107	70v on 80v #572	1.25	1.25
		Nos. 619-622 (4)	2.95	2.95

Service Organizations A114

Hong Kong '94: 25v, Kiwanis Intl., Charity Races, vert. 60v, Lions Intl. Twin Otter on mercy mission. 75v, Rotary Intl. fighting malaria, vert. 150v, Red Cross blood donar service. 200v, Emblems of service organizations.

Perf. 14x15, 15x14
1994, Feb. 18   Litho.   Wmk. 373
623	A114	25v multicolored	.40	.40
624	A114	60v multicolored	1.10	1.10
625	A114	75v multicolored	1.25	1.25
626	A114	150v multicolored	2.50	2.50
		Nos. 623-626 (4)	5.25	5.25

Souvenir Sheet
627	A114	200v multicolored	3.50	3.50

Intl. Year of the Family — A115

1994, Mar. 2   Perf. 14
628	A115	25v vio & rose brn	.40	.40
629	A115	60v ver & dk grn	1.00	1.00
630	A115	90v green & sepia	1.40	1.40
631	A115	150v brn & vio bl	2.50	2.50
		Nos. 628-631 (4)	5.30	5.30

Shell Type of 1993

60v, Cyprea argus. 70v, Conus marmoreus. 85v, Lambis chiragra. 155v, Chicoreus brunneus.

1994, May 31   Litho.   Perf. 12
632	A112	60v multicolored	1.40	1.40
633	A112	70v multicolored	1.40	1.40
634	A112	85v multicolored	2.10	2.10
635	A112	155v multicolored	3.75	3.75
		Nos. 632-635 (4)	8.65	8.65

Tourism — A116

Designs: a, 25v, Slit gong (drum), traditional hut. b, 75v, Volcano, boats. c, 90v, Sailboats, airplane, green palm lorikeet. d, 200v, Helicopter, woman with tray of fruit.

1994, July 27   Litho.   Perf. 13½
636	A116	Strip of 4, #a.-d.	8.00	8.00

Anemonefish — A117

1994, Aug. 16   Litho.   Perf. 12
637	A117	55v Pink	2.10	2.10
638	A117	70v Clark's	2.75	2.75
639	A117	80v Red & black	2.90	2.90
640	A117	140v Orange-fin	5.25	5.25
a.		Souvenir sheet of 4	5.50	5.50
		Nos. 637-640 (4)	13.00	13.00

Philakorea '94 (#640a).

ICAO, 50th Anniv. — A118

Designs: 25v, 1950 Qantas Catalina. 60v, 1956 Tai Douglas DC3. 75v, 1966 New Hebrides Airways Drover. 90v, 1994 Air Vanuatu Boeing 737.

1994, Dec. 7

641	A118	25v multicolored	.60	.60
642	A118	60v multicolored	1.60	1.60
643	A118	75v multicolored	1.90	1.90
644	A118	90v multicolored	2.50	2.50
		Nos. 641-644 (4)	6.60	6.60

Hibiscus A119

1995, Feb. 1   Litho.   Perf. 12

645	A119	25v The Path	.45	.45
646	A119	60v Old Frankie	1.20	1.20
647	A119	90v Fijian white	1.75	1.75
648	A119	200v Surf rider	4.00	4.00
		Nos. 645-648 (4)	7.40	7.40

Lizards A120

Designs: 25v, Emoia nigromarginata. 55v, Nactus multicarinatus. 70v, Lepidodactylus. 80v, Emoia caerulocauda. 140v, Emoia sanfordi.

1995, Apr. 12

649	A120	25v multicolored	.50	.50
650	A120	55v multicolored	1.20	1.20
651	A120	70v multicolored	1.50	1.50
652	A120	80v multicolored	1.60	1.60
653	A120	140v multicolored	3.00	3.00
		Nos. 649-653 (5)	7.80	7.80

Shell Type of 1993

25v, Epitonium scalare. 55v, Strombus latissimus. 90v, Conus bullatus. 200v, Pterynotus pinnatus.

1995, June 1

654	A112	25v multicolored	.60	.60
655	A112	55v multicolored	1.25	1.25
656	A112	90v multicolored	2.00	2.00
657	A112	200v multicolored	4.75	4.75
		Nos. 654-657 (4)	8.60	8.60

Anniversaries — A121

Designs: 25v, Girls wearing traditional head pieces. 55v, Stylized picture of natives dancing, vert. 60v, Children, doves, natl. flag, UN flag, vert. 75v, Embroidered tapestry of native, vert. 90v, Troops parading. 140v, Group in traditional ceremony.

Perf. 14x13½, 13½x14

1995, July 28   Litho.

658	A121	25v multicolored	.50	.50
659	A121	55v multicolored	1.00	1.00
660	A121	60v multicolored	1.00	1.00
661	A121	75v multicolored	1.50	1.50
662	A121	90v multicolored	1.60	1.60

663	A121	140v multicolored	2.50	2.50
a.		Souvenir sheet of 1	4.25	4.25
		Nos. 658-663 (6)	8.10	8.10

UN, 50th anniv. (#660). Singapore 95 (#663a). Others, independence, 15th anniv.

World War II Type of 1992

60v, SB2C Helldiver. 70v, Spitfire Mk VIII. 75v, F4U-1A Corsair. 80v, PV1 Ventura. 140v, Japanese surrender, USS Missouri.

1995, Sept. 1   Litho.   Perf. 12½

664	A105	60v multicolored	2.75	2.75
665	A105	70v multicolored	3.00	3.00
666	A105	75v multicolored	3.00	3.00
667	A105	80v multicolored	3.50	3.50
		Nos. 664-667 (4)	12.25	12.25

Souvenir Sheet

Perf. 13½

667A	A105	140v multicolored	9.00	9.00

No. 667A for Singapore 95.

Artifacts — A122

Ambae money mat and: a, 25v, Rambaramp mortuary effigy, Malakula. b, 60v, Wusi pot, Espiritu Santo. c, 75v, Slit gong, Efate Island. d, 90v, Tapa cloth, Erromango Island.
Nos. 668e, 668f, like No. 668d.

1995, Nov. 22   Litho.   Perf. 13½x13

668	A122	Strip of 4, #a.-d.	5.50	5.50
e.		90v Perf. 14	1.50	1.50
f.		Souvenir sheet, #668e	2.75	2.75

No. 668f, 9th Asian Intl. Philatelic Exhibition, Beijing.
Issued: Nos. 668e, 668f, Dec. 1995.
See No. 720.

Fishing A123

1996, Feb. 1   Litho.   Perf. 14

669	A123	55v Cast net	1.00	1.00
670	A123	75v Reef	1.25	1.25
671	A123	80v Deep water, vert.	1.25	1.25
672	A123	140v Game, vert.	2.50	2.50
		Nos. 669-672 (4)	6.00	6.00

Flying Foxes A124

No. 673, Notopteris macdonaldi, facing left. No. 674, Pteropus anetianus, green leaves on tree, vert. No. 675, Pteropus anetianus, diff., vert. No. 676, Notopteris macdonaldi, diff.
No. 677, vert: a, 90v, Pteropus tonganus. b, 140v, Pteropus tonganus, diff.

1996, Apr. 3   Litho.   Perf. 14

673	A124	25v multicolored	.70	.55
674	A124	25v multicolored	.70	.55
675	A124	25v multicolored	.70	.55
676	A124	25v multicolored	.70	.55
		Nos. 673-676 (4)	2.80	2.20

Souvenir Sheet

677	A124	Sheet of 2, #a.-b.	5.25	5.25

World Wildlife Fund (Nos. 673-676). 9th Asian Intl. Philatelic Exhibition (No. 677).

UNICEF, 50th Anniv. A125

Unwmk.

1996, June 5   Litho.   Perf. 14

678	A125	55v Immunizations	1.10	1.10
679	A125	60v Breast feeding	1.40	1.40

Radio, Cent. A126

60v, Airplane, radio signal. 75v, Radio Vanuatu. 80v, Guglielmo Marconi. 90v, Ship, radio signal.

1996, June 5   Perf. 14½

680	A126	60v multicolored	1.00	1.00
681	A126	75v multicolored	1.20	1.20
682	A126	80v multicolored	1.25	1.25
683	A126	90v multicolored	1.50	1.50
a.		Block of 4, #680-683	6.50	6.50

Modern Olympic Games, Cent. — A127

Designs: 25v, Marie Kapalu, Tawai Keiruan, Baptiste Firiam, Tava Kalo, 1996 athletes from Vanuatu. 70v, 1996 Athletes in training. 75v, 1950's Athletes. 200v, 1896 Athletes.

1996, July 17   Litho.   Perf. 14

684	A127	25v multicolored	.45	.45
685	A127	70v multicolored	1.25	1.25
686	A127	75v multicolored	1.25	1.25
687	A127	200v multicolored	3.75	3.75
		Nos. 684-687 (4)	6.70	6.70

Christmas A128

Children of various races holding candles in front of churches: a, 25v, Presbyterian, Roman Catholic. b, 60v, Church of Christ. c, 75v, 7th Day Adventist, Apostolic. d, 90v, Anglican.

1996, Sept. 11   Litho.   Perf. 14

688	A128	Strip of 4, #a.-d.	4.50	4.50

No. 688 is a continuous design.

Hibiscus A129

1996, Nov. 13   Litho.   Perf. 13½

689	A129	25v Lady Cilento	.50	.50
690	A129	60v Kinchen's Yellow	1.25	1.25
691	A129	90v D.J. O'Brien	1.75	1.75
692	A129	200v Cuban Variety	3.75	3.75
a.		Sheet of 2, #689, #692	6.00	6.00
		Nos. 689-692 (4)	7.25	7.25

Hong Kong '97. No. 692a issued 2/12/97.

Diving A130

Designs: 70v, Coral Garden. 75v, Lady of the President Coolidge. 90v, "Boris," Queensland grouper. 140v, Wreck of the President Coolidge.

1997, Jan. 15   Litho.   Perf. 14½x14

693	A130	70v multicolored	1.25	1.25
694	A130	75v multicolored	1.25	1.25
695	A130	90v multicolored	1.50	1.50
696	A130	140v multicolored	2.50	2.50
a.		Souvenir sheet, #694, 696	6.00	6.00
b.		Souvenir sheet, #693-696	12.00	12.00
		Nos. 693-696 (4)	6.50	6.50

Pacific '97 (#696a).

Birds A131

25v, Sharp-tailed sandpiper. 55v, Crested tern. 60v, Little pied cormorant. 75v, Brown booby. 80v, Reef heron. 90v, Red-tailed tropic bird.

1997, June 4   Litho.   Perf. 13½x14

697	A131	25v multi	.55	.55
698	A131	55v multi	1.10	1.10
699	A131	60v multi	1.20	1.20
700	A131	75v multi	1.40	1.40
701	A131	80v multi, vert.	1.40	1.40
702	A131	90v multi, vert.	1.75	1.75
		Nos. 697-702 (6)	7.40	7.40

Air Vanuatu, 10th Anniv. A132

Designs: 25v, Pilot at controls. 60v, Airplane being serviced, cargo loaded. 90v, Serving drinks to passengers. 200v, Passengers leaving plane upon arrival at Vanuatu.

1997, Apr. 2   Perf. 14½x14

703	A132	25v multicolored	.45	.45
704	A132	60v multicolored	1.10	1.10
705	A132	90v multicolored	1.75	1.75
706	A132	200v multicolored	3.75	3.75
		Nos. 703-706 (4)	7.05	7.05

No. 704 is 81x31mm.

Thomas A. Edison (1847-1931) — A133

Designs: 60v, Light bulb, Edison. 70v, Hydro dam, Santo. 200v, Port Vila by dusk.

1997, Aug. 27   Litho.   Perf. 12

707		60v multicolored	1.00	1.00
708		70v multicolored	1.25	1.25
709		200v multicolored	3.50	3.50
a.		A133 Block of 3, #707-709 + label	7.25	7.25

No. 709 is 80x30mm.

Fish — A134

Designs: 25v, Yellow-faced angelfish. 55v, Flame angelfish. 60v, Lemonpeel angelfish. 70v, Emperor angelfish. 140v, Multi-barred angelfish.

1997, Nov. 12   Litho.   Perf. 14x13½

710	A134	25v multicolored	.45	.45
711	A134	55v multicolored	1.00	1.00
712	A134	60v multicolored	1.20	1.20
713	A134	70v multicolored	1.25	1.25
714	A134	140v multicolored	2.50	2.50
		Nos. 710-714 (5)	6.40	6.40

Architecture in Vanuatu A135

Designs: 30v, Fale-Espiritu Santo. 65v, Natl. Cultural Center. 80v, University of the South Pacific. 200v, Chief's Nakamal.

1998, Feb. 11   Litho.   Perf. 14½x14

715	A135	30v multicolored	.45	.45
716	A135	65v multicolored	1.00	1.00
717	A135	80v multicolored	1.20	1.20
718	A135	200v multicolored	3.00	3.00
		Nos. 715-718 (4)	5.65	5.65

Diana, Princess of Wales (1961-97)
Common Design Type

Various portraits: a, 75v. b, 85v. c, 145v.

1998, Mar. 31   Litho.   Perf. 14½x14

718A	CD355	95v multicolored	1.50	1.50
		Sheet of 4		
719	CD355	#a.-c., 718A	6.50	6.50

No. 719 sold for 400v + 50v, with surtax from international sales being donated to The Diana, Princess of Wales Memorial Fund and surtax from national sales being donated to designated local charity.

Artifacts Type of 1995

Tribal masks: a, 30v, South West Malakula. b, 65v, North Ambrym. c, 75v, Gana Island Banks. d, 85v, Uripiv Island, Malakula. e, 95v, Vao Island, Malakula, and Central South Pentecost.

1998, June 3   Litho.   Perf. 14½

720	A122	Strip of 5, #a.-e.	7.25	7.25

Butterflies — A136

30v, Danaus plexippus. 60v, Hypolimnas bolina. 65v, Eurema hecabe. 75v, Nymphalidae. 95v, Precis villida. 205v, Tirumala hamata.

**1998, July 23   Litho.   Die Cut
Self-Adhesive**

721	A136	30v multicolored	.55	.55
722	A136	60v multicolored	1.10	1.10
723	A136	65v multicolored	1.25	1.25
724	A136	75v multicolored	1.60	1.60
725	A136	95v multicolored	1.90	1.90
726	A136	205v multicolored	3.25	3.25
a.		Souvenir sheet of 1	5.00	5.00
		Nos. 721-726 (6)	9.65	9.65

Singpex '98 (#726a).

Volcanoes — A137

30v, Yasur, Tanna. 60v, Marum & Benbow, Ambrym. 75v, Gaua. 80v, Lopevi. 145v, Ambae.

1998, Oct. 23   Litho.   Perf. 15x14

728	A137	30v multicolored	.45	.45
729	A137	60v multicolored	.90	.90
730	A137	75v multicolored	1.20	1.20
731	A137	80v multicolored	1.20	1.20
732	A137	145v multicolored	2.25	2.25
		Nos. 728-732 (5)	6.00	6.00

Early Explorers A138

Explorer, ship: 34v, Pedro Fernandez de Quiros, San Pedro y Paulo, 1606. 73v, Louis-Antoine de Bougainville, Boudeuse, 1768. 84v, Capt. James Cook, HMS Resolution, 1774. 90v, Jean-Fancois de Galaup de la Perousse, Astrolabe, 1788. 96v, Jules Sebastien-Cesar Dumont d'Urville, Astrolabe, "1788."

1999, Feb. 17   Litho.   Perf. 14

733	A138	34v multicolored	.50	.50
734	A138	73v multicolored	1.60	1.60
735	A138	84v multicolored	1.90	1.90
a.		Souv. sheet, #733-735	3.75	3.75
736	A138	90v multicolored	1.90	1.90
737	A138	96v multicolored	2.00	2.00
a.		Souv. sheet, #734, 736-737	5.50	5.50
		Nos. 733-737 (5)	7.90	7.90

No. 735a was released for Australia '99 World Stamp Expo on 3/19/99; No. 737a for PhilexFrance 99.

Birds — A139

34v, Vanuatu kingfisher. 67v, Shining cuckoo. 73v, Peregrine falcon. 107v, Rainbow lorikeet.

1999, May 12   Litho.   Perf. 14

738	A139	34v multicolored	.75	.75
739	A139	67v multicolored	1.25	1.25
		Booklet, 5 #739	7.00	
740	A139	73v multicolored	1.50	1.50
741	A139	107v multicolored	2.25	2.25
a.		Sheet of 1	4.75	4.75
b.		Sheet of 1 with China 1999 emblem in margin	5.75	5.75
		Nos. 738-741 (4)	5.75	5.75

Issued: #741b, 8/18.

Nos. 601, 603-605, 607, 608 Surcharged

Perf. 14½x14, 14x14½

1998-2000   Litho.

742	A111	1v on 100v #608	.25	.25
742A	A111	2v on 45v #601	.25	.25
743	A111	2v on 55v #603	.25	.25
744	A111	3v on 60v #604	.25	.25
744A	A111	3v on 75v #606	.25	.25

745	A111	4v on 45v #601	.25	.25
745A	A111	5v on 70v #605		
745B	A111	34v on 20v #598	.50	.50
745C	A111	67v on 300v #609	1.00	1.00
745D	A111	73v on 80v #607		
		Nos. 742-745D (10)	3.00	3.00

Issued: No. 742, No. 742A, 743, 744, 745, 745A, 12/18/98; No. 744A, 4/27/99; Nos. 745B, 745C, 745D, 2/17/00.

Ceremonial Dancers — A140

1v, Banks Islands. 2v, Small Nambas, Laman-Malakula. 3v, Small Nambas, Malakula. 5v, Smol Bag Theatre. 107v, South West Bay, Malakula. 200v, Big Nambas, Malakula. 500v, Pentecost.

1999, July 14   Perf. 14

746	A140	1v multicolored	.25	.25
747	A140	2v multicolored	.25	.25
748	A140	3v multicolored	.25	.25
749	A140	5v multicolored	.25	.25
750	A140	107v multicolored	1.60	1.60
751	A140	200v multicolored	3.25	3.25
752	A140	500v multicolored	7.75	7.75
		Nos. 746-752 (7)	13.60	13.60

See Nos. 788-791.

Poisonous Fish — A141

Designs: 34v, Pterois antennata. 84v, Pterois antennata, diff. 90v, Pterois volitans. 96v, Pterois volitans, diff.

1999, Oct. 13   Litho.   Perf. 14¼

753	A141	34v multi	.70	.70
754	A141	84v multi	1.75	1.75
755	A141	90v multi	2.00	2.00
756	A141	96v multi	2.25	2.25
		Nos. 753-756 (4)	6.70	6.70

Millennium A142

Designs: a, 34v, Fish. b, 68v, Girl, land diver, vert. c, 84v, Fetish, vert. d, 90v, Bird, flowers. e, 96v, Man with conch shell.

1999, Dec. 1   Perf. 14½

757	A142	Sheet of 5, #a.-e.	7.00	7.00

Souvenir Sheet

Queen Mother, 100th Birthday — A143

a, 107v, As child. b, 100v, As old woman.

Litho. with Foil Application

2000, May 22   Perf. 13¼

758	A143	Sheet of 2, #a-b	5.50	5.50

The Stamp Show 2000, London.

Intelsat A144

Designs: 10v, Launch vehicle. 34v, Port Vila ground station. 100v, Intelsat 802 over Vaunatu. 225v, Intelsat and Tam Tam drum.

Litho. with Foil Application

**2000, June 21   Die Cut Perf. 10
Self-Adhesive**

759-762	A144		7.00	7.00
762a		Souvenir sheet, #760, 762	5.25	5.25

World Stamp Expo 2000, Anaheim (#762a).

Independence, 20th Anniv., UN Peace Year — A145

Artwork: 34v, Abstract painting by Sero Kuautonga. 67v, Tapa cloth by Moses Pita. 73v, Tapestry by Juliet Pita. 84v, Natora wood carving by Emmannuel Watt. 90v, Watercolor by Joseph John.

2000, July 29   Litho.   Perf. 13¾x13¼

763-767	A145	Set of 5	8.00	8.00
		Booklet, 5 #764	6.50	

2000 Summer Olympics, Sydney — A146

Designs: 56v, Runner. 67v, Weight lifter. 90v, High jumper. 96v, Boxer.

2000, Sept. 15   Perf. 13¼x13

768-771	A146	Set of 4	5.50	5.50
		Booklet, 5 #769	6.00	

Dolphins — A147

34v, Common. 73v, Spotted. 84v, Spinner. 107v, Bottlenose.

2000, Nov. 30   Litho.   Perf. 12½

772-775	A147	Set of 4	6.50	6.50
775a		Souvenir sheet, #774-775	5.50	5.50

Hong Kong 2001 Stamp Exhibition (#775a).

Birds — A148

Designs: 35v, Cardinal honeyeater. 60v, Vanuatu white-eye. 90v, Santo Mountain starling. 100v, Royal parrotfinch. 110v, Vanuatu Mountain honeyeater.

2001, Feb. 1	Litho.		Perf. 14	
776-780	A148	Set of 5	10.50	10.50
780a	Horiz. strip, #776-780		10.50	10.50

Exports — A149

Designs: 35v, Vanilla. 75v, Cacao. 90v, Coffee. 110v, Copra.

2001, Apr. 11		Perf. 13¼x13	
781-784	A149 Set of 4	6.50	6.50

Whales
A150

Designs: 60v, Sperm. 80v, Humpback, vert. 90v, Blue.

	Perf. 14½x14¾, 14¾x14½		
2001, July 18		Litho.	
785-787	A150 Set of 3	6.00	6.00
787a	Souvenir sheet, #785-787, perf. 14½	6.25	6.25

See New Caledonia No. 874.

Ceremonial Dancers Type of 1999

Designs: 35v, Snake dance, Banks Islands, horiz. 100v, Toka Dance, Tanna, horiz. 300v, Rom Dance, Ambryn, horiz. 1000v, Brasive Dance, Futuna, horiz.

2001, Sept. 12	Litho.	Perf. 13x13¼	
788	A140 35v multi	.75	.75
789	A140 100v multi	2.10	2.10
790	A140 300v multi	6.25	6.25

Litho. With Foil Application			
791	A140 1000v multi	20.00	20.00
	Nos. 788-791 (4)	29.10	29.10

Sand
Drawings — A151

Various sand drawings and: a, Four people on beach. b, Man standing in canoe in water. c, Man sitting on canoe, man rowing canoe. d, Canoe, shelter.

	Perf. 12¾x13½		
2001, Nov. 28		Litho.	
792	A151 60v multi	1.00	1.00
792A	A151 90v multi	1.50	1.50
792B	A151 110v multi	1.90	1.90
792C	A151 135v multi	2.40	2.40
	d. Horiz. strip of 4 + central label	9.00	9.00

Intl. Year of
Ecotourism
A152

Designs: Nos. 793, 798a, 35v, Mount Yasur, Pentecost Island land diver, dancers. Nos. 794, 798b, 60v Dancers, man making kava. Nos. 795, 798c, 75v, Siri Falls, flowers, birds, vert. Nos. 796, 798d, 110v, Kayakers, scuba

---

diver, vert. Nos. 797, 798e, 135v, Beach bungalows, tourists.

2002, Jan. 30	Litho.	Perf. 14	
Stamps + Label			
793-707	A152 Set of 5	8.75	8.75

Souvenir Sheet
Without Labels

	Perf. 14½x14¾		
798	A152 Sheet of 5, #a-e	8.75	8.75

Nos. 793, 794, and 797 are 38x26mm and Nos. 795-796 are 26x38mm, while Nos. 798a, 798b, and 798e are 37x25mm and Nos. 798c-798d are 25x37mm.

Horses
A153

Designs: 35v, Working horses. 60v, Cattle roundup. 75v, Horse racing. 80v, Tourism and horses. 200v, Wild Tanna horse.

2002, Mar. 27		Perf. 14¾x14	
799-803	A153 Set of 5	8.25	8.25
803a	Souvenir sheet of 1	4.25	4.25
803b	Souvenir sheet of 1 with Philakorea 2002 emblem	4.25	4.25

Issued: No. 803b, 7/31/02.

Soccer
A154

Designs: 35v, Children's soccer. 80v, Under 17 soccer. 110v, Women's soccer. 135v, International soccer.

2002, May 31	Litho.	Perf. 13¾	
804-807	A154 Set of 4	7.00	7.00

Value is for stamps with surrounding selvage.

Reforestation — A155

No. 808: a, Girl with seedling of Artocarpus atilis. b, Boy and man planting seedling of Endospermum medullosum. c, Canoe carver with Gyrocarpus americanus log. d, Mother and child with Dracontomelon vitiense fruit.

	Serpentine Die Cut		
2002, July 31		Litho.	
Self-Adhesive			
808	Horiz. strip of 4	6.75	
a.	A155 35v multi	.80	.80
b.	A155 60v multi	1.40	1.40
c.	A155 90v multi	1.90	1.90
d.	A155 110v multi	2.50	2.50

Dugongs
A156

Designs: 35v, Pair nuzzling. 75v, Pair swimming. 80v, One swimming. 135v, One on ocean floor.

2002, Sept. 25	Litho.	Perf. 13¾	
812-815	A156 Set of 4	6.25	6.25
815a	Souvenir sheet, #814-815	7.00	7.00

Orchids — A157

Designs: 35v, Dendrobium gouldii. 60v, Dendrobium polysema. 90v, Dendrobium spectabile. 110v, Flickingeria comata.

2002, Nov. 27	Litho.	Perf. 13¼	
816-819	A157 Set of 4	6.25	6.25

Year of
Cattle — A158

Cattle Breeds: 35v, Limousin. 80v, Charolais 110v, Simmental. 135v, Red Brahman.

2003, Jan. 29		Perf. 13	
820-823	A158 Set of 4	7.50	7.50

Pentecost
Island Land
Divers — A159

Designs: 35v, Diver on platform. 80v, Diver in air. 110v, Dancers, platform. 200v, Diver and platform (35x90mm).

2003, Mar. 26		Perf. 13¾x13¼	
824-827	A159 Set of 4	9.50	9.50
827a	Souvenir sheet of 1	5.25	5.25

Snorkeling
A160

Various people snorkeling: 35v, 80v, 90v, 110v, 135v. 80v and 90v are vert.

2003, May 28	Litho.	Perf. 13¾	
828-832	A160 Set of 5	7.50	7.50
832a	Souvenir sheet, #828-832, perf. 13¼	8.25	8.25

Natanggura
Palm — A161

Half of palm nut and: 35v, Man planting palm tree, carved dolphins. 80v, Man weaving thatch for roof, carved turtle. 90v, Carver, carved lizard. 135v, Carvers, carved fish.

2003, July 23		Perf. 13¾x13¼	
833-836	A161 Set of 4	5.75	5.75

Opening of
Underwater Post
Office in May
2003 — A162

2003, Sept. 24		Perf. 13¾	
837	A162 90v multi	2.25	2.25

Sea
Horses — A163

Designs: 60v, Hippocampus kuda. 90v, Hippocampus histrix. 200v, Hippocampus bargibanti.

2003, Sept. 24			
838-840	A163 Set of 3	6.00	6.00
840a	Souvenir sheet of 1	4.50	4.50

Moths
A164

Designs: 35v, Daphnis hypothous. 90v, Hippotion celerio. 110v, Euchromia creusa. 135v, Eudocima salaminia.

2003, Nov. 26		Perf. 13½	
841-844	A164 Set of 4	6.50	6.50

Activities at
Underwater Post
Office — A165

Designs: 35v, Workers placing mail in bag. 80v, Swimmer placing mail in mail box. 110v, Swimmer at counter. 220v, Clerk at counter, swimmer near mail box.

2004, Jan. 30		Perf. 13¾x13½	
845-848	A165 Set of 4	8.25	8.25
848a	Souvenir sheet of 1	4.50	4.50

2004 Hong Kong Stamp Expo (#848a).

Starfish
A166

Designs: 35v, Protoreaster nodulosus. 60v, Linckia laevigata. 90v, Fromia monilis. 250v, Echinaster callosus.

Serpentine Die Cut
2004, Apr. 28   Litho.
Self-Adhesive
849-852   A166   Set of 4   8.25   8.25

Red-tailed Tropicbird A167

Designs: 35v, Adult and juvenile. 50v, Adult and chick, vert. 75v, Adult flying above juvenile, vert. 135v, Adult in flight. 200v, Adult pair.

2004, July 14   Litho.   Perf. 13¾
853-857   A167   Set of 5   10.50   10.50
857a   Souvenir sheet, #853-857, perf. 13½   11.50   11.50

Musket Cove to Port Vila Yacht Race, 25th Anniv. — A168

Various yachts: 35v, 80v, 90v, 200v. 80v and 200v are vert.

2004, Sept. 18   Perf. 14¼
858-861   A168   Set of 4   10.00   10.00
861a   Souvenir sheet of 1   5.25   5.25

See Fiji Nos. 1024-1027

Miniature Sheet

Marine Life — A169

No. 862: a, Red and black anemonefish. b, Longfin bannerfish. c, Goldman's sweetlips. d, Green turtle. e, Clark's anemonefish. f, Harlequin sweetlips. g, Yellowtail coris. h, Emperor angelfish. i, Hairy red hermit crab, leaf oyster. j, Spotfin lionfish. k, Yellow-lipped sea krait. l, Clam.

Serpentine Die Cut 13¼
2004, Nov. 24   Litho.
Self-Adhesive
862   A169   35v Sheet of 12, #a-l   11.00   11.00

Christmas A170

Serpentine Die Cut 13
2004, Nov. 24   Self-Adhesive
863   A170   80v multi   2.25   2.25

Sunsets A171

Designs: 60v, Sailboat. 80v, Man with raised arm, vert. 90v, Sailboats, vert. 135v, Man blowing conch shell.

2005, Jan. 19   Perf. 14x14½, 14½x14
864-867   A171   Set of 4   9.25   9.25

Miniature Sheet

Lapita People — A172

No. 868: a, 50v, Man holding tool, vert. b, 70v, People cleaning fish. c, 110v, People tending fire and carrying animal to fire. d, 200v, Women making baskets, mother and child, vert.

2005, Mar. 2   Perf. 13¼
868   A172   Sheet of 4, #a-d   11.50   11.50

Pacific Explorer 2005 World Stamp Expo, Sydney.

Volcano Post A173

Mail box on Mount Yasur and: 35v, Five tourists. 80v, Native woman. 100v, Three postal workers. 250v, Postal worker removing mail.

2005, May 31   Litho.   Perf. 14x14¼
869-872   A173   Set of 4   9.25   9.25
872a   Souvenir sheet of 1   5.50   5.50

Souvenir Sheet

Independence, 25th Anniv. — A174

No. 873: a, 35v, Vanuatu natives celebrating. b, 50v, Soldiers raising Vanuatu flag, 1980. c, 400v, Children and statue of family.

2005, July 30   Litho.   Perf. 13
873   A174   Sheet of 3, #a-c   12.50   12.50

Miniature Sheet

Corals — A175

No. 874: a, Lace coral. b, Star coral. c, Sun coral (Tubastraea sp.). d, Plate coral. e, Brown anthelia. f, Bubble coral. g, Flowerpot coral. h, Cup coral. i, Daisy coral. j, Sun coral (Tubastraea diaphana). k, Mushroom-feather coral. l, Sun coral (Tubastraea micrantha).

Serpentine Die Cut 13½x13¼
2005, Sept. 7   Litho.
Self-Adhesive
874   A175   35v Sheet of 12, #a-l   11.00   11.00

Landscapes — A176

Designs: 80v, Horse and rider on beach. 90v, Palm trees. 110v, Waterfall. 135v, Harbor.

2005, Nov. 16   Litho.   Perf. 14¼x14
875-878   A176   Set of 4   11.00   11.00

Miniature Sheet

Reef Shells — A177

No. 879: a, Crocus clam. b, Pearl oyster. c, Gold-ringer cowrie. d, Cock-a-comb oyster. e, Tiger cowrie. f, Textile cone. g, Marlinspike. h, Vibex cowrie. i, Erosa cowrie. j, Scorpion conch. k, Honey cowrie. l, Umbilical ovula.

Serpentine Die Cut 13½
2006, Feb. 8   Self-Adhesive
879   A177   35v Sheet of 12, #a-l   11.00   11.00

Queen Elizabeth II, 80th Birthday A178

Queen: 50v, As young woman in Army uniform. 100v, Without hat. No. 882, 110v, With blue hat. No. 883, 200v, With yellow hat.
No. 884: a, 110v, Like 100v. b, 200v, Like No. 882.

2006, Apr. 21   Litho.   Perf. 14
With White Frames
880-883   A178   Set of 4   8.00   8.00

Souvenir Sheet
Without White Frames
884   A178   Sheet of 2, #a-b   5.75   5.75

Souvenir Sheet

Arrival in Vanuatu of Pedro Fernandez de Quiros, 400th Anniv. — A179

2006, May 10   Perf. 13¼
885   A179   350v multi   7.50   7.50

2006 World Cup Soccer Championships, Germany — A180

Various soccer players, 2006 World Cup emblem on soccer jersey: 35v, 80v, 110v, 135v.

2006, June 9   Litho.   Die Cut
Self-Adhesive
886-889   A180   Set of 4   7.00   7.00
889a   Souvenir sheet, #886-889   7.00   7.00

Flowers A181

Designs: 5v, Passiflora foetida. 10v, Hibiscus rosa-sinensis. 20v, Cereus undatus. 40v, Strelitzia reginae. 50v, Spathodea campanulata. 70v, Delonix regia. 90v, Hibiscus hilaceus. 100v, Nymphaea sp. 150v, Plumeria obtusa. 500v, Allamanda cathartica. 1000v, Thunbergia grandiflora.

Serpentine Die Cut 11¾
2006, July 1   Self-Adhesive
890   A181   5v multi   .25   .25
891   A181   10v multi   .25   .25
892   A181   20v multi   .35   .35
893   A181   40v multi   .65   .65
894   A181   50v multi   .80   .80
895   A181   70v multi   1.10   1.10
896   A181   100v multi   1.60   1.60
897   A181   150v multi   2.50   2.50
898   A181   500v multi   8.00   8.00
899   A181   1000v multi   16.50   16.50

Inscribed "International Post" at Left
900   A181   5v multi   .25   .25
901   A181   10v multi   .25   .25
902   A181   20v multi   .35   .35
903   A181   50v multi   .80   .80
904   A181   90v multi   1.40   1.40
905   A181   100v multi   1.60   1.60
906   A181   500v multi   8.00   8.00
907   A181   1000v multi   16.50   16.50
   Nos. 890-907 (18)   61.15   61.15

Miniature Sheet

Worldwide Fund for Nature (WWF) — A182

No. 908: a, 70v, Giant grouper and coral. b, 90v, Giant grouper and smaller fish. c, 100v, Juvenile giant groupers. d, 150v, Giant grouper, smaller fish, diff.

2006, Oct. 4   Litho.   Perf. 13¼
908   A182   Sheet, 2 each #a-d   13.50   13.50

Shipwreck of the SS President Coolidge — A183

Designs: 90v, Diver, corals. 100v, Divers, fish. 130v, Shipwreck, fish. 150v, Ship sinking, sailors leaving ship (85x30mm).
No. 913: a, 90v, Like #909. b, 100v, Like #910. c, 130v, Like #911. d, 150v, Like #912.

2006, Nov. 29   Litho.   Perf. 13¼
Stamps Inscribed "International Post"
909-912   A183   Set of 4   8.50   8.50
Souvenir Sheet
Stamps Without "International Post"
913   A183   Sheet of 4, #a-d   8.50   8.50

Reef Heron
A184

Reef heron: 10v, With wings extended. 20v, Standing on land, vert. 50v, With fish in bill, vert. 70v, Head. 250v, Chicks.

2007, Feb. 9   **Litho.**   **Perf. 14½**
914-918 A184   Set of 5   8.00 8.00
918a   Souvenir sheet, #914-918   8.00 8.00

Diving at Million Dollar Point
A185

Designs: Nos. 919, 923a, 90v, Divers near submerged jeep. Nos. 920, 923b, 100v, Divers near submerged truck, vert. (42x60mm). Nos. 921, 923c, 130v, Diver, diff. Nos. 922, 923d, 150v, Diver, lionfish.

2007, Apr. 18   **Perf. 13¼**
Stamps Inscribed "International Post"
919-922 A185   Set of 4   8.50 8.50
Souvenir Sheet
Stamps Without "International Post"
923 A185   Sheet of 4, #a-d   8.50 8.50

Fruit — A186

Designs: 30v, Bananas. 40v, Watermelon. 70v, Limes. 100v, Papayas. 250v, Coconuts.

2007, June 27   **Serpentine Die Cut**
Self-Adhesive
924-928 A186   Set of 5   9.50 9.50

James A. Michener (1907-97), Writer
A187

Michener: 40v, With pen. 90v, At typewriter. 130v, With island natives. 350v, Holding book.

2007, Aug. 22   **Perf. 14½**
929-932 A187   Set of 4   11.50 11.50

Banded Iguana — A188

Designs: 50v, Two iguanas, two flowers. 70v, Iguana on branch. 100v, Iguana. 250v, Iguana on flower bud.

Serpentine Die Cut 15
2007, Nov. 7   **Litho.**
Self-Adhesive
933-936 A188   Set of 4   9.25 9.25
936a   Souvenir sheet, #936 000   7.75 7.75

Air Vanuatu, 20th Anniv. — A189

Designs: 40v, Three airplanes at airport. 90v, Boeing 737-800. 130v, Boeing 737-300. 180v, Twin Otter. 250v, ATR 42.

2007-08   **Serpentine Die Cut 15**
937 A189   40v multi   .75 .75
938 A189   90v multi   1.75 1.75
939 A189   130v multi   2.50 2.50
940 A189   180v multi   3.50 3.50
941 A189   250v multi   4.75 4.75
  Nos. 937-941 (5)   13.25 13.25

First flight of Boeing 737-800 (#938). Issued: 40v, 130v, 180v, 250v, 11/23; 90v, 1/17/08.

Coconut Crabs
A190

Crab on: 60v, Beach. 500v, Tree, vert.

Perf. 10½x13¼, 13¼x13½
2008, Feb. 20   **Litho.**
942-943 A190   Set of 2   13.00 13.00
943a   Souvenir sheet, #942-943   13.00 13.00

Miniature Sheet

2008 Summer Olympics, Beijing — A191

No. 944: a, 10v, Archery. b, 40v, Athletics. c, 60v, Table tennis. d, 90v, Weight lifting

2008, June 18   **Litho.**   **Perf. 12**
944 A191   Sheet of 4, #a-d   4.25 4.25

Underwater Post Office — A192

Designs: 40v, Underwater postal workers carrying sacks of mail, fish with postcard. 80v, Postal worker, fish with letters. 100v, Postal workers in raft, fish with mail. 200v, Underwater post office, fish and marine life with letters.

2008, July 30   **Litho.**   **Die Cut**
Self-Adhesive
945-948 A192   Set of 4   8.50 8.50

Tourism — A193

Scenes and website addresses of: No. 949, 90v, Vanuatu Tourism. No. 950, 90v, Breakas Beach Resort. No. 951, 90v, Iririki Island Resort and Spa. No. 952, 90v, Le Lagon Resort, No. 953, 90v, The Melanesian Hotel. No. 954, 90v, Le Meridien Resort Spa and Casino. No. 955, 90v, Sebel Hotel.

2008, Aug. 27   **Perf. 15x14¾**
949-955 A193   Set of 7   13.00 13.00

Miniature Sheet

Nudibranchs — A194

No. 956: a, Risbecia tryoni. b, Phyllidia coelestis. c, Flabellina rubrolineata. d, Chromodoris lochi. e, Chromodoris elisabethina. f, Jorunna funebris. g, Glossodoris rufomarginata. h, Phyllidia ocellata. i, Chromodoris geometrica. j, Phyllidia madangensis. k, Hexabranchus sanguineus. l, Glossodoris atromarginata.

Serpentine Die Cut 13¼
2008, Oct. 8   **Self-Adhesive**
956 A194   40v Sheet of 12, #a-l   8.50 8.50

Birds — A195

Designs: 45v, Eastern reef heron. 100v, Great crested tern. 130v, White-tailed tropicbird. 250v, Fairy tern.

2008, Nov. 26   **Litho.**   **Perf. 14½x15**
957-960 A195   Set of 4   9.00 9.00
960a   Souvenir sheet of 1 #960   5.00 5.00

Romance in Vanuatu — A196

Couples in Vanuatu, website addresses for: No. 961, 90v, Bride and groom wearing flowers (Events Vanuatu). No. 962, 90v, Bride and groom with wine glasses (Events Vanuatu). No. 963, 90v, Man and woman sitting on beach (Air Vanuatu). No. 964, 90v, Man and woman sitting on chaise lounges (Breakas Beach Resort). No. 965, 90v, Man and woman at table (White Grass Ocean Resort).

2009, Jan. 28   **Litho.**   **Die Cut**
Self-Adhesive
961-965 A196   Set of 5   7.00 7.00

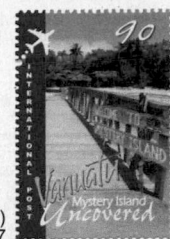

Mystery (Inyeug) Island — A197

Designs: Nos. 966, 970a, 90v, Boat dock. Nos. 967, 970b, 100v, Snorkelers and boat, horiz. Nos. 968, 970c, 130v, Sailboat and trees, horiz. Nos. 969, 970d, 200v, Man and woman on outrigger canoe on beach.

2009, Mar. 28   **Litho.**   **Perf. 14**
Stamps Inscribed "International Post"
966-969 A197   Set of 4   8.25 8.25
Souvenir Sheet
Stamps Without "International Post"
970 A197   Sheet of 4, #a-d   8.25 8.25

Peonies
A198

2009, Apr. 10   **Litho.**   **Perf. 13¼**
971 A100   100v multi   1.75 1.75

Printed in sheets of 8.

Plumeria Flowers — A199

Various plumeria flowers: 90v, 100v, 130v, 150v.

2009, May 14   **Perf. 14½x14**
972-975 A199   Set of 4   8.00 8.00

Souvenir Sheet

Hong Kong 2009 Intl. Stamp Exhibition — A200

2009, May 14   **Perf. 13½**
976 A200   Sheet of 2, Pitcairn Islands #685a, Vanuatu #976a   8.50 8.50
a.   150v Two pandas   4.25 4.25

No. 976 sold for 310v and New Zealand $5, and is identical to Pitcairn Islands No. 685.

Souvenir Sheet

First Contact Between Russia and Vanuatu, 200th Anniv. — A201

No. 977 — Map and: a, 130v, Russian Admiral V. M. Golovnin. b, 350v, Russian ship, "Diana."

2009, July 28   **Perf. 13¼**
977 A201   Sheet of 2, #a-b   8.50   8.50

Charles Darwin (1809-82),
Naturalist — A202

No. 978 — Darwin, birds and: a, Tortoises. b, Iguanas.

2009, Sept. 2   **Perf. 13¼x13½**
978 A202   200v Horiz. pair, #a-b,   7.50   7.50
      + central label

Worldwide Fund for Nature
(WWF) — A203

No. 979 — Beach thick-knee: a, Adult on nest, bird in flight. b, Adult and chick on ground, two birds in flight. c, Two adults at water's edge, bird in flight. d, Adult on beach, bird in flight.

2009, Nov. 25   **Litho.**   **Perf. 13¼**
979   Horiz. strip of 4   8.00   8.00
  a.   A203 50v multi   1.00   1.00
  b.   A203 90v multi   1.60   1.60
  c.   A203 130v multi   2.50   2.50
  d.   A203 150v multi   2.75   2.75

No. 979 was printed in sheets containing two strips.

Souvenir Sheet

New Year 2010 (Year of the Tiger) — A204

2010, Feb. 14   **Perf. 13¼**
980 A204   250v multi   5.00   5.00

Miniature Sheet

Butterflies — A205

No. 981: a, Calopsilia pomona. b, Papilio godeffroyi. c, Hypolimnas octocula. d, Doleschallia bisaltide. e, Acraea andromacha. f, Danaus affinis.

2010, Apr. 14   **Die Cut**
Self-Adhesive
981 A205   100v Sheet of 6, #a-
       f   11.00   11.00

Tourism — A206

Designs: 40v, Dugong off Epi Island. 140v, Snake Dance, Banks Island, horiz. 160v, Iririki Resort, Efate Island, horiz. 190v, Mt. Yasur Volcano, Tanna Island, horiz.

Perf. 13¼x13¾, 13¾x13¼
2010, Apr. 30
982 A206   40v multi   .75   .75
  a.   Perf. 14   .75   .75

Inscribed "International Post" at Left
983 A206   140v multi   2.75   2.75
984 A206   160v multi   3.00   3.00
985 A206   190v multi   3.50   3.50
    Nos. 982-985 (4)   10.00   10.00

Miniature Sheet
Perf. 14
986   Sheet of 4, #982a,
       986a-986c   10.50   10.50
  a.   A206 140v Like #983, without
     "International Post" at left   2.75   2.75
  b.   A206 160v Like #984, without
     "International Post" at left   2.90   2.90
  c.   A206 190v Like #985, without
     "International Post" at left   3.75   3.75
    Expo 2010, Shanghai (#986).

Cats — A207

Color of cat: 10v, White. 100v, Black and white. 160v, Brown and white. 190v, Gray and white.

2010, July 14   **Perf. 14½x14**
987-990 A207   Set of 4   8.50   8.50

Souvenir Sheet

2010 Youth Olympics,
Singapore — A208

2010, Aug. 14   **Perf. 13¼**
991 A208   500v multi   8.50   8.50

"Smile
With Us"
A209

Designs: No. 992, 20v, Man, statues in background. No. 993, 20v, Two women. No. 994, 20v, Three children. No. 995, 20v, Fish. No. 996, 20v, Dugong. No. 997, 100v, Woman. No. 998, 100v, Divers at Underwater Post Office. No. 999, 100v, Island. No. 1000, 100v, Dolphin. No. 1001, 100v, Airplane.

2010, Dec. 15   **Perf. 13½**
992-1001 A209   Set of 10   11.00   11.00
  996a   Horiz. strip of 5, #992-996   1.75   1.75
  1001a   Horiz. strip of 5, #997-1001   9.00   9.00

Turtles
A210

No. 1002: a, Green turtles, "International Post" at left. b, Green turtles, "International Post" at right. c, Hawksbill turtle, "International Post" at left. d, Hawksbill turtles, "International Post" at right.

2011, Jan. 26   **Perf. 13½x13¼**
1002   Horiz. strip of 4 + cen-
      tral label   7.75   7.75
  a.-d.   A210 100v Any single   1.75   1.75

Tanna
Coffee — A211

Designs: No. 1003, 100v, Short black. No. 1004, 100v, Long black. 140v, Latte. 160v, Cappuccino.

2011, Mar. 23   **Perf. 14½x14**
1003-1006 A211   Set of 4   9.75   9.75

Worldwide Fund for Nature
(WWF) — A212

No. 1007 — Massena's lorikeet: a, Bird facing left. b, Bird on branch. c, Two birds on branch. d, Bird on palm frond.

2011, May 25   **Litho.**   **Perf. 14**
1007   Horiz. strip of 4   8.50   8.50
  a.   A212 40v multi   .80   .80
  b.   A212 60v multi   1.25   1.25
  c.   A212 140v multi   2.90   2.90
  d.   A212 160v multi   3.25   3.25
  e.   Sheet of 8, 2 each #1007a-
     1007d   17.50   17.50

Green and
Golden Bell
Frog — A213

Designs: 45v, Frog on branch. 70v, Frog in flower. 140v, Three frogs in flower. 200v, Frog on cut branch.

2011, July 27   **Perf. 14¼**
1008-1011 A213   Set of 4   9.00   9.00
  1011a   Souvenir sheet of 2,
     #1010-1011   7.00   7.00

Beaches
A214

Designs: No. 1012, 100v, Airplane on beach of Eratap Island, birds. No. 1013, 100v, Trees near Champagne Beach, Espiritu Santo Island, turtles. 140v, Woman on beach at

Havannah Harbor, Efate Island, shells. 160v, Beach on Pele Island, fish.

2011, Sept. 28   **Perf. 14x14½**
1012-1015 A214   Set of 4   10.00   10.00

A gritty substance has been applied to the beach portions of the stamp designs.

Flowers — A215

Designs: No. 1016, 100v, Heliconia psittacorum. No. 1017, 100v, Heliconia rostrata. 140v, Strelitzia reginae. 180v, Heliconia caribaea variety.

2011, Dec. 7   **Perf. 14½x14**
1016-1019 A215   Set of 4   10.50   10.50

Dragonflies
A216

Designs: 40v, Yellow-striped flutterer. 90v, Globe skimmer. 140v, Fiery skimmer. 250v, Painted grasshawk.

2012, Feb. 22   **Perf. 14¼**
1020-1023 A216   Set of 4   11.00   11.00
  1023a   Souvenir sheet of 2,
     #1021, 1023   7.00   7.00

Diplomatic Relations Between Vanuatu and People's Republic of Chin, 30th Anniv. — A217

2012, Mar. 26   **Perf. 12**
1024 A217   90v multi   1.75   1.75

Birds — A218

Designs: 10v, Southern shrikebill. 20v, Silvereyes. 40v, Red-bellied fruuit doves. 50v, Pacific imperial pigeon. 70v, Long-tailed trillers. 90v, Vanuatu scrubfowl. 100v, Streaked fantails. 140v, Dark brown honeyeater. 160v, Vanuatu petrels. 400v, Ruddy turnstones. 500v, Purple swamphens. 1000v, Striated mangove heron. 40v and 70v lack blue triangle and airplane.

2012, May 2   **Litho.**   **Perf. 14¼**
1025 A218   10v multi   .25   .25
1026 A218   20v multi   .40   .40
1027 A218   40v multi   .80   .80
1028 A218   50v multi   1.00   1.00
1029 A218   70v multi   1.40   1.40
1030 A218   90v multi   1.75   1.75
1031 A218   100v multi   2.00   2.00
1032 A218   140v multi   3.00   3.00
1033 A218   160v multi   3.25   3.25
1034 A218   400v multi   8.00   8.00
1035 A218   500v multi   10.00   10.00
1036 A218   1000v multi   20.00   20.00
  a.   Souvenir sheet of 12,
     #1025-1036   52.50   52.50
    Nos. 1025-1036 (12)   51.85   51.85

Reign Of Queen Elizabeth II, 60th Anniv. — A219

No. 1037 — Queen Elizabeth II: a, 250v, On horse. b, 300v, Waving.

2012, June 1   **Perf. 13¼x13½**
1037	Horiz. pair + central label	11.00	11.00
a.	A219 250v multi	5.00	5.00
b.	A219 300v multi	6.00	6.00

Kiwanis Charity Race Day A220

Kiwanis emblem and various race horses: 35v, 50v, 150v, 250v.

Perf. 14x14¼
2012, July 12   **Litho.**   **Unwmk.**
1038-1041   A220   Set of 4   10.50   10.50

Nov. 14, 2012 Partial Solar Eclipse A221

People in boats and diagram of position of Sun and Moon at various times during eclipse: 40v, 60v, 160v, 180v.

Perf. 14x14¼
2012, Oct. 31   **Litho.**   **Unwmk.**
1042-1045   A221   Set of 4   9.75   9.75

Vanuatu Red Cross Society, 30th Anniv. A222

Vanuatu Red Cross Society emblem, anniversary emblem and: 60v, Workers removing boxes from small boat. 100v, Hand under water running from faucet.

Perf. 14x14¼
2012, Dec. 5   **Litho.**   **Wmk. 387**
1046-1047   A222   Set of 2   3.50   3.50

Greetings A223

Designs: 80v, Children and flowers. 100v, Snorkeler, fish, coral reef. 140v, Volcano. 160v, Aerial view of islands, butterflies.

Wmk. 387
2012, Dec. 5   **Litho.**   **Perf. 14½**
1048-1051   A223   Set of 4   10.50   10.50

Sam's Animal Welfare Association — A224

Various dogs and people: 40v, 60v, 160v, 200v.

Perf. 14x14¼
2013, Feb. 27   **Litho.**   **Wmk. 387**
1052-1055	A224	Set of 4	10.00	10.00
1055a		Souvenir sheet of 2, #1054-1055	8.00	8.00

Worldwide Fund for Nature (WWF) A225

Various depictions of orange spot filefish.

Wmk. 387
2013, Mar. 28   **Litho.**   **Perf. 14**
1056	Horiz. strip of 4	9.00	9.00
a.	A225 30v multi	.65	.65
b.	A225 70v multi	1.60	1.60
c.	A225 100v multi	2.25	2.25
d.	A2225 200v multi	4.50	4.50

Printed in sheets of 8 containing 2 each #1056a-1056d.

Waterfalls — A226

Designs: 40v, Siri Falls, Gaua. 100v, Big Wota Falls, Northern Maewo. 140v, Saser Twin Falls, Vanua Lava. 160v, Mele Cascades, Efate.

Perf. 14¼x14
2013, June 26   **Litho.**   **Wmk. 387**
1057-1060   A226   Set of 4   9.25   9.25

Birth of Prince George of Cambridge A227

Designs: 40v, Duke of Cambridge holding Prince George. 60v, Duchess of Cambridge holding Prince George. 100v, Duke and Duchess of Cambridge, Prince George. 250v, Prince George.

Perf. 13¾x13¼
2013, Sept. 18   **Litho.**   **Unwmk.**
1061-1064   A227   Set of 4   9.50   9.50

Christmas A228

Santa Claus: 40v, In hammock. 100v, Snorkeling near underwater post office, vert. 160v, In sleigh above island, vert. 250v, Looking at card in Vanuatu post office lobby.

Perf. 13½
2013, Nov. 6   **Litho.**   **Unwmk.**
1065-1068   A228   Set of 4   12.00   12.00

Souvenir Sheet

Underwater Post Office, 10th Anniv. — A229

Unwmk.
2013, Dec. 11   **Litho.**   **Perf. 14**
1069   A229   350v multi   7.50   7.50

Submarine Cable Between Fiji and Vanuatu — A230

No. 1070: a, Workers, ship and cable with floats. b, Divers examining cable. c, Electronic cables plugged into machine.

Litho. With Foil Application
2014, Jan. 15   **Perf. 14½x14**
1070	Horiz. strip of 6 + central label, #1070a-1070c, Fiji #1304a-1304c	14.50	14.50
a.	A230 40v multi	.65	.65
b.	A230 130v multi	2.10	2.10
c.	A230 190v multi	3.25	3.25

No. 1070 sold for 750v in Vanuatu and $13.30 in Fiji. See Fiji No. 1304.

Wan Smolbag International Theater Festival, 25th Anniv. — A231

Art for: 10v, *9 Long 1 Step Wan* music compact disc. 40v, Film *Vanua-tai. . .of Land and Sea.* 120v, Television show *Love Patrol.* 300v, Film *Las Kad.*

2014, May 7   **Litho.**   **Perf. 14x14¼**
1071-1074   A231   Set of 4   10.00   10.00

Cocktail Glasses and Flowers A232

Flower and cocktail glass containing: 70v, Fire. 100v, Underwater post office. 180v, Woman drinking at beach. 250v, Sailboat at sea.

2014, July 23   **Litho.**   **Die Cut**
Self-Adhesive
1075-1078   A232   Set of 4   13.00   13.00

Extreme Sports — A233

Designs: 50v, Kiteboarding. 120v, People riding off-road buggies, vert. 160v, Parasailing, vert. 190v, Jet boating.

2014, Oct. 29   **Litho.**   **Perf. 14½**
1079-1082   A233   Set of 4   10.50   10.50

Nelson Mandela (1918-2013), President of South Africa — A234

Flags of South Africa and Vanuatu, various pictures of Mandela and quotes starting with: 40v, "Action without vision. . ." 120v, "Education is the most powerful weapon. . ." 150v, "Sport has the power to inspire. . ." 200v, "Forgiveness liberates the soul. . ."

2014, Dec. 5   **Litho.**   **Perf. 14x14¼**
1083-1086   A234   Set of 4   10.50   10.50

Items Made in Vanuatu — A235

Designs: 20v, Items made by ACTIV Association. 80v, Venui Vanilla. 150v, Health and beauty products by The Summit. 300v, Jewelry by Vanuatu Bijouterie.

2015, Mar. 11   **Litho.**   **Perf. 14½x14**
1087-1090   A235   Set of 4   10.50   10.50

Restaurants — A236

Designs: No. 1091, 120v, Eratap. No. 1092, 120v, Francesca's. No. 1093, 120v, The Havannah. No. 1094, 120v, L'Houstalet.

2015, Oct. 28   **Litho.**   **Perf. 14x14½**
1091-1094   A236   Set of 4   8.75   8.75

2016 Summer Olympics, Rio de Janeiro A237

Designs: 40v, Table tennis, taekwondo. 90v, Rowing, beach volleyball. 150v, Boxing, rowing. 200v, Rowing, judo.

2016, May 11   **Litho.**   **Perf. 14x14¼**
1095-1098   A237   Set of 4   8.75   8.75

Swimming Holes — A238

Designs: 10v, Matevulu Blue Hole, Santo Island. 100v, Riri Blue Hole, Santo Island. 180v, Nanda Blue Hole, Santo Island. 250v, Blue Lagoon, Efate Island.

2017, July 19   Litho.   Perf. 14
| 1099-1102 | A238 | Set of 4 | 10.50 | 10.50 |

Miniature Sheet

2017 Pacific Mini Games, Port Vila — A239

No. 1103: a, 20v, Boxing. b, 20v, Beach volleyball. c, 30v, Women's netball. d, 30v, 3-on-3 basketball. e, 30v, Tennis. f, 40v, Soccer. g, 40v, Table tennis. h, 60v, Archery. i, 80v, Golf. j, 80v, Weight lifting. k, 90v, Judo. l, 130v, Shot put. m, 150v, Rugby sevens. n, 180v, Karate.

2017, Nov. 25   Litho.   Perf. 14¼x14
| 1103 | A239 | Sheet of 14, #a-n | 18.00 | 18.00 |

New Year 2018 (Year of the Dog) — A240

Designs: 180v, Two dogs. 350v, One dog.

2018, Feb. 1   Litho.   Perf. 13¼
| 1104-1105 | A240 | Set of 2 | 10.00 | 10.00 |
| 1105a | | Souvenir sheet of 2, #1104-1105 | 10.00 | 10.00 |

New Year 2019 (Year of the Pig) — A241

Designs: 180v, Pig and piglets. 350v, Stylized pig and piglets, diff.

2018, Dec. 10   Litho.   Perf. 13¼
| 1106-1107 | A241 | Set of 2 | 9.25 | 9.25 |

SEMI-POSTAL STAMPS

No. 324 Surcharged

Nos. 414-418 Surcharged

Wmk. 373 (No. B1), 384
Perf. 14x13½, 14x14½

1987, May 12   Litho.
B1	A60	20v +10v on 2v	1.00	1.00
B2	CD337	20v +10v	1.00	1.00
B3	CD337	35v +15v	1.75	1.75
B4	CD337	45v +20v	1.90	1.90
B5	CD337	55v +25v	3.75	3.75
B6	CD337	100v +50v	4.00	4.00
		Nos. B1-B6 (6)	13.40	13.40

Old value of #B1 obliterated by 2 horizontal bars. Surcharge indicated by text "Surcharge +10."

VATICAN CITY

ˈva-ti-kən ˈsi-tē

LOCATION — Western Italy, directly outside the western boundary of Rome
GOVT. — Independent state subject to certain political restrictions under a treaty with Italy
AREA — 108.7 acres
POP. — 870 (1999 est.)

100 Centesimi = 1 Lira
100 Cents = 1 Euro (2002)

Catalogue values for unused stamps in this country are for Never Hinged items, beginning with Scott 68 in the regular postage section, Scott C1 in the airpost section, Scott E3 in the special delivery section, and Scott J7 in the postage due section.
Certificates for often forged or never hinged high value items are advised.

Watermarks

Wmk. 235 — Crossed Keys

Wmk. 277 — Winged Wheel

Papal Arms — A1

Pope Pius XI — A2

Unwmk.
1929, Aug. 1   Engr.   Perf. 14
Surface-Colored Paper
1	A1	5c dk brn & pink	.25	.25
2	A1	10c dk grn & lt grn	.25	.35
3	A1	20c violet & lilac	.75	.65
4	A1	25c dk bl & lt bl	.95	.75
5	A1	30c indigo & yellow	1.10	.90
6	A1	50c ind & sal buff	1.60	.90
7	A1	75c brn car & gray	2.25	1.50

Photo.
White Paper
8	A2	80c carmine rose	1.60	.50
9	A2	1.25 l dark blue	2.60	1.10
10	A2	2 l olive brown	5.25	2.25
11	A2	2.50 l red orange	4.50	3.75
12	A2	5 l dk green	5.25	12.00
13	A2	10 l olive blk	11.00	17.00
		Nos. 1-13,E1-E2 (15)	74.85	75.35
		Set, never hinged	265.00	

The stamps of Type A1 have, in this and subsequent issues, the words "POSTE VATICANE" in rows of colorless letters in the background.
For surcharges and overprints see Nos. 14, 35-40, 61-67, J1-J6, Q1-Q13.

No. 5 Surcharged in Red

1931, Oct. 1
| 14 | A1 | 25c on 30c ind & yel | 3.00 | 2.25 |
| | | Never hinged | 10.00 | |

Arms of Pope Pius XI — A5

Vatican Palace and Obelisk — A6

Vatican Gardens — A7

Pope Pius XI A8

St. Peter's Basilica A9

1933, May 31   Engr.   Wmk. 235
19	A5	5c copper red	.25	.25
a.	Imperf., pair		600.00	825.00
20	A6	10c dk brn & blk	.25	.25
21	A6	12½c dp grn & blk	.25	.25
22	A6	20c orange & blk	.25	.25
a.	Vertical pair imperf. between and at bottom		750.00	
23	A6	25c dk olive & blk	.25	.25
a.	Imperf., pair		425.00	600.00
24	A7	30c blk & dk brn	.25	.25
25	A7	50c vio & dk brn	.25	.25
26	A7	75c brn red & dk brn	.25	.25
27	A7	80c rose & dk brn	.25	.25
28	A8	1 l violet & blk	7.50	7.50
29	A8	1.25 l dk bl & blk	22.50	13.50
30	A8	2 l dk brn & blk	52.50	37.50
31	A8	2.75 l dk vio & blk	67.50	90.00
32	A9	5 l blk brn & dk grn	.25	.25
33	A9	10 l dk bl & dk grn	.25	.30
34	A9	20 l blk & dp grn	.40	.50
		Nos. 19-34,E3-E4 (18)	153.85	152.70
		Set, never hinged	620.00	

Nos. 8-13 Surcharged in Black

No. 36   No. 36a

1934, June 16   Unwmk.
35	A2	40c on 80c	40.00	20.00
36	A2	1.30 l on 1.25 l	180.00	125.00
a.	Small figures "30" in "1.30"	24,000.	16,000.
	Never hinged	30,000.	
37	A2	2.05 l on 2 l	240.00	125.00
a.	No comma btwn. 2 & 0	1,000.	800.00
	Never hinged	2,000.	
38	A2	2.55 l on 2.50 l	225.00	250.00
a.	No comma btwn. 2 & 5	800.00	900.00
	Never hinged	1,600.	
39	A2	3.05 l on 5 l	500.00	450.00
40	A2	3.70 l on 10 l	450.00	550.00
a.	No comma btwn. 3 & 7	—	—
		Nos. 35-40 (6)	1,635.	1,520.
		Set, never hinged	3,750.	

A second printing of Nos. 36-40 was made in 1937. The 2.55 l and 3.05 l of the first printing and 1.30 l of the second printing sell for more.
The status of No. 40a has been questioned. The editors would like to examine an authenticated example of this variety.
Forged surcharges of Nos. 35-40 are plentiful.

Tribonian Presenting Pandects to Justinian I A10

Pope Gregory IX Promulgating Decretals A11

1935, Feb. 1   Photo.
41	A10	5c red orange	4.50	4.50
42	A10	10c purple	4.50	4.50
43	A10	25c green	22.50	22.50
44	A11	75c rose red	50.00	42.50
45	A11	80c dark brown	45.00	37.50
46	A11	1.25 l dark blue	50.00	47.50
		Nos. 41-46 (6)	176.50	154.00
		Set, never hinged	1,000.	

Intl. Juridical Congress, Rome, 1934.

Doves and Bell — A12

Allegory of Church and Bible — A13

St. John Bosco — A14

St. Francis de Sales — A15

1936, June 22
47	A12	5c blue green	1.50	1.50
48	A13	10c black	1.50	1.50
49	A14	25c yellow green	37.50	15.00
50	A12	50c rose violet	1.50	1.50
51	A13	75c rose red	47.50	60.00
52	A14	80c orange brn	2.60	3.00
53	A15	1.25 l dark blue	3.00	3.00
54	A15	5 l dark brown	3.00	7.50
		Nos. 47-54 (8)	98.10	93.00
		Set, never hinged	360.00	

World Exposition of the Catholic Press, 1936.

Crypt of St. Cecilia in Catacombs of St. Calixtus A16

Basilica of Sts. Nereus and Achilleus in Catacombs of St. Domitilla A17

1938, Oct. 12   **Perf. 14**

55	A16	5c bister brown	1.00	1.00
56	A16	10c deep orange	1.00	1.00
57	A16	25c deep green	1.00	1.00
58	A17	75c deep rose	10.00	10.00
59	A17	80c violet	20.00	20.00
60	A17	1.25 l blue	25.00	25.00
		Nos. 55-60 (6)	58.00	58.00
		Set, never hinged	200.00	

Intl. Christian Archaeological Congress, Rome, 1938.

Interregnum Issue

Nos. 1-7 Overprinted in Black

1939, Feb. 20   **Perf. 14**

61	A1	5c dk brn & pink	26.00	7.50
62	A1	10c dk grn & lt grn	.75	.25
63	A1	20c violet & lilac	.75	.25
64	A1	25c dk bl & lt bl	3.25	5.00
a.		Pair, one without ovpt.	3,000.	
66	A1	50c indigo & sal buff	1.25	.25
67	A1	75c brn car & gray	1.25	.25
		Nos. 61-67 (7)	34.50	13.75
		Set, never hinged	135.00	

> **Catalogue values for unused stamps in this section, from this point to the end of the section, are for Never Hinged items.**

Coronation of Pope Pius XII — A18

1939, June 2   **Photo.**

68	A18	25c green	3.00	.40
69	A18	75c rose red	.70	.70
70	A18	80c violet	8.50	4.00
71	A18	1.25 l deep blue	.70	.70
		Nos. 68-71 (4)	12.90	5.80

Coronation of Pope Pius XII, Mar. 12, 1939.

Arms of Pope Pius XII — A19

Pope Pius XII
A20   A21

Wmk. 235

1940, Mar. 12   **Engr.**   **Perf. 14**

72	A19	5c dark carmine	.45	.25
a.		Imperf., pair	1,100.	
73	A20	1 l purple & blk	.45	.25
74	A21	1.25 l slate bl & blk	.45	.25
a.		Imperf., pair	1,100.	1,200.
75	A20	2 l dk brn & blk	2.00	2.00
76	A21	2.75 l dk rose vio & blk	2.50	2.50
		Nos. 72-76 (5)	5.85	5.25

See Nos. 91-98. For surcharges see Nos. 102-109.

A22

Picture of Jesus inscribed "I have Compassion on the Multitude."

1942, Sept. 1   **Photo.**   **Unwmk.**

77	A22	25c dk blue green	.25	.25
78	A22	80c chestnut brown	.25	.25
79	A22	1.25 l deep blue	.25	.25
		Nos. 77-79 (3)	.75	.75

See Nos. 84-86, 99-101.

A23

Consecration of Archbishop Pacelli by Pope Benedict XV.

1942, Jan. 16

80	A23	25c myr grn & gray grn	.25	.25
81	A23	80c dk brn & yel grn	.25	.25
82	A23	1.25 l sapphire & vio bl	.25	.25
a.		Name and value panel omitted		
83	A23	5 l vio blk & gray blk	.35	.25
		Nos. 80-83 (4)	1.10	1.00

25th anniv. of the consecration of Msgr. Eugenio Pacelli (later Pope Pius XII) as Archbishop of Sardes.

Type of 1942
Inscribed MCMXLIII

1944, Jan. 31

84	A22	25c dk blue green	.25	.25
85	A22	80c chestnut brown	.25	.25
86	A22	1.25 l deep blue	.25	.25
		Nos. 84-86 (3)	.75	.75

Raphael Sanzio — A24

Designs: 80c, Antonio da Sangallo. 1.25 l, Carlo Maratti. 10 l, Antonio Canova.

1944, Nov. 21   **Wmk. 235**   **Photo.**

87	A24	25c olive & green	.35	.25
88	A24	80c cl & rose vio	.60	.50
a.		Dbl. impression of center	1,800.	
89	A24	1.25 l bl vio & dp bl	.80	.40
a.		Imperf., pair	1,900.	2,100.
90	A24	10 l bister & ol brn	2.00	2.00
		Nos. 87-90 (4)	3.75	3.15

400th anniv. of the Pontifical Academy of the Virtuosi of the Pantheon.

Types of 1940

1945, Mar. 5   **Engr.**   **Unwmk.**

91	A19	5c gray	.25	.25
a.		Imperf., pair	360.00	

92	A19	30c brown	.25	.25
a.		Imperf., pair	475.00	
93	A19	50c dark green	.25	.25
94	A21	1 l brown & blk	.25	.25
95	A21	1.50 l rose car & blk	.25	.25
a.		Imperf., pair	475.00	
96	A21	2.50 l dp ultra & blk	.25	.25
a.		Imperf., pair	475.00	
97	A20	5 l rose vio & blk	.30	.25
98	A20	20 l gray grn & blk	.40	.40
		Nos. 91-98,E5-E6 (10)	3.45	3.65

Nos. 91-96 exist in pairs imperf. between, some vertical, some horizontal. Value, each pair $150.

Type of 1942
Inscribed MCMXLIV
Wmk. 277

1945, Sept. 12   **Photo.**   **Perf. 14**

99	A22	1 l dk blue green	.25	.25
100	A22	3 l dk carmine	.25	.25
a.		Jesus image omitted	225.00	225.00
101	A22	5 l deep ultra	.25	.25
a.		Jesus image omitted	225.00	225.00
		Nos. 99-101 (3)	.75	.75

Nos. 99-101 exist in pairs imperf. between, both horizontal and vertical. Value, each pair $140.

Pairs imperf. horizontally exist of 3 lire (value $150) and 5 lire (value $200).

Nos. 91 to 98 Surcharged with New Values and Bars in Black or Blue

Two types of 25c on 30c:
I — Surcharge 16mm wide.
II — Surcharge 19mm wide.

Two types of 1 l on 50c:
I — Surcharge bars 5mm wide.
II — Bars 4mm wide.

1946, Jan. 9   **Unwmk.**   **Perf. 14**

102	A19	20c on 5c	.25	.25
a.		Inverted surcharge	975.00	975.00
103	A19	25c on 30c (I)	.25	.25
a.		Type II	.40	.25
b.		Inverted surcharge (II)	975.00	975.00
104	A19	1 l on 50c (I)	.25	.25
a.		Type II	11.50	6.00
105	A21	1.50 l on 1 l (Bl)	.25	.25
a.		Double surcharge	450.00	

106	A21	3 l on 1.50 l	.25	.25
107	A21	5 l on 2.50 l	.50	.30
a.		Double surcharge	450.00	
108	A20	10 l on 5 l	1.75	.60
109	A20	30 l on 20 l	4.25	2.00
		Nos. 102-109,E7-E8 (10)	18.75	9.65

Nos. 102, 105-109 exist in horizontal pairs, imperf. between. Value, each pair $150.

Vertical pairs imperf. between exist of Nos. 102, 106-107 (value, each $150) and of No. 104a (value $250).

Nos. 102-108 exist in pairs, one without surcharge. Value, Nos. 102-105, each pair $600.; Nos. 106-108, each pair $900.

St. Vigilio Cathedral, Trent — A28

St. Angela Merici — A29

Designs: 50c, St. Anthony Zaccaria. 75c, St. Ignatius of Loyola. 1 l, St. Cajetan Thiene. 1.50 l, St. John Fisher. 2 l, Christoforo Cardinal Madruzzi. 2.50 l, Reginald Cardinal Pole. 3 l, Marello Cardinal Cervini. 4 l, Giovanni Cardinal del Monte. 5 l, Emperor Charles V. 10 l, Pope Paul III.

Perf. 14, 14x13½
1946, Feb. 21　Photo.　Unwmk.
Centers in Dark Brown

110	A28	5c olive bister	.25	.25
111	A29	25c purple	.25	.25
112	A29	50c brown orange	.25	.25
113	A29	75c black	.25	.25
114	A29	1 l dk violet	.25	.25
115	A29	1.50 l red orange	.25	.25
116	A29	2 l yellow green	.25	.25
117	A29	2.50 l deep blue	.25	.25
118	A29	3 l brt carmine	.25	.25
119	A29	4 l ocher	.25	.25
120	A29	5 l brt ultra	.25	.25
121	A29	10 l dp rose car	.25	.25
a.		Imperf. pair	1,900.	
		Nos. 110-121,E9-E10 (14)	3.50	3.50

Council of Trent (1545-63), 400th anniv.
Vertical pairs imperf. between exist of Nos. 110-114, 116-118 (value, each pair $100); No. 121 (value, each pair $150).
Horizontal pairs imperf. between exist of #121 (value $325); #119 (value $275).

Basilica of St. Agnes — A40

Basilica of the Holy Cross in Jerusalem A41

Pope Pius XII A42

Basilicas: 3 l, St. Clement, 5 l, St. Prassede. 8 l, St. Mary in Cosmedin. 16 l, St. Sebastian. 25 l, St. Lawrence. 35 l, St. Paul. 40 l, St. Mary Major.

Perf. 14, 14x13½
1949, Mar. 7　Photo.　Wmk. 235

122	A40	1 l dark brown	.25	.25
123	A40	3 l violet	.25	.25
124	A40	5 l deep orange	.25	.25
a.		Perf. 14x13½	18.50	7.50
125	A40	8 l dp blue grn	.25	.25

Perf. 14, 13½x14

126	A41	13 l dull green	3.25	3.25
127	A41	16 l dk olive brn	.35	.30
a.		Perf. 14	.50	.30
128	A41	25 l car rose	6.50	.65
129	A41	35 l red violet	30.00	10.00
a.		Perf. 13½x14	47.50	10.00
130	A41	40 l blue	.35	.30
a.		Perf. 13½x14	.40	.30

Engr.
Perf. 14

131	A42	100 l sepia	3.00	3.00
		Nos. 122-131,E11-E12 (12)	109.45	50.50

All values come in two perfs except the 100 l.
Nos. 127, 128 exist imperf horizontally, Nos. 125-126 exist imperf vertically. Value in pairs $200 each pair.
Nos. 130-131 exist imperf.

Jesus Giving St. Peter the Keys to Heaven — A43

Cathedrals of St. Peter, St. Paul, St. John Lateran and St. Mary Major — A44

Pope Boniface VIII Proclaiming Holy Year in 1300 — A45

Pope Pius XII in Ceremony of Opening the Holy Door — A46

Wmk. 277
1949, Dec 21　Photo.　Perf. 14

132	A43	5 l red brn & brn	.25	.25
133	A44	6 l ind & yel brn	.25	.25
134	A45	8 l ultra & dk grn	.85	.55
135	A46	10 l green & slate	.25	.25
136	A43	20 l dk grn & red brn	1.40	.30
137	A44	25 l sepia & dp blue	.75	.25
138	A45	30 l grnsh blk & rose lil	2.50	1.10
139	A46	60 l blk brn & brn rose	1.40	1.10
		Nos. 132-139 (8)	7.65	4.05

Holy Year, 1950.

Palatine Guard and Statue of St. Peter — A47

1950, Sept. 12

140	A47	25 l sepia	7.50	4.50
141	A47	35 l dark green	3.50	3.50
142	A47	55 l red brown	2.00	3.75
		Nos. 140-142 (3)	13.00	11.75

Centenary of the Palatine Guard.

Pope Pius XII Making Proclamation A48

Crowd at St. Peter's Basilica — A49

1951, May 8　Unwmk.

143	A48	25 l chocolate	11.00	1.00
144	A49	55 l bright blue	4.75	12.00

Proclamation of the Roman Catholic dogma of the Assumption of the Virgin Mary, Nov. 1, 1950.

A50

Pope Pius X — A51

Perf. 14x13½
1951, June 3　Photo.　Wmk. 235
Background of Medallion in Gold

145	A50	6 l purple	.25	.25
146	A50	10 l Prus green	.40	.25
147	A51	60 l blue	7.00	5.50
148	A51	115 l brown	22.50	22.50
		Nos. 145-148 (4)	30.15	28.50

Council of Chalcedon A52

Pope Leo I Remonstrating with Attila the Hun — A53

1951, Oct. 31　Engr.　Perf. 14x13½

149	A52	5 l dk gray green	.50	.40
a.		Pair, imperf. horiz.	900.00	
150	A53	25 l red brown	3.50	2.00
a.		Horiz. pair, imperf. btwn.	2,250.	2,250.
151	A52	35 l carmine rose	8.00	4.00
152	A53	60 l deep blue	25.00	11.00
153	A52	100 l dark brown	42.50	37.50
		Nos. 149-153 (5)	79.50	54.90

Council of Chalcedon, 1500th anniv.

No. 126 Surcharged with New Value and Bars in Carmine
1952, Mar. 15　Perf. 14

154	A41	12 l on 13 l dull grn	2.00	1.00
a.		Perf. 13½x14	2.00	1.00
b.		Pair, one without surcharge	750.00	750.00
c.		Surcharge inverted	750.00	
d.		As "a," surcharge double	750.00	

Roman States Stamp and Stagecoach — A54

1952, June 9　Engr.　Perf. 13

155	A54	50 l sep & dp bl, cr	5.00	4.50
a.		Souvenir sheet	160.00	160.00

1st stamp of the Papal States, cent.
#155a contains 4 stamps similar to #155, with papal insignia and inscription in purple. Singles from the souvenir sheet differ slightly from #155. The colors are closer to black and blue, and the cream tone of the paper is visible on the back.

St. Maria Goretti — A55

Perf. 13½x14
1953, Feb. 12　Photo.　Wmk. 235

156	A55	15 l dp brown & vio	4.75	2.50
157	A55	35 l dp rose & brn	3.50	2.50

Martyrdom of St. Maria Goretti, 50th anniv.

St. Peter — A56

Designs: 5 l, Pius XII and Roman sepulcher. 10 l, St. Peter and Tomb of the Apostle. 12 l, Sylvester I and Constantine Basilica. 20 l, Julius II and Bramante's plans. 25 l, Paul III and the Apse. 35 l, Sixtus V and dome. 45 l, Paul V and facade. 60 l, Urban VIII and the canopy. 65 l, Alexander VII and colonnade. 100 l, Pius VI and the sacristy.

Perf. 13½x13, 14
1953, Apr. 23　Engr.

158	A56	3 l dk red brn & blk	.25	.25
159	A56	5 l slate & blk	.25	.25
160	A56	10 l dk green & blk	.25	.25
161	A56	12 l chestnut & blk	.25	.25
162	A56	20 l violet & blk	.25	.25
163	A56	25 l dk brown & blk	.25	.25
164	A56	35 l dk carmine & blk	.25	.25
165	A56	45 l olive brn & blk	.25	.25
166	A56	60 l dk blue & blk	.25	.25
167	A56	65 l car rose & blk	.25	.25
168	A56	100 l rose vio & blk	.25	.25
		Nos. 158-168,E13-E14 (13)	3.35	3.25

Nos. 158, 163 and 165 exist imperf. Value $900 each pair.

St. Clare of Assisi — A57

Unwmk.
1953, Aug. 12　Photo.　Perf. 13

169	A57	25 l aqua, yel brn & vio brn	2.00	1.50
170	A57	35 l brn red, yel brn & vio brn	16.00	11.00

Death of St. Clare of Assisi, 700th anniv.

Virgin Mary and St. Bernard A58

1953, Nov. 10

171	A58	20 l ol grn & dk vio brn	.75	.75
172	A58	60 l brt bl & ol grn	7.50	5.50

Death of St. Bernard of Clairvaux, 800th anniv.

Peter Lombard
Medal — A59

1953, Dec. 29
173 A59 100 l lil rose, bl, dk
    grn & yel   37.50 20.00
  Peter Lombard, Bishop of Paris 1159.

Pope Pius XI and Vatican City — A60

1954, Feb. 12   **Wmk. 235**
174 A60 25 l bl, red brn & cr   1.25 1.00
175 A60 60 l yel brn & dp bl   3.50 3.00
  Signing of the Lateran Pacts, 25th anniv.

Pope
Pius IX
A61

Portraits: (At left) — 6 l, 20 l, Pope Pius IX. (At right) — 4 l, 12 l, 35 l, Pope Pius XII.

1954, May 26   **Engr.**   *Perf. 13*
176 A61   3 l violet   .25 .25
177 A61   4 l carmine   .25 .25
178 A61   6 l plum   .25 .25
179 A61 12 l blue green   1.00 .25
180 A61 20 l red brown   .90 .85
181 A61 35 l ultra   2.00 2.00
    Nos. 176-181 (6)   4.65 3.85
  Marian Year; centenary of the dogma of the Immaculate Conception.

St. Pius X — A62

1954, May 29   **Photo.**
Colors (except background): Yellow and Plum
182 A62 10 l dark brown   .30 .25
183 A62 25 l violet   2.50 1.50
184 A62 35 l dk slate gray   4.50 3.25
    Nos. 182-184 (3)   7.30 5.00
  Canonization of Pope Pius X, May 20, 1954. #182-184 exist imperf. Value, each pair $800.

Basilica of
St. Francis
of Assisi
A63

1954, Oct. 1   **Photo.**   *Perf. 14*
185 A63 20 l dk vio gray & cr   2.00 1.60
186 A63 35 l dk brown & cream   1.50 1.50
  Consecration of the Basilica of St. Francis of Assisi, 200th anniv.

St.
Augustine
A64

1954, Nov. 13
187 A64 35 l blue green   1.10 .90
188 A64 50 l redsh brown   1.75 1.75
  1600th birth anniv. of St. Augustine.

Madonna of the
Gate of Dawn,
Vilnius — A65

1954, Dec. 7
189 A65 20 l pink & multi   1.40 .85
190 A65 35 l blue & multi   9.00 6.50
191 A65 60 l multicolored   13.50 8.50
    Nos. 189-191 (0)   23.90 15.85
  Issued to mark the end of the Marian Year.

St. Boniface
and Fulda
Abbey
A66

1955, Apr. 28   **Engr.**   *Perf. 13*
192 A66 10 l grnsh gray   .25 .25
193 A66 35 l violet   .60 .60
  a.   Imperf., pair   525.00
194 A66 60 l brt blue green   .75 .70
    Nos. 192-194 (3)   1.60 1.55
  1200th death anniv. of St. Boniface. No. 193 also exists imperf horizontally and vertically. Value $275 each pair.

Pope Sixtus II and St.
Lawrence — A67

      Wmk. 235
1955, June 27   **Photo.**   *Perf. 14*
195 A67 50 l carmine   4.25 2.00
196 A67 100 l deep blue   2.75 2.00
  Fra Angelico (1387-1455), painter. Design is from a Fra Angelico fresco. No. 196 exists imperf. Value, pair $400.

Pope
Nicholas V — A68

1955, Nov. 28
197 A68 20 l grnsh bl & ol brn   .30 .25
198 A68 35 l rose car & ol brn   .40 .30
199 A68 60 l yel grn & ol brn   .75 .40
    Nos. 197-199 (3)   1.45 .95
  Death of Pope Nicholas V, 500th anniv.

St. Bartholomew and
Church of
Grottaferrata — A69

1955, Dec. 29
200 A69 10 l brown & gray   .25 .25
201 A69 25 l car rose & gray   .50 .30
202 A69 100 l dk green & gray   2.00 1.50
    Nos. 200-202 (3)   2.75 2.05
  900th death anniv. of St. Bartholomew, abbot of Grottaferrata.

Capt. Gaspar
Roust — A70

6 l, 50 l, Guardsman. 10 l, 60 l, Two drummers.

1956, Apr. 27   **Engr.**   *Perf. 13*
203 A70   4 l dk carmine rose   .25 .25
204 A70   6 l deep orange   .25 .25
205 A70 10 l deep ultra   .25 .25
206 A70 35 l brown   .55 .40
207 A70 50 l violet   .75 .60
208 A70 60 l blue green   .85 .65
    Nos. 203-208 (0)   2.90 2.40
  450th anniv. of the Swiss Papal Guard.

St. Rita of
Cascia — A71

1956, May 19   **Photo.**   *Perf. 14*
209 A71 10 l gray green   .25 .25
210 A71 25 l olive brown   .55 .55
211 A71 35 l ultra   .35 .35
    Nos. 209-211 (3)   1.15 1.15
  500th death anniv. of St. Rita of Cascia.

Pope Paul III
Confirming
Society of
Jesus — A72

1956, July 31   **Engr.**   *Perf. 13*
212 A72 35 l dk red brown   .50 .50
213 A72 60 l blue gray   .95 .95
  400th death anniv. of St. Ignatius of Loyola, founder of the Society of Jesus.

St. John of
Capistrano
A73

1956, Oct. 30   *Perf. 14*
214 A73 25 l slate blk & grn   2.10 1.25
215 A73 35 l dk brn car & brn   .75 .75
  5th cent. of the death of St. John of Capistrano, leader in the war against the Turks.

Black Madonna
of Czestochowa
A74

1956, Dec. 20
216 A74 35 l dk blue & blk   .25 .25
217 A74 60 l green & ultra   .45 .45
218 A74 100 l brn & dk car rose   .90 .80
    Nos. 216-218 (3)   1.60 1.50
  300th anniv. of the proclamation of the Madonna of Czestochowa as "Queen of Poland."

St. Domenico
Savio — A75

6 l, 60 l, Sts. Domenico Savio and John Bosco.

1957, Mar. 21   **Wmk. 235**   *Perf. 13½*
219 A75   4 l red brown   .25 .25
220 A75   6 l brt carmine   .25 .25
221 A75 25 l green   .25 .25
222 A75 60 l ultra   1.20 .95
    Nos. 219-222 (4)   1.95 1.70
  Death cent. of St. Domenico Savio.

Cardinal
Capranica
and College
A76

Design: 10 l, 100 l, Pope Pius XII.

1957, June 27   **Engr.**   *Perf. 13*
223 A76   5 l dk carmine rose   .25 .25
224 A76 10 l pale brown   .25 .25
225 A76 35 l grnsh black   .25 .25
226 A76 100 l ultra   .50 .50
    Nos. 223-226 (4)   1.25 1.25
  500th anniv. of Capranica College, oldest seminary in the world.

Pontifical
Academy of
Science
A77

1957, Oct. 9   **Photo.**   *Perf. 14*
227 A77 35 l dk blue & green   .55 .55
228 A77 60 l brown & ultra   .75 .55
  Pontifical Academy of Science, 20th anniv.

Mariazell
A78

High
Altar — A79

1957, Nov. 14   Engr.   Perf. 13½

229	A78	5 l	green	.25	.25
230	A79	15 l	slate	.25	.25
231	A79	60 l	ultra	.70	.25
232	A79	100 l	violet	.90	.85
		Nos. 229-232 (4)		2.10	1.60

Mariazell shrine, Austria, 800th anniv.

Apparition of the Virgin Mary — A80

Designs: 10 l, 35 l, Sick man and basilica. 15 l, 100 l, St. Bernadette.

Perf. 13x14

1958, Feb. 21   Wmk. 235

233	A80	5 l	dark blue	.25	.25
234	A80	10 l	blue green	.25	.25
235	A80	15 l	reddish brown	.25	.25
236	A80	25 l	rose carmine	.25	.25
237	A80	35 l	gray brown	.25	.25
238	A80	100 l	violet	.25	.25
		Nos. 233-238 (6)		1.50	1.50

Centenary of apparition of the Virgin Mary at Lourdes and the establishment of the shrine.

Pope Pius XII — A81

60 l, 100 l, Vatican pavilion at Brussels fair.

1958, June 19   Engr.   Perf. 13

| 239 | A81 | 35 l | claret | .30 | .25 |

Perf. 13x14

240	A81	60 l	fawn	.55	.55
241	A81	100 l	violet	1.75	1.25
242	A81	300 l	ultra	1.40	1.10
a.		Souvenir sheet of 4, #239-242		20.00	15.00
		Nos. 239-242 (4)		4.00	3.15

Universal and Intl. Exposition, Brussels.

Statue of Pope Clement XIII by Canova — A82

Statues: 10 l, Clement XIV. 35 l, Pius VI. 100 l, Pius VII.

1958, July 2   Perf. 14

243	A82	5 l	brown	.25	.25
244	A82	10 l	carmine rose	.25	.25
245	A82	35 l	blue gray	.25	.25
246	A82	100 l	dark blue	.85	.85
		Nos. 243-246 (4)		1.60	1.60

Antonio Canova (1757-1822), sculptor.

Interregnum Issue

St. Peter's Keys and Papal Chamberlain's Insignia — A83

1958, Oct. 21   Wmk. 235
Photo.   Perf. 14

247	A83	15 l	brn blk, *yel*	1.40	1.00
248	A83	25 l	brown black	.25	.25
249	A83	60 l	brn blk, *pale vio*	.25	.25
		Nos. 247-249 (3)		1.90	1.50

Pope John XXIII — A84

Design: 35 l, 100 l, Coat of Arms.

1959, Apr. 2   Photo.   Perf. 14

250	A84	25 l	car rose, bl & buff	.25	.25
251	A84	35 l	multicolored	.25	.25
252	A84	60 l	rose car, bl & ocher	.25	.25
253	A84	100 l	multicolored	.25	.25
		Nos. 250-253 (4)		1.00	1.00

Coronation of Pope John XXIII, 11/4/58.

Pope Pius XI — A85

1959, May 25   Wmk. 235   Perf. 14

| 254 | A85 | 30 l | brown | .25 | .25 |
| 255 | A85 | 100 l | violet blue | .25 | .25 |

Lateran Pacts, 30th anniversary.

St. Lawrence — A86

Portraits of Saints: 25 l, Pope Sixtus II. 50 l, Agapitus. 60 l, Filicissimus. 100 l, Cyprianus. 300 l, Fructuosus.

1959, May 25

256	A86	15 l	red, brn & yel	.25	.25
257	A86	25 l	lilac, brn & yel	.25	.25
258	A86	50 l	Prus bl, blk & yel	.25	.25
259	A86	60 l	ol grn, brn & bis	.25	.25
260	A86	100 l	maroon, brn & yel	.25	.25
261	A86	300 l	bis brn & dk brn	.50	.35
		Nos. 256-261 (6)		1.75	1.60

Martyrs of Emperor Valerian's persecutions.

Radio Tower and Archangel Gabriel — A87

1959, Oct. 27   Photo.   Perf. 14

| 262 | A87 | 25 l | rose, org yel & dk brn | .25 | .25 |
| 263 | A87 | 60 l | multicolored | .25 | .25 |

2nd anniv. of the papal radio station, St. Maria di Galeria.

St. Casimir, Tower of Gediminas and Cathedral, Vilnius A88

1959, Dec. 14   Engr.   Wmk. 235

| 264 | A88 | 50 l | brown | .25 | .25 |
| 265 | A88 | 100 l | dull green | .25 | .25 |

500th anniv. (in 1958) of the birth of St. Casimir, patron saint of Lithuania.

Nativity by Raphael — A89

1959, Dec. 14   Engr.   Perf. 13½

266	A89	15 l	dark gray	.25	.25
267	A89	25 l	magenta	.25	.25
268	A89	60 l	bright ultra	.25	.25
		Nos. 266-268 (3)		.75	.75

St. Antoninus — A90

25 l, 110 l, St. Antoninus preaching.

Perf. 13x14

1960, Feb. 29   Wmk. 235

269	A90	15 l	ultra	.25	.25
270	A90	25 l	turquoise	.25	.25
271	A90	60 l	brown	.30	.25
272	A90	110 l	rose claret	.60	.35
		Nos. 269-272 (4)		1.40	1.10

5th cent. of death of St. Antoninus, bishop of Florence.

Transept of Lateran Basilica — A91

1960, Feb. 29   Photo.   Perf. 14

| 273 | A91 | 15 l | brown | .25 | .25 |
| 274 | A91 | 60 l | black | .40 | .25 |

Roman Diocesan Synod, February, 1960.

Flight into Egypt by Fra Angelico — A92

Designs: 10 l, 100 l, St. Peter Giving Alms to the Poor, by Masaccio. 25 l, 300 l, Madonna of Mercy, by Piero della Francesca.

1960, Apr. 7   Wmk. 235   Perf. 14

275	A92	5 l	green	.25	.25
276	A92	10 l	gray brown	.25	.25
277	A92	25 l	deep carmine	.25	.25
278	A92	60 l	lilac	.25	.25
279	A92	100 l	ultra	1.40	1.25
280	A92	300 l	Prus green	.80	.50
		Nos. 275-280 (6)		3.20	2.75

World Refugee Year, 7/1/59-6/30/60.

Cardinal Sarto's Departure from Venice — A93

35 l, Pope John XXIII praying at coffin of Pope Pius X. 60 l, Body of Pope Pius X returning to Venice.

1960, Apr. 11   Engr.   Perf. 13½

281	A93	15 l	brown	.25	.25
282	A93	35 l	rose carmine	.75	.60
283	A93	60 l	Prus green	1.75	1.50
		Nos. 281-283 (3)		2.75	2.10

Return of the body of Pope Pius X to Venice.

Feeding the Hungry A94

"Acts of Mercy," by Della Robbia: 10 l, Giving drink to the thirsty. 15 l, Clothing the naked. 20 l, Sheltering the homeless. 30 l, Visiting the sick. 35 l, Visiting prisoners. 40 l, Burying the dead. 70 l, Pope John XXIII.

1960, Nov. 8   Photo.   Perf. 14
Centers in Brown

284	A94	5 l	red brown	.25	.25
285	A94	10 l	green	.25	.25
286	A94	15 l	slate	.25	.25
287	A94	20 l	rose carmine	.25	.25
288	A94	30 l	violet blue	.25	.25
289	A94	35 l	violet brown	.25	.25
290	A94	40 l	red orange	.25	.25
291	A94	70 l	ocher	.25	.25
		Nos. 284-291,E15-E16 (10)		2.50	2.50

Holy Family by Gerard van Honthorst A95

1960, Dec. 6   Wmk. 235   Perf. 14

292	A95	10 l	slate grn & slate blk	.25	.25
293	A95	15 l	sepia & ol blk	.25	.25
294	A95	70 l	grnsh bl & dp bl	.30	.25
		Nos. 292-294 (3)		.80	.75

St. Vincent de Paul — A96

Designs: 70 l, St. Louisa de Marillac. 100 l, St. Louisa and St. Vincent.

1960, Dec. 6

295	A96	40 l	dull violet	.25	.25
296	A96	70 l	dark gray	.30	.25
297	A96	100 l	dk red brown	.70	.30
		Nos. 295-297 (3)		1.25	.80

Death of St. Vincent de Paul, 300th anniv.

St. Meinrad — A97

Designs: 40 l, Statue of Our Lady of Einsiedeln. 100 l, Einsiedeln monastery, horiz.

1961, Feb. 28   *Perf. 14*

298	A97	30 l dark gray	.40	.25
299	A97	40 l lt violet	.75	.40
300	A97	100 l brown	1.50	1.00
	Nos. 298-300 (3)		2.65	1.65

Death of St. Meinrad, 1,100th anniv.; Einsiedeln Abbey, Switzerland.

Pope Leo the Great Defying Attila — A98

Wmk. 235

1961, Apr. 6   Photo.   *Perf. 14*

301	A98	15 l rose brown	.25	.25
302	A98	70 l Prus green	.25	.25
303	A98	300 l brown black	1.75	.55
	Nos. 301-303 (3)		2.25	1.05

Death of Pope Leo the Great (St. Leo Magnus), 1,500th anniv. The design is from a marble bas-relief in St. Peter's Basilica.

St. Paul Arriving in Rome, 61 A.D. — A99

10 l, 30 l, Map showing St. Paul's journey to Rome. 20 l, 200 l, First Basilica of St. Paul, Rome.

1961, June 13   Wmk. 235   *Perf. 14*

304	A99	10 l Prus green	.25	.25
305	A99	15 l dl red brn & gray	.25	.25
306	A99	20 l red org & gray	.25	.25
307	A99	30 l blue	.25	.25
308	A99	75 l org brn & gray	.30	.30
309	A99	200 l blue & gray	1.40	1.00
	Nos. 304-309 (6)		2.70	2.30

Arrival of St. Paul in Rome, 1,900th anniv.

1861 and 1961 Mastheads A100

70 l, Editorial offices. 250 l, Rotary press.

1961, July 4

310	A100	40 l red brn & blk	.25	.25
311	A100	70 l blue & blk	.50	.35
312	A100	250 l yellow & blk	2.00	1.25
	Nos. 310-312 (3)		2.75	1.85

Centenary of L'Osservatore Romano, Vatican's newspaper.

St. Patrick's Purgatory, Lough Derg — A101

10 l, 40 l, St. Patrick, marble sculpture.

Wmk. 235

1961, Oct. 6   Photo.   *Perf. 14*

313	A101	10 l buff & slate grn	.25	.25
314	A101	15 l blue & sepia	.25	.25
315	A101	40 l yellow & bl grn	.25	.25
316	A101	150 l Prus bl & red brn	.45	.30
	Nos. 313-316 (4)		1.20	1.05

Death of St. Patrick, 1,500th anniv.

Arms of Roncalli Family — A102

Designs: 25 l, Church at Sotto il Monte. 30 l, Santa Maria in Monte Santo, Rome. 40 l, Church of San Carlo al Corso, Rome (erroneously inscribed with name of Basilica of Sts. Ambrosius and Charles, Milan). 70 l, Altar, St. Peter's, Rome. 115 l, Pope John XXIII.

1961, Nov. 25

317	A102	10 l gray & red brn	.25	.25
318	A102	25 l ol bis & sl grn	.25	.25
319	A102	30 l vio bl & pale pur	.25	.25
320	A102	40 l lilac & dk blue	.25	.25
321	A102	75 l gray grn & org brn	.30	.25
322	A102	115 l choc & slate	.40	.30
	Nos. 317-322 (6)		1.70	1.55

80th birthday of Pope John XXIII.

"The Adoration" by Lucas Chen — A103

1961, Nov. 25   Center Multicolored

323	A103	15 l bluish green	.25	.25
324	A103	40 l gray	.25	.25
325	A103	70 l pale lilac	.25	.25
	Nos. 323-325 (3)		.75	.75

Christmas.

Draining of Pontine Marshes Medal by Pope Sixtus V, 1588 — A104

40 l, 300 l, Map of Pontine Marshes showing 18th cent. drainage under Pope Pius VI.

1962, Apr. 6   Wmk. 235   *Perf. 14*

326	A104	15 l dark violet	.25	.25
327	A104	40 l rose carmine	.25	.25
328	A104	70 l brown	.25	.25
329	A104	300 l dull green	.40	.30
	Nos. 326-329 (4)		1.15	1.05

WHO drive to eradicate malaria.

"The Good Shepherd" A105

Wheatfield (Luke 10:2) — A106

1962, June 2   Photo.

330	A105	10 l lilac & black	.25	.25
331	A106	15 l blue & ocher	.25	.25
332	A105	70 l lt green & blk	.25	.30
333	A106	115 l fawn & ocher	1.40	1.00
334	A105	200 l brown & black	1.60	1.25
	Nos. 330-334 (5)		3.75	3.05

Issued to honor the priesthood and to stress its importance as a vocation.

"The Good Shepherd" is a fourth-century statue in the Lateran Museum, Rome.

St. Catherine of Siena — A107

1962, June 12

335	A107	15 l brown	.25	.25
336	A107	60 l brt violet	.30	.25
337	A107	100 l blue	.45	.40
	Nos. 335-337 (3)		1.00	.90

Canonization of St. Catherine of Siena, 500th anniv. The portrait is from a fresco by Il Sodoma, Church of St. Dominic, Siena.

Paulina M. Jaricot — A108

1962, July 5   Portrait Multicolored

338	A108	10 l pale violet	.25	.25
339	A108	50 l dull green	.25	.25
340	A108	150 l gray	.45	.40
	Nos. 338-340 (3)		.95	.90

Paulina M. Jaricot (1799-1862), founder of the Society for the Propagation of the Faith.

Sts. Peter and Paul A109

Design: 40 l, 100 l, "The Invincible Cross," relief from sarcophagus.

Wmk. 235

1962, Sept. 25   Photo.   *Perf. 14*

341	A109	20 l lilac & brown	.25	.25
342	A109	40 l lt brown & blk	.25	.25
343	A109	70 l bluish grn & brn	.25	.25
344	A109	100 l sal pink & blk	.25	.25
	Nos. 341-344 (4)		1.00	1.00

6th Congress of Christian Archeology, Ravenna, Sept. 23-28.

"Faith" by Raphael — A110

Designs: 10 l, "Hope." 15 l, "Charity." 25 l, Arms of Pope John XXIII and emblems of the Four Evangelists. 30 l, Ecumenical Congress meeting in St. Peter's. 40 l, Pope John XXIII on throne. 60 l, Statue of St. Peter. 115 l, The Holy Ghost as a dove (symbolic design).

Photo.; Center Engr. on 30 l

1962, Oct. 30

345	A110	5 l brt blue & blk	.25	.25
346	A110	10 l green & blk	.25	.25
347	A110	15 l ver & sepia	.25	.25
348	A110	25 l ver & slate	.25	.25
349	A110	30 l lilac & blk	.25	.25
350	A110	40 l dk carmine & blk	.25	.25
351	A110	60 l dk grn & dp org	.25	.25
352	A110	115 l crimson	.25	.25
	Nos. 345-352 (8)		2.00	2.00

Vatican II, the 21st Ecumenical Council of the Roman Catholic Church, which opened Oct. 11, 1962. Nos. 345-347 show "the Three Theological Virtues" by Raphael.

Nativity Scene A111

Set in India, following a design by Marcus Toano.

1962, Dec. 4   Center Multicolored

353	A111	10 l gray	.25	.25
354	A111	15 l brown	.25	.25
355	A111	90 l dull green	.30	.25
	Nos. 353-355 (3)		.80	.75

Miracle of the Loaves and Fishes by Murillo — A112

Design: 40 l, 200 l, "The Miraculous Catch of Fishes" by Raphael.

Wmk. 235

1963, Mar. 21   Photo.   *Perf. 14*

356	A112	15 l brn & dk brn	.25	.25
357	A112	40 l rose red & blk	.25	.25
358	A112	100 l blue & dk brn	.25	.25
359	A112	200 l bl grn & blk	.25	.25
	Nos. 356-359 (4)		1.00	1.00

FAO "Freedom from Hunger" campaign.

Pope John XXIII — A113

1963, May 8

360	A113	15 l red brown	.25	.25
361	A113	160 l black	.40	.25

Awarding of the Balzan Peace Prize to Pope John XXIII.

Interregnum Issue

Keys of St. Peter and Papal Chamberlain's Insignia — A114

1963, June 15   Wmk. 235   *Perf. 14*

362	A114	10 l dk brown	.25	.25
363	A114	40 l dk brown, *yel*	.25	.25
364	A114	100 l dk brown, *vio*	.25	.25
	Nos. 362-364 (3)		.75	.75

Pope Paul VI — A115

Design: 40 l, 200 l, Arms of Pope Paul VI.

1963, Oct. 16 Engr. Perf. 13x14
365 A115 15 l black .25 .25
366 A115 40 l carmine .25 .25
367 A115 115 l redsh brown .25 .25
368 A115 200 l slate blue .40 .40
Nos. 365-368 (4) 1.15 1.00
Coronation of Pope Paul VI, June 30, 1963.

St. Cyril — A116

Designs: 70 l, Map of Hungary, Moravia and Poland, 16th century. 150 l, St. Methodius.

Wmk. 235
1963, Nov. 22 Photo. Perf. 14
369 A116 30 l violet black .25 .25
370 A116 70 l brown .30 .25
371 A116 150 l rose claret .40 .25
Nos. 369-371 (3) .95 .75
1100th anniv. of the beginning of missionary work among the Slavs by Sts. Cyril and Methodius. The pictures of the saints are from 16th century frescoes in St. Clement's Basilica, Rome.

African Nativity Scene — A117

1963, Nov. 22
372 A117 10 l brn & pale brn .25 .25
373 A117 40 l ultra & brown .25 .25
374 A117 100 l gray olive & brn .25 .25
Nos. 372-374 (3) .75 .75
The design is after a sculpture by the Burundi artist Andreas Bukuru.

Church of the Holy Sepulcher, Jerusalem A118

15 l, Pope Paul VI. 25 l, Nativity Church, Bethlehem. 160 l, Well of the Virgin Mary, Nazareth.

1964, Jan. 4 Wmk. 235 Perf. 14
375 A118 15 l black .25 .25
376 A118 25 l rose brown .25 .25
377 A118 70 l brown .25 .25
378 A118 160 l ultra .25 .25
Nos. 375-378 (4) 1.00 1.00
Visit of Pope Paul VI to the Holy Land, Jan. 4-6.

St. Peter from Coptic Church at Wadi-es-Sebua, Sudan — A119

Design: 20 l, 200 l, Trajan's Kiosk, Philae.

1964, Mar. 10 Photo.
379 A119 10 l ultra & red brn .25 .25
380 A119 20 l multicolored .25 .25
381 A119 70 l gray & red brn .25 .25
382 A119 200 l gray & multi .25 .25
Nos. 379-382 (4) 1.00 1.00
UNESCO world campaign to save historic monuments in Nubia.

Pietà by Michelangelo A120

Designs: 15 l, 100 l, Pope Paul VI. 250 l, Head of Mary from Pietà.

1964, Apr. 22 Wmk. 235 Perf. 14
383 A120 15 l violet blue .25 .25
384 A120 50 l dark brown .25 .25
385 A120 100 l slate blue .25 .25
386 A120 250 l chestnut .25 .25
Nos. 383-386 (4) 1.00 1.00
New York World's Fair, 1964-65.

Isaiah by Michelangelo A121

10 l, Michelangelo, after Jacopino del Conte. 25 l, Isaiah. 30 l, Delphie Sibyl. 40 l, Jeremiah. 150 l, Joel.

1964, June 16 Engr. Perf. 13½x14
387 A121 10 l multicolored .25 .25
388 A121 25 l multicolored .25 .25
389 A121 30 l multicolored .25 .25
390 A121 40 l multicolored .25 .25
391 A121 150 l multicolored .25 .25
Nos. 387-391 (5) 1.25 1.25
Michelangelo Buonarroti (1475-1564). Designs are from the Sistine Chapel.

The Good Samaritan A122

Perf. 14x13½
1964, Sept. 22 Engr. Wmk. 235
392 A122 10 l red brown & red .25 .25
393 A122 30 l dark blue & red .25 .25
394 A122 300 l gray & red .25 .25
Nos. 392-394 (3) .75 .75
Cent. (in 1963) of the founding of the Intl. Red Cross.

Birthplace of Cardinal Nicolaus Cusanus A123

Design: 200 l, Cardinal's sepulcher, Church of San Pietro in Vincoli, Rome.

1964, Nov. 16 Wmk. 235
395 A123 40 l dull blue grn .25 .25
396 A123 200 l rose red .30 .25
German cardinal Nicolaus Cusanus (Nicolaus Krebs of Kues) (1401-1464).

Japanese Nativity Scene by Kimiko Koseki — A124

1964, Nov. 16 Photo. Perf. 14
397 A124 10 l multicolored .25 .25
a. Yellow omitted
398 A124 15 l black & multi .25 .25
399 A124 135 l bister & multi .25 .25
Nos. 397-399 (3) .75 .75

Pope Paul VI and Map of India and Southeast Asia — A125

Designs: 15 l, Pope Paul VI at prayer. 25 l, Eucharistic Congress altar, Bombay, horiz. 60 l, Gateway of India, Bombay, horiz.

1964, Dec. 2
400 A125 15 l dull violet .25 .25
401 A125 25 l green .25 .25
402 A125 60 l brown .25 .25
403 A125 200 l dull violet .25 .25
Nos. 400-403 (4) 1.00 1.00
Trip of Pope Paul VI to India, Dec. 2-5, 1964.

Uganda Martyrs — A126

Various groups of Martyrs of Uganda.

Perf. 13½x14
1965, Mar. 16 Engr. Wmk. 235
404 A126 15 l Prus green .25 .25
405 A126 20 l brown .25 .25
406 A126 30 l ultra .25 .25
407 A126 75 l black .25 .25
408 A126 100 l rose red .25 .25
409 A126 160 l violet .25 .25
Nos. 404-409 (6) 1.50 1.50
Canonization of 22 African martyrs, 10/18/64.

Dante by Raphael — A127

Designs: 40 l, Dante and the 3 beasts at entrance to the Inferno. 70 l, Dante and Virgil at entrance to Purgatory. 200 l, Dante and Beatrice in Paradise. (40 l, 70 l, 200 l, by Botticelli.)

Photogravure and Engraved
1965, May 18 Perf. 13½x14
410 A127 10 l bis brn & dk brn .25 .25
411 A127 40 l rose & dk brn .25 .25
412 A127 70 l lt grn & dk brn .25 .25
413 A127 200 l pale bl & dk brn .25 .25
Nos. 410-413 (4) 1.00 1.00
Birth of Dante Alighieri, 700th anniv.

St. Benedict by Perugino — A128

Design: 300 l, View of Monte Cassino.

1965, July 2 Photo. Perf. 14
414 A128 40 l brown .25 .25
415 A128 300 l dark green .30 .25
Conferring of the title Patron Saint of Europe upon St. Benedict by Pope Paul VI; restoring of the Abbey of Monte Cassino.

Pope Paul VI Addressing UN Assembly — A129

30 l, 150 l, UN Headquarters and olive branch.

1965, Oct. 4 Wmk. 235 Perf. 14
416 A129 20 l brown .25 .25
417 A129 30 l sapphire .25 .25
418 A129 150 l olive green .25 .25
419 A129 300 l rose violet .25 .25
Nos. 416-419 (4) 1.00 1.00
Visit of Pope Paul VI to the UN, NYC, Oct. 4.

Peruvian Nativity Scene — A130

1965, Nov. 25 Engr. Perf. 13½x14
420 A130 20 l rose claret .25 .25
421 A130 40 l red brown .25 .25
422 A130 200 l gray green .25 .25
Nos. 420-422 (3) .75 .75

Cartographer A131

Designs: 5 l, Pope Paul VI. 10 l, Organist. 20 l, Painter. 30 l, Sculptor. 40 l, Bricklayer. 55 l, Carpenter. 75 l, Plowing farmer. 90 l, Blacksmith. 130 l, Scholar.

1966, Mar. 8 Photo. Perf. 14
423 A131 5 l sepia .25 .25
424 A131 10 l violet .25 .25
425 A131 15 l brown .25 .25
426 A131 20 l gray green .25 .25
427 A131 30 l brown red .25 .25
428 A131 40 l Prus green .25 .25
429 A131 55 l dark blue .25 .25
430 A131 75 l dk rose brown .25 .25
431 A131 90 l carmine rose .25 .25
432 A131 130 l black .25 .25
Nos. 423-432,E17-E18 (12) 3.00 3.00
The Pope's portrait is from a bas-relief by Enrico Manfrini; the arts and crafts designs

are bas-reliefs by Mario Rudelli from the chair in the Pope's private chapel.

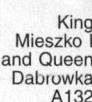

King Mieszko I and Queen Dabrowka A132

Designs: 25 l, St. Adalbert (Wojciech) and Cathedrals of Wroclaw and Gniezno. 40 l, St. Stanislas, Skalka Church, Wawel Cathedral and Castle, Cracow. 50 l, Queen Jadwiga (Hedwig), Holy Gate with Our Lady of Mercy, Vilnius, and Jagellon University Library, Cracow. 150 l, Black Madonna of Czestochowa, cloister and church of Bright Mountain, Czestochowa, and St. John's Cathedral, Warsaw. 220 l, Pope Paul VI blessing students and farmers.

Perf. 14x13½
1966, May 3		**Engr.**	**Wmk. 235**	
433	A132	15 l	black	.25 .25
434	A132	25 l	violet	.25 .25
435	A132	40 l	brick red	.25 .25
436	A132	50 l	claret	.25 .25
437	A132	150 l	slate blue	.25 .25
438	A132	220 l	brown	.25 .25
	Nos. 433-438 (6)			1.50 1.50

Millenium of Christianization of Poland.

Pope John XXIII Opening Vatican II Council — A133

Designs: 15 l, Ancient Bible on ornate display stand. 55 l, Bishops celebrating Mass. 90 l, Pope Paul VI greeting Patriarch Athenagoras I. 100 l, Gold ring given to participating bishops. 130 l, Pope Paul VI carried in front of St. Peter's.

1966, Oct. 11		**Photo.**	**Perf. 14**	
439	A133	10 l	red & black	.25 .25
440	A133	15 l	brown & green	.25 .25
441	A133	55 l	blk & brt rose	.25 .25
442	A133	90 l	slate grn & blk	.25 .25
443	A133	100 l	green & ocher	.25 .25
444	A133	130 l	orange brn & brn	.25 .25
	Nos. 439-444 (6)			1.50 1.50

Conclusion of Vatican II, the 21st Ecumenical Council of the Roman Catholic Church, Dec. 8, 1965.

Nativity, Sculpture by Scorzelli — A134

1966, Nov. 24		**Wmk. 235**	**Perf. 14**	
445	A134	20 l	plum	.25 .25
446	A134	55 l	slate green	.25 .25
447	A134	225 l	yellow brown	.25 .25
	Nos. 445-447 (3)			.75 .75

St. Peter, Fresco, Catacombs, Rome — A135

Designs: 20 l, St. Paul, fresco from Catacombs, Rome. 55 l, Sts. Peter and Paul, glass painting, Vatican Library. 90 l, Baldachin by

Bernini, St. Peter's, Rome. 220 l, Interior of St. Paul's, Rome.

Perf. 13½x14
1907, June 15		**Photo.**	**Unwmk.**	
448	A135	15 l	multi	.25 .25
449	A135	20 l	multi	.25 .25
450	A135	55 l	multi	.25 .25
451	A135	90 l	multi	.25 .25
452	A135	220 l	multi	.25 .25
	Nos. 448-452 (5)			1.25 1.25

Martyrdom of the Apostles Peter and Paul, 1,900th anniv.

Cross, People and Globe — A136

1967, Oct. 13		**Wmk. 235**	**Perf. 14**	
453	A136	40 l	carmine rose	.25 .25
454	A136	130 l	brt blue	.25 .25

3rd Congress of Catholic Laymen, Rome, Oct. 11-18.

Sculpture of Shepherd Children of Fatima — A137

Designs: 50 l, Basilica at Fatima. 200 l, Pope Paul VI praying before statue of Virgin of Fatima.

1967, Oct. 13			**Perf. 13½x14**	
455	A137	30 l	multi	.25 .25
456	A137	50 l	multi	.25 .25
457	A137	200 l	multi	.25 .25
	Nos. 455-457 (3)			.75 .75

Apparition of the Virgin Mary to 3 shepherd children at Fatima, 50th anniv.

Christmas Issue

Nativity, 9th Century Painting on Wood — A138

1967, Nov. 28		**Photo.**	**Unwmk.**	
458	A138	25 l	purple & multi	.25 .25
459	A138	55 l	gray & multi	.25 .25
460	A138	180 l	green & multi	.25 .25
	Nos. 458-460 (3)			.75 .75

Pope Paul VI — A139

Designs: 55 l, Monstrance from fresco by Raphael. 220 l, Map of South America.

1968, Aug. 22		**Wmk. 235**	**Perf. 14**	
461	A139	25 l	blk & dk red brn	.25 .25
402	A139	55 l	blk, gray & ocher	.25 .25
463	A139	220 l	blk, lt bl & sep	.25 .25
	Nos. 461-463 (3)			.75 .75

Visit of Pope Paul VI to the 39th Eucharistic Congress in Bogotá, Colombia, Aug. 22-25.

Holy Infant of Prague — A140

Engraved and Photogravure
1968, Nov. 28			**Perf. 13½x14**	
464	A140	20 l	plum & pink	.25 .25
465	A140	50 l	vio & pale vio	.25 .25
466	A140	250 l	dk bl & lt bluish gray	.25 .25
	Nos. 464-466 (3)			.75 .75

The Resurrection, by Fra Angelico de Fiesole — A141

Easter Issue
Perf. 13½x14
1969, Mar. 6		**Engr.**	**Wmk. 235**	
467	A141	20 l	dk carmine & buff	.25 .25
468	A141	90 l	green & buff	.25 .25
469	A141	180 l	ultra & buff	.25 .25
	Nos. 467-469 (3)			.75 .75

Common Design Types pictured following the introduction.

Europa Issue
Common Design Type
Perf. 13½x14
1969, Apr. 28		**Photo.**	**Wmk. 235**	
	Size: 36½x27mm			
470	CD12	50 l	gray & lt brn	.25 .25
471	CD12	90 l	vermilion & lt brn	.25 .25
472	CD12	130 l	olive & lt brn	.25 .25
	Nos. 470-472 (3)			.75 .75

Pope Paul VI with African Children — A142

Designs: 55 l, Pope Paul VI and African bishops. 250 l, Map of Africa with Kampala, olive branch and compass rose.

Perf. 13½x14
1969, July 31		**Photo.**	**Wmk. 235**	
473	A142	25 l	bister & brown	.25 .25
474	A142	55 l	dk red & brown	.25 .25
475	A142	250 l	multicolored	.25 .25
	Nos. 473-475 (3)			.75 .75

Visit of Pope Paul VI to Uganda, 7/31-8/2.

Pope Piuo IX — A143

Designs: 50 l, Chrismon, emblem of St. Peter's Circle. 220 l, Pope Paul VI.

Perf. 13½x14
1969, Nov. 18		**Engr.**	**Wmk. 235**	
476	A143	30 l	red brown	.25 .25
477	A143	50 l	dark gray	.25 .25
478	A143	220 l	deep plum	.25 .25
	Nos. 476-478 (3)			.75 .75

Centenary of St. Peter's Circle, a lay society dedicated to prayer, action and sacrifice.

Mt. Fuji and EXPO '70 Emblem — A144

EXPO '70 Emblem and: 25 l, EXPO '70 emblem. 40 l, Osaka Castle. 55 l, Japanese Virgin and Child, by Domoto in Osaka Cathedral. 90 l, Christian Pavilion.

1970, Mar. 16		**Photo.**	**Unwmk.**	
479	A144	25 l	gold, red & blk	.25 .25
480	A144	40 l	red & multi	.25 .25
481	A144	55 l	brown & multi	.25 .25
402	A144	90 l	gold & multi	.25 .25
483	A144	110 l	blue & multi	.25 .25
	Nos. 479-483 (5)			1.25 1.25

EXPO '70 Intl. Exhibition, Osaka, Japan, Mar. 15-Sept. 13.

Centenary Medal, Jesus Giving St. Peter the Keys — A145

Designs: 50 l, Coat of arms of Pope Pius IX. 180 l, Vatican I Council meeting in St. Peter's, obverse of centenary medal.

Engr. & Photo.; Photo. (50 l)
1970, Apr. 29			**Perf. 13x14**	
484	A145	20 l	orange & brown	.25 .25
485	A145	50 l	multicolored	.25 .25
486	A145	180 l	ver & brn	.30 .25
	Nos. 484-486 (3)			.80 .75

Centenary of the Vatican I Council.

Christ, by Simone Martini A146

25 l, Christ with Crown of Thorns, by Rogier van der Weyden. 50 l, Christ, by Albrecht Dürer. 90 l, Christ, by El Greco. 180 l, Pope Paul VI.

1970, May 29		**Photo.**	**Perf. 14x13**	
487	A146	15 l	gold & multi	.25 .25
488	A146	25 l	gold & multi	.25 .25
489	A146	50 l	gold & multi	.25 .25
490	A146	90 l	gold & multi	.25 .25
491	A146	180 l	gold & multi	.25 .25
	Nos. 487-491 (5)			1.25 1.25

Ordination of Pope Paul VI, 50th anniv.

Adam, by Michelangelo; UN Emblem — A147

UN Emblem and: 90 l, Eve, by Michelangelo. 220 l, Olive branch.

1970, Oct. 8　Photo.　Perf. 13x14

492	A147	20 l multi	.25	.25
493	A147	90 l multi	.25	.25
494	A147	220 l multi	.25	.25
		Nos. 492-494 (3)	.75	.75

25th anniversary of the United Nations.

Pope Paul VI — A148

Designs: 55 l, Holy Child of Cebu, Philippines. 100 l, Madonna and Child, by Georg Hamori, Darwin Cathedral, Australia. 130 l, Cathedral of Manila. 220 l, Cathedral of Sydney.

1970, Nov. 26　Photo.　Unwmk.

495	A148	25 l multi	.25	.25
496	A148	55 l multi	.25	.25
497	A148	100 l multi	.25	.25
498	A148	130 l multi	.25	.25
499	A148	220 l multi	.25	.25
		Nos. 495-499 (5)	1.25	1.25

Visit of Pope Paul VI to the Far East, Oceania and Australia, Nov. 26-Dec. 5.

Angel Holding Lectern — A149

Sculptures by Corrado Ruffini: 40 l, 130 l, Crucified Christ surrounded by doves. 50 l, like 20 l.

1971, Feb. 2　　　Perf. 13x14

500	A149	20 l multicolored	.25	.25
501	A149	40 l dp orange & multi	.25	.25
502	A149	50 l purple & multi	.25	.25
503	A149	130 l multicolored	.25	.25
		Nos. 500-503 (4)	1.00	1.00

Intl. year against racial discrimination.

Madonna and Child by Francesco Ghissi — A150

Paintings: Madonna and Child, 40 l, by Sassetta (Stefano di Giovanni); 55 l, Carlo Crivelli; 90 l, by Carlo Maratta. 180 l, Holy Family, by Ghisberto Ceracchini.

1971, Mar. 26　Photo.　Perf. 14

504	A150	25 l gray & multi	.25	.25
505	A150	40 l gray & multi	.25	.25
506	A150	55 l gray & multi	.25	.25
507	A150	90 l gray & multi	.25	.25
508	A150	180 l gray & multi	.25	.25
		Nos. 504-508 (5)	1.25	1.25

St. Dominic, Sienese School — A151

Portraits of St. Dominic: 55 l, by Fra Angelico. 90 l, by Titian. 180 l, by El Greco.

1971, May 25　Unwmk.　Perf. 13x14

509	A151	25 l multi	.25	.25
510	A151	55 l multi	.25	.25
511	A151	90 l multi	.25	.25
512	A151	180 l multi	.25	.25
		Nos. 509-512 (4)	1.00	1.00

St. Dominic de Guzman (1170-1221), founder of the Dominican Order.

St. Stephen, from Chasuble, 1031 — A152

180 l, Madonna as Patroness of Hungary, 1511.

1971, Nov. 25

513	A152	50 l multi	.25	.25
514	A152	180 l black & yellow	.30	.25

Millenium of the birth of St. Stephen (975?-1038), king of Hungary.

Bramante A153

Designs: 25 l, Bramante's design for dome of St. Peter's. 130 l, Design for spiral staircase.

1972, Feb. 22　Engr.　Perf. 13½x14

515	A153	25 l dull yellow & blk	.25	.25
516	A153	90 l dull yellow & blk	.25	.25
517	A153	130 l dull yellow & blk	.25	.25
		Nos. 515-517 (3)	.75	.75

Bramante (real name Donato d'Agnolo; 1444-1514), architect.

St. Mark in Storm, 12th Century Mosaic — A154

Map of Venice, 1581 — A155

Design: 180 l, St. Mark's Basilica, Painting by Emilio Vangelli.

Unwmk.

1972, June 6　Photo.　Perf. 14

518	A154	25 l lt brown & multi	.25	.25
519	A155	Block of 4	1.00	.60
a.-d.		50 l, UL, UR, LL, LR, each	.25	.25
520	A154	180 l lt blue & multi	1.10	.65
a.		Souvenir sheet, #518-520	2.50	2.50
		Nos. 518-520 (3)	2.35	1.50

UNESCO campaign to save Venice.

Gospel of St. Matthew, 13th Century, French A156

Illuminated Initials from: 50 l, St. Luke's Gospel, Biblia dell'Aracoeli 13th century, French. 90 l, Second Epistle of St. John, 14th century, Bologna. 100 l, Apocalypse of St. John, 14th century, Bologna. 130 l, Book of Romans, 14th century, Central Italy.

1972, Oct. 11　　Perf. 14x13½

521	A156	30 l multi	.25	.25
522	A156	50 l multi	.25	.25
523	A156	90 l multi	.25	.25
524	A156	100 l multi	.25	.25
525	A156	130 l multi	.35	.25
		Nos. 521-525 (5)	1.35	1.25

Intl. Book Year. Illustrations are from illuminated medieval manuscripts.

Luigi Orione A157

Design: 180 l, Lorenzo Perosi and music from "Hallelujah."

1972, Nov. 28　Photo.　Perf. 14x13½

526	A157	50 l rose, lilac & blk	.25	.25
527	A157	180 l orange, grn & blk	.30	.25

Secular priests Luigi Orione (1872-1940), founder of CARITAS, Catholic welfare organization; and Lorenzo Perosi (1872-1956), composer.

Cardinal Bessarion A158

40 l, Reading Bull of Union between the Greek and Latin Churches, 1439, from bronze door of St. Peter's. 130 l, Coat of arms from tomb, Basilica of Holy Apostles, Rome.

Perf. 13x14

1972, Nov. 28　Wmk. 235　Engr.

528	A158	40 l dull green	.25	.25
529	A158	90 l carmine	.25	.25
530	A158	130 l black	.25	.25
		Nos. 528-530 (3)	.75	.75

Johannes Cardinal Bessarion (1403?-1472), Latin Patriarch of Constantinople, who worked for union of the Greek and Latin Churches. Portrait by Cosimo Rosselli in Sistine Chapel.

Eucharistic Congress Emblem — A159

Designs: 75 l, Head of Mary (Pietá), by Michelangelo. 300 l, Melbourne Cathedral.

1973, Feb. 27　Photo.　Unwmk.

531	A159	25 l violet & multi	.25	.25
532	A159	75 l olive & multi	.25	.25
533	A159	300 l multicolored	.50	.40
		Nos. 531-533 (3)	1.00	.90

40th Intl. Eucharistic Congress, Melbourne, Australia, Feb. 18-25.

St. Teresa — A160

Designs: 25 l, St. Teresa's birthplace, Alençon. 220 l, Lisieux Basilica.

1973, May 23　Engr. & Photo.

534	A160	25 l black & pink	.25	.25
535	A160	55 l black & yellow	.25	.25
536	A160	220 l black & lt blue	.25	.25
		Nos. 534-536 (3)	.75	.75

St. Teresa of Lisieux and of the Infant Jesus (1873-1897), Carmelite nun.

Copernicus A161

Designs: 20 l, 100 l, View of Torun.

1973, June 19　Engr.　Perf. 14

537	A161	20 l dull green	.25	.25
538	A161	50 l brown	.25	.25
539	A161	100 l lilac	.25	.25
540	A161	130 l dark blue	.30	.25
		Nos. 537-540 (4)	1.05	1.00

Nicolaus Copernicus (1473-1543), Polish astronomer.

St. Wenceslas A162

90 l, Arms of Prague Diocese. 150 l, Spire of Prague Cathedral. 220 l, St. Adalbert.

1973, Sept. 25　Photo.　Perf. 14

541	A162	20 l shown	.25	.25
542	A162	90 l multicolored	.25	.25
543	A162	150 l multicolored	.25	.25
544	A162	220 l multicolored	.35	.25
		Nos. 541-544 (4)	1.10	1.00

Millenium of Prague Latin Episcopal See.

St. Nerses Shnorali — A163

25 l, Church of St. Hripsime. 90 l, Armenian khatchkar, a stele with cross and inscription.

Engr. & Litho.

1973, Nov. 27　　Perf. 13x14

545	A163	25 l tan & dk brown	.25	.25
546	A163	90 l lt violet & blk	.25	.25
547	A163	180 l lt green & sepia	.35	.25
		Nos. 545-547 (3)	.85	.75

Armenian Patriarch St. Nerses Shnorali (1102-1173).

Noah's Ark, Rainbow and Dove
(Mosaic) — A164

Design: 90 l, Lamb drinking from stream,
and Tablets of the Law (mosaic).

1974, Apr. 23   Litho.   Perf. 13x14
548 A164 50 l gold & multi   .25 .25
549 A164 90 l gold & multi   .30 .25
Centenary of the Universal Postal Union.

"And There was
Light" — A165

Designs: 25 l, Noah's Ark, horiz. 50 l, The
Annunciation. 90 l, Nativity (African). 180 l,
Hands holding grain (Spanish inscription: The
Lord feeds his people), horiz. Designs chosen
through worldwide youth competition in con-
nection with 1972 Intl. Book Year.

Perf. 13x14, 14x13
1974, Apr. 23   Photo.
550 A165 15 l brown & multi   .25 .25
551 A165 25 l yellow & multi   .25 .25
552 A165 50 l blue & multi   .25 .25
553 A165 90 l green & multi   .25 .25
554 A165 180 l rose & multi   .25 .25
     Nos. 550-554 (5)   1.25 1.25
"The Bible: the Book of Books."

St. Thomas
Aquinas
Teaching — A166

Designs: 50 l, Students (left panel). 220 l,
Students (right panel). Designs from a painting
in the Convent of St. Mark in Florence, by an
artist from the School of Fra Angelico.

**Sizes: 50 l, 220 l, 20x36mm, 90 l,
26x36mm**

Engr. & Litho.
1974, June 18   Unwmk.   Perf. 13x14
555 A166 50 l dk brown & gold   .25 .25
556 A166 90 l dk brown & gold   .25 .25
557 A166 220 l dk brown & gold   .40 .25
  a. Strip of 3, #555-557   .90 .75
St. Thomas Aquinas (1225-1274), scholastic philosopher.

St. Bonaventure
A167

Woodcuts: 40 l, Civita Bagnoregio. 90 l, Tree
of Life (13th century).

1974, Sept. 26   Photo.   Perf. 13x14
558 A167 40 l gold & multi   .25 .25
559 A167 90 l gold & multi   .25 .25
560 A167 220 l gold & multi   .30 .25
     Nos. 558-560 (3)   .80 .75
St. Bonaventure (Giovanni di Fidanza; 1221-
1274), scholastic philosopher.

Christ, St. Peter's
Basilica — A168

Pope Paul VI
Giving his
Blessing — A169

Holy Year 1975: 10 l, Christus Victor, Sts.
Peter and Paul. 30 l, Christ. 40 l, Cross sur-
mounted by dove. 50 l, Christ enthroned. 55 l,
St. Peter. 90 l, St. Paul. 100 l, St. Peter. 130 l,
St. Paul. 220 l, Arms of Pope Paul VI. Designs
of 10 l, 25 l, are from St. Peter's; 30 l, 40 l,
from St. John Lateran; 50 l, 55 l, 90 l, from St.
Mary Major; 100 l, 130 l, from Ol. Paul outside
the Walls.

1974, Dec. 19   Photo.   Perf. 13x14
561 A168 10 l multi   .25 .25
562 A168 25 l multi   .25 .25
563 A168 30 l multi   .25 .25
564 A168 40 l multi   .25 .25
565 A168 50 l multi   .25 .25
566 A168 55 l multi   .25 .25
567 A168 90 l multi   .25 .25
568 A168 100 l multi   .25 .25
569 A168 130 l multi   .25 .25
570 A169 220 l multi   .25 .25
571 A169 250 l multi   .30 .25
     Nos. 561-571 (11)   2.80 2.75

Pentecost, by El
Greco — A170

1975, May 22   Engr.   Perf. 13x14
572 A170 300 l car rose & org   .60 .40

Fountain, St. Peter's Square — A171

Fountains of Rome: 40 l, Piazza St. Martha,
Apse of St. Peter's. 50 l, Borgia Tower and St.
Peter's. 90 l, Belvedere Courtyard. 100 l,
Academy of Sciences. 200 l, Galleon.

Litho. & Engr.
1975, May 22   Perf. 14
573 A171 20 l buff & blk   .25 .25
574 A171 40 l pale violet & blk   .25 .25
575 A171 50 l salmon & blk   .25 .25
576 A171 90 l pale citron & blk   .25 .25
577 A171 100 l pale green & blk   .25 .25
578 A171 200 l pale blue & blk   .25 .25
     Nos. 573-578 (6)   1.55 1.50
European Architectural Heritage Year.

Miracle of
Loaves and
Fishes, Gilt
Glass
A172

Designs: 150 l, Painting of Christ, from
Comodilla Catacomb. 200 l, Raising of Lazarus. All works from 4th century.

Perf. 14x13½
1975, Sept. 25   Photo.   Unwmk.
579 A172 30 l multi   .25 .25
580 A172 150 l brown & multi   .25 .25
581 A172 200 l green & multi   .25 .30
     Nos. 579-581 (3)   .75 .80
9th Intl. Congress of Christian Archaeology.

Investiture
of First
Librarian
Bartolomeo
Sacchi by
Pope
Sixtus IV
A173

Designs: 100 l, Pope Sixtus IV and books in
old wooden press, from Latin Vatican Codex
2044, vert. 250 l, Pope Sixtus IV visiting
Library, fresco in Hospital of the Holy Spirit.
Design of 70 l is from fresco by Melozzo di
Forli in Vatican Gallery.

Perf. 14x13½, 13½x14
1975, Sept. 25   Litho. & Engr.
582 A173 70 l gray & lilac   .25 .25
583 A173 100 l lt yellow & grn   .25 .25
584 A173 250 l gray & red   .30 .30
     Nos. 582-584 (3)   .80 .80
Founding of the Vatican Apostolic Library,
500th anniv.

Mt.
Argentario
Monastery
A174

St. Paul of the
Cross, by Giovanni
Della Porta — A175

Design: 300 l, Basilica of Sts. John and Paul
and burial chapel of Saint.

1975, Nov. 27   Photo.   Perf. 14x13½
585 A174 50 l multi   .25 .25
586 A175 150 l multi   .25 .25
587 A174 300 l multi   .30 .25
     Nos. 585-587 (3)   .80 .75
Bicentenary of death of St. Paul of the
Cross, founder of the Passionist religious
order in 1737.

Praying Women,
by Fra
Angelico — A176

International Women's Year: 200 l, Seated
women, by Fra Angelico.

1975, Nov. 27   Perf. 13½x14
588 A176 100 l multi   .25 .25
589 A176 200 l multi   .30 .25

Virgin and
Child in
Glory, by
Titian
A177

Design: 300 l, The Six Saints, by Titian.
Designs from "The Madonna in Glory with the
Child Jesus and Six Saints."

1976, May 13   Engr.   Perf. 14x13½
590 A177 100 l rose magenta   .25 .25
591 A177 300 l rose magenta   .30 .25
  a. Pair, #590-591   .75 .60
Titian (1477-1576), painter.

A178

Designs: 150 l, Eucharist, wheat and globe.
200 l, Hands Holding Eucharist. 400 l, Hungry
mankind reaching for the Eucharist.

1976, July 2   Photo.   Perf. 13½x14
592 A178 150 l gold, red & bl   .25 .25
593 A178 200 l gold & blue   .25 .25
594 A178 400 l gold, grn & brn   .30 .25
     Nos. 592-594 (3)   .80 .75
41st Intl. Eucharistic Congress, Philadelphia, PA, Aug. 1-8.

A179

Details from Transfiguration by Raphael: 30
l, Moses Holding Tablets. 40 l, Transfigured
Christ. 50 l, Prophet Elijah with book. 100 l,
Apostles John and Peter. 150 l, Group of
women. 200 l, Landscape.

1976, Sept. 30   Photo.   Perf. 13½x14
595 A179 30 l ocher & multi   .25 .25
596 A179 40 l red & multi   .25 .25
597 A179 50 l violet & multi   .25 .25
598 A179 100 l multicolored   .25 .25
599 A179 150 l green & multi   .25 .25
600 A179 200 l ocher & multi   .25 .25
     Nos. 595-600 (6)   1.50 1.50

St.
John's
Tower
A180

Roman Views: 100 l, Fountain of the Sacrament. 120 l, Fountain at entrance to the gardens. 180 l, Basilica, Cupola of St. Peter's and
Sacristy. 250 l, Borgia Tower and Sistine
Chapel. 300 l, Apostolic Palace and Courtyard
of St. Damasius.

Litho. & Engr.
1976, Nov. 23   Perf. 14
601 A180 50 l gray & black   .25 .25
602 A180 100 l salmon & dk brn   .25 .25
603 A180 120 l citron & dk grn   .25 .25
604 A180 180 l pale gray & blk   .25 .25
605 A180 250 l yellow & brn   .25 .25
606 A180 300 l pale lilac & mag   .25 .25
     Nos. 601-606 (6)   1.50 1.50

The Lord's Creatures A181

70 l, Brother Sun. 100 l, Sister Moon and Stars. 130 l, Sister Water. 170 l, Praise in infirmities and tribulations. 200 l, Praise for bodily death. Designs are illustrations by Duilio Cambellotti for "The Canticle of Brother Sun," by St. Francis.

1977, Mar. 10　Photo.　Perf. 14x13½
607	A181	50 l multi	.25	.25
608	A181	70 l multi	.25	.25
609	A181	100 l multi	.25	.25
610	A181	130 l multi	.25	.25
611	A181	170 l multi	.25	.25
612	A181	200 l multi	.25	.25
		Nos. 607-612 (6)	1.50	1.50

St. Francis of Assisi, 750th death anniv.

Sts. Peter and Paul A182

Design: 350 l, Pope Gregory XI and St. Catherine of Siena. Designs are after fresco by Giorgio Vasari.

1977, May 20　Engr.　Perf. 14
613	170 l black		.30	.25
614	350 l black		.45	.25
a.	A182 Pair, #613-614		.85	.60

Return of Pope Gregory XI from Avignon, 600th anniv.

Dormition of the Virgin — A183

Design: 400 l, Virgin Mary in Heaven. Both designs after miniatures in Latin manuscripts, Vatican Library.

1977, July 5　Photo.　Perf. 13½x14
615	A183	200 l multi	.30	.25
616	A183	400 l multi	.55	.30

Feast of the Assumption.

The Nile Deity, Roman Sculpture — A184

Sculptures: 120 l, Head of Pericles. 130 l, Roman Couple Joining Hands. 150 l, Apollo Belvedere, head. 170 l, Laocoon, head. 350 l, Apollo Belvedere, torso.

1977, Sept. 29　　　Perf. 14x13½
617	A184	50 l multi	.25	.25
618	A184	120 l multi	.25	.25
619	A184	130 l multi	.25	.25
620	A184	150 l multi	.25	.25
621	A184	170 l multi	.25	.25
622	A184	350 l multi	.25	.25
		Nos. 617-622 (6)	1.50	1.50

Classical sculptures in Vatican Museums.

Creation of Man and Woman — A185

Designs: 70 l, Three youths in the furnace. 100 l, Adoration of the Kings. 130 l, Raising of Lazarus. 200 l, The Good Shepherd. 400 l, Chrismon, Cross, sleeping soldiers (Resurrection). Designs are bas-reliefs from Christian sarcophagi, 250-350 A.D., found in Roman excavations.

1977, Dec. 9　Photo.　Perf. 14x13½
623	A185	50 l multi	.25	.25
624	A185	70 l multi	.25	.25
625	A185	100 l multi	.25	.25
626	A185	130 l multi	.25	.25
627	A185	200 l multi	.25	.25
628	A185	400 l multi	.25	.25
		Nos. 623-628 (6)	1.50	1.50

Madonna with the Parrot and Rubens Self-portrait A186

1977, Dec. 9　　　Perf. 13½x14
629	A186	350 l multi	.50	.50

Peter Paul Rubens (1577-1640).

Pope Paul VI, by Lino Bianchi Barriviera A187

Design: 350 l, Christ's Face, by Pericle Fazzini and arms of Pope Paul VI.

1978, Mar. 9　Photo.　Perf. 14
630	A187	350 l multi	.40	.30
631	A187	400 l multi	.45	.40

80th birthday of Pope Paul VI.

Pope Pius IX (1792-1878) A188

Designs: 130 l, Arms of Pope Pius IX. 170 l, Seal of Pius IX, used to sign definition of Dogma of Immaculate Conception.

1978, May 9　Litho. & Engr.　Perf. 13x14
632	A188	130 l multi	.25	.25
633	A188	170 l multi	.25	.25
634	A188	200 l multi	.30	.25
		Nos. 632-634 (3)	.80	.75

Interregnum Issues

Keys of St. Peter and Papal Chamberlain's Insignia — A189

1978, Aug. 23　Photo.　Perf. 14
635	A189	120 l purple & lt green	.25	.25
636	A189	150 l purple & salmon	.25	.25
637	A189	250 l purple & yellow	.25	.25
		Nos. 635-637 (3)	.75	.75

Keys of St. Peter and Papal Chamberlain's Insignia — A190

1978, Oct. 12　Photo.　Perf. 14
638	A190	120 l black & multi	.25	.25
639	A190	200 l black & multi	.25	.25
640	A190	250 l black & multi	.25	.25
		Nos. 638-640 (3)	.75	.75

Pope John Paul I, Pope from Aug. 26 to Sept. 28, 1978 — A191

Pope John Paul I: 70 l, Sitting on his throne. 250 l, Walking in Vatican garden. 350 l, Giving blessing, horiz.

1978, Dec. 11　　　Perf. 13x14, 14x13
641	A191	70 l multi	.25	.25
642	A191	120 l multi	.25	.25
643	A191	250 l multi	.25	.25
644	A191	350 l multi	.30	.30
		Nos. 641-644 (4)	1.05	1.05

Arms of Pope John Paul II A192

Designs: 250 l, Pope John Paul II raising hand in blessing. 400 l, Jesus giving keys to St. Peter.

1979, Mar. 22　Litho. & Engr.　Perf. 14x13
645	A192	170 l black & multi	.25	.25
646	A192	250 l black & multi	.30	.30
647	A192	400 l black & multi	.55	.45
		Nos. 645-647 (3)	1.10	1.00

Inauguration of pontificate of Pope John Paul II.

Martyrdom of St. Stanislas — A193

Designs: 150 l, St. Stanislas appearing to the people. 250 l, Gold reliquary, 1504, containing saint's head. 500 l, View of Cracow Cathedral.

1979, May 18　Photo.　Perf. 14
648	A193	120 l multi	.25	.25
649	A193	150 l multi	.25	.25
650	A193	250 l multi	.30	.30
651	A193	500 l multi	.50	.50
		Nos. 648-651 (4)	1.30	1.30

900th anniversary of martyrdom of St. Stanislas (1030-1079), patron saint of Poland.

St. Basil the Great Instructing Monk — A194

St. Basil the Great, 16th cent. of death: 520 l, St. Basil the Great visiting the sick.

1979, June 25　Engr. & Photo.　Perf. 13½x14
652	A194	150 l multi	.25	.25
653	A194	520 l multi	.55	.50

Father Secchi, Solar Protuberance, Spectrum and Meteorograph — A195

Father Angelo Secchi (1818-1878), astronomer, solar protuberance, spectrum and: 220 l, Spectroscope. 300 l, Telescope.

1979, June 25　Litho. & Engr.　Perf. 14x13½
654	A195	180 l multi	.25	.25
655	A195	220 l multi	.25	.25
656	A195	300 l multi	.30	.30
		Nos. 654-656 (3)	.80	.80

Vatican City A196

Papal Arms and Portraits: 70 l, Pius XI. 120 l, Pius XII. 150 l, John XXIII. 170 l, Paul VI. 250 l, John Paul I. 450 l, John Paul II.

1979, Oct. 11　Photo.　Perf. 14x13½
657	A196	50 l multi	.25	.25
658	A196	70 l multi	.25	.25
659	A196	120 l multi	.25	.25
660	A196	150 l multi	.25	.25
661	A196	170 l multi	.25	.25
662	A196	250 l multi	.25	.25
663	A196	450 l multi	.40	.40
		Nos. 657-663 (7)	1.90	1.90

Vatican City State, 50th anniversary.

Infant, by Andrea Della Robbia, IYC Emblem — A197

IYC Emblem and Della Robbia Bas Reliefs, Hospital of the Innocents, Florence.

1979, Nov. 27　Engr. & Photo.　Perf. 13½x14
664	A197	50 l multi	.25	.25
665	A197	120 l multi	.25	.25
666	A197	200 l multi	.25	.25
667	A197	350 l multi	.30	.25
		Nos. 664-667 (4)	1.05	1.00

International Year of the Child.

Abbot Desiderius Giving Codex to St. Benedict — A198

Illuminated Letters and Illustrations, Codices, Vatican Apostolic Library: 100 l, St. Benedict writing the Rule. 150 l, Page from the Rule. 220 l, Death of St. Benedict. 450 l, Montecassino (after painting by Paul Bril).

1980, Mar. 21 Photo. *Perf. 14x13½*
668	A198	80 l multi	.25	.25
669	A198	100 l multi	.25	.25
670	A198	150 l multi	.25	.25
671	A198	220 l multi	.25	.25
672	A198	450 l multi	.40	.30
	Nos. 668-672 (5)		1.40	1.30

St. Benedict of Nursia (patron saint of Europe), 1500th birth anniversary.

Bernini, Medallion Showing Baldacchino in St. Peter's — A199

Gian Lorenzo Bernini (1598-1680), Architect (Self-portrait and Medallion): 170 l, St. Peter's Square with third wing (never built). 250 l, Bronze chair, Doctors of the Church. 350 l, Apostolic Palace stairway.

1980, Oct. 16 Litho. *Perf. 14x13½*
673	A199	80 l multicolored	.25	.25
674	A199	170 l multicolored	.25	.25
675	A199	250 l multicolored	.30	.25
676	A199	350 l multicolored	.35	.25
	Nos. 673-676 (4)		1.15	1.00

St. Albertus Magnus on Mission of Peace — A200

1980, Nov. 18 Litho. *Perf. 13½x14*
677	A200	300 l shown	.40	.40
678	A200	400 l As bishop	.50	.40

St. Albertus Magnus, 700th death anniv.

Communion of the Saints — A201

1980, Nov. 18 *Perf. 14x13½*
679	A201	250 l shown	.35	.25
680	A201	500 l Christ and saints	.50	.50

Feast of All Saints.

Guglielmo Marconi and Pope Pius XI, Vatican Radio Emblem, Vatican Arms A202

Designs: 150 l, Microphone, Bible text. 200 l, St. Maria di Galeria Radio Center

antenna, Archangel Gabriel statue. 600 l, Pope John Paul II.

1981, Feb. 12 Photo. *Perf. 14x13½*
681	A202	100 l shown	.25	.25
682	A202	150 l multicolored	.25	.25
683	A202	200 l multicolored	.25	.25
684	A202	600 l multicolored	.50	.50
	Nos. 681-684 (4)		1.25	1.25

Vatican Radio, 50th anniversary.

Virgil Seated at Podium, Vergilius Romanus — A203

1981, Apr. 23 Litho. *Perf. 14*
685	A203	350 l multicolored	.30	.30
686	A203	600 l multicolored	.50	.50
	Set, with labels		1.75	1.75

2000th birth anniversary of Virgil. Issued in sheets of 16 stamps plus 9 labels.

Congress Emblem A204

Congress Emblem and: 150 l, Virgin appearing to St. Bernadette. 200 l, Pilgrims going to Lourdes. 500 l, Bishop and pilgrims.

1981, June 22 Photo.
687	A204	80 l multicolored	.25	.25
688	A204	150 l multicolored	.25	.25
689	A204	200 l multicolored	.25	.30
690	A204	500 l multicolored	.50	.50
	Nos. 687-690 (4)		1.25	1.30

42nd Intl. Eucharistic Congress, Lourdes, France, July 16-23.

Intl. Year of the Disabled A205

1981, Sept. 29 Photo. *Perf. 14x13½*
691	A205	600 l multicolored	.65	.60

Jan van Ruusbroec, Flemish Mystic, 500th Birth Anniv. — A206

Litho. & Engr.

1981, Sept. 29 *Perf. 13½x14*
692	A206	200 l shown	.25	.25
693	A206	300 l Portrait	.30	.25

1980 Journeys of Pope John Paul II — A207

50 l, Papal arms. 100 l, Map of Africa. 120 l, Crucifix. 150 l, Baptism. 200 l, African bishop. 250 l, Visiting sick. 300 l, Notre Dame, France. 400 l, UNESCO speech. 600 l, Christ of the

Andes, Brazil. 700 l, Cologne Cathedral, Germany. 900 l, John Paul II.

1981, Dec. 3 Photo. *Perf. 13½x14½*
694	A207	50 l multicolored	.25	.25
695	A207	100 l multicolored	.25	.25
696	A207	120 l multicolored	.25	.25
697	A207	150 l multicolored	.25	.25
698	A207	200 l multicolored	.25	.25
699	A207	250 l multicolored	.30	.30
700	A207	300 l multicolored	.30	.30
701	A207	400 l multicolored	.35	.35
702	A207	600 l multicolored	.50	.50
703	A207	700 l multicolored	.65	.65
704	A207	900 l multicolored	.95	.95
a.	Complete booklet, 8 each #694, 695, 698, 699 ('82)		27.50	
	Nos. 694-704 (11)		4.30	4.30

700th Death Anniv. of St. Agnes of Prague — A208

Designs: 700 l, Handing order to Grand Master of the Crosiers of the Red Star. 900 l, Receiving letter from St. Clare.

1982, Feb. 16 Photo. *Perf. 13½x14*
705	A208	700 l multicolored	.75	.75
706	A208	900 l multicolored	1.10	1.10

Pueri Cantores — A209

Luca Della Robbia (1400-1482), Sculptor: No. 708, Pueri Cantores, diff. No. 709, Virgin in Prayer (44x36mm).

Photo. & Engr.

1982, May 21 *Perf. 14*
707	A209	1000 l multicolored	.80	.75
708	A200	1000 l multicolored	.80	.75
709	A209	1000 l multicolored	.80	.75
a.	Strip of 3, #707-709		3.50	3.25

St. Teresa of Avila (1515-1582) A210

Sketches of St. Teresa by Riccardo Tommasi-Ferroni.

1982, Sept. 23 Photo.
710	A210	200 l multicolored	.25	.25
711	A210	600 l multicolored	.50	.50
712	A210	1000 l multicolored	1.10	1.10
	Nos. 710-712 (3)		1.85	1.85

Christmas A211

Nativity Bas-Reliefs: 300 l, Wit Stwosz, Church of the Virgin Mary, Cracow. 450 l, Enrico Manfrini.

Photo. & Engr.

1982, Nov. 23 *Perf. 14*
713	A211	300 l multicolored	.40	.40
714	A211	450 l multicolored	.55	.55

400th Anniv. of Gregorian Calendar — A212

Sculpture Details, Tomb of Pope Gregory XIII, St. Peter's Basilica: 200 l, Surveying the globe. 300 l, Receiving Edict of Reform. 700 l, Presenting edict.

1982, Nov. 23 Engr. *Perf. 13½x14*
715	A212	200 l multicolored	.25	.25
716	A212	300 l multicolored	.35	.35
717	A212	700 l multicolored	.80	.80
a.	Souvenir sheet of 3, #715-717		2.25	2.25
	Nos. 715-717 (3)		1.40	1.40

Souvenir Sheets

The Papacy and Art, US 1983 Exhibition — A213

1983, Mar. 10 Litho. *Perf. 13½x14*
718	A213	Sheet of 6	3.25	2.00
a.	100 l Greek Vase		.30	.25
b.	200 l Italian vase		.30	.25
c.	250 l Female terra-cotta bust		.40	.35
d.	300 l Marcus Aurelius bust		.40	.35
e.	350 l Bird fresco		.50	.40
f.	400 l Pope Clement VIII vestment		.50	.40

1983, June 14 Litho. *Perf. 13½x14*
719	A213	Sheet of 6	3.50	3.50
a.	100 l Horse's head, Etruscan terra cotta		.35	.30
b.	200 l Horseman, Greek fragment		.35	.30
c.	300 l Male head, Etruscan		.45	.40
d.	400 l Apollo Belvedere head		.45	.40
e.	500 l Moses, Roman fresco		.55	.45
f.	1000 l Madonna and Child, by Bernardo Daddi		.60	.45

1983, Nov. 10 Litho. *Perf. 13½x14*
720	A213	Sheet of 6	3.75	3.75
a.	150 l Greek cup, Oedipus and the Sphinx		.40	.35
b.	200 l Etruscan bronze statue of a child		.40	.35
c.	350 l Emperor Augustus marble statue		.50	.45
d.	400 l Good Shepherd marble statue		.50	.45
e.	500 l St. Nicholas Saving a ship by G. da Fabriano		.60	.50
f.	1200 l The Holy face by G. Rouault		.75	.60

Vatican Collection: The Papacy and Art - US 1983 exhibition, New York, Chicago, San Francisco.

Extraordinary Holy Year, 1983-84 (1950th Anniv. of Redemption) A214

Sketches by Giovanni Hajnal.

1983, Mar. 10   **Photo. & Engr.**
721	A214	300 l	Crucifixion	.30 .25
722	A214	350 l	Christ the Redeemer	.30 .25
723	A214	400 l	Pope	.40 .40
724	A214	2000 l	Holy Spirit	2.00 1.75
		Nos. 721-724 (4)		3.00 2.65

Theology, by Raphael (1483-1517) A215

Allegories, Room of the Segnatura.

1983, June 14
725	A215	50 l	shown	.25 .25
726	A215	400 l	Poetry	.35 .25
727	A215	500 l	Justice	.50 .50
728	A215	1200 l	Philosphy	1.40 1.25
		Nos. 725-728 (4)		2.50 2.25

Gregor Johann Mendel (1822-1884), Biologist — A216

Phases of pea plant hybridization.

Photo. & Engr.
1984, Feb. 28   **Perf. 14x13½**
729	A216	450 l	multicolored	.45 .40
730	A216	1500 l	multicolored	1.75 1.25

St. Casimir of Lithuania (1458-1484) — A217

1984, Feb. 28   **Perf. 14**
731	A217	550 l	multicolored	.55 .50
732	A217	1200 l	multicolored	1.60 1.25

Pontifical Academy of Sciences — A218

1984, June 18   **Litho. & Engr.**
733	A218	150 l	shown	.25 .25
734	A218	450 l	Secret Archives	.50 .40
735	A218	550 l	Apostolic Library	.75 .55
736	A218	1500 l	Observatory	1.75 1.50
		Nos. 733-736 (4)		3.25 2.70

Papal Journeys A218a

1984-85   **Photo.**   **Perf. 13½x14½**
737	A218a	50 l	Pakistan	.25 .25
738	A218a	100 l	Philippines	.25 .25
739	A218a	150 l	Guam	.25 .25

740	A218a	250 l	Japan	.25 .25
741	A218a	300 l	Alaska	.30 .30
742	A218a	400 l	Africa	.35 .30
743	A218a	450 l	Portugal	.40 .40
a.		Bklt. pane, 4ea #738, 741-743 + 4 labels ('85)		10.00
		Complete booklet, #743a		10.00
744	A218a	550 l	Grt. Britain	.80 .60
745	A218a	1000 l	Argentina	1.00 .90
746	A218a	1500 l	Switzerland	1.75 1.25
747	A218a	2500 l	San Marino	3.00 2.50
748	A218a	4000 l	Spain	6.00 4.75
		Nos. 737-748 (12)		14.60 12.00

Issued: Nos. 737-748, 10/2/84; No. 743a, 3/14/85.

St. Damasus I (b. 304) A219

St. Damasus I and: 200 l, Sepulchre of Sts. Marcellinus and Peter. 500 l, Epigraph of St. Januarius. 2000 l, Basilica, Church of the Martyrs Simplicius, Faustinus and Beatrice.

1984, Nov. 27 **Photo.** **Perf. 14x13½**
749	A219	200 l	multicolored	.35 .25
750	A219	500 l	multicolored	.70 .50
751	A219	2000 l	multicolored	2.25 2.00
		Nos. 749-751 (3)		3.30 2.75

St. Methodius (d. 885) — A220

St. Methodius and: 500 l, Madonna and Christ. 600 l, St. Cyril, carrying the body of St. Clement I. 1700 l, Sts. Benedict and Cyril, patrons of Europe.

Photo. & Engr.
1985, May 7   **Perf. 13½x14**
752	A220	500 l	multicolored	.50 .30
753	A220	600 l	multicolored	.70 .50
754	A220	1700 l	multicolored	2.25 1.50
		Nos. 752-754 (3)		3.45 2.30

St. Thomas More (1477-1535) — A221

St. Thomas More (from a portrait by Hans Holbein) and: 250 l, map of British Isles. 400 l, Frontispiece of Utopia. 2000 l, Frontispiece of Domenico Regi's biography of More.

Litho. & Engr.
1985, May 7   **Perf. 14x13½**
755	A221	250 l	multicolored	.40 .25
756	A221	400 l	multicolored	.50 .40
757	A221	2000 l	multicolored	2.60 2.00
		Nos. 755-757 (3)		3.50 2.65

St. Gregory VII (c. 1020-85) A222

Designs: 150 l, Eagle from Byzantine door, St. Paul's Basilica, Rome. 450 l, St. Gregory blessing. 2500 l, Sarcophagus.

Perf. 13½x14, 14x13½
1985, June 18   **Photo.**
758	A222	150 l	multi, vert.	.25 .25
759	A222	450 l	multi, vert.	.60 .45
760	A222	2500 l	multicolored	2.75 2.50
		Nos. 758-760 (3)		3.60 3.20

43rd Intl. Eucharistic Congress — A223

Emblem, host, cross and: 100 l, Outline map of Africa. 400 l, Altar and Assembly of Bishops. 600 l, African chalice. 2300 l, African Christian family.

Photo. & Engr.
1985, June 18   **Perf. 13½x14**
761	A223	100 l	multicolored	.25 .25
762	A223	400 l	multicolored	.45 .40
763	A223	600 l	multicolored	.55 .55
764	A223	2300 l	multicolored	2.60 2.00
		Nos. 761-764 (4)		3.85 3.20

Concordat Agreement Ratification A224

1985, Oct. 15 **Photo.** **Perf. 14x13½**
765	A224	400 l	Papal arms, map of Italy	.60 .50

Coaches A225

1985, Oct. 15   **Litho. & Engr.**
766	A225	450 l	dp lil rose & int bl	.45 .35
767	A225	1500 l	brt bl & dp lil rose	1.50 1.25
a.		Souvenir sheet of 2, #766-767, perf. 13½x12½		3.25 3.25

Italia '85.

Intl. Peace Year 1986 — A226

Biblical and gospel texts: 50 l, Isaiah 2:4. 350 l, Isaiah 52:7. 450 l, Matthew 5:9. 650 l, Luke 2:14. 2000 l, Message for World Peace, speech of Pope John Paul II, Jan. 1, 1986.

1986, Apr. 14   **Photo.**   **Perf. 14**
768	A226	50 l	multicolored	.25 .25
769	A226	350 l	multicolored	.35 .30
770	A226	450 l	multicolored	.60 .40
771	A226	650 l	multicolored	.80 .60
772	A226	2000 l	multicolored	2.25 1.75
		Nos. 768-772 (5)		4.25 3.30

Vatican City — A227

1986, Apr. 14   **Perf. 13½x14**
773	A227	Block of 6		5.00 4.00
a.-f.		550 l, any single		.70 .40

UNESCO World Heritage Campaign. No. 773 has continuous design.

Patron Saints of the Sick — A228

Designs: No. 774, St. Camillus de Lellis rescuing invalid during Tiber flood, by Pierre Subleyras (1699-1749). No. 775, St. John of God with invalids, by Gomez Moreno (1834-1918). 2000 l, Pope John Paul II visiting the sick.

Litho. & Engr.
1986, June 12   **Perf. 13½x14**
774	A228	700 l	multicolored	.80 .60
775	A228	700 l	multicolored	.80 .60
776	A228	2000 l	multicolored	2.50 1.90
		Nos. 774-776 (3)		4.10 3.10

Pontifical Academy of Sciences, 50th Anniv. A229

School of Athens (details), by Raphael: 1500 l, Scribes. 2500 l, Students learning math.

Litho. & Engr.
1986, Oct. 2   **Perf. 14x13½**
777	A229	1500 l	multicolored	1.75 1.50
778	A229	2500 l	multicolored	3.00 2.50

Conversion of St. Augustine (354-430) in 387 — A230

Religious art: 300 l, St. Augustine reading St. Paul's Epistles, fresco by Benozzo Gozzoli (1420-1498), Church of St. Augustine, San Gimignano. 400 l, Baptism of St. Augustine, painting by Bartolomeo di Gentile (1470-1534), Vatican Art Gallery. 500 l, Ecstasy of St. Augustine, fresco by Benozzo Gozzoli, Church of St. Augustine. 2200 l, St. Augustine, detail of Disputa del Sacramento, fresco by Raphael (1483-1520), Room of the Segnatura, Apostolic Palace.

1987, Apr. 7 **Photo.** **Perf. 13½x14**
779	A230	300 l	multicolored	.40 .30
780	A230	400 l	multicolored	.55 .45
781	A230	500 l	multicolored	.65 .50
782	A230	2200 l	multicolored	3.00 2.25
		Nos. 779-782 (4)		4.60 3.50

A231

Seals: 700 l, Church of Riga, 1234-1269. 2400 l, Marian Basilica of the Assumption, Aglona, 1780.

1987, June 2 **Photo.** **Perf. 13½x14**
783	A231	700 l	multicolored	1.25 .95
784	A231	2400 l	multicolored	3.25 2.75

Christianization of Latvia, 800th anniv.

Christianization Anniversaries A232

Designs: 200 l, Christ, statue in the Lithuanian Chapel, Vatican Crypt. 700 l, Two Angels and Our Lady Holding the Body of Christ, by a Lithuanian artist. 3000 l, Lithuanian shrine.

1987, June 2   **Perf. 13½x14**

785	A232	200 l multicolored	.30	.25
786	A232	700 l multicolored	1.00	.75
787	A232	3000 l multicolored	3.25	2.75
		Nos. 785-787 (3)	4.55	3.75

Christianization of Lithuania, 600th anniv.

OLYMPHILEX '87, Rome, Aug. 29-Sept. 9 — A233

Details of mosaic from the Baths of Caracalla: 400 l, Judge. 500 l, Athlete. 600 l, Athlete, diff. 2000 l, Athlete, diff.

Litho. & Engr.

1987, Aug. 29   **Perf. 14**

788	A233	400 l multicolored	.40	.30
789	A233	500 l multicolored	.50	.40
790	A233	600 l multicolored	.60	.50
791	A233	2000 l multicolored	3.00	2.25
		Nos. 788-791 (4)	4.50	3.45

Souvenir Sheet

792		Sheet of 4 + 4 labels	4.25	4.25
a.	A233	400 l like No. 788	.40	.30
b.	A233	500 l like No. 789	.50	.40
c.	A233	600 l like No. 790	.60	.50
d.	A233	2000 l	2.75	2.25

Stamps from souvenir sheet have a Greek border in blue surrounding vignettes (pictured). Nos. 788-791 have single line border in blue. No. 792 has 4 labels picturing the papal arms, a goblet, a crown and the exhibition emblem.

Inauguration of the Philatelic and Numismatic Museum — A235

Designs: 400 l, Philatelic department, Vatican City, No. 1. 3500 l, Numismatic department, 1000-lire coin of 1986.

1987, Sept. 29   **Photo.**   **Perf. 14x13½**

793	A235	400 l multicolored	.50	.45
794	A235	3500 l multicolored	4.50	3.75

Journeys of Pope John Paul II, 1985-86 A236

Designs: 50 l, Venezuela, Peru, Ecuador and Trinidad & Tobago, 1985. 250 l, The Netherlands, Luxembourg, Belgium, 1985. 400 l, Togo, Ivory Coast, Cameroun, Central Africa, Zaire, Kenya and Morocco, 1985. 500 l, Liechtenstein, 1985. 600 l, India, 1986. 700 l, Colombia, St. Lucia, 1986. 2500 l, France, 1986. 4000 l, Bangladesh, Singapore, Fiji, New Zealand, Australia and Seychelles, 1986.

1987, Oct. 27   **Photo.**   **Perf. 14x13½**

795	A236	50 l multicolored	.30	.25
796	A236	250 l multicolored	.50	.30
797	A236	400 l multicolored	.60	.40
798	A236	500 l multicolored	.80	.50
799	A236	600 l multicolored	1.00	.80
800	A236	700 l multicolored	1.50	1.00
801	A236	2500 l multicolored	5.50	4.25
802	A236	4000 l multicolored	8.50	7.00
		Nos. 795-802 (8)	18.70	14.50

A237

Transfer of St. Nicholas Relics from Myra to Bari, 900th anniv.: 500 l, Arrival of relics at Bari. 700 l, Act of charity, three impoverished women. 3000 l, Miraculous rescue of ship.

1987, Dec. 3   **Perf. 13½x14**

803	A237	500 l multicolored	1.00	1.00
804	A237	700 l multicolored	1.50	1.25
805	A237	3000 l multicolored	11.50	8.00
		Nos. 803-805 (3)	14.00	10.25

St. Nicholas of Bari (c. 270-352), bishop of Myra. Legend of Santa Claus originated because of his charitable works. Printed in sheets of 8 + 16 se-tenant labels picturing Santa Claus.

A238

Children and: 500 l, Sister of the Institute of the Daughters of Mary Help of Christians. 1000 l, St. John Bosco. 2000 l, Salesian lay brother. Printed in a continuous design.

1988, Apr. 19   **Photo.**

806		Strip of 3	5.25	4.00
a.	A238	500 l multicolored	.45	.40
b.	A238	1000 l multicolored	.75	.50
c.	A238	2000 l multicolored	1.25	1.25

St. John Bosco (1815-1888), educator.

A239

50 l, Annunciation. 300 l, Nativity. 500 l, Pentecost. 750 l, Assumption. 1000 l, Mother of the Church. 2400 l, Refuge of Sinners.

1988, June 16   **Photo.**   **Perf. 13½x14**

807	A239	50 l multicolored	.25	.25
808	A239	300 l multicolored	.30	.25
809	A239	500 l multicolored	.50	.40
810	A239	750 l multicolored	.90	.60
811	A239	1000 l multicolored	1.25	.80
812	A239	2400 l multicolored	2.75	1.75
		Nos. 807-812 (6)	5.95	4.05

Marian Year, 1987-88.

A240

Baptism of the Rus' of Kiev, Millennium: 450 l, "Prince St. Vladimir the Great," from a 15th cent. icon. 650 l, Cathedral of St. Sophia, Kiev. 2500 l, "Mother of God in Prayor," from a mosaic at the cathedral.

1988, June 16

813	A240	450 l multicolored	.60	.45
814	A240	650 l multicolored	.85	.65
815	A240	2500 l multicolored	3.00	2.25
		Nos. 813-815 (3)	4.45	3.35

Paintings by Paolo Veronese (1528-1588) — A241

Designs: 550 l, Marriage of Cana (Madonna and Christ) the Louvre, Paris. 650 l, Self-portrait of the Artist, Villa Barbaro of Maser, Treviso. 3000 l, Marriage of Cana (woman and two men).

Perf. 13½x14, 14x13½

1988, Sept. 29   **Photo. & Engr.**

816	A241	550 l multi, vert.	.75	.45
817	A241	650 l multicolored	.85	.55
818	A241	3000 l multi, vert.	4.00	2.50
		Nos. 816-818 (3)	5.60	3.50

Christmas A242

Luke 2:14 and: 50 l, Angel facing LR. 400 l, Angel facing UR. 500 l, Angel facing LL. 550 l, Shepherds. 850 l, Nativity. 1500 l, Magi.

1988, Dec. 12   **Photo.**   **Perf. 13½x14**

819	A242	50 l multicolored	.25	.25
820	A242	400 l multicolored	.45	.30
821	A242	500 l multicolored	.60	.35
822	A242	550 l multicolored	.70	.40
823	A242	850 l multicolored	1.00	.60
824	A242	1500 l multicolored	1.50	1.00
		Nos. 819-824 (6)	4.50	2.90

Souvenir Sheet

825		Sheet of 6	5.00	5.00
a.	A242	50 l gold & multi	.25	.25
b.	A242	400 l gold & multi	.40	.30
c.	A242	500 l gold & multi	.50	.35
d.	A242	550 l gold & multi	.70	.40
e.	A242	850 l gold & multi	1.00	.60
f.	A242	1500 l gold & multi	1.50	1.00

No. 825 has continuous design.

Feast of the Visitation, 600th Anniv. — A243

Illuminations: 550 l, The Annunciation. 750 l, The Visitation (Virgin and St. Elizabeth). 2500 l, Mary, Elizabeth and infants.

1989, May 5   **Photo.**   **Perf. 13½x14**

826	A243	550 l multicolored	.75	.40
827	A243	750 l multicolored	.90	.55
828	A243	2500 l multicolored	2.75	1.90
		Nos. 826-828 (3)	4.40	2.85

Souvenir Sheet

Gregorian Egyptian Museum, 150th Anniv. — A244

Designs: 400 l, Apis. 650 l, Isis and Apis dicephalous bust. 750 l, Statue of the physician Ugiahorresne. 2400 l, Pharaoh Mentuhotep.

Litho. & Engr.

1989, May 5   **Perf. 14x13½**

829	A244	Sheet of 4	4.75	4.75
a.		400 l multicolored	.30	.25
b.		650 l multicolored	.40	.25
c.		750 l multicolored	.55	.45
d.		2400 l multicolored	1.50	1.25

A245

Birds from engravings by Eleazar Albin in *Histoire Naturelle des Oiseaux*, 1750 — 100 l, Parrot. 150 l, Green woodpecker. 200 l, Crested and common wrens. 350 l, Kingfisher. 500 l, Red grosbeak of Virginia. 700 l, Bullfinch. 1500 l, Lapwing plover. 3000 l, French teal.

1989, June 13   **Photo.**   **Perf. 12**

Granite Paper

830	A245	100 l multicolored	.25	.25
831	A245	150 l multicolored	.25	.25
832	A245	200 l multicolored	.25	.25
833	A245	350 l multicolored	.45	.25
834	A245	500 l multicolored	.65	.30
835	A245	700 l multicolored	.90	.45
836	A245	1500 l multicolored	2.00	1.00
837	A245	3000 l multicolored	4.00	2.00
		Nos. 830-837 (8)	8.75	4.75

A246

Symbols of the Eucharist.

Photo. & Engr.

1989, Sept. 29   **Perf. 13½x14**

838	A246	550 l shown	.70	.40
839	A246	850 l multi, diff.	1.00	.65
840	A246	1000 l multi, diff.	1.25	.75
841	A246	2500 l multi, diff.	3.25	1.90
		Nos. 838-841 (4)	6.20	3.70

44th Intl. Eucharistic Cong., Seoul, Oct. 5-8.

Ecclesiastical Hierarchy in the US, Bicent. — A247

Designs: 450 l, Basilica of the Assumption of the Blessed Virgin Mary, Baltimore. 1350 l, John Carroll (1735-1815), 1st bishop of Baltimore and the US. 2400 l, Cathedral of Mary Our Queen, Baltimore.

1989, Nov. 9　　Photo.　　Perf. 12

842	A247	450 l multicolored	.60	.40
843	A247	1350 l multicolored	1.75	1.25
844	A247	2400 l multicolored	3.25	2.00
		Nos. 842-844 (3)	5.60	3.65

Papal Journeys 1988
A248

Papal arms, Pope John Paul II and maps: 50 l, Uruguay, Bolivia, Peru and Paraguay, May 7-19. 550 l, Austria, June 23-27. 800 l, Zimbabwe, Botswana, Lesotho, Swaziland and Mozambique, Sept. 10-19. 1000 l, France, Oct. 8-11. 4000 l, Pastoral visits in Italy, 1978-1988.

1989, Nov. 9　　　　　　　Perf. 14x13½

845	A248	50 l multicolored	.25	.25
846	A248	550 l multicolored	.80	.50
847	A248	800 l multicolored	1.10	.70
848	A248	1000 l multicolored	1.50	.90
849	A248	4000 l multicolored	5.75	3.50
		Nos. 845-849 (5)	9.40	5.85

St. Angela Merici (c. 1474-1540)
A249

Designs: 700 l, The vision of the mystical stair, Prophecy of the Ursulines. 800 l, Evangelical counsel. 2800 l, Ursulines mission continued.

1990, Apr. 5　　Photo.　　Perf. 13½x14

850	A249	700 l multicolored	1.10	.80
851	A249	800 l multicolored	1.25	.95
852	A249	2800 l multicolored	4.25	3.25
		Nos. 850-852 (3)	6.60	5.00

Caritas Intl., 40th Anniv.
A250

Designs: 450 l, Abraham. 650 l, Three visitors. 800 l, Abraham and Sarah. 2000 l, Three visitors at Abraham's table.

1990, June 5　　Photo.　　Perf. 12x11½
Granite Paper

853	A250	450 l multicolored	.75	.45
854	A250	650 l multicolored	1.25	.70
855	A250	800 l multicolored	1.50	.85
856	A250	2000 l multicolored	3.00	2.00
		Nos. 853-856 (4)	6.50	4.00

Souvenir Sheet

857		Sheet of 4	7.00	7.00
a.	A250	450 l like #853	.70	.60
b.	A250	650 l like #854	1.10	.90
c.	A250	800 l like #855	1.25	1.00
d.	A250	2000 l like #856	3.25	2.25

Nos. 853-856 have a single line border in gold. Nos. 857a-857d have no border line.

No. 857 with "Pro Terremotati 1997" overprinted in sheet margin exists in limited quantities, sold for 8000 l to assist earthquake victims in Umbria and Marche, but was not officially issued by Vatican postal authorities. It was sold in a folder depicting St. Francis of Assisi. Value $30.

A251

300 l, Ordination of St. Willibrord. 700 l, Stay in Antwerp. 3000 l, Leaving belongings, death.

1990, June 5　　　　　　　Perf. 13½x14

858	A251	300 l multicolored	.50	.30
859	A251	700 l multicolored	1.00	.70
860	A251	3000 l multicolored	4.00	3.25
		Nos. 858-860 (3)	5.50	4.25

1300th anniv. of ministry of St. Willibrord.

A252

Diocese of Beijing-Nanking, 300th Anniv.: 500 l, Lake Beijing. 750 l, Church of the Immaculate Conception, Beijing, 1650. 1500 l, Lake Beijing, diff. 2000 l, Church of the Redeemer, Beijing, 1703.

1990, Oct. 2

861	A252	500 l multicolored	.70	.45
862	A252	750 l multicolored	1.10	.70
863	A252	1500 l multicolored	2.25	1.40
864	A252	2000 l multicolored	2.75	1.90
		Nos. 861-864 (4)	6.80	4.45

Christmas
A253

Details from painting by Sebastiano Mainardi.

1990, Nov. 27　　Photo.　　Perf. 13

865	A253	50 l Choir of Angels	.25	.25
866	A253	200 l St. Joseph	.30	.30
867	A253	650 l Holy Child	1.10	1.10
868	A253	750 l Madonna	1.25	1.25
869	A253	2500 l Nativity scene, vert.	4.00	4.00
		Nos. 865-869 (5)	6.90	6.90

Paintings of the Sistine Chapel — A254

Different details from lunettes: 50 l, 100 l, Eleazar. 150 l, 250 l, Jacob. 350 l, 400 l, Josiah. 500 l, 650 l, Asa. 800 l, 1000 l, Zerubbabel. 2000 l, 3000 l, Azor.

1991, Apr. 9　　Photo.　　Perf. 11½
Granite Paper

870	A254	50 l multicolored	.25	.25
871	A254	100 l multicolored	.25	.25
a.		Booklet pane of 6	.75	
872	A254	150 l multicolored	.25	.25
a.		Booklet pane of 6	1.25	
873	A254	250 l multicolored	.30	.30
874	A254	350 l multicolored	.40	.40
875	A254	400 l multicolored	.50	.50
876	A254	500 l multicolored	.65	.65
877	A254	650 l multicolored	.85	.85
a.		Booklet pane of 6	5.50	
		Complete booklet, #871a, 872a, 877a	7.50	
878	A254	800 l multicolored	.90	.90
879	A254	1000 l multicolored	1.25	1.25
880	A254	2000 l multicolored	2.50	2.50
881	A254	3000 l multicolored	3.75	3.75
		Nos. 870-881 (12)	11.85	11.85

Encyclical Rerum Novarum, Cent.
A255

Arms of Pope Leo XIII and: 600 l, Title page of Encyclical. 750 l, Allegory of Church's interest in workers, employers. 3500 l, Pope Leo XIII (1878-1903).

1991, May 23　　Engr.　　Perf. 14x13½

882	A255	600 l blue & dk grn	.90	.85
883	A255	750 l sage grn & rose car	1.10	1.00
884	A255	3500 l brt pur & dk bl	5.00	4.50
		Nos. 882-884 (3)	7.00	6.35

Vatican Observatory, Cent. — A256

Designs: 750 l, Astrograph for making photographic sky map, 1891. 1000 l, Zeiss Double Astrograph, Lake Castelgandolfo, 1935, horiz. 3000 l, New telescope, Vatican Observatory, Mt. Graham, Arizona, 1991.

Perf. 11½x12, 12x11½
1991, Oct. 1　　　　　　　　　Photo.
Granite Paper

885	A256	750 l multicolored	1.25	1.10
886	A256	1000 l multicolored	1.75	1.50
887	A256	3000 l multicolored	4.75	5.00
		Nos. 885-887 (3)	7.75	7.60

Canonization of St. Bridget, 600th Anniv. — A257

Designs: 1500 l, Receiving Madonna's revelations. 2000 l, Receiving Christ's revelations.

1991, Oct. 1　　　　　　　Perf. 12½x13

888	A257	1500 l multicolored	2.50	2.25
889	A257	2000 l multicolored	3.50	3.25

Journeys of Pope John Paul II, 1990 — A258

Pope John Paul II and: 200 l, Cathedral of Immaculate Conception, Ouagadougou, Burkina Faso. 550 l, St. Vitus' Cathedral, Prague. 750 l, Our Lady of Guadaloupe's Basilica, Mexico. 1500 l, Ta' Pinu Sanctuary, Gozo. 3500 l, Cathedral of Christ the King, Gitega, Burundi.

Litho. & Engr.
1991, Nov. 11　　　　　　Perf. 13½x14

890	A258	200 l green & multi	.40	.40
891	A258	550 l org brn & multi	.90	.90
892	A258	750 l claret & multi	1.25	1.25
893	A258	1500 l dk brn & multi	2.50	2.50
894	A258	3500 l grn bl & multi	6.00	6.00
		Nos. 890-894 (5)	11.05	11.05

West Africa, Jan. 25-Feb. 1 (200 l); Czechoslovakia, Apr. 21-22 (550 l); Mexico, Curacao, May 6-14 (750 l); Malta, May 25-27 (1500 l); Tanzania, Burundi, Rwanda, Ivory Coast, Sept. 1-10 (3500 l).

A259

Special Assembly for Europe of Synod of Bishops: 300 l, Colonnade of St. Peter's Basilica. 500 l, St. Peter's Basilica and Square. 4000 l, Colonnade of St. Peter's Basilica, Apostolic Palace.

1991, Nov. 11　　Engr.　　Perf. 12½x13

895		300 l olive & blk	.50	.50
896		500 l olive & blk	.90	.90
897		4000 l olive & blk	6.00	6.00
a.	A259	Strip of 3, #895-897	8.00	8.00

No. 897a has continous design.

A260

Discovery and Evangelization of America, 500th Anniv.: 500 l, Christopher Columbus. 600 l, Saint Peter Claver. 850 l, La Virgen de los Reyes Catolicos. 1000 l, Bishop Bartolome de las Casas. 2000 l, Father Junipero Serra.
Charts: 1500 l, New World. 2500 l, Old World.

1992, Mar. 24　　Photo.　　Perf. 11½x12
Granite Paper

898	A260	500 l multicolored	.75	.75
899	A260	600 l multicolored	.90	.90
900	A260	850 l multicolored	1.25	1.25
901	A260	1000 l multicolored	1.50	1.50
902	A260	2000 l multicolored	3.00	3.00
		Nos. 898-902 (5)	7.40	7.40

Souvenir Sheet
Perf. 12

903	A260	Sheet of 2	8.00	8.00
a.		1500 l multicolored	2.25	2.25
b.		2500 l multicolored	3.75	3.75

Piero Della Francesca (d. 1492), Painter — A261

Frescoes: 300 l, 750 l (detail), Our Lady of Childbirth. 1000 l, 3000 l (detail), Resurrection.

1992, May 15　　Photo.　　Perf. 13½x14

904	A261	300 l multicolored	.40	.40
905	A261	750 l multicolored	1.10	1.10
906	A261	1000 l multicolored	1.40	1.40
907	A261	3000 l multicolored	4.25	4.25
		Nos. 904-907 (4)	7.15	7.15

St. Giuseppe Benedetto Cottolengo (1786-1842)
A262

St. Giuseppe Benedetto Cottolengo: 650 l, Comforting the sick. 850 l, With Little House of Divine Providence.

1992, May 15　　　　　　　Perf. 11½x12
Granite Paper

908	A262	650 l multicolored	1.00	1.00
909	A262	850 l multicolored	1.40	1.40

A263

Plants of the New World: a, Frumentum indicum. b, Solanum pomiferum. c, Opuntia. d, Cacaos, cacavifera. e, Solanum tuberosum, capsicum, mordens. f, Ananas sagitae folio.

1992, Sept. 15   Photo.   Perf. 11½x12
Granite Paper
910	Block of 6	8.25	8.25
a.-f.	A263 850 l any single	1.10	1.10

A264

1992, Oct. 12   Perf. 12½x13
911	A264	700 l	multicolored	1.25 1.10

4th General Conference of the Latin American Episcopacy.

Christmas
A265

Mosaics from Basilica of St. Maria Maggiore, Rome: 600 l, The Annunciation. 700 l, Nativity. 1000 l, Adoration of the Magi. 1500 l, Presentation to the Temple.

1992, Nov. 24   Photo.   Perf. 11½
Granite Paper
912	A265	600 l	multicolored	1.10 .95
913	A265	700 l	multicolored	1.25 1.10
914	A265	1000 l	multicolored	1.50 1.40
915	A265	1500 l	multicolored	3.00 2.75
	Nos. 912-915 (4)			6.85 6.20

St. Francis Healing Man from Ilerda, by Giotto di Bondone (1266-1337) — A266

1993, Jan. 9   Litho.   Perf. 13½x14
916	A266	1000 l	multi + label	2.10 1.75

Prayer Meeting for Peace in Europe, Assisi.

Architecture of Vatican City and Rome — A267

Buildings: 200 l, St. Peter's Basilica, Vatican City. 300 l, St. John Lateran Basilica, Rome. 350 l, St. Mary Major's Basilica, Rome. 500 l, St. Paul's Basilica, Rome. 600 l, Apostolic Palace, Vatican. 700 l, Lateran Apostolic Palace, Rome. 850 l, Papal Palace, Castel Gandolfo.

1000 l, Chancery Palace, Rome. 2000 l, Palace of the Propagation of the Faith, Rome. 3000 l, St. Calixtus Palace, Rome.

1993, Mar. 23   Photo.   Perf. 12x11½
Granite Paper
917	A267	200 l	multicolored	.25 .25
a.	Booklet pane of 4			1.10
918	A267	300 l	multicolored	.40 .40
a.	Booklet pane of 4			1.60
919	A267	350 l	multicolored	.50 .50
a.	Booklet pane of 4			2.00
920	A267	500 l	multicolored	.65 .65
a.	Booklet pane of 4			2.75
	Complete booklet, #917a, 918a, 919a, 920a			7.50
921	A267	600 l	multicolored	.80 .80
922	A267	700 l	multicolored	.95 .95
923	A267	850 l	multicolored	1.00 1.00
924	A267	1000 l	multicolored	1.25 1.25
925	A267	2000 l	multicolored	2.60 2.60
926	A267	3000 l	multicolored	3.75 3.75
	Nos. 917-926 (10)			12.15 12.15

A268

Congress emblem, Vatican arms and: 500 l, Cross, grape vines. 700 l, Cross, hands breaking bread. 1500 l, Hands lifting chalice. 2500 l, Wheat, banner.

1993, May 22   Litho.   Perf. 14x13½
927	A268	500 l	multicolored	.60 .60
928	A268	700 l	multicolored	.90 .90
929	A268	1500 l	multicolored	1.90 1.90
930	A268	2500 l	multicolored	3.00 3.00
	Nos. 927-930 (4)			6.40 6.40

45th Intl. Eucharistic Congress, Seville.

A269

Traditio Legis Sarcophagus, St. Peter's Basilica: a, 200 l, Sacrifice of Isaac. b, 750 l, Apostle Peter receiving law from Jesus, Apostle Paul. c, 3000 l, Christ watching servant pouring water on Pilate's hands.

1993, May 22   Engr.   Perf. 13½x14
931	A209	Triptych, #a.-c.		5.25 5.25

Ascension Day, May 20.

Contemporary Art — A270

Europa: 750 l, Crucifixion, by Felice Casorati (1886-1963). 850 l, Rouen Cathedral, by Maurice Utrillo (1883-1955).

1993, Sept. 29   Photo.   Perf. 13
932	A270	750 l	multicolored	.95 .95
933	A270	850 l	multicolored	1.00 1.00

Death of St. John of Nepomuk, 600th Anniv. — A271

2000 l, Buildings in Prague, Charles Bridge.

1993, Sept. 29   Litho.   Perf. 13½x14
934	A271	1000 l	multicolored	1.40 1.25
935	A271	2000 l	multicolored	2.75 2.50

Travels of Pope John Paul II — A272

Visits to: 600 l, Senegal, Gambia, Guinea. 1000 l, Angola, St. Thomas and Prince. 5000 l, Dominican Republic.

1993, Nov. 23   Photo.   Perf. 12x11½
Granite Paper
936	A272	600 l	multicolored	.75 .75
937	A272	1000 l	multicolored	1.50 1.50
938	A272	5000 l	multicolored	7.00 7.00
	Nos. 936-938 (3)			9.25 9.25

Hans Holbein the Younger (1497?-1543), Painter — A273

Details or entire paintings: 700 l, 1000 l, Madonna of Solothurn. 1500 l, Self-portrait.

Litho. & Engr.
1993, Nov. 23   Perf. 13½x14
939	A273	700 l	multicolored	.90 .90
940	A273	1000 l	multicolored	1.50 1.50
941	A273	1500 l	multicolored	2.25 2.25
	Nos. 939-941 (3)			4.65 4.65

Synod of Bishops, Special Assembly for Africa A274

Designs: 850 l, Stylized crosier, dome with cross, vert. 1000 l, Crucifix, dome of St. Peter's Basilica, crosiers, African landscape.

Perf. 12½x13, 13x12½
1994, Apr. 8   Photo.
942	A274	850 l	multicolored	1.25 1.25
943	A274	1000 l	multicolored	1.50 1.50

The Restored Sistine Chapel — A275

Frescoes, by Michelangelo: Creation of the Sun and Moon: No. 944, Sun. No. 945, God pointing toward moon. Creation of Man: No. 946, Adam, No. 947, God. Original Sin: No. 948, Adam, Eve taking apple from serpent. No. 949, Adam, Eve forced from Garden of Eden. The Flood: No. 950, People on dry ground. No. 951, People on stone outcropping.

4000 l, Detail of Last Judgment, Christ and the Virgin.

1994, Apr. 8   Photo.   Perf. 11½
944	A275	350 l	multicolored	.40 .40
945	A275	350 l	multicolored	.40 .40
a.	A275 Pair, #944-945			1.00 1.00
946	A275	500 l	multicolored	.60 .60
947	A275	500 l	multicolored	.60 .60
a.	A275 Pair, #946-947			1.50 1.50
948	A275	1000 l	multicolored	1.50 1.50
949	A275	1000 l	multicolored	1.50 1.50
a.	A275 Pair, #948-949			2.50 2.50
950	A275	2000 l	multicolored	4.00 4.00
951	A275	2000 l	multicolored	3.00 3.00
a.	A275 Pair, 950-951			8.00 8.00
	Nos. 944-951 (8)			12.00 12.00

Souvenir Sheet
Perf. 12
952	A275	4000 l	multicolored	6.25 6.25

No. 952 contains one 36x54mm stamp.

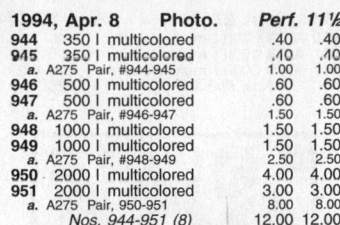

European Inventions, Discoveries — A276

Europa: 750 l, Progess from wheel to atom traced by white thread. 850 l, Galileo in center of solar system, scientific instruments.

1994, May 31   Litho.   Perf. 13x13½
953	A276	750 l	multicolored	.95 .95
954	A276	850 l	multicolored	1.10 1.10

Intl. Year of the Family — A277

Stained glass: 400 l, God creating man and woman. 750 l, Family under names of four Evangelists. 1000 l, Parents teaching son. 2000 l, Young man comforting elderly couple.

1994, May 31   Photo.   Perf. 13x14
955	A277	400 l	multicolored	.50 .50
956	A277	750 l	multicolored	.95 .95
957	A277	1000 l	multicolored	1.40 1.40
958	A277	2000 l	multicolored	2.50 2.50
	Nos. 955-958 (4)			5.35 5.35

Giovanni da Montecorvino (1247-1328), Missionary — A278

1994, Sept. 27   Litho.   Perf. 14
959	A278	1000 l	multicolored	1.75 1.75

Evangelization of China, 700th anniv.

13th Intl. Convention of Christian Archaeology, Split, Croatia — A279

Mosaics from Euphrasian Basilica, Parentium, Croatia, 6th Cent.: 700 l, Bishop Euphrasius, Archdeacon Claudius, Claudius' son. 1500 l, Madonna and Child, two angels. 3000 l, Christ, Apostles Peter & Paul.

1994, Sept. 27   **Perf. 13x14**
960 A279   700 l multicolored   1.00   1.00
961 A279   1500 l multicolored   2.00   2.00
962 A279   3000 l multicolored   4.25   4.25
    Nos. 960-962 (3)   7.25   7.25

Travels of Pope John Paul II — A280

Designs: 600 l, Benin, Uganda, Sudan. 700 l, Albania. 1000 l, Spain. 2000 l, Jamaica, Mexico, US. 3000 l, Lithuania, Latvia, Estonia.

1994, Nov. 18   **Engr.**   **Perf. 13**
963 A280   600 l multicolored   .85   .85
964 A280   700 l multicolored   1.00   1.00
965 A280   1000 l multicolored   1.40   1.40
966 A280   2000 l multicolored   2.75   2.75
967 A280   3000 l multicolored   4.25   4.25
    Nos. 963-967 (5)   10.25   10.25

Christmas
A281

The Nativity, by Il Tintoretto: 700 l, The Holy Family. No. 969, The Holy Family, two women. No. 970, Adoration of the shepherds.

1994, Nov. 18   **Photo.**   **Perf. 11½**
    Granite Paper
968 A281   700 l multicolored   1.00   1.00
    Size: 45x27mm
969 A281   1000 l multicolored   1.40   1.40
970 A281   1000 l multicolored   1.40   1.40
    a.   Pair, #969-970   3.00   3.00
    Nos. 968-970 (3)   3.80   3.80

Peace and Freedom
A282

1995, Mar. 25   **Photo.**   **Perf. 14x13**
971 A282   750 l shown   .90   .90
972 A282   850 l Hands clasp, dove   1.00   1.00
    Europa.

Shrine of Loreto, 700th Anniv. — A283

Details of artworks from vaults of Sacristy: 600 l, St. Mark's, Angel with chalice, by Melozzo da Forli. 700 l, St. Mark's, Angel with lamb, by da Forli. 1500 l, 2500 l, St. John's, Music making angels, by Luca Signorelli.
    No. 977, Marble carving showing Holy House of Loreto.

1995, Mar. 25   **Perf. 11½**
973 A283   600 l multicolored   .75   .75
974 A283   700 l multicolored   .85   .85
975 A283   1500 l multicolored   2.00   2.00
976 A283   2500 l multicolored   4.00   4.00
    Nos. 973-976 (4)   7.60   7.60
    Souvenir Sheet
977 A283   3000 l multicolored   3.75   3.75
    No. 977 contains one 36x36mm stamp.

Radio, Cent. A284

Designs: 850 l, Guglielmo Marconi, transmitting equipment. 1000 l, Archangel Gabriel, Pope John Paul II, Marconi broadcasting station, Vatican City.

1995, June 8   **Photo.**   **Perf. 14**
978 A284   850 l multicolored   1.25   1.25
979 A284   1000 l multicolored   1.75   1.75
    See Germany No. 1990, Ireland Nos. 973-974, Italy Nos. 2038-2039, San Marino Nos. 1336-1337.

A285

European Nature Conservation Year (Scenes in Vatican Gardens & Castel Gandolfo: 200 l, Fountain of the Triton, arches of rhyncospernum jasminoides. 300 l, Avenue of roses, Palazzo Barberini. 400 l, Statue of Apollo Citaredo. 550 l, Ruins of Domitian's Villa, Avenue of roses. 750 l, Acer negundo, Viale dell'Osservatorio. 1500 l, Belvedere garden. 2000 l, Fountain of the Eagle, Quercus ilex. 3000 l, Avenue of cypresses, equestrian statue.

1995, June 8   **Perf. 12**
    Granite Paper
980 A285   200 l multicolored   .25   .25
981 A285   300 l multicolored   .35   .35
    a.   Booklet pane of 3   1.00
982 A285   400 l multicolored   .50   .50
    a.   Booklet pane of 3   1.50
983 A285   550 l multicolored   .70   .70
    a.   Booklet pane of 3   2.25
984 A285   750 l multicolored   .90   .90
    a.   Booklet pane of 3   2.75
     Complete booklet, #981a, 982a, 983a, 984a   7.50
985 A285   1500 l multicolored   1.90   1.90
986 A285   2000 l multicolored   2.50   2.50
987 A285   3000 l multicolored   3.75   3.75
    Nos. 980-987 (8)   10.85   10.85

A286

Paintings of peace, by Paolo Guiotto: 550 l, Small hearts flying from large heart. 750 l, Stylized faces. 850 l, Doves in flight. 1250 l, Lymph reaching to smallest branches. 2000 l, Explosion of colors, people.

1995, Oct. 3   **Photo.**   **Perf. 13½x13**
988 A286   550 l multicolored   .65   .65
989 A286   750 l multicolored   .85   .85
990 A286   850 l multicolored   1.00   1.00
991 A286   1250 l multicolored   1.40   1.40
992 A286   2000 l multicolored   2.25   2.25
    Nos. 988-992 (5)   6.15   6.15
    UN, 50th anniv.

A287

St. Anthony of Padua (1195-1231): 750 l, St. John of God (1495-1550). 3000 l, St. Philip Neri (1515-95).

    Litho. & Engr.
1995, Oct. 3   **Perf. 13½x14**
993 A287   500 l green & brown   .65   .65
994 A287   750 l violet & green   .95   .95
995 A287   3000 l magenta & black   3.75   3.75
    Nos. 993-995 (3)   5.35   5.35

A288

Scenes depicting life of Jesus Christ from illuminated manuscripts: 400 l, The Annunciation. 850 l, Nativity. 1250 l, Flight into Egypt. 2000 l, Jesus among the teachers.

1995, Nov. 20   **Photo.**   **Perf. 12x11½**
    Granite Paper
996 A288   400 l multicolored   .50   .50
997 A288   850 l multicolored   1.10   1.10
998 A288   1250 l multicolored   1.60   1.60
999 A288   2000 l multicolored   2.50   2.50
    Nos. 996-999 (4)   5.70   5.70
    Towards the Holy Year 2000.

Travels of Pope John Paul II
A289

Designs: 1000 l, Giving greeting in Croatia, statue of Blessed Lady, Zagreb Cathedral. 2000 l, In Italy, lighthouse in Genoa, Orvieto Cathedral, Valley of Temples in Agrigento.

1995, Nov. 20   **Litho.**   **Perf. 14½x14**
1000 A289   1000 l multicolored   1.50   1.50
1001 A289   2000 l multicolored   3.00   3.00

Religious Anniversaries
A290

Designs: 1250 l, Angel holding crosses, Union of Brest-Litovsk, 400th anniv. 2000 l, Cross with branches, Latin episcopal mitre, Byzantine mitre, Union of Uzhorod, 350th anniv.

1996, Mar. 16   **Photo.**   **Perf. 13½x14**
1002 A290   1250 l multicolored   1.60   1.60
1003 A290   2000 l multicolored   2.50   2.50

A291

Marco Polo's Return from China, 700th Anniv. — A292

Designs from miniatures, Bodleian Library, Oxford: 350 l, Marco Polo delivering Pope Gregory X's letter to Great Khan. 850 l, Great Khan dispensing alms to poor in Cambaluc. 1250 l, Marco Polo receiving golden book from Great Khan. 2500 l, Marco Polo in Persia listening to story of three Kings who go to Bethlehem to adore Jesus.
    2000 l, Stylized portrait of Marco Polo drawn from first printed edition of "Il Milione."

1996, Mar. 15   **Perf. 11½**
    Granite Paper
1004 A291   350 l multicolored   .45   .45
1005 A291   850 l multicolored   1.10   1.10
1006 A291   1250 l multicolored   1.60   1.60
1007 A291   2500 l multicolored   3.25   3.25
    Nos. 1004-1007 (4)   6.40   6.40
    Souvenir Sheet
    Perf. 12x11½
1008 A292   2000 l black   2.50   2.50

A293

Famous Women: 750 l, Gianna Baretta Molla (1922-62), physician. 850 l, Sister Edith Stein (1891-1942).

1996, May 7   **Engr.**   **Perf. 13x14**
1009 A293   750 l blue   1.25   1.25
1010 A293   850 l brown   1.50   1.50

A294

Modern Olympic Games, Cent.: a, Statue of athlete. b, Athlete's torso. c, Hand. d, Statue of athlete reaching upward. e, Hercules.

1996, May 7   **Photo.**   **Perf. 13**
1011   Strip of 5   10.00   10.00
    a.-e.   A294 1250 l any single   1.40   1.40

Ordination of Pope John Paul II, 50th Anniv. A295

Designs: 500 l, Wawel Cathedral, Krakow. 750 l, Pope John Paul II giving blessing. 1250 l, Basilica of St. John Lateran, Rome.

1996, Oct. 12   **Litho.**   **Perf. 14**
1012 A295   500 l multicolored   .65   .65
1013 A295   750 l multicolored   1.00   1.00
1014 A295   1250 l multicolored   2.00   2.00
    Nos. 1012-1014 (3)   3.65   3.65

Life of Jesus Christ from Illuminated Manuscripts A296

Designs: 550 l, Baptism of Jesus at River Jordan. 850 l, Temptation in the desert. 1500 l, Cure of the leper. 2500 l, Jesus the teacher.

1996, Oct. 12   Photo.   Perf. 12x11½
1015	A296	550 l multicolored	.75	.75
1016	A296	850 l multicolored	1.50	1.25
1017	A296	1500 l multicolored	3.00	2.50
1018	A296	2500 l multicolored	5.00	3.50
		Nos. 1015-1018 (4)	10.25	8.00

Christmas — A297

Nativity, by Murillo (1618-82).

1996, Nov. 20   Litho.   Perf. 13½
1019	A297	750 l multicolored	2.00	1.50

St. Celestine V (1215-96) A298

No. 1021, St. Alfonso Maria De'Liguori (1696-1787).

1996, Nov. 20   Perf. 13½x14
1020	A298	1250 l multicolored	1.60	1.60
1021	A298	1250 l multicolored	1.60	1.60

Travels of Pope John Paul II, 1995 A299

Designs: 250 l, Jan. 11-21, Philippines, Papua New Guinea, Australia, Sri Lanka. 500 l, May 20-22, Czech Republic, Poland. 750 l, June 3-4, Belgium. 1000 l, June 30-July 3, Slovakia. 2000 l, Sept. 14-20, Cameroun, South Africa, Kenya. 5000 l, Oct. 4-9, UN headquarters, NY, US.

1996, Nov. 20   Perf. 14x13½
1022	A299	250 l blue & multi	.35	.35
1023	A299	500 l blue green & multi	.65	.65
1024	A299	750 l green & multi	1.00	1.00
1025	A299	1000 l brown & multi	1.25	1.25
1026	A299	2000 l gray & multi	2.50	2.50
1027	A299	5000 l pink & multi	6.75	6.75
		Nos. 1022-1027 (6)	12.50	12.50

Papal Carriages and Automobiles A300

Designs: 50 l, Touring carriage. 100 l, Graham Paige. 300 l, Festive traveling carriage. 500 l, Citroen Lictoria VI. 750 l, Grand touring carriage. 850 l, Mercedes Benz. 1000 l, Festive half carriage. 1250 l, Mercedes Benz 300SEL. 2000 l, Touring carriage, diff. 4000 l, Fiat "Pope mobile."

1997, Mar. 20   Photo.   Perf. 12
Granite Paper
1028	A300	50 l multicolored	.25	.25
1029	A300	100 l multicolored	.25	.25
a.		Booklet pane of 4	.75	
1030	A300	300 l multicolored	.35	.35
a.		Booklet pane of 4	1.40	
1031	A300	500 l multicolored	.60	.60
a.		Booklet pane of 4	2.50	
1032	A300	750 l multicolored	.90	.90
a.		Booklet pane of 4	3.75	
		Complete booklet, #1029a, 1030a, 1031a, 1032a	8.50	
1033	A300	850 l multicolored	1.00	1.00
1034	A300	1000 l multicolored	1.25	1.25
1035	A300	1250 l multicolored	1.75	1.75
1036	A300	2000 l multicolored	2.50	2.50
1037	A300	4000 l multicolored	5.00	5.00
		Nos. 1028-1037 (10)	13.85	13.85

A301

Swiss Guard: 750 l, Guard in traditional attire. 850 l, Guard in armor with sword in front of iron gate.

1997, Mar. 20   Litho.   Perf. 13½
1038	A301	750 l multicolored	.90	.90
1039	A301	850 l multicolored	1.00	1.00
a.		Strip of 2 + 2 labels	1.90	1.90

Europa.

A302

1997, Apr. 23   Engr.   Perf. 14
1040	A302	850 l deep violet	1.60	1.60

St. Adalbert (956-997). See Germany No. 1964, Poland No. 3337, Czech Republic No. 3012, Hungary No. 3560.

"Looking at the Classics," Museum Exhibition — A304

Pictures from texts of Latin and Greek classics: 500 l, Aristotle observing and describing various species from man to insect, from his "De Historia Animalium." 750 l, Bacchus riding dragon, from "Metamorphoses" by Ovid. 1250 l, General haranguing his soldiers, from "Iliad" by Homer. 2000 l, Hannibal leaving Canne, two horsemen, foot soldier, from "Ab Urbe Condita" by Titus Livius.

Masks from "Comedies," by Terence: No. 1045: a, Man, woman. b, Two women. c, Two men.

1997, Apr. 23   Photo.   Perf. 14
1041	A303	500 l multicolored	.60	.60
1042	A303	750 l multicolored	.90	.90
1043	A303	1250 l multicolored	1.50	1.50
1044	A303	2000 l multicolored	2.40	2.40
		Nos. 1041-1044 (4)	5.40	5.40

Perf. 13½
1045	A304	1000 l Sheet of 3, #a.-c.	4.00	4.00

A305

46th Intl. Eucharistic Congress, Wroclaw, Poland: 650 l, Elements of the Eucharist, chalice, consecrated Host, arms of Wroclaw. 1000 l, The Last Supper, fish, Congress emblem. 1250 l, Wroclaw Cathedral, sheaf of wheat, holy spirit descending on church. 2500 l "IHS" symbol of Christ on cross, doves, world with two hands on it.

1997, May 27   Photo.   Perf. 13
1046	A305	650 l multicolored	.75	.70
1047	A305	1000 l multicolored	1.25	1.10
1048	A305	1250 l multicolored	1.50	1.40
1049	A305	2500 l multicolored	3.25	2.75
		Nos. 1046-1049 (4)	6.75	5.95

A306

1997, Sept. 15   Litho.   Perf. 13x14
1050	A306	900 l multicolored	.90	.70

Pope Paul VI (1897-1978).
No. 1050 was printed se-tenant with 4 labels. Value $2.00.

St. Ambrose (d. 397) — A307

1997, Sept. 15   Photo.   Perf. 13x14
1051	A307	800 l multicolored	1.50	1.25

Towards the Holy Year 2000 — A308

Illustrations of Christ's miracles: 400 l, Healing of paralyzed man. 800 l, Calming of the tempest. 1300 l, Multiplication of bread and fish. 3600 l, Peter's confession and conferment of primacy.

1997, Sept. 15   Perf. 12
Granite Paper
1052	A308	400 l multicolored	.60	.50
1053	A308	800 l multicolored	1.25	1.00
1054	A308	1300 l multicolored	2.50	2.00
1055	A308	3600 l multicolored	7.00	6.00
		Nos. 1052-1055 (4)	11.35	9.50

1996 Travels of Pope John Paul II — A309

Designs: 400 l, Central & South America, Feb. 5-12. 900 l, Tunisia, Apr. 14. 1000 l, Slovenia , May 17-19. 1300 l, Germany, June 21-23. 2000 l, Hungary, Sept. 6-7. 4000 l, France, Sept. 19-22.

1997, Nov. 11   Litho.   Perf. 14x13½
1056	A309	400 l multicolored	.50	.50
1057	A309	900 l multicolored	1.00	1.00
1058	A309	1000 l multicolored	1.50	1.50
1059	A309	1300 l multicolored	2.00	2.00
1060	A309	2000 l multicolored	3.00	3.00
1061	A309	4000 l multicolored	6.00	6.00
		Nos. 1056-1061 (6)	14.00	14.00

Christmas — A310

Detail from "The Nativity," by Benozzo Gozzoli (1420-97).

1997, Nov. 11   Photo.   Perf. 14
1062	A310	800 l multicolored	1.60	1.40

Feasts of Sts. Peter and Paul, June 29th — A311

1998, Mar. 24   Photo.   Perf. 13
1063	A311	800 l St. Peter	.90	.90
1064	A311	900 l St. Paul	1.00	1.00

Europa.

The Popes of the Holy Years 1300-1525 A312

Designs: 200 l, Boniface VIII, 1300. 400 l, Clement VI, 1350. 500 l, Boniface IX, 1390, 1400. 700 l, Martin V, 1423. 800 l, Nicholas V, 1450. 900 l, Sixtus IV, 1475. 1300 l, Alexander VI, 1500. 3000 l, Clement VII, 1525.

1998, Mar. 24   Litho.   Perf. 14
1065	A312	200 l multicolored	.30	.30
1066	A312	400 l multicolored	.50	.50
1067	A312	500 l multicolored	.65	.65
1068	A312	700 l multicolored	.85	.85
1069	A312	800 l multicolored	1.00	1.00
1070	A312	900 l multicolored	1.25	1.25
1071	A312	1300 l multicolored	1.75	1.75
1072	A312	3000 l multicolored	3.75	3.75
		Nos. 1065-1072 (8)	10.05	10.05

Nos. 1065-1072 were each printed se-tenant with a label picturing the respective papal arms.

See Nos. 1095-1102, 1141-1150.

Face on
Shroud — A313

2500 l, Cathedral of Turin.

Litho. & Engr.

1998, May 19			**Perf. 13½x14**	
1073	A313	900 l multicolored	1.00	1.00
1074	A313	2500 l multicolored	3.00	3.00

Exposition of the Shroud of Turin.

A314

Frescoes of Angels, by Melozzo da Forli (1438-94), Basilica of Sts. Apostles, Rome: Angels playing various musical instruments.

1998, May 19		**Photo.**	**Perf. 12**	
		Granite Paper		
1075	A314	450 l multicolored	.65	.65
1076	A314	650 l multicolored	.80	.80
1077	A314	800 l multicolored	1.00	1.00
1078	A314	1000 l multicolored	1.25	1.25
1079	A314	1300 l multicolored	2.00	2.00
1080	A314	2000 l multicolored	2.75	2.75
		Nos. 1075-1080 (6)	8.45	8.45

Towards
Holy Year
2000
A315

Episodes from the Life of Christ: 500 l, Triumphal entry into Jerusalem. 800 l, Washing of the feet. 1300 l, The Last Supper. 3000 l, Crucifixion.

1998, May 19			**Perf. 12**	
		Granite Paper		
1081	A315	500 l multicolored	.60	.60
1082	A315	800 l multicolored	.90	.90
1083	A315	1300 l multicolored	1.75	1.75
1084	A315	3000 l multicolored	3.50	3.50
		Nos. 1081-1084 (4)	6.75	6.75

Italia
'98
A316

1998, Oct. 23		**Photo.**	**Perf. 14**	
1085	A316	800 l Pope John Paul II	1.40	1.40

See Italy No. 2259 and San Marino No. 1430.

The Good
Shepherd — A317

1998, Oct. 25			**Perf. 12 Vert.**	
		Granite Paper		
		Booklet Stamp		
1086	A317	900 l multicolored	1.30	1.30
a.		Booklet pane of 5	6.50	
		Complete booklet, #1086a	6.50	

Italia '98.

Christian
Sculptures
A318

Designs: a, 600 l, Peter's denial. b, 900 l, Praying woman. c, 1000 l, Christ and the Cyrenean. 2000 l, Christ with the Cross and Two Apostles.

Granite Paper

1998, Oct. 25			**Perf. 12**	
1087	A318	Sheet of 4, #a.-d.	6.50	6.50

Italia '98. Margin is embossed.

Christmas — A319

1998, Dec. 1		**Litho.**	**Perf. 14x13½**	
1088	A319	800 l multicolored	1.10	1.00

See Croatia No. 381.

1997 Travels of
Pope John Paul
II — A320

Designs: 300 l, Sarajevo, 4/12-13/97. 600 l, Prague, 4/25-27/97. 800 l, Beirut, 5/10-11/97. 900 l, Poland, 5/21-6/10/97. 1300 l, Paris, 8/21-24/97. 5000 l, Rio de Janeiro, 10/2-6/97.

1998, Dec. 1			**Perf. 12½**	
1089	A320	300 l brown	.40	.40
1090	A320	600 l green	.75	.75
1091	A320	800 l brown	1.25	1.25
1092	A320	900 l violet blue	1.50	1.50
1093	A320	1300 l org brn	1.75	1.75
1094	A320	5000 l org brn	6.50	6.50
		Nos. 1089-1094 (6)	12.15	12.15

Popes of the Holy Years Type of 1998

Popes: 300 l, Julius III, 1550. 600 l, Gregory XIII, 1575. 800 l, Clement VIII, 1600. 900 l, Urban VIII, 1625. 1000 l, Innocent X, 1650. 1300 l, Clement X, 1675. 1500 l, Innocent XII, 1700. 2000 l, Benedict XIII, 1725.

1999, Mar. 23		**Litho.**	**Perf. 14**	
1095	A312	300 l multicolored	.55	.55
1096	A312	600 l multicolored	1.00	1.00
1097	A312	800 l multicolored	1.75	1.75
1098	A312	900 l multicolored	2.00	2.00
1099	A312	1000 l multicolored	2.25	2.25
1100	A312	1300 l multicolored	2.50	2.50
1101	A312	1500 l multicolored	3.00	3.00
1102	A312	2000 l multicolored	4.00	4.00
		Nos. 1095-1102 (8)	17.05	17.05

Nos. 1095-1102 were each printed se-tenant with a label picturing the respective papal arms.

Flowers from
Vatican Gardens
and Papal Villa,
Castelgandolfo
A321

Europa: 800 l, John Paul II Rose. 900 l, Water lilies.

1999, Mar. 23		**Litho.**	**Perf. 12½x13**	
1103	A321	800 l multicolored	1.00	1.00
1104	A321	900 l multicolored	1.25	1.25
a.		Pair, #1103-1104 + label	3.50	3.50

Padre Pio de Pietrelcina (1887-1968) — A322

#1106: a, 1st church, San Giovanni Rotondo. b, New church, San Giovanni Rotondo. c, Like #1105.

1999, Apr. 27		**Litho.**	**Perf. 14x13**	
1105	A322	800 l multicolored	1.25	1.25
		Souvenir Sheet		
		Perf. 13x13½		
1106	A322	Sheet of 3	2.10	2.10
a.		300 l multi, vert.	.35	.35
b.		600 l multi, vert.	.70	.70
c.		900 l multi	1.00	1.00

Nos. 1106a-1106b are 30x40mm, No. 1106c is 60x40mm.

A323

Holy Places in Palestine — A324

Nos. 1107-1111: 19th cent. watercolors, Pontifical Lateran University Library.

Map of Holy Land from "Geographia Blaviana," 17th cent — #1112: a, Mediterranean Sea, denomination, LL. b, Mediterranean Sea, denomination LR. c, Red Sea, Holy Land. d, Inscription identifying map.

1999, May 25		**Photo.**	**Perf. 11½**	
		Granite Paper		
1107	A323	200 l Bethlehem	.25	.25
1108	A323	500 l Nazareth	.55	.55
1109	A323	800 l Lake of Tiberias	.85	.85
1110	A323	900 l Jerusalem	1.25	1.25
1111	A323	1300 l Mount Tabor	1.60	1.60
		Nos. 1107-1111 (5)	4.50	4.50
		Perf. 12x11¾		
1112	A324	1000 l Sheet of 4, #a.-d.	11.00	11.00

Towards
Holy Year
2000
A325

Events from life of Christ: 400 l, Deposition from the Cross. 700 l, Resurrection. 1300 l, Pentecost. 3000 l, Last Judgement.

1999, May 25			**Perf. 12x11¾**	
		Granite Paper		
1113	A325	400 l multicolored	.45	.45
1114	A325	700 l multicolored	.75	.75
1115	A325	1300 l multicolored	1.40	1.40
1116	A325	3000 l multicolored	3.25	3.25
		Nos. 1113-1116 (4)	5.85	5.85

Kosovo 1999 — A326

1999, May 25			**Perf. 12¼**	
		Granite Paper		
1117	A326	3600 l black	4.75	4.75

Proceeds from sale of stamp benefits victims of the fighting in Kosovo.

1998 Travels of
Pope John Paul
II — A327

600 l, Cuba, June 21-26. 800 l, Nigeria, Mar. 21-23. 900 l, Austria, June 19-21. 1300 l, Croatia, Oct. 2-4. 2000 l, Italy, Oct. 20.

1999, Oct. 12		**Litho.**	**Perf. 14x13½**	
1118	A327	600 l multicolored	1.00	1.00
1119	A327	800 l multicolored	1.10	1.10
1120	A327	900 l multicolored	1.25	1.25
1121	A327	1300 l multicolored	2.00	2.00
1122	A327	2000 l multicolored	3.00	3.00
		Nos. 1118-1122 (5)	8.35	8.35

Council of
Europe, 50th
Anniv. — A328

1999, Oct. 12		**Photo.**	**Perf. 11¾**	
		Granite Paper		
1123	A328	1200 l multicolored	1.50	1.50

Christmas
A329

The Birth of Christ, by Giovanni di Pietro: 500 l, Joseph (detail). 800 l, Christ (detail). 900 l, Mary (detail). 1200 l, Entire painting.

		Perf. 13¼x12½		
1999, Nov. 24			**Litho.**	
1124	A329	500 l multi	.75	.75
1125	A329	800 l multi	1.25	1.25
1126	A329	900 l multi	1.50	1.50
1127	A329	1200 l multi	1.75	1.75
		Nos. 1124-1127 (4)	5.25	5.25

Opening of the Holy Door for Holy Year 2000 A330

Various panels of Holy Door. Stamps on No. 1136 lack white border.

1999, Nov. 24   Photo.   Perf. 11¾x12
Granite Paper

1128	A330	200 l multi	.30	.30
1129	A330	300 l multi	.35	.35
1130	A330	400 l multi	.45	.45
1131	A330	500 l multi	.60	.60
1132	A330	600 l multi	.70	.70
1133	A330	800 l multi	.90	.90
1134	A330	1000 l multi	1.50	1.50
1135	A330	1200 l multi	2.25	2.25
	Nos. 1128-1135 (8)		7.05	7.05

Souvenir Sheet

1136		Sheet of 8, #a.-h.	10.00	10.00
a.	A330	200 l Like #1128	.30	.30
b.	A330	300 l Like #1129	.40	.40
c.	A330	400 l Like #1130	.50	.50
d.	A330	500 l Like #1131	.60	.60
e.	A330	600 l Like #1132	.70	.70
f.	A330	800 l Like #1133	1.00	1.00
g.	A330	1000 l Like #1134	1.25	1.25
h.	A330	1200 l Like #1135	1.50	1.50

Holy Year 2000 — A331

Designs: 800 l, St. Peter's Basilica. 1000 l, Basilica of St. John Lateran. 1200 l, Basilica of St. Mary Major. 2000 l, Basilica of St. Paul.

2000, Feb. 4   Photo.   Perf. 11¾
Granite Paper

1137	A331	800 l multi	1.00	.80
1138	A331	1000 l multi	1.40	1.25
1139	A331	1200 l multi	1.75	1.40
1140	A331	2000 l multi	2.50	2.25
	Nos. 1137-1140 (4)		6.65	5.70

Popes of the Holy Year Type of 1998

Designs: 300 l, Benedict XIV, 1750. 400 l, Pius VI, 1775. 500 l, Leo XII, 1825. 600 l, Pius IX, 1875. 700 l, Leo XIII, 1900. 800 l, Pius XI, 1925. 1200 l, Pius XII, 1950. 1500 l, Paul VI, 1975. No. 1149, John Paul II with miter, 2000. No. 1150, John Paul II with hand on chin, 2000.

2000, Feb. 4   Litho.   Perf 13¾

1141	A312	300 l multi + label	.50	.50
1142	A312	400 l multi + label	.75	.75
1143	A312	500 l multi + label	1.00	1.00
1144	A312	600 l multi + label	1.25	1.25
1145	A312	700 l multi + label	1.50	1.50
1146	A312	800 l multi + label	1.75	1.75
1147	A312	1200 l multi + label	2.25	2.25
1148	A312	1500 l multi + label	2.50	2.50
1149	A312	2000 l multi + label	5.50	5.50
	Nos. 1141-1149 (9)		17.00	17.00

Souvenir Sheet

1150	A312	2000 l multi	2.00	2.00

No. 1150 contains one label.

Christianity in Iceland, 1000th Anniv. A332

2000, Feb. 4   Perf. 13¼x13¾

1151	A332	1500 l multi	2.10	2.10

See Iceland Nos. 900-901.

Europa, 2000
Common Design Type

2000, May 9   Litho.   Perf. 13¼x13

1152	CD17	1200 l multi	1.25	1.25

Printed in sheets of 10, with left and right side selvage of Priority Mail etiquettes.

Pope John Paul II, 80th Birthday — A333

800 l, Pope. 1200 l, Black Madonna of Jasna Gora. 2000 l, Pope's silver cross.

2000, May 9   Engr.   Perf. 13x12¾

1153	A333	800 l purple	1.00	1.00
1154	A333	1200 l dark blue	1.75	1.50
1155	A333	2000 l green	3.00	2.50
	Nos. 1153-1155 (3)		5.75	5.00

See Poland Nos. 3520-3522.

Restored Sistine Chapel Frescoes — A334

Designs: 500 l, The Calling of St. Peter and St. Andrew, by Domenico Ghirlandaio. 1000 l, The Trials of Moses, by Sandro Botticelli. 1500 l, The Donation of the Keys, by Pietro Perugino. 3000 l, The Worship of the Golden Calf, by Cosimo Rosselli.

Perf. 11½x11¾
2000, May 9   Photo.   Blue Frame
Granite Paper

1156	A334	500 l multi	1.00	.75
1157	A334	1000 l multi	1.50	1.25
1158	A334	1500 l multi	2.25	2.00
1159	A334	3000 l multi	5.00	3.50
	Nos. 1156-1159 (4)		9.75	7.50

See Nos. 1172-1175, 1215-1218.

20th World Youth Day — A335

Various photos of Pope John Paul II and youth.

Perf. 13¾x13¼
2000, June 19   Litho.
Color of Cross

1160	A335	800 l red	1.00	1.00
1161	A335	1000 l green	1.25	1.10
1162	A335	1200 l violet	1.50	1.25
1163	A335	1500 l orange	2.25	1.75

Booklet Stamp
Self-Adhesive
Serpentine Die Cut 12

1164	A335	1000 l green	1.25	1.25
a.		Booklet of 4 + 4 labels	6.00	
	Nos. 1160-1164 (5)		7.25	6.35

47th Intl. Eucharistic Congress A336

2000, June 19   Perf. 13x12½

1165	A336	1200 l multi	1.50	1.50

Beatification of Pope John XXIII — A337

2000, Sept. 1   Photo.   Perf. 13¼x14

1166	A337	1200 l multi	1.60	1.60

1999 Travels of Pope John Paul II — A338

#1167: a, Mexico, 1/22-28. b, Romania, 5/7-9. c, Poland, 6/17. d, Slovenia, 9/19. e, India and Georgia, 11/5-9.

2000, Sept. 1   Perf. 11¾
Granite Paper

1167		Horiz. strip of 5	7.00	7.00
a.-e.	A338	1000 l Any single	1.00	1.00

Christmas A339

Frescoes in Basilica of St. Francis, Assisi, by Giotto: 800 l, Nativity. 1200 l, Infant Jesus. 1500 l, Mary. 2000 l, Joseph.

2000, Nov. 7   Photo.   Perf. 11¾x11½
Granite Paper

1168-1171	A339	Set of 4	9.00	7.00

Sistine Chapel Restoration Type of 2000

Paintings: 800 l, The Baptism of Christ, by Pietro Perugino. 1200 l, The Passage of the Red Sea, by Blagio d'Antonio. 1500 l, The Punishment of Korah and the Stoning of Moses and Aaron, by Sandro Botticelli. 4000 l, The Sermon on the Mount, by Cosimo Rosselli.

Perf. 11½x11¾
2001, Feb. 15   Photo.
Granite Paper
Red Frame

1172-1175	A334	Set of 4	9.75	8.00

Christian Conversion of Armenia, 1700th Anniv. — A340

Scenes from illuminated code of 1569: 1200 l, St. Gregory prepares to give King Tiridates human features. 1500 l, St. Gregory makes Agatangel write history of Armenians. 2000 l, St. Gregory and King Tiridates meet Emperor Constantine and Pope Sylvester I.

2001, Feb. 15   Perf. 11¾
Granite Paper

1176-1178	A340	Set of 3	6.00	6.00

Year of Dialogue Among Civilizations A341

2001, May 22   Litho.   Perf. 14¼x14

1179	A341	1500 l multi	1.75	1.75

Europa — A342

Designs: 800 l, Hands holding water above earth. 1200 l, Hand catching water.

2001, May 22   Perf. 13½x13¼

1180-1181	A342	Set of 2	1.75	1.75

Giuseppe Verdi (1010-1901), Composer A343

Verdi and: 800 l, Score from Nabucco. 1500 l, Costumes from Aida. 2000 l, Scenery from Othello.

2001, May 22   Perf. 13¼x14¼

1182-1184	A343	Set of 3	5.50	5.50

2000 Travels of Pope John Paul II — A344

Designs: 500 l, Mount Sinai, Feb. 26. 800 l, Mount Nebo, Mar. 20. 1200 l, The Last Supper, Mar. 23. 1500 l, Holy Sepulchre, Mar. 26. 5000 l, Fatima, May 12. 3000 l, Western Wall.

2001, Sept. 25   Litho.   Perf. 13¼

1185-1189	A344	Set of 5	12.00	12.00

Souvenir Sheet
Perf. 13¼x14

1190	A344	3000 l multi	4.00	4.00

No. 1190 contains one 35x26mm stamp.

Remission of Debts of Poor Countries A345

Various panels by Carlo di Camerino: 200 l, 400 l, 800 l, 1000 l, 1500 l.

2001, Sept. 25   Photo.   Perf. 13

1191-1195	A345	Set of 5	5.25	5.25

Giuseppe Toniolo Institute for Higher Studies, 80th Anniv. — A346

Litho. & Embossed

2001, Nov. 22			Perf. 12¾	
1196	A346	1200 l red & blue	1.75	1.75

Etruscan Museum Gold Objects — A347

Designs: 800 l, Parade fibula. 1200 l, Earrings. 1500 l, Vulci fibula. 2000 l, Head of Medusa.

2001, Nov. 22		Photo.	Perf. 13½	
1197-1200	A347	Set of 4	8.00	8.00

Christmas A348

Artwork by Egino G. Weinert: 800 l, The Annunciation. 1200 l, The Nativity. 1500 l, Adoration of the Magi.

2001, Nov. 22		Litho.	Perf. 13x13¼	
1201-1203	A348	Set of 3	4.75	3.75
1202a		Booklet pane of 4 + 4 etiquettes	7.00	
		Booklet, #1202a	7.00	

100 Cents = 1 Euro (€)

Depictions of Virgin Mary in Vatican Basilica — A349

Designs: 8c, Our Lady of Women in Labor. 15c, Our Lady with People Praying. 23c, Our Lady at the Tomb of Pius XII. 31c, Our Lady of the Fever. 41c, Our Lady of the Slap. 52c, Mary Immaculate. 62c, Our Lady Help of Christians. 77c, Virgin of the Deesis. €1.03, L'Addolorata. €1.55, Presentation of Mary at the Temple.

2002, Mar. 12		Litho.	Perf. 13¼x13	
1204	A349	8c multi	.30	.30
1205	A349	15c multi	.40	.40
1206	A349	23c multi	.60	.50
1207	A349	31c multi	.65	.60
1208	A349	41c multi	1.00	.80
1209	A349	52c multi	1.25	1.10
1210	A349	62c multi	1.60	1.25
1211	A349	77c multi	2.00	1.75
1212	A349	€1.03 multi	2.75	2.50
1213	A349	€1.55 multi	4.50	4.00
		Nos. 1204-1213 (10)	15.05	13.20

Pontifical Ecclesiastical Academy, 300th Anniv. — A350

No. 1214: a, Pope Clement XI. b, Academy building (46x33mm). c, Pope John Paul II.

2002, Mar. 12		Engr.	Perf. 13¼x13	
1214	A350	Horiz. strip of 3	6.00	6.00
a.-c.		77c Any single	1.80	1.80

Sistine Chapel Restoration Type of 2000

Designs: 26c, The Temptation of Christ, by Sandro Botticelli. 41c, The Last Supper, by Cosimo Rosselli. 77c, Moses' Journey in Egypt, by Pietro Perugino. €1.55, The Last Days of Moses, by Luca Signorelli.

2002, June 13			Perf. 11½x11¾	
		Granite Paper		**Photo.**
1215-1218	A334	Set of 4	7.75	7.75

Europa — A351

Christ and the Circus, by Aldo Carpi: 41c, Entire painting. 62c, Detail.

2002, June 13			Perf. 13¼	
1219-1220	A351	Set of 2	2.40	2.40

Roman States Postage Stamps, 150th Anniv. — A352

Designs: 41c, Regina Viarum, Roman States #11. 52c, Cassian Way, Roman States #25. €1.03, Vatican walls, Vatican City #2. €1.55, St. Peter's Basilica.

2002, June 13		Set of 3	Perf. 13x13¼	
1221-1223	A352	Set of 3	5.00	5.00
		Souvenir Sheet		
		Perf.		
1224	A352	€1.55 multi	4.00	4.00

No. 1224 contains one 31mm diameter stamp.

St. Leo IX (1002-54), Pope A353

Designs: 41c, Portrait. 62c, In procession, receiving papal miter. €1.29, Reading from scroll, as prisoner of Normans.

2002, Sept. 26		Litho.	Perf. 13x13¼	
1225-1227	A353	Set of 3	6.00	6.00

Cimabue (1240-1302), Artist — A354

Designs: 26c, Crucifix. 62c, Jesus Christ. 77c, Virgin Mary. €1.03, St. John.

2002, Sept. 26		Photo.	Perf. 13¼x14	
1228-1231	A354	Set of 4	7.00	7.00

Nativity, by Pseudo Ambrogio di Baldese — A355

2002, Nov. 21		Photo.	Perf. 13	
1232	A355	41c multi	1.10	1.10

See New Zealand No. 1834.

2001 Travels of Pope John Paul II — A356

Designs: 41c, Greece, Syria and Malta, May 4-9. 62c, Ukraine, June 23-27. €1.55, Armenia and Kazakhstan, Sept. 22-27.

2002, Nov. 21		Litho.	Perf. 13x13¼	
1233-1235	A356	Set of 3	6.50	6.50
1234a		Booklet pane, 4 #1234 + 4 etiquettes	6.50	
		Booklet, #1234a	6.50	

A357

Pontificate of John Paul II, 25th Anniv. — A358

No. 1236: a, Election as Pope, 1978. b, In Poland, 1979. c, In France, 1980. d, Assassination attempt, 1981. e, At Fatima, Portugal, 1982. f, Extraordinary Holy Year, 1983. g, At Quirinale Palace, Rome, 1984. h, World Youth Day, 1985. i, At synagogue, Rome, 1986. j, Pentecost vigil, 1987. k, At European Parliament, Strasbourg, France, 1988. l, Meeting with Mikhail Gorbachev, 1989. m, At Guinea-Bissau leper colony, 1990. n, At European Bishops' Synod, 1991. o, Publication of Catechism of the Catholic Church, 1992. p, Praying for the Balkans in Assisi, 1993. q, At Sistine Chapel, 1994. r, At UN Headquarters for 50th anniv. celebrations, 1995. s, In Germany, 1996. t, In Sarajevo, Bosnia & Herzegovina, 1997. u, In Cuba, 1998. v, Opening Holy Doors, 1999. w, World Youth Day, 2000. x, Closing Holy Doors, 2001. y, Addressing Italian Parliament, 2002.

2003, Mar. 20		Litho.	Perf. 13x13¼	
1236		Sheet of 25	27.50	27.50
a.-y.		A357 41c Any single	1.00	.95

Etched on Silver Foil
Die Cut Perf. 12½x13
Self-Adhesive

2003, Mar. 20				
1237	A358	€2.58 Pope John Paul II	9.00	9.00

Cancels can be easily removed from No. 1237.
See Poland Nos. 3668-3669.

Martyrdom of St. George, 1700th Anniv. A359

2003, May 6		Litho. & Engr.	Perf. 13	
1238	A359	62c multi	1.90	1.90

Europa — A360

Poster art for: 41c, 1975 Holy Year. 62c, Exhibition of Slav codices, incunabula and rare books at Sistine Hall, 1985.

2003, May 6		Litho.	Perf. 13¼x13	
1239-1240	A360	Set of 2	2.40	2.40

Masterpieces by Beato Angelico in Niccolina Chapel — A361

Designs: 41c, Diaconal Consecration of St. Lawrence. 62c, St. Stephen Preaching. 77c, Trial of St. Lawrence. €1.03, Stoning of St. Stephen.

2003, May 6		Photo.	Perf. 13¼	
1241-1244	A361	Set of 4	7.00	7.00

Beatification of Mother Teresa of Calcutta — A362

2003, Sept. 23		**Perf. 13½x13¼**		**Litho.**
1245	A362	41c multi + label	1.25	1.25

Printed in sheets of 5 + 5 different labels. Value $7.00

19th Century Artists — A363

Designs: 41c, Blessed Are the Pure at Heart, by Paul Gauguin. 62c, The Pietà, by Vincent van Gogh.

Perf. 13¼x13½

2003, Sept. 23   Photo.
1246 A363 41c multi   1.10 1.00
1247 A363 62c multi   1.75 1.50
   a.   Booklet pane of 4 + 4 etiquettes   7.00 —
    Complete booklet, #1247a   7.00

Animals in Vatican Basilica Art A364

Designs: 21c, Dragon. 31c, Camel. 77c, Horse. €1.03, Leopard.

2003, Sept. 23
1248-1251 A364   Set of 4   6.00 5.50

Canonization of Josemaría Escrivá de Balaguer, Oct. 6, 2003 — A365

2003, Nov. 18   Litho.   Perf. 14x13¼
1252 A365 41c multi   1.10 1.10

2002 Travels of Pope John Paul II — A366

Designs: 62c, Bulgaria and Azerbaijan, May 22-26. 77c, Canada, Guatemala and Mexico, July 23-Aug. 2. €2.07, Poland, Aug. 16-19.

2003, Nov. 18   Perf. 13x13¼
1253-1255 A366   Set of 3   9.00 9.00

Christmas A367

2003, Nov. 18
Stamp With White Border
1256 A367 41c multi   1.60 1.60
Souvenir Sheet
Stamp Without White Border
1257 A367 41c multi   1.75 1.75
Death of Pope Paul VI, 25th anniv. (#1257).

St. Pius V (1504-72) A368

Altarpiece by Grazio Cossoli in Chapel of the Rosary, Santa Croce di Bosco Marengo: 4c, Detail depicting St. Pius V and flag. €2, Entire altarpiece.

Litho. & Silk Screened
2004, Mar. 18   Perf. 13¼x13¼
1258-1259 A368   Set of 2   5.50 5.50

2003 Travels of Pope John Paul II — A369

Designs: 60c, Spain, May 3-4. 62c, Bosnia & Herzegovina, June 22. 80c, Croatia, June 5-9. €1.40, Slovakia, Sept. 11-14.

2004, Mar. 18   Litho.
1260-1263 A369   Set of 4   9.00 9.00

EMISSIONE CONGIUNTA

VISITE PASTORALI DEL SANTO PADRE   GIOVANNI PAOLO II IN POLONIA

CITTA' DEL VATICANO - POLONIA

Papal Visits to Poland — A370

No. 1264, 45c: a, Pope with hand on chin. b, Pope praying. c, Pope carrying crucifix. d, Pope with crucifix against head.
No. 1265, 62c: a, Pope holding crucifix, diff. b, Pope with arm raised. c, Pope, wearing white, seated. d, Pope, wearing red cape, seated.

Litho. (Labels Litho. & Embossed)
2004, Mar. 18
Sheets of 4, #a-d, + 8 Labels
1264-1265 A370   Set of 2   13.00 13.00
See Poland Nos. 3724-3725.

Children AIDS Victims — A371

2004, June 3   Photo.   Perf. 13¼x13
1266 A371 45c multi + label   1.50 1.50
Printed in sheets of 6 + 6 stamp-sized labels (with different text) and 1 large central label.

Europa — A372

Paintings of: 45c, Men on horses. 62c, People in garden.

2004, June 3   Litho.   Perf. 12¾x13¼
1267-1268 A372   Set of 2   2.60 2.60

Flags and One-Euro Coins — A373

2004, June 3   Litho.   Perf. 13½
1269 A373 4c Austria   .25 .25
1270 A373 8c Belgium   .25 .25
1271 A373 15c Finland   .35 .35
1272 A373 25c France   .60 .60
1273 A373 30c Germany   .70 .70
1274 A373 40c Greece   .95 .95
1275 A373 45c Vatican City   1.10 1.10
1276 A373 60c Ireland   1.40 1.40
1277 A373 62c Italy   1.50 1.50
1278 A373 70c Luxembourg   1.75 1.75
1279 A373 80c Monaco   1.90 1.90
1280 A373 €1 Netherlands   2.40 2.40
1281 A373 €1.40 Portugal   3.50 3.50
1282 A373 €2 San Marino   4.75 4.75
1283 A373 €2.80 Spain   6.75 6.75
   Nos. 1269-1283 (15)   28.15 28.15

48th Intl. Eucharistic Congress A374

Designs: 45c, Hands breaking bread over chalice. 65c, Hand raising eucharist.

2004, Sept. 16   Litho.   Perf. 13x13¼
1284-1285 A374   Set of 2   3.00 3.00

Contemporary Religious Art in Vatican Museum Collection — A375

Designs: 45c, Still Life with Bottles, by Giorgio Morandi. 60c, The Fall of an Angel, by Marino Marini. 80c, Landscape with Houses, by Ezio Pastorio. 85c, Tuscan Countryside, by Giulio Cesare Vinzio.

2004, Sept. 16   Photo.   Perf. 14x13¼
1286 A375 45c multi   1.10 1.10
1287 A375 60c multi   1.50 1.50
   a.   Perf. 13½x13¼   1.75 1.75
   b.   Booklet pane of 4 #1287a + 4 etiquettes   7.00 —
    Complete booklet, #1287b   7.00
1288 A375 80c multi   2.25 2.25
1289 A375 85c multi   2.50 2.50
   Nos. 1286-1289 (4)   7.35 7.35

Petrarch (1304-74), Poet A376

2004, Nov. 18   Photo.   Perf. 13¼x13
1290 A376 60c multi   1.60 1.60

Christmas A377

2004, Nov. 18   Litho.   Perf. 13¼
1291 A377 80c multi   2.25 2.25

Interregnum Issue

Arms of St. Peter and Papal Chamberlain's Insignia — A378

Inscription colors: 60c, Blue. 62c, Red. 80c, Green.

2005, Apr. 12   Litho.   Perf. 13½x13
1292-1294 A378   Set of 3   8.25 8.25

Pope Benedict XVI — A379

Pope Benedict XVI wearing: 45c, Stole. 62c, White vestments. 80c, Miter.

2005, June 2   Litho.   Perf. 13¼x13
1295-1297 A379   Set of 3   5.25 5.25
Coronation of Pope Benedict XVI, Apr. 19, 2005.

20th World Youth Day A380

2005, June 2
1298 A380 62c multi   1.50 1.50
See Germany No. 2343.

Europa A381

Ceramic plates depicting fish painted by Pablo Picasso with background colors of: 62c, Orange. 80c, Blue.

2005, June 2   Perf. 12½
1299-1300 A381   Set of 2   4.00 4.00

Ratification of Modifications to Italy-Vatican Concordat, 20th Anniv. — A382

Arms of Vatican City and Italy and: 45c, Pen. €2.80, Map.

2005, June 9   Photo.   Perf. 13¼
1301-1302 A382 Set of 2   8.00 8.00
See Italy Nos. 2677-2678.

Resurrection of Christ, by Perugino — A383

Various painting details: 60c, 62c, 80c, €1. €2.80, Jesus Christ.

2005, June 9   Perf. 14x13¼
1303-1306 A383 Set of 4   7.50 7.50
Souvenir Sheet
Perf. 13¼x13¾
1307 A383 €2.80 multi   7.25 7.25
No. 1307 contains one 29x60mm stamp.

Dinner at Emmaus, by Primo Conti A384

2005, Nov. 10 Litho. Perf. 13x13¼
1308 A384 62c multi   1.50 1.50
Eleventh General Assembly of the Synod of Bishops.

2004 Journeys of Pope John Paul II — A385

Designs: 45c, Bern, Switzerland, June 5-6. 80c, Lourdes, France, Aug. 14-15. €2, Loreto, Italy, Sept. 5.

2005, Nov. 10
1309-1311 A385 Set of 3   8.00 8.00

The Annunciation, by Raphael — A386

Designs: Nos. 1312, 1314a, Drawing of Angel, Painting of Virgin Mary. Nos. 1313, 1314b, Painting of Angel, drawing of Virgin Mary.

Litho. & Engr.
2005, Nov. 10   Perf. 13x13¼
1312 A386 62c multi   1.60 1.60
1313 A386 €1 multi   2.75 2.75

Souvenir Sheet
1314 A386 €1.40 Sheet of 2,
          #a-b   7.00 7.00
See France No. 3153.

Swiss Papal Guards, 500th Anniv. A387

Designs: 62c, Guard and drummers. 80c, Guards and St. Peter's Basilica.

2005, Nov. 22 Litho. Perf. 14x14¼
1315-1316 A387 Set of 2   3.50 3.50
Nos. 1315-1316 each issued in sheets of 6. See Switzerland Nos. 1224-1225.

Christmas A388

Details from Adoration of the Shepherds, by François Le Moyne: 45c, Shepherds and sheep. 62c, Angel. 80c, Madonna and Child.

2005, Nov. 22   Perf. 13¼x13
1317-1319 A388 Set of 3   4.75 4.75
1319a   Booklet pane of 4 #1319   8.00
         Complete booklet, #1319a   8.00

Europa A389

Designs: 62c, Praying hands, church, mosque and synagogue. 80c, Handshake, classroom.

2006, Mar. 16 Litho. Perf. 13x13¼
1320-1321 A389 Set of 2   3.50 3.50

Jesuits A390

Designs: 45c, Blessed Peter Faber (1506-46). 60c, St. Ignatius of Loyola (1491-1556). €2, St. Francis Xavier (1506-52).

2006, Mar. 16
1322-1324 A390 Set of 3   7.50 7.50

Andrea Mantegna (c. 1430-1506), Painter A391

Designs: 60c, Madonna and Child. 85c, Saints Gregory and John the Baptist. €1, Saints Peter and Paul.
No. 1328 — San Zeno Polyptych: a, Country name at right. b, Country name at left.

2006, Mar. 16   Photo.   Perf. 12¾
1325-1327 A391 Set of 3   6.00 6.00
Souvenir Sheet
Perf. 13¼x13
1328 A391 €1.40 Sheet of 2,
          #a-b   7.00 7.00
No. 1328 contains two 21x37mm stamps.

Wolfgang Amadeus Mozart (1756-91), Composer A392

Litho. & Engr.
2006, June 22   Perf. 14x14¼
1329 A392 80c multi   2.25 2.25

2005 Travels of Pope Benedict XVI — A393

Designs: 62c, National Eucharistic Congress, Bari, Italy, May 21-29. €1.40, World Youth Day, Cologne, Germany, Aug. 16-21.

2006, June 22 Litho. Perf. 13¼x13
1330-1331 A393 Set of 2   5.25 5.25

St. Peter's Basilica, 500th Anniv. — A394

No. 1332, 45c — 1506 medallion depicting: a, Allegory of architecture (denomination at LL). b, Architect Donato Bramante (denomination at UR).
No. 1333, 60c — 1506 medallion depicting: a, Pope Julius II (denomination at LL). b, Bramante's plan for St. Peter's Basilica (denomination at UR).

Litho. & Embossed
2006, June 22   Perf. 14
Horiz. Pairs, #a-b
1332-1333 A394 Set of 2   6.00 6.00

Intl. Year of Deserts and Desertification — A395

Designs: 62c, Flowers, child on parched earth. €1, Trees, child and cattle.

2006, Oct. 12 Litho. Perf. 13½x13¼
1334-1335 A395 Set of 2   4.25 4.25

Diplomatic Relations Between Vatican City and Singapore, 25th Anniv. — A396

Designs: 85c, Merlion and St. Peter's Basilica. €2, Flags of Singapore and Vatican City.

2006, Oct. 12   Perf. 13½x13
1336-1337 A396 Set of 2   7.50 7.50
See Singapore Nos. 1232-1233.

Vatican Musum, 500th Anniv. A397

Heads from Laocoon sculpture: 60c, Son of Laocoon. 65c, Laocoon. €1.40, Son of Laocoon, diff. €2.80, Laocoon, horiz.

Litho. & Embossed
2006, Oct. 12   Perf. 13x13¼
1338-1340 A397 Set of 3   7.00 7.00
Souvenir Sheet
Perf. 13 Horiz.
1341 A397 €2.80 multi   8.00 8.00
No. 1341 contains one 80x30mm stamp.

Christmas A398

Stained glass from Pope's private chapel: 60c, Shepherds. 65c, Holy Family. 85c, Magi and Star of Bethlehem.

2006, Oct. 12 Litho. Perf. 13¼x13
1342-1344 A398 Set of 3   5.50 5.50
1343a   Booklet pane of 4 #1343   7.00
         Complete booklet, #1343a   7.00

St. Francis of Paola (1416-1507) — A399

Details from sculpture: 60c, Head of St. Francis. €1, Angel.

2007, Mar. 16 Litho. Perf. 13x13¼
1345-1346 A399 Set of 2   4.25 4.25

Pope Benedict XVI, 80th
Birthday — A400

Pope Benedict XVI: 60c, Wearing zucchetto.
65c, Without head covering. 85c, Wearing
miter.

2007, Mar. 16   **Perf. 13¼x13**
Stamp + Label
1347-1349 A400   Set of 3   5.75 5.75

Europa
A401

Designs: 60c, Scouts reading map, Scout
holding chick. 65c, Scouts around campfire.

2007, June 12   **Perf. 13x13¼**
1350-1351 A401   Set of 2   3.50 3.50
Scouting, cent.

Christian
Museum,
250th Anniv.
A402

Designs: 85c, Gilded glass depicting Saints
Peter and Paul, silver vase. €2, Bronze lamp
with monogram of Christ, silver bottle.

2007, June 12
1352-1353 A402   Set of 2   8.00 8.00

Carlo
Goldoni
(1707-93),
Playwright
A403

Goldoni and: 60c, Bridge, man, harlequin.
85c, Church, man, woman.
€2.80, Goldoni holding book.

2007, June 12   **Perf. 13x13¼**
1354-1355 A403   Set of 2   4.00 4.00
Souvenir Sheet
Perf. 13
1356 A403   €2.80 multi   7.75 7.75
No. 1356 contains one 45x33mm stamp and
was sold with side portions of the sheet folded
to produce an effect like a theater curtain.

New Philatelic and Numismatic
Museum A404

No. 1357: a, Vatican City #37, 576, 1013,
1296. b, Four Vatican City coins.

Litho. & Embossed
2007, Sept. 20   **Perf. 14**
1357 A404   60c Horiz. pair, #a-b   3.50 3.50

Treaty of
Rome,
50th Anniv.
A405

Stars and: 15c, Atomium, Brussels. 30c, Eiffel Tower, Paris. 60c, Brandenburg Gate, Berlin. 65c, Plaza, Rome. €1, Castle, Luxembourg. €4, Buildings and bridges, Amsterdam.
€2.80, Mother and child.

2007, Sept. 20 **Litho.** **Perf. 13x13¼**
1358-1363 A405   Set of 6   19.00 19.00
Souvenir Sheet
Perf. 13x13¼ on 2 Sides
1364 A405   €2.80 multi   8.00 8.00
No. 1364 contains one 40x37mm stamp.

St. Elizabeth of
Hungary (1207-
31)
A406

2007, Nov. 20   **Perf. 13¾**
1365 A406   65c multi   1.90 1.90

2006 Travels of
Pope Benedict
XVI — A407

Travels: 60c, Poland, May 25-28. 65c,
Valencia, Spain, July 8-9. 85c, Germany, Sept.
9-14. €1.40, Turkey, Nov. 28-Dec. 1.

2007, Nov. 20   **Perf. 13¼x13**
1366-1369 A407   Set of 4   9.75 9.75
Booklet Stamp
Self-Adhesive
1370 A407   85c Like #1368   2.50 2.50
  a. Booklet pane of 4   10.00

Christmas
A408

Vatican arms and nave paintings in St.
Andrew's Church, Luqa, Malta, by Giuseppe
Calì: 60c, Madonna and Child. 65c, Holy Fam-
ily with Women and Young Girl. 85c, Infant
Jesus and Young Girl.

2007, Nov. 20
1371-1373 A408   Set of 3   6.25 6.25
See Malta Nos. 1319-1321.

Europa
A409

Designs: 60c, Envelope with cachet and
cancels. 85c, Handwritten letter, Pope Benedict XVI.

2008, Mar. 6 **Litho.** **Perf. 13¾**
1374-1375 A409   Set of 2   4.00 4.00

Sistine Chapel Paintings by
Michelangelo, 500th Anniv. — A410

Designs: 5c, Libyan. 10c, Eritrean. 25c, Delphic Sibyl. 60c, Sibyl Cumana. 65c, Daniel.
85c, Jonah. €2, Ezekiel. €5, Zaccharias.

2008, Mar. 6   **Perf. 13x13¼**
1376 A410   5c multi   .25   .25
1377 A410   10c multi   .30   .30
1378 A410   25c multi   .75   .75
1379 A410   60c multi   1.75 1.75
1380 A410   65c multi   1.90 1.90
1381 A410   85c multi   2.40 2.40
1382 A410   €2 multi   5.50 5.50
1383 A410   €5 multi   14.00 14.00
  Nos. 1376-1383 (8)   26.85 26.85

23rd
World
Youth Day
A411

2008, May 15 **Litho.** **Perf. 13¾**
1384 A411   €1 multi   3.25 3.25

Visit of Pope
Benedict XVI to
United
Nations — A412

2008, May 15
1385 A412   €1.40 multi   4.25 4.25

49th Eucharistic Congress,
Quebec — A413

Designs: 60c, Wedding at Cana, Washing of
the Feet, Last Supper. 85c, Crucifixion, Resurrection, Disciples of Emmaus.

2008, May 15   **Perf. 13¾x13¼**
1386-1387 A413   Set of 2   4.50 4.50

Apparition of the
Virgin Mary at
Lourdes, 150th
Anniv. — A414

Designs: 65c, Pilgrims at Lourdes. 85c, Virgin Mary, Lourdes.

2008, May 15 **Litho.** **Perf. 13x13¼**
1388-1389 A414   Set of 2   9.50 9.50
Nos. 1388-1389 each were printed in sheets
of 4.

2007 Travels of
Pope Benedict
XVI — A415

Travels: 65c, Brazil, May 9-14. 85c, Austria,
Sept. 7-9.

Litho. & Engr.
2008, Sept. 17   **Perf. 12¾**
1390-1391 A415   Set of 2   4.75 4.75

Pauline
Year — A416

Designs: 60c, Conversion of St. Paul. 65c,
St. Paul preaching. 85c, St. Paul imprisoned.

2008, Sept. 17 **Litho.** **Perf. 13¼x13**
1392-1394 A416   Set of 3   6.00 6.00

Postal Convention Between Vatican
City and Sovereign Military Order of
Malta
A417

2008, Nov. 13 **Litho.** **Perf. 13⅛**
1395 A417   €2.50 multi + label 7.00 7.00

Andrea Palladio
(1508-80),
Architect — A418

Designs: 65c, San Giorgio Maggiore
Church, Venice. 85c, Villa Rotonda, Vicenza,
Italy.
€2.80, Palladio.

2008, Nov. 13   **Perf. 13¼x14**
1396-1397 A418   Set of 2   4.00 4.00
Souvenir Sheet
1398 A418   €2.80 multi   7.25 7.25

Christmas
A419

Designs: 60c, Adoration of the Magi, by
Raphael. 65c, Nativity, by Albrecht Dürer.

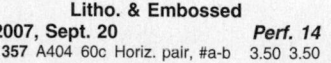

2008, Nov. 13 Litho. Perf. 13x13¼
1399-1400 A419 Set of 2 3.25 3.25

Booklet Stamp
Self-Adhesive
Serpentine Die Cut 12½

1401 A419 60c multi 1.60 1.60
a. Booklet pane of 4 6.50
See Germany Nos. B1008-B1009.

Gibraltar Shrine to Our Lady of Europe, 700th Anniv. — A420

2009, Feb. 10 Litho. Perf. 14x14¾
1402 A420 85c multi 2.25 2.25

Printed in sheets of 4. See Gibraltar No. 1182.

A421

Vatican City State, 80th Anniv. — A422

Popes: No. 1403, 65c, Pius XI. No. 1404, 65c, Pius XII. No. 1405, 65c, John XXIII. No. 1406, 65c, Paul VI. No. 1407, 65c, John Paul I. No. 1408, 65c, John Paul II. No. 1409, Benedict XVI. €2.80, Vatican City map.

2009, Feb. 10 Perf. 13½x14
1403-1409 A421 Set of 7 11.50 11.50

Souvenir Sheet
1410 A422 €2.80 gray & blk 8.00 8.00

Europa A423

Paintings from Astronomical Observations series by Donato Creti: 60c, The Sun. 65c, Saturn.

2009, May 20 Litho. Perf. 14¼
1411-1412 A423 Set of 2 3.50 3.50
Intl. Year of Astronomy.

St. Frances of Rome (1384-1440) — A424

Designs: 85c, St. Frances healing a poor man with an injured arm. €1, Miracle of the grapes.

2009, May 20 Perf. 13¼
1413-1414 A424 Set of 2 5.25 5.25

World Book and Copyright Day — A425

Pontifical Biblical Institute, Cent. — A426

75th Intl. Federationo of Library Associations and Institutions General Conference, Milan — A427

2009, May 20 Perf. 14x14¾
1415 A425 60c multi 1.75 1.75
1416 A426 85c multi 2.40 2.40
1417 A427 €1.40 multi 4.00 4.00
Nos. 1415-1417 (3) 8.15 8.15

Guglielmo Cardinal Massaja (1809-89), Missionary in Africa — A428

2009, Sept. 23 Litho. Perf. 13¾
1418 A428 60c brown 1.75 1.75

2008 Travels of Pope Benedict XVI A429

Travels: 65c, France, Sept. 12-15. 85c, United States, Apr. 15-21. €1, Australia, July 12-21.

2009, Sept. 23
1419-1421 A429 Set of 3 8.00 8.00

A430

A431

The Disputation of the Holy Sacrament, by Raphael, 500th Anniv. — A432

Designs: Nos. 1422-1424, Various painting details. €3.30, Entire painting.

2009, Sept. 23 Perf. 14
1422 A430 65c multi 1.90 1.90
1423 A431 65c multi 1.90 1.90
1424 A432 65c multi 1.90 1.90
Nos. 1422-1424 (3) 5.70 5.70

Souvenir Sheet
Perf. 13¾
1425 A432 €3.30 multi 9.75 9.75

No. 1425 contains one 35x50mm stamp.

Italian Language Day — A433

2009, Oct. 21 Photo. Perf. 13¼x13
1426 A433 60c multi + label 1.90 1.90

Printed in sheets of 5 + 5 labels. See Italy No. 2966; San Marino No. 1801.

Composers — A434

Designs: 65c, George Frideric Handel (1685-1759). 85c, Joseph Haydn (1732-1809). €5, Felix Mendelssohn Bartholdy (1809-47).

2009, Oct. 24 Litho. Perf. 14¾x14
1427-1429 A434 Set of 3 19.50 19.50

Convocation of Second Vatican Council, 50th Anniv. — A435

Litho. & Embossed
2009, Nov. 4 Perf. 14
1430 A435 60c multi 1.90 1.90

Louis Braille (1809-52), Educator of the Blind A436

2009, Nov. 4 Perf. 14¾x14
1431 A436 65c multi 2.00 2.00

Christmas A437

Madonna and Child Enthroned with Two Angels and Saints Joachim and Anne, by Francesco Melanzio: 60c, Detail. 65c, Entire painting.

2009, Nov. 4 Litho. Perf. 12½
1432 A437 60c multi 1.90 1.90
1433 A437 65c multi 2.00 2.00
a. Booklet pane of 4 8.00 8.00
Complete booklet, #1433a 8.00

Easter — A438

Litho. & Engr.
2010, Mar. 5 Perf. 13x12¾
1434 A438 65c multi 2.00 2.00

Sandro Botticelli (1445-1510), Painter — A439

Details of Sistine Chapel paintings: 60c, Women from *The Temptation of Christ.* 85c, Woman holding walking stick from *The Life of Moses.* €1.45, Woman carrying basket on head from *The Life of Moses.*

2010, Mar. 5 Litho. Perf. 13¾x13½
1435-1437 A439 Set of 3 8.25 8.25

The Deposition, by Caravaggio (1573-1610) A440

2010, June 22 Litho. Perf. 13¼x14
1438 A440 65c multi 1.75 1.75

Europa
A441

Illustrations from *The Bible Narrated for Children*: 60c, Adam and Eve in the Garden of Eden. 65c, Jesus and children.

2010, June 22			**Perf. 13**	
1439-1440	A441	Set of 2	3.25	3.25

Sacerdotal Year — A442

Designs: €1.40, St. John Vianney (1786-1859) and priests. €1.50, The Good Shepherd, sheep and wolf.

2010, June 22			**Perf. 13¾x13½**	
1441-1442	A442	Set of 2	8.25	8.25

Father Matteo Ricci (1552-1610), Missionary to China — A443

Designs: 5c, Ricci and Xu Guangqi, Chinese court official. €3.30, Ricci.

2010, June 22			**Perf. 14¾x14**	
1443-1444	A443	Set of 2	9.50	9.50

Pope Leo XIII (1810-1903) A444

2010, Sept. 20		**Litho.**	**Perf. 14¾x14**	
1445	A444	65c multi	1.90	1.90

Composers A445

Designs: 65c, Frédéric Chopin (1810-49). €1, Robert Schumann (1810-56). €4.40, Chopin and Schumann, horiz. (65x16mm).

2010, Sept. 20			**Perf. 13x12¾**	
1446	A445	65c multi	2.00	2.00
1447	A445	€1 multi	3.00	3.00
		Perf. 12¾ at Top		
1448	A445	€4.40 multi + label	12.50	12.50
	Nos. 1446-1448 (3)		*17.50*	*17.50*

Reopening of the Vatican Library A446

Designs: 65c, Crucified Christ. 85c, Sts. Cosmas and Damian. €3.90, Medallion depicting Pope Sixtus V, vert.

2010, Sept. 20			**Perf. 14x13½**	
1449	A446	65c multi	2.00	2.00
1450	A446	85c multi	2.50	2.50
		Imperf		
1451	A446	€3.90 multi	14.00	14.00
	Nos. 1449-1451 (3)		*18.50*	*18.50*

No. 1451 is printed as a miniature book made up of two pieces of paper of different sizes. Both pieces of paper are printed on both sides, and are glued together. The cover of the book is the longer of the two pieces of paper, and is folded into three parts. The stamp, the front cover of the book, is the middle part of this piece of paper. The gum, applied to the left of the stamp, becomes the book's back cover when the longer piece of paper is folded. The title page of *De Nuptiis Philologiae et Mercurii* is to the right of the stamp, and is the book's first page. Text and illustrations are on the reverse of this picture and the stamp, and another picture depicting text and the seal of the Vatican Library is printed on the back of the gum. The second piece of paper, folded in half to constitute four pages of the book, has text and illustrations, and is glued to the back of longer sheet where the fold between the stamp and the photo is found. Values are for the complete item.

Approval of the Franciscan Rule, 800th Anniv. — A447

2010, Nov. 15		**Litho.**	**Perf. 12¾**	
1452	A447	65c multi	2.00	2.00

Writers — A448

Scenes from works by: 60c, Anton Chekhov (1860-1904). 65c, Leo Tolstoy (1828-1910).

2010, Nov. 15			**Perf. 14¼x14¾**	
1453-1454	A448	Set of 2	3.75	3.75

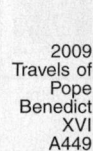

2009 Travels of Pope Benedict XVI A449

Travels: 10c, Cameroun and Angola, Mar. 17-23. 65c, Holy Land, May 8-15. 85c, Czech Republic, Sept. 26-28.

2010, Nov. 15			**Perf. 13x13¼**	
1455-1457	A449	Set of 3	4.75	4.75

See Israel No. 1837.

Christmas A450

Paintings: 60c, The Birth of Jesus, by Gheorghe Tattarascu. 65c, The Nativity and Adoration of the Shepherds, by the School of Murillo.

2010, Nov. 15			**Perf. 13¼**	
1458	A450	60c multi	1.75	1.75
1459	A450	65c multi	1.90	1.90

Booklet Stamps
Self-Adhesive
Serpentine Die Cut 12½

1460	A450	60c multi	1.75	1.75
a.		Booklet pane of 4	7.00	
1461	A450	65c multi	1.90	1.90
a.		Booklet pane of 4	7.75	

See Romania Nos. 5218-5219.

Easter A451

2011, Mar. 21			**Perf. 12¾**	
1462	A451	75c multi	2.25	2.25

Father Eusebio Kino (1645-1711), Missionary in Mexico — A452

2011, Mar. 21			**Perf. 14¼x14¾**	
1463	A452	€1.60 maroon & black	4.75	4.75

A453

Unification of Italy, 150th Anniv. — A454

Designs: No. 1464, 60c, Milan Cathedral and Lombardy-Venetia #6. No. 1465, 60c, Modena Cathedral and Modena #3. No. 1466, 60c, Uffizi Gallery, Palazzo Vecchio, Florence and Tuscany #4. No. 1467, 60c, San Carlo Square, Turin and Sardinia #1. No. 1468, 60c, Mt. Vesuvius and Naples, Two Sicilies #3, 13. No. 1469, 60c, Baptistry, Parma and Parma #4.

€1.50, Piazza del Popolo, Rome.

2011, Mar. 21			**Perf. 12½**	
1464-1469	A453	Set of 6	11.00	11.00
		Souvenir Sheet		
1470	A454	€1.50 multi	5.00	5.00

See Italy No. 3046.

Beatification of Pope John Paul II — A455

2011, Apr. 12			**Perf. 13**	
1471	A455	75c multi	2.50	2.50

Printed in sheets of 6. See Poland No. 4009.

World Youth Day, Madrid — A456

2011, June 21			**Perf. 14x13½**	
1472	A456	75c multi	2.10	2.10

See Spain No. 3797.

Europa — A457

Detail from *The Journey of Moses into Egypt*, by Perugino: a, 60c, "Europa" at UL. b, 75c, "Europa" at UR.

2011, June 21			**Perf. 13¾**	
1473	A457	Horiz. pair, #a-b	4.00	4.00
		Intl. Year of Forests.		

Ordination of Pope Benedict XVI, 60th Anniv. — A458

Designs: No. 1474, 75c, Shell, photograph from ordination as priest, June 29, 1951. No. 1475, 75c, Bear, photograph from installation as bishop, May 28, 1977. No. 1476, 75c, St. Corbninian, photograph from installation as cardinal, June 27, 1977. No. 1477, 75c, Papal arms, photograph from installation as pope, Apr. 19, 2005.

2011, June 21			**Perf. 13½x13¾**	
1474-1477	A458	Set of 4	9.00	9.00

Miniature Sheet

L'Osservatore Romano (Official Vatican Newspaper), 150th Anniv. — A459

No. 1478 — Front pages of newspaper announcing election of Pope: a, Leo XIII. b, Pius X. c, Benedict XV. d, Pius XI. e, Pius XII. f, John XXIII. g, Paul VI. h, John Paul I. i, John Paul II. j, Benedict XVI.

2011, June 21   *Perf. 14x14¾*
1478 A459 60c Sheet fo 10,
   #a-j   18.50 18.50

Mater et Magistra, Encyclical by Pope John XXIII, 50th Anniv. A460

2011, Sept. 2   *Perf. 13¾*
1479 A460 60c multi   1.75 1.75

Room of Heliodorus Frescoes by Raphael, 500th Anniv. — A461

Details from The Expulsion of Heliodorus from the Temple. 75c, Left side of fresco. €1.60, Right side of fresco.

2011, Sept. 2   *Perf. 14¼*
1480-1481 A461   Set of 2   7.00 7.00

Rudjer Boskovic (1711-87), Astronomer, and Dome of St. Peter's Basilica — A462

2011, Sept. 13
1482 A462 €3.30 multi   10.00 10.00
   See Croatia No. 810.

Composers A463

Designs: 75c, Franz Liszt (1811-86). €1.60, Gustav Mahler (1860-1911).

2011, Nov. 18   Litho.   *Perf. 14x14¾*
1483-1484 A463   Set of 2   6.50 6.50

2010 Travels of Pope Benedict XVI A464

Travels: 60c, Malta, Apr. 17-18. 75c, Portugal, May 11-14. €1.40, Cyprus, June 4-6. €1.60, United Kingdom, Sept. 16-19. €2, Spain, Nov. 6-7.

2011, Nov. 18   *Perf. 13¼*
1485-1489 A464   Set of 5   18.00 18.00

Christmas A465

Designs: 60c, Madonna and Child, Saints Benedict and Francis. 75c, Infant Jesus and animals.

2011, Nov. 18   *Perf. 13¼*
1490 A465 60c multi   1.75 1.75
1491 A465 75c multi   2.00 2.00

Booklet Stamp
Self-Adhesive
Serpentine Die Cut 12½x12¼
1492 A465 75c multi   2.00 2.00
   a.   Booklet pane of 4   8.00

Easter — A466

2012, Mar. 1   *Perf. 14¼x14¾*
1493 A466 75c multi   2.00 2.00

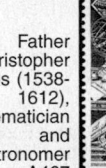

Father Christopher Clavius (1538-1612), Mathematician and Astronomer A467

2012, Mar. 1   *Perf. 14¼*
1494 A467 €1.60 black & red   4.50 4.50

Madonna of Foligno, by Raphael A468

Sistine Madonna, by Raphael A469

2012, Mar. 1   *Perf. 13¼*
1495 A468 60c multi   1.75 1.75
1496 A469 75c multi   2.25 2.25
Souvenir Sheets
1497 A468 €1.40 multi   4.00 4.00
1498 A469 €2.40 multi   7.00 7.00
   See Germany No. 2666.

St. Joan of Arc (c. 1412-31) — A470

Litho. & Engr.
2012, May 11   *Perf. 13*
1499 A470 75c multi   2.00 2.00
   See France No. 4220.

Seventh World Meeting of Families, Milan — A471

2012, May 11   Litho.   *Perf. 13¼x14*
1500 A471 €1.50 multi   4.00 4.00

Europa — A472

Designs: No. 1501, 75c, Dome of St. Peter's Basilica. No. 1502, 75c, Dove in stained-glass window, St. Peter's Basilica.

2012, May 11
1501-1502 A472   Set of 2   4.00 4.00

50th Intl. Eucharistic Congress, Dublin A473

Designs: 75c, Celtic cross from the Rock of Cashel, Tipperary, Ireland. €1, Ardagh Chalice.

2012, May 11   *Perf. 14¾x14*
1503-1504 A473   Set of 2   4.75 4.75

Pope John Paul I (1912-78) A474

2012, Sept. 13   *Perf. 14x13¾*
1505 A474 75c multi   2.00 2.00
   No. 1505 was printed in sheets of 6.

Vatican Secret Archives, 400th Anniv. — A475

No. 1506: a, Pope Benedict XVI. b, Sealed document. c, Pope Paul V.

2012, Sept. 13   *Perf. 13¾x13½*
1506 A475 75c Horiz. strip of 3,
   #a-c   6.00 6.00
   No. 1506 was printed in sheets containing four strips.

Souvenir Sheet

Battle of the Milvian Bridge, 1700th Anniv. — A476

2012, Sept. 13   *Perf. 14x13½*
1507 A476 €4.40 multi   11.50 11.50
   See Italy No. 3136.

2011 Travels of Pope Benedict XVI A477

Travels: 60c, Croatia, June 4-5. 75c, San Marino, June 19. €1.40, Spain, Aug. 18-21. €1.60, Germany, Sept. 22-25. €2, Benin, Nov. 18-20.

2012, Nov. 6   *Perf. 13½*
1508-1512 A477   Set of 5   17.50 17.50

Christmas A478

Stained-glass windows by János Hajnal depicting: 60c, Annunciation. 75c, Holy Family and shepherd.

2012, Nov. 6   *Perf. 13¾*
1513-1514 A478   Set of 2   3.50 3.50
1514a   Booklet pane of 8, 4 each
     #1513-1514   14.00 —
     Complete booklet, #1514a   14.00

Souvenir Sheet

Restoration of the Colonnade of St. Peter's Square — A479

No. 1515 — Papal arms of: a, Alexander VII. b, Benedict XVI.

Litho. With Foil Application
2012, Nov. 20   *Perf. 13¾*
1515 A479 €10 Sheet of 2,
   #a-b   57.50 57.50

Inscription in sheet margin "Officium Philatelicum et Nomismaticum" could be personalized.

Sculpture of Risen Christ, by Pericle Fazzini A480

Perf. 13¼x13½
2013, Feb. 28   Litho.
1516 A480 85c multi   2.25 2.25
Easter.

Year of Faith — A481

No. 1517 — Details from Faith, by Raphael: a, Putto, denomination at LL (20x38mm). b, Putto, denomination at LR (20x38mm). c, Faith with chalice and host (30x38mm).

2013, Feb. 28   Perf. 13½x13¾
1517 A481   Horiz. strip of 3   6.00 6.00
a.-b.   60c Either single   1.60 1.60
c.   €1 multi   2.60 2.60

Souvenir Sheet

Mass of Bolsena, by Raphael — A482

2013, Feb. 28   Perf. 13½x13¾
1518 A482 €4.80 multi   12.50 12.50
Miracle of Bolsena, 750th anniv.

Interregnum Issue

Angel and Sede Vacante Arms — A483

Background colors: 70c, Blue green. 85c, Blue. €2, Gray. €2.50, Yellow.

2013, Mar. 1   Perf. 13¼x13
1519-1522 A483   Set of 4   16.00 16.00

Pope Francis — A484

Various photographs of Pope Francis: 70c, 85c, €2, €2.50.

2013, May 2   Perf. 13¼x14
1523-1526 A484   Set of 4   16.00 16.00
See Argentina No. 2682, Italy No. 3179.

Giuseppe Gioachino Belli (1791-1863), Poet — A485

2013, May 2   Perf. 14x14¾
1527 A485 €1 multi   2.60 2.00

World Youth Day — A486

2013, May 2   Perf. 13¼x13
1528 A486 €1.90 multi   5.00 5.00

Europa — A487

Vatican City postal van and: 70c, St. Peter's Basilica. 85c, Globe.

2013, May 2
1529-1530 A487   Set of 2   4.00 4.00

Pope John XXIII (1881-1963) A488

2013, June 12   Perf. 14x13½
1531 A488 85c multi   2.25 2.25
No. 1531 was printed in sheets of 9.

Edict of Milan, 1700th Anniv. A489

Frescoes from the Oratory of St. Sylvester, Rome, depicting Pope Sylvester I and Emperor Constantine: 70c, 85c, €2.50.
€1.90, Pope Sylvester I showing icon depicting Sts. Peter and Paul to Emperor Constantine.

2013, June 12   Perf. 13x13¼
1532-1534 A489   Set of 3   11.00 11.00
Souvenir Sheet
1535 A489 €1.90 multi   5.25 5.25
See Italy No. 3178.

Souvenir Sheet

Mission of Sts. Cyril and Methodius to Slavic Lands, 1150th Anniv. — A490

Litho. & Engr.
2013, June 12   Perf. 11¾
1536 A490 €1.90 multi   5.25 5.25
See Bulgaria No. 4647, Czech Republic No. 3573, Slovakia No. 666.

Composers A491

Designs: 70c, Giuseppe Verdi (1813-1901). 85c, Richard Wagner (1813-83).

2013, Aug. 30   Litho.   Perf. 14x14¾
1537-1538 A491   Set of 2   4.25 4.25

Popes of the Renaissance A492

Designs: 70c, Pope Julius II (1443-1513). €2, Pope Leo X (1475-1521).

2013, Aug. 30   Perf. 13¾x13½
1539-1540 A492   Set of 2   7.25 7.25

Raoul Follereau (1903-77), Journalist, and Lepers A493

2013, Nov. 7   Litho.   Perf. 13¾
1541 A493 €2 multi   5.50 5.50
World Leprosy Day.

2012 Travels of Pope Benedict XVI A494

Travels: 70c, Mexico and Cuba, Mar. 23-29. 85c, Lebanon, Sept. 14-16.

2013, Nov. 7   Litho.   Perf. 14x13¾
1542 A494 70c multi   1.90 1.90
1543 A494 85c multi   2.40 2.40
a.   Booklet pane of 4, 2 each
   #1542-1543   8.75 —
   Complete booklet, #1543a   8.75

Santa Maria di Nardò Cathedral, Lecce, Italy, 600th Anniv. — A495

Cathedral frescoes depicting: 5c, St. Augustine. 10c, Our Lady of Health. 15c, Madonna del Giglio. 25c, St. Nicholas of Myra. 45c, Christ Pantocrator.

2013, Nov. 7   Litho.   Perf. 13x13¼
1544-1548 A495   Set of 5   2.75 2.75

Christmas A496

Paintings by Pinturicchio: 70c, Nativity. 85c, Adoration of the Magi.

2013, Nov. 7   Litho.   Perf. 13¼x13¾
1549-1550 A496   Set of 2   4.25 4.25
Nos. 1549-1550 each were printed in sheets of 8 + central label. See Finland (Aland Islands) Nos. 349-350.

27th Intl. Book Fair, Turin — A497

2014, Mar. 21   Litho.   Perf. 13
1551 A497 70c multi   2.00 2.00

Easter — A498

2014, Mar. 21   Litho.   Perf. 13¾
1552 A498 85c multi   2.40 2.40

Start of Second Year of Reign of Pope Francis — A499

Various photographs of Pope Francis with denomination in: 70c, Red. 85c, Blue. €2, Green. €2.50, Bister.

2014, Mar. 21   Litho.   Perf. 13½x13
1553-1556 A499   Set of 4   17.00 17.00
See Philippines No. 3519.

Canonization of Pope John XXIII — A500

2014, Mar. 21   Litho.   Perf. 13¼
1557 A500 70c multi   2.00 2.00
See Italy No. 3228.

Souvenir Sheet

Canonization of Popes John Paul II
and John XXIII — A501

No. 1558: a, Pope John Paul II. b, Pope
John XXIII.

Perf. 11½x11¼ Syncopated
2014, Mar. 21   Litho.
1558 A501 €1 Sheet of 2, #a-b   5.50 5.50
See Poland No. 4112.

A502

Canonization of Pope John Paul
II — A503

Perf. 11½x11¾ Syncopated
2014, Mar. 21   Litho.
1559 A502 85c multi   2.40 2.40
Souvenir Sheets
Perf. 11¼x11½ Syncopated
1560 A503 €1.90 multi   5.25 5.25
Engr.
1561 A503 €2.50 bister   7.00 7.00
See Poland Nos. 4113-4115.

Charlie Chaplin
(1889-1977), Film
Actor — A504

2014, May 20   Litho.   Perf. 13½
1562 A504 70c multi   1.90 1.90

Face of Christ, by
El Greco (1541-
1614)
A505

2014, May 20   Litho.   Perf. 14¾x14
1563 A505 85c multi   2.40 2.40

Europa — A506

Pipe organ from: 70c, Basilica of St. John
Lateran. 85c, St. Peter's Basilica.

2014, May 20   Litho.   Perf. 13¾
1564-1565 A506   Set of 2   4.25 4.25

Emperor
Charlemagne
(742-814) — A507

Charlemagne: 85c, On horse. €1.90, With
orb and scepter.

2014, May 20   Litho.   Perf. 13¾
1566-1567 A507   Set of 2   7.50 7.50

Souvenir Sheet

Donato Bramante (1444-1514),
Architect — A508

No. 1568: a, €1.20, Bramante (38mm diameter). b, €3.60, Bramante Staircase, Octagonal Courtyard of the Belvedere (30x40mm).

Perf. (#1568a), Perf. 14¼ (#1568b)
2014, May 20   Litho.
1568 A508 Sheet of 2, #a-b   13.00 13.00

Saint Camillus Amongst the Plague-
Stricken, by Sebastiano
Conca — A509

2014, Aug. 28   Litho.   Perf. 13¼
1569 A509 70c multi   1.90 1.90
St. Camillus de Lellis (1550-1614), founder
of the Order of the Ministers of the Sick.

Richard Strauss
(1864-1949),
Composer
A510

2014, Aug. 28   Litho.   Perf. 13¾
1570 A510 70c multi   1.90 1.90

Beatification of
Pope Paul VI
(1897-1978)
A511

2014, Aug. 28   Litho.   Perf. 13¼x13
1571 A511 70c multi   1.90 1.90
No. 1571 was issued in sheets of 4.

Statue of St.
Pius X (1835-
1914), by Pier
Enrico
Astorri — A512

2014, Aug. 28   Litho.   Perf. 13
1572 A512 €2 multi   5.25 5.25

Synod of
Ayutthaya,
350th
Anniv.
A513

2014, Aug. 28   Litho.   Perf. 13¾
1573 A513 €2 multi   5.25 5.25
See Thailand No. 2822.

Fall of the
Berlin Wall,
25th
Anniv. — A514

Designs: 85c, Old woman holding chisel
against wall. €3.60, Rainbow.

2014, Aug. 28   Litho.   Perf. 14¼
1574 A514 85c multi   2.25 2.25
Souvenir Sheet
1575 A514 €3.60 multi   9.50 9.50

William Shakespeare (1564-1616),
Writer — A515

2014, Nov. 21   Litho.   Perf. 13¾
1576 A515 85c multi   2.10 2.10

Pauline Chapel Paintings by
Michelangelo (1475-1564) — A516

Designs: 70c, Crucifixion of Saint Peter.
85c, Conversion of Saint Paul.

Perf. 11½x11¾
2014, Nov. 21   Litho.
1577-1578 A516   Set of 2   4.00 4.00

2013
Travels of
Pope
Francis
A517

Travels: 70c, Rio de Janeiro, Brazil, July 22-
29. 85c, Lampedusa, Cagliari and Assisi, Italy,
July 8, vert.

2014, Nov. 21   Litho.   Perf. 13¾
1579 A517 70c multi   1.75 1.75
1580 A517 85c multi   2.10 2.10
  a. Booklet pane of 4   8.50
        Complete booklet, #1580a 8.50

Nativity, by
Raúl Soldi
(1905-94)
A518

2014, Nov. 21   Litho.   Perf. 13½
1581 A518 85c multi   2.10 2.10
Christmas. See Argentina No. 2754.

Easter — A519

2015, Feb. 15   Litho.   Perf. 13¾
1582 A519 80c multi   1.75 1.75

Public
Display of
the Shroud
of Turin
A520

2015, Feb. 19   Litho.   Perf. 13¾
1583 A520 95c multi   2.10 2.10

International Year of Light — A521

2015, Feb. 19   Litho.   Perf. 13¼
1584 A521 €2.15 multi   4.75 4.75

Pope Francis — A522

Various photographs of Pope Francis: 80c, 95c, €2.30, €3.

2015, Feb. 19 Litho. *Perf. 14x14¾*
1585-1588 A522 Set of 4 16.00 16.00

St. John Bosco (1815-88) A523

2015, May 19 Litho. *Perf. 12½*
1589 A523 80c multi 1.75 1.75

See Italy No. 3304.

International Telecommunication Union, 150th Anniv. — A524

2015, May 19 Litho. *Perf. 13½*
1590 A524 €2.15 multi 4.75 4.75

Europa — A525

Toys: 80c, Teddy bear, train, toy soldiers in Papal gendarmes uniforms. 95c, Toy soldiers in Swiss Guards uniforms, blocks, marble.

2015, May 19 Litho. *Perf. 13¾x13½*
1591-1592 A525 Set of 2 4.00 4.00

Souvenir Sheet

Events of 1945, 70th Anniv. — A526

No. 1593: a, End of World War II. b, Founding of the United Nations.

2015, May 19 Litho. *Perf. 13¼*
1593 A526 €2 Sheet of 2, #a-b 9.00 9.00

Eighth World Meeting of Families, Philadelphia — A527

2015, Sept. 2 Litho. *Perf. 13¾*
1594 A527 €2.30 multi 5.25 5.25

Armenian Religious Figures — A528

No. 1595: a, St. Gregory of Narek (951-1003). b, Blessed Ignatius Maloyan (1869-1915).

2015, Sept. 2 Litho. *Perf. 13¾*
1595 A528 €1 Horiz. pair, #a-b 4.50 4.50

Cent. of proclamation of St. Gregory of Narek as Doctor of the Church and martyrdom of Maloyan. No. 1595 printed in sheets containing two pairs.

Synod of Bishops, 50th Anniv. A529

Designs: 80c, Pope Paul VI and bishops. 95c, Pope Francis and family.

2015, Sept. 2 Litho. *Perf. 13x13¼*
1596-1597 A529 Set of 2 4.00 4.00

14th General Assembly of the Synod of Bishops (No. 1597).

2014 Travels of Pope Francis A530

Travels: No. 1598, 95c, Tirana, Albania, Sept. 21. No. 1599, 95c, Strasbourg, France, Nov. 25. No. 1600, 95c, Istanbul, Turkey, Nov. 28-30. €2.30, Seoul, South Korea, Aug. 13-18.

€3, Jerusalem, Israel, May 24-26.

2015, Sept. 2 Litho. *Perf. 14¾x14*
1598-1601 A530 Set of 4 12.00 12.00

Souvenir Sheet

Perf. 13¼

1602 A530 €3 multi 6.75 6.75

No. 1602 contains one 52x40mm stamp. See Israel No. 2075.

St. Colombanus of Bobbio (c. 543-615) — A531

2015, Nov. 19 Litho. *Perf. 14x14¾*
1603 A531 95c multi 2.00 2.00

Pope Innocent XII (1615-1700) A532

2015, Nov. 19 Litho. *Perf. 13¾*
1604 A532 95c multi 2.00 2.00

St. Philip Neri (1515-95) and St. Teresa of Avila (1515-82) — A533

Perf. 13¼x13½
2015, Nov. 19 Litho.
1605 A533 €2.30 multi 5.00 5.00

Vatican Observatory, Castel Gondolfo, 80th Anniv. — A534

Designs: 80c, Pope Pius XI (1857-1939), Papal Palace, Castel Gondolfo, Schmidt telescope. 95c, Pope Francis, Moon, refractor telescope.

2015, Nov. 19 Litho. *Perf. 13¾*
1606-1607 A534 Set of 2 3.75 3.75

Holy Year of Mercy — A535

Designs: 80c, Pope Francis, Holy Door, cross. 95c, Immaculate Conception.

2015, Nov. 19 Litho. *Perf. 13¼x13*
1608-1609 A535 Set of 2 3.75 3.75

Christmas A536

Illustration of Nativity from Codices Urbinates Latini 239: 80c, Entire scene. 95c, Detail.

Perf. 11¼x11½ Syncopated
2015, Nov. 19 Litho.
1610-1611 A536 Set of 2 3.75 3.75
1611a Booklet pane of 4 #1611 8.00 —
Complete booklet, #1611a 8.00

Easter — A537

No. 1612 — Stained-glass windows from Church of St. Angela Mercini, Milan: a, 95c, Crucifixion. b, €1, Resurrection.

2016, Feb. 1 Litho. *Perf. 14x14¾*
1612 A537 Pair, #a-b 4.25 4.25

Printed in sheets containing two pairs.

51st International Eucharistic Congress, Cebu City, Philippines A538

Designs: 95c, Holy Child of Cebu. €1, Cebu Cathedral, Philippines.

2016, Feb. 1 Litho. *Perf. 13¾*
1613-1614 A538 Set of 2 4.25 4.25

Jubilee of Mercy — A539

Designs: 95c, People distributing bread on seashore. €1, People at well.

2016, Feb. 1 Litho. *Perf. 13¼x13*
1615-1616 A539 Set of 2 4.25 4.25

Pope Francis — A540

Varioius photographs of Pope Francis with denomination color of: 95c, Green. €1, Blue. €2.30, Orange. €3, Red.

2016, Feb. 1 Litho. *Perf. 13¼x13*
1617-1620 A540 Set of 4 16.00 16.00
1620a Souvenir sheet of 4, #1617-1620 16.00 16.00

Europa A541

2016, May 10 Litho. *Perf. 13¾*
1621 A541 95c multi 2.25 2.25

Think Green Issue.

Vatican Gendarmerie, 200th Anniv. — A542

Designs: 95c, Papal gendarme in ceremonial uniform. €1, Gendarme in current uniform.

2016, May 10 **Litho.** **Perf. 14x14¾**
1622-1623 A542 Set of 2 4.50 4.50

Jubilee of Mercy A543

Designs: 95c, Clothing the naked. €1, Sheltering the homeless.

2016, May 10 **Litho.** **Perf. 14¾x14**
1624-1625 A543 Set of 2 4.50 4.50

World Youth Day, Cracow, Poland A544

Designs: €1, Pope Francis and youths. €4.50, Pope Francis.

Perf. 11¼x11½
2016, May 10 **Photo.**
1626 A544 €1 multi 2.40 2.40

Souvenir Sheet
Photo. & Engr.
Perf. 11¼x11
1627 A544 €4.50 multi 10.50 10.50
No. 1627 contains one 54x41mm stamp. See Poland Nos. 4223-4224.

Canonization of St. Teresa of Calcutta (Mother Teresa) — A545

2016, Sept. 2 **Litho.** **Perf. 13¾**
1628 A545 95c multi 2.10 2.10

Pope Innocent III (1160-1216) A546

2016, Sept. 13 **Litho.** **Perf. 13x13¼**
1629 A546 95c multi 2.10 2.10

St. Maximilian Kolbe (1894-1941) A547

2016, Sept. 13 **Litho.** **Perf. 13¼x13**
1630 A547 €1 multi 2.25 2.25

Election of Virgin Mary as Patroness of Luxembourg, 350th Anniv. — A548

2016, Sept. 13 **Engr.** **Perf. 13x13¼**
1631 A548 €1 multi 2.25 2.25
See Luxembourg No. 1441.

Jubilee of Mercy A549

Designs: 95c, Visiting the imprisoned. €1, Visiting the sick.

2016, Sept. 13 **Litho.** **Perf. 13x13¼**
1632-1633 A549 Set of 2 4.50 4.50

Souvenir Sheet

2015 Travels of Pope Francis — A550

2016, Sept. 13 **Litho.** **Perf. 13x13¼**
1634 A550 €4 multi 9.00 9.00

St. Dominic (1170-1221), Founder of the Dominican Order — A551

2016, Nov. 17 **Litho.** **Perf. 13¼x13**
1635 A551 95c multi 2.10 2.10
Dominican Order, 800th anniv.

Pope Francis, 80th Birthday A552

2016, Nov. 17 **Litho.** **Perf. 13x13¼**
1636 A552 €1 multi 2.25 2.25
No. 1636 was printed in sheets of 4.

Jubilee of Mercy A553

Designs: 95c, Symbols of burial of the dead. €1, Jesus Christ and Holy Door.

2016, Nov. 17 **Litho.** **Perf. 14¾x14**
1637-1638 A553 Set of 2 4.25 4.25

Christmas A554

Nativity ceramic by Giovanni della Robbia. 95c, Holy Family with St. Francis and St. Anthony of Padua. €1, Infant Jesus.

2016, Nov. 17 **Litho.** **Perf. 13¾x14**
1639 A554 95c multi 2.10 2.10
1640 A554 €1 multi 2.25 2.25
a. Booklet pane of 4 9.00 —
Complete booklet, #1640a 9.00

Lithuanian Grand Duke Vytautas and Bishop Motiejus — A555

2017, Feb. 10 **Litho.** **Perf. 13¾**
1641 A555 €1 sil & multi 2.10 2.10
Diocese of Samogitia, Lithuania, 600th anniv. See Lithuania No. 1100.

Pope Alexander VII (1599-1667), His Coat of Arms and St. Peter's Square — A556

Francesco Borromini (1599-1667), Architect, and Church of Sant'Ivo alla Sapienza — A557

2017, Feb. 10 **Litho.** **Perf. 13¾**
1642 A556 95c multi 2.00 2.00
1643 A557 €1 multi 2.10 2.10

Pope Francis — A558

Various photographs of Pope Francis: 95c, €1, €2.30, €3.

2017, Feb. 10 **Litho.** **Perf. 13¼**
1644-1647 A558 Set of 4 15.50 15.50

Risen Christ From Flemish Tapestry by Pieter van Aelst — A559

Perf. 14¼x14½
2017, Feb. 10 **Litho.**
Stamp With White Frame
1648 A559 €1 multi 2.10 2.10
Souvenir Sheet
Stamp Without White Frame
Perf. 13x13¼
1649 A559 €4.50 multi 9.50 9.50
Easter. No. 1649 contains one 40x60mm stamp.

Pope Emeritus Benedict XVI, 90th Birthday — A560

2017, May 4 **Litho.** **Perf. 13½x13**
1650 A560 95c multi 2.10 2.10
No. 1650 was printed in sheets of 4.

Cardinal Domenico Bartolucci (1917-2013), Director of Sistine Chapel Choir — A561

2017, May 4 **Litho.** **Perf. 13x13¼**
1651 A561 95c multi 2.10 2.10

Apparition of the Virgin Mary at Fatima, Portugal, Cent. — A562

2017, May 4 **Litho.** **Perf. 13¼x13**
1652 A562 €2.55 multi 5.75 5.75

Martyrdom of Saints Peter and Paul, 1950th Anniv. — A563

Designs: 95c, St. Peter, rooster and keys. €1, St. Paul, book and sword.

2017, May 4   Litho.   Perf. 13¾
1653-1654 A563   Set of 2   4.25 4.25

Europa
A564

Designs: 95c, Castel Gandolfo and Vatican Observatory. €1, Palace of Belvedere, Vatican City.

2017, May 4   Litho.   Perf. 13x10¼
1655-1656 A564   Set of 2   4.25 4.25

St. Frances Xavier Cabrini (1850-1917), Founder of the Missionary Sisters of the Sacred Heart of Jesus — A565

2017, Sept. 7   Litho.   Perf. 14¼
1657 A565 95c multi   2.25 2.25

Father Lorenzo Milani (1923-67), Educator of Poor in Italy A566

2017, Sept. 7   Litho.   Perf. 13¼x13
1658 A566 95c multi   2.25 2.25

Lay People, Children and St. Marcellino Champagnat (1789-1840) Founder of Marist Brothers — A567

2017, Sept. 7   Litho.   Perf. 13¼x13
1659 A567 €1 multi   2.40 2.40

Marist Brothers, 200th anniv.

Publication of "Populorum Progressio" Encyclical by Pope Paul VI, 50th Anniv. — A568

2017, Sept. 7   Litho.   Perf. 14
1660 A568 €1 multi   2.40 2.40

No. 1660 was printed in sheets of 4.

Souvenir Sheet

Congregation for Oriental Churches, Cent. — A569

2017, Sept. 7   Litho.   Perf. 12 at Top
1661 A569 €2.55 multi   6.00 6.00

2016 Travels of Pope Francis A570

Travels: No. 1662, 95c, Mexico, Feb. 12-18. No. 1663, 95c, Lesbos, Greece, Apr. 16. No. 1664, 95c, Armenia, June 24-26. No. 1665, 95c, Poland, July 27-31. No. 1666, 95c, Georgia and Azerbaijan, Sept. 30-Oct ? No. 1667, 05c, Sweden, Oct. 31-Nov. 1.

2017, Nov. 23   Litho.   Perf. 13x13¼
1662-1667 A570   Set of 6   13.50 13.50

Protestant Reformation, 500th Anniv. — A571

2017, Nov. 23   Litho.   Perf. 13x13¼
1668 A571 €1 gold & multi   2.40 2.40

St. Francis de Sales (1567-1622) A572

2017, Nov. 23   Litho.   Perf. 13¼x13
1669 A572 €2.55 multi   6.25 6.25

Christmas
A573

Designs: 95c, Annunciation. €1, Madonna and Child.

2017, Nov. 23   Litho.   Perf. 13¼x13
1670 A573 95c multi   2.25 2.25
a.   Booklet pane of 4 + 4 labels   9.00 —
       Complete booklet, #1670a   9.00
1671 A573 €1 multi   2.40 2.40

See Monaco Nos. 2908-2909.

Easter — A574

2018, Feb. 6   Litho.   Perf. 13¾
1672 A574 95c multi   2.40 2.40

Blessed Giuseppe Puglisi (1937-1993), Palermo Priest Killed by Mafia — A575

2018, Feb. 6   Litho.   Perf. 13¼x13
1673 A575 €1 multi   2.50 2.50

Pope Francis — A576

2017 photographs of Pope Francis: 95c, Celebrating Palm Sunday. €1, Holding pastoral staff. €2.30, Wearing miter on pastoral visit. €3, Holding candle.

2018, Feb. 6   Litho.   Perf. 13¼
1674-1677 A576   Set of 4   18.00 18.00
1677a   Souvenir sheet of 4,
           #1674-1677   18.00 18.00

The Adoration of the Magi (Detail), by Domenico Ghirlandaio A577

2018, May 3   Litho.   Perf. 13¼
1678 A577 95c multi   2.25 2.25

Centesimus Annus Pro Pontifice Foundation, 25th anniv.

Dome of Santa Maria del Fiore Cathedral, Florence, 600th Anniv. A578

2018, May 3   Litho.   Perf. 13x13¼
1679 A578 €1 multi   2.40 2.40

No. 1679 was printed in sheets of 4.

Bridges
A579

Designs: 95c, St. Peter and Ponte Sant'Angelo, Rome. €1, St. John Nepomuk and Charles Bridge, Prague.

2018, May 3   Litho.   Perf. 13¾
1680-1681 A579   Set of 2   4.75 4.75

Europa.

Vatican Museum Statues — A580

Designs: 10c, Belvedere Apollo. 15c, Augustus of Prima Porto. 30c, Charity With Four Putti, by Gian Lorenzo Bernini. 95c, Perseus Triumphant, by Antonio Canova.

2018, May 3   Litho.   Perf. 13¼x13
1682-1685 A580   Set of 4   3.75 3.75

European Year of Cultural Heritage.

Souvenir Sheet

Old Church Slavonic Liturgical Language, 1150th Anniv. — A581

2018, May 3   Litho. & Engr.   Perf. 13
1686 A581 €5.95 multi   14.50 14.50

See Slovakia No. 791

St. Pio of
Pietrelcina
(1887-1968)
A582

2018, Sept. 6   Litho.   Perf. 14x13¼
1687 A582 €1.10 multi   2.60 2.60

No. 1687 was printed in sheets of 4.

15th Ordinary
General
Assembly of the
Synod of
Bishops — A583

2018, Sept. 6   Litho.   Perf. 13¾
1688 A583 €1.15 multi   2.75 2.75

Popes — A584

Designs: €1.10, Pope Paul VI (1897-1978).
€1.15, Pope John Paul I (1912-78).

2018, Sept. 6   Litho.   Perf. 13¾
1689-1690 A584 Set of 2   5.25 5.25

Canonization of Pope Paul VI.

Scientists — A585

Designs: €1.10, Father Angelo Secchi
(1818-78), astronomer. €1.15, Maria Gaetana
Agnesi (1718-99), mathematician.

2018, Sept. 6   Litho.   Perf. 13¼x13
1691-1692 A585 Set of 2   5.25 5.25

Our Lady of Good Health Viewed
From the Grand Canal, by Canaletto
(1697-1768) — A586

Mary with the Child Venerated by St.
Mark and St. Luke, by Tintoretto
(1518-94) — A587

2018, Sept. 6 Litho. Perf. 13¾x13¼
1693 A586 €1.10 multi   2.60 2.60
Souvenir Sheet
Perf. 14x13½ on 3 Sides
1694 A587 €2.60 multi   6.00 6.00

Gioachino Rossini
(1792-1868),
Composer
A588

2018, Nov. 9   Litho.   Perf. 13¼x13
1695 A588 €2.40 multi   5.50 5.50

Universal
Declaration of
Human Rights,
70th
Anniv. — A589

No. 1696: a, €1.10, Peace dove. b, €1.15,
Man and woman.

2018, Nov. 9   Litho.   Perf. 13¼x13
1696 A589   Pair, #a-b   5.25 5.25

Popes
A590

Designs: €1.10, St. Adeodatus I (570-618).
€1.15, St. Zosimus (d. 418).

2018, Nov. 9   Litho.   Perf. 13x13¼
1697-1698 A590 Set of 2   5.25 5.25

Souvenir Sheet

Pope Francis and Hands — A591

2018, Nov. 9   Litho.   Perf. 14x13¼
1699 A591 €1.15 multi   2.60 2.60

2017 travels of Pope Francis.

Christmas
A592

Designs: €1.10, Virgin Mary and angel.
€1.15, Madonna and Child.

2018, Nov. 9   Litho.   Perf. 14x13¾
1700-1701 A592 Set of 2   5.25 5.25
1701a   Booklet pane of 4, 2 each
             #1700-1701   10.50   —
             Complete booklet, #1701a 10.50

Pope
Francis — A593

Color of vestments: €1.10, White. €1.15,
Purple. €2.40, Red. €3, Green.

2019, Feb. 11   Litho.   Perf. 13¾
1702-1705 A593 Set of 4   17.50 17.50

Easter — A594

2019, Feb. 11   Litho.   Perf. 13¼
1706 A594 €1.10 multi   2.50 2.50

World Youth
Day,
Panama
A595

2019, Feb. 11   Litho.   Perf. 13x13¼
1707 A595 €2.60 multi   6.00 6.00

Souvenir Sheet

Italo-Albanese Eparchy of Lungro,
Cent. — A596

2019, Feb. 11   Litho.   Perf.
1708 A596 €2.40 multi   5.50 5.50

Lateran Treaty, 90th Anniv. — A597

No. 1709: a, Pope Pius XI (1857-1939). b.
Pope Francis.

2019, Feb. 11   Litho.   Perf. 13¼x14
1709 A597   Pair, #a-b   5.25 5.25
  a.   €1.10 multi   2.50 2.50
  b.   €1.15 multi   2.60 2.60

No. 1709 was printed in sheets containing
two pairs.

Conciliation Hall, Lateran Palace, Site of Signing of the Lateran Treaty — A598

Serpentine Die Cut 11
2019, Feb. 11   **Litho.**
Self-Adhesive
1710 A598 €1.10 gold & multi   2.50 2.50

A self-adhesive embroidered €8.40 stamp depicting the Papal Arms and commemorating the 90th anniversary of the Lateran Pacts and formation of the Vatican City State was offered only in a folder containing an unused example and a used example on cover. The folder sold for €28.

Bambino Gesù Pediatric Hospital, Rome, 150th Anniv. — A599

2019, Mar. 19   **Litho.**   **Perf. 13¼x13**
1711 A599 €1.10 multi   2.50 2.50
See Italy No.

Giuseppe Diana (1958-94), Priest Murdered by the Camorra — A600

2019, Mar. 19   **Litho.**   **Perf. 13¼x13**
1712 A600 €1.10 multi   2.50 2.50

Europa — A601

Designs: €1.10, Mallard duck. €1.15, Pigeon.

Perf. 13¾x13½
2019, Mar. 19   **Litho.**
1713-1714 A601 Set of 2   5.00 5.00

Marshal Józef Pilsudski (1867-1935) and Pope Benedict XV (1854-1922) A602

Perf. 11x11½ Syncopated
2019, Mar. 29   **Litho.**
1715 A602 €1.15 multi   2.60 2.60
Diplomatic relations between Vatican City and Poland, cent. See Poland No. 4408.

SEMI-POSTAL STAMPS

Holy Year Issue

Cross and Orb
SP1   SP2

1933 Unwmk. Engr. Perf. 13x13½
B1 SP1 25c + 10c green   4.75 4.75
B2 SP1 75c + 15c scarlet   8.25 16.50
B3 SP2 80c + 20c red brown   30.00 22.50
B4 SP2 1.25 l + 25c ultra   9.00 17.00
   Nos. B1-B4 (4)   52.00 60.75
Set, never hinged   190.00

> Catalogue values for unused stamps in this section, from this point to the end of the section, are for Never Hinged items.

Shrine of Our Lady of Mentorella, Italy, 1500th Anniv. — SP3

2010, Mar. 5   **Litho.**   **Perf. 14¼x14¾**
B5 SP3 65c +20c multi   2.25 2.25
Printed in sheets of 6. Surtax for Haitian earthquake relief.

AIR POST STAMPS

> Catalogue values for unused stamps in this section are for Never Hinged items.

Statue of St. Peter AP1

Dove of Peace over Vatican AP2

Elijah's Ascent into Heaven AP3

Our Lady of Loreto and Angels Moving the Holy House AP4

Wmk. 235
1938, June 22 Engr. Perf. 14
C1 AP1 25c brown   .30 .25
C2 AP2 50c green   .30 .25
C3 AP3 75c lake   .30 .30
C4 AP4 80c dark blue   .30 .45
C5 AP1 1 l violet   .90 .50
C6 AP2 2 l ultra   1.60 .80
C7 AP3 5 l slate blk   3.50 2.50
C8 AP4 10 l dk brown vio   3.50 2.50
   Nos. C1-C8 (8)   10.70 7.55

Dove of Peace Above St. Peter's Basilica — AP5   House of Our Lady of Loreto — AP6

Birds Circling Cross — AP7

1947, Nov. 10   **Photo.**
C9 AP5 1 l rose red   .25 .25
C10 AP6 4 l dark brown   .25 .25
C11 AP5 5 l brt ultra   .25 .25
C12 AP7 15 l brt purple   2.25 2.10
C13 AP6 25 l dk blue green   5.25 2.75
C14 AP7 50 l dk gray   7.50 5.25
C15 AP7 100 l red orange   35.00 9.00
   Nos. C9-C15 (7)   50.75 19.85
Nos. C13-C15 exist imperf. Value, each pair €1,000.

Archangel Raphael and Young Tobias AP8

1948, Dec. 28 Engr. Perf. 14
C16 AP8 250 l sepia   55.00 10.00
C17 AP8 500 l ultra   585.00 375.00
Set, hinged   440.00

Angels and Globe AP9

1949, Dec. 3
C18 AP9 300 l ultra   30.00 12.50
C19 AP9 1000 l green   150.00 82.50
Set, hinged   95.00
UPU, 75th anniversary.

Franciscus Gratianus — AP10

1951, Dec. 20   **Perf. 14x13**
C20 AP10 300 l deep plum   350.00 220.00
C21 AP10 500 l deep blue   45.00 20.00
Set, hinged   240.00
Publication of unified canon laws, 800th anniv.

Dome of St. Peter's Basilica — AP11

1953, Aug. 10   **Perf. 13**
C22 AP11 500 l chocolate   35.00 9.00
C23 AP11 1000 l deep ultra   105.00 20.00
Set, hinged   47.50
See Nos. C33-C34.

Archangel Gabriel by Melozzo da Forli — AP12

Archangel Gabriel: 10 l, 35 l, 100 l, Annunciation by Pietro Cavallini. 15 l, 50 l, 300 l, Annunciation by Leonardo da Vinci.

1956, Feb. 12   **Wmk. 235**
C24 AP12 5 l gray black   .25 .25
C25 AP12 10 l blue green   .25 .25
C26 AP12 15 l deep orange   .25 .25
C27 AP12 25 l dk car rose   .25 .25
C28 AP12 35 l carmine   .25 .25
C29 AP12 50 l olive brown   .25 .25
C30 AP12 60 l ultra   2.75 2.25
C31 AP12 100 l orange brown   .25 .25
C32 AP12 300 l deep violet   .75 .75
   Nos. C24-C32 (9)   5.25 4.75

Type of 1953
1958   **Perf. 13½**
C33 AP11 500 l grn & bl grn   7.50 4.00
  a. Perf. 14   4,000. 1,200.
C34 AP11 1000 l dp mag   .75 .75
  a. Perf. 14   .75 .75

Obelisk of St. John Lateran — AP13

Obelisks, Rome: 10 l, 60 l, St. Mary Major. 15 l, 100 l, St. Peter. 25 l, 200 l, Piazza del Popolo. 35 l, 500 l, Trinita dei Monti.

1959, Oct. 27 Engr. Perf. 13½x14
C35 AP13 5 l dull violet   .25 .25
C36 AP13 10 l blue green   .25 .25
C37 AP13 15 l dk brown   .25 .25
C38 AP13 25 l slate grn   .25 .25
C39 AP13 35 l ultra   .25 .25
C40 AP13 50 l yellow grn   .25 .25
C41 AP13 60 l rose carmine   .25 .25
C42 AP13 100 l bluish black   .25 .25
C43 AP13 200 l brown   .25 .25
C44 AP13 500 l orange brn   .30 .25
   Nos. C35-C44 (10)   2.55 2.50

Archangel Gabriel by Filippo Valle — AP14

1962, Mar. 13   **Wmk. 235**
C45 AP14 1000 l brown   1.25 .75
C46 AP14 1500 l dark blue   1.75 1.25

Jet over St. Peter's Cathedral AP15

Designs: 40 l, 200 l, Radio tower and statue of Archangel Gabriel (like A87). 90 l, 500 l,

Aerial view of St. Peter's Square and Vatican City.

1967, Mar. 7   Photo.   Perf. 14
C47	AP15	20 l brt violet	.25	.25
C48	AP15	40 l black & pink	.25	.25
C49	AP15	90 l sl bl & dk gray	.25	.25
C50	AP15	100 l black & salmon	.25	.25
C51	AP15	200 l vio blk & gray	.25	.25
C52	AP15	500 l dk brn & lt brn	.25	.25
		Nos. C47-C52 (6)	1.50	1.50

Archangel Gabriel by Fra Angelico — AP16

1968, Mar. 12   Engr.   Perf. 13½x14
C53	AP16	1000 l dk car rose, *cr*	1.00	.75
C54	AP16	1500 l black, *cr*	1.75	1.50

St. Matthew, by Fra Angelico AP17

The Evangelists, by Fra Angelico from Niccolina Chapel: 300 l, St. Mark. 500 l, St. Luke. 1000 l, St. John.

Engr. & Photo.
Perf. 14x13½
1971, Sept. 30   Unwmk.
C55	AP17	200 l blk & pale grn	.25	.25
C56	AP17	300 l black & bister	.25	.25
C57	AP17	500 l black & salmon	.85	.60
C58	AP17	1000 l black & pale lil	1.00	.75
		Nos. C55-C58 (4)	2.35	1.85

AP18

Seraph, mosaic from St. Mark's Basilica, Venice.

Litho. & Engr.
1974, Feb. 21   Perf. 13x14
C59	AP18	2500 l multicolored	2.50	2.00

AP19

Last Judgment, by Michelangelo: 500 l, Angel with Trumpet. 1000 l, Ascending figures. 2500 l, Angels with trumpets.

Litho. & Engr.
1976, Feb. 19   Perf. 13x14
C60	AP19	500 l sal, bl & brn	1.25	1.10
C61	AP19	1000 l sal, bl & brn	1.50	1.10
C62	AP19	2500 l sal, bl & brn	2.00	1.50
		Nos. C60-C62 (3)	4.75	3.70

Radio Waves, Antenna, Papal Arms AP20

1978, July 11   Engr.   Perf. 14x13
C63	AP20	1000 l multicolored	1.00	.70
C64	AP20	2000 l multicolored	2.00	1.40
C65	AP20	3000 l multicolored	3.00	1.90
		Nos. C63-C65 (3)	6.00	4.00

10th World Telecommunications Day.

Pope John Paul II Shaking Hands, Arms of Dominican Republic AP21

Litho. & Engr.
1980, June 24   Perf. 14x13½
C66	AP21	200 l shown	.25	.25
C67	AP21	300 l Mexico	.30	.30
C68	AP21	500 l Poland	.60	.60
C69	AP21	1000 l Ireland	1.10	1.10
C70	AP21	1500 l US	1.75	1.75
C71	AP21	2000 l UN	2.00	2.00
C72	AP21	3000 l with Dimitrios I, Turkey	3.50	3.50
		Nos. C66-C72 (7)	9.50	9.50

Issued: 3000 l, Sept. 18; others June 24.

World Communications Year — AP22

Designs: 2000 l, Moses Explaining The Law to the People by Luca Signorelli. 5000 l, Paul Preaching in Athens, Tapestry of Raphael design.

1983, Nov. 10   Perf. 14
C73	AP22	2000 l multicolored	3.00	3.00
C74	AP22	5000 l multicolored	6.75	6.75

Journeys of Pope John Paul II, 1983-84 AP23

Designs: 350 l, Central America, the Caribbean, 1983. 450 l, Warsaw Cathedral, Our Lady of Czestochowa, Poland, 1983. 700 l, Statue of Our Lady, Lourdes, France, 1983. 1000 l, Mariazell Sanctuary, St. Stephen's Cathedral, Austria, 1983. 1500 l, Asia, the Pacific, 1984. 2000 l, Einsiedeln Basilica, St. Nicholas of Flue, Switzerland, 1984. 2500 l, Quebec's Notre Dame Cathedral, five crosses of the Jesuit martyrs, Canada, 1984. 5000 l, Saragossa, Spain, Dominican Republic and Puerto Rico, 1984.

1986, Nov. 20 Photo. Perf. 14x13½
C75	AP23	350 l multicolored	.50	.50
C76	AP23	450 l multicolored	.65	.65
C77	AP23	700 l multicolored	1.00	1.00
C78	AP23	1000 l multicolored	1.50	1.50
C79	AP23	1500 l multicolored	2.25	2.25
C80	AP23	2000 l multicolored	3.25	3.25
C81	AP23	2500 l multicolored	4.00	4.00
C82	AP23	5000 l multicolored	8.00	8.00
		Nos. C75-C82 (8)	21.15	21.15

Papal Journeys Type of 1986

Designs: 450 l, Horseman, shepherdess, St. Peter's Basilica, Cathedral of Santiago in Chile, and the Sanctuary of Our Lady of Lujan, Argentina. 650 l, Youths and the Cathedral of Speyer, Federal Republic of Germany. 1000 l, St. Peter's Basilica, Altar of Gdansk, flowers

and thorns. 2500 l, Crowd and American skyscrapers. 5000 l, Tepee at Fort Simpson, Canada, and American Indians.

1988, Oct. 27 Photo. Perf. 14x13½
C83	AP23	450 l multicolored	.65	.65
C84	AP23	650 l multicolored	.95	.95
C85	AP23	1000 l multicolored	1.50	1.50
C86	AP23	2500 l multicolored	3.50	3.50
C87	AP23	5000 l multicolored	7.25	7.25
		Nos. C83-C87 (5)	13.85	13.85

Uruguay, Chile and Argentina, Mar. 30-Apr. 14, 1987 (450 l); Federal Republic of Germany, Apr. 30-May 4, 1987 (650 l); Poland, June 8-14, 1987 (1000 l); US, Sept. 10-19, 1987 (2500 l); and Canada, Sept. 20, 1987 (5000 l).

Journeys of Pope John Paul II, 1989 AP24

500 l, Africa. 1000 l, Scandinavia. 3000 l, Santiago de Compostela, Spain. 5000 l, Asia.

1990, Nov. 27 Photo. Perf. 12
Granite Paper
C88	AP24	500 l multicolored	.80	.80
C89	AP24	1000 l multicolored	1.60	1.60
C90	AP24	3000 l multicolored	5.00	5.00
C91	AP24	5000 l multicolored	8.00	8.00
		Nos. C88-C91 (4)	15.40	15.40

Madagascar, Reunion, Zambia and Malawi, Apr. 28-May 6 (500 l); Norway, Iceland, Finland, Denmark and Sweden, June 1-10 (1000 l); Korea, Indonesia and Mauritius, Oct. 6-16 (5000 l).

Travels of Pope John Paul II, 1991 AP25

1992, Nov. 24 Photo. Perf. 14
C92	AP25	500 l multicolored	.65	.65
C93	AP25	1000 l multicolored	1.40	1.40
C94	AP25	4000 l multicolored	5.25	5.25
C95	AP25	6000 l multicolored	8.00	8.00
		Nos. C92-C95 (4)	15.30	15.30

Portugal, May 10-13 (500 l); Poland, June 1-9 (1000 l); Poland, Hungary, Aug. 13-20 (4000 l); Brazil, Oct. 12-21 (6000 l).

SPECIAL DELIVERY STAMPS

Pius XI SD1

Unwmk.
1929, Aug. 1   Photo.   Perf. 14
E1	SD1	2 l carmine rose	20.50	15.00
E2	SD1	2.50 l dark blue	17.00	18.50

For overprints see Nos. Q14-Q15.

> Catalogue values for unused stamps in this section, from this point to the end of the section, are for Never Hinged items.

Aerial View of Vatican City SD2

1933, May 31   Wmk. 235   Engr.
E3	SD2	2 l rose red & brn	.35	.35
E4	SD2	2.50 l dp blue & brn	.35	*.55*

1945, Mar. 2   Unwmk.
E5	SD2	3.50 l dk car & ultra	.50	.50
E6	SD2	5 l ultra & green	.75	1.00

Nos. E5 and E6 Srchd. with New Values and Bars in Black
1945, Dec. 29
E7	SD2	6 l on 3.50 l dk car & ultra	5.50	2.75
E8	SD2	12 l on 5 l ultra & grn	5.50	2.75

Vertical pairs imperf. between exist of No. E7 (value $150) and No. E8 (value $200).

Bishop Matteo Giberti SD3

Design: 12 l, Gaspar Cardinal Contarini.

1946, Feb. 21   Photo.
Centers in Dark Brown
E9	SD3	6 l dark green	.25	.25
E10	SD3	12 l copper brown	.25	.25

See note after No. 121.
Nos. E9-E10 exist imperf (No. E10 value pair $1,900.) and part perf. (Value, pair $150.00).

St. Peter's Basilica SD5

Design: 80 l, Basilica of St. John.

1949, Mar. 7 Wmk. 235 Perf. 14
E11	SD5	40 l slate gray	15.00	4.50
a.		Perf. 13½x14	32.50	8.00
E12	SD5	80 l chestnut brown	50.00	27.50
a.		Perf. 13½x14	55.00	32.50

St. Peter and His Tomb — SD6

85 l, Pius XII and Roman sepulcher.

Perf. 13½x13, 14
1953, Apr. 23   Engr.
E13	SD6	50 l blue grn & dk brn	.25	.25
E14	SD6	85 l dp orange & dk brn	.35	.25

Arms of Pope John XXIII SD7

1960   Photo.   Perf. 14
E15	SD7	75 l red & brown	.25	.25
E16	SD7	100 l dk blue & brown	.25	.25

Pope Paul VI by Enrico Manfrini — SD8

Design: 150 l, Papal arms.

1966, Mar. 8   Wmk. 235   Perf. 14

E17	SD8	150 l black brown	.25	.25
E18	SD8	180 l brown	.25	.25

POSTAGE DUE STAMPS

Nos. 1-3 Overprinted in Black and Brown

1931, Oct. 1   Unwmk.   Perf. 14

J1	A1	5c dk brown & pink	.35	.75
a.		Double frame	—	
J2	A1	10c dk grn & lt grn	.35	.75
a.		Frame omitted	5,250.	
J3	A1	20c violet & lilac	1.90	2.25

No. 5 Surcharged

J4	A1	40c on 30c indigo & yel	2.25	6.00

Nos. 10-11 Surcharged

J5	A2	60c on 2 l olive brn	40.00	30.00
J6	A2	1.10 l on 2.50 l red org	11.00	22.50
		Nos. J1-J6 (6)	55.85	62.25
		Set, never hinged	235.00	

In addition to the surcharges, #J4-J6 are overprinted with ornamental frame as on #J1-J3.

No. J5 is valued in the grade of fine.

> **Catalogue values for unused stamps in this section, from this point to the end of the section, are for Never Hinged items.**

Papal Arms — D1

Unwmk.

1945, Aug. 16   Typo.   Perf. 14

J7	D1	5c black & yellow	.25	.25
J8	D1	20c black & lilac	.25	.25
J9	D1	80c black & salmon	.25	.25
J10	D1	1 l black & green	.25	.25
J11	D1	2 l black & blue	.25	.25
J12	D1	5 l black & gray	.25	.25
a.		Imperf., pair	150.00	150.00
		Nos. J7-J12 (6)	1.50	1.50

A second type of Nos. J7-J12 exists, in which the colored lines of the background are thicker.

The 20c and 5 lire exist in horizontal pairs imperf. vertically. Value, each $100.

The 20c exists in horizontal pairs imperf. between. Value $275.

Papal Arms — D2

Perf. 13½x13

1954, Apr. 30   Wmk. 235   Engr.

J13	D2	4 l black & rose	.25	.25
J14	D2	6 l black & green	.30	.30
J15	D2	10 l black & yellow	.25	.25
J16	D2	20 l black & blue	.55	.55
J17	D2	50 l black & ol brn	.25	.25
J18	D2	70 l black & red brn	.25	.25
		Nos. J13-J18 (6)	1.85	1.85

Papal Arms — D3

Photo. & Engr.

1968, May 28   Wmk. 235   Perf. 14

J19	D3	10 l black, grysh bl	.25	.25
J20	D3	20 l black, pale bl	.25	.25
J21	D3	50 l black, pale lil rose	.25	.25
J22	D3	60 l black, gray	.25	.25
J23	D3	100 l black, dull yel	.25	.25
J24	D3	180 l black, bluish lil	.25	.25
		Nos. J19-J24 (6)	1.50	1.50

PARCEL POST STAMPS

Nos. 1-7 Overprinted

1931, Oct. 1   Unwmk.   Perf. 14

Q1	A1	5c dk brown & pink	.25	.55
Q2	A1	10c dk grn & lt grn	.25	.55
Q3	A1	20c violet & lilac	7.50	2.60
Q4	A1	25c dk bl & lt bl	11.00	5.50
Q5	A1	30c indigo & yel	7.50	5.50
Q6	A1	50c indigo & sal buff	7.50	5.50
Q7	A1	75c brn car & gray	1.50	5.50
a.		Inverted overprint	750.00	

Nos. 8-13 Overprinted

Q8	A2	80c carmine rose	1.10	5.50
Q9	A2	1.25 l dark blue	1.50	5.50
Q10	A2	2 l olive brown	1.10	5.50
a.		Inverted overprint	750.00	900.00
Q11	A2	2.50 l red orange	1.90	5.50
a.		Double overprint	750.00	
b.		Inverted overprint	1,350.	
Q12	A2	5 l dark green	1.90	5.50
Q13	A2	10 l olive black	1.50	5.50
a.		Double overprint	950.00	

Nos. E1-E2 Overprinted Vertically

Q14	SD1	2 l carmine rose	1.50	5.50
Q15	SD1	2.50 l dark blue	1.50	5.50
a.		Inverted overprint	750.00	
		Nos. Q1-Q15 (15)	47.50	69.70
		Set, never hinged	160.00	

VENEZUELA

ˌve-nə-ˈzwā-lə

LOCATION — Northern coast of South America, bordering on the Caribbean Sea
GOVT. — Republic
AREA — 352,143 sq. mi.
POP. — 23,203,466 (1999 est.)
CAPITAL — Caracas

100 Centavos = 8 Reales = 1 Peso
100 Centesimos = 1 Venezolano (1879)
100 Centimos = 1 Bolivar (1880)

Watermark

Wmk. 346

Catalogue values for unused stamps in this country are for Never Hinged items, beginning with Scott 743 in the regular postage section, Scott B2 in the semipostal section, Scott C709 in the airpost section, and Scott E1 in the special delivery section.

Coat of Arms — A1

Fine Impression
No Dividing Line Between Stamps

		Unwmk.	
1859, Jan. 1		**Litho.**	**Imperf.**
1	A1 ½r yellow	60.00	12.00
a.	½r orange	—	
b.	Greenish paper	225.00	
2	A1 1r blue	450.00	15.00
a.	Half used as ½r on cover		7,500.
3	A1 2r red	42.50	15.00
a.	2r dull rose red	55.00	17.00
b.	Half used as 1r on cover		1,250.
c.	Greenish paper	225.00	140.00
	Nos. 1-3 (3)	552.50	42.00

Coarse Impression

			Thick Paper
1859-62			
4	A1 ½r orange ('61)	12.00	4.00
a.	½r yellow ('59)	500.00	30.00
b.	½r olive yellow	750.00	35.00
c.	Bluish paper	575.00	
d.	½r dull rose (error)	250,000.	350,000.
5	A1 1r blue ('62)	20.00	12.50
a.	1r pale blue	35.00	15.00
b.	1r dark blue	35.00	15.00
c.	Half used as ½r on cover		7,500.
d.	Bluish paper	200.00	
6	A1 2r red ('62)	45.00	80.00
a.	2r dull rose	55.00	80.00
b.	Tête bêche pair	10,000.	
c.	Half used as 1r on cover		400.00
d.	Bluish paper	225.00	
	Nos. 4-6 (3)	77.00	96.50

In the fine impression, the background lines of the shield are more sharply drawn. In the coarse impression, the shading lines at each end of the scroll inscribed "LIBERTAD" are usually very heavy. Stamps of the coarse impression are closer together, and there is usually a dividing line between them.

Nos. 1-3 exist on thick paper and on bluish paper. Nos. 1-6 exist on pelure paper.

The greenish paper varieties (Nos. 1b and 3c) and the bluish paper varieties were not regularly issued.

Arms — A2

1862		**Litho.**	
7	A2 ¼c green	20.00	200.00
8	A2 ½c dull lilac	8.00	240.00
a.	½c violet	40.00	210.00
9	A2 1c gray brown	42.50	400.00
	Nos. 7-9 (3)	70.50	840.00

Counterfeits are plentiful. Forged cancellations abound on Nos. 7-17.

Eagle — A3

1863-64			
10	A3 ½c pale red ('64)	55.00	400.00
a.	½c red	60.00	400.00
11	A3 1c slate ('64)	62.50	160.00
12	A3 ½r orange	7.75	3.50
13	A3 1r blue	17.00	8.50
a.	1r pale blue	30.00	13.00
b.	Half used as ½r on cover		750.00
14	A3 2r green	23.00	20.00
a.	2r deep yellow green	30.00	20.00
b.	Quarter used as ½r on cover		7,500.
c.	Half used as 1r on cover		2,000.

Counterfeits exist.

1865		**Redrawn**	
15	A3 ½r orange	4.00	2.50

The redrawn stamp has a broad "N" in "FEDERACION." "MEDIO REAL" and "FEDERACION" are in thin letters. There are 52 instead of 49 pearls in the circle.

No. 15 in yellow is a postal forgery.

A4

1865-70			
16	A4 ½c yel grn ('67)	275.00	300.00
17	A4 1c bl grn ('67)	275.00	250.00
18	A4 ½r brn vio (thin paper)	9.50	2.00
19	A4 ½r lil rose ('70)	9.50	3.25
a.	½r brownish rose	9.50	3.00
b.	Tête bêche pair	200.00	600.00
20	A4 1r vermilion	45.00	15.00
a.	Half used as ½r on cover		500.00
21	A4 2r yellow	160.00	77.50
a.	Half used as 1r on cover		3,000.
	Nos. 16-21 (6)	774.00	647.75

This issue is known unofficially rouletted.
Postal forgeries exist of the ½r.
One quarter of #21 used as ½r is a postal forgery.
For overprints see Nos. 37-48.

Overprinted in Very Small Upright Letters "Bolivar Sucre Miranda — Decreto de 27 de Abril de 1870", or "Decreto de 27 de Junio 1870" in Slanting Letters

Simón Bolívar — A5

(The "Junio" overprint is continuously repeated, in four lines arranged in two pairs, with the second line of each pair inverted.)

Un	1	Siete	7
Dos	2	Nueve	9
Tres	3	Quince	15
Cuatro	4	Veinte	20
Cinco	5	Cincuenta	50

1871-76		**Litho.**	
22	A5 1c yellow	1.50	.40
a.	1c orange	2.10	.45
b.	1c brown orange ('76)	2.10	.30
c.	1c pale buff ('76)	2.10	.45
d.	Laid paper	1.00	.75
23	A5 2c yellow	2.00	.45
a.	2c orange	4.00	.45
b.	2c brown orange	3.50	.75

---

c.	2c pale buff ('76)	3.50	.45
d.	Laid paper	3.50	.55
e.	Frame inverted	4,000.	3,000.
24	A5 3c yellow	3.00	.75
a.	3c orange	3.00	1.40
b.	3c pale buff ('76)	5.50	1.75
25	A5 4c yellow	4.00	.75
a.	4c orange	4.50	1.25
b.	4c brown orange ('76)	4.50	1.25
c.	4c buff ('76)	4.50	1.25
26	A5 5c yellow	4.00	.75
a.	5c orange	4.00	.90
b.	5c pale buff ('76)	4.00	.90
c.	Laid paper	7.50	.90
27	A5 1r rose	4.00	2.00
a.	1r pale red	4.00	2.00
b.	Laid paper	6.00	2.50
c.	Half used as ½r on cover		1,500.
28	A5 2r rose	4.50	2.00
a.	2r pale red	4.50	2.00
b.	Laid paper	12.00	2.50
29	A5 3r rose	6.00	2.00
a.	3r pale red	6.00	2.00
30	A5 5r rose	5.75	1.00
a.	5r pale red	5.75	1.00
31	A5 7r rose	22.50	4.00
a.	7r pale red	22.50	4.00
32	A5 9r green	22.50	4.25
a.	9r olive green	22.50	6.00
33	A5 15r green	55.00	8.50
a.	15r gray green ('76)	55.00	8.50
b.	Frame inverted	8,000.	6,500.
34	A5 20r green	77.50	20.00
a.	Laid paper	110.00	35.00
35	A5 30r green	375.00	110.00
a.	30r gray green ('76)	600.00	160.00
b.	Double overprint		
36	A5 50r green	1,200.	300.00
a.	50r gray green ('76)		
	Nos. 22-34 (13)	212.25	46.85
	Nos. 22-35 (14)	587.25	156.85

These stamps were made available for postage and revenue by official decree, and were the only stamps sold for postage in Venezuela from Mar., 1871 to Aug., 1873.

Due to lack of canceling handstamps, the majority of stamps were canceled with pen marks. Fiscal cancellations were also made with the pen. The values quoted are for pen-canceled stamps.

Different settings were used for the different overprints. Stamps with the upright letters were issued in 1871. Those with the slanting letters in one double line were issued in 1872-73. Those with the slanting overprint in two double lines were issued starting in 1874 from several different settings, those of 1877-78 showing much coarser impressions of the design than the earlier issues. The 7r and 9r are not known with this overprint. Stamps on laid paper (1875) are from a separate setting.

Stamps and Types of 1866-67 Overprinted in Two Lines of Very Small Letters Repeated Continuously

Overprinted "Estampillas de Correo — Contrasena"

1873, July 1			
37	A4 ½r pale rose	70.00	13.00
a.	½r rose	70.00	13.00
b.	Inverted overprint	175.00	75.00
c.	Tête bêche pair	3,000.	2,000.
38	A4 1r vermilion	85.00	25.00
a.	Inverted overprint	—	
b.	Half used as ½r on cover		5,500.
39	A4 2r yellow	300.00	125.00
a.	Inverted overprint	—	
b.	Half used as 1r on cover		12,000.
	Nos. 37-39 (3)	455.00	163.00

Overprinted "Contrasena — Estampillas de Correo"

1873, Nov.			
40	A4 1c gray lilac	30.00	32.50
a.	Inverted overprint	6.50	17.00
41	A4 2c green	125.00	90.00
a.	Inverted overprint	40.00	50.00
b.	As "a," half used as 1c on cover		7,500.
42	A4 ½r rose	72.50	13.00
a.	Inverted overprint	30.00	4.00
b.	½r light rose	60.00	11.00
43	A4 1r vermilion	85.00	23.00
a.	Inverted overprint	35.00	9.00
b.	Half used as ½r on cover		300.00
44	A4 2r yellow	325.00	160.00
a.	Inverted overprint	110.00	50.00
b.	Half used as 1r on cover		10,000.
	Nos. 40-44 (5)	637.50	318.50

Overprinted "Contrasena — Estampilla de Correos"

1875			
45	A4 ½r rose	85.00	10.00
a.	Inverted overprint	125.00	25.00
b.	Double overprint	160.00	90.00
46	A4 1r vermilion	160.00	15.00
a.	Inverted overprint	200.00	80.00
b.	Tête bêche pair	3,500.	3,000.
c.	Half used as ½r on cover		3,500.

Overprinted "Estampillas de correo — Contrasena"

1876-77			
47	A4 ½r rose	77.50	9.25
a.	½r pink	65.00	7.50
b.	Inverted overprint	65.00	7.50
c.	Both lines of overprint read "Contrasena"	75.00	17.50
d.	Both lines of overprint read "Estampillas de correo"	75.00	17.50
e.	Double overprint	125.00	35.00
48	A4 1r vermilion ('77)	92.50	23.00
a.	Inverted overprint	85.00	24.00
b.	Tête bêche pair	2,250.	2,500.
c.	Half used as ½r on cover		

On Nos. 47 and 48 "correo" has a small "c" instead of a capital. Nos. 45 and 46 have the overprint in slightly larger letters than the other stamps of the 1873-76 issues.

Overprinted "Decreto de 27 Junio 1870" Twice, One Line Inverted

Simón Bolívar

A6 　　　　A7

1879			**Imperf.**
49	A6 1c yellow	4.00	1.00
a.	1c orange	5.00	1.50
b.	1c olive yellow	5.50	1.75
50	A6 5c yellow	3.50	.50
a.	5c orange	2.50	.75
b.	Double overprint	20.00	10.00
51	A6 10c blue	5.00	.50
52	A6 30c blue	7.75	1.00
53	A6 50c blue	7.75	1.00
54	A6 90c blue	40.00	12.00
55	A7 1v rose red	77.50	18.00
56	A7 3v rose red	130.00	55.00
57	A7 5v rose red	225.00	77.50
	Nos. 49-57 (9)	500.50	166.50

In 1879 and the early part of 1880 there were no regular postage stamps in Venezuela and the stamps inscribed "Escuelas" were permitted to serve for postal as well as revenue purposes. Postally canceled stamps are extremely scarce. Values quoted are for stamps with cancellations of banks or business houses or with pen cancellations. Stamps with pen marks removed are sometimes offered as unused stamps, or may have fraudulent postal cancellations added.

Nos. 49-57 exist without overprint. These are proofs.

A8 　　　　A9

1880			**Perf. 11**
58	A8 5c yellow	1.50	.50
a.	5c orange	1.50	.50
b.	Printed on both sides	150.00	85.00
59	A8 10c yellow	2.50	.60
a.	10c orange	2.50	.60
60	A8 25c yellow	2.50	.60
a.	25c orange	2.75	.70
b.	Printed on both sides	110.00	52.50
c.	Impression of 5c on back	175.00	90.00
61	A8 50c yellow	4.75	.80
a.	50c orange	5.25	.85
b.	Half used as 25c on cover		
c.	Printed on both sides	150.00	90.00
d.	Impression of 25c on back	150.00	90.00
62	A9 1b pale blue	12.00	1.40
63	A9 2b pale blue	17.00	1.75
64	A9 5b pale blue	40.00	5.75
a.	Half used as 2½b on cover		
65	A9 10b rose red	200.00	70.00
66	A9 20b rose red	1,200.	200.00
67	A9 25b rose red	5,000.	500.00
	Nos. 58-65 (8)	280.25	81.40

See note on used values below No. 57.

Bolívar — A10

1880   Litho.   Perf. 11
Thick or Thin Paper

68	A10	5c blue	15.00	7.25
a.		Printed on both sides	225.00	140.00
69	A10	10c rose	20.00	12.00
a.		10c carmine	20.00	12.00
b.		Double impression	90.00	75.00
c.		Horiz. pair, imperf. btwn.	75.00	75.00
70	A10	10c scarlet	20.00	12.00
a.		Horiz. pair, imperf. btwn.	75.00	75.00
71	A10	25c yellow	15.00	7.25
b.		Thick paper	20.00	10.00
72	A10	50c brown	92.50	40.00
a.		50c deep brown	92.50	40.00
b.		Printed on both sides	225.00	140.00
c.		Half used as 25c on cover		5,000.
73	A10	1b green	140.00	50.00
a.		Horiz. pair, imperf. btwn.	300.00	300.00
		Nos. 68-73 (6)	302.50	128.50

Nos. 68 to 73 were used for the payment of postage on letters to be sent abroad and the Escuelas stamps were then restricted to internal use.

Counterfeits of this issue exist in a great variety of shades as well as in wrong colors. They are on thick and thin paper, white or toned, and imperf. or perforated 11, 12 and compound. They are also found tête bêche. Counterfeits of Nos. 68 to 72 inclusive often have a diagonal line across the "S" of "CENTS" and a short line from the bottom of that letter to the frame below it. Originals of No. 73 show parts of a frame around "BOLIVAR."

Simón Bolívar
A11   A12

A13   A14

A15

1882, Aug. 1   Engr.   Perf. 12

74	A11	5c blue	.70	.35
75	A12	10c red brown	.70	.35
76	A13	25c yellow brown	1.10	.40
a.		Printed on both sides	50.00	27.50
77	A14	50c green	2.40	.70
a.		Half used as 25c on cover		500.00
78	A15	1b violet	4.50	1.75
		Nos. 74-78 (5)	9.40	3.55

Nos. 75-78 exist imperf. Value, set $32.50.
See Nos. 88, 92-95. For surcharges and overprints see Nos. 100-103, 108-112.

A16   A17

A18   A19

A20   A21

A22   A23

1882-88

79	A16	5c blue green	.25	.25
80	A17	10c brown	.25	.25
81	A18	25c orange	.25	.25
82	A19	50c blue	.25	.25
83	A20	1b vermilion	.25	.25
84	A21	3b dull vio ('88)	.25	.25
85	A22	10b dark brn ('88)	1.25	.80
86	A23	20b plum ('88)	1.50	.95
		Nos. 79-86 (8)	4.25	3.25

By official decree, dated Apr. 14, 1882, stamps of types A11 to A15 were to be used for foreign postage and those of types A16 to A23 for inland correspondence and fiscal use.
Issue date: Nos. 79-83, Aug. 1.
See Nos. 87, 89-91, 96-99. For surcharges and overprints see Nos. 104-107, 114-122.

1887-88   Litho.   Perf. 11

87	A16	5c gray green	.45	.30
88	A13	25c yellow brown	55.00	22.50
89	A18	25c orange	.70	.45
90	A20	1b orange red ('88)	4.75	.90
		Nos. 87-90 (4)	60.90	24.15

Perf. 14

91	A16	5c gray green	95.00	40.00

Stamps of type A16, perf. 11 and 14, are from a new die with "ESCUELAS" in smaller letters. Stamps of the 1887-88 issue, perf. 12, and a 50c dark blue, perf. 11 or 12, are believed by experts to be from printer's waste.
Counterfeits of No. 91 have been made by perforating printers waste of No. 96.

Rouletted 8

92	A11	5c blue	40.00	17.00
93	A13	25c yel brown	15.00	10.00
94	A14	50c green	15.00	10.00
95	A15	1b purple	30.00	20.00
		Nos. 92-95 (4)	100.00	57.00

1887-88

96	A16	5c green	.25	.25
97	A18	25c orange	.25	.25
98	A19	50c dark blue	1.25	1.10
99	A21	3b purple ('88)	3.50	3.50
		Nos. 96-99 (4)	5.25	5.10

The so-called imperforate varieties of Nos. 92 to 99, and the pin perforated 50c dark blue, type A19, are believed to be from printer's waste.

Stamps of 1882-88 Handstamp Surcharged in Violet

1892   Perf. 12

100	A11	25c on 5c blue	40.00	40.00
101	A12	25c on 10c red brn	16.00	16.00
102	A13	1b on 25c yel brn	16.00	16.00
103	A14	1b on 50c green	20.00	20.00
		Nos. 100-103 (4)	92.00	92.00

See note after No. 107.

1892

104	A16	25c on 5c bl grn	10.00	6.00
105	A17	25c on 10c brown	10.00	6.00
106	A18	1b on 25c orange	15.00	12.00
107	A19	1b on 50c blue	23.00	12.00
		Nos. 104-107 (4)	58.00	36.00

Counterfeits of this surcharge abound.

Stamps of 1882-88 Overprinted in Red or Black

1893

108	A11	5c blue (R)	.55	.25
a.		Inverted overprint	3.25	3.25
b.		Double overprint	16.00	16.00
109	A12	10c red brn (Bk)	.90	.90
a.		Inverted overprint	4.00	4.00
b.		Double overprint	16.00	16.00
110	A13	25c yel brn (R)	.80	.50
a.		Inverted overprint	5.25	5.25
b.		Double overprint	16.00	16.00
c.		25c yel brn (Bk)	500.00	500.00
111	A14	50c green (R)	1.25	.80
a.		Inverted overprint	5.25	5.25
b.		Double overprint	27.50	27.50
112	A15	1b pur (R)	3.25	1.20
a.		Inverted overprint	10.00	10.00
		Nos. 108-112 (5)	6.75	3.55

1893

114	A16	5c bl grn (R)	.25	.25
a.		Inverted overprint	3.25	3.25
b.		Double overprint	5.25	5.25
115	A17	10c brn (R)	.25	.25
a.		Inverted overprint	3.25	3.25
116	A18	25c org (R)	.25	.25
a.		Inverted overprint	3.25	3.25
117	A18	25c org (Bk)	5.75	2.75
a.		Inverted overprint	8.25	5.00
118	A19	50c blue (R)	.25	.25
a.		Inverted overprint	3.25	3.25
119	A20	1b ver (Bk)	.60	.40
a.		Inverted overprint	4.00	4.00
120	A21	3b dl vio (R)	.90	.40
a.		Inverted overprint	8.25	8.25
121	A22	10b dk brn (R)	3.50	2.25
a.		Double overprint	10.00	10.00
b.		Inverted overprint	20.00	20.00
122	A23	20b plum (Bk)	3.00	3.00
a.		Double overprint	10.00	20.00
		Nos. 114-122 (9)	14.75	9.80

Counterfeits exist.

Simón Bolívar — A24

1893   Engr.

123	A24	5c red brn	.90	.25
124	A24	10c blue	3.25	1.25
125	A24	25c magenta	15.00	.50
126	A24	50c brn vio	4.25	.55
127	A24	1b green	5.75	1.25
		Nos. 123-127 (5)	29.15	3.80

Many shades exist in this issue, but their values do not vary.

Simón Bolívar — A25

1893

128	A25	5c gray	.25	.25
129	A25	10c green	.25	.25
130	A25	25c blue	.25	.25
131	A25	50c orange	.25	.25
132	A25	1b red vio	.25	.25
133	A25	3b red	.55	.25
134	A25	10b dl vio	.90	.80
135	A25	20b red brn	4.25	2.75
		Nos. 128-135 (8)	6.95	5.05

By decree of Nov. 28, 1892, the stamps inscribed "Correos" were to be used for external postage and those inscribed "Instruccion" were for internal postage and revenue purposes.
For surcharge see No. 230.

Until July 1, 1895, revenue stamps inscribed "Escuelas" or "Instruccion," fiscal stamps for the collection of taxes for primary schools, were used as both revenue stamps and as postage stamps. After that date, they were no longer to be used for postal purposes, but their use was permitted when supplies of regular postage stamps were temporarily exhausted. See Nos. AR1-AR86.

Landing of Columbus A26

1893   Perf. 12

136	A26	25c magenta	11.00	.60

4th cent. of the discovery of the mainland of South America, also participation of Venezuela in the Intl. Exhib. at Chicago in 1893.

Map of Venezuela A27

1896   Litho.

137	A27	5c yel grn	3.00	2.75
a.		5c apple green	3.00	2.75
138	A27	10c blue	4.00	5.50
139	A27	25c yellow	4.00	5.50
a.		25c orange	4.00	5.50
b.		Tête bêche pair	125.00	125.00
140	A27	50c rose red	55.00	25.00
a.		50c red	52.50	52.50
b.		Tête bêche pair	375.00	375.00
141	A27	1b violet	40.00	27.50
		Nos. 137-141 (5)	106.00	66.25

Gen. Francisco Antonio Gabriel de Miranda (1752-1816).
These stamps were in use from July 4 to Nov. 4, 1896. Later usage is known.
There are many forgeries of this issue. They include faked errors, imperforate stamps and many tête bêche. The paper of the originals is thin, white and semi transparent. The gum is shiny and crackled. The paper of the reprints is often thick and opaque. The gum is usually dull, smooth, thin and only slightly adhesive.

Bolívar — A28

1899-1901   Engr.

142	A28	5c dk grn	1.00	.25
143	A28	10c red	1.25	.40
144	A28	25c blue	1.50	.55
145	A28	50c gray blk	2.00	1.00
146	A28	50c org ('01)	1.75	.50
147	A28	1b yel grn	32.50	15.00
149	A28	2b orange	400.00	225.00
		Nos. 142-147,149 (7)	440.00	242.70

Stamps of 1899 Overprinted in Black

1900

150	A28	5c dk grn	1.25	.40
a.		Inverted overprint	4.75	4.75
151	A28	10c red	1.25	.40
a.		Inverted overprint	6.50	6.50
b.		Double overprint	10.50	10.50
152	A28	25c blue	7.75	1.25
a.		Inverted overprint	13.00	13.00
153	A28	50c gray blk	4.00	.55
a.		Inverted overprint	12.00	12.00
154	A28	1b yel grn	1.75	.80
a.		Double overprint	13.00	13.00
b.		Inverted overprint	12.00	12.00

155	A28	2b orange	2.75	2.25
a.		Inverted overprint	35.00	35.00
b.		Double overprint	32.50	32.50
		Nos. 150-155 (6)	18.75	5.65

Initials are those of R. T. Mendoza. Counterfeit overprints exist, especially of inverted and doubled varieties.

Bolivar Type of 1899-1903 Overprinted

1900

156	A28	5c dk grn	750.00	750.00
157	A28	10c red	750.00	750.00
158	A28	25c blue	600.00	600.00
159	A28	50c yel orange	23.00	1.60
160	A28	1b slate	1.25	1.00
a.		Without overprint	7,000.	—
		Nos. 156-160 (5)	2,124.	2,103.

Nos. 156-158 Overprinted

1900, Aug. 14

161	A28	5c green	8.00	.55
162	A28	10c red	7.00	1.00
163	A28	25c blue	8.00	1.00
		Nos. 161-163 (3)	23.00	2.55

Inverted Overprint

161a	A28	5c	9.25	9.25
162a	A28	10c	9.25	9.25
163a	A28	25c	12.00	12.00
		Nos. 161a-163a (3)	30.50	30.50

Overprint exists on each value without "Castro" or without "1900."

Type of 1893 Surcharged

1904, Jan.   Perf. 12

230	A25	5c on 50c green	.80	.60
a.		"Vele"	23.00	23.00
b.		Surcharge reading up	1.00	.50
c.		Double surcharge	18.00	18.00

Gen. José de Sucre — A35

1904-09   Engr.

231	A35	5c bl grn	.50	.25
232	A35	10c carmine	.55	.25
233	A35	15c violet	.90	.40
234	A35	25c dp ultra	6.50	.40
235	A35	50c plum	1.00	.50
236	A35	1b plum	1.10	.50
		Nos. 231-236 (6)	10.55	2.30

Issue date: 15c, Dec. 1909. Others, July 1, 1904.

Pres. Cipriano Castro — A37

1905, July 5   Litho.   Perf. 11½

245	A37	5c vermilion	3.25	3.25
a.		5c carmine	5.00	5.00

246	A37	10c dark blue	5.50	4.25
247	A37	25c yellow	2.00	1.50
		Nos. 245-247 (3)	10.75	9.00

National Congress. Issued for interior postage only. Valid only for 90 days.

Various part-perforate varieties of Nos. 245-247 exist. Value, $15-$30.

Liberty — A38

1910, Apr. 19   Engr.   Perf. 12

249	A38	25c dark blue	13.00	.70

Centenary of national independence.

Francisco de Miranda A39   Rafael Urdaneta A40

Bolívar — A41

1911   Litho.   Perf. 11½x12

250	A39	5c dp grn	.50	.25
251	A39	10c carmine	.50	.25
252	A40	15c gray	5.75	.40
253	A40	25c dp bl	3.25	.60
a.		Imperf., pair	40.00	50.00
254	A41	50c purple	3.50	.40
255	A41	1b yellow	3.50	1.50
		Nos. 250-255 (6)	17.00	3.40

The 50c with center in blue was never issued although examples were postmarked by favor.

The centers of Nos. 250-255 were separately printed and often vary in shade from the rest of the design. In a second printing of the 5c and 10c, the entire design was printed at one time.

1913   Redrawn

255A	A40	15c gray	3.50	2.25
255B	A40	25c deep blue	2.00	.65
255C	A41	50c purple	2.00	.65
		Nos. 255A-255C (3)	7.50	3.55

The redrawn stamps have two berries instead of one at top of the left spray; a berry has been added over the "C" and "S" of "Centimos"; and the lowest leaf at the right is cut by the corner square.

Simón Bolívar — A42

1914, July   Engr.   Perf. 13½, 14, 15

256	A42	5c yel grn	37.50	.55
257	A42	10c scarlet	35.00	.50
258	A42	25c dark blue	5.75	.25
		Nos. 256-258 (3)	78.25	1.30

Simón Bolívar — A43

Different frames.

Printed by the American Bank Note Co.

1915-23   Perf. 12

259	A43	5c green	4.25	.25
260	A43	10c vermilion	10.00	.60
261	A43	10c claret ('22)	10.00	.90
262	A43	15c dull ol grn	9.25	.60
263	A43	25c ultra	6.50	.25
a.		25c blue	13.00	.60
264	A43	40c dull green	23.00	11.50
265	A43	50c dp violet	6.50	.80
266	A43	50c ultra ('23)	17.00	4.75
267	A43	75c lt blue	57.50	23.00
a.		75c greenish blue	57.50	23.00
268	A43	1b dark gray	35.00	5.25
		Nos. 259-268 (10)	179.00	47.90

See Nos. 269-285. For surcharges see Nos. 307, 309-310.

Type of 1915-23 Issue Re-engraved Printed by Waterlow & Sons, Ltd.

1924-39   Perf. 12½

269	A43	5c orange brn	.55	.25
a.		5c yellow brown	.55	.25
b.		Horiz. pair, imperf. between	25.00	40.00
270	A43	5c green ('39)	12.00	1.00
271	A43	7½c yel grn ('39)	1.25	.40
272	A43	10c dk green	.25	.25
273	A43	10c dk car ('39)	4.00	.25
274	A43	15c olive grn	2.25	.50
275	A43	15c brown ('27)	.30	.25
276	A43	25c ultra	2.25	.25
277	A43	25c red ('28)	.25	.25
a.		Horiz. pair, imperf. btwn.	50.00	85.00
278	A43	40c dp blue ('25)	.55	.25
279	A43	40c slate bl ('39)	7.75	1.25
280	A43	50c dk blue	.55	.25
281	A43	50c dk pur ('39)	7.75	.85
282	A43	1b black	.55	.25
283	A43	3b yel org ('25)	1.75	.95
284	A43	3b red org ('39)	12.00	4.25
285	A43	5b dull vio ('25)	16.00	8.50
		Nos. 269-285 (17)	70.00	19.95

Perf. 14

269c	A43	5c	7.00	2.00
272a	A43	10c	7.00	2.00
274a	A43	15c	8.25	2.75
276a	A43	25c	12.00	4.75
280a	A43	50c	35.00	14.00
282a	A43	1b	42.50	27.00
		Nos. 269c-282a (6)	111.75	52.50

The re-engraved stamps may readily be distinguished from the 1915 issue by the perforation and sometimes by the colors. The designs differ in many minor details which are too minute for illustration or description.

Bolívar and Sucre A44

1924, Dec. 1   Perf. 11½x12, 12   Litho.

286	A44	25c grayish blue	2.75	.55

Redrawn

286A	A44	25c ultra	3.50	.85

Centenary of the Battle of Ayacucho.

The redrawn stamp has a whiter effect with less shading in the faces. Bolivar's ear is clearly visible and the outline of his aquiline nose is broken.

A45   A46

Revenue Stamps Surcharged in Black or Red

1926   Perf. 12, 12½

287	A45	5c on 1b ol grn	.65	.40
a.		Double surcharge	8.00	8.00
b.		Pair, one without surcharge	12.00	12.00
c.		Inverted surcharge	8.00	8.00
288	A46	25c on 5c dk brn (R)	.65	.40
a.		Inverted surcharge	8.00	8.00
b.		Double surcharge	8.00	8.00

View of Ciudad Bolívar and General J.V. Gómez — A47

1928, July 21   Litho.   Perf. 12

289	A47	10c deep green	1.00	.65
a.		Imperf., pair	40.00	

25th anniversary of the Battle of Ciudad Bolívar and the foundation of peace in Venezuela.

Simón Bolívar — A48

1930, Dec. 9

290	A48	5c yellow	1.00	.35
291	A48	10c dark blue	1.00	.25
292	A48	25c rose red	1.00	.25
		Nos. 290-292 (3)	3.00	.85

Imperf., Pairs

290a	A48	5c	5.25	5.25
291a	A48	10c	6.50	6.50
292a	A48	25c	10.50	10.50

Death centenary of Simón Bolívar (1783-1830), South American liberator.

Nos. 290-292 exist part-perforate, including pairs imperf. between, imperf. horiz., imperf. vert. Value range, $6-12.

Simón Bolívar — A49

Various Frames
Bluish Winchester Security Paper

1932-38   Engr.   Perf. 12½

293	A49	5c violet	.50	.25
294	A49	7½c dk green ('37)	1.10	.40
295	A49	10c green	.65	.25
296	A49	15c yellow	1.50	.25
297	A49	22½c dp car ('38)	3.50	.50
298	A49	25c red	1.25	.25
299	A49	37½c ultra ('36)	4.50	2.00
300	A49	40c indigo	4.50	.25
301	A49	50c olive grn	4.50	.40
302	A49	1b lt blue	6.00	.70
303	A49	3b brown	47.50	13.00
304	A49	5b yellow brn	65.00	17.50
		Nos. 293-304 (12)	140.50	35.75

For surcharges see Nos. 308, 318-319, C223.

Arms of Bolívar — A50

1933, July 24   Litho.   Perf. 11

306	A50	25c brown red	3.00	2.40
a.		Imperf., pair	32.50	32.50

150th anniv. of the birth of Simón Bolívar. Valid only to Aug. 21.

Stamps of 1924-32 Surcharged in Black — (Blocks of Surcharge in Color of stamps)

1933

307	A43	7½c on 10c grn	.50	.25
a.		Double surcharge	2.50	2.50
b.		Inverted surcharge	4.25	4.25
308	A49	22½c on 25c (#298)	2.00	.85
309	A43	22½c on 25c (#277)	1.50	1.50
a.		Double surcharge	10.00	10.00
310	A43	37½c on 40c dp bl	2.00	.95
a.		Double surcharge	11.50	11.50
b.		Inverted surcharge	10.00	10.00
		Nos. 307-310 (4)	6.00	3.55

Nurse and
Child — A51

River
Scene — A52

Gathering Cacao
Pods — A53

Cattle
Raising
A54

Plowing
A55

Perf. 11, 11½ or Compound

1937, July 1   **Litho.**
311 A51   5c deep violet   .55   .35
312 A52   10c dk slate grn   .55   .25
313 A53   15c yellow brn   1.00   .55
314 A51   25c cerise   1.00   .35
315 A54   50c yellow grn   6.50   4.25
316 A55   3b red orange   12.00   7.75
317 A51   5b lt brown   23.00 15.00
   Nos. 311-317 (7)   44.60 28.50

Nos. 311-317 exist imperforate. Value for set $75. Nos. 311-315 exist in pairs, imperf. between; value range, $20-$30.

For overprints and surcharges see Nos. 321-324, 345, 376-377, 380-384.

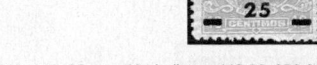

No. 300 Surcharged
in Black

1937, July   **Perf. 12½**
318 A49   25c on 40c indigo   7.75   .95
   a.   Double surcharge   16.00 16.00
   b.   Inverted surcharge   13.00 13.00
   c.   Triple surcharge   32.50 32.50

No. 300 Surcharged

319 A49   25c on 40c indigo 440.00 350.00
   a.   Double surcharge

A56

1937, Oct. 28   **Litho.**   **Perf. 10½**
320 A56   25c blue   1.25   .45

Acquisition of the Port of La Guaira by the Government from the British Corporation, June 3, 1937. Exists imperf. See Nos. C64-C65.

A redrawn printing of No. 320, with top inscription beginning "Nacionalización . . ." was prepared but not issued. Value, $40.

For surcharge see No. 385.

Stamps of 1937
Overprinted in Black

1937, Dec. 17   **Perf. 11, 11½**
321 A51   5c deep violet   5.75   3.25
322 A52   10c dk slate grn   1.75   .75
   a.   Inverted overprint   13.00 13.00
323 A51   25c cerise   1.50   .55
   a.   Inverted overprint   16.00 16.00
324 A55   3b red orange   376.00 225.00
   Nos. 321-324 (4)   384.00 229.55

Part-perforate pairs exist of Nos. 321-322 and 324. Value range, $12.50 to $125.

See Nos. C66-C78.

Gathering Coffee
Beans — A57

Simón
Bolívar — A58

Post Office,
Caracas — A59

1938   **Engr.**   **Perf. 12**
325 A57   5c green   .40   .25
326 A57   5c deep green   .40   .25
327 A58   10c car rose   .70   .25
328 A58   10c dp rose   .70   .25
329 A59   15c dk violet   1.40   .25
330 A59   15c olive grn   .85   .25
331 A58   25c lt blue   .40   .25
332 A58   25c dk blue   .40   .25
333 A58   37½c dk blue   8.50 4.00
334 A58   37½c lt blue   2.75   .85
335 A59   40c sepia   20.00 7.75
336 A59   40c black   17.00 7.75
337 A57   50c olive grn   27.50 7.75
338 A57   50c dull violet   9.25   .85
339 A58   1b dp brown   12.00 5.50
340 A58   1b black brown   17.00 1.50
341 A57   3b orange   92.50 50.00
342 A59   5b black   15.00 7.75
   Nos. 325-342 (18)   226.75 95.70

See Nos. 400, 412.

Teresa
Carreño — A60

1938, June 12   **Perf. 11½x12**
343 A60   25c blue   5.75   .60

Teresa Carreno, Venezuelan pianist, whose remains were repatriated Feb. 14, 1938.

For surcharge see No. 386.

Bolívar Statue — A61

1938, July 24   **Perf. 12**
344 A61   25c dark blue   6.50   .60

"The Day of the Worker."
For surcharge see No. 387.

Type of 1937
Surcharged in Black

1938   **Litho.**   **Perf. 11, 11½**
345 A51   40c on 5b lt brn   8.50   4.50
   a.   Inverted surcharge   21.00 21.00

Gen. José I. Paz
Castillo, Postmaster of
Venezuela, 1859 — A62

1939, Apr. 19   **Engr.**   **Perf. 12½**
348 A62   10c carmine   2.50   .70

80th anniv. of the first Venezuelan stamp.

View of
Ojeda
A63

1939, June 24   **Photo.**
349 A63   25c dull blue   9.25   .75

Founding of city of Ojeda.

Cristóbal
Mendoza — A64

1939, Oct. 14   **Engr.**   **Perf. 13**
350 A64   5c green   .40   .25
351 A64   10c dk car rose   .40   .25
352 A64   15c dull lilac   1.00   .25
353 A64   25c brt ultra   .80   .25
354 A64   37½c dark blue   15.00 6.25
355 A64   50c lt olive grn 16.00 4.00
356 A64   1b dark brown   6.50 3.50
   Nos. 350-356 (7)   40.10 14.75

Mendoza (1772-1839), postmaster general.

Diego Urbaneja — A65

1940-43   **Perf. 12**
357 A65   5c Prus green   .55   .25
357A A65 7½c dk bl grn ('43) .80   .30
358 A65   15c olive   .95   .30
359 A65   37½c deep blue   1.50   .70
360 A65   40c violet blue   1.10   .35
361 A65   50c violet   6.50 1.75
362 A65   1b dk violet brn   3.50   .90
363 A65   3b scarlet   9.50 3.75
   Nos. 357-363 (8)   24.40 8.30

See Nos. 399, 408, 410-411. For surcharges see Nos. 396, C226.

Battle of
Carabobo,
1821 — A67

1940, June 13
365 A67   25c blue   6.75   .80

Birth of General JoséAntonio Páez, 150th anniv.

"Crossing the
Andes" by Tito
Salas — A68

1940, June 13
366 A68   25c dark blue   6.75   .80

Death cent. of General Francisco Santander.

Monument and
Urn containing
Ashes of Simón
Bolívar — A69

Bed where Simón
Bolívar was
Born — A70

Designs: 15c, "Christening of Bolivar" by Tito Salas. 20c, Bolivar's birthplace, Caracas. 25c, "Bolivar on Horseback" by Salas. 30c, Patio of Bolivar House, Caracas. 37½c, Patio of Bolivar's Birthplace. 50c, "Rebellion of 1812" by Salas.

1940-41
367 A69   5c turq green   .25   .25
368 A70   10c rose pink   .25   .25
369 A69   15c olive   .60   .25
370 A70   20c blue ('41)   1.00   .25
371 A69   25c lt blue   .60   .25
372 A70   30c plum ('41)   1.50   .25
373 A70   37½c dk blue   3.00 1.00
374 A70   50c purple   2.00   .50
   Nos. 367-374 (8)   9.20 3.00

110th anniv. of the death of Simón Bolívar. See Nos. 397, 398, 403, 405-407, 409. For surcharges see Nos. 375, 401-402, C224, C237-C238.

No. 371 Surcharged
In Black

1941
375 A69   20c on 25c lt blue .60   .25
   a.   Inverted surcharge 10.00 10.00

Nos. 311-312
Overprinted in Black

1941   *Perf. 11½*
376 A51   5c deep violet   2.00   .50
   a.   Double overprint   10.00   8.25
   b.   Vert. pair, imperf. btwn.   14.00   14.00
   c.   Inverted overprint   20.00   16.00
377 A52   10c dk slate grn   1.00   .30
   a.   Double overprint   13.00   13.00

Symbols of
Industry — A77

1942, Dec. 17   **Litho.**   *Perf. 12*
378 A77   10c scarlet   1.10   .25
   a.   Imperf., pair   22.50   22.50

Grand Industrial Exposition, Caracas.

Caracas
Cathedral — A78

1943   **Engr.**
379 A78   10c rose carmine   .75   .25
See No. 404.

Stamps of 1937
Overprinted in Black

1943   *Perf. 11, 11½*
380 A51   5c deep violet   16.00   9.50
381 A52   10c dk slate grn   6.00   4.00
382 A54   50c yellow green   8.00   4.50
383 A55   3b red orange   45.00   22.00
   Nos. 380-383 (4)   75.00   40.00

Issued for sale to philatelists & sold only in sets.

Stamps of 1937-38
Surcharged in Black

1943   *Perf. 11½, 10½, 12*
384 A51   20c on 25c cerise   30.00   30.00
385 A56   20c on 25c blue   77.50   77.50
386 A60   20c on 25c dk blue   15.00   15.00
387 A61   20c on 25c dk blue   15.00   15.00
   a.   Inverted surcharge   42.50   42.50
   Nos. 384-387 (4)   137.50   137.50

Issued for sale to philatelists & sold only in sets.

Souvenir Sheet

A79

1944, Aug. 22   **Litho.**   *Perf. 12*
Flags in Red, Yellow, Blue & Black
388 A79   Sheet of 4   35.00   35.00
   a.   5c Prussian green   3.00   .80
   b.   10c rose   4.50   .80
   c.   20c ultramarine   4.50   1.75
   d.   1b rose lake   6.00   2.25

80th anniv. of Intl. Red Cross and 37th anniv. of Venezuela's joining.
No. 388 exists imperf. Value $60.

Antonio José de
Sucre — A80

1945, Mar. 3   **Engr.**   **Unwmk.**
389 A80   5c orange yellow   2.10   1.10
390 A80   10c dark blue   3.25   1.75
391 A80   20c rose pink   4.25   1.75
   Nos. 389-391,C206-C215 (13)   33.55   22.30

Birth of Antonio de Sucre, 150th anniv.

Andrés   Gen. Rafael
Bello — A81   Urdaneta — A82

1946, Aug. 24
392 A81   20c deep blue   .65   .35
393 A82   20c deep blue   .65   .35
   Nos. 392-393,C216-C217 (4)   3.50   1.20

80th anniversary of the death of Andrés Bello (1780?-1865), educator and writer, and the centenary of the death of Gen. Rafael Urdaneta.

Allegory of the
Republic — A83

1946, Oct. 18   **Litho.**   *Perf. 11½*
394 A83   20c light blue   .80   .35
   Nos. 394,C218-C221 (5)   5.60   3.85

Anniversary of Revolution of October, 1945. Exists imperf.

Anti-tuberculosis Institute,
Maracaibo — A84

1947, Jan. 12
395 A84   20c ultra & yellow   .80   .35
   Nos. 395,C228-C231 (5)   6.90   5.15

12th Pan-American Health Conf., Caracas, Jan. 1947. Exists imperf. and part perf.

No. 362 Surcharged in
Green

396 A65   15c on 1b dk vio brn   .70   .30
   a.   Inverted surcharge   6.00   5.00
   Nos. 396,C223-C227 (6)   30.50   23.95

Types of 1938-40

1947   **Engr.**
397 A69   5c green   .25   .25
398 A70   30c black   1.00   .50
399 A65   40c red violet   .95   .25
400 A59   5b deep orange   40.00   18.00
   Nos. 397-400 (4)   42.20   19.00

In 1947 a decree authorized the use of 5c and 10c revenue stamps of the above type for franking correspondence. Other denominations were also used unofficially.
For surcharges see Nos. 876-883.

Nos. 398 and 373
Surcharged in Red

1947   **Unwmk.**   *Perf. 12*
401 A70   5c on 30c black   .40   .25
   a.   Inverted surcharge   5.00   5.00
402 A70   5c on 37½c dk bl   .45   .25
   a.   Inverted surcharge   5.00   5.00

Types of 1938-43

1947-48
403 A69   5c brt ultra   .25   .25
404 A78   10c red   .25   .25
405 A69   15c rose car   .50   .25
406 A69   25c violet   .40   .25
407 A70   30c dk vio brn ('48)   .50   .25
408 A65   40c orange ('48)   .50   .25
409 A70   50c olive green   .95   .25
410 A65   1b deep blue   1.75   .25
411 A65   3b gray   3.50   .90
412 A59   5b chocolate   13.00   5.00
   Nos. 403-412 (10)   21.60   7.90

M. S.
Republica
de
Venezuela
A85

**Imprint: "American Bank Note
Company"**

1948-50   **Engr.**   *Perf. 12*
413 A85   5c blue   .25   .25
414 A85   7½c red org ('49)   .70   .40
   a.   Booklet pane of 20
415 A85   10c car rose   .55   .25
   a.   Booklet pane of 10
416 A85   15c gray ('50)   .55   .25
417 A85   20c sepia   .40   .25
418 A85   25c violet ('49)   .55   .25
419 A85   30c orange ('50)   3.75   2.25
420 A85   37½c brown ('49)   1.75   1.40
421 A85   40c olive ('50)   2.50   1.75
422 A85   50c red violet ('49)   .70   .25
423 A85   1b gray green   1.75   .55
   Nos. 413-423 (11)   13.45   7.85

Grand Colombian Merchant Fleet. See Nos. 632-634, C256-C271, C554-C556. For surcharges see Nos. 450-451.

Santos
Michelena — A86

1949, Apr. 25   *Perf. 12½*
424 A86   5c ultra   .25   .25
425 A86   10c carmine   .40   .25
426 A86   20c sepia   1.60   .60
427 A86   1b green   5.75   3.00
   Nos. 424-427,C272-C277 (10)   16.50   9.70

Centenary of the death of Santos Michelena, Finance Minister, and the 110th anniversary of the Postal Convention of Bogota.

Christopher
Columbus — A87

1949-50   **Engr.**
428 A87   5c deep ultra   .45   .25
429 A87   10c carmine   1.50   .50
430 A87   20c dark brown   1.75   .60
431 A87   1b green   4.75   2.10
   Nos. 428-431,C278-C283 (10)   18.45   8.65

450th anniversary (in 1948) of Columbus' discovery of the American mainland.
Issued: 5c, 10c, 1949; 20c, 1b, Jan. 1950.

Arms of
Venezuela
A88

1948
432 A88   5c blue   1.40   .70
433 A88   10c red   1.75   .80

The 20c and 1b, type A88, and six similar air post stamps were prepared but not issued. Value, set of 8, about $125.

Gen. Francisco de
Miranda — A89

1950, Mar. 28   **Unwmk.**   *Perf. 12*
434 A89   5c blue   .25   .25
435 A89   10c green   .40   .25
436 A89   20c sepia   .85   .35
437 A89   1b rose carmine   4.00   1.75
   Nos. 434-437 (4)   5.50   2.60

Bicentenary of birth of General Francisco de Miranda.

Map and Population
Chart — A90

1950, Sept. 1
438 A90   5c blue   .25   .25
439 A90   10c gray   .25   .25
440 A90   15c sepia   .25   .25
441 A90   25c green   .45   .25
442 A90   30c red   .55   .25

443	A90	50c violet	1.10	.45
444	A90	1b red brown	2.75	1.40
		Nos. 438-444,C302-C310 (16)	12.00	7.50

8th National Census of the Americas.

Alonso de Ojeda — A91

1950, Dec. 18   Photo.   Perf. 11½

445	A91	5c deep blue	.25	.25
446	A91	10c deep red	.30	.25
447	A91	15c slate gray	.35	.25
448	A91	20c ultra	1.40	.55
449	A91	1b blue green	5.50	2.75
		Nos. 445-449 (5)	7.80	4.05
		Nos. 445-449,C316-C321 (11)	15.65	7.80

450th anniversary (in 1949) of the discovery of the Gulf of Maracaibo.

Nos. 414 and 420 Surcharged in Black

1951   Unwmk.   Perf. 12

450	A85	5c on 7½c red org	.30	.25
451	A85	10c on 37½c brn	.30	.25
a.		Inverted surcharge	16.00	16.00

Telegraph Stamps Surcharged in Black or Red

Grayish Security Paper

1951, June   Engr.

452		5c on 5c brown	.25	.25
453		10c on 10c green	.25	.25
454		20c on 1b blk (R)	.50	.25
455		25c on 25c carmine	.65	.25
456		30c on 2b ol grn (R)	.90	.70
		Nos. 452-456 (5)	2.55	1.70

The 5c and 10c surcharges include quotation marks on each line and values are expressed "Bs. 0.05" etc.

Bolivar Statue, New York — A92

1951, July 13   Perf. 12

457	A92	5c green	.25	.25
458	A92	10c car rose	.40	.25
459	A92	20c ultra	.40	.25
460	A92	30c slate gray	.50	.25
461	A92	40c deep green	.70	.25
462	A92	50c red brown	1.50	.50
463	A92	1b gray black	4.75	2.50
		Nos. 457-463 (7)	8.50	4.25
		Nos. 457-463,C322-C329 (15)	21.65	9.50

Relocation of the equestrian statue of Simon Bolivar in NYC, Apr. 19, 1951.

Arms of Carabobo and "Industry" — A93

1951   Unwmk.   Photo.   Perf. 11½

464	A93	5c green	.25	.25
465	A93	10c red	.25	.25
466	A93	15c brown	1.40	.25
467	A93	20c ultra	2.00	.25
468	A93	25c orange brn	2.25	.25
469	A93	30c blue	5.00	2.00
470	A93	35c purple	19.00	16.00
		Nos. 464-470 (7)	30.05	19.00

Issue dates: 5c, 10c, Oct. 8; others, Oct. 29.

Arms of Zulia and "Industry"

471	A93	5c green	.25	.25
472	A93	10c red	.95	.25
473	A93	15c brown	2.10	.95
474	A93	20c ultra	2.75	1.25
475	A93	50c brown org	16.00	12.00
476	A93	1b dp gray grn	5.50	2.10
477	A93	5b rose violet	12.00	8.00
		Nos. 471-477 (7)	39.50	24.70

Issued: 5c, 10c, Sept. 8; others, Sept. 20.

Arms of Anzoategui and Globe

478	A93	5c green	.25	.25
479	A93	10c red	.25	.25
480	A93	15c brown	2.25	1.00
481	A93	20c ultra	3.75	.25
482	A93	40c red orange	7.75	3.75
483	A93	45c rose violet	22.50	1.25
484	A93	3b blue gray	8.75	4.25
		Nos. 478-484 (7)	45.40	10.85

Issue date: Nov. 9.

Arms of Caracas and Buildings

485	A93	5c green	1.25	.25
486	A93	10c red	1.75	.25
487	A93	15c brown	4.25	1.00
488	A93	20c ultra	8.50	1.00
489	A93	25c orange brn	11.50	2.25
490	A93	30c blue	11.00	2.50
491	A93	35c purple	110.00	62.50
		Nos. 485-491 (7)	148.25	69.65

Issued: 5c, 10c, June 20; others, Aug. 6.

Arms of Tachira and Agricultural Products

492	A93	5c green	.25	.25
493	A93	10c red	.95	.25
494	A93	15c brown	1.75	.60
495	A93	20c ultra	4.25	1.10
496	A93	50c brown org	260.00	3.25
497	A93	1b dp gray grn	4.25	1.50
498	A93	5b dull purple	10.50	6.00
		Nos. 492-498 (7)	281.90	12.85

Issue date: Aug. 9.

Arms of Venezuela and Statue of Simon Bolivar

499	A93	5c green	1.00	.25
500	A93	10c red	.85	.25
501	A93	15c brown	7.50	1.50
502	A93	20c ultra	7.50	1.00
503	A93	25c orange brn	12.50	2.75
504	A93	30c blue	12.50	2.75
505	A93	35c purple	65.00	50.00
		Nos. 499-505 (7)	106.85	58.40

Issue date: Aug. 6.

Arms of Miranda and Agricultural Products

1952

506	A93	5c green	.25	.25
507	A93	10c red	.25	.25
508	A93	15c brown	1.75	.25
509	A93	20c ultra	1.90	.25
510	A93	25c orange brn	2.50	1.10
511	A93	30c blue	4.25	1.90
512	A93	35c purple	26.00	18.00
		Nos. 506-512 (7)	36.80	21.80

Arms of Aragua and Stylized Farm

513	A93	5c green	.25	.25
514	A93	10c red	.25	.25
515	A93	15c brown	1.90	.25
516	A93	20c ultra	1.90	.25
517	A93	25c orange brn	4.25	1.10
518	A93	30c blue	4.25	1.90
519	A93	35c purple	22.50	17.50
		Nos. 513-519 (7)	35.20	21.30

Issue date: 20c, 30c, Mar. 24.

Arms of Lara, Agricultural Products and Rope

520	A93	5c green	.25	.25
521	A93	10c red	.25	.25
522	A93	15c brown	1.00	.25
523	A93	20c ultra	2.40	.25
524	A93	25c orange brn	2.75	1.75

525	A93	30c blue	5.25	1.40
526	A93	35c purple	21.00	13.00
		Nos. 520-526 (7)	32.80	16.95

Issue date: 20c, 30c, Mar. 24.

Arms of Bolivar and Stylized Design

527	A93	5c green	.25	.25
528	A93	10c red	.25	.25
529	A93	15c brown	.95	.25
530	A93	20c ultra	2.10	.25
531	A93	40c red orange	8.00	2.75
532	A93	45c rose violet	20.00	14.00
533	A93	3b blue gray	9.50	6.25
		Nos. 527-533 (7)	40.95	23.80

Issue date: 20c, Mar. 24.

Arms of Sucre, Palms and Seascape

534	A93	5c green	.25	.25
535	A93	10c red	.25	.25
536	A93	15c brown	2.40	.25
537	A93	20c ultra	2.40	.25
538	A93	40c red orange	8.00	2.10
539	A93	45c rose violet	27.50	17.50
540	A93	3b blue gray	7.00	4.75
		Nos. 534-540 (7)	47.70	25.15

Arms of Trujillo Surrounded by Stylized Tree

541	A93	5c green	.25	.25
542	A93	10c red	.25	.25
543	A93	15c brown	2.50	.25
544	A93	20c ultra	2.50	.60
545	A93	50c brown orange	15.00	7.25
546	A93	1b dp gray green	3.50	1.25
547	A93	5b dull purple	9.00	4.50
		Nos. 541-547 (7)	32.90	14.20

Map of Delta Amacuro and Ship

1953-54

548	A93	5c green	.25	.25
549	A93	10c red	.25	.25
550	A93	15c brown	.90	.25
551	A93	20c ultra	1.50	.25
552	A93	40c red orange	4.75	3.00
553	A93	45c rose violet	22.50	13.50
554	A93	3b blue gray	6.00	4.50
		Nos. 548-554 (7)	36.05	21.80

Issue date: 20c, Feb. 13.

Arms of Falcon and Stylized Oil Refinery

555	A93	5c green	.25	.25
556	A93	10c red	.25	.25
557	A93	15c brown	1.40	.25
558	A93	20c ultra	1.40	.25
559	A93	50c brown orange	7.25	3.50
560	A93	1b dp gray grn	4.50	2.75
561	A93	5b dull purple	13.50	7.25
		Nos. 555-561 (7)	28.45	14.30

Issue date: 20c, Feb. 13.

Arms of Guarico and Factory

562	A93	5c green	.25	.25
563	A93	10c red	.25	.25
564	A93	15c brown	1.10	.25
565	A93	20c ultra	1.25	.25
566	A93	40c red orange	6.50	4.00
567	A93	45c rose violet	16.00	7.75
568	A93	3b blue gray	6.50	3.50
		Nos. 562-568 (7)	31.75	16.05

Issue date: 20c, Feb. 13.

Arms of Merida and Church

569	A93	5c green	.25	.25
570	A93	10c red	.25	.25
571	A93	15c brown	.85	.25
572	A93	20c ultra	2.10	.25
573	A93	50c brown orange	9.00	4.00
574	A93	1b dp gray green	2.50	1.75
575	A93	5b dull purple	9.00	5.25
		Nos. 569-575 (7)	23.85	11.80

Issue date: 20c, Feb. 2.

Arms of Monagas and Horses

576	A93	5c green	.25	.25
577	A93	10c red	.25	.25
578	A93	15c brown	1.10	.25
579	A93	20c ultra	1.60	.90
580	A93	40c red orange	7.50	2.75
581	A93	45c rose violet	22.50	13.50
582	A93	3b blue gray	9.25	7.50
		Nos. 576-582 (7)	42.35	25.25

Arms of Portuguesa and Forest

583	A93	5c green	.25	.25
584	A93	10c red	.25	.25
585	A93	15c brown	.65	.25
586	A93	20c ultra	1.40	.25
587	A93	50c brown org	7.25	4.75
588	A93	1b dp gray grn	1.90	.80
589	A93	5b dull purple	8.00	5.25
		Nos. 583-589 (7)	19.60	11.60

Issue date: 5c, 10c, Feb. 2.

Map of Amazonas and Orchid

590	A93	5c green	1.40	.25
591	A93	10c red	1.40	.25
592	A93	15c brown	3.00	.25
593	A93	20c ultra	8.50	.85
594	A93	40c red orange	10.00	3.00
595	A93	45c rose violet	16.00	7.75
596	A93	3b blue gray	24.00	8.50
		Nos. 590-596 (7)	64.30	20.70

Issue date: Jan. 1954.

Arms of Apure, Horse and Bird

597	A93	5c green	.25	.25
598	A93	10c red	.25	.25
599	A93	15c brown	1.60	.25
600	A93	20c ultra	8.50	.25
601	A93	50c brown org	11.00	8.50
602	A93	1b dp gray grn	3.50	3.00
603	A93	5b dull purple	21.00	12.00
		Nos. 597-603 (7)	46.00	24.30

Issue date: Jan. 1954.

Arms of Barinas, Cow and Horse

604	A93	5c green	.25	.25
605	A93	10c red	.25	.25
606	A93	15c brown	.55	.25
607	A93	20c ultra	3.75	.55
608	A93	50c brown org	4.50	2.75
609	A93	1b dp gray grn	1.10	.55
610	A93	5b dull purple	10.00	5.00
		Nos. 604-610 (7)	20.30	9.45

Issue date: Jan. 1954.

Arms of Cojedes and Cattle

611	A93	5c green	.25	.25
612	A93	10c red	.25	.25
613	A93	15c brown	.25	.25
614	A93	20c ultra	.25	.25
615	A93	25c orange brown	4.00	1.10
616	A93	30c blue	6.25	1.75
617	A93	35c purple	7.75	6.25
		Nos. 611-617 (7)	18.80	9.90

Issue date: Dec. 17, 1953.

Arms of Nueva Esparta and Fish

618	A93	5c green	.25	.25
619	A93	10c red	.25	.25
620	A93	15c brown	1.40	.25
621	A93	20c ultra	1.60	.25
622	A93	40c red orange	7.25	2.75
623	A93	45c rose vio	17.50	10.00
624	A93	3b blue gray	8.00	5.50
		Nos. 618-624 (7)	36.15	19.05

Issue date: Jan. 1954.

Arms of Yaracuy and Tropical Foliage

625	A93	5c green	1.50	.25
626	A93	10c red	.25	.25
627	A93	15c brown	1.10	.25
628	A93	20c ultra	1.75	.25
629	A93	25c orange brn	2.50	1.10
630	A93	30c blue	2.75	.95
631	A93	35c purple	6.50	4.25
		Nos. 625-631 (7)	16.30	7.10
		Nos. 464-631 (168)	1,264.	514.15

Issue date: Jan. 1954.
See Nos. C338-C553.

Ship Type of 1948-50, Redrawn

Coil Stamps
Imprint: "Courvoisier S.A."

1952   Unwmk.   Photo.   Perf. 11½x12

632	A85	5c green	1.50	.25
633	A85	10c car rose	2.50	.25
634	A85	15c gray	9.00	.25
		Nos. 632-634,C554-C556 (6)	22.50	1.50

Juan de Villegas and Cross of Father Yepez — A94

1952, Sept. 14   Perf. 11½

635	A94	5c green	.25	.25
636	A94	10c red	1.25	.25
637	A94	20c dk gray bl	1.90	.60
638	A94	40c dp org	9.00	3.50
639	A94	50c brown	4.75	2.00
640	A94	1b violet	9.00	2.40
		Nos. 635-640 (6)	26.15	9.00
		Nos. 635-640,C557-C564 (14)	38.00	13.80

Founding of the city of Barquisimeto by Juan de Villegas, 400th anniv.

Virgin of Coromoto and Child — A95

1952-53   Perf. 11½x12

Size: 17x26mm

641	A95	1b rose pink	8.00	1.25

Size: 26½x41mm
642 A95 1b rose pink ('53)   6.00 1.25
Size: 36x55mm
643 A95 1b rose pink ('53)   2.75 .95
Nos. 641-643 (3)   16.75 3.45

300th anniv. of the appearance of the Virgin Mary to a chief of the Coromoto Indians. Issue date: No. 641, Oct. 6.

Telegraph Stamps Surcharged in Black or Red

1952, Nov. 24   Engr.   Perf. 12
Grayish Security Paper
644   5c on 25c car   .30 .25
645   10c on 1b blk (R)   .30 .25

Surcharged

1952, Dec.
646   20c on 25c car   .35 .25
647   30c on 2b ol grn   2.10 1.40
648   40c on 1b blk (R)   .85 .45
649   50c on 3b red org   2.75 1.60
Nos. 646-649 (4)   6.05 3.70

Post Office, Caracas — A96

Perf. 13x12½
1953-54   Unwmk.   Photo.
650 A96   5c green   .25 .25
  a.   Bklt. pane of 10
651 A96   7½c brt green   .35 .25
652 A96   10c rose carmine .25 .25
  a.   Bklt. pane of 10
653 A96   15c gray   .40 .25
654 A96   20c ultra   .25 .25
655 A96   25c magenta   .40 .25
656 A96   30c blue   1.90 .25
657 A96   35c brt red vio   .85 .25
658 A96   40c orange   1.25 .40
659 A96   45c violet   1.90 .65
660 A96   50c red orange   1.25 .40
Nos. 650-660 (11)   9.05 3.45

Issued: 20c, 30c, 45c, 3/11; 7½c, 25c, 50c, 6/53; 5c, 10c, 2/54; 15c, 1954.
See Nos. C565-C575, C587-C589.

A96a

Type of 1953-54 Inscribed "Republica de Venezuela"

1955
661 A96a   5c green   .25 .25
662 A96a   10c rose car   .25 .25
663 A96a   15c gray   .25 .25
664 A96a   20c ultra   .25 .25
665 A96a   30c blue   .65 .40
666 A96a   35c brt red vio   .65 .25
667 A96a   40c orange   1.00 .25
668 A96a   45c violet   1.25 .50
Nos. 661-668 (8)   4.55 2.40
Nos. 661-668,C597-C606 (18) 13.65 6.55

Arms of Valencia and Industrial Scene — A97

1955, Mar. 26   Engr.   Perf. 12
669 A97   5c brt grn   .25 .25
670 A97   20c ultra   .40 .25
671 A97   25c reddish brn   .65 .25
672 A97   50c vermilion   1.00 .25
Nos. 669-672,C590-C596 (11) 5.10 2.75

Founding of Valencia del Rey, 400th anniv.

Coat of Arms — A98

1955, Dec. 9   Unwmk.   Perf. 11½
673 A98   5c green   1.10 .25
674 A98   20c ultra   3.75 .25
675 A98   25c rose car   3.00 .25
676 A98   50c orange   3.75 .25
Nos. 673-676,C607-C612 (10) 19.90 3.50

1st Postal Convention, Caracas, 2/9-15/54.

Book and Map of the Americas — A99

1956   Photo.   Perf. 11½
Granite Paper
677 A99   5c lt grn & bluish grn   .25 .25
678 A99   10c lil rose & rose vio   .25 .25
679 A99   20c ultra & dk bl   .25 .25
680 A99   30c gray & lil gray   .55 .25
681 A99   30c lt bl & bl   .55 .25
682 A99   40c bis brn & brn   .65 .25
683 A99   50c ver & red brn   1.40 .65
684 A99   1b lt pur & vio   2.25 1.10
Nos. 677-684 (8)   6.15 3.25
Nos. 677-684,C629-C635 (15) 10.80 5.15

Book Festival of the Americas, 11/15-30/56.

Simon Bolivar — A100

Engraved, Center Embossed
1957-58   Unwmk.   Perf. 13½
685 A100   5c brt bl grn   .25 .25
686 A100   10c red   .25 .25
687 A100   20c lt slate bl   .40 .25
688 A100   25c rose lake   .40 .25
689 A100   30c vio blue   .50 .25
690 A100   40c red orange   .75 .25
691 A100   50c orange yel   1.10 .55
Nos. 685-691 (7)   3.65 2.05
Nos. 685-691,C636-C642 (14) 7.40 3.45

150th anniv. of the Oath of Monte Sacro and the 125th anniv. of the death of Simon Bolivar (1783-1830).
Issued: 10c, 50c, 1958; others, 11/15/57.

Hotel Tamanaco, Caracas A101

1957-58   Engr.   Perf. 13
692 A101   5c green   .25 .25
693 A101   10c carmine   .25 .25
694 A101   15c black   .25 .25
695 A101   20c dark blue   .30 .25
696 A101   25c dp claret   .30 .25
697 A101   30c dp ultra   .50 .25
698 A101   35c purple   .30 .25
699 A101   40c orange   .40 .25
700 A101   45c rose violet   .50 .25
701 A101   50c yellow   .70 .25
702 A101   1b dk slate grn 1.10 .45
Nos. 692-702 (11)   4.85 2.95
Nos. 692-702,C643-C657 (26) 14.65 7.30

Issued: 5c, 10c, Oct. 10, 1957; others, 1958.
For surcharge see No. 878.

Main Post Office, Caracas — A102

1958, May 14   Litho.   Perf. 14
703 A102   5c emerald   .25 .25
704 A102   10c rose red   .25 .25
705 A102   15c gray   .25 .25
706 A102   20c lt bl   .25 .25
707 A102   35c red lilac   .25 .25
708 A102   45c brt vio   1.25 .85
709 A102   50c yellow   .30 .25
710 A102   1b lt ol grn   .75 .40
Nos. 703-710 (8)   3.55 2.75
Nos. 703-710,C658-C670 (21) 15.80 10.85

See Nos. 748-750, C658-C670, C786-C792.
For surcharges see Nos. 865, C807, C856-C861.

Main Post Office, Caracas A103

1958, Nov. 17   Engr.   Perf. 11½x12
711 A103   5c green   .25 .25
712 A103   10c rose red   .40 .25
713 A103   15c black   .60 .25
Nos. 711-713,C671-C673 (6) 2.45 1.50

Arms of Merida — A104

1958, Oct. 9   Photo.   Perf. 14x13½
714 A104   5c green   .25 .25
715 A104   10c bright red   .25 .25
716 A104   15c greenish gray .25 .25
717 A104   20c blue   .25 .25
718 A104   25c magenta   .45 .25
719 A104   30c violet   .25 .25
720 A104   35c light purple .30 .25
721 A104   40c orange   .65 .25
722 A104   45c deep rose lilac .35 .25
723 A104   50c bright yellow .55 .25
724 A104   1b gray green   1.60 .55
Nos. 714-724 (11)   5.15 3.05
Nos. 714-724,C674-C689 (27) 13.90 7.50

400th anniversary of the founding of the city of Merida. For surcharge see No. 873.

Arms of Trujillo, Bolivar Monument and Trujillo Hotel — A105

1959, Nov. 17   Unwmk.   Perf. 14
725 A105   5c emerald   .25 .25
726 A105   10c rose   .25 .25
727 A105   15c gray   .25 .25
728 A105   20c blue   .25 .25
729 A105   25c brt pink   .35 .25
730 A105   30c lt ultra   .50 .25
731 A105   35c lt pur   .50 .25
732 A105   45c rose lilac   .65 .35
733 A105   50c yellow   .65 .25
734 A105   1b lt ol grn   1.60 .85
Nos. 725-734 (10)   5.25 3.20
Nos. 725-734,C690-C700 (21) 10.95 5.95

Founding of the city of Trujillo, 400th anniv.

Stadium A106

1959 Mar. 10   Litho.   Perf. 13½
735 A106   5c brt grn   .35 .25
736 A106   10c rose pink   .35 .25
737 A106   20c blue   .60 .25
738 A106   30c dk bl   .70 .25
739 A106   50c red lilac   1.10 .25
Nos. 735-739 (5)   3.10 1.25
Nos. 735-739,C701-C705 (10) 5.55 2.45

8th Central American and Caribbean Games, Caracas, Nov. 29-Dec. 14, 1958.
#735-739 exist imperf. Value, pair $25.

Stamp of 1859, Mailman and José Ignacio Paz Castillo A107

Stamp of 1859 and: 50c, Mailman on horseback and Jacinto Gutierrez. 1b, Plane, train and Miguel Herrera.

1959, Sept. 15   Engr.   Perf. 13½x14
740 A107   25c org yel   .50 .25
741 A107   50c blue   .50 .25
742 A107   1b rose red   1.25 .45
Nos. 740-742,C706-C708 (6) 3.90 1.85

Centenary of Venezuelan postage stamps.

Catalogue values for unused stamps in this section, from this point to the end of the section, are for Never Hinged items.

Alexander von Humboldt — A108

1960, Feb. 9   Unwmk.   Perf. 13½
743 A108   5c grn & yel grn .45 .25
744 A108   30c vio bl & vio 1.40 .35
745 A108   40c org & brn org 1.75 .55
Nos. 743-745,C709-C711 (6) 7.35 2.15

Centenary of the death of Alexander von Humboldt, German naturalist and geographer.

Post Office Type of 1958
1960, July   Litho.   Perf. 14
748 A102   25c yellow   .25 .25
749 A102   30c light blue   .25 .25
750 A102   40c fawn   .55 .25
Nos. 748-750 (3)   1.05 .75

Newspaper, 1808, and View of Caracas, 1958 — A109

1960, June 6 **Litho.** **Perf. 14**
751 A109 10c rose & blk .55 .25
752 A109 20c lt blue & blk .95 .25
753 A109 35c lilac & blk 1.40 1.00
Nos. 751-753,C712-C714 (6) 9.15 3.75

150th anniv. (in 1958) of the 1st Venezuelan newspaper, Gazeta de Caracas.

Agustin Codazzi A110

1960, June 15 **Engr.** **Unwmk.**
754 A110 5c brt green .25 .25
755 A110 15c gray 1.10 .25
756 A110 20c blue .85 .25
757 A110 45c purple 1.10 .50
Nos. 754-757,C715-C720 (10) 9.35 3.70

Centenary (in 1959) of the death of Agustin Codazzi, geographer.
For surcharges see Nos. 869, C884.

National Pantheon — A111

Pantheon in Bister

1960, May 9 **Litho.**
758 A111 5c emerald .25 .25
759 A111 20c brt blue .60 .25
760 A111 25c light olive .95 .25
761 A111 30c dull blue 1.10 .30
762 A111 40c fawn 1.60 .55
763 A111 45c lilac 1.50 .55
Nos. 758-763 (6) 6.00 2.15
Nos. 758-763,C721-C734 (20) 27.95 7.75

For surcharges see Nos. C894-C895.

Andres Eloy Blanco, Poet (1896-1955) A112

1960, May 21 **Unwmk.** **Perf. 14**
Portrait in Black
764 A112 5c emerald .30 .25
765 A112 30c dull blue .40 .25
766 A112 50c yellow .85 .30
Nos. 764-766,C735-C737 (6) 5.25 1.85

For surcharge see No. C874.

Independence Meeting of April 19, 1810, Led by Miranda — A113

1960, Aug. 19 **Litho.** **Perf. 13½**
Center Multicolored
767 A113 5c brt green .65 .25
768 A113 20c blue 1.40 .35

769 A113 30c violet blue 1.75 .45
Nos. 767-769,C738-C740 (6) 8.25 2.35

150th anniversary of Venezuela's Independence.
See Nos. 812-814, C804-C806. For surcharge see No. C893.

Drilling for Oil — A114

1960, Aug. 26 **Engr.** **Perf. 14**
770 A114 5c grn & slate grn 2.75 .95
771 A114 10c dk car & brn .90 .35
772 A114 15c gray & dull pur 1.25 .45
Nos. 770-772,C741-C743 (6) 8.40 3.00

Issued to publicize Venezuela's oil industry.

Luisa Cáceres de Arismendi A115

Unwmk.
1960, Oct. 21 **Litho.** **Perf. 14**
Center Multicolored
773 A115 20c light blue 1.40 .40
774 A115 25c citron 1.00 .40
775 A115 30c dull blue 1.40 .55
Nos. 773-775,C744-C746 (6) 9.50 3.40

Death of Luisa Càceres de Arismendi, 94th anniv.

José Antonio Anzoategui — A116

1960, Oct. 29 **Engr.**
776 A116 5c emerald & gray ol .35 .25
777 A116 15c ol gray & dl vio .50 .25
778 A116 20c blue & gray vio .70 .25
Nos. 776-778,C747-C749 (6) 4.35 2.05

140th anniversary (in 1959) of the death of General José Antonio Anzoategui.

Antonio José de Sucre — A117

Unwmk.
1960, Nov. 18 **Litho.** **Perf. 14**
Center Multicolored
779 A117 10c deep rose .45 .25
780 A117 15c gray brown .50 .25
781 A117 20c blue .85 .40
Nos. 779-781,C750-C752 (6) 5.85 2.40

130th anniversary of the death of General Antonio José de Sucre.

Bolivar Peak, Merida — A118

Designs: 15c, Caroni Falls, Bolivar. 35c, Guacharo caves, Monagas.

1960, Mar. 22 **Perf. 14**
782 A118 5c emerald & grn 1.00 1.00
783 A118 15c gray & dk gray 3.25 3.25
784 A118 35c rose lil & lil 2.75 2.75
Nos. 782-784,C753-C755 (6) 13.75 13.75

Buildings and People — A119

1961 **Litho.** **Unwmk.**
Building in Orange
785 A119 5c emerald .25 .25
786 A119 10c carmine .25 .25
787 A119 15c gray .25 .25
788 A119 20c blue .25 .25
789 A119 25c lt red brown .25 .25
790 A119 30c dull blue .25 .25
791 A119 35c red lilac .35 .25
792 A119 40c fawn .55 .25
793 A119 45c brt violet .70 .30
794 A119 50c yellow .55 .25
Nos. 785-794 (10) 3.65 2.55

1960 national census. See #C756-C770.
For surcharge see No. 866.

Rafael Maria Baralt — A120

1961, Mar. 11 **Engr.** **Perf. 14**
795 A120 5c grn & slate grn .25 .25
796 A120 15c gray & dull red brn .50 .25
797 A120 35c rose lilac & lt vio .75 .25
Nos. 795-797,C771-C773 (6) 4.30 1.95

Rafael Maria Baralt, statesman, death cent.

Yellow-headed Parrot — A121

1961, Sept. 6 **Litho.** **Perf. 14½**
798 A121 30c shown 1.25 .50
799 A121 40c Snowy egret 1.90 .50
800 A121 50c Scarlet ibis 3.00 .90
Nos. 798-800,C776-C778 (6) 9.55 4.25

Juan J. Aguerrevere — A122

1961, Oct. 21 **Unwmk.** **Perf. 14**
801 A122 25c dark blue .35 .25
a. Souvenir sheet, imperf. 2.50 2.50

Centenary of the founding of the Engineering Society of Venezuela, Oct. 28, 1861.
No. 801a sold for 1b.
No. 801a exists with "Valor: Bs 1,00" omitted at lower left corner. Value, $7.

Battle of Carabobo, 1821 — A123

1961, Dec. 1 **Perf. 14**
Center Multicolored
802 A123 5c emerald & blk .25 .25
803 A123 40c brown & blk .70 .25
Nos. 802-803,C779-C784 (8) 15.20 5.00

140th anniversary of Battle of Carabobo.

Oncidium Papilio Lindl — A124

Orchids: 10c, Caularthron bilamellatum. 20c, Stanhopea Wardii Lodd. 25c, Catasetum pileatum. 30c, Masdevallia tovarensis. 35c, Epidendrum Stamfordianum Batem, horiz. 50c, Epidendrum atropurpureum Willd. 3b, Oncidium falcipetalum Lindl.

Perf. 14x13½, 13½x14
1962, May 30 **Litho.** **Unwmk.**
Orchids in Natural Colors
804 A124 5c black & orange .25 .25
805 A124 10c blk & brt grnsh bl .25 .25
806 A124 20c black & yel grn .55 .25
807 A124 25c black & lt blue .80 .25
808 A124 30c black & olive .90 .25
809 A124 35c black & yellow 1.00 .25
810 A124 50c black & gray 1.10 .35
811 A124 3b black & vio 6.75 2.75
Nos. 804-811 (8) 11.60 4.65
Nos. 804-811,C794-C803 (18) 28.10 10.10

For surcharges see Nos. 872, C885-C887.

Independence Type of 1960
Signing Declaration of Independence.

1962, June 11 **Perf. 13½**
Center Multicolored
812 A113 5c emerald .25 .25
813 A113 20c blue .50 .25
814 A113 25c yellow .75 .30
a. Souv. sheet, #812-814, imperf 3.25 3.25
Nos. 812-814,C804-C806 (6) 5.80 2.10

150th anniv. of the Venezuelan Declaration of Independence, July 5, 1811.
No. 814a sold for 1.50b.

Shot Put A125

1962, Nov. 30 **Litho.** **Perf. 13x14**
815 A125 5c shown .30 .25
816 A125 10c Soccer .30 .25
817 A125 25c Swimming .40 .25
a. Souv. sheet, #815-817, imperf 3.50 3.50
Nos. 815-817,C808-C810 (6) 3.95 2.20

1st Natl. Games, Caracas, 1961. The stamps are arranged so that two pale colored edges of each stamp join to make a border around blocks of four.
No. 817a sold for 1.40b.
For surcharge see No. C899.

Vermilion Cardinal — A126

Birds: 10c, Great kiskadee. 20c, Glossy black thrush. 25c, Collared trogons. 30c, Swallow tanager. 40c, Long-tailed sylph. 3b, Black-necked stilt.

1962, Dec. 14 *Perf. 14x13½*
Birds in Natural Colors, Black Inscription

818	A126	5c brt yellow grn	.25	.25
819	A126	10c violet blue	.25	.25
820	A126	20c lilac rose	.50	.25
821	A126	25c dull brown	.60	.25
822	A126	30c lemon	.75	.25
823	A126	40c lilac	1.00	.30
824	A126	3b fawn	7.00	3.00
		Nos. 818-824 (7)	10.35	4.55
		Nos. 818-824,C811-C818 (15)	27.95	11.45

For surcharges see Nos. 868, C880-C882.

Malaria Eradication Emblem, Mosquito and Map — A127

Lithographed and Embossed
Perf. 13½x14
1962, Dec. 20 **Wmk. 346**
825 A127 50c brown & black .80 .30

WHO drive to eradicate malaria. See Nos. C819-C819a.

White-tailed Deer A128

Designs: 10c, Collared peccary. 35c, Collared titi (monkey). 50c, Giant Brazilian otter. 1b, Puma. 3b, Capybara.

Perf. 13½x14
1963, Mar. 13 **Litho.** **Unwmk.**
Multicolored Center; Black Inscriptions

826	A128	5c green	.25	.25
827	A128	10c orange	.25	.25
828	A128	35c red lilac	.25	.25
829	A128	50c blue	.55	.25
830	A128	1b rose brown	2.75	1.40
831	A128	3b yellow	5.50	3.50
		Nos. 826-831 (6)	9.55	5.90
		Nos. 826-831,C820-C825 (12)	23.75	11.00

For surcharges see #870-871, C888-C889.

Fisherman and Map of Venezuela — A129

1963, Mar. 21
832 A129 25c pink & ultra .25 .25
Nos. 832,C826-C827 (3) 1.80 1.30

FAO "Freedom from Hunger" campaign.

Cathedral of Bocono — A130

1963, May 30 **Wmk. 346**
833 A130 50c brn, red & grn, *buff* .75 .25

400th anniversary of the founding of Bocono. See No. C828.

St. Peter's Basilica, Rome A131

1963, June 11 *Perf. 14x13½*
834 A131 35c dk bl, brn & buff .45 .25
835 A131 45c dk grn, red brn & buff .50 .25
Nos. 834-835,C829-C830 (4) 3.45 1.35

Vatican II, the 21st Ecumenical Council of the Roman Catholic Church.

National Flag — A132

1963, July 29 **Unwmk.** *Perf. 14*
836 A132 30c gray, red, yel & bl 1.00 .25

Centenary of Venezuela's flag and coat of arms. See No. C831.

Lake Maracaibo Bridge — A133

Perf. 13½x14
1963, Aug. 24 **Wmk. 346**
837 A133 30c blue & brown .45 .25
838 A133 35c bluish grn & brn .50 .25
839 A133 80c blue grn & brn 1.10 .45
Nos. 837-839,C832-C834 (6) 6.65 2.55

Opening of bridge over Lake Maracaibo. For surcharge see No. 875.

Map, Soldier and Emblem — A134

1963, Sept. 10 **Unwmk.**
840 A134 50c red, bl & grn, *buff* .75 .25

25th anniversary of the armed forces. See No. C835. For surcharge see No. C862.

Dag Hammarskjold and World Map — A135

Perf. 14x13½
1963, Sept. 25 **Unwmk.**
841 A135 25c dk bl, bl grn & ocher .30 .25
842 A135 55c grn, grnsh bl & ocher 1.10 .40
Nos. 841-842,C836-C837 (4) 4.40 1.85

"1st" anniv. of the death of Dag Hammarskjold, Secretary General of the UN, 1953-61.
See #C837a. For surcharges see #867, C875-C876.

Dr. Luis Razetti — A136

1963, Oct. 10 **Litho.**
843 A136 35c blue, ocher & brn .60 .25
844 A136 45c mag, ocher & brn .90 .25
Nos. 843-844,C838-C839 (4) 4.50 2.40

Dr. Luis Razetti, physician, birth cent.

Dr. Francisco A. Risquez — A137

Design: 20c, Dr. Carlos J. Bello.

1963, Dec. 31 *Perf. 11½x12*
845 A137 15c multicolored .50 .25
846 A137 20c multicolored .70 .25
Nos. 845-846,C840-C841 (4) 2.70 1.50

Cent. of the Intl. Red Cross.

Oil Field Workers — A138

10c, Oil refinery. 15c Crane & building construction. 30c, Cactus, train & truck. 40c, Tractor.

1964, Feb. 5 **Litho.** *Perf. 14x13½*
847	A138	5c multi	.25	.25
848	A138	10c multi	.25	.25
849	A138	15c multi	.30	.25
850	A138	30c multi	.50	.25
851	A138	40c multi	.55	.25
		Nos. 847-851 (5)	1.85	1.25
		Nos. 847-851,C842-C846 (10)	3.35	2.10

Department of Industrial Development, cent.

Pedro Gual — A139

1964, Mar. 20 **Unwmk.** *Perf. 14*
852 A139 40c lt olive green .60 .25
853 A139 50c lt red brown .80 .30
Nos. 852-853,C847-C848 (4) 3.50 1.40

Pedro Gual (1784-1862), statesman.

Carlos Arvelo — A140

1964, Apr. 17 **Engr.** *Perf. 14x13½*
854 A140 1b dull bl & gray 1.50 .55

Centenary of the death of Dr. Carlos Arvelo (1784-1862), chief physician of Bolivar's revolutionary army, director of Caracas Hospital, rector of Central University and professor of pathology.
For surcharge see No. 874.

Foundry Ladle and Molds A141

1964, May 22 *Perf. 14x13½*
855 A141 20c multicolored .40 .25
856 A141 50c multicolored .75 .25
Nos. 855-856,C849-C850 (4) 4.15 1.60

Orinoco Steel Mills.

Romulo Gallegos, Novelist, 80th Birthday — A142

Unwmk.
1964, Aug. 3 **Litho.** *Perf. 12*
857 A142 5c dk & lt green .25 .25
858 A142 10c bl & pale bl .25 .25
859 A142 15c dk & lt red lil .40 .25
Nos. 857-859,C852-C854 (6) 2.90 1.55

Angel Falls, Bolivar State A143

Tourist Publicity: 10c, Tropical landscape, Sucre State. 15c, San Juan Peaks, Guarico. 30c, Net fishermen, Anzoategui. 40c, Mountaineer, Merida.

1964, Oct. 22 *Perf. 13½x14*
860	A143	5c multi	.25	.25
861	A143	10c multi	.25	.25
862	A143	15c multi	.25	.25
863	A143	30c multi	.55	.25
864	A143	40c multi	.80	.25
		Nos. 860-864 (5)	2.10	1.25

Issues of 1958-64 Surcharged in Black, Dark Blue or Lilac

1965
865 A102 5c on 1b (#710) .60 .25
866 A119 10c on 45c (#793) .25 .25
867 A135 15c on 55c (#842) .25 .25
868 A126 20c on 3b (#824) .25 .25
869 A110 25c on 45c (#757) (DB) .25 .25

870	A128	25c on 1b (#830)	.40 .25
871	A128	25c on 3b (#831)	.45 .25
872	A124	25c on 3b (#811) (L)	.25 .25
873	A104	30c on 1b (#724)	.40 .25
874	A140	40c on 1b (#854)	.90 .25
875	A133	60c on 80c (#839)	1.25 .40
		Nos. 865-875 (11)	5.25 2.90

Lines of surcharge arranged variously; old denomination obliterated with bars on Nos. 867, 870-872. See Nos. C856-C899.

Revenue Stamps of 1947 Surcharged in Red or Black

Imprint: "American Bank Note Co."

1965 Engr. Perf. 12, 13½ (No. 882)

876	R1	5c on 5c emerald	.30 .25
877	R1	5c on 20c red brn	.30 .25
878	R1	10c on 10c brn ol	.30 .25
879	R1	15c on 40c grn	.30 .25
880	R1	20c on 3b dk bl (R)	.50 .25
881	R1	25c on 5b vio bl (R)	1.00 .35
882	R1	25c on 5b vio bl (R) (Imprint: "Bundesdruckerei Berlin")	.50 .25
883	R1	60c on 3b dk bl (R)	1.25 .35
		Nos. 876-883 (8)	4.45 2.20

Type R1 is illustrated above No. 401.

John F. Kennedy and Alliance for Progress Emblem A144

1965, Aug. 20 Photo. Perf. 12x11½

884	A144	20c gray	.50 .25
885	A144	40c bright lilac	.80 .25
		Nos. 884-885,C900-C901 (4)	3.65 1.40

Map of Venezuela and Guiana by Codazzi, 1840 — A145

Maps of Venezuela and Guiana: 15c, by Juan M. Restrepo, 1827, horiz. 40c, by L. de Surville, 1778.

1965, Nov. 5 Litho. Perf. 13½

886	A145	5c multi	.25 .25
887	A145	15c multi	.40 .25
888	A145	40c multi	.70 .25
a.		Souv. sheet, #886-888, imperf	8.00 8.00
		Nos. 886-888,C905-C907 (6)	3.45 1.65

Issued to publicize Venezuela's claim to part of British Guiana.
No. 888a sold for 85c.

Protesilaus Leucones — A146

Various Butterflies in Natural Colors
Black Inscriptions

1966, Jan. 25 Litho. Perf. 13½x14

889	A146	20c lt olive grn	1.25 .25
890	A146	30c lt yellow grn	2.50 .25
891	A146	50c yellow	3.75 .30
		Nos. 889-891,C915-C917 (6)	14.50 2.30

Ship and Map of Atlantic Ocean A147

1966, Mar. 10 Litho. Perf. 13½x14

892	A147	60c brown, bl & blk	2.25 .70

Bicentenary of the first maritime mail.

"El Carite" Dance — A148

Various Folk Dances

Perf. 14x13½

1966, Apr. 5 Litho. Unwmk.

893	A148	5c gray & multi	.25 .25
894	A148	10c orange & multi	.25 .25
895	A148	15c lemon & multi	.35 .25
896	A148	20c lilac & multi	.45 .25
897	A148	25c brt pink & multi	.55 .35
898	A148	35c yel grn & multi	.70 .40
		Nos. 893-898,C919-C924 (12)	11.45 4.70

Type of Air Post Stamps and

Arturo Michelena, Self-portrait A149

Paintings: 1b, Penthesileia, battle scene. 1.05b, The Red Cloak.

Perf. 12½x12, 12x12½

1966, May 12 Litho. Unwmk.

899	A149	95c sepia & buff	.90 .65
900	AP74	1b multi	1.10 .65
901	AP74	1.05b multi	1.40 .65
		Nos. 899-901,C927-C929 (6)	7.05 3.60

Arturo Michelena (1863-1898), painter. Miniature sheets of 12 exist.

Construction Worker and Map of Americas — A150

Designs: 20c, as 10c. 30c, 65c, Labor monument. 35c, Machinery worker and map of Venezuela. 50c, Automobile assembly line.

1966, July 6 Litho. Perf. 14x13½

902	A150	10c yellow & blk	.25 .25
903	A150	20c lt grnsh bl & blk	.30 .25
904	A150	30c lt blue & vio	.30 .25
905	A150	35c lemon & olive	.45 .25
906	A150	50c brt rose & claret	.60 .30
907	A150	65c salmon pink & brn	.80 .35
		Nos. 902-907 (6)	2.70 1.65

2nd Conference of Ministers of Labor of the Organization of American States.

Velvet Cichlid A151

1966, Aug. 31 Litho. Perf. 13½x14

908	A151	15c shown	.30 .25
909	A151	25c Perch cichlid	.40 .25
910	A151	45c Piranha	1.00 .35
		Nos. 908-910,C933-C935 (6)	6.50 2.20

Nativity — A152

1966, Dec. 9 Litho. Perf. 13½x14

911	A152	65c violet & blk	1.00 .40

Christmas 1966.

Satellite, Radar, Globe, Plane and Ship A153

1966, Dec. 28 Perf. 13½x14

912	A153	45c multi	.80 .30

Ministry of Communications, 30th anniv.

Rubén Dario — A154

1967 Litho.

913	A154	70c gray bl & dk bl	1.25 .65

Rubén Dario (pen name of Felix Rubén Garcia Sarmiento, 1867-1916), Nicaraguan poet, newspaper correspondent and diplomat.

Old Building and Arms, University of Zulia A155

Perf. 13½x14

1967, Apr. 21 Unwmk.

914	A155	80c gold, blk & car	1.25 .65

University of Zulia founding, 75th anniv.

Front Page and Printing Press — A156

1968, June 27 Photo. Perf. 14x13½

915	A156	1.50b emer, blk & brn	1.75 .80

Newspaper Correo del Orinoco, 150th anniv.

Boll Weevil A157

Insect Pests: 20c, Corn borer, vert. 90c, Tobacco caterpillar.

Perf. 14x13½, 13½x14

1968, Aug. 30 Litho.

916	A157	20c multicolored	.50 .25
917	A157	75c olive & multi	1.50 .25
918	A157	90c multicolored	2.10 .35
		Nos. 916-918,C989-C991 (6)	7.10 1.60

Guayana Substation A158

Designs: 45c, Guaira River Dam, horiz. 50c, Macagua Dam and power plant, horiz. 80c, Guri River Dam and power plant.

1968, Nov. 8 Litho.

919	A158	15c fawn & multi	.25 .25
920	A158	45c dl yel & multi	.70 .25
921	A158	50c bl grn & multi	.90 .35
922	A158	80c blue & multi	1.40 .75
		Nos. 919-922 (4)	3.25 1.60

Electrification program.

House and Piggy Bank A159

1968, Dec. 6 Litho. Perf. 13½x14

923	A159	45c blue & multi	.80 .35

National Savings System.

Nursery and Child Planting Tree A160

Designs: 15c, Child planting tree (vert.; this design used as emblem on entire issue). 30c, Waterfall, vert. 45c, Logging. 55c, Fields and village, vert. 75c, Palambra (fish).

Perf. 14x13½, 13½x14

1968, Dec. 19 Litho.

924	A160	15c multicolored	.35 .25
925	A160	20c multicolored	.35 .25
926	A160	30c multicolored	.40 .25
927	A160	45c multicolored	.55 .25
928	A160	55c multicolored	1.25 .35
929	A160	75c multicolored	.85 .25
		Nos. 924-929 (6)	3.75 1.60
		Nos. 924-929,C1000-C1005 (12)	10.55 4.05

Issued to publicize nature conservation.

Colorada Beach, Sucre A161

Designs: 45c, Church of St. Francis of Yare, Miranda. 90c, Stilt houses, Zulia.

Map of Venezuela and Guiana by Codazzi, 1840 — A145

1969, Jan. 24   **Perf. 13½x14**
930 A161 15c multicolored   .25 .25
931 A161 45c multicolored   .75 .25
932 A161 90c multicolored   1.10 .75
Nos. 930-932,C1006-C1008 (6)   3.55 3.85

Tourist publicity. For souvenir sheet see No. C1007a.

Bolivar Addressing Congress of
Angostura — A162

1969, Feb. 15   **Litho.**   **Perf. 11**
933 A162 45c multicolored   .85 .35

Sesquicentennial of the Congress of Angostura (Ciudad Bolivar).

Martin Luther
King,
Jr. — A163

1969, Apr. 1   **Litho.**   **Perf. 13½**
934 A163 1b bl, red & dk brn   1.10 .30

Rev. Dr. Martin Luther King, Jr. (1929-1968), American civil rights leader and recipient of the Nobel Peace Prize, 1964.

Tabebuia
A164

Trees: 65c, Erythrina poeppigiana. 90c, Platymiscium.

1969, May 30   **Litho.**   **Perf. 13½x14**
935 A164 50c multicolored   .75 .25
936 A164 65c gray & multi   1.00 .25
937 A164 90c pink & multi   1.50 .40
Nos. 935-937,C1009-C1011 (6)   5.35 1.65

Issued to publicize nature conservation.

Still Life with Pheasant, by
Rojas — A165

Paintings by Cristobal Rojas (1858-1890): 25c, On the Balcony, vert. 45c, The Christening. 50c, The Empty Place (family). 60c, The Tavern. 1b, Man's Arm, vert.

Perf. 14x13½, 13½x14
1969, June 27   **Litho.**   **Unwmk.**
Size: 32x42mm, 42x32mm
938 A165 25c gold & multi   .25 .25
939 A165 35c gold & multi   .55 .25
940 A165 45c gold & multi   .90 .30
941 A165 50c gold & multi   1.00 .35
942 A165 60c gold & multi   1.40 .45
Perf. 11
Size: 26x53mm
943 A165 1b gold & multi   1.90 .70
Nos. 938-943 (6)   6.00 2.30

ILO
Emblem
A166

1969, July 28   **Perf. 13½**
944 A166 2.50b fawn & blk   2.50 1.50

50th anniv. of the ILO.

Charter
and Coat
of Arms
A167

Industrial
Complex
A168

1969, Aug. 26   **Litho.**   **Perf. 13½**
945 A167 45c ultra & multi   .85 .30
946 A168 1b multicolored   1.25 .40

Industrial development.

House with
Arcade,
Carora — A169

Designs: 25c, Ruins of Pastora Church. 55c, Chapel of the Cross. 65c, House of Culture.

1969, Sept. 8   **Perf. 13x14½**
947 A169 20c multicolored   .25 .25
948 A169 25c multicolored   .40 .25
949 A169 55c multicolored   .90 .30
950 A169 65c multicolored   1.25 .45
Nos. 947-950 (4)   2.80 1.25

400th anniversary of city of Carora.

Simon Bolivar in
Madrid — A170

Designs: 10c, Bolivar's wedding, Madrid, 1802, horiz. 35c, Bolivar monument. Madrid.

Perf. 13½x14, 14x13½
1969, Oct. 28   **Litho.**
951 A170 10c multicolored   .25 .25
952 A170 15c brn red & blk   .45 .25
953 A170 35c multicolored   .60 .25
a.   Souvenir sheet of 2   2.50 2.50
Nos. 951-953 (3)   1.30 .75

Bolivar's sojourn in Spain. No. 953a contains 2 imperf. stamps similar to Nos. 952-953 with simulated perforation. Sold for 75c.

"Birds in the Woods" — A171

Design: 45c, "Children in Summer Camp." Both designs are after children's paintings.

1969, Dec. 12   **Litho.**   **Perf. 12½**
954 A171 5c emerald & multi   .25 .25
955 A171 45c red & multi   .90 .40

Issued for Children's Day.

Map of
Great
Colombia
A172

1969, Dec. 16   **Litho.**   **Perf. 11½**
956 A172 45c multicolored   .70 .25

150th anniversary of the founding of the State of Great Colombia.

St.
Anthony's,
Clarines
A173

Churches: 30c, Church of the Conception, Caroni. 40c, St. Michael's, Burbusay. 45c, St. Anthony's, Maturin. 75c, St. Nicholas, Moruy. 1b, Coro Cathedral.

1970, Jan. 15   **Perf. 14**
957 A173 10c pink & multi   .25 .25
958 A173 30c emerald & multi   .30 .25
959 A173 40c yellow & multi   .65 .25
960 A173 45c gray bl & multi   .90 .30
a.   Souvenir sheet of 1, imperf.   2.00 2.00
961 A173 75c yellow & multi   1.25 .45
962 A173 1b orange & multi   1.50 .55
Nos. 957-962 (6)   4.85 2.05

Colonial architecture.
No. 960a sold for 75c.

A174

Design: Seven Hills of Valera.

1970, Feb. 13   **Litho.**   **Perf. 13x14½**
963 A174 95c multicolored   1.25 .40

Sesquicentennial of the city of Valera.

A175

Flowers: 20c, Monochaetum Humboldtianum. 25c, Symbolanthus vasculosis. 45c, Cavedishia splendens. 1b, Befaria glauca.

1970, July 29   **Litho.**   **Perf. 14x13½**
964 A175 20c multicolored   .50 .25
965 A175 25c multicolored   .80 .25
966 A175 45c multicolored   1.10 .40
967 A175 1b multicolored   1.60 .55
Nos. 964-967,C1049-C1052 (8)   8.50 2.75

Battle of
Boyaca, by
Martin Tovar
y Tovar
A176

1970, Aug. 7   **Perf. 13½x14**
968 A176 30c multicolored   .50 .25

150th anniversary of Battle of Boyaca.

Our Lady of
Belén de San
Mateo — A177

Designs: 35c, Pastoral Cross of Archbishop Silvestre Guevera y Lira, 1867. 40c, Our Lady of Valle. 90c, Virgin of Chiquinquira. 1b, Our Lady of Socorro de Valencia.

1970, Sept. 1   **Perf. 14x13½**
969 A177 35c gray & multi   .60 .25
970 A177 40c gray & multi   .70 .25
971 A177 60c gray & multi   1.00 .40
a.   Souvenir sheet of 1, imperf.   1.75 1.75
972 A177 90c gray & multi   1.25 .55
973 A177 1b gray & multi   1.60 .65
Nos. 969-973 (5)   5.15 2.10

The designs are from sculptures and paintings in various Venezuelan churches.
No. 971a sold for 75c.

Venezuela No. 22 and EXFILCA
Emblem — A178

Designs: 20c, EXFILCA emblem and flags of participating nations, vert. 70c, Venezuela No. C13 and EXFILCA emblem, vert.

1970, Nov. 28   **Litho.**   **Perf. 11**
974 A178 20c yellow & multi   .40 .25
975 A178 25c dk blue & multi   .45 .25
976 A178 70c brown & multi   .90 .40
a.   Souvenir sheet of 1, imperf.   1.75 1.75
Nos. 974-976 (3)   1.75 .90

EXFILCA 70, 2nd Interamerican Philatelic Exhibition, Caracas, Nov. 27-Dec. 6. No. 976a is a hexagon with each side 50mm long. Sold for 85c.

Guardian Angel, by
Juan Pedro
Lopez — A179

1970, Dec. 1   **Litho.**   **Perf. 14½x13½**
977 A179 45c dull yellow & multi   .70 .30

Christmas 1970.

Jet and 1920 Plane A180

1970, Dec. 10   *Perf. 13x14*
978 A180 5c blue & multi   .40 .25
Venezuelan Air Force, 50th anniversary.

Question Mark Full of Citizens — A181

1971, Apr. 30   **Litho.**   *Perf. 14x13½*
Light Green, Red & Black
979   Block of 4   4.00 2.25
   a. A181 30c frame L & I   .95 .45
   b. A181 30c frame T & R   .95 .45
   c. A181 30c frame L & B   .95 .45
   d. A181 30c frame B & R   .95 .45

National Census, 1971. Sheet of 20 contains 5 No. 979 and 5 blocks of 4 labels. See No. C1054.

Battle of Carabobo A182

1971, June 21   *Perf. 13½x14*
980 A182 2b blue & multi   2.10 1.25
Sesquicentennial of Battle of Carabobo.

Map of Federal District — A183

State maps. 25c, 55c, 85c, 90c, vert.

1971   **Litho.**   *Perf. 13½x14, 14x13½*
981 A183 5c shown   .40 .25
982 A183 15c Monagas   .40 .25
983 A183 20c Nueva Esparta   .40 .25
984 A183 25c Portuguesa   .40 .25
985 A183 45c Sucre   .45 .25
986 A183 55c Tachira   .55 .25
987 A183 65c Trujillo   .65 .25
988 A183 75c Yaracuy   .75 .30
989 A183 85c Zulia   .95 .30
990 A183 90c Amazonas   1.50 .30
991 A183 1b Federal Depen-
     dencies   1.60 .55
   Nos. 981-991 (11)   8.05 3.20
Nos. 981-991,C1035-C1048 (25) 19.20 6.85

Issued: 5c, 7/15; 15c, 20c, 8/16; 25c, 45c, 9/15; 55c, 65c, 10/15; 75c, 85c, 11/15; 90c, 1b, 12/15.

Madonna and Child — A184

Design: #993, Madonna & Jesus in manger.

1971, Dec. 1   *Perf. 11*
992 A184 25c multicolored   .60 .25
993 A184 25c multicolored   .60 .25
   a. Pair, #992-993   1.40 .60
Christmas 1971. Printed checkerwise.

Luis Daniel Beauperthuy A185

1971, Dec. 10   *Perf. 14x13½*
994 A185 1b vio bl & multi   1.25 .60
Dr. Luis Daniel Beauperthuy, scientist.

Globe in Heart Shape — A186

1972, Apr. 7   **Litho.**   *Perf. 14x13½*
995 A186 1b red, ultra & blk   1.00 .60
"Your heart is your health," World Health Day 1972.

Flags of Americas and Arms of Venezuela A187

Designs: 4b, Venezuelan flag. 5b, National anthem. 10b, Araguaney, national tree. 15b, Map, North and South America. All show flags of American nations in background.

1972, May 16   **Litho.**   *Perf. 14x13½*
996 A187 3b multicolored   4.00 1.00
997 A187 4b multicolored   4.25 1.75
998 A187 5b multicolored   4.75 2.25
999 A187 10b multicolored   9.00 3.00
1000 A187 15b multicolored   13.00 4.25
   Nos. 996-1000 (5)   35.00 12.25
"Venezuela in America."

Parque Central Complex A188

#1002, Front view ("Parque Central" on top).
#1003, Side view ("Parque Central" at right).

1972, July 25   *Perf. 11½*
1001 A100 30c yellow & multi   .25 .25
1002 A188 30c blue & multi   .25 .25
1003 A188 30c red & multi   .25 .25
   a. Strip of 3, #1001-1003   1.40 1.40

Completion of "Parque Central" middle-income housing project, Caracas.

Mahatma Gandhi — A189

1972, Oct. 2   **Litho.**   *Perf. 13½x14*
1004 A189 60c multicolored   1.25 .40

103rd birthday of Mohandas K. Gandhi (1869-1948), leader in India's fight for independence, advocate of non-violence.

Children Playing Music — A190

Christmas: #1006, Children roller skating.

1972, Dec. 5   **Litho.**   *Perf. 13½x14*
1005   30c multicolored   .25 .25
1006   30c multicolored   .25 .25
   a. A190 Pair, #1005-1006   1.00 1.00

Indigo Snake A191

Snake: 15c, South American chicken snake. 25c, Venezuelan lance-head. 30c, Coral snake. 60c, Casabel rattlesnake. 1b, Boa constrictor.

1972, Dec. 15   **Litho.**   *Perf. 13½x14*
1007 A191 10c black & multi   .50 .35
1008 A191 15c black & multi   .50 .35
1009 A191 25c black & multi   .70 .35
1010 A191 30c black & multi   .80 .35
1011 A191 60c black & multi   1.50 .40
1012 A191 1b black & multi   2.25 .60
   Nos. 1007-1012 (6)   6.25 2.40

Copernicus — A192

Designs: 5c, Model of solarcentric system. 15c, Copernicus' book "De Revolutionibus."

1973, Feb. 19   **Litho.**   *Perf. 13½x14*
1013   5c multicolored   .25 .25
1014   10c multicolored   .35 .25
1015   15c multicolored   .50 .25
   a. A192 Strip of 3, #1013-1015   1.60 .00

Sun — A193

Designs: Planetary system.

Size: 26½x29mm

1973   **Litho.**   *Perf. 13½*
1016 A193 5c shown   .25 .25
1017 A193 5c Earth   .25 .25
1018 A193 20c Mars   .55 .25
1019 A193 20c Saturn   .40 .25
1020 A193 30c Asteroids   .45 .25
1021 A193 40c Neptune   .55 .25
1022 A193 50c Venus   .80 .40
1023 A193 60c Jupiter   .95 .45
1024 A193 75c Uranus   1.10 .55
1025 A193 90c Pluto   1.40 .80
1026 A193 90c Moon   2.00 .80
1027 A193 1b Mercury   2.25 .95

Size: 27x55mm
Perf. 12
1028 A193 10c Orbits and Sat-
     urn   .25 .25
1029 A193 15c Sun, Mercury,
     Venus, Earth   .40 .25
1030 A193 15c Jupiter, Uranus,
     Neptune, Pluto   .45 .25
   a. Strip of 3, #1028-1030   1.10 1.10
   Nos. 1016-1030 (15)   12.05 6.20

10th anniversary of Humboldt Planetarium. No. 1030a has continuous design showing solar system.
Issue dates: Nos. 1016, 1018, 1021, 1023-1025, Mar. 15; others Mar. 30.

OAS Emblem, Map of Americas — A194

1973, Apr. 30   **Litho.**   *Perf. 13½x14*
1031 A194 60c multicolored   .65 .30
Organization of American States, 25th anniv.

José Antonio Paez — A195

Street of the Lancers, Puerto Cabello — A196

Designs: 10c, Paez in uniform. 30c, Paez and horse, from old print. 2b, Paez at Battle of Centauro, horiz. 10c, 2b are after contemporary paintings.

1973   *Perf. 14x13½, 13½x14*
1032 A195 10c gold & multi   .25 .25
1033 A195 30c red, blk & gold   .35 .25
1034 A195 50c bl, vio bl & dk brn   .60 .25
1035 A196 1b multicolored   1.25 .60
1036 A195 2b gold & multi   2.10 1.25
   Nos. 1032-1036 (5)   4.55 2.70

Gen. José Antonio Paez (1790-1873), leader in War of Independence, President of Venezuela. The 1b for the sesquicentenary of the fall of Puerto Cabello.
Issue dates: Nos. 1033-1034, May 6; Nos. 1032, 1036, June 13; No. 1035, Nov. 8.

José P. Padilla, Mariano Montilla, Manuel Manrique — A197

1b, Naval battle. 2b, Line-up for naval battle.

1973, July 27   Litho.   Perf. 12½
1037 A197 50c multicolored   .35   .25
1038 A197 1b multicolored   1.00   .45
1039 A197 2b multicolored   2.00 1.00
    Nos. 1037-1039 (3)   3.35 1.70
150th anniv. of the Battle of Maracaibo.

Bishop Ramos de Lora — A198

1973, Aug. 1   Photo.   Perf. 14x13½
1040 A198 75c gold & dk brn   .60   .25
Sesquicentennial of the birth of Ramos de Lora (1722-1790), first Bishop of Merida de Maracaibo and founder of the Colegio Seminario, the forerunner of the University of the Andes.

Plane, Ship, Margarita Island — A199

1973, Sept. 8   Litho.   Perf. 14x13½
1041 A199 5c multicolored   .50   .25
Establishment of Margarita Island as a free port.

Map of Golden Road and Waterfall — A200

Designs (Road Map and): 10c, Scarlet macaw. 20c, Church ruins. 50c, 60c, Indian mountain sanctuary. 90c, Colonial church. 1b, Flags of Venezuela and Brazil.

1973, Oct. 1   Litho.   Perf. 13
1042 A200 5c black & multi   .25   .25
1043 A200 10c black & multi   .25   .25
1044 A200 20c black & multi   .80   .25
1045 A200 50c black & multi   .85   .35
1046 A200 60c black & multi   .85   .35
1047 A200 90c black & multi   1.30   .40
1048 A200 1b black & multi   1.60   .55
    Nos. 1042-1048 (7)   5.90 2.40
Completion of the Golden Road from Santa Elena de Uairen, Brazil, to El Dorado, Venezuela.
Issued: 50c, 60c, Oct. 30; others Oct. 1.

Gen. Paez Dam and Power Station — A201

1973, Oct. 14   Perf. 14x13½
1049 A201 30c multicolored   .50   .25
Opening of the Gen. José Antonio Paez Dam and Power Station.

Child on Slide — A202

Designs: No. 1051, Fairytale animals. No. 1052, Children's book. No. 1053, Children disembarking from plane for vacation.

1973, Dec. 4   Litho.   Perf. 12
1050 A202 10c multicolored   .40   .25
1051 A202 10c multicolored   .40   .25
1052 A202 10c multicolored   .40   .25
1053 A202 10c multicolored   .40   .25
    Nos. 1050-1053 (4)   1.60 1.00
Children's Foundation Festival.

King Following Star — A203

Christmas: No. 1055, Two Kings.

1973, Dec. 5   Litho.   Perf. 14x13½
1054   30c multicolored   .55   .25
1055   30c multicolored   .55   .25
  a. A203 Pair, #1054-1055   1.40 1.40

Regional Map of Venezuela A204

1973, Dec. 13   Perf. 13½x14
1056 A204 25c multicolored   .75   .25
Introduction of regionalization.

Handicraft A205

Designs: 35c, Industrial park. 45c, Cog wheels and chimney.

1973, Dec. 18   Perf. 14x13½
1057 A205 15c blue & multi   .25   .25
1058 A205 35c multicolored   .30   .25
1059 A205 45c yellow & multi   .50   .25
    Nos. 1057-1059 (3)   1.05   .75
Progress in Venezuela and jobs for the handicapped.

Map of Carupano and Revelers — A206

1974, Feb. 22   Perf. 13½x14
1060 A206 5c multicolored   .60   .25
10th anniversary of Carupano Carnival.

Congress Emblem — A207

1974, May 20   Litho.   Perf. 13½
1061 A207 50c multicolored   .60   .25
9th Venezuelan Engineering Congress, Maracaibo, May 19-25.

Waves and "M" A208

Designs: Under-water photographs of deep-sea fish and marine life.

1974, June 20   Litho.   Perf. 12½
1062 A208 15c multicolored   .50   .25
1063 A208 35c multicolored   .70   .25
1064 A208 75c multicolored   .95   .30
1065 A208 80c multicolored   .95   .40
    Nos. 1062-1065 (4)   3.10 1.20
3rd UN Conference on the Law of the Sea, Caracas, June 20-Aug. 29.

Pupil and New School — A209

"Pay your Taxes" Campaign: 10c, 15c, 20c, like 5c. 25c, 30c, 35c, 40c, Suburban housing development. 45c, 50c, 55c, 60c, Highway and overpass. 65c, 70c, 75c, 80c, Playing field (sport). 85c, 90c, 95c, 1b, Operating room. All designs include Venezuelan coat of arms, coins and banknotes.

1974   Perf. 13½
1066 A209 5c blue & multi   .25   .25
1067 A209 10c ultra & multi   .25   .25
1068 A209 15c violet & multi   .25   .25
1069 A209 20c lilac & multi   .25   .25
1070 A209 25c multicolored   .25   .25
1071 A209 30c multicolored   .65   .25
1072 A209 35c multicolored   .25   .25
1073 A209 40c olive & multi   .45   .25
1074 A209 45c multicolored   .45   .25
1075 A209 50c green & multi   .45   .25
1076 A209 55c multicolored   .80   .40
1077 A209 60c multicolored   .65   .30
1078 A209 65c bister & multi   1.50   .60
1079 A209 70c multicolored   .70   .25
1080 A209 75c multicolored   .80   .30
1081 A209 80c brown & multi   .80   .30
1082 A209 85c ver & multi   .80   .30
1083 A209 90c multicolored   1.00   .30

1084 A209 95c multicolored   1.75   .95
1085 A209 1b multicolored   1.00   .40
    Nos. 1066-1085 (20)   13.30 6.60

Bolivar at Battle of Junin A210

1974, Aug. 6   Litho.   Perf. 13½x14
1086 A210 2b multicolored   2.00 1.00
Sesquicentennial of the Battle of Junin.

Globe and UPU Emblem — A211

50c, Postrider, sailing ship, steamer and jet.

1974, Oct. 9   Perf. 12
1087 A211 45c dk blue & multi   .45   .25
1088 A211 50c black & multi   .55   .25
Centenary of Universal Postal Union. No. 1088 has a white background.

Rufino Blanco-Fombona — A212

Portraits of Blanco-Fombona and his books.

1974, Oct. 16   Litho.   Perf. 12½
1089 A212 10c gray & multi   .25   .25
1090 A212 30c yellow & multi   .25   .25
1091 A212 45c multicolored   .45   .25
1092 A212 90c buff & multi   .70   .35
    Nos. 1089-1092 (4)   1.65 1.10
Centenary of the birth of Rufino Blanco-Fombona (1874-1944), writer.

Children A213

1974, Nov. 29   Litho.   Perf. 13½
1093 A213 70c blue & multi   .60   .25
Children's Foundation Festival.

General Sucre — A214

Globe with South American Map and Flags — A215

Battle of Ayacucho — A216

1b, Map of South America with battles marked.

1974, Dec. 9   Perf. 14x13½, 13½x14
1094 A214 30c multicolored   .25   .25
1095 A215 50c multicolored   .40   .35
1096 A215   1b multicolored   .85   .40
1097 A216   2b multicolored   1.75   .85
    Nos. 1094-1097 (4)   3.25 1.85

Sesquicentennial of the Battle of Ayacucho.

Adoration of the Shepherds, by J. B. Mayno — A217

1974, Dec. 16   Photo.   Perf. 14x13½
1098 30c Shepherd   .35   .30
1099 30c Madonna & Child   .35   .30
  a. A217 Pair, #1098-1099   1.00 1.00

Christmas 1974.

Road Building, 1905 and El Ciempies Overpass, 1972 — A219

Designs: 20c, 1b, Jesus Muñoz Tebar, first Minister of Public Works. 25c, Bridges on Caracas-La Guaira Road, 1912 and 1953. 40c, View of Caracas, 1874 and 1974. 70c, Tucacas Railroad Station, 1911, and projected terminal, 1974. 80c, Anatomical Institute, Caracas, 1911, and Social Security Hospital, 1909. 85c, Quinnari River Bridge, 1804, and Orinoco River Bridge, 1967.

1974, Dec. 18   Litho.   Perf. 12½
1100 A219   5c ultra & multi   .25   .25
1101 A219 20c ocher & blk   .30   .05
1102 A219 25c blue & multi   .35   .25
1103 A219 40c yellow & multi   .35   .25
1104 A219 70c green & multi   1.75   .30
1105 A219 80c multicolored   1.40   .35

1106 A219 85c orange & multi   1.75   .35
1107 A219   1b red & black   1.90   .60
    Nos. 1100-1107 (8)   8.05 2.60
Centenary of the Ministry of Public Works.

Women and IWY Emblem — A220

1975, Oct. 8   Litho.   Perf. 13½x14
1108 A220 90c multicolored   .60   .35
International Women's Year.

Scout Emblem and Tents — A221

1975, Nov. 11   Litho.   Perf. 13½x14
1109 A221 20c multicolored   .25   .25
1110 A221 80c multicolored   .60   .30
    14th World Boy Scout Jamboree, Lille-hammer, Norway, July 29-Aug. 7.

Adoration of the Shepherds — A222

1975, Dec. 5   Litho.   Perf. 13½x14
1111 30c multicolored   .40   .40
1112 30c multicolored   .40   .40
  a. A222 Pair, #1111-1112   1.40 1.40

Christmas 1975.

Bolivar's Tomb — A224

Design: 1.05b, National Pantheon.

1976, Feb. 2   Engr.   Perf. 14x13½
1113 A224   30c gray & ultra   .25   .25
1114 A224 1.05b sepia & car   .75   .30
Centenary of National Pantheon.

Bolivia Flag Colors A225

1976, Mar. 22   Litho.   Perf. 13½
1115 A225 60c multicolored   .60   .25
Sesquicentennial of Bolivia's independence.

Aerial Map Survey — A226

1976, Apr. 8   Perf. 13½x12½
1116 A226 1b black & vio bl   1.00   .35
Natl. Cartographic Institute, 40th anniv.

Gen. Ribas' Signature A227

José Felix Ribas A228

1976, Apr. 26   Photo.   Perf. 12½x13
1117 A227 40c red & green   .40   .25
    Perf. 13½
1118 A228 55c multicolored   .60   .25
    Gen. José Felix Ribas (1775-1815), independence hero, birth bicentenary.

Musicians of the Chacao School, by Armandio Darrios — A229

Lamas's Colophon A230

1976, May 13   Litho.   Perf. 13½
1119 A229 75c multicolored   1.25   .80
    Photo.   Perf. 12½x13
1120 A230 1.25b buff, red & gray   .70   .35
José Angel Lamas (1775-1814), composer, birth bicentenary.

Bolivar, by José Maria Espinoza — A231

1976   Engr.   Perf. 12
    Size: 18x22½mm
1121 A231   5c green   .25   .25
1122 A231 10c lilac rose   .25   .25
1123 A231 15c brown   .25   .25
1124 A231 20c black   .25   .25
1125 A231 25c yellow   .25   .25
1126 A231 30c violet bl   .25   .25
1127 A231 45c dk purple   .25   .25
1128 A231 50c orange   .25   .25
1129 A231 65c blue   .35   .25
1130 A231   1b vermilion   .45   .35

    Size: 26x32mm
    Perf. 12x11½
1131 A231   2b gray   .90   .35
1132 A231   3b violet blue   1.40   .55
1133 A231   4b yellow   1.75   .75
1134 A231   5b orange   2.10 1.00
1135 A231 10b dull purple   5.00 2.00
1136 A231 15b blue   7.25 2.75
1137 A231 20b vermilion   9.25 3.75
    Nos. 1121-1137 (17)   30.45 13.75
Issued: 5c-1b, May 17; 2b-20b, July 15.

    Coil Stamps
1978, May 22   Perf. 13½ Horiz.
    Size: 18x22½mm
1138 A231   5c green   .30   .25
1139 A231 10c lilac rose   .30   .25
1140 A231 15c brown   .30   .25
1141 A231 20c black   .30   .25
1142 A231 25c yellow   .30   .25
1143 A231 30c violet blue   .35   .25
1144 A231 45c dk purple   .45   .25
1144A A231 50c orange   .60   .25
1144B A231 65c blue   .75   .25
1144C A231   1b vermilion   1.25   .25
    Nos. 1138-1144C (10)   4.90 2.50

Black control number on back of every fifth stamp.
See Nos. 1305-1307, 1362-1366, 1401-1409, 1482, 1484, 1487, 1490. Compare with designs A405-A406.

Maze A232

Central University A233

Faculty Emblems A234

1976, June 1   Litho.   Perf. 12½x13
1145 A232 30c multicolored   .25   .25
1146 A233 50c yel, org & blk   .35   .25
1147 A234 90c black & yellow   .70   .45
    Nos. 1145-1147 (3)   1.30   .95
Central University of Venezuela, 250th anniv.

"Unity" — A235

Designs: 45c, 1.25b, similar to 15c.

1976, June 29   Litho.   Perf. 12½
1148 A235 15c multicolored   .25   .25
1149 A235 45c multicolored   .35   .25
1150 A235 1.25b multicolored   .70   .45
    Nos. 1148-1150 (3)   1.30   .95
Amphictyonic Cong. of Panama, Sesqui.

Washington, US Bicent. Emblem A236

US Bicentennial Emblem and: No. 1152, Jefferson. No. 1153, Lincoln. No. 1154, F. D. Roosevelt. No. 1155, J. F. Kennedy.

1976, July 4   Engr.   Perf. 14

1151	A236	1b red brn & blk	.70	.35
1152	A236	1b green & blk	.70	.35
1153	A236	1b purple & blk	.70	.35
1154	A236	1b blue & blk	.70	.35
1155	A236	1b olive & blk	.70	.35
	Nos. 1151-1155 (5)		3.50	1.75

American Bicentennial.

Valve — A237

Computer drawings of valves & pipelines.

1976, Nov. 8   Photo.   Perf. 12½x14

1156	A237	10c multicolored	.25	.25
1157	A237	30c multicolored	.25	.25
1158	A237	35c multicolored	.30	.25
1159	A237	40c multicolored	.30	.25
1160	A237	55c multicolored	.40	.25
1161	A237	90c multicolored	.70	.25
	Nos. 1156-1161 (6)		2.20	1.50

Nationalization of the oil industry.

Nativity, by Barbaro Rivas — A238

1976, Dec. 1   Litho.   Perf. 13x14

1162	A238	30c multicolored	.60	.30

Christmas 1976.

Ornament A239

Lithographed and Embossed

1976, Dec. 15   Perf. 14x13½

1163	A239	60c yellow & black	.60	.25

Declaration of Bogota (economic agreements of Andean countries), 10th anniv.

Coat of Arms of Barinas — A240

1977, May 25   Photo.   Perf. 12½x13

1164	A240	50c multicolored	.60	.25

400th anniv. of the founding of Barinas.

Crucified Christ, Patron Saint of La Grita — A241

1977, Aug. 6   Litho.   Perf. 13

1165	A241	30c multicolored	.50	.25

Founding of La Grita, 400th anniv. (in 1976).

Symbolic City — A242

1977, Aug. 26   Litho.   Perf. 13½

1166	A242	1b multicolored	.65	.30

450th anniversary of the founding of Coro.

Communications Symbols — A243

1977, Sept. 30   Litho.   Perf. 13½x14

1167	A243	85c multicolored	.65	.25

9th Interamerican Postal and Telecommunications Staff Congress, Caracas, Sept. 26-30.

Cable Connecting with TV, Telephone and Circuit Box — A244

1977, Oct. 12   Litho.   Perf. 14

1168	A244	95c multicolored	.95	.25

Inauguration of Columbus underwater cable linking Venezuela and the Canary Islands.

"Venezuela" A245

Designs: "Venezuela" horizontal on 50c, 1.05b; reading up on 80c, 1.25b; reading down on 1.50b.

1977, Nov. 26   Photo.   Perf. 13½x13

1169	A245	30c brt yel & blk	.25	.25
1170	A245	50c dp org & blk	.35	.25
1171	A245	80c gray & blk	.60	.25
1172	A245	1.05b red & blk	.80	.25
1173	A245	1.25b yel & blk	.90	.25
1174	A245	1.50b gray & blk	1.10	.35
	Nos. 1169-1174 (6)		4.00	1.60

Iron industry nationalization, 1st anniv.

Juan Pablo Duarte — A246

1977, Dec. 8   Engr.   Perf. 11x13

1175	A246	75c black & lilac	.55	.25

Duarte (1813-76), leader in liberation struggle.

Nativity, Colonial Sculpture — A247

1977, Dec. 15   Litho.   Perf. 13

1176	A247	30c green & multi	.40	.25

Christmas 1977.

OPEC Emblem — A248

1977, Dec. 20

1177	A248	1.05b brt & lt bl & blk	.90	.25

50th Conference of Oil Producing and Exporting Countries, Caracas.

Bicyclist A249

1978, Jan. 16   Litho.   Perf. 13½x13

1178	A249	5c Racing bicyclists	.25	.25
1179	A249	1.25b shown	1.00	.25

World Bicycling Championships, San Cristobal, Tachira, Aug. 22-Sept. 4.

Profiles A250

1978, Apr. 21   Litho.   Perf. 13½x14

1180	A250	70c blk, gray & lil	.65	.25

Language Day.
Issued in tete-beche pairs. Value $1.25.

Magnetic Computer Tape and Satellite A251

1978, May 17   Litho.   Perf. 14

1184	A251	75c violet blue	.75	.25

10th World Telecommunications Day.

"1777-1977" — A252

Goya's Carlos III as Computer Print — A253

1978, June 23   Litho.   Perf. 12

1185	A252	30c multicolored	.25	.25
1186	A253	1b multicolored	.55	.25

200th anniversary of Venezuelan unification.

Bolivar Bicentenary

Juan Vicente Bolivar y Ponte, Father of Simon Bolivar — A254

The Oath on Monte Sacro, Rome, by Tito Salas — A255

Designs: 30c, Bolivar as infant in nursemaid's arms (detail from design of No. 1189). No. 1189, Baptism of the Liberator, by Tito Salas, 1929.

1978, July 24   Engr.   Perf. 12½

1187	A254	30c emerald & blk	.25	.25
1188	A254	1b multicolored	.55	.25

Souvenir Sheet

Litho.

Perf. 14

1189	A255	Sheet of 5	40.00	40.00
a.		50c, single stamp	1.50	1.50

1978, Dec. 17   Engr.   Perf. 12½

Designs: 30c, Bolivar at 25. 1b, Simon Rodriguez. No. 1192, shown. (Bolivar's tutor).

1190	A254	30c multicolored	.25	.25
1191	A254	1b rose red & blk	.45	.25

Souvenir Sheet

Litho.

Perf. 14

1192	A255	Sheet of 5	24.00	24.00
a.		50c, single stamp	1.10	1.10

Size of souvenir sheet stamps: 20x24mm. Size of #1189: 154x130mm; #1192: 130x155mm.

1979, July 24   Engr.   Perf. 12½

Designs: 30c, Alexander Sabes Petion, president of Haiti. 1b, Bolivar's signature. No. 1195: a, Partial map of Jamaica, horiz. b, Partial map of Jamaica, vert. c, Bolivar, 1816. d, Luis Brion. e, Petion.

1193	A254	30c org, vio & blk	.30	.25
1194	A254	1b red org & blk	.45	.25

Souvenir Sheet

Litho.

Perf. 14

1195	A255	Sheet of 5	3.25	3.25
a.-e.		50c, any single	.35	.35

Size of souvenir sheet stamps: 26x20, 20x26mm.

1979, Dec. 17   Engr.   Perf. 12½

Designs: 30c, Bolivar. 1b, Slave. No. 1198, Freeing of the Slaves, by Tito Salas. (30c, 1b, details from design of No. 1198.)

1196	A254	30c multicolored	.25	.25
1197	A254	1b multicolored	.30	.25

Souvenir Sheet

Litho.

Perf. 14

1198	A255	Sheet of 5	5.50	5.50
a.		50c, single stamp	1.10	1.10

Simon Bolivar, birth centenary. Size of souvenir sheet stamps: 22x28mm.
See Nos. 1228-1230, 1264-1266, 1276-1284, 1294-1296, 1317-1322.

"T" and "CTV" — A256

Designs: Different arrangement of letters "T" and "CTV" for "Confederacion de Trabajeros Venezolanos."

1978, Sept. 27 Photo. *Perf. 13x13½*
1199 Strip of 5 .90 .90
a.-e. A256 30c, single stamp .25 .25
1200 Strip of 5 1.90 1.90
a.-e. A256 95c, single stamp .30 .25
Workers' Day.

Symbolic Design — A257

1978, Oct. 3 Litho. *Perf. 14*
1201 A257 50c dark brown .75 .30
Rafael Rangel, physician and scientist, birth centenary.

Drill Head, Tachira Oil Field Map — A258

"P" as Pipeline A259

1978, Nov. 2 Litho. *Perf. 13½*
1202 A258 30c multicolored .25 .25
1203 A259 1.05b multicolored .95 .30
Centenary of oil industry.

Star — A260

1978, Dec. 6 Litho. *Perf. 14*
1204 A260 30c multicolored .60 .25
Christmas 1978.

"P T" — A261

1979, Feb. 8 Litho. *Perf. 12½*
1205 A261 75c black & red .40 .25
Creation of Postal and Telegraph Institute.

"Dam Holding Back Water" A262

1979, Feb. 15 Photo. *Perf. 13½*
1206 A262 2b silver, gray & blk .90 .45
Guri Dam, 10th anniversary.

San Martin, by E. J. Maury — A263

60c, San Martin, by Mercedes. 70c, Monument, Guayaquil. 75c, San Martin's signature.

1979, Feb. 25 *Perf. 12½x13*
1207 A263 40c blue, blk & yel .25 .25
1208 A263 60c blue, blk & yel .30 .25
1209 A263 70c blue, blk & yel .40 .25
1210 A263 75c blue, blk & yel .40 .25
Nos. 1207-1210 (4) 1.35 1.00
José de San Martin (1778-1850), South American liberator.

"Rotary" — A264

1979, Aug. 7 Litho. *Perf. 14x13½*
1211 A264 85c gold & blk .70 .25
Rotary Club of Caracas, 50th anniversary.

Our Lady of Coromoto Appearing to Children A265

Engraved and Lithographed
1979, Aug. 23 *Perf. 13*
1212 A265 55c black & dp org .65 .25
Canonization of Our Lady of Coromoto, 25th anniv.

London Residence, Coat of Arms, Miranda — A266

1979, Oct. 23 Litho. *Perf. 14½x14*
1213 A266 50c multicolored .50 .25
Francisco de Miranda (1750-1810), Venezuelan independence fighter.

O'Leary, Maps of South America and United Kingdom A267

1979, Nov. 6
1214 A267 30c multicolored .50 .25
Daniel O'Leary (1801-1854), general, writer.

IYC Emblem and: 79c, Boy holding nest. 80c, Boys in water, bridge.

A269

1979, Dec. 1 Litho. *Perf. 13*
1217 A269 30c multicolored .50 .25
Christmas 1979.

Caudron Bomber, EXFILVE Emblem A270

EXFILVE Emblem and: No. 1219, Stearman biplane. No. 1220, UH-1H helicopter. No. 1221, CF-5 jet fighter.

1979, Dec. 15 *Perf. 11x11½*
1218 A270 75c multicolored .40 .25
1219 A270 75c multicolored .40 .25
1220 A270 75c multicolored .40 .25
1221 A270 75c multicolored .40 .25
a. Block of 4, #1218-1221 1.75 1.00
Venezuelan Air Force, 59th anniv.; EXFILVE 79, 3rd Natl. Philatelic Exhibition, Dec. 7-17.

IPOSTEL Emblem, World Map A271

1979, Dec. 27 *Perf. 11½*
1222 A271 75c multicolored .50 .25
Postal and Telegraph Institute, introduction of new logo.

Queen Victoria, Hill — A272

1980, Feb. 13 Litho. *Perf. 12½*
1223 A272 55c multicolored .50 .25
Sir Rowland Hill (1795-1879), originator of penny postage.

Dr. Augusto Pi Suner, Physiologist, Birth Centenary — A273

1980, Mar. 14 Litho. *Perf. 11½*
1224 A273 80c multicolored .50 .25

Spanish Seed Leaf — A274

1979, Nov. 20 Litho. *Perf. 14½x14*
1215 A268 70c lt blue & blk .25 .25
1216 A268 80c multicolored .40 .25
International Year of the Child.

Lithographed and Engraved
1980, Mar. 27 *Perf. 13*
1225 A274 50c multicolored .60 .25
Pedro Loefling (1729-56), Swedish botanist.

Juan Lovera (1778-1841), Artist — A275

1980, May 25 Litho. *Perf. 13½*
1226 A275 60c blue & dp org .25 .25
1227 A275 75c violet & org .30 .25

Bolivar Types of 1978
30c, Signing of document. 1b, House of Congress. #1230, Angostura Congress, by Tito Salas.

1980, July 24 Engr. *Perf. 12½*
1228 A254 30c multicolored .25 .25
1229 A254 1b multicolored .50 .25

Souvenir Sheet
Litho.
Perf. 14
1230 A255 Sheet of 5 4.00 4.00
a. 50c, single stamp .25 .25
Simon Bolivar (1783-1830), revolutionary. Size of souvenir sheet stamps: 25x20mm, 20x25mm.

Dancing Girls, by Armando Reveron — A276

1980, Aug. 17 Litho. *Perf. 13*
1231 A276 50c shown .25 .25
Size: 25x40mm
1232 A276 65c Portrait .55 .30
Armando Reveron (1889-1955), artist.

Bernardo O'Higgins — A277

Lithographed and Engraved
1980, Aug. 22 *Perf. 13x14*
1233 A277 85c multicolored .75 .30
Bernardo O'Higgins (1776-1842), Chilean soldier and statesman.

School Ship Simon Bolivar A278

Frigate Mariscal Sucre A279

Perf. 11½ (#1234), 11x11½

1980, Sept. 13			Litho.	
1234	A278	1.50b shown	1.25	.40
1235	A279	1.50b shown	1.25	.40
1236	A279	1.50b Submarine Picua	1.25	.40
1237	A279	1.50b Naval Academy	1.25	.40
		Nos. 1234-1237 (4)	5.00	1.60

"Picuda" is misspelled on stamp.

Workers Holding OPEC Emblem A280

20th Anniv. of OPEC (Organization of Petroleum Exporting Countries): #1239, Emblem.

1980, Sept. 14		Litho.	Perf. 12x11½	
1238	A280	1.50b multicolored	.75	.30
1239	A280	1.50b multicolored	.75	.30

Death of Simon Bolivar A281

1980, Dec. 17	Litho.	Perf. 11x11½	
1240	A281	2b multicolored	1.60	.50

Simon Bolivar, 150th anniversary of death.

A282

Lithographed and Engraved

1980, Dec. 17		Perf. 13x12½	
1241	A282	2b multicolored	.90	.40

Gen. José Antonio Sucre, 150th anniv. of death.

A283

1980, Dec. 19	Litho.	Perf. 14x13½	
1242	A283	1b Nativity by Rubens	.60	.35

Christmas 1980.

Helen Keller's Initials (Written and Braille) — A284

Lithographed and Embossed

1981, Feb. 12		Perf. 12½	
1243	A284	1.50b multicolored	.90	.35

Helen Keller (1880-1968), blind and deaf writer and lecturer.

John Baptiste de la Salle — A285

1981, May 15	Litho.	Perf. 11½x11	
1244	A285	1.25b multicolored	.55	.25

Christian Brothers' 300th anniv.

San Felipe City, 250th Anniv. — A286

1981, May 1		Perf. 11½	
1245	A286	3b multicolored	1.10	.50

Municipal Theater of Caracas Centenary A287

1981, June 28	Litho.	Perf. 12	
1246	A287	1.25b multicolored	2.00	.35

A288

1981, Sept. 15	Litho.	Perf. 11½	
1247	A288	2b multicolored	.60	.25

UPU membership centenary.

A289

1981, Oct. 14		Litho.	
1248	A289	1b multicolored	.50	.25

11th natl. population and housing census.

A290

1981, Dec. 3	Litho.	Perf. 11½	
1249	A290	95c multicolored	.50	.25

9th Bolivar Games, Barquismeto.

Transportation — A291

1981, Dec. 5		Photo.	Perf. 13x14	
1250	A291	1b 19th Cent. Bicycle	.55	.35
1251	A291	1.05b Locomotive, 1926	.55	.35
1252	A291	1.25b Buick, 1937	.95	.50
1253	A291	1.50b Coach	1.25	.60
		Nos. 1250-1253 (4)	3.30	1.80

See Nos. 1289-1292, 1308-1311.

Christmas 1981 A292

1981, Dec. 21	Litho.	Perf. 11½	
1254	A292	1b multicolored	.50	.25

50th Anniv. of Natural Science Society — A293

1982, Jan. 21		Perf. 11½	
1255	A293	1b Mt. Autana	.45	.25
1256	A293	1.50b Sarisarinama	.70	.40
1257	A293	2b Guacharo Cave	.90	.45
		Nos. 1255-1257 (3)	2.05	1.10

20th Anniv. of Constitution A294

1982, Jan. 28	Photo.	Perf. 13x13½	
1258	A294	1.85b gold & blk	.90	.35

A295

1982, Feb. 19	Litho.	Perf. 13½	
1259	A295	3b multicolored	1.40	.60

20th anniv. of agricultural reform.

A296

1982, Mar. 12	Litho.	Perf. 13½	
1260	A296	1b blue & dk blue	.75	.25

Jules Verne (1828-1905), science fiction writer.

Natl. Anthem Centenary (1981) A297

1982, Mar. 26		Perf. 11½	
1261	A297	1b multicolored	.65	.25

1300th Anniv. of Bulgaria — A298

1982, June 2	Litho.	Perf. 13½	
1262	A298	65c multicolored	.60	.35

6th Natl. 5-Year Plan, 1981-85 — A299

1982, June 11			
1263	A299	2b multicolored	.50	.25

Bolivar Types of 1978

30c, Juan José Rondon. 1b, José Antonio Anzoategui.

1982, July 24		Engr.	Perf. 12½	
1264	A254	30c multicolored	.50	.30
1265	A254	1b multicolored	.50	.30

Souvenir Sheet

			Litho.	Perf. 14	
1266	A255	Sheet of 5		4.50	4.50
a.-e.		50c, any single		.30	.30

Single stamps of No. 1266 show details from Battle of Boyaca, by Martin Tovar y Tovar. Size of souvenir sheet stamps: 19x26mm, 26x19mm.

Cecilio Acosta (1818-1881), Writer — A299a

1982, Aug. 13   Litho.   Perf. 11½
1266F A299a 3b multicolored   .65   .35

Aloe
A300

1982, Oct. 14   Photo.   Perf. 13
1267 A300 1.05b shown   .75   .40
1268 A300 2.55b Tortoise   1.90   .40
1269 A300 2.75b Tara amarilla tree   2.10   .40
1270 A300   3b Guacharo bird   2.50   .45
    Nos. 1267-1270 (4)   7.25 1.65

Andres Bello (1781-1865), Statesman and Reformer — A301

1982, Nov. 20   Litho.   Perf. 12
1271 A301 1.05b multicolored   .45   .25
1272 A301 2.55b multicolored   .95   .30
1273 A301 2.75b multicolored   .95   .30
1274 A301   3b multicolored   1.25   .35
    Nos. 1271-1274 (4)   3.60 1.20

Christmas 1982 — A302

Design: Holy Family creche figures by Francisco J. Cardozo, 18th cent.

Photogravure and Engraved
1982, Dec. 7   Perf. 13½
1275 A302 1b multicolored   .40   .25

Bolivar Types of 1978

No. 1276, Victory Monument, Carabobo. No. 1277, Monument to the Meeting plaque. No. 1278, Antonio de Sucre. No. 1279, Jose Antonio Paez. No. 1280, Sword hilt, 1824. No. 1281, Guayaquil Monument.

1982-83   Engr.   Perf. 12½
1276 A254 30c multicolored   .25   .25
1277 A254 30c multicolored   .25   .25
1278 A254 30c multicolored   .25   .25
1279 A254 1b multicolored   .35   .25
1280 A254 1b multicolored   .35   .25
1281 A254 1b multicolored   .35   .25
    Nos. 1276-1281 (6)   1.80 1.50

Souvenir Sheets
Litho.
Perf. 14
1282 A255   Sheet of 5   5.00 5.00
    a.-e. 50c, any single   .30   .30
1283 A255   Sheet of 5   5.00 5.00
    a.-e. 50c, any single   .30   .30
1284 A255   Sheet of 5   5.00 5.00
    a.-e. 50c, any single   .30   .30

No. 1282: Battle of Carabobo by Martin Tovar y Tovar; No. 1283, Monument to the Meeting; No. 1284, Battle of Ayacucho, by Martin Tovar y Tovar.
Issue dates: Nos. 1276-1277, 1279, 1281-1283, Dec. 17; others, Apr. 18, 1983.

Gen. Jose Francisco Bermudez — A303

Antonio Nicolas Briceno, Liberation Hero A304

Perf. 13x13½, 15x14
1982, Dec. 23   Litho.
1285 A303 3b multicolored   1.60   .50
1286 A304 3b multicolored   1.60   .50

25th Anniv. of 1958 Reforms A305

1983, Jan. 23   Perf. 10½x10
1287 A305 3b multicolored   1.00   .45

A306

1983, Mar. 20   Photo.   Perf. 13½x13
1288 A306 4b olive & red   1.00   .45
25th anniv. of Judicial Police Technical Dept.

Transportation Type of 1981
Perf. 13½x14½
1983, Mar. 28   Photo.
1289 A291 75c Lincoln, 1923   1.10   .45
1290 A291 80c Locomotive, 1889   1.10   .45
1291 A291 85c Willys truck, 1927   1.40   .45
1292 A291 95c Cleveland motorcycle, 1920   1.40   .45
    Nos. 1289-1292 (4)   5.00 1.80

A307

1983, May 17   Photo.   Perf. 13x12½
1293 A307 2.85b multicolored   .75   .40
World Communications Year.

Bolivar Types of 1978

Designs: 30c; Flags of Colombia, Peru, Chile, Venezuela, and Buenos Aires. 1b; Equestrian Statue of Bolivar.

Photo. & Engr. (#1294), Engr. (#1295)
1983, July 25   Perf. 12½
1294 A254 30c multicolored   .35   .25
1295 A254 1b multicolored   .50   .25

Souvenir Sheet
Litho.
Perf. 14
1296 A255   Sheet of 5   5.00 4.75
    a.-e. 50c, any single   .25   .25

Single stamps of No. 1296 show details of "The Liberator on the Silver Mountain of Potosi" Size of souvenir sheet stamps, 20x25mm.

A308   9th Pan-American Games — A309

Designs: #1303a, baseball. b, cycle wheel. c, boxing glove. d, soccer ball. e, target.

Lithographed and Engraved
1983, Aug. 25   Perf. 13
1297 A308 2b shown   .50   .25
1298 A308 2b Swimming   .50   .25
1299 A308 2.70b Cycling   .60   .40
1300 A308 2.70b Fencing   .60   .40
1301 A308 2.85b Runners   .75   .50
1302 A308 2.85b Weightlifting   .75   .50
    Nos. 1297-1302 (6)   3.70 2.30

Souvenir Sheet
1303   Sheet of 5   16.00 16.00
    a.-e. A309 1b, any single   16.00 16.00
#1303 for Copan '83. Size: 167x101mm.

25th Anniv. of Cadafe (State Electricity Authority) — A310

1983, Oct. 27   Litho.   Perf. 14
1304 A310 3b multicolored   1.40   .65

Redrawn Bolivar Type of 1976
1983, Sept. 29   Engr.   Perf. 12
Size: 26x32mm
1305 A231 25b blue green   11.50   5.50
1306 A231 30b brown   13.50   6.75
1307 A231 50b brt rose lilac   20.00 11.50
    Nos. 1305-1307 (3)   45.00 23.75

Transportation Type of 1981
Various views of Caracas Metro.

1983, Dec.   Photo.   Perf. 13½x14½
1308 A291 55c multicolored   .70   .45
1309 A291 75c multicolored   .70   .45
1310 A291 95c multicolored   .70   .45
1311 A291 2b multicolored   1.50   .65
    Nos. 1308-1311 (4)   3.60 2.00

Christmas 1983 A311

1983, Dec. 1   Litho.   Perf. 13x14
1312 A311 1b Nativity   .50   .35

Scouting Year (1982) A312

Lithographed and Engraved
1983, Dec. 14   Perf. 12½x13
1313 A312 2.25p Pitching tent   .60   .35
1314 A312 2.55b Planting tree   .60   .35
1315 A312 2.75b Mountain climbing   .75   .35
1316 A312   3b Camp site   .75   .35
    Nos. 1313-1316 (4)   2.70 1.40

Bolivar Types of 1978

Designs: No. 1317, Title page of "Opere de Raimondo Montecuccoli" (most valuable book in Caracas University Library). No. 1318, Pedro Gual, Congress of Panama delegate, 1826. No. 1319, Jose Maria Vargas (b. 1786), University of Caracas pres. No. 1320, José Faustino Sanchez Carrion, Congress of Panama delegate, 1826.

1984   Engr.   Perf. 12½
1317 A254 30c multicolored   .25   .25
1318 A254 30c multicolored   .25   .25
1319 A254 1b multicolored   .25   .25
1320 A254 1b multicolored   .25   .25
    Nos. 1317-1320 (4)   1.00 1.00

Souvenir Sheets
Litho.
Perf. 14
1321 A255   Sheet of 5   4.75 4.50
    a.-e. 50c, any single   .30   .30
1322 A255   Sheet of 5   5.25 5.25
    a.-e. 50c, any single   .30   .30

Single stamps of No. 1321 show details of Arts, Science and Education, fresco by Hector Poleo; 1322, Map of South America, 1829. Size of souvenir sheet stamps: 20x30mm; 27x20mm.
Issued: #1317, 1319, 1321, 1/19; others, 1/20.

Radio Waves — A313

1984, Jan. 30   Litho.   Perf. 14x13
1323 A313 2.70b multicolored   .65   .25
Radio Club of Venezuela, 50th anniv.

Intelligentsia for Peace — A314

1984, Jan. 31
1324 A314 1b Doves   .30   .25
1325 A314 2.70b Profile   .60   .25
1326 A314 2.85b Flower, head   .60   .25
    Nos. 1324-1326 (3)   1.50   .75

President Romulo Gallegos (1884-1969) A315

Gallegos: No. 1327, Portrait as a young man in formal dress. No. 1328, Portrait, 1948.

1984-85   Litho.   Perf. 11½
1327 A315 1.70b royal bl, dl bl,
                 beige & blk   .65 .40
1328 A315 1.70b ocher, org brn &
                 buff   .65 .40

Issued: #1327, 10/12/84; #1328, 1/18/85. See Nos. 1335-1336.

Pan-American Union of Engineering Associations, 18th Convention A316

1984, Oct. 28
1329 A316 2.55b pale buff, dk bl   .65 .25

Christmas 1984 A317

1984, Dec. 3
1330 A317 1b multicolored   .50 .25

Pope John Paul II, Statue of the Virgin of Caracas A318

1985, Jan. 26   Litho.   Perf. 12
1331 A318 1b multicolored   1.75 .45

Papal visit, 1985.

Pascua City Bicent. A319

1985, Feb. 10
1332 A319 1.50b multicolored   .60 .35

Dr. Mario Briceno-Iragorry (b. 1897), Historian — A320

1985, Oct.   Litho.   Perf. 12
1333 A320 1.25b silver & ver   .50 .25

Natl. St. Vincent de Paul Soc., Cent. — A321

1985, July
1334 A321 1b dk ol bis, ver & buff   .60 .25

Gallegos Memorial Type of 1984-85
  Designs: Gallegos, diff.

1985, Aug. 8
1335 A315 1.70b gray grn, dk gray
                 grn & dl gray grn   .35 .25
1336 A315 1.70b grn, sage grn & dl
                 grn   .35 .25

Dated 1984.

Latin American Economic System, 10th Anniv. A322

1985, Aug. 15
1337 A322 4b black & red   2.00 .85

Miniature Sheet

Virgin Mary, Birth Bimillennium — A323

Statues: a, Virgin of the Divine Shepherd. b, Chiquinquira Madonna. c, Coromoto Madonna. d, Valley Madonna. e, Virgin of Perpetual Succor. f, Virgin of Peace. g, Immaculate Conception Virgin. h, Soledad Madonna. i, Virgin of Consolation. j, Nieves Madonna.

1985, Sept. 9
1338 A323   Sheet of 10   7.00 7.00
a.-j.   1b, any single   .40 .25

OPEC, 25th Anniv. A324

1985, Sept. 13
1339 A324 6b multicolored   1.75 .80

Opening of the Museum of Contemporary Art, Caracas — A325

1985, Oct. 24   Perf. 13½
1340 A325 3b multicolored   .90 .45

Dated 1983.

UN, 40th Anniv. A326

1985, Nov. 15   Perf. 12
1341 A326 10b brt blue & ver   2.25 1.40

Intl. Youth Year A327

1985, Nov. 26
1342 A327 1.50b multicolored   .60 .25

Christmas 1985 — A328

Nativity: a, Sheperds. b, Holy Family, Magi. Se-tenant in a continuous design.

1985, Dec. 2
1343 A328   Pair   1.75 1.75
a.-b.   2b, any single   .85 .25

Dr. Luis Maria Drago (b. 1859), Politician A329

1985, Dec. 20   Perf. 13½
1344 A329 2.70b tan, ver & sepia   .70 .50

Dated 1984.

Miniature Sheet

Natl. Oil Industry, 10th Anniv. — A330

Designs: a, Industry emblem. b, Isla Oil Refinery. c, Bariven oil terminal. d, Pequiven refinery. e, Corpoven drilling rig. f, Maraven offshore rig. g, Intevep labs. h, Meneven refinery. i, Lagoven refinery. j, Emblem, early drilling rig.

1985, Dec. 13   Perf. 12
1345 A330   Sheet of 10   12.00 12.00
a.-b.   1b multi   .25 .25
c.-d.   2b multi   .55 .25
e.-f.   3b multi   1.00 .35
g.-h.   4b multi   1.25 .40
i.-j.   5b multi   1.50 .50

Simon Bolivar Memorial Coins — A331

1985, Dec. 18
1346 A331 2b multicolored   .50 .35
1347 A331 2.70b multicolored   .70 .45
1348 A331 3b multicolored   .80 .50
   Nos. 1346-1348 (3)   2.00 1.30

Dated 1984.

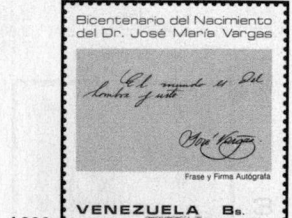

Guayana Development Corp., 25th Anniv. — A332

2b, Guayana City. 3b, Orinoco Steel Mill. 5b, Raul Leoni-Guri Hydro-electric Dam.

1985, Dec. 27
1349 A332 2b multicolored   .50 .40
1350 A332 3b multicolored   .85 .50
1351 A332 5b multicolored   1.40 .90
   Nos. 1349-1351 (3)   2.75 1.80

A333

Dr. Jose Vargas (1786-1854) — A334

Designs: No. 1352a, Handwriting and signature. b, Portrait, 1874, by Martin Tovar y Tovar. c, Statue, Palace of the Academies. d, Flags, EXFILBO '86 emblem. e, Vargas do Caracas Hospital. f, Frontispiece of lectures manual, 1842. g, Portrait, 1986, by Alirio Palacios. h, Gesneria vargasii. i, Bolivar-Vargas commemorative medal, 1955, 6th Natl. Medical Sciences Cong. j, Portrait, anonymous, 19th cent. No. 1353a, Portrait, facing front. b, Portrait, facing left, Nos. 1352a, 1352d, 1352e, 1352h and 1352i have horizontal vignettes.

Miniature Sheet
1986, Mar. 10   Litho.   Perf. 12
1352   Sheet of 10   11.00 11.00
a.-j.   A333 3b, any single   .90 .40
Souvenir Sheet
Imperf
1353 A334   Sheet of 2   13.50 13.50
a.-b.   15b, any single   6.00 1.00

EXFILBO '86, Mar. 10-17, Caracas, 1st Bolivarian exhibition.

Youths Painting School Wall A335

1986, May 12   Perf. 12
1354 A335 3b shown   .75 .35
1355 A335 5b Repairing desk   1.25 .35

Founding and maintenance of educational institutions.

Francisco Miranda's Work for American Liberation, Bicent. (1981)
A336

Lithographed and Engraved

1986, Apr. 18			**Perf. 13**	
1356	A336	1.05h multicolored	.50	.25

Dated 1983.

INDULAC, 45th Anniv.
A337

2.55b, Milk trucks, vert. 2.70b, Map, vert. 3.70b, Milk processing plant.

1986, June 27		**Litho.**	**Perf. 12**	
1357	A337	2.55b multicolored	.60	.25
1358	A337	2.70b multicolored	.60	.25
1359	A337	3.70b multicolored	.80	.25
		Nos. 1357-1359 (3)	2.00	.75

Industria Lactea (INDULAC), Venezuelan milk processing company.

Miniature Sheet

Viasa Venezuelan Airlines, 25th Anniv. — A338

a, Commemorative coin. b, Douglas DC-8 ascending. c, DC-8 taxiing. d, Boeing 747 in flight. e, DC-10 tails. f, Map of hemispheres. g, DC-10 taking off. h, Rear of DC-10 & DC8 on runway. i, DC-9 over mountains. j, Crew in cockpit.

1986, Aug. 11		**Litho.**	**Perf. 12**	
1360	A338	Sheet of 10	9.00	9.00
a.-e.		3b, any single	.55	.40
f.-j.		3.25b, any single	.60	.40

Miniature Sheet

Romulo Betancourt (1908-1981), President — A339

a, i, Portrait with natl. flag. b, j, Seated in armchair, smoking pipe. c, h, Wearing hat, text. d, f, Wearing sash of office. e, g, Reading.

1986, Sept. 28

1361	A339	Sheet of 10	10.00	10.00
a.-e.		2.70b, any single	.50	.25
f.-j.		3b, any single	.60	.25

Redrawn Bolivar Type of 1976

1986, Sept. 29		**Litho.**	**Perf. 12½**	
1362	A231	25c red	.50	.35
1363	A231	50c blue	.50	.35
1364	A231	75c pink	.50	.35
1365	A231	1b orange	.50	.35
1366	A231	2b brt yellow grn	.60	.35
		Nos. 1362-1366 (5)	2.60	1.75

Nos. 1362-1366 inscribed Armitano.
For surcharges see Nos. 1453-1464.

Re-opening of Zulia University, 40th Anniv. — A340

1986, Sept. 29

1367	A340	2.70b shown	.45	.35
1368	A340	2.70b Library entrance	.45	.35
a.		Pair, #1367-1368	1.00	1.00

11th Congress of Architects, Engineers and Affiliated Professionals — A341

1986, Oct. 3

1369		1.40b multicolored	.40	.25
1370		1.55b multicolored	.40	.25
a.	A341	Pair, #1369-1370	.85	.85

Fauna and Flora A342

70c, Priodontes maximus. 85c, Espeletia angustifolia. 2.70b, Crocodylus intermedius. 3b, Brownea grandiceps.

1986, Sept. 12		**Photo.**	**Perf. 13½**	
1371	A342	70c multicolored	.70	.60
1372	A342	85c multicolored	.70	.60
1373	A342	2.70b multicolored	.70	.60
1374	A342	3b multicolored	.90	.65
		Nos. 1371-1374 (4)	3.00	2.45

Miniature Sheet

State Visit of Pope John Paul II — A343

1986, Oct. 22 **Perf. 12**

1375	A343	Sheet of 10	7.50	7.50
a.		1b Pope, mountains	.25	.25
b.		2b Bridge	.40	.25
c.		3b Kissing the ground	.50	.25
d.		3b Statue of Our Lady	.50	.25
e.		4b Crosier, buildings	.70	.25
f.		5.25b Waterfall	.95	.30

#1375 contains 2 each #1375a-1375b, 1375e-1375f and one each #1375c-1375d.

Miniature Sheet

Children's Foundation, 20th Anniv. — A344

Children's drawings: a, Three children. b, Hearts, children, birds. c, Child, animals. d, Animals, house. e, Landscape. f, Child, flowers on table. g, Child holding ball. h, Children, birds. i, Lighthouse, port. j, Butterfly in flight.

1986, Nov. 10

1376	A344	Sheet of 10	5.50	5.50
a.-e.		2.55b, any single	.40	.25
f.-j.		2.70b, any single	.40	.25

Christmas — A345

Creche figures carved by Eliecer Alvarez.

1986, Nov. 10

1377		2b shown	.40	.25
1378		2b Virgin and child	.40	.25
a.	A345	Pair, #1377-1378	.90	.90

City Police, 25th Anniv. — A346

Emblem and: a, Emergency medical aid, helicopter. b, Security at sporting event. c, Bar code. d, Cadets in front of police academy. e, Motorcycle policeman.

1986, Dec. 10

1379		Strip of 5	4.00	4.00
a.-e.	A346	2.70b, any single	.50	.25

Folk Art A347

Lithographed and Engraved

1987, Jan. 31 **Perf. 13**

1380	A347	2b Musical instrument	.70	.25
1381	A347	2b Fabric	.70	.25
1382	A347	3b Ceramic pot	.90	.25
1383	A347	3b Basket work	.90	.25
		Nos. 1380-1383 (4)	3.20	1.00

Dated 1983. Nos. 1380, 1382 show Pre-Hispanic art.

Discovery of the Tubercle Bacillus by Robert Koch, Cent. (in 1982)
A348

Lithographed and Engraved

1987, Feb. 27 **Perf. 14x14½**

1384	A348	2.55b multicolored	1.60	.25

Dated 1983.

Miniature Sheet

Easter 1987 — A349

Paintings and sculpture: a, Arrival of Jesus in Jerusalem. b, Christ at the Column. c, Jesus of Nazareth. d, The Descent. e, The Solitude. f, The Last Supper. g, Christ Suffering. h, The Crucifixion. i, Christ Entombed. j, The Resurrection.

1987, Apr. 2 **Litho.** **Perf. 12**

1385	A349	Sheet of 10	17.50	17.50
a.-e.		2b, any single	1.00	.25
f.-j.		2.25h, any single	1.10	.25

World Neurochemistry Congress — A350

3b, Bolivar and Bello, outdoor sculpture by Marisol Escobar. 4.25b, Retinal neurons.

1987, May 8 **Litho.** **Perf. 12**

1386	A350	3b multicolored	.50	.25
1387	A350	4.25b multicolored	.70	.25
a.		Pair, #1386-1387	3.00	3.00

Miniature Sheet

Tourism — A351

Hotels: a, f, Barquisimeto Hilton. b, g, Lake Hotel Intercontinental, Maracaibo. c, h, Macuto Sheraton, Caraballeda. d, i, Melia Caribe, Caraballeda. e, j, Melia, Puerto la Cruz.

1987, May 29		**Litho.**		**Perf. 12**
1388	A351	Sheet of 10	13.00	13.00
a.-e.		6b, any single	.70	.25
f.-j.		6.50b, any single, diff.	.70	.25

Natl. Institute of Canalization, 35th Anniv. — A352

2b, Map of Amazon territory waterways. 4.25b, Apure and Bolivar states waterways.

1987, June 25		**Litho.**		**Perf. 12**
1389	A352	2b multicolored	.30	.25
1390	A352	4.25b multicolored	.50	.30
g.		Pair, #1389-1390	1.25	1.25

Vicente Emilio Sojo (1887-1974), Composer — A352a

2b, Academy of Fine Arts, Caracas. 4b, Sojos directing choir. 5b, Hymn to Bolivar score. 6b, Sojo, score on blackboard. 7b, Portrait, signature.

1987, July 1		**Litho.**		**Perf. 12**
1390A		Strip of 5	37.50	37.50
b.	A352a 2b tan & sepia		1.25	1.25
c.	A352a 4b tan & sepia		2.00	1.40
d.	A352a 5b tan & sepia		2.00	1.40
e.	A352a 6b tan & sepia		3.25	2.00
f.	A352a 7b tan & sepia		4.00	2.00

Printed in sheets of 10 containing two strips of five, black control number (UR).

Simon Bolivar University, 20th Anniv. A353

Designs: a, Bolivar statue by Roca Rey, 1973. b, Outdoor sculpture of solar panels by

---

Alejandro Otero, 1972. c, Rectory, 1716. d, Laser. e, Owl, sculpture, 1973.

1987, July 9		**Litho.**		**Perf. 12**
1391		Strip of 5	15.00	15.00
a.	A353 2b multicolored		.50	.25
b.	A353 3b multicolored		.75	.25
c.	A353 4b multicolored		1.00	.25
d.	A353 5b multicolored		1.25	.50
e.	A353 6b multicolored		1.50	.50

Miniature Sheet

Ministry of Transportation and Communication — A354

Designs: a, Automobiles. b, Ship. c, Train, Cathedral. d, Letters, telegraph key. e, Communication towers. f, Highway. g, Airplane. h, Locomotive, rail caution signs. i, Satellite dish. j, Satellite in orbit.

1987, July 16			
1392	A354 Sheet of 10	9.00	9.00
a.-e.	2b any single	.25	.25
f.-j.	2.25b any single	.25	.25

Nos. 1392a and 1392f, 1392b and 1392g, 1392c and 1392h, 1392d and 1392i, 1392e and 1392j have continuous designs.

Miniature Sheet

Venezuela Navigation Company, 70th Anniv. — A355

Designs: a, Corporate headquarters. b, Fork lift. c, Ship's Superstructure. d, Engine room. e, The Zulia. f, The Guarico. g, Ship's officer on the bridge. h, Bow of supertanker. i, Loading dock. j, Map of sea routes.

1987, July 31		**Litho.**		**Perf. 12**
1393	A355 Sheet of 10		6.25	6.25
a.-b.	2b, any single		.25	.25
c.-d.	3b, any single		.25	.25
e.-f.	4b, any single		.30	.25
g.-h.	5b, any single		.40	.25
i.-j.	6b, any single		.25	.25

Nos. 1393a, 1393c, 1393e, 1393g and 1393i in vertical strip; No. 1393b, 1393d, 1393f, 1393h and 1393j in vertical strip.

Miniature Sheet

Natl. Guard, 50th Anniv. — A356

a, f, Air-sea rescue. b, g, Traffic control. c, h, Environment and nature protection. d, i, Border control. e, j, Industrial security.

1987, Aug. 6			
1394	A356 Sheet of 10	40.00	40.00
a.-e.	2b, any single	.75	.25
f.-j.	4b, any single	1.50	.50

Discovery of America, 500th Anniv. (in 1992) A357

20th cent. paintings (details): 2b, Departure from Port of Palos, by Jacobo Borges. 7b, Discovery of America, by Tito Salas. 11.50b, El Padre de las Casas, Protector of the Indians, by Salas. 12b, Trading in Venezuela at the Time of the Conquest, by Salas. 12.50b, Defeat of Guaicaipuro, by Borges.

1987, Oct.		**Litho.**		**Perf. 12**
1395		Strip of 5	11.00	11.00
a.	A357 2b multi		.25	.25
b.	A357 7b multi		.60	.30
c.	A357 11.50b multi		1.00	.45
d.	A357 12b multi		1.10	.55
e.	A357 12.50b multi		1.25	.55

Christmas 1987 — A358

Paintings and sculpture representing the Spanish Colonial School, 18th cent.: 2b, *The Annunciation*, by Juan Pedro Lopez (1724-1787). 3b, *Nativity*, by Jose Francisco Rodriguez (1767-1818). 5.50b, *Adoration of the Magi*, anonymous. 6b, *Flight into Egypt*, by Lopez.

1987, Nov. 17		**Litho.**		**Perf. 12**
1396		Block of 4	6.75	6.75
a.	A358 2b multi		.25	.25
b.	A358 3b multi		.25	.25
c.	A358 5.50b multi		.50	.30
d.	A358 6b multi		.60	.30

Miniature Sheet

Sidor Mills, 25th Anniv. — A359

Natl. steel production: a-d, Exterior view of steel plant (in a continuous design). e, Tower bearing the SIDOR emblem. f, Furnaces and molten steel flowing down gutters. g, Pooring steel rods. h, Slab mill. i, Steel rod production, diff. j, Anniv. emblem.

1987, Nov. 23			
1397	A359 Sheet of 10	11.00	11.00
a.	2b multi	.25	.25
b.	6b multi	.80	.40
c.	7b multi	.95	.50
d.	11.50b multi	1.50	.75
e.	12b black	1.75	.80
f.	2b multi	.25	.25
g.	6b multi	.80	.40
h.	7b multi	.95	.50
i.	11.50b multi	1.50	.75
j.	12b multi	1.75	.80

Meeting of 8 Latin American Presidents, 1st Anniv. — A360

1987, Nov. 26			
1398	A360 6b multicolored	.80	.40

Pequiven Petrochemical Co., 10th Anniv. — A361

1987, Dec. 1			
1399	Strip of 5	7.75	7.75
a.	A361 2b Plastics	.25	.25
b.	A361 6b Refined oil products	.60	.30
c.	A361 7b Fertilizers	.70	.30
d.	A361 11.50b Installations	1.10	.55
e.	A361 12b Expansion	1.25	.60

St. John Bosco (1815-88) A362

Portrait of Bosco and: 2b, Map, children. 3b, National Church, Caracas. 4b, Vocational training (printer's apprentice). 5b, Church of Mary Auxiliadora. 6b, Missionary school (nun teaching children).

1987, Dec. 8			
1400	Strip of 5	4.00	4.00
a.	A362 2b multicolored	.25	.25
b.	A362 3b multicolored	.30	.25
c.	A362 4b multicolored	.40	.25
d.	A362 5b multicolored	.45	.25
e.	A362 6b multicolored	.60	.30

Redrawn Bolivar Type of 1976

1987, Dec. 31		**Litho.**	**Perf. 12½**
1401	A231 3b emerald grn	.35	.25
1402	A231 4b gray	.50	.25
1403	A231 5b vermilion	.65	.25
1404	A231 10b dark olive bister	1.50	.50
1405	A231 15b rose claret	2.50	.90
1406	A231 20b bright blue	3.00	1.10
1407	A231 25b olive bister	4.00	1.75
1408	A231 30b dark violet	4.75	1.90
1409	A231 50b carmine	7.75	3.00
	Nos. 1401-1409 (9)	25.00	9.90

Nos. 1401-1409 inscribed Armitano.

29th Assembly of Inter-American Development Bank Governors — A363

1988, Mar. 18   Litho.   Perf. 12
1410 A363 11.50b multi   1.50   .80

Miniature Sheet

Republic Bank, 30th Anniv. — A364

Bank functions and finance projects: a, Personal banking at branch. b, Capital for labor. c, Industrial projects. d, Financing technology. e, Exports and imports. f, Financing agriculture. g, Fishery credits. h, Dairy farming development. i, Construction projects. j, Tourism trade development.

1988, Apr. 11
1411 A364 Sheet of 10   10.00 10.00
  a.-e. 2b any single   .35   .25
  f.-j. 6b any single   .50   .25

No. 1411 contains two strips of five.

Anti-Polio Campaign Day of Victory, May 25 — A365

Design: Polio victims pictured on bronze relief, Rotary and campaign emblems.

1988, May 20   Litho.   Perf. 12
1412 A365 11.50b multi   1.40   .65

Carlos Eduardo Frias (1906-1986), Founder of the Natl. Publicity Industry — A366

1988, May 27   Litho.   Perf. 12
1414 A366 Pair   3.00   3.00
  a.   4b multi   .35   .35
  b.   10b multi   .75   .45

Publicity Industry, 50th anniv.

Venalum Natl. Aluminum Corp., 10th Anniv. — A367

Designs: 2b, Factory interior. 6b, Electric smelter. 7b, Aluminum pipes. 11.50b, Aluminum blocks moved by crane. 12b, Soccer team, aluminum equipment on playing field.

1988, June 10
1415 Strip of 5   7.50   7.50
  a. A367 2b multi   .30   .25
  b. A367 6b multi   .80   .25
  c. A367 7b multi   .90   .25
  d. A367 11.50b multi   1.50   .55
  e. A367 12b multi   1.50   .55

Nature Conservation — A368

Birds: 2b, Carduelis cucullata. 6b, Eudocimus ruber. 11.50b, Harpia harpyja. 12b, Phoenicopterus ruber ruber. 12.50b, Pauxi pauxi.

1988, June 17   Litho.   Perf. 12
1416 Strip of 5   7.50   7.50
  a. A368 2b multi   .25   .25
  b. A368 6b multi   .60   .25
  c. A368 11.50b multi   1.10   .45
  d. A368 12b multi   1.25   .40
  e. A368 12.50b multi   1.25   .45

Army Day — A369

Military uniforms: a, Simon Bolivar in dress uniform, 1828. b, Gen.-in-Chief Jose Antonio Paez in dress uniform, 1821. c, Liberation Army division gen., 1810. d, Brig. gen., 1820. e, Artillery corpsman, 1836. f, Alferez Regiment parade uniform, 1988. g, Division Gen. No. 1 dress uniform, 1988. h, Line Infantry Regiment, 1820. i, Promenade Infantry, 1820. j, Light Cavalry, 1820.

1988, June 20
1417 Sheet of 10   15.00 15.00
  a., f. A369 2b multi   .30   .25
  b., g. A369 6b multi   .75   .25
  c., h. A369 7b multi   .90   .25
  d., i. A369 11.50b multi   1.50   .45
  e., j. A369 12b multi   1.60   .45

Scabbard, Sword and Signature A370

Paintings by Tito Salas: 4.75b, The General's Wedding. 6b, Portrait. 7b, Battle of Valencia. 12b, Retreat from San Carlos.

1988, July 1   Litho.   Perf. 12
1418 Strip of 5   7.50   7.50
  a. A370 2b shown   .35   .25
  b. A370 4.75b multi   .65   .25
  c. A370 6b multi   .75   .25
  d. A370 7b multi   1.25   .30
  e. A370 12b multi   2.75   .45

General Rafael Urdaneta (b. 1788).

General Santiago Marino (b. 1788), by Martin Tovar y Tovar — A371

1988, July
1419 A371 4.75b multi   .65   .35

1988 Summer Olympics, Seoul — A372

1988, Aug. 2
1420 A372 12b multi   1.75   .70

Electric Industry, Cent. A373

Buildings, 1888: 2b, 1st Office. 4.75b, Jaime Carrillo and electrical plant. 10b, Bolivar Plaza. 11.50b, Baralt Theater. 12.50b, Central Thermoelectric Plant, Ramon Lagoon, 1988.

1988, Oct. 25   Litho.   Perf. 12
1421 Strip of 5   6.50   6.50
  a. A373 2b multi   .25   .25
  b. A373 4.75b multi   .40   .25
  c. A373 10b multi   .80   .35
  d. A373 11.50b multi   .90   .45
  e. A373 12.50b multi   1.00   .45

Christmas — A374

Designs: 4b, Nativity (left side), by Tito Salas, 1936. 6b, Christ child, anonymous, 17th cent. 15b, Nativity (right side).

1988, Dec. 9
1422 4b multi   .40   .25
1423 6b multi   .70   .30
1424 15b multi   1.90   .90
  a. A374 Strip, #1423, 2 ea #1422,
       1424   5.00   5.00

Miniature Sheet

Marian Year — A375

Icons: a, Our Lady of Copacabana, Bolivia. b, Our Lady of Chiquinquira, Colombia. c, Our Lady of Coromoto, Venezuela. d, Our Lady of the Clouds, Ecuador. e, Our Lady of Antigua, Panama. f, Our Lady of the Evangelization, Peru. g, Our Lady of Lujan, Argentina. h, Our Lady of Altagracia, Dominican Republic. i, Our Lady of Aparecida, Brazil. j, Our Lady of Guadalupe, Mexico.

1988, Aug. 15   Litho.   Perf. 12
1425 A375 Sheet of 10   12.50 12.50
  a.-e. 4.75b any single   .50   .25
  f.-j. 6b any single   .55   .35

Juan Manuel Cagigal Observatory, Cent. — A376

Designs: 2b, Bardou refracting telescope. 4.75b, Universal theodolite AUZ-27. 6b, Bust of Cagigal. 11.50b, Boulton cupola and night sky over Caracas in September. 12b, Satellite photographing Hurricane Allen.

1989, Sept. 5
1426 Strip of 5   6.75   6.75
  a. A376 2b multicolored   .25   .25
  b. A376 4.75b multicolored   .45   .25
  c. A376 6b multicolored   .60   .30
  d. A376 11.50b multicolored   1.00   .50
  e. A376 12b multicolored   1.10   .60

Comptroller-General's Office, 50th Anniv. — A377

1988, Oct. 14   Litho.   Perf. 12
1427 A377 10b multi   1.10   .60

Portrait of Founder Juan Pablo Rojas Paul, by Cristobal Rojas, 1890 — A378

6b, Commemorative medal.

1989, Oct. 21   Litho.   Perf. 12
1428 A378 6b multi   .60   .35
1429 A378 6.50b shown   .65   .35
  a.   Pair, #1428-1429   1.50   1.50

Natl. History Academy, cent.

Portrait of Ricardo — A379

Paintings: No. 1430, Simon Bolivar and Dr. Mordechay Ricardo. No. 1430A, The Octagon. Nos. 1430-1430A printed in continuous design completing the painting The Liberator in Curacao, by John de Pool.

1989, Jan. 27   Litho.   Perf. 12
1430   A379 10b multi   .75   .40
1430A A379 10b multi   .75   .40
1430B A379 11.50b shown   1.10   .50
  c.   Strip of 5, #1430B, 2 ea
         #1430-1430A   9.25   9.25

Convention
with Holy See,
25th
Anniv. — A380

Designs: a, Raul Leoni, constitutional president, 1964-69. b, Cardinal Quintero, archbishop of Caracas, 1960-80. c, Arms of Cardinal Lebrun, archbishop of Caracas since 1980. d, Arms of Luciano Storero, titular archbishop of Tigimma. e, Pope Paul VI.

1989, May 4   Litho.   Perf. 12
1431　　Strip of 5　　　　5.00　5.00
a.-b.　A380 4b any single　　.40　.25
c.-d.　A380 12b any single　1.00　.75
e.　A380 16b any single　1.40　1.00

Bank of
Venezuela,
Cent.
A381

Designs: a, *Cocoa Harvest,* by Tito Salas, 1946. b, *Teaching a Boy How to Grow Coffee,* by Salas, 1946. c, Bank headquarters, Caracas. d, Archive of the Liberator, Caracas. e, Aforestation campaign (seedling). f, Aforestation campaign (five youths planting seedlings). g, 50-Bolivar bank note (left side). h, 50-Bolivar bank note (right side). i, 500-Bolivar bank note (left side). j, 500-Bolivar bank note (right side).

1989, Aug. 1
1432　　Sheet of 10　　12.50　12.50
a.-f.　A381 4b any single　.35　.25
g.-j.　A381 8b any single　.85　.50

Nos. 1432g-1432h and 1432i-1432j printed in continuous designs.

America
Issue — A382

UPAE emblem and pre-Columbian votive bisque artifacts: 6b, Vessel. 24b, Statue of a man.

1989
1433　A382　6b multicolored　.80　.25
1434　A382　24b multicolored　3.50　1.75
a.　Pair, #1433-1434　6.00　6.00

Miniature Sheet

Christmas
A383

Denomination at top: a, Shepherds, sheep. c, Angel appears to 3 shepherds. e, Holy Family. g, Two witnesses. i, Adoration of the kings. Denomination at bottom: b, like a. d, like c. f, like e. h, like g. j, like i.

1989   Litho.   Perf. 12
1435　　Sheet of 10　　11.50　11.50
a.-b.　A383 5b any single　.40　.25
c.-f.　A383 6b any single　.45　.25
g.-h.　A383 12b any single　1.00　.45
i.-j.　A383 15b any single　1.10　.60

Miniature Sheets

Bank of Venezuela Foundation, 20th
Anniv. — A384

Tree and arms:　No. 1436: a, Tabebuia chrysantha, national. b, Ceiba pentandra, Federal District. c, Myrospermum frutescens, Anzoategui. d, Pithecellobium saman, Aragua. e, Cedrela odorata, Barinas. f, Diptenyx punctata, Bolivar. g, Licania pyrofolia, Apure. h, Sterculia apetala, Carabobo.
No. 1437: a, Tabebuia rosea, Cojedes. b, Prosopis juliflora, Falcon. c, Copernicia tectorum, Guarico. d, Erythrina poeppigiana, Merida. e, Brawnea leucantha, Miranda. f, Mauritia flexuosa, Monagas. g, Malpighia glabra, Lara. h, Guaicum officinale, Nueva Esparta.
No. 1438: a, Swietenia macrophylla, Portuguesa. b, Platymiscium diadelphum, Sucre. c, Prumnopitys montana de Laub, Tachira. d, Roystonea venezuelana, Yaracuy. e, Cocos nucifera, Zulia. f, Hevea benthamiana, Federal Territory of Amazonas. g, Erythrina fusca, Trujillo. h, Rhizophora mangle, Territory of the Amacuro Delta.

1990, June 27   Litho.   Perf. 12
1436　A384　Sheet of 8 + 2 labels　22.50　22.50
a.-f.　10b any single　.65　.35
g.　40b multicolored　2.50　1.25
h.　50b multicolored　3.25　1.60
1437　A384　Sheet of 8 + 2 labels　22.50　22.50
a.-f.　10b any single　.65　.35
g.　40b multicolored　2.50　1.25
h.　50b multicolored　3.25　1.60
1438　A384　Sheet of 8 + 2 labels　22.50　22.50
a.-f.　10b any single　.65　.35
g.　40b multicolored　2.50　1.25
h.　50b multicolored　3.25　1.60

Central
Bank of
Venezuela,
50th Anniv.
A385

Designs: a, Santa Capilla Headquarters, 1943. b, Headquarters, 1967. c, Left half of 500b Bank Note, 1940. d, Right half of 500b Bank Note, 1940. e, Sun of Peru decoration, 1825. f, Medals Ayacucho, 1824, Boyaca, 1820 and Liberators of Quito, 1822. g, Swords of Peru, 1825. h, Cross pendant, Bucaramanga, 1830. i, Medallion of George Washington, 1826. j, Portrait of Gen. O'Leary.

1990, Oct. 15
1439　　Sheet of 10　　15.00　15.00
a.-f.　A385 10b any single　.70　.40
g.-h.　A385 15b any single　1.00　.50
i.　A385 40b multicolored　2.75　1.40
j.　A385 50b multicolored　3.50　1.75

University
of Zulia,
Cent.
A386

Designs: a, Dr. Francisco Ochoa, founder. b, Dr. Jesus E. Lossada, President, 1946-47. c, Soil conservation. d, Developing alternative automotive fuels. e, Organ transplants.

1990, Sept. 18   Litho.   Perf. 12
1440　　Strip of 5　　　8.00　8.00
a.-b.　A386 10b any single　.50　.30
c.-d.　A386 15b any single　.75　.35
e.　A386 20b multicolored　1.10　.55

Christmas
A387

Paintings: a, St. Joseph and Child by Juan Pedro Lopez. b, The Nativity by Lopez. c, The Return from Egypt by Matheo Moreno. d, The Holy Family by unknown artist. e, The Nativity (oval painting) by Lopez.

1990, Nov. 25
1441　　Strip of 5　　　7.50　7.50
a.-c.　A387 10b any single　.50　.30
d.-e.　A387 20b any single　1.10　.55

OPEC, 30th
Anniv. — A388

a, Globe. b, Square emblem. c, Circular emblem. d, Diamond emblem. e, Flags.

1990, Dec. 21   Litho.   Perf. 12
1442　　Strip of 5　　　8.00　8.00
a.-b.　A388 10b any single　.70　.40
c.　A388 20b multicolored　1.50　.75
d.　A388 30b multicolored　2.10　1.00
e.　A388 40b multicolored　2.75　1.50

America
Issue — A389

1990, Dec. 12   Litho.   Perf. 12
1443　A389　10b Lake dwelling　1.50　.65
1444　A389　40b Coastline　4.00　2.25
a.　Pair, #1443-1444　6.00　6.00

Exflive '90, Caracas — A389a

Designs: 40b, Bank of Venezuela 1000b note. 50b, Bank of Caracas 100b note.

1990, Nov. 16   Litho.   Imperf.
1444B　A389a 40b multicolored　3.50　3.50
1444C　A389a 50b multicolored　4.50　4.50

No. 1444B, Bank of Venezuela, cent. No. 1444C, Bank of Caracas, cent.

St. Ignatius of
Loyola (1491-
1556)
A390

Designs: a, Jesuit quarters, Caracas. b, Death mask. c, Statue by Francisco de Vergara, 18th century. d, Statue of Our Lady of Montserrat, 11th century.

1991, Apr. 12   Litho.   Perf. 12
1445　　Strip of 4 + label　12.50　12.50
a.-b.　A390 12b any single　.55　.30
c.　A390 40b multicolored　2.00　.90
d.　A390 50b multicolored　2.25　1.10

Venezuelan-American Cultural Center,
50th Anniv. — A391

Designs: a, Elisa Elvira Zuloaga (1900-1980), painter & engraver. b, Gloria Stolk (1912-1979), writer. c, Caroline Lloyd (1924-1980), composer. d, Jules Waldman (1912-1990), publisher. e, William Coles (1908-1978), attorney.

1991, July 4   Litho.   Perf. 12
1446　　Strip of 5　　　12.50　12.50
a.-c.　A391 12b any single　.55　.30
d.　A391 40b multicolored　2.00　1.00
e.　A391 50b multicolored　2.25　1.10

Miniature Sheet

Orchids — A392

Designs: No. 1447a, 12b, Acineta alticola. b, 12b, Brassavola nodosa. c, 12b, Brachionidium brevicaudatum. d, 12b, Bifrenaria maguirei. e, 12b, Odontoglossum spectatissimum. f, 12b, Catasetum macrocarpum. g, 40b, Mendocella jorisiana. h, 40b, Cochleanthes discolor. i, 50b, Maxillaria splendens. j, 50b, Pleurothallis dunstervillei. No. 1448, Cattleya violacea.

1991, Aug. 22   Litho.   Perf. 12
1447　A392　Sheet of 10,
　　　　#a.-j.　18.00　18.00

Souvenir Sheet

1448　A392 50b multicolored　18.00　18.00

No. 1448 contains one 42x37mm stamp. Nos. 1447-1448 exist imperf. Values: No. 1447 $55; No. 1448 $25.
See Nos. 1499-1500, 1508-1509.

Democratic Action Party, 50th Anniv. — A393

Designs: a, People voting. b, Agricultural reform. c, Students and teachers. d, Nationalization of the petroleum industry.

1991, Sept. 13   Litho.   Perf. 12
1449 A393 12b Block of 4, #a.-d. 3.25 3.25

America Issue A394

1991, Oct. 24
1450 A394 12b Terepaima Chief .60 .30
1451 A394 40b Paramaconi Chief 2.40 1.50
a.   Pair, #1450-1451 4.50 4.50

Nos. 1450-1451 also exist imperf.

Children's Foundation, 25th Anniv. — A395

Children's drawings: a, 12b, Children in house. b, 12b, Playground. c, 12b, Carnival. d, 12b, Woman and girl walking by pond. e, 12b, Boy in hospital. f, 12b, Five children around tree. g, 40b, Two girls in colorful room. h, 40b, Classroom. i, 50b, Three children. j, 50b, Four children dancing.

1991, Oct. 31   Litho.   Perf. 12
1452 A395 Sheet of 10, #a.-j. 17.00 17.00

Nos. 1362-1364
Surcharged

1991   Litho.   Perf. 12½
1453 A231 5b on 25c red .30 .25
1454 A231 5b on 75c pink .30 .25
1455 A231 10b on 25c red .55 .30
1456 A231 10b on 75c pink .55 .00
1457 A231 12b on 50c blue .70 .40
1458 A231 12b on 75c pink .70 .40
1459 A231 20b on 50c blue 1.10 .55
1460 A231 20b on 75c pink 1.10 .55
1461 A231 40b on 50c blue 2.10 1.10
1462 A231 40b on 75c pink 2.10 1.10
1463 A231 50b on 50c blue 2.75 1.40
1464 A231 50b on 75c pink 2.75 1.40
    Nos. 1453-1464 (12) 15.00 8.00

Christmas A396

Children's art work: a, 10b, Wise men. b, 12b, Holy Family. c, 20b, Statues of Holy Family. d, 25b, Shepherds. e, 30b, Holy Family, cow, donkey.

1991, Nov. 14   Litho.   Perf. 12
1465 A396 Strip of 5, #a.-e. 6.75 6.75

Souvenir Sheet

Exfilve '91, Caracas — A397

1991, Nov. 29   Litho.   Perf. 12
1466 A397 50b No. 136 3.50 3.50

Discovery of America, 500th Anniv. (in 1992) A398

a, 12b, Coat of arms of Columbus. b, 12b, Santa Maria. c, 12b, Map by Juan de la Cosa. d, 40b, Sighting land. e, 50b, Columbus with Queen Isabella and King Ferdinand II.

1991, Dec. 12   Litho.   Perf. 12
1468 A398 Strip of 5, #a.-e. 6.25 6.25

1992, Mar. 15
Designs: No. 1469a, 12b, Emblem for discovery of America Commission. b, 12b, Venezuelan pavillion, Expo '92. c, 12b, 15th century map of Spain. d, 12b, Portrait of Columbus, by Susy Dembo. e, 12b, Encounter, by Ivan Jose Rojas. f, 12b, 0x500 America, by Annella Armas. g, 40b, Imago-Mundi, by Alessandro Grechi. h, 40b, Long Journey, by Gloria Fiallo. i, 50b, Playa Dorado, by Carlos Riera. j, 50b, Irminaoro, by Erasmo Sanches Cedeno. No. 1470, Untitled work, by Muaricio Sanchez.

1469 A398   Sheet of 10,
           #a.-j. 18.00 18.00
1470 A398 50b multicolored 4.50 4.50

Expo '92, Seville. No. 1470 contains one 38x42mm stamp.

Protection of Nature — A399

Turtles: No. 1471a, Geochelone carbonaria, facing left. b, Geochelone carbonaria, facing right. c, Podocnemis expansa, facing left. d, Podocnemis expansa, swimming.

1992, June 12   Litho.   Perf. 12
1471 A399 12b Block of 4, #a.-d. 10.00 6.00

World Wildlife Fund.
No. 1471 also exists imperf.

Miniature Sheet

Beatification of Josemaria Escriva — A400

Designs: a, 18b, Teaching in Venezuela, 1975. b, 18b, Celebrating mass. c, 10b, Parents, Jose Escriva and Dolores Albas. d, 18b, Text with autograph. e, 18b, Kissing feet of Madonna. f, 18b, Commemorative medallion. g, 60b, With Pope Paul VI. h, 60b, At desk, writing. i, 75b, Portrait. j, 75b, Portrait in St. Peter's Square, 1992.

1992, Oct. 2   Litho.   Perf. 12
1472 A400 Sheet of 10, #a.-j. 18.00 18.00

Electrification of Southern Regions A401

Designs: a, 12b, Roof of native hut. b, 12b, Transmission lines and towers. c, 12b, Horses running through pond. d, 40b, Workmen under tower. e, 50b, Baskets, crafts.

1992, July 15   Litho.   Perf. 12
1473 A401 Strip of 5, #a.-e. 6.00 6.00

Miniature Sheet

Artwork, by Mateo Manaure — A402

Color of background: a, 12b, Red. b, 12b, Red violet. c, 12b, Gray. d, 12b, Violet brown. e, 40b, Brown. f, 40b, Blue. g, 50b, Blue violet. h, 50b, Black.

1993, July 23
1474 A402   Sheet of 8, #a.-h. +
            2 labels 8.50 8.50

Bank of Maracaibo, 110th anniv.

Discovery of America, 500th Anniv. — A403

Paintings: a, 18b, The Third Trip, by Elio Caldera. b, 60b, Descontextura, by Juan Pablo Nascimiento.

1992, Nov. 20   Litho.   Perf. 12
1476 A403 Pair, #a.-b. 4.00 4.00

Christmas A404

Artwork by Lucio Rivas: a, 18b, Adoration of the Shepherds. b, 75b, Adoration of the Magi. 100b, Flight into Egypt.

1992, Dec. 3   Litho.   Perf. 12
1477 A404 Pair, #a.-b. 3.50 3.50

Souvenir Sheet
1478 A404 100b multicolored 4.00 4.00

No. 1478 contains one 42x38mm stamp.

A405   A406

A407

Designs: 1b, 2b, Simon Bolivar. 5b, Natl. Pantheon. 10b, Victory Monument, Carabobo. 20b, Jose Antonio Paez. 25b, Luisa Caceres de Arismendi. 35b, Ezequiel Zamora. 40b, Cristobal Mondoza. No. 1490, Central University. No. 1491, Jose Felix Ribas. No. 1494, Manuel Piar. 200b, Simon Bolivar.

1993-94   Litho.   Perf. 12½
Size: 18x22mm
1479 A405 1b silver .35 .25
1480 A405 2b greenish
           blue .35 .25
1482 A406 5b red .35 .25
1484 A406 10b violet .35 .25
1487 A407 20b olive green .75 .35
1488 A407 25b red brown .55 .45
1488A A407 35b brt yel grn .85 .55
1489 A407 40b lt blue .90 .65
1490 A406 50b orange 2.00 .85
1491 A407 50b lilac rose 1.25 .90

1493	A407	100b brown	4.00	2.00
1494	A407	100b dark blue	2.50	1.40
1496	A407	200b brown	5.00	2.75
		Nos. 1479-1496 (13)	19.20	10.90

Nos. 1479-1493 inscribed Armitano.
See Nos. 1548-1562.

Orchid Type of 1991

Miniature Sheet

Designs: a, 20b, Cattleya percivaliana. b, 20b, Anguloa ruckeri. c, 20b, Chondrorhyncha flaveola. d, 20b, Stenia pallida. e, 20b, Zygosepalum lindeniae. f, 20b, Maxillaria triloris. g, 80b, Stanhopea wardii. h, 80b, Oncidium papilio. i, 100b, Oncidium hastilabium. j, 100b, Sobralia cattleya. 150b, Polycycnis muscifera.

1993, Apr. 1   Litho.   Perf. 12
1499	A392	Sheet of 10, #a.-j.	18.00	18.00

Souvenir Sheet
1500	A392	150b multicolored	7.50	7.50

Miniature Sheet

Settlement of Tovar Colony, 150th Anniv. — A408

Designs: a, 24b, Woman. b, 24b, Children. c, 24b, Catholic Church, 1862. d, 24b, Statue of St. Martin of Tours, 1843. e, 24b, Fruits and vegetables. f, 24b, School, 1916. g, 80b, Home of founder, Augustin Codazzi, 1845. h, 80b, House of colony director, Alexander Benitz, 1845. i, 100b, Breidenbach Mill, 1860. j, 100b, Parade.

1993, Apr. 12   Litho.   Perf. 12
1501	A408	Sheet of 10, #a.-j.	18.00	18.00

Miniature Sheet

19th Pan-American Railways Conference — A409

Designs: a, 24b, Tucacas steam locomotive. b, 24b, Halcon steam locomotive on Las Mostazas Bridge, 1894. c, 24b, Maracaibo locomotive. d, 24b, Tender, rail cars, Palo Grande Station. e, 24b, Fiat diesel locomotive, 1957. f, 24b, GP-9-L diesel locomotive, 1957. g, 80b, GP-15-L diesel locomotive, 1982. h, 80b, Metro subway train, Caracas. i, 100b, Electric locomotive. j, 100b, Passenger cars of electric train.

1993, May 25   Litho.   Perf. 12
1502	A409	Sheet of 10, #a.-j.	22.50	22.50

Nos. 1502c-1502d, 1502i-1502j are continuous designs.

A410

World Day to Stop Smoking: a, 24b, Shown. b, 80b, "No smoking" emblem.

1993, May 27   Litho.   Perf. 12½x12
1503	A410	Pair, #a.-b.	4.00	4.00

A411

America Issue: a, 24b, Amazona barbadensis. b, 80b, Ara macao.

1993, Oct. 7   Litho.   Perf. 12
1504	A411	Pair, #a.-b.	6.75	6.75

Miniature Sheets

Native Indians — A412

Designs: No. 1505a, 1b, Two Yanomami children with painted bodies, spear. b, 1b, Yanomami woman preparing food. c, 40b, Two Panare children performing in Katyayinto ceremony. d, 40b, Panare man with nose flute. e, 40b, Taurepan man in canoe. f, 40b, Taurepan girl weaving. g, 40b, Piaroa woman with infant. h, 40b, Piaroa dancers wearing war masks. i, 100b, Hoti man blowing flute. j, 100b, Hoti woman carrying baby, basket over back. 150b, Child blowing traditional whistle.

1993, Nov. 25   Litho.   Perf. 12
1505	A412	Sheet of 10, #a.-j.	12.00	12.00

Souvenir Sheet
1506	A412	150b multicolored	4.50	4.50

Christmas A413

Nativity scene: a, f, 24b, Joseph. b, g, 24b, Madonna and Child. c, h, 24b, Shepherd boy, wise man holding gift, lambs. d, i, 80b, Wise man with hands folded, boy. e, j, 100b, Wise man presenting gift, boy with hands folded.

1993, Nov. 30
1507	A413	Sheet of 10, #a.-j.	15.00	15.00

Nos. 1507f-1507j are black, magenta & buff.

Orchid Type of 1991

Miniature Sheet

Designs: a, 35b, Chrysocycnis schlimii. b, 35b, Galeandra minax. c, 35b, Oncidium falcipetalum. d, 35b, Oncidium lanceanum. e, 40b, Sobralia violacea linden. f, 40b, Sobralia infundibuligera. g, 80b, Mendoncella burkei. h, 80b, Phragmipedium caudatum. i, 100b, Phragmipedium kaieteurum. j, 200b, Stanhopea grandiflora. 150b, Epidendrum elongatum.

1994, May 19   Litho.   Perf. 12
1508	A392	Sheet of 10, #a.-j.	18.00	18.00

Souvenir Sheet
1509	A392	150b multicolored	3.75	3.75

No. 1509 contains one 42x37mm stamp.

Miniature Sheet of 10

FEDECAMARAS (Federal Council of Production & Commerce Associations), 50th Anniv. — A414

a, 35b; f, 80b, Anniversary emblem. b, 35b; e, 80b, Luis Gonzalo Marturet (1914-64), 1st president. c, 35b; d, 80b, FEDECAMARAS emblem.

1994, July 17   Litho.   Perf. 12
1510	A414	#c, f, 2 ea #a-b, d-e	13.50	13.50

Judicial Service A415

1994, Sept. 13   Litho.   Perf. 12
1511	A415	100b multicolored	1.75	1.75

Miniature Sheet

Christmas — A416

Paintings: a, 35b, g, 80b, The Nativity, by follower of Jose Lorenzo de Alvarado. b, 35b, h, 80b, Birth of Christ, 19th cent. c, 35b, i, 80b, The Nativity, diff., by follower of Jose Lorenzo de Alvarado. d, 35b, j, 80b, Adoration of the Magi, 17th cent.. e, 35b, f, 80b, Birth of Christ, by School of Tocuyo.

1994, Dec. 1
1512	A416	Sheet of 10, #a.-j.	13.50	13.50

Miniature Sheet

Antonio Jose de Sucre (1795-1830) — A417

Designs: No. 1513a, 25b, Portrait. b, 25b, Dona Mariana Carcelen Y Larrea Marquesa de Solanda. c, 35b, Top of equestrian monument. d, 35b, Bottom of monument. e, 40b, Painting of Battle of Pichincha, mountains at top. f, 40b, Painting of Battle of Pichincha, battle scent. g, 80b, Painting of Battle of Ayacucho, soldiers on horseback. h, 80b, Painting of Battle of Ayacucho, dead soldiers. i, 100b, Painting of Surrender at Ayachucho, general signing document. j, 100b, Painting of Surrender at Ayacucho, seated general at right. 150b, Portion of mural, Carabobo, by Pedro Centeno Vallenilla.

1995, Feb. 2
1513	A417	Sheet of 10, #a.-j.	13.50	13.50

Souvenir Sheet
1514	A417	150b multicolored	3.50	3.50

Postal Transportation — A418

a, 35b, Post office van. b. 80b, Airplane.

1995, Mar. 22   **Litho.**   *Perf. 12*
1515 A418 Pair, #a.-b.   2.50 2.50
No. 1515 issued in sheets of 10 stamps.

Miniature Sheet

St. Jean-Baptiste de La Salle (1651-
1719), Educator — A419

Denomination LR: a, 100b, Portrait. b, 35b,
Students with microscope, academic education. c, 80b, Soccer players, sports education.
d, 35b, Scouts at camp, citizenship education.
e, 80b, La Salle College, Caracas.
Denomination LL: f, like #1516e. g, like
#1516d. h, like #1516b. i, like #1516c. j, like
#1516a.

1995, May 15
1516 A419 Sheet of 10, #a.-j.   11.00 11.00

Miniature Sheet

Founding of Salesian Order,
Cent. — A420

Designs: a, 35b, St. John Bosco (1815-88),
priest with child. b, 35b, Lonely child,
Madonna and Child. c, 35b, Man running
machine tool. d, 35b, Young men working with
electronic instruments. e, 35b, Baseball game.
f, 35b, Basketball game. g, 80b, People working in fields. h, 80b, Man looking at chili peppers. i, 100b, Young tribal natives receiving
religious training. j, 100b, Tribal native.

1995, Apr. 26
1517 A420 Sheet of 10, #a.-j.   11.00 11.00

Miniature Sheet

Orchids — A421

Designs: a, 35b, Maxillaria guareimensis. b,
35b, Paphinia lindeniana. c, 50b, Catasetum
longifolium. d, 50b, Anguloa clowesii. e, 35b,
Coryanthes biflora. f, 35b, Catasetum
pileatum. g, 80b, Maxillaria histrionica. h, 80b,
Sobralia ruckeri. i, 35b, Mormodes con-
volutum. j, 35b, Huntleya lucida.
150b, Catasetum barbatum.

1995, May 31   **Litho.**   *Perf. 12*
1518 A421 Sheet of 10, #a.-j.   12.00 12.00
Souvenir Sheet
1519 A421 150b multicolored   3.50 3.50
No. 1519 contains one 42x36mm stamp.
See #1534-1535, 1563-1564, 1587-1588.

CAF (Andes
Development
Corporation),
25th
Anniv. — A422

1995, June 7
1520 A422 80b multicolored   1.60 1.60

Miniature Sheet

Beatification of Mother Maria of San
Jose — A423

Designs: a, 35b, In formal habit. b, 35b,
Pope John Paul II. c, 35b, As young woman
distributing Bibles. d, 35b, Doing embroidery

work. e, 35b, Statue of Madonna, altar. f, 35b,
Kneeling in devotions. g, 80b, Walking with
Sisters in hospital. h, 80b, With patient in hos-
pital. i, 100b, Working with children. j, 100b,
Helping person seated along road.

1995, July 2
1521 A423 Sheet of 10, #a.-j.   11.00 11.00
Nos. 1521a-1521b, 1521c-1521d, 1521e-
1521f, 1521g-1521h, 1521i-1521j are each
continuous designs.

UN, 50th Anniv. — A424

Designs: a, People from different countries
unfurling UN flag. b, Emblem on UN flag.

1995, June 26
1522 A424 50b Pair, #a.-b.   3.25 3.25

Gen. José Gregorio Monagas (1795-
1858), President, Liberator of the
Slaves — A425

a, Portrait. b, Slave family with opened
chains.

1995, July 26   **Litho.**   *Perf. 12*
1523 A425 50b Pair, #a.-b.   2.40 2.40

Slave Rebellion, Bicent. — A426

Jose Leonardo Chirino and: a, Liberty leading the people (after Delacroix). b, Revolutionaries with weapons.

1995, Aug. 16
1524 A426 50b Pair, #a.-b.   2.50 2.50

Venezuelan
Red Cross,
Cent.
A427

Designs: a, 100b, Red Cross flag. b, 80b,
Carlos J. Bello Hospital. c, 35b, Surgery
scene. d, 35b, Rescue workers carrying victim. e, 35b, Care givers with child.

1995, Aug. 30
1525 A427 Strip of 5, #a.-e.   6.00 6.00

America Issue — A428

Environmental protection: a, 35b, Trees,
lake. b, 80b, Flowers, hillside.

1995, Sept. 13   **Litho.**   *Perf. 12*
1526 A428 Pair, #a.-b.   3.50 3.50
No. 1526 was issued in sheets of 10 stamps.
No. 1526 exists in two types: the heavy border at top is above "America" only: the heavy
line extends over the denomination. Values the
same.

Miniature Sheet

Native Aboriginals — A429

No. 1527: a, 25b, Kuana man seated on post. b, 25b, Kuana woman using stones to do laundry. c, 35b, Guahibo people, one playing flute. d, 35b, Guahibo shaman with child. e, 50b, Uruak man with tree branch. f, 50b, Uruak woman cooking. g, 80b, Warao woman spinning twine. h, 80b, Warao man, woman in boat. i, 100b, Bari men with bows, arrows. j, 100b, Bari man rubbing sticks to make fire. 150b, Young boy with bird.

1995, Oct. 18
1527	A429		Sheet of 10,	
			#a.-j.	16.00 16.00

Souvenir Sheet
1528	A429	150b multicolored	5.00 5.00

See Nos. 1541-1542.

Miniature Sheet

Christmas — A431

Designs: a, 35b, The Annunciation. b, 35b, Being turned away at the inn. c, 100b, Birth of Christ in the stable. d, 35b, Angel appearing to shepherds. e, 35b, Three Magi. f, 40b, Christmas pageant. g, 40b, Children skating. h, 100b, Christmas presents. i, 40b, Women preparing food for holidays. j, 40b, Children, mother preparing food for holidays.

1995, Nov. 15
1530	A431	Sheet of 10, #a.-j.	10.00 10.00

Nos. 1530f-1530g, and 1530i-1530j are each continuous designs.

Miniature Sheet

Petroleum Industries of South America (PDVSA), 20th Anniv. — A432

a, 35b, PDVSA emblem, 7 petroleum company emblems. b, PDVSA emblem, 6 petroleum company emblems. c, 80b, Oil derrick. d, 80b, Refinery. e, 35b, Oil tanker crossing under bridge. f, 35b, Worker, orimulsion tanks. g, 35b, Two people examining carbon. h, 35b, Semi truck hauling petrochemicals. i, 35b, Filling station. j, 35b, Gas storage tanks.

1995, Dec. 13   Litho.   Perf. 12
1531	A432	Sheet of 10, #a.-j.	11.00 11.00

Miniature Sheet

Town of El Tocuyo, 450th Anniv. — A433

Designs: a, 35b, City arms. b, 35b, Workers in sugar cane field. c, Church of Our Lady of Immaculate Conception. d, Statue of Madonna inside church. e, 35b, Ruins of Temple of Santa Domingo. f, 35b, House of Culture. g, 80b, Cactus, vegetation. h, 80b, Cactus up close. i, 100b, Dancers with swords. j, 100b, Man playing guitar.

1995, Dec. 5
1532	A433	Sheet of 10, #a.-j.	11.00 11.00

Miniature Sheet

Vist of Pope John Paul II — A434

Statues of various saints, Pope and: a, 25b, Children. b, 25b, Man, woman. c, 40b, Man, woman, baby. d, 40b, Elderly man. e, 50b, Woman, boy. f, 50b, Sick person. g, 60b, Man in prison. h, 60b, Working man. i, 100b, People of various career fields. j, 100b, Priests, nuns.
200b, Pope John Paul II holding crucifix.

1996, Jan. 26
1533	A434	Sheet of 10, #a.-j.	12.00 12.00

Souvenir Sheet
1533K	A434	200b multicolored	6.50 6.50

Miniature Sheet

Electricity in Caracas, Cent. — A430

Designs: a, 35b, Ricardo Zuloaga, early pioneer. b, 35b, Early electric plant. c, 35b, Substation. d, 35b, 1908 Electric trams. e, 35b, Electric lampposts mandated by Congress, 1908. f, 35b, Lampposts, Bolivar Plaza. g, 80b, Electrical repairman. h, 80b, Lighted cross, Avila. i, 100b, Teresa Carreño Cultural Complex. j, 100b, Ricardo Zuloaga main generator plant.

1995, Nov. 6
1529	A430	Sheet of 10, #a.-j.	11.00 11.00

Orchid Type of 1995

Designs: a, Epidendrum fimbriatum. b, Myoxanthus reymondii. c, Catasetum pileatum. d, Ponthieva maculata. e, Maxillaria triloris. f, Scaphosepalum breve. g, Cleistes rosea. h, Maxillaria sophronitis. i, Catasetum discolor. j, Oncidium ampliatum.
200b, Odontoglossum naevium.

1996, May 31   Litho.   Perf. 12
1534	A421	60b Sheet of 10, #a.-j.	11.00 11.00

Souvenir Sheet
1535	A421	200b multicolored	6.50 6.50

1996 Summer Olympic Games, Atlanta A435

Designs: a, Emblem of Olympic Committee. b, Swimmer. c, Boxer. d, Cyclist. e, Medal winners.

1996, June 28   Litho.   Perf. 12
1536	A435	130b Strip of 5, #a.-e.	9.00 9.00

No. 1536 was issued in a sheet of 10 stamps.

Maiquetia Intl. Airport, 25th Anniv. — A436

Designs: a, Symbol of automation. b, Map of airport flight routes. c, La Guaira Airdrome, 1929. d, Maiqueitia Airport, 1944. e, Simon Bolivar Airport, 1972. f, Interior view of terminal. g, Airport police, control tower. h, Airport firetruck. i, Airplane at terminal, Simon Bolivar Airport. j, Airplane on taxiway, Simon Bolivar Airport.

1996, Aug. 4
1537 A436 80b Sheet of 10,
   #a-j   12.50 12.50

America Issue — A437

Traditional costumes: a, 60b, Women's. b, 130b, Men's.

1996, Sept. 10
1538 A437 Pair, #a.-b.   3.75 3.75
No. 1538 was issued in sheets of 10 stamps.

Mario Briceño-Iragorry (1897-1958) — A438

Portraits: a, As young man, Trujillo, 1913. b, At University of Mérida, 1919. c, As politician, 1944. d, As writer, 1947. e, As older man, Caracas, 1952.

1996, Sept. 24
1539 A438 80b Strip of 5, #a.-e. 6.50 6.50
No. 1539 was issued in sheets of 10 stamps.

Caracas Rotary Club, 70th Anniv. — A439

1996, Oct. 3
1540 A439 50b multicolored   .85 .85
No. 1540 was issued in sheets of 10.

Native Aboriginal Type of 1995

Designs: a, 80b, Yukpa boy working in garden. b, 80b, Paraujanos girl carrying fruit. c, 80b, Kinaroes man, woman bundling cattailo. d, 80b, Motilon man with bananas. e, 80b, Chaque mother carrying infant on back. f, 100b, Guajiros man, young woman fixing hair. g, 100b, Mucuchi man carrying pack on back. h, 100b, Mape man with bow and arrow. i, 100b, Macoa working with grain, painted faces. j, 100b, Yaruros man weaving.
200b, Woman breastfeeding infant.

1996, Oct. 11
1541 A429 Sheet of 10, #a.-j. 13.50 13.50
       Souvenir Sheet
1542 A429 200b multicolored   3.25 3.25

Souvenir Sheet

Taipei '96, Intl. Philatelic Exhibition — A440

1996, Oct. 21   Litho.   Perf. 12
1543 A440 200b Ara chloroptera 7.50 7.50

José Gregorio Hernández (1864-1908), Physician — A441

a, As young boy. b, As student, anatomy drawing. c, Praying, Madonna statue. d, Thinking of the needy. e, In research study. f, As professor of university. g, Comforting sick patient. h, Empty chair at academy. i, Vargas Hospital, statue, portrait of Hernández. j, Hospital named after Hernández, statue.
200b, Portrait of Hernández.

1996, Oct. 26   Litho.   Perf. 12
1544 A441 60b Sheet of 10,
   #a.-j.   7.00 7.00
       Souvenir Sheet
1545 A441 200b multicolored 2.75 2.75
No. 1545 contains one 42x36mm stamp.

Christmas — A442

Designs: a, 60b, Child setting up Nativity scene. b, 60b, Three men with guitars, woman. c, 60b, Rooster, people making music. d, 60b, People with painted faces dancing, singing. e, 60b, Men, woman playing drums, instruments. f, 80b, Exchanging gifts of food. g, 80b, Family at table, looking at gift of

---

food. h, 80b, Child in hammock, presents. i, 80b, Parading replica of infant Jesus. j, 80b, Kissing feet of Christ Child.

1996, Nov. 7
1546 A442 Sheet of 10, #a.-j. 6.50 6.50

Andrés Eloy Blanco (1896-1955), Politician, Writer — A443

Designs: a, As adolescent. b, As Caracas city official, government building. c, With family. d, With democratic founders. e, As politician, building. f, As President of Constituent Assembly, building. g, As "Poet of Pueblo." h, Lincoln Memorial, as Chancellor of the Republic. i, Author of writings on Spain, sailing ship. j, Map of Spain, sailing ships, conquistador on horseback.

1997, Feb. 17   Litho.   Perf. 12
1547 A443 100b Sheet of 10,
   #a.-j.   9.00 9.00

Simon Bolivar (1783-1830) — A444

1997, Mar. 7 Litho. Perf. 13½x13
1548 A444 15b olive   .25   .25
1549 A444 20b brown org   .25   .25
1550 A444 40b dark brown   .40   .40
1551 A444 50b rose claret   .60   .60
1552 A444 70b deep violet   .85   .85
1553 A444 90b deep blue   1.25 1.25
1554 A444 200b dp grn bl   2.25 2.25
1555 A444 300b dp bl grn   3.00 3.00
1556 A444 400b gray   4.50 4.50
1557 A444 500b pale sepia 5.25 5.25
1558 A444 600b pale brown 5.75 5.75
1559 A444 800b pale vio brn 7.25 7.25
1560 A444 900b slate blue   7.50 7.50
1561 A444 1000b dk org brn 8.00 8.00
1562 A444 2000b olive bister 15.00 15.00
  Nos. 1548-1562 (15)   62.10 62.10

Orchid Type of 1995

Designs: a, Phragmipedium lindleyanum. b, Zygosepalum labiosum. c, Acacallis cyanea. d, Maxillaria camaridii. e, Scuticaria steelei. f, Aspasia variegata. g, Comparettia falcata. h, Scapyglottis stellata. i, Maxillaria ruffescens. j, Vanilla pompona.
250b, Rodriguezia lanceolata.

1997, May 30   Perf. 12
1563 A421 165b Sheet of 10,
   #a.-j.   15.00 15.00
       Souvenir Sheet
1564 A421 250b multicolored 3.50 3.50
No. 1564 contains one 42x37mm stamp.

Independence Conspiracy of Gual and España, Bicent. — A445

#1565, José María España, proclamation for independence being read. #1566, España under arrest. #1567, Manuel Gual, soldiers. #1568, Gual fleeing through door, sailing ship, standing on Trinidad. #1569, Revolutionary flag, sailing ship.

1997, July 16
1565 A445 165b multicolored 1.50 1.50
1566 A445 165b multicolored 1.50 1.50
   a.   Pair, #1565-1566   3.00 3.00
1567 A445 165b multicolored 1.50 1.50
   a.   Pair, #1566-1567   3.00 3.00
1568 A445 165b multicolored 1.50 1.50
   a.   Pair, #1567-1568   3.00 3.00
1569 A445 165b multicolored 1.50 1.50
   a.   Pair, #1565, 1569   3.00 3.00
   b.   Pair, #1568-1569   3.00 3.00

Printed in sheet of 10 containing one each #1566a, 1567a, 1568a, 1569a-1569b. Value $16.

Treaty of Tlatelolco Banning Use of Nuclear Weapons in Latin America, 30th Anniv. — A446

Various stylized designs representing devastation resulting from use of nuclear weapons: a.-e., White inscriptions. f.-j., Black inscriptions.

1997, July 31
1570 A446 140b Sheet of 10,
   #a.-j.   15.00 15.00

Stories for Children — A447

"The Rabbit and the Tiger:" a, Rabbit, tiger carrying satchel. b, Watching rat figure digging. c, Watching turtle on his back. d, Rabbit. e, Rat in net, rabbit. f, Tiger, house, rat. g, Bird, rat, rabbit, bee, beehive. h, Rabbit, turtle. i, Tiger with stick over shoulder. j, Tiger with mouth open, bees.
250b, Rabbit, tiger.

1997, Aug. 7
1571 A447 55b Sheet of 10,
#a.-j.   8.00 8.00

Souvenir Sheet

1572 A447 250b multicolored   3.25 3.25

No. 1572 contains one 42x37mm stamp.
The reverse of Nos. 1571a-1571j are each
inscribed with parts of the childrens' story.

Unexpected
Adventures
of a
Postman
A448

America Issue: 110b, Giving letter to woman
with dog. 280b, With motor scooter in rain.

1997, Aug. 29   Litho.   Perf. 12
1573 A448 110b multicolored   2.00 2.00
1574 A448 280b multicolored   3.50 3.50
  a.   Pair, #1573-1574   7.25 7.25

No. 1574a was issued in sheets of 10
stamps.

Villa of Anauco Villa, Bicent. — A449

Designs: a, Inscription. b, Main entrance. c,
Entrance corridor. d, Interior patio. e, Exterior
corridor leading to kitchen. f, Kitchen. g, Stairs
leading to balcony. h, Coach house. i, Stable.
j, Outside stable, water trough.

1997, Sept. 23
1575 A449 110b Sheet of 10,
#a.-j.   11.00 11.00

Independence in India, 50th
Anniv. — A450

Designs: a, 165b, Jawaharlal Nehru. b,
200b, Sardar Patel, flag. c, 165b, Congressional building. d, 200b, Gandhi. e, 165b, Puri-
fication at the Ganges. f, 200b, Rabindranath
Tagore. g, 165b, Motion picture industry. h,
200b, Traditional music. i, 165b, Insat-1B
meteorological satellite. j, 200b, Use of modern technology.
  250b, Minarets of Taj Majal.

1997, Oct. 2
1576 A450 Sheet of 10, #a.-j. 20.00 20.00
Souvenir Sheet
1577 A450 250b multicolored   3.25 3.25

Heinrich von
Stephan
(1831-97)
A451

a, 110b, Portrait. b, 280b, UPU emblem.

1997, Oct. 9   Litho.   Perf. 12
1578 A451 Pair, #a.-b.   3.75 3.75

Wicker-work — A452

No. 1579: a, Red basket, Ye'Kuana. b, With
handles, Ye'Kuana. c, Round, Ye'Kuana. d,
Tray, Panare. e, Backpack, Pemon. f, With carrying strap, Yanomami. g, Round (dk brown),
diff., Ye'Kuana. h, Tray, Ye'Kuana. i, Oval tray,
Panare. j, Wide mouth, Warao.
  250b, Square box with lid, Ye'Kuana.

1997, Oct. 24   Perf. 12
1579 A452 140b Sheet of 10,
#a.-j.   15.00 15.00

Souvenir Sheet

1580 A452 250b multicolored   4.00 4.00

No. 1580 contains one 42x37mm stamp.

Christmas
A453

a, Annunciation. b, Mary, St. Elizabeth. c,
No room at the inn. d, Nativity. e, Annunciation
to shepherds. f, Adoration of the shepherds. g,
Magi following star. h, Adoration of the Magi. i,
Presentation of Christ child in temple. j, Flight
into Egypt.

1997, Oct. 31
1581 A453 110b Sheet of 10,
#a.-j.   11.00 11.00

7th Summit of
Latin American
Chiefs of State
and
Government,
Isla de
Margarita
A454

a, 165b, j, 200b, Social justice. b, 165b, i,
200b, Free elections. c, 165b, h, 200b, Summit
emblem. d, 165b, g, 200b, Truthful information.
e, 165b, f, 200b, Human rights.

1997, Nov. 5
1582 A454 Sheet of 10, #a.-
j.   18.00 18.00

Diocese of
Zulia, Cent.
A455

Churches: a, Convent. b, Church of St. Ann.
c, Reliquary, Chiquinquira. d, Basilica of Chi-
quinquira and St. John of God. e, Church,
Aranza. f, Cathedral, Maracaibo. g, Cathedral,
Machiques. h, Archbishop's seal. i, Cathedral,
Cabimas. j, Cathedral of the Virgin, San
Carlos.

1997, Dec. 16
1583 A455 110b Sheet of 10,
#a.-j.   10.00 10.00

Democracy in Venezuela, 40th
Anniv. — A456

Designs: a, Commemorative emblem. b,
Popular decision. c, Public education. d, Social
development. e, Freedom of expression. f,
Capital, constitution. g, Popular culture. h, Civil
rights. i, Environmental protection. j, Social
and civic participation.

1998, Feb. 19   Litho.   Perf. 12
1584 A456 110b Sheet of 10,
#a.-j.   12.00 12.00

Discovery of Margarita Island, 500th
Anniv. — A457

Map of Margarita Islands and: a, 200b,
Angel Rock. b, 265b, Christopher Columbus,
ship. c, 200b, Simon Bolivar. d, 200b, Pearl
diver. e, 265b, Statue of the Virgin del Valle,
church. f, 100b, Mending fish net, fishermen in
boats. g, 200b, Gen. Santiago Marino. h,
100b, Petronila Mata, cannon. i, 200b, Gen.
Juan Bautista Arismendi. j, 100b, Parrot.
  250b, Women weeping at the Lagoon of
Martyrs, horiz.

1998, Mar. 26   Litho.   Perf. 12
1585 A457 Sheet of 10, #a.-j. 17.00 17.00
Souvenir Sheet
1586 A457 250b multicolored   3.25 3.25

No. 1586 contains one 42x37mm stamp.

Orchid Type of 1995

a, Oncidium orthostates. b, Epidendrum
praetervisum. c, Odontoglossum schilleranum.
d, Bletia lansbergii. e, Caularthron bicornutum.
f, Darwiniera bergoldii. g, Houlletia tigrina. h,

Pleurothallis acuminata. i, Elleanthus lupulinus. j, Epidendrum ferrugineum. 250b, Pleurothallis immersa.

1998, May 29
1587 A421 185b Sheet of 10,
#a.-j.   18.00 18.00

Souvenir Sheet

1588 A421 250b multicolored   3.25 3.25
No. 1588 contains one 42x37mm stamp.

Henri Pittier Natl. Park, 60th Anniv. — A458

Fauna: a, 140b, Crax pauxi. b, 150b, Spizaetus ornatus. c, 200b, Touit collaris. d, 200b, Trogon collaris. e, 350b, Cyanocorax yncas. f, 140b, Tersina viridis. g, 150b, Phyllomedusa trinitatis. h, 200b, Morpho peleides. i, 200b, Acrocinus longimanus. j, 350b, Dynastes hercules.

1998, July 17
1589 A458 Sheet of 10, #a.-j.   20.00 20.00

Comptroller General of the Republic, 60th Anniv. — A459

Designs: a, 140b, Gumersindo Torres Millet, founding Comptroller. b, 140b, Luis Antonio Pietri Yépez, first Comptroller of the democracy. c, 140b, View of capitol dome. d, 140b, Colors of flag (service to society). e, 200b, Simon Bolivar, coins. f, 200b, Various numbers on green background. g, 350b, Newspaper headlines (inform the public). h, 350b, Statue of justice (uphold law). i, 350b, Text of duties of the Comptroller General. j, 350b, Emblem, the 6th Assembly of the Latin American and Caribbean States Comptrollers.

1998, July 29
1590 A459 Sheet of 10, #a.-j.   20.00 20.00

Organization of the American States (OAS), 50th Anniv. — A460

a, 140b, Logo of the anniversary. b, 140b, OAS emblem. c, 350b, Flags forming double helix, US flag at center left. d, 150b, Deactivating land mine. e, 150b, Defending human rights. f, 200b, Simon Bolivar. g, 200b, Scroll, quill pen, inkwell. h, 350b, Flags forming double helix, Venezuelan flag at center right. i, 200b, Road sign with map of Americas. j, 200b, Mountain climbers.

1998, July 30
1591 A460 Sheet of 10, #a.-j.   17.50 17.50

Expo '98, Lisbon A461

Designs: a, 140b, Bird, turtle, crab. b, 140b, Fishermen throwing net from boat. c, 150b, Seashells, turtle. d, 150b, Fish. e, 200b, Marine life, denomination UR. f, 200b, Marine

---

life, denomination LR. g, 200b, Man riding through river on horse. h, 200b, Cattle in river, monkey. i, 350b, Two sea birds. j, 350b, Monkey, waterfall, flower.

1998, July 31
1592 A461 Sheet of 10, #a.-j.   20.00 20.00

18th Central American and Caribbean Games, Maracaibo A462

Figures: a, 150b, Running. b, 200b, Playing basketball. c, 150b, Bowling. d, 200b, Boxing. e, 150b, Cycling. f, 200b, Fencing. g, 150b, Performing gymnastics. h, 200b, Weight lifting. i, 150b, Swimming. j, 200b, Playing tennis.

1998, Aug. 4
1593 A462 Sheet of 10, #a.-j.   15.00 15.00

Discovery of Venezuela, 500th Anniv. — A463

Designs: a, 350b, Christopher Columbus. b, 200b, Juan de la Cosa (1460?-1510), map. c, 200b, Huts built on stilts in water. d, 150b, Women of three different races. e, 140b, 13th cent. artifact. f, 350b, Alonso de Ojeda (1465-1515), map. g, 200b, Detail of map of Jodocus Hondius. h, 200b, Modern city. i, 150b, Various people of modern Venezuela. j, 140b, Statues of Catholic king and queen.

1998, Aug. 10
1594 A463 Sheet of 10, #a.-j.   18.00 18.00

Landing of Christoper Columbus, and Exploration of Amerigo Vespucci, 500th Anniv. A464

1998, Aug. 12
1595 A464 400b multicolored   3.50 3.50
See Italy No. 2252.

Treaty of Amazon Cooperation, 20th Anniv. A465

Designs: a, Casiquiare River, denomination LR. b, Casiquiare River, denomination LL. c, Bactris gasipaes. d, Neblinaria celiae. e, Paracheidon axelrodi. f, Dendrobates leucomelas. g, Nocthocrax urumutum. h, Speothos venaticus. i, Cocuy mountain. j. Neblina Mountains.

1998, Aug. 20
1596 A465 200b Sheet of 10,
#a.-j.   18.00 18.00

Children's Story — A466

Cockroach Martinez and Perez Rat: a, Cockroach. b, Burro. c, Parrot. d, Insects with camera, pad. e, Cat. f, Cockroach, pig. g, Goat. h, Cockroach, rat. i, Rat. j, Cockroach, bird.
350b, Cockroach.

1998, Aug. 21   Litho.   Perf. 12
1597 A466 130b Sheet of 10,
#a.-j.   10.00 10.00

Souvenir Sheet

1598 A466 350b multicolored   4.00 4.00

State of Israel, 50th Anniv. — A467

a, 350b, Menorah. b, 350b, Moses, Ten Commandments. c, 200b, Theodore Herzl. d, 200b, King David. e, 140b, Blowing of Shofar. f, 350b, Torah. g, 350b, Praying at Wailing Wall. h, 200b, David Ben Gurion. i, 200b, Knesset. j, 140b, Book Museum.

1998, Sept. 15
1599 A467 Sheet of 10, #a.-j.   20.00 20.00

Souvenir Sheet

Comptroller General, 60th Anniv. — A468

1998, Sept.
1600 A468 480b multicolored   4.50 4.50

UPU, 125th Anniv. A469

a, 100b, Customer at window, clerks at left. b, 100b, Scanning bar code, woman at right. c, 100b, Electronic mail. d, 100b, Hybrid mail. e, 100b, Business mail. f, 300b, Like "a," clerks at right. g, 300b, Like "b," woman at left. h, 300b, Like "c," large monitor at right. i, 300b, Like "d," woman at right. j, 300b, Like "e," building with stacks at loft.

1998, Sept. 29
1601 A469 Sheet of 10, #a.-j.   10.00 10.00

Legendary Caciques A470

---

a, Caruao. b, Manaure. c, Guacamayo. d, Tapiaracay. e, Mamacuri. f, Maniacuare. g, Mara. h, Chacao. i, Tamanaco. j, Tiuna.
500b, Indian.

1998, Oct. 9
1602 A470 420b Sheet of 10,
#a.-j.   22.50 22.50

Souvenir Sheet

1603 A470 500b multicolored   4.00 4.00

Evangelism in Venezuela, 500th Anniv. — A471

No. 1604: a, 100b, Fr. Francisco de Córdoba, Fr. Juan Garcés. b, 100b, Fr. Matías Ruíz Blanco. c, 100b, Fr. Vincente de Requejada. d, 100b, Fr. José Gumilla. e, 100b, Fr. Antonio Gonzáles de Acuña. f, 300b, Fr. Pedro de Córdoba. g, 300b, Fr. Francisco de Pamplona. h, 300b, Fr. Bartolomé Díaz. i, 300b, Fr. Filipe Salvador Gilij. j, 300b, Don Mariano Martí.
350b, Emblem of Papal Nuncio.

1998, Oct. 24   Litho.   Perf. 12
1604 A471 Sheet of 10, #a.-j.   13.50 13.50

Souvenir Sheet

1605 A471 350b multicolored   3.50 3.50
No. 1605 contains one 42x37mm stamp.

Special Olympics, 30th Anniv. A472

180b: a, Carrying torch. b, Giving hug. c, Soccer players. d, Girl holding small flag. e, Girl performing gymnastics.
420b: f, Swimmer. g, Coach walking with athletes. h, Hitting volleyball. i, Particpants cheering. j, Coach instructing girl in softball.

1998, Oct. 30   Litho.   Perf. 12
1606 A472 Sheet of 10, #a.-j.   15.00 15.00

Christmas A473

Children standing in front of windows — 180b: a, Girl holding sparkler. b, Boy holding artist's brush, ornament. c, Girl with kite. d, Boy with pinwheel. e, Girls playing musical instruments.

420b: f, Boy on wagon. g, Girl with yo-yo, doll. h, Boy with bell. i, Girl with spool and thread. j, Boy on skateboard.

1998, Nov. 4
1607 A473 Sheet of 10, #a.-j. 15.00 15.00

America Issue — A474

Famous women: a, 180b, Teresa de la Parra (1889-1936), writer. b, 420b, Teresa Carreño (1853-1917), pianist.

1998, Nov. 23
1608 A474 Pair, #a.-b. 3.75 3.75

William H. Phelps (1875-1965), Ornithologist — A475

Portrait of Phelps and — 200b: a, Cephalopterus ornatus. b, Topaza pella. c, Grallaria excelsa phelpsi. d, Chrysolampis mosquitus. e, Tangara xanthogastra phelpsi.
300b: f, Radio transmitter. g, Mt. Phelps. h, Baseball and glove. i, Phelps Library. j, Cash register.

1998, Dec. 4
1609 A475 Sheet of 10, #a.-j. 16.00 16.00

Msgr. Jesús Manuel Jáuregui Moreno (1848-1905) — A476

Designs: a, Portrait as younger man. b, Christ on the cross. c, Our Mother of Angels Church. d, Madonna and Child. e, Portrait as older man.

1999, Jan. 30 Litho. Perf. 12
1610 A476 500b Strip of 5, #a.-e. 12.00 12.00

Holy Sacrament for the Consecration of the Republic of Venezuela, Cent. — A477

No. 1612: a, Man, elderly woman. b, Priest. c, Ostensorium (top). d, Boy with basketball, girl. e, Man, woman holding baby. f, Lady doctor. g, Woman. h, Ostensorium (base). i, Soldier. j, Native man holding spear.
500b, Hands of priest holding the Host.

1999, June 16 Litho. Perf. 12
1611 A477 250b Sheet of 10, #a.-j. 12.00 12.00
Souvenir Sheet
1612 A477 500b multicolored 2.25 2.25
No. 1612 contains one 42x37mm stamp.

Souvenir Sheet

Andino Parliament, 20th Anniv. — A478

1999 Litho. Perf. 12
1613 A478 500b multi 3.00 3.00

Christmas A479

a, 500b, Betrothal of Joseph, Mary. b, 500b, Annunciation. c, 500b, Elizabeth, Mary. d, 500b, The search for lodging in Bethlehem. e, 500b, Birth of Jesus. f, 300b, Vision of the shepherds. g, 300b, Magi following star. h, 300b, Adoration of the Magi. i, 300b, Flight into Egypt. j, 300b, Slaughter of the innocents.

1999, Nov. 5 Perf. 12x12¼
1614 A479 Sheet of 10, #a.-j. 24.00 24.00

Souvenir Sheet

Expo 2000, Hanover — A480

2000, July 8 Litho. Perf. 12
1615 A480 650b multi 4.00 4.00

2nd Summit of Heads of State and Government of OPEC Countries — A481

No. 1616 — Sites in Venezuela: a, 300b, Angel Falls. b, 300b, Llanos, Cojedes. c, 300b, Quebrada Jaspe. d, 300b, Morichal Largo. e, 300b, Auyantepuy, Carrao River. f, 400b, Lake Maracaibo. g, 400b, Humboldt Peak. h, 400b, Mochima. i, 400b, Morichal Largo River. j, 400b, Auyantepuy, from Uruyen.
No. 1617, 550b: a, Saudi Arabia. b, Algeria. c, United Arab Emirates. d, Indonesia. e, Iraq. f, Iran. g, Kuwait. h, Libya. i, Nigeria. j, Qatar.

2000, Sept. 26 Litho. Perf. 12
Sheets of 10, #a-j
1616-1617 A481 Set of 2 70.00 70.00

Christmas — A482

No. 1618: a, 300b, Angel and "Gloria." b, 300b, Angel and "a." c, 650b, Angel and "Dios." d, 300b, Angel and "en los." e, 300b, Angel and "Cielos." f, 300b, Shepherd and lamb. g, 550b, Joseph. h, 650b, Jesus. i, 550b, Mary. j, 300b, Woman with water jar.

2000, Nov. 29
1618 A482 Sheet of 10, #a-j 30.00 30.00

America Issue, A New Millennium Without Arms — A483

No. 1619: a, 300b, Finger in gun barrel. b, 650b, Man in heaven.

2000, Dec. 14
1619 A483 Vert. pair, #a-b 6.50 6.50

Educational Building and Endowment Foundation, 25th Anniv. — A484

No. 1620 — School buildings in: a, Caracas. b, Vargas State. c, Portuguesa State. d, Mérida State. e, Yaracuy State.

2001, May 9 Litho. Perf. 12
1620 Horiz. strip of 5 9.50 9.50
a.-c. A484 300b Any single 1.60 1.60
d.-e. A484 400b Any single 2.10 2.10

Orchids — A485

No. 1621: a, 200b, Galeottia jorisiana. b, 200b, Lycaste longipetala. c, 300b, Coryanthes albertinae. d, 300b, Hexisea bidentata. e, 400b, Lycaste macrophylla. f, 400b, Masdevallia maculata. g, 550b, Ada aurantiaca. h,

550f, Kefersteinia graminea. ì, 550b, Sobralia liliastrum. j, 550b, Gongora maculata. 650b, Masdevallia tovarensis.

2001, May 25
1621 A485 Sheet of 10, #a-j 30.00 30.00
Souvenir Sheet
1622 A485 650b multi 7.00 7.00

Blessed Josemaría Escrivá de Balaguer (1902-75), Founder of Opus Dei — A486

No. 1623: a, 300b, Portrait. b, 300b, Bell of Nuestra Senora de los Angeles Church. c, 300b, Figure of Infant Jesus. d, 300b, Escrivá with men. e, 550b, Escrivá with women. f, 550f, Escrivá receiving doctorate, 1972. g, 550b, Escrivá with children, 1975. h, 300b, Commemorative plaque, Caracas Cathedral. i, 550b, Color portrait. j, 300b, Beatification ceremony, St. Peter's Square, Vatican City.

2001, June 8
1623 A486 Sheet of 10, #a-j 32.50 32.50

Battle of Carabobo, 180th Anniv. — A487

No. 1624: a, Thomas I. Ferriar. b, Bolívar in Buenavista, by Martín Tovar y Tovar. c, Quote by Simón Bolívar. d, Commemorative column. e, Pedro Camejo. f, José Antonio Páez, by Tovar y Tovar. g, Santiago Mariño, by Tovar y Tovar. h, Simón Bolívar, by M. Eberstein. i, Manuel Cedeño, by Tito Salas. j, Ambrosio Plaza, by Salas.

2001, June 22
1624 A487 Sheet of 10 32.50 32.50
a.-e. 400b Any single 1.40 1.40
f.-j. 600b Any single 1.90 1.90

Christmas — A488

Holy Family and angel with: a, 200b, Clarinet. b, 200b, Guitar. c, 220b, Lute. d, 220b, Trumpet. e, 280b, Violin. f, 280b, Harp. g, 400b, Bagpipes. h, 400b, Pan pipes. i, 500b, Drum. j, 500b, Stringed instrument.

2001, Nov. 30 Litho. Perf. 12
1625 A488 Sheet of 10, #a-j 24.00 24.00

Navigational
Signaling,
160th
Anniv. — A489

Navigational aids: a, Margarita Aqueduct buoy. b, BNFA buoy. c, Punta Brava lighthouse. d, Punta Macolla lighthouse. e, Los Roques lighthouse. f, Isla Redonda lighthouse. g, Punta Faragoza lighthouse. h, Punta Ballena lighthouse. i, Punta Tigre lighthouse. j, Recalada de Güiria lighthouse.

2002, May 10	Litho.	Perf. 12	
1626	Sheet of 10	25.00	25.00
a.-b.	A489 300b Either single	1.00	1.00
c.-f.	A489 450b Any single	1.40	1.40
g.-j.	A489 500b Any single	1.50	1.50

Symbolic Incorporation of Guacaipuro
into National Pantheon — A490

No. 1627: a, Tiaora and Caycape, sisters of Guacaipuro. b, Guacaipuro defeats Pedro de Miranda. c, Guacaipuro defeated by Juan Rodriguez Suárez. d, Killing in the gold mines. e, Death of Juan Rodriguez Suárez. f, Guacaipuro's escape from cabin fire. g, Death of Guacaipuro. h, Urquía, companion of Guacaipuro. i, Baruta, first son of Guacaipuro. j, Guacaipuro, Cacique of the Teques and Caracas people.

2002, Oct. 29	Litho.	Perf. 12	
1627	Sheet of 10	14.00	14.00
a.	A490 200b multi	.60	.60
b.-g.	A490 300b any single	.75	.75
h.	A490 350b multi	.90	.90
i.	A490 400b multi	1.00	1.00
j.	A490 500b multi	1.25	1.25

Mission Robinson — A491

No. 1628: a, Toddler. b, Boy reading. c, Simón Bolívar and torch. d, Simón "Robinson" Rodriguez, Bolívar's teacher. e, Rodriguez

and Eiffel Tower. f, Bolívar and flag. g, Bolívar and Rodriguez reading. h, Bolívar standing and Rodriguez seated. i, Rodriguez, men and women reading. j, Indians reading.

2003, Sept. 19	Litho.	Perf. 12x12¼	
1628	A491 Sheet of 10	8.50	8.50
a.-d.	300b Any single	.40	.40
e.-f.	400b Either single	.60	.60
g.-j.	500b Any single	.75	.75

Agricultural, Fishery and Forestry
Fund (FONDAFA) — A492

No. 1629: a, Cattle drive. b, Farmer plowing field. c, Row of tractors. d, Farmer tending crops. e, Corn in field. f, Boats. g, Ear of corn. h, Farmer in tractor in field. i, Cacao pods. j, Cacao beans.

2003, Nov. 7	Litho.	Perf. 12	
1629	A492 Sheet of 10	7.50	7.50
a.-f.	300b Any single	.40	.40
g.-h.	400b Either single	.60	.60
i.-j.	500b Either single	.75	.75

National Urban Development Fund
(FONDUR), 28th Anniv. — A493

No. 1630: a, Barinas. b, Portuguesa. c, Carabobo. d, Miranda. e, Sucre. f, Trujillo. g, Táchira. h, Vargas. i, FONDUR emblem. j, Lara.

2003, Dec. 16	Litho.	Perf. 14¼	
1630	A493 Sheet of 10	7.50	7.50
a.-f.	300b Any single	.50	.50
g.-h.	400b Either single	.75	.75
i.-j.	500b Either single	.90	.90

Natl. Urban Transportation Fund
(FONTUR), 12th Anniv. — A494

No. 1631: a, Av. Uruguay, Lara. b, Carretera del Páramo, Merida. c, Av. Cumanan-Cumanacoa, Sucre. d, Carratera Santa Lucia, Barinas. e, Francisco Fajardo Expressway, Caracas. f, Students. g, Paraiso Tunnel, Caracas. h, VIVEX Module. i, Row of buses. j, Av. Cruz Paredes, Barinas.

2003, Dec. 18	Litho.	Perf. 14¼	
1631	A494 Sheet of 10	9.00	9.00
a.-c.	300b Any single	.60	.60
d.-f.	400b Any single	.75	.75
g.-j.	500b Any single	1.00	1.00

Natl. Telecommunications Commission
(CONATEL) — A495

No. 1632: a, Three Amazonian children, two dogs and hammock. b, Caracas and mountain. c, Amazonian children with spears. d, Snow-covered Bolivar Peak. e, Amazonian child in canoe aiming arrow. f, Medina Beach. g, Amazonian children aiming arrows skyward. h, Angel Falls. i, Amazonian children making baskets. j, Coro Dunes.

2003, Dec. 23	Litho.	Perf. 12	
1632	A495 Sheet of 10	9.00	9.00
a.-d.	300b Any single	.60	.60
e.-f.	400b Either single	.80	.80
g.-h.	500b Either single	1.00	1.00
i.-j.	600b Either single	1.25	1.25

Foundation for the Development of
Community and Municipal
Reconstruction (FUNDACOMUN),
42nd Anniv. — A496

No. 1633: a, Miranda. b, Trujillo. c, Mérida. d, Falcón. e, Vargas. f, Esparta. g, Caracas, denomination at left. h, Caracas, denomination at right. i, Barinas. j, Lara.

2004, Mar. 10	Litho.	Perf. 12	
1633	A496 Sheet of 10	9.00	9.00
a.-c.	300b Any single	.60	.60
d.-f.	400b Any single	.80	.80
g.-j.	500b Any single	.90	.90

Barrio Adentro Mission — A497

No. 1634: a, Houses on hillside, people in doorway. b, Woman, house, ladder, people in alley. c, Woman, mother and child. d, Family, children. e, Boys playing baseball, boat. f, People near fence, man with cap. g, Man, sand dunes. h, Man with guitar, cows. i, Mountain, woman, cross and statue. j, Indians, river.

2004, Mar. 24		Perf. 12	
1634	A497 Sheet of 10	14.00	14.00
a.-b.	300b Either single	.40	.40
c.-f.	500b Any single	.60	.60
g.	750b multi	1.00	1.00
h.-i.	1500b Either single	1.90	1.90
j.	1700b multi	2.00	2.00

Souvenir Sheet

Design: 1000b, Man pushing wheelbarrow, horiz.

1634K	A497 1000b multi	3.00	3.00

No. 1634K contains one 41x36mm stamp.

National Housing Institute
(INAVI) — A498

No. 1635: a, Apartment block 6, El Silencio. b, El Pilar. c, Central section of apartment block 1, El Silencio. d, La Quiboreña. e, Apartment block 7, El Silencio. f, Santa Ana. g, Apartment block 144, El Silencio. h, La Quiracha. i, Architectural drawings of Caracas buildings. j, Los Peregrinos.

2004, May 28	Litho.	Perf. 12	
1635	A498 Sheet of 10	7.50	7.50
a.-c.	300b Any single	.45	.45
d.-f.	400b Any single	.70	.70
g.-j.	500b Any single	.80	.80

National Aquatic Areas and Islands Institute (INEA) — A499

No. 1636: a, INEA emblem. b, INEA emblem and headquarters. c, Marine firefighters. d, Firetruck, marine firefighter moving drum. e, Sunken tugboat Gran Roque. f, Underwater view of Gran Roque. g, Tugboats. h, Large ships at port. i, Starfish, religious statue. j, Boats and birds.

2004, June 15

1636	A499	Sheet of 10	15.00	15.00
a.-b.		300b Either single	.45	.45
c.-f.		500b Any single	.80	.80
g.		600b multi	1.00	1.00
h.		1000b multi	1.60	1.60
i.		1500b multi	2.40	2.40
j.		1700b multi	2.75	2.75

A500

Latin American Parliament, 40th Anniv. — A501

No. 1637: a, Latin American Parliament emblem, 40th anniversary emblem. b, 40th anniversary emblem. c, Latin American Parliament flag and 40th anniversary emblem. d, Flags of member nations. e, Flags and Andrés Townsend Ezcurra. f, Flags and Luis Beltrán Prieto Figueroa. g, Flags and Nelson Carneiro. h, Plenary meeting room, Venezuela. i, Assembly hall, Sao Paolo. j, Latin American Parliament Building, Sao Paolo.

No. 1638: a, Latin American Parliament emblem. b, 40th Anniversary emblem. c, Mérida Session emblem. d, Charter of Social Rights. e, Flags and map of Latin America. f, Flag and map of Panama. g, Táchira Session emblem. h, Bird with ball and chain (social

debt). i, Simón Bolivar. j, Constitutional Hypothesis.

2004, July 12

1637	A500	Sheet of 10	12.50	12.50
a.-c.		300b Any single	.45	.45
d.-e.		450b Either single	.75	.75
f.-g.		500b Either single	.80	.80
h.-i.		1500b Either single	2.25	2.25
j.		1700b multi	2.40	2.40
1638	A501	Sheet of 10	12.50	12.50
a.-c.		300b Any single	.45	.45
d.-e.		450b Either single	.75	.75
f.-g.		500b Either single	.80	.80
h.-i.		1500b Either single	2.25	2.25
j.		1700b multi	2.40	2.40

CVG Edelca, 40th Anniv. — A502

No. 1639: a, Macagua Hydroelectric Station and Dam,, Ciudad Guayana. b, Electric transmission towers and lines. c, Electrical power equipment. d, Room, Guri. e, Native people. f, Guri Hydroelectric Station and Dam. g, Streetlights near Macagua Hydroelectric Station and Dam. h, Solar tower, by Alejandro Otero. i, Dam, Ecomuseum, Caroní. j, Gran Sabana.

No. 1640, Guri Hydroelectric Station and Dam.

2004, July 29

1639	A502	Sheet of 10	10.00	10.00
a.-b.		300b Either single	.45	.45
c.		400b multi	.70	.70
d.-g.		500b Any single	.80	.80
h.		600b multi	.90	.90
i.		1000b multi	1.40	1.40
j.		1500b multi	2.25	2.25

Souvenir Sheet

1640	A502	1000b multi	4.50	4.50

No. 1640 contains one 41x36mm stamp.

United Nations Population Fund — A503

No. 1641 — Inscriptions: a, Los y las adolescentes . . . b, El comporttmiento . . . c, Las niñas tienen . . . d, Los seres humanos . . . e, Promovamos el empoderamiento . . . f, Los derechjos reproductivos . . . g, Por una maternidad sin riesgo. h, El derecho al desarrollo . . . i, Eliminemos la violencia . . . j, El condón protege vidas.

2004, Sept. 15

1641	A503	Sheet of 10	12.50	12.50
a.-d.		500b Any single	.80	.80
e.-j.		1000b Any single	1.40	1.40

National Parks Institute (INPARQUES) — A504

No. 1642 — Parks and: a, Food. b, Education. c, Recreation. d, Water. e, Landscapes. f, Biodiversity. g, Conservation. h, Electricity. i, Tourism. j, Ethnic people.

2004, Oct. 11 Litho. Perf. 14¼x14½

1642	A504	Sheet of 10	10.00	10.00
a.-b.		300b Either single	.45	.45
c.		400b multi	.70	.70
d.-g.		500b Any single	.80	.80
h.		600b multi	.90	.90
i.		1000b multi	1.60	1.60
j.		1500b multi	2.25	2.25

National Tax and Customs Administration (SENIAT) — A505

No. 1643 — Inscriptions: a, Aporte a la educación, cultura y deporte (children). b, Aporte a la salud. c, Dile no al contrabando. d, Con tus tributos . . . e, Aporte a la educación, cultura y deporte (baseball players). f, Construcción de futuras . . . g, Aporte a la vialidad. h, Bienvenidos a un país . . . i, Aporte a la educación, cultura y deporte (building and palm tree). j, Aporte a la educación, cultura y deporte (modern building and sculpture).

2004, Oct. 15 Litho. Perf. 12

1643	A505	Sheet of 10	13.00	13.00
a.-d.		500b Any single	.90	.90
e.-j.		1000b Any single	1.40	1.40

A506

Banco Federal — A507

No. 1644: a, Cerro El Avila, Caracas, 1945. b, Nuevo Circo, Caracas, 1970. c, Plaza Venezuela, Caracas, 1943. d, Sculpture by Francisco Narváez, Caracas, 1940. e, Baralt Theater, Maracaibo, 1883. f, Los Próceres, Caracas, 1956. g, El Paraíso Horse Track, Caracas, 1908. h, Bullfighter Luis Sánchez Olivares, Caracas, 1950. i, Funicular, Mérida, 1954. j, Angel Falls, Bolivar State, 1937. k, Banco Federal emblem, gold star. l, Banco Federal Building (sepia). m, Lake Bridge, Maracaibo, 1962. n, Virgin of Coromoto (sepia). o, El Silencio, Caracas, 1945.

No. 1645: a, San Fernando de Apure Church. b, Caracas Cathedral. c, Coro Cathedral. d, Santa Inés de Cumaná Cathedral. e, Our Lady of Chiquinquirá Basilica. f, Our Lady of Coromoto Basilica. g, St. Rose of Lima Church, Ortíz. h, Mérida Cathedral. i, Our Lady of the Assumption Cathedral. j, San Cristóbal Cathedral. k, Banco Federal emblem, silver star. l, Banco Federal Building (full color). m, Barquisimeto Cathedral. n, Virgin of Coromoto (full color). o, Valencia Cathedral.

2005, Jan. 20 Litho. Perf. 14¼x14½

1644	A506	Sheet of 15	15.00	15.00
a.-e.		300b Any single	.45	.45
f.-h.		400b Any single	.60	.60
i.-j.		600b Either single	.90	.90
k.-l.		750b Either single	1.20	1.20
m.-n.		1000b Either single	1.60	1.60
o.		1700b multi	2.40	2.40
1645	A507	Sheet of 15	15.00	15.00
a.-e.		300b Any single	.45	.45
f.-h.		400b Any single	.60	.60
i.-j.		600b Either single	.90	.90
k.-l.		750b Either single	1.20	1.20
m.-n.		1000b Either single	1.60	1.60
o.		1700b multi	2.40	2.40

Christmas — A508

No. 1646 — Creche figures from various states: a, Bolívar. b, Falcón. c, Mérida. d, Aragua. e, Miranda. f, Miranda, diff. g, Falcón, diff. h, Zulia. i, Bolívar, diff. j, Trujillo.

2004, Dec. 23		Perf. 12	
1646	A508 Sheet of 10	12.50	12.50
a.-b.	300b Either single	.50	.50
c.-d.	400b Either single	.60	.60
e.	600b multi	.90	.90
f.-g.	750b Either single	1.20	1.20
h.-i.	1000b Either single	1.60	1.60
j.	1700b multi	2.40	2.40

Souvenir Sheet

Incan and Modern Mail
Deliverers — A509

2004		Perf. 12	
1647	A509 1000b multi	4.50	4.50

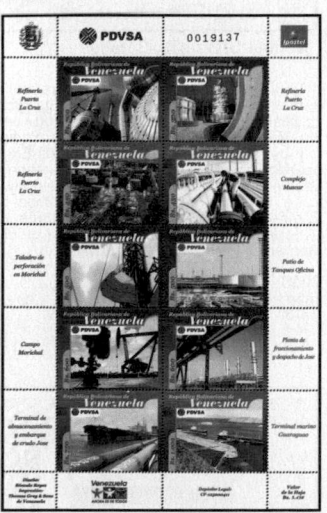

Petróleos de Venezuela, S. A. — A510

No. 1648: a, Crane above turbines, Puerto La Cruz Refinery. b, Night view of tower Puerto La Cruz Refinery. c, Aerial view of Puerto La Cruz refinery. d, Man inspecting pipes. e, Crane and Venezuelan flag. f, Storage tanks. g, Oil wells. h, Refinery towers. i, Oil tanker and pipes. j, Tankers at Guaraguao Marine Terminal.

2004, Nov. 24	Litho.	Perf. 14¼	
1648	A510 Sheet of 10	10.00	10.00
a.-b.	300b Either single	.50	.50
c.-d.	450b Either single	.65	.65
e.-f.	500b Either single	.75	.75
g.-h.	600b Either single	1.00	1.00
i.	750b multi	1.20	1.20
j.	1000b multi	1.60	1.60

Mountains — A511

Designs: No. 1649, Bolivar Peak, Venezuela. No. 1650, Mt. Damavand, Iran.

2004	Litho.	Perf. 13	
1649	A511 1700b multi	3.00	3.00
1650	A511 1700b multi	3.00	3.00
a.	Horiz. pair, #1649-1650	6.50	6.50

No. 1650 has "Republica Bolivariana de Venezuela" overprinted in black over vignette. No. 1650 exists without overprint. Nos. 1649 and 1650 without overprint were prepared for issue in 2004 but No. 1649 and 1650 with overprint were not placed on sale until 2006.

Caracas Municipal Symphony
Orchestra, 25th Anniv. — A512

No. 1651: a, French horns. b, Bass (in blue) and bow. c, Violin and bow. d, Marimba. e, Timpani. f, Clarinets. g, Flutes. h, Oboes. i, Trumpets. j, Trombone.

2005	A512	Perf. 12	
1651	A512 Sheet of 10	18.00	18.00
a.-d.	500b Any single	.75	.75
e.-h.	1000b Any single	1.60	1.60
i.-j.	2000b Either single	3.00	3.00

16th World Youth and Student
Festival — A513

No. 1652: a, Festival emblems from 1947-59. b, Festival emblems from 1962-2005. c, Festival emblem and joined arms. d, Festival emblem and text of Simón Bolívar's Vow of Monte Sacro. e, Festival emblem and Bolívar with outstretched arm, signature of Bolívar. f, Festival emblem and broken chain. g, Festival emblem, Bolívar. h, Festival emblem, dove. i, Festival emblem, dove, globe and hands. j, Festival emblem and hands.
1000b, Festival emblem and Bolívar with outstretched arm, horiz.

2005, Aug. 5	Litho.	Perf. 12	
1652	A513 Sheet of 10	8.50	8.50
a.-d.	300b Any single	.50	.50
e.-i.	500b Any single	.75	.75
j.	1500b multi	2.25	2.25

Souvenir Sheet
Perf. 12x11¾

1653	A513 1000b multi	4.00	4.00

No. 1653 contains one 41x36mm stamp.

IPOSTEL — A514

No. 1654: a, IPOSTEL emblem, flag, Caracas Post Office. b, Postal vans. c, IPOSTEL emblem on envelope, Caracas Post Office. d, Postal motorcycles. e, Carmelitas Post Office. f, Airplane, postal bicycles. g, Falcón Post Office. h, Mail carriers. i, Zulia Post Office. j, Postal workers in San Martín.

No. 1655: a, Man, IPOSTEL emblem, letters. b, Postal worker, mail sacks. c, Mail on conveyor belt. d, Mail carriers with parcels. e, Postal workers sorting mail. f, Postal workers at Ribas Mission. g, Mail sacks. h, Doctor, medical equipment at Barrio Adentro Mission. i, Postal worker and postal machinery. j, Forklift and Mercal emblem.

2005, Oct. 10		Perf. 12	
1654	A514 Sheet of 10	15.00	15.00
a.-b.	300b Either single	.50	.50
c.-d.	400b Either single	.60	.60
e.-f.	600b Either single	.85	.85
g.-i.	1700b Any single	2.40	2.40
j.	2000b multi	2.90	2.90
1655	A514 Sheet of 10	15.00	15.00
a.-b.	300b Either single	.50	.50
c.-d.	400b Either single	.60	.60
e.-f.	600b Either single	.85	.85
g.-i.	1700b Any single	2.40	2.40
j.	2000b multi	2.90	2.90

Central Bank of Venezuela, 65th
Anniv. — A515

No. 1656: a, Bank emblem. b, Caracas branch. c, Maracaibo branch. d, Venezuela Mint. e, Children's economic educational program. f, Numismatic Museum. g, Plaza Juan Pedro López. h, Gold bars. i, Bank notes and printing plates. j, Coins.

2005, Oct. 20		Perf. 12½x13½	
1656	A515 Sheet of 10	15.00	15.00
a.-b.	300b Either single	.50	.50
c.-d.	400b Either single	.60	.60
e.-f.	600b Either single	.85	.85
g.-h.	1500b Either single	2.10	2.10
i.-j.	1700b Either single	2.40	2.40

Christmas — A516

No. 1657 — Angel with: a, h, Long-necked stringed instrument with bow. b, j, Lute. c, Harp. d, g, Maracas. e, i, Stringed instrument with bow. f, Horn.

2005, Dec. 1		Perf. 12	
1657	A516 Sheet of 10	15.00	15.00
a.-c.	400b Any single	.65	.65
d.-f.	600b Either single	1.00	1.00
g.-h.	1000b Either single	1.60	1.60
i.	1500b multi	2.25	2.25
j.	2000b multi	3.25	3.25

National Guard — A517

No. 1658: a, Villa Zoila. b, Troops and building with ornate roof. c, Troops and automobiles. d, Troops saluting. e, Helicopter. f, Troops in inflatable raft. g, Three guardsmen at industrial site. h, Two guardsmen inspecting boxes. i, Guardsman with drug-sniffing dog. j, Guardsman, children.

2006, Feb. 23			
1658	A517 Sheet of 10	15.00	15.00
a.-d.	300b Any single	.50	.50
e.-f.	400b Either single	.60	.60
g.-h.	1500b Either single	2.25	2.25
i.-j.	2000b Either single	3.00	3.00

Banco Guayana, 50th Anniv. — A518

No. 1659 — Shimaraña people: a, People with painted faces. b, Archer and man with spear. c, Canoes on water. d, Women near dock. e, Man in canoe, woman's face. f, Children. g, Bow fishermen. h, Men, child, waterfall. i, Child. j, Women, dancer and river.

2006, Mar. 16

1659	A518	Sheet of 10	17.00	17.00
a.-b.		300b Either single	.50	.50
c.-f.		500b Any single	.75	.75
g.-h.		1700b Either single	2.50	2.50
i.-j.		2000b Either single	2.90	2.90

National Tax and Customs Administration (SENIAT) — A519

No. 1660 — Customs buildings in: a, Valencia. b, Puerto Cabello. c, Paraguachón. d, Santa Elena de Uairén. e, Maiquetía (in day). f, Maiquetía (at night). g, Ureña. h, Táchira. i, Barcelona. j, La Guaira.

2006, Mar. 22

1660	A519	Sheet of 10	17.00	17.00
a.-b.		400b Either single	.60	.60
c.-d.		500b Either single	.75	.75
e.-f.		700b Either single	1.00	1.00
g.-h.		1000b Either single	1.40	1.40
i.-j.		2000b Either single	3.00	3.00

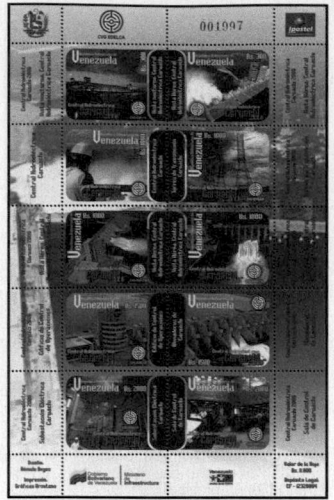

Carauchi Hydroelectric Dam Project — A520

No. 1661: a, Dam at night. b, Aerial view of dam. c, Worker at dam. d, Power lines. e, Aerial view of dam, water flowing to right. f, Aerial view of dam, water flowing straight ahead, descriptive text at left. g, Control tower. h, Spillway. i, Electrical substation. j, Control room.

No. 1662 — Rescued animals: a, Iguana iguana. b, Caluromys philander. c, Paleosuchus palpebrosus. d, Geochelone carbonaria. e, Cebus olivaceus. f, Choloepus didactylus. g, Tupinambis teguixin. h, Lora bejuca. i, Coendou prehensilis. j, Tamandua tetradactyla.

No. 1663, Aerial view of dam, water flowing straight ahead, descriptive text at top.

2006, Apr. 6

1661	A520	Sheet of 10	20.00	20.00
a.-b.		300b Either single	.50	.50
c.-f.		1000b Any single	1.60	1.60
g.-h.		1500b Either single	2.25	2.25
i.-j.		2000b Either single	3.50	3.50
1662	A520	Sheet of 10	20.00	20.00
a.-b.		300b Either single	.50	.50
c.-f.		1000b Any single	1.60	1.60
g.-h.		1500b Either single	2.25	2.25
i.-j.		2000b Either single	3.25	3.25

Souvenir Sheet

1663	A520	1000b multi	4.50	4.50

No. 1663 contains one 42x37mm stamp.

141st Extraordinary Meeting of OPEC — A521

No. 1664 — Petroleum facilities, meeting emblem and: a, "OPEP". b, Flag of United Arab Emirates flag. c, Flag of Libya. d, Flag of Iraq. e, Flag of Saudi Arabia. f, Flag of Indonesia. g, Flag of Nigeria. h, Flag of Algeria. i, Flag of Iran. j, Flag of Qatar. k, Flag of Venezuela. l, Flag of Kuwait.

2006, June 1

1664	A521	Sheet of 12	20.00	20.00
a.-b.		300b Either single	.60	.60
c.-h.		500b Any single	.75	.75
i.-j.		1500b Either single	2.25	2.25
k.-l.		2000b Either single	3.00	3.00

Caracas Mass Transit — A522

No. 1665: a, Train on Yellow line. b, Yellow line station. c, Plaza Venezuela Station. d, Three trains. e, Train switches. f, Line 4 Tunnel. g, Metro bus. h, Control room. i, Construction of Line 4 Nuevo Circo Station. j, Art by Jesús Soto, Chacaíto Station.

2006, July 2

1665	A522	Sheet of 10	25.00	25.00
a.-b.		300b Either single	.60	.60
c.-d.		500b Either single	.90	.90
e.-f.		1500b Either single	2.50	2.50
g.-j.		2000b Any single	3.25	3.25

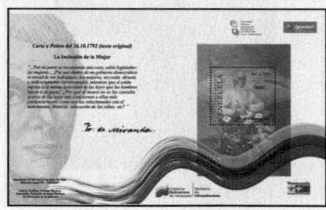

Francisco de Miranda University — A523

No. 1666, vert.: a, Miranda on horse. b, Miranda facing left. c, Nose, mouth and hand of Miranda. d, Statue of Miranda, Venezuelan flag. e, Miranda holding flag. f, Miranda at Venezuelan independence ceremonies. g, Miranda. h, Statues of Miranda. i, Miranda facing right. j, Miranda writing letter, ship.

No. 1667, Like #1666j.

2006, July 28

1666	A523	Sheet of 10	17.50	17.50
a.-d.		300b Any single	.60	.60
e.-f.		500b Either single	.90	.90
g.-h.		1500b Either single	2.50	2.50
i.-j.		2000b Either single	3.25	3.25

Souvenir Sheet

1667	A523	1500b multi	2.50	2.50

No. 1666 contains ten 35x45mm stamps.

Children's Art — A524

No. 1668: a, Flag of Liberty, by Elimar Sanchez. b, Miranda (Miranda and broken chain), by Gabriel Solano. c, Miranda and Catalina, by Elikarina Sánchez. d, Musical Aspects of Miranda (G clef), by Josmelys Díaz. e, Miranda Playing, by Nasser Sultan. f, Miranda and His Dreams, by Cynthia Urbina. g, Flag of Miranda, by Janem Sultan. h, Miranda Thinking, by Luis Miguel Martínez. i, Miranda and His Family, by Vianny Gonella. j, Diary of Miranda, by José A. Martínez.

2006

1668	A524	Sheet of 10	17.50	17.50
a.-d.		300b Any single	.60	.60
e.-f.		500b Either single	.80	.80
g.-h.		1500b Either single	2.40	2.40
i.-j.		2000b Either single	3.25	3.25

Souvenir Sheet

CVG EDELCA, 43rd Anniv. — A525

2006

1669	A525	3500b multi	6.50	6.50

Central University, Caracas — A526

No. 1670: a, Exterior of Engineering Library. b, Interior of Engineering Library. c, Electrical Engineering Building. d, School of Engineering, Metallurgy and Material Sciences, Sculpture by Harry Abend. e, School of Civil Engineering. f, School of Chemical Engineering, Petroleum and Geology, Mines and Geophysics. g, Mural by Alejandro Otero at School of Engineering. h, Machinery at Institute of Materials and Structural Models. i, Fluid Mechanics Institute. j, Aulas Auditorium.

2006

1670	A526	Sheet of 10	32.50	32.50
a.-d.		400b Any single	.60	.60
e.-f.		600b Either single	.90	.90
g.-h.		3000b Either single	4.50	4.50
i.-j.		5000b Either single	7.50	7.50

Modern Art — A527

No. 1671: a, Esfera Japón. b, Biface Naranja. c, Repetición y Progresión. d, Repetición Optica No. 2. e, Composición Dinámica. f,

Muro Optico. g, Pardelas Interferentes. h, Espiral. i, Ambivalencia Dicembre. j, Estructura Cinética.

1500b, Espiral, diff.

2006

1671	A527	Sheet of 10	14.00	14.00
a.-b.		300b Either single	.60	.60
c.-f.		500b Any single	.80	.80
g.-j.		1000b Any single	1.75	1.75

Souvenir Sheet

1672	A527	1500b multi	4.25	4.25

No. 1671 contains ten 45x35mm stamps.

Transportation — A528

No. 1673: a, Airplane in flight. b, Simón Bolívar Intl. Airport, Maiquetía. c, Highway, Ayacucho. d, Highway, Barquisimeto. e, José Antonio Páez Highway. f, Caracas — La Guaira Viaduct. g, Line 3, Caracas Metro. h, Line 4, Caracas Metro. i, Maracaibo Metro. j, Teques Metro. k, Valencia Metro. l, Caracas — Tuy Medio tram.

2006

1673	A528	Sheet of 12	27.50	27.50
a.-g.		300b Any single	.60	.60
h.-j.		2000b Any single	3.25	3.25
k. l.		3000b Either single	4.50	4.50

A529

Christmas — A530

No. 1674: a, Musicians. b, Toy. c, Top. d, Holiday table setting. e, Food. f, Letter to Baby Jesus. g, Illuminated cross. h, Yo-yo. i, Yo-yo, top and toy. j, Envelope with Holy Family.

No. 1675: a, Nativity. b, Food. c, Letter to Baby Jesus. d, IPOSTEL emblem with Holy Family.

2006

1674	A529	Sheet of 10	16.00	16.00
a.-b.		300b Either single	.50	.50
c.-d.		450b Either single	.70	.70
e.-f.		550b Either single	.85	.85
g.-h.		1000b Either single	1.50	1.50
i.		2000b multi	2.90	2.90
j.		3000b multi	4.25	4.25
1675	A530	Sheet of 4	7.50	7.50
a.-b.		300b Either single	.50	.50
c.		1000b multi	1.50	1.50
d.		2000b multi	2.90	2.90

Miniature Sheets

A531

A532

A533

2007 Copa America Soccer Tournament, Venezuela — A533

No. 1676: a, Mascot Guaky and soccer ball. b, City University Olympic Stadium, Caracas. c, José E. Pachencho Stadium, Maracaibo. d, Metropolitan Stadium, Lara. e, Agustín Tovar "La Carolina" Stadium, Barinas. f, General J. A. Anzoátegui Stadium, Puerto La Cruz. g, Cachamay Total Entertainment Center, Ciudad Guayana. h, Metropolitan Stadium, Mérida. i, Monumental Stadium, Maturín. j,

Multisport Stadium, Pueblo Nuevo San Cristóbal.

No. 1677 — Mascots: a, Guaky Jugador. b, Guaky Inspector. c, Guaky Bombero. d, Guaky Doctor. e, Guaky Futbolista. f, Guaky Obrero. g, Guaky Sembrador. h, Guaky Militar. i, Guaky Policia. j, Guaky Jugador, diff.

No. 1678 — Mascot Guaky and emblem of soccer governing body of: a, Venezuela. b, Brazil. c, Argentina. d, Mexico. e, Colombia. f, Chile. g, Peru. h, Uruguay. i, Ecuador. j, Bolivia. k, Paraguay. l, United States.

2007, June 18   Litho.   Perf. 12

1676	A531	Sheet of 10	25.00	25.00
a.-b.		300b Either single	.50	.50
c.-f.		400b Any single	.65	.65
g.-h.		2000b Either single	3.00	3.00
i.		3000b multi	4.00	4.00
j.		5000b multi	7.00	7.00
1677	A532	Sheet of 10	25.00	25.00
a.-b.		300b Either single	.50	.50
c.-f.		400b Any single	.65	.65
g.-h.		2000b Either single	3.00	3.00
i.		3000b multi	4.00	4.00
j.		5000b multi	7.00	7.00
1678	A533	Sheet of 12	25.00	25.00
a.-d.		300b Any single	.50	.50
e.-h.		400b Any single	.65	.65
i.-j.		2000b Either single	2.50	2.50
k.		3000b multi	4.00	4.00
l.		5000b multi	6.50	6.50
		Nos. 1676-1678 (3)	75.00	75.00

Intelligence and Prevention Service (DISIP), 38th Anniv. — A534

No. 1679 — DISIP emblem and: a, El Helicoide (Headquarters Building), denomination in red, "Venezuela" in dark blue. b, Model of El Helicoide, denomination in dark blue, "Venezuela" in orange. c, Model of El Helicoide, denomination in yellow. d, El Helicoide being built, denomination in red, "Venezuela" in green. e, Cupola of El Helicoide, denomination in orange. f, Auditorium of El Helicoide, denomination in light blue, "Venezuela" in red. g, El Helicoide, denomination in green. h, El Helicoide, denomination in red. i, Garden outside El Helicoide. j, Plaza Bolívar.

3500b, El Helicoide, denomination in yellow.

2007, June 21

1679	A534	Sheet of 10	25.00	25.00
a.-f.		300b Any single	.50	.50
g.-h.		2000b Either single	3.00	3.00
i.		3000b multi	4.00	4.00
j.		5000b multi	7.00	7.00

Souvenir Sheet

1680	A534	3500b multi	6.00	6.00

No. 1680 contains one 42x37mm stamp.

Miniature Sheet

Simón Bolívar Center, Caracas — A535

No. 1681: a, Muses de los Niños. b, Juan Pablo II buildings. c, Torres del Silencio. d, Palacio de Justicia. e, Parque Central building. f, Museo de Arte Contemporaneo de Caracas. g, Avenida Bolívar. h, Paseo Vargas. i, Teresa Carreño Theater. j, Cristobal Rojas.

2007, July 19

1681	A535	Sheet of 10	20.00	20.00
a.-d.		300b Any single	.40	.40
e.-f.		450b Either single	.55	.55
g.-h.		2000b Either single	2.75	2.75
i.		3000b multi	3.75	3.75
j.		5000b multi	6.75	6.75

Miniature Sheet

Christmas — A536

No. 1682 — Art: a, Resplendent God, by Hugo Rivero. b, Creole Christmas, by Vidalia González. c, Christmas Door, by Soccoro Peraza. d, Christmas, wood carvings by Orlando Campos. e, Christmas, wood carving by Tomás Flores. f, Christmas Wish, by Alberto Allup. g, St. Joseph, Virgin and Child, by Baldomero Higuera. h, Christmas, by Edgar Vegas. i, Holy Family, by Margarita Pérez de Lamanna. j, Merry Christmas, by Ana Teresa Pesce.

2007, Dec. 10

1682	A536	Sheet of 10	12.50	12.50
a.-d.		500b Any single	.65	.65
e.-h.		1000b Any single	1.40	1.40
i.-j.		1500b Either single	1.95	1.95

Miniature Sheet

Venezuelan Institute for Scientific Investigations (IVIC) — A537

No. 1683 — IVIC emblem and: a, Quimbiotec Blood Products Plant. b, Beatriz Roche Children's Band. c, Academic medal. d, Cubagua gargoyle. e, Advance Studies Center graduates. f, Bolívar and Bello Plaza. g, Molecular model. h, Investigative laboratory. i, Marcel Roche Library. j, Samuel Robinson Apartments.

No. 1684 — Artwork by: a, Linda Morales. b, Alberto Allup. c, Freddy Simoza. d, Orlando Campos.

2007, Dec. 14
1683	A537	Sheet of 10	15.00	15.00
a.-d.		500b Any single	.65	.65
e.-h.		1000b Any single	1.40	1.40
i.-j.		2000b Either single	2.75	2.75

Souvenir Sheet
| 1684 | A537 | 500b Sheet of 4, #a-d | 4.25 | 4.25 |

Miniature Sheet

Coins and Banknotes of Revalued Currency — A538

No. 1685: a, Coins and banknotes. b, 1 centimo coin. c, 5 centimo coin. d, 10 centimo coin. e, 12½ centimo coin. f, 25 centimo coin. g, 50 centimo coin. h, 1 bolivar coin. i, Francisco de Miranda and Inia geoffrensis from 2 bolivar banknote. j, Pedro Camejo and Priodontes maximus from 5 bolivar banknote. k, Guaicaipuro and Harpia harpyja from 10 bolivar banknote. l, Luisa Cáceres de Arismendi and Eretmochelys imbricata from 20 bolivar banknote. m, Simón Rodríguez and Tremarctos ornatus from 50 bolivar banknote. n, Simon Bolivar and Carduelis cucullata from 100 bolivar banknote.

2008, May 7 **Litho.** **Perf. 12**
1685	A538	Sheet of 14	13.50	13.50
a.-d.		40c Any single	.45	.45
e.-f.		50c Either single	.50	.50
g.-h.		60c Either single	6.00	6.00
i.-j.		1b Either single	1.00	1.00
k.-l.		1.50b Either single	1.50	1.50
m.-n.		2b Either single	2.10	2.10

Miniature Sheet

2008 Summer Olympics, Beijing — A539

No. 1686: a, Swimming. b, Weight lifting. c, Women's wrestling. d, Fencing.

2008, June 20 **Perf. 12**
| 1686 | A539 | 1b Sheet of 4, #a-d | 4.50 | 4.50 |

Miniature Sheet

Sites in Caracas — A540

No. 1687: a, Palacio de las Academias. b, Sabana Grande Boulevard. c, Plaza El Venezolano. d, Abra Solar. e, Carmelitas Post Office. f, Plaza O'Leary. g, City Hall (Palacio Municipal). h, Reflecting pool (Paseo Monumental Los Próceres). i, Casona Anauco Arriba. j, Plaza Bolívar.

3b, Reflecting pool (Paseo Monumental Los Próceres).

2008, Oct. 9 **Litho.** **Perf. 12**
1687	A540	Sheet of 10	24.00	24.00
a.-b.		30c Either single	.40	.40
c.-d.		40c Either single	.50	.50
e.-f.		60c Either single	.70	.70
g.-h.		1.50b Either single	1.60	1.60
i.		5b multi	5.50	5.50
j.		10b multi	11.00	11.00

Souvenir Sheet
| 1688 | A540 | 3b multi | 4.00 | 4.00 |

Miniature Sheet

Portraits of Simon Bolivar — A541

No. 1689 — Portraits by: a, José M. Espinosa. b, Pierre Colf. c, Tito Salas. d, José Gil de Castro. e, Angel Zeballos. f, Gil de Castro, diff. g, Salas, diff. h, Juan Lovera. i, Unknown artist. j, Salas, diff. k, Salas, diff. l, Daniel Hernández.

2008 **Litho.** **Perf. 12**
1689	A541	Sheet of 12	25.00	25.00
a.-d.		30c Any single	.40	.40
e.-g.		50c Any single	.60	.60
h.-j.		1.50b Any single	1.60	1.60
k.		3b multi	3.50	3.50
l.		10b multi	11.00	11.00

Miniature Sheet

Christmas — A542

No. 1690: a, Four people wearing hats, baby. b, Children giving letters to baby Jesus. c, Woman in kitchen. d, Family eating holiday meal. e, Boy and girl with toys. f, Boys flying kite. g, Choir and musicians. h, Three children at small creche. i, Musicians. j, Children playing, house decorated with Christmas lights.

2008, Dec. 1 **Litho.** **Perf. 12**
1690	A542	Sheet of 10	16.00	16.00
a.-c.		30c Any single	.35	.35
d.-e.		40c Either single	.45	.45
f.-g.		1b Either single	1.10	1.10
h.		2b multi	2.10	2.10
i.		3b multi	3.00	3.00
j.		5b multi	5.00	5.00

Miniature Sheet

Simón Bolívar Satellite — A543

No. 1691: a, Parts of satellite. b, Arm of satellite folded up. c, Satellite on scaffolds. d, Scaffolds and sign. e, Launch pad. f, Satellite dishes. g, Lift-off. h, Satellite dishes and control building. i, Satellite dish and control room. j, Satellite in space.

2009, Jan. 8
1691	A543	Sheet of 10	25.00	25.00
a.-b.		30c Either single	.40	.40
c.-d.		60c Either single	.65	.65
e.-f.		1b Either single	1.10	1.10
g.		2b multi	2.10	2.10
h.-i.		3b Either single	3.00	3.00
j.		8b multi	8.50	8.50

Miniature Sheet

Protection of Children on the Internet — A544

No. 1692: a, Two boys at laptop computer. b, Two children at desktop computers. c, Man at computer. d, Two children at laptop computer, diff. (children at right). e, Two boys at laptop computer, diff. (children at left). f, Child at computer with adult watching. g, Group of children in computer classroom. h, Boy with finger at ear near computer. i, Man and woman in field with computer. j, Laptop computer showing children on screen.

2009, May 15
1692	A544	Sheet of 10	20.00	20.00
a.-b.		30c Either single	.35	.35
c.-f.		50c Any single	.50	.50
g.-h.		2b Either single	2.10	2.10
i.		4b multi	4.00	4.00
j.		6.50b multi	7.00	7.00

Francisco de Miranda (1750-1816), Revolutionist in Venezuela and France — A545

2009, Oct. 15
1693	A545	1.50b multi	1.60	1.60
a.		Souvenir sheet of 1, imperf.	3.00	3.00

See France No. 3729.

Miniature Sheets

Venezuelan Declaration of Independence, 200th Anniv. (in 2011) — A546

A547

Signers of the Venezuelan Declaration of Independence — A548

No. 1694: a, Part 7 of Declaration of Independence. b, Part 8. c, Part 9. d, Part 4. e, Part 5. f, Part 6. g, Part 2. h, Part 3. i, Part 1. j, Signatures. k, Signatures, diff. l, Simon Bolivar and map of North and South America.

No. 1695: a, Francisco de Miranda. b, Francisco Hernández. c, Salvador Delgado. d, Juan José de Maya. e, Juan Antonio Díaz Argote. f, Felipe Fermín Paul. g, Manuel Vicente Maya. h, Juan Toro. i, Francisco Policarpo Ortiz. j, Gabriel Pérez de Pagola. k, José María Ramírez. l, Fernando Toro.

No. 1696: a, Gabriel de Ponte. b, Lino de Clemente. c, Ramón Ignacio Méndez. d, Francisco Javier Ustáriz. e, Isidoro Antonio López Méndez. f, El Marqués del Toro. g, Juan Antonio Rodriguez Domínguez. h, José de Sata y Busy. i, José Vicente de Unda. j, Antonio Nicolás Briceño.

2009	Litho.	Perf. 12	
1694	A546 Sheet of 12	24.00	24.00
a.-c.	30c Any single	.35	.35
d.-f.	50c Any single	.50	.50
g.-h.	1b Either single	1.10	1.10
i.-j.	2b Either single	2.10	2.10
k.	3.50b multi	3.50	3.50
l.	9.50b multi	10.00	10.00
1695	A547 Sheet of 12	24.00	24.00
a.-c.	30c Any single	.35	.35
d.-f.	50c Any single	.50	.50
g.-h.	1b Either single	1.10	1.10
i.-j.	2b Either single	2.10	2.10
k.	3.50b multi	3.50	3.50
l.	9.50b multi	10.00	10.00
1696	A548 Sheet of 10	24.00	24.00
a.	30c multi	.35	.35
b.-c.	50c Either single	.50	.50
d.-f.	1b Any single	1.10	1.10
g.-h.	2b Either single	2.10	2.10
i.	3.50b multi	3.50	3.50
j.	9.50b multi	10.00	10.00
	Nos. 1694-1696 (3)	72.00	72.00

Miniature Sheets

History of the Venezuelan Flag — A549

No. 1697 — Flag from: a, 1797. b, 1800. c, 1806 (Sun and Moon). d, 1806 (yellow, blue and red stripes). e, 1810. f, 1811. g, 1817 (7 stars). h, 1817 (8 stars). i, 1819. j, 1821 (arms in upper left corner).

No. 1698 — Flag from: a, 1821. b, 1830. c, 1836. d, 1859 (7 stars). e, 1859 (20 stars). f, 1863. g, 1905. h, 1930. i, 1954. j, 2006.

2009	Litho.	Perf. 12	
1697	A549 Sheet of 10	15.00	15.00
a.-b.	40c Either single	.45	.45
c.	50c multi	.50	.50
d.	60c multi	.60	.60
e.-f.	1b Either single	1.10	1.10
g.-h.	2b Either single	2.10	2.10
i.-j.	3b Either single	2.90	2.90
1698	A549 Sheet of 10	15.00	15.00
a.-b.	40c Either single	.45	.45
c.	50c multi	.50	.50
d.	60c multi	.60	.60
e.-f.	1b Either single	1.10	1.10
g.-h.	2b Either single	2.10	2.10
i.-j.	3b Either single	2.90	2.90

Miniature Sheets

History of the Venezuelan Coat of Arms — A550

No. 1699 — Arms from: a, 1591. b, 1811 (sun and banner). c, 1811 (dated 19 Abril de 1810). d, 1811 (dated 1811). e, 1812 (with 7 stars). f, 1812 (eagle with shield). g, 1819. h, 1821 (with eagle). i, 1821 (fasces and cornucopias). j, 1822.

No. 1700 — Arms from: a, 1830. b, 1834. c, 1836. d, 1856. e, 1863. f, 1871. g, 1905. h, 1930. i, 1954. j, 2006.

2009	Litho.	Perf. 12	
1699	A550 Sheet of 10	15.00	15.00
a.-b.	40c Either single	.45	.45
c.	50c multi	.50	.50
d.	60c multi	.60	.60
e.-f.	1b Either single	1.10	1.10
g.-h.	2b Either single	2.10	2.10
i.-j.	3b Either single	2.90	2.90
1700	A550 Sheet of 10	15.00	15.00
a.-b.	40c Either single	.45	.45
c.	50c multi	.50	.50
d.	60c multi	.60	.60
e.-f.	1b Either single	1.10	1.10
g.-h.	2b Either single	2.10	2.10
i.-j.	3b Either single	2.90	2.90

Miniature Sheet

Ayacucho Library, 35th Anniv. — A551

No. 1701 — Map color: a, Bister. b, Dark green. c, Dark blue. d, Lilac. e, Gray brown. f, Light blue. g, Yellow. h, Apple green. i, Brownish lilac. j, Gray.

2009	Litho.	Perf. 12	
1701	A551 Sheet of 10	22.50	22.50
a.-d.	30c Any single	.35	.35
e.-f.	2b Either single	2.10	2.10
g.-h.	3.50b Either single	3.50	3.50
i.-j.	4b Either single	4.00	4.00

Miniature Sheet

Christmas — A552

No. 1702 — Religious art by: a, Lidoska Pirela. b, Miguel Marsán. c, Thays Arteaga. d, Gustavo Martínez. e, Orlando Campos. f, Daniel Sanseviero. g, Hugo Rivero. h, Edgar Vegas. i, Liliana Benítez. j, Alberto Allup.

2009			
1702	A552 Sheet of 10	30.00	30.00
a.-d.	30c Any single	.50	.50
e.-g.	50c Any single	.80	.80

h.	3.10b multi	5.00	5.00
i.	4.20b multi	7.00	7.00
j.	6.50b multi	10.00	10.00

Miniature Sheets

A553

Signers of the Venezuelan Declaration of Independence — A554

No. 1703: a, Juan Germán Roscio. b, Fernando Peñalver. c, Martín Tovar Ponte. d, Ignacio Fernández. e, José Angel Alamo. f, Luis Ignacio Mendoza. g, Nicolás de Castro. h, Ignacio Ramón Briceño. i, Francisco Javier Yánes. j, Gabriel de Alcalá.

No. 1704: a, Mariano de la Cova. b, Juan Bermúdez. c, Francisco Isnardi. d, Manuel Plácido Maneiro. e, Juan Pablo Pacheco. f, José Luis Cabrera. g, Manuel Palacio. h, Juan Nepomuceno Quintana. i, Luis José de Cazorla. j, Francisco Javier de Mayz.

2009		Perf. 12	
1703	A553 Sheet of 10	30.00	30.00
a.-b.	30c Either single	.45	.45
c.	50c multi	.65	.65
d.-f.	1b Any single	1.25	1.25
g.-h.	2b Either single	2.50	2.50
i.	3.50b multi	4.50	4.50
j.	9.50b multi	12.50	12.50
1704	A554 Sheet of 10	30.00	30.00
a.-b.	30c Either single	.45	.45
c.-d.	50c Either single	.65	.65
e.-f.	1b Either single	1.25	1.25
g.-h.	2b Either single	2.50	2.50
i.	3.50b multi	4.50	4.50
j.	9.50b multi	12.50	12.50

Miniature Sheet

Bolivarian Militia — A555

No. 1705 — General Command Building: a, Domed and crenellated tower. b, Columns and balcony. c, Flag above main entrance. d, Round crenellated tower in foreground. e, Round crenellated tower in background. f, Rectangular tower. g, Columns and Plaza of Honor. h, Militia members, round crenellated tower in background. i, Building. j, Building and flag.

2010, Apr. 21			
1705	A555 Sheet of 10	19.00	19.00
a.-c.	1b Any single	.55	.55
d.-f.	2b Any single	1.10	1.10
g.-h.	4.50b Either single	2.25	2.25
i.	6b multi	3.00	3.00
j.	10.50b multi	6.00	6.00

Miniature Sheet

Prominent Figures of the First Republic of Venezuela — A556

No. 1706: a, Juan Germán Roscio (1763-1821). b, José Félix Ribas (1775-1815). c, Francisco Espejo (1758-1814). d, Isidoro López Méndez (1767-1834). f, José Félix Sosa (1773-1814). g, Martín Tovar Ponte (1772-1843). h, Francisco Javier Ustáriz (1772-1814). i, Francisco Salias (1785-1834). j, José Cortés de Madariaga (1766-1826).

2010, Apr. 28			
1706	A556 Sheet of 10	21.00	21.00
a.-b.	1b Either single	.60	.60
c.-f.	2.50b Any single	1.50	1.50
g.-i.	4b Any single	2.25	2.25
j.	12b multi	7.00	7.00

Manuela Sáenz (c. 1797-1856), Mistress of Simón Bolívar — A557

2010, May 24

1707	A557 2.50b multi	2.50	2.50

See Ecuador No. 2007.

Miniature Sheet

Scenes From Independence Day Military Parade — A558

No. 1708: a, National flag (Bandera Nacional). b, Athletes on float (Atletas). c, Women from cultural group wearing yellow and green dresses (Agrupaciones Culturales). d, People from cultural group wearing masks, red and white costumes (Agrupaciones Culturales). e, Women from cultural group wearing headdresses and white blouses (Agrupaciones Culturales). f, Indigenous people (Etnias Indígenas). g, People carrying flags (Estandartes FANB). h, Two uniformed men and white horse (Réplica de la Espada del Libertador). i, Soldiers from Venezuela Military Academy marching (Academia Militar de Venezuela). j, Sailors from Naval School (Escuela Naval). k, Students from Military Aviation School (Escuela de Aviación Militar). l, Students from National Guard Officer's Training School (EFOFAC). m, Students from Military Technical School (Escuela Técnica Militar). n, Male members of Bolivarian Militia wearing red pants (Milicia Bolivariana). o, Female members of Bolivarian Militia wearing white boots (Milicia Bolivariana). p, Rural militia (Milicia Campesina). q, AMX-30 tank. r, C-90 Escorpión tank. s, Dragón 300 armored fighting vehicle. t, E-11 Urutu armored personnel carrier. u, Oto Melara armored personnel carrier. v, Sultán tank. w, AMX-13 tank. x, Tank of Mechanized Infantry with banner (Infantería Mecanizada del Ejército). y, Members of Brazil delegation. z, Members of Cuba delegation. aa, Members of Bolivia delegation. ab, Members of Nicaragua delegation. ac, Members of Argentina delegation. ad, Members of Ecuador delegation. ae, Members of Belarus delegation. af, Members of Dominican Republic delegation. ag, Members of Parachute battalion (Batallón de Paracaidistas). ah, Members of Caribbean Batallion (Batallón de Caribes). ai, Members of Forest Batallion (Batallón de Selva). aj, Special Forces wearing jungle camouflage with hoods (Fuerzas Especiales). ak, Special Forces members, man with black ski cap at right (Fuerzas Especiales). al, Special Forces members with open mouths and camouflage painted faces, white gun straps (Fuerzas Especiales). am, Special Forces members wearing red berets (Fuerzas Especiales). an, Special Forces members with fully-painted faces, black gun straps (Fuerzas Especiales). ao, Sukhoi 30MK2 jet. ap, F-16 jet. aq, K-8 jet. ar, MI-26T Panare helicopter. as, MI-35M Caribe helicopter. at, MI-17V5

Pemón helicopter. au, Sikorsky AS-61D heli-copter. av, Mounted sqadron (Escuadrón de Caballería.

2010, Aug. 9
1708	A558	Sheet of 48	25.00	25.00
	a.-x.	30c Any single	.35	.35
	y.-av.	1b Any single	.65	.65

Organization of Petroleum Exporting Countries (OPEC), 50th Anniv. — A559

No. 1709 — Paintings: a, Sembradores, by Ender Cepeda. b, Y Por Fin Nos Tocó Un Chorrito de Petróleo, by Soccorro Salinas. c, Cartografía Soberana, by Saúl Huerta. d, Serie Atardecer en Campos Petroleros, by Ernesto León. e, Como Caída del Cielo, by Rosa Contreras. f, Marea, by Morella Jurado. g, Julio, by Omar Carreño. h, Del Reventón al Barril Dorado, by Gabriel Bracho. i, Petróleo Nuestro de Cada Día, by Manuel Quintana Castillo. j, El Pozo y Las Ocho Estrellas, by Paúl Del Río.

12p, 50th anniversary emblem, horiz.

2010, Sept. 14
1709	A559	Sheet of 10	21.00	21.00
	a.-c.	30c Any single	.30	.30
	d.-e.	50c Either single	.30	.30
	f.-g.	3b Either single	1.50	1.50
	h.	8b multi	4.00	4.00
	i.-j.	10b Either single	5.00	5.00

Souvenir Sheet
| 1710 | A559 | 12b multi | | 7.50 | 7.50 |

No. 1710 contains one 42x37mm stamp.

Miniature Sheet

Central Bank of Venezuela Art Collection, 70th Anniv. — A560

No. 1711 — Paintings: a, Venezuela, by Armando Reverón. b, Formas en Equilibio N-1, by Angel Hurtado. c, Bananeros, by Camille Pissarro. d, La Pareja, by Armando Barrias. e, Left half of El Avila Visto Desde el Country Club (trees at left), by Manuel Cabré. f, Right half of El Avila Visto Desde el Country Club (trees at right), by Cabré.

2010, Nov. 24
1711	A560	Sheet of 6	21.00	21.00
	a.-b.	30c Either single	.30	.30
	c.	5b multi	2.50	2.50
	d.	8b multi	4.00	4.00
	e.-f.	12.50b Either single	6.50	6.50

Miniature Sheet

Christmas — A561

No. 1712: a, Nativity. b, Satellite over the three Magi. c, Musicians. d, Cable car, buildings on mountainside, children playing. e, Woman and man at market. f, Fireworks over building. g, Teacher and children in school room, boy working at computer. h, Father and son opening Christmas gift. i, Father and son outside of candy store. j, Child on blanket in plaza, people, bus.

2010, Dec. 7
1712	A561	Sheet of 10	21.00	21.00
	a.-c.	30c Any single	.30	.30
	d.-e.	60c Either single	.35	.35
	f.-g.	4.50b Either single	2.25	2.25
	h.	6.50b multi	3.25	3.25
	i.-j.	10b Either single	5.00	5.00

Miniature Sheet

Venezuelan Antarctic Program — A562

No. 1713: a, Members of first expedition, 2008. b, Scientists taking measurements. c, Members of third expedition, 2010. d, Line of expedition members in snowstorm. e, Iceberg adrift. f, Antarctic base buildings, iceberg. g, Members of second expedition, 2009. h, Giant petrel. i, Penguins and ship, Barrientos Island. j, Whale at surface.

2010, Dec. 21   **Perf. 12¼x12**
1713	A562	Sheet of 10	27.50	27.50
	a.-b.	30c Either single	.40	.40
	c.-d.	40c Either single	.40	.40
	e.-f.	60c Either single	.60	.60
	g.	6.50b multi	4.00	4.00
	h.-i.	8.50b Either single	5.00	5.00
	j.	13.50b multi	7.50	7.50

America Issue (National Symbols) — A563

2011, Feb. 21   **Perf. 14¼**
| 1714 | A563 | 2b multi | 1.25 | 1.25 |

Miniature Sheet

Army Day — A564

No. 1715 — Uniform of: a, Batallón Bravos de Apure. b, Guardia de Honor del Libertador. c, Soldado Llanero. d, Batallón de Rifles. e, Batallón Tiradores de la Guardia. f, Cazadores Britanicos. g, Dragones de la Guardia. h, Husares de Páez. i, General de División Patriota. j, Campaña del Libertador.

2011, June 27   **Perf. 12**
1715	A564	Sheet of 10	24.00	24.00
	a.-b.	30c Either single	.30	.30
	c.-e.	40c Any single	.30	.30
	f.-g.	1.50b Either single	.90	.90
	h.	6.50b multi	4.00	4.00
	i.	10b multi	6.00	6.00
	j.	15.60b multi	9.00	9.00

Reunion of the Patriotic Society, by Tito Salas — A565

The Pantheon of Heroes, by Arturo Michelena — A566

No. 1716: a, Woman in black dress at right (left fifth of painting). b, Three men seated on bench at right, man at lectern in foreground (fourth fifth of painting). c, Bearded man standing at right (right fifth of painting). d, Woman with white dress in foreground at table (second fifth of painting). e, As "a." f, As "b." g, Three men seated on bench at left, lectern in foreground (middle fifth of painting). h, As "d." i, As "b." j, As "g."

2011, June 27   **Perf. 12**
1716	A565	Sheet of 10	30.00	30.00
	a.-c.	30c Any single	.30	.30
	d.-e.	60c Either single	.40	.40
	f.	1.50b multi	.90	.90
	g.-h.	8.50b Either single	5.00	5.00
	i.-j.	12.50b Either single	7.00	7.00

Souvenir Sheet
| 1717 | A566 | 18b multi | 11.00 | 11.00 |

Miniature Sheet

Central Bank of Venezuela Gold Coin Collection — A567

No. 1718: a, Reverse of 1975 Venezuela 1000b coin depicting arms. b, Reverse of 1886 Venezuela 100b coin depicting arms. c, Obverse of 1851 United States $20 coin depicting Liberty. d, Reverse of 1851 United States $20 coin depicting Great Seal. e, Obverse of 1886 Venezuela 100b coin depicting Simón Bolívar. f, Obverse of 1975 1000b coin depicting bird.

2011, Oct. 25
1718	A567	Sheet of 6	30.00	30.00
	a.	40c multi	.35	.35
	b.	60c multi	.40	.40
	c.-d.	5.50b Either single	2.75	2.75
	e.	13b multi	7.50	7.50
	f.	20b multi	11.00	11.00

Stained Glass Windows at Supreme Justice Tribunal, by Alirio Rodríguez — A568

No. 1719 — Detail from window numbered: a, 1/10. b, 6/10. c, 2/10. d, 7/10. e, 3/10. f, 8/10. g, 4/10. h, 9/10. i, 5/10. j, 10/10. 25b, Detail from different window.

2011, Dec. 14
1719	A568	Sheet of 10	30.00	30.00
	a.-b.	30c Either single	.35	.35
	c.-d.	40c Either single	.35	.35
	e.-f.	1.50b Either single	1.00	1.00
	g.-h.	6.50b Either single	4.00	4.00
	i.	12b multi	9.00	9.00
	j.	15.60b multi	12.00	12.00

Souvenir Sheet
| 1720 | A568 | 25b multi | 17.50 | 17.50 |

Souvenir Sheet

Simón Bolívar (1783-1830) — A569

2012, Sept. 27
| 1721 | A569 | 25b multi | 17.50 | 17.50 |

New Bolívar Mausoleum, Caracas.

Miniature Sheet

Luis Zambrano (1901-90),
Inventor — A570

No. 1722 — Zambrano: a, Facing forward, wearing hat. b, Facing left, without hat. c, Fancing forward, without hat. d, Facing right, without hat. e, Working on machine with two men. f, Standing in front of machine. g, Touching wheel. h, Putting rod in machine. i, Wearing cap. j, Standing next to machine.

2012

1722	A570	Sheet of 10	25.00 25.00
a.-b.		30c Either single	.35 .35
c.-d.		40c Either single	.35 .35
e. f.		1.50b Either single	1.00 1.00
g.		4b multi	3.00 3.00
h.-i.		6.50b Either single	5.00 5.00
j.		12.50b multi	10.00 10.00

Miniature Sheet

Pres. Hugo Chávez (1954-
2013) — A571

No. 1723 — Pres. Chávez: a, Touching crucifix. b, Wearing beret and uniform, saluting. c, Hugging Venezuelan flag. d, Visiting school children. e, Hugging elderly woman. f, Holding flagpole. g, Shaking hands with person in crowd. h, Pointing finger. i, Wearing beret and uniform. j, Holding microphone.
20b, Wearing sash and necklace, vert.

2013, Apr. 9

1723	A571	Sheet of 10	15.00 15.00
a.-d.		30c Any single	.35 .35
e.		40c multi	.35 .35
f.-g.		1.50b Either single	.60 .60
h.		4.20b multi	1.60 1.60
i.		11.70b multi	4.25 4.25
j.		14b multi	5.00 5.00

Souvenir Sheet

1724	A571	20b multi	0.00 8.00

No. 1724 contains one 37x42mm stamp.

Miniature Sheet

Correos Carmelitas Building,
Caracas — A572

No. 1725: a, 50c, Black-and-white photograph. b, 50c, Color photograph of builing painted yellow. c, 20b, Black-and-white photograph of different corner of building. d, 34b, Color photograph of building painted red.

2014, Jan. 28   Litho.   Perf. 12

1725	A572	Sheet of 4	18.00 18.00
a.-b.		50c Either single	.25 .25
c.		20b multi	6.50 6.50
d.		34b multi	11.00 11.00

America Issue — A570

No. 1726 — Pres. Hugo Chávez (1954-2013): a, Waving. b, Holding map of South America.

2014, Mar. 5   Litho.   Perf. 12

1726	A573	Pair	4.25 4.25
a.		1b multi	.25 .25
b.		12.50b multi	4.00 4.00

Works of the Revolution — A574

No. 1727: a, Estadio Monumental de Maturín (soccer stadium). b, Tractor in field. c, Latin American Infantile Cardiological Hospital. d, Metrocable cable car. e, Bridge over Orinoco River. f, Buildings, Ciudad Caribia. g, Miranda Satellite. h, Children with computers (Canaima Education Project).

2014, Dec. 18   Litho.   Perf. 12

1727		Horiz. strip of 8	57.00 57.00
a.	A574	30c multi	.25 .25
b.	A574	40c multi	.25 .25
c.	A574	50c multi	.25 .25
d.	A574	3.50b multi	1.10 1.10
e.	A574	15.60b multi	5.00 5.00
f.	A574	25b multi	8.00 8.00
g.	A574	31.50b multi	10.00 10.00
h.	A574	100b multi	32.00 32.00

Miniature Sheet

Serge Raynaud de la Ferrière (1916-62), Founder of Universal Great Brotherhood — A575

Various photograhphs of Ferrière: a, 30c. b, 40c. c, 50c. d, 80c. e, 12.50b. f, 25b. g, 34.50b. h, 50b. i, 100b. j, 200b.

2015, May 12   Litho.   Perf. 12

1728	A575	Sheet of 10, #a-j	15.00 15.00

Miniature Sheet

Pedro Camejo (1790-1821), Soldier in War of Independence Known as "Negro Primero" — A576

No. 1729 — Bust or statue of Camejo and various works or art or buildings: a, 30c. b, 50c. c, 4b. d, 9b. e, 15b. f, 38b. g, 45b. h, 80b. i, 100b. j, 200b.

2015, June 29   Litho.   Perf. 12

1729	A576	Sheet of 10, #a-j	17.00 17.00

Miniature Sheet

Cacao Farming and
Processing — A577

No. 1730: a, 2b, Emblem of Chocolate Expoferia Internacional. b, 2b. Yellow cacao pods. c, 8b, Cacao buds and growing pods. d, 28b, Brown cacao pod and cocoa beans in sack. e, 37b, Farmer harvesting cacao pod. f, 40b, Opened cacao pod. g, 52b, Yellow and Green cacao pods on tree. h, 69b, Venezuelan flag, wrapped chocolate candy bars. i, 140b, Cacao flowers. j, 184b, Drying of cocoa beans and building.

2015, Oct. 1   Litho.   Perf. 12

1730	A577	Sheet of 10, #a-j	13.50 13.50

Campaign to
End Violence
Against
Women
— A578

2015, Nov. 25   Litho.   Perf. 12

1731	A578	338b multi	5.00 5.00

See Dominican Republic No. 1583, Ecuador No. 2173, Guatemala No. 717, El Salvador No.

Flora and Fauna — A579

No. 1732 — Inscription: a, 50c, Sabana de Barinas. b, 10b, Reforestación del Parque Nacional Macarao. c, 46b, Arbol flamboyant (Delonix regia). d, 71b, Corocora colorada (Eudocimus ruber). e, 94b, Caimán del Orinoco (Cocodylus intermedius). f, 110b, Cangrejo Ermitaño (Coenobita clypeatus). g, 250b, Arbol araguaney (Handroanthus chrysanthus). h, 458b, Tortuga arrau (Podocnemis expansa).

2016, Oct. 13   Litho.   Perf. 12

1732	A579	Block of 8, #a-h	9.00 9.00

Christmas — A580

No. 1733 — Art by: a, 10b, Darianna Castillo. b, 20b, Romna Medina. c, 50b, Katherin Chacón. d, 70b, Dervis Nuñez. e, 90b, Pedro Crespo (Pan de Jamon, grapes, ensalada de gallina). f, 100b, Crespo (roast ham, hallacas). g, 300b, Enriqueta Aguiar. h, 500b, Mirelis Rojas.

2016, Dec. 1   Litho.   Perf. 12

1733	A580	Block of 8, #a-h	10.00 10.00

Miniature Sheet

Biotechnology Organizations, 10th Anniv. — A581

No. 1734: a, 10b, Crop irrigation. b, 20b, Field and trees. c, 40b, Emblem of Comprehensive Dairy Development Program (PIDEL). d, 50b, Emblem of National Foundation for Development of Biotechnology (NADBIO) e, 100b, Emblem of National Environment Ecology Education Program (PROECO). f, 150b, NADBIO and words. g, 160b, Two cows. h, 220b, Calf. i, 320b, Technician at microscope. j, 500b, Cattle at feed trough.

2017, Mar. 27   Litho.   Perf. 12
1734 A581   Sheet of 10, #a-j   8.00 8.00

Ezequiel Zamora (1817-60), Soldier
A582

2017, May 19   Litho.   Perf. 12
1735 A582 500b multi   2.50 2.50

POSTAL FISCAL STAMPS

Nos. 128-135 Overprinted

1900			Perf. 12	
AR1	A25	5c gray	.25	.25
a.		Overprint inverted	8.00	8.00
AR2	A25	10c deep green	.25	.25
a.		Overprint inverted	8.00	8.00
AR3	A25	25c blue	.25	.25
a.		Overprint inverted	8.00	8.00
AR4	A25	50c orange	.25	.25
a.		Overprint inverted	8.00	8.00
AR5	A25	1b red violet	.30	.25
a.		Overprint inverted	8.00	8.00
AR6	A25	3b red orange	.50	.25
a.		Overprint inverted	8.00	8.00
AR7	A25	10b dull violet	1.25	.25
AR8	A25	20b red brown	7.50	7.50
		Nos. AR1-AR8 (8)	10.55	9.75

Type of 1893 Postage Stamps in Changed Colors Overprinted

1900			Perf. 12	
AR9	A25	5c orange	.25	.25
AR10	A25	10c deep blue	.25	.25
AR11	A25	25c plum	.25	.25
AR12	A25	50c bright green	1.00	.25
AR13	A25	1b gray black	10.00	1.75
AR14	A25	3b red brown	2.00	1.00
AR15	A25	10b vermilion	12.00	3.50
AR16	A25	20b deep violet	20.00	5.00
		Nos. AR9-AR16 (8)	45.75	12.25

Type of 1893 Postage Stamps in Changed Colors Overprinted

1901				
AR17	A25	1b gray black	.75	.50

Type of 1893 in Changed Colors

1901				
AR18	A25	5c orange	.25	.25
AR19	A25	10c vermilion	.25	.25
AR20	A25	10c blue	.25	.25
AR21	A25	25c Prussian blue	.25	.25
AR22	A25	50c yellow green	.25	.25
AR23	A25	1b gray black	10.00	2.50
AR24	A25	3b red brown	.25	.25
AR25	A25	10b vermilion	.50	.45
AR26	A25	20b deep violet	1.00	.65
		Nos. AR18-AR26 (9)	13.00	5.10

Simón Bolivar — PF1

1904, July		Engr.	Perf. 12	
AR27	PF1	5c green	.25	.25
AR28	PF1	10c gray	.25	.25
AR29	PF1	25c vermilion	.25	.25
AR30	PF1	50c yel org	.25	.25
AR31	PF1	1b claret	3.00	.40
AR32	PF1	3b blue	.50	.25
AR33	PF1	10b bluish gray	.75	.50
AR34	PF1	20b deep carmine	1.75	.50
		Nos. AR27-AR34 (8)	7.00	2.65

National Figures — PF2

5c, José Vargas (1786-1854), Independence leader and provisional president. 10c, De Avila. 25c, Miguel José Sanz, revolutionary jurist and educator. 50c, Antonio Guzman Blanco (1829-99), jurist, president. 1b, Andres Bello. 2b, Martin S. Sanabria (1831-1904), educator, cabinet minister. 3b, José Antonio Paez (1790-1873), revolutionary leader. 10b, Antonio José de Sucre known as the "Gran Mariscal de Ayacucho." 20b, Simón Bolívar, military and political leader.

1911		Litho.	Perf. 11½x12	
AR35	PF2	5c blue	.25	.25
AR36	PF2	10c pale yel & org	.25	.25
AR37	PF2	25c gray	.25	.25
AR38	PF2	50c scarlet	.25	.25
AR39	PF2	1b green	.25	.25
AR40	PF2	2b brown	.90	.50
AR41	PF2	3b blue violet	.90	.50
AR42	PF2	10b lilac	1.75	.75
AR43	PF2	20b brown blue	1.75	1.10
		Nos. AR35-AR43 (9)	6.55	4.10

Simón Bolívar — PF3

1914		Engr.	Perf. 14	
AR44	PF3	5c lilac	.25	.25
AR45	PF3	10c olive green	.25	.25
AR46	PF3	25c red brown	1.00	.25
AR47	PF3	50c rose carmine	1.50	.50
AR48	PF3	1b violet brown	1.50	.50
AR49	PF3	2b bister	3.25	1.50
AR50	PF3	3b gray blue	3.25	.50
AR51	PF3	10b orange brown	10.00	3.25
AR52	PF3	20b gray black	6.50	2.25
		Nos. AR44-AR52 (9)	27.50	9.00

PF4   PF5

Antonio José de Sucre — PF6

1915			Perf. 12	
AR53	PF4	5c brown	.25	.25
AR54	PF5	10c blue	.25	.25
AR55	PF5	25c carmine	3.25	.25
AR56	PF5	50c red brown	.25	.25
AR57	PF4	1b green	.40	.25
AR58	PF4	2b gray brown	2.25	.25
AR59	PF6	3b violet	.25	.25
AR60	PF6	10b gray black	20.00	2.25
AR61	PF6	20b orange	.25	.25
		Nos. AR53-AR61 (9)	27.15	4.25

Type of 1915 in Changed Colors and

PF7

Antonio José de Sucre — PF8

1922				
AR62	PF5	10c green	.25	.25
AR63	PF7	20c light blue	.25	.25
AR64	PF4	1b olive brown	.25	.25
AR65	PF4	2b carmine	.25	.25
AR66	PF6	10b yellow	.35	.25
AR67	PF8	50b claret	.60	.25
		Nos. AR62-AR67 (6)	1.95	1.50

 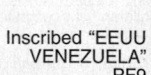

Inscribed "EEUU VENEZUELA" PF9

Pale Blue Security Imprint "EEUU VENEZUELA" on Face of Paper

1947		Engr.	Perf. 12	
AR68	PF9	5c green	.25	.25
AR69	PF9	10c yellow brown	.25	.25
AR70	PF9	20c red brown	.25	.25
AR71	PF9	40c green	.45	.25
AR72	PF9	50c light blue	.45	.25
AR73	PF9	1b violet	.45	.25
AR74	PF9	2b blue	.60	.45
AR75	PF9	3b blue	.60	.45
AR76	PF9	10b orange	4.50	2.50
		Nos. AR68-AR76 (9)	7.80	4.90

Nos. AR67-AR71, AR75 and AR76 overprinted, see Nos. 876-883.

Inscribed "REPUBLICA DE VENEZUELA" PF10

Pale Blue Security Imprint "REPUBLICA DE VENEZUELA" on Face of Paper

1956				
AR77	PF10	5c green	.25	.25
AR78	PF10	10c yellow brown	.25	.25
AR79	PF10	20c red brown	.25	.25
AR80	PF10	40c green	.25	.25
AR81	PF10	50c blue	.45	.25
AR82	PF10	1b violet	.60	.40
AR83	PF10	2b deep violet	1.00	.85
AR84	PF10	3b dark blue	1.40	.85
AR85	PF10	5b ultramarine	2.50	1.75
AR86	PF10	10b orange	4.50	2.50
		Nos. AR77-AR86 (10)	11.45	7.60

SEMI-POSTAL STAMPS

A 5c green stamp of the Cruzada Venezolana Sanitaria Social portraying Simon Bolivar was overprinted "EE. UU. DE VENEZUELA CORREOS" in 1937.
It is stated that 50,000 stamps without control numbers on back were sold by post offices and 147,700 with control numbers on back were offered for sale by the Society at eight times face value.

Bolívar Funeral Carriage SP1

Unwmk.
1942, Dec. 17   Engr.   Perf. 12
B1 SP1 20c + 5c blue   6.00 .65

Cent. of the arrival of Simón Bolívar's remains in Caracas. The surtax was used to erect a monument to his memory. See Nos. CB1-CB2.

> Catalogue values for unused stamps in this section, from this point to the end of the section, are for Never Hinged items.

Red Cross Nurse — SP2

1975, Dec. 15   Litho.   Perf. 14
B2 SP2 30c + 15c multi   .40 .25
B3 SP2 50c + 25c multi   .60 .40

Surtax for Venezuelan Red Cross.

Carmen América Fernandez de Leoni — SP3

Children in Home — SP4

1976, June 7   **Litho.**   **Perf. 13½**
B4   SP3   30c + 15c multi   .30 .25
B5   SP4   50c + 25c multi   .50 .35

Surtax was for the Children's Foundation, founded by Carmen América Fernandez de Leoni in 1966.

Patient — SP5

1976, Dec. 8   **Litho.**   **Perf. 14**
B6   SP5   10c + 5c multi   .25 .25
B7   SP5   30c + 10c multi   .25 .25

Surtax was for Anti-tuberculosis Society.

AIR POST STAMPS

Air post stamps of 1930-42 perforated "GN" (Gobierno Nacional) were for official use.

Airplane and Map of Venezuela — AP1

1930   **Unwmk.**   **Litho.**   **Perf. 12**
C1   AP1   5c bister brn   .25 .25
C2   AP1   10c yellow   .25 .25
   a.   10c salmon   32.50 32.50
C3   AP1   15c gray   .25 .25
C4   AP1   25c lilac   .25 .25
C5   AP1   40c olive grn   .25 .25
   a.   40c slate blue   45.00
   b.   40c slate green   45.00
C6   AP1   75c dp red   .30 .25
C7   AP1   1b indigo   .45 .25
C8   AP1   1.20b blue grn   .70 .35
C9   AP1   1.70b dk blue   .90 .45
C10   AP1   1.90b blue grn   .90 .50
C11   AP1   2.10b dk blue   1.75 .65
C12   AP1   2.30b vermilion   1.75 .50
C13   AP1   2.50b dk blue   1.75 .50
C14   AP1   3.70b blue grn   1.75 1.10
C15   AP1   10b dull vio   5.25 2.40
C16   AP1   20b gray grn   8.00 4.50
   Nos. C1-C16 (16)   24.75 12.70

Issued: 10b, 6/8; 20b, 6/16; others, 4/5.
Nos. C1-C16 exist imperforate or partly perforated. Value, imperf set $200.
See Nos. C119-C126.

Airplane and Map of Venezuela — AP2

Bluish Winchester Security Paper

1932, July 12   **Engr.**   **Perf. 12½**
C17   AP2   5c brown   .40 .25
C18   AP2   10c org yel   .40 .25
C19   AP2   15c gray lilac   .40 .25
C20   AP2   25c violet   .40 .25
C21   AP2   40c ol grn   .80 .25
C22   AP2   70c rose   .55 .25
C23   AP2   75c red org   1.00 .25
C24   AP2   1b dk bl   1.10 .25
C25   AP2   1.20b green   2.40 .85
C26   AP2   1.70b red brn   4.75 .55
C27   AP2   1.80b ultra   2.40 .35
C28   AP2   1.90b green   6.00 3.50
C29   AP2   1.95b blue   6.50 2.75
C30   AP2   2b blk brn   4.00 2.25
C31   AP2   2.10b blue   9.50 6.00
C32   AP2   2.30b red   4.00 2.40
C33   AP2   2.50b dk bl   6.00 1.40
C34   AP2   3b dk vio   6.00 .85
C35   AP2   3.70b emerald   8.00 6.00
C36   AP2   4b red org   6.00 1.40
C37   AP2   5b black   6.50 2.40
C38   AP2   8b dk car   13.00 4.75

C39   AP2   10b dk vio   26.00 8.00
C40   AP2   20b grnsh slate   60.00 20.00
   Nos. C17-C40 (24)   176.10 65.45

Pairs imperf. between exist of the 1b (value $150); the 25c and 4b (value $300 each).

Air Post Stamps of 1932 Surcharged in Black

1937, June 4
C41   AP2   5c on 1.70b red brn   11.00 7.00
C42   AP2   10c on 3.70b emer   11.00 7.00
C43   AP2   15c on 4b red org   5.00 3.50
C44   AP2   25c on 5b blk   5.00 3.50
C45   AP2   1b on 8b dk car   4.00 3.50
C46   AP2   2b on 2.10b bl   30.00 23.00
   Nos. C41-C46 (6)   66.00 47.50

Various varieties of surcharge exist, including double and triple impressions. No. C43 exists in pair imperf. between; value $30 unused, $50 used.

Allegory of Flight AP3

Allegory of Flight AP4

National Pantheon at Caracas AP5

Airplane — AP6

Perf. 11, 11½ and Compound

1937, July 1   **Litho.**
C47   AP3   5c brn org   .30 .40
C48   AP4   10c org red   .25 .25
C49   AP5   15c gray blk   .60 .40
C50   AP6   25c dk vio   .60 .40
C51   AP4   40c yel grn   1.10 .55
C52   AP3   70c red   1.10 .40
C53   AP5   75c bister   2.50 1.30
C54   AP3   1b dk gray   1.50 .55
C55   AP4   1.20b pck grn   6.50 4.25
C56   AP3   1.80b dk ultra   3.25 2.00
C57   AP3   1.95b lt ultra   10.00 7.75
C58   AP6   2b chocolate   4.25 2.75
C59   AP6   2.50b gray bl   11.50 11.50
C60   AP4   3b lt vio   6.50 4.50
C61   AP3   3.70b rose red   11.50 15.00
C62   AP5   10b red vio   25.00 15.00
C63   AP3   20b gray   30.00 23.00
   Nos. C47-C63 (17)   116.45 90.00

All values exist imperf, and all except the 3.70b part-perf.
Counterfeits exist.
For overprints & surcharges see Nos. C66-C78, C114-C118, C164-C167, C169-C172, C174-C180.

AP7

1937, Oct. 28   **Perf. 11**
C64   AP7   70c emerald   1.40 .55
C65   AP7   1.80b ultra   2.25 1.00

Acquisition of the Port of La Guaira by the Government from the British Corporation, June 3, 1937. Nos. C64-C65 exist imperf. Value, set $275.

A redrawn printing of Nos. C64-C65, with lower inscription beginning "Nacionalización..." was prepared but not issued. Value, $40 each.
For overprints see Nos. C168, C173.

Air Post Stamps of 1937 Overprinted in Black

1937, Dec. 17   **Perf. 11, 11½**
C66   AP4   10c org red   1.00 .70
   a.   Inverted overprint   15.00 12.00
C67   AP6   25c dk vio   2.00 1.00
C68   AP4   40c yel grn   2.00 1.40
C69   AP3   70c red   1.50 1.00
   a.   Inverted overprint   15.00 14.00
   b.   Double overprint   20.00 16.00
C70   AP3   1b dk gray   2.00 1.40
   a.   Inverted overprint   16.00 13.00
   b.   Double overprint   13.00
C71   AP4   1.20b pck grn   30.00 20.00
   a.   Inverted overprint   77.50
C72   AP3   1.80b dk ultra   5.75 2.40
C73   AP5   1.95b lt ultra   7.75 4.25
   a.   Inverted overprint   60.00 40.00
C74   AP6   2b chocolate   50.00 23.00
   a.   Inverted overprint   100.00 90.00
   b.   Double overprint   82.50 82.50
C75   AP6   2.50b gray bl   50.00 19.00
   a.   Double overprint   70.00
   b.   Inverted overprint   100.00 82.50
C76   AP4   3b lt vio   30.00 12.00
C77   AP6   10b red vio   72.50 40.00
C78   AP3   20b gray   77.50 47.50
   a.   Double overprint   150.00 150.00
   Nos. C66-C78 (13)   332.00 173.65

Counterfeit overprints exist on #C77-C78.

View of La Guaira AP8

National Pantheon AP9

Oil Wells AP10

1938-39   **Engr.**   **Perf. 12**
C79   AP8   5c green   1.00 .50
C80   AP8   5c dk grn   .25 .25
C81   AP9   10c car rose   1.40 .80
C82   AP9   10c scarlet   .25 .25
C83   AP8   12½c dull vio   .60 .55
C84   AP10   15c slate vio   3.00 1.25
C85   AP10   15c dk bl   .85 .25
C86   AP8   25c dk bl   3.00 1.25
C87   AP8   25c bis brn   .25 .25
C88   AP10   30c vio ('39)   2.00 .25
C89   AP9   40c dk vio   3.50 1.25
C90   AP10   40c redsh brn   2.50 .25
C91   AP8   45c Prus grn ('39)   1.00 .25

C92   AP9   50c blue ('39)   1.25 .25
C93   AP10   70c car rose   .85 .25
C94   AP8   75c bis brn   6.00 2.00
C95   AP8   75c ol bis   1.40 .25
C96   AP10   90c red org ('39)   1.00 .25
C97   AP9   1b ol & bis   7.00 2.75
C98   AP9   1b dk vio   1.25 .25
C99   AP10   1.20b orange   20.00 5.75
C100   AP10   1.20b green   2.00 .55
C101   AP8   1.80b ultra   2.00 .55
C102   AP9   1.90b black   5.50 2.75
C103   AP9   1.95b lt bl   4.25 2.50
C104   AP8   2b ol gray   45.00 15.00
C105   AP8   2b car rose   1.75 .70
C106   AP9   2.50b red brn   45.00 20.00
C107   AP9   2.50b orange   10.00 2.75
C108   AP10   3b bl grn   20.00 4.75
C109   AP10   3b ol gray   5.50 2.00
C110   AP10   3.70b gray blk   7.75 5.50
C111   AP10   5b red brn ('39)   7.75 2.00
C112   AP9   10b vio brn   20.00 2.40
C113   AP10   20b red org   57.50 25.00
   Nos. C79-C113 (35)   292.35 105.55

See Nos. C227a, C235-C236, C254-C255.
For surcharge see No. C227.

Nos. C51, C56, C58-C59, C61 Surcharged

1938, Apr. 15   **Perf. 11, 11½**
C114   AP3   5c on 1.80b   .85 .60
   a.   Inverted surcharge   12.50 7.50
C115   AP6   10c on 2.50b   3.00 1.40
   a.   Inverted surcharge   10.00 7.50
C116   AP6   15c on 2b   1.40 1.10
C117   AP4   25c on 40c   1.75 1.40
C118   AP6   40c on 3.70b   3.50 3.25
   Nos. C114-C118 (5)   10.50 7.75

Plane & Map Type of 1930
White Paper; No Imprint

1938-39   **Engr.**   **Perf. 12½**
C119   AP1   5c dk grn ('39)   .25 .25
C120   AP1   10c org yel ('39)   .55 .25
C121   AP1   12½c rose vio ('39)   1.10 .85
C122   AP1   15c dp bl   .95 .25
C123   AP1   25c brown   1.10 .25
C124   AP1   40c olive ('39)   2.75 .40
C125   AP1   70c rose car ('39)   20.00 7.75
C126   AP1   1b dk bl ('39)   7.75 3.00
   Nos. C119-C126 (8)   34.45 13.00

Monument to Sucre — AP11

Monuments at Carabobo AP12   AP13

1938, Dec. 23   **Perf. 13½**
C127   AP11   20c brn blk   .80 .30
C128   AP12   30c purple   1.20 .30
C129   AP13   45c dk bl   1.75 .25
C130   AP11   50c lt ultra   1.50 .25
C131   AP13   70c dk car   26.00 7.50
C132   AP12   90c red org   2.50 .75
C133   AP13   1.35b gray blk   3.00 1.00
C134   AP11   1.40b slate gray   12.00 2.75
C135   AP12   2.25b green   6.00 2.00
   Nos. C127-C135 (9)   54.75 15.10

For surcharge see No. C198.

Simón Bolívar and Carabobo Monument AP14

1940, Mar. 30 — Perf. 12

C136	AP14	15c blue	.75	.25
C137	AP14	20c olive bis	.75	.25
C138	AP14	25c red brn	2.75	.40
C139	AP14	40c blk brn	2.25	.25
C140	AP14	1b red lilac	5.00	.55
C141	AP14	2b rose car	11.00	1.40
		Nos. C136-C141 (6)	22.50	3.10

"The Founding of Grand Colombia" AP15

1940, June 13

C142	AP15	15c copper brown	1.25	.45

Founding of the Pan American Union, 50th anniv.

Statue of Simón Bolívar, Caracas — AP16

1940-44

C143	AP16	5c dk grn ('42)	.25	.25
C144	AP16	10c scar ('42)	.25	.25
C145	AP16	12½c dull purple	.75	.30
C146	AP16	15c blue ('43)	.50	.25
C147	AP16	20c bis brn ('44)	.50	.25
C148	AP16	25c bis brn ('42)	.50	.25
C149	AP16	30c dp vio ('43)	.50	.25
C150	AP16	40c blk brn ('43)	.65	.25
C151	AP16	45c turq grn ('43)	.65	.25
C152	AP16	50c blue ('44)	.65	.25
C153	AP16	70c rose pink	2.00	.30
C154	AP16	75c ol bis ('43)	7.75	1.60
C155	AP16	90c red org ('43)	1.25	.30
C156	AP16	1b dp red lil ('43)	.65	.25
C157	AP16	1.20b dp yel grn ('43)	2.50	.75
C158	AP16	1.35b gray blk ('42)	10.50	3.50
C159	AP16	2b rose pink ('43)	2.00	.25
C160	AP16	3b ol blk ('43)	3.25	.75
C161	AP16	4b black	2.50	.75
C162	AP16	5b red brn ('44)	20.00	8.00
		Nos. C143-C162 (20)	57.60	19.00

See Nos. C232-C234, C239-C253. For surcharges see Nos. C225, C873.

Nos. C48, C50-C65 Overprinted

Resellado 1943

Perf. 11, 11½ & Compound

1943, Dec. 21

C164	AP4	10c orange red	2.00	.90
C165	AP6	25c dk violet	2.00	.90
C166	AP4	40c yellow grn	2.00	.90
C167	AP3	70c red	2.00	.90
C168	AP7	70c emerald	2.00	.90
C169	AP5	75c bister	2.00	.90
C170	AP4	1b dk gray	2.00	.90
C171	AP4	1.20b peacock grn	5.00	1.60
C172	AP3	1.80b dk ultra	5.00	1.60
C173	AP7	1.80b dk ultra	5.00	2.50
C174	AP5	1.95b lt ultra	6.00	3.25
C175	AP4	2b chocolate	6.00	3.25
C176	AP5	2.50b gray blue	5.00	3.25
C177	AP4	3b lt violet	6.00	3.25
C178	AP6	3.70b rose red	52.50	45.00
C179	AP5	10b red violet	12.00	10.00
C180	AP3	20b gray	27.50	20.00
		Nos. C164-C180 (17)	144.00	100.00
		Set, never hinged	275.00	

Issued for sale to philatelists. Nos. C164-C169 were sold only in sets.
Nearly all are known with invtd. ovpt.

Flags of Venezuela and the Red Cross — AP17

Flags in red, yellow, blue and black

1944, Aug. 22 — Litho. — Perf. 12

C181	AP17	5c gray green	.25	.25
C182	AP17	10c magenta	.25	.25
C183	AP17	20c brt blue	.25	.25
C184	AP17	30c violet bl	.40	.25
C185	AP17	40c chocolate	.55	.25
C186	AP17	45c apple green	1.75	.45
C187	AP17	90c orange	1.60	.45
C188	AP17	1b gray black	2.40	.45
		Nos. C181-C188 (8)	7.45	2.60
		Set, never hinged	12.00	

80th anniv. of the Intl. Red Cross and 37th anniv. of Venezuela's joining the organization. Nos. C181-C188 exist imperf. and part perf. Value, imperf set $30.

Baseball Players — AP18

"AEREO" in dark carmine

1944, Oct. 12

C189	AP18	5c dull vio brn	.30	.25
C190	AP18	10c gray green	.50	.25
C191	AP18	20c ultra	.50	.25
C192	AP18	30c dull rose	1.00	.40
C193	AP18	45c rose violet	2.00	.70
C194	AP18	90c red orange	3.50	1.40
C195	AP18	1b dark gray	4.00	1.40
C196	AP18	1.20b yellow grn	9.25	7.25
C197	AP18	1.80b ocher	12.00	9.25
		Nos. C189-C197 (9)	33.05	21.15
		Set, never hinged	55.00	

7th World Amateur Baseball Championship Games, Caracas.
Nos. C189-C197 exist imperf. and all but 1b exist part perf. Value, imperf set $75.
Various errors of "AEREO" overprint exist.

No. C134 Surcharged in Black

Habilitado 1944 VALE Bs. 0.30

1944, Nov. 17 — Perf. 13½

C198	AP11	30c on 1.40b	.50	.50
a.		Double surcharge	35.00	35.00
b.		Inverted surcharge	13.50	13.50

Charles Howarth — AP19

1944, Dec. 21 — Unwmk. — Perf. 12

C199	AP19	5c black	.25	.25
C200	AP19	10c purple	.25	.25
C201	AP19	20c sepia	.40	.25
C202	AP19	30c dull green	.55	.25
C203	AP19	1.20b bister	2.50	2.40
C204	AP19	1.80b deep ultra	4.50	2.90
C205	AP19	3.70b rose	6.00	4.75
		Nos. C199-C205 (7)	14.45	11.05
		Set, never hinged	20.00	

Cent. of founding of 1st cooperative shop in Rochdale, England, by Charles Howarth. Nos. C199-C205 exist imperf. and part perf.

Antonio José de Sucre — AP20

1945, Mar. 3 — Engr.

C206	AP20	5c orange	.25	.25
C207	AP20	10c violet	.25	.25
C208	AP20	20c grnsh blk	.25	.25
C209	AP20	30c brt green	.25	.25
C210	AP20	40c olive	1.10	1.10
C211	AP20	45c black brn	1.60	1.10
C212	AP20	90c redsh brn	2.10	1.10
C213	AP20	1b dp red lil	2.10	1.10
C214	AP20	1.20b black	6.25	5.25
C215	AP20	2b yellow	10.00	7.25
		Nos. C206-C215 (10)	24.15	17.90
		Set, never hinged	40.00	

150th birth anniv. of Antonio Jose de Sucre, Grand Marshal of Ayacucho.

Type of 1946

1946, Aug. 24 — Perf. 12

C216	A81	30c Bello	1.10	.25
C217	A82	30c Urdaneta	1.10	.25
		Set, never hinged	2.75	

Allegory of Republic — AP23

Perf. 11½

1946, Oct. 18 — Litho. — Unwmk.

C218	AP23	15c dp violet bl	.40	.25
C219	AP23	20c bister brn	.40	.25
C220	AP23	30c dp violet	.50	.35
C221	AP23	1b brt rose	3.50	2.75
		Nos. C218-C221 (4)	4.80	3.60
		Set, never hinged	8.00	

Anniversary of the Revolution of October, 1945. Exist imperf. and part perf.

Nos. 297, 371, C152 and 362 Surcharged in Black

J. R. G. AEREO Vale Bs. 0.15 1946

1947, Jan. — Perf. 12

C223	A49	10c on 22½c dp car	.25	.25
a.		Inverted surcharge	7.00	5.00
C224	A69	15c on 25c lt bl	.40	.25
C225	AP16	20c on 50c blue	.40	.25
a.		Inverted surcharge	9.00	7.00
C226	A65	70c on 1b dk vio brn	.75	.45
a.		Inverted surcharge	9.00	5.00

Type of 1938 Surcharged in Black

J. R. G. AEREO Vale Bs. 20 1946

C227	AP10	20b on 20b org red	28.00	22.50
a.		Surcharge omitted	92.50	40.00
		Nos. C223-C227 (5)	29.80	23.70
		Set, never hinged	40.00	

"J. R. G." are the initials of "Junta Revolucionaria de Gobierno."
Also exist: 20c on #C143, 10c on #371.

Anti-tuberculosis Institute, Maracaibo — AP24

1947, Jan. 12 — Litho.

Venezuela Shown on Map in Yellow

C228	AP24	15c dark blue	.45	.35
C229	AP24	20c dark brown	.45	.35
C230	AP24	30c violet	.45	.35
C231	AP24	1b carmine	4.75	3.75
		Nos. C228-C231 (4)	6.10	4.80
		Set, never hinged	16.00	

12th Pan-American Health Conf., Caracas, Jan. 1947.
Nos. C228-C231 exist imperf., part perf. and with yellow omitted.

Types of 1938-40

1947, Mar. 17 — Engr.

C232	AP16	75c orange	7.50	4.50
C233	AP16	1b brt ultra	.70	.25
C234	AP16	3b red brown	17.50	8.00
C235	AP10	5b scarlet	15.00	5.00
C236	AP9	10b violet	20.00	7.50
		Nos. C232-C236 (5)	60.70	25.25
		Set, never hinged	100.00	

On Nos. C235 and C236 the numerals of value are in color on a white table.

No. 370 Surcharged in Black

AEREO Vale Bs. 0.05 1947

1947, June 20

C237	A70	5c on 20c blue	.40	.25
C238	A70	10c on 20c blue	.40	.25
a.		Inverted surcharge	5.00	5.00
		Set, never hinged	1.00	

Types of 1938-44

1947-48 — Engr.

C239	AP16	5c orange	.25	.25
C240	AP16	10c dk green	.25	.25
C241	AP16	12½ bister brn	.45	.45
C242	AP16	15c gray	.25	.25
C243	AP16	20c violet	.25	.25
C244	AP16	25c dull green	.25	.25
C245	AP16	30c brt ultra	.45	.25
C246	AP16	40c green ('48)	.25	.25
C247	AP16	45c vermilion	.45	.25
C248	AP16	50c red violet	.25	.25
C249	AP16	70c dk car	1.00	.45
C250	AP16	75c purple ('48)	.65	.45
C251	AP16	90c black	1.00	.30
C252	AP16	1.20b red brn ('48)	1.25	.50
C253	AP16	3b dp blue	1.75	.50
C254	AP10	5b olive grn	9.25	5.00
C255	AP9	10b yellow	8.25	4.75
		Nos. C239-C255 (17)	26.25	14.45
		Set, never hinged	60.00	

On Nos. C254 and C255 the numerals of value are in color on a white tablet.
Issue dates: 5c, 10c, Oct. 8. 15c, Dec. 2, 40c, 75c, 1.20b, May 10, 1948. Others, Oct. 27, 1947.

M. S. Republica de Venezuela — AP25

Imprint: "American Bank Note Company"

1948-50 — Unwmk. — Perf. 12

C256	AP25	5c red brown	.25	.25
C257	AP25	10c deep green	.25	.25
C258	AP25	15c brown	.25	.25
C259	AP25	20c violet brn	.35	.25
C260	AP25	25c brown black	.35	.25
C261	AP25	30c olive green	.35	.25
C262	AP25	45c blue green	.65	.35
C263	AP25	50c gray black	1.00	.55
C264	AP25	70c orange	1.75	.55
C265	AP25	75c brt ultra	3.00	.75
C266	AP25	90c car lake	1.75	1.75
C267	AP25	1b purple	2.40	1.75
C268	AP25	2b gray	2.50	1.75
C269	AP25	3b emerald	9.75	5.50
C270	AP25	4b deep blue	4.50	5.50
C271	AP25	5b orange red	18.00	8.25
		Nos. C256-C271 (16)	47.10	27.55

Issued to honor the Grand-Colombian Merchant Fleet. See Nos. C554-C556.
Issued: 5c, 10c, 15c, 25c, 30c, 1b, 7/9/48; 45c, 75c, 5b, 5/11/50; others, 3/9/49.
For surcharges see Nos. C863-C864.

Santos
Michelena
AP26

1949, Apr. 25

C272	AP26	5c orange brn	.25	.25
C273	AP26	10c gray	.25	.25
C274	AP26	15c red orange	.50	.50
C275	AP26	25c dull green	1.00	.80
C276	AP26	30c plum	1.00	.80
C277	AP26	1b violet	5.50	3.00
		Nos. C272-C277 (6)	8.50	5.60
		Set, never hinged	12.00	

See note after No. 427.

Christopher
Columbus
AP27

1948-49   Unwmk.   Perf. 12½

C278	AP27	5c brown ('10)	.30	.25
C279	AP27	10c gray	.30	.30
C280	AP27	15c orange ('49)	.65	.30
C281	AP27	25c green ('49)	1.25	.65
C282	AP27	30c red vio ('49)	1.50	.95
C283	AP27	1b violet ('49)	6.00	2.75
		Nos. C278-C283 (6)	10.00	5.20
		Set, never hinged	16.00	

See note after No. 431.

AP28

Symbols of global air mail.

1950   Perf. 12

C284	AP28	5c red brown	.25	.25
C285	AP28	10c dk green	.25	.25
C286	AP28	15c olive brn	.25	.25
C287	AP28	25c olive gray	.40	.30
C288	AP28	30c olive grn	.55	.30
C289	AP28	50c black	.40	.25
C290	AP28	60c brt ultra	1.10	.60
C291	AP28	90c carmine	1.40	.75
C292	AP28	1b purple	1.90	.50
		Nos. C284-C292 (9)	6.50	3.45
		Set, never hinged	10.50	

75th anniv. of the UPU.
Issue dates: 5c, Jan. 28. Others, Feb. 19.

AP29

Araguaney, Venezuelan national tree.

Foliage in Yellow

1950, Aug. 25   Photo.   Perf. 11½

C293	AP29	5c orange brn	.45	.25
C294	AP29	10c blue grn	.45	.25
C295	AP29	15c deep plum	.90	.25
C296	AP29	25c dk gray grn	5.50	1.60
C297	AP29	30c red orange	7.00	2.00
C298	AP29	50c dark gray	3.50	.45
C299	AP29	60c deep blue	5.50	1.00
C300	AP29	90c red	9.00	2.00
C301	AP29	1b rose violet	13.50	2.50
		Nos. C293-C301 (9)	45.80	10.30
		Set, never hinged	160.00	

Issued to publicize Forest Week, 1950.

Census Type of 1950

1950, Sept. 1   Engr.   Perf. 12

C302	A90	5c olive gray	.25	.25
C303	A90	10c green	.25	.25
C304	A90	15c olive green	.25	.25
C305	A90	25c gray	.45	.45
C306	A90	30c orange	.65	.30
C307	A90	50c lt brown	.45	.25
C308	A90	60c ultra	.45	.25
C309	A90	90c rose carmine	1.40	.65
C310	A90	1b violet	1.75	1.75
		Nos. C302-C310 (9)	5.90	4.40
		Set, never hinged	10.00	

Signing Act of Independence — AP31

1950, Nov. 17

C311	AP31	5c vermilion	.60	.25
C312	AP31	10c red brown	.60	.25
C313	AP31	15c violet	.85	.25
C314	AP31	30c brt blue	1.00	.40
C315	AP31	1b green	5.00	2.40
		Nos. C311-C315 (5)	8.05	3.55
		Set, never hinged	10.00	

200th anniversary of the birth of Gen. Francisco de Miranda.

Alonso de Ojeda Type of 1950

1950, Dec. 18   Photo.   Perf. 11½

C316	A91	5c orange brn	.25	.25
C317	A91	10c cerise	.30	.25
C318	A91	15c black brn	.55	.25
C319	A91	25c violet	.60	.30
C320	A91	30c orange	1.25	.50
C321	A91	1b emerald	5.00	2.50
		Nos. C316-C321 (6)	7.95	4.05
		Set, never hinged	12.00	

Bolivar Statue Type of 1951

1951, July 13   Engr.   Perf. 12

C322	A92	5c purple	.70	.25
C323	A92	10c dull green	.80	.25
C324	A92	20c olive gray	.80	.25
C325	A92	25c olive green	.90	.25
C326	A92	30c vermilion	1.10	.55
C327	A92	40c lt brown	1.10	.55
C328	A92	50c gray	2.50	1.00
C329	A92	70c orange	3.50	2.50
		Nos. C322-C329 (8)	11.40	5.60
		Set, never hinged	15.00	

Queen Isabella
I — AP34

1951, Oct. 12   Photo.   Perf. 11½

C330	AP34	5c dk green & buff	.45	.25
C331	AP34	10c dk red & cream	.45	.25
C332	AP34	20c dp blue & gray	.75	.25
C333	AP34	30c dk blue & gray	.75	.25
a.		Souv. sheet of 4, #C330-C333	14.00	15.00
		Never hinged	24.00	
		Nos. C330-C333 (4)	2.40	1.00
		Set, never hinged	8.00	

500th anniv. of the birth of Queen Isabella I of Spain.

Bicycle Racecourse — AP35

1951, Dec. 18   Engr.   Perf. 12

C334	AP35	5c green	.80	.25
C335	AP35	10c rose carmine	.80	.25
C336	AP35	20c redsh brown	1.00	.70
C337	AP35	30c blue	1.30	1.00
a.		Souv. sheet, #C334-C337	20.00	24.00
		Never hinged	32.50	
		Nos. C334-C337 (4)	3.90	2.20
		Set, never hinged	6.50	

3rd Bolivarian Games, Caracas, Dec. 1951.

Arms of Carabobo and
"Industry" — AP36

1951   Photo.   Perf. 11½

C338	AP36	5c blue green	2.50	1.10
C339	AP36	7½c gray green	3.25	1.90
C340	AP36	10c car rose	2.50	1.10
C341	AP36	15c dark brown	3.25	1.10
C342	AP36	20c gray blue	3.50	1.10
C343	AP36	30c deep blue	9.50	1.60
C344	AP36	45c magenta	4.75	1.60
C345	AP36	60c olive brown	9.00	3.50
C346	AP36	90c rose brown	20.00	11.00
		Nos. C338-C346 (9)	58.25	24.00

Issue date: Oct. 29.

Arms of Zulia and "Industry"

C347	AP36	5c blue green	1.25	.60
C348	AP36	10c car rose	1.25	.60
C349	AP36	15c dark brown	1.90	.60
C350	AP36	30c deep blue	12.50	4.00
C351	AP36	60c olive	7.50	1.25
C352	AP36	1.20b brown car	25.00	16.00
C353	AP36	3b blue gray	8.75	2.40
C354	AP36	5b purple brn	12.50	6.25
C355	AP36	10b violet	20.00	12.50
		Nos. C347-C355 (9)	90.65	44.20

Issued: 5b, 9/8; 5c, 3b, 10b, 10/8; others, 10/29.

Arms of Anzoategui

C356	AP36	5c blue green	1.50	.85
C357	AP36	10c car rose	1.50	.85
C358	AP36	15c dk brown	2.00	.85
C359	AP36	25c sepia	2.40	.85
C360	AP36	30c deep blue	6.25	3.50
C361	AP36	50c henna brn	6.25	1.75
C362	AP36	60c olive brn	9.00	1.10
C363	AP36	1b purple	11.00	3.50
C364	AP36	2b violet gray	19.00	7.75
		Nos. C356-C364 (9)	58.90	21.00

Issue date: Nov. 9.

Arms of Caracas and Buildings

C365	AP36	5c blue green	2.75	1.10
C366	AP36	7½c gray green	8.00	3.50
C367	AP36	10c car rose	1.90	1.10
C368	AP36	15c dk brown	19.00	2.50
C369	AP36	20c gray blue	12.50	2.50
C370	AP36	30c deep blue	21.00	4.75
C371	AP36	45c magenta	12.50	2.75
C372	AP36	60c olive brn	42.50	5.75
C373	AP36	90c rose brn	25.00	20.00
		Nos. C365-C373 (9)	145.15	43.95

Issue date: Aug. 6.

Arms of Tachira and Agricultural Products

C374	AP36	5c blue green	.90	.90
C375	AP36	10c car rose	.90	.90
C376	AP36	15c dk brown	2.50	.90
C377	AP36	30c deep blue	32.50	3.75
C378	AP36	60c olive brn	26.00	3.75
C379	AP36	1.20b brown car	26.00	18.00
C380	AP36	3b blue gray	8.50	3.75
C381	AP36	5b purple brn	15.00	7.75
C382	AP36	10b violet	20.00	15.00
		Nos. C374-C382 (9)	132.30	54.70

Issue date: Aug. 9.

Arms of Venezuela and Bolivar Statue

C383	AP36	5c blue green	1.75	.90
C384	AP36	7½c gray green	4.50	2.75
C385	AP36	10c car rose	13.50	.90
C386	AP36	15c dk brown	10.00	2.75
C387	AP36	20c gray blue	13.50	2.25
C388	AP36	30c deep blue	24.50	4.75
C389	AP36	45c magenta	11.00	2.00
C390	AP36	60c olive brn	50.00	10.00
C391	AP36	90c rose brn	32.50	22.50
		Nos. C383-C391 (9)	161.25	48.80

Issue date: Aug. 6.

Arms of Miranda and Agricultural Products

1952

C392	AP36	5c bl grn	1.00	.70
C393	AP36	7½c gray grn	1.75	1.00
C394	AP36	10c car rose	1.00	.70
C395	AP36	15c dk brn	2.10	.70
C396	AP36	20c gray blue	3.00	.85
C397	AP36	30c deep blue	6.00	1.40
C398	AP36	45c magenta	5.50	.70
C399	AP36	60c olive brn	10.50	1.90
C400	AP36	90c rose brn	45.00	27.50
		Nos. C392-C400 (9)	75.85	35.45

Issue date: 7½c, 15c, 20c, 30c, Mar. 24.

Arms of Aragua and Stylized Farm

C401	AP36	5c blue green	2.50	.90
C402	AP36	7½c gray grn	2.25	1.25
C403	AP36	10c car rose	1.25	.90
C404	AP36	15c dk brown	7.75	1.10
C405	AP36	20c gray blue	3.75	1.10
C406	AP36	30c deep blue	11.00	1.25
C407	AP36	45c magenta	8.50	1.10
C408	AP36	60c olive brn	18.00	1.75
C409	AP36	90c rose brn	67.50	35.00
		Nos. C401-C409 (9)	122.50	44.35

Issue date: 7½c, 15c, 20c, 30c, Mar. 24.

Arms of Lara, Agricultural Products and Hope

C410	AP36	5c blue green	2.25	.80
C411	AP36	7½c gray grn	2.00	1.10
C412	AP36	10c car rose	1.10	.80
C413	AP36	15c dk brown	3.50	.80
C414	AP36	20c gray blue	5.50	.80
C415	AP36	30c deep blue	11.00	1.60
C416	AP36	45c magenta	5.50	1.40
C417	AP36	60c olive brn	11.00	2.50
C418	AP36	90c rose brn	60.00	40.00
		Nos. C410-C418 (9)	101.85	49.80

Issue date: 7½c, 15c, 20c, 30c, Mar. 24.

Arms of Bolivar and Stylized Design

C419	AP36	5c blue green	11.50	1.25
C420	AP36	10c car rose	1.00	.70
C421	AP36	15c dark brown	1.75	.70
C422	AP36	25c sepia	1.40	.70
C423	AP36	30c deep blue	8.00	3.25
C424	AP36	50c henna brn	5.40	1.40
C425	AP36	60c olive brn	9.00	1.75
C426	AP36	1b purple	8.00	1.40
C427	AP36	2b violet gray	18.00	6.25
		Nos. C419-C427 (9)	64.05	17.40

Issue date: 15c, 30c, Mar. 24.

Arms of Sucre, Palms and Seascape

C428	AP36	5c blue green	1.00	.65
C429	AP36	10c car rose	.65	.65
C430	AP36	15c dk brown	1.40	.65
C431	AP36	25c sepia	27.50	.65
C432	AP36	30c deep blue	9.25	2.75
C433	AP36	50c henna brn	4.25	1.00
C434	AP36	60c olive brn	5.25	2.10
C435	AP36	1b purple	6.75	1.60
C436	AP36	2b violet gray	15.00	7.50
		Nos. C428-C436 (9)	71.05	17.55

Issue date: 15c, 30c, Mar. 24.

Arms of Trujillo Surrounded by Stylized Tree

C437	AP36	5c blue green	11.00	.70
C438	AP36	10c car rose	.80	.40
C439	AP36	15c dk brown	3.00	.40
C440	AP36	30c deep blue	13.50	2.25
C441	AP36	60c olive brn	9.75	2.10
C442	AP36	1.20b rose red	8.75	5.00
C443	AP36	3b blue gray	4.25	3.10
C444	AP36	5b purple brn	9.25	3.50
C445	AP36	10b violet	16.00	8.25
		Nos. C437-C445 (9)	76.30	25.70

Issue date: 5c, 30c, Mar. 24.

Map of Delta Amacuro and Ship

1953-54

C446	AP36	5c bl grn	1.25	.85
C447	AP36	10c car rose	.85	.85
C448	AP36	15c dk brn	1.90	.96
C449	AP36	25c sepia	2.75	1.25
C450	AP36	30c dp bl	11.00	3.25
C451	AP36	50c hn brn	5.50	1.25
C452	AP36	60c ol brn	8.25	2.50
C453	AP36	1b purple	10.50	3.50
C454	AP36	2b vio gray	17.50	13.00
		Nos. C446-C454 (9)	59.50	27.41

Issue date: 15c, 30c, Feb. 13.

Arms of Falcon and Stylized Oil Refinery

C455	AP36	5c bl grn	1.00	.50
C456	AP36	10c car		.50
		rose	.50	.50
C457	AP36	15c dk brn	1.00	.50
C458	AP36	30c dp bl	8.25	2.25
C459	AP36	60c ol brn	6.25	1.75
C460	AP36	1.20b rose		
		red	7.75	7.25
C461	AP36	3b bl gray	8.25	4.50
C462	AP36	5b pur		
		brn	13.50	9.25
C463	AP36	10b violet	13.50	10.50
Nos. C455-C463 (9)			60.00	37.00

Issue date: 10c, 15c, 30c, Feb. 13.

Arms of Guarico and Factory

C464	AP36	5c blue		
		grn	1.10	.80
C465	AP36	10c car		
		rose	.80	.80
C466	AP36	15c dk brn	1.75	.80
C467	AP36	25c sepia	2.50	1.10
C468	AP36	30c dp bl	11.00	4.25
C469	AP36	50c hn brn	5.50	1.75
C470	AP36	60c ol brn	6.25	2.50
C471	AP36	1b purple	11.00	2.50
C472	AP36	2b vio		
		gray	16.00	8.25
Nos. C464-C472 (9)			55.90	22.75

Issue date: 15c, 30c, Feb. 13.

Arms of Merida and Church

C473	AP36	5c bl grn	.95	.80
C474	AP36	10c car		
		rose	.80	.80
C475	AP36	15c dk brn	1.50	.80
C476	AP36	30c dp bl	14.00	3.25
C477	AP36	60c ol brn	7.00	1.90
C478	AP36	1.20b rose		
		red	12.00	7.00
C479	AP36	3b bl gray	7.00	3.25
C480	AP36	5b pur		
		brn	13.50	7.00
C481	AP36	10b violet	19.00	12.00
Nos. C473-C481 (9)			75.75	36.80

Issue date: 10c, Feb. 2.

Arms of Monagas and Horses

C482	AP36	5c bl grn	1.10	.85
C483	AP36	10c car		
		rose	.85	.85
C484	AP36	15c dk brn	1.75	.85
C485	AP36	25c sepia	1.25	.85
C486	AP36	30c dp bl	16.00	4.25
C487	AP36	50c hn brn	6.50	2.10
C488	AP36	60c ol brn	7.50	2.10
C489	AP36	1b purple	11.00	2.75
C490	AP36	2b vio		
		gray	15.00	7.50
Nos. C482-C490 (9)			60.95	22.10

Issue date: 10c, Feb. 2.

Arms of Portuguesa and Forest

C491	AP36	5c bl grn	4.00	1.25
C492	AP36	10c car		
		rose	.95	.95
C493	AP36	15c dk brn	2.40	.95
C494	AP36	30c dp bl	12.00	5.50
C495	AP36	60c ol brn	8.75	2.25
C496	AP36	1.20b rose		
		red	20.00	12.00
C497	AP36	3b bl gray	7.00	4.00
C498	AP36	5b pur		
		brn	12.50	7.00
C499	AP36	10b violet	18.00	15.00
Nos. C491-C499 (9)			85.60	48.90

Issue date: 5c, 10c, 30c, Feb. 2.

Map of Amazonas and Orchid

C500	AP36	5c bl grn	9.25	2.10
C501	AP36	10c car		
		rose	2.10	2.10
C502	AP36	15c dk brn	9.25	2.10
C503	AP36	25c sepia	19.00	2.10
C504	AP36	30c dp bl	47.50	4.75
C505	AP36	50c hn brn	37.50	8.25
C506	AP36	60c ol brn	47.50	8.25
C507	AP36	1b purple	190.00	27.50
C508	AP36	2b vio		
		gray	75.00	32.50
Nos. C500-C508 (9)			437.10	89.65

Issue date: Jan. 1954

Arms of Apure, Horse and Bird

C509	AP36	5c bl grn	1.60	.80
C510	AP36	10c car		
		rose	.80	.80
C511	AP36	15c dk brn	1.60	.80
C512	AP36	30c dp bl	6.25	2.75
C513	AP36	60c ol brn	5.75	1.40
C514	AP36	1.20b brn		
		car	9.75	7.00
C515	AP36	3b bl gray	4.75	3.00
C516	AP36	5b pur		
		brn	11.50	5.50
C517	AP36	10b violet	16.00	11.50
Nos. C509-C517 (9)			59.00	33.55

Issue date: Jan. 1954.

Arms of Barinas, Cow and Horse

C518	AP36	5c bl grn	.50	.50
C519	AP36	10c car		
		rose	.50	.50
C520	AP36	15c dk brn	1.90	.50
C521	AP36	30c dp		
		blue	6.50	2.50
C522	AP36	60c ol brn	6.50	1.25
C523	AP36	1.20b brn		
		car	9.00	4.75
C524	AP36	3b bl gray	5.75	3.50
C525	AP36	5b pur		
		brn	9.75	3.25
C526	AP36	10b violet	14.00	10.00
Nos. C518-C526 (9)			54.40	26.75

Issue date: Jan. 1954.

Arms of Cojedes and Cattle

C527	AP36	5c bl grn	7.75	1.10
C528	AP36	7½c gray		
		grn	2.00	1.10
C529	AP36	10c car		
		rose	.60	.60
C530	AP36	15c dk brn	.60	.60
C531	AP36	20c gray bl	1.50	.60
C532	AP36	30c dp		
		blue	10.50	1.50
C533	AP36	45c mag	3.75	.90
C534	AP36	60c ol brn	7.75	1.25
C535	AP36	90c rose		
		brn	9.25	5.25
Nos. C527-C535 (9)			43.70	12.90

Issue date: Dec.

Arms of Nueva Esparta and Fish

C536	AP36	5c bl grn	1.25	.65
C537	AP36	10c car		
		rose	.65	.65
C538	AP36	15c dk brn	2.10	.65
C539	AP36	25c sepia	3.50	.85
C540	AP36	30c dp bl	7.50	1.60
C541	AP36	50c hn brn	7.50	1.60
C542	AP36	60c ol brn	7.50	1.00
C543	AP36	1b purple	11.00	2.50
C544	AP36	2b vio		
		gray	15.00	7.50
Nos. C536-C544 (9)			56.00	17.00

Issue date: Jan. 1954.

Arms of Yaracuy and Tropical Foliage

C545	AP36	5c bl grn	2.00	.75
C546	AP36	7½c gray		
		grn	24.50	22.50
C547	AP36	10c car		
		rose	1.10	.75
C548	AP36	15c dk brn	2.25	.75
C549	AP36	20c gray bl	3.75	.75
C550	AP36	30c dp bl	7.50	1.90
C551	AP36	45c mag	5.25	1.10
C552	AP36	60c ol brn	5.25	1.90
C553	AP36	90c rose		
		brn	14.00	9.50
Nos. C545-C553 (9)			65.60	39.90
Nos. C338-C553 (216)			2,272.	841.61

Issue date: Jan. 1954.

Ship Type of 1948-50 Redrawn
Coil Stamps
Imprint: "Courvoisier S.A."

1952   **Unwmk.**   **Perf. 12x11½**

C554	AP25	5c rose brn	2.00	.25
C555	AP25	10c org red	3.25	.25
C556	AP25	15c ol brn	4.25	.25
Nos. C554-C556 (3)			9.50	.75

Barquisimeto Type of 1952

1952, Sept. 14   **Photo.**   **Perf. 11½**

C557	A94	5c blue green	.25	.25
C558	A94	10c car rose	.25	.25
C559	A94	20c dk blue	.40	.25
C560	A94	25c black brn	.60	.25
C561	A94	30c ultra	.75	.25
C562	A94	40c brown org	3.50	1.50
C563	A94	50c dk ol grn	1.40	.40
C564	A94	1b purple	4.75	2.00
Nos. C557-C564 (8)			11.90	5.15

Caracas Post Office Type of 1953-54

1953, Mar. 11   **Perf. 12½**

C565	A96	7½c yellow grn	.25	.25
C566	A96	15c dp plum	.25	.25
C567	A96	20c slate	.25	.25
C568	A96	25c sepia	.50	.25
C569	A96	40c plum	.50	.25
C570	A96	45c rose vio	.50	.25
C571	A96	50c red orange	.75	.25
C572	A96	70c dk sl grn	1.50	.75
C573	A96	75c dp ultra	5.25	1.10
C574	A96	90c brown org	1.25	.60
C575	A96	1b violet blue	1.25	.60
Nos. C565-C575 (11)			12.25	4.80

See Nos. C587-C589, C597-C606.

Simon Rodriguez — AP39

1954, Feb. 28   **Perf. 11½**

C576	AP39	5c blue green	1.50	.25
C577	AP39	10c car rose	1.50	.25
C578	AP39	20c gray blue	1.50	.25
C579	AP39	45c magenta	1.50	1.50
C580	AP39	65c gray green	3.50	6.00
Nos. C576-C580 (5)			9.50	8.25
Set, never hinged			24.00	

Centenary of the death of Simon Rodriguez, scholar and tutor of Bolivar.

Quotation from Bolivar's Manifesto of 1824 — AP40

1954, Mar. 1   **Unwmk.**

C581	AP40	15c blk & brn buff	1.50	.25
C582	AP40	25c dk red brn &		
		gray	1.50	.25
C583	AP40	40c dk red brn &		
		red org	1.50	.25
C584	AP40	65c black & blue	1.50	1.00
C585	AP40	80c dk red brn &		
		rose	1.50	.65
C586	AP40	1b pur & rose lil	3.50	.50
Nos. C581-C586 (6)			11.00	2.90
Set, never hinged			27.50	

10th Inter-American Conf., Caracas, Mar. 1954.

P.O. Type of 1953

1954, Feb.   **Photo.**   **Perf. 12½**

C587	A96	5c orange	.25	.25
C588	A96	30c red brown	1.25	1.25
C589	A96	60c bright red	1.25	2.00
Nos. C587-C589 (3)			2.75	3.50
Set, never hinged			7.00	

Valencia Arms Type of 1955

1955, Mar. 26   **Engr.**   **Perf. 12**

C590	A97	5c blue green	.25	.25
C591	A97	10c rose pink	.25	.25
C592	A97	20c ultra	.25	.25
C593	A97	25c gray	.25	.25
C594	A97	40c violet	.35	.25
C595	A97	50c vermilion	.35	.25
C596	A97	60c olive green	.50	.25
Nos. C590-C596 (7)			2.20	1.75
Set, never hinged			6.00	

P.O. Type of 1953 Inscribed: "Republica de Venezuela"

1955   **Photo.**   **Perf. 12½**

C597	A96a	5c orange	.25	.25
C598	A96a	10c olive brn	.25	.25
C599	A96a	15c deep plum	.25	.25
C600	A96a	20c slate	.25	.25
C601	A96a	30c red brn	.25	.25
C602	A96a	40c plum	.75	.40
C603	A96a	45c rose violet	.75	.60
C604	A96a	70c dk slate grn	1.75	1.25
C605	A96a	75c deep ultra	1.00	.75
C606	A96a	90c brown org	.75	.40
Nos. C597-C606 (10)			6.25	4.65
Set, never hinged			9.50	

Caracas Arms Type of 1955

1955, Dec. 9   **Unwmk.**   **Perf. 11½**

C607	A98	5c yellow org	.60	.25
C608	A98	15c claret brn	.60	.25
C609	A98	25c violet blk	.60	.25
C610	A98	40c red	1.75	.25
C611	A98	50c red orange	1.75	.25
C612	A98	60c car rose	1.75	1.25
Nos. C607-C612 (6)			7.05	2.50
Set, never hinged			16.00	

University Hospital, Caracas AP43

5c, 10c, 15c, 70c, O'Leary School, Barinas. 25c, 30c, 80c, University Hospital, Caracas. 40c, 45c, 50c, 1b, Caracas-La Guaira Highway. 60c, 65c, 75c, 2b, Towers of Simon Bolivar Center.

1956-57   **Unwmk.**   **Perf. 11½**

C613	AP43	5c orange	1.00	.25
C614	AP43	10c sepia	1.00	.25
C615	AP43	15c claret brown	1.00	.25
C616	AP43	20c dark blue	1.00	.25
C617	AP43	25c gray black	1.00	.25
C618	AP43	30c henna brown	1.50	.25
C619	AP43	40c bright crimson	1.50	.30
C620	AP43	45c brown violet	1.50	.30
C621	AP43	50c deep orange	1.50	.30
C622	AP43	60c olive green	1.50	.30
C623	AP43	65c bright blue	2.50	.30
C624	AP43	70c blue green	2.50	.30
C625	AP43	75c ultra	2.50	.45
C626	AP43	80c carmine rose	2.50	.30
C627	AP43	1b plum	2.50	.30
C628	AP43	2b dark car rose	2.50	.95
Nos. C613-C628 (16)			27.50	5.25
Set, never hinged			42.50	

Issued: 20c, 40c, 45c, 50c, 1b, 11/5/56; others, 1957.

Book and Flags of American Nations — AP44

1956-57   **Granite Paper**

C629	AP44	5c orange & brn	.35	.25
C630	AP44	10c brn & pale brn	.35	.25
C631	AP44	20c blue & sapphire	.35	.25
C632	AP44	25c gray vio & gray	.35	.25
C633	AP44	40c rose red & pale		
		pur	.35	.25
C634	AP44	45c vio brn & gray		
		brn	.35	.25
C635	AP44	60c olive & gray ol	.85	.80
Nos. C629-C635 (7)			2.95	2.30
Set, never hinged			17.50	

Book Festival of the Americas, 11/15-30/56. Issued: 5c, 40c, 11/15; others, 2/7/57.

Bolivar Type of 1957-58
Engraved; Center Embossed

1957-58   **Unwmk.**   **Perf. 13½**

C636	A100	5c orange	.25	.25
C637	A100	10c olive gray	.25	.25
C638	A100	20c blue	.35	.25
C639	A100	25c gray black	.40	.25
C640	A100	40c rose red	.35	.25
C641	A100	45c rose lilac	.40	.25
C642	A100	65c yellow brn	.75	.45
Nos. C636-C642 (7)			2.75	1.95
Set, never hinged			6.00	

Issued: 45c, 1958; others, Nov. 15, 1957.

Tamanaco Hotel Type of 1957-58

1957-58   **Engr.**   **Perf. 13**

C643	A101	5c dull yellow	.25	.25
C644	A101	10c brown	.25	.25
C645	A101	15c chocolate	.25	.25
C646	A101	20c gray blue	.25	.25
C647	A101	25c sepia	.25	.25
C648	A101	30c violet bl	.25	.25
C649	A101	40c car rose	.25	.25
C650	A101	45c claret	.25	.25
C651	A101	50c red org	.25	.25
C652	A101	60c yellow grn	.25	.25
C653	A101	65c orange brn	1.10	.90
C654	A101	70c slate	.60	.45
C655	A101	75c grnsh blue	.65	.55
C656	A101	1b dk claret	.65	.55
C657	A101	2b dk gray	1.10	.70
Nos. C643-C657 (15)			6.60	5.65
Set, never hinged			13.00	

Issue dates: 5c, 10c, Oct. 10; others, 1958. For surcharge see No. C878.

Post Office Type of 1958

1958, May 14   **Litho.**   **Perf. 14**

C658	A102	5c dp yellow	.25	.25
C659	A102	10c brown	.25	.25
C660	A102	15c red brn	.25	.25
C661	A102	20c lt blue	.25	.25
C662	A102	25c lt gray	.25	.25

C663	A102	30c lt ultra	.25	.25
C664	A102	40c brt yel grn	.25	.25
C665	A102	50c red orange	.25	.25
C666	A102	60c rose pink	.25	.25
C667	A102	65c red	.25	.25
C668	A102	90c violet	.40	.25
C669	A102	1b lilac	.50	.25
C670	A102	1.20b bister brn	6.50	6.00
		Nos. C658–C670 (13)	9.90	9.00
		Set, never hinged	23.00	

See Nos. C786–C792. For surcharges see Nos. C856–C861.

Post Office Type of 1958
Coil Stamps

1958		**Engr.**	**Perf. 11½x12**	
C671	A103	5c deep yellow	.25	.25
C672	A103	10c brown	.25	.25
C673	A103	15c dark brown	.35	.25
		Nos. C671–C673 (3)	.85	.75
		Set, never hinged	1.25	

Merida Type of 1958

1958, Oct. 9		**Photo.**	**Perf. 13½**	
C674	A104	5c orange yellow	.25	.25
C675	A104	10c gray brown	.25	.25
C676	A104	15c dull red brn	.25	.25
C677	A104	20c chalky blue	.25	.25
C678	A104	25c brown gray	.25	.25
C679	A104	30c violet bl	.25	.25
C680	A104	40c rose car	.25	.25
C681	A104	50c brt lilac	.35	.25
C682	A104	50c red orange	.35	.25
C683	A104	60c lt olive grn	.25	.25
C684	A104	65c hennna brn	.85	.75
C685	A104	70c gray black	.50	.50
C686	A104	75c brt grnsh bl	1.00	1.20
C687	A104	80c brt vio bl	.60	.55
C688	A104	90c blue green	.60	.60
C689	A104	1b lilac	.75	.75
		Nos. C674–C689 (16)	6.90	6.85
		Set, never hinged	13.00	

Trujillo Type of 1959

1958, Nov. 17		**Photo.**	**Perf. 14**	
C690	A105	5c orange yel	.25	.25
C691	A105	10c lt brown	.25	.25
C692	A105	15c redsh brown	.25	.25
C693	A105	20c lt blue	.25	.25
C694	A105	25c pale gray	.25	.25
C695	A105	30c lt vio blue	.25	.25
C696	A105	40c brt yel grn	.35	.25
C697	A105	50c red orange	.35	.25
C698	A105	60c lilac rose	.50	.35
C699	A105	65c vermilion	1.50	1.25
C700	A105	1b lilac	1.00	.65
		Nos. C690–C700 (11)	5.20	4.25
		Set, never hinged	10.00	

Emblem — AP45

1959, Mar. 10		**Litho.**	**Perf. 13½**	
C701	AP45	5c yellow	.25	.25
C702	AP45	10c red brown	.25	.25
C703	AP45	15c orange	.25	.25
C704	AP45	30c gray	.50	.45
C705	AP45	50c green	.75	.55
		Nos. C701–C705 (5)	2.00	1.75
		Set, never hinged	3.75	

8th Central American and Caribbean Games, Caracas, Nov. 29-Dec. 14, 1958. Exist imperf. Value, pair $25.

Stamp Centenary Type of 1959

Stamp of 1859 and: 25c, Mailman and José Ignacio Paz Castillo. 50c, Mailman on horseback and Jacinto Gutierrez. 1b, Plane, train and Miguel Herrera.

1959, Sept. 15		**Engr.**	**Perf. 13½**	
C706	A107	25c orange yel	.30	.25
C707	A107	50c blue	.45	.25
C708	A107	1b rose red	.90	.45
		Nos. C706–C708 (3)	1.65	.95
		Set, never hinged	6.00	

Catalogue values for unused stamps in this section, from this point to the end of the section, are for Never Hinged items.

Alexander von Humboldt Type of 1960

1960, Feb. 9			**Unwmk.**	
C709	A108	5c ocher & brn	.45	.25
C710	A108	20c brt bl & turq bl	1.40	.45
C711	A108	40c ol & ol grn	2.00	.50
		Nos. C709–C711 (3)	3.85	1.00

Newspaper Type of 1960

1960, June 11		**Litho.**	**Perf. 14**	
C712	A109	5c yellow & blk	2.75	1.10
C713	A109	15c lt red brn & blk	1.40	.40
C714	A109	65c salmon & blk	2.10	.75
		Nos. C712–C714 (3)	6.25	2.25

Agustin Codazzi Type of 1960

1960, June 15			**Engr.**	
C715	A110	5c yel org & brn	.25	.25
C716	A110	10c brn & dk brn	.40	.25
C717	A110	25c gray & blk	.55	.25
C718	A110	30c vio bl & sl	1.25	.25
C719	A110	50c org brn & brn	2.00	.50
C720	A110	70c gray ol & ol gray	3.25	.95
		Nos. C715–C720 (6)	7.70	2.45

For surcharge see No. C884.

National Pantheon Type of 1960

1960, May 9			**Litho.**	
		Pantheon in Bister		
C721	A111	5c dp bister	.25	.25
C722	A111	10c red brown	.25	.25
C723	A111	15c fawn	.40	.25
C724	A111	20c lt brown	.55	.25
C725	A111	25c gray	3.25	.40
C726	A111	30c lt vio bl	3.25	.65
C727	A111	40c brt yel grn	.55	.25
C728	A111	45c lt violet	.85	.25
C729	A111	60c deep pink	1.20	.45
C730	A111	65c salmon	1.20	.45
C731	A111	70c gray	1.75	.65
C732	A111	75c chalky blue	4.75	1.20
C733	A111	80c lt ultra	2.40	.95
C734	A111	1.20b bister brn	2.75	1.25
		Nos. C721–C734 (14)	23.40	7.50

For surcharges see Nos. C894–C895.

Andres Eloy Blanco Type of 1960

1960, May 21			**Perf. 14**	
		Portrait in Black		
C735	A112	20c blue	.50	.25
C736	A112	75c grnsh blue	1.75	.40
C737	A112	90c brt violet	1.60	.40
		Nos. C735–C737 (3)	3.85	1.05

For surcharge see No. C874.

Independence Type of 1960

1960, Aug. 19		**Litho.**	**Perf. 13½**	
		Center Multicolored		
C738	A113	50c orange	.80	.40
C739	A113	75c brt grnsh blue	2.00	.65
C740	A113	90c purple	1.60	.75
		Nos. C738–C740 (3)	4.40	1.80

Oil Refinery AP46

1960, Aug. 26		**Engr.**	**Perf. 14**	
		Unwmk.		
C741	AP46	30c dk bl & sl bl	1.40	.40
C742	AP46	40c yel grn & ol	1.60	.45
C743	AP46	50c org & red brn	1.75	.60
		Nos. C741–C743 (3)	4.75	1.45

Issued to publicize Venezuela's oil industry.

Luisa Cáceres de Arismendi Type of 1960

1960, Oct. 21		**Litho.**	**Perf. 14**	
		Center Multicolored		
C744	A115	5c bister	1.10	.40
C745	A115	10c redsh brown	1.50	.65
C746	A115	60c rose carmine	2.75	.80
		Nos. C744–C746 (3)	5.35	1.85

José Antonio Anzoategui Type of 1960

1960, Oct. 29			**Engr.**	
C747	A116	25c gray & brown	.75	.25
C748	A116	40c yel grn & ol gray	1.25	.35
C749	A116	45c rose cl & dl pur	1.25	.45
		Nos. C747–C749 (3)	3.25	1.05

Antonio José de Sucre Type of 1960

1960, Nov. 18		**Litho.**	**Perf. 14**	
		Unwmk.		
		Center Multicolored		
C750	A117	25c gray	1.00	.40
C751	A117	30c violet blue	1.40	.55
C752	A117	50c brown orange	1.75	.75
		Nos. C750–C752 (3)	4.15	1.70

Type of Regular Issue, 1960

Designs: 30c, Bolivar Peak. 50c, Caroni Falls. 65c, Guacharo caves.

1960, Mar. 22			**Perf. 14**	
C753	A118	30c vio bl & blk bl	2.75	2.75
C754	A118	50c brn org & brn	2.75	2.75
C755	A118	65c red org & red brn	2.75	2.75
		Nos. C753–C755 (3)	8.25	8.25

Cow's Head, Grain, Man and Child — AP47

1961, Feb. 6		**Litho.**	**Unwmk.**	
		Cow and Inscription in Black		
C756	AP47	5c yellow	.25	.25
C757	AP47	10c brown	.25	.25
C758	AP47	15c redsh brn	.25	.25
C759	AP47	20c dull blue	.25	.25
C760	AP47	25c gray	.25	.25
C761	AP47	30c violet bl	.25	.25
C762	AP47	40c yellow grn	.45	.25
C763	AP47	45c lilac	.45	.25
C764	AP47	50c orange	.45	.25
C765	AP47	60c cerise	.65	.25
C766	AP47	65c red orange	.80	.40
C767	AP47	70c gray	1.20	.55
C768	AP47	75c brt grnsh bl	1.00	.45
C769	AP47	80c brt violet	1.20	.40
C770	AP47	90c violet	1.60	.80
		Nos. C756–C770 (15)	9.30	5.10

9th general census & 3rd agricultural census. Issued: 5-15c, 30c, 60-65c, 75-80c, 2/6; others, 4/6.
For surcharges see Nos. C865–C866.

Rafael Maria Baralt Type of 1961

1961, Mar. 11		**Engr.**	**Perf. 14**	
C771	A120	25c gray & sepia	.80	.40
C772	A120	30c dk blue & vio	.90	.45
C773	A120	40c yel grn & ol grn	1.25	.55
		Nos. C771–C773 (3)	2.95	1.40

Arms of San Cristobal — AP48

1961, Apr. 10			**Litho.**	
		Arms in Original Colors		
C774	AP48	5c orange & blk	.25	.25
C775	AP48	55c yel grn & blk	.85	.30

400th anniversary of San Cristobal.
For surcharge see No. C879.

Bird Type of 1961

Birds: 5c, Troupial. 10c, Golden cock of the rock. 15c, Tropical mockingbird.

1961, Sept. 6		**Unwmk.**	**Perf. 14½**	
C776	A121	5c multicolored	1.60	1.10
C777	A121	10c multicolored	.80	.60
C778	A121	15c multicolored	1.00	.65
		Nos. C776–C778 (3)	3.40	2.35

Charge, Battle of Carabobo — AP49

1961, Dec. 1		**Litho.**	**Perf. 14**	
		Center Multicolored		
C779	AP49	50c black & ultra	.75	.25
C780	AP49	1.05b black & org	1.75	.50
C781	AP49	1.50b blk & lil rose	2.00	.50
C782	AP49	1.90b black & lilac	2.50	1.00
C783	AP49	2b black & gray	3.25	1.00
C784	AP49	3b black & grnsh bl	4.00	1.25
		Nos. C779–C784 (6)	14.25	4.50

140th anniversary of Battle of Carabobo. For surcharges see Nos. C867–C870.

Arms of Cardinal Quintero AP50

1962, Mar. 1			**Unwmk.**	
C785	AP50	5c lilac rose	.50	.25
a.		Souv. sheet of 1, imperf.	4.00	3.50

1st Venezuelan Cardinal, José Humberto Quintero.
No. C785a, issued Mar. 23, sold for 1b.

Post Office Type of 1958

1962, Apr. 12		**Litho.**	**Perf. 13½x11**	
C786	A102	35c citron	.25	.25
C787	A102	55c gray olive	.45	.25
C788	A102	70c bluish green	.75	.30
C789	A102	75c brown orange	.90	.25
C790	A102	80c fawn	.90	.35
C791	A102	85c deep rose	1.40	.50
C792	A102	95c lilac rose	.95	.45
		Nos. C786–C792 (7)	5.60	2.35

For surcharges see Nos. C856–C861.

Archbishop Rafael Arias Blanco — AP51

1962, May 10			**Perf. 10½**	
C793	AP51	75c red lilac	.80	.30

4th anniversary (in 1961) of the anti-communist pastoral letter of the Archbishop of Caracas, Rafael Arias Blanco.

Orchid Type of 1962

Orchids: 5c, Oncidium volvox. 20c, Cycnoches chlorochilon. 25c, Cattleya Gaskelliana. 30c, Epidendrum difforme, horiz. 40c, Catasetum callosum Lindl, horiz. 50c, Oncidium bicolor Lindl, horiz. 1b, Brassavola nodosa Lindl, horiz. 1.05b, Epidendrum lividum Lindl. 1.50b, Schomburgkia undulata Lindl. 2b, Oncidium zebrinum.

Perf. 14x13½, 13½x14				
1962, May 30		**Litho.**	**Unwmk.**	
		Orchids in Natural Colors		
C794	A124	5c blk & lt grn	.25	.25
C795	A124	20c black	.25	.25
C796	A124	25c black & fawn	.60	.25
C797	A124	30c black & pink	.25	.25
C798	A124	40c black & yel	.60	.25
C799	A124	50c black & lil	.95	.40
C800	A124	1b blk & pale rose	1.25	.60
C801	A124	1.05b blk & dp org	4.75	2.00
C802	A124	1.50b blk & pale vio	4.50	2.25
C803	A124	2b blk & org brn	5.00	2.75
		Nos. C794–C803 (10)	18.70	9.25

For surcharges see Nos. C885–C887.

Independence Type of 1960

Signing Declaration of Independence.

1962, June 11			**Perf. 13½**	
		Center Multicolored		
C804	A113	55c olive	.65	.25
C805	A113	1.05b brt rose	2.10	.85
C806	A113	1.50b purple	1.75	.80
a.		Souv. sheet of 3, #C804-C806, imperf.	5.00	5.00
		Nos. C804–C806 (3)	4.50	1.90

No. C806a, issued Oct. 13, sold for 4.10b.
A buff cardboard folder exists with impressions of Nos. 812-814, C804-C806. Perforation is simulated. Sold for 6.60b. Value $10.
For surcharge see No. C893.

No. 710 Srchd. in Rose Carmine "BICENTENARIO DE UPATA 1762-1962 RESELLADO AEREO VALOR Bs. 2,00"

1962, July 7 — *Perf. 13½x14*

C807 A102 2b on 1b lt ol grn — 2.50 1.20

Upata, a village in the state of Bolivar, 200th anniv.

National Games Type of 1962
Perf. 13x14

1962, Nov. 30 — Unwmk. — Litho.

C808	A125	40c Bicycling	.50	.30
C809	A125	75c Baseball	.95	.40
C810	A125	85c Woman athlete	2.00	.95
a.		Souv. sheet of 3, #C808-C810 imperf.	4.50	4.50
		Nos. C808-C810 (3)	3.45	1.65

See note after No. 817.
No. C810a sold for 3b.
For surcharge see No. C899.

Bird Type of 1962

Birds: 5c, American kestrel. 20c, Black-bellied tree duck, horiz. 25c, Amazon kingfisher. 30c, Rufous-tailed chachalaca. 50c, Black-and-yellow troupial. 55c, White-naped night-jar. 2.30b, Red-crowned woodpecker. 2.50b, Black-moustached quail-dove.

1962, Dec. 14 — Perf. 14x13½, 13½x14
Birds in Natural Colors;
Black Inscription

C811	A126	5c car rose	.25	.25
C812	A126	20c brt blue	.60	.25
C813	A126	25c lt gray	.70	.25
C814	A126	30c lt olive	.80	.30
C815	A126	50c violet	1.25	.45
C816	A126	55c dp orange	2.10	.80
C817	A126	2.30b dl red brn	6.00	3.50
C818	A126	2.50b orange yel	6.00	4.00
		Nos. C811-C818 (8)	17.70	9.80

For surcharges see Nos. C880-C882.

Malaria Eradication Emblem, Mosquito and Map — AP52

Lithographed and Embossed
Perf. 13½x14

1962, Dec. 20 — Wmk. 346

C819	AP52	30c green & blk	.75	.35
a.		Souv. sheet of 2, #825, C819, imperf.	4.00	4.00

WHO drive to eradicate malaria. No. C819a sold for 2b.

Animal Type of Regular Issue

5c, Spectacle bear, vert. 40c, Paca. 50c, Three-toed sloths. 55c, Great anteater. 1.50b, South American tapirs. 2b, Jaguar.

Multicolored Center; Black Inscriptions
Perf. 14x13½, 13½x14

1963, Mar. 13 — Litho. — Unwmk.

C820	A128	5c yellow	.25	.25
C821	A128	40c brt green	.80	.25
C822	A128	50c lt violet	1.10	.40
C823	A128	55c brown olive	1.40	.45
C824	A128	1.50b gray	4.00	2.00
C825	A128	2b ultra	6.75	3.25
		Nos. C820-C825 (6)	14.30	6.60

For surcharges see Nos. C888-C889.

Freedom from Hunger Type of 1963

40c, Map, shepherd. 75c, Map, farmer.

1963, Mar. 21

C826	A129	40c lt yel grn & dl red	.65	.40
C827	A129	75c yellow & brown	.90	.65

Arms of Bocono — AP53

1963, May 30 — Wmk. 346

C828 AP53 1b multicolored — 2.00 .65

400th anniversary of the founding of Bocono. For surcharge see No. C892.

Papal and Venezuelan Arms AP54

1963, June 11 — Perf. 14x13½
Arms Multicolored

C829	AP54	80c light green	1.25	.35
C830	AP54	90c gray	1.25	.50

Vatican II, the 21st Ecumenical Council of the Roman Catholic Church.
For surcharges see Nos. C871-C872.

Arms of Venezuela — AP55

1963, July 29 — Unwmk. — Perf. 14

C831 AP55 70c gray, red, yel & bl — 1.25 .50

Cent. of Venezuela's flag and coat of arms. For surcharge see No. C883.

Lake Maracaibo Bridge AP56

Wmk. 346
1963, Aug. 24 — Litho. — Perf. 14

C832	AP56	90c grn, brn & ocher	1.50	.50
C833	AP56	95c blue, brn & och	1.50	.60
C834	AP56	1b ultra, brn & och	1.25	.50
		Nos. C832-C834 (3)	4.25	1.60

Opening of bridge over Lake Maracaibo. For surcharges see Nos. C897-C898.

Armed Forces Type of 1963

1963, Sept. 10 — Unwmk.

C835 A134 1b red & bl, *buff* — 2.00 1.00

For surcharge see No. C862.

Hammarskjold Type of 1963

1963, Sept. 25 — Unwmk. — Perf. 14

C836	A135	80c dk bl, lt ultra & ocher	1.25	.50
C837	A135	90c dk bl, bl & ocher	1.75	.70
a.		Souv. sheet of 4, #841-842, C836-C837, imperf.	5.25	5.25

No. C837a sold for 3b.
For surcharges see Nos. C875-C876.

Dr. Luis Razetti, Physician, Birth Cent. — AP57

1963, Oct. 10 — Engr.

C838	AP57	95c dk blue & mag	1.50	.90
C839	AP57	1.05b dk brn & grn	1.50	1.00

For surcharges see Nos. C890-C891.

Red Cross Type of 1963

Designs: 40c, Sir Vincent K. Barrington. 75c, Red Cross nurse and child.

1963, Dec. 31 — Litho. — Perf. 11½x12

C840	A137	40c multicolored	.55	.40
C841	A137	75c multicolored	.95	.60

Development Type of 1964

Designs: 5c, Loading cargo. 10c, Tractor and corn. 15c, Oil field workers. 20c, Oil refinery. 50c, Crane and building construction.

1964, Feb. 5 — Unwmk. — Perf. 14x13½

C842	A138	5c multicolored	.25	.25
C843	A138	10c multicolored	.25	.25
C844	A138	15c multicolored	.25	.25
C845	A138	20c multicolored	.25	.25
C846	A138	50c multicolored	.65	.40
		Nos. C842-C846 (5)	1.65	1.40

Cent. of the Dept. of Industrial Development and to publicize the Natl. Industrial Expo.

Pedro Gual Type of 1964

1964, Mar. 20 — Perf. 14x13½

C847	A139	75c dull blue green	.85	.40
C848	A139	1b bright pink	1.25	.45

Blast Furnace and Map of Venezuela AP58

1964, May 22 — Litho. — Perf. 13½x14

C849	AP58	80c multi	1.25	.45
C850	AP58	1b multi	1.75	.65

Issued to publicize the Orinoco steel mills.

Arms of Ciudad Bolivar — AP59

1964, May 22 — Perf. 10½

C851 AP59 1b multi — 1.75 1.00

Bicentenary of Ciudad Bolivar.

AP60

1964, Aug. 3 — Unwmk. — Perf. 11½

C852	AP60	30c bister brn & yel	.45	.25
C853	AP60	40c plum & pink	.70	.25
C854	AP60	50c brn & tan	1.00	.40
		Nos. C852-C854 (3)	2.15	.90

80th birthday of novelist Romulo Gallegos.

AP61

1964, Nov. 11 — Litho. — Perf. 14x13½

C855 AP61 1b orange & dk vio — 1.50 .65

Eleanor Roosevelt and 15th anniv. (in 1963) of the Universal Declaration of Human Rights. For surcharge see No. C896.

Issues of 1947-64 Srchd. in Black, Dark Blue, Red, Carmine or Lilac with New Value and "RESELLADO / VALOR"

1965

C856	A102	5c on 55c (#C787)	.55	.25
C857	A102	5c on 70c (#C788)	.55	.25
C858	A102	5c on 80c (#C790)	.55	.25
C859	A102	5c on 85c (#C791)	.55	.25
C860	A102	5c on 90c (#C668)	.55	.25
C861	A102	5c on 95c (#C792)	.55	.25
C862	A134	5c on 1b (#C835)	.75	.25
C863	AP25	10c on 3b (#C269) (C)	.55	.25
C864	AP25	10c on 4b (#C270) (C)	.95	.25
C865	AP47	10c on 70c (#C767) (C)	.60	.25
C866	AP47	10c on 90c (#C770) (C)	.55	.25
C867	AP49	10c on 1.05b (#C780)	.80	.25
C868	AP49	10c on 1.90b (#C782)	.55	.25
C869	AP49	10c on 2b (#C783)	.60	.25
C870	AP49	10c on 3b (#C784)	.60	.25
C871	AP54	10c on 80c (#C829)	.55	.25
C872	AP54	10c on 90c (#C830)	.55	.25
C873	AP16	15c on 3b (#C253)	.60	.25
C874	A112	15c on 90c (#C737)	.55	.25
C875	A135	15c on 80c (#C836)	.55	.25
C876	A135	15c on 90c (#C837)	.55	.25
C877	AP59	15c on 1b (#C851)	.60	.25
C878	A101	20c on 2b (#C657) (R)	.75	.25
C879	AP48	20c on 55c (#C775) (DB)	.60	.25
C880	A126	20c on 55c (#C816)	.80	.25
a.		25c on 55c (#C816)		
C881	A126	20c on 2.30b (#C817)	.60	.25
C882	A126	20c on 2.50b (#C818)	.80	.25
C883	AP55	20c on 70c (#C831)	.80	.25
C884	A110	25c on 70c (#C720) (DB)	.85	.25
C885	A124	25c on 1.05b (#C801) (L)	.60	.25
C886	A124	25c on 1.50b (#C802) (L)	.60	.25
C887	A124	25c on 2b (#C803) (L)	.80	.25
C888	A128	25c on 1.50b (#C824)	.80	.25
C889	A128	25c on 2b (#C825)	.80	.25
C890	AP57	25c on 95c (#C838)	.75	.25
C891	AP57	25c on 1.05b (#C839)	.80	.25
C892	AP53	30c on 1b (#C828)	1.00	.25
C893	A113	40c on 1.05b (#C805) (DB)	.80	.25
C894	A111	50c on 65c (#C730) (DB)	.55	.25
C895	A111	50c on 1.20b (#C734) (DB)	1.00	.25
C896	AP61	50c on 1b (#C855)	.60	.25
C897	AP56	60c on 90c (#C832)	1.40	.40
C898	AP56	60c on 95c (#C833)	1.10	.25
C899	A125	75c on 85c (#C810)	1.25	.40
		Nos. C856-C899 (44)	31.25	11.30

Lines of surcharge arranged variously on Nos. C856-C899. Old denominations obliterated with bars on Nos. C862, C871-C873, C875-C877, C883, C885-C887, C889, C892, C896-C898. Vertical surcharge on Nos. C865-C866, C871-C872, C874, C878, C896.

Kennedy Type of 1965

1965, Aug. 20 Photo. *Perf. 12x11½*

C900	A144 60c lt grnsh bl	1.10	.40
C901	A144 80c red brn	1.25	.50

Medical Federation Emblem — AP62

1965, Aug. 24 Litho. *Perf. 13½x14*

C902	AP62 65c red org & blk	1.60	.75

20th anniversary of the founding of the Medical Federation of Venezuela.

Unisphere and Venezuela Pavilion AP63

1965, Aug. 31 *Perf. 14x13½*

C903	AP63 1b multi	1.25	.35

New York World's Fair, 1964-65.

Andrés Bello (1780?-1865), Educator and Writer — AP64

Perf. 14x13½
1965, Oct. 15 Litho. Unwmk.

C904	AP64 80c dk brn & org	1.50	.75

Map Type of 1965

Maps of Venezuela and Guiana: 25c, Map of Venezuela and Guiana by J. Cruz Cano, 1775. 40c, Map stamp of 1896 (No. 140). 75c, Map by the Ministry of the Exterior, 1965 (all horiz.).

1965, Nov. 5 *Perf. 13½*

C905	A145 25c multi	.45	.25
C906	A145 40c multi	.70	.25
C907	A145 75c multi	1.00	.40
a.	Souv. sheet of 3, #C905-C907, imperf.	14.00	14.00
	Nos. C905-C907 (3)	2.15	.90

#C907a, issued June 7, 1966, sold for 1.65b.

ITU Emblem and Telegraph Poles AP65

1965, Nov. 19 Litho. *Perf. 13½x14*

C908	AP65 75c blk & ol grn	1.00	.40

Cent. of the ITU.

Simon Bolivar and Quotation AP66

1965, Dec. 9 *Perf. 14x13½*

C909	AP66 75c lt bl & dk brn	1.00	.40

Sesquicentennial of Bolivar's Jamaica letter, Sept. 6, 1815.

Children Riding Magic Carpet and Three Kings on Camels — AP67

1965, Dec. 16 *Perf. 13½x14*

C910	AP67 70c yel & vio bl	1.50	.75

Children's Festival, 1965 (Christmas).

Fermin Toro — AP68

1965, Dec. 22 *Perf. 14x13½*

C911	AP68 1b blk & org	1.25	.55

Death centenary of Fermin Toro (1808-1865), statesman and writer.

Winston Churchill — AP69

1965, Dec. 29 *Perf. 14½x13*

C912	AP69 1b lilac & blk	1.50	.55

Sir Winston Spencer Churchill (1874-1965), statesman and World War II leader.

ICY Emblem, Arms of Venezuela and UN Emblem AP70

1965, Dec. 30 *Perf. 13½x14*

C913	AP70 85c gold & vio blk	1.50	.55

International Cooperation Year, 1965.

OAS Emblem and Map of America — AP71

1965, Dec. 31 *Perf. 14x13½*

C914	AP71 50c bl, blk & gold	1.25	.45

Organization of American States, 75th anniv.

Butterfly Type of 1966

1966, Jan. 25 Litho. *Perf. 13½x14*
Various Butterflies in Natural Colors; Black Inscriptions

C915	A146 65c lilac	1.75	.40
C916	A146 85c blue	2.50	.50
C917	A146 1b salmon pink	2.75	.60
	Nos. C915-C917 (3)	7.00	1.50

Farms of 1936 and 1966 — AP72

1966, Mar. 1 *Perf. 14x13½*

C918	AP72 55c blk, yel & emer	1.10	.40

30th anniversary of the Ministry for Agriculture and Husbandry.

Dance Type of 1966

Various folk dances.

1966, Apr. 5 Litho. *Perf. 14*

C919	A148 40c bl & multi	.85	.35
C920	A148 50c multi	1.00	.40
C921	A148 60c vio & multi	.70	.25
C922	A148 70c multi	1.60	.50
C923	A148 80c red & multi	1.75	.65
C924	A148 90c ocher & multi	1.90	.80
	Nos. C919-C924 (6)	7.80	2.95

Title Page "Popule Meus" AP73

1966, Apr. 15 *Perf. 13½x14*

C925	AP73 55c yel grn, blk & bis	.80	.45
C926	AP73 95c dp mag, blk & bis	1.00	.60

150th anniv. (in 1964) of the death of José Angel Lamas, composer of natl. anthem.

Circus Scene, by Michelena — AP74

Paintings by Michelena: 1b, Miranda in La Carraca. 1.05b, Charlotte Corday.

Perf. 12x12½
1966, May 12 Litho. Unwmk.

C927	AP74 95c multi	1.00	.75
C928	AP74 1b multi	1.25	.75
C929	AP74 1.05b multi	1.40	.75
	Nos. C927-C929 (3)	3.65	2.25

Cent. of the birth of Arturo Michelena (1863-1898), painter. Miniature sheets of 12 exist. See Nos. 900-901.

Abraham Lincoln — AP75

1966, May 31 *Perf. 13½x14*

C930	AP75 1b gray & blk	1.25	.75

Dr. José Gregorio Hernandez AP76

1966, July 29 Litho. *Perf. 14x13½*

C931	AP76 1b brt bl & vio bl	1.60	.65

Centenary (in 1964) of the birth of Dr. José Gregorio Hernandez, physician.

Dr. Manuel Dagnino and Hospital AP77

1966, Aug. 16 Litho. *Perf. 13½x14*

C932	AP77 1b sl grn & yel grn	1.50	.55

Founding of Chiquinquira Hospital, cent.

Fish Type of 1966

Fish: 75c, Pearl headstander, vert. 90c, Swordtail characine. 1b, Ramirez's dwarf cichlid.

Perf. 14x13½, 13½x14
1966, Aug. 31

C933	A151 75c multi	1.60	.50
C934	A151 90c grn & multi	1.60	.50
C935	A151 1b multi	1.60	.50
	Nos. C933-C935 (3)	4.80	1.50

Rafael Arevalo Gonzalez — AP78

1966, Sept. 13 Litho. *Perf. 13½x14*

C936	AP78 75c yel bis & blk	1.40	.55

Centenary of the birth of Rafael Arevalo Gonzalez, journalist.

Simon Bolivar, 1816 — AP79

Bolivar Portraits: 25c, 30c, 35c, by José Gil de Castro, 1825. 40c, 50c, 60c, Anonymous painter, 1825. 80c, 1.20b, 4b, Anonymous painter, c. 1829.

Imprint: "Bundesdruckerei Berlin 1966"

1966		**Multicolored Center**		
C937	AP79	5c lem & blk	.25	.25
C938	AP79	10c lt ol grn & blk	.25	.25
C939	AP79	20c grn & blk	.25	.25
C940	AP79	25c salmon & blk	.25	.25
C941	AP79	30c pink & blk	.25	.25
C942	AP79	35c dl rose & blk	.30	.25
C943	AP79	40c bis brn & blk	.25	.25
C944	AP79	50c org brn & blk	.45	.25
C945	AP79	60c brn red & blk	.45	.25
C946	AP79	80c brt bl & blk	.90	.35
C947	AP79	1.20b dl bl & blk	1.40	.65
C948	AP79	4b vio bl & blk	4.50	2.75
		Nos. C937-C948 (12)	9.50	6.00

Issued to honor Simon Bolivar.
Issue dates: Nos. C937-C939, Aug. 15; Nos. C940-C942, Sept. 29; others, Oct. 14.
See Nos. C961-C972.

"Justice" — AP80

1966, Nov. 3   Litho.   Perf. 14x13½
C949 AP80 50c pale lil & red lil   1.00 .40

50th anniversary of the Academy of Political and Social Sciences.

Angostura Bridge, Orinoco River — AP81

1967, Jan. 6   Litho.   Perf. 13½x14
C950 AP81 40c multi   .50 .25

Issued to commemorate the opening of the Angostura Bridge over the Orinoco River.

Pavilion of Venezuela AP82

1967, Apr. 28   Litho.   Perf. 11x13½
C951 AP82 1b multi   1.25 .40

EXPO '67, International Exhibition, Montreal, Apr. 28-Oct. 27, 1967.

Statue of Chief Guaicaipuro AP83

Constellations over Caracas, 1567 and 1967 — AP84

Designs: 45c, Captain Francisco Fajardo. 55c, Diego de Losada, the Founder. 65c, Arms of Caracas. 90c, Map of Caracas, 1578. 1b, Market on Plaza Mayor, 1800.

1967   Litho.   Perf. 14x13½, 13½x14
C952 AP83 15c multi   .25 .25
C953 AP83 45c gold, car & brn   .45 .25
C954 AP83 55c multi   .55 .25
C955 AP84 60c blk, ultra & sil   .60 .25
C956 AP83 65c multi   .80 .30
C957 AP84 90c multi   .95 .35
C958 AP84 1b multi   1.10 .45
    Nos. C952-C958 (7)   4.70 2.10

400th anniv. of the founding of Caracas (1st issue). See Nos. C977-C982 (2nd issue).
Two souvenir sheets each contain single stamps similar to Nos. C952-C953, but with simulated perforation. Sold for 1b each. Size: 80x119mm. Value $45 each.
Issued: 55c, 65c, July 28; others, July 12.

Gen. Francisco Esteban Gomez — AP85

1967, July 31   Litho.   Perf. 14x13½
C959 AP85 90c multi   1.25 .55

150th anniversary, Battle of Matasiete.

Juan Vicente González — AP86

1967, Oct. 18   Litho.   Perf. 14x13½
C960 AP86 80c ocher & blk   1.25 .40

Centenary of the death (in 1866) of Juan Vicente González, journalist.

Bolivar Type of 1966
Imprint: "Druck Bruder Rosenbaum. Wien"

1967-68   Litho.   Perf. 13½x14
Multicolored Center
C961 AP79   5c lemon & blk   .25 .25
C962 AP79 10c lemon & blk   .25 .25
C963 AP79 20c grn & blk   .35 .25
C964 AP79 25c salmon & blk   .30 .25
C965 AP79 30c pink & blk   .35 .25
C966 AP79 35c dl rose & blk   .35 .25
C967 AP79 40c bis brn & blk   .60 .25
C968 AP79 50c org brn & blk   4.75 .35
C969 AP79 60c brn red & blk   2.10 .90
C970 AP79 80c brt bl & blk   1.25 .50
C971 AP79 1.20b dl bl & blk   1.75 .35
C972 AP79   4b vio bl & blk   4.75 1.90
    Nos. C961-C972 (12)   17.05 5.75

Issue dates: 20c, 30c, 50c, Nov. 24; 5c, 25c, 40c, Feb. 5, 1968; others, Aug, 28, 1967.

Child with Pinwheel AP87

1967, Dec. 15   Litho.   Perf. 14x13½
C973 AP87 45c multi   .60 .25
C974 AP87 75c multi   .80 .30
C975 AP87 90c multi   1.00 .35
    Nos. C973-C975 (3)   2.40 .90

Children's Festival.

Madonna with the Rosebush, by Stephan Lochner AP88

1967, Dec. 19
C976 AP88 1b multi   1.60 .70

Christmas 1967.

Palace of the Academies, Caracas — AP89

Views of Caracas: 50c, St. Theresa's Church, vert. 70c, Federal Legislature. 75c, University City. 85c, El Pulpo highways crossing. 2b, Avenida Libertador.

1967, Dec. 28   Perf. 13½x14, 14x13½
C977 AP89 10c multi   .25 .25
C978 AP89 50c lil & multi   .35 .25
C979 AP89 70c multi   .65 .25
C980 AP89 75c multi   .75 .25
C981 AP89 85c multi   .80 .30
C982 AP89 2b multi   2.25 .85
    Nos. C977-C982 (6)   5.05 2.15

400th anniv. of Caracas (2nd issue).

Dr. José Manuel Nuñez Ponte (1870-1965), Educator — AP90

1968, Mar. 8   Litho.   Perf. 14
C983 AP90 65c multi   .75 .35

De Miranda and Printing Press AP91

Designs (Miranda Portraits and): 35c, Parliament, London. 45c, Arc de Triomphe, Paris. 70c, Portrait, vert. 80c, Portrait bust and Venezuelan flags, vert.

Perf. 13½x14, 14x13½
1968, June 20   Litho.
C984 AP91 20c yel brn, grn & brn   .35 .25
C985 AP91 35c multi   .55 .25
C986 AP91 45c lt bl & multi   1.00 .40
C987 AP91 70c multi   1.25 .35
C988 AP91 80c multi   1.50 .55
    Nos. C984-C988 (5)   4.65 1.80

General Francisco de Miranda (1750?-1816), revolutionist, dictator of Venezuela.

Insect Type of 1968
Insect Pests: 5c, Red leaf-cutting ant, vert. 15c, Sugar cane beetle, vert. 20c, Leaf beetle.

Perf. 14x13½, 13½x14
1968, Aug. 30   Litho.
C989 A157 5c multi   .50 .25
C990 A157 15c multi   1.00 .25
C991 A157 20c gray & multi   1.50 .25
    Nos. C989-C991 (3)   3.00 .75

Three Keys — AP92

1968, Oct. 17   Litho.   Perf. 14x13½
C992 AP92 95c yel, vio & dk grn   1.40 .50

Natl. Comptroller's Office, 30th anniv.

Fencing — AP93

Designs: 5c, Pistol shooting, vert. 15c, Running. 75c, Boxing. 5b, Sailing, vert.

Perf. 14x13½, 13½x14
1968, Nov. 6   Litho.   Unwmk.
C993 AP93 5c vio, bl & blk   .50 .30
C994 AP93 15c multi   .60 .30
C995 AP93 30c yel grn, dk grn & blk   .75 .30
C996 AP93 75c multi   1.40 .40
C997 AP93 5b multi   5.25 1.90
    Nos. C993-C997 (5)   8.50 3.20

19th Olympic Games, Mexico City, 10/12-27.

Holy Family, by Francisco José de Lerma — AP94

1968, Dec. 4   Litho.   Perf. 14x13½
C998 AP94 40c multi   .75 .25

Christmas 1968.

Dancing Children and Stars — AP95

1968, Dec. 13   Litho.   Perf. 14x13½
C999 AP95 80c vio & org   1.10 .50

Issued for the 5th Children's Festival.

Conservation Type of 1968
Designs: 15c, Marbled wood-quail, vert. 20c, Water birds, vert. 30c, Woodcarvings and tools, vert. 90c, Brown trout. 95c, Valley and road. 1b, Red-eyed vireo feeding young bronzed cowbird.

Perf. 13½x14, 14x13½
1968, Dec. 19   Litho.
C1000 A160 15c multi   .45 .35
C1001 A160 20c multi   .45 .35
C1002 A160 30c multi   .55 .35
C1003 A160 90c multi   1.50 .45
C1004 A160 95c multi   2.25 .65
C1005 A160 1b multi   1.60 .55
    Nos. C1000-C1005 (6)   6.80 2.70

Tourist Type of 1969
Designs: 15c, Giant cactus and desert, Falcon. 30c, Hotel Humboldt, Federal District. 40c, Cable car and mountain peaks, Merida.

1969, Jan. 24   Perf. 13½x14
C1006 A161 15c multi   .30 .25
C1007 A161 30c multi   .35 .25
    a.   Souv. sheet of 2, #931, C1007, imperf.   2.10 2.10
C1008 A161 40c multi   .60 .25
    Nos. C1006-C1008 (3)   1.25 .75

Tree Type of 1969
Trees: 5c, Cassia grandis. 20c, Trip/aris caracasana. 25c, Samanea saman.

1969, May 30   Litho.   Perf. 13½x14
C1009 A164 5c lt grn & multi   .50 .25
C1010 A164 20c org & multi   .75 .25
C1011 A164 25c lt vio & multi   .85 .25
    Nos. C1009-C1011 (3)   2.10 .75

Alexander von
Humboldt, by
Joseph
Stieler — AP96

1969, Sept. 12   Photo.   *Perf. 14*
C1012 AP96 50c multi   .80 .25
Alexander von Humboldt (1769-1859), naturalist and explorer.

Map of
Maracaibo,
1562 — AP97

20c, Ambrosio Alfinger, Alfonso Pacheco, Pedro Maldonado, horiz. 40c, Maracaibo coat of arms. 70c, University Hospital. 75c, Monument to the Indian Mara. 1b, Baralt Square, horiz.

Perf. 13½x13, 13x13½
1969, Sept. 30   Litho.
C1013 AP97 20c lil & multi   .35 .25
C1014 AP97 25c org & multi   .40 .25
C1015 AP97 40c multi   .45 .25
C1016 AP97 70c grn & multi   1.00 .35
C1017 AP97 75c brn & multi   1.25 .40
C1018 AP97 1b multi   1.40 .50
    Nos. C1013-C1018 (6)   4.85 2.00
400th anniversary of Maracaibo.

Astronauts
Neil A.
Armstrong,
Edwin E.
Aldrin, Jr.,
Michael
Collins and
Moonscape
AP98

1969, Nov. 18   Litho.   *Perf. 12½*
C1019 AP98 90c multi   1.60 .65
  a.   Souv. sheet of 1, imperf.   3.25 3.25
    See note after US No. C76.

Virgin with the
Rosary, 17th
Century
AP99

Christmas: 80c, Holy Family, Caracas, 18th Cent.

1969, Dec. 1   Litho.   *Perf. 12½*
C1020 AP99 75c gold & multi   .90 .35
C1021 AP99 80c gold & multi   1.10 .45
  a.   Pair, #C1020-C1021   2.40 2.40

Simon Bolivar,
1819, by M. N.
Bate — AP100

Bolivar Portraits: 45c, 55c, like 15c. 65c, 70c, 75c Drawing by Francois Roulin, 1828. 85c, 90c, 95c, Charcoal drawing by José Maria Espinoza, 1828. 1b, 1.50b, 2b, Drawing by Espinoza, 1830.

1970, Mar. 16   Litho.   *Perf. 14x13½*
C1022 AP100 15c multi   .25 .25
C1023 AP100 45c bl & multi   .45 .25
C1024 AP100 55c org & multi   .60 .25
C1025 AP100 65c multi   .60 .30
C1026 AP100 70c bl & multi   .70 .40
C1027 AP100 75c org & multi   .95 .40
C1028 AP100 85c multi   1.10 .40
C1029 AP100 90c bl & multi   1.10 .45
C1030 AP100 95c org & multi   1.25 .50
C1031 AP100 1b multi   1.25 .50
C1032 AP100 1.50b bl & multi   1.40 .55
C1033 AP100 2b multi   3.00 1.75
    Nos. C1022-C1033 (12)   12.65 6.00
Issued to honor Simon Bolivar (1783-1830), liberator and father of his country.

General
Antonio
Guzmán
Blanco and
Dr. Martin
J. Sanabria
AP101

1970, June 26   Litho.   *Perf. 13*
C1034 AP101 75c brt grn & multi   .80 .35
Free obligatory elementary education, cent.

Map of Venezuela with Claim to Part
of Guyana — AP102

State map and arms. 55c, 90c, vert.

Perf. 13½x14, 14x13½
1970-71   Litho.
C1035 AP102 5c shown   .35 .25
C1036 AP102 15c Apure   .35 .25
C1037 AP102 20c Aragua   .40 .25
C1038 AP102 20c Anzoategui   .45 .25
C1039 AP102 25c Barinas   .45 .25
C1040 AP102 25c Bolivar   .45 .25
C1041 AP102 45c Carabobo   .65 .25
C1042 AP102 55c Cojedes   .70 .25
C1043 AP102 65c Falcon   .75 .25
C1044 AP102 75c Guárico   .90 .25
C1045 AP102 85c Lara   1.10 .30
C1046 AP102 90c Mérida   1.10 .30
C1047 AP102 1b Miranda   1.10 .40
C1048 AP102 2b Delta
                Amacuro
                Territory   2.40 .95
    Nos. C1035-C1048 (14)   11.15 4.45

Issued: 5c, 7/15; 15c, #C1037, 1/18; #C1038-C1039, 2/15/71; #C1040, 45c, 3/15/71; 55c, 65c, 4/15; 75c, 85c, 5/15/71; 90c, 1b, 6/15/71; 2b, 7/15/71.

Flower Type of 1970

Flowers: 20c, Epidendrum secundum. 25c, Oyedaea verbesinoides. 45c, Heliconia villosa. 1b, Macleania nitida.

1970, July 29   Litho.   *Perf. 14x13½*
C1049 A175 20c multi   .50 .25
C1050 A175 25c multi   .60 .25
C1051 A175 45c multi   1.50 .35
C1052 A175 1b multi   1.90 .45
    Nos. C1049-C1052 (4)   4.50 1.30

Caracciolo
Parra Olmedo
AP104

1970, Nov. 16   Photo.   *Perf. 12½*
C1053 AP104 20c bl & multi   .30 .25
Sesquicentennial of birth of Caracciolo Parra Olmedo (1819-1900), professor of law, rector of University of Merida.

Census Chart — AP105

1971, Apr. 30   Litho.   *Perf. 13½x14*
C1054   Block of 4   5.00 2.50
  a.   AP105 70c, frame L & T   .90 .35
  b.   AP105 70c, frame T & R   .90 .35
  c.   AP105 70c, frame L & B   .90 .35
  d.   AP105 70c, frame B & R   .90 .35
    See note after No. 979.

Cattleya Gaskelliana — AP106

Orchids: 20c, Cattleya percivaliana, vert. 75c, Cattleya mossiae, vert. 90c, Cattleya violacea. 1b, Cattleya lawrenciana.

Perf. 14x13½, 13½x14
1971, Aug. 25
C1055 AP106 20c blk & multi   .55 .25
C1056 AP106 25c blk & multi   .80 .25
C1057 AP106 75c blk & multi   1.50 .50
C1058 AP106 90c blk & multi   2.10 .80
C1059 AP106 1b blk & multi   2.25 .90
    Nos. C1055-C1059 (5)   7.20 2.70
40th anniversary of Venezuelan Society of Natural History. Issued in sheets of 5 stamps and one label with Society emblem in blue. Value $37.50.

Draft of
Constitution
Superimposed
on Capitol
AP107

1971, Dec. 29   Litho.   *Perf. 13½*
C1060 AP107 90c multi   .80 .40
Anniversary of 1961 Constitution.

AIR POST SEMI-POSTAL STAMPS

King Vulture
SPAP1

Unwmk.
1942, Dec. 17   Engr.   *Perf. 12*
CB1 SPAP1 15c + 10c org brn   2.25 .60
CB2 SPAP1 30c + 5c violet   2.25 .75
    Set, never hinged   7.50
    See note after No. B1.

SPECIAL DELIVERY STAMPS

**Catalogue values for unused
stamps in this section are for
Never Hinged items.**

SD1

Perf. 12½
1949, Mar. 9   Unwmk.   Engr.
E1 SD1 30c red   .75 .30

SD2

Wmk. 116
1961, Apr. 7   Litho.   *Perf. 13½*
E2 SD2 30c orange   .76 .25

REGISTRATION STAMPS

Bolívar — R1

1899, May Unwmk. Engr. *Perf. 12*
F1 R1 25c yellow brown   3.25 2.75

No. F1 Overprinted

1900
F2 R1 25c yellow brown   2.00 2.00
  a.   Inverted overprint   32.50 32.50
  b.   Double overprint   40.00 40.00
Counterfeit overprints exist, especially of the varieties.

OFFICIAL STAMPS

Coat of Arms — O1

Lithographed, Center Engraved

1898, May 1	Unwmk.		Perf. 12	
O1	O1	5c bl grn & blk	.80	.55
O2	O1	10c rose & blk	.95	.85
O3	O1	25c bl & blk	1.50	1.40
O4	O1	50c yel & blk	2.50	2.25
O5	O1	1b vio & blk	2.75	2.50
	Nos. O1-O5 (5)		8.50	7.55

Nos. O4 and O5
Handstamp
Surcharged in
Magenta or Violet

1899, Nov.

O6	O1	5c on 50c yel & blk	4.75	4.50
O7	O1	5c on 1b vio & blk	20.00	18.00
O8	O1	25c on 50c yel & blk	20.00	18.00
O9	O1	25c on 1b vio & blk	12.00	11.00
	Nos. O6-O9 (4)		56.75	51.50

Inverted Surcharge

O6a	O1	5c on 50c	15.00	15.00
O7a	O1	5c on 1b	40.00	40.00
O8a	O1	25c on 50c	32.50	32.50
O9a	O1	25c on 1b	32.50	32.50
	Nos. O6a-O9a (4)		120.00	120.00

Nos. O6-O9 exist with double surcharge.
Value each $18.50-$37.50.
Many of the magenta overprints have become violet. There are intermediate shades.
Counterfeit overprints exist.

Coat of Arms — O3

1900 Litho., Center Engr.

O14	O3	5c bl grn & blk	.40	.40
O15	O3	10c rose & blk	.55	.55
O16	O3	25c bl & blk	.55	.55
O17	O3	50c yel & blk	.55	.55
O18	O3	1b dl vio & blk	.65	.65
	Nos. O14-O18 (5)		2.70	2.70

O4

Imprint: "American Bank Note Co., N.Y."

1904, July Engr.

O19	O4	5c emerald & blk	.25	.25
O20	O4	10c rose & blk	.65	.65
O21	O4	25c blue & blk	.65	.65
O22	O4	50c red brn & blk	4.25	4.25
a.		50c claret & black	4.25	4.25
O23	O4	1b red brn & blk	2.00	2.00
a.		1b claret & black	2.00	2.00
	Nos. O19-O23 (5)		7.80	7.80

No Stars Above
Shield — O5

1912 Lithographed in Caracas

O24	O5	5c grn & blk	.55	.30
O25	O5	10c car & blk	.55	.30
O26	O5	25c dk bl & blk	.55	.30
O27	O5	50c pur & blk	.55	.40
a.		Center double	19.00	
O28	O5	1b yel & blk	1.30	.80
	Nos. O24-O28 (5)		3.50	2.10

Perforated Initials

After 1925, Venezuela's official stamps consisted of regular postage stamps, some commemoratives and air post stamps of 1930-42 punched with "GN" (Gobierno Nacional) in large perforated initials.

LOCAL STAMPS FOR THE PORT OF CARUPANO

In 1902 Great Britain, Germany and Italy, seeking compensation for revolutionary damages, established a blockade of La Guaira and seized the custom house. Carúpano, a port near Trinidad, was isolated and issued the following provisionals. A treaty effected May 7, 1903, referred the dispute to the Hague Tribunal.

A1

A2

1902 Typeset Imperf.

1	A1	5c purple, orange	27.00	
2	A2	10c black, orange	40.00	
a.		Tête bêche pair	82.50	
3	A1	25c purple, green	32.50	
4	A1	50c green, yellow	85.00	
5	A1	1b blue, rose	120.00	
	Nos. 1-5 (5)		304.50	

A3

1902

6	A3	1b black, yellow	200.00	
a.		Tête bêche pair		

A4

1903 Handstamped

7	A4	5c carmine, yellow	45.00	45.00
8	A4	10c green, yellow	92.50	92.50
9	A4	25c green, orange	45.00	45.00
10	A4	50c blue, rose	45.00	45.00
11	A4	1b violet, gray	45.00	45.00
12	A4	2b carmine, green	45.00	45.00
13	A4	5b violet, blue	45.00	45.00
	Nos. 7-13 (7)		362.50	362.50

Dangerous counterfeits exist of Nos. 1-13.

LOCAL STAMPS FOR THE STATE OF GUAYANA

Revolutionary
Steamship
"Banrigh" — A1

Control Mark

Control Mark on Block of 4

1903 Typo. Perf. 12

1	A1	5c black, gray	19.00	19.00
2	A1	10c black, orange	47.50	47.50
3	A1	25c black, pink	19.00	19.00
4	A1	50c black, blue	30.00	30.00
5	A1	1b black, straw	25.00	25.00
	Nos. 1-5 (5)		140.50	140.50

Nos. 1-5 can be found with or without the illustrated control mark which covers four stamps.

Counterfeits include the 10c and 50c in red and are from different settings from the originals. They are on papers differing in colors from the originals. All 5c on granite paper are bogus.

Coat of
Arms
A2

1903

11	A2	5c black, pink	40.00	
12	A2	10c black, orange	50.00	
13	A2	25c black, gray blue	40.00	
a.		25c black, blue	40.00	
14	A2	50c black, straw	40.00	
15	A2	1b black, gray	30.00	
	Nos. 11-15 (5)		200.00	

Postally used examples are very scarce, as are examples having 9 ornaments in horizontal borders. Nos. 11-15 pen canceled sell for same values as unused.

See note on controls after No. 5.

Counterfeits exist of Nos. 11-15. Stamps with 10 ornaments in horizontal borders are counterfeits.

Nos. 1-5, 11-15 were issued by a group of revolutionists and had a limited local use. The dates on the stamps commemorate the declaration of Venezuelan independence and a compact with Spain against Joseph Bonaparte.

VIET NAM

vē-'et-'näm

LOCATION — In eastern Indo-China
GOVT. — Kingdom
AREA — 123,949 sq. mi.
POP. — 77,311,210 (1999 est.)
CAPITAL — Hanoi

Viet Nam, which included the former French territories of Tonkin, Annam and Cochin China, became an Associated State of the French Union in 1949. The Communist Viet Minh obtained control of Northern Viet Nam in 1954, and the republic of South Viet Nam was established in October, 1955.

100 Cents (Xu) = 1 Piaster (Dong)

Catalogue values for unused stamps in this country are for Never Hinged items, beginning with Scott 27 in the regular postage section, Scott B2 in the semipostal section, Scott C1 in the airpost section, Scott J1 in the postage due section, and Scott M1 in the military section.

Bongour
Falls,
Dalat — A1

Emperor Bao-
Dai — A2

Designs: 20c, 2pi, 10pi, Imperial palace, Hué. 30c, 15pi, Lake, Hanoi. 50c, 1pi, Temple, Saigon.

Perf. 13x13½, 13½x13
Unwmk.

1951, June 6-Oct. 23			Photo.	
1	A1	10c olive green	.25	.25
2	A1	20c deep plum	.50	.25
3	A1	30c blue	.50	.40
4	A1	50c red	1.00	.25
5	A1	60c brown	.50	.25
6	A1	1pi chestnut brn	.50	.25
7	A2	1.20pi yellow brn	3.50	2.00
8	A1	2pi purple	1.00	.25
9	A2	3pi dull blue	3.50	.25
10	A1	5pi green	2.75	.30
11	A1	10pi crimson	6.50	.35
12	A1	15pi red brown	22.50	2.50
13	A2	30pi blue green	50.00	3.00
	Nos. 1-13 (13)		93.00	10.30
	Set, never hinged		175.00	

Souvenir booklets exist comprising five gummed sheets of 1 containing Nos. 1, 2, 6, 9, 12, together with commemorative inscriptions. Value, $125.

Empress Nam-
Phuong — A3

1952, Aug. 15 Perf. 12½

14	A3	30c dk pur, yel & brn	.60	.35
15	A3	50c blue, yel & brn	.80	.45
16	A3	1.50pi ol grn, yel & brn	1.75	.30
	Nos. 14-16 (3)		3.15	1.10
	Set, never hinged		6.00	

For surcharge see No. B1.

Globe and Lightning Bolt — A4

1952, Aug. 24   Engr.   Perf. 13
17   A4   1pi greenish blue   2.00   1.25
　　　　Never hinged   6.00

Viet Nam's admission to the ITU, 1st anniv.

Coastal Scene and UPU Emblem — A5

1952, Sept. 12
18   A5   5pi red brown   1.75   1.50
　　　　Never hinged   3.50

Viet Nam's admission to the UPU, 1st anniv.

Bao-Dai and Pagoda of Literature, Hanoi — A6

1952, Nov. 10   Perf. 12
19   A6   1.50pi rose violet   1.75   1.25
　　　　Never hinged   3.50

39th birthday of Emperor Bao-Dai.

Crown Prince Bao-Long in Annamite Costume — A7

70c, 80c, 100pi, Prince in Annamite costume. 90c, 20pi, 50pi, Prince in Western uniform.

1954, June 15   Perf. 13
20   A7   40c aqua   .25   .40
21   A7   70c claret   .25   .40
22   A7   80c black brown   .25   .40
23   A7   90c dark green   .40   1.25
24   A7   20pi rose pink   1.25   2.25
25   A7   50pi violet   4.00   7.00
26   A7   100pi blue violet   6.00   17.50
　　　Nos. 20-26 (7)   12.40   29.20
Set, never hinged, brown gum   22.50
Set, never hinged, white gum   40.00

REPUBLIC OF VIET NAM

(South Viet Nam)

(Viet Nam Cong Hoa)

GOVT. — Republic
AREA — 66,280 sq. mi.
POP. — 19,600,000 (est. 1973)
CAPITAL — Saigon

Catalogue values for unused stamps in this section, from this point to the end of the section, are for Never Hinged items. Because of the tropical conditions, never hinged stamps must also be free of wrinkles, toning, and any other disturbance.

Mythological Turtle — A8

Unwmk.
1955, July 20   Engr.   Perf. 13
27   A8   30c claret   1.25   .50
28   A8   50c dark green   3.75   1.75
29   A8   1.50pi bright blue   3.00   1.25
　　　Nos. 27-29 (3)   8.00   3.50

Refugees on Raft — A9

1955, Oct. 11
30   A9   70c crimson rose   1.00   1.00
31   A9   80c brown violet   3.00   3.00
32   A9   1pi indigo   5.50   5.50
33   A9   20pi vio, red brn & org   16.00   16.00
34   A9   35pi dk bl, blk brn & yel   25.00   25.00
35   A9   100pi dk grn, brn vio & org   65.00   65.00
　　　Nos. 30-35 (6)   115.50   115.50

1st anniv. of the flight of the North Vietnamese.

No. 34 is inscribed "Chiên-Dich-Huynh-Dê" (Operation Brotherhood) below design. See No. 54.

Post Office, Saigon — A10

1956, Jan. 10   Perf. 12
36   A10   60c bluish green   1.25   1.00
37   A10   90c violet   2.25   1.25
38   A10   3pi red brown   4.50   2.50
　　　Nos. 36-38 (3)   8.00   4.75

5th anniv. of independent postal service.
For overprints see Nos. 51-53.

Pres. Ngo Dinh Diem — A11

1956   Engr.   Perf. 13x13½
39   A11   20c orange ver   .40   .25
40   A11   30c rose lilac   .75   .40
41   A11   50c brt carmine   .40   .40
42   A11   1pi violet   .75   .40
43   A11   1.50pi violet   1.10   .50
44   A11   3pi black brown   1.90   .60
45   A11   4pi dark blue   2.60   .70
46   A11   5pi red brown   3.00   .75
47   A11   10pi blue   3.75   1.25
48   A11   20pi gray black   7.50   2.25
49   A11   35pi green   18.00   4.00
50   A11   100pi brown   37.50   19.00
　　　Nos. 39-50 (12)   77.65   30.50

Nos. 36-38 Overprinted

1956, Aug. 6   Perf. 12
51   A10   60c bluish green   .90   .60
52   A10   90c violet   1.50   .60
53   A10   3pi red brown   2.00   .90
　　　Nos. 51-53 (3)   4.40   2.10

The overprint reads: "Government Post Office Building."

No. 34 Overprinted

1956, Aug. 6
54   A9   35pi dk bl, blk brn & yel   9.00   6.00

Bamboo — A12

1956, Oct. 26   Litho.   Perf. 13x13½
55   A12   50c scarlet   1.10   1.10
56   A12   1.50pi rose violet   1.10   1.10
57   A12   2pi brt green   1.50   1.50
58   A12   4pi deep blue   3.00   3.00
　　　Nos. 55-58 (4)   6.70   6.70

1st anniv. of the Republic.

Children — A13

1956, Nov. 7   Engr.   Perf. 13½x14
59   A13   1pi lilac rose   .60   .40
60   A13   2pi blue green   .85   .40
61   A13   6pi purple   1.25   .40
62   A13   35pi violet blue   8.50   2.75
　　　Nos. 59-62 (4)   11.20   3.95

"Operation Brotherhood."

Hunters on Elephants — A14

Design: 90c, 2pi, 3pi, Mountain dwelling.

1957, July 7   Photo.   Perf. 13
63   A14   20c yellow grn & pur   .75   .45
64   A14   30c bister & dp mag   .80   .55
65   A14   90c yel grn & dk brn   1.00   .65
66   A14   2pi green & ultra   1.75   .70
67   A14   3pi blue vio & brn   2.25   .80
　　　Nos. 63-67 (5)   6.55   3.15

Loading Cargo — A15

1957, Oct. 21   Perf. 13½x13
68   A15   20c rose violet   .25   .25
69   A15   40c lt olive grn   .30   .25
70   A15   50c lt carmine rose   .40   .40

71   A15   2pi ultra   1.10   .45
72   A15   3pi brt green   1.40   .55
　　　Nos. 68-72 (5)   3.45   1.90

9th Colombo Plan Conference, Saigon.

Torch, Map and Constitution — A16

1957, Oct. 26   Litho.   Perf. 13x13½
73   A16   50c black, green & sal   .25   .25
74   A16   80c black, brt bl & mag   .30   .25
75   A16   1pi black, bl grn & brt car   .40   .40
76   A16   4pi blk, ol grn & fawn   .75   .45
77   A16   5pi blk, grnsh bl & cit   .75   .55
78   A16   10pi black, ultra & rose   1.50   .75
　　　Nos. 73-78 (6)   3.95   2.65

Republic of South Viet Nam, 2nd anniv.

Farmers, Tractor and Village — A17

1958, July 7   Engr.   Perf. 13½
79   A17   50c yellow green   .35   .25
80   A17   1pi deep violet   .40   .25
81   A17   2pi ultra   .85   .45
82   A17   10pi brick red   2.25   .75
　　　Nos. 79-82 (4)   3.85   1.70

4th anniv. of the government of Ngo Dinh Diem.

Girl and Lantern — A18

1958, Sept. 27
83   A18   30c yellow   .30   .25
84   A18   50c dk carmine rose   .40   .25
85   A18   2pi dp carmine   .60   .40
86   A18   3pi blue green   1.00   .45
87   A18   4pi lt olive green   1.25   .50
　　　Nos. 83-87 (5)   3.55   1.85

Children's Festival.

A19

1958, Oct. 26   Perf. 13½
88   A19   1pi dull red brown   .40   .25
89   A19   2pi bluish green   .75   .25
90   A19   4pi rose carmine   1.00   .45
91   A19   5pi rose lilac   1.50   .75
　　　Nos. 88-91 (4)   3.65   1.70

Issued for United Nations Day.

Most South Viet Nam stamps from 1958 onward exist imperforate in issued and trial colors, and also in small presentation sheets in issued colors.

UNESCO
Building,
Paris — A20

1958, Nov. 3   **Perf. 12½x13**
92 A20 50c ultra   .45   .25
93 A20 2pi bright red   .75   .25
94 A20 3pi lilac rose   1.00   .40
95 A20 6pi violet   1.40   .60
    Nos. 92-95 (4)   3.60 1.50
   UNESCO Headquarters in Paris opening, 11/3.

Torch and UN
Emblem — A21

1958, Dec. 10   **Engr.**   **Perf. 13½**
96 A21 50c dark blue   .30   .25
97 A21 1pi brown carmine   .45   .25
98 A21 2pi yellow green   .65   .40
99 A21 6pi rose violet   1.10   .60
    Nos. 96-99 (4)   2.50 1.50
   Signing of the Universal Declaration of Human Rights, 10th anniv.

Cathedral of
Hué — A22

Thien Mu
Pagoda,
Hué — A23

National
Museum
A24

50c, 2pi, Palace of Independence, Saigon.

1958-59   **Perf. 13½**
100 A22 10c dk blue gray   .25   .40
101 A23 30c green ('59)   .40   .75
102 A24 40c dk green ('59)   .70   .65
103 A24 50c green ('59)   .80   .80
104 A24 2pi grnsh blue ('59)   2.00   1.75
105 A23 4pi dull purple ('59)   2.50   2.00
106 A23 5pi dk carmine ('59)   2.75   2.00
107 A22 6pi orange brown   3.25   2.00
    Nos. 100-107 (8)   12.65 10.35

Trung Sisters
on Elephants
A25

1959, Mar. 14   **Photo.**   **Perf. 13**
108 A25 50c multicolored   1.50   .75
109 A25 2pi ocher, grn & bl   2.25   1.20
110 A25 3pi emerald, vio & bis   2.75   1.50
111 A25 6pi multicolored   5.50   2.25
    Nos. 108-111 (4)   12.00 5.70
   Sisters Trung Trac and Trung Nhi who resisted a Chinese invasion in 40-44 A.D.

Symbols of
Agrarian
Reforms
A26

1959, July 7   **Engr.**   **Perf. 13**
112 A26 70c lilac rose   .35   .25
113 A26 2pi dk grn & Prus bl   .50   .25
114 A26 3pi olive   .90   .35
115 A26 6pi dark red & red   1.75   1.10
    Nos. 112-115 (4)   3.50 1.95
   5th anniv. of Ngo Dinh Diem's presidency.

Diesel Engine
and Map of North
and South Viet
Nam — A27

1959, Aug. 7
116 A27 1pi lt violet & grn   .75   .75
117 A27 2pi gray & green   1.40   1.10
118 A27 3pi grnsh bl & grn   2.10   1.50
119 A27 4pi maroon & grn   3.00   2.25
    Nos. 116-119 (4)   7.25 5.60
   Re-opening of the Saigon-Dongha Railroad.

Volunteer
Road
Workers
A28

1959, Oct. 26
120 A28 1pi org brn, ultra & grn   .70   .30
121 A28 2pi violet, org & grn   1.10   .45
122 A28 4pi dk bl, bl & bis   2.10   .50
123 A28 5pi bister, brn & ocher   2.60   .85
    Nos. 120-123 (4)   6.50 2.10
   4th anniv. of the constitution, stressing communal development.

Boy Scout — A29

1959, Dec.   **Engr.**   **Perf. 13**
124 A29 3pi brt yellow grn   .60   .30
125 A29 4pi deep lilac rose   1.25   .30
126 A29 8pi dk brn & lil rose   2.10   .65
127 A29 20pi Prus bl & bl grn   3.75   1.10
    Nos. 124-127 (4)   7.70 2.30
   National Boy Scout Jamboree.

Symbols of
Family and
Justice
A30

1960
128 A30 20c emerald   .80   .80
129 A30 30c brt grnsh blue   .85   .85
130 A30 2pi orange & maroon   1.60   1.60
131 A30 6pi car & rose vio   1.75   1.75
    Nos. 128-131 (4)   5.00 5.00
   Issued to commemorate the family code.

Refugee
Family and
WRY
Emblem
A31

1960, Apr. 7   **Engr.**   **Perf. 13**
132 A31 50c brt lilac rose   .45   .25
133 A31 3pi brt green   .55   .30
134 A31 4pi scarlet   .65   .40
135 A31 5pi dp violet blue   .80   .60
    Nos. 132-135 (4)   2.45 1.55
   World Refugee Year, 7/1/59-6/30/60.

Henri
Dunant — A32

1960, May 8   **Cross in Carmine**
136 A32 1pi dark blue   .45   .30
137 A32 3pi green   1.40   .35
138 A32 4pi crimson rose   1.90   .50
139 A32 6pi dp lilac rose   2.25   .65
    Nos. 136-139 (4)   6.00 1.80
   Centenary (in 1959) of the Red Cross idea.

Model
Farm
A33

1960, July 7   **Perf. 13**
140 A33 50c ultra   .50   .25
141 A33 1pi dark green   .60   .30
142 A33 3pi orange   1.00   .35
143 A33 7pi bright pink   1.60   .65
    Nos. 140-143 (4)   3.70 1.55
   Establishment of communal rice farming.

Girl With
Basket of
Rice and
Rice Plant
A34

1960, Nov. 21
144 A34 2pi emerald & green   .80   .40
145 A34 4pi blue & ultra   1.20   .60
   Conf. of the UN FAO, Saigon, Nov. 1960.

Map and Flag of
Viet Nam — A35

1960, Oct. 26   **Engr.**   **Perf. 13**
146 A35 50c grnsh bl, car & yel   .45   .25
147 A35 1pi ultra, car & yel   .55   .30
148 A35 3pi purple, car & yel   .95   .40
149 A35 7pi yel grn, car & yel   1.60   .60
    Nos. 146-149 (4)   3.55 1.55
   Fifth anniversary of the Republic.

Agricultural Development Center,
Tractor and Plow — A36

1961, Jan. 3   **Perf. 13**
150 A36 50c red brown   .40   .25
151 A36 70c rose lilac   .55   .30
152 A36 80c rose red   .65   .40
153 A36 10pi bright pink   4.00   1.00
    Nos. 150-153 (4)   5.60 1.95

Plant and
Child — A37

1961, Mar. 23   **Perf. 13**
154 A37 70c light blue   .45   .25
155 A37 80c ultra   .60   .30
156 A37 4pi olive bister   .70   .45
157 A37 7pi grnsh bl & yel grn   1.25   .70
    Nos. 154-157 (4)   3.00 1.70
   Child protection.

Pres. Ngo Dinh
Diem — A38

1961, Apr. 29   **Perf. 13**
158 A38 50c brt ultra   .80   .50
159 A38 1pi red   1.40   .90
160 A38 2pi lilac rose   1.50   1.10
161 A38 4pi brt violet   2.40   1.75
    Nos. 158-161 (4)   6.10 4.25
   Second term of Pres. Ngo Dinh Diem.

Boy, Girl
and
Flaming
Torch
A39

1961, July 7   **Engr.**   **Perf. 13**
162 A39 50c red   .35   .25
163 A39 70c bright pink   .35   .30
164 A39 80c ver & maroon   .45   .40
165 A39 8pi dp claret & mag   1.40   .75
    Nos. 162-165 (4)   2.55 1.70
   Issued for Youth Day.

Saigon-Bien Hoa Highway
Bridge — A40

1961, July 28
166 A40 50c yellow green   .45   .25
167 A40 1pi orange brown   .65   .30
168 A40 2pi dark blue   .75   .40
169 A40 5pi brt red lilac   1.75   .45
    Nos. 166-169 (4)   3.60 1.40
   Opening of Saigon-Bien Hoa Highway.

Alexandre de Rhodes A41

1961, Sept. 5

170	A41	50c rose carmine	.35	.25
171	A41	1pi claret	.50	.30
172	A41	3pi bister brown	.55	.40
173	A41	6pi emerald	1.60	.65
		Nos. 170-173 (4)	3.00	1.60

Alexandre de Rhodes (1591-1660), Jesuit missionary who introduced Roman characters to express the Viet Nam language.

Young Man with Torch, Sage, Pagoda — A42

1961, Oct. 26 Perf. 13

174	A42	50c orange ver	.40	.25
175	A42	1pi brt green	.55	.30
176	A42	3pi rose red	.80	.40
177	A42	8pi rose lilac & brn	1.90	.75
		Nos. 174-177 (4)	3.65	1.70

Moral Rearmament of Youth Movement.

Temple Dedicated to Confucius — A43

1961, Nov. 4 Engr.

178	A43	1pi brt green	.50	.25
179	A43	2pi rose red	.75	.30
180	A43	5pi olive	1.90	.65
		Nos. 178-180 (3)	3.15	1.05

15th anniversary of UNESCO.

Earth Scraper Preparing Ground for Model Village — A44

1961, Dec. 11 Perf. 13

181	A44	50c dark green	.60	.25
182	A44	1pi Prus bl & car lake	.70	.30
183	A44	2pi olive grn & brn	.90	.40
184	A44	10pi Prus blue	3.25	.65
		Nos. 181-184 (4)	5.45	1.60

Agrarian reform program.

Man Fighting Mosquito and Emblem — A45

1962, Apr. 7 Perf. 13

185	A45	50c brt lilac rose	.45	.25
186	A45	1pi orange	.45	.30
187	A45	2pi emerald	.60	.40
188	A45	6pi ultra	1.50	.65
		Nos. 185-188 (4)	3.00	1.60

WHO drive to eradicate malaria.

Postal Check Center, Saigon — A46

1962, May 15 Engr. Perf. 13

189	A46	70c dull green	.30	.25
190	A46	80c chocolate	.35	.30
191	A46	4pi lilac rose	.85	.35
192	A46	7pi rose red	2.00	.65
		Nos. 189-192 (4)	3.50	1.45

Inauguration of postal checking service.

Madonna of Vang — A47

1962, July 7

193	A47	50c violet & rose red	.40	.25
194	A47	1pi red brn & indigo	.60	.30
195	A47	2pi brown & rose car	1.00	.40
196	A47	8pi green & dk blue	2.50	.65
		Nos. 193-196 (4)	4.50	1.60

Catholic shrine of the Madonna of Vang.

Armed Guards and Village A48

1962, Oct. 26

197	A48	50c bright red	.35	.25
198	A48	1pi yellow green	.65	.30
199	A48	1.50pi lilac rose	1.00	.40
200	A48	7pi ultra	2.25	.65
		Nos. 197-200 (4)	4.25	1.60

"Strategic village" defense system.

Gougah Waterfall, Dalat — A49

1963, Jan. 3

201	A49	60c orange red	1.00	.30
202	A49	1pi bluish black	1.50	.45

62nd birthday of Pres. Ngo Dinh Diem; Spring Festival.

Trung Sisters' Monument and Vietnamese Women — A50

1963, Mar. 1 Engr.

203	A50	50c green	.25	.25
204	A50	1pi dk carmine rose	.40	.30
205	A50	0pi lilac rose	.60	.45
206	A50	8pi violet blue	1.25	.60
		Nos. 203-206 (4)	2.50	1.60

Issued for Women's Day.

Farm Woman with Grain A51

1963, Mar. 21 Perf. 13

207	A51	50c red	.40	.25
208	A51	1pi dk car rose	.45	.30
209	A51	3pi lilac rose	.65	.45
210	A51	5pi violet	1.00	.65
		Nos. 207-210 (4)	2.50	1.65

FAO "Freedom from Hunger" campaign.

Common Defense Emblem — A52

1963, July 7 Engr. Perf. 13

211	A52	30c bister	.50	.25
212	A52	50c lilac rose	.70	.25
213	A52	3pi brt green	.95	.30
214	A52	8pi red	1.50	.65
		Nos. 211-214 (4)	3.65	1.45

Common defense effort. The inscription says: "Personalism-Common Progress."

Emblem — A53

1963, Oct. 26 Perf. 13

215	A53	50c rose red	.35	.25
216	A53	1pi emerald	.50	.30
217	A53	4pi purple	1.00	.40
218	A53	5pi orange	1.75	.60
		Nos. 215-218 (4)	3.60	1.55

The fighting soldiers of the Republic.

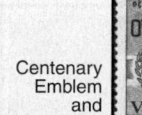

Centenary Emblem and Map — A54

1963, Nov. 17 Engr.
Cross in Deep Carmine

219	A54	50c Prus blue	.35	.25
220	A54	1pi deep carmine	.70	.30
221	A54	3pi orange yellow	1.60	.40
222	A54	6pi brown	2.25	.65
		Nos. 219-222 (4)	4.90	1.60

Centenary of International Red Cross.

Constitution and Scales — A55

1963, Dec. 10 Perf. 13

223	A55	70c orange	.30	.25
224	A55	1pi brt rose	.45	.30
225	A55	3pi green	.65	.40
226	A55	8pi ocher	1.25	.60
		Nos. 223-226 (4)	2.65	1.55

15th anniv. of the Universal Declaration of Human Rights.

Danhim Hydroelectric Station — A56

1964, Jan. 15 Engr.

227	A56	40c rose red	.30	.25
228	A56	1pi bister brown	.45	.30
229	A56	3pi violet blue	.75	.40
230	A56	8pi olive green	1.50	.60
		Nos. 227-230 (4)	3.00	1.55

Inauguration of the Danhim Hydroelectric Station.

Atomic Reactor A57

1964, Feb. 3 Perf. 13

231	A57	80c olive	.35	.25
232	A57	1.50pi brown orange	.55	.30
233	A57	3pi chocolate	.75	.45
234	A57	7pi brt blue	.70	.75
		Nos. 231-234 (4)	2.35	1.75

Peaceful uses of atomic energy.

Compass Rose, Barograph and UN Emblem — A58

1964, Mar. 23 Engr.

235	A58	50c bister	.25	.25
236	A58	1pi vermilion	.25	.25
237	A58	1.50pi rose claret	.60	.40
238	A58	10pi emerald	1.50	.70
		Nos. 235-238 (4)	2.50	1.60

4th World Meteorological Day, Mar. 23.

South Vietnamese Gesturing to North Vietnamese; Map — A59

1964, July 20 Perf. 13

239	A59	30c dk grn, ultra & mar	.95	.25
240	A59	50c dk car rose, yel & blk	1.10	.30
241	A59	1.50pi dk bl, dp org & blk	1.50	.65
		Nos. 239-241 (3)	3.55	1.20

10th anniv. of the Day of National Grief, July 20, 1954, when the nation was divided into South and North Viet Nam.

Hatien Beach — A60

1964, Sept. 7 — Engr. — Perf. 13½

242	A60	20c bright ultra	.35	.25
243	A60	3pi emerald	1.50	.40

Revolutionists and "Nov. 1" — A61

Designs: 80c, Soldier breaking chain. 3pi, Broken chain and date: "1-11 1963," vert.

1964, Nov. 1 — Engr. — Perf. 13

244	A61	50c red lilac & indigo	.40	.25
245	A61	80c violet & red brn	.50	.30
246	A61	3pi dk blue & red	1.10	.70
		Nos. 244-246 (3)	2.00	1.25

Anniv. of November 1963 revolution.

Temple, Saigon A62

Designs: 1pi, Royal tombs, Hué. 1.50pi, Fishermen and sailboats at Phan-Thiet beach. 3pi, Temple, Gia-Dhin.

1964-66 — Size: 35½x26mm — Perf. 13

247	A62	50c fawn, grn & dl vio	.45	.25
248	A62	1pi olive bis & ind	.70	.30
249	A62	1.50pi ol gray & dk sl grn	.85	.40
250	A62	3pi vio, dk sl grn & cl	1.60	.65
		Nos. 247-250 (4)	3.60	1.60

Coil Stamp
Size: 23x17mm

250A	A62	1pi ol bis & ind ('66)	6.00	3.50

Issue date: Nos. 247-250, Dec. 2, 1964.

Hung Vuong and Au Co with their Children A63

1965, Apr. — Engr. — Perf. 13

251	A63	3pi car lake & org red	2.50	.45
252	A63	100pi brown vio & vio	12.00	3.50

Mythological founders of Viet Nam, c. 2000 B.C.

ITU Emblem, Insulator and TV Mast — A64

1965, May 17 — Engr.

253	A64	1pi olive, dp car & bister	.50	.30
254	A64	3pi henna brn, car & lil	1.50	.45

ITU, centenary.

Buddhist Wheel of Life and Flames — A65

1.50pi, Wheel, lotus blossom and world map, horiz. 3pi, Wheel and Buddhist flag.

Inscribed: "Phat-Giao" (Buddhism)

1965, May 15 — Perf. 13

255	A65	50c dark carmine	.90	.25
256	A65	1.50pi dk blue & ocher	1.20	.30
257	A65	3pi dk blue & dk brn	1.50	.45
		Nos. 255-257 (3)	3.60	1.00

Anniversary of Buddha's birth.

ICY Emblem and Women of Various Races — A66

1965, June 26

258	A66	50c bluish blk & bis	.60	.25
259	A66	1pi dk brn & brn	.90	.30
260	A66	1.50pi dark red & gray	1.50	.45
		Nos. 258-260 (3)	3.00	1.00

International Cooperation Year.

Ixora — A67

Flowers: 80c, Orchid. 1pi, Chrysanthemum. 1.50pi, Lotus, horiz. 3pi, Plum blossoms.

1965, Sept. 10 — Engr. — Perf. 13

261	A67	70c grn, slate grn & red	.35	.25
262	A67	80c dk brn, lil & sl grn	.50	.30
263	A67	1pi dk blue & yellow	.65	.40
264	A67	1.50pi sl grn, dl grn & gray	.85	.45
265	A67	3pi slate grn & org	1.60	.75
		Nos. 261-265 (5)	3.95	2.15

Student, Dormitory and Map of Thu Duc — A68

1965, Oct. 15 — Perf. 13

266	A68	50c dark brown	.25	.25
267	A68	1pi bright green	.40	.25
268	A68	3pi crimson	.60	.30
269	A68	7pi dark blue violet	1.25	.55
		Nos. 266-269 (4)	2.50	1.35

Issued to publicize higher education.

Farm Boy and Girl, Pig and 4-T Emblem A69

4pi, Farm boy with chicken, village and 4-T flag.

1965, Nov. 25 — Engr. — Perf. 13

270	A69	3pi emerald & dk red	1.20	.25
271	A69	4pi dull violet & plum	1.75	.30

10th anniv. of the 4-T Clubs and the National Congress of Young Farmers.

Basketball A70

Designs: 1pi, Javelin. 1.50pi, Hand holding torch, athletic couple. 10pi, Pole vault.

1965, Dec. 14 — Engr. — Perf. 13

272	A70	50c dk car & brn org	.45	.25
273	A70	1pi brn org & red brn	.65	.30
274	A70	1.50pi brt green	1.00	.40
275	A70	10pi red lil & brn org	2.40	.75
		Nos. 272-275 (4)	4.50	1.70

Radio Tower — A71

Radio tower, telephone dial, map of Viet Nam.

1966, Apr. 24 — Engr. — Perf. 13

276	A71	3pi brt blue & brn	.45	.25
277	A71	4pi purple, red & blk	.55	.30

Saigon microwave station.

Loading Hook and Globe — A72

1966, June 22 — Engr. — Perf. 13

278	A72	3pi gray & dk car rose	.35	.25
279	A72	4pi olive & dk purple	.45	.30
280	A72	6pi brt grn & dk blue	.80	.40
		Nos. 278-280 (3)	1.60	.95

Appreciation of the help given by the free world.

Hands Reaching for Persecuted Refugees A73

1966, July 20

281	A73	3pi brn, vio brn & olive	.40	.25
282	A73	7pi claret, vio brn & dk pur	1.00	.30

Refugees from communist oppression.

Paper Soldiers, Votive Offering A74

Designs: 1.50pi, Man and woman making offerings. 3pi, Floating candles in paper boats. 5pi, Woman burning paper offerings.

1966, Aug. 30 — Engr. — Perf. 13

283	A74	50c red, blk & bis brn	.65	.25
284	A74	1.50pi brown, emer & grn	1.00	.30
285	A74	3pi rose red & lake	1.40	.40
286	A74	5pi org brn, bis & dk brn	2.00	.65
		Nos. 283-286 (4)	5.05	1.60

Wandering Souls Festival.

Oriental Two-string Violin A75

Vietnamese Instruments: 3pi, Woman playing 16-string guitar. 4pi, Musicians playing two-string guitars. 7pi, Woman and boy playing flutes.

1966 — Engr. — Perf. 13
Size: 35½x26mm

287	A75	1pi brown red & brn	.75	.25
288	A75	3pi rose lilac & pur	1.10	.30
289	A75	4pi rose brown & brn	1.50	.40
290	A75	7pi dp blue & vio bl	2.25	.65
		Nos. 287-290 (4)	5.60	1.60

Coil Stamp
Size: 23x17mm

290A	A75	3pi rose lil & pur	8.00	3.00
b.		Booklet pane of 5	45.00	
		Complete booklet, 2 #290Ab	140.00	

Nos. 287-290 were issued Sept. 28. Complete booklet contains two vertical strips of 5 with selvage at either end. These strips were also sold loose without booklet cover.

WHO Building, Geneva, and Flag — A76

Designs: 50c, WHO Building and emblem, horiz. 8pi, WHO flag and building.

1966, Oct. 12 — Engr. — Perf. 13

291	A76	50c purple & carmine	.45	.25
292	A76	1.50pi red brn, vio bl & blk	.65	.30
293	A76	8pi grnsh bl, vio bl & brn	1.40	.80
		Nos. 291-293 (3)	2.50	1.35

Opening of WHO Headquarters, Geneva.

Hand Holding Spade, and Soldiers A77

Soldier and Workers — A78

Designs: 1.50pi, Flag, workers. 4pi, Soldier and cavalryman.

1966, Nov. 1 — Engr. — Perf. 13

294	A77	80c dull brn & red brn	.35	.25
295	A77	1.50pi car rose, yel & brn	.65	.30

296	A78	3pi brown & slate grn	1.25	.40
297	A78	4pi lilac, black & brn	1.75	.65

Nos. 294-297 (4) 4.00 1.60

3rd anniv. of the revolution against the government of Pres. Ngo Dinh Diem.

Symbolic Tree and UNESCO Emblem — A79

Designs: 3pi, Globe and olive branches. 7pi, Symbolic temple, horiz.

1966, Dec. 15 Engr. *Perf. 13*

298	A79	1pi pink, brn & dk car	.75	.25
299	A79	3pi dp bl, grn & brn org	1.00	.30
300	A79	7pi grnsh bl, dk bl & red	1.75	.65

Nos. 298-300 (3) 3.50 1.20

20th anniv. of UNESCO.

Bitter Melon A80

1967, Jan. 12 Engr. *Perf. 13*

301	A80	50c Cashew, vert.	1.25	.25
302	A80	1.50pi shown	1.60	.30
303	A80	3pi Sweetsop	2.00	.40
304	A80	20pi Areca nuts	5.00	.65

Nos. 301-304 (4) 9.85 1.60

Phan-Boi-Chau — A81

Designs: 20pi, Phan-Chau-Trinh portrait and addressing crowd.

1967, Mar. 24 Engr. *Perf. 13*

305	A81	1pi mar, red brn & dk brn	75	25
306	A81	20pi vio, slate grn & blk	2.00	.80

Issued to honor Vietnamese patriots.

Woman Carrying Produce A82

Labor Day: 1pi, Market scene. 3pi, Two-wheeled horse cart. 8pi, Farm scene with water buffalo.

1967, May 1 Engr. *Perf. 13*

307	A82	50c vio bl, dk bl & ultra	.25	.25
308	A82	1pi sl grn & dull pur	.30	.30
309	A82	3pi dk carmine	.50	.35
310	A82	8pi brt car rose & pur	.95	.60

Nos. 307-310 (4) 2.00 1.50

Potter, Vases and Lamp — A83

Weavers and Potters A84

Designs: 1.50pi, Vase and basket. 35d, Bag and lacquerware.

1967, July 22 Engr. *Perf. 13*

311	A83	50c red brn, grn & ultra	.25	.25
312	A83	1.50pi grnsh bl, car & blk	.50	.30
313	A84	3pi red, vio & org brn	1.00	.40
314	A83	35pi bis brn, blk & dk red	3.25	1.40

Nos. 311-314 (4) 5.00 2.35

Issued to publicize Vietnamese handicrafts.

Wedding Procession A85

1967, Sept. 18 Engr. *Perf. 13*

315	A85	3pi rose cl, dk vio & red	1.25	.45

Symbols of Stage, Music and Art — A86

Litho. & Engr.

1967, Oct. 27 *Perf. 13*

316	A86	10pi bl gray, blk & red	1.50	.55

Issued to publicize the Cultural Institute.

"Freedom and Justice" A87

Balloting A88

"Establishment of Democracy" — A89

1967, Nov. 1 Photo.

317	A87	4pi mag, brn & ocher	.80	.25
318	A88	5pi brown, yel & blk	1.25	.30
319	A89	30pi dl lil, indigo & red	2.50	.65

Nos. 317-319 (3) 4.55 1.20

National Day; general elections.

Pagoda and Lions Emblem A90

1967, Dec. 5 Photo. *Perf. 13½x13*

320	A90	3pi multicolored	1.75	1.00

50th anniversary of Lions International.

Teacher with Pupils and Globe — A91

1967, Dec. 10 *Perf. 13x13½*

321	A91	3pi tan, blk, yel & car	1.75	.65

International Literacy Day, Sept. 8, 1967.

Tractor and Village — A92

Rural Construction Program: 9pi, Bulldozer and home building. 10pi, Wheelbarrow, tractor and new building. 20pi, Vietnamese and Americans working together.

1968, Jan. 26 Photo. *Perf. 13½*

322	A92	1pi multicolored	.25	.25
323	A92	9pi lt blue & multi	1.00	.25
324	A92	10pi multicolored	1.25	.30
325	A92	20pi yel, red lil & blk	1.75	.65

Nos. 322-325 (4) 4.25 1.45

WHO Emblem — A93

1968, Apr. 7 Photo. *Perf. 13½*

326	A93	10pi gray grn, blk & yel	2.00	1.00

WHO, 20th anniversary.

Flags of Viet Nam's Allies — A94

Designs: 1.50pi, Flags surrounding SEATO emblem. 3pi, Flags, handclasp, globe and map of Viet Nam. 50pi, Flags and handclasp.

1968, June 22 Photo. *Perf. 13½*

327	A94	1pi multicolored	.55	.25
328	A94	1.50pi multicolored	1.10	.30
329	A94	3pi multicolored	2.00	.40
330	A94	50pi multicolored	6.50	.95

Nos. 327-330 (4) 10.15 1.90

Issued to honor Viet Nam's allies.

Three-wheeled Truck and Tractor — A95

Private Property Ownership: 80c, Farmer, city man and symbols of property. 2pi, Three-wheeled cart, taxi and farmers. 30pi, Taxi, three-wheeled cart and tractor in field.

Inscribed: "HUU-SAN-HOA CONG-NHAN VA NONG-DAN"

1968, Nov. 1 Photo. *Perf. 13½*

331	A95	80c multicolored	.25	.25
332	A95	2pi steel blue & multi	.30	.30
333	A95	10pi orange brn & multi	.95	.45
334	A95	30pi gray blue & multi	2.75	1.25

Nos. 331-334 (4) 4.25 2.25

Human Rights Flame — A96

Men of Various Races — A97

1968, Dec. 10 Photo. *Perf. 13½*

335	A96	10pi multicolored	.70	.30
336	A97	16pi purple & multi	1.40	.40

International Human Rights Year.

UNICEF Emblem, Mother and Child — A98

6pi, Children flying kite with UNICEF emblem.

1968, Dec. 11

337	A98	6pi multicolored	1.00	.50
338	A98	16pi multicolored	2.00	.80

Workers and Train — A99

1.50pi, 3pi, Crane, train, map of Viet Nam.

1968, Dec. 15

339	A99	1.50pi multicolored	.70	.25
340	A99	3pi org, vio bl & grn	1.00	.30
341	A99	9pi multicolored	1.50	.40
342	A99	20pi multicolored	2.40	.65

Nos. 339-342 (4) 5.60 1.60

Reopening of Trans-Viet Nam Railroad.

Farm Woman — A100

Vietnamese Women: 1pi, Merchant. 3pi, Nurses, horiz. 20pi, Three ladies.

1969, Mar. 23   Engr.   Perf. 13
343 A100 50c vio bl, lil & ocher   .30   .25
344 A100 1pi grn, bis & dk brn   .50   .30
345 A100 3pi brown, blk & bl   .70   .40
346 A100 20pi lilac & multi   1.50   .60
       Nos. 343-346 (4)   3.00 1.55

Soldiers and Civilians A101

Family Welcoming Soldier A102

1969, June 1   Photo.   Perf. 13
347 A101 2pi multicolored   .45   .25
348 A102 50pi multicolored   2.25   .60

Pacification campaign.

Man Reading Constitution, Scales of Justice A103

Voters, Torch and Scales A104

1969, June 9
349 A103 1pi yel org, yel & blk   .25   .25
350 A104 20pi multicolored   3.00   .50

Constitutional democracy. Phrase on both stamps: "Democratic and Governed by Law."

Mobile Post Office — A105

Mobile Post Office: 3pi, Window service. 4pi, Child with letter. 20pi, Crowd at window and postmark: "15, 12, 67."

1969, July 10
351 A105 1pi multicolored   .25   .25
352 A105 3pi multicolored   .60   .30
353 A105 4pi multicolored   .75   .45
354 A105 20pi ocher & multi   1.50   .75
       Nos. 351-354 (4)   3.10 1.75

Installation of the first mobile post office in Viet Nam.

Mnong-gar Woman A106

1pi, Djarai woman. 50pi, Bahnar man.

1969, Aug. 29   Photo.   Perf. 13
355 A106 1pi brt pink & multi   1.00   .40
356 A106 6pi sky blue & multi   1.75   .65
357 A106 50pi gray & multi   7.25   .95
       Nos. 355-357 (3)   10.00 2.00

Ethnic minorities in Viet Nam.

Civilians Becoming Soldiers A107

General Mobilization: 3pi, Bayonet training. 5pi, Guard duty. 10pi, Farewell.

Inscribed: "TONG BONG VIEN"

1969, Sept. 20
358 A107 1.50pi orange & multi   .55   .25
359 A107 3pi purple & multi   1.10   .30
360 A107 5pi blk, red & ocher   1.75   .40
361 A107 10pi pink & multi   2.25   .65
       Nos. 358-361 (4)   5.65 1.60

ILO Emblem and Globe — A108

1969, Oct. 29   Photo.   Perf. 13
362 A108 6pi blue grn, blk &
                    gray   .75   .30
363 A108 20pi red, blk & gray   1.25   .45

ILO, 50th anniversary.

Pegu House Sparrow — A109

Birds: 6pi, Moluccan munia. 7pi, Great hornbill. 30pi, Old world tree sparrow.

1970, Jan. 15   Photo.   Perf. 12½x14
364 A109 2pi blue & multi   1.00   .35
365 A109 6pi orange & multi   3.00   .70
366 A109 7pi org brn & multi   4.00   .70
367 A109 30pi blue & multi   14.00 2.10
       Nos. 364-367 (4)   22.00 3.85

Burning House and Family — A110

Design: 20pi, Family fleeing burning house and physician examining child.

1970, Jan. 31   Photo.   Perf. 13
368 A110 10pi multicolored   1.25   .25
369 A110 20pi multicolored   2.00   .30

Mau Than disaster, 1968.

Vietnamese Costumes — A111

Traditional Costumes: 1pi, Man, woman and priest, vert. 2pi, Seated woman with fan. 100pi, Man and woman.

Inscribed: "Y-PHUC CO TRUYEN"

1970, Mar. 13   Photo.   Perf. 13
370 A111 1pi lt brown & multi   .35   .25
371 A111 2pi pink & multi   .45   .30
372 A111 3pi ultra & multi   .55   .40
373 A111 100pi multicolored   5.50 1.50
       Nos. 370-373 (4)   6.85 2.45

Issued for the Trung Sisters' Festival.

Building Workers, Pagodas and Bridge A112

Rebuilding of Hué: 20pi, Concrete mixers and scaffolds.

1970, June 10   Litho. & Engr.
374 A112 6pi multicolored   .75   .30
375 A112 20pi rose lil, brn & bis 1.50 .45

Plower in Rice Field — A113

1970, Aug. 29   Perf. 13
376 A113 6pi multicolored   1.50   .45

"Land to the Tiller" agricultural reform program.

New Building and Scaffold A114

Construction Work — A115

1970, Sept. 15   Engr.   Perf. 13
377 A114 8pi pale ol & brn org   .75   .30
378 A115 16pi brn, indigo & yel 1.50 .45

Reconstruction after 1968 Tet Offensive.

Productivity Year Emblem A116

1970, Oct. 3
379 A116 10pi multicolored   1.25   .45

Asian Productivity Year.

Nguyen-Dinh-Chieu — A117

1970, Nov. 16   Engr.   Perf. 13½
380 A117 6pi dull vio, red & brn .80   .30
381 A117 10pi grn, red & dk brn 1.25   .45

Nguyen-Dinh-Chieu (1822-1888), poet.

Education Year Emblem — A118

Litho. & Engr.
1970, Nov. 30   Perf. 13
382 A118 10pi pale brn, yel & blk 1.50 .65

International Education Year.

Parliament Building A119

Design: 6pi, Senate Building.

1970, Dec.
383 A119 6pi lt bl, cit & dk brn .50   .30
384 A119 10pi multicolored   1.00   .45

6pi issued Dec. 8 for the 6th Cong.; 10pi issued Dec. 9 for the 9th General Assembly of the Asian Interparliamentary Union.

Dancers — A120

Designs: Various Vietnamese dancers and musicians. 6pi and 7pi horizontal.

1971, Jan. 12
385 A120 2pi ultra & multi   .70   .30
386 A120 6pi pale green & multi 1.75   .35
387 A120 7pi pink & multi   2.10   .45
388 A120 10pi brown org & multi 2.50   .50
       Nos. 385-388 (4)   7.05 1.60

For surcharge see No. 500.

Farmers and Law — A121

Agrarian Reform Law: 3pi, Tractor and law, dated 26.3.1970. 16pi, Farmers, people rejoicing and law book.

1971, Mar. 26   Engr.   Perf. 13
389 A121 2pi vio bl, dk brn &
                    dl org   .35   .25
   a.   Dated "1970"   40.00
390 A121 3pi pale grn, brn &
                    dk bl   .55   .30
391 A121 16pi multicolored   2.50   .45
       Nos. 389-391 (3)   3.40 1.00

No. 389 is dated "1971."

For surcharge see No. 482.

Courier on Horseback A122

Design: 6pi, Mounted courier with flag.

Engr. & Photo.
1971, June 6   Perf. 13
392 A122 2pi violet & multi   .35   .30
393 A122 6pi tan & multi   1.90   .45

Postal history.

Military and Naval Operations on Vietnamese Coast — A123

1971, June 19
394 A123 3pi multi + label   1.00   .45
395 A123 40pi multi + label   5.00 1.00

Armed Forces Day.

Deer — A124

1971, Aug. 20   **Engr.**
396 A124 9pi shown   1.25 .35
397 A124 30pi Tiger   3.75 .90

Rice Harvest
A125

30pi, Threshing and winnowing rice and rice plants. 40pi, Bundling and carrying rice.

Litho. & Engr.
1971, Sept. 28   **Perf. 13**
398 A125 1pi multicolored   .40 .30
399 A125 30pi sal pink, dk pur & blk   2.10 .75
400 A125 40pi sepia, yel & grn   2.50 .80
    Nos. 398-400 (3)   5.00 1.85

For surcharge see No. 496.

Inauguration
of UPU
Building,
Bern — A126

1971, Nov. 9   **Engr.**   **Perf. 13**
401 A126 20pi green & multi   1.75 .50

Fish — A127

Various Fish; 2pi vertical.

1971, Nov. 16   **Photo. & Engr.**
402 A127 2pi multicolored   1.10 .30
403 A127 10pi violet & multi   2.25 .45
404 A127 100pi lilac & multi   17.00 2.00
    Nos. 402-404 (3)   20.35 2.75

Mailman and
Woman on
Water Buffalo
A128

Rural Mail: 10pi, Bird carrying letter. 20pi, Mailman with bicycle delivering mail to villagers.

Inscribed: "PHAT TRIEN BUU-CHINH NONG THON"

1971, Dec. 20   **Perf. 13**
405 A128 5pi multicolored   .65 .30
406 A128 10pi multicolored   1.10 .45
407 A128 20pi multicolored   1.75 .60
    Nos. 405-407 (3)   3.50 1.35

Trawler
Fishermen,
and
Fish — A129

Publicity for Fishing Industry: 7pi, Net fishing from boat. 50d, Trawler with seine.

1972, Jan. 2   **Engr.**   **Perf. 13**
408 A129 4pi pink, blk & blue   .40 .25
409 A129 7pi lt blue, blk & red   .65 .30
410 A129 50pi multicolored   3.50 1.00
    Nos. 408-410 (3)   4.55 2.15

King Quang Trung
(1752-1792) — A130

1972, Jan. 28   **Perf. 13½**
411 A130 6pi red & multi   1.00 .35
  a.   Booklet pane of 10   90.00
412 A130 20pi black & multi   3.00 1.20

No. 411a is imperf. horizontally.

Road
Workers
A131

1972, Feb. 4
413 A131 3pi multicolored   .50 .30
414 A131 8pi multicolored   1.00 .45

Community development.

Rice Farming
A132

1972, Mar. 26   **Engr.**   **Perf. 13½**
415 A132 1pi shown   .25 .25
416 A132 10pi Wheat farming   2.00 .30

Farmers' Day.

Plane over
Dalat — A133

1972, Apr. 18   **Engr. & Photo.**
417 A133 10pi shown   2.00 .50
418 A133 10pi over Ha-tien   2.00 .50
419 A133 10pi over Hue   2.00 .50
420 A133 10pi over Saigon   2.00 .50
  a.   Block of 4, #417-420   10.00 7.50
421 A133 25pi like No. 417   4.50 .75
422 A133 25pi like No. 418   4.50 .75
423 A133 25pi like No. 419   4.50 .75
424 A133 25pi like No. 420   4.50 .75
  a.   Block of 4, #421-424   20.00 12.50
    Nos. 417-424 (8)   26.00 5.00

20 years Air Viet Nam.

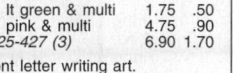

Scholar
A134

20pi, Teacher, pupils. 50pi, Scholar, scroll.

1972, May 5   **Engr. & Litho.**
425 A134 5pi multicolored   .40 .30
Engr.
426 A134 20pi lt green & multi   1.75 .50
427 A134 50pi pink & multi   4.75 .90
    Nos. 425-427 (3)   6.90 1.70

Ancient letter writing art.

Armed
Farmer — A135

6pi, Civilian rifleman & Self-defense Forces emblem, horiz. 20pi, Man, woman training with rifles.

Engr. & Litho.
1972, June 15   **Perf. 13**
428 A135 2pi brt rose & multi   1.10 .35
429 A135 6pi multicolored   1.50 .50
430 A135 20pi lt violet & multi   2.40 .60
    Nos. 428-430 (3)   5.00 1.45

Civilian Self-defense Forces.

Hands
Holding
Safe — A136

1972, July 10
431 A136 10pi lt blue & multi   1.75 .30
432 A136 25pi lt green & multi   3.25 .45

Treasury Bonds campaign.

Frontier
Guard — A137

Designs: 10pi, 3 guards and horse, horiz. 40pi, Marching guards, horiz.

Engr. & Litho.
1972, Aug. 14   **Perf. 13**
433 A137 10pi olive & multi   1.00 .30
434 A137 30pi buff & multi   1.50 .50
435 A137 40pi lt blue & multi   2.50 .70
    Nos. 433-435 (3)   5.00 1.50

Historic frontier guards.

Soldier Helping
Wounded
Man — A138

Designs: 16pi, Soldier on crutches and flowers. 100pi, Veterans' memorial, map and flag.

1972, Sept. 1
436 A138 9pi olive & multi   1.25 .35
437 A138 16pi yellow & multi   1.75 .45
438 A138 100pi lt blue & multi   6.00 1.40
    Nos. 436-438 (3)   9.00 2.20

For surcharge see No. 483.

Tank,
Memorial,
Flag and
Map — A139

Soldiers and Map of
Viet Nam — A140

1972, Nov. 25   **Litho.**   **Perf. 13**
439 A139 5pi multicolored   6.50 .30
440 A140 10pi ultra & multi   9.50 .45

Victory at Binh-Long.

Book Year
Emblem and
Globe — A141

Designs: 4pi, Emblem, books circling globe. 5pi, Emblem, books and globe.

1972, Nov. 30
441 A141 2pi dp carmine & multi   .55 .25
442 A141 4pi blue & multi   1.25 .30
443 A141 5pi yellow bister & multi   1.60 .45
    Nos. 441-443 (3)   3.40 1.00

International Book Year.

Liberated
Vietnamese
Family — A142

1973, Feb. 18   **Litho.**   **Perf. 13**
444 A142 10pi yellow & multi   2.00 1.20

To celebrate the 200,000th returnee.

Soldiers Raising
Vietnamese
Flag — A143

Design: 10pi, Victorious soldiers and map of demilitarized zone, horiz.

1973, Feb. 24   **Litho.**   **Perf. 13**
445 A143 3pi lilac & multi   .80 .75
446 A143 10pi yellow grn & multi   2.00 1.50

Victory at Quang Tri.

Satellite,
Storm over
Viet
Nam — A144

1973, Mar. 23   **Litho.**   **Perf. 12½x12**
447 A144 1pi lt blue & multi   1.25 .60

World Meteorological Day.
For surcharge see No. 497.

Farmers with
Tractor,
Symbol of
Law — A145

Farmer Plowing with Water Buffalos
A146

Pres. Thieu Holding Agrarian Reform Law
A147

1973, Mar. 26   Litho.   Perf. 12½x12
448 A145 2pi lt green & multi .... 3.00 .60
449 A146 5pi orange & multi .... 3.00 .60
   Perf. 11
450 A147 10pi blue & multi *115.00 30.00*
   Nos. 448-450 (3) 121.00 31.20

3rd anniv. of the agrarian reform law; 5-year plan for rural development.
   Value for No. 450 is for stamp with first day cancel. Commercially used examples are worth substantially more.
   See No. 475.

INTERPOL Emblem and Headquarters
A148

2pi, INTERPOL emblem. 25pi, INTERPOL emblem, side view of Headquarters.

1973, Apr. 8   Litho.   Perf. 12½x12
451 A148 1pi olive & multi .... .45 .25
452 A148 2pi yellow & multi .... .75 .30
453 A148 25pi ocher, lilac & brn .... 3.25 .45
   Nos. 451-453 (3) 4.45 1.00

Intl. Criminal Police Org., 50th anniv.
For surcharge see No. 498.

ITU Emblem and Waves
A149

2pi, Globe and waves. 3pi, ITU emblem.

1973, May 17
454 A149 1pi dull blue & multi .... .40 .25
455 A149 2pi brt blue & multi .... .65 .30
456 A149 3pi orange & multi .... 1.10 .45
   Nos. 454-456 (3) 2.15 1.00

World Telecommunications Day.
For surcharge see No. 499.

Globe, Hand Holding House — A150

Men Building Pylon — A151

Design: 10pi, Fish in net, symbols of agriculture, industry and transportation.

1973, Nov. 6   Litho.   Perf. 12x12½
457 A150 8pi gray & multi .... .90 .25
458 A150 10pi vio bl, blk & gray .... 1.40 .30
459 A151 15pi blk, org & lil rose .... 1.75 .45
   Nos. 457-459 (3) 4.05 1.00

National development.
For surcharge see No. 514.

Water Buffalos
A152

1973, Dec. 20   Litho.   Perf. 12½x12
460 A152 5pi shown .... 2.50 .50
461 A152 10pi Water buffalo .... 3.50 .75

Human Rights Flame, Three Races
A153

Design: 100pi, Human Rights flame, scales and people, vert.

1973, Dec. 29   Perf. 12½x12, 12x12½
462 A153 15pi ultra & multi .... .50 .25
463 A153 100pi green & multi .... 2.75 .50

25th anniv. of Universal Declaration of Human Rights.

"25" and WHO Emblem
A154

Design: 15pi, WHO emblem, diff.

1973, Dec. 31   Perf. 12½x12
464 A154 8pi orange, bl & brn .... .80 .30
465 A154 15pi lt brn, bl & brt pink .... 1.20 .45

25th anniversary of WHO.
For surcharge see No. 515.

Sampan Ferry
A155

Design: 10pi, Sampan ferry (different).

1974, Jan. 13   Litho.   Perf. 14x13½
466 A155 5pi lt blue & multi .... 1.25 .30
467 A155 10pi yellow grn & multi .... 2.00 .70

Sampan ferry women.

Soldiers of 7 Nations
A156

American War Memorial
A157

Map of South Viet Nam and Allied Flags — A158

Design: No. 469, Soldiers and flags of South Viet Nam, Korea, US, Australia New Zealand, Thailand and Philippines. Same flags shown on 8pi and 60pi.

1974, Jan. 28   Perf. 12½x12, 12x12½
468 A156 8pi multicolored .... .65 .25
469 A156 15pi lt brown & multi .... 1.40 .30
470 A157 15pi multicolored .... 1.40 .30
471 A158 60pi multicolored .... 4.00 .60
   Nos. 468-471 (4) 7.45 1.45

In honor of South Viet Nam's allies.
For surcharge see No. 516.

Trung Sisters on Elephants Fighting Chinese
A159

1974, Feb. 27   Litho.   Perf. 12½x12
472 A159 8pi green, citron & blk .... 1.00 .25
473 A159 15pi dp orange & multi .... 1.50 .30
474 A159 80pi ultra, pink & blk .... 3.50 .45
   Nos. 472-474 (3) 6.00 1.00

Trung Trac and Trung Nhi, queens of Viet Nam, 39-43 A.D. Day of Vietnamese Women.

Pres. Thieu Type of 1973 and

Farmers Going to Work — A160

Woman Farmer Holding Rice — A161

1974, Mar. 26   Litho.   Perf. 14
475 A147 10pi blue & multi .... 1.50 .30
   Perf. 12½x12, 12x12½
476 A160 20pi yellow & multi .... 1.50 .45
477 A161 70pi blue & multi 12.00 1.50
   Nos. 475-477 (3) 15.00 2.25

Agriculture Day. Size of No. 475 is 31x50mm, No. 450 is 34x54mm and printed on thick paper. No. 475 has been extensively redrawn and first line of inscription in bottom panel changed to "26 THANG BA."
   Value for No. 477 is for stamp with first day cancel. Commercially used examples are worth substantially more.

Hung Vuong with Bamboo Tallies
A162

Flag Inscribed: Hung Vuong, Founder of Kingdom
A163

1974, Apr. 2   Perf. 14x13½
478 A162 20pi yellow & multi .... 1.50 .30
479 A163 100pi olive & multi .... 4.50 .45

Hung Vuong, founder of Vietnamese nation and of Hông-Bang Dynasty (2879-258 B.C.).

National Library
A164

New National Library Building: 15pi, Library, right facade and Phoenix.

1974, Apr. 14
480 A164 10pi orange, brn & blk .... .80 .75
481 A164 15pi multicolored .... 1.20 .90

Nos. 391 and 437 Srchd. with New Value and Two Bars in Red

1974   Perf. 13
482 A121 25pi on 16pi multi 10.00 2.75
483 A138 25pi on 16pi multi 5.00 2.25

Memorial Tower, Saigon — A165

Globe, Crane Lifting Crate — A167

Crane with Flags, Globe and Map of Viet Nam — A166

Perf. 12x12½, 12½x12½
1974, June 22   Litho.
484 A165 10pi blue & multi .... .75 .35
485 A166 20pi multicolored .... 1.75 .45
486 A167 60pi yellow & multi .... 4.50 .60
   Nos. 484-486 (3) 7.00 1.40

International Aid Day.

Sun and Views of Saigon, Dalat Hué
A168

Cau-Bong Bridge, Nha Trang
A169

Thien-Mu Pagoda, Hué — A170

1974, July 12   Perf. 14x13½, 13½x14
487 A168 5pi blue & multi .... 1.10 .30
488 A169 10pi blue & multi .... 1.10 .60
489 A170 15pi yellow & multi 1.90 1.00
   Nos. 487-489 (3) 4.10 1.90

Tourist publicity.

Rhynchostylis Gigantea — A171

Orchids: 20pi, Cypripedium caliosum, vert. 200pi, Dendrobium nobile.

1974, Aug. 18
490	A171	10pi blue & multi	.35	.40
491	A171	20pi yellow & multi	.40	.45
492	A171	200pi bister & multi	6.50	1.25
		Nos. 490-492 (3)	7.25	2.10

Hands Passing Letter, UPU Emblem A172

UPU Emblem and Woman — A173

UPU Cent.: 30pi, World map, bird, UPU emblem.

Perf. 12½x12, 12x12½
1974, Oct. 9   **Litho.**
493	A172	20pi ultra & multi	.35	.30
494	A172	30pi orange & multi	.85	.45
495	A173	300pi gray & multi	2.75	1.25
		Nos. 493-495 (3)	3.95	2.00

Nos. 398, 447, 451, 454, 387 Srchd. with New Value and Two Bars in Red
1974-75
496	A125	25pi on 1pi multi	16.00	5.00
497	A144	25pi on 1pi multi	16.00	5.00
498	A148	25pi on 1pi multi	16.00	5.00
499	A149	25pi on 1pi multi	22.50	9.00
500	A120	25pi on 7pi multi	19.00	5.00
		Nos. 496 500 (5)	89.50	29.00

Issued: #496, 498, 1/1/75; others, 11/18/74.

Hien Lam Pavilion, Hué A174

Throne, Imperial Palace, Hué A175

Water Pavilion, Hué A176

1975, Jan. 5   **Litho.**   *Perf. 14x13½*
501	A174	25pi multicolored	1.40	1.40
502	A175	30pi multicolored	1.75	1.75
503	A176	60pi multicolored	2.10	2.10
		Nos. 501-503 (3)	5.25	5.25

Historic sites.

Symbol of Youth, Children Holding Flower — A177

Family and Emblem A178

1975, Jan. 14   *Perf. 11½*
504	A177	20pi blue & multi	2.50	.35

Perf. 12½x12
505	A178	70pi yellow & multi	2.50	.35

Intl. Conf. on Children & Natl. Development.

Unicorn Dance A179

Boy Lighting Firecracker A180

Bringing New Year Gifts and Wishes — A181

Perf. 14x13½, 13½x14
1975, Jan. 26   **Litho.**
506	A179	20pi multicolored	2.50	.35
507	A180	30pi blue & multi	3.00	.50
508	A181	100pi bister & multi	7.00	1.00
		Nos. 506-508 (3)	12.50	1.85

Lunar New Year, Tet.

A182

A184

Designs: 25pi, Military chief from play "San Hau." 40pi, Scene from "Tam Ha Nam Duong." 100pi, Warrior Luu-Kim-Dinn.

1975, Feb. 23
509	A182	25pi rose & multi	1.25	.45
510	A183	40pi lt green & multi	2.10	.45
511	A184	100pi violet & multi	7.50	.75
		Nos. 509-511 (3)	10.85	1.65

National theater.

Produce, Map of Viet Nam, Ship — A185

Irrigation Project A186

1975, Mar. 26   Litho.   *Perf. 12½x12*
512	A185	10pi multicolored	1.75	.75
513	A186	50pi multicolored	4.50	1.20

Agriculture Day; 5th anniv. of Agrarian Reform Law.

Nos. 457, 464, 468 Srchd. with New Value and Two Bars in Red
1975
514	A150	10pi on 8pi multi	30.00	10.00
515	A154	10pi on 8pi multi	19.00	6.00
516	A156	20pi on 8pi multi	9.00	4.00
		Nos. 514-516 (3)	58.00	20.00

In the 1980's a number of South Viet Nam stamps appeared on the market. These apparently had been printed before the collapse of the Republic but saw no postal use. These include, but are not limited to, sets of two for western electric and for rural electric, one each for history, library, New Year and cows, a set of three for transportation and a set of four for economic development.

SEMI-POSTAL STAMPS

Type of 1952 Surcharged in Carmine

Perf. 12x12½
1952, Nov. 10   **Unwmk.**
B1	A3	1.50pi + 50c bl, yel & brn	3.50	2.75
		Never hinged	7.50	

The surtax was for the Red Cross.

Sabers and Flag — SP1

1952, Dec. 21   Engr.   *Perf. 13*
B2	SP1	3.30pi + 1.70pi dp claret	2.25	2.00

The surtax was for the Wounded Soldiers' Aid Organization.

X-ray Camera and Patient SP2

1960, Aug. 1   *Perf. 13*
B3	SP2	3pi + 50c bl grn & red	1.40	.75

The surtax was for the Anti-Tuberculosis Foundation.

AIR POST STAMPS

AP1

AP2

Perf. 13½x12½
1952-53   Unwmk.   Photo.
C1	AP1	3.30pi dk brn red & pale yel grn	1.00	.50
C2	AP1	4pi brown & yellow	1.25	.35
C3	AP1	5.10pi dk vio bl & sal pink	1.25	.75
C4	AP2	6.30pi yellow & car	1.50	.85
		Nos. C1-C4 (4)	5.00	2.45

Issued: #C2, 11/24/53; others, 3/8/52.

Dragon AP3

Fish — AP4

1952, Sept. 3   Engr.   Perf. 13

C5	AP3	40c red	1.40	.35
C6	AP3	70c green	2.40	.50
C7	AP3	80c ultra	2.40	.50
C8	AP3	90c brown	2.40	.50
C9	AP4	3.70pi deep magenta	5.25	.75
		Nos. C5-C9 (5)	13.85	2.60

Nos. C5-C9 exist imperforate in a souvenir booklet. Value, $175.

South Viet Nam

Phoenix — AP5

1955, Sept. 7

C10	AP5	4pi violet & lil rose	3.25	2.25

Crane
Carrying
Letter
AP6

1960, Dec. 20.   Perf. 13

C11	AP6	1pi olive	.90	.45
C12	AP6	4pi green & dk blue	2.10	.60
C13	AP6	5pi ocher & purple	2.50	.75
C14	AP6	10pi deep magenta	4.50	1.20
		Nos. C11-C14 (4)	10.00	3.00

POSTAGE DUE STAMPS

Catalogue values for unused stamps in this section, from this point to the end of the section, are for Never Hinged items. Because of the tropical conditions, never hinged stamps must also be free of wrinkles, toning, and any other disturbance.

Temple Lion — D1

Perf. 13x13½

1952, June 16   Typo.   Unwmk.

J1	D1	10c red & green	.70	.60
J2	D1	20c green & yellow	1.00	.80
J3	D1	30c purple & orange	1.25	1.00
J4	D1	40c dk grn & sal rose	1.60	1.25
J5	D1	50c dp carmine & gray	2.10	1.75
J6	D1	1pi blue & silver	3.25	3.00
		Nos. J1-J6 (6)	9.90	8.40

South Viet Nam

Dragon — D2

1955-56

J7	D2	2pi red vio & org	.40	.30
J8	D2	3pi violet & grnsh bl	.55	.40
J9	D2	5pi violet & yellow	.60	.45
J10	D2	10pi dk green & car	.90	.65
J11	D2	20pi red & brt grn ('56)	2.00	1.50
J12	D2	30pi brt grn & yel ('56)	3.00	2.25
J13	D2	50pi dk red brn & yel ('56)	6.00	4.50
J14	D2	100pi pur & yel ('56)	12.00	9.00
		Nos. J7-J14 (8)	25.45	19.05

Nos. J11-J14 inscribed "BUU-CHINH" instead of "TIMBRE-TAXE."

Atlas Moth — D3

Design: 3pi, 5pi, 10pi, Three butterflies.

1968, Aug. 20   Photo.   Perf. 13½x13

J15	D3	50c multicolored	2.25	.90
J16	D3	1pi multicolored	2.75	1.00
J17	D3	2pi multicolored	5.00	2.00
J18	D3	3pi multicolored	6.75	3.00
J19	D3	5pi multicolored	12.00	4.75
J20	D3	10pi multicolored	18.00	6.75
		Nos. J15-J20 (6)	46.75	18.40

Nos. J15-J18 Srchd. with New Value and Two Bars in Red

1974, Oct. 1

J21	D3	5pi on 3pi multi	2.00	1.50
J22	D3	10pi on 50c multi	2.00	1.50
J23	D3	40pi on 1pi multi	2.00	1.50
J24	D3	60pi on 2pi multi	2.00	1.50
		Nos. J21-J24 (4)	8.00	6.00

MILITARY STAMPS

Catalogue values for unused stamps in this section, from this point to the end of the section, are for Never Hinged items. Because of the tropical conditions, never hinged stamps must also be free of wrinkles, toning, and any other disturbance.

Soldier
Guarding
Village
M1

Rouletted 7½

1961, June   Unwmk.   Litho.

M1	M1	och, brn, dk grn & blk	4.00	1.50

1961, Sept.   Typo.

M2	M1	org yel, dk grn & brn	4.00	1.50

Bottom inscription on No. M1 is black, brown on No. M2.

Battle and
Refugees
M2

1969, Feb. 22   Litho.   Imperf.

M3	M2	red & green	70.00	80.00
a.		Booklet pane of 10	700.00	

VIET NAM, DEMOCRATIC REPUBLIC
(North Viet Nam)

LOCATION — In eastern Indo-China
GOVT. — Republic
AREA — 61,293 sq. mi.
POP. — 18,800,000 (1968 est.)
CAPITAL — Hanoi

Beginning in 1946, the Communist Viet Minh fought the French in a guerrilla war that ended with the French defeat at Dien Bien Phu in 1954. In an agreement signed in Geneva on July 21, 1954, Viet Nam was partitioned at the 17th parallel. The government in Hanoi controlled the north, and engaged in another protracted military campaign against American and South Vietnamese forces that led to the official

---

reunification of the country under Communist control on July 2, 1976.

100 cents = 1 Dong
100 Xu = 1 Dong (1959)

All stamps are without gum unless otherwise indicated. Values for stamps with gum are for Never Hinged items.

Watermark

Wmk. 376 — "R de C"

VIET MINH ISSUES

Stamps and Types of Indo-China Overprinted or Surcharged

No. 236 Overprinted

Printing Methods and Perfs as Before

1945-46   Without Gum

1L1	A41	1pi yel grn (Yersin)	7.50	19.00

Nos. 238-239 (Rhodes) Ovptd.

1L2	A43	15c dk vio brn, perf. 11½	3.00	4.00
a.		Perf. 12	3.00	4.00
b.		Perf. 11½, green overprint	10.00	10.00
1L3	A43	30c org brn, perf. 11½	3.00	3.00
a.		Perf. 13½	6.00	6.00
b.		Perf. 12	30.00	—

No. 242 Overprinted

1L4	A44	50c dl red (Athlete)	20.00	25.00

No. 241 Ovptd.

1L5	A44	10c dk vio brn & yel (Athlete)	8.00	10.00

Nos. 218-222 (Petain) Overprinted

1L6	A32	3c olive brn, perf. 11½	3.00	3.00
a.		Perf. 12x14	10.00	
b.		Perf. 14	30.00	
1L7	A32	6c rose red	3.00	3.00
1L8	A32	10c dull grn (R)	5.00	5.00
1L9	A32	40c dk bl (R)	5.00	10.00
1L10	A32	40c slate bl (R)	10.00	20.00
		Nos. 1L6-1L10 (5)	26.00	41.00

Nos. 245-246 and Type (Pavie) Overprinted

1L11	A46	4c org yel	3.00	3.00
1L12	A46	10c dl grn	5.00	6.00
1L13	A46	20c dark red	3.00	3.00
		Nos. 1L11-1L13 (3)	11.00	12.00

No. 165A Overprinted

1L14	A22	25c dk bl (Planting Rice, R), top line 18 mm wide	80.00	90.00
a.		Top line 20 mm wide	67.50	9.00

Nos. 1L14-1L14a issued with gum.

No. 232 (Courbet) Overprinted

1L15	A39	3c lt brn	2.00	2.00
1L16	A39	6c car rose	2.00	2.00

No. 261 (Lagree) Overprinted Vertically

1L17	A52	40c brt bl	5.00	15.00

Nos. 253-255 (Doumer) Overprinted

1L18	A50	2c red vio	2.00	2.00
1L19	A50	4c org brn	2.00	2.00
1L20	A50	10c dull grn	3.00	3.00
a.		"HANH-PHUC" inverted	22.00	—
		Nos. 1L18-1L20 (3)	7.00	7.00

No. 217 (Petain) Overprinted | Nos. 256-258 (Charner) Overprinted

1L21 A32 1c olive brn 2.00 2.00
1L22 A51 10c green 3.00 3.00
1L23 A51 20c red 5.00 15.00
1L24 A51 1pi pale yel grn 10.00 25.00
Nos. 1L21-1L24 (4) 20.00 45.00

No. 230 and Type (Genouilly) Overprinted

1L25 A37 5c dull brown 2.00 2.00
1L26 A37 6c carmine rose 3.50 3.50

No. 210-212 (Sihanouk) Surcharged

1L27 A28 5d on 1c red org (Bl) 45.00 45.00
1L28 A28 10d on 6c violet (R) 50.00 50.00
1L29 A28 15d on 25c dp ultra (R) 50.00 50.00
Nos. 1L27-1L29 (3) 145.00 145.00

Nos. 225-226 (Sihanouk) Surcharged

No. 1L30 | No. 1L31

1L30 A34 50xu on 1c reddish brn 4.00 —
1L31 A35 2d on 6c car rose 30.00 —

Nos. 213-214 (Elephant) Surcharged

1L32 A29 2d on 3c red brn (G) 45.00 45.00
1L33 A29 4d on 6c crim (G) 45.00 45.00

Nos. 247-248 (Pasquier) Surcharged Vertically

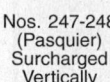

1L34 A47 1d on 5c brn vio 3.00 4.00
1L35 A47 2d on 10c dl grn 4.00 5.00

No. B30 (Cathedral) Surcharged

1L36 SP7 5d on 15c+60c brn pur 40.00 40.00

Nos. 259-260 (Lagree) Surcharged Vertically

1L37 A52 30xu on 1c dl gray brn (R) 3.00 —
1L38 A52 3d on 15c dl rose vio 6.00 —

Nos. 243-244 (La Grandiere) Surcharged

1L39 A45 1d on 5c dk brn (Bl) 8.00 8.00
1L40 A45 4d on 1c dull brn 4.00 6.00

Type of 1943 (Garnier) Srchd.

1L41 A42 30xu on 15c dp plum (R) 2.00 3.00

No. 237 (Garnier) Surcharged with New Value, "VIET-NAM DAN CHU CONG HOA BUU-CHINH," Wavy & Straight Line Obliterators
1L42 A42 5d on 1c dull ol bis 6.00 —

Nos. 249-252 (De Lanessan, Van Vollenhoven) Surcharged

No. 1L43

No. 1L44

No. 1L45

No. 1L46

1L43 A49 50xu on 1c ol brn 5.00 6.00
1L44 A48 60xu on 1c ol brn 5.00 5.00
1L45 A48 1.60d on 10c green 3.00 4.00
1L46 A49 3d on 15c dp reddish pur (Bl) 4.00 6.00
Nos. 1L43-1L46 (4) 17.00 21.00

Nos. B30-B31 (Cathedral) Surcharged

1L47 SP7 2d on 15c+60c pur brn 25.00 —
1L48 SP7 3d on 40c+1.10pi blue 25.00 —

No. 234 (Yersin) Surcharged

1L49 A41 +2d on 6c car rose 5.00 —

No. 233 (Behaine) Surcharged

1L50 A40 +3d on 20c dull red 9.00 9.00

No. 215 (Saigon Fair) Surcharged

1L51 A30 +4d on 6c car rose 5.00 6.00

No. 229 (Natl. Revolution) Surcharged

1L52 A36 +4d on 6c car rose 10.00 —

Nos. 213-214 Surcharged

1L53 A29 +5d on 3c reddish brown 8.00 10.00
1L54 A29 +10d on 6c crimson 8.00 12.00

Nos. 216, 224 Surcharged

1L55 A31 30xu +3d on 6c (Nam-Phuong) 2.00 3.00
Perf. 13½
1L56 A33 30xu +3d on 6c (Bao-Dai) 2.50 3.00
a. Perf. 12 30.00

Ho Chi Minh — VM1

1946 Litho. Unwmk. Perf. 11½
Without Gum
1L57 VM1 1h green 1.00 1.00
1L58 VM1 3h brt rose red 1.00 1.00
1L59 VM1 9h yellow bister 1.00 1.00

With Added Inscription

1L60 VM1 4h +6h Prus blue 2.50 5.00
1L61 VM1 6h +9h dp pur 2.50 5.00
Nos. 1L57-1L61 (5) 8.00 13.00

Ho Chi Minh — VM2

1948 Typo. Perf. 7 Rough
Thin, Rough, Brown Paper
1L62 VM2 2d brown, *buff* 20.00 160.00
1L63 VM2 5d red, *buff* 20.00 160.00

For surcharge and overprints see Nos. 50, O6-O7.

DEMOCRATIC REPUBLIC OF VIET NAM

From 1945-2002, all stamps are without gum unless otherwise indicated. Values for stamps with gum are for Never Hinged items.

Many North Vietnamese stamps are roughly perforated, especially issues before 1958.

Ho Chi Minh, Map of Vietnam — A1

1951-55 Unwmk. Litho. Imperf.
1	A1	100d brown	20.00	20.00
a.		Perf. 11¼ ('55)	20.00	20.00
2	A1	100d green	20.00	20.00
a.		Perf. 11¼ ('55)	20.00	20.00

Perf. 11¼
3	A1	200d red	20.00	20.00
a.		Imperf. ('55)	20.00	20.00
		Nos. 1-3 (3)	60.00	60.00

Nos. 1-3 printed on thin semi-transparent paper.
Nos. 1-3 used values are for cto. Postally used examples are worth about 5 times these values.
Counterfeits exist.
For surcharges, see Nos. 9-14, 36-38, and note before No. J1.

Blacksmith — A2

1953-55 Perf. 11¼
4	A2	100d violet	4.00	3.00
5	A2	500d brown	6.00	8.00

Issued: 100d, 6/53. 500d, 2/55.

Georgi Malenkov, Ho Chi Minh, Mao Tse-tung and Flags — A3

1954-55 Perf. 11¼
6	A3	50d brown & red, brnish	25.00	25.00
7	A3	100d red	25.00	25.00
8	A3	100d yellow & red, brnish	30.00	30.00
		Nos. 6-8 (3)	80.00	80.00

Issued: 50d, 10/54; #7, 1/54; #8, 4/55.
No. 7 printed on thin, white paper.

Nos. 1-3 Surcharged in Red or Blue

1954, Oct. Imperf.
9	A1	10d on 100d brown	22.50	32.50
10	A1	10d on 100d green	22.50	32.50

Perf. 11
11	A1	20d on 200d red (Bl)	22.50	42.50
		Nos. 9-11 (3)	67.50	107.50

Nos. 1-3 Surcharged in Black, Red or Blue

1954, Oct. Imperf.
12	A1	10d on 100d brown (Bk, R or Bl)	26.00	35.00
13	A1	10d on 100d green (Bk, R or Bl)	26.00	35.00

Perf. 11
14	A1	20d on 200d red (Bk or Bl)	60.00	75.00
		Nos. 12-14 (3)	112.00	145.00

Nos. 9-14 exist with counterfeit surcharges, counterfeit surcharges on counterfeit stamps, and with fantasy surcharges.

Victory at Dien Bien Phu A4

1954-56 Perf. 11¼
17	A4	10d red brn & yel brn	25.00	25.00
a.		Imperf	110.00	110.00
18	A4	50d red & org yel	20.00	7.50
a.		Imperf	20.00	15.00
19	A4	150d brown & blue	20.00	10.00
a.		Imperf	20.00	15.00
		Nos. 17-19 (3)	65.00	42.50

Issued: Imperfs, 10/54; others, 1956. See #O5.
Used values for Nos. 17-19 are for postally used examples. The 10d exists cto, perf or imperf. Value about 1/10 those shown above.

Liberation of Hanoi — A5

1955, Jan. 1 Perf. 11½
20	A5	10d lt blue & bl	6.50	6.50
21	A5	50d dk grn & grn	8.00	8.00
22	A5	150d rose & brn red	10.00	12.00
		Nos. 20-22 (3)	24.50	26.50

Nos. 20-22 used values are for postally used examples. Cto stamps are worth about $1 each.

Land Reform A6

1955-56 Perf. 11¼
23	A6	5d lt green	18.00	4.75
24	A6	10d gray	18.00	4.75
25	A6	20d orange	18.00	6.00
26	A6	50d rose	18.00	6.00
27	A6	100d lt brown	37.50	6.00
		Nos. 23-27 (5)	109.50	27.50

Issued: 100d, 12/55; 20d, 50d, 2/56; others, 6/56. See Nos. O8-O9.

Return of Government to Hanoi — A7

1956, Mar. 1 Perf. 11¼
28	A7	1000d violet	47.50	12.00
29	A7	1500d dk blue	65.00	12.00
30	A7	2000d turquoise	65.00	12.00
31	A7	3000d blue green	80.00	12.00
		Nos. 28-31 (4)	257.50	48.00

Counterfeits exist, often imperf and offered as proofs.

Re-opening of Hanoi-China Railroad — A8

1956, Mar. 1
32	A8	100d dark blue	20.00	6.00
33	A8	200d blue green	20.00	6.00
34	A8	300d violet	40.00	6.00
35	A8	500d lilac brown	47.50	6.00
		Nos. 32-35 (4)	127.50	24.00

Counterfeits exist, often imperf and offered as proofs.

Nos. 1-3 Surcharged

1954, Oct. Imperf.
36	A1	10d on 100d brown	25.00	40.00
37	A1	10d on 100d green	25.00	—

Perf. 11
38	A1	20d on 200d red	15.00	15.00
		Nos. 36-38 (3)	65.00	55.00

Nos. 36-38 exist with counterfeit surcharges, counterfeit surcharges on counterfeit stamps, and with fantasy surcharges.

Tran Dang Ninh (1910-55), Guerrilla Leader A9

1956, July Litho. Perf. 11¼
39	A9	5d bl grn & pale grn	4.50	2.00
40	A9	10d lilac & rose	4.50	2.00
41	A9	20d gr brn & dk gray	5.50	3.00
42	A9	100d dk blue pale bl	6.50	3.50
		Nos. 39-42 (4)	21.00	10.50

Nos. 39-42 used values are for postally used. CTO value, set $2.50.

Mac Thi Buoi (1927-51), Guerrilla Leader A10

1956, Nov. 3 Perf. 11½
43	A10	1000d rose & lilac rose	47.50	15.00
44	A10	2000d brown & bister	90.00	24.00
45	A10	4000d bl grn & green	190.00	35.00
46	A10	5000d ultra & lt blue	240.00	60.00
		Nos. 43-46 (4)	567.50	134.00

Nos. 43-46 used values are for postally used. Cto value, set $40.
Counterfeits exist, often imperf and offered as proofs.

Bai Thuong Dam — A11

1956-58 Perf. 11¼
47	A11	100d vio bl & lil brn	10.00	6.50
a.		Perf 13	11.00	9.50
48	A11	200d lilac & gr grn	11.00	6.50
a.		Perf 13	12.50	11.00
49	A11	300d rose & lil brn	16.00	12.00
a.		Perf 13	12.50	11.00
		Nos. 47-49 (3)	37.00	25.00

Nos. 47-49 used values are for postally used. CTO values: Nos. 47-49, set $4; Nos. 47a-49a, set $5.50.
Issued: #47-49, 12/15/56; #47a-49a, 1958.

No. 1L63 Surcharged

1956, Dec. Typo. Perf. 7 Rough
50	VM2	50d on 5d org red, brnish	40.00	50.00
a.		50d on 5d dp red, brnish	90.00	100.00

Reprints and counterfeits exist.

Nam Dinh Textile Mill — A13

1957, Mar. Litho. Perf. 12½
51-53	A13	100d, 200d, 300d, set of 3	25.00	2.50
51a		Perf. 11½	6.00	6.00
51b		Imperf	12.00	12.00
51c		Perf. 11½x12½	6.50	6.50
51d		Imperf x perf 11½	12.00	12.00

Nos. 51-53 used values are for cto. Postally used value, set $25.

Ho Chi Minh — A14

1957 Perf. 12½
54-57	A14	20d, 60d, 100d, 300d, set of 4	20.00	2.00

Nos. 54-57 used values are for cto. Postally used value, set $8.
Issued: 20d, 60d, 12/13; others, 5/19.

Fourth World Trade Union Congress, Leipzig A15

1957, Aug. 1 Perf. 12½
58	A15	300d red violet	8.00	.75

No. 58 used value is for cto. Postally used value $5.50.
See Nos. O17-O20.

Democratic Republic, 12th Anniv. A16

1957, Sept. 2   *Perf. 13*
59-60 A16 20d, 100d, set of 2   10.00 2.00
    Nos. 59-60 used values are for cto. Postally used value, set $5.50.

Presidents Voroshilov, Ho Chi Minh — A17

1957, Nov. 7   *Perf. 12½*
61-63 A17 100d, 500d, set of
     1000d, 3   40.00 30.00
    Russian revolution, 40th anniv.

    Used values from No. 64 on are for cto stamps. Postally used examples are worth substantially more.

Anti-illiteracy Campaign — A18

1958, Jan. 6   *Perf. 12½*
64-66 A18 50d, 150d, 1000d,
     set of 3   30.00 2.00

A19

1958, Mar. 8
67-68 A19 150d, 500d, set of 2 30.00 2.50
    Physical education.

A20

1958, May 1
69-70 A20 50d, 150d, set of 2 10.00 1.10
    May Day.

Fourth Intl. Congress of Democratic Women, Vienna A21

1958, May   *Typo.*
71 A21 150d blue   7.00 .75

A22

A22a

    A22: #72, 150d, #75, 2000d, Basket, lace & cup, vert.
    A22a: #73, 150d, #74, 1000d, Potter.

1958   *Litho.*
72-75 A22, A22a Set of 4   22.00 2.00
    Arts & Crafts Fair, Hanoi.
    Issued: Nos. 72, 75, 6/26; others, 8/19.

Building the Reunification Railway — A23

1958, July 20
76-77 A23 50d, 150d, set of 2   7.00 .75

August Revolution, 13th Anniv. A24

1958, Aug. 19
78-79 A24 150d, 500d, set of 2   7.00 1.10

Resistance Movement in South Viet Nam, 13th Anniv. A25

1958, Sept. 23
80-81 A25 50d, 150d, set of 2   8.00 .75

A26

1958, Oct.
82 A26 150d grnsh blue & blk   2.25 .40
    Tran Hung Dao (1253-1300).

A27

    Hanoi Engineering Plant.

1958, Nov. 7   *Engr.*   *Perf. 11½*
83 A27 150d brown   2.50 .40

Mutual Aid Teams — A28

1958, Nov. 7
84-85 A28 150d, 500d, set of 2   12.00 2.75

Ngoc Son Temple (Temple of Jade) — A29

1958, Dec. 1   *Photo.*   *Perf. 12*
86-87 A29 150d, 2000d, set of
     2   20.00 3.00

Rattanware Cooperative A30

1958, Dec. 31
88 A30 150d greenish blue   2.75 .65

Ha Long Bay — A31

1959, Feb. 8
89-90 A31 150d, 350d, set of 2   6.00 2.00

Cam Pha Coal Mines — A32

1959, Mar. 3   *Engr.*   *Perf. 11½*
91 A32 150d blue   6.00 .40

Trung Sisters — A33

1959, Mar. 14   *Litho.*   *Perf. 11*
92-93 A33 5xu, 8xu, set of 2   7.00 1.10

World Peace Movement, 10th Anniv. — A34

1959, Apr. 15
94 A34 12xu purple, *rose*   1.25 .50

Xuan Quang Dam A35

1959, May 1
95-96 A35 6xu, 12xu, set of 2   6.00 .70

Phu Loi Massacre A36

1959, May 15
97-98 A36 12xu, 20xu, set of 2   5.50 .70

Hien Luong Bridge — A37

1959, July 20
99 A37 12xu black & carmine   2.50 .65

Me Tri Radio Station — A38

1959, Aug. 10
100-101 A38 3xu, 12xu, set of 2   3.50 1.00

Shooting A39

Swimming — A39a

Wrestling — A39b

1959, Sept. 2
102 A39   1xu lt blue & dk blue   1.10 .35
103 A39a 6xu multicolored   1.90 .35
104 A39b 12xu brown rose   3.50 .35
    Nos. 102-104 (3)   6.50 1.05

People's
Republic of
China, 10th
Anniv. — A40

1959, Oct. 1
105 A40 12xu multicolored   4.00   .70

Fruits — A41

Designs: 3xu, Coconuts. 12xu, Bananas.
30xu, Pineapple.

1959, Nov. 20
106-108 A41 Set of 3   6.00 1.00

People's
Army, 15th
Anniv.
A42

1959, Dec. 22
109 A42 12xu multicolored   2.25   .35

A43

1960, Jan. 6
110-111 A43 2xu, 12xu, set of 2   4.25   .70
Vietnamese Workers' Party, 30th Anniv.

A44

Ethnic costumes: 2xu, Ede. 10xu, Meo. No.
114, 12xu, Tay. No. 115, 12xu, Thai.

1960, Jan. 6
112-115 A44 Set of 4   7.50 2.00

Census
A45

Designs: 1xu, People. 12xu, Transmitting
tower, dam, buildings, workers.

1960, Feb. 20
116-117 A45 Set of 2   3.25 1.00
No. 117 is 37x26mm.

Intl.
Women's
Day, 50th
Anniv.
A46

1960, Mar. 8
118 A46 12xu multicolored   1.75   .70

A47

1960, Apr. 5
119-120 A47 4xu, 12xu, set of
2   40.00 20.00
Hung Vuong Temple.

A48

1960, Apr. 22
121-122 A48 5xu, 12xu, set of
2   5.00 1.00
121a   Souv. sheet of 1, olive
    brown & blue, imperf.   65.00 65.00
Lenin. No. 121a exists on brownish paper.

Election of National
Assembly
Delegates — A49

1960, May 3   **Perf. 11**
123 A49 12xu multicolored, *rose* 1.50   .45

A50

1960, May 8
124-125 A50 8xu, 12xu, set of 2   3.50   .65
Viet Nam Red Cross.

A51

Ho Chi Minh, 70th Birthday: Nos. 128, 130,
Ho with children.

1960, May 19
126 A51   4xu green & purple   1.50   .35
127 A51 12xu pink & brown   2.25   .35
128 A51 12xu multicolored   2.25   .35
    Nos. 126-128 (3)   6.00 1.05
Souvenir Sheets
Imperf
129 A51 10xu yel bis & brn,
    rose   12.00   —
130 A51 10xu multicolored   11.00   —
    No. 128 is 25x39mm.

New
Constitution
A52

1960, July 7
131 A52 12xu lemon & gray   2.50 1.00

National
Day, 15th
Anniv.
A53

1960, Sept. 2
132-133 A53 4xu, 12xu, set of 2   6.00   .65

Development — A54

Designs: No. 134, Classroom. No. 135,
Plowing. No. 136, Factory.

1960, Sept. 2
134-136 A54 12xu Set of 3   10.00 1.00

3rd Vietnamese Communist Party
Congress — A55

1960, Sept. 4
137-138 A55 1xu, 12xu, set of 2   5.00   .65

World Federation of Trade Unions,
15th Anniv. — A56

1960, Oct. 3
139 A56 12xu black & vermilion   4.25   .35

Hanoi, 950th
Anniv.
A57

1960, Oct. 10   **Litho.**   **Perf. 11**
140-141 A57 8xu, 12xu, set of
2   6.00   .65
141a   Souv. sheet of 1, imperf.   15.00 12.00
    No. 141a exists on brownish paper.

15 Years' Achievements
Exhibition — A58

1960, Oct. 20
142-143 A58 2xu, 12xu, set of 2   3.00   .65

World Federation of Democratic Youth,
15th Anniv. — A59

1960, Nov. 10
144 A59 12xu multicolored   2.75   .35

Trade
Unions,
2nd Natl.
Congress
A60

1961, Feb. 10
145 A60 12xu multicolored, *rose* 2.00   .35

Vietnamese
Women's Union, 3rd
Natl.
Congress — A61

1961, Mar. 8   **Tinted Paper**
146-147 A61 6xu, 12xu, set of 2   5.00 1.25

Animals — A62

Designs: 12xu, Rusa unicolor. 20xu,
Helarctos malynus. 50xu, Elephas maximus.
1d, Hylobates leucogenys.

1961, Mar. 8
148-151 A62 Set of 4   25.00 3.50
    Imperf., #148-151   60.00 60.00

Ly Tu Trong — A63

1961, Mar. 18
152-153 A63 2xu, 12xu, set of 2   2.75   .75
Youth Labor Union, 3rd Congress.

Young Pioneers, 20th Anniv. — A64

1961, May 2
154-155 A64 1xu, 12xu, set of 2 3.50 .75

Intl. Red Cross — A65

1961, May 8
156-157 A65 6xu, 12xu, set of 2 6.00 .70

Intl. Children's Day — A66

1961, June 1 **Perf. 11**
158-159 A66 4xu, 12xu, set of 2 4.25 .70

Yuri Gagarin's Space Flight A67

1961, June 15
160-161 A67 6xu, 12xu, set of
2 15.00 2.00
Imperf., #160-161 20.00 —

Hanoi, Hue and Saigon A68

1961, July 20
162-163 A68 12xu, 3d, set of 2 14.00 1.00

A69

1961, July 20
164-165 A69 12xu, 2d, set of 2 7.00 1.00
Imperf., #164-165
Reunification campaign.

A70

1961, Aug. 21
166-167 A70 2xu, 12xu, set of 2 4.50 .70
Geological exploration.

Savings Campaign A71

1961, Aug. 21
168-169 A71 3xu, 12xu, set of 2 4.50 .70

Ancient Towers — A72

Designs: 6xu, Thien Mu, Hue. 10xu, Pen Brush, Bac Ninh. No. 172, 12xu, Binh Son, Vinh Phuc. No. 173, 12xu, Cham, Phan Rang.

1961, Sept. 12
170-173 A72 Set of 4 9.00 3.75
Imperf., #170-173 12.00 12.00

A73

6xu, 12xu, Gherman Titov's Space Flight.

1961, Oct. 17
174-175 A73 Set of 2 6.00 .80
Imperf., #174-175 10.00 10.00

A74

1961, Oct. 17
176 A74 12xu vermilion & black 3.50 .40
22nd Communist Party Congress, Moscow.

Port of Haiphong — A75

1961, Nov. 7
177-178 A75 5xu, 12xu, set of 2 9.00 .80

A76

Musicians: No. 179, 12xu, Flutist. No. 180, 12xu, Cymbalist. 30xu, Dancer with fan. 50xu, Guitarist.

1961, Nov. 18 **Perf. 13½**
179-182 A76 Set of 4 16.00 2.00
Imperf., #179-182 20.00 20.00
182a Souvenir sheet, #179-182 50.00 50.00
Stamps on No. 182a are se-tenant and perfed on outside edges of the strip of 4.

5th World Trade Union Congress, Moscow A77

1961, Dec. 4 **Perf. 11**
183 A77 12xu dp red lil & gray 2.00 .45

Natl. Resistance, 15th Anniv. A78

1961, Dec. 4
184-185 A78 4xu, 12xu, set of 2 2.25 .65

Tet Holiday — A79

Designs: 6xu, Sow, piglets. 12xu, Poultry.

1962, Jan. 16 **Litho.**
186-187 A79 Set of 2 9.00 1.50

Tet Tree-Planting Festival — A80

1962, Jan. 16
188-189 A80 12xu, 40xu, set of 2 5.00 .80

Crops — A81

Designs: 2xu, Camellia sinensis. 6xu, Illicium verum. No. 192, 12xu, Coffea arabica. No. 193, 12xu, Ricinus communis. 30xu, Rhus succedanea.

1962, Mar. 1
190-194 A81 Set of 5 15.00 2.50

Folk Dances — A82

Designs: No. 195, 12xu, Rong Chieng. No. 196, 12xu, Bamboo. 30xu, Hat. 50xu, Parasol.

1962, Mar. 20 Photo. **Perf. 11½x12**
195-198 A82 Set of 4 20.00 2.25
Imperf., #195-198 20.00 20.00
Souvenir Sheet
199 A82 30xu like #195 16.00 16.00

First Five Year Plan — A83

Designs: 1xu, Kim Lien Apartments, Hanoi. 3xu, State farm. 8xu, Natl. Institute of Hydraulics.

1962, Apr. 10 Litho. **Perf. 11**
200-202 A83 Set of 3 4.00 1.25

A84

Flowers: No. 203, 12xu, Hibiscus rosa sinensis. No. 204, 12xu, Plumeria acutifolia. 20xu, Chrysanthemum indicum. 30xu, Nelumbium nuciferum. 50xu, Ipomoea pulchella.

Perf. 12½x11½
1962, Apr. 10 **Photo.**
203-207 A84 Set of 5 20.00 3.00
Imperf., #203-207 25.00 25.00
206a Souvenir sheet of 1 12.00 12.00

A85

1962, May 4 Litho. **Perf. 11**
208 A85 12xu multicolored 3.00 .50
3rd Natl. Heroes of Labor Congress.

Harrow A86

Dai Lai Lake A87

1962, May 25
209-210 A86-A87 6xu, 12xu set of 2 4.00 .80

Visit by Gherman Titov
A88

Titov: 12xu, Waving at children. 20xu, Receiving medal from Ho Chi Minh. 30xu, Wearing space suit.

1962, June 12
211-213 A88 Set of 3   7.00   1.50
     Imperf., #211-213   12.00   12.00

Anti-Malaria Campaign
A89

1962, July 9
214-216 A89   8xu, 12xu, 20xu, set of 3   7.50   1.50

War for Reunification — A90

1962, July 20
217 A90 12xu multicolored   2.50   .40

Ba Be Lake — A91

Design: No. 219, Ban Gioc Falls, vert.

1962, Aug. 14
218-219 A91 12xu Set of 2   4.00   .90

A stamp picturing a weight lifter exists, but was not released. Values: mint $120; used $130.

King Quang Trung (1752-92) — A92

1962, Sept. 16
220-221 A92 3xu, 12xu, set of 2   3.50   .70

Nguyen Trai (1380-1442) — A93

1962, Sept. 19
222-223 A93 3xu, 12xu, set of 2   3.50   .70

Food Crops
A94

Designs: 1xu, Peanuts. 4xu, Beans. 6xu, Sweet potatoes. 12xu, Corn. 30xu, Cassava.

1962, Oct. 10
224-228 A94 Set of 5   9.00   4.75
     Imperf., #224-228

Animal Husbandry
A95

Designs: 2xu, Feeding poultry. No. 230, 12xu, Feeding pigs. No. 231, 12xu, Cattle grazing. No. 232, 12xu, Tending water buffalo.

1962, Nov. 28
229-232 A95 Set of 4   6.00   1.75

A stamp commemorating the 45th anniversary of the Russian Revolution exists, but was not issued. Value $200.

First Five Year Plan
A96

#233, Evening classes. #234, Clearing land.

1962, Dec. 28
233-234 A96 12xu Set of 2   3.50   .70

Flights of Vostok 3 and 4 — A97

12xu, Pavel Popovich, Vostok 4. 20xu, Andrian Nikolayev, Vostok 3. 30xu, Rockets lifting-off, vert.

1962, Dec. 28   *Perf. 11*
235-237 A97 Set of 3   6.00   1.25
     Imperf., #235-237   12.00   12.00

Guerrilla — A98

1963, Jan. 15
238-239 A98 5xu, 12xu, set of 2   3.00   .70

Hoang Hoa Tham (1846-1913)
A99

1963, Feb. 10
240-241 A99 6xu, 12xu, set of 2   3.00   .90

A100

First Five Year Plan
A100a

Designs: No. 242, Fertilizing rice paddy. No. 243, Lam Thao superphosphate plant.

1963, Feb. 25
242-243 A100-A100a 12xu Set of 2   3.50   .75

Karl Marx — A101

1963, Mar. 14
244-245 A101 3xu, 12xu, set of 2   3.00   .65
Nos. 244-245 are printed on greenish and rose toned paper respectively.

Fidel Castro, Vietnamese Soldiers
A102

1963, Apr. 17
246 A102 12xu multicolored   2.00   .50

May Day
A103

1963, May 8
247 A103 12xu multicolored   1.75   .45

A104   Intl. Red Cross, Cent. — A105

Design: No. 249, Child, syringe.

1963, May 8
248 A104 12xu grn, blk & red   1.50   .35
249 A104 12xu grn, red & blk   1.50   .35
250 A105 20xu multicolored   2.50   .35
     Nos. 248-250 (3)   5.50   1.05

Mars 1 Spacecraft — A106

6xu, 12xu (#252), Mars 1 approaching Mars. 12xu (#253), 20xu, Mars 1 entering orbit, vert.

1963, May 21
251-254 A106 Set of 4   7.50   1.50
     Imperf., #251-254   15.00   15.00

Fishing Industry
A107

Designs: No. 255, Trawler, offshore fish. No. 256, Freshwater fish.

1963, July 3
255-256 A107 12xu Set of 2   9.00   .75

Ho Chi Minh, Nguyen Van Hien — A108

1963, July 20
257 A108 12xu multicolored   2.00   .35

Flights of Vostok 3, 4
A109

Designs: 12xu, Rockets in orbit. 20xu, Nikolayev. 30xu, Popovich.

1963, Aug. 11
258-260 A109 Set of 3   6.00   1.10
     Imperf., #258-260   12.00   12.00

First Five Year Plan for Chemical Industry
A110

Designs: 3xu, Viet Tri Insecticide Factory. 12xu, Viet Tri Chemical Factory.

1963, Aug. 11
261-262 A110 Set of 2   3.00   .60

Fish
A111

Designs: No. 263, 12xu, Cyprinus carpio. No. 264, 12xu, Myloharyngodon piceus. No. 265, 12xu, Hypophthalmichthys molitrix. 20xu, Ophiocephalus caqua. 30xu, Tilapia mossambica.

1963, Sept. 10
263-267 A111 Set of 5   13.00   3.00
     Imperf., #263-267   20.00   20.00
   a. Souvenir Sheet 0f 1, #266   60.00

A112

Birds: #268, 12xu, Francolinus stephenson. #269, 12xu, Acridotheres cristatellus. #270, 12xu, Halcyon smyrneusis. 20xu, Diardigallus diardi, horiz. 30xu, Egretta. 40xu, Psittacula aloxandri.

Perf. 11½x12, 12x11½

1963, Oct. 15   **Photo.**
268-273   A112   Set of 6   32.50   3.50
    Imperf., #268-273   45.00   45.00

Souvenir Sheet
274   A112 50xu Sheet of 1, like
       #272   80.00   80.00

A113

1963, Oct. 20   **Litho.**   **Perf. 11**
275   A113 12xu multicolored   1.75   .35
World Federation of Trade Unions Congress for Viet Nam.

GANEFO Games A114

#276, 12xu, Swimming. #277, 12xu, Volleyball, vert. #278, 12xu, Soccer, vert. 30xu, High jump.

1963, Nov. 10
276-279   A114   Set of 4   5.00   1.50
    Imperf., #276-279   6.00   6.00

A115

Flowers: 6xu, Rauwolfia verticillata. No. 281, 12xu, Sophora japonica. No. 282, 12xu, Fibraurea tinctoria. No. 283, 12xu, Chenopodium ambrosioides. 20xu, Momordica cochinchinensis.

1963, Dec. 3
280-284   A115   Set of 5   7.50   2.00
    Imperf., #280-284   10.00   10.00

A116

1963, Dec. 20
285   A116 12xu multicolored   2.00   .35
World Day for Viet Nam.

A117

First Five Year Plan — A118

6xu, Molten cast iron. #287, 12xu, Thai Nguyen Steel & Iron Works. #288, 12xu, Power lines.

1964, Jan. 25   **Litho.**
286-288   A117-A118   Set of 3   3.50   1.40

Intl. Quiet Sun Year — A119

1964, Jan. 25
289-290   A119 12xu, 50xu, set
           of
           2   5.00   .80
    Imperf., #289-290   17.50   17.50

Flights of Vostok 5 and 6 A120

#291, 12xu, Rockets in orbit. #292, 12xu, Valery Bykovsky. 30xu, Valentina Tereshkova.

1964, Mar. 25
291-293   A120   Set of 3   5.00   1.00
    Imperf., #291-293   12.00   12.00

A stamp commemorating the anniversary of the founding of the People's Democratic Republic of Korea was printed but not issued.

A121

Flowers: No. 294, 12xu, Persica vulgaris. No. 295, 12xu, Hibiscus mutabilis. No. 296, 12xu, Passiflora hispida. No. 297, 12xu, Saraca dives. 20xu, Michelia champaca. 30xu, Camellia amplexicaulis.

1964, Apr. 10   **Perf. 11½x12**
294-299   A121   Set of 6   13.00   2.00
    Imperf., #294-299   15.00   15.00

A122

Costumes: 6xu, Peasant, 19th cent. No. 301, 12xu, Woman wearing large hat, 19th cent. No. 302, 12xu, Woman carrying hat.

1964, Apr. 27   **Perf. 11**
300-302   A122   Set of 3   4.00   1.00

Battle of Dien Bien Phu, 10th Anniv. A123

Designs: 3xu, Artillery. 6xu, Machine gun emplacement. Nos. 305, 307c, Bomb disposal. Nos. 306, 307d, Farmer on tractor.

1964, May 7
303   A123   3xu red & black   .80   .35
304   A123   6xu blue & black   1.20   .35
305   A123   12xu yel org & blk   2.00   .35
306   A123   12xu red lilac &
            black   2.00   .35
    Nos. 303-306 (4)   7.50   1.60
    Imperf., #303-306   12.00   12.00

Souvenir Sheet
Imperf
307   Sheet of 4   15.00   15.00
   a.   A123 3xu orange & black
   b.   A123 6xu yellow green & black
   c.   A123 12xu red, black & orange
   d.   A123 12xu blue & black

Ham Rong Bridge — A124

1964, May 17
308   A124 12xu multicolored   2.50   .35

Wild Animals A125

Designs: No. 309, 12xu, Panthera tigris, vert. No. 310, 12xu, Pseudaxis axis, vert. No. 311, 12xu, Tapirus indicus. 20xu, Bubalus bubalis. 30xu, Rhinoceros bicornis. 40xu, Bibos banteng.

1964, June 2   **Perf. 10½**
309-314   A125   Set of 6   20.00   2.25
    Imperf., #309-314   25.00   25.00

Geneva Agreement on Viet Nam, 10th Anniv. A126

Intl. Labor Federation Committee United with People of South Viet Nam — A127

1964, July 20   **Perf. 11**
315-316   A126-A127 12xu Set of
            2   2.75   .70

Nam Bac Ninh Pumping Station A128

1964, Aug. 25
317   A128 12xu blue gray & black   1.75   .35

Liberation of Hanoi, 10th Anniv. — A129

6xu, People cheering soldiers in truck. 12xu, Construction, hammerhead crane.

1964, Oct. 10
318-319   A129   Set of 2   3.00   .70

Natl. Defense Games — A130

Designs: 5xu, Rowing. No. 321, 12xu, Parachuting, vert. No. 322, 12xu, Gliders, vert. No. 323, 12xu, Shooting.

1964, Oct. 18
320-323   A130   Set of 4   5.50   2.25

Fruits — A131

Designs: No. 324, 12xu, Mangifera indica. No. 325, 12xu, Guarcinia mangostana. No. 326, 12xu, Nephelium litchi. 20xu, Anona squamosa. 50xu, Citrus medica.

1964, Oct. 31   **Photo.**   **Perf. 11½x12**
324-328   A131   Set of 5   10.00   2.00
    Imperf., #324-328   12.00   12.00

World Solidarity Conference — A132

Designs: a, Ba Dinh Hall. b, Vietnamese soldier shaking hands with foreign people. c, Fist, planes, submarine.

1964, Nov. 25   **Litho.**   **Perf. 11**
329   A132 12xu Strip of 3, #a.-c.   4.00   3.00

People's Army, 20th Anniv. A133

Designs: No. 330, Soldiers, flag. No. 331a, Coast guards. No. 331b, Mounted border guards, vert.

1964, Dec. 22
330 A133 12xu multicolored   1.25   .35
331 A133 12xu Pair, #a.-b.   2.50 2.50
    Nos. 330-331 (2)   3.75 2.85

Cuban Revolution, 6th Anniv. — A134

Designs: a, Vietnamese, Cuban flags. b, Cuban revolutionaries.

1965, Jan. 1
332 A134 12xu Pair, #a.-b.   4.00   .75

Economic & Cultural Development of Mountain Region — A135

Designs: 2xu, 3xu, Women pollinating corn. 12xu, Girls walking to school.

1965, Feb. 28
333-335 A135 Set of 3   2.50 1.00
        Imperf., #333-335

A136

Vietnamese Worker's Party, 35th Anniv. — A137

Politicians: No. 336a, Le Hong Phong. b, Tran Phu. c, Hoang Van Thu. d, Ngo Gia Tu. e, Nguyen Van Cu.
No. 337a, Party flag. b, Worker, soldier.

1965, Feb. 3   Litho.   Perf. 11
336 A136 6xu Strip of 5, #a.-
          e.   15.00 15.00
337 A137 12xu Pair, #a.-b.   15.00 15.00
    Nos. 336-337 (2)   30.00 30.00
    Issued: No. 336, 2/3; No. 337, 1/30.

Transportation Ministers Conference, Hanoi — A138

12xu, 30xu, Nguyen Van Troi, locomotive.

1965, Mar. 23
338-339 A138 Set of 2   7.50   .70
        Imperf., #338-339
Vignette on No. 339 is mirror image of No. 338.

Flight of Voskhod 1 — A139

20xu, Cosmonauts Komarov, Feoktistov, Yegorov, rocket, globe. 1d, Cosmonauts, rocket.

1965, Mar. 30
340-341 A139 Set of 2   8.00   .70
        Imperf., #340-341   10.00 10.00

Lenin, 95th Birth Anniv. A140

1965, Apr. 22   Litho.
342-343 A140 8xu, 12xu, set of 2 3.00   .70

A141

1965, May 19
344-345 A141 6xu, 12xu, set of 2 3.00   .70
Ho Chi Minh, 75th birthday.

A142

1965, May 19
346 A142 12xu multicolored   2.00   .35
6th Afro-Asian Conference, 10th anniv.

Trade Union Conference, Hanoi — A143

Designs: No. 347, Workers solidarity. No. 348, Soldiers, vert. No. 349, Naval battle.

1965, June 2
347-349 A143 12xu Set of 3   4.50 1.10

Wild Animals — A144

Designs: No. 350, 12xu, Martes flavigula. No. 351, 12xu, Chrotogale owstoni. No. 352, 12xu, Manis pentadactyla. No. 353, 12xu,

Presbytis delacouri, vert. 20xu, Petaurista lylei, vert. 50xu, Nycticebus pygmaeus, vert.

1965, June 24   Photo.   Perf. 12
350-355 A144 Set of 6   17.00 2.25
        Imperf., #350-355   25.00 25.00

A145

1965, July 1   Perf. 11½x11
356 A145 12xu multicolored   3.25   .35
6th Socialist Postal Ministers Conference.

A146

Nguyen Van Troi (1940-64). Denominations: 12xu, 50xu, 4d.

1965, July 20   Litho.   Perf. 11
357-359 A146 Set of 3   8.00 2.40

A147

Insects — A148

Designs: No. 360, 12xu, Tessaratoma papillosa. No. 361, 12xu, Rhynchocoris humeralis. No. 362, 12xu, Poeciliocoris latus.
No. 363, 12xu, Tosena melanoptera. 20xu, Cicada. 30xu, Fulgora candelaria.

1965, July 24   Photo.
360-362 A147 Set of 3   4.00 1.00
363-365 A148 Set of 3   10.00 1.00
        Nos. 360-365 (6)   12.00 2.50
        Imperf., #360-365   18.00 18.00

August Revolution, 20th Anniv. A149

1965, Aug. 19   Litho.
366-367 A149 6xu, 12xu, set of 2 3.00   .70

Crustaceans — A150

Designs: No. 368, 12xu, Penaeus indicus. No. 369, 12xu, Scylla serrata. No. 370, 12xu, Metapenaeus joyneri. No. 371, 12xu, Neptunus. 20xu, Palinurus japonicus. 50xu, Uca marionis.

1965, Aug. 19
368-373 A150 Set of 6   17.00 2.00
        Imperf., #368-373   22.50 22.50

500th US Warplane Shot Down — A151

1965, Aug. 30
374 A151 12xu gray green & lilac 5.50 4.00

A152

Completion of 1st Five-Year Plan — A153

#375, Foundry worker. #376, Electricity, irrigation. #377, Public health, education. #378, Students, children playing. #379, Factory worker. #380, Agricultural workers.

1965
375-377 A152 12xu Set of 3   2.75 1.25
378-380 A153 12xu Set of 3   2.75 1.25
        Imperf., #375-380
    Issued: #375-377, 9/2; #378-380, 12/25.

Nghe An, Ha Tinh Uprising, 35th Anniv. — A154

1965, Sept. 12
381-382 A154 10xu, 12xu, set of
             2   2.50   .80
        Imperf., #381-382

Friendship Between Viet Nam,
People's Republic of China, 16th
Anniv. — A155

Designs: No. 383, Youth holding flags,
Friendship Gate. No. 384, Children waving
flags, walking through Gate, vert.

1965, Oct. 1
383-384 A155 12xu Set of 2   10.00 1.75

Flight of Voskhod 2 — A156

#385, 12xu, Konstantin Tsiolkovsky, Sputnik
I. #386, 12xu, Voskhod 2, A. Leonov, P.
Belyayev. #387, 50xu, Yuri Gagarin. #388,
50xu, Leonov walking in space.

1965, Oct. 5
385-388 A156 Set of 4   8.00 3.25
     Imperf., #385-388

A157

Norman R. Morrison, US anti-war demonstration.

1965, Nov. 22
389 A157 12xu black & red   2.50   .35

A158

Nguyen Du (1765-1820), poet: No. 390,
12xu, Birthplace. No. 391, 12xu, Museum.
20xu, Volume of poems entitled Kieu. 1d,
Scene from Kieu.

1965, Nov. 25
390-393 A158 Set of 4   6.00 1.50

A159

Designs: No. 394, 12xu, Ho Chi Minh. No.
395, 12xu, Karl Marx. No. 396, 12xu, Lenin.
50xu, Frederich Engels.

Litho. & Engr. (#394), Litho.
1965, Nov. 28   **Perf. 11½**
394-397 A159 Set of 4   6.00 1.50
     Nos. 395-397 have white border.

Butterflies
A160

#398, 12xu, Cethosia cyane. #399, 12xu,
Zelides sarpedon. #400, 12xu, Cethosia.
#401, 12xu, Apatura ambica. 20xu, Papilio
paris. 30xu, Tros aristolochiae.

1965, Nov. 18   **Litho.   Perf. 11**
398-403 A160 Set of 6   20.00 2.25
     Imperf., #398-403   55.00 55.00

South Viet Nam Natl. Liberation Front,
5th Anniv. — A161

1965, Dec. 20
404 A161 12xu lilac   2.00   .35
     Imperf.

1st General Elections, 20th
Anniv. — A162

1966, Jan. 6
405 A162 12xu black & red   2.00   .35

A163

Orchids: No. 406, 12xu, Vanda teres. No.
407, 12xu, Dendrobium meschatum. No. 408,
12xu, Dendrobium nobile. No. 409, 12xu, Dendrobium crystallinum. 20xu, Vandopsis
gigantea. 30xu, Dendrobium.

1966, Jan. 10   **Perf. 12**
406-411 A163 Set of 6   12.00 2.50
     Imperf., #406-411   20.00 20.00

A164

1966, Jan. 18   **Perf. 11**
412 A164 12xu multicolored   2.50   .35
     Imperf.
     New Year 1966 (Year of the Horse).

Reptiles
A165

#413, 12xu, Physignathus cocincinus. #414,
12xu, Gekko gecko. #415, 12xu, Trionyx
sinensis. #416, 12xu, Testudo elongata. 20xu,
Varanus salvator. 40xu, Eretmochelys
imbricata.

1966, Feb. 25   **Perf. 12x11½**
413-418 A165 Set of 6   12.00 2.25
     Imperf., #413-418   20.00 20.00

Natl.
Sports
A166

Designs: No. 419, Archery. No. 420, Wrestling. No. 421, Spear fighting.

1966, Mar. 25   **Perf. 11**
419-421 A166 12xu Set of 3   4.25 1.10

6xu, 12xu, 1d stamps for running,
swimming and shooting were printed
but not issued.

Youth Labor
Union, 35th
Anniv. A167

1966, Mar. 26
422 A167 12xu multicolored   1.75   .50

1000th US Warplane Shot
Down — A168

1966, Apr. 29
423 A168 12xu multicolored   6.00 4.00

May
Day — A169

1966, May 1
424 A169 6xu multicolored   1.75   .35

Defending Con Co Island — A170

1966, June 1
425 A170 12xu multicolored   2.00   .35

A171

1966, June 1
426 A171 12xu red & black   1.75   .35
     Young Pioneers, 25th anniv.

A172

Designs: 3xu, View of Yenan. 12xu, Ho Chi
Minh, Mao Tse-Tung.

1966, July 1
427-428 A172 Set of 2   4.00   .70
     Imperf., #427-428
     Chinese Communist Party, 45th anniv.

A173

Luna 9: 12xu, Flight path to moon. 50xu, In
lunar orbit.

1966, Aug. 5
429-430 A173 Set of 2   5.00 1.25
     Imperf., #429-430   10.00 10.00

A174

1966, Oct. 14
431 A174 12xu multicolored   10.00 3.00

With Additional Inscription: "NGAY 14.10.1966"

431A A174 12xu multicolored 15.00 3.75
Imperf., #431-431A

1500th US warplane shot down.

Victory in Dry Season Campaign — A175

Designs: 1xu, 12xu (No. 433), Woman guerrilla carrying guns. 12xu (No. 434), Soldier escorting prisoners of war.

1966, Oct. 15
432-434 A175 Set of 3 4.00 1.25
Imperf., #432-434

See also No. 618A.

Vietnamese Women's Union, 20th Anniv. A176

1966, Oct. 20
435 A176 12xu orange & black 2.00 .35
Imperf.

Birds A177

Designs: No. 436, 12xu, Pitta moluccensis. No. 437, 12xu, Psarisomus dolhousiae. Nos. 438, 12xu, Alcedo atthis, vert. No. 439, 12xu, Oriolus chinensis, vert. 20xu, Upupa epops, vert. 30xu, Oriolus traillii.

1966, Oct. 31 Perf. 12x12½, 12½x12
436-441 A177 Set of 6 10.00 2.50
Imperf., #436-441 25.00 25.00

GANEFO Asian Games — A178

Designs: No. 442, Soccer. No. 443, Shooting. No. 444, Swimming. No. 445, Running.

1966, Nov. 25 Perf. 11
442-445 Set of 4 7.50 1.25
Imperf., #442-445 10.00 10.00
443a A178 12xu Pair, #442-443 3.50
445a A178 30xu Pair, #444-445 4.50
Nos. 443a-445a (2) 8.00

Ho Chi Minh's Appeal for Natl. Resistance, 20th Anniv. — A179

Designs: No. 446, Flags, workers. No. 447, Soldiers, workers, ships.

1967, Jan. 30
446-447 A179 12xu Set of 2 2.25 .80
See Nos. 501-504.

Rice Harvest A180

1967, Jan. 30
448 A180 12xu multicolored 1.75 .35

Bamboo A181

No. 449, 12xu, Bambusa arundinaceu. No. 450, 12xu, Arundinaria rolleana. No. 451, 12xu, Arundinaria racemosa. No. 452, 12xu, Bambusa bingami. 30xu, Bambusa nutans. 50xu, Dendrocalamus patellaris.

1967, Feb. 2 Perf. 12x11½
449-454 A181 Set of 6 8.50 2.25
Imperf., #449-454 10.00 10.00

Wild Animals — A182

Designs: No. 455, 12xu, Cuon rutilans. No. 456, 12xu, Arctictis binturong. No. 457, 12xu, Arctonyx collaris. 20xu, Viverra zibetha. 40xu, Macaca speciosa. 50xu, Neofelis nebulosa.

1967, Mar. 26 Litho. Perf. 12
455-460 A182 Set of 6 11.00 2.25
Imperf., #455-460 12.00 12.00

2000th US Aircraft Shot Down — A183

1967, June 5 Perf. 11
461-462 A183 6xu, 12xu, set of 2 7.50 3.00

Fish A184

#463, 12xu, Saurida filamentosa. #464, 12xu, Scomberomorus niphonius. #465, 12xu, Haplogenys mucronatus. 20xu, Lethrinus haematopterus. 30xu, Formio niger. 50xu, Lutianus erythropterus.

1967, July 25 Perf. 12
463-468 A184 Set of 6 9.50 2.25
Imperf., #463-468 13.00 13.00

A185

Launch of 1st Chinese ballistic missile: 12xu, Missile, flag, agricultural scene. 30xu, Missile, Gate of Heavenly Peace.

1967, July 25 Perf. 11
469-470 A185 Set of 2 7.00 2.50
Imperf., #469-470

A186

Russian October Revolution, 50th anniv.: 6xu, Lenin, revolutionary soldiers. No. 472a, 12xu, Lenin, armed mob. No. 472b, 12xu, Lenin, Marx, Vietnamese soldiers. 20xu, Cruiser Aurora.

1967, Oct. 15
471-473 A186 Set of 4 3.50 1.25
No. 472 is printed se-tenant.

2500th US Warplane Shot Down — A187

Design: No. 475, Plane in flames, vert.

1967, Nov. 6
474-475 A187 12xu Set of 2 7.50 3.50
Nos. 474-475 exist imperf. Value, set $40.

1st Chinese Hydrogen Bomb Test — A188

Designs: 12xu, Atomic symbol, Gate of Heavenly Peace. 20xu, Chinese lantern, atomic symbol, dove.

1967, Nov. 20
476-477 A188 Set of 2 6.50 1.50
Imperf., #476-477 30.00 30.00
No. 477 is 30x35mm.

A189

#478, 12xu, Rifle fire from trenches. #479, 12xu, Militia with captured US pilot. #480, 12xu, Factory anti-aircraft unit. #481, 12xu,

Naval anti-aircraft unit. 20xu, Aerial dog-fight. 30xu, Heavy anti-aircraft battery.

1967, Dec. 19 Perf. 12
478-483 A189 Set of 6 5.00 2.25

Chickens — A190

Designs: No. 484, 12xu, White spotted cock, hen. No. 485, 12xu, Black hens. No. 486, 12xu, Bantam cock, hen. No. 487, 12xu, Bantam cock. 20xu, Fighting cocks. 30xu, Exotic hen. 40xu, Hen, chicks from Ho region. 50xu, Dong Cao's cock, hen.

1968, Feb. 29
484-491 A190 Set of 8 10.00 2.75
Imperf., #484-491 15.00 15.00

Victories of 1966-67 — A191

No. 492: a, Soldier attacking US tank. b, Gunner firing on US ships. c, Burning stockade. d, Soldier firing mortar.
No. 493: a, Attacking US artillery. b, Escorting US prisoners. c, Interrogating refugees. d, Civilian demonstration.

1968, Mar. 5 Perf. 11
492-493 A191 12xu Blocks of 4, set of 2 6.00 6.00
Imperf., #492-493

Maxim Gorki (1868-1936) — A192

1968, Mar. 5
494 A192 12xu brown & black 1.75 .35
Imperf.

Roses — A193

Designs: No. 495, 12xu, Pale red. No. 496, 12xu, Orange. No. 497, 12xu, Pink. 20xu, Yellow, 30xu, Dark red. 40xu, Lilac.

1968, Apr. 25 Photo. Perf. 11½x12
495-500 A193 Set of 6 9.00 2.25
Imperf., #495-500 15.00 15.00

Ho Chi Minh's Appeal for Resistance Type

Values and colors: No. 501, 6xu, greenish blue and yellow. No. 502, 12xu, vermilion. No. 503, 12xu, bright blue. No. 504, 12xu, brownish lilac.

1968, Apr. 25 Litho. Perf. 11
Size: 25x17mm
501-504 A179 6xu, 12xu Set of 4 6.00 .75
Imperf., #501-504

Ho Chi Minh, Flag
A195

1968, May 19
505 A195 12xu brown & red 1.60 .40
Imperf.

Karl Marx — A196

1968, May 19
506 A196 12xu olive grn & blk 1.75 .35

3000th US Warplane Shot Down A197

#507: a, 12xu, Anti-aircraft machine gunners. b, 12xu, Women firing anti-aircraft gun.
#508: a, 40xu, Vietnamese plane shooting down US plane. b, 40xu, Anti-aircraft missile.

1968, June 25
507-508 A197 Set of 2 pairs 12.00 4.50
Imperf., #507-508

Handicrafts — A198

6xu, Rattan products. #510, 12xu, Ceramics. #511, 12xu, Bamboo products. 20xu, Ivory carving. 30xu, Lacquerware. 40xu, Silverware.

1968, July 5 *Perf. 12*
509-514 A198 Set of 6 5.50 2.00
Imperf., #509-514 12.50 12.50

Martial Arts A199

Designs: No. 515, 12xu, Saber fencing. No. 516, 12xu, Stick fighting. No. 517, 12xu, Dagger fighting. 30xu, Unarmed combat. 40xu, Chinese war sword fighting. 50xu, Duel with swords, shields.

1968, Oct. 25
515-520 A199 Set of 6 9.00 2.25
Imperf., #515-520 16.00 16.00

Architecture — A200

Designs: No. 521, 12xu, Khue Van tower, vert. No. 522, 12xu, Bell tower, Keo pagoda, vert. 20xu, Covered bridge, Thay pagoda. 30xu, One-pillar pagoda, Hanoi, vert. 40xu, Gateway, Ninh Phuc pagoda. 50xu, Tay Phuong pagoda.

1968, Nov. 15
521-526 A200 Set of 6 6.00 2.50
Imperf., #521-526 10.00 10.00

Foreign Solidarity with Viet Nam — A201

#527, 12xu, Latin American guerrilla, vert. #528, 12xu, Cuban, Vietnamese militia. 20xu, Asian, African, Latin American soldiers. vert.

1968, Dec. 15 Wmk. 376 *Perf. 12½*
With Gum
527-529 A201 Set of 3 4.00 2.25

Scenes of War A202

Artworks: No. 530, 12xu, Defending the mines. No. 531, 12xu, Plowman with rifle, vert. 30xu, Repairing railway track. 40xu, Wreckage of US aircraft.

1968, Dec. 15 Wmk. 376 *Perf. 12½*
With Gum
530-533 A202 Set of 4 4.00 2.50

Victories in South Viet Nam — A203

#534, 12xu, Tay Nguyen throwing grenade. #535, 12xu, Gun crews, Tri Thien. #536, 12xu, Nam Ngai shooting down US aircraft. 40xu, Insurgents, Tay Ninh, destroyed US armor. 50xu, Guerrillas preparing bamboo spike booby traps.

1969, Feb. 16 Unwmk. *Perf. 11½*
534-538 A203 Set of 5 5.00 1.75

Timber Industry A204

Designs: 6xu, Loading timber trucks. No. 540, 12xu, Log raft running rapids. No. 541,

12xu, Launch towing log raft. No. 542, 12xu, Elephant hauling timber. No. 543, 12xu, Forest protection. 20xu, Water buffalo hauling log. 30xu, Hauling logs by overhead cable.

1969, Apr. 10
539-545 A204 Set of 7 7.50 2.50
Imperf., #539-545 15.00 15.00

Scenes of War — A205

Designs: No. 546, 12xu, Young guerrilla. No. 547, 12xu, Scout on patrol. 20xu, Female guerrilla, vert. 30xu, Halt at way station. 40xu, After a skirmish. 50xu, Liberated hamlet.

Perf. 12½x11½, 11½x12½
1969, June 20
546-551 A205 Set of 6 7.00 2.25
Imperf., #546-551 14.00 14.00

Tet Offensive Battles — A206

Designs: 8xu, 12xu (No. 553), Ben Tre. No. 554, 12xu, Mortar crew, Khe Sanh. No. 555, 12xu, Two soldiers, flag, Hue, vert. No. 556, 12xu, Soldier running toward US Embassy, Saigon, vert.

1969, Sept. 20 *Perf. 11*
552-556 A206 Set of 5 3.50 2.25
Imperf., #552-556

Liberation of Hanoi, 15th Anniv. A207

#557, Soldier with flamethrower. #558, Children constructing toy buildings.

1969, Oct. 10
557-558 A207 12xu Set of 2 3.25 .65
Imperf., #557-558

A208

1969, Nov. 20
559 A208 12xu brn, blk & red 2.50 .35
Imperf.
Bertrand Russell Intl. War Crimes Tribunal, Stockholm and Roskilde.

A209

Fruits: No. 560, 12xu, Papaya. No. 561, 12xu, Grapefruit. 20xu, Tangerines. 30xu, Oranges. 40xu, Lychee nuts. 50xu, Persimmons.

1969, Nov. 20 *Perf. 12*
560-565 A209 Set of 6 5.50 2.00
Imperf., #560-565 8.50 8.50

Viet Nam Labor Party, 40th Anniv. — A210

Designs: No. 566, Nguyen Ai Quoc. No. 567, Ho Chi Minh. No. 568, Le Hong Phong. No. 569, Tran Phu. No. 570, Nguyen Van Cu.

1970, Feb. 3 *Perf. 11*
566-570 A210 12xu Set of 5 4.00 2.75

Nos. 568-570 are 10x25mm. Nos. 566-567 issued in vert. or horiz. se-tenant pairs. Nos. 568-570 issued in horizontal strips of 3.

Children's Activities — A211

Designs: No. 571, 12xu, Playing with toys. No. 572, 12xu, Three boys at kindergarten. No. 573, 20xu, Tending a garden. No. 574, 20xu, Tending water buffaloes. 30xu, Feeding chickens. 40xu, Piano, violin duet. 50xu, Flying model airplane. 60xu, Walking to school.

1970, Mar. 8 *Perf. 12*
571-578 A211 Set of 8 6.50 2.75

For overprints see Nos. 2181-2188.

Lenin, Birth Centenary A212

Designs: 12xu, Making speech. 1d, Portrait.

1970, Apr. 22 *Perf. 11*
579-580 A212 Set of 2 4.00 .65
Imperf., #579-580

Shells A213

No. 581, 12xu, Oc con lon. No. 582, 12xu, Oc xa cu. 20xu, Oc tien. 1d, Oc tu va.

1970, Apr. 26 *Perf. 12½x12*
581-584 A213 Set of 4 6.00 1.25
Imperf., #581-584 11.50 10.00

Ho Chi Minh — A214

12xu (#585, 588c, 588g), In 1930 (full face, no beard). 12xu (#586, 588b, 588f), In 1945 (facing right, beard). 2d, 6xu, (#587, 588a, 588e), In 1969 (full face, beard).

1970, May 19　　　　　　*Perf. 11*
585-587　A214　Set of 3　　　4.00　1.10
　Imperf., #585-587
Souvenir Sheets of 3
Imperf
588　Types of #585-587, #a.-c.,
　　orange background　　　8.00　7.00
588D　Types of #585-587, #e.-g.,
　　pale lilac background　　8.00　7.00

Stamps in souvenir sheets have white backgrounds. The 6xu stamp is larger than the 2d stamp. Nos. 588a and 588e, 588c and 588g are different colors.

Vietcong Flag A215

1970, June 6
589　A215　12xu multicolored　　1.50　.35
Formation of Revolutionary Provisional Government of South Viet Nam, 1st anniv.

Fruits and Vegetables A216

#590, 12xu, Watermelon. #591, 12xu, Pumpkin. 20xu, Cucumber. 50xu, Zucchini. 1d, Melon.

1970, July 15　　　　　　*Perf. 12*
590-594　A216　Set of 5　　　5.00　1.75
　Imperf., #590-594　　　　12.00　12.00

Consumer Industries — A217

#595, Coal miners, truck. #596, Power linesman, vert. #597, Textile worker, soldier, vert. #598, Stoker, power plant, vert.

Perf. 12x11½, 11½x12
1970, Aug. 25　　　　**Litho. & Engr.**
595-598　A217　12xu Set of 4　　4.00　1.25

Agriculture A218

1970, Aug. 25　　**Litho.**　　*Perf. 11*
599　A218　12xu multicolored　　2.00　.35

Democratic Republic of Viet Nam, 25th Anniv. — A219

Famous people: #600, 12xu, Vo Thi Sau facing firing squad. #601, 12xu, Nguyen Van Troi, captors. #602, 12xu, Phan Din Giot attacking pillbox. #603, 12xu, Ho Chi Minh. 20xu, Nguyen Viet Xuan, troops in battle. 1d, Nguyen Van Be attacking tank with mine.

1970-71
600-605　A219　Set of 6　　　4.00　3.50
　Imperf., #600-605
　　No. 603 is 41x28mm.
　Issued 9/2-71: Nos. 600, 603, 604; 3/71: Nos. 601, 602, 605.

Indo-Chinese People's Summit Conf. — A220

1970, Oct. 25
606　A220　12xu multicolored　　2.00　.35
　Imperf.

Bananas A221

Designs: No. 607, 12xu, Tay. No. 608, 12xu, Tieu. 50xu, Ngu. 1d, Mat.

1970, Oct. 25　　　　　　*Perf. 12*
607-610　A221　Set of 4　　　4.25　1.25
　Imperf., #607-610　　　　12.00　12.00

Friedrich Engels — A222

1970, Nov. 28　　　　　　*Perf. 11*
611-612　A222　12xu, 1d set of 2　2.50　.70

Snakes A223

Designs: 12xu, Akistrodon ciatus. 20xu, Calliophis macclellandii. 50xu, Bungarus faciatus. 1d, Trimeresurus gramineus.

1970, Nov. 30　**Photo.**　*Perf. 12x11½*
613-616　A223　Set of 4　　　6.00　.70
　Imperf., #613-616　　　　17.50　17.50

Natl. Liberation Front of South Viet Nam, 10th Anniv. — A224

Design: 6xu, Mother and child, flag, vert.

1970, Dec. 20　　**Litho.**　　*Perf. 11*
617-618　A224　Set of 2　　　2.50　.70
　Imperf., #617-618

Victory Type of 1966
1971, Mar.?
618A　A175　2xu black & orange　2.00　.35

Launching of 1st Chinese Satellite, 1st Anniv. — A225

1971, Apr. 10
619-620　A225　12xu, 50xu Set of
　　2　　　　　　　　　　　4.00　.70
　Imperf., #619-620

Ho Chi Minh A226

Denominations: 1xu, 3xu, 10xu, 12xu.

1971, May 19
621-624　A226　Set of 4　　　5.50　1.25
　Imperf., #621-624
624a　　Souvenir sheet of 1, imperf.　6.00　5.00
No. 624a contains one 52x52mm stamp.

Tay Son Uprising, Bicent. — A227

1971, May 25
625-626　A227　6xu, 12xu, set of 2　3.00　.70
　Imperf., #625-626

Marx, Music for The Internationale — A228

1971, June 20　　　　　*Perf. 12½*
627　A228　12xu org, blk & red　1.50　.35
　Imperf.
　Paris Commune, cent.

Hai Thuong Lan Ong, Physician, 250th Birth Anniv. A229

1971, July 1
628-629　A229　12xu, 50xu Set of
　　2　　　　　　　　　　　3.50　.70
　Imperf., #628-629

Statues from Tay Phuong Pagoda A230

Designs: No. 630, 12xu, Vasumitri. No. 631, 12xu, Kapimala. No. 632, 12xu, Dhikaca. No. 633, 12xu, Sangkayasheta. 30xu, Bouddha Nandi. 40xu, Rahulata. 50xu, Sangha Nandi. 1d, Cakyamuni.

1971, July 30　　**Photo.**　　*Perf. 12*
630-637　A230　Set of 8　　　12.00　2.75
　Imperf., #630-637　　　　20.00　20.00

Ho Chi Minh Working Youth Union, 40th Anniv. A231

1971, Sept. 7　　**Litho.**　　*Perf. 11*
638　A231　12xu multicolored　　1.50　.35
　Imperf.

Flight of Luna 16 — A232

Luna 16: No. 639a, 12xu, Return from Moon. No. 639b, 12xu, Flight to Moon. 1d, On Moon.

1971, Sept. 17
639-640　A232　Set of 3　　　4.00　1.10
　Imperf., #639-640　　　　15.00　15.00
　　No. 639 is se-tenant.

Designs: No. 641, 12xu, Landing on Moon, vert. No. 642 12xu, On Moon. 1d, Lunakhod 1 crossing lunar crevasse.

Flight of Luna 17 A233

1971, Oct. 15

| 641-643 | A233 | Set of 3 | | 4.00 | 1.10 |
| | | Imperf., #641-643 | | 15.00 | 15.00 |

Five Tigers A234

Folk paintings: No. 644, 12xu, White tiger. No. 645, 12xu, Red tiger. No. 646, 12xu, Yellow tiger. 40xu, Green tiger. 50xu, Black tiger. 1d, Five tigers.

1971, Nov. 25   *Perf. 12*

| 644-649 | A234 | Set of 6 | | 8.00 | 2.00 |
| | | Imperf., #644-649 | | 18.00 | 18.00 |

Size: 90x119mm

Imperf

| 650 | A234 | 1d multicolored | 14.00 | 12.00 |

Chinese Communist Party, 50th Anniv. A235

1971, Dec. 1   *Perf. 11*

| 651 | A235 | 12xu multicolored | 1.50 | .35 |

Mongolian People's Republic, 50th Anniv. — A236

1971, Dec. 25

| 652 | A236 | 12xu multicolored | 1.50 | .35 |

Folk Engravings from Dong Ho — A237

#653a, 12xu, Traditional wrestling. #653b, 12xu, Drum procession. #654a, 12xu, Gathering coconuts, vert. #654b, 12xu, Jealousy, vert. 40xu, Wedding of mice. 50xu, Frog school.

1972, Jan. 30

| 653-656 | A237 | Set of 6 | | 9.00 | 4.25 |
| | | Imperf., #653-656 | | 10.00 | 10.00 |

No. 653 is tete-beche.
The 30xu in design of #654a is a proof.

3rd Natl. Trade Unions Congress A238

Designs: 1xu, Workers facing right. 12xu, Workers facing left.

1972, May 1

| 657-658 | A238 | Set of 2 | | 2.00 | .70 |
| | | Imperf., #657-658 | | 10.00 | 10.00 |

Natl. Resistance, 25th Anniv. — A239

Designs: No. 659, Munitions worker. No. 660, Soldier in battle. No. 661, Woman in paddy field. No. 662, Text of Ho Chi Minh's appeal.

1972, May 5

| 659-662 | A239 | 12xu Set of 4 | | 3.00 | 1.25 |
| | | Imperf., #659-662 | | 20.00 | 20.00 |

Ho Chi Minh's Birthplace A240

Design: No. 664, Home in Hanoi.

1972, May 19

| 663-664 | A240 | 12xu Set of 2 | | 2.50 | .70 |
| | | Imperf., #663-664 | | 5.00 | 5.00 |

A241

1972, June 20

| 665-666 | A241 | 12xu Set of 2 | | 5.00 | 2.00 |
| | | Imperf., #665-666 | | | |

3500th US warplane shot down.
Added inscription on No. 666 reads "NGAY 20.4.1972."

Georgi Dimitrov (1882-1949), Bulgarian politician: No. 668, Dimitrov at Leipzig Court, 1933.

A242

1972, Aug. 15

| 667-668 | A242 | 12xu Set of 2 | | 2.50 | .70 |
| | | Imperf., #667-668 | | 5.00 | 5.00 |

Birds — A243

Designs: No. 669, 12xu, Lobivanellus indicus. No. 670, 12xu, Anas falcata. 30xu, Bubulcus ibis. 40xu, Gallicrex cinerea. 50xu, Prophyria porphyrio. 1d, Leptoptilos dubius.

1972, Oct. 12   *Perf. 12*

| 669-674 | A243 | Set of 6 | | 10.00 | 2.00 |
| | | Imperf., #669-674 | | 20.00 | 20.00 |

A244

4000th US warplane shot down: No. 676, Gunner holding rocket.

1972, Oct. 17   *Perf. 11*

| 675-676 | A244 | 12xu Set of 2 | 7.00 | 1.25 |
| | | Imperf., #675-676 | 9.00 | |

A245

Tay Nguyen folk dances: #677, 12xu, Drum. #678, 12xu, Umbrella. #679, 12xu, Shield. 20xu, Horse. 30xu, Ca Dong. 40xu, Rice pounding. 50xu, Khaen. 1d, Cham rong.

1972, Dec. 20   *Perf. 12*

| 677-684 | A245 | Set of 8 | | 7.00 | 2.50 |
| | | Imperf., #677-684 | | 9.00 | 9.00 |

Flight of Soyuz 11 A246

Designs: 12xu, Soyuz 11 docking with Salyut laboratory. 1d, Soyuz 11 cosmonauts.

1972, Dec. 30   *Perf. 11*

| 685-686 | A246 | Set of 2 | | 3.00 | .70 |
| | | Imperf., #685-686 | | 20.00 | 20.00 |

Wild Animals — A247

Designs: 12xu, Cuon alpinus. 30xu, Panthera pardus. 50xu, Felis bengalensis. 1d, Lutra lutra.

1973, Feb. 15   *Perf. 12½*

| 687-690 | A247 | Set of 4 | | 6.50 | 1.50 |
| | | Imperf., #687-690 | | 20.00 | 20.00 |

Copernicus A248

Copernicus and: No. 691a, 12xu, Armillary sphere. No. 691b, 12xu, Sun. 30xu, Signature, vert.

1973, Feb. 19   *Perf. 11*

| 691-692 | A248 | Set of 3 | 4.00 | 1.75 |
| | | Imperf., #691-692 | | |

Engravings on Ngoc Lu Bronze Drums — A249

Designs: No. 693, Drummers (Nha Danh Trong). No. 694, Pounding rice (Nha Gia Gao). No. 695, Dancers (Mua). No. 696, War canoe (Thuyen). No. 697, Birds (Chim, Thu).

1973, Apr. 12

| 693-697 | A249 | 12xu Set of 5 | | 4.00 | 1.75 |
| | | Imperf., #693-697 | | | |

Wild Animals — A250

Designs: 12xu, Tragulus javanicus. 30xu, Capricornis sumatraensis. 50xu, Sus scrofa. 1d, Moschus moschiferus.

1973, May 25   *Perf. 12x12½*

| 698-701 | A250 | Set of 4 | | 5.00 | 1.25 |
| | | Imperf., 698-701 | | 14.00 | 14.00 |

Birds A251

#702, 12xu, Pycnonotus jocosus. #703, 12xu, Megalurus palustris. 20xu, Capsychus saularis. 40xu, Rhipidura albicollis. 50xu, Parus major. 1d, Zosterops japonica.

1973, July 15   *Perf. 12*

| 702-707 | A251 | Set of 6 | | 6.75 | 2.10 |
| | | Imperf., 702-707 | | 15.00 | 15.00 |

Disabled Soldiers
A252   A252a

1973, July 27   *Perf. 11*
708-709 A252, A252a 12xu Set
    of 2   .80   .80
    Imperf., #708-709

Nos. 708-709 were issued for the use of disabled soldiers.

Three
Readiness
Youth
Movement
A253

Designs: No. 710, Road building. No. 711, Open-air class. No. 712, On the march.

1973, Sept. 2
710-712 A253 12xu Set of 3   2.00 1.10
    Imperf., #710-712

Democratic People's Republic of Korea, 25th Anniv. — A254

1973, Sept. 9
713 A254 12xu multicolored   1.50 .35
    Imperf.

4181st US
Warplane
Shot Down
A255

Designs: No. 714, 12xu, US B-52 hit by air attack. No. 715, 12xu, US B-52, fighter crashing over Haiphong Harbor. No. 716, 12xu, Anti-aircraft battery. 1d, Aircraft wreckage caught in fishing net.

1973, Oct. 10
714-717 A255 Set of 4   9.00 1.75
    Imperf., #714-717

Flowers — A256

6xu, 12xu (#719), Chrysanthemum (Cuc). #720, 12xu, Rose. #721, 12xu, Dahlia. #722, 12xu, Chrysanthemum (Bach mi). #723, 12xu, Chrysanthemum (Dai doa).

1974, Jan. 15
718-723 A256 Set of 6   45.00
    Imperf., #718-723   75.00

Nos. 718-723 may not have been officially released.

Elephants
A257

#724, 12xu, Hauling logs. #725, 12xu, War elephant. 40xu, Setting logs in place. 50xu, Circus elephant. 1d, Carrying war supplies.

1974, Feb. 10   *Perf. 11½*
724-728 A257 Set of 5   6.50 1.75
    Imperf., #724-728   12.00 12.00

Victory at Dien Bien Phu, 20th Anniv. — A258

Designs: a, Dien Bien Phu soldier's badge. b, Soldier waving victory flag.

1974, May 7   *Perf. 11*
729 A258 12xu Pair, #a.-b.   2.50 .70
    Imperf.   5.00 5.00

Three Responsibilities Women's Movement — A259

Designs: a, Armed worker, peasant. b, Female textile worker.

1974, June 1
730 A259 12xu Pair, #a.-b.   2.50 1.10
    Imperf.

A260

Chrysanthemums: No. 731, 12xu, Brown. No. 732, 12xu, Yellow (Vang). 20xu, Ngoc Khong Tuoc. 30xu, White. 40xu, Kim. 50xu, Hong mi. 60xu, Gam. 1d, Lilac.

1974, June 20   *Perf. 12x12½*
731-738 A260 Set of 8   7.00 4.00
    Imperf., #731-738   9.00 9.00

A261

Industrial plants: No. 739, 12xu, Corchorus capsularis. No. 740, 12xu, Cyperus tojet jormis. 30xu, Morus alba.

1974, Aug. 15   *Perf. 11*
739-741 A261 Set of 3   3.75 1.10
    Imperf., #739-741   10.00 10.00

Liberation of Hanoi, 20th Anniv. — A262

Designs: a, Woman laying bricks. b, Soldier holding child waving flag.

1974, Oct. 10
742 A262 12xu Pair, #a.-b.   2.00 .70

Solidarity with
Chilean
Revolution
A263

Designs: No. 743, Pres. Salvador Allende, flag. No. 744, Pablo Neruda, poet.

1974, Oct. 15
743-744 A263 12xu Set of 2   2.50 .70
    Imperf., #743-744   5.00 5.00

Marine Life — A264

Designs: No. 745, 12xu, Rhizostoma. No. 746, 12xu, Loligo. 30xu, Haleotis. 40xu, Pteria martensii. 50xu, Sepia officinalis. 1d, Palinurus japonicus.

1974, Oct. 25   *Perf. 12½*
745-750 A264 Set of 6   7.00 2.10
    Imperf., #745-750   10.00 10.00

People's Republic of Albania, 30th Anniv. — A265

Designs: a, Natl. arms. b, Albanian, Vietnamese flags, women.

1974, Nov. 29   *Perf. 11*
752 A265 12xu Pair, #a.-b.   2.25 .70
    Imperf.

Paris Agreement on Vietnam, 2nd Anniv. — A266

Designs: No. 753, Intl. Conference on Viet Nam in session, 5-line inscription. No. 754, Signing of Paris Agreement, 4-line inscription.

1975, Jan. 27
753-754 A266 12xu Set of 2   2.50 .70
    Imperf.

Medicinal
Plants — A267

Designs: No. 755, 12xu, Costus speciosus. No. 756, 12xu, Curcuma zedoaria. No. 757, 12xu, Rosa laevigata. 30xu, Erythrina indica. 40xu, Lilium brownii. 50xu, Hibiscus sagittifolius. 60xu, Papaver somniferum. 1d, Belamcanda chinensis.

1975, Feb. 8   *Perf. 11½x12*
755-762 A267 Set of 8   7.00 2.75
    Imperf., #755-762   12.50 12.50

Vietnamese Labor Party, 45th Anniv. — A268

Designs: No. 763, 12xu, Tran Phu. No. 764, 12xu, Le Hong Phong. No. 765, 12xu, Nguyen Van Cu. No. 766, 12xu, Ngo Gia Tu. 60xu, Ho Chi Minh in 1924, vert.

1975, Feb. 3   *Perf. 11*
763-767 A268 Set of 5   6.00 1.25
    Imperf., #763-767   10.00 10.00

A269

Fruit: No. 768, 12xu, Achras sapota. No. 769, 12xu, Persica vulgaris. 20xu, Eugenia jambos. 30xu, Chrysophyllum cainito. 40xu, Lucuma mamosa. 50xu, Prunica granitum. 60xu, Durio ziberthinus. 1d, Prunus salicina.

1975, Apr. 25   *Perf. 12x12½*
768-775 A269 Set of 8   6.50 2.50
    Imperf., 768-775   12.00 12.00

A270

No. 776, 12xu. No. 777, 60xu.

1975, May 19   *Perf. 11*
776-777 A270 Set of 2   3.50 1.10
    Imperf., #776-777   10.00 10.00

Ho Chi Minh, 85th birthday.

People's
Republic
of
Poland,
30th
Anniv.
A271

1975, July 5
778-781 A271 1xu, 2xu, 3xu,
12xu, set of 4   3.00   .80
Imperf., #778-781

Flags
A272

Natl. Arms — A273

Flag of North Viet Nam and: No. 782,
Draped flag. No. 783, Flag with star & crescent.
No. 784, DDR flag and handshake.

1975
782-785 A272-A273 12xu Set of
4   7.00   .80
Imperf., #782-784

People's Republic of China, 25th anniv.
(#782), Republic of Algeria, 20th anniv.
(#783), German Democratic Republic, 25th
anniv. (#784), liberation of Hungary, 30th
anniv. (#785).
Issued: No. 782, 7/5; Nos. 783-785, 8/15.

Independence, 30th Anniv. — A274

#786, Flag. #787, Natl. arms. #788-789, Ho
Chi Minh proclaiming independence.

1975, Sept. 2
786-788 A274 12xu Set of 3   3.50   1.10

Souvenir Sheet
Imperf

789 A274 20xu multi   20.00 15.00

No. 789 contains one 45x30mm stamp.

Reptiles
A275

#790, 12xu, Dermochelys coriacea. #791,
12xu, Physignathus cocincinus. 20xu,
Hydrophis brookii. 30xu, Platysternum
megacephalum. 40xu, Leiolepis belliana.
50xu, Python molurus. 60xu, Naja hannah. 1d,
Draco maculatus.

1975, Nov. 25   **Perf. 12**
790-797 A275 Set of 8   8.00   2.50
Imperf., #790-797   15.00 15.00

Butterflies — A276

#798, 12xu, Pathysa antiphates. #799,
12xu, Danaus plexippus. 20xu, Cynautocera
papilionaria. 30xu, Maenas salaminia. 40xu,
Papilio machaon. 50xu, Ixias pyrene. 60xu,
Eusemia vetula. 1d, Eriboea.

1976, Jan. 6
798-805 A276 Set of 8   8.00   2.50
Imperf., #798-805   22.50 22.50

No. 799 misspelled "Danais."

Lan Hoang
Thao Orchid
A277

1976, Jan. 25   **Perf. 11**
806-807 A277 6xu, 12xu, set of 2 4.00 1.25

See Nos. 854-855.

Wild Animals
A278

#808, 12xu, Callosciurus erythraeus. #809,
12xu, Paguma larvata. 20xu, Macaca mulatta.
30xu, Hystrix hodgsoni. 40xu, Nyctereutes
procyonoides. 50xu, Selenarctos thibetanus.
60xu, Panthera pardus. 1d, Cynocephalus
variegatus.

1976, Mar. 20   **Perf. 12**
808-815 A278 Set of 8   6.50 2.25
Imperf., #808-815   15.00 15.00

A279

A279a

No. 816, Map, hand placing ballot in ballot
box. Nos. 817, 818, Map, voters.

1976, Apr. 10   **Perf. 11**
816 A279 6xu rose red & yel   .75   .35
817 A279a 6xu brown & red   .75   .35
818 A279a 12xu lt blue & red   2.00   .40
Imperf., #816-818
    Nos. 816-818 (3)   3.50 1.10

1st Elections to Unified Natl. Assembly.
Size of Nos. 817-818 is 35x22mm.
Identical stamps inscribed "Mien Nam Viet
Nam" are National Front issues. Same values.

Unified
Natl.
Assembly,
1st
Session
A280

Design: 12xu, Inscribed "Doc Lap Thong
Nhat Chu Nghia Xa Hoi."

1976, June 24
819-820 A280 6xu, 12xu, set of 2 2.50   .70

Identical stamps inscribed "Mien Nam Viet
Nam" are National Front issues. Same values.

A281

1976, June 24   **Perf. 12x12½**
821 A281 12xu multicolored   1.50   .35

Reunification of Viet Nam.

A282

Orchids: No. 822, 12xu, Habenaria
rhodocheila. No. 823, 12xu, Dendrobium
devonianum. 20xu, Dendrobium tortile. 30xu,
Doritis pulcherrima. 40xu, Dendrobium
farmeri. 50xu, Dendrobium aggregatum. 60xu,
Eria pannea. 1d, Paphiopedilum concolor.

1976, June 24   **Perf. 12**
822-829 A282 Set of 8   8.00 1.50
Imperf., #822-829   12.00 12.00

DEMOCRATIC REPUBLIC
OF VIET NAM
(After Unification)

AREA — 128,000 sq. mi.
POP. — 77,311,210 (1999 est.)
CAPITAL — Hanoi

Vietnamese Red Cross, 30th
Anniv. — A283

1976, July 27   **Perf. 11**
830 A283 12xu multicolored   2.00   .35
Imperf.

Fish — A284

#831, 12xu, Lutjanus sebae. #832, 12xu,
Dampieria melanotaenia. 20xu, Therapon
theraps. 30xu, Amphiprion bifasciatus. 40xu,
Abudefduf sexfasciatus. 50xu, Heniochus
acuminatus. 60xu, Amphiprion macrostoma.
1d, Symphorus spilurus.

1976, Aug. 15   **Perf. 12**
831-838 A284 Set of 8   5.50 2.50
Imperf., #831-838   10.00 10.00

Viet Nam
Worker's
Party, 4th
Natl.
Congress
A285

1976, Nov. 12   **Perf. 11**
839-844 A285 2, 3, 5, 10, 12,
20xu, set of 6   3.50 2.25

Viet Nam Communist Party, 4th Natl.
Congress — A286

Designs: a, Agriculture, industry. b, Ho Chi
Minh, worker, farmer, soldier, scientist.

Design size: 24.5mmx35mm

1976, Dec. 10
845 A286 12xu Pair, #a.-b.   2.00   .70
Imperf.

See Nos. 951-954.

Unification of Viet
Nam — A287

1976, Dec. 14
846-847 A287 6xu, 12xu, set of 2 2.00   .70
Imperf., #846-847   4.50

General Offensive, 1975 — A288

Designs: 2xu, 50xu, Liberation of Buon Me
Thuot. 3xu, 1d, Tanks liberating Da Nang. 6xu,
2d, Tank, soldiers liberating Presidential palace, Saigon.

1976, Dec. 14
848-853 A288 Set of 6   4.50 2.25

**Lan Hoang Thao Orchid Type of
1976 Inscribed "VIET NAM" and
"1976"**

1976, Dec.   **Litho.**   **Perf. 11**
854-855 A277 6xu, 12xu Set of
2   *25.00 15.00*

Dragonflies — A289

#856, 12xu, Ho. #857, 12xu, Bao. 20xu,
Canh dom. 30xu, Nuong. 40xu, Suoi. 50xu,
Canh vang. 60xu, Canh khoang. 1d, Canh
den.

1977, Jan. 25   *Perf. 12*
856-863   A289   Set of 8   6.00   1.00
    Imperf., #856-863   13.00   13.00

A290

Rare Birds: 12xu (#864), 60xu, Buceros bicornis. 12xu (#865), Ptilolaemus tickelli. 20xu, Berenicornis comatus. 30xu, Aceros undulatus. 40xu, Anthracoceros malabaricus. 50xu, Anthracoceros malayanus. 1d, Aceros nipalensis.

1977, Apr. 15
864-871   A290   Set of 8   6.00   1.75
    Imperf., #864-871   9.00   9.00

A291

Bronze drum and: 4xu, Thang Long Tower. 5xu, Map. 12xu, Lotus blossom. 50xu, Flag.

1977, Apr. 25   *Perf. 11*
872-875   A291   Set of 4   4.50   1.75
    Imperf., #872-875

Natl. Assembly general elections, 1st anniv.

Beetles
A292

#876, 12xu, Black-spotted (Dom den). #877, 12xu, Yellow-spotted (Lang vang). 20xu, Veined (Van gach). 30xu, Green (Nhung xanh). 40xu, Green-spotted (Hoa xanh). 50xu, Black (Van den). 60xu, Leopard skin (Da bao). 1d, Nine-spotted (Chin cham).

1977, June 15   *Perf. 12½x12*
876-883   A292   Set of 8   6.00   1.50
    Imperf., #876-883   12.00   12.00

Wildflowers
A293

Designs: No. 884, 12xu, Thevetia peruviana. No. 885, 12xu, Broussonetia papvrifera. 20xu, Aleurites montana. 30xu, Cerbera manghes. 40xu, Cassia multijuga. 50xu, Cassia nodosa. 60xu, Hibiscus schizopetalus. 1d, Lagerstroesnia speciosa.

1977, Aug. 19   *Perf. 12x12½*
884-891   A293   Set of 8   4.50   1.50
    Imperf., #884-891   10.00   10.00

A294

Dahlias: 6xu (#892), 12xu (#894), Pink. 6xu (#893), 12xu (#895), Orange.

1977, Sept. 10   *Perf. 11*
892-895   A294   Set of 4   4.00   .60
    See Nos. 921-924.

A295

Children drawing map of unified Viet Nam. Denominations: 4xu, 5xu, 10xu, 12xu, 30xu each have different colored border.

1977, Sept. 10
896-900   A295   Set of 5   4.00   1.50

Goldfish
A296

Designs: No. 901, 12xu, Dong nai. No. 902, 12xu, Velvet (Hoa nhung). 20xu, Blue Chinese (Tau xanh). 30xu, Dragon-eyed (Mat bong). 40xu, Cam trang. 50xu, Five-colored (Ngu sac). 60xu, Dong nai. 1d, Thap cam.

1977, Oct. 20   *Perf. 12*
901-908   A296   Set of 8   6.50   1.25
    Imperf., #901-908   12.00   12.00

A297

Russian October Revolution, 60th anniv.: 12xu (No. 909, olive background), 12xu (No. 910, blue background), Ho Chi Minh, Lenin banner. 50xu, Mother holding child with flag. 1d, Workers, farmers, Moscow Kremlin, cruiser Aurora.

1977, Nov. 7
909-912   A297   Set of 4   3.25   1.25

A298

Songbirds: 12xu, Gracula religiosa. No. 914, 20xu, Garrulax canorus. No. 915, 20xu, Streptopelia chinensis. 30xu, Linius schach. 40xu, Garrulax formosus. 50xu, Garrulax chinensis. 60xu, Acridotheres cristatellus. 1d, Garrulax yersini.

1978, Jan. 25
913-920   A298   Set of 8   5.50   1.75
    Imperf., #913-920   12.00   12.00

Cultivated Flower Type of 1977

5xu, 10xu, Sunflower. 6xu, 12xu, Pansy.

1978, Mar. 20   *Perf. 11*
921-924   A294   Set of 4   4.00   .60

Intl. Children's Day (June 1977) — A299

1978, Mar. 20
925   A299   12xu multicolored   1.50   .35

Sports
A300

#926, 12xu, Discus. #927, 12xu, Long jump. 20xu, Hurdles. 30xu, Hammer throw. 40xu, Shot put. 50xu, Javelin. 60xu, Running. 1d, High jump.

1978, Apr. 10   *Perf. 11½*
926-933   A300   Set of 8   4.00   1.25
    Imperf., #926-933   10.00   10.00

A301

4th Viet Nam Trade Union Cong.: #934, Trade Union emblem. #935, Ho Chi Minh, workers.

1978, May 1   *Perf. 11*
934-935   A301   10xu Set of 2   2.25   .70

A302

10xu, Ho Chi Minh conducting orchestra. 12xu, Ho Chi Minh's mausoleum, horiz.

1978, May 15
936-937   A302   Set of 2   2.25   .70
    No. 937 is 39x23mm.

Young Pioneers' Cultural Palace, Hanoi — A303

1978, May 29
938   A303   10xu multicolored   1.50   .35
    Intl. Children's Day.

Sculptures from Tay Phuong Pagoda — A304

Designs: No. 939, 12xu, Sanakavasa. No. 940, 12xu, Parsva. No. 941, 12xu, Punyasas. No. 942, 20xu, Kumarata. No. 943, 20xu, Nagarjuna. 30xu, Yayata. 40xu, Cadiep. 50xu, Ananda. 60xu, Buddhamitra. 1d, Asvagmosa.

1978, July 1   *Perf. 12*
939-948   A304   Set of 10   7.50   1.50
    Imperf., #939-948   20.00   20.00

Cuban Revolution, 25th Anniv. — A305

1978, July 20   *Perf. 11*
949-950   A305   6xu, 12xu Set of 2   2.50   .70

Types of 1976

6xu (No. 951), 12xu (No. 953), like #845a. 6xu (No. 952), 12xu (No. 954), like #845b.

Design size: 18.5mmx23mm

1978, Aug. 15
951-954   A286   Set of 4   3.50   1.75

Space Exploration, 20th Anniv. — A306

#955, 12xu, Sputnik. #956, 12xu, Venera 1. 30xu, Spacecraft docking. 40xu, Molniya 1. 60xu, Soyuz. 2d, Cosmonauts Gubarev, Grechko.

1978, Aug. 28   *Perf. 12½x12*
955-960   A306   Set of 6   4.50   1.50
    Imperf., #955-960   9.50   9.50

World Telecommunications Day — A307

Designs: a, Printed circuit. b, ITU emblem.

1978, Sept. 25 **Perf. 11**
962 A307 12xu Pair, #a.-b. 2.50 .70
Imperf. 18.00 18.00

20th Congress of Socialist Postal Ministers — A308

1978, Sept. 25
963 A308 12xu multicolored 1.50 .35

Chrysanthemums — A309

No. 964, 12xu, Tim. No. 965, 12xu, Kim tien. 20xu, Hong. 30xu, Van tho. 40xu, Vang. 50xu, Thuy tim. 60xu, Vang mo. 1d, Nau do.

1978, Oct. 1 **Perf. 12**
964-971 A309 Set of 8 5.00 1.25
Imperf., #964-971 10.00 10.00

Dinosaurs A310

Designs: No. 972, 12xu, Plesiosaurus. No. 973, 12xu, Brontosaurus. 20xu, Iguanodon. 30xu, Tyrannosaurus rex. 40xu, Stegosaurus. 50xu, Mosasaurus. 60xu, Triceratops. 1d, Pteranodon.

1979, Jan. 1 **Litho.** **Perf. 11½**
972-979 A310 Set of 8 10.00 1.25
Imperf., #972-979 17.00 17.00

No. 977 misspelled "Mozasaurus."

A311

1979, Jan. 1 **Perf. 11**
980 A311 12xu multicolored 1.50 .35
Imperf. 5.00 5.00
Socialist Republic of Cuba, 20th anniv.

A312

Quang Trung's victory over the Chinese, 190th Anniv.: #981, Battle plan. #982, Quang Trung.

1979, Feb. 1
981-982 A312 12xu Set of 2 2.50 .70
a. Perf 12, #981-982 20.00

Albert Einstein, Physicist A313

Designs: No. 983, 12xu, Einstein. No. 984, 60xu, Equation, sun, planets.

1979, Mar. 14
983-984 A313 12xu, 60xu, set of 2 8.50 .50

Domestic Animals — A314

10xu, Ram. 12xu, Ox. 20xu, Ewe, lamb. 30xu, White water buffalo, vert. 40xu, Cow. 50xu, Goat. 60xu, Water buffalo, calf. 1d, Young goat, kid.

1979, Mar. 20 **Perf. 12**
985-992 A314 Set of 8 5.00 1.25
Imperf., #985-992 9.00 9.00

Five Year Plan (1976-80) — A315

#993, 998, Map, emblem. #994, 999, Factory worker. #995, 1000, Peasant woman, tractor. #996, 1001, Soldier. #997, 1002, Man, atom, compass.

1979 **Perf. 11**
993-997 A315 6xu Set of 5 5.00 1.50
998-1002 A315 12xu Set of 5 5.00 3.50
1000a Perf. 12
Nos. 993-1002 (2) 10.00 5.00

Issued: Nos. 993-997, 5/1. Nos. 998-1002, 6/1. Nos. 993, 996-1002 on toned paper.

Philaserdica '79, Intl. Stamp Exhibition, Sofia, Bulgaria A316

1979, May 27 **Perf. 12**
1003-1004 12xu, 30xu Set of 2 2.00 .70

Intl. Year of the Child — A317

12xu, Ho Chi Minh, children. 20xu, Nurse, mother, child. 50xu, Children with glider, painting supplies. 1d, Girls of different races.

1979, June 1 **Perf. 11**
1005-1008 A317 Set of 4 4.00 1.25

Ornamental Birds — A318

#1009, 12xu, Lophura diardi. #1010, 12xu, Tragopan temminckii. 20xu, Phasianus colchicus. 30xu, Lophura edwardsi. 40xu, Lophura nycthemera, vert. 50xu, Polyplectron germaini, vert. 60xu, Rheinhardia ocellata, vert. 1d, Pavo muticus, vert.

1979, June 16 **Perf. 12**
1009-1016 A318 Set of 8 6.50 1.75
Imperf., #1009-1016 12.00 12.00

Orchids A319

Designs: No. 1017, 12xu, Dendrobium heterocacpum. No. 1018, 12xu, Cymbidium hybridum. 20xu, Rhynchostylis gigantea. 30xu, Dendrobium mobile. 40xu, Aerides falcatum. 50xu, Paphiopedilum callosum. 60xu, Vanda teres. 1d, Dendrobium phalaenopsis.

1979, Aug. 10 **Perf. 12**
1017-1024 A319 Set of 8 6.50 1.75
Imperf., #1017-1024 12.00 12.00

Cats A320

Designs: No. 1025, 12xu, Meo tam the. No. 1026, 12xu, Meo muop, vert. 20xu, Meo khoang, vert. 30xu, Meo dom van. 40xu, Meo muop dom, vert. 50xu, Meo vang, vert. 60xu, Meo xiem. 1d, Meo van am.

1979, Nov. 10
1025-1032 A320 Set of 8 5.50 2.75
Imperf., #1025-1032 12.00 12.00

Vietnamese People's Army, 25th Anniv. — A321

a, People greeting soldiers. b, Frontier guards.

1979, Dec. 22 **Perf. 11**
1033 A321 12xu Pair, #a.-b. 3.00 .75

Roses — A322

Designs: 1xu, 12xu (No. 1036), Red, pink roses. 2xu, 12xu (No. 1037), Single pink rose.

1980, Jan. 1
1034-1037 A322 Set of 4 4.00 1.25
See Nos. 1084-1085.

Aquatic Flowers A323

#1038, 12xu, Nelumbium nuciferum. #1039, 12xu, Nymphala stellata. 20xu, Ipomola reptans. 30xu, Nymphoides indicum. 40xu, Jussiala repens. 50xu, Eichhornia crassipes. 60xu, Monochoria voginalis. 1d, Nelumbo nucifera.

1980, Jan. 15 **Perf. 12½**
1038-1045 A323 Set of 8 4.75 1.25
Imperf., #1038-1045 9.00 9.00

Vietnamese Communist Party, 50th Anniv. — A324

Designs: No. 1046a, Ho Chi Minh proclaiming independence, 1945. No. 1046b, Peasants with banner, improvised weapons. No. 1047a, Map, soldiers, tanks storming palace. No. 1047b, Soldiers waving flag at Dien Bien Phu. 2d, Ho Chi Minh, soldiers and workers.

1980, Feb. 3 **Perf. 11**
1046 A324 12xu Pair, #a.-b. 1.00 .65
1047 A324 20xu Pair, #a.-b. 1.00 .65
1048 A324 2d multicolored 2.00 .35
Nos. 1046-1048 (3) 4.00 1.65

Lenin, 110th Anniv. of Birth A325

1980, Apr. 22 **Perf. 12**
1049-1051 A325 6xu, 12xu, 1d, set of 3 3.00 1.75

1980 Summer Olympics, Moscow A326

#1052, 12xu, Hurdles. #1053, 12xu, Running. 20xu, Team handball. 30xu, Soccer. 40xu, Wrestling. 50xu, Gymnastics, horiz. 60xu, Swimming, horiz. 1d, Sailing, horiz.

1980, May 1 **Perf. 12x12½, 12½x12**
1052-1059 A326 Set of 8 5.00 1.25
Imperf., #1052-1059 10.00 10.00

A327

Ho Chi Minh, 90th anniv. of birth: 12xu, In 1924. 40xu, As president.

1980, May 19　　　　**Perf. 11**
1060-1061　A327　Set of 2　　　2.25　1.00

A328

1980, June 15
1062　A328　5xu multicolored　　1.25　.35
Intl. Children's Day.

Intercosmos '80, Soviet-Vietnamese Space Mission — A329

Designs: No. 1063, 12xu, Cosmonauts. No. 1064, 12xu, Soyuz 37 atop booster. 20xu, Soyuz 37. 40xu, Soyuz docking with Salyut space station. 1d, Soyuz firing retro-rockets. 2d, Parachute landing. 3d, Cosmonauts, Soyuz-Salyut station.

1980, July 24　　　**Perf. 12x12½**
1063-1068　A329　Set of 6　　5.25　1.00
　　Imperf., #1063-1068　　9.00　9.00
Souvenir Sheet
1069　A329　3d multicolored　　8.00　8.00
　　Imperf.　　　　　　　9.00　9.00

Saltwater Fish — A330

Designs: No. 1070, 12xu, Rhincodon typus. No. 1071, 12xu, Galeocerdo cuvier. 20xu, Orectolobus japonicus. 30xu, Heterodontus zebra. 40xu, Dasyatis uarnak. 50xu, Pristis microdon. 60xu, Sphyrna lewini. 1d, Myliobatis tobijei.

1980, Aug. 1　　　　**Perf. 12**
1070-1077　A330　Set of 8　　5.50　1.75
　　Imperf., #1070-1077　　10.00　10.00

A331

Post and Telecommunications Office, 35th Anniv.: 12xu, Ho Chi Minh reading newspaper. 20xu, Ho Chi Minh talking on telephone. 50xu, Kim Dong carrying bird in cage. 1d, Dish antenna.

1980, Aug. 15　**Litho.**　**Perf. 12½**
1078-1081　A331　Set of 4　　3.50　1.25

A332

Natl. Telecommunications Day: No. 1082, Telephone switchboard operator. No. 1083, Train, map.

1980, Aug. 25　**Perf. 11, 12 (#1083)**
1082-1083　A332　12xu　Set of 2　2.50　.70

Rose Type of 1980
No. 1084, Pink. No. 1085, Red and pink.

1980, Aug. 25　　　　**Perf. 11**
Size: 20x24mm
1084-1085　A322　12xu　Set of 2　3.50　.40
For surcharge see Nos. 1384A-1385.

Republic of Vietnam, 35th Anniv. — A333

Designs: No. 1086, 12xu, Ho Chi Minh. No. 1087, 12xu, Natl. arms. 40xu, Pac Bo Cave. 1d, Source of Lenin River, horiz.

1980, Sept. 2　　　　**Perf. 12½**
1086-1089　A333　Set of 4　　4.00　1.25

A334

Natl. emblems: 6xu, Arms. No. 1091, 12xu, Flag, horiz. No. 1092, 12xu, Anthem.

1980, Sept. 20　　　**Perf. 12**
1090-1092　A334　Set of 3　　3.50　1.25

A335

Nguyen Trai, 600th birth anniv.: 12xu, Nguyen Trai. 50xu, Books, horiz. 1d, Ho Chi Minh reading commemorative stele, Con Son.

1980, Oct. 6　　　　**Perf. 11**
1093-1095　A335　Set of 3　　3.00　1.25
For surcharge see No. 1386.

A336

Natl. Women's Union, 50th Anniv.: #1096, Ho Chi Minh, women. #1097, Group of 4 women.

1980, Oct. 20
1096-1097　A336　12xu　Set of 2　1.50　.70

A337

Flowers: No. 1098, 12xu, Ipomoea pulchella. No. 1099, 12xu, Biguoniaceae venusta. 20xu, Petunia hybrida. 30xu, Trapaeolum majus. 40xu, Thunbergia grandiflora. 50xu, Anlamanda cathartica. 60xu, Campsis radicans. 1d, Bougainivillaea spectabilis.

1980, Nov. 20　　　　**Perf. 12½**
1098-1105　A337　Set of 8　　5.00　1.25
　　Imperf., #1098-1105　　10.00　10.00

Ornamental Fish — A338

Designs: No. 1106, 12xu, Betta splendens. No. 1107, 12xu, Symphysodon aequifasciata. 20xu, Poecilobrycon eques. 30xu, Gyrinocheilus aymonieri. 40xu, Barbus tetrazona. 50xu, Pterophyllum eimekei. 60xu, Xiphophorus helleri. 1d, Trichopterus sumatranus.

1981, Jan. 15　　　　**Perf. 12**
1106-1113　A338　Set of 8　　6.00　3.00
　　Imperf., #1106-1113　　10.00　9.00

26th Soviet Communist Party Congress A339

20xu, Rocket, book. 50xu, Young people, flag.

1981, Feb. 23　　　　**Perf. 11**
1114-1115　A339　Set of 2　　3.50　.70

Animals from Cuc Phuona Natl. Forest — A340

#1116, 12xu, Hylobates concolor. #1117, 12xu, Macaca speciosa. 20xu, Selenarctos thibetanus. 30xu, Cuon alpinus. 40xu, Sus scrofa. 50xu, Cervus unicolor. 60xu, Panthera pardus. 1d, Panthera tigris.

1981, Apr. 10　　　**Perf. 12½x12**
1116-1123　A340　Set of 8　　7.50　1.50
　　Imperf., #1116-1123　　11.00　11.00

Doves A341

#1124, 12xu, Treron sieboldi. #1125, 12xu, Ducula aenea, vert. 20xu, Streptopelia tranquebarica, vert. 30xu, Macropygia unchall, vert. 40xu, Ducula badia, vert. 50xu, Treron apicauda. 60xu, Chalcophaps indica. 1d, Seimun treron seimundi.

1981, June 5　　　　**Perf. 12**
1124-1131　A341　Set of 8　　6.00　3.00
　　Imperf., #1124-1131　　10.00　9.00

Nectar-sucking Birds — A342

Designs: No. 1132, 20xu, Aethopyga siparaja. No. 1133, 20xu, Anthreptes singalensis. 30xu, Aethopyga saturata. 40xu, Aethopyga gouldiae. No. 1136, 50xu, Nectarinia chalcostetha. No. 1137, 50xu, Nectarinia hypogrammica. 60xu, Nectarinia sperata. 1d, Aethopyga nipalensis.

1981, Aug. 5　　　**Perf. 12½x12**
1132-1139　A342　Set of 8　　5.00　1.75
　　Imperf., #1132-1139　　10.00　10.00

A343

1981, Aug. 5　　　　**Perf. 11**
1140　A343　12xu　Lotus flower　2.00　.35

A343a

Design: Factory militiawoman.

1981, Aug. 5
1140A　A343a　12xu　yel & multi　20.00　.75
　　See Nos. M30-M31.

A344

Fruit: No. 1141, 20xu, Elaeagnus latifolia. No. 1142, 20xu, Fortunella japonica. 30xu, Nephelium lappaceum. 40xu, Averrhoa bilimbi. No. 1145, 50xu, Ziziphus mauritiana. No. 1146, 50xu, Fragaria vesca. 60xu, Bouea oppositifolia. 1d, Syzygium aqueum.

1981, Oct. 12   *Perf. 12*
1141-1148 A344 Set of 8   5.00 1.25
   Imperf., #1141-1148   8.00

A345

Planting trees: No. 1149, Ho Chi Minh. No. 1150, Three people.

1981, Nov. 15   *Perf. 11*
1149-1150 A345 30xu Set of 2   2.00 .50
   Tree planting festival.

Bulgaria, 1300th Anniv. A346

1982, May 7   *Perf. 11*
1151-1153 A346   30xu, 50xu, 2d, set of 3   3.50 1.10

Wild Animals — A347

Designs: No. 1154, 30xu, Orangutan. No. 1155, 30xu, Bison bonasus. No. 1156, 40xu, Kangaroo. No. 1157, 40xu, Hippopotamus. No. 1158, 50xu, Rhinoceros sondaicus. No. 1159, 50xu, Giraffe. 60xu, Zebra. 1d, Lion.

1981, Dec. 9   *Perf. 12½x12*
1154-1161 A347 Set of 8   5.00 1.50
   Imperf., #1154-1161   10.00 10.00

A348

World Food Day: 30xu, 50xu, Woman holding sheaf of rice. 2d, FAO emblem, horiz.

1982, Jan. 26   *Perf. 11*
1162-1164 A348 Set of 3   2.50 1.10

A349

1982, Feb. 19
1165-1166 A349 50xu, 5d, Set of 2   3.75 1.75

10th World Trade Unions Congress, Havana, Cuba.

5th Vietnamese Communist Party Congress — A350

Designs: No. 1167, 30xu, Ho Chi Minh. No. 1168, 30xu, Hammer, sickle. No. 1169, 30xu, Worker, dam. 50xu, Women harvesting rice. 1d, Ho Chi Minh.

1982
1167-1170 A350   Set of 4   4.50 1.50
Imperf
Size: 99x61 mm
1171 A350 1d multicolored   60.00 60.00
   Issued: Nos. 1167-1168, 1171, 2/15; Nos. 1169-1170, 3/27.

Bees & Wasps A351

Designs: No. 1172, 20xu, Ong bove. No. 1173, 20xu, Ong van xanh. 30xu, To vo nau. 40xu, Ong vang. No. 1176, 50xu, Ong dau nau. No. 1177, 50xu, To vo xanh. 60xu, Ong bau. 1d, Ong mat.

1982, Feb. 20   *Perf. 12*
1172-1179 A351 Set of 8   5.00 1.50
   Imperf., #1172-1179   10.00 10.00

Soccer A352

#1180, 30xu, 3 players. #1181, 30xu, 2 players. #1182, 40xu, Striped background. #1183, 40xu, grass background. #1184, 50xu, Vertically striped background. #1185, 50xu, Horizonally striped background. 60xu, 1d, Various soccer scenes.

1982, Apr. 15
1180-1187 A352 Set of 8   5.00 1.25
   Imperf., #1180-1187   10.00 10.00

For overprints see Nos. 2142-2149.

A353

Vietnamese Red Cross, 35th Anniv.: 1d, Red Cross emblem.

1982, May 15   *Perf. 11*
1188-1189 A353 Set of 2   2.50 .70

A354

5th Natl. Women's Congress: No. 1190, Congress emblem, three women with arms raised. No. 1191, Congress emblem, faces of three women.

1982, May 19   *Perf. 12*
1190-1191 A354 12xu Set of 2   2.50 .75

A355

Birds of Prey: No. 1192, 30xu, Microhierax melanoleucos. No. 1100, 00xu, Falco tinnunculus. 40xu, Aviceda leuphotes. No. 1195, 50xu, Icthyophaga nana. No. 1196, 50xu, Milvus korschun. 60xu, Neohierax harmandi, horiz. No. 1198, 1d, Elanus caeruleus, horiz. No. 1199, 1d, Circaetus gallicus.

1982, June 10
1192-1199 A355 Set of 8   8.00 1.75
   Imperf., #1192-1199   16.00 16.00

A356

1982, May 16   *Perf. 11*
1200-1201 A356 30xu, 3d, set of 2   4.00 2.00
   Imperf., #1200-1201   45.00

Georgi Dimitrov (1882-1949), Bulgarian Communist leader.

Dahlias A357

Designs (last word or two of Vietnamese inscription): No. 1202, 30xu, Da cam. No. 1203, 30xu, Do. 40xu, Canh se. No. 1205, 50xu, Do nhung. No. 1206, 50xu, Vang. 60xu, Do tuoi. No. 1208, 1d, Bien. No. 1209, 1d, Trang. Various flowers.

1982, July 15   *Perf. 12x12½*
1202-1209 A357 Set of 8   6.00 2.25
   Imperf., #1202-1209   12.00 12.00

1982 World Cup Soccer Championships, Spain — A358

#1210, 50xu, Ball at bottom right. #1211, 50xu, Ball at right in air. #1212, 50xu, Ball at bottom center. #1213, 1d, 1 player. #1214, 1d, 3 players. 2d, 2 players.

1982, July 25   *Perf. 12x12½*
1210-1215 A358 Set of 6   5.50 2.25
   Imperf., #1210-1215   10.00 10.00

A359

1982, Apr. 22   *Perf. 11*
1216 A359 30xu Natl. defense   1.50 .70
   See No. M32.

A360

1982, Aug. 15
1217 A360 30xu multicolored   1.50 .35
   Cuban victory at Giron (Bay of Pigs), 20th anniv.

World Environment Day — A361

#1219, Ho Chi Minh, children planting tree.

1982, Aug. 15
1218-1219 A361 30xu Set of 2   2.00 .70
   Imperf., #1218-1219   40.00

A362

1982, Sept. 20
1220 A362 30xu multicolored   1.50 .35
   Rabindranath Tagore (1861-1941), poet.

A363

Insects: No. 1221, 30xu, Catacanthus incarnatus. No. 1222, 30xu, Sycanus falleni. 40xu, Nezara viridula. No. 1224, 50xu, Lohita grandis. No. 1225, 50xu, Helcomeria spinosa. 60xu, Chrysocoris stollii. No. 1227, 1d, Pterygamia srayi. No. 1228, 1d, Tiarodes ostentans.

1982, Sept. 25   *Perf. 12x12½*
1221-1228   A363   Set of 8   5.50   1.75
   Imperf., #1221-1228   11.00   11.00

Russian Revolution, 65th Anniv. — A364

Design: No. 1230, Lenin, workers.

1982, Nov. 7   *Perf. 11*
1229-1230   A364   30xu   Set of 2   2.00   .70

9th South East Asian Games, New Delhi, India A365

#1231, 30xu, Table tennis. #1232, 30xu, Swimming. 1d, Wrestling. 2d, Shooting.

1982, Nov. 19
1231-1234   A365   Set of 4   4.50   1.50

Fish A366

Designs: No. 1235, 30xu, Samaris cristatus. No. 1236, 30xu, Tephrinectes sinensis. No. 1237, 40xu, Psettodes erumei. No. 1238, 40xu, Zebrias zebra. No. 1239, 50xu, Cynoglossus puncticeps. No. 1240, 50xu, Pardachirus pavoninus. 60xu, Brachirus orientalis. 1d, Psettina iijimae.

1982, Dec. 15   *Perf. 12*
1235-1242   A366   Set of 8   5.50   1.50
   Imperf., #1235-1242   12.00   12.00

Socialist Ideals — A367

#1243, 30xu, Agriculture. #1244, 30xu, Industry. 1d, Natl. defense. 2d, Health & education.

1982, Dec. 25   *Perf. 11*
1243-1246   A367   Set of 4   5.50   1.50

Founding of Soviet Union, 60th Anniv. A368

1982, Dec. 30
1247   A368   30xu multicolored   2.50   .40
   Imperf., #1247   35.00

Sampans A369

Designs: 30xu, Docked. 50xu, With striped sails. 1d, Sampans on Red River. 3d, With white sails. 5d, With patched sail. 10d, Fast sampan, horiz.

1983, Jan. 10   *Perf. 12½*
1248-1253   A369   Set of 6   6.00   2.00
   Imperf., #1248-1253   12.00   12.00

Locomotives — A370

30xu, Class 231-300. 50xu, Class 230-000. 1d, Class 140-601. 2d, Class 241-000. 3d, Class 141-500. 5d, Class 150-000. 8d, Class 40-300.

1983, Feb. 20   *Perf. 13*
1254-1260   A370   Set of 7   7.50   2.50
   Imperf., #1254-1260   15.00   15.00

1st Manned Balloon Flight, Bicent. A371

Balloons: 30xu, Montgolfier. 50xu, Yellow. 1d, CA-11. 2d, Hot-air. 3d, Over harbor. 5d, Le Geant. 8d, Ascending. 10d, Montgolfier, diff.

1983, Mar. 25   *Litho.*   *Perf. 12½*
1261-1267   A371   Set of 7   6.75   2.00
   Imperf., #1261-1267   15.00   15.00
Souvenir Sheet   *Perf. 13*
1268   A371   10d Sheet of 1   5.00   1.50
   No. 1268 contains one 32x40mm stamp.

Discovery of Tubercle Bacillus, Cent. — A372

1983, Mar. 25   *Perf. 11*
1269   A372   5d multicolored   3.00   .75

Laos-Cambodia-Viet Nam Summit — A373

1983, Mar. 25
1270-1271   A373   50xu, 5d   Set of 2   2.50   .75
   Imperf., #1270-1271   40.00

Cosmonauts — A374

Designs: 30xu, Gubarev, Remek. No. 1273, 50xu, Klimuk, Hermaszewski. No. 1274, 50xu, Bykovsky, Jahn. No. 1275, 1d, Rukavishnikov, Ivanov. No. 1276, 1d, Farcas, Kubasov. No. 1277, 2d, Mendez, Romanenko. No. 1278, 2d, Gorbatko, Tuan. 5d, Dzhanibekov, Gurragcha. 8d, Popov, Prunariu. No. 1281, Gagarin.

1983, Apr. 1   *Perf. 12½x12*
1272-1280   A374   Set of 9   6.00   2.00
   Imperf., #1272-1280   12.50   12.50
Souvenir Sheet
1281   A374   10d multicolored   6.00   1.50
   No. 1281 contains one 36x28mm stamp.

Reptiles A375

Designs: No. 1282, 30xu, Teratolepis fasciata. No. 1283, 30xu, Chamaeleo jacksoni. No. 1284, 50xu, Uromastyx acanthinurus. No. 1285, 80xu, Heloderma suspectum. 1d, Cameleo menle. 2d, Amphibolurus barbatus. 5d, Chlamydosaurus kingi. 10d, Phrynosoma coronatum.

1983, Apr. 5   *Perf.*
1282-1289   A375   Set of 8   7.50   3.00
   Imperf., #1282-1289   15.00   15.00

Raphael (1483-1520), Painter — A375a

Designs: 30xu, Virgin Mother Seated on Chair. 50xu, Granduca, the Virgin Mother. 1d,

Sistine Madonna. 2d, Marriage of Maria. 3d, The Gardener. 5d, Woman with Veil. 8d, 10d, Self-Portrait.

1983, Apr. 30   *Perf. 12½*
1289A-1289G   A375a   Set of 7   7.50   2.00
   Imperf., #1289A-1289G   10.00   10.00
Souvenir Sheet   *Perf. 13*
1289H   A375a   10d multicolored   6.00   1.50

Chess Pieces — A376

Designs: 30xu, Vietnamese pawns. 50xu, Indian elephant. 1d, Scottish knight, bishop. 2d, Indian elephant, diff. 3d, Knight. 5d, Sailing ship. 8d, Jester, elephant. 10d, Modern pawns.

1983, May 9   *Perf. 13*
1290-1296   A376   Set of 7   6.00   2.00
   Imperf., #1290-1296   17.00   17.00
Souvenir Sheet
1297   A376   10d multicolored   6.00   1.50
   No. 1297 contains one 28x36mm stamp.

Souvenir Sheet

TEMBAL '83 World Stamp Exhibition, Basel — A377

1983, May 21   *Perf. 13*
1298   A377   10d multicolored   4.50   1.50

1984 Summer Olympics, Los Angeles A378

Designs: 30xu, Long jump. 50xu, Running. 1d, Javelin. 2d, High jump, horiz. 3d, Hurdles, horiz. 5d, Shot put. 8d, Pole vault. 10d, Discus.

1983, June 13   *Litho.*   *Perf. 13*
1299-1305   A378   Set of 7   6.00   2.00
   Imperf., #1299-1305
Souvenir Sheet
1306   A378   10d Sheet of 1   6.25   1.50
   No. 1306 contains one 32x40mm stamp.
   The issuance of this set has been questioned.

Souvenir Sheet

Brasiliana '83, Rio de Janeiro — A379

1983, July 20 *Perf. 13*
1307 A379 10d Rhamphastos
toco 10.00 2.50

Butterflies
A380

Designs: No. 1308, 30xu, Leptocircus meges. No. 1309, 30xu, Terias hecabe. No. 1310, 40xu, Zetides agamemnon. No. 1311, 40xu, Nyctalemon patroclus. No. 1312, 50xu, Papilio chaon. No. 1313, 50xu, Precis almana. 60xu, Thauria lathyi. 1d, Kallima inachus.

1983, July 30 *Litho. Perf. 12*
1308-1315 A380 Set of 8 7.50 3.00
Imperf., #1308-1315 16.00 16.00

Souvenir Sheet

Bangkok '83 — A381

1983, Aug. 4 *Perf. 13*
1316 A381 10d multicolored 10.00 1.50

Karl Marx
(1818-1883)
A382

No. 1317, 50xu. No. 1318, 10d,

1983, Oct. 10 *Perf. 11*
1317-1318 A382 Set of 2 4.50 1.25
Imperf., #1317-1318 *50.00*

Phu Dong Sports Festival A383

1983, Oct. 10
1319-1320 A383 30xu, 1d, Set of
2 3.50 .70

World
Food Day
A384

Design: 50xu, Infant, fish. 4d, Family.

1983, Oct. 10 *Perf. 12½*
1321-1322 A384 Set of 2 3.00 .70
Imperf., #1321-1322 7.00

Mushrooms
A385

#1323, 50xu, Flammulina velutipes. #1324, 50xu, Pleurotus ostreatus. #1325, 50xu, Cantharellus cibarius. #1326, 50xu, Coprinus atramentarius. 1d, Volvariella volvacea. 2d, Agaricus silvaticus. 5d, Morchella esculenta. 10d, Amanita caesarea.

1983, Oct. 10 *Perf. 12x12½*
1323-1330 A385 Set of 8 9.00 3.00
Imperf., #1323-1330 14.50

For overprints see Nos. 2150-2157.

World Communications Year — A386

50xu, Letter carrier. 2d, Mail sorting room. 8d, Switchboard operators. #1334, 10d, Radio operator, antenna. #1335, 10d, Telephone, letter, dish antenna, ship.

1983, Sept. 30 *Perf. 12½*
1331-1334 A386 Set of 4 5.75 1.50
Souvenir Sheet
Perf. 13
1335 A386 10d Sheet of 1 3.00 1.50

5th Natl. Trade Unions
Congress — A387

50xu, Woman with flowers, Vietnam-Soviet Union Friendship Cultural Building. 2d, 30d, Welder.

1983, Nov. 16 *Perf. 11*
1336-1338 A387 Set of 3 7.50 1.50

Water Birds
A388

Designs: No. 1339, 50xu, Ciconia nigra. No. 1340, 50xu, Ardea cinerea. No. 1341, 50xu, Ardea purpurea. No. 1342, 50xu, Ibis leucocephalus. 1d, Grus grus. 2d, Platalea minor. 5d, Nycticorax nycticorax. 10d, Anastomus oscitans.

1983, Nov. 20 *Perf. 12x12½*
1339-1346 A388 Set of 8 9.00 3.00
Imperf., #1339-1346 18.00 18.00

No. 1343 inscribed "Grus grue."

World Peace
Conference,
Prague — A389

Designs: 50xu, Shown. 3d, 5d, 20d, Hands, globe, dove.

1983, Dec. 19 *Perf. 11*
1347-1350 A389 Set of 4 9.00 2.00

1984 Winter Olympics, Sarajevo,
Yugoslavia — A390

#1351, 50xu, Cross-country skiing, vert. #1352, 50xu, Biathlon, vert. 1d, Speed skating, vert. 2d, Bobsled, vert. 3d, Hockey. 5d, Ski jumping. 6d, Slalom skiing. 10d, Pairs figure skating.

1984, Jan. 30 *Perf. 12½*
1351-1357 A390 Set of 7 5.50 2.00
Imperf., #1351-1357 15.00 15.00
Souvenir Sheet
1358 A390 10d multicolored 3.75 1.50

No. 1358 contains one 40x32mm stamp.

Soviet Union-Vietnamese Projects,
1978-83 — A391

Designs: 20xu (No. 1359), 4d, Hoa Binh Hydro-electric project. 20xu (No. 1360), Vietnamese-Soviet Cultural Palace. 50xu, Thang Long Bridge.

1984, Jan. 31 **With Gum** *Perf. 11*
1359-1362 A391 Set of 4 55.00

Endangered Animals — A392

Designs: No. 1363, 50xu, Felis marmorata. No. 1364, 50xu, Panthera tigris. No. 1365, 50xu, Panthera pardus. No. 1366, 1d, Hylobates lar. No. 1367, 1d, Nycticebus coucang. No. 1368, 2d, Elephas indidus. No. 1369, 2d, Bos gaurus.

1984, Feb. 26 *Perf. 12½x12*
1363-1369 A392 Set of 7 5.00 1.00
Imperf., #1363-1369 12.00 12.00

A393

Wildflowers: No. 1370, 50xu, Banhinia variegata. No. 1371, 50xu, Caesalpinia pulcherrima. 1d, Cassia fistula. 2d, Delonix regia. 3d, Artagotrys uncinatus. 5d, Corchorus olitorius. 8d, Banhinia grandiflora.

1984, Mar. 15 *Perf. 12x12½*
1370-1376 A393 Set of 7 5.75 2.50
Imperf., #1370-1376 11.50 11.50
Souvenir Sheet
1377 A393 10d Delonix regia 4.00 1.50

Location of inscriptions differs on Nos. 1373, 1377.

A394

Orchids: No. 1378, 50xu, Cymbidium. No. 1379, 50xu, Brasse callleya. 1d, Callleya Dianx. 2d, Cymbidium, diff. 3d, Cymbidium hybridum. 5d, Phoenix winged orchids. 8d, Yellow Queen orchids.

1984, Mar. 28 *Perf. 13*
1378-1384 A394 Set of 7 8.00 2.00
Imperf., #1378-1384 16.00 16.00

Nos. 1084-1085, 1093 Surcharged

a b

1984, Apr. 25 *Perfs. as before*
1384A A322(a) 50xu on 12xu
#1084 6.00 6.00
1385 A322(a) 50xu on 12xu
#1085 6.00 6.00
1386 A335(b) 50xu on 12xu
#1093 4.00 4.00

Souvenir Sheet

Espana '84, Madrid — A395

1984, Apr. 27   *Perf. 12½*
1387 A395 10d Ciconia ciconia   6.50 2.50

Victory at Dien Bien Phu, 30th Anniv. A396

No. 1388, 50xu; No. 1395, 10d, Ho Chi Minh, generals, battle map. #1389, 50xu, Troops, truck. No. 1390, 1d, Civilians carrying provisions. No. 1391, 2d, Men-hauling artillery. No. 1392, 3d, Anti-aircraft battery. No. 1393, 5d, Troops attacking enemy base. No. 1394, 8d, Troops waving flag.

1984, May 7   *Perf. 12½*
1388-1394 A396   Set of 7   4.50 2.00
Souvenir Sheet
1395   A396 10d multicolored 4.50 1.50

Souvenir Sheet

UPU Congress, Hamburg '84 — A397

1984, June 19   *Perf. 13*
1396 A397 10d Junkers JU-52
3M   4.50 1.50

Fish
A398

Designs: No. 1397, 30xu, Cypselurus spilopterus. No. 1398, 30xu, Ostracion cornutus. 50xu, Diodon hystrix. 80xu, Chelmon rostratus. 1d, Antennarius tridens. 2d, Pterois russelli. 5d, Mola mola. 10d, Minous monodactylus.

1984, June 25   Litho.   *Perf. 12*
1397-1404 A398   Set of 8   7.25 3.00
          Imperf., #1397-1404   12.00 12.00

Ornamental Fish — A399

Designs: No. 1405, 50xu, Trichogaster trichopterus. No. 1406, 50xu, Brachydanio rerio. 1d, Macropodus opercularis. 2d, Gymnocorymbus ternetzi. 3d, Hyphessobrycon serpae. 5d, Labeo bicolor. 8d, Batta splendens.

1984, June 29   *Perf. 12½*
1405-1411 A399   Set of 7   6.00 3.00
          Imperf., #1405-1411   12.00 12.00

Vietnamese Trade Union Movement, 55th Anniv. — A400

Designs: No. 1412a, 50xu, House at 15 Hang Non St., Hanoi, vert. No. 1412b, 50xu, Nguyen Duc Canh, vert. 1d, Striking workers. 2d, Ho Chi Minh visiting factory. 3d, Hanoi Mechanical Engineering plant. 5d, Intl. trade union movement.

1984, July 20   *Perf. 11*
1412-1416 A400   Set of 6   3.50 2.25
Souvenir Sheet
Imperf
1417   A400 2d like #1414 11.00 11.00

No. 1412 printed se-tenant. No. 1417 contains one 45x38mm stamp.

Rock Formations, Ha Long Bay — A401

#1418, 50xu, Hang-Bo Nau. #1419, 50xu, Nui Yen Ngua. #1420, 50xu, Hon Dua. #1421, 50xu, Hang Con Gai. #1422, 1d, Hon Coc. #1423, 1d, Hon Ga Choi. 2d, Hon Dinh Huong. 3d, Hon Su Tu. 5d, Hon Am. 8d, Nui Bai Tho.

1984, July 30   *Perf. 12½x12*
1418-1427 A401   Set of 10   6.50 2.50
          Imperf., #1418-1427   14.00 14.00

Dinosaurs — A402

#1428, 50xu, Styracosaurus. #1429, 50xu, Diplodocus. #1430, 1d, Corythosaurus. #1431, 1d, Rhamphyorhynchus. 2d, Seymouria. 3d, Allosaurus. 5d, Dimetrodon. 8d, Brachiosaurus.

1984, Aug. 30
1428-1435 A402   Set of 8   13.50 3.00
          Imperf., #1428-1435   27.00 27.00

Viet Nam-Laos-Cambodia
Friendship — A403

1984, Aug. 30   *Perf. 11*
1436-1437 A403 50xu, 10d, set
          of 2 6.00 .80

Souvenir Sheet

Ausipex '84, Melbourne, Australia — A404

1984, Sept. 20   *Perf. 13*
1438 A404 10d Koala   9.00 1.50

Viet Nam-Cambodia Friendship Agreement, 5th Anniv. — A405

50xu, 3d, People, pagoda, statue. 50d, Dancers.

1984, Sept. 30   *Perf. 11*
1439-1441 A405   Set of 3   10.00 4.00
          Imperf., #1439-1441   50.00

Liberation of Hanoi, 30th Anniv. A406

Designs: 50xu, Thang Long Bridge. 1d, Khue Van Gateway. 2d, Ho Chi Minh mausoleum.

1984, Oct. 5
1442-1444 A406   Set of 3   3.50 1.25
          Imperf., #1442-1444   35.00

Vintage Automobiles — A407

#1445, 50xu, Vis-a-Vis, vert. #1446, 50xu, Duc. 1d, Tonneau. 2d, Double phaeton. 3d, Landaulet. 5d, Torpedo. 6d, Coupe de Ville.

1984, Oct. 30   *Perf. 12½x13, 13x12½*
1445-1451 A407   Set of 7   5.00 2.50
          Imperf., #1445-1451   10.00 10.00

Lenin (1870-1924)
A408

Paintings of Lenin: 50xu, At his desk. 1d, Standing with revolutionaries. 3d, Speaking at factory. 5d, Meeting with farmers.

1984, Nov. 15   *Perf. 12x12½*
1452-1455 A408   Set of 4   3.00 1.50
          Imperf., #1452-1455   6.00 6.00

UNICEF
A409

Paintings: 30xu, Woman, soldiers. 50xu, Mother, children. 1d, Miner, family. 3d, Young girl, vert. 5d, Children playing on ground. 10d, Women, child, vert.

1984, Dec. 7   *Perf. 12*
1456-1461 A409   Set of 6   5.50 2.75
          Imperf., #1456-1461   10.00 10.00

A410

50xu, 30d. Frontier Forces, 25th anniv.

1984, Dec. 15   *Perf. 11*
1462-1463 A410   Set of 2   10.00 1.90
          Imperf., #1462-1463
          See No. M39.

A411

Flora and Fauna: 20xu, Bubalus bubalis. 30xu, Felis marmorata. No. 1466, 50xu, Hibiscus rosa-sinensis. No. 1467, 50xu, Ailurus fulgens. No. 1468, 50xu, Rosa centifolia. No. 1469, 50xu, Betta splendens. No. 1470, 1d, Chrysanthemum sinense. No. 1471, 1d, Nymphaea ampla. No. 1472, 1d, Pelecanus onocrotalus. No. 1473, 1d, Panthera tigris. No. 1474, 2d, Nycticebus coucang. No. 1475, 2d, Macaca fascicularis. No. 1476, 2d, Dalia coccinea. 5d, Gekko gecko. 10d, Rhytidoceros bicornis.

1984, Dec.   *Perf. 12½x12*
1464-1478 A411   Set of 15   10.00 4.00
          Imperf., #1464-1478   15.00

No. 1466 inscribed "Hybiscus." No. 1470 inscribed "Chrysanthemun."

A412

1985   **Perf. 11**
1479-1480 A412 3d, 5d, set of 2   2.75   .80
          Imperf., #1479-1480   30.00

New Year 1985 (Year of the Buffalo).
Issued: 3d, 1/21; 5d, 4/30.

A413

1985, Apr. 26   **Perf. 11**
1481 A413 2d Ho Chi Minh   1.10   .40
      Imperf.   20.00

Vietnamese Communist Party, 55th anniv.

Military
Victory in
South Viet
Nam, 10th
Anniv.
A414

Designs: 1d, Soldiers advancing forward.
2d, 10d, Ho Chi Minh, tank, soldiers. 4d, Construction worker. 5d, Map, women.

1985, Apr. 30   **Perf. 12½**
1482-1485 A414 Set of 4   3.50 1.50
          Souvenir Sheet
          Perf. 13
1486 A414 10d multicolored   3.75 1.75
      Imperf.   10.00

Cactus
A415

Designs: No. 1487, 50xu, Echinocereus
knippelianus. No. 1488, 50xu, Lemaireocereus
thurberi. 1d, Notocactus haselbergii. 2d,
Parodia chrysacanthion. 3d, Pelecyphora
pseudopectinata. 5d, Rebutia frebrighii. 8d,
Lobivia aurea.

1985, Mar. 30   **Perf. 11½**
1487-1493 A415 Set of 7   7.00 2.50
          Imperf., #1487-1493   15.00 15.00

Vietnamese People's Army, 40th
Anniv. — A416

Designs: No. 1494, 50xu, Ho Chi Minh. No.
1495, 50xu, Taking oath on flag. 1d, Anti-aircraft missile. 2d, Soldiers, civilians working
together. 3d, Tank entering grounds of presidential palace, Saigon. 5d, Soldier demonstrating use of rifle. 8d, Officers, soldiers, map.
10d, Four soldiers representing branches of
military.

1984, Dec. 22   **Perf. 12½**
1494-1500 A416 Set of 7   5.50 3.00
          Souvenir Sheet
1501 A416 10d multi   4.00 1.50

End of World War
II, 40th
Anniv. — A417

Designs: 1d, 10d, Victory Monument. 2d,
Vietnamese soldier. 4d, Dove, falling American eagle. 5d, Child, doves.

1985, June 5   **Perf. 12x12½**
1502-1505 A417 Set of 4   3.50 1.50
          Imperf., #1502-1505   15.00 15.00

1506 A417 10d multicolored   3.25 1.50

Liberation of
Haiphong, 30th
Anniv. — A418

Designs: 2d, Long Chau Lighthouse. 5d, An
Duong Bridge, horiz.
10d, To Hieu (1912-44), vert.

1985, May 13   **Perf. 11**
1507-1508 A418 Set of 2   2.50   .80
          Imperf., #1507-1508   45.00
          Souvenir Sheet
          Imperf
1509 A418 10d multicolored   3.50 1.50

Ho Chi Minh, 95th Birth
Anniv. — A419

Ho Chi Minh: 1d, At battlefield. 2d, Reading.
4d, 10d, Portrait, vert. 5d, Writing.

1985, July 6   **Perf. 12½**
1510-1513 A419 Set of 4   4.00 2.00
          Souvenir Sheet
          Perf. 13
1514 A419 10d multicolored   5.00 1.40
No. 1514 contains one 30x36mm stamp.

Motorcycles, Cent. — A420

Designs: No. 1515, 1d, 1895, Germany. No.
1516, 1d, 1898 tricycle, France. No. 1517, 2d,
1913 Harley-Davidson, US. No. 1518, 2d,
1918 Cleveland, US. 3d, 1935 Simplex, US.
4d, 1984 Minarelli, Italy. 6d, 1984 Honda,
Japan. 10d, 1984 Honda racing bike.

1985, June 28   **Perf. 13**
1515-1521 A420 Set of 7   5.50 2.75
          Imperf., #1515-1521   13.00 13.00
          Souvenir Sheet
1522 A420 10d multicolored   5.00 1.40
No. 1522 contains one 32x40mm stamp.

Argentina '85, Buenos Aires — A421

Wild animals: No. 1523, 1d, Aptenodytes
pennati, vert. No. 1524, 1d, Dolichotis
patagonum, vert. No. 1525, 2d, Panthera
onca. No. 1526, 2d, Hydrochoerys capibara.
3d, Peterocnemia pennata, vert. 4d, Priodontes giganteus. 6d, Voltur gryphus. 10d,
Lama glama, horiz.

1985, July 5   **Perf. 12½**
1523-1529 A421 Set of 7   10.00 2.50
          Imperf., #1523-1529   18.00 18.00
          Souvenir Sheet
          With Gum
          Perf. 13
1530 A421 10d multicolored   12.50 1.50
No. 1530 contains one 40x32mm stamp.

12th World
Youth and
Students
Festival,
Moscow
A422

No. 1531, 2d, Youth carrying flags, globe.
No. 1532, 2d, Workers, power transmission
lines. 4d, Lighthouse, coastal defense. 5d, Intl.
festival.

1985, June 20   **Perf. 12½**
1531-1534 A422 Set of 4   4.25 1.50
          Imperf., #1531-1534   17.50 17.50
          Souvenir Sheet
          With Gum
          Perf. 13
1535 A422 10d like #1531   5.00 1.25

Marine Life
A423

#1536, 3d, Nadoa tuberculata. #1537, 3d,
Luidia maculata. #1538, 3d, Stichopus chloro-
notus. #1539, 3d, Holothuria monacaria.
#1540, 4d, Astropyga radiata. #1541, 4d,
Astropecten scoparius. #1542, 4d, Linckia
laevigata.

1985, July 30   **Perf. 12**
1536-1542 A423 Set of 7   7.00 2.75
          Imperf., #1536-1542   19.00 19.00

Socialist
Republic of Viet
Nam, 40th
Anniv. — A424

Designs: 2d, Construction. 3d, Hands shaking, doves. 5d, Flag, military forces. No. 1567,
10d, Flag, Ho Chi Minh.

1985, Aug. 28   **Perf. 12½**
1543-1546 A424 Set of 4   4.50 1.90
          Imperf., #1543-1546   20.00 20.00
          Souvenir Sheet
          Perf. 13
1547 A424 10d like #1543   3.00 3.00
No. 1547 contains one 32x40mm stamp.

Vietnamese Police Force, 40th
Anniv. — A425

1985, Aug. 30   **Perf. 11**
1548 A425 10d multicolored   4.00   .40
      Imperf.   18.00
          See No. M41.

1st Natl.
Sports
Festival
A426

Designs: 5d, Gymnastics. 10d, Gymnastics,
running, swimming.

1985, Aug. 30
1549-1550 A426 Set of 2   4.50   .80
          Imperf., #1549-1550   40.00

German Railways, 150th
Anniv. — A427

Various locomotives: #1551, 1d, Facing left.
#1552, 1d, Facing right. #1553, 2d, Facing left.
#1554, 2d, Facing right. 3d, 4d, 6d.

1985, Sept. 13   **Perf. 12½**
1551-1557 A427 Set of 7   6.25 2.50
          Imperf., #1551-1557   10.00 10.00
          Souvenir Sheet
          With Gum
          Perf. 13
1558 A427 10d multicolored   3.75 1.50
No. 1558 contains one 32x40mm stamp.

Vietnamese Geological Survey, 30th
Anniv. — A428

#1559, Drilling rigs. #1560, Aerial survey.

1985, Oct. 5   **Perf. 11**
1559-1560 A428 1d Set of 2   2.50   .80

Italia '85
A429

Vintage Italian cars: No. 1561, 1d, 1922 Alfa
Romeo. No. 1562, 1d, 1932 Bianchi Berlina.
No. 1563, 2d, 1928 Isotta Fraschini. No. 1564,
2d, 1930 Bugatti. No. 1565, 3d, 1912 Itala. 4d,

1934 Lancia Augusta. 6d, 1927 Fiat Convertable (top up). 10d, 1927 Fiat Convertable (top down).

1985, Oct. 25 **Perf. 13**
1561-1567 A429 Set of 7 5.50 2.25
 Imperf., #1561-1567 17.50 17.50
Souvenir Sheet
With Gum
1568 A429 10d multicolored 6.00 1.25
 No. 1568 contains one 40x32mm stamp.

Whales
A430

Designs: No. 1569, 1d, Balaenoptera musculus. No. 1570, 1d, Balaena borealis. No. 1571, 2d, Orcinus orca. No. 1572, 2d, Delphinus. 3d, Megaptera boops. 4d, Balaenoptera physalus. 6d, Eubalaena glacialis.

1985, Nov. 15
1569-1575 A430 Set of 7 8.00 2.50
 Imperf., #1569-1575 20.00 20.00

1986 World Cup Soccer
Championships, Mexico City — A431

Various soccer plays: No. 1576, 1d, From behind goal. No. 1577, 1d, Goalie from side. No. 1578, 2d, From behind goal. No. 1579, 2d, From in front of goal, vert. 3d, vert. 4d, vert. 6d, vert.

1985, Nov. 30
1576-1582 A431 Set of 7 5.00 1.75
 Imperf., #1576-1582 12.00 12.00
Souvenir Sheet
Perf. 13
1583 A431 10d multicolored 4.00 1.25
 No. 1583 contains one 40x32mm stamp.

People's
Democratic
Republic of
Laos, 10th
Anniv. — A432

a, Woman, dove. b, Woman dancing, natl. arms.

1985, Dec. 2 **Perf. 11**
1584 A432 1d Pair, #a.-b. 3.00 1.50

Traditional Musical
Instruments — A433

#1585, 1d, Stone chimes. #1586, 1d, Large bronze drum. #1587, 2d, Flutes. #1588, 2d, Large red drum. 3d, Monochord. 4d, Moon-shaped lute. 6d, Vietnamese two-string violin.

1985, Dec. 5 **Perf. 12½x12**
1585-1591 A433 Set of 7 5.75 2.75
 Imperf., #1585-1591 12.00 12.00

A434

Socialist Republic of Viet Nam, 40th Anniv.: No. 1592, 10d, Industry. No. 1593, 10d, Agriculture. 20d, Public health. 30d, Education.

1985, Dec. 6 **Perf. 11**
1592-1595 A434 Set of 4 30.00 15.00

A435

1986, Jan. 6 **Litho.** **Perf. 11**
1596-1597 A435 50xu, 1d Set of 2 2.25 .80
 1st Natl. Elections, 40th anniv.

A436

1986, Jan. 6
1598 A436 1d multicolored 1.50 .45
 UN 40th anniv.

A437

Halley's Comet: No. 1599, 2d, Edmond Halley. No. 1600, 2d, Isaac Newton. 3d, Rocket, flags. 5d, Comet.

1986, Feb. 24 **Perf. 12½**
1599-1602 A437 Set of 4 5.00 1.50
 Imperf., #1599-1602 12.00 12.00

A438

Soviet Communist Party, 27th Congress: 50xu, Kremlin, map. 1d, Lenin banner.

1986, Feb. 25 **Perf. 11**
1603-1604 A438 Set of 2 2.50 .80
 Imperf., #1603-1604 40.00

Map of Battle of
Xuong
Giang — A439

1986, Mar. 1
1605 A439 1d multicolored 1.50 .40
 Le Loi, 600th birth anniv.

1986 World
Cup Soccer
Championships,
Mexico
City — A440

Various soccer players in action: No. 1606, 1d, Viet Nam at left. No. 1607, 1d, Viet Nam at right. 2d, Viet Nam at left. No. 1609, 3d, Viet Nam at left. No. 1610, 3d, Viet Nam at right. No. 1611, 5d, Viet Nam at left. No. 1612, 5d, Viet Nam at right.

1986, Mar. 3 **Perf. 12½**
1606-1612 A440 Set of 7 4.50 2.50
 Imperf., #1606-1612 9.00 9.00
Souvenir Sheet
Perf. 13
1613 A440 10d multicolored 4.50 1.25
 No. 1613 contains one 40x32mm stamp.

1st
Manned
Space
Flight,
25th
Anniv.
A441

#1614, 1d, Konstantin Tsiolkovsky. #1615, 1d, Rocket on transporter. 2d, Yuri Gagarin. #1617, 3d, Valentina Tereshkova, vert. #1618, 3d, Alexei Leonov. #1619, 5d, Apollo-Soyuz, crews. #1620, 5d, Soyuz, Salut space station. 10d, Cosmonauts, vert.

1986, Apr. 12 **Perf. 13**
1614-1620 A441 Set of 7 4.50 2.25
 Imperf., #1614-1620 10.00 10.00
Souvenir Sheet
1621 A441 10d multicolored 5.00 1.25
 No. 1621 contains one 32x40mm stamp.

Ernst Thalmann (1886-1944), German
Politician — A442

1986, Apr. 16 **Perf. 11**
1622 A442 2d red & black 1.50 .40
 Imperf. 20.00

May Day — A443

1986, May 1
1623-1624 A443 1d, 5d, Set of 2 2.25 .40
 Imperf., #1623-1624 40.00

Vancouver Expo '86 — A444

Airplanes: No. 1625, 1d, Hawker Hart. No. 1626, 1d, Curtiss Jenny. 2d, PZL-P23. No. 1628, 3d, Yakovlev Yak-11. No. 1629, 3d, Fokker Dr.1. No. 1630, 5d, Boeing P-12 (1920). No. 1631, 5d, Nieuport-Delage NiD.29C1 (1929).

1986, Sept. 30 **Perf. 13**
1625-1631 A444 Set of 7 5.50 2.00
 Imperf., #1625-1631 10.00 10.00

Dam-Strengthening Committee, 40th
Anniv. — A445

1986, May 22 **Perf. 11**
1632 A445 1d carmine 1.50 .45
 Imperf. 20.00

Bonsai — A446

Designs: No. 1633, 1d, Ficus glomerata. No. 1634, 1d, Ficus benjamina. 2d, Ulmus tonkinensis. No. 1636, 3d, Persica vulgaris. No. 1637, 3d, Streblus asper. No. 1638, 5d, Pinus khasya. No. 1639, 5d, Podocarpus macrophyllus. 10d, Serissa foetida, horiz.

1986, Dec. 10 **Perf. 12x12½**
1633-1639 A446 Set of 7 6.00 2.75
 Imperf., #1633-1639 15.00 15.00
Souvenir Sheet
Perf. 12½x12
1640 A446 10d multicolored 4.00 4.00

Domestic Cats — A447

Various cats (Background colors): No. 1641, 1d, blue green. No. 1642, 1d, red. 2d, blue. No. 1644, 3d, brown. No. 1645, 3d, blue. No. 1646, 5d, violet. No. 1647, 5d, red, vert.

Perf. 13x12½, 12½x13

1986, June 16
1641-1647 A447 Set of 7   7.50   2.75
    Imperf., #1641-1647   16.00   16.00

Traditional
Houses
A448

Designs: No. 1648, 1d, Thai den. No. 1649, 1d, Nung. 2d, Thai trang. No. 1651, 3d, Tay. No. 1652, 3d, Hmong. No. 1653, 5d, Dao. No. 1654, 5d, Tay nguyen, vert.

Perf. 12½x12, 12x12½

1986, June 20
1648-1654 A448 Set of 7   6.00   2.75
    Imperf., #1648-1654   15.00   15.00
Souvenir Sheet
Perf. 12x12½

1655 A448 10d like #1654   3.50   1.25

Postal Service,
40th
Anniv. — A449

Designs: No. 1656, 2d, Telecommunications. No. 1657, 2d, Map, letter carrier. 4d, Soldiers, Nguyen Thi Nghia. 5d, Dish antenna.

1986, Aug. 15   **Perf. 13**
1656-1659 A449 Set of 4   3.25   1.25
    Imperf., #1656-1659   22.50   22.50

A450

Birds: No. 1660, 1d, Merops apiaster. No. 1661, 1d, Cissa chinensis. 2d, Pteruthius erythropterus. No. 1663, 3d, Garrulax leucolophus. No. 1664, 3d, Psarisomus dalhousiae, horiz. No. 1665, 5d, Cyanopica cyanus, horiz. No. 1666, 5d, Motacilla alba. 10d, Copsychus malabaricus.

1986, Aug. 28   **Perf. 13**
1660-1666 A450 Set of 7   5.00   2.75
    Imperf. #1660-1666   12.00   12.00
Souvenir Sheet
Perf. 12½

1667 A450 10d multicolored   5.25   1.25

No. 1667 contains one 32x40mm stamp. Stockholmia '86.

A451

Domestic fowl: No. 1668, 1d, Plymouth Rock. No. 1669, 1d, Maleagris gallopavo. No. 1670, 2d, Ri. No. 1671, 2d, White Plymouth rock. No. 1672, 3d, Leghorn. No. 1673, 3d, Rhode Island red. No. 1674, 3d, Rhode ri. 5d, Gray Plymouth rock hen.

1986, Sept. 15   **Perf. 12x12½**
1668-1675 A451 Set of 8   6.00   3.00
    Imperf., #1668-1675   13.50   13.50

11th Intl. Trade Unions
Congress — A452

1986, Sept. 16   **Perf. 12½**
1676 A452 1d blue & red   1.50   .40

Artifacts, Hung-Voung Period — A453

Designs: No. 1677, 1d, Seated figure, vert. No. 1678, 1d, Knife hilt in form of female figure, vert. 2d, Bronze axe. No. 1680, 3d, Bronze axe, diff. No. 1681, 3d, Bronze bowl. No. 1682, 5d, Bronze pot (round). No. 1683, 5d, Bronze vase (open top).

1986, Oct. 15   **Perf. 12x12½, 12½x12**
1677-1683 A453 Set of 7   5.00   2.75
    Imperf., #1677-1683   11.00   11.00
Souvenir Sheet
Perf. 12x12½

1684 A453 10d like #1677   4.25   4.25

Vietnamese
Red Cross,
40th
Anniv. — A454

1986, Oct. 20   **Perf. 12½**
1685 A454 3d rose & greenish
      blue   1.50   .40

Sailing Ships — A455

Various sail and oar-powered ships (sail colors): #1686, 1d, bl, grn, yel. #1687, 1d, org. 2d, yel. #1689, 3d, pur & red. #1690, 3d, bl. #1691, 5d, bl, brn, org. #1692, 5d, org.

Perf. 12½x12, 12½x13 (#1688)

1986, Oct. 20
1686-1692 A455 Set of 7   6.00   1.50
    Imperf., #1686-1692   15.00

No. 1688 is 38x47mm.

Butterflies — A456

Designs: No. 1693, 1d, Catopsilia scylla. No. 1694, 1d, Euploea midamus. 2d, Appias nero. No. 1696, 3d, Danaus chrysippus. No. 1697, 3d, Papilio polytes stichius. No. 1698, 5d, Euploea diocletiana. No. 1699, 5d, Charaxes polyxena.

1987, June 30   **Perf. 12½**
1693-1699 A456 Set of 7   6.00   2.00
    Imperf., #1693-1699   13.00

No. 1696 misspelled "Danais."

Vietnamese Communist Party, 6th
Congress — A457

1d, Construction projects. 2d, Natl. defense. 4d, Ho Chi Minh. 5d, Intl. cooperation.

1986, Nov. 20   **Perf. 11**
1700-1703 A457 Set of 4   5.50   1.50
1700a-1703a   Perf. 12½   50.00   50.00
1702b   Perf. 11x12½   27.50   27.50
Souvenir Sheet
Imperf

1704 A457 10d like #1700   4.50   1.25

Insects
A458

Designs: No. 1705, 1d, Poecilocoris nepalensis. No. 1706, 1d, Bombus americanorum. 2d, Romalea microptera. No. 1708, 3d, Chalcocoris rutilans. No. 1709, 3d, Chrysocoris sellatus. No. 1710, 5d, Paranthrene palmi. No. 1711, 5d, Crocisa crucifera. 10d, Anabrus simplex.

1987, June 30   **Perf. 12½**
1705-1711 A458 Set of 7   5.50   2.75
    Imperf., #1705-1711   12.50   12.50
Souvenir Sheet

1712 A458 10d multicolored   5.00   1.25

No. 1712 contains one 32x40mm stamp.

Intl. Peace
Year — A459

1986, Dec. 7   **Perf. 11**
1713-1714 A459 1d, 3d, Set of 2   2.50   .80

Handicrafts — A460

Designs: No. 1715, 1d, Round dish. No. 1716, 1d, Rattan handbag. 2d, Rattan foot stool. No. 1718, 3d, Bamboo hand basket. No. 1719, 3d, Muong pannier. No. 1720, 5d, Rattan basket with shoulder straps. No. 1721, 5d, Rattan basket with lid. 10d, Tall rattan basket.

1986, Dec. 10   **Perf. 11½**
1715-1721 A460 Set of 7   5.00   2.75
    Imperf., #1715-1721   9.00   9.00
Souvenir Sheet

1722 A460 10d multicolored   3.50   3.50

A461

1986, Dec. 18   **Perf. 11**
1723 A461 2d blue green & fawn   1.50   .40

Natl. Resistance, 40th anniv.

A462

Endangered flora: No. 1724, 1d, Fokienia hodginsii. No. 1725, 1d, Amentotaxus yunnanensis. 2d, Pinus kwangtungensis. No. 1727, 3d, Taxus chinensis. No. 1728, 3d, Cupressus torulosa. No. 1730, 5d, Ducampopinus krempfii. No. 1730, 5d, Tsuga yunnanensis. 10d, Abies nukiangensis.

1986, Dec. 26   **Perf. 12x12½**
1724-1730 A462 Set of 7   5.00   2.75
    Imperf., #1724-1730   11.00   11.00
Souvenir Sheet

1731 A462 10d multicolored   4.25   1.25

Elephants — A463

#1732, 1d, Two elephants. #1733, 1d, Female, calf. #1734, 3d, Elephant. #1735, 1d, Elephant facing, vert. #1736, 5d, Man riding elephant, vert. #1737, 5d, Four elephants.

1987, Mar. 10   **Perf. 12½**
1732-1737 A463 Set of 6   7.50   1.50
    Imperf., #1732-1737   13.50   13.50

No. 1737 is 68x27mm.

Vietnamese
Legends
A464

Designs: a, Son Tinh. b, My Nuong. c-e, Battle between Mountain Genie and Water Genie. f-h, Celebration.

1987, Jan. 20   **Perf. 12**
1738 A464 3d Strip of 8, #a.-h.   7.00   3.50
    Imperf.   12.50   12.50

New Year 1987
(Year of the
Cat) — A465

1987, Jan. 6   *Perf. 11*
1739 A465 3d red lilac   3.00   .45

Natl.
Events
A466

Ho Chi Minh and: 10d, August revolution,
Aug. 19, 1945. 20d, Proclaiming independence, Sept. 9, 1945. 30d, Victory at Dien
Bien Phu, July 7, 1954. 50d, Capture of Saigon, Apr. 30, 1975.

1987, Apr. 12   *Perf. 11*
1740-1743 A466   Set of 4   6.25 1.50

A467

Champa art: 3d, Temple, Da Nang. 10d,
Tower, Na Trang. 15d, Temple, Da Nang (side
view). 20d, Dancing girl. 25d, Bust of woman.
30d, Girl playing flute. 40d, Dancing girl, diff.

1987, June 30   *Perf. 12x12½*
1744-1750 A467   Set of 7   7.25 2.75
   Imperf., #1744-1750   9.50 9.50
       Souvenir Sheet
1751 A467 50d like #1749   4.00 4.00

A468

Various flowering cacti: 5d, 10d, 15d, 20d,
25d, 30d, 40d.

1987, Dec. 30   *Perf. 12½*
1752-1758 A468   Set of 7   5.00 2.00
   Imperf., #1752-1758   17.50
       Souvenir Sheet
         Perf. 13
1759 A468 50d multicolored   5.00 1.25

Global Population Reaches 5
Billion — A469

1987, July 11   *Perf. 13*
1760 A469 5d multicolored   1.50   .45

World Wildlife
Fund — A470

Designs: No. 1761, 5d, Concolor gibbon.
No. 1762, 5d, Douc monkeys. 15d, Black concolor gibbon. 40d, Douc monkey.

1987, Sept. 23   *Perf. 12½*
1761-1764 A470   Set of 4   9.00 2.00
   Imperf., #1761-1764   40.00

A471

Western high plateau costumes: 5d, Male
Bana. No. 1766, 20d, Female Bana. No. 1767,
20d, Female Gia Rai. No. 1768, 30d, Male Gia
Rai. No. 1769, 30d, Male Ede. 40d, Female
Ede.

1987, July 25   *Perf. 12x12½*
1765-1770 A471   Set of 6   7.00 2.50
   Imperf., #1765-1770   15.00

A472

1987, July 27   *Perf. 13*
1771 A472 5d multicolored   1.50   .40
    Day of the Invalids, 40th anniv.

Postal
Trade
Union,
40th
Anniv.
A473

Designs: 5d, Letter carrier, jet, truck, train.
30d, Switchboard operator.

1987, Aug. 30
1772-1773 A473   Set of 2   2.10 1.20

A474

Paintings by Picasso: No. 1774, 3d, *The
Three Musicians.* No. 1775, 20d, War. No.
1776, 20d, Peace. No. 1777, 30d, Child with
Dove, vert. No. 1778, 30d, Portrait of Gertrude
Stein, vert. 40d, Guernica. 50d, Child as
Harlequin.

1987, Dec. 30   *Perf. 12½*
1774-1779 A474   Set of 6   5.75 1.75
   Imperf., #1774-1779   12.00
       Souvenir Sheet
1780 A474 50d multicolored   5.00 1.50
   No. 1779 is 44x27mm. No. 1780 contains
one 40x32mm stamp.

Coral — A475

Designs: 5d, Epanouis. 10d, Acropora. 15d,
Rhizopsammia. 20d, Acropora, diff. 25d, Alcy-
one, 30d, Corollum. 40d, Cristatella.

1987, Oct. 30   *Perf. 12x12½*
1781-1787 A475   Set of 7   7.00 2.75
   Imperf., #1781-1787   14.00

Intl. Year
for
Housing
for the
Homeless
A476

1987, Sept. 23   *Perf. 13*
1788 A476 5d greenish bl & blk   1.50   .40

Russian
Revolution, 70th
Anniv. — A477

Designs: 5d, 65d, Industry, agriculture. 20d,
Lenin. 30d, Construction. 50d, Ho Chi Minh.

1987, Oct. 6   *Perf. 13*
1789-1792 A477   Set of 4   3.50 1.50
       Souvenir Sheet
1793 A477 65d multicolored   4.00 4.00

Hafnia
'87
A478

Seaplanes: 5d, PBY-5. 10d, LeO H-246.
15d, Dornier DO-18. 20d, Short Sunderland.
25d, Rohrbach Rostra. 30d, Chetverikov ARK-
3. 40d, CANT Z-509. 50d, Curtiss H-16.

1987, Dec. 30   *Perf. 13*
1794-1800 A478   Set of 7   5.00 2.00
   Imperf., #1794-1800   12.50
       Souvenir Sheet
1801 A478 50d multicolored   4.50 1.25
   No. 1801 contains one 40x32mm stamp.

Czechoslovakia-Viet Nam Friendship
Agreement, 10th Anniv. — A479

10d, Handshake. 50d, Flags, buildings.

1987, Oct. 31
1802-1803 A479   Set of 2   3.25   .80
   Imperf., 1802-1803   17.50

Viet Nam-Soviet Union
Cooperation — A480

Designs: 5d, Industry. 50d, Buildings.

1987, Nov. 3
1804-1805 A480   Set of 2   3.50   .80

Mushrooms
A481

Designs: 5d, Polyporellus squamosus. 10d,
Clitocybe geotropa. 15d, Tricholoma terreum.
20d, Russula aurata. 25d, Collybia fusipes.
30d, Cortinarius violaceus. 40d, Boletus
aereus.

1987, Dec. 30   *Perf. 12½*
1806-1812 A481   Set of 7   5.00 2.00
   Imperf., #1806-1812   11.50

Peace
A482

1987, Nov. 10   *Perf. 13*
1813 A482 10d multicolored   1.40   .40

Afro-Asian Solidarity Committee
(AAPSO), 30th Anniv. — A483

10d, Hands, dove. 30d, Map, hands, vert.

1987, Nov. 30
1814-1815 A483   Set of 2   2.25   .80
   Imperf., #1814-1815   20.00

Victory Over US Bombing Campaign, 15th Anniv. — A484

Designs: 10d, B-52 wreckage. 30d, Children with flowers, wreckage.

1987, Dec. 26
1816-1817 A484 Set of 2 2.75 .80
 Imperf., #1816-1817 27.50

Productivity
A485

Designs: 5d, Consumer goods. 20d, Agriculture. 30d, Export products.

1987, Dec. 30
1818-1820 A485 Set of 3 3.25 1.20

Hoang Sa, Truong Sa Islands A486

Designs: 10d, Ship, sailor. 100d, Maps.

1988, Jan. 19
1821-1822 A486 Set of 2 5.25 .90
 Imperf., #1821-1822 17.50

Roses — A487

Various roses: 5d, 10d, 15d, 20d, 25d, 30d, 40d.

1988, Jan. 20 *Perf. 12½*
1823-1829 A487 Set of 7 5.00 2.75
 Imperf., #1823-1829 15.00
 Souvenir Sheet
 Perf. 13
1830 A487 50d multicolored 4.50 1.25

Tropical Fish A488

Designs: 5d, Red betta splendens. 10d, Labeo bicolor. 15d, Puntis tetrazona. 20d, Brachydania albolineatus. 25d, Puntis conchonius. 30d, Betta splendens, diff. 40d, Botia leicontei.

1988, Jan. 20 *Perf. 13*
1831-1837 A488 Set of 7 5.00 2.00
 Imperf., #1831-1837 12.00

Intl. Red Cross, Red Crescent, 125th Anniv. — A489

1988, Feb. 17
1838 A489 10d multicolored 1.25 .40
 Imperf. 12.00

Battle of Bach Dang, 700th Anniv. A490

80d, Fleet of ships. 200d, Battle scene.

1988, Apr. 8
1839-1840 A490 Set of 2 5.00 .90

Tourism A491

5d, One-pillar pagoda. 10d, Bach Dang River. 15d, Thien Mu Tower, Hue. 20d, Hgu Hanh Mountain, Da Nang. 25d, Nha Trang beach. 30d, Pren Waterfalls. 40d, Market, Ben Thanh. 50d, Cleft Rocks, Quang Ninh.

1988, Apr. 20 *Perf. 12½x12*
1841-1847 A491 Set of 7 5.25 2.00
 Imperf., #1841-1847 9.00
 Souvenir Sheet
1848 A491 50d multicolored 3.50 1.25

Water Lilies — A492

Designs: 5d, Nymphaea lotus. No. 1850, 10d, Nymphaea pubescens. No. 1851, 10d, Nymphaea nouchali. No. 1852, 20d, Nymphaea rubra. No. 1853, 20d, Nymphaea gigantea. 30d, Nymphaea laydekeri. 50d, Nymphaea capensis.

1988, Apr. 24 *Perf. 12x12½*
1849-1855 A492 Set of 7 5.75 2.00
 Imperf., #1849-1855 12.00

Offshore Oil Drilling — A493

1988, Apr. 28 *Perf. 13*
1856 A493 1000d multicolored 8.50 8.50
 Imperf. 15.00

A494

Parrots: No. 1857, 10d, Ara araruna. No. 1858, 10d, Psittacula himalayana. No. 1859, 20d, Aprosmictus erythropterus. No. 1860, 20d, Ara chloroptera. No. 1861, 30d, Ara militaris. No. 1862, 30d, Psittacula alexandri. 50d, Loriculus vernalis. 80d, Ara chloroptera, diff.

1988, May 5 *Perf. 12x12½*
1857-1863 A494 Set of 7 6.00 2.75
 Imperf., #1857-1863 17.50
 Souvenir Sheet
1864 A494 80d multicolored 4.00 1.25

A495

Membership in Council of Mutual Economic Assistance, 10th Anniv.: 200d, Map. 300d, Headquarters building.

1988, May 29 *Perf. 13*
1865-1866 A495 Set of 2 5.50 1.25
 Imperf. 20.00

A496

1988, June 1
1867 A496 60d multicolored 1.25 .80
 Imperf. 10.00

Vaccinations against disease.

Problems of Peace and Socialism Magazine, 30th Anniv. — A497

1988, July 20
1868 A497 20d multicolored 1.25 .40
 Imperf. 10.00

A498

1988, Aug. 20
1869 A498 150d multicolored 1.75 .40
 Imperf. 10.00

Pres. Ton Duc Thang, birth cent.

A499

6th Vietnamese Trade Union Congress: 50d, Emblem. 100d, Workers.

1988, Aug. 28
1870-1871 A499 Set of 2 2.00 .80
 Imperf., #1870-1871 20.00

Children's Paintings A500

#1872, 10d, My Family. #1873, 10d, My House. #1874, 20d, Fishing. #1875, 20d, Flying Kites. #1876, 30d, Girl playing guitar, animals. #1877, 30d, Children in rain, vert. 50d, Girl holding dove, vert. 80d, Family, diff., vert.

Perf. 12½x12, 12x12½
1988, Sept. 25
1872-1878 A500 Set of 7 5.25 2.50
 Imperf., #1872-1878 12.50
 Souvenir Sheet
 Perf. 12x12½
1879 A500 80d multicolored 4.00 1.25

Hydroelectric Plants — A501

Designs: 2000d, Tri An. 3000d, Hoa Binh.

1988, Sept. 27 *Perf. 13*
1880-1881 A501 Set of 2 10.00 5.50
 Imperf., #1880-1881 20.00

A502

1988, Nov. 3 *Perf. 13½x13*
1882 A502 50d multicolored 2.00 .45
 Imperf. 17.50

Viet Nam-USSR Friendship Agreement, 10th anniv.

A503

Designs: 100d, Fidel Castro. 300d, Flags, Vietnamese, Cuban people.

1988, Dec. 27
1883-1884　A503　Set of 2　　2.25　.80
　　Imperf., #1883-1884　　15.00

Cuban revolution, 30th anniv.

Wild Animals A504

Designs: No. 1885, 10d, Bos banteng. No. 1886, 10d, Bos gaurus. No. 1887, 20d, Axis porcinus. No. 1888, 20d, Tapirus indicus. No. 1889, 30d, Capricornis sumatrensis. No. 1890, 30d, Sus scrofa. 50d, Bubalus bubalus. 80d, Rhinoceros sodaicus.

1988, Dec. 30　　　　　**Perf. 12½**
1885-1891　A504　Set of 7　5.00　2.00
　　Imperf., #1885-1891　　15.00
　　　　Souvenir Sheet
1892　A504　80d multicolored　5.00　4.00
　　Imperf.　　20.00

Locomotives — A505

Designs: No. 1893, 20d, Kiha 80, Japan. No. 1894, 20d, LRC, Canada. No. 1895, 20d, Hitachi, Japan. No. 1896, 20d, BL-85, USSR. No. 1897, 30d, RC-1, Sweden. No. 1898, 30d, DR-1A, USSR. 50d, T3-136, USSR. 80d, SCNF Z6400.

1988, Dec. 30　　　　　**Perf. 13**
1893-1899　A505　Set of 7　5.00　2.25
　　Imperf., #1893-1899　　12.00
　　　　Souvenir Sheet
1900　A505　80d multicolored　4.50　1.25
　　Imperf.　　7.00

No. 1900 contains one 40x32mm stamp.

A506

Fruits, vegetables: No. 1901, 10d, Lagenaria siceraria. No. 1902, 10d, Momordica charantia. No. 1903, 20d, Solanum melongena. No. 1904, 20d, Cucurbita moschata. No. 1905, 30d, Luffa cylindrica. No. 1906, 30d, Benincasa hispida. 50d, Lycopercicon esculentum.

1988, Dec. 30　　　　　**Perf. 12x12½**
1901-1907　A506　Set of 7　5.50　2.75
　　Imperf., #1901-1907　　10.50

A507

Various project spacecraft: No. 1908, 10d, Mars. No. 1909, 10d, Moon. No. 1910, 20d, Saturn. No. 1911, 20d, Inter-planetary. No. 1912, 30d, Venus. No. 1913, 30d, Earth orbital space station. 50d, Cosmos house. 80d, Lander docking with orbiter.

1988, Dec. 30　　　　　**Perf. 13**
1908-1914　A507　Set of 7　4.75　1.50
　　Imperf., #1908-1914　　17.00
　　　　Souvenir Sheet
1915　A507　80d multicolored　4.50　1.25
　　　　　Cosmos Day.
No. 1915 contains one 32x40mm stamp.

Shells A508

Designs: No. 1916, 10d, Conus miles. No. 1917, 10d, Strombus lentiginosus. No. 1918, 20d, Nautilus. No. 1919, 20d, Bursa rana. No. 1920, 30d, Turbo petholatus. No. 1921, 30d, Oliva erythros. 50d, Mitra eriscopalis. 80d, Tonna tessellata.

1988, Dec. 30　　　　　**Perf. 12½x12**
1916-1922　A508　Set of 7　5.00　2.50
　　Imperf., #1916-1922　　10.00
　　　　Souvenir Sheet
1923　A508　80d multicolored　4.00　1.25

India '89 — A509

Butterflies: No. 1924, 50d, Anaea echemus. No. 1925, 50d, Ascia monuste. No. 1926, 50d, Juniona evarete. No. 1927, 100d, Phoebis avellaneda. No. 1928, 100d, Eurema proterpia. 200d, Papilio palamedes. 300d, Danaus plexippus. 400d, Parides gundlachiamus.

1989, Jan. 7　　　　　**Perf. 12½**
1924-1930　A509　Set of 7　6.50　2.75
　　Imperf., #1924-1930　　13.50
　　　　Souvenir Sheet
1931　A509　400d multicolored　4.00　1.25

No. 1931 contains one 40x32mm stamp. Nos. 1924-1930 printed with se-tenant label.

Natl. Day of Cambodia, 10th Anniv. — A510

Designs: 100d, Soldiers, women working in field. 500d, Viet Nam-Cambodia friendship.

1989, Jan. 7　　　　　**Perf. 13x13½**
1932-1933　A510　Set of 2　2.25　1.20
　　Imperf., #1932-1933　　21.00

India '89 — A511

Designs: No. 1934, 100d, Science, technology. No. 1935, 100d, Agriculture, industry. 300d, Asoka pillar. 600d, Nehru (1889-1964).

1989, Jan. 20　　　　　**Perf. 13**
1934-1937　A511　Set of 4　3.00　1.50

Battle of Dong Da, Bicent. — A512

Designs: 100d, Festival. 1000d, Quang Trung defeating Qing invaders.

1989, Feb. 10　　　　　**Perf. 13**
1938-1939　A512　Set of 2　3.00　1.50
　　Imperf., #1938-1939　　20.00

Inter-Parliamentary Union, Cent. — A513

Designs: 100d, Vietnamese membership, 10th anniv. 200d, Centennial emblem.

1989, Mar. 1
1940-1941　A513　Set of 2　2.25　.60

Fishing Boats — A513a

Boats from: No. 1942, 10d, Quang Nam. No. 1943, 10d, Quang Tri. No. 1944, 20d, Thua Thien. No. 1945, 20d, Da Nang (sail furled). No. 1946, 30d, Da Nang (under sail). No. 1947, 30d, Quang Tri (under sail). 50d, Hue.

1989, Mar. 20　　　　　**Perf. 12½x12**
1942-1948　A513a　Set of 7　5.50　2.25
　　Imperf., #1942-1948　　12.00

Helicopters — A514

#1949, 10d, Kamov KA-26. #1950, 10d, Boeing Vertol 234. #1951, 20d, Mil MI-10(V10). #1952, 20d, MBB BO 105. #1953, 30d, Kawasaki Hughes 369HS. #1954, 30d, Bell 206B Jet Ranger, 50d, Mil MI-8. 80d, Puma SA330.

1989, Apr. 12　　　　　**Perf. 12½**
1949-1955　A514　Set of 7　4.75　1.90
　　Imperf., #1949-1955　　14.00
　　　　Souvenir Sheet
1956　A514　80d multicolored　3.00　1.25
　　Imperf.　　10.00

No. 1956 contains one 40x32mm stamp.

Bicycles A515

#1957, 10d, Bowden Spacelander. #1958, 10d, Rabasa Derbi. #1959, 20d, Huffy. #1960,

20d, Rabasa Derbi. #1961, 30d, VMX-PL. #1962, 30d, Premier. 50d, Columbia RX5.

1989, May 1　　　　　**Perf. 13**
1957-1963　A515　Set of 7　5.00　1.90
　　Imperf., #1957-1963　　10.00

Turtles — A516

No. 1964, 10d, Cuora trifasciata. No. 1965, 10d, Testudo elegans. No. 1966, 20d, Eretmochelys imbricata. No. 1967, 20d, Platysternon megacephalum. No. 1968, 30d, Dermochelys coriacea. No. 1969, 30d, Chelonia mydas. 50d, Caretta caretta. 80d, Caretta caretta, diff.

1989, May 1　　　　　**Perf. 12½**
1964-1970　A516　Set of 7　7.00　2.25
　　Imperf., #1964-1970　　13.50
　　　　Souvenir Sheet
1971　A516　80d multicolored　6.00　1.25
　　Imperf.　　17.00

Finlandia '88 (#1971).

Poisonous Snakes — A517

Designs: No. 1972, 10d, Trimeresurus popeorum. No. 1973, 10d, Trimeresurus mucrosquamatus. No. 1974, 20d, Bungarus fasciatus. No. 1975, 20d, Bungarus candidus. No. 1976, 30d, Calliophis maclellandii. No. 1977, 30d, Ancistrodon acutus. 50d, Ophiophagus hannah, vert.

1989, May 1
1972-1978　A517　Set of 7　5.00　1.90
　　Imperf., #1972-1978　　10.00

Pairs Figure Skating — A518

Various figure skaters: No. 1979, 10d, "Viet Nam" at left. No. 1980, 10d, "Viet Nam" at right. No. 1981, 20d, "Viet Nam" at left. No. 1982, 20d, "Viet Nam" at right, horiz. No. 1983, 30d, "Viet Nam" at left. No. 1984, 30d, "Viet Nam" at right, horiz. 50d, "Viet Nam" at left, horiz.

1989, May 29　　　　　**Perf. 13**
1979-1985　A518　Set of 7　4.50　1.50
　　Imperf., #1979-1985　　11.00
　　　　Souvenir Sheet
　　　　　With Gum
1986　A518　80d multi, horiz.　4.00　1.25
　　Imperf.　　10.00

No. 1986 contains one 40x32mm stamp.

A519

1989, June 5　　　　　**Perf. 13**
1987　A519　100d buff　1.25　.25

Post & Telecommunications.

A520

Ceramics, Li-Tran Period: 50d, Pitcher. No. 1989, 100d, Bowl. No. 1990, 100d, Jug. 200d, Jug, diff. 300d, Vase.

1989, July 1   *Perf. 12*
1988-1992 A520 Set of 5   3.75 1.50
  Imperf., #1988-1992   8.00

Legend of Giong
A521

Designs: 50d, Mother nursing infant. No. 1994, 100d, Giong meets imperial messenger. No. 1995, 100d, Giong riding iron horse, people following. 200d, Giong pulling up bamboo trees. 300d, Giong flying into sky.

1989, July 1   *Perf. 12½x12*
1993-1997 A521 Set of 5   3.50 1.50
  Imperf., #1993-1997   7.25

French Revolution, Bicent. — A522

Designs: 100d, Emblem. 500d, Liberty leading the people, after Delacroix.

1989, July 14   *Perf. 13½x13*
1998-1999 A522 Set of 2   2.50 .80
  Imperf., #1998-1999   12.00

PHILEXFRANCE '89 — A523

Paintings: No. 2000, 50d, Oath of the Tennis Court, by David. No. 2001, 50d, Capture of Louis XVI, horiz. No. 2002, 50d, Liberty, Equality, Fraternity, horiz. No. 2003, 100d, Storming the Bastille. No. 2004, 100d, Death of Marat, by David. 200d, Child and Rabbit, by Prud'hon. 300d, Slave Market, by Gerome, horiz. 400d, Liberty Leading the People, by Delacroix.

1989, July 14   *Perf. 13*
2000-2006 A523 Set of 7   5.00 2.25
  Imperf., #2000-2006   10.00
Souvenir Sheet
2007 A523 400d multicolored   3.50 1.25
No. 2007 contains one 33x44mm stamp.

1989 World Cup Soccer
Championships, Italy — A524

Soccer plays: No. 2008, 50d, Dribbling. No. 2009, 50d, Tackling. No. 2010, 50d, Goalie. No. 2011, 100d, Dribbling, diff. No. 2012, 100d, Dribbling, diff., vert. 200d, Preparing to kick, vert. 300d, Heading ball, vert. 400d, Heading ball, diff., vert.

Perf. 13x12½, 12½x13
1989, Aug. 27
2008-2014 A524 Set of 7   4.50 1.75
  Imperf., #2008-2014   11.00
Souvenir Sheet
Perf. 13
2015 A524 400d multicolored   3.50 1.25
No. 2015 contains one 32x40mm stamp.

Dogs
A525

#2016, 50d, Dachshund. #2017, 50d, Beagle. #2018, 50d, English setter, vert. #2019, 100d, German short-haired pointer, vert. #2020, 100d, Dassel hounds. 200d, German sheperd, vert. 300d, Beagle, diff.

1989, Aug. 20   *Perf. 12½*
2016-2022 A525 Set of 7   5.50 1.75
  Imperf., #2016-2022   10.00
No. 2020 is 68x28mm.

Horses
A526

#2023, 50d, Tennessee Walking. #2024, 50d, Appaloosa. #2025, 50d, Tersky. #2025, 100d, Kladruber. #2026, 100d, Welsh cob. 200d, Pinto. 300d, Pony and bridle.

1989, Sept. 23   *Perf. 13*
2023-2029 A526 Set of 7   4.50 1.75
  Imperf., #2023-2029   10.00
No. 2029 is 68x28mm.

Flowers — A527

No. 2030, 50d, Paphiopedilum siamense. No. 2031, 50d, Fuchsia fulgens. No. 2032, 100d, Hemerocallis fulva. No. 2033, 100d, Gloriosa superba. 200d, Strelitzia reginae. 300d, Iris.

1989, Sept. 23   *Perf. 12½*
2030-2035 A527 Set of 6   5.50 1.50
  Imperf., #2030-2035   11.50

German Democratic Republic, 40th
Anniv. — A528

1989, Oct. 7   *Perf. 13*
2036 A528 200d multicolored   1.25 .40

Immunization Campaign — A529

#2037, Woman receiving vaccination. #2038, Child receiving oral vaccine. #2039, Clinic.

1989, Oct. 20
2037-2039 A529 100d Set of 3   2.50 .90

Drawings of Everyday Life, 19th Cent. — A530

Designs: 50d, Assembling plow. No. 2041, 100d, Harrowing. No. 2042, 100d, Irrigating. 200d, Fertilizing. 300d, Harvesting.

1989, Oct. 28   *Perf. 12x12½*
2040-2044 A530 Set of 5   3.75 1.50
  Imperf., #2040-2044   8.50

Horse Paintings, by Xu Beihong (1895-1953)
A531

Various horses: 100d, 200d, 300d, 500d horiz., 800d, 1000d, 1500d.

1989, Dec. 22   *Perf. 13*
2045-2051 A531 Set of 7   4.25 1.50
  Imperf., #2045-2051   9.00
Imperf
Size: 117x72mm
2052 A531 2000d multicolored   7.50 1.25
  Imperf.   14.00

Vietnamese Communist Party, 60th
Anniv. — A532

Designs: 100d, Ho Chi Minh, tank. 500d, Workers, refinery, field.

1990, Feb. 3   **Litho.**   *Perf. 13*
2053-2054 A532 Set of 2   2.50 1.20
  Imperf., #2053-2054   6.50

Ducks — A533

a, 100d, Anas platyrhynchos hybrid. b, 300d, Anas penelope. c, 500d, Anas platyrhynchos. d, 1000d, Anas erythrorhyncha. e, 2000d, Anas platyrhynchos, diff. f, 3000d, Anas undulata.

1990, Feb. 15
2055 A533 Block of 6, #a.-f.   4.75 1.50
  Imperf.   12.50

Trucks
A534

100d, Mack. 200d, Volvo F89. 300d, Tatra 915 S1. 500d, Hino KZ30000. 1000d, Iveco. 2000d, Leyland DAF Super Comet. 3000d, Kamaz 53212.

1990, Feb. 20
2056-2062 A534 Set of 7   3.75 1.50
  Imperf., #2056-2062   6.25

Architectural Sites, Hue — A535

#2063, 100d, Tu Duc's Mausoleum. #2064, 100d, Hien Nhon Arch. 200d, Ngo Mon Gate. 300d, Thien Mu Temple. 400d, Palace, gateway.

1990, Feb. 20   *Perf. 12½x12*
2063-2066 A535 Set of 4   3.50 1.50
Souvenir Sheet
2067 A535 400d multicolored   3.50 1.20

Goldfish — A536

100d, Bulging-eyed, horiz. 300d, Telescopic-eyed, horiz. 500d, Red-headed, horiz. 1000d, Double-tailed. 2000d, Rainbow. 3000d, Comet.

1990, Mar. 20   *Perf. 13*
2068-2073 A536 Set of 6   4.50 1.50
  Imperf., #2068-2073   10.00

Paintings
A537

London '90: 100d, Antonia Zarate, by Goya. 200d, Girl Holding a Paper Fan, by Renoir.

300d, Janet Grizel, by John Russell. 500d, Love Untieing the Belt of Beauty, by Sir Joshua Reynolds. 1000d, Portrait of a Woman, by George Romney. 2000d, Portrait of Madame Ginoux, by Van Gogh. 3000d, Woman in Blue, by Gainsborough. 3500d, Woman in a Straw Hat, by Van Gogh.

1990, Apr. 10
2074-2080	A537	Set of 7	4.50	1.50
	Imperf., #2074-2080			9.00
	Souvenir Sheet			
2081	A537	3500d multicolored	3.00	1.50
	Imperf.			5.00

1990 World Cup Soccer Championships, Italy — A538

Various soccer players in action: 100d, 200d, 300d, 500d, 1000d, 2000d, 3000d.

1990, Apr. 19
2082-2088	A538	Set of 7	4.00	1.50
	Imperf., #2082-2088			25.00
	Souvenir Sheet			
2089	A538	3500d multicolored	3.00	1.25

No. 2089 contains one 32x40mm stamp. For overprints see Nos. 2189-2196.

Cats — A539

Various cats: 100d, horiz., 200d, 300d, horiz., 500d, 1000d, horiz., 2000d, 3000d.

1990, May 5
2090-2096	A539	Set of 7	4.50	1.50
	Imperf., #2090-2096			6.00
	Souvenir Sheet			
2097	A539	3500d multicolored	4.00	1.25
	Imperf.			5.00

No. 2097 contains one 44x33mm stamp. Belgica '90 (#2097).

Dogs — A540

Various dogs: 100d, 200d, 300d, 500d, 1000d, 2000d, 3000d.

1990, May 15
2098-2104	A540	Set of 7	4.25	1.50
	Imperf., #2098-2194			7.00
	Souvenir Sheet			
2105	A540	3500d Collies	3.25	1.25
	Imperf.			7.50

New Zealand '90.

Ho Chi Minh (1890-1969) A541

Ho Chi Minh and: 100d, Lenin. 300d, Soldiers waving flag. 500d, Hand holding rifle, dove. 1000d, Map. 2000d, Child, dove. 3000d, Stylized globe. 3500d, Flag.

1990, May 17   *Perf. 13*
2106-2111	A541	Set of 6	4.00	4.00
	Imperf., #2106-2111			6.00
	Souvenir Sheet			
	Perf. 12½x13			
2112	A541	3500d multicolored	4.00	4.00

No. 2112 contains one 33x44mm stamp.

Dinosaurs — A542

100d, Gorgosaurus. 500d, Ceratosaurus. 1000d, Ankylosaurus. 2000d, Ankylosaurus, diff. 3000d, Edaphosaurus.

1990, June 1   *Perf. 13*
2113-2117	A542	Set of 5	5.25	2.25
	Imperf., #2113-2117			15.00

Columbus' Discovery of America, 500th Anniv. — A543

Designs: 50d, Fleet. No. 2119, 100d, Columbus presenting gifts to natives. No. 2120, 100d, Columbus, priest at Rabida. No. 2121, 100d, Columbus at Court of Ferdinand, Isabella. No. 2122, 200d, Map of Caribbean. No. 2123, 500d, Columbus, arms. 300d, Map of Atlantic. 500d, Teotihuacan pot.

1990, June 10   *Perf. 12½*
2118-2124	A543	Set of 7	5.50	5.50
	Imperf., #2118-2124			20.00
	Souvenir Sheet			
2125	A543	500d multicolored	3.00	3.00

No. 2125 contains one 40x32mm stamp. For overprints see Nos. 2313-2320.

Sailing Ships A544

Designs: 100d, Viking longship. 500d, Caravel. No. 2128, 1000d, Carrack, 14th-15th cent. No. 2129, 1000d, Flit. No. 2130, 1000d, Carrack, 15th cent., vert. 2000d, Galleon, vert. 3000d, Galleon, diff. 4200d, Egyptian barge.

1990, June 10   *Perf. 13*
2126-2132	A544	Set of 7	5.00	1.50
	Imperf., #2126-2132			14.00
	Souvenir Sheet			
	Perf. 13x12½			
2133	A544	4200d multicolored	3.00	1.50

No. 2133 contains one 44x33mm stamp.

11th Asian Games, Beijing — A545

Designs: 100d, High jump. 200d, Basketball. 300d, Table tennis. 500d, Volleyball. 1000d, Rhythmic gymnastics. 2000d, Tennis. 3000d, Judo. 3500d, Hurdles.

1990, June 20   *Perf. 13*
2134-2140	A545	Set of 7	4.00	4.00
	Imperf., #2134-2140			12.00
	Souvenir Sheet			
	Perf. 12½x13			
2141	A545	3500d multicolored	3.00	3.00

No. 2141 contains one 33x44mm stamp.

Nos. 1180-1187 Ovptd. in Red, Green and Black

1990, June 22   *Perf. 12*
2142-2149	A352	Set of 8	10.00

1990 World Cup Soccer Championships, Italy.

Nos. 1323-1330 Ovptd. in Black and Red

1990, June 22   *Perf. 12x12½*
2150-2157	A385	Set of 8	10.00

Tourism.

Modern Ships A546

100d, Freighter. 300d, Container ship. 500d, Cruise ship. 1000d, Liquified natural gas tanker. 2000d, Ro-Ro ship. 3000d, Ferry.

1990, July 20   *Perf. 13*
2158-2163	A546	Set of 6	4.25	2.25
	Imperf., #2158-2163			7.50

Post & Telecommunications Dept., 45th Anniv. — A547

Designs: 100d, Dove, ship, plane. 1000d, Satellite antenna.

1990, Aug. 15   *Perf. 13x13½*
2164-2165	A547	Set of 2	2.00
	Imperf., #2164-2165		4.00

Socialist Republic of Viet Nam, 45th Anniv. — A548

Designs: 100d, Flag, construction projects. 500d, Map, tank, soldiers. 1000d, "VI," ship, communications network. 3000d, Workers, oil rigs. 3500d, Ho Chi Minh.

1990, Sept. 1   *Perf. 13*
2166-2169	A548	Set of 4	3.00	
	Imperf., #2166-2169			6.00
	Souvenir Sheet			
	Perf. 12½x13			
2170	A548	3500d multicolored		2.75

No. 2170 contains one 33x44mm stamp. Sixth Vietnamese Communist Party Congress (#2168).

Airships A549

Designs: 100d, Henry Gifford, 1871. 200d, Lebandy, 1910. 300d, Graf Zeppelin. 500d, R-101, 1930. 1000d, Soviet, 1936. 2000d, Tissandier, 1883. 3000d, US Navy. 3500d, "Zodiac," 1931.

1990, Sept. 10   *Perf. 12½*
2171-2177	A549	Set of 7	4.50	
	Imperf., #2171-2177			11.00
	Souvenir Sheet			
2178	A549	3500d multicolored	2.50	1.00
	Imperf.			7.50

No. 2178 contains one 40x32mm stamp. Helvetia '90, Stamp World London '90.

Fable of Thach Sanh — A550

Designs: a, 100d, Thach Sanh carrying bundles of wood. b, 300d, Ly Thong. c, 500d, Thach Sanh killing python. d, 1000d, Thach Sanh shooting arrow at eagle. e, 2000d, Thach Sanh in prison. f, 3000d, Thach Sanh, princess.

1990, Sept. 20   *Perf. 13*
2179	A550	Block of 6, #a.-f.	6.00	
	Imperf.			8.00

Asian-Pacific Postal Training Center, 20th Anniv. — A551

1990, Sept. 25
2180	A551	150d multicolored	1.00	
	Imperf.			20.00

Nos. 571-578 Ovptd. with Red Cross in Red & "FOR THE FUTURE GENERATION" in various Languages in Black

Language: No. 2181, 12xu, Japanese. No. 2182, 12xu, Italian. No. 2183, 20xu, German. No. 2184, 20xu, Vietnamese. 30xu, English. 40xu, Russian. 50xu, French. 60xu, Spanish.

1990, Sept. 25   *Perf. 12*
2181-2188	A211	Set of 8	10.00

Position of overprint varies. Use of these stamps at stated face value is unlikely.

Nos. 2082-2089 Ovptd.

1990, Sept. 25   *Perf. 13*
2189-2195 A538 Set of 7   10.00
Souvenir Sheet
2196 A538 3500d multicolored   8.00

Vietnamese Women's Federation, 60th Anniv. — A552

Designs: 100d, Woman carrying rifle. 500d, Women working in field, laboratory.

1990, Oct. 10
2197-2198 A552 Set of 2   2.00
   Imperf., #2197-2198   5.00

Correggio (1494-1534), Painter — A553

Various paintings of the Madonna and Child: No. 2199, 50xu, shown. No. 2200, 50xu, diff. 1d, 2d, 3d, 5d, 6d.

1990, Nov. 13   *Perf. 12½*
2199-2205 A553 Set of 7   4.50
Souvenir Sheet
2206 A553 10d multicolored   4.50
No. 2206 contains one 32x40mm stamp. Dated "1984." Use of these stamps at stated face value is unlikely.

Protection of Forests — A554

Designs: 200d, Water conservation, healthy forest. 1000d, SOS, prevent forest fires.

1990, Nov. 15   *Perf. 13*
2207-2208 A554 Set of 2   1.50   .30
   Imperf., #2207-2208   6.00

A555

Poisonous mushrooms: 200d, Amanita pantherina. 300d, Amanita phalloides. 1000d, Amanita virosa. 1500d, Amanita muscaria.

2000d, Russula emetica. 3000d, Boletus satanas.

1991, Jan. 21
2209-2214 A555 Set of 6   4.50 2.00
   Imperf., #2209-2214   9.50

A555a

1992 Summer Olympics, Barcelona: 200d, Sailing. 300d, Boxing. 400d, Cycling. 1000d, High jump. 2000d, Equestrian. No. 2220, 3000d, Judo. No. 2221, 3000d, Wrestling, horiz. 5000d, Soccer, horiz.

1991, Jan. 31
2215-2221 A555a Set of 7   4.00 2.00
   Imperf., #2215-2221   7.00
Souvenir Sheet
2222 A555a 5000d multicolored   3.00 1.25
   Imperf., #2222   7.00
No. 2222 contains one 44x33mm stamp.

Nguyen Binh Khiem (1491-1585), Writer — A556

1991, Feb. 15
2223 A556 200d multicolored   1.50   .25
   Imperf.   3.25

Discovery of America, 500th Anniv. — A557

Sailing ships: 200d, Marisiliana. No. 2225, 400d, Venetian. No. 2226, 400d, Cromster, vert. No. 2227, 2000d, Nina. No. 2228, 2000d, Pinta. 3000d, Howker, vert. 5000d, Santa Maria.
6500d, Portrait of Columbus.

1991, Feb. 22
2224-2230 A557 Set of 7   5.50 2.00
   Imperf., #2224-2230   6.00
Souvenir Sheet
2231 A557 6500d multicolored   2.75 1.25
   Imperf.   7.00

Golden Heart Charity — A558

Women wearing traditional costumes: 200d, 500d, 1000d, 5000d.

1991, Feb. 26
2232-2235 A558 Set of 4   4.00 1.25
   Imperf., #2232-2235   9.00

Sharks A559

Designs: 200d, Carcharhinus melanopterus. 300d, Carcharhinus amblyrhynchos. 400d, Triakis semifasciata. 1000d, Sphyrna mokarran. 2000d, Triaenodon obesus. No. 2241, 3000d, Carcharias taurus. No. 2242, 3000d, Carcharhinus leucas.

1991, Apr. 6
2236-2242 A559 Set of 7   7.50 2.00
   Imperf., #2236-2242   14.00

Endangered Birds — A560

World Wildlife Fund: 200d, Grus vipio. 300d, Grus antigone chick, vert. 400d, Grus japonensis, vert. 1000d, Grus antigone, adults, vert. 2000d, Grus nigricollis, vert. No. 2248, 3000d, Balearica regulorum, vert. No. 2249, 3000d, Bugeranus leucogerranus.

1991, Apr. 20
2243-2249 A560 Set of 7   7.00 2.00
   Imperf., #2243-2249   20.00

Shellfish A561

Designs: 200d, 1000d, 2000d, Palinurus, all diff. 300d, Alpheus bellulus. 400d, Periclemenes brevicarpalis. No. 2255, 3000d, Astacus. No. 2256, 3000d, Palinurus, diff.

1991, Apr. 20
2250-2256 A561 Set of 7   5.00 2.00
   Imperf., #2250-2256   9.00

Young Pioneers, 50th Anniv. — A562

Designs: 200d, shown. 400d, UN Convention on Children's Rights.

1991, May 15
2257-2258 A562 Set of 2   1.50   .65
   Imperf., #2257-2258   4.50

Rally Cars A563

#2259, 400d, Lada. #2260, 400d, Nissan. 500d, Ford Sierra RS Cosworth. 1000d, Suzuki. 2000d, Mazda 323 4WD. #2264, 3000d, Lancia. #2265, 3000d, Peugeot. 5000d, Peugeot 405.

1991, May 24
2259-2265 A563 Set of 7   5.00 2.25
     7.50
Souvenir Sheet
2266 A563 5000d multicolored   2.25 1.25
   Imperf.   5.00
No. 2266 contains one 44x33mm stamp.

Locomotives — A564

#2267, 400d, Puffing Billy, 1811, vert. #2268, 400d, Fusee, 1829, vert. 500d, Stevens, 1825. 1000d, Crampton #80, 1852. 2000d, Locomotion, 1825. #2272, 3000d, Saint-Lo, 1844. #2273, 3000d, Coutances, 1855. 5000d, Atlantic, 1843.

1991, May 25
2267-2273 A564 Set of 7   5.00
     8.00
Souvenir Sheet
2274 A564 5000d multicolored   2.50
   Imperf.   6.00
No. 2274 contains one 33x44mm stamp.

Frogs A565

World Wildlife Fund: 200d, Dendrobates leucomelas. 400d, Rana esculenta. 500d, Mantella aurantiaca. 1000d, Dendrobates tinctorius. 2000d, Hyla halowelli. No. 2280, 3000d, Agalychnis callidryas. No. 2281, 3000d, Hyla aurea.

1991, June 12
2275-2281 A565 Set of 7   8.50 2.50
   Imperf., #2275-2281   25.00

7th Vietnamese Communist Party Congress — A566

Designs: 200d, Ho Chi Minh, buildings. 300d, Workers. 400d, Mother, children.

1991, May 15
2282-2284 A566 Set of 3   1.25   .65
   Imperf., #2282-2284   4.50

Vietnamese Communist Party, 60th Anniv. — A566a

1991, June 24   *Litho.*   *Perf. 13*
2284A A566a 100d red   2.00 2.00
   Imperf.   6.50

1992
Winter
Olympics,
Albertville
A567

Designs: 200d, Speed skating, vert. 300d, Free-style skiing, vert. 400d, Bobsled. 1000d, Biathlon. 2000d, Slalom skiing. No. 2290, 3000d, Cross-country skiing, vert. No. 2291, 3000d, Ice dancing, vert. 5000d, Hockey, vert.

1991, July 15
2285-2291 A567 Set of 7   5.00 2.00
    Imperf., #2285-2291   5.00
Souvenir Sheet
2292 A567 5000d multicolored   2.50 1.25
    Imperf.
No. 2292 contains one 33x44mm stamp.

Prehistoric Animals — A568

Designs: a, 200d, Arsinoitherium zitteli. b, 500d, Elephas primigenius. c, 1000d, Baluchitherium. d, 2000d, Deinotherium giganteum. e, 3000d, Brontops. f, 3000d, Uinatherium.

1991, July 26
2293 A568 Block of 6, #a.-f.   5.00 4.00
    Imperf., #2293   5.00

A569

Golden Heart Charity: 200d, Eye, folded hands. 3000d, Tennis player in wheelchair.

1991, Dec. 19
2294-2295 A569 Set of 2   2.00 .70

A570

Chess pieces: 200d, Pawn. 300d, Knight. 1000d, Rook. 2000d, Queen. No. 2300, 3000d, Bishop. No. 2301, 3000d, King. 5000d, Pawn, Knight, King.

1991, Aug. 20
2296-2301 A570 Set of 6   5.50 2.00
    Imperf., #2296-2301   6.75
Souvenir Sheet
2302 A570 5000d multicolored   2.25 1.25
    Imperf.   5.00
No. 2302 contains one 33x44mm stamp.

PHILANIPPON '91 — A571

Butterflies: 200d, Attacus atlas. 400d, Morpho cypris. 500d, Troides rotschildi. No. 2306, 1000d, Papilio demetrius. No. 2307, 1000d, Vanessa atalanta. 3000d, Papilio weiskei. 5000d, Apatura ilia substituta. 5500d, Heliconius melpomene.

1991, Aug. 29
2303-2309 A571 Set of 7   4.50 2.25
    Imperf., #2303-2309   5.00
Souvenir Sheet
2310 A571 5500d multicolored   4.50 1.25
    Imperf.   7.00
No. 2310 contains one 44x33mm stamp.

Post and Telecommunications
Research Institute, 25th
Anniv. — A572

3500d, Communications network, horiz.

1991, Aug.
2311 A572 200d multicolored   1.25 .25
    Imperf.   4.50
Souvenir Sheet
2312 A572 3500d multicolored   2.25 1.25
    Imperf.   5.00
No. 2312 contains one 44x33mm stamp.

Nos. 2118-2125 Ovptd. in Red

1992, Jan. 15   **Perf. 12½**
2313-2319 A543 Set of 7   7.50 2.75
Souvenir Sheet
2320 A543 500d multicolored   4.50 1.40

7th Vietnamese
Communist Party
Congress
A574

200d, Workers, industry, agriculture, atomic energy symbol. 2000d, Map of Asia, hands clasped.

1992, Feb. 3   **Litho.**   **Perf. 13**
2322-2323 A574 Set of 2   2.00 1.75

1992 Winter Olympics,
Albertville — A575

Designs: 200d, Biathlon. 2000d, Hockey. 4000d, Slalom skiing. 5000d, Pairs figure skating. 6000d, Downhill skiing.

1992, Feb. 5
2324-2328 A575 Set of 5   4.50 1.75

Miniature Sheet

Columbus' Discovery of America,
500th Anniv. — A576

Designs: a, 4000d, Columbus, flag. b, 6000d, Columbus, natives. c, 8000d, Aboard ship. d, 3000d, Two sailing ships. e, 400d, Columbus' fleet setting sail.
11,000d, Columbus with Ferdinand and Isabella.

1992, Feb. 12
2329 A576 #a.-f. + label   4.00 2.00
    Imperf
    Size: 102x70mm
2330 A576 11,000d multicolored   3.50 1.25

Airplanes — A577

Designs: 400d, Tupolev TU-154M. 500d, Concorde. 1000d, Airbus A-320. 3000d, Airbus A340-300. 4000d, Boeing Dash 8-400. 5000d, Boeing 747-200. 6000d, McDonnell-Douglas MD-11CF.

1992, Mar. 6   **Perf. 13**
2331-2337 A577 Set of 7   4.25 2.25

A578

Intl. Decade for Natural Disaster Reduction: 400d, Storm system, weather forecasting equipment. 4000d, Man taking water depth readings.

1992, Mar. 23
2338-2339 A578 Set of 2   2.00 .50

A579

1992 Summer Olympics, Barcelona: 400d, Archery. 600d, Volleyball. 1000d, Wrestling. 3000d, Fencing. 4000d, Running. 5000d, Weight lifting. 6000d, Field hockey. 10,000d, Basketball.

1992, Mar. 28
2340-2346 A579 Set of 7   4.50 2.00
Souvenir Sheet
2347 A579 10,000d multicolored   3.00 1.25
No. 2347 contains one 32x43mm stamp.

Motorcycles — A580

Designs: 400d, 5000d, Suzuki 500F. 500d, Honda CBR 600F. 1000d, Honda HRC 500F. 3000d, Kawasaki 250F, vert. 4000d, Suzuki RM 250F, vert. 6000d, BMW 1000F. 10,000d, Suzuki RM 250F, diff.

1992, Apr. 8
2348-2354 A580 Set of 7   6.00 2.00
Souvenir Sheet
2355 A580 10,000d multicolored   4.25 1.25
No. 2355 contains one 33x44mm stamp.

Intl.
Space
Year
A581

400d, Space shuttle launch, vert. 500d, Launch of shuttle Columbia, vert. 3000d, Columbia in space. 4000d, Space station, shuttle Hermes. 5000d, Shuttle Hermes. 6000d, Astronauts, Hubble space telescope, vert.

1992, Apr. 12
2356-2361 A581 Set of 6   4.25 2.00

Saigon
Post
Office,
Cent.
A582

200d, Main entrance. 10,000d, Facade.

1992, Apr. 30   **Perf. 13**
2362 A582 200d multicolored   1.00 .25
    Imperf.   10.00
Souvenir Sheet
    Perf. 13½
2363 A582 10,000d multicolored   3.00 1.25
No. 2363 contains one 43x32mm stamp.

European Cup
Soccer
Championships
A583

Various soccer players in action: 200d,
2000d, 4000d, 5000d, 6000d.

1992, May 14   **Perf. 13**
2364-2368 A583 Set of 5   4.75 2.00
Souvenir Sheet
2369 A583 9000d multicolored   3.00 1.25
No. 2369 contains one 44x33mm stamp.

Spanish
Paintings
A584

Designs: 400d, Childhood of the Virgin, by
Zurbaran. 500d, Woman with a Jug, by Murillo.
1000d, Portrait of Maria Aptrickaia, by Velaz-
quez. 3000d, Holy Family with St. Katherine,
by de Ribera. 4000d, Madonna and Child with
Saints Agnes and Thekla, by El Greco. 5000d,
Woman with a Jug, by Goya. 6000d, The
Naked Maja, by Goya, horiz. 10,000d, Three
Women, by Picasso, horiz.

1992, May 30
2370-2376 A584 Set of 7   4.25 2.00
Souvenir Sheet
2377 A584 10,000d multicolored   3.00 1.25
No. 2377 contains one 44x33mm stamp.
Expo '92, Seville (#2377).

UN Conference on Environmental
Protection, 20th Anniv. — A585

Designs: 200d, Clean, polluted water.
4000d, Graph comparing current development
pattern with environmentally safe pattern.

1992, June 1
2378-2379 A585 Set of 2   2.00 .50

A586

Lighthouses: 200d, Cu Lao Xanh. 3000d,
Can Gio. 5000d, Vung Tau. 6000d, Long
Chau.

1992, June 14   **Perf. 13½x13**
2380-2383 A586 Set of 4   10.00 1.40
Genoa '92.

Flowers — A587

Designs: 200d, Citrus maxima. 2000d, Nerium indicum. 4000d, Ixora coccinea. 5000d,
Cananga oborata. 6000d, Cassia surattensis.

1992, June 28   **Perf. 13**
2384-2388 A587 Set of 5   4.00 1.40

Birds — A588

Designs: 200d, Ducula spilorrhoa. 2000d,
Petrophassa ferruginea. 4000d, Columba livia.
5000d, Lopholaimus antarcticus. 6000d,
Streptopelia senegalensis, horiz.

1992, July 3
2389-2393 A588 Set of 5   4.50 1.40

Rodents — A589

Designs: 200d, 500d, Cavia porcellus, horiz.
3000d, Hystrix indica, horiz. 4000d, Gerbillus
gerbillus. 5000d, Petaurista petaurista. 6000d,
Oryctolagus cuniculus.

1992, July 26
2394-2399 A589 Set of 6   4.50 2.00

Disabled
Soldiers Day,
45th Anniv.
A590

1992, July 27
2400 A590 200d multicolored   1.00 .25
Imperf.   12.50

3rd
Phu
Dong
Games
A591

1992, Aug. 1
2401 A591 200d multicolored   1.00 .25

Betta Splendens — A592

Various fish: 200d, 500d, 3000d, 4000d,
5000d, 6000d.

1992, Aug. 15
2402-2407 A592 Set of 6   4.50 2.00

1984
Summer
Olympics,
Los
Angeles
A592a

Designs: No. 2407A, 50xu, Gymnastics. No.
2407B, 50xu, Soccer, vert. 1d, Wrestling. 2d,
Volleyball, vert. 3d, Hurdles. 5d, Basketball,
vert. 8d, Weight lifting.
10d, Running, vert.

1992, Sept. 1   **Litho.**   **Perf. 12½**
2407A-2407G A592a Set of 7   5.00 5.00
Souvenir Sheet
2407H A592a 10d multi   5.00 5.00
Nos. 2407A-2407G were prepared in 1984
but were not released at that time, because of
Viet Nam's boycott of the 1984 Summer
Olympics.

Intl. Planned Parenthood Federation,
40th Anniv. — A593

Designs: 200d, Map showing member's
locations, vert. 4000d, Anniv. emblem, map.

1992, Oct. 1
2408-2409 A593 Set of 2   2.00 .50

Hanoi
Medical
School,
90th
Anniv.
A594

Designs: 200d, Medical students. 5000d,
Alexandre Yersin, school.

1992, Nov. 20
2410-2411 A594 Set of 2   2.50 .50

SOS Children's
Villages — A595

Designs: 200d, Adult sheltering child.
5000d, Women, children inside house.

1992, Dec. 22
2412-2413 A595 Set of 2   2.00 .50
Imperf., #2412-2413   10.00

17th Southeast Asian Games,
Singapore — A596

1993, Jan. 1
2414 A596 200d multicolored   1.00 .25
Imperf.   12.50

Bees
A597

Designs: 200d, Apis dorsata. 800d, Apis
koschevnikovi. 1000d, Apis laboriosa. 2000d,
Apis cerana japonica. 5000d, Apis cerana cerana. 10,000d, Apis mellifera, vert.

1993, Jan. 15
2415-2420 A597 Set of 6   5.00 2.00
Imperf., #2415-2420   9.00

Fable of Tam
Cam — A598

Designs: 200d, Returning from river. 800d,
Vision of old man by goldfish pool. 1000d,
With unsold rice at market. 3000d, Trying on
slipper for prince. 4000d, Rising from lotus
flower. 10,000d, Royal couple.

1993, Jan. 18
2421-2426 A598 Set of 6   6.50 2.00
Imperf., #2421-2425   17.00

New Year
1993 (Year of
the Rooster)
A599

200d, 5000d, Rooster, hen and chicks.

1993, Jan. 20
2427-2428 A599 Set of 2   2.50 .50
Imperf. #2427-2428   12.50

Medicinal
Plants
A600

Designs: 200d, Atractylodes macrocephala.
No. 2430, 1000d, Lonicera japonica. No. 2431,
1000d, Quisqualis indica. 3000d, Rehmannia
glutinosa. 12,000d, Gardenia jasminoides.

1993, Feb. 27
2429-2433 A600 Set of 5   6.50 1.50

Communications
A601

200d, Map, communications equipment. 2500d, Map, Hong Kong-Sri Racha Cable route.

1993, Mar. 1
2434-2435　A601　Set of 2　　1.50　.30

Asian Animals A602

200d, Ailuropoda melanoleuca. 800d, Panthera tigris. 1000d, Elephas maximus. 3000d, Rhinoceros unicornis. 4000d, Hylobates leucogenys. #2441, 10,000d, Neofelis nebulosa. #2442, 10,000d, Bos sauveli.

1993, Mar. 10
2436-2441　A602　Set of 6　　6.50　2.00
　　Imperf., #2436-2441　　19.00
Souvenir Sheet
Perf. 13½
2442　A602　10,000d multicolored　4.00　1.25

1994 World Cup Soccer Championships, U.S. — A603

Various soccer players in action.

1993, Mar. 30　　　　**Perf. 13**
2443-2445　A603　200d, 1500d,
　　　　　　　　7000d, set of
　　　　　　　　3　　　　3.00　.65

Transportation — A604

Designs: 200d, Wheelbarrow. 800d, Buffalo cart. 1000d, Rickshaw, top up. 2000d, Rickshaw with passenger. 5000d, Rickshaw, top down. 10,000d, Horse-drawn carriage.

1993, Apr. 6
2446-2451　A604　Set of 6　　5.00　2.00
　　Imperf., #2446-2451　　17.50

500Kv Electricity Lines — A605

1993, May 1
2452-2453　300d, 400d, set of 2　1.75　.30

Polska '93 — A606

Paintings: 200d, Sunflowers, by Van Gogh. No. 2455, 1000d, Young Woman, by Mogidliani. No. 2456, 1000d, Couple in Forest, by Rousseau. 5000d, Harlequin with Family, by Picasso. No. 2458, 10,000d, Female Model, by Matisse, horiz. No. 2459, 10,000d, Portrait of Dr. Gachet, by Van Gogh.

1993, May 7　　　　　**Perf. 13**
2454-2458　A606　Set of 5　　5.00　1.25
　　Imperf., #2454-2458　　5.50
Souvenir Sheet
Perf. 12½
2459　A606　10,000d multicolored　5.00　1.25
　No. 2459 contains one 32x43mm stamp.

Da Lat, Cent. A607

Orchids: 400d, Paphiopedilum hirsutissimum. No. 2461, 1000d, Paphiopedilum malipoense. No. 2462, 1000d, Paphiopedilum gratrixianum. 12,000d, Paphiopedilum hennisianum.

1993, June 15　　　　**Perf. 13**
2460-2463　A607　Set of 4　　5.00　1.50
　　Imperf., #2460-2463　　9.00

Asian Architecture — A608

Landmark buildings from: 400d, Thailand, vert. 800d, Indonesia, vert. 1000d, Singapore, vert. No. 2467, 2000d, Malaysia. No. 2468, 2000d, Cambodia. 6000d, Laos. 8000d, Brunei.
　10,000d, Thai Binh, Viet Nam, vert.

1993, July 10　　　　**Litho.**
2464-2470　A608　Set of 7　　4.75　1.50
　　Imperf., #2464-2470　　10.00
Souvenir Sheet
Perf. 14x13½
2471　A608　10,000d multicolored　4.00　1.50

7th Trade Union Congress — A608a

Designs: 400d, Industry, communications. 5000d, Hand holding hammer, doves, flowers.

1993, July 28　**Litho.**　**Perf. 13**
2471A-2471B　A608a　Set of 2　4.50　.40

Crabs A609

Designs: 400d, Scylla serrata. 800d, Portunus sanguinotentus. 1000d, Charybdis bimaculata. 2000d, Paralithodes brevipes. 5000d, Portunus pelagicus. 10,000d, Lithodes turritus.

1993, July 30
2472-2477　A609　Set of 6　　6.50　1.50
　　Imperf., #2472-2477　　9.00

Stamp Day A610

5000d, Hand holding stamped envelope.

1993, Aug. 15
2478-2479　A610　Set of 2　　2.25　.40

Miniature Sheet

Tennis — A611

Women tennis players: a, 400d. c, 1000d. Male tennis players: b, 1000d. d, 12,000d.

1993, Sept. 20
2480　A611　#a.-d. + 2 labels　5.50　3.50

A613

Costumes: 400d, Lo Lo. 800d, Thai. 1000d, Dao Do. 2000d, H'mong. 5000d, Kho Mu. No. 2488, 10,000d, Kinh.
　No. 2489, 10,000d, Precious gem stones.

1993, Oct. 1　　　　**Perf. 13**
2483-2488　A613　Set of 6　　4.50　1.75
Souvenir Sheet
Perf. 13½
2489　A613　10,000d multicolored　5.25　1.25
　Bangkok '93. Issued: Nos. 2483-2488, 10/1/93. No. 2489, 10/10/93.
　No. 2489 contains one 43x32mm stamp.

A614

New Year 1994 (Year of the Dog): Various dogs.

1994, Jan. 1
2490-2491　A614　400d, 6000d,
　　　　　　　　set of 2　　2.50　.45
　　Imperf., #2490-2491　　4.00

Flowers A615

#2492, 400d, Prunus persica. #2493, 400d, Chrysanthemum morifolium. #2494, 400d, Rosa chinensis. 15,000d, Delonix regia.

1994
2492-2495　A615　Set of 4　　5.50　1.60
　Issued: #2492, 1/4; 15,000d, 4/30; #2493, 7/30; #2494, 10/10.

Chess A616

Designs: 400d, Anatoly Karpov. 1000d, Gary Kasparov. 2000d, Bobby Fischer. 4000d, Emanuel Lasker. No. 2500, 10,000d, Jose Capablanca.
　No. 2501, 10,000d, King.

1994, Jan. 20
2496-2500　A616　Set of 5　　4.50　1.50
　　Imperf., #2496-2500　　8.00
Souvenir Sheet
2501　A616　10,000d multicolored　3.25　1.25
　　Imperf.　　　　　5.25

Hong Kong '94 — A617

Festivals: 400d, Hoi Lim. 800d, Cham. 1000d, Tay Nguyen. 12,000d, Nam Bo.

1994, Feb. 18
2502-2505　A617　Set of 4　　3.75　1.25
　　Imperf., #2502-2505　　6.75

A618

Various opera masks: 400d, 500d, 2000d, 3000d, 4000d, 7000d.

1994, Mar. 15
2506-2511　A618　Set of 6　　4.25　1.50
　　Imperf., #2506-2511　　8.50

A619

Various gladiolus hybridus: 400d, 2000d, 5000d, 8000d.

1994, Mar. 30
2512-2515　A619　Set of 4　　3.75　1.25
　　Imperf., #2512-2515　　6.75

Japanese Paintings — A620

Paintings by: 400d, Utamaro. 500d, Harunobu. 1000d, Hokusai. 2000d, Hiroshige. 3000d, Hokusai, diff. 4000d, Utamaro, diff. 8000d, Choki.

1994, Apr. 9
2516-2522 A620 Set of 7   6.50 1.75
   Imperf., #2516-2522   12.00

Insects — A621

Designs: 400d, Cicindela aurulenta. 1000d, Harmonia octomaculata. 6000d, Cicindela tennipes. 7000d, Collyris.

1994, June 15
2523-2526 A621 Set of 4   4.00 1.25
   Imperf., #2523-2526   6.75

Victory at Dien Bien Phu, 40th Anniv. A622

Designs: 400d, Soldiers dragging equipment. 3000d, Celebration.

1994, May 7
2527-2528 A622 Set of 2   1.00 .45
   Imperf., #2527-2528   1.40

Newspaper "Young Pioneers," 40th Anniv. A623

1994, May 15   **Perf. 13x13½**
2529 A623 400d red & black   .60 .25

Crocodiles — A625

Designs: 400d, Crocodylus porosus. 600d, Alligator mississippiensis. 2000d, Crocodylus niloticus. 3000d, Alligator sinensis. 4000d, Caiman yacare. 9000d, Crocodylus johnsoni. 10,000d, Caiman crocodilus.

1994, June 1   **Perf. 13x13½**
2532-2537 A625 Set of 6   5.00 1.75
   Imperf., #2532-2537   8.00
Souvenir Sheet
Perf. 13½
2538 A625 10,000d multicolored   3.75 1.25
   Imperf.   7.00

No. 2538 contains one 43x32mm stamp.

1994 World Cup Soccer Championships, US — A626

Various soccer players in action: 400d, 600d, 1000d, 2000d, 3000d, 11,000d.

1994, Apr. 20   **Perf. 13**
2539-2544 A626 Set of 6   4.75 1.10
   Imperf., #2539-2544   8.00
Souvenir Sheet
Perf. 13½
2545 A626 10,000d multicolored   3.00 1.10
   Imperf.   5.00

No. 2545 contains one 32x43mm stamp.

Yersin's Discovery of Plague Bacillus, Cent. A627

1994, June 15   **Perf. 13x13½**
2546 A627 400d multicolored   .85 .25

UPU, 120th Anniv. A629

Designs. 400d, UPU emblem, "120." 5000d, World map. 10,000d, UPU emblem, "P," vert.

1994, Aug. 10   **Perf. 13**
2551-2552 A629 Set of 2   1.50 .45
   Imperf., #2551-2552   2.50
Souvenir Sheet
Perf. 14x13½
2553 A629 10,000d multicolored   4.25 1.25
   Imperf.   6.00

PHILAKOREA '94 — A630

Birds: 400d, Numenius arquata. 600d, Oceanites oceanicus. 1000d, Fregata minor. 2000d, Morus capensis. 3000d, Lunda cirrhata. 11,000d, Larus belcheri. 10,000d, Collocalia fuciphaga.

1994, Aug. 16   **Perf. 13x13½**
2554-2559 A630 Set of 6   5.00 1.50
   Imperf., #2554-2559   8.00
Souvenir Sheet
Perf. 13½
2560 A630 10,000d multicolored   4.50 1.25
   Imperf.   7.50

No. 2560 contains one 43x32mm stamp.

Bamboo A631

Bamboo: 400d, Bambusa blumeana. 1000d, Phyllostachys aurea. 2000d, Bambusa vulgaris. 4000d, Tetragonocalamus quadrangularis. 10,000d, Bambusa venticosa.

1994, Aug. 17   **Perf. 13½x13**
2561-2565 A631 Set of 5   1.50 1.50
   Imperf., #2561-2565   9.00

Singpex '94.

A632

Various bridges: 400d, 900d, 8000d.

1994, Sept. 20   **Perf. 13x13½**
2566-2568 A632 Set of 3   2.75 .90

Children's Future A634

Designs: 400d+100d, Boy helping girl in wheelchair with kite. 2000d, Children dancing, vert.

1994, Oct. 10   **Litho.**   **Perf. 13**
2572-2573 A634 Set of 2   1.00 .40
   Imperf., #2572-2573   10.00

A636

People's Army, 50th Anniv.: 400d, People in formation. 1000d, Soldiers, battle map. 2000d, Ho Chi Minh, child. 4000d, Anti-aircraft battery.

1994, Dec. 22
2576-2579 A636 Set of 4   2.25 .75

A637

Intl. Olympic Committee, Cent.: 400d, Flags. 6000d, Pierre de Coubertin.

1994, June 25   **Perf. 13**
2580-2581 A637 Set of 2   2.75 .90

ICAO, 50th Anniv. A638

Jets: 400d, In flight. 3000d, On ground.

1994, Dec. 7
2582-2583 A638 Set of 2   1.25 .40

Trams A639

Designs: 400d, With overhead conductor. 900d, Paris tram. 8000d, Philadelphia mail.

1994, Oct. 10   **Litho.**   **Perf. 13x13½**
2584-2586 A639 Set of 3   2.25 .75

Liberation of Hanoi, 40th Anniv. A640

Designs: 400d, Greeting soldiers. 2000d, Workers, students, modern technology.

1994, Oct. 10
2587-2588 A640 Set of 2   1.25 .40

New Year 1995 (Year of the Boar) A641

Stylized boars: 400d, Adult, five young. 8000d, One eating.

1995, Jan. 2   **Litho.**   **Perf. 13**
2589-2590 A641 Set of 2   2.50 .65
   Imperf., #2589-2590   12.50

A642

Birds: No. 2591, 400d, Pluvialis apricarla, horiz. No. 2592, 400d, Philetairus socius, horiz. No. 2593, 400d, Oxyruncus cristatus, horiz. No. 2594, 400d, Pandion haliaetus. No. 2595, 5000d, Cariama cristata.

1995, Jan. 20   **Perf. 13x13½, 13½x13**
2591-2595 A642 Set of 5   2.25 .75

A number has been reserved for a souvenir sheet with this set.

A643

Traditional women's attire: 400d, Young women, bicycle. 3000d, Bride. 5000d, Girl in formal dress holding hat.

1995, Feb. 1   **Perf. 13**
2597-2599 A643 Set of 3   2.50 .75
   Imperf., #2597-2599   12.50

Vietstampex '95 — A644

1995, Feb. 18
2600 A644 5500d multicolored   2.25 .50

Owls — A645

Designs: 400d, Ketupa zeylonensis. 1000d, Strix aluco. 2000d, Strix nebulosa. 5000d, Strix seloputo. 10,000d, Otus leucotis. 12,500d, Tyto alba.

1995, Mar. 1   *Perf. 13½x13*
2601-2605 A645 Set of 5   5.00   1.50
Souvenir Sheet
Perf. 14x13½
2606 A645 12,500d multicolored   5.50   1.10
    Imperf.   6.75

Fish
A646

Designs: 400d, Pomacanthus arcuatus. 1000d, Rhinecanthus rectangulus. 2000d, Pygoplites diacanthus. 4000d, Pomacanthus ciliaris. 5000d, Balistes vetula. 9000d, Balistes conspicillum.

1995, Mar. 20   *Perf. 13*
2607-2612 A646 Set of 6   4.00   1.50

Lenin, 125th Birth Anniv. — A647

1995, Apr. 22   *Litho.*   *Perf. 13*
2613 A647 400d red & black   .60   .25

End of World War II, 50th Anniv.
A648

1995, May 2   *Litho.*   *Perf. 13*
2614 A648 400d multicolored   1.00   .25

A649

1996 Summer Olympics, Atlanta: 400d, Hammer throw. 3000d, Cycling. 4000d, Running. 10,000d, Pole vault. 12,500d, Basketball.

1995, Apr. 5   *Litho.*   *Perf. 13*
2615-2618 A649 Set of 4   4.00   1.40
Souvenir Sheet
2619 A649 12,500d multicolored   3.50   1.10

A650

Various balloons: 500d, 1000d, 2000d, 3000d, 4000d, 5000d, 7000d.

1995, May 5
2620-2626 A650 Set of 7   6.50   1.50
  Finlandia '95, Intl. Philatelic Exhibition, Helsinki.

Miniature Sheets

Tapirus Indicus — A651

No. 2627a, 400d, With young. b, 1000d, Facing left. c, 2000d, Walking right. d, 4000d, Mouth open, left.
No. 2528a, 4000d, Facing right. b, 4000d, Eating leaves. c, 5000d, In water. d, 6000d, Head protruding out of water.

1995, Apr. 25
2627 A651 Sheet of 4, #a.-d.   4.25   3.00
2628 A651 Sheet of 4, #a.-d.   6.00   3.50
  World Wildlife Fund (#2627).

Miniature Sheet

Parachutes — A652

No. 2629: a, 400d, One parachutist descending from sky. b, 2000d, Two descending. c, 3000d, One about to touch ground. d, 9000d, Three men on ground with open parachute.

1995, May 24
2629 A652 Sheet of 4, #a.-d.   4.00   2.00

Rhododendrons — A653

Designs: 400d, Fleuryi. 1000d, Sulphoreum. 2000d, Sinofalconeri. 3000d, Lyi. 5000d, Ovatum. 9000d, Tanastylum.

1995, June 30
2630-2635 A653 Set of 6   4.50   1.50

Miniature Sheet

Native Folktale — A654

a, 400d, Brothers and their parents. b, 1000d, Mother saying farewell to her departing sons. c, 3000d, One brother is transformed into a statue. d, 10,000d, Both brothers transformed into statues.

1995, July 20   *Litho.*   *Perf. 13*
2636 A654 Sheet of 4, #a.-d.   4.25   2.75

A655

400d, Statue of a woman holding child. 3000d, Three women of different races, emblem, horiz.

1995, Aug. 5
2637-2638 A655 Set of 2   1.25   .40
  Women's Federation of Viet Nam: 65th anniv. (#2637), 1995 Intl. Women's Conf., Beijing (#2638).

A656

1995, July 26
2639 A656 400d multicolored   .35   .25
  Admission to Assoc. of Southeast Asian Nations (ASEAN).

Natl. Day — A657

#2640, 400d, Ho Chi Minh, people waving flags, dove of peace. #2641, 400d, Ho Chi Minh holding child. #2642, 1000d, Communist symbol, bridge, electrical wire, Ho Chi Minh Mausoleum. #2643, 1000d, Ho Chi Minh, silhouettes of soldiers, building with flags flying. #2644, 2000d, Soldiers, natl. flag. #2645, 2000d, Antenna, satellite dish, van, olive branch, people on motorcycles.

1995, Aug. 14
2640-2645 A657 Set of 6   3.50   .90
  Viet Nam Labor Party, 65th anniv. (No. 2640). Ho Chi Minh, 105th birth anniv. (No. 2641). Evacuation of French troops from North Viet Nam, 40th anniv. (No. 2642). End of war in Viet Nam, 20th anniv. (No 2643). Natl.

army, 50th anniv. (No. 2644). Post and Telecommunications Service, 50th anniv. (No. 2645).

Sir Rowland Hill (1795-1879)
A658

Design: 4000d, Hill, "penny black."

1995, Aug. 15
2646 A658 4000d multicolored   1.25   .25

Natl. Sports Games — A659

1995, Aug. 30
2647 A659 400d multicolored   .75   .25

Singapore '95 — A660

Orchids: 400d, Paphiopedilum druryi. 2000d, Dendrobium orcraceum. 3000d, Vanda. 4000d, Cattelya. 5000d, Paphiopedilum hirsutissimum. 6000d, Christenosia vietnamica haeger. 12,500d, Angraecum sesquipedale.

1995, Sept. 1
2648-2653 A660 Set of 6   6.50   1.40
Souvenir Sheet
2654 A660 12,500d multicolored   5.50   1.25
  No. 2654 contains one 32x43mm stamp.

Asian Sites — A661

Designs: 400d, Buildings, monuments, tombs, Hue, Viet Nam. 3000d, Zigzag bridge, West Lake, Hangzhou, China. 4000d, Temple, Macao. 5000d, Peak tram, Hong Kong. 6000d, Pagoda, Peace Memorial Park, Taipei, Taiwan.

1995, Sept. 6
2655-2659 A661 Set of 5   4.75   1.25

UN, 50th Anniv.
A662

1995, Oct. 10
2660 A662 2000d multicolored   .75   .25

Total Solar Eclipse, Oct. 10, 1995 A663

1995, Dec. 23   **Litho.**   **Perf. 13**
2661 A663 400d multicolored   1.00   .30

Paintings of Women A664

Designs: 400d, Woman in white dress, flowers, by To Ngoc Van (1906-54) (4-1). 2000d, Washing hair, by Tran Van Can (1906-94) (4-2). 6000d, Standing beside vase of flowers, by To Ngoc Van (4-3). 8000d, Two women, by Tran Van Can (4-4).

1995, Nov. 15   **Litho.**   **Perf. 13**
2662-2665 A664   Set of 4   3.50 3.00

New Year 1996 (Year of the Rat) — A665

Stylized rats: 400d, One carrying fan, one riding horse. 8000d, Four carrying one in palanquin. 13,000d, Marching in parade, carrying banner.

1996, Jan. 2   **Litho.**   **Perf. 13**
2666 A665 400d multicolored   .35 .25
2667 A665 8000d multicolored   2.00 1.25
    Souvenir Sheet
2668 A665 13,000d multi, vert.   3.00 1.50
   No. 2668 contains one 32x43mm stamp.

Dinosaurs — A666

Designs: 400d, Tsintaosaurus. 1000d, Archaeopteryx. 2000d, Psittacosaurus. 3000d, Hypsilophodon. 13,000d, Parasaurolophus.

1996, Mar. 6
2669-2673 A666   Set of 5   4.25 3.00

Kingfishers A667

Designs: 400d, Halcyon smyrnensis. 1000d, Megaceryle alcyon. 2000d, Alcedo Atthis. 4000d, Halcyon coromanda. 12,000d, Ceryle rudis.

1996, Mar. 11
2674-2678 A667   Set of 5   4.50 3.00

Flowers A668

Various flowers: No. 2679, 400d, brown (5-1). No. 2680, 400d, claret (5-2). No. 2681, 400d, green (5-3). No. 2682, 400d, blue (5-4). No. 2683, 5000d, red (5-5), vert.

    Perf. 13x13½, 13½x13
1996, Jan. 10   **Litho.**
2679-2683 A668   Set of 5   1.50 1.10

8th Vietnamese Communist Party Congress — A669

Designs: 400d, Ho Chi Minh (2-1). 3000d, Stylized dove, satellite dish, electrical towers, hammer & sickle, building, olive branch (2-2).

1996, Feb. 3   **Perf. 13**
2684-2685 A669   Set of 2   .75 .60

Asian Sites — A670

Monuments and statues in: 400d, Hanoi. 2000d, Thailand. 3000d, Bhubanesvar, India. 4000d, Kyoto, Japan. 10,000d, Borobudur, Java.

1996, Apr. 10   **Litho.**   **Perf. 13**
2686-2690 A670   Set of 5   4.00 3.00
    See Nos. 2773-2777.

Statues — A671

Various statues of men in traditional costumes of early warriors: 400d, 600d, 1000d, 2000d, 3000d, 5000d, 6000d, 8000d.

1996, Feb. 10   **Litho.**   **Perf. 13½x13**
2691-2698 A671   Set of 8   5.00 4.00
    Imperf., #2691-2698   15.00

Central Committee, 50th Anniv. — A672

1996, May 22   **Perf. 13**
2699 A672 400d multicolored   .30 .25

UNICEF, 50th Anniv. A673

Designs: 400d, Children of different races, cultures. 7000d, Plant, emblem, water droplets containing representations of education, drinking water, medicine, food.

1996, May 15
2700-2701 A673   Set of 2   2.25 1.50

Red Cross of Viet Nam, 50th Anniv. A674

1996, May 8   **Perf. 13½**
2702 A674 3000d Quotation, Ho Chi Minh   .75 .50

A675

Traditional Musical Instruments: a, 400d, Mandolin. b, 3000d, Bow and string instrument. c, 4000d, Square-shaped guitar-like instrument. d, 9000d, Zither.

1996, Apr. 24   **Perf. 13½x13**
2703 A675 Sheet of 4, #a.-d.   3.50 1.75
    China '96 Intl. Philatelic Exhibition.

A676

Insects: 400d, Cincindela japonica. 500d, Calodema wallacei. 1000d, Mylabris oculata. 4000d, Chrysochroa buqueti. 5000d, Ophioniea nigrofasciata. 12,000d, Carabus tauricus.

1996, May 20   **Perf. 13**
2704-2709 A676   Set of 6   5.00 3.50

1996 Summer Olympic Games, Atlanta A677

Designs: 2000d, Soccer. 4000d, Sailing. 5000d, Field hockey.

1996, July 8
2710-2712 A677   Set of 3   2.75 1.50

Euro '96, European Soccer Championships, Great Britain — A678

Designs: a, 400d, Net, goalie. b, 8000d, Player making shot on goal.

1996, June 1
2713 A678   Pair, #a.-b.   2.00 1.00
    No. 2713 is a continuous design.

Aircraft A679

400d, Airbus A320. 1000d, AN-72. 2000d, MD-11F. 6000d, RJ-85. 10,000d, B747-400F. 13,000d, Space shuttle carried by Boeing 747.

1996, June 1   Set of 5   4.25 3.00
2714-2718 A679
    Souvenir Sheet
    Perf. 13½
2719 A679 13,000d multicolored   2.50 2.00

Stamp Day A680

1996, Aug. 15   **Perf. 13**
2720 A680 400d No. 1L57 (1-1)   .30 .25

Paintings by Nguyen Sang (1923-88) A681

400d, Woman, vase of flowers (2-1). 8000d, Soldiers returning from battle (2-2).

1996, Sept. 10   **Perf. 13**
2721-2722 A681   Set of 2   1.75 1.00

Hue School, Cent. — A682

400d, Women walking beside entrance (2-1). 3000d, View of portals, building (2-2).

1996, Sept. 5
2723-2724 A682   Set of 2   .75 .45

Mushrooms
A683

Designs: 400d, Aleuria aurantia. 500d, Morchella conica. 1000d, Anthurus archeri. 4000d, Laetiporus serlphureus. 5000d, Filoboletus manipularis. 12,000d, Tremiscus helvelloides.

1996, Aug. 26   **Litho.**   *Perf. 13*
2725-2730 A683 Set of 6   5.00 4.00

Wild Animals — A684

Designs: a, 400d, Pygathrix nemacus. b, 2000d, Panthera tigris. c, 4000d, Rhinoceros sondaicus. d, 10,000d, Balearica regulorum.

1996, Oct. 10   **Litho.**   *Perf. 13*
2731 A684 Sheet of 4, #a.-d.   4.00 4.00

Taipei '96.

Campaign Promoting Iodized Salt — A685

1996, Nov. 2   **Litho.**   *Perf. 13*
2732 A685 400d multicolored   .55 .30

Natl. Liberation Movement, 50th Anniv. — A686

1996, Dec. 19
2733 A686 400d multicolored   .40 .30

Fruit — A687

Designs: No. 2734, Hylocereus undatus. No. 2735, Durio zibethinus. No. 2736, Persea americana. No. 2737, Garcinia mangostana. No. 2738, Nephelium lappacheum.

1997, Jan. 2   *Perf. 13x13½*
2734-2738 A687 400d Set of 5   *2.00* .75

New Year 1997 (Year of the Ox) — A688

Stylized oxen: 400d, Adult, calf. 8000d, Adult.

1997, Jan. 8   **Litho.**   *Perf. 13*
2739-2740 A688 Set of 2   2.50 1.50
   Imperf., #2739-2740   12.50

8th Vietnamese Communist Party Congress — A689

1997, Feb. 3
2741 A689 400d multicolored   .60 .30

Goldfish A690

Various carassius auratus: 400d, 1000d, 5000d, 7000d, 8000d.

1997, Feb. 5
2742-2746 A690 Set of 5   4.00 3.00
   Imperf., #2742-2746   14.50

Souvenir Sheet
Perf. 13½x14
2747 A690 14,000d multicolored   3.50 1.50

No. 2747 contains one 43x32mm stamp. Hong Kong '97 (#2747).

Sculptures from Ly Dynasty — A691

Designs: 400d, Serpents in round figure, vert. 1000d, Dragon head, vert. 3000d, People playing instruments. 5000d, Gargoyle. 10,000d, Dragon-head bowl.

1997, Mar. 5
2748-2752 A691 Set of 5   4.00 2.50
   Imperf., #2748-2752   14.50

Scenes — A692

Designs: 400d, Lake, people in park, Hà Tay. 5000d, Footbridge over river, Lai Chau. 7000d, Houses, fog, trees, Lào Cai.

1997, Mar. 20
2753-2755 A692 Set of 3   3.00 2.00

Huynh Thuc Khang (1876-1947) — A693

1997, Apr. 21   **Litho.**   *Perf. 13½x13*
2756 A693 400d multi   .35 .30

Disabled People in Sports — A694

1000d, Tennis. 6000d, Shooting.

1997, Apr. 27   *Perf. 13*
2757-2758 A694 Set of 2   1.60 1.20

Wild Animals A695

400d, Chrotogale owstoni. 3000d, Lutra lutra. 4000d, Callosciurus erythraeus. 10,000d, Felis bangalensis.

1997, May 2
2759-2762 A695 Set of 4   3.50 2.75

A696

1997, May 19
2763 A696 400d Women's Union   .50 .30

A697

Lilium longiflorum (Lilies): 400d, Red. 1000d, White. 5000d, Pink & white. 10,000d, Orange.

1997, Apr. 15   **Litho.**   *Perf. 13*
2764-2767 A697 Set of 4   3.50 2.50

PACIFIC 97 — A698

Suspension bridges: 400d, Golden Gate, San Francisco. 5000d, Raippaluoto. 10,000d, Seto.

1997, May 12
2768-2770 A698 Set of 3   3.25 2.50

Children A699

400d, UN Convention on the Rights of the Child. 5000d, Breast milk is better.

1997, June 1   **Litho.**   *Perf. 13*
With Gum
2771-2772 A699 Set of 2   1.25 1.00

Asian Sites Type of 1996

Designs: 400d, Pagoda, Hanoi, Viet Nam. 1000d, Ruins of Persepolis, Iran. 3000d, Statue of woman, Iraq. 5000d, Sacred Rock, Kyaikto, Burma. 10,000d, Statue of Buddha lying down, Sr. Lanka.

1997, June 20   **Litho.**   *Perf. 13*
2773-2777 A670 Set of 5   4.00 3.00

Women's Costumes A700

Various costumes: 400d, Woman holding umbrella, San Chay. 2000d, Woman sewing, wearing jacket tied with sash, Dao quain trang. 5000d, Woman pumping water from well provided by UNICEF, Phù Lá. 10,000d, Woman holding hands in air, Kho Me.

1997, July 8
2778-2781 A700 Set of 4   3.50 2.50

A701

1997, July 11
2782 A701 400d multicolored   4.00 .40
Prevention of AIDS.

ASEAN, 30th
Anniv. — A702

1997, Aug. 8   Litho.   *Perf. 13*
2783 A702 400d multicolored   .35   .25

Monument to War Martyrs & Invalids,
50th Anniv. — A703

1997, July 25
2784 A703 400d multicolored   .35   .35

Hibiscus — A704

a, 1000d, Hibiscus rosa sinensis. b, 3000d,
Hibiscus schizopetalus. c, 5000d, Hibiscus
syriacus (pink). d, 9000d, Hibiscus syriacus
(yellow).

1997, Aug. 1
2785 A704 Sheet of 4, #a.-d.   3.50 2.50

A705

1997, Aug. 26   Litho.   *Perf. 13*
2786 A705 400d multicolored   .40   .30
Post and Telecommunications Union, 50th
anniv.

A706

Sea horses: 400d, 1000d, Hippocampus
(diff.). 3000d, Hippocampus guttulatus. 5000d,
Hippocampus kelloggi. 6000d, Hippocampus
japonicus. 7000d, Hippocampus
hippocampus.

1997, Sept. 4
2787-2792 A706 Set of 6   4.50 4.00

19th Southeast
Asian
Games — A707

1997, Oct. 11   Litho.   *Perf. 13*
2793 A707 5000d multicolored   1.10   .90

Handicrafts
A708

Designs: No. 2794, 400d, Lamp. No. 2795,
400d, Two baskets. No. 2796, 400d, Swan-
shaped basket. No. 2797, 400d, Deer-shaped
basket. 2000d, Basket with handle.

1998, Jan. 1   Litho.   *Perf. 13*
2794-2798 A708 Set of 5   1.10   .80

7th Francophone Summit,
Hanoi — A709

1997, Sept. 24   Litho.   *Perf. 13½x13*
2799 A709 5000d multicolored   2.75 2.00

Birds
A710

400d, Syrmaticus ellioti. 3000d, Lophura
diardi. 5000d, Phasianus cholchicus. 6000d,
Chrysolophus amherstiae. 8000d, Polyplectron germaini.
14,000d, Lophura imperialis.

1997, Oct. 15   *Perf. 13*
2800-2804 A710 Set of 5   4.50 4.00
     Souvenir Sheet
     Perf. 13½
2805 A710 14,000d multicolored   2.50 2.50
No. 2805 contains one 43x30mm stamp.

New Year
1998 (Year of
the Tiger)
A711

Stylized tigers: 400d, Adult with young.
8000d, Adult.

1998, Jan. 5   *Perf. 13*
2806-2807 A711 Set of 2   2.00 1.50

Sites in
Vietnam
A712

Designs: No. 2808, 400d, Rocks, lake, Ninh
Thuan. No. 2809, 400d, Lake, cavern, Quang
Binh. 10,000d, Village of Quang Nam.

1998, Feb. 2
2808-2810 A712 Set of 3   2.00 1.50

Communist
Manifesto, 150th
Anniv. — A713

1998, Feb. 3
2811 A713 400d multicolored   .10   .30

Bonsai
A714

#2812, 400d, Limonia acidissima. #2813,
400d, Deeringia polysperma. #2814, 400d,
Pinus merkucii, vert. 4000d, Barringtonia
acutangula, vert. 6000d, Ficus elastica, vert.
10,000d, Wrightia religiosa, vert.
No. 2818, Adenium obesum.

1998, Mar. 2
2812-2817 A714 Set of 6   4.00 3.00
     Souvenir Sheet
     Perf. 13½
2818 A714 14,000d multicolored   2.50 2.00
No. 2818 contains one 43x32mm stamp.

Tet Offensive,
30th
Anniv. — A715

1998, Jan. 30   Litho.   *Perf. 13*
2819 A715 400d multicolored   .40   .30

Opera — A716

Designs: a, 400d, Thi kính bi oan. b, 1000d,
Thi mâu lên chúa. c, 2000d, Thi mâu-gia nô. d,
4000d, Thi me dôp-Xa trúong. e, 6000d, Thi
kính hi phat va. f, 9000d, Thi kính xin sua.

1998, Apr. 20
2820 A716 Sheet of 6, #a.-f   4.50 3.50

Raptors
A717

Designs: No. 2821, 400d, Pernis apivorus.
No. 2822, 400d, Spizaetus ornatus. No. 2823,
400d, Accipiter gentilis. 3000d, Buteo buteo.
5000d, Circus melanoleucas. 12,000d,
Haliaeetus albicilla.

1998, May 4   Litho.   *Perf. 13*
2821-2826 A717 Set of 6   4.25 3.00

Ho Chi Minh
City (Saigon),
300th
Anniv. — A718

400d, Tank, natl. flag, Ho Chi Minh as young
man, building. 5000d, Monument to Ho Chi
Minh, symbols of industry, communications,
and transportation.
14,000d, Statue of Nguyen Huu Canh
(1650-1700), general.

1998, Apr. 30
2827-2828 A718 Set of 2   2.00   .90
     Souvenir Sheet
     Perf. 14x13½
2828A A718 14,000d multi   —   —

Orchids
A719

Designs: 400d, Paphiopedilum appletoni-
anum. 6000d, Paphiopedilum helenae.

1998, May 18   Litho.   *Perf. 13½*
2829-2830 A719 Set of 2   2.00 1.00

Children's
Paintings
A720

UNICEF: 400d, Children, mother in front of
home. 5000d, Children on playground.

1998, June 1   *Perf. 13*
2831-2832 A720 Set of 2   1.25   .90

1998 World Cup Soccer
Championships, France — A721

Various soccer plays: 400d, 5000d, 7000d.

1998, June 10
2833-2835　A721　Set of 3　　　　2.50　2.00

Sculptures of
the Tran
Dynasty
A722

Ornate designs: No. 2836, 400d, Serpent.
No. 2837, 400d, Two people. 1000d, Shown.
8000d, Person. 9000d, Face.

1998, June 15　Litho.　**Perf. 13**
2836-2840　A722　Set of 5　　3.75 2.75

Martial
Arts
A723

1998, July 13
2841　A723　2000d multicolored　　.90　.50

Intl. Year
of the
Ocean
A724

1998, Aug. 1　Litho.　**Perf. 13**
2842　A724　400d multicolored　1.75　.30

Stamp
Day — A725

1998, Aug. 15
2843　A725　400d Bell's telephone　.60　.30

Ton Duc Thang
(1888-1980)
A726

1998, Aug. 20
2844　A726　400d multicolored　　.60　.30

Moths
A727

Designs: No. 2845, 400d, Antheraea helferi.
No. 2846, 400d, Attacus atlas. 4000d, Argema
mittrei, vert. 10,000d, Argema maenas, vert.

1998, Aug. 22
2845-2848　A727　Set of 4　　4.00 2.50

Paintings by Te
Bach Thach (Qi
Baishi; 1863-
1957)
A728

Various paintings: 400d, Dragonfly & Lotus.
1000d, Chrysanthemum, Cock & Hens.
2000d, Shrimps, 1948. 4000d, Crabs. 6000d,
Lotus & Mandarin Ducks. 9000d, Shrimps,
1949.

1998, Sept. 16
2849-2854　A728　Set of 6　　4.75 3.25

Legend
of the
Lake
A729

Designs: No. 2855, Turtle with sword leading boat. No. 2856, Lake.

1998, Oct. 10
2855-2856　A729　400d Set of 2　1.60　.50

Le Thanh Tong (1442-1497) — A730

1998, Oct. 12
2857　A730　400d multicolored　　.65　.30

Souvenir Sheet

Italia '98, Intl. Philatelic
Exhibition — A731

Milan Cathedral.

1998, Oct. 6　　　**Perf. 13½**
2858　A731　16,000d multicolored　3.50 2.00

8th Trade
Union
Congress
A732

1998, Oct. 15　Litho.　**Perf. 13**
2859　A732　400d multicolored　　.60　.30

Quy Nhon City, 396th Anniv., Binh
Dinh Province, Cent. — A733

1998, Oct. 20
2860　A733　400d multicolored　　.60　.30

Buoi-Chu Van An Secondary School,
90th Anniv. — A734

Designs: 400d, Students outside school.
5000d, Students listening to speaker.

1998, Nov. 20
2861-2862　A734　Set of 2　　1.25　.90

6th ASEAN
Congress,
Hanoi — A735

1998, Dec.　Litho.　**Perf. 13**
2863　A735　1000d multicolored　.90　.40

Cuban Revolution, 40th Anniv. (in
1999) — A736

1998, Dec.　Litho.　**Perf. 13**
2864　A736　400d multicolored　　.60　.30

A737

Paintings: 400d, Birds, tree, flowers
(Spring). 1000d, Flowers, ducks (Summer).
3000d, Flowers, rooster (Fall). 12,000d, Tree,
flowers, deer & fawn (Winter).

1999, Jan. 4　Litho.　**Perf. 13½x13**
2865-2868　A737　Set of 4　　4.00 2.00

A738

New Year 1999 (Year of the Cat): 400d, Cat
holding tree branch. 8000d, Two cats.
13,000d, Kittens, ball.

1999, Jan. 6　　　**Perf. 13½**
2869-2870　A738　Set of 2　　2.00 1.40
Souvenir Sheet
2871　A738　13,000d multicolored　3.00 2.00

No. 2871 contains one 32x43mm stamp.

Kites — A739

400d, Large bird with long tail. 5000d, Crescent-shaped. 7000d, Bird with long legs.

1999, Feb. 16　Litho.　**Perf. 13½x13**
2872-2874　A739　Set of 3　　3.00 1.50

Australia
'99,
World
Stamp
Expo
A740

Various sailing vessels: #2875, 400d, (4-1).
#2876, 400d, (4-2). 7000d, (4-3). 9000d, (4-4).

1999, Mar. 10　Litho.　**Perf. 13**
2875-2878　A740　Set of 4　　3.50 2.00

Medicinal
Plants
A741

Designs: No. 2879, 400d, Kaempferia
galanga. No. 2880, 400d, Tacca chantrieri,
vert. No. 2881, Alpinia galanga, vert. 6000d,

Typhonium trilobatum, vert. 13,000d, Asarum maximum, vert.

1999, Mar. 15
2879-2883 A741 Set of 5   4.25 2.25

Opera Masks
A742

Various masks: 400d (6-1). 1000d (6-2). 2000d (6-3). 5000d (6-4). 6000d (6-5). 10,000d (6-6).

1999, Apr. 16   **Perf. 13½**
2884-2889 A742 Set of 6   4.75 3.50

IBRA '99,
World
Philatelic
Exhibition,
Nuremberg
A743

Octopuses: No. 2890, 400d, Octopus gibertianus. No. 2891, 400d, Philonexis catenulata. 4000d, Paroctopus yendol. 12,000d, Octopus vulgaris.

1999, Apr. 20
2890-2893 A743 Set of 4   3.75 2.25

Landscape Paintings of Southern Viet Nam — A744

#2894, 400d, Sun over lake, Cà Mau. #2895, 400d, Rocks protruding out of water, Kien Giang. 12,000d, Traditional huts, Bac Lieu.

1999, May 4   **Perf. 13**
2894-2896 A744 Set of 3   3.00 1.50

Asia-Pacific Telecommunity, 20th Anniv. — A745

1999, May 10   **Litho.**   **Perf. 13x13¼**
2897 A745 400d multi   2.25 1.50

Woodpeckers
A746

Designs: 400d, Chrysocolaptes lucidus. 1000d, Picumnus innominatus. 3000d, Picus rabieri. 13,000d, Blythipicus pyrrhotis.

1999, May 18   **Litho.**   **Perf. 13**
2898-2901 A746 Set of 4   4.25 2.50

UNICEF
A747

Designs: 400d, Girl, hand. 5000d, Boy carrying factory.

1999, June 1   **Litho.**   **Perf. 13**
2902-2903 A747 Set of 2   1.50 .50

Architecture of Late 19th and Early 20th Centuries — A748

Designs: No. 2904, 400d, Government Office Building, Hanoi (3-1). No. 2905, 400d, History Museum, Ho Chí Minh City (3-2). 12,000d, Duc Ba Cathedral (3-3). 15,000d, Theater, Hanoi.

1999, June 10   **Perf. 13**
2904-2906 A748 Set of 3   2.75 1.50
     Souvenir Sheet
     Perf. 13½x14
2907 A748 15,000d multi   3.50 2.00

PhilexFrance '99 (No. 2907). No. 2907 contains one 44x32mm stamp.

Intl.
Day to
Stop
Drug
Abuse
A749

1999, June 24   **Litho.**   **Perf. 13**
2908 A749 400d multicolored   .60 .25

Da
Rang
Bridge,
Phu
Yen
A750

1999, July 1   **Litho.**   **Perf. 13**
2909 A750 400d multi   .75 .30

Le Dynasty Sculptures — A751

Designs: No. 2910, 1000d, Man Against Tiger (5-1). No. 2911, 1000d, Phoenix (5-2). 3000d, Playing Chess, vert. (5-3). 7000d, Hostler, vert. (5-4). 9000d, Dragon (5-5).

1999, July 1
2910-2914 A751 Set of 5   7.00 5.00

Birth of World's
Six Billionth
Person — A752

1999, Aug. 2
2915 A752 400d multi   .90 .25

Chinese Landscapes — A753

Designs: 400d, Park, Beijing (4-1). 2000d, Scenic overlook, Anhwei (4-2). 3000d, Park, Shandong, (4-3). 10,000d, Park, Beijing, diff. (4-4). 14,000d, Great Wall of China.

1999, Aug. 16   **Perf. 13**
2916-2919 A753 Set of 4   4.25 2.50
     Souvenir Sheet
     Perf. 13½x14
2920 A753 14,000d multi   3.50 2.50

China 1999 World Philatelic Exhibition (No. 2920). No. 2920 contains one 43x32mm stamp.

Boat
Races
A754

Races from regions: 400d, North (3-1). 2000d, Central (3-2). 10,000d, South (3-3).

1999, Sept. 10   **Perf. 13**
2921-2923 A754 Set of 3   3.00 2.00

Women's
Costumes
A755

Various costumes. #2924, 400d (3-1). #2925, 400d (3-2). #2926, 12,000d (3-3).

1999, Sept. 10
2924-2926 A755 Set of 3   3.50 2.00

Buffalo
Fighting
Festivals
A756

Fighting buffaloes: 400d, (2-1). 5000d, (2-2).

1999, Sept. 15
2927-2928 A756 Set of 2   2.00 .75

Ngo Quyen (898-944),
General — A757

1999, Oct. 21
2929 A757 400d multi   .90 .30

Nguyen Van
Sieu (1799-
1872), Teacher,
Writer — A758

1999, Nov. 2   **Litho.**   **Perf. 13**
2930 A758 400d multi   .00 .00

Tran Xuan Soan (1849-1923), Anticolonial Leader — A759

1999, Nov. 24
2931 A759 400d multi   .90 .30

United Nations Development
Program — A760

Designs: 400d, Mother and child, farmer, fisherman. 5000d, Villagers, buildings.

1999, Dec. 3
2932-2933 A760 Set of 2   2.75 1.00

Viet Nam in the
20th
Century — A761

Designs; No. 2934, 400d, Founding of Viet Nam Communist Party (6-1). No. 2935, 400d, Ho Chi Minh's declaration of country's independence (6-2). No. 2936, 1000d, Conquest of South Viet Nam (6-3). No. 2937, 1000d, People, dam, high tension wire tower, atom (6-4). 8000d, People, satellite, satellite dish, dam, high tension wire tower (6-5). 12,000d, Organizations Viet Nam belongs to (6-6).

2000, Jan. 1   **Litho.**   **Perf. 13**
     With Gum
2934-2939 A761 Set of 6   6.00 3.00
2939a   Sheet, #2934-2939, without   9.50 4.00
     gum

New Year 2000 (Year of the Dragon) A762

Dragon: 400d, Facing right (2-1). 8000d, Facing right (2-2).

2000, Jan. 3　With Gum　Perf. 13½
2940-2941　A762　Set of 2　　　3.50　1.50

Intl. Year of Culture and Peace A763

2000, Jan. 18　　　　With Gum
2942　A763　400d multi　　　.90　.30

Viet Nam Communist Party, 70th Anniv. — A764

#2943, Ho Chi Minh (1890-1969), Pres. (8-1). #2944, Tran Phu (1904-31), 1st Gen. Sec. (8-2). #2945, Le Hong Phong (1902-42), Gen. Sec. (8-3). #2946, Ha Huy Tap (1902-41), Gen. Sec. (8-4). #2947, Nguyen Van Cu (1912-41), Gen. Sec. (8-5). #2948, Truong Chinh (1907-88), Gen. Sec. (8-6). #2949, Le Duan (1907-86), Gen. Sec. (8-7). #2950, Nguyen Van Linh (1915-98), Gen. Sec. (8-8).

2000, Feb. 2　With Gum　Perf. 13
2943-2950　A764　400d Set of 8　　3.50　1.00

Cockfighting — A765

Postures: No. 2951, 400d, Song long cuoc (4-1). No. 2952, 400d, Long vu da dao (4-2). 7000d, Song long phuong hoang (4-3). 9000d, Nhan o giap chien (4-4).

2000, Feb. 8　Litho.　Perf. 13
2951-2954　A765　Set of 4　　　4.25　2.50
　　　Imperf., #2951-2954　　　　6.50

Bangkok 2000 Stamp Exhibition A766

Palanquins: 400d, Imperial court roofed palanquin (3-1). 7000d, Palanquin without roof (3-2). 8000d, Roofed palanquin (3-3). 15,000d, Palanquin in procession.

2000, Mar. 10　　　　With Gum
2955-2957　A766　Set of 3　　　4.25　2.50
　　　Souvenir Sheet
2958　A766　15,000d multi　　　4.00　2.50

Legend of Lac Long Quan and Au Co — A767

Designs: No. 2959, 400d, Lang Long Quan and Au Co marry (6-1). No. 2960, 400d, Au Co, gives birth to 100 sons (6-2). 500d, Au Co takes 50 children to forest (6-3). 3000d, Lac Long Quan takes 50 children to sea (6-4). 4000d, Eldest son, Hung Vuong ascends to throne (6-5). 11,000d, Vietnamese ethnic groups as descendents (6-6).

2000, Apr. 4　　　　Perf. 13½
2959-2964　A767　Set of 6　　　5.50　3.50

Souvenir Sheet

The Stamp Show 2000, London — A768

No. 2965 — Fire engines: a, 400d, Iveco Magirus, Germany. b, 1000d, Hino, Japan. c, 5000d, ZIL 103E, Russia. d, 12,000d, FPS.32 Camiva, France.

2000, May 15　　　　Perf. 13
2965　A768　Sheet of 4, #a-d　6.00　3.00

Worldwide Fund for Nature A769

Pseudoryx nghetinhensis: No. 2966, 400d, Head, vine (4-1). No. 2967, 400d, In grass (4-2). 5000d, Near pond (4-3). 10,000d, Head, mountains (4-4).

2000, May 18　With Gum　Perf. 13½
2966-2969　A769　Set of 4　　　4.50　2.50
2969a　　　Sheet, 2 each #2966-2969　9.75　5.00

Ho Chi Minh (1890-1969) A770

2000, May 19　With Gum　Perf. 13
2970　A770　400d multi　　　.90　.30

World Stamp Expo 2000, Anaheim A771

Water puppets: No. 2971, 400d, Chu teu (6-1). No. 2972, 400d, Fairy (6-2). No. 2973, 400d, Man plowing field (6-3). 3000d, Female

peasant (6-4). 9000d, Drummer (6-5). 11,000d, Fisherman (6-6).

2000, June 28　　　　Perf. 13½
2971-2976　A771　Set of 6　　　6.00　3.50

50th Vietnam Youth Volunteers' Day — A772

2000, July 15　With Gum　Perf. 13
2977　A772　400d multi　　　.90　.30

Phu Dong Natl. Youth Sports Festival A773

2000, July 20　　　　With Gum
2978　A773　400d multi　　　.90　.30

Fish A774

Designs: No. 2979, 400d, Cephalopholis miniatus (6-1). No. 2980, 400d, Pomacanthus imperator (6-2). No. 2981, 400d, Epinephelus merra (6-3). 4000d, Zancius cornutus, vert. (6-4). 6000d, Chaetodon ephippium, vert. (6-5). 12,000d, Heniochus acuminatus, vert. (6-6). 15,000d, Chaetodon lunula.

2000, Aug. 7　　　　Perf. 13
2979-2984　A774　Set of 6　　　6.00　3.00
　　　Souvenir Sheet
　　　Perf. 13½x13¾
2985　A774　15,000d multi　　　4.00　2.00

Post and Telegraph Dept., 55th Anniv. A775

2000, Aug. 15　With Gum　Perf. 13
2986　A775　400d multi　　　.75　.30

People's Police, 50th Anniv. A776

Designs: 400d, Ho Chi Minh, five policemen. 2000d, Policeman checking documents, vert.

2000, Aug. 19　Litho.　Perf. 13
　　　With Gum
2987-2988　A776　Set of 2　　　1.00　.55

Gen. Nguyen Tri Phuong, 200th Anniv. of Birth — A777

2000, Aug. 31　With Gum　Perf. 13½
2989　A777　400d multi　　　.90　.30

UN Right of the Child Conference, 10th Anniv. — A778

Emblem and: 400d, Boy and girl. 5000d, Five children, vert.

2000, Sept. 8　　　　Perf. 13
2990-2991　A778　Set of 2　　　1.75　1.00

2000 Summer Olympics, Sydney — A779

Designs: 400d, Running. 6000d, Shooting. 7000d, Taekwondo, vert.

2000, Sept. 15
2992-2994　A779　Set of 3　　　3.00　2.25

Gen. Tran Hung Dao, 700th Anniv. of Death. — A780

2000, Sept. 17　　　　With Gum
2995　A780　400d multi　　　.90　.30

Birds — A781

Designs: No. 2996, 400d, Leiothrix argentauris. No. 2997, 400d, Pitta ellioti. No. 2998, 400d, Pomatorinus ferruginosus. 5000d, Dicrurus paradiceus, vert. 7000d, Melanochlora sultanea, vert. 10,000d, Stachyris striolata, vert.

2000, Sept. 28　　　　Perf. 13½
2996-3001　A781　Set of 6　　　6.00　4.00
　　　Souvenir Sheet
　　　Perf. 13½x13¾
3002　A781　15,000d Trena puella　5.00　2.50

No. 3002 contains one 42x31mm stamp. España 2000 Intl. Philatelic Exhibition (No. 3002).

Vietnam Philately Association, 40th Anniv. — A782

2000, Oct. 6 **With Gum** *Perf. 13*
3003 A782 400d No. 821 .90 .30

Farmer's Association, 70th Anniv. — A783

2000, Oct. 14 **With Gum**
3004 A783 400d multi .90 .30

Women's Union, 70th Anniv. A784

2000, Oct. 14 **With Gum**
3005 A784 400d multi .90 .30

Hanoi, 990th Anniv. A785

Designs: 400d, Building, and Ly Thai To, founder of Hanoi. 3000d, Temple, two people, monuments. 10,000d, Peasants with goods, building. 15,000d, People and doves.

2000, Oct. 15 *Perf. 13*
3006-3008 A785 Set of 3 3.50 2.25
Souvenir Sheet
Perf. 13½x13¾
3009 A785 15,000d multi 4.00 2.50

Bats — A786

Designs: No. 3010, 400d, Scotomanes ornatus. No. 3011, 400d, Pteropus lylei. 2000d, Rhinolophus paradoxolophus. 6000d, Eonycteris spelaea. 11,000d, Cynopterus sphinx.

2000, Oct. 14 *Perf. 13*
3010-3014 A786 Set of 5 2.25 3.00

Fatherland Front, 70th Anniv. — A787

2000, Oct. 18 **With Gum**
3015 A787 400d multi .90 .30

6th Natl. Emulation Congress A788

Designs: 400d, People at work. 3000d, Symbols of industry, vert.

2000, Nov. 10 **With Gum**
3016-3017 A788 Set of 2 1.25 .75

Flowers A789

Designs: 400d, Oxyspora sp. 5000d, Melanstoma villosa, vert.

With Gum
2000, Nov. 15 *Perf. 13½*
3018-3019 A789 Set of 2 2.75 1.00

Hon Khoai Uprising, 60th Anniv. A790

2000, Dec. 13 **With Gum** *Perf. 13*
3020 A790 400d multi .80 .30

Advent of New Millennium A791

2001, Jan. 1 **With Gum**
3021 A791 400d multi .80 .30

New Year 2001 (Year of the Snake) A792

Snake and: 400d, Pink flowers. 8000d, Yellow flowers.

2001, Jan. 1 **With Gum** *Perf. 13½*
3022-3023 A792 Set of 2 2.50 1.60

Hong Kong 2001 Stamp Exhibition — A793

Fish: 400d, Toxotes microlepis. 800d, Cosmocheilus harmandi. 2000d, Anguilla bicolor pacifica. 3000d, Chitala ornata. 7000d, Megalops cyprinoides. 8000d, Probarbus jullieni.

2001, Jan. 18 **Litho.** *Perf. 13*
3024-3029 A793 Set of 6 6.00 3.00

Nobel Prize, Cent. A794

2001, Jan. 27 **With Gum** *Perf. 13½*
3030 A794 400d multi .60 .30

Four Seasons — A795

No. 3031: a, 400d, Peach blossoms and birds (spring). b, 800d, Cotton rose and pheasant (summer). c, 4000d, Chrysanthemum and phoenix (autumn). d, 10,000d, Pine tree and cranes (winter).

With Gum
2001, Feb. 1 *Perf. 13¼x13*
3031 A795 Sheet of 4, #a-d 5.50 2.50

Wild Fruits — A796

Designs: No. 3032, 400d, Rubus cochinchinensis. No. 3033, 400d, Rhizophora mucronata. No. 3034, 400d, Podocarpus neriifolius. No. 3035, 400d, Magnolia pumila. 15,000d, Taxus chinensis.

2001, Feb. 8 **With Gum** *Perf. 13½*
3032-3036 A796 Set of 5 4.00 2.25

Landscapes — A797

Designs: No. 3037, 400d, Co Tien Mountain (3-1). No. 3038, 400d, Dong Pagoda, Yen Tu Mountain (3-2). 10,000d, King Dinh Temple (3-3).

2001, Feb. 23 *Perf. 13*
3037-3039 A797 Set of 3 3.50 1.50

Nhan Dan Newspaper, 50th Anniv. — A798

2001, Mar. 11 **With Gum**
3040 A798 400d multi .80 .30

Rubies Found in Tan Huong A799

Designs: 400d, 1960-gram ruby. 6000d, 2160-gram "Viet Nam Star."

2001, Mar. 20 **With Gum**
3041-3042 A799 Set of 2 3.00 1.00

Ho Chi Minh Youth Union, 70th Anniv. — A800

2001, Mar. 26 **Litho.** *Perf. 13*
With Gum
3043 A800 400d multi .70 .30

9th Communist Party Congress — A801

Designs: 400d, Ho Chi Minh, flag, map (2-1). 3000d, Hammer and sickle, Ngoc Lu bronze drum head, symbols of technology, vert (2-2).

2001, Apr. 18 **With Gum**
3044-3045 A801 Set of 2 1.10 .55

Fauna in Cat Tien Natl. Park — A802

Designs: 400d, Arborophila davidi (4-1). 800d, Stichophthalma uemurai (4-2). 3000d, Rhinoceros sondaicus (4-3). 5000d, Crocodylus siamensis (4-4).

2001, Apr. 3 *Perf. 13½*
3046-3049 A802 Set of 4 3.50 2.00

Mushrooms A803

Designs: No. 3050, 400d, Phallus indusiatus (7-1). No. 3051, 400d, Aseroe arachnoidea (7-2). No. 3052, 400d, Phallus tenuis (7-3). 2000d, Phallus impudicus (7-4). 5000d, Phallus rugulosus (7-5). 6000d, Simblum periphragmoides (7-6). 7000d, Mutinus bambusinus (7-7).

2001, May 2
3050-3056 A803   Set of 7   6.00 3.50

Mushrooms Type of 2001

Design: 13,000d,   Pseudocolus schellenbergiae.

2001, May 2   Litho.   Perf. 13½x13¾
3057 A803 13,000d multi   5.50 2.50
No. 3057 contains one 42x31mm stamp.

Ho Chi Minh Young Pioneer's League, 60th Anniv. — A804

2001, May 15   Litho.   Perf. 13
With Gum
3058 A804 400d multi   .70   .30

Viet Minh Front, 60th Anniv. A805

2001, May 19   **With Gum**
3059 A805 400d multi   .70   .30

Campaign Against Smoking — A806

2001, May 30   **Perf. 13¼x13½**
With Gum
3060 A806 800d multi   .90   .45

Children A807

Designs: 400d, Two children, UNICEF emblem. 5000d, Five children, UN emblem.

2001, June 1   **Perf. 13½**
3061-3062 A807   Set of 2   2.10 1.00
Children's safety day (#3061); UN Special Session on Children, Washington, DC (#3062).

Diesel Locomotives — A808

Designs: No. 3063, 400d, D18E (6-1). No. 3064, 400d, D4H (6-2). 800d, D11H (6-3).

2000d, D5H (6-4). 6000d, D9E (6-5). 7000d, D12E (6-6).

2001, June 5   **Perf. 13**
3063-3068 A808   Set of 6   5.50 3.00
Souvenir Sheet
Perf. 13½x13¾
3069 A808 13,000d D11H, diff.   4.25 2.25
No. 3069 contains one 43x32mm stamp.

Orchids A809

Designs: No. 3070, 800d, Vanda sp. (6-1). No. 3071, 800d, Dendrobium lowianum (6-2). No. 3072, 800d, Phajus wallichii (6-3). No. 3073, 800d, Habenaria medioflexa (6-4). No. 3074, 800d, Arundina graminifolia, vert. (6-5). 12,000d, Calanthe clavata, vert. (6-6).

Perf. 13½x13¼, 13¼x13½
2001, July 5   **With Gum**
3070-3075 A809   Set of 6   4.25 2.75

Phila Nippon '01 — A810

Butterflies: No. 3076, 800d, Troides aeacus (6-1). No. 3077, 800d, Inachis io (6-2). No. 3078, 800d, Ancyluris formosissima (6-3). 5000d, Cymothoe sanguris (6-4). 7000d, Taenaris selene (6-5). 10,000d, Trogonoptera brookiana (6-6).
13,000d, Atrophaneura horishanus, vert.

2001, July 16   **Perf. 13½x13¼**
3076-3081 A810   Set of 6   6.50 3.50
Souvenir Sheet
Perf. 13¾x13½
3082 A810 13,000d multi   6.50 2.25
No. 3082 contains one 32x42mm stamp.

2002 World Cup Soccer Championships, Japan and Korea — A811

No. 3083: a, 800d, Player with red shirt. b, 3000d, Player with white shirt.

2001, July 24   With Gum   Perf. 13
3083 A811   Horiz. pair, #a-b   2.75 1.50

Musical Instruments — A812

Designs: No. 3084, 800d, Ho gáo (6-1). No. 3085, 800d, Kenh (6-2). No. 3086, 800d, Dàn tú, vert. (6-3). 2000d, Dàn t'rung, vert. (6-4). 6000d, Trong kinang, vert . (6-5). 9000d, Tính tau, vert. (6-6).

Perf. 13x13¼, 13¼x13
2001, Aug. 4   **Litho.**
3084-3089 A812   Set of 6   6.00 3.00

Year of Dialogue Among Civilizations — A813

2001, Oct. 9   Litho.   Perf. 13¼x13½
With Gum
3090 A813 800d multi   1.25   .40

Tran Huy Lieu (1901-69), Writer — A814

2001, Nov. 5   **Perf. 13x12¾**
With Gum
3091 A814 800d multi   .90   .40

Nam Cao (1917-51), Writer A815

2001, Nov. 30   **Perf. 13x13¼**
With Gum
3092 A815 800d multi   .90   .45

A816   A817

2001   **With Gum   Perf. 13½**
3093 A816 800d multi   .40   .25
3094 A817 3000d multi   1.25   .45

New Year 2002 (Year of the Horse) A818

Horse facing: 800d, Right. 8000d, Left. 14,000d, Horse galloping.

2002, Jan. 2   With Gum   Perf. 13½
3095-3096 A818   Set of 2   3.25 1.10
Souvenir Sheet
Perf. 13½x13¼
3097 A818 14,000d multi   4.25 2.50
No. 3097 contains one 42x31mm stamp.

Opera Costumes A819

Designs: No. 3098, 1000d, Giáp Tuong Nam (6-1). No. 3099, 1000d, Giáp Tuong Nu (6-2). 2000d, Giáp Tuong Phan Dien (6-3). 3000d, Long Chan (6-4). 5000d, Giáp Tuong Phien (6-5). 9000d, Lung Xiem Quan Giáp (6-6).

2002, Jan. 15   **Perf. 13**
3098-3103 A819   Set of 6   6.00 3.25

Vo Thi Sáu, Heroine, 50th Anniv. of Death A820

2002, Jan. 23   **Perf. 13x13¼**
3104 A820 1000d multi   .90   .40

Program Implementation of 9th Communist Party Congress A821

Designs: 800d, Map, satellite, buildings, dam, power lines, bridge, computer keyboard (2-1). 3000d, Flag, building, doves, people (2-2).

2002, Feb. 1   **Perf. 13¼x13**
With Gum
3105-3106 A821   Set of 2   1.40   .65

Cacti — A822

Designs: No. 3107, 1000d, Echinocereus albatus (5-1). No. 3108, 1000d, Echinocereus delaetii (5-2). No. 3109, 1000d, Cylindropuntia bigelowii (5-3). 5000d, Echinocereus triglochidatus (5-4). 10,000d, Epiphyllum truncatum (5-5).

2002, Feb. 18   **Perf. 13¼x13½**
3107-3111 A822   Set of 5   5.00 2.50

Victor Hugo (1802-85), French Writer A823

2002, Feb. 26   **Perf. 13x13¼**
With Gum
3112 A823 1000d multi   .90   .45

A824

2002, Feb. 21   Litho.   Perf. 13x13¼
With Gum
3113 A824 800d multi   .90   .45

Birds — A825

Designs: 600d, Actinodura sodangorum (6-1). No. 3115, 800d, Garrulax ngoclinhensis (6-2). No. 3116, 800d, Garrulax pectoralis (6-3). No. 3117, 800d, Pomatorhinus hypoleucos (6-4). 5000d, Minla ignotincta (6-5). 8000d, Minla cyanouroptera (6-6).

2002, Mar. 15   Litho.   Perf. 13½
With Gum
3114-3119 A825 Set of 6   6.00 2.75

Landscapes A826

Designs: No. 3120, 800d, Ganh Son, Binh Thuan (3-1). No. 3121, 800d, Dawn over Tung Estuary, Quang Tri (3-2). 10,000d, Sa Huynh Harbor, Quang Ngai (3-3).

2002, Mar. 15   With Gum
3120-3122 A826 Set of 3   4.25 2.00

Primates — A827

Designs: 600d, Trachypithecus poliocephalus (8-1). 800d, Trachypithecus delacouri (8-2). 1000d, Rhinopithecus avunculus (8-3). 2000d, Pygathrix cinerea (8-4). 4000d, Nomascus concolor (8-5). 5000d, Trachypithecus laotum hatinhensis (8-6). 7000d, Trachypithecus phayrei (8-7). 9000d, Pygathrix nemaeus (8-8).

2002, Apr. 10
3123-3130 A827 Set of 8   6.50 4.50
3130a   Souvenir sheet, #3123-
           3130 + label   6.50 4.50

Bui Thi Xuan, 200th Anniv. of Death — A828

2002, Apr. 13   With Gum   Perf. 13
3131 A828 1000d multi   .90 .45

Souvenir Sheet

2002 World Cup Soccer Championships, Japan and Korea — A829

Color of player or players: a, 1000d, Blue. b, 2000d, Red. c, 5000d, Red violet. d, 7000d, Green.

2002, June 1   With Gum   Litho.
3132 A829 Sheet of 4, #a-d   4.00 2.75

Flowers — A830

Designs: 600d, Paphiopedilum concolor (7-1). 800d, Sterculia lanceolata (7-2). 1000d, Schefflera alongensis (7-3). 2000d, Hibiscus tiliaceus (7-4). 3000d, Mussaenda glabra (7-5). 5000d, Boniodendron parviflorum (7-6). 9000d, Bauhinia ornata.

2002, June 5
3133-3139 A830 Set of 7   6.00 3.25

Chau Van Liem, Communist Party Leader, Cent. of Birth — A831

2002, June 28   Litho.   Perf. 13
With Gum
3140 A831 800d multi   .90 .45

Stamp Day — A832

2002, July 1   Perf. 13x12¾
With Gum
3141 A832 800d multi + label   .90 .45

Tay Nguyen Province A833

2002, July 10   Litho.   Perf. 13
With Gum
3142 A833 800d multi   .90 .40

Soft-shell Turtles A834

Designs: 800d, Pelochelys bibroni (4-1). 2000d, Pelodiscus sinensis. 5000d, Palea steindachneri. 9000d, Trionyx cartilagineus.

2002, July 15   Litho.   Perf. 13½
3143-3146 A834 Set of 4   6.00 2.60
3146a   Souvenir sheet, 2 each
           #3143-3146   10.00 5.25

Viet Nam — Laos Diplomatic Relations, 40th Anniv. A835

2002, July 18   With Gum   Perf. 13
3147 A835 800d multi   .75 .45

Civil Aircraft A836

Designs: 800d, Super King Air B200 in air (4-1). 2000d, Fokker 70 (4-2). 3000d, ATR-72 (4-3). 8000d, Boeing 767-300 (4-4). 14,000d, Super King Air B200 on ground.

2002, Aug. 1   With Gum   Perf. 13
3148-3151 A836 Set of 4   5.00 2.25
Souvenir Sheet
Perf. 13½x13¾
3152 A836 14,000d multi   4.50 2.25

Autumn Festival Lanterns A837

Designs: No. 3153, 800d, Den Ong Sao (4-1). No. 3154, 800d, Den Ong Su (4-2). 2000d, Den Con Tho Om Trang (4-3). 7000d, Den Xep (4-4).

2002, Aug. 16   With Gum   Perf. 13½
3153-3156 A837 Set of 4   2.75 1.50

Viet Nam Posts and Telecommunications Trade Union, 55th Anniv. — A838

2002, Aug. 23   With Gum   Perf. 13
3157 A838 800d multi   .90 .40

Bridges — A839

Designs: No. 3158, 800d, Cau Long Bien (4-1). No. 3159, 800d, Cau Song Han (4-2). 2000d, Cau Truong Tien (4-3). 10,000d, Cau My Thuan (4-4).

2002, Sept. 27   Perf. 13x13¼
With Gum
3158-3161 A839 Set of 4   4.50 2.00

Communist Party's Ideology and Culture Commission, 72nd Anniv. — A840

2002, Oct. 10   With Gum   Perf. 13
3162 A840 800d multi   .90 .40

Hanoi Medical University, Cent. A841

2002, Nov. 15   With Gum
3163 A841 800d multi   .90 .40

Teachers' Day — A842

2002, Nov. 20   With Gum
3164 A842 800d multi   .90 .40

New Year 2003 (Year of the Ram) — A843

Various goats with background colors of: 800d, Rose pink (2-1). 8000d, Orange (2-2).

2002, Dec. 15   Perf. 13½
With Gum
3165-3166 A843 Set of 2   2.25 1.25

Viet Nam — South Korea Diplomatic Relations, 10th Anniv. — A844

Pagoda from: No. 3167, 800d, Viet Nam (2-1). No. 3168, 800d, South Korea (2-2).

2002, Dec. 21   With Gum   Perf. 13
3167-3168 A844 Set of 2   1.25 .65

Starting with the 2003 issues, stamps are gummed unless otherwise indicated.

Landscapes — A845

Designs: 800d, Rung Cao Su, Bình Phuoc (3-1). 3000d, Ao Bà Om, Trà Vinh (3-2). 7000d, Mot nhanh song Rach Gam-Xoài Mút, Tien Giang (3-3).

2003, Feb. 1   **Litho.**   **Perf. 13**
3169-3171 A845   Set of 3   2.50   1.40

Viet Nam Culture Program, 60th Anniv. — A846

2003, Feb. 3
3172 A846 800d multi   .90   .30

Viet Nam Cinema Association, 50th Anniv. — A847

2003, Mar. 1
3173 A847 1000d multi   .90   .40

Khanh Hoa Province, 350th Anniv. A848

2003, Mar. 25
3174 A848 800d multi   .90   .30

Cycle Rickshaws A849

Cycle rickshaws from: 800d, Hanoi. 3000d, Ho Chi Minh City. 8000d, Haiphong.

2003, Apr. 1
3175-3177 A849   Set of 3   2.50   1.60

Adventures of the Cricket — A850

2003, May 1   **Perf. 13¼x13½**
3178   Horiz. strip of 6   4.50   2.60
   a.   A850 800d Toi là út...   .30   .25
   b.   A850 1000d Chang bao...   .35   .25

   c.   A850 2000d Toi an han...   .45   .25
   d.   A850 3000d Toi và Trui...   .65   .40
   e.   A850 5000d Mot ngày...   1.10   .70
   f.   A850 8000d Tu nay the...   1.75   1.10

Animals in Ba Vi National Park — A851

Designs: No. 3179, 800d, Manis pentadactyla (4-1). No. 3180, 800d, Petaurista petaurista (4-2). 5000d, Selenarctos thibetanus (4-3). 10,000d, Capricornis sumatraensis (4-4).

2003, June 5   **Perf. 13½**
3179-3182 A851   Set of 4   4.50   2.25

22nd South East Asian Games, Viet Nam — A852

Designs: 800d, Soccer (4-1). 2000d, Hurdles (4-2). 3000d, Kayaking (4-3). 7000d, Wrestling (4-4).
10,000d, Games emblem, mascot, stadium.

2003, July 1   **Perf. 13**
3183-3186 A852   Set of 4   4.00   1.75
Souvenir Sheet
Perf. 13½x13¾
3187 A852 10,000d multi   4.00   1.50

Ninth Congress of Viet Nam Federation of Trade Unions — A853

2003, July 28   **Perf. 13**
3188 A853 800d multi   .90   .25

Camellias — A854

Designs: 800d, Camellia petelotii (4-1). 1000d, Camellia rubriflora (4-2). 5000d, Camellia vietnamensis (4-3). 6000d, Camellia gilberti (4-4).

2003, Sept. 1   **Perf. 13½**
3189-3192 A854   Set of 4   3.00   1.75
Bangkok 2003 World Philatelic Exhibition.

Orchids A855

Designs: 800d, Paphiopedilum dianthum (2-1). 8000d, Pleione bulbocodioides (2-2).

2003, Oct. 1   **Perf. 13**
3193-3194 A855   Set of 2   3.25   1.10

Asian Elephants A856

Designs: 800d, Elephant with trunk extended (4-1). 1000d, Elephants and riders (4-2). 2000d, Elephant with trunk down (4-3). 8000d, Two elephants (4-4)

2003, Oct. 1   **Perf. 13½**
3195-3198 A856   Set of 4   4.50   1.50
3198a   Miniature sheet, 2 each
     #3195-3198   9.00   3.00

My Son World Heritage Site — A857

Various ruins: 800d, (3-1). 3000d, (3-2). 8000d (3-3).
10,000d, Temple (43x32mm).

2003, Dec. 1   **Perf. 13x13¼**
3199-3201 A857   Set of 3   4.50   2.00
Souvenir Sheet
Perf. 13½x13¾
3202 A857 10,000d multi   3.25   2.00

New Year 2004 (Year of the Monkey) A858

Monkeys and: 800d, Apple tree (2-1). 8000d, Palm leaf (2-2).

2003, Dec. 1   **Perf. 13½**
3203-3204 A858   Set of 2   2.25   1.10

Ngo Gia Tu (1908-35), Leader of 1926 Strike — A859

2003, Dec. 30   **Perf. 13¼x13**
3205 A859 800d multi   .85   .25

Congratulations A860

Designs: 800d, Flowers (2-1). 8000d, Bird with envelope (2-2).

2004, Jan. 1   **Perf. 13 Syncopated**
3206-3207 A860   Set of 2   2.10   1.10

Shells A861

Designs: 800d, Murex trocheli (3-1). 3000d, Murex haustellum (3-2). 8000d, Chicoreus ramosus (3-3).

2004, Feb. 1   **Perf. 13**
3208-3210 A861   Set of 3   4.00   1.50

Bamboo Lamps — A862

Various lamps with background colors of: 400d, Yellow (3-1). 1000d, Pale green (3-2). 7000d, Buff (3-3).

Perf. 13 Syncopated
2004, Mar. 1   **Litho.**
3211-3213 A862   Set of 3   2.75   1.10
See Nos. 3352-3363.

Hué, UNESCO World Heritage Site — A863

Designs: 800d, Pavilion of Edicts (3-1). 4000d, Ngo Mon Gate (3-2). No. 3216, 8000d, Hien Lam Pavilion (3-3).
No. 3217, 8000d, Thai Hoa Palace.

2004, Apr. 1   **Perf. 13**
Stamp + Label
3214-3216 A863   Set of 3   2.50   1.75
Souvenir Sheet
Perf. 13½x13¾
3217 A863 8000d multi   3.50   1.00
No. 3217 contains one 42x31mm stamp.

Tran Phu (1904-31), Communist Leader — A864

2004, May 1   **Perf. 13**
3218 A864 800d multi   .70   .25

Battle of Dien Bien Phu, 50th Anniv. A865

Designs: 800d, Soldier, flowers (2-1). 5000d, Dancer, flowers.
8000d, Three dancers, flowers.

2004, May 4   **Perf. 13**
3219-3220 A865   Set of 2   1.90   .75
Souvenir Sheet
Perf. 13½x13¾
3221 A865 8000d multi   2.50   1.00

FIFA (Fédération Internationale de Football Association), Cent. — A866

2004, May 21   *Perf. 13*
3222 A866 800d multi   1.25 .25

Thieu Nien Newspaper, 50th Anniv. — A867

2004, June 1
3223 A867 800d multi   .85 .25

Bonsai — A868

Designs: 800d, Ficus microcarpa (4-1). 2000d, Premna serratifolia (4-2). 3000d, Ficus pilosa (4-3). 8000d, Ficus religiosa (4-4).

2004, July 1
3224-3227 A868   Set of 4   4.50 1.75
2004 World Stamp Championship, Singapore.

2004 Summer Olympics, Athens — A869

Designs: 800d, Hurdles (4-1). 1000d, Swimming, horiz. (4-2). 6000d, Shooting, horiz. (4-3). 7000d, Taekwondo (4-4).

2004, Aug. 1
3228-3231 A869   Set of 4   3.50 1.90

Naming of Country as Viet Nam, Bicent. A870

Designs: 800d, Citadel, Hué, lotus flower (2-1). 5000d, Ho Chi Minh, flag (2-2).

2004, Sept. 2
3232-3233 A870   Set of 2   1.60 .75

World Summit on the Information Society, Geneva — A871

2004, Oct. 9
3234 A871 1000d multi   .85 .25

Liberation of Hanoi From French, 50th Anniv. — A872

2004, Oct. 10
3235 A872 800d multi   .85 .25

Dak Lak Province, Cent. — A873

2004, Nov. 22
3236 A873 800d multi   1.00 .25

Hoi An, UNESCO World Heritage Site — A874

Designs: 800d, Chua Cau. 8000d, Hoi Quán Phúc Kien.

Perf. 13¼x13¾ Syncopated
2004, Dec. 1
3237 A074 000d multi   1.25 .25
Souvenir Sheet
Perf. 13½x13¾
3238 A874 8000d multi   3.00 1.50
No. 3238 contains one 42x31mm stamp.

New Year 2005 (Year of the Rooster) A875

Designs: 800d, Rooster (2-1). 8000d, Hen and chicks.

2004, Dec. 15   *Perf. 13*
3239-3240 A875   Set of 2   2.50 1.10
3240a   Souvenir sheet, #3239-3240   2.75 1.50

Viet Nam Communist Party, 75th Anniv. — A876

2005, Feb. 3
3241 A876 800d multi   .75 .25

Gia Lai Province A877

Perf. 13¼x13¾ Syncopated
2005, Mar. 16   *Litho.*
3242 A877 800d multi   .85 .25

Nha Trang Bay — A878

Designs: 800d, Boat near shore (2-1). 8000d, Road near shore (2-2).

2005, Apr. 2   *Perf. 13x12¾*
Stamp + Label
3243-3244 A878   Set of 2   1.90 1.40

Worldwide Fund for Nature (WWF) A879

Various views of Chrotogale owstoni: 800d, (4-1). 3000d, (4-2). 5000d, (4-3). 8000d, (4-4).

2005, May 2   *Perf. 13½*
3245-3248 A879   Set of 4   3.50 3.25
    Imperf., #3245-3248   9.50
3248a   Souvenir sheet #3245-3248, perf. 13x13½   4.25 3.50

Liberation of Haiphong, 50th Anniv. — A880

Designs: 800d, Burning airplanes at Cat Bi Airport, Haiphong harbor (2-1). 5000d, Nam Trieu Port (2-2).

2005, May 6   *Perf. 13x12¾*
Stamp + Label
3249-3250 A880   Set of 2   2.75 .75

People's Police, 60th Anniv. A881

Medals and: 800d, Marching police, statue of Ho Chi Minh (2-1). 10,000d, Police helping civilians (2-2).

2005, Aug. 10   *Perf. 13*
3251-3252 A881   Set of 2   1.90 1.40

Posts and Telecommunications Dept., 60th Anniv. — A882

2005, Aug. 15   *Perf. 13*
Background Color
3253 A882 800d beige   .90 .25
Souvenir Sheet
Perf. 13½x13¾
3254 A882 8000d gray   1.75 1.25

August Revolution, 60th Anniv. — A883

Crowd with flags in: 1000d, Hanoi (3-1). 2000d, Hué (3-2). 4000d, Saigon (3-3).

2005, Aug. 19   *Perf. 13*
3255-3257 A883   Set of 3   1.50 .90
3257a   Souvenir sheet, #3255-3257   1.50 .90

Traditional Dress and Houses of Ethnic Groups — A884

No. 3258: a, Ba-na (54-1). b, Bo Y (54-2). c, Brau (54-3). d, Bru-Van Kieu (54-4). e, Cham (54-5). f, Cho-ro (54-6). g, Chu-ru (54-7). h, Chut (54-8). i, Co (54-9). j, Cong (54-10). k, Co-ho (54-11). l, Co Lao (54-12). m, Co-tu (54-13). n, Dao (54-14). o, E-de (54-15). p, Gia-rai (54-16) q, Giay (54-17). r, Gie-Trieng (54-18). s, Ha Nhi (54-19). t, Hoa (54-20). u, Hre (54-21). v, Khang (54-22). w, Khmer (54-23). x, Kho-mu (54-24). y, Kinh (54-25). z, La Chi (54-26). aa, La Ha (54-27). ab, La Hu (54-28). ac, Lao (54-29). ad, Lo Lo (54-30). ae, Lu (54-31). af, Ma (54-32). ag, Mang (54-33). ah, Mnong (54-34). ai, Mong (54-35). aj, Muong (54-36). ak, Ngai (54-37). al, Nung (54-38). am, O Du (54-39). an, Pa Then (54-40). ao, Phu La (54-41). ap, Pu Peo (54-42). aq, Ra-glai (54-43). ar, Ro-mam (54-44). as, San Chay (54-45). at, San Diu (54-46). au, Si La (54-47). av, Ta-oi (54-48). aw, Tay (54-49). ax, Thai (54-50). ay, Tho (54-51). az, Xinh-mun (54-52). ba, Xo-dang (54-53). bb, Xtieng (54-54).

Perf. 13¾x13¼ Syncopated
2005, Aug. 30
3258   Sheet of 54 + 2 labels   15.00 15.00
a.-bb.   A884 800d Any single   .25 .25
    Complete booklet, #3258a-3258bb   15.00

Thang Long (Hanoi), 1000th Anniv. A885

People reenacting battles and: 800d, Statue of Gen. Quang Trung, building (3-1). 5000d, Statue of Independence Fighters, building (3-2). No. 3261, 8000d, Statue of Victory Against B-52's, Long Bien Bridge (3-3).
No. 3262, Government officials on dais in Ba Dinh Square.

2005, Oct. 10 Litho. *Perf. 13*
3259-3261 A885 Set of 3 2.75 1.75
Souvenir Sheet
Perf. 13½x13¾
3262 A885 8000d multi 2.50 1.50

New Year 2006 (Year of the Dog) A886

Designs: 800d, Dog and puppies (2-1). 8000d, Dog (2-2).

2005, Dec. 1 *Perf. 13*
3263-3264 A886 Set of 2 2.50 1.10
3264a Souvenir sheet, #3263-3264 3.00 1.25

National Coat of Arms, 50th Anniv. A887

2006, Jan. 16 *Perf. 13*
3265 A887 1000d multi .85 .25

10th Vietnamese Communist Party Congress A888

2006, Feb. 3
3266 A888 800d multi .85 .25

Prime Minister Pham Van Dong (1906-2000) — A889

2006, Mar. 1
3267 A889 800d multi .85 .25

Wolfgang Amadeus Mozart (1756-91), Composer — A890

2006, Mar. 1
3268 A890 2000d multi 1.50 .35

Léopold Senghor (1906-2001), First President of Senegal — A891

2006, Mar. 20 Litho. *Perf. 13*
3269 A891 800d multi .85 .25

BirdLife International A892

Designs: 800d, Lophura edwardsi (5-1). 2000d, Arborophila davidi (5-2). 3000d, Lophura hatinhensis (5-3). 5000d, Polyplectron germaini (5-4, 49x23mm). 8000d, Rheinardia ocellata (5-5, 49x23mm).

Perf. 13¼x14 Syncopated, 13¼x13½ Syncopated (#3273-3274)
2006, Apr. 1
3270-3274 A892 Set of 5 4.50 4.50
3274a Souvenir sheet, #3270-3274 4.50 4.50

2006 World Cup Soccer Championships, Germany — A893

Designs: 800d, One player (1-2). 10,000d, Two players (2-2).

2006, May 1 Litho. *Perf. 13¼x13*
3275-3276 A893 Set of 2 2.50 2.50

Phong Nha - Ke Bang National Park World Heritage Site — A894

Designs: 800d, Bi Ky Cave (3-1). 4000d, Xuyen Son Cave (3-2). 8000d, Nuoc Moc Stream (3-3).
12,000d, Tien Cave, vert.

2006, June 1 *Perf. 13x12¾*
3277-3279 A894 Set of 3 7.50 2.50
Souvenir Sheet
Perf. 13¾x13½
3280 A894 12,000d multi 4.00 2.50
No. 3280 contains one 32x43mm stamp.

Animals in Ben En Botanical Gardens A895

Designs: 800d, Nycticebus bengalensis (4-1). 1000d, Neofelis nebulosa, horiz. (4-2). 7000d, Cuon alpinus, horiz. (4-3). 10,000d, Nomascus leucogenys (4-4).
12,000d, Physignathus cocincinus, horiz.

2006, July 1 *Perf. 13¼x13, 13x13¼*
3281-3284 A895 Set of 4 3.50 3.50
Souvenir Sheet
Perf. 13½x13¾
3285 A895 12,000d multi 3.00 2.50

Flowers — A896

Designs: 800d, Momordica cochinchinensis (4-1). 3000d, Telosma cordata (4-2). 5000d, Momordica charantia (4-3). 8000d, Luffa cylindrica (4-4).

2006, Aug. 1 *Perf. 13*
3286-3289 A896 Set of 4 3.25 3.25

Asia-Pacific Economic Cooperation Summit — A897

2006, Sept. 16
3290 A897 8000d multi 2.25 2.00

Cooperation Between Viet Nam and European Union — A898

2006, Oct. 1 *Perf. 13x13¼*
3291 A898 800d multi 1.00 .25

New Year 2007 (Year of the Pig) A899

Designs: 800d, Pig and piglets (2-1). 8000d, Pig (2-2).

2006, Dec. 15 *Perf. 13*
3292-3293 A899 Set of 2 2.25 2.00

Tran Te Xuong (1870-1907), Poet — A900

2007, Jan. 20 Litho. *Perf. 13x13¼*
3294 A900 1000d multi .70 .40

Implementation of Resolutions of 10th Communist Party Congress — A901

Perf. 13½x13¼ Syncopated
2007, Feb. 3
3295 A901 800d multi .70 .40

Truong Chinh (1907-88), General Secretary of Communist Party — A902

2007, Feb. 9 *Perf. 13x13¼*
3296 A902 800d multi .70 .40

Le Duan (1907-86), First Secretary of Communist Party — A903

2007, Apr. 7
3297 A903 800d multi .70 .40

Dugong Dugon — A904

Various depictions of Dugong dugon: 800d, (4-1). 1000d, (4-2). 7000d, (4-3). 9000d, (4-4).

2007, Aug. 1 Litho. *Perf. 13*
3298-3301 A904 Set of 4 4.25 2.25

Association of South East Asian Nations (ASEAN), 40th Anniv. — A905

Designs: No. 3302, 800d, Secretariat Building, Bandar Seri Begawan, Brunei (10-1). No. 3303, 800d, National Museum of Cambodia (10-2). No. 3304, 800d, Fatahillah Museum, Jakarta, Indonesia (10-3). No. 3305, 800d, Typical house, Laos (10-4). No. 3306, 800d, Malayan Railway Headquarters Building, Kuala Lumpur, Malaysia (10-5). No. 3307, 800d, Yangon Post Office, Myanmar (Burma) (10-6). No. 3308, 800d, Malacañang Palace, Philippines (10-7). No. 3309, 800d, National Museum of Singapore (10-8). No. 3310, 800d, Vimanmek Mansion, Bangkok, Thailand (10-9). No. 3311, 800d, Presidential Palace, Hanoi, Viet Nam (10-10).

2007, Aug. 8 Litho. *Perf. 13x13¼*
3302-3311 A905 Set of 10 5.00 1.25
3311a Miniature sheet of 10, #3302-3311 5.50 1.25

See Brunei No. 607, Burma No. 370, Cambodia No. 2339, Indonesia Nos. 2120-2121, Laos Nos. 1717-1718, Malaysia No. 1170, Philippines Nos. 3103-3105, Singapore No. 1265, and Thailand No. 2315.

Tay Nguyen Tribal Gongs A906

Various tribal members using gongs: 800d, (3-1). 5000d, (3-2). 8000d, (3-3). 12,000d, Man holding gong.

2007, Nov. 21   Litho.   Perf. 13x13¼
3312-3314 A906   Set of 3   3.00 1.75

Souvenir Sheet
3314A A906 12,000d multi   3.00 1.50

New Year 2008 (Year of the Rat) — A907

Designs: 800d, Rat at left (2-1). 8000d, Rat at right (2-2).

2007, Dec. 1   Perf. 13½
3315-3316 A907   Set of 2   2.00 1.10

Ho Chi Minh (1890-1969) A908

Perf. 13¼x13½
2007, Dec. 31   Litho.
3317 A908 1000d dk red & pink   .30 .25
3318 A908 3000d dk & lt green   .50 .30
3319 A908 4000d dk & lt blue   .90 .50
   Nos. 3317-3319 (3)   1.70 1.05

Vietnamese Cuisine — A909

Designs: 800d, Nem rán (2-1). 9000d, Pho bò (2-2).

2008, Feb. 1   Perf. 13x13¼
3320-3321 A909   Set of 2   1.75 1.25

Orchids A910

Designs: 800d, Calanthe densiflora (4-1). 2000d, Ludisia discolor (4-2). 6000d, Spathoglottis affinis (4-3). 8000d, Calanthe argenteo-striata (4-4).

2008, Mar. 1   Litho.   Perf. 13½
3322-3325 A910   Set of 4   3.00 2.10

2008 Summer Olympics, Beijing — A911

Designs: 800d, Wushu (4-1). 3000d, Swimming (4-2). 5000d, Taekwondo (4-3). 9000d, Canoeing (4-4).

Perf. 14x13½ Syncopated
2008, Mar. 15   Litho.
3326-3329 A911   Set of 4   3.25 2.25

Cyprinus Carpio — A912

Various depictions of Cyprinus carpio: 800d, (3-1). 6000d, (3-2). 8000d, (3-3).

2008, Apr. 1   Perf. 13
3330-3332 A912   Set of 3   2.75 1.90

Vinasat-1 Satellite A913

2008, Apr. 19   Perf. 13½
3333 A913 800d multi   .75 .25

Vietnamese Court Music, UNESCO Masterpiece of Intangible Heritage — A914

Inscriptions: 800d, Dai nhac, Bien khanh (3-1). 4000d, Tieu nhac, Dàn Nguyet và Nhi (3-2). 8000d, Luc cúng hoa dang, Kèn Bóp và Sáo (3-3). 9000d, Dai nhac trong le te.

2008, June 3   Litho.   Perf. 13x12¾
3334-3336 A914   Set of 3   2.75 1.60

Souvenir Sheet
Perf. 13x12¾ Syncopated
3337 A914 9000d multi   2.25 1.10
No. 3337 contains one 40x28mm stamp.

Tran Quy Cáp (1870-1908), Progressive Movement Leader — A915

2008, June 8   Litho.   Perf. 13
3338 A915 1000d multi   .60 .25

Binh Thuan Province A916

2008, Sept. 1   Perf. 13x12¾
3339 A916 800d multi   .60 .25

Seascapes of France and Viet Nam — A917

Designs: 800d, Strait of Bonifacio, France (2-1). 14,000d, Along Bay, Viet Nam (2-2).

2008, Oct. 15
3340-3341 A917   Set of 2   3.00 1.75
See France Nos. 3519-3520.

Lady Trieu's Rebellion, A.D. 248 — A918

Perf. 13¼x13½ Syncopated
2008, Oct. 20
3342 A918 1000d multi   .60 .25

Flowers A919

Designs: 800d, Ceiba chodatii (2-1). 10,000d, Nelumbo nucifera (2-2).

2008, Oct. 25   Perf. 13
3343-3344 A919   Set of 2   2.00 1.40
See Argentina Nos. 2508-2509.

Fruit — A920

Designs: 2000d, Durio zibetinus (2-1). 8000d, Hylocereus undatus (2-2).

2008, Nov. 18   Litho.   Perf. 13½
3345-3346 A920   Set of 2   2.00 1.25
See Singapore Nos. 1352-1353.

New Year 2009 (Year of the Ox) — A921

Designs: 2000d, Ox (2-1). 9000d, Ox and calf (2-2).

2008, Dec. 1   Litho.   Perf. 13½
3347-3348 A921   Set of 2   2.00 1.40
3348a   Souvenir sheet, #3347-3348   2.50 1.40

Nguyen Khuyen (1835-1909), Poet — A922

2009, Feb. 2   Litho.   Perf. 13¼x13
3349 A922 2000d multi   .50 .50

Charles Darwin (1809-82), Naturalist A923

2009, Feb. 12   Perf. 13
3350 A923 2000d multi   .75 .50

Border and Coast Guard's Day — A924

2009, Mar. 3   Perf. 13¼x13
3351 A924 2000d multi   .50 .50

Bamboo Lamps Type of 2004
Perf. 13 Syncopated
2009, May 15   Litho.
Background Color
Design of No. 3211
3352 A862   1200d yellow (12-1)   .25 .25
3353 A862   2000d lt green (12-2)   .25 .25
3354 A862   2500d blue (12-3)   .40 .30
3355 A862   4500d gray blue (12-4)   .60 .50

Design of No. 3212
3356 A862   5000d gray green (12-5)   .65 .55
3357 A862   6500d brn vio (12-6)   1.00 .75
3358 A862   9500d violet (12-7)   1.25 1.10
3359 A862   10,500d red (12-8)   1.50 .75

Design of No. 3213
3360 A862   13,500d fawn (12-9)   1.25 1.00
3361 A862   14,500d brn yel (12-10)   1.50 1.40
3362 A862   17,500d drab (12-11)   2.50 1.75
3363 A862   18,500d olive grn (12-12)   2.50 1.90
   Nos. 3352-3363 (12)   13.65 10.50

Opening of the Ho Chi Minh Trail, 50th Anniv. A925

2009, May 19   Perf. 13
3364 A925 2000d multi   .60 .30

Praying Mantises
A926

Designs: 1500d, Mantis religiosa (2-1). 12,500d, Tenodera aridiforia (2-2).

2009, July 1   Litho.   *Perf. 13½*
3365-3366   A926   Set of 2   2.00 1.60

Rhododendrons — A927

Designs: 500d, Rhododendron fortunei (4-1). 1200d, Rhododendron simsii (4-2). 4500d, Rhododendron sp. (4-3). 14,500d, Enkianthus quinqueflorus (4-4).

Perf. 13¼x13¾ Syncopated
2009, Aug. 1
3367-3370   A927   Set of 4   4.00 2.40

Fish
A928

Designs: 2000d, Botia macracanthus (4-1). 3000d, Trichopsis pumila (4-2). 6500d, Cynolebias elongatus (4-3). 10,500d, Centropyge flavissima (4-4). 14,500d Scleropages formosus.

2009, Sept. 1   *Perf. 13*
3371-3374   A928   Set of 4   3.25 2.75
Souvenir Sheet
Perf. 13½x13¾
3375   A928   14,500d multi   3.50 1.75

New Year 2010 (Year of the Tiger) A929

Tiger: 2000d, Walking (2-1). 8500d, Sitting (2-2).

2009, Dec. 1   Litho.   *Perf. 13x13¼*
3376-3377   A929   Set of 2   2.25 1.25

Viet Nam Communist Party, 80th Anniv. — A930

2010, Feb. 2   Litho.   *Perf. 13¼x13*
3378   A930   2000d multi   .60 .25

Frédéric Chopin (1810-49), Composer — A931

2010, Feb. 22   Litho.   *Perf. 13*
3379   A931   2000d multi   .60 .25

Intl. Women's Day A932

2010, Mar. 3   Litho.   *Perf. 13x13¼*
3380   A932   3000d multi   .70 .40

Pres. Ho Chi Minh (1890-1969) A933

2010, May 16   Litho.   *Perf. 13*
3381   A933   2000d multi   .50 .30

BirdLife International — A934

Birds: 2000d, Tringa guttifer. 6500d, Calidris pygmeus. 8500d, Larus saundersi. 14,500d, Rynchops albicollis.

2010, May 25   Litho.   *Perf. 13x13¼*
3382-3384   A934   Set of 3   2.50 2.00
Souvenir Sheet
Perf. 13½x13¾
3385   A934   14,500d multi   2.50 1.60

Nguyen Huu Tho (1910-96), Acting President — A935

2010, July 10   *Perf. 13x13¼*
3386   A935   2000d multi   .50 .40

Ta Quang Buu (1910-86), Minister of Higher and Secondary Professional Education — A936

2010, July 27
3387   A936   2000d multi   .50 .40

Fairy Lilies — A937

Designs: 3500d, Zephyranthes carinata. 10,500d, Zephyranthes ajax.

Perf. 14x13½ Syncopated
2010, July 30
3388-3389   A937   Set of 2   2.50 2.50
Bangkok 2010 Intl. Philatelic Exhibition.

Worldwide Fund for Nature (WWF) — A938

Prionailurus viverrinus: 2000d, At water's edge, facing right. 2500d, In water with fish in mouth. 4500d, Standing on rocks, facing left. 10,500d, Sitting.

2010, Aug. 1   Litho.   *Perf. 13*
3390-3393   A938   Set of 4   3.50 3.25
3393a   Miniature sheet of 8, 2 each #3390-3393   7.00 7.00

Hanoi, 1000th Anniv. A939

Dragon and: 2000d, Banner, Hanoi Flag Tower. 2500d, Quan Chuong City Gate, National Conference Center, apartment buildings. 4500d, Long Bien Bridge, Nhật Tân Bridge. 6500d, Hanoi Train Station, Noi Bài Airport. 14,000d, Highways, graduate, computer operators, vert.

2010, Oct. 2   *Perf. 13x13¼*
3394-3397   A939   Set of 4   2.75 2.75
Souvenir Sheet
Perf. 13¾x13½
3398   A939   14,000d multi   2.50 2.50

Viet Nam Stamp Association, 50th Anniv. — A940

2010, Oct. 3   *Perf. 13x13¼*
3399   A940   2000d multi   .70 .40

Viet Nam Membership in Association of South East Asian Nations (ASEAN), 15th Anniv. — A941

2010, Oct. 27
3400   A941   8500d multi   1.50 1.50

New Year 2011 (Year of the Cat) — A942

Cat: 2000d, Sitting. 10,500d, Lying down.

2010, Dec. 1   *Perf. 13½*
3401-3402   A942   Set of 2   2.25 2.25

Diplomatic Relations Between Viet Nam and Cuba, 50th Anniv. A943

2010, Dec. 2
3403   A943   2000d multi   .50 .40

11th Congress of Vietnamese Communist Party — A944

2011, Jan. 5   *Perf. 13¼x13*
3404   A944   2000d multi   .50 .40

UNESCO Intangible Heritage Quan Ho Bac Ninh Folk Songs — A945

Singers: 3000d, Two men with umbrella, two women with hats. 4500d, Two men and two women seated, horiz. 10,500d, Two men with umbrella in boat, two women holding hats. 12,500d, Men and women in boat, horiz.

2011, Jan. 15   *Perf. 13¼x13, 13x13¼*
3405-3407   A945   Set of 3   1.90 1.90
Souvenir Sheet
Perf. 13½x13¾
3408   A945   12,500d multi   1.40 1.40

Ho Chi Minh Communist Youth Union, 80th Anniv. — A946

2011, Mar. 26   Litho.   *Perf. 13*
3409   A946   2000d multi   .90 .30

Phú Yên, 400th Anniv. — A947

2011, Mar. 31   **Perf. 13x12¾**
3410 A947 2000d multi   .70 .30

Fauna in Ba Be National Park A948

Designs: 2000d, Muntiacus muntjac (4-1). 3500d, Gorsachius magnificus (4-2). 6000d, Acanthosaura lepidogaster (4-3). 8500d, Pyxidea mouhoti (4-4). 14,500d, Catopuma temminckii.

2011, May 15   **Perf. 13**
3411-3414 A948   Set of 4   2.50 2.50
Souvenir Sheet
Perf. 13½x13¾
3415 A948 14,500d multi   1.50 1.50

Ho Chi Minh 's Departure From Viet Nam, Cent. — A949

2011, June 5   **Perf. 13**
3416 A949 2000d multi   .40 .30

Ernest Hemingway (1899-1961), Writer A950

2011, July 2   **Perf. 13½**
3417 A950 10,500d multi   1.25 1.25

Dragonflies A951

Designs: 2000d, Lyriothemis mortoni (4-1). 2500d, Trithemis aurora (4-2). 6500d, Rhyothemis obsolescens (4-3). 10,500d, Ictinogomphus decoratus (4-4).

2011, July 11   **Perf. 13½**
3418-3421 A951   Set of 4   2.75 2.75
PhilaNippon '11 Intl. Philatelic Exhibition, Yokohama.

Tran Van Giau (1911-2010), Revolutionary Activist — A952

2011, Sept. 6   **Perf. 13**
3422 A952 2000d multi   .40 .30

Decade for Road Safety — A953

Designs: 2000d, Traffic light, police officer teaching students traffic signs (2-1). 6500d, People crossing street in crosswalk (2-2).

2011, Oct. 1   **Litho.**
3423-3424 A953   Set of 2   1.50 1.25

Mikhail Lomonosov (1711-65), Scientist — A954

2011, Nov. 19
3425 A954 8500d multi   1.25 1.25

New Year 2012 (Year of the Dragon) A955

Dragon with background color of: 2000d, Bright pink (2-1). 10,500d, Olive green (2-2).

2011, Dec. 1   **Perf. 13x13¼**
3426-3427 A955   Set of 2   1.75 1.75

One-Pillar Pagoda, Hanoi — A956   Keo Pagoda, Vu Thu — A957

Bridge Pagoda, Hoi An — A958

Perf. 13¾x13½ Syncopated
2012, Jan. 16
3428 A956   2000d rose carmine   .30 .25
3429 A956   3000d green   .40 .35
3430 A957   3500d brn orange   .45 .40
3431 A957   4500d red lilac   .60 .60

Perf. 13½x13¾ Syncopated
3432 A958   6500d blue   .90 .80
3433 A958   10,500d red   1.40 1.25
    Nos. 3428-3433 (6)   3.00 3.00

Ao Dais — A959

Designs: 2500d, Woman in brown ao dai with hat (4-1). 3000d, Woman in orange ao dai, woman in red ao dai (4-2). 6000d, Woman in red ao dai holding hat, woman in blue ao dai (4-3). 10,500d, Woman in blue ao dai standing, woman in purple ao dai seated (4-4).

2012, Mar. 8   **Perf. 13**
3434-3437 A959   Set of 4   3.00 3.00

Campaign Against Tuberculosis — A960

2012, Mar. 24
3438 A960 2000d multi   .40 .30

Asian Pacific Postal Union, 50th Anniv. A961

2012, Apr. 1
3439 A961 3000d multi   .60 .40

Bears A962

Designs: 2000d, Ursus thibetanus (4-1). 4500d, Ursus malayanus (4-2). 8500d, Ursus malayanus, diff. (4-3). 10,500d, Ursus thibetanus, diff. (4-4). 14,500d, Ursus thibetanus, diff.

2012, Apr. 1   **Perf. 13x13¼**
3440-3443 A962   Set of 4   3.00 3.00
Souvenir Sheet
Perf. 13½x13¾
3444 A962 14,500d multi   2.00 1.75

Tiled Covered Bridges — A963

Bridge in: 2000d, Huong Thuy (3-1). 3000d, Kim Son (3-2). 12,000d, Hai Hau (3-3).

2012, Apr. 8   **Perf. 13**
3445-3447 A963   Set of 3   2.50 2.00

Nguyen Huy Tuong (1912-60), Writer — A964

2012, May 6   **Perf. 13x13¼**
3448 A964 2000d multi   .40 .30

Ton That Tung (1912-82), Physician — A965

2012, May 10
3449 A965 2000d multi   .40 .30

Plumeria Flowers A966

Designs: 2500d, Plumeria rubra (2-1). 8500d, Plumeria obtusa (2-2).

2012, May 15
3450-3451 A966   Set of 2   1.50 1.50

Pham Hung (1912-88), Politician — A967

2012, June 11   **Perf. 13**
3452 A967 2000d multi   .40 .30

Nguyen Van Cu (1912-41), Communist Party General Secretary — A968

2012, July 9
3453 A968 2000d multi   .40 .30

2012 Summer Olympics, London A969

Designs: 2000d, Weight lifting (4-1). 3500d, Fencing (4-2). 8500d, Gymnast on pommel horse (4-3). 12,000d, Taekwondo (4-4).

2012, July 12   **Perf. 13½**
3454-3457 A969   Set of 4   3.00 3.00

Flags, Laotian Prime Minister Kaysone Phomivane and Vietnamese President Ho Chi Minh — A970

Buildings in Laos and Viet Nam — A971

2012, July 18   **Perf. 13**
3458 A970   2000d multi   .25   .25
3459 A971   12,000d multi   1.60   1.60

See Laos Nos. 1860-1861.

Monument to Heroic Mothers, Thach Phu — A972

2012, July 27   **Perf. 13¼x13**
3460 A972   2000d multi   .40   .30

Vo Chi Cong (1912-2011), Politician — A973

2012, Aug. 7   **Perf. 13**
3461 A973   2000d multi   .40   .30

Vu Trong Phung (1912-39), Writer — A974

2012, Oct. 20   **Perf. 13¼x13**
3462 A974   2000d multi   .40   .30

Nguyen Thi Minh Khai (1910-41), Communist Party Leader — A975

2012, Nov. 23   **Perf. 13x13¼**
3463 A975   2000d multi   .40   .30

New Year 2013 (Year of the Snake) A976

Various snakes and flowers in: 2000d, Orange (2-1). 10,500d, Red violet (2-2).

2012, Dec. 1   **Perf. 13½**
3464-3465 A976   Set of 2   2.00   1.25

Huynh Tan Phat (1913-89), Politician — A977

2013, Feb. 15   **Litho.**   **Perf. 13**
3466 A977   2000d multi   .40   .25

Vovinam (Vietnamese Martial Arts) — A978

Various combatants with frame color of: 2000d, Orange yellow (3-1). 6500d, Lilac (3-2). 8500d, Green (3-3).

2013, Mar. 1   **Litho.**   **Perf. 13**
3467-3469 A978   Set of 3   2.50   1.75

Orchids — A979

Designs: 2000d, Dendrobium aphyllum (3-1). 2500d, Dendrobium chrysotoxum (3-2). 17,500d, Dendrobium draconis (3-3).

2013, Apr. 1   **Litho.**   **Perf. 13**
3470-3472 A979   Set of 3   2.50   2.10

Lighthouses A980

Designs: 2000d, Diêm Diên Lighthouse (4-1). 3000d, Quang Ngai Lighthouse (4-2). 6000d, Dai Lanh Lighthouse (4-3). 14,500d, Kê Gà Lighthouse (4-4).

2013, May 15   **Litho.**   **Perf. 13¼x13**
3473-3476 A980   Set of 4   2.50   2.50

Birds in Xuân Thuy National Park A981

Designs: 2000d, Platalea minor (4-1). 3500d, Limnodromus semipalmatus (4-2). 6500d, Anas clypeata (4-3). 10,500d, Vanellus cinereus (4-4). 15,000d, Pelecanus philippensis.

2013, June 1   **Litho.**   **Perf. 13**
3477-3480 A981   Set of 4   3.25   2.25
     Souvenir Sheet
3481 A981   15,000d multi   2.50   1.50

Musical Instruments A982

Designs: 2000d, Ta lu (3-1). 4500d, Kloong put, horiz. (3-2). 12,000d, Goong (3-3).

2013, July 15   **Litho.**   **Perf. 13**
3482-3484 A982   Set of 3   3.50   1.75

Birds A983

Designs: 2000d, Gallus gallus (2-1). 10,500d, Polyplectron bicalcaratum (2-2).

2013, Sept. 12   **Litho.**   **Perf. 13x13¼**
3485-3486 A983   Set of 2   1.75   1.25

Diplomatic relations between Viet Nam and Singapore, 40th anniv. See Singapore Nos. 1626-1627.

Tran Dai Nghia (1913-97), Military Engineer — A984

2013, Sept. 13   **Litho.**   **Perf. 13**
3487 A984   2000d multi   .40   .25

Alexandre Yersin (1863-1943), Bacteriologist — A985

Yersin as: 2000d, Young man (2-1). 18,500d, Older man (2-2).

2013, Sept. 22   **Litho.**   **Perf. 13**
3488-3489 A985   Set of 2   2.50   2.00

See France Nos. 4480-4481.

Rudolf Diesel (1858-1913), Inventor — A986

2013, Sept. 29   **Litho.**   **Perf. 13¼x13**
3490 A986   2000d multi   .40   .25

Tran Huu Tuóc (1913-83), Physician — A987

2013, Oct. 13   **Litho.**   **Perf. 13x13¼**
3491 A987   2000d multi   .40   .25

New Year 2014 (Year of the Horse) A988

Horse with background color of: 2000d, Orange (2-1). 10,500d, Red violet (2-2).

2013, Dec. 1   **Litho.**   **Perf. 13½**
3492-3493 A988   Set of 2   1.75   1.25

This stamp depicting Nguyen Chi Thanh, released Dec. 31, 2013, was a gift for standing order customers. It was not made available for sale. Value, $1.25.

Tree Frogs A989

Designs: 3000d, Rhacophorus puerensis (5-1). 4500d, Rhacophorus annamensis (5-2). 6000d, Rhacophorus robertingeri (5-3). 8000d, Rhacophorus kio (5-4). 10,000d, Rhacophorus rhodopus (5-5).

2014, Apr. 1   **Litho.**   **Perf. 13**
3494-3498 A989   Set of 5   4.50   3.00

Battle of Dien Bien Phu, 60th Anniv. A990

2014, May 5   **Litho.**   **Perf. 13**
3499 A990   3000d multi   .60   .30

Ca Trù Singing, UNESCO Intangible Cultural Heritage A991

Various musicians and singers: 3000d, (3-1). 8500d, (3-2). 10,500d (3-3). 16,000d, Ca trù musicians and singers, diff.

2014, June 1   Litho.   *Perf. 13*
3500-3502 A991   Set of 3   2.25 1.60
Souvenir Sheet
Perf. 13½x13¾
3503 A991 16,000d multi   2.00 1.50

Ngo Mon (Gate of Noon), Hué — A992

Opera House, Ho Chi Minh City — A993

Main Post Office, Ho Chi Minh City — A994

Perf. 13½x13¾ Syncopated
2014, July 1   Litho.
3504 A992   3000d purple   .40 .30
3505 A992   6000d emerald   .75 .55
3506 A993   6500d blue   .80 .60
3507 A993   8000d brown   .90 .75
3508 A994   10,000d red   1.25 .95
3509 A994   12,000d ol brn   1.50 1.10
    Nos. 3504-3509 (6)   5.60 4.25

Endangered Primates A995

Designs: 3000d, Rhinopithecus avunculus (4-1). 5500d, Trachypithecus poliocephalus (4-2). 8500d, Pygathrix cinerea (4-3). 12,500d, Trachypithecus delacouri (4-4). 18,000d, Nomascus nasutus.

2014, Aug. 11   Litho.   *Perf. 13*
3510-3513 A995   Set of 4   4.00 2.75
Souvenir Sheet
Perf. 13¾x13½
3514 A995 18,000d multi   2.50 1.75
25th Intl. Primatological Society Congress, Hanoi.

Truong Dinh (1820-64), Anti-Colonial Military Leader — A996

2014, Aug. 20   Litho.   *Perf. 13*
3515 A996 3000d multi   .60 .30

Lê Trong Tan (1914-86), General — A997

2014, Oct. 1   Litho.   *Perf. 13*
3516 A997 3000d multi   .60 .30

New Year 2015 (Year of the Goat) A998

Goats and flowers with background color of: 3000d, Yellow (2-1). 10,500d, Pink (2-2).

2014, Dec. 1   Litho.   *Perf. 13½*
3517-3518 A998   Set of 2   1.75 1.25

Trang An UNESCO World Heritage Site — A999

Designs: 3000d, Den vua Dinh Tiên Hoàng (Co dô Hoa Lu) (3-1). 7000d, Sông Ngô Dong (Tam Coc - Bích Dong) (3-2). 12,000d, Hang Toi (Tràng An) (3-3). 14,000d, Ceremony at temple.

2015, Jan. 23   Litho.   *Perf. 13x13¼*
3519-3521 A999   Set of 3   2.75 2.10
Souvenir Sheet
Perf. 13½x13¾
3522 A999 14,000d multi   1.40 1.40
No. 3522 contains one 43x32mm stamp.

Worship of Hung Kings UNESCO Intangible Cultural Heritage — A1000

Designs: 3000d, Gate, procession (3-1). 7000d, Incense stick holder, worshipers (3-2). 8500d, Rice cakes, worshipers (3-3). 14,000d, Temple.

2015, Apr. 23   Litho.   *Perf. 13*
3523-3525 A1000   Set of 3   2.00 1.75
Souvenir Sheet
Perf. 13½x13¾
3526 A1001 14,000d multi   1.40 1.40

General Hoang Van Thai (1915-86) A1002

2015, May 7   Litho.   *Perf. 13*
3527 A1002 3000d multi   .60 .30

Nguyen Van Linh (1915-98), Communist Party General Secretary — A1003

2015, July 1   Litho.   *Perf. 13*
3528 A1003 3000d multi   .60 .30

Flags and Emblems of Association of South East Asian Nations A1004

2015, Aug. 7   Litho.   *Perf. 13½*
3529 A1004 3000d multi   .60 .30
    a.   Miniature sheet of 10   6.00 6.00
See Brunei No. 656, Burma Nos. 417-418, Cambodia No. , Indonesia No. 2428, Laos No. , Malaysia No. 1562, Philippines No. 3619, Singapore No., Thailand No. 2875.

Viet Nam Posts and Telecommunications, 70th Anniv. — A1005

2015, Aug. 14   Litho.   *Perf. 13*
3530 A1005 3000d multi   .60 .30

Climate Change A1006

Designs: No. 3531, 3000d, Leaf (4-1). No. 3532, 3000d, Wind generator, satellite dish, satellite, helicopter, ship (4-2). 4500d, Wind generator, buildings, foliage (4-3). 12,000d, Globe clock, hands (4-4).

2015, Oct. 14   Litho.   *Perf. 13*
3531-3534 A1006   Set of 4   2.50 2.00

Beetles A1007

Designs: No. 3535, 3000d, Odontolabis cuvera fallaciosa (4-1). No. 3536, 3000d, Cheirotonus battareli (4-2). 4500d, Dorcus titanus westermanni (4-3). 8000d, Jumnos ruckeri tonkinensis (4-4).

2015, Oct. 20   Litho.   *Perf. 13½*
3535-3538 A1007   Set of 4   2.50 1.75
3538a   Souvenir sheet of 4,   2.25 1.75
    #3535-3538

New Year 2016 (Year of the Monkey) A1008

Flowers and: 3000d, Monkey (2-1). 10,500d, Adult and juvenile monkeys (2-2).

2015, Dec. 1   Litho.   *Perf. 13½*
3539-3540 A1008   Set of 2   1.75 1.25

A1009

Nguyen Du (1765-1820), Poet — A1010

2015, Dec. 5   Litho.   *Perf. 13*
3541 A1009   3000d multi   .60 .30
Souvenir Sheet
Perf. 13¾x13½
3542 A1010 15,000d multi   1.75 1.40

Civil Aviation Department, 60th Anniv. — A1011

2016, Jan. 10   Litho.   *Perf. 13*
3543 A1011 3000d multi   .50 .30
    Complete booklet, 10 #3543   5.00

12th Congress of Viet Nam Communist Party — A1012

2016, Jan. 18   Litho.   *Perf. 13*
3544 A1012 3000d multi   .50 .30

Xuan Dieu (1916-85), Poet A1013

2016, Feb. 2   Litho.   *Perf. 13*
3545 A1013 3000d multi   .50   .30

Barringtonia Asiatica — A1014

Designs: 3000d, Flowers (2-1). 6000d, Plant near coast (2-2).

2016, Apr. 2   Litho.   *Perf. 13*
3546-3547 A1014   Set of 2   1.10   .80
3547a   Souvenir sheet of 4, 2 each #3546-3547   2.25   1.60

William Shakespeare (1564-1616), Writer A1015

2016, Apr. 23   Litho.   *Perf. 13½*
3548 A1015 3000d multi   .50   .30
  Complete booklet, 10 #3548   5.00

Relations Between Portugal and Viet Nam, 500th Anniv. A1016

Flags of Portugal and Viet Nam and: 3000d, Vietnamese ceramic vessel, view of Hoi An (2-1). 12,000d, Portuguese ceramic plate, view of Lisbon (2-2).

2016, July 1   Litho.   *Perf. 13*
3549-3550 A1016   Set of 2   1.75   1.40
See Portugal Nos. 3803-3804.

Diplomatic Relations Between Thailand and Viet Nam, 40th Anniv. — A1017

Designs: 3000d, Vietnamese figurines in boat (2-1). 10,500d, Thai figurines in boat (2-2).

2016, Aug. 6   Litho.   *Perf. 13*
3551 A1017   3000d multi   .30   .30
3552 A1017   10,500d multi   .95   .95
  a.   Souvenir sheet of 4, 2 each #3551-3552   2.50   2.50
  Complete booklet, 4 #3551, 4 #3552   5.00
See Thailand No. 2927.

Worldwide Fund for Nature (WWF) — A1018

Aonyx cinerea: No. 3553, 3000d, Two otters in water (4-1). No. 3554, 3000d, Otter eating fish (4-2). 4500d, Two otters on shore (4-3). 8500d, Two otters on rocks. (4-4).

2016, Sept. 1   Litho.   *Perf. 13*
3553-3556 A1018   1.75   1.75
3556a   Souvenir sheet of 8, 2 each #3553-3556   3.50   3.50
  Complete booklet, 2 each #3553-3556   3.50

Fifth Asian Beach Games, Da Nang — A1019

Designs: 3000d, Beach volleyball (2-1). 8500d, Rowing (2-2).

2016, Sept. 24   Litho.   *Perf. 13*
Stamp + Label
3557-3558 A1019   Set of 2   .85   .85
3558a   Miniature sheet of 8, 4 each #3557-3558, + 8 labels   3.50   3.50
  Complete booklet, #3558a   3.50

Dò'n Ca Tài Tu Musicians (UNESCO Intangible Cultural Heritage List) — A1020

Various musicians: 3000d, On rug by tree (3-1). 4500d, On boats (3-2). 8000d, On rug in front of building (3-3).
12,000d, Two singers.

2016, Oct. 10   Litho.   *Perf. 13x12¾*
3559-3561 A1020   Set of 3   1.40   1.40
Souvenir Sheet
Perf. 13½x13¾
3562 A1020   12,000d multi   1.10   1.10
No. 3562 contains one 43x32mm stamp.

Jack London (1876-1916), Writer — A1021

2016, Nov. 22   Litho.   *Perf. 13x13¼*
3563 A1021 3000d multi   .50   .30
  Complete booklet, 10 #3563   5.00

New Year 2017 (Year of the Rooster) A1022

Designs: 3000d, One rooster (2-1). 10,500d, Two roosters (2-2).

2016, Dec. 20   Litho.   *Perf. 13½*
3564-3565 A1022   Set of 2   1.40   1.25
  Complete booklet, 4 each #3564-3565   5.50

National Tourism Day — A1023

Designs: 3000d, Terraced fields, Lào Cai (2-1). 10,500d, Monument on peak of Fanispan (2-2).

2017, Feb. 13   Litho.   *Perf. 13¼x13*
3566-3567 A1023   Set of 2   1.25   1.25

Markets — A1024

Designs: 3000d, Cho Vùng Cao (3-1). 4500d, Cho Làng (3-2). 6000d, Cho Sông Nuóc (3-3).

2017, Mar. 1   Litho.   *Perf. 13x12¾*
3568-3570 A1024   Set of 3   1.25   1.25

General Van Tien Dung (1917-2002) — A1025

2017, Apr. 28   Litho.   *Perf. 13*
3571 A1025 3000d multi   .30   .30

Panax Vietnamensis — A1026

Ginseng root and ginseng plant with: 3000d, Red flower. 12,000d, Flower.

2017, June 10   Litho.   *Perf. 13*
3572 A1026   3000d multi   .30   .30
  Complete booklet, 10 #3572   3.00
Souvenir Sheet
Perf. 13½x13¾
3573 A1026   12,000d multi   1.10   1.10

Nelumbo Nucifera A1027

2017, Aug. 8   Litho.   *Perf. 13*
3574 A1027 3000d multi   .30   .30
  Complete booklet, 10 #3574   3.00
Association of Southeast Asian Nations, 50th anniv.

General Vo Nguyen Giáp (1911-2013) — A1028

2017, Aug. 25   Litho.   *Perf. 13*
3575 A1028 3000d multi   .30   .30
  Complete booklet, 10 #3575   3.00
Souvenir Sheet
Perf. 13½x13¾
3576 A1028 12,000d multi   1.10   1.10

Artifacts From Hanoi Citadel UNESCO World Heritage Site — A1029

Various artifacts with frame color of: No. 3577, 3000d, Flesh (3-1). No. 3578. 3000d, Light blue (3-2). 8000d, Light yellow green (3-3).
12,000d, Artifact, diff.

2017, Oct. 10   Litho.   *Perf. 13*
3577-3579 A1029   Set of 3   1.25   1.25
Souvenir Sheet
Perf. 13¾x13½
3580 A1029 12,000d multi   1.10   1.10

Asia-Pacific Economic Cooperation Economic Leaders Meeting, Da Nang — A1030

2017, Nov. 6   Litho.   *Perf. 13*
3581 A1030 3000d multi   .30   .30
  Complete booklet, 10 #3581   3.00

Russian October Revolution, Cent. — A1031

2017, Nov. 7   Litho.   *Perf. 13*
3582 A1031 3000d multi   .30   .30
  Complete booklet, 10 #3582   3.00

Trung Vuong High School. Hanoi, Cent. — A1032

2017, Nov. 11   Litho.   *Perf. 13*
3583 A1032 3000d multi   .30   .30
  Complete booklet, 10 #3583   3.00

New Year 2018 (Year of the Dog) A1033

Designs: 3000d, Dog (2-1). 10,500d, Dog and puppy (2-2).

2017, Dec. 1   Litho.   Perf. 13½
3584-3585 A1033   Set of 2   1.25 1.25
    Complete booklet, 4 #3584, 4
    #3585   5.00

Phan Boi Châu (1867-1940), Founder of Reformation Society — A1034

Perf. 13¼x13½
2017, Dec. 26   Litho.
3586 A1034 3000d multi   .30 .30

Sanchi Stupa, India A1035

Pho Minh Pagoda, Viet Nam — A1036

2018, Jan. 25   Litho.   Perf. 13
3587 A1035 3000d multi   .30 .30
3588 A1036 10,500d multi   .95 .95

See India Nos. 2992-2993.

Tet Offensive, 50th Anniv. — A1037

2018, Feb. 8   Litho.   Perf. 13
3589 A1037 3000d multi   .30 .30

Nguyen Binh (1918-66), Poet A1038

2018, Feb. 13   Litho.   Perf. 13
3590 A1038 3000d multi   .30 .30
Souvenir Sheet
Perf. 13½x13¾
3591 A1038 12,000d multi   1.10 1.10

Bauhinia Variegata A1039

Flowers with denomination at: 3000d, LL (2-1). 8500d, LR (2-2). 14,000d, Flowers, vert.

2018, Mar. 1   Litho.   Perf. 13
3592-3593 A1039   Set of 2   1.00 1.00
    Complete booklet, 4 each #3592,
    3593   4.00
Souvenir Sheet
Perf. 13¾x13½
3594 A1039 14,000d multi   1.25 1.25

Dr. Martin Luther King, Jr. (1929-68), Civil Rights Leader A1040

2018, Apr. 4   Litho.   Perf. 13½
3595 A1040 3000d multi   .30 .30
    Complete booklet, 10 #3595   3.00

Karl Marx (1818-83), Political Theorist A1041

2018, May 5   Litho.   Perf. 13½
3596 A1041 3000d multi   .30 .30
    Complete booklet, 10 #3596   3.00

Anti-Smoking Campaign A1042

2018, May 31   Litho.   Perf. 13½
3597 A1042 3000d multi   .30 .30
    Complete booklet, 10 #3597   3.00

Marine Life A1043

Designs: No. 3598, 3000d, Nautilus pompilius (4-1). No. 3599, 3000d, Trochus niloticus (4-2). No. 3600, 3000d, Tridacna maxima (4-3). 10,500d, Mauritia scurra (4-4). 12,000d, Charonia tritonis.

2018, June 23   Litho.   Perf. 13
3598-3601 A1043   Set of 4   1.75 1.75
3601a   Booklet pane of 8, 2 each
            #3598-3601   3.50 —
    Complete booklet, #3601a   3.50
Souvenir Sheet
Perf. 13½x13¾
3602 A1043 12,000d multi   1.10 1.10

Citadel of the Ho Dynasty UNESCO World Heritage Site A1044

Designs: 3000d, East Gate (3-1). 4500d, West Gate (3-2). 6000d, North Gate (3-3). 12,000d, South Gate.

2018, June 27   Litho.   Perf. 13
3603-3605 A1044   Set of 3   1.25 1.25
Souvenir Sheet
Perf. 13½x13¾
3606 A1044 12,000d multi   1.10 1.10

Tra Co Communal House, Mong Cai — A1045

2018, July 12   Litho.   Perf. 13
3607 A1045 3000d multi   .30 .30
    Complete booklet, 10 #3607   3.00

Fauna of Kon Ka Kinh National Park A1046

Designs: No. 3608, 3000d, Garrulax konkakinhensis (4-1). No. 3609, 3000d, Acanthosaura nataliae, vert. (4-2). 6500d, Muntiacus truongsonensis (4-3). 10,500d, Pyrops spinolae, vert (4-4).

2018, Aug. 18   Litho.   Perf. 13
3608-3611 A1046   Set of 4   2.00 2.00
3611a   Souvenir sheet of 4, #3608-
            3611, perf. 13½x13¾,
            13¾x13½   2.00 2.00

Bronze Belt Buckle A1047

Bronze Jar — A1048

Bronze Sword A1049

Bronze Lantern A1050

2018, Oct. 1   Litho.   Perf. 13½
3612 A1047 3000d multi   .25 .25
3613 A1048 4000d multi   .35 .35
3614 A1049 6000d multi   .55 .55
3615 A1050 8000d multi   .70 .70
    a.   Block or horiz. strip of 4,
            #3612-3615   1.90 1.90
    Complete booklet, 2 each
    #3612-3615   3.80 3.80
    Nos. 3612-3615 (4)   1.85 1.85

National treasures from the Dong Son Bronze Age culure.

Nguyen Trung Truc (1838-68), Anti-Colonial Militia Leader, and Sinking of French Ship L'Espérance — A1051

2018, Oct. 6   Litho.   Perf. 13
3616 A1051 3000d multi   .25 .25

Nguyen Hong (1918-82), Writer A1052

2018, Nov. 5   Litho.   Perf. 13
3617 A1052 4000d multi   .35 .35

New Year 2010 (Year of the Pig) — A1053

Pig with head at: 4000d, Right (2-1). 15,000d, Left (2-2).

2018, Dec. 1   Litho.   Perf. 13½
3618-3619 A1053   Set of 2   1.75 1.75
3619a   Souvenir sheet of 8, 4 each
            #3618-3619   7.00 7.00
    Complete booklet, 4 each #3618,
    3619   7.00

Nelson Mandela (1918-2013), President of South Africa — A1054

2018, Dec. 5   Litho.   Perf. 13
3620 A1054 4000d multi   .35 .35
    Complete booklet, 10 #3620   3.50

Diep Minh Chau (1919-2002),
Sculptor — A1055

2019, Feb. 10   Litho.   *Perf. 13*
3621 A1055 4000d multi   .35   .35

Hanoi Summit Meeting of U.S. Pres.
Donald Trump and North Korean
Chairman Kim Jong Un
A1056

2019, Feb. 26   Litho.   *Perf. 13*
3622 A1056 4000d multi   .35   .35
     Complete booklet, 10 #3622   3.50
  a. Miniature sheet of 8   3.00   3.00

SEMI-POSTAL STAMPS

World Communications Year — SP1

No. B1, Hands holding envelope with ITU
emblem. No. B2, Satellite dish antenna.

Unwmk.
1983, Nov. 1   Litho.   *Perf. 11*
B1-B2 SP1 50xu +10xu Set of 2 3.50   .80

AIR POST STAMP

AP1

Unwmk.
1959, Nov. 20   Litho.   *Perf. 11*
C1 AP1 20xu blue & black   9.00   2.00

POSTAGE DUE STAMPS

Democratic Republic of Viet Nam
Nos. 1-4 exist with handstamps of "TT"
in a diamond. It is unclear to the editors
if these stamps were used.

D1

1955   Typo.   *Perf. 11½*
J14 D1 50d brown & yellow   10.00   6.00

D2

1958, Dec. 1   Litho.   *Perf. 12½*
J15 D2 10d purple & red   .65   .60
J16 D2 20d orange & aqua   1.50   1.00
J17 D2 100d gray blue & red   3.00   2.50
J18 D2 300d olive grn & red   4.50   3.50
   Nos. J15-J18 (4)   9.65   7.60

MILITARY STAMPS

M1

Perf. 12½
1958, May 1   Litho.   Unwmk.
M1 M1 multicolored   12.00   4.50

Invalids in
Field
Paddy
M2

1959-60   Litho.   *Perf. 11*
M2 M2 org brn & brown   4.00   1.00
M3 M2 grey blue & olive   6.00   1.75
   Nos. M2-M3 (2)   10.00   2.75
Issued: No. M2, 3/14/59; No. M3, 7/27/60.

Soldier, Train — M3

1959, July 1
M4 M3 turq blue & black   4.00   1.50

Frontier
Guard — M4

1961, Jan. 3
M5 M4 multicolored   13.50   8.00

Naval
Patrol
M5

1962, June 15
M6 M5 multicolored   4.75   2.00

Military Medal,
Invalid's
Badge — M6

1963, Sept. 10
M7 M6 12xu multicolored   3.75   3.75

Rifleman
M7

1964, Aug.
M8 M7 multicolored   4.00   4.00

Rifleman Jumping
Wall — M8

1965
M9   M8 red & black   4.00   4.00
M10 M8 yellow green & black   4.00   4.00
   Nos. M9-M10 (2)   8.00   8.00
Issued: No. M9, 7/1; No. M10, 12/25.

Soldier,
Guerrilla
Woman
M9

1966-67
M11 M9 greenish blue & vio bl   8.00   8.00
Redrawn with two boats at right
M12 M9 olive & brown bl   13.50 12.00
Issued: No. M11, 9/25; No. M12, 6/26/67.

Badge of
People's
Army — M10

1967, Oct. 10
M13 M10 multicolored   2.75   1.50

M11

1968, Nov. 10
M14 M11 lilac   4.50   1.25

M12

1969, Nov. 15
M15 M12 red & brown red   2.00   1.25

M13

1971, Apr. 27
M16 M13 yellow, brown & red   2.00   1.25

Nguyen
Van Be
M14

Design: No. M18, Nguyen Viet Xuan.

1971, Oct. 30   *Perf. 11*
M17 M14 multicolored   1.75   1.25
           Perf. 12½
M18 M14 black, pink & buff   2.50   1.10
M19 M14 black & green   2.50   1.10

M15

M16

1973, Dec. 22   *Perf. 11*
M20 M15 blue, black & buff   1.25   .50
  a. Perf. 12½   4.50   4.50
M22 M16 olive, red & black   1.25   .50
  a. Perf. 12½   4.50   4.50

Disabled
Veteran in
Factory
M17

No. M24, Invalid's Badge, open book, vert.

1976, July 27
M23-M24 M17 Set of 2   3.50   1.50

Soldier,
Map — M18

1976, Oct. 21
M25 M18 red & black   1.25   1.25

Pilot — M19

No. M27, Tank driver. No. M28, Seaman.

1978
M26-M28 M19 Set of 3   5.00 2.00
Issued: No. M26, 6/3; others, 10/10.

M20

Designs: a, Pilot. b, Badge of People's Army.

1979, Dec. 22
M29 M20 Vertical pair, #a.-b.   3.50 3.50

Types A343a, A359 and

Ho Chi
Minh — M21

#M30, Factory militiawoman. #M31, Soldier, woman pointing. #M32, Militiawoman.

1981, Aug. 5
M30 A343a salmon & multi   1.25 .75
M31 A343a green & multi   1.25 .75
M32 A359   blue & multi   1.25 .75
M33 M21   blue & tan   1.25 .75
  Nos. M30-M33 (4)   5.00 3.00
Size of No. M32: 13x18mm.

M22

1982, Nov. 9
M34 M22 pink & greenish blue   1.75 1.00

M23

1983, Apr. 30
M35 M23 multicolored   2.25 1.10

Victory at
Dien Bien
Phu, 30th
Anniv.
M24

1984, May 5   **Litho.**
M37 M24 multicolored   1.75 .75

Disabled
Soldier
Teaching
Class — M25

1984, Nov. 10
M38 M25 tan & brown   2.00 .75

Frontier Forces Type of 1984
1984, Dec. 15
M39 A410 multicolored   1.50 .75

M26

1984, Dec. 22
M40 M26 multicolored   2.00 .50

Policemen
and
Women
M27

1985, Aug. 30
M41 M27 multicolored   2.00 .60

M28

1986, Oct. 1
M42 M28 olive brown & black   1.50 .75

M29

1987, Sept. 23
M43 M29 carmine and tan   2.00 1.00

OFFICIAL STAMPS

Harvesting
Rice — O1

Denominations in grams or kilograms of rice. Dated 1952.

Perf. 11¼
1953, July   Litho.   Unwmk.
O1 O1 600g rose   9.50 3.00
O2 O1 1kg ol brown   0.50 4.00
O3 O1 2kg orange   9.00 12.00
O4 O1 5kg gray   15.00 15.00
  Nos. O1-O4 (4)   43.00 34.00

Dien Bien Phu Type of 1954
1954-56   **Perf. 11**
O5 A4 600g sepia & ocher   18.00 12.50
No. O5 exists perf 6, Value $60; and also imperf, Value $18.
Issued: #O5, 10/54; perf 6, 12/54; imperf, 1956.

Nos. 1L62-1L63
Overprinted

1955   Typo.   Perf. 7 Rough
O6-O7 VM2 100g on 2d,
           100g on
           5d, set of
           2   375.00 300.00

Land Reform Type of 1955-56
Inscribed "SU VU" Above Value
1955   Litho.   Perf. 11
O8-O9 A6 40d, 80d, set of 2   35.00 20.00

Cu Chinh
Lan (1930-
1952)
O3

Denominations: 20d, 80d, 100d, 500d, 1000d, 2000d, 3000d.

1956, June   Litho.   Perf. 11½
O10-O16 O3 Set of 7   210.00 200.00

4th World Trade Union Congress
Type of 1957
Inscribed "SU VU" Above Value
1957, Aug. 1   Perf. 12½
O17-O20 A15 20d, 40d, 80d,
             100d, set of 4   17.50 15.00

One-Pillar
Pagoda — O4

1957-58
O21 O4 150d green and brown
O22 O4 150d orange and slate
  Nos. O21-O22 (2)   22.50 10.00
Nos. O21-O22 exist with and without imprint and designer's name. Issued: No. O21, 12/22/57; No. O22, 3/12/58.

Craft Fair,
Hanoi — O5

1958, May 30
O23-O24 O5 150d, 200d, set of
            2   7.00 5.50

1st World
Congress of
Young
Workers,
Prague —
O6

1958, June 26
O25 O6 150d lt olive green & red   3.00 1.75

Soldier,
Factory,
Crops — O7

1958, Aug. 19
O26-O28 O7 50, 150, 200d, set
            of 3   10.00 7.00

Opening of
New Hanoi
Stadium
O8

1958, Dec. 31
O29-O32 O8 10d, 20d, 80d,
            150d, set of 4   8.50 4.75

Planting Rice — O9

1962, Sept. 1   Perf. 11
O33-O35 O9 3, 6, 12xu, set of 3   3.00 2.50

Rural
Mail
Service
O10

1966, July 1   Perf. 11
O36-O37 O10 3xu, 6xu, set of 2   3.00 1.00

VIRGIN ISLANDS

ˈvər-jən ˈī-ləndz

LOCATION — West Indies, southeast of Puerto Rico
GOVT. — British colony
AREA — 59 sq. mi.
POP. — 19,107 (1997)
CAPITAL — Road Town

The British Virgin Islands constituted one of the presidencies of the former Leeward Islands colony until it became a colony itself in 1956. For many years stamps of Leeward Islands were used concurrently.

The Virgin Islands group is divided between Great Britain and the United States. See Danish West Indies.

12 Pence = 1 Shilling
20 Shillings = 1 Pound
100 Cents = 1 Dollar (1951)
100 Cents = 1 US Dollar (1962)

Catalogue values for unused stamps in this country are for Never Hinged items, beginning with Scott 88 in the regular postage section and Scott O1 in the officials section.

Values for unused stamps are for examples with original gum as defined in the catalogue introduction. However, Nos. 1-2c are valued without gum as the vast majority of examples are found thus.

Virgin and Lamps — A1

St. Ursula — A2

A3

A4

1866   Litho. Unwmk.   Perf. 12
Toned or White Paper

1	A1	1p green		55.00	65.00
a.		Toned paper		57.50	67.50
c.		Perf. 15x12, toned paper		6,000.	7,000.
2	A3	6p rose		65.00	100.00
a.		Large "V" in "VIRGIN"		325.00	425.00
b.		White paper		92.50	125.00
c.		As "a," white paper		425.00	500.00

Examples offered as No. 1c frequently have forged perfs.

1867-70   Perf. 15

3	A1	1p blue grn ('70)		70.00	75.00
4	A1	1p yel grn ('68)		87.50	87.50
a.		Toned paper		95.00	87.50
5	A2	4p lake, buff		50.00	65.00
a.		4p lake, rose		60.00	82.50
6	A3	6p rose		625.00	625.00
a.		Toned paper ('68)		325.00	375.00
7	A4	1sh rose red & blk		300.00	300.00
a.		Toned paper		400.00	400.00
b.		Double lined frame		275.00	350.00

---

c.	As "b," bluish paper		250.00	350.00
	Colored Margins			
8	A4	1sh rose & blk	82.50	95.00
a.		White paper	100.00	115.00
b.		Bluish paper	750.00	900.00
c.		Central figure omitted	225,000.	
	Nos. 3-8 (6)		1,215.	1,248.

Examples of No. 8c have perfs. trimmed on one or two sides.

1878   Wmk. 1   Perf. 14

9	A1	1p green	95.00	115.00

See #16-17, 19-20. For surcharge see #18.

Queen Victoria — A5

1880   Typo.

10	A5	1p green	82.50	100.00
11	A5	2½p red brown	125.00	140.00

1883-84   Wmk. 2

12	A5	½p yellow	95.00	95.00
13	A5	½p green	6.75	17.50
a.		Imperf., pair	1,750.	
14	A5	1p rose	50.00	55.00
15	A5	2½p ultra ('84)	4.25	16.00
	Nos. 12-15 (4)		156.00	183.50

No. 13a probably is a plate proof.

1887   Litho.

16	A2	4p brick red	36.00	67.50
a.		4p brown red	45.00	72.50
17	A3	6p violet	20.00	55.00

No. 8 Handstamp Surcharged in Violet

1888   Unwmk.   Perf. 15

18	A4	4p on 1sh dp rose & blk, toned paper	145.00	160.00
a.		Double surcharge	8,500.	
b.		Inverted surcharge	55,000.	
c.		White paper	200.00	225.00

1889   Wmk. 2   Perf. 14

19	A1	1p carmine	4.00	10.00
20	A4	1sh brown	42.50	65.00
a.		1sh black brown	75.00	100.00

St. Ursula with Sheaf of Lilies — A7

1899   Engr.

21	A7	½p yellow grn	4.25	.60
a.		"PFNNY"	90.00	125.00
b.		"F" without cross bar	90.00	125.00
c.		Horiz. pair, imperf. between	13,000.	
22	A7	1p red	6.00	2.00
23	A7	2½p ultra	13.00	3.00
24	A7	4p chocolate	6.00	22.50
a.		"PENCF"	750.00	1,100.
25	A7	6p dark violet	8.00	3.00
26	A7	7p slate green	14.00	6.50
27	A7	1sh ocher	25.00	37.50
28	A7	5sh dark blue	85.00	95.00
	Nos. 21-28 (8)		161.25	170.10

Edward VII — A8

1904   Typo.   Wmk. 3

29	A8	½p violet & bl grn	1.00	.60
30	A8	1p violet & scar	3.25	.55
31	A8	2p violet & bis	7.75	4.00
32	A8	2½p violet & ultra	4.25	2.00
33	A8	3p violet & blk	6.00	2.50
34	A8	6p violet & brn	4.75	2.50
35	A8	1sh green & scar	7.75	7.25

36	A8	2sh6p green & blk	45.00	55.00
37	A8	5sh green & ultra	55.00	75.00
	Nos. 29-37 (9)		134.75	149.40

Numerals of 2p, 3p, 1sh and 2sh6p of type A8 are in color on plain tablet.

George V — A9

Die I

For description of dies I and II see "Dies of British Colonial Stamps" in Table of Contents.

1913   Ordinary Paper

38	A9	½p green	4.25	7.00
39	A9	1p scarlet	10.00	12.00
40	A9	2p gray	8.50	32.50
41	A9	2½p ultra	10.00	10.00

Chalky Paper

42	A9	3p vio, yel	3.00	7.00
43	A9	6p dl vio & red vio	11.00	22.50
44	A9	1sh blk, green	3.50	11.00
45	A9	2sh6p blk & red, bl	55.00	60.00
46	A9	5sh grn & red, yel	50.00	140.00
	Nos. 38-46 (9)		155.25	302.00

Numerals of 2p, 3p, 1sh and 2sh6p of type A9 are in color on plain tablet.

1921   Die II   Wmk. 4

47	A9	½p green	17.50	65.00
48	A9	1p carmine	10.00	40.00

For overprints see Nos. MR1-MR2.

Colony Seal — A10

1922   Wmk. 3

49	A10	3p violet, yel	1.00	17.50
50	A10	1sh black, emerald	1.00	17.50
51	A10	2sh6p blk & red, bl	6.00	12.50
52	A10	5sh grn & red, yel	52.50	120.00
	Nos. 49-52 (4)		60.50	167.50

1922-28   Wmk. 4

53	A10	½p green	1.00	3.00
54	A10	1p rose red	.80	.80
55	A10	1p violet ('27)	2.00	7.00
56	A10	1½p rose red ('27)	2.00	3.00
57	A10	1½p fawn ('28)	2.75	1.50
58	A10	2p gray	1.40	6.50
59	A10	2½p ultra	7.00	25.00
60	A10	2½p orange ('23)	1.40	2.50
61	A10	3p dl vio, yel	2.50	12.00
62	A10	5p dl lil & ol grn	6.00	50.00
63	A10	6p dl vio & red vio	2.10	6.50
a.		6p brown lilac & red violet	2.10	7.00
64	A10	1sh blk, emer ('28)	3.00	20.00
65	A10	2sh6p blk & red, bl ('28)	20.00	60.00
66	A10	5sh grn & red, yel ('23)	25.00	75.00
	Nos. 53-66 (14)		76.95	272.80

The ½, 1, 2 and 2½p are on ordinary paper, the others on chalky.
Numerals of 1½p of type A10 are in color on plain tablet.

Common Design Types pictured following the introduction.

Silver Jubilee Issue
Common Design Type

1935, May 6   Engr.   Perf. 11x12

69	CD301	1p car & dk blue	1.50	7.50
70	CD301	1½p black & ultra	1.50	6.50
71	CD301	2½p ultra & brn	4.00	6.25
72	CD301	1sh brn vio & ind	18.00	35.00
	Nos. 69-72 (4)		25.00	55.25
	Set, never hinged		32.50	

Coronation Issue
Common Design Type

1937, May 12   Perf. 11x11½

73	CD302	1p dark carmine	.90	2.75
74	CD302	1½p brown	.75	2.75
75	CD302	2½p deep ultra	.55	1.40
	Nos. 73-75 (3)		2.20	6.90
	Set, never hinged		2.75	

King George VI and Seal of the Colony — A11

1938-47   Photo.   Perf. 14

76	A11	½p green	.90	.90
77	A11	1p scarlet	1.25	1.00
78	A11	1½p red brown	1.50	1.25
79	A11	2p gray	1.50	1.25
80	A11	2½p ultra	2.00	1.50
81	A11	3p orange	1.25	1.00
82	A11	6p deep violet	3.50	1.00
83	A11	1sh olive bister	2.50	2.00
84	A11	2sh6p sepia	11.00	5.00
85	A11	5sh rose lake	11.00	6.00
86	A11	10sh brt blue ('47)	6.00	11.00
87	A11	£1 gray blk ('47)	7.00	25.00
	Nos. 76-87 (12)		49.40	56.90
	Set, never hinged		75.00	

1938   Chalky Paper

76a	A11	½p green	.85	3.50
77a	A11	1p scarlet	3.15	2.00
78a	A11	1½p red brown	3.50	6.50
79a	A11	2p gray	3.50	2.50
80a	A11	2½p ultramarine	2.50	1.80
81a	A11	3p orange	4.25	1.10
82a	A11	6p deep violet	6.50	2.75
83a	A11	1sh olive bister	12.00	4.50
84a	A11	2sh6p sepia	12.00	5.50
85a	A11	5sh rose lake	36.00	12.00

Catalogue values for unused stamps in this section, from this point to the end of the section, are for Never Hinged items.

Peace Issue
Common Design Type
Perf. 13½x14

1946, Nov. 1   Engr.   Wmk. 4

88	CD303	1½p red brown	.25	.25
89	CD303	3p orange	.25	.25

Silver Wedding Issue
Common Design Types

1949, Jan. 3   Photo.   Perf. 14x14½

90	CD304	2½p brt ultra	.25	.25

Engr.; Name Typo.
Perf. 11½x11

91	CD305	£1 gray black	16.00	22.00

UPU Issue
Common Design Types

Engr.; Name Typo. on Nos. 93 & 94

1949, Oct. 10   Perf. 13½, 11x11½

92	CD306	2½p ultra	.40	2.40
93	CD307	3p deep orange	1.25	2.50
94	CD308	6p red lilac	.50	.50
95	CD309	1sh olive	.45	.50
	Nos. 92-95 (4)		2.60	5.90

University Issue
Common Design Types

1951   Engr.   Perf. 14x14½

96	CD310	3c red brn & gray blk	.40	2.25
97	CD311	12c purple & black	1.10	1.50

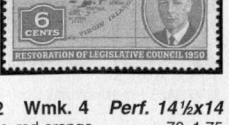

Map of the Islands
A12

1951, Apr. 2   Wmk. 4   Perf. 14½x14

98	A12	6c red orange	.70	1.75
99	A12	12c purple	1.25	1.00
100	A12	24c olive grn	.70	1.25
101	A12	$1.20 carmine	3.50	1.50
	Nos. 98-101 (4)		6.15	5.50

Restoration of the Legislative Council, 1950.

Sombrero Lighthouse — A13

Map of Jost van Dyke — A14

Designs: 3c, Sheep. 4c, Map, Anegada. 5c, Cattle. 8c, Map, Virgin Gorda. 12c, Map, Tortola. 24c, Badge of the Presidency. 60c, Dead Man's Chest. $1.20, Sir Francis Drake Channel. $2.40, Road Town. $4.80, Map, Virgin Islands.

1952, Apr. 15   Perf. 12½x13, 13x12½

102	A13	1c gray black	.40	2.00
103	A14	2c deep green	.85	.25
104	A14	3c choc & gray blk	.45	1.25
105	A14	4c red	.70	1.60
106	A14	5c gray blk & rose lake	1.40	.70
107	A14	8c ultra	.85	1.25
108	A14	12c purple	1.25	1.60
109	A13	24c dk brown	1.00	.25
110	A14	60c blue & ol grn	4.00	11.00
111	A14	$1.20 ultra & blk	6.00	12.00
112	A14	$2.40 hn brn & dk grn	15.00	16.00
113	A14	$4.80 rose car & bl	19.00	19.00
		Nos. 102-113 (12)	50.90	66.90

Coronation Issue
Common Design Type

1953, June 2   Perf. 13½x14

114	CD312	2c dk green & blk	.40	1.00

Map of Tortola — A15

Brown Pelican A16

Designs: 1c, Virgin Islands sloop. 2c, Nelthrop Red Poll bull. 3c, Road Harbor. 4c, Mountain travel. 5c, St. Ursula. 8c, Beach scene. 12c, Boat launching. 24c, White Cedar tree. 60c, Skipjack tuna. $1.20, Treasury Square. $4.80, Magnificent frigatebird.

Perf. 13x12½

1956, Nov. 1   Engr.   Wmk. 4

115	A15	½c claret & blk	.45	.25
116	A15	1c dk bl & grnsh bl	1.90	1.10
117	A15	2c black & ver	.40	.25
118	A15	3c olive & brt bl	.40	.45
119	A15	4c blue grn & brn	.45	.45
120	A15	5c gray	.50	.25
121	A15	8c dp ultra & org	.75	.65
122	A15	12c car & brt ultra	2.50	1.10
123	A15	24c dull red & grn	1.25	1.00
124	A15	60c yel org & dk bl	10.00	12.00
125	A15	$1.20 car & yel grn	2.75	11.00

Perf. 12x11½

126	A16	$2.40 vio brn & dl yel	37.50	16.00
127	A16	$4.80 grnsh bl & dk brn	40.00	16.00
		Nos. 115-127 (13)	98.85	60.50

Types of 1956 Surcharged

Perf. 13x12½

1962, Dec. 10   Wmk. 314

128	A15	1c on ½c	.25	.25
129	A15	2c on 1c	1.25	.25
130	A15	3c on 2c	.25	.25
131	A15	4c on 3c	.25	.25
132	A15	5c on 4c	.25	.25
133	A15	8c on 8c	.35	.35
134	A15	10c on 12c	.45	.45
135	A15	12c on 24c	.65	.65
136	A15	25c on 60c	3.25	1.25
137	A15	70c on $1.20	.70	3.25

Perf. 12x11½

138	A16	$1.40 on $2.40	10.00	5.00
139	A16	$2.80 on $4.80	10.00	5.00
		Nos. 128-139 (12)	27.65	17.20

Freedom from Hunger Issue
Common Design Type

1963, June 4   Photo.   Perf. 14x14½

140	CD314	25c lilac	.50	.50

Red Cross Centenary Issue
Common Design Type

Wmk. 314

1963, Sept. 2   Litho.   Perf. 13

141	CD315	2c black & red	.25	1.00
142	CD315	25c ultra & red	.55	.25

Shakespeare Issue
Common Design Type

1964, Apr. 23   Photo.   Perf. 14x14½

143	CD316	10c ultramarine	.15	.45

Bonito — A17

Map of Tortola Island — A18

2c, Seaplane at Soper's Hole. 3c, Brown pelican. 4c, Dead Man's Chest (mountain). 5c, Road Harbor. 6c, Fallen Jerusalem Island. 8c, The Baths, Virgin Gorda. 10c, Map of Virgin Islands. 12c, Ferry service, Tortola—St. Thomas. 15c, The Towers. 25c, Plane at Beef Island Airfield. $1, Virgin Gorda Island. $1.40, Yachts, Tortola. $2.80, Badge.

Perf. 13x12½

1964, Nov. 2   Engr.   Wmk. 314

144	A17	1c gray ol & dk bl	.35	2.40
145	A17	2c rose red & ol	.35	.45
146	A17	3c grnsh bl & sep	4.25	2.40
147	A17	4c carmine & blk	1.10	2.40
148	A17	5c green & blk	.90	1.60
149	A17	6c orange & blk	.35	1.40
150	A17	8c pink & blk	.35	1.00
151	A17	10c lt violet & mar	1.60	.45
152	A17	12c vio bl & Prus grn	2.75	3.50
153	A17	15c gray & yel grn	.45	3.50
154	A17	25c pur & yel grn	13.00	3.50

Perf. 13x13½
Size: 27x30½mm

155	A18	70c bister brn & blk	5.25	8.00
156	A18	$1 red brn & yel grn	4.25	3.00
157	A18	$1.40 rose & blue	24.00	13.00

Perf. 11½x12
Size: 27x37mm

158	A18	$2.80 rose lilac & blk	26.00	13.00
		Nos. 144-158 (15)	84.95	59.60

For surcharges & overprints see Nos. 173-175, 190-191.

ITU Issue
Common Design Type

Perf. 11x11½

1965, May 17   Litho.   Wmk. 314

159	CD317	4c yellow & bl grn	.25	.25
160	CD317	25c blue & org yel	.60	.60

Intl. Cooperation Year Issue
Common Design Type

1965, Oct. 25   Wmk. 314   Perf. 14½

161	CD318	1c blue grn & cl	.25	.25
162	CD318	25c lt violet & grn	.40	.25

Churchill Memorial Issue
Common Design Type

1966, Jan. 24   Photo.   Perf. 14
Design in Black, Gold and Carmine Rose

163	CD319	1c brt blue	.25	.25
164	CD319	2c green	.25	.25
165	CD319	10c brown	.40	.40
166	CD319	25c violet	1.00	1.00
		Nos. 163-166 (4)	1.90	1.90

Royal Visit Issue
Common Design Type

1966, Feb. 22   Litho.   Perf. 11x12

167	CD320	4c violet blue	.25	.25
168	CD320	70c dk car rose	1.50	1.50

Stamps of 1866 — A19

Designs: 5c, R.M.S. Atrato, 1866. 25c, Beechcraft mail plane on Beef Island Airfield and 6p stamp (No. 2). 60c, Landing mail at Road Town, 1866, and 1p stamp (No. 1).

Perf. 12½x13

1966, Apr. 25   Wmk. 314

169	A19	5c grn, yel, red & blk	.30	.25
170	A19	10c yel, grn, red, blk & rose	.30	.25
171	A19	25c lt grn, bl, red, blk & rose	.55	.75
172	A19	60c bl, red, blk, & grn	1.00	1.50
		Nos. 169-172 (4)	2.15	2.75

Centenary of Virgin Islands postage stamps.

No. 155 Surcharged

No. 157 Surcharged

No. 158 Surcharged

Perf. 13x12½, 11½x12

1966, Sept. 15   Engr.   Wmk. 314

173	A18	50c on 70c	2.00	2.00
174	A18	$1.50 on $1.40	3.75	3.75
175	A18	$3 on $2.80	3.75	3.75
		Nos. 173-175 (3)	9.50	9.50

UNESCO Anniversary Issue
Common Design Type

1966, Dec. 1   Litho.   Perf. 14

176	CD323	2c "Education"	.25	.25
177	CD323	12c "Science"	.25	.25
178	CD323	60c "Culture"	.90	.80
		Nos. 176-178 (3)	1.40	1.30

Map and Seal of Virgin Islands A20

Wmk. 314

1967, Apr. 18   Photo.   Perf. 14½

179	A20	2c gold, grn & org	.25	.25
180	A20	10c gold, rose red, grn & org	.25	.25
181	A20	25c gold, red brn, grn & org	.25	.25
182	A20	$1 gold, bl, grn & org	.45	.45
		Nos. 179-182 (4)	1.20	1.20

Introduction of new constitution.

Map of Virgin Islands, Bermuda and C.S. Mercury — A21

10c, Communications center, Chalwell, Virgin Islands. 50c, Cable ship Mercury.

1967, Sept. 14   Wmk. 314   Perf. 14½

183	A21	4c green & multi	.25	.25
184	A21	10c dp plum & multi	.25	.25
185	A21	50c bister & multi	.60	.60
		Nos. 183-185 (3)	1.10	1.10

Completion of the Bermuda-Tortola, Virgin Islands, telephone link.

Blue Marlin A22

Designs: 10c, Sergeant fish (cobia). 25c, Peto fish (Wahoo). 40c, Fishing boat, map of Virgin Islands and fishing records.

Perf. 12½x12

1968, Jan. 2   Photo.   Wmk. 314

186	A22	2c multicolored	.25	1.00
187	A22	10c multicolored	.25	.25
188	A22	25c multicolored	.40	.40
189	A22	40c multicolored	.75	.75
		Nos. 186-189 (4)	1.65	2.40

Game fishing in Virgin Islands waters.

Nos. 151 and 154 Ovptd. "1968 / INTERNATIONAL / YEAR FOR / HUMAN RIGHTS"

1968, July 1   Engr.   Perf. 13x12½

190	A17	10c lt violet & maroon	.25	.25
191	A17	25c purple & green	.40	.40

Martin Luther King, Bible and Sword A23

1968, Oct. 15   Litho.   Perf. 14

192	A23	4c dl org, vio & blk	.35	.35
193	A23	25c dl org, gray grn & blk	.45	.45

Martin Luther King, Jr. (1929-68), American civil rights leader.

DHC-6 Twin Otter A24

Designs: 10c, Hawker Siddeley 748. 25c, Hawker Siddeley Heron. $1, Badge from cap of Royal Engineers.

1968, Dec. 16   Unwmk.   Perf. 14
194	A24	2c brn red & multi	.25	1.00
195	A24	10c grnsh bl, blk & red	.40	.25
196	A24	25c ultra, lt bl, org & blk	.45	.25
197	A24	$1 green & multi	.50	2.00
		Nos. 194-197 (4)	1.60	3.50

Opening of enlarged Beef Island Airport.

Long John Silver and Jim Hawkins — A25

Scenes from Treasure Island: 10c, Jim's escape from the pirates, horiz. 40c, The fight with Israel Hands. $1, Treasure trove, horiz.

Perf. 13½x13, 13x13½
1969, Mar. 18   Photo.   Wmk. 314
198	A25	4c dp car & multi	.30	.25
199	A25	10c multicolored	.35	.25
200	A25	40c ultra & multi	.40	.30
201	A25	$1 black & multi	.75	1.00
		Nos. 198-201 (4)	1.80	1.80

Robert Louis Stevenson (1850-94). The Virgin Islands were used as the setting for "Treasure Island."

Tourist and Rock Grouper — A26

Tourist Publicity: 10c, Yachts in Road Harbor, Tortola, horiz. 20c, Tourists on beach in Virgin Gorda National Park, horiz. $1, Pipe organ cactus and woman tourist.

1969, Oct. 20   Litho.   Perf. 12½
202	A26	2c multicolored	.25	.55
203	A26	10c multicolored	.25	.25
204	A26	20c multicolored	.35	.25
205	A26	$1 multicolored	.90	1.50
		Nos. 202-205 (4)	1.75	2.55

Carib Canoe A27

Ships: 1c, Santa Maria. 2c, H.M.S. Elizabeth Bonaventure. 3c, Dutch buccaneer, 1660. 4c, Thetis (1827 merchant ship). 5c, Henry Morgan's ship. 6c, Frigate Boreas. 8c, Schooner L'Eclair, 1804. 10c, H.M.S. Formidable. 12c, H.M.S. Nymph burning. 15c, Packet Windsor Castle fighting French privateer. 25c, Frigate Astrea, 1808. 50c, H.M.S. Rhone. $1, Tortola sloop. $2, H.M.S. Frobisher. $3, Booker Line Viking (cargo ship). $5, Hydrofoil Sun Arrow.

Wmk. 314 Sideways
1970, Feb. 16   Perf. 14½
206	A27	½c brn & ocher	.25	1.50
207	A27	1c bl, lt grn & vio	.25	.50
208	A27	2c red brn, org & gray	.45	.75
209	A27	3c ver, bl & brn	.35	1.00
210	A27	4c brn, bl & vio bl	.35	.40
211	A27	5c grn, pink & blk	.35	.25
212	A27	6c lil, grn & blk	.45	.25
213	A27	8c lt ol, yel & brn	.55	.30
214	A27	10c ocher, bl & brn	.60	.40
215	A27	12c sep, yel & dp cl	.70	1.25
216	A27	15c org, grnsh bl & brn	3.75	.55

217	A27	25c bl, grnsh gray & pur	3.75	1.50
218	A27	50c rose car, lt grn & brn	3.00	1.60
219	A27	$1 brn, sal pink & dk grn	3.75	3.50
220	A27	$2 gray & yel	7.50	7.00
221	A27	$3 brn, ol bis & dk bl	3.00	5.00
222	A27	$5 lil & gray	3.00	5.00
		Nos. 206-222 (17)	32.05	30.75

For overprints see Nos. 235-236.

1973, Oct. 17   Wmk. 314 Upright
206a	A27	½c	.85	5.75
209a	A27	3c	2.00	2.25
210a	A27	4c	2.00	4.25
211a	A27	5c	2.00	2.10
214a	A27	10c	2.40	2.40
215a	A27	12c	3.25	3.25
		Nos. 206a-215a (6)	12.50	20.00

Wmk. 314 Sideways
1974, Nov. 11   Perf. 13½
207a	A27	1c	1.25	2.25
214b	A27	10c	2.50	2.25
215b	A27	12c	2.50	3.50
216a	A27	15c	3.50	3.25
		Nos. 207a-216a (4)	9.75	11.25

"A Tale of Two Cities," by Dickens A28

Charles Dickens: 10c, "Oliver Twist." 25c, "Great Expectations."

1970, May 4   Litho.   Perf. 14½
223	A28	5c blk, gray & pink	.25	.25
224	A28	10c blk, pale yel grn & blue	.35	.35
225	A28	25c blk, yel & lt yel grn	.50	.95
		Nos. 223-225 (3)	1.10	1.55

Hospital Visitor A29

10c, Girl Scouts receiving 1st aid training at lake side. 25c, Red Cross & Virgin Islands coat of arms.

1970, Aug. 10   Wmk. 314   Perf. 14
226	A29	4c multicolored	.25	.25
227	A29	10c multicolored	.40	.25
228	A29	25c multicolored	.75	.75
		Nos. 226-228 (3)	1.40	1.25

Centenary of British Red Cross.

Mary Read — A30

Pirates: 10c, George Lowther. 30c, Edward Teach (Blackbeard). 60c, Henry Morgan.

1970, Nov. 16   Wmk. 314   Perf. 14
229	A30	½c dp rose & multi	.25	.25
230	A30	10c blue grn & multi	.30	.25
231	A30	30c ultra & multi	.80	.80
232	A30	60c multicolored	1.25	1.30
		Nos. 229-232 (4)	2.60	2.60

Children Spelling out "UNICEF" A31

1971, Dec. 13
233	A31	15c tan & multi	.25	.25
234	A31	30c lt blue & multi	.30	.30

25th anniv. of UNICEF.

Nos. 210 and 217 Dated "1972" and Ovptd. "VISIT OF / H.R.H. / THE / PRINCESS MARGARET"
1972, Mar. 7   Perf. 14½
235	A27	4c multicolored	.40	.40
236	A27	25c multicolored	.85	.85

Seaman, 1800 — A32

10c, Boatswain, 1787-1807. 30c, Captain, 1795-1812. 60c, Admiral in full dress uniform, 1787-95.

1972, Mar. 17   Perf. 14x13½
237	A32	½c yellow & multi	.25	.25
238	A32	10c brt pink & multi	.35	.35
239	A32	30c orange & multi	.80	.80
240	A32	60c blue & multi	1.75	1.75
		Nos. 237-240 (4)	3.15	3.15

INTERPEX, 14th Intl. Stamp Exhib., NYC, Mar. 17-19.

Silver Wedding Issue, 1972
Common Design Type

Design: Queen Elizabeth II, Prince Philip, sailfish and "Sir Winston Churchill" yacht.

1972, Nov. 24   Photo.   Perf. 14x14½
241	CD324	15c ultra & multi	.25	.25
242	CD324	25c Prus blue & multi	.25	.25

Allison Tuna A33

1972, Dec. 12   Litho.   Perf. 13½x14
243	A33	½c Wahoo	.25	.25
244	A33	½c Blue marlin	.25	.25
a.		Horiz. or vert. pair, #243-244	.25	.25
245	A33	15c shown	.45	.45
246	A33	25c White marlin	.70	.70
247	A33	50c Sailfish	1.15	1.15
248	A33	$1 Dolphin	2.00	2.00
a.		Souvenir sheet of 6, #243-248	11.00	11.00
		Nos. 243-248 (6)	4.80	4.80

Game fish.

Lettsom House and Medal — A34

Themes from Quaker History: ½c, Dr. John Coakley Lettsom, vert. 15c, Dr. William Thornton, vert. 30c, US Capitol, Washington, DC, and Dr. Thornton who designed it. $1, Library Hall, Philadelphia, and William Penn.

1973, Mar. 9   Litho.   Perf. 13½
249	A34	½c rose & multi	.25	.25
250	A34	10c multicolored	.25	.25
251	A34	15c multicolored	.25	.25
252	A34	30c ultra & multi	.35	.35
253	A34	$1 multicolored	.75	.75
		Nos. 249-253 (5)	1.85	1.85

INTERPEX, 15th Intl. Phil. Exhib., NYC, Mar. 9-11.

Hummingbirds on 1c Coin — A35

Coins and Beach Scenes: 5c, Zenaida doves. 10c, Kingfisher. 25c, Mangrove cuckoos. 50c, Brown pelicans. $1, Magnificent frigate birds.

1973, June 30   Wmk. 314   Perf. 14½
254	A35	1c orange & multi	.25	.45
255	A35	5c lt blue & multi	.25	.25
256	A35	10c pale ultra & multi	.65	.25
257	A35	25c yellow & multi	.75	.25
258	A35	50c lt violet & multi	1.25	1.50
259	A35	$1 ultra & multi	1.75	2.25
		Nos. 254-259 (6)	4.90	4.95

New Virgin Islands coinage.

Princess Anne's Wedding Issue
Common Design Type

1973, Nov. 16   Wmk. 314   Perf. 14
260	CD325	5c citron & multi	.25	.25
261	CD325	50c blue grn & multi	.25	.25

Virgin and Child, by Bernardino Pintoricchio — A36

Christmas (Paintings of the Virgin and Child by): 3c, Lorenzo Credi. 25c, Carlo Crivelli. 50c, Bernardino Luini.

1973, Dec. 7   Perf. 14x14½
262	A36	½c lt green & multi	.25	.25
263	A36	3c rose & multi	.25	.25
264	A36	25c ocher & multi	.25	.25
265	A36	50c lt blue & multi	.30	.30
		Nos. 262-265 (4)	1.05	1.05

Arms of French Minesweeper Canopus — A37

1974, Mar. 22   Wmk. 314   Perf. 14
266	A37	5c shown	.25	.25
267	A37	18c USS Saginaw	.30	.30
268	A37	25c HMS Rothesay	.35	.35
269	A37	50c HMCS Ottawa	.50	.50
a.		Souvenir sheet of 4, #266-269	1.75	1.75
		Nos. 266-269 (4)	1.40	1.40

INTERPEX Phil. Exhib., NYC, Mar. 22-24.

Famous Explorers — A38

1974, Aug. 19   Perf. 14½
270	A38	5c Columbus	.25	.25
271	A38	10c Sir Walter Raleigh	.25	.25
272	A38	25c Sir Martin Frobisher	.35	.35
273	A38	40c Sir Francis Drake	.65	.65
a.		Souvenir sheet of 4, #270-273	1.60	1.60
		Nos. 270-273 (4)	1.50	1.50

Sea
Shells
A39

1974, Sept. 30   **Perf. 13x13½**
274	A39	5c Trumpet triton	.30	.30
275	A39	18c West Indian murex	.70	.70
276	A39	25c Bleeding tooth	1.00	1.00
277	A39	75c Virgin Island latirus	2.50	2.50
a.		Souvenir sheet of 4, #274-277	5.00	5.00
		Nos. 274-277 (4)	4.50	4.50

St. Mary, Aldermanbury,
London, — A40

Design: 50c, St. Mary, Fulton, Missouri.

1974, Nov. 30   **Wmk. 373**   **Perf. 14**
278	A40	10c multicolored	.25	.25
279	A40	50c multicolored	.45	.45
a.		Souvenir sheet of 2, #278-279	.90	.90

Sir Winston Churchill (1874-1965).

Figurehead from
"Boreas" — A41

Figureheads: 18c, The Golden Hind. 40c, Crowned lion from the "Superb." 85c, Warrior, from the "Formidable."

Perf. 13½x13
1975, Mar. 14   **Wmk. 314**
280	A41	5c multicolored	.25	.25
281	A41	18c multicolored	.30	.30
282	A41	40c multicolored	.50	.50
283	A41	85c multicolored	1.15	1.15
a.		Souv. sheet of 4, #280-283, perf. 14	2.75	2.75
		Nos. 280-283 (4)	2.20	2.20

INTERPEX, 17th Phil. Exhib., NYC, Mar. 14-16.

Rock
Beauty
A42

Fish: 1c, Squirrelfish. 3c, Queen triggerfish. 5c, Blue angelfish. 8c, Stoplight parrotfish. 10c, Queen angelfish. 12c, Nassau grouper. 13c, Blue tang. 15c, Sergeant major. 18c, Jewfish. 20c, Bluehead wrasse. 25c, Gray angelfish. 60c, Glasseye snapper. $1, Blue chromis. $2.50, French angelfish. $3, Queen parrotfish. $5, Four-eye butterflyfish.

1975   **Wmk. 373**   **Perf. 14**
Inscribed "1975" Below Design
284	A42	½c shown	.25	.25
285	A42	1c multicolored	.55	.65
286	A42	3c multicolored	1.50	1.75
287	A42	5c multicolored	.35	.45
288	A42	8c multicolored	.35	.45
289	A42	10c multicolored	.35	.45
290	A42	12c multicolored	.55	.65
291	A42	13c multicolored	.55	.65
292	A42	15c multicolored	.55	.65
293	A42	18c multicolored	1.25	1.50
294	A42	20c multicolored	.75	.95
295	A42	25c multicolored	1.60	1.90
296	A42	60c multicolored	1.90	2.40
297	A42	$1 multicolored	2.75	3.25
298	A42	$2.50 multicolored	3.50	5.50
299	A42	$3 multicolored	3.75	5.50
300	A42	$5 multicolored	4.00	6.00
		Nos. 284-300 (17)	24.50	32.95

Issue dates: $5, Aug. 15. Others, June 16.

1977
Inscribed "1977" Below Design
284a	A42	½c multicolored	.55	.55
287a	A42	5c multicolored	1.00	1.00
288a	A42	8c multicolored	1.00	1.00
289a	A42	10c multicolored	1.00	1.00
290a	A42	12c multicolored	1.40	1.40
291a	A42	13c multicolored	1.40	1.40
292a	A42	15c multicolored	1.40	1.40
294a	A42	20c multicolored	2.00	2.00
		Nos. 284a-294a (8)	9.75	9.75

St.
Georges
Parish
School
A43

Designs: 25c, Legislative Council Building. 40c, Mace and gavel of Legislative Council. 75c, Scroll with dates of historical events.

1975, Nov. 27   **Litho.**   **Wmk. 373**
301	A43	5c ultra & multi	.25	.25
302	A43	25c green & multi	.25	.25
303	A43	40c ocher & multi	.25	.25
304	A43	75c ultra & multi	.25	.25
		Nos. 301-304 (4)	1.00	1.00

Restoration of Legislative Council, 25th anniv.

Copper
Mine
Point
A44

Historic Sites: 18c, Dr. Thornton's Ruin, Pleasant Valley. 50c, Callwood distillery. 75c, The Dungeon.

1976, Mar. 12   **Litho.**   **Perf. 14½**
305	A44	5c red & multi	.25	.25
306	A44	18c red & multi	.25	.25
307	A44	50c red & multi	.40	.40
308	A44	75c red & multi	.60	.60
		Nos. 305-308 (4)	1.50	1.50

Massachusetts Brig Hazard — A45

Designs: 22c, American Privateer Spy. 40c, Continental Navy Frigate Raleigh. 75c, Frigate Alliance and HMS Trepasy.

1976, May 29   **Wmk. 373**   **Perf. 14**
309	A45	8c multicolored	.30	.25
310	A45	22c multicolored	.65	.45
311	A45	40c multicolored	1.00	1.00
312	A45	75c multicolored	1.75	1.75
a.		Souvenir sheet of 4, #309-312	6.50	6.50
		Nos. 309-312 (4)	3.70	3.45

American Bicentennial.

Government House, Tortola — A46

Designs: 15c, Government House, St. Croix, vert. 30c, Flags of US and British Virgin Islands, vert. 75c, Arms of British and US Virgin Islands.

1976, Oct. 29   **Litho.**   **Perf. 14**
313	A46	8c green & multi	.25	.25
314	A46	15c green & multi	.25	.25
315	A46	30c green & multi	.25	.25
316	A46	75c green & multi	.55	.55
		Nos. 313-316 (4)	1.30	1.30

US and British Virgin Islands Friendship Day, 5th anniversary.

Holy
Bible — A47

8c, Queen visiting Agricultural Station, Tortola, 1966. 60c, Presentation of Holy Bible.

1977, Feb. 7   **Perf. 14x13½**
317	A47	8c silver & multi	.25	.25
318	A47	30c silver & multi	.25	.25
319	A47	60c silver & multi	.75	.75
		Nos. 317-319 (3)		

25th anniv. of the reign of Elizabeth II.
For overprints see Nos. 324-326.

Virgin Islands Chart, 1739 — A48

18th Century Maps of Virgin Islands: 22c, 1758. 30c, 1775. 75c, 1779.

1977, June 12   **Wmk. 373**   **Perf. 13½**
320	A48	8c multicolored	.30	.25
321	A48	22c multicolored	.65	.60
322	A48	30c multicolored	.90	.80
323	A48	75c multicolored	1.00	1.90
		Nos. 320-323 (4)	3.75	3.55

Type of 1977 Inscribed "ROYAL VISIT"

Designs: 5c, Queen visiting Agricultural Station, Tortola, 1966. 25c, Holy Bible. 50c, Presentation of Holy Bible.

1977, Oct. 26   **Litho.**   **Perf. 14x13½**
324	A47	5c yel brn & multi	.25	.25
325	A47	25c dk blue & multi	.25	.25
326	A47	50c purple & multi	.40	.40
		Nos. 324-326 (3)	.90	.90

Caribbean visit of Queen Elizabeth II.

Divers Checking
Equipment — A49

Tourist publicity: 5c, Cup coral inside bow of "Rhone." 8c, Sponge growing on superstructure of "Rhone." 22c, Sponge and cup coral. 30c, Scuba diver searching for sponges in cave. 75c, Marine life.

1978, Feb. 10   **Wmk. 373**   **Perf. 13½**
327	A49	½c multicolored	.25	.25
328	A49	5c multicolored	.25	.25
329	A49	8c multicolored	.25	.25
330	A49	22c multicolored	.55	.25
331	A49	30c multicolored	.75	.75
332	A49	75c multicolored	1.10	1.10
		Nos. 327-332 (6)	3.15	2.85

Corals
A50

1978, Feb. 27   **Perf. 14**
333	A50	8c Fire	.35	.35
334	A50	15c Staghorn	.40	.40
335	A50	40c Brain	.75	.75
336	A50	75c Elkhorn	1.50	1.50
		Nos. 333-336 (4)	3.00	3.00

Elizabeth II Coronation Anniversary Issue
Common Design Types
Souvenir Sheet
1978, June 2   **Unwmk.**   **Perf. 15**
337		Sheet of 6	1.80	1.80
a.		CD326 50c Falcon of the Plantagenets	.30	.30
b.		CD327 50c Elizabeth II	.30	.30
c.		CD328 50c Iguana	.30	.30

No. 337 contains 2 se-tenant strips of Nos. 337a-337c, separated by horizontal gutter.

Lignum
Vitae
A51

Flowering Trees: 22c, Ginger thomas. 40c, Dog almond. 75c, White cedar.

1978, Sept. 4   **Litho.**   **Perf. 13x13½**
338	A51	8c multicolored	.25	.25
339	A51	22c multicolored	.40	.40
340	A51	40c multicolored	.50	.50
341	A51	75c multicolored	.60	.60
a.		Souvenir sheet of 4, #338-341	1.25	1.25
		Nos. 338-341 (4)	1.75	1.75

Eurema
Lisa
A52

Butterflies: 22c, Dione vanillae. 30c, Heliconius charitonius. 75c, Hemiargus hanno.

1978, Dec. 4   **Wmk. 373**   **Perf. 14**
342	A52	5c multicolored	.25	.25
343	A52	22c multicolored	.75	.75
a.		Sheet of 9, 6 #342, 3 #343	3.25	3.25
344	A52	30c multicolored	1.00	1.80
345	A52	75c multicolored	2.75	2.25
		Nos. 342-345 (4)	4.75	5.05

Spiny
Lobsters
A53

Conservation: 15c, Iguana, vert. 22c, Hawksbill turtle. 75c, Black coral, vert.

1979, Feb. 10   **Litho.**
346	A53	5c multicolored	.25	.25
347	A53	15c multicolored	.40	.25
348	A53	22c multicolored	.60	.25
349	A53	75c multicolored	1.25	1.25
a.		Souvenir sheet of 4, #346-349	3.25	3.25
		Nos. 346-349 (4)	2.50	2.00

Strawberry
Cactus — A54

Native Cacti: 5c, Snowy cactus. 13c, Barrel cactus. 22c, Tree cactus. 30c, Prickly pear. 75c, Dildo cactus.

1979, May 7　Wmk. 373　Perf. 14

350	A54	½c multicolored	.25	.25
351	A54	5c multicolored	.25	.25
352	A54	13c multicolored	.35	.35
353	A54	22c multicolored	.50	.50
354	A54	30c multicolored	.55	.55
355	A54	75c multicolored	.90	.90
		Nos. 350-355 (6)	2.80	2.80

West Indies Girl and Church — A55

Children and IYC Emblem: 10c, African boy and dancers. 13c, Asian girl and children playing. $1, European girl and bicycle.

1979, July 9　　　　　Perf. 14x14½

356	A55	5c multicolored	.25	.25
357	A55	10c multicolored	.25	.25
358	A55	13c multicolored	.25	.25
359	A55	$1 multicolored	.35	.35
a.		Souvenir sheet of 4, #356-359	1.25	1.25
		Nos. 356-359 (4)	1.10	1.10

International Year of the Child.

No. 118 — A56

Rowland Hill's Signature and: 13c, Virgin Islands No. 11, horiz. 75c, Unissued Great Britain 2d stamp, 1910, horiz. $1, Virgin Islands No. 8c.

1979, Oct. 1　Photo.　Perf. 13½

360	A56	5c multicolored	.25	.25
361	A56	13c multicolored	.25	.25
362	A56	75c multicolored	.60	.60
		Nos. 360-362 (3)	1.10	1.10

Souvenir Sheet

363	A56	$1 multicolored	.90	.90

Sir Rowland Hill (1795-1879), originator of penny postage.
For overprints see Nos. 389-390.

Pencil Urchin — A57

½c, Calcified algae. 1c, Purple-tipped sea anemone. 3c, Starfish. 8c, Triton's trumpet. 10c, Christmas tree worms. 13c, Flamingo tongue snails. 15c, Spider crab. 18c, Sea squirts. 20c, True tulip. 25c, Rooster tail conch. 30c, Fighting conch. 60c, Mangrove crab. $1, Coral polyps. $2.50, Peppermint shrimp. $3, West Indian murex. $5, Carpet anemone.

"1979" or "1980" Below Design

1979-80　　Litho.　　Perf. 14

364	A57	½c multicolored	.75	2.50
365	A57	1c multicolored	1.00	2.50
366	A57	3c multicolored	1.50	2.50
367	A57	5c shown	1.75	2.00
368	A57	8c multicolored	1.75	1.50
369	A57	10c multicolored	.50	1.00
370	A57	13c multicolored	2.00	.75
371	A57	15c multicolored	.75	.75
372	A57	18c multicolored	2.25	4.25
373	A57	20c multicolored	1.00	1.90
374	A57	25c multicolored	1.75	4.00
375	A57	30c multicolored	3.00	1.90

376	A57	60c multicolored	2.00	3.00
377	A57	$1 multicolored	1.75	4.00
378	A57	$2.50 multicolored	1.75	3.75
379	A57	$3 multicolored	1.75	4.00
380	A57	$5 multicolored	1.75	4.00
		Nos. 364-380 (17)	27.00	44.30

Issued: 5, 8, 10, 15, 20, 25c, $2.50, $3, 12/17/79; others, 4/1/80. Date of year of issue below design.
For overprints see Nos. O1-O15.

"1982" Below Design

1982, Aug. 27　　　　Chalky Paper

367a	A57	5c multicolored	1.15	1.15
368a	A57	8c multicolored	1.15	1.15
370a	A57	13c multicolored	2.25	2.25
371a	A57	15c multicolored	2.25	2.25
373a	A57	20c multicolored	2.00	2.00
375a	A57	30c multicolored	3.00	3.00
		Nos. 367a-375a (6)	11.80	11.80

Rotary Athletic Meet, Tortola, Emblem A58

22c, Paul P. Harris. 60c, Mount Sage National Park. $1, Anniversary emblem.

1980, Mar. 3　Litho.　Perf. 13½x14

381	A58	8c shown	.25	.25
382	A58	22c multicolored	.25	.25
383	A58	60c multicolored	.40	.40
384	A58	$1 multicolored	.70	.70
a.		Souvenir sheet of 4, #381-384	1.75	1.75
		Nos. 381-384 (4)	1.60	1.60

Rotary International, 75th anniv.

Brown Booby, London 1980 Emblem A59

25c, Magnificent frigatebird. 50c, White-tailed tropic bird. 75c, Brown pelican.

1980, May 6　Wmk. 373　Perf. 14

385	A59	20c shown	.25	.25
386	A59	25c multicolored	.35	.35
387	A59	50c multicolored	.60	.60
388	A59	75c multicolored	.80	.80
a.		Souvenir sheet of 4, #385-388	2.00	2.00
		Nos. 385-388 (4)	2.00	2.00

London 80 Intl. Stamp Exhib., May 6-14.

Nos. 361-362 Overprinted

1980, July 7　Photo.　Perf. 13½

389	A56	13c multicolored	.25	.25
390	A56	75c multicolored	.45	.45

Sir Francis Drake — A60

1980, Sept. 26　Litho.　Perf. 14½

391	A60	8c shown	.45	.45
392	A60	15c Queen Elizabeth I	.75	.75
393	A60	30c Drake knighted	.90	.90
394	A60	75c Golden Hinde	1.90	1.90
a.		Souvenir sheet of 4, #391-394	4.00	4.00
		Nos. 391-394 (4)	4.00	4.00

400th anniv. of circumnavigation of the world.

Jost Van Dyke A61

1980, Dec. 1　Wmk. 373　Perf. 14

395	A61	2c shown	.25	.25
396	A61	5c Peter Island	.25	.25
397	A61	13c Virgin Gorda	.25	.25
398	A61	22c Anegada	.35	.35
399	A61	30c Norman Island	.40	.40
400	A61	$1 Tortola	.75	.75
a.		Souvenir sheet of 1	1.50	1.50
		Nos. 395-400 (6)	2.25	2.25

Dancing Lady — A62

1981, Mar. 3　Litho.　Perf. 11

401	A62	5c shown	.25	.25
402	A62	20c Love in the mist	.25	.25
403	A62	22c Red pineapple	.25	.25
404	A62	75c Dutchman's pipe	.85	.85
405	A62	$1 Maiden apple	.85	.85
		Nos. 401-405 (5)	2.45	2.45

Royal Wedding Issue
Common Design Type

1981, July 22　Litho.　Perf. 14

406	CD331	10c Bouquet	.25	.25
407	CD331	35c Charles, Queen Mother	.25	.25
408	CD331	$1.25 Couple	.60	.60
		Nos. 406-408 (3)	1.10	1.10

#406-408 each se-tenant with decorative label.

Duke of Edinburgh's Awards, 25th Anniv. — A63

1981, Sept. 16　Wmk. 373　Perf. 14

409	A63	10c Stamp collecting	.25	.25
410	A63	15c Running	.25	.25
411	A63	50c Camping	.30	.30
412	A63	$1 Duke of Edinburgh	.40	.40
		Nos. 409-412 (4)	1.20	1.20

Intl. Year of the Disabled A64

1981, Oct. 19　Litho.　Perf. 14

413	A64	15c Children	.25	.25
414	A64	20c Fort Charlotte Children's Center	.30	.30
415	A64	30c Playing music	.35	.35
416	A64	$1 Center, diff.	.75	.75
		Nos. 413-416 (4)	1.65	1.65

A65

Virgin and Child (Christmas): Details from Adoration of the Shepherds, by Rubens. 50c, horiz.

1981, Nov. 30　Litho.　Perf. 14

417	A65	5c multicolored	.25	.25
418	A65	15c multicolored	.25	.25
419	A65	30c multicolored	.50	.50
420	A65	$1 multicolored	1.50	1.50
		Nos. 417-420 (4)	2.50	2.50

Souvenir Sheet

421	A65	50c multicolored	2.50	2.50

A66

Hummingbirds on local flora: 15c, Green-throated carib, erythrina. 30c, Same, bougainvillea. 35c, Antillean crested hummingbird, granadilla passiflora. $1.25, Same, hibiscus.

1982, Apr. 15　Litho.　Perf. 14x14½

422	A66	15c multicolored	.80	.50
423	A66	30c multicolored	1.00	1.00
424	A66	35c multicolored	1.20	1.20
425	A66	$1.25 multicolored	2.50	2.50
		Nos. 422-425 (4)	5.50	5.20

10th Anniv. of Lions Club of Tortola — A67

1982, May 3　　　　Perf. 13½x14

426	A67	10c Helping disabled	.30	.25
427	A67	20c Headquarters	.40	.30
428	A67	30c Map	.55	.30
429	A67	$1.50 Emblem	1.75	2.00
a.		Souvenir sheet of 4, #426-429	3.00	3.00
		Nos. 426-429 (4)	3.00	2.85

Princess Diana Issue
Common Design Type

1982, July 1　Litho.　Perf. 14

430	CD333	10c Arms	.25	.25
431	CD333	35c Diana	.35	.35
432	CD333	50c Wedding	.50	.50
433	CD333	$1.50 Portrait	1.90	1.90
		Nos. 430-433 (4)	3.00	3.00

10th Anniv. of Air BVI (Natl. Airline) A68

1982, Sept. 10　Wmk. 373　Perf. 14

434	A68	10c Douglas DC-3	.30	.30
435	A68	15c Britten-Norman Islander	.55	.55
436	A68	60c Hawker-Siddeley	2.40	2.40
437	A68	75c Planes	2.75	2.75
		Nos. 434-437 (4)	6.00	6.00

Scouting Year A69

8c, Emblem, Flag raising. 20c, Cub scout, nature study. 50c, Kayak, sea scout. $1, Camp Brownsea Is., Baden-Powell.

1982, Nov. 18

438	A69	8c multicolored	.25	.25
439	A69	20c multicolored	.35	.35
440	A69	50c multicolored	.90	.90
441	A69	$1 multicolored	1.40	1.40
		Nos. 438-441 (4)	2.90	2.90

Commonwealth Day — A70

1983, Mar. 14   Perf. 13½x14

442	A70	10c Legislature in session	.25	.25
443	A70	30c Wind surfing	.30	.30
444	A70	35c Globe	.35	.35
445	A70	75c Flags	1.25	1.25
		Nos. 442-445 (4)	2.15	2.15

Nursing Week A71

10c, Florence Nightingale (1820-1910), vert. 30c, Nurse, assistant, vert. 60c, Public health. 75c, Peebles Hospital.

1983, May 9   Litho.   Perf. 14½

446	A71	10c multicolored	.60	.25
447	A71	30c multicolored	1.00	.45
448	A71	60c multicolored	1.90	1.25
449	A71	75c multicolored	1.90	1.75
		Nos. 446-449 (4)	5.40	3.70

Boat Building A72

1983, July 25   Perf. 14

450	A72	15c First stage	.35	.35
451	A72	25c 2nd stage	.55	.55
452	A72	50c Launching	1.10	1.10
453	A72	$1 First voyage	2.00	2.00
a.		Souvenir sheet of 4, #450-453	4.00	4.00
		Nos. 450-453 (4)	4.00	4.00

Manned Flight Bicentenary — A73

1983, Sept. 15   Wmk. 373   Perf. 14

454	A73	10c Grumman Goose	.25	.25
455	A73	30c De Havilland Heron	.50	.50
456	A73	60c EMB Bandeirante	1.15	1.15
457	A73	$1.25 Hawker-Siddeley 748	2.10	2.10
		Nos. 454-457 (4)	4.00	4.00

Christmas — A74

Raphael Paintings: 8c, Madonna & Child with Infant Baptist. 15c, La Belle Jardiniere. 50c, Madonna del Granduca. $1, Terranuova Madonna.

1983, Nov. 7   Litho.   Perf. 14½

458	A74	8c multicolored	.25	.25
459	A74	15c multicolored	.25	.25
460	A74	50c multicolored	.80	.80
461	A74	$1 multicolored	1.60	1.60
a.		Souvenir sheet of 4, #458-461	3.50	3.50
		Nos. 458-461 (4)	2.90	2.90

World Chess Federation, 60th Anniv. — A75

10c, Local tournament. 35c, Chess pieces, vert. 75c, 1980 Olympiad, Winning board, vert. $1, Gold medal.

1984, Feb. 20   Litho.   Perf. 14

462	A75	10c multicolored	1.00	1.00
463	A75	35c multicolored	1.75	1.75
464	A75	75c multicolored	4.25	4.25
465	A75	$1 multicolored	6.75	6.75
		Nos. 462-465 (4)	13.75	13.75

Lloyd's List Issue
Common Design Type

15c, Port Purcell, Tortola. 25c, Boeing 747. 50c, Shipwreck of RMS Rhone. $1, Booker Viking.

1984, Apr. 16   Litho.   Perf. 14½x14

466	CD335	15c multicolored	.35	.35
467	CD335	25c multicolored	.65	.65
468	CD335	50c multicolored	1.25	1.25
469	CD335	$1 multicolored	2.00	2.00
		Nos. 466-469 (4)	4.25	4.25

Souvenir Sheet

UPU Congress — A76

1984, May 16   Wmk. 373   Perf. 14

470	A76	$1 Emblem, jet, mailboat	2.75	2.75

1984 Summer Olympics A77

1984, July 3

471	A77	15c Runners	.40	.40
472	A77	15c Runner	.40	.40
a.		Pair, #471-472	1.25	1.25
473	A77	20c Wind surfers	.50	.50
474	A77	20c Wind surfer	.50	.50
a.		Pair, #473-474	1.50	1.50
475	A77	30c Yachts	.60	.60
476	A77	30c Yacht	.60	.60
a.		Pair, #475-476	2.00	2.00
		Nos. 471-476 (6)	3.00	3.00

Souvenir Sheet

477	A77	$1 Torch bearer, vert.	2.50	2.50

Festival (Slavery Abolition Sesquicentennial) — A78

Designs: No. 478: a, Steel band. b, Calypso dancers. c, Dancers (men). d, Woman in traditional dress. e, Parade float.
No. 479 (Sail color of boat(s) in foreground): a, Green & white. b, Red & white, white, purple & white. c, white, yellow & white, blue & white. d, Yellow, red & white. e, Purple & white, white.
Nos. 478 and 479 each in continuous design.

1984, Aug. 14   Perf. 13½x14

478		Strip of 5, Parade	1.50	1.50
a.-e.	A78	10c, any single	.25	.25
479		Strip of 5, Regatta	3.00	3.00
a.-e.	A78	30c, any single	.45	.45

Local Boats A79

1984, Nov. 15   Wmk. 373   Perf. 13

480	A79	10c Sloop	.70	.40
481	A79	35c Fishing boat	1.10	1.10
482	A79	60c Schooner	1.30	1.30
483	A79	75c Cargo boat	1.30	1.60
a.		Souvenir sheet of 4, #480-483	4.50	4.50
		Nos. 480-483 (4)	4.40	4.40

Four stamps picturing Michael Jackson were printed. The designs were not acceptable to the Virgin Islands so they were not issued. A number of stamps had been distributed in advance for publicity purposes.

New Coinage A80

1985, Jan. 15   Litho.   Perf. 14½

484	A80	1c Hawksbill Turtle	.25	.25
485	A80	5c Bonito	.25	.25
486	A80	10c Great Barricuda	.25	.25
487	A80	25c Blue Marlin	.55	.55
488	A80	50c Dolphin	1.15	1.25
489	A80	$1 Spotfin Butterfly Fish	2.25	2.25
a.		Miniature sheet of 6, #484-489	5.00	5.00
		Nos. 484-489 (6)	4.70	4.80

Birds — A81

1985, July 3   Wmk. 373   Perf. 14

490	A81	1c Boatswain bird	1.00	2.00
491	A81	2c Night gaulin	1.00	2.00
492	A81	5c Rain bird	1.50	1.50
493	A81	8c Mockingbird	1.50	2.50
494	A81	10c Chinchary	1.75	.50
495	A81	12c Wild pigeon	2.00	1.00
496	A81	15c Bittlin	2.50	1.00
497	A81	18c Blach witch	2.75	3.00
498	A81	20c Pond shakey	2.50	1.25
499	A81	25c Killy-killy	2.50	1.25
500	A81	30c Thrushie	2.50	1.00
501	A81	35c Marmi dove	2.50	1.00
502	A81	40c Little gaulin	3.00	1.25
503	A81	50c Ground dove	3.25	1.25
504	A81	60c Blue gaulin	3.75	4.50
505	A81	$1 Pimleco	4.75	5.50
506	A81	$2 White booby	5.25	8.00
507	A01	$3 Cow bird	7.25	12.50
508	A81	$5 Turtle dove	8.75	15.00
		Nos. 490-508 (19)	60.00	66.00

For overprints see Nos. O16-O34.

1987, Oct. 28   Wmk. 384

494a	A81	10c	.90	.90
496a	A81	15c	1.30	1.30
498a	A81	20c	1.80	1.80
499a	A81	25c	2.25	2.25
501a	A81	35c	2.75	2.75
505a	A81	$1	8.00	8.00
507a	A81	$3	23.00	23.00
		Nos. 494a-507a (7)	40.00	40.00

Queen Mother, 85th Birthday — A82

Portraits.

1985, Aug. 20   Litho.   Perf. 12½

509	A82	10c Facing right	.25	.25
510	A82	10c Facing left	.25	.25
a.		Pair, #509-510	.30	.30
511	A82	25c Facing right	.25	.25
512	A82	25c Facing left	.25	.25
a.		Pair, #511-512	.55	.55
513	A82	50c Facing right	.40	.40
514	A82	50c Facing forward	.40	.40
a.		Pair, #513-514	.85	.85
515	A82	75c Facing right	.60	.60
516	A82	75c Facing forward	.60	.60
a.		Pair, #515-516	1.25	1.25
		Nos. 509-516 (8)	3.00	3.00

Souvenir Sheets

1985-86   Litho.   Perf. 13x12½

517		Sheet of 2	2.25	2.25
a.-b.	A82	$1 dull grn & multi	1.10	1.10
518		Sheet of 2	3.00	3.00
a.-b.	A82	$1 orange & multi	1.50	1.50
519		Sheet of 2	7.50	7.50
a.-b.	A82	$2.50 dl yel & multi	3.75	3.75

Issued: #517, 12/18/85; #518-519, 2/18/86.
For overprints see Nos. 528-531.

Audubon Birth Bicent. — A83

1985, Dec. 17   Perf. 15

520	A83	5c Seaside sparrow	.25	.25
521	A83	30c Passenger pigeon	.50	.50
522	A83	50c Yellow-breasted chat	.85	.85
523	A83	$1 American kestrel	1.40	1.40
		Nos. 520-523 (4)	3.00	3.00

Exists imperf.

Cruise Ships A84

1986, Jan. 27

524	A84	35c Flying Cloud	.75	.75
525	A84	50c Newport Clipper	1.10	1.10
526	A84	75c Cunard Countess	1.75	1.75
527	A84	$1 Sea Goddess	2.50	2.50
		Nos. 524-527 (4)	6.10	6.10

Nos. 511-512,
515-516 Ovptd.

1986, Apr. 17   Litho.   Perf. 12½

528	A82	25c on No. 511	.50	.50
529	A82	25c on No. 512	.50	.50
530	A82	75c on No. 515	1.75	1.75
531	A82	75c on No. 516	1.75	1.75
		Nos. 528-531 (4)	4.50	4.50

Queen Elizabeth II, 60th
Birthday — A85

12c, Portrait, 1958. 35c, Maundy service.
$1.50, Contemporary photograph. $2, Canberra, 1982, vert.
$3, Contemporary photograph, diff.

Perf. 13x12½, 12½x13

1986, Apr. 21   Litho.

532	A85	12c multicolored	.25	.25
533	A85	35c multicolored	.25	.25
534	A85	$1.50 multicolored	.60	.60
535	A85	$2 multicolored	.90	.90
		Nos. 532-535 (4)	2.00	2.00

Souvenir Sheet

536	A85	$3 multicolored	4.25	4.25

Stamps with blue ribbons and frames omitted were from stock sold when the printer was liquidated.

Wedding of Prince Andrew and Sarah
Ferguson — A86

1986, July 23   Perf. 12½

537	A86	35c Couple, vert.	.45	.45
538	A86	35c Sarah, vert.	.45	.45
539	A86	$1 Andrew	.75	.75
540	A86	$1 Sarah, diff.	.75	.75
		Nos. 537-540 (4)	2.40	2.40

Stamps of the same denomination exist setenant.

Nos. 537-540 overprinted "Congratulations to T.R.H. The Duke & Duchess of York" were not issued.

Traditional Rum Production — A87

1986, July 30   Perf. 14

541	A87	12c Harvesting sugar cane	.50	.50
542	A87	40c Grinding	2.00	2.00
543	A87	60c Distillery	3.25	3.25
544	A87	$1 Transport	5.25	5.25
		Nos. 541-544 (4)	11.00	11.00

Souvenir Sheet

545	A87	$2 Up Spirits ceremony, 19th cent.	6.50	6.50

Souvenir Sheet

Wedding of Prince Andrew and Sarah
Ferguson — A88

1986, Oct. 15   Litho.   Perf. 13x12½

546	A88	$4 multicolored	3.75	3.75

Cable-Laying Ships — A89

1986, Oct. 15   Wmk. 380   Perf. 12½

547	A89	35c Sentinel	.65	.65
548	A89	35c Retriever	.65	.65
a.		Pair, #547-548	1.30	1.30
549	A89	60c Cable Enterprise	1.10	1.10
550	A89	60c Mercury	1.10	1.10
a.		Pair, #549-550	2.25	2.25
551	A89	75c Recorder	1.25	1.25
552	A89	75c Pacific Guardian	1.25	1.25
a.		Pair, #551-552	2.50	2.50
553	A89	$1 Great Eastern	1.75	1.75
554	A89	$1 Cable Venture	1.75	1.75
a.		Pair, #553-554	3.50	3.50
		Nos. 547-554 (8)	9.50	9.50

Souvenir Sheets

555		Sheet of 2	1.30	1.30
a.-b.		A89 40c, like #547-548	.65	.65
556		Sheet of 2	1.60	1.60
a.-b.		A89 50c, like #549-550	.80	.80
557		Sheet of 2	2.50	2.50
a.-b.		A89 80c, like #551-552	1.25	1.25
558		Sheet of 2	4.75	4.75
a.-b.		A89 $1.50, like #553-554	2.25	2.25

Cable and wireless in the islands, 20th anniv. Exists Imperf. Value, set of 4 sheets $50.

Souvenir Sheets

Statue of Liberty, Cent. — A90

Various views of the statue.

1986, Dec. 15   Litho.   Perf. 14

559	A90	50c multicolored	.60	.60
560	A90	75c multicolored	1.00	1.00
561	A90	90c multicolored	1.10	1.10
562	A90	$1 multicolored	1.30	1.30
563	A90	$1.25 multicolored	1.60	1.60
564	A90	$1.50 multicolored	1.90	1.90
565	A90	$1.75 multicolored	2.25	2.25
566	A90	$2 multicolored	2.40	2.40
567	A90	$2.50 multicolored	3.25	3.25
		Nos. 559-567 (9)	15.40	15.40

A91

Shipwrecks — A92

12c, Spanish galleon, 18th cent. 35c, HMS Astrea, 1808. 75c, RMS Rhone, 1867. $1.50, SS Rocus, 1929.
$2.50, Brig Volvart, 1918.

1987, Apr. 15   Perf. 14

572	A91	12c multicolored	.85	.85
573	A91	35c multicolored	2.40	2.40
574	A91	75c multicolored	4.75	4.75
575	A91	$1.50 multicolored	10.00	10.00
		Nos. 572-575 (4)	18.00	18.00

Souvenir Sheet

576	A92	$2.50 multicolored	16.00	16.00

Natl. Flags,
Outline
Maps — A93

1987, May 28

577	A93	10c Montserrat	.25	.25
578	A93	15c Grenada	.55	.55
579	A93	20c Dominica	.80	.80
580	A93	25c St. Kitts-Nevis	1.00	1.00
581	A93	35c St. Vincent and Grenadines	1.25	1.25
582	A93	50c Virgin Isls.	1.90	1.90
583	A93	75c Antigua & Barbuda	2.75	2.75
584	A93	$1 St. Lucia	4.00	4.00
		Nos. 577-584 (8)	12.50	12.50

11th Meeting of the Organization of Eastern Caribbean States.

Botanical
Gardens — A94

1987, Aug. 12   Wmk. 384

585	A94	12c Spider lily	.75	.75
586	A94	35c Barrel cactus	2.25	2.25
587	A94	$1 Wild plantain	3.25	3.25
588	A94	$1.50 Little butterfly orchid	9.25	9.25
		Nos. 585-588 (4)	15.50	15.50

Souvenir Sheet

589	A94	$2.50 White cedar	4.50	4.50

Postal
Service
Bicent.
A95

Designs: 10c, 18th Cent. packet, #7 canceled "A13." 20c, Map of the islands, #22 canceled "A91." 35c, Tortola Post Office and Customs House, and #5 canceled "Tortola De 20 61." $1.50, Mail plane and #154 canceled "Road town No 2 64 Tortola W.I." $2.50, Late 19th cent. steam packet and #10 canceled "A Tortola Ap 12 70."

1987, Dec. 17   Litho.   Perf. 14½

590	A95	10c multicolored	.70	.70
591	A95	20c multicolored	1.40	1.40
592	A95	35c multicolored	2.25	2.25
593	A95	$1.50 multicolored	10.00	10.00
		Nos. 590-593 (4)	14.35	14.35

Souvenir Sheet

594	A95	$2.50 multicolored	7.00	7.00

Paintings by
Titian — A96

10c, Salome, 1512. 12c, Man with the Glove, c. 1520-22. 20c, Fabrizio Salvaresio, 1558. 25c, Daughter of Roberto Strozzi, 1542. 40c, Pope Julius II. 50c, Bishop Ludovico Beccadelli, 1552. 60c, Philip II. $1, Empress Isabella of Portugal, 1548. #603, Emperor Charles V at Muhlberg, 1548. #604, Pope Paul III & His Grandsons, 1546.

Perf. 13½x14

1988, Aug. 11   Unwmk.

595	A96	10c multicolored	.65	.65
596	A96	12c multicolored	.70	.70
597	A96	20c multicolored	.90	.90
598	A96	25c multicolored	1.00	1.00
599	A96	40c multicolored	1.60	1.60
600	A96	50c multicolored	1.75	1.75
601	A96	60c multicolored	1.90	1.90
602	A96	$1 multicolored	2.50	2.50
		Nos. 595-602 (8)	11.00	11.00

Souvenir Sheet

603	A96	$2 multicolored	10.00	10.00
604	A96	$2 multicolored	10.00	10.00

1st Annual Open Chess
Tournament — A97

35c, Pawn & Transporter aircraft over Sir Francis Drake Channel. $1, King & Jose Raul Capablanca (1888-1942), Cuban chess master and world champion from 1921-27. $2, Match scene.

1988, Aug. 25   Unwmk.   Perf. 14

605	A97	35c multicolored	4.00	4.00
606	A97	$1 multicolored	11.50	11.50

Souvenir Sheet

607	A97	$2 multicolored	12.50	12.50

1988
Summer
Olympics,
Seoul
A98

1988, Sept. 8

608	A98	12c Hurdling	.65	.65
609	A98	20c Windsurfing	1.10	1.10
610	A98	75c Basketball	3.75	3.75
611	A98	$1 Tennis	4.00	4.00
		Nos. 608-611 (4)	9.50	9.50

Souvenir Sheet

612	A98	$2 Running	5.25	5.25

Intl. Red Cross, 125th Anniv. A99

Safety warnings and steps in administering cardiopulmonary resuscitation (CPR): 12c, "Don't swim alone." 30c, "No swimming during electrical storms." 60c, "Don't eat before swimming." $1, "Proper equipment for boating." No. 617a, Turn victim on back. No. 617b, Position victim's chin so breathing passages are not blocked. No. 617c, Mouth-to-mouth resuscitation. No. 617d, Chest compressions. Nos. 617a-617d vert.

1988, Sept. 26

613	A99	12c multicolored	.80	.80
614	A99	30c multicolored	2.00	2.00
615	A99	60c multicolored	3.75	3.75
616	A99	$1 multicolored	6.50	6.50
		Nos. 613-616 (4)	13.05	13.05

Souvenir Sheet

617		Sheet of 4	6.25	6.25
a.-d.		A99 50c any single	1.10	1.10

#617a-617d has a continuous design.

Visit of Princess Alexandra — A100

Various photographs of the princess.

1988, Nov. 9   Litho.   Perf. 14

618	A100	40c shown	2.75	2.75
619	A100	$1.50 multi, diff.	6.00	6.00

Souvenir Sheet

620	A100	$2 multi, diff.	8.00	8.00

World Wildlife Fund — A101

Brown pelicans, Pelecanus Occidentalis: 10c, Pelican in flight. 12c, Perched. 15c, Close-up of head. 35c, Swallowing fish.

1988, Nov. 15

621	A101	10c multicolored	1.50	1.50
622	A101	12c multicolored	1.75	1.75
623	A101	15c multicolored	2.00	2.00
624	A101	35c multicolored	4.00	4.00
		Nos. 621-624 (4)	9.25	9.25

Reptiles, Marine Mammals and Birds — A102

20c, Anegada rock iguana. 40c, Virgin gorda dwarf gecko. 60c, Hawksbill turtle. $1, Humpback whale. #629, Northern shoveler, American widgeon & ring-necked ducks. #630, Trunk turtle.

1988, Nov. 15

625	A102	20c multicolored	1.50	1.50
626	A102	40c multicolored	2.00	2.00
627	A102	60c multicolored	3.00	3.00
628	A102	$1 multicolored	7.00	7.00
		Nos. 625-628 (4)	13.50	13.50

Souvenir Sheets

629	A102	$2 multicolored	11.50	11.50
630	A102	$2 multicolored	6.50	6.50

Spring Regatta A103

Various yachts.

1989, Apr. 7   Litho.   Perf. 14

631	A103	12c multi, diff., vert.	.45	.45
632	A103	40c shown	1.40	1.40
633	A103	75c multi, diff., vert.	2.00	2.00
634	A103	$1 multi, diff.	3.00	3.00
		Nos. 631-634 (4)	6.85	6.85

Souvenir Sheet

635	A103	$2 multi, diff., vert.	7.00	7.00

Pre-Columbian Societies and Their Customs — A104

1989, May 18

636	A104	10c Hammock	.75	.75
637	A104	20c Making a fire	.95	.95
638	A104	25c Carvers	1.10	1.10
639	A104	$1.50 Arawak family	5.25	5.25
		Nos. 636-639 (4)	8.05	8.05

Souvenir Sheet

640	A104	$2 Ritual	10.00	10.00

Discovery of America 500th anniv. (in 1992).

1st Moon Landing, 20th Anniv. A105

Highlights of the Apollo 11 mission: 15c, Lunar surface, mission emblem. 30c, Buzz Aldrin conducting solar wind experiment. 65c, Raising American flag. $1, Recovery of crew after splashdown. $2, Portrait of crew.

1989, Sept. 28   Litho.   Perf. 14

641	A105	15c multicolored	1.00	1.00
642	A105	30c multicolored	1.75	1.75
643	A105	65c multicolored	3.50	3.50
644	A105	$1 multicolored	5.00	5.00
		Nos. 641-644 (4)	11.25	11.25

Souvenir Sheet
Perf. 13½x14

645	A105	$2 multicolored	11.00	11.00

No. 645 contains one 37x46mm stamp.

Methodist Church, 200th Anniv. A106

Designs: 12c, Black Harry, Nathaniel Gilbert preaching. 25c, Book symbolizing role of the church in education. 35c, East End Methodist Church, 1810. $1.25, John Wesley, modern youth choir. $2, Thomas Coke.

1989, Oct. 24   Perf. 14

646	A106	12c multicolored	.50	.50
647	A106	25c multicolored	1.10	1.10
648	A106	35c multicolored	1.60	1.60
649	A106	$1.25 multicolored	5.75	5.75
		Nos. 646-649 (4)	8.95	8.95

Souvenir Sheet

650	A106	$2 multicolored	8.00	8.00

1990 World Cup Soccer Championships, Italy — A107

Various athletes.

1989, Nov. 6

651	A107	5c shown	.65	.65
652	A107	10c multi, diff.	.65	.65
653	A107	20c multi, diff.	1.25	1.25
654	A107	$1.75 multi, diff.	10.00	10.00
		Nos. 651-654 (4)	12.55	12.55

Souvenir Sheet

655	A107	$2 Natl. team	10.00	10.00

Princess Alexandra, Sunset House — A108

Royal Yacht Britannia — A109

b, Princess Margaret, Government House. c, Hon. Angus Ogilvy, Little Dix Bay Hotel. d, Princess Diana & her children, Necker Island Resort.

1990, May 3   Litho.   Perf. 14

656		Min. sheet of 4	13.00	13.00
a.-d.		A108 50c any single	1.25	1.25

Souvenir Sheet

657	A109	$2 multicolored	14.00	14.00

Stamp World London '90.

Audubon's Shearwater — A110

12c, Red-necked pigeon. 20c, Common gallinule. 25c, Green heron. 40c, Yellow warbler. 60c, Smooth-billed ani. $1, Antillean crested hummingbird. $1.25, Black-faced grassquit. No. 666, Egg of royal tern. No. 667, Egg of red-billed tropicbird.

1990, May 15

658	A110	5c shown	1.50	1.50
659	A110	12c multicolored	2.25	2.25
660	A110	20c multicolored	2.50	2.50
661	A110	25c multicolored	2.50	2.50
662	A110	40c multicolored	2.75	2.75
663	A110	60c multicolored	3.00	3.00
664	A110	$1 multicolored	3.00	3.00
665	A110	$1.25 multicolored	3.00	3.00
		Nos. 658-665 (8)	20.50	20.50

Souvenir Sheets

666	A110	$2 multicolored	6.75	6.75
667	A110	$2 multicolored	6.75	6.75

Blue Tang A111

1990, June 18

668	A111	10c shown	.60	.60
669	A111	35c Glasseye	2.40	2.40
670	A111	50c Slippery Dick	3.50	3.50
671	A111	$1 Porkfish	6.75	6.75
		Nos. 668-671 (4)	13.25	13.25

Souvenir Sheet

672	A111	$2 Yellowtail snapper	6.25	6.25

A112

1990, Aug. 30   Litho.   Perf. 14

673	A112	12c multicolored	.40	.40
674	A112	25c multi, diff.	.85	.85
675	A112	60c multi, diff.	2.25	2.25
676	A112	$1 multi, diff.	3.00	3.00
		Nos. 673-676 (4)	6.50	6.50

Souvenir Sheet

677	A112	$2 multi, diff.	4.75	4.75

Queen Mother, 90th birthday.

A113

Various soccer players.

1990, Dec. 10   Litho.   Perf. 14

678	A113	12c multicolored	.45	.45
679	A113	20c multi, diff.	.80	.80
680	A113	50c multi, diff.	1.90	1.90
681	A113	$1.25 multi, diff.	4.00	4.00
		Nos. 678-681 (4)	7.15	7.15

Souvenir Sheet

682	A113	$2 multi, diff.	5.75	5.75

World Cup Soccer Championships, Italy.

1992 Summer Olympics, Barcelona A114

1990, Dec. 20   Litho.   Perf. 14

683	A114	12c Judo	.65	.65
684	A114	40c Yachting	2.10	2.10
685	A114	60c Hurdles	3.25	3.25
686	A114	$1 Show jumping	5.50	5.50
		Nos. 683-686 (4)	11.50	11.50

Souvenir Sheet

687	A114	$2 Windsurfing	5.50	5.50

Copper Mine Ruins A115

10c, Cyathea arborea, vert. 35c, Mt. Healthy windmill ruin, vert. $2, Baths, Virgin Gorda.

1991, Mar. 1 Litho. Perf. 14

688	A115	10c multicolored	.50	.50
689	A115	25c shown	1.25	1.25
690	A115	35c multicolored	2.00	2.00
691	A115	$2 multicolored	9.25	9.25
		Nos. 688-691 (4)	13.00	13.00

National Park Trust.

Flowers — A116

1c, Haiti Haiti. 2c, Lobster claw. 5c, Frangipani. 10c, Autograph tree. 12c, Yellow allamanda. 15c, Lantana. 20c, Jerusalem thorn. 25c, Turk's cap. 30c, Swamp immortelle. 35c, White cedar. 40c, Mahoe tree. 45c, Pinguin. 50c, Christmas orchid. 70c, Lignum vitae. $1, African tulip tree. $2, Beach morning glory. $3, Organ pipe cactus. $5, Tall ground orchid. $10, Ground orchid.

1991-92 Litho. Perf. 14
No Date Imprint Below Design

692	A116	1c multicolored	.25	.25
693	A116	2c multicolored	.25	.25
694	A116	5c multicolored	.25	.25
695	A116	10c multicolored	.25	.25
696	A116	12c multicolored	.25	.25
697	A116	15c multicolored	.40	.40
698	A116	20c multicolored	.55	.55
699	A116	25c multicolored	.65	.65
700	A116	30c multicolored	.75	.75
701	A116	35c multicolored	.85	.85
702	A116	40c multicolored	1.00	1.00
703	A116	45c multicolored	1.10	1.10
704	A116	50c multicolored	1.25	1.25
a.		Perf 12	2.00	2.00
705	A116	70c multicolored	1.75	1.75
706	A116	$1 multicolored	2.50	2.50
a.		Perf 12	3.25	3.25
707	A116	$2 multicolored	5.00	5.00
a.		Perf 12	6.50	6.50
708	A116	$3 multicolored	7.25	7.25
a.		Perf 12½x11½	10.00	10.00
709	A116	$5 multicolored	10.00	10.00
710	A116	$10 multicolored	21.00	21.00
		Nos. 692-710 (19)	55.30	55.30

Issued: 1c-$5, 5/1/91; $10, 5/92; Nos. 704a, 706a, 707a, 708a, 8/95.
For overprints see Nos. O37-O51.

1995, June 1 Wmk. 373 Sideways
Inscribed "1995" Below Design

695b	A116	10c multicolored	.60	1.60
697b	A116	15c multicolored	.80	.50
700b	A116	30c multicolored	.85	.60
701b	A116	35c multicolored	1.00	.65
703b	A116	45c multicolored	1.20	1.00
704b	A116	50c multicolored	2.75	2.10
707b	A116	$2 multicolored	3.75	6.00
709b	A116	$5 multicolored	10.50	14.00
		Nos. 695b-709b (8)	21.45	26.45

Butterflies — A117

5c, Cloudless sulphur. 10c, Flambeau. 15c, Caribbean buckeye. 20c, Gulf fritillary. 25c, Polydamus swallowtail. 30c, Little sulphur. 35c, Zebra. $1.50, Malachite.
No. 719, Monarch, horiz. No. 720, Red rim, horiz.

Unwmk.
1991, June 28 Litho. Perf. 14

711	A117	5c multicolored	.50	.50
712	A117	10c multicolored	.50	.50
713	A117	15c multicolored	.85	.85
714	A117	20c multicolored	1.25	1.25
715	A117	25c multicolored	1.40	1.40
716	A117	30c multicolored	1.75	1.75
717	A117	35c multicolored	2.10	2.10
718	A117	$1.50 multicolored	8.75	8.75
		Nos. 711-718 (8)	17.10	17.10

Souvenir Sheets

719	A117	$2 multicolored	8.75	8.75
720	A117	$2 multicolored	8.75	8.75

Voyages of Discovery A118

Ships of explorers: 12c, Ferdinand Magellan, 1519-1521. 50c, Rene-Robert de la Salle, 1682. 75c, John Cabot, 1497-1498. $1, Jacques Cartier, 1534. $2, Columbus' ship, 1493 woodcut, vert.

1991, Sept. 20 Litho. Perf. 14

721	A118	12c multicolored	2.00	2.00
722	A118	50c multicolored	3.00	3.00
723	A118	75c multicolored	3.75	3.75
724	A118	$1 multicolored	5.00	5.00
		Nos. 721-724 (4)	13.75	13.75

Souvenir Sheet

725	A118	$2 multicolored	10.00	10.00

Vincent Van Gogh (1853-1890), Painter — A119

Paintings: 15c, Cottage with Decrepit Barn and Stooping Woman. 30c, Paul Gauguin's Armchair, vert. 75c, Breton Women. $1, Vase with Red Gladioli, vert. $2, The Dance Hall in Arles (detail).

1991, Nov. 1 Perf. 13

726	A119	15c multicolored	1.25	1.25
727	A119	30c multicolored	1.75	1.75
728	A119	75c multicolored	4.50	4.50
729	A119	$1 multicolored	5.75	5.75
		Nos. 726-729 (4)	13.25	13.25

Souvenir Sheet

730	A119	$2 multicolored	12.50	12.50

Christmas A120

Entire paintings or details by Quinten Massys: 15c, The Virgin and Child Enthroned. 30c, The Virgin and Child Enthroned, diff. 60c, The Adoration of the Magi. $1, Virgin in Adoration. No. 735, The Virgin Standing with Angels. No. 736, The Adoration of the Magi.

1991, Dec. 12 Litho. Perf. 12

731	A120	15c multicolored	1.25	1.25
732	A120	30c multicolored	1.75	1.75
733	A120	60c multicolored	3.50	3.50
734	A120	$1 multicolored	4.75	4.75
		Nos. 731-734 (4)	11.25	11.25

Souvenir Sheets
Perf. 14½

735	A120	$2 multicolored	7.00	7.00
736	A120	$2 multicolored	7.00	7.00

Mushrooms — A121

12c, Agaricus bisporus, vert. 30c, Lentinus edodes. 45c, Hyrocybe autoconica, vert. $1, Gymnopilus chrysopellus. $2, Pleurotus ostreatus.

1992, Jan. 15 Perf. 14

737	A121	12c multicolored	1.75	1.75
738	A121	30c multicolored	2.10	2.10
739	A121	45c multicolored	3.25	3.25
740	A121	$1 multicolored	5.50	5.50
		Nos. 737-740 (4)	12.60	12.60

Souvenir Sheet

741	A121	$2 multicolored	15.00	15.00

Queen Elizabeth II's Accession to the Throne, 40th Anniv.
Common Design Type

1992, Feb. 6 Litho. Perf. 14

742	CD348	12c multicolored	.40	.40
743	CD348	45c multicolored	1.50	1.50
744	CD348	60c multicolored	2.10	2.10
745	CD348	$1 multicolored	3.50	3.50
		Nos. 742-745 (4)	7.50	7.50

Souvenir Sheet

746	CD348	$2 multicolored	8.00	8.00

Discovery of America, 500th Anniv. A122

10c, Queen Isabella. 15c, Columbus' fleet. 20c, Columbus' second coat of arms. 30c, Landing Monument on Watling Island, Columbus' signature. 45c, Columbus. 50c, Flag of Ferdinand & Isabella, Columbus landing on Watling Island. 70c, Convent at La Rabida. $1.50, Replica of Santa Maria at New York World's Fair, 1964-65. #755, Columbus' 2nd fleet. #756, Map.

1992, May 26 Litho. Perf. 14

747	A122	10c multi, vert.	.90	.90
748	A122	15c multi	1.60	1.60
749	A122	20c multi, vert.	1.60	1.60
750	A122	30c multi	1.60	1.60
751	A122	45c multi, vert.	2.25	2.25
752	A122	50c multi	2.25	2.25
753	A122	70c multi, vert.	2.50	2.50
754	A122	$1.50 multi	3.75	3.75
		Nos. 747-754 (8)	16.45	16.45

Souvenir Sheets

755	A122	$2 multicolored	7.50	7.50
756	A122	$2 multicolored	7.50	7.50

1992 Summer Olympics, Barcelona — A123

1992, Aug. Litho. Perf. 14

757	A123	15c Basketball	2.50	2.50
758	A123	30c Tennis	2.75	2.75
759	A123	60c Volleyball	3.00	3.00
760	A123	$1 Soccer	3.25	3.25
		Nos. 757-760 (4)	11.50	11.50

Souvenir Sheet

761	A123	$2 Olympic flame	14.00	14.00

Ministerial Government, 25th Anniv. — A124

Designs: 12c, Social progress and development. 15c, Map of Virgin Islands. 45c, Administration complex. $1.30, International finance.

1993, Apr. Litho. Perf. 14

762	A124	12c multicolored	.35	.35
763	A124	15c multicolored	.40	.40
764	A124	45c multicolored	1.25	1.25
765	A124	$1.30 multicolored	3.75	3.75
		Nos. 762-765 (4)	5.75	5.75

Tourism A125

15c, Swimming from anchored yacht. 30c, Sailboat. 60c, Scuba diver in pink wetsuit. $1, Snorkelers, anchored boat.
#770: a, Trimaran, vert. b, Scuba diver, vert.

1993, Apr. Litho. Perf. 14

766	A125	15c multi	1.50	1.50
767	A125	30c multi, vert.	2.00	2.00
768	A125	60c multi	2.50	2.50
769	A125	$1 multi, vert.	3.00	3.00
		Nos. 766-769 (4)	9.00	9.00

Souvenir Sheet

770	A125	$1 Sheet of 2, #a.-		
		b.	9.00	9.00

Miniature Sheet

Coronation of Queen Elizabeth II, 40th Anniv. A126

No. 771: a, 12c, Official coronation photograph. b, 45c, Dove atop Rod of Equity and Mercy. c, 60c, Royal family. d, $1, Recent color photo.

1993, June 2 Litho. Perf. 13½x14

771	A126	Sheet, 2 each #a.-		
		d.	12.00	12.00

A souvenir sheet containing a $2 stamp was not an authorized issue. Value $18.

Discovery of Virgin Islands, 500th Anniv. A127

3c, Ferdinand and Isabella supporting Columbus. 12c, Departure of Columbus. 15c, Departure of second voyage. 25c, Arms, flag of British Virgin Islands. 30c, Columbus, Santa Maria. 45c, Columbus' second fleet at sea. 60c, Rowing ashore. $1, Landing of Columbus. #781, Natives watching ships. #782, Columbus, two ships of his fleet.

1993, Sept. 24 Litho. Perf. 14

773	A127	3c multicolored	.30	.30
774	A127	12c multicolored	.40	.40
775	A127	15c multicolored	.55	.55
776	A127	25c multicolored	.85	.85
777	A127	30c multicolored	1.10	1.10
778	A127	45c multicolored	1.50	1.50
779	A127	60c multicolored	2.10	2.10
780	A127	$1 multicolored	3.50	3.50
		Nos. 773-780 (8)	10.30	10.30

Souvenir Sheets

781	A127	$2 multicolored	7.50	7.50
782	A127	$2 multicolored	7.50	7.50

Secondary Education and Library Services, 50th Anniv. — A128

Designs: 5c, Historical documents. 10c, Sporting activities. 15c, Stanley W. Nibbs, educator, vert. 20c, Bookmobile. 30c, Norwell E. Harrigan, educator, vert. 35c, Public library's annual summer program. 70c, Text. $1, High school.

1993, Dec.   **Litho.**
Perf. 14x13½, 13½x14

783	A128	5c multicolored	.50	.50
784	A128	10c multicolored	2.50	2.50
785	A128	15c multicolored	.70	.70
786	A128	20c multicolored	1.00	1.00
787	A128	30c multicolored	1.60	1.60
788	A128	35c multicolored	1.90	1.90
789	A128	70c multicolored	3.00	3.00
790	A128	$1 multicolored	3.25	3.25
		Nos. 783-790 (8)	14.45	14.45

Anegada Ground Iguana — A129

5c, Crawling right. 10c, Head up to right. 15c, View from behind. 45c, Head up to left. $2, Head.

1994, Jan.   **Litho.**   *Perf. 14*

791	A129	5c multicolored	.90	.90
792	A129	10c multicolored	.90	.90
793	A129	15c multicolored	1.25	1.25
794	A129	45c multicolored	2.00	2.00
		Nos. 791-794 (4)	5.05	5.05

Souvenir Sheet

795	A129	$2 multicolored	6.25	6.25

World Wildlife Fund.

Rotary Club of Virgin Islands, 25th Anniv. A130

Designs: 15c, Disaster relief airlift. 45c, Kids, Sea "Kats." 50c, Donated hospital equipment. 90c, Paul P. Harris (1868-1947), founder of Rotary Intl.

1994, June 3   **Litho.**   *Perf. 14*

796	A130	15c multicolored	.60	.60
797	A130	45c multicolored	1.35	1.35
798	A130	50c multicolored	1.50	1.50
799	A130	90c multicolored	2.50	2.50
		Nos. 796-799 (4)	5.95	5.95

Miniature Sheet of 6

First Manned Moon Landing, 25th Anniv. — A131

Designs: No. 800a, Anniversary emblem. b, Lunar landing training vehicle. c, Apollo 11 lift-off, July 16, 1969. d, Lunar module Eagle in flight. e, Moon landing site approached by Eagle. f, 1st step on Moon, July 20, 1969. No. 801, Mission patch, crew signatures.

1994, Sept. 30   **Litho.**   *Perf. 14*

800	A131	50c #a.-f.	15.00	15.00

Souvenir Sheet

801	A131	$2 multicolored	14.00	14.00

A132

Previous champions: 15c, Argentina, 1978. 35c, Italy, 1982. 50c, Argentina, 1986. $1.30, W. Germany, 1990.
$2, US flag, World Cup trophy, horiz.

1994, Dec. 16   **Litho.**   *Perf. 14*

802	A132	15c multicolored	1.50	1.50
803	A132	35c multicolored	2.00	2.00
804	A132	50c multicolored	2.25	2.25
805	A132	$1.30 multicolored	5.50	5.50
		Nos. 802-805 (4)	11.25	11.25

Souvenir Sheet

806	A132	$2 multicolored	14.00	14.00

1994 World Cup Soccer Championships, US.

UN, 50th Anniv.
Common Design Type

Designs: 15c, Peugeot P4 all-purpose light vehicle. 30c, Foden medium tanker. 45c, Sisu all-terrain vehicle. $2, Westland Lynx AH7 helicopter.

Wmk. 373

1995, Oct. 24   **Litho.**   *Perf. 14*

807	CD353	15c multicolored	.45	.45
808	CD353	30c multicolored	.90	.90
809	CD353	45c multicolored	1.60	1.60
810	CD353	$2 multicolored	4.50	4.50
		Nos. 807-810 (4)	7.45	7.45

A133

Anegada Flamingos.

Wmk. 373

1995, Nov. 15   **Litho.**   *Perf. 13*

811	A133	15c Juveniles	.50	.50
812	A133	20c Adults	.75	.75
813	A133	60c Adult feeding	2.25	2.25
814	A133	$1.45 Adult feeding chick	4.00	4.00
		Nos. 811-814 (4)	7.50	7.50

Souvenir Sheet

815	A133	$2 Chicks	8.50	8.50

Christmas — A134

Children's paintings: 12c, House with palm trees. 50c, Santa in boat. 70c, Red house, Christmas tree, presents. $1.30, Dove of peace.

Wmk. 384

1995, Dec. 1   **Litho.**   *Perf. 14*

816	A134	12c multicolored	2.00	2.00
817	A134	50c multicolored	2.75	2.75
818	A134	70c multicolored	3.75	3.75
819	A134	$1.30 multicolored	5.50	5.50
		Nos. 816-819 (4)	14.00	14.00

Island Scenes A135

Designs: 15c, Seine fishing. 35c, Sandy Spit, Jost Van Dyke. 90c, Map of Jost Van Dyke. $1.50, Foxy's wooden boat regatta.

1996, Feb. 14   **Litho.**   *Wmk. 373*
Perf. 13½x13

820	A135	15c multicolored	1.50	1.50
821	A135	35c multicolored	1.60	1.60
822	A135	90c multicolored	3.50	3.50
823	A135	$1.50 multicolored	5.50	5.50
		Nos. 820-823 (4)	12.10	12.10

See Nos. 892-896.

Queen Elizabeth II, 70th Birthday
Common Design Type

Queen in various attire, scenes of Virgin Islands: 10c, Government House. 30c, Legislative Council Chambers. 45c, Road Harbor. $1.50, Map of Virgin Islands.
$2, Wearing royal crown.

1996, Apr. 22   **Litho.**   *Wmk. 373*
Perf. 13½x14

824	CD354	10c multicolored	.30	.30
825	CD354	30c multicolored	1.00	1.00
826	CD354	45c multicolored	1.50	1.50
827	CD354	$1.50 multicolored	4.25	4.25
		Nos. 824-827 (4)	7.05	7.05

Souvenir Sheet
Perf. 13x13½

828	CD354	$2 multicolored	4.25	4.25

Modern Olympic Games, Cent. A136

Wmk. 373

1996, May 22   **Litho.**   *Perf. 13*

829	A136	20c Hurdles	.65	.65
830	A136	35c Volleyball	1.25	1.25
831	A136	50c Swimming	1.40	1.40
832	A136	$1 Sailing	2.50	2.50
		Nos. 829-832 (4)	5.80	5.80

CAPEX '96 A137

Vintage automobiles: 15c, 1934 Mercedes-Benz 500KA Cabriolet. 40c, 1934 Citroen 12. 60c, 1932 Cadillac V-8 Sport Phaeton. $1.35, 1934 Rolls Royce Phantom II.
$2, 1932 Ford Sport Coupe.

Wmk. 373

1996, June 8   **Litho.**   *Perf. 13½*

833	A137	15c multicolored	.35	.35
834	A137	40c multicolored	1.00	1.00
835	A137	60c multicolored	1.75	1.75
836	A137	$1.35 multicolored	3.75	3.75
		Nos. 833-836 (4)	6.85	6.85

Souvenir Sheet

837	A137	$2 multicolored	4.25	4.25

UNICEF, 50th Anniv. A138

Goals of UNICEF for the year 2000: 10c, Educate the child. 15c, Children first. 30c, Children have rights. 45c, No more polio.

1996, Sept. 16   *Wmk. 373*
Perf. 14x14½

838	A138	10c multicolored	.45	.45
830	A100	15c multicolored	.70	.70
840	A138	30c multicolored	1.60	1.60
841	A138	45c multicolored	1.75	1.75
		Nos. 838-841 (4)	4.50	4.50

Girl Guiding in Virgin Islands, 25th Anniv. — A139

Designs: 10c, Rainbows, arts and crafts. 15c, Brownies, community service. 30c, Guides, campfire. 45c, Rangers, H.M. Queen's birthday parade. $2, Lady Baden-Powell, world chief guide.

Wmk. 373

1996, Dec. 30   **Litho.**   *Perf. 13½*

842	A139	10c multicolored	.25	.25
843	A139	15c multicolored	.40	.40
844	A139	30c multicolored	.70	.70
845	A139	45c multicolored	1.00	1.00
846	A139	$2 multicolored	3.50	3.50
		Nos. 842-846 (5)	5.85	5.85

Game Fish A140

1997, Jan. 6   **Wmk. 384**   *Perf. 14*

847	A140	1c Mackerel	.25	.25
848	A140	10c Wahoo	.25	.25
849	A140	15c Barracuda	.35	.35
850	A140	20c Tarpon	.50	.50
851	A140	25c Tiger shark	.60	.60
852	A140	35c Sailfish	.85	.85
853	A140	40c Dolphin	.95	.95
854	A140	50c Blackfin tuna	1.25	1.25
855	A140	60c Yellowfin tuna	1.50	1.50
856	A140	75c Kingfish	1.75	1.75
857	A140	$1.50 White marlin	3.50	3.50
a.		Souvenir sheet of 1, wmk. 373	4.50	4.50
858	A140	$1.85 Amberjack	4.50	4.50
859	A140	$2 Bonito	4.75	4.75
860	A140	$5 Bonefish	12.00	12.00
861	A140	$10 Blue marlin	24.00	24.00
		Nos. 847-861 (15)	57.00	57.00

No. 857a, Hong Kong '97.
See Nos. 1020-1023.

Queen Elizabeth II and Prince Philip, 50th Wedding Anniv. — A141

#862, Prince with horse. #863, Queen Elizabeth II. #864, Queen riding in open carriage. #865, Prince Philip. #866, Queen holding hat down, Prince. #867, Prince Charles on polo pony.
$2, Queen, Prince riding in open carriage, horiz.

Wmk. 373

1997, July 10   **Litho.**   *Perf. 13*

862		30c multicolored	.70	.70
863		30c multicolored	.70	.70
a.	A141	Pair, #862-863	1.75	1.75
864		45c multicolored	1.00	1.00
865		45c multicolored	1.00	1.00
a.	A141	Pair, #864-865	2.50	2.50
866		70c multicolored	1.50	1.50
867		70c multicolored	1.50	1.50
a.	A141	Pair, #866-867	4.00	4.00
		Nos. 862-867 (6)	6.40	6.40

Souvenir Sheet

868	A141	$2 multicolored	4.50	4.50

Crabs
A142

Wmk. 373

1997, Sept. 11		**Litho.**	***Perf. 13***	
869	A142	12c Fiddler	.40	.40
870	A142	15c Coral	.60	.60
871	A142	35c Blue	1.50	1.50
872	A142	$1 Giant hermit	3.00	3.00
		Nos. 869-872 (4)	5.50	5.50

Souvenir Sheet

873	A142	$2 Arrow	5.00	5.00

Orchids — A143

Designs: a, 20c, Psychilis macconnelliae. b, 50c, Tolumnia prionochila. c, 60c, Tetramicra canaliculata. d, 75c, Liparis elata. $2, Dendrobium crumenatum, vert.

Wmk. 373

1997, Nov. 26		**Litho.**	***Perf. 14***	
874	A143	Strip of 4, #a.-d.	7.00	7.00

Souvenir Sheet

875	A143	$2 multicolored	4.50	4.50

World Voyage of Sir Francis
Drake — A144

Portions of map and: No. 876: a, Francis Drake. b, Drake Coat of Arms. c, Queen Elizabeth I. d, Christopher & Marigold. e, Golden Hinde. f, Swan. g, Cacafuego. h, Elizabeth. i, Maria. j, Drake's Astrolabe. k, Golden Hinde beakhead. l, 16th cent. compass rose.
$2, Modern ship named, "Sir Francis Drake."

1997, Dec. 13			***Perf. 14½***	
876	A144	40c Sheet of 12, #a.-l.	20.00	20.00

Souvenir Sheet

877	A144	$2 multicolored	5.00	5.00

Diana, Princess of Wales (1961-97)
Common Design Type

Portraits: a, 15c. b, 45c. c, 70c. d, $1.

		Perf. 14½x14		
1998, Mar. 31		**Litho.**	**Wmk. 373**	
878	CD355	Sheet of 4, #a.-d.	4.50	4.50

No. 878 sold for $2.30 + 20c, with surtax from international sales being donated to the Princess Diana Memorial Fund and surtax from national sales being donated to designated local charity.

Royal Air Force, 80th Anniv.
Common Design Type of 1993 Reinscribed

Designs: 20c, Fairey IIIF. 35c, Supermarine Scapa. 50c, Westland Sea King HAR3. $1.50, BAe Harrier GR7.
No. 883: a, Curtiss H.12 Large America. b, Curtiss JN-4A. c, Bell Airacobra. d, Boulton-Paul Defiant.

		Perf. 13½x14		
1998, Apr. 1		**Litho.**	**Wmk. 373**	
879	CD350	20c multicolored	.50	.50
880	CD350	35c multicolored	1.00	1.00
881	CD350	50c multicolored	1.50	1.50
882	CD350	$1.50 multicolored	3.50	3.50
		Nos. 879-882 (4)	6.50	6.50

Souvenir Sheet

883	CD350	75c Sheet of 4, #a.-d.	8.50	8.50

Marine
Life — A145

Designs: 15c, Fingerprint cyphoma. 30c, Long spined sea urchin. 45c, Split crown feather duster worm. $1, Upside down jelly. $2, Giant anemone.

1998, May 20		**Wmk. 384**	***Perf. 14½***	
884	A145	15c multicolored	1.00	1.00
885	A145	30c multicolored	1.40	1.40
886	A145	45c multicolored	2.10	2.10
887	A145	$1 multicolored	3.75	3.75
		Nos. 884-887 (4)	8.25	8.25

Souvenir Sheet

888	A145	$2 multicolored	6.00	6.00

No. 888 is a continuous design.

Childrens'
Art
Festival
A146

Wmk. 373

1998, Aug. 25		**Litho.**	***Perf. 14***	
889	A146	30c Girl in yellow & red, vert.	1.00	1.00
890	A146	45c Dancer, vert.	1.60	1.60
891	A146	$1.30 shown	4.50	4.50
		Nos. 889-891 (3)	7.10	7.10

Island Scenes Type of 1996

Designs: 12c, Salt pond. 30c, Shipwreck, HMS Rhone. 70c, Traditional house. $1.45, Salt Island. $2, Gathering salt.

1998, Oct. 28				
892	A135	12c multicolored	1.50	1.50
893	A135	30c multicolored	2.00	2.00
894	A135	70c multicolored	2.50	2.50
895	A135	$1.45 multicolored	4.00	4.00
		Nos. 892-895 (4)	10.00	10.00

Souvenir Sheet

896	A135	$2 multicolored	9.00	9.00

Anniversaries and Events — A147

5c, Classes in computer training, woodworking, electronics. 15c, Students playing musical instruments. 30c, Chapel, Mona Campus, Jamaica. 45c, Plaque on wall, university crest. 50c, Dr. John Coakley Lettsom, map of Little Jost Van Dyke island. $1, Crest of the Medical Society of London, building.

Wmk. 384

1998, Dec. 14		**Litho.**	***Perf. 14***	
897	A147	5c multicolored	.25	.25
898	A147	15c multicolored	.40	.40
899	A147	30c multicolored	.90	.90
900	A147	45c multicolored	1.25	1.25
901	A147	50c multicolored	1.50	1.50
902	A147	$1 multicolored	1.75	1.75
		Nos. 897-902 (6)	6.05	6.05

Comprehensive education in Virgin Islands, 30th anniv. (#897-898). University of West Indies, 50th anniv. (#899-900). Founding of the Medical Society of London by Dr. John Coakley Lettsom, 225th anniv. (#901-902).

Lizards
A148

Designs: 5c, Rock iguana. 35c, Pygmy gecko. 60c, Slippery back skink. $1.50, Wood slave gecko.

No. 907: a, Doctor lizard. b, Yellow-bellied lizard. c, Man lizard. d, Ground lizard.

		Perf. 14½x14		
1999, Apr. 30		**Litho.**	**Wmk. 373**	
903	A148	5c multicolored	.30	.30
904	A148	35c multicolored	1.10	1.10
905	A148	60c multicolored	2.00	2.00
906	A148	$1.50 multicolored	2.75	2.75
		Nos. 903-906 (4)	6.15	6.15

Sheet of 4

907	A148	75c #a.-d.	6.50	6.50

Wedding of Prince Edward and Sophie Rhys-Jones
Common Design Type

		Perf. 13¾x14		
1999, June 15		**Litho.**	**Wmk. 384**	
908	CD356	20c Separate portraits	1.25	1.25
909	CD356	$3 Couple	6.25	6.25

1st Manned Moon Landing, 30th Anniv.
Common Design Type

Designs: 10c, Apollo 11 on launch pad. 40c, Second stage fires. 50c, Artist's rendition of Apollo 11 on moon. $2, Astronauts transfer to lunar module. $2.50, Looking at earth from moon.

		Perf. 14x13¾		
1999, July 20		**Litho.**	**Wmk. 384**	
910	CD357	10c multicolored	.25	.25
911	CD357	40c multicolored	1.10	1.10
912	CD357	50c multicolored	1.40	1.40
913	CD357	$2 multicolored	4.00	4.00
		Nos. 910-913 (4)	6.75	6.75

Souvenir Sheet
Perf. 14

914	CD357	$2.50 multicolored	5.00	5.00

No. 914 contains one 40mm circular stamp.

Shells — A149

Designs: 25c, Measle cowrie. 35c, West Indian top shell. 75c, Zigzag scallop. $1, West Indian fighting conch.
No. 919: a, 5c, Sunrise tellin. b, 10c, King helmet. c, 25c, Like No. 915. d, 35c, Like No. 916. e, 75c, Like No. 917. f, $1, Like No. 918.

Wmk. 373

1999, Nov. 1		**Litho.**	***Perf. 14¼***	
915	A149	25c multi	.90	.90
916	A149	35c multi	1.50	1.50
917	A149	75c multi	2.50	2.50
918	A149	$1 multi	3.00	3.00
919	A149	Strip of 6, #a.-f.	15.00	15.00
		Nos. 915-919 (5)	22.90	22.90

Vignette extends to the top perforations on Nos. 915-918, but does not on stamps from No. 919.

Christmas
A150

Churches: 20c, Zion Hill Methodist. 35c, Fat Hogs Bay Seventh Day Adventist. 50c, Ruins of Kingstown St. Philip's Anglican. $1, Road Town St. William's Catholic.

		Perf. 13¼x13		
1999, Dec. 16		**Litho.**	**Wmk. 373**	
920	A150	20c multi	.50	.50
921	A150	35c multi	.85	.85
922	A150	50c multi	1.25	1.25
923	A150	$1 multi	2.00	2.00
		Nos. 920-923 (4)	4.60	4.60

British Monarchs — A151

a, Henry VII. b, Lady Jane Grey. c, Charles I. d, William III. e, George III. f, Edward VII.

Wmk. 373

2000, Feb. 29		**Litho.**	***Perf. 14***	
924	A151	60c Sheet of 6, #a.-f.	8.25	8.25

The Stamp Show 2000, London.

Prince William, 18th Birthday
Common Design Type

William: 20c, As toddler, on chest. 40c, As toddler, standing. 50c, With ski cap & goggles. 60c, Wearing suits & striped shirts. $1, Wearing sweater & bow tie.

		Perf. 14¼x13¾, 13¾x14¼		
2000, June 21		**Litho.**	**Wmk. 373**	
Stamps With White Border				
925	CD359	20c multi	.50	.50
926	CD359	40c multi, vert.	1.00	1.00
927	CD359	50c multi, vert.	1.50	1.50
928	CD359	$1 multi	2.50	2.50
		Nos. 925-928 (4)	5.50	5.50

Souvenir Sheet
Stamps Without White Border
Perf. 14¼

929		Sheet of 5	9.00	9.00
a.	CD359	20c multi	.50	.50
b.	CD359	40c multi	1.00	1.00
c.	CD359	50c multi	1.25	1.25
d.	CD359	60c multi	1.60	1.60
e.	CD359	$1 multi	2.50	2.50

Queen Mother,
100th
Birthday — A152

Various photos. Frame color: 15c, Lilac. 35c, Light green. 70c, Pink. $1.50, Light blue.

Wmk. 373

2000, Aug. 4		**Litho.**	***Perf. 13¾***	
930-933	A152	Set of 4	7.50	7.50

Flowering Plants
and
Trees — A153

10c, Red hibiscus. 15c, Pink oleander. 35c, Yellow bell. 50c, Yellow & white frangipani. 75c, Flamboyant. $2, Bougainvillea.

2000, Sept. 7			***Perf. 13½x13¾***	
934-939	A153	Set of 6	10.00	10.00

Millennium — A154

Virgin Islands history: 5c, Site of Emancipation Proclamation. 20c, Nurse Mary Louise Davies. 30c, Cheyney University, US, founded by Richard Humphreys. 45c, Enid Leona Scatliffe, former chief education officer. 50c, H. Lavity Stoutt Community College. $1 Sir J. Olva Georges.
$2, Victoria Cross of Pvt. Samuel Hodge, vert.

Wmk. 373

2000, Nov. 16   Litho.   Perf. 14
940-945 A154 Set of 6   5.75 5.75

Souvenir Sheet
946 A154 $2 multi   4.75 4.75

Restoration of the Legislative Council,
50th Anniv. — A155

Virgin Islands Councilmen: 10c, Dr. Q. William Osbourne & Arnando Scatliffe. 15c, H. Robinson O'Neal & A. Austin Henley. 20c, Wilfred W. Smith & John C. Brudenell-Bruce. 35c, Howard R. Penn & I. G. Fonseca. 50c, Carlton L. de Castro & Theodolph H. Faulkner. 60c, Willard W. Wheatley. $1, H. Lavity Stoutt.

2000, Nov. 22
947-953 A155 Set of 7   7.00 7.00

Souvenir Sheet

New Year 2001 (Year of the
Snake) — A156

No. 954: a, 50c, White-crowned dove. b, 50c, Bar-tailed cuckoo dove.

2001, Feb. 1   Perf. 14½
954 A156 Sheet of 2, #a-b   6.00 6.00

Hong Kong 2001 Stamp Exhibition.

Visiting Royal Navy Ships A157

Designs: 35c, HMS Wistaria, 1923-30. 50c, HMS Dundee, 1934-35. 60c, HMS Eurydice, 1787. 75c, HMS Pegasus, 1787. $1, HMS Astrea, 1807. $1.50 HM Yacht Britannia, 1966.

Wmk. 373

2001, Sept. 28   Litho.   Perf. 14
955-960 A157 Set of 6   17.50 17.50

Nobel Prizes,
Cent. — A158

Nobel laureates: 10c, Fridtjof Nansen, Peace, 1922. 20c, Albert Einstein, Physics, 1921. 25c, Sir Arthur Lewis, Economics, 1979. 40c, Saint-John Perse, Literature, 1960. 70c, Mother Teresa, Peace, 1979. $2, Christian Lous Lange, Peace, 1921.

2001, Oct. 5
961-966 A158 Set of 6   15.00 15.00

**Reign Of Queen Elizabeth II, 50th
Anniv. Issue**
Common Design Type

Designs: Nos. 967, 971a, 15c, Princess Elizabeth in uniform. Nos. 968, 971b, 50c, In 1977. Nos. 969, 971c, 60c, Holding flowers. Nos. 970, 971d, 75c, In 1996. No. 971e, $1, 1955 portrait by Annigoni (38x50mm).

Perf. 14¼x14½, 13¾ (#971e)

2002, Feb. 6   Litho.   Wmk. 373

With Gold Frames
967 CD360 15c multicolored   .60   .60
968 CD360 50c multicolored   1.90 1.90
969 CD360 60c multicolored   2.00 2.00
970 CD360 75c multicolored   2.00 2.00
     Nos. 967-971 (4)   6.50 6.50

Souvenir Sheet
Without Gold Frames
971 CD360 Sheet of 5, #a-e   10.00 10.00

Reptiles in Guinness Book Of World Records A159

Designs: 5c, Estuarine crocodile. 20c, Reticulated python. 30c, Komodo dragon. 40c, Boa constrictor. $1, Dwarf caiman. $2, Sphaerodactylus parthenopion. $1.50, Head of Sphaerodactylus parthenopion.

Perf. 13¼x13

2002, June 10   Litho.   Wmk. 373
972-977 A159 Set of 6   11.50 11.50
977a   Sheet of 6, #972-977   11.50 11.50

Souvenir Sheet
978 A159 $1.50 multi   5.00 5.00

Queen Mother Elizabeth (1900-2002)
Common Design Type

Designs: 20c, Wearing tiara (black and white photograph). 60c, Wearing dark blue hat. Nos. 981, 983a, $2, Wearing hat (black and white photograph). Nos. 982, 983b, $3, Wearing pink hat.

Perf. 13¾x14¼

2002, Aug. 5   Litho.   Wmk. 373
With Purple Frames
979 CD361 20c multicolored   .50   .50
980 CD361 60c multicolored   1.50 1.50
981 CD361 $2 multicolored   4.50 4.50
982 CD361 $3 multicolored   6.00 6.00
     Nos. 979-982 (4)   12.50 12.50

Souvenir Sheet
Without Purple Frames
Perf. 14½x14¼
983 CD361 Sheet of 2, #a-b   11.00 11.00

Royal Navy Ships A100

Designs: 20c, HMS Invincible and HMS Argo. 35c, HMS Boreas and HMS Solebay. 50c, HMS Coventry. $3, HMS Argyll.

Wmk. 373

2002, Aug. 30   Litho.   Perf. 14
984-987 A160 Set of 4   14.50 14.50

Island Scenes Type of 1996

Designs: 5c, Spring Bay. 40c, Devils Bay. 60c, The Baths. 75c, St. Thomas Bay. $1, Savannah and Pond Bay. $2, Trunk Bay.

2002, Sept. 13
988-993 A135 Set of 6   11.00 11.00

West Indian Whistling Duck — A161

Designs: Nos. 994, 998a, 10c, Duckling and eggs. Nos. 995, 998b, 35c, Duck standing on rock, vert. Nos. 996, 998c, 40c, Duck in water, vert. Nos. 997, 998d, 70c, Two ducks. No. 998e, $2, Duck's head.

Perf. 14¼x13¾, 13¾x14¼

2002, Dec.   Litho.   Wmk. 373
Stamps With Brown Border
994-997 A161 Set of 4   5.00 5.00

Souvenir Sheet
Stamps Without Brown Border
**Perf. 14¼x14½ (Horiz. stamps), 14½
(Vert. stamps)**
998 A161 Sheet of 5, #a-e   8.00 8.00

Birdlife International.

Anniversaries and Events — A162

No. 999, 10c: a, Sprinters. b, Cyclists.
No. 1000, 35c: a, Laser class sailboats. b, Women's long jump.
No. 1001, 50c: a, Bareboat class sailboats. b, Racing Cruiser class sailboats.
No. 1002, $1.35: a, Carlos and Esme Downing, founders of Island Sun newspaper. b, Island Sun newspaper and emblem.

Wmk. 373

2003, Mar. 13   Litho.   Perf. 13½
Horiz. pairs, #a-b
999-1002 A162 Set of 4   11.00 11.00

2002 Commonwealth Games (#999); Admission to Olympic Games, 20th anniv. (#1000); Spring Regatta, 30th anniv. (#1001); Island Sun newspaper, 40th anniv. (#1002).

Head of Queen Elizabeth II
Common Design Type
Wmk. 373

2003, June 2   Litho.   Perf. 13¾
1003 CD362 $5 multi   10.00 10.00

**Coronation of Queen Elizabeth II,
50th Anniv.**
Common Design Type

Designs: Nos. 1004, 1006a, 15c, Queen in gown. Nos. 1005, 1006b, $5, Royal Family on Buckingham Palace balcony.

Perf. 14¼x14½

2003, June 2   Litho.   Wmk. 373
Vignettes Framed, Red Background
1004 CD363 15c multi   .50   .50
1005 CD363 $5 multi   12.00 12.00

Souvenir Sheet
**Vignettes Without Frame, Purple
Panel**
1006 CD363 Sheet of 2, #a-
              b   12.50 12.50

Prince William, 21st Birthday
Common Design Type

Designs: 50c, William in polo uniform at right. $2, William on polo pony at left.

Wmk. 373

2003, June 21   Litho.   Perf. 14¼
With Gray Frames
1007 CD364 50c multi   1.00 1.00
1008 CD364 $2 multi   4.00 4.00

Without Gray Frames
1009   Horiz. pair   5.00 5.00
  a. CD364 50c multi   1.00 1.00
  b. CD364 $2 multi   4.00 4.00
     Nos. 1007-1009 (3)   10.00 10.00

Powered Flight, Cent. — A163

Designs: 15c, Douglas DC-4. 20c, Boeing Stearman "Kaydet." 35c, B-25 J Mitchell. 40c, F-4B Phantom. 70c, CH-47 Chinook helicopter. $2, AH-64 Apache helicopter.

Perf. 13¼x13¾

2003, Nov. 15   Litho.   Wmk. 373
Stamp + Label
1010-1015 A163 Set of 6   12.50 12.50

Christmas — A164

Details from Arrival of the English Ambassadors, by Vittore Carpaccio: 20c, Men standing near railing and pillar. 40c, Men, ships in background. $2.50, Seated man. No. 1019a (36x36mm), Kneeling man delivering message.

Perf. 13¾x13½

2003, Dec. 15   Litho.   Wmk. 373
1016-1018 A164 Set of 3   8.00 8.00

Souvenir Sheet
1019 A164 Sheet, #1016-
            1018, 1019a   9.50 9.50
  a. $1 multi, perf. 13½x13¼   3.00 3.00

Game Fish Type of 1997
Serpentine Die Cut 12½ on 3 Sides
2004, July 1   Litho.   Unwmk.
Self-Adhesive
Booklet Stamps
Size: 21x17mm
1020 A140 15c Barracuda   .30   .30
  a. Booklet pane of 4   1.20
1021 A140 20c Tarpon   .40   .40
  a. Booklet pane of 4   1.60
1022 A140 35c Sailfish   .70   .70
  a. Booklet pane of 4   2.80
      Complete booklet, #1020a,
      1022a   4.00
1023 A140 40c Dolphin   .80   .80
  a. Booklet pane of 3 + label 2.40
      Complete booklet, #1021a,
      1023a   5.25
     Nos. 1020-1023 (4)   2.20 2.20

Fruit — A165

2004, July 20   Wmk. 373   Perf. 13¾
Inscribed "2004" Below Design
1024 A165 15c Pomegranates   .30   .30
1025 A165 20c Cashews   .40   .40
1026 A165 35c Tamarinds   .70   .70
1027 A165 40c Soursop   .80   .80
1028 A165 50c Mangos   1.00 1.00
1029 A165 $2 Guavaberries   4.00 4.00
1030 A165 $5 Mamee apples   10.00 10.00
     Nos. 1024-1030 (7)   17.20 17.20

See Nos. 1042-1049.

2007
Inscribed "2007" Below Design
1025a A165 20c multicolored   .40   .40
1026a A165 35c multicolored   .70   .70
1028a A165 50c multicolored   1.00 1.00
1029a A165 $2 multicolored   4.00 4.00
     Nos. 1025a-1029a (4)   6.10 6.10

Virgin Islands Festival, 50th Anniv. — A166

Designs: 10c, Parade. 60c, Horse race. $1, Kayak race. $2.35, Festival Queen.

Wmk. 373

2004, Oct. 26   Litho.   Perf. 13¼
1031-1034 A166 Set of 4   10.00 10.00

Sports — A167

Designs: 75c, Women soccer players. $1, Runner.

2004, Dec. 30   **Perf. 14**
1035-1036 A167   Set of 2   4.50 4.50

FIFA (Fédération Internationale de Football Association), cent.; 2004 Summer Olympics, Athens.

Caribbean Endemic Bird Festival A168

Designs: 5c, Black and white warbler. 25c, Worm-eating warbler. 35c, Yellow warbler. 50c, Prothonotary warbler.
No. 1041: a, 10c, Prairie warbler. b, 15c, Yellow-rumped warbler. c, 40c, Black-throated blue warbler. d, 60c, Cape May warbler. e, 75c, Northern parula. f, $2.75, Palm warbler.

     Wmk. 373
2005, July 8   **Litho.**   **Perf. 13¾**
1037-1040 A168   Set of 4   3.50 3.50
1041 A168   Miniature sheet,
   #1037-1040,
   1041a-1041f   14.00 14.00

   Fruit Type of 2004
2005, Aug. 25   **Wmk. 373**
   Inscribed "2005" Below Design
1042 A165   1c Hog plum   .25 .25
  a.   Inscribed "2007"   .25 .25
1043 A165   10c Coco plum   .25 .25
1044 A165   25c Sugar apple   .50 .50
1045 A165   60c Papaya   1.25 1.25
1046 A165   75c Custard ap-
     ple   1.50 1.50
1047 A165 $1 Otaheite
     gooseberry   2.00 2.00
1048 A165 $1.50 Guava   3.00 3.00
1049 A165 $10 Passion fruit   20.00 20.00
   Nos. 1042-1049 (8)   28.75 28.75

Pope John Paul II (1920-2005) A169

     Wmk. 373
2005, Aug. 18   **Litho.**   **Perf. 14**
1050 A169 75c multi   3.00 3.00

Worldwide Fund for Nature (WWF) — A170

Various depictions of Virgin Islands tree boa: 20c, 30c, 70c, $1.05.

     Wmk. 373
2005, Sept. 15   **Litho.**   **Perf. 14**
1051-1054 A170   Set of 4   6.50 6.50
  1054a   Miniature sheet, 2 each
   #1051-1054   13.00 13.00

Battle of Trafalgar, Bicent. — A171

Designs: 5c, HMS Colossus. 25c, HMS Boreas. 75c, HMS Victory. $3, Admiral Horatio Nelson, vert.
$2.50, HMS Colossus and French ship.

2005, Oct. 18   **Perf. 14x14¾, 14¾x14**
1055-1058 A171   Set of 4   18.00 18.00
    Souvenir Sheet
     Perf. 13½
1059 A171 $2.50 multi   11.50 11.50
No. 1059 contains one 44x44mm stamp.

Christmas A172

Flora: 15c, Century plant. 35c, Poinsettia, horiz. 60c, Inkberry. $2.50, Snow on the mountain, horiz.

2005, Nov. 3   **Perf. 14¾x14, 14x14¾**
1060-1063 A172   Set of 4   11.00 11.00

Anniversaries A173

Designs: 20c, Social Security, 25th anniv. 40c, ZBVI radio station, 40th anniv. 50c, Beef Island Airstrip, 50th anniv. $1, Rotary International, cent.

     Wmk. 373
2005, Nov. 16   **Litho.**   **Perf. 13¾**
1064-1067 A173   Set of 4   7.50 7.50

Queen Elizabeth II, 80th Birthday A174

Queen: 15c, As young woman, in uniform. 75c, Wearing white hat. No. 1070, $1.50, Wearing large earrings. No. 1071, $2, Wearing gray hat with large brim.
No. 1072: a, $1.50, Like 75c. b, $2, Like #1070.

     Perf. 14¼x14
2006, July 17   **Litho.**   **Wmk. 373**
   Stamps With White Frames
1068-1071 A174   Set of 4   12.50 12.50
    Souvenir Sheet
   Stamps Without White Frames
1072 A174   Sheet of 2, #a-b   10.00 10.00

Red Cross Buildings A175

Designs: 20c, New building. $3, Previous building.

     Wmk. 373
2007, Aug. 1   **Litho.**   **Perf. 14**
1073-1074 A175   Set of 2   7.00 7.00

Royal Air Force, 90th Anniv. A176

Designs: 18c, Supermarine Spitfire. 20c, Avro Lancaster. 35c, Douglas C-47 Dakota. 60c, Handley Page Halifax. $1.25 Westland Lysander.
$2.50, Spitfire patrolling D-Day beaches.

     Wmk. 373
2008, Apr. 1   **Litho.**   **Perf. 14**
1075-1079 A176   Set of 5   9.00 9.00
    Souvenir Sheet
1080 A176 $2.50 multi   6.00 6.00

Princess Diana (1961-97) A177

Princess Diana in: 60c, Black dress. $3.50, Red dress.

2008, Apr. 7   **Perf. 13¾**
1081 A177   60c multi   1.25 1.25
    Souvenir Sheet
     Perf. 14¼
1082 A177 $3.50 multi   7.25 7.25
No. 1082 contains one 42x57mm stamp.

Rev. Charles Wesley (1707-88), Hymn Writer — A178

Designs: 20c, Arms. 50c, Wesley. $1.75, Wesley, diff.

2008, May 1   **Perf. 14**
1083-1085 A178   Set of 3   5.00 5.00

2008 Summer Olympics, Beijing A179

Designs: 15c, Bamboo, runner. 18c, Dragon, yachting. 20c, Lanterns, runner. $1, Fish, yachting.

2008, Aug. 1   **Perf. 13½**
1086-1089 A179   Set of 4   4.00 4.00

Ministerial Government — A180

Arms and: 18c, Mace in House of Assembly, mace head. 35c, House of Assembly, entrance arch. 60c, Henry O. Creque, Ivan Dawson. $2, Paul Wattley, Terrance B. Lettsome.

2008, Aug. 21   **Perf. 14x14¾**
1090-1093 A180   Set of 4   6.50 6.50

End of World War I, 90th Anniv. — A181

Designs: 75c, Sanctuary Wood Cemetery, Ypres, Belgium, horiz. 80c, Somme Battlefield, France, horiz. 90c, Lone Pine Cemetery, Gallipoli, Turkey, horiz. $1, War Memorial, Vauquois, France. $1.15, Theipval Memorial, France, horiz. $1.25, Menin Gate, Ypres, Belgium, horiz.
$2, Wreath of Remembrance.

     Wmk. 406
2008, Sept. 16   **Litho.**   **Perf. 14**
1094-1099 A181   Set of 6   13.00 13.00
    Souvenir Sheet
1100 A181 $2 multi   5.00 5.00

J. R. O'Neal Botanic Gardens — A182

Designs: 20c, Climbing pandanus. 35c, True aloe. 50c, Crown of thorns. $1, Red-eared slider (turtle).
$2.50, Fountain.

     Wmk. 373
2009, Mar. 27   **Litho.**   **Perf. 14**
1101-1104 A182   Set of 4   6.00 6.00
    Souvenir Sheet
1105 A182 $2.50 multi   6.00 6.00

Ships and Explorers A183

Designs: 15c HMS Ark Royal. 20c, Whydah. 60c, Santa Maria. 70c, RMS Rhone. 90c, Golden Hind. $1.95, HMY Britannia.
$2, Christopher Columbus, vert.

     Wmk. 406
2009, May 25   **Litho.**   **Perf. 14**
1106-1111 A183   Set of 6   11.00 11.00
    Souvenir Sheet
1112 A183 $2 multi   5.50 5.50

Naval Aviation, Cent. A184

Victoria Cross recipients: 18c, Lieutenant Robert Hampton Gray. 35c, Lieutenant Commander Eugene Esmonde. 60c, Flight Squadron Lieutenant Rex Warneford. 90c, Squadron Commander Richard Bell Davies. $2, HMS Illustrious.

2009, June 30
1113-1116 A184   Set of 4   6.00 6.00

Souvenir Sheet
1117 A184 $2 multi   5.50 5.50

Nos. 1113-1116 each were printed in sheets of 8 + central label.

Space Exploration A185

Designs: 50c, Goddard Rocket Shop, Roswell, New Mexico, 1940. 75c, Vertol VZ-2, 1960. $1, Apollo 11 on launch pad, 1969. $1.25, Space Shuttle flight STS-126 on launch pad, 2008. $2.30, Docking procedure, International Space Station.
$3, Lunar Rover on Moon, painting by Capt. Alan Bean, vert.

2009, July 20   Perf. 13¼
1118-1122 A185   Set of 5   15.00 15.00

Souvenir Sheet
Perf. 13x13¼
1123 A185 $3 multi   7.50 7.50

No. 1123 contains one 40x60mm stamp. Nos. 1118-1122 each were printed in sheets of 6.

Scouting in the Virgin Islands, 75th Anniv. (in 2007) — A185a

2009   Litho.   Wmk. 373   Perf. 14
1123A A185a 40c multi   — —

Coral Reefs A186

Designs: 20c, Sea turtle. 35c, Fish. 50c, Seahorse, vert. 60c, Shell. $1.50, Coral reef.

Wmk. 406
2010, Mar. 29   Litho.   Perf. 12½
1124-1128 A186   Set of 5   7.50 7.50

Construction of New North Sound Post Office Substation A187

Designs: 20c, John E. George, Sub-postmaster. 50c, New post office substation, horiz. $2, Old post office substation, horiz.

Wmk. 406
2010, May 3   Litho.   Perf. 12½
1129-1131 A187   Set of 3   5.50 5.50

East End Methodist Church, 200th Anniv. A188

Designs: 20c, Church bell. 50c, Church in 2010. 60c, Church in 1977. $2, Church in early 19th cent.

Wmk. 406
2010, Nov. 10   Litho.   Perf. 13¼
1132-1135 A188   Set of 4   6.75 6.75

Sailability — A189

Various sailors and sailboats with country name and lower panels in: 5c, Dark red. 20c, Violet blue. 25c, Purple. 40c, Green. 50c, Red. $1.50, Orange red.

Wmk. 406
2011, Feb. 24   Litho.   Perf. 12½
1136-1141 A189   Set of 6   6.00 6.00

2011 Spring Regatta A190

Various sailboats with country name and lower panels in: 15c, Green. 35c, Blue, vert. 50c, Olive green, vert. $2, Olive brown.

2011, Mar. 1
1142-1145 A190   Set of 4   6.00 6.00

Souvenir Sheet

Wedding of Prince William and Catherine Middleton — A191

Perf. 14¾x14
2011, Apr. 29   Wmk. 406
1146 A191 $5 multi   10.00 10.00

Coronation of Queen Elizabeth II, 60th Anniv. — A192

Queen Elizabeth II: 20c, And Prince Philip at coronation, 1953. 50c, With Prince Philip on

1966 Virgin Islands visit. $1.50, Walking in Virgin Islands, 1977. $2, With Prince Philip, 2013.

2013, Oct. 1   Perf. 13¼x13¾
1147-1150 A192   Set of 4   8.50 8.50

Worldwide Fund for Nature (WWF) — A193

Antillean crested hummingbird: Nos. 1151, 1155a, 35c, Two birds on branch. Nos. 1152, 1155b, 40c, Bird in nest. Nos. 1153, 1155c, 75c, Bird in flight near flowers. Nos. 1154, 1155d, $1.50, Head of bird.
$5, Bird in flight near flowers, diff.

Unwmk.
2014, Jan. 30   Litho.   Perf. 14
Stamps With White Frames
1151-1154 A193   Set of 4   6.00 6.00
Stamps Without White Frames
1155 A193   Strip of 4, #a-d   6.00 6.00

Souvenir Sheet
Perf. 14x14¾
1156 A193 $5 multi   10.00 10.00

No. 1156 contains one 48x32mm stamp.

Royal Christenings A194

Photographs of British royalty with christened infants: 50c, Queen Elizabeth II, 1926. 75c, Prince Charles, 1948. $2, Prince William, 1982. $2.50, Prince George, 2013.

2014, Sept. 25   Litho.   Perf. 13x13¼
1157-1160 A194   Set of 4   11.50 11.50

Magna Carta, 800th Anniv. A195

Designs: 15c, King John approving Magna Carta. 20c, Statue of Justice. 75c, Magna Carta, field of cattails. $2.35, Arms of Virgin Islands, King John.

Perf. 13¼x13½
2015, June 15   Litho.
1161-1164 A195   Set of 4   7.00 7.00

Queen Elizabeth II, 90th Birthday — A196

Photograph of Queen Elizabeth II taken in: 20c, 1940s. 40c, 1977. $1, 1972. $2, 1999. $4, Queen Elizabeth II in 1954.

2016, Apr. 21   Litho.   Perf. 14
1165-1168 A196   Set of 4   7.25 7.25

Souvenir Sheet
1169 A196 $4 multi   8.00 8.00

Queen Elizabeth II, 90th Birthday A197

Queen Elizabeth II wearing: $10, Pink jacket and hat. $90, Light green jacket and hat.

2016, Dec. 9   Litho.   Perf. 13½
1170 A197 $10 multi   20.00 20.00
1171 A197 $90 multi   180.00 180.00

Marine Life A198

Designs: 10c, Grooved brain coral. 15c, Spiny flower coral. 18c, Elkhorn coral. 40c, Flamingo tongue. 50c, Cushion sea star. 60c, Queen conch. 80c, Caribbean reef squid. $1, Pederson cleaner shrimp. $1.50, Branching vase sponge. $2.50, Common octopus. $5, Spotted eagle ray. $10, Bottlenose dolphins.

2017, July 5   Litho.   Perf. 13¼x13½
1172 A198 10c multi   .25 .25
1173 A198 15c multi   .30 .30
1174 A198 18c multi   .40 .40
1175 A198 40c multi   .80 .80
1176 A198 50c multi   1.00 1.00
1177 A198 60c multi   1.25 1.25
1178 A198 80c multi   1.60 1.60
1179 A198 $1 multi   2.00 2.00
1180 A198 $1.50 multi   3.00 3.00
1181 A198 $2.50 multi   5.00 5.00
1182 A198 $5 multi   10.00 10.00
1183 A198 $10 multi   20.00 20.00
    Nos. 1172-1183 (12)   45.60 45.60

Turtles A199

Designs: 4c, Hawksbill turtle hatchlings. 15c, Head of Green turtle. 20c, Green turtle. 75c, Hawksbill turtle. $2.75, Head of Green turtle, diff.
$5, Head of Hawksbill turtle.

2017, Sept. 6   Litho.   Perf. 13¼x13½
1184-1188 A199   Set of 5   8.00 8.00
1188a   Vert. strip of 5, #1184-   8.00 8.00
          1188

Souvenir Sheet
1189 A199 $5 multi   10.00 10.00

No. 1185 was only printed in sheets containing four No. 1188a. Nos. 1184, 1186-1188 were each additionally printed in sheets of 10.

Fish A200

Designs: 5c, Coney fish. 15c, Balloon fish. 35c, Queen triggerfish. 90c, Red hind. $2, Queen angelfish.
$5, Scrawled filefish.

2017, Nov. 8   Litho.   Perf. 13¼x13½
1190-1194 A200   Set of 5   7.00 7.00
1194a   Vert. strip of 5, #1190-   7.00 7.00
          1194

Souvenir Sheet
1195 A200 $5 multi   10.00 10.00

No. 1191 was only printed in sheets containing four No. 1194a. Nos. 1190, 1192-1194 were each additionally printed in sheets of 10.

Wedding of Prince Harry and Meghan Markle
A201

Various photographs of couple: 20c, Prince Harry at left. 50c, Prince Harry at right. $1, On wedding day, standing. $2.50, On wedding day, in coach. $5, Couple kissing, vert.

Perf. 13¼x13½

2018, Sept. 13		**Litho.**		
1196-1199	A201	Set of 4	8.50	8.50

Souvenir Sheet

Perf. 13½x13¼

1200	A201	$5 multi	10.00	10.00

WAR TAX STAMPS

Regular Issue of 1913 Overprinted

1916-17		**Wmk. 3**	**Perf. 14**	
		Die I		
MR1	A9	1p scarlet	.55	8.00
a.		1p carmine	2.50	25.00
MR2	A9	3p violet, *yellow*	7.00	26.00

OFFICIAL STAMPS

> Catalogue values for unused stamps in this section are for Never Hinged items.

Nos. 365-368, 370-380 Overprinted "OFFICIAL" in Silver

1985, July		**Litho.**	**Perf. 14**	
O1	A57	1c multi	.30	1.25
O2	A57	3c multi	.45	1.25
O3	A57	5c multi	.45	.45
O4	A57	8c multi	.55	.60
O5	A57	13c multi	.80	.75
O6	A57	15c multi	.80	.75
O7	A57	18c multi	.90	1.50
O8	A57	20c multi	.90	.80
O9	A57	25c multi	1.25	2.00
O10	A57	30c multi	1.40	1.00
O11	A57	60c multi	2.00	2.50
O12	A57	$1 multi	3.25	3.75
O13	A57	$2.50 multi	5.75	8.00
O14	A57	$3 multi	7.00	10.00
O15	A57	$5 multi	9.50	11.50
		Nos. O1-O15 (15)	35.30	46.10

Nos. 364-380 overprinted in gold and Nos. 364, 369 overprinted in silver exist but were not issued by the Virgin Islands.

Nos. 490-508 Ovptd. "OFFICIAL"

1986		**Litho.**	**Perf. 14**	
O16	A81	1c multicolored	.75	2.00
O17	A81	2c multicolored	.50	2.00
O18	A81	5c multicolored	1.50	2.25
O19	A81	8c multicolored	.70	3.00
O20	A81	10c multicolored	1.50	2.25
O21	A81	12c multicolored	1.75	.50
O22	A81	15c multicolored	1.75	.50
O23	A81	18c multicolored	.85	.90
O24	A81	20c multicolored	1.50	1.25
O25	A81	25c multicolored	1.75	1.25
O26	A81	30c multicolored	1.75	1.25
O27	A81	35c multicolored	1.50	1.25
O28	A81	40c multicolored	1.50	1.25
O29	A81	50c multicolored	1.40	2.00
O30	A81	60c multicolored	1.75	2.50
O31	A81	$1 multicolored	2.75	3.50
O32	A81	$2 multicolored	3.00	4.50
O33	A81	$3 multicolored	7.50	9.50
O34	A81	$5 multicolored	12.00	12.00
		Nos. O16-O34 (19)	45.70	53.65

Issue: 1, 5, 10, 15, 20-35c, $5, 7/3; others, 1/28.

Nos. 694-695, 698, 701-706, 708 Ovptd. "OFFICIAL"

1991, Sept.		**Litho.**	**Perf. 14**	
O37	A116	5c multicolored	.75	.75
O38	A116	10c multicolored	.75	.75
O41	A116	20c multicolored	.75	.75

O44	A116	35c multicolored	1.40	1.40
O45	A116	40c multicolored	1.50	1.50
O46	A116	45c multicolored	1.75	1.75
O47	A116	50c multicolored	1.90	1.90
O48	A116	70c multicolored	2.75	2.75
O49	A116	$1 multicolored	3.75	3.75
O51	A116	$3 multicolored	7.00	9.50
		Nos. O37-O51 (10)	22.30	24.80

Ovpt. on Nos. O37-O51 is 19mm long. Used values are for c-t-o examples.
Nos. O37-O38, O41, O44-O49, O51 were not available unused until mid-1992.
This set was never used in the Virgin Islands.

Nos. 694-695, 698, 700-706, 708 Ovptd. "OFFICIAL"

1992		**Litho.**	**Perf. 14**	
O55	A116	5c multicolored	.25	.25
O56	A116	10c multicolored	.25	.25
O59	A116	20c multicolored	.75	.75
O61	A116	30c multicolored	1.25	1.25
O62	A116	35c multicolored	1.40	1.40
O63	A116	40c multicolored	1.50	1.50
O64	A116	45c multicolored	1.75	1.75
O65	A116	50c multicolored	1.90	1.90
O66	A116	70c multicolored	2.75	2.75
O67	A116	$1 multicolored	3.75	3.75
O69	A116	$3 multicolored	11.50	11.50
		Nos. O55-O69 (11)	27.05	27.05

Ovpt. on Nos. O55-O56, O59, O61-O67, O69 is 15½mm long.

WALLIS & FUTUNA ISLANDS

'wä-ləs and fə-'tü-nə
'ī-lənds

LOCATION — Group of islands in the South Pacific Ocean, northeast of Fiji
GOVT. — French Overseas Territory
AREA — 106 sq. mi.
POP. — 15,129 (1999 est.)
CAPITAL — Mata-Utu, Wallis Island

100 Centimes = 1 Franc

Catalogue values for unused stamps in this country are for Never Hinged items, beginning with Scott 127 in the regular postage section, Scott B9 in the semipostal section, Scott C1 in the airpost section, and Scott J37 in the postage due section.

New Caledonia Stamps of 1905-28 Overprinted in Black or Red

1920-28		**Unwmk.**	**Perf. 14x13½**	
1	A16	1c black, *green*	.25	.30
a.		Double overprint	175.00	
2	A16	2c red brown	.25	.30
3	A16	4c blue, *org*	.40	.50
4	A16	5c green	.40	.50
5	A16	5c dull blue ('22)	.40	.55
6	A16	10c rose	.40	.65
7	A16	10c green ('22)	.50	.90
8	A16	10c red, *pink* ('25)	2.00	2.25
9	A16	15c violet	.90	1.10
10	A17	20c gray brown	.60	1.25
11	A17	25c blue, *grn*	1.25	1.50
12	A17	25c red, *yel* ('22)	.80	1.00
13	A17	30c brown, *org*	1.50	2.00
14	A17	30c dp rose ('22)	1.25	1.75
15	A17	30c red orange ('25)	.60	.85
16	A17	30c lt green ('27)	1.75	3.25
17	A17	35c black, *yel* (R)	.75	1.00
18	A17	40c rose, *grn*	1.10	1.50
19	A17	45c violet brn, *pnksh*	1.40	2.00
20	A17	50c red, *org*	1.40	2.10
21	A17	50c dark blue ('22)	1.50	2.40
22	A17	50c dark gray ('25)	2.00	3.25
23	A17	65c deep blue ('28)	4.75	7.50
24	A17	75c olive green	1.90	2.60

Nos. 113, 115-116 Overprinted

25	A18	1fr blue, *yel grn*	3.50	5.25
a.		Triple overprint	240.00	
b.		Double overprint	240.00	
c.		Pair, one stamp without overprint	600.00	
26	A18	1.10fr orange brn ('28)	4.00	7.25
27	A18	2fr carmine, *bl*	5.50	8.50
28	A18	5fr black, *org* (R)	11.00	17.00
		Nos. 1-28 (28)	52.05	79.00

No. 9 Surcharged in Various Colors

1922				
29	A16	0.01c on 15c violet (Bk)	.60	.95
30	A16	0.02c on 15c violet (Bl)	.60	.95
31	A16	0.04c on 15c violet (G)	.60	.95
32	A16	0.05c on 15c violet (R)	.60	.95
		Nos. 29-32 (4)	2.40	3.80

Stamps and Types of 1920 Surcharged in Black or Red

1924-27				
33	A18	25c on 2fr car, *bl*	.90	1.00
34	A18	25c on 5fr black, *org*	.90	1.00
35	A17	65c on 40c rose red, *grn* ('25)	1.50	2.00
36	A17	85c on 75c ol grn ('25)	1.20	1.60
37	A17	90c on 75c dp rose ('25)	1.50	2.75
38	A18	1.25fr on 1fr dp bl (R; '26)	1.00	1.40
39	A18	1.50fr on 1fr dp bl, *bl* ('27)	3.50	5.50
a.		Double surcharge	320.00	
b.		Surcharge omitted	290.00	
40	A18	3fr on 5fr red vio ('27)	5.75	8.00
a.		Surcharge omitted	250.00	
b.		Double surcharge	325.00	
41	A18	10fr on 5fr ol, *lav* ('27)	27.50	42.50
42	A18	20fr on 5fr vio rose, *yel* ('27)	32.50	50.00
		Nos. 33-42 (10)	76.25	115.75

New Caledonia Stamps and Types of 1928-40 Overprinted as in 1920

1930-40		**Perf. 13½, 14x13, 14x13½**		
43	A19	1c brn vio & indigo	.25	.25
a.		Double overprint	200.00	
b.		Imperf.	50.00	
44	A19	2c dk brn & yel grn	.25	.25
a.		Imperf.	50.00	
45	A19	3c brn vio & ind ('40)	.25	.25
46	A19	4c org & Prus grn	.25	.25
47	A19	5c Prus bl & dp ol	.25	.40
48	A19	10c gray lil & dk brn	.25	.40
49	A19	15c yel brn & dp bl	.25	.40
50	A19	20c brn red & dk brn	.50	.70
51	A19	25c dk grn & dk brn	1.00	1.25
52	A20	30c gray grn & bl grn	1.00	1.25
53	A20	35c Prus grn & dk grn ('38)	1.10	1.25
a.		Without overprint	200.00	
54	A20	40c brt red & olive	.95	1.10
55	A20	45c dp bl & red org	1.00	1.25
56	A20	45c bl grn & dl grn ('40)	1.00	1.00
57	A20	50c violet & grn	1.00	1.10
58	A20	55c bl vio & rose red ('38)	1.75	2.75
59	A20	60c vio bl & car ('40)	.25	.90
60	A20	65c org brn & bl	1.50	2.00
61	A20	70c dp rose & brn ('38)	1.40	1.60
62	A20	75c Prus bl & ol gray	2.40	3.00
63	A20	80c dk cl & grn ('38)	1.40	1.60
64	A20	85c green & brown ('38)	3.50	4.00
65	A20	90c dp red & brt red	1.90	2.75
66	A20	90c ol grn & rose red ('39)	1.10	1.25
67	A21	1fr dp ol & sal red ('38)	4.00	4.75
68	A21	1fr rose red & dk car ('38)	1.60	2.75
69	A21	1fr brn red & green ('40)	.40	.80
70	A21	1.10fr dp grn & brn	26.00	40.00
71	A21	1.25fr brn red & grn ('33)	3.00	3.50
72	A21	1.25fr rose red & dk car ('39)	1.10	1.25
73	A21	1.40fr dk bl & red org ('40)	1.10	1.40
74	A21	1.50fr dp bl & bl	1.25	1.50
75	A21	1.60fr dp grn & brn ('40)	1.60	2.00
76	A21	1.75fr dk bl & red org ('33)	15.00	16.00
77	A21	1.75fr vio bl ('38)	1.90	2.75
78	A21	2fr red org & brn	1.25	1.90
79	A21	2.25fr vio & brn ('39)	1.75	2.40
80	A21	2.50fr brn & lt brn ('40)	1.50	2.40
81	A21	3fr magenta & brn	1.40	2.00
82	A21	5fr dk bl & brn	1.75	2.60
83	A21	10fr vio & brn, *pnksh*	2.25	3.50
84	A21	20fr red & brn, *yel*	3.75	5.25
		Nos. 43-84 (42)	95.10	127.70

For overprints see Nos. 94-126.
For types A19 and A21 of New Caledonia, with "RF," overprinted as above, see Nos. 126A-126F.

Common Design Types pictured following the introduction.

Colonial Exposition Issue
Common Design Types

1931, Apr. 13		**Engr.**	**Perf. 12½**	
Name of Country Typo. in Black				
85	CD70	40c deep green	7.75	8.75
86	CD71	50c violet	7.75	8.75
87	CD72	90c red orange	7.75	8.75
88	CD73	1.50fr dull blue	7.75	8.75
		Nos. 85-88 (4)	31.00	35.00

Colonial Arts Exhibition Issue
Common Design Type
Souvenir Sheet

1937			**Imperf.**	
89	CD78	3fr red violet	19.00	37.50
		Never hinged	35.00	
a.		Inscription inverted	3,500.	

New York World's Fair Issue
Common Design Type

1939, May 10		**Engr.**	**Perf. 12½x12**	
90	CD82	1.25fr carmine lake	2.50	3.00
91	CD82	2.25fr ultramarine	2.50	3.00

Petain Issue
New Caledonia Nos. 216A-216B Ovptd. in Lilac or Red

1941		**Engr.**	**Perf. 12½x12**	
92	A21a	1fr bluish green (L)	1.10	
93	A21a	2.50fr dark blue (R)	1.10	

Nos. 92-93 were issued by the Vichy government in France, but were not placed on sale in Wallis & Futuna.
For surcharges, see Nos. B8A-B8B.

Nos. 43-69, 71, 74, 77-78, 80-84 with Additional Overprint in Black

1941-43			**Perf. 14x13½**	
94	A19	1c	2.50	2.50
95	A19	2c	2.50	2.50
96	A19	3c	80.00	80.00
97	A19	4c	3.25	3.25
98	A19	5c	3.25	3.25
99	A19	10c	3.25	3.25
100	A19	15c	3.75	3.75
101	A19	20c	4.50	4.50
102	A19	25c	4.50	4.50
103	A20	30c	4.50	4.50
104	A20	35c	3.25	3.25
105	A20	40c	4.00	4.00
106	A20	45c #55	4.00	4.00
107	A20	45c #56	90.00	90.00
108	A20	50c	3.50	3.50
109	A20	55c	3.50	3.50
110	A20	60c	80.00	80.00
111	A20	65c	3.50	3.50
112	A20	70c	3.50	3.50
113	A20	75c	5.00	5.00
114	A20	80c	3.25	3.25
115	A20	85c	4.00	4.00
116	A20	90c #65	3.50	3.50
117	A21	1fr #68	4.00	4.00
118	A21	1.25fr #71	4.00	4.00
119	A21	1.50fr	3.25	3.25
120	A21	1.75fr #77	3.25	3.25
121	A21	2fr	4.00	4.00
122	A21	2.50fr	160.00	160.00
123	A21	3fr	3.25	3.25
124	A21	5fr	8.00	8.00
125	A21	10fr	60.00	60.00
126	A21	20fr	95.00	95.00
		Nos. 94-126 (33)	667.75	667.75

Types of New Caledonia Without "RF" overprinted as in 1920

1944				
126A	A19	10c gray lil & dk brn		1.25
126B	A19	15c yel brn & dp bl		1.40
126C	A21	1fr brn red & grn		2.00
126D	A21	1.50fr blue		2.50
126E	A21	10fr vio & brn, *pnksh*		2.50
126F	A21	20fr red & brn, *yel*		2.75
		Nos. 126A-126F (6)		12.40

Nos. 126A-126F were issued by the Vichy government in France, but were not placed on sale in Wallis & Futuna.

Catalogue values for unused stamps in this section, from this point to the end of the section, are for Never Hinged items.

Ivi Poo, Bone Carving in Tiki Design A1

1944		**Unwmk.** **Photo.**	**Perf. 11½x12**	
127	A1	5c lt brown	.40	.40
128	A1	10c dp gray blue	.40	.40
129	A1	25c emerald	.40	.40
130	A1	30c dull orange	.40	.40
131	A1	40c dk slate grn	1.40	1.40
132	A1	80c brown red	1.25	1.25
133	A1	1fr red violet	.50	.50
134	A1	1.50fr red	.65	.65
135	A1	2fr gray black	.70	.70
136	A1	2.50fr brt ultra	.90	.90
137	A1	4fr dark purple	1.25	1.25
138	A1	5fr lemon yellow	1.50	1.50
139	A1	10fr chocolate	2.00	2.00
140	A1	20fr deep green	2.00	2.00
		Nos. 127-140 (14)	13.75	13.75

Nos. 127, 129 and 136 Surcharged in Black or Carmine

1946				
141	A1	50c on 5c lt brown	.65	.65
142	A1	60c on 5c lt brown	.65	.65
143	A1	70c on 5c lt brown	.65	.65
144	A1	1.20fr on 5c lt brown	.65	.65
145	A1	2.40fr on 25c emerald	.95	.95
146	A1	3fr on 25c emerald	.95	.95
147	A1	4.50fr on 25c emerald	1.90	1.90
148	A1	15fr on 2.50fr (C)	2.00	2.00
		Nos. 141-148 (8)	8.40	8.40

Military Medal Issue
Common Design Type
Engraved and Typographed

1952, Dec. 1			**Perf. 13**	
149	CD101	2fr multicolored	7.25	7.25

Wallis Islander A2

1957, June 11		**Unwmk.** **Engr.**	**Perf. 13**	
150	A2	3fr dk purple & lil rose	1.00	1.00
151	A2	9fr bl, dl lil & vio brn	1.90	1.90
		See Nos. 753a, 753c.		

Imperforates

Most Wallis and Futuna stamps from 1957 onward exist imperforate in issued and trial colors, and also in small presentation sheets in issued colors.

Flower Issue
Common Design Type

Design: 5fr, Montrouziera, horiz.

1958, Aug. 4   Photo.   Perf. 12½x12
152 CD104 5fr multicolored   3.25 3.25

Human Rights Issue
Common Design Type

1958, Dec. 10   Engr.   Perf. 13
153 CD105 17fr brt bl & dk bl   4.50 4.50

Women Making Tapa Cloth — A3

Kava Ceremony A4

17fr, Dancers. 19fr, Dancers with paddles.

1960, Sept. 19   Engr.   Perf. 13
154 A3 5fr dk brown, grn & org
          brn   1.50 1.50
155 A4 7fr dk brown & Prus
          grn   2.25 2.25
156 A4 17fr ultra, claret & grn   3.00 3.00
157 A3 19fr claret & slate   3.00 3.00
     Nos. 154-157 (4)   9.75 9.75

For No. 157 with surcharge, see No. 174. See No. 753b

Map of South Pacific — A4a

1962, July 18   Photo.   Perf. 13x12
158 A4a 16fr multicolored   3.75 3.75

5th South Pacific Conf., Pago Pago, 1962.

Sea Shells — A5

1962-63   Engr.   Perf. 13
Size: 22x36mm
159 A5 25c Triton   1.00 1.00
160 A5 1fr Mitra episcopalis   1.00 1.00
161 A5 2fr Cypraecassis rufa   1.75 1.75
162 A5 4fr Murex tenuspina   3.00 3.00
163 A5 10fr Oliva erythrostoma   7.00 7.00
164 A5 20fr Cyprae tigris   10.50 10.50
     Nos. 159-164,C18 (7)   36.75 31.25

Red Cross Centenary Issue
Common Design Type

1963, Sept. 2   Unwmk.   Perf. 13
165 CD113 12fr red lil, gray & car 4.00 4.00

Human Rights Issue
Common Design Type

1963, Dec. 10   Engr.
166 CD117 29fr dk red & ocher   7.00 7.00

Philatec Issue
Common Design Type

1964, Apr. 15   Unwmk.   Perf. 13
167 CD118 9fr dk sl grn, grn &
          red   3.00 3.00

Queen Amelia and Ship "Queen Amelia" A6

1965, Feb. 15   Photo.   Perf. 12½x13
168 A6 11fr multicolored   6.75 6.75

WHO Anniversary Issue
Common Design Type

1968, May 4   Engr.   Perf. 13
169 CD126 17fr bl grn, org & lil   5.75 5.75

Human Rights Year Issue
Common Design Type

1968, Aug. 10   Engr.   Perf. 13
170 CD127 19fr dk pur, org brn &
          brt mag   3.25 3.25

Outrigger Canoe A7

1969, Apr. 30   Photo.   Perf. 13
171 A7 1fr multicolored   1.10 1.10
     Nos. 171,C31-C35 (6)   32.10 18.85

ILO Issue
Common Design Type

1969, Nov. 24   Engr.   Perf. 13
172 CD131 9fr orange, brn & bl   2.75 2.75

UPU Headquarters Issue
Common Design Type

1970, May 20   Engr.   Perf. 13
173 CD133 21fr lil rose, ind & ol
          bis   3.25 3.25

No. 157 Surcharged

1971   Engr.   Perf. 13
174 A3 12fr on 19fr   1.30 1.25

Weight Lifting — A8

1971, Oct. 25
175 A8 24fr shown   5.25 5.25
176 A8 36fr Basketball   6.50 6.50
     Nos. 175-176,C37-C38 (4)   23.25 19.75

4th South Pacific Games, Papeete, French Polynesia, Sept. 8-19.

De Gaulle Issue
Common Design Type

Designs: 30fr, Gen. de Gaulle, 1940. 70fr, Pres. de Gaulle, 1970.

1971, Nov. 9   Engr.   Perf. 13
177 CD134 30fr blue & black   8.00 6.25
178 CD134 70fr blue & black   12.00 10.00

Child's Outrigger Canoe A9

Designs: 16fr, Children's canoe race. 18fr, Outrigger racing canoe.

1972, Oct. 16   Photo.   Perf. 13x12½
Size: 35½x26½mm
179 A9 14fr dk green & multi   8.00 4.25
180 A9 16fr dk plum & multi   8.00 4.25
181 A9 18fr blue & multi   12.00 6.25
     Nos. 179-181,C41 (4)   63.00 39.75

Outrigger sailing canoes.

Rhinoceros Beetle A10

Insects: 25fr, Cosmopolites sordidus (beetle). 35fr, Ophideres fullonica (moth). 45fr, Dragonfly.

1974, July 29   Photo.   Perf. 13
182 A10 15fr ol & multi   3.25 2.10
183 A10 25fr ol & multi   4.00 3.00
184 A10 35fr gray bl & multi   7.75 4.00
185 A10 45fr multicolored   7.75 6.00
     Nos. 182-185 (4)   22.75 15.10

Georges Pompidou (1911-74), Pres. of France — A11

1975, Dec. 1   Engr.   Perf. 13
186 A11 50fr ultra & slate   6.25 5.50

Battle of Yorktown and George Washington — A12

American Bicentennial: 47fr, Virginia Cape Battle and Lafayette.

1976, June 28   Engr.   Perf. 13
187 A12 19fr blue, red & olive   2.40 1.40
188 A12 47fr blue, red & maroon   4.50 4.00

For overprints see Nos. 205-206.

Conus Ammiralis — A13

Sea Shells: 23fr, Cyprae assellus. 43fr, Turbo petholatus. 61fr, Mitra papalis.

1976, Oct. 1   Engr.   Perf. 13
189 A13 20fr multicolored   2.50 2.00
190 A13 23fr multicolored   2.50 2.00
191 A13 43fr multicolored   4.75 4.00
192 A13 61fr ultra & multi   7.00 6.50
     Nos. 189-192 (4)   16.75 14.50

Father Chanel and Poi Church — A14

32fr, Father Chanel and map of islands.

1977, Apr. 28   Litho.   Perf. 12
193 A14 22fr multicolored   1.60 1.40
194 A14 32fr multicolored   2.10 1.50

Return of the ashes of Father Chanel, missionary.

Bowl, Mortar and Pestle A15

Handicrafts: 25fr, Wooden bowls and leather bag. 33fr, Wooden comb, club, and boat model. 45fr, War clubs, Futuna. 69fr, Lances.

1977, Sept. 26   Litho.   Perf. 12½
195 A15 12fr multicolored   1.00 .75
196 A15 25fr multicolored   1.90 1.00
197 A15 33fr multicolored   2.10 1.25
198 A15 45fr multicolored   2.75 1.75
199 A15 69fr multicolored   3.75 3.00
     Nos. 195-199 (5)   11.50 7.75

Post Office, Mata Utu — A16

50fr, Sia Hospital, Mata Utu. 57fr, Administration Buildings, Mata Utu. 63fr, St. Joseph's Church, Sigave. 120fr, Royal Palace, Mara Utu.

1977, Dec. 12   Litho.   Perf. 13
200 A16 27fr multicolored   1.60 1.40
201 A16 50fr multicolored   2.40 1.80
202 A16 57fr multicolored   2.50 1.80
203 A16 63fr multicolored   3.50 2.75
204 A16 120fr multicolored   8.00 4.50
     Nos. 200-204 (5)   18.00 12.25

Nos. 187-188 Overprinted

1978, Jan. 20   Engr.   Perf. 13
205 A12 19fr multicolored   3.00 2.50
206 A12 47fr multicolored   6.00 4.00

Bicentenary of the arrival of Capt. Cook in the Hawaiian Islands.

Cruiser Triomphant — A17

Warships: 200fr, Destroyers Cap des Palmes and Chevreuil. 280fr, Cruiser Savorgnan de Brazza.

1978, June 18 Photo. Perf. 13x12½
207	A17	150fr multicolored	9.00	6.25
208	A17	200fr multicolored	12.50	9.00
209	A17	280fr multicolored	17.00	12.50
		Nos. 207-209 (3)	38.50	27.75

Free French warships serving in the Pacific, 1940-1944.

Solanum Seaforthianum — A18

Flowers: 24fr, Cassia alata. 29fr, Gloriosa superba. 36fr, Hymenocallis littoralis.

1978, July 11 Photo. Perf. 13
210	A18	16fr multicolored	1.20	.90
211	A18	24fr multicolored	1.45	1.00
212	A18	29fr multicolored	2.00	1.40
213	A18	36fr multicolored	3.50	1.80
		Nos. 210-213 (4)	8.15	5.10

Gray Egret — A19

Birds: 18fr, Red-footed booby. 28fr, Brown booby. 35fr, White tern.

1978, Sept. 5 Photo. Perf. 13
214	A19	17fr multicolored	1.50	.90
215	A19	18fr multicolored	2.10	1.00
216	A19	28fr multicolored	2.60	1.40
217	A19	35fr multicolored	3.50	1.60
		Nos. 214-217 (4)	9.70	4.90

Traditional Patterns — A20

Designs: 55fr, Corpus Christi procession. 59fr, Chief's honor guard.

1978, Oct. 3
218	A20	53fr multicolored	2.50	1.80
219	A20	55fr multicolored	3.50	2.10
220	A20	59fr multicolored	4.00	2.50
		Nos. 218-220 (3)	10.00	6.40

Human Rights Flame A21

1978, Dec. 10 Litho. Perf. 12½
221	A21	44fr multicolored	1.50	1.30
222	A21	56fr multicolored	2.50	1.80

30th anniversary of Universal Declaration of Human Rights.

Fishing Boat — A22

Designs: 30fr, Weighing young tuna. 34fr, Stocking young tunas. 38fr, Measuring tuna. 40fr, Angler catching tuna. 48fr, Adult tuna.

1979, Mar. 19 Litho. Perf. 12
223	A22	10fr multicolored	.65	.50
224	A22	30fr multicolored	1.25	.90
225	A22	34fr multicolored	1.35	1.00
226	A22	38fr multicolored	2.25	1.40
227	A22	40fr multicolored	2.75	2.00
228	A22	48fr multicolored	3.75	2.00
a.		Souv. sheet of 6, #223-228 + 3 labels	25.00	25.00
		Nos. 223-228 (6)	12.00	7.80

Tuna tagging by South Pacific Commission. For surcharge see No. 261.

Boy with Raft and IYC Emblem — A23

Design: 58fr, Girl on horseback.

1979, Apr. 9 Photo. Perf. 13
229	A23	52fr multicolored	1.75	1.30
230	A23	58fr multicolored	2.25	1.70

International Year of the Child.

Bombax Ellipticum — A24

64fr, Callophyllum. 76fr, Pandanus odoratissimus.

1979, Apr. 23 Litho. Perf. 13
231	A24	50fr multicolored	1.75	1.40
232	A24	64fr multicolored	3.00	1.80
233	A24	76fr multicolored	3.50	2.50
		Nos. 231-233 (3)	8.25	5.70

Green and Withered Landscapes — A25

1979, May 28 Photo. Perf. 13
234	A25	22fr multicolored	1.50	1.10

Anti-alcoholism campaign.

Flowers — A26

20fr, Crinum moorei hook. 42fr, Passiflora. 62fr, Canna indica.

1979, July 16 Photo. Perf. 12½x13
235	A26	20fr multicolored	.80	.65
236	A26	42fr multicolored	1.75	1.10
237	A26	62fr multicolored	2.40	1.75
		Nos. 235-237 (3)	4.95	3.50

See Nos. 279-281.

Swimming — A27

1979, Aug. 27 Engr. Perf. 13
238	A27	31fr shown	1.90	1.40
239	A27	39fr High jump	2.40	1.80

6th South Pacific Games, Suva, Fiji, Aug. 27-Sept. 8.

Flower Necklaces — A28

Design: 140fr, Coral necklaces.

1979, Aug. 27 Litho.
240	A28	110fr multicolored	3.75	2.75
241	A28	140fr multicolored	4.25	3.50

Trees and Birds, by Sutita — A29

Paintings by Local Artists: 65fr, Birds and Mountain, by M. A. Pilioko, vert. 78fr, Festival Procession, by Sutita.

1979, Oct. 8 Perf. 13x12½, 12½x13
242	A29	27fr multicolored	1.25	1.10
243	A29	65fr multicolored	2.25	1.50
244	A29	78fr multicolored	3.50	2.25
		Nos. 242-244 (3)	7.00	4.85

Marine Mantis A30

Marine Life: 23fr, Hexabranchus sanguineus. 25fr, Spondylus barbatus. 43fr, Gorgon coral. 45fr, Linckia laevigata. 63fr, Tridacna squamosa.

1979, Nov. 5 Photo. Perf. 13x12½
245	A30	15fr multicolored	1.00	.75
246	A30	23fr multicolored	1.50	.90
247	A30	25fr multicolored	1.50	1.00
248	A30	43fr multicolored	2.25	1.10
249	A30	45fr multicolored	2.40	1.25
250	A30	63fr multicolored	4.50	2.50
		Nos. 245-250 (6)	13.15	7.50

See #294-297. For surcharge see #272.

Transportation Type of 1979

1980, Feb. 29 Litho. Perf. 13
251	AP32	1fr like No. C87	.25	.25
252	AP32	3fr like No. C88	.30	.25
253	AP32	5fr like No. C89	.30	.30
		Nos. 251-253 (3)	.85	.80

Radio Station and Tower — A31

1980, Apr. 21 Litho. Perf. 13
254	A31	47fr multicolored	2.25	1.40

Radio station FR3, 1st anniversary.

Jesus Laid in the Tomb, by Maurice Denis — A32

1980, Apr. 28 Perf. 13x12½
255	A32	25fr multicolored	1.45	.90

Easter 1980.

Gnathodentex Mossambicus — A33

27fr, Pristipomoides filamentosus. 32fr, Etelis carbunculus. 51fr, Cephapholis wallisi. 59fr, Aphareus rutilans.

1980, Aug. 25 Litho. Perf. 12½x13
256	A33	23fr multi	1.10	.90
257	A33	27fr multi	1.50	1.00
258	A33	32fr multi	2.25	1.40
259	A33	51fr multi	3.25	2.40
260	A33	59fr multi	3.75	2.75
a.		Vert. strip of 5, Nos. 256-260	13.00	13.00

No. 228 Surcharged

1980, Sept. 29   Litho.   Perf. 12
261 A22 50fr on 48fr multi   3.00 1.80

Sydpex 80 Philatelic Exhibition, Sydney.

13th World Telecommunications Day — A34

1981, May 17   Litho.   Perf. 12½
262 A34 49fr multicolored   1.60 1.10

Pierre Curie and Laboratory Equipment — A35

1981, May 25   Litho.   Perf. 13
263 A35 56fr multicolored   2.00 1.40

Pierre Curie (1859-1906), discoverer of radioactivity.

Conus Textile A36

Marine life: 28fr, Favites. 30fr, Cyanophycees. 31fr, Ceratium vultur. 35fr, Amphiprion frenatus. 55fr, Comatule.

1981, June 22   Perf. 12½x13
264 A36 28fr multicolored   1.00 .90
265 A36 30fr multicolored   1.10 .90
266 A36 31fr multicolored   1.50 .90
267 A36 35fr multicolored   1.75 1.10
268 A36 40fr shown   2.10 1.40
269 A36 55fr multicolored   2.50 1.60
 a.   Vert. strip of 6, Nos. 264-269   11.00 11.00

No. 269a is from sheet of 24.

60th Anniv. of Anti-tuberculin Vaccine (Developed by Calmette and Guerin) — A37

1981, July 28   Litho.   Perf. 13
270 A37 27fr multicolored   1.10 .90

Intl. Year of the Disabled — A38

1981, Aug. 17
271 A38 42fr multicolored   2.00 1.20

No. 245 Surcharged in Red

1981, Sept.   Photo.   Perf. 13x12½
272 A30 5fr on 15fr multi   .80 .35

Thomas Edison (1847-1931) and his Phonograph, 1878 — A39

1981, Sept. 5   Engr.   Perf. 13
273 A39 59fr multicolored   1.90 1.40

Battle of Yorktown, 1781 (American Revolution) — A40

1981, Oct. 19   Engr.   Perf. 13
274 A40 66fr Admiral de Grasse   2.00 1.80
275 A40 74fr Sea battle, vert.   3.00 2.75

200-Mile Zone Surveillance — A41

60fr, Patrol boat Dieppoise. 85fr, Protet.

1981, Dec. 4   Litho.   Perf. 13
276 A41 60fr multicolored   1.60 1.40
277 A41 85fr multicolored   2.25 2.10

TB Bacillus Centenary — A42

1982, Mar. 24   Litho.   Perf. 13
278 A42 45fr multicolored   1.75 1.40

Flower Type of 1979 in Changed Colors

1982, May 3   Photo.   Perf. 12½x13
279 A26 1fr like No. 235   .25 .25
280 A26 2fr like No. 236   .30 .25
281 A26 3fr like No. 237   .30 .30
 Nos. 279-281 (3)   .85 .80

PHILEXFRANCE '82 Intl. Stamp Exhibition, Paris, June 11-21 — A43

1982, May 12   Engr.   Perf. 13
282 A43 140fr like No. 25   3.25 2.75

Acanthe Phippium A44

68fr, Acanthe phippium, diff. 70fr, Spathoglottis pacifica. 83fr, Mussaenda raiateensis, Orchids and rubiaceae.

1982, May 24   Litho.   Perf. 12½x13
283 A44 34fr shown   1.00 .90
284 A44 68fr multicolored   1.90 1.75
285 A44 70fr multicolored   2.40 1.75
286 A44 83fr multicolored   2.40 2.25
 Nos. 283-286 (4)   7.70 6.65

Scouting Year A45

1982, June 21   Perf. 12½
287 A45 80fr Baden-Powell   2.40 1.75

Cypraea Talpa A46

Porcelaines shells.

1982, June 28   Perf. 12½x13
288 A46 10fr shown   .30 .30
289 A46 15fr Cypraea vitellus   .70 .30
290 A46 25fr Cypraea argus   .85 .65
291 A46 27fr Cypraea carneola   1.10 .75
292 A46 40fr Cypraea mappa   1.40 1.10
293 A46 50fr Cypraea tigris   1.75 1.25
 Nos. 288-293 (6)   6.10 4.35

Marine Life Type of 1979

1982, Oct. 1   Photo.   Perf. 13x12½
294 A30 32fr Gorgones milithea   1.25 .75
295 A30 35fr Linckia laevigata   1.75 1.10
296 A30 46fr Hexabranchus sanguineus   2.00 1.50
297 A30 63fr Spondylus barbatus   2.50 2.25
 Nos. 294-297 (4)   7.50 5.60

St. Teresa of Jesus of Avila (1515-1582) — A48

1982, Nov. 8   Engr.   Perf. 13
298 A48 31fr multicolored   1.40 .75

See No. 315.

Traditional House A49

1983, Jan. 20   Litho.   Perf. 13
299 A49 19fr multicolored   .70 .50

Gustave Eiffel (1832-1923), Architect — A50

1983, Feb. 14   Engr.   Perf. 13
300 A50 97fr multicolored   3.00 2.75

Thai Dancer, 19th Cent. — A51

1983, June 28   Engr.   Perf. 13
301 A51 92fr multicolored   2.75 1.80

BANGKOK '83 Intl. Stamp Show, Aug. 4-13.

A52

1983, Aug. 25   Litho.   Perf. 13x13½
302 A52 20fr multicolored   .65 .50

World Communications Year.

Cone Shells A53

10fr, Conus tulipa. 17fr, Conus capitaneus. 21fr, Conus virgo. 22fr, Strombus lentiginosus. 25fr, Lambis chiragra. 35fr, Strombus dentatus. 39fr, Conus vitulinus. 43fr, Lambis scorpius. 49fr, Strombus aurisdianae. 52fr, Conus marmoreus. 65fr, Conus leopardus. 76fr, Lambis crocata.

1983-84   Litho.   Perf. 13½x13
303 A53 10fr multicolored   .25 .25
304 A53 17fr multicolored   .65 .50
305 A53 21fr multicolored   .65 .50
306 A53 22fr multicolored   .55 .50
307 A53 25fr multicolored   .65 .60
308 A53 35fr multicolored   1.15 .75
309 A53 39fr multicolored   1.00 .90
310 A53 43fr multicolored   1.40 .90
311 A53 49fr multicolored   1.75 1.40
312 A53 52fr multicolored   1.50 1.40
313 A53 65fr multicolored   1.60 1.60
314 A53 76fr multicolored   2.10 1.60
 Nos. 303-314 (12)   13.25 10.90

Issued: 22, 25, 35, 43, 49, 76fr, 3/23/84; others, 10/14/83.

No. 298 Redrawn with Espana '84 Emblem

1984, Apr. 27   Engr.   *Perf. 13*
315 A48 70fr multicolored   1.90 1.40

Denis Diderot (1713-1784), Philosopher A54

100fr, Portrait, encyclopedia title page.

1984, May 11
316 A54 100fr multicolored   2.60 1.75

Nature Protection (Whale) A55

1984, June 5   Litho.   *Perf. 13x12½*
317 A55 90fr Orcina orca   3.25 1.75

4th Pacific Arts Festival — A56

1984, Nov. 30   Litho.   *Perf. 13*
318 A56 160fr Islanders   3.75 2.50

Lapita Pottery — A57

Ethno-Archaeological Museum: Excavation site, reconstructed ceramic bowl.

1985, Jan. 16   Litho.   *Perf. 13*
319 A57 53fr multicolored   1.50 .90

Seashells A58

1985, Feb. 11
320 A58 2fr Nautilus pompilius   .25 .25
321 A58 3fr Murex bruneus   .25 .25
322 A58 41fr Casmaria erinaceus   1.30 .90
323 A58 47fr Conus vexillum   1.60 1.00
324 A58 56fr Harpa harpa   2.10 1.10
325 A58 71fr Murex ramosus   2.50 1.60
    Nos. 320-325 (6)   8.00 5.10

Victor Hugo, Author (1802-1885) A59

1985, Mar. 7   Engr.
326 A59 89fr multicolored   2.60 1.60

Bat — A60

1985, Apr. 29   Litho.
327 A60 38fr multicolored   1.60 1.10

Intl. Youth Year — A61

1985, May 20   Litho.   *Perf. 12½x13*
328 A61 64fr Children   1.60 1.10

UN, 40th Anniv. — A61a

1985, July 12   Engr.   *Perf. 13*
328A A61a 49fr Prus grn, dk ultra & red   1.50 .90

Pierre de Ronsard (1524-1585), Poet — A62

1985, Sept. 16   Engr.   *Perf. 13*
329 A62 170fr brt bl, sep & brn   5.00 3.50

Dr. Albert Schweitzer — A63

1985, Nov. 22   Engr.   *Perf. 13*
330 A63 50fr blk, dk red lil & org brn   2.00 1.25

World Food Day — A64

1986, Jan. 23   Litho.   *Perf. 12½x13*
331 A64 39fr Breadfruit   1.25 .75

Flamboyants — A65

1986, Feb. 13   *Perf. 13x12½*
332 A65 38fr multicolored   1.25 1.00

Seashells A66

1986, Apr. 24   Litho.   *Perf. 13½x13*
333 A66 4fr Lambis truncata   .30 .30
334 A66 5fr Charonia tritonis   .30 .30
335 A66 10fr Oliva miniacea   .45 .35
336 A66 18fr Distorsio anus   .65 .65
337 A66 25fr Mitra mitra   .95 .75
338 A66 107fr Conus distans   3.00 2.25
    Nos. 333-338 (6)   5.65 4.60

Also exists in se-tenant strips of 6 from sheet of 24.

1986 World Cup Soccer Championships, Mexico — A67

1986, May 20   *Perf. 13x12½*
339 A67 95fr multicolored   2.75 1.80

UNICEF.

Discovery of Horn Islands, 370th Anniv. — A68

No. 340: a, 8fr, William Schouten, ship. b, 9fr, Jacob LeMaire, ship. c, 155fr, Map of Alo & Alofi.

1986, June 19   Engr.   *Perf. 13*
340 A68   Strip of 3, #a.-c.   6.00 4.75

James Watt (1736-1819), Inventor, and Steam Engine — A69

1986, July 11
341 A69 74fr blk & dk red   2.00 1.50

Minesweeper La Lorientaise — A70

7fr, Corvette Commandant Blaison, vert. 120fr, Frigate Balny.

1986, Aug. 7
342 A70   6fr shown   .60 .50
343 A70   7fr multicolored   .65 .50
344 A70 120fr multicolored   3.25 2.75
    Nos. 342-344 (3)   4.50 3.75

Rose Laurel — A71

1986, Oct. 2   Litho.   *Perf. 13x12½*
345 A71 97fr multi   2.60 2.00

Virgin and Child, by Sandro Botticelli A72

1986, Dec. 12   Litho.   *Perf. 12½x13*
346 A72 250fr multicolored   6.25 4.50

Christmas.

Butterflies — A73

1987, Apr. 2   Litho.   *Perf. 12½*
347 A73 2fr Papilio montrouzieri   .40 .35
348 A73 42fr Belenois java   .90 .70
349 A73 46fr Delias ellipsis   1.75 .75
350 A73 50fr Danaus pumila   2.25 .95
351 A73 52fr Luthrodes cleotas   2.40 1.00
352 A73 59fr Precis villida   2.80 1.50
    Nos. 347-352 (6)   10.50 5.25

World Wrestling Championships — A74

1987, May 26   Litho.   *Perf. 12½*
353 A74 97fr multi   3.00 1.90

For overprint see No. 360.

Seashells
A75

1987, June 24　　Litho.　　*Perf. 13*
354 A75　3fr Cymatium pileare　.25　.25
355 A75　4fr Conus textile　.25　.25
356 A75　28fr Cypraea mauritiana　1.00　.75
357 A75　44fr Bursa bubo　1.30　1.00
358 A75　48fr Cypraea tes-
　　　　　　tudinaria　1.40　1.10
359 A75　78fr Cypraecassis rufa　2.10　1.50
　　　Nos. 354-359 (6)　6.30　4.85
　Also exists in se-tenant strips of 6 from
sheet of 24.

No. 353
Overprinted

1987, Aug. 29　　Litho.　　*Perf. 12½*
360 A74　97fr multicolored　3.00　2.40
　　　OLYMPHILEX '87, Rome.

Bust of a Girl, by
Auguste Rodin
(1840-1917)
A76

1987, Sept. 15　　Engr.　　*Perf. 13*
361 A76 150fr plum　4.50　2.75
　　　See No. 390.

World Post Day — A77

1987, Oct. 9　　Litho.　　*Perf. 13*
362 A77 116fr multicolored　2.90　1.80

Birds — A78

1987, Oct. 28　　　*Perf. 13x12½*
363 A78　6fr Anas superciliosa　.35　.35
364 A78　19fr Pluvialis dominica　.70　.50
365 A78　47fr Gallicolumba stairi　1.40　.95
366 A78　56fr Arenaria interpres　1.90　1.00
367 A78　64fr Rallus philippensis　2.00　1.10
368 A78　68fr Limosa lapponica　2.25　1.30
　　　Nos. 363-368 (6)　8.60　5.20

Francis Carco (1886-1958),
Poet — A79

　Design: Carco and views of the Moulin de la
Galette and Place du Tertre, Paris.

1988, Jan. 29　　Litho.　　*Perf. 13*
369 A79 40fr multicolored　2.00　.95

Jean-Francois de Galaup (1741-
c.1788), Comte de La Perouse,
Explorer — A80

　Design: Ships L'Astrolabe and La Boussole,
portrait of La Perouse.

1988, Mar. 21　　Engr.　　*Perf. 13*
370 A80 70fr org brn, dark blue &
　　　　olive grn　2.75　2.40

Intl. Red Cross
and Red
Crescent
Organizations,
125th
Anniv. — A81

1988, July 4　　Engr.　　*Perf. 13*
371 A81 30fr blk, dark red & brt
　　　　blue grn　1.75　1.00

1988 Summer Olympics, Seoul — A82

1988, Sept. 1　　Engr.　　*Perf. 13*
372 A82　11fr Javelin　.70　.50
373 A82　20fr Women's volleyball　.95　.70
374 A82　60fr Windsurfing　2.00　1.50
375 A82　80fr Yachting　2.90　1.90
　a.　Souv. sheet of 4, #372-375 + 2
　　　labels, gutter between　8.25　8.25
　　　Nos. 372-375 (4)　6.55　4.60

Intl. Maritime Organization Emblem
and Frigate F727 Admiral
Charner — A83

1989, Jan. 26　　Litho.　　*Perf. 13*
376 A83 26fr multi　1.00　.70

Jean Renoir (1894-1979), Film
Director, and Scene from The Grand
Illusion — A84

1989, Feb. 16　　Engr.　　*Perf. 13*
377 A84 24fr brt lil rose, dark vio
　　　　brn & brt org　1.35　.75

Antoine Becquerel (1788-1878),
Physicist — A85

**　　　*Perf. 13x12½***
1988, Nov. 9　　Engr.　　Unwmk.
378 A85 18fr blk & dark ultra　1.05　.50

Futuna Hydroelectric Plant — A86

**　　Wmk. 385**
1989, Apr. 13　　Litho.　　*Perf. 13½*
379 A86 25fr multi　.95　.50

A87

**　　Unwmk.**
1988, Oct. 26　　Litho.　　*Perf. 13*
380 A87 17fr multi　.95　.50
　　　World Post Day.

A88

1989, May 17　　　*Perf. 12½x13*
381 A88 21fr multi　.95　.50
　　　World Telecommunications Day.

Fresco
A89

1989, June 8　　　*Perf. 12½*
382 A89 22fr multi　1.00　.50

PHILEXFRANCE '89 — A90

Declaration of Human Rights and
Citizenship, Bicent. — A91

1989, July 7　　Litho.　　*Perf. 13*
383 A90　29fr multi　.90　.70
384 A91 900fr multi　18.50 14.00
　a.　Souv. sheet of 2, #383-384 +
　　　label　25.00 25.00
　No. 384 is airmail. No. 384a sold for 1000fr.

World Cycling Championships — A92

1989, Sept. 14　　Engr.　　*Perf. 13*
385 A92 10fr blk, red brn & emer　.65　.45

World Post Day — A93

**　　Unwmk.**
1989, Oct. 18　　Litho.　　*Perf. 13*
386 A93 27fr multicolored　.95　.50

Landscape — A94

1989, Nov. 23　　Litho.　　*Perf. 13*
387 A94 23fr multicolored　1.10　.70

Star of
Bethlehem
A95

1990, Jan. 9   Litho.   Perf. 12½
388 A95 44fr multicolored   1.60 1.00

Fossilized
Tortoise
A96

1990, Feb. 15   Litho.   Perf. 12½x13
389 A96 48fr multicolored   2.75 1.40

Sculpture by
Auguste Rodin
(1840-1917)
A97

1990, Mar. 15   Engr.   Perf. 13
390 A97 200fr royal blue   5.50 4.00

1990 World Cup Soccer
Championships, Italy — A98

1990, Apr. 16   Litho.
391 A98 59fr multicolored   1.75 1.10

Orchids
A99

1990, May 17   Litho.   Perf. 12½
392 A99 78fr multicolored   2.50 1.50

·Mother's Day

Phaeton — A100

1990, July 16   Perf. 13
393 A100 300fr multicolored   7.75 4.50
394 A100 600fr Island   16.00 8.50

Moana II — A101

1990, Aug. 16   Engr.   Perf. 13
395 A101 40fr shown   1.25   .95
396 A101 50fr Moana III   1.75 1.00

Native Huts
A102

1990, Sept. 17   Litho.   Perf. 13x12½
397 A102 28fr multicolored   .95   .50

Stamp Day
A103

1990, Oct. 16   Litho.   Perf. 12½
398 A103 97fr multicolored   2.25 1.00

Wallis Island
Pirogue — A104

1990, Nov. 16   Litho.   Perf. 13x12½
399 A104 46fr multicolored   1.75   .95

Best Wishes — A105

1990, Dec. 17   Litho.   Perf. 13x12½
400 A105 100fr multicolored   3.00 1.90

Patrol Boats — A106

1991   Engr.   Perf. 13
401 A106 42fr La Moqueuse   1.40   .95
402 A106 52fr La Glorieuse   1.75 1.00
   Issue dates: 42fr, Jan. 7; 52fr, Mar. 4.

A107

1991, Feb. 4   Litho.   Perf. 13
403 A107   7fr Breadfruit picker   .30   .30
404 A107 54fr Taro planter   1.75 1.00
405 A107 62fr Spear fisherman   1.90 1.20
406 A107 72fr Native warrior   2.25 1.30
407 A107 90fr Kailao dancer   2.75 1.75
  a. Souv. sheet of 5, #403-407   9.50 9.50
     Nos. 403-407 (5)   8.95 5.55

  Issued: 7fr, 9/2; 54fr, 5/13; 62fr, 4/1; 72fr,
2/4; 90fr, 11/4.
  No. 407a sold for 300fr.

Doctors
Without
Borders,
20th Anniv.
A108

1991, Feb. 18   Litho.   Perf. 13½
408 A108 55fr multicolored   1.75 1.00

Ultralight Aircraft — A108a

1991, June 24
409 A108a 85fr multicolored   2.75 1.80

Portrait of Jean by Auguste Renoir
(1841-1919) — A109

1991, July 8   Photo.   Perf. 12½x13
410 A109 400fr multicolored   9.75 8.00

**Litho.
Die Cut
Self-Adhesive**
411 A109 400fr multicolored   10.00 8.00

Overseas Territorial Status, 30th
Anniv. — A110

1991, July 29   Litho.   Perf. 13
412 A110 102fr multicolored   2.75 1.80

Feast of the Assumption — A111

1991, Aug. 15   Perf. 13x12½
413 A111 30fr multicolored   1.30   .70

Amnesty
Intl., 30th
Anniv.
A113

1991, Oct. 7   Perf. 13x12½
414 A113 140fr bl, vio & yel   4.00 2.75

Central Bank for Economic
Cooperation, 50th Anniv. — A114

1991, Dec. 2   Litho.   Perf. 13
415 A114 10fr multicolored   .50   .35

Flowers
A115

  1fr, Monetto allamanda catharttica. 4fr,
Hibiscus rosa sinensis. 80fr, Ninuphar.

1991, Dec. 2   Perf. 12½x13, 13x12½
416 A115   1fr multi   .25   .25
417 A115   4fr multi, vert.   .65   .35
418 A115 80fr multi   2.50 1.50
     Nos. 416-418 (3)   3.40 2.10

Christmas — A116

1991, Dec. 16   Litho.   Perf. 13
419 A116 60fr multicolored   1.90 1.20

Maritime Surveillance — A117

1992, Jan. 20   Litho.   Perf. 13
420 A117 48fr multicolored   1.60 1.00

1992 Winter Olympics,
Albertville — A118

1992, Feb. 17   Litho.   *Perf. 13*
421 A118 150fr multicolored   4.00 2.75

Canada '92, Intl. Philatelic Exposition,
Montreal — A119

1992, Mar. 25   Engr.   *Perf. 13*
422 A119 35fr blk, violet & red   1.25 .70

1992 Summer Olympics,
Barcelona — A120

1992, Apr. 15   Engr.   *Perf. 13*
423 A120 106fr bl grn, grn & bl   3.25 2.25

Granada '92, Intl. Philatelic
Exposition — A121

1992, Apr. 17   Engr.   *Perf. 12½x12*
424 A121 100fr multicolored   3.00 2.00

Expo '92, Seville — A122

1992, Apr. 20   *Perf. 13*
425 A122 200fr bl grn, ol & red
     brn   5.00 3.75

Chaetodon Ephippium — A123

Designs: 22fr, Chaetodon auriga. 23fr, Heniochus monoceros. 24fr, Pygoplites diacanthus. 25fr, Chaetodontoplus conspicillatus. 26fr, Chaetodon unimaculatus. 27fr, Siganus punctatus. 35fr, Zebrasoma veliferum. 45fr, Paracanthurus hepatus. 53fr, Siganus vulpinus.

1992-93   Litho.   *Perf. 13*
426 A123 21fr multicolored   1.15 .50
427 A123 22fr multicolored   1.15 .50
428 A123 23fr multicolored   1.15 .50
429 A123 24fr multicolored   1.40 .70
430 A123 25fr multicolored   1.40 .70
431 A123 26fr multicolored   1.40 .70
432 A123 27fr multicolored   1.40 .80
433 A123 35fr multicolored   1.50 .80
434 A123 45fr multicolored   1.60 .95
435 A123 53fr multicolored   1.75 1.25
   Nos. 426-435 (10)   13.90 7.40

   Issued: 21fr, 26fr, 5/18; 22fr, 7/27; 25fr, 7/27; 23fr, 24fr, 9/14; 35fr, 45fr, 6/21/93; 27fr, 53fr, 9/6/93.

Natives — A125

a, 3 warriors. b, 2 warriors. c, Warrior, 2 boats. d, 2 spear fisherman. e, 3 fisherman.

1992, June 15   Litho.   *Perf. 12*
436 A125 70fr Strip of 5, #a.-e.   11.25 9.00
   f.   Souvenir sheet of 5, #a.-e.   11.25 11.25

#436 has continuous design. #436f sold for 450fr.

Support
Ship, "La
Garonne"
A126

1992, Oct. 12   Litho.   *Perf. 12*
437 A126 20fr multicolored   .75 .50

L'Idylle D'Ixelles,
by Auguste
Rodin (1840-
1917)
A127

1992, Nov. 17   Engr.   *Perf. 13*
438 A127 300fr lilac & dk blue   8.00 6.00

Miribilis
Jalapa
A128

1992, Dec. 7   Litho.   *Perf. 12½*
439 A128 200fr multicolored   5.50 3.75

Maritime Forces of the Pacific — A129

1993, Jan. 27   Litho.   *Perf. 13x12½*
440 A129 130fr multicolored   3.50 2.75

School
Art — A130

1993, Feb. 22   Litho.   *Perf. 12*
441 A130 56fr multicolored   1.90 1.40

   See Nos. 451-452.

Birds
A131

Designs: 50fr, Rallus philippensis swindellsi. 60fr, Porphyrio porphyrio. 110fr, Ptilinopus greyi.

1993, Mar. 20   *Perf. 13½*
442 A131 50fr multicolored   1.50 1.00
443 A131 60fr multicolored   1.75 1.50
444 A131 110fr multicolored   3.25 1.90
   Nos. 442-444 (3)   6.50 4.40

Mother's
Day
A132

1993, May 30   Litho.   *Perf. 12½*
445 A132 95fr Hibiscus   2.00 1.75
446 A132 120fr Siale   2.75 2.75

Admiral Antoine d'Entrecasteaux
(1737-1793), French
Navigator — A133

1993, July 12   Engr.   *Perf. 13*
447 A133 170fr grn bl, red brn &
     blk   4.00 3.25

Taipei '93 — A134

1993, Aug. 14   Litho.   *Perf. 13x12½*
448 A134 435fr multicolored   9.25 9.25

Churches — A135

1993, Aug. 15   *Perf. 13*
449 A135 30fr Tepa, Wallis   .80 .80
450 A135 30fr Vilamalia, Futuna   .80 .80

School Art Type of 1993
1993   Litho.   *Perf. 13x13½, 13½x13*
451 A130 28fr Stylized trees   .80 .55
452 A130 52fr Family, vert.   1.30 1.00
   Issue dates: 28fr, Oct. 18. 52fr, Nov. 8.

Christmas
A136

1993, Dec, 6   *Perf. 13*
453 A136 80fr multicolored   2.00 1.60

Traditional
Arts and
Crafts
Exhibition
A137

1994, Mar. 24   Litho.   *Perf. 12½*
454 A137 80fr multicolored   2.40 1.60

Liberation of Paris, 50th
Anniv. — A138

1994, Apr. 21   Engr.   *Perf. 13*
455 A138 110fr black, blue & red   3.00 2.00

Satellite Communications — A139

1994, June 23   Litho.
456 A139 10fr multicolored   1.00 1.00

1994 World Cup Soccer
Championships, U.S. — A140

1994, June 23
457 A140 105fr multicolored   2.75 2.00

Princesses Ouveennes, 1903 — A141

1994, July 21 Engr. Perf. 13
458 A141 90fr blue grn, blk & red 2.25 1.50

Symbols of Playing Cards Suits — A142

1994, Aug. 25 Litho. Perf. 13
459 A142 40fr multicolored 1.40 .70

Ultra-Light Aircraft — A143

1994, Aug. 25
460 A143 5fr multicolored .35 .35

Coconut — A144

1994, Oct. 13 Litho. Perf. 13
461 A144 36fr multicolored 1.25 .70

Parrots A145

1994, Nov. 17 Litho. Perf. 13x13½
462 A145 62fr multicolored 2.00 1.25

Grand Lodge of France, Cent. — A146

1994, Nov. 24 Engr. Perf. 13
463 A146 250fr multicolored 6.50 4.50

Preparing Traditional Meal — A147

1995, Jan. 25 Litho. Perf. 13
464 A147 80fr multicolored 2.40 1.40

Aerial View of Islands A148

1995, Feb. 21 Perf. 13x13½, 13½x13
465 A148 85fr Nukulaelae 1.75 1.25
466 A148 90fr Nukufetau, vert. 2.00 1.40
467 A148 100fr Nukufotu, Nukuloa 2.10 1.90
    Nos. 465-467 (3) 5.85 4.55

Mua College — A149

1995, Apr. 11 Perf. 12
468 A149 35fr multicolored 1.20 .70

UN, 50th Anniv. — A150

1995, June 26 Litho. Perf. 13½
469 A150 55fr multicolored 1.75 1.00

10th South Pacific Games — A151

1995, Aug. 1 Litho. Perf. 13
470 A151 70fr multicolored 1.90 1.40

Local Plants — A152

1995, Oct. 24 Litho. Perf. 13½x13
471 A152 20fr Breadfruit tree .55 .55
472 A152 60fr Tarot 1.30 1.00
473 A152 65fr Kava 1.60 1.40
    Nos. 471-473 (3) 3.45 2.95
    See Nos. 478-481, 484-485.

Tapa — A153

1995, Dec. 12 Litho. Perf. 13
474 A153 25fr Native life, vert. .80 .70
475 A153 26fr Fish, sea shells .90 .70

Mothers from the Islands — A154

1996, Jan. 14 Litho. Perf. 13½x13
476 A154 80fr multicolored 1.90 1.50

Golf A155

1996, Jan. 24 Perf. 13
477 A155 95fr multicolored 3.25 2.00

Local Plant Type of 1995
1996 Litho. Perf. 13½x13
478 A152 27fr Cananga odorata .85 .70
479 A152 28fr Mahoaa 1.10 .70
480 A152 45fr Hibiscus 1.10 .80
481 A152 52fr Ufi 1.30 1.00
    Nos. 478-481 (4) 4.35 3.20
    Issued: #479, 481, 3/14; #478, 480, 6/20.

Sanglants Swamp — A156

1996, June 26 Perf. 13
482 A156 53fr multicolored 1.60 1.00

Chess — A157

1996, July 17
483 A157 110fr multicolored 2.40 2.00

Local Plant Type of 1995
Designs: 30fr, 48fr, Calladium.

1996, Sept. 17 Litho. Perf. 13½x13
Background Color
484 A152 30fr blue green .80 .70
485 A152 48fr lilac 1.15 .90

Francoise Perroton, Missionary — A158

1996, Oct. 25 Perf. 13
486 A158 50fr multicolored 1.40 1.00

UNICEF, 50th Anniv. A159

1996, Dec. 4 Litho. Perf. 13
487 A159 25fr multicolored .80 .70

CPS, 50th Anniv. A160

1997, Feb. 6 Litho. Perf. 13
488 A160 7fr multicolored .30 .30

Royal Standards A161

1997, Feb. 14 Litho. Perf. 13x13½
489 A161 56fr King Lavelua 1.40 1.00
490 A161 60fr King Tulagaifo 1.40 1.00
491 A161 70fr King Tuisigave 1.75 1.00
    Nos. 489-491 (3) 4.55 3.00

Brasseur de Kava — A162

1997, Apr. 17 Perf. 13½x13
492 A162 170fr multicolored 4.25 2.75

Island Scenes A163

Designs: 10fr, Old man telling stories to children seated around campfire. 36fr, Braiding mat, vert. 40fr, Preparing "Kai'umu" (feast).

Perf. 13x13½, 13½x13

1997, May 20   **Litho.**
493 A163 10fr multicolored   .30 .30
494 A163 36fr multicolored   1.00 .80
495 A163 40fr multicolored   1.10 .80
        Nos. 493-495 (3)   2.40 1.90

Green
Lagoon
Turtles
A164

1997, June 18   **Perf. 13x13½**
496 A164 62fr Crawling ashore   1.60 1.00
497 A164 80fr Swimming   2.00 1.40

Festival of Avignon — A165

1997, July 31   **Litho.**   **Perf. 13**
498 A165 160fr multicolored   4.00 2.40

Berlin
Handicapped
Sports
Festival — A166

1997, Aug. 12
499 A166 35fr multicolored   1.10 .70

D'Uvéa Karate Club — A167

1997, Oct. 15   **Litho.**   **Perf. 13x13½**
500 A167 24fr multicolored   .90 .50

Fight Against
AIDS — A168

1997, Dec. 1   **Litho.**   **Perf. 13**
501 A168 5fr multicolored   1.00 .35

Christmas — A169

1997, Dec. 24
502 A169 85fr Nativity   2.10 1.50

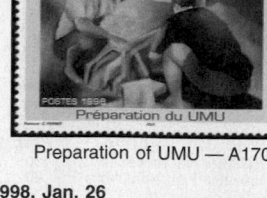

Preparation of UMU — A170

1998, Jan. 26
503 A170 800fr multicolored   16.50 11.00

Orchids — A171

70fr, Vanda T.M.A. 85fr, Cattleya bow bells.
90fr, Arachnis. 105fr, Cattleya.

1998, Feb. 18   **Perf. 13**
504 A171 70fr multi, vert.   1.50 1.00
505 A171 85fr multi   1.90 1.25
506 A171 90fr multi, vert.   1.90 1.25
507 A171 105fr multi   2.50 1.50
        Nos. 504-507 (4)   7.80 5.00

Telecom 2000 — A172

1998, Mar. 24   **Litho.**   **Perf. 13**
508 A172 7fr multicolored   .25 .25

Fishing — A173

Designs: 50fr, Fisherman casting net into
lagoon. 52fr, Fisherman sorting catch.

1998, May 26   **Litho.**   **Perf. 13**
509 A173 50fr multicolored   1.40 .70
510 A173 52fr multicolored   1.40 .70

1998 World Cup Soccer
Championships, France — A174

1998, June 10
511 A174 80fr multicolored   2.00 1.40

Insects
A175

1998, July 21   **Litho.**   **Perf. 13x13½**
512 A175 36fr Dragonfly   .80 .50
513 A175 40fr Cicada   .85 .70

Coral — A176

Various corals: a, 4fr. b, 5fr. c, 10fr. d, 15fr.

1998   **Litho.**   **Perf. 13x13½**
514 A176 Strip of 4, #a.-d.   1.25 1.25

52nd Autumn Philatelic Salon — A177

1998, Nov. 5   **Litho.**   **Perf. 13½**
515 A177 175fr multicolored   4.00 2.50

World Fight
Against
AIDS
A178

1998, Dec. 1   **Perf. 13**
516 A178 62fr multicolored   1.60 1.00

Islet of
Nuku
Taakimoa
A179

1999, Mar. 22   **Litho.**   **Perf. 13**
517 A179 130fr multicolored   3.00 1.80
        See No. 594.

Souvenir Sheet

Lagoon Life — A180

a, 20fr, Various fish. b, 855fr, Fish, diver.

1999, May 17   **Litho.**   **Perf. 13**
518 A180 Sheet of 2, #a.-b.   18.00 18.00

PhilexFrance '99, World Philatelic
Exhibition — A181

1999, July 2   **Litho.**   **Perf. 13**
519 A181 200fr multicolored   4.50 3.25

French Senate, Bicent. — A182

1999, Sept. 20   **Engr.**   **Perf. 13**
520 A182 125fr multicolored   3.00 2.00

Territorial Assembly Building — A183

1999, Aug. 23   **Litho.**
521 A183 17fr multicolored   .45 .35

Pandanus
A184

1999, Oct. 18
522 A184 25fr multicolored   .70 .45

Man
Making
Canoe
A185

1999, Nov. 8
523 A185 55fr multicolored   1.50 .80

French Postage Stamps, 150th
Anniv. — A186

1999, Dec. 1
524 A186 65fr Wallis & Futuna
#86 1.60 1.00

Millennium — A187

2000, Jan. 1 **Litho.** *Perf. 13*
525 A187 350fr multicolored 7.50 4.50

Mata'utu
Cathedral
A188

2000, Apr. 28 **Photo.** *Perf. 13x13¼*
526 A188 300fr multicolored 7.00 3.75

Patrol Boat "La Glorieuse" — A189

2000, June 5 **Engr.** *Perf. 13x12¾*
527 A189 155fr multicolored 4.00 2.40

Sosefo Papilio
Makape, First
Senator — A190

2000, June 19 *Perf. 12¾x13*
528 A190 115fr multicolored 2.90 1.50

Overseas Broadcasting
Institute — A191

2000, July 3 *Perf. 13x12½*
529 A191 200fr multicolored 5.25 2.50

Taro
Cultivation
A192

2000, July 27 **Litho.** *Perf. 13*
530 A192 275fr multicolored 6.25 3.50

Souvenir Sheet

2000 Summer Olympics,
Sydney — A193

Traditional games, 85fr: a, Spear throwing.
b, Sailing. c, Rowing. d, Volleyball.

2000, Sept. 15 **Litho.** *Perf. 13*
531 A193 #a-d + 2 labels 9.00 9.00

8th Pacific
Arts
Festival
A194

2000, Oct. 23 *Perf. 13x13¼*
532 A194 330fr multicolored 7.75 4.50

Fish — A195

No. 533: a, Coryphaena hippurus. b, Caranx
melanpygyus. c, Thunnus albacares.

2000, Nov. 9 **Litho.** *Perf. 13*
533 Vert. strip of 3 + 2 labels 7.75 7.75
a.-c. A195 115fr Any single 2.40 1.75

Canonization of St. Marcellin
Champagnat, 1st Anniv. — A196

2000, Nov. 13
534 A196 380fr multicolored 9.50 5.00

Talietumu Archaeological Site — A197

2000, Dec. 1 *Perf. 13x13½*
535 A197 205fr multicolored 5.25 2.75

Christmas
A198

2000, Dec. 25 *Perf. 13*
536 A198 225fr multicolored 5.75 2.75

Ship "Jacques Cartier" — A199

2001, Feb. 26 **Engr.** *Perf. 13*
537 A199 225fr multicolored 5.50 2.75

Campaign Against
Alcoholism
A200

2001, Mar. 14 **Litho.** *Perf. 13¼x13*
538 A200 75fr multicolored 2.00 1.00

Souvenir Sheet

Les Tapas de Wallis et Futuna

Tapas — A201

Tapa with: a, Large diamond, shells, map of
islands. b, Triangles and diamonds. c, Scenes
of native life, fish, shells, boat. d, Overlapping
ovals.

2001, Apr. 14 *Perf. 13*
539 A201 90fr Sheet of 4, #a-d, +
2 labels 9.00 9.00

Children's Drawings of
Flowers — A202

2001, May 31
540 Horiz. strip of 4 7.00 7.00
a. A202 50fr multi 1.25 1.25
b. A202 55fr multi 1.25 1.25
c. A202 95fr multi 2.10 2.10
d. A202 100fr multi 2.10 2.10

Territorial
Status, 40th
Anniv.
A203

2001, July 29 **Litho.** *Perf. 13*
541 A203 165fr multicolored 4.00 2.00

Installation
of Mediator,
1st Anniv.
A204

2001, Sept. 26
542 A204 800fr multicolored 16.50 10.00

Year of
Dialogue
Among
Civilizations
A205

2001, Oct. 9
543 A205 390fr multicolored 15.00 5.00

5th Autumn
Salon — A206

Birds: a, Dacula pacifica. b, Vini australis. c,
Tyto alba.

2001, Nov. 8
544 Vert. strip of 3 + 2
labels 10.00 10.00
a.-c. A206 150fr Any single 3.00 3.00

Children's Drawings of Fruit A207

No. 545, 65fr: a, Custard apple (pomme canelle). b, Breadfruit (fruit de pain).
No. 546, 65fr: a, Pineapple. b, Mango.

2001, Aug. 22   Litho.   Perf. 13
Vert. Pairs, #a-b
545-546 A207   Set of 2 pairs   6.50 5.00
  a.   Vert. strip of 4, #545-546   7.00 5.00

Tomb of Futuna King Fakavelikele — A208

2001, Dec. 28   Litho.   Perf. 13
547 A208 325fr multicolored   7.00 3.75

Finemui-Teesi College — A209

2002, Jan. 29   Perf. 13x13½
548 A209 115fr multicolored   2.75 1.40

Intl. Women's Day — A210

2002, Mar. 5   Litho.   Perf. 13
549 A210 800fr Queen Aloisia   16.50 10.00

Arms of Bishop Pompallier A211

2002, Apr. 19   Engr.   Perf. 13¼
550 A211 500fr multicolored   11.00 6.50

Uvea Firefighters A212

Serpentine Die Cut
2002, Apr. 28   Photo.
Self-Adhesive
551 A212 85fr multicolored   2.10 1.40

2002 World Cup Soccer Championships, Japan and Korea — A213

2002, May 31   Litho.   Perf. 13
552 A213 65fr multicolored   1.75 1.00

World Environment Day — A214

2002, June 5   Perf. 13x13½
553 A214 330fr multicolored   6.50 4.00

Traditional Buildings A215

Designs: No. 554, 50fr, Building with overhanging roof. No. 555, 50fr, Open-air shelter, vert. No. 556, 55fr, Building with two entry ways. No. 557, 55fr, Building with ladder to roof, vert.

2002, Aug. 9   Engr.   Perf. 13¼
554-557 A215   Set of 4   5.75 2.50

Discovery of the Horn Islands, 1616 A216

No. 558: a, Jacob Lemaire and compass rose. b, Map of Futuna and Alofi Islands. c, William Schouten and ship.

2002, Aug. 30   Litho.   Perf. 13x13¼
558   Horiz. strip of 3   9.50 9.50
  a.-c. A216 125fr any single   3.00 3.00
  d.   Souvenir sheet, #558   9.00 9.00

Landscapes A217

No. 559: a, Utua Bay. b, Liku Bay. c, Kingfisher at Vele. d, Aka'Aka Bay.

2002, Sept. 20
559   Horiz. strip of 4   9.50 9.50
  a.   A217 95fr multi   2.00 1.50
  b.   A217 100fr multi   2.25 1.50
  c.   A217 105fr multi   2.25 1.60
  d.   A217 135fr multi   3.00 1.75

Enygrus Bibroni — A218

2002, Oct. 28   Litho.   Perf. 13¼x13
560 A218 75fr multicolored   1.90 .75

Fish A219

No. 561: a, Dendrochirus biocellatus. b, Discordipina griessingeri. c, Antennacius nummifer. d, Novaculichthys taeniourus.

2002, Nov. 7   Perf. 13x13¼
561   Vert. strip of 4 + 3 labels   9.00 9.00
  a.-d. A219 110fr Any single   2.00 1.75

Best Wishes A220

2002, Dec. 5
562 A220 140fr multicolored   3.00 1.40

Last Avro Lancaster Flight to Wallis, 40th Anniv. A221

2003, Jan. 26   Perf. 13
563 A221 135fr multicolored   3.25 1.75

St. Valentine's Day — A222

2003, Feb. 14   Perf. 13
564 A222 85fr multicolored   1.75 1.00

Introduction of the Euro, 1st Anniv. A223

2003, Feb. 17   Perf. 12½x12¾
565 A223 125fr multicolored   3.00 1.80
  Values are for examples with surrounding selvage.

Alain Gerbault (1893-1941), Circumnavigator, Aboard Boat "Firecrest" — A224

2003, Mar. 6   Engr.   Perf. 13¼
566 A224 600fr grn & ol grn   12.00 8.00

Postal Art — A225

Various designs.

2003, Mar. 31   Litho.   Perf. 13
567   Horiz. strip of 5   2.40 2.40
  a.   A225 5fr multi   .25 .25
  b.   A225 10fr multi   .30 .25
  c.   A225 15fr multi   .35 .35
  d.   A225 20fr multi   .55 .25
  e.   A225 40fr multi   .80 .40

Coral Reefs A226

Various views.

2003, Apr. 10   Perf. 13x13¼
568   Horiz. strip of 4   10.00 10.00
  a.   A226 95fr multi   1.75 1.75
  b.   A226 105fr multi   1.90 1.90
  c.   A226 110fr multi   2.00 2.00
  d.   A226 115fr multi   2.10 2.10

St. Pierre Chanel (1803-41), Martyred Missionary A227

2003, Apr. 28   Engr.   Perf. 12¼
569 A227 130fr multicolored   2.60 1.80

2003 Census — A228

2003, June 12   Litho.   Perf. 13
570 A228 55fr multicolored   1.90 .70

Pacific Legends
A229

Legend of the Coconut Palm: 30fr, Eel. 50fr, Coconut palms, split coconut. 60fr, Split and whole coconuts. 70fr, Coconut palms and clouds.

2003, July 28 Litho. *Perf. 13x13¼*
571		Horiz. strip of 4	5.00	5.00
a.	A229	30fr multi	.65	.40
b.	A229	50fr multi	1.00	.75
c.	A229	60fr multi	1.05	.85
d.	A229	70fr multi	1.40	.95
e.		Souvenir sheet, #571a-571d	5.25	5.25

Still Life with Maori Statuette, by Paul Gauguin (1848-1903) A230

No. 573a: Study of Heads of Tahitian Women, by Gauguin.

2003 *Perf. 13*
572	A230	100fr multicolored	2.75	1.60

Souvenir Sheet
573		Sheet, #572, 573a	5.50	5.50
a.	A230	100fr multi	2.75	2.25

Issued: No. 572, 7/01; No. 573, 8/20. See New Caledonia No. 929.

Futuna Waterfalls — A231

2003, Aug. 6 *Perf. 13¼x13*
574	A231	115fr multicolored	2.75	1.75

Frigate Le Nivose A232

2003, Sept. 15 Engr. *Perf. 13¼*
575	A232	325fr multicolored	8.00	4.00

Bishop Alexandre Poncet (1884-1973) A233

2003, Sept. 18 Engr. *Perf. 13¼*
576	A233	205fr multicolored	4.00	3.00

Arms of Bishop Pierre Bataillon (1810-77) — A234

2003, Oct. 1 Litho. *Perf. 13¼*
577	A234	500fr multicolored	12.50	7.00

2003 Rugby World Cup, Australia A235

2003, Oct. 10 *Perf. 13*
578	A235	65fr multicolored	1.50	.85

Parinari Insularum A236

2003, Nov. 6 Litho. *Perf. 13¼x13*
579	A236	250fr multicolored	5.00	3.50

Goddess Havea Hikule'o — A237

2004, Jan. 8
580	A237	85fr multicolored	2.00	1.40

People in Canoe A238

2004, Jan. 13 *Perf. 13*
581	A238	75fr multicolored	1.90	1.25

Miniature Sheet

Campaign Against Dengue Fever — A239

No. 582: a, 5fr, Mosquito, crying man. b, 10fr, Mosquitos, man. c, 20fr, Mosquitos, trash. d, 30fr, Mosquitos, sleeping child.

Perf. 13¼x12¾
2004, Feb. 18 Litho.
582	A239	Sheet of 4, #a-d	1.75	1.75

Badminton A240

2004, Mar. 12 *Perf. 13¼x13*
583	A240	55fr multicolored	1.40	1.25

Kava Drinkers A241

2004, Mar. 31 *Perf. 13x13¼*
584	A241	205fr multicolored	4.00	4.00

Flora A242

2004, Apr. 22 *Perf. 13*
585		Horiz. strip of 4 + central label	2.50	2.50
a.	A242	15fr Colocasia esculenta	.30	.30
b.	A242	25fr Carrica papaya	.50	.50
c.	A242	35fr Artocarpus altilus	.70	.70
d.	A242	40fr Dioscorea sp.	.80	.80

Dispatch Boat Savorgnan de Brazza A243

Gourdou-Leseurre GL 832 Hy No. 5 and Wallis Island — A244

2004, May 12 Engr. *Perf. 13¼*
586	A243	300fr multi	6.00	6.00
587	A244	380fr multi	7.50	7.50

Souvenir Sheet
Litho.
588		Sheet of 2	13.00	13.00
a.	A243	300fr multi	5.75	5.75
b.	A244	380fr multi	7.25	7.25

First flight over Wallis Island, 68th anniv.

Seaweeds — A245

2004, June 26 Litho. *Perf. 13*
589		Horiz. strip of 3 + 2 alternating labels	10.00	10.00
a.	A245	105fr Turbinaria ornata	1.60	1.60
b.	A245	155fr Padina melomelo	2.40	2.40
c.	A245	175fr Tubinaria concoides	2.75	2.75
d.		Miniature sheet of 6 + 9 labels	20.00	

No. 589 was issued in sheets of 15 with 10 labels.

Miniature Sheet

Flowers — A246

No. 590: a, Hibiscus rosa-sinensis. b, Cananga odorata. c, Plumeria rubra. d, Ipomeapes caprae. e, Gardenia taitensis.

Serpentine Die Cut 14
2004, June 26 Photo.
Self-Adhesive
590	A246	Sheet of 5	10.00	10.00
a.-d.		85fr Any single	1.90	1.90
e.		115fr multi	2.40	2.40

Salon du Timbre 2004, Paris.

Ninth Pacific Arts Festival, Palau A247

2004, July 22 Litho. *Perf. 13x13¼*
591	A247	200fr multicolored	4.00	4.00

Pili'uli Lizard — A248

2004, July 26 *Perf. 13*
592	A248	100fr multicolored	2.50	2.10

Arms of Monsignor Louis Elloy (1829-78) A249

2004, Sept. 6 Engr. *Perf. 13¼*
593	A249	500fr multicolored	10.00	10.00

No. 517 Redrawn
2004, Nov. 10 Litho. *Perf. 13*
594	A179	115fr multi	2.50	2.50

No. 594 shows a 115fr denomination below an obliterated 130fr denomination, the denomination shown on No. 517. This new denomination is not overprinted. No. 594 also has a 2004 year date, rather than an obliterated 1999 year date.

A250

Traditional Houses — A251

2004, Nov. 11   **Perf. 13¼x13**
595 A250   95fr multicolored   1.90   1.90
596 A251   130fr multicolored   2.75   2.75

Nos. 595-596 were printed in sheets containing four of each stamp plus a large central label.

Miniature Sheet

Cone Shells — A252

No. 597: a, Conus eburneus. b, Conus imperialis. c, Conus generalis. d, Gastridium textile.

2005, Jan. 26   **Perf. 13x13¼**
597 A252   55fr Sheet of 4, #a-d   5.75   5.00

Miniature Sheet

Stories and Legends — A253

No. 598: a, 65fr, Whale, bird, crab, eel, turtle. b, 65fr, Fish, octopus, dolphin, butterfly. c, 75fr, Boy, waves, G clef and musical notes. d, 75fr, Musical notes, butterflies.

2005, Jan. 31   **Perf. 13**
598 A253   Sheet of 4, #a-d   6.75   6.75

Pirogue A254

2005, Feb. 25   Litho.   Perf. 13x13¼
599 A254   330fr multicolored   7.00   7.00

Francophone Week — A255

2005, Mar. 17
600 A255   135fr multicolored   3.00   3.00

Printed in sheets of 10 + 5 labels. See New Caledonia No. 959.

Family Budget Inquiry A256

2005, Mar. 31   **Perf. 12¾**
601 A256   205fr multicolored   4.50   4.50

Values are for stamps with surrounding selvage.

Warriors — A257

2005, Apr. 19   **Perf. 13½x13**
602   Horiz. strip of 5   2.75   2.75
   a.   A257   5fr blk, red & maroon   .25   .25
   b.   A257   10fr blk, bl & vio blue   .25   .25
   c.   A257   20fr blk, pur & indigo   .40   .40
   d.   A257   30fr blk & red   .45   .45
   e.   A257   50fr blk, lt grn & emerald   .80   .80

Traditional Cricket A258

2005, May 16   **Perf. 13**
603 A258   190fr multicolored   4.00   4.00

Butterflies — A259

No. 604: a, 40fr, Papilio montrouzieri. b, 60fr, Danaus pumila.

2005, June 30   **Perf. 13x13¼**
604 A259   Horiz. pair, #a-b   2.25   2.25

Warrior With Spear — A260

2005, July 14   **Self-Adhesive**
Booklet Stamp
605 A260   115fr multicolored   2.50   2.40
   a.   Booklet pane of 10   25.00

Historical Images of Wallis Island — A261

2005, July 14   Engr.   Perf. 13x13¼
606   Horiz. pair + central label   7.50   7.50
   a.   A261   155fr Village scene   3.50   3.25
   b.   A261   175fr Family, house   4.00   3.75

First Noumea to Hihifo Flight, 58th Anniv. — A262

2005, Aug. 19
607 A262   380fr multi   8.00   8.00

Souvenir Sheet

Chelomia Mydas — A263

No. 608 — Green turtle: a, Adult entering water. b, Hatchlings entering water. c, Head. d, Swimming underwater.

2005, Aug. 19   Litho.   Perf. 13x13¼
608 A263   85fr Sheet of 4, #a-d   8.50   8.50

Arms of Monsignor Jean Armand Lamaze (1833-1906) A264

2005, Oct. 5   Engr.   Perf. 13¼
609 A264   500fr multi   10.50   10.00

Spattoglottis Cinguiculata — A265

2005, Oct. 30   Litho.   Perf. 13
610 A265   100fr multi   2.00   2.00

Printed in sheets of 10 + 5 labels.

Design of Wallis and Futuna Islands No. 4 — A266

Design of Wallis and Futuna Islands No. 87 — A267

2005, Nov. 10   Litho.   Perf. 13x13¼
611 A266   150fr multi   4.00   3.00
612 A267   150fr multi   4.00   3.00

59th Autumn Philatelic Show.

Native Child A268

2006, Mar. 29   Litho.   Perf. 13x13¼
613 A268   75fr multi   1.75   1.60

Monarchical Flags — A269

Designs: 55fr, Kingdom of Uvea. 65fr, Kingdom of Sigave. 85fr, Kingdom of Alo.

Self-Adhesive
Booklet Stamps

2006   Litho.   Serpentine Die Cut 11
614 A269   55fr multi   1.20   1.20
   a.   Booklet pane of 10   12.00
615 A269   65fr multi   1.40   1.40
   a.   Booklet pane of 10   14.00
616 A269   85fr multi   1.75   1.75
   a.   Booklet pane of 10   18.00

Issued: 55fr, 6/17; 65fr, 4/18; 85fr, 3/29.

Haka Mai — A270

2006   **Perf. 13¼x13**
617 A270   190fr multi   4.00   4.00

Removal of Christ from the Cross, by Jean Soane Michon (1926-68) A271

2006, May 31 Litho. *Perf. 13¼x13*
618 A271 400fr multi 8.00 8.00

2006 World Cup Soccer Championships, Germany A272

2006, June 9
619 A272 100fr multi 2.25 2.10

Mata Vai A273

Mata Tai A274

2006, June 17 *Perf. 13x13¼*
620 A273 140fr multi 3.00 3.00
621 A274 200fr multi 4.25 4.25

Historical Images From the 19th Century — A275

2006, July 13 Engr. *Perf. 13x13¼*
622 Horiz. pair + central label 15.00 15.00
a. A275 330fr Girls dancing 7.00 7.00
b. A275 380fr Mua Church 8.00 8.00

Stamp Day — A276

2006, Aug. 5 Litho. *Perf. 13¼x13*
623 A276 150fr multi 3.50 3.25

Twin Otter Airplane "Ville de Paris", 20th Anniv. — A277

2006, Aug. 7 *Perf. 13*
624 A277 30fr multi 1.00 .65

Territorial Rugby Committee — A278

2006, Sept. 9 *Perf. 12¾x13½*
625 A278 10fr multi 1.00 .25

Uhilamoafa Gravesite A279

2006, Sept. 12 *Perf. 13x13¼*
626 A279 290fr multi 6.00 6.00

Arms of Monsignor Joseph Félix Blanc (1872-1962) A280

2006, Oct. 5 Engr. *Perf. 13¼*
627 A280 500fr multi 10.50 10.50

Tagaloa, Polynesian Deity — A281

2006, Nov. 8 Litho. *Perf. 13½x13*
628 A281 150fr multi 3.50 3.50

Tapas A282

No. 629: a, Tapas design (shown). b, Mako à Ono. c, Tauasu à Leava. d, Tapas design, diff.

Litho. & Engr.
2006, Nov. 8 *Perf. 13x13¼*
629 Vert. strip of 4 + central label 8.00 8.00
a.-d. A282 85fr Any single 1.90 1.90

Souvenir Sheet

Christmas — A283

2006, Nov. 8 Litho. *Perf. 13*
630 A283 225fr multi 5.25 5.25

Pio Cardinal Taofinu'u (1923-2006) A284

2007, Jan. 19 Engr. *Perf. 12½x13*
631 A284 800fr multi 20.00 17.50

Telemedicine A285

2007, Feb. 28 Litho. *Perf. 13¼x13*
632 A285 5fr multi .75 .25

Audit Office, Bicent. A286

2007, Mar. 19 Engr. *Perf. 13¼*
633 A286 105fr multi 2.50 2.40

Woman A287

2007, Mar. 22 Litho. *Perf. 13*
634 A287 75fr multi 1.75 1.75

First Noumea-Hihifo Air Service, 50th Anniv. — A288

2007, Apr. 30 Engr. *Perf. 13x12½*
635 A288 290fr multi 6.75 6.75

Fish — A289

2007, May 22 Litho. *Perf. 12¾x13¼*
636 Horiz. pair 2.00 2.00
a. A289 40fr Eviota .90 .90
b. A289 50fr Trimma 1.10 1.10

Secretary General of the Pacific Community, 60th Anniv. — A290

2007, June 28 Litho. *Perf. 13*
637 A290 155fr multi 3.50 3.50

Lolesio Tuita, Javelin Thrower A291

2007, July 30 Engr. *Perf. 12½x13*
638 A291 330fr purple & red 7.50 7.50

Buildings — A292

No. 639; a, House, Tamana. b, Sanctuary of Pierre Chanel, Poi.

2007, July 31 Engr. *Perf. 13x13¼*
639 Horiz. pair with central label 9.00 9.00
a. A292 190fr brown 4.25 4.25
b. A292 200fr brown 4.75 4.75

Discovery of Uvea Island by Samuel Wallis, 240th Anniv. — A293

2007, Aug. 3 Litho.
640 A293 225fr multi 5.25 5.25
a. Souvenir sheet of 1 5.50 5.50

No. 640a sold for 240fr.

Legends of Lomipeau A294

No. 641 — People and: a, Togitapu Island. b, Uvea Island.

2007, Aug. 3
641 Horiz. pair 1.25 1.25
 a. A294 20fr multi .50 .50
 b. A294 30fr multi .75 .75

Arms of Monsignor Armand Olier (1851-1911) A295

2007, Oct. 22 Engr. Perf. 13¼
642 A295 500fr multi 12.00 12.00

Emblem of Handisport A296

2007, Oct. 11 Photo. Perf. 12¾
643 A296 10fr multi .25 .25
 Values are for stamps with surrounding selvage.

2007 Rugby World Cup Championships, France — A297

2007, Oct. 20 Litho. Perf. 13
644 A297 205fr multi 5.00 5.00
 Printed in sheets of 10 + label.

Dances — A298

Designs: No. 645, 100fr, Mio dance, Futuna. No. 646, 100fr, Kailao Tokotoko dance, Wallis.

2007, Nov. 10 Litho. Perf. 13¼x13
645-646 A298 Set of 2 5.00 5.00

Connection to the Internet, 10th Anniv. A299

2008, Mar. 3 Litho. Perf. 13x13¼
647 A299 55fr multi 1.30 1.30
 Printed in sheets of 10 + central label.

Coral Reef A300

2008, Mar. 7
648 A300 95fr multi 2.00 2.00

Islands — A301

No. 649: a, Uvea. b, Futuna and Alofi, horiz.

Perf. 13¼x13 (#649a), 13x13¼ (#649b)
2008, Mar. 7
649 A301 85fr Pair, #a-b 3.50 3.50
 Printed in sheets containing four of each stamp.

Women and Hibiscus Flowers — A302

2008, Mar. 7 Perf. 13
650 A302 65fr multi 1.75 1.75
 Printed in sheets of 10 + 5 labels.

2008 Summer Olympics, Beijing A303

2008, June 14 Perf. 13x13¼
651 A303 75fr multi 2.00 2.00

Intl. Year of Planet Earth — A304

2008, June 14 Perf. 13
652 A304 190fr multi 5.00 5.00
Souvenir Sheet
653 A304 200fr multi 5.25 5.25

King Tomasi Kulimoetoke II (1918-2007) A305

2008, July 29 Engr. Perf. 13¼
654 A305 380fr orange brown 9.75 9.75

Aglaia Psilopetala A306

2008, July 30 Litho. Perf. 13
655 A306 105fr multi 2.75 2.75

Historical Images of Futuna — A307

No. 656: a, Women braiding straw. b, Boats returning to island.

2008, July 30 Engr. Perf. 13x13¼
656 Horiz. pair with central
 label 6.75 6.75
 a. A307 110fr brown 2.75 2.75
 b. A307 155fr brown 4.00 4.00

Stained-glass Windows of Lano Church — A308

Designs: 100fr, St. Theresa. 140fr, St. Peter Chanel.

2008, July 31 Litho. Perf. 13
657-658 A308 Set of 2 6.00 6.00

Pirogue Hulls A309

Various painted pirogue hulls.

2008, Aug. 18 Perf. 13x13¼
659 Horiz. strip of 4 2.75 2.75
 a. A309 5fr multi .25 .25
 b. A309 20fr multi .50 .50
 c. A309 40fr multi .95 .95
 d. A309 50fr multi 1.10 1.10

Lolesio Tuita Stadium A310

2008, Oct. 28
660 A310 55fr multi 1.25 1.25

Arms of Monsignor Alexandre Poncet (1884-1973) A311

2008, Oct. 28 Engr. Perf. 13¼
661 A311 500fr multi 11.00 11.00

World Youth Day — A312

2008, Nov. 8 Litho. Perf. 13¼x13
662 A312 10fr multi .25 .25

Pigs — A313

No. 663 — Pigs on farm with denomination at: a, UL. b, UR.

2008, Nov. 8 Perf. 13x13¼
663 A313 115fr Horiz. pair, #a-b 5.00 5.00

Fifth French Republic, 50th Anniv. A314

2008, Nov. 8 Engr. Perf. 13¼
664 A314 225fr multi 5.00 5.00

Louis Braille (1809-52), Educator of the Blind — A315

2009, Mar. 7 Engr. Perf. 12¾x13
665 A315 330fr multi 7.50 7.50

Bougainvillea Spectabilis — A316

Flowers with background colors of: No. 666, 55fr, Black. No. 667, 55fr, Green. No. 668, 55fr, Red. No. 669, 55fr, White.

2009, May 4   Litho.   *Perf. 13*
666-669 A316   Set of 4   5.25 5.25

Gobies — A317

No. 670: a, Akihito futuna. b, Stiphodon rubromaculatus.

2009, May 7   *Perf. 12¾x13¼*
670   Horiz. pair   3.00 3.00
a.-b. A317 65fr Either single   1.50 1.50

St. Theresa of Lisieux (1873-97) A318

Phil@poste at bottom in: No. 671, White (brown border at bottom). No. 672, Black (brown border at top).

2009, June 27   *Perf. 13½x13*
671 A318 140fr multi   3.25 3.25
672 A318 140fr multi   3.25 3.25

New Year 2009, (Year of the Ox) — A319

2009, June 30   *Perf. 13¼x13*
673 A319 95fr multi   2.25 2.25

Pétanque Playing in Wallis & Futuna Islands — A320

2009, July 31
674 A320 105fr multi   2.50 2.50

Arms of Bishop Michel Darmancier (1918-84) A321

2009, Oct. 30   Engr.   *Perf. 13¼*
675 A321 500fr multi   12.50 12.50

Historical Images — A322

No. 676: a, France House. b, Army of Wallisians.

2009, Nov. 5   *Perf. 13x13¼*
676   Horiz. pair + central label   9.50 9.50
a.-b. A322 190fr Either single   4.75 4.75

Man Preparing Kava — A323

2009, Nov. 12   Litho.   *Perf. 13¼x13*
677 A323 115fr multi   3.00 3.00

Eiffel Tower on Tapa Cloth — A324

2009, Dec. 8   *Perf. 13x13¼*
678 A324 85fr brown & black   2.10 2.10

Wallis & Futuna Islands as French Overseas Territory, 50th Anniv. — A325

2009, Dec. 27   Engr.   *Perf. 13¼*
679 A325 205fr multi   5.00 5.00

Arrival of First Doctors on Futuna Island, 50th Anniv. — A326

2010, Jan. 3   Litho.   *Perf. 13*
680 A326 800fr multi   18.50 18.50

Gobies — A327

2010, Feb. 19   *Perf. 12¾x13¼*
681   Horiz. pair   2.75 2.75
a. A327 50fr Sicyopus sasali   1.25 1.25
b. A327 65fr Stenogobius keletaona   1.50 1.50

A328

A329

A330

Coral Reefs A331

2010, Mar. 12   Litho.   *Perf. 13x13¼*
682   Horiz. strip of 4   2.40 2.40
a. A328 10fr multi   .25 .25
b. A329 20fr multi   .45 .45
c. A330 30fr multi   .70 .70
d. A331 40fr multi   .95 .95

Easter — A332

2010, Apr. 2
683 A332 135fr multi   3.25 3.25

Mother's Day A333

2010, May 28   *Perf. 13*
684 A333 105fr multi   2.25 2.25

Renewable Energy — A334

No. 685: a, Solar panels on ground. b, Solar panels on roof.

2010, June 11
685   Horiz. pair + central label   16.50 16.50
a.-b. A334 400fr Either single   8.25 8.25

Arms of Bishop Lolesio Fuahea — A335

2010, July 16   Engr.   *Perf. 13¼*
686 A335 500fr multi   11.00 11.00

First Flight to Vele, 40th Anniv. — A336

2010, Aug. 24   Litho.   *Perf. 13¼x13*
687 A336 100fr multi   2.25 2.25

Traditional Group Fishing — A337

2010, Sept. 24
688 A337 205fr brown   4.75 4.75

Depictions of the Elements — A338

No. 689: a, Water. b, Fire.

2010, Oct. 15   *Perf. 13*
689 A338 150fr Horiz. pair, #a-b   7.00 7.00

Souvenir Sheet

Cardisoma Carnifex — A338a

No. 689C: d, 95fr, Denomination at LL. e, 130fr, Denomination at UR.

2010, Nov. 6   Litho.   Perf. 13¼x13
689C A338a   Sheet of 2, #d-e   5.25 5.25

Christmas
A339

2010, Dec. 24   Litho.   Perf. 13
690 A339 95fr multi   2.25 2.25

Cicada — A340

2011, Jan. 17
691 A340 55fr multi   1.25 1.25

Arms of Bishop Ghislain Marie Raoul Suzanne de Rasilly — A341

2011, Feb. 19   Engr.   Perf. 13¼
692 A341 500fr multi   12.00 12.00

French Navy Ship Jacques Cartier, Relief Ship for Victims of Tropical Cyclone Tomas A342

2011, Mar. 31   Litho.   Perf. 13
693 A342 600fr multi   14.50 14.50

St. Peter Chanel (1803-41) — A343

2011, Apr. 28
694 A343 75fr multi   1.75 1.75

Birds — A344

No. 695: a, 5fr, Vini australis (30x40mm). b, 20fr, Melipphage foulehaio (30x40mm). c, 115fr, Lalage maculosa futunae (60x40mm).

2011, May 28   Perf. 13¼x13
695 A344   Horiz. strip of 3, #a-c 3.50 3.50

Campaign Against Alcohol — A345

2011, June 28
696 A345 130fr multi   3.25 3.25

Georges Pompidou (1911-74), President of France A346

2011, July 5   Perf. 13x13¼
697 A346 1000fr multi   24.00 24.00

Territorial Statute, 50th Anniv. — A347

2011, July 16
698 A347 380fr multi   9.25 9.25

Souvenir Sheet

Pacific Games, Noumea, New Caledonia — A348

No. 699: a, 10fr, Track. b, 190fr, Sailing.

2011, Aug. 24
699 A348   Sheet of 2, #a-b   4.75 4.75

Tapa Cloth Designs — A349

Designs: 40fr, Flowers and diamonds. 50fr, Shells.

2011, Sept. 24
700-701 A349   Set of 2   2.10 2.10

Wallis Open Air Market, 1st Anniv. — A350

2011, Oct. 2
702 A350 30fr multi   .70 .70

Historical Images — A351

No. 703: a, Marriage in Mua. b, Marist Sisters, Sofala.

2011, Nov. 4
703   Horiz. pair + central label 6.25 6.25
a.   A351 110fr brown   2.50 2.50
b.   A351 155fr brown   3.75 3.75

Ninth Pacific Mini-Games, Wallis and Futuna Islands — A352

2012, Jan. 25
704 A352 65fr multi   1.50 1.50

Tekena — A353

Fai Koka
A354

2012, Feb. 17
705 A353 75fr multi   1.75 1.75
706 A354 115fr multi   2.60 2.60

First Territorial Assembly — A355

2012, Mar. 4
707 A355 200fr multi   4.50 4.50

Corals A356

Various corals.

2012, Apr. 17   Perf. 13x13¼
708   Horiz. strip of 4   3.25 3.25
a.   A356 10fr multi   .25 .25
b.   A356 30fr multi   .70 .70
c.   A356 40fr multi   .90 .90
d.   A356 55fr multi   1.25 1.25

Arrival of Americans, 70th Anniv. — A357

2012, May 28   Perf. 13
709 A357 55fr multi   1.25 1.25

Lavelua, King of Uvea, and Chieftains, Circa 1900 — A358

2012, June 21   Engr.   Perf. 13x13¼
710 A358 380fr bl grn & blk   8.00 8.00

Poetry of the
Seas — A359

2012, July 16   **Litho.**   *Perf. 13*
711 A359 35fr multi   .75 .75

Opening of New Payment
Office — A360

2012, July 27
712 A360 135fr multi   3.00 3.00

Reconstruction of Futuna Upper
Administration Delegation
Building — A361

2012, Sept. 5
713 A361 95fr multi   2.10 2.10

2013 Oceania Pétanque Tournament,
Wallis & Futuna Islands — A362

2012, July 7   **Litho.**
714 A362 25fr multi   .55 .55

Arms of Bishop
Guillaume
Douarre (1810-
53) — A363

2012, Oct. 18   **Engr.**   *Perf. 13¼*
715 A363 500fr multi   11.00 11.00

Second Vatican Council, 50th
Anniv. — A364

2012, Oct. 11   **Litho.**   *Perf. 13*
716 A364 290fr multi   6.25 6.25

Shells
A365

Various shells.

2012, Nov. 8   *Perf. 13x13¼*
717   Horiz. strip of 4   3.50 3.50
   a.   A365 5fr multi   .25 .25
   b.   A365 25fr multi   .55 .55
   c.   A365 35fr multi   .75 .75
   d.   A365 85fr multi   1.90 1.90

Bishop Lolesio
Fuahea (1927-
2011), First
Wallis & Futuna
Islands Bishop
Born in Oceania
A366

2012, Dec. 2   **Engr.**   *Perf. 13¼x13*
718 A366 1000fr multi   22.00 22.00

A367

Ocean
Garden — A368

2013, Jan. 17   **Litho.**   *Perf. 13*
719 A367 85fr multi   2.00 2.00
720 A368 85fr multi   2.00 2.00

Bats — A369

2013, Feb. 20   **Litho.**   *Perf. 13*
721 A369 55fr multi   1.25 1.25

Hervé Loste
(1926-94),
Politician — A370

2013, Mar. 5   **Litho.**   *Perf. 13*
722 A370 800fr multi   17.50 17.50

State High School, 20th
Anniv — A371

2013, Mar. 10   **Litho.**   *Perf. 13*
723 A371 65fr multi   1.40 1.40

First Session of Mata-Utu Tribunal,
50th Anniv. — A372

2013, Apr. 5   **Litho.**   *Perf. 13*
724 A372 190fr multi   4.25 4.25

Discovery of
Horn Island
(Futuna Island),
400th Anniv. (in
2016) — A373

2013, May 19   **Litho.**   *Perf. 13*
725 A373 330fr multi   7.50 7.50

Story
Telling
A374

Traditional
Dancers
A375

2013, June 14   **Litho.**   *Perf. 13x13¼*
726 A374 105fr multi   2.40 2.40
727 A375 140fr multi   3.25 3.25

Petelo Sanele Vakalima, Javelin
Thrower — A376

2013, July 3   **Litho.**   *Perf. 13*
728 A376 75fr multi   1.75 1.75

Sister Marie
Françoise
Perroton (1796-
1873),
Missionary
A377

2013, Aug. 10   **Engr.**   *Perf. 13¼x13*
729 A377 400fr beige & blk   9.00 9.00

2013 Pacific Mini-
Games, Mata-
Utu — A378

No. 730 — Red lizard mascot: a, Serving
volleyball, map of Wallis Island. b, Diving for
volleyball, map of Futuna Island, horiz. c, Sailing, map of Futuna Island, horiz. d, Weight
lifting, map of Futuna Island, horiz. e, Playing
rugby, map of Wallis Island. f, Making
Taekwondo kick, map of Wallis Island. g, Paddling outrigger canoe, map of Futuna Island,
horiz. h, Throwing javelin, map of Wallis
Island.

Litho. & Silk-screened
2013, Sept. 2   *Serpentine Die Cut 11*
Self-Adhesive
730   Booklet pane of 8   15.50
   a.-h.   A378 85fr Any single   1.90 1.90

Bishop Alexandre Poncet (1884-
1973) — A379

2013, Sept. 18   **Engr.**   *Perf. 13x13¼*
731 A379 150fr black   3.50 3.50

Landscapes of Shores of Wallis
Island — A380

Designs. 55fr, Fisherman in surf. 65fr,
Beach, tree at right.

2013, Oct. 25   **Litho.**   *Perf. 13*
732-733 A380   Set of 2   2.75 2.75

Flowers — A381

Designs: No. 734, 165fr, Hyacinth (jacinth).
No. 735, 165fr, Red jasmine (frangipanier).

2013, Nov. 5   **Litho.**   *Perf. 13*
734-735 A381   Set of 2   7.50   7.50

Christmas
A382

2013, Dec. 1   **Litho.**   *Perf. 13*
736 A382 175fr multi   4.00   4.00

New Banknotes — A383

Designs: 50fr, 500-franc banknote. 90fr,
1000-franc banknote. 115fr, 5000-franc banknote. 800fr, 10,000-franc banknote.

2014, Jan. 24   **Litho.**   *Perf. 13*
737-740 A383   Set of 4   24.00   24.00

Cyrthandra
Futunae — A384

2014, Feb. 18   **Litho.**   *Perf. 13*
741 A384 95fr multi   2.25   2.25

Fai Koka — A385

2014, Mar. 5   **Litho.**   *Perf. 13*
742 A385 95fr multi   2.25   2.25

Canonization of
Popes — A386

Designs: No. 743, 100fr, Pope John XXIII.
No. 744, 100fr, Pope John Paul II.

2014, Apr. 27   **Litho.**   *Perf. 13¼x13*
743-744 A386   Set of 2   4.75   4.75

Chapel and
Shrine to
St. Peter
Chanel,
Poi — A387

2014, Apr. 28   **Litho.**   *Perf. 13*
745 A387 130fr multi   3.00   3.00

Mother's
Day — A388

2014, May 23   **Litho.**   *Perf. 13¼x13*
746 A388 115fr multi   2.60   2.60

2014 Oceania Weight Lifting
Championships, Noumea, New
Caledonia — A389

2014, May 27   **Litho.**   *Perf. 13*
747 A389 20fr multi   .45   .45

Turtles In Water — A390

2014, June 16   **Litho.**   *Perf. 13*
748 A390 65fr multi   1.50   1.50

2014 World Cup Soccer
Championships, Brazil — A391

2014, July 12   **Litho.**   *Perf. 13*
749 A391 330fr multi   7.50   7.50

Talietumu Archaeological Site — A392

2014, Aug. 6   **Litho.**   *Perf. 13*
750 A392 75fr multi   1.75   1.75

Miniature Sheet

Tapa Cloths — A393

No. 751 — Tapa cloth: a, With geometric
design, denomination at UR. b, Depicting people seated around kava bowl. c, With stripes
and diamonds, denominations at UL. d,
Depicting canoe, shells, trees and house in
octagons.

2014, Sept. 5   **Litho.**   *Perf. 13*
751 A393 85fr Sheet of 4, #a-d   7.25   7.25

American
Village
Near Gahi
A394

2014, Oct. 3   **Litho.**   *Perf. 13x13¼*
752 A394 400fr brown   8.50   8.50

Miniature Sheet

Old Stamps — A395

No. 753 — Old stamps redrawn in different
sizes: a, Stamp like #150. b, Stamp like #155.
c, Stamp like #151. d, Stamp like #B9.

2014, Nov. 6   **Litho.**   *Perf. 13x13¼*
753 A395   Sheet of 9, #753a-
     753c, 6 #753d   30.00   30.00
   a.   3fr multi   .25   .25
   b.   7fr multi   .25   .25
   c.   9fr multi   .25   .25
   d.   225fr red   4.75   4.75

Paintings — A396

No. 754 — Painting by: a, 40fr, Nicolai
Michoutouchkine. b, 205fr, Aloi Pilioko.

2014, Nov. 8   **Litho.**   *Perf. 13x13¼*
754 A396 Vert. pair, #a-b   5.25   5.25

Benjamin Brial
(1923-2004),
Politician — A397

2014, Nov. 12   **Litho.**   *Perf. 13*
755 A397 340fr multi   7.00   7.00

Christmas
A398

2014, Dec. 23   **Litho.**   *Perf. 13x13¼*
756 A398 85fr multi   1.75   1.75

Women
and
Children
A399

2015, Jan. 29   **Litho.**   *Perf. 13x13¼*
757 A399 85fr multi   1.60   1.60

Boat Near Beach on Wallis
Island — A400

2015, Feb. 18   **Litho.**   *Perf. 13*
758 A400 85fr multi   1.60   1.60

Kamilo Gata
(1949-2004),
Politician — A401

2015, Mar. 27   **Litho.**   *Perf. 13x13¼*
759 A401 600fr multi   11.00   11.00

St. Peter Chanel (1803-41), Missionary A402

2015, Apr. 28   Litho.   *Perf. 13*
760   A402   55fr multi   1.10   1.10

Orchids — A403

Various orchids: 75fr, 100fr.

2015, May 21   Litho.   *Perf. 13*
761-762   A403   Set of 2   4.00   4.00

Emblem of Territorial Committee for Olympics and Sport A404

2015, June 24   Litho.   *Perf. 13*
763   A404   55fr multi   1.00   1.00

Pirogue A405

2015, July 13   Litho.   *Perf. 13¼*
764   A405   400fr multi   7.50   7.50

Traditional Women's Clothing A406

2015, Aug. 31   Litho.   *Perf. 13x13¼*
765   A406   330fr multi   6.25   6.25

A407

A408

Lano College, 40th Anniv. A409

2015, Sept. 3   Litho.   *Perf. 13x13¼*
766   Horiz. strip of 3   6.75   6.75
  a.   A407 55fr multi   1.00   1.00
  b.   A408 90fr multi   1.75   1.75
  c.   A409 205fr multi   4.00   4.00

Fugalei, Kaviki and Luaniva Islands — A410

2015, Nov. 5   Litho.   *Perf. 13*
767   A410   700fr multi   12.50   12.50

Christmas A411

2015, Nov. 23   Litho.   *Perf. 13*
768   A411   250fr multi   4.50   4.50

Souvenir Sheet

Cone Shells — A412

2016, Jan. 29   Litho.   *Perf. 13*
769   A412   Sheet of 2   5.00   5.00
  a.   125fr Conus floccatus   2.25   2.25
  b.   150fr Conus bullatus   2.75   2.75

Manuia Mobile Phone Service — A413

2016, Feb. 14   Litho.   *Perf. 13x13¼*
770   A413   500fr multi   9.25   9.25

Clipper Ship Flying Cloud — A414

2016, Mar. 25   Litho.   *Perf. 13*
771   A414   300fr multi   5.75   5.75

Eke Dancers A415

2016, May 4   Litho.   *Perf. 13x13¼*
772   A415   105fr multi   2.00   2.00

2016 Festival of Pacific Arts, Guam — A416

2016, May 30   Litho.   *Perf. 13*
773   A416   330fr multi   6.25   6.25

Saber Dancer A417

2016, June 6   Litho.   *Perf. 13*
774   A417   135fr multi   2.60   2.60

Campaign Against Diabetes — A418

2016, July 13   Litho.   *Perf. 13*
775   A418   115fr multi   2.25   2.25

Traditional Fishing, Nukuafo A419

2016, July 26   Engr.   *Perf. 13*
776   A419   800fr dull purple   15.00   15.00

Twin Otter Airplane "Ville de Paris", 30th Anniv. A421

2016, Nov. 3   Litho.   *Perf. 13x13¼*
778   A421   105fr multi   1.90   1.90

World Post Day — A422

2016, Nov. 3   Litho.   *Perf. 13¼x13*
779   A422   205fr multi   3.75   3.75

Souvenir Sheet

Birds — A423

No. 780: a, Fregata ariel. b, Ptilinopus porphyraceus, vert. c, Phaethon rubricauda.

Perf. 13x13¼, 13¼x13 (#780b)
2016, Nov. 30   Litho.
780   A423   95fr Sheet of 3, #a-c   5.25   5.25

Christmas A424

2016, Dec. 20   Litho.   *Perf. 13x13¼*
781   A424   100fr multi   1.75   1.75

Wallis and Futuna Islands Marianne Sculpture A425

2017, Jan. 31   Litho.   *Perf. 13¼x13*
782   A425   95fr multi   1.75   1.75

Visit of French President François Hollande to Wallis and Futuna Islands — A426

2017, Feb. 22   Litho.   *Perf. 13*
783   A426   290fr multi   5.25   5.25

International Women's Day — A427

2017, Mar. 8   Litho.   *Perf. 13*
784   A427   290fr multi   5.25   5.25

St. Peter Chanel (1803-41), Missionary on Futuna Island A428

2017, Apr. 28   Litho.   *Perf. 13*
785   A428   300fr multi   5.50   5.50

Fire Dancer — A429

2017, May 26   Litho.   *Perf. 13*
786   A429   65fr multi   1.25   1.25

Megaptera Novaeangliae and Map of Wallis and Futuna Islands — A430

2017, June 7   Litho.   *Perf. 13*
787   A430   400fr multi   7.75   7.75
World Environment Day.

SEMI-POSTAL STAMPS

French Revolution Issue
Common Design Type
Unwmk.
1939, July 5   Photo.   *Perf. 13*
Name and Value Typo. in Black

B1	CD83	45c + 25c green	16.00 *22.00*
B2	CD83	70c + 30c brown	16.00 *22.00*
B3	CD83	90c + 35c red org	16.00 *22.00*
B4	CD83	1.25fr + 1fr rose pink	16.00 *22.00*
B5	CD83	2.25fr + 2fr blue	16.00 *22.00*
		Nos. B1-B5 (5)	80.00 *110.00*
		Set, never hinged	150.00

New Caledonia Nos. B10 and B12 Ovptd. "WALLIS ET FUTUNA" in Blue or Red, and Common Design Type

1941   Photo.   *Perf. 13½*

B6	SP2	1fr + 1fr red	1.75
B7	CD86	1.50fr + 3fr maroon	1.75
B8	SP3	2.50fr + 1fr dark blue	1.75
		Nos. B6-B8 (3)	5.25
		Set, never hinged	9.00

Nos. B6-B8 were issued by the Vichy government in France, but were not placed on sale in Wallis & Futuna.

Nos. 92-93 Srchd. in Black or Red

1944   Engr.   *Perf. 12x12½*

B8A	50c + 1.50fr on 2.50fr deep blue (R)	1.90
B8B	+ 2.50fr on 1fr green	1.90

Colonial Development Fund.
Nos. B8A-B8B were issued by the Vichy government in France, but were not placed on sale in Wallis & Futuna.

> **Catalogue values for unused stamps in this section, from this point to the end of the section, are for Never Hinged items.**

Red Cross Issue
Common Design Type
1944   Photo.   *Perf. 14½x14*
B9   CD90   5fr + 20fr red orange   3.00   3.00

The surtax was for the French Red Cross and national relief. See No. 753d.

AIR POST STAMPS

> **Catalogue values for unused stamps in this section are for Never Hinged items.**

Victory Issue
Common Design Type
Perf. 12½
1946, May 8   Unwmk.   Engr.
C1   CD92   8fr dark violet   2.25   1.90

Chad to Rhine Issue
Common Design Types
1946

C2	CD93	5fr dark violet	1.40 1.10
C3	CD94	10fr dk slate grn	1.60 1.30
C4	CD95	15fr violet brn	1.60 1.30
C5	CD96	20fr brt ultra	2.40 1.75
C6	CD97	25fr brown orange	2.75 2.10
C7	CD98	50fr carmine	4.00 2.90
		Nos. C2-C7 (6)	13.75 10.45

New Caledonia Nos. C21-C22 Overprinted in Blue

1949, July 4   *Perf. 13x12½, 12½x13*

C8	AP2	50fr yel & rose red	8.50 7.00
C9	AP3	100fr yel & red brn	15.00 12.00

The overprint on No. C9 is in three lines.

UPU Issue
Common Design Type
1949, July 4   Engr.   *Perf. 13*
C10   CD99   10fr multicolored   11.00   8.25

Liberation Issue
Common Design Type
1954, June 6
C11   CD102   3fr sepia & vio brn   11.00   8.25

Father Louis Marie Chanel — AP1

1955, Nov. 21   Unwmk.   *Perf. 13*
C12   AP1   14fr dk grn, grnsh bl & ind   2.75   1.40

Issued in honor of Father Chanel, martyred missionary to the Islands.

View of Mata-Utu, Queen Amelia and Msgr. Bataillon — AP2

33fr, Map of islands and sailing ship.

1960, Sept. 19   Engr.   *Perf. 13*

C13	AP2	21fr blue, brn & grn	4.50 4.00
C14	AP2	33fr ultra, choc & bl grn	6.75 6.00

For No. C14 with surcharge, see No. C36.

Shell Diver — AP3

1962, Sept. 20   Unwmk.   *Perf. 13*
C16   AP3   100fr bl, grn & dk red   19.00   15.00

Telstar Issue
Common Design Type
1962, Dec. 5
C17   CD111   12fr dk pur, mar & bl   3.75   3.75

Sea Shell Type of Regular Issue
1963, Apr. 1   Engr.
Size: 26x47mm
C18   A5   50fr Harpa ventricosa   12.50   7.00

Javelin Thrower — AP4

1964, Oct. 10   Engr.   *Perf. 13*
C19   AP4   31fr emer, ver & vio brn   19.00   19.00

18th Olympic Games, Tokyo, Oct. 10-25.

ITU Issue
Common Design Type
1965, May 17   Unwmk.   *Perf. 13*
C20   CD120   50fr multicolored   16.00   16.00

Mata-Utu Wharf — AP5

1965, Nov. 26   Engr.   *Perf. 13*
C21   AP5   27fr brt bl, sl grn & red brn   4.50   4.50

French Satellite A-1 Issue
Common Design Type
Designs: 7fr, Diamant rocket and launching installations. 10fr, A-1 satellite.

1966, Jan. 17   Engr.   *Perf. 13*

C22	CD121	7fr crim, red & car lake	3.25 3.25
C23	CD121	10fr car lake, red & crim	3.75 3.75
a.		Strip of 2, #C22-C23 + label	8.50 8.50

French Satellite D-1 Issue
Common Design Type
1966, June 2   Engr.   *Perf. 13*
C24   CD122   10fr lake, bl grn & red   3.50   3.50

WHO Headquarters, Geneva, and Emblem — AP6

1966, July 5   Photo.   *Perf. 12½x13*
C25   AP6   30fr org, maroon & bl   3.50   3.50
New WHO Headquarters, Geneva.

Girl and Boy Reading; UNESCO Emblem — AP7

1966, Nov. 4   Engr.   *Perf. 13*
C26   AP7   50fr green, org & choc   5.75   4.25
20th anniv. of UNESCO.

Athlete and Pattern AP8

Design: 38fr, Woman ballplayer and pattern.

1966, Dec. 8   Engr.   *Perf. 13x12½*

C27	AP8	32fr bl, dp car & blk	4.25 3.00
C28	AP8	38fr emer & brt pink	4.75 4.00

2nd South Pacific Games, Nouméa, 12/8-18.

Samuel Wallis' Ship and Coast of Wallis Island — AP9

1967, Dec. 16   Photo.   *Perf. 13*
C29   AP9   12fr multicolored   6.50   4.75
Bicentenary of the discovery of Wallis Island.

Concorde Issue
Common Design Type

1969, Apr. 17	**Engr.**		**Perf. 13**	
C30	CD129 20fr black & plum		15.00	10.00

Man Climbing Coconut Palm — AP10

32fr, Horseback rider. 38fr, Men making wooden stools. 50fr, Spear fisherman & man holding basket with fish. 100fr, Women sorting coconuts.

1969, Apr. 30	**Photo.**		**Perf. 13**	
C31	AP10 20fr multi		2.50	1.50
C32	AP10 32fr multi		4.25	2.00
C33	AP10 38fr multi		4.50	2.50
C34	AP10 50fr multi		7.25	4.50
C35	AP10 100fr multi		12.50	7.25
	Nos. C31-C35 (5)		31.00	17.75

No. C14 Surcharged with New Value and Three Bars

1971	**Engr.**		**Perf. 13**	
C36	AP2 21fr on 33fr multi		4.00	4.00

Pole Vault — AP11

1971, Oct. 25	**Engr.**		**Perf. 13**	
C37	AP11 48fr shown		4.75	3.00
C38	AP11 54fr Archery		6.75	5.00

4th South Pacific Games, Papeete, French Polynesia, Sept. 8-19.

South Pacific Commission Headquarters, Noumea — AP12

1972, Feb. 5	**Photo.**		**Perf. 13**	
C39	AP12 44fr blue & multi		5.75	4.25

South Pacific Commission, 25th anniv.

Round House and Festival Emblem — AP13

1972, May 15	**Engr.**		**Perf. 13**	
C40	AP13 60fr dp car, grn & pur		7.50	5.00

South Pacific Festival of Arts, Fiji, May 6-20.

Canoe Type of Regular Issue

Design: 200fr, Outrigger sailing canoe race, and island woman.

1972, Oct. 16	**Photo.**		**Perf. 13x12½**	
			Size: 47½x28mm	
C41	A9 200fr multicolored		35.00	25.00

La Pérouse and "La Boussole" — AP14

Explorers and their Ships: 28fr, Samuel Wallis and "Dolphin." 40fr, Dumont D'Urville and "Astrolabe." 72fr, Bougainville and "La Boudeuse."

1973, July 20	**Engr.**		**Perf. 13**	
C42	AP14 22fr brn, slate & car		11.00	6.00
C43	AP14 28fr sl grn, dl red & bl		12.50	6.00
C44	AP14 40fr brn, ind & ultra		15.00	9.25
C45	AP14 72fr brown, bl & pur		18.00	12.50
	Nos. C42-C45 (4)		56.50	33.75

Charles de Gaulle — AP15

1973, Nov. 9	**Engr.**		**Perf. 13**	
C46	AP15 107fr brn org & dk brn		15.00	11.00

Pres. Charles de Gaulle (1890-1970).

Red Jasmine AP16

Flowers from Wallis: 17fr, Hibiscus tiliaceus. 19fr, Phaeomeria magnifica. 21fr, Hibiscus rosa oinensis. 23fr, Allamanda cathartica. 27fr, Barringtonia. 39fr, Flowers in vase.

1973, Dec. 6	**Photo.**		**Perf. 13**	
C47	AP16 12fr shown		1.30	1.25
C48	AP16 17fr multicolored		2.00	1.90
C49	AP16 19fr multicolored		2.60	1.90
C50	AP16 21fr multicolored		3.50	2.10
C51	AP16 23fr multicolored		4.50	2.50
C52	AP16 27fr multicolored		5.25	3.00
C53	AP16 39fr multicolored		7.25	6.25
	Nos. C47-C53 (7)		26.40	18.90

UPU Emblem and Symbolic Design — AP17

1974, Oct. 9	**Engr.**		**Perf. 13**	
C54	AP17 51fr multicolored		6.50	4.75

Centenary of Universal Postal Union.

Holy Family, Primitive Painting AP18

1974, Dec. 9	**Photo.**		**Perf. 13**	
C55	AP18 150fr multicolored		13.00	10.00

Christmas 1974.

Tapa Cloth — AP19

Tapa Cloth: 24fr, Village scene. 36fr, Fish & marine life. 80fr, Marine life, map of islands, village scene.

1975, Feb. 3	**Photo.**		**Perf. 13**	
C56	AP19 3fr multicolored		1.00	.65
C57	AP19 24fr multicolored		2.00	1.50
C58	AP19 36fr multicolored		3.25	2.25
C59	AP19 80fr multicolored		6.75	5.25
	Nos. C56-C59 (4)		13.00	9.65

DC-7 in Flight — AP20

1975, Aug. 13	**Engr.**		**Perf. 13**	
C60	AP20 100fr multicolored		7.25	5.50

First regular air service between Nouméa, New Caledonia, and Wallis.

Volleyball AP21

1975, Nov. 10	**Photo.**		**Perf. 13**	
C61	AP21 26fr shown		1.90	1.20
C62	AP21 44fr Soccer		2.60	1.90
C63	AP21 56fr Javelin		4.25	2.90
C64	AP21 105fr Spear fishing		8.25	6.50
	Nos. C61-C64 (4)		17.00	12.50

5th South Pacific Games, Guam, Aug. 1-10.

Lalolalo Lake, Wallis — AP22

Landscapes: 29fr, Vasavasa, Futuna. 41fr, Sigave Bay, Futuna. 68fr, Gahi Bay, Wallis.

1975, Dec. 1	**Litho.**		**Perf. 13**	
C65	AP22 10fr grn & multi		1.50	.95
C66	AP22 29fr grn & multi		2.50	1.75
C67	AP22 41fr grn & multi		3.50	2.40
C68	AP22 68fr grn & multi		4.75	3.75
	Nos. C65-C68 (4)		12.25	8.85

Concorde, Eiffel Tower and Sugar Loaf Mountain — AP23

1976, Jan. 21	**Engr.**		**Perf. 13**	
C69	AP23 250fr multi		21.00	20.00

1st commercial flight of supersonic jet Concorde from Paris to Rio, Jan. 21.
For overprint see No. C73.

Hammer Throw and Stadium — AP24

39fr, Diving, Stadium and maple leaf.

1976, Aug. 2	**Engr.**		**Perf. 13**	
C70	AP24 31fr multi		2.75	2.25
C71	AP24 39fr multi		4.00	3.50

21st Olympic Games, Montreal, Canada, July 17-Aug. 1.

De Gaulle Memorial AP25

Photogravure and Embossed

1977, June 18			**Perf. 13**	
C72	AP25 100fr gold & multi		8.75	7.50

5th anniversary of dedication of De Gaulle Memorial at Colombey-les-Deux-Eglises.

No. C69 Ovptd. in Dark Brown "PARIS NEW-YORK / 22.11.77 / 1er VOL COMMERCIAL"

1977, Nov. 22	**Engr.**		**Perf. 13**	
C73	AP23 250fr multicolored		19.00	17.50

Concorde, 1st commercial flight, Paris-NY.

Balistes Niger — AP26

Fish: 35fr, Amphiprion akindynos. 49fr, Pomacanthus imperator. 51fr, Zanclus cornutus.

1978, Jan. 31	**Litho.**		**Perf. 13**	
C74	AP26 26fr multi		1.75	.75
C75	AP26 35fr multi		2.75	1.00
C76	AP26 49fr multi		3.50	1.25
C77	AP26 51fr multi		4.25	3.25
	Nos. C74-C77 (4)		12.25	6.25

Map of Wallis and Uvea
Islands — AP27

300fr, Map of Futuna and Alofi Islands, horz.

1978, Mar. 7   **Engr.**
C78 AP27 300fr vio bl & grnsh
                bl   15.00 12.50
C79 AP27 500fr multi   20.00 19.00

Father Bataillon, Churches on Wallis
and Futuna Islands — AP28

72fr, Monsignor Pompallier, map of Wallis,
Futuna and Alofi Islands, outrigger canoe.

1978, Apr. 28 Litho.   Perf. 13x12½
C80 AP28 60fr multi   2.50 1.75
C81 AP28 72fr multi   2.75 2.00
First French missionaries on Wallis and
Futuna Islands.

ITU Emblem — AP29

1978, May 17   Litho.   Perf. 13
C82 AP29 66fr multi   3.00 2.25
10th World Telecommunications Day.

Nativity and Longhouse — AP30

1978, Dec. 4   Photo.   Perf. 13
C83 AP30 160fr multi   7.75 5.50
Christmas 1978.

Popes Paul VI, John Paul I, St.
Peter's, Rome — AP31

37fr, Pope Paul VI. 41fr, Pope John Paul I.

Perf. 12½x13, 13x12½
1979, Jan. 31   **Litho.**
C84 AP31 37fr multi, vert.   1.75 1.40
C85 AP31 41fr multi, vert.   2.00 1.75
C86 AP31 105fr multi   4.25 3.50
      Nos. C84-C86 (3)   8.00 6.65
In memory of Popes Paul VI and John Paul I.

Monoplane
of UTA
Airlines
AP32

68fr, Freighter Muana. 80fr, Hihifo Airport.

1979, Feb. 28   **Perf. 13x12½**
C87 AP32 46fr multi   1.50 .95
C88 AP32 68fr multi   1.75 1.50
C89 AP32 80fr multi   2.75 2.00
      Nos. C87-C89 (3)   6.00 4.45
Inter-Island transportation.
See Nos. 251-253.

France No. 67 and Eole Weather
Satellite — AP33

70fr, Hibiscus & stamp similar to #25. 90fr,
Rowland Hill & Penny Black. 100fr, Birds,
Kano School, Japan 17th cent. & Japan #9.

1979, May 7   Photo.   Perf. 13
C90 AP33 5fr multi   .90 .65
C91 AP33 70fr multi, vert.   3.00 1.90
C92 AP33 90fr multi   3.50 2.50
C93 AP33 100fr multi   4.50 3.75
      Nos. C90-C93 (4)   11.90 8.80
Sir Rowland Hill (1795-1879), originator of
penny postage.

Cross of Lorraine and People — AP34

1979, June 18   Engr.   Perf. 13
C94 AP34 33fr multi   2.25 1.75

Map of
Islands,
Arms of
France
AP35

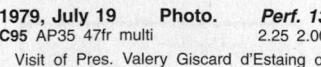

1979, July 19   Photo.   Perf. 13
C95 AP35 47fr multi   2.25 2.00
Visit of Pres. Valery Giscard d'Estaing of
France.

Capt. Cook, Ships and Island — AP36

1979, July 28
C96 AP36 130fr multi   6.50 4.25
Capt. James Cook (1728-1779).

Telecom Emblem, Satellite, Receiving
Station — AP37

1979, Sept. 20   Litho.   Perf. 13
C97 AP37 120fr multi   4.50 3.50
3rd World Telecommunications Exhibition,
Geneva, Sept. 20-26.

Virgin of
the
Crescent
Moon, by
Albrecht
Durer
AP38

1979, Dec. 17   Engr.   Perf. 13
C98 AP38 180fr red & blk   7.50 6.25
Christmas 1979. See No. C163.

Rotary International, 75th
Anniversary — AP39

1980, Feb. 29   Litho.   Perf. 13
C99 AP39 86fr multi   4.75 3.50

Rochambeau
and Troops, US
Flag,
1780 — AP40

1980, May 27   Engr.   Perf. 13
C100 AP40 102fr multi   4.50 3.50
Rochambeau's landing at Newport, RI
(American Revolution), bicentenary.

National Day, 10th
Anniversary — AP41

1980, July 15   Litho.   Perf. 13
C101 AP41 71fr multi   2.25 1.50

Transatlantic Airmail Flight, 50th
Anniversary — AP42

1980, Sept. 22   Engr.   Perf. 13
C102 AP42 122fr multi   4.50 3.50

Fleming,
Penicillin
Bacilli — AP43

1980, Oct. 20
C103 AP43 101fr multi   4.00 2.50
Alexander Fleming (1881-1955), discoverer
of penicillin, 25th death anniversary.

Charles De Gaulle, 10th Anniversary
of Death — AP44

1980, Nov. 9   Engr.   Perf. 13
C104 AP44 200fr sep & dk ol
                  grn   8.00 7.25

Virgin and Child with St. Catherine, by
Lorenzo Lotto — AP45

1980, Dec. 20   Litho.   Perf. 13x12½
C105 AP45 150fr multi   4.50 3.50
Christmas 1980.

Alan B. Shepard
and Spacecraft
AP46

20th Anniv. of Space Flight: 44fr, Yuri
Gagarin.

1981, May 11   Litho.   *Perf. 13*
C106 AP46 37fr multi   1.20   .95
C107 AP46 44fr multi   1.60 1.40

Vase of Flowers, by Paul Cezanne
(1839-1906) — AP47

Design: 135fr, Harlequin, by Pablo Picasso.

1981, Oct. 22   Litho.   *Perf. 12½x13*
C108 AP47 50fr multi   2.40 1.40
C109 AP47 135fr multi   4.75 3.00

Espana '82 World Cup
Soccer — AP48

1981-82   Engr.   *Perf. 13*
C110   AP48 120fr blk, brn & grn 3.75 2.25
C110A AP48 120fr lil, brn & ol
grn   3.75 3.00

Issued: #C110, 11/16/81; #C110A,5/13/82.
For overprint see No. C115.

Christmas 1981 — AP49

1981, Dec. 21   Litho.   *Perf. 12½*
C111 AP49 180fr multi   5.50 4.25

Tapestry,
by Pilioho
Aloi
AP50

1982, Feb. 22   Litho.   *Perf. 12½x13*
C112 AP50 100fr multi   2.90 2.50

Boats at Collioure, by George Braque
(1882-1963) — AP51

1982, Apr. 13   Litho.   *Perf. 12½x13*
C113 AP51 300fr multi   7.50 5.25

Alberto Santos-Dumont (1873-1932),
Aviation Pioneer — AP52

1982, July 24
C114 AP52 95fr multi   3.25 2.40

**No. C110 Overprinted with Winner's
Name in Blue**
1982, Aug. 26   Engr.   *Perf. 13*
C115 AP48 120fr multi   4.00 3.00

Italy's victory in 1982 World Cup.

French Overseas Possessions Week,
Sept. 18-25 — AP53

1982, Sept. 17   Litho.
C116 AP53 105fr Beach   2.50 2.25

Day of the
Blind — AP54

1982, Oct. 18   Engr.
C117 AP54 130fr red & blue   3.25 2.00

Christmas
1982
AP55

Adoration of the Virgin, by Correggio.

1982, Dec. 20   Litho.   *Perf. 12½x13*
C118 AP55 170fr multi   4.25 3.00

Wind Surfing
(1984 Olympic
Event) — AP56

1983, Mar. 4   Litho.   *Perf. 13*
C119 AP56 270fr multi   6.50 4.75

World UPU Day — AP57

1983, Mar. 30   Litho.   *Perf. 13*
C120 AP57 100fr multi   2.75 1.75

Manned Flight
Bicentenary
AP58

1983, Apr. 25   Litho.   *Perf. 13*
C121 AP58 205fr Montgolfiere 5.50 4.00

Cat, 1926,
by Foujita
(d. 1968)
AP59

1983, May 20   Litho.   *Perf. 12½x13*
C122 AP59 102fr multi   0.75 2.00

Pre-Olympic
Year — AP60

1983, July 5   Engr.   *Perf. 13*
C123 AP60 250fr Javelin   5.50 4.50

Alfred Nobel (1833-1896) — AP61

1983, Aug. 1   Engr.   *Perf. 10*
C124 AP61 150fr multi   4.00 2.75

Nicephore Niepce (1765-1833),
Photography Pioneer — AP62

1983, Sept. 20   Engr.   *Perf. 13*
C125 AP62 75fr dk grn & rose
vio   2.50 1.75

Raphael (1483-1520), 500th Birth
Anniv. — AP63

1983, Nov. 10   Litho.   *Perf. 12½x13*
C126 AP63 167fr The Triumph of
Galatea   4.25 3.00

Pandanus
AP64

1983, Nov. 30   Litho.   *Perf. 13*
C127 AP64 137fr multi   3.50 3.00

Christmas
1983
AP65

Sistine Madonna, by Raphael.

1983, Dec. 22   Litho.   Perf. 12½x13
C128 AP65 200fr multi   5.00 4.00

Steamer Commandant Bory — AP66

1984, Jan. 9   Perf. 13
C129 AP66 67fr multi   2.25 1.40

1984 Summer Olympics — AP67

1984, Feb. 3   Litho.   Perf. 13
C130 AP67 85fr Weight lifting   2.40 1.75

Frangipani
Blossoms
AP68

1984, Feb. 28   Perf. 12½
C131 AP68 130fr multi   3.25 2.25

Easter
1984
AP69

1984, Apr. 17   Litho.   Perf. 12½x13
C132 AP69 190fr Descent from
            the Cross   4.50 3.25

Homage to
Jean
Cocteau
AP70

1984, June 30   Litho.   Perf. 13
C133 AP70 150fr Portrait   4.00 2.90

Soano Hoatau
Tiki Sculpture
AP71

1984, July 26
C134 AP71 175fr multi   4.25 3.50

Portrait of Alice,
by Modigliani
(1884-1920)
AP72

1984, Aug. 20
C135 AP72 140fr multi   3.50 2.50

Ausipex
'84 — AP73

1984, Sept. 21   Litho.   Perf. 12½x13
C136 AP73 180fr Pilioko Tapestry   4.50 3.00
    Se-tenant with label showing exhibition
    emblem.

Local Dances, by Jean
Michon — AP74

1984, Oct. 11   Photo.   Perf. 13
C137 AP74 110fr multi   3.25 2.00

Altar
AP75

1984, Nov. 5   Litho.   Perf. 13x12½
C138 AP75 52fr Mount Lulu
            Chapel   1.50 1.10

Christmas 1984 — AP76

1984, Dec. 21   Litho.   Perf. 13x12½
C139 AP76 260fr Tropical Nativity 6.25 4.00

Pilioko Tapestry — AP77

1985, Apr. 3   Litho.   Perf. 13x12½
C140 AP77 500fr multi   10.00 6.50

The Post in
1926, by
Utrillo
AP78

1985, June 17   Litho.   Perf. 12½x13
C141 AP78 200fr multi   5.00 4.00

Wallis Island Pirogue — AP79

1985, Aug. 9   Perf. 13
C142 AP79 350fr multi   7.50 5.00

Ship Jacques
Cartier — AP80

1985, Oct. 2   Engr.   Perf. 13x13½
C143 AP80 51fr Prus bl, brt bl &
            dk bl   1.40 1.10

Portrait of a
Young
Woman, by
Patrice
Nielly
AP81

1985, Oct. 28   Litho.   Perf. 12½x13
C144 AP81 245fr multi   6.00 4.50

Nativity, by
Jean
Michon
AP82

1985, Dec. 19   Litho.   Perf. 12½x13
C145 AP82 330fr multi   7.75 6.50

Halley's Comet — AP83

1986, Mar. 6   Litho.   Perf. 13
C146 AP83 100fr multi   2.60 1.75

Cure of Ars, Birth
Bicent. — AP84

1986, Mar. 28   Litho.   Perf. 12½x13
C147 AP84 200fr multi   5.00 4.25

French Overseas Territory Status, 25th
Anniv. — AP85

90fr, Queen Amelia. 137fr, July 30 Law,
Journal of the Republic.

1986, July 29   Engr.   Perf. 13
C148 AP85 90fr multicolored   2.25 2.25
C149 AP85 137fr multicolored   3.75 3.75
    a.   Strip of 2, #C148-C149 + label 6.00 6.00
    Queen Amelia's request to France for pro-
    tection, cent.

World Post Day — AP86

1986, Oct. 9 Litho. *Perf. 13*
C150 AP86 270fr multi 6.25 4.00

Statue of Liberty, Cent. — AP87

1986, Oct. 31 Engr.
C151 AP87 205fr multi 6.50 5.00

Poi Basilica, 1st Anniv. — AP88

230fr, Fr. Chanel, basilica.

1987, Apr. 30 Litho. *Perf. 13*
C152 AP88 230fr multicolored 5.50 3.75

Telstar Transmitting to Pleumeur-Bodou, France — AP89

1987, May 17 Engr. *Perf. 13*
C153 AP89 200fr gray, brt bl & brn org 5.25 3.75
World Communications Day, 25th anniv. of Telstar.

Piccard, Bathyscaphe Trieste and Stratospheric Balloon — AP90

1987, Aug. 21 Engr. *Perf. 13*
C154 AP90 135fr brt ol grn, dk bl & brt bl 4.00 3.00
Auguste Piccard (1884-1962), physicist.

Arrival of First Missionary, 150th Anniv. — AP91

Design: 260fr, Monsignor Bataillon's arrival in 1837, ship and the islands.

1987, Nov. 8 Engr. *Perf. 13*
C155 AP91 260fr brt blue, blk & blue grn 6.25 5.00

Christmas 1987 — AP92

1987, Dec. 15 Litho. *Perf. 13x12½*
C156 AP92 300fr multi 6.50 5.00

Garros and Bleriot Aircraft — AP93

1988, Feb. 18 Engr. *Perf. 13*
C157 AP93 600fr multi 17.50 10.50
Roland Garros (1888-1918), aviator and tennis player.

Self-portrait with Lace Cravat, by Maurice Quentin de La Tour (1704-88) AP94

1988, Apr. 8 Litho.
C158 AP94 500fr multi 13.00 9.50

World Telecommunications Day — AP95

1988, May 5 Litho. *Perf. 12½x13*
C159 AP95 100fr multi 2.50 1.90

South Pacific Episcopal Conference — AP96

1988, June 1 Litho. *Perf. 13*
C160 AP96 90fr Map, bishop 2.25 1.75

Christmas — AP97

Unwmk.
1988, Dec. 15 Litho. *Perf. 13*
C161 AP97 400fr multi 11.00 7.00

Royal Throne — AP98

1989, Mar. 11
C162 AP98 700fr multi 16.00 10.50

Type of 1979
Virgin of the Crescent Moon, by Albrecht Durer

1989, Dec. 21 Engr. *Perf. 13½x13*
C163 AP38 800fr plum 19.00 13.00
Christmas 1989.

Clement Ader (1841-1926), Aviation Pioneer — AP100

1990, June 9 Engr. *Perf. 13*
C164 AP100 56fr multicolored 2.00 1.40
First anniversary of Wallis-Tahiti air link.

Gen. Charles de Gaulle (1890-1979) — AP101

1990, Nov. 22 *Perf. 12½x13*
C165 AP101 1000fr multi 24.50 19.00

Father Louis Marie Chanel, 150th Death Anniv. — AP102

1991, Apr. 28 Litho. *Perf. 13*
C166 AP102 235fr multicolored 6.50 4.25

French Open Tennis Championships, Cent. — AP103

1991, May 24 Engr. *Perf. 13x12½*
C167 AP103 250fr blk, grn & org 7.50 5.50

Wolfgang Amadeus Mozart, Death Bicent. AP104

1991, Sept. 23 Engr. *Perf. 13*
C168 AP104 500fr multicolored 13.00 9.50

World Columbian Stamp Expo '92, Chicago — AP105

1992, May 22 Litho. *Perf. 13x12½*
C169 AP105 100fr multicolored 3.00 2.25

1992, July 15 *Perf. 13*
C170 AP105 800fr multicolored 19.00 13.00
Genoa '92.

First French Republic, Bicent. — AP106

1992, Aug. 17 Engr. *Perf. 13*
C171 AP106 350fr blk, bl & red 9.75 7.50

Louvre Museum, Bicent. — AP107

1993, Apr. 12 Engr. *Perf. 13*
C172 AP107 315fr blue, dk blue & red 7.50 5.50

Nicolaus Copernicus, Heliocentric
Solar System — AP108

1993, May 7   Engr.   Perf. 13
C173 AP108 600fr multicolored 15.00 9.25
  Polska '93.

Second Year of First French Republic,
Bicent. — AP109

1993, Sept. 22   Engr.   Perf. 13
C174 AP109 400fr bl, blk & red   9.50 7.50

Wallis Island Landscape — AP110

1994, Jan. 26   Litho.   Perf. 13
C175 AP110 400fr multicolored 11.00 7.50

Hong Kong '94 — AP111

1994, Feb. 18   Litho.   Perf. 14x13½
C176 AP111 700fr multicolored 17.50 12.00

South Pacific Geography
Day — AP112

1994, May 4   Litho.   Perf. 13
C177 AP112 85fr multicolored   2.40 1.75
  See New Caledonia No. C259.

European Stamp
Salon,
Paris — AP113

1994, Sept. 22   Litho.   Perf. 13
C178 AP113 300fr multicolored   8.00 5.00

Antoine de Saint-Exupery (1900-44),
Aviator, Author — AP114

1994, Oct. 27   Engr.   Perf. 13
C179 AP114 800fr multicolored 22.00 15.00

Christmas
AP115

1994, Dec. 15   Litho.   Perf. 13
C180 AP115 150fr multicolored   4.00 3.00

Louis Pasteur (1822-95) — AP116

1995, Mar. 25   Litho.   Perf. 13
C181 AP116 350fr multicolored   8.50 4.75

AP117

1995, Apr. 19   Perf. 13½x13
C182 AP117 115fr multicolored   2.75 1.90
  University Teacher's Training Institute of the
Pacific. See French Polynesia No. 656 and
New Caledonia No. 710.

AP118

1995, May 17   Perf. 13
C183 AP118 200fr Painting of
              Cocoa Nuts   4.50 3.00

Intl. Youth Year, 10th Anniv. — AP119

1995, July 25   Litho.   Perf. 13
C184 AP119 450fr multicolored 10.00 6.25

Singapore '95 — AP120

1995, Aug. 24   Litho.   Perf. 13
C185 AP120 500fr multicolored 11.00 6.75

Motion Pictures, Cent. — AP121

Lumiere Brothers, film strip.

1995, Sept. 19
C186 AP121 600fr multicolored 13.00 8.50

Charles de Gaulle (1890-
1970) — AP122

1995, Nov. 14   Engr.   Perf. 13
C187 AP122 315fr multicolored   8.00 5.50

7th Va'a (Outrigger Canoe) World
Championship, Noumea, New
Caledonia — AP123

1996, Apr. 24   Litho.   Perf. 13
C188 AP123 240fr multicolored   6.00 4.25

Sisia
College — AP124

1996, May 22   Litho.   Perf. 13½x13
C189 AP124 235fr multicolored   6.00 4.25

Radio, Cent. — AP125

1996, July 25   Engr.   Perf. 13
C190 AP125 550fr multicolored   13.00 9.25

Modern Olympic Games,
Cent. — AP126

1996, Aug. 20   Engr.   Perf. 13
C191 AP126 1000fr blk & dk bl 25.00 17.00

50th
Autumn
Stamp
Salon
AP127

1996, Oct. 24   Litho.   Perf. 13
C192 AP127 175fr multicolored   4.75 3.00

Campaign
to Control
Alcoholism
AP128

1996, Nov. 19   Perf. 13x13½
C193 AP128 260fr multicolored   6.00 4.25

Natl. Center for Scientific Research AP129

1997, Mar. 14   Litho.   Perf. 13
C194 AP129 400fr Lapita pottery   8.00 5.50

HIHIFO Air Service — AP130

1997, July 8   Litho.   Perf. 13
C195 AP130 130fr multicolored   3.25 2.10

Sundown Over the Lagoon — AP131

1997, Sept. 22   Litho.   Perf. 13½x13
C196 AP131 300fr multicolored   7.75 4.25

51st Autumn Stamp Salon — AP132

350fr, #C194, 492, 497, 486, C104, C185, 475, C192, C188, 464, 493.
1000fr, Hemispheres, #486, 475, 464, C185, C175, 493, C184, 492, C192, 497, C188, C194, Winged Victory of Samothrace.

1997, Nov. 6   Litho.   Perf. 13
C197 AP132 350fr multi   7.20 4.75
   Imperf
C198 AP132 1000fr multi   20.80 24.00

Marshal Jacques Leclerc (1902-47) — AP133

1997, Nov. 28   Litho.   Perf. 13
C199 AP133 800fr multicolored   18.00 11.50

Alphonse Daudet (1840-97), Writer — AP134

1997, Dec. 16   Litho.   Perf. 13
C200 AP134 710fr multi   18.00 10.00

Alofi Beach — AP135

1998, Apr. 21   Litho.   Perf. 13
C201 AP135 315fr multicolored   7.50 4.25

Cricket AP136

1998, Sept. 22   Litho.   Perf. 13x13½
C202 AP136 106fr multicolored   2.75 1.40

Paul Gauguin (1848-1903) — AP137

1998, Oct. 27   Litho.   Perf. 13
C203 AP137 700fr multicolored   16.50 9.25

Garden of Happiness — AP138

1998, Nov. 17
C204 AP138 460fr multicolored   11.00 7.25

Polynesian Dancing AP139

1998, Dec. 15   Litho.   Perf. 13
C205 AP139 250fr multicolored   6.50 3.50

Kava Porter AP140

1999, Jan. 18
C206 AP140 600fr multicolored   13.00 8.00

Shells AP141

95fr, Epitonium scalare. 100fr, Cassis cornuta. 110fr, Charonia tritonis. 115fr, Lambis lambis.

1999, Feb. 15
C207 AP141 95fr multi, vert.   2.25 1.75
C208 AP141 100fr multi, vert.   2.40 1.75
C209 AP141 110fr multi   2.40 1.75
C210 AP141 115fr multi   3.00 1.75
   Nos. C207-C210 (4)   10.05 7.00

Finemui — AP142

1999, Apr. 19   Engr.   Perf. 12¾
C211 AP142 900fr multicolored   20.00 11.50

Birds of Nuku Fotu AP143

a, 10fr, Airgrettes. b, 20fr, Audubon's. c, 26fr, Fregates. d, 54fr, Paille en queue.

1999, June 14   Litho.   Perf. 13x13¾
C212 AP143 Strip of 4, #a.-d.   3.25 2.50

Wind Song — AP144

1999, Nov. 22   Engr.   Perf. 13
C213 AP144 325fr multi   7.50 4.50

Sunrise Over a Lagoon AP145

1999, Dec. 20   Litho.
C214 AP145 500fr multi   11.00 7.50

First Transport Flight to Futuna, 30th Anniv. — AP146

2000, Aug. 24   Litho.   Perf. 13
C215 AP146 350fr multi   9.00 4.50

AIR POST SEMI-POSTAL STAMPS

New Caledonia Nos. CB2-CB3 overprinted "ILES WALLIS ET FUTUNA"

1942, June 22   Engr.   Perf. 13
CB1 SPAP1 1.50fr + 3.50fr green   2.00
CB2 SPAP1 2fr + 6fr yellow brown   2.00

Native children's welfare fund. Nos. CB1-CB2 were issued by the Vichy government in France, but were not placed on sale in Wallis & Futuna.

Colonial Education Fund

New Caledonia No. CB4 Common Design Type overprinted "ILES WALLIS ET FUTUNA"

1942, June 22
CB3 CD86a 1.20fr + 1.80fr blue & red   2.00

No. CB3 was issued by the Vichy government in France, but was not placed on sale in Wallis & Futuna.

POSTAGE DUE STAMPS

Postage Due Stamps of New Caledonia, 1906, Overprinted in Black or Red

1920		**Unwmk.**	**Perf. 13½x14**	
J1	D2	5c ultra, *azure*	1.00	1.00
J2	D2	10c brn, *buff*	1.10	1.10
J3	D2	15c grn, *grnsh*	1.10	1.10
J4	D2	20c blk, *yel* (R)	1.50	1.50
a.		Double overprint	200.00	
J5	D2	30c carmine rose	1.50	1.50
J6	D2	50c ultra, *straw*	2.40	2.40
J7	D2	60c olive, *azure*	2.90	2.90
a.		Double overprint	200.00	
J8	D2	1fr grn, *cream*	3.75	3.75
		Nos. J1-J8 (8)	15.25	15.25

Type of 1920 Issue Surcharged

1927				
J9	D2	2fr on 1fr brt vio	12.50	12.50
J10	D2	3fr on 1fr org brn	12.50	12.50

Postage Due Stamps of New Caledonia, 1928, Overprinted as in 1920

1930				
J11	D3	2c sl bl & dp brn	.25	.25
a.		Double surcharge	200.00	
b.		Imperf.	200.00	
J12	D3	4c brn red & bl grn	.25	.25
J13	D3	5c red org & bl blk	.25	.25
J14	D3	10c mag & Prus bl	.25	.25
J15	D3	15c dl grn & scar	.35	.35
J16	D3	20c maroon & ol grn	.75	.75
J17	D3	25c bis brn & sl bl	.75	.75
J18	D3	30c bl grn & ol grn	1.40	1.40

J19	D3	50c lt brn & dk red	.85	.85
J20	D3	60c mag & brt rose	1.40	1.40
J21	D3	1fr dl bl & Prus grn	1.40	1.40
J22	D3	2fr dk red & ol grn	1.40	1.40
J23	D3	3fr vio & brn	1.40	1.40
		Nos. J11-J23 (13)	10.70	10.70

Postage Due Stamps
of 1930 with
Additional Overprint
in Black

1943

J24	D3	2c sl bl & dp brn	35.00	35.00
J25	D3	4c brn red & bl grn	35.00	35.00
J26	D3	5c red org & bl blk	35.00	35.00
J27	D3	10c mag & Prus bl	35.00	35.00
J28	D3	15c dl grn & scar	37.50	37.50
J29	D3	20c mar & ol grn	37.50	37.50
J30	D3	25c bis brn & sl bl	37.50	37.50
J31	D3	30c dk red & ol grn	37.50	37.50
J32	D3	50c lt brn & dk red	37.50	37.50
J33	D3	60c brt rose	40.00	40.00
J34	D3	1fr dl bl & Prus grn	40.00	40.00
J35	D3	2fr dk red & ol grn	40.00	40.00
J36	D3	3fr violet & brn	40.00	40.00
		Nos. J24-J36 (13)	487.50	487.50

Catalogue values for unused stamps in this section, from this point to the end of the section, are for Never Hinged items.

Thalassoma Lunare — D1

Fish: 1fr, Zanclus cornutus, vert. 5fr, Amphiprion percula.

Perf. 13x13½

1963, Apr. 1		**Typo.**	**Unwmk.**	
J37	D1	1fr yel org, bl & blk	.60	.60
J38	D1	3fr red, grnsh bl & grn	1.90	2.40
J39	D1	5fr org, bluish grn & blk	3.00	3.50
		Nos. J37-J39 (3)	5.50	6.50

Nos. J37-J39 were reprinted in 1982 on white paper in slightly different shades.

WESTERN UKRAINE

ˈwes-tərn yü-ˈkrān

LOCATION — In Eastern Central Europe

GOVT. — A former short-lived independent State

A provisional government was established in 1918 in the eastern part of Austria-Hungary but the area later came under Polish administration.

100 Shahiv (Sotykiv) = 1 Hryvnia
100 Heller = 1 Krone

Forgeries of almost all Western Ukraine stamps are plentiful. Particularly dangerous forgeries have been noted for the Kolomyia Issue and for the First and Second Stanyslaviv Issues.

Lviv Issue

Austria Nos. 145-146, 148, 169 Overprinted

Nos. 1-4A are handstamped with an octagonal overprint that reads "ZAKHIDNO UKR. NARODNA REPUBLYKA" ("Western Ukrainian National Republic"), framing the image of a rearing crowned lion.

1918, Nov. 20

1	A37	3h bright vio	60.00	425.00
a.		Inverted overprint	150.00	
2	A37	5h light green	50.00	325.00
a.		Inverted overprint	150.00	
3	A37	10h magenta	50.00	325.00
a.		Inverted overprint	150.00	
4	A42	20h dark green	50.00	350.00
a.		Inverted overprint	150.00	
4A	A42	20h light green	240.00	900.00
		Nos. 1-4A (5)	450.00	2,325.

This issue was in circulation for only two days before Lviv was captured by the Poles on Nov. 22. No examples of Nos. 1-4A used in Lviv are known.

The Western Ukrainian National Republic (ZUNR) government evacuated to the city of Ternopil, which became the provisional capital. ZUNR postal operations were set up in other Western Ukrainian cities, and the Lviv Issue was used in Stanyslaviv (earliest known cancellation date, Dec. 8), Khodoriv and Kolomyia.

Nos. 1-4 exist in pairs with both normal and inverted overprints. Value $325.

Overprints in other colors (green, red and violet) are known, but these are probably proofs. Violet-black overprints are likely transitional color impressions.

Kolomyia Issue

Austria Nos. 168, 145, 147, 149 Surcharged

Kolomyia is the main town of the Pokutia region of southwestern Ukraine. Cut off from ZUNR postal officials by wartime conditions and in urgent need of basic value stamps, the Kolomyia postmaster obtained permission from the District Military Command to surcharge remaining Austrian postage stamps to either 5 or 10 sotyks, the equivalent of 5 or 10 heller. These stamps were produced on Dec. 10, under very strict security, by preparing two distinct plates (one for each value) that overprinted 25 stamps at a time (5x5 quarter sections of the Austrian 100-stamp panes). The stamps were placed on sale two days later.

1918, Dec. 12   Unwmk.   Perf. 12½

5	A42	5sot on 15h dl red	90.00	120.00
a.		Inverted overprint	600.00	725.00
b.		Double overprint	1,500.	1,600.
6	A37	10sot on 3h vio	90.00	120.00
7	A37	10sot on 6h dp org	1,650.	1,250.
8	A37	10sot on 12h lt bl	1,750.	1,500.
		Nos. 5-8 (4)	3,580.	2,990.

10 sotyk on 15 heller values are essays; only six were produced.

All inverted surcharges on Nos. 6-8 are forgeries. Double surcharges are forgeries.

First Stanyslaviv Issue

Austrian Stamps of 1916-18 Surcharged in Shahiv (shown) and Hryvnia Currency

At the end of December, 1918, the national government again moved, this time to the city of Stanyslaviv (present-day Ivano-Frankivsk). A shortage of qualified postal personnel resulted in a considerable delay in the creation of new ZUNR postage stamps. In the interim, remaining unoverprinted Austrian stamps were used. Finally, on March 18, 1919, 20 different available Austrian definitive stamps were typograph surcharged at the Weidenfeld Printing Shop in Stanyslaviv.

1919, Mar. 18

9	A37	3sh on 3h bright vio	17.00	22.50
10	A37	5sh on 5h light green	17.00	22.50
11	A37	6sh on 6h deep orange	32.50	55.00
12	A37	10sh on 10h mag	27.50	40.00

13	A37	12sh on 12h lt blue	27.50	37.50
a.		Double overprint	300.00	425.00
b.		Double overprint, one on reverse	500.00	210.00
14	A42	15sh on 15h dull red	27.50	37.50
15	A42	20sh on 20h dp grn	27.50	37.50
16	A42	30sh on 30h dull violet	250.00	250.00
17	A39	40sh on 40h ol green	27.50	50.00
18	A39	50sh on 50h dk grn	27.50	37.50
19	A39	60sh on 60h deep blue	27.50	37.50
20	A39	80sh on 80h org brown	27.50	37.50
a.		Inverted overprint	300.00	425.00
21	A39	1hr on 1k car, yel	40.00	45.00
22	A40	2hr on 2k lt blue	40.00	50.00
23	A40	3hr on 3k claret (on #161)	3,250.	3,250.
24	A40	3hr on 3k car rose (on #165)	100.00	125.00
25	A40	3hr on 3k car rose (on #173)	100.00	150.00
26	A40	4hr on 4k dk grn (on #162)	800.00	700.00
27	A40	4hr on 4k yel grn (on #166)	75.00	55.00
28	A40	10hr on 10k deep violet	800.00	800.00
a.		Double overprint	3,000.	3,500.
		Nos. 9-28 (20)	5,742.	5,840.

The 25sh on 25h, type A42, in both light and dull blue shades, never received this overprint. All such stamps are fantasies.

Second Stanyslaviv Issue

The overprinting of a second issue of postage stamps in Stanyslaviv was undertaken in early May. Stamps from several different Austrian stamp series were utilized to create four distinct sets. Most of the stamps available were Austrian postage due, charity or field post stamps.

Postage Due Stamps of Bosnia, 1904 Surcharged but without Asterisks

1919, May 5

29	D1	1sh on 1h blk, red & yel	35.00	40.00
a.		Inverted overprint	100.00	65.00
b.		Double overprint	90.00	90.00
30	D1	2sh on 2h blk, red & yel	15.00	15.00
a.		Inverted overprint	85.00	150.00
31	D1	3sh on 3h blk, red & yel	25.00	50.00
a.		Inverted overprint	25.00	45.00
32	D1	4sh on 4h blk, red & yel	150.00	150.00
a.		Inverted overprint	200.00	200.00
b.		Double overprint	300.00	300.00
33	D1	5sh on 5h blk, red & yel	3,250.	3,500.
34	D1	6sh on 6h red & yel	650.00	650.00
a.		Inverted overprint	900.00	900.00
b.		Double overprint	750.00	750.00
35	D1	7sh on 7h blk, red & yel	25.00	27.50
a.		Inverted overprint	37.50	42.50
36	D1	8sh on 8h blk, red & yel	30.00	35.00
a.		Inverted overprint	50.00	60.00
b.		Vertical overprint	750.00	950.00
c.		As "b," double overprint	950.00	1,100.
37	D1	10sh on 10h blk, red & yel	1,250.	1,400.
38	D1	15sh on 15h blk, red & yel	625.00	625.00
a.		Inverted overprint	950.00	800.00
39	D1	20sh on 20h blk, red & yel	6,250.	
a.		Double overprint	7,750.	17,000.
40	D1	50sh on 50h blk, red & yel	350.00	375.00
a.		Inverted overprint	500.00	600.00

Nos. 29-40 were created by overprinting Bosnian 1904 postage due stamps, which had been brought to Stanyslaviv by a Ukrainian military officer returning from the Serbian front. The same printing cliché was used as for the First Stanyslaviv Issue, but the asterisk obliterators were removed.

Most of the overprinting was made using 50-stamp panes (half of a sheet). After one half of the pane (25 positions) was overprinted, it would apparently be turned over and its second half overprinted with the same 25-position block, but as an inverted impression. After overprinting, the pane was torn into two equal 25-stamp halves.

A corrected block was utilized in overprinting, resulting in two types of surcharges on No. 29 (shahiv to shaha) and on Nos. 32, 34 and 38 (shahiv to shahi).

Austrian Military Semipostal Stamps of 1918 Srchd.

41	MSP7	10sh on 10h gray green	150.00	150.00
a.		Inverted overprint	150.00	160.00
b.		Double overprint	175.00	210.00
42	MSP8	20sh on 20h mag	125.00	110.00
a.		Inverted overprint	120.00	120.00
b.		Double overprint	160.00	180.00
43	MSP7	45sh on 45h blue	100.00	110.00
a.		Inverted overprint	100.00	120.00

Nos. 41-43 were printed in the same manner as Nos. 29-40.

Austrian Military Stamps of 1917 Srchd.

44	M3	1sh on 1h grnsh blue	950.00	950.00
45	M3	2sh on 2h red orange	100.00	100.00
a.		Inverted overprint	125.00	125.00
b.		Double overprint	210.00	210.00
46	M3	3sh on 3h olive gray	175.00	200.00
a.		Double overprint	750.00	750.00
47	M3	5sh on 5h olive grn	275.00	275.00
48	M3	6sh on 6h vio	150.00	175.00
49	M3	10sh on 10h org brn	900.00	1,000.
50	M3	12sh on 12h blue	550.00	600.00
a.		Inverted overprint	650.00	725.00
51	M3	15sh on 15h brt rose	500.00	600.00
a.		Inverted overprint	625.00	725.00
52	M3	20sh on 20h red brown	16.50	20.00
a.		Inverted overprint	82.50	140.00
b.		Double overprint	47.50	55.00
53	M3	25sh on 25h ultra	3,250.	3,900.
54	M3	30sh on 30h slate	1,000.	1,200.
55	M3	40sh on 40h ol bister	950.00	950.00
56	M3	50sh on 50h dp grn	9.00	9.00
a.		Inverted overprint	20.00	20.00
b.		Double overprint	55.00	55.00
57	M3	60sh on 60h car rose	950.00	950.00
58	M3	80sh on 80h dull blue	32.50	32.50
a.		Inverted overprint	80.00	85.00
59	M3	90sh on 90h dk vio	950.00	1,000.
60	M4	2hr on 2k rose, straw	17.50	20.00
a.		Inverted overprint	35.00	37.50
b.		Imperforate	3,000.	
61	M4	3hr on 3k blue, grn	22.50	30.00
a.		Inverted overprint	40.00	40.00
b.		Double overprint	60.00	65.00
62	M4	4hr on 4k rose, grn	22.50	25.00
a.		Inverted overprint	100.00	100.00
b.		Double overprint	60.00	65.00
63	M4	10hr on 10k dl vio, gray	35,000.	35,000.

Two examples of No. 63 were printed, and neither was ever postally used. The "used" example was cut from a document prepared by the Western Ukrainian economic bureau (Ekonomat) to display the stamps that made up the First, Second and Third Stanyslaviv issues. The specimen stamps on this document were tied with a double-ring bureau cancel that somewhat resembles a regular double-ring postal cancellation.

About half of this issue, where several sheets were available for printing, was overprinted in the manner of Nos. 29-43.

Austrian Stamps of 1916-18 Surcharged

64	A38	15sh on 36h vio (on #J61)	350.00	450.00
a.		Double overprint	450.00	500.00

65	A38	50sh on 42h choc (on #J63)	5,000.	5,500.
66	A37	3sh on 3h brt violet (on #145)	375.00	375.00
67	A37	5sh on 5h lt green (on #146)	375.00	375.00
a.		Inverted overprint	650.00	650.00
68	A37	6sh on 6h deep org (on #147)	725.00	725.00
69	A37	10sh on 10h mag (on #148)	210.00	210.00
a.		Inverted overprint	250.00	250.00
70	A37	12sh on 12h lt blue (on #149)	425.00	425.00
71	A38	15sh on 15h rose red (on #150)	375.00	375.00
a.		Inverted overprint	650.00	650.00
72	A42	15sh on 15h dull red (on #168)	400.00	400.00
73	A42	30sh on 30h dull vio (on #171)	375.00	375.00
a.		Double overprint	650.00	650.00
74	A39	40sh on 40h ol grn (on #154)	300.00	300.00
75	M3	50sh on 50h dp grn (on #M61)	475.00	475.00

The two bars in the surcharge were originally created to obliterate the "PORTO" on Nos. 64 and 65 but were subsequently retained for Nos. 66-75.

Third Stanyslaviv Issue

Austrian Stamps of 1916-18 Overprinted

1919, May

76	A37	3h brt violet	.50	1.00
77	A37	5h light green	.50	1.00
78	A37	6h deep orange	.50	1.00
79	A37	10h magenta	.50	1.00
80	A37	12h light blue	.50	1.00
81	A42	15h dull red	.50	1.00
82	A42	20h deep green	.50	1.00
83	A42	25h blue	.50	1.00
84	A42	30h dull vio	.50	1.00
85	A39	40h olive green	.75	1.25
86	A39	50h dark green	.75	1.25
87	A39	60h deep blue	.75	1.25
88	A39	80h orange brn	1.00	1.25
89	A39	90h red violet	1.00	1.60
90	A39	1k car, yel	1.25	4.00
91	A40	2k light blue	2.00	6.00
92	A40	3k carmine rose	2.50	7.50
93	A40	4k yellow grn	12.00	16.00
94	A40	10k deep violet	16.00	50.00
		Nos. 76-94 (19)	42.50	99.10

Issued: 3h-10h, 15h, 25h-40h, 60h-1k, 5/8; balance of set, 5/13.

A definitive set for Western Ukraine was ordered from the Austrian State Printing Office in March, 1919. Because of the time involved in designing and printing these stamps, Nos. 76-94 were overprinted in Vienna as a provisional issue and were delivered in two shipments. Because travel into and out of Stanyslaviv was becoming more difficult as the month wore on, it was not known whether or not the second shipment, which included the higher values, would arrive. Because of this, the Fourth Stanyslaviv Issue, Nos. 95-103, were overprinted locally.

Fourth Stanislaviv Issue

Austrian Military Stamps of 1917-18 Surcharged in Black

1919, May   *Perf. 12½*

95	M3	2hr on 2k rose, straw	15.00	15.00
a.		Perf 11½	130.00	150.00
96	M3	3hr on 2k rose, straw	13.00	16.00
a.		Perf 11½	130.00	160.00
97	M3	3hr on 3k grn, blue	125.00	175.00
a.		"5" instead of "3" at left in overprint	1,500.	
98	M3	4hr on 2k rose, straw	15.00	16.00
99	M3	4hr on 4k rose, grn	1,300.	1,900.
100	M3	5hr on 2k rose, straw	20.00	22.50
a.		Inverted surcharge	300.00	
101	M3	10hr on 50h dp grn	35.00	40.00
a.		Double surcharge	175.00	

Austrian Postage Due Stamps of 1916 Srchd., but without Rosettes and Numerals

102	D5	1hr ultra	140.00	210.00
103	D5	5hr ultra	1,400.	2,100.

REGISTRATION STAMPS

Kolomyia Issue

RS1

Without Gum

1918-19   **Unwmk.**   **Typeset**   *Imperf.*

F1	RS1	30sot black, rose	250.00	175.00
F2	RS1	50sot black, rose ('19)	150.00	160.00

No. F1 was printed on Dec. 10 and issued Dec. 12, 1918, along with the regular Kolomyia Issue (Nos. 5-8). On Dec. 19, the ZUNR government approved an increase in the registered letter rate to 50 sotyks, effective January 1, 1919. Because of communication disruptions, the Kolomyia post office did not learn of this decree until about January 7, when it ordered new values in the higher denomination (No. F2). F1 continued to be used, usually in combination with 20h of Austrian stamps, until supplies were exhausted, at which point No. F2 was put into use. A second printing of the 50sot value was made in late March. Variations in paper color — from light pink to deep rose — as well as paper thickness occurred in the 30-sot and both of the 50-sot printings.

Nos. F1-F2a were typographed in vertical panes of five stamps by the Wilhelm Brauner Print Ship in Kolomyia.

Forgeries exist.

OCCUPATION STAMPS

Romanian Occupation of Pokutia

Only the stamps listed below were officially created. Soon after the Romanian occupation ended on Aug. 20, 1919, the C.M.T. handstamps fell into the hands of speculators, and some 37 other Austrian stamps were overprinted. None of these privately-created stamps are known on authentic covers.

Austrian Stamps Surcharged in Dark Violet Blue

1919, June 14   **Unwmk.**   *Perf. 12½*
On Stamps of 1916-18

N1	A37	40h on 5h lt grn	4.50	5.50
N2	A42	60h on 15h dl red	5.50	6.50
N3	A42	60h on 20h dp grn	2.25	3.25
a.		Inverted overprint	3,000.	
b.		Double overprint	25.00	
N4	A42	60h on 25h blue	12.00	13.00
a.		Inverted overprint	60.00	
b.		Double overprint	82.50	
N5	A42	60h on 30h dl vio	14.00	15.00
N6	A39	1k 20h on 60h dk grn	5.50	6.50
N7	A39	1k 20h on 60h dp bl	10.00	12.00

N8	A39	1k 20h on 1k car, yel	19.00	21.00

On Austrian Postage Due Stamps of 1910-1917

N9	D4	40h on 5h rose red	21.00	22.50
N10	D3	1k 20h on 25h car	175.00	350.00
N11	D4	1k 20h on 25h rose red	175.00	350.00
N12	D4	1k 20h on 30h rose red	1,400.	1,400.
N13	A38	1k 20h on 50h on 42h choc	1,500.	1,500.

Arms of Kiev

Arms of Ukraine

Arms of Galicia

First Definitive Issue, May 1919: Lithographed at the Austrian State Printing Office on unwatermarked white paper. Inscribed: "Ukrainska Narodnia Republyka Zakhidnia Oblast." ("Ukrainian National Republic Western Province"). Set of 12 values (four of each design), perf 11½ or imperf. Not issued. Value, set of 12: perf $350; imperf $550.

Second Definitive Issue, May 1919: Lithographed at the Austrian State Printing Office on unwatermarked white paper. Inscribed: "Ukrainska Narodnia Respublika Z.O." ("Ukrainian National Republic W(estern) P(rovince)"). Design incorporates the heraldic arms of Ukraine (trident), Kiev (Archangel Michael) and Lviv (lion rampant). 10, 20 and 50 sotyk values imperf; 1 and 10 krone values perf 11½. Not issued. Value, set of 5, $6. Also exists on cream-colored paper.

WEST IRIAN

(Irian Barat)
(West New Guinea)

Stamps formerly listed under West Irian now appear in Volume 1, following United Nations, and Volume 3, following Indonesia.

YEMEN

ˈye-mən

LOCATION — Arabian Peninsula, south of Saudi Arabia and bordering on the Red Sea
GOVT. — Republic
AREA — 204,000 sq. mi. (est.)

POP. — 16,942,230 (1999 est.)
CAPITAL — Sana'a (San'a)

40 Bogaches = 1 Imadi
40 Bogaches = 1 Riyal (1962)
100 Fils = 1 Riyal (1975)

The Yemen Arab Republic and the People's Republic of Yemen planned a 30-month unification process scheduled for completion by November 1992. While government ministries merged, both currencies remained valid.

> **Catalogue values for unused stamps in this country are for Never Hinged items, beginning with Scott 44 in the regular postage section, Scott C1 in the airpost section.**

Watermarks

Wmk. 127 — Quatrefoils

Wmk. 258 — Arabic Characters and Y G Multiple

Wmk. 277 — Winged Wheel

For Domestic Postage

A1

Crossed Daggers and Arabic Inscriptions
A2

1926   **Unwmk.**   **Typo.**   *Imperf.*
Laid Paper
Without Gum

1	A1	2½b black	60.00	60.00
2	A1	2½b black, orange	60.00	60.00
3	A2	5b black	60.00	60.00
		Nos. 1-3 (3)	180.00	180.00

No. 2 is known rouletted 7½ or 9.

Type A1 differs from A2 primarily in the inscription in the left dagger blade.

All come on wove paper. Beware of forgeries, especially those on wove paper.

Replica sheets of Nos. 1-3 exist on horizontally laid, watermarked paper. The sheets are marked on the reverse with "CRC / FAC" in san serif font. Any stamps removed from these replica sheets will contain this marking from 1-4 times on the reverse.

For Foreign and Domestic Postage

Arabic Inscriptions
A3   A4

1930-31		**Wmk. 127**		*Perf. 14*	
7	A3	½b orange ('31)		.35	.30
8	A3	1b green		.70	.50
9	A3	1b yellow grn ('31)		.35	.30
10	A3	2b olive grn		.90	.55
11	A3	2b olive brn ('31)		.55	.50
12	A3	3b dull vio ('31)		.70	.55
13	A3	4b red		.75	1.00
14	A3	4b deep rose ('31)		1.00	.85
15	A3	5b slate gray ('31)		1.25	.90
16	A4	6b dull blue		2.75	1.75
17	A4	6b dp ultra ('31)		1.75	1.25
18	A4	8b lilac rose ('31)		2.00	1.40
19	A4	10b lt brown		5.00	3.50
20	A4	10b brn org ('31)		2.75	1.75
21	A4	20b yel grn ('31)		8.50	7.00
22	A4	1i red brn & lt bl		25.00	14.00
23	A4	1i lil rose & yel grn ('31)		20.00	14.00
		Nos. 7-23 (17)		74.30	50.10

Some values exist imperforate.
For surcharges and overprints see Nos. 30, 59-62, 166-167, 169-171, 174-176, 246-246Q.

Flags of Saudi Arabia, Yemen and Iraq — A5

1939	**Litho.**	**Wmk. 258**	*Perf. 12½*	
24	A5	4b dl rose & ultra	1.00	.70
25	A5	6b slate bl & ultra	1.25	.90
26	A5	10b fawn & ultra	1.75	1.50
27	A5	14b olive & ultra	3.00	2.75
28	A5	20b yel grn & ultra	4.25	3.50
29	A5	1i claret & ultra	9.00	8.50
		Nos. 24-29 (6)	20.25	17.85

2nd anniv. of the Arab Alliance. Nos. 24-29 exist imperforate. Value, set, $20.
For overprints see Nos. C29-C29D.

a   b

c   d

---

e

Five types of surcharge:
All genuine surcharges are 12-13mm x 15-16mm and were made from steel handstamps.
a. "YEMEN" ½mm from left frameline and ½mm above bottom frameline.
b. "YEMEN" ½mm from left frameline and 1½mm above bottom frameline.
c. "YEMEN" 1½mm from left frameline and ½mm above bottom frameline. Found only on Types A13 and D1.
d. Arabic "4" at the center of the surcharge has been replaced with two vertical strokes. Usually blurred and found only on Type A9.
e. Arabic "4" has been replaced by a pair of crescents. Found only on Type A13.
Values of surcharged stamps are for ordinary examples. Clear, legible surcharges command a premium. Beware of fraudulent rubber-stamped surcharges in violet or grey black ink.

1939	**Wmk. 127**		*Perf. 14*	
No. 7 Handstamped Type "a" in Black				
30	A3	4b on ½b orange	*15.00*	*15.00*

See Nos. 44-48, 59-67, 82, 86-87.

A6

1940	**Wmk. 258**	**Litho.**	*Perf. 12½*	
31	A6	½b ocher & ultra	.40	.30
32	A6	1b lt grn & rose red	.40	.30
33	A6	2b bis brn & vio	.50	.30
34	A6	3b dl vio & ultra	.50	.30
35	A6	4b rose & yel grn	.50	.30
36	A6	5b dk gray grn & bis brn	.60	.35
37	A7	6b ultra & yel org	.75	.35
38	A7	8b claret & dull bl	.90	.60
39	A7	10b brn org & yel grn	1.10	.75
40	A7	14b gray grn & vio	1.25	.90
41	A7	18b emerald & blk	1.75	1.50
42	A7	20b yel ol & cerise	2.75	2.00
43	A7	1i vio rose, yel grn & brn red	6.50	4.25
		Nos. 31-43 (13)	17.90	12.20
		Set, never hinged	25.00	

No. 36 was used as a 4b stamp in 1957.
For surcharges see Nos. 44-47.

> **Catalogue values for unused stamps in this section, from this point to the end of the section, are for Never Hinged items.**

Nos. 31-34, 36 Handstamped Type "a" in Black

1945-48			*Perf. 12½*	
44	A6	4b on ½b	4.50	3.50
45	A6	4b on 1b ('48)	4.00	4.50
46	A6	4b on 2b ('48)	4.50	5.00
47	A6	4b on 3b ('48)	5.00	5.00
48	A6	4b on 5b ('46)	4.50	3.50
1949-51				
Handstamp Type "b" in Black				
44a	A6	4b on ½b ('51)	4.00	3.00
45a	A6	4b on 1b ('49)	4.00	3.50
46a	A6	4b on 2b ('49)	4.50	3.50
47a	A6	4b on 3b ('49)	5.00	3.50

Forged surcharges exist.

A8

1946		**Frames in Emerald**		
49	A8	4b black	1.75	.85
50	A8	6b lilac rose	2.50	1.50
51	A8	10b ultra	3.50	1.90
52	A8	14b olive green	6.00	3.25
		Nos. 49-52 (4)	13.75	7.50

Opening of Mutawakkili Hospital. Exist imperforate. Value, set $40.
For overprints see Nos. 168, 172-173.

Mocha Coffee Tree — A9   Palace, San'a — A10

1947-58	**Unwmk.**	**Engr.**	*Perf. 12½*	
53	A9	½b yellow brown	.25	.25
54	A9	1b purple	.70	.40
55	A9	2b ultra	1.40	.90
56	A10	4b red	2.25	1.25
57	A10	5b gray blue	2.50	1.50
58	A9	6b yellow green ('58)	3.50	2.00
		Nos. 53-58 (6)	10.60	6.30

No. 58 was printed in 1947 but not officially issued until June, 1958.
Additional values, prepared but not issued, were 10b, 20b and 1i, with views of palaces superimposed on flag, and palace square. These were looted from government storehouses during the 1948 revolution and a number of copies later reached collectors. Values, set: unused $20; used (cto) $15.
For surcharges see Nos. 63-65.

Admission of Yemen to the U.N.
10 postage, 5 airmail and 5 postage due stamps for the Admission of Yemen to the UN were not officially issued for use on domestic mail. Pictured on some of the stamps were Truman, Roosevelt, Churchill and the Statue of Liberty. Value, unused: 10v postage, $35; 5v air post, $22; 5v postage due, $14. Covers, scarce and all philatelic, exist to foreign destinations. A few local-use covers are also known.

Nos. 9, 11, 12 and 15 Handstamped Type "a" in Black

1949		**Wmk. 127**	*Perf. 14*	
59	A3	4b on 1b yellow grn	10.00	8.00
60	A3	4b on 2b olive brn	35.00	30.00
61	A3	4b on 3b dull vio	12.00	10.00
62	A3	4b on 5b slate gray	12.00	10.00

Handstamped type "b" were unauthorized.

Nos. 53-55 Handstamped Types "a" and "b" in Black

1949		**Unwmk.**	*Perf. 12½*	
63	A9(b)	4b on ½b yel brn	6.00	6.00
64	A9(a)	4b on 1b purple	5.00	5.00
a.		Handstamp type "b"	5.00	5.00
b.		Handstamp type "d"	20.00	15.00
65	A9(a)	4b on 2b ultra	6.00	6.00
a.		Handstamp type "b"	6.00	6.00
b.		Handstamp type "d"	20.00	10.00

Nos. J1-J2 Handstamped Type "b" in Black

1953			**Wmk. 258**	
66	D1	4b on 1b org & yel grn	20.00	25.00
a.		Handstamp type "c"	35.00	40.00
67	D1	4b on 2b org & yel grn	20.00	25.00
a.		Handstamp type "c"	25.00	30.00

Types "a" and "b" exist inverted, double or horizontal.
Forged surcharges exist.

Parade Ground, San'a — A13

Mosque, San'a — A14

Designs: 5b, Flag of Yemen. 6b, Flag & eagle. 8b, Mocha coffee branch. 14b, Walled city of San'a. 20b, 1i, Ta'iz & its citadel.

1951	**Wmk. 277**	**Photo.**	*Perf. 14*	
68	A13	1b dark brown	.30	.25
69	A13	2b red brown	.60	.25
70	A13	3b lilac rose	.75	.35
71	A14	5b blue & red	1.25	.60
72	A14	6b dk pur & red	1.40	.65
73	A13	8b dk bl & gray grn	1.50	.75
74	A14	10b rose lilac	1.25	.85
75	A14	14b blue green	2.25	1.00
76	A14	20b rose red	3.25	1.75
77	A14	1i violet	7.50	3.00
		Nos. 68-77 (10)	20.05	9.45
		Nos. 68-77,C3-C9 (17)	44.70	17.70

No. 71 was used as a 4b stamp in 1956. For surcharges see Nos. 82, 86-87.

Palace of the Rock, Wadi Dhahr — A15

Design: 20b, Walls of Ibb.

Engraved and Photogravure

1952	**Unwmk.**		*Perf. 14½, Imperf.*	
78	A15	12b choc, bl & dl grn	6.00	6.00
79	A15	20b dp car, bl & brn	9.00	9.00
		Nos. 78-79,C10-C11 (4)	31.00	28.00

Flag and View of San'a (Palace in Background) — A16

1952

80	A16	1i red brn, car & gray	12.50	12.50

4th anniv. of the accession of King Ahmed, Feb. 18, 1948. See Nos. 81, C12-C13.

1952		**Palace in Foreground**		
81	A16	30b red brn, car & dk grn	11.00	11.00

Victory of Mar. 13, 1948. See No. C13.

No. 69 Handstamped Type "b" in Black

1951 (?)		**Wmk. 277**	*Perf. 14*	
82	A13	4b on 2b red brown	7.50	10.00
a.		Handstamp type "c"	11.00	14.00

Surcharge exists without left frameline. Forged surcharges exist. See Nos. 86-87.

Leaning Minaret,
Mosque of
Ta'iz — A17

1954 **Photo.** **Unwmk.**
83 A17 4b deep orange 1.25 .40
84 A17 6b deep blue 2.00 .60
85 A17 8b deep blue green 2.50 1.50
Nos. 83-85,C14-C16 (6) 19.50 6.65

Accession of King Ahmed I, 5th anniv.

**Nos. 68 and 70 Handstamped Type
"b" in Black**

1955 **Wmk. 277** **Perf. 14**
86 A13 4b on 1b dk brown 6.50 9.00
a. Handstamp type "c" 20.00 10.00
b. Handstamp type "e" — —
87 A13 4b on 3b lilac rose 9.50 12.50

Yemen Gate,
San'a — A18

1956-57 **Wmk. 277** **Perf. 14**
87A A18 1b lt brown 1.00 .75
87B A18 5b blue green 1.25 .75
87C A18 10b dark blue ('57) 1.50 .85
Nos. 87A-87C (3) 3.75 2.35

Nos. 87A-87C were prepared for official
use, but issued for regular postage. The 1b
and 5b were used as 4b stamps. A 20b and 1-
imadi of type A18 were not issued. Value
unused $25., used (CTO) $15.

Arab Postal Union Issue

Globe — A19

Perf. 13½x13
1957-58 **Wmk. 195** **Photo.**
88 A19 4b yellow brown 1.00 .90
89 A19 6b green ('58) 1.40 1.10
90 A19 16b violet ('58) 2.00 1.50
Nos. 88-90 (3) 4.40 3.50

Arab Postal Union founding, July 1, 1954.

Telecommunications Issue

Globe,
Radio and
Telegraph
A20

1959, Mar. **Wmk. 318** **Perf. 13x13½**
91 A20 4b vermilion 1.50 1.00
Arab Union of Telecommunications.
Exists imperf. Value $4.50.

United Arab States Issue

Flags of
UAR and
Yemen
A21

1959, Mar. 13
92 A21 1b dl red brn & blk .35 .25
93 A21 2b dk blue & blk .45 .35
94 A21 4b sl grn, car & blk .65 .50
Nos. 92-94,C17-C19 (6) 6.95 5.05

First anniversary of United Arab States.
No. 94 exists imperf. Value $10.

In 1959 four special sets of stamps
were distributed abroad. They honored
Human Rights (4v), Yemeni stamps
(6v), Automatic Telephone Service (5v)
and King Ahmed's Reign (4v). They
were overprinted on stamps of either
the 1940 issue (type A6) or the 1931
issue (type A4). Although not regularly
sold at post offices in Yemen, several
values from these sets do appear on
covers that passed through normal postal channels. Some values are known
with inverted or doubled overprints.

Arab League Center Issue

Arab
League
Center,
Cairo
A22

Perf. 13x13½
1960, Mar. 22 **Wmk. 328**
95 A22 4b dull green & blk .90 .90
Opening of the Arab League Center and the
Arab Postal Museum in Cairo.
Exists imperf. Value $10.

Refugees
Pointing
to Map of
Palestine
A23

1960, Apr. 7 **Photo.**
96 A23 4b brown 1.00 .75
97 A23 6b yellow green 1.50 1.25

World Refugee Year, 7/1/59-6/30/60.
Exist imperf. Value, set $25.
In 1961 a souvenir sheet was issued containing a 4b gray and 6b sepia in type A18,
imperf. Black marginal inscription, "YEMEN
1960," repeated in Arabic. Size: 103x85mm.
Value $35.

Torch
and
Olympic
Rings
A24

1960, Dec. **Unwmk.** **Perf. 14x14½**
98 A24 2b black & lil rose .40 .25
99 A24 4b black & yellow .60 .40
100 A24 6b black & orange 1.00 .60
101 A24 8b brn blk & bl grn 1.50 1.00
102 A24 20b dk bl, org & vio 4.00 2.50
Nos. 98-102 (5) 7.50 4.75

17th Olympic Games, Rome, 8/25-9/11.
Exist imperf. Value $75.
An imperf. souvenir sheet exists, containing
one example of No. 99. Size: 100x60mm.
Value $80.

UN Emblem Breaking Chains — A25

1961 **Unwmk.** **Perf. 14x14½**
103 A25 1b violet .25 .25
104 A25 2b green .30 .25
105 A25 3b grnsh blue .40 .25
106 A25 4b brt ultra .50 .35
107 A25 6b brt lilac .60 .50

108 A25 14b rose brown .80 .60
109 A25 20b brown 1.50 1.25
Nos. 103-109 (7) 4.35 3.45

15th anniversary (in 1960) of UN.
Exist imperf. Value, set $14.
An imperf. souvenir sheet exists, containing
one example of No. 106. Blue marginal
inscription. Size: 100x60mm. Value $15.
For overprints see Nos. 137-143.

Cranes
and
Ship,
Hodeida
A26

1961, June **Litho.** **Perf. 13x13½**
110 A26 4b multicolored .75 .40
111 A26 6b multicolored 1.25 .75
112 A26 16b multicolored 2.40 1.25
Nos. 110-112 (3) 4.40 2.40

Opening of deepwater port at Hodeida.
An imperf. souvenir sheet exists, containing
one each of Nos. 110-112. Size: 160x130mm.
Value $7.
For overprints see Nos. 177, 180.

Alabaster Funerary
Mask — A27

Designs (ancient sculptures from Marib,
Sheba): 2b, Horned animal's head, symbolizing Moon God (limestone). 4b, Bronze head
of an Emperor 1st or 2nd century. 8b, Statue
of Emperor Dhamar Ali. 10b, Statue of a child,
2nd or 3rd century (alabaster). 12b, Stairs in
court of Temple of the Moon God. 20b, Alabaster relief, boy riding monster. 1i, Woman
with grapes, relief.

1961, Oct. 14 **Photo.** **Perf. 11½**
Granite Paper
113 A27 1b salmon, blk & gray .35 .25
114 A27 2b purple & gray .50 .25
115 A27 4b pale brn, gray &
blk .70 .25
116 A27 8b brt pink & blk .85 .25
117 A27 10b yellow & blk 1.00 .40
118 A27 12b lt vio bl & blk 1.75 .50
119 A27 20b gray & blk 2.00 .75
120 A27 1i gray ol & blk 4.00 1.25
Nos. 113-120,C20-C21 (10) 14.40 5.15

Exist imperf. Value, set (10), $25.
For overprints see Nos. 144-145, 147, 151,
153, 156-158, C24, C25.

Imam's New Palace,
San'a — A28

8b, Side view of Imam's palace, San'a,
horiz. 10b, Palace of the Rock (Dar al-Hajar).

1961, Nov. 15 **Unwmk.**
121 A28 4b black & lt bl grn .35 .25
122 A28 8b blk, brt pink & grn .75 .45
123 A28 10b black, sal & grn .85 .50
Nos. 121-123,C22-C23 (5) 5.05 2.05

Exist imperf. Value, set (5) $6.
For overprints see #148, 152, 154, C24A,
C25A.

Hodeida-San'a Road — A29

1961, Dec. 25 **Litho.** **Perf. 13½x13**
124 A29 4b multicolored .75 .25
125 A29 6b multicolored .90 .40
126 A29 10b multicolored 1.50 .50
Nos. 124-126 (3) 3.15 1.15

Opening of the Hodeida-San'a highway. A
miniature sheet exists containing one each of
Nos. 124-126, imperf. Size: 159x129mm.
Value $7.
For overprints see Nos. 178-179.

Trajan's Kiosk, Philae, Nubia — A30

1962, Mar. 1 **Photo.** **Perf. 11x11½**
127 A30 4b dk red brown 3.00 1.50
128 A30 6b blue green 4.00 2.00

Issued to publicize UNESCO's help in safe-
guarding the monuments of Nubia. Exist
imperf. on toned paper with printer's imprint.
Value, set $12.50.
A souvenir sheet exists, containing one
each of #127-128, imperf. on white paper with
printer's imprint at the bottom of the sheet.
Size: 100x88½mm. Value $10.

Arab League
Building, Cairo, and
Emblem — A31

1962, Mar. 22 **Perf. 13½x13**
129 A31 4b dark green .70 .25
130 A31 6b deep ultra .85 .40

Arab League Week, Mar. 22-28.
A souvenir sheet exists, containing one
each of Nos. 129-130, imperf. Size:
94x80mm. Value $3.50.
For overprints see Nos. 164-165.

Nurses,
Mother and
Child — A32

Designs: 4b, Nurse weighing child. 6b,
Vaccination. 10b, Weighing infant.

1962, June 20 **Unwmk.** **Perf. 11½**
131 A32 2b multicolored .60 .25
132 A32 4b multicolored .85 .30
133 A32 6b multicolored 1.00 .40
134 A32 10b multicolored 1.75 .50
Nos. 131-134 (4) 4.20 1.45

Issued for Child Welfare.
Exist imperf. Value, set $5.
For overprints see Nos. 146, 149-150, 155.

Malaria Eradication Emblem — A33

1962, July 20 *Perf. 13½x13*
135 A33 4b black & dp org .70 .40
136 A33 6b dk brown & grn 1.00 .60

WHO drive to eradicate malaria. An imperf. souvenir sheet contains one each of Nos. 135-136. Size: 95x79mm. Value $12.50.

No. 136 has laurel leaves added and inscription rearranged.

For overprints see Nos. 189-190.

Nos. 103-109 Overprinted

Perf. 14x14½
1962, Nov. 7 Photo. Unwmk.
137 A25 1b violet 1.50 1.50
138 A25 2b green 1.50 1.50
139 A25 3b greenish blue 1.50 1.50
140 A25 4b brt ultra 1.50 1.50
141 A25 6b brt lilac 1.50 1.50
142 A25 14b rose brown 1.50 1.50
143 A25 20b brown 1.50 1.50
Nos. 137-143 (7) 10.50 10.50

Exist imperf. and with inverted overprint.

Yemen Arab Republic
Nos. 113-123 and 131-134 Ovptd. in Dark Green or Dark Red

a

b

1963, Jan. 1 *Perf. 11½*
144 A27 (a) 1b No. 113 (G) .25 .25
145 A27 (a) 2b No. 114 .25 .25
146 A32 (b) 2b No. 131 .35 .35
147 A32 (b) 4b No. 115 (G) .35 .35
148 A28 (a) 4b No. 121 .50 .50
149 A32 (b) 4b No. 132 (G) .50 .50
150 A32 (b) 6b No. 133 .65 .65
151 A27 (a) 8b No. 116 (G) .65 .65
152 A28 (b) 8b No. 122 (G) .90 .90
153 A27 (a) 10b No. 117 .90 .90
154 A28 (a) 10b No. 123 1.60 1.60
155 A32 (b) 10b No. 134 (G) 1.60 1.60
156 A27 (a) 12b No. 118 1.25 1.25
157 A27 (a) 20b No. 119 1.80 1.80
158 A27 (a) 1i No. 120 5.00 5.00
Nos. 144-158,C24-C25A (19) 24.10 24.10

Nos. 144-158, C24-C25A exist imperf. Value, set $45.

Proclamation of the Republic — A34

1963, Mar. 15 *Perf. 11x11½*
159 A34 4b shown .55 .55
160 A34 6b Flag, tank .85 .85

An imperf. souvenir sheet containing Nos. 159-160 exists. Value $10.
See Nos. C26-C28.

UN Freedom From Hunger Campaign — A35

1963, Mar. 21 *Perf. 11½x11, 11x11½*
162 A35 4b Milk cow, horiz. .90
163 A35 6b shown 1.25

An imperf. souvenir sheet of 2 containing one each Nos. 162-163 exists. Value $12.
For overprints see Nos. 218-218A.

Nos. 129-130 Ovptd. in Dark Red

1963, Sept. 1 *Perf. 13½x13*
164 A31 4b dark green 6.00 6.00
165 A31 6b deep ultra 6.00 6.00

Nos. 98-100 Overprinted in Black or Red

1963 Unwmk. *Perf. 14x14½*
165A A24 2b black & lil rose 5.00 5.00
165B A24 4b black & yellow (R) 5.00 5.00
165C A24 6b black & orange (R) 5.00 5.00
Nos. 165A-165C (3) 15.00 15.00

Nos. 15-16, 18-23, 50-52 Ovptd. in Black

a

b

1963, Sept. 1
166 A3 (a) 5b No. 15 1.25 1.25
167 A4 (a) 6b No. 16 1.60 1.60
168 A8 (b) 6b No. 50 1.60 1.60
169 A4 (a) 8b No. 18 1.80 1.80
170 A4 (a) 10b No. 19 2.25 2.25
171 A4 (a) 10b No. 20 2.25 2.25
172 A8 (b) 10b No. 51 2.25 2.25
173 A8 (b) 14b No. 52 6.25 6.25
174 A4 (a) 20b No. 21 2.50 2.50
175 A4 (a) 1i No. 22 6.25 6.25
176 A4 (a) 1i No. 23 4.75 4.75
Nos. 166-176 (11) 32.75 32.75

Nos. 111-112 and 125-126 Ovptd. in Black

Perf. 13x13½, 13½x13
1963, Sept. 1 Litho. Unwmk.
177 A26 6b No. 111 1.75 1.75
178 A29 6b No. 125 1.75 1.75
179 A29 10b No. 126 2.50 2.50
180 A26 16b No. 112 2.50 2.50
Nos. 177-180 (4) 8.50 8.50

On Nos. 178-179 the bars eliminate old inscription with text of overprint positioned below and to the right of them, on Nos. 177 and 180, the text is slightly left below the bars.
Imperf. souvenir sheets of 2 exist containing Nos. 177 and 180 or Nos. 178-179. Value $20 each.

1st Anniv. of the Revolution — A36

2b, Flag, torch, candle, vert. 6b, Flag, grain, chain, vert.

Perf. 11½x11, 11x11½
1963, Sept. 26 Photo.
186 A36 2b multicolored .35 .30
187 A36 4b shown .55 .45
188 A36 6b multicolored .90 .70
Nos. 186-188 (3) 1.80 1.45

Imperf. souvenir sheet exists containing one each Nos. 186-188. Value $5.

Red Cross, Centennial — A36a

1963, October Photo. *Perf. 13½x13*
188A A36a ⅛b bl, blk & red .25 .25
188B A36a ⅛b lil brn, blk & red .25 .25
188C A36a ⅛b ol grey, blk & red .25 .25
188D A36a 4b vio, black & red .75 .35
188E A36a 8b ocher, blk & red 1.00 .50
188F A36a 20b grn, blk & red 2.00 1.00
Nos. 188A-188F (6) 4.50 2.60

Nos. 188A-188F exist imperf. Value $12. An imperf. souvenir sheet of 2 exists containing one each Nos. 188D-188E. Value $7.50.

Nos. 135-136 Ovptd. in Black

UN Declaration of Human Rights, 15th Anniv. — A37

1963, Dec. 10 *Perf. 13½*
191 A37 4b orange & dk brn vio .40 .40
192 A37 6b blue grn & blk .60 .60

Nos. 191-192 exist imperf. Value $6.50. An imperf. souvenir sheet of 2 exists containing one each Nos. 191-192. Value $9.

Olympic Sports — A37a

1964, Mar. 30 Photo. *Perf. 12*
192A A37a ¼b Darts .25 .25
192B A37a ½b Table tennis .25 .25
192C A37a ½b Running, vert. .25 .25
192D A37a 1b Volleyball, vert. .45 .40
192E A37a 1½b Soccer, vert. .45 .40
192F A37a 4b Horse racing .65 .50
192G A37a 20b Pole vault 1.35 1.25
i. Souvenir sheet of 1 4.00 4.00
192H A37a 1r Basketball, vert. 2.75 1.50
Nos. 192A-192H (8) 6.40 4.80

Nos. 192F-192H are airmail. Nos. 192A-192H exist imperf. Value $25. An imperf. souvenir sheet containing 1 No. 192F exists. Value $4.

Bagel Spinning and Weaving Factory Inauguration — A38

2b, Factory, bobbin, spool, cloth. 4b, Loom machine. 6b, Factory, spool, bolt of cloth.

1964, Apr. 10 *Perf. 11x11½, 11½x11*
193 A38 2b multicolored .25 .25
193A A38 4b mutlicolored .30 .25
193B A38 6b multicolored .40 .35
193C A38 16b shown 1.10 1.40
Nos. 193-193C (4) 2.05 2.25

Nos. 193-193B vert. An imperf. souvenir sheet of one exists containing No. 193C. Value $3.
No. 193C is air mail.

Hodeida Airport Inauguration — A39

1964, Apr. 30 *Perf. 11½x11*
194 A39 4b Runway .40 .35
194A A39 6b Runway, terminal .55 .50
194B A39 10b Aircraft, terminal, ship at sea .75 .55
Nos. 194-194B (3) 1.70 1.40

An imperf. souvenir sheet of one exists containing No. 194B. Value $3.

1964 New York World's Fair — A39a

Designs: ¼b, 1b, 20b, Manhattan skyline, Sana'a. ½b, 4b, Empire State Building, minaret. ½b, 16b, Statue of Liberty, ship loading cranes.

1964, May 10 **Perf. 12**
195	A39a	¼b brown & multi	.25	.25
195A	A39a	½b grey & multi	.25	.25
195B	A39a	½b dk bl green & multi	.30	.25
195C	A39a	1b dk grey & multi	.45	.35
195D	A39a	4b dk grey & multi	.80	.50
195E	A39a	16b brown & multi	1.50	1.00
195F	A39a	20b red vio & multi	2.00	1.50
		Nos. 195-195F (7)	5.55	4.10

Nos. 195E-195F are airmail. An imperf. souvenir sheet containing 1 No. 195F exists. Value $4.

For overprints see Nos. 220-220F.

1964 Summer Olympic Games, Tokyo — A39b

Designs: ¼b, 12b, Globe and flags. ½b, 6b, Torch. ½b, 20b, Discus thrower. 1b, Yemen flag. 1½b, Swimmers, horiz.

1964, June 1 **Perf. 12**
196	A39b	¼b multicolored	.25	.25
196A	A39b	½b multicolored	.25	.25
196B	A39b	½b multicolored	.30	.25
196C	A39b	1b multicolored	.40	.30
196D	A39b	1½b multicolored	.50	.35
196E	A39b	4b multicolored	.70	.60
196F	A39b	6b multicolored	.80	.75
196G	A39b	12b multicolored	1.50	1.25
196H	A39b	20b multicolored	2.25	2.00
i.		Souvenir sheet of 1	5.00	5.00
		Nos. 196-196H (9)	6.95	6.00

Exist imperf. Value, set $25.
Nos. 196E-196H are airmail.

Boy Scouts A39c

Designs: ¼b, 4b, Raising flag. ½b, 1b, 6b, Scouts, tents. ½b, 16b, Bugler. 1½b, 20b, Campfire.

1964, June 20
197	A39c	¼b multicolored	.25	.25
197A	A39c	½b multicolored	.25	.25
197B	A39c	½b multicolored	.25	.25
197C	A39c	1b multicolored	.35	.25
197D	A39c	1½b multicolored	.50	.35
197E	A39c	4b multicolored	.60	.35
197F	A39c	16b multicolored	.70	.50
197G	A39c	16b multicolored	1.50	1.25
i.		Souvenir sheet of 1	4.00	4.00
197H	A39c	20b multicolored	2.25	1.75
		Nos. 197-197H (9)	6.65	5.20

Exist imperf. Value, set $20. An imperf. souvenir sheet containing 1 No. 197H exists. Value, $4.

Nos. 197E-197H are airmail.

Animals — A39d

Designs: ¼b, Baboons. ½b, Arabian horses. ½b, 12b, Zebu. 1b, 20b, Lions. 1½b, 4b, Gazelles.

1964, Aug. 15 **Photo.** **Perf. 12x11½**
198	A39d	¼b lilac & brown	.25	.25
198A	A39d	½b blue & dk brn	.25	.25
198B	A39d	½b org & brn	.25	.25
198C	A39d	1b blue & brn	.25	.25
198D	A39d	1½b multicolored	.40	.25
198E	A39d	4b multicolored	.65	.40

198F	A39d	12b multicolored	1.50	1.00
198G	A39d	20b multicolored	3.00	1.25
		Nos. 198-198G (8)	6.55	3.90

Exist imperf. Value, set $15.
Nos. 198F-198G are airmail. See Nos. J9-J11.

Flowers — A39e

Designs: ¼b, shown. ½b, Crinum. ½b, 12b, Poinsettia. 1b, 4b, Hybrid tea. 1½b, 20b, Peppermint.

1964, Aug. 15 **Photo.** **Perf. 11½x12**
199	A39e	¼b multicolored	.25	.25
199A	A39e	½b multicolored	.25	.25
199B	A39e	½b grn, red & yel	.25	.25
199C	A39e	1b multicolored	.35	.25
199D	A39e	1½b red, grn & blk	.45	.25
199E	A39e	4b multicolored	.65	.40
199F	A39e	12b dk grn, red & yel	1.50	1.00
199G	A39e	20b multicolored	3.00	1.25
		Nos. 199-199G (8)	6.70	3.90

Exist imperf. Value, set $12. Nos. 199E-199G are airmail. See Nos. J12-J14.

Sana'a Intl. Airport Inauguration — A40

1964, Oct. 1
200	A40	1b shown	.35	.35
201	A40	2b Terminal, runway, aircraft	.35	.35
202	A40	4b like 2b	.35	.35
203	A40	8b like 1b	.70	.70
		Nos. 200-203 (4)	1.75	1.75

An imperf. souvenir sheet of two exists containing one each Nos. 202 and C30. Value $4. See No. C30.

Arab Postal Union, 10th Anniv. — A41

1964, Oct. 15 **Perf. 13½**
204	A41	4b multicolored	.65	.55

See No. C31.

2nd Arab Summit Conference — A42

1964, Nov. 30
205	A42	4b shown	.65	.55
206	A42	6b Conference emblem, map	.85	.70

An imperf. souvenir sheet of 2 exists containing one each Nos. 205-206. Value $2.50.
For overprints see Nos. 222-222A.

2nd Anniv. of the Revolution — A43

1964, Dec. 30
207	A43	2b Torch, map	.35	.25
208	A43	4b Revolutionary	.60	.35
209	A43	6b Flag, 2 candles, map	.65	.45
		Nos. 207-209 (3)	1.60	1.05

An imperf. souvenir sheet of one exists containing No. 209. Value $2.50.

Birds — A43a

Designs: ¼b, Reef Heron. ½b, Arabian red-legged partridge. ¾b, Eagle owl, vert. 1b, Hammer kop. 1½b, Yemen linnets. 4b, Hoopoes. 6b, Amethyst starlings. 8b, Bald ibis, vert. 12b, Arabian woodpecker, vert. 20b, Bateleur, vert. 1r, Bruce's green pigeon.

Perf. 15x14½, 14½x15
1965, Jan. 30 **Photo.**
Background Color
209A	A43a	¼b light violet	.50	.25
209B	A43a	½b brown olive	.75	.25
209C	A43a	¾b grey	.75	.25
209D	A43a	1b olive green	1.00	.40
209E	A43a	1½b rose	1.00	.40
209F	A43a	4b light blue	2.00	.75
209G	A43a	6b blue	2.00	.75
209H	A43a	8b bistre	2.00	1.00
209I	A43a	12b green	3.00	1.50
209J	A43a	20b orange	4.00	2.00
209K	A43a	1r blue green	6.00	3.00
		Nos. 209A-209K (11)	23.00	10.55

Souvenir Sheet
Imperf
209L	A43a	20b rose	15.00	15.00

Nos. 209A-209K exist imperf. Value, set $35.
Nos. 209H-209L are airmail. For overprints see Nos. 221-221B.

Deir Yassin Massacre — A44

1965, Apr. 30 **Perf. 11x11½**
210	A44	4b red lil & deep blue	.75	.50

See No. C32.

Intl. Telecommunications Union (ITU), Cent. — A45

1965, May 17 **Perf. 11x11½, 11½x11**
211	A45	4b red & pale blue, vert.	.65	.35
212	A45	6b org brn & grn	.90	.50

A souvenir sheet of 1 exists containing #212. Value $4.

Burning of Algiers Library, 3rd Anniv. A46

1965, July 7 **Perf. 11½x11**
213	A46	4b sepia, red & grn	.60	.40

See No. C33.

3rd Anniv. of the Revolution A47

1965, Sept. 26
214	A47	4b Tractor, corn, grain	.70	.40
214A	A47	6b Tractor, tower, buildings	.90	.50

An imperf. souvenir sheet of one exists containing No. 214A. Value $3.

Intl. Cooperation Year — A48

1965, Oct. 15 **Perf. 11x11½**
215	A48	4b shown	.70	.55
215A	A48	6b UN building, New York	1.00	.60

Nos. 215-215A exist imperf. Value $5. An imperf. souvenir sheet of one exists containing No. 215A. Value $4.

Pres. John F. Kennedy — A48a

Kennedy and: Nos. 216, 216D, Rocket in flight. Nos. 210A, 216G, Launch pads. Nos. 216B-216C, Lift-off. 4b, Capsule in space. 8b, Splash down.

1965, Nov. 29 **Photo.** **Perf. 12x11½**
216	A48a	¼b multicolored	.25	.25
216A	A48a	¼b multicolored	.25	.25
216B	A48a	¼b multicolored	.25	.25
216C	A48a	¼b multicolored	.25	.25
216D	A48a	½b multicolored	.25	.25
216E	A48a	4b multicolored	.70	.60
216F	A48a	8b multicolored	1.60	1.25
216G	A48a	12b multicolored	3.00	1.75
		Nos. 216-216G (8)	6.55	4.85

Nos. 216F-216G are airmail. Nos. 216-216G exist imperf. Value $12.50. Imperf. souvenir sheets of Nos. 216E-216F exist. Value $5 each.

Astronauts and Cosmonauts — A48b

Spacecraft and: Nos. 217, 8b, Pavel Belyayev. Nos. 217A, 4b, Alexei Leonov. Nos. 217B, 217D, M. Scott Carpenter. Nos. 217C, 16b, Virgil I. "Gus" Grissom. No. 217H, James McDivitt, Edward White.

1965, Dec. 29 Photo. Perf. 11½x12

217	A48b	¼b multicolored	.25	.25
217A	A48b	¼b multicolored	.25	.25
217B	A48b	½b multicolored	.25	.25
217C	A48b	½b multicolored	.25	.25
217D	A48b	½b multicolored	.25	.25
217E	A48b	4b multicolored	.75	.35
217F	A48b	8b multicolored	1.50	1.40
217G	A48b	16b multicolored	2.75	2.75
	Nos. 217-217G (8)		6.25	5.75

Souvenir Sheet

Imperf

217H	A48b	16b multicolored	12.50	12.50

Exist imperf. Value, set $11.
Nos. 217E-217H are airmail. For overprints see Nos. 225-225H, 229-229D.

Nos. 162-163 Overprinted in Black

a

b

1966, Jan. 15 Perf. 11½x11, 11x11½

218	A35 (a)	4b sal rose & golden brn	.90	.90
218A	A35 (b)	6b bpr pur & yel	1.25	1.25

An imperf. souvenir sheet of two exists containing Nos. 218-218A. Value $8.

Telecommunications — A48c

Designs: No. 219, Light signals. No. 219A, Samuel F.B. Morse, telegraph. No. 219B, Early telephone. No. 219C, Philipp Reis, Thomas Edison, early telephone system. No. 219D, Television camera, antenna. No. 219E, Radar dish. No. 219F, Fax machine. No. 219G, Satellite.

1966, Jan. 29 Photo. Perf. 12x11½

219	A48c	¼b red & black	.25	.25
219A	A48c	¼b grnish bl & blk	.25	.25
219B	A48c	¼b yel brn & blk	.25	.25
219C	A48c	½b org red & blk	.25	.25
219D	A48c	½b violet & black	.25	.25
219E	A48c	4b yel grn & blk	.75	.35
219F	A48c	6b drab & black	1.25	.65
219G	A48c	20b blue & black	2.50	1.25
	Nos. 219-219G (8)		5.75	3.50

Nos. 219E-219G are airmail. Nos. 291-219G exist imperf. Value $10. An imperf. souvenir sheet containing 1 No. 219G exists. Value $6.

Nos. 195-195F Overprinted in Black

1966, Feb. 10 Photo. Perf. 12

220	A39a	¼b brown & multi	.50	.50
220A	A39a	½b grey & multi	.50	.50
220B	A39a	½b dk bl grn & multi	.50	.50
220C	A39a	1b dk grey & multi	.75	.75
220D	A39a	4b dk grey & multi	1.25	1.25

220E	A39a	16b brown & multi	3.00	3.00
220F	A39a	20b red vio & multi	4.50	4.50
	Nos. 220-220F (7)		11.00	11.00

Nos. 220E-220F are airmail. An imperf. souvenir sheet containing 1 No. 220F exists. Value $10.

Nos. 209A-209C Overprinted in Black or Red

1966, Mar. 5 Photo. Perf. 12x11½

Background Color

221	A43a	¼b light violet	.75	.65
221A	A43a	½b brown olive	.75	.65
221B	A43a	¾b grey (R)	1.10	.75
	Nos. 221-221B (3)		2.60	2.05

Nos. 205-206
Ovptd. in Red or
Black

1966, Mar. 20 Perf. 13½

222	A42	4b dark green (R)	.60	.40
222A	A42	6b orange brown	.75	.50

An imperf. souvenir sheet of two exists containing Nos. 222-222A ovptd. in bright pink (4b) or black (6b) with additional inscription at bottom "CASABLANCA / 1965." Value $3.50.

Builders
of World
Peace
A49

Designs: Nos. 223, 223C, Dag Hammerskjold. Nos. 223A, 4b, John F. Kennedy. Nos. 223B, 223D, Jawaharlal Nehru. 6b, Mohammed Abdel Khaliq Hussana. 10b, U Thant. 12b, Pope Paul VI.

1966, Mar. 25 Photo. Perf. 12

223	A49	¼b green	.25	.25
223A	A49	¼b orange brown	.25	.25
223B	A49	¼b dark grey	.25	.25
223C	A49	½b red brown	.25	.25
223D	A49	½b violet brown	.25	.25
223E	A49	4b claret	.75	.35

Size:51x38mm

223F	A49	6b bl grn & brn	1.00	.50
223G	A49	10b blue & brown	1.25	.65
223H	A49	12b red lilac & brn	2.00	1.00
	Nos. 223-223H (9)		6.25	3.75

Exist imperf. Value, set $9. Nos. 223F-223H are airmail.
Two imperf. souvenir sheets, 4b and 8b, exist. Values $4 and $6, respectively.

1966, May 5 Photo. Perf. 12½

224	A50	¼b Rooster	.30	.25
224A	A50	¼b Rabbit	.30	.25
224B	A50	¼b Donkey	.30	.25
224C	A50	½b Cat	.40	.25
224D	A50	½b Sheep	.40	.25
224E	A50	4b Camel	1.00	.50
	Nos. 224-224E (6)		2.70	1.75

Souvenir Sheet

Imperf

224F	A50	22b Sheep, chickens, geese	4.00	3.00

Nos. 224-224E exist imperf. Value, set $7. No. 224F is airmail.

Nos. 217-217H
Overprinted in
Black and Red

Luna IX

1966, May 20 Photo. Perf. 11½x12

225	A48b	¼b multicolored	.25	.25
225A	A48b	¼b multicolored	.25	.25
225B	A48b	¼b multicolored	.25	.25
225C	A48b	½b multicolored	.25	.25
225D	A48b	½b multicolored	.25	.25
225E	A48b	4b multicolored	.45	.30
225F	A48b	8b multicolored	1.00	.70
225G	A48b	16b multicolored	1.50	1.25
	Nos. 225-225G (8)		4.20	3.45

Souvenir Sheet

Imperf

225H	A48b	16b multicolored	8.00	8.00

Nos. 225-225G exist imperf. Value, set $7.50. Nos. 225E-225H are airmail.

Traffic Day — A52

1966, June 30 Perf. 11x11½

227	A52	4b green & ver	.65	.45
228	A52	6b green & ver	.75	.50

Nos. 227-228 exist imperf. Value $3. An imperf. souvenir sheet of No. 228 exists. Value $3.50.

Nos. 217-217D
Surcharged in
Black

Surveyor I.

1966, Aug. 15 Photo. Perf. 11½x12

229	A48b	1b on ¼b multi	.65	.50
229A	A48b	¼b multicolored	.65	.50
229B	A48b	½b multicolored	.65	.70
229C	A48b	½b multicolored	.65	.70
229D	A48b	½b multicolored	1.60	1.25
	Nos. 229-229D (5)		4.20	3.45

A53

Revolution, 6th
Anniv. — A53a

1966, Sept. Photo. Perf. 11½

230	A53	2b multicolored	1.50	1.25

Perf. 11x11¼

230A	A53a	4b multicolored	1.75	1.25
230B	A53a	6b Factory, tractor, wheat, corn	2.75	1.75
	Nos. 230-230B (3)		6.00	4.25

An imperf. souvenir sheet containing 1 each of Nos. 230A-230B exists. Value $20.

New WHO Headquarters,
Geneva — A54

WHO Headquarters, flowers and: Nos. 231, 4b, Galen (129-199). Nos. 231A, 8b, Hippocrates (460-370 BC). Nos. 231B, 16b, Ibn Sina (Avicenna) (980-1037).

1966, Nov. 1 Litho. Perf. 12½

231	A54	¼b multicolored	.25	.25
231A	A54	¼b multicolored	.25	.25
231B	A54	¼b multicolored	.25	.25
231C	A54	4b multicolored	.50	.25
231D	A54	8b multicolored	1.00	.50
231E	A54	16b multicolored	2.00	1.00
	Nos. 231-231E (6)		4.25	2.50

Nos. 231C-231E are airmail. Nos. 231-231E exist imperf. Value $10 An imperf. souvenir sheet of 1 No. 231E exists. Value $8.

1966, May 29 Photo. Perf. 11

Background Color

226	A51	¼b light green	.25	.25
226A	A51	¼b violet	.25	.25
226B	A51	¼b dull rose	.25	.25
226C	A51	½b green	.25	.25
226D	A51	½b orange red	.25	.25
226E	A51	4b blue	.45	.25
226F	A51	5b bistre	.60	.30
226G	A51	20b gold	1.90	1.00
	Nos. 226-226G (8)		4.20	2.80

Nos. 226-226G exist imperf. Value $8. An imperf souvenir sheet containing 1 No. 226G exists. Value $6.

World Cup Soccer Championship,
London — A51

Domesticated Animals — A50

Gemini 6 and 7 Flights A55

Designs: No. 232, Astronauts. No. 232A, Lift off. No. 232B, Spacecraft, Earth. ½b, 2b, Spacecraft in orbit. ½b, 8b, Splash down. 12b, Rendevous.

1966, Dec. 1 Photo. Perf. 12½
Background Color

232	A55	¼b rose	.25	.25
232A	A55	¼b olive bistre	.25	.25
232B	A55	¼b blue	.25	.25
232C	A55	½b light blue	.25	.25
232D	A55	½b blue green	.25	.25
232E	A55	2b bistre	.50	.25
232F	A55	8b blue	1.00	.50
232G	A55	12b violet	1.50	.75
		Nos. 232-232G (8)	4.25	2.75

Nos. 232F-232G are airmail. Nos. 232-232G exist imperf. Value $9. An imperf. souvenir sheet containing 1 No. 232G exists. Value $6.

Nos. 232-232G Overprinted in Red

1966, Dec. 25 Photo. Perf. 12½
Background Color

233	A55	¼b rose	.25	.25
233A	A55	¼b olive bistre	.25	.25
233B	A55	¼b blue	.25	.25
233C	A55	½b light blue	.25	.25
233D	A55	½b blue green	.25	.25
233E	A55	2b bistre	.45	.30
233F	A55	8b blue	1.60	1.10
233G	A55	12b violet	2.00	1.40
		Nos. 233-233G (8)	5.30	4.05

Nos. 233F-233G are airmail. Nos. 233-233G exist imperf. Value $8. An imperf. souvenir sheet containing 1 No. 233G exists. Value $6.

Fruit A56

1967, Feb. 10 Litho. Perf. 12½x12

234	A56	¼b Figs	.25	.25
234A	A56	¼b Red apples	.25	.25
234B	A56	½b Purple grapes	.25	.25
234C	A56	½b Dates	.25	.25
234D	A56	½b Apricots	.25	.25
234E	A56	2b Yellow apples	.55	.30
234F	A56	4b Oranges	.70	.40
234G	A56	6b Bananas	.90	.50
234H	A56	8b Green figs	1.10	.65
234I	A56	10b Green grapes	1.35	.75
		Nos. 234-234I (10)	5.85	3.85

Exist imperf. Value, set $9. Nos. 234G-234I are airmail. See Nos. J23-J25.

Arab League Day — A57

1967, July Photo. Perf. 11x11½

235	A57	4b violet & brown	.50	.25
235A	A57	6b dk violet & brown	.75	.40
235B	A57	8b dk violet & brown	1.25	.65
235C	A57	20b dk bl grn & brn	2.00	1.00
235D	A57	40b dk bl grn & blk	4.00	2.00
		Nos. 235-235D (5)	8.50	4.30

Gamal el-Din el-Afghani (1839-97), advocate of Arab unity.

Intl. Labor Organization (ILO) — A58

1967, Aug. Photo. Perf. 11½x11

236	A58	2b vio & dk blue	.40	.25
236A	A58	4b car & dk bl grn	.60	.30
236B	A58	6b grn & dp red lilac	1.00	.50
236C	A58	8b vio bl & ol bis	1.50	.75
		Nos. 236-236C (4)	3.50	1.80

An imperf. souvenir sheet containing 1 10b No. 236C exists. Value $6.

Agriculture — A59

1967, Sept. Photo. Perf. 11½x11

237	A59	1b multicolored	.25	.25
237A	A59	2b multicolored	.30	.25
237B	A59	4b multicolored	.35	.25
237C	A59	6b multicolored	.50	.25
237D	A59	8b multicolored	.85	.45
237E	A59	10b multicolored	1.25	.65
237F	A59	12b multicolored	1.50	.75
237G	A59	16b multicolored	1.75	.85
237H	A59	20b multicolored	2.50	1.25
237I	A59	40b multicolored	4.00	2.00
		Nos. 237-237I (10)	13.25	6.95

Nos. 237-237E Overprinted in Black

1967, Sept.

238	A59	1b multicolored	.40	.25
238A	A59	2b multicolored	.60	.30
238B	A59	4b multicolored	1.00	.50
238C	A59	6b multicolored	1.50	.75
238D	A59	8b multicolored	2.00	1.00
238E	A59	10b multicolored	2.50	1.25
		Nos. 238-238E (6)	8.00	4.05

Fifth Anniv. of the Revolution.

Paintings by Flemish Masters A60

Designs: ¼b, Village Wedding by Bruegel. ½b, The Doctor G. Zeile by Van Orley. ½b, H. Fourment and Her Children by Rubens. 3b, The King is Drinking by Jordaens. 6b, Self-Portrait by Van Dyck.

1967, Oct. Photo. Perf. 13½

239	A60	¼b gold & multi	.25	.25
239A	A60	½b gold & multi	.25	.25
239B	A60	½b gold & multi	.25	.25
239C	A60	3b gold & multi	1.25	.25
239D	A60	6b gold & multi	3.00	.55
		Nos. 239-239D (5)	5.00	1.55

Nos. 239C-239D are airmail. An imperf. souvenir sheet containing 1 No. 239D exists. Value, $6. Nos. 239-239D exist imperf. with silver frames.

Flemish Painting Type

Paintings by Florentine Masters: ¼b, Portrait of a Young Man by Raphael. ½b, E. de Toledo and Her Son by A. Bronzino. ½b, Simoneta Vespucci by P. Di Cosimo. 3b, The Delphic Sibyl by Michelangelo. 6b, Spring by Botticelli.

1967, Nov. 17 Photo. Perf. 13½

240	A60	¼b gold & multi	.25	.25
240A	A60	½b gold & multi	.25	.25
240B	A60	½b gold & multi	.25	.25
240C	A60	3b gold & multi	1.25	.25
240D	A60	6b gold & multi	3.00	.55
		Nos. 240-240D (5)	5.00	1.55

Nos. 240C-240D are airmail. An imperf. souvenir sheet containing 1 No. 240D exists. Value, $6. Nos. 240-240D exist imperf. with silver frames.

Flemish Painting Type

Paintings by Spanish Masters: ¼b, The Infanta Margarita by Velazquez. ½b, The Knock-Kneed Man by Ribera. ½b, The Beggar by Murillo. 3b, A Knight by El Greco. 6b, The Grape Gathering by Goya.

1967, Nov. 17 Photo. Perf. 13½

241	A60	¼b gold & multi	.25	.25
241A	A60	½b gold & multi	.25	.25
241B	A60	½b gold & multi	.25	.25
241C	A60	3b gold & multi	1.25	.25
241D	A60	6b gold & multi	3.00	.55
		Nos. 241-241D (5)	5.00	1.55

Nos. 241C-241D are airmail. An imperf. souvenir sheet containing 1 No. 241D exists. Value, $6. Nos. 241-241D exist imperf. with silver frames.

1968 Winter Olympic Games, Grenoble A61

Sports: ¼b, Cross-country skiing. ½b, Figure skating. ½b, Bobsled. 3b, Ice hockey. 6b, Slalom skiing.

1967, Dec. 9 Photo. Perf. 11½

242	A61	¼b multicolored	.25	.25
242A	A61	½b multicolored	.25	.25
242B	A61	½b multicolored	.25	.25
242C	A61	3b multicolored	1.20	.25
242D	A61	6b multicolored	3.50	.55
		Nos. 242-242D (5)	5.45	1.55

An imperf. souvenir sheet containing 1 No. 242D exists. 9.50. Value, $. Nos. 242-242D exist imperf. with different colors.

Paintings by Paul Gauguin — A62

Paintings: No. 243e, Woman in white dress. No. 243f, Woman lying on beach. No. 243Ag, Self-portrait. No. 243Ah, Nevermore. No. 243Bi, Girls from Pouldu. No. 243Bj, Girls from Bretagne. No. 243Ck, La Lune et la Terre. No. 243Cl, Angela. No. 243Dm, Woman. No. 243Dn, Two women.

1968, June Litho. Perf. 13½

243	A62	¼b Pair, #e.-f.	.40	.25
243A	A62	½b Pair, #g.-h.	.40	.25
243B	A62	½b Pair, #i.-j.	.40	.25
243C	A62	3b Pair, #k.-l.	2.00	.50
243D	A62	6b Pair, #m.-n.	3.50	1.00
		Nos. 243-243D (5)	6.70	2.25

Nos. 243C-243D are airmail. Nos. 243-243D exist imperf. with gold frames. Value, $9. An imperf. souvenir sheet containing 1 No. 243D exists with either silver or gold frame. Value, each $9.

Paintings by Gaugin Type

Paintings by Van Gogh: No. 244e, Julien Tanguy. No. 244f, Joseph Roulin. No. 244Ag, Sunflowers. No. 244Ah, Church in Auvers. No. 244Bi, Armand Roulin. No. 244Bj, La Berceuse (Madam Roulin). No. 244Ck, Une Arlésienne an Mouemé. No. 244Cl, Marguerite Gachet at piano. No. 244Dm, L'Arlésienne. No. 244Dn, Self-portrait.

1968, June Litho. Perf. 13½

244	A62	¼b Pair, #e.-f.	.40	.25
244A	A62	½b Pair, #g.-h.	.40	.25
244B	A62	½b Pair, #i.-j.	.40	.25
244C	A62	3b Pair, #k.-l.	2.00	.50
244D	A62	6b Pair, #m.-n.	3.50	1.00
		Nos. 244-244D (5)	6.70	2.25

Nos. 244C-244D are airmail. Nos. 244-244D exist imperf. with gold frames. Value, $9. An imperf. souvenir sheet containing 1 No. 244D exists with either silver or gold frame. Value, each $9.

Paintings by Gaugin Type

Paintings by Rubens: No. 245e, Head of a little girl. No. 245f, Child's head (Holy Family detail). No. 245Ag, Portrait of a Negro. No. 245Ah, Thomas, Count of Arundel. No. 245Bi, Self-Portrait. No. 245Bj, Isabelle Brandt. No. 245Ck, Woman in a Hat. No. 245Cl, Helene Fourment. No. 245Dm, Rubens' sons. No. 245Dn, The Holy Family.

1968, June Litho. Perf. 13½

245	A62	¼b Pair, #e.-f.	.40	.25
245A	A62	½b Pair, #g.-h.	.40	.25
245B	A62	½b Pair, #i.-j.	.40	.25
245C	A62	3b Pair, #k.-l.	2.00	.50
245D	A62	6b Pair, #m.-n.	3.50	1.00
		Nos. 245-245D (5)	6.70	2.25

Nos. 245C-245D are airmail. Nos. 245-245D exist imperf. with gold frames. Value, $9. An imperf. souvenir sheet containing 1 No. 245D exists with either silver or gold frame. Value, each $9.

Nos. 7-23 Overprinted in Black or Red

1968 Wmk. 127 Perf. 14

246	A3	½b on No. 7	.75	
246A	A3	1b on No. 8 (R)	.75	
246B	A3	1b On No. 9 (R)	.75	
246C	A3	2b on No. 10 (R)	1.00	
246D	A3	2b On No. 11	1.00	
246E	A3	3b on No. 12	1.25	
246F	A3	4b On No. 13	1.25	
246G	A3	4b on No. 14	1.25	
246H	A3	5b On No. 15 (R)	2.00	
246I	A4	6b on No. 16 (R)	2.00	
246J	A4	6b On No. 17 (R)	2.00	
246K	A4	8b On No. 18	10.00	
246L	A4	10b on No. 19	3.00	
246M	A4	10b On No. 20	3.00	

246N	A4	20b On No. 21	4.00	
246O	A4	1i On No. 22	7.00	
246P	A4	1i On No. 23	7.00	

Nos. 246-246P (17) 48.00

No. 246 exists with a red overprint. No. 246H is known with an inverted overprint.

Flemish Painting Type of 1967

Paintings of Horses: ¼b, Righteous Judge and Warrior of God by Hugo Van Eyck. ⅛b, The Virgin and the Unicorn by Zampieri (Domenichino). ½b, The Prince Baltsar Carlos by Velazquez. 3b, Roman Slave with Horses by Gericault. 6b, The Hunt by Ucello.

1968, July 10		**Photo.**	**Perf. 13½**	
247	A60	¼b gold & multi	.25	.25
247A	A60	⅛b gold & multi	.25	.25
247B	A60	½b gold & multi	.25	.25
247C	A60	3b gold & multi	1.75	.35
247D	A60	6b gold & multi	3.00	.65

Nos. 247-247D (5) 5.50 1.75

Nos. 247C-247D are airmail. An imperf. souvenir sheet containing 1 No. 247D exists. Value, $11. Nos. 247-247D exist imperf. with silver frames. Value, $7.

Flemish Painting Type of 1967

Paintings by Raphael: ¼b, La Velata. ⅛b, Angelo Doni. ½b, Plato and Aristotle. 3b, A Man. 6b, A Young Woman.

1968, July 10		**Photo.**	**Perf. 13½**	
248	A60	¼b gold & multi	.25	.25
248A	A60	⅛b gold & multi	.25	.25
248B	A60	½b gold & multi	.25	.25
248C	A60	3b gold & multi	1.75	.35
248D	A60	6b gold & multi	3.00	.55
e.		Souvenir sheet of 1	4.00	

Nos. 248-248D (5) 5.50 1.55

Nos. 248C-248D are airmail. An imperf. souvenir sheet of No. 248De exists. Nos. 248-248D exist imperf. with silver frames. Value, $7.

Flemish Painting Type of 1967

Paintings by Rembrandt: ¼b, Jan Six. ⅛b, Saskia. ½b, Mars. 3b, H. Stoffels. 6b, Self-portrait.

1968, July 10		**Photo.**	**Perf. 13½**	
249	A60	¼b gold & multi	.25	.25
249A	A60	⅛b gold & multi	.25	.25
249B	A60	½b gold & multi	.25	.25
249C	A60	3b gold & multi	1.75	.35
249D	A60	6b gold & multi	3.00	.55
e.		Souvenir sheet of 1	4.00	

Nos. 249-249D (5) 5.50 1.55

Nos. 249C-249D are airmail. An imperf. souvenir sheet of No. 249De exists. Nos. 249-249D exist imperf. with silver frames. Value, $7.

Revolution, 6th Anniversary — A63

President and: 2b, Fighters. 4b, Flag. 6b, Roses, vert.

1968, July		**Litho.**	**Perf. 12¾**	
250	A63	2b multicolored	.40	.25
250A	A63	4b multicolored	.60	.30
250B	A63	6b multicolored	1.00	.50

Nos. 250-250B (3) 2.00 1.05

Nos. 250-250B exist imperf. Value $2. An imperf souvenir sheet of No. 250B exists. Value $3.50.

Gold Medalists, 1968 Winter Olympic Games — A64

Various Olympic Gold Medals and: ¼b, Peggy Fleming, USA. ⅛b, Franco Nones, Italy. ½b, Jiri Raska, Czechosovakia. 2b, Hockey Team, USSR. 3b, Jean Claude Killy, France. 4b, Erhard Keller, Germany.

1968, Sept. 10		**Litho.**	**Perf. 13½**	
251	A64	¼b multicolored	.25	.25
251A	A64	⅛b multicolored	.25	.25
251B	A64	½b multicolored	.25	.25
251C	A64	2b multicolored	1.00	.25
251D	A64	3b multicolored	1.40	.25
251E	A64	4b multicolored	2.00	.30

Nos. 251-251E (6) 5.15 1.55

Nos. 251D-251E are airmail. No. 251E exists in perf. and imperf. souvenir sheets of one. Nos. 251-251E exist imperf. with light blue borders. Value, $7.

1968 Summer Olympic Games, Mexico City — A65

Ancient Greek art and artifacts of Mexico: ¼b, Greek man, sculpture. ⅛b, Woman on bull, jade mask. ½b, Three people, jaguar. 2b, Two warriors, large carving. 3b, Chariot, mask. 4b, Rider and 2 people, sculpture. No. 252F, Three warriors, Central University City Campus site.

1968, Sept. 30		**Litho.**	**Perf. 13½**	
252	A65	¼b multicolored	.25	.25
252A	A65	⅛b multicolored	.25	.25
252B	A65	½b multicolored	.25	.25
252C	A65	2b multicolored	1.20	.25
252D	A65	3b multicolored	1.50	.25
252E	A65	4b multicolored	1.75	.30

Nos. 251-251E (6) 2.15 1.55

Souvenir Sheet

252F	A65	¼b multicolored	7.00	1.50

Nos. 252D-252F are airmail. No. 252F contains one 88x35mm stamp. Nos. 252-252F exist imperf. with silver frames. Values: set $7; souvenir sheet, $12.

Olympic Medals Type of 1968

Olympic Gold Medals from: ¼b, 1896, 1908, 1912. ⅛b, 1920, 1924. ½b, 1928, 1932. 2b, 1936, 1948, 1952. 3b, 1956, 1960, 1964. 4b, 1968, 1972.

1968, Oct. 18		**Litho.**	**Perf. 13½**	
253	A64	¼b multicolored	.25	.25
253A	A64	⅛b multicolored	.25	.25
253B	A64	½b multicolored	.25	.25
253C	A64	2b multicolored	.90	.25
253D	A64	3b multicolored	1.20	.25
253E	A64	4b multicolored	1.75	.30

Nos. 253-253E (6) 4.60 1.55

Nos. 253D-253E are airmail. No. 253E exists in perf. and imperf. souvenir sheets of one. Nos. 253-253E exist imperf. with light blue borders. Value, $5.

Arms of Winter Olympic Games Host Cities — A66

Designs: ¼b, Ancient ski. ⅛b, Chamonix, 1924; St. Moritz, 1928; Lake Placid, 1932. ½b, Garmisch 1936; St. Moritz, 1948; Oslo, 1952. 2b, Cortina, 1956; Squaw Valley, 1960; Innsbruck, 1964. 3b, Grenoble, 1968. 4b,Sapporo, 1972.

1968, Nov. 23		**Litho.**	**Perf. 13½**	
254	A66	¼b multicolored	.25	.25
254A	A66	⅛b multicolored	.25	.25
254B	A66	½b multicolored	.25	.25
254C	A66	2b multicolored	.60	.25
254D	A66	3b multicolored	1.20	.25
254E	A66	4b multicolored	1.75	.30

Nos. 254-254E (6) 4.30 1.55

Nos. 254D-254E are airmail. A perf. and imperf. souvenir sheet containing one each of Nos. 254D-254E exist. Values: perf $7; imperf $14. Nos. 254-254E exist perf. and imperf. with light blue borders. Value, $5.

Arms of Olympic Host Cities Type

Arms of Summer Olympic Games Host Cities: ¼b, Athens, 1896; London, 1908; Stockholm, 1912. ⅛b, Antwerp, 1920; Paris, 1924. ½b, Amsterdam, 1928; Los Angeles, 1932; Berlin, 1936. 2b, London, 1948; Helsinki, 1952. 3b, Melbourne, 1956; Rome, 1960; Tokyo, 1964. 4b, Mexico City, 1968; Munich, 1972.

1968, Dec. 22		**Litho.**	**Perf. 13½**	
255	A66	¼b multicolored	.25	.25
255A	A66	⅛b multicolored	.25	.25
255B	A66	½b multicolored	.25	.25
255C	A66	2b multicolored	.60	.25
255D	A66	3b multicolored	1.20	.25
255E	A66	4b multicolored	1.75	.30

Nos. 255-255E (6) 4.30 1.55

Nos. 255D-255E are airmail. A perf. and imperf. souvenir sheet containing one No. 255E exists. Values: perf $7; imperf. $14. Nos. 255-255E exist perf. and imperf. with light blue borders. Value, $5.

Intl. Human Rights Figures A67

Designs: ¼b, 10b, Dr. Christiaan Barnard with patient, horiz. ½b, 2b, Dag Hammarskjold. ¾b, Dr. Barnard. 1b, 4b, Rev. Martin Luther King. 6b, 14b, Robert F. and John F. Kennedy, horiz. 8b, Dr. Barnard with heart, horiz. 12b, 16b, Dr. King and Abraham Lincoln, horiz.

1968		**Litho.**	**Perf. 12½**	
256	A67	¼b multicolored	.25	.25
256A	A67	½b multicolored	.25	.25
256B	A67	¾b multicolored	.25	.25
256C	A67	1b multicolored	.25	.25
256D	A67	2b multicolored	.90	.25
256E	A67	4b multicolored	.75	.25
256F	A67	6b multicolored	1.50	.35
256G	A67	8b multicolored	2.00	.35
256H	A67	10b multicolored	2.75	.50
256I	A67	12b multicolored	2.75	.55
256J	A67	14b multicolored	2.00	.65
256K	A67	16b multicolored	2.50	.65

Nos. 256-256K (12) 16.15 4.55

Nos. 256-256K exist imperf. Value: set, $20. Three imperf. souvenir sheets exist; a 10b with Robert and John Kennedy, a 16b with King and LIncoln and a 20b with Dr. Barnard. Value, 3 sheets, $20.

Cultural Olympiad, Mexico City — A68

Paintings in the Louvre, Paris: ¼b, Madeleine by Van Der Weyden. ⅛b, The Gypsy by Frans Hals. ½b, Balthasar Castiglionne by Raphael. 2b, The Lacemaker by Vermeer. 3b, Women and Child by Da Vinci. 4b, Madonna and Child by Botticelli. No. 257F, Mona Lisa by Da Vinci.

1969, Feb. 19		**Litho.**	**Perf. 13½**	
257	A68	¼b silver & multi	.25	.25
257A	A68	⅛b silver & multi	.25	.25
257B	A68	½b silver & multi	.25	.25
257C	A68	2b silver & multi	.90	.25
257D	A68	3b silver & multi	1.20	.25
257E	A68	4b silver & multi	1.75	.30

Nos. 257-257E (6) 4.60 1.55

Souvenir Sheet

257F	A68	4b gold & multi	7.00	3.50

Nos. 257D-257F are airmail. Value: set, $6. Nos. 257-257E exist with gold frames. No. 257F has an orange yellow background and exists imperf., as well as both perf and imperf with a blue green background. No. 257C is iinscribed The Embroiderer. No. 257E is inscribed Woman and Child.

Cultural Olympiad Type

Paintings in the Uffizi Gallery, Florence: ¼b, Battista Sforza by Piero Della Francesca. ⅛b, Francesco delle Opere by Perugino. ½b, Francesco Maria della Rovere by Raphael. 2b, Isabel Brandt by Rubens. 3b, Don Garcia de Médicis by Bronzino. 4b, The Birth of Venus (detail) by Botticelli No. 257F, Alegoria della Primavera by Botticelli.

1969, Mar. 29		**Litho.**	**Perf. 13½**	
258	A68	¼b gold & multi	.25	.25
258A	A68	⅛b gold & multi	.25	.25
258B	A68	½b gold & multi	.25	.25
258C	A68	2b gold & multi	1.20	.25
258D	A68	3b gold & multi	1.50	.25
258E	A68	4b gold & multi	1.75	.30

Nos. 258-258E (6) 5.20 1.55

Souvenir Sheet

258F	A68	4b gold & multi	7.00	3.50

Nos. 258D-258F are airmail. Nos. 258-258E exist with gold frames. Value: set, perf or imperf, $6. No. 258F has a red background and exists imperf, as well as perf and imperf with a red orange frame. Value, $14.

Cultural Olympiad Type

Paintings in the Prado, Madrid: ¼b, Charles the First, of England by Van Dyck. ⅛b, The Story of Nastaglio by Botticelli. ½b, Maria Ruthwen by Van Dyck. 2b, Portrait of a Man by Dürer. 3b, Young Girl by Raphael. 4b, Self-portrait by Dürer. No. 257F, A Maja Vestida by Goya.

1969, May 2		**Litho.**	**Perf. 13½**	
259	A68	¼b silver & multi	.25	.25
259A	A68	⅛b silver & multi	.25	.25
259B	A68	½b silver & multi	.25	.25
259C	A68	2b silver & multi	1.20	.25
259D	A68	3b silver & multi	1.50	.25
259E	A68	4b silver & multi	1.75	.30

Nos. 259-259E (6) 5.20 1.55

Souvenir Sheet

259F	A68	4b silver & multi	7.00	3.50

Nos. 259D-259F are airmail. Value: set, $6. Nos. 259-259E exist with bronze frames. No. 258F exists imperf. Value, $14.

Discoveries of the Universe — A69

Spacecraft and Astronomers: No. 260, Vanguard, Ptolemy. No. 260A, Sputnik III, Copernicus. No. 260B, Lunik, Michelangelo. No. 260C, Explorer VI, Tycho Brahe. 3b, Lunik III, Galileo. 6b, Lunik II, Kepler. 10b, Explorer VII, Newton. 14b, Apollo 8.

1969, May 26		**Litho.**	**Perf. 13½**	
260	A69	¼b silver & multi	.25	.25
260A	A69	¼b silver & multi	.25	.25
260B	A69	½b silver & multi	.25	.25
260C	A69	⅛b silver & multi	.75	.35
260D	A69	3b silver & multi	1.25	.65
260E	A69	6b silver & multi	1.25	.65
260F	A69	10b silver & multi	2.00	1.00

Nos. 260-260F (7) 5.00 3.00

Souvenir Sheet

260G	A69	14b multicolored	6.00	3.00

Nos. 260E-260G are airmail. Nos. 260-260F exist imperf. with lilac-silver frames. A 14b imperf. souvenir sheet with Soyuz 4-5 and Apollo 8 exists.

Discoveries of the Universe Type

Old and New Space Travel: No. 261, Wan Pou, Pioneer IV, Pioneer V. No. 261A, Lucion di Samosa, Sputnik V, Explorer 10, Venus I. No. 261B, Cyrano de Bergerac, Mariner II, Mariner III. No. 261C, Jules Verne, Mariner IV. 2b, Nicolar Kibaltchich, Zond II. 4b, Rocket Lift-off, Venus II, Venus III, Luna X. 22b, Lunar lander, Venus IV. No. 261G, Apollo 9.

1969, July 3   Litho.   Perf. 13½

261	A69	¼b silver & multi	.25	.25
261A	A69	¼b silver & multi	.25	.25
261B	A69	½b silver & multi	.25	.25
261C	A69	½b silver & multi	.25	.25
261D	A69	2b silver & multi	.90	.35
261E	A69	4b silver & multi	1.20	.35
261F	A69	22b silver & multi	2.75	1.10
		Nos. 261-261F (7)	5.85	2.80

Souvenir Sheet

261G	A69	6b multicolored	7.00	2.00

Nos. 261D-261G are airmail. Nos. 261-261F exist imperf. with gold frames. Value: set, $7. A 6b imperf. souvenir sheet with Apollo 9 and a space station exists.

Intl. Labor Organization — A70

1969, Aug. 4   Litho.   Perf. 13½

262	A70	1b Stonemason	.25	.25
262A	A70	2b Blacksmith	.35	.25
262B	A70	3b Teacher	.50	.25
262C	A70	4b Printer	.60	.30
262D	A70	6b Polisher	.75	.35
262E	A70	8b Foundry worker	1.00	.50
262F	A70	10b Farrier	1.25	.60
		Nos. 262-262F (7)	4.70	2.50

Nos. 262D-262F are airmail. Nos. 262-262F exist imperf.

Discoveries of the Universe Type

Spacecraft: No. 263, Mercury Atlas 3, Vostok I, Vostok II, Mercury Atlas 6. No. 263A, Mercury Atlas 8, Vostok III & IV, Mercury Atlas 9, Vostok VI. No. 263B, Voskhod II, Voskhod I, Gemini 3, Gemini 4. No. 263C, Gemini 5-9. 3b, Apollo 8-9. 6b, Soyuz III, Soyuz I, Apollo 7-8. 10b, Gemini 10-12, Apollo 7. No. 263G, Vostok I, Mercury.

1969, Aug. 25   Litho.   Perf. 13½

263	A69	¼b multicolored	.25	.25
263A	A69	¼b multicolored	.25	.25
263B	A69	½b multicolored	.25	.25
263C	A69	½b multicolored	.25	.25
263D	A69	3b multicolored	.90	.35
263E	A69	6b multicolored	1.20	.50
263F	A69	10b multicolored	2.75	.75
		Nos. 263-263F (7)	5.85	2.60

Souvenir Sheet

263G	A69	6b multicolored	7.00	3.00

Nos. 263D-263G are airmail. No. 263G contains one 82x43mm stamp. Nos. 263-263F exist imperf. with light yellow green frames. A 6b imperf. souvenir sheet with Apollo 10 exists.

Napoloen, Birth Bicentennial — A71

Napoleon: ¼b, As artillery lieutenant. ½b, As lieutenant colonel, 1792. ½b, As consul. ¾b, On his way to Augsburg. 4b, Crossing over the St. Bernard. 8b, In 1814. 10b, At the height of his career. No. 264G, At his coronation, 1804.

1969, Sept. 16   Litho.   Perf. 13½

264	A71	¼b silver & multi	.35	.25
264A	A71	¼b silver & multi	.35	.25
264B	A71	b silver & multi	.40	.25
264C	A71	¾b silver & multi	.40	.25
264D	A71	4b silver & multi	1.50	.75

264E	A71	8b silver & multi	2.00	1.00
264F	A71	10b silver & multi	2.50	1.25
		Nos. 264-264F (7)	7.50	4.00

Souvenir Sheet

264G	A71	4b multicolored	7.00	2.00

Nos. 264D-264G are airmail. No. 264G contains one 46x69mm stamp. Value, $12. An imperf. 4b souvenir sheet showing a Napoleon bicentennial medal exists. Nos. 264-264F exist imperf. with lilac-silver frames. Value: set, $7.50.

Revolution, 7th Anniv. — A71a

Designs: 2b, Map of Yemen, vert. 4b, Parliament. 6b, Worker, soldier, farmer and student.

1969, Sept. 26   Perf. 13

264H	A71a	2b multicolored	.30	.30
264I	A71a	4b multicolored	.60	.60
264J	A71a	6b multicolored	1.25	1.25
		Nos. 264H-264J (3)	2.15	2.15

Nos. 264H-264J exist imperf. Value: set, $4. Nos. 264J also exists in an imperf. souvenir sheet. Value, $7.

Discoveries of the Universe Type

Lunar Research: No. 265, Soyuz IV & V, Apollo 10. No. 265A, Apollo 11. No. 265D, Planned Lunar trips. No. 265C, Lunar surface vehicles. 2b, Lunar vehicles, diff. 4b, Moon base and vehicles. 22b, Soviet lunar project, Apollo 11. No. 265G, Apollo 11.

1969, Oct. 10   Litho.   Perf. 13½

265	A69	¼b multicolored	.25	.25
265A	A69	¼b multicolored	.25	.25
265B	A69	½b multicolored	.25	.25
265C	A69	½b multicolored	.25	.25
265D	A69	2b multicolored	.30	.25
265E	A69	4b multicolored	.90	.30
265F	A69	22b multicolored	2.50	1.00
		Nos. 265-265F (7)	4.70	2.55

Souvenir Sheet

265G	A69	14b multicolored	9.00	2.00

Nos. 265D-265G are airmail. No. 263G contains one 63x49mm stamp. Nos. 265-265F exist imperf. with light orange frames. Value: set, $5. A 14b imperf. souvenir sheet with Apollo 11 plaque and astronauts exists. Value, $12.

Cultural Olympiad Type

Paintings in the National Gallery, Washington, DC: ¼b, David by Del Castagno. ½b, Elena Grimaldi by Van Dyck. ½b, Girl with her Dueña by Murillo. 2b, Agostina by Corot. 3b, Ginevra Bentivoglio by Ercole Roberti. 4b, Balthasar Coymans by Frans Hals. No. 266F, Ginevra de Benci by Da Vinci.

1969, Nov.   Litho.   Perf. 13½

266	A68	¼b lilac silver & multi	.25	.25
266A	A68	¼b lilac silver & multi	.25	.25
266B	A68	½b lilac silver & multi	.25	.25
266C	A68	2b lilac silver & multi	.90	.25
266D	A68	3b lilac silver & multi	1.20	.25
266E	A68	4b lilac silver & multi	1.75	.30
		Nos. 266-266E (6)	4.60	1.55

Souvenir Sheet

266F	A68	4b gold & multi	9.00	2.00

Nos. 266D-266F are airmail. Nos. 266-266E exist with gold frames. Value, $6. No. 266F contains one 36x69mm stamp. No. 266F exists with a red background instead of blue green and also exists imperf.

Cultural Olympiad Type

Paintings in the National Gallery, London: ¼b, Portrait of a Woman by Van Der Weyden. ½b, Portrait of a Young Man by Antonello da Messina. ½b, Portrait of a Young Girl by Mabuoc. 2b, The Crab Saleswoman by Hogarth. 3b, Baron Schwiter by Delacroix. 4b, Portrait of an Old Woman by Cézanne. No. 266F, Morning Promenade by Gainsborough.

1969, Dec.   Litho.   Perf. 13½

267	A68	¼b bluish sil & multi	.25	.25
267A	A68	½b bluish sil & multi	.25	.25
267B	A68	½b bluish sil & multi	.25	.25
267C	A68	2b bluish sil & multi	.90	.25

267D	A68	3b bluish sil & multi	1.20	.25
267E	A68	4b bluish sil & multi	1.75	.30
		Nos. 267-267E (6)	4.60	1.55

Souvenir Sheet

267F	A68	4b gold & multi	7.00	2.00

Nos. 267D-267F are airmail. Nos. 267-267E exist with bronze frames. Value: set, $5. No. 267F contains one 35x74mm stamp. No. 267F exists with an orange yellow background instead of greenish blue and also exists imperf.

Famous French Leaders A72

HISTORY OF FRANCE

Designs: 1¾b, Clovis I. 2b, Charlemagne. 2¼b, Jeanne d'Arc. 2½b, Louis XIV. 3½b, Napoleon I. 5b, Georges Clemenceau. 6b, 10b, Charles de Gaulle.

1969   Litho.   Perf. 13½

268	A72	1¾b gold & multi	.50	.25
268A	A72	2b gold & multi	.60	.25
268B	A72	2¼b gold & multi	.65	.25
268C	A72	2½b gold & multi	.70	.25
268D	A74	3½b gold & multi	.90	.30
268E	A72	5b gold & multi	1.20	.35
268F	A72	6b gold & multi	1.50	.45
		Nos. 268-268F (7)	6.05	2.10

Souvenir Sheet

268G	A72	10b multicolored	11.00	2.00

Nos. 268-268F exist imperf. with silver frames. Value $7.50. Nos. 268D-268G are airmail. No. 268G contains one 50x83mm stamp. A 10b imperf. souvenir sheet exists depicting DeGaulle, Jeanne d'Arc and Napoleon. Value $12.

Art Treasures of Tutankhamen — A73

Tutankhamun: ¼b, Stone bust. ½b, Alabaster bust. ½b, Painted bust. 2b, Painted statue. 3b, Gold Mask. 4b, Painted head.

1970, May 20   Litho.   Perf. 13½

269	A73	¼b lilac silver & multi	.25	.25
269A	A73	¼b lilac silver & multi	.25	.25
269B	A73	½b lilac silver & multi	.25	.25
269C	A73	2b lilac silver & multi	1.20	.30
269D	A73	3b lilac silver & multi	1.75	.35
269E	A73	4b lilac silver & multi	2.00	.45
		Nos. 269-269E (6)	5.70	1.85

Nos. 269D-269E are airmail. Perf. and imperf. souvenir sheets containing 1 No. 269E exist. Values: perf, $7.50; imperf, $9. These sheets were also overprinted in Red or Green for Roma '70. Values: perf, $7.50; imperf, $9. Nos. 269-269E exist imperf with silver frames. Value, $6.

Art Treasures Type

Treasures of Siam: ¼b, Bronze Buddha head. ½b, Stone Buddha head. ½b, Statue from Angkor. 2b, Spirit of Echiffre. 3b, King Pisei. 4b, Buddha on Naga.

1970   Litho.   Perf. 13½

270	A73	¼b lilac silver & multi	.25	.25
270A	A73	½b lilac silver & multi	.25	.25
270B	A73	½b lilac silver & multi	.25	.25
270C	A73	2b lilac silver & multi	.90	.30
270D	A73	3b lilac silver & multi	1.20	.35
270E	A73	4b lilac silver & multi	1.75	.45
			4.60	1.85

Nos. 270D-270E are airmail. Perf. and imperf. souvenir sheets containing 1 No. 270E exist. Values: perf, $7.50; imperf, $9. Nos. 270-270E exist imperf with silver frames. Value, $6.

Art Treasures Type

Treasures of Japan: Various paintings.

1970   Litho.   Perf. 13½

271	A73	¼b lilac silver & multi	.25	.25
271A	A73	½b lilac silver & multi	.25	.25
271B	A73	½b lilac silver & multi	.25	.25
271C	A73	2b lilac silver & multi	.90	.25
271D	A73	3b lilac silver & multi	1.20	.35
271E	A73	4b lilac silver & multi	1.75	.45
f.		Souvenir sheet of 1, silver & multi	7.50	2.00
		Nos. 271-271E (6)	4.60	1.85

Nos. 271D-271E, 271Ef are airmail. No. 271Ef has red Expo '70 imprint in the sheet margin. Nos. 271-271E exist imperf with silver frames. No. 271Ef exists imperf. Values: set, $5.50; souvenir sheet, $9.

Expo '70, Osaka, Japan — A74

Various traditional Japanese puppets.

1970, Mar. 15   Litho.   Perf. 13½

272	A74	¼b gold & multi	.35	.25
272A	A74	½b gold & multi	.35	.25
272B	A74	½b gold & multi	.35	.25
272C	A74	2b gold & multi	.90	.35
272D	A74	3b gold & multi	1.75	.45
272E	A74	4b gold & multi	2.25	.55
		Nos. 272-272E (6)	5.95	2.10

Nos. 272D-272E are airmail. Nos. 272-272E exist with silver frames (Values: perf, $4; imperf, $7), and imperf. with gold frames (Values: perf, $5.50; imperf, $6). Perf. and imperf. souvenir sheets containing 1 No. 272E exist. Values: perf, $7.50; imperf., $11.

World Cup Soccer Championships, Mexico — A75

1970, Apr. 4   Litho.   Perf. 13½

273	A75	Sheet of 9 + label	7.00	2.75
c.		1¾b Uruguay 1930	.35	.25
d.		2b Italy 1934	.45	.25
e.		2¼b France 1938	.50	.25
f.		2½b Brazil 1950	.50	.25
g.		3½b Switzerland 1954	.60	.30
h.		5b Sweden 1968	.60	.30

i.	6b Chile 1962	.60	.30
j.	7b England 1966	.70	.35
k.	8b Mexico 1970	.80	.40

Souvenir Sheets

273A A75	4b Pele	*9.00*	
273B A75	4b Beckenbauer	*10.00*	

Nos. 273g-273k, 273A-273B are airmail. No. 273B exists imperf.

No. 273k and the adjacent label exist with the name ISRAEL showing and also with the name covered with a black overprint.

Opening of New UPU Headquarters, Bern, Switzerland — A76

Country Views and Europa Stamp Designs: 1½b, Austria, Luxembourg, 1956-57 designs. 1¾b, Belgium, Spain, 1958-59 designs. 2¼b, Greece, Portugal, 1960-61 designs. 2½b, Norway, Denmark, 1962-63 designs. 5b, Switzerland, Netherlands, 1964-65 designs. 7b, France, England, 1965-66 Designs. 8b, Germany, Italy, 1968-69 designs. 10b, New UPU Headquarters, 1970 design, UPU emblem.

1970, May 5　Litho.　Perf. 13½

274 A76	Sheet of 8	5.00	2.25
b.	1½b multicolored	.40	.25
c.	1¾b multicolored	.40	.25
d.	2¼b multicolored	.40	.25
e.	2½b multicolored	.40	.25
f.	5b multicolored	.50	.30
g.	7b multicolored	.65	.30
h.	8b multicolored	.75	.35
i.	10b multicolored	1.00	.50

Souvenir Sheet

274A A76	10b Liechtenstein 356	*9.00*	2.00

Nos. 274g-274i, 274A are airmail. No. 274 exists imperf with light orange borders. Value, $7. No. 274A contains one 50x50mm stamp. An imperf. 10b souvenir sheet showing Luxembourg 320 exists. Value, $9.

Apollo 12 — A77

Stages of Apollo 12 Mission: 1b, Lift-off. 1¼b, In Lunar orbit. 1½b, LM approaches landing site. 1½b, 32 hours on Lunar surface. 4b, Lift-off from the Moon. 4½b, Return to Earth. 7b, Splash down. No. 275A, Astronauts on Lunar surface.

1970, May 11　Litho.　Perf. 13½

275 A77	Sheet of 7 + label	5.50	2.25
b.	1b multicolored	.40	.25
c.	1¼b multicolored	.40	.25
d.	1½b multicolored	.40	.25
e.	1½b multicolored	.40	.25
f.	4b multicolored	.65	.30
g.	4½b multicolored	.75	.30
h.	7b multicolored	1.25	.65

Souvenir Sheet

275A A77	4b multicolored	*5.00*	

Nos. 274f-275h, 275A are airmail. No. 275 exists imperf with yellow and gold borders. Value, $6. No. 275A contains one 72x56mm stamp. An imperf 4b souvenir sheet exists with the lunar scene reflected in astronaut's helmet.

World Cup Soccer Championships, Mexico — A78

1970, May 20　Litho.　Perf. 13½

276 A78	Sheet of 6	5.50	2.00
c.	¼b Soviet team	.50	.25
d.	⅓b Brazilian team	.50	.25
e.	½b English team	.50	.25
f.	¾b Italian team	.50	.25
g.	4b German team	.60	.30
h.	4½b Mexican team	.60	.30

Souvenir Sheets

276A A78	6b Stadium	*9.00*	
276B A78	6b Two players	*12.00*	

Nos. 276g-276h, 276A-276B are airmail. Nos. 276A-276B each contain a 57x58mm stamp, and exist imperf. No. 276 exists imperf. with silver borders.

World Cup Soccer Championships, Mexico — A79a

No. 277: Various soccer players, pre-Columbian sculptures. Nos. 277A-277B, Players, World Cup trophy, soccer ball.

1970, May 31　Litho.　Perf. 13½

277 A79a	Sheet of 6	4.50	2.00
c.	1b olive grn & multi	.50	.25
d.	1¼b blue & multi	.50	.25
e.	1½b red lil & multi	.50	.25
f.	1½b grn & multi	.50	.25
g.	3b pink & multi	.60	.30
h.	10b org & multi	.60	.30

Souvenir Sheets

277A A79a	10b grn & multi	*6.00*	
277B A79a	10b red & multi	*8.50*	

Nos. 277g-277h, 277A-277B are airmail. Nos. 277A contains an 85x30mm stamp. No. 277B contains a 49x62mm stamp and exists imperf. No. 277 exists imperf. with light orange background. Value $5. No. 277B also exists imperf. Value $15.

Space '70 Interplanetary Travel A79b

Interplanetary Stations: 1¾b, McDonnell Douglas project 1975-80. 2b, McDonnel Douglas project 1980-85. No. 278A contains one 67x43mm stamp. An imperf 10b souvenir sheet exists with the a space workshop 1975 design. Value, $7.

1970, July 21　Litho.　Perf. 13½

278 A79b	Sheet of 7 + label	4.50	2.25
b.	1¾b silver & multi	.40	.25
c.	2b silver & multi	.40	.25
d.	2½b silver & multi	.40	.25
e.	2½b silver & multi	.40	.25
f.	5b silver & multi	.60	.30
g.	8b silver & multi	.80	.40
h.	10b silver & multi	1.00	.50

Souvenir Sheet

278A A79b	10b multicolored	*6.00*	

Nos. 278f-278h, 278A are airmail. No. 278 exists imperf with gold borders. Value, $5. No. 278A contains one 67x43mm stamp. An imperf 10b souvenir sheet exists with the a space workshop 1975 design. Value, $7.

Opening of New UPU Headquarters, Bern, Switzerland — A79c

New UPU Headquarters and: ⅓b, Post coach. 1¼b, Train. 1½b, Early mail truck. 2b, Biplane. 3½b, Zeppelin. 4½b, Jet plane. 6b, Satellite. No. 279A, Zeppelin and post coach.

1970, Aug. 25　Litho.　Perf. 13½

279 A79c	Sheet of 7 + label	4.50	2.25
b.	⅓b silver & multi	.40	.25
c.	1¼b silver & multi	.40	.25
d.	1½b silver & multi	.40	.25
e.	2b silver & multi	.40	.25
f.	3½b silver & multi	.60	.30
g.	4½b silver & multi	.80	.40
h.	6b silver & multi	1.00	.50

Souvenir Sheet

279A A79c	6b multicolored	*7.00*	

Nos. 279f-279h, 279A are airmail. No. 279 exists imperf with gold borders. Value, $5. No. 279A contains one 44x64mm stamp. An imperf 6b souvenir sheet exists with the a satellite design. Value, $10.

Philympia London 1970 — A79d

Landmarks and stamps: ¼b, Ruins, Greece 163. ½b, Stadium, France 201. ¾b, Statue of Liberty, US719. 1b, Windsor Castle, Great Britain 274. 3b, Statue of She wolf suckling Romulus and Remus, Italy 807. 4b, Tower, Yemen 242C. No. 280A, UPU Headquarters, Germany B89.

1970, Sept. 10　Litho.　Perf. 13½

280 A79d	Sheet of 6	4.25	2.25
b.	¼b greenish silver & multi	.30	.25
c.	½b greenish silver & multi	.35	.25
d.	¾b greenish silver & multi	.40	.25
e.	1b greenish silver & multi	.50	.25
f.	3b greenish silver & multi	.85	.40
g.	4b greenish silver & multi	1.10	.55

Souvenir Sheet

280A A79d	4b multicolored	*7.00*	

Nos. 280g, 280A are airmail. No. 280 exists imperf with brownish silver borders. No. 280A contains one 45x51mm stamp, and also exists imperf. An imperf 4b souvenir sheet exists with Mexico C311.

Revolution, 8th Anniv. — A79e

Still Life Paintings by: No. 281b, Courbet. c, No. 281A, Linared. d, Fantin-Latour. e, Renoir, vert. f, Beert, vert.

1970, Sept. 26　Litho.　Perf. 13

281 A79e	Strip of 5	3.00	
b.-f.	A79e ¼b any single		.60

Souvenir Sheet

281A A79e	10b multicolored	*4.50*	

No. 281 was issued in sheets of 4 strips and also exists imperf.

Arab League, 25th Anniv. — A79f

1970, Oct. 5　Photo.　Perf. 11½x11

282 A79f	5b org, grn & dark pur	.35	—
282A A79f	7b blue, grn & brn	.75	—
282B A79f	16b dark olive grn, grn & chalky blue	1.75	—

Nos. 282-282B exist imperf. A perf. souvenir sheet of one exists containing No. 282B. Value, $4.

Munich, 1972 Summer Olympic Games Host City — A79g

City Landmarks: 1b, Glyptothek. 1¾b, Wittelsbach Fountain. 2½b, Maximilianeum. 3b, National Theater. 3½b, Propylaea. 8b, Nymphenburg Castle. 10b, City Hall. No. 283A, Munich Olympic Tower, vert.

1970, Oct. 15　Litho.　Perf. 13½

283 A79g	Sheet of 7 + label	4.50	2.25
b.	1b multicolored	.40	.25
c.	1¾b multicolored	.45	.25
d.	2½b multicolored	.45	.25
e.	3b multicolored	.50	.25
f.	3½b multicolored	.50	.25
g.	8b multicolored	.80	.40
h.	10b multicolored	.90	.45

Souvenir Sheet

283A A79g	10b multicolored	*3.50*	

Nos. 283g-283h, 283A are airmail. No. 283 exists imperf with olive inscriptions at top. Value, $5. No. 283A contains one 30x96mm stamp. An imperf 10b souvenir sheet exists with the Marienplatz.

Sapporo, 1972 Winter Olympic Games Host City — A79h

City Landmarks: 1½b, Sapporor City. 2½b, Olympic Skating Center. 4½b, Makomanai Indoor Ice Arena. 5b, Main Stadium. 7b, Olympic Village. 8b, Bobsled and Luge Courses. 10b, Olympic Jump Hill. No. 283A, Ski Jumper, vert.

1970, Nov. 16　Litho.　Perf. 13½

284 A79h	Sheet of 7 + 2 labels	4.00	2.25
b.	1½b silver & multi	.30	.25
c.	2½b silver & multi	.30	.25
d.	4½b silver & multi	.45	.25
e.	5b silver & multi	.45	.25
f.	7b silver & multi	.60	.30
g.	8b silver & multi	.60	.30

h. 10b multicolored .80 .40

Souvenir Sheet

284A A79h 4b multicolored 5.00

Nos. 284g-284h, 284A are airmail. No. 284 exists imperf with gold frames and inscriptions. No. 284A contains one 54x74mm stamp. An imperf 4b souvenir sheet exists with a map and speed skater.

German Olympic Medalists — A79i

Medalists: No. 285, 1896-1908 medalists. No. 285A, 1908-1932 medalists. No. 285B, 1936-1956 medalists. No. 285C, 1956-1964 medalists. No. 285D, 1968 medalists, Sapporo & Munich emblems. No. 285E, Summer Olympic medals.

1970, Dec. 15   Litho.   Perf. 13½

285	A79i	¼b	red lilac & multi	.25 .25
285A	A79i	½b	red lilac & multi	.25 .25
285B	A79i	½b	red lilac & multi	.25 .25
285C	A79i	1½b	red lilac & multi	.25 .25
285D	A79i	6b	red lilac & multi	3.00 1.25
		Nos. 285-285D (5)		4.00 2.25

Souvenir Sheet

285E A79i 6b multicolored 7.00 1.75

Nos. 285D-285E are airmail. No. 285E contains 1 54x54mm stamp and exists imperf. Value, \$9. Nos. 285-285D exist imperf. Value, \$6.

Gamel Abdel Nasser (1918-1970)
A79j

Nassar and: No. 286, Sukarno. No. 286A, Nehru. No. 286B, Arif. No. 286C, Hammarskjold. No. 286D, Eisenhower. No. 286E, Abdarrahman al-Iryani. No. 286F, Farmer. No. 286G, Suez Canal. No. 286H, Industrial site. No. 286I, Aswan High Dam. No. 286J, Oil field. No. 286K, Abu Simbel. No. 286L, World map.
No. 286M, Nassar.

1971, Jan. 6   Litho.   Perf. 11

286	A79j	¼b	multicolored	.25 .25
286A	A79j	¼b	multicolored	.25 .25
286B	A79j	¼b	multicolored	.25 .25
286C	A79j	¼b	multicolored	.25 .25
286D	A79j	½b	multicolored	.25 .25
286E	A79j	½b	multicolored	1.00 .50
286F	A79j	1b	multicolored	.35 .25
286G	A79j	2b	multicolored	.40 .25
286H	A79j	5b	multicolored	.50 .25
286I	A79j	7b	multicolored	.65 .30
286J	A79j	10b	multicolored	1.00 .50
286K	A79j	16b	multicolored	1.35 .75
		Nos. 286-286K (12)		6.50 4.05

Souvenir Sheets

286L	A79j	5b	multicolored	3.00 1.00
286M	A79j	16b	multicolored	7.50

No. 286E is 85x81mm. Nos. 286F-286K, 286M are airmail. Nos. 286-286K exist imperf. No. 286M contains one 59x40mm stamp.

Intl. Sports Contribute to World Peace
A79k

Sports: ¼b, No. 287, Athens, Pierre de Coubertin. ½b, No. 287A, Skier, hurdler. ½b, No. 287B, Figure skater, weightlifter. 2b, Biathlon, Equestrian. 3b, Speed skater, high jump. Nos. 287E-287Ef, Ski jumping, gymnastics.

1971, Jan. 15   Litho.   Perf. 13½

287	A79k	¼b	blk, yel & gold	.25 .25
287A	A79k	½b	blk, grn & gold	.25 .25
287B	A79k	½b	blk, pink & gold	.25 .25
287C	A79k	2b	blk, pur & gold	.50 .25
287D	A79k	3b	blk, yel grn & gold	.75 .35
287E	A79k	4b	blk, blue & gold	1.00 .50
		f. Souvenir sheet of 1		5.00 1.50
		Nos. 287-287E (6)		3.00 1.85

Nos. 287D-287E are airmail. No. 287Ef exists imperf. Nos. 287-287E, 287Ef exist imperf with silver borders. Value: set, \$4.50; souvenir sheet, \$9.

Munich, Olympic Host City — A79l

Composer, opera scenes — No. 288: ½b, Handel, Agrippina. 1¼b, Wagner, Tristan & Isolde. 1¾b, Verdi, Othello. 2¼b, Berg, Lulu. 4½b, Orff, Prometheus. 5b, Wagner, Die Meistersinger. 6b, Mozart, Marriage of Figaro. No. 288A, Richard Wagner (1813-1883), vert.

1971, Feb. 15   Litho.   Perf. 13½

288	A79l	Sheet of 7 + 2 labels		4.50 2.00
b.		½b multicolored		.40 .25
c.		1¼b multicolored		.40 .25
d.		1¾b multicolored		.50 .25
e.		2¼b multicolored		.50 .25
f.		4½b multicolored		.60 .30
g.		5b multicolored		.60 .30
h.		6b multicolored		.75 .35

Souvenir Sheet

288A A79l 6b multicolored 7.00 1.50

Nos. 288g-288h, 288A are airmail. No. 288 exists with light green inscription at top. No. 288A contains one 50x56mm stamp. A 6b imperf. souvenir sheet exists with a portrait of Mozart.

Paintings in Pinakothek Gallery,
Munich — A79m

Paintings — No. 289: ¼b, Sebastian by Holbein. ½b, Count Philippe by Grein. ¾b, Young Man by Dürer. 1½b, O. Krel by Dürer. 2b, Susanna in the Bath by Altdorfer. 4b, C. Fugger by Amberger. 7b, C. Schuch by Leibl. No. 289A, Count Otto von Wittelsbach, horiz.

1971, Mar. 15   Litho.   Perf. 13½

289	A79m	Sheet of 7 + label		4.50
b.		¼b multicolored		.40 .25
c.		½b multicolored		.40 .25
d.		¾b multicolored		.50 .25
e.		1½b multicolored		.45 .25
f.		2b multicolored		.45 .25
g.		4b multicolored		.70 .35
h.		7b multicolored		.90 .45

Souvenir Sheet

289A A79m 4b multicolored 7.00 2.00

Nos. 289g-289h, 289A are airmail. No. 289A contains one 66x46mm stamp. No. 288 exists imperf with inscriptions in light red. A 4b imperf. souvenir sheet exists with Suzanne in the Bath.

Art Type of 1970

Chinese Paintings: ¼b, The Hall of Green Country by Yuan Kiang. ½b, Lady at Her Dressing Table by Sou Han. ½b, The Bodhisattva Wen Tchou. 2b, Gatherer of Simples

at Tchen Wei by Wou Li. 3b, Buddha by Ting Yun. 4b, Li T'ie Kouai by Yen Houei.

1971, Apr. 8   Litho.   Perf. 13½

290	A73	¼b	lilac silver & multi	.25 .25
290A	A73	½b	lilac silver & multi	.25 .25
290B	A73	½b	lilac silver & multi	.25 .25
290C	A73	2b	lilac silver & multi	.80 .25
290D	A73	3b	lilac silver & multi	1.25 .35
290E	A73	4b	lilac silver & multi	1.50 .50
		f. Souvenir sheet of 1		7.00 1.50
		Nos. 290-290E (6)		4.30 1.85

Nos. 290D-290E, 290Ef are airmail. Stamp in No. 290Ef has white borders. No. 290Ef exists imperf. Value, \$9.

UN, 25th
Anniv.
A79n

1971, Apr. 4   Photo.   Perf. 11½x11

291	A79n	5b	dk ol grn, grn & dk vio	.55 .45
291A	A79n	7b	bl, grn & dk bl	.90 .75

Exist imperf. Value \$6.

Souvenir Sheet
Imperf

291B A79n 16b multicolored 2.00 1.50

Winter Olympic Games, Sapporo
A79o

Early Winter Sports: ¼b, Woman on sled. ½b, Skier with bow. 1b, Woman on sled, diff. 1½b, Archer on ice skates. 2b, Man on ice skates. 3b, Woman on ice skates. 4b, Man on skis. No. 292A, Sapporo Games emblem, snowflakes, horiz.

1971, Apr. 15   Litho.   Perf. 13¼

292	A79o	Sheet of 7 + label		3.75 2.25
b.		¼b silver & multi		.40 .25
c.		½b silver & multi		.40 .25
d.		1b silver & multi		.40 .25
e.		1½b silver & multi		.50 .25
f.		2b silver & multi		.60 .30
g.		3b silver & multi		.80 .40
h.		4b silver & multi		.80 .40

Souvenir Sheet

292A A79o 10b multicolored 5.00 1.25

Nos. 292g-292h, 292A are airmail. No. 292A contains one 66x61mm stamp. No. 292 exists imperf with grayish green borders. A 10b imperf. souvenir sheet exists with Snow Festival.

Summer Olympic Games, Munich
A79p

Early Summer Sports: ½b, Swimming. 1b, Stone throwing. 1½b, Walking, diff. 1¾b, Wrestling. 2¼b, Crossbow. 4½b, Jousting. 7b,

Handball. 10b, Gymnastics. No. 293A, Stone throwing, vert.

1971, May 15   Litho.   Perf. 13½

293	A79p	Sheet of 8		4.50 2.25
b.		½b gold & multi		.30 .25
c.		1b gold & multi		.30 .25
d.		1½b gold & multi		.30 .25
e.		1¾b gold & multi		.40 .25
f.		2¼b gold & multi		.40 .30
g.		4½b gold & multi		.70 .35
h.		7b gold & multi		.90 .45
i.		10b gold & multi		1.25 .65

Souvenir Sheet

293A A79p 10b multicolored 5.00 1.50

Nos. 293g-293i, 293A are airmail. No. 293A contains one 44x78mm stamp. No. 293 exists imperf with silver borders. A 10b imperf. souvenir sheet exists with swimmers.

Conquest of Mars — A79q

Stages of Mars exploration: ¼b, Assembly of Photon rocket in Earth orbit. ½b, Lunar Base, preparations for Mars mission. ½b, Photon rocket in Lunar orbit. ¾b, Departure for Mars. 3b, In orbit around Phobos. 3½b, Three men on Mars. 6b, Upper stage of Photon rocket returns to Earth. No. 294A, Daedalus, rocket shuttle, Phobos, Mars.

1971, June 15   Litho.   Perf. 13½

294	A79q	Sheet of 7 + label		4.00 2.25
b.		¼b orange & multi		.40 .25
c.		½b orange & multi		.40 .25
d.		½b orange & multi		.40 .25
e.		¾b orange & multi		.40 .25
f.		3b orange & multi		.60 .30
g.		3½b orange & multi		.70 .35
h.		6b orange & multi		.90 .45

Souvenir Sheet

294A A79q 6b multicolored 5.00 1.50

Nos. 294f-294h, 294A are airmail. No. 294A contains one 70x51mm stamp. No. 294 exists imperf with light blue borders. A 6b imperf. souvenir sheet exists with Galileo.

Ludwig van Beethoven, Birth Bicent.
A79r

Designs: No. 295h, Recital with Beethoven. No. 295i, Chamber music evening. No. 295j, Portrait of Beethoven, Schubert at piano. No. 295k, View of Bonn. No. 295l, View of Vienna. No. 295m, Beethoven's study. 1b, Birth of Beethoven. 2b, Josephine von Brunswick. 5b, Young Beethoven. 7b, 10b, 16b, Beethoven at piano, various.

1971, June 23   Litho.   Perf. 12

295	A79r	Sheet of 3		1.50
h.		¼b bl, blk & grn		.50
i.		¼b org, blk & pink		.50
j.		½b blue & multi		.50
295A	A79r	Sheet of 3 + 3 labels		1.50
k.		¼b multicolored		.50
l.		¼b multicolored		.50
m.		½b multicolored		.50
295B	A79r	1b	multicolored	.40
295C	A79r	2b	multicolored	.50
295D	A79r	5b	multicolored	.60
295E	A79r	7b	multicolored	.80
295F	A79r	10b	multicolored	.80
295G	A79r	16b	multicolored	1.00
		Nos. 295-296G (8)		7.10

No. 295A contains 2 80x49mm stamps and 1 40x49mm stamp. Imperf. 5b and 16b souvenir sheets exist.
Nos. 295B-295G are airmail.

Art Type of 1970

Indian Paintings: ¼b, Ibrahim Adil Shah II of Bijapur. ½b, Head of Apsaras. ½b, Kamodi Ragini. 2b, Virahini. 3b, Krishna and Radha. 4b, Girls Swimming in a Lotus Pond.

1971, Apr. 8   **Litho.**   **Perf. 13½**
296	A73	¼b lilac silver & multi	.25	.25
296A	A73	½b lilac silver & multi	.25	.25
296B	A73	½b lilac silver & multi	.25	.25
296C	A73	2b lilac silver & multi	.90	.25
296D	A73	3b lilac silver & multi	1.20	.35
296E	A73	4b lilac silver & multi	1.75	.50
	f.	Souvenir sheet of 1	7.00	1.50
		Nos. 296-296E (6)	4.60	1.85

Nos. 296D-296E, 296Ef are airmail. Stamp in No. 296Ef has white borders. No. 296Ef exists imperf.

Olympic Sailing, Kiel, Germany
A79s

Olympic sailing yachts: ¼b, 16.5m class, blue spinnaker. ½b, 5.5m class. 1¼b, 16.5m class, white spinnaker.2b, Belouga class. 3b, Flying Dutchman class. 4b, Finn class. No. 297A, Finn class, diff.

1971, Sept. 1   **Litho.**   **Perf. 13½**
297	A79s	Sheet of 6	4.00	1.65
	b.	¼b lilac silver & multi	.40	.25
	c.	½b lilac silver & multi	.40	.25
	d.	1¼b lilac silver & multi	.40	.25
	e.	2b lilac silver & multi	.60	.30
	f.	3b lilac silver & multi	.65	.30
	g.	4b lilac silver & multi	.80	.40

Souvenir Sheet

297A	A79s	4b multicolored	7.00	1.50

Nos. 297g, 297A are airmail. No. 297A contains one 42x64mm stamp and also exists imperf. No. 297exists imperf with gold borders.

1972 Winter Olympic Games, Sapporo
A79t

Olympic Sports: ½b, Downhill skiing. ¾b, Women's figure skating. 1¼b, 2-man bobsled. 1¾b, Speed skating. 2¼b, Ski jumping. 3½b, Cross-country skiing. 6b, Pairs figure skating. No. 298A, Ski jumping, diff.

1971, Oct. 2   **Litho.**   **Perf. 13½**
298		Sheet of 7 + label	4.50
	b.	½b silver & multi	.45
	c.	¾b silver & multi	.45
	d.	1¼b silver & multi	.45
	e.	1¾b silver & multi	.60
	f.	2¼b silver & multi	.60
	g.	3½b silver & multi	.75
	h.	6b silver & multi	1.00

Souvenir Sheet

298A	A79t	6b multicolored	5.00	1.25

Nos. 298g-298h, 298A are airmail. No. 298A contains one 73x50mm stamp. No. 298 exists imperf with gray violet borders. Value, $5. A 6b imperf. souvenir sheet exists with Sapporo emblems. Value, $9.

Art Type of 1970

Persian Paintings: ¼b, Murakka Gulshan. ½b, Shanname de Baisonghor. ½b, Djami al Tawarikh (drummers). 2b, Murakka Gulshan (fighting bear) . 3b, Djami al Tawarikh (kneeling). 4b, Shanname de Baisonghor (musicians).

1971, Oct. 15   **Litho.**   **Perf. 13½**
299	A73	¼b lilac silver & multi	.25	.25
299A	A73	½b lilac silver & multi	.25	.25
299B	A73	½b lilac silver & multi	.25	.25
299C	A73	2b lilac silver & multi	.90	.25
299D	A73	3b lilac silver & multi	1.20	.35
299E	A73	4b lilac silver & multi	2.00	.50
	f.	Souvenir sheet of 1	7.00	1.50
		Nos. 299-299E (6)	4.85	1.85

Nos. 299D-299E, 299Ef are airmail. Stamp in No. 299Ef has white borders and exists imperf.

1972 Summer Olympic Games,
Munich — A79u

Olympic Sports: ¾b, Women's hurdles. 1½b, Discus. 2½. Equestrian. 3½b, Gymnastics. 5b, Shooting. 6b, Rowing. 8b, Diving. No. 300A, Sprinter at start.

1971, Nov. 4   **Litho.**   **Perf. 13½**
300	A79u	Sheet of 7 + label	4.00	2.25
	b.	¾b gold & multi	.40	.25
	c.	1½b gold & multi	.40	.25
	d.	2½b gold & multi	.50	.25
	e.	3½b gold & multi	.50	.25
	f.	5b gold & multi	.60	.30
	g.	6b gold & multi	.60	.30
	h.	8b gold & multi	.75	.35

Souvenir Sheet

300A	A79u	6b multicolored	7.00	1.25

Nos. 300g-300h, 300A are airmail. No. 300A contains one 44x59mm stamp. No. 300 exists imperf with silver gray borders. A 6b imperf. souvenir sheet exists with equestrian design.

Olympic Medalists Type of 1970 in Diamond Shape

Italian Medalists: No. 301, 1908-1924 medalists. No. 301A, 1928-1936 medalists. No. 301B, 1952-1956 medalists. No. 301C, 1960-1968 medalists. No. 301D, 1968 medalists, Sapporo, Munich emblems. No. 301E, Emblesm of Rome, Tokyo and Munich Games.

1971, Dec. 3   **Litho.**   **Perf. 13½**
301	A79i	¼b silver & multi	.25	.25
301A	A79i	¼b silver & multi	.25	.25
301B	A79i	½b silver & multi	.25	.25
301C	A79i	½b silver & multi	.25	.25
301D	A79i	22b silver & multi	3.00	1.25
		Nos. 301-301D (5)	4.00	2.25

Souvenir Sheet

301E	A79i	14b multicolored	7.00	1.75

Nos. 301D-301E are airmail. No. 301E contains 1 54x54mm stamp. Nos. 301-301D exist imperf. with light green borders. Value, $3.50. A 14b imperf. souvenir sheet with different Olympic emblems exists. Value, $9.

Revolution, 9th Anniv. — A79v

Designs: 7b, View of Sana'a. 18b, Military parade. 24b, Mosque in Sana'a.

1972, Feb. 29   **Perf. 13**
302	A79v	7b multi	1.10
302A	A79v	18b multi	2.25
302B	A79v	24b multi	3.25
		Nos. 302-302B (3)	6.60

An imperf souvenir sheet containing No. 302B exists. Value $3.50.

Arab Postal
Union, 25th
Anniv. —
A79w

1972, Mar. 18   **Perf. 13**
303	A79v	3b multi	.40
303A	A79w	7b multi	.80
303B	A79w	10b multi	1.50
		Nos. 303-303B (3)	2.70

A 16b souvenir sheet also exists. Value $2.50.

Olympic Medalists Type of 1970 in Diamond Shape

French Medalists: 2b, 1896-1912 medalists. 3b, 1920-1932 medalists. 4b, 1936-1964 medalists. 10b, 1968 medalists, Sapporo, Munich emblems. No. 304D, Olympic Stadia from Tokyo, Mexico City and Munich Games.

1972, Apr. 4   **Litho.**   **Perf. 13½**
304	A79i	2b bl grey & multi	.35	.25
304A	A79i	3b bl grey & multi	.60	.30
304B	A79i	4b bl grey & multi	.90	.35
304C	A79i	10b bl grey & multi	2.25	.75
		Nos. 304-304C (4)	4.10	1.65

Souvenir Sheet

304D	A79i	4b multicolored	7.00	1.50

Nos. 304B-304D are airmail. No. 304D contains 1 50x33mm stamp. Nos. 304-304C exist imperf. with light blue borders. Value, $5. A 4b imperf. souvenir sheet with different Olympic venues exists. Value, $10.

Art Treasures — A79x

Designs: 1b, Azure stone vase, 1583. 1¼b, Siren of the "Nautilus Cup," 1822. 1½b, Neptune vase. 1½b, Emperor Rudolph II's crown, 1602. 3b, Statue of Balthazar, 1724. 4½b, Catherine the Great's carriage, 1779. 7b, Statue of St. George. 6b, The Bath of Diana.

1972, July 31   **Litho.**   **Perf. 13x13½**
305	A79x	1b bluish sil & multi	.25	.25
305A	A79x	1¼b bluish sil & multi	.30	.25
305B	A79x	1½b bluish sil & multi	.35	.25
305C	A79x	1½b bluish sil & multi	.45	.25
305D	A79x	3b bluish sil & multi	.85	.30
305E	A79x	4½b bluish sil & multi	1.40	.40
305F	A79x	7b bluish sil & multi	1.50	.50
		Nos. 305-305F (7)	5.10	2.20

Souvenir Sheet

305G	A79x	6b multicolored	5.00	2.00

Nos. 305D-305F are airmail. An imperf 6b souvenir sheets with a Jasper Cup, Florence, exists. Value, $9.

10th anniv. of
Revolution
A80

1972, Nov. 25   **Photo.**   **Perf. 13**
306	A80	7b lt blue, blk & multi	.75	.50
307	A80	10b gray, blk & multi	1.00	.65
		Nos. 306-307,C40 (3)	5.75	4.65

For surcharge see No. 318.

25th Anniv. of
WHO — A81

1972, Dec. 1   **Litho.**
308	A81	2b lt yel grn & multi	.30	.35
308A	A81	21b sky blue & multi	2.00	1.40
308B	A81	37b red lilac & multi	4.00	2.25
		Nos. 308-308B (3)	6.30	4.00

For surcharge see No. 341A.

Burning of Al-Aqsa Mosque, 2nd
Anniv. — A82

1972, Jan. 1   **Photo.**   **Perf. 13½**
309	A82	7b lt bl, blk & multi	1.00	.60
309A	A82	18b lt bl, blk & multi	2.00	1.10
		Nos. 309-309A,C41 (3)	6.00	4.20

For surcharges see Nos. 319, 341.

25th Anniv. of UNICEF — A83

1973, Jan. 15   **Photo.**   **Perf. 13**
310	A83	7b lt bl, blk & multi	1.10	.65
310A	A83	10b lt bl, blk & multi	1.60	.80
		Nos. 310-310A,C42 (3)	4.60	2.95

For surcharge see No. C46.

UPU Cent. — A84

1974, Nov. 20   Photo.   Perf. 14
311   A84 10b multicolored   .60   .40
311A A84 30b multicolored   1.25 1.50
311B A84 40b multicolored   1.75 1.90
    Nos. 311-311B (3)   3.60 3.80

For surcharge see No. 341B.

10th World Hunger Program — A85

1975, Feb. 5   Litho.   Perf. 13½
313   A85 10b multicolored   .50   .25
314   A85 30b multicolored   1.50 1.00
315   A85 63b multicolored   3.00 2.00
    Nos. 313-315 (3)   5.00 3.25

12th Anniv. of Revolution A86

1975, Sept. 25
316   A86 25f Janad Mosque   .60   .35
317   A86 75f Althawra Hospital   1.90   .65

Nos. 306, 309 Surcharged in Black with New Values and Bars

1975, Nov. 15   Photo.   Perf. 13½
318   A80 75f on 7b   —   —
319   A82 278f on 7b   —   —

Telephone Cent. — A87

1976, Mar. 10   Litho.   Perf. 14½
320   A87 25f brt pink & blk   .55   .55
321   A87 75f lt grn & blk   1.60 1.60
322   A87 160f lt bl & blk   2.75 2.75
    a. Souvenir sheet of 1   3.50 3.00
    Nos. 320-322 (3)   4.90 4.90

No. 322a exists both perf. and imperf. Same value.

Coffee Bean Branch — A88

1976, Apr. 25   Perf. 14
323   A88 1f dull lilac   .25   .25
324   A88 3f pale gray   .25   .25
325   A88 5f lt bl grn   .25   .25
326   A88 10f bis brn   .25   .25
327   A88 25f golden brn   .30   .25
328   A88 50f brt plum   .65   .40
329   A88 75f dull pink   1.25   .60

Size: 22x30mm
Perf. 14½
330   A88 1r sky blue   2.00   .70
331   A88 1.50r red lilac   3.00 1.40
332   A88 2r light grn   4.75 1.40
333   A88 5r yel org   12.00 3.00
    Nos. 323-333 (11)   24.95 8.75

For surcharges see Nos. 403-407, 592.

2nd Anniv. of Reformation Movement — A89

1976, June 13   Photo.   Perf. 12x12½
334   A89 75f Industrial Park   1.50 1.50
335   A89 135f Forestry   2.50 2.50

Souvenir Sheet
336   A89 135f Forestry   3.50 3.50

No. 336 contains one stamp (32x47mm).

14th Anniv. of Revolution — A90

Designs: 25f, Natl. Institute of Public Administration. 75f, Housing and population census. 160f, Sanaa University emblem.

1976, Sept. 26   Photo.   Perf. 12x12½
337   A90 25f buff & multi   .65   .65
338   A90 75f yel bis & multi   1.75 1.75
339   A90 160f pale grn & multi   3.25 3.25
    Nos. 337-339 (3)   5.65 5.65

Souvenir Sheet
340   A90 160f pale grn & multi   5.00 5.00

No. 340 contains one stamp (33x49mm).

No. 309 Surcharged in Black

1976
341   A82 75f on 7b   —   —

Nos. 308A, 311B Surcharged in Black or Red

1976   Photo.   Perf. 14
341A A81 75f on 21b (R)   —   —
341B A84 160f on 40b   —   —

Size and location of surcharge varies.

3rd Anniv. of Correction Movement — A91

1977   Photo.   Perf. 14
342   A91 25f Dish antenna   .45   .30
343   A91 75f Computer, technician   1.25   .65
    a. Miniature sheet of 1   4.00 4.00

15th Anniv. of September Revolution — A92

1977   Photo.   Perf. 13½
344   A92 25f Sa'ada-San'a Road   .45   .35
345   A92 75f Television, Transmitting tower   1.25   .85
346   A92 160f like 25f   2.50 2.00
    a. Souvenir sheet of 1   5.00 5.00
    Nos. 344-346 (3)   4.20 3.20

25th Anniv. of Arab Postal Union — A93

1978   Perf. 14
347   A93 25f lt yel grn & multi   .90   .75
348   A93 60f bis & multi   2.25 1.60
    a. Miniature sheet of 1   5.00 4.50

Pres. Hamdi — A94

1978   Perf. 11½
349   A94 25f dk grn & blk   .35   .35
350   A94 75f ultra & blk   1.25 1.10
351   A94 160f brn & blk   2.50 1.90
    a. Miniature sheet of 1   5.00 5.00
    Nos. 349-351 (3)   4.10 3.35

30th Anniv. of ICAO (1977) A95

1979, Nov. 15   Photo.   Perf. 13½
352   A95 75f multi   2.10 1.00
353   A95 135f multi   3.25 1.60
    a. Miniature sheet of 1   5.00 4.50

Book, World Map, Arab Achievements — A96

1979, Dec. 1   Perf. 14
354   A96 25f multi   .60   .35
355   A96 75f multi   1.50 1.00
    a. Souvenir sheet of 1   3.75 3.25

A97

1980, Jan. 1
356   A97 75f multi   2.00 1.00
357   A97 135f multi, horiz.   3.00 1.60
    a. Miniature sheet of 1   5.00 4.50

12th World Telecommunications Day, May 17, 1979.

A98

Dome of the Rock.

1980   Photo.   Perf. 14
358   A98 5f brt bl & multi   .50   .35
359   A98 10f yel & multi   1.00   .65

Palestinian fighters and their families.

Argentina World Cup — A99

World Cup emblem and various players.

1980, Mar. 30
360   A99 25f gold & multi   .60   .40
361   A99 30f gold & multi   .60   .30
362   A99 35f gold & multi   .75   .40
363   A99 50f gold & multi   1.05   .50
    Nos. 360-363,C49-C52 (8)   9.80 4.80

Issued in sheets of 8.
Exist imperf. (Value, set $70) and in souvenir sheets (Value, set $60).

International Year of the Child — A100

1980, Apr. 1   Perf. 13½
364   A100 25f Girl, bird   1.75 .50
365   A100 50f Girl, bird, diff.   2.50 .80
366   A100 75f Boy, butterfly, flower 2.60 1.25
    Nos. 364-366,C53-C55 (6)   18.85 6.80

Issued in sheets of 6.
Exist imperf. (Value, set $60) and in souvenir sheets (Value, set $60).

World Scouting Jamboree — A101

25f, Fishing. 35f, Troup, aircraft. 40f, Mounted bugler, flag. 50f, Telescope, night sky.

1980, May 1　　**Perf. 13½x14**
367	A101	25f multicolored	.60	.30
368	A101	35f multicolored	1.40	.50
369	A101	40f multicolored	1.40	.50
370	A101	50f multicolored	1.50	.65
	Nos. 367-370,C56-C58 (7)		13.05	5.35

Issued in sheets of 6.
Exist imperf. (Value, set $60) and in souvenir sheets (Value, set $60).

Argentina 1978 World Cup
Winners — A102

World cup emblem and various soccer players.

1980, June 1　　**Perf. 14**
371	A102	25f gold & multi	.60	.25
372	A102	30f gold & multi	.90	.30
373	A102	35f gold & multi	.90	.40
374	A102	50f gold & multi	1.35	.40
	Nos. 371-374,C59-C62 (8)		12.00	4.35

Exist imperf. (Value, set $60) and in souvenir sheets (Value, set $60).

Hegira, 1400th Anniv. — A102a

Designs: 160f, Outside view.

1980, July 1　　**Perf. 13½**
375	A102a	25f blk & multi	.40	.25
376	A102a	75f car rose & multi	1.40	.60
377	A102a	160f blk & multi	2.40	.75
a.	Miniature sheet of 1		5.00	4.00
	Nos. 375-377 (3)		4.20	1.60

18th Anniv.
of
September
Revolution
A103

A104

1980, Sept. 26　　**Perf. 13½**
378	A103	25f multi	.35	.25
379	A104	75f multi	1.10	.65

Souvenir Sheet
380	100f multi	3.00	2.00

No. 380 contains one stamp combining designs A103 and A104 (42x34mm).

Al Aqsa
Mosque
A105

Mosques: 25f, Al-Rawda entrance. 100f, Al-Nabwi. 160f, Al-Haram.

1980, Nov. 6　　**Photo.**　　**Perf. 13½**
381	A105	25f multi	.40	.25
382	A105	75f multi	.90	.50
383	A105	100f multi	2.25	.65
384	A105	160f multi	3.00	1.00
	Nos. 381-384 (4)		6.55	2.40

Souvenir Sheet
385	160f multi	6.00	3.25

Islamic Postal Systems Week and Hegira. No. 385 contains one stamp (109x47mm) combining designs of Nos. 382-384.

Intl. Palestinian
Solidarity
Day — A106

1980, Nov. 29
386	A106	25f lt bl & multi	.30	.25
387	A106	75f ver & multi	.90	.90

Inscribed 1979.

9th Arab Archaeological
Conference — A107

1981, Mar. 1　　**Perf. 13½**
388	A107	75f Al Aamiriya Mosque	1.00	.60
389	A107	125f Al Hadi Mosque	1.40	.85
a.	Souvenir sheet of 2, #388-389		3.00	3.00

1980 World
Tourism
Conference,
Manila
A108

1981, Apr. 1
390	A108	25f shown	.25	.25
391	A108	75f Mosque, houses	.55	.30
392	A108	100f Columns, horiz.	.70	.45
393	A108	135f Bridge	.80	.60
394	A108	160f View of San'a, horiz.	1.20	.60
a.	Miniature sheet of 1		5.00	5.00
	Nos. 390-394 (5)		3.50	2.20

Sir Rowland Hill (1795-1879), Postage
Stamp Inventor — A109

25f, Portrait, UPU emblem. 30f, Emblem, stamp of 1963. 50f, Portrait, stamps. 75f, Portrait, globe, jet. 100f, Portrait, stamp collection. 150f, Jets, No. 322.
No. 401, Portrait, vert. No. 402, Portrait, diff.

1981, Sept. 15　　**Litho.**　　**Perf. 14**
395	A109	25f multicolored	.90	.50
396	A109	30f multicolored	1.05	.70
397	A109	50f multicolored	1.50	1.00
398	A109	75f multicolored	2.40	1.75
399	A109	100f multicolored	3.25	2.00
400	A109	150f multicolored	6.00	3.00
	Nos. 395-400 (6)		15.10	8.95

Souvenir Sheets
401	A109	200f multicolored	10.00

Imperf
402	A109	200f multicolored	20.00

Nos. 398-402 are airmail.
Nos. 395-400 exist imperf and in souvenir sheets (Value, set $45).

Nos. 323-327 Surcharged

1981
403	A88	125f on 1f	1.25	.70
404	A88	150f on 3f	1.50	.85
405	A88	325f on 5f	3.50	2.00
406	A88	350f on 10f	4.00	2.00
407	A88	375f on 25f	4.25	2.50
	Nos. 403-407 (5)		14.50	8.05

20th Anniv. of Yemen Airways — A110

1983, Apr. 1　　**Litho.**　　**Perf. 14**
408	A110	75f yel & multi	1.00	.50
409	A110	125f red & multi	1.75	.80
410	A110	325f bl & multi	4.00	2.00
	Nos. 408-410 (3)		6.75	3.30

Folk Costumes — A111

No. 411, Woman carrying waterjar. No. 412, Women, sheep. No. 413, Man, donkeys. No. 414, Man in town square. No. 415, Women, child, well. No. 416, Scholar. No. 417, Woman on beach. No. 418, Camel-drawn plow. No. 419, Woman. No. 420, Man.

1983, May 1
411	A111	50f multicolored	2.50	1.20
412	A111	50f multicolored	2.50	1.20
413	A111	50f multicolored	2.50	1.20
414	A111	50f multicolored	2.50	1.20
415	A111	75f multicolored	3.75	2.00
416	A111	75f multicolored	3.75	2.00
417	A111	75f multicolored	3.75	2.00
418	A111	75f multicolored	3.75	2.00
	Nos. 411-418 (8)		25.00	12.80

Souvenir Sheets
419	A111	200f multicolored	8.00

Imperf
420	A111	200f multicolored	8.00

#411-414 vert. #415-420 are airmail.
Nos. 411-418 exist imperf. (Value, set $60) and in souvenir sheets (Value, set $60).

Sept. 26th Revolution, 20th Anniv.
(1982) — A112

1983, Sept. 26　　**Litho.**　　**Perf. 14**
421	A112	100f Communications	1.25	.75
422	A112	150f Literacy	1.75	1.10
423	A112	325f Educational development	4.00	2.40
a.	Souvenir sheet of 2, #422, 423		8.00	
424	A112	400f Independence	6.00	3.00
	Nos. 421-424 (4)		13.00	7.25

World Communications Year — A113

1983, Dec. 15
425	A113	150f lt bl & multi	2.50	1.20
426	A113	325f lt grn & multi	5.00	2.75
a.	Souvenir sheet of 1		9.00	

Sept. 26 Revolution, 21st
Anniv. — A114

1984, Apr. 1　　**Litho.**　　**Perf. 14**
427	A114	100f shown	1.75	.85
428	A114	150f Fist, statue	2.00	1.25
429	A114	325f Gate, tank	4.00	2.00
a.	Souvenir sheet of 1		8.00	
	Nos. 427-429 (3)		7.75	4.10

Israel
Aggression
Day — A115

1984, Sept. 7
430	A115	150f multi	1.75	.75
431	A115	325f multi	4.50	2.25

Size: 91x120mm

Imperf
432	A115	325f multi	25.00
	Nos. 430-432 (3)	31.25	3.00

Sept. 26 Revolution, 22nd
Anniv. — A116

1985, Oct. 1
433	A116	50f Triumphal Arch	.75	.35
434	A116	150f San'a Castle walls	2.00	1.25
435	A116	325f Stadium, Govt. Palace, San'a	4.50	2.50
a.	Souvenir sheet of 1		8.00	
	Nos. 433-435 (3)		7.25	4.10

Intl. Anti-Apartheid Year (1978) — A117

1985, Jan. 1
436	A117	150f dp ver & multi	2.00	.90
437	A117	325f grn & multi	4.75	2.40
a.		Souvenir sheet of 1	9.00	

Intl. Civil Aviation Org., 40th Anniv. A118

1985, Sept. 20
438	A118	25f multi	.40	.25
439	A118	50f multi	.60	.25
440	A118	150f multi	1.50	.75
441	A118	325f multi	3.50	1.50
a.		Souvenir sheet of 1	6.00	8.00
		Nos. 438-441 (4)	6.00	2.75

Arabsat Satellite, 1st Anniv. A119

1986, Apr. 15   Litho.   Perf. 14
442	A119	150f multi	2.75	1.25
443	A119	325f multi	6.00	2.50
a.		Souvenir sheet of 1	9.50	

World Telecommunications, 120th Anniv. — A120

1986, May 1
444	A120	150f multi	2.75	1.25
445	A120	325f multi	6.00	2.50
a.		Souvenir sheet of 1	9.00	

General People's Conference, 2nd Anniv. — A121

1986, May 1
446	A121	150f multi	2.75	1.25
447	A121	325f multi	5.00	2.50
a.		Souvenir sheet of 1	6.00	5.00

A122

1986, July 1
448	A122	150f multi	7.25	1.25
449	A122	325f multi	5.00	2.50
a.		Souvenir sheet of 1	6.00	5.00

15th Islamic Foreign Ministers' Conference, San'a, Dec. 18-22, 1984.

A123

1986, Oct. 1
450	A123	150f multi	2.50	1.25
451	A123	325f multi	4.50	2.25
a.		Souvenir sheet of 1	6.00	5.00

UN 40th anniv.

Arab League, 39th Anniv. A124

1986, Nov. 15
452	A124	150f multi	2.75	1.50
453	A124	325f multi	5.00	3.00

Natl. Arms A125

1987, Sept. 26   Litho.   Perf. 14
454	A125	100f multi	1.00	.30
455	A125	150f multi	1.40	.70
456	A125	425f multi	4.00	2.00
a.		Souvenir sheet of 1	4.50	3.50
457	A125	450f multi	4.50	2.25
		Nos. 454-457 (4)	10.90	5.25

Sept. 26th Revolution, 25th anniv. For surcharge see No. 593.

Intl. Youth Year (1985) A126

1987, Oct. 15   Perf. 13x13½
458	A126	150f multi	2.00
459	A126	425f multi	4.00
a.		Souvenir sheet of 1	5.00

For surcharge see No. C150.

Drilling of the Republic's First Oil Well, 1984 A127

1987, Nov. 1   Perf. 14
460	A127	150f Oil derrick	2.50
461	A127	425f Derrick, refinery	4.00
a.		Souvenir sheet of 1	5.00

For surcharge see No. C151.

General Population and Housing Census, 1986 A128

1987, Dec. 1
462	A128	150f multi	2.50	1.25
463	A128	425f multi	4.50	2.25
a.		Souvenir sheet of 1	5.50	3.00

For surcharge see No. C152.

1986 World Cup Soccer Championships, Mexico — A129

Designs: 100f, 150f, Match scenes, vert. 425f, Match scene and Pique, character trademark.

1988, Jan. 1   Litho.   Perf. 14
464	A129	100f multi	1.00	.60
465	A129	150f multi, diff.	1.50	1.00
466	A129	325f multi	3.50	1.50
a.		Souvenir sheet of 1	6.00	3.00
		Nos. 464-466 (3)	6.00	3.10

For surcharge see No. C153.

17th Scouting Conference, San'a — A130

1988, Mar. 1   Litho.   Perf. 14
467	A130	25f Skin diving	.35	.25
468	A130	30f Table tennis	.45	.25
469	A130	40f Tennis	.55	.30
470	A130	50f Two scouts, flag	.65	.30
471	A130	60f Volleyball	.75	.35
472	A130	100f Tug-of-war	1.20	.60
473	A130	150f Basketball	1.75	.75
474	A130	425f Archery	5.00	2.00
		Nos. 467-474 (8)	10.70	4.80

Souvenir Sheet
475	A130	425f Scout, emblem, hand sign	5.50	4.00

For surcharge see No. C154.

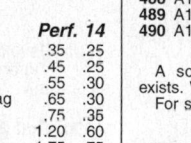

San'a Preservation — A131

1988, May 1   Litho.   Perf. 14
476	A131	25f multicolored	.45	.25
477	A131	50f multicolored	.85	.45
478	A131	100f multicolored	1.40	.70
479	A131	150f multicolored	1.90	1.00
480	A131	425f multicolored	4.50	2.25
a.		Souvenir sheet of 1	6.00	5.00
		Nos. 476-480 (5)	9.10	4.65

For surcharge see No. 594.

Battle of Hattin, 800th Anniv. in 1987 A132

1988   Litho.   Perf. 14
482	A132	150f multicolored	2.75	1.40
483	A132	425f multicolored	6.75	3.50
a.		Souvenir sheet	10.00	10.00

For surcharge see No. C155.

Arab Telecommunication Day, 1987 — A133

1988
484	A133	100f multicolored	1.50	.75
485	A133	150f multicolored	2.25	1.10
486	A133	425f multicolored	5.25	2.50
a.		Souvenir sheet	9.00	9.00
		Nos. 484-486 (3)	9.00	4.35

For surcharge see No. C156.

A134

Sept. 26 Revolution, 26th Anniv. — A134a

1989, Sept. 30
487	A134	300f multicolored	1.25	.60
488	A134	375f multicolored	1.75	1.00
489	A134a	850f multicolored	3.50	1.75
490	A134a	900f multicolored	3.50	1.75
		Nos. 487-490 (4)	10.00	5.10

A souvenir sheet containing one #488 exists. Value, $10.
For surcharges see Nos. 595, 605.

A135

October 14 Revolution, 25th Anniv. — A135a

1989, Oct. 14
491	A135	300f multicolored	1.25	.60
492	A135	375f multicolored	1.75	.85
493	A135a	850f multicolored	3.50	1.75
494	A135a	900f multicolored	1.75	
		Nos. 491-494 (4)	8.25	3.20

A souvenir sheet containing one #492 exists. Value, $10.
For surcharges see Nos. 596, 606.

1988 Summer Olympics, Seoul A136

Game emblem and various events: 300f, Table tennis, basketball, track, boxing. 375f, Soccer game. 850f, Soccer, judo, vert. 900f, Torch bearer.

1989, Nov. 10   Litho.   Perf. 13x13½
495 A136 300f multicolored   1.50   .75
496 A136 375f multicolored   2.00 1.00
  a.   Souvenir sheet   10.00 7.50
497 A136 850f multicolored   5.00 2.50
498 A136 900f multicolored   5.00 2.50
    Nos. 495-498 (4)   13.50 6.75

For surcharges see Nos. 597, 607.

Palestinian
Uprising
A137

375f, Flag raising, vert. 850f, Burning barricades. 900f, Man waving flag, vert.

1989, Dec. 9   Perf. 13x13½, 13½x13
499 A137 300f shown   2.00 1.00
500 A137 375f multicolored   3.00 1.50
  a.   Souvenir sheet of 1   17.50 8.50
501 A137 850f multicolored   5.50 2.75
502 A137 900f multicolored   7.00 3.50
    Nos. 499-502 (4)   17.50 8.75

For surcharges see Nos. 598, 608.

Arab Cooperation Council — A138

1990, Feb. 16   Litho.   Perf. 13x13½
504 A138 300f multicolored   1.25   .65
505 A138 375f multicolored   1.75   .90
  a.   Souvenir sheet   12.00 9.00
506 A138 850f multicolored   3.50 1.75
507 A138 900f multicolored   3.50 1.75
    Nos. 504-507 (4)   10.00 5.05

For surcharges see Nos. 599, 609.

First
Exported
Oil — A139

1990, Mar. 15   Perf. 14
508 A139 300f multicolored   1.25   .60
509 A139 375f multicolored   2.00 1.00
  a.   Souvenir sheet   10.00 5.00
510 A139 850f multi, diff.   4.00 2.00
511 A139 900f like 850f   4.00 2.00
    Nos. 508-511 (4)   11.25 5.60

For surcharges see Nos. 600, 610.

Arab Scout
Movement,
75th Anniv.
A140

300f, Scouts holding globe. 850f, Oil rig, scouts, globe.

1990, June 15   Litho.   Perf. 13x13½
512 A140 300f multicolored   1.25   .60
513 A140 375f like No. 512   1.40   .70
  a.   Souvenir sheet of 1   7.00 1.90
514 A140 850f multicolored   3.00 1.50
515 A140 900f like No. 514   3.50 1.75
    Nos. 512-515 (4)   9.15 4.55

For surcharges see Nos. 601, 611.

Arab Board for
Medical
Specializations,
10th
Anniv. — A141

1990, Apr. 15   Photo.   Perf. 13½x13
516 A141 300f brt grn & multi   1.25   .60
517 A141 375f lt bl & multi   1.50   .75
  a.   Sheet of 1, perf. 12½   5.00 2.50
518 A141 850f lt org & multi   3.25 1.60
519 A141 900f lt vio & multi   3.50 1.75
    Nos. 516-519 (4)   9.50 4.70

For surcharges see Nos. 602, 612.

Immunization Campaign — A142

300f, 375f, Mother feeding infant, vert.

1990, May 15   Perf. 13½x13, 13x13½
520 A142 300f lt bl & multi   1.40   .70
521 A142 375f lt org & multi   2.00 1.00
  a.   Sheet of 1, perf. 12½   11.00 6.00
522 A142 850f lt bl grn & multi   4.00 2.00
523 A142 900f lt lake & multi   4.00 2.00
    Nos. 520-523 (4)   11.40 5.70

No. 521a contains one 26x37mm stamp.
For surcharges see Nos. 603, C157.

UN Development
Program, 40th
Anniv. — A144

1990, Oct. 24   Litho.   Perf. 12
532 A144 150f multicolored   1.00   .50

For surcharge see No. 622.

Ducks
A145

1990, Sept. 18   Litho.   Perf. 12
533 A145   10f Pintail swimming   .25   .25
534 A145   20f Wigeon   .25   .25
535 A145   25f Ruddy shelduck   .25   .25
536 A145   40f Gadwall   .30   .25
537 A145   75f Shelduck, male   .50   .30
538 A145 150f Shoveler   1.00   .50
539 A145 600f Teal   4.00 2.00
    Nos. 533-539 (7)   6.55 3.80

Souvenir Sheet
540 A145 460f Pintail in flight   8.00 4.00

For surcharge see No. 623.

Moths and
Butterflies
A146

5f, Dirphia multicolor. 20f, Automeris io. 25f, Papilio machaon. 40f, Bhutanitis lidderdalii. 55f, Prepona demophon muson. 75f, Agarista agricola. 700f, Attacus edwardsii.
460f, Daphnis nerii, vert.

1990, Nov. 3   Perf. 12½x12
541 A146   5f multicolored   .25   .25
542 A146   20f multicolored   .25   .25
543 A146   25f multicolored   .25   .25
544 A146   40f multicolored   .35   .25
545 A146   55f multicolored   .45   .30
546 A146   75f multicolored   .55   .30
547 A146 700f multicolored   3.75 2.00
    Nos. 541-547 (7)   5.85 3.60

Souvenir Sheet
Perf. 12x12½
548 A146 460f multicolored   7.50 4.50

Prehistoric
Animals
A147

Perf. 12x12½, 12½x12
1990, Nov. 27
549 A147   5f Protembolotheri-
       um, vert.   .25   .25
550 A147   10f Diatryma, vert.   .25   .25
551 A147   35f Mammuthus   .25   .25
552 A147   40f Edaphosaurus   .30   .25
553 A147   55f Dimorphodon   .40   .30
554 A147   75f Phororhacos   .50   .30
555 A147 700f Ichthyosaurus,
       vert.   3.25 1.75
    Nos. 549-555 (7)   5.20 3.35

Size: 61x90mm
Imperf
556 A147 460f Tyrannosaurus,
       vert.   4.00 2.50

A148

Various domestic cats.

1990, Dec. 26   Perf. 12x12½
557 A148   5f multicolored   .25   .25
558 A148   15f multicolored   .25   .25
559 A148   35f multicolored   .25   .25
560 A148   55f multicolored   .35   .30
561 A148   60f multicolored   .35   .30
562 A148 150f multicolored   .75   .60
563 A148 600f multicolored   2.75 1.50
    Nos. 557-563 (7)   4.95 3.45

Size: 70x90mm
Imperf
564 A148 460f multicolored   5.00 2.50

A149

Mushrooms: 50f, Boletus aestivalis. 60f, Suillus luteus. 80f, Gyromitra esculenta. 100f, Leccinum scabrum. 130f, Amanita muscaria. 200f, Boletus erythropus. 300f, Leccinum testaceoscabrum.
460f, Stropharia aeruginosa.

1991, Mar. 18   Litho.   Perf. 12x12½
565 A149   50f multicolored   .30   .25
566 A149   60f multicolored   .40   .25
567 A149   80f multicolored   .50   .30
568 A149 100f multicolored   .65   .35
569 A149 130f multicolored   .90   .45
570 A149 200f multicolored   1.50   .55
571 A149 300f multicolored   2.00   .60
    Nos. 565-571 (7)   6.25 2.75

Size: 70x90mm
Imperf
572 A149 460f multicolored   3.00

Unified
Yemen
Republic,
1st Anniv.
A150

Designs: 300f, 375f, Eagle crest. 850f, 900f, Hand holding flag, map, sun.

1991, May 22   Perf. 13x13½
573 A150 300f pink & multi   .65   .35
574 A150 375f grn bl multi   .85   .45
  a.   Sheet of 1, perf. 12½   2.25 1.50
575 A150 850f lt bl & multi   2.00   .65
576 A150 900f bl grn & multi   2.00   .80
    Nos. 573-576 (4)   5.50 2.25

No. 574a contains one 37x27mm stamp.
For surcharges see #604, 613, 624, 627.

Unity Agreement
Signed Nov. 30,
1989 — A151

Designs: 300f, 375f, 850f, Fist, flag, map.

1991, May 22   Perf. 13½x13
577 A151 225f multicolored   .45   .25
578 A151 300f multicolored   .70   .35
579 A151 375f multicolored   .90   .50
  a.   Sheet of 1, perf. 12½   2.75 1.50
580 A151 850f multicolored   1.40   .70
581 A151 850f multiccolored   1.75   .90
    Nos. 577-581 (5)   5.20 2.70

No. 579a contains one 27x37mm stamp.
For surcharges see #614, 617-619, 625.

World Anti-Smoking Day — A153

Designs: 300f, 375f, 850f, Man facing skull smoking cigarette.

1991, May 31   Perf. 13x13½
582 A153 225f multicolored   .45   .25
583 A153 300f multicolored   .70   .35
584 A153 375f multicolored   1.00   .50
  a.   Sheet of 1, perf. 12½   3.50 1.75
585 A153 650f multicolored   1.50   .75
586 A153 850f multicolored   2.00 1.00
    Nos. 582-586 (5)   5.65 2.85

No. 584a contains one 36x26mm stamp.
For surcharges see Nos. 615, 620, 626.

United
Nations,
45th Anniv.
A154

1991, June 26   Perf. 13x13½
587 A154   5r multicolored   1.40   .70
588 A154   8r multicolored   1.75   .90
589 A154   10r multicolored   2.50 1.25
590 A154   12r multicolored   2.75 1.40
    Nos. 587-590 (4)   8.40 4.25

Souvenir Sheet
Perf. 12½
591 A154   6r multicolored   2.50 1.50

No. 591 contains one 37x28mm stamp.

Nos. 329, 456, 480, 489-490, 493-494, 497-498, 501-502, 506-507, 510-511, 514-515, 518-519, 523, 575-576, 581 & 586 Surcharged, "Rials" Spelled Out

1993, Jan. 1 Perfs., Etc. as Before

592	A88	5r on 75f #329	5.75	
593	A125	8r on 425f #456	6.50	
594	A131	8r on 425f #480	6.50	
595	A134a	10r on 900f #490	6.50	
596	A135a	10r on 900f #494	6.50	
597	A136	10r on 900f #498	6.50	
598	A137	10r on 900f #502	6.50	
599	A138	10r on 900f #507	6.50	
600	A139	10r on 900f #511	6.50	
601	A140	10r on 900f #515	6.50	
602	A141	10r on 900f #519	6.50	
603	A142	10r on 900f #523	6.50	
604	A150	10r on 900f #576	6.50	
605	A134a	12r on 850f #489	7.25	
606	A135a	12r on 850f #493	7.25	
607	A136	12r on 850f #497	7.25	
608	A137	12r on 850f #501	7.25	
609	A138	12r on 850f #506	7.25	
610	A139	12r on 850f #510	7.25	
611	A140	12r on 850f #514	7.25	
612	A141	12r on 850f #518	7.25	
613	A150	12r on 850f #575	7.25	
614	A151	12r on 850f #581	7.25	
615	A153	12r on 850f #586	7.25	
		Nos. 592-615 (24)	163.50	

Size and location of surcharge varies.

Yemen (PDR) Nos. 441, 443, 447, and Yemen Nos. 577-578, 583 Srchd. Type a or — c

1993 Perfs., Etc. as Before

616	A139(a)	50r on 500f #447	100.00	
617	A151(a)	50r on 225f #577	175.00	
618	A151(c)	50r on 225f #577	—	
a.		Pair, #617-618		
619	A151(a)	100r on 300f #578	175.00	
620	A153(a)	100r on 300f #583	225.00	
621	A139(a)	200r on 5f #441	250.00	
a.		3-Line surcharge		
621B	A139(a)	200r on 20f #443	250.00	

Size and location of surcharge varies.

Yemen Republic Nos. 532, 538, 573-574, 579, & 584 Srchd. — a

1993, Sept. 1 Perfs., Etc. as Before

622	A144(a)	50r on 150f #532	25.00	20.00
623	A145(a)	50r on 150f #538	25.00	20.00
623A	A153(a)	50r on 225f #582	300.00	200.00
624	A150(a)	50r on 375f #574	27.50	20.00
625	A151(a)	50r on 375f #579	27.50	25.00
626	A153(a)	50r on 375f #584	27.50	25.00
627	A150(a)	100r on 300f #573	50.00	25.00

Size and location of surcharge varies.
No. 623 exists with a surcharge similar to surcharge "c."

Yemen People's Democratic Republic Nos. 75, 84B, 204, 208, 216, 232, 235, 244, 267, 335-336, 347, 425, 436-437, 439 & Types Surcharged Type a and

b

1993, Sept. 1 Perfs., Etc. as Before

628	A25(a)	8r on 110f #84B	4.75	
629	A63(a)	8r on 110f #204	4.75	
630	A64(a)	8r on 110f #208	4.75	
631	A66(a)	8r on 110f #216	4.75	
632	A72(a)	8r on 110f #232	4.75	
633	A74(a)	8r on 110r #235	4.75	
634	A76(a)	8r on 110r #244	16.00	
635	A86(a)	8r on 110f #267	4.75	
636	A105(a)	100r on 2d #347	60.00	
637	A137(a)	100r on 300f #439	60.00	
638	A24(a)	200r on 5f #75	100.00	
639	(b)	200r on 15f Soyuz 10 & Salyut 1	100.00	
640	A105(b)	200r on 15f #335	100.00	
641	(b)	200r on 20f Apollo 8	100.00	
642	A105(b)	200r on 20f #336	100.00	
643	A131(a)	200r on 20f #425	240.00	
644	A134(a)	200r on 75f #436	100.00	
645	A135(a)	200r on 250f #437	100.00	

Size and location of surcharge varies.
No. 582 exists with a 50r type "b" surcharge.
No. 636 exists with a surcharge similar to surcharge "c."
Nos. 630, 641 without surcharge have not been listed in the Scott Catalogue.

Yemen Unity, 4th Anniv. — A155

Various views of govt. building, San'a.

1994, Sept. 27 Litho. Perf. 13½x14

646	A155	3r multicolored	.65	.35
647	A155	5r multicolored	1.20	.50
648	A155	8r multicolored	1.75	.75
649	A155	20r multicolored	4.50	2.00
		Nos. 646-649 (4)	8.10	3.60

Souvenir Sheet

650	A155	20r multi, diff.	5.00	3.00

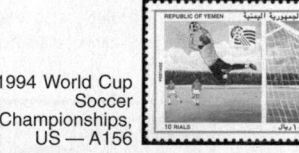

1994 World Cup Soccer Championships, US — A156

2r, Player in yellow shirt dribbling ball, vert. 6r, Player in striped shirt dribbling, vert. 10r, Goal keeper. No. 654, Heading ball, vert. No. 655, Tackling.

1994, Oct. 1 Perf. 14x13½, 13½x14

651	A156	2r multicolored	.55	.25
652	A156	6r multicolored	1.50	.60
653	A156	10r multicolored	2.50	1.00
654	A156	12r multicolored	3.00	1.25
		Nos. 651-654 (4)	7.55	3.10

Souvenir Sheet

655	A156	12r multicolored	3.50	2.50

World Day of Environmental Protection — A157

1995, Oct. 15 Litho.

656	A157	15r Arabian leopard	1.40	.90
657	A157	20r Caracal lynx	1.60	1.00
658	A157	30r Guinea fowl, horiz.	2.40	1.25
		Nos. 656-658 (3)	5.40	3.15

Souvenir Sheet

659	A157	50r Partridge, horiz.	5.25	3.50

FAO, 50th Anniv. — A158

Emblem, field, hand holding: 10r, Plant. 25r, Seed. 30r, Fish. 50r, Grain.

1995, Oct. 16 Perf. 14x13½

660	A158	10r violet & multi	.90	.50
661	A158	25r claret & multi	1.75	.75
662	A158	30r light blue & multi	2.50	1.00
		Nos. 660-662 (3)	5.15	2.25

Souvenir Sheet

663	A158	50r dark blue & multi	2.00	

A159

UN, 50th anniv.: Various views of Aden Dam.

1995, Oct. 24 Perf. 14x13½, 13½x14

664	A159	10r multi	1.00	.60
665	A159	20r multi	2.00	.85
666	A159	25r multi, horiz.	2.50	1.25
		Nos. 664-666 (3)	5.50	2.70

Souvenir Sheet

667	A159	50r multi, horiz.	5.00	3.00

A160

Naseem Hamed Kashmem, world boxing champion: 10r, With champion belts. 20r, Up close. 25r, Boxing opponent, horiz. 30r, Holding up arm as winner, trainer.
50r, Boxing opponent, diff., horiz.

1995, Nov. 29 Perf. 14x13½, 13½x14

668	A160	10r multicolored	1.00	.40
669	A160	20r multicolored	2.00	.65
670	A160	25r multicolored	2.50	.80
671	A160	30r multicolored	3.00	1.00
		Nos. 668-671 (4)	8.50	2.85

Souvenir Sheet

672	A160	50r multicolored	5.00	3.00

Souvenir Sheet

CHINA '96, 9th Asian Intl. Philatelic Exhibition — A161

1996, May 18 Litho. Perf. 11½

673	A161	80r Shanghai	7.50	4.50

1996 Summer Olympic Games, Atlanta — A162

1996, July 19 Perf. 14x13½, 13½x14

674	A162	20r Wrestling, vert.	.90	.40
675	A162	50r High jump	1.90	1.20
676	A162	60r Running, vert.	2.10	1.40
677	A162	70r Gymnastics, vert.	2.75	1.75
678	A162	100r Judo, vert.	4.50	2.00
		Nos. 674-678 (5)	12.15	6.75

Souvenir Sheet

679	A162	150r Javelin, vert.	10.00	6.50

Landmarks A163

10r, 70r, 250r, Popular Heritage Museum, Seiyoan. 15r, 40r, 60r, 500r, Rook Palace, Wadi Dhahr, vert. 20r, 100r, 200r, Old Sana'a City. 30r, 50r, 150r, 300r, Al-Mohdhar Minaret, Tarim, vert.

Perf. 13½x14, 14x13½

1996, Sept. 26 Litho.

680	A163	10r org yel & multi	.50	.25
681	A163	15r grn yel & multi	.75	.25
682	A163	20r lt blue & multi	1.00	.35
683	A163	30r blue & multi	1.25	.40
684	A163	40r salmon & multi	1.75	.55
685	A163	50r green & multi	2.25	.70
686	A163	60r lilac & multi	3.00	.85
687	A163	70r violet & multi	3.50	1.00
688	A163	100r yellow & multi	4.50	1.40
689	A163	150r orange & multi	6.00	1.90
690	A163	200r rose & multi	8.00	2.40
691	A163	250r gray & multi	10.00	2.75
692	A163	300r red & multi	12.50	3.25
693	A163	500r yellow & multi	20.00	4.75
		Nos. 680-693 (14)	75.00	20.80

Birds — A164

Designs: 20r, Tyto alba. 50r, Alectoris philbyi. 60r, Gypaetus barbatus. 70r, Alectoris melanocephala. 100r, Chlamydotis undulata. 150r, Ixobrychus minutus, vert.

1996, Oct. 14 Litho. Perf. 13½x14

694	A164	20r multicolored	.65	.40
695	A164	50r multicolored	1.60	.80
696	A164	60r multicolored	2.10	1.00

697 A164 70r multicolored   2.25 1.40
698 A164 100r multicolored   3.00 2.00
   Nos. 694-698 (5)   9.60 5.60
          Souvenir Sheet
          Perf. 14x13½
699 A164 150r multicolored   7.50 4.50

Rare Plants in
Yemen — A165

Designs: 20r, Parodia masii. 50r, Notocatus
cristata. 60r, Adenium obesum socotranum.
70r, Dracaena cinnabari. 100r, Mammillaria
erythrosperma.
150r, Parodia maasii, diff.

1996, Nov. 30   **Perf. 13½x14**
700 A165 20r multicolored   .65   .40
701 A165 50r multicolored   1.50   .80
702 A165 60r multicolored   1.80 1.00
703 A165 70r multicolored   2.10 1.40
704 A165 100r multicolored   3.00 2.00
   Nos. 700-704 (5)   9.05 5.60
          Souvenir Sheet
705 A165 150r multicolored   7.00 4.50

A166

Fish: 20r, Heniochus acuminatus. 50r, 150r,
Cheilinus undulatus. 60r, Zebrasoma
xanthurum. 70r, Pomacanthus imperator.
100r, Pomacanthus vanthometopon.

1996, Nov. 30
706 A166 20r multicolored   .70   .40
707 A166 50r multicolored   1.50 1.00
708 A166 60r multicolored   1.90 1.25
709 A166 70r multicolored   2.75 1.75
710 A166 100r multicolored   3.50 2.50
   Nos. 706-710 (5)   10.35 6.90
          Souvenir Sheet
711 A166 150r multicolored   8.50 4.50

A167

UNICEF, 50th Anniv.: 20r, Children with
books. 50r, Girls clapping hands. 60r, Mother,
child. 70r, Mother, three children.
150r, Child making jewelry, horiz.

1996, Dec. 11   **Perf. 14x13½**
712 A167 20r multicolored   .75   .35
713 A167 50r multicolored   1.50   .70
714 A167 60r multicolored   1.80   .85
715 A167 70r multicolored   2.10 1.40
   Nos. 712-715 (4)   6.15 3.15
          Souvenir Sheet
          Perf. 13½x14
716 A167 150r multicolored   6.00 4.00

1998 World Cup Soccer
Championships, France — A168

Various soccer plays.

1998, June 10 Litho.   Perf. 13x13½
717 A168 10r multicolored   .40   .25
718 A168 15r multicolored   .65   .30
719 A168 35r multicolored   1.40   .65
720 A168 65r multicolored   2.25 1.10

721 A168 75r multicolored   2.50 1.25
 a.   Souvenir sheet, #717-721   8.00 4.00
   Nos. 717-721 (5)   7.20 3.55

Birds
A169

Designs: 10r, Ardeotis arabs. 15r, Neophron
percnopterus. 35r, Coracias abyssinicus. 65r,
Cinnyricinclus leucogaster. 75r, Melierax
metabates.

1998, Sept. 26   Litho.   Perf. 13
722-726 A169 Set of 5   8.00 4.00
726a   Sheet of 5, #722-726   9.00 5.00

Universal
Declaration
of Human
Rights,
50th Anniv.
A170

15r, Hands in air. 35r, Hands clasped in
handshake. 100r, Hands reaching out.

1998, Oct. 12
727-729 A170 Set of 3   6.00 3.00
729a   Sheet of 3, #727-729   6.00 4.50

First
General
Conference
of Yemeni
Immigrants
(in 1999)
A171

Emblem &: 60r, Dhows. 90r, Fort, camel.

2000, May 16   Litho.   Perf. 14½x14
730-731 A171 Set of 2   4.50 3.00
731a   Souvenir sheet, #730-731   5.50 4.00

Tenth National
Day — A172

Background colors: 30r, Light green. 50r,
Rose lilac. 70r, Light blue. 150r, Orange.

2000, May 22   **Perf. 14x14½**
732-734 A172 Set of 3   6.00 4.00
          Souvenir Sheet
735 A172 150r multi   6.00 4.00

Plants of
Socotra — A173

Designs: 30r, Euphorbia abdalkuri. 70r,
Dendrosicyos socotranus. 80r, Caralluma
socotrana. 120r, Dracaena cinnabari.
300r, Exacum affine.

2000, July 15
736-739 A173 Set of 4   9.00 5.00
          Souvenir Sheet
740 A173 300r multi   10.00 8.00

2000 Summer
Olympics,
Sydney — A174

Designs: 50r, Judo. 70r, Runner. 80r, Hurdler. 100r, Shooting.
300r, Tennis.

2000, Sept. 15
741-744 A174 Set of 4   8.00 5.00
          Souvenir Sheet
745 A174 300r multi   9.50 8.00

Antiquities — A175

Designs: 30r, Stone idols, 3000 B.C. 70r,
Statue of Ma'adi Karib, 800 B.C. 100r, Horned
griffin, Royal Palace of Shabwa, 300. 120r,
Statue of King of Awsan Yasduq Eil, 100 B.C.
320r, Stele with bull's head, 100 B.C., horiz.

2002, June 15   Litho.   Perf. 13x12¾
746-749 A175 Set of 4   8.50 8.50
          Souvenir Sheet
          Imperf
750 A175 320r multi   8.50 8.50
   No. 750 contains one 41x26mm stamp.

2002 World Cup Soccer
Championships, Japan and
Korea — A176

Soccer players with background colors of:
30r, Bister, vert. 70r, Green. 100r, Blue, vert.
120r, Red brown, vert.
No. 755: a, Player's foot and ball. b, World
Cup trophy.

2002, May 31   Perf. 13x12¾, 12¾x13
751-754 A176 Set of 4   8.50 8.50
          Souvenir Sheet
          Perf.
755 A176 160r Sheet of 2, #a-b   8.50 8.50
   No. 755 contains two 28mm diameter
stamps.

Scouting in
Yemen,
75th Anniv.
A177

Designs: 30r, Scout escorting man across
street. 60r, Scout digging. 70r, Scouts in
rowboat.
160r, Scout saluting, vert.

2002, Apr. 30   **Perf. 12¾x13**
756-758 A177 Set of 3   4.25 4.25
          Souvenir Sheet
          Perf. 13x13¼
759 A177 160r multi   5.50 4.25
   No. 759 contains one 16x26mm stamp.

Palestinian
Intifada — A178

Designs: 30r, Frightened child. 60r, Bleeding child.
90r, Dome of the Rock, horiz.

2002, Apr. 27   **Perf. 13x12¾**
760-761 A178 Set of 2   2.50 2.50
          Imperf
          Size: 111x78mm
762 A178 90r multi   2.50 2.50

Poets — A179

Designs: Nos. 763, 30r, 765, 60r, 767a, 70r,
Hussain Al-Muhdhar (1931-2000). Nos. 764,
30r, 766, 60r, 767b, 70r, Abdullah Al-Baradony
(1929-99).

2002, June 30   Litho.   Perf. 13x12¾
763-766 A179 Set of 4   4.50 4.50
          Souvenir Sheet
          Perf. 13x13¼
767 A179 70r Sheet of 2, #a-b   3.50 3.50
   No. 767 contains two 16x28mm stamps.

Revolution, 40th
Anniv. — A180

Background colors: 30r, Dull green. 60r,
Rose.
90r, Lilac.

2002, Sept. 26   **Perf. 13x12¾**
768-769 A180 Set of 2   2.25 2.25
          Imperf
          Size: 110x76mm
770 A180 90r multi   2.50 2.25

World Under-17 Soccer
Championships, Finland — A181

Various soccer players with background
color of: 30r, Red violet. 50r, Golden brown.
70r, Blue. 100r, Green.
250r, Soccer team and stadium.

2003, Aug. 13   Litho.   Perf. 12¾x13
771-774 A181 Set of 4   6.00 6.00
          Imperf
          Size: 109x74mm
775 A181 250r multi   6.00 6.00

Antiquities — A182

Various sculptures with background colors of: 20r, Pale yellow. 40r, Lilac. 50r, Light green. 150r, Pink.
260r, Black, horiz.

2003, Sept. 26   *Perf. 13x12¾*
776-779 A182   Set of 4   6.00 6.00
Souvenir Sheet
Perf. 12¾x13
780 A182 260r multi   6.00 6.00

Traditional Women's Clothing — A183

Various women with panel colors of: 30r, Purple. 60r, Yellow green. 70r, Dark green. 100r, Red violet. 150r, Brown.
410r, Purple background, horiz.

2003, Oct. 14   *Perf. 13x12¾*
781-785 A183   Set of 5   9.00 9.00
Souvenir Sheet
Perf. 12¾x13
786 A183 410r multi   9.00 9.00

Children's Art — A184

Designs: 20r, Girl with flower on globe, vert. 30r, Dove over buildings, vert. 40r, Dove holding swing, vert. 50r, Children in field. 60r, Animals in field. 70r, Street and park.

2003, Oct. 15   *Perf. 13x12¾, 12¾x13*
787-792 A184   Set of 6   6.00 6.00

Sana'a, 2004 Arabic Cultural Capital — A185

Various buildings with frame colors of: 30r, White. 50r, Purple. 70r, Black. 100r, Dark brown. 150r Red brown.
400r, Buildings, horiz.

2003, Nov. 30   *Perf. 13x12¾*
793-797 A185   Set of 5   9.00 9.00
Souvenir Sheet
Perf. 12¾x13
798 A185 400r multi   9.00 9.00

FIFA (Fédération Internationale de Football Association), Cent. — A186

2004, May 21   Litho.   Perf. 13x12¾
799 A186 100r multi   2.25 2.25
Dated 2005. Stamps did not appear in marketplace until 2005.

2004 Summer Olympics, Athens — A187

Designs: 70r, Running. 80r, Shooting. 100r, Swimming.
250r, Equestrian.

2004, Aug. 13
800-802 A187   Set of 3   5.50 5.50
Souvenir Sheet
803 A187 250r multi   5.50 5.50
Dated 2005. Stamps did not appear in marketplace until 2005.

Telecommunications and Technology — A188

Designs: 60r, Computer chips, "@" symbol, keyboard. 70r, Computer and stylized people, vert. 100r, Yemen Mobile emblem, vert. 400r, Like 70r, vert.

Perf. 12¾x13, 13x12¾
2004, Sept. 26
804-806 A188   Set of 3   5.00 5.00
Souvenir Sheet
807 A188 400r multi   9.00 9.00
Dated 2005. Stamps did not appear in marketplace until 2005.

Spiders A189

No. 808: a, Tidarren argo. b, Scelidomachus socotranus. c, Habrocestum albopunctatum. d, Rafalus insignipalpis. e, Latrodectus hystrix. f, Atrophothele socotrana.
300r, Like No. 808b.

2004, Oct. 14   *Perf. 12¾x13*
808   Horiz. strip of 6   6.50 6.50
a.-f. A189 50r Any single   1.00 1.00
Souvenir Sheet
809 A189 300r multi   6.50 6.50
Dated 2005. Stamps did not appear in marketplace until 2005.

Traditional Men's Clothing — A190

Men wearing various outfits with background colors of: 50r, Light yellow. 60r, Green. 70r, Pink. 100r, Blue.
360r, Orange brown.

2004, Oct. 30   *Perf. 13x12¾*
810-813 A190   Set of 4   6.50 6.50
Souvenir Sheet
814 A190 360r multi   8.00 8.00
Dated 2005. Stamps did not appear in marketplace until 2005.

Handicrafts A191

No. 815: a, Knife maker holding hammer. b, Textile worker piecing fabric. c, Jeweler. d, Weaver at loom.
3004, Like No. 815a.

2004, Nov. 30
815   Horiz. strip of 4   6.50 6.50
a.-d. A191 70r multi   1.60 1.60
Souvenir Sheet
816 A191 300r multi   6.50 6.50
Dated 2005. Stamps did not appear in marketplace until 2005.

15th National Day — A192

Emblem and: 30r, Industrial plant. 60r, Dam and reservoir. 70r, Man holding flag.
90r, Buildings.

2005, May 22
817-819 A192   Set of 3   3.50 3.50
Souvenir Sheet
820 A192 90r multi   2.00 2.00

United Nations, 60th Anniv. — A193

Symbols of eight goals for a better Yemen: No. 821, 40r, Pregnant woman and doctor. No. 822, 40r, Woman, infant and doctor. No. 823, 40r, Woman reading book. No. 824, 40r, Mosquito, AIDS ribbon, medicine and bottle. No. 825, 40r, Man depositing trash in can, tree, smiling sun. 80r, Goats, hat seller and child. 100r, Woman, man and balance. 120r, Handshake.
130r, UN anniversary emblem.

2005, Oct. 24   Litho.   Perf. 13x12¾
821-828 A193   Set of 8   11.00 11.00

Size: 111x83mm
Imperf
829 A193 130r multi   3.00 3.00
No. 829 contains one perforated label lacking a denomination.

Flowers A194

Various flowers: 50r, 80r, 110r, 130r, 140r, 150r, 300r.

Perf. 13¼x13¾   **Litho.**
830-835 A194   Set of 6   13.50 13.50
Souvenir Sheet
836 A194 300r multi   6.00 6.00

Insects A195

Designs: No. 837, 50r, Cheilomenes lunata yemenensis. No. 838, 50r, Pharoscymnus c-luteus. No. 839, 50r, Hippodamia variegata. No. 840, 50r, Cheilomenes propinqua vicina. No. 841, 50r, Brumoides nigrifrons. No. 842, 50r, Serangium buettikeri.
250r, Pharoscymnus c-luteus, diff.

2007, Sept. 26   *Perf. 13¾x13¼*
837-842 A195   Set of 6   6.00 6.00
Souvenir Sheet
843 A195 250r multi   5.00 5.00

Mosques A196

Designs: 50r, Mosque of Prophethood, Hadhramaut. 80r, Al Ameria Mosque, Radaa. 100r, Queen Arwa Mosque, Jebla. 110r, Al Ashrafiah Mosque, Taiz. 120r, Al Aidarous Mosque, Aden. 200r, Al Bukiriah Mosque, Sana'a.
300r, Unidentified mosque.

2007, Oct. 14   *Perf. 13¼x13¾*
844-849 A196   Set of 6   13.50 13.50
Souvenir Sheet
850 A196 300r multi   6.00 6.00

Citadels and Castles A197

Designs: 50r, Thulaa Citadel, Amran. 80r, Al Tawama Citadels, Hadhramaut. 100r, Serah Castle, Aden. 110r, Sumarah Castle, Ibb. 130r, Al Qahira Castle, Taiz.
300r, Unidentified castle.

2007, Oct. 14
851-855 A197   Set of 5   9.50 9.50
Souvenir Sheet
856 A197 300r multi   6.00 6.00

Marine Life A198

Designs: 50r, Parupeneus marconema. 80r, Sarda orientalis. 100r, Carcharhinus melanopterus. 110r, Plectorhinchus schotaf. 130r, Panulirus homarus. 160r, Seriola rivoliana. 300r, Panulirus homarus, diff.

2007, Nov. 30
857-862 A198 Set of 6   13.00 13.00
Souvenir Sheet
863 A198 300r multi   6.00 6.00

Yemeni Onyx A199

Various set and unset onyx stones: 50r, 80r, 100r, 110r, 120r, 130r, 140r, 160r. 250r, Set and unset onyx stones.

2007, Nov. 30   *Perf. 13¾x13¼*
864-871 A199 Set of 8   18.00 18.00
Souvenir Sheet
872 A199 250r multi   5.00 5.00

Natl. Day of Human Rights A200

Globe, flag, dove, human rights emblem with background color of: 110r, Red violet. 130r, Blue. 250r, Dove and flag, vert.

2007, Dec. 10   *Perf. 13¼x13¾*
873-874 A200 Set of 2   5.00 5.00
Souvenir Sheet
Perf. 13¾x13¼
875 A200 250r multi   5.00 5.00

Yasser Arafat (1929-2004), Palestinian Leader — A201

Palestinian Authority flag and Arafat: 120r, With hand raised. 300fr, With hands not shown, horiz.

2008, Nov. 4   **Litho.**   *Perf. 13x12¾*
876 A201 120r multi   2.50 2.50
Size: 110x70mm
Imperf
877 A201 300r multi   6.00 6.00

Opening of Al-Saleh Mosque, Sana'a A202

Mosque: 80r, Pillars, ceiling and chandeliers. 100r, Interior wall. 120r, Exterior. 300r, Exterior, diff.

2008, Nov. 22   *Perf. 12¾x13*
878-880 A202 Set of 3   6.00 6.00
Size: 109x70mm
Imperf
881 A202 300r multi   6.00 6.00

Gaza — A203

Designs: 60r, Man, boy carrying Palestinian flag. 100r, Barbed wire, children looking through hole in wall, horiz. 120r, Dove and chain.

2009, May 22   *Perf. 13¼x13, 13x13¼*
882-883 A203 Set of 2   3.25 3.25
Souvenir Sheet
884 A203 120r multi   2.50 2.50

Ancient Coins A204

Various ancient coins: 50r, 60r, 70r, 80r, 100r, 120r. 60r and 80r are vert. 120r is 50x50mm diamond-shaped stamp.

2009, May 22   *Perf. 13x13¼, 13¼x13*
885-889 A204 Set of 5   7.50 7.50
Souvenir Sheet
Perf. 13¼
890 A204 120r multi   2.50 2.50

Ancient Jewelry — A205

Designs: 50r, Bracelet and ring. 60r, Bracelet, horiz. 80r, Necklace and earrings. 100r, Bracelets, horiz. 120r, Necklace. 140r, Bracelets, diff., horiz. 150r, Belt, horiz.

2009, May 22   *Perf. 13¼x13, 13x13¼*
891-896 A205 Set of 6   11.00 11.00
Souvenir Sheet
897 A205 150r multi   3.00 3.00

Horses A206

Designs: 60r, Head of brown horse with white blaze. 80r, Black horse. 100r, Brown horse with white blaze. 120r, Brown horse with white mane. 140r, White horse.150r, Head of brown horse with white blaze, diff. 200r, Dappled gray horse, vert.

2009, May 22   *Perf. 13x13¼*
898-903 A206 Set of 6   13.00 13.00
Souvenir Sheet
Perf. 13¼x13
904 A206 200r multi   4.25 4.25

Souvenir Sheet

Arab Postal Day — A207

No. 905 — Emblem and: a, World map, pigeon. b, Camel caravan.

2009, May 22   *Perf. 12¾*
905 A207 100r Sheet of 2, #a-b   4.25 4.25

Tarim, 2010 Capital of Islamic Culture A208

Designs: 50r, Palace, yellow and red panel. 60r, Minaret, yellow and green panel. 80r, Al Kaff Palace, orange panel. 100r, Qasr al-Qubba Hotel, black panel. 200r, Palace at night, yellow and brown frame.

2010, Mar. 1   **Litho.**   *Perf. 13¼*
906-909 A208 Set of 4   3.50 3.50
Souvenir Sheet
910 A208 200r multi   4.75 4.75

National Day — A209

20th anniversary emblem and background colors of: 60r, Brown and red brown. 80r, Yellow and brown. 200r, Emblem, horiz.

2010, May 22   **Litho.**   *Perf. 13*
911-912 A209 Set of 2   3.00 3.00
Souvenir Sheet
913 A209 200r multi   4.25 4.25

2010 World Cup Soccer Championships, South Africa — A210

2010 World Cup emblem, World Cup and various South African stadiums hosting matches: 50r, 60r, 80r, 100r. No. 918, vert.: a, 50r, 2010 World Cup emblem. b, 100r, World Cup.

2010, June 11
914-917 A210 Set of 4   7.75 7.75
Souvenir Sheet
918 A210 Sheet of 2, #a-b   4.75 4.75

Yemeni Janbiahs (Daggers) A211

Various daggers in sheaths: 50r, 60r, 80r, 100r, 120r. 60r and 100r are vert. 200r, Dagger, diff.

2010, July 21   *Perf. 12¾*
919-923 A211 Set of 5   8.50 8.50
Souvenir Sheet
924 A211 200r multi   4.25 4.25

20th Gulf Cup of Nations Soccer Tournament, Aden — A212

Soccer player at LL and: 60r, Emblem depicting soccer ball, map of Arabian Peninsula. 80r, Soccer players in posed photograph. 100r, Gulf Cup, ring of flags. 120r, Stadium. 150r, Tournament emblem. 250r, Soccer ball with tournament emblem depicting soccer ball and map of Arabian Peninsula.

2010, Nov. 22   *Perf. 13¼*
925-929 A212 Set of 5   7.25 7.25
Souvenir Sheet
930 A212 250r multi   3.50 3.50

AIR POST STAMPS

Catalogue values for unused stamps in this section are for Never Hinged items.

Plane over San'a AP1

1947   **Unwmk.**   **Engr.**   *Perf. 12½*
C1 AP1 10b bright blue   6.00 2.00
C2 AP1 20b olive green   10.00 2.50

Views Type of Regular Issue

6b, 8b, View of San'a. 10b, Mocha coffee tree. 12b, Palace of the Rock, Wadi Dhahr. 16b, Palace, Ta'iz. 20b, 1i, Parade Ground, San'a.

1951   **Wmk. 277**   **Photo.**   *Perf. 14*
C3 A14   6b blue   1.40 .50
C4 A14   8b dark brown   1.75 .60
C5 A14 10b dark green   2.25 1.40
C6 A13 12b dark blue   2.50 .80
C7 A14 16b lilac rose   3.00 .80
C8 A13 20b orange brown   3.75 1.25
C9 A13   1i dark red   10.00 3.00
    Nos. C3-C9 (7)   24.65 8.35

Nos. C3 and C4 were used provisionally in 1957 for registry and foreign ordinary mail.

Type of Regular Issue

Designs: 12b, Palace of the Rock, Wadi Dhahr. 20b, Walls of Ibb.

Engraved and Photogravure
1952   **Unwmk.**   *Perf. 14½, Imperf.*
C10 A15 12b grnsh blk, bl & brn   8.00 6.50
C11 A15 20b indigo, bl & brn   8.00 6.50

Flag-and-View Type
1952
C12 A16   1i dk brn, car & brt ultra   18.00 18.00

1952   **Palace in Foreground**
C13 A16 30b yel grn, car & gray   11.00 11.00

Leaning Minaret, Mosque of Ta'iz — AP6

1954   Photo.   Perf. 14

C14	AP6	10b scarlet	3.25	.90
C15	AP6	12b dull blue	4.00	1.25
C16	AP6	20b olive bister	6.50	2.00
		Nos. C14-C16 (3)	13.75	4.15

Accession of King Ahmed I, 5th anniv.

Type of Regular Issue

1959   Wmk. 318   Perf. 13x13½

C17	A21	6b orange & blk	1.00	.70
C18	A21	10b red & blk	1.75	1.25
C19	A21	16b brt violet & red	2.75	2.00
		Nos. C17-C19 (3)	5.50	3.95

In 1959, four values of the 1931 issue and three values of the 1930 issue overprinted Air Mail 1959 were distributed. Although these stamps were not regularly sold in Yemeni post offices, several values of these sets were used on airmail covers going abroad. Several of these stamps exist with inverted or doubled overprints.

Antiquities of Marib Type

Designs: 6b, Columns, Temple of the Moon God. 16b, Control tower and spillway of 2,700-year-old dam of Marib.

Perf. 11½

1961, Oct. 14   Unwmk.   Photo.

| C20 | A27 | 6b lt bl grn & blk | .85 | .25 |
| C21 | A27 | 16b lt blue & blk | 2.40 | 1.00 |

Exist imperf.
For overprints see Nos. C24, C25.

Buildings Type

6b, Bab al-Yemen, main gate of San'a, horiz. 16b, Palace of the Rock (Dar al-Hajar).

1961, Nov. 15

| C22 | A28 | 6b blk, lt bl & grn | .85 | .25 |
| C23 | A28 | 16b blk, rose & grn | 2.25 | .60 |

For overprints see Nos. C24A, C25A.

Nos. C20-C23 Ovptd. Like Nos. 144-158 in Dark Red or Black

Perf. 11½

1963, Jan. 1   Photo.   Unwmk.

C24	A27 (a)	6b No. C20	.90	.90
C24A	A28 (b)	6b No. C22	.90	.90
C25	A27 (a)	16b No. C21	2.75	2.75
C25A	A28 (a)	16b No. C23 (B)	3.00	3.00

Proclamation of the Republic Type

1963, Mar. 15   Perf. 11x11½, 11½x11

C26	A34	8b Bayonette, torch	1.50	1.50
C27	A34	10b Jet, torch, tank	2.00	2.00
C28	A34	16b Flag, chain, torch	2.75	2.75
		Nos. C27-C28 horiz.		

An imperf. souvenir sheet containing one No. C28 exists. Value $10.

Nos. 25-29
Ovptd. in Black

Wmk. 258

1963, Sept. 1   Litho.   Perf. 12½

C29	A5	6b slate blue & ultra	1.50	1.50
C29A	A5	10b fawn & ultra	1.90	1.90
C29B	A5	14b olive & ultra	2.25	2.25
C29C	A5	20b yel grn & ultra	3.00	3.00
C29D	A5	1i claret & ultra	6.50	6.50
		Nos. C29-C29D (5)	15.15	15.15

Exist imperf. Value, set $25.

Spacecraft — AP6a

Various spacecraft.

1963, Dec. 5   Photo.   Perf. 13

C29E	AP6a	¼b multicolored	.70	.50
C29F	AP6a	½b multicolored	.70	.50
C29G	AP6a	½b multicolored	.70	.50
C29H	AP6a	4b multicolored	1.50	1.25
C29I	AP6a	20b multicolored	5.00	5.00
		Nos. C29E-C29I (5)	8.60	7.75

Exist imperf. Value, set $15. An imperf. souvenir sheet containing C29I also exists. Value $7.

Nos. C29E-C29G Overprinted in Black, Red Brown or Brown

1964-1966   Photo.   Perf. 13

C29J	AP6a	¼b On No. C29E	1.25	1.25
C29K	AP6a	¼b On No. C29E (RB)	2.50	2.50
C29L	AP6a	½b On No. C29F	1.25	1.25
C29M	AP6a	½b On No. C29F (RB)	2.50	2.50
C29N	AP6a	½b On No. C29G	1.25	1.25
C29O	AP6a	½b On No. C29G (Br)	5.00	5.00
		Nos. C29J-C29O (6)	13.75	13.75

Issued: Nos. C29J, C29L, C29N, 12/6/64. Nos. C29K, C29M, 1965. No. C29O, 1966. Imperf. examples of Nos. C29H-C29I exist with the red brown overprint.

San'a Intl. Airport Type

Perf. 11½x11

1964, Oct. 1   Photo.   Unwmk.

| C30 | A40 | 6b Sun, buildings, air-craft | .70 | .70 |

See note after No. 203.

APU 10th Anniv. Type

1964, Oct. 15   Perf. 13½

| C31 | A41 | 6b blue grn & blk | 1.00 | .80 |

An imperf. souvenir sheet of one exists containing No. C31. Value $3.

Deir Yassin Massacre Type

1965, Apr. 30   Perf. 11x11½

| C32 | A44 | 6b ver & brt org | 1.00 | .50 |

Library Type

1965, July 7   Perf. 11½x11

| C33 | A46 | 6b sepia, red & int blue | .75 | .50 |

An imperf. souvenir sheet of one exists containing No. C33. Value $2.50.

Butterflies — AP6b

Various butterflies.

1966, May 5   Photo.   Perf. 12½

C33A	AP6b	6b multicolored	2.50	.90
C33B	AP6b	8b multicolored	3.00	1.00
C33C	AP6b	10b multicolored	3.50	1.50
C33D	AP6b	16b multicolored	5.50	2.00
		Nos. C33A-C33D (4)	14.50	5.40

Nos. C33A-C33D exist imperf. Value $20.

1968 Winter Olympic Games, Grenoble — AP6c

1967, Nov. 11   Litho.   Perf. 13¼

C33E	AP6c	5b gold & multi	1.05	.45
C33F	AP6c	10b gold & multi	2.10	.70
C33G	AP6c	15b gold & multi	3.25	1.00
		Nos. C33E-C33G (3)	6.40	2.15

Exist imperf. in silver. Perf. and imperf. souvenir sheets containing one No. C33G exist in both gold and silver. Value, each $30.

Konrad Adenauer (1876-1967)   AP6d

1968, June   Litho.   Perf. 11

C33H	AP6d	5b gold & black	1.90	.45
C33I	AP6d	10b gold, blk & grn	3.75	.75
C33J	AP6d	15b gold, blk & blue	5.50	1.00
		Nos. C33H-C33J (3)	11.15	2.20

Exist imperf. in silver. Value, $18. Perf. and imperf. souvenir sheets containing one No. C33J exist in both gold and silver. Value, each $18.

Red Crescent Organization — AP6e

1968   Litho.   Perf. 11

C33K	AP6e	5b gold & multi	.90	
C33L	AP6e	10b gold & multi	1.75	
C33M	AP6e	15b gold & multi	2.75	
		Nos. C33K-C33M (3)	5.40	

Exist imperf. in silver. Value, $7. An imperf. souvenir sheet containing one No. C33M exists in both silver and gold. Value, each $9.
For surcharge see No. C39A.

Vladimir Komarov (1927-1967), Soviet Cosmonaut — AP6f

1968   Litho.   Perf. 13½

C33N	AP6f	5b gold & multi	1.00	
C33O	AP6f	10b gold & multi	2.00	
C33P	AP6f	15b gold & multi	3.00	
		Nos. C33N-C33P (3)	6.00	

Exist imperf. in silver. Value, $7. An imperf. souvenir sheet containing one No. C33P exists in gold. Value, $14.

Nos. C33H-C33J Overprinted in Black for Refugees

1968   Litho.   Perf. 11

C33Q	AP6d	5b gold & black	1.50	
C33R	AP6d	10b gold, blk & grn	3.00	
C33S	AP6d	15b gold, blk & blue	4.50	
		Nos. C33Q-C33S (3)	9.00	

Exist imperf. in silver. Perf. and imperf. souvenir sheets containing one No. C33S exist in both gold and silver.

1968 Summer Olympic Games, Mexico City — AP6g

1968, July 2   Litho.   Perf. 13½

C33T	AP6g	5b gold & multi	1.00	.45
C33U	AP6g	10b gold & multi	2.00	.75
C33V	AP6g	15b gold & multi	3.00	1.25
		Nos. C33T-C33V (3)	6.00	2.45

Exist imperf. in silver. Value, $7. Imperf. souvenir sheets containing one No. C33V exists in gold and silver.
For surcharge see No. C39B. Value, each $9.

Universal Declaration of Human Rights, 20th Anniv. — AP6h

1968, Oct. 20   Litho.   Perf. 13½

C33W	AP6g	5b gold & multi	1.00	
C33X	AP6g	10b gold & multi	2.00	
C33Y	AP6g	15b gold & multi	3.00	
		Nos. C33W-C33Y (3)	6.00	

Exist imperf. in silver. Value, $7. An imperf. souvenir sheet containing one No. C33Y exists in gold. Value, $10.
For surcharge see No. C39C.

Lenin's Birth Centenary AP7

1970, Aug. 15   Litho.   Perf. 12x12½
C34 AP7 6b Public speech   1.40 1.10
C35 AP7 16b Meeting with Arab
                delegates   3.00 1.90

8th Anniv. of the Revolution — AP8

1971, Jan. 24   Perf. 13
C36 AP8 5b Country estate   .75
C37 AP8 7b Workers   1.10
C38 AP8 16b Handshake, flag,
                flowers, open
                book   1.50
        Nos. C36-C38 (2)   2.25

A souv. sheet of 1 exists containing. No.
C38. Value $5.

No. C38 Overprinted in Black

1971, Jan. 24
C39 AP8 16b multicolored   5.00 3.00

**Nos. C33L, C33V and C33X
Surcharged in Black**

1971, Jan. 24   Perf. 13
C39A AP6e 40b On 10b
                #C33L, "40"
                is 4.5mm
                high
    d.   "40" is 3.5mm high
C39B AP6g 60b On 15b
                #C33V
    f.   Missing "B" in surcharge
C39C AP6h 80b On 10b
                #C33X
    e.   Missing "B" in surcharge

Revolution Type

1972, Nov. 25   Photo.   Perf. 13
C40 A80 21b lilac, blk & multi   4.00 3.50
For surcharge see No. C46A.

Al-Aqsa Mosque Type

1973, Jan. 1   Photo.   Perf. 13½
C41 A82 24b lt bl, blk & multi   3.00 2.50
    a.   Min. sheet of 1, imperf. 3.00 2.50

UNICEF Type

1973, Jan. 15   Photo.   Perf. 13
C42 A83 18b lt bl, blk & multi   1.90 1.50
    a.   Min. sheet of 1, imperf. 3.25 2.50
For surcharge see No. C46.

11th Anniv. of Revolution AP10

1973, Sept. 26   Photo.   Perf. 14
C43 AP10 7b Bank   .50 .35
C44 AP10 10b Cement factory   .65 .55
C45 AP10 18b Hospital   1.50 1.10
        Nos. C43-C45 (3)   2.65 2.00
For surcharges see Nos. C47-C48.

**Nos. C40, C42, C43, C45
Surcharged in Black or Red with
New Value and Bars**

1975, Nov. 15
C46   A83 75f on 18b lt bl, blk
                & multi   —   —
C46A A80 75f on 21b #C40
                (R)   —   —
C47   AP10 90f on 7b multi   —   —
C48   AP10 120f on 18b multi   —   —
    a.   Overprinted in black

Argentina 1978 World Cup Type

World cup emblem and various soccer
players.

1980, Mar. 30   Photo.   Perf. 14
C49 A99 60f gold & multi   1.25 .60
C50 A99 75f gold & multi   1.50 .70
C51 A99 80f gold & multi   1.80 .90
C52 A99 100f gold & multi   2.25 1.00
        Nos. C49-C52 (4)   4.55 3.20

Two 225f souvenir sheets exist. Value, perf.
$12, imperf. $15.

IYC Type

1980, Apr. 1   Perf. 13½
C53 A100 80f Girl, bird   3.50 1.25
C54 A100 100f Boy, butterfly,
                flower   3.50 1.25
C55 A100 150f Boy, butterfly,
                flower, diff.   5.00 1.75
        Nos. C53-C55 (3)   10.50 4.25

Two 200f souvenir sheets exist. Value $12
each.

Scouting Type of 1980

1980, May 1   Photo.   Perf. 13½x14
C56 A101 60f Bicycling   2.00 .80
C57 A101 75f Fencing   2.40 1.10
C58 A101 120f Butterfly catching 3.75 1.50
        Nos. C56-C58 (3)   8.15 3.40

Two 300f souvenir sheets exist. Value $15
each.

Argentina 1978 Winners' Type

World cup emblem and various soccer
players.

1980, June 1   Photo.   Perf. 14
C59 A102 60f gold & multi   1.50 .50
C60 A102 75f gold & multi   2.10 .65
C61 A102 80f gold & multi   2.25 .75
C62 A102 100f gold & multi   2.40 1.10
        Nos. C59-C62 (4)   5.50 3.00

Two 225f souvenir sheets exist. Value $12
each.

19th Anniv. of Sept. 26th Revolution (1981) — AP11

1982, Jan. 25   Litho.   Perf. 14
C63 AP11 75f Map   .75 .35
C64 AP11 125f Map in sunset   1.00 .50
C65 AP11 325f Dove in natl. col-
                ors   3.00 2.00
    a.   Souvenir sheet of 1   8.00 8.00
C66 AP11 400f Jets   4.00 2.00
        Nos. C63-C66 (4)   8.75 4.85

Al-Hasan Ibn Al-Hamadani, Writer — AP12

1982, Feb. 1
C67 AP12 125f green & multi   1.25 .60
C68 AP12 325f blue & multi   3.25 1.50

Souvenir Sheet
C69 AP12 375f multi   9.00 9.00

No. C69 contains one stamp (36x46mm).
For surcharge see No. C138.

World Food Day — AP13

Designs: No. C76a, Eggplants. No. C76b,
Tomatoes. No. C76c, Beets, peas. No. C76d,
Cauliflower, carrots. No. C77a, Dove. No.
C77b, Water birds. No. C77c, Fish. No. C77d,
Geese.

1982, Mar. 1   Litho.   Perf. 14
C70 AP13 25f Rabbits   1.25 .45
C71 AP13 50f Rooster, Hens   1.50 .90
C72 AP13 60f Turkeys   1.75 1.00
C73 AP13 75f Sheep   2.50 1.25
C74 AP13 100f Cattle   3.50 1.50
C75 AP13 125f Deer   4.00 1.90
        Nos. C70-C75 (6)   14.50 7.00

Souvenir Sheets
C76   Sheet of 4   10.00
    a.-d.   AP13 100f, any single 2.50
C77   Sheet of 4   10.00
    a.-d.   AP13 125f, any single 2.50

For surcharges see Nos. C139, C144.
Nos. C70-C75 exist imperf. (Value, set $50)
and in souvenir sheets (Value, set $45).

1980 Summer Olympics, Moscow AP14

1982, Apr. 1
C78 AP14 25f Gymnastics   1.25 .50
C79 AP14 50f Pole vault   1.50 .65
C80 AP14 60f Javelin   1.75 .75
C81 AP14 75f Running   2.50 1.00
C82 AP14 100f Basketball   3.50 1.50
C83 AP14 125f Soccer   4.00 1.75
        Nos. C78-C83 (6)   14.50 6.15

Nos. C78-C81 exist imperf. (Value, set $50)
and in souvenir sheets (Value, set $45).
Two souvenir sheets of 4 exist: 100f, picturing boxing, wrestling, canoeing, swimming
(Value $12.50), and 125f, picturing weight lift-
ing, discus, long jump, fencing (Value $15).
For surcharges see Nos. C140, C145.

Aviation — AP15

Various space and aircraft.

1982, May 21
C86 AP15 25f multi   1.25 .50
C87 AP15 50f multi   1.50 .60
C88 AP15 60f multi   1.75 .75
C89 AP15 75f multi   2.50 1.00
C90 AP15 100f multi   3.50 1.40
C91 AP15 125f multi   4.00 1.60
        Nos. C86-C91 (6)   14.50 5.85

Nos. C86-C91 exist imperf. (Value set, $50)
and in souvenir sheets (Value, set $45).
Two souvenir sheets of 4 exist, 100f and
125f, picturing various aircraft and satellites.
Values $12.50 and $15, respectively.
For surcharges see Nos. C141, C146.

Intl. Year of the Disabled — AP16

Designs: Nos. C94-C99, Diff. flowers.
No. C100a, Emblem, natl. flag. b, Emblem
on globe. c, Natl. colors, UN emblems. d, Disabled man, gifts, nurse.
No. C101a, Flags, globe and nurse. b, UN
emblems, natl. flag. c, Emblem, disabled man.
d, UN emblem, nurse.

1982, June 1
C94 AP16 25f multi   1.25 .60
C95 AP16 50f multi   1.50 .75
C96 AP16 60f multi   1.75 .90
C97 AP16 75f multi   2.50 1.25
C98 AP16 100f multi   3.50 1.75
C99 AP16 125f multi   4.00 2.00
        Nos. C94-C99 (6)   14.50 7.25

Souvenir Sheets
C100   Sheet of 4   12.50
    a.-d.   AP16 100f, any single 3.00
C101   Sheet of 4   15.00
    a.-d.   AP16 125f, any single 3.50

Nos. C94-C99 exist imperf. (Value, set $50)
and in souvenir sheets (Value, set $45).
For surcharge see No. C147.

Telecommunications Progress — AP17

Designs: 25f, FNRR communication center.
50f, Dish receivers, satellite, globe. 60f,
Broadcast towers, dish receivers. 75f, Receivers, birds over plain. 100f, Receivers, satellite,
telegraph key. No. C107, Receivers, passenger jet, Earth.
No. C108a, Receivers, Earth. b, Earth, television, flag and camera. c, Computer. d, Skyscraper, Earth, telephone.
No. C109a, Receivers, satellite, ship. b,
Communication center, bolts of energy,
receivers. c, Receivers, jet, ship, train, car,
carriage. d, Radar.

1982, July 1   Litho.   Perf. 14
C102 AP17 25f multi   1.00 .50
C103 AP17 50f multi   1.25 .60
C104 AP17 60f multi   1.50 .75
C105 AP17 75f multi   2.25 1.00
C106 AP17 100f multi   3.25 1.50
C107 AP17 125f multi   3.75 1.75
        Nos. C102-C107 (6)   13.00 6.10

Souvenir Sheets

C108	Sheet of 4	10.00
a.-d.	AP17 100f any single	2.50
C109	Sheet of 4	12.00
a.-d.	AP17 100f any single	3.00

Nos. C102-C107 exist imperf. (Value, set $50) and in souvenir sheets (Value, set $45). For surcharges see Nos. C142, C148.

TB Bacillus Centenary — AP18

1982, Aug. 1   Litho.   Perf. 14

C110	AP18	25f multi	1.00	.50
C111	AP18	50f multi	1.25	.60
C112	AP18	60f multi	1.50	.75
C113	AP18	75f multi	2.25	1.00
C114	AP18	100f multi	3.25	1.50
C115	AP18	125f multi	3.75	1.75
	Nos. C110-C115 (6)		13.00	6.10

Souvenir Sheets

C116	Sheet of 4, Fruit	14.00
a.	AP18 100f, any single	3.50
C117	Sheet of 4, Flowers	14.00
a.	AP18 125f, any single	3.50

Nos. C110-C115 exist imperf. (Value, set $20) and in souvenir sheets (Value, set $40). For surcharges see Nos. C143, C149.

1982 World Cup Soccer Championships, Spain — AP19

Various soccer plays.

1982, Sept. 1   Perf. 14

C118	AP19	25f multi	1.25	.50
C119	AP19	50f multi	1.50	.60
C120	AP19	60f multi	1.75	.75
C121	AP19	75f multi	2.50	1.00
C122	AP19	100f multi	3.50	1.50
C123	AP19	125f multi	4.00	1.75
	Nos. C118-C123 (6)		14.50	6.10

Nos. C118-C123 exist imperf. (Value, set $50) and in souvenir sheets (Value, set $72).

Palestinian Children's Day — AP20

1982, Oct. 20

C126	AP20	75f Boy	1.50	1.00
C127	AP20	125f Girl	2.50	2.00
C128	AP20	325f Boy and girl	6.00	4.00
a.	Souvenir sheet of 1		8.00	8.00
	Nos. C126-C128 (3)		10.00	7.00

Arab Postal Union, 30th Anniv. — AP21

1982, Dec. 1

C129	AP21	75f yellow & multi	1.25	1.00
C130	AP21	125f green & multi	2.25	1.75
C131	AP21	325f magenta & multi	4.00	2.00
a.	Souvenir sheet of 1		8.00	8.00
	Nos. C129-C131 (3)		7.50	4.75

1984 Summer Olympics, Los Angeles — AP22

1984, Nov. 15

C132	AP22	20f Wrestling	.60	.25
C133	AP22	30f Boxing	.90	.30
C134	AP22	40f Running	1.25	.50
C135	AP22	60f Hurdling	1.50	.70
C136	AP22	150f Pole vault	2.25	1.10
C137	AP22	325f Javelin throw	3.50	1.75
	Nos. C132-C137 (6)		10.00	4.60

Nos. C132-C137 exist imperf. (Value, set $50) and in souvenir sheets (Value, set $50). Two souvenir sheets of four 75f stamps exist picturing water sports, gymnastics, weightlifting, shot put and discus throwing. Value $12.50 each.

No. C67 Surcharged Nos. 459, 461, 463, 466, 474, 483, 486, 522, C73, C75, C81, C83, C89, C91, C97, C105, C107, C113 & C115 Surcharged with New Value and "AIR MAIL"

1993, Jan. 1   Perfs, etc. as Before

C138	AP12	3r on 125f #C67	
C139	AP13	3r on 125f #C75	
C140	AP14	3r on 125f #C83	
C141	AP15	3r on 125f #C91	
C142	AP17	3r on 125f #C107	
C143	AP18	3r on 125f #C115	
C144	AP13	5r on 75f #C73	
C145	AP14	5r on 75f #C81	
C146	AP15	5r on 75f #C89	
C147	AP16	5r on 75f #C97	
C148	AP17	5r on 75f #C105	
C149	AP18	5r on 75f #C113	
C150	A126	8r on 425f #460	
C151	A127	8r on 425f #461	
C152	A128	8r on 425f #463	
C153	A129	8r on 425f #466	
C154	A130	8r on 425f #474	
C155	A132	8r on 425f #483	
C156	A133	8r on 425f #486	
C157	A142	12r on 850f #522	

Size and location of surcharge varies.

POSTAGE DUE STAMPS

D1

1942   Litho.   Wmk. 258   Perf. 12½

J1	D1	1b org & yel grn	.25	.25
J2	D1	2b org & yel grn	.25	.25
J3	D1	4b org & yel grn	.45	.45
J4	D1	6b org & brt ultra	.55	.55
J5	D1	8b org & brt ultra	.80	.80
J6	D1	10b org & brt ultra	1.00	1.00

J7	D1	12b org & brt ultra	1.50	1.50
J8	D1	20b org & brt ultra	3.00	3.00
	Nos. J1-J8 (8)		7.80	7.80

Yemen had no postage due system. Nos. J1-J8 were used for regular postage. See Nos. 66-67 for surcharge.

Animals Type of Regular Issue Inscribed "Postage Due"

1964, Aug. 15   Photo.   Perf. 12x11½

J9	A39d	4b Gazelles	1.75	.60
J10	A39d	12b Buffalo	3.50	1.50
J11	A39d	20b Arabian horse	6.50	2.50
	Nos. J9-J11 (3)		11.75	4.60

Flower Type of Regular Issue Inscribed "Postage Due"

1964, Sept. 1   Photo.   Perf. 11½x12

J12	A39e	4b Like No. 199C	1.40	1.00
J13	A39e	12b Like No. 199B	3.50	2.00
J14	A39e	20b Like No. 199D	5.00	3.50
	Nos. J12-J14 (3)		9.90	6.50

Nos. 209G-209K Overprinted in Black

Perf. 14x14½, 14½x15

1966, Mar. 5   Photo.

J15	A43a	6b On No. 209G	4.00	2.50
J16	A43a	8b On No. 209H	4.25	3.00
J17	A43a	12b On No. 209I	6.00	3.50
J18	A43a	20b On No. 209J	10.00	6.50
J19	A43a	1r On No. 209K	20.00	12.50
	Nos. J15-J19 (5)		44.25	28.00

World Cup Soccer Type of Regular Issue Inscribed "Postage Due"

Designs: No. J20, Goalie defending shot on goal. No. J21, Three players. No. J22, Jules Rimet Cup emblem.

1966, May 29   Litho.   Perf. 11

J20	A51	4b multicolored	1.75	1.25
J21	A51	5b multicolored	3.00	2.00
J22	A51	20b multicolored	6.00	4.00
	Nos. J20-J22 (3)		10.75	7.25

Fruit Type of Regular Issue Inscribed "Postage Due"

1967, Feb. 10   Litho.   Perf. 12½x12

J23	A56	6b Bananas	1.60	1.25
J24	A56	8b Figs	2.50	1.75
J25	A56	10b Green grapes	3.50	2.25
	Nos. J23-J25 (3)		7.60	5.25

Two stamps of this design were released in 1968 or 1978. While they have been called postal tax stamps, questions about their status and use exist. The editors would like more information about these stamps and would like to examine unused and on cover examples.

YEMEN, PEOPLE'S DEMOCRATIC REPUBLIC OF

'pē-pəls ri-'pə-blik of 'ye-mən

LOCATION — Southern Arabia
GOVT. — Republic

AREA — 111,074 sq. mi.
POP. — 2,030,000 (est. 1981)
CAPITAL — Aden

The People's Republic of Southern Yemen was proclaimed Nov. 30, 1967, when the Federation of South Arabia achieved independence. It consisted of the former British colony of Aden and the protectorates. The name was changed to People's Democratic Republic of Yemen on Nov. 30, 1970. See South Arabia.

The Yemen Arab Republic and the People's Republic of Yemen planned a 30-month unification process scheduled for completion by November 1992. While government ministries merged, both currencies remained valid. A civil war in 1994 delayed the merger.

1,000 Fils = 1 Dinar

Catalogue values for all unused stamps in this country are for Never Hinged items.

People's Republic of Southern Yemen

South Arabia Nos. 3-16 Overprinted in Red or Blue

Nos. 1-10

Nos. 11-14

Perf. 14½x14

1968, Apr. 1   Photo.   Unwmk.

1	A1	5f blue	.25	.25
2	A1	10f lt vio bl	.25	.25
3	A1	15f bl grn	.25	.25
4	A1	20f green	.25	.25
5	A1	25f org brn (B)	.25	.25
6	A1	30f lemon	.25	.25
7	A1	35f red brn (B)	.35	.25
8	A1	50f rose red (B)	.45	.35
9	A1	65f lt yel grn	.60	.40
10	A1	75f rose car (B)	.75	.55
11	A2	100f multi (B)	1.10	.70
12	A2	250f multi	2.25	1.40
13	A2	500f multi (B)	4.50	2.75
14	A2	1d vio & multi	10.00	7.00
	Nos. 1-14 (14)		21.50	14.90

Globe and Flag A1

Designs: 15f, Revolutionist with broken chain and flames, vert. 50f, Aden Harbor. 100f, Cotton picking.

1968, May 25   Litho.   Perf. 13x12½

15	A1	10f multi	.25	.25
16	A1	15f multi	.25	.25
17	A1	50f multi	.55	.55
18	A1	100f multi	1.50	1.50
	Nos. 15-18 (4)		2.55	2.55

Independence Day, Nov. 30, 1967.

Girl Scouts at Campfire A2

Designs: 25f, Three Girl Scouts, vert. 50f, Three Girl Scout leaders.

Perf. 13½
1968, Sept. 21   Litho.   Unwmk.
19   A2 10f ultra & sepia   .50   .50
20   A2 25f org brn & Prus bl   .75   .75
21   A2 50f yel, bl & brn   1.40 1.40
    Nos. 19-21 (3)   2.65 2.65
Girl Scout movement in Southern Yemen, established 1966 (in Aden).

Revolutionary — A3

"Freedom-Socialism-Unity" — A4

Design: 30f, Radfan Mountains where first revolutionary fell.

1968, Oct. 14   Unwmk.   Perf. 13
22   A3 20f brn & lt bl   .30   .30
23   A3 30f grn & brn   .45   .45
24   A4 100f ver & yel   1.10 1.10
    Nos. 22-24 (3)   1.85 1.85
Revolution Day (revolution of Oct. 14, 1963).

King of Ausan,
Alabaster
Statue — A5

Antiquities of Southern Yemen: 35f, African-type sculpture of a man. 50f, Winged bull, Assyrian-type bas-relief, horiz. 65f, Bull's head (Moon God), alabaster plaque, 230 B.C., horiz.

1968, Dec. 28   Litho.   Perf. 13
25   A5 5f olive & bister   .25   .25
26   A5 35f maroon & lt bl   .50   .50
27   A5 50f bister & blue   1.10 1.10
28   A5 65f lt grnsh bl & lilac 1.40 1.40
    Nos. 25-28 (4)   3.25 3.25

A6

Martyr Monument, Steamer Point, Aden.

1969, Feb. 11   Litho.   Perf. 13
29   A6 15f yellow & multi   .25   .25
30   A6 35f emerald & multi   .25   .25
31   A6 100f orange & multi   1.50 1.50
    Nos. 29-31 (3)   2.00 2.00
Issued for Martyr Day.

A7

Albert Thomas Monument, Geneva, and ILO emblem.

1969, June 1   Litho.   Perf. 13
32   A7 10f brt grn, blk & lt brn .25   .25
33   A7 35f car rose, blk & lt brn .70   .60
50th anniv. of the ILO, and to honor founder Albert Thomas.

Classroom — A8

1969, Sept. 8   Litho.   Perf. 13
34   A8 35f orange & multi   .50   .35
35   A8 100f yellow & multi   1.40 1.25
International Literacy Day, Sept. 8.

Mahatma
Gandhi — A9

1969, Sept. 27   Litho.   Perf. 13
36   A9 35f lt ultra & vio brn   1.75   .60
Mohandas K. Gandhi (1869-1948), leader in India's fight for independence.

Family
A10

1969, Oct. 1
37   A10 25f lt grn & multi   .50   .40
38   A10 75f car rose & multi   1.40   .90
Issued for Family Day.

UN Headquarters, NYC — A11

1969, Oct. 24   Perf. 13
39   A11 20f rose red & multi   .50   .35
40   A11 65f emer & multi   1.40   .70
Issued for United Nations Day.

Map and Flag of Southern
Yemen — A12

40f, 50f, Tractors, flag (agricultural progress).

1969, Nov. 30   Litho.   Unwmk.
Size: 41x24½mm
41   A12 15f multi   .25   .25
42   A12 35f multi   .45   .25
Size: 37x37mm
43   A12 40f blue & multi   .55   .45
44   A12 50f brown & multi   .90   .60
    Nos. 41-44 (4)   2.15 1.55
Second anniversary of independence.

Map of Arab League Countries, Flag
and Emblem — A13

1970, Mar. 22   Unwmk.   Perf. 13
45   A13 35f lt bl & multi   .85   .35
25th anniversary of the Arab League.

Lenin — A14

1970, Apr. 22   Litho.   Perf. 13
46   A14 75f multi   1.50   .60
Lenin (1870-1924), Russian communist leader.

Fighter — A15

Designs: 35f, Underground soldier and plane destroyed on ground. 50f, Fighting people hailing Arab liberation flag, horiz.

1970, May 15
47   A15 15f grn, red & blk   .25   .25
48   A15 35f grn, bl, red & blk   .55   .55
49   A15 50f grn, blk & red   .85   .70
    Nos. 47-49 (3)   1.65 1.50
Issued for Palestine Day.

UPU Headquarters, Bern — A16

1970, May 22   Litho.   Perf. 13
50   A16 15f org & brt grn   .60   .25
51   A16 65f yel & car rose   1.40   .60
New UPU Headquarters in Bern.

Yemeni
Costume — A17

Regional Costumes: 15f, 20f, Women's costumes. 50f, Three men of Aden.

1970, July 2   Litho.   Perf. 13
52   A17 10f yel & multi   .40   .25
53   A17 15f lt lil & multi   .40   .25
54   A17 20f lt bl & multi   .65   .25
55   A17 50f multi   1.25   .45
    Nos. 52-55 (4)   2.70 1.20

Camel and Calf — A18

Designs: 25f, Goats. 35f, Arabian oryx. 65f, Socotra dwarf cows.

1970, Aug. 31   Litho.   Perf. 13
56   A18 15f dk brn & multi   .40   .25
57   A18 25f car rose & multi   .65   .45
58   A18 35f ultra & multi   1.20   .75
59   A18 65f brt grn & multi   2.00 1.25
    Nos. 56-59 (4)   4.25 2.70

A19

35f, Natl. Front Organization Headquarters. 50f, Farm worker, 1970, battle scene, 1963.

1970, Oct. 14   Litho.   Perf. 13
Size: 41½x29½mm
60   A19 25f multi   .40   .25
Size: 56½x27mm
61   A19 35f multi   .50   .45
Size: 41x24½mm
62   A19 50f multi   1.90 1.25
    Nos. 60-62 (3)   2.80 1.95
7th anniversary of Oct. 14 Revolution.

UN Headquarters, Emblem — A20

1970, Oct. 24   Litho.   Perf. 13
63   A20 10f org & bl   .45   .25
64   A20 65f brt pink & bl   1.50   .80
25th anniversary of the United Nations.

People's Democratic Republic of Yemen

Temples at Philae — A21

1971, Feb. 1   Litho.   Perf. 13½x13
65	A21	5f violet & multi	.25	.25
66	A21	35f blue & multi	.65	.40
67	A21	65f green & multi	1.60	.90
		Nos. 65-67 (3)	2.50	1.55

UNESCO campaign to save the monuments in Nubia.

Scales, Book and Sword A22

1971, Mar. 1   Perf. 13x12½
68	A22	10f brt pink & multi	.25	.25
69	A22	15f brt grn & multi	.25	.25
70	A22	35f lt ultra & multi	.65	.65
71	A22	50f rose & multi	.85	.85
		Nos. 68-71 (4)	2.00	2.00

First Constitution, 1971.

Men of 3 Races, Human Rights Emblem A23

1971, Mar. 21
72	A23	20f lt bl & multi	.25	.25
73	A23	35f grn & multi	.75	.75
74	A23	75f lt vio & multi	1.10	1.10
		Nos. 72-74 (3)	2.10	2.10

Intl. year against racial discrimination.

Map and Flag — A24

"Brothers' Blood" Tree, Socotra Island — A25

1971-77   Litho.   Perf. 13½
75	A24	5f yel & multi	.25	.25
76	A24	10f grn & multi	.25	.25
77	A24	15f yel & multi	.25	.25
78	A24	20f org & multi	.25	.25
79	A24	25f bl & multi	.25	.25
80	A24	35f red org & multi	.35	.25
81	A24	40f vio & multi	.50	.25
82	A24	50f yel grn & multi	.65	.45
82A	A24	60f red & multi	1.40	.60
83	A24	65f pale vio & multi	.90	.65
84	A24	80f org brn & multi	1.00	.80
84A	A24	90f ol & multi	1.40	.75

Perf. 13
84B	A25	110f brn & multi	2.00	.95
85	A25	125f ultra & multi	1.60	1.50
86	A25	250f org & multi	2.90	2.00
87	A25	500f multi	6.00	4.00
88	A25	1d grn & multi	13.50	8.00
		Nos. 75-88 (17)	33.45	21.45

Issued: #82A, 84A-84B, 10/17/77; others, 4/1/71.

See Nos. 332-333. For surcharges see Yemen Nos. 628, 638.

Machine Gun and Map — A26

Designs: 45f, Woman fighter and flame, horiz. 50f, Fighter, factories and rainbow.

1971, June 9   Litho.   Perf. 12½x13
89	A26	15f multi	.25	.25
90	A26	45f green & multi	.65	.45
91	A26	50f multi	1.10	.75
		Nos. 89-91 (3)	2.00	1.45

Armed revolution in the Arabian Gulf.

Arms with Wrench and Cogwheel — A27

25f, Torch, factories, symbols. 65f, Windmill.

1971, June 22
92	A27	15f blue & multi	.25	.25
93	A27	25f multi	.75	.55
94	A27	65f multi	1.25	.75
		Nos. 92-94 (3)	2.25	1.55

2nd anniversary of the revolution of June 22, 1969 (Corrective Movement).

A 20f picturing a fighter holding rifle and flag, with flag colors transposed, was withdrawn on day of issue.

Revolutionary Emblem — A28

40f, Map of southern Arabia & flag of republic.

1971, Sept. 26
95	A28	10f yellow & multi	.25	.25
96	A28	40f lt grn & multi	.75	.55

9th anniv. of the revolution of Sept. 26.

Gamal Abdel Nasser — A29

1971, Sept. 28   Litho.   Perf. 12½x13
97	A29	65f multi	1.25	.75

1st anniv. of the death of Gamal Abdel Nasser (1918-1970), President of Egypt.

UNICEF Emblem, Children of the World — A30

1971, Dec. 11   Perf. 13x13½
98	A30	15f org, car & blk	.25	.25
99	A30	40f lt ultra, car & blk	.40	.35
100	A30	50f yel grn, car & blk	.70	.55
		Nos. 98-100 (3)	1.35	1.15

25th anniv. of UNICEF.

Pigeons A31

Birds: 40f, Partridge. 65f, Partridge and guinea fowl. 100f, European kite.

1971, Dec. 22   Perf. 13½x13
101	A31	5f bl, blk & car	.35	.25
102	A31	40f salmon & multi	1.25	.60
103	A31	65f brt grn, blk & car	3.00	1.10
104	A31	100f yel, blk & car	5.25	2.25
		Nos. 101-104 (4)	9.85	4.20

Dhow under Construction A32

Design: 80f, Dhow under sail, vert.

1972, Feb. 15   Perf. 13½x13, 13x13½
105	A32	25f bl, brn & yel	.75	.45
106	A32	80f lt bl & multi	2.40	1.60

Band — A33

Designs: 25f, 40f, 80f, Various folk dances.

1972, Apr. 8   Litho.   Perf. 13
107	A33	10f lt grn & multi	.25	.25
108	A33	25f org & multi	.35	.25
109	A33	40f red & multi	.80	.45
110	A33	80f blue & multi	1.50	.90
		Nos. 107-110 (4)	2.90	1.85

Palestinian Fighter and Barbed Wire — A34

1972, May 15
111	A34	5f emerald & multi	.30	.25
112	A34	20f blue & multi	.60	.35
113	A34	65f org ver & multi	1.50	.85
		Nos. 111-113 (3)	2.40	1.45

Struggle for Palestine liberation.

Militia Women on Parade A35

Design: 25f, Policemen on parade.

1972, June 20   Litho.   Perf. 13½
114	A35	25f lt bl & multi	.60	.25
115	A35	80f bl grn & multi	2.50	1.50
a.		Souv. sheet of 2, #114-115	9.00	9.00

Police Day. No. 115a sold for 150f.

Start of Bicycle Race A36

15f Parade of young women. 40f, Yemeni Guides & Scouts on parade. 80f, Acrobats, vert.

1972, July 20   Litho.   Perf. 13½
116	A36	10f lt bl & multi	.40	.25
117	A36	15f multi	.55	.25
118	A36	40f buff & multi	1.00	.60
119	A36	80f lt ultra & multi	1.60	.90
		Nos. 116-119 (4)	3.55	2.00

Turtle A37

1972, Sept. 2   Litho.   Perf. 13
120	A37	15f shown	.90	.25
121	A37	40f Sailfish	1.10	.70
122	A37	65f Kingfish	1.75	.90
123	A37	125f Spiny lobster	3.25	1.60
		Nos. 120-123 (4)	7.00	3.45

Book Year Emblem A38

1972, Sept. 9
124	A38	40f red, ultra & yel	.75	.50
125	A38	65f org, ultra & yel	1.25	.80

International Book Year 1972.

Farm Couple and Fields A39

1972, Nov. 23   Litho.   Perf. 13
126	A39	10f orange & multi	.25	.25
127	A39	25f rose lilac & multi	.70	.45
128	A39	40f red & multi	1.25	.80
		Nos. 126-128 (3)	2.20	1.50

Lands Day, publicizing land reforms.

Militia — A40

20f, Soldier guarding village. 65f, Industrial, agricultural and educational progress, vert.

1972, Dec. 2　Litho.　Perf. 13
129　A40　5f multi　　.25　.25
130　A40　20f multi　　.25　.25
131　A40　65f multi　　1.60　1.60
　a.　Souv. sheet of 3, #129-131, im-
　　　perf.　　　　　　4.00　4.00
　Nos. 129-131 (3)　　2.10　2.10

5th anniversary of independence.

Census
Chart
A41

1973, Apr. 3　Litho.　Perf. 12½x13½
132　A41　25f org, emer & ol　.25　.25
133　A41　40f rose, bl & vio　1.25　1.25

Population census 1973.

WHO
Emblem
and
"25" — A42

5f, "25" and WHO emblem, vert. 125f, "25" and WHO emblem.

1973, Apr. 7　Perf. 14x12½, 12½x14
134　A42　5f multicolored　　.25　.25
135　A42　20f shown　　　　.25　.25
136　A42　125f multicolored　2.10　2.10
　Nos. 134-136 (3)　　　2.60　2.60

25th anniv. of the WHO.

Elephant
Bay
A43

Tourist Publicity: 20f, Taweels Tanks Reservoir, vert. 25f, Shibam Town. 100f, Al-Mohdar Mosque, Tarim.

1973, June 9　Litho.　Perf. 13
137　A43　20f multi　　.25　.25
138　A43　25f multi　　.25　.25
139　A43　40f multi　　1.50　1.50
140　A43　100f multi　　1.75　1.75
　Nos. 137-140 (4)　　3.75　3.75

Office Buildings and Slum,
Aden — A44

Design: 80f, Intersection, Aden, vert.

1973, Aug. 4　Litho.　Perf. 13
141　A44　20f multi　　.25　.25
142　A44　80f multi　　1.75　1.75

Nationalization of buildings.

Army
Unit
A45

People's Army: 20f, Four marching soldiers. 40f, Sailors on parade. 80f, Tanks.

1973, Sept. 1
143　A45　10f multi　　.25　.25
144　A45　20f multi　　.25　.25
145　A45　40f multi　　1.00　1.00
146　A45　80f multi　　1.40　1.40
　Nos. 143-146 (4)　　2.90　2.90

FAO
Emblem,
Loading
Food
A46

Design: 80f, Workers and grain sacks.

1973, Dec. 19　Litho.　Perf. 13
147　A46　20f blue & multi　.25　.25
148　A46　80f blue & multi　1.50　.90

World Food Program, 10th anniversary.

Letter and
UPU
Emblem
A47

UPU Emblem
and Yemeni
Flag — A48

Map of Yemen,
UPU
Emblem — A49

UPU cent.: 20f, "100" formed by people, and UPU emblem.

1974, Oct. 9　Litho.　Perf. 12½x13½
149　A47　5f multi　　.25　.25
150　A47　20f multi　　.45　.25
151　A48　40f multi　　.70　.70
152　A49　125f multi　　1.40　1.25
　Nos. 149-152 (4)　　2.80　2.45

Irrigation System — A50

Progress in Agriculture: 20f, Bulldozer pushing soil. 100f, Tractors plowing field.

1974　Litho.　Perf. 13
153　A50　10f multi　　.25　.25
154　A50　20f multi　　.25　.25
155　A50　100f multi　　1.50　1.50
　Nos. 153-155 (3)　　2.00　2.00

Lathe
Operator — A51

Industrial progress: 40f, Printers. 80f, Women textile workers, horiz.

1975, May 1　Litho.　Perf. 13
156　A51　10f multi　　.25　.25
157　A51　40f multi　　.60　.60
158　A51　80f multi　　1.20　1.00
　Nos. 156-158 (3)　　2.05　1.85

Yemeni
Woman — A52

Designs: Various women's costumes.

1975, Nov. 15　Litho.　Perf. 11½x12
159　A52　5f blk & ocher　　.25　.25
160　A52　10f blk & vio　　.25　.25
161　A52　15f blk & olive　　.25　.25
162　A52　25f blk & rose lil　.45　.45
163　A52　40f blk & Prus bl　.75　.75
164　A52　50f blk & org brn　1.10　1.10
　Nos. 159-164 (6)　　3.05　3.05

Women
Factory
Workers,
IWY
Emblem
A53

1975, Dec. 30　Litho.　Perf. 12x11½
165　A53　40f blk & salmon　.60　.60
166　A53　50f blk & yel grn　1.00　1.00

International Women's Year 1975.

Soccer Player
and
Field — A54

Designs: Different scenes from soccer.

1976, Apr. 1　Litho.　Perf. 11½x12
167　A54　5f lt bl & brn　　.25　.25
168　A54　40f yel & green　　.70　.70
169　A54　80f salmon & vio　1.10　1.10
　Nos. 167-169 (3)　　2.05　2.05

Rocket Take-off
from
Moon — A55

15f, Alexander Satalov. 40f, Lunokhod on moon, horiz. 65f, Valentina Tereshkova, rocket.

Perf. 11½x12, 12x11½
1976, Apr. 17　　　　Litho.
170　A55　10f multi　　.25　.25
171　A55　15f multi　　.25　.25
172　A55　40f multi　　1.00　1.00
173　A55　65f multi　　1.25　1.25
　Nos. 170-173 (4)　　2.75　2.75

Soviet cosmonauts and space program.

Traffic
Policemen
A56

1977, Apr. 16　Litho.　Perf. 14
174　A56　25f red & blk　　.60　.60
175　A56　60f yel & blk　　1.25　1.25
176　A56　75f grn & blk　　1.50　1.50
177　A56　110f dp bl & blk　2.00　2.00
　Nos. 174-177 (4)　　5.35　5.35

Traffic change to right side of road.

APU
Emblem — A57

1977, Apr. 12　Litho.　Perf. 13½
178　A57　20f lt bl & multi　.25　.25
179　A57　60f gray & multi　.80　.80
180　A57　70f lt grn & multi　1.00　1.00
181　A57　90f bl grn & multi　1.10　1.10
　Nos. 178-181 (4)　　3.15　3.15

Arab Postal Union, 25th anniversary.

Congress
Decree
and Red
Star
A58

Designs: 25f, Pres. Salim Rubi'a Ali, Council members Ali Nasser Muhamed and Abdul Farta Ismail. 65f, Women's militia on parade. 95f, Aerial view of textile mill.

1977, May　Photo.　Perf. 13
182　A58　25f grn, gold & dk brn　.25　.25
183　A58　35f red, gold & lt bl　.50　.50
184　A58　65f bl, gold & lil　1.00　1.00
185　A58　95f org, gold & grn　1.10　1.10
　Nos. 182-185 (4)　　2.85　2.85

Unification Congress, 1st anniversary.

Afrivoluta
Pringlei
A59

Shells: 60f, Festilyria duponti, vert. 110f, Conus splendidulus. 180f, Cypraea 4broderipii.

1977, July 16　Litho.　Perf. 13½
186　A59　60f multi　　.95　.70
187　A59　90f multi　　1.40　.70
188　A59　110f multi　　2.40　1.40
189　A59　180f multi　　3.25　2.40
　Nos. 186-189 (4)　　8.00　5.20

Emblem and Flag — A60

Designs: 20f, Man with broken chain. 90f, Pipeline, agriculture and industry. 110f, Flag, symbolic tree and hands holding tools.

1977, Nov. 30   Litho.   Perf. 13½
190	A60	5f blk & multi	.25	.25
191	A60	20f blk & multi	.25	.25
192	A60	90f blk & multi	.50	.25
193	A60	110f blk & multi	.85	.40
	Nos. 190-193 (4)		1.85	1.15

10th anniversary of independence.

Dome of the Rock A61

1978, May 15   Perf. 12
194	A61	5f multi	2.00	.40

Palestinian fighters & families. See #264A.

Festival Emblem and "CUBA" — A62

Designs: 60f, Festival emblem. 90f, Festival emblem as flower. 110f, Festival emblem, dove, young man and woman.

1978, June 22   Litho.   Perf. 14
195	A62	5f multi	.25	.25
196	A62	60f multi	.65	.40
197	A62	90f multi	.85	.45
198	A62	110f multi	1.10	.70
	Nos. 195-198 (4)		2.85	1.80

11th World Youth Festival, Havana.

Silver Ornaments — A63

Designs: Various silver ornaments.

1978, July 22   Litho.   Perf. 13½
199	A63	10f blk & multi	.25	.25
200	A63	15f blk & multi	.25	.25
201	A63	20f blk & multi	.25	.25
202	A63	60f blk & multi	.25	.25
203	A63	90f blk & multi	1.00	.65
204	A63	110f blk & multi	1.50	.75
	Nos. 199-204 (6)		3.50	2.40

For surcharge see Yemen No. 629.

Yemeni Musical Instruments — A64

1978, Aug. 26   Perf. 14
205	A64	35f Almarfaai	.40	.25
206	A64	60f Almizmar	.90	.35
207	A64	90f Alqnboos	1.60	.45
208	A64	110f Simsimiya	2.00	.80
	Nos. 205-208 (4)		4.90	1.85

For surcharge see Yemen No. 630.

"V" for Vanguard A65

1978, Oct. 11   Litho.   Perf. 14
209	A65	5f multi	.25	.25
210	A65	20f multi	.25	.25
211	A65	60f multi	.40	.25
212	A65	180f multi	.85	.50
	Nos. 209-212 (4)		1.75	1.25

1st Conf. of Vanguard Party, Oct. 11-13.

Man with Palm, Factories — A66

Designs: 10f, Palm branches, broken chains, horiz. 60f, Candle and "15." 110f, Woman and man with rifle, "15."

1978, Oct. 14   Perf. 14
213	A66	10f multi	.25	.25
214	A66	35f multi	.25	.25
215	A66	60f multi	.45	.25
216	A66	110f multi	.75	.45
	Nos. 213-216 (4)		1.70	1.20

15th Revolution Day.
For surcharge see Yemen No. 631.

Child, Map of Arabia and IYC Emblem — A67

1979, Mar. 20   Litho.   Perf. 13½
217	A67	15f multi	.25	.25
218	A67	20f multi	.25	.25
219	A67	60f multi	.60	.25
220	A67	90f multi	1.10	.70
	Nos. 217-220 (4)		2.20	1.45

International Year of the Child.

Sickle, Star, Tractor, Wheat and Dove — A68

Designs: 35f, Pylon, star, compass, wheat and hammer. 60f, Students, worker and clock. 90f, Woman with raised arms, doves and star.

1979, June 22   Litho.   Perf. 14
221	A68	20f multi	.25	.25
222	A68	35f multi	.25	.25
223	A68	60f multi	.40	.25
224	A68	90f multi	.55	.25
	Nos. 221-224 (4)		1.45	1.00

Corrective Movement, 10th anniversary.

Yemen #52, Hill A69

Hill and: 110f, Yemen #56. 250f, Aden #12.

1979, Aug. 27   Litho.   Perf. 14
225	A69	90f multi	.60	.25
226	A69	110f multi	.75	.45

Souvenir Sheet
227	A69	250f multi	2.25	2.25

Sir Rowland Hill (1795-1879), originator of penny postage.

Book, World Map, Arab Achievements — A70

1979, Sept. 26   Litho.   Perf. 14
228	A70	60f multi	1.00	.45

Party Emblem — A71

1979, Oct. 13   Perf. 14½x14
229	A71	60f multi	.70	.25

Yemeni Socialist Party, 1st anniversary.

Cassia Adenesis — A72

Flowers: 90f, Nerium oleander. 110f, Calligonum comosum. 180f, Adenium obesium.

1979, Nov. 30   Litho.   Perf. 13½
230	A72	20f multi	.25	.25
231	A72	90f multi	.90	.50
232	A72	110f multi	1.50	.75
233	A72	180f multi	1.90	.90
	Nos. 230-233 (4)		4.55	2.40

For surcharge see Yemen No. 632.

First Anniv. of Iranian Revolution — A73

1980, Feb. 12   Litho.   Perf. 13½
234	A73	60f multi	1.10	1.10

Dido A74

1980, Mar. 5   Litho.   Perf. 13½
235	A74	110f shown	1.00	.50
236	A74	180f Anglia	1.50	.70
237	A74	250f India	2.00	.90
	Nos. 235-237 (3)		4.50	2.10

For surcharge see Yemen No. 633.

Basket Maker, London 1980 Emblem — A75

1980, May 6   Litho.   Perf. 14
238	A75	60f shown	.25	.25
239	A75	90f Hubble bubble pipe maker	.65	.25
240	A75	110f Weaver	.90	.55
241	A75	250f Potter	2.00	1.10
	Nos. 238-241 (4)		3.80	2.15

London 1980 Intl. Stamp Exhib., May 6-14.

Hemprich's Skink — A76

1980, May 8   Litho.   Perf. 14
242	A76	20f shown	.25	.25
243	A76	35f Mole viper	.60	.25
244	A76	110f Carter's day gecko	1.50	.60
245	A76	180f Cobra	2.50	1.25
	Nos. 242-245 (4)		4.85	2.35

For surcharge see Yemen No. 634.

Misha and Olympic Emblem — A77

1980, July 19   Litho.   Perf. 12½x12
246	A77	110f multi	1.10	.65

For overprint see No. 287.

Farmers
Armed — A78

50f, Armed farmers working, horiz. 110f,
Sickle (wheat) and fist.

1980, Oct. 17   *Perf. 13½*
247 A78 50f multicolored   .50   .25
248 A78 90f shown   .75   .50
249 A78 110f multicolored   1.00   .70
   Nos. 247-249 (3)   2.25 1.45

10th anniversary of farmers' uprising.

110th Birth
Anniversary of
Lenin — A79

1980, Nov. 7   Litho.   *Perf. 12*
250 A79 35f multi   .50   .50

Douglas DC-3 — A80

1981, Mar. 11   Litho.   *Perf. 13½*
251 A80 60f shown   .25   .25
252 A80 90f Boeing 707   1.50   .35
253 A80 250f DHC Dash 7   3.50 1.60
   Nos. 251-253 (3)   5.25 2.10

Democratic Yemen Airlines, 10th anniv.

Ras
Boradli
Earth
Satellite
Station
A82

1981, June 22   Litho.   *Perf. 12*
257 A82 60f multi   1.25   .65

Conocarpus
Lancifolius — A83

1981, Aug. 1   Litho.   *Perf. 12*
258 A83 90f shown   .95   .25
259 A83 180f Ficus vasta   1.75 1.10
260 A83 250f Maerua crassifolia 2.75 1.40
   Nos. 258-260 (3)   5.45 2.75

Supreme People's
Council, 10th
Anniv. — A84

1981, Aug. 18   Litho.   *Perf. 15x14½*
261 A84 180f multi   1.50   .90

Desert Fox — A85

1981, Sept. 26   Litho.   *Perf. 14½*
262 A85 50f shown   .70   .25
263 A85 90f South Arabian
          leopard   1.40   .70
264 A85 250f Ibex   3.25 1.60
   Nos. 262-264 (3)   5.35 2.55

No. 194 Redrawn

1981, Oct. 15   Litho.   *Perf. 12*
Size: 25x27mm
264A A61 5f multi   1.00   .45

Denomination in upper right.

Tephrosia
Apollinea — A86

1981, Nov. 30   Litho.   *Perf. 13½*
265 A86 50f shown   .25   .25
266 A86 90f Citrullus colo-
          cynthis   1.00   .25
267 A86 110f Aloe sqarrosa   1.40   .25
268 A86 250f Lawsonia inermis   3.50 2.00
   Nos. 265-268 (4)   6.15 2.75

For surcharge see Yemen No. 635.

Intl. Year
of the
Disabled
A87

1981, Dec. 12   Litho.   *Perf. 14½*
269 A87 50f multi   .40   .25
270 A87 100f multi   1.00   .50
271 A87 150f multi   1.50   .85
   Nos. 269-271 (3)   2.90 1.60

TB Bacillus Centenary — A88

1982, Mar. 24   Litho.   *Perf. 14½*
272 A88 50f multi   4.50   .75

30th
Anniv. of
Arab
Postal
Union
A89

1982, Apr. 12   Litho.   *Perf. 14*
273 A89 100f multi   1.25   .75

1982
World Cup
A90

Designs: Various soccer players.

1982, June 13   Litho.   *Perf. 14*
274 A90 50f multi   .65   .25
275 A90 100f multi   1.20   .65
276 A90 150f multi   2.00 1.25
277 A90 200f multi   2.60 1.40
   a.   Souv. sheet of 4, #274-277   6.50 6.50
   Nos. 274-277 (4)   6.45 3.55

For overprints see Nos. 281-284.

60th
Anniv. of
USSR
A93

1982, Dec. 22   Litho.   *Perf. 12½x12*
280 A93 50f Flags, arms   .65   .45

**Nos. 274-277, 277a Ovptd. with
Emblem and "WORLD CUP /
WINNERS / 1982 / 1st ITALY / 2nd
W-GERMANY / 3rd POLAND / 4th
FRANCE" in Blue**

1982, Dec. 30   Litho.   *Perf. 14*
281 A90 50f multi   .25   .25
282 A90 100f multi   1.50 1.50
283 A90 150f multi   2.25 2.25
284 A90 200f multi   2.50 2.50
   a.   Souvenir sheet of 4, #281-284   7.00 7.00
   Nos. 281-284 (4)   6.50 6.50

Palestinian
Solidarity
A94

1983, Apr. 10   *Perf. 13½x14½*
285 A94 50f Yasser Arafat   1.00   .60
286 A94 100f Arafat, Dome of the
          Rock   3.00 1.00
   a.   Souvenir sheet of 1, imperf.   3.00 3.00

**No. 246 Ovptd. with TEMBAL '83
Emblem in Yellow**

1983, May 21   *Perf. 12½x12*
287 A77 110f multi   4.75 2.50

World Communications Year — A95

Designs: 50f, Correspondent, postrider,
ship. 100f, Postman, coach, telegraph. No.
290, Telephones, bus. 200f, Telecommunications. No. 292, Montage.

1983, June 10   *Perf. 13x13½*
288 A95 50f blk & brt bl   .25   .25
289 A95 100f multi   1.50 1.50
290 A95 150f multi   2.40 2.40
291 A95 200f multi   2.75 2.75
   Nos. 288-291 (4)   6.90 6.90
Souvenir Sheet
292 A95 150f multi   3.00 3.00

Pablo Picasso (1881-1973),
Painter — A96

Paintings: No. 293, The Poor Family, 1903.
No. 294, Woman with Crow. No. 295a, The
Gourmet. No. 295b, Woman with Child on
Beach. No. 295c, Sitting Beggar. No. 296,
The Soler Family, horiz.

1983, July 25   *Perf. 14*
293 A96 50f multi   1.00   .30
294 A96 100f multi   2.00   .90
Souvenir Sheets
295   Sheet of 3   13.50 13.50
   a.   A96 50f multi   1.75 1.75
   b.   A96 100f multi   4.50 4.50
   c.   A96 150f multi   6.50 6.50
296 A96 150f multi   8.00 8.00

23rd Pre-Olympics Games,
1984 — A97

1983, July 30
297 A97 25f Show jumping   1.00   .35
298 A97 50f Show jumping,
          diff.   1.40   .65
299 A97 100f Three-day event   2.50 1.25
   Nos. 297-299 (3)   4.90 2.25
Souvenir Sheets
300   Sheet of 4   13.50 13.50
   a.   A97 20f Bay, vert.   2.50 2.50
   b.   A97 40f Gray, vert.   2.50 2.50
   c.   A97 60f Bay, diff., vert.   3.25 3.25
   d.   A97 80f Arabian   4.50 4.50
301 A97 200f Show jumping,
          diff., vert.   9.75 9.75

Locomotives — A98

1983, Aug. 24   *Perf. 14½x15*
302 A98 25f P8 steam en-
          gine, 1905   1.25   .50
303 A98 50f 880 steam, 1915   2.25   .90
304 A98 100f GT 2-4-4, 1923   3.50 1.75
   Nos. 302-304 (3)   7.00 3.15
Souvenir Sheets
305   Sheet of 3   20.00 20.00
   a.   A98 40f D51 steam, 1936   4.75 4.75
   b.   A98 60f 45 Series, 1937   4.75 4.75
   c.   A98 100f PT 47, 1948   9.00 9.00
306 A98 200f P36, 1950   20.00 20.00

Ships — A99

1983, Sept. 15   Perf. 14
307 A99 50f Europa   .60   .50
308 A99 100f World Discoverer   3.00 1.75

Miniature Sheet
309   Sheet of 4   18.00 18.00
a.   A99 20f Kruzenstern   1.75 1.75
b.   A99 40f Grossherzogin Elisa-
           beth   3.50 3.50
c.   A99 60f Sedov   5.50 5.50
d.   A99 80f Dar Pomorza   7.50 7.50

Souvenir Sheet
310 A99 200f Gorch Foch   16.00 15.00

Natl. Revolution, 20th Anniv. A100

1983, Oct. 15   Litho.   Perf. 13½x13
312 A100 50f shown   .90   .45
313 A100 100f Flag, freedom
             fighter   2.00 1.00

1st Manned Flight, Bicent. — A101

Balloons: 100f, La Montgolfiere prototype. No. 316a, Lunardi's. No. 316b, Charles and Robert's. No. 316c, Wiseman's. No. 316d, Blanchard and Jeffries's. 200f, Five-balloon craft.

1983, Oct. 25   Perf. 14
314 A101 50f shown   1.25   .50
315 A101 100f multi   2.50 1.00

Souvenir Sheets
316   Sheet of 4   13.50 13.50
a.   A101 20f multi   3.00 3.00
b.   A101 40f multi   3.00 3.00
c.   A101 60f multi   3.00 3.00
d.   A101 80f multi   4.00 4.00
317 A101 200f multi   13.50 13.50

1984 Winter Olympics, Sarajevo A102

50f, Men's downhill skiing. 100f, Two-man bobsled.

1983, Dec. 28   Litho.   Perf. 14
318 A102 50f multicolored   .90   .40
319 A102 100f multicolored   1.75   .80

Souvenir Sheets
320   Sheet of 3   9.00 9.00
a.   A102 40f Ski jumping   3.00 3.00
b.   A102 60f Figure skating   3.00 3.00
c.   A102 100f Two-man bobsled   3.00 3.00
321 A102 200f Ice hockey   9.00 9.00

1984 Summer Olympics, Los Angeles — A103

1984, Jan. 24
322 A103 25f Fencing   .45   .25
323 A103 50f Fencing, diff.   .90   .45
324 A103 100f Fencing, diff.   1.40   .75
     Nos. 322-324 (3)   2.75 1.45

Souvenir Sheets
325   Sheet of 4   11.00 11.00
a.   A103 20f Gymnastics   2.75 2.75
b.   A103 40f Water polo   2.75 2.75
c.   A103 60f Wrestling   2.75 2.75
d.   A103 80f Show jumping   2.75 2.75
326 A103 200f Show jumping,
             diff.   11.00 11.00

Space Flights — A104

Designs: 15f, Soyuz 10 and Salyut 1 docking, 1971. 20f, Apollo 8 circling Moon, 1968. 50f, Apollo 11 Moon landing, 1969. 100f, Apollo-Soyuz mission, 1975. 200f, Space Shuttle Columbia.

1984, Apr. 16   Litho.   Perf. 14
327-330 A104 Set of 4   3.00 2.00

Souvenir Sheet
331 A104 200f multi   7.00 5.50

Nos. 83 and 84B Surcharged with Black Squares

1984, May 26   Litho.   Perf. 13½, 13
332 A24 50f on 65f multi   1.00   .60
333 A25 100f on 110f multi   2.25 1.00

Fish — A105

10f, Abalistes stellaris. 15f, Caranx speciocus. 20f, Pomadasys maculatus. 25f, Chaetodon fasciatus. 35f, Pomacanthus imperator. 50f, Rastrelliger kanagurta. 100f, Euthynnus affinis. 150f, Heniochus acuminatus. 200f, Pomacanthus maculosus. 250f, Pterois russellii. 400f, Argyrops spinifer. 500f, Dasyatis uarnak. 1d, Epinephalus chlorostigma. 2d, Drepane longimana.

1984, Nov. 25   Litho.   Perf. 11½
334 A105 10f multicolored   .25   .25
335 A105 15f multicolored   .25   .25
336 A105 20f multicolored   .30   .25
337 A105 25f multicolored   .45   .25
338 A105 35f multicolored   .70   .25
339 A105 50f multicolored   1.00   .25
340 A105 100f multicolored   2.00   .45
341 A105 150f multicolored   3.00   .90
342 A105 200f multicolored   4.00 1.00
343 A105 250f multicolored   5.50 1.75
344 A105 400f multicolored   9.00 2.40
345 A105 500f multicolored   11.00 3.25
346 A105 1d multicolored   24.00 7.50
347 A105 2d multicolored   52.50 15.00
     Nos. 334-347 (14)   113.95 33.75

For surcharges see Yemen Nos. 636, 640, 642.

Natl. Literacy Campaign A106

1985, Feb. 27   Perf. 12
350 A106 50f Girls writing   1.40   .75
351 A106 100f Hand, fountain
             pen, vert.   2.90 1.20

Victory Parade, Red Square, Moscow, 1945 — A107

1985, May 9   Perf. 12x12½
352 A107 100f multi   1.75   .80

Defeat of Nazi Germany, end of World War II, 40th anniv.

12th World Youth and Students Festival — A108

1985, Aug. 3   Perf. 12
353 A108 50f Emblem   1.50   .70
354 A108 100f Hand holding em-
             blem   3.00 1.25

UNESCO World Heritage Campaign — A109

1985, Aug. 29
355 A109 50f Shiham city   .90   .50
356 A109 50f Close-up of build-
             ings   .90   .50
357 A109 100f Windows   1.90 1.90
358 A109 100f Door   1.90 1.90
     Nos. 355-358 (4)   5.60 4.80

Nos. 355-357 horiz.

Natl. Socialist Party, 3rd Gen. Cong. — A110

1985, Oct. 10
359 A110 25f Energy   .70   .45
360 A110 50f Industry   1.25   .60
361 A110 100f Agriculture   2.40 1.00
     Nos. 359-361 (3)   4.35 2.05

UN Child Survival Campaign — A111

1985, Nov. 28
362 A111 50f Mother feeding
             child   .90   .70
363 A111 50f Holding child   .90   .70
364 A111 100f Feeding child, diff. 1.90 1.25
365 A111 100f Breastfeeding   1.90 1.25
     Nos. 362-365 (4)   5.60 3.90

World Food Day — A112

1986, Jan. 30
366 A112 20f Almihdar Mosque,
             Aden   .90   .25
367 A112 180f Palm trees   4.00 1.75

UN Food and Agriculture Org., 40th anniv.

Lenin, Red Square, Moscow A113

1986, Feb. 25   Perf. 12x12½
368 A113 75f multi   1.75   .70
369 A113 250f multi   4.00 2.00

27th Soviet Communist Party Cong., Moscow.

Costumes Worn at the 1984 Brides Dance Festival — A114

Designs: No. 370, Bride wearing red and green costume, face markings. No. 371, Violet costume. No. 372, Veiled bride. No. 373, Unveiled bride. No. 374, Groom holding dagger. No. 375, Groom holding rifle.

1986, Feb. 27
370 A114 50f multi   .80   .50
371 A114 50f multi   .80   .50
372 A114 50f multi   .80   .50
373 A114 100f multi   1.50 1.25
374 A114 100f multi   1.50 1.25
375 A114 100f multi   1.50 1.25
     Nos. 370-375 (6)   6.90 5.25

Revolution Martyrs A115

1986, Oct. 15   Litho.   Perf. 12
376	A115	75f Abdul Fattah Ismail	1.10	.70
377	A115	75f Ali Shayaa Hadi	1.10	.70
378	A115	75f Saleh Musleh Kasim	1.10	.70
379	A115	75f Ali Ahmed N. Antar	1.10	.70
		Nos. 376-379 (4)	4.40	2.80

UN Child Survival Campaign A116

Infant Immunization Program: 20f, Immunizing pregnant woman. 75f, Immunizing infant. 140f, Oral immunization. 150f, Infant, girl, pregnant woman.

1987, Apr. 7   Litho.   Perf. 12
380	A116	20f multicolored	.35	.25
381	A116	75f multicolored	1.10	.70
382	A116	140f multicolored	2.25	1.00
383	A116	150f multicolored	2.25	1.25
		Nos. 380-383 (4)	5.95	3.20

1st Socialist Party General Conference — A117

1987, July 30   Litho.   Perf. 12
384	A117	75fr multi	1.10	.45
385	A117	150fr multi	2.25	1.00

October Revolution, Russia, 70th Anniv. — A118

1987, Nov. 7   Litho.   Perf. 12½x12
386	A118	250f multi	4.50	2.25

Monuments, Ancient City of Shabwa — A119

25f, Royal palace and court. 75f, Palace, diff. 140f, Winged lion bas-relief on stone capital. 150f, The Moon, legend on bronze tablet.

1987, Nov. 18   Perf. 12
387	A119	25f multicolored	.45	.25
388	A119	75f multicolored	1.10	.55
389	A119	140f multicolored	2.00	1.10
390	A119	150f multicolored	2.25	1.25
		Nos. 387-390 (4)	5.80	3.15
		Nos. 387-388 horiz.		

Natl. Independence, 20th Anniv. — A120

Designs: 5f, Students walking to school. 75f, Family, apartments. 140f, Workers, oil derrick, thermal plant. 150f, Workers, soldier, Workers' Party headquarters.

1987, Nov. 29   Perf. 12x12½
391	A120	25f multi	.35	.25
392	A120	75f multi	1.00	.45
393	A120	140f multi	2.00	.90
394	A120	150f multi	2.25	1.00
		Nos. 391-394 (4)	5.60	2.60

September 26th Revolution, 25th Anniv. A121

1988, Feb. 27   Litho.   Perf. 13
395	A121	75f Revolution monument, San'a	1.10	.45

WHO, 40th Anniv. A122

40f, Sanitary public water supply, vert. 75f, No smoking. 140f, Child immunization. 250f, Health care for all by the year 2000.

1988, Apr. 7   Litho.   Perf. 12
396	A122	40f multicolored	.45	.30
397	A122	75f multicolored	1.00	.35
398	A122	140f multicolored	1.75	.70
399	A122	250f multicolored	2.75	1.25
		Nos. 396-399 (4)	5.95	2.60

1988 Summer Olympics, Seoul A125

1988, Sept. 17   Litho.   Perf. 12x12½
406	A125	40f Weight lifting	.55	.25
407	A125	75f Running	1.00	.45
408	A125	140f Boxing	2.25	1.10
409	A125	150f Soccer	2.40	1.25
		Nos. 406-409 (4)	6.20	3.05

1st Freedom Fighter Killed at the Liberation Front, Radfan Mountains A126

25f, Freedom fighters, flag, vert. 300f, Anniv. emblem, vert.

Perf. 12½x12, 12x12½
1988, Oct. 12   Litho.
410	A126	25f multicolored	.35	.25
411	A126	75f shown	1.00	.35
412	A126	300f multicolored	4.00	1.75
		Nos. 410-412 (3)	5.35	2.35

October 14th Revolution, 25th anniv.

Indigenous Birds A127

40f, Treron waalia. 50f, Coracias caudatus lorti, vert. 75f, Upupa epops, vert. 250f, Chlamydotis undulata macqueenii.

1988, Nov. 5   Perf. 12x12½, 12½x12
413	A127	40f multicolored	.60	.60
414	A127	50f multicolored	.80	.55
415	A127	75f multicolored	1.40	.80
416	A127	250f multicolored	3.75	2.00
		Nos. 413-416 (4)	6.55	3.95

Handicrafts — A128

Designs: 25f, Incense brazier. 75f, Cage-shaped dress form. 150f, Shell and wicker lidded basket. 250f, Wicker basket.

1988, Nov. 29   Litho.   Perf. 12½x12
417	A128	25f multi	.25	.25
418	A128	75f multi	1.00	.45
419	A128	150f multi	1.75	1.00
420	A128	250f multi	3.25	1.75
		Nos. 417-420 (4)	6.25	3.45

Aden Harbor and Yemen Port Authority, Cent. A129

1988, Dec. 5   Perf. 12x12½
421	A129	75f Old harbor facility	1.50	.50
422	A129	300f New facility	4.50	2.10

Preservation of San'a City, a Site on the UNESCO World Heritage List — A130

1988, Dec. 15   Perf. 12x12½, 12½x12
423	A130	75f shown	1.00	.70
424	A130	250f City view, diff., vert.	4.00	1.75

World Wildlife Fund — A131

1989, May 18   Litho.   Perf. 12½x12
425	A131	20f Sand cat	1.50	.25
426	A131	25f Cat's head	1.50	.30
427	A131	50f Fennec fox	3.00	.50
428	A131	75f Fox's head	4.00	.80
		Nos. 425-428 (4)	10.00	1.85

For surcharge see Yemen No. 643.

Military Forces — A132

Developments of the corrective movement.

1989, Aug. 15   Perf. 12x12½
429	A132	25f shown	.35	.25
430	A132	35f Industry	.45	.25
431	A132	40f Agriculture	.55	.25
		Nos. 429-431 (3)	1.35	.75

June 22 Corrective Movement, 20th anniv.

Abdul Fattah Ismail — A133

1989, Aug. 28
432	A133	75f multi	.75	.75
433	A133	150f multi	1.50	1.25

50th Birthday of Abdul Fattah Ismail, 1st secretary-general of the natl. Socialist Party.

Ali Anter Yemeni Pioneer Organization, 15th Anniv. — A134

10f, Drawing by Abeer Anwer. 25f, Girl in pioneer uniform. 75f, Parade, Aden.

Perf. 12x12½, 12½x12
1989, Sept. 29   Litho.
434	A134	10f multicolored	.25	.25
435	A134	25f multicolored	.35	.25
436	A134	75f multicolored	.90	.55
		Nos. 434-436 (3)	1.50	1.05
		Nos. 434-435 vert.		

For surcharge see Yemen No. 644.

Nehru and the Taj Mahal — A135

1989, Nov. 14   Photo.   Perf. 14
437	A135	250f blk & golden brn	3.50	1.50

Jawaharlal Nehru, 1st prime minister of independent India.
For surcharge see Yemen No. 645.

Seventy-Day Siege of San'a, 1967-68 — A136

1989, Oct. 25   Litho.   Perf. 12x12½
438	A136	150f multicolored	4.50	2.50

Coffee Plant — A137

1989, Dec. 20
439	A137	300f multicolored	5.00	2.50

For surcharge see Yemen No. 637.

Seera Rock, Aden, and the Arc de Triomphe, Paris A138

1989, Dec. 29   Litho.   Perf. 12½x12
440   A138   250f multicolored   4.25   2.50
French Revolution, bicent.

World Cup Soccer Championships, Italy — A139

Character trademark, soccer plays and flags of participants: 5f, US, Belgium, 1930. 10f, Switzerland, Holland, 1934. 20f, Italy, France, 1938. 35f, Sweden, Spain, 1950. 50f, Federal Republic of Germany, Austria, 1954. Brazil, England, 1958. 500f, Russia, Uruguay, 1962. No. 448, Soccer game.

1990, Apr. 30   Litho.   Perf. 12½x12
441   A139   5f multicolored   .25   .25
442   A139   10f multicolored   .25   .25
443   A139   20f multicolored   .25   .25
444   A139   35f multicolored   .30   .30
445   A139   50f multicolored   .35   .35
446   A139   60f multicolored   .40   .40
447   A139   500f multicolored   4.00   1.00
      Nos. 441-447 (7)   5.80   2.80
      Souvenir Sheet
448   A139   340f multicolored   3.00   3.00

For surcharges see Yemen Nos. 616, 621-621B.

YUGOSLAVIA

yü-gō-'slä-vē-ə

LOCATION — Southern Europe, bordering on the Adriatic Sea
GOVT. — Republic
AREA — 39,500 sq. mi. (est)
POP. — 11,206,847 (1999 est.)
CAPITAL — Belgrade

On December 1, 1918, Bosnia and Herzegovina, Croatia, Dalmatia, Montenegro, Serbia and Slovenia united to form a kingdom which was later called Yugoslavia. A republic was proclaimed November 29, 1945. Other listings may be found under all.

100 Heller = 1 Krone (Bosnia & Herzegovina)

100 Filler = 1 Krone (Croatia-Slavonia)

100 Paras = 1 Dinar (General Issues)

> Catalogue values for unused stamps in this country are for Never Hinged items, beginning with Scott 410 in the regular postage section, Scott C50 in the airpost section, Scott F1 in the registered letter section, Scott J67 in the postage due section, Scott RA1 in the postal tax section, and Scott RAJ1 in the postal tax due section.

> Counterfeits exist of most of the 1918-19 overprints for Bosnia and Herzegovina, Croatia-Slavonia and Slovenia.

BOSNIA AND HERZEGOVINA

Stamps of Bosnia and Herzegovina, 1910, Overprinted or Surcharged in Black or Red

a

b

c

1918		Unwmk.	Perf. 12½	
1L1	A4(a)	3h olive green	.40	.80
1L2	A4(b)	5h dk grn (R)	.40	.40
1L3	A4(a)	10h carmine	.40	.40
1L4	A4(a)	20h dk brn (R)	.40	.40
1L5	A4(a)	25h deep blue (R)	.40	.40
1L6	A4(b)	30h green	.40	.40
1L7	A4(b)	40h orange	.40	.40
1L8	A4(b)	45h brown red	.40	.40
1L9	A4(a)	50h dull violet	.55	.80
1L10	A4(a)	60h on 50h dl vio	.40	.40
1L11	A4(b)	80h on 6h org brown	.40	.40
1L12	A4(a)	90h on 35h myr green	.40	.40
1L13	A5(c)	2k gray green	.40	.40
1L14	A4(b)	3k on 3h ol grn	2.00	2.75

1L15	A5(c)	4k on 1k mar	4.00	4.75
1L16	A4(b)	10k on 2h vio	6.00	6.75
		Nos. 1L1-1L16 (16)	17.35	20.25

Inverted and double overprints and assorted varieties exist on the stamps for Bosnia and Herzegovina.

Bosnian Girl — A1

1918		Typo.	Perf. 11½	
1L17	A1	2h ultramarine	.40	.40
1L18	A1	6h violet	.80	1.20
1L19	A1	10h rose	.40	.40
1L20	A1	20h green	.40	.40
		Nos. 1L17-1L20 (4)	2.00	2.40

Imperforate stamps of this type (A1) are newspaper stamps of Bosnia.
For surcharges see Nos. 1L21-1L22, 1L43-1L45.

Bosnia and Herzegovina Nos. P1-P2 (Nos. 1L17-1L18, Imperf.) Srchd.

1918			Imperf.	
1L21	A1	3h on 2h ultra	.40	.40
a.		Double surcharge	14.00	
1L22	A1	5h on 6h violet	.40	.40
a.		Double surcharge	14.00	

Stamps of Bosnia and Herzegovina, 1906-17, Ovptd. or Srchd. in Black or Red

d

e

f

1919			Perf. 12½	
1L25	A23(d)	3h claret	.40	.80
1L26	A23(e)	5h green	.40	.40
1L27	A23(e)	10h on 6h dark gray	.40	.40
1L28	A24(d)	20h on 35h myr green	.40	.40
1L29	A23(e)	25h ultra	.40	.40
1L30	A23(e)	30h orange red	.40	.40
1L31	A24(d)	45h olive brn	.40	.40
1L32	A27(e)	45h on 80h org brown	.40	.40
a.		Perf. 11½	1.40	1.60
1L33	A24(e)	50h slate blue	100.00	100.00
1L34	A24(e)	50h on 72h dk blue (R)	.40	.40
1L35	A24(d)	60h brown violet	.40	.40
1L36	A27(e)	80h orange brown	.40	.40
a.		Perf. 11½	35.00	30.00
1L37	A27(d)	90h dark violet	.40	.40
a.		Perf. 11½	3.50	2.75
1L38	A5(f)	2k gray green	.40	.40
a.		Imperf.	35.00	
b.		Perf. 9½	4.50	5.00
1L39	A26(d)	3k car, green	.40	.55
1L40	A28(d)	4k car, green	1.75	2.50
1L41	A26(d)	5k dk vio, gray	1.75	2.75
1L42	A28(d)	10k dk vio, gray	3.25	4.00
		Nos. 1L25-1L42 (18)	112.35	115.40

Nos. 1L32, 1L36, 1L37, 1L40 and 1L42 have no bars in the overprint.
Nos. 1L25 to 1L42 exist with inverted overprint or surcharge.

Bosnia and Herzegovina Nos. P2-P4 (Nos. 1L18-1L20, Imperf.) Srchd.

1920			Imperf.	
1L43	A1	2h on 6h violet	200.00	180.00
1L44	A1	2h on 10h rose	50.00	50.00
1L45	A1	2h on 20h green	10.00	10.00
		Nos. 1L43-1L45 (3)	260.00	240.00

SEMI-POSTAL STAMPS ISSUES FOR BOSNIA AND HERZEGOVINA

Leading Blind Soldier — SP1

Wounded Soldier — SP2

Semi-Postal Stamps of Bosnia and Herzegovina, 1918 Overprinted

1918		Unwmk.	Perf. 12½, 13	
1LB1	SP1	10h greenish bl	.80	1.00
a.		Overprinted as No. 1LB2	52.50	52.50
1LB2	SP2	15h red brown	2.00	2.00
a.		Overprinted as No. 1LB1	47.50	47.50

Bosnian Semi-Postal Stamps of 1916 Overprinted like No. 1LB2

1LB3	SP1	5h green	125.00	175.00
a.		Overprinted as No. 1LB1	375.00	375.00
1LB4	SP2	10h magenta	100.00	125.00
		Nos. 1LB1-1LB4 (4)	227.80	303.00

Inverted and double overprints exist on Nos. 1LB1-1LB4.

Regular Issue of Bosnia, 1906 Surcharged in Black

Mail Wagon SP3

Bridge at Mostar SP4

Scene near Sarajevo — SP5

1919				
1LB5	SP3	10h + 10h on 40h org red	1.25	2.00
1LB6	SP4	20h + 10h on 20h dk brown	.60	1.75
1LB7	SP5	45h + 15h on 1k mar	4.75	4.75
		Nos. 1LB5-1LB7 (3)	6.60	8.50

Nos. 1LB5-1LB7 exist with surcharge inverted. Value each $7.50.

SPECIAL DELIVERY STAMPS ISSUES FOR BOSNIA AND HERZEGOVINA

Lightning
SD1   SD2

Bosnian Special Delivery Stamps Overprinted in Black

1918		Unwmk.	Perf. 12½, 13	
1LE1	SD1	2h vermilion	6.00	6.00
a.		Inverted overprint	35.00	
b.		Overprinted as No. 1LE2	47.50	47.50
1LE2	SD2	5h deep green	3.25	3.25
a.		Inverted overprint	18.00	
b.		Overprinted as No. 1LE1	47.50	47.50

POSTAGE DUE STAMPS ISSUES FOR BOSNIA AND HERZEGOVINA

Postage Due Stamps of Bosnia and Herzegovina, 1916, Overprinted in Black or Red

a

b

1918		Unwmk.	Perf. 12½, 13	
1LJ1	D2 (a)	2h red	.25	.25
1LJ2	D2 (b)	4h red	.55	.55
1LJ3	D2 (a)	5h red	.25	.25
1LJ4	D2 (b)	6h red	.90	.90
1LJ5	D2 (a)	10h red	.25	.25
1LJ6	D2 (b)	15h red	6.75	6.75
1LJ7	D2 (a)	20h red	.25	.25
1LJ8	D2 (b)	25h red	.55	.55
1LJ9	D2 (a)	30h red	.55	.55
1LJ10	D2 (b)	40h red	.25	.25
1LJ11	D2 (a)	50h red	1.20	1.20

c

d

1LJ12	D2 (c)	1k dark blue (R)	.55	.55
1LJ13	D2 (c)	3k dark blue (R)	.40	.40
		Nos. 1LJ1-1LJ13 (13)	12.70	12.70

Nos. 1LJ1-1LJ13 exist with overprint double or inverted. Value $3 to $7.
Nos. 1LJ1-1LJ11 exist with type "b" overprint instead of type "a," and vice versa. Value, each $10.

Stamps of Bosnia and Herzegovina, 1900-04, Surcharged

e

f

1919				
1LJ14	A2 (e)	2h on 35h blue	.55	.80
1LJ15	A2 (e)	5h on 45h grnsh bl	.95	1.20
1LJ16	A2 (f)	10h on 10 red	.25	.25
1LJ17	A2 (e)	15h on 40h org	.40	.50
1LJ18	A2 (f)	20h on 5h green	.25	.25
1LJ19	A2 (e)	25h on 20h pink	.40	.55

1LJ20	A2 (f)	30h on 30h bis brn		.40	.55
1LJ21	A2 (e)	1k on 50h red lil		.25	.55
1LJ22	A2 (e)	3k on 25h blue		.50	.55

Postage Due Stamps of Bosnia and Herzegovina, 1904 Surcharged

g   h

1LJ23	D1 (g)	40h on 6h blk, red & yel		.25	.25
1LJ24	D1 (h)	50h on 8h blk, red & yel		.25	.25
1LJ25	D1 (h)	200h blk, red & grn		8.00	6.75
1LJ26	D1 (h)	4k on 7h blk, red & yel		.40	.55
		Nos. 1LJ14-1LJ26 (13)		12.85	13.00

Nos. 1LJ14-1LJ26 exist with overprint double or inverted. Value, $3 to $6.

CROATIA-SLAVONIA

Stamps of Hungary Overprinted in Blue

A1

1918   **Wmk. 137**   **Perf. 15**
On Stamps of 1913

2L1	A1	6f olive green	1.10	2.00
2L2	A1	50f lake, *blue*	1.20	2.00

A2   A3

On Stamps of 1916

2L3	A2	10f violet	100.00	140.00
2L4	A3	15f red	100.00	140.00

A4

On Hungary Nos. 106-107 White Numerals

2L4A	A4	10f rose	1,600.	1,600.
2L5	A4	15f violet	150.00	150.00
a.		Inverted overprint	—	

On Stamps of 1916-18 Colored Numerals

2L6	A4	2f brown orange	.40	.40
2L7	A4	3f red lilac	.40	.40
2L8	A4	5f green	.40	.40
2L9	A4	6f greenish blue	.40	.40
2L10	A4	10f rose red	16.00	12.00
2L11	A4	15f violet	.40	.40
2L12	A4	20f gray brown	.40	.40
2L13	A4	25f dull blue	.40	.40
2L14	A4	35f brown	.40	.40
2L15	A4	40f olive green	.40	.80

The overprints and surcharges for Croatia-Slavonia exist inverted, double, double inverted, in wrong colors, on wrong stamps, on back, in pairs with one lacking overprint, etc.

A5

A6

2L16	A5	50f red vio & lilac	.40	.40
2L17	A5	75f brt bl & pale bl	.40	.40
2L18	A5	80f grn & pale grn	.40	.40
2L19	A6	1k red brown & cl	.40	.40
2L20	A6	2k olive brn & bis	.40	.40
2L21	A6	3k dark vio & ind	.40	.40
2L22	A6	5k dk brn & lt brn	2.50	3.00
2L23	A6	10k vio brn & vio	16.00	16.00

Stamps of Hungary Overprinted in Blue, Black or Red

No. 2L24   No. 2L27

2L24	A7	10f scarlet (Bl)	.40	.40
2L25	A7	20f dark brown (Bk)	.40	.40
2L26	A7	25f deep blue (R)	.40	.80
2L27	A8	40f olive green (Bl)	.40	.40
		Nos. 2L6-2L27 (22)	42.10	39.40

Many other stamps of the 1913-18 issues of Hungary, the Semi-Postal Stamps of 1915-16 and Postage Due Stamps were surreptitiously overprinted but were never sold through the post office.

Freedom of Croatia-Slavonia
A9

1918   **Unwmk.**   **Litho.**   **Perf. 11½**

2L28	A9	10f rose	6.50	4.00
2L29	A9	20f violet	6.50	4.00
2L30	A9	25f blue	12.00	8.00
2L31	A9	45f greenish blk	95.00	55.00
		Nos. 2L28-2L31 (4)	120.00	71.00

Independence of Croatia, Slavonia and Dalmatia.
#2L28-2L31 exist imperforate, but were not officially issued in this condition.
Excellent counterfeits of #2L28-2L31 exist.

Allegory of Freedom   Youth with Standard
A10   A11

Falcon, Symbol of Liberty — A12

1919   **Perf. 11½**

2L32	A10	2f brn orange	.25	.40
2L33	A10	3f violet	.25	.50
2L34	A10	5f green	.25	.25
2L35	A11	10f red	.25	.25
2L36	A11	20f black brown	.25	.25
2L37	A11	25f deep blue	.25	.25
2L38	A11	45f dark ol grn	.25	.25
2L39	A12	1k carmine rose	.25	.25
2L40	A12	3k dark violet	.80	.95
2L41	A12	5k deep brown	1.20	.80
		Nos. 2L32-2L41 (10)	4.00	4.15

Perf. 12½

2L32a	A10	2f	2.90	2.90
2L33a	A10	3f	2.90	2.90
2L34a	A11	5f	15.00	15.00
2L35a	A11	10f	2.90	2.90
2L36a	A11	20f	2.90	2.90
		Nos. 2L32a-2L36a (5)	26.60	26.60

#2L32-2L41 exist imperf. Value, set $25.

SEMI-POSTAL STAMPS ISSUES FOR CROATIA-SLAVONIA

SP1   SP2

SP3

1918   **Wmk. 137**   **Perf. 15**

2LB1	SP1	10f + 2f rose red	.40	2.75
2LB2	SP2	15f + 2f dull violet	.40	.40
2LB3	SP3	40f + 2f brn carmine	.40	.85
		Nos. 2LB1-2LB3 (3)	1.20	4.00

SPECIAL DELIVERY STAMP ISSUE FOR CROATIA-SLAVONIA

SD1

Hungary No. E1 Overprinted in Black

1918   **Wmk. 137**   **Perf. 15**

2LE1	SD1	2f gray green & red	.25	.25

POSTAGE DUE STAMPS ISSUES FOR CROATIA-SLAVONIA

D1

Postage Due Stamps of Hungary Overprinted in Blue

1918   **Wmk. Crown (136)**   **Perf. 15**

2LJ1	D1	50f green & blk	650.00	650.00

Wmk. Double Cross (137)

2LJ2	D1	1f green & red	40.00	40.00
a.		Inverted overprint		
2LJ3	D1	2f green & red	1.20	1.20
2LJ4	D1	10f green & red	1.20	1.20
2LJ5	D1	12f green & red	160.00	160.00
2LJ6	D1	15f green & red	.80	.80
2LJ7	D1	20f green & red	.80	.80
2LJ8	D1	30f green & red	2.00	2.00
2LJ9	D1	50f green & blk	65.00	65.00
		Nos. 2LJ2-2LJ9 (8)	271.00	271.00

NEWSPAPER STAMPS ISSUES FOR CROATIA-SLAVONIA

N1

Hungary No. P8 Overprinted in Black

1918   **Wmk. 137**   **Imperf.**

2LP1	N1	(2f) orange	.40	.40

N2

1919   **Litho.**   **Unwmk.**

2LP2	N2	2f yellow orange	.25	1.20

SLOVENIA

Chain Breaker
A1   A2

3, 5, 10, 15f: Chain on right wrist is short, extending only about half way to the frame.
10f: Numerals are 8¼mm high.
20, 25, 30, 40f: Distant mountains show faintly between legs of male figure.
40f: Numerals 7mm high. The upright strokes of the "4" extend to the same height; the "0" is 3mm wide.

1919   **Unwmk.**   **Perf. 11½**
Lithographed at Ljubljana
Fine Impression

3L1	A1	3f violet	.25	.25
3L2	A1	5f green	.25	.25
3L3	A1	10f carmine rose	.40	.25
3L4	A1	15f blue	.25	.25
3L5	A2	20f brown	.65	.25
3L6	A2	25f blue	.30	.25
3L7	A2	30f lilac rose	.30	.25
3L8	A2	40f bister	.30	.25
		Nos. 3L1-3L8 (8)	2.70	2.00

Various stamps of this series exist imperforate and part perforate. Many shades exist.
See Nos. 3L9-3L17, 3L24-3L28. For surcharges see Nos. 3LJ15-3LJ32.

Allegories of Freedom
A3   A4

King Peter I — A5

3, 5, 15f: The chain on the right wrist touches the bottom tablet.
10f: Numerals are 7½mm high.
15f: Curled end of loin cloth appears above letter "H" in the bottom tablet.
20, 25, 30, 40f: The outlines of the mountains have been redrawn and they are more distinct than on the lithographed stamps.
40f: Numerals 8mm high. The left slanting stroke of the "4" extends much higher than the main vertical stroke. The "0" is 2½mm wide and encloses a much narrower space than on the lithographed stamp.

1919-20   **Perf. 11½**
Typographed at Ljubljana and Vienna
Coarse Impression

3L9	A1	3f violet	.25	.25
3L10	A1	5f green	.30	.25
3L11	A1	10f red	.25	.25
3L12	A1	15f blue	1.60	.25
3L13	A2	20f brown	.55	.25

3L14	A2	25f blue	.50	.25
3L15	A2	30f carmine rose	.55	.25
3L16	A2	30f dp red	2.75	.90
3L17	A2	40f orange	.55	.25
3L18	A3	50f green	.55	.25
a.		50f dark green	.55	.25
b.		50f olive green	3.50	1.10
3L19	A3	60f dark blue	.85	.25
a.		60f violet blue	.85	.25
3L20	A4	1k vermilion	.55	.25
a.		1k red orange	.55	.25
3L21	A4	2k blue	.55	.25
a.		2k dull ultramarine	.90	.25
3L22	A5	5k brown lake	.80	.25
a.		5k lake	12.00	1.60
b.		5k dull red	.60	.25
3L23	A5	10k deep ultra	3.25	.90
		Nos. 3L9-3L23 (15)	13.85	5.05

Nos. 3L9-3L23 exist imperf. Value, set $90. Many of the series exist part perforate. Many shades exist of lower values. See Nos. 3L29-3L32, 3L40-3L41.

Serrate Roulette 13½

3L24	A1	5f light grn	.25	.25
3L25	A1	10f carmine	.25	.25
3L26	A1	15f slate blue	.30	.25
3L27	A2	20f dark brown	.65	.25
a.		Serrate x straight roul.	.65	.25
3L28	A2	30f car rose	.30	.25
a.		Serrate x straight roul.	.70	.25
3L29	A3	50f green	.30	.25
3L30	A3	60f dark blue	.95	.40
a.		60f violet blue	2.25	1.10
3L31	A4	1k vermilion	1.40	.40
a.		1k rose red	1.40	.40
3L32	A4	2k blue	9.00	2.75
		Nos. 3L24-3L32 (9)	13.40	5.05

Roulette x Perf. 11½

3L24a	A1	5f	150.00	150.00
3L25a	A1	10f	55.00	55.00
3L26a	A1	15f	175.00	175.00
3L28b	A2	30f	55.00	55.00
3L29a	A3	60f	5.25	4.00
3L30b	A3	60f	55.00	55.00
3L31b	A4	1k	55.00	55.00

Thick Wove Paper

1920   **Litho.**   **Perf. 11½**

3L40	A5	15k gray green	7.25	14.50
3L41	A5	20k dull violet	1.40	2.40

On Nos. 3L40-3L41 the horizontal lines have been removed from the value tablets. They are printed over a background of pale brown wavy lines.

Chain Breaker — A7   Freedom — A8

King Peter I — A9   Pale red wavy lines

Dinar Values:
Type I — Size: 21x30½mm.
Type II — Size: 22x32½mm.

Thin to Thick Wove Paper

1920   *Serrate Roulette 13½*

3L42	A7	5p olive green	.25	.25
3L43	A7	10p green	.25	.25
3L44	A7	15p brown	.25	.25
3L45	A7	20p carmine	.40	.40
3L46	A7	25p chocolate	.40	.25
3L47	A8	40p dark violet	.25	.25
3L48	A8	45p yellow	.25	.25
3L49	A8	50p dark blue	.25	.25
3L50	A8	60p red brown	.25	.25
3L51	A9	1d brown red (I)	.25	.25

Perf. 11½

3L52	A9	2d gray vio (II)	.25	.25
3L53	A9	4d grnsh black (I)	.30	.30
3L54	A9	6d olive brn (II)	.25	.25
3L55	A9	10d brown red (II)	.30	.80
		Nos. 3L42-3L55 (14)	3.90	4.25

The 2d and 6d have a background of pale red wavy lines, the 10d of gray lines. Counterfeits exist of No. 3L45.

POSTAGE DUE STAMPS ISSUES FOR SLOVENIA

D1

Ljubljana Print
Numerals 9½mm high

1919   **Litho.**   **Unwmk.**   **Perf. 11½**

3LJ1	D1	5f carmine	.25	.25
3LJ2	D1	10f carmine	.25	.25
3LJ3	D1	20f carmine	.25	.25
3LJ4	D1	50f carmine	.25	.25

Nos. 3LJ1-3LJ4 were also printed in scarlet and dark red.

Numerals 8mm high

3LJ5	D1	1k dark blue	.45	.30
3LJ6	D1	5k dark blue	.65	.50
3LJ7	D1	10k dark blue	.90	.75
		Nos. 3LJ1-3LJ7 (7)	3.00	2.55

Vienna Print

1920   **Numerals 11 to 12 mm high**

3LJ8	D1	5f red	.25	.25
3LJ9	D1	10f red	.25	.25
3LJ10	D1	20f red	.25	.25
3LJ11	D1	50f red	1.25	.85

Numerals 7mm high

3LJ12	D1	1k Prussian blue	1.10	.70
a.		1k dark blue	5.00	4.50
3LJ13	D1	5k Prussian blue	1.60	1.25
a.		5k dark blue	8.00	6.75
3LJ14	D1	10k Prussian blue	3.75	3.25
a.		10k dark blue	14.00	15.00
		Nos. 3LJ8-3LJ14 (7)	8.45	6.80

Nos. 3LJ8-3LJ14 exist imperf. Value, set $40.

No. 3L4 Surcharged in Red

1920   **On Litho. Stamps**   **Perf. 11½**

3LJ15	A1	5p on 15f blue	.25	.25
3LJ16	A1	10p on 15f blue	.60	.80
3LJ17	A1	20p on 15f blue	.25	.25
3LJ18	A1	50p on 15f blue	.25	.25
		Nos. 3LJ15-3LJ18 (4)	1.35	1.55

Nos. 3L7, 3L12, 3L26, 3L28, 3L28a Surcharged in Dark Blue

3LJ19	A2	1d on 30f lil rose	.25	.25
3LJ20	A2	3d on 30f lil rose	.25	.25
3LJ21	A2	8d on 30f lil rose	1.60	.80
		Nos. 3LJ19-3LJ21 (3)	2.10	1.30

On Typographed Stamps

3LJ22	A1	5p on 15f pale bl	12.00	2.50
3LJ23	A1	10p on 15f pale bl	35.00	25.00
3LJ24	A1	20p on 15f pale bl	11.00	4.00
3LJ25	A1	50p on 15f pale bl	6.00	7.00
		Nos. 3LJ22-3LJ25 (4)	64.00	38.50
3LJ26	A1	5p on 15f slate bl	2.75	.50
3LJ27	A1	10p on 15f slate bl	8.50	3.25
3LJ28	A1	20p on 15f slate bl	2.75	.50
3LJ29	A1	50p on 15f slate bl	2.75	.50
3LJ30	A2	1d on 30f dp rose	2.75	.65
a.		Serrate x straight roulette	7.00	4.50
3LJ31	A2	3d on 30f dp rose	5.75	1.75
a.		Serrate x straight roulette	8.00	5.50
3LJ32	A2	8d on 30f dp rose	125.00	6.50
a.		Serrate x straight roulette	125.00	7.50
		Nos. 3LJ26-3LJ32 (7)	150.25	13.65

The para surcharges were printed in sheets of 100, ten horizontal rows of ten. There were: 5p three rows, 10p one row, 20p three rows, 50p three rows. The dinar surcharges were in a setting of 50, arranged in vertical rows of

five. There were: 1d five rows, 3d three rows, 8d two rows.

NEWSPAPER STAMPS ISSUES FOR SLOVENIA

Eros — N1

Ljubljana Print

1919   **Unwmk.**   **Litho.**   **Imperf.**

3LP1	N1	2f gray	.25	.25
3LP2	N1	4f gray	.25	.40
3LP3	N1	6f gray	3.50	4.00
3LP4	N1	10f gray	.25	.25
3LP5	N1	30f gray	.25	.40
		Nos. 3LP1-3LP5 (5)	4.50	5.30

See Nos. 3LP6-3LP13. For surcharges see Nos. 3LP14-3LP23, 4LB1-4LB5.

N2

1920   **Vienna Print**

3LP6	N2	2f gray	.25	.25
3LP7	N2	4f gray	6.50	10.00
3LP8	N2	6f gray	1.75	2.75
3LP9	N2	10f gray	14.00	21.00
3LP10	N2	2f blue	.25	.30
3LP11	N2	4f blue	.25	.25
3LP12	N2	6f blue	125.00	125.00
3LP13	N2	10f blue	.25	.25
		Nos. 3LP6-3LP13 (8)	148.25	159.80

Nos. 3LP1, 3LP10 Surcharged

a   b

On Ljubljana Print

3LP14	N1 (a)	2p on 2f gray	.25	.40
3LP15	N1 (a)	4p on 2f gray	.25	.40
3LP16	N1 (a)	6p on 2f gray	.40	.65
3LP17	N1 (b)	10p on 2f gray	.65	.80
3LP18	N1 (b)	30p on 2f gray	.65	.85

On Vienna Print

3LP19	N1 (a)	2p on 2f blue	.25	.25
3LP20	N1 (a)	4p on 2f blue	.25	.25
3LP21	N1 (a)	6p on 2f blue	.25	.25
3LP22	N1 (b)	10p on 2f blue	.25	.25
3LP23	N1 (b)	30p on 2f blue	.25	.25
		Nos. 3LP14-3LP23 (10)	3.45	4.35

The five surcharges were arranged in a setting of 100, in horizontal rows of ten. There were: 2p three rows, 4p three rows, 6p two rows, 10p one row and 30p one row. The sheets were perforated 11½ horizontally between the groups of the different values.

SEMI-POSTAL STAMPS ISSUE FOR CARINTHIA PLEBISCITE

SP1

Nos. 3LP2, 3LP1 Surcharged With Various Designs in Dark Red

1920

4LB1	SP1	5p on 4f gray	.25	.25
4LB2	SP1	15p on 4f gray	.25	.25
4LB3	SP1	25p on 4f gray	.25	.55
4LB4	SP1	45p on 2f gray	.25	1.20
4LB5	SP1	50p on 2f gray	.25	1.40
4LB6	SP1	2d on 2f gray	2.00	6.00
		Nos. 4LB1-4LB6 (6)	3.25	9.65

Nos. 4LB1 to 4LB6 have a different surcharge on each stamp but each includes the letters "K.G.C.A." which signify Carinthian Governmental Commission, Zone A.

Sold at three times face value for the benefit of the Plebiscite Propaganda Fund.

GENERAL ISSUES

For Use throughout the Kingdom

King Alexander — A1   King Peter I — A2

Unwmk.

1921, Jan. 16   **Engr.**   **Perf. 12**

1	A1	2p olive brown	.25	.25
2	A1	5p deep green	.25	.25
3	A1	10p carmine	.25	.25
4	A1	15p violet	.25	.25
5	A1	20p black	.25	.25
6	A1	25p dark blue	.25	.25
7	A1	50p olive green	.25	.25
8	A1	60p vermilion	.25	.25
9	A1	75p purple	.25	.25
10	A2	1d orange	.25	.25
11	A2	2d olive bister	.30	.25
12	A2	4d dark green	.60	.25
13	A2	5d carmine rose	2.50	.25
14	A2	10d red brown	12.00	3.80
		Nos. 1-14 (14)	17.90	3.80
		Set, never hinged	32.50	

Exist imperf. Value, set $125. For surcharge see No. 27.

Nos. B1-B3 Surcharged in Black, Brown, Green or Blue

a

b

1922-24

15	SP1(a)	1d on 10p	.25	.25
16	SP2(b)	1d on 15p ('24)	.25	.25
17	SP3(a)	1d on 25p (Br)	.25	.25
18	SP2(b)	3d on 15p (G)	.80	.25
a.		Blue surcharge	1.20	1.20
19	SP2(b)	8d on 15p (G)	1.60	.25
a.		Double surcharge	35.00	30.00
b.		9d on 15p (error)	130.00	
20	SP2(b)	20d on 15p	10.00	1.00
21	SP2(b)	30d on 15p (Bl)	27.50	2.50
		Nos. 15-21 (7)	40.65	4.75
		Set, never hinged	60.00	

A3

1923, Jan. 23   Engr.
22	A3	1d red brown		2.00	.25
23	A3	5d carmine		3.75	.25
24	A3	8d violet		6.75	.25
25	A3	20d green		27.50	.75
26	A3	30d red orange		72.50	2.75
		Nos. 22-26 (5)		112.50	4.25
		Set, never hinged		250.00	

For surcharge see No. 28.

Nos. 8 and 24
Surcharged in Black
or Blue

1924, Feb. 18
27	A1	20p on 60p ver		.25	.25
28	A3	5d on 8d violet (Bl)		8.00	.60
		Set, never hinged		17.50	

The color of the surcharge on No. 28 varies, including blue, blue black, greenish black and black.

A4   A5

1924, July 1   Perf. 14
29	A4	20p black		.25	.25
30	A4	50p dark brown		.25	.25
31	A4	1d carmine		.25	.25
32	A4	2d myrtle green		.25	.25
33	A4	3d ultramarine		.25	.25
34	A4	5d orange brown		1.40	.25
35	A5	10d dark violet		12.50	.25
36	A5	15d olive green		7.50	.25
37	A5	20d vermilion		7.50	.25
38	A5	30d dark green		7.50	1.25
		Nos. 29-38 (10)		37.65	3.50
		Set, never hinged		80.00	

No. 33 Surcharged

1925, June 5
39	A4	25p on 3d ultramarine		.35	.25
40	A4	50p on 3d ultramarine		.35	.25
		Set, never hinged		1.60	

King Alexander — A6

1926-27   Typo.   Perf. 13
41	A6	25p deep green		.25	.25
42	A6	50p olive brown		.25	.25
43	A6	1d scarlet		.25	.25
44	A6	2d slate black		.25	.25
45	A6	3d slate blue		.30	.25
46	A6	4d red orange		.50	.25
47	A6	5d violet		.80	.25
48	A6	8d black brown		5.25	.25
49	A6	10d olive brown		4.00	.25
50	A6	15d brown ('27)		15.00	.25
51	A6	20d dark vio ('27)		17.50	.25
52	A6	30d orange ('27)		65.00	.45
		Nos. 41-52 (12)		109.35	3.20
		Set, never hinged		240.00	

For overprints and surcharges see Nos. 53-62, 87-101, B5-B16.

Nos. B7-B16
Overprinted over the
Red Surcharge

1928, July
53	A6	1d scarlet		.25	.25
a.		Surcharge "0.50" inverted			
54	A6	2d black		.50	.25
55	A6	3d deep blue		.80	.50
56	A6	4d red orange		2.00	.60
57	A6	5d bright vio		1.60	.25
58	A6	8d black brown		6.50	.95
59	A6	10d olive brown		12.50	.25
60	A6	15d brown		95.00	3.00
61	A6	20d violet		47.50	3.00
62	A6	30d orange		125.00	9.50
		Nos. 53-62 (10)		291.65	18.55
		Set, never hinged		725.00	

King Alexander — A7

With Imprint at Foot

1931-34   Perf. 12½
63	A7	25p black		.25	.25
64	A7	50p green		.25	.25
65	A7	75p slate green		.40	.25
66	A7	1d red		.25	.25
67	A7	1.50d pink		.80	.25
68	A7	1.75d dp rose ('34)		1.60	.35
69	A7	3d slate blue		6.00	.25
70	A7	3.50d ultra ('34)		2.40	.35
71	A7	4d deep orange		3.00	.25
72	A7	5d purple		3.00	.25
73	A7	10d dark olive		12.00	.25
74	A7	15d deep brown		12.00	.25
75	A7	20d dark violet		24.00	.25
76	A7	30d rose		12.00	.45
		Nos. 63-76 (14)		77.95	3.90
		Set, never hinged		175.00	

Type of 1931 Issue
Without Imprint at Foot

1932-33
77	A7	25p black		.25	.25
78	A7	50p green		.25	.25
79	A7	1d red		.25	.25
80	A7	3d slate bl ('33)		1.00	.25
81	A7	4d deep org ('33)		3.50	.25
82	A7	5d purple ('33)		5.25	.25
83	A7	10d dk olive ('33)		17.00	.25
84	A7	15d deep brn ('33)		27.50	.25
85	A7	20d dark vio ('33)		35.00	.25
86	A7	30d rose ('33)		45.00	.35
		Nos. 77-86 (10)		135.00	2.60
		Set, never hinged		225.00	

See Nos. 102-115.

Nos. 41 to 52
Overprinted

1933, Sept. 5   Perf. 13
87	A6	25p deep green		.25	.25
88	A6	50p olive brown		.25	.25
89	A6	1d scarlet		.75	.25
90	A6	2d slate black		3.25	.70
91	A6	3d slate blue		3.00	.25
92	A6	4d red orange		2.00	.25
93	A6	5d violet		4.00	.25
94	A6	8d black brown		9.25	1.40
95	A6	10d olive brown		16.00	.25
96	A6	15d brown		24.00	1.75
97	A6	20d dark violet		32.50	.80
98	A6	30d orange		32.50	.80
		Nos. 87-98 (12)		127.75	7.20
		Set, never hinged		240.00	

Semi-Postal Stamps of 1926
Overprinted like Nos. 87 to 98 and
Four Bars over the Red Surcharge
of 1926

1933, Sept. 5
99	A6	25p green		.80	.25
100	A6	50p olive brown		.80	.25
101	A6	1d scarlet		2.40	.50
		Nos. 99-101 (3)		4.00	1.00
		Set, never hinged		8.00	

Nos. 99-101 exist with double impression of bars. Value, each $5.50 unused, $4.50 used.

King Alexander Memorial Issue
Type of 1931-34 Issues
Borders in Black

1934, Oct. 17
102	A7	25p black		.25	.25
103	A7	50p green		.25	.25
104	A7	75p slate green		.25	.25
105	A7	1d red		.25	.25
106	A7	1.50d pink		.25	.25
107	A7	1.75d deep rose		.25	.25
108	A7	3d slate blue		.25	.25
109	A7	3.50d ultramarine		.25	.25
110	A7	4d deep orange		.40	.25
111	A7	5d purple		.60	.25
112	A7	10d dark olive		2.00	.25
113	A7	15d deep brown		4.00	.25
114	A7	20d dark violet		12.00	.25
115	A7	30d rose		10.00	.40
		Nos. 102-115 (14)		31.00	3.65
		Set, never hinged		50.00	

Cyrillic Characters
Latin and Cyrillic inscriptions are transposed within some sets. In some sets some stamps are inscribed in Latin, others in Cyrillic. This will be mentioned only if it is necessary to identify otherwise identical stamps.

King Peter II — A10

1935-36   Perf. 13x12½
116	A10	25p brown black		.25	.25
117	A10	50p yel orange		.25	.25
118	A10	75p turq green		.25	.25
119	A10	1d brown red		.25	.25
120	A10	1.50d scarlet		.25	.25
121	A10	1.75d cerise		.25	.25
122	A10	2d magenta ('36)		.25	.25
123	A10	3d brn orange		.25	.25
124	A10	3.50d ultramarine		.40	.25
125	A10	4d yellow grn		1.20	.25
126	A10	4d slate blue ('36)		.25	.25
127	A10	10d bright vio		1.20	.25
128	A10	15d brown		1.20	.25
129	A10	20d bright blue		4.75	.25
130	A10	30d rose pink		2.40	.25
		Nos. 116-130 (15)		13.40	3.75
		Set, never hinged		25.00	

For overprints see Nos. N12, N14, N29.

King
Alexander — A11

1935, Oct. 9   Perf. 12½x11½, 11½
131	A11	75p turq green		.35	.40
132	A11	1.50d scarlet		.35	.40
133	A11	1.75d dark brown		.40	.80
134	A11	3.50d ultramarine		2.25	2.50
135	A11	7.50d rose carmine		1.50	2.25
		Nos. 131-135 (5)		4.85	6.35

Death of King Alexander, 1st anniv.

Nikola Tesla — A12

1936, May 28   Litho.   Perf. 12½x11½
136	A12	75p yel grn & dk brn		.40	.25
137	A12	1.75d dull blue & indigo		.40	.25
		Set, never hinged		2.00	

80th birthday of Nikola Tesla (1856-1943), electrical inventor.

Memorial Church,
Oplenac — A13

1937, July 1
138	A13	3d Prussian grn		1.00	.50
a.		Perf. 12½		15.00	24.00
		Never hinged		30.00	
139	A13	4d dark blue		1.00	1.20
		Set, never hinged		4.00	

"Little Entente," 16th anniversary.

Coats of Arms
of Yugoslavia,
Greece,
Romania and
Turkey — A14

Perf. 11, 11½, 12½

1937, Oct. 29   Photo.
140	A14	3d peacock grn		1.50	.40
141	A14	4d ultramarine		2.00	1.40
		Set, never hinged		5.75	

Balkan Entente.
Some of the varieties of perfs are scarce.

King Peter II — A16

1939-40   Typo.   Perf. 12½
142	A16	25p black ('40)		.25	.25
143	A16	50p orange ('40)		.25	.25
144	A16	1d yellow grn		.25	.25
145	A16	1.50d red		.25	.25
146	A16	2d dp mag ('40)		.25	.25
147	A16	3d dull red brn		.25	.25
148	A16	4d ultra		.25	.25
148A	A16	5d dk blue ('40)		.25	.25
148B	A16	5.50d dk vio brn ('40)		.50	.25
149	A16	6d slate blue		1.00	.25
150	A16	8d sepia		1.20	.25
151	A16	12d bright vio		1.75	.25
152	A16	16d dull violet		2.40	.25
153	A16	20d blue ('40)		2.40	.25
154	A16	30d brt pink ('40)		5.50	.55
		Nos. 142-154 (15)		16.75	4.05
		Set, never hinged		35.00	

For overprints and surcharges see Nos. N1-N11, N13, N15-N28, N30-N35, Croatia 1-25, Serbia 2N1-2N30.

Arms of Yugoslavia, Greece, Romania
and Turkey
A17   A18

1940, June 1
155	A17	3d ultramarine		.95	.55
156	A18	3d ultramarine		.95	.55
a.		Pair, #155-156		7.00	13.50
157	A17	4d dark blue		.95	.55
158	A18	4d dark blue		.95	.55
a.		Pair, #157-158		7.00	13.50
		Nos. 155-158 (4)		0.80	2.20
		Set, never hinged		7.50	
		Pairs, never hinged		30.00	

Balkan Entente.

Bridge at Obod A19

1940, Sept. 29   **Litho.**
159   A19   5.50d slate grn & pale
         blue   2.25   3.50
     Never hinged   4.00

Zagreb Phil. Exhib.; 500th anniv. of Johann Gutenberg's invention of printing. The first press in the Yugoslav area was located at Obod in 1493.

Issues for Federal Republic

Serbia Nos. 2N37, 2N39 Srchd. in Green or Vermilion

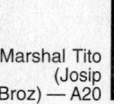

Overprinted with Pale Green Network

1944, Dec.   **Unwmk.**   **Perf. 11½**
159A   OS4   5d (3d + 2d) rose
         pink   .25   .25
159B   OS4   10d (7d + 3d) dk sl
         grn (V)   .25   .25

Similar Srch. on Serbia Nos. 2N37-2N39

1945, Jan. 24   **Without Network**
159C   OS4   5d (3d + 2d) rose
         pink   .25   .25
159D   OS4   10d (7d + 3d) dk sl
         grn (V)   .25   .25
159E   OS4   25d (4d + 21d) ultra
         (Bk)   .25   .25
     Nos. 159C-159E (3)   .75   .75

Marshal Tito (Josip Broz) — A20

1945   **Photo.**   **Perf. 12½**
160   A20   25p bright bl grn   .25   .25
161   A20   50p deep green   .25   .25
162   A20   1d crimson rose   1.20   .25
163   A20   2d dark car rose   .25   .25
164   A20   4d deep blue   .25   .25
165   A20   5d deep green   .25   .40
166   A20   6d dark purple   .25   .25
167   A20   9d orange brown   .35   .25
168   A20   10d deep rose   .25   .40
169   A20   20d orange   1.75   1.60
170   A20   25d dark purple   .25   .25
171   A20   30d deep blue   .25   .25
     Nos. 160-171 (12)   5.55   4.65
     Set, never hinged   9.00

Prohor Pcinski Monastery — A21

1945, Aug. 2   **Typo.**   **Perf. 11½**
172   A21   2d red   2.00   2.00
     Never hinged   4.00

Formation of the Popular Antifascist Chamber of Deputies of Macedonia, Aug. 2, 1944.

Partisans A22   A23

Marshal Tito — A24   City of Jajce — A25

Partisan Girl and Flag — A26

1945, Oct. 10   **Litho.**   **Perf. 12½**
173   A22   50p olive gray   .25   .25
174   A22   1d blue green   .25   .25
175   A23   1.50d orange brown   .25   .25
176   A24   2d scarlet   .25   .25
177   A24   3d red brown   1.75   .25
178   A24   4d dark blue   .30   .25
179   A25   5d dark yel grn   1.00   .25
180   A26   6d black   .45   .25
181   A26   9d deep plum   .40   .25
182   A23   12d ultramarine   .90   .25
183   A23   16d blue   .70   .25
184   A23   20d orange ver   1.60   .25
     Nos. 173-184 (12)   8.10   3.00
     Set, never hinged   17.50

See Nos. 211-214. For surcharges and overprints see Nos. 202-203, 273-292, 286-289, Istria 42, 44, 46, 48, 50, Trieste 5-14.

"Labor" and "Agriculture" A27   A28

1945, Nov. 29   **Photo.**   **Perf. 12**
185   A27   2d brn carmine   1.75   3.50
186   A28   2d brn carmine   1.75   3.50
187   A27   4d deep blue   1.75   3.50
188   A28   4d deep blue   1.75   3.50
189   A27   6d dk slate grn   1.75   3.50
190   A28   6d dk slate grn   1.75   3.50
191   A27   9d red orange   1.75   3.50
192   A28   9d red orange   1.75   3.50
193   A27   16d bright ultra   1.75   3.50
194   A28   16d bright ultra   1.75   3.50
195   A27   20d dark brown   1.75   3.50
     a.   Souv. sheet of 2, #191, 195,
         perf. 11½   13.50   25.00
196   A28   20d dark brown   1.75   3.50
     a.   Souv. sheet of 2, #192, 196,
         perf. 11½   13.50   25.00
     Nos. 185-196 (12)   21.00   42.00
     Set, never hinged   42.50
     Se-tenant pairs, #185-196 (6)   30.00   30.00
     Se-tenant pairs, never
         hinged   60.00

Constitution for the Democratic Federation of Yugoslavia, Nov. 29, 1945.

Parade of Armed Forces — A31

1946, May 9   **Unwmk.**   **Perf. 12½**
199   A31   1.50d org yel & red   .45   .60
200   A31   2.50d cerise & red   .95   .85
201   A31   5d blue & red   3.00   1.75
     Nos. 199-201 (3)   4.40   3.20
     Set, never hinged   8.50

Victory over fascism, 1st anniv.

Type of 1945 Surcharged with New Values in Black

1946, Apr. 1
202   A26   2.50d on 6d bright red   .40   .25
203   A26   8d on 9d orange   .50   .25
     Set, never hinged   1.75

Svetozar Markovic — A32

1946, Sept. 22
204   A32   1.50d blue green   .75   .35
205   A32   2.50d dp red lilac   .85   .50
     Set, never hinged   2.50

Markovic, Serbian socialist, birth cent.

People's Theater, Sofia A33

...

Sigismund Monument, Warsaw — A35

Designs: 1d, Prague. 2½d, Victory Monument, Belgrade. 5d, Spassky Tower, Kremlin.

1946, Dec. 8   **Litho.**   **Perf. 11½**
206   A33   ½d dk brn & yel brn   2.00   4.00
207   A33   1d grnsh blk & emer   2.00   4.00
208   A35   1½d dk car rose &
         rose   2.00   4.00
209   A35   2½d hn brn & brn org   2.00   4.00
210   A35   5d dark bl & blue   2.00   4.00
     Nos. 206-210 (5)   10.00   20.00
     Set, never hinged   20.00

Pan-Slavic Congress, Belgrade, Dec. 1946.

Types of 1945

1947, Jan. 15   **Litho.**   **Perf. 12½**
211   A26   2.50d red orange   .35   .25
212   A25   3d dull red   .50   .25
213   A25   5d dark blue   1.40   .25
214   A26   8d orange   .90   .25
     Nos. 211-214 (4)   3.15   1.00
     Set, never hinged   6.00

Gorski Vijenac — A38   Peter P. Nyegosh — A39

1947, June 8   **Typo.**
215   A38   1.50d Prus grn & blk   .50   .80
216   A39   2.50d ol bis & dk car   .50   .80
217   A38   5d blue & black   .50   .80
     Nos. 215-217 (3)   1.50   2.40
     Set, never hinged   2.50

Centenary of the Montenegrin national epic "Gorski Vijenac" (Wreath of Mountains) by Nyegosh.

Girls' Physical Training Classes — A40

Girl Runner — A41

Physical Culture Parade A42

1947, June 15   **Litho.**   **Perf. 11**
218   A40   1.50d brown   1.00   1.00
219   A41   2.50d red   1.00   1.00
220   A42   4d violet blue   1.00   1.00
     Nos. 218-220 (3)   3.00   3.00
     Set, never hinged   6.00

Natl. sports meet, Belgrade, 6/15-22/47.

Map and Star — A43

1947, Sept. 16   **Typo.**
231   A43   2.50d dp car & dark bl   .40   .80
232   A43   5d org brn & dk grn   .40   .80
     Set, never hinged   1.60

Annexation of Julian Province.

Music and One-string Gusle A44

Vuk Karadzic — A45

1947, Sept. 27   **Perf. 11½x12, 12½**
233   A44   1.50d green   .40   .80
234   A45   2.50d orange red   .40   .80
235   A44   5d violet blue   .40   .80
     Nos. 233-235 (3)   1.20   2.40
     Set, never hinged   2.40

Centenary of Serbian literature.

Symbols of Industry and Agriculture, Map and Flag — A46

1948, Apr. 8 — Litho. — Perf. 12½

236	A46	1.50d grn, bl & salmon	1.40	2.00
237	A46	2.50d red brn, bl & salmon	1.40	2.00
238	A46	5d dk bl, bl & salmon	1.40	2.00
		Nos. 236-238 (3)	4.20	6.00
		Set, never hinged	8.00	

International Fair, Zagreb, May 8-17.

Danube River Scene — A47

1948, July 30 — Unwmk.

239	A47	2d green	2.50	4.25
240	A47	3d carmine	2.50	4.25
241	A47	5d blue	2.50	4.25
242	A47	10d brown orange	2.50	4.25
		Nos. 239-242 (4)	10.00	17.00
		Set, never hinged	17.50	

Danube Conference, Belgrade.

Marchers with Party Flag — A48

1948, July 21 — Perf. 11½, 12½

243	A48	2d dark green	.40	.40
244	A48	3d dark red	.60	1.20
245	A48	10d dark blue vio	.60	.80
		Nos. 243-245 (3)	1.60	2.40
		Set, never hinged	3.25	

5th Congress of the Communist Party in Yugoslavia, July 21, 1948.

Laurent Kosir — A49

1948, Aug. 21 — Perf. 12½

246	A49	3d claret	.40	.40
247	A49	5d blue	.40	.40
248	A49	10d red orange	.40	.40
249	A49	12d dull green	.40	.40
		Nos. 246-249 (4)	1.60	1.60
		Set, never hinged	3.25	

80th death anniv. of Laurent Kosir, recognized by Yugoslavia as inventor of the postage stamp.

Arms of Bosnia and Herzegovina A50

Arms of Yugoslavia A51

1948, Nov. 29 — Perf. 12½, 12x11½
Arms of Yugoslav Peoples Republics

250	A50	3d green	.40	.80
251	A50	3d rose lil (Macedonia)	.40	.80
252	A50	3d gray bl (Serbia)	.40	.80
253	A50	3d gray (Montenegro)	.40	.80
254	A50	3d rose (Croatia)	.40	.80
255	A50	3d orange (Slovenia)	.40	.80
256	A51	10d deep carmine	.60	1.40
		Nos. 250-256 (7)	3.00	6.20
		Set, never hinged	6.00	

The Cyrillic and Latin inscriptions are transposed on Nos. 252, 253 and 255.

Franc Presern — A52

1949, Feb. 8 — Photo. — Perf. 11½

257	A52	3d dark blue	.30	.25
258	A52	5d brown orange	.30	.25
259	A52	10d olive black	1.00	.80
		Nos. 257-259 (3)	1.60	1.30
		Set, never hinged	2.75	

Death cent. of Franc Presern, poet.

Ski Jump, Planica — A53

Ski Jumper — A54

Perf. 12½x11½

1949, Mar. 20 — Litho.

260	A53	10d magenta	.40	1.00
261	A54	10d slate gray	.80	1.10
		Set, never hinged	2.40	

Intl. Ski Championships, Planica, Mar. 13-20.

Soldiers — A55

Farmers — A56

Arms and Flags of Macedonia and Yugoslavia — A57

1949, Aug. 2 — Perf. 12½

262	A55	3d carmine rose	.30	.65
263	A56	5d dull blue	.40	.80
264	A57	12d red brown	2.00	2.75
		Nos. 262-264 (3)	2.70	4.20
		Set, never hinged	4.20	

Liberation of Macedonia, 5th anniv.
It is reported that No. 264 was not sold to the public at post offices.
For overprints see Nos. C30-C32.

Postal Communications A58

UPU, 75th anniversary: 5d, Plane, locomotive and stagecoach, horiz.

1949, Sept. 8 — Unwmk.

265	A58	3d red	1.60	3.25
266	A58	5d blue	.40	.80
267	A58	12d brown	.40	.80
		Nos. 265-267 (3)	2.40	4.85
		Set, never hinged	4.75	

For overprints see Trieste Nos. 15-16.

Locomotives A60

1949, Dec. 15 — Photo.

269	A60	2d Early steam	1.25	2.00
270	A60	3d Modern steam	1.25	2.00
271	A60	5d Diesel	1.25	2.00
272	A60	10d Electric	25.00	24.00
		Nos. 269-272 (4)	28.75	30.00
		Set, never hinged	52.50	

Centenary of Yugoslav railroads.
For overprints see Trieste Nos. 17-20.

Official Stamps Nos. O7 and O8 Surcharged

1949 — Typo.

272A	O1	3d on 8d chocolate	.50	.40
272B	O1	3d on 12d violet	.50	.40
		Set, never hinged	2.00	

Stamps of 1945 and 1947 Overprinted or Surcharged in Black

a

b

c

d

1949 — Litho.

273	A22	(a) 50p olive gray	.25	.25
274	A22	(a) 1d blue green	.25	.25
275	A24	(b) 2d scarlet	.25	.25
276	A26	(c) 3d on 8d orange	.25	.25
277	A25	(d) 3d dull red	.25	.25
278	A25	(d) 5d dark blue	.25	.25
279	A23	(a) 10d on 20d org ver	.45	.25
280	A23	(a) 12d ultramarine	.40	.25
281	A22	(a) 16d blue	.60	.25
282	A23	(a) 20d orange ver	.60	.25
		Nos. 273-282 (10)	3.55	2.50
		Set, never hinged	6.00	

On No. 279 the surcharge includes a rule below "JUGOSLAVIJA" and "D 10" with two bars over "20D."
See Nos. 286-289.

Surveying for Highway A61

Bridge, Map and Automobile A62

Highway Completion Symbolized A63

1950, Jan. 16 — Photo. — Perf. 12½

283	A61	2d blue green	.55	.80
284	A62	3d rose brown	.55	.80
285	A63	5d violet blue	.80	1.20
		Nos. 283-285 (3)	1.90	2.80
		Set, never hinged	3.75	

Completion of Belgrade-Zagreb highway, Dec. 1949.

Types of 1945 Overprinted in Black

1950 — Unwmk. — Perf. 12½

286	A22	(a) 1d brownish org	.40	.25
287	A24	(b) 2d blue green	.40	.25
288	A25	(d) 3d rose pink	.60	.25
289	A25	(d) 5d blue	.60	.25
		Nos. 286-289 (4)	2.00	1.00
		Set, never hinged	4.00	

Marshal Tito — A64

1950, Apr. 30 — Engr.

290	A64	3d red	1.00	.80
291	A64	5d dull blue	1.00	.80
292	A64	10d brown	10.00	20.00
293	A64	12d olive black	1.25	2.40
		Nos. 290-293 (4)	13.25	24.00
		Set, never hinged	24.00	

Labor Day, May 1.

Child Eating — A65

1950, June 1 — Photo.

294	A65	3d brown red	.80	.45
		Never hinged	1.60	

Issued to publicize Children's Day, June 1.

Boy and Model Plane — A66

Designs: 3d, Glider aloft. 5d, Parachutists. 10d, Aviatrix. 20d, Glider on field.

1950, July 2 — Engr.

295	A66	2d dark green	1.60	3.25
296	A66	3d brown red	1.60	3.25
297	A66	5d violet	1.60	3.25
298	A66	10d chocolate	1.60	3.25
299	A66	20d ultramarine	12.00	24.00
		Nos. 295-299 (5)	18.40	37.00
		Set, never hinged	37.50	

Third Aviation Meet, July 2-11.

Map and Chess Symbols — A67

3d, Rook and ribbon. 5d, Globe and chess board. 10d, Allegory of international chess. 20d, View of Dubrovnik, knight and ribbon.

1950, Aug. 20   Photo.   Perf. 11½
300	A67	2d red brn & rose brown	.45	.80
301	A67	3d blk brn, gray brn & dl yellow	.45	.80
302	A67	5d dk grn, bl & buff	1.10	.80
303	A67	10d cl, bl & org yel	1.10	2.00
304	A67	20d dk bl, bl & org yellow	22.00	22.50
		Nos. 300-304 (5)	25.10	26.90
		Set, never hinged	50.00	

Intl. Chess Matches, Dubrovnik, Aug. 1950.

Electrification — A68

Designs: 50p, Metallurgy. 2d, Agriculture. 3d, Construction. 5d, Fishing. 7d, Mining. 10d, Fruitgrowing. 12d, Lumbering. 16d, Gathering sunflowers. 20d, Livestock raising. 30d, Book manufacture. 50d, Loading ship.

1950-51   Unwmk.   Engr.   Perf. 12½
305	A68	50p dk brn ('51)	.25	.25
306	A68	1d blue green	.25	.25
307	A68	2d orange	.25	.25
308	A68	3d rose red	.25	.25
309	A68	5d ultramarine	.60	.25
310	A68	7d gray	.60	.25
311	A68	10d chocolate	.60	.25
312	A68	12d vio brn ('51)	2.00	.25
313	A68	16d vio bl ('51)	1.75	.30
314	A68	20d ol grn ('51)	1.75	.30
314A	A68	30d red brn ('51)	4.00	.55
315	A68	50d violet ('51)	21.00	24.00
		Nos. 305-315 (12)	33.30	27.10
		Set, never hinged	55.00	

See Nos. 343-354, 378-384A. For overprints see Trieste Nos. 68-75, 90-92.

Coal and Logs for Export — A69

1950, Sept. 23   Photo.
316	A69	3d red brown	.80	.25
		Never hinged	1.60	

Zagreb International Fair, 1950.

Early Sailing Vessel "Dubrovnik" A70

Designs: 3d, Partisans in boat. 5d, Loading freighter. 10d, Transatlantic ship "Zagreb." 12d, Sailboats. 20d, Naval gun and ship.

1950, Nov. 29
317	A70	2d brown violet	.25	.25
318	A70	3d orange brown	.25	.25
319	A70	5d dull green	.25	.25
320	A70	10d chalky blue	.30	.25
321	A70	12d dark blue	.80	.30
322	A70	20d red brown	10.00	2.90
		Nos. 317-322 (6)	11.85	4.20
		Set, never hinged	20.00	

Yugoslav navy.

Partisans with Flag — A71

1951, Mar. 27   Engr.
323	A71	3d red & red brn	3.50	3.50
		Never hinged	7.50	

Yugoslavia's resistance to Nazi Germany, 10th anniv.

Stane Rozman A72

5d, Post-boy during Slovene insurrection.

1951, Apr. 27   Photo.
324	A72	3d brown red	.25	.25
325	A72	5d dark blue	.60	.40
		Set, never hinged	1.60	

Slovene insurrection, 10th anniv.

Children Painting A73

1951, June 3
326	A73	3d red	.80	.25
		Never hinged	1.60	

Issued to publicize Children's Day, June 3.

Zika Jovanovich — A74

Serbian Revolutionists A75

1951, July 7
327	A74	3d brown red	.30	.45
328	A75	5d deep blue	.55	.90
		Set, never hinged	1.60	

Serbian insurrection, 10th anniv.

Sava Kovacevich A76

Kovacevich Leading Revolutionists A77

1951, July 13
329	A76	3d rose pink	.40	.50
330	A77	5d light blue	1.00	1.10
		Set, never hinged	2.60	

Montenegrin insurrection, 10th anniv.

Monument to Marko Oreskovich A78

1951, July 27
331	A78	3d shown	.45	.50
332	A78	5d Monument to wounded	.70	.90
		Set, never hinged	2.00	

Croatian insurrection, 10th anniv.

Sium Bolaj — A79

Revolutionists A80

1951, July 27
333	A79	3d rose brown	.40	.50
334	A80	5d blue	.75	.90
		Set, never hinged	2.00	

Revolution in Bosnia and Herzegovina, 10th anniv.

Primoz Trubar — A81

12d, Marko Marulic. 20d, Tsar Stefan Duschan.

1951, Sept. 9   Engr.
335	A81	10d slate gray	3.25	6.50
336	A81	12d brown orange	3.25	6.50
337	A81	20d violet	10.00	20.00
		Nos. 335-337 (3)	16.50	33.00
		Set, never hinged	32.50	

Yugoslav cultural anniversaries.
For overprints see Trieste Nos. 40-41.

National Handicrafts — A82

1951, Sept. 15   Litho.   Perf. 11½
338	A82	3d multicolored	1.75	1.20
		Never hinged	2.50	

Zagreb International Fair, 1951.

Mirce Acev — A83

Monument at Skopje A84

1951, Oct. 11
339	A83	3d deep plum	.40	.40
340	A84	5d indigo	.80	1.20
		Set, never hinged	2.50	

Macedonian insurrection, 10th anniv.

Soldier and Emblem — A85

1951, Dec. 22   Photo.   Perf. 12½
341	A85	15d deep carmine	.25	.25
		Never hinged	.50	

Army Day. See No. C54.

Peter P. Nyegosh — A86

1951, Nov. 29   Engr.
342	A86	15d deep claret	2.00	.80
		Never hinged	3.25	

Death centenary of Nyegosh. See note after No. 217.

Types of 1950-51

Designs: 15d, Gathering sunflowers. 25d, Agriculture. 35d, Construction. 75d, Lumbering. 100d, Metallurgy.

1951-52   Engr.
343	A68	1d gray ('52)	.25	.25
344	A68	2d rose car ('52)	.25	.25
345	A68	5d orange ('52)	.80	.25
346	A68	10d emerald ('52)	4.00	.25
347	A68	15d rose car ('52)	20.00	.25
348	A68	20d purple	2.00	.25
349	A68	25d yel brn ('52)	8.75	.25
350	A68	30d blue	1.00	.25
351	A68	35d red brn ('52)	1.50	.25
352	A68	50d greenish bl	.80	.25
353	A68	75d purple ('52)	2.00	.25
354	A68	100d sepia ('52)	4.00	.25
		Nos. 343-354 (12)	45.35	3.00
		Set, never hinged	90.00	

No. 349 exists with and without printer's inscriptions at bottom, with stamps differing slightly.

Marshal Tito

A87   A88

1952, May 25 — Photo. — Perf. 11½

355	A87	15d shown	.40 .80
356	A88	28d shown	.40 .80
357	A87	50d Tito facing left	19.00 30.00
		Nos. 355-357 (3)	19.80 31.60
		Set, never hinged	40.00

60th birthday of Marshal Tito.

Child with Ball — A89

1952, June 1 — Litho. — Perf. 12½

358	A89	15d bright rose	3.00 3.00
		Never hinged	6.00

Issued to publicize Children's Day, June 1.
For overprint see Trieste No. 60.

Girl Gymnast — A90

1952, July 10 — Perf. 12½

359	A90	5d shown	.40 .25
360	A90	10d Runner	.60 .25
361	A90	15d Swimmer	.60 .25
362	A90	28d Boxer	1.40 .80
363	A90	50d Basketball	2.00 4.50
364	A90	100d Soccer	24.00 27.50
		Nos. 359-364 (6)	29.00 33.55
		Set, never hinged	55.00

15th Olympic Games, Helsinki, 1952.
Nos. 359-364 exist imperf. Value $800.
For overprints see Trieste Nos. 51-56.

Split, Dalmatia — A91

1952, Sept. 10 — Litho.

365	A91	15d shown	.40 .80
366	A91	28d Naval scene	.80 1.75
367	A91	50d St. Stefan	9.00 14.00
		Nos. 365-367 (3)	10.20 16.55
		Set, never hinged	20.00

Yugoslav navy, 10th anniv.
For overprints see Trieste Nos. 57-59.

Belgrade, 16th Century A92

1952, Sept. 14 — Engr. — Perf. 11½

368	A92	15d violet brn	6.00 10.00
		Never hinged	10.00

1st Yugoslav Phil. Exhib., Sept. 14-20. Sold only at the exhibition.

Marching Workers and Congress Flag — A93

1952, Nov. 2 — Perf. 11½

369	A93	15d red brown	.60 1.20
370	A93	15d dark vio blue	.60 1.20
371	A93	15d dark brown	.60 1.20
372	A93	15d blue green	.60 1.20
		Nos. 369-372 (4)	2.40 4.80
		Set, never hinged	5.00

6th Yugoslav Communist Party Congress, Zagreb.
For overprints see Trieste Nos. 61-64.

Nikola Tesla — A94

1953, Jan. 7 — Unwmk.

373	A94	15d brown carmine	.40 .25
374	A94	30d chalky blue	2.00 .65
		Set, never hinged	4.00

Death of Nikola Tesla, 10th anniv.
For overprints see Trieste Nos. 66-67.

Woman Pouring Water — A95

Designs: 30d, Hands holding two birds. 50d, Woman holding Urn.

1953, Mar. 24 — Litho. — Perf. 11½

375	A95	15d dark olive green	.40 .65
376	A95	30d chalky blue	.90 .65
377	A95	50d henna brown	8.75 4.50
		Nos. 375-377 (3)	10.05 5.80
		Set, never hinged	20.00

Issued to honor the United Nations.
See Nos. RA19 and RAJ16. For overprints see Trieste Nos. 76-78.

Types of 1950-52

1953-55 — Litho. — Perf. 12½

8d, Mining. 17d, Livestock raising.

378	A68	1d dull gray	.40 .25
379	A68	2d carmine	1.00 .25
380	A68	5d orange	3.50 .25
381	A68	8d blue	2.50 .25
382	A68	10d yellow green	4.00 .25
383	A68	12d lt vio brown	20.00 .25
384	A68	15d rose red	8.00 .25
384A	A68	17d vio brn ('55)	1.50 .25
		Nos. 378-384A (8)	40.90 2.00
		Set, never hinged	75.00

For overprints see Trieste Nos. 68-75, 90-92.

Automobile Climbing Mt. Lovcen — A96

30d, Motorcycle & auto at Opatija. 50d, Racers leaving Belgrade. 70d, Auto near Mt. Triglav.

1953, May 10 — Photo. — Perf. 12½

385	A96	15d sal & dp plum	.25 .25
386	A96	30d bl & dark blue	.25 .25
387	A96	50d ocher & choc	.60 .40
388	A96	70d lt bl grn & ol grn	15.00 4.75
		Nos. 385-388 (4)	16.10 5.65
		Set, never hinged	35.00

Intl. Automobile & Motorcycle Races, 1953.

President Tito — A97

1953, June 28 — Engr. — Unwmk.

389	A97	50d deep purple	6.00 8.00
		Never hinged	12.00

Marshal Tito's election to the presidency, Jan. 14, 1953.
For overprint see Trieste No. 83.

Star and Flag-encircled Globe — A98

1953, July 25 — Engr.; Star Typo.

390	A98	15d gray & green	1.50 2.40
		Never hinged	5.00

38th Esperanto Cong., Zagreb, 7/25-8/1.
For overprint see Trieste No. 84.

Macedonian Revolutionary A99 — Nicolas Karev A100

1953, Aug. 2 — Litho.

391	A99	15d dark red brown	.30 .65
392	A100	30d dull green	1.75 3.50
		Set, never hinged	4.00

Macedonian Insurection of 1903, 50th anniv.

Family — A101

1953, Sept. 6 — Photo.

393	A101	15d deep green	27.50 25.00
		Never hinged	50.00

Liberation of Istria and the Slovene coast, 10th anniv.
For overprint see Trieste No. 85.

Branko Radicevic — A102

1953, Oct. 1 — Engr.

394	A102	15d lilac	2.50 2.00
		Never hinged	5.00

10th death anniv. of Branko Radicevic, poet.
For overprint see Trieste No. 86.

View of Jajce — A103

Designs: 30d, First meeting place. 50d, Marshal Tito addressing Assembly.

1953, Nov. 29 — Perf. 12½x12

395	A103	15d dark green	.40 .80
396	A103	30d rose car	.60 1.20
397	A103	50d dark brown	4.00 8.00
		Nos. 395-397 (3)	5.00 10.00
		Set, never hinged	10.00

2nd Assembly of the Natl. Republic of Yugoslavia, 10th anniv.
For overprints see Trieste Nos. 87-89.

Wildlife A104

Lammergeier A105

1954, June 30 — Photo. — Perf. 11½

398	A104	2d Ground squirrel	.25 .25
399	A104	5d Lynx	.25 .25
400	A104	10d Red deer	.40 .25
401	A104	15d Brown bear	.50 .25
402	A104	17d Chamois	.80 .25
403	A104	25d White pelican	1.20 .40
404	A105	30d shown	1.20 .40
405	A105	35d Black beetle	1.60 .55
406	A105	50d Bush cricket	6.00 2.00
407	A105	65d Adriatic lizard	10.00 10.00
408	A105	70d Salamander	8.00 10.00
409	A105	100d Trout	24.00 32.50
		Nos. 398-409 (12)	54.20 57.10
		Set, never hinged	125.00

See Nos. 497-505. For overprints see Trieste Nos. 93-104.

> **Catalogue values for unused stamps in this section, from this point to the end of the section, are for Never Hinged items.**

Ljubljana, 17th Century A106

1954, July 29 — Engr.

410	A106	15d multicolored	13.00 13.00

2nd Yugoslav Phil. Exhib., July 29-Aug. 8. Sold for 50d, which included admission to the exhibition.

Revolutionary Flag — A107

30d, Cannon. 50d, Revolutionary seal. 70d, Karageorge.

1954, Oct. 3 — Engr. & Typo. — Perf. 12½

411	A107	15d shown	1.60 .45
412	A107	30d multi	2.25 .80
413	A107	50d multi	5.00 1.10
414	A107	70d multi	32.50 15.00
		Nos. 411-414 (4)	41.35 17.35

1st Serbian insurrection, 150th anniv.
For overprints see Trieste Nos. 105-108.

Vatroslav
Lisinski — A108

30d, Andrea Kacic-Miosic. 50d, Jure Vega. 70d, Jovan Jovanovic-Zmaj. 100d, Philip Visnic.

1954, Dec. 25   **Engr.**

415	A108	15d dark green	2.75	1.00
416	A108	30d chocolate	2.75	1.60
417	A108	50d dp claret	3.75	3.00
418	A108	70d indigo	7.50	7.00
419	A108	100d purple	19.00	19.00
		Nos. 415-419 (5)	35.75	31.60

Scene from "Robinja" — A109

"A Midsummer Night's Dream" A110

1955   **Photo.**   *Perf. 12x11½, 12½*
Glazed Paper

420	A109	15d brown lake	1.50	.90
421	A110	30d dark blue	5.25	3.00

Festival at Dubrovnik.

Dragon Emblem of Ljubljana — A111

1955   **Engr.**   *Perf. 12½*

422	A111	15d dk grn & brn	6.25	2.25

1st Intl. Exhib. of Graphic Arts, Ljubljana, July 3-Sept. 3.

Symbol of Sign Language A112

1955, Aug. 23

423	A112	15d rose lake	2.50	.60

2nd World Congress of Deaf Mutes, Zagreb, Aug. 23-27.

Hops — A113

Medicinal Plants.

1955, Sept. 24   **Photo.**   *Perf. 11½*

424	A113	5d shown	.25	.25
425	A113	10d Tobacco	.25	.25
426	A113	15d Poppy	.25	.25
427	A113	17d Linden	.25	.25
428	A113	25d Chamomile	.25	.25
429	A113	30d Salvia	.60	.30
430	A113	50d Dog rose	4.00	2.00
431	A113	70d Gentian	7.00	2.75
432	A113	100d Adonis	30.00	19.00
		Nos. 424-432 (9)	42.85	25.30

"Peace" Statue, New York — A114

1955, Oct. 24   **Litho.**   *Perf. 12½*

433	A114	30d lt bl & blk	1.50	1.10

United Nations, 10th anniversary.

Woman and Dove — A115

1955, Nov. 29   **Engr.**

434	A115	15d dull violet	.80	.55

10th anniv. of the "New Yugoslavia."

St. Donat, Zadar — A116

Cornice, Cathedral at Sibenik A117

Yugoslav Art: 10d, Relief of a King, Split. 15d, Griffin, Studenica Monastery. 20d, Figures, Trogir Cathedral. 25d, Fresco, Sopocani Monastery. 30d, Tombstone, Radimlje. 40d, Ciborium, Kotor Cathedral. 50d, St. Martin from Tryptich, Dubrovnik. 70d, Figure, Belec Church. 100d, Rihard Jakopic, self-portrait. 200d, "Peace" Statue, New York.

1956, Mar. 24   **Photo.**   *Perf. 11½*

435	A116	5d blue vio	.45	.25
436	A116	10d slate grn	.45	.25
437	A116	15d olive brn	.45	.25
438	A116	20d brown car	.45	.25
439	A116	25d black brn	.45	.25
440	A116	30d dp claret	.45	.25
441	A117	35d olive grn	1.00	.25
442	A117	40d red brown	1.75	.50
443	A116	50d olive brn	2.50	.70
444	A116	70d dk green	9.25	6.75
445	A116	100d dark pur	32.50	20.00
446	A116	200d deep blue	77.50	32.50
		Nos. 435-446 (12)	127.20	62.20

13th Century Tower, Zagreb A118

1956, Apr. 20   **Engr.**   *Perf. 11½*
Chalky Paper

447	A118	15d vio brn, bis brn & gray	1.00	.25
a.		Miniature sheet of 4	9.00	

3rd Yugoslavia Phil. Exhib. (JUFIZ III), Zagreb, May 20-27. No. 447a was sold at the exhibition, tipped into a folder, for 75 dinars. See No. C56.

Induction Motor — A119

Perf. 11½x12½

1956, July 10   **Photo.**

448	A119	10d shown	.50	.25
449	A119	15d Transformer	.60	.25
450	A119	30d Electronic controls	1.10	.50
451	A119	50d Nikola Tesla	4.00	2.00
		Nos. 448-451 (4)	6.20	3.00

Birth cent. of Nikola Tesla, inventor.

Sea Horse — A120

Paper Nautilus A121

Designs: 20d, European rock lobster. 25d, "Sea Prince." 30d, Sea perch. 35d, Red mullet. 50d, Scorpion fish. 70d, Wrasse. 100d, Dory.

1956, Sept. 10   *Perf. 11½*
Granite Paper
Animals in Natural Colors

452	A120	10d bright grn	.50	.30
453	A121	15d ultra & blk	.50	.30
454	A121	20d deep blue	.50	.30
455	A121	25d violet blue	.80	.30
456	A121	30d brt grnsh bl	.85	.30
457	A121	35d dk bl green	1.75	.30
458	A121	50d indigo	6.50	1.90
459	A121	70d slate grn	8.00	4.00
460	A121	100d dark blue	32.50	20.00
		Nos. 452-460 (9)	51.90	27.70

Runner A122

Designs: 15d, Paddling kayak. 20d, Skiing. 30d, Swimming. 35d, Soccer. 50d, Water polo. 70d, Table tennis. 100d, Sharpshooting.

1956, Oct. 24   **Litho.**   *Perf. 12½*
Design and Inscription in Bister

461	A122	10d dk carmine	.80	.35
462	A122	15d dark blue	.80	.35
463	A122	20d ultramarine	1.50	.70
464	A122	30d olive grn	1.50	.70
465	A122	35d dark brown	1.50	.70
466	A122	50d green	1.50	.70
467	A122	70d brn violet	50.00	22.50
468	A122	100d dark red	50.00	22.50
		Nos. 461-468 (8)	107.60	48.50

16th Olympic Games, Melbourne, 11/22-12/8.

Centaury — A123

Medicinal Plants: 15d, Belladonna. 20d, Autumn crocus. 25d, Marsh mallow. 30d, Valerian. 35d, Woolly Foxglove. 50d, Aspidium. 70d, Green Winged Orchid. 100d, Pyrethrum.

Granite Paper
Flowers in Natural Colors

1957, May 25   **Photo.**   *Perf. 11½*

469	A123	10d dk bl & grn	.25	.25
470	A123	15d violet	.25	.25
471	A123	20d lt grn & brn	.25	.25
472	A123	25d dp cl & dk bl	.50	.25
473	A123	30d lil rose & claret	.90	.25
474	A123	35d dk gray & dl pur	1.50	.25
475	A123	50d dp grn & choc	2.50	.75
476	A123	70d pale brn & grn	4.50	1.60
477	A123	100d gray & brown	14.00	6.00
		Nos. 469-477 (9)	24.65	9.85

See #538-546, 597-605, 689-694, 772-777.

Hand Holding Factory A124

1957, June 25   **Engr.**   *Perf. 12½*

478	A124	15d dark car rose	.40	.25
479	A124	30d violet blue	1.40	.80

Congress of Workers' Councils, Belgrade, June 25. Exist imperf.

2nd Gymnastic Meet, Zagreb, July 10-14 — A125

Various gymnastic positions.

1957, July 1   **Photo.**

480	A125	10d ol grn & blk	.25	.25
481	A125	15d brn red & blk	.25	.25
482	A125	30d Prus bl & blk	.80	.25
483	A125	50d brn & black	3.75	1.25
		Nos. 480-483 (4)	5.05	2.00

Montenegro A126

Natl. Costumes: 15d, Macedonia. 30d, Croatia. 50d, Serbia. 70d, Bosnia and Herzegovina. 100d, Slovenia. 50d, 70d, 100d vert.

1957, Sept. 24   **Typo.**   *Perf. 12½*
Background in Bister Brown

484	A126	10d dk brn, ultra & red	.40	.25
485	A126	15d dk brn, blk & red	.40	.25
486	A126	30d dk brn, grn & red	.40	.25
487	A126	50d dk brn & green	1.00	.25
488	A126	70d dk brn & black	1.40	.50
489	A126	100d dk brn, grn & red	6.50	3.25
		Nos. 484-489 (6)	10.10	4.75

Revolutionists
A127

Lithographed and Engraved
1957, Nov. 7 **Perf. 11½x12½**
490 A127 15d ocher & red 1.00 .75
Russian Revolution, 40th anniv.

Simon
Gregorcic — A128

Famous Yugoslavs: 30d, Anton Linhart, dramatist and historian. 50d, Oton Kucera, physicist. 70d, Stevan Mokranjac, composer. 100d, Jovan Sterija Popovic, writer

1957, Dec. 3 **Engr.** **Perf. 12½**
491 A128 15d sepia .45 .40
492 A128 30d indigo .60 .40
493 A128 50d reddish brn 1.25 .40
494 A128 70d dl violet 9.00 4.75
495 A128 100d olive grn 15.00 8.00
Nos. 491-495 (5) 26.30 13.95

"Young Man on
Fire" — A129

1958, Apr. 22 **Photo.**
496 A129 15d deep plum .80 .25
Union of Yugoslav Communists, 7th congress, Ljubljana, Apr. 22.

Types of 1954
Game birds.

1958, May 25 **Perf. 11½**
Granite Paper
Birds in Natural Colors
497 A104 10d Mallard .30 .25
498 A104 15d Capercaillie .30 .25
499 A104 20d Ring-necked
pheasant .30 .25
500 A104 25d Coot .30 .25
501 A104 30d Water rail .70 .25
502 A105 35d Great bustard 1.25 .25
503 A104 50d Rock partridge 4.50 1.25
504 A104 70d Woodcock 8.25 3.25
505 A105 100d Eurasian crane 17.50 7.50
Nos. 497-505 (9) 33.40 13.50

Stylized
Bird — A130

1958, June 14 **Engr.** **Perf. 12½**
506 A130 15d bluish black .80 .25
Opening of Postal Museum, Belgrade. Exists imperf.

Flag and
Laurel
A131

1958, July 1 **Unwmk.**
507 A131 15d brn carmine .50 .30
15th anniv. of victory over Germans at Sutjeska, Bosnia.

Onufrio Well,
Dubrovnik
A132

1958, Aug. 10 **Litho.** **Perf. 12½**
508 A132 15d black & brn 1.50 .30
Marin Drzic, dramatist, 450th birth anniv.

Sisak Steel
Works — A133

Titograd Hotel and
Open-Air
Theater — A134

Industrial Progress Designs: 2d, Crude oil production. 5d, Shipbuilding. 10d, Sisak steel works. 15d, Jablanica hydroelectric works. 17d, Lumber industry. 25d, Overpass, Zagreb-Ljubljana highway. 30d, Litostroy turbine factory. 35d, Lukavac coke plant. 50d, Bridge at Skopje. 70d, Railroad station, Sarajevo. 100d, Triple bridge, Ljubljana. 200d, Mestrovic station, Zagreb. 500d, Parliament, Belgrade.

1958 **Typo.** **Perf. 12½ Horiz.**
509 A133 10d green 14.00 6.00
510 A133 15d orange ver 14.00 6.00

Engr. **Perf. 12½**
511 A133 2d olive .25 .25
512 A133 5d brown red .25 .25
513 A133 10d green .40 .25
514 A133 15d orange ver .40 .25
515 A133 17d deep claret .40 .25
516 A133 25d slate .40 .25
517 A133 30d blue black .40 .25
518 A133 35d rose red .40 .25
519 A134 40d car rose .45 .25
520 A134 50d bright bl .50 .25
521 A134 70d orange ver 1.25 .25
522 A134 100d green 4.75 .25
523 A134 200d red brown 4.50 .25
524 A134 500d intense bl 8.50 .30
Nos. 511-524 (14) 22.85 3.55

Nos. 509-510 are coil stamps.
See #555-562, 627-645, 786-789, 830-840.

Ocean
Exploration
A135

1958, Oct. 24 **Unwmk.**
525 A135 15d brown violet .50 .25
Intl. Geophysical Year, 1957-58. Exists imperf. See #C58.

White and
Black Hands
Holding
Scales
A136

1958, Dec. 10 **Perf. 12½**
526 A136 30d steel blue 1.50 1.00
Universal Declaration of Human Rights, 10th anniv.

Dubrovnik
A137

Tourist attractions: #528, Bled. #529, Postojna grotto. #530, Ohrid. #531, Opatija. #532, Plitvice National Park. #533, Split. #534, Sveti Stefan. #535, Exhibition Hall, Belgrade.

1959, Feb. 16 **Litho.** **Perf. 12½**
527 A137 10d crim rose & cit .25 .25
528 A137 10d lt grn & lt vio bl .25 .25
529 A137 15d grnsh bl & pur .25 .25
530 A137 15d grn & bright bl .25 .25
531 A137 20d lt grn & grnsh bl .25 .25
532 A137 20d ol bis & brt grn .25 .25
533 A137 30d yel org & purple 1.40 .25
534 A137 30d lt vio bl & gray ol 1.40 .25
535 A137 70d gray & grnsh bl 4.50 2.25
Nos. 527-535 (9) 8.80 4.25

Nos. 527, 530, 532 and 534 are inscribed in Cyrillic characters. See #650-658, 695-700

Red
Flags — A138

1959, Apr. 20 **Unwmk.** **Perf. 12½**
536 A138 20d multicolored .50 .25
Yugoslav Communist Party, 40th anniv.

Dubrovnik,
15th
Century
A139

1959, May 24 **Engr.** **Perf. 11½**
537 A139 20d yel grn, dk grn &
bl 10.00 3.50
4th Yugoslavia Phil. Exhib. (JUFIZ IV), Dubrovnik.

Flower Type of 1957
Medicinal Plants: 10d, Lavender. 15d, Black Alder. 20d, Scopolia. 25d, Monkshood. 30d, Bilberry. 35d, Juniper. 50d, Primrose. 70d, Pomegranate. 100d, Jimson weed.

1959, May 25 **Photo.**
Granite Paper
Flowers in Natural Colors
538 A123 10d lt bl & dk blue .25 .25
539 A123 15d brt yel & car .25 .25
540 A123 20d dk ol bis & mar .25 .25
541 A123 25d ap grn & dk pur .25 .25
542 A123 30d pink & dk bl .25 .25
543 A123 35d bis brn & vio bl 1.25 .25
544 A123 50d brn & green 3.00 .40
545 A123 70d yel & ocher 4.00 .65
546 A123 100d lt brn & brn 8.50 4.00
Nos. 538-546 (9) 18.00 6.55

Tug of
War — A140

Sports: 15d, High jump and runners. 20d, Ring and parallel bar exercises. 35d, Women gymnasts. 40d, Sailors doing gymnastics. 55d, Field ball and basketball. 80d, Swimming. 100d, Festival emblem, vert.

1959, June 26 **Litho.** **Perf. 12½**
547 A140 10d dk sl grn &
ocher .25 .25
548 A140 15d vio bl & sepia .25 .25
549 A140 20d ol bis & dl lil .25 .25
550 A140 35d deep cl & gray .25 .25
551 A140 40d violet & gray .25 .25
552 A140 55d sl grn & ol bis .50 .25
553 A140 80d indigo & olive 3.25 .50
554 A140 100d pur & bister 7.00 3.50
Nos. 547-554 (8) 12.00 5.50

Physical Culture Festival. Exist imperf.

Types of 1958; Designs as before
Designs: 8d, Lumber industry. 15d, Overpass, Zagreb-Ljubljana highway. 20d, Jablanica hydroelectric works. 40d, Titograd Hotel. 55d, Bridge at Skopje. 80d, Railroad Station, Sarajevo.

1959 **Typo.** **Perf. 12½ Horizontally**
555 A133 15d green 2.50 1.10
556 A133 20d orange ver 3.00 1.10

Engr. **Perf. 12½**
557 A133 8d deep claret .40 .25
558 A133 15d green .55 .25
559 A133 20d orange ver .95 .25
560 A134 40d bright blue 2.25 .25
561 A134 55d carmine rose 3.50 .25
562 A134 80d orange ver 6.00 .25
Nos. 557-562 (6) 13.65 1.50

Nos. 555-556 are coil stamps.

Fair
Emblem — A141

1959, Sept. 5 **Litho.** **Unwmk.**
563 A141 20d lt vio bl & blk 2.00 1.00
50th International Fair at Zagreb.

Athletics — A142

1960, Apr. 25 **Perf. 12½**
564 A142 15d shown .40 .40
565 A142 20d Swimming .40 .40
566 A142 30d Skiing .40 .40
567 A142 35d Wrestling .40 .40
568 A142 40d Bicycling .40 .40
569 A142 55d Yachting .40 .40
570 A142 80d Horseback riding 5.00 3.50
571 A142 100d Fencing 5.00 3.50
Nos. 564-571 (8) 12.40 9.40

17th Olympic Games.

Hedgehog
A143

1960, May 25　Photo.　Perf. 12x11½
Animals in Natural Colors

572	A143	15d shown	.30	.30
573	A143	20d Red squirrel	.30	.30
574	A143	25d Pine marten	.30	.30
575	A143	30d Hare	.70	.70
576	A143	35d Red fox	.70	.70
577	A143	40d Badger	.70	.70
578	A143	55d Wolf	1.50	1.50
579	A143	80d Roe deer	1.50	1.50
580	A143	100d Wild boar	4.00	4.00
		Nos. 572-580 (9)	10.00	10.00

See Nos. 663-671.

Lenin, 90th Birth
Anniv. — A144

1960, June 22　Engr.　Perf. 12½
581　A144　20d dk grn & slate grn　.25　.25

Atomic
Accelerator
A145

1960, Aug. 23　　　Unwmk.

582	A145	15d shown	8.00	8.00
583	A145	20d Generator	8.00	8.00
584	A145	40d Nuclear reactor	8.00	8.00
		Nos. 582-584 (3)	24.00	24.00

Nuclear energy exposition, Belgrade. Exist
imperf.

Serbian National
Theater, Novi
Sad — A146

Designs: 20d, Woman from Croatian play.
40d, Edward Rusijan and early plane. 55d,
Symbolic hand holding fruit. 80d, Atom and
UN emblem.

1960, Oct. 24　　　Perf. 12½

585	A146	15d gray black	.75	.75
586	A146	20d brown	.75	.75
587	A146	40d dark gray blue	.75	.75
588	A146	55d dull claret	1.00	1.00
589	A146	80d dark green	1.00	1.00
		Nos. 585-589 (5)	4.25	4.25

Serbian Natl. Theater, Novi Sad, cent.
(#585); Croatian Natl. Theater, Zagreb, cent.
(#586); 1st flight in Yugoslavia, 50th anniv.
(#587); 15th anniv. of the Yugoslav Republic
(#588); UN, 15th anniv. (#589).
Exist imperf.

Ivan Cankar,
Writer — A147

Famous Yugoslavs: 20d, Silvije Strahimir
Kranjcevic, poet. 40d, Paja Jovanovic, painter.
55d, Dura Jaksic, writer and painter. 80d,
Mihajlo Pupin, electro-technician. 100d,
Rudjer Boscovich, mathematician.

1960, Dec. 24　Engr.　Perf. 12½

590	A147	15d dark green	.35	.30
591	A147	20d henna brown	.35	.30
592	A147	40d olive bister	.35	.30
593	A147	55d magenta	.35	.30
594	A147	80d dark blue	.35	.30
595	A147	100d Prussian bl	.35	.30
		Nos. 590-595 (6)	2.10	1.80

Exist imperf.

International
Atomic Energy
Commission
Emblem — A148

Engr. & Litho.
1961, May 15　　　Perf. 12½
596　A148　25d multicolored　.50　.25
Intl. Nuclear Electronic Conf., Belgrade.

Flower Type of 1957
Medicinal plants: 10d, Yellow foxglove. 15d,
Marjoram. 20d, Hyssop. 25d, Scarlet haw.
40d, Rose mallow. 50d, Soapwort. 60d, Clary.
80d, Blackthorn. 100d, Marigold.

1961, May 25　Photo.　Perf. 11½
Granite Paper
Flowers in Natural Colors

597	A123	10d lt bl & grnsh bl	.30	.30
598	A123	15d gray & chnt	.30	.30
599	A123	20d buff & green	.30	.30
600	A123	25d lt vio & vio	.30	.30
601	A123	40d lt ultra & ultra	.30	.30
602	A123	50d lt bl & blue	.30	.30
603	A123	60d beige & dk car rose	.30	.30
604	A123	80d lt grn & green	.30	.30
605	A123	100d redsh brn & choc	12.00	9.00
		Nos. 597-605 (9)	14.40	11.40

Victims' Monument,
Kragujevac — A149

Monuments: 15d, Stevan Filipovic, Valjevo.
20d, Relief from Insurrection, Bozansko
Grahovo. 60d, Victory, Nova Gradiska. 100d,
Marshal Tito, Titovo Uzice.

Granite Paper
Gold Frames and Inscriptions
1961, July 3　　　Perf. 12x12½

606	A149	15d crimson & brn	.25	.25
607	A149	20d brn & ol bis	.25	.25
608	A149	25d bl grn & gray olive	.25	.25
609	A149	60d violet	.25	.25
610	A149	100d indigo & black	.25	.25
		Nos. 606-610 (5)	1.25	1.25

Souvenir Sheet
Imperf
611　A149　500d indigo & black　125.00　125.00
Natl. Insurrection, 20th anniv.

Men of
Five
Races
A150

National Assembly Building,
Belgrade — A151

1961, Sept. 1　Litho.　Perf. 11½
613　A150　25d brown　.25　.25
Engr.
614　A151　50d blue green　.25　.25
Nos. 613-614,C59-C60 (4)　3.40　2.35

Miniature Sheet
Imperf
615　A150　1000d claret　20.00　17.50
Conference of Non-aligned Nations, Belgrade, Sept. 1961.

St. Clement, 14th
Century Wood
Sculpture — A152

1961, Sept. 10　Engr.　Perf. 12½
616　A152　25d sepia & olive　2.00　.65
12th Intl. Congress for Byzantine Studies.

Serbian
Women
A153

Regional Costumes: 25d, Montenegro. 30d,
Bosnia and Herzegovina. 50d, Macedonia.
65d, Croatia. 100d, Slovenia.

1961, Nov. 28　　　Litho.

617	A153	15d beige, brn & red	.25	.25
618	A153	25d beige, red brn & black	.25	.25
619	A153	30d beige, brn & dk red	.25	.25
620	A153	50d multicolored	.25	.25
621	A153	65d brn, red & yel	.60	.25
622	A153	100d multicolored	1.60	.75
		Nos. 617-622 (6)	3.20	2.00

Luka
Vukalovic — A154

1961, Dec. 15　　　Engr.
623　A154　25d slate blue　.25　.25
Centenary of Herzegovina insurrection.

Hands with
Flower and
Rifle — A155

1961, Dec. 22
624　A155　25d red & vio blue　.25　.25
20th anniversary of Yugoslav army.

Miladinov
Brothers
A156

1961, Dec. 25　　　Litho.
625　A156　25d buff & claret　.25　.25
Centenary of Macedonian folksong "Koder";
Dimitri and Konstantin Miladinov, brothers who
collected and published folksongs. Monument
is at Struga.

Types of 1958; Designs as before
Designs: 5d, Shipbuilding. 8d, Lumber
industry. 10d, Sisak steel works. 15d, Over-
pass. 20d, Jablanica hydroelectric works. 25d,
Cable factory, Svetozarevo. 30d, Litostroy tur-
bine factory. 40d, Lukavac coke plant. 50d,
Zenica steel works. 65d, Sevojno copper
works. 100d, Crude oil production. 150d,
Titograd hotel. 200d, Bridge, Skopje. 300d,
Railroad station, Sarajevo. 500d, Triple bridge,
Ljubljana. 1000d, Mestrovic station, Zagreb.
2000d, Parliament, Belgrade.

1961-62　Typo.　Perf. 12½ Horiz.

627	A133	10d dark red brn	7.50	.55
628	A133	15d emerald	12.00	.30

Engr.　Perf. 12½

629	A133	5d dull orange	.25	.25
630	A133	8d gray	.25	.25
631	A133	10d dk red brn	.25	.25
632	A133	15d emerald	.25	.25
633	A133	20d violet blue	.50	.25
634	A133	25d vermilion	.25	.25
635	A133	30d red brown	6.50	.25
636	A133	40d dp cl ('62)	.25	.25
637	A133	50d gray blue	1.60	.25
638	A133	65d green	.25	.25
639	A133	100d yel olive	3.25	.25
640	A134	150d carmine ('62)	.75	.25
641	A134	200d slate grn ('62)	.75	.25
642	A134	300d olive ('62)	1.50	.25
643	A134	500d dull violet	1.25	.25
644	A134	1000d bister brn	4.50	.25
645	A134	2000d claret	10.00	.40
		Nos. 629-645 (17)	32.35	4.40

Nos. 627-628 are coil stamps. For
surcharges see Nos. 786, 789.

Isis of
Kalabsha — A157

Design: 50d, Ramses II, Abu Simbel.

1962, Apr. 7　Engr.　Perf. 12½

646	A157	25d grnsh blk, cream	.25	.25
647	A157	50d brown, buff	.25	.25

15th anniv. (in 1961) of UNESCO.

Joy of
Motherhood by
Frano
Krsinic — A158

1962, Apr. 7
648　A158　50d black, cream　.30　.25
15th anniv. (in 1961) of UNICEF.

Anopheles Mosquito — A159

1962, Apr. 7   **Unwmk.**
649 A159 50d black, *gray*   .40 .25

WHO drive to eradicate malaria.

Scenic Type of 1959

Tourist attractions: #650, Portoroz. #651, Jajce. #652, Zadar. #653, Popova Sapka. #654, Hvar. #655, Bay of Kotor. #656, Danube, Iron Gate. #657, Rab. #658, Zagreb.

1962, Apr. 24   **Litho.**
650 A137 15d ol & chlky bl   .25 .25
651 A137 15d blue grn & bis   .25 .25
652 A137 25d blue & red brn   .25 .25
653 A137 25d dk bl & pale bl   .25 .25
654 A137 30d blue & brn org   .25 .25
655 A137 30d gray & chlky bl   .25 .25
656 A137 50d ol & grnsh bl   .90 .25
657 A137 50d blue & olive   .90 .25
658 A137 100d dk grn & gray bl   7.50 3.00
Nos. 650-658 (9)   10.80 5.00

#651, 653, 655-656 are inscribed in Cyrillic. Exist imperf.

Marshal Tito, by Augustincic A160

Design: 50d, 200d, Sideview of bust by Antun Augustincic.

1962, May 25   **Engr.**   **Perf. 12½**
659 A160 25d dark green   1.00 .80
660 A160 50d dark brown   1.00 .80
661 A160 100d dark blue   1.00 .80
662 A160 200d greenish blk   1.00 .80
   a.   Souv. sheet of 4, #659-662,
     imperf.   35.00 35.00
Nos. 659-662 (4)   4.00 3.20

70th birthday of Pres. Tito (Josip Broz).

Animal Type of 1960

Designs: 15d, Crested newt. 20d, Fire salamander. 25d, Yellow-bellied toad. 30d, Pond frog. 50d, Pond turtle. 65d, Lizard. 100d, Emerald lizard. 150d, Leopard snake. 200d, European viper (adder).

1962, June 8   **Photo.**   **Perf. 12x11½**

Animals in Natural Colors
663 A143 15d green   .50 .50
664 A143 20d purple   .50 .50
665 A143 25d chocolate   .50 .50
666 A143 30d violet blue   .50 .50
667 A143 50d dark red   .50 .50
668 A143 65d bright grn   .50 .50
669 A143 100d black   1.25 1.25
670 A143 150d brown   1.25 1.25
671 A143 200d car rose   12.50 7.00
Nos. 663-671 (9)   18.00 12.50

Pole Vault — A161

Sports: 25d, Woman discus thrower, horiz. 30d, Long distance runners, horiz. 50d, Javelin thrower, horiz. 65d, Shot put. 100d, Women runners, horiz. 150d, Hop, step and jump. 200d, High jump, horiz.

Athletes in Black

1962, July 10   **Litho.**   **Perf. 12½**
672 A161 15d blue   .35 .25
673 A161 25d magenta   .35 .25
674 A161 30d emerald   .35 .25
675 A161 50d red   .35 .25

676 A161 65d vio blue   .35 .25
677 A161 100d green   .70 .25
678 A161 150d orange   3.50 .40
679 A161 200d orange brn   9.50 .80
Nos. 672-679 (8)   15.45 2.70

7th European Athletic Championships, Belgrade, Sept. 12-16. See No. C61.

Child at Play — A162

Litho. & Engr.

1962, Oct. 1   **Perf. 12½**
680 A162 25d red & black   .30 .25

Issued for Children's Week.

Gold Mask, Trebeniste, 5th Century B.C. — A163

Bathing the Infant Christ, Fresco, Decani Monastery — A164

Yugoslav Art Treasures: 25d, Horseman and bird, bronze vase (5th cent. B.C.). 50d, God Kairos, marble relief. 65d, "The Pigeons of Nerezi," fresco (12th cent.). 150d, Archangel Gabriel, icon (14th cent.).

1962, Nov. 28   **Photo.**
681 A163 25d Prus bl, blk &
     gold   .25 .25
682 A163 30d gold, saph & blk   .25 .25
683 A164 50d dk grn, brn &
     gold   .25 .25
684 A164 65d multicolored   .25 .25
685 A164 100d multicolored   .50 .50
686 A163 150d multicolored   1.00 1.00
Nos. 681-686 (6)   2.50 2.50

Parched Earth and Wheat — A165

1963, Mar. 21   **Engr.**   **Perf. 12½**
687 A165 50d dark brn, *tan*   .40 .40

FAO "Freedom from Hunger" campaign.

Dr. Andrija Mohorovicic and UN Emblem — A166

1963, Mar. 23   **Unwmk.**
688 A166 50d dk blue, *gray*   .40 .40

UN 3rd World Meteorological Day, Mar. 23. Dr. Mohorovicic (1857-1936) was director of the Zagreb meteorological observatory.

Flower Type of 1957

Medicinal Plants: 15d, Lily of the valley. 25d, Iris. 30d, Bistort. 50d, Henbane. 65d, St. John's wort. 100d, Caraway.

1963, May 25   **Photo.**   **Perf. 11½**

Granite Paper
Flowers in Natural Colors
689 A123 15d gray grn & grn   .25 .25
690 A123 25d lt bl, ultra & pur   .25 .25
691 A123 30d gray & black   .25 .25
692 A123 50d redsh brn & red
     brn   .25 .25
693 A123 65d pale brn & brn   .65 .65
694 A123 100d slate & blk   3.50 2.75
Nos. 689-694 (6)   5.15 4.40

Scenic Type of 1959

Tourist attractions: 15d, Pula. 25d, Vrnjacka Banja. 30d, Crikvenica. 50d, Korcula. 65d, Durmitor mountain. 100d, Ljubljana.

1963, June 6   **Litho.**   **Perf. 12½**
695 A137 15d multicolored   .25 .25
696 A137 25d multicolored   .25 .25
697 A137 30d multicolored   .25 .25
698 A137 50d multicolored   .25 .25
699 A137 65d multicolored   .25 .25
700 A137 100d multicolored   1.50 .40
Nos. 695-700 (6)   2.75 1.65

Partisans on the March, by Djordje Andrejevic-Kun — A167

Sutjeska (Gorge) — A168

Design: No. 702A, As 15d, but inscribed "Vis 1944-1964." 50d, Partisans in battle.

Engr. & Litho.; Litho. (No. 702)
1963-64   **Perf. 12½, 11½**
701 A167 15d gray & dk sl grn   .25 .25
702 A168 25d dark slate grn   .25 .25
702A A167 25d gray & dark car
     rose   .45 .45
703 A167 50d tan & purple   .25 .25
Nos. 701-703 (4)   1.20 1.20

20th anniv. of the Partisan Battle of Sutjeska (Nos. 701, 702-703); 20th anniv. of the arrival of the Yugoslav General Staff on the island of Vis (No. 702A).
Issued: #702A, 7/27/64; others, 7/3/63.

Gymnast on Vaulting Horse — A169

1963, July 6   **Litho.**   **Perf. 12½**
704 A169 25d shown   .40 .40
705 A169 50d Parallel bars   .80 .40
706 A169 100d Rings   1.20 .40
Nos. 704-706 (3)   2.40 1.20

5th Gymnastics Europa Prize.

Mother, by Ivan Mestrovic A170

Sculptures by Mestrovic (1883-1962): 50d, "Reminiscences" (woman). 65d, Head of Kraljevic Marko. 100d, Indian on Horseback.

1963, Sept. 28   **Engr.**
707 A170 25d brown, *buff*   .25 .25
708 A170 50d sl green, *grnsh*   .25 .25
709 A170 65d grnsh blk, *grysh*   .25 .25
710 A170 100d black, *grayish*   1.00 .75
Nos. 707-710 (4)   1.75 1.50

Children with Toys — A171

1963, Oct. 5   **Litho.**
711 A171 25d multicolored   .40 .25

Issued for Children's Week.

Soldier with Gun and Flag — A172

Litho. & Engr.
1963, Oct. 20   **Perf. 12½**
712 A172 25d ver, tan & gold   .50 .35

Yugoslavian Democratic Federation, 20th anniv.

Relief from Tombstone, Herzegovina A173

Art through the centuries: 30d, Horseback trio, Split Cathedral. 50d, King & queen on horseback, Beram Church, Istria. 65d, Archangel Michael, Dominican monastery, Dubrovnik. 100d, Man pouring water, fountain, Ljubljana. 150d, Archbishop Eufrasie, mosaic, Porec Basilica, Istria.

1963, Nov. 29   **Photo.**
713 A173 25d multi   .25 .25
714 A173 30d multi, horiz.   .25 .25
715 A173 50d multi, horiz.   .25 .25
716 A173 65d multi   .25 .25
717 A173 100d multi   .25 .25
718 A173 150d multi   .95 .75
Nos. 713-718 (6)   2.20 2.00

Issued for the Day of the Republic.

Dositej Obradovic A174

Famous Yugoslavians: 30d, Vuk Stefanovic Karadzic, reformer of Serbian language. 50d, Franc Miklosic, Slovenian philologist. 65d, Ljudevit Gaj, reformer of Croatian language. 100d, Peter Petrovich Nyegosh, Montenegrin prince, bishop and poet.

Variously Toned Paper

1963, Dec. 10   **Engr.**
719 A174 25d black   .25 .25
720 A174 30d black   .25 .25
721 A174 50d black   .25 .25
722 A174 65d black   1.00 .25
723 A174 100d black   1.00 .50
Nos. 719-723 (5)   2.75 1.50

Vanessa Io — A175

Butterflies & Moths: 30d, Vanessa antiopa. 40d, Daphnis nerii. 50d, Parnassius apollo. 150d, Saturnia pyri. 200d, Papilio machaon.

1964, May 25   Photo.   Perf. 12½

724	A175	25d multicolored	.40	.40
725	A175	30d multicolored	.40	.40
726	A175	40d multicolored	.40	.40
727	A175	50d multicolored	.40	.40
728	A175	150d multicolored	4.00	4.00
729	A175	200d multicolored	4.00	4.00
		Nos. 724-729 (6)	9.60	9.60

Fireman Rescuing Child — A176

1964, June 14   Litho.

730	A176	25d red & black	.25	.25

Centenary of voluntary firemen. Exists imperf.

Runner A177

1964, July 1   Unwmk.   Perf. 12½

731	A177	25d shown	.25	.25
732	A177	30d Boxing	.25	.25
733	A177	40d Rowing	.25	.25
734	A177	50d Basketball	.25	.25
735	A177	150d Soccer	5.00	1.00
736	A177	200d Water polo	5.00	1.00
		Nos. 731-736 (6)	11.00	3.00

18th Olympic Games, Tokyo, Oct. 10-25.

UN Flag over Scaffolding A178

25d, Upheaval of the earth & scaffolding.

1964, July 26   Engr.

737	A178	25d red brown	.25	.25
738	A178	50d blue	.25	.25

Earthquake at Skopje; 1st anniv.

Serbian Women — A179

Regional Costumes: 30d, Slovenia. 40d, Bosnia and Herzegovina. 50d, Croatia. 150d, Macedonia. 200d, Montenegro.

Costumes Multicolored

1964, Aug. 5   Litho.

740	A179	25d violet & brn	.65	.65
741	A179	30d slate & green	.65	.65
742	A179	40d redsh brn & blk	.65	.65

743	A179	50d blue & black	.65	.65
744	A179	150d dl grn & sepia	2.75	2.75
745	A179	200d tan, red & brn	2.75	2.75
		Nos. 740-745 (6)	8.10	8.10

Exist imperf.

Friedrich Engels — A180

Litho. & Engr.

1964, Sept. 27   Perf. 11½

746	A180	25d shown	.25	.25
747	A180	50d Karl Marx	.25	.25

1st Socialist Intl., London, Sept. 28, 1864. Exist imperf.

Children at Play — A181

1964, Oct. 4   Litho.   Perf. 12½

748	A181	25d ver, pink & gray grn	.40	.40

Issued for Children's Week. Exists imperf.

The Victor by Ivan Mestrovic — A182

1964, Oct. 20   Engr.   Perf. 11½

749	A182	25d bister & blk	.25	.25

Liberation of Belgrade, 20th anniv.

Initial from Evangel of Hilandar — A183

Art through the centuries: 30d, Initial from Evangel of Miroslav (musician). 40d, Detail from Cetinje octavo, 1494 (saint with scroll). 50d, Miniature from Evangel of Trogir, 13th cent. (female saint). 150d, Miniature from Hrvoye Missal, 15th cent. (knight on horseback). 200d, Miniature from 14th cent. manuscript (symbolic fight), horiz.

Perf. 11½x12, 12x11½

1964, Nov. 29   Photo.   Unwmk.

750	A183	25d multicolored	.25	.25
751	A183	30d multicolored	.25	.25
752	A183	40d multicolored	.25	.25
753	A183	50d multicolored	.25	.25
754	A183	150d multicolored	.25	.25
755	A183	200d multicolored	.25	.25
		Nos. 750-755 (6)	1.50	1.50

Issued for Day of the Republic.

Hand, "Liberty and Equality" — A184

50d, Dove over factory, "Peace and Socialism." 100d, Smokestacks, "Building Socialism."

1964, Dec. 7   Perf. 12

756	A184	25d multicolored	.25	.25
757	A184	50d multicolored	.25	.25
758	A184	100d multicolored	.40	.25
		Nos. 756-758 (3)	.90	.75

Yugoslav Communist League, 8th congress.

Table Tennis Player — A185

1965, Apr. 15   Litho.   Perf. 12½

759	A185	50d shown	4.00	4.00
760	A185	150d Player at left	4.00	4.00

28th Table Tennis Championships, Ljubljana, Apr. 15-25. Exist imperf.

Titograd — A186

1965, May 8   Engr.

761	A186	25d shown	.25	.25
762	A186	30d Skopje	.25	.25
763	A186	40d Sarajevo	.25	.25
764	A186	50d Ljubljana	.50	.50
765	A186	150d Zagreb	.50	.50
766	A186	200d Belgrade	.65	.65
		Nos. 761-766 (6)	2.40	2.40

Liberation of Yugoslavia from the Nazis, 20th anniv. Exist imperf.

Young Pioneer — A187

1965, May 10   Litho. & Engr.

767	A187	25d blk & tan, *buff*	.25	.25

Young Pioneer Games "20 Years of Freedom." Exists imperf.

ITU Emblem and Television Tower — A188

1965, May 17   Engr.

768	A188	50d dark blue	.50	.40

ITU, centenary.

Iron Gate, Danube — A189

Arms of Yugoslavia and Romania and Djerdap Dam — A190

50d, Iron Gate hydroelectric plant and dam.

1965, May 20   Litho.   Perf. 12½x12

769	A189	25d (30b) lt gray bl & dp bl grn	.25	.25
770	A189	50d (55b) lt gray bl & car lake	.40	.25

Miniature Sheet

Perf. 13½x13

771	A190	Sheet of 4	4.25	4.25
a.		100d multicolored	.35	.35
b.		150d multicolored	.70	.70

Nos. 769-771 were issued simultaneously by Yugoslavia and Romania to commemorate the start of the construction of the Iron Gate hydroelectric plant. Nos. 769-770 were valid for postage in both countries.

No. 771 contains one each of Nos. 771a, 771b and Romania Nos. 1747a and 1747b. Only Nos. 771a and 771b were valid in Yugoslavia. Sold for 500d.

See Romania Nos. 1745-1747.

Flower Type of 1957

Medicinal Plants: 25d, Milfoil. 30d, Rosemary. 40d, Inula. 50d, Belladonna. 150d, Mint. 200d, Foxglove.

1965, May 25   Photo.   Perf. 11½

Granite Paper

Flowers in Natural Colors

772	A123	25d deep carmine	.30	.30
773	A123	30d olive bister	.30	.30
774	A123	40d red brown	.30	.30
775	A123	50d dark blue	.30	.30
776	A123	150d violet blue	.35	.35
777	A123	200d purple	2.00	2.00
		Nos. 772-777 (6)	3.55	3.55

Intl. Cooperation Year Emblem A191

1965, June 26   Litho.   Perf. 12½

778	A191	50d dk bl & dull bl	.25	.25

Sibenik — A192

1965, July 6   Unwmk.   Perf. 12½

779	A192	25d Rogaska Slatina	.40	.40
780	A192	30d shown	.40	.40
781	A192	40d Prespa Lake	.40	.40
782	A192	50d Prizren	.40	.40
783	A192	150d Scutari	1.20	1.20
784	A192	200d Sarajevo	2.00	2.00
		Nos. 779-784 (6)	4.80	4.80

Cat — A193

1965, Oct. 3   Litho.   Perf. 12½
785 A193 30d maroon & brt yel   .45 .25

Issued for Children's Week. Exists imperf.

Nos. 630 and 634 Surcharged in Maroon and Type of 1958

Designs: 20d, Jablanica hydroelectric works. 30d, Litostroy turbine factory.

1965   Engr.   Perf. 12½
786 A133 5d on 8d gray   1.00 .50
787 A133 20d emerald   .50 .25
788 A133 30d red orange   .80 .25
789 A133 50d on 25d vermilion   1.00 .50
        Nos. 786-789 (4)   3.30 1.50

Branislav
Nusic — A194

Famous Yugoslavs: 50d, Antun Gustav Matos, poet. 60d, Ivan Mazuranic, writer. 85d, Fran Levstik, writer. 200d, Josif Pancic, physician and botanist. 500d, Dimitrije Tucovic, political writer.

1965, Nov. 28   Engr.
Variously Toned Paper
790 A194 30d dull red   .25 .25
791 A194 50d indigo   .25 .25
792 A194 60d brown   .25 .25
793 A194 85d dark blue   .25 .25
794 A194 200d dk olive grn   .25 .25
795 A194 500d deep claret   .60 .45
        Nos. 790-795 (6)   1.85 1.70

Marshal Tito — A195

1966, Feb. 4   Litho.   Perf. 12½
796 A195 20p bluish grn   .40 .25
797 A195 30p rose pink   .55 .25

Exists imperf.

Rowing
A196

1966, Mar. 1   Engr.
798 A196 30p dk car rose   .25 .25
799 A196 50p dk purple   .25 .25
800 A196 1d gray green   .25 .25
801 A196 3d dk red brn   1.75 1.75
802 A196 5d dark blue   1.75 1.75
        Nos. 798-802 (5)   4.25 4.25

25th Balkan Games; World ice hockey championship; 2nd rowing championships.

"T" from 15th
Century
Psalter — A197

Art through the Centuries (Initials from Medieval Manuscripts): 50p, Cyrillic "V," Divosh Evangel, 14th cent. 60p, "R," Gregorius I, Libri moralium, 12th cent. 85p, Cyrillic "P," Miroslav Evangel, 12th cent. 2d, Cyrillic "B," Radomir Evangel, 13th cent. 5d, "F," Passional, 11th cent.

1966, Apr. 25   Photo.   Perf. 12
803 A197 30p multicolored   .25 .25
804 A197 50p multicolored   .25 .25
805 A197 60p multicolored   .25 .25
806 A197 85p multicolored   .25 .25
807 A197 2d multicolored   .25 .25
808 A197 5d multicolored   .80 .40
        Nos. 803-808 (6)   2.05 1.65

Radio Amateurs'
Emblem — A198

1966, May 23   Engr.   Perf. 12½x12
809 A198 85p dark blue   2.50 1.20

Union of Yugoslav Radio Amateurs, 20th anniv.; Intl. Congress of Radio Amateurs, Opatija, 5/23-28.

Stag Beetle — A199

Beetles: 50p, Floral beetle. 60p, Oil beetle. 85p, Ladybird. 2d, Rosalia alpina. 5d, Aquatic beetle.

1966, May 25   Photo.   Perf. 12x12½
810 A199 30p gray, blk & bis   .30 .25
811 A199 50p gray, emer & blk   .30 .25
812 A199 60p bluish blk, sl grn & gray   .30 .25
813 A199 85p dl org, dp org & black   .30 .25
814 A199 2d gray, ultra & blk   .30 .25
815 A199 5d tan, brn & blk   .55 .25
        Nos. 810-815 (6)   2.05 1.50

Serbia No. 2,
1866 — A200

Litho. & Engr.
1966, June 25   Perf. 12½
816 A200 30p shown   .25 .25
817 A200 50p No. 3   .25 .25
818 A200 60p No. 4   .25 .25
819 A200 85p No. 5   .25 .25
820 A200 2d No. 6   .45 .35
        Nos. 816-820 (5)   1.45 1.35

Souvenir Sheet
Imperf
821 A200 10d No. 1   2.00 2.00

Serbia's first postage stamps, cent.

Leather Shield
with Farmer,
Soldier and
Woman — A201

1966, July 2   Perf. 12½
822 A201 20p pale grn, gold & red brown   .25 .25
823 A201 30p buff, gold & dp mag   .25 .25
824 A201 85p lt gray, gold & Prus bl   .25 .25
825 A201 2d lt bl, gold & vio   .25 .25
        Nos. 822-825 (4)   1.00 1.00

25th anniversary of National Revolution.

Bishop
Strossmayer and
Franjo
Racki — A202

1966, July 15
826 A202 30p dl ol, blk & buff   .25 .25

Centenary of Academy of Arts and Sciences, founded by Bishop Josip Juraj Strossmayer with Racki as first president.

Mostar Bridge,
Neretva
River — A203

1966, Sept. 24   Engr.   Perf. 12½
827 A203 30p rose claret   4.00 1.60

400th anniversary of Mostar Bridge.

Medieval
View of
Sibenik
A204

1966, Sept. 24
828 A204 30p deep plum   .25 .25

900th anniversary of Sibenik.

Girl — A205

1966, Oct. 2   Litho.
829 A205 30p ultra, org, red & blk   1.50 1.50

Issued for Children's Week.

Shipbuilding — A206

Designs: 10p, Sisak steel works. 15p, Overpass. 20p, Jablonica hydroelectric works. 30p, Litostroy turbine factory. 40p, Lukavac coke factory. 50p, Zenica steel works. 60p, Cable factory, Svetozarevo. 65p, Sevojno copper works. 85p, Lumber industry. 1d, Crude oil production.

1966   Engr.   Perf. 12½
830 A206 5p dull orange   1.00 1.00
831 A206 10p brown   1.00 1.00
832 A206 15p vio blue   1.00 1.00
833 A206 20p emerald   .25 .25
834 A206 30p vermilion   .75 .25
835 A206 40p dp claret   1.00 1.00
836 A206 50p gray blue   1.00 1.00
837 A206 60p red brown   1.00 1.00
838 A206 65p green   1.00 1.00
839 A206 85p dl purple   1.00 1.00
840 A206 1d yel olive   2.00 2.00
        Nos. 830-840 (11)   11.00 10.50

Issued: 5, 15p, 6/10; 10, 40, 50p, 6/8; 20, 30p, 4/28; 60, 65, 85p, 5/12; 1d, 6/18.
Nos. 830, 832 and 840 exist imperf.
For surcharge see No. 1322.

UNESCO
Emblem — A207

1966, Nov. 4   Litho.
841 A207 85p violet blue   .25 .25

20th anniversary of UNESCO.

Santa Claus — A208

Designs: 15p, Stylized winter landscape. 30p, Stylized Christmas tree.

1966, Nov. 25   Litho.   Perf. 12½
842 A208 15p org & dk bl   .25 .25
843 A208 20p org & purple   .25 .25
844 A208 30p org & sl grn   .25 .25

1966, Dec. 23   Photo.   Perf. 12½
845 A208 15p gold & dk bl   .30 .25
846 A208 20p gold & red   .30 .25
847 A208 30p gold & green   .30 .25
        Nos. 842-847 (6)   1.65 1.50

Nos. 842-847 issued for New Year, 1967.

Wolf's Head
Coin of Durad
I, 1373 — A209

Medieval Coins: 50p, ½d of King Stefan, c. 1461 (arms of Bosnia). 60d, Dinar of Serbia (portrait of Durad Brankovic). 85p, Dinar of Ljubljana, c. 1250 (heraldic eagle). 2d, Dinar of Split, c. 1403-1413 (shield with arms of Duke Hrvoje Vukcic). 5d, Dinar of Emperor Stefan Dusan, c. 1346-1355 (Emperor on horseback).

1966, Nov. 28   Photo.
Coins in Silver, Gray and Black
848 A209 30p ver & blk   .25 .25
849 A209 50p ultra & blk   .25 .25
850 A209 60p magenta & blk   .25 .25
851 A209 85p violet & blk   .25 .25
852 A209 2d dk ol bis & blk   .25 .25
853 A209 5d brt grn & blk   .55 .35
        Nos. 848-853 (6)   1.80 1.60

Medicinal
Plants — A210

1967, May 25   Photo.   Perf. 11½
Granite Paper

854	A210	30p Arnica	.25	.25
855	A210	50p Flax	.25	.25
856	A210	85p Oleander	.25	.25
857	A210	1.20d Gentian	.25	.25
858	A210	3d Laurel	.25	.25
859	A210	5d African rue	.80	.80
		Nos. 854-859 (6)	2.05	2.05

Youth Day, May 25.

Marshal Tito — A211

Size: 20x27½mm

1967, May 25   Engr.   Perf. 12½

860	A211	5p orange	.25	.25
861	A211	10p dk red brown	.25	.25
862	A211	15p dk vio blue	.25	.25
863	A211	20p green	.25	.25
864	A211	30p vermilion	.25	.25
865	A211	40p black	.25	.25
866	A211	50p Prussian grn	.25	.25
867	A211	60p lilac	.25	.25
868	A211	85p deep blue	.25	.25
869	A211	1d plum	.25	.25
		Nos. 860-869 (10)	2.50	2.50

75th birthday of Pres. Tito. Sheets of 15.
Nos. 860-869 were reissued in 1967 with slight differences including thinner paper and slightly darker shades.
See #924-939. For surcharge see #1414.

Coil Stamps

1968-69   Photo.   Perf. 12½ Horiz.

869A	A211	20p green	.30	.25
869B	A211	30p vermilion	.40	.25
869C	A211	50p vermilion ('69)	.30	.25
		Nos. 869A-869C (3)	1.00	.75

EXPO Emblem,
Sputnik 1 and
Explorer 1 — A212

Spacecraft: 50p, Tiros, Telstar and Molniya. 85p, Luna 9 and lunar satellite. 1.20d, Mariner 4, and Venera 3. 3d, Vostok, Gemini and Agena Rocket. 5d, Astronaut walking in space.

1967, June 26   Photo.   Perf. 11½

870	A212	30p ultra & multi	.25	.25
871	A212	50p yel & multi	.25	.25
872	A212	85p slate & multi	.25	.25
873	A212	1.20d multicolored	.25	.25
874	A212	3d vio & multi	.25	.25
875	A212	5d blue & multi	2.75	2.75
		Nos. 870-875 (6)	4.00	4.00

EXPO '67, Montreal, Apr. 28-Oct. 27; 18th Congress of the Intl. Astronautical Federation, Belgrade. Exist imperf.

ITY Emblem, St.
Tripun's Church,
Kotor — A213

Designs (ITY Emblem and): 50p, Municipal Building, Maribor. 85p, Cathedral, Trogir. 1.20d, Fortress gate, Nis. 3d, Drina Bridge, Visegrad. 5d, Daut-pasha's Bath, Skopje.

1967, July 17   Engr.

876	A213	30p slate bl & lt ol	.25	.25
877	A213	50p brn & dl vio	.25	.25
878	A213	85p dk bl & dp claret	.25	.25
879	A213	1.20d dp claret & brn	.25	.25
880	A213	3d brn & slate grn	.35	.25
881	A213	5d slate grn & brn	3.00	.45
		Nos. 876-881 (6)	4.35	1.70

Issued for International Tourist Year, 1967.

Partridge — A214

1967, Sept. 22   Photo.   Perf. 14

882	A214	30p shown	.30	.30
883	A214	50p Pike	.30	.30
884	A214	1.20d Red deer	.50	.50
885	A214	5d Peregrine falcon	1.25	1.25
		Nos. 882-885 (4)	2.35	2.35

Intl. Fishing and Hunting Exposition and Fair, Novi Sad.

Congress
Emblem with
Sputnik 1
A215

Litho. & Engr.

1967, Sept. 25   Perf. 12½
886 A215 85p dk bl, lt bl & gold   .25 .25

18th Congress of the Intl. Astronautical Federation, Belgrade, Sept. 25-30.

Old Theater and
Castle,
Ljubljana — A216

1967, Sept. 29   Engr.   Perf. 12½
887 A216 30p sepia & dk grn   .25 .25

Centenary of Slovene National Theater.

Child's Drawing:
Winter
Scene — A217

1967, Oct. 2   Litho.
888 A217 30p multicolored   .50 .25

International Children's Week, Oct. 2-8.

Lenin by
Mestrovic
A218

1967, Nov. 7   Engr.   Perf. 12½

889	A218	30p dark purple	.25	.25
890	A218	85p olive gray	.25	.25

Souvenir Sheet
Imperf
891 A218 10d magenta   8.00 8.00

Russian October Revolution, 50th anniv.
Nos. 889-890 exist imperf.

4-Leaf Clover — A219

30p, Chimney sweep. 50p, Horseshoe & flower.

Dated "1968"

1967, Nov. 15   Photo.   Perf. 14

892	A219	20p shown	.25	.25
893	A219	30p Chimney sweep	.25	.25
894	A219	50p Horseshoe, flower	.25	.25
		Nos. 892-894 (3)	.75	.75

New Year 1968. See Nos. 957-959.

The Young Sultana, by Vlaho
Bucovac — A220

Paintings: 85p, The Watchtower, by Dura Jaksic. 2d, Visit to the Family, by Josip Petkovsek. 3d, The Cock Fight, by Paja Jovanovic. 5d, "Spring" (woman and children), by Ivana Kobilca.

Perf. 11½x12, 12x11½
1967, Nov. 28   Engr. & Litho.

895	A220	85p multi, vert.	1.00	.30
896	A220	1d multi	1.00	.30
897	A220	2d multi	1.00	.30
898	A220	3d multi	1.00	.30
899	A220	5d multi, vert.	5.00	2.50
		Nos. 895-899 (5)	9.00	3.70

Issued for the Day of the Republic, Nov. 29.
See Nos. 942-946, 995-1000.

Ski Jump — A221

Sport: 1d, Figure skating pair. 2d, Downhill skiing. 5d, Ice hockey.

1968, Feb. 5   Engr.   Perf. 12½

900	A221	50p dk bl & dk pur	.40	.25
901	A221	1d brn & sl green	.40	.25
902	A221	2d sl grn & lake	.70	.40
903	A221	5d sl grn & dk bl	5.50	3.00
		Nos. 900-903 (4)	7.00	3.90

10th Winter Olympic Games, Grenoble, France, Feb. 6-18.

Annunciation
A222

Medieval Icons: 50p, Madonna, St. George's Church, Prizren. 1.50d, St. Sava and St. Simeon. 2d, Christ's descent into hell, Ohrid. 3d, Crucifixion, St. Clement's Church, Ohrid. 5d, Madonna, Church of Our Lady of the Bell Tower, Split.

1968, Apr. 20   Photo.   Perf. 13½

906	A222	50p gold & multi	.25	.25
907	A222	1d gold & multi	.25	.25
908	A222	1.50d gold & multi	.25	.25
909	A222	2d gold & multi	.35	.25
910	A222	3d gold & multi	.50	.40
911	A222	5d gold & multi	1.10	1.00
		Nos. 906-911 (6)	2.70	2.40

European
Bullfinch — A223

Finches: 1d, Goldfinch. 1.50d, Chaffinch. 2d, European greenfinch. 3d, Red crossbill. 5d, Hawfinch.

Birds in Natural Colors

1968, May 25   Photo.   Perf. 11½

912	A223	50p bister	.40	.40
913	A223	1d rose lake	.40	.40
914	A223	1.50d gray blue	.40	.40
915	A223	2d deep orange	.40	.40
916	A223	3d olive green	.45	.45
917	A223	5d pale violet	6.50	3.25
		Nos. 912-917 (6)	8.55	5.30

Issued for Youth Day. Exist imperf.

800-meter Race
for
Women — A224

1d, Basketball. 1.50d, Gymnast on vaulting horse. 2d, Rowing. 3d, Water polo. 5d, Wrestling.

Litho. & Engr.

1968, June 28   Perf. 12½

918	A224	50p dk brn & dk red brown	.40	.40
919	A224	1d Prus bl & blk	.40	.40
920	A224	1.50d slate & dk brn	.40	.40
921	A224	2d bis & sl grn	1.50	.40
922	A224	3d blk brn & ind	1.50	.40
923	A224	5d dk grn & vio blk	16.00	5.00
		Nos. 918-923 (6)	20.20	7.00

19th Olympic Games, Mexico City, 10/12-27.

Tito Type of 1967

1968-72   Engr.   Perf. 12½
Size: 20x27½mm

924	A211	20p dark blue	1.25	.25
925	A211	25p lake	.25	.25
926	A211	30p green	.25	.25
927	A211	50p vermilion	.75	.25
928	A211	70p black	.30	.25
929	A211	75p slate grn	.40	.25
930	A211	80p olive	2.00	.25
930A	A211	80p red org ('72)	.40	.25
931	A211	90p olive	.30	.25
932	A211	1.20d dark blue	.50	.25
932A	A211	1.20d sl grn ('72)	.25	.25
933	A211	1.25d deep blue	.25	.25
934	A211	1.50d slate grn	.40	.25

Size: 20x30½mm

935	A211	2d sepia	2.50	.25
936	A211	2.50d Prussian grn	1.60	.25
937	A211	5d deep plum	1.40	.25

938	A211	10d violet blk	3.00	.35
939	A211	20d bluish black	4.25	.45
		Nos. 924-939 (18)	20.20	4.80

The shading of the background of Nos. 924-939 has been changed from the 1967 issue to intensify the contrast around the portrait.

Cannon and Laurel Wreath — A225

1968, Aug. 2   Photo.   Perf. 12½
940 A225 50p org brn & gold   .25 .25

65th anniversary of the Ilinden uprising.

Mother Nursing Twins, Fresco by Jan of Kastav — A226

1968, Sept. 9   Litho.
941 A226 50p black & multi   .25 .25

Annexation of Istria and the Slovene Coast to Yugoslavia, 25th anniv. Exists imperf.

Painting Type of 1967

Paintings: 1d, Lake Klansko, by Marko Pernhart. 1.50d, Bavarian Landscape, by Milan Popovic. 2d, Porta Terraferma, Zadar, by Ferdo Quiquerez. 3d, Mt. Triglav seen from Bohinj, by Anton Karinger. 6d, Studenica Monastery, by Djordje Krstic.

Engr. & Litho.

1968, Oct. 3   Perf. 14x13½
942 A220 1d gold & multi   .25 .25
943 A220 1.50d gold & multi   .25 .25
944 A220 2d gold & multi   .25 .25
945 A220 3d gold & multi   .30 .25
946 A220 5d gold & multi   2.40 .70
| | | *Nos. 942-946 (5)* | 3.45 | 1.70 |

Exist imperf.

Aleksa Santic (1868-1924), Poet — A227

1968, Oct. 5   Engr.   Perf. 12½
947 A227 50p dark blue   .25 .25

"Going for a Walk" — A228

1968, Oct. 6   Litho.
948 A228 50p multicolored   .25 .25

Issued for Children's Week.

Karl Marx (1818-1883), by N. Mitric — A229

1968, Oct. 11   Engr.
949 A229 50d dk car rose   .25 .25

Old Theater and Belgrade Castle — A230

1968, Nov. 22   Engr.   Perf. 12½
950 A230 50p ol brn & sl grn   .25 .25

Serbian National Theater, Belgrade, cent.

Hasan Brkic — A231

Portraits: 75p, Ivan Milutinovic. 1.25d, Rade Koncar. 2d, Kuzman Josifovski. 2.50d, Tone Tomsic. 5d, Mosa Pijade.

1968, Nov. 28   Engr.   Perf. 12½
951 A231 50p violet black   .25 .25
952 A231 75p black   .25 .25
953 A231 1.25d red brown   .25 .25
  a. Souv. sheet, 2 ea #951-953   15.00 15.00
954 A231 2d bluish black   .25 .25
955 A231 2.50d slate green   .25 .25
956 A231 5d claret   .25 .50
  a. Souv. sheet, 2 ea #954-956   15.00 15.00
| | | *Nos. 951-956 (6)* | 2.50 | 1.75 |

2nd Assembly of the National Republic of Yugoslavia, 25th anniv.
No. 954 exists imperf. Value $100.
Nos. 953a and 956a exist imperf.

New Year's Type of 1967

1968, Nov. 25   Photo.   Perf. 14
Dated "1969"
957 A219 20p Four-leaf clover   .25 .25
958 A219 30p Chimney sweep   .25 .25
959 A219 50p Horseshoe, flower   .25 .25
| | | *Nos. 957-959 (3)* | .75 | .75 |

Issued for New Year 1969.

The Family, by J. Soldatovic A232

1968, Dec. 10   Engr.   Perf. 12½
960 A232 1.25d dark blue   .25 .25

International Human Rights Year.

ILO Emblem — A233

Litho. & Engr.

1969, Jan. 27   Perf. 12½
961 A233 1.25d red & black   .25 .25

ILO, 50th anniv.

Dove, Hammer and Sickle Emblem — A234

75p, Graffiti "TITO" & 5-pointed star. 1.25d, 5-pointed crystal. 10d, Marshal Tito in 1943.

Engr. & Photo.

1969, Mar. 11   Perf. 12½
962 A234 50p black & red   .25 .25
963 A234 75p ol bis & blk   .25 .25
964 A234 1.25d red & black   .25 .25
| | | *Nos. 962-964 (3)* | .75 | .75 |

Souvenir Sheet

964A   Sheet of 9   9.00 9.00
  b. A234 10d brown, engr.   5.00 5.00

Communist Federation of Yugoslavia, 50th anniv.; 9th party congress.
No. 964A contains 4 No. 962, 2 each Nos. 963-964, 964b.
Nos. 962-964A exist imperf.

St. Nikita, from Manasija Monastery A235

Frescoes from Monasteries: 75p, Apostles, Zakopani. 1.25d, Crucifixion, Studenica. 2d, Wedding at Cana, Kalenic. 3d, Angel at the Grave, Milseva. 5d, Pietá, Nerezi.

1969, Apr. 7   Photo.   Perf. 13½
965 A235 50p gold & multi   .25 .25
966 A235 75p gold & multi   .25 .25
967 A235 1.25d gold & multi   .25 .25
968 A235 2d gold & multi   .25 .25
969 A235 3d gold & multi   .45 .45
970 A235 5d gold & multi   2.00 .90
| | | *Nos. 965-970 (6)* | 3.45 | 2.35 |

Roman Memorial and View of Ptuj A236

1969, Apr. 23   Engr.   Perf. 11½
971 A236 50p violet brown   .25 .25

1900th anniv. of Ptuj, the Roman Petovio. Issued in sheets of 9 (3x3).

Vasil Glavinov — A237

1969, May 8   Perf. 12x12½
972 A237 50p ocher & rose lilac   .25 .25

Vasil Glavinov, Macedonian socialist, birth cent. Issued in sheets of 9 (3x3).

Thin-leafed Peony — A238

Medicinal Plants: 75p, Coltsfoot. 1.25d, Primrose. 2d, Hellebore. 2.50d, Violets. 5d, Anemones.

Flowers in Natural Colors

1969, May 25   Photo.   Perf. 11½
973 A238 50p yellow brn   .25 .25
974 A238 75p dull purple   .25 .25
975 A238 1.25d blue   .25 .25
976 A238 2d brown   .25 .25
977 A238 2.50d plum   .25 .25
978 A238 5d green   2.75 2.75
| | | *Nos. 973-978 (6)* | 4.00 | 4.00 |

Exist imperf.
See Nos. 1056-1061, 1140-1145.

Eber, by Vasa Ivankovic — A239

Paintings of Sailing Ships: 1.25d, Tare, by Franasovic. 1.50d, Brig Sela, by Vasa Ivankovic. 2.50d, Dubrovnik galleon, 16th century. 3.25d, Madre Mimbelli, by Antoine Roux. 5d, The Virgin Saving Seamen from Disaster, 16th century ikon.

1969, July 10   Photo.   Perf. 11½
979 A239 50p gold & multi   .25 .25
980 A239 1.25d gold & multi   .25 .25
981 A239 1.50d gold & multi   .25 .25
982 A239 2.50d gold & multi   .25 .25
983 A239 3.25d gold & multi   .55 .35
984 A239 5d gold & multi   2.75 2.25
| | | *Nos. 979-984 (6)* | 4.30 | 3.55 |

Dubrovnik Summer Festival, 20th anniv. Exist imperf.

11th World Games for the Deaf, Belgrade, Aug. 9-16 — A240

1969, Aug. 9   Engr.   Perf. 12½
985 A240 1.25d dp claret & dl vio   .40 .25

Lipice Horse A241

Horses: 75p, Bosnian mountain horse. 3.25d, Ljutomer trotter. 5d, Half-breed.

1969, Sept. 26   Photo.   Perf. 11½
986 A241 75p multicolored   .25 .25
987 A241 1.25d olive & multi   .25 .25
988 A241 3.25d brn & multi   .30 .25
989 A241 5d multicolored   3.00 1.50
| | | *Nos. 986-989 (4)* | 3.80 | 2.25 |

Zagreb Veterinary College, 50th anniv. Exist imperf.

Children and Birds, by Tanja Vucanik, 13 years A242

1969, Oct. 5   **Litho.**   *Perf. 12½*
990 A242 50p org, blk & gray   .25 .25
Issued for Children's Week.

Arms of Belgrade — A243

Arms: #992, Skopje (bridge & mountain). #993, Titograd (bridge & fortifications).

1969   **Litho.**   *Perf. 12½*
991 A243 50p gold & multi   .25 .25
992 A243 50p gold & multi   .25 .25
993 A243 50p gold & multi   .25 .25
   Nos. 991-993 (3)   .75 .75
Liberation of capitals of the Federated Republics, 25th anniv. See Nos. 1017-1020.

Josip Smodlaka A244

1969, Nov. 9   **Engr.**
994 A244 50p dark blue   .25 .25
Smodlaka (1869-1956), leader in Yugoslavia's fight for independence.

Painting Type of 1967
Paintings of Nudes: 50p, The Little Gypsy with the Rose, by Nikola Martinoski. 1.25d, Girl on a Red Chair, by Sava Sumanovic. 1.50d, Woman Combing her Hair, by Marin Tartaglia. 2.50d, Olympia, by Miroslav Kraljevic. 3.25d, The Bather, by Jovan Bijelic. 5d, Woman on a Couch, by Matej Sternen.

Photo. & Engr.
1969, Nov. 29   *Perf. 13½*
995 A220 50p multi, vert.   .25 .25
996 A220 1.25d multi, vert.   .25 .25
997 A220 1.50d multi, vert.   .25 .25
998 A220 2.50d multi   .35 .30
999 A220 3.25d multi, vert.   .50 .40
1000 A220 5d multi   3.00 2.75
   Nos. 995-1000 (6)   4.60 4.20
Exist imperf.

University of Ljubljana, 50th Anniv. A245

1969, Dec. 9   **Engr.**   *Perf. 11½*
1001 A245 50p slate grn   .25 .25

Seal of Zagreb University A246

Photo. & Engr.
1969, Dec. 17   *Perf. 12½*
1002 A246 50p gold, bl & brn   .25 .25
University of Zagreb, 300th anniv.

Common Design Types pictured following the introduction.

Europa Issue, 1969
Common Design Type
1969, Dec. 20   **Photo.**   *Perf. 11½*
1003 CD12 1.25d grnsh gray, buff & brn   1.25 1.25
1004 CD12 3.25d rose lil, gray & dk bl   2.75 2.75
Yugoslavia's admission to CEPT. Exist imperf.

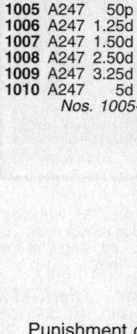

Jovan Cvijic, Geographer A247

Famous Yugoslavs: 1.25d, Dr. Andrija Stampar, hygienist. 1.50d, Joakim Krcovski, author. 2.50d, Marko Miljanov, Montenegrin patriot-hero. 3.25d, Vaca Pelagic, socialist. 5d, Oton Zupancic, Slovenian poet.

1970, Feb. 16   **Engr.**   *Perf. 12½*
1005 A247 50p reddish brn   .25 .25
1006 A247 1.25d brnsh black   .25 .25
1007 A247 1.50d lilac   .25 .25
1008 A247 2.50d slate grn   .25 .25
1009 A247 3.25d reddish brn   .25 .25
1010 A247 5d blue vio   .25 .25
   Nos. 1005-1010 (6)   1.50 1.50

Punishment of Dirce, Pulj — A248

Mosaics from the 1st-4th Centuries: 1.25d, Cerberus, Bitola, horiz. 1.50d, Angel of the Annunciation, Porec. 2.50d, Hunters, Gamzigard. 3.25d, Bull and cherry tree, horiz. 5d, Virgin and Child enthroned, Porec.

1970, Mar. 16   **Photo.**   *Perf. 13½*
1011 A248 50p gold & multi   .25 .25
1012 A248 1.25d gold & multi   .25 .25
1013 A248 1.50d gold & multi   .25 .25
1014 A248 2.50d gold & multi   .30 .25
1015 A248 3.25d gold & multi   .55 .35
1016 A248 5d gold & multi   1.50 1.50
   Nos. 1011-1016 (6)   3.10 2.85
Exist imperf.

Arms Type of 1969
#1017, Sarajevo (arcade). #1018, Zagreb (castle). #1019, Ljubljana (dragon and tower). #1020a, Yugoslavia (embossed coat of arms.)

1970   **Litho.**   *Perf. 12½*
1017 A243 50p gold & multi   .25 .25
1018 A243 50p gold & multi   .25 .25
1019 A243 50p gold & multi   .25 .25
   Nos. 1017-1019 (3)   .75 .75

Souvenir Sheet
1020   Sheet of 7   15.00 15.00
   a.   A243 12d gold & black   12.50 12.50
Liberation of Yugoslavia, 25th anniv. No. 1020 contains Nos. 991-993, 1017-1019, 1020a + 2 labels.
Issued: #1017, Apr. 6; #1018, May 8; #1019, May 9; #1020, May 15.

Lenin (1870-1924), by S. Stojanovic A249

Design: 1.25d, Lenin sculpture facing left.

1970, Apr. 22   **Engr.**
1021 A249 50p rose lilac   .25 .25
1022 A249 1.25d blue gray   .25 .25

Basketball A250

1970, Apr. 25
1023 A250 1.25d plum   .25 .25
6th World Basketball Championships, Ljubljana, May 10-23. Exists imperf.

Europa Issue, 1970
Common Design Type
1970, May 4   **Photo.**   *Perf. 11½*
   Size: 32½x23mm
1024 CD13 1.25d lt bl, dk bl & lt grnsh bl   .40 .40
1025 CD13 3.25d rose lil, plum & gray   .40 .40
Exist imperf.

Istrian Shorthaired Hound A251

Yugoslav Breeds of Dogs: 1.25d, Yugoslav tricolor hound. 1.50d, Istrian hard-haired hound. 2.50d, Balkan hound. 3.25d, Dalmatian. 5d, Shara mountain dog.

1970, May 25   **Photo.**   *Perf. 11½*
   Granite Paper
1026 A251 50p tan & multi   .25 .25
1027 A251 1.25d olive & multi   .25 .25
1028 A251 1.50d violet & multi   .25 .25
1029 A251 2.50d slate & multi   .25 .25
1030 A251 3.25d multi   .45 .25
1031 A251 5d multi   2.00 2.00
   Nos. 1026-1031 (6)   3.45 3.25
Exist imperf.

Telegraph Circuit — A252

1970, June 20   **Litho.**   *Perf. 12½*
1032 A252 50p henna brn, gold & blk   .25 .25
Telegraph service in Montenegro, cent.

Bird — A253

1970, Oct. 5
1033 A253 50p multicolored   .25 .25
Issued for Children's Week, Oct. 5-11.

Stylized Gymnast — A254

1970, Oct. 22   **Engr.**
1034 A254 1.25d car & slate   .25 .25
17th World Gymnastics Championships, Ljubljana, Oct. 22-27.

UN Emblem and Hand Holding Dove, by Makoto A255

Litho. & Engr.
1970, Oct. 24   *Perf. 11½*
1035 A255 1.25d dk brn, blk & gold   .25 .25
25th anniversary of the United Nations.

Ascension, by Teodor D. Kracum A256

Baroque Paintings: 75p, Abraham's Sacrifice, by Federiko Benkovic. 1.25d, Holy Family, by Francisek Jelovsek. 2.50d, Jacob's Ladder, by Hristofor Zefarovic. 3.25d, Baptism of Christ, by unknown Serbian painter. 5.75d, The Coronation of Mary, by Tripo Kokolja.

Engr. & Photo.
1970, Nov. 28   *Perf. 13½x14*
1036 A256 50p gold & multi   .25 .25
1037 A256 75p gold & multi   .25 .25
1038 A256 1.25d gold & multi   .25 .25
1039 A256 2.50d gold & multi   .25 .25
1040 A256 3.25d gold & multi   .45 .25
1041 A256 5.75d gold & multi   .75 .70
   Nos. 1036-1041 (6)   2.20 1.95
Exist imperf.

Alpine Rhododendron — A257

European Nature Protection Year emblem and: 3.25d, Bearded vulture.

1970, Dec. 14   Photo.   Perf. 11½
1042 A257 1.25d multi   3.00   3.00
1043 A257 3.25d multi   10.00 10.00
Sheets of 9.

Frano Supilo — A258

Litho. & Engr.
1971, Jan. 25   Perf. 12½
1044 A258 50p black & buff   .25   .25
Supilo (1870-1917), Croat leader for independence from Austria-Hungary. Sheets of 9.

British, French, Canadian, Italian Satellites A259

75p, Satellite. 1.25d, Automated moon exploration. 2.50d, Various spacecraft. 3.25d, 1st experimental space station. 5.75d, Astronauts on moon.

1971, Feb. 8   Photo.   Perf. 13½
1045 A259 50p multi   .25   .25
1046 A259 75p multi   .25   .25
1047 A259 1.25d multi   .25   .25
1048 A259 2.50d multi, horiz.   .25   .25
1049 A259 3.25d multi, horiz.   .25   .25
1050 A259 5.75d multi, horiz.   1.10 1.10
     Nos. 1045-1050 (6)   2.35 2.35
"Space in the service of science." Sheets of 9.

Proclamation of the Commune, Town Hall, Paris — A260

Litho. & Engr.
1971, Mar. 18   Perf. 11½
1051 A260 1.25d bis brn & gray brn   .25 .25
Centenary of the Paris Commune. Exist imperf.

Europa Issue, 1971
Common Design Type
1971, May 4   Photo.   Perf. 11½
Size: 33x23mm
1052 CD14 1.50d Prus bl, pale
                   grn & dk bl   .25   .25
1053 CD14 4d mag, pink & dk
                   mag   .25   .25
Exist imperf.

Circles — A261

1971, May 5   Perf. 13½
1054 A261 50p shown   .50   .25
1055 A261 1.25d 20 circles   1.40   .70
2nd Congress of Managers of Autonomous States.

Flower Type of 1969
Medicinal Plants: 50p, Common mallow. 1.50d, Common buckthorn. 2d, Water lily. 2.50d, Poppy. 4d, Wild chicory. 6d, Physalis.

1971, May 25   Photo.   Perf. 11½
Flowers in Natural Colors
1056 A238 50p lt ultra   .25   .25
1057 A238 1.50d olive bis   .25   .25
1058 A238 2d dull blue   .25   .25
1059 A238 2.50d dark car   .30   .25
1060 A238 4d dp bister   .65   .65
1061 A238 6d org brown   4.00 4.00
     Nos. 1056-1061 (6)   5.70 5.65
Exist imperf.

Prince Lazar, Fresco, Lazarica Church — A262

1971, June 28   Photo.   Perf. 13½
1062 A262 50p gray & multi   .25   .25
600th anniversary of founding of Krusevac by Prince Lazar Hrebeljanovic (1329-1389).

View of Krk — A263

Views: 5p, Krusevo. 10p, Castle & mosque, Gradacac. 20p, Church & bridge, Bohinj. 35p, Shore & mountains, Omis. 40p, Peje. 50p, Memorial column, Krusevac. 60p, Logar Valley. 75p, Bridge & church, Bohinj. 80p, Church, Piran. 1d, Street, Bitolj. 1.20d, Minaret, Pocitelj. 1.25d, 1.50d, Gate tower, Hercegnovi. 2d, Cathedral & City Hall Square, Novi Sad. 2.50d, Crna River.

1971-73   Engr.   Perf. 13
1063   A263 5p orange ('73)   .25   .25
1064   A263 10p brown ('72)   .25   .25
1065   A263 20p vio blk ('73)   .25   .25
1066   A263 30p ol gray ('72)   .25   .25
  a.   30p green   1.00   .25
1067   A263 35p brn car ('73)   .25   .25
1068   A263 40p black ('72)   .25   .25
1069   A263 50p vermilion   1.50   .25
1070   A263 50p green ('72)   .25   .25
1071   A263 60p purple ('72)   .25   .25
1072   A263 75p slate green   .25   .25
1073   A263 80p rose red
                         ('72)   1.50   .25
1073A A263 1d violet brn   1.50   .45
1073B A263 1.20d sl grn ('72)   2.00   .25
1073C A263 1.25d deep blue   1.10   .25
1073D A263 1.50d bluish blk
                         ('73)   .25
                                   .25   .25
1073E A263 2d blue ('72)   1.00   .25
1073F A263 2.50d dl pur ('73)   1.00   .25
     Nos. 1063-1073F (17)   12.10 4.45
Issued with and without fluorescent bars. See type A323. See Nos. 1482-1486, 1599-1600, 1602-1603, 1717. For surcharges see Nos. 1413, 1711-1712, 1765-1766, 1769.

Tourist Issue

Emperor Constantine, 4th Century — A264

Antique Bronzes excavated in Yugoslavia: 1.50d, Boy with fish. 2d, Hercules, replica after Lysippus. 2.50d, Satyr. 4d, Head of Aphrodite. 6d, Citizen of Emona, 1st century tomb.

1971, Sept. 20   Photo.   Perf. 13½
1074 A264 50p rose & multi   .25   .25
1075 A264 1.50d multicolored   .25   .25
1076 A264 2d multicolored   .25   .25
1077 A264 2.50d lem & multi   .25   .25
1078 A264 4d ocher & multi   .25   .25
1079 A264 6d multicolored   .25   .25
     Nos. 1074-1079 (6)   1.50 1.50
Sheets of 9.

UNICEF Emblem, Children in Balloon — A265

1971, Oct. 4   Litho.   Perf. 13x13½
1080 A265 50p multicolored   .25   .25
Children's Week, Oct. 3-10.

Woman in Serbian Costume, by Katarina Ivanovic A266

Portraits, 19th Century: 1.50d, The Merchant Ivanisevic, by Anastasije Bocaric. 2d, Ana Kresic, by Vjekoslav Karas. 2.50d, Pavle Jagodic, by Konstantin Danil. 4r, Luiza Pesjakova, by Mihael Stroj. 6d, Old Man and view of Ljubljana, by Matevz Langus.

Engraved and Photogravure
1971, Nov. 29   Perf. 13½x14
1081 A266 50p gold & multi   .25   .25
1082 A266 1.50d gold & multi   .25   .25
1083 A266 2d gold & multi   .25   .25
1084 A266 2.50d gold & multi   .25   .25
1085 A266 4d gold & multi   .25   .25
1086 A266 6d gold & multi   .80   .80
     Nos. 1081-1086 (6)   2.05 2.05
See Nos. 1120-1125.

Letter with Postal Code, Map of Yugoslavia — A267

1971, Dec. 15   Photo.   Perf. 13½x14
1087 A267 50p ultra & multi   .25   .25
Introduction of postal code system.

Damjan Gruev (1871-1906), Macedonian Revolutionist A268

1971, Dec. 22   Engr.   Perf. 12½
1088 A268 50p dark blue   .25   .25

11th Winter Olympic Games, Sapporo, Japan, Feb. 3-13 A269

Engr. & Typo.
1972, Feb. 3   Perf. 11½
1089 A269 1.25d Speed skating   .25   .25
1090 A269 6d Slalom   2.50 1.25
Sheets of 9.

First Page of Statute of Dubrovnik A270

Lithographed and Engraved
1972, Mar. 15   Perf. 13½
1091 A270 1.25d gold & multi   .25   .25
700th anniversary of the Statute of Dubrovnik, a legal code given by Prince Marko Justiniani.

Ski Jump Track, Planica — A271

1972, Mar. 21   Perf. 11½
1092 A271 1.25d blk, lt bl & grn   .25   .25
World Ski Jump Championships, Planica, Mar. 22-26.

Water Polo and Olympic Rings — A272

1972, Apr. 17   Litho.   Perf. 12½x12
1093 A272 50p shown   .25   .25
1094 A272 1.25d Basketball   .25   .25
1095 A272 2.50d Butterfly stroke   .25   .25
1096 A272 3.25d Boxing   .25   .25
1097 A272 5d Running   .25   .25
1098 A272 6.50d Yachting   .40   .40
     Nos. 1093-1098 (6)   1.65 1.65
20th Olympic Games, Munich, Aug. 26-Sept. 10. Sheets of 9.

Europa Issue 1972
Common Design Type
1972, May 4   Photo.   Perf. 11½
1100 CD15 1.50d bl, grn & yel   .60   .60
1101 CD15 5d brt rose, mag
                   & org   .60   .60

Wall Creeper — A275

878

Birds: 1.25d, Little bustard. 2.50d, Red-billed chough. 3.25d, Spoonbill. 5d, Eagle owl. 6.50d, Rock ptarmigan.

1972, May 8
Birds in Natural Colors
1102	A275	50p gray violet	.25	.25
1103	A275	1.25d ocher	.25	.25
1104	A275	2.50d gray olive	.25	.25
1105	A275	3.25d light plum	.35	.35
1106	A275	5d red brown	.65	.65
1107	A275	6.50d violet	2.50	2.50
Nos. 1102-1107 (6)			4.25	4.25

Nature protection.

Marshal Tito, by Bozidar Jakac — A276

1972, May 25   Litho.   Perf. 12½
1108	A276	50p cream & dk brn	.25	.25
1109	A276	1.25d gray & indigo	.50	.25

Souvenir Sheet
Imperf
1110	A276	10d gray & blk brn	2.75	2.75

80th birthday of Pres. Tito. Sheets of 9. No. 1110 printed in blocks of 4.

First Locomotive Built in Serbia, 1882 — A277

5d, Modern Yugoslavian electric locomotive.

1972, June 12   Photo.   Perf. 11½
1111	A277	1.50d multicolored	.25	.25
1112	A277	5d multicolored	.80	.30

Intl. Railroad Union, 50th anniv. Exist imperf.

Glider A278

1972, July 8   Photo.   Perf. 12½
1113	A278	2d bl gray, gold & blk	.25	.25

13th World Gliding Championships, Vrsac Airport, July 9-23. Sheets of 9. Exists imperf.

Pawn on Chessboard — A279

6d, Chessboard, emblems of King and Queen.

1972, Sept. 18   Perf. 11½
1114	A279	1.50d multi	.25	.25
1115	A279	6d multi	1.25	.70

20th Men's and 5th Women's Chess Olympiad, Skopje, Sept.-Oct. Sheets of 9.

Boy on Rocking Horse — A280

1972, Oct. 2   Litho.   Perf. 12½
1116	A280	80p org & multi	.25	.25

Children's Week, Oct. 2-8.

Goce Delchev — A281

1972, Oct. 16   Perf. 13
1117	A281	80p yel grn & blk	.25	.25

Delchev (1872-1903), Macedonian freedom fighter.

Grga Martic, by Ivan Mestrovic A282

1972, Nov. 3   Perf. 12½
1118	A282	80p red, yel grn & blk	.25	.25

Brother Grga Martic (1822-1905), Franciscan administrator, educator and poet.

Serbian National Library, Belgrade A283

1972, Nov. 25   Engr.   Perf. 11½x12
1119	A283	50p chocolate	.25	.25

140th anniversary of the Serbian National Library and opening of new building.

Painting Type of 1971
Still-Life Paintings: 50p, by Milos Tenkovic, horiz. 1.25d, by Jozef Pekovsek. 2.50d, by Katarina Jovanovic, horiz. 3.25d, by Konstantin Danil, horiz. 5d, by Nikola Masic. 6.50d, by Celestin Medovic, horiz.

Perf. 14x13½, 13½x14
1972, Nov. 28   Engr. & Photo.
1120	A266	50p gold & multi	.25	.25
1121	A266	1.25d gold & multi	.25	.25
1122	A266	2.50d gold & multi	.25	.25
1123	A266	3.25d gold & multi	.25	.25
1124	A266	5d gold & multi	.25	.25
1125	A266	6.50d gold & multi	.70	.50
Nos. 1120-1125 (6)			1.95	1.75

Exist imperf.

Battle of Stubica, by Krsto Hegedusic — A284

6d, Battle of Krsko, by Gojmir Anton Kos.

1973, Jan. 29   Photo.   Perf. 11½
1126	A284	2d gold & multi	.30	.25
1127	A284	6d gold & multi	1.25	.70

Croatian-Slovenian Rebellion, 400th anniv. (2d); Beginning of the peasant rebellions in Slovenia, 500th anniv. (6d). Sheets of 9.

Radoje Domanovic (1873-1908), Serbian Writer — A285

1973, Feb. 3   Litho.   Perf. 12½
1128	A285	80p tan & brn	.40	.25

Sheets of 9.

Skofja Loka A286

1973, Feb. 15   Perf. 11½
1129	A286	80p brown & buff	.30	.25

Millennium of the founding of Skofja Loka. Sheets of 9.

Novi Sad, by Peter Demetrovic — A287

Old Engravings: 1.25d, Zagreb, by Josef Szeman. 2.50d, Kotor, by Pierre Mortier. 3.25d, Belgrade, by Mancini. 5d, Split, by Louis-Francois Cassas. 6.50d, Kranj, by Matthaus Merian.

Engraved and Photogravure
1973, Mar. 15   Perf. 13½
1130	A287	50p gold, buff & blk	.25	.25
1131	A287	1.25d gold, gray & black	.25	.25
1132	A287	2.50d gold & blk	.25	.25
1133	A287	3.25d gold & blk	.25	.25
1134	A287	5d gold, buff & blk	.25	.25
1135	A287	6.50d gold & blk	.25	.25
Nos. 1130-1135 (6)			1.50	1.50

Nos. 1130-1131, 1133-1135 exist imperf.

Championship Poster A288

1973, Apr. 5   Litho.   Perf. 13½x13
1136	A288	2d multicolored	.40	.40

32nd Intl. Table Tennis Championships, Sarajevo, Apr. 5-15. Sheets of 9.

Europa Issue, 1973
Common Design Type
1973, Apr. 30   Photo.   Perf. 11½
Size: 32½x23mm
1138	CD16	2d dk bl, lil & lt grn	.35	.30
1139	CD16	5.50d pur, cit & sal pink	.80	.80

Sheets of 9.

Flower Type of 1969
Medicinal Plants: 80p, Birthwort. 2d, Globe thistles. 3d, Olive branch. 4d, Corydalis. 5d, Mistletoe. 6d, Comfrey.

1973, May 25   Photo.   Perf. 11½
Flowers in Natural Colors
1140	A238	80p orange & grn	.25	.25
1141	A238	2d dl bl & blue	.25	.25
1142	A238	3d olive & blk	.25	.25
1143	A238	4d yel grn & grn	.25	.25
1144	A238	5d org & sepia	.40	.40
1145	A238	6d lilac & grn	1.75	1.75
Nos. 1140-1145 (6)			3.15	3.15

Anton Jansa (1734-1773), Teacher, Apiculturist and Bee — A291

1973, Aug. 25   Engr.   Perf. 12½
1147	A291	80p black	.40	.25

Sheets of 9.

Championship Badge A292

1973, Sept. 1   Litho.   Perf. 13½x13
1148	A292	2d multicolored	.30	.25

World water sport championships (swimming, water polo, water jumps, figure swimming), Belgrade, Sept. 1-9. Sheets of 9.

"Greeting the Sun," by Ivan Vucovic A293

1973, Oct. 1   Perf. 12½
1149	A293	80p multicolored	1.20	.80

Children's Week, Oct. 1-7. Sheets of 9.

Post Horn — A294

Coil Stamps
1973-77   Photo.   Perf. 14½x14
1150	A294	30p brown	.25	.25
1151	A294	50p gray blue	.25	.25
1152	A294	80p rose red ('74)	.40	.25
1153	A294	1d yel grn ('77)	.40	.25
1154	A294	1.20d pink ('74)	.30	.25
1155	A294	1.50d rose ('77)	.40	.25
Nos. 1150-1155 (6)			2.00	1.50

Juraj Dalmatinac, Sculptor, Architect, 500th Anniv. of Death — A295

1973, Oct. 8   Litho.   Perf. 12½
1158	A295	80p grnsh gray & ol blk	.25	.25

Sheets of 9.

Nadezda Petrovic (1873-1915), Self-Portrait — A296

Lithographed and Engraved
1973, Oct. 12 **Perf. 11½**
1159 A296 2d gold & multi .30 .25
Sheets of 9.

Interior, by Marko Celebonovic — A297

Paintings of Interiors by Yugoslav artists: 2d, St. Duja, by Emanuel Vidovic. 3d, Room with Slovak Woman, by Marino Tartaglia. 4d, Painter with Easel, by Miljenko Stancic. 5d, Studio, by Milan Konjovic. 6d, Tavern in Stara Loka, by France Slana.

1973, Oct. 20 **Photo.** **Perf. 13½**
1160 A297 80p gold & multi .25 .25
1161 A297 2d gold & multi .25 .25
1162 A297 3d gold & multi .25 .25
1163 A297 4d gold & multi .25 .25
1164 A297 5d gold & multi .25 .25
1165 A297 6d gold & multi .45 .40
Nos. 1160-1165 (6) 1.70 1.65
Sheets of 9.

Dragojlo Dudic — A298

Lithographed and Engraved
1973, Nov. 29 **Perf. 12½**
Gray and Indigo
1166 80p shown .25 .25
1167 80p Strahil Pindzur .25 .25
1168 80p Boris Kidric .25 .25
1169 80p Radoje Dakic .25 .25
Gray and Plum
1170 2d Josip Mazar-Sosa .25 .25
1171 2d Zarko Zrenjanin .25 .25
1172 2d Emin Duraku .25 .25
1173 2d Ivan-Lola Ribar .25 .25
a. A298 Sheet of 8, #1166-1173 2.00 2.00

Republic Day, Nov. 29, honoring national heroes who perished during WWII.

Memorial, by O. Boljka, Ljubljana A299

Winged Globe, by D. Dzamonja, at Podgaric A300

Sculptures: 4.50d, Tower by D. Dzamonja, at Kozara. 5d, Memorial, by B. Grabulovski, at Belcista. 10d, Abstract, by M. Zivkovic, at Sutjeska. 50d, Stone "V," by Zivkovic, at Kragujevac.

1974 **Engr.** **Perf. 12½**
1174 A299 3d slate grn .65 .25
1175 A299 4.50d brn lake 1.00 .25
1176 A299 5d dark vio .90 .25
b. Perf. 13½ 6.00 .40
1177 A300 10d slate grn 1.60 .40
1178 A300 20d dull pur 3.25 .25
1179 A300 50d indigo 4.00 1.00
Nos. 1174-1179 (6) 11.40 2.40
Exist imperf.

1978-82 **Litho.**
1176a A299 5d 2.25 .25
1177a A300 10d ('81) 2.25 .50
1178a A300 20d ('81) 3.25 .50
1179a A300 50d ('82) 4.00 1.00
Nos. 1176a-1179a (4) 11.75 2.25

Metric Measure A301

1974, Jan. 10 **Litho.** **Perf. 13**
1180 A301 80p plum & multi .25 .25
Centenary of introduction of metric system.

European Ice Skating Championships, Jan. 29-Feb. 2, Zagreb — A302

1974, Jan. 29
1181 A302 2d multicolored .65 .25
Exists imperf.

Diligence, 1874 A303

Litho. & Engr.
1974, Feb. 25 **Perf. 11½**
1182 A303 80p shown .25 .25
1183 A303 2d New UPU head-quarters .25 .25
1184 A303 8d Jet plane .25 .25
Nos. 1182-1184 (3) .75 .75
Centenary of the Universal Postal Union.

Montenegro No. 1 — A304

Litho. & Engr.
1974, Mar. 11 **Perf. 13**
1185 A304 80p shown .25 .25
1186 A304 6d Montenegro No. 7 .30 .25
Centenary of first Montenegrin postage stamps.

Marshal Tito — A305

1974 **Litho.** **Perf. 13**
1193 A305 50p green .25 .25
a. Perf. 13x12½ .40 .25
1196 A305 80p vermilion .25 .25
1198 A305 1.20d slate green .25 .25
1201 A305 2d gray blue .25 .25
a. Perf. 13x12½ .40 .25
b. Perf. 13¼x13½
Nos. 1193-1201 (4) 1.00 1.00
Issued with and without fluorescence.
For surcharge see No. 1415.

Lenin, by Nandor Glid — A306

1974, Apr. 20 **Litho.** **Perf. 13**
1204 A306 2d blk & silver .25 .25
50th death anniv. of Lenin.

Lepenski Vir Statue, c. 4950 B.C. — A307

Europa: 6d, Widow & Child, by Ivan Mestrovic.

1974, Apr. 29 **Photo.** **Perf. 11½**
1205 A307 2d multicolored .40 .40
1206 A307 6d multicolored 1.20 1.20
Exist imperf.

Great Tit — A308

1974, May 25 **Photo.** **Perf. 11½**
1207 A308 80p shown .25 .25
1208 A308 2d Rose .25 .25
1209 A308 6d Cabbage butterfly 1.40 1.10
Nos. 1207-1209 (3) 1.90 1.60
Youth Day. Issued in sheets of 9.

Congress Poster — A309

1974, May 27 **Litho.** **Perf. 11½**
1210 A309 80p gold & multi .25 .25
1211 A309 2d silver & multi .25 .25
1212 A309 6d ocher & multi .40 .40
Nos. 1210-1212 (3) .90 .90
10th Congress of Yugoslav League of Communists, Belgrade, May 27-30.

Radar Ground Station, Ivanjica — A311

1974, June 7 **Engr.** **Perf. 13**
1214 A311 80p shown .25 .25
1215 A311 6d Intelsat IV .50 .25
Opening of first satellite ground station in Yugoslavia at Ivanjica. Sheets of 9.

Games Emblem and Soccer Cup — A312

1974, June 13 **Litho.** **Perf. 13**
1216 A312 4.50d vio bl & multi 1.25 .90
World Cup Soccer Championship, Munich, June 13-July 7. Sheets of 9.

Klek Mountain, Edelweiss, Mountaineers' Emblem — A313

1974, June 15
1217 A313 2d grn & multi .25 .25
Mountaineering in Yugoslavia, cent. Sheets of 9. Exists imperf. Value $40.

Children's Dance, by Jano Knjazovic — A314

Paintings: 2d, "Crucified Rooster," by Ivan Generalic, vert. 5d, Laundresses, by Ivan Lackovic, vert. 8d, Dance, by Janko Brasic.

1974, Sept. 9 **Photo.** **Perf. 11½**
1218 A314 80p multi .30 .30
1219 A314 2d multi .30 .30
1220 A314 5d multi .30 .30
1221 A314 8d multi .75 .75
Nos. 1218-1221 (4) 1.65 1.65
Yugoslav primitive art.

Cock and Flower, by Kaca Milinojsin A315

Designs (Children's Paintings): 3.20d, Girl and Boy, by Ewa Medrzecka, vert. 5d, Cat and Kitten, by Jelena Anastasijevic.

1974, Oct. 7 **Litho.** **Perf. 13**
1222 A315 1.20d multi .25 .25
1223 A315 3.20d multi .25 .25
1224 A315 5d multi .25 .25
Nos. 1222-1224 (3) .75 .75
Children's Week, Oct. 1-7, and Joy of Europe meeting in Belgrade. Sheets of 9.

Library and Primoz Trubar Statue
A316

1974, Oct. 21   Engr.   Perf. 13
1225 A316 1.20d black   .25 .25
Natl. University Library, Ljubljana, 200th anniv. Exists imperf.

White Peonies, by Petar Dobrovic
A317

Paintings of Flowers by Yugoslav artists: 2d, Carnations, by Vilko Gecan. 3d, Flowers, still-life, by Milan Konjovic. 4d, White Vase, by Sava Sumanovic. 5d, Larkspur, by Stane Kregar. 8d, Roses, by Petar Lubarda.

1974, Nov. 28   Photo.   Perf. 11½
1226 A317 80p gold & multi   .25 .25
1227 A317 2d gold & multi   .25 .25
1228 A317 3d gold & multi   .25 .25
1229 A317 4d gold & multi   .25 .25
1230 A317 5d gold & multi   .25 .25
1231 A317 8d gold & multi   .80 .80
    Nos. 1226-1231 (6)   2.05 2.05
Sheets of 9.

Title Page and View of Belgrade
A318

1975, Jan. 8   Litho.   Perf. 13
1232 A318 1.20d citron   .25 .25
  a.   Perf. 12½   30.00 30.00
Sesquicentennial of the first publication of Matica Srpska, literary journal.

Map of Europe and Dove — A319

1975, Jan. 30   Perf. 12x11½
1233 A319 3.20d bl & multi   .25 .25
1234 A319 8d multi   .50 .25
Interparliamentary Union for European Cooperation and Security, 2nd Conference, Belgrade, Jan. 31-Feb. 6. Exist imperf.

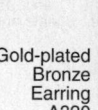

Gold-plated Bronze Earring
A320

Antique jewelry in Yugoslav museums: 2.10d, Silver bracelet, 18th cent. 3.20d, Silver gilt belt buckle, 18th cent. 5d, Silver ring with Nike cameo, 14th cent. 6d, Silver necklace, 17th cent. 8d, Bronze gilt bracelet, 14th cent.

1975, Feb. 25   Photo.   Perf. 14x13
1235 A320 1.20d multi   .25 .25
1236 A320 2.10d multi   .25 .25
1237 A320 3.20d multi   .25 .25
1238 A320 5d multi   .25 .25
1239 A320 6d multi   .25 .25
1240 A320 8d multi   .40 .40
    Nos. 1235-1240 (6)   1.65 1.65

Svetozar Markovic, by Stevan Bodnarov
A321

1975, Feb. 26   Engr.   Perf. 13
1241 A321 1.20d blue blk   .50 .25
Markovic (1846-1875), writer and poet.

Fettered Woman, by Frano Krsinic
A322

1975, Mar. 8   Photo.   Perf. 14½x14
1242 A322 3.20d gold & sepia   .25 .25
International Women's Year.

Street, Ohrid — A323

Views: 25p, Budva. 75p, City Hall, Rijeka (Fiume). Nos. 1245, 1246, Street, Ohrid. 1.50d, Church, Bihac. 2.10d, Street and fountain, Hvar. 3.20d, Skofja Loka. 3.40d, Main Square, Vranje. 4.90d, Mosque, Perast.

No Inscription at Bottom

1975-77   Litho.   Perf. 13
1243 A323 25p carmine ('76)   1.20 .25
1244 A323 75p purple ('76)   .80 .25
1245 A323 1d dull purple   .25 .25
1246 A323 1d dl grn ('76)   .40 .25
  a.   Perf. 13x12½   .40 .25
1247 A323 1.50d rose red ('76)   1.20 .25
  a.   Perf. 13x12½   24.00 24.00
1248 A323 2.10d gray green   .25 .25
1249 A323 3.20d dull blue   .25 .25
1250 A323 3.40d gray grn ('77)   .80 .25
  a.   Perf. 13x12½   1.60 .25
1251 A323 4.90d dl bl ('76)   2.75 .25
    Nos. 1243-1251 (9)   7.90 2.25

See Nos. 1487-1491, 1598, 1601, 1603A, 1713, 1718-1719. For surcharges see Nos. 1382-1383, 1481, 1502, 1545, 1550, 1594-1597A, 1764, 1767-1768, 1770-1771, 1964, 1973.
Nos. 1243, 1246, 1247 exist imperf. Value each, $20.

Europa Issue

Still Life with Eggs, by Mosa Pijade
A325

Painting: 8d, Three Graces, by Ivan Radovic.

1975, Apr. 28
1252 A325 3.20d gold & multi   .40 .40
1253 A325 8d gold & multi   .40 .40
Exist imperf.

Srem Front Fighters' Monument, by Dusan Dzamonja
A326

1975, May 9   Litho.   Perf. 13½
1254 A326 3.20d red & multi   .30 .25
Victory over Fascism in WWII; liberation of Yugoslavia, 30th anniv.

Garland Flower — A327

1975, May 24   Photo.   Perf. 14x14½
1255 A327 1.20d shown   .25 .25
1256 A327 2.10d Garden balsam   .25 .25
1257 A327 3.20d Rose mallow   .25 .25
1258 A327 5d Geranium   .25 .25
1259 A327 6d Crocus   .25 .25
1260 A327 8d Oleander   1.00 1.00
    Nos. 1255-1260 (6)   2.25 2.25
Youth Day.

Kayak — A328

1975, June 20   Litho.   Perf. 13½
1261 A328 3.20d grnsh bl & multi   .25 .25
9th World Championship of Wild Water Racing, Radika River, June 24-25, and 14th World Championship of Canoe-Slalom, Treska River, June 28-29.

Ambush, Herzegovinian Insurgents, by Ferdo Quiquerez — A329

1975, July 9   Photo.   Perf. 13½x14½
1262 A329 1.20d gold & multi   .25 .25
Bosnian & Herzegovinian Uprising, cent.

Stjepan Mitrov Ljubisa (1824-1878)
A330

Yugoslav writers: 2.10d, Ivan Prijatelj (1875-1937). 3.20d, Jakov Ignjatovic (1824-89). 5d, Dragojla Jarnevic (1813-75). 6d, Svetozar Corovic (1875-1919). 8d, Ivana Brlic-Mazuranic (1874-1938).

1975, Sept. 16   Litho.   Perf. 13
1263 A330 1.20d brick red & blk   .25 .25
1264 A330 2.10d dl grn & blk   .25 .25
1265 A330 3.20d ol bis & blk   .25 .25
1266 A330 5d brn org & blk   .25 .25
1267 A330 6d yel grn & blk   .25 .25
1268 A330 8d Prus bl & blk   .30 .30
    Nos. 1263-1268 (6)   1.55 1.55

"Joy of Europe" Children's Meeting, Oct. 2-7, Belgrade
A331

Children's drawings.

1975, Oct. 1   Litho.   Perf. 13½
1269 A331 3.20d Young Lion   .25 .25
1270 A331 6d Baby Carriage   .70 .65

Peace Dove
A332

1975, Oct. 10
1271 A332 3.20d multi   .25 .25
1272 A332 8d multi   .45 .45
European Security and Cooperation Conference, Helsinki, July 30-Aug. 1. Exist imperf.

Red Cross, "100", Map of Yugoslavia
A333

8d, Red Cross, people seeking help.

1975, Nov. 1   Litho.   Perf. 13½x13
1273 A333 1.20d red & multi   .25 .25
1274 A333 8d red & multi   .25 .25
Centenary of Red Cross in Yugoslavia.

Soup Kitchen, by Dorde Andrejevic-Kun
A334

Social paintings by 20th century Yugoslav artists: 2.10d, People at the Door, by Vinko Grdan. 3.20d, Drunks in Coach, by Marijan Detoni, horiz. 5d, Workers' Lunch, by Tone Kralj, horiz. 6d, Water Wheel, by Lazar Licenoski. 8d, The Hanging, by Krsto Hegedusic.

Perf. 14½x13½, 13½x14½
1975, Nov. 28   Photo.
1275 A334 1.20d gold & multi   .25 .25
1276 A334 2.10d gold & multi   .25 .25
1277 A334 3.20d gold & multi   .25 .25
1278 A334 5d gold & multi   .25 .25
1279 A334 6d gold & multi   .25 .25
1280 A334 8d gold & multi   .30 .30
    Nos. 1275-1280 (6)   1.55 1.55
Sheets of 9. No. 1277 exists imperf.

Diocletian's Palace, 304 A.D. — A335

3.20d, House of Ohrid, 19th cent., vert. 8d, Gracanica Monastery, Kosovo, 1321.

1975, Dec. 10   Engr.   Perf. 13½
1281 A335 1.20d dark brown   .25 .25
1282 A335 3.20d bluish black   .25 .25
1283 A335 8d dk vlo brown   .25 .25
     Nos. 1281-1283 (3)   .75 .75
European Architectural Heritage Year 1975.
Sheets of 9. Exist imperf.

12th Winter Olympic Games, Feb. 4-15, Innsbruck, Austria A336

1976, Feb. 4   Engr.   Perf. 13½
1284 A336 3.20d Ski jump   .25 .25
1285 A336 8d Pair figure skating   .70 .40
     Exist imperf.

Red Flag — A337

1976, Feb. 14   Litho.
1286 A337 1.20d red & multi   .25 .25
"Red Flag" workers demonstration, Kragujevac, Feb. 15, 1876. Exists imperf. Value $32.50.

Svetozar Miletic (1826-1901), Lawyer, Founder of United Serbian Youth — A338

1976, Feb. 23   Perf. 13½x13
1287 A338 1.20d grnsh gray & dl grn .25 .25

Borislav "Bora" Stankovic, (1876-1927), Writer A339

1976, Mar. 31   Litho.   Perf. 13½x13
1288 A339 1.20d lem, ol & mar   .25 .25
     Sheets of 9.

Europa Issue

King Matthias, by Jakob Pogorelec, 1931 — A340

1976, Apr. 26   Photo.   Perf. 11½
1289 A340 3.20d shown   .25 .25
1290 A340 8d Bowl, 14th cent   .25 .25

Ivan Cankar (1876-1918), Slovenian Writer A341

1976, May 8   Litho.   Perf. 13½x13
1291 A341 1.20d orange & plum   .25 .25

Train on Viaduct in Bosnia A342

Design: 8d, Train on viaduct in Montenegro.

1976, May 15   Engr.   Perf. 13½
1292 A342 3.20d deep magenta   .25 .25
1293 A342 8d deep blue   .40 .40
Inauguration of the Belgrade-Bar railroad.

Hawker Dragonfly A343

Fresh-water Fauna: 2.10d, Winkle. 3.20d, Rudd. 5d, Green frog. 6d, Ferruginous duck. 8d, Muskrat.

1976, May 25   Litho.
1294 A343 1.20d yel & multi   .40 .40
1295 A343 2.10d bl & multi   .40 .40
1296 A343 3.20d vio & multi   .40 .40
1297 A343 5d multicolored   .80 .80
1298 A343 6d multicolored   .80 .80
1299 A343 8d multicolored   2.75 2.75
     Nos. 1294-1299 (6)   5.55 5.55
Youth Day. Exist imperf.

Vladimir Nazor, Croatian Writer, Birth Cent. — A344

1976, May 29   Perf. 13
1300 A344 1.20d pale lil & dl bl   .25 .25

Battle of Vucji Dol, 1876 A345

1976, June 16   Litho.   Perf. 13
1301 A345 1.20d gold, brn & buff   .25 .25
Liberation of Montenegro from Turkey, cent. Exists imperf.

Serbian Pitcher A346

Water Pitchers: 2.10d, Slovenia. 3.20d, Bosnia-Herzegovina. 5d, Vojvodina 6d, Macedonia. 8d, Kosovo.

1976, June 22   Photo.   Perf. 14x13
1302 A346 1.20d dk car & multi   .25 .25
1303 A346 2.10d olive & multi   .25 .25
1304 A346 3.20d red & multi   .25 .25
1305 A346 5d brown & multi   .25 .25
1306 A346 6d dk grn & multi   .25 .25
1307 A346 8d dk bl & multi   .35 .35
     Nos. 1302-1307 (6)   1.60 1.60
     Exist imperf.

Tesla Monument, Belgrade, and Niagara Falls — A347

1976, July 10   Engr.   Perf. 13
1308 A347 5d slate grn & indigo   .50 .25
Nikola Tesla (1856-1943), electrical engineer and inventor. Sheets of 9. Exists imperf.

21st Olympic Games, July 17-Aug. 1, Montreal, Canada, A348

1976, July 17
1309 A348 1.20d Long jump   .25 .25
1310 A348 3.20d Team handball   .25 .25
1311 A348 5d Target shooting   .25 .25
1312 A348 8d Single scull rowing 2.00 1.50
     Nos. 1309-1312 (4)   2.75 2.25
     Sheets of 9.

World Map and Peace Dove A349

1976, Aug. 16   Litho.   Perf. 13
1313 A349 4.90d multi   .30 .25
5th Summit Conference of Non-Aligned Countries, Colombo, Sri Lanka, Aug. 9-19. Sheets of 9.
Exists imperf. Value $25.

Children's Train — A350

Children's drawings: 4.90d, Navy Day (submarine).

1976, Oct. 2   Litho.   Perf. 13
1314 A350 4.90d multi   .25 .25
1315 A350 8d multi   .30 .30
"Joy of Europe" Children's Meeting, Belgrade, Oct. 2-7.
No. 1315 exists imperf.

Herzegovinian Fugitives, by Uros Predic — A351

Historical paintings by 19th-20th century Yugoslav painters: 1.20d, Battle of the Montenegrins, by Djura Jaksic, vert. 2.10d, Nikola S. Zrinjski at Siget, by Oton Ivekovic, vert. 5d, Uprising at Razlovci, by Borko Lazeski. 6d, Enthroning of Slovenian Duke at Gospovetsko Field, by Anton Gojmir Kos. 8d, Break-through at Solun Front, by Veljko Stanojevic.

Perf. 13½x12½, 12½x13½
1976, Nov. 29   Photo.
1316 A351 1.20d gold & multi   .25 .25
1317 A351 2.10d gold & multi   .25 .25
1318 A351 3.20d gold & multi   .25 .25
1319 A351 5d gold & multi   .25 .25
1320 A351 6d gold & multi   .25 .25
1321 A351 8d gold & multi   .80 .80
     Nos. 1316-1321 (6)   2.05 2.05
     Sheets of 9.

No. 839 Surcharged with New Value and 3 Bars in Rose
1976, Dec. 8   Engr.   Perf. 12½
1322 A206 1d on 85p dl pur   .40 .25

Mateja Nenadovic A352

1977, Feb. 4   Photo.   Perf. 13½x14
1323 A352 4.90d multicolored   .30 .25
Prota Mateja Nenadovic (1777-1854), Serbian Duke, archbishop and writer.

Rajko Zinzifov — A353

1977, Feb. 10   Litho.   Perf. 13x13½
1324 A353 1.50d brn & sepia   .25 .25
Rajko Zinzifov (1839-1877), writer.

Phlox — A354

Flowers: 3.40d, Lily. 4.90d, Bleeding heart. 6d, Zinnia. 8d, Spreading marigold. 10d, Horseshoe geranium.

1977, Mar. 8   Perf. 13½x13
1325 A354 1.50d multi   .25 .25
1326 A354 3.40d multi   .25 .25
1327 A354 4.90d multi   .25 .25
1328 A354 6d multi   .30 .25
1329 A354 8d multi   .30 .25
1330 A354 10d multi   1.00 .80
     Nos. 1325-1330 (6)   2.35 2.05
     Exists imperf.

Croatian Music Institute, Zagreb, 150th Anniv. A355

1977, Apr. 4   Engr.   Perf. 13
1331 A355 4.90d bl & sepia   .40 .40

Alojz Kraigher — A356

1977, Apr. 11   Litho.   Perf. 13½
1332 A356 1.50d lemon & brn   .30 .25
Kraigher (1877-1959), Slovenian writer.

Boka Kotorska, by Milo Milunovic A357

10d, Zagorje in November, by Ljubo Babie.

1977, May 4   Photo.   Perf. 11½
1333 A357 4.90d gold & multi   .40   .40
1334 A357 10d gold & multi   .40   .40
Europa. Issued in sheets of 9.

Marshal Tito, by Omer Mujadzic A358

1977, May 25   Perf. 11½x12
1335 A358 1.50d gold & multi   .25   .25
1336 A358 4.90d gold & multi   .25   .25
1337 A358 8d gold & multi   .30   .30
    Nos. 1335-1337 (3)   .80   .80
85th birthday of Pres. Tito. Sheets of 9. Exists imperf.

Mountain Range and Gentian — A359

Design: 10d, Plitvice Lakes Falls, trees, robin and environmental protection emblem.

1977, June 6   Litho.   Perf. 13x13½
1338 A359 4.90d multicolored   .25   .25
1339 A359 10d multicolored   .70   .50
World Environment Day.

Petar Kocic (1877-1916), Writer A360

1977, June 15   Perf. 13½
1340 A360 1.50d pale grn & brn   .30   .25

Map of Europe and Peace Dove A361

1977, June 15   Litho.   Perf. 13½
1341 A361 4.90d multi   .25   .25
1342 A361 10d multi   1.00   1.00
Security and Cooperation Conference, Belgrade, June 15.

Child on Float — A362

Children's drawings: 10d, Fruit picking.

1977, Oct. 3   Litho.   Perf. 13½
1343 A362 4.90d multi   .25   .25
1344 A362 10d multi   .50   .40
"Joy of Europe" Children's Meeting.

Sava Congress Center, Belgrade A363

1977, Oct. 4   Litho.   Perf. 13½
1345 A363 4.90d bl & multi   .25   .25
1346 A363 10d car & multi   1.00   1.00
European Security and Cooperation Conference, Belgrade.
Exist imperf. Value, each $125.

Exhibition Emblem — A364

1977, Oct. 20   Litho.   Perf. 13½
1347 A364 4.90d gold & multi   .30   .25
Balkanfila 1977, 6th Intl. Phil. Exhib. of Balkan Countries, Belgrade, Oct. 24-30.

Double Flute and Shepherd A365

Landscape and Musician: 3.40d, 4.90d, 6d, Various string instruments. 8d, Bagpipes. 10d, Panpipes.

1977, Oct. 25   Engr.   Perf. 13½
1348 A365 1.50d och & red brn   .25   .25
1349 A365 3.40d green & brn   .25   .25
1350 A365 4.90d dk brn & yel   .25   .25
1351 A365 6d bl & red brn   .25   .25
1352 A365 8d brick red & sep   .25   .25
1353 A365 10d sl grn & bis   .50   .50
    Nos. 1348-1353 (6)   1.75   1.75
Musical instruments from Belgrade Ethnographical Museum.

Ivan Vavpotic, Self-portrait A366

Self-portraits of Yugoslav artists: 3.40d, Mihailo Vukotic. 4.90d, Kosta Hakman. 6d, Miroslav Kraljevic. 8d, Nikola Martinovski. 10d, Milena Pavlovic-Barili.

Perf. 13½x12½

1977, Nov. 26   Photo.
1354 A366 1.50d gold & multi   .25   .25
1355 A366 3.40d gold & multi   .25   .25
1356 A366 4.90d gold & multi   .25   .25
1357 A366 6d gold & multi   .25   .25
1358 A366 8d gold & multi   .25   .25
1359 A366 10d gold & multi   .65   .65
    Nos. 1354-1359 (6)   1.90   1.90

Festival of Testaccio, by Klovic — A367

Julija Klovic, by El Greco — A368

1978, Jan. 14   Photo.   Perf. 13½
1360 A367 4.90d multicolored   .25   .25
1361 A368 10d multicolored   .25   .25
Julija Klovic (1498-1578), Croat miniaturist.

Stampless Cover, Banaviste to Kubin, 1869 — A369

Designs: 3.40d, Mailbox. 4.90d, Ericsson telephone, 1900. 10d, Morse telegraph, 1844.

1978, Jan. 28   Perf. 13x14
1362 A369 1.50d multicolored   .25   .25
1363 A369 3.40d multicolored   .25   .25
1364 A369 4.90d multicolored   .25   .25
1365 A369 10d multicolored   .25   .25
    Nos. 1362-1365 (4)   1.00   1.00
Post Office Museum, Belgrade.

Battle of Pirot A370

1978, Feb. 20   Litho.   Perf. 13½
1366 A370 1.50d gold, blk & sl grn   1.75   1.75
Centenary of Serbo-Turkish War. Exists imperf. Value $40.

Airplanes A371

1978, Apr. 24   Litho.   Perf. 13½
1367 A371 1.50d S-49A, 1949   .25   .25
1368 A371 3.40d Galeb, 1961   .25   .25
1369 A371 4.90d Utva-75, 1976   .25   .25
1370 A371 10d Orao, 1974   .80   .80
    Nos. 1367-1370 (4)   1.55   1.55
Aeronautical Day. Exist imperf. Value, each $35.

Europa Issue

View of Golubac A372

10d, St. Naum Monastery, Ohrid.

1978, May 3   Photo.   Perf. 11½
1371 A372 4.90d shown   .25   .25
1372 A372 10d multicolored   .40   .40
Exist imperf.

Boxing Glove — A373

1978, May 5   Litho.   Perf. 13½
1373 A373 4.90d multicolored   .35   .25
Amateur Boxing Championships. Exists imperf. Value $35.

Honeybee — A374

Bees of Yugoslavia: 3.40d, Halictus scabiosae. 4.90d, Blue carpenter bee. 10d, Large earth bumblebee.

1978, May 25   Photo.   Perf. 11½
1374 A374 1.50d multi   .25   .25
1375 A374 3.40d multi   .25   .25
1376 A374 4.90d multi   .25   .25
1377 A374 10d multi   .95   .95
    Nos. 1374-1377 (4)   1.70   1.70
Exist imperf.

Filip Filipovic (1878-1938), Radovan Radovic (1878-1906), Revolutionaries — A375

1978, June 19   Litho.   Perf. 13½
1378 A375 1.50d dk pur & dl ol   .25   .25

Marshal Tito — A376

Congress Emblem — A377

1978, June 20
1379 A376 2d red & multi   .25   .25
1380 A377 4.90d red & multi   .30   .25
Souvenir Sheet
Imperf
1381 A376 15d red & multi   3.00   3.00
11th Congress of Yugoslav League of Communists, Belgrade, June 20-23.

Nos. 1379-1380 exist imperf. Value, each $35.

Nos. 1246, 1248 Surcharged with New Value and Two Bars in Brown

1978	Litho.	Perf. 13
1382	A323	2d on 1d	10.00	.25
1383	A323	3.40d on 2.10d	.40	.25

Issue dates: #1382, July 17; #1383, Aug 1.

Conference Emblem over Belgrade — A378

1978, July 25	Photo.	Perf. 13½
1384	A378	4.90d bl & lt blue	.30	.25

Conference of Foreign Ministers of Nonaligned Countries, Belgrade, July 25-29. Exists imperf. Value $35.

Championship Emblem — A379

1978, Aug. 10	Litho.	Perf. 13½x13
1385	A379	4.90d multicolored	.30	.25

14th Kayak and Canoe Still Water Championships, Lake Sava, Aug. 10-14.

Mt. Triglav, North Rock — A380

1978, Aug. 26	Photo.	Perf. 14
1386	A380	2d multicolored	.25	.25

Bicentenary of first ascent of Mt. Triglav by Slovenian climbers.

Black Lake, Mt. Durmitor A381

1978, Sept. 20
| 1387 | A381 | 4.90d shown | .25 | .25 |
| 1388 | A381 | 10d Tara River | .55 | .30 |

Protection of the environment.

Night Sky A382

1978, Sept. 30	Litho.	Perf. 13x12½
1389	A382	4.90d bl blk, blk & gold	.30	.25

29th Congress of International Astronautical Federation, Dubrovnik, Oct. 1-8.

People in Forest A383

Children's drawings: 10d, Family around pond.

1978, Oct. 2		Perf. 13½x13
1390	A383	4.90d multi	.35	.25
1391	A383	10d multi	.65	.45

"Joy of Europe" Children's Meeting.

Seal on Insurrection Declaration A384

1978, Oct. 5		Perf. 13½
1392	A384	2d gold, brn & blk	.25	.25

Centenary of Kresna uprising. Exists imperf. Value $40.

Teachers' Training Institute, Sombor, Bicent. A385

1978, Oct. 16
| 1393 | A385 | 2d multicolored | .25 | .25 |

Exists imperf.

Croatian Red Cross, Cent. A386

1978, Oct. 21
| 1394 | A386 | 2d lt bl, blk & red | .25 | .25 |

Metallic Sculpture XXII, by Dusan Dzamonja A387

Modern Sculptures: 3.40d, Circulation in Space I, by Vojin Bakic, vert. 4.90d, Tectonic Octopode, by Olga Jevric, vert. 10d, Tree of Life, by Drago Trsar.

Perf. 13½x13, 13x13½

1978, Nov. 4		Litho.
1395	A387	2d multicolored	.25	.25
1396	A387	3.40d multicolored	.25	.25
1397	A387	4.90d multicolored	.25	.25
1398	A387	10d multicolored	.35	.35
	Nos. 1395-1398 (4)		1.10	1.10

Crossing of Neretva Pass, by Ismet Mujezinovic A388

1978, Nov. 10		Litho.	Perf. 13
1399	A388	2d multicolored	.25	.25

35th anniversary of Battle of Neretva. Exists imperf.

Workers Leaving Factory, by Marijan Detoni — A389

Engravings: 3.40d, Workers, by Maksim Sedej. 4.90d, Lumberjacks, by Daniel Ozmo. 6d, Meal Break, by Pivo Karamatijevic. 10d, Hanged Man and Raped Woman, by Djordje Andrejevic Kun.

1978, Nov. 28	Photo.	Perf. 14x13½
1400	A389	2d gold, blk & buff	.25	.25
1401	A389	3.40d gold & black	.25	.25
1402	A389	4.90d gold, yel & blk	.25	.25
1403	A389	6d gold, buff & blk	.25	.25
1404	A389	10d gold, cr & blk	.70	.50
	Nos. 1400-1404 (5)		1.70	1.50

Republic day.

Larch Cone — A390

1978, Dec. 11	Photo.	Perf. 13x12½
1405	A390	1.50d shown	.25	.25
1406	A390	1.50d Red squirrel	.25	.25
1407	A390	2d Sycamore leaves	.25	.25
1408	A390	2d Red deer	.25	.25
a.	Bkt. pane of 8		1.25	
1409	A390	3.40d Alder leaves	.25	.25
1410	A390	3.40d Partridge	.25	.25
1411	A390	4.90d Oak leaves	.25	.25
1412	A390	4.90d Grouse	.25	.25
a.	Bkt. pane of 8		3.25	
	Nos. 1405-1412 (8)		2.00	2.00

New Year 1979. Nos. 1405-1412 printed se-tenant in sheets of 25.
No. 1408a contains 4 each of Nos. 1407-1408; No. 1412a 2 each of Nos. 1409-1412, with background colors changed. Exist imperf.

Nos. 1064, 868, 1198 Surcharged with New Value and Bars

1978	Engr.; Litho.	Perf. 12½, 13½
1413	A263	35p on 10p brown	1.60	.30
1414	A211	60p on 85p dp bl	1.60	.30
1415	A305	80p on 1.20d sl grn	1.60	.30
	Nos. 1413-1415 (3)		4.80	.90

First Masthead of Politika A391

1979, Jan. 25	Litho.	Perf. 13½
1416	A391	2d gold & black	.25	.25

Politika daily newspaper, 75th anniv. Exists imperf. Value $35.

Red Flags and Emblem — A392

1979, Feb. 15
| 1417 | A392 | 2d red & gold | .25 | .25 |

11th Meeting of Self-managers, Kragujevac, Feb. 15-16. Exists imperf. Value $40.

Child and IYC Emblem — A393

1979, Mar. 1	Photo.	Perf. 11½x12
1418	A393	4.90d gold vio & bl	.45	.30

International Year of the Child. Exists imperf.

Sabre, Mace, Koran Pouch A394

Old Weapons: 3.40d, Pistol and ramrod, Montenegro. 4.90d, Short carbine and powder horn, Slovenia and Croatia. 10d, Oriental rifle and cartridge pouch.

1979, Mar. 26	Photo.	Perf. 14
1419	A394	2d multicolored	.25	.25
1420	A394	3.40d multicolored	.25	.25
1421	A394	4.90d multicolored	.25	.25
1422	A394	10d multicolored	.50	.50
	Nos. 1419-1422 (4)		1.25	1.25

5-Pointed Star, Hammer and Sickle — A395

1979, Apr. 20	Photo.	Perf. 13½
1423	A395	2d multicolored	.25	.25
1424	A395	4.90d multicolored	.25	.25

Communist and Communist Youth Leagues, 60th anniversary. Exist imperf. Value, each used, $25.

Cyril and Methodius University and Emblem A396

1979, Apr. 24		Litho.
1425	A396	2d multicolored	.25	.25

Sts. Cyril and Methodius University, Skopje, 30th anniv.

19th Century Belgrade, by C. Goebel A397

Europa: 10d, Postilion and Ljubljana, 17th century, by Jan van der Heyden.

1979, Apr. 30	Photo.	Perf. 11½
1426	A397	4.90d multicolored	.40	.40
1427	A397	10d multicolored	.40	.40

Blue Sow Thistles — A398

Flowers: 3.40d, Anemones. 4.90d, Astragalus. 10d, Alpine trifolium.

1979, May 25   Photo.   Perf. 13½
1428	A398	2d multicolored	.25	.25
1429	A398	3.40d multicolored	.25	.25
1430	A398	4.90d multicolored	.25	.25
1431	A398	10d multicolored	.75	.75
		Nos. 1428-1431 (4)	1.50	1.50

Milutin Milankovic, by Paja Jovanovic — A399

1979, May 28
1432	A399	4.90d multi	.35	.25

Milutin Milankovic (1879-1958), scientist.

Kosta Abrasevic (1879-1898), Poet — A400

1979, May 29   Litho.   Perf. 13½x13
1433	A400	2d org, blk & gray	.25	.25

Exists imperf. Value, used $40.

Eight-Oared Shell A401

1979, Aug. 28   Litho.   Perf. 13
1434	A401	4.90d multicolored	.40	.25

9th World Rowing Championship, Lake Bled. Exist imperf. Value $40.

8th Mediterranean Games, Sept. 15-29, Split — A402

1979, Sept. 10
1435	A402	2d Games Emblem	.25	.25
1436	A402	4.90d Mascot	.25	.25
1437	A402	10d Map, Flags	.30	.30
		Nos. 1435-1437 (3)	.80	.80

Exist imperf. Value, each $30.

Seal, 15th Century A403

1979, Sept. 14   Perf. 12½
1438	A403	2d multicolored	.25	.25

Zagreb Postal Service, 450th anniversary. Exists imperf. Value $35.

Lake Palic — A404

Environment Protection: 10d, Lakefront, Prokletije Mountains.

1979, Sept. 20   Photo.   Perf. 14x13½
1439	A404	4.90d multicolored	.25	.25
1440	A404	10d multicolored	.65	.40

Bank and Fund Emblems A405

Engr. & Photo.
1979, Oct. 1   Perf. 13½
1441	A405	4.90d multicolored	.25	.25
1442	A405	10d multicolored	.40	.40

Meeting of the World Bank and International Monetary Fund, Belgrade, Oct. 2-5. Exist imperf. Value, each $25.

"Joy of Europe" A406

Children's drawings.

1979, Oct. 2   Litho.
1443	A406	4.90d shown	.25	.25
1444	A406	10d Child in yard	.45	.45

Exist imperf. Value, each $40.

Mihailo Pupin (1854-1935), Physicist, Inventor — A407

1979, Oct. 9   Perf. 13x13½
1445	A407	4.90d multicolored	.40	.25

Marko Cepenkov A408

1979, Nov. 15   Litho.   Perf. 13½
1446	A408	2d multicolored	.25	.25

Cepenkov (1829-1920), Macedonian folklorist. Exists imperf.

Pristina University, 10th Anniversary A409

1979, Nov. 17
1447	A409	2d multicolored	.25	.25

Exists imperf. Value, used $40.

Radovan Portal, Trogir Cathedral A410

Romanesque Sculptures: 3.40d, Choir stall, Cathedral of Split. 4.90d, Triforium, Church of the Resurrection, Decani. 6d, Buvina Portal, Cathedral of Split. 10d, Western portal, Church of Our Lady, Studenica.

1979, Nov. 28   Photo.
1448	A410	2d multi	.25	.25
1449	A410	3.40d multi	.25	.25
1450	A410	4.90d multi	.25	.25
1451	A410	6d multi	.25	.25
1452	A410	10d multi	.35	.35
		Nos. 1448-1452 (5)	1.35	1.35

Exist imperf.

Sarajevo University, 30th Anniversary A411

1979, Dec. 1   Litho.
1453	A411	2d multicolored	.25	.25

Exists imperf. Value, used $40.

Duro Dakovic and Nikola Hecimovic, Communist Revolutionaries, 50th Death Annivs. — A412

1979, Dec. 10
1454	A412	2d multicolored	.25	.25

Exists imperf. Value, used $40.

Sidewheeler Deligrad, 1862-1914 — A413

10d, Sidewheeler Serbia, 1917-72.

1979, Dec. 14
1455	A413	4.90d shown	.50	.60
1456	A413	10d multicolored	1.00	1.00

Danube Conference. Exist imperf. Value, each $60.

Milton Manaki and Camera A414

1980, Jan. 21   Litho.   Perf. 13½
1457	A414	2d pur, yel & brn	.25	.25

Manaki (1880-1964), photographer and documentary film maker.

Edward Kardelj, by Zdenko Kalin — A415

1980, Jan. 26
1458	A415	2d multicolored	.25	.25

Kardelj (1910-1979), labor movement leader. Exists imperf. Value, used $40.

No. 1458 Overprinted in Red

1980, Jan. 26
1459	A415	2d multicolored	.25	.25

Ploce renamed Kardeljevo. Exists imperf. Value, used $40.

13th Winter Olympic Games, Feb. 12-24, Lake Placid, NY — A416

1980, Feb. 13
1460	A416	4.90d Speed skating	.25	.25
1461	A416	10d Cross-country skiing	1.40	1.40

Exist imperf.

University of Belgrade, 75th Anniversary A417

1980, Feb. 27
1462	A417	2d multicolored	.25	.25

22nd Summer Olympic Games, July 19-Aug. 3, Moscow A418

1980, Apr. 21
1463	A418	2d Fencing	.25	.25
1464	A418	3.40d Bicycling	.25	.25
1465	A418	4.90d Field hockey	.25	.35
1466	A418	10d Archery	.50	.50
		Nos. 1463-1466 (4)	1.25	1.35

Marshal Tito, by Antun Augustincic A419

Europa: 13d, Tito, by Djordje Prudnikov.

1980, Apr. 28   Photo.   Perf. 11½
Granite Paper
1467	A419	4.90d multi	.25	.25
1468	A419	13d multi	1.00	1.00

Exist imperf. Value, each $15.

Marshal Tito, by Bozidar Jakac — A420

1980, May 4   Litho.   Perf. 13½
1469	A420	2.50d purplish blk	.25	.25
a.		Perf. 10½	.30	.30
1470	A420	4.90d gray black	.60	.60

Marshal Tito (1892-1980) memorial. Issued in sheets of 8 plus label.

Exist imperf. Value, each $25.

Sava Kovacevic (1905-1943),
Revolutionary — A421

1980, May 11   Litho.   Perf. 13½
1471 A421 2.50d multicolored   .25 .25

Wood Baton and Letter A422

1980, May 14
1472 A422 2d multicolored   .25 .25
1st Tito Youth Relay Race, 35th anniv.
Exists imperf. Value $35.

Flying Gunard — A423

1980, May 24   Photo.   Perf. 12
1473 A423   2d shown   .25 .25
1474 A423   3.40d Loggerhead tur-
            tle   .25 .25
1475 A423   4.90d Sea swallow   .30 .30
1476 A423   10d Dolphin   2.25 2.25
       Nos. 1473-1476 (4)   3.05 3.05

Emperor Trajan Decius Coin, 3rd Cent. — A424

3rd Century Roman Coins (Illyrian Emperors): 3.40d, Aurelianus. 4.90d, Probus. 10d, Diocletianus.

1980, June 10
1477 A424   2d multicolored   .25 .25
1478 A424   3.40d multicolored .25 .25
1479 A424   4.90d multicolored .30 .25
1480 A424   10d multicolored   .50 .30
       Nos. 1477-1480 (4)   1.30 1.05

No. 1247 Surcharged with New Value and Bars

1980, June 17   Litho.   Perf. 13½
1481 A323 2.50d on 1.50d   .40 .25

Types of 1971-77

Views: 5p, Krusevac. 10p, Gradacac. 20p, Church and bridge, Bohinj. 30p, Krk. 35p, Omis. 40p, Pec. 60p, Logar Valley. 2.50d, Kragujevac. 3.50d, Vrsac. 5.60d, Travnik. 8d, Dubrovnik.

Perf. 13½, 13¼x12½ (#1487), 13¼ (#1486A)

1978-81
1482 A263   5p deep orange   .40 .25
1483 A263   10p brown   .40 .40
1483A A263   20p purple ('78) .80 .55
1484 A263   30p olive gray   .40 .25
1485 A263   35p brown red   .80 .55
1486 A263   40p gray   .40 .25
1486A A263   60p purple   .40 .25
1487 A323   2.50d rose red   .80 .25
1488 A323   2.50d bl gray ('81) .35 .25
1489 A323   3.50d red org ('81) .25 .25
1490 A323   5.60d gray grn ('81) .25 .25
1491 A323   8d gray ('81)   .25 .25
       Nos. 1482-1491 (12)   5.50 3.75

No. 1483A has all three numerals in denomination the same size. On No. 1065 "20" is taller than first "0."

Perf. 13¼x12½
1482a A263   5p   1.25 .25
1483b A263   10p   .60 .60
1483Ac A263 20p   .80 .55
1484a A263   30p   .80 .40
1485a A263   35p   1.25 .80
1486b A263   40p   .55 .25
1486Ac A263 60p   .55 .40
1487a A323   2.50d .60 .25
1488a A320   2.50d .25 .25
1489a A323   3.50d .25 .25
1490a A323   5.60d .25 .25
1491a A323   8d   .60 .25
       Nos. 1482a-14891a (12) 7.65 4.50

400th Anniversary of Lipica Stud Farm — A425

1980, June 25
1493 A425 2.50d black   .25 .25

A426

1980, June 27   Perf. 13½
1494 A426 2.50d magenta & red   .25 .25
Tito, Basic Law of Self-management, 30th anniv.

A427

1980, June 28   Perf. 13
1495 A427 2.50d light green   .25 .25
University of Novi Sad, 20th anniv.

Mljet National Park — A428

1980, Sept. 5   Photo.   Perf. 14
1496 A428 4.90d shown   .25 .25
1497 A428 13d Galicica Natl.
          Park   .25 .25
European Nature Protection Year.

Minerals — A429

1980, Sept. 10   Litho.   Perf. 13½
1498 A429 2.50d Pyrrhotine   .35 .35
1499 A429 3.40d Dolomite   .35 .35
1500 A429 4.90d Sphalerite   .35 .35
1501 A429 13d Wulfenite   .80 .80
       Nos. 1498-1501 (4)   1.85 1.85

No. 1244 Surcharged with New Value and Bars

1980, Oct. 15   Litho.   Perf. 13
1502 A323 5d on 75p purple   2.00 .25

View of Kotor, UNESCO Emblem A430

1980, Sept. 23   Perf. 13½
1503 A430 4.90d multicolored   .25 .25
21st UNESCO General Conf., Belgrade,

Children in Garden A431

Joy of Europe Children's Festival: 13d, 3 faces.

1980, Oct. 2   Perf. 13½x13
1504 A431 4.90d multi   .25 .25
1505 A431 13d multi   .35 .35

Dove over Madrid Meeting Hall — A432

Lithographed and Engraved
1980, Nov. 11   Perf. 13½
1506 A432 4.90d dk grn & bl grn .25 .25
1507 A432 13d dk brn & yel
          brown   .40 .40
European Security Conference, Madrid.

Federal Flag of Yugoslavia A433

Republic Day: Socialist Republic flags. Nos. 1508-1515 se-tenant. No. 1511 has Latin letters.

1980, Nov. 28   Litho.   Perf. 12½
1508 A433 2.50d Bosnia & Her-
          zegovina   .25 .25
1509 A433 2.50d Croatia   .25 .25
1510 A433 2.50d shown   .25 .25
1511 A433 2.50d Yugoslavia   .25 .25
1512 A433 2.50d Macedonia   .25 .25
1513 A433 2.50d Montenegro   .25 .25
1514 A433 2.50d Serbia   .25 .25
1515 A433 2.50d Slovenia   .25 .25
       Nos. 1508-1515 (8)   2.00 2.00

Woman with Straw Hat — A434

Paintings: 3.40d, Atelier No. 1, by Gabriel Stupica. 4.90d, To the Glory of the Sutjeska Fighters, by Ismet Mujezinovic. 8d, Serenity, by Marino Tartaglia. 13d, Complaint, by Milos Vuskovic.

1980, Dec. 16   Perf. 13½
1516 A434 2.50d multi   .25 .25
1517 A434 3.40d multi   .25 .25
1518 A434 4.90d multi   .25 .25
1519 A434 8d multi, vert.   .25 .25
1520 A434 13d multi, vert.   .80 .80
       Nos. 1516-1520 (5)   1.80 1.80

Ivan Ribar (1881-1968), Politician — A435

1981, Jan. 21   Litho.   Perf. 13½
1521 A435 2.50d rose red & blk .25 .25

Cementusa Hand Bomb A436

Partisan Weapons: 5.60d, Rifle. 8d, 52-mm Cannon. 13d, Man-powered tank.

1981, Feb. 16
1522 A436 3.50d brick red & blk .25 .25
1523 A436 5.60d grn & blk   .25 .25
1524 A436 8d bis brn & blk   .25 .25
1525 A436 13d rose vio & blk   .50 .50
       Nos. 1522-1525 (4)   1.25 1.25

Monastery of the Virgin, Eleousa, 900th Anniversary A437

1981, Mar. 3
1526 A437 3.50d multicolored   1.10 1.10
Exists imperf. Value $35.

36th World Table Tennis Championship, Novi Sad, Apr. 14-26 — A438

1981, Apr. 14   Litho.   Perf. 13½
1527 A438 8d multicolored   .25 .25
Exists imperf.

Europa Issue

Wedding in Herzegovina, by Nikola Arsenovic A439

Paintings by Nikola Arsenovic (1823-85): 13d, Witnesses at a Wedding.

1981, May 5   Photo.   Perf. 12
Granite Paper
1528 A439 8d multicolored   .30 .25
1529 A439 13d multicolored   .30 .25

Dimitrije Tucovic and Slavija Square, Belgrade A440

1981, May 13   Litho.   Perf. 13½
1530 A440 3.50d bl vio & red   .25 .25
Tucovic (1881-1914), Socialist leader. Exists imperf.

Marshal Tito, by Milivoje Unkovic — A441

1981, May 25 Photo. Perf. 11½x12
Granite Paper
1531 A441 3.50d gold & dk brn   .40 .40
Marshal Tito's 89th birth anniversary. Exists imperf.

Sunflower — A442

1981, May 28 Photo. Perf. 11½
Granite Paper
1532 A442 3.50d shown   .25 .25
1533 A442 5.60d Hops   .25 .25
1534 A442 8d Corn   .30 .25
1535 A442 13d Wheat   .55 .35
Nos. 1532-1535 (4)   1.35 1.10
Exist imperf.

3rd Autonomous Enterprises Cong. — A443

1981, June 16 Litho. Perf. 13½
1536 A443 3.50d multicolored   .25 .25

Djordje Petrov (1864-1921), Macedonian Revolutionary A444

1981, June 22
1537 A444 3.50d bister & black   .25 .25

National Insurrection, 40th Anniv. A445

1981, July 4 Perf. 12½
1538 A445 3.50d red org & tan   .25 .25
1539 A445 8d red org & tan   .25 .25
Souvenir Sheet
Imperf
1540 A445 30d Tito monument   1.25 1.25

800th Anniv. of Varazdin A446

1981, Aug. 20 Litho. Perf. 13½
1541 A446 3.50d multicolored   .25 .25

Parliament Building, Belgrade — A447

1981, Sept. 1
1542 A447 8d red & blue   .25 .25
Belgrade Conference of Non-Aligned Countries, 20th anniv.

Serbian Printing Office, 150th Anniv. A448

1981, Sept. 15
1543 A448 3.50d pale rose & dk bl .25 .25

Fran Levstik (1831-1887), Writer A449

1981, Sept. 28 Perf. 12x11½
1544 A449 3.50d dl red & gray   .25 .25

No. 1251 Surcharged with New Value and Bars
1981, Oct. Perf. 13
1545 A323 5d on 4.90d dl bl   .80 .25
 a. Perf. 13x12½   1.60 .40

Joy of Europe Children's Festival A450

1981, Oct. 2
1546 A450 8d Barnyard   .25 .25
1547 A450 13d Skiers   .25 .25

125th Anniv. of European Danube Commission — A451

8d, Tugboat Karlovac. 13d, Train hauling boat, Sip Canal.

1981, Oct. 28 Litho. Perf. 13½
1548 A451 8d multicolored   .25 .25
1549 A451 13d multicolored   .70 .70
Nos. 1548-1549 exist imperf. Value, set $75.

No. 1250a Surcharged with New Value and Bars
1981, Oct. 9 Litho. Perf. 13x12½
1550 A323 3.50d on 3.40d gray grn   1.75 .30
 a. on #1250   .40 .25

Savings Bank of Yugoslavia, 60th Anniv. — A452

1981, Oct. 31 Perf. 11½x12
1551 A452 3.50d multicolored   .25 .25

Intl. Inventions Conference A453

1981, Nov. 4 Perf. 13½
1552 A453 8d red & gold   .25 .25

Nature Protection — A454

8d, Plant, Ruguvo Gorge. 13d, Lynx, Prokletjie Mountains.

1981, Nov. 14
1553 A454 8d multicolored   .25 .25
1554 A454 13d multicolored   .75 .75

August Senoa (1838-1881), Writer — A455

1981, Dec. 12 Perf. 11½x12
1555 A455 3.50d dl gray vio & gldn brn   .25 .25

Still Life with a Fish, by Jovan Bijelic (1886-1964) — A456

Paintings of Animals: 5.60d, Raven, by Milo Milunovic (1897-1967). 8d, Bird on Blue Background, by Marko Celebonovic (b. 1902). 10d, Horses, by Peter Lubarda (1907-1974). 13d, Sheep, by Nikola Masic (1852-1902).

1981, Dec. 29 Photo. Perf. 13½
1556 A456 3.50d multi   .25 .25
1557 A456 5.60d multi   .25 .25
1558 A456 8d multi   .25 .25
1559 A456 10d multi   .25 .25
1560 A456 13d multi   .55 .55
Nos. 1556-1560 (5)   1.55 1.55

40th Anniv. of Foca Regulations A457

1982, Jan 14 Litho. Perf. 13½
1561 A457 3.50d Mosa Pijade   .25 .25

60th Anniv. of Communist Newspaper Borba A458

1982, Feb. 19 Litho.
1562 A458 3.50d red & blk   .25 .25

500th Anniv. of City of Cetinje — A459

1982, Mar. 10
1563 A459 3.50d dull red brn   .25 .25

Capt. Ivo Visin (1806-1868), Boka Kotorska's Map — A460

1982, May 5 Photo. Perf. 11½
1564 A460 8d shown   .40 .40
1565 A460 15d Ship Splendido   .40 .40
Europa, 1st Yugoslavian circumnavigation, 1852-1859.

Male House Sparrow A461

5.60d, Female house sparrow. 8d, Male field sparrow. 15d, Female field sparrow.

1982, May 24 Litho. Perf. 13½
1566 A461 3.50d shown   .25 .25
1567 A461 5.60d multicolored   .25 .25
1568 A461 8d multicolored   .25 .25
1569 A461 15d multicolored   2.40 2.40
Nos. 1566-1569 (4)   3.15 3.15
See Nos. 1687-1690.

90th Birth Anniv. of Marshal Tito — A462

1982, May 25 Photo. Perf. 11½x12
Granite Paper
1570 A462 3.50d multicolored   .25 .25

1982 World
Cup — A463

Designs: Soccer ball in various positions.

1982, June 12   **Perf. 11½**
Granite Paper

1571		Sheet of 4	1.60	1.60
a.	A463	3.50d multicolored	.25	.25
b.	A463	5.60d multicolored	.25	.25
c.	A463	8d multicolored	.25	.25
d.	A463	15d multicolored	.25	.25

12th
Congress of
Yugoslavian
Communists'
League,
Belgrade,
June 26-29
A464

1982 June 26   **Litho.**   **Perf. 13½**

1572	A464	3.50d orange & red	.25	.25
1573	A464	8d gray & red	.25	.25

Souvenir Sheet
Perf. 12½

1574		Sheet of 2	.80	.80
a.	A464	10d like 3.50d	.25	.25
b.	A464	20d like 8d	.55	.55

Exists imperf. Value $250.

Dura Jaksic
(1832-1878),
Writer, Painter
A465

1982, July 27   **Litho.**   **Perf. 14**

1575	A465	3.50d Self-portrait	.25	.25

1982 World Championships Held in
Yugoslavia — A466

1982, July 30   **Perf. 13½**

1576	A466	8d Gymnastics	.80	.25
1577	A466	8d Kayak	.80	.25
1578	A466	8d Weightlifting	.80	.25
		Nos. 1576-1578 (3)	2.40	.75

Ivan Zajc (1832-
1914), Composer
and Conductor
A467

1982, Aug. 3

1579	A467	4d brown	.25	.25

Breguet
XIX and
Potez XXV
A468

6.10d, Super Galeb G-4. 8.80d, Armed
boat. 15d, Rocket gun boat.

1982, Sept. 1   **Litho.**   **Perf. 13½**

1580	A468	4d shown	.25	.25
1581	A468	6.10d multicolored	.25	.25
1582	A468	8.80d multicolored	.25	.25
1583	A468	15d multicolored	.50	.50
		Nos. 1580-1583 (4)	1.25	1.25

40th anniv. of Air Force/Anti-aircraft
Defense and Navy.

Spruce
Branch,
Tara
Natl.
Park
A469

15d, Mediterranean monk seal, Kornati.

1982, Sept. 3

1584	A469	8.80d shown	.25	.25
1585	A469	15d multicolored	.60	.60

14th Joy of Europe Children's
Festival — A470

1982, Oct. 2

1586	A470	8.80d Traffic	.25	.25
1587	A470	15d In the Bath	.55	.55

Small
Onofrio's
Fountain,
15th Cent.
A471

1982, Oct. 23

1588	A471	8.80d multi	.25	.25

16th Universal Federation of Travel Agents'
Assoc. Cong., Dubrovnik, Oct. 24-30.

600th Anniv.
of
Hercegnovi
A472

1982, Oct. 28

1589	A472	4d multicolored	.50	.50

14th Winter
Olympic
Games,
Sarajevo,
Feb. 8-19,
1984 — A473

4d, Bridge, Miljacka River. 6.10d, Minaret,
Mosque. 8.80d, Evangelical Church. 15d,
Street.

1982, Nov. 20   **Perf. 12½**

1590	A473	4d multicolored	.25	.25
1591	A473	6.10d multicolored	.25	.25
1592	A473	8.80d multicolored	.50	.50
1593	A473	15d multicolored	1.10	1.10
		Nos. 1590-1593 (4)	2.10	2.10

**Nos. 1488a and 1489a Surcharged
In Red, Blue, Black or Red Violet
with Two Bars or Shield**

1982-83   **Litho.**   **Perf. 13x12½**

1594	A323	30p on 2.50d (R)	.50	.25
1595	A323	50p on 2.50d (Bl)	1.20	.25
1596	A323	60p on 2.50d ('83)	.50	.25

1597	A323	1d on 3.50d	.25	.25
1597A	A323	2d on 2.50d (RV)	1.60	.25
		Nos. 1594-1597A (5)	4.05	1.25

Perf. 13

1594a	A323	30p on #1488	.40	.25
1595a	A323	50p on #1488	.25	.25
1596a	A323	60p on #1488	1.00	.25
1597b	A323	1d on #1489	.65	.25
		Nos. 1594a-1597b (4)	2.30	1.00

Types of 1971-77

Designs: 3d, Skofja Loka. 4d, Pocitelj. 5d,
Osijek. 6.10d, like 2.10d. 8.80d, Hercegnovi.
10d, Sarajevo. 16.50d, Ohrid.

1982-83   **Litho.**   **Perf. 13x12½**

1598	A323	3d gray bl	.25	.25
1599	A263	4d red org	.25	.25
1600	A263	5d grnsh bl ('83)	.40	.25
1601	A323	6.10d olive grn	.60	.25
1602	A263	8.80d gray	.40	.25

Perf. 13½

1603	A263	10d red lil ('83)	.25	.25
1603A	A323	16.50d dl bl ('83)	.25	.25
		Nos. 1598-1603A (7)	2.40	1.75

Type styles of Nos. 1600, 1603-1603A differ
somewhat from illustrations.
No. 1600 exists imperf. Value $35.

Perf. 13

1598a	A323	3d	.50	.25
1599a	A323	4d	.50	.25
1600a	A323	5d	.40	.25
1601a	A323	6.10d	.80	.25
1602a	A323	8.80d	1.20	.25
1603b	A323	10d	1.10	.25
1603c	A323	16.50d	1.25	.30
		Nos. 1598a-1603c (7)	5.75	1.80

40th Anniv.
of Anti-
Fascist
Council
A474

1982, Nov. 26   **Perf. 13½**

1604	A474	4d Bihac, 1942	.25	.25

The Manuscript, by Janez Bernik (b.
1933) — A475

4d, Prophet on Golden Background, by Joze
Ciuha (b. 1924). 6.10d, Journey to the West,
by Andrej Jemec (b. 1934). 8.80d, Black Comb
with Red Band, by Riko Debenjak (b. 1908).
15d, The Vitrine, by Adriana Maraz (b. 1931).

1982, Nov. 27

1605	A475	4d multi, vert.	.25	.25
1606	A475	6.10d multi, vert.	.25	.25
1607	A475	8.80d multi, vert.	.25	.25
1608	A475	10d multi	.25	.25
1609	A475	15d multi	.55	.55
		Nos. 1605-1609 (5)	1.55	1.55

Uros Predic
(1857-1953),
Painter — A476

1982, Dec. 7

1610	A476	4d multicolored	.25	.25

Union of Pioneers,
40th Anniv. — A477

1982, Dec. 27   **Perf. 12**

1611	A477	4d multicolored	.25	.25

Articles from
Museum of
Applied Art,
Belgrade
A478

Designs: 4d, Lead pitcher, Gnjilane, 16th
cent. 6.10d, Silver-plated jug, Macedonia, 18th
cent. 8.80d, Goblet, 16th cent., Dalmatia. 15d,
Mortar, 15th cent., Kotor.

1983, Feb. 19

1612	A478	4d multicolored	.25	.25
1613	A478	6.10d multicolored	.25	.25
1614	A478	8.80d multicolored	.25	.25
1615	A478	15d multicolored	.40	.30
		Nos. 1612-1615 (4)	1.15	1.05

Mount
Jalovec — A479

1983, Feb. 26

1616	A479	4d blue & lt bl	.25	.25

Slovenian Mountaineering Soc., 90th anniv.

Serbian
Telephone
Service
Centenary
A480

1983, Mar. 15

1617	A480	3d Ericsson phone	.25	.25

25th Anniv. of
Intl. Org. for
Maritime
Navigation
(OMI) — A481

1983, Mar. 17   **Perf. 13½x14**

1618	A481	8.80d multi	.25	.25

Edible
Mushrooms
A482

4d, Agaricus campestris. 6.10d, Morchella
vulgaris. 8.80d, Boletus edulis. 15d,
Cantharellus cibarius.

1983, Mar. 21   **Perf. 14**

1619	A482	4d multi	.30	.30
1620	A482	6.10d multi	.30	.30
1621	A482	8.80d multi	.30	.30
1622	A482	15d multi	1.20	1.20
		Nos. 1619-1622 (4)	2.10	2.10

Rijeka Railway, 110th Anniv. — A483

No. 1623, Steam engine series 401. No. 1624, Thyristor locomotive 442.

1983, Apr. 5
| 1623 | A483 | 4d multi | .25 | .25 |
| 1624 | A483 | 23.70d on 8.80d multi | .50 | .50 |

No. 1624 not issued without surcharge.

Boro and Ramiz Monument, Landovica A484

1983, Apr. 10
| 1625 | A484 | 4d multi | .25 | .25 |

Boro Vukmirovic and Ramiz Sadiku, revolutionary martyrs, 40th death anniv.

Ivo Andric (1892-1975), Poet, 1961 Nobel Prize Winner A485

8.80d, Medal, Travnik Chronicle text. 20d, Portrait, Bridge, Drina River.

1983, May 5   Photo.   Perf. 11½
Granite Paper
| 1626 | A485 | 8.80d multicolored | .40 | .40 |
| 1627 | A485 | 20d multicolored | .40 | .40 |

Europa.

50th Intl. Agricultural Fair, Novi Sad — A486

1983, May 13   Litho.   Perf. 14
| 1628 | A486 | 4d Combine harvester | .25 | .25 |

40th Anniv. of Battle of Sutjeska A487

3d, Assault, by Pivo Karamatijevic.

1983, May 14   Perf. 12½
| 1629 | A487 | 3d multicolored | .25 | .25 |

A488

1983, May 25   Perf. 13½
| 1630 | A488 | 4d Tito, Parliament | .25 | .25 |
| a. | | Perf. 12½ | 1.00 | 1.00 |

30th anniv. of election of Pres. Tito.

A489

4d, First mail and passenger car. 16.50d, Mountain road, Kotor.

1983, May 27
| 1631 | A489 | 4d multi | .25 | .25 |
| 1632 | A489 | 16.50d multi | .25 | .25 |

80th anniv. of automobile service in Montenegro.

A490

1983, June 5   Perf. 14
| 1633 | A490 | 23.70d multi | .25 | .25 |

UN Conference on Trade and Development, 6th session, Belgrade, June 6-30.

Engraving by Valvasor — A491

1983, June 7   Perf. 12½
| 1634 | A491 | 4d multicolored | .25 | .25 |

Town of Pazin millennium.

Triumphal Arch, Titograd A492

100d, Memorial to S. Filipovic, Valjevo, vert.

1983, June 9   Perf. 12½
1635	A492	100d multicolored	2.50	.25
a.		Perf. 13x13½	1.40	
1636	A492	200d shown	2.00	.95
a.		Perf. 13½x13	3.75	.95

Skopje Earthquake, 20th Anniv. — A493

1983, July 26   Litho.   Perf. 12½
| 1637 | A493 | 23.70d deep magenta | .25 | .25 |
| a. | | Perf. 13½ | .80 | .45 |

For surcharge, see No. 1715.

Sculpture by Ivan Mestrovic — A494

1983, Aug. 15
| 1638 | A494 | 6d multicolored | .25 | .25 |

European Nature Protection — A495

16.50d, Gentian, Kopaonik National Park. 23.70d, Chamois, Perucica Gorge.

1983, Sept. 10   Litho.   Perf. 13
| 1639 | A495 | 16.50d multi | .35 | .35 |
| 1640 | A495 | 23.70d multi | .65 | .65 |

See Nos. 1685-1686.

Joy of Europe — A496

Children's Paintings: 16.50d, Bride and Bridegroom by Verna Paunkonik. 23.70d, Andres and his Mother by Marta Lopez-Ibor.

1983, Oct. 3   Litho.   Perf. 13½
| 1641 | A496 | 16.50d multi | .25 | .25 |
| 1642 | A496 | 23.70d multi | .65 | .65 |

A497

1983, Oct. 17   Litho.   Perf. 12½
| 1643 | A497 | 5d multicolored | .25 | .25 |

Kragujevac High School sesquicentenary.

A498

1983, Oct. 17   Litho.   Perf. 13½
| 1644 | A498 | 5d multicolored | .25 | .25 |

Timok Uprising centenary.

14th Winter Olympic Games, Sarajevo, Feb. 8-19, 1984 A499

1983, Nov. 25   Engr.   Perf. 13½
1645	A499	4d Ski jump	.25	.25
1646	A499	4d Slalom	.25	.25
1647	A499	16.50d Bobsledding	.25	.25
1648	A499	16.50d Downhill skiing	.25	.25
1649	A499	23.70d Speed skating	.50	.50
1650	A499	23.70d Hockey	.50	.50
		Nos. 1645-1650 (6)	2.00	2.00

Souvenir Sheet
Imperf
| 1651 | A499 | 50d Emblem | 1.75 | 1.75 |

Nos. 1645-1651 exist imperf.

Jovan Jovanovic Zmaj (1833-1904), Poet, Neven Masthead A500

1983, Nov. 24   Litho.   Perf. 12½
| 1652 | A500 | 5d multicolored | .25 | .25 |

Peasant Wedding, by Pieter Brueghel A501

Paintings: No. 1654, Susanna with the Old Men, by the "Master of the Prodigal Son." No. 1655, Allegory of Wisdom and Strength, by Paolo Veronese (1528-1588). No. 1656, Virgin Mary from Salamanca, by Robert Campin (1375-1444). No. 1657, St. Ann with Madonna and Jesus, by Albrecht Dürer (1471-1528).

1983, Nov. 26   Perf. 14
1653	A501	4d multi	.25	.25
1654	A501	16.50d multi	.25	.25
1655	A501	16.50d multi	.25	.25
1656	A501	23.70d multi	.55	.55
1657	A501	23.70d multi	.80	.80
		Nos. 1653-1657 (5)	2.10	2.10

View of Jajce — A502

1983, Nov. 28   Perf. 13x12½
| 1658 | A502 | 5d multicolored | .25 | .25 |

Souvenir Sheet
Imperf
| 1659 | A502 | 30d Tito | .80 | .80 |

40th anniv. of Second Session of the Antifascist Council of the Natl. Liberation of Yugoslavia, Jajce, Nov. 29-30.

World Communications Year — A503

1983, Dec. 10   Perf. 13½
| 1660 | A503 | 23.70d multi | .25 | .25 |

Koco Racin (1908-1943), Writer — A504

1983, Dec. 22
| 1661 | A504 | 5d multicolored | .25 | .25 |

Politika Front Page, Oct. 28, 1944 — A505

1984, Jan. 25   Litho.   Perf. 12½
| 1662 | A505 | 5d red & black | .25 | .25 |

80th anniv. of Politika newspaper and 40th anniv. in Yugoslavia.

Veljko Petrovic (1884-1967), Poet — A506

1984, Feb. 4   Litho.   Perf. 13½
| 1663 | A506 | 5d multicolored | .25 | .25 |

1984
Winter
Olympics
A507

1984, Feb. 8

1664	A507	4d	Biathlon	.25	.25
1665	A507	4d	Giant slalom	.25	.25
1666	A507	5d	Bobsledding	.25	.25
1667	A507	5d	Slalom	.25	.25
1668	A507	16.50d	Speed skating	.40	.40
1669	A507	16.50d	Hockey	.40	.40
1670	A507	23.70d	Ski jumping	.45	.45
1671	A507	23.70d	Downhill skiing	.45	.45
		Nos. 1664-1671 (8)		2.70	2.70

Souvenir Sheets
Imperf

1672	A507	50d	Flame, rings	1.40	1.40
1673	A507	100d	Flame, map	2.75	2.75

No. 1664-1671 exist imperf.

Natl. Heroines
A508

Designs: a, Marija Bursac (1902-43). b, Jelena Cetkovic (1916-43). c, Nada Dimic (1923-42). d, Elpida Karamandi (1920-42). e, Toncka Cec Olga (1906-1943). f, Spasenija Babovic Cana (1907-77). g, Jovanka Radivojevic Kica (1922-43). h, Sonja Marinkovic (1916-41).

1984, Mar. 8   Litho.   Perf. 14

1674		Sheet of 8 + label	3.50	3.50
a.-h.	A508	5d any single	.25	.25

Slovenia
Monetary
Institute,
40th Anniv.
A509

1984, Mar. 12   Perf. 12½

1675	A509	5d Bond, note	.25	.25

Railroad Service in Serbia (Belgrade-Nis) Centenary — A510

5d, Train, Central Belgrade Station.

1984, Apr. 9   Perf. 13

1676	A510	5d multicolored	.25	.25

Jure Franko,
Giant Slalom
Silver Medalist,
1984 — A511

1984, Apr. 28

1677	A511	23.70d multi	.80	.80

Yugoslavia's first Winter Olympic medalist.

Europa (1959-84)
A512

1984, Apr. 30   Perf. 13½

1678	A512	23.70d multi	.40	.40
1679	A512	50d multi	.80	.80

1984 Summer
Olympics, Los
Angeles
A513

1984, May 14

1680	A513	5d	Basketball	.55	.55
1681	A513	16.50d	Diving	.55	.55
1682	A513	23.70d	Equestrian	.55	.55
1683	A513	50d	Running	2.00	2.00
		Nos. 1680-1683 (4)		3.65	3.65

Marshal
Tito — A514

1984, May 25   Perf. 13

1684	A514	5d brown red	.25	.25

Nature Type of 1983

Designs: 26d, Centaurea gloriosa (flower), Biokovo Mountain Park. 40d, Anophthalmus (insect), Pekel Cave, Savinja Valley.

1984, June 11   Litho.   Perf. 13½

1685	A495	26d multicolored	.50	.25
1686	A495	40d multicolored	.80	.40

Bird Type of 1982

4d, Great black-backed gull. 5d, Black-headed gull. 16.50d, Herring gull. 40d, Common tern.

1984, June 28

1687	A461	4d multicolored	.40	.40
1688	A461	5d multicolored	.40	.40
1689	A461	16.50d multicolored	.40	.40
1690	A461	40d multicolored	3.50	1.50
		Nos. 1687-1690 (4)	4.70	2.70

19th Cent.
Cradles
A515

1984, Sept. 1   Litho.   Perf. 12½

1691	A515	4d Bosnia & Herzegovina	.25	.25
1692	A515	5d Montenegro	.25	.25
1693	A515	26d Macedonia	.40	.40
1694	A515	40d Serbia	.65	.65
		Nos. 1691-1694 (4)	1.55	1.55

Olive Tree,
Mirovica
A516

1984, Sept. 1

1695	A516	5d multi	.25	.25

Joy of
Europe — A517

Children's Drawings: 26d, Traditional costumes. 40d, Girl with doll carriage.

1984, Oct. 2   Litho.   Perf. 14

1696	A517	26d multicolored	.35	.35
1697	A517	40d multicolored	.90	.90

City of
Virovitica,
750th
Anniv.
A518

5d, Engraving, 17th cent.

1984, Oct. 4   Perf. 13½

1698	A518	5d multicolored	.25	.25

Map, Concentric
Waves — A519

1984, Oct. 10

1699	A519	6d Prus bl & brt grn	.25	.25

Radio and telegraph service in Montenegro, 80th anniv.

Veterans
Conference
A520

1984, Oct. 18

1700	A520	26d multicolored	.90	.90
1701	A520	40d multicolored	1.20	1.20

Conf. of Veterans on Security, Disarmament & Cooperation in Europe, Belgrade, 10/18-20.

Liberation of
Belgrade, 40th
Anniv. — A521

1984, Oct. 20

1702	A521	6d "40," arms	.25	.25

Miloje Milojevic
(1884-1946),
Composer
A522

1984, Oct. 27

1703	A522	6d Portrait, score	.25	.25

Medals Events,
1984 Summer
Olympics
A522a

Designs: a, Wrestling. b, Running. c, Field hockey. d, Shot put. e, Soccer. f, Basketball. g, Netball. h, Rowing.

1984, Nov. 14   Litho.   Perf. 13½

1704		Sheet of 8	4.00	4.00
a.-h.	A522a	26d any single	.25	.25

The Tahitians, by Gauguin — A523

Paintings by Foreign Artists in Yugoslav Museums: 6d, Portrait of Madame Tatichek, by Ferdinand Waldmuller (1793-1865). No. 1706, The Bathers, by Renoir (1841-1919). No. 1707, At the Window, by Henri Matisse (1869-1954). 40d, Ballerinas, by Edgar Degas (1834-1917).

Perf. 13½x14, 14x13½

1984, Nov. 15

1705	A523	6d multi, vert.	.25	.25
1706	A523	26d multi, vert.	.25	.25
1707	A523	26d multi, vert.	.25	.25
1708	A523	38d multi	.50	.50
1709	A523	40d multi	.80	.80
		Nos. 1705-1709 (5)	2.05	2.05

Nova
Macedonia
Newspaper,
40th Anniv.
A523a

1984, Nov. 29   Perf. 13½

1710	A523a	6d 1st & recent editions	.25	.25

Nos. 1602, 1599 and
1637 Surcharged in
Red Brown or Black

Types of 1975 and

Exhibition
Center,
Zagreb
A524

Bird, Jet,
Landscape
A525

Designs: 6d, Kikinda. 26d, Korcula. 38d, Maribor. 70d, Trumpeter monument, riverside buildings in Zagreb. 1000d, bird, tail of jet on airfield.

**Perf. 13½x12½, 13 (#1713, 1717),
12½ (#1715)**

1984-86   Litho.

1711	A263	2d on 8.80d	1.75	1.75
a.		on #1602a	.40	.25
1712	A263	6d on 4d (RBr)	.40	.25
a.		on #1599a	.55	.40
1713	A323	6d lt red brn	.40	.25
a.		Perf. 13x12½	.80	.25
1715	A493	20d on 23.70d	.40	.25
1717	A263	26d dp ultra	.40	.25
a.		Perf. 13x12½	.50	.25

1718	A323	38d dp lil rose	1.60	.25
a.		Perf. 13	.40	.25
1719	A323	70d brt ultra ('85)	1.25	.55
b.		Perf. 13	.55	.45

Perf. 14

1719A	A524	100d brt org yel & vio	.65	.35

Perf. 12½

1720	A525	500d redsh brn & multi ('85)	3.75	1.40
a.		Perf. 13¼	1.75	.65
1721	A525	1000d org brn & multi ('85)	5.50	2.90
a.		Perf. 13½	2.10	1.25
		Nos. 1711-1721 (10)	16.10	8.20

Type styles for Nos. 1717-1718 differ somewhat from illustration.
For surcharge, see No. 1973.

Museum Exhibits - Fossils
A526

5d, Aturia aturi. 6d, Pachyophis woodwardi. 33d, Chaetodon hoeferi. 60d, Homo sapiens neanderthalensis.

1985, Feb. 4   Litho.   Perf. 12½

1722	A526	5d multi	.25	.25
1723	A526	6d multi	.25	.25
1724	A526	33d multi	.40	.40
1725	A526	60d multi	.90	.90
		Nos. 1722-1725 (4)	1.80	1.80

40th Anniv., Monument Protection
A527

1985, Feb. 20   Litho.   Perf. 12½

1726	A527	6d Hopovo church	.25	.25

Ski Jumping at Planica, 50th Anniv. — A528

1985, Mar. 15   Litho.   Perf. 13½

1727	A528	6d Three herons in flight	4.75	2.40

European Nature Conservation
A529

1985, Mar. 30   Perf. 14

1728	A529	42d Pandion haliaetus	1.25	.80
1729	A529	60d Upupa epops	2.40	1.25

Audubon birth bicentenary, European Information Center for Nature Protection.

A530

Fresco of St. Methodius, St. Naum Monastery, Ohrid.

1985, Apr. 6   Litho.   Perf. 11½x12

1730	A530	10d multicolored	1.75	.80

St. Methodius (d. 885), archbishop of Pannonia and Moravia.

A531

1985, Apr. 16   Litho.   Perf. 12½

1731	A531	6d Clasped hands	.25	.25

Osimo Agreements, 10th anniv. Yugoslavia-Italy political and economic cooperation.

Josip Slavenski (1896-1955), Composer
A532

Europa: 60d, Portrait, block flute, darabukka. 80d, Balkanophonia score, signature.

1985, Apr. 29   Perf. 14

1732	A532	60d multi	.40	.40
1733	A532	80d multi	.80	.80

Joachim Vujic, by Dimitrije Avramovic (1815-1855)
A533

1985, May 8   Perf. 12x11½

1734	A533	10d multi	.25	.25

Joachim Vujic Theater, Kragujevac, 150th anniv.

Liberation from German Occupation Forces, 40th Anniv. — A534

1985, May 9   Perf. 13½

1735	A534	10d shown	.25	.25
1736	A534	10d Order of Natl. Liberation	.25	.25

Franjo Kluz (1912-1944), Rudi Cajavec (1911-1942), Breguet-19 Fighter — A535

1985, May 21   Perf. 13x12½

1737	A535	10d multi	.25	.25

Air Force Day.

Pres. Tito (1892-1980)
A536

1985, May 25   Perf. 13½

1738	A536	10d Portrait	.50	.25

Cres-Losinj Municipal Tourism Bureau, Cent. — A537

1985, June 12

1739	A537	10d Map, town arms, villa	.65	.65

UN 40th Anniv. — A538

1985, June 26   Litho.   Perf. 12½

1740	A538	70d Emblem, rainbow	.25	.25

Rowing — A539

1985, June 29   Litho.   Perf. 13½

1741	A539	70d multicolored	.40	.40

Souvenir Sheet

1742	A539	100d Course map, arms	1.40	1.40

Intl. European-Danube Rowing Regatta, 30th anniv.

Nautical Tourism — A540

1985, July 1   Litho.

1743	A540	8d Sailboat	.80	.80
1744	A540	10d Windsurfing	.80	.80
1745	A540	50d Sailboat, diff.	.80	.80
1746	A540	70d Sailboat, diff.	2.50	2.50
		Nos. 1743-1746 (4)	4.90	4.90

F1B Class Motorized Model Plane
A541

1985, Aug. 10   Litho.   Perf. 12½x13

1747	A541	70d multicolored	.50	.40

Free Flight World Championships, Livno, Aug. 12-18.

Algae — A542

8d, Corallina officinalis. 10d, Desmarestia viridis. 50d, Fucus vesiculosus. 70d, Padina pavonia.

1985, Sept. 20   Perf. 14

1748	A542	8d multicolored	.25	.25
1749	A542	10d multicolored	.25	.25
1750	A542	50d multicolored	.30	.30
1751	A542	70d multicolored	1.50	1.50
		Nos. 1748-1751 (4)	2.30	2.30

Intl. Federation of Stomatologists, 73rd Congress, Belgrade, Sept. 21-28 — A543

1985, Sept. 21   Perf. 12x11½

1752	A543	70d multicolored	.40	.40

Children's Drawings
A544

Designs: 50d, Children in a Horse-drawn Cart, by Branka Lukic, age 14, Yugoslavia. 70d, Children in Field, by Suzanne Straathof, age 9, Netherlands.

1985, Oct. 2   Perf. 14

1753	A544	50d multicolored	.40	.40
1754	A544	70d multicolored	1.25	1.25

Croatian Natl. Theater, Zagreb, 125th Anniv.
A545

1985, Nov. 23   Perf. 12½

1755	A545	10d Facade detail	.25	.25

Miladin Popovic — A546

1985, Nov. 26   Perf. 11½x12

1756	A546	10d Portrait	.25	.25

Popovic (1910-1945), revolutionary.

Natl. Coat of Arms — A547

1985, Nov. 28   *Perf. 13½*
1757   A547   10d multicolored   .25   .25

Souvenir Sheet
Imperf
1758   A547   100d multicolored   1.00 1.00

Socialist Federal Republic of Yugoslavia, 40th anniv. No. 1758 contains one stamp 18x27mm.

Royal Procession, by Iromie Wijewardena, Sri Lanka — A548

Paintings from the Art Gallery of Non-aligned Countries, Titograd: 10d, Return from Hunting, by Mama Cangare, Mali. No. 1761, Drum of Coca, by Agnes Ovando Sanz De Franck, Bolivia. No. 1762, The Cock, by Mariano Rodriguez, Cuba, vert. 70d, Three Women, by Quamrul Hassan, Bangladesh, vert.

1985, Dec. ?   *Perf. 14*
1759   A548   8d multicolored   .25   .25
1760   A548   10d multicolored   .25   .25
1761   A548   50d multicolored   .25   .25
1762   A548   50d multicolored   .25   .25
1763   A548   70d multicolored   1.40 1.40
    Nos. 1759-1763 (5)   2.40 2.40

Nos. 1243, 1482, 1485a, 1490, 1491, 1713a, 1717a, 1603A and 1718 Srchd. in Light Red Brown, Brown or Dark Brown

1985-86   **Litho.**   *Perf. 13½, 13½x12½*
1764   A323   1d on 25p (B)   .80   .25
1765   A263   2d on 5p (DB)   .40   .25
  a.   on #1482a   .40   .25
1766   A263   3d on 35p (DB)   .25   .25
  a.   on #1485a   .25   .25
1767   A323   4d on 5.60d (B)   .25   .25
  b.   on #1490   .80   .50
1767A   A323   5d on 8d (B)   .40   .25
  c.   on #1491a   .80   .80
1768   A323   8d on 6d   .25   .25
  a.   on #1713   .25   .25
1769   A263   20d on 26d   .25   .25
  a.   on #1717   7.00 4.00
1770   A323   50d on 16.50d (B)   .80   .40
  a.   on #1603c   .80   .40
1771   A323   70d on 38d   .80   .50
    Nos. 1764-1771 (9)   4.20 2.65

Issued: #1767A, 3/17/86; others, 12/85.

Natl. Automobile Assoc., 40th Anniv. A549

1986, Feb. 25   *Perf. 12½*
1772   A549   10d Car   .25   .25
1773   A549   70d Helicopter   .80   .80

Tara River, Montenegro A550

1986, Mar. 3   *Perf. 14*
1774   A550   100d Canyon   .40   .40
1775   A550   150d Bridge   .80   .80

European nature protection. Sheets of 9.

Studenica Monastery, 800th Anniv. — A551

1986, Mar. 15   *Perf. 13½*
1776   A551   10d Chapel of Our Lady   .55   .40

A552

Various soccer plays.

1986, Apr. 5   **Litho.**   *Perf. 14*
1777   A552   70d multi   .65   .65
1778   A552   150d multi   .80   .80

1986 World Cup Soccer Championships, Mexico.

Arrival of St. Clement in Ohrid, 1100th Anniv. A553

1986, Apr. 12   *Perf. 12½*
1779   A553   10d Township model   5.00 5.00

Europa Issue

Brain, Mushroom Cloud — A554

1986, Apr. 28   *Perf. 14*
1780   A554   100d shown   .40   .40
1781   A554   200d Injured deer   1.20 .80

European Men's Senior Judo Championships, Belgrade, May 8-11 — A555

1986, May 7   *Perf. 12½*
1782   A555   70d multi   .50   .40

Natl. Costumes — A556

a, Slovenia. b, Vojvodina. c, Croatia. d, Macedonia. e, Serbia. f, Montenegro. g, Kosovo. h, Bosnia & Herzegovina.

Yachts, Moscenika Draga Bay — A557

1986, May 22   **Litho.**   *Perf. 12x13*
Booklet Stamps
1783   Bklt. pane of 8   4.50
  a.-h.   A556 50d any single   .55   .55

1986, May 23   *Perf. 14*
1784   A557   50d multi   .25   .25
1785   A557   80d multi, diff.   .40   .40

Souvenir Sheet
Imperf
1786   A557   100d multi   3.25 3.25

European Sailing Championships, Croatia, May 29-June 7, Flying Dutchman Class. No. 1786 contains one stamp 22x28mm.

Marshal Tito — A557a

1986, May 24   *Perf. 13x12½*
1787   A557a   10d multicolored   .25   .25

Moths and Butterflies A558

1986, May 26   *Perf. 14*
1788   A558   10d Eudia pavonia   .80   .80
1789   A558   20d Inachis io   .80   .80
1790   A558   50d Parnassius apollo   .80   .80
1791   A558   100d Apatura iris   1.60 1.60
    Nos. 1788-1791 (4)   4.00 4.00

Ancient Manuscripts A558a

Designs: 10d, Evangelical, 18th cent. 20d, Leontijevo Evangelical, 16th cent. 50d, Astrological, Mesopotamia, 15th cent. 100d, Hebrew Haggadah, Spain, 14th cent.

1986, June 12   **Litho.**   *Perf. 14*
1792   A558a   10d multicolored   .25   .25
1793   A558a   20d multicolored   .25   .25
1794   A558a   50d multicolored   .40   .40
1795   A558a   100d multicolored   .80   .65
    Nos. 1792-1795 (4)   1.70 1.55

A559

A560

Designs: 20d, Postman on motorcycle. 30d, Postman, resident. 40d, Forklift, mail pallets. 50d, Mail train. 60d, Man posting letters in mailbox. 93d, Open envelope and greetings telegram form. 100d, Postman, mail van. No. 1803, Computer operator facing right. No. 1804, 140d, Computer operator facing left. 120d, Woman sending love letter. 200d, Freighter in high seas. 500d, Postal employee sorting mail. 1000d, Woman at telephone station. 2000d, Aircraft, hemispheres on world map. 30d, 60d, 93d, 106d, 120d, 140d, 500d, 1000d vert.

Perf. 13½, 12½x13½ (20d, 40d, 50d), 14 (100d)

1986-88   **Litho.**
1796   A559   20d brt pink   .40   .25
  a.   Perf. 13   .40   .25
1797   A559   30d lt brn vio   .40   .25
  a.   Perf. 13x12½   .80   .25
1798   A559   40d brt red   .40   .25
  a.   Perf. 13   .40   .25
1799   A559   50d violet   .40   .25
  a.   Perf. 13   .25   .25
1800   A559   60d lt sage grn   .40   .25
1801   A559   93d ultra   .40   .25
1802   A559   100d dl magenta   .80   .30
1803   A559   106d rose red   .40   .25
1804   A559   106d brn org   .40   .25
1805   A559   120d dull blue grn   .25   .25
1806   A559   140d dull rose   .25   .25
1807   A559   200d greenish bl   1.00 .40
  a.   Perf. 12½   2.00 1.60
  b.   Perf. 12½x13½   6.00 2.00
1808   A559   500d deep blue & beige   .40   .40
1809   A559   500d chalky blue & yel   .25   .25
1810   A559   1000d vio & blue grn   .25   .25
  b.   Perf. 12½   .55   .50
1810A   A560   2000d brt blue, red & brt vio   1.00 .50
    Nos. 1796-1810A (16)   7.40 4.60

Size of No. 1802: 19½x18mm.
Issued: 20d, 3/17; 50d, 200d, 6/4; 40d, 7/17; 100d, 6/12; 30d, 7/26; 60d, 6/5/87; #1803, 12/10/87; 93d, 12/16/87; #1804, 1/22/88; #1808, 4/29/88; 1000d, 7/21/88; 20d, 140d, 2000d, #1809, 9/5/88.
See Nos. 1935-1945, 2004-2007, 2013-2015, 2021. For surcharges see Nos. 1877, 1912-1913, 1947-1948, 1972, 1974-1975, 2017, 2019, 2048-2051, 2053.

13th Communist Federations Congress (SKJ) A561

1986, June 25   *Perf. 12½*
1811   A561   10d shown   .25   .25
1812   A561   20d Star   .25   .25

Souvenir Sheet
Imperf
1813   A561   100d Tito   .80   .80

Trubar, Abecedarian Manuscript Title Page A562

1986, June 28   **Litho.**   *Perf. 12½x13*
1814   A562   20d multi   .55   .40

Primoz Trubar (1508-1568), Slovenian philologist and religious reformer.

Serbian Natl. Theater, Novi Sad, 125th Anniv. — A563

1986, July 28   *Perf. 14*
1815 A563 40d Thalia   .25 .25

Rugovo Dance, Kosovo Province — A564

1986, Sept. 10
1816 A564 40d multi   .25 .25

1987 Universiade Games, Zagreb, July 8-19 — A565

1986, Sept. 22   *Perf. 13½*
1817 A565 30d Volleyball   .35 .35
1818 A565 40d Canoeing   .35 .35
1819 A565 100d Gymnastics   .55 .55
1820 A565 150d Fencing   .80 .80
   Nos. 1817-1820 (4)   2.05 2.05

18th Joy of Europe Youth Conference A566

Children's drawings: 100d, Dove, by Tanja Faletic, 14. 150d, Buildings, by Johanna Kraus, 12, DDR.

1986, Oct. 2   *Perf. 14*
1821 A566 100d multicolored   .55 .55
1822 A566 150d multicolored   .80 .80

Rotary Switching Apparatus, Village of Bled — A567

1986, Oct. 4   *Perf. 13½*
1823 A567 40d multicolored   .25 .25

Telephone exchanges connected with automatic switching equipment, 50th anniv.

INTERPOL 55th General Assembly, Belgrade, Oct. 6-13 — A568

1986, Oct. 6   *Perf. 14*
1824 A568 150d multicolored   .40 .40

Intl. Brigades, 50th Anniv. — A569

1986, Oct. 21   *Perf. 13½*
1825 A569 40d multicolored   .25 .25

Intl. Peace Year — A570

1986, Nov. 20
1826 A570 150d multicolored   .50 .50

Serbian Academy of the Arts and Sciences, Cent. A571

1986, Nov. 1   **Photo.**   *Perf. 13½*
1827 A571 40d multicolored   .25 .25

Paintings by Foreign Artists in the Museum of Contemporary Art, Skopje — A572

No. 1828, Still Life, by Frantisek Muzika, Czechoslovakia. #1829, Disturance, by Rafael Canogar, England. #1830, Iol, by Victor Vasarely, France. #1831, Portrait, by Bernard Buffet, France. #1832, Woman's Head, by Pablo Picasso, Spain.

1986, Dec. 10   **Litho.**   *Perf. 14*
1828 A572 30d multi   .25 .25
1829 A572 40d multi   .25 .25
1830 A572 100d multi, vert.   .40 .40
1831 A572 100d multi, vert.   .40 .40
1832 A572 150d multi, vert.   .65 .65
   Nos. 1828-1832 (5)   1.95 1.95

Wildlife Conservation A573

30d, Lutra lutra. 40d, Ovis musimon. 100d, Cervus elaphus. 150d, Ursus arctos.

1987, Jan. 22   **Litho.**   *Perf. 13½x14*
1833   Strip of 4 + label   8.00 8.00
  a.   A573 30d multi   .65 .65
  b.   A573 40d multi   .65 .65
  c.   A573 100d multi   .65 .65
  d.   A573 150d multi   .65 .65

   Label pictures nature reserve.

Rudjer Boscovich (1711-1787), Scientist, and Solar Eclipse over Brera Observatory, Italy — A574

1987, Feb. 13   *Perf. 14*
1834 A574 150d multicolored   .50 .40

European Nature Protection — A575

1987, Mar. 9
1835 A575 150d shown   1.00 1.00
1836 A575 400d Triglav glacial lake   1.50 1.50

1987 World Alpine Skiing Championships, Crans Montana — A576

1987, Mar. 20   **Litho.**   *Perf. 14*
1837 A576 200d multicolored   2.40 2.40

   No. 1837 printed in sheets of 8 plus center label.

Natl. Civil Aviation, 60th Anniv. A577

1987, Mar. 20   *Perf. 14*
1838 A577 150d POTEZ-29   .55 .55
1839 A577 400d DC-10   1.20 1.20

Each printed in sheets of 8 plus center label.

Kole Nedelkovski (1912-1941), Poet, Revolutionary A578

1987, Apr. 2   *Perf. 13½*
1840 A578 40d multicolored   .25 .25

Liberation of Montenegro from Turkey, 125th Anniv. A579

1987, Apr. 16   *Perf. 13½*
1841 A579 40d Battle flags, folk guitar   .25 .25

Slovenian Communist Party, Cebine, 50th Anniv. — A580

1987, Apr. 18   *Perf. 14*
1842 A580 40d multicolored   .25 .25

Europa Issue

Tito Bridge, Krk — A581

1987, Apr. 30   **Litho.**   *Perf. 14*
1843 A581 200d shown   .40 .40
1844 A581 400d Bridges over canal   .80 .80

Fruit Trees — A582

1987, May 15   **Litho.**   *Perf. 14*
1845 A582 60d Almond   .30 .30
1846 A582 150d Pear   .90 .90
1847 A582 200d Apple   1.10 1.10
1848 A582 400d Plum   2.25 2.25
   Nos. 1845-1848 (4)   4.55 4.55

Tito, 1930, by Mosa Pijade — A583

1987, May 25
1849 A583 60d multi   .30 .25

   50th anniv. of Tito's assumption of Yugoslavian communist party leadership.

Vuk Stefanovik Karadzic (1787-1864), Linguist and Historian — A584

60d, Bust by Petar Ubavkic, his Trsic residence & Vienna. 200d, Portrait by Uros Knezevic, & alphabet from Karadzic's Serbian Dictionary, 1818.

1987, June 10
1850 A584 60d multi   .25 .25
1851 A584 200d multi   .40 .40

Zrenjanin Postal Service, 250th Anniv. A585

1987, June 22   *Perf. 13½*
1852 A585 60d multi   .25 .25

UNIVERSIADE '87, Zagreb, July 8-19 — A586

1987, July 8   Litho.   Perf. 13½
1853	A586	60d Hurdling	.25	.25
1854	A586	150d Basketball	.40	.40
1855	A586	200d Balance beam	.55	.55
1856	A586	400d Swimming	1.25	1.25
		Nos. 1853-1856 (4)	2.45	2.45

Each printed in sheets of eight plus label.

Fire Fighting A587

1987, July 20   Perf. 14
1857	A587	60d Canadair CL-215 spraying forest	.25	.25
1858	A587	200d Fire boat	.25	.25

Each printed in sheets of eight plus label.

Monument, Anindol Park, Samobor — A588

1987, Aug. 1   Perf. 13½
1859	A588	60d multi	.25	.25

Communist Party of Croatia, 50th anniv.

Sabac High School, 150th Anniv. A589

1987, Sept. 10   Litho.   Perf. 13½
1860	A589	80d multi	.25	.25

Exhibition Emblem, Balkan Peninsula, Flowers A590

Clock Tower, Petrovaradin Fortress and Novi Sad — A591

1987, Sept. 19   Perf. 14
1861	A590	250d multi	.40	.40

Souvenir Sheet
Imperf
1862	A591	400d multi	1.00	1.00

BALKANFILA XI, Novi Sad, Sept. 19-26.

19th Joy of Europe Conference A592

Children's drawings: 250d, Girls in forest, by Bedic Aranka, Juguoslavia. 400d, Scarecrow, by Schaffer Ingeborg, Austria.

1987, Oct. 2   Litho.   Perf. 14
1863	A592	250d multi	.75	.75
1864	A592	400d multi	.80	.80

Printed in sheets of nine.

Bridges A593

80d, Arslanagica, Trebinje, 16th cent. 250d, Terzija, Djakovica, 15th cent.

1987, Oct. 15
1865	A593	80d multi	.40	.40
1866	A593	250d multi	.40	.40

Ship, Dunav-Tisa Channel A594

1987, Oct. 20   Perf. 13½
1867	A594	80d multi	.25	.25

City of Titov Vrbas, 600th anniv.

Astronomical and Meteorological Observatory, Belgrade, Cent. — A595

1987, Nov. 21   Perf. 14
1868	A595	80d multi	.25	.25

St. Luke the Evangelist, by Raphael A596

Paintings by foreign artists in national museums: 200d, Infanta Maria Theresa, by Velazquez. 250d, Nicholas Rubens, Painter's Son, by Rubens. 400d, Louis Laure Sennegon, Painter's Niece, by Jean-Baptiste-Camille Corot (1796-1875).

1987, Nov. 28
1869	A596	80d shown	.25	.25
1870	A596	200d multi	.40	.40
1871	A596	250d multi	.40	.40
1872	A596	400d multi	1.10	1.10
		Nos. 1869-1872 (4)	2.15	2.15

Traditional Competitions A597

80d, Bull fighting. 200d, Ljubicevo Horse Games. 250d, Moresca game. 400d, Sinj iron ring.

1987, Dec. 10
1873	A597	80d multi	.25	.25
1874	A597	200d multi	.40	.40
1875	A597	250d multi	.40	.40
1876	A597	400d multi	1.50	1.50
		Nos. 1873-1876 (4)	2.55	2.55

No. 1800 Surcharged

1987, Sept. 22   Perf. 13½
1877	A559	80d on 60d sg grn	.40	.25

Vinodol Codex, City of Vinodolski, Coat of Arms — A598

1988, Jan. 6   Litho.   Perf. 14
1878	A598	100d multi	.25	.25

Vinodol Codex, 700th anniv.

Intl. Women's Golden Fox Skiing Championships, 25th Anniv. — A599

1988, Jan. 30
1879	A599	350d Slalom, emblem, Mirobor City	.25	.25

Printed in sheets of eight plus center label.

World Wildlife Fund — A600

Brown bears (Ursus arctos).

1988, Feb. 1
1880	A600	70d Cub	2.40	1.60
1881	A600	80d Cubs	2.40	1.60
1882	A600	200d Adult, head	2.40	1.60
1883	A600	350d Adult	9.00	4.75
		Nos. 1880-1883 (4)	16.20	9.55

1988 Winter Olympics, Calgary — A601

1988, Feb. 13   Perf. 14x13½
1884	A601	350d Slalom	.85	.85
1885	A601	1200d Ice hockey	1.25	1.25

Each printed in sheets of 8 plus center label.

Souvenir Sheet

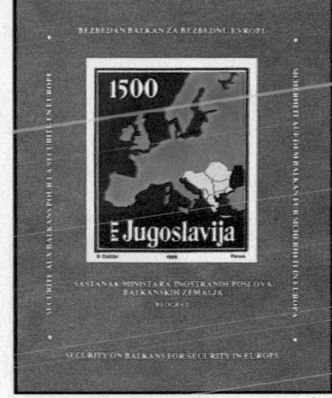

Map of Europe Highlighting Balkan Nations — A602

1988, Feb. 24   Litho.   Imperf.
1886	A602	1500d multi	1.75	1.75

Congress of Foreign Affairs Ministers from the Balkan Countries, Belgrade, Feb. 24-26.

1988 Summer Olympics, Seoul — A603

South Korean Landscape — A604

1988, Mar. 21   *Perf. 14x13½*
1887 A603 106d Basketball   .55   .55
1888 A603 450d High jump   .55   .55
1889 A603 500d Pommel horse   .55   .55
1890 A603 1200d Boxing   .55   .55
    Nos. 1887-1890 (4)   2.20 2.20
Souvenir Sheet
Imperf
1891 A604 1500d multi   2.00 2.00
   Nos. 1887-1890 printed in sheets of 8 plus center label.

Europa Issue

Telecommunications — A605

1988, Apr. 30   **Litho.**   *Perf. 13½x14*
1892 A605 450d shown   .45   .45
1893 A605 1200d Transportation   .80   .80

Sea Shells — A606

   106d, Gibbula magus. 550d, Pecten jacobaeus. 600d, Tonna galea. 1000d, Argonauta argo.

1988, May 14
1894 A606 106d multicolored   .65   .50
1895 A606 550d multicolored   .65   .50
1896 A606 600d multicolored   1.00   .80
1897 A606 1000d multicolored   1.50   .80
    Nos. 1894-1897 (4)   3.80 2.60

Trial of Tito and Five Comrades, 60th Anniv. — A607

1988, May 25
1898 A607 106d black & brn   .25   .25

Palace of Princess Ljubica of Serbia, 1st University Building A608

1988, June 14   **Litho.**   *Perf. 13½*
1899 A608 106d multi   .25   .25
   Belgrade University, 150th anniv.

Flowers — A609

   600d, Phelypaea boissieri. 1000d, Campanula formanekiana.

1988, July 2   *Perf. 14*
1900 A609 600d multicolored   .80   .80
1901 A609 1000d multicolored   1.25 1.25
   European Nature Protection.

Esperanto, Cent. — A610

1988, July 14   *Perf. 13½*
1902 A610 600d dull vio & ol grn   .80   .55
   Printed in sheets of 8 plus center label.

Cargo Ships — A611

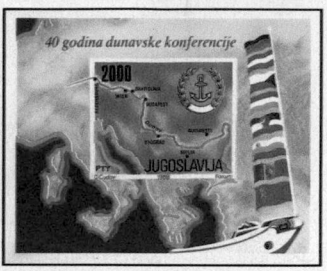

Map of the Danube Basin — A612

1988, Aug. 18   **Litho.**   *Perf. 14*
1903 A611 1000d multi   .50   .50
Souvenir Sheet
Imperf
1904 A612 2000d multi   3.25 3.25
   Danube Conference, 40th anniv.

13th European Junior Basketball Championships, Aug. 21-28 — A613

1988, Aug. 20   *Perf. 14*
1905 A613 600d multi   .40   .40

1st Horse Race in Belgrade, 125th Anniv. — A614

1988, Aug. 27
1906 A614 140d Thoroughbred racing   .40   .40
1907 A614 600d Steeplechase   .80   .80
1908 A614 1000d Harness racing   1.20 1.20
    Nos. 1906-1908 (3)   2.40 2.40

Museum of Bosnia and Herzegovina, Sarajevo, Cent. A615

   140d, Museum, Bosnian bellflower.

1988, Sept. 10   *Perf. 13½*
1909 A615 140d multicolored   .25   .25

Anti-Cancer and AIDS Campaigns A616

   140d, Arm, lobster claw. 1000d, Blood, scream.

1988, Sept. 24   *Perf. 14*
1910 A616 140d multicolored   .25   .25
1911 A616 1000d multicolored   .65   .65

Nos. 1801 and 1804 Surcharged

1988, July   **Litho.**   *Perf. 13½*
1912 A559 120d on 93d ultra   .25   .25
1913 A559 140d on 106d brn org   .25   .25

Joy of Europe Youth Conference A617

   Portraits of girls by: 1000d, P. Ranosovic. 1100d, Renoir.

1988, Oct. 1   **Litho.**   *Perf. 14*
1914 A617 1000d multi   .65   .65
1915 A617 1100d multi   .80   .80
    See Nos. 1987-1988.

Slovenski Academy, 50th Anniv. — A618

1988, Oct. 13   **Litho.**   *Perf. 14*
1916 A618 200d multi   .25   .25

Museum Exhibits and Places of Origin A618a

   200d, Wood bassinet, traditional wedding (Galicka). #1918, Embroidery, man and woman wearing folk costumes of Vojvodina. #1919, Scimitar, flintlock, man & woman wearing folk costumes of Kotor (Bokelji). 1100d, Masks (Kurenti).

1988, Oct. 18
1917 A618a 200d multi, vert.   .65   .65
1918 A618a 1000d shown   .65   .65
1919 A618a 1000d multi, vert.   .65   .65
1920 A618a 1100d multi   .65   .65
    Nos. 1917-1920 (4)   2.60 2.60

Woman with Lyre, 4th Cent. B.C. — A618b

   Grecian terra cotta figurines: #1922, Eros & Psyche, 2nd cent. BC. #1923, Seated woman, 3rd cent. BC. 1100d, Woman by Stele, 3rd cent. BC.

1988, Oct. 28
1921 A618b 200d multi   .50   .50
1922 A618b 1000d multi   .50   .50
1923 A618b 1000d multi   .50   .50
1924 A618b 1100d multi   .50   .50
    Nos. 1921-1924 (4)   2.00 2.00

Peter II (1813-1851), Prince Bishop and Poet — A618c

   Portraits and: 200d, Cetinje Monastery and frontispiece of his principal work. 1000d, Njegos Mausoleum.

1988, Nov. 1
1925 A618c 200d multi   .25   .25
1926 A618c 1000d multi   .55   .55

Postal Service Types of 1986 and

Telephone Receiver and Telephone Card — A619

Bird, Posthorn, Simulated Stamp — A620

Propeller Plane, Two Arrows and Map — A621

   Designs: 170d, 300d, Flower, envelope, mailbox and simulated stamp. 220d, PTT emblem on simulated stamp, mail coach. 800d, Postman on motorcycle. No. 1941, Postman, resident. No. 1942, Mail train. No. 1943, Envelopes, satellite dish. No. 1944, Earth, telecommunications satellite. 100,000d, Bird, open envelope, flower. 170d, 220d, 300d, 2000d, 5000d, No. 1941 vert.

1988-89   **Litho.**   *Perf. 13¼*
1935 A559 170d dl grn   .40   .25
1936 A559 220d brn org   .40   .25
1937 A559 300d ver   .40   .25
1938 A559 800d brt ultra   .25   .25
1939 A619 2000d multi   .25   .25
1940 A620 5000d dk red & ultra   .80   .40
1941 A559 10,000d org & brt lil   .55   .55
1942 A559 20,000d lt ol grn & lt red brn   .55   .55

Perf. 13½
1943 A560 10,000d multi   1.25   .55
1944 A560 20,000d multi   .80   .55
1944A A621 50,000d org & dl bl   1.00   .40
1945 A560 100,000d org & dl grn   .25   .25
    Nos. 1935-1945 (12)   6.90 4.50

Perf. 12½
1937a A559 300d   .40   .25
1938a A559 800d   .25   .25
1939a A619 2000d   .25   .25
1940a A620 5000d   .80   .40
1941a A559 10,000d   .25   .25
1942a A559 20,000d   .25   .25
    Nos. 1937a-1941a (5)   1.95 1.40

   Issued: 1988 — 170d, 11/17; 220d, 12/6;
   1989 — 300d, 5/11; 800d, 2000d, 7/20; 5000d, 1/20; #1941, 11/28; #1942, 12/8; #1943, 3/20; #1944, 7/19; 50,000d, 11/8; 100,000d, 12/4.
   See Nos. 2008-2009, 2017, 2052. For surcharges see Nos. 1972, 1974, 2048.

Yugoslavia, 70th Anniv. — A622

1988, Dec. 1   Litho.   Perf. 14
1946 A622 200d Krsmanovic Hall,
Belgrade   .25 .25

Nos. 1805-1806 Surcharged
1988   Litho.   Perf. 13½
1947 A559 170d on 120d   .80 .25
1948 A559 220d on 140d   .80 .25

Issued: #1947, Dec. 21; #1948, Dec. 15.

Miniature Sheet

Victory of Yugoslavian Athletes at the
1988 Summer Olympics,
Seoul — A623

Medals and events: a, Women's air pistol.
b, Team handball. c, Table tennis. d, Wrestling.
e, Double sculls. f, Basketball. g, Water polo.
h, Boxing.

1988, Dec. 31   Litho.   Perf. 14
1949 A623 Sheet of 8 + label   3.00 3.00
a.-h.   500d any single   .30 .25

Ivan Gundulic
(1589-1638),
Poet — A624

1989, Jan. 7   Perf. 13½
1950 A624 220d multi   .40 .25

World Wildlife
Fund — A625

Ducks.

1989, Feb. 23   Litho.   Perf. 14
1951   Strip of 4 + label   14.00 8.00
a. A625 300d Anas platyrhynchos 1.25 .50
b. A625 2100d Anas crecca   3.50 1.75
c. A625 2200d Anas acuta   3.50 1.75
d. A625 2200d Anas clypeata   3.50 1.75

Printed in sheets of 20+5 labels. Label pictures WWF emblem.

Publication of The Glory of the Duchy
of Kranjska, by Johann Valvasor
(1641-1693), 300th Anniv.
A626

1989, Mar. 10   Perf. 13½
1952 A626 300d Portrait   .25 .25

Flowering
Plants — A627

300d, Bulbocodium vernum. 2100d,
Nymphaea alba. 2200d, Fritillaria degeniana,
vert. 3000d, Orchis simia, vert.

1989, Mar. 20   Perf. 14
1953 A627 300d multi   1.00 1.00
1954 A627 2100d multi   1.00 1.00
1955 A627 2200d multi   1.00 1.00
1956 A627 3000d multi   1.00 1.00
Nos. 1953-1956 (4)   4.00 4.00

6th World Air-Gun Championships,
Sarajevo, Apr. 27-30 — A628

1989, Apr. 26
1957 A628 3000d multi   .50 .50

Europa
1989 — A629

1989, Apr. 29
1958 A629 3000d shown   .80 .80
1959 A629 6000d Marbles   .80 .80

15th European
Trophy for Natl.
Athletic Club
Champions,
Belgrade, June 3-
4 — A630

1989, June 1   Litho.   Perf. 13½
1960 A630 4000d Pole vault   .80 .80
Printed in sheets of 8+label picturing flags of
participating nations.

Yugoslavia
Motorcycle
Grand Prix,
Rijeka, June
9-11 — A631

Various race scenes.

1989, June 9   Perf. 14
1961 A631 500d multi   .25 .25
1962 A631 4000d multi   .40 .40

Souvenir Sheet
Perf. 14x13½
1963 A631 6000d multi   1.50 1.50
No. 1963 contains one 54x35 stamp.

No. 1246 Surcharged
1989, Apr. 6   Litho.   Perf. 13
1964 A323 100d on 1d dull grn   .40 .25
a.   Perf. 13x12½   .40 .40

Tito — A632

1989, May 25   Perf. 13½x14
1965 A632 300d multi   .25 .25

Early
Adriatic
Ships
A633

a, Ancient Greek galley. b, Roman galley. c,
Crusade galleon, 13th cent. d, Nava of
Dubrovnik, 16th cent. e, French ship, 17th
cent. f, Vessels, 18th cent. 3000d, View of
Dubrovnik seaport, called Ragusa in Italian,
from a 17th cent. engraving.

1989, June 10   Perf. 13½
1966   Block of 6   2.00 1.50
a.-f.   A633 1000d any single   .30 .25
Souvenir Sheet
1967 A633 3000d multi   .75 .35
No. 1967 contains one 75x32mm stamp.
Nos. 1966-1967 printed se-tenant and sold
folded in booklet cover.

26th European Basketball
Championships — A634

Map of Europe, basketball and flags of: No.
1968, France, Yugoslavia, Greece, Bulgaria.
No. 1969, Netherlands, Italy, Russia, Spain.

1989, June 20   Litho.   Perf. 13½x14
1968 A634 2000d multi   .25 .25
1969 A634 2000d multi   .25 .25
Nos. 1968-1969 exist with setenant label.

Defeat of the Serbians at the Battle of
Kosovo, 1389 — A635

1989, June 28
1970 A635 500d multi   .25 .25

Danilovgrad
Library, Cent. —
A636

1989, July 15   Litho.   Perf. 13½
1971 A636 500d multi   .25 .25

**Nos. 1797, 1719, 1935, 1936
Surcharged**
1989
1972 A559 400d on 30d lt brn vio   .80 .25
1973 A323 700d on 70d brt ultra   .80 .25
1974 A559 700d on 170d dull
green   .80 .25
1975 A559 700d on 220d brn org   .80 .25
Nos. 1972-1975 (4)   3.20 1.00

Issued: #1975, 7/19; #1974, 8/10; #1972,
8/23; #1973, 12/13.

Kulin Ban
Charter,
800th
Anniv.
A638

1989, Aug. 29   Litho.   Perf. 14
1976 A638 500d multi   .25 .25

World Rowing
Championships
A639

1989, Sept. 2   Perf. 13½
1977 A639 10,000d multi   .50 .50

Interparliamentary Union,
Cent. — A640

Architecture: No. 1978, Parliament, London
(emblem at R). No. 1979, Notre Dame Cathedral (emblem at L).

1989, Sept. 4   Perf. 13½x14
1978 A640 10,000d multi   .40 .40
1979 A640 10,000d multi   .40 .40

A641

View of Belgrade and Maps
BEOGRAD '89 — A642

Architecture & antiquities of non-aligned
summit host cities: #1980, Belgrade '61, Cairo

'64. #1981, Lusaka '70, Algiers '73. #1982, Colombo '76, Havana '79. #1983, New Delhi '83, Harare '76.

1989, Sept. 4
1980	A641	10,000d multi	.25	.25
1981	A641	10,000d multi	.25	.25
1982	A641	10,000d multi	.25	.25
1983	A641	10,000d multi	.25	.25
		Nos. 1980-1983 (4)	1.00	1.00

Souvenir Sheet
Perf. 14
1984	A642	20,000d multi	1.25	1.25

European Nature Protection A643

8000d, Paeonia officinalis, Brezovica-Jazinac Lake. 10,000d, Paeonia corallina, Mirusa Canyon.

1989, Sept. 11 **Perf. 14**
1985	A643	8000d multi	.40	.40
1986	A643	10,000d multi	.40	.40

Joy of Europe Type of 1988
Portraits of children: No. 1987, Child with Lamb, by Jovan Popovic. No. 1988, Girl Feeding Dog, by Albert Cuyp (1620-1691).

1989, Oct. 2 **Litho.** **Perf. 14**
1987	A617	10,000d multi	.50	.50
1988	A617	10,000d multi	.50	.50

Karpos Uprising, 300th Anniv. — A644

1989, Oct. 20 **Litho.** **Perf. 13½**
1989	A644	1200d ver & dark brn	.25	.25

No. 1833c, Cancellation, Quill Pen, Wax Seals and Seal Device on Parchment A645

1989, Oct. 31 **Perf. 14**
1990	A645	1200d multicolored	.25	.25

Stamp Day.

Museum Exhibits A646

1989, Nov. 2
1991	A646	1200d Pack-saddle maker	.25	.25
1992	A646	14,000d Cooper	.55	.55
1993	A646	15,000d Winegrower	.80	.80
1994	A646	30,000d Weaver	1.40	1.40
		Nos. 1991-1994 (4)	3.00	3.00

Religious Paintings — A647

2100d, Apostle Matthew, vert. 21,000d, St. Barbara, vert. 30,000d, The Fourth Day of Creation. 50,000d, The Fifth Day of Creation.

1989, Nov. 28 **Litho.** **Perf. 14**
1997	A647	2100d multicolored	.25	.25
1998	A647	21,000d multicolored	.40	.40
1999	A647	30,000d multicolored	.80	.80
2000	A647	50,000d multicolored	1.25	1.25
		Nos. 1997-2000 (4)	2.70	2.70

A648

League of Communists 14th Congress — A649

1990, Jan. 20 **Litho.** **Perf. 13½x14**
2001	A648	10,000d Star	.30	.25
2002	A648	50,000d Computer	.55	.55

Souvenir Sheet
Imperf
2003	A649	100,000d Star, diff.	1.25	1.25

Postal Service Types of 1986-88
10p, Man posting letters in mailbox. 20p, Postal employee sorting mail. 30p, Postman, resident. 40p, Woman at telephone station. 1d, Mail train. 2d, Ship & envelope. 3d, Flower, mailbox, envelope & simulated stamp. 5d, Airplane, letters, map of Europe. 10d, Bird, open envelope, flower. 20d, Woman at telephone station.
Designs for other values as before.
10p, 20p, 30p, 40p, 3d, 5d vert.

1990 **Perf. 12½**
2004	A559	10p br yel grn & vio	.50	.25
2005	A559	20p red vio & org	.50	.25
2006	A559	30p org & yel grn	.25	.25
2007	A559	40p blue grn & red vio	.25	.25
2008	A620	50p pur & blue grn	.30	.25
2009	A619	60p red org & brt vio	.30	.25
2013	A559	1d rose lil & greenish bl	.50	.25
2014	A559	2d red lil & blue	.90	.25
2015	A559	3d org & dl blue	.90	.30
2017	A619	5d ultra & grnsh blue	.90	.45
2019	A559	10d red org & vio bl	1.75	1.40
		Nos. 2004-2019 (11)	7.05	4.15

Issued: 10p, 20p, 2/9; 30p, 40p, 1/24; 50p, 1/29; 60p, 2/6; 2d, 2/14; 3d, 2/22; 5d, 1/31; 1d, 5/24; 10d, 6/12.
For surcharges see Nos. 2049-2053, 2168//2176.

1990-92 **Perf. 13¼**
2004a	A559	10p br yel grn & vio	.50	.25
2005a	A559	20p red vio & org	1.40	.70
2006a	A559	30p org & yel grn	.25	.25
2007a	A559	40p blue grn & red vio	.25	.25
2008a	A620	50p pur & blue grn	.30	.25
2009a	A619	60p red org & brt vio	.30	.30
2013a	A559	1d rose lil & greenish bl	1.75	1.25
2014a	A559	2d red lil & blue	.65	.45
2015a	A559	3d org & dl blue>	2.50	2.25
2017a	A619	5d ultra & grnsh blue	1.25	1.00
2019a	A559	10d red org & vio bl	7.50	5.50
2021	A559	20d car rose & org	.45	.25
		Nos. 2004a-2021 (12)	17.10	12.70

Issued: 30p, 40p, 1/24; 50p, 1/29; 5d, 1/31; 60p, 2/6; 10p, 20p, 2/9; 2d, 2/14; 3d, 2/22; 10d, 6/12; 1d, 7/2; 20d, 1/27/92.
For surcharges see Nos. 2049a-2053a, 2168//2176.

Anti-smoking Campaign A650

1990, Jan. 31 **Litho.** **Perf. 13½x13**
2034	A650	10d gry & yel brn	.90	.90

Protected Fish — A651

1990, Feb. 15 **Perf. 13½**
2035		Strip of 4 + label	8.00	8.00
a.	A651	1d Esox lucius	1.25	1.25
b.	A651	5d Silurus glanis	1.25	1.25
c.	A651	10d Lota lota	1.25	1.25
d.	A651	15d Perca fluviatilis	1.25	1.25

Zabljak Fortress, Illuminated Manuscript, Coat of Arms — A652

1990, Mar. 9 **Perf. 14x13½**
2036	A652	50p multicolored	1.20	1.20

Enthronement of Djuradj Crnojevic, 500th anniv.

ITU, 125th Anniv. A653

1990, Mar. 23
2037	A653	6.50d Telegrapher, computer	.90	.90

1990 World Cup Soccer Championships, Italy — A654

1990, Apr. 16
2038	A654	6.50d shown	1.40	1.40
2039	A654	10d multi, diff.	1.40	1.40

Europa 1990 — A655

Post offices: 6.50d, PTT Central, Skopje. 10d, Telecommunications Central, Belgrade.

1990, Apr. 23 **Perf. 13½x14**
2040	A655	6.50d multicolored	1.60	1.60
2041	A655	10d multicolored	1.60	1.60

A656

1990, Apr. 30 **Litho.** **Perf. 13½**
2042	A656	6.50d multicolored	1.00	1.00

Labor Day, cent.

A657

Eurovision Song Contest: 10d, Conductor, musical score.

1990, May 5 **Perf. 14x13½**
2043	A657	6.50d multicolored	1.10	1.10
2044	A657	10d multicolored	1.20	1.20

No. 2043 exists with setenant label.

Tennis — A658

1990, May 15 **Litho.** **Perf. 14**
2045	A658	6.50d multicolored	1.40	1.40
2046	A658	10d multicolored	1.40	1.40

Tito — A659

1990, May 25 **Perf. 13½x14**
2047	A659	50p multicolored	.30	.30

Nos. 1938, 2004-2009a Surcharged

No. 2048   No. 2049

1990-91 **Litho.** **Perf. 12½**
2048	A559	50p on 800d (#1938a)	.45	.25
a.		Perf 13¼ (#1938)	.45	.25
2049	A559	50p on 20p (#2005)	.45	.25
a.		Perf 13¼ (#2005a) ('91)	3.50	2.75

2050 A559 1d on 30p (#2006) .45 .25
  a. Perf 13¼ (#2006a) 3.50 3.25
2051 A559 2d on 40p (#2007), I .90 .45
  a. Type II, perf. 13¼ (#2007a) 1.40 .90
  b. Type I, perf. 13¼ (#2007a) 2.25 2.25
2052 A619 5d on 60p (#2009) .45 .25
  a. Perf 13¼ (#2009a) 4.50 1.75
2053 A559 10d on 10p (#2004) .45 .25
  a. Perf 13¼ (#2004a) 1.00 .55
   Nos. 2048-2053 (6) 3.15 1.70

Type II surcharge has 3 instead of 2 bars obliterating old value, new denomination is at bottom of stamp.

Issued: #2048, 2048a, 5/24; #2050, 8/7; #2049, 2049a, 9/18; #2051-2051b, 10/2; #2050a, 1/4/91; #2053, 2053a, 12/12/91; #2052, 2052a, 12/17/91.

Public Postal Service in Serbia, 150th Anniv. A660

1990, May 25
2056 A660 50p multicolored 2.25 1.50

Pigeons A661

1990, June 8   **Perf. 13½**
2057 A661 50p multicolored .55 .55
2058 A661 5d multicolored 1.10 1.10
2059 A661 6.50d multi, vert. 1.10 1.10
2060 A661 10d multi, vert. 2.75 2.75
   Nos. 2057-2060 (4) 5.50 5.50

Mercury Mine at Idrija, 500th Anniv. — A662

Designs: 6.50d, Miners at work, ca. 1490.

1990, June 22   **Perf. 13½x14**
2061 A662 50p multicolored .25 .25
2062 A662 6.50d multicolored 1.00 1.00

Newspaper "Vjesnik," 50th Anniv. — A663

1990, June 23   **Perf. 13½**
2063 A663 60p multicolored .70 .70

Serbian Migration, 300th Anniv. — A664

1990, Sept. 20   **Perf. 14**
2064 A664 1d shown .25 .25
2065 A664 6.50d Caravan .90 .90

European Track & Field Championships, Split — A665

1990, Aug. 27   **Perf. 13½**
2067 A665 1d Start of race .60 .60
2068 A665 6.50d Runners' feet .90 .90

Souvenir Sheet

2069 A665 10d Runners 2.25 2.25

No. 2069 contains one 54x35mm stamp. A 50p exists but no information on its postal category is available.

Joy of Europe A666

Paintings: 6.50d, Children by I. Kobilca. 10d, William III of Orange as a Child by A. Hanneman, vert.

1990, Oct. 2   **Litho.**   **Perf. 14**
2070 A666 6.50d multicolored 1.10 1.10
2071 A666 10d multicolored 1.50 1.50

Souvenir Sheets

29th Chess Olympics, Novi Sad — A667

1990, Oct. 2   **Perf. 11½**
   Granite Paper
2072 A667 Sheet of 4 8.00 8.00
  a. 1d Pawns, knight, bishop, king
    & queen 1.10 1.10
  b. 5d Rook, bishop, knight 1.10 1.10
  c. 6.50d King, bishop, knght,
    pawn 1.10 1.10
  d. 10d Chess pieces 1.10 1.10

     Imperf

2073 A667 Sheet of 4 8.00 8.00
  a. 1d like No. 2072a 1.10 1.10
  b. 5d like No. 2072b 1.10 1.10
  c. 6.50d like No. 2072c 1.10 1.10
  d. 10d like No. 2072d 1.10 1.10

No. 2073 has blue margin inscriptions. Emblems on Nos. 2072a-2072d are in silver, those on Nos. 2073a-2073d are in gold.

Stamp Day A668

1990, Oct. 2   **Perf. 14**
2074 A668 2d multicolored .60 .55

150th anniv. of the Penny Black.

European Nature Protection A669

1990, Nov. 16   **Litho.**   **Perf. 14**
2075 A669 6.50d Vransko Lake 1.10 1.10
2076 A669 10d Gyps fulvus 1.50 1.50

Frescoes — A670

Designs: 2d, King Milutin, Monastery of Our Lady, Ljeviska. 5d, Saint Sava, Mileseva Monastery. 6.50d, Saint Elias, Moraca Monastery. 10d, Jesus Christ, Sopocani Monastery.

1990, Nov. 28
2077 A670 2d multicolored .45 .45
2078 A670 5d multicolored .95 .95
2079 A670 6.50d multicolored .95 .95
2080 A670 10d multicolored 1.40 1.40
   Nos. 2077-2080 (4) 3.75 3.75

Dr. Bozo Milanovic (1890-1980), Religious and Political Leader A671

1990, Dec. 20   **Litho.**   **Perf. 13½**
2081 A671 2d multicolored .30 .30

Religious Carvings A672

Designs: 2d, Christ in the temple. 5d, Nativity scene. 6.50d, Flight from Egypt, horiz. 10d, Entry into Jerusalem, horiz.

1990, Dec. 24   **Perf. 13½x14, 14x13½**
2082 A672 2d gld, brn, & blk .45 .45
2083 A672 5d gld, brn, & blk .70 .70
2084 A672 6.50d gld, brn, & blk .90 .90
2085 A672 10d gld, brn, & blk 1.10 1.10
   Nos. 2082-2085 (4) 3.15 3.15

Protected Birds — A673

1991, Jan. 31   **Litho.**   **Perf. 14x13½**
2086 Strip of 4 + label 9.00 9.00
  a. A673 2d Vanellus vanellus 1.10 1.10
  b. A673 5d Lanius senator 1.10 1.10
  c. A673 6.50d Grus grus 1.10 1.10
  d. A673 10d Mergus merganser 1.10 1.10

Flora — A674

2d, Crocus kosaninii. 6d, Crocus scardicus. 7.50d, Crocus rujanesis. 15d, Crocus adamii.

1991, Feb. 20
2087 A674 2d multicolored .45 .45
2088 A674 6d multicolored .55 .55
2089 A674 7.50d multicolored .60 .60
2090 A674 15d multicolored 2.00 2.00
   Nos. 2087-2090 (4) 3.60 3.60

Bishop Josip J. Strossmayer (1815-1905), Founder of Academy of Arts and Sciences A675

1991, Mar. 4   **Litho.**   **Perf. 13½x14**
2091 A675 2d multicolored 1.10 .60

Academy of Arts and Sciences, 125th Anniv.

Wolfgang Amadeus Mozart, Composer A676

1991, Mar. 20   **Perf. 14**
2092 A676 7.50d multicolored .90 .60

Otto Lilienthal's First Glider Flight, Cent. — A677

Designs: 7.50d, Edvard Rusjan (1886-1911), pilot, aircraft designer. 15d, Otto Lilienthal (1848-1896), aviation pioneer.

1991, Apr. 1
2093 A677 7.50d multicolored 1.10 1.10
2094 A677 15d multicolored 1.40 1.40

Printed in sheets of 8 plus label.

Lhotse I, Himalayas, South Face First Climbed by Tomo Cesen, 1990 — A678

1991, Apr. 24   **Perf. 14x13½**
2095 A678 7.50d multicolored .90 .55

Europa A679

Designs: 7.50d, Telecommunications satellite. 15d, Satellite, antenna, telephone.

1991, May 6   **Perf. 14**
2096 A679 7.50d multicolored .90 .90
2097 A679 15d multicolored 1.75 1.75

Franciscan Monastery, Trsat, 700th Anniv. — A680

1991, May 10   Litho.   Perf. 13½x14
2098 A680 3.50d multicolored   .80   .25

Governments of Danube River Region Conf., Belgrade — A681

15d, Danube River shipping. 20d, Course of Danube, landmarks, regional animals.

1991, May 15   Perf. 13½
2099 A681 7.50d multicolored   1.00 1.00
2100 A681 15d multicolored   1.50 1.50
Souvenir Sheet
2101 A681 20d multicolored   9.00 9.00
No. 2101 contains one 55x35mm stamp.

Opening of Karavanke Tunnel — A682

Designs: 4.50d, Passage Over Karavanke by J. Valvasor, 17th century. 11d, Entrance to new Karavanke Tunnel.

1991, June 1   Perf. 14x13½
2102 A682 4.50d multicolored   .60   .60
2103 A682 11d multicolored   .90   .90

Basketball, Cent. — A683

1991, June 15   Perf. 13½x14
2104 A683 11d shown   1.10 1.10
2105 A683 15d Nets, "100"   1.10 1.10

Yugoslavian Insurrection, 50th Anniv. — A684

Designs: 4.50d, Partisan Memorial Medal, 1941. 11d, Medal for Courage.

1991, July 4   Litho.   Perf. 14
2106 A684 4.50d multicolored   .35   .35
2107 A684 11d multicolored   .70   .70
Yugoslav Natl. Army, 50th Anniv.

Tin Ujevic (1891-1955), Writer — A685

1991, July 5   Perf. 13½
2108 A685 4.50d multicolored   .60   .45

Jacobus Gallus (1550-1591), Composer A686

1991, July 18
2109 A686 11d multicolored   .60   .60

Lighthouses of Adriatic and Danube — A687

Designs: a, Savudrija, 1818. b, Sveti Ivan na pucini, 1853. c, Porer, 1833. d, Stoncica, 1865. e, Olipa, c. 1842. f, Glavat, 1884. g, Veli rat, 1849. h, Vir, 1881. i, Tajerske sestrice, 1876. j, Razanj, 1875. k, Derdap-Danube. l, Tamis-Danube.

1991, July 25   Litho.   Perf. 13½
2110 A687 10d Bklt. pane of 12, #a.-l.   12.00 12.00

Sremski Karlovci High School, Bicent. — A688

1991, Sept. 12   Litho.   Perf. 14
2111 A688 4.50d multicolored   .45   .30

European Nature Protection A689

11d, Palingenia longicauda. 15d, Phalacrocorax pygmaeus.

1991, Sept. 24   Perf. 13½x14
2112 A689 11d multicolored   .90   .90
2113 A689 15d multicolored   .90   .90

A690

1991, Sept. 28   Perf. 14
2114 A690 4.50d multicolored   .45   .30
Town of Subotica, 600th anniv.

A691

Paintings: 15d, Little Dubravka, by Jovan Bijelic (1886-1964). 30d, Little Girl with a Cat by Mary Cassatt (1845-1926).

1991, Oct. 2
2115 A691 15d multicolored   .70   .70
2116 A691 30d multicolored   1.10 1.10
Joy of Europe.

33rd Intl. Apicultural Congress, APIMONDIA '91 — A692

1991, Sept. 28   Litho.   Perf. 13½x14
2117 A692 11d multicolored   1.10   .90

Stamp Day, Monument to Prince Michael Obrenovich, Serbia #1 — A693

1991, Oct. 31   Perf. 14
2118 A693 4.50d multicolored   .60   .25
First Serbia Postage Stamps, 125th Anniv.

Museum Exhibits A694

Flags and medals: 20d, Vucjido battle flag, medal for courage. 30d, Grahovac battle flag and medal. 40d, Montenegrin state flag, medal for bravery. 50d, Montenegrin court flag, medal of Petrovich Nyegosh Dynasty.

1991, Nov. 28   Perf. 13½x14
2119 A694 20d multicolored   .25   .25
2120 A694 30d multicolored   .45   .45
2121 A694 40d multicolored   .60   .60
2122 A694 50d multicolored   .90   .90
    Nos. 2119-2122 (4)   2.20 2.20

Illustrations from Ancient Manuscripts A695

Designs: 20d, Angel carrying Sun around Earth, 17th cent. 30d, Celnica Gospel, menology for April, 14th cent. 40d, Angel from the Annunciation, 13th cent. 50d, Mary Magdalene, 12th cent.

1991, Dec. 12
2123 A695 20d multicolored   .25   .25
2124 A695 30d multicolored   .45   .45
2125 A695 40d multicolored   .60   .60
2126 A695 50d multicolored   .90   .90
    Nos. 2123-2126 (4)   2.20 2.20

Gotse Deltchev (1872-1903), Macedonian Revolutionary A696

1992, Jan. 29   Litho.   Perf. 13½
2127 A696 5d multicolored   2.25 2.25

Red Star, European and World Soccer Champions A697

1992, Jan. 29   Litho.   Perf. 14x13½
2128 A697 17d multicolored   2.00 2.00

A698

1992, Feb. 8   Perf. 14x13½
2129 A698 80d Ski jumping   1.75 1.75
2130 A698 100d Freestyle skiing   1.75 1.75
1992 Winter Olympics, Albertville.

A699

Protected Animals: a, 50d, Lepus europaeus. b, 60d, Pteromys volans. c, 80d, Dryomys nitedula. d, 100d, Cricetus cricetus.

1992, Mar. 10   Litho.   Perf. 14
2131 A699 Strip of 4, #a.-d. + label   8.00 8.00

Madonna and Child, 14th century, Pec — A700

1992, Mar. 14   Perf. 13½x14
2132 A700 80d multicolored   1.00 1.00
Promotion of Breastfeeding.

Ski Association of Montenegro — A701

1992, Mar. 25   *Perf. 14x13½*
2133 A701 8d multicolored   5.00 5.00
Skiing in Montenegro, cent.

1860 Fountain, Belgrade — A702   A702a

A702b   A702c

A702d   A702e

A702f   A702g

A702h   A702i

A702j

5d, Griffins, 14th cent. #2136, #2139, Fisherman Fountain, Belgrade, like #2137. 300d, Kalemegdan Fountain, Belgrade. 500d, Fountain, Sremski Karlovci. #2142, Symbols of Miroslav-Evangelium, 12th cent. 3000d, Fountain, Studenica. 5000d, Fountain, Oplenzu. 10,000d, 500,000d, Health spa, Vrnjacka Banja. 50,000d, Envelopes over map of Europe. #2147, Airplane. #2148, Health spa, Bukovacka Banja.

Inscribed "1992" or "1993"

1992-93	Litho.	*Perf. 13¼*	
2135 A702a	5d brn & olive	1.00	.25
2136 A702	50d dk bl & lt bl	.45	.25
2137 A702	50d violet	.45	.35
2138 A702	100d lil rose & pink	.45	.25
2139 A702	100d dk grn & lt grn	.25	.25
2140 A702b	300d brn & red brn	.45	.25
2141 A702c	500d dk ol & pale org	.90	.25
a.	Perf. 12½	1.75	1.75
2142 A702d	(A) red, 18x22mm	1.75	.45
a.	Perf. 12½	4.00	.45
b.	Inscribed "1996," Perf. 13¼	2.25	2.25
c.	Inscribed "1996," perf. 12½	.90	.25

d.	Inscribed "1997," perf. 12½	1.50	.25
e.	Inscribed "2002," perf. 12½	5.00	1.50
2143 A702e	3000d red brn	.45	.25
a.	Perf. 12½	2.75	2.25
2144 A702f	5000d vio & yel brn	.45	.25
a.	Perf 12½	3.50	2.75
2145 A702g	10,000d vio bl & grn bl	1.00	.25
2146 A702h	50,000d gray & gray bl	.45	.25
a.	Perf. 12½	1.10	.90
2147 A702i	100,000d red & bl	.90	.45
a.	Perf. 12½	1.10	.90
2148 A702j	100,000d brn red & brn	.90	.25
2149 A702g	500,000d bl & vio	.45	.25
Nos. 2135-2149 (15)		10.30	4.25

Issued: #2137, 4/1/92; #2139, 5/6/92; 5d, 11/24/92; #2136, 12/15/92; #2138, 12/22/92; 300d, 12/3/92; 500d, 1/14/93; #2142, 4/5/93; #2142a, 1993; #2143, 4/23/93; 5000d, 3/18/93; 10,000d, 11/9/93; 50,000d, 6/10/93; 100,000d, 6/28/93; 100,000d, 12/6/93; 500,000d, 8/10/93.
No. 2142 was valued at 3000d on day of issue.
See No. 2386. For surcharges see Nos. 2220A-2220I, 2253-2254.

Sinking of the Titanic, 80th Anniv. — A703

1992, Apr. 14   *Perf. 14*
2152 A703 150d multicolored   .90 .90

Expo '92, Seville A704

1992, Apr. 20
2153 A704 150d multicolored   .90 .90

Discovery of America, 500th Anniv. — A705

300d, Columbus, ship. 500d, Columbus' fleet. 1200d, Ships in port.

1992, May 5   Litho.   *Perf. 13½x14*
2154 A705 300d multicolored   4.50 4.50
2155 A705 500d multicolored   4.50 4.50

Souvenir Sheet
Perf. 14x13½
2156 A705 1200d multicolored   13.50 13.50
Europa. No. 2156 contains one 54x34mm stamp.

1992 Summer Olympics, Barcelona — A706

1992, May 20   *Perf. 14x13½*
2157 A706 500d Pistol shooting   .90 .90
2158 A706 500d Water polo   .90 .90
2159 A706 500d Tennis   .90 .90
2160 A706 500d Handball   .90 .90
Nos. 2157-2160 (4)   3.60 3.60

European Soccer Championships — A707

Various soccer plays.

1992, June 1   *Perf. 13½*
2161 A707 1000d shown   1.60 1.60
2162 A707 1000d multicolored   1.60 1.60

Domestic Cats — A708

Designs: No. 2163, Red Persian. No. 2164, White Persian. No. 2165, Yellow tabby. No. 2166, British blue short-hair.

1992, June 25   Litho.   *Perf. 13½x14*
Background Color
Cyrillic Letters
2163 A708 1000d blue   1.60 1.60
2164 A708 1000d purple   1.60 1.60
Latin Letters
2165 A708 1000d dark purple   1.60 1.60
2166 A708 1000d brown   1.60 1.60
Nos. 2163-2166 (4)   6.40 6.40

Steam Locomotives A709

Designs: a, JDZ 162. b, JDZ 151. c, JDZ 73. d, JDZ 83. e, JDZ 16. f, Prince Nicholas' coach.

1992, July 3   Litho.   *Perf. 14*
2167 A709 1000d Booklet pane of 6, #a.-f.   15.00 15.00

Nos. 2005//2017a Surcharged

1992		*Perfs., Etc. as Before*	
2168 A559	2d on 30p #2006	.90	.50
a.	Perf 13¼ (#2006a)	1.75	1.00
2169 A559	5d on 20p #2005	1.75	.25
2170 A559	5d on 40p #2007	.90	.50
a.	Perf 13¼ (#2007a)	1.75	1.00
2171 A620	10d on 50p #2008	1.75	.25
2172 A621	10d on 5d #2017a	.90	.25
2173 A559	20d on 1d #2013	3.00	.90
a.	Perf 13¼ (#2013a)	1.75	.90
2174 A621	20d on 5d type of #2017, yel, bl & grn bl	1.00	.50
2175 A559	50d on 2d #2014	10.00	5.00
a.	Perf 13¼ (#2014a)	1.75	.25
2176 A559	100d on 3d #2015	6.00	2.00
a.	Perf 13¼ (#2015a)	3.50	.25
Nos. 2168-2176 (9)		26.20	10.15

Issued: #2168, 2170, 10/26; #2169, 9/12; #2171, 9/17; #2172, 10/29; #2173, 2175-2176, 8/6; #2174, 11/9.

World Chess Champions A710

1992, Sept. 14   Litho.   *Perf. 14*
2177 A710 500d Bobby Fischer   1.75 1.75
2178 A710 500d Boris Spassky   1.75 1.75

Telephone Service in Vojvodina, Cent. A711

1892 Telephone, buildings of Novi Sad, Subotica and Zrenjanin.

1992, Oct. 1
2179 A711 10d multicolored   1.40 1.40

Stamp Day A712

Design: Montenegro #7, musician.

1992, Oct. 2
2180 A712 50d multicolored   1.00 .90

European Art — A713

Europa: No. 2181, Ballet Dancer, by Edgar Degas (1834-1917). No. 2182, Painting of young man, by U. Knezevic.

1992, Oct. 2
2181 A713 500d multicolored   1.40 1.40
2182 A713 500d multicolored   1.40 1.40

European Nature Protection A714

1992, Nov. 14   *Perf. 13½*
2183 A714 500d Tetrao urogallus   4.00 4.00
2184 A714 500d Pelecanus onocrotalus   4.00 4.00

Publisher Srpska Knjizevna Zadruga, Cent. — A715

1992, Nov. 20   *Perf. 14*
2185 A715 100d multicolored   1.00 1.00

Traditional Architecture — A716

Designs: No. 2186, Ancient hut, Zlatibor region. No. 2187, Round house, Morava region. No. 2188, House, on stone cliff, Metohija region. No. 2189, Large estate house, Vojvodina region.

1992, Dec. 12
2186	A716	500d multicolored	.80	.80
2187	A716	500d multicolored	.80	.80
2188	A716	500d multicolored	.80	.80
2189	A716	500d multicolored	.80	.80
		Nos. 2186-2189 (4)	3.20	3.20

Icons, Mosaics — A717

#2190, St. Petka, St. Petka Church, Belgrade. #2191, St. Vasilije-Ostronoski, St. Vasilije-Ostronoski Church, Montenegro. #2192, Mosaic of Simeon Nemanja with model of Blessed Virgin Church, Studenica. #2193, Mosaic of St. Lazar with model of Ravanica Monastery.

1992, Dec. 15
2190	A717	500d multi	1.00	1.00
2191	A717	500d multi	1.00	1.00
2192	A717	500d multi, vert.	1.00	1.00
2193	A717	500d multi, vert.	1.00	1.00
		Nos. 2190-2193 (4)	4.00	4.00

Aviation in Yugoslavia, 80th Anniv. — A718

1992, Dec. 24
2194	A718	500d Bleriot XI	1.10	1.10

Diocletian's Reformation of the Roman Empire, 1700th Anniv. — A719

Design: Detail of Roman fresco.

1993, Jan. 28　Litho.　Perf. 13½
2195	A719	1500d multicolored	1.10	1.10

State Museum, Cetinje, Cent. — A720

1993, Feb. 12　　Perf. 14
2196	A720	2500d multicolored	1.10	1.10

Marine Life — A721

Designs: a, Acipenser sturio. b, Scorpaena scrofa. c, Xiphias gladius. d, Tursiops truncatus.

1993, Mar. 20　　Perf. 13½
2197	A721	10,000d Strip of 4, #a.-d. + label	8.00	8.00

Serbian Money — A722

#2198, Ancient document, 10 para coins. #2199, 5 dinar banknotes, 5 dinar coins.

1993, Mar. 30
2198	A722	10,000d multicolored	1.40	1.40
2199	A722	10,000d multicolored	1.40	1.40

Restablishment of Serbian monetary system, 125th anniv. (No. 2198). Restoring dinars as Serbian currency, 120th anniv. (No. 2199).

Famous People A723

Designs: No. 2200, Milos Crnjanski (1893-1977), writer, journalist. No. 2201, Nicola Tesla (1856-1943), physicist. No. 2202, Mihailo Petrovic (1868-1943), mathematician. No. 2203, Aleksa Santic (1868-1924), poet.

1993, Apr. 1
2200	A723	40,000d multicolored	1.40	1.40
2201	A723	40,000d multicolored	1.40	1.40
2202	A723	40,000d multicolored	1.40	1.40
2203	A723	40,000d multicolored	1.40	1.40
		Nos. 2200-2203 (4)	5.60	5.60

Joy of Europe — A724

Children's paintings: No. 2204, Girl holding flowers, children, dove, by M. Markovski. No. 2205, Angels, birds, by J. Rugovac.

1993, Apr. 5
2204	A724	50,000d multicolored	1.40	1.40
2205	A724	50,000d multicolored	1.75	1.75

Contemporary Art — A725

Europa: No. 2206, Nude with a Mirror, by M. Milunovic. No. 2207, Composition, by M.P. Barili.

1993, May 5
2206	A725	95,000d multicolored	2.75	2.75
2207	A725	95,000d multicolored	2.75	2.75

A726

A727

A728

A729

A730

Ancient Fortresses: No. 2208, Sutorina, Montenegro. No. 2209, Kalemegdan, Belgrade. No. 2210, Medun, Montenegro. No. 2211, Petrovaradin, near Novi Sad. No. 2212, Bar, Montenegro. No. 2213, Golubac.

1993, July 9　　Booklet Stamps
2208	A726	900,000d multi	1.00	1.00
2209	A727	900,000d multi	1.00	1.00
2210	A728	900,000d multi	1.00	1.00
2211	A729	900,000d multi	1.00	1.00
2212	A730	900,000d multi	1.00	1.00
2213	A730	900,000d multi	1.00	1.00
a.		Booklet pane, #2208-2213	6.00	
		Complete booklet, #2213a	6.00	

Flowers A731

Colors of various flowers in vases: No. 2214, Yellow, white. No. 2215, Orange, red. No. 2216, Purple, pink, white. No. 2217, Mixed.

1993, July 10　　Perf. 14
2214	A731	1,000,000d multi	1.40	1.40
2215	A731	1,000,000d multi	1.40	1.40
2216	A731	1,000,000d multi	1.40	1.40
2217	A731	1,000,000d multi	1.40	1.40
		Nos. 2214-2217 (4)	5.60	5.60

Electrification of Serbia, Cent. A732

1993, July 28　　Perf. 13½
2218	A732	2,500,000d multi	.70	.65

European Nature Protection A733

Designs: No. 2219, Garrulus glandarius. No. 2220, Oriolus oriolus.

1993, Sept. 30
2219	A733	300,000,000d multi	6.25	6.25
2220	A733	300,000,000d multi	6.25	6.25

Nos. 2147a, 2135, 2144, 2136 and 2140 Srchd.

No. 2143 Surcharged

1993　　　　Perf. 13¼
2220A	A702i	10d on 100,000d	.90	.90
b.		Perf 12½	1.75	.25
2220B	A702a	50d on 5d	1.00	.25
2220C	A702f	100d on 5000d	1.00	.25
2220D	A702	500d on 50d	1.00	.25
2220E	A702e	1000d on 3000d	1.00	.60
f.		Perf 12½	1.00	.25
2220F	A702b	10,000d on 300d	1.00	.25
2220G	A702a	50,000d on 5d	2.75	.75
		Nos. 2220A-2220G (7)	8.65	3.25

Issued: 50,000d, 11/9/93; others, 10/18/93. Size and location of surcharge varies.
No. 2220G was created by applying three additional "0"s to the "50" surcharge on No. 2220B.

A734

Cooperation on the Danube River — A735

Designs: No. 2221, Ships on river. No. 2222, Ship going down river. 20,000d, Map showing location of Danube River.

1993, Oct. 20　　Perf. 14
2221	A734	15,000d multicolored	1.40	1.40
2222	A734	15,000d multicolored	1.40	1.40

Souvenir Sheet
2223	A735	20,000d multicolored	2.75	2.75

Post Office in Jagodina, 150th Anniv. A736

1993, Oct. 30　　Perf. 13½
2224	A736	12,000d multicolored	1.50	1.00

Stamp Day.

Joy of Europe — A737

Paintings: No. 2225, Boy with Cat, by Sava Sumanovic (1896-1942). No. 2226, Circus Rider, by Georges Rouault (1871-1958).

1993, Nov. 26
2225	A737	2,000,000d multi	1.40	1.40
2226	A737	2,000,000d multi	1.40	1.40

Icons in Monasteries A738

Designs: No. 2227, The Annunciation, Mileseva. No. 2228, Nativity, Studenica. No. 2229, Madonna and Child, Bogorodica Ljeviska. No. 2230, Flight into Egypt, Oplenac.

1993, Dec. 15
2227	A738	400,000,000d multi	1.00	1.00
2228	A738	400,000,000d multi	1.00	1.00
2229	A738	400,000,000d multi	1.00	1.00
2230	A738	400,000,000d multi	1.00	1.00
	Nos. 2227-2230 (4)		4.00	4.00

Traditional Houses — A739

#2231, A-frame huts, Savardak, horiz. #2232, Watchtower. #2233, Stone house on edge of river. #2234, Crmnicka house, Bar, horiz.

1993, Dec. 31
2231	A739	50d multicolored	1.00	1.00
2232	A739	50d multicolored	1.00	1.00
2233	A739	50d multicolored	1.00	1.00
2234	A739	50d multicolored	1.00	1.00
	Nos. 2231-2234 (4)		4.00	4.00

Publication of Oktoechos, 500th Anniv. — A740

1994, Jan. 17   Litho.   Perf. 13½
2235	A740	1000d Text	.80	.80
2236	A740	1000d Liturgists	.80	.80

Raptors A741

Designs: a, Neophron percnopterus. b, Falco cherrug. c, Buteo rufinus. d, Falco naumanni.

1994, Feb. 7
2237	A741	80p Strip of 4, #a.- d. + label	22.50	22.50

Intl. Mimosa Festival, Herceg-Novi A742

1994, Feb. 28
2238	A742	80p multicolored	1.40	1.40

Natl. Museum, Belgrade, 150th Anniv. A743

Design: No. 2240, National Theater, Belgrade, 125th anniv., portrait of Prince Milos Obrenovic.

1994, Mar. 19
2239	A743	80p multicolored	1.40	1.40
2240	A743	80p multicolored	1.40	1.40

1994 Winter Olympics, Lillehammer — A744

a, Speed skater. b. Olympic rings, flame. c, Skier.

1994, Apr. 11
2241	A744	60p Strip of 3, #a.-c.	3.25	3.25

Europa A745

Map of flight route and: 60p, Kodron C61, automobile. 1.80d, Kodron C61 in air over Belgrade.

1994, May 5
2242	A745	60p multicolored	1.75	1.75
2243	A745	1.80d multicolored	2.25	2.25

First night flight Paris-Belgrade-Bucharest-Istanbul, piloted by Louis Guidon, 1923.

Burning of Relics of Holy Sava, 400th Anniv. A746

1994, May 10   Perf. 14
2244	A746	60p multicolored	1.75	1.75

1994 World Cup Soccer Championships, U.S. — A747

60p, Three players with arms raised in victory. 1d, Three players down on ground.

1994, June 10   Perf. 13½
2245	A747	60p multicolored	1.40	1.40
2246	A747	1d multicolored	1.40	1.40

A748

1994, July 8
2247	A748	60p Basset hound	1.40	1.40
2248	A748	60p Maltese	1.40	1.40
2249	A748	60p Welsh terrier	1.40	1.40
2250	A748	1d Husky	1.40	1.40
	Nos. 2247-2250 (4)		5.60	5.60

A749

1994, July 20
2251	A749	60p multicolored	1.40	1.40

Assembly of Eastern Orthodox Christian nations.

Protecting the Ecology of Montenegro A750

1994, July 28
2252	A750	50p Tcherna Gora Park	1.40	1.40

Nos. 2148, 2145 Surcharged

1994, July 15   Perf. 13½
2253	A702j	10p on 100,000d	.50	.50
2254	A702g	50p on 10,000d	.90	.65

A751

Monasteries: 1p, Moraca, 13th cent. 5p, Gracanica, 14th cent. 10p, Ostrog. No. 2258-2259, Lazarica, 14th cent. 50p, Studenica, 12th cent. 1d, Sopocani, 13th cent.

Inscribed "1994"

1994   Litho.   Perf. 13¼
2255	A751	1p bister & purple	1.40	.25
a.		Perf 12½, Inscr. "1997"	1.40	.25
2256	A751	5p yel brn & blue	1.40	.25
a.		Perf 12½, Inscr. "1998"	1.40	.25
2257	A751	10p magenta & slate	.55	.25
a.		Perf 12½, Inscr. "1998"	.55	.25
2258	A751	20p lil rose & pale vio	.90	.25
2259	A751	20p pale car & gray	35.00	.25
a.		Perf 12½, Inscr. "1998"	1.75	.25
2260	A751	50p deep pur & mag	.55	.25
a.		Inscribed "1997"	.55	.25
b.		As "a," perf 12½	.55	.25
2261	A751	1d blue & org brown	1.40	.50
a.		Perf 12½, Inscr. "1997"	1.40	.50
	Nos. 2255-2261 (7)		41.20	2.00

UNESCO (#2260-2261).

Issued: 1p, 5p, #2258, 1d, 8/15; #2259, 9/10; 10p, 50p, 11/10.
Nos. 2262-2271 are unassigned.
For surcharges, see Serbia Nos. 195, 260-261.

A752

1994, Sept. 10
2272	A752	50p multicolored	.90	.90

St. Arsenius Seminary, Sremski Karlovci, bicent.

European Nature Protection A753

Designs: 1d, Fishing pier, Reka Bojana. 1.50d, Lake, Belgrade.

1994, Sept. 20
2273	A753	1d multicolored	2.75	2.75
2274	A753	1.50d multicolored	2.75	2.75

Painting by U. Knezevic — A754

1994, Oct. 5   Perf. 14
2275	A754	1d multicolored	1.75	1.75

Joy of Europe.

Sailing Ships in Bottles — A755

a, Revenge, 1585. b, Grand yacht, 1678. c, Santa Maria, 15th cent. d, Nava, 15th cent. e, Mayflower, 1615. f, Carrack, 14th cent.

1994, Oct. 27   Perf. 13½
2276	A755	50p Bklt. pane of 6, #a.-f.	6.00	6.00
	Complete booklet, #2276		6.00	

Stamp Day — A756

1994, Oct. 31
2277	A756	50p multicolored	4.00	4.00

Drawings on Gravestones
A757

#2278, Man holding umbrella, purse. #2279, 2 men. #2280, Cemetery, stone with man on horse, inscriptions. #2281, Fence, 2 gravestones, cross, man.

1994, Nov. 25
2278	A757	50p multicolored	.80	.80
2279	A757	50p multicolored	.80	.80
2280	A757	50p multicolored	.80	.80
2281	A757	50p multicolored	.80	.80
		Nos. 2278-2281 (4)	3.20	3.20

Religious Art — A758

#2282, The Annunciation, by D. Bacevic. #2283, Adoration of the Magi, by N. Neskovic. #2284, Madonna and Child, by T.N. Cesljar. #2285, St. John Baptizing Christ, by T. Kracun.

1994, Dec. 15
2282	A758	60p multicolored	.80	.80
2283	A758	60p multicolored	.80	.80
2284	A758	60p multicolored	.80	.80
2285	A758	60p multicolored	.80	.80
		Nos. 2282-2285 (4)	3.20	3.20

Natl. Symbols
A759

1995, Jan. 26   Litho.   Perf. 13½
2286	A759	1d Flag	1.50	1.50
2287	A759	1d Arms	1.50	1.50

Sheets of 8

World Chess Champions — A760

#2288: a, Wilhelm Steinitz (1836-1900), Austria. b, Silhouettes of chessman. c, Emmanuel Lasker (1868-1941), Germany. d, Knight. e, Chessman, row of pawns at top. f, José Raúl Capablanca (1888-1942), Cuba. g, Chessman, rook at left. h, Alexander Alekhine (1892-1946), Russia.

#2289: a, Max Euwe, Netherlands. b, Board, pawn in center. c, Mikhail M. Botvinik, Soviet Union. d, Board, queen in middle. e, Board, bishop, knight. f, Vassili Smyslov, Soviet Union. g, Silhouette of knight, rook queen, chessboard. h, Mikhail N. Tal, Soviet Union.

1995
2288	A760	60p #a.-h. + label	10.00	10.00
2289	A760	60p #a.-h. + label	10.00	10.00

Issued: No. 2288, 2/28; No. 2289, 9/1.

Red Star Army Sport Club, 50th Anniv.
A761

1995, Mar. 4
2290	A761	60p bl, red & bister	1.75	1.75

Protection of Nature
A762

a, Salamandra salamandra. b, Triturus alpestris. c, Rana graeca. d, Pelobates syriacus balcanicus.

1995, Mar. 23
2291	A762	60p Strip of 4, #a.-d. + label	10.00	10.00

A763

1995, Apr. 20
2292	A763	60p multicolored	1.50	1.50

Radnicki Soccer Club, Belgrade, 75th anniv.

A764

Europa: 60p, Eagle, mountains. 1.90d, Girl on tricycle, elderly man, woman on park bench, horiz.

1995, May 6
2293	A764	60p multicolored	3.00	2.50
2294	A764	1.90d multicolored	3.00	2.50

A765

1995, May 9
2295	A765	60p multicolored	1.50	1.50

End of World War II, 50th anniv.

A766

1995, May 28
2296	A766	60p multicolored	2.00	2.00

Opening of Vukov-Denkmal Subway Station, Belgrade.

Draba Bertiscea
A767

a, shown. b, Plants, diff. c, Flowers, mountain. d, Plants on rock, stems at right.

1995, June 12
2297	A767	60p Strip of 4, #a.-d. + label	10.00	10.00

European Nature Protection
A768

Designs: 60p, Eremophila alpestris balcanica. 1.90d, Rhinolophus blasii.

1995, July 10
2298	A768	60p multicolored	2.00	2.00
2299	A768	1.90d multicolored	2.50	2.50

Slovakian Folk Festival, by Zuzka Medvedova (1897-1985), Painter — A769

1995, Aug. 3
2300	A769	60p multicolored	1.25	1.25

Volleyball, Cent. — A770

1995, Sept. 10
2301	A770	90d multicolored	1.25	1.25

Church of St. Luke, Kotor, 800th Anniv. — A771

1995, Sept. 20
2302	A771	80p multicolored	1.25	1.25

Motion Pictures, Cent.
A772

Designs: 1.10d, Newsreel showing coronation of King Peter II. 2.20d, Auguste and Louis Jean Lumière, film projector.

1995, Oct. 3
2303	A772	1.10d dk brn, lt red brn	1.50	1.50
2304	A772	2.20d dk brn, lt red brn	1.50	1.50

Army Sports Club "Partisan," 50th Anniv. — A773

1995, Oct. 4
2305	A773	80p multi + label	1.25	1.25

UN, 50th Anniv. — A774

1995, Oct. 24
2306	A774	1.10d multicolored	1.25	1.25

Stamp Day — A775

1995, Oct. 31
2307	A775	1.10d multicolored	1.00	1.00

Joy of Europe — A776

Paintings: 1.10d, Young boy by Milos Tenkovic. 2.20d, Young girl by Pierre Bonnard.

1995, Nov. 26
2308	A776	1.10d multicolored	1.50	1.50
2309	A776	2.20d multicolored	1.50	1.50

Children's Day.

Souvenir Sheet

JUFIZ VIII, Natl. Philatelic Exhibition, Budva — A777

Design: Montenegro #37, Serbia #6.

1995, Dec. 13   Perf. 14
2310	A777	2.50d Sheet of 1 + label	2.00	2.0

Christmas
A778

Contemporary religious paintings: No. 2311, Flight into Egypt, by Z. Halupova. No. 2312, Nativity, by D. Milojevic, vert. No. 2313, Outdoor Christmas scene, by M. Rasic, vert. No. 2314, Indoor traditional Christmas scene, by J. Brasic.

1995, Dec. 26   **Perf. 13½**
2311 A778 1.10d multicolored   .50 .50
2312 A778 1.10d multicolored   .50 .50
2313 A778 2.20d multicolored   1.00 1.00
2314 A778 2.20d multicolored   1.00 1.00
   Nos. 2311-2314 (4)   3.00 3.00

Airplanes
A779

1995, Dec. 26
2315 A779 1.10d Saric No. 1   .50 .50
2316 A779 1.10d Douglas DC-3   .50 .50
2317 A779 2.20d Fizir FN   1.00 1.00
2318 A779 2.20d Caravelle   1.00 1.00
   Nos. 2315-2318 (4)   3.00 3.00

Battle of Mojkovac, 80th Anniv. — A780

Design: Montenegrins on mountain.

1996, Jan. 6
2319 A780 1.10d multicolored   .50 .50

Birth of Sava Sumanovic, Cent. A781

Design: 1927 Painting, "Drink Boat."

1996, Jan. 22
2320 A781 1.10d multicolored   .50 .50

Insects — A782

a, Pyrgomorphela serbica. b, Calosoma sycopanta. c, Formica rufa. d, Ascalaphus macaronius.

1996, Feb. 15
2321 A782 2.20d Strip of 4, #a.-
    d. + label   7.00 7.00
   Protection of nature.

A783

Churches.

1996, Feb. 29   **Litho.**   **Perf. 12½**
2322 A783 5d Ljeviska   2.00 1.50
2323 A783 10d Zica   4.00 3.00
2324 A783 20d Decani   8.00 6.00
   Nos. 2322-2324 (3)   14.00 10.50

Chess Champions — A784

Designs: a, Tigran Petrosian, Soviet Union. b, Chess pieces, sundial, chess board. c, Boris Spassky, Soviet Union. d, Chess pieces, board, clock showing two time zones. e, Garry Kasparov, Soviet Union. f, Chess pieces, hand holding hour glass. g, Bobby Fischer, US. h, Chess pieces, six clocks. i, Anatoly Karpov, Soviet Union.

1996, Mar. 15   **Litho.**   **Perf. 13½**
2325 A784 1.50d Sheet of 9, #a.-
    i.   6.00 6.00

Olympic Games, Cent. A786

1.50d, Discus throwers. 2.50d, Runners.

Perf. 13½x13¼
1996, Mar. 30   **Litho.**
2326 A786 1.50d multi   .75 .75
2327 A786 2.50d multi   1.25 1.25

1996 Summer Olympics, Atlanta — A787

1996, Apr. 12
2328 A787 1.50d shown   1.50 1.50
2329 A787 1.50d Basketball   1.50 1.50
2330 A787 1.50d Handball   1.50 1.50
2331 A787 1.50d Volleyball   1.50 1.50
2332 A787 1.50d Shooting   1.50 1.50
2333 A787 1.50d Water polo   1.50 1.50
   Nos. 2328-2333 (6)   9.00 9.00

1996 Summer Olympic Games, Atlanta — A787a

1996, Apr. 12   **Litho.**   **Perf. 13**
2334 A787a 5d Sheet of 1 + la-
    bel   2.00 2.00

Stamp Day — A788

1996, Apr. 30   **Litho.**   **Perf. 13½**
2335 A788 1.50d Railway mail
    car   .60 .60

Famous Women Writers — A789

Europa: 2.50d, Isidora Sekulic (1877-1958). 5d, Desanka Maksimovic (1898-1993).

1996, May 7   **Litho.**   **Perf. 13½**
2336 A789 2.50d multicolored   2.00 2.00
2337 A789 5d multicolored   2.00 2.00

Serbian Red Cross, 120th Anniv. A790

1996, May 8
2338 A790 1.50d Dr. Vladan
    Djordjevic   .60 .60

Architectural Education in Yugoslavia, 150th Anniv. — A791

1996, June 1   **Litho.**   **Perf. 13½**
2339 A791 1.50d multicolored   .60 .60

European Nature Protection A792

2.50d, Platalea leucorodia. 5d, Plegadis falcinellus.

1996, June 28
2340 A792 2.50d multicolored   1.00 1.00
2341 A792 5d multicolored   2.00 2.00

Prince Peter I Petrovic at Battle of Martinici, 1796 — A793

Design: 2.50d, Prince's Guard at Battle of Kruse (1796), by Valerio, vert.

1996, July 22
2342 A793 1.50d multicolored   .50 .50
2343 A793 2.50d multicolored   1.00 1.00

Horse Racing, Ljubicevo A794

1996, Sept. 2   **Litho.**   **Perf. 13½**
2344 A794 1.50d shown   .50 .50
2345 A794 2.50d 3 horses racing   1.00 1.00

Fauna — A795

Designs: a, 1.50d, Probosciger aterrimus. b, 2.50d, Goura scheepmakeri. c, 1.50d, Equus burchelli. d, 2.50d, Panthera tigris.

1996, Sept. 25
2346 A795 Strip of 4, #a.-d. +
    label   8.00 8.00
   Belgrade Zoo, 60th anniv.

Children's Day — A796

1996, Oct. 2
2347 A796 1.50d multicolored   .70 .70
2348 A796 2.50d Bird   1.25 1.25

Medalists, 1996 Summer Olympic Games A797

Designs: No. 2349, Shooting, bronze. No. 2350, Shooting, gold. No. 2351, Volleyball, bronze. No. 2352, Basketball, silver.

1996, Oct. 31   **Litho.**   **Perf. 13½**
2349 A797 2.50d multicolored   1.40 1.40
2350 A797 2.50d multicolored   1.40 1.40
2351 A797 2.50d multicolored   1.40 1.40
2352 A797 2.50d multicolored   1.40 1.40
   Nos. 2349-2352 (4)   5.60 5.60

Savings Accounts, 75th Anniv. — A798

1996, Oct. 31   **Litho.**   **Perf. 13½**
2353 A798 1.50d multicolored   .70 .70

Soccer in Yugoslavia, Cent. — A799

1996, Nov. 8   **Litho.**   **Perf. 13½**
2354 A799 1.50d multicolored   .70 .70

Archaeological Finds — A800

Sculptures: No. 2355, God of Autumn. No. 2356, Mother with child. No. 2357, Head of woman. No. 2358, Redheaded goddess.

1996, Nov. 25
2355 A800 1.50d multicolored   .60 .50
2356 A800 1.50d multicolored   .60 .50
2357 A800 2.50d multicolored   1.00 .75
2358 A800 2.50d multicolored   1.00 .75
   Nos. 2355-2358 (4)   3.20 2.50

A801

Christmas (Paintings): No. 2359, Annunciation. No. 2360, Mother of God with Christ. No. 2361, Birth of Christ. No. 2362, Palm Sunday.

1996, Dec. 10

2359	A801	1.50d multicolored	.60	.50
2360	A801	1.50d multicolored	.60	.50
2361	A801	2.50d multicolored	1.00	.75
2362	A801	2.50d multicolored	1.00	.75
		Nos. 2359-2362 (4)	3.20	2.50

A802

1997, Jan. 24　　Litho.　　Perf. 13½

2363	A802	1.50d multicolored	.60	.60

Radomir Putnik Voivode, 150th birth anniv.

25th Intl. Film Festival, Belgrade A803

1997, Jan. 31

2364	A803	1.50d multicolored	.70	.70

Protected Birds — A804

Designs: No. 2365, Dendrocopos major. No. 2366, Nucifraga caryocatactes. No. 2367, Parus cristatus. No. 2368, Erithacus rubecula.

1997, Feb. 21

2365	A804	1.50d multicolored	.60	.60
2366	A804	2.50d multicolored	.60	.60
2367	A804	1.50d multicolored	.90	.90
2368	A804	2.50d multicolored	.90	.90
a.	Strip of 4, #2365-2368 + label		7.00	7.00

A805

1997, Mar. 17　　Litho.　　Perf. 13

2369	A805	1.50d multicolored	1.00	1.00

St. Achilleus Church, 700th Anniv.

A806

Design: Prince Peter I Petrovic (1747-1830), Bishop of Montenegro.

1997, Apr. 3　　　　　　Perf. 13½

2370	A806	1.50d multicolored	1.00	1.00

A807

1997, Apr. 19

2371	A807	2.50d multicolored	1.25	1.25

10th Belgrade Marathon.

A808

1997, Apr. 22　　Litho.　　Perf. 13½

2372	A808	2.50d multicolored	1.25	1.25

Serbian Medical Assoc., 125th anniv.

Air Mail Being Loaded at Night A809

1997, May 3

2373	A809	2.50d multicolored	1.25	1.25

Stamp Day.

Tennis Tournaments in Yugoslavia — A810

Stylized designs: No. 2374, Player, large racket overhead, Budva. No. 2375, Player with ball flying from racket, Belgrade. No. 2376, Player with racket out in front, Novi Sad.

1997, May 8

2374	A810	2.50d multi + label	1.25	1.25
2375	A810	2.50d multi + label	1.25	1.25
2376	A810	2.50d multi + label	1.25	1.25
		Nos. 2374-2376 (3)	3.75	3.75

Stories and Legends A811

Europa: 2.50d, Shackled Bach Chelik surrounded by creatures. 6d, Bach Chelik in chains, prince fighting with him, princess, castle.

1997, May 30　　　　　　Perf. 11½

2377	A811	2.50d multicolored	2.00	2.00
2378	A811	6d multicolored	2.00	2.00

Each issued in sheets of 8 + label.

European Nature Protection A812

2.50d, Cerambyx cerdo. 6d, Quercus robur.

1997, June 5

2379	A812	2.50d multicolored	1.00	1.00
2380	A812	6d multicolored	2.00	2.00

Stanislav Binicki (1872-1947) A813

1997, June 7　　　　　　Perf. 13½

2381	A813	2.50d multicolored	1.00	1.00

Printing of Gorski Vijenac, 150th Anniv. — A814

1997, June 7

2382	A814	2.50d multicolored	1.00	1.00

Flowers — A815

Designs: a, 1.50d, Pelargonium grandiflorum. b, 2.50d, Saintpaulia ionantha. c, 1.50d, Hydrangea macrophylla. d, 2.50d, Oncidium varicosum.

1997, Sept. 10　　Litho.　　Perf. 13

2383	A815	Strip of 4, #a.-d. + label	7.00	7.00

Souvenir Sheet

JUFIZ IX, 9th Natl. Philatelic Exhibition — A816

Design: Sculpture, by Dragomir Arambasic, in front of art gallery.

1997, Sept. 10　　　　　　Perf. 14

2384	A816	5d multicolored	2.50	2.50

A817

1997, Sept. 24　　　　Perf. 13½x14

2385	A817	2.50d multicolored	1.00	1.00

Serbian Chemical Society, cent.

**Type of 1993
Size: 18x18mm**

1997, Oct. 2　　　　　　Perf. 14

2386	A702d	(A) like #2142	1.00	.25
a.	Dated "1999"		1.00	.25

A818

Joy of Europe children's art works: 2.50d, 5d, Busts of people formed from collage of various food products.

1997, Oct. 2

2387	A818	2.50d multicolored	1.00	1.00
2388	A818	5d multicolored	2.00	2.00

"May Assembly in Sremski Karlivoci," by Pavle Simic — A819

1997, Oct. 10　　Litho.　　Perf. 14

2389	A819	2.50d multicolored	1.00	1.00

Matica Srpska Gallery, 150th anniv.

A820

Museum exhibits: No. 2390, Two-headed statuette. No. 2391, Parade helmet. No. 2392, Terra cotta statuette. No. 2393, Virgin icon.

1997, Nov. 12

2390	A820	1.50d multicolored	.50	.50
2391	A820	1.50d multicolored	.50	.50
2392	A820	2.50d multicolored	1.00	1.00
2393	A820	2.50d multicolored	1.00	1.00
		Nos. 2390-2393 (4)	3.00	3.00

A821

Icons (Chelandari Serbian Monastery, Mount Athos): No. 2394, Christ. No. 2395, Madonna and Child, 12th cent. No. 2396, Madonna and Child, 13th cent. No. 2397, 3-handed Madonna.

Granite Paper

1997, Dec. 2   *Perf. 11½*
2394 A821 1.50d multicolored   .50 .50
2395 A821 1.50d multicolored   .50 .50
2396 A821 2.50d multicolored   1.00 1.00
2397 A821 2.50d multicolored   1.00 1.00
   Nos. 2394-2397 (4)   3.00 3.00

A822

1998, Jan. 20   **Litho.**   *Perf. 13½*
2398 A822 1.50d Savina   *1.00 1.00*
2399 A822 2.50d Donji Brceli   *1.00 1.00*
   Monasteries of Montenegro.

A823

1998, Feb. 6   *Perf. 14*
2400 A823 2.50d Figure skater   2.00 2.00
2401 A823 6d Skier   2.00 2.00
   1998 Winter Olympic Games, Nagano.

Horses
A824

   Designs: a, 1.50d, Two running. b, 2.50d, Arabian up close. c, 1.50d, Thoroughbred. d, 2.50d, Thoroughbred running on race track.

1998, Feb. 26   **Litho.**   *Perf. 12x11½*
2402 A824   Strip of 4, #a.-d. +
      label   10.00 10.00

Intl.
Women's
Day
A825

1998, Mar. 7   *Perf. 13½*
2403 A825 2.50d multicolored   1.00 1.00

Yugoslav
Airlines
Assoc., 50th
Anniv.
A826

1998, Apr. 24
2404 A826 2.50d multicolored   1.00 1.00

Europa — A827

Paintings: 6d, "Dressing the Bride," by Paja Jovanovic (1859-1957). 9d, "Bishop's Congratulations," by Pero Pocek (1878-1963).

1998, May 4   *Perf. 12*
   Granite Paper
2405 A827 6d multicolored   3.00 3.00
2406 A827 9d on 2.50d, multi   3.00 3.00
   No. 2406 was not issued without the silver surcharge.

1998 World Cup
Soccer
Championships,
France — A828

1998, May 15   **Litho.**   *Perf. 13½*
2407 A828 6d shown   1.75 1.75
2408 A828 9d Soccer players,
      diff.   2.75 2.75

Souvenir Sheet

Danube Commission, 50th
Anniv. — A829

1998, May 19   *Perf. 14*
2409 A829 9d multicolored   4.00 4.00

European
Nature
Protection
A830

   Designs: 6d, Heracium blecicii. 9d, Mola mola, vert.

1998, June 17   **Litho.**   *Perf. 13¾*
2410 A830 6d multi   1.25 1.25
2411 A830 9d multi   1.75 1.75
   Each stamp was printed in sheets of 8 + label.

Famous People of
Serbia — A831

   a, Djura Jaksic (1832-78), poet, painter. b, Nadezda Petrovic (1873-1915), painter. c, Radoje Domanovic (1873-1908), writer. d, Vasilije Mokranjac (1923-1984), composer. e, Streten Stojanovic (1898-1960), sculptor. f, Milan Konjovic (1898-1993), painter. g, Desanka Maksimovic (1898-1993), poet. h, Ivan Tabakovic (1898-1977), painter.

1998, June 30   **Litho.**   *Perf. 12*
   Granite Paper
   Sheet of 8 + label
2412 A831 1.50d #a.-h.   3.25 3.25

Souvenir Sheet

Yugoslavia, Winner of World
Basketball Championships — A832

1998, Aug. 21   *Perf. 13½*
2413 A832 10d multicolored   8.00 8.00

Protected Animals — A833

   a, 2d, Martes martes. b, 2d, Anthropoides virgo. c, 5d, Lynx lynx. d, 5d, Loxia curvirostra.

1998, Sept. 2
2414 A833   Strip of 4, #a.-d. +
      label   9.00 9.00

Breaking of
the
Thessaloniki
Front, 80th
Anniv.
A834

   Designs: No. 2415, 5d, Soldiers and cannons. No. 2416, 5d, Soldiers with machine guns, binoculars.

1998, Sept. 15   **Engr.**   *Perf. 13½*
2415-2416 A834   Set of 2   3.50 3.50

Stamp
Day — A835

1998, Sept. 28
2417 A835 6d Prussian blue   1.40 1.40
   Serbian Philatelic Society, 50th anniv.

Joy of Europe
Children's
Drawings
A836

   Designs: 6d, Fish. 9d, Fish, diff.

1998, Oct. 2   **Litho.**   *Perf. 13¾*
2418-2419 A836   Set of 2   3.50 3.50

Development of the Railway — A837

Trains: a, 1847. b, 1900. c, 1920. d, 1930. e, Diesel locomotive. f, 1990.

1998, Nov. 3   **Litho.**   *Perf. 13½*
2420 A837 2.50d Booklet pane of
      6, #a.-f.   9.00 9.00
   Complete booklet, #2420   9.50

Paintings of
Sailing
Ships,
Maritime
Museum,
Kotor
A838

   #2421, Veracruz, 1873. #2422, Pierino, 1883. #2423, Draghetto, 1865. #2424, Group of ships.

1998, Nov. 11   *Perf. 12*
   Granite Paper
2421 A838 2d multicolored   .50 .50
2422 A838 2d multicolored   .50 .50
2423 A838 5d multicolored   1.50 1.50
2424 A838 5d multicolored   1.50 1.50
   Nos. 2421-2424 (4)   4.00 4.00

Chelandari Monastery, 800th
Anniv. — A839

   Views of monastery: No. 2425, Looking from center of complex, two trees. No. 2426, Group of taller buildings. No. 2427, Aerial view. No. 2428, Looking across group of buildings, crosses on turrets.

1998, Dec. 9   *Perf. 14*
2425 A839 2d multicolored   .50 .50
2426 A839 2d multicolored   .50 .50
2427 A839 5d multicolored   1.25 1.25
2428 A839 5d multicolored   1.25 1.25
   Nos. 2425-2428 (4)   3.50 3.50

Third Meeting
of Southeast
European
Postal
Ministers
A840

1998, Dec. 17   **Litho.**   *Perf. 14*
2429 A840 5d multicolored   *3.00 3.00*

Souvenir Sheet

Yugoslavia, Silver Medalist at 1998
World Volleyball
Championships — A841

1998, Dec. 19   *Perf. 13½*
2430 A841 10d multicolored   50.00 50.00

Post and Telecommunications
Museum, Belgrade, 75th
Anniv. — A842

#2431, Postrider. #No. 2432, Antique telegraph equipment, museum building.

1998, Dec. 21   **Engr.**
2431 A842 5d olive brown & slate   1.00 1.00
2432 A842 5d red & brown   1.00 1.00

Serbian
Monasteries
A843

1999, Jan. 14   **Litho.**   **Perf. 13¾**
2433 A843 2d Visoki Decani   .60 .60
2434 A843 5d Grachanica   1.60 1.60

Farm Animals
A844

Designs: a, 2d, Pigs. b, 6d, Goat. c, 2d, Oxen. d, 6d, Long-horn sheep.

1999, Feb. 5   **Litho.**   **Perf. 13½**
2435 A844 Strip of 4, #a.-d. +
    label   7.00 7.00

A845

1999, Feb. 24   **Litho.**   **Perf. 13¼**
2436 A845 6d Scouting   2.00 2.00

A846

1999, Mar. 27
2437 A846 6d brown & buff   1.40 1.40
Yugoslav Bar Association, 70th anniv.

Target
A847   A848

1999   **Perf. 12¼x12½**
2438 A847 (A) black   5.00 3.00
2439 A848 (A) black & red   20.00 12.00
Issued: No. 2438, 3/27; No. 2439, 4/7. Nos. 2438-2439 sold for 2.04d when issued.

World Table Tennis Championships,
Belgrade — A849

1999, Apr. 9   **Perf. 13¼**
Player colors
2440 A849 6d blue & red   2.00 2.00
2441 A849 6d green & red   2.00 2.00

A850

Europa, National Parks and Reserves: 6d, Falcon, trees, mountains, Kopaonik Natl. Park. 15d, Flowers, mountains, Lovcen Natl. Park.

1999, May 5   **Photo.**   **Perf. 11¾**
Granite Paper
2442 A850 6d multicolored   6.00 6.00
2443 A850 15d multicolored   6.00 6.00
Each printed in shhets of 8 + 1 central label.

A851

European Nature Protection: 6d, Shovel, spider web. 15d, Thumb squeezing earth.

1999, May 13   **Perf. 11¾x12**
2444 A851 6d multicolored   2.50 2.50
2445 A851 15d multicolored   2.50 2.50

Mushrooms
A852

Designs: a, Amanita virosa. b, Amanita pantherina. c, Hypholoma fasciculare. d, Ramaria pallida.

1999, June 18   **Litho.**   **Perf. 11¾x12**
Granite Paper
2446 A852 6d Strip of 4, #a.-
    d., + central la-
    bel   10.00 10.00
Central labels differ on sheet.

Famous Montenegrins — A853

Designs: a, Stjepan Mitrov Ljubisa (1824-78). b, Marko Milanov (1833-1901). c, Pero Pocek (1878-1963). d, Risto Stijovic (1894-1974). e, Milo Milunovic (1897-1967). f, Petar Lubarda (1907-74). g, Vuko Radovic (1911-96). h, Mihailo Lalic (1914-92).

1999, June 30   **Perf. 13¼**
2447 A853 2d Sheet of 8, #a.-h.,
    + central label   3.25 3.25

UPU, 125th
Anniv.
A854

1999, Sept. 15   **Perf. 13¼**
2448 A854 6d shown   1.00 1.00
2449 A854 12d Envelopes cir-
    cling globe   2.00 2.00

Joy of Europe
Children's
Drawings
A855

1999, Oct. 1   **Perf. 13¾**
2450 A855 6d Lion   1.00 1.00
2451 A855 15d Family, vert.   2.50 2.50

Frédéric Chopin
(1810-49),
Composer
A856

1999, Oct. 15   **Perf. 13¼**
2452 A856 10d multi   2.25 2.25

No. 2438,
Mastheads of
"Filatelista"
A857

1999, Oct. 18
2453 A857 10d multi   1.50 1.50
Stamp Day.

A858

Bridges
Destroyed by
NATO Air
Strikes
A859

Bridges: #2454, Varadinski. #2455, Ostruznica. #2456, Murino. #2457, Grdelica. #2458, Bistrica. #2459, Zezeljev.

1999, Oct. 29   **Perf. 13¾**
2454 A858 2d shown   .90 .90
2455 A859 2d shown   .90 .90
2456 A859 2d multi   .90 .90
2457 A859 6d multi   .90 .90
2458 A859 6d multi   .90 .90
2459 A859 6d multi   .90 .90
   Nos. 2454-2459 (6)   5.40 5.40

Millennium
A860

a, 6d, Roman altars, statue of Jupiter. b, 6d, Sculpture of Emperor Trajan and army leaders, mosaic, lamp, lead mirror. c, 6d, Mosaic of Dionysius, arch. d, 6d, Hagia Sophia, mosaic of Madonna and Child, Emperor Constantine. e, 6d, Large cross, candle, fibula, pot. f, 6d, Church, boats, manuscript. g, 15d, Nativity and crucifixion of Christ, boats, farmers.

1999, Nov. 19
2460 A860   Booklet pane of 7,
    #a.-g., + 2 labels   9.00 9.00
   Complete booklet, #2460   9.00
Size of #2460g: 105x55mm.

A861

Bomb Damage
A862

#2461, Bolnice. #2462, Telecommunications complex. #2463, Refinery. #2464, Bolnice, diff. #2465, Telecommunications complex, diff. #2466, Television complex.

1999, Nov. 27   **Litho.**   **Perf. 13¾**
2461 A861 2d shown   .50 .50
2462 A862 2d shown   .50 .50
2463 A862 2d multi   .50 .50
2464 A862 6d multi   1.00 1.00
2465 A862 6d multi   1.00 1.00
2466 A862 6d multi   1.00 1.00
   Nos. 2461-2466 (6)   4.50 4.50

A863

Frescoes of Poganovo Monastery,
500th Anniv. — A864

Design A863 has Latin letters, A864 has Cyrillic letters.

1999, Dec. 23

2467	A863	6d shown	.80 .80
2468	A864	6d shown	.80 .80
2469	A863	6d Fresco, diff.	.80 .80
2470	A864	6d Fresco, diff.	.80 .80
		Nos. 2467-2470 (4)	3.20 3.20

A865

Gold Prospectors in Pec River — A866

Design A865 has Latin letters, A866 has Cyrillic letters.

1999, Dec. 30

2471	A865	6d shown	.80 .80
2472	A866	6d shown	.80 .80
2473	A865	6d Prospectors, diff.	.80 .80
2474	A866	6d Prospectors, diff.	.80 .80
		Nos. 2471-2474 (4)	3.20 3.20

Krusedol Monastery A867

2000, Jan. 13   Perf. 13¼

2475	A867	10d shown	1.50 1.50
2476	A867	10d Rakovac Monastery	1.50 1.50

Yugoslavian Archives, 50th Anniv. A868

2000, Jan. 21

2477	A868	10d multi	25.00 25.00

Butterflies — A869

No. 2478: a, Nymphalis antiopa. b, Parnalius polyxena. c, Limenitis populi. d, Melanargia galathea.

2000, Feb. 25   Litho.   Perf. 13¾

2478		Horiz. strip of 4 + central label	18.00 18.00
a.-d.	A869	10d Any single	2.50 2.50

Worldwide Fund for Nature — A870

No. 2478: Perdix perdix: a, Pair in snow. b, Pair facing right. c, Bird on nest. d, Pair, one facing left.

2000, Mar. 14   Litho.   Perf. 12x11¾

2479	A870	10d Strip of 4, #a.-d., + central label	12.00 12.00

Damage from NATO Airstrikes A871

Various destroyed buildings. Colors: 10d, Blue. 20d, Brown.

2000, Mar. 24   Engr.   Perf. 13¼

2480-2481	A871	Set of 2	5.00 5.00

Souvenir Sheet

JUFIZ X Philatelic Exhibition, Belgrade — A872

2000, May 2   Litho.

2482	A872	15d multi	50.00 50.00

Nature Protection A873

Designs: No. 2483, 30d, Feeding chicks by hand. No. 2484, 30d, Map of Europe in tree's leaves, vert.

Perf. 12x11¾, 11¾x12

2000, May 4   Litho.

2483-2484	A873	Set of 2	4.00 4.00

Europa — A874

"2000" and: No. 2485, 30d, Astronaut on moon. No. 2486, 30d, Star and mountains.

2000, May 9   Perf. 11¾x12

2485-2486	A874	Set of 2	8.00 8.00

European Soccer Championships A875

Inscriptions in: No. 2487, 30d, Cyrillic letters. No. 2488, 30d, Latin letters.

2000, May 20   Litho.   Perf. 13¾

2487-2488	A875	Set of 2	6.00 6.00

Postal Services in Serbia, 160th Anniv. — A876

2000, June 7   Litho.   Perf. 13¾

2489	A876	10d multi	2.00 2.00

2000 Summer Olympics, Sydney — A877

Map of Australia and: 6d, Kangaroo. 12d, Emu. 24d, Koala and soccer ball. 30d, Parrot.

2000, June 28

2490-2493	A877	Set of 4	7.00 7.00

Stamp Day — A878

2000, Sept. 26   Perf. 13¼

2494	A878	10d multi	4.50 4.50

"Joy of Europe" A879

Children's art: 30d, Cows. 40d, Cranes, vert.

2000, Oct. 2

2495-2496	A879	Set of 2	3.50 3.50

World Teachers' Day — A880

2000, Oct. 5

2497	A880	10d multi	20.00 20.00

13th Apiarists Congress A881

2000, Oct. 6

2498	A881	10d multi	5.00 5.00

Medals Won at 2000 Summer Olympics A882

Designs: No. 2499, 20d, Water polo (bronze). No. 2500, 20d, Shooting (silver). 30d, Volleyball, vert.

2000, Oct. 23   Perf. 13¾

2499-2500	A882	Set of 2	3.00 3.00

Souvenir Sheet

2501	A882	30d multi	20.00 20.00

No. 2501 contains one 35x46mm stamp.

Millennium — A883

No. 2502: a, Ships. b, Papermaking. c, Galileo and telescopes. d, Steam locomotive and steamship. e, Nikola Tesla, invention of the telephone. f, Astronaut, outer space settlement. g, Ships, airplanes, balloons, horses.

2000, Nov. 2   Litho.   Perf. 13¾

2502	A883	Booklet pane of 7 + 2 labels	6.00 —
a.-f.		12d Any single	.60 .60
g.		40d multi	2.00 2.00
		Booklet, #2502	6.00

Size of No. 2502g: 105x55mm.

Nativity Fresco, Pec — A884

2000, Nov. 7   Litho.   Perf. 13¾

2503	A884	A multi	3.50 .50

No. 2503 sold for 3.56d on day of issue.

Serb Clothing From the 1900s — A885

Designs: 6d, Vest, Jagodina. 12d, Dresses, Metochija. 24d, Blouse, Pec. 30d, Vest, Kupres.

2000, Dec. 7

2504-2507	A885	Set of 4	3.00 3.00

Montenegrin Religious Art — A886

Designs: 6d, Madonna and Child, 1573-74. 12d, Nativity, 1666-67. 24d, St. Luke, 1672-73. 30d, Madonna and Child, 1642.

2000, Dec. 19

2508-2511	A886	Set of 4	3.00 3.00

A887

A887a

2000, Dec. 29 Litho. Perf. 13¾
2512 A887 6d multi .50 .50
2513 A887a 12d multi .50 .50
Resumption of Yugoslavia's membership in Organization for Security and Cooperation in Europe (#2512), and United Nations (#2513).

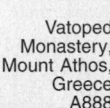

Vatoped Monastery, Mount Athos, Greece A888

Esfigmen Monastery, Mount Athos, Greece A889

2001, Jan. 26 Litho. Perf. 13¼
2514 A888 10d multi .55 .55
2515 A889 27d multi 1.60 1.60

Matica Srpska, 175th Anniv. — A890

2001, Feb. 16 Perf. 13¾
2516 A890 15d multi 1.10 1.10

Animals — A891

No. 2517: a, Felis leo. b, Ursus maritimus. c, Macaca fuscata. d, Spheniscus humboldti.

2001, Feb. 23
2517 Horiz. strip of 4 + central label 7.25 7.25
a. A891 6d multi .45 .45
b. A891 12d multi .90 .90
c. A891 24d multi 1.10 1.10
d. A891 30d multi 1.40 1.40

Women's World Chess Champions — A892

No. 2518: a, Vera Menchik (1927-44). b, Lyudmila Rudenko (1950-53). c, Yelisavyeta

---

Bykova (1953-56, 1958-62). d, Olga Rubtsova (1956-58). e, Nona Gaprindashvili (1962-78). f, Maia Chiburdanidze (1978-91). g, Zsuzsa Polgar (1996-99). h, Xie Jun (1991-96, 1999-2000).

2001, Mar. 8 Perf. 13¼
2518 A892 10d Sheet of 8, #a-h, + label 4.50 4.50

Famous Men — A893

Designs: 50d, Stevan Mokranjac (1856-1914), composer. 100d, Nikola Tesla (1856-1943), inventor.

2001, Mar. 19 Perf. 13¾
2519-2520 A893 Set of 2 7.25 7.25

Flowers A894

No. 2521: a, Hibiscus syriacus. b, Nerium oleander. c, Lapageria rosea. d, Sorbus aucuparia.

2001, Apr. 13 Perf. 12x11¾
2521 Horiz. strip of 4 + central label 6.50 6.50
a. A894 6d multi .35 .35
b. A894 12d multi .55 .55
c. A894 24d multi 1.00 1.00
d. A894 30d multi 1.40 1.40

Europa — A895

Designs: 30d, Vratna River. 45d, Jerme Canyon.

2001, May 4 Perf. 11¾x12
2522-2523 A895 Set of 2 6.75 6.75

Serbian Mountaineering Association, Cent. — A896

2001, June 8 Perf. 13¼
2524 A896 15d multi 1.25 1.25

European Nature Protection A897

Designs: 30d, Bird on branch, Lake Ludasko. 45d, Stork flying above Begej River.

2001, June 22 Perf. 12x11¾
2525-2526 A897 Set of 2 3.75 3.75

14th Cent. Book Illumination A898

2001, July 2 Perf. 13¼
2527 A898 E multi 1.60 1.60
Sold for 28.70d on day of issue.

Souvenir Sheet

Yugoslavian Victory in European Water Polo Championships — A899

2001, July 5 Perf. 13¾
2528 A899 30d multi 6.50 6.50

Souvenir Sheet

Serbiafila XII Stamp Exhibition — A900

2001, Sept. 8
2529 A900 30d multi 2.50 2.50

Solar Energy — A901

2001, Sept. 19 Perf. 13¼
2530 A901 15d multi 1.60 1.60

Danube Commission A902

Designs: 30d, Ships, hands raising bridge. 45d, Ship, hand, clock.

2001, Sept. 20 Perf. 13¾
2531-2532 A902 Set of 2 5.50 5.50

Joy of Europe — A903

Paintings: 30d, Child, by Marko Chelebonovic. 45d, Girl Under a Fruit Tree, by Beta Vukanovic.

2001, Oct. 2 Perf. 13¼
2533-2534 A903 Set of 2 5.50 5.50

Yugoslavian Victories in European Sports Championships A904

Designs: No. 2535, 30d, Men's basketball. No. 2536, 30d, Men's volleyball.

2001, Oct. 11
2535-2536 A904 Set of 2 45.00 45.00

Intl. Federation of Philately (FIP), 75th Anniv. A905

2001, Oct. 24
2537 A905 15d multi 1.60 1.60
Stamp Day.

Minerals A906

2001, Nov. 2 Perf. 13¾
2538 Horiz. strip of 4 + central label 5.00 5.00
a. A906 7d Antimonite 1.10 1.10
b. A906 14d Calcite 1.10 1.10
c. A906 26.20d Quartz 1.10 1.10
d. A906 28.70d Calcite and galenite 1.10 1.10

Pljevlja Gymnasium, Cent. — A907

2001, Nov. 18 Perf. 13¼
2539 A907 15d multi 2.25 2.25

Public Telephone Booths in Serbia, Cent. — A908

2001, Nov. 20
2540 A908 15d multi 1.40 1.40

Christmas A910

Paintings of the Birth of Jesus Christ: 7d, 14d, 26.20d, 28.70d.

2001, Dec. 1 Perf. 13¾
2541-2544 A910 Set of 4 4.50 4.50

Junior World Ice Hockey Championships, Belgrade — A911

2002, Jan. 5   **Perf. 13¼**
2545 A911 14d multi   10.00 10.00

2002 Winter Olympics, Salt Lake City — A912

Designs: 28.70d, Skier. 50d, Four-man bobsled, vert.

2002, Jan. 25   **Perf. 13¼**
2546-2547 A912   Set of 2   25.00 25.00

Jovan Karamata (1902-67), Mathematician A913

2002, Feb. 1
2548 A913 14d multi   10.00 10.00

Birds — A914

No. 2549: a, Saxicola torquata. b, Saxicola rubetra. c, Parus caeruleus. d, Turdus philomelos.

2002, Feb. 22
2549   Horiz. strip of 4 +   10.00 10.00
    central label
  a. A914 7d multi   .65 .65
  b. A914 14d multi   1.50 1.50
  c. A914 26.20d multi   3.00 3.00
  d. A914 28.70d multi   0.50 3.50

Easter — A915

Designs: 7d, Crucifixion, fresco from Studenica Monastery, 1208. 14d, King Milutin's Veil, 1300. 26.20d, Christ's Descent to Hell, silverwork, 1540. 28.70d, Easter egg, Pec Patriarchy, 1980.

2002, Mar. 7   **Perf. 13¾**
2550-2553 A915   Set of 4   9.00 9.00

Bunjevac Women's Clothing — A916

Woman with: 7d, White blouse. 28.70d, Kerchief.

2002, Mar. 29   **Perf. 13¼**
2554-2555 A916   Set of 2   4.50 4.50

Zarko Tomic-Sremac (b. 1900), World War II Hero — A917

2002, Apr. 15
2556 A917 14d multi   12.50 12.50

Danube Fish — A918

No. 2557: a, Rutilus rutilus. b, Acipenser ruthenus. c, Huso huso. d, Stizostedion lucioperca.

2002, Apr. 25   **Litho.**   **Perf. 13¼**
2557   Horiz. strip of 4 +   18.00 18.00
    central label
  a. A918 7d multi   1.50 1.50
  b. A918 14d multi   2.50 2.50
  c. A918 26.20d multi   5.00 5.00
  d. A918 28.70d multi   5.00 5.00

Europa A919

Designs: 28.70d, Trapeze artists. 50d, Tiger trainer.

2002, May 3   **Perf. 13¾**
2558-2559 A919   Set of 2   11.00 11.00

Europa Type
Souvenir Sheet

Design: 45d, Trained horse act.

2002, May 3   **Litho.**   **Perf. 13¾**
2560 A919 45d multi   60.00 60.00

No. 2560 contains one 46x35mm stamp.

Civil Aviation in Yugoslavia, 75th Anniv. A920

Designs: 7d, Potez-29. 28.70d, Boeing 737-300.

Perf. 13¼ Syncopated
2002, June 17   **Litho.**
2561-2562 A920   Set of 2   30.00 30.00

Types of 1993 and 2001
Size: 19x21mm (#2563)

2002, July 25   **Litho.**   **Perf. 12½**
2563 A702d A blue   3.00 1.50

Perf. 13¼
"E" in Green
2564 A898 E multi   7.50 4.50

Nos. 2563-2564 were intended for use in Montenegro and were sold there for 13c and 52c in euro currency respectively. The stamps were valid for use in the Serbian section of Yugoslavia.

European Nature Protection A921

Designs: 28.70d, Tara National Park. 50d, Golija Nature Park.

Perf. 13¼ Syncopated
2002, June 28   Set of 2   **Litho.**
2565-2566 A921   9.00 9.00

Mills — A922

Designs: 7d, Windmill, Melenci. 28.70d, Water mill, Lyuberada.

2002, Sept. 14
2567-2568 A922   Set of 2   9.00 9.00

Liberation of Niskic, 125th Anniv. — A923

2002, Sept. 18   **Perf. 13¾**
2569 A923 14d multi   10.00 9.00

Souvenir Sheet

Victory in 2002 World Basketball Championships — A924

2002, Sept. 20
2570 A924 30d multi   10.00 10.00

Souvenir Sheet

JUFIZ XI Philatelic Exhibition — A925

2002, Sept. 23
2571 A925 30d multi   8.00 8.00

Joy of Europe — A926

Children's art: 28.70d, Boat. 50d, Bird.

2002, Oct. 2
2572-2573 A926   Set of 2   8.50 8.50

Moraca Monastery, 750th Anniv. — A927

2002, Oct. 10
2574 A927 16d multi   20.00 12.00

Nos. 2255-2256 Srchd. in Black or Violet

2002   **Perfs., etc., as Before**
2575 A751   50p on 5p #2256   2.50 1.25
    multi
2576 A702g   1d on 10,000d   7.50 6.00
    #2145
2577 A751   12d on 1p #2255   6.00 4.00
    multi (V)
  Nos. 2575-2577 (3)   16.00 11.25

Issued: No. 2575, 10/17; No. 2576, 11/28; No. 2577, 12/19.
For stamp like No. 2577, but with black surcharge, see Serbia and Montenegro No. 260.

Intl. Federation of Stamp Dealers Associations, 50th Anniv. — A928

2002, Oct. 24   **Litho.**   **Perf. 13¾**
2578 A928 16d multi   7.50 7.50

Serbian Folk Costumes — A929

Paintings of costumes by Olga Benson in Ethnographic Institute of Serbian Academy of Sciences and Arts: a, Man, Kusadak. b, Woman with red headdress, Belgrade. c, Man, Novo Selo. d, Woman in profile, Belgrade.

2002, Nov. 8   **Perf. 13¾**
2579   Horiz. strip of 4, + cen-   8.00 8.00
    tral label
  a. A929 16d multi   1.00 1.00
  b. A929 24d multi   2.00 2.00
  c. A929 26.20d multi   2.00 2.00
  d. A929 28.70d multi   2.00 2.00

Christmas A930

Religious art: 12d, Nativity, Stavronikita Monastery, Mount Athos, Greece, 1546. 16d, Nativity, Chilandari Monastery, Mount Athos, Greece, c. 1618. 26.20d, Nativity, Tretyakov

Gallery, Moscow, 15th cent. 28.70d, Adoration of the Magi, by Sandro Botticelli.

2002, Dec. 2
2580-2583 A930 Set of 4   7.00 7.00

Abandoned Dogs — A931

Various dogs.

2003, Jan. 31   **Perf. 13¾**
2584   Horiz. strip of 4, + central label   5.00 5.00
   a. A931 16d multi   .50 .50
   b. A931 24d multi   1.25 1.25
   c. A931 26.20d multi   1.25 1.25
   d. A931 28.70d multi   1.25 1.25

> Yugoslavia became Serbia & Montenegro on Feb. 4, 2003. See Serbia & Montenegro for subsequent issues.

SEMI-POSTAL STAMPS

Giving Succor to Wounded SP1

Wounded Soldier SP2

Symbolical of National Unity — SP3

Unwmk.
1921, Jan. 30   **Engr.**   **Perf. 12**
B1 SP1 10p carmine   .25 .25
B2 SP2 15p violet brown   .25 .25
B3 SP3 25p light blue   .25 .25
   Nos. B1-B3 (3)   .75 .75

Nos. B1-B3 were sold at double face value, the excess being for the benefit of invalid soldiers.
Exist imperf. Value $35.
For surcharges see Nos. 15-21.

This overprint was applied to 500,000 examples of No. B1 in 1923 and they were given to the Society for Wounded Invalids (Uprava Ratnih Invalida) which sold them for 2d a piece. These overprinted stamps had no franking power, but some were used through ignorance.

Regular Issue of 1926-27 Surcharged in Dark Red

1926, Nov. 1   **Perf. 13**
B5 A6 25p + 25p green   .25 .25
B6 A6 50p + 50p olive brn   .25 .25
B7 A6 1d + 50p scarlet   .25 .25
B8 A6 2d + 50p black   .25 .25
B9 A6 3d + 50p slate blue   .25 .25
B10 A6 4d + 50p red org   .30 .25
B11 A6 5d + 50p brt vio   .50 .25
B12 A6 8d + 50p black brn   1.00 .25
B13 A6 10d + 1d olive brn   2.00 .25
B14 A6 15d + 1d brown   8.00 1.00
B15 A6 20d + 1d dark vio   12.00 .55
B16 A6 30d + 1d orange   27.50 3.25
   a. Double surcharge
   Nos. B5-B16 (12)   52.55 7.05
   Set, never hinged   105.00

The surtax on these stamps was intended for a fund for relief of sufferers from floods.
For overprints see Nos. 99-101.

Cathedral at Duvno SP4

King Tomislav SP6

Kings Tomislav and Alexander SP5

Perf. 12½, 11½x12
1929, Nov. 1   **Typo.**
B17 SP4 50p (+ 50p) olive green   .25 .25
B18 SP5 1d (+ 50p) red   .60 .40
B19 SP6 3d (+ 1d) blue   1.60 1.10
   Nos. B17-B19 (3)   2.45 1.75
   Set, never hinged   4.75

Millenary of the Croatian kingdom. The surtax was used to create a War Memorial Cemetery in France and to erect a monument to Serbian soldiers who died there.
No. B18 exists imperf. Value $400.

View of Dobropolje SP7

War Memorial — SP8

View of Kajmaktchalan SP9

1931, Apr. 1   **Perf. 12½, 11½**
B20 SP7 50p + 50p blue grn   .25 .25
B21 SP8 1d + 1d scarlet   .25 .25
B22 SP9 3d + 3d deep blue   .25 .25
   Nos. B20-B22 (3)   .75 .75

The surtax was added to a fund for a War Memorial to Serbian soldiers who died in France during World War I.

SP10

SP12

SP11

Black Overprint

1931, Nov. 1   **Perf. 12½, 11½x12**
B23 SP10 50p (+ 50p) olive grn   .25 .25
B24 SP11 1d (+ 50p) red   .25 .25
B25 SP12 3d (+ 1d) blue   .30 .30
   Nos. B23-B25 (3)   .80 .80

Surtax for War Memorial fund.

Rower on Danube at Smederevo SP13

Bled Lake SP14

Danube near Belgrade SP15

View of Split Harbor SP16

Zagreb Cathedral — SP17

Prince Peter — SP18

1932, Sept. 2   **Litho.**   **Perf. 11½**
B26 SP13 75p + 50p dl grn & lt blue   .75 1.50
B27 SP14 1d + ½d scar & lt blue   .75 1.50
B28 SP15 1½d + ½d rose & green   1.00 2.00
B29 SP16 3d + 1d bl & lt bl   2.00 3.00
B30 SP17 4d + 1d red org & lt blue   9.00 20.00

B31 SP18 5d + 1d dl vio & lilac   9.00 17.00
   Nos. B26-B31 (6)   22.50 45.00
   Set, never hinged   45.00

European Rowing Championship Races, Belgrade.

King Alexander — SP19

1933, May 25   **Typo.**   **Perf. 12½**
B32 SP19 50p + 25p black   6.00 12.00
B33 SP19 75p + 25p yel grn   6.00 12.00
B34 SP19 1.50d + 50p rose   6.00 12.00
B35 SP19 3d + 1d bl vio   6.00 12.00
B36 SP19 4p + 1d dk grn   6.00 12.00
B37 SP19 5d + 1d orange   6.00 12.00
   Nos. B32-B37 (6)   36.00 72.00
   Set, never hinged   72.50

11th Intl. Congress of P.E.N. (Poets, Editors and Novelists) Clubs, Dubrovnik, May 25-27.
The labels at the foot of the stamps are printed in either Cyrillic or Latin letters and each bears the amount of a premium for the benefit of the local P.E.N. Club at Dubrovnik.

Prince Peter — SP20

1933, June 28
B38 SP20 75p + 25p slate grn   .25 .25
B39 SP20 1½d + ½d deep red   .25 .25

60th anniv. meeting of the National Sokols (Sports Associations) at Ljubljana, July 1.

Eagle Soaring over City — SP22

1934, June 1   **Perf. 12½**
B40 SP22 75p + 25p green   5.00 9.50
B41 SP22 1.50d + 50p car   7.50 10.00
B42 SP22 1.75d + 25p brown   12.50 10.50
   Nos. B40-B42 (3)   25.00 30.00
   Set, never hinged   50.00

20th anniversary of Sokols of Sarajevo.

Athlete and Eagle — SP23

1934, June 1
B43 SP23 75p + 25p Prus grn   2.40 4.75
B44 SP23 1.50d + 50p car   2.40 4.75
B45 SP23 1.75d + 25p choc   10.00 14.50
   Nos. B43-B45 (3)   14.80 24.00
   Set, never hinged   27.50

60th anniversary of Sokols of Zagreb.

Mother and Children
SP24   SP25

Perf. 12½x11½

1935, Dec. 25   Photo.
B46 SP24 1.50d + 1d dk brn & brown   1.25   1.20
   a.   Perf. 11½   12.00   14.50
B47 SP25 3.50d + 1.50d bright ultra & bl   2.00   2.90
   Set, never hinged   6.50
The surtax was for "Winter Help."

Queen Mother Marie — SP26

1936, May 3   Litho.
B48 SP26 75p + 25p grnsh bl   .25   .40
B49 SP26 1.50d + 50p rose pink   .25   .45
B50 SP26 1.75d + 75p brown   1.25   1.25
B51 SP26 3.50d + 1d brt bl   1.60   2.75
   Nos. B48-B51 (4)   3.35   4.85
   Set, never hinged   6.50

Prince Regent Paul — SP27

1936, Sept. 20   Typo.
B52 SP27 75p + 50p turq grn & red   .40   *.35*
B53 SP27 1.50d + 50p cer & red   .40   *.35*
   Set, never hinged   1.60
Surtax for the Red Cross.

Princes Tomislav and Andrej
SP28   SP29

Perf. 11½x12½, 12½x11½

1937, May 1
B54 SP28 25p + 25p red brn   .25   .25
B55 SP28 75p + 75p emerald   .25   .40
B56 SP29 1.50d + 1d org red   .30   .65
B57 SP29 2d + 1d magenta   .60   1.20
   Nos. B54-B57 (4)   1.40   2.50
   Set, never hinged   2.40

Souvenir Sheet

National Costumes — SP30

1937, Sept. 12   Perf. 14
B57A SP30 Sheet of 4   4.75   10.00
   Never hinged   9.50
   b.   1d blue green   1.00   1.75
   c.   1.50d bright violet   1.00   1.75
   d.   2d rose red   1.00   1.75
   e.   4d dark blue   1.00   1.75

1st Yugoslavian Phil. Exhib., Belgrade. Sold only at the exhibition post office at 15d each.

SP31   SP32

Perf. 11½x12½, 12½x11½

1938, May 1   Photo.
B58 SP31 50p + 50p dark brn   .25   .30
B59 SP32 1d + 1d dk green   .25   .35
B60 SP31 1.50d + 1.50d scar   .50   .40
B61 SP32 2d + 2d magenta   1.25   .80
   Nos. B58-B61 (4)   2.25   1.85
   Set, never hinged   4.00

Surtax for the benefit of Child Welfare. For overprints see Nos. B75-B78.

Bridge and Anti-aircraft Lights — SP33

1938, May 28   Perf. 11½x12½
B62 SP33 1d + 50p dk grn   .40   .80
B63 SP33 1.50d + 1d scarlet   .60   1.20
   a.   Perf. 11½   17.50   27.50
B64 SP33 2d + 1d rose vio   1.25   2.40
   a.   Perf. 11½   18.00   35.00
B65 SP33 3d + 1.50d dp bl   2.00   4.00
   Nos. B62-B65 (4)   4.25   8.40
   Set, never hinged   8.00

Intl. Aeronautical Exhib., Belgrade.

Cliff at Demir-Kapiya — SP34

Modern Hospital SP35

Runner Carrying Torch — SP36   Alexander I — SP37

Perf. 11½x12½, 12½x11½

1938, Aug. 1
B66 SP34 1d + 1d slate grn & dp grn   .45   .40
B67 SP35 1.50d + 1.50d scar   .70   .55
B68 SP36 2d + 2d claret & dp rose   1.60   3.25
B69 SP37 3d + 3d dp bl   1.60   3.25
   Nos. B66-B69 (4)   4.35   7.45
   Set, never hinged   9.00

The surtax was to raise funds to build a hospital for railway employees.

Runner   Shot-Putter
SP38   SP41

Hurdlers SP39

Pole Vaulter SP40

1938, Sept. 11
B70 SP38 50p + 50p org brn   1.50   3.00
B71 SP39 1d + 1d sl grn & dp grn   1.50   3.00
B72 SP40 1.50d + 1.50d rose & dk mag   1.50   3.00
B73 SP41 2d + 2d dk blue   3.00   6.00
   Nos. B70-B73 (4)   7.50   15.00
   Set, never hinged   16.00

Ninth Balkan Games.

Stamps of 1938 Overprinted in Black

a   b

1938, Oct. 1
B75 SP31(a) 50p + 50p dk brn   .40   .55
B76 SP32(b) 1d + 1d dk grn   .40   .80
B77 SP31(a) 1.50d + 1.50d scar   .60   1.20
B78 SP32(b) 2d + 2d mag   1.25   2.40
   Nos. B75-B78 (4)   2.65   4.95
   Set, never hinged   5.25

Surtax for the benefit of Child Welfare.

Postriders SP43

1d+1d, Rural mail delivery. 1.50d+1.50d, Mail train. 2d+2d, Mail bus. 4d+4d, Mail plane.

1939, Mar. 15   Photo.   Perf. 11½
B79 SP43 50p + 50p buff, bis & brown   .35   .75
B80 SP43 1d + 1d sl grn & dp green   .35   .75
B81 SP43 1.50d + 1.50d red, cop red & brn car   2.50   2.50
B82 SP43 2d + 2d dp plum & rose lilac   2.50   3.50
B83 SP43 4d + 4d ind & sl bl   3.00   5.00
   Nos. B79-B83 (5)   8.70   12.50
   Set, never hinged   17.00

Centenary of the present postal system in Yugoslavia. The surtax was used for the Railway Benevolent Association.
The Cyrillic and Latin inscriptions are transposed on Nos. B82 and B83.

Child Eating SP48

Children at Seashore — SP49

Boy Planing Board SP50

Children in Crib — SP51

1939, May 1   Perf. 12½
B84 SP48 1d + 1d blk & dp bl green   .50   1.00
B85 SP49 1.50d + 1.50d org brn & sal   2.00   3.25
   a.   Perf. 11½   80.00   160.00
B86 SP50 2d + 2d mar & vio rose   1.40   2.90
B87 SP51 4d + 4d ind & royal blue   1.40   2.90
   Nos. B84-B87 (4)   5.30   10.05
   Set, never hinged   10.50

The surtax was for the benefit of Child Welfare.

Czar Lazar of Serbia — SP52

Milosh Obilich — SP53

1939, June 28   Perf. 11½
B88 SP52 1d + 1d sl grn & bl grn   1.60   1.60
B89 SP53 1.50d + 1.50d mar & brt car   1.60   1.60
   Set, never hinged   6.50

Battle of Kosovo, 550th anniversary.

Training Ship "Jadran" SP54

Designs: 1d+50p, Steamship "King Alexander." 1.50d+1d, Freighter "Triglan." 2d+1.50d, Cruiser "Dubrovnik."

1939, Sept. 6   **Engr.**

B90	SP54	50p + 50p brn org	.40	.80
B91	SP54	1d + 50p dull grn	.80	1.60
B92	SP54	1.50d + 1d dp rose	1.25	2.40
B93	SP54	2d + 1.50d dark bl	2.00	4.00
		Nos. B90-B93 (4)	4.45	8.80
		Set, never hinged		9.00

Yugoslav Navy and Merchant Marine. The surtax aided a Marine Museum.

Nos. B90-B93 also exist with a small "S" engraver's mark. Set value NH, $160. Location of the mark: On No. B90, above the base of the bowsprit. On No. B91, at the top of the smoke plume just below the "B" in the country name. On No. B92, at the top left of the large numeral "1". On No. B93, in the curve of the numeral "2".

Motorcycle and Sidecar — SP58

Racing Car SP59

Motorcycle SP60

Racing Car SP61

1939, Sept. 3   **Photo.**

B94	SP58	50p + 50p multi	.50	.80
B95	SP59	1d + 1d multi	1.00	1.60
B96	SP60	1.50d + 1.50d multi	1.40	2.40
B97	SP61	2d + 2d multi	2.50	4.00
		Nos. B94-B97 (4)	5.40	8.80
		Set, never hinged		10.50

Automobile and Motorcycle Races, Belgrade. The surtax was for the Race Organization and the State Treasury.

Unknown Soldier Memorial SP62

1939, Oct. 9   **Perf. 12½**

B98	SP62	1d + 50p sl grn & green	1.00	1.60
B99	SP62	1.50d + 1d red & rose red	1.00	1.60
B100	SP62	2d + 1.50d dp cl & vio rose	1.25	2.40
B101	SP62	3d + 2d dp bl & bl	2.50	4.00
		Nos. B98-B101 (4)	5.75	9.60
		Set, never hinged		11.00

Assassination of King Alexander, 5th anniv. The surtax was used to aid World War I invalids.

Postman Delivering Mail — SP64

Postman Emptying Mail Box — SP65

Parcel Post Delivery Wagon SP66

Parcel Post SP67

Repairing Telephone Wires — SP68

1940, Jan. 1

B102	SP64	50p + 50p brn & deep org	.60	1.00
B103	SP65	1d + 1d sl grn & blue grn	.60	1.00
B104	SP66	1.50d + 1.50d red brn & scar	1.00	2.40
B105	SP67	2d + 2d dl vio & red lilac	1.25	2.40
B106	SP68	4d + 4d sl bl & bl	4.00	6.50
		Nos. B102-B106 (5)	7.45	13.30
		Set, never hinged		14.50

The surtax was used for the employees of the Postal System in Belgrade.

Croats' Arrival at Adriatic in 640 SP69

King Tomislav — SP70

Death of Matija Gubec — SP71

Anton and Stjepan Radic SP72

Map of Yugoslavia SP73

1940, Mar. 1   **Typo.**   **Perf. 11½**

B107	SP69	50p + 50p brn org	.40	.55
B108	SP70	1d + 1d green	.40	.55
B109	SP71	1.50d + 1.50d brt red	1.25	.55
B110	SP72	2d + 2d dk cerise	2.00	2.40
B111	SP73	4d + 2d dark blue	2.00	2.75
		Nos. B107-B111 (5)	6.05	6.80
		Set, never hinged		12.00

The surtax was used for the benefit of postal employees in Zagreb.

Children Playing in Snow SP74

Children at Seashore — SP75

1940, May 1   **Photo.**   **Perf. 11½, 12½**

B112	SP74	50p + 50p brn org & org yellow	.25	.40
B113	SP75	1d + 1d sl grn & dk green	.25	.40
B114	SP74	1.50d + 1.50d brn red & scarlet	.60	.80
B115	SP75	2d + 2d mar & vio rose	1.00	1.60
		Nos. B112-B115 (4)	2.10	3.20
		Set, never hinged		4.00

The surtax was for Child Welfare.

Nos. C11-C14 Surcharged in Carmine

Perf. 11½x12½, 12½x11½

1940, Dec. 23

B116	AP6	50p + 50p on 5d	.25	.25
B117	AP7	1d + 1d on 10d	.25	.40
	a.	Perf. 12½	40.00	40.00
B118	AP8	1.50d + 1.50d on 20d	.80	1.40
B119	AP9	2d + 2d on 30d	.90	1.75
		Nos. B116-B119 (4)	2.20	3.80
		Set, never hinged		4.00

The surtax was used to fight tuberculosis. For surcharges see Nos. NB1-NB4.

St. Peter's Cemetery, Ljubljana — SP76

Croatian, Serbian and Slovenian SP77   Chapel at Kajmaktchalan SP78

Memorial at Brezje SP79

1941, Jan. 1   **Perf. 12½**

B120	SP76	50p + 50p gray grn & yel green	.25	.40
B121	SP77	1d + 1d brn car & dl rose	.25	.40
B122	SP78	1.50d + 1.50d myr grn & bl green	.60	1.25
B123	SP79	2d + 2d gray bl & pale lilac	1.00	2.00
		Nos. B120-B123 (4)	2.10	4.05
		Set, never hinged		

Surtax for the Ljubljana War Veterans Assoc.

Kamenita Gate, Zagreb — SP80

13th Century Cathedral, Zagreb — SP81

1941, Mar. 16   **Engr.**   **Perf. 11½**

B124	SP80	1.50d + 1.50d choc	.60	1.25
B125	SP81	4d + 3d blue blk	.60	1.25
		Set, never hinged		2.75

2nd Philatelic Exhibition of Croatia, at Zagreb, Mar. 16-27.

Nos. B124-B125 exist perf. 9½ on right side. Value, each $32.50.

No. B124 exists with "S" engraver's mark located next to the lower left window of the building. Value NH $80.

1941, Apr.

B126	SP80	1.50d + 1.50d bl black	12.00	24.00
B127	SP81	4d + 3d choc	12.00	24.00
		Set, never hinged		55.00

Regional philatelic exhibition at Slavonski Brod. Nos. B126-B127 with gold overprint, "Nezavisna Drzava Hrvatska," are Croatia Nos. B1-B2.

Nos. B126-B127 exist perf. 9½ on right side. Value, each $40 unused, $80 never hinged, $80 used.

No. B126 exists with "S" engraver's mark located next to the lower left window of the building. Value NH $425.

Issues for Federal Republic

Carrying
Wounded
Soldier — SP82

Child — SP83

1945, Sept. 15   Typo.   Perf. 11½
B131 SP82 1d + 4d deep ultra   .50   .80
B132 SP83 2d + 6d scarlet   .50   .80
Set, never hinged   1.90

The surtax was for the Red Cross.

Russia,
Yugoslavia
Flags
SP84

1945, Oct. 20   Photo.   Unwmk.
B133 SP84 2d + 5d multi   .80 1.60
Never hinged   1.60

Liberation of Belgrade, 1st anniv.
Exist imperf. Value $50 unused, $100 never hinged.

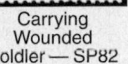

Communications
Symbols — SP85

1946, May 10   Perf. 12½
B134 SP85 1.50d + 1d emer   1.60 3.25
B135 SP85 2.50d + 1.50d car rose   1.60 3.25
B136 SP85 5d + 2d gray bl   1.60 3.25
B137 SP85 8d + 3.50d dl brn   1.60 3.25
Nos. B134-B137 (4)   6.40 13.00
Set, never hinged   12.00

1st PTT Congress since liberation, May 10.

Flag and Young
Laborers — SP86

Flag in Red or Carmine and Deep or Dark Blue

1946, Aug. 1   Litho.
B138 SP86 50p + 50p brn & buff   1.00 1.60
B139 SP86 1.50d + 1d dk grn & lt green   1.00 1.60
B140 SP86 2.50d + 2d rose vio & rose lilac   1.00 1.60
B141 SP86 5d + 3d gray bl & blue   1.00 1.60
Nos. B138-B141 (4)   4.00 6.40
Set, never hinged   8.00

The surtax aided railroad reconstruction carried out by Yugoslav youths.

Handstand on
Horizontal
Bar — SP87

1947, Sept. 5   Perf. 11½
B142 SP87 1.50d + 50p dark grn   1.50 1.50
B143 SP87 2.50d + 50p carmine   1.50 1.50
B144 SP87 4d + 50p brt blue   1.60 1.60
Nos. B142-B144 (3)   4.50 4.50
Set, never hinged   9.00

1947 Balkan Games, Sept. 5-7, Ljubljana.

Young
Railway
Laborers
SP88

1947, Sept. 25   Typo.   Perf. 11½x12
B145 SP88 1d + 50p orange   .60   .75
B146 SP88 1.50d + 1d yel green   .60   .75
B147 SP88 2.50d + 1.50d car lake   .60   .75
B148 SP88 5d + 2d deep blue   .60   .75
Nos. B145-B148 (4)   2.40 3.00
Set, never hinged   4.75

The surtax was for youth brigades employed in the construction of the Samac-Sarajevo railway.

Symbolizing
Protection of
"B.C.G."
Vaccine
SP89

Dying Serpent
SP91

"Illness" and
"Recovery"
SP90

1948, Apr. 1   Litho.   Perf. 12½
B149 SP89 1.50d + 1d sl blk & red   .40   .80
B150 SP90 2.50d + 2d grnsh gray, ol blk & red   .40   .80
B151 SP91 5d + 3d dk bl & car   .40   .80
Nos. B149-B151 (3)   1.20 2.40
Set, never hinged   2.40

Fight against tuberculosis. The surtax was for the Yugoslav Red Cross.

Juro
Daniclc
SP92

Portraits: 2.50d+1d, Franjo Racki. 4d+2d, Josip J. Strossmayer.

1948, July 28   Perf. 11
B152 SP92 1.50d + 50p blk green   .80   .80
B153 SP92 2.50d + 1d dark red   .80   .80
B154 SP92 4d + 2d dark blue   .80   .80
Nos. B152-B154 (3)   2.40 2.40
Set, never hinged   4.75

Yugoslav Academy of Arts and Sciences, Zagreb, 80th anniv. The surtax was for the Academy.

Shot Put — SP93

1948, Sept. 10   Perf. 12½
B155 SP93 2d + 1d shown   .40   .80
B156 SP93 3d + 1d Hurdles   .40   .80
B157 SP93 5d + 2d Pole vault   1.00 1.25
Nos. B155-B157 (3)   1.80 2.85
Set, never hinged   3.50

Balkan and Central Europe Games, 1948. On sale 4 days.

AIR POST STAMPS

Dubrovnik
AP1

Lake Bled
AP2

Falls of
Jaice — AP3

Church at
Oplenac — AP4

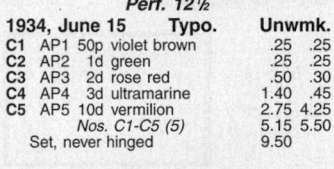

Bridge at
Mostar — AP5

Perf. 12½
1934, June 15   Typo.   Unwmk.
C1 AP1 50p violet brown   .25   .25
C2 AP2 1d green   .25   .25
C3 AP3 2d rose red   .50   .30
C4 AP4 3d ultramarine   1.40 .45
C5 AP5 10d vermilion   2.75 4.25
Nos. C1-C5 (5)   5.15 5.50
Set, never hinged   9.50

King Alexander Memorial Issue

No. 4 Overprinted in
Black

1935, Jan. 1
C6 AP4 3d ultramarine   3.25 4.75
Never hinged   6.50

St. Naum
Convent — AP6

Port of
Rab — AP7

Sarajevo
AP8

Ljubljana
AP9

Perf. 11½x12½, 12½x11½

1937, Sept. 12   Photo.
C7   AP6 50p brown   .25   .25
  a.   Perf. 12½   .25   .25
C8   AP7 1d yellow grn   .25   .25
  a.   Perf. 12½   .25   .25
C9   AP8 2d blue gray   .25   .25
  a.   Perf. 12½   .25   .25
C10 AP9 2.50d rose red   .25   .25
  a.   Perf. 12½   .25   .25
C11 AP6 5d brn violet   .25   .25
C12 AP7 10d brown lake   .50   .25
  a.   Perf. 12½   .70   .25
C13 AP8 20d dark green   5.25 8.00
  a.   Perf. 12½   .70 1.00
C14 AP9 30d ultramarine   18.00 27.50
  a.   Perf. 12½   1.00 1.75
Nos. C7-C14 (8)   25.00 37.00
Nos. C7-C14, never hinged   47.50
Nos. C7a-C14a, never hinged   5.50

For surcharges see Nos. B116-B119, NB1-NB4, NC1-NC8.

Cathedral
of Zagreb
AP10

Bridge at
Belgrade
AP11

1940, Aug. 15   Litho.   Perf. 12½
C15 AP10 40d Prus grn & pale green   4.50 3.50
C16 AP11 50d slate bl & gray bl   4.50 5.00
Set, never hinged   17.50

For overprints see Nos. NC9-NC10.

Issues for Federal Republic

Plane over
Terrace of
Kalimegdan,
Belgrade
AP12

Plane over
Dubrovnik
AP13

1947, Apr. 21   Typo.   Perf. 11½
Cyrillic Inscription at Top
C17 AP12 50p ol gray & brn vio   .25   .25
C18 AP13 1d mag & ol gray   .25   .25
C19 AP12 2d blue & black   .25   .25
C20 AP13 5d green & gray   .25   .25
C21 AP12 10d olive bis & choc   .25   .25
C22 AP13 20d ultra & olive   .60 1.25

Roman Inscription at Top
C23 AP12 50p ol gray & brn vio   .25   .25
C24 AP13 1d mag & ol gray   .25   .25
C25 AP12 2d blue & black   .25   .25
C26 AP13 5d green & gray   .25   .25
C27 AP12 10d olive bis & choc   .25   .25
C28 AP13 20d ultra & olive   .60 1.25
Nos. C17-C28 (12)   3.70 5.00
Set, never hinged   4.75

Sheets of each denomination contain alternately stamps with Cyrillic or Roman inscription at top. Value, 6 se-tenant pairs: unused $24; never hinged $47.50.

Laurent
Kosir and
Birthplace
AP14

1948, Aug. 27 — Engr.
C29 AP14 15d red violet .60 1.25
Never hinged 1.25

Kosir, recognized by Yugoslavia as inventor of the postage stamp, 80th death anniv. Issued in sheets of 25 stamps and 25 labels.

Nos. 262 to 264 Overprinted in Blue or Carmine

1949, Aug. 25 — Unwmk. — Perf. 12½
C30 A55 3d carmine rose 5.50 8.00
C31 A56 5d dull blue (C) 5.50 8.00
C32 A57 12d red brown 5.50 8.00
Nos. C30-C32 (3) 16.50 24.00
Never hinged 32.50

Liberation of Macedonia, 5th anniv.
It is reported that No. C32 was not sold to the public at the post office.

Souvenir Sheet

Electric Train AP15

Perf. 11½x12½
1949, Dec. 15 — Photo.
C33 AP15 10d lilac rose 90.00 105.00
Never hinged 175.00
a. Imperf. 90.00 105.00
Never hinged 175.00

Centenary of Yugoslav railroads.
For overprint see Trieste No. C17.

Iron Gate, Derdap AP16

Belgrade AP17

Designs: 2d, Cascades, Plitvice. 3d, Carniola. 6d, Roman bridge, Mostar. 10d, Ohrid. 20d, Gulf of Kotor. 30d, Dubrovnik. 50d, Bled.

Perf. 12½
1951, June 16 — Unwmk. — Engr.
C34 AP16 1d deep org .25 .25
C35 AP16 2d dk green .25 .25
C36 AP16 3d dark red .25 .25
C37 AP16 6d ultra 2.00 4.00
C38 AP16 10d dark brn .25 .25
C39 AP16 20d grnsh blk .40 .25
C40 AP16 30d dp claret 1.00 .25
C41 AP16 50d dk purple 1.40 .25
C42 AP17 100d dk gray bl 27.50 9.00
Nos. C34-C42 (9) 33.30 14.75
Set, never hinged 65.00

Souvenir Sheet
Imperf
C43 AP17 100d red brn 90.00 175.00
Never hinged 175.00

See Nos. C50-C53. For overprints see Nos. C44, C49, Trieste C22-C32.

Roman Bridge Type of 1951 Overprinted "ZEFIZ 1951" in Carmine
1951, June 16 — Perf. 12½
C44 AP16 6d dark green 4.00 3.75
Never hinged 8.00

Nos. C43-C44 were issued for Zagreb Philatelic Exhibition, June 16-26.

View on Mt. Kopaonik — AP18

Perf. 12½
1951, July — Unwmk. — Photo.
C45 AP18 3d shown 1.00 2.00
C46 AP18 5d Mt. Triglav 1.00 2.00
C47 AP18 20d Mt. Kalnik 35.00 50.00
Nos. C45-C47 (3) 37.00 54.00
Set, never hinged 70.00

Intl. Union of Mountaineers, 12th Assembly, Bled, July 13-18.

Plane and Parachutists — AP19

1951, Aug. 16 — Engr.
C48 AP19 6d carmine 2.00 2.00

Type of 1951 Overprinted in Carmine

C49 AP16 50d blue 32.50 40.00

First World Parachute Championship, Bled, Aug. 16-20.
Nos. C48-C49, never hinged $65.

> Catalogue values for unused stamps in this section, from this point to the end of the section, are for Never Hinged items.

Types of 1951

Designs: 5d, Cascades, Plitvice. 100d, Carniola. 200d, Roman bridge, Mostar.

1951-52
C50 AP16 5d yel brn ('52) .40 .25
C51 AP16 100d green 1.75 .25
C52 AP16 200d deep car ('52) 2.50 .30
C53 AP17 500d blue vio ('52) 8.00 .40
Nos. C50-C53 (4) 12.65 1.20

Marshal Tito, Tank, Factory and Planes AP20

1951, Dec. 22 — Unwmk.
C54 AP20 150d deep blue 12.00 10.00

Army Day, Dec. 22; 10th anniv. of the formation of the 1st military unit of "New" Yugoslavia.

Star and Flag-encircled Globe — AP21

1953, July 30 — Engr.
C55 AP21 300d bl & grn 190.00 190.00

38th Esperanto Congress, Zagreb, 7/25-8/1. For overprint see Trieste No. C21.

13th Century Tower, Zagreb AP22

1956, May 20 — Perf. 11½
Chalky Paper
C56 AP22 30d gray, vio bl & org red 3.25 1.40

Yugoslav Intl. Phil. Exhib., JUFIZ III, Zagreb, May 20-27.

Workers and Cogwheel — AP23

1956, June 15 — Photo.
Glossy Paper
C57 AP23 30d car rose & blk 2.50 2.50

10th anniversary of technical education.

Moon and Earth with Satellites — AP24

1958, Oct. 24 — Engr. — Perf. 12½
C58 AP24 300d dark blue 12.00 4.50

Intl. Geophysical Year, 1957-58.

Types of Regular Issue, 1961
1961, Sept. 1 — Perf. 11½
C59 A150 250d dark purple .90 .60
C60 A151 500d violet blue 2.00 1.25

Type of Athletic Regular Issue, 1962
Souvenir Sheet

Design: Army Stadium, Belgrade.

1962, Sept. 12 — Litho. — Imperf.
C61 A161 600d vio & blk 16.00 16.00

7th European Athletic Championships, Belgrade, Sept. 12-16.

REGISTERED LETTER STAMPS

> Catalogue values for unused stamps in this section are for Never Hinged items.

RL1

1993, June 28 — Litho. — Perf. 13¼
F1 RL1 (R) ultra 1.60 .40
a. Perf. 12½ 6.50 .55
b. Dated "1997" 6.50 .40

No. F1 was valued at 11,000d on day of issue. No. F1b issued 2/97.
For surcharge, see Serbia Nos. 194, 274.

Type of 1993
2002, July 25 — Litho. — Perf. 12½
F2 RL1 R red 2.00 1.50

No. F2 was intended for use in Montenegro and was sold there for 39c in euro currency. The stamp was valid for use in the Serbian section of Yugoslavia.

POSTAGE DUE STAMPS

King Alexander — D1

1921 — Typo. — Unwmk. — Perf. 11½
Red or Black Surcharge
J1 D1 10p on 5p green (R) .25 .25
J2 D1 30p on 5p green (Bk) .25 .25
Set, never hinged .65

D2 D3

1921-22 — Typo. — Perf. 11½, Rough
J3 D2 10p rose .25 .25
J4 D2 30p yellow green .25 .25
J5 D2 50p violet .25 .25
J6 D2 1d brown .30 .25
J7 D2 2d blue .40 .25
J8 D3 5d orange 2.00 .25
J9 D3 10d violet brown 6.00 .45
a. Cliche of 10p in sheet of 10d 190.00
J10 D3 25d pink 35.00 1.60
J11 D3 50d green 30.00 1.60
Nos. J3-J11 (9) 74.45 5.15
Set, never hinged 140.00

1924 — Perf. 9, 10½, 11½, Clean-cut
J12 D3 10p rose red .25 .25
J13 D3 30p yellow green .35 .40
J14 D3 50p violet .25 .25
J15 D3 1d brown .25 .25
J16 D3 2d deep blue .50 .25
J17 D3 5d orange 1.60 .25
J18 D3 10d violet brown 10.00 .25
J19 D3 25d pink 65.00 1.25
J20 D3 50d green 47.50 1.25
Nos. J12-J20 (9) 125.70 4.40
Set, never hinged 240.00

Nos. J19-J20 do not exist perf 9. Nos. J18-J20 do not exist perf 11½.

Nos. J19-J20 Surcharged

1928
J21 D3 10d on 25d pink 3.25 .40
J22 D3 10d on 50d green 3.25 .40
a. Inverted surcharge 30.00 18.00
Set, never hinged 13.00

A second type of "1" in surcharge has flag projecting horizontally. Value, each: $24 never hinged; $12 unused; $3.25 used.

Coat of Arms — D4

1931 Typo. Perf. 12½
With Imprint at Foot
J23	D4	50p violet	1.40	.25
J24	D4	1d deep magenta	3.00	.25
J25	D4	2d deep blue	9.50	.25
J26	D4	5d orange	2.00	.25
J27	D4	10d chocolate	10.00	1.25

Nos. J23-J27 (5) 25.90 2.25
Set, never hinged 47.50

For overprints see Nos. NJ1-NJ13, Croatia 26-29, J1-J5.

1932 Without Imprint at Foot
J28	D4	50p violet	.25	.25
J29	D4	1d deep magenta	.25	.25
J30	D4	2d deep blue	.25	.25
J31	D4	5d orange	.25	.25
J32	D4	10d chocolate	.25	.25

Nos. J28-J32 (5) 1.25 1.25

Numeral of Value — D5

Overprint in Green, Blue or Maroon
1933 Perf. 9, 10½, 11½
J33	D5	50p vio (G)	.25	.25
a.		Perf. 10½		.30
J34	D5	1d brown (Bl)	.25	.25
a.		Perf. 10½	2.00	1.40
J35	D5	2d blue (M)	.25	.25
a.		Perf. 10½	1.00	1.25
J36	D5	5d orange (Bl)	.80	.25
J37	D5	50d violet brn (Bl)	4.00	.25

Nos. J33-J37 (5) 5.55 1.25
Set, never hinged 10.50

Issues for Federal Republic

Redrawn Type OD5, German Occupation of Serbia, Overprinted in Black

1945 Unwmk. Perf. 12½
| J37A | OD5 | 10d red | .60 | .55 |
| J37B | OD5 | 20d ultramarine | .60 | .55 |

Set, never hinged 2.40

In the redrawn design the eagle is replaced by a colorless tablet.

Coat of Arms — D6

1945 Litho. Perf. 12½
Numerals in Black
J38	D6	2d brown violet	.25	.25
J39	D6	3d violet	.25	.25
J40	D6	5d green	.25	.25
J41	D6	7d orange brown	.25	.25
J42	D6	10d rose lilac	.25	.25
J43	D6	20d blue	.25	.25
J44	D6	30d light bl grn	.40	.35
J45	D6	40d rose red	.40	.40

Numerals in Color of Stamp
J46	D6	1d blue green	.25	.25
J47	D6	1.50d blue	.25	.25
J48	D6	2d vermilion	.40	.25
J49	D6	3d violet brown	.40	.25
J50	D6	4d rose violet	.60	.25

Nos. J38-J50 (13) 4.20 3.50
Set, never hinged 6.50

For overprints see Nos. J64-J66.

Torches and Star — D7

1946-47 Typo. Unwmk.
J51	D7	50p dp orange ('47)	.25	.25
J52	D7	1d orange	.25	.25
J53	D7	2d dark blue	.25	.25
J54	D7	3d yellow green	.25	.25
J55	D7	5d bright purple	.25	.25
J56	D7	7d crimson	.80	.25
J57	D7	10d brt pink ('47)	.80	.25
J58	D7	20d rose lake ('47)	2.00	.55

Nos. J51-J58 (8) 4.85 2.30
Set, never hinged 8.00

See Nos. J67-J79. For overprints see Trieste Nos. J1-J5, J11-J18.

Nos. J47, J49 and J50 Overprinted in Black

1950 Litho.
J64	D6	1.50d blue	.25	.25
J65	D6	3d violet brown	.25	.25
J66	D6	4d rose violet	.25	.30

Nos. J64-J66 (3) .75 .80
Set, never hinged 1.25

> Catalogue values for unused stamps in this section, from this point to the end of the section, are for Never Hinged items.

Type of 1946-47
1951-52 Typo. Perf. 12½
J67	D7	1d brown ('52)	.40	.25
J68	D7	2d emerald	.40	.25
J69	D7	5d blue	.55	.25
J70	D7	10d scarlet	1.25	.25
J71	D7	20d purple	2.00	.25
J72	D7	30d org yel ('52)	4.00	.25
J73	D7	50d ultramarine	16.00	.40
J74	D7	100d dp plum ('52)	55.00	2.00

Nos. J67-J74 (8) 79.60 3.90

For overprints see Istria Nos. J20-J24, Trieste J11-J18.

1962 Litho. Perf. 12½
J75	D7	10d red orange	3.25	.25
J76	D7	20d purple	3.25	.25
J77	D7	30d orange	6.75	.25
J78	D7	50d ultramarine	32.50	.80
J79	D7	100d rose lake	20.00	1.25

Nos. J75-J79 (5) 65.75 2.80

OFFICIAL STAMPS

Issues for Federal Republic

Arms of the Federated People's Republic — O1

Perf. 12½
1946, Nov. 1 Unwmk. Typo.
O1	O1	50p orange	.25	.25
O2	O1	1d blue green	.25	.25
O3	O1	1.50d olive green	.25	.25
O4	O1	2.50d red	.25	.25
O5	O1	4d yellow brown	.40	.25
O6	O1	5d deep blue	.60	.25
O7	O1	8d chocolate	1.25	.25
O8	O1	12d violet	1.40	.25

Nos. O1-O8 (8) 4.65 2.00
Set, never hinged 8.00

For surcharges see Nos. 272A-272B, Istria 43, 45, 47, 49, 51.

POSTAL TAX STAMPS

> Catalogue values for unused stamps in this section are for Never Hinged items.

The tax was for the Red Cross or The Olympic Fund unless otherwise noted.

Red Cross Emblem — PT1

Unwmk.
1933, Sept. 17 Litho. Perf. 13
RA1 PT1 50p dark blue & red .65 .25

Obligatory on inland letters during Red Cross Week, Sept. 17-23. See No. RAJ1.

Dr. Vladen Djordjevic — PT2

1936, Sept. 20 Typo. Perf. 12
RA2 PT2 50p brn blk & red .40 .25

Obligatory on inland letters during Red Cross Week, Sept. 20-26.

Aiding the Wounded PT3

1938, Sept. 18 Litho. Perf. 12½
RA3 PT3 50p dk bl, red, yel & grn .40 .25

1940, Sept. 15 Redrawn
RA4 PT3 50p slate blue & red .55 .25

The inscription at the upper right of this stamp and the numerals of value are in smaller characters.
Obligatory on all letters during the second week of September.

Issues for Federal Republic

Ruined Dwellings — PT4

1947, Jan. 1 Litho. Perf. 12½
RA5 PT4 50p brn & scarlet .25 .25

See No. RAJ2. For overprints see Trieste Nos. RA1, RAJ1.

Red Cross Nurse — PT5

1948, Oct. 1
RA6 PT5 50p dk vio bl & red .25 .25
See No. RAJ3.

Nurse and Child — PT6

1949, Nov. 5
RA7 PT6 50p red & brown .25 .25

See No. RAJ4. For overprints see Trieste Nos. RA2, RAJ2.

Nurse Holding Book — PT7

1950, Oct. 1
RA8 PT7 50p dark green & red .25 .25
Obligatory Oct. 1-8, 1950.
See No. RAJ6.

Hands Raising Red Cross Flag — PT8

1951, Oct. 7
RA9 PT8 50p vio bl & red .25 .25
Obligatory Oct. 7-14.
For overprints see Trieste Nos. RA3, RAJ3.

Nurse — PT9

1952, Oct. 5 Photo. Perf. 12½
RA10 PT9 50p gray & carmine .25 .25
For overprint see Trieste No. RA4.

Child Receiving Blood Transfusion — PT10

1953, Oct. 25 Litho.
RA11 PT10 2d red vio & red .40 .25
See No. RAJ8. For overprints see Trieste Nos. RA5, RAJ5.

Youths Carrying Flags — PT11

1954, Nov. 1
RA12 PT11 2d gray grn & red .40 .25
See Nos. RAJ9.

Infant — PT11a

1954, Oct. 4
RA12A PT11a 2d brn & salmon   1.25   .65
The tax was for Children's Week.

Girl — PT12

1955, Oct. 2   Unwmk.   *Perf. 12½*
RA13 PT12 2d dull red   .40   .25
The tax was for child welfare.
See No. RAJ10.

Nurse Opening
Window — PT13

1955, Oct. 31
RA14 PT13 2d vio blk & red   .25   .25
See No. RAJ11.

Ruins in the
Snow — PT14

1956, May 6   *Perf. 12½*
RA15 PT14 2d sepia & red   .30   .25
See No. RAJ12.

Children and
Goose — PT15

1956, Sept. 30
RA16 PT15 2d gray green   .40   .25
The tax was for child welfare.
See No. RAJ13.

Plane over
Temporary
Shelter — PT16

1957, May 5   Litho.
RA17 PT16 2d lt bl, blk & car   .30   .25
See No. RAJ14.

Girl and Boy
Pioneers
PT17

1957, Sept. 30   Unwmk.   *Perf. 12½*
RA18 PT17 2d rose & gray   .30   .25
Children's Week. Obligatory Oct. 2-6.
See No. RAJ15.

Woman Pouring
Water — PT17a

1958, May 4   *Perf. 12½x12*
RA19 PT17a 2d multicolored   .40   .25
Issued to honor the United Nations.
On No. RA19 the UN emblem has been left
out, Cyrillic inscriptions at left added, country
name in Latin letters.
See Nos. 375-377; No. RAJ16.

Playing
Children — PT18

1958, Oct. 5   Litho.   *Perf. 12½*
RA20 PT18 2d brt yel & black   .25   .25
Children's Week, Oct. 5-11.

Helping Hand
and
Family — PT19

1959, May 3
RA21 PT19 2d blue vio & red   .30   .25
Red Cross centenary. Obligatory May 3-9.
See No. RAJ18.

Blackboard,
Flower and
Fish — PT20

1959, Oct. 5   Unwmk.
RA22 PT20 2d ocher & dp gray grn   .30   .25
Children's Week. Obligatory on domestic
mail, Oct. 5-11.
See No. RAJ19.

"Reconstruction"
PT21

1960, May 8   *Perf. 12½*
RA23 PT21 2d slate & red   .30   .25
Obligatory May 8-14. See No. RAJ20.

Girl and
Toys — PT22

1960, Oct. 2   Litho.   *Perf. 12½*
RA24 PT22 2d red   .25   .25
Issued for Children's Week. Obligatory on
domestic mail Oct. 2-8.
See No. RAJ21.

Blood Donor
Symbolism
PT23

1961, May 7
RA25 PT23 2d multicolored   .30   .25
Obligatory May 7-13. Exists imperf. Value
$14.
See No. RAJ22.

Bird Holding
Flower
PT24

1961, Oct. 1
RA26 PT24 2d orange & violet   .25   .25
Children's Week. Exists imperf. Obligatory
on domestic mail, Oct. 1-7.
See No. RAJ23.

Bandages and Symbols of Home,
Industry, Weather, Transportation, Fire
and Flood — PT25

1962, Apr. 30   *Perf. 12½*
RA27 PT25 5d red brn, gray &
red   .25   .25
Obligatory on domestic mail May 6-12.
See No. RAJ24.

Centenary
Emblem — PT26

1963, May 5   Unwmk.   *Perf. 12½*
RA28 PT26 5d dl yel, red & gray   .30   .25
Intl. Red Cross, centenary. Exists imperf.
Obligatory on all domestic mail during Red
Cross Week, May 5-11.
See No. RAJ25.

Parachute Drop of
Supplies, Yugoslav
Flag — PT27

1964, Apr. 27   Litho.
RA29 PT27 5d blue, rose & dk bl   .25   .25
Obligatory on domestic mail, May 3-9.

Children in
Circle — PT28

1965, May 2   Litho.   *Perf. 12½*
RA30 PT28 5d tan & red   .25   .25
Obligatory on domestic mail, May 2-8.

Arrows
PT29

1966, Apr. 28   Litho.   *Perf. 12½*
RA31 PT29 5p gray & multi   .25   .25
Obligatory on domestic mail, May 1-7.

Crosses and
Flower
PT30

1967, Apr. 28   Litho.   *Perf. 12½*
RA32 PT30 5p vio, red & yel grn   .25   .25
Exists imperf.

Honeycomb and
Red
Cross — PT31

1968, Apr. 30   Litho.   *Perf. 12*
RA33 PT31 5p multicolored   .25   .25
Obligatory on all domestic mail May 5-11.

Aztec Calendar Stone and Olympic Rings — PT32

1968, Oct. 12　　　　**Perf. 12½**
RA34 PT32 10p black & multi　　　.25　.25

Red Cross, Hands and Globe — PT33

1969, May 18　Litho.　Perf. 12
RA35 PT33 20p red org, dl red & blk　　.25　.25

Globe, Olympic Torch and Rings — PT34

1969, Nov. 24　Litho.　Perf. 11¼
RA36 PT34 10p gold & multi　　4.50　.25
　a.　　Perf. 9　　　12.00　1.90
Yugoslav Olympic Committee, 50th anniv. Exists imperf. Value $125.

Symbolic Flower and People PT35

1970, Apr. 27　Litho.　Perf. 13
RA37 PT35 20p vio bl, org & red　.25　.25

Olympic Flag — PT36

1970, June 10　Litho.　Perf. 13x13½
RA38 PT36 10p multicolored　　.25　.25

Red Cross Encircling Globe PT37

1971, Apr. 26　Litho.　Perf. 12½
RA39 PT37 20p blue, yel & red　　.25　.25

Olympic Rings and Disk — PT38

1971, June 15　Litho.　Perf. 12½
RA40 PT38 10p blue & black　　.25　.25

Red Cross and Hemispheres PT39

1972, Apr. 27　　　Perf. 13½x13
RA41 PT39 20p red & multi　　.25　.25

Olympic Rings, TV Tower, Munich and Sapporo Emblems — PT40

1972, May　　　Perf. 13x13½
RA42 PT40 10p ultra & multi　　.25　.25

Red Cross, Crescent and Lion Emblems — PT41

1973, Apr. 24　Litho.　Perf. 13x13½
RA43 PT41 20p blue & multi　　.25　.25

Globe and Olympic Rings — PT42

1973, June 1　Litho.　Perf. 13x13½
RA44 PT42 10p multicolored　　.25　.25

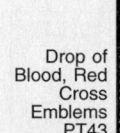

Drop of Blood, Red Cross Emblems PT43

1974, Apr. 25　Litho.　Perf. 13
RA45 PT43 20p red & multi　　.25　.25

Olympic Rings PT44

1974, June 1　Litho.　Perf. 13
RA46 PT44 10p blue & multi　　.25　.25

Red Cross, Hands PT45

1975, Apr. 23　Photo.　Perf. 11½
RA47 PT45 20p blue, car & blk　.25　.25

Olympic Rings — PT46

1975, June 2　Litho.　Perf. 13½
RA48 PT46 10p multicolored　　.25　.25

Ruin and Clock — PT47

1975, July 26　Litho.　Perf. 13x13½
RA49 PT47 30p gray, blk & dk bl　.25　.25
Solidarity Week, July 26-Aug. 1. See Nos. RA61-RA62.

Red Crescent, Red Cross, Red Lion — PT48

1976, May 8　Photo.　Perf. 12½x13
RA50 PT48 20p multicolored　　.80　.55

1984 Olympics PT49

1976, July 26　Litho.　Perf. 13½
RA51 PT49 10p intense blue　　.25　.25

Fight Tuberculosis, Red Cross — PT50

1977, Sept. 14　　　Photo.
RA52 PT50 50p multicolored　　2.00　.80
RA53 PT50　1d multicolored　　2.00　.80
　　Exist imperf.

1984 Olympics PT51

1977, Dec. 17　　　Perf. 13½x13
RA54 PT51 10p multicolored　　.25　.25

Postal Tax Stamps for use in a particular republic or republics fall beyond the scope of this catalogue and are not listed. These stamps, issued since 1977, were not intended for nationwide use. Some of these issues have designs which are similar to stamps used nationwide, most notably those using variations of the Ruin and Clock (PT47) design. Most others show the Red Cross or the Tuberculosis Cross.

Red Crescent, Red Cross, Red Lion — PT52

1978, May 7　Litho.　Perf. 13½
RA55 PT52 20p on 1d bl & red　.50　.25
RA56 PT52　1d blue & red　　.30　.25

1984 Olympics PT53

1978, Sept.
RA57 PT53 30p multicolored　　.35　.25

8th Mediterranean Games, Split, Sept. 15-29 — PT54

1979, Mar. 1　Photo.　Perf. 13½x13
RA58 PT54 1d violet　　　.25　.25
RA59 PT54 1d greenish blue　.25　.25

Red Cross Week PT55

1979, May 6　　　Perf. 13½
RA60 PT55 1d multicolored　　.25　.25

**Ruin and Clock Type of 1975
Inscribed "1.-7.VI"**
1979, June 1
RA61 PT47 30p blk & intense bl　.25　.25
　　Solidarity Week.

**Ruin and Clock Type of 1975
Inscribed "1.-7.VI"**
1980, June 1　Litho.　Perf. 13x13½
RA62 PT47 1d black & blue　　.25　.25
　　Solidarity Week, June 1-7.

Olympic Week — PT57

1979, Oct. 15　Photo.　Perf. 14
RA63 PT57 30p blue & red　　.25　.25

Sculpture, Red Cross — PT58

1980, May 4 Litho. *Perf. 13½*
RA64 PT58 1d multicolored .35 .30

Olympic Week — PT59

1980, Oct. 20 *Perf. 14*
RA65 PT59 50p multicolored .40 .25

SPENS '81, Novi Sad — PT60

1980, Dec. 20 *Perf. 13½*
RA66 PT60 1d multicolored .25 .25

Red Cross — PT61

1981, May 4 Photo.
RA67 PT61 1d multicolored .25 .25

Fight Tuberculosis, Red Cross — PT62

1981, Sept. 14
RA68 PT62 1d multicolored .25 .25

Handshake PT63

1982, May Litho. *Perf. 13*
RA69 PT63 1d black & red .25 .25

Robert Koch PT64

1983, Sept. 18 Litho. *Perf. 13*
RA70 PT64 1d multicolored .25 .25
For surcharge see No. RA76.

Fight Tuberculosis, Red Cross — PT65

1983, Sept. 14 Litho. *Perf. 13½*
RA71 PT65 1d bluish grn, blk & red .25 .25
RA72 PT65 2d bluish grn, blk & red .25 .25

1984 Winter Olympics, Sarajevo PT66

1983, Oct. 20 Litho. *Perf. 12½*
RA73 PT66 2d greenish blue .25 .25

PLANICA 50 — PT67

1985, Apr. 1 Photo. *Perf. 14*
RA74 PT67 2d brt ultra & blue .25 .25

Ruin, Clock and Red Cross — PT68

1987, June 1 Litho. *Perf. 10*
RA75 PT68 30d multicolored .25 .25
Solidarity Week, June 1-7.

No. RA70 Surcharged in Silver

1988, Sept. 14 Litho. *Perf. 13*
RA76 PT64 12d on 1d multi 8.00 8.00

Intl. Red Cross, 125th Anniv. — PT69

1989, May 8 Litho. *Perf. 12x11*
Without Gum
RA77 PT69 20d bl, sil & red .40 .40
RA78 PT69 80d bl, sil & red .40 .40
RA79 PT69 150d bl, sil & red .40 .40
RA80 PT69 160d bl, sil & red .40 .40
Nos. RA77-RA80 (4) 1.60 1.60
Souvenir folders with perf. or imperf. miniature sheets of 4 sold for 3200d.

Ruin, Clock and Red Cross — PT70

Building, Clock and Red Cross — PT71

1989, June 1 *Perf. 10*
Without Gum
RA81 PT70 250d red & silver .55 .40
Roulette 10
RA82 PT71 400d brt bl gray & red 1.00 .50
Souvenir folders with perf. or imperf. miniature sheets containing one 45x65mm stamp like RA81 sold for 3200d.

Fight TB, Red Cross — PT72

1989, Sept. 14 *Rough Perf. 10½*
Without Gum
RA83 PT72 20d black & red .30 .30
RA84 PT72 200d black & red .30 .30
RA85 PT72 250d black & red .30 .30
RA86 PT72 400d black & red .30 .30
RA87 PT72 650d black & red .30 .30
Nos. RA83-RA87 (5) 1.50 1.50

Red Cross — PT73

1990, May 8 *Perf. 13½*
Without Gum
RA88 PT73 10p green & red .80 .25
Perf. 12½
RA89 PT73 20p green & red .80 .25
a. Perf. 13½ .80 .25
RA90 PT73 30p green & red .80 .25
Nos. RA88-RA90 (3) 2.40 .75

Flowers — PT74

Macedonian Red Cross, 45th Anniv. — PT75

1990, May 8 *Perf. 10*
Without Gum
RA91 PT74 20p shown .25 .25
RA92 PT74 20p multi, diff. .25 .25
RA93 PT75 20p multicolored .25 .25
a. Block of 3 + label, #RA91-RA93 .80 .80
Souvenir folders with perf. or imperf. miniature sheets of 3 + label sold for 4d.

PT76

1990, Sept. 14 Litho. *Perf. 10*
Without Gum
RA94 PT76 20p blue, org & red .40 .40
RA95 PT76 25p blue, yel & red .40 .40
RA96 PT76 50p blue, yel & red .40 .40
Nos. RA94-RA96 (3) 1.20 1.20
Fight tuberculosis, Red Cross.

PT77

1991, Sept. 14 Litho. *Perf. 12½*
Without Gum
RA97 PT77 1.20d dk bl, yel & red .30 .30
RA98 PT77 2.50d multicolored .30 .30
Required on mail 9/14-21/91.

PT78

1994, May 8 Litho. *Perf. 13½*
RA99 PT78 10p multicolored 1.00 .50
No. RA99 was required on mail 5/8-15/94.

PT79

1994, Sept. 14 Litho. *Perf. 13x13½*
RA100 PT79 10p multicolored 1.00 .50
No. RA100 was required on mail 9/14-21/94.

PT80

1995, May 8 Litho. *Perf. 13½x13*
RA101 PT80 10p multicolored 1.00 .50
No. RA101 was required on mail 5/8-15/95.

PT81

1995, Sept. 9 Litho. *Perf. 13½x13*
RA102 PT81 10p Wilhelm Röntgen 1.00 .50
Fight Tuberculosis. No. RA102 was required on mail 9/9-14/95.

PT82

1996, May 8 Litho. Perf. 12x12½
RA103 PT82 15p multicolored .40 .30
No. RA103 was required on mail 5/8-15/96.

PT83

1996, Sept. Litho. Perf. 12x12½
RA104 PT83 20p multicolored 2.00 .40

PT84

1997, May 8 Litho. Perf. 13
RA105 PT84 20p multicolored 5.00 1.00
No. RA105 was required on mail 5/8-15/97.

Milutin Rankovic
(1880-1967),
Artist — PT85

1997, Sept. 14 Litho. Perf. 14
RA106 PT85 20p multicolored .40 .40
Fight Tuberculosis. No. RA106 was required on mail 9/14-21/97.

PT86

1998, May 8 Litho. Perf. 13¾
RA107 PT86 20p multicolored .40 .40
No. RA107 was required on mail 5/8-15/98.

Red Cross — PT87

1999, May 8 Litho. Perf. 13¾
RA108 PT87 1d multi 2.00 .50
No. RA108 was required on mail 5/8-5/15/99.

Red Cross — PT88

1999, Sept. 14
RA109 PT88 1d multi 7.00 .70
No. RA109 was required on mail 9/14-9/21/99.

POSTAL TAX DUE STAMPS

> Catalogue values for unused stamps in this section are for Never Hinged items.

The tax of Nos. RAJ1-RAJ9, RAJ11-RAJ12, RAJ14 and RAJ18 was for the Red Cross.

Inscribed "PORTO."

Type of Postal Tax Stamp, 1933
1933 Unwmk. Litho. Perf. 12½
RAJ1 PT1 50p dull grn & red 1.00 .25
 a. Perf. 11½ 20.00 8.00

Type of Postal Tax Stamp, 1947
1947
RAJ2 PT4 50p blue grn & scar .50 .25
For surcharge see Trieste No. RAJ1.

Type of Postal Tax Stamp, 1948
1948
RAJ3 PT5 50p dark grn & red .40 .25

Type of Postal Tax Stamp, 1949
1949
RAJ4 PT6 50p red & violet .55 .25
For overprint see Trieste No. RAJ2.

Cross and Map of
Yugoslavia — PTD2

1950 Unwmk. Perf. 12½
RAJ5 PTD2 50p red brown & red .40 .25
Exists imperf.

Type of Postal Tax Stamp, 1951
1951
RAJ6 PT8 50p emerald & red .40 .25
For overprint see Trieste No. RAJ3.

Red Cross — PTD3

1952 Unwmk. Photo. Perf. 12½
RAJ7 PTD3 50p gray & car .65 .25
For overprint see Trieste No. RAJ4.

Type of Postal Tax Stamp, 1953
1953 Litho.
RAJ8 PT10 2d yel brown & red .80 .40
For overprints see Trieste Nos. RAJ5.

Type of Postal Tax Stamp, 1954
1954 Litho.
RAJ9 PT11 2d lilac & red ('54) .75 .30

Types of Postal Tax Stamps, 1955
1955 Litho.
RAJ10 PT12 2d yel grn ('55) .55 .25
RAJ11 PT13 2d dk vio brn & red ('55) .80 .25

Types of Postal Tax Stamps, 1956
1956 Litho.
RAJ12 PT14 2d blue grn & red ('56) .55 .25
RAJ13 PT15 2d violet brn ('56) .55 .25

Types of Postal Tax Stamps, 1957
1957 Litho.
RAJ14 PT16 2d gray, blk & car ('57) .55 .25
RAJ15 PT17 2d lt bl, bis & grn ('57) .55 .25

Redrawn Type of Regular Issue, 1953
1958 Perf. 12½x12
RAJ16 A95 2d multicolored .80 .40
See Nos. O75-O77; No. RA19.

Child With
Toy — PTD4

1958 Litho. Perf. 12½
RAJ17 PTD4 2d lt ultra & blk .55 .25
Issued for Children's Week, Oct. 5-11.

Type of Postal Tax Stamp, 1959
1959
RAJ18 PT19 2d yel org & red .55 .25

Type of Postal Tax Stamp, 1959
Design: Tree, cock and wheat.
1959
RAJ19 PT20 2d ocher & red brn .40 .25

Type of Postal Tax Stamp, 1960
1960
RAJ20 PT21 2d vio brn & red .50 .25

Type of Postal Tax Stamp, 1960
Design: Boy, tools and ball.
1960
RAJ21 PT22 2d Prussian blue .30 .25

Type of Postal Tax Stamp, 1961
1961, May 7
RAJ22 PT23 2d multicolored .30 .25

Type of Postal Tax Stamp, 1961
1961, Oct. 1
RAJ23 PT24 2d apple grn & brn .30 .25

Type of Postal Tax Stamp, 1962
1962, Apr. 30
RAJ24 PT25 5d brn red, bl & red .30 .25

Type of Postal Tax Stamp, 1963
1963, May 5
RAJ25 PT26 5d red org, red & gray .50 .25

OFFICES ABROAD

> Catalogue values for unused stamps in this section are for Never Hinged items.

King Peter II — A1

1943 Unwmk. Typo. Perf. 12½
1K1 A1 2d dark blue .40 4.00
1K2 A1 3d slate .40 4.00
1K3 A1 5d carmine .40 4.00
1K4 A1 10d black .40 4.00
 Nos. 1K1-1K4 (4) 1.60 16.00
For surcharges see Nos. 1KB1-1KB4.

V. Vodnik — A2

Peter Nyegosh — A3

3d, Ljudovit Gaj. 4d, Vuk Stefanovic Karadzic. 5d, Bishop Joseph Strossmayer. 10d, Karageorge.

1943, Dec. 1 Engr. Perf. 12½x13
1K5 A2 1d rod org & black .40 8.25
1K6 A3 2d yel green & blk .80 8.50
1K7 A2 3d dp ultra & blk .80 8.75
1K8 A3 4d dk pur & brn blk 1.60 9.25
1K9 A2 5d brn vio & brn blk 1.60 9.75
1K10 A3 10d brn & brown blk 5.50 10.00
 Nos. 1K5-1K10 (6) 10.70 54.50

**Souvenir Sheet
Center in Black**
1K11 Sheet of 6, #1K5-1K10 65.00

25th anniv. of the Union of Liberated Yugoslavia. Valid on ships of the Yugoslav Navy and Mercantile Marine.
Nos. 1K5-1K10 overprinted diagonally "1945" in London were not issued. In 1950, they were sold by the Yugoslav Government without postal validity. Later they appeared with the additional overprint of the outline of a plane at upper left in carmine or black.

OFFICES ABROAD SEMI-POSTAL STAMPS

Nos. 1K1-1K4
Surcharged in
Orange or Black

1943 Unwmk. Perf. 12½
1KB1 A1 2d + 12.50d dk bl 2.40 8.25
1KB2 A1 3d + 12.50d slate 2.40 8.25
1KB3 A1 5d + 12.50d car (Bk) 2.40 8.25
1KB4 A1 10d + 12.50d black 2.40 8.25
 Nos. 1KB1-1KB4 (4) 9.60 33.00
The surtax was for the Red Cross.

LJUBLJANA

(Lubiana, Laibach)
Italian Occupation

Under Italian occupation in 1941, the western half of Slovenia was known as the Province of Ljubljana (Lubiana to the Italians, Laibach to the Germans) and a quisling administration was set up under the profascist General Rupnik.

100 Centesimi = 1 Lira

Yugoslavia Nos. 127,
128, 142-154
Overprinted in Black

1941 Unwmk. Perf. 12½, 13x12½
N1 A16 25p black 3.25 4.00
N2 A16 50p orange 3.25 4.00
N3 A16 1d yellow grn 3.25 4.00
N4 A16 1.50d red 3.25 4.00
N5 A16 2d dp magenta 3.25 4.00
N6 A16 3d dl red brn 3.25 4.00
N7 A16 4d ultra 3.25 4.00
N8 A16 5d dark blue 3.25 4.00
N9 A16 5.50d dk vio brn 3.25 4.00
N10 A16 6d slate blue 4.75 9.50
N11 A16 8d sepia 4.75 9.50
N12 A10 10d bright vio 4.75 9.50
N13 A16 12d brt violet 12.00 14.50
N14 A10 15d brown 325.00 525.00
N15 A16 16d dl violet 12.00 14.50
N16 A16 20d blue 24.00 32.50
N17 A16 30d brt pink 52.50 95.00
 Nos. N1-N17 (17) 469.00 746.00
 Set, never hinged 1,100.

Yugoslavia Nos. 127, 142-154 Overprinted in Black

N18	A16	25p black	3.25	3.25
N19	A16	50p orange	3.25	3.25
N20	A16	1d yellow grn	3.25	3.25
N21	A16	1.50d red	3.25	3.25
N22	A16	2d dp magenta	3.25	3.25
N23	A16	3d dl red brn	3.25	3.25
N24	A16	4d ultra	3.25	3.25
N25	A16	5d dark blue	3.25	3.25
N26	A16	5.50d dk vio brn	3.25	3.25
N27	A16	6d slate blue	3.25	3.25
N28	A16	8d sepia	3.25	3.25
N29	A10	10d brt violet	6.50	4.00
N30	A16	12d bright vio	3.25	3.25
N31	A16	16d dl violet	6.50	4.00
N32	A16	20d blue	20.00	27.50
N33	A16	30d brt pink	110.00	140.00

Yugoslavia Nos. 145, 148 Surcharged in Black

N34	A16	50p on 1.50d red	1.60	2.00
N35	A16	1d on 4d ultra	1.60	2.00
		Nos. N18-N35 (18)	185.20	218.50
		Set, never hinged	400.00	

German Occupation

Stamps of Italy, 1929-42, Overprinted or Surcharged in Blue, Carmine, Black or Green

a　　　　　　b

c

1944		**Wmk. 140**	**Perf. 14**
N36	A90(a)	5c ol brown	.25	5.50
N37	A92(b)	10c dark brn	.25	5.50
N38	A93(a)	15c sl grn (C)	.25	5.50
N39	A91(b)	20c rose red	.25	5.50
N40	A94(a)	25c dp grn (C)	.25	5.50
N41	A95(b)	30c ol brown	.25	5.50
N42	A93(a)	35c dp bl (C)	.40	5.50
N43	A95(b)	50c purple (C)	.25	7.00
N44	A94(a)	75c rose red	.25	10.50
N45	A94(b)	1 l deep vio	.25	10.50
N46	A94(a)	1.25 l dp bl (C)	.25	4.00
N47	A92(b)	1.75 l red org	6.00	24.00
N48	A93(a)	2 l car lake	.25	7.00
N49	A90(c)	2.55 l on 5c ol brn (Bk)	2.40	12.00
N50	A94(a)	5 l on 25c dp grn	2.40	20.00
N51	A93(b)	10 l purple	10.00	55.00
N52	A91(a)	20 l on 20c rose red (G)	12.00	65.00
N53	A93(b)	25 l on 2 l car lake (G)	10.00	125.00
N54	A92(a)	50 l on 1.75 l red org (C)	40.00	400.00
		Nos. N36-N54 (19)	85.95	778.50
		Set, never hinged	175.00	

Krizna Jama — A1

Cerknica Lake — A2

Designs: 20c, Railroad Bridge, Borovnica. 25c, Landscape near Ljubljana. 50c, Church, Ribnica. 75c, View, Ljubljana. 1 l, Old Castle, Ljubljana. 1.25 l, Kocevje (Gottschee). 1.50 l, Borovnica Falls. 2 l, Castle, Konstanjevnica. 2.50 l, Castle, Turjak. 3 l, Castle, Zuzemperk. 5 l, View of Krk. 10 l, View of Otolac. 20 l, Farm, Carniola. 30 l, Castle and church, Tabor.

Perf. 10½x11½, 11½x10½

1945		**Photo.**	**Unwmk.**
N55	A1	5c black	.40	4.00
N56	A2	10c red orange	.40	4.00
N57	A2	20c brn carmine	.40	4.00
N58	A2	25c dk sl green	.40	4.00
N59	A1	50c deep violet	.40	4.00
N60	A2	75c vermilion	.40	4.00
N61	A2	1 l dark ol grn	.40	4.00
N62	A1	1.25 l dark blue	.40	8.00
N63	A2	1.50 l olive black	.40	8.00
N64	A2	2 l ultramarine	.60	9.50
N65	A2	2.50 l brown	.60	9.50
N66	A1	3 l brt red vio	1.50	16.00
N67	A2	5 l dk red brn	1.60	16.00
N68	A2	10 l slate green	3.25	72.50
N69	A2	20 l sapphire	20.00	250.00
N70	A1	30 l rose pink	95.00	950.00
		Nos. N55-N70 (16)	126.15	1,368.
		Set, never hinged	240.00	

SEMI-POSTAL STAMPS

Italian Occupation

Yugoslavia Nos. B116-B119 with Additional Ovpt. in Black

Perf. 11½x12½, 12½x11½

1941			**Unwmk.**
NB1	AP6	50p + 50p on 5d	9.50	14.50
NB2	AP7	1d + 1d on 10d	9.50	14.50
NB3	AP8	1.50d + 1.50d on 20d	9.50	14.50
NB4	AP9	2d + 2d on 30d	9.50	14.50
		Nos. NB1-NB4 (4)	38.00	58.00
		Set, never hinged	90.00	

German Occupation

Italy Nos. E14 & E15 Srchd. in Red

1944		**Wmk. 140**	
NB5	SD4	1.25 l + 50 l green	35.00	600.00
NB6	SD4	2.50 l + 50 l dp org	35.00	600.00

The surtax aided the Red Cross.

Italy Nos. E4 & E15 Srchd. in Blue or Green

NB7	SD4	1.25 l + 50 l grn (B)	35.00	600.00
NB8	SD4	2.50 l + 50 l dp org	35.00	600.00
		Nos. NB5-NB8 (4)	140.00	2,400.
		Set, never hinged	275.00	

The surtax aided the Homeless Relief Fund. The German and Slovenian inscriptions in the surcharges are transposed on Nos. NB6 and NB8.

Italy Nos. C12-C14, C16-C18 Srchd. in Blue or Red

Nos. NB9, NB11　　Nos. NB10, NB12, NB14

No. NB13

1944			**Wmk. 140**
NB9	AP4	25c + 10 l dk grn	14.00	400.00
NB10	AP3	50c + 10 l ol brn	14.00	400.00
NB11	AP5	75c + 20 l org brn	14.00	400.00
NB12	AP5	1 l + 20 l pur	14.00	400.00
NB13	AP6	2 l + 20 l dp bl (R)	14.00	400.00
NB14	AP3	5 l + 20 l dk grn	14.00	400.00
		Nos. NB9-NB14 (6)	84.00	2,400.
		Set, never hinged	175.00	

The surcharge aided orphans.

Italy Nos. C12-C14, C16-C18 Srchd. in Blue or Red

Nos. NB15, NB17　　Nos. NB16, NB18, NB20

No. NB19

NB15	AP4	25c + 10 l dk grn	14.00	400.00
NB16	AP3	50c + 10 l ol brn	14.00	400.00
NB17	AP5	75c + 20 l org brn	14.00	400.00
NB18	AP5	1 l + 20 l pur	14.00	400.00
NB19	AP6	2 l + 20 l dp bl (R)	14.00	400.00
NB20	AP3	5 l + 20 l dk grn	14.00	400.00
		Nos. NB15-NB20 (6)	84.00	2,400.
		Set, never hinged	175.00	

The surcharge was for winter relief.

AIR POST STAMPS

Italian Occupation

Yugoslavia Nos. C7-C16 Ovptd. like Nos. NB1-NB4

Perf. 12½, 12½x11½, 11½x12½

1941			**Unwmk.**
NC1	AP6	50p brown	11.00	11.00
NC2	AP7	1d yel grn	11.00	11.00
NC3	AP8	2d bl gray	12.50	12.50
NC4	AP9	2.50d rose red	12.50	12.50
NC5	AP6	5d brn vio	20.00	20.00
NC6	AP7	10d brn lake	20.00	20.00
NC7	AP8	20d dark grn	55.00	55.00
NC8	AP9	30d ultra	87.50	95.00
NC9	AP10	40d Prus grn & pale grn	300.00	360.00
NC10	AP11	50d sl bl & gray bl	240.00	240.00
a.		Inverted overprint	950.00	
		Nos. NC1-NC10 (10)	769.50	837.00
		Set, never hinged	1,800.	

German Occupation

Italy Nos. C12-C14, C16-C19 Overprinted Types "a" and "b" in Carmine, Green or Blue

1944		**Wmk. 140**	**Perf. 14**
NC11	AP4(a)	25c dk grn (C)	10.00	40.00
NC12	AP3(b)	50c ol brn (C)	10.00	125.00
NC13	AP5(a)	75c org brn (G)	10.00	40.00
NC14	AP5(b)	1 l pur (C)	10.00	125.00
NC15	AP6(a)	2 l dp bl (Bl)	10.00	87.50
NC16	AP3(b)	5 l dk grn (C)	10.00	125.00
NC17	AP3(a)	10 l dp car (G)	10.00	87.50
		Nos. NC11-NC17 (7)	70.00	630.00

AIR POST SPECIAL DELIVERY STAMP

German Occupation

Italy #CE3 Ovptd. Type "b" in Blue

1944		**Wmk. 140**	**Perf. 14**
NCE1	APSD2	2 l gray blk	10.00	87.50

SPECIAL DELIVERY STAMP

German Occupation

Italy #E14 Ovptd. Type "b" in Green

1944		**Wmk. 140**	**Perf. 14**
NE1	SD4	1.25 l green	10.00	24.00

POSTAGE DUE STAMPS

Italian Occupation

Yugoslavia Nos. J28-J32 Overprinted in Black Like Nos. N1-N17

1941		**Unwmk.**	**Perf. 12½**
NJ1	D4	50p violet	4.00	4.00
NJ2	D4	1d rose	4.00	4.00
NJ3	D4	2d deep blue	4.00	4.00
NJ4	D4	5d orange	12.00	22.50
NJ5	D4	10d chocolate	12.00	22.50
		Nos. NJ1-NJ5 (5)	36.00	57.00
		Set, never hinged	80.00	

Same Overprinted in Black

NJ6	D4	50p violet	4.00	8.00
NJ7	D4	1d deep magenta	4.00	8.00
NJ8	D4	2d deep blue	8.00	9.50
NJ9	D4	5d orange	55.00	110.00
NJ10	D4	10d chocolate	21.00	40.00
		Nos. NJ6-NJ10 (5)	92.00	175.50

Same Overprinted in Black

NJ11	D4	50p violet	4.00	4.00
NJ12	D4	1d deep magenta	6.50	6.50
NJ13	D4	2d deep blue	55.00	110.00
		Nos. NJ11-NJ13 (3)	65.50	120.50

German Occupation

Postage Due Stamps of Italy, 1934, Overprinted or Surcharged in Various Colors

d　　　　　　e

f　　　　　　g

1944		Wmk. 140		Perf. 14	
NJ14	D6(d)	5c brown (Br)		2.40	80.00
NJ15	D6(d)	10c blue (Bl)		2.40	80.00
NJ16	D6(d)	20c rose red (R)		1.25	8.00
NJ17	D6(e)	25c green (G)		1.25	8.00
NJ18	D6(f)	30c on 50c vio (Bk)		1.25	8.00
NJ19	D6(d)	40c on 5c brn (Bl)		1.25	8.00
NJ20	D6(d)	50c violet (V)		1.25	8.00
NJ21	D7(e)	1 l red orange (R)		2.40	80.00
NJ22	D7(d)	2 l green (Bl)		2.40	80.00
		Nos. NJ14-NJ22 (9)		15.85	360.00

Fiume-Kupa Zone
Italian Occupation

Four issues of 1941-42 consist of overprints on Yugoslav stamps of 1939-41: (a.) 14 stamps overprinted "ZONA OCCUPATO FIUMANO KUPA" and "ZOFK ZOFK ZOFK." (b.) 3 stamps overprinted as illustrated. (c.) 1 stamp surcharged "MEMENTO AVDERE SEMPER." "L1," etc. (d.) 3 stamps overprinted in arch: "Pro Maternite e Infanzia."

ISSUES FOR ISTRIA AND THE SLOVENE COAST (ZONE B)

Grapes — A1

Olive Branch — A2

Sailboat, Pola — A3

Designs: 50c, Donkey. Nos. 25-26, Ruined home. 2 l, Duino Castle. 5 l, Birthplace of Vladimir Gortan. 10 l, Plowing. Nos. 33-34, Tuna. 30 l, Viaduct at Solkan, Soca River.

	Perf. 11½, 12, 10½x11½				
1945-46				Photo.	
23	A1	25c dark green		.40	1.00
24	A1	50c red brown		.25	.25
25	A1	1 l green		.25	.25
26	A1	1 l red		.25	.25
27	A2	1.50 l olive brown		.25	.25
28	A2	2 l dk Prus grn		.25	.25
29	A3	4 l red		.25	.25
30	A3	4 l bright blue		.25	.40
31	A3	5 l gray black		.25	.25
32	A3	10 l brown		.25	.25
33	A3	20 l blue		1.60	.85
34	A3	20 l dark violet		3.50	5.25
35	A3	30 l magenta		1.40	.80
		Nos. 23-35 (13)		9.15	10.30
		Set, never hinged		16.00	

The first (Ljubljana) printing is perf. 10½x11½ and consists of Nos. 23-24, 26-28, 30-32, 34-35. The second (Zagreb) printing is perf. 12 and consists of Nos. 23-25, 27-29, 31-33, 35. The third (Belgrade) printing is perf. 11½ and consists of Nos. 25, 28, 40-41.
See Nos. 40-41. For surcharges see Nos. 36-37, J1-J19.

Nos. 33 and 35 Surcharged with New Values and Bars in Black

1946		Unwmk.		Perf. 11½	
36	A3	1 l on 20 l blue		.60	1.25
37	A3	2 l on 30 l magenta		.60	1.25
		Set, never hinged		2.40	

Types of 1945
Design: 3 l, Duino Castle

1946, Nov. 30					
40	A2	3 l crimson		1.50	1.75
41	A3	6 l ultra		3.25	4.00
		Set, never hinged		9.25	

Types of Yugoslavia & Official Stamps of 1946 Surcharged in Black

On A26

On O1

1947		Unwmk.		Perf. 12½	
42	A26	1 l on 9d lilac rose		.25	.40
43	O1	1.50 l on 50p blue		.25	.40
44	A26	2 l on 9d lilac rose		.25	.40
45	O1	3 l on 50p blue		.25	.40
46	A26	5 l on 9d lilac rose		.25	.40
47	O1	6 l on 50p blue		.25	.40
48	A26	10 l on 9d lilac rose		.25	.40
49	O1	15 l on 50p blue		.25	.55
50	A26	20 l on 9d lilac rose		.25	.90
51	O1	50 l on 50p blue		.25	.90
		Nos. 42-51 (10)			5.15
		Set, never hinged		2.00	

POSTAGE DUE STAMPS

Nos. 23, 24 34 and 35 Surcharged in Black

1945		Unwmk.		Perf. 10½x11½	
J1	A3	50c on 20 l dk vio		.30	1.00
J2	A1	1 l on 25c dk grn		6.00	2.00
J3	A3	2 l on 30 l magenta		.90	2.40
J4	A1	4 l on 50c red brn		.70	.65
J5	A1	8 l on 50c red brn		.70	.65
J6	A1	10 l on 50c red brn		4.00	1.90
J7	A1	20 l on 50c red brn		4.50	3.25
		Nos. J1-J7 (7)		17.10	11.85
		Set, never hinged		32.50	

Nos. 25 and 35 Surcharged in Black

1945				Perf. 12	
J8	A1	1 l on 1 l green		.25	.40
J9	A1	2 l on 1 l green		.25	.40
J10	A1	4 l on 1 l green		.30	.40
J11	A3	10 l on 30 l magenta		2.50	2.00
J12	A3	20 l on 30 l magenta		4.00	4.50
J13	A3	30 l on 30 l magenta		4.00	4.50
		Nos. J8-J13 (6)		11.30	12.20

The surcharges are arranged to fit the designs of the stamps.

No. 23 Surcharged in Black

1946					
J14	A1	1 l on 25c dark green		.40	.55
J15	A1	2 l on 25c dark green		.70	.80
J16	A1	4 l on 25c dark green		.40	.55

No. 33 Surcharged in Black

J17	A3	10 l on 20 l blue		2.25	1.75
J18	A3	20 l on 20 l blue		5.50	4.50
J19	A3	30 l on 20 l blue		5.25	5.25
		Nos. J14-J19 (6)		14.50	13.40
		Set, never hinged		25.00	

Type of Yugoslavia Postage Due Stamps, 1946, Surcharged in Black

1947					
J20	D7	1 l on 1d brt blue grn		.25	.50
J21	D7	2 l on 1d brt blue grn		.25	.50
J22	D7	6 l on 1d brt blue grn		.25	.50
J23	D7	6 l on 1d brt blue grn		.25	.50
J24	D7	30 l on 1d brt blue grn		.25	.65
		Nos. J20-J24 (5)		1.25	2.65
		Set, never hinged		1.75	

TRIESTE, ZONE A
See listing under Italy, Vol. 3.

TRIESTE

A free territory (1947-1954) on the Adriatic Sea between Italy and Yugoslavia. In 1954 the territory was divided, Italy acquiring the northern section and seaport, Yugoslavia the southern section (Zone B).

> **Catalogue values for all unused stamps in this country are for Never Hinged items.**

ZONE B

Issued by the Yugoslav Military Government
100 Centesimi = 1 Lira
100 Paras = 1 Dinar (1949)

See Istria and the Slovene Coast (Zone B) for preceding issues of 1945-47.

Stylized Gymnast and Arms of Trieste — A1

1948	Unwmk. Litho.		Perf. 10½x11	
	Inscriptions in:			
1	A1	100 l Italian	8.00	4.00
2	A1	100 l Croatian	8.00	4.00
3	A1	100 l Slovene	8.00	4.00
a.	Strip of 3, #1-3		95.00	65.00
	Nos. 1-3 (3)		24.00	12.00

May Day.

Clasped Hands, Hammer and Sickle — A2

1949		Photo.		Perf. 11½x12½	
4	A2	10 l grnsh blk & ol grn		.80	.80

Labor Day, May 1, 1949.
"V.U.J.A. S.T.T." are the initials of "Vojna Uprava Jugoslovenske Armije, Slobodna Teritorija Trsta" (Military Administration Yugoslav Army, Free Territory of Trieste).

Stamps of Yugoslavia, 1945-47 Overprinted in Carmine or Ultramarine

1949, Aug. 15				Perf. 12½	
5	A22	50p ol gray		.40	.30
6	A22	1 d bl grn		.40	.30
7	A24	2d scar (U)		.40	.30
8	A25	3d dl red (U)		.40	.30
9	A24	4d dk bl		.80	.30
10	A25	5d dk bl		.80	.30
11	A26	9d rose vio (U)		5.50	.80
12	A23	12d ultra		5.50	4.00
13	A22	16d blue		8.00	4.75
14	A23	20d org ver (U)		16.00	6.50
		Nos. 5-14 (10)		38.20	17.85

The letters of the overprint are set closer and in one line on Nos. 7 and 9.

Yugoslavia Nos. 266 and 267 Overprinted in Carmine

Burelage in Color of Stamp

1949					
15	A58	5d blue		10.50	8.00
16	A58	12d brown		10.50	8.00

75th anniv. of the UPU.

Yugoslavia, Nos. 269 to 272, Overprinted in Carmine

1950					
17	A60	2d bl grn		4.00	.80
18	A60	3d car rose		4.00	.80
19	A60	5d blue		4.00	2.40
20	A60	10d dp org		16.00	8.00
		Nos. 17-20 (4)		28.00	12.00

Workers Carrying Tools and Flag — A3

1950, May 1				Photo.	
21	A3	3d violet		.55	.55
22	A3	10d carmine		1.00	1.00

Labor Day, May 1, 1950.

Peasant on Ass — A4

Designs: 1d, Cockerel. 2d, Goose. 3d, Bees and honeycomb. 5d, Oxen. 10d, Turkey. 15d, Goats. 20d, Silkworms.

1950   Unwmk.   Perf. 12½

23	A4	50p dk gray	.40	.40
24	A4	1d brn car	.40	.40
25	A4	2d dp bl	.40	.40
26	A4	3d org brn	.40	.40
27	A4	5d aqua	3.25	.40
28	A4	10d brown	3.25	.40
29	A4	15d violet	20.00	8.00
30	A4	20d dk grn	8.00	4.00
		Nos. 23-30 (8)	36.10	14.40

1951

31	A4	1d orange brown	1.25	.40
32	A4	3d rose brown	1.60	.40

Worker A5

1951, May 1

33	A5	3d dark red	.80	.40
34	A5	10d brown olive	1.25	.80

Labor Day.

Pietro Paolo Vergerio — A7

1951, Oct. 21   Litho.

37	A7	5d blue	1.00	1.00
38	A7	10d claret	1.00	1.00
39	A7	20d sepia	1.00	1.00
		Nos. 37-39 (3)	3.00	3.00

Types of Yugoslavia, 1951, Overprinted "STT VUJA"

1951, Nov.

40	A81	10d brn org (V)	1.00	.70
41	A81	12d grnsh blk (C)	1.00	.70

Bicycle Race — A8

1952   Photo.

42	A8	5d shown	.40	.40
43	A8	10d Soccer	.40	.40
44	A8	15d Rowing	.40	.40
45	A8	28d Sailing	1.60	1.25
46	A8	50d Volleyball	3.25	2.40
47	A8	100d Diving	10.00	4.00
		Nos. 42-47 (6)	16.05	8.85

Marshal Tito
A9   A10

1952, May 25   Perf. 11½

48	A9	15d dk brn	2.50	1.25
49	A10	28d red brn	2.50	2.00
50	A9	50d dk gray grn	4.75	2.75
		Nos. 48-50 (3)	9.75	6.00

60th birthday of Marshal Tito.

Types of Yugoslavia 1952 Overprinted in Carmine

1952, July 26   Perf. 12½

51	A90	5d dk brn & sal, cr	1.60	.40
52	A90	10d dk grn & grn	1.60	.40
53	A90	15d dk brn & bl, lil	1.60	.40
54	A90	28d dk brn & buff, cr	1.60	1.60
55	A90	50d dk brn & buff, yel	14.00	9.50
56	A90	100d ind & lil, pink	32.50	27.50
		Nos. 51-56 (6)	52.90	39.80

15th Olympic Games, Helsinki, 1952. Nos. 52, 54, 56 inscribed in Cyrillic characters. The added "N" in "VUJNA" stands for "Narodna" (Peoples'). See note after No. 4. Nos. 51-56 exist imperf. Value of set, $950, unused or used.

Yugoslavia Nos. 365 to 367 Overprinted in Carmine

1952, Sept. 13

57	A91	15d deep claret	3.25	2.75
58	A91	28d dark brown	4.00	2.75
59	A91	50d gray	4.75	2.75
		Nos. 57-59 (3)	12.00	8.25

Formation of the Yugoslav navy, 10th anniv.

Yugoslavia No. 358 Overprinted in Blue

1952, June 22

60	A89	15d bright rose	1.60	.80

Children's Week.

Yugoslavia Nos. 369-372 Overprinted in Blue or Carmine

1952, Nov. 4

61	A93	15d red brn (Bl)	1.00	.65
62	A93	15d dk vio bl	1.00	.65
63	A93	15d dk brn	1.00	.65
64	A93	15d bl grn	1.00	.65
		Nos. 61-64 (4)	4.00	2.60

Issued to publicize the 6th Yugoslavia Communist Party Congress, Zagreb, 1952.

Anchovies and Starfish — A11

1952   Unwmk.   Photo.   Perf. 11x11½

65	A11	15d red brown	4.00	4.00
a.		Souvenir sheet, imperf.	55.00	55.00

Capodistria Phil. Exhib., Nov. 29-Dec. 7. No. 65a contains a 50d dark blue green stamp. Sold for 85d.

Yugoslavia Types of 1952 Overprinted in Various Colors

1953, Feb. 3   Perf. 12½

66	A94	15d brn carmine (Bl)	.40	.40
67	A94	30d chalky blue (R)	1.60	1.60

10th anniv. of the death of Nikola Tesla.

Stamps or Types of Yugoslavia Overprinted in Various Colors

1953

68	A68	1d gray	9.50	7.25
69	A68	2d car (V)	.80	.40
70	A68	3d rose red (R)	.80	.40
71	A68	5d orange	.40	.40
72	A68	10d emerald (G)	.80	.40
73	A68	15d rose red (V)	1.60	.80
74	A68	30d blue (Bl)	4.00	2.40
75	A68	50d grnsh bl (Bl)	8.00	4.00
		Nos. 68-75 (8)	25.90	16.05

Nos. 69, 71 and 73 are lithographed. See Nos. 90-92.

Yugoslavia Nos. 375-377 Overprinted in Various Colors

1953, Apr. 21   Perf. 11½

76	A95	15d dk ol grn (O)	.25	.25
77	A95	30d chalky blue (O)	.40	.40
78	A95	50d henna brown	1.10	1.10
		Nos. 76-78 (3)	1.75	1.75

Issued in honor of the United Nations.

Automobile Climbing Mt. Lovcen — A12

Various automobiles and motorcycles.

1953, June 2   Perf. 12½

79	A12	15d ocher & choc	.40	.40
80	A12	30d lt bl grn & ol grn	.40	.40
81	A12	50d salmon & dp plum	.40	.40
82	A12	70d bl & dk bl	2.75	2.00
		Nos. 79-82 (4)	3.95	3.20

Intl. Automobile and Motorcycle Races, 1953.

Yugoslavia Types of 1953 Overprinted in Carmine

1953, July 8   Engr.

83	A97	50d gray grn (C)	4.00	4.00

Tito's election to the presidency, 1/14/53.

Yugoslavia No. 390 Overprinted in Carmine

1953, July 31

84	A98	15d gray & grn (C)	2.00	2.00

38th Esperanto Cong., Zagreb, July 25-Aug. 1, 1953. See No. C21.

Yugoslavia Types of 1953 Overprinted in Carmine

1953, Sept. 5

85	A101	15d blue (C)	4.00	4.00

Liberation of Istria & the Slovene coast, 10th anniv.

Yugoslavia Types of 1953 Overprinted in Carmine

1953, Oct. 3

86	A102	15d black & gray (C)	1.60	1.25

Cent. of the death of Branko Radicevic, poet.

Stamps or Types of Yugoslavia Overprinted in Various Colors

1953, Nov. 29   Perf. 12½x12

87	A103	15d gray vio (V)	1.10	.80
88	A103	30d claret (Br)	1.10	.80
89	A103	50d dl bl grn (Dk Bl)	1.10	.80
		Nos. 87-89 (3)	3.30	2.40

10th anniv. of the 1st republican legislative assembly of Yugoslavia.

Yugoslavia Nos. 380, 382, 384 Overprinted in Various Colors

1954, Mar. 5 — Perf. 12½

90	A68	5d org (V)	1.00	.40
91	A68	10d yel grn (C)	.80	.40
92	A68	15d rose red (G)	1.00	.40
		Nos. 90-92 (3)	2.80	1.20

Overprinted in Carmine

1954 — Photo. — Perf. 11½

93	A104	2d red brn, sl & cr	.80	.40
94	A104	5d gray & dk yel brn	.80	.40
95	A104	10d ol grn & dk org brn	.80	.40
96	A104	15d dp bl grn & dk org brn	.80	.40
97	A104	17d gray brn, dk brn & cr	.80	.40
98	A104	25d bis, gray bl & org yel	.80	.40
99	A105	30d lil & dk brn	.80	.40
100	A105	35d rose vio & bl blk	.80	.80
101	A105	50d yel grn & vio brn	1.60	1.25
102	A105	65d org brn & gray blk	4.75	3.25
103	A105	70d bl & org brn	12.00	6.50
104	A105	100d brt bl & blk brn	32.50	25.00
		Nos. 93-104 (12)	57.25	39.60

Yugoslavia Types of 1954 Overprinted in Various Colors

1954, Oct. 8 — Perf. 12½

105	A107	15d mar, red, ocher & dk bl (Bk)	.80	.55
106	A107	30d dk bl, grn, sal buff & choc (G)	.80	.55
107	A107	50d brn, bis & red (G)	.80	.55
108	A107	70d dk grn, gray grn & choc (R)	1.60	1.25
		Nos. 105-108 (4)	4.00	2.90

150th anniv. of the 1st Serbian insurrection.

AIR POST STAMPS

AP1

Perf. 12½x11½

1948, Oct. 17 — Photo. — Unwmk.

C1	AP1	25 l gray	1.10	.80
C2	AP1	50 l orange	1.10	.80

Economic Exhib. at Capodistria, Oct. 17-24.

Fishermen AP2

Farmer and Pack Mule — AP3

Mew over Chimneys AP4

1949, June 1 — Perf. 11½

C3	AP2	1 l grnsh bl	.40	.40
C4	AP3	2 l red brn	.80	.40
C5	AP2	5 l blue	.80	.40
C6	AP3	10 l purple	2.40	2.00
C7	AP2	25 l brown	6.50	4.00
C8	AP3	50 l ol grn	8.00	4.00
C9	AP4	100 l deep brown	14.50	6.50
		Nos. C3-C9 (7)	33.40	17.70

Italian inscriptions on Nos. C5 and C6, Croatian on No. C7, Slavonic on No. C8. Nos. C3-C4 exist imperf. Value, each $150.

Nos. C3-C9 Surcharged in Various Colors

No. C14

No. C15

No. C16

1949, Nov. 5

C10	AP2	1d on 1 l (Bk)	.40	.40
C11	AP3	2d on 2 l (Br)	.80	.40
C12	AP2	5d on 5 l (Bl)	.80	.40
C13	AP3	10d on 10 l (V)	.80	.40
C14	AP2	15d on 25 l (Br)	16.00	9.50
C15	AP3	20d on 50 l (Gr)	8.00	3.25
C16	AP4	30d on 100 l (Bk)	9.50	4.00
		Nos. C10-C16 (7)	36.30	18.35

On Nos. C14 and C15 the original value is obliterated by a framed block, on No. C16 by four parallel lines.

Yugoslavia No. C33 Overprinted in Carmine and Lilac Rose Network
Souvenir Sheet

1950 — Perf. 11½x12½

C17	AP15	10d lilac rose	200.00	160.00
a.		Imperf.	200.00	160.00

Main Square, Capodistria AP5

Lighthouse, Pirano — AP6

Design: 25d, Hotel, Portorose.

1952 — Unwmk. — Photo. — Perf. 12½

C18	AP5	5d brown	12.00	12.00
C19	AP6	15d brt bl	8.00	8.00
C20	AP5	25d green	8.00	8.00
		Nos. C18-C20 (3)	28.00	28.00

75th anniv. (in 1949) of the UPU.

Type of 1953 Yugoslavia Overprinted in Carmine

1953, July 31

C21	AP21	300d vio & grn	250.00	250.00

38th Esperanto Cong., Zagreb, 7/25-8/1. Sheets of 12 (12,000 stamps) and sheets of 8 (3,000 stamps in light violet and green). A private red overprint was applied marginally to 250 sheets of 8: "Esperantski Kongres — 38 — a Universala Kongreso de Esperanto — Congresso del Esperanto."

Air Post Stamps of Yugoslavia in New Colors Overprinted in Various Colors

1954			**Engr.**	
C22	AP16	1d dp pur gray	.80	.40
C23	AP16	2d brt grn (G)	.80	.40
C24	AP16	3d red brn (Br)	.80	.40
C25	AP16	5d chocolate	.80	.40
C26	AP16	10d bl grn	.80	.40
C27	AP16	20d brn (Br)	.80	.40
C28	AP16	30d blue	.80	.40
C29	AP16	50d olive blk	.80	.60
C30	AP16	100d scar (R)	2.50	2.50
C31	AP16	200d dk bl vio (Bl)	4.75	4.00
		Perf. 11x11½		
C32	AP17	500d orange (Br)	27.50	20.00
		Nos. C22-C32 (11)	41.15	29.90

POSTAGE DUE STAMPS

Yugoslavia Nos. J51 to J55 Overprinted "S T T VUJA" in Two Lines in Ultramarine or Carmine

1949 — Unwmk. — Perf. 12½

J1	D7	50p dp org	.80	.40
J2	D7	1d orange	.80	.40
J3	D7	2d dk bl (C)	.80	.40
J4	D7	3d yel grn (C)	1.60	.40
J5	D7	5d brt pur (C)	4.00	1.60
		Nos. J1-J5 (5)	8.00	3.20

Croakers D1

Anchovies D2

1950 — Photo.

J6	D1	50p brn org	4.00	.80
J7	D1	1d dp ol grn	4.00	1.60
J8	D2	2d dk grnsh bl	4.00	1.60
J9	D2	3d dk vio bl	4.00	1.60
J10	D2	5d plum	20.00	6.50
		Nos. J6-J10 (5)	36.00	12.10

Yugoslavia Nos. J67-J74 Overprinted "STT VUJNA" in Blue or Carmine

1952

J11	D7	1d brown (Bl)	.40	.40
J12	D7	2d emerald	.40	.40
J13	D7	5d blue	.40	.40
J14	D7	10d scar (Bl)	.40	.40
J15	D7	20d purple	.40	.40
J16	D7	30d org yel (Bl)	.40	.40
J17	D7	50d ultra	.40	.40
J18	D7	100d dp plum (Bl)	13.50	8.00
		Nos. J11-J18 (8)	16.30	10.80

POSTAL TAX STAMPS

Yugoslavia No. RA5 Surcharged in Blue

1948 — Unwmk. — Perf. 12½

RA1	PT4	2 l on 50p brn & scar	32.50	32.50

Obligatory on all mail from May 22-30.

Yugoslavia No. RA7 Overprinted in Black

1950, July 3

RA2	PT6	50p brn & red	2.40	1.25

Yugoslavia No. RA9 Overprinted in Black

1951

RA3	PT8	50p vio bl & red	24.00	16.00

Yugoslavia No. RA10 Overprinted in Carmine

1952

RA4	PT9	50p gray & carmine	1.60	.80

Type of 1953 Yugoslavia Overprinted in Blue

1953

RA5	PT10	2d org brn & red	1.60	.80

The tax of Nos. RA1-RA5 was for the Red Cross.

POSTAL TAX DUE STAMPS

Yugoslavia No. RAJ2 Surcharged Like No. RA1 in Scarlet

1948	Unwmk.	Perf. 12½

RAJ1 PT4 2 l on 50p bl grn & scar   260.00   240.00

Yugoslavia No. RAJ4 Overprinted in Black

1950, July 3
RAJ2 PT6 50p vio & red   2.40   1.25

Yugoslavia No. RAJ6 Overprinted in Black

1951
RAJ3 PT8 50p emer & red   240.00   225.00

Yugoslavia No. RAJ7 Overprinted in Orange

1952
RAJ4 PTD3 50p gray & car   1.60   1.00

Type of 1953 Yugoslavia Overprinted in Blue

1953
RAJ5 PT10 2d brt car & red   1.60   1.00

ZAIRE

zä-'ir

(Congo Democratic Republic)

LOCATION — Central Africa
GOVT. — Republic
AREA — 905,365 sq. mi.
POP. — 50,481,305 (1999 est.)
CAPITAL — Kinshasa

Congo Democratic Republic changed its name to Republic of the Zaire in November 1971. Issues before that date are listed in Vol. 2 under Congo Democratic Republic.

100 Sengi = 1 Li-Kuta
100 Ma-Kuta = 1 Zaire
100 Centimes = 1 Franc (July 1998)

> **Catalogue values for all unused stamps in this country are for Never Hinged items.**

> **From 1971 through 1997, imperforates exist of almost all issues. Exceptions are Nos. 756-772, 850-860, 991-999 and 1259-1442.**

UNICEF Emblem, Child Care — A143

UNICEF Emblem and: 14k, Map of Africa showing Zaire. 17k, Boy in African village.

1971, Dec. 18		Unwmk.

750	A143	4k gold & multi	.50	.25
751	A143	14k lt bl, gold, red & grn	1.25	.75
752	A143	17k gold & multi	2.00	1.10
		Nos. 750-752 (3)	3.75	2.10

25th anniv. of UNICEF. For surcharge see No. 1327.

Pres. Mobutu, MPR Emblem A144

1972	Photo.	Perf. 11½

753	A144	4k multi	4.00	2.50
754	A144	14k multi	4.00	2.50
755	A144	22k multi	4.00	2.50
		Nos. 753-755 (3)	12.00	7.50

5th anniv. of the People's Revolutionary Movement (MPR). For surcharge see #1308.

Zaire Arms — A145   Pres. Joseph D. Mobutu — A146

1972	Litho.	Perf. 14

756	A145	10s red org & blk	.25	.25
757	A145	40s brt bl & multi	.25	.25
758	A145	50s citron & multi	.25	.25

		Perf. 13		
759	A146	1k sky bl & multi	.25	.25
760	A146	2k org & multi	.25	.25
761	A146	3k multi	.25	.25
762	A146	4k emer & multi	.25	.25
763	A146	5k multi	.25	.25
764	A146	6k multi	.25	.25
765	A146	8k cit & multi	.40	.25
766	A146	9k multi	.50	.25
767	A146	10k lt lil & multi	.55	.25
768	A146	14k multi	.75	.30
769	A146	17k multi	.90	.40
770	A146	20k yel & multi	1.25	.50
771	A146	50k multi	3.00	1.00
772	A146	100k fawn & multi	6.00	2.50
		Nos. 756-772 (17)	15.60	7.70

For surcharges and overprints see Nos. 860, 1328, O1-O11.

Same, Denominations in Zaires

1973, Feb. 21
773	A146	0.01z sky bl & multi	.25	.25
774	A146	0.02z org & multi	.25	.25
775	A146	0.03z multi	.25	.25
776	A146	0.04z multi	.25	.25
777	A146	0.10z multi	.40	.25
778	A146	0.14z multi	.60	.55
		Nos. 773-778 (6)	2.00	1.80

Inga Dam A147

1973, Jan. 25	Litho.	Perf. 13½

790	A147	0.04z multi	.35	.25
791	A147	0.14z pink & multi	.45	.35
792	A147	0.18z yel & multi	.80	.55
		Nos. 790-792 (3)	1.60	1.15

Completion of first section of Inga Dam Nov. 24, 1972.

World Map A148

1973, June 23	Photo.	Perf. 12½x12

793	A148	0.04z lil & multi	.25	.25
794	A148	0.07z multi	.35	.25
795	A148	0.18z multi	.85	.50
		Nos. 793-795 (3)	1.45	1.00

3rd Intl. Fair at Kinshasa, June 23-July 8. The dark brown ink of the inscription was applied by a thermographic process and varnished, producing a shiny, raised effect.

Hand and INTERPOL Emblem — A149

1973, Sept. 28	Litho.	Perf. 12½

| 796 | A149 | 0.06z multi | .45 | .25 |
| 797 | A149 | 0.14z multi | .95 | .50 |

50th anniversary of International Criminal Police Organization.

Leopard with Soccer Ball on Globe A150

1974, July 17	Photo.	Perf. 11½x12

798	A150	1k multi	.25	.25
799	A150	2k multi	.25	.25
800	A150	3k multi	1.00	.30
801	A150	4k multi	1.25	.45
802	A150	5k multi	1.50	.60
803	A150	14k multi	4.50	1.10
a.		Souvenir sheet, 1 #803	37.50	—
		Nos. 798-803 (6)	8.75	2.95

World Cup Soccer Championship, Munich, June 13-July 7.

Foreman-Ali Fight — A151

1974, Nov. 9	Litho.	Perf. 12x12½

804	A151	1k multi	.25	.25
805	A151	4k multi	.25	.25
806	A151	6k multi	.35	.30
807	A151	14k multi	.75	.50
808	A151	20k multi	1.10	.90
		Nos. 804-808 (5)	2.70	2.20

World Heavyweight Boxing Championship match between George Foreman and Muhammad Ali, Kinshasa, Oct. 30 (postponed from Sept. 25).

Same, Type of 1974, Denominations in Zaires and Inscribed in Various Colors

1975, Aug.	Litho.	Perf. 12x12½

809	A151	0.01z multi (R)	.25	.25
810	A151	0.04z multi (Br)	.25	.25
811	A151	0.06z multi (Bk)	.30	.25
812	A151	0.14z multi (G)	.65	.50
813	A151	0.20z multi (Bk)	1.25	.90
		Nos. 809-813 (5)	2.70	2.20

Judge, Lawyers, IWY Emblem A152

1975, Dec.	Photo.	Perf. 11½

814	A152	1k dull blk & multi	.40	.25
815	A152	2k dp rose & multi	.50	.25
816	A152	4k dull grn & multi	1.00	.35
817	A152	14k violet & multi	2.25	.50
		Nos. 814-817 (4)	4.15	1.35

International Women's Year 1975.

Waterfall — A153

1975	Photo.	Perf. 11½

818	A153	1k multicolored	.30	.25
819	A153	2k lt blue & multi	.40	.25
820	A153	3k multicolored	.50	.30
821	A153	4k salmon & multi	1.40	.65
822	A153	5k green & multi	1.50	.65
		Nos. 818-822 (5)	4.10	2.10

12th General Assembly of the Intl. Union for Nature Preservation (U.I.C.N.), Kinshasa, Sept. 1975.

Okapis A154

1975
823	A154	1k blue & multi	.60	.25
824	A154	2k yellow grn & multi	.90	.25
825	A154	3k brown red & multi	1.50	.30
826	A154	4k green & multi	2.40	.50
827	A154	5k yellow & multi	3.25	.60
		Nos. 823-827 (5)	8.65	1.90

Virunga National Park, 50th anniversary.

Siderma Maluku Industry A155

Designs: 1k, Sozacom apartment building, vert. 3k, Matadi flour mill, vert. 4k, Women parachutists. 8k, Pres. Mobutu visiting Chairman Mao, vert. 10k, Soldiers working along the Salongo. 14k, Pres. Mobutu addressing UN Gen. Assembly, Oct. 1974. 15k, Celebrating crowd.

1975
828	A155	1k ocher & multi	.50	.25
829	A155	2k yel grn & multi	.75	.25
830	A155	3k multi	1.00	.25

831	A155	4k multi	1.50 .25
832	A155	8k dk brn & multi	1.75 .35
833	A155	10k sep & multi	2.00 .50
834	A155	14k bl & multi	5.00 .75
835	A155	15k org & multi	7.00 1.00
		Nos. 828-835 (8)	19.50 3.60

10th anniversary of new government.

Tshokwe
Mask — A156

Designs: 2k, 4k, Seated woman, Pende. 7k, like 5k. 10k, 14k, Antelope mask, Suku. 15k, 18k, Kneeling woman, Kongo. 20k, 25k, Kuba mask.

1977, Jan. 8		Photo.	Perf. 11½
836	A156	2k multi	.25 .25
837	A156	4k multi	.25 .25
838	A156	5k gray & multi	.25 .25
839	A156	7k multi	.25 .25
840	A156	10k multi	.30 .25
841	A156	14k multi	.45 .25
842	A156	15k multi	.55 .25
843	A156	18k multi	.65 .35
844	A156	20k multi	1.25 .40
845	A156	25k vio & multi	1.50 .80
		Nos. 836-845 (10)	5.70 3.30

Wood carving and masks of Zaire.

Map of Zaire,
UPU
Emblem — A157

1977, Apr.		Litho.	Perf. 13½
846	A157	1k org & multi	.35 .25
847	A157	4k dk bl & multi	1.00 .25
848	A157	7k ol grn & multi	1.75 .30
849	A157	50k brn & multi	6.50 4.00
		Nos. 846-849 (4)	9.60 4.80

Cent. of UPU (in 1974).

Congo Stamps of 1968-1971 Srchd. with New Value, Bars and "REPUBLIQUE DU ZAIRE"

1977

850	A126	1k on 10s (#642)	.70 .35
851	A122	2k on 9.6k (#618)	.70 .35
852	A140	10k on 10s (#735)	2.50 .75
853	A134	25k on 10s (#703)	2.75 .50
854	A127	40k on 9.6k (#652)	3.75 2.00
855	A135	48k on 10s (#713)	7.50 3.00
		Nos. 850-855 (6)	17.90 6.95

Congo Nos. 644, 643, 635, 746 Srchd. with New Value, Bars and "REPUBLIQUE DU ZAIRE" in Black or Carmine, Zaire No. 757 Srchd.

1977

856	A126	5k on 30s	1.00 .35
857	A126	10k on 15s (C)	1.00 .35
858	A124	20k on 9.60k	2.25 .75
859	A141	30k on 12k	3.75 .75
860	A145	100k on 40s (C)	9.50 3.00
		Nos. 856-860 (5)	17.50 5.20
		Nos. 850-860 (11)	29.15 17.70

Nos. 850-860 exist with a number of overprint color varieties, as well as with inverted and double overprint errors.

Souvenir Sheet

Adoration of the Kings, by
Rubens — A158

1977, Dec. 19		Photo.	Perf. 13½
861	A158	5z multi	140.00 110.00

Christmas 1977.

Pantodon
Buchholzi
A159

Fish: 70s, Aphyosemion striatum. 55, Ctenopoma fasciolatum. 8k, Malapterurus electricus. 10k, Hemichromis bimaculatus. 30k, Marcusenius isidori. 40k, Synodontis nigriventris. 48k, Julidochromis ornatus. 100k, Nothobranchius brieni. 250k, Micralestes interruptus.

1978, Jan. 23		Litho.	Perf. 14
862	A159	30s multi	.25 .25
863	A159	70s multi	.25 .25
864	A159	5k multi	.25 .25
865	A159	8k multi	.35 .30
866	A159	10k multi	.55 .35
867	A159	30k multi	1.25 .75
868	A159	40k multi	1.75 1.00
869	A159	48k multi	2.00 1.25
870	A159	100k multi	5.50 2.75
		Nos. 862-870 (9)	12.15 7.15

Souvenir Sheet
Perf. 13½

871	A159	250k multi	14.00 14.00

No. 871 contains one 46x35mm stamp. For surcharges see Nos. 1294, 1311.

Soccer Game,
Argentina-France
A160

Various Soccer Games and Jules Rimet Cup: 3k, Austria-Brazil. 7k, Scotland-Iran. 9k, Netherlands-Peru. 10k, Hungary-Italy. 30k, Fed. Rep. of Germany-Mexico. 50k, Tunisia-Poland. 100k, Spain-Sweden. 500k, Rimet Cup, Games' emblem and cartoon of soccer player, horiz.

1978, Aug. 7		Litho.	Perf. 12½
872	A160	1k multi	.25 .25
873	A160	3k multi	.25 .25
874	A160	7k multi	.25 .25
875	A160	9k multi	.25 .25
876	A160	10k multi	.25 .25
877	A160	20k multi	.40 .25
878	A160	50k multi	1.10 .60
879	A160	100k multi	2.25 1.25
		Nos. 872-879 (8)	5.00 3.35

Souvenir Sheets

880	A160	500k blue & multi	25.00 25.00
881	A160	500k red & multi	25.00 25.00

11th World Cup Soccer Championship, Argentina, June 1-25. Nos. 880-881 contain one stamp each (47x36mm). Stamp of No. 880 has blue frameline. Stamp of No. 881 has red frame line.
For surcharge see No. 1259.

Mama
Mobutu — A161

1978, Oct. 23		Photo.	Perf. 12
882	A161	8k multi	.30 .30

Mama Mobutu (1941-77), wife of Pres. Mobutu.

Pres. Joseph D.
Mobutu — A162

**Frame Color
Granite Paper**

1978		Photo.	Perf. 12
883	A162	2k blue	.25 .25
884	A162	5k bister	.25 .25
885	A162	6k Prussian blue	.25 .25
886	A162	8k red brown	.25 .25
887	A162	10k emerald	.25 .25
888	A162	25k red	.25 .25
889	A162	48k purple	.40 .30
890	A162	1z green	.80 .50
		Nos. 883-890 (8)	2.70 2.30

See Nos. 1053, 1065-1066. For surcharges see Nos. 1313, 1333-1336.

Souvenir Sheet

Elizabeth II in Westminster
Abbey — A163

1978, Dec. 11		Photo.	Perf. 13½
891	A163	5z multi	12.00 12.00

Coronation of Queen Elizabeth II, 25th anniv.

Souvenir Sheet

Albrecht Dürer, Self-portrait — A164

1978, Dec. 18			Perf. 13
892	A164	5z multi	12.00 12.00

Albrecht Dürer (1471-1528), German painter and engraver.

Leonardo da Vinci and his
Drawings — A165

History of Aviation: 70s, Planes of Wright Brothers, 1905, and Santos Dumont, 1906. 1k, Bleriot XI, 1909, and Farman F-60, 1909. 5k, Junkers G-38, 1929, and Spirit of St. Louis, 1927. 8k, Sikorsky S-42B, 1934 and Macchi-Castoldi MC-72, 1934. 10k, Boeing 707, 1960, and Fokker F-VII, 1935. 50k, Apollo XI, 1969, and Concorde, 1976. 75k, Helicopter and Douglas DC-10, 1971. 5z, Giffard's balloon, 1852, and Hindenburg LZ 129, 1936.

1978, Dec. 28		Litho.	Perf. 13
893	A165	30s multi	.25 .25
894	A165	70s multi	.25 .25
895	A165	1k multi	.25 .25
896	A165	5k multi	.05 .25
897	A165	8k multi	.40 .25
898	A165	10k multi	.75 .25
899	A165	50k multi	3.25 1.00
900	A165	75k multi	4.25 1.25
		Nos. 893-900 (8)	9.75 3.75

Souvenir Sheet
Perf. 11½

901	A165	5z multi	16.00 16.00

For overprint and surcharges see Nos. 993, 1173-1181, 1291, 1295.

Pres. Mobutu, Map of Zaire, N'tombe
Dancer — A166

Pres. Mobutu & Map: 3k, Bird. 4k, Elephant. 10k, Diamond and cotton boll. 14k, Hand holding torch. 17k, Leopard's head and Victoria Regia lily. 25k, Finzia waterfall. 50k, Wagenia fishermen.

1979, Feb.		Litho.	Perf. 14x13½
902	A166	1k multicolored	.25 .25
903	A166	3k multicolored	.25 .25
904	A166	4k multicolored	.25 .25
905	A166	10k multicolored	.25 .25
a.		Souvenir sheet of 4, #902-905	13.00
906	A166	14k multicolored	.25 .25
907	A166	17k multicolored	.40 .25
908	A166	25k multicolored	.60 .40
909	A166	50k multicolored	1.25 .85
a.		Souvenir sheet of 4, #906-909	13.00
		Nos. 902-909 (8)	3.50 2.75

Zaire (Congo) River expedition.

A stamp similar to design No. A166, depicting Pres. Mobutu and a flag and printed on gold foil, exists. Value, $50.

Phylloporus
Ampliporus
A167

Mushrooms: 5k, Engleromyces goetzei. 8k, Scutellinia virungae. 10k, Pycnoporus sanguineus. 30k, Cantharellus miniatescens. 40k, Lactarius phlebonemus. 48k, Phallus indusiatus. 100k, Ramaria moelleriana.

1979, Mar.   Photo.   Perf. 13½x13
910	A167	30s multicolored	.30	.25
911	A167	5k multicolored	.35	.30
912	A167	8k multicolored	.55	.40
913	A167	10k multicolored	.85	.50
914	A167	30k multicolored	1.75	1.25
915	A167	40k multicolored	2.50	1.50
916	A167	48k multicolored	4.25	2.00
917	A167	100k multicolored	6.25	3.50
		Nos. 910-917 (8)	16.80	9.70

For surcharges see Nos. 1296, 1298, 1312, 1361-1362, 1365-1366, 1368-1369, 1372, 1375.

Souvenir Sheets

Pope John XXIII (1881-1963) — A168

Popes: No. 919, Paul VI (1897-1978). No. 920, John Paul I (1912-78).

1979, June 25   Litho.   Perf. 11½
918	A168	250k multi	5.00	5.00
919	A168	250k multi	5.00	5.00
920	A168	250k multi	5.00	5.00
		Nos. 918-920 (3)	15.00	15.00

Boy Beating
Drum — A169

IYC Emblem on Map of Zaire and: 10k, 20k, Girl, diff. 50k, Boy. 100k, Boys. 300k, Mother and child. 10z, Mother and children, horiz.

1979, July 23   Litho.   Perf. 12½
921	A169	5k multi	.25	.25
922	A169	10k multi	.25	.25
923	A169	20k multi	.40	.25
924	A169	50k multi	.90	.50
925	A169	100k multi	1.90	1.00
926	A169	300k multi	5.25	2.50
		Nos. 921-926 (6)	8.95	4.75

Souvenir Sheet
| 927 | A169 | 10z multi | 14.00 | 10.50 |

International Year of the Child.
For surcharges see Nos. 997, 999, 1299, 1306.

Globe and
Drummer
A170

1979, July 23
928	A170	1k multi	.25	.25
929	A170	9k multi	.25	.25
930	A170	90k multi	.70	.50
931	A170	100k multi	.80	.55
		Nos. 928-931 (4)	2.00	1.55

Souvenir Sheet
| 932 | A170 | 500k multi | 5.00 | 5.00 |

6th International Fair, Kinshasa. No. 932 contains one 52x31mm stamp.
For overprint & surcharge see #996, 1320.

Globe and
School
Desk — A171

1979, Dec. 24   Litho.   Perf. 13
| 933 | A171 | 10k multi | .30 | .25 |

Intl. Bureau of Education, Geneva, 50th anniv.

Adoration of the Kings,
Memling — A172

1979, Dec. 24   Imperf.
| 934 | A172 | 5z multi | 6.00 | 6.00 |

Christmas 1979.

"Puffing
Billy,"
1814, Gt.
Britain
A173

1.50k, Buddicom No. 33, 1843, France. 5k, "Elephant," 1835, Belgium. 8k, No. 601, 1906, Zaire. 50k, "Slieve Gullion 440," Ireland. 75k, "Black Elephant," Germany. 2z, Type 1-15, Zaire. 5z, "Golden State," US.
10z, Type E.D.75, Zaire.

1980, Jan. 14   Litho.   Perf. 13½x13
935	A173	50s shown	.25	.25
936	A173	1.50k multicolored	.25	.25
937	A173	5k multicolored	.25	.25
938	A173	8k multicolored	.25	.25
939	A173	50k multicolored	.75	.25
940	A173	75k multicolored	1.10	.75
941	A173	2z multicolored	2.25	1.90
942	A173	5z multicolored	6.00	6.00
		Nos. 935-942 (8)	11.10	9.90

Souvenir Sheet
| 943 | A173 | 10z multicolored | 15.00 | 15.00 |

For overprints and surcharges see Nos. 991-992, 994, 1325.

Hill,
Belgian
Congo
No. 257
A174

1980, Jan. 28   Perf. 13½x14
944	A174	2k No. 5	.25	.25
945	A174	4k No. 13	.25	.25
946	A174	10k No. 24	.25	.25
947	A174	20k No. 38	.25	.25
948	A174	40k No. 111	.40	.25
949	A174	150k No. B29	1.25	1.00
950	A174	200k No. 198	1.50	1.25
951	A174	250k shown	1.90	1.50
		Nos. 944-951 (8)	6.05	5.00

Souvenir Sheet
| 952 | A174 | 10z No. 198 | 11.00 | 11.00 |

Sir Rowland Hill (1795-1879), originator of penny postage.
For overprint and surcharge see Nos. 998, 1329.

Albert Einstein
(1879-1955),
Theoretical
Physicist
A175

1980, Feb. 18   Perf. 13
953	A175	40s multi	.25	.25
954	A175	2k multi	.25	.25
955	A175	4k multi	.25	.25
956	A175	15k multi	.25	.25
957	A175	50k multi	.40	.40
958	A175	300k multi	1.60	1.90
		Nos. 953-958 (6)	3.00	2.40

Souvenir Sheet
| 959 | A175 | 5z multi, diff. | 4.50 | 4.50 |

For surcharges see Nos. 1285, 1290, 1304.

Salvation Army Brass Players — A176

50s, Booth Memorial Hospital, NYC. 4.50k, Commissioner George Railton sailing for US mission. 10k, Mobile dispensary, Masina. 20k, Gen. Evangeline Booth, officer holding infant, vert. 75k, Outdoor well-baby clinic. 1.50z, Disaster relief. 2z, Parade, vert. 10z, Gen. & Mrs. Arnold Brown.

1980, Mar. 3   Perf. 11
960	A176	50s multi	.25	.25
961	A176	4.50k multi	.25	.25
962	A176	10k multi	.25	.25
963	A176	20k multi	.25	.25
964	A176	40k multi	.35	.25
965	A176	75k multi	.55	.25
966	A176	1.50z multi	1.10	.55
967	A176	2z multi	1.60	.80
		Nos. 960-967 (8)	4.60	2.85

Souvenir Sheet
| 968 | A176 | 10z multi | 9.00 | 9.00 |

Salvation Army cent. in US. No. 968 contains one 53x38mm stamp and 2 labels.

A set of nine stamps and one souvenir sheet for the 1980 Olympic Games in Moscow was prepared but not issued. Value, set $140.

Souvenir Sheets

Visite de Sa Sainteté le Pape Jean Paul II
au Zaïre — Mai 1980

Pope John Paul II — A177

1980, May 2   Litho.   Perf. 11½
| 969 | A177 | 10z multi | 17.50 | 17.50 |

Visit of Pope John Paul II to Zaire, May.

Baia Castle, by Antonio Pitloo — A178

1980, May 5
| 970 | A178 | 10z multi | 6.00 | 6.00 |

20th International Philatelic Exhibition, Europa '80, Naples, Apr. 26-May 4.

A179

50k, Woman, line-drawing. 100k, Plutiarch. 500k, Kneeling man, sculpture, vert.

Perf. 12½x13, 13x12½
1980, May 24   Litho.
971	A179	50k multicolored	.25	.25
972	A179	100k multicolored	.50	.40
973	A179	500k multicolored	2.50	1.75
a.		Souvenir sheet of 3	6.00	6.00
		Nos. 971-973 (3)	3.25	2.40

Rotary Intl., 75th anniv. No. 973a contains 3 stamps similar to Nos. 971-973, size: 55x35, 35x55mm. Exists imperf.
For surcharge see No. 1313.

Tropical Fish — A180

1k, Chaetodon collaris. 5k, Zebrasoma veliferum. 10k, Euxiphipops xanthometapon. 20k, Pomacanthus annularis. 50k, Centropyge oriculus. 150k, Oxymonacanthus longirostris. 200k, Balistoides niger. 250k, Rhinecanthus aculeatus.
5z, Baliste ondule.

1980, Oct. 20   Litho.   Perf. 14x13½

974	A180	1k multicolored	.25	.25
975	A180	5k multicolored	.25	.25
976	A180	10k multicolored	.25	.25
977	A180	20k multicolored	.25	.25
978	A180	50k multicolored	.60	.40
979	A180	150k multicolored	1.40	.55
980	A180	200k multicolored	1.90	.70
981	A180	250k multicolored	2.25	1.00
		Nos. 974-981 (8)	7.15	3.65

Souvenir Sheet

981A	A180	5z multicolored	4.75	4.75

For surcharge see No. 1307.

Exhibition Emblem, Congo
#365 — A181

1980, Dec. 6   Litho.   Perf. 13

982		Block or strip of 4	2.00	1.75
a.	A181	1z denomination at UR, shown	.45	.35
b.	A181	1z denomination at UL, Belgium #511	.45	.35
c.	A181	1z denomination at UR, like #982b	.45	.35
d.	A181	1z denomination at UL, like #982a	.45	.35
983		Block or strip of 4	4.00	3.00
a.	A181	2z denomination at UR, Congo #432	.95	.60
b.	A181	2z denomination at UL, Belguim # B835	.95	.60
c.	A181	2z denomination at UR, like #983b	.95	.60
d.	A181	2z denomination at UL, like #983a	.95	.60
984		Block or strip of 4	6.00	4.50
a.	A181	3z denomination at UR, Zaire #755	1.40	.90
b.	A181	3z denomination at UL, Belgium # B878	1.40	.90
c.	A181	3z denomination at UR, like #984b	1.40	.90
d.	A181	3z denomination at UL, like #984a	1.40	.90
985		Block or strip of 4	8.50	6.00
a.	A181	4z denomination at UR, Congo #572	1.75	1.10
b.	A181	4z denomination at UL, Belgium # B996	1.75	1.10
c.	A181	4z denomination at UR, like #985b	1.75	1.10
d.	A181	4z denomination at UL, like #985a	1.75	1.10
		Nos. 982-985 (4)	20.50	15.25

PHIBELZA, Belgium-Zaire Phil. Exhib.
For surcharge see No. 1342.

Map of
Africa,
King
Leopold I
A182

Belgian independence sesquicentennial:
75k, Stanley expedition, Leopold II. 100k,
Colonial troops, Albert I. 145k, Protected animals, Leopold III. 270k, Visit of King Baudouin
and Queen Fabiola.

1980, Dec. 13   Photo.   Perf. 14

986	A182	10k multi	.45	.25
987	A182	75k multi	1.40	.45
988	A182	100k multi	2.00	.60
989	A182	145k multi	2.50	.80
990	A182	270k multi	4.50	1.25
		Nos. 986-990 (5)	10.85	3.35

For surcharges see Nos. 1326, 1331, 1345,
1357, 1408-1412, 1426.

**Nos. 935, 936, 898, 939, 900, 931,
925, 951, Overprinted in Red, Silver
or Black: 20e Anniversaire-
Independence / 1960-1980**

1980, Dec. 13   Litho.

991	A173	50s multi	.25	.25
992	A173	1.50k multi	.25	.25
993	A165	10k multi	.25	.25
994	A173	50k multi	.40	.25
995	A165	75k multi	.60	.25
996	A170	100k multi (S)	.90	.50
997	A169	1z on 5z on 100k multi (B)	1.00	.50
998	A174	250k multi	2.00	1.00

999	A169	5z on 100k multi (B)	4.75	2.50
		Nos. 991-999 (9)	10.40	5.75

20th anniversary of independence. For
surcharges see Nos. 1300, 1316.

Nativity
A183

1980, Dec. 24   Perf. 13

1000	A183	10k Shepherds and angels	.25	.25
1001	A183	75k Flight into Egypt	1.00	.40
1002	A183	80k Three kings	1.00	.40
1003	A183	145k shown	1.75	.60
		Nos. 1000-1003 (4)	4.00	1.65

Souvenir Sheet

1004	A183	10z Church, nativity	5.50	5.50

Christmas 1980. No. 1004 contains one
49x33mm stamp. Exists imperf. For
surcharges see Nos. 1301, 1317-1318.

Postal Clerk
Sorting Mail,
by Norman
Rockwell
A184

Designs: Saturday Evening Post covers by
Norman Rockwell.

1981, Apr. 27   Litho.   Perf. 14

1005	A184	10k multi	.25	.25
1006	A184	20k multi	.25	.25
1007	A184	50k multi	.40	.25
1008	A184	80k multi	.65	.35
1009	A184	100k multi	.70	.40
1010	A184	125k multi	1.10	.45
1011	A184	175k multi	1.25	.65
1012	A184	200k multi	1.40	.75
		Nos. 1005-1012 (8)	6.00	3.35

For surcharges see Nos. 1262, 1265, 1269,
1275, 1281, 1354.

First
Anniv.
of Visit
of Pope
John
Paul II
A185

Scenes of Pope's visit. 50k, 500k, vert.

1981, May 2   Perf. 13

1013	A185	5k multi	.25	.25
1014	A185	10k multi	.25	.25
1015	A185	50k multi	.35	.30
1016	A185	100k multi	1.00	.50
1017	A185	500k multi	5.50	2.50
1018	A185	800k multi	7.75	4.25
		Nos. 1013-1018 (6)	15.10	8.05

For surcharges see #1190-1194, 1292,
1302, 1343.

Soccer
Players — A186

Designs: Soccer scenes.

1981, July 6   Litho.   Perf. 12½

1019	A186	2k multi	.25	.25
1020	A186	10k multi	.25	.25
1021	A186	25k multi	.25	.25
1022	A186	90k multi	.50	.25
1023	A186	2z multi	1.00	.55
1024	A186	3z multi	1.60	.85
1025	A186	6z multi	2.75	1.50
1026	A186	8z multi	4.50	3.00
		Nos. 1019-1026 (8)	11.10	6.90

Souvenir Sheet

1027		Sheet of 2	6.00	6.00
a.		A186 5z like #1019	2.75	2.75
b.		A186 5z like #1025	2.75	2.75

ESPANA '82 World Cup Soccer Championship. For surcharges see Nos. 1287, 1303,
1309, 1321.

Intl. Year of the Disabled — A187

2k, Archer. 5k, Ear, sound waves. 10k,
Amputee. 18k, Cane braille, sunglasses. 50k,
Boy with leg braces. 150k, Sign language.
500k, Hands. 800k, Dove.

1981, Nov. 2   Litho.   Perf. 14x14½

1028	A187	2k multicolored	.25	.25
1029	A187	5k multicolored	.25	.25
1030	A187	10k multicolored	.25	.25
1031	A187	18k multicolored	.25	.25
1032	A187	50k multicolored	.25	.25
1033	A187	150k multicolored	.60	.30
1034	A187	500k multicolored	1.50	1.25
1035	A187	800k multicolored	2.75	2.00
		Nos. 1028-1035 (8)	6.10	4.80

For surcharges see Nos. 1288, 1293, 1305,
1314.

Souvenir Sheet

Birth Sesqui. of Heinrich von
Stephan, UPU Founder — A188

Photogravure and Engraved

1981, Dec. 21   Perf. 11½x12

1036	A188	15z purple	8.00	8.00

Christmas
1981 — A189

Designs: 25k, 1z, 1.50z, 3z, 5z, Various
children. 10z, Holy Family, horiz.

1981, Dec. 21   Litho.   Perf. 14

1037	A189	25k multi	.25	.25
1038	A189	1z multi	.70	.25
1039	A189	1.50z multi	.80	.35

1040	A189	3z multi	1.75	.75
1041	A189	5z multi	2.75	1.25
		Nos. 1037-1041 (5)	6.25	2.85

Souvenir Sheet

1042	A189	10z multi	5.50	5.50

13th World Telecommunications Day
(1981) — A190

Designs: Symbols of communications and
health care delivery.

1982, Feb. 8   Litho.   Perf. 13

1043	A190	1k multi	.25	.25
1044	A190	25k multi	.25	.25
1045	A190	90k multi	.30	.25
1046	A190	1z multi	.30	.25
1047	A190	1.70z multi	.55	.45
1048	A190	3z multi	1.10	.75
1049	A190	4.50z multi	1.60	1.10
1050	A190	5z multi	1.75	1.25
		Nos. 1043-1050 (8)	6.10	4.55

For surcharges see Nos. 1270, 1282.

**Pres. Mobutu Type of 1978
Frame Color
Granite Paper**

1902   Photo.   Perf. 12

1053	A162	50k purple	.25	.25
1055	A162	2z bister	.75	.25
1056	A162	5z Prussian blue	2.25	1.25
		Nos. 1053-1056 (3)	3.25	1.75

20th Anniv. of African Postal Union
(1981) — A191

1982, Mar. 8   Litho.   Perf. 13

1057	A191	1z yel grn & gold	.50	.40

For surcharges see Nos. 1348, 1352.

1982
World
Cup
A192

Designs: Flags and players of finalists.

1982

1058	A192	2k multi	.25	.25
1059	A192	8k multi	.25	.25
1060	A192	25k multi	.25	.25
1061	A192	50k multi	.25	.25
1062	A192	90k multi	.30	.25
1063	A192	1z multi	.45	.30
1064	A192	1.45z multi	.55	.45
1065	A192	1.70z multi	.85	.70
1066	A192	3z multi	1.40	1.10
1067	A192	3.50z multi	1.90	1.40
1068	A192	5z multi	3.00	2.10
1069	A192	6z multi	3.25	2.50
		Nos. 1058-1069 (12)	12.70	9.80

Souvenir Sheet

1070	A192	10z multi	7.50	7.50

Issued: #1058-1069, July 6; #1070, Sept. 21.
For surcharges see #1289, 1315, 1322,
1344, 1435 and footnote after #1336.

9th Conference of Heads of State of Africa and France, Kinshasa, Oct. — A193

1982, Oct. 8   Litho.   Perf. 13
1071	A193	75k multi	.25	.25
1072	A193	90k multi	.25	.25
1073	A193	1z multi	.25	.25
1074	A193	1.50z multi	.25	.25
1075	A193	3z multi	.75	.60
1076	A193	5z multi	1.75	1.25
1077	A193	8z multi	2.00	1.75
		Nos. 1071-1077 (7)	5.50	4.60

For surcharges see Nos. 1268, 1271, 1280, 1283, 1347, 1351.

Animals from Virunga Natl. Park — A194

1982, Nov. 5
1078	A194	1z Lions	.30	.25
1079	A194	1.70z Buffalo	1.00	.75
1080	A194	3.50z Elephants	2.25	1.50
1081	A194	6.50z Antelope	4.00	2.75
1082	A194	8z Hippopotamus	5.75	3.25
1083	A194	10z Monkeys	6.50	4.00
1084	A194	10z Leopard	6.50	4.25
a.		Pair, #1083-1084 + label	18.00	18.00
		Nos. 1078-1084 (7)	26.30	16.75

#1084a has continuous design.
For surcharge see No. 1430.

Scouting Year — A195

1982, Nov. 29   Photo.   Perf. 11½
Granite Paper
1085	A195	90k Camp	.35	.30
1086	A195	1.70z Campfire	.90	.55
1087	A195	3z Scout	1.50	1.00
1088	A195	5z First aid	3.25	1.75
1089	A195	8z Flag signals	6.00	3.25
		Nos. 1085-1089 (5)	12.00	6.85

Souvenir Sheet
| 1090 | A195 | 10z Baden-Powell | 11.00 | 11.00 |

For surcharges see Nos. 1207-1214.

Local Birds — A196

25k, Quelea quelea. 50k, Ceyx picta. 90k, Tauraco persa. 1.50z, Charadrius tricollaris. 1.70z, Cursorius temminckii. 2z, Campethera bennettii. 3z, Podiceps ruficollis. 3.50z, Kaupifalco monogrammicus. 5z, Limnocorax flavirostris. 8z, White-headed vulture.

1982, Dec. 6   Litho.   Perf. 13
1091	A196	25k multicolored	.25	.25
1092	A196	50k multicolored	.25	.25
1093	A196	90k multicolored	.60	.25
1094	A196	1.50z multicolored	.65	.40
1095	A196	1.70k multicolored	.70	.40
1096	A196	2z multicolored	.95	.60
1097	A196	3z multicolored	1.50	.80
1098	A196	3.50z multicolored	1.60	.85
1099	A196	5z multicolored	2.50	1.25
1100	A196	8z multicolored	3.75	2.10
		Nos. 1091-1100 (10)	12.75	7.15

All except 3.50z, 8z horiz.
For surcharges see Nos. 1263, 1266, 1272, 1276, 1278, 1284, 1425, 1432, 1438, 1440.

Souvenir Sheet

Christmas — A197

15z, Adoration of the Magi, by van der Goes.

1982, Dec. 20   Photo.   Perf. 13½
| 1101 | A197 | 15z multicolored | 8.00 | 8.00 |

Quartz A198

2k, Malachite, vert. 75k, Gold. 1z, Uraninite. 1.50z, Bournonite, vert. 3z, Cassiterite. 6z, Dioptase, vert. 8z, Cuprite, vert. 10z, Diamonds.

1983, Feb. 13   Photo.   Perf. 11½
Granite Paper
1102	A198	2k multicolored	.30	.25
1103	A198	45k shown	.40	.25
1104	A198	75k multicolored	.75	.25
1105	A198	1z multicolored	1.25	.25
1106	A198	1.50z multicolored	1.75	.80
1107	A198	3z multicolored	3.50	1.50
1108	A198	6z multicolored	6.00	3.00
1109	A198	8z multicolored	8.00	4.00
		Nos. 1102-1109 (8)	21.95	10.30

Souvenir Sheet
| 1110 | A198 | 10z multicolored | 10.00 | 10.00 |

For surcharges see Nos. 1324, 1330, 1332, 1346.

TB Bacillus Centenary — A199

1983, Feb. 21   Litho.   Perf. 13
1111	A199	80k multi	.25	.25
1112	A199	1.20z multi	.40	.35
1113	A199	3.60z multi	1.40	1.00
1114	A199	9.60z multi	4.00	2.25
		Nos. 1111-1114 (4)	6.05	3.85

For surcharges see Nos. 1319, 1356, 1358, 1360, 1433, 1436, 1441.

Kinshasa Monuments — A200

50k, Zaire Diplomat, vert. 1z, Echo of Zaire. 1.50z, Messengers, vert. 3z, Shield of Revolution, vert. 5z, Weeping Woman. 10z, Militant, vert.

1983, Apr. 25
1115	A200	50k multicolored	.25	.25
1116	A200	1z multicolored	.25	.25
1117	A200	1.50z multicolored	.35	.25
1118	A200	3z multicolored	.65	.50
1119	A200	5z multicolored	1.10	.90
1120	A200	10z multicolored	2.40	2.00
		Nos. 1115-1120 (6)	5.00	4.15

For surcharges see Nos. 1267, 1279, 1349-1350.

ITU Plenipotentiaries Conference, Nairobi, Sept. 1982 — A201

Various satellites, dish antennae and maps.

1983, June 13   Litho.   Perf. 13
1121	A201	2k multi	.25	.25
1122	A201	4k multi	.25	.25
1123	A201	25k multi	.25	.25
1124	A201	1.20z multi	.40	.25
1125	A201	2.05z multi	.65	.35
1126	A201	3.60z multi	1.00	.60
1127	A201	6z multi	1.75	1.00
1128	A201	8z multi	2.50	1.40
		Nos. 1121-1128 (8)	7.05	4.35

For surcharges see Nos. 1260-1261, 1264, 1273-1274, 1277, 1355, 1359, 1429, 1434, 1437, 1439, 1442.

Christmas 1983 — A202

Raphael Paintings; No. 1129: a, Virgin and Child. b, Holy Family. c, Esterhazy Madonna. d, Sistine Madonna. No. 1130: a, La Belle Jardiniere. b, Virgin of Alba. c, Holy Family, diff. d, Virgin and Child, diff.

1983, Dec. 26   Photo.   Perf. 13½x13
1129		Sheet of 4	4.50	4.50
a.-d.	A202	10z, any single	.85	.75
1130		Sheet of 4	5.00	5.00
a.-d.	A202	15z, any single	1.00	.75

Garamba Park — A203

10k, Darby's Eland. 15k, Eagles. 3z, Servals. 10z, White rhinoceros. 15z, Lions. 37.50z, Warthogs. No. 1137, Koris bustards. No. 1138, Crowned cranes.

1984, Apr. 2   Litho.   Perf. 13
1131	A203	10k multi	.25	.25
1132	A203	15k multi	.35	.25
1133	A203	3z multi	.60	.25
1134	A203	10z multi	2.25	1.25
1135	A203	15z multi	2.75	1.75
1136	A203	37.50z multi	6.25	4.25
1137	A203	40z multi	7.00	4.50
1138	A203	40z multi	7.00	4.50
a.		Pair, #1137-1138 + label	16.00	16.00
		Nos. 1131-1138 (8)	26.45	17.00

Nos. 1137-1138 are narrower, 49x34mm, with continuous design.
For surcharge see No. 1428.

World Communications Year — A204

Designs: 10k, Computer operator, Congo River ferry. 15k, Communications satellite. 8.50z, Engineer, Congo River Bridge. 10z, Satellite, ground receiving station. 15z, TV camerawoman filming crowed crane. 37.50z, Satellite, dish antennas. 80z, Switchboard operator, bus.

1984, May 14   Litho.   Perf. 13x12½
1139	A204	10k multi	.25	.25
1140	A204	15k multi	.25	.25
1141	A204	8.50z multi	.65	.65
1142	A204	10z multi	.70	.70
1143	A204	15z multi	1.10	1.10
1144	A204	37.50z multi	2.75	2.75
1145	A204	80z multi	5.75	5.75
		Nos. 1139-1145 (7)	11.45	11.45

Hypericum Revolutum A205

Local flowers: 15k, Borreria dibrachiata. 3z, Disa erubescens. 8.50z, Scaevola plumieri. 10z, Clerodendron thompsonii. 15z, Thumbergia erecta. 37.50z, Impatiens niamniamensis. 100z, Canarina eminii.

1984, May 28   Photo.   Perf. 14x13½
1146	A205	10k multi	.25	.25
1147	A205	15k multi	.25	.25
1148	A205	3z multi	.25	.25
1149	A205	8.50z multi	.80	.80
1150	A205	10z multi	.90	.90
1151	A205	15z multi	1.25	1.25
1152	A205	37.50z multi	3.25	3.25
1153	A205	100z multi	9.00	9.00
		Nos. 1146-1153 (8)	15.95	15.95

1984 Summer Olympics A206

1984, June 5   Litho.   Perf. 13
1154	A206	2z Basketball	.25	.25
1155	A206	3z Equestrian	.35	.35
1156	A206	10z Running	1.10	1.10
1157	A206	15z Long jump	1.60	1.60
1158	A206	20z Soccer	2.75	2.75
		Nos. 1154-1158 (5)	6.05	6.05

Souvenir Sheet
Perf. 11½
| 1159 | A206 | 50z Kayak | 5.50 | 5.50 |

No. 1159 contains one 31x49mm stamp.
For surcharge see No. 1427.

Manned Flight Bicent. — A207

10k, Montgolfiere, 1783. 15k, Charles & Robert, 1783. 3z, Gustave, 1783. 5z, Santos-Dumont III, 1899. 10z, Stratospheric balloon,

1934. 15z, Zeppelin LZ-129, 1936. 37.50z, Double Eagle II, 1978. 80z, Hot air balloons.

1984, June 28		Litho.	Perf. 14	
1100	A207	10k multi	.25	.25
1161	A207	15k multi	.25	.25
1162	A207	3z multi	.25	.25
1163	A207	5z multi	.50	.40
1164	A207	10z multi	.90	.75
1165	A207	15z multi	1.40	1.00
1166	A207	37.50z multi	3.25	2.75
1167	A207	80z multi	7.25	6.50
		Nos. 1160-1167 (8)	14.05	12.15

For surcharges see Nos. 1413-1420.

Okapi — A208

1984, Oct. 15		Litho.	Perf. 13	
1168	A208	2z Grazing	1.25	.65
1169	A208	3z Resting	2.00	.70
1170	A208	8z Mother and young	3.75	2.25
1171	A208	10z In water	6.00	4.25
		Nos. 1168-1171 (4)	13.00	7.80

Souvenir Sheet
Perf. 11½

1172	A208	50z like 10z	5.25	5.25

World Wildlife Fund. No. 1172 contains one 36x51mm stamp, margin continues the design of the 10z without emblem.

Nos. 893-900 Surcharged in Silver Over Black Bar and With One of Three Different Sabena Airlines Emblems and "1925 1985" in Silver

1985, Feb. 19			Perf. 13	
1173	A165	2.50z on 30s #893	.35	.25
1174	A165	5z on 5k #896	.90	.50
1175	A165	6z on 70s #894	1.00	.60
1176	A165	7.50z on 1k #895	1.10	.70
1177	A165	8.50z on 10k #898	1.40	.90
1178	A165	10z on 8k #897	1.75	1.25
1179	A165	12.50z on 75k #900	2.00	1.75
1180	A165	30z on 50k #899	3.75	3.25
		Nos. 1173-1180 (8)	12.25	9.20

No. 901 Surcharged in Silver Over Black Bar and With Silver Text "60e ANNIVERSAIRE/1re LIASON AERIENNE/BRUXELLES-KINSHASAL/PAR EDMOND THIEFFRY"
Souvenir Sheet

1985, Feb. 19			Perf. 11½	
1181	A165	50z on 5z #901	70.00	70.00

OLYMPHILEX '85, Lausanne — A209

1985, Apr. 19			Perf. 13	
1182	A209	1z Swimming	.25	.25
1183	A209	2z Soccer, vert.	.25	.25
1184	A209	3z Boxing	.25	.25
1185	A209	4z Basketball, vert.	.25	.25
1186	A209	5z Equestrian	.40	.40
1187	A209	10z Volleyball, vert.	.85	.85
1188	A209	15z Running	1.25	1.25
1189	A209	30z Cycling, vert.	2.50	2.50
		Nos. 1182-1189 (8)	6.00	6.00

Nos. 1013-1018, 969 Ovptd. and Surcharged with 1 or 2 Gold Bars and "AOUT 1985" in Gold or Black

1985, Aug. 15			Perf. 13, 11½	
1190	A185	2z on 5k	.25	.25
1191	A185	3z on 10k	.35	.35
1192	A185	5z on 50k	.60	.60
1192A	A185	10z on 100k	1.40	1.40
1192B	A185	15z on 500k	1.90	1.90
1193	A185	40z on 800k	5.50	5.50
		Nos. 1190-1193 (6)	10.00	10.00

Souvenir Sheet

1194	A177	50z on 10z (B)	12.00	12.00

Second visit of Pope John Paul II.

Audubon Birth Bicent. — A210

Illustrations of North American bird species by John Audubon: 5z, Great egret. 10z, Yellow-beaked duck. 15z, Small heron. 25z, White-fronted duck.

1985, Oct. 1			Perf. 13	
1195	A210	5z multicolored	1.25	.60
1196	A210	10z multicolored	1.90	1.10
1197	A210	15z multicolored	4.00	1.50
1198	A210	25z multicolored	6.50	3.00
		Nos. 1195-1198 (4)	13.65	6.20

For surcharges see Nos. 1421-1424.

Natl. Independence, 25th Anniv. — A211

1985, Oct. 23		Photo.	Perf. 12	
		Granite Paper		
1200	A211	5z multi	.25	.25
1201	A211	10z multi	.45	.45
1202	A211	15z multi	.70	.70
1203	A211	20z multi	1.10	1.10
		Nos. 1200-1203 (4)	2.50	2.50

Souvenir Sheet
Perf. 11½

1204	A211	50z multi	2.50	2.50

UN, 40th Anniv. A212

1985, Nov. 26				
1205	A212	10z Flags, vert.	.50	.50
1206	A212	50z Emblem, UN building	2.75	2.75

Nos. 1087-1088, 1085-1086, 1089-1090 Surcharged

1985, Dec. 2			Perf. 11½	
		Granite Paper		
1207	A195	3z on 3z multi	.60	.60
1208	A195	5z on 5z multi	.85	.85
1209	A195	7z on 90k multi	1.10	1.10
1210	A195	10z on 90k multi	1.60	1.60
1211	A195	15z on 1.70z multi	2.50	2.50

1212	A195	20z on 8z multi	3.50	3.50
1213	A195	50z on 90k multi	8.75	8.75
		Nos. 1207-1213 (7)	18.90	18.90

Souvenir Sheet

1214	A195	50z on 10z multi	12.00	12.00

Intl. Youth Year.

Souvenir Sheet

Virgin and Child, by Titian — A213

Photogravure and Engraved

1985, Dec. 23			Perf. 13½	
1215	A213	100z brown	7.00	7.00

Christmas 1985.

Natl. Transit Authority, 50th Anniv. — A214

1985, Dec. 31			Perf. 13	
1216	A214	7z Kokolo mail ship	.25	.25
1217	A214	10z Steam locomotive	.40	.40
1218	A214	15z Luebo ferry	.60	.60
1219	A214	50z Stanley locomotive	2.00	1.50
		Nos. 1216-1219 (4)	3.25	2.75

Postage Stamp, Cent. A215

Stamps on stamps: 7z, Belgian Congo No. 30. 15z, Belgian Congo No. B28. 20z, Belgian Congo No. 226. 25z, Zaire No. 1059. 40z, Zaire No. 1152. 50z, Zaire No. 883 and Belgium No. 1094.

1986, Feb. 23			Perf. 13	
1220	A215	7z multi	.40	.30
1221	A215	15z multi	.65	.50
1222	A215	20z multi	1.00	.75
1223	A215	25z multi	1.10	1.00
1224	A215	40z multi	1.75	1.25
		Nos. 1220-1224 (5)	4.90	3.80

Souvenir Sheet
Perf. 11½

1225	A215	50z multi	3.25	3.25

No. 1225 contains one 50x35mm stamp.

Beatification of Sister Anuarite Nengapeta, Aug. 15, 1985 — A216

1986, Feb. 21		Litho.	Perf. 13	
1226	A216	10z Pope John Paul II	.80	.50
1227	A216	15z Sr. Anuarite	1.10	.70
1228	A216	25z Both portraits	1.60	1.10
		Nos. 1226-1228 (3)	3.50	2.30

Souvenir Sheet
Imperf

1229	A216	100z Both portraits, triangular	5.00	5.00

Nos. 1226-1227 vert. No. 1229 contains one quadrilateral stamp, size: 30x36x60mm.
For surcharges see Nos. 1370-1371, 1373, 1376-1377.

Congo Stamp Cent. — A217

1986, Feb. 22		Litho.	Perf. 13	
1230	A217	25z Belgian Congo No. 3	1.25	1.00

Imperfs exist. Value $5.
See Belgium No. 1236.

Indigenous Reptiles A218

2z, Dasypeltis scaber. 5z, Agama agama. 10z, Python regius. 15z, Chamaeleo dilepis. 25z, Dendroaspis jamesoni. 50z, Naja nigricolis.

1987, Feb. 11		Litho.	Perf. 13	
1231	A218	2z multicolored	.25	.25
1232	A218	5z multicolored	.25	.25
1233	A218	10z multicolored	.50	.50
1234	A218	15z multicolored	1.00	.65
1235	A218	25z multicolored	1.40	1.00
1236	A218	50z multicolored	2.50	2.50
		Nos. 1231-1236 (6)	5.90	5.15

Christmas 1987 — A219

Paintings (details) by Fra Angelico: 50z, Virgin and Child, center panel of the Triptych of Cortona, 1435. 100z, The Nativity. 120z, Virgin and Child with Angels and Four Saints, Fiesole Retable. 180z, Virgin and Child with Six Saints, Annalena Retable.

1987, Dec. 24		Litho.	Perf. 13	
1237	A219	50z multi	.75	.75
1238	A219	100z multi	1.75	1.75
1239	A219	120z multi	2.25	2.25
1240	A219	180z multi	3.25	3.25
		Nos. 1237-1240 (4)	8.00	8.00

French Revolution, Bicent. — A220

Designs: 50z, Declaration of the Rights of Man and Citizen. 100z, Abstract art. 120z, Globe showing Africa, South America.

1989		Litho.	Perf. 13½x14½	
1241	A220	40z multicolored	.55	.50
1242	A220	50z multicolored	.65	.60
1243	A220	100z multicolored	1.40	1.25
1244	A220	120z multicolored	2.00	1.60
	Nos. 1241-1244 (4)		4.60	3.95

REGIDESCO, 50th Anniv. — A221

40z, Administration bldg. 50z, Modern factory. 75z, Water works. 120z, Woman drawing water.

1989				
1245	A221	40z multicolored	.40	.40
1246	A221	50z multicolored	.50	.50
1247	A221	75z multicolored	.75	.75
1248	A221	120z multicolored	1.40	1.25
	Nos. 1245-1248 (4)		3.05	2.90

Fight Against AIDS — A222

Designs: 40z, Bowman firing arrow through SIDA. 80z, "SIDA" on Leopard. 150z, World map with AIDS symbols.

1989				
1249	A222	30z multicolored	1.00	.90
1250	A222	40z multcilored	1.25	1.25
1251	A222	80z multicolored	2.75	2.50
	Nos. 1249-1251 (3)		5.00	4.65

Souvenir Sheet
Perf. 14

| 1252 | A222 | 150z multicolored | 4.75 | 4.75 |

Tourist Attractions — A223

40z, Waterfalls of Venus. 60z, Rural village. 100z, Kivu Lake. 120z, Niyara Gongo Volcano. 300z, Kisantu Botanical Gardens, vert.

1990		Litho.	Perf. 13½x14½	
1253	A223	40z multicolored	.55	.55
1254	A223	60z multicolored	.85	.85
1255	A223	100z multicolored	1.40	1.40
1256	A223	120z multicolored	1.75	1.75
	Nos. 1253-1256 (4)		4.55	4.55

Souvenir Sheet
Perf. 14½

| 1257 | A223 | 300z multicolored | 4.50 | 4.50 |

Souvenir Sheet

Christmas — A224

1990		Litho.	Perf. 14	
1258	A224	500z multicolored	5.00	5.00

Various 1971-1983 Stamps Surcharged in Gold

1990		Perfs., Etc. as Before		
1259	A160	20z on 20k #877	.60	.60
1260	A201	40z on 2k #1121	.60	.60
1261	A201	40z on 4k #1122	.60	.60
1262	A184	40z on 10k #1005	.60	.60
1263	A196	40z on 25k #1091	.60	.60
1264	A201	40z on 25k #1123	.60	.60
1265	A184	40z on 50k #1007	.60	.60
1266	A196	40z on 50k #1092	.60	.60
1267	A200	40z on 50k #1115	.60	.60
1268	A193	40z on 75k #1071	.60	.60
1269	A184	40z on 80k #1008	.60	.60
1270	A190	40z on 90k #1045	.60	.60
1271	A193	40z on 90k #1072	.60	.60
1272	A196	40z on 90k #1093	.60	.60
1273	A201	80z on 2k #1121	1.50	1.50
1274	A201	80z on 4k #1122	1.50	1.50
1275	A184	80z on 10k #1005	1.50	1.50
1276	A196	80z on 25k #1091	1.50	1.50
1277	A201	80z on 25k #1123	1.50	1.50
1278	A196	80z on 50k #1092	1.50	1.50
1279	A200	80z on 50k #1115	1.50	1.50
1280	A193	80z on 75k #1071	1.50	1.50
1281	A184	80z on 80k #1008	1.50	1.50
1282	A190	80z on 90k #1045	1.50	1.50
1283	A193	80z on 90k #1072	1.50	1.50
1284	A196	80z on 90k #1093	1.50	1.50
1285	A175	100z on 40s #953	2.10	2.10
1287	A186	100z on 2k #1019	2.10	2.10
1288	A187	100z on 2k #1028	2.10	2.10
1289	A192	100z on 2k #1058	2.10	2.10
1290	A175	100z on 4k #955	2.10	2.10
1291	A165	100z on 5k #896	2.10	2.10
1292	A185	100z on 5k #1013	2.10	2.10
1293	A187	100z on 5k #1029	2.10	2.10
1294	A159	100z on 8k #865	2.10	2.10
1295	A165	100z on 8k #897	2.10	2.10
1296	A167	100z on 8k #912	2.10	2.10
1298	A167	100z on 10k #913	2.10	2.10
1299	A169	100z on 10k #922	2.10	2.10
1300	A165	100z on 10k #993	2.10	2.10
1301	A183	100z on 10k #1000	2.10	2.10
1302	A185	100z on 10k #1014	2.10	2.10
1303	A186	100z on 10k #1020	2.10	2.10
1304	A175	100z on 15k #956	2.10	2.10
1305	A187	100z on 18k #1031	2.10	2.10
1306	A169	100z on 20k #923	2.10	2.10
1307	A180	100z on 20k #977	2.10	2.10
1308	A144	100z on 22k #755	2.10	2.10
1309	A186	100z on 25k #1021	2.10	2.10
1311	A159	100z on 48k #869	2.10	2.10
1312	A167	100z on 48k #916	2.10	2.10
1313	A179	100z on 50k #971	2.10	2.10
1314	A187	100z on 50k #1032	2.10	2.10
1315	A192	100z on 50k #1061	2.10	2.10
1316	A165	100z on 75k #995	2.10	2.10
1317	A183	100z on 75k #1001	2.10	2.10
1318	A183	100z on 80k #1002	2.10	2.10
1319	A199	100z on 80k #1111	2.10	2.10
1320	A170	100z on 90k #930	2.10	2.10
1321	A186	100z on 90k #1022	2.10	2.10
1322	A192	100z on 90k #1062	2.10	2.10
1324	A198	300z on 2k #1102	6.50	6.50
1325	A173	300z on 8k #938	6.50	6.50
1326	A182	300z on 10k #986	6.50	6.50
1327	A143	300z on 14k #751	6.50	6.50
1328	A146	300z on 17k #769	6.50	6.50
1329	A174	300z on 20k #947	6.50	6.50
1330	A198	300z on 45k #1103	6.50	6.50
1331	A182	300z on 75k #987	6.50	6.50
1332	A198	300z on 75k #1104	6.50	6.50
1333	A162	500z on 8k #886	11.50	11.50
1334	A162	500z on 10k #887	11.50	11.50
1335	A162	500z on 25k #888	11.50	11.50
1336	A162	500z on 48k #889	11.50	11.50
	Nos. 1259-1336 (74)		204.40	204.40

Size and location of surcharge varies. Some surcharges show "z" before numeral.
100z on #1060 was surcharged in error. Value, $20.

Various 1980-1983 Stamps Surcharged

1991		Perfs., Etc., as Before		
1342	A181	1000z on 1z #982a-982d	2.00	2.00
1343	A185	1000z on 100k #1016	.35	.35
1344	A192	1000z on 1z #1063	.35	.35
1345	A182	2000z on 100k #988	.70	.70
1346	A198	2000z on 1z #1105	.70	.70
1347	A193	2500z on 1z #1073	1.40	1.40
1348	A191	3000z on 1z #1057	2.00	2.00
1349	A200	4000z on 1z #1116	2.75	2.75
1350	A200	5000z on 1z #1116	4.00	4.00
1351	A193	10,000z on 1z #1073	5.25	5.25
1352	A191	15,000z on 1z #1057	8.00	8.00
	Nos. 1342-1352 (11)		27.50	27.50

Size and location of surcharge varies.

The editors have received from a collector mint stamps bearing the surcharges shown below. There is conflicting data as to the validity of these surcharges, and anyone with information on them is asked to contact the new issues editor.

12 - 6 - 92
6ᵉ ANNIVERSAIRE DE OFFICE NATIONAL DU TOUR.SME

1.000 000 Z

12-3-92 INAUGURATION STATION POMPAGE
600.000 Z.

Du 8 au 15 - 6 - 92
2ᵉ Conférence Addis - Abeba
Virus VIH 1 - et VIH 2
EN AFRIQUE
10.000.000 Z

30.000.000 Z
Conference Nationale Souveraine 9 mars - 4 decembre 1991 - 1992

15.000.000 Z.
Conférence Nationale Souveraine 3 mars - 4 décembre 1991 - 1992

Nos. 989, 1010, 1112, 1124 Srchd.

1992, Aug. 18		Perfs., Etc. as Before		
1354	A184	50th z on 125k #1010	.60	.60
1355	A201	100th z on 1.20z #1124	.80	.80
1356	A199	150th z on 1.20z #1112	1.40	1.40
1357	A182	200th z on 145k #989	1.75	1.75
1358	A199	250th z on 1.20z #1112	2.25	2.25
1359	A201	300th z on 1.20z #1124	2.75	2.75
1360	A199	500th z on 1.20z #1112	4.50	4.50
	Nos. 1354-1360 (7)		14.05	14.05

Size and location of surcharge varies.

#1361-1366

#1368-1374

1993, Oct. 29   Photo.   Perf. 13½x13
1361	A167	500th z on 30s		
		#910	.75	.75
1362	A167	500th z on 5k		
		#911	.90	.90
1365	A167	750th z on 8k		
		#912	1.00	1.00
1366	A167	750th z on 10k		
		#913	1.25	1.25
1368	A167	1 mil z on 30k		
		#914	1.50	1.50
1369	A167	1 mil z on 40k		
		#915	1.50	1.50
1370	A167	5 mil z on 48k		
		#916	7.50	7.50
1371	A167	10 mil z on 100k		
		#917	15.00	15.00
		Nos. 1361-1371 (8)	29.40	29.40

Nos. 1226-
1229 Srchd. in
Black or Red

1993, Oct. 29   Litho.   Perf. 13
1373	A216	3 mil z on 10z		
		#1226	3.00	3.00
1374	A216	3 mil z on 10z		
		#1226 (R)		
1375	A216	5 mil z on 15z		
		#1227	4.75	4.75
1376	A216	10 mil z on 25z		
		#1228	9.25	9.25

Souvenir Sheet
Imperf
1377	A216	10 mil z on 100z		
		#1229	13.00	13.00

Size and location of surcharge varies.

Natl.
Game
Parks,
50th
Anniv.
A225

1993   Litho.   Perf. 13
1403	A225	30k Cape eland	.30	.25
1404	A225	50k Elephants	.30	.25
1405	A225	1.50z Giant eland	1.25	1.00
1406	A225	3.50z White rhinoceros	3.00	2.00
1407	A225	5z Bongo	4.00	2.50
		Nos. 1403-1407 (5)	8.85	6.00

For surcharge see No. 1431.

Nos. 986-900 Surcharged

1994, Apr. 23   Photo.   Perf. 14
1408	A182	30k on 10k	.75	.75
1409	A182	50k on 75k	1.25	1.25
1410	A182	1.50z on 100k	3.75	3.75
1411	A182	3.50z on 145k	7.50	7.50
1412	A182	5z on 270k	11.50	11.50
		Nos. 1408-1412 (5)	24.75	24.75

Nos. 1160-1167 Surcharged
1994, Apr. 23   Litho.   Perf. 14
1413	A207	30k on 10k	.75	.75
1414	A207	50k on 15k	1.00	1.00
1415	A207	1.50z on 3z	2.50	2.50
1416	A207	2.50z on 5z	3.75	3.75
1417	A207	3.50z on 10z	5.50	5.50
1418	A207	5z on 15z	8.00	8.00
1419	A207	7.50z on 37.50z	12.50	12.50
1420	A207	10z on 80z	17.50	17.50
		Nos. 1413-1420 (8)	51.50	51.50

Nos. 1195-1198 Surcharged

1994, Apr. 23   Litho.   Perf. 13
1421	A210	50k on 5z	1.75	1.75
1422	A210	1.50z on 10z	5.00	5.00
1423	A210	3.50z on 15z	9.50	9.50
1424	A210	5z on 25z	19.00	19.00
		Nos. 1421-1424 (4)	35.25	35.25

**Nos. 990, 1079, 1094, 1097, 1113,
1125-1126, 1133, 1155, & 1404
Surcharged in Gold**

1994, Aug. 31   Perfs., Etc. as Before
1425	A196	20z on 3z #1097	.40	.40
1426	A182	40z on 270k #990	.40	.40
1427	A203	50z on 3z #1133	.50	.50
1428	A206	75z on 3z #1155	.60	.60
1429	A201	100z on 2.05z		
		#1125	.75	.75
1430	A194	150z on 1.70z		
		#1079	1.25	1.25
1431	A225	200z on 50k #1404	1.50	1.50
1432	A196	250z on 1.50z		
		#1094	1.75	1.75
1433	A199	300z on 3.60z		
		#1113	2.00	2.00
1434	A201	500z on 3.60z		
		#1126	3.25	3.25
		Nos. 1425-1434 (10)	12.40	12.40

Size and location of surcharge varies.

**Nos. 1067, 1094, 1113, 1125-1126
Surcharged in Gold**

No.
1435

No. 1437

1996   Perfs., Etc. as Before
1435	A192	100z on 3.50z		
		#1067	.50	.50
1436	A199	500z on 3.60z		
		#1113	.50	.50
1437	A201	1000z on 2.05z		
		#1125	.50	.50
1438	A196	2500z on 1.50z		
		#1094	1.75	1.75
1439	A201	5000z on 1.50z		
		#1126	3.25	3.25
1440	A196	6000z on 1.50z		
		#1094	3.50	3.50
1441	A199	15,000z on 3.60z		
		#1113	9.00	9.00
1442	A201	25,000z on 3.60z		
		#1126	17.50	17.50
		Nos. 1435-1442 (8)	36.50	36.50

1996
Summer
Olympic
Games,
Atlanta
A226

1000z, Equestrian. 12,500z, Boxing.
25,000z, Table tennis. 35,000z, Basketball,
vert. 50,000z, Tennis.

1996, July 29   Litho.   Perf. 11½
1444	A226	1000z multi	.25	.25
1445	A226	12,500z multi	1.00	1.00
1446	A226	25,000z multi	3.00	3.00
1447	A226	35,000z multi	4.00	4.00
1448	A226	50,000z multi	4.75	4.75
		Nos. 1444-1448 (5)	13.00	13.00

Insects &
Spiders
A227

No. 1449: a, Lasius niger. b, Calopterygides. c, Peucetia. d, Sphecides.

1996   Litho.   Perf. 13½
1449	A227	15,000z Sheet of 4,		
		#a.-d.	15.00	15.00

Minerals
A228

No. 1450: a, Uraninite. b, Malachite. c,
Ruby. d, Diamond.
No. 1452, Uranotile, cuprosklodowskite,
horiz.

1996
1450	A228	40,000z Sheet of		
		4, #a.-d.	27.50	27.50

Souvenir Sheet
1452	A228	105,000z multi	20.00	20.00

No. 1452 exists overprinted in silver for
Hong Kong Exposition '97.
A number has been reserved for an additional sheet with this set.

Raptors
A229

No. 1453: a, Congo eagle. b, Crowned
eagle. c, Melierax metabates. d, Urotriorchis
macrourus.

1996
1453	A229	50,000z Sheet of 4,		
		#a.-d.	30.00	30.00

Butterflies
A230

No. 1454: a, Cymothoe sangaris. b, Colotis
zoe. c, Physcaeneura leda. d, Charaxes
candiope.

1996
1454	A230	70,000z Sheet of 4,		
		#a.-d.	37.50	37.50

The validity of Nos. 1455-1481 and
other stamps from the same time period
has been questioned. The editors are
attempting to find out more about these
stamps.

1998 World Cup Soccer
Championships, France — A231

Numbers on players: No. 1455, #12. No.
1456, none. No. 1457, #7. No. 1458, #3.
No. 1459: a, British player. b, Brazilian
player.
No. 1460: a-d, Like #1455-1458, but with
part of World Cup Trophy behind each player.

1996
1455-1458	A231	35,000z Set		
		of 4	14.00	14.00

Souvenir Sheets
1459	A231	105,000z Sheet of		
		2, #a.-b.	20.00	20.00
1460	A231	35,000z Sheet of 4,		
		#a.-d.	14.00	14.00

No. 1459 contains 2 42x39mm stamps.
See Nos. 1467-1476.

World
Wildlife
Fund —
A231a

No. 1466 — Pan paniscus: a, With young. b,
Two in trees. c, Holding vines. d, Head.

1997
1466	A231a	20,000z Block of		
		4, #a.-d.	20.00	20.00

1998 World Cup Soccer Championships Type of 1996

African soccer players: No. 1467, 20,000z, Soccer ball at his right. No. 1468, 20,000z, Ball at head. No. 1469, 20,000z, Yellow uniform. No. 1470, 20,000z, Ball on knee.

German soccer players, soccer ball on stamp at: No. 1471, 50,000z. No. 1472, 50,000z, LL. No. 1473, 50,000z, LR. No. 1474, 50,000z, UL.

Nos. 1475a-1475d, 1476a-1476d are like Nos. 1467-1474 but with part of World Cup Trophy behind each player.

1996	Litho.		Perf. 13½	
1467-1470	A231	Set of 4	9.00	9.00
1471-1474	A231	Set of 4	20.00	20.00

Souvenir Sheets

1475	A231	20,000z Sheet of 4,		
		#a.-d.	9.00	9.00
1476	A231	50,000z Sheet of 4,		
		#a.-d.	20.00	20.00

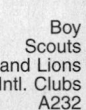

Boy Scouts and Lions Intl. Clubs A232

No. 1477 — Diceros bicornis: a, Walking forward. b, Walking left, left leg up. c, Facing left. d, Holding head up.

No. 1478 — Panthera leo: a, Cubs. b, Adult male. c, Adult male facing forward, mouth open. d, Adult female on fallen tree.

No. 1479 — Loxodonta africana: a, Walking right, trunk in air. b, Reaching up to tree limb with trunk. c, Walking right, trunk down. d, Mother with calf.

105,000z, Hippopotamus amphibus.

1997	Litho.		Perf. 13x13½	
1477	A232	40,000z Sheet of		
		4, #a.-d.	13.00	13.00
1478	A232	50,000z Sheet of		
		4, #a.-d.	17.50	17.50
1479	A232	70,000z Sheet of		
		4, #a.-d.	24.00	24.00

Souvenir Sheet

| 1480 | A232 | 105,000z multi | 12.00 | 12.00 |

Boy Scouts (#1477, 1479-1480). Lions Intl. Clubs (#1478).

Jacqueline Kennedy Onassis (1929-94) — A233

Various portraits.

1997	Litho.		Perf. 13½	
1481	A233	15,000z Sheet of 9,		
		#a.-i.	17.50	17.50

No. 1481 also exists imperf.

Stamps from this country are now being released under the previous name, "Republique Democratique du Congo," or Congo Democratic Republic, despite the resumption of civil war. We will continue to list these stamps under the country's name of Zaire until the situation is resolved.

Diana, Princess of Wales (1961-97) — A234

No. 1482: a, Wearing tiara. b, In white jacket. c, In white hat. d, In polka dotted dress. e, Scarf around neck. f, Low cut evening dress.

No. 1483: a, Wearing tiara. b, Hand under chin. c, Leaning chin on both hands. d, One-shoulder-covered outfit.

No. 1484; a, Red & black dress. b, White jacket, pearls. c, Profile view. d, Wearing tiara.

No. 1485, Black evening dress. No. 1486, 400,000z, Holding flowers.

1998, Aug. 6	Litho.		Perf. 14	
1482	A234	50,000z Sheet of 6, #a.-f.	13.50	7.75
1483	A234	100,000z Sheet of 4, #a.-d.	17.50	10.50
1484	A234	125,000z Sheet of 4, #a.-d.	24.00	14.50

Souvenir Sheets

| 1485-1486 | A234 | Set of 2 | 50.00 | 25.00 |

Mother Teresa (1910-97) — A235

1998, Aug. 6				
1487	A235	50,000z shown	2.25	1.50

Souvenir Sheet

| 1488 | A235 | 325,000z Portrait, diff. | 11.50 | 7.50 |

No. 1487 was issued in sheets of 6.

100 Centimes = 1 Franc (1998)

Native Dwelling — A236

Arms — A237

Inauguration of Pres. Laurent Kabila — A238

Designs: 1.25fr, Troops and civilians in Kinshasa. 3fr, Flag, crowd, Pres. Kabila breaking chain with sword, horiz.
2.50fr, Gun, arrow, handshake, tractor. 3.50fr, Pres. Kabila.

1999, May 12	Litho.		Perf. 14	
1489	A236	25c multi	.25	.25
1490	A237	50c multi	.55	.55
1491	A238	75c multi	.80	.80
1492	A238	1.25fr multi	1.75	1.75
1493	A238	3fr multi	3.25	3.25
		Nos. 1489-1493 (5)	6.60	6.60

Souvenir Sheets

| 1494 | A238 | 2.50fr multi | 2.60 | 2.60 |
| 1495 | A238 | 3.50fr multi | 3.75 | 3.75 |

Conquest of Kinshasa by troops of Laurent Kabila, 2nd anniv.

Chinese Zodiac Animals — A239

No. 1496: a, Rat. b, Ox. c, Tiger. d, Rabbit. e, Dragon. f, Snake. g, Horse. h, Ram. i, Monkey. j, Cock. k, Dog. l, Boar.

1999, Aug. 20			Perf. 13¼x13½	
1496	A239	78c Sheet of 12, #a-l	27.50	17.50

A240

A241

A242

A243

Outlaws of the Marsh — A244

No. 1497 — Sheet with text starting with "The historical novel. . .": a, 1.45fr, Men fighting. b, 1.50fr, Man uprooting tree. c, 1.60fr, Man with sword in snowstorm. d, 1.70fr, Man with sword, other men at bridge. e, 1.80fr, Three men at table.

No. 1498 — Sheet with text starting with "The main theme. . .": a, 1.45fr, Men and baskets. b, 1.50fr, Man threatening another man with sword. c, 1.60fr, Man attacking tiger. d, 1.70fr, People watching men in martial arts battle. e, 1.80fr, Battling horsemen.

No. 1499 — Sheet with text starting with "The common people. . .": a, 1.45fr, Men fighting in boat. b, 1.50fr, Man with sword fighting man with hatchets. c, 1.60fr, Men near fortified wall. d, 1.70fr, Men fighting on cobblestone street. e, 1.80fr, Archer on horseback at doorway.

No. 1500 — Sheet with text starting with "Today, it is thought. . .": a, 1.45fr, Man seated and other man standing near table. b, 1.50fr, Man setting fire to building. c, 1.60fr, Man in room. d, 1.70fr, Man lifting another man in a battle. e, 1.80fr, Man holding torn scroll.

1999, Aug. 20			Perf. 13¼	
		Sheets of 5, #a-e		
1497-1500	A240	Set of 4	60.00	45.00

Souvenir Sheets

Perf. 13¼x13½

1501	A241	10fr multi	17.50	17.50
1502	A242	10fr multi	17.50	17.50
1503	A243	10fr multi	17.50	17.50
1504	A244	10fr multi	17.50	17.50

A245

A246

African Flora and Fauna — A247

Designs: 1fr, Telophorus quadricolor. 1.50fr, Panthera pardus. No. 1507, 2fr, Colotis protomedia. No. 1508, 2fr, Kobus vardoni. No. 1509, 3fr, Canarina abyssinica. No. 1510, 3fr, Smutsia temminckii.

7.80fr, Lion.

No. 1512: a, Okapi. b, Bird, rainbow, waterfalls. c, Giraffe, rainbow, waterfalls. d, Giraffe, waterfall mist. e, Mandrill. f, Chimpanzee. g, Leopard. h, Butterflies. i, Hippopotamus. j, Bird in water. k, Flowers. l, Antelope.

No. 1513: a, Sun. b, Pieris citrina. c, Merops apiaster. d, Lanius collurio. e, Ploceus cucullatus. f, Charaxes pelias. g, Charaxes eupale. h, Giraffa camelopardalis. i, Galago moholi. j, Strelitzia reginae. k, Gazella thomsoni. l, Upupa epops.

No. 1514, 10fr, Taurotragus oryx. No. 1515, 10fr, Hippopotamus amphibus.

No. 1516, 10fr, Warthog.

Perf. 14, 14¼x14¾ (#1511), 14¼x14 (#1516)

2000, Feb. 28

1505-1510	A245	Set of 6	14.50	14.50
1511	A246	7.80fr multi	8.00	8.00
1512	A247	1fr Sheet of 12, #a-l	12.50	12.50
1513	A245	1.50fr Sheet of 12, #a-l	20.00	20.00

Souvenir Sheets

1514-1515	A245	Set of 2	20.00	20.00
1516	A247	10fr multi	10.00	10.00

No. 1516 contains one 42x57mm stamp.

Wild Felines and Canines — A248

No. 1517, 1.50fr: a, Felis bengalensis. b, Felis aurata. c, Felis caracal. d, Felis conoclor. e, Felis nigripes. f, Panthera leo. g, Neofelis nebulosa. h, Felis wiedii. i, Acinonyx jubatus. j, Felis pardina. k, Felis yagouaroundi. l, Felis serval.

No. 1518, 2fr: a, Canis mesomelas. b, Otocyon megalotis. c, Speothos venaticus. d, Canis latrans. e, Cuon alpinus. f, Fennecus zerda. g, Urocyon cinereoargenteus. h, Canis lupus. i, Vulpes macrotis. j, Chrysocyon brachyurus. k, Nyctereutes procyonoides. l, Vulpes vulpes.

No. 1519, 10fr, Panthera pardus. No. 1520, 10fr, Alopex lagopus.

2000, Feb. 28 *Perf. 14*

Sheets of 12, #a-l

1517-1518	A248	Set of 2	40.00	40.00

Souvenir Sheets

1519-1520	A248	Set of 2	17.00	17.00

Millennium A249

2000, June 10

1521		Horiz. strip of 3	12.00	12.00
a.		A249 4.50fr multi	1.25	1.25
b.		A249 9fr multi	3.25	3.25
c.		A249 15fr multi	5.00	5.00

Printed in sheets containing two strips.

A250 A251

Birds A252

Designs: No. 1522, 3fr, Alopochen aegyptiacus. No. 1523, 3fr, Ardeola ibis. No. 1524, 4.50fr, Oena capensis. No. 1525, 4.50fr, Lybius torquatus. No. 1526, 9fr, Falco tinnunculus. No. 1527, 9fr, Corythaelo cristata.

No. 1528, 4.50fr, Psephotus chrysopterygius chrysopterygius. 8fr, Amazona aestiva. No. 1530, 8.50fr, Are nobilis cumanensis. No. 1531, 9fr, Agapornis roseicollis.

No. 1532, 8.50fr, Loriculus ornata. No. 1533, 9fr, Polytrus guauvunibi.

No. 1534, 9fr: a, Euplectes orix. b, Euplectes ardens. c, Oriolus auratus. d, Plocens cucullatus. e, Amandava subflava. f, Nectarina senegalensis.

No. 1535, 9fr: a, Halcyon malimbicus. b, Tachymarptis melba. c, Haliaeetus vocifer. d, Ardea purpurea. e, Balaeniceps rex. f, Balearica regulorum.

No. 1536: a, Ertoxeres aquila. b, Aglaiolepus kinde. c, Archilochus calobris. d, Trochlus polytaus. e, Chaliostigma herrani. f, Ensifera. g, Chrysolampus mosquitus. h, Phorethornus syrmatophorus. i, Calypre hetervare.

No. 1537, 5fr: a, Eos squamata squamata. b, Aratinga guarouba. c, Aratinga aurea. d, Psuedeos fuscata. e, Agapornis fischeri. f, Aratinga nana nana. g, Aratinga mitrata. h, Trichoglossus haematodus rubitorquis. i, Cacatua galerita galerita.

No. 1538, 5fr: a, Ara macao. b, Neophema elegans. c, Loriculus vernalis. d, Aratinga solstitialis. e, Pionites melancephala. f, Bolborhynchus lineola. g, Ara severa. h, Psephotus chrysopterygius dissimilis. i, Ara militaris.

No. 1539, 15fr, Actophilornis atricanus, horiz. No. 1540, 20fr, Ceryle rudis, horiz. No. 1541, 15fr, Opopsitta diophthalma. No. 1542, 15fr, Ara ararrauna, horiz. No. 1543, 15fr, Coeligena torgoata. No. 1544, 20fr, Campylopterus hemileicurus.

2000, Aug. 16 *Perf. 14*

1522-1527	A250	Set of 6	15.00	15.00
1528-1531	A251	Set of 4	13.50	13.50
1532-1533	A253		7.75	7.75

Sheets of 6, #a-f

1534-1535	A250	Set of 2	47.50	47.50
1536	A252	4.50fr Sheet of 9, #a-i	18.00	18.00

Sheets of 9, #a-i

1537-1538	A251	Set of 2	40.00	40.00

Souvenir Sheets

1539-1540	A250	Set of 2	16.00	16.00
1541-1542	A251	Set of 2	13.50	13.50
1543-1544	A252	Set of 2	16.00	16.00

Types of 1996 and Unissued Stamps Surcharged

A253

A253a

A253b

A253c

A253d

Designs: 10fr on 70,000z, Colotis zoe. 15fr on 25,000z, Bulbophyllum falcatum. 25fr on 20,000z, Scutellosaurus. 35fr on 15,000z, Sphecides. 45fr on 100,000z, Diamond. 50fr on 35,000z, Termitomyces auranticus. 70fr on 50,000z, Melierax metabates. 100fr on 40,000z, Malachite. 150fr on 25,000z, Panda.

No. 1545 surcharged as A253. No. 1548 surcharged as A253d. No. 1551 surcharged as A253a. No. 1552 surcharged as A253b.

2000 *Litho.* *Perf. 13¼*

1545	A230	10fr on 70,000z multi	7.25	7.25
1546	A253	15fr on 25,000z multi	7.25	7.25
1547	A253a	25fr on 20,000z multi	7.25	7.25
1548	A227	35fr on 15,000z multi	7.25	7.25
1549	A253b	45fr on 100,000z multi	7.25	7.25
1550	A253c	50fr on 35,000z multi	7.25	7.25
1551	A229	70fr on 50,000z multi	7.25	7.25
1552	A228	100fr on 40,000z multi	7.25	7.25
1553	A253d	150fr on 25,000z multi	7.25	7.25

Location of surcharges varies. All surcharged stamps have white margins.

A254

Trains — A255

Designs: 1fr, Missouri-Kansas-Texas Line locomotive. 2fr, Spremberg steam locomotive. No. 1556, 3fr, King Class, Great Western Railway. No. 1557, 3fr, Crocodile locomotive. 5fr, Inner-city trains, Great Britain. 6fr, Big Boy, Union Pacific.

No. 1560, 4.50fr: a, Class SU, 2-6-2, Russia. b, Prussian locomotive. c, Zimbabwe locomotive. d, Hunslet 2-8-2, Peru. e, London, Midland & Scottish Railway locomotive. f, London Northeastern Railway locomotive.

No 1561, 8fr: a, Denver & Rio Grande Western Railroad locomotive. b, Mikado 2-8-2, Louisville & Nashville. c, Mogul, Rio Grande. d, New York Central Railway locomotive. e, Sumpter Valley Railway steam locomotive. f, Three-truck Shay No. 7.

No. 1562, 9.50fr: a, Compagnie du Nord locomotive, France. b, Union Pacific locomotive. c, Great Northern Railway locomotive. d, Liverpool & Manchester Railway locomotive. e, Patentee 2-2-2, London & Birmingham. f, Puffing Billy.

No. 1563, 10fr: a, Chicago, Rock Island & Pacific Railway locomotive. b, Powhattan Arrow, Norfolk & Western. c, Class S-1, New York Central Hudson River Railway. d, Reading Railroad locomotive. e, Great Bear, Great Western Railway. f, Bi-polar, Chicago, Milwaukee, St. Paul & Pacific Railway.

No. 1564, 5fr: a, Beyer-Garratt 50 4-8-2+2-8-4 locomotive. b, Locomotive Express 4-6-2. c, 780CV electric locomotive. d, Electric locomotive on curve. e, Class 2-10-0 Locomotive 56001. f, Electric locomotive on straight track. g, Class 2-8-4 Locomotive 284. h, Class G 6/6 electric locomotive.

No. 1565, 8.50fr: a, Class B-B electric locomotive AE4/4. b, Class EX, Paris-Lyon-Mediterranean. c, Big Boy. d, Tourist car. e, Class 4-8-4 GS-4. f, Class 46 electric locomotive. g, Class-4-6-0 County. h, Class DA Diesel-electric locomotive.

No. 1566, 15fr, New York Central & Hudson River Railway locomotive. No. 1567, 20fr, Mohawk & Hudson Railroad locomotive. No. 1568, 20fr, Broadway Limited, Pennsylvania Railroad. No. 1569, 20fr, Trans-Europe Express.

No. 1570, 20fr, Deltic electric locomotive, Great Britain. No. 1571, 20fr, Diesel-electric locomotive, Canada Pacific.

2001, Jan. 15 *Litho.* *Perf. 14*

1554-1559	A254	Set of 6	11.50	11.50

Sheets of 6, #a-f

1560-1563	A254	Set of 4	65.00	65.00

Sheets of 8, #a-h

1564-1565	A255	Set of 2	45.00	45.00

Souvenir Sheets

1566-1569	A254	Set of 4	32.50	32.50
1570-1571	A255	Set of 2	14.00	14.00

Ships A256

Designs: 2.50fr, Clipper. 5fr, Arab bum. 20fr, Flemish galley. 21.70fr, Trabaccolo, vert. 30fr, Dutch galliot. 45.80fr, Japanese coaster.

No. 1578, 10fr: a, Trireme. b, Roman caudicaria. c, 13th cent. warship. d, Byzantine galley. e, Lateneer. f, 14th century cog. g, Arab dhow. h, Hanseatic cog. i, Portuguese galley.

No. 1579, 10fr: a, Egyptian sailing ship. b, Egyptian rowing craft. c, Egyptian seagoing ship. d, Greek galley. e, Etruscan merchantman f, Etruscan fishing skiff. g, Greek merchantman. h, Minoan passenger ship. i, Roman harbor boat.

No. 1580, 10fr: a, Flemish galleon. b, English galleon. c, Carrack. d, Chinese war galley. e, Venetian galley. f, Polacre. g, Hemmena. h, Venetian bragozzo. i, Schooner.

No. 1581, 25fr, Viking drakkar. No. 1582, 25fr, Portuguese caravel, vert. No. 1583, 25fr, HMS Endeavour, vert.

2001, June 22 *Perf. 14*

1572-1577	A256	Set of 6	14.00	14.00

Sheets of 9, #a-i

1578-1580	A256	Set of 3	30.00	30.00

Souvenir Sheets

Perf. 13¾

1581-1583	A256	Set of 3	16.00	16.00

No. 1581 contains one 50x38mm stamp; Nos. 1582-1583 each contain one 38x50mm stamp.

History of Aviation — A257

No. 1584: a, Montgolfier balloon (36x61mm). b, Boxkite and Tiger Moth airplanes (36x61mm). c, Gladiator. d, Eurofighter. e, Mosquito. f, Chipmunk.

No. 1585: a, Blackburn and Spartan Arrow airplanes (36x61mm). b, Tiger Moth. c, Lightning. d, Vulcan B2. e, Tornado.

No. 1586, 25fr, Fox Moth and Avro 540K airplanes. No. 1587, 25fr, Avro 504K and Fox Moth airplanes.

2001, June 22   **Perf. 14¼**
1584 A257 10fr Sheet of 6, #a-
     f   10.00 10.00
1585 A257 10fr Sheet of 6,
     #1584a,
     1585a-1585e   10.00 10.00
Souvenir Sheets
Perf. 14¼x14½
1586-1587 A257 Set of 2   12.00 12.00

First Zeppelin Flight, Cent. — A258

No. 1588: a, LZ-6. b, LZ-7. c, US Navy airship Akron. c, Lindstrand HS-110 Pittsburgh Tribune-Review airship.

No. 1589, 100fr, LZ-130 Graf Zeppelin II. No. 1590, 100fr, LZ-1.

2001, June 22   **Perf. 14**
1588 A258 60fr Sheet of 4, #a-
     d   27.50 27.50
Souvenir Sheets
1589-1590 A258 Set of 2   22.50 22.50

Butterflies — A259

Designs: 5fr, Striped policeman. 21.70fr, Brown-veined white. 45fr, Common dotted border. 45.80fr, Cabbage. 50fr, African migrant. 51.80fr, Mocker swallowtail.

No. 1597, 6fr, horiz.: a, Common grass blue. b, Golden tiger. c, Palla. d, Blue diadem. e, African giant swallowtail. f, African leaf. g, Gold-banded forester. h, Small harvester.

No. 1598, 6fr, horiz.: a, Guinea fowl. b, Forest queen. c, Sweet potato acraea. d, Wanderer. e, Evening brown. f, African ringlet. g, Plain tiger. h, Monarch.

No. 1599, 8fr, horiz.: a, Broad-bordered grass yellow. b, Crimson tip. c, Orange-banded protea. d, Azure hairstreak. e, Marshall's false monarch. f, Blue swallowtail. g, Figtree blue. h, Grass jewel.

No. 1600, 25fr, Long-tailed blue, horiz. No. 1601, 25fr, Chief, horiz. No. 1602, 25fr, Large spotted acraea, horiz.

2001, June 22
1591-1596 A259 Set of 6   25.00 25.00
Sheets of 8, #a-h
1597-1599 A259 Set of 3   37.50 37.50
Souvenir Sheets
1600-1602 A259 Set of 3   17.50 17.50

Flowers and Insects — A260

Designs; 20fr, Aconite, Brazilian frog-hopper. 21.70fr, Larkspur, Mexican cicada. 25fr, Blue orchid, dragonfly. 45.80fr, Spotted blossom orchid, buck moth.

No. 1607, 10fr, horiz.: a, Rein orchids, tiger moth. b, Ivy, Siamese wasp. c, Pink lady's slipper, goat weed emperor. d, Gletscher-petersbart, velvet ant. e, Licorice, viceroy butterfly. f, Grass pink, aphid. g, Ranunculus, spider wasp. h, Clamshell orchid, tropical bee. i, Bog orchids, mayfly.

No. 1608, 10fr, horiz.: a, Common lantana, red-spotted purple butterfly. b, Deep purple lilac, zebra swallowtail. c, Mt. Fujiyama, ruddy copper butterfly. d, Pinafore pink, red admiral butterfly. e, Argemone mexicana, purple hairstreak butterfly. f, Soapwort, sulphur butterfly. g, Lungwort, Buckeye butterfly. h, Wild thyme, pipevine swallowtail. i, Loeselia mexicana, banded purple butterfly.

No. 1609, 10fr, horiz.: a, Cymbidium Stanley Fouraker Highlander, scarlet tiger moth. b, Cymbidium Sparkle "Ruby Lips," Sumatran carpenter bee. c, Dendrobium Sussex, ant lion. d, Cymbidium Vieux Rose Loch Lomond, nachahmend butterfly. e, Cymbidium, cicada-killer wasp. f, Dendrobium Mousmee, spechosoma wasp. g, Arachnis flos-aeris, green lacewing. h, Paphiopedilum, seven-spot ladybug. i, Eulophia quartiniana, damselfly.

No. 1610, 25fr, Jolly Jocker pansy, monarch butterfly, horiz. No. 1611, 25fr, Pink peony, wasp (inscribed erroneously like No. 1610), horiz. No. 1612, 25fr, Plumbago capensis, honey bee, horiz.

2001, June 22   **Perf. 14**
1603-1606 A260 Set of 4   13.00 13.00
Sheets of 9, #a-i
Perf. 14¼x14½
1607-1609 A260 Set of 3   32.50 32.50
Souvenir Sheets
1610-1612 A260 Set of 3   16.00 16.00
Nos. 1607-1609 each contain nine 37x30mm stamps; Nos. 1610-1612 each contain one 50x37mm stamp.

Tintin in Africa — A261

Designs: 190fr, Tintin with hand above eyes. 461fr, Tintin in car with dog and native.

2001, Dec. 31   **Photo.**   **Perf. 11½**
1613 A261 190fr multi   2.50 2.50
Souvenir Sheet
1614 A261 461fr multi   7.00 7.00
No. 1614 contains one 48x38mm stamp. Examples of No. 1613 with a red overprint for Expo 2010 Shanghai were never put on sale at Congolese post offices.
Imperfs exist. Value: 1613, $15; 1614, $30.
See Belgium Nos. 1875-1876.

Millennium — A261a

Designs: No. 1614A, Patrice Lumumba (1925-61), first Prime Minister of Democratic Republic of the Congo, and Congolese flag. No. 1614B, Neil Armstrong (1930-2012), first man on Moon. No. 1614C, Agricultural worker, farm field and cow. No. 1614D, Congolese drummer and satellite dish. No. 1614E, Dr. Albert Schweitzer (1875-1965), humanitarian and 1952 Nobel Peace laureate. No. 1614F, Dr. Martin Luther King, Jr. (1929-68), civil rights leader and 1964 Nobel Peace laureate. No. 1614G, Nurse examining infant. No. 1614H, Train, ferry and Congolese people in canoe. No. 1614I, Teacher, map and school children. No. 1614J, Aerial view of city.

No. 1614K: l, Charles de Gaulle (1890-1970), president of France. m, Miner and crystals. n, Albert Einstein (1879-1955), physicist. o, Pres. John F. Kennedy (1917-63), p, Mohandas K. Gandhi (1869-1948), Indian nationalist leader. q, Congolese dancer and drummers. r, Congolese art. s, Soccer players. t, Pope John Paul II (1920-2005). u, King Baudouin of Belgium (1930-93).

2001		**Litho.**	**Perf. 11½**
1614A	A261a 22fr multi	—	—
1614B	A261a 22fr multi	—	—
1614C	A261a 22fr multi	—	—
1614D	A261a 22fr multi	—	—
1614E	A261a 42fr multi	—	—
1614F	A261a 42fr multi	—	—
1614G	A261a 42fr multi	—	—
1614H	A261a 43fr multi	—	—
1614I	A261a 43fr multi	—	—
1614J	A261a 47fr multi	—	—

Miniature Sheet
1614K   Sheet of 20, #1614A-
     1614J, 1614l-1614u   —   —
l.-m   A261a 22fr Either single   —   —
n.   A261a 42fr multi   —   —
o.-p.   A261a 43fr Either single   —   —
q.-r.   A261a 43fr Either single   —   —
s.   A261a 47fr multi   —   —
t.   A261a 48fr multi   —   —
u.   A261a 90fr multi   —   —

Nos. 1614A-1614J were each issued in sheets of 20.

Native Handicrafts A262

Designs: 10fr, Tabwa buffalo mask. 50fr, Kongo bedpost. 60fr, Loi drum. 150fr, Kuba royal statue, vert. 200fr, Tshokwe mask, vert. 300fr, Luba mask, vert.

2002, Mar. 7   **Litho.**   **Perf. 11½**
1615-1620 A262 Set of 6   13.00 13.00

Lions A263

Designs: 50fr, Lioness and cub. 75fr, Lion and dead animal. 150fr, Lioness and cubs at water's edge. 250fr, Lion and lioness. 300fr, Lion leaping in water.

2002, Mar. 7   **Litho.**   **Perf. 11½**
1621-1625 A263 Set of 5   13.50 13.50

Flowers — A264

Designs: 25fr, Gloriosa rothschildiana. 50fr, Aworthia cooperi. 125fr, Lithops aucampiae. 250fr, Angraecum sesquipedale. 500fr, Lampranthus coccineus.

2002   **Litho.**   **Perf. 11½**
1626-1629 A264 Set of 4   4.75 4.75
Souvenir Sheet
1630 A264 500fr multi   5.75 5.75

Minerals A265

Designs: 190fr, Beryl, vert. 340fr, Willemite mimetite. 410fr, Quartz chlorite. 445fr, Allophane copper. 455fr, Rhodochrosite, vert. 480fr, Zircon.

Perf. 11½x11¼
2002, Aug. 30   **Litho.**
1631 A265 190fr multi   2.25 2.25
1632 A265 340fr multi   4.00 4.00
1633 A265 410fr multi   5.00 5.00
1634 A265 445fr multi   5.25 5.25
1635 A265 455fr multi   5.25 5.25
1636 A265 480fr multi   5.75 5.75
An additional stamp was issued in the set. The editors would like to examine it.

Worldwide Fund for Nature (WWF) — A266

Designs: 20fr, Head of gorilla. 190fr, Adult and juvenile gorillas. 390fr, Gorilla in grass, vert. 455fr, Gorilla eating grass, vert. 1000fr, Head of gorilla, diff.

2002, Aug. 30   **Litho.**   **Perf. 11¾**
1638-1641 A266 Set of 4   15.00 15.00
Souvenir Sheet
1642 A266 1000fr multi   —   —

Pres. Joseph Kabila A267

Background color: 195fr, Blue green. 350fr, 800fr, Light blue. 1500fr, Gold.

2002, Dec. 10   **Litho.**   **Perf. 13¼**
1643-1644 A267 Set of 2   5.00 2.00
Souvenir Sheets
1645 A267 800fr multi   7.50 7.50
Litho. & Embossed With Foil Application
1646 A267 1500fr gold & multi   16.00 16.00
Nos. 1645-1646 each contain one 42x50mm stamp.

Numerous stamps on a variety of topics having year dates of 2002-2012 and inscription "Republique Democratique du Congo" apparently were not available in the Congo.

AIDS Prevention — A268

AIDS ribbon and text: 320fr, "Une vraie femme ne vend pas son amour propre pour des cadeaux ou de l'argent," head of woman, woman refusing gift from man. 470fr, "Une vraie femme pense à son avenir avant de penser à faire l'amour," head of woman, weomen at school. 490fr, "Je l'aime. Je la protège avec Prudence," man and woman. 530fr, "Un vrai homme ne forcerait jamais une femme à faire l'amour," head of man, men and woman in argument. 550fr, "Un vrai homme ne sera pas forcé à faire l'amour par ses amis," head of man, group of men and woman. 000fr, "Roulez protege," AIDS ribbon on truck. 800fr, "Les apparences sont souvent trompeuses." 1000fr, "Prudence, l'amour de l'avenir."

2016	Litho.	Perf. 13¼x13
1647-1652	A268	Set of 6	—	—

Souvenir Sheets
Size: 120x86mm

| 1653 | A268 | 800fr multi | — | — |

Size: 86x121mm

| 1654 | A268 | 1000fr multi | — | — |

Nos. 1649 and 1652 are dated "2005," but Nos. 1647-1652 apparently were not put on sale in the Democratic Republic of Congo until 2016.

OFFICIAL STAMPS

Nos. 756-772
Overprinted

1975	Litho.	Perf. 14
O1	A145	10s red org & blk	.25	.25
O2	A145	40s multi	.25	.25
O3	A145	50s multi	.25	.25
		Perf. 13		
O4	A146	1k multi	.25	.25
O5	A146	2k multi	.25	.25
O6	A146	3k multi	.25	.25
O7	A146	4k multi	.30	.25
O8	A146	5k multi	.30	.25
O9	A146	6k multi	.45	.25
O10	A146	8k multi	.65	.25
O11	A146	9k multi	.65	.25
O12	A146	10k multi	.80	.25
O13	A146	14k multi	1.25	.40
O14	A146	17k multi	1.50	.45
O15	A146	20k multi	1.50	.60
O16	A146	50k multi	3.75	1.50
O17	A146	100k multi	12.50	4.00
		Nos. O1-O17 (17)	25.15	9.95

"SP" are the initials of "Service Public."

ZAMBEZIA
zam-'bē-zē-ə

LOCATION — A former district of the Mozambique Province in Portuguese East Africa
GOVT. — Part of the Portuguese East Africa Colony

The districts of Quelimane and Tete were created from Zambezia. Eventually stamps of Mozambique came into use. See Quelimane and Tete.

1000 Reis = 1 Milreis

King Carlos
A1   A2
Perf. 11½, 12½, 13½

1894		Typo.	Unwmk.	
1	A1	5r yellow	.70	.60
2	A1	10r red violet	1.00	.80
3	A1	15r chocolate	2.00	1.20
a.		Perf. 12½	160.00	115.00
4	A1	20r lavender	2.00	1.20
5	A1	25r blue green	3.25	2.10
a.		Perf. 11½	30.00	30.00
6	A1	50r lt blue	3.00	2.10
7	A1	75r carmine	7.75	6.00
a.		Perf. 11½	120.00	85.00
8	A1	80r yellow grn	7.00	4.50
9	A1	100r brown, buff	6.00	3.25
10	A1	150r car, rose	5.25	5.25
11	A1	200r dk blue, bl	9.00	5.25
a.		Perf. 11½	1,350.	1,000.
b.		Perf. 13½	60.00	45.00

12	A1	300r dk bl, salmon	15.00	7.75
a.		Perf. 11½	60.00	32.00
		Nos. 1-12 (12)	64.70	40.00

For surcharges and overprints see Nos. 36-47, 73-74, 77-81, 84-88.

1898-1903			Perf. 11½

Name and Value in Black or Red (500r)

13	A2	2½r gray	.80	.60
14	A2	5r orange	.80	.60
15	A2	10r lt green	1.30	1.00
16	A2	15r brown	1.75	1.40
17	A2	15r gray grn ('03)	2.10	2.10
18	A2	20r gray violet	1.75	1.40
19	A2	25r sea green	1.75	1.40
20	A2	25r carmine ('03)	1.75	1.40
21	A2	50r blue	1.75	1.40
22	A2	50r brown ('03)	4.00	3.50
23	A2	65r dull bl ('03)	11.50	9.25
24	A2	75r rose	16.00	7.00
25	A2	75r lilac ('03)	5.00	3.50
26	A2	80r violet	7.75	4.25
27	A2	100r dk bl, bl	3.50	2.50
28	A2	115r org brn, pink ('03)	13.00	7.75
29	A2	130r brn, straw ('03)	13.00	7.75
30	A2	150r brn, buff	8.50	4.25
31	A2	200r red vio, pnksh	8.50	4.25
32	A2	300r dk bl, rose	9.25	4.25
33	A2	400r dull bl, straw ('03)	20.00	11.50
34	A2	500r blk, bl ('01)	20.00	8.50
35	A2	700r vio, yelsh ('01)	25.00	11.00
		Nos. 13-35 (23)	178.75	100.15

For surcharges and overprints see Nos. 49-68, 72, 82-83, 93-107.

Stamps of 1894
Surcharged

1902			Perf. 11½, 12½
36	A1	65r on 10r red vio	13.50	10.00
37	A1	65r on 15r choc	13.50	10.00
38	A1	65r on 20r lav	13.50	10.00
39	A1	65r on 300r bl, sal	13.50	10.00
40	A1	115r on 5r yel	13.50	10.00
41	A1	115r on 25r bl grn	13.50	10.00
42	A1	115r on 80r yel grn	13.50	10.00
43	A1	130r on 75r car	10.00	10.00
44	A1	130r on 150r car, rose	8.50	6.50
45	A1	400r on 50r lt bl	3.00	3.25
46	A1	400r on 100r brn, buff	3.00	3.50
47	A1	400r on 200r bl, bl	3.00	3.50

Same Surcharge on No. P1

48	N1	130r on 2½r brn	13.50	10.00
		Nos. 36-48 (13)	135.50	106.75

Stamps of 1898
Overprinted

1902			Perf. 11½
49	A2	15r brown	4.00	2.00
50	A2	25r sea green	4.00	1.60
51	A2	50r blue	4.00	1.60
52	A2	75r rose	8.25	4.00
		Nos. 49-52 (4)	20.25	9.20

No. 23 Surcharged in Black

1905			
53	A2	50r on 65r dull blue	8.50	5.00

Stamps of 1898-1903
Overprinted in
Carmine or Green

1911				
54	A2	2½r gray	.50	.30
55	A2	5r orange	.50	.30
56	A2	10r light green	.60	.35
a.		Inverted overprint	21.00	21.00
57	A2	15r gray green	.60	.35
58	A2	20r gray violet	.85	.50
59	A2	25r carmine (G)	2.50	1.20
60	A2	50r brown	.60	.60
61	A2	75r lilac	1.60	1.00
62	A2	100r dk bl, bl	1.60	1.00
63	A2	115r org brn, pink	1.60	1.00
64	A2	130r brown, straw	1.60	1.00
65	A2	200r red vio, pnksh	1.60	1.00
66	A2	400r dull bl, straw	3.00	1.75
67	A2	500r blk & red, bl	3.00	1.75
68	A2	700r violet, yelsh	3.50	2.50
		Nos. 54-68 (15)	23.65	14.60

Stamps of 1902-05
Overprinted in
Carmine or Green

1914			Without Gum	
72	A2	50r on 65r dl bl	4,000.	1,300.
73	A1	115r on 5r yellow	2.50	1.50
74	A1	115r on 25r bl grn	2.50	1.50
75	A1	115r on 80r yel grn	2.50	1.50
76	N1	130r on 2½r brn (G)	2.50	2.50
a.		Carmine overprint	22.50	22.50
77	A1	130r on 75r car	3.00	1.50
a.		Perf. 12½	7.00	7.00
78	A1	130r on 150r car, rose	3.00	1.50
79	A1	400r on 50r lt bl	3.00	3.00
a.		Perf. 12½	15.50	15.50
80	A1	400r on 100r brn, buff	4.00	2.50
81	A1	400r on 200r bl, bl	4.00	3.00

On Nos. 51-52

82	A2	50r blue	2.10	1.75
83	A2	75r rose	2.10	1.75
		Nos. 73-83 (11)	31.20	21.00

Preceding Issues
Overprinted in
Carmine

1915				
On Surcharged Issue of 1902				
84	A1	115r on 5r yellow	1.15	.85
85	A1	115r on 25r bl grn	1.15	.85
86	A1	115r on 80r lt grn	1.15	.85
87	A1	130r on 75r carmine	1.15	.85
a.		Perf. 12½	7.00	4.75
88	A1	130r on 150r car, rose	1.15	.85
92	N1	130r on 2½r (down)	1.15	.85

On Nos. 51, 53

93	A2	50r blue	1.15	.85
a.		"Republica" inverted	15.00	15.00
94	A2	50r on 65r dull bl	4.25	4.50
		Nos. 84-94 (8)	12.30	10.45

Stamps of 1898-1903
Overprinted Locally
in Carmine

1917			Without Gum	
95	A2	2½r gray	2.10	2.25
96	A2	5r orange	10.50	6.50
97	A2	10r light green	10.50	6.50
98	A2	15r gray green	10.50	6.50
99	A2	20r gray violet	10.50	6.50
100	A2	25r sea green	17.50	15.00
101	A2	100r blue, blue	6.00	4.25
102	A2	115r org brn, pink	6.00	4.25
103	A2	130r brown, straw	6.00	4.25
104	A2	200r red vio, pnksh	6.00	4.25
105	A2	400r dull bl, straw	6.00	4.25
106	A2	500r blk & red, bl	6.00	5.75
107	A2	700r vio, yelsh	13.50	9.25
		Nos. 95-107 (13)	111.10	79.50

NEWSPAPER STAMP

N1

1894	Unwmk.	Typo.	Perf. 12½
P1	N1	2½r brown	.60	.35

For overprints and surcharges see Nos. 76, 92.

ZAMBIA

'zam-bē-ə

LOCATION — Southern Africa
GOVT. — Republic
AREA — 290,586 sq. mi.
POP. — 9,663,535 (1999 est.)
CAPITAL — Lusaka

The former British protectorate of Northern Rhodesia became an independent republic Oct. 24, 1964, taking the name Zambia. See Northern Rhodesia; see Rhodesia and Nyasaland.

12 Pence = 1 Shilling
20 Shillings = 1 Pound
100 Ngwee = 1 Kwacha (1968)

> Catalogue values for all unused stamps in this country are for Never Hinged items.

Pres. Kenneth D. Kaunda, Victoria Falls — A1

College of Further Education, Lusaka — A2

Perf. 14½x14, 14x14½
1964, Oct. 24   Photo.   Unwmk.

1	A1	3p shown	.25	.25
2	A2	6p shown	.30	.25
3	A1	1sh3p Barotse dancer	.40	.30
		Nos. 1-3 (3)	.95	.80

Zambia's independence, Oct. 24, 1964.

Farmer and Silo A3

X-Ray Technician A4

Designs: 2p, Chinyau dancer. 3p, Woman picking cotton. 4p, Angoni bull. 6p, Communications by drum and teletype. 9p, Redwood blossoms and factory. 1sh, Night fishing on Lake Tanganyika. 1sh3p, Woman tobacco worker. 2sh, Tonga basket maker and child. 2sh6p, Elephants in Luangwa Valley Game Reserve. 5sh, Child and school. 10sh, Copper mining. £1, Makishi dancer.

1964, Oct. 24   Photo.   Perf. 14½
Size: 23x19mm, 19x23mm

4	A3	½p emerald, blk & red	.25	.25
5	A4	1p ultra, blk & brn	.25	.25
6	A4	2p orange, brn & red	.25	.25
7	A4	3p red & black	.25	.25
8	A3	4p orange & black	.25	.25

Perf. 13½x14½, 14½x13½
Size: 32x23mm, 23x32mm

9	A3	6p Prus grn, brn & org	.25	.25
10	A3	9p ultra, brn & dk car rose	.25	.25
11	A3	1sh blue, bis & blk	.25	.25
12	A4	1sh3p dk bl, ver, blk & yel	.25	.25
13	A4	2sh org, blk, brn & ultra	.30	.25
14	A3	2sh6p org yel & blk	.75	.40
15	A3	5sh emerald, blk & yel	1.00	.55
16	A3	10sh orange & blk	3.50	3.50
17	A4	£1 red, blk, brn & yel	2.00	3.50
		Nos. 4-17 (14)	9.80	10.45

ITU Emblem, Old and New Communication Equipment — A5

1965, July 26   Photo.   Perf. 14

18	A5	6p brt lilac & gold	.25	.25
19	A5	2sh6p gray & gold	1.00	1.50

Cent. of the ITU.

ICY Emblem A6

1965, July 26   Perf. 14

20	A6	3p grnsh blue & gold	.25	.25
21	A6	1sh3p ultra & gold	.50	.50

International Cooperation Year, 1965.

Pres. Kaunda and State House, Lusaka — A7

Clematopsis — A8

Designs: 6p, Fireworks over Independence Stadium. 2sh6p, Tithonia diversifolia.

Perf. 13½x14½
1965, Oct. 18   Unwmk.

22	A7	3p multicolored	.25	.25
23	A7	6p ind, yel & brt pink	.25	.25

Perf. 14

24	A8	1sh3p pink, yel & brn	.25	.25
25	A8	2sh6p brt grn, dp org & brn	.25	.25
		Nos. 22-25 (4)	1.00	1.00

1st anniv. of independence, Oct. 24.

Inauguration of WHO Headquarters, Geneva — A9

1966, May 18   Perf. 14

26	A9	3p rose brn, brt bl & gold	.25	.25
27	A9	1sh3p vio bl, brt bl & gold	.90	.90

University of Zambia — A10

1966, July 12   Photo.   Perf. 14

28	A10	3p brt green & gold	.25	.25
29	A10	1sh3p brt purple & gold	.30	.25

University of Zambia opening, Mar. 17.

National Assembly Building — A11

1967, May 2   Unwmk.   Perf. 14

30	A11	3p slate & bronze	.25	.25
31	A11	6p yellow grn & bronze	.30	.25

Completion of National Assembly Building.

Lusaka Airport — A12

1967, Oct. 2   Photo.   Perf. 13½x14½

32	A12	6p vio blue & bronze	.25	.25
33	A12	2sh6p brown & bronze	.75	.75

Opening of Lusaka International Airport.

Symbols of Agriculture A13

Radio, Telephone and Television — A14

Designs: 4p, Emblem of Zambia Youth Service. 1sh, Map showing locations of Zambia coalfields. 1sh6p, Map showing Zambia-Tanzania Road.

Perf. 14½x13½, 13½x14½
1967, Oct. 23

34	A14	4p gray, red & gold	.25	.25
35	A13	6p lt vio bl, gold & blk	.25	.25
36	A14	9p dull blue, sil & blk	.30	.35
37	A14	1sh gold, red, blk & vio bl	.50	.25
38	A13	1sh6p bl grn, ultra, gold & blk	.75	1.25
		Nos. 34-38 (5)	2.05	2.35

Issued to publicize National Development.

Lusaka Cathedral — A15

Baobab Tree — A16

Designs: 3n, Zambia Airways plane. 5n, National Museum, Livingstone. 8n, Vimbuza dancer. 10n, Woman tobacco picker. 15n, Nudaurelia zambesina butterfly. 20n, Crowned cranes. 25n, Angoni warrior. 50n, Chokwe dancer. 1k, Railroad bridge, Kafue River. 2k, Eland.

Perf. 13½x14½, 14½x13½
1968, Jan. 16   Photo.
Size: 26x22mm, 22x26mm

39	A15	1n bronze & multi	.25	.25
a.		Booklet pane of 6	1.40	
b.		Booklet pane of 4	1.40	
40	A16	2n bronze & multi	.25	.25
41	A16	3n bronze & multi	.25	.25
a.		Booklet pane of 6	1.40	
b.		Booklet pane of 4	1.40	
42	A16	5n sepia & bronze	.25	.25
43	A16	8n bronze & multi	.25	.25
44	A16	10n bronze & multi	.25	.25

Size: 32x26mm, 26x32mm

45	A15	15n bronze & multi	2.50	.25
46	A16	20n bronze & multi	4.00	.25
47	A16	25n bronze & multi	.50	.25
48	A15	50n bronze, org & blk	.45	.25
49	A15	1k dk blue & brnz	4.00	.30
50	A15	2k copper & blk	3.00	1.25
		Nos. 39-50 (12)	15.95	4.05

Used values of Nos. 48-50 are for canceled-to-order stamps. Postally used examples sell for more.

Map of Zambia, Arrow Pointing to Ndola — A17

Perf. 14½x14
1968, June 29   Photo.   Unwmk.

51	A17	15n brt green & gold	.35	.35

Zambia Trade Fair at Ndola.

Children and Human Rights Flame — A18

WHO Emblem A19

Children A20

Photogravure; Gold Impressed
1968, Oct. 23   Perf. 14½x14

52	A18	3n ultra, dk bl & gold	.30	.30
53	A19	10n brt violet & gold	.30	.30
54	A20	25n brt blue, blk & gold	.40	.60
		Nos. 52-54 (3)	1.00	1.20

Intl. Human Rights Year; 20th anniv. of WHO; 21st anniv. of UNICEF (25n).

Copper Miner — A21

Design: 25n, Worker poling furnace, horiz.

Perf. 14½x13½
1969, June 18   Photo.

55	A21	3n dp violet & copper	.30	.25
56	A21	25n yellow, blk & copper	1.25	1.10

50th anniv. of the ILO.

Map of Africa with Zambia — A22

10n, Waterbucks, Kafue National Park, horiz. 15n, Golden perch, Kasaba Bay, horiz. 25n, Carmine bee-eater, Luangwa Valley.

Perf. 13½x14, 14x13½

1969, Oct. 23   **Photo.**
57	A22	5n ultra, yel & copper	.25	.25
58	A22	10n copper & multi	.30	.25
59	A22	15n copper & multi	.55	.35
60	A22	25n copper & multi	1.40	1.40
		Nos. 57-60 (4)	2.50	2.25

International Year of African Tourism.

Nimbus III Weather Satellite — A23

1970, Mar. 23   **Litho.**   **Perf. 13x11**
61	A23	15n multicolored	.65	.65

Issued for World Meteorological Day.

"Clean Water" — A24

Designs: 15n, "Nutrition" (infant on scale). 25n, Children's immunization and Edward Jenner, M.D.

1970, July 4   **Litho.**   **Perf. 13x12½**
62	A24	3n multicolored	.25	.25
63	A24	15n multicolored	.55	.55
64	A24	25n multicolored	1.00	1.00
		Nos. 62-64 (3)	1.80	1.80

Issued to publicize preventive medicine and the "Under Five" children's clinics.

Mural by Gabriel Ellison A25

1970, Sept. 8   **Litho.**   **Perf. 14x14½**
65	A25	15n multicolored	.55	.55

Opening of the Conf. of Non-Aligned Nations in Mulungushi Hall (decorated with murals by Mrs. Ellison) in Zambia.

Ceremonial Axe — A26

Traditional Crafts: 5n, Clay pipe bowl with antelope head. 15n, Makishi mask, vert. 25n, The Kuomboka Ceremony (dancers and ceremonial boat).

1970, Nov. 30   **Litho.**   **Perf. 14x14½**
Size: 34x25mm
66	A26	3n dp lil rose & multi	.25	.25
67	A26	5n dp org, blk & sepia	.25	.25

Perf. 13x13½
Size: 30x45½mm
68	A26	15n dp lil rose & multi	.60	.60

Perf. 12½
Size: 71½x23½mm
69	A26	25n violet, blue & multi	.95	.95
a.		Souvenir sheet of 4, #66-69	10.50	10.50
		Nos. 66-69 (4)	2.05	2.05

Dag Hammarskjold and UN General Assembly — A27

Hammarskjold and: 10n, Downed plane. 15n, Dove with olive branch. 25n, Plaque and flowers.

1971, Sept. 18   **Perf. 13½**
70	A27	4n brown & multi	.25	.25
71	A27	10n yellow grn & multi	.25	.25
72	A27	15n blue & multi	.35	.35
73	A27	25n plum & multi	.55	.55
		Nos. 70-73 (4)	1.40	1.40

10th anniv. of the death of Dag Hammarskjold, (1905-61) Secretary-General of the UN, near Ndola, Zambia.

Red-Breasted Bream — A28

10n, Green-headed bream. 15n, Tiger fish.

1971, Dec. 10
74	A28	4n shown	.30	.30
75	A28	10n multicolored	.85	.80
76	A28	15n multicolored	2.00	1.10
		Nos. 74-76 (3)	3.15	2.20

Christmas.

Cheetah — A29

Soil Conservation A30

1972, Mar. 15   **Perf. 13½x14**
77	A29	4n shown	.25	.25
78	A29	10n Lechue	.55	.55

Perf. 14x13½
79	A30	15n Cape porcupine	.80	.85
80	A30	25n Elephant	2.00	1.40
		Nos. 77-80 (4)	3.60	3.05

Conservation Year.

1972, June 30   **Litho.**   **Perf. 14x13½**

10n, Forest conservation. 15n, Water conservation (river view). 25n, Woman in corn field.

Size: 18½x45mm
81	A30	4n shown	.25	.25
82	A30	10n multicolored	.35	.35

Perf. 13½x14
83	A29	15n multicolored	.60	.60
84	A29	25n multicolored	1.10	1.10
		Nos. 81-84 (4)	2.30	2.30

Souvenir Sheet
85		Sheet of 4	10.00	13.50
a.		A30 10n Giraffe and zebra	1.40	1.90
b.		A30 10n Rhinoceros	1.40	1.90
c.		A30 10n Hippopotamus and deer	1.40	1.90
d.		A30 10n Lion	1.40	1.90

Conservation Year. Stamp size: 27x50mm.

1972, Sept. 22   **Perf. 13½x14**

4n, Zambian flowers. 10n, Citrus swallowtails and roses. 15n, Bee. 25n, Locusts in corn field.
All horizontal.

Size: 48x35mm
86	A30	4n multicolored	.75	.75
87	A30	10n multicolored	2.10	2.10
88	A30	15n multicolored	3.00	3.00
89	A30	25n multicolored	4.50	4.50
		Nos. 86-89 (4)	10.35	10.35

Conservation Year.

Mary and Joseph Going to Bethlehem — A31

9n, Holy Family. 15n, Adoration of the shepherds. 25n, Kings following the star.

1972, Dec. 1   **Litho.**   **Perf. 14**
90	A31	4n shown	.25	.25
91	A31	9n multicolored	.25	.25
92	A31	15n multicolored	.25	.25
93	A31	25n multicolored	.35	.35
		Nos. 90-93 (4)	1.10	1.10

Christmas.

Broken Hill Man A32

Designs: 4n, Oudenodon and rubidgea (artist's conception; vert.), 10n, Zambiasaurus. 15n, Skull of Luangwa Drysdalii. 25n, Glossoptoris (seed).

Perf. 14x13½, 14

1973, Feb. 1   **Litho.**
Size: 29x45mm
94	A32	4n org ver & multi	.65	.35

Size: 37½x21mm
95	A32	9n org ver & multi	.95	.75
96	A32	10n apple grn & multi	1.10	.95
97	A32	15n lilac & multi	1.50	1.25
98	A32	25n orange brn & multi	2.40	2.40
		Nos. 94-98 (5)	6.60	5.70

Fossils from Luangwa area (except 9n), over 200 million years old.

Meeting of Stanley and Livingstone at Ujiji — A33

4n, Livingstone, the missionary. 9n, Livingstone at Victoria Falls. 10n, Livingstone stopping slave traders. 15n, Livingstone, the physician. 25n, Portrait & tree in Chitumbu, marking burial place of heart.

1973, May 1   **Perf. 13x13½**
99	A33	3n multicolored	.25	.25
100	A33	4n multicolored	.25	.25
101	A33	9n multicolored	.40	.40
102	A33	10n multicolored	.45	.45
103	A33	15n multicolored	.70	.70
104	A33	25n multicolored	1.10	1.10
		Nos. 99-104 (6)	3.15	3.15

Dr. David Livingstone (1813-73), medical missionary and explorer.

Parliamentary Mace — A34

1973, Sept. 24   **Litho.**   **Perf. 13½x14**
105	A34	9n tan & multi	.40	.40
106	A34	15n gray & multi	.75	.75
107	A34	25n brt green & multi	1.00	1.00
		Nos. 105-107 (3)	2.15	2.15

Third Commonwealth Conference of Speakers and Presiding Officers, Lusaka.

Vaccination — A35

WHO Emblem and: 4n, Mother washing infant, vert. 9n, Nurse weighing infant, vert. 15n, Child eating cereal and fruit.

1973, Oct. 16   **Litho.**   **Perf. 14**
108	A35	4n blue & multi	52.50	35.00
109	A35	9n orange & multi	.30	.30
110	A35	10n brt grn & multi	.40	.40
111	A35	15n violet & multi	.50	.50
		Nos. 108-111 (4)	53.70	36.20

WHO, 25th anniv.

A36

A37

Birth of the Second Republic: 4n, UNIP flag. 9n, United National Independence Party Headquarters, Lusaka. 10n, Army band. 15n, Women dancing and singing. 25n, President's parliamentary chair.

1973, Dec. 13   **Litho.**   **Perf. 14x13½**
112	A36	4n multicolored	12.00	7.50
113	A36	9n multicolored	.25	.25
114	A36	10n multicolored	.30	.30
115	A36	15n multicolored	.45	.45
116	A37	25n multicolored	.75	.75
		Nos. 112-116 (5)	13.75	9.25

Pres. Kaunda and his Home During Struggle for Independence — A38

4n, Pres. Kaunda at Mulungushi. 15n, Pres. Kaunda holding torch of freedom.

1974, Apr. 28   Litho.   Perf. 14½x14
117	A38	4n multi, vert.	.50	.50
118	A38	9n multi	.60	.60
119	A38	15n multi	.90	.90
	Nos. 117-119 (3)		2.00	2.00

50th birthday of Pres. Kenneth Kaunda.

Nakambla Sugar Estate — A39

Designs: 4n, Local market. 9n, Kapiri glass factory. 10n, Kafue hydroelectric plant. 15n, Kafue Bridge. 25n, Conference of Non-aligned Nations, Lusaka, 1970.

1974, Oct. 24   Litho.   Perf. 13½x14
120	A39	3n multicolored	.25	.25
121	A39	4n multicolored	.25	.25
122	A39	9n multicolored	.30	.30
123	A39	10n multicolored	.35	.35
124	A39	15n multicolored	.50	.50
125	A39	25n multicolored	.80	.80
	Nos. 120-125 (6)		2.45	2.45

Souvenir Sheet
126		Sheet of 4	6.00	10.00
a.	A39	15n Academic education	1.20	1.90
b.	A39	15n Teacher Training College	1.20	1.90
c.	A39	15n Technical education	1.20	1.90
d.	A39	15n University of Zambia	1.20	1.90

10th anniversary of indepencence.

Mobile Post Office — A40

UPU Emblem and: 9n, Rural mail service by Zambia Airways. 10n, Modern Post Office, Chipata. 15n, Ndola Postal Training Center.

1974, Nov. 15
127	A40	4n multicolored	.25	.25
128	A40	9n multicolored	.25	.25
129	A40	10n multicolored	.25	.25
130	A40	15n multicolored	.30	.30
	Nos. 127-130 (4)		1.05	1.05

Centenary of Universal Postal Union.

Radar by Day A41

1974, Dec. 16
131	A41	4n shown	.25	.25
132	A41	9n Radar by night	.45	.40
133	A41	15n Radar at dawn	.75	.70
134	A41	25n Radar station	1.20	1.20
	Nos. 131-134 (4)		2.65	2.55

Inauguration of Mwembeshi Earth Station, Oct. 21, 1974.

Rhinoceros and Calf — A42

Peanut Harvest — A43

2n, Guinea fowl. 3n, Zambian dancers. 4n, Fish eagle. 5n, Bridge, Victoria Falls. 8n, Sitatunga. 9n, Elephant, Kasaba Bay Resort. 10n, Giant pangolin. 15n, Zambezi River source, Monument. 25n, Tobacco field. 50n, Flying doctor service. 1k, Lady Ross's touraco. 2k, Village scene.

1975, Jan. 3   Litho.   Perf. 13½x14
135	A42	1n shown	.55	.55
136	A42	2n multicolored	.55	.55
137	A42	3n multicolored	.25	.40
138	A42	4n multicolored	1.00	.25
139	A42	5n multicolored	1.00	1.00
140	A42	8n multicolored	1.00	.90
141	A42	9n multicolored	1.25	.85
142	A42	10n multicolored	.25	.25

Perf. 13
143	A43	15n multicolored	.35	.25
144	A43	20n shown	1.00	1.40
145	A43	25n multicolored	1.60	.65
146	A43	50n multicolored	4.00	3.00
147	A43	1k multicolored	5.75	2.50
148	A43	2k multicolored	4.00	6.00
	Nos. 135-148 (14)		22.55	18.55

For surcharges see #188-191, 319.

Map of Namibia (South-West Africa) — A44

1975, Aug. 26   Litho.   Perf. 14x13½
149	A44	4n green & dk green	.25	.25
150	A44	9n dk blue & gray bl	.25	.25
151	A44	15n yellow & orange	.35	.55
152	A44	25n orange & dp orange	.40	1.10
	Nos. 149-152 (4)		1.25	2.15

Namibia Day.

Sprinkler Irrigation — A45

Designs: 9n, Sprinkler irrigation over rows of vegetables. 15n, Furrow irrigation.

1975, Dec. 16   Litho.   Perf. 13
153	A45	4n multicolored	.25	.25
154	A45	9p multicolored	.35	.50
155	A45	15n multicolored	.60	1.10
	Nos. 153-155 (3)		1.20	1.85

Intl. Commission on Irrigation and Drainage, 25th anniv.

Julbernardia Paniculata — A46

Trees of Zambia: 4n, Sycamore fig. 9n, Baikiaea plurijuga. 10n, Colophospermum. 15n, Uapaca kirkiana. 25n, Pterocarpus angolensis.

1976, Mar. 22   Litho.   Perf. 13
156	A46	3n multicolored	.30	.30
157	A46	4n multicolored	.30	.30
158	A46	9n multicolored	.45	.45
159	A46	10n multicolored	.45	.45
160	A46	15n multicolored	.70	.70
161	A46	25n multicolored	.85	.85
	Nos. 156-161 (6)		3.05	3.05

World Forestry Day, Mar. 21.

TAZARA Passenger Train — A47

9n, Train carrying copper. 10n, Clearing the bush. #164, Train carrying heavy machinery. #166b, Track laying. 20n, Reinforcing railroad track. #165, Train carrying various goods. #166d, Completed tracks.

1976, Dec. 10   Litho.   Perf. 13
162	A47	4n multicolored	.25	.25
163	A47	9n multicolored	.55	.55
164	A47	15n multicolored	.90	.90
165	A47	25n multicolored	1.50	1.50
	Nos. 162-165 (4)		3.20	3.20

Souvenir Sheet
Perf. 13½x14
166		Sheet of 4	3.75	3.75
a.	A47	10n multicolored	.35	.35
b.	A47	15n multicolored	.55	.50
c.	A47	20n multicolored	.65	.55
d.	A47	25n multicolored	.90	.70

Completion of Tanzania-Zambia Railroad.

Kayowe Dance — A48

1977, Jan. 18   Litho.   Perf. 13½x14
167	A48	4n shown	.25	.25
168	A48	9n Lilombola dance	.25	.25
169	A48	15n Initiation ceremony	.40	.40
170	A48	25n Munkhwele dance	.50	.50
	Nos. 167-170 (4)		1.40	1.40

2nd World Black and African Festival, Lagos, Nigeria, Jan. 15-Feb. 12.

Grimwood's Longclaw — A49

Birds of Zambia: 9n, Shelley's sunbird. 10n, Black-cheeked lovebird. 15n, Locust finch. 20n, White-chested tinkerbird. 25n, Chaplin's barbet.

1977, July 1   Litho.   Perf. 14½
171	A49	4n multicolored	.40	.25
172	A49	9n multicolored	.65	.60
173	A49	10n multicolored	.80	.60
174	A49	15n multicolored	1.60	1.90
175	A49	20n multicolored	1.75	2.25
176	A49	25n multicolored	2.00	2.75
	Nos. 171-176 (6)		7.20	8.35

Children Playing with Blocks A50

Designs: 9n, Women of various races dancing in circle. 15n, Black and white girls with young bird.

1977, Oct. 20   Litho.   Perf. 14x14½
177	A50	4n multicolored	.25	.25
178	A50	9n multicolored	.25	.25
179	A50	15n multicolored	.35	.35
	Nos. 177-179 (3)		.85	.85

Combat racism and racial discrimination.

"Glory to God in the Highest" A51

Christmas: 9n, Nativity. 10n, Three Kings and camel. 15n, Presentation at the Temple.

1977, Dec. 20   Litho.   Perf. 14
180	A51	4n multicolored	.25	.25
181	A51	9n multicolored	.25	.25
182	A51	10n multicolored	.25	.25
183	A51	15n multicolored	.25	.25
	Nos. 180-183 (4)		1.00	1.00

Elephant and Road Check A52

Designs: 18n, Waterbuck and Kafue River boat patrol. 28n, Warthog and helicopter surveillance of National Parks. 32n, Cheetah and armed wildlife guards in Parks and Game Management Areas.

1978, Aug. 1   Litho.   Perf. 14x14½
184	A52	8n multicolored	.30	.30
185	A52	18n multicolored	.60	.60
186	A52	28n multicolored	.95	.95
187	A52	32n multicolored	1.15	1.15
	Nos. 184-187 (4)		3.00	3.00

Anti-poaching Campaign of Zambia Wildlife Conservation Society, Aug. 1978.

Nos. 141, 137, 145 and 143 Srchd. with New Value and 2 Bars
1979, Mar. 15   Perf. 13½x14, 13
188	A42	8n on 9n multi	.60	.25
189	A42	10n on 3n multi	.25	.25
190	A43	18n on 25n multi	.25	.25
191	A43	28n on 15n multi	.25	.25
	Nos. 188-191 (4)		1.35	1.00

Kayowe Dance A53

Designs: 32n, Kutambala dance. 42n, Chitwansombo drummers. 58n, Lilombola dance.

1979, Aug. 1
192	A53	18n multicolored	.30	.30
193	A53	32n multicolored	.35	.35
194	A53	42n multicolored	.35	.35
195	A53	58n multicolored	.50	.50
	Nos. 192-195 (4)		1.50	1.50

Commonwealth Summit Conf., Lusaka, Aug. 1-9.

"Why the Zebra is Hornless" — A54

Children's Stories: 18n, Kalulu and the Tug of War. 42n, How the Tortoise got his Shell. 58n, Kalulu and the Lion.

1979, Sept. 21   Litho.   Perf. 14
196	A54	18n multicolored	.25	.25
197	A54	32n multicolored	.40	.55
198	A54	42n multicolored	.45	.75
199	A54	58n multicolored	.55	1.00
a.		Souvenir sheet of 4, #196-199	2.50	2.50
		Nos. 196-199 (4)	1.65	2.55

International Year of the Child.

Girls of Different Races Holding Emblem A55

Anti-Apartheid Year (1978): 32n, Boys and toy car. 42n, Infants and butterfly. 58n, Children and microscope.

1979, Nov. 16   Litho.   Perf. 14½x15
200	A55	18n multicolored	.25	.25
201	A55	32n multicolored	.35	.35
202	A55	42n multicolored	.55	.55
203	A55	58n multicolored	.70	.70
		Nos. 200-203 (4)	1.85	1.85

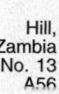

Hill, Zambia No. 13 A56

Hill and: 32n, Mailman & bicycle. 42n, No. Rhodesia #75. 58n, Mailman & oxcart.

1979, Dec. 20   Litho.   Perf. 14½
204	A56	18n multicolored	.30	.25
205	A56	32n multicolored	.40	.50
206	A56	42n multicolored	.40	.65
207	A56	58n multicolored	.45	1.10
a.		Souvenir sheet of 4, #204-207	2.40	3.25
		Nos. 204-207 (4)	1.55	2.50

Sir Rowland Hill (1795-1879), originator of penny postage.

Nos. 204-207a Overprinted "LONDON 1980"

1980, Mar 6   Litho.   Perf. 15
208	A56	18n multicolored	.25	.40
209	A56	32n multicolored	.30	.55
210	A56	42n multicolored	.40	.70
211	A56	58n multicolored	.60	.85
a.		Souvenir sheet of 4	3.00	4.00
		Nos. 208-211 (4)	1.55	2.50

London 80 Intl. Stamp Exhib., May 6-14.

Anniverary Emblem on Map of Zambia — A57

1980, June 18   Litho.   Perf. 14
212	A57	8n multicolored	.25	.25
213	A57	32n multicolored	.45	.45
214	A57	42n multicolored	.55	.55
215	A57	58n multicolored	.70	.70
a.		Souvenir sheet of 4, #212-215	2.40	2.40
		Nos. 212-215 (4)	1.95	1.95

Rotary International, 75th anniversary.

Running A58

1980, July 19   Litho.   Perf. 13
216	A58	18n shown	.25	.25
217	A58	32n Boxing	.45	.45
218	A58	42n Soccer	.55	.55

219	A58	58n Swimming	.75	.75
a.		Souvenir sheet of 4, #216-219	2.75	2.75
		Nos. 216-219 (4)	2.00	2.00

22nd Summer Olympic Games, Moscow, July 19-Aug. 3.

Zaddach's Forester — A59

1980, Sept. 22
220	A59	18n shown	.40	.25
221	A59	32n Northern highflier	.65	.60
222	A59	42n Zambezi skipper	.95	.95
223	A59	58n Modest blue	1.30	2.10
a.		Souvenir sheet of 4, #220-223	8.00	8.00
		Nos. 220-223 (4)	3.30	3.90

Coat of Arms — A60

1980, Sept. 27   Litho.   Perf. 14½
224	A60	18n multicolored	.25	.25
225	A60	32n multicolored	.40	.45
226	A60	42n multicolored	.50	.65
227	A60	58n multicolored	.60	1.25
		Nos. 224-227 (4)	1.75	2.60

26th Commonwealth Parliamentary Association Conference, Lusaka.

A61

Nativity and St. Francis of Assisi (stained glass window), Ndola Church.

1980, Oct.   Litho.   Perf. 14
228	A61	8n multicolored	.25	.25
229	A61	28n multicolored	.60	.90
230	A61	32n multicolored	.60	.90
231	A61	42n multicolored	.80	1.25
		Nos. 228-231 (4)	2.25	3.30

Christmas and 50th anniv. of Catholic Church in Copperbelt (central Zambia).

Trichilia Emetica Seed Pods, Musikili A62

Seed Pods: 18n, Afzelia quanzensis, Mupapa. 28n, Erythrina abyssinica, Mulunguti. 32n, Combretum collinum, Mulama.

1981, Mar. 21   Litho.   Perf. 14
232	A62	8n shown	.25	.25
233	A62	18n multicolored	.30	.35
234	A62	28n multicolored	.35	.70
235	A62	32n multicolored	.35	1.15
		Nos. 232-235 (4)	1.25	2.45

World Forestry Day.

ITU Emblem — A63

Designs: 18n, 32n, WHO emblem.

1981, May 15   Litho.   Perf. 14½
236	A63	8n multicolored	.50	.50
237	A63	18n multicolored	.65	.65
238	A63	28n multicolored	.75	.75
239	A63	32n multicolored	.85	.85
		Nos. 236-239 (4)	2.75	2.75

13th World Telecommunications Day (8n, 28n).

Mask Maker — A64

2n, Blacksmiths. 5n, Potter. 8n, Straw basket fishing. 10n, Roof thatching. 12n, Picking mushrooms ('83). 18n, Millet grinding. 28n, Royal Barge paddler. 30n, Makishi tightrope dancer. 35n, Tonga-ila granary, house. 42n, Cattle herding. 50n, Traditional healer. 75n, Carrying water jugs ('83). 1k, Grinding corn ('83). 2k, Woman smoking pipe.

1981-83
240	A64	1n shown	.25	.25
241	A64	2n multicolored	.25	.25
242	A64	5n multicolored	.25	.25
243	A64	8n multicolored	.25	.25
244	A64	10n multicolored	.25	.25
244A	A64	12n multicolored	3.50	2.75
245	A64	18n multicolored	.50	.25
246	A64	28n multicolored	.70	.25
247	A64	30n multicolored	.70	.25
248	A64	35n multicolored	.75	.25
249	A64	42n multicolored	.75	1.50

Perf. 14
Size: 37x25mm
250	A64	50n multicolored	.75	.25
251	A64	75n multicolored	.75	.90
252	A64	1k multicolored	.75	.90
253	A64	2k multicolored	.75	.90
		Nos. 240-253 (15)	11.15	9.45

For surcharges see Nos. 358, 372, 499-506, 596.

Kankobele — A65

Designs: Traditional musical instruments.

1981, Sept. 30   Litho.   Perf. 14½
254	A65	8n shown	.45	.25
255	A65	18n Inshingili	.55	.45
256	A65	28n Ilimba	.80	1.40
257	A65	32n Bango	.80	1.60
		Nos. 254-257 (4)	2.60	3.70

Bornite — A66

Designs: Rocks and minerals.

1982, Jan. 5   Litho.   Perf. 14
258	A66	8n Banded Ironstone	1.30	.30
259	A66	18n Cobaltocalcite	2.60	1.10
260	A66	28n Amazonite	3.50	3.00
261	A66	32n Tourmaline	3.75	4.00
262	A66	42n Uranium ore	4.00	5.25
		Nos. 258-262 (5)	15.15	13.65

1982, July 1   Litho.   Perf. 14
263	A66	8n shown	1.05	.35
264	A66	18n Chalcopyrite	2.50	1.40
265	A66	28n Malachite	3.00	3.75
266	A66	32n Azurite	3.00	3.75
267	A66	42n Vanadinite	3.75	4.50
		Nos. 263-267 (5)	13.30	13.75

Scouting Year A67

8n, Scouts, flag. 18n, Baden-Powell. 28n, Horned buffalo, patrol pennant. 1k, Eagle, conservation badge.

1982, Mar. 30   Litho.   Perf. 14
268	A67	8n multicolored	.35	.35
269	A67	18n multicolored	.35	.35
270	A67	28n multicolored	.35	.35
271	A07	1k multicolored	2.10	2.60
a.		Souvenir sheet of 4, #268-271	4.75	5.50
		Nos. 268-271 (4)	3.15	3.65

Drilling Rig, 1926 A68

Steam locomotives.

1983, Jan. 26   Perf. 14x14½
272	A68	8n shown	.55	.30
273	A68	18n Class B6, 1910	.85	.85
274	A68	28n Borsig engine, 1925	1.35	2.00
275	A68	32n 7th class, 1900	1.75	2.50
		Nos. 272-275 (4)	4.50	5.65

Commonwealth Day — A68a

1983, Mar. 10   Litho.   Perf. 14
276	A68a	12n Cotton picking	.25	.25
277	A68a	18n Miners	.25	.25
278	A68a	28n Ritual pot, dancers	.25	.35
279	A68a	1k Victoria Falls, purple-crested lorie	2.75	3.75
		Nos. 276-279 (4)	3.50	4.60

Local Flowers — A69

1983, May 26   Litho.   Perf. 14
280	A69	12n Eulophia cucullata	.25	.25
281	A69	28n Kigelia africana	.45	.60
282	A69	35n Protea gaguedi	.55	.75
283	A69	50n Leonotis nepotifolia	1.05	2.25
a.		Souvenir sheet of 4, #280-283, perf. 12x12½	2.75	4.00
		Nos. 280-283 (4)	2.30	3.85

Thornicroft's Giraffes — A70

28n, Cookson's wildebeest. 35n, Black lechwe. 1k, Yellow-backed duiker.

1983, July 21	Litho.	*Perf. 14*		
284	A70	12n shown	.65	.65
285	A70	28n multicolored	.85	.85
286	A70	35n multicolored	1.20	1.20
287	A70	1k multicolored	2.40	3.25
		Nos. 284-287 (4)	5.10	5.95

Tiger Fish
A71

1983, Sept. 29	Litho.	*Perf. 14*		
288	A71	12n shown	.55	.25
289	A71	28n Silver Barbel	.85	.70
290	A71	35n Spotted Squeaker	.95	2.00
291	A71	38n Red Breasted Bream	1.10	2.00
		Nos. 288-291 (4)	3.45	4.95

For surcharge see No. 597.

Christmas — A72

1983, Dec. 12	Litho.	*Perf. 14x14½*		
292	A72	12n Annunciation	.25	.25
293	A72	28n Shepherds	.30	.30
294	A72	35n Three Kings	.35	.75
295	A72	38n Flight into Egypt	.40	1.00
		Nos. 292-295 (4)	1.30	2.30

40th Anniv.
of Intl. Civil
Aviation
Org. — A73

1984, Jan. 26	Litho.	*Perf. 14*		
296	A73	12n Boeing 737, 1983	.25	.25
297	A73	28n Beaver, 1954	.45	.45
298	A73	35n Short Solent Flying Boat, 1948	.55	.55
299	A73	1k DH-66, 1931	1.75	2.50
		Nos. 296-299 (4)	3.00	3.75

60th
Birthday of
Pres.
Kaunda
A74

12n, Receiving greetings. 28n, Swearing in, 1983, vert. 60n, Planting cherry tree. 1k, Opening Natl. Assembly, vert.

Perf. 14½x14, 14x14½

1984, Apr. 28			Litho.	
300	A74	12n multicolored	.30	.30
301	A74	28n multicolored	.45	.45
302	A74	60n multicolored	.90	2.00
303	A74	1k multicolored	1.10	2.50
		Nos. 300-303 (4)	2.75	5.25

1984 Summer
Olympics — A75

1984, July 18	Litho.	*Perf. 14*		
304	A75	12n Soccer	.25	.25
305	A75	28n Running	.50	.50
306	A75	35n Hurdles	.55	.65
307	A75	50n Boxing	.75	1.25
		Nos. 304-307 (4)	2.05	2.65

Reptiles
A76

1984, Sept. 5	Litho.	*Perf. 14*		
308	A76	12n Gabon viper	.35	.30
309	A76	28n Chameleon	.65	.55
310	A76	35n Nile crocodile	.75	.65
311	A76	1k Blue-headed agama	1.75	2.25
a.		Souvenir sheet of 4, #308-311	4.75	4.75
		Nos. 308-311 (4)	3.50	3.75

20th Anniv. of Independence — A77

1984, Oct. 22	Litho.	*Perf. 14*		
312	A77	12n Pres. Kaunda, Mulungushi Rock	.30	.30
313	A77	28n Freedom Statue	.40	.50
314	A77	1k Produce	1.30	2.00
		Nos. 312-314 (3)	2.00	2.80

Local Mushrooms
A78

12n, Amanita flammeola. 28n, Amanita zambiana. 32n, Termitomyces letestui. 75n, Cantharellus miniatescens.

1984, Dec. 12	Litho.	*Perf. 14x14½*		
315	A78	12n multicolored	1.25	1.25
316	A78	28n multicolored	1.35	1.35
317	A78	32n multicolored	2.10	2.10
318	A78	75n multicolored	4.00	4.00
		Nos. 315-318 (4)	8.70	8.70

For surcharge see No. 600.

**No. 146 Surcharged with New Value
and Two Bars**

1985, Mar. 5	Litho.	*Perf. 13½*		
319	A43	5k on 50n multi	2.50	3.00

Primates
A79

1985, Apr. 25	Litho.	*Perf. 14*		
320	A79	12n Chacma baboon	.60	.60
321	A79	20n Moloney's monkey	.80	.80
322	A79	45n Blue monkey	1.75	1.75
323	A79	1k Vervet monkey	2.60	3.25
		Nos. 320-323 (4)	5.75	6.40

For surcharge see No. 604.

SADCC,
5th Anniv.
A80

1985, July 9	Litho.	*Perf. 14*		
324	A80	20n Map	.80	.80
325	A80	45n Mining	2.10	2.10
326	A80	1k Mulungushi Hall	2.10	2.60
		Nos. 324-326 (3)	5.00	5.50

Southern African Development Coordination Conference.
For surcharge see No. 605.

Queen
Mother,
85th
Birthday
— A81

25n, Portrait in blue, age 80. 45n, Queen Consort at Clarence House, 1963. 55n, With Elizabeth II and Princess Margaret. 5k, With royal family, christening of Prince Henry, 1984.

1985, Aug. 2				
327	A81	25n multi, vert.	.25	.25
328	A81	45n multi, vert.	.25	.25
329	A81	55n multi	.25	.25
330	A81	5k multi	1.25	2.00
		Nos. 327-330 (4)	2.00	2.75

For surcharges see Nos. 401, 406, 410, 414, 595, 606, 611.

National Anniversaries — A81a

#330A, Pres. Kenneth Kaunda, Mulungushi Rock. #330B, Kaunda, agricultural products. #330C, Freedom statue, flags.

Die Cut Perf. 10

1985, Oct. 23			Embossed	
330A-330C	A81a	5k gold	18.00	18.00

United National Independence Party, 26th anniv. (No. 330A); Independence, 20th anniv. (Nos. 330B-330C).

Postal and Telecommunications Corp.,
10th Anniv. — A82

20n, Lusaka P.O., 1958. 45n, Livingstone P.O., 1950. 55n, Kalomo P.O., 1902. 5k, Transcontinental Telegraph, 1900.

1985, Dec. 12			*Perf. 13½x13*	
331	A82	20n multicolored	.60	.60
332	A82	45n multicolored	.90	.90
333	A82	55n multicolored	1.00	1.00
334	A82	5k multicolored	3.25	4.25
		Nos. 331-334 (4)	5.75	6.75

For surcharges see Nos. 590-593.

UN, 40th
Anniv. — A83

1985, Dec. 19			*Perf. 14*	
335	A83	20n Boy in cornfield	.35	.35
336	A83	45n Emblem	.60	.60
337	A83	1k Pres. Kaunda, 1970	1.15	1.50
338	A83	2k Charter signing, 1945	1.75	2.25
		Nos. 335-338 (4)	3.85	4.70

For surcharges see #594, 607.

Beetles
A84

35n, Mylabris tricolor. 1k, Phasgonocnema melanianthe. 1.70k, Amaurodes passerinii. 5k, Ranzania petersiana.

1986, Mar. 20				
339	A84	35n multicolored	.25	.25
340	A84	1k multicolored	.40	.45
341	A84	1.70k multicolored	.65	.75
342	A84	5k multicolored	2.10	2.25
		Nos. 339-342 (4)	3.40	3.70

For surcharges see #609, 612.

> Common Design Types
> pictured following the introduction.

**Queen Elizabeth II 60th Birthday
Common Design Type**

Designs: 35n, At the Flower Ball, Savoy Hotel, London, 1951. 1.25k, With Prince Andrew at Lusaka Airport, Commonwealth Conf., 1979. 1.70k, With Dr. Kaunda observing natl. anthem. 1.95k, Wearing Queen Mary tiara, state visit to Luxembourg, 1976. 5k, Visiting Crown Agents' offices, 1983.

1986, Apr. 21		Wmk. 384	*Perf. 14*	
343	CD337	35n scar, blk & sil	.25	.25
344	CD337	1.25k ultra & multi	.30	.30
345	CD337	1.70k grn, blk & sil	.35	.35
346	CD337	1.95k vio & multi	.35	.35
347	CD337	5k rose vio & multi	.50	.50
		Nos. 343-347 (5)	1.75	1.75

For surcharges see Nos. 402, 405, 407, 411, 415.

**Royal Wedding Issue, 1986
Common Design Type**

Designs: 1.70k, Sarah Ferguson kissing Prince Andrew. 5k, Andrew in informal dress.

1986, July 23	Litho.	*Perf. 14*		
348	CD338	1.70k multicolored	.30	.30
349	CD338	5k multicolored	.80	1.00

1986 World Cup
Soccer
Championships,
Mexico — A85

Various soccer plays.

1986, June 27	Litho.	*Perf. 14½*		
350	A85	35n multicolored	.90	.90
351	A85	1.25k multicolored	2.00	2.00
352	A85	1.70k multicolored	2.40	2.40
353	A85	5k multicolored	3.50	3.50
		Nos. 350-353 (4)	8.80	8.80

For surcharges see Nos. 403, 408, 412, 416.

Halley's Comet A86

Designs: 1.25k, Edmond Halley (1656-1742), by Henry Pegram. 1.70k, Giotto space probe approaching comet. 2k, Youth, astronomer. 5k, Halley's map of the southern constellations.

1986, July 4
354	A86	1.25k multicolored	.90	.90
355	A86	1.70k multicolored	1.05	1.05
356	A86	2k multicolored	1.50	1.50
357	A86	5k multicolored	3.00	3.00
		Nos. 354-357 (4)	6.45	6.45

For surcharges see Nos. 404, 409, 413, 417.

#244A Surcharged in Light Red Brown

1986, July   Litho.   Perf. 14½
358	A64	20n on 12n multi	15.00	.50

Christmas A87

Children's drawings.

1986, Dec. 15   Litho.   Perf. 14
359	A87	35n Nativity	.40	.40
360	A87	1.25k Magi	1.40	1.40
361	A87	1.60k Nativity	1.75	1.75
362	A87	5k Angel, house, tree	3.50	3.50
		Nos. 359-362 (4)	7.05	7.05

For surcharges see #602, 608.

Tazara Railroad, 10th Anniv. A88

Locomotive traveling various railway lines.

1986, Dec. 22
363	A88	35n Overpass, Kasama	.25	.25
364	A88	1.25k Tunnel 21 vicinity	.40	.40
365	A88	1.70k Tunnels 6 7	.65	.65
366	A88	5k Mpika Station grade separation	1.05	1.05
		Nos. 363-366 (4)	2.25	2.25

University of Zambia A89

Designs: 35n, Pres. Kaunda shaking council member's hand. 1.25k, University crest, vert. 1.60k, University statue. 5k, Kaunda laying university building cornerstone, vert.

1987, Jan. 27   Litho.   Perf. 14
367	A89	35n multicolored	.35	.35
368	A89	1.25k multicolored	.75	.75
369	A89	1.60k multicolored	.85	.85
370	A89	5k multicolored	3.00	4.25
		Nos. 367-370 (4)	4.95	6.20

No. 137 Surcharged in Blue

1987   Perf. 14½
372	A64	25n on 8n multi	.65	.45

Municipal Arms — A90

1987, Mar. 26   Perf. 14
373	A90	35n Kitwe	.25	.25
374	A90	1.25k Ndola	.30	.30
375	A90	1.70k Lusaka	.40	.40
376	A90	20k Livingstone	3.00	3.00
		Nos. 373-376 (4)	3.95	3.95

For surcharge see No. 603.

Birds — A91

25n, Long-toed fluff tail. 30n, Miombo pied barbet. 35n, Black-and-rufous swallow. 50n, Slaty egret. 1k, Bradfield's hornbill. 1.25k, Margaret's batis. 1.60k, Red-and-blue sunbird. 1.70k, Boehm's bee-eater. 1.95k, Gorgeous bush shrike. 2k, Shoebill. 5k, Taita falcon.

1987-88   Perf. 11x13
Size: 20x25½mm
377	A91	25n multicolored	3.50	3.50
378	A91	30n multicolored	.30	.30
379	A91	35n multicolored	3.50	3.50

Size: 25x38½mm
Perf. 14
380	A91	50n multicolored	.30	.30
381	A91	1k multicolored	3.50	3.50
382	A91	1.25k multicolored	3.50	3.50
383	A91	1.60k multicolored	3.50	3.50
384	A91	1.70k multicolored	3.75	3.75
385	A91	1.95k multicolored	3.75	3.75
386	A91	2k multicolored	.50	.50
387	A91	5k multicolored	4.50	4.50
		Nos. 377-387 (11)	30.60	30.60

Surcharged

No. 390

No. 392

No. 388, Yellow swamp warbler. No. 389, Olive-flanked robin.

Size: 20x25½mm
388	A91	20n on 1n multi	.35	.35
389	A91	75n on 2n multi	.35	.35
390	A91	1.65k on 30n #378	.35	.35

Size: 25x38½mm
Perf. 14
391	A91	10k on 50n #380	2.25	2.25
392	A91	20k on 2k #386	3.00	3.00
		Nos. 388-392 (5)	6.30	6.30

Issued: #377, 379, 381-385, 387, 9/14/87; #391-392, 3/10/88; others 10/8/87.
Nos. 388-389 not issued without overprint.
See Nos. 433-435, 527-540. For surcharges see Nos. 490, 492-498.

Look-out Tree, Livingstone — A92

1.25k, Rafting, Zambezi River. 1.70k, Walking safari, Luangwa Valley. 10k, White pelicans.

1987, June 30   Perf. 14
393	A92	35n shown	.35	.35
394	A92	1.25k multicolored	.40	.40
395	A92	1.70k multicolored	1.75	1.75
396	A92	10k multicolored	6.00	6.00
		Nos. 393-396 (4)	8.50	8.50

Zambia Airways, 20th Anniv. A93

1987, Sept. 21
397	A93	35n De Havilland Beaver	.80	.80
398	A93	1.70k DC-10	1.75	1.75
399	A93	5k DC-3	4.00	4.00
400	A93	10k Boeing 707	6.25	6.25
		Nos. 397-400 (4)	12.80	12.80

Issues of 1985-86 Surcharged in Gold or Black

1987, Sept. 14   Perfs. as Before
401	A81	3k on 25n #327		
		(G)	1.40	1.40
402	CD337	3k on 35n #343	1.05	1.05
403	A85	3k on 35n #350	1.40	1.40
404	A86	3k on 1.25k #354		
		(G)	2.40	2.40
405	CD337	4k on 1.25k #344	1.30	1.30
406	A81	6k on 45n #328	2.40	2.40
407	CD337	6k on 1.70k #345	1.90	1.90
408	A85	6k on 1.25k #351	2.40	2.40
409	A86	6k on 1.70k #355		
		(G)	3.75	3.75
410	A81	10k on 55n #329		
		(G)	3.50	3.50
411	CD337	10k on 1.95k #346	3.50	3.50
412	A85	10k on 1.70k #352	3.50	3.50
413	A86	10k on 2k #356		
		(G)	6.50	6.50
414	A81	20k on 5k #330		
		(G)	6.75	6.75
415	CD337	20k on 5k #347	6.75	6.75
416	A85	20k on 5k #353	6.75	6.75
417	A86	20k on 5k #357		
		(G)	12.00	12.00
		Nos. 401-417 (17)	67.25	67.25

World Food Day — A94

Cattle.

1987, Oct. 1   Perf. 14½x15
418	A94	35n Friesian-Holstein	.25	.25
419	A94	1.25k Simmental	.40	.40
420	A94	1.70k Sussex	.40	.40
421	A94	20k Brahma	1.90	1.90
		Nos. 418-421 (4)	2.95	2.95

Traditional Heritage — A95

Zambian people.

1987, Oct. 20   Perf. 13x12½
422	A95	35n Mpoloto Ne Mikobango	.25	.25
423	A95	1.25k Zintaka	.30	.30
424	A95	1.70k Mufuluhi	.45	.45
425	A95	10k Ntebwe	1.15	1.15
426	A95	20k Kubangwa Aa Mbulunga	2.10	2.10
		Nos. 422-426 (5)	4.25	4.25

World Wildlife Fund — A96

Wild Cats — A97

50n, Black lechwe drinking water. 2k, Adults and young, horiz. 2.50k, Running, horiz. 10k, Male, diff.
No. 431, Cheetah. No. 432, Caracal.

1987, Dec. 21   Litho.   Perf. 14
427	A96	50n multicolored	1.50	1.50
428	A96	2k multicolored	2.75	2.75
429	A96	2.50k multicolored	2.75	2.75
430	A96	10k multicolored	6.00	6.00
		Nos. 427-430 (4)	13.00	13.00

Souvenir Sheets
431	A97	20k multicolored	9.00	9.00
432	A97	20k multicolored	9.00	9.00

Bird Type of 1987

1987   Litho.   Perf. 11x13
433	A91	5n Black-tailed cisticola	.35	.35
434	A91	10n White-winged starling	.35	.35
435	A91	40n Wattled crane	.35	.35
		Nos. 433-435 (3)	1.05	1.05

For surcharge see No. 491.

Intl. Fund for Agricultural Development (IFAD), 10th Anniv. — A98

1988, Apr. 2   Perf. 14
436	A98	50n Cassava crop	.25	.25
437	A98	2.50k Net fishing	.55	.55
438	A98	2.85k Cattle breeding	.65	.65
439	A98	10k Coffee picking	2.10	2.10
		Nos. 436-439 (4)	3.55	3.55

A99

1988, Sept. 12   Litho.   Perf. 12½
440	A99	50n Breast-feeding	.25	.25
441	A99	2k Growth monitoring	.55	.55
442	A99	2.85k Immunization	.65	.65
443	A99	10k Oral rehydration	2.10	2.10
		Nos. 440-443 (4)	3.55	3.55

UN child survival campaign.

A100

1988, Oct. 10   Litho.   Perf. 12½x13
444 A100 50n Asbestos cement .25 .25
445 A100 2.35k Textiles .50 .50
446 A100 2.50k Tea .55 .55
447 A100 10k Poultry 2.00 2.00
   Nos. 444-447 (4) 3.30 3.30

Preferential Trade Area Fair.

Intl. Red Cross and Red Crescent
Organizations, 125th Annivs. — A101

1988, Oct. 20   Perf. 14
448 A101 50n Famine relief .25 .25
449 A101 2.50k Giving first aid .55 .55
450 A101 2.85k Teaching first aid .70 .70
451 A101 10k Jean-Henri Du-
   nant 2.60 2.60
   Nos. 448-451 (4) 4.10 4.10

Endangered Species — A102

1988, Dec. 5   Litho.   Perf. 14
452 A102 50n Aardvark .30 .30
453 A102 2k Pangolin .65 .65
454 A102 2.85k Wild dog .85 .85
455 A102 20k Black rhinoceros 7.00 7.00
   Nos. 452-455 (4) 8.80 8.80

1988
Summer
Olympics,
Seoul
A103

1988, Dec. 30   Litho.   Perf. 14
456 A103 50n Boxing .25 .25
457 A103 2k Running .45 .45
458 A103 2.50k Hurdling .55 .55
459 A103 20k Soccer 4.00 4.00
   Nos. 456-459 (4) 5.25 5.25

Souvenir Sheets
460 A103 30k Tennis 5.25 5.25
461 A103 30k Martial arts 5.25 5.25

Frogs and
Toads
A104

1989, Jan. 25   Litho.   Perf. 12½
462 A104 50n Red toad .25 .25
463 A104 2.50k Puddle frog .70 .70
464 A104 2.85k Marbled reed
   frog .85 .85
465 A104 10k Young reed frogs 2.75 2.75
   Nos. 462-465 (4) 4.55 4.55

Bats
A105

50n, Common slit-faced. 2.50k, Little free-
tailed. 2.85k, Hildebrandt's horseshoe. 10k,
Peters' epauletted fruit.

1989, Mar. 22   Litho.   Perf. 12½x13
466 A105 50n multi .25 .25
467 A105 2.50k multi .70 .70
468 A105 2.85k multi .85 .85
469 A105 10k multi 2.75 2.75
   Nos. 466-469 (4) 4.55 4.55

A106

1989, May 2   Litho.   Perf. 12½
470 A106 50n Map of
   Zambia .90 .25
471 A106 6.85k Peace dove 3.50 3.50
472 A106 7.85k Papal arms 4.00 4.00
473 A106 10k Victoria Falls 6.00 6.00
   Nos. 470-473 (4) 14.40 13.75

State visit of Pope John Paul II, May 2-4.
For surcharges see #614, 616.

Edible Wild
Fruits — A107

50n, Parinari curatellifolia. 6.50k, Uapaca
kirkiana. 6.85k, Ficus capensis. 10k, Borassus
aethiopum.

1989, July 26   Litho.   Perf. 14½x15
474 A107 50n multicolored .25 .25
475 A107 6.50k multicolored 1.60 2.10
476 A107 6.85k multicolored 1.60 2.10
477 A107 10k multicolored 3.00 3.50
   Nos. 474-477 (4) 6.45 7.95

For surcharges see #613, 615.

Grasshoppers — A108

1989, Nov. 8   Litho.   Perf. 14x13½
478 A108 70n Phamphagid .25 .25
479 A108 10.40k Pyrgomorphid 2.10 2.25
480 A108 12.50k Brown katydid 2.50 2.75
481 A108 15k Bush locust 3.00 3.75
   Nos. 478-481 (4) 7.85 9.00

No. 480 misspelled "Catydid."

Christmas — A109

Flowers.

1989, Dec. 6   Litho.   Perf. 14½
482 A109 70n Fireball .25 .25
483 A109 10.40k Flame lily 1.30 1.40
484 A109 12.50k Foxglove lily 1.90 2.10
485 A109 20k Vlei lily 3.00 3.50
   Nos. 482-485 (4) 6.45 7.25

Stamp
World
London
'90
A110

Designs: 1.20k, Lusaka Main P.O., van,
mailman, bicycle. 19.50k, Zambia #220.
20.50k, Rhodesia and Nyasaland #164A,
Northern Rhodesia #1. 50k, Great Britain #1,
Maltese Cross cancel in red.

Unwmk.
1990, May 2   Litho.   Perf. 14
486 A110 1.20k multicolored .30 .30
487 A110 19.50k multicolored 3.25 3.25
488 A110 20.50k multicolored 3.25 3.25
489 A110 50k multicolored 6.50 6.50
   Nos. 486-489 (4) 13.30 13.30

Nos. 379, 381-387, 433 Surcharged

No. 492   No. 497

1989, July 1   Perf. 11x13
490 A91 70n on 35n #379 1.00 .25
491 A91 3k on 5n #433 1.25 .40

Size: 25x38½mm
Perf. 14
492 A91 8k on 1.25k #382 1.50 1.00
493 A91 9.90k on 1.70k #384 1.75 1.75
494 A91 10.40k on 1.60k #383 1.75 1.75
495 A91 12.50k on 1k #381 2.00 2.00
496 A91 15k on 1.95k #385 2.00 2.00
497 A91 20k on 2k #386 3.00 3.00
498 A91 20.35k on 5k #387 3.00 3.00
   Nos. 490-498 (9) 17.25 15.15

**Nos. 242, 244-245, 247-248 251, 253
Surcharged in Black, Orange
Brown, Red Brown, or Violet**

a   b

c

1989   Perf. 14½
Size: 22x26mm
499 A64(a) 1.20k on 35n
   #248 (OB) .25 .25
500 A64(b) 3.75k on 5n #242 .40 .40
501 A64(b) 8.11k on 10n
   #244 1.00 1.00
502 A64(b) 9k on 30n
   #247 1.00 1.00
Size: 37x25mm
Perf. 14
503 A64(b) 10k on 75n
   #251 1.00 1.00
504 A64(c) 18.50k on 2k #253 2.00 2.00
Size: 22x26mm
Perf. 14½
505 A64(a) 19.50k on 12n
   #244A
   (RB) 4.00 4.00

506 A64(a) 20.50k on 18n
   #245 (V) 2.00 1.75
   Nos. 499-506 (8) 11.65 11.40
Issued: #500-504, 7/1; others, 11/1.

World Cup Soccer
Championships,
Italy — A111

Soccer players in various positions.

1990, July 7   Litho.   Perf. 14
507 A111 1.20k multicolored .25 .25
508 A111 18.50k multicolored 2.50 2.50
509 A111 19.50k multicolored 2.50 2.50
510 A111 20.50k multicolored 2.50 2.50
   Nos. 507-510 (4) 7.75 7.75

Souvenir Sheet
510A A111 50k multicolored 13.00 13.00

Southern African Development Coordination Conf. (SADCC), 10th
Anniv. — A112

Map of SADCC members and: 1.20k, Truck.
19.50k, Telecommunications. 20.50k,
Regional cooperation. 50k, Coal transport by
cable car.

1990, July 23   Perf. 12½
511 A112 1.20k multicolored .30 .25
512 A112 19.50k multicolored 2.25 2.25
513 A112 20.50k multicolored 2.25 2.25
514 A112 50k multicolored 7.50 7.50
   Nos. 511-514 (4) 12.30 12.25

Independence, 26th Anniv. — A113

1.20k, Agriculture. 19.50k, Shoe factory.
20.50k, Satellite communications. 50k, Mother
and child statue.

1990, Oct. 23   Litho.   Perf. 14
515 A113 1.20k multicolored .25 .25
516 A113 19.50k multicolored 1.25 1.25
517 A113 20.50k multicolored 1.40 1.40
518 A113 50k multicolored 3.00 3.00
   Nos. 515-518 (4) 5.90 5.90

Small Carnivores — A114

1990, Nov. 12
519 A114 1.20k Genet .30 .30
520 A114 18.50k Civet 3.00 3.00
521 A114 19.50k Serval 3.25 3.25
522 A114 20.50k African wild
   cat 3.50 3.50
   Nos. 519-522 (4) 10.05 10.05

Intl. Literacy
Year — A115

Children's stories — 1.20k, Bird and the
Snake. 18.50k, Hare and the Leopard. 19.50k,
Mouse and Lion. 20.50k, Hare and the Hippo.

1991, Jan. 11   Litho.   Perf. 14
523	A115	1.20k multi	.30	.30
524	A115	18.50k multi	1.90	1.90
525	A115	19.50k multi	2.75	2.75
526	A115	20.50k multi	3.00	3.00
		Nos. 523-526 (4)	7.95	7.95

Bird Type of 1987

10n, Livingstone's flycatcher. 15n, Bar-
winged weaver. 30n, Purple-throated cuckoo
shrike. No. 530, Red-billed helmet shrike.
1.20k, Western bronze-naped pigeon. 15k,
Corn crake. 20k, Dickinson's grey kestrel. 50k,
Denham's bustard.

1990-91   Litho.   Perf. 11x13
527	A91	10n multicolored	1.00	.50
528	A91	15n multicolored	1.00	.50
529	A91	30n multicolored	1.75	.50
530	A91	50n multicolored	1.75	.50
531	A91	50n like #527	1.75	.70
532	A91	1k like #528	2.00	.30
533	A91	1.20k multicolored	2.00	.30
534	A91	2k like #529	2.00	.75
535	A91	3k like #530	2.00	.75
536	A91	5k like #533	2.25	.75

Size: 25x38½mm
Perf. 14
537	A91	15k multicolored	1.75	.70
538	A91	20k multicolored	3.25	2.00
539	A91	20.50k like #538	1.75	1.00
540	A91	50k multicolored	2.75	2.25
		Nos. 527-540 (14)	27.00	11.50

Issued: #533, 1k, 2k, 3k, 5k, 20k, 5/7/91;
others, 10/30.

Soy Beans — A116

1k, Woman cooking. 2k, Soy bean seed. 5k,
Woman feeding child. 20k, Malnourished,
healthy children. 50k, Pres. Kaunda, child.

1991, June 28   Litho.   Perf. 13½
548	A116	1k multicolored	.25	.25
549	A116	2k multicolored	.25	.25
550	A116	5k multicolored	.25	.25
551	A116	20k multicolored	1.75	1.75
552	A116	50k multicolored	3.25	3.25
		Nos. 548-552 (5)	5.75	5.75

United Church of Zambia / Rotary Foundation Project.

St. Ignatius of
Loyola (1491-
1556), Founder of
Jesuit
Order — A117

1k, Chilubula Church near Kasama. 2k,
Chikuni Church near Monze. 20k, Bishop
Joseph Du Pont. 50k, St. Ignatius of Loyola.

1991, July 18   Litho.   Perf. 13½
553	A117	1k multicolored	.30	.30
554	A117	2k multicolored	.30	.30
555	A117	20k multicolored	2.75	2.75
556	A117	50k multicolored	5.00	5.00
		Nos. 553-556 (4)	8.35	8.35

Flowering
Trees
A118

1k, Baobab. 2k, Dichrostachys cinerea. 10k,
Sterospermum kunthianum. 30k, Azanza
garckeana.

1991, Nov. 29   Litho.   Perf. 13½
557	A118	1k multicolored	.25	.25
558	A118	2k multicolored	.35	.25
559	A118	10k multicolored	2.00	1.50
560	A118	30k multicolored	3.75	3.75
		Nos. 557-560 (4)	6.35	5.75

**Queen Elizabeth II's Accession to
the Throne, 40th Anniv.**
Common Design Type
Perf. 14x13½
1992, Feb. 2   Litho.   Wmk. 373
561	CD349	4k multicolored	.25	.25
562	CD349	32k multicolored	1.10	1.10
563	CD349	35k multicolored	1.25	1.25
564	CD349	38k multicolored	1.25	1.25
565	CD349	50k multicolored	1.75	1.75
		Nos. 561-565 (5)	5.60	5.60

For surcharges see Nos. 690-692.

Orchids — A119

1k, Disa hamatopetala. 2k, Eulophia paivae-
ana. 5k, Eulophia quartiniana. 20k, Aerangis
verdickii.

Perf. 13x13½
1992, Feb. 28   Unwmk.
566	A119	1k multi	.60	.25
567	A119	2k multi	.60	.25
568	A119	5k multi	1.00	.60
569	A119	20k multi	4.75	4.75
		Nos. 566-569 (4)	6.95	5.85

Masks — A120

1992, Mar. 10
570	A120	1k Kasinja	.30	.30
571	A120	2k Chizaluke	.30	.30
572	A120	10k Mwanapweu	1.25	1.00
573	A120	30k Maliya	3.25	3.75
		Nos. 570-573 (4)	5.10	5.35

Antelopes
A121

1992, Sept. 14   Litho.   Perf. 14
574	A121	4k Bushbuck	.25	.25
575	A121	40k Eland	1.40	.85
576	A121	45k Roan antelope	1.40	.85
577	A121	100k Sable antelope	2.75	3.75
		Nos. 574-577 (4)	5.80	5.70

Airmail
Services,
75th
Anniv.
A122

1992, Nov. 24   Litho.   Perf. 14
578	A122	4k DH66 Hercules	.35	.30
579	A122	40k VC10	2.25	.95
580	A122	45k C Class flying boat	2.25	.95
581	A122	100k DC10	3.75	5.00
		Nos. 578-581 (4)	8.60	7.20

1992 Summer
Olympics,
Barcelona — A123

1992, Dec. 28
582	A123	10k 400-meter hurdles	.25	.25
583	A123	40k Boxing	.85	.55
584	A123	80k Judo	1.75	1.75
585	A123	100k Cycling	4.25	4.25
		Nos. 582-585 (4)	7.10	6.80

Christmas — A124

1992, Dec. 23   Litho.   Perf. 14
586	A124	10k Wise men	.25	.25
587	A124	80k Nativity scene	1.75	1.75
588	A124	90k Angels singing	2.00	2.00
589	A124	100k Angel, shepherds	2.00	2.00
a.		Souvenir sheet of 4, #586-589	12.00	12.00
		Nos. 586-589 (4)	6.00	6.00

For surcharges see Nos. 658-659.

Nos. 331-334 Surcharged

1991, Mar. 4   Litho.   Perf. 13½x13
590	A82	2k on 20n #331	35.00	5.75
591	A82	2k on 45n #332	.75	5.75
592	A82	2k on 55n #333	—	5.75
593	A82	2k on 5k #334	17.50	5.75

Stamps of 1981-89
Surcharged in
Black or Gold

Perfs. as Before
1991, July 5   Litho.
594	A83	2k on 20n #335	10.00	6.00
595	A81	2k on 25n #327 (G)	10.00	6.00
596	A64	2k on 28n #246	—	
597	A71	2k on 28n #289	—	
598	A73	2k on 28n #297	—	
600	A78	2k on 32n #317	30.00	8.00
601	CD337	2k on 35n #343	—	20.00
602	A87	2k on 35n #359	75.00	6.00
603	A90	2k on 35n #373	45.00	6.00
604	A79	2k on 45n #322	45.00	6.00
605	A80	2k on 45n #325	60.00	6.00
606	A81	2k on 45n #328	90.00	6.00
607	A83	2k on 45n #336	47.50	6.00
608	A87	2k on 1.60k #361	80.00	6.00
609	A84	2k on 1.70k #341	47.50	6.00
611	A81	2k on 5k #330	17.50	6.00
612	A84	2k on 5k #342	17.50	6.00
613	A107	2k on 6.50k #475	47.50	6.00
614	A106	2k on 6.85k #471	62.50	6.00
615	A107	2k on 6.85k #476	17.50	6.00
616	A106	2k on 7.85k #472	90.00	6.00

Numbers have been reserved for additional
surcharges in this set.

Waterfalls
A125

1993, Sept. 30   Litho.   Perf. 13½
617	A125	50k Nkundalila	.35	.35
618	A125	200k Chishimba	1.40	1.40
619	A125	250k Chipoma	1.75	1.75
620	A125	300k Lumangwe	2.50	2.50
		Nos. 617-620 (4)	6.00	6.00

For surcharges, see Nos. 1011-1014.

Healthy
Hearts — A126

1993, Oct. 20   Litho.   Perf. 14½
| 621 | A126 | O Runner | 1.10 | 1.10 |
| 622 | A126 | P Heart | 1.10 | 1.10 |

No. 621 sold for 50k and No. 622 sold for
80k on date of issue.

Sunbirds
A127

Designs: 20k, Bronze. 50k, Violet-backed.
No. 625, Marico. No. 626, Eastern double-collared. 100k, Scarlet-chested. 150k, Ban-
nerman's blue-headed. 200k, Oustalet's.
250k, Red and blue. 300k, Olive. 350k, Green-
headed. 400k, Scarlet tufted malachite. 500k,
Yellow-bellied. 800k, Copper. 1000k, Orange-
tufted. 1500k, Black. 2000k, Green-throated.

1993, May 30   Litho.   Perf. 13
623	A127	20k multicolored	.25	.25
624	A127	50k multicolored	.25	.25
625	A127	O multicolored	.25	.25
626	A127	P multicolored	.30	.30
627	A127	100k multicolored	.35	.35
628	A127	150k multicolored	.55	.55
629	A127	200k multicolored	.65	.65
630	A127	250k multicolored	.80	.80
631	A127	300k multicolored	.90	.90
632	A127	350k multicolored	1.10	1.10
633	A127	400k multicolored	1.25	1.25
634	A127	500k multicolored	1.50	1.50
635	A127	800k multicolored	2.50	2.50
636	A127	1000k multicolored	3.25	3.25
637	A127	1500k multicolored	5.00	5.00
638	A127	2000k multicolored	6.75	6.75
		Nos. 623-638 (16)	25.65	25.65

Nos. 625 sold for 50k and 626 sold for 80k
on date of issue.
For surcharge, see Nos. 997, 1090.

Snakes — A128

1994, Sept. 28 Litho. Perf. 14
639	A128	50k Tiger snake	.25	.25
640	A128	200k Egyptian cobra	1.60	1.60
641	A128	300k African python	2.50	2.50
642	A128	500k Green mamba	4.25	4.25
		Nos. 639-642 (4)	8.60	8.60

For surcharges, see Nos. 996, 1007-1010, 1175.

ILO, 75th Anniv. — A129

1995, Apr. 3 Litho. Perf. 14
643	A129	100k Road rehabilitation	.60	.60
644	A129	450k Block making	2.00	2.00

For surcharge see No. 781A.

Christmas Angels — A130

1995, Aug. 29 Perf. 14½x14
645	A130	100k shown	.40	.25
646	A130	300k With animals	1.10	.60
647	A130	450k Blowing horn, birds	1.25	1.25
648	A130	500k Playing drum	1.60	1.60
		Nos. 645-648 (4)	4.35	3.70

For surcharge, see No. 998.

UN, 50th Anniv. A131

1995, Dec. 30 Litho. Perf. 11½
Granite Paper
649	A131	700k multicolored	1.90	1.90

For surcharges, see Nos. 1038, 1121, 1152.

Natl. Monuments A132

Designs: 100k, David Livingstone. 300k, Mbereshi Mission. 450k, Von Lettow-Vorbeck. 500k, Niamkolo Church.

1996, Feb. 21 Litho. Perf. 14
650	A132	100k multicolored	.30	.25
651	A132	300k multicolored	.75	.75
652	A132	450k multicolored	1.25	1.25
653	A132	500k multicolored	1.50	1.50
		Nos. 650-653 (4)	3.80	3.75

For surcharges, see Nos. 870A, 1015-1018.

World Wildlife Fund A133

Designs: 200k, Saddle-billed stork. 300k, Black-cheeked lovebird. 500k, Two black-cheeked lovebirds. 900k, Saddle-billed stork with young.

1996, Nov. 27 Litho. Perf. 14x14½
654	A133	200k multicolored	.50	.50
655	A133	300k multicolored	.65	.65
656	A133	500k multicolored	1.00	1.00
657	A133	900k multicolored	1.75	1.75
a.		Sheet of 4, #654-657	125.00	125.00
		Nos. 654-657 (4)	3.90	3.90

For surcharges, see Nos. 1003-1006.

Nos. 587-588 Surcharged

1996 Litho. Perf. 14
658	A124	(0) on 90k #588	1.75	1.75
659	A124	900k on 80k #587	3.00	3.00

No. 658 was valued at 500k on day of issue. Size and location of surcharge varies.

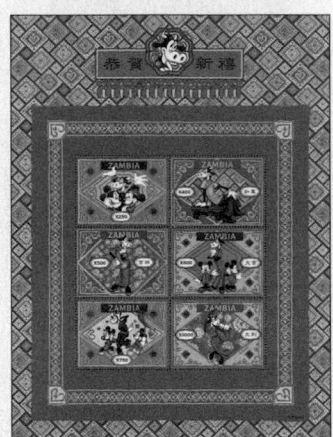

New Year 1997 (Year of the Ox) — A134

Disney characters posing for portrait in Chinese scene, vert.: #660: a, Clarabelle seated. b, Holding scroll. c, Playing musical instrument. d, On bicycle. e, Minnie, Mickey, Clarabelle. f, Holding mirror.
No. 661: a, 250k, Faces of Minnie, Mickey, Clarabelle Cow. b, 400k, Clarabelle seated. c, 500k, Clarabelle standing. d, 600k, Mickey, Clarabelle, Minnie dressed in Chinese outfits. e, 750k, Minnie, Clarabelle, Mickey dancing. f, 1000k, Clarabelle with parasol.

1997, Jan. 28 Litho. Perf. 14x13½
660	A134	500k Sheet of 6, #a.-f.	8.50	8.50
661	A134	Sheet of 6, #a.-f.	8.50	8.50

No. 660 contains six 35x61mm stamps.

Endangered Species — A135

Species of the world, each 500k: No. 662: a, Spider monkey. b, Manatee. c, Jaguar. d, Puerto Rican parrot. d, Green sea turtle. e, Harpy eagle.
Species of Africa, each 1000k: No. 663a, Black rhinoceros. b, Leopard. c, Chimpanzee. d, Zebra (Grants). e, Mountain gorilla. f, African elephant.
Each, 3000k: No. 664, Lion (African). No. 665, Margay cat.

1997, Feb. 12 Perf. 14
662	A135	Sheet of 6, #a.-f.	7.50	7.50
663	A135	Sheet of 6, #a.-f.	15.00	15.00

Souvenir Sheets
664-665	A135	Set of 2	11.00	11.00

Deng Xiaoping (1904-97) — A136

Various portraits of Deng Xiaoping and: 800k, Flags, map of Hong Kong. 1000k, Flag, Hong Kong harbor. 2000k, Hong Kong at night, countdown clock. 2500k, World map with China highlighted.

1997, May 26 Litho. Perf. 14
666	A136	800k multicolored	2.50	2.50
667	A136	1000k multicolored	3.50	3.50

Souvenir Sheets
668	A136	2000k multicolored	5.00	5.00
669	A136	2500k multicolored	6.00	6.00

Nos. 666-667 were issued in sheets of 3 each. No. 669 contains one 72x47mm stamp.

Trains — A137

Locomotives: 200k, Suburban tank, Eastern Railway, France. 300k, Streamlined express, Belgian Natl. Railways. 500k, "Mountain" type express, Union Pacific Railroad. 900k, 2-8-2 "Mikado," Kenya & Uganda Railway. 1000k, 4-6-0 "Royal Scot," LM & S Railway. 1500k, 4-6-0 "Lord Nelson" type, Southern Railway.
No. 676, each 500k: a, Express, German State Railways. b, Express, "Duke of Abercorn," NCC (LMSR), Ireland. c, Heavy freight tank, Netherlands Railways. d, Express, Austrian Federal Railways. e, "Governor" class, Gold Coast Railways. f, 4-8-4 Express, Canadian Natl. Railways.
Each 3000k: No. 677, Diesel-electric passenger, Royal Siamese State Railways. No. 678, "Pacific" type, South African Railways.

1997, June 2
670-675	A137	Set of 6	6.50	6.50
676	A137	Sheet of 6, #a.-f.	6.25	6.25

Souvenir Sheets
677-678	A137	Set of 2	11.00	11.00

Butterflies and Moths — A138

300k, No. 683a, Gaudy commodore. 500k, No. 683b, African moon moth. 700k, No. 683c, Emperor moth. No. 682, 900k, Emperor swallowtail.

1997, Aug. 8 Litho. Perf. 14
679-682	A138	Set of 4	11.00	11.00
683	A138	900k Sheet of 4, #a.-c., #682	17.50	17.50

Queen Elizabeth II and Prince Philip, 50th Wedding Anniv. — A139

No. 684, each 500k: a, Queen Elizabeth II. b, Royal arms. c, Queen wearing crown,

Prince in uniform. d, Queen, Prince riding in open carriage. e, Buckingham Palace. f, Prince waving.
3200k, Queen, Prince waving from balcony.

1997, Aug. 26 Litho. Perf. 14
684	A139	Sheet of 6, #a.-f.	8.00	8.00

Souvenir Sheet
685	A139	3200k multicolored	8.00	8.00

Paul P. Harris (1868-1947), Founder of Rotary, Intl. — A140

1000k, First Rotarians, Silvester Schiele, Harris, Hiram Shorey, Gus Loehr, portrait of Harris.
3200k, Zambian interactors with retirees.

1997, Aug. 27
686	A140	1000k multicolored	4.75	4.75

Souvenir Sheet
687	A140	3200k multicolored	6.25	6.25

Heinrich von Stephan (1831-97), Founder of UPU — A141

Each 1000k, Portrait of Von Stephan and: #688a, World Postal Congress, Berne, 1874. #688b, UPU emblem. #688c, Savannah, paddle steamer, 1819.
3200k, Von Stephan, Prussian postilion, 1715.

1997, Aug. 28
688	A141	Sheet of 3, #a.-c.	6.75	6.75

Souvenir Sheet
689	A141	3200k multicolored	5.75	5.75

Nos. 562-564 Surcharged

1997, Sept. 19 Litho. Perf. 14x13½
690	CD349	500k on 35k	1.75	.75
691	CD349	(0) on 32k	1.75	.90
692	CD349	900k on 38k	3.50	3.50
		Nos. 690-692 (3)	7.00	5.15

No. 691 was valued at 600k on day of issue.

Owls — A142

300k, #697b, Verreaux's eagle owl. 500k, #697c, Pel's fishing owl. 700k, #697a, Barn owl. #696, Spotted eagle owl.

1997, Dec. 18 — Litho. — Perf. 14

693	A142	300k multicolored	.80 .80
694	A142	500k multicolored	1.40 1.40
695	A142	700k multicolored	2.00 2.00
696	A142	900k multicolored	2.40 2.40
		Nos. 693-696 (4)	6.60 6.60

Sheet of 4

697	A142	900k #a.-c., #696	10.00 10.00

Christmas — A143

Entire paintings or details, sculpture: No. 698, 50k, Winged Victory of Samothrace. No. 699, 50k, Ognissanti Madonna, by Giotto. No. 700, 100k, Angel, by Antonio Pollaiuolo. No. 701, 100k, Angel of the Annunciation, by Jacopo da Pontormo. No. 702, 500k, No. 703, 1000k, The Virgin and Child Enthroned Among Angels and Saints, by Benozzo Gozzoli.
Each 3200k: No. 704, All of the Rebel Angels, detail, by Rubens. No. 705, The Resurrection of the Dead, by Joseph Christian.

1997, Dec. 18 — Litho. — Perf. 14

698-703	A143	Set of 6	5.75 5.75

Souvenir Sheets

704-705	A143	Set of 2	11.50 11.50

No. 704 incorrectly inscribed "The Virgin and Child Enthroned Among Angels and Saints, by Bonozzo Gozzoli."

Diana, Princess of Wales (1961-97) — A144

Various portraits with color of sheet margin: No. 706, Pale green. No. 707, Pale yellow.
Each 2500k: No. 708, Touching hand of blind man (in sheet margin). No. 709, With Barbara Bush (in sheet margin).

1997

706	A144	500k Sheet of 6, #a.-f.	9.00 9.00
707	A144	700k Sheet of 6, #a.-f.	11.00 11.00

Souvenir Sheets

708-709	A144	Set of 2	10.50 10.50

PAPU (Pan African Postal Union), 18th Anniv. A145

Designs: 500k, Kobus leche kafuensis. (O), Dove carrying letter over map. 900k, Emblem of dove carrying letter.

1998 — Perf. 14½

710	A145	500k multicolored	1.40 1.40
711	A145	(O) multicolored	1.75 1.75
712	A145	900k multicolored	2.25 2.25
		Nos. 710-712 (3)	5.40 5.40

No. 711 was valued at 600k on day of issue. For surcharges, see Nos. 1019-1021.

Mahatma Gandhi (1869-1948) — A146

Portraits of Gandhi: 250k, As law student in London, 1888. 500k, With Nehru, 1946. No. 715, (O), In front of Red Fort, New Dehli. 900k, At prayer.
2000k, Gandhi at 2nd Round Table Conference, London, 1931.

1998, Jan. 30 — Litho. — Perf. 13½

713-716	A146	Set of 4	16.00 16.00

Souvenir Sheet

717	A146	2000k multicolored	13.00 13.00

No. 715 was valued at 600k on day of issue. Nos. 713, 715-717 are vert.
For surcharges, see Nos. 911-912.

Flowers — A147

Designs: No. 718, Lantana camara. No. 719, Clusia rosea. No. 720, Nymphaea hybrida. No. 721, Portulaca grandiflora.
No. 722: a, Hibiscus rosa-sinensis. b, Plumeria. c, Erythrina variegata. d, Bauhinia blakeana. e, Carissa grandiflora. f, Cordia sebestena. g, Couroupita guianensis. h, Eustoma grandiflorum. i, Passiflora.
3200k, Strelitzia reginae, horiz.

1998, Feb. 27 — Litho. — Perf. 14

718-721	A147	500k Set of 4	5.00 5.00
722	A147	500k Sheet of 9, #a.-i.	11.00 11.00

Souvenir Sheet

723	A147	3200k multicolored	16.00 16.00

New Year 1998 (Year of the Tiger) — A148

Chinese symbols and stylized tigers, each 700k: No. 724: a, Looking right. b, Looking left. c, Facing forward, denomination UL. d, Facing forward, denomination UR.
1500k, Tiger, symbols on both sides.

1998 — Litho. — Perf. 14

724	A148	Sheet of 4, #a.-d.	6.25 6.25

Souenir Sheet

725	A148	1500k multicolored	4.00 4.00

Sites of India — A149

Designs: a, Taj Mahal, Agra. b, Gateway to India, Calcutta. c, Great Imambara Mosque, Lucknow.

1998

726	A149	900k Sheet of 3, #a.-c.	7.25 7.25

Art of India — A150

No. 727, each 700k: a, Ragmala, School of Mewar, 17th cent. b, Babur Nama, Mogul School, 16th cent. c, Hamza Nama, Mogul School, 16th cent. d, Meghamallar, School of Mewar, 16th cent.
2500k, Hindola Raga, School of Deccan, 17th-18th cent.

1998

727	A150	Sheet of 4, #a.-d.	8.25 8.25

Souvenir Sheet

728	A150	2500k multicolored	8.00 8.00

1998 World Cup Soccer Championships, France — A151

No. 729, each 450k: a, Albert, Belgium. b, Bebeto, Brazil. c, Beckenbauer, W. Germany. d, Littbarski, W. Germany. e, Juninho, Brazil. f, Lineker, England. g, Lato, Poland. h, McCoist, Scotland.
No. 730, each 500k: a, Maier, W. Germany, 1974. b, Bellini, Brazil, 1958. c, Kempes, Argentina, 1978. d, Nazassi, Uruguay, 1930. e, Pele, Brazil, 1970. f, Beckenbauer, W. Germany, 1974. g, Combi, Italy, 1934. h, Zoff, Italy, 1982.
No. 731, each 500k: a, Koano, Rep. of Ireland. b, Seaman, England. c, Like #729b. d, Futre, Portugal. e, Ravanelli, Italy. f, Weah, Liberia. g, Bergkamp, Holland. h, Raducioiu, Romania.
Each 3200k: No. 732, Juninho, Brazil. No. 733, Romario, Brazil, horiz. No. 734, McCoist, Scotland, horiz.

1998, Apr. 17 — Perf. 13½x14, 14x13½
Sheets of 8, #a-h, + Label

729	A151	multi	5.25 5.25
730-731	A151	Set of 2	13.00 13.00

Souvenir Sheets

732-734	A151	Set of 3	13.50 13.50

Parrots — A152

No. 735, each 500k: a, Rainbow lorikeet. b, Budgerigar, blossom-headed parakeet. c, Blue-yellow macaw. d, Blue-crowned parrot. e, Golden conure. f, Sulphur-crested cockatoo.
No. 736, each 1000k: a, Ara ararauna. b, Ara chloropterd. c, Pale-headed rosellas. d, Northern rosella. e, Gang-gang cockatoo. f, Palm cockatoo.
Each 3200k: No. 737, Mulga parakeet. No. 738, Major Mitchell cockatoo, horiz.

1998, June 1 — Litho. — Perf. 14

735	A152	Sheet of 6, #a.-f.	6.00 6.00
736	A152	Sheet of 6, #a.-f.	12.00 12.00

Souvenir Sheets

737-738	A152	Set of 2	18.00 18.00

Mushrooms — A153

No. 739, 250k, Red-tufted wood tricholoma. No. 740, 250k, Chlorophyllum molybdites. No. 741, 450k, Stuntz's psilocybe. No. 742, 450k, Lepista sordida. No. 743, 500k, Lepiota. No. 744, 500k, Rosy gomphidius. No. 745, 900k, Cantharellus cybrina. No. 746, 900k, Olive-capped boletus. No. 747, 1000k, Showy volvaria. No. 748, 1000k, Sooty brown waxy cap.
No. 749, each 900k: a, Leller's boletus. b, Short-stemmed russula. c, Anise-scented clitocybe. d, Dung roundhead. e, Oak-loving collybia. f, Wine-red stropharia.
No. 750, each 900k: a, Flat-topped mushroom. b, Alice Eastwood's boletus. c, Pitted milky cap. d, Short-stemmed slippery jask. e, Rose-red russula. f, Zeller's tricholoma.
Each 3200k: No. 751, Honey mushroom. No. 752, Velvet-stemmed flammulina.

1998, July 1

739-748	A153	Set of 10	22.50 22.50

Sheets of 6

749-750	A153	Set of 2	22.50 22.50

Souvenir Sheets

751-752	A153	Set of 2	18.00 18.00

Nos. 749-752 are continuous designs.

Traditional Stories — A154

No. 755, each 2000k: a, like #753. b, like #754.

1998, Dec. 2 — Litho. — Perf. 14

753	A154	300k Luchela nganga	.90 .90
754	A154	500k Kasuli	1.40 1.40

Souvenir Sheet

755	A154	Sheet of 2, #a.-b.	6.00 6.00

Christmas.

Orchids A155

Designs, vert: No. 756, 100k, Paphiopedilum callosum. No. 757, 100k, Phaius tankervilleae. No. 758, 500k, Paphiopedilum fairrieanum. No. 759, 500k, Barkeria lindleyana. No. 760, 1000k, Laelia flava. No. 761, 1000k, Masdervallia unifloria, masdervallia angulifera.
No. 762, each 900k: a, Acacallis cyanea. b, Miltoniopsis phalaenopsis. c, Dendrobium bellatulum. d, Polystachya campyloglossa. e, Pleione bulbocodioides. f, Rhynchostylis gigantea. g, Cattleya lawrenceana. h, Sopbrolaelia. i, Laelia tenebrosa.
No. 763, each 900k: a, Acacallis cyanea, diff. b, Epidendrum gastropodium. c, Laelia rubescens. d, Paphiopedilum dayanum. e, Laelia lobata. f, Dendrobium crepidatum. g, Cattleya nobilior. h, Dendrobium johnsoniae. i, Trichopilia fragrans.
Each 4000k: No. 764, Cattleya maxima, vert. No. 765, Cattleya violacea.

1998, Dec. 23

756-761	A155	Set of 6	5.50 5.50

Sheets of 9

762-763	A155	Set of 2	17.50	17.50

Souvenir Sheets

764-765	A155	Set of 2	13.00	13.00

Classic Cars A156

Designs: 300k, Ferrari Daytona 365 GTB/4. 500k, Austin Healey Sprite. 900k, Gordon Keeble. 1000k, Alvis TD.

No. 770: a, Mercedes-Benz 300Sl. b, Chevrolet Corvair. c, AC Cobra 427. d, Aston Martin DB5. e, BMW 2002 Turbo. f, Cadillac Eldorado Brougham.

No. 771: a, Mercedes-Benz 280SE 3.5. b, Aston Martin DB2. c, Volkswagen Beetle. d, Lancia Aurelia B20 GT. e, Lamborghini 350 GT. f, Cisitalia 202 Coupe.

No. 771G: h, 1995 Ferrari 750 Pinnafarina. i, 1997 Federrari 312T2/77. j, 1983 Ferrari 208 Turbo. k, 1962 Ferrari Dino 268 SP. l, 1994 Ferrari F355 Berlinetta. m, Ferrari 250 GTE Coupe 2+2 California.

Each 4000k: No. 772, Citroen Light 15. No. 773, Austin Healey MKII 3000.

1998, Dec. 23

766-769	A156	Set of 4	5.00	5.00

Sheets of 6, #a-f

770-771G	A156	900k Set of 3	17.50	17.50

Souvenir Sheets

772-773	A156	Set of 2	17.50	17.50

New Year 1999 (Year of the Rabbit) — A157

Various rabbits, denomination at — #774 (each 700k): a, LL. b, LR. c, LL (scratching). d, LR (nose near ground).
2000k, Rabbit, vert.

1999, Jan. 4

774	A157	Sheet of 4, #a.-d.	4.75	4.75

Souvenir Sheet

775	A157	2000k multicolored	4.50	4.50

Trains A158

Locomotives: No. 776, (0), U20C Diesel electric, 1967. No. 777, 800k, 7th Class No. 70, 1900. No. 778, 800k, 15A Class Beyer-Garrat No. 401, 1950. No. 779, 900k, HP diesel electric, 1966. No. 780, 900k, 20th Class No. 708, 1954.
4000k, 7th Class No. 955, 1892.

1999, Feb. 1   Litho.   Perf. 14½

776-780	A158	Set of 5	6.25	6.25

Souvenir Sheet

781	A158	4000k multicolored	4.50	4.50

No. 776 was valued at 600k on day of issue.

No. 643 Surcharged

Methods and Perfs as Before

1999, June 1

781A	A129	500k on 100k multi	

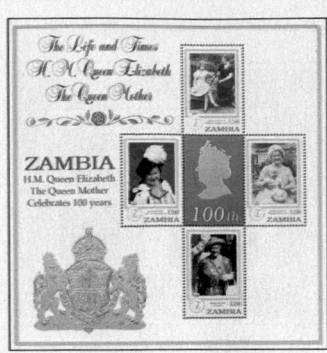

Queen Mother (b. 1900) — A159

No. 782: a, With Princess Elizabeth, 1936. b, Lady of the Garter. c, With Prince Andrew, 1960. d, At Ascot.
5000k, Wedding photograph, 1923.

1999, Sept. 1   Perf. 14

782	A159	2000k Sheet of 4, #a.-d., + label	9.50	9.50

Souvenir Sheet

Perf. 13¾

783	A159	5000k multicolored	6.50	6.50

No. 783 contains one 38x51mm stamp.

Dinosaurs A160

Designs: 50k, Dimetrodon. 100k, Deinonychus. 500k, Protoceratops. 900k, Heterodontosaurus. 1000k, Oviraptor. 1800k, Psittacosaurus.

No. 790, each 900k: a, Stegosaurus. b, Triceratops. c, Brontosaurus. d, Gallimimus. e, Saurolophus. f, Lambeosaurus. g, Centrosaurus. h, Edmontonia. i, Parasaurolophus.

No. 791, each 900k: a, Ceratosaurus. b, Daspletosaurus. c, Baryonyx. d, Ornitholestes. e, Troodon. f, Coelophysis. g, Tyrannosaurus. h, Allosaurus. i, Compsognathus.

Each 4000k: No. 792, Saltasaurus, vert. No. 793, Stygimoloch, vert.

1999, Sept. 27   Litho.   Perf. 14

784-789	A160	Set of 6	4.50	4.50

Sheets of 9

790-791	A160	Set of 2	14.50	14.50

Souvenir Sheets

792-793	A160	Set of 2	9.00	9.00

Johann Wolfgang von Goethe (1749-1832), German Poet — A161

No. 794, each 2000k: a, A drinking party in Amerbach's cellar. b, Goethe and Friedrich von Schiller. c, Faust falls in love with Margaret.
5000k, Angel.

1999, Oct. 4   Litho.   Perf. 14

794	A161	Sheet of 3, #a.-c.	5.00	5.00

Souvenir Sheet

795	A161	5000k org brn & brn	4.50	4.50

A162

Cats: 50k, White Devon Rex. 100k, Red Persian. 500k, Chartreux. 900k, Brown tabby Maine Coon.

No. 800, each 1000k, horiz.: a, Tortie point Himalayan. b, Blue mackerel tabby Scottish Fold. c, Chocolate lynx point Balinese. d, Havana Brown. e, Seal point Ragdoll. f, Silver shaded Persian.

No. 801, each 1000k, horiz.: a, Red spotted tabby Exotic Shorthair. b, Blue tortie smoke Persian. c, Brown classic tabby longhaired Scottish Fold. d, Spotted tabby American Bobtail. e, Silver spotted tabby Ocicat. f, Blue British Shorthair.

Each 4000k: No. 802, Silver tabby longhair Persian, horiz. No. 803, Tabby point Siamese.

1999, Oct. 18

796-799	A162	Set of 4	1.60	1.60

Sheets of 6, #a.-f.

800-801	A162	Set of 2	9.50	9.50

Souvenir Sheets

802-803	A162	Set of 2	7.00	7.00

A163

Dogs: 100k, Welsh corgi. 500k, Shetland sheepdog. 900k, Italian greyhound. 1000k, Tibetan spaniel.

No. 808, each 1000k, horiz.: a, Dalmatian. b, Shetland sheepdogs. c, Bearded collie. d, Eskimo. e, Basenji. f, Saluki.

No. 809, each 1000k, horiz.: a, Norwegian elkhound. b, Flat-coated retriever. c, St. Bernard. d, Basset hound, Pembroke Welsh corgi. e, Pembroke Welsh corgi, Pointer. f, Petit Basset Griffon Vendeen.

Each 4000k: No. 810, Whippet. No. 811, Rottweiler.

1999, Oct. 18

804-807	A163	Set of 4	2.25	2.25

Sheets of 6, #a.-f.

808-809	A163	Set of 2	9.50	9.50

Souvenir Sheets

810-811	A163	Set of 2	7.00	7.00

11th Intl. Conference on AIDS in Africa, Lusaka — A164

Designs: 500k, Emblem, waterfalls. 900k, Emblem, close-up view of waterfalls.

1999, Oct. 20

812-813	A164	Set of 2	2.00	2.00

Paintings by Zhang Daqian (1899-1983) — A165

No. 814, each 500k: a, Water Lily in the Rain. b, Chinghai Tribal Girl and a Black Hound. c, Taking a Nap. d, Monkey and Old Tree. e, Bird and Tree of Chin-Chang Mountain. f, Watching Waterfalls. g, On the Way to Switzerland and Austria. h, A Boat Brings the Wine. i, Brown Landscape. j, Nice Autumn.

No. 815: a, 1000k, White Water Lily, horiz. b, 2000k, Cloudy Waterfalls and Summer Mountain, horiz.

1999, Oct. 21   Perf. 13

814	A165	Sheet of 10, #a.-j.	3.75	3.75
815	A165	Sheet of 2, #a.-b.	2.10	2.10

China 1999 World Philatelic Exhibition, 22nd UPU Congress, Beijing. #815 contains two 52x39mm stamps.

A166

Flora & Fauna A167

Designs: 50k, Leatherback turtle. 100k, American kestrel. No. 818, 500k, Great blue heron. 900k, Mesene phareus. 1000k, Laeliocattleya. 1800k, Papilio cresphontes.

Each 500k: No. 822, Cairn's birdwing. No. 823, Pintail. No. 824, Rose. No. 825, Gray tree frog.

No. 826, each 700k: a, White-tailed tropicbird. b, Sooty tern. c, Laughing gull. d, Black skimmer. e, Brown pelican. f, Bottle-nosed dolphin. g, Common dolphin. h, Man in sailboat. i, Blue tang. j, Southern stingray. k, Hammerhead shark. l, Mako shark.

No. 827, each 700k: a, Heliconia. b, Purple-throated Carib. c, St. Vincent parrot. d, Bananaquit. e, prepona meander. f, Unidentified butterfly. g, Hawksbill turtle. h, Black-necked stilt. i, Banded butterflyfish. j, Porkfish. k, Seahorse. l, Chain moray eel.

No. 828: a, Baltimore oriole. b, Chipmunk. c, Blue jay. d, Monarch butterfly. e, Gray heron. f, Mallard. g, Canadian otter. h, American lotus. i, Fowler's toad. j, Bluegill sunfish. k, Rainbow trout. l, Terrapin.

Each 4000k: No. 829, Amazona guildingii. No. 830, Bottle-nosed dolphin, diff. No. 831, Fuchsia. No. 832, Red-banded pereute.

1999, Oct. 27

816-821	A166	Set of 6	4.25	4.25
822-825	A167	Set of 4	2.00	2.00

Sheets of 12, #a.-l.

826-827	A166	Set of 2	12.00	12.00
828	A167	700k multi	6.00	6.00

Souvenir Sheets

829-830	A166	Set of 2	7.50	7.50
831-832	A167	Set of 2	7.50	7.50

IBRA '99 — A168

Trains: 1000k, Crampton. 3200k, Post standard 2-8-4 tank locomotive.

1999   **Perf. 14x14¾**
833-834   A168   Set of 2   3.00   3.00

Souvenir Sheets

PhilexFrance '99 — A169

Each 5000k: #835, Paris-Orleans Railway 4-4-0. #836, paris, Lyon & Mediterranean Railway 2-4-2.

1999   **Perf. 14¼**
835-836   A169   Set of 2   7.50   7.50

Wedding of Prince Edward and Sophie Rhys-Jones — A170

No. 837: a, 500k, Sophie. b, 900k, Couple. c, 100k, Edward.
3000k, Couple kissing.

1999   **Perf. 14**
837   A170   Sheet of 3, #a.-c.   1.75   1.75

Souvenir Sheet
838   A170   3000k multi   2.10   2.10

Birds — A171

Designs: 50k, Blacksmith plover. 100k, Sacred ibis. 200k, Purple gallinule. 250k, Purple heron. 300k, Glossy ibis. 400k, Marabou stork. 450k, African spoonbill. 500k, African finfoot. O, No. 847, Knot-billed duck. 600k, Darter. 700k, African skimmer. 800k, Spurwinged goose. 900k, Hammerkop. 1000k, White pelican. 1500k, Black-winged stilt. 2000k, Black-crowned night heron.

1999, Dec. 20   Litho.   Perf. 14½x15
839-854   A171   Set of 16   14.00   14.00

No. 847 sold for 500k on day of issue. Design size of No. 847 is 30½mm wide. See Nos. 927-930.

Flowers — A172

Various flowers making up a photomosaic of Princess Diana, each 1000k.

1999, Dec. 31   **Perf. 13¾**
855   A172   Sheet of 8, #a.-h.   8.00   8.00

Millennium — A173

Highlights of 1950-2000: a, Venice Biennale shows Jackson Pollock and Abstract Expressionism. b, James Watson and Francis Crick piece together the structure of DNA. c, Edmund Hillary reaches the summit of Mount Everest. d, Jonas Salk's polio vaccine. e, Ghana achieves independence. f, Yuri Gagarin becomes 1st man in space. g, Rachel Carson and the beginning of the environmental movement. h, Indira Gandhi becomes Prime Minister of India. i, 1st successful heart transplant. j, Apollo 11 lands on moon. k, Microprocessor developed. l, Richard Nixon visits People's Republic of China. m, Qin Shi Huang Mausoleum discovered. n, Stephen Hawking proposes new ideas about the universe and black holes. o, Margaret Thatcher elected 1st female Prime Minister of Great Britain. p, Mikhail Gorbachev becomes leader of Soviet Union. q, Fall of the Berlin Wall. r, Nelson Mandela elected Pres. of South Africa.

2000, Feb. 7   **Perf. 12¾x12½**
856   A173   500k Sheet of 18, #a.-r., + label   8.00   8.00

Butterflies A174

400k, Papilio antimachus. 450k, Amauris niavius. 500k, Charaxes smaragdalis. 800k, Charaxes zelica. 900k, Cymothoe confusa. 1000k, #862, Labobunea ansorgei.
No. 863, each 1000k: a, Palla ussheri. b, Euphaedra aureola. c, Graphium cyrnus nuscyrus. d, Salamis cacta. e, Salamis parhassus. f, Charaxes pelias.

No. 864, each 1000k: a, Large Spotted Acraea. b, Palla (orange wings). c, Palla (blue wings). d, Gold-banded Forester (white wings). o, Figtree blue. f, Gold-banded Forester (pink wings).
No. 865, each 1500k: a, Colotis ione. b, Charaxes acraeoides. c, Euphaedra edwardsi. d, Colotis phisadia. e, Charaxes lydiae. f, Euphaedra eupaulus.
No. 866, each 1500k: a, Papilio zalmoxis. b, Amauris niavius. c, Salamis cytora. d, Salamis temora. e, Charaxes eupale. f, Cymothoe hypatha.
Each 5000k: No. 867, Euphaedra ceres. No. 868, Cymothoe fumana. No. 869, Euphaedra spatiosa. No. 870, Euryphene gambiae.

2000, Feb. 8   **Perf. 14**
857-862   A174   Set of 6   5.00   5.00

Sheets of 6, #a.-f.
863-864   A174   Set of 2   8.50   8.50
865-866   A174   Set of 2   12.50   12.50

Souvenir Sheets
867-870   A174   Set of 4   16.00   16.00

No. 650
Surcharged

Method and Perf. as Before
2000, Apr. 11
870A   A132   700k on 100k multi

Orchids — A175

No. 871, each 1500k: a, Paphiopedilum sioux. b, Phalaenopsis amabilis hybrid. c, Thelymitza ixioides. d, Phalaenopsis schilleriana.
No. 872, each 1500k: a, Miltoniopsis pansy orchid. b, Paphiopedilum venustum. c, Odontoglossum grande. d, Vanda sanderiana alba. e, Phalaenopsis violacea. f, Pleione alishan.
No. 873, each 1500k: a, Cyrtorchis arcuata. b, Cymbioiella rhodochila. c, Unidentified orchid. d, Eulophia quartiana. e, Augraecum montanum. f, Polystacha vulcanica.
No. 874, each 1500k, vert.: a, Catasetum splendens. b, Miltonia spectabilis. c, Stenia pallida. d, Cozacias spatulata. e, Eriopsis sceptzum. f, Paphinia cristata.
Each 5000k: No. 875, Cattleya hybrid. No. 876, Brachycorythis kalbreyeri.

2000, May 16   Litho.   Perf. 14
871   A175   Sheet of 4, #a.-d.   5.00   5.00

Sheets of 6, #a.-f.
872-874   A175   Set of 3   20.00   20.00

Souvenir Sheets
875-876   A175   Set of 2   9.00   9.00

The Stamp Show 2000, London.

Popes — A176

No. 877: a, Liberius, 352-66. b, Linus, 67-76. c, Lucius I, 253-54. d, Marcellinus, 296-304. e, Mark, 336. f, Pius I, 140-155.
No. 878: a, Simplicius, 468-83. b, Siricius, 384-99. c, Stephen I, 254-57. d, Urban I, 222-30. e, Zephyrinus, 199-217. f, Zosimus, 417-18.
No. 879, Silverius, 536-37. No. 880, Vigilius, 537-55.

2000, July 7   Litho.   Perf. 13¾
Sheets of 6, #a-f
877-878   A176   1500k Set of 2   11.00   11.00

Souvenir Sheets
879-880   A176   5000k Set of 2   8.00   8.00

Birds — A177

400k, Great Indian hornbill. 500k, Cockatiel. 600k, Amazonian umbrellabird. 1000k, Unidentified bird. 2000k, Rainbow lorikeet.
No. 886: a, Green aracari. b, Eclectus parrot. c, Crimson topaz. d, King bird of paradise. e, keel-billed toucan. f, Australian king parrot. g, Sailboat. h, Hyacinth macaw.
No. 887: a, Resplendent quetzal. b, Carmine bee-eater. c, Wattled false sunbird. d, Palm trees. e, Sulphur-crested cockatoo. f, Great blue turaco. g, Crimson rosella. h, Malabar pied hornbill.
No. 888: a, Yellow-crowned amazon. b, Green turaco. c, Butterfly and palm trees. d, Plate-billed mountain toucan. e, Scarlet macaw. f, Blue and yellow macaw. g, Guianan cock of the rock. h, Palm cockatoo.
No. 889, Red-crested pochard. No. 890, Toco toucan, horiz. No. 891, Blue and yellow macaw, horiz.

2000, Sept. 8   **Perf. 14**
881-885   A177   Set of 5   3.25   3.25

Sheets of 8, #a-h
886-888   A177   1500k Set of 3   25.00   25.00

Souvenir Sheets
889-891   A177   5000k Set of 3   10.50   10.50

Birds — A178

Designs: 700k, Red-backed shrike. 800k, Golden pipet. No. 894, 1200k, Orange-breasted sunbird. No. 895, 1400k, Eurasian goldfinch. 1500k, Red-crested turaco. 3000k, Carmine bee-eater.
No. 898, 1000k: a, Gouldian finch. b, Parrot finch. c, Purple grenadier. d, Red bishop. e, Red-crested cardinal. f, Spectacled monarch. g, Crimson chat. h, Necklaced laughing thrush. i, Chestnut-backed jewel babbler.
No. 899, 1200k: a, Lovely cotinga. b, Andean cock-of-the-rock. c, Orange-bellied

leafbird. d, Pin-tailed manakin. e, Pin-tailed broadbill. f, Rufous motmot. g, American goldfinch. h, Double-barred finch. i, Golden-breasted starling.

No. 900, 1400k: a, Campo oriole. b, Hooded warbler. c, Purple honeycreeper. d, Blue-faced honeyeater. e, Scarlet tanager. f, Green-headed tanager. g, Blue-breasted fairy wren. h, Banded pitta. i, Wire-tailed manakin.

No. 901, 5000k, Pin-tailed sandgrouse. No. 902, 5000k, Black bustard.

2000, Sept. 8　　Litho.　　Perf. 14
892-897　A178　Set of 6　　　5.75　5.75
Sheets of 9, #a-i
898-900　A178　Set of 3　　21.50　21.50
Souvenir Sheets
901-902　A178　Set of 2　　　7.00　7.00

African Creation Legends A179

Designs: Nos, 903, 906a, 600k, Creation in Clay. Nos. 904, 906b, 1000k, The Chameleon and the Lizard. Nos. 905, 906c, 1400k, Why the Stones Do Not Die.

Perf. 14¼x14½
2000, Nov. 10　　　　　　Litho.
903-905　A179　Set of 3　　　1.60　1.60
With Brown Frame
906　A179　Horiz. strip of 3, #a-c　1.60　1.60
Souvenir Sheet
No Frame Around Stamp
907　A179　3500k The Rooster in
　　　　　　　　the Sky　　　1.90　1.90

No. 906 issued in sheets of 9 stamps. For surcharge, see No. 1106.

Common Market for Eastern and Southern Africa A180

Designs: 600k, Map of member nations. 700k, Truck crossing border. 1000k, Exchange of money and sale of goods at border.

2000
908-910　A180　Set of 3　　　2.25　2.25

Nos. 713-714 Surcharged

2000　Method and Perf. as Before
911　A146　1200k on 250k multi
912　A146　1500k on 500k multi

UN High Commissioner for Refugees, 50th Anniv. — A181

Designs: 700k, Children receiving food. 1500k, Woman carrying child.

Perf. 13¾x14¼
2001, Mar. 13　　　　　　Litho.
915-916　A181　Set of 2　　　1.60　1.60

A182

Animals — A183

Designs: 500k, African buffalo. 1000k, Cheetah, vert. No. 919, 2000k, Female elephant. 3200k, Ruffed lemur, vert.

No. 921, 2000k: a, Crimson-breasted shrike. b, Common bee-eater. c, Blue monkey. d, Chimpanzee. e, Bush baby. f, Genet.

No. 922, 2000k, horiz.: a, Defassa waterbuck. b, Crowned crane. c, Red hartebeest. d, Pygmy hippopotamus. e, White rhinoceros. f, Giant forest hog.

No. 923, 2000k, horiz.: a, Cheetah. b, Three adult, one young impala. c, Four adult impalas. d, Warthog. e, Two lions. f, Four lions.

No. 924, 6000k, Bull elephant. No. 925, 6000k, Black rhinoceros. No. 926, 6000k, Zebras, vert.

Perf. 13¼x13½, 13½x13¼
2001, Mar. 30
917-920　A182　Set of 4　　　4.75　4.75
Sheets of 6, #a-f
921-923　A183　Set of 3　　22.50　22.50
Souvenir Sheets
924-926　A182　Set of 3　　11.00　11.00

Bird Type of 1999

Designs: No. 927, O, Knob-billed duck. No. 928, A, Blacksmith plover. No. 929, B, Sacred ibis. No. 930, C, Purple gallinule.

Perf. 14½x14¾
2001, Mar. 19　　　　　　Litho.
927-930　A171　Set of 4　　　3.50　3.50

Nos. 927-930 each sold for 700k, 1200k, 1400k, and 1500k respectively on day of issue. No. 927 is dated "2000" and has a design width of 31½mm. No. 847 has no date and has a design width of 30½mm.

For surcharges, see Nos. 1119, 1120, 1147, 1148, 1178, 1179, 1182.

Total Solar Eclipse, June 21 — A184

Eclipse and: 1000k, Woman. 1500k, Bird. 1700k, Lizard. 1800k, Elephant and man. 2200k, Man.

2001, June 1　　Litho.　　Perf. 13¾
931-935　A184　Set of 5　　　5.00　5.00

Phila Nippon '01, Japan — A185

Designs: No. 936, 500k, Senya Nakamura as Toknatsu, by Kiyomasu Torii I. No. 937, 500k, Kantaro Sanjo II and Monosuke Ichikawa I, by Okumura Masanobu, 1720. No. 938, 1000k, Kantaro Sanjo and Monosuke Ichikawa, by Masanobu, c. 1730. No. 939, 1000k, Standing Figure of a Woman, by Kiyomasu Torii I. 1500k, Ono no Komachi, by Masanobu. 1800k, Dog Bringing a Love Letter, by Shigenaga.

No. 942, 3200k: a, Matsue Nakamura as a Cat Woman, by Shunsho. b, Kantaro Sanjo With Branch of Bamboo, by Kiyomasu Torii I. c, Kinsaku Yamashika I as Peddler, by Kiyomasu Torii I. d, Portrait of an Actor, by Shunsho.

No. 943, 3200k: a, Kumetaro Nakamura I, by Shunsho. b, Actor in Female Role, by Kiyomasu Torii I. c, Kikunojo Segawa Leaning on Sugoroku Board, by Kiyomasu Torii I. d, Gennosuke Ichikawa as a Wakashu, by Kiyomasu Torii I.

No. 944, 6000k, Akashi of the Tamaya, by Ryukoku Hishikawa. No. 945, 6000k, Events of Year in the Floating World, by Moroshige, horiz.

2001, July 4　　　　　　Perf. 14
936-941　A185　Set of 6　　　4.00　4.00
Sheets of 4, #a-d
942-943　A185　Set of 2　　14.00　14.00
Souvenir Sheets
944-945　A185　Set of 2　　　6.50　6.50

SOS Children's Village A186

2001, July 30
946　A186　2500k multi　　　1.60　1.60

Royal Navy Submarines, Cent. — A187

No. 947, horiz.: a, HMS Tabard. b, HMS Opossum. c, HMS Unicorn. d, HMS Churchill. e, HMS Victorious. f, HMS Triumph.

6000k, Lieutenant Commander Malcolm David Wanklyn.

2001, July 30
947　A187　2000k Sheet of 6, #a-f　8.00　8.00
Souvenir Sheet
948　A187　6000k multi　　　4.25　4.25

Giuseppe Verdi (1813-1901), Opera Composer — A188

No. 949 — Actors in Falstaff : a, Benjamin Luxon (without hat). b, Luxon (with hat). c, Paul Plishke. d, Anne Collin.
8000k, Falstaff.

2001, July 30
949　A188　4000k Sheet of 4, #a-d　9.50　9.50
Souvenir Sheet
950　A188　8000k multi　　　5.50　5.50

Monet Paintings — A189

No. 951, horiz.: a, The Promenade at Argenteuil. b, View of the Argenteuil Plain from the Sannois Hills. c, The Seine at Argenteuil. d, The Basin at Argenteuil.
6000k, Rouen Cathedral Portal, Overcast Weather.

2001, July 30　　　　　　Perf. 13¾
951　A189　1500k Sheet of 4, #a-d　6.50　6.50
Souvenir Sheet
952　A189　6000k multi　　　6.50　6.50

Mao Zedong (1893-1976) — A190

No. 953 — Mao in: a, 1918. b, 1945. c, 1937.
4000k, Portrait.

2001, July 30
953　A190　3200k Sheet of 3, #a-c　7.00　7.00
Souvenir Sheet
954　A190　4000k multi　　　5.00　5.00

Queen Victoria (1819-1901) — A191

No. 955: a, As child. b, Wearing black dress. c, With child. d, With Prince Albert. e, Wearing crown and red sash. f, Wearing red dress. 7000k, Portrait.

2001, July 30   **Perf. 14**
955 A191 2000k Sheet of 6, #a-f   7.25 7.25
Souvenir Sheet
956 A191 7000k multi   6.00 6.00

Queen Elizabeth II, 75th Birthday — A192

No. 957: a, As infant. b, As child. c, As child, in garden. d, Wearing hat. 8000k, Wearing green and black hat.

2001, July 30
957 A192 4000k Sheet of 4, #a-d   8.00 8.00
Souvenir Sheet
958 A192 8000k multi   6.00 6.00
No. 957 contains four 28x42mm stamps.

First Zeppelin Flight, Cent. — A193

No. 959: a, LZ-1. b, Parseval PL25. c, LZ-3. d, Baldwin. e, LZ-129. f, Norge Nobile N1. No. 960, 700k, Graf Zeppelin, vert.

2001, July 30
959 A193 2000k Sheet of 6, #a-f   7.50 7.50
Souvenir Sheet
960 A973 700k multi   .40 .40
No. 960 contains one 38x51mm stamp.

Pres. F. J. T. Chiluba — A194

Chiluba: 1000k, Recieving Master's degree. 1500k, Signing forms. 1700k, With arm raised, horiz. 6000k, Receiving Master's degree, diff.

2001   **Litho.**   **Perf. 14**
961-963 A194   Set of 3   3.75 3.75
Souvenir Sheet
964 A194 6000k multi   5.50 5.50

Nobel Prizes, Cent. (in 2001) — A195

No. 965, 2000k — Peace laureates: a, Norman E. Borlaug, 1970. b, Lester B. Pearson, 1957. c, Intl. Red Cross, 1944. d, Anwar Sadat, 1978. e, Georges Pire, 1958. f, Linus Pauling, 1962.

No. 966, 2000k — Literature laureates: a, Isaac Bashevis Singer, 1978. b, Gao Xingjian, 2000. c, Claude Simon, 1985. d, Naguib Mahfouz, 1988. e, Camilo Jose Cela, 1989. f, Czeslaw Milosz, 1980.

No. 967, 2000k — Literature laureates: a, Seamus Heaney, 1995. b, Toni Morrison, 1993. c, Günter Grass, 1999. d, Wislawa Szymborska, 1996. e, Dario Fo, 1997. f, José Saramago, 1998.

No. 968, 6000k, George C. Marshall, Peace, 1953. No. 969, 6000k, Gerard Debreu, Economics, 1983. No. 970, 6000k, Robert W. Fogel, Economics, 1993.

2002, Feb. 11   **Litho.**   **Perf. 14**
Sheets of 6, #a-f
965-967 A195   Set of 3   17.50 17.50
Souvenir Sheets
968-970 A195   Set of 3   9.00 9.00

Souvenir Sheet

New Year 2002 (Year of the Horse) — A196

2002, Feb. 18   **Perf. 13¼**
971 A196 5000k multi   3.00 3.00

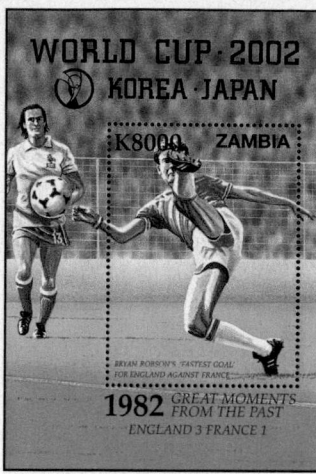

2002 World Cup Soccer Championships, Japan and Korea — A197

No. 972, 2000k: a, Poster from 1954 World Cup, Switzerland. b, Stanly Matthews and English flag. c, Scottish player and flag. d, Belgian player and flag. e, Player and Daejon World Cup Stadium, Korea, horiz.

No. 973, 2000k: a, Ferenc Puskas and Hungarian flag. b, Poster from 1962 World Cup, Chile. c, Spanish player and flag. d, English player and flag. e, Player and Jeonju World Cup Stadium, Korea, horiz.

No. 974, 8000k, Bryan Robson's goal against France, 1982. No. 975, 8000k, Salenko's fifth goal against Cameroon, 1994, horiz.

2002, Feb. 26   **Perf. 14**
Sheets of 5, #a-e
972-973 A197   Set of 2   9.75 9.75
Souvenir Sheets
974-975 A197   Set of 2   8.00 8.00
Size of Nos. 972a-972d, 973a-973d: 28x42mm.

United We Stand — A198

2002, Feb.   **Perf. 13½x13¼**
976 A198 3200k multi   1.60 1.60
Issued in sheets of 4.

Reign of Queen Elizabeth, 50th Anniv. — A199

No. 977: a, Wearing blue and white hat. b, Without hat. c, Wearing scarf. d, Wearing tiara. 7500k, With Prince Philip.

2002, July 15   **Litho.**   **Perf. 14¼**
977 A199 3200k Sheet of 4, #a-d   6.50 6.50
Souvenir Sheet
978 A199 7500k multi   4.00 4.00

2002 Winter Olympics, Salt Lake City A200

Designs: 1000k, Ice hockey. 3200k, Cross-country skiing.

2002, July 30   **Perf. 13¼x13¾**
979-980 A200   Set of 2   2.50 2.50

20th World Scout Jamboree, Thailand — A201

No. 981, horiz.: a, Troop hiking. b, Knot tying. c, Archery. d, Fire making. 8000k, Camping.

2002, July 30   **Perf. 14**
981 A201 3200k Sheet of 4, #a-d   6.75 6.75
Souvenir Sheet
982 A201 8000k multi   4.50 4.50

Intl. Year of Mountains — A202

No. 983: a, Mt. Whitney, US. b, Mt. Aconcagua, Argentina and Chile. c, Mt. Mönch, Switzerland. d, Mt. Ararat, Turkey. 9000k, Mt. Everest, Nepal and China.

2002, July 30
983 A202 1500k Sheet of 4, #a-d 3.75 3.75
Souvenir Sheet
984 A202 9000k multi   5.00 5.00

Birds — A203

Designs: 700k, Bee-eater. 1200k, Blue-cheeked bee-eater. 1400k, Boehn's bee-eater. 1500k, Little bee-eater.

2002, Aug. 12
985-988 A203   Set of 4   4.25 4.25
See Nos. 1027-1030. For surcharge, see No. 1091.

Flowers, Butterflies and Mushrooms — A204

No. 989, 2500k — Flowers: a, Camel's foot. b, Christmas bells. c, Impala lily. d, Everlasting. e, Anomatheca grandiflora. f, Soldier lily.
No. 990, 2500k — Butterflies: a, False monarch. b, Golden piper. c, Blue pansy. d, Christmas tree acraea. e, Grass yellow. f, Gold-spotted sylph.
No. 991, 2500k — Mushrooms: a, Copper trumpet. b, King bolete. c, Death cap. d, Fly agaric. e, Chanterelle. f, Deadly fiber cap.
No. 992, 8000k, Arum lily. No. 993, 8000k, African monarch butterfly. No. 994, 8000k, Stump brittle-head mushrooms.

2002, Sept. 9   **Litho.**
Sheets of 6, #a-f
989-991 A204   Set of 3   20.00 20.00
Souvenir Sheets
992-994 A204   Set of 3   15.00 15.00

Nos. 624, 629, 645 Surcharged

Methods & Perfs as Before
2002, July 1
996 A128   250k on 50k #639   — —
997 A127   300k on 50k #624   — —
998 A130   1000k on 100k #645   — —

Coronation of Queen Elizabeth II, 50th Anniv. — A205

No. 999: a, Wearing crown and pearl necklace. b, Wearing tiara and jeweled necklace. c, Wearing pink and black hat.
10,000k, Wearing flowered dress and hat.

2003, May 19   **Litho.**   **Perf. 14**
999 A205   5000k Sheet of 3, #a-c   7.25 7.25
Souvenir Sheet
1000 A205   10,000k multi   5.00 5.00

Prince William, 21st Birthday — A206

No. 1001: a, Wearing bow tie. b, Wearing blue shirt and tie. c, Wearing yellow and black sports shirt.
10,000k, Wearing sweater.

2003, May 19
1001 A206   5000k Sheet of 3, #a-c   7.25 7.25
Souvenir Sheet
1002 A206   10,000k multi   5.00 5.00

Nos. 654-657 Srchd.

Nos. 639-642 Surcharged

Nos. 617-620 Surcharged

Nos. 650-653 Surcharged

Nos. 710-712 Surcharged

Methods & Perfs. as Before
2003, June 26
1003 A133   1000k on 200k #654   25.00 25.00
1004 A133   1000k on 300k #655   25.00 25.00
1005 A133   1000k on 500k #656   25.00 25.00
1006 A133   1000k on 900k #657   25.00 25.00
1007 A128   1700k on 50k #639   1.00 1.00
1008 A128   1700k on 200k #640   1.00 1.00
1009 A128   1700k on 300k #641   1.00 1.00
1010 A128   1700k on 500k #642   1.00 1.00
1011 A125   1800k on 50k #617   1.10 1.10
1012 A125   1800k on 200k #618   1.10 1.10
1013 A125   1800k on 250k #619   1.10 1.10
a.   Inverted surcharge   35.00 —
1014 A125   1800k on 300k #620   1.10 1.10
1015 A132   2200k on 100k #650   1.25 1.25
1016 A132   2200k on 300k #651   1.25 1.25
1017 A132   2200k on 450k #652   1.25 1.25
1018 A132   2200k on 500k #653   1.25 1.25
1019 A145   2500k on 500k #710   1.50 1.50
a.   Inverted surcharge   35.00 —
1020 A145   2500k on (O) #711   1.50 1.50
1021 A145   2500k on 900k #712   1.50 1.50
Nos. 1003-1021 (19)   117.90 117.90
Location of surcharges vary on Nos. 1019-1021.

Miniature Sheet

New Year 2003 (Year of the Ram) — A207

No. 1022 — Background colors: a, Green. b, Blue violet. c, Maroon. d, Purple.

2003, July 30   **Litho.**   **Perf. 13¼**
1022 A207   3200k Sheet of 4, #a-d   6.50 6.50

Intl. Year of Fresh Water — A208

No. 1023: a, Cabora Bassa Dam. b, Lake Kariba. c, Mana Pools National Park.
10,000k, Victoria Falls.

2003, July 30   **Perf. 13½x13¼**
1023 A208   5000k Sheet of 3, #a-c   7.50 7.50
Souvenir Sheet
1024 A208   10,000k multi   5.00 5.00

Powered Flight, Cent. — A209

No. 1025: a, Avro 547A. b, Avro 504O with floats. c, Avro 584 Avrocet. d, Avro 504M. 10,000k, Avro 621 Tutor Replica.

2003, July 30   **Perf. 14**
1025 A209   4000k Sheet of 4, #a-d   7.75 7.75
Souvenir Sheet
1026 A209   9000k multi   5.00 5.00

Bird Type of 2002

Designs: 1000k, White-fronted bee-eaters. 1200k, Little bee-eaters. 1500k, Blue-cheeked bee-eater. 1800k, Boehn's bee-eater.

2003, Dec. 26   **Perf. 13¼**
Size: 25x20mm
1027-1030 A203   Set of 4   2.50 2.50

For surcharges, see Nos. 1089, 1109, 1143, 1177.

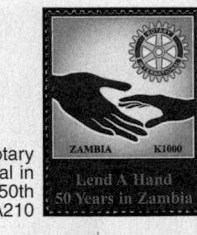

Rotary International in Zambia, 50th Anniv. — A210

Design: 1000k, Rotary emblem and hands. 1200k, Rotary emblem.

2003, Nov. 21   **Litho.**   **Perf. 13**
1031 A210   1000k multi   — —
1032 A210   1200k multi   — —

For surcharges, see Nos. 1107, 1123, 1154.

Miniature Sheet

Birds — A211

No. 1033: a, 500k, African fish eagles, national bird of Zimbabwe. b, 750k, Cattle egrets, national bird of Botswana. c, 1000k, African fish eagles, national bird of Zambia. d, 1100k, Peregrine falcons, national bird of Angola. e, 1500k, Bar-tailed trogons. f, 1700k, African fish eagles, national bird of Namibia. g, 1800k, Purple-crested louries, national bird of Swaziland. h, 2200k, Blue cranes, national bird of South Africa.

2004, Oct. 11   **Litho.**   **Perf. 14**
1033 A211   Sheet of 8, #a-h   4.50 4.50

See Botswana Nos. 792-793, Namibia No. 1052, South Africa No. 1342, Swaziland Nos. 727-735, and Zimbabwe No. 975.

Independence, 40th Anniv. — A212

Design: 1500k, Vimbuza dancer. 1800k, Kayowe dancer. 2700k, Ngoma dancer. 3300k, Ukishi dancer.

2004, Oct. 23 Litho. Perf. 13x13¼
1034	A212	1500k multi	— —
1035	A212	1800k multi	— —
1036	A212	2700k multi	— —
1037	A212	3300k multi	— —

For surcharges, see Nos. 1112, 1144, 1176.

No. 649 Surcharged

Methods and Perfs As Before
2004, Dec. 28
Granite Paper
1038	A131	1000k on 700k #649	1.50 1.50

Mammals
A213

Designs: No. 1039, 2250k, Acionyx jubatus. No. 1040, 2250k, Phacochoerus aethiopicus. No. 1041, 2250k, Giraffa camelopardalis. 2700k, Syncerus caffer.
No. 1043, vert.: a, Panthera pardus. b, Pan troglodytes. c, Lycaon pictus. d, Equus burchelli.
10,000k, Diceros bicornis, vert.

2005, June 27 Litho. Perf. 14
1039-1042	A213	Set of 4	4.25 4.25
1043	A213	3300k Sheet of 4, #a-d	5.75 5.75

Souvenir Sheet
1044	A213	10,000k multi	4.50 4.50

Insects — A214

Designs: 1500k, Fornasinius russus. No. 1046, 2250k, Goliathus giganteus. No. 1047, 2250k, Macrorhina. 2700k, Chelorrhina polyphemus.
No. 1048: a, Sternotomis virescens. b, Cicindela regalis. c, Goliathus meleagris. d, Mecosasms explanta.
10,000k, Meloid.

2005, June 27
1045-1048	A214	Set of 4	3.75 3.75
1049	A214	3300k Sheet of 4, #a-d	5.75 5.75

Souvenir Sheet
1050	A214	10,000k multi	4.50 4.50

Butterflies — A215

Designs: No. 1051, 2250k, Ropalo ceres. No. 1052, 2250k, Morpho portis nymphalidae. No. 1053, 2250k, Phyllocnistls cltrella. 2700k, H. misippus.
No. 1055: a, Colotis evippe. b, Papilio lormieri. c, Papilio dardanus. d, Papilio zalmoxis.
10,000k, Epiphora albida druce.

2005, June 27
1051-1054	A215	Set of 4	4.25 4.25

1055	A215	3300k Sheet of 4, #a-d	5.75 5.75

Souvenir Sheet
1056	A215	10,000k multi	4.50 4.50

Orchids — A216

Designs: No. 1057, 1500k, Disa draconis. No. 1058, 1500k, Disa uniflora. No. 1059, 1500k, Disa uniflora orange. 2700k, Phalaenopsis penetrate.
No. 1061: a, Ansellia africana (yellow flower). b, Ansellia africana (spotted flower). c, Cattleya lueddemanniana. d, Laelia tenebrosa.
10,000k, Cymbidium.

2005, June 27
1057-1060	A216	Set of 4	3.25 3.25
1061	A216	3300k Sheet of 4, #a-d	5.75 5.75

Souvenir Sheet
1062	A216	10,000k multi	4.50 4.50

Jesuits in Zambia, Cent. A217

Designs: 1500k, Bishop Paul Lungu, Map of Zambia. 2550k, Father Torrend, Kasisi Church. 2700k, Father Moreau, Chikuni Church. 3300k, St. Ignatius of Loyola.

2005, June 25 Litho. Perf. 13¼x13
1063-1066	A217	Set of 4	4.50 4.50
1066a		Souvenir sheet, #1063-1066	4.50 4.50

Dag Hammarskjöld (1905-61), UN Secretary General A218

Background color: 1500k, Dark blue. 2700k, Blue green.

2005, July 29 Litho. Perf. 13½
1067-1068	A218	Set of 2	6.50 6.50
1068a		Souvenir sheet of 2, #1067-1068	6.50 6.50

For surcharge, see No. 1145.

Pope John Paul II (1920-2005) and Pres. Jimmy Carter — A219

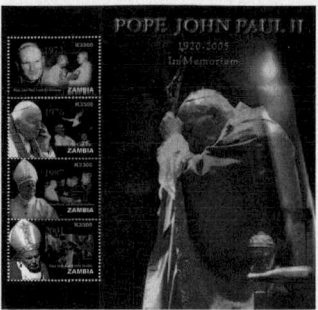

Pope John Paul II — A220

No. 1070: a, With Sri Chinmoy. b, With boy and dove. c, With Schneider brothers. d, Visiting Ukraine.

2005, Aug. 22 Litho. Perf. 12¾
1069	A219	7000k multi	3.00 3.00
1070	A220	3300k Sheet of 4, #a-d	5.75 5.75

No. 1069 was printed in sheets of 4.

A221

Railroads, 200th Anniv. — A222

No. 1071: a, Chinese Class KF 4-8-4. b, Indian Class WP 4-6-2. c, Irish 800 Class 4-6-0. d, French 241A Class 4-8-2.
No. 1072, 1700k: a, British Rail Class 4MT 2-6-4T. b, South African Railways Class 12A. c, Cuban sugar plantation locomotive. d, LNER A4 Pacific facing right. e, LNER A4 Pacific facing left. f, GWR City of Truro 4-4-0. g, British Rail HST Intercity 125. h, Eurostar. i, LNER A3 Flying Scotsman.
No. 1073, 1700k: a, Southern Railway King Arthur Class 4-6-0. b, Berkshire at Kaiiman's Bridge. c, Indian Railways WT Class 2-84 Suburban Tank steam locomotive. d, Ladders on shell of railway car being built. e, Worker on knees inside railway car. f, Yellow staircase next to railway car. g, Workers looking at undercarriage of raised railway car. h, Railway car between blue machinery. i, Model of steam locomotive.
No. 1074, 1700k: a, Great Western Hall Class 4-6-0. b, Argentinian 15B Class 4-8-0. c, Mallet Meter Gauge steam locomotive. d, Worker cutting track. e, Worker and pulley. f, Workers in cherrypicker. g, Workers on tracks and in cherrypickers. h, Workers pouring cement. i, Track workers.
No. 1075, Finnish Class HV2 4-6-0.
No. 1076, 8000k, Orient Express. No. 1077, 8000k, Edinburgh to London train. No. 1078, 800k, Bernina Express.

2005, Aug. 22
1071	A221	4200k Sheet of 4, #a-d	7.50 7.50

Sheets of 9, #a-i
1072-1074	A222	Set of 3	20.00 20.00

Souvenir Sheets
1075	A221	8000k multi	3.50 3.50
1076-1078	A222	Set of 3	10.50 10.50

David Livingstone at Victoria Falls, 150th Anniv. A223

Designs: 1500k, Livingstone, Victoria Falls. 2700k, Statue of Livingstone, railroad bridge.

2006, Jan. 20 Litho. Perf. 13x13¼
1079-1080	A223	Set of 2	2.60 2.60

For surcharges, see Nos. 1113, 1150.

Franciscan Conventuals in Zambia, 75th Anniv. A224

Design: 2250k, Sister Moon. 2700k, Brother Sun. 3300k, Sister Water.

2006, July 8 Litho. Perf. 13¼x13
1082	A224	2250k multi	— —
1083	A224	2700k multi	— —
1084	A224	3300k multi	— —

An additional stamp was issued in this set. The editors would like to examine any examples.

Queen Elizabeth II, 80th Birthday — A225

No. 1085 — Queen: a, Wearing crown. b, Wearing necklace. c, Wearing necklace and jacket. d, With Princess Anne.
6500k, Wearing green hat.

2006, Aug. 8 Litho. Perf. 13¼
1085	A225	3200k Sheet of 4, #a-d	6.50 6.50

Souvenir Sheet
1086	A225	6500k multi	3.25 3.25

Scouting, Cent. (in 2007) — A226

No. 1087, vert. — Scouting emblem, doves, Lord Robert Baden-Powell and background colors of: a, Pink and lilac. b, Yellow and orange. c, Blue and light blue. d, Light green and green.
6500k, Purple and red.

2006, Aug. 8
1087	A226	3200k Sheet of 4, #a-d	6.50 6.50

Souvenir Sheet
1088	A226	6500k multi	3.25 3.25

Nos. 623, 987 and 1028 Surcharged

Methods and Perfs As Before
2007
1089 A203 1500k on 1200k
   #1028   .70 .70
1090 A127 1850k on 20k #623 .95 .95
1091 A203 3300k on 1400k #987 1.60 1.60
  Nos. 1089-1091 (3)   3.25 3.25

  Issued: Nos. 1089, 1091, 3/19; No. 1090, 5/30.

Miniature Sheet

Tazara Railway, 30th Anniv. (in 2006) — A227

  No. 1092: a, Map of Tanzania and Zambia, waterfall, mountain, people waving, and men signing agreement. b, Men and train, elephant and antelope. c, Dar es Salaam Station, sign and wreaths with Chinese inscriptions. d, New Kapiri Mposhi Station, people near train. e, Train, bridge and tunnel, zebra and giraffe. f, Train on bridge, lion and lioness.

2007, May 28   Litho.   Perf. 12
1092 A227 1500k Sheet of 6, #a-
  f   4.75 4.75

Mammals A228

  Designs: 1500k, Bat-eared fox. 2250k, Spotted hyena. 2700k, Aardwolf. 3300k, Side-striped jackal.

2007, June 29   Perf. 13¼x13
1093-1096 A228 Set of 4   5.25 5.25
1096a Souvenir sheet, #1093-1096 6.00 6.00

  For surcharges, see Nos. 1110, 1114, 1122, 1146, 1149, 1151, 1153.

National Animals A229

  Designs: 1500k, Buffalo (Zambia). 1800k, Nyala (Malawi). 2250k, Nyala (Zimbabwe). 2700k, Burchell's zebra (Botswana). 3300k, Oryx (Namibia).

Litho. With Foil Application
2007, Oct. 9   Perf. 13¾
1097-1101 A229 Set of 5   6.25 6.25

  See Botswana No. 838, Malawi No. 752, Namibia Nos. 1141-1142, Zimbabwe Nos. 1064-1068.

Miniature Sheet

2008 Summer Olympics, Beijing — A230

  No. 1102: a, Soccer. b, Hurdles. c, Boxing. d, Swimming.

2008, June 8   Litho.   Perf. 12
1102 A230 2000k Sheet of 4, #a-
  d   5.00 5.00

Worldwide Fund for Nature (WWF) — A231

  No. 1103 — Greater kudu: a, Two males battling. b, Female and calf. c, Male drinking. d, Female and tree branches.

2008, June 30   Perf. 13¼
1103   Horiz. strip or block
    of 4   7.25 7.25
 a.-d. A231 3000k Any single 1.75 1.75
 e. Miniature sheet of 8, 2 each
    #1103a-1103d   14.50 14.50

Muhammad Ali, Boxer — A232

  No. 1104 — Ali: a, In fighting stance without boxing gloves. b, Looking right. c, With gloved fist at chest level. d, With gloved fist near head. e, Pointing. f, Holding Olympic torch.
  3200k, Ali wearing crown, with arms raised, and boxing.

2008   Perf. 14
1104 A232 500k Sheet of 6, #a-
  f   1.90 1.90
Souvenir Sheet
Perf. 13½x13¾
1105 A232 3200k multi   1.90 1.90

  No. 1105 contains one 38x50mm stamp. Nos. 1104-1105 were said to have been released in 1998, but did not appear in the marketplace until 2008.

No. 905 Surcharged

Method and Perf. As Before
2008, July 22
1106 A179 1500k on 1400k #905 .90 .90

No. 1032 Surcharged

Method and Perf. As Before
2009, Feb. 17
1107 A210 1500k on 1200k
   #1032   1.50 1.50

Peonies A233

2009, Apr. 10   Litho.   Perf. 13¼
1108 A233 2000k multi   .75 .75
  Printed in sheets of 8.

No. 1030 Surcharged

Method and Perf. As Before
2009, May 29
1109 A203 1500k on 1800k
   #1030   1.50 1.50

No. 1094 Surcharged

No. 1068 Surcharged

No. 1036 Surcharged

No. 1080 Srchd.

No. 1095 Surcharged

2009   Method and Perf. As Before
1110 A228 3300k on 2250k
   #1094   7.75 7.75
1111 A218 3500k on 2700k
   #1068

1112 A212 3800k on 2700k
   #1036   — —
1113 A223 4050k on 2700k
   #1080   — —
1114 A228 4950k on 2700k
   #1095   — —

  Issued: Nos. 1110-1111, 1113, 5/29, Nos. 1112, 1114, 12/1.
  For surcharges, see Nos. 1150, 1151.

2010 World Cup Soccer Championships, South Africa — A234

  Soccer players, ball, 2010 World Cup mascot and flag of: Nos. 1115, 1118e, 2500k, Zambia. Nos. 1116, 1118h, 4050k, Namibia. Nos. 1117, 1118i, 4950k, South Africa. No. 1118: a, 900k, Lesotho. b, 1000k, Mauritius. c, 2050k, Botswana. d, 2250k, Zimbabwe. f, 3500k, Malawi. g, 3800k, Swaziland.

2010, Apr. 9   Litho.   Perf. 13½
On Plain Paper With Olive Brown Background
1115-1117 A234 Set of 3   5.00 5.00
On Gold-faced Paper
1118 A234 Sheet of 9, #a-i 11.00 11.00

  See Botswana Nos. 896-905, Lesotho No. , Malawi No. 753, Mauritius No. 1086, Namibia No. 1188, South Africa No. 1403, Swaziland Nos. 794-803, and Zimbabwe Nos.1112-1121.
  For surcharge, see No. 1155.
  A single sheetlet of 9 omnibus issues exist containing 1118a. See footnote under Namibia 1188.

Nos. 649, 928, 929, 1032 and 1094 Surcharged

K10,000

Methods and Perfs As Before
2010 ?
1119	A171	2500k on A #928	—	—
1120	A171	2500k on B #929	—	—
1121	A131	5000k on 700k #649	—	—
1122	A228	10,000k on 2250k #1094	—	—
1123	A210	10,000k on 1200k #1032	—	—

Issued: No. 1120, 11/12/10.
For surcharges, see Nos. 1147, 1148, 1152, 1153, 1154.

Animals — A237

Designs: No. 1137, Boehm's bush squirrel. No. 1140, Sun squirrel.

2012, Oct.   Litho.   Perf. 14
1137	A237	3500k multi	—
1140	A237	3500k multi	—

Sixteen additional stamps were issued in this set. The editors would like to examine any examples.

Miniature Sheet

Dr. David Livingstone (1813-73), African Missionary and Explorer — A239

No. 1142: a, 25k, Livingstone. b, 30k, Map of northern Zambia, rhinoceros. c, 40k, Map of southwestern Zambia, hippopotamus, antelope. d, 50k, Map of southeastern Zambia, lion.

2013, Mar. 19   Litho.   Perf. 13¼x13
1142	A239	Sheet of 4, #a-d	54.00	54.00

Nos. 1028, 1036, 1068, 1095-1096, 1113-1114, 1119-1123 Surcharged

No. 1143

Methods and Perfs As Before
2013
1143	A203	1.50k on 1200k #1028	—	—
1144	A212	1.50k on 2700k #1036	—	—
1145	A218	1.50k on 2700k #1068	—	—
1146	A228	1.50k on 2700k #1095	—	—
1147	A171	2.50k on 2500k on A #1119	—	—
1148	A171	2.50k on 2500k on B #1120	—	—
1149	A228	3.80k on 2475k on 3300k #1096	—	—
1150	A223	4.05k on 4050k on 2700k #1113	—	—
1151	A228	4.95k on 4950k on 2700k #1114	—	—
1152	A131	5k on 5000k on 700k #1121	—	—
1153	A228	10k on 10,000k on 2250k #1122	—	—
1154	A210	10k on 10,000k on 1200k #1123	—	—

No. 1116 Surcharged

K4.05

Methods and Perfs. As Before
2013, July 25
1155	A234	4.05k on 4050k #1116	—

Surcharge on No. 1155 is on the selvage surrounding the stamp. An additional stamp was issued in this set. The editors would like to examine any example of it.

In 2014, Zambia declared as "illegal" 31 souvenir sheets of one depicting various topics including famous women, actresses, birds, Elvis Presley, mammals, bats, dogs, turtles, and a sheet of 4 and a souvenir sheet depicting the birth of Prince George of Cambridge.

Nos. 639, 928-930, 1030, 1035 Surcharged

K 1.50

K 1.50

K 1.50

K 2.50

K 2.50

K4.95

Methods and Perfs. As Before
2014, May 2
1175	A128	1.50k on 50k #639	—	
1176	A212	1.50k on 1800k #1035	—	—
1177	A203	1.50k on 1800k #1030	—	—
1178	A171	2.50k on A #928	1.75	
1179	A171	2.50k on B #929	1.75	
1182	A171	4.95k on C #930	3.25	3.25

Three additional surcharges were issued in this set. The editors would like to examine any examples.

A240

Red Flag Canal, People's Republic of China, 50th Anniv. — A241

No. 1184: a, Workers marching to site. b, Waterway under mountain, horiz. c, Building, horiz. d, Workers dangling from cables.
No. 1185: a, Zambian Pres. Kenneth Kaunda. b, Chinese Vice-Premier Li Xiannian.

2014, June 13   Litho.   Perf. 13¼
1184	A240	7.50k Sheet of 4, #a-d, + label	9.75	9.75

Souvenir Sheet
Perf. 12
1185	A241	15k Sheet of 2, #a-b	9.75	9.75

Animals — A243

Designs: No. 1187, Black rhinoceros. No. 1194, Lion. No. 1201, Leopard.

2014, June 26   Litho.   Perf. 14
1187	A243	1k multi	—
1194	A243	2.50k multi	—
1201	A243	4.95k multi	—

Fifteen additional stamps were issued in this set. The editors would like to examine any examples.

Miniature Sheets

Independence, 50th Anniv. — A247

No. 1214 — Dr. Kenneth Kaunda, first President of Zambia: a, With Queen Elizabeth II. b, With British Prime Minister Margaret Thatcher. c, With Archbishop of Canterbury. d, At Independence ceremony. e, With African leaders.
No. 1215: a, Pres. Kaunda. b, Pres. Frederick Chiluba (1943-2011). c, Pres. Levy Mwanawasa (1948-2008). d, Pres. Rupiah Banda. e, Pres. Michael Sata (1937-2014).
No. 1216 — Pres. Sata: a, At inauguration. b, Addressing United Nations.

Litho. With Foil Application
2014, Oct. 23   Perf. 13¼
1214	A247	10k Sheet of 5, #a-e	18.00	18.00
1215	A247	10k Sheet of 5, #a-e	18.00	18.00

Souvenir Sheet
1216	A247	10k Sheet of 2, #a-b	7.25	7.25

Four strips of five stamps were also issued with this set. The editors would like to examine any examples of the strips.

No. 905 Surcharged

K10.00

Method and Perf. As Before
2017 ?
1217	A179	10k on 1400k #905	—

K5.00

No. 1064 Surcharged

Method and Perf. As Before
2018 ?
1224	A217	5k on 2550k #1064	—

POSTAGE DUE STAMPS

Type of Northern Rhodesia
Perf. 12½
1964, Oct. 24   Litho.   Unwmk.
J1	D2	1p orange	.25	1.10
J2	D2	2p dark blue	.25	1.10
J3	D2	3p rose claret	.25	1.40
J4	D2	4p violet blue	.35	1.75
J5	D2	6p purple	.50	2.25
J6	D2	1sh emerald	1.50	8.00
		Nos. J1-J6 (6)	3.10	15.60

ZANZIBAR

ˈzan-zə-ˌbär

LOCATION — Group of islands about twenty miles off the coast of Tanganyika in East Africa
GOVT. — Republic
AREA — 1,044 sq. mi. (approx.)
POP. — 354,360 (est. 1967)
CAPITAL — Zanzibar

Before 1895, unoverprinted stamps of India were used in Zanzibar. Zanzibar was a British protectorate until Dec. 10, 1963, when it became independent. After a revolt in January, 1964, a republic was established. Zanzibar joined Tanganyika Apr. 26, 1964, to form the United Republic of Tanganyika and Zanzibar (later renamed Tanzania). See Tanzania.

12 Pies = 1 Anna
16 Annas = 1 Rupee
100 Cents = 1 Rupee (1908)
100 Cents = 1 Shilling (1935)

Catalogue values for unused stamps in this country are for Never Hinged items, beginning with Scott 201 in the regular postage section and Scott J18 in the postage due section.

Watermarks

Wmk. 47 —
Multiple Rosette

Wmk. 71 —
Rosette

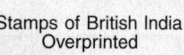

Stamps of British India Overprinted

Zanzibar

On Stamps of 1882-95

	1895	Wmk. Star (39)	Perf. 14	
		Blue Overprint		
1	A17	½a green	30,000.	6,250.
2	A19	1a violet brn	3,500.	600.
a.		"Zanzidar"		28,500.

	1895-96		**Black Overprint**	
3	A17	½a green	5.00	5.00
a.		"Zanzibar"	1,450.	800.00
b.		"Zanibar"	1,450.	1,900.
c.		"Zapzibar"		
4	A19	1a violet brn	5.25	4.25
a.		"Zanzidar"	—	4,000.
b.		"Zanibar"	1,900.	2,250.
5	A20	1a6p bister brn	5.50	4.25
a.		"Zanzidar"	4,500.	1,200.
b.		"Zanibar"	2,000.	
c.		"Zanzibar"	1,800.	1,750.
d.		"Zapzibar"	125.00	125.00
6	A21	2a ultra	10.00	9.00
a.		"Zanzidar"	8,500.	3,500.
b.		"Zanibar"	6,750.	2,750.
c.		"Zapzibar"	150.00	160.00
d.		Double overprint	310.00	
7	A28	2a6p green	10.00	5.50
a.		"Zanzidar"	8,500.	1,800.
b.		"Zanibar"	800.00	1,400.
c.		"Zanzidar"		
d.		"Zanzidar"	1,250.	
8	A22	3a orange	13.50	17.50
a.		"Zanzidar"	1,150.	2,150.
b.		"Zanibar"	7,500.	4,750.
9	A23	4a olive grn	22.50	20.00
a.		"Zanzidar"	11,500.	4,750.
10	A25	8a red vio	45.00	30.00
a.		"Zanzidar"	11,500.	9,000.
11	A26	12a vio, *red*	20.00	11.50
a.		"Zanzidar"	11,500.	5,000.
12	A27	1r gray	125.00	100.00
a.		"Zanzidar"	10,500.	6,750.
13	A29	1r car rose & grn	22.50	40.00
a.		Vertical overprint	475.00	
14	A30	2r brn & rose	125.00	*135.00*
a.		"Zanziba"	32,500.	
b.		Inverted "r"	4,500.	5,500.

---

c.		Pair, one without overprint		
15	A30	3r grn & brn	95.00	*105.00*
a.		"Zanziba"	32,500.	
b.		Inverted "r"	6,750.	6,750.
c.		Double overprint, one albino		
			1,550.	
16	A30	5r vio & blue	105.00	*125.00*
a.		"Zanziba"	32,500.	
b.		Inverted "r"	5,000.	7,250.
c.		Dbl. ovpt., one invtd.	950.00	

On Stamp of 1873-76
Wmk. Elephant's Head (38)

17	A14	6a bister	22.50	12.50
a.		"Zanziba"	11,500.	4,000.
b.		"Zanzibarr"	7,240.	4,750.
c.		"Zaniba"	900.00	1,400.
d.		"Zapzibar"		
e.		Double overprint		
		Nos. 3-17 (15)	631.75	624.50

Double and triple overprints, with one overprint albino, and color varieties exist for most of the 1-17 overprints. For detailed listings, see *Scott Classic Specialized Catalogue.*

Nos. 4-6 Surcharged

a

b

c

d

e

f

	1896		**Wmk. Star (39)**	
			Black Surcharge	
18	(a)	2½a on 1a	200.00	110.00
19	(b)	2½a on 1a	525.00	350.00
20	(c)	2½a on 1a	225.00	125.00
			Red Surcharge	
21	(a)	2½a on 1a	275.00	725.00
22	(b)	2½a on 1a	500.00	1,050.
23	(c)	2½a on 1a	310.00	725.00
24	(d)	2½a on 1a6p	85.00	60.00
a.		"Zanzibar"	1,700.	1,450.
b.		"Zanzibar"	5,250.	2,250.
24C	(b)	2½a on 1a6p	250.00	550.00
25	(c)	2½a on 1a6p	145.00	350.00
26	(d)	2½a on 1a6p	200.00	175.00
27	(e)	2½a on 1a6p	475.00	400.00
27A	(f)	2½a on 1a6p	27,500.	18,000.
28	(a)	2½a on 2a	160.00	360.00
28A	(b)	2½a on 2a	340.00	625.00
29	(c)	2½a on 2a	180.00	425.00
30	(d)	2½a on 2a	80.00	47.50
31	(e)	2½a on 2a	225.00	125.00
31A	(f)	2½a on 2a	5,750.	2,800.

Certain type varieties are found in the word "Zanzibar" on Nos. 1 to 31A viz: Inverted "q" for "b," broken "p" for "n," "i" without dot, small second "z" and tall second "z." These varieties are found on all values from ½a to 1r inclusive and the tall "z" is also found on the 2r, 3r and 5r.

Double and triple "Zanzibar" with one or two overprints albino exist for most of the 18-31 overprints. For detailed listings, see *Scott Classic Specialized Catalogue.*

Stamps of British East Africa, 1896, Overprinted in Black or Red

	1896		**Wmk. Crown and C A (2)**	
32	A8	½a yellow grn	42.50	25.00
33	A8	1a carmine	47.50	19.00
a.		Double overprint	825.00	1,000.
34	A8	2½a dk blue (R)	100.00	52.50
35	A8	4½a orange	55.00	65.00
36	A8	5a dark ocher	70.00	45.00
37	A8	7½a lilac	60.00	70.00
			Nos. 32-37 (6)	375.00	276.50

A2

Sultan Seyyid Hamed-bin-Thwain
A3

	1896, Sept. 20		**Engr.**	**Wmk. 71**	
38	A2	½a	yel grn & red	4.50	2.25
39	A2	1a	indigo & red	4.00	1.75
40	A2	2a	red brn & red	4.75	.85
41	A2	2½a	ultra & red	17.50	1.60
42	A2	3a	slate & red	20.00	10.00
43	A2	4a	dk green & red	14.00	6.00
44	A2	4½a	orange & red	8.75	8.25
45	A2	5a	bister & red	9.25	5.75
a.		Half used as 2½a on cover			4,900.
46	A2	7½a	lilac & red	8.25	8.25
47	A2	8a	ol gray & red	13.50	9.00
48	A3	1r	ultra & red	26.00	12.00
49	A3	2r	green & red	32.50	13.00
50	A3	3r	violet & red	36.00	13.00
51	A3	4r	lake & red	27.50	20.00
52	A3	5r	blk brn & red	38.00	20.00
			Nos. 38-52 (15)	264.50	131.70

No. 43 Surcharged in Red
1897

53	A2 (a)	2½a on 4a	100.00	55.00
54	A2 (b)	2½a on 4a	325.00	300.00
55	A2 (c)	2½a on 4a	120.00	82.50
		Nos. 53-55 (3)	545.00	437.50

	1898		**Engr.**	**Wmk. 47**	
56	A2	½a	yel grn & red	1.75	.45
57	A2	1a	indigo & red	6.00	1.40
58	A2	2a	red brn & red	11.00	2.25
58A	A2	2½a	ultra & red	5.50	.45
59	A2	3a	slate & red	9.50	1.10
60	A2	4a	dk grn & red	4.25	2.00
60A	A2	4½a	orange & red	17.00	1.25
61	A2	5a	bister & red	24.00	2.50
61A	A2	7½a	lilac & red	21.00	3.00
61B	A2	8a	ol gray & red	22.50	3.25
			Nos. 56-61B (10)	122.50	17.65

A4

Sultan Seyyid Hamoud-bin-Mahommed-bin-Said — A5

	1899-1901				
62	A4	½a	yel grn & red	3.00	.65
63	A4	1a	indigo & red	5.00	.25
64	A4	1a	car & red ('01)	4.75	.25
65	A4	2a	red brn & red	5.75	1.50
66	A4	2½a	ultra & red	5.75	1.10
67	A4	3a	slate & red	8.00	3.25
68	A4	4a	dk green & red	8.00	7.00
69	A4	4½a	orange & red	20.00	9.50
70	A4	4½a	ind & red ('01)	22.00	14.50
71	A4	5a	bister & red	8.25	3.50
72	A4	7½a	lilac & red	8.25	*9.50*
73	A4	8a	ol gray & red	8.25	*7.25*
			Wmk. 71		
74	A5	1r	ultra & red	26.00	17.50
75	A5	2r	green & red	29.00	25.00
76	A5	3r	violet & red	50.00	*52.50*
77	A5	4r	lilac rose & red	75.00	*77.50*
78	A5	5r	gray brown & red	85.00	110.00
			Nos. 62-78 (17)	372.00	340.75

For surcharges see Nos. 94-98.

A6

Monogram of Sultan Ali bin Hamoud — A7

	1904, June 8		**Typo.**	**Wmk. 47**	
79	A6	½a	emerald	3.00	1.00
80	A6	1a	rose red	3.00	.25
81	A6	2a	bister brown	5.00	.50
82	A6	2½a	ultra	5.00	.40
83	A6	3a	gray	6.00	2.50
84	A6	4a	blue green	4.50	1.75
85	A6	4½a	black	5.75	2.75
86	A6	5a	ocher	7.50	2.50
87	A6	7½a	violet	9.25	8.75
88	A6	8a	olive green	6.75	6.75
89	A7	1r	ultra & red	37.50	27.50
90	A7	2r	green & red	45.00	55.00
91	A7	3r	violet & red	65.00	100.00
92	A7	4r	magenta & red	75.00	120.00
93	A7	5r	olive & red	75.00	120.00
			Nos. 79-93 (15)	353.25	449.65

Nos. 69-70, 72-73 Surcharged in Black or Lake

g

h

i

	1904				
94	A4 (g)	1a on 4½a	5.00	*6.25*
95	A4 (g)	1a on 4½a (L)	7.00	*24.00*
96	A4 (h)	2a on 4a (L)	19.00	*24.00*
97	A4 (i)	2½a on 7½a	17.50	*25.00*
a.		"Hlaf"	16,000.	
b.		Thin open "w" in overprint	85.00	105.00
c.		Serif on foot of "f" in overprint	150.00	180.00
98	A4 (i)	2½a on 8a	32.50	*40.00*
a.		"Hlaf"	15,000.	10,000.
b.		Thin open "w" in overprint	85.00	105.00
c.		Serif on foot of "f" in overprint	250.00	300.00
		Nos. 94-98 (5)	81.00	119.25

Sultan Ali bin Hamoud
A8

A9

A10

Palace of the Sultan — A11

	1908-09		**Engr.**	**Wmk. 47**	
99	A8	1c	gray ('09)	2.75	.35
100	A8	3c	yellow grn	17.00	.25
101	A8	6c	carmine	11.00	.25
102	A8	10c	org brn ('09)	7.25	3.00
103	A8	12c	violet	19.00	3.75
104	A9	15c	ultra & pur	21.00	.45

105	A9	25c	brown	8.75	1.10
106	A9	50c	dp green	13.00	8.00
107	A9	75c	slate ('09)	16.00	20.00
108	A10	1r	yellow green	45.00	14.00
109	A10	2r	violet	25.00	21.00
110	A10	3r	yellow brown	45.00	62.50
111	A10	4r	red	75.00	100.00
112	A10	5r	blue	77.50	115.00
113	A11	10r	brn & dk grn	230.00	375.00
114	A11	20r	yel grn & blk	675.00	875.00
115	A11	30r	dk brn & blk	775.00	1,100.
116	A11	40r	org brn & blk	975.00	
117	A11	50r	lilac & blk	875.00	
118	A11	100r	blue & blk	1,350.	
119	A11	200r	black & brn	1,850.	
			Nos. 99-112 (14)	383.25	349.65

It is probable that Nos. 118 and 119 were used only for fiscal purposes.

Sultan Khalifa bin Harub — A12

Dhow — A13

Dhow — A14

1913   **Perf. 14**

120	A12	1c	gray	.50	.75
121	A12	3c	yellow grn	1.50	.75
122	A12	6c	carmine	1.75	.25
123	A12	10c	brown	1.25	3.75
124	A12	12c	violet	1.50	.50
125	A12	15c	ultra	4.25	1.10
126	A12	25c	black brn	1.60	3.00
127	A12	50c	dk green	5.00	8.25
128	A12	75c	dk gray	3.25	7.25
129	A13	1r	yellow grn	29.00	21.00
130	A13	2r	dk violet	22.50	42.50
131	A13	3r	orange	27.50	67.50
132	A13	4r	red	45.00	92.50
133	A13	5r	blue	57.50	57.50
134	A14	10r	brown & grn	230.00	440.00
135	A14	20r	yel grn & blk	400.00	725.00
136	A14	30r	dk brn & blk	425.00	875.00
137	A14	40r	orange & blk	725.00	1,150.
138	A14	50r	dull vio & blk	725.00	1,250.
139	A14	100r	blue & blk	1,000.	
140	A14	200r	black & brn	1,450.	
			Nos. 120-134 (15)	432.10	746.60

1914-22   **Wmk. 3**

141	A12	1c	gray	.90	.50
142	A12	3c	yellow grn	1.40	.25
143	A12	6c	carmine	1.25	.25
144	A12	8c	vio, yel ('22)	1.75	7.75
145	A12	10c	dk grn, yel ('22)	.95	.40
146	A12	15c	ultra	1.75	8.75
148	A12	50c	dark green	5.25	8.25
149	A12	75c	deep gray	3.50	37.50
150	A13	1r	yellow grn	5.75	4.00
151	A13	2r	dark violet	20.00	21.00
152	A13	3r	brown org	27.50	52.50
153	A13	4r	red	34.00	95.00
154	A13	5r	blue	19.00	72.50
155	A14	10r	brown & grn	225.00	775.00
			Nos. 141-155 (14)	348.00	1,084.

1921-29   **Wmk. 4**

156	A12	1c	gray	.30	12.50
157	A12	3c	yellow grn	4.50	7.75
158	A12	3c	orange ('22)	.40	.25
159	A12	4c	green ('22)	.65	3.25
160	A12	6c	carmine	.45	.55
161	A12	6c	vio, bl ('22)	.50	.25
162	A12	10c	lt brown	.85	16.50
163	A12	12c	violet	.55	.35
164	A12	12c	carmine ('22)	.55	.50
165	A12	15c	ultra	.80	15.50
166	A12	20c	dk blue ('22)	1.25	.40
167	A12	25c	black brn	1.10	32.50
168	A12	50c	blue green	4.25	8.25
169	A12	75c	dark gray	3.25	65.00
170	A13	1r	yellow grn	7.25	4.00
171	A13	2r	dk violet	4.50	15.50
172	A13	3r	ocher	6.75	8.50
173	A13	4r	red	17.50	50.00
174	A13	5r	blue	27.00	75.00
175	A14	10r	brown & grn	240.00	525.00
176	A14	20r	green & blk	450.00	825.00
177	A14	30r	dk brn & blk ('29)	350.00	750.00
			Nos. 156-175 (20)	322.40	841.55

Sultan Khalifa bin Harub ("CENTS" with Serifs) — A15

1926-27

184	A15	1c	brown	1.10	.25
185	A15	3c	yellow org	.35	.25
186	A15	4c	deep green	.35	.50
187	A15	6c	dark violet	.35	.25
188	A15	8c	slate	1.10	5.50
189	A15	10c	olive green	1.10	.45
190	A15	12c	deep red	3.25	.25
191	A15	20c	ultra	.65	.40
192	A15	25c	violet, yel	17.00	3.00
193	A15	50c	claret	5.00	.50
194	A15	75c	olive brown	40.00	42.50
			Nos. 184-194 (11)	70.25	53.85

> Catalogue values for unused stamps in this section, from this point to the end of the section, are for Never Hinged items.

"CENTS" without Serifs — A16

Dhow — A17

Dhow — A18

1936   **Perf. 14**

201	A16	5c	deep green	.25	.25
202	A16	10c	black	.25	.25
203	A16	15c	carmine	.30	1.25
204	A16	20c	brown org	.25	.25
205	A16	25c	violet, yel	.25	.25
206	A16	30c	ultra	.25	.25
207	A16	40c	black brown	.25	.25
208	A16	50c	claret	.50	.25
209	A17	1sh	yellow grn	.75	.25
210	A17	2sh	dark violet	3.50	2.50
211	A17	5sh	red	24.00	8.00
212	A17	7.50sh	blue	40.00	37.50
213	A18	10sh	brn & grn	40.00	32.50
			Nos. 201-213 (13)	110.55	83.75

For overprints see Nos. 222-223.

A19

1936, Dec. 9

214	A19	10c	olive grn & blk	4.00	.35
215	A19	20c	red violet & blk	6.00	2.75
216	A19	30c	deep ultra & blk	16.00	1.00
217	A19	50c	red orange & blk	17.50	6.75
			Nos. 214-217 (4)	43.50	10.85
			Set, hinged	25.00	

Reign of Sultan Khalifa bin Harub, 25th anniv.

A20

Dhow & Map Showing Zanzibar & Muscat.

Perf. 14

1944, Nov. 20   **Engr.**   **Wmk. 4**

218	A20	10c	violet blue	1.00	5.25
219	A20	20c	brown orange	1.50	3.75
220	A20	50c	Prus green	1.50	.40
221	A20	1sh	dull purple	1.50	1.50
			Nos. 218-221 (4)	5.50	10.90

200th anniv. of the Al Busaid Dynasty.

Nos. 202 and 206 Overprinted in Red

1946, Nov. 11

222	A16	10c	black	.25	.50
223	A16	30c	ultra	.40	.50

Victory of the Allied Nations in WW II.

Common Design Types pictured following the introduction.

Silver Wedding Issue
Common Design Types

1949, Jan. 10   **Photo.**   **Perf. 14x14½**

224	CD304	20c	orange	.60	1.50

Engraved; Name Typographed
Perf. 11½x11

225	CD305	10sh	light brown	29.00	36.50

UPU Issue
Common Design Types
Engr.; Name Typo. on 30c, 50c
Perf. 13½, 11x11½

1949, Oct. 10   **Wmk. 4**

226	CD306	20c	red orange	.45	3.75
227	CD307	30c	indigo	2.50	2.00
228	CD308	50c	red lilac	1.25	3.25
229	CD309	1sh	blue green	1.25	4.50
			Nos. 226-229 (4)	5.45	13.50

Sultan Khalifa bin Harub — A21

Seyyid Khalifa Schools A22

Perf. 12x12½, 13x12½

1952, Aug. 26   **Engr.**

230	A21	5c	black	.25	.25
231	A21	10c	red orange	.25	.25
232	A21	15c	green	2.00	3.00
233	A21	20c	carmine	.75	.75
234	A21	25c	plum	1.10	.25
235	A21	30c	blue green	1.10	.25
236	A21	35c	ultra	1.00	5.00
237	A21	40c	chocolate	1.00	2.00
238	A21	50c	purple	3.25	.25
239	A22	1sh	choc & bl grn	.75	.25
240	A22	2sh	claret & ultra	3.00	2.75
241	A22	5sh	carmine & blk	3.00	6.50
242	A22	7.50sh	emer & gray	27.50	27.50
243	A22	10sh	gray blk & rose red	12.00	15.00
			Nos. 230-243 (14)	56.95	64.00

Sultan Khalifa bin Harub — A23

1954, Aug. 26   **Perf. 12½x12**

244	A23	15c	green	.25	.25
245	A23	20c	scarlet	.25	.25
246	A23	30c	ultra	.25	.25
247	A23	50c	purple	.30	.30
248	A23	1.25sh	brown orange	.50	.75
			Nos. 244-248 (5)	1.55	1.80

The frames differ on Nos. 245 and 247. Sultan Khalifa bin Harub, 76th birth anniv.

Cloves — A24

Dhows A25

Sultan's Barge — A26

Malindi Minaret Mosque — A27   Kibweni Palace — A28

Sultan Khalifa bin Harub and: 25c, 35c, and 50c Map showing location of Zanzibar. 1sh, 2sh, Dimbani Mosque.

Perf. 11½ (A24), 11x11½ (A25), 14x13½ (A26), 13½x14 (A27), 13x13½ (A28)

1957, Aug. 26   **Engr.**   **Wmk. 314**

249	A24	5c	dull grn & org	.25	.25
250	A24	10c	rose car & brt grn	.25	.25
251	A26	15c	dk brn & grn	.25	3.25
252	A26	20c	ultra	.25	.25
253	A25	25c	blk & brn org	.25	1.50
254	A25	30c	int blk & rose car	.25	1.50
255	A26	35c	brt grn & ind	.30	.25
256	A27	40c	int blk & redsh brn	.25	.25
257	A26	50c	dull grn & bl	.35	.30
258	A27	1sh	int blk & brt	.00	.00
259	A25	1.25sh	rose car & dk grn	4.00	.45
260	A27	2sh	dull grn & org	4.00	2.50
261	A28	5sh	ultra	6.00	2.50
262	A28	7.50sh	green	15.00	4.50
263	A28	10sh	rose carmine	16.00	6.50
			Nos. 249-263 (15)	47.70	24.55

Sultan Seyyid Abdulla bin Khalifa — A29

Designs as before with portrait of Sultan Seyyid Abdulla bin Khalifa.

Perf. 11½ (A29), 11x11½ (A25), 14x13½ (A26), 13½x14 (A27)

1961, Oct. 17   **Engr.**   **Wmk. 314**

264	A29	5c	dull grn & org	.40	1.10
265	A29	10c	rose car & brt grn	.40	.25
266	A25	15c	dk brn & grn	.90	3.75
267	A26	20c	ultra	.40	.45
268	A26	25c	blk & brn org	1.75	1.75
269	A25	30c	int blk & rose car	3.25	3.00
270	A26	35c	brt grn & in-digo	3.00	5.00
271	A27	40c	int blk & redsh brn	.40	.25
272	A26	50c	dull grn & bl	3.25	.25
273	A27	1sh	int blk & brt	.50	1.50
274	A25	1.25sh	rose car & dk grn	3.00	6.50

| 275 | A27 | 2sh dull grn & org | 1.00 | 3.75 |

Perf. 13x13½

276	A28	5sh ultra	4.00	10.00
277	A28	7.50sh green	3.75	19.00
278	A28	10sh rose carmine	3.75	11.00
279	A28	20sh dk brown	19.00	30.00
		Nos. 264-279 (16)	48.75	97.55

For overprints see Nos. 285-300.

Freedom from Hunger Issue

Common Design Type with Portrait of Sultan Seyyid Abdulla bin Khalifa

1963, June 4   Photo.   Perf. 14x14½

| 280 | CD314 | 1.30sh sepia | 1.50 | .80 |

Independent State

Sultan Seyyid Jamshid bin Abdulla and Zanzibar Clove — A30

Designs: 50c, "To Prosperity," arch and sun. 1.30sh, "Religious Tolerance," composite view of churches and mosques, horiz. 2.50sh, "Towards the Light," Mangapwani Cave.

Perf. 12½

1963, Dec. 10   Photo.   Unwmk.

281	A30	30c multicolored	.25	.25
282	A30	50c multicolored	.30	.30
283	A30	1.30sh multicolored	.40	2.00
284	A30	2.50sh multicolored	.50	2.00
		Nos. 281-284 (4)	1.45	4.55

Zanzibar's independence, Dec. 10, 1963. For overprints see Nos. 301-304.

Republic

Nos. 264-279 Overprinted

1964, Feb. 28   As Before

285	A29	5c dull grn & org	.25	.25
286	A29	10c rose car & brt grn	.25	.25
287	A25	15c dk brn & grn	.25	.25
288	A26	20c ultra	.25	.25
289	A26	25c blk & brn org	.35	.25
290	A25	30c int blk & rose car	.25	.25
291	A26	35c brt grn & ind	.35	.25
292	A27	40c int blk & redsh brn	.25	.25
293	A26	50c dull grn & blue	.35	.25
294	A27	1sh int blk & brt car	.30	.25
295	A25	1.25sh rose car & dk grn	2.25	.90
296	A27	2sh dull grn & org	.85	.45
297	A28	5sh ultra	.85	.50
298	A28	7.50sh green	1.25	7.00
299	A28	10sh rose carmine	2.00	7.00
300	A28	20sh dark brown	3.00	8.50
		Nos. 285-300 (16)	13.05	26.85

The overprint was applied in England. It is in 2 lines on 40c and 1sh to 20sh. "Jamhuri" means "republic."

Overprint Handstamped

285a	A29	5c	1.00	.60
286a	A29	10c	1.00	.60
287a	A25	15c	1.50	2.00
288a	A26	20c	1.00	.50
289a	A26	25c	1.75	.25
290a	A25	30c	1.00	.50
291a	A26	35c	1.75	1.00
292a	A27	40c	1.00	1.00
293a	A26	50c	1.75	.25
294a	A27	1sh	1.50	1.25
295a	A25	1.25sh	1.25	1.50
296a	A27	2sh	2.50	1.50
297a	A28	5sh	2.00	1.75
298a	A28	7.50sh	2.50	1.75
299a	A28	10sh	2.50	2.50
300a	A28	20sh	3.00	6.00
		Nos. 285a-300a (16)	27.00	22.60

This overprint was applied locally. It has one line of serifed letters. These are found diagonal, vertical, horizontal, double and inverted.

See Nos. 301a-304b. Other stamps with this overprint, including postage dues, were unofficial.

Nos. 281-284 Overprinted

1964, Feb. 28   As Before

301	A30	30c multi	.25	.25
302	A30	50c multi	.25	.25
303	A30	1.30sh multi	.30	.25
304	A30	2.50sh multi	.40	.60
a.		Green omitted	150.00	
		Nos. 301-304 (4)	1.20	1.35

One-line overprint on 1.30sh.

Overprint Handstamped

301a	A30	30c	1.00	1.00
302a	A30	50c	.40	.35
303a	A30	1.30sh	1.00	.80
304b	A30	2.50sh	1.50	1.50
c.		Green omitted	350.00	
		Nos. 301a-304b (4)	3.90	3.65

See note after No. 300a.

Moorish Arch, Ax, Sword and Spear — A31

Designs: 10c, 20c, Arch and arrow piercing chain. 25c, 40c, Man with rifle. 30c, Man breaking chain. 1sh, Man, flag and sun. 1.30sh, Hands breaking chain and cloves, horiz. 2sh, Hands waving flag, horiz. 5sh, Map of Zanzibar and Pemba and flag, horiz. 10sh, Flag and map of Zanzibar and Pemba. 20sh, Flag of Zanzibar, horiz

Perf. 13x13½, 13½x13

1964, June 21   Litho.   Unwmk.

305	A31	5c multicolored	.40	.25
306	A31	10c multicolored	.40	.25
307	A31	15c multicolored	.40	.25
308	A31	20c multicolored	.50	.25
309	A31	25c multicolored	.50	.25
310	A31	30c multicolored	.40	.25
311	A31	40c multicolored	.60	.25
312	A31	50c multicolored	.40	.25
313	A31	1sh multicolored	.50	.25
314	A31	1.30sh multicolored	.30	1.25
315	A31	2sh multicolored	.50	.50
316	A31	5sh multicolored	1.25	3.00
317	A31	10sh multicolored	5.25	4.00
318	A31	20sh multicolored	5.00	20.00
		Nos. 305-318 (14)	16.40	31.00

Soldier and Maps of Zanzibar and Pemba A32

Reconstruction A33

Perf. 13½x13, 13x13½

1965, Jan. 12   Unwmk.

319	A32	20c green & yel grn	.25	.25
320	A33	30c dk brn & ocher	.25	.25
321	A33	1.30sh vio blue & blue	.25	.25
322	A33	2.50sh purple & rose	.75	.50
		Nos. 319-322 (4)	1.50	1.25

First anniversary of the revolution.

Zanzibar and Tanzania

Rice Planting A34

Design: 30c, 1.30sh, Hands holding rice.

Perf. 13x12½

1965, Oct. 17   Litho.   Unwmk.

323	A34	20c blue & blk brn	.25	1.00
324	A34	30c brt pink & blk brn	.25	1.00
325	A34	1.30sh org & blk brn	.35	2.25
326	A34	2.50sh emer & blk brn	.55	4.00
		Nos. 323-326 (4)	1.40	8.25

Issued to publicize agricultural development.

Symbols of Trade, Agriculture, Industry and Education — A35

Designs: 50c, 2.50sh, Soldier and sunburst.

1966, Jan. 12   Litho.   Perf. 12½x13

327	A35	20c ultra, red & gray	.25	.25
328	A35	50c black & yel	.25	.25
329	A35	1.30sh multicolored	.30	.25
330	A35	2.50sh black & org	.60	1.00
		Nos. 327-330 (4)	1.40	1.85

2nd anniv. of the revolution of Jan. 12, 1964.

Pres. Abeid Amani Karume and Vice-Pres. Abdulla Kassim Hanga — A36

Design: 50c, 1.30sh, Flag, laurel and hands holding Flame of the Union (inscribed: Jamhuri Tanzania Zanzibar).

1966, Apr. 26   Photo.   Perf. 13½x13

331	A36	30c multicolored	.25	.25
332	A36	50c multicolored	.25	.25
333	A36	1.30sh multicolored	.35	.30
334	A36	2.50sh multicolored	.60	1.25
		Nos. 331-334 (4)	1.45	2.05

Union of Tanganyika and Zanzibar, 2nd anniv.

Logging A37

10c, 1sh, Clove trees & man. 15c, 40c, Cabinetmaker. 20c, 5sh, Lumumba College & book. 25c, 1.30sh, Farmer & tractor. 30c, 2sh, Volunteer farm workers. 50c, 10sh, Street scene, vert.

Perf. 13x12½, 12½x13

1966, June 5   Litho.

335	A37	5c lemon & vio brn	.70	.80
336	A37	10c brt grn & vio brn	.70	.80
337	A37	15c vio brn & bl	.70	.80
338	A37	20c vio bl & org	.70	.25
339	A37	25c vio brn & yel	.70	.30
340	A37	30c vio brn & dl yel	.80	.25
341	A37	40c vio brn & rose	.90	.25
342	A37	50c green & yel	.90	.25
343	A37	1sh ultra & vio brn	.90	.25
344	A37	1.30sh lt bl grn & vio brn	1.00	3.25
345	A37	2sh brt grn & vio brn	1.00	.60
346	A37	5sh ver & gray	1.50	6.00
347	A37	10sh red brn & yel	2.50	20.00
348	A37	20sh brt pink & vio brn	5.00	35.00
		Nos. 335-348 (14)	18.00	68.80

Symbols of Education — A38

1966, Sept. 25   Perf. 13½x13

349	A38	50c blue, blk & org	.25	1.00
350	A38	1.30sh blue, blk & yel grn	.30	1.75
351	A38	2.50sh blue, blk & pink	.80	4.00
		Nos. 349-351 (3)	1.35	6.75

Introduction of free education.

People and Flag A39

Design: 50c, 1.30sh, Vice-President Abdulla Kassim Hanga, flag and crowd, vert.

Perf. 14x14½, 14½x14

1967, Feb. 5   Litho.   Unwmk.

352	A39	30c multicolored	.25	1.00
353	A39	50c multicolored	.25	1.00
354	A39	1.30sh multicolored	.25	1.25
355	A39	2.50sh multicolored	.40	3.00
		Nos. 352-355 (4)	1.15	6.25

10th anniversary of Afro-Shirazi Party.

Volunteer Workers A40

Perf. 12½x12

1967, Aug. 20   Photo.   Unwmk.

| 356 | A40 | 1.30sh multicolored | .30 | 2.50 |
| 357 | A40 | 2.50sh multicolored | .55 | 6.50 |

Volunteer (Young) Workers Brigade.

All Zanzibar stamps were withdrawn July 1, 1968, and replaced with current Kenya, Uganda and Tanzania stamps.

In 2013, Tanzania denounced as "illegal" stamps bearing the name "Zanzibar" that had been recently introduced into the philatelic marketplace.

POSTAGE DUE STAMPS

D1

Rouletted 10

1931		**Typeset**		**Unwmk.**	
		Thin Paper			
		Without Gum			
J1	D1	1c blk, *orange*		12.50	150.00
J2	D1	2c blk, *orange*		5.50	80.00
J3	D1	3c blk, *orange*		5.75	65.00
J3A	D1	6c blk, *orange*			8,000.
J4	D1	9c blk, *orange*		3.25	40.00
J4A	D1	12c blk, *orange*		15,000.	12,000.
J4B	D1	12c blk, *green*		1,600.	675.00
J5	D1	15c blk, *orange*		3.25	42.50
J6	D1	18c blk, *orange*		27.50	90.00
a.		18c black, *salmon*		5.50	75.00
J7	D1	20c blk, *orange*		4.50	80.00
J8	D1	21c blk, *orange*		4.00	50.00
J8A	D1	25c blk, *orange*		19,000.	17,000.
J8B	D1	25c blk, *magenta*		3,250.	1,500.
J9	D1	31c blk, *orange*		11.00	115.00
J10	D1	50c blk, *orange*		24.00	250.00
J11	D1	75c blk, *orange*		80.00	600.00

The variety "cent.s" occurs once on each sheet of Nos. J3 to J11 inclusive. For more detailed listings, see the *Scott Classic Specialized* catalog.

D2

1931-33			**Rouletted 5**		
		Thick Paper			
J12	D2	2c blk, *salmon*		27.50	40.00
J13	D2	3c blk, *rose*		4.00	67.50
J14	D2	6c blk, *yellow*		4.00	40.00
J15	D2	12c blk, *blue*		5.00	32.50
J16	D2	25c blk, *pink*		11.00	145.00
J17	D2	25c blk, *dull violet*		27.50	87.50
		Nos. J12-J17 (6)		79.00	412.50

Catalogue values for unused stamps in this section, from this point to the end of the section, are for Never Hinged items.

D3

1936	D3	**Typo.**	**Wmk. 4**		**Perf. 14**
J18	D3	5c violet		8.50	14.00
J19	D3	10c carmine		7.25	3.25
J20	D3	20c green		2.50	6.75
J21	D3	30c brown		18.00	24.00
J22	D3	40c ultra		10.00	30.00
J23	D3	1sh gray		15.50	37.50
		Nos. J18-J23 (6)		61.75	115.50

Chalky paper was introduced in 1956 for the 5c, 30c, 40c, 1sh, and in 1962 for the 10c, 20c. Value for set of 6, unused $3.25, used $110. See note after No. 300a.

ZIMBABWE

zim-'bä-bwē

LOCATION — Southeastern Africa, bordered by Zambia, Mozambique, South Africa, and Botswana
GOVT. — Republic
AREA — 150,872 sq. mi.
POP. — 11,163,160 (1999 est.)
CAPITAL — Harare

Formerly Rhodesia, the Republic of Zimbabwe was established April 18, 1980.

100 Cents = 1 Dollar

Catalogue values for all unused stamps in this country are for Never Hinged items.

Morganite A69   Black Rhinoceros A70

Odzani Falls — A71

Perf. 14½, 14½x14 (A70)

1980			**Litho.**		
414	A69	1c shown		.25	.30
415	A69	3c Amethyst		.25	.30
416	A69	4c Garnet		.25	.25
417	A69	5c Citrine		.25	.25
418	A69	7c Blue topaz		.25	.25
419	A70	9c shown		.25	.25
420	A70	11c Lion		.25	.25
421	A70	13c Warthog		.25	.25
422	A70	15c Giraffe		.25	.25
423	A70	17c Zebra		.25	.25
424	A71	21c shown		.25	.25
425	A71	25c Goba Falls		.00	.30
426	A71	30c Inyangombe Falls		.30	.45
426A	A71	40c Bundi Falls		3.00	4.25
427	A71	$1 Bridal Veil Falls		.40	1.60
428	A71	$2 Victoria Falls		.50	3.00
		Nos. 414-428 (16)		7.25	12.45

Rotary International, 75th Anniversary — A72

1980, June 18			**Perf. 14½**	
429	A72	4c multicolored	.25	.25
430	A72	13c multicolored	.25	.25
431	A72	21c multicolored	.30	.25
432	A72	25c multicolored	.35	.35
a.		Souvenir sheet of 4, #429-432	1.40	1.40
		Nos. 429-432 (4)	1.15	1.10

Olympic Rings A73

1980, July 19				
433	A73	17c multicolored	.45	.45

22nd Summer Olympic Games, Moscow, July 19-Aug. 3.

Gatooma Post Office, 1912 A74

Post Offices: 7c, Salisbury, 1912. 9c, Umtali, 1901. 17c, Bulawayo, 1895.

1980		**Litho.**		**Perf. 14½**
434	A74	5c multicolored	.25	.25
435	A74	7c multicolored	.25	.25
436	A74	9c multicolored	.25	.25
437	A74	17c multicolored	.25	.26
a.		Souvenir sheet of 4, #434-437	1.00	1.00
		Nos. 434-437 (4)	1.00	1.00

Post Office Savings Bank, 75th anniv.

Intl. Year of the Disabled — A75

Designs: Various disabilities. Nos. 438-441 form a continuous design.

1981, Sept. 23		**Litho.**		**Perf. 14½**
438	A75	5c multicolored	.25	.25
439	A75	7c multicolored	.25	.25
440	A75	11c multicolored	.25	.25
441	A75	17c multicolored	.30	.30
		Nos. 438-441 (4)	1.05	1.05

Natl. Tree Day — A76

1981, Dec. 4				
442	A76	5c Msasa	.25	.25
443	A76	7c Mopane	.25	.25
444	A76	21c Flat-crowned acacia	.45	.45
445	A76	30c Pod mahogany	.75	.75
		Nos. 442-445 (4)	1.70	1.70

Rock Paintings A77

Designs: 9c, Khoisan figures, Gwamgwadza Cave. 11c, Kudus, human figures, Epworth Mission. 17c, Diana's Vow, Rusape. 21c, Giraffes, Gwamgwadza Cave. 25c, Warthog, Mucheka Cave. 30c, Hunters, Shinzwini Shelter.

1982, Mar. 17		**Litho.**		**Perf. 14½**
446	A77	9c multicolored	.80	.25
447	A77	11c multicolored	1.00	.25
448	A77	17c multicolored	1.25	.40
449	A77	21c multicolored	1.40	.40
450	A77	25c multicolored	1.60	1.60
451	A77	30c multicolored	1.75	2.75
		Nos. 446-451 (6)	7.80	5.65

Scouting Year — A78

1982, July 21				
452	A78	9c Emblem	.30	.25
453	A78	11c Campfire	.35	.25
454	A78	21c Map reading	.50	.40
455	A78	30c Baden Powell	.65	.65
		Nos. 452-455 (4)	1.80	1.55

TB Bacillus Centenary A79

1982, Nov. 17				**Perf. 14½**
456	A79	11c Koch	.80	40
457	A79	30c Scientist examining slide	1.20	1.75

Commonwealth Day — A80

Sculptures: 9c, Wing Woman, by Henry Mudzengerere, vert. 11c, Telling Secrets, by Joseph Ndandarika. 30c, Hornbill Man, by John Takawira. $1, The Chief, by Nicholas Mukomberanwa, vert.

1983, Mar. 14				**Perf. 14½**
458	A80	9c multicolored	.25	.25
459	A80	11c multicolored	.25	.25
460	A80	30c multicolored	.25	.25
461	A80	$1 multicolored	.40	1.25
		Nos. 458-461 (4)	1.15	2.00

World Plowing Contest, May — A81

No. 463, mechanized plowing.

1983, May 13		**Litho.**		**Perf. 14½**
462	A81	Pair	.60	.60
a.-b.		21c, any single	.25	.25
463	A81	Pair	.80	.80
a.-b.		30c, any single	.25	.25

World Communications Year — A82

Means of communication and transportation. Nos. 464-467 vert.

1983, Oct. 12		**Litho.**		**Perf. 14½**
464	A82	9c Mailman	.25	.25
465	A82	11c Signaling airplane	.25	.25
466	A82	15c Telephone operators	.30	.25
467	A82	17c Reading newspapers	.40	.25
468	A82	21c Truck on highway	.50	.50
469	A82	30c Train	.65	.90
		Nos. 464-469 (6)	2.35	2.40

Zimbabwe Intl. Trade Fair, Bulawayo, May 5-13 — A83

1984, Apr. 11		**Litho.**		**Perf. 14½**
470	A83	9c shown	.25	.25
471	A83	11c Globe	.25	.25
472	A83	30c Emblem	.45	.45
		Nos. 470-472 (3)	.95	.95

1984 Summer Olympics A84

Children's Drawings.

1984, July 18   Litho.   Perf. 14½
473	A84	11c Bicycling	.60	.60
474	A84	21c Swimming	.50	.50
475	A84	30c Running	.60	.60
476	A84	40c Hurdles	.70	1.50
		Nos. 473-476 (4)	2.40	3.20

Heroes' Day A85

1984, Aug. 8   Litho.   Perf. 14½
477	A85	9c Heroes	.25	.25
478	A85	11c Monument, vert.	.25	.25
479	A85	17c Statue, vert.	.30	.30
480	A85	30c Bas-relief	.50	.90
		Nos. 477-480 (4)	1.30	1.70

Fish Eagle — A86

1984, Oct. 10   Litho.   Perf. 14½
481	A86	9c shown	.60	.25
482	A86	11c Long crested eagle	.65	.25
483	A86	13c Bateleur	.70	.70
484	A86	17c Black eagle	.90	.90
485	A86	21c Martial eagle	1.25	1.25
486	A86	30c African hawk eagle	1.50	2.00
		Nos. 481-486 (6)	5.60	5.35

Superheat Engine No. 86, Mashonaland Railways, 1918 — A87

Steam locomotives: 11c, Engine No. 190, North British Locomotive Co., 1926. 17c, Engine No. 424, Beyer Peacock & Co., 1950. Engine No. 726, Beyer Peacock & Co., 1957.

1985, May 15   Litho.
487	A87	9c multicolored	.80	.50
488	A87	11c multicolored	1.10	.50
489	A87	17c multicolored	1.60	1.00
490	A87	30c multicolored	3.25	3.25
		Nos. 487-490 (4)	6.75	5.25

INTELSAT V A88

57c, Mazowe Earth Satellite Station.

Perf. 14½x14, 14½
1985, July 8   Litho.
| 491 | A88 | 26c multicolored | 1.60 | 1.60 |

Size: 62x23mm
| 492 | A88 | 57c multicolored | 4.00 | 4.00 |

Zimbabwe Bird and Tobacco — A89

Agriculture and industry.

Perf. 14¾x14½
1985, Aug. 21   Litho.
493	A89	1c shown	.25	.25
a.		Perf 14¼x13¾ ('88)	30.00	2.00
494	A89	3c Corn	.25	.25
a.		Perf 14¼x13¾ ('88)	10.00	2.00
495	A89	4c Cotton	.25	.25
a.		Perf 14¼x13¾ ('88)	40.00	2.00
496	A89	5c Tea	.50	.25
a.		Perf 14¼x13¾ ('88)	40.00	2.00
497	A89	10c Cattle	.30	.25
a.		Perf 14¼x13¾ ('88)	20.00	2.00
498	A89	11c Birchenough Bridge	.75	.25
499	A89	12c Stamp mill	1.25	.25
500	A89	13c Gold production	3.00	.25
a.		Perf 14¼x13¾ ('88)	20.00	4.00
501	A89	15c Coal mining	2.75	.25
a.		Perf 14¼x13¾ ('88)	40.00	4.00
502	A89	17c Amethyst mining	3.00	1.25
503	A89	18c Electric train	2.25	2.75
504	A89	20c Kariba Dam	1.50	.25
a.		Perf 14¼x13¾ ('88)	20.00	4.00
505	A89	23c Elephants	4.50	.45
506	A89	25c Zambezi River sunset	.65	.90
a.		Perf 14¼x13¾ ('88)	—	20.00
507	A89	26c Baobab tree	.65	.30
508	A89	30c Great Zimbabwe ruins	.75	.70
509	A89	35c Folk dancing	.60	.30
510	A89	45c Crushing corn	1.25	.60
511	A89	57c Wood carving	.75	.70
512	A89	$1 Mbira drum	1.25	1.00
a.		Perf 14¼x13¾ ('88)	—	25.00
513	A89	$2 Mule-drawn scotch cart	2.00	3.00
514	A89	$5 Natl. coat of arms	2.25	4.50
		Nos. 493-514 (22)	30.70	18.35

Natl. Archives, 50th Anniv. A90

Designs: 12c, Gatsi Rusere (c. 1589-1623), ruler of Mashonaland and Zambezi area; mutapa, 17th cent. 18c, Lobengula, ruler of Ndebele State (1870-94), sketch by E. A. Maund, 1889; 1888 Moffat Treaty and elephant seal. 26c, Archives exhibition hall. 35c, Archives building.

1985, Sept. 18   Perf. 14½
515	A90	12c multicolored	.25	.25
516	A90	18c multicolored	.30	.30
517	A90	26c multicolored	.45	.45
518	A90	35c multicolored	.65	.65
		Nos. 515-518 (4)	1.65	1.65

UN Decade for Women A91

1985, Nov. 13
519	A91	10c Computer operator	.70	.70
520	A91	17c Nurse, child	1.00	1.00
521	A91	26c Engineer	1.75	1.75
		Nos. 519-521 (3)	3.45	3.45

Harare Conference Center — A92

1986, Jan. 29   Litho.   Perf. 14½
| 523 | A92 | 26c Facade | 1.00 | 1.00 |
| 524 | A92 | 35c Interior | 1.75 | 1.75 |

Southern African Development Coordination Conference — A93

1986, Apr. 1   Perf. 14½
525	A93	12c Grain elevators	.50	.50
526	A93	18c Rhinoceros	2.60	2.60
527	A93	26c Map, jet	2.60	2.60
528	A93	35c Map, flags	2.75	2.75
		Nos. 525-528 (4)	8.45	8.45

Moths — A94

12c, Jackson's emperor. 18c, Oleander hawk. 26c, Zaddach's emperor. 35c, Southern marbled emperor.

1986, June 18   Litho.   Perf. 14½x14
529	A94	12c multicolored	1.60	1.60
530	A94	18c multicolored	2.10	2.10
531	A94	26c multicolored	2.75	2.75
532	A94	35c multicolored	3.25	3.25
		Nos. 529-532 (4)	9.70	9.70

8th Non-aligned Summit Conference A95

1986, Aug. 28   Litho.   Perf. 14½x14
| 533 | A95 | 26c Victoria Falls | 2.75 | 2.75 |

Size: 66x26mm
Perf. 14½
| 534 | A95 | $1 Great Zimbabwe Enclosure | 6.50 | 6.50 |

Motoring Cent. A96

1986, Oct. 8   Perf. 14½
535	A96	10c Sopwith, 1921	.75	.75
536	A96	12c Gladiator, 1902	.75	.75
537	A96	17c Douglas, 1920	1.10	1.10
538	A96	26c Ford Model-A, 1930	1.75	1.75
539	A96	35c Schacht, 1909	2.25	2.25
540	A96	40c Benz Velocipede, 1886	2.25	2.25
		Nos. 535-540 (6)	8.85	8.85

A97

UN Child Survival Campaign: a, Growth monitoring. b, Breast-feeding. c, Oral rehydration. d, Immunization.

1987, Feb. 11   Litho.   Perf. 14x14½
| 541 | | Block of 4 | 8.50 | 8.50 |
| a.-d. | | A97 12c any single | 1.90 | 1.90 |

A98

Indigenous owls.

1987, Apr. 15   Perf. 14½
542	A98	12c Barred	2.75	2.75
543	A98	18c Pearl-spotted	3.25	3.25
544	A98	26c White-faced	3.75	3.75
545	A98	35c Scops	4.75	4.75
		Nos. 542-545 (4)	14.50	14.50

Natl. Girl Guides Movement, 75th Anniv. — A99

1987, June 24
546	A99	15c Commitment	.75	.75
547	A99	23c Adventure	.90	.90
548	A99	35c Service	1.10	1.10
549	A99	$1 Intl. friendship	2.50	2.50
		Nos. 546-549 (4)	5.25	5.25

Duikers and Population Maps — A100

1987, Oct. 7   Perf. 14½x14
550	A100	15c Common gray	.60	.60
551	A100	23c Zebra	.75	.75
552	A100	25c Yellow-backed	.80	.80
553	A100	30c Blue	.90	.90
554	A100	35c Jentink's	1.00	1.00
555	A100	38c Red	1.10	1.10
		Nos. 550-555 (6)	5.15	5.15

Insects A101

1988, Jan. 12   Litho.   Perf. 14½
556	A101	15c Praying mantis	.75	.25
557	A101	23c Scarab beetle	1.00	.50
558	A101	35c Short-horned grasshopper	1.50	1.50
559	A101	45c Giant shield bug	1.75	2.00
		Nos. 556-559 (4)	5.00	4.25

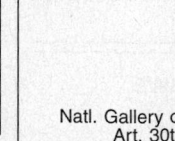

Natl. Gallery of Art, 30th Anniv. — A102

Sculpture and paintings: 15c, Cockerel, by Arthur Azevedo. 23c, Changeling, by Bernard Matemera. 30c, Spirit Python, by Henry Munyaradzi. 35c, Spirit Bird Carrying People, by Thomas Mukarobgwa, horiz. 38c, The Song of the Shepherd Boy, by George Nene, horiz. 45c, War Victim, by Joseph Muzondo, horiz.

Perf. 14x14½, 14½x14
1988, Apr. 14   Litho.
560	A102	15c multicolored	.25	.25
561	A102	23c multicolored	.25	.25
562	A102	30c multicolored	.40	.40
563	A102	35c multicolored	.60	.60

564 A102 38c multicolored .60 .60
565 A102 45c multicolored .70 .70
Nos. 560-565 (6) 2.80 2.80

Aloes and Succulents A103

15c, Aloe cameronii bondana. 23c, Orbeopsis caudata. 25c, Euphorbia wildii. 30c, Euphorbia fortissima. 35c, Aloe aculeata. 38c, Huernia zebrina.

1988, July 14 **Perf. 14½**
566 A103 15c multicolored .35 .35
567 A103 23c multicolored .55 .55
568 A103 25c multicolored .55 .55
569 A103 30c multicolored .60 .60
570 A103 35c multicolored .60 .70
571 A103 38c multicolored .75 .85
Nos. 566-571 (6) 3.40 3.60

Ducks — A104

1988, Oct. 6 **Litho.** **Perf. 14½x14**
572 A104 15c White-faced duck .75 .25
573 A104 23c Pygmy goose .85 .25
574 A104 30c Hottentot teal .90 .85
575 A104 35c Knob-billed duck 1.00 1.40
576 A104 38c White-backed duck 1.00 1.50
577 A104 45c Maccoa 1.60 2.75
Nos. 572-577 (6) 6.10 7.00

Geckos A105

1989, Jan. 10 **Litho.** **Perf. 14½**
578 A105 15c O'Shaughnessy's banded .80 .25
579 A105 23c Tiger rock .90 .40
580 A105 35c Tasman's 1.50 1.25
581 A105 45c Bibron's 1.75 2.00
Nos. 578-581 (4) 4.95 3.90

Wildflowers A106

1989, Apr. 12 **Litho.** **Perf. 14½**
582 A106 15c Spotted-leaved arum-lily .45 .10
583 A106 23c Grassland vlei-lily .50 .25
584 A106 30c Manica protea .55 .40
585 A106 35c Flame lily .65 .40
586 A106 38c Poppy hibiscus .70 .50
587 A106 45c Blue sesbania .80 .65
Nos. 582-587 (6) 3.65 2.30

Fish A107

15c, Red-breasted bream. 23c, Chessa. 30c, Eastern bottle-nose. 35c, Vundu. 38c, Largemouth black bass. 45c, Tiger fish.

1989, July 12 **Litho.** **Perf. 14½**
588 A107 15c multicolored .50 .25
589 A107 23c multicolored .70 .25
590 A107 30c multicolored .75 .50
591 A107 35c multicolored .75 .50
592 A107 38c multicolored .80 .80
593 A107 45c multicolored 1.00 1.50
Nos. 588-593 (6) 4.50 3.80
See Nos. 696-701.

Endangered Species A108

1989 **Litho.** **Perf. 14½x14**
594 A108 15c Black rhinoceros 1.25 .40
595 A108 23c Cheetah 1.25 .45
596 A108 30c Wild dog 1.40 .90
597 A108 35c Pangolin 1.40 1.25
598 A108 38c Brown hyena 1.50 2.00
599 A108 45c Roan antelope 1.60 2.50
Nos. 594-599 (6) 8.40 7.50

Achievements, 1980-1990 A109

1990, Apr. 17 **Litho.** **Perf. 14½x14**
600 A109 15c Unity accord .45 .25
601 A109 23c Conference center .50 .25
602 A109 30c Education .55 .80
603 A109 35c Satellite dish .05 .90
604 A109 38c Sports stadium .65 .90
605 A109 45c Agriculture 1.00 2.50
Nos. 600-605 (6) 3.80 5.60

City of Harare, Cent. A110

15c, Runhare house, 1986. 23c, Market hall, 1894. 30c, Charter house, 1959. 35c, Supreme Court, 1927. 38c, Standard Chartered Bank, 1911. 45c, Town house, 1933.

1990, July 11 **Litho.** **Perf. 14½**
606 A110 15c multicolored .40 .25
607 A110 23c multicolored .60 .25
608 A110 30c multicolored .05 .45
609 A110 35c multicolored .75 .90
610 A110 38c multicolored .75 1.00
611 A110 45c multicolored .90 1.50
Nos. 606-611 (6) 4.05 4.35

36th Commonwealth Parliamentary Conf. — A111

1990, Sept. 17
612 A111 35c Speaker's mace .75 .40
613 A111 $1 Speaker's chair 1.75 2.25

Animals — A112

Hand Crafts — A113

Transportation — A114

1c, Tiger fish. 2c, Helmeted guineafowl. 3c, Scrub hare. 4c, Pangolin. 5c, Greater kudu. 9c, Black rhinoceros. 15c, Head rest. 20c, Hand axe. 23c, Gourd, water pot. 25c, Snuff box. 26c, Winnowing basket. 30c, Grinding stone. 33c, Riding bicycles. 35c, Buses. 38c, Train. 45c, Motorcycle, trailer. $1, Jet. $2, Tractor-trailer truck.

Perf. 14, 14½x14 (#620-625), 14¼ (#626-631)

1990, Jan. 2 **Litho.**
614 A112 1c multicolored .25 .25
  a. Perf 14¾x14½ 1.00 .25
615 A112 2c multicolored 1.00 .25
  a. Perf 14¾x14½ 1.25 .25
616 A112 3c multicolored .25 .25
  a. Perf 14¾x14½ 1.00 .25
617 A112 4c multicolored .45 .25
  a. Perf 14x13½ .90 .25
  b. Perf 14¾x14½
618 A112 5c multicolored .45 .45
  a. Perf 14¾x14½ 1.00 .25
619 A112 9c multicolored 1.50 .40
  a. Perf 14¾x14½ 1.50 .40
620 A113 15c multicolored .30 .25
621 A113 20c multicolored .25 .25
622 A113 23c multicolored .25 .25
623 A113 25c multicolored .25 .25
624 A113 26c multicolored .60 .40
625 A113 30c multicolored .40 .40
626 A114 33c multicolored 1.20 .40
627 A114 35c multicolored 1.40 .45
628 A114 38c multicolored 1.75 .45
629 A114 45c multicolored 1.20 .45
630 A114 $1 multicolored 2.10 .90
631 A114 $2 multicolored 1.90 1.60
Nos. 614-631 (18) 15.50 7.90

Animals A115

1991, Jan. 15 **Litho.** **Perf. 14½x14**
632 A115 15c Small-spotted genet 1.00 .25
633 A115 23c Red squirrel 1.10 .30
634 A115 35c Night ape 1.50 1.25
635 A115 45c Bat-eared fox 2.00 1.50
Nos. 632-635 (4) 5.60 3.30

A116

Traditional musical instruments.

1991, Apr. 16 **Litho.** **Perf. 14½**
636 A116 15c Hosho .50 .25
637 A116 23c Mbira .55 .25
638 A116 30c Ngororombe .60 .40
639 A116 35c Chipendani .70 .70
640 A116 38c Marimba .70 .80
641 A116 45c Ngoma .80 1.10
Nos. 636-641 (6) 3.85 3.50

Wild Fruits — A117

1991, July 17 **Litho.** **Perf. 14x14½**
642 A117 20c Snot-apple .50 .25
643 A117 39c Marula .55 .30
644 A117 51c Mobola plum .60 .70
645 A117 60c Water berry .70 .75
646 A117 65c Northern dwaba berry .75 .75
647 A117 77c Mahobohobo .90 1.00
Nos. 642-647 (6) 4.00 3.75
See Nos. 870-875.

A118

20c, Bridal Veil Falls. 39c, Conference Emblem. 51c, Chinhoyi Caves. 60c, Kariba Dam Wall. 65c, Victoria Falls. 77c, Balancing Rocks.

1991, Oct. 16 **Litho.** **Perf. 14½**
648 A118 20c multi .75 .60
649 A118 39c multi .80 .60
650 A118 51c multi .90 .80
651 A118 60c multi 1.10 1.10
652 A118 65c multi 1.20 1.20
653 A118 77c multi 1.50 1.30
Nos. 648-653 (6) 6.25 5.60
Commonwealth Heads of Government meeting, Harare.

Wild Cats A119

1992, Jan. 8 **Litho.** **Perf. 14½**
654 A119 20c Lion 1.00 .25
655 A119 39c Leopard 1.50 .50
656 A119 60c Cheetah 2.25 1.75
657 A119 77c Serval 2.50 2.00
Nos. 654-657 (4) 7.25 4.50

Mushrooms A120

Designs: 20c, Amanita zambiana. 39c, Boletus edulis. 51c, Termitomyces. 60c, Cantharellus densifolius. 65c, Cantharellus longisporus. 77c, Cantharellus cibarius.

1992, Apr. 8 **Litho.** **Perf. 14x14½**
658 A120 20c multicolored .50 .25
659 A120 39c multicolored .75 .50
660 A120 51c multicolored .90 .90
661 A120 60c multicolored 1.00 1.00
662 A120 65c multicolored 1.10 1.10
663 A120 77c multicolored 1.25 1.50
Nos. 658-663 (6) 5.50 5.25

Birds — A121

25c, Blackeyed bulbul. 59c, Fiscal shrike. 77c, Forktailed drongo. 90c, Cardinal woodpecker. 98c, Yellowbilled hornbill. $1.16, Crested francolin.

1992, July 17   Litho.   Perf. 14½
664	A121	25c multi	.80	.25
665	A121	59c multi	1.10	.45
666	A121	77c multi	1.25	.80
667	A121	90c multi	1.40	.95
668	A121	98c multi	1.40	.95
669	A121	$1.16 multi	1.50	1.40
		Nos. 664-669 (6)	7.45	4.80

Butterflies A122

25c, Foxy charaxes. 59c, Orange & lemon. 77c, Emperor swallowtail. 90c, Blue pansy. 98c, African monarch. $1.16, Gaudy commodore.

1992, Oct. 15   Litho.   Perf. 14½x14
670	A122	25c multicolored	.90	.25
671	A122	59c multicolored	1.50	.50
672	A122	77c multicolored	1.60	1.00
673	A122	90c multicolored	2.25	1.50
674	A122	98c multicolored	2.25	1.60
675	A122	$1.16 multicolored	2.50	2.00
		Nos. 670-675 (6)	11.00	6.85

Minerals A123

1993, Jan. 12   Litho.   Perf. 14½x14
676	A123	25c Autunite	1.25	.25
677	A123	59c Chromite	1.50	.55
678	A123	77c Azurite	1.75	1.00
679	A123	90c Coal	2.50	1.50
680	A123	98c Gold	2.50	1.75
681	A123	$1.16 Emerald	3.00	2.25
		Nos. 676-681 (6)	12.50	7.30

Owls — A124

25c, Wood owl. 59c, Pels fishing owl. 90c, Spotted eagle owl. $1.16, Giant eagle owl.

1993, Apr. 6   Litho.   Perf. 14½
682	A124	25c multicolored	2.00	1.00
683	A124	59c multicolored	2.50	1.50
684	A124	90c multicolored	4.00	4.50
685	A124	$1.16 multicolored	5.00	6.00
		Nos. 682-685 (4)	13.50	13.00

Household Pottery A125

1993, July 13   Litho.   Perf. 14½x14
686	A125	25c Hadyana	.60	.30
687	A125	59c Chirongo	.80	.40
688	A125	77c Mbiya	.90	.80
689	A125	90c Pfuko	1.00	1.00
690	A125	98c Tsaya	1.00	1.00
691	A125	$1.16 Gate	1.20	1.20
		Nos. 686-691 (6)	5.50	4.70

Orchids — A126

35c, Polystachya dendrobiflora. $1, Diaphananthe subsimplex. $1.50, Ansellia gigantea. $1.95, Vanilla polyepis.

1993, Oct. 12   Litho.   Perf. 14½
692	A126	35c multicolored	.75	.60
693	A126	$1 multicolored	1.75	1.25
694	A126	$1.50 multicolored	2.50	2.50
695	A126	$1.95 multicolored	3.00	3.00
		Nos. 692-695 (4)	8.00	7.35

Fish Type of 1989

1994, Jan. 20   Litho.   Perf. 14½
696	A107	35c Hunyani salmon	.45	.25
697	A107	$1 Barbel	.75	.25
698	A107	$1.30 Rainbow trout	.85	.60
699	A107	$1.50 Mottled eel	.90	.65
700	A107	$1.65 Mirror carp	1.00	.80
701	A107	$1.95 Robustus bream	1.05	1.00
		Nos. 696-701 (6)	5.00	3.55

City of Bulawayo, Cent. A127

1994, Apr. 5   Litho.   Perf. 14½
702	A127	35c City Hall	.25	.25
703	A127	80c Cresta Churchill Hotel	.40	.25
704	A127	$1.15 High Court	.50	.45
705	A127	$1.75 Douslin House	.60	.75
706	A127	$1.95 Goldfields Building	.75	1.00
707	A127	$2.30 Parkade Centre	1.00	1.25
		Nos. 702-707 (6)	3.50	3.95

Export Flowers — A128

1994, July 12   Litho.   Perf. 14½
708	A128	35c Strelitzia	.45	.25
709	A128	80c Protea	.70	.25
710	A128	$1.15 Phlox	.85	.60
711	A128	$1.75 Chrysanthemum	1.00	1.40
712	A128	$1.95 Lillum	1.25	2.25
713	A128	$2.30 Rose	1.50	2.75
		Nos. 708-713 (6)	5.75	7.50

Christmas — A129

Designs: 35c, Archangel Gabriel, Virgin Mary. 80c, Mary, Joseph on way to Bethlehem. $1.15, Nativity scene. $1.75, Angel pointing way to shepherds. $1.95, Magi following star. $2.30, Madonna and child.

A130

1c, Corn. 2c, Sugar cane. 3c, Sunflowers. 4c, Sorghum. 5c, Mine workers. 10c, Underground mining. 20c, Coal mining. 30c, Chrome smelting. 40c, Opencast mining. 45c, Underground drilling. 50c, Gold smelting. 70c, Boggie Clock Tower. 80c, Masvingo Watchtower. $1, Hanging tree. $2, Cecil House. $5, The Toposcope. $10, Paper House.

1995-96   Litho.   Perf. 14
720	A130	1c multicolored	.25	.50
721	A130	2c multicolored	.25	.50
722	A130	3c multicolored	.25	.50
723	A130	4c multicolored	.25	.50
724	A130	5c multicolored	.50	.50
725	A130	10c multicolored	.75	.50
726	A130	20c multicolored	1.25	.50
727	A130	30c multicolored	1.50	.50
728	A130	40c multicolored	1.75	.50
728A	A130	45c multicolored	1.75	.40
729	A130	50c multicolored	1.75	.40
730	A130	70c multicolored	.30	.30
731	A130	80c multicolored	.30	.30
732	A130	$1 multicolored	.40	.30
733	A130	$2 multicolored	.50	.50
734	A130	$5 multicolored	.50	1.50
735	A130	$10 multicolored	1.75	1.75
		Nos. 720-735 (17)	14.00	9.95

Issued: 45c, 6/3/96; others, 1/17/95.

Insects A131

35c, Spider-hunting wasp. $1.15, Emperor dragonfly. $1.75, Foxy charaxes. $2.30, Antlion.

1995, Apr. 4   Litho.   Perf. 14½
736	A131	35c multicolored	.60	.25
737	A131	$1.15 multicolored	1.15	.55
738	A131	$1.75 multicolored	1.50	2.00
739	A131	$2.30 multicolored	2.00	2.75
		Nos. 736-739 (4)	5.25	5.55

6th All Africa Games, Harare — A132

1995, July 11   Litho.   Perf. 14x14½
740	A132	35c Soccer	.40	.25
741	A132	80c Track	.50	.25
742	A132	$1.15 Boxing	.55	.30
743	A132	$1.75 Swimming	.80	1.00
744	A132	$1.95 Field hockey	2.00	1.75
745	A132	$2.30 Volleyball	1.75	2.00
		Nos. 740-745 (6)	6.00	5.55

UN, 50th Anniv. — A133

1995, Oct. 17   Litho.   Perf. 14½
746	A133	35c Health	.25	.25
747	A133	$1.15 Environment	.50	.50
748	A133	$1.75 Food distribution	.60	.60
749	A133	$2.30 Education	.85	.85
		Nos. 746-749 (4)	2.20	2.20

Flowering Trees — A134

1996, Jan. 24   Litho.   Perf. 14½
750	A134	45c Fernandoa	.30	.25
751	A134	$1 Round leaf mukwa	.50	.25
752	A134	$1.50 Luckybean tree	.70	.60
753	A134	$2.20 Winter cassia	.85	1.00
754	A134	$2.50 Sausage tree	.90	1.40
755	A134	$3 Sweet thorn	1.00	1.75
		Nos. 750-755 (6)	4.25	5.25

Dams of Zimbabwe A135

1996, Apr. 9   Litho.   Perf. 14½
756	A135	45c Mazvikadei	.25	.25
757	A135	$1.50 Mutirikwi	.50	.50
758	A135	$2.20 Ncema	.75	1.00
759	A135	$3 Odzani	1.00	1.50
		Nos. 756-759 (4)	2.50	3.25

Scenic Views A136

Designs: 45c, Matusadonha Natl. Park. $1.50, Juliasdale Rocky Outcrops. $2.20, Honde Valley. $3, Finger Rocks, Morgenster Mission.

1996, July 18   Litho.   Perf. 14½
760	A136	45c multicolored	.25	.25
761	A136	$1.50 multicolored	.50	.50
762	A136	$2.20 multicolored	.75	1.00
763	A136	$3 multicolored	1.00	1.50
		Nos. 760-763 (4)	2.50	3.25

Wood Carvings A137

1996, Oct. 15   Litho.   Perf. 14½
764	A137	45c Frog	.25	.25
765	A137	$1.50 Tortoise	.40	.25
766	A137	$1.70 Kudu	.50	.50
767	A137	$2.20 Chimpanzee	.65	.90
768	A137	$2.50 Porcupine	.70	1.00
769	A137	$3 Rhinoceros	.75	1.25
		Nos. 764-769 (6)	3.25	4.15

Cattle A138

1997, Jan. 7   Litho.   Perf. 14½
770	A138	45c Mashona cow	.30	.25
771	A138	$1.50 Tuli cow	.75	.25
772	A138	$2.20 Nkoni bull	.95	1.00
773	A138	$3 Brahman bull	1.25	1.75
		Nos. 770-773 (4)	3.25	3.25

Convention on Intl. Trade in Endangered Species of Flora and Fauna (CITES) — A139

1997, Apr. 15   Litho.   Perf. 14½
774	A139	45c Cycad	.25	.25
775	A139	$1.50 Peregrine falcon	1.00	.75
776	A139	$1.70 Pangolin	.25	.50
777	A139	$2.20 Black rhinoceros	1.00	1.00
778	A139	$2.50 Elephant	1.00	1.00
779	A139	$3 Python	.75	2.00
		Nos. 774-779 (6)	4.25	5.50

Aspects of Rural Life A140

1997, July 22   Litho.   Perf. 14½
780	A140	65c Carving	.25	.25
781	A140	$1 Winnowing	.25	.25
782	A140	$2.40 Dancing	.50	.60
783	A140	$2.50 Plowing	.50	.70
784	A140	$3.10 Stamping	.60	.90
785	A140	$4.20 Fetching water	.90	1.30
		Nos. 780-785 (6)	3.00	4.00

Zimbabwe Railway, Cent. A141

65c, Passenger coach. $1, 12th Class, No. 257. $2.40, 16A Class, No. 605. $2.50, El 1, No. 4107. $3.10, Jack Tar. $4.20, DE 2, No. 1211.

1997, Oct. 28   Litho.   Perf. 14½
786	A141	65c multicolored	.35	.35
787	A141	$1 multicolored	.35	.35
788	A141	$2.40 multicolored	.50	.70
789	A141	$2.50 multicolored	.60	.70
790	A141	$3.10 multicolored	.60	1.00
791	A141	$4.20 multicolored	.80	1.25
		Nos. 786-791 (6)	3.10	4.35

Wildlife A142

65c, Aardwolf. $2.40, Large gray mongoose. $3.10, Clawless otter. $4.20, Antbear (Aardvark).

1998, Jan. 20   Litho.   Perf. 14½
792	A142	65c multicolored	.40	.25
793	A142	$2.40 multicolored	.50	.60
794	A142	$3.10 multicolored	.60	1.00
795	A142	$4.20 multicolored	.75	1.50
		Nos. 792-795 (4)	2.25	3.35

Apiculture A143

Designs: $1.20, Honeybee on flower. $4.10, Queen, worker, drone. $4.70, Queen, retinue. $5.60, Rural beekeeper. $7.40, Commercial beekeepers. $9.90, Products of the hive.

1998, Apr. 14   Litho.   Perf. 14
796	A143	$1.20 multicolored	.35	.25
797	A143	$4.10 multicolored	.50	.50
798	A143	$4.70 multicolored	.50	.50
799	A143	$5.60 multicolored	.65	.75

800	A143	$7.40 multicolored	.90	1.00
801	A143	$9.90 multicolored	1.10	1.25
		Nos. 796-801 (6)	4.00	4.25

Fossils A144

1998, July 21   Litho.   Perf. 14½
802	A144	$1.20 Fossil fish	.80	.25
803	A144	$5.60 Allosaurus footprints	1.10	.70
804	A144	$7.40 Massospondylus	1.50	1.25
805	A144	$9.90 Fossil wood	1.75	1.75
		Nos. 802-805 (4)	5.15	3.95

Birds — A145

Designs: $1.20, Yellow-bellied sunbird. $4.10, Lesser blue-eared starling. $4.70, Greyhooded kingfisher. $5.60, Mombo gray tit. $7.40, Chirinda apalis. $9.90, Swynnerton's robin.

1998, Oct. 20   Litho.   Perf. 14
806	A145	$1.20 multicolored	.50	.25
807	A145	$4.10 multicolored	.75	.40
808	A145	$4.70 multicolored	.75	.50
809	A145	$5.60 multicolored	1.00	1.00
810	A145	$7.40 multicolored	1.00	1.25
811	A145	$9.90 multicolored	1.25	1.50
		Nos. 806-811 (6)	5.25	4.90

UPU, 125th Anniv. — A146

$1.20, Counter services at Post Office and Philatelic Bureau. $5.60, Postman delivering mail on bicycle. $7.40, 19th cent. runner, EMS, PTC delivery today. $9.90, Harare Central Sorting Office.

1999, Jan. 19   Litho.   Perf. 14
812	A146	$1.20 multicolored	.25	.25
813	A146	$5.60 multicolored	.50	.25
814	A146	$7.40 multicolored	1.25	.70
815	A146	$9.90 multicolored	.50	.75
		Nos. 812-815 (4)	2.50	1.95

A147

Wild cats of Zimbabwe.

1999, Mar. 16   Litho.   Perf. 14
816	A147	$1.20 Serval	.40	.25
817	A147	$5.60 Cheetah	.65	.45
818	A147	$7.40 Caracal	.95	1.05
819	A147	$9.90 Leopard	1.25	1.50
		Nos. 816-819 (4)	3.25	3.25

A148

Owls.

1999, June 8   Litho.   Perf. 14¼
820	A148	$1.20 Cape eagle owl	.50	.30
821	A148	$5.60 Grass owl	1.00	.80
822	A148	$7.40 Barn owl	1.00	1.00
823	A148	$9.90 Marsh owl	1.50	1.50
		Nos. 820-823 (4)	4.00	3.40

Tourist Activities A149

1999, Aug. 10   Litho.   Perf. 14¼x14
824	A149	$2 Canoeing	.25	.25
825	A149	$6.70 Rock climbing	.60	.50
826	A149	$7.70 Microlighting	.65	.60
827	A149	$9.10 White water rafting	.80	.80
828	A149	$12 Scenic view	1.00	1.25
829	A149	$16 Viewing game	1.25	2.00
		Nos. 824-829 (6)	4.55	5.40

A150

Christmas: $2, Christmas time — Family time. $6.70, Christmas time in Africa. $7.70, Joy to you this Christmas. $9.10, Christmas time — Flame lily time. $12, Glory to God & Peace on Earth. $16, The House of Christmas.

1999, Oct. 12   Litho.   Perf. 14x14¼
830	A150	$2 multi	.25	.25
831	A150	$6.70 multi	.35	.25
832	A150	$7.70 multi	.35	.30
833	A150	$9.10 multi	.50	.45
834	A150	$12 multi	.75	1.00
835	A150	$16 multi	1.00	1.30
		Nos. 830-835 (6)	3.20	3.60

A151

Designs: 1c, Nyala. 10c, Construction. 30c, Timber. 50c, Tobacco auction floors. 70c, Harare Central Sorting Office. 80c, New international airport, Harare. $1, Westgate Shopping Complex. $2, Nile crocodile. $3, Pungwe water project. $4, Zebra. $5, Mining. $7, National University of Science and Technology. $10, Ostrich. $15, Cape parrot. $20, Leather products. $30, Lilac-breasted roller. $50, Victoria Falls. $100, Tokwe Mukorsi Dam.

2000, Jan. 25   Litho.   Perf. 14¾
836	A151	1c multi	.25	.25
837	A151	10c multi	.25	.25
838	A151	30c multi	.25	.25
839	A151	50c multi	.25	.25
840	A151	70c multi	.25	.40
841	A151	80c multi	.70	.50
842	A151	$1 multi	.25	.30
843	A151	$2 multi	.70	.30
844	A151	$3 multi	.25	.25
845	A151	$4 multi	1.00	.25
846	A151	$5 multi	1.10	.30
847	A151	$7 multi	.25	.40
848	A151	$10 multi	1.50	.65
849	A151	$15 multi	1.50	1.10
850	A151	$20 multi	.60	.80
851	A151	$30 multi	2.50	1.25
852	A151	$50 multi	1.60	1.60
853	A151	$100 multi	2.25	3.00
		Nos. 836-853 (18)	15.45	12.10

Sports — A152

2000, Apr. 25   Litho.   Perf. 14
854	A152	$2 Basketball	.25	.25
855	A152	$6.70 Lawn tennis	.50	.45
856	A152	$7.70 Netball	.50	.50
857	A152	$9.10 Weight lifting	.50	.60
858	A152	$12 Taekwondo	.75	.60
859	A152	$16 Diving	1.00	1.00
		Nos. 854-859 (6)	3.50	3.60

Dr. Joshua Nkomo (1917-99), Vice-President A153

Designs: $2, $12, Wearing suit. $9.10, $16, Wearing headdress.

2000, June 27   Litho.   Perf. 14x14¼
Background Color
860	A153	$2 blue	.25	.25
861	A153	$9.10 green	.80	1.00
862	A153	$12 red	1.10	1.25
863	A153	$16 orange	1.25	1.75
		Nos. 860-863 (4)	3.40	4.25

Organizations Combating Disease A154

Designs: $2, Ministry of Health. $6.70, Rehabilitation and Prevention of Tuberculosis (RAPT). $7.70, New Start centers. $9.10, Riders for Health. $12, Natl. Aids Coordination Program (NACP). $16, Rotary Intl.

2000, July 18   Litho.   Perf. 14¼x14
864	A154	$2 multi	.30	.30
865	A154	$6.70 multi	.50	.50
866	A154	$7.70 multi	.50	.50
867	A154	$9.10 multi	.60	.60
868	A154	$12 multi	.75	.75
869	A154	$16 multi	1.10	1.00
		Nos. 864-869 (6)	3.75	3.65

Wild Fruits Type of 1991

$2, Masawu. $6.70, Spiny monkey orange. $7.70, Bird plum. $9.10, Shakama plum. $12, Wild medlar. $16, Wild custard apple.

2000, Oct. 24   Litho.   Perf. 14x14½
870-875	A117	Set of 6	3.50	3.50

Aviation A155

Designs: $8, Boeing 737-200. $12, BAe Hawk MK 60. $14, Hawker Hunter FGA-9. $16, Cessna/Reims F-337. $21, Aerospatiale Alouette III helicopter. $28, Boeing 767-200ER.

2001, Jan. 31   Litho.   Perf. 14¼
876-881	A155	Set of 6	5.50	5.50

Total Solar Eclipse, June 21, 2001 — A156

Designs: $8, Solar prominences. $21, Eclipse path over Africa. $28, Eclipse phases (62x24mm).

Perf. 14¼x14, 14½ ($28)
2001, Apr. 24   Litho.
882-884	A156	Set of 3	3.00	3.00

Folklore — A157

Designs: $8, The Hare Who Rode Horseback. $12, The Hippo Who Lost His Hair. $13, The Lion Who Was Saved by a Mouse. $16, The Bush Fowl Who Wakes the Sun. $21, The Chameleon Who Came Too Late. $28, The Tortoise Who Collected Wisdom.

2001, July 24   Litho.   Perf. 14x14¼
885-890 A157   Set of 6   4.50 4.50
  a. Souvenir sheet, #885-890   6.00 6.00

Heroes' Acre — A158

Designs: $8, Main entrance gate. $16, Statue of the Unknown Soldier. $21, General view. $28, Aerial view.

2001, Aug. 7   Litho.   Perf. 14¼x14
891-894 A158   Set of 4   3.00 3.00

Year of Dialogue Among Civilizations A159

Winning stamp design entry in: $8, National competition (Three Faces, by Nation Mandla Mguni). $21, International competition.

2001, Oct. 16   Litho.   Perf. 14¼
895-896 A159   Set of 2   2.50 2.50

Butterflies A160

Designs: $12, Large blue charaxes. $20, Painted lady. $25, Yellow pansy. $30, Gold-banded forester. $35, Sapphire. $45, Clear-spotted acrea.

2001, Dec. 6   Litho.   Perf. 14¼x14
897-902 A160   Set of 6   7.50 7.50
  902a Souvenir sheet, #897-902   7.50 7.50

Craftsmanship A161

Designs: $12, Knitting and crocheting. $20, Art and design. $25, Basket making. $30, Pottery. $35, Wood carving. $45, Sculpture.

2002, Jan. 22
903-908   Set of 6   7.00 7.00

Gemstones A162

Designs: $12, Agate. $25, Aquamarine. $35, Diamond. $45, Emerald.

2002, Apr. 23   Litho.   Perf. 14¼x14
909-912 A162   Set of 4   7.50 7.50

Childline A163

Children's art: $12, Children embracing. $25, Girl on phone. $35, Teddy bear. $45, Arm with phone receiver.

2002, June 4   Litho.   Perf. 14¼x14
913-916 A163   Set of 4   6.00 6.00

First Lady Sally Mugabe (1931-92) — A164

Various portraits: $20, $50, $70, $90.

2002, Aug. 6   Perf. 14x14¼
917-920 A164   Set of 4   7.00 7.00

Children's Stamp Design Contest Winners A165

Designs: $20, Mail runner and bicycle at post office, by Agreement Ngwenya. $70, Mail runner and airplane, by Kudzai Chikomo.

2002, Oct. 8   Litho.   Perf. 14¼
921-922 A165   Set of 2   4.50 4.50

Wild Flowers A166

Designs: $20, Dissotis princeps. $35, Leonotis nepetifolia. $40, Hibiscus vitifolius. $50, Boophane disticha. $70, Pycnostachys urticifolia. $90, Gloriosa superba.

2002, Oct. 22   Perf. 14¼x14
923-928 A166   Set of 6   11.00 11.00
  928a Souvenir sheet, #923-928   12.00 12.00

History Society of Zimbabwe, 50th Anniv. — A167

Map of Zimbabwe and: $30, Society emblem. $80, Hourglass, books, diploma. $110, People listening to speaker. $140, Old building.

2003, Jan. 28   Litho.   Perf. 14¼x14
929-932 A167   Set of 4   5.50 5.50

Harare Intl. Festival of the Arts — A168

Designs: $30, Festival emblem. $80, Emblem and flower. $110, Eye and flowers. $140, Emblem and flowers.

2003, Apr. 22   Litho.   Perf. 14x14¼
933-936 A168   Set of 4   4.25 4.25

Type of 2000

Designs: ($100), Bateleur eagle. $500, Goliath heron. $1000, White rhinoceros. $5000, Cheetah.

2003, June 24   Litho.   Perf. 14¾
937 A151 ($100) multi   1.00 1.00
938 A151 $500 multi   1.00 1.00
939 A151 $1000 multi   2.00 2.00
940 A151 $5000 multi   5.00 5.00
  Nos. 937-940 (4)   9.00 9.00

No. 937 is inscribed "Standard Postage."

Spiders A169

Designs: $150, Baboon spider. $200, Rain spider. $600, Black widow spider. $900, Wolf spider. $1250, Violin spider. $1600, Wall spider.

2003, July 30   Perf. 14¼
941-946 A169   Set of 6   8.50 8.50
  946a Souvenir sheet, #941-946   8.50 8.50

Women Empowerment A170

Woman in cap and gown with: $300, Globe, hoe and briefcase. $2100, Traditional woman.

2003, Oct. 14   Litho.   Perf. 14¼
947-948 A170   Set of 2   4.00 4.00

Endangered Medicinal Herbs — A171

Designs: $200, Wild verbena. $500, Pimpernel. $1000, African arrowroot. $3000, Bird pepper. $4200, Wild garlic. $5400, Cleome.

2003, Oct. 28   Perf. 14¼x14¼
949-954 A171   Set of 6   14.00 14.00
  a. Miniature sheet, #949-954   17.00 17.00

Environmental Awareness A172

Designs: $500, Environment Africa. $3000, Sondela. $4200, Water Africa. $5400, Tree Africa.

2004, Feb. 17   Litho.   Perf. 14¼x14
955-958 A172   Set of 4   14.00 14.00

Medals — A173

Designs: $1500, Zimbabwe Independence Medal. $9000, Bronze Cross of Zimbabwe. $13,000, Silver Cross of Zimbabwe. $16,500, Gold Cross of Zimbabwe.

2004, Apr. 6   Litho.   Perf. 14¼
959-962 A173   Set of 4   40.00 40.00

Aloes — A174

Designs: $1500, Aloe ballii. $3,000, Aloe rhodesiana. $9000, Aloe greatheadii. $10,000, Aloe ortholopha. $13,000, Aloe inyangensis. $16,500, Aloe arborescens.

2004, July 20   Litho.   Perf. 14x14¼
963-968 A174   Set of 6   15.00 15.00
  968a Miniature sheet, #963-968   17.00 17.00

Co-Vice President Simon Vengai Muzenda (1922-2003) A175

Background colors: $2300, Red. $12,000, Yellow. $17,000, Green. $22,000, Gray.

2004, Sept. 20   Litho.   Perf. 14x14¼
969-972 A175   Set of 4   15.00 15.00

Conservation A176

Winning art in conservation stamp design contest: $4600, Butterfly, by Kingston Chigidhani. $33,500, Hands and wildlife, by Kudzai Chikomo.

2004, Oct. 26   Litho.   Perf. 14¼x14
973-974 A176   Set of 2   7.00 7.00

Miniature Sheet

Birds — A177

No. 975: a, $500, African fish eagles, national bird of Zambia. b, $1000, Purple-crested louries, national bird of Swaziland. c, $2300, African fish eagles, national bird of Zimbabwe. d, $3000, Blue cranes, national bird of South Africa. e, $5000, Cattle egrets, national bird of Botswana. f, $9000, Peregrine falcons, national bird of Angola. g, $12,000,

Bar-tailed trogons. h, $17,000, African fish eagles, national bird of Namibia.

2004, Oct. 11   Litho.   Perf. 14
975 A177   Sheet of 8, #a-h   45.00 45.00

See Botswana Nos. 792-793, Namibia No. 1052, South Africa No. 1342, Swaziland Nos. 727-735, and Zambia No. 1033.

Birds — A178

Designs: $500, Black-collared barbet. $5000, Gray-headed bush shrike. Z, Red-headed weaver. $10,000, Golden-breasted bunting. $20,000, Cut-throat finch. A, Cabanis's bunting. E, Miombo double-collared sunbird. R, Crested barbet. $50,000, Heuglin's robin. $100,000, Giant kingfisher.

2005, Feb. 8   Litho.   Perf. 14¾x14½
976 A178 $500 multi   1.00 1.00
977 A178 $5000 multi   2.00 2.00
978 A178   Z multi   2.50 2.50
979 A178 $10,000 multi   3.00 3.00
980 A178 $20,000 multi   5.50 5.50
981 A178   A multi   8.00 8.00
982 A178   E multi   11.00 11.00
983 A178   R multi   13.00 13.00
984 A178 $50,000 multi   13.00 13.00
985 A178 $100,000 multi   26.00 26.00
    Nos. 976-985 (10)   85.00 85.00

On day of issue No. 978 sold for $6900, No. 981 sold for $30,000, No. 982 sold for $40,000, and No. 983 sold for $50,000.

Clouds
A179

Designs: $6900, Cirrus. $13,800, Nimbostratus. $30,000, Altocumulus. $40,000, Cumulonimbus.

2005, Apr. 26   Perf. 14¼
986-989 A179   Set of 4   22.50 22.50

Snakes
A180

Designs: $6900, Banded Egyptian cobra. $13,800, Puff adder. $20,000, Boomslang. $25,000, Mozambique spitting cobra. $30,000, Gaboon viper. $40,000, Black mamba.

2005, July 12   Litho.   Perf. 14¼x14
990-995 A180   Set of 6   18.00 18.00
995a   Miniature sheet, #990-995   25.00 25.00

Governmental
Officials — A181

Designs: $6900, Josiah Tongogara (1940-79), Chief of Defense. $13,800, Herbert Chitepo (1923-75), Director of Public Prosecutions. $30,000, Bernard Chidzero (1927-2002), Minister of Economic Planning. $50,000, Moven Mahachi (1948-2001), Minister of various departments.

2005, Aug. 4   Litho.   Perf. 14x14¼
996-999 A181   Set of 4   10.00 10.00

UNESCO
World
Heritage
Sites
A182

Designs: Z, Soapstone Zimbabwe bird, Great Zimbabwe National Park. $15,500, Wall, Khami Ruins. $52,000, Elephant, Mana Pools National Park. $62,000, Victoria Falls.

2005, Oct. 6   Litho.   Perf. 14¼
1000-1003 A182   Set of 4   20.00 20.00
1003a   Souvenir sheet, #1000-1003   25.00 25.00

No. 1000 sold for $10,250 on day of issue.

World AIDS
Day — A183

Designs: $18,000, Cooking pot, field tender, care for the ill. $30,000, Children teaching AIDS prevention.

2005, Dec. 1   Litho.   Perf. 14¼x14
1004-1005 A183   Set of 2   8.75 8.75

Food — A184

Designs: $25,000, Mushrooms. $35,000, Rapoko, corn and sorghum. $50,000, Pumpkin, watermelon, spiny cucumber. $150,000, Wild fruits. $250,000, Herbs. $300,000, Sweet potato, cassava, peanuts.

2006, Jan. 17   Litho.   Perf. 14x14¼
1006-1011 A184   Set of 6   10.00 10.00
1011a   Miniature sheet, #1006-1011   14.00 14.00

Pope John Paul
II (1920-2005)
A185

Pope: $25,000, Wearing crucifix. $250,000, Holding crucifix.

2006, Feb. 9
1012-1013 A185   Set of 2   10.00 10.00
1013a   Souvenir sheet, #1012-1013   12.00 12.00

Water
Conservation
A186

Designs: $30,000, Faucet and pail. $225,000, Flood irrigation system. $375,000, Lions at waterhole. $450,000, Kariba Dam.

2006, Apr. 25   Litho.   Perf. 14x14¼
1014-1017 A186   Set of 4   18.50 18.50

National
Heroes — A187

Flag and: $60,000, Leopold T. Takawira (1916-70), first vice-president of Zimbabwe African National Union. $350,000, Simon C. Mazorodze (1933-81), health minister. $500,000, Herbert M. Ushewokunze (1933-95), government minister. $650,000, Tichafa S. Parirenyatwa (1927-62), deputy president of Zimbabwe African People's Union.

2006, July 25   Litho.   Perf. 14x14¼
1018-1021 A187   Set of 4   15.00 15.00

Huts — A188

Designs: $100, One hut. $800, Three huts.

2006, Oct. 24   Litho.   Perf. 14¼x14
1022-1023 A188   Set of 2   12.00 12.00
1023a   Souvenir sheet, #1022-1023   10.00 10.00

Bridges
A189

Designs: Z, Mpudzi River Bridge. $450, Victoria Falls Bridge. $600, Limpopo River Bridge. $750, Otto Beit Bridge. $800, Kariba Barrage Bridge. $1000, Birchenough Bridge.

2006, Oct. 24
1024-1029 A189   Set of 6   25.00 25.00
1029a   Souvenir sheet, #1024-1029   30.00 30.00

No. 1024 sold for $100 on day of issue.

Trees — A190

Designs: $150, Ziziphuus mauritania. $600, Schlerochra birrea. $750, Jatropha carcus. $1000, Uaparca kirkiana.

2006, Dec. 1   Litho.   Perf. 14x14¼
1030-1033 A190   Set of 4   18.00 18.00
1033a   Souvenir sheet, #1030-1033   18.00 18.00

Birds — A191

Designs: $50, Hoopoe. $100, Cattle egret. $500, Malachite kingfisher. $1000, Little bee-eater. $2000, Purple-crested lorie. $5000, Purple gallinule. $10,000, African jacana. $20,000, Ground hornbill. $50,000, Gorgeous bush shrike. $100,000, Secretary bird.

Perf. 14¾x14½
2007, Feb. 20   Litho.
1034 A191 $50 multi   .25 .25
1035 A191 $100 multi   .25 .25
1036 A191 $500 multi   .25 .25
1037 A191 $1000 multi   .35 .35
1038 A191 $2000 multi   .65 .65
1039 A191 $5000 multi   1.75 1.75
1040 A191 $10,000 multi   3.25 3.25
1041 A191 $20,000 multi   6.50 6.50
1042 A191 $50,000 multi   12.00 12.00
1043 A191 $100,000 multi   25.00 25.00
a.   Souvenir sheet, #1034-1043   65.00 65.00
    Nos. 1034-1043 (10)   50.25 50.25

Scouting,
Cent. — A192

Scouting emblem and: $400, Great Zimbabwe Ruins. $1500, Map of Zimbabwe. $2000, Centenary emblem. $2500, Map of Africa.

2007, Feb. 20   Perf. 14x14¼
1044-1047 A192   Set of 4   15.00 15.00

Women
A193

Designs: $7500, Mbuya Nehanda (?-1898), colonial resistance organizer. $29,000, Queen Lozikeyi (c. 1855-1919). $35,000, Mother Patrick (1863-1900), educator. $45,000, Amai Sally Mugabe (1932-92), First Lady.

2007, July 10   Perf. 14¼
1048-1051 A193   Set of 4   9.00 9.00

Beginning in 2007, Zimbabwean currency began to experience extreme hyperinflation. Starting with Nos. 1052-1055, most stamps are non-denominated, inscribed "Z" for surface-rate letters sent within Zimbabwe, "A" for letters sent to the rest of Africa by air, "E" for letters sent to Europe by air, and "R" for letters sent to the rest of the world by air, with letters being up to 20 grams in weight. Press release information about these stamps probably was printed in advance of their issuance, so it is unknown if the stamps were actually sold to local customers for the rates implied by the release on the stated day of issue at post offices in Zimbabwe. As the Zimbabwean dollar and denominated stamps daily became more and more worthless (with a reissuance of new Zimbabwe dollars eliminating 10 zeroes on Aug. 1, 2008, and yet again eliminating 12 zeroes on Feb. 2, 2009), the editors cannot easily determine selling prices for these stamps.

National
Heroes — A194

Designs: Z, Jason Ziyaphapha Moyo (1927-77), second vice-president of Zimbabwe African People's Union. A, Maurice T. Nyagumbo (1924-89), Zimbabwe African National Union senior minister of political affairs. E, Guy Clutton-Brock (1906-95), founder of Cold Comfort Farm Society. R, Chief Rekayi Tangwena (c. 1910-84), senator.

2007, Aug. 9   Litho.   Perf. 14x14¼
1052-1055 A194   Set of 4   15.00 —

On day of issue, Nos. 1052-1055 reportedly sold for $3,000, $12,000, $17,000, and $20,000, respectively.

Butterflies
A195

Designs: Z, Mother-of-pearl. A, Citrus swal-lowtail. E, Orange tip. R, Blue charaxes. $50,000, Crimson tip. $100,000, Painted lady.

2007, Sept. 18
1056-1061 A195   Set of 6   20.00   —
a. Souvenir sheet, #1056-1061   25.00   —

On day of issue, Nos. 1056-1059 reportedly sold for $7,500, $29,000, $35,000, and $45,000, respectively.

Life of
Children — A196

Winning art in stamp design contest: Z, Boy studying, by John Ndhlovu. $100,000, Mother feeding baby, by Fungai Madzima.

2007, Oct. 9
1062-1063 A196   Set of 2   15.00   —
a. Souvenir sheet, #1062-1063   15.00   —

On day of issue, Nos. 1062 reportedly sold for $7,500.

National
Animals
A197

Designs: Z, Buffalo (Zambia). A, Nyala (Malawi). E, Burchell's zebra (Botswana). R, Oryx (Namibia). $100,000, Nyala (Zimbabwe).

Litho. With Foil Application
2007, Oct. 9   **Perf. 13¾**
1064-1068 A197   Set of 5   13.00   —
a. Souvenir sheet, #1064-1068   20.00   —

On day of issue, Nos. 1064-1067 reportedly sold for $7,500, $29,000, $35,000, and $45,000, respectively. See Botswana No. 838, Malawi No. 752, Namibia Nos. 1141-1142, Zambia Nos. 1097-1101.

St. Valentine's
Day — A198

Designs: Z, Heart. A, Cupid. E, Card (5 hearts). R, Rose.

2008, Jan. 24   Litho.   Perf. 14x14¼
1069-1072 A198   Set of 4   13.00   —
a. Souvenir sheet, #1069-1072   13.00   —

On day of issue, Nos. 1069-1072 reportedly sold for $25,000, $100,000, $170,000, and $240,000, respectively.

Rodents
A199

Designs: Z, Striped mouse. A, Water rat. E, Angoni vlei rat. R, Woodland dormouse. $5,000,000, Bushveld gerbil. $10,000,000, Namaqua rock mouse.

2008, Apr. 24   **Perf. 14¼**
1073-1078 A199   Set of 6   15.00   —
a. Souvenir sheet, #1073-1078   20.00   —

On day of issue, Nos. 1073-1076 reportedly sold for $550,000, $1,900,000, $3,150,000, and $4,600,000, respectively.

National
Heroes — A200

Designs: Z, Johanna Nkomo (1927-2003), wife of Joshua Nkomo. A, Ruth Lottie Nomonde Chinamano (1925-2005), political activist. E, Dr. Swithun Tachiona Mombeshora (1945-2003), National president of Red Cross. R, Willie Dzawanda Musarurwa (1927-90), journalist.

2008, Aug. 5   **Perf. 14x14¼**
1079-1082 A200   Set of 4   20.00   —

On day of issue, release information states that Nos. 1079-1082 were to be sold for $250,000,000, $50,000,000,000, $90,000,000,000, and $110,000,000,000, respectively, but the stamps were issued after the Aug. 1 revaluation of the currency eliminating 10 zeroes from the denominations.

In December 2008, Zimbabwe's hyperinflation was calculated by *Forbes Asia* at 6.5 times 10 to the 108th power. By the middle of January 2009, virtually all transactions in Zimbabwe were being conducted in foreign currencies, despite law that mandated that the Zimbabwe dollar be used in transactions between parties not having a government license allowing them to conduct transactions in foreign currencies. On January 29, Zimbabwe's finance minister finally made the use of foreign currencies legal for any transactions in Zimbabwe. On February 2, the government revalued the Zimbabwe dollar for the final time, and finally suspended its use on April 12. Selling prices for stamps listed below are stated in US currency, the primary foreign currency used in the country, as well as the currency used in philatelic press releases.

2008
Summer
Olympics,
Beijing
A201

Emblem of the Zimbabwe Olympic Committee and: Z, Water Cube. A, National Stadium (Bird's Nest). E, Olympic pool. R, Flag of Zimbabwe, medals won by Zimbabwe Olympic athletes.

2009, Jan. 20   Litho.   Perf. 14¼
1083-1086 A201   Set of 4   10.00 10.00

On day of issue, Nos. 1083-1086 reportedly sold in US currency for 50c, $1, $1.50, and $2. respectively.

Paintings
A202

Designs: Zb, Cardoor Scape, bu Cosmos Shiridzinomwa. Zs, Countryside, by James Jali. No. 1089, A, Mountains, by George Churu. No. 1090, A, Barn, by Hilary Kashiri. E, Backyard 1, by Freddy Tauro. R, X in the Land, by Admire Kamudzengere.

2009, Apr. 21
1087-1092 A202   Set of 6   10.00 10.00
1092a   Souvenir sheet of 6,
          #1087-1092   11.00 11.00

On day of issue, Nos. 1087-1092 sold in US currency for 20c, 25c, 50c, 50c, 75c and $1, respectively.

Wildlife
A203

Designs: Zb, Leopard. Zs, Black rhinoceros. No. 1095, A, African buffalo. No. 1096, A, Lion. E, African elephant. R, All five animals.

2009, June 23
1093-1098 A203   Set of 6   14.00 14.00
1098a   Souvenir sheet of 6,
          #1093-1098   15.00 15.00

On day of issue, Nos. 1093-1098 sold in US currency for 20c, 25c, 50c, 50c, 75c and $1, respectively.

National
Heroes — A204

Flag of Zimbabwe and: Zb, Vitalis Musungwa Gava Zvinavashe (1943-2009), commander of Zimbabwe Defense Forces. Zs, Garikayi Hlomayi Settled Magadzire (1937-96), leader of Zimbabwe National Farmers' Union. A, George Bodzo Nyandoro (1926-94), Minister of Lands, Natural Resources and Rural Development. E, Border "Madzibaba" Gezi (1964-2001), Minister of Youth, Gender and Employment Creation. R, Seugeant Masotsha Ndlovu (1890-1982), union leader.

2009, Aug. 4   **Perf. 14x14¼**
1099-1103 A204   Set of 5   12.00 12.00

On day of issue, Nos. 1099-1103 sold in US currency for 20c, 25c, 50c, 75c and $1, respectively.

Christmas
A205

Rural churches: Z, St. Barbara's Catholic Church, Kariba. A, Regina Coeli Catholic Church. E, Elim Evangelical Church, Katerere. R, Free Presbyterian Church, Mbuma.

2009, Dec. 15   **Perf. 14¼**
1104-1107 A205   Set of 4   8.00   8.00
a. Souvenir sheet, #1104-1107 8.50   8.50

On day of issue, Nos. 1104-1107 sold in US currency for 25c, 50c, 75c and $1, respectively.

Zimbabwe, Africa's Paradise — A206

Winning art in stamp design contest by: Z, Fredy Tembo. A, Munashe M. Patsanza. E, Methembe Dhlamini. R, Kudzai Chikomo.

2010, Jan. 19
1108-1111 A206   Set of 4   10.00 10.00
1111a   Souvenir sheet of 4,
          #1108-1111   11.00 11.00

On day of issue, Nos. 1108-1111 sold in US currency for 25c, 50c, 75c and $1 respectively.

2010 World Cup Soccer
Championships, South Africa — A207

Soccer players, ball, 2010 World Cup mascot and flag of: Nos. 1112, 1121a, 10c, Namibia. Nos. 1113, 1121b, 15c, South Africa. Nos. 1114, 1121c, 25c, Zimbabwe. Nos. 1115, 1121d, Z, Botswana. Nos. 1116, 1121e, 50c, Malawi. Nos. 1117, 1121f, A, Mauritius. Nos. 1118, 1121g, 75c, Swaziland. Nos. 1119, 1121h, E, Lesotho. Nos. 1120, 1120i, R, Zambia.

2010, Apr. 9   Litho.   Perf. 13½
On Plain Paper With Olive Brown Background
1112-1120 A207   Set of 9   15.00 15.00
On Gold-faced Paper
1121 A207   Sheet of 9, #a-i   15.00 15.00

On day of issue, Nos. 1115 and 1121d sold for 25c, Nos. 1117 and 1121f sold for 50c, Nos. 1119 and 1121h sold for 75c, and Nos. 1120 and 1121i sold for $1.
See Botswana Nos. 896-905, Lesotho No. , Malawi No. 753, Mauritius No. 1086, Namibia No. 1188, South Africa No. 1403, Swaziland Nos. 794-803, and Zambia Nos. 1115-1118.
Single sheetlets of 9 omibus issues exist containing No. 1121a. See footnote under Namibia 1188.

Vice-President
Joseph Wilfred
Msika (1923-
2009)
A208

Zimbabwe flag and various photographs of Msika with panel color of: Z, Yellow. A, Black. E, Dark red. R, Green.

2010, July 27   Litho.   Perf. 14x14¼
1122-1125 A208   Set of 4   8.50   8.50

On day of issue, Nos. 1122-1125 sold for 25c, 50c, 75c and $1, respectively.

Pan-African Postal
Union, 30th
Anniv. — A209

2010, Dec. 28   **Perf. 14¼**
1126 A209 Z multi   1.00   .50

No. 1126 sold for 50c on day of issue.

Railroad
Stations
A210

Station in: 25c, Harare. 30c, Kadoma. 85c, Bulawayo. $1, Mutare.

2011, May 26   **Perf. 14¼x14**
1127-1130 A210   Set of 4   6.50   6.50

National Heroes — A211

Designs: 25c, Tarcissius Malan George Silundika (1929-81), governmental minister. 30c, Julia Zvobgo (1937-2004), politician. 85c, Ariston Maguranyanga Chambati (1934-95), politician. $1, Joseph Luke Culverwell (1918-93), governmental minister.

2011, July 27   **Perf. 14x14¼**
1131-1134 A211 Set of 4   6.50 6.50

Huts — A212

Designs: 25c, Shona hut. 30c, Ndebele hut. 85c, Manyika hut. $1, Tonga hut.

2011, Nov. 29   **Perf. 14½x14**
1135-1138 A212 Set of 4   6.50 6.50
1138a   Sheet of 4, #1135-1138   6.50 6.50

A213

Sculptures — A214

Designs: 5c, 50c, Tobacco Wither, by Henry Munyaradzi. 25c, Family, by Bernard Matemera. 30c, Mother and Daughters, by Victor Mutongwizo. 75c, $1.50, Bird Carrying Spirit People, by Thomas Mukarobgwa. 85c, Wounded Kudu, by Bakali Manzi. $1, Witch and Her Mate, by Sylvester Mubayi.

2012, Mar. 27   **Litho.**   **Perf. 14¼**
1139 A213 5c multi   .25 .25
1140 A213 25c multi   .75 .75
1141 A213 30c multi   .75 .75
1142 A213 50c multi   1.25 1.00
a.   Souvenir sheet of 4, #1139-1142   3.75 3.75

Perf. 14¼x14
1143 A214 75c multi   1.75 2.00
1144 A214 85c multi   2.00 2.25
1145 A214 $1 multi   2.00 2.25
1146 A214 $1.50 multi   3.50 3.75
a.   Souvenir sheet of 4, #1143-1146   10.00 10.00
    Nos. 1139-1146 (8)   12.25 13.00

National Heroes — A215

Designs: 30c, Solomon Tapfunmaneyi Ruzambo Mujuru (1945-2011), army officer and politician. 75c, Eddison Jonas Mudadirwa Zvobgo (1935-2004), governmental minister.

85c, Welshman Mabhena (1924-2010), politician. $1, Robson Dayford Manyika (1936-85), governmental minister.

2012, July 24   **Perf. 14x14¼**
1147-1150 A215 Set of 4   7.00 7.00

Road Safety Campaign A216

Inscriptions: 30c, Light up 5:30 PM. 75c, Speed/drunk driving. 85c, Obey the code. $1, Visibility.

2012, Aug. 28   **Perf. 14¼x14**
1151-1154 A216 Set of 4   7.00 7.00

Ants and Termites A217

Designs: 5c, Honeydew ant. No. 1156, 30c, Philidris ant. No. 1157, 30c, Leaf cutter ant. 75c, Termite and Matabele soldier ant. 85c, Carpenter ant. $1, Termite habitat.

2012, Nov. 20
1155-1160 A217 Set of 6   8.50 8.50
1160a   Souvenir sheet of 6, #1155-1160   8.50 8.50

Children's Art — A218

Designs: 30c, Children and rainbow. $1, Corn, mortar, pestle, bowl, head.

2013, Mar. 26
1161-1162 A218 Set of 2   3.00 3.00

Landa John Nkomo (1934-2013), Co-Vice-President A219

Sculpture at Heroes Acre, national flag and: 30c, Nkomo as young man. 75c, Nkomo as older man. 85c, Like 30c. $1, Like 75c.

2013, July 30   **Perf. 14x14¼**
1163-1166 A219 Set of 4   8.50 8.50

Women's Hairstyles A220

Designs: 30c, Tonga-Musila. 75c, Shona-Bumhu. 85c, Ndebele-Isicholo. $1, Shangaan-Bhibho.

2013, Dec. 17   **Litho.**   **Perf. 14¼x14**
1167-1170 A220 Set of 4   7.50 7.50
1170a   Souvenir sheet of 4, #1107-1170   7.50 7.50

Export Crops — A221

Designs: 30c, Flowers. 75c, Cotton. 85c, Tea. $1, Tobacco.

2014, Mar. 11   **Litho.**   **Perf. 14¼x14**
1171-1174 A221 Set of 4   10.00 10.00
1174a   Souvenir sheet of 4, #1171-1174   10.00 10.00

Transportation History — A222

Designs: 25c, Donkey-drawn sled, 1890s. No. 1176, 30c, Winston Churchill Train, 1929. No. 1177, 30c, 1928 Model A Ford Phaeton. 75c, De Havilland DH Fox Moth, 1932. 85c, 1946 Bristol Bus. $1, Ox-drawn cart, 1964.

2014, June 3   **Litho.**   **Perf. 14¼**
1175-1180 A222 Set of 6   9.00 9.00

National Heroes — A223

Designs: 30c, Sabrina Gabriel Mugabe (1929-2010), politician and sister of Pres. Robert Mugabe. 75c, Kumbirai Manyika Kangai (1938-2013), governmental minister. 85c, Stephen Kenneth Sesulelo Vuma (1936-97), politician. $1, Eric Nyakudya Gwanzura (1924-2013), politician.

2014, July 29   **Litho.**   **Perf. 14x14¼**
1181-1184 A223 Set of 4   7.00 7.00

World Post Day — A224

Designs: 30c, Ancient post runner. 75c, Post rider on horse. 85c, Harare Main Post Office. $1, Post bus.

2014, Oct. 9   **Litho.**   **Perf. 14¼x14**
1185-1188 A224 Set of 4   7.00 7.00

Frogs A225

Designs: 30c, Swynnerton's reed frog. 75c, Giant bullfrog. 85c, Bushveld rain frog. $1, Inyanga river frog.

2014, Dec. 9   **Litho.**   **Perf. 14¼**
1189-1192 A225 Set of 4   7.00 7.00
1192a   Souvenir sheet of 4, #1189-1192, imperf.   7.00 7.00

Ruins — A226

Designs: 40c, Chisvingo Ruins. 75c, Dhlo Dhlo Ruins. 85c, Khami Ruins. $1, Nalatale Ruins.

2015, Feb. 24   **Litho.**   **Perf. 14¼**
1193-1196 A226 Set of 4   7.00 7.00
1196a   Souvenir sheet of 4, #1193-1196   7.00 7.00

Victoria Falls — A227

Designs: 10c, Victoria Falls Bridge. 15c, Elephant interaction. 20c, View inside the rain forest. 25c, Makishi dancers. 40c, Zambezi whitewater rafters. 60c, Victoria Falls train station. 75c, Big Tree. 80c, Masks and curios. 85c, Statue of David Livingstone. $1, View of Victoria Falls from Devil's Cataract.

2015, Apr. 30   **Litho.**   **Perf. 14x14¼**
1197 A227 10c multi   .25 .25
1198 A227 15c multi   .30 .30
1199 A227 20c multi   .40 .40
1200 A227 25c multi   .50 .50
1201 A227 40c multi   .80 .80
1202 A227 60c multi   1.25 1.25
1203 A227 75c multi   1.50 1.50
1204 A227 80c multi   1.60 1.60
1205 A227 85c multi   1.75 1.75
1206 A227 $1 multi   2.00 2.00
a.   Souvenir sheet of 10, #1197-1206   10.50 10.50
    Nos. 1197-1206 (10)   10.35 10.35

National Heroes — A228

Designs: 40c, Sunny Ntombiyelanga Takawira (1927-2010), politician. 75c, David Isheunesu Godi Karimanzira (1947-2011), Minister of Education. 85c, Nolan Chipo Makombe (1932-98), Parliament Speaker. $1, Nathan Marwirakuwa Shamuyarira (1929-2014), Minister of Information.

2015, July 30   **Litho.**   **Perf. 14x14¼**
1207-1210 A228 Set of 4   7.00 7.00

Handicrafts A229

Designs: 40c, Basketry. 75c, Batik fabrics. 85c, Pottery. $1, Metal sculptures.

2015, Sept. 29   **Litho.**   **Perf. 14¼x14**
1211-1214 A229 Set of 4   7.00 7.00

Historic Hotels — A230

Designs: 40c, Leopard Rock Hotel. 75c, Bulawayo Club. 85c, Victoria Falls Hotel. $1, Meikles Hotel.

2015, Nov. 28   Litho.   Perf. 14¼x14
1215-1218   A230   Set of 4   7.50 7.50

Bank Buildings
A231

Designs: 40c, Standard Bank Ltd. Building, Harare, 1912. 75c, Standard Bank Building, Chegutu, early 1900s. 85c, Barclays Bank Building, Bulawayo, 1912. $1, African Banking Corp. Building, Kadoma, 1913.

2016, Mar. 22   Litho.   Perf. 14¼x14
1219-1222   A231   Set of 4   7.50 7.50

National
Heroes — A232

Governmental ministers: 40c, Victoria Fikile Chitepo (1927-2016). 75c, Enos Chamunorwa Chikowore (1936-2005). 85c, Josiah Mushore Chinamano (1925-84). $1, Enos Mzombi Nkala (1932-2013).

2016, July 28   Litho.   Perf. 14x14¼
1223-1226   A232   Set of 4   8.00 8.00

Campaign
Against
Pollution
A233

Types of pollution: 10c, Water. 30c, Soil. 40c, Rubbish. 75c, Noise. 85c, Air. $1, Toxic waste.

2016, Aug. 30   Litho.   Perf. 14½x14
1227-1232   A233   Set of 6   8.00 8.00

Recreational
Fishing
A234

Designs: 40c, Tiger fish. 75c, Largemouth bass. 85c, Fishermen on Lake Mutirikwi. $1, Fishermen on Lake Manyame.

2017, Jan. 30   Litho.   Perf. 14¼x14
1233-1236   A234   Set of 4   6.00 6.00
1236a   Souvenir sheet of 4,
     #1233-1236, imperf.   6.00 6.00

Dairy
Cows
A235

Breed of cow: 40c, Ayrshire. 75c, Holstein. 85c, Jersey. $1, Red Dane.

2017, Aug. 22   Litho.   Perf. 14¼
1237-1240   A235   Set of 4   6.00 6.00
1240a   Souvenir sheet of 4,
     #1237-1240, imperf.   6.00 6.00

National
Heroes — A236

Sculpture at Heroes Acre, national flag and: 40c, Cephas George Msipa (1931-2016), politician. 75c, Felix Ngwarati Muchemwa (1945-2016), brigadier general. 85c, Godfrey Guwa Chidyausiku (1947-2017), Chief Justice. $1, Dr. Charles Munhamu Botsio Utete (1938-2016), politician.

2018, Feb. 5   Litho.   Perf. 14x14¼
1241-1244   A236   Set of 4   6.00 6.00

Postal officials of Zimbabwe have declared as "illegal" sheets of 4 dated 2009 and 2010 depicting butterflies, sheets of 6 and 9 dated 2011 depicting fire trucks, sheets of 4 and souvenir sheets dated 2015 depicting World Championship ice hockey players, and 76 other souvenir sheets depicting various themes.

Promotion of
Zimbabwe for
Businesses
A237

Zimbabwe Pres. Emmerson D. Mnangagwa: 40c, With South African Pres. Cyril Ramaphosa. 75c, Speaking at African Continental Free Trade Area Business Forum. 85c, With International Monetary Fund Managing Director Christine Lagarde. $1, With People's Repubic of China Pres. Xi Jinping.

2018, July 18   Litho.   Perf. 14
1245-1248   A237   Set of 4   6.00 6.00
1248a   Souvenir sheet of 4,
     #1245-1248, imperf.   6.00 6.00

Ladybugs — A238

Designs: 40c, Seven-spotted ladybug. 75c, Black-and-yellow-spotted ladybug. 85c, Twenty-spotted ladybug. $1, Ladybug in flight.

2018, Oct. 15   Litho.   Perf. 14
1249-1252   A238   Set of 4   6.00 6.00
1252a   Souvenir sheet of 4,
     #1249-1252, imperf.   6.00 6.00

POSTAGE DUE STAMPS

D1

1981   Litho.   Perf. 14½
J20   D1   1c emerald   .40 1.10
J21   D1   2c ultramarine   .40 1.10
J22   D1   5c lilac   .50 1.40
J23   D1   6c yellow   .65 2.00
J24   D1   10c red   1.40 4.25
    Nos. J20-J24 (5)   3.35 9.85

For surcharge see No. J30.

D2

1985, Aug. 21   Litho.   Perf. 14½
J25   D2   1c pale orange   .40 .75
J26   D2   2c lilac rose   .40 .75
J27   D2   6c light green   .40 .75
J28   D2   10c tan   .40 .75
J29   D2   13c bright blue   .40 .75
    Nos. J25-J29 (5)   2.00 3.75

No. J24
Surcharged

1990, Jan. 2   Litho.   Perf. 14½
J30   D1   25c on 10c #J24   11.00 11.00

D3

1995, Jan. 17   Litho.   Perf. 14½
J31   D3   1c yellow   .35 .35
J32   D3   2c yellow orange   .35 .35
J33   D3   5c rose lilac   .35 .35
J34   D3   10c pale blue   .35 .35
J35   D3   25c violet   .35 .35
J36   D3   40c green   .35 .35
J37   D3   60c orange   .35 .35
J38   D3 $1 brown   .55 .55
    Nos. J31-J38 (8)   3.00 3.00

D4

Bird sculpture.

2000, Jan. 25   Litho.   Perf. 14½
J39   D4   1c blk, lt grn & grn   .25 .25
J40   D4   10c blk, lt blue & blue   .25 .25
J41   D4   50c blk; lt brn & brn   .25 .25
J42   D4 $1 blk, pink & red   .25 .25
J43   D4 $2 blk, lt yel & yel   .25 .25
J44   D4 $5 blk, lil & red vio   .25 .25
J45   D4 $10 blk, lt ver & ver   .55 .55
    Nos. J39-J45 (7)   2.05 2.05

ZULULAND

ˈzü-₍ˌ₎lü-ˌland

LOCATION — Northeastern part of Natal, South Africa
GOVT. — British Colony, 1887-1897
AREA — 10,427 sq. mi.
POP. — 230,000 (estimated 1900)
CAPITAL — Eshowe

   12 Pence = 1 Shilling
   20 Shillings = 1 Pound

Stamps of Great Britain
Overprinted

1888-93   Wmk. 30   Perf. 14
1   A54   ½p vermilion   8.75 3.00
2   A40   1p violet   30.00 6.75
3   A56   2p green & red   32.50 55.00
4   A57   2½p vio, bl ('91)   45.00 24.00
5   A58   3p violet, yel   34.00 25.00
6   A59   4p green & brn   62.50 77.50
7   A61   5p lil & bl ('93)   110.00 160.00
8   A62   6p vio, rose   25.00 20.00
9   A63   9p blue & lil ('92)   125.00 135.00
10   A65   1sh green ('92)   160.00 175.00

Wmk. 31
11   A51   5sh rose ('92)   725.00 800.00
   Nos. 1-10 (10)   632.75 681.25
Dangerous forgeries exist. Expertization is recommended for used examples of No. 11.

Natal No. 66
Overprinted

1888-94   Wmk. 2
12   A14   ½p green, no period   32.50 55.00
   a.   Period after "Zululand"   62.50 97.50
   b.   As "a," double overprint   1,450. 1,600.
   d.   As "a," pair, one without
     ovpt.   7,500.

The varieties formerly listed as Nos. 12c and 12e, No. 12a with inverted overprint and No. 12 with double overprint, are now considered to be forgeries.

Natal No. 71 Ovptd. Like Nos. 1-11
13   A11   6p violet ('94)   70.00 62.50

A1

1891
14   A1   1p lilac   5.00 3.75

By proclamation of the Governor of Zululand, dated June 27th, 1891, No. 14 was declared to be a postage stamp.

A2

1894-96   Typo.
15   A2   ½p lilac & grn   8.00 7.50
16   A2   1p lilac & rose   7.00 3.25
17   A2   2½p lilac & blue   16.00 12.00
18   A2   3p lilac & brn   11.00 4.00
19   A2   6p lilac & blk   24.00 25.00
20   A2   1sh green   52.50 45.00
21   A2   2sh6p grn & blk
     ('96)   95.00 115.00
22   A2   4sh grn & car
     rose   160.00 240.00
23   A2   £1 violet, red   675.00 725.00
24   A2   £5 vio & blk,
     red   5,750. 1,900.
   Overprinted "SPECIMEN"   500.00
   Nos. 15-23 (9)   1,049. 1,177.
   Nos. 15-23 ovptd.
   "SPECIMEN"   525.00

Numerals of Nos. 19-24 are in color on plain tablet. Dangerous forgeries of No. 24 exist. Expertization is recommended for used examples of No. 24.

Purple or violet cancellations are not necessarily revenue cancels. 14 of the 17 post offices and agencies used violet as well as black postal cancellations.

Zululand was annexed to Natal in Dec. 1897 and separate stamps were discontinued June 30, 1898.

Scott Advantage Stock Sheets

Take advantage of the specialty engineered Scott stock sheets that fit directly into you Scott National or country album. These high-quality stock sheets are available in multiple pockets that will fit your needs!

- Stock sheets match album pages in every respect, including size, border and color. Pages are punched to fit perfectly in your binder.

- These sheets are ideal for storing minor varieties and collateral material – a great place to keep new issues until the next supplement is available!

- Clear acetate pockets on heavyweight pages provide protection for your valuable stamps.

Retail Price $21.99   AA* Price $19.99

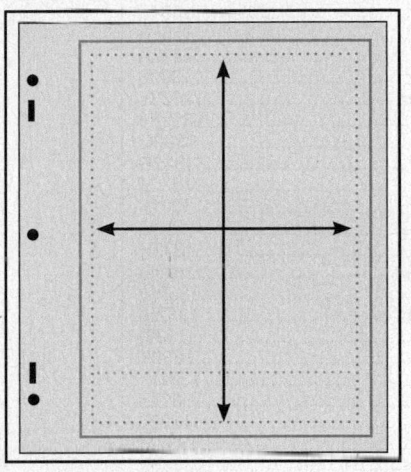

190 mm pocket width

Number of Pockets	Pocket Size	National	Specialty
1 Pocket	242mm	AD11	AD21
2 Pockets	119mm	AD12	AD22
3 Pockets	79mm	AD13	AD23
4 Pockets	58mm	AD14	AD24
5 Pockets	45mm	AD15	AD25
6 Pockets	37mm	AD16	AD26
7 Pockets	34mm	AD17	AD27
8 Pockets	31mm	AD18	AD28

190 mm pocket width

www.AmosAdvantage.com/ScottCatalogs

Call 800-572-6885

Outside U.S. & Canada call: (937) 498-0800

Vols. 6A-6B Number Additions, Deletions & Changes

Number in 2019 Catalogue	Number in 2020 Catalogue

Sierra Leone

new	859c
new	860c
new	861c
new	862c
new	863c
new	859d
new	860d
new	861d
new	862d
new	863d
new	864d
new	1259a
new	1332A
1332A	1332B
1332Am	1332Bn
new	1332Bo
1332B	1332C
1332C	1332D
1332D	1332E
1332E	1332F
1332F	1332G
1332G	1332H
1332H	1332I
new	1332Iq
1332Hn	1332Ip
1332I	1332J
1332J	1332K
1332Jo	1332Kr
new	1332Ks
1332K	1332L
1332L	1332M
1332Lp	1332Mt
new	1332Mu
1546b	1546c
1546Ae	1546Ai
1546Af	1546Aj
1546Ag	1546Ak
1546Bb	1546Bl
1546Be	1546Bm
1546Bf	1546Bn
1546Bg	1546Bo

South Africa

new	23k
new	23m
new	50c

Swaziland

new	J14a
new	J15a

Switzerland

new	220a

Thailand

new	194a
new	198a
new	283a
new	284a
new	285b
new	285Ac
new	286a
new	287a
new	288a
new	291a
new	292a
new	293a

Thrace

new	N8d
new	N10f
new	N11c
new	N75a
new	NJ1c
new	NJ2c
new	NJ3c

Turkey

B120a	deleted

Vatican City

40a	deleted

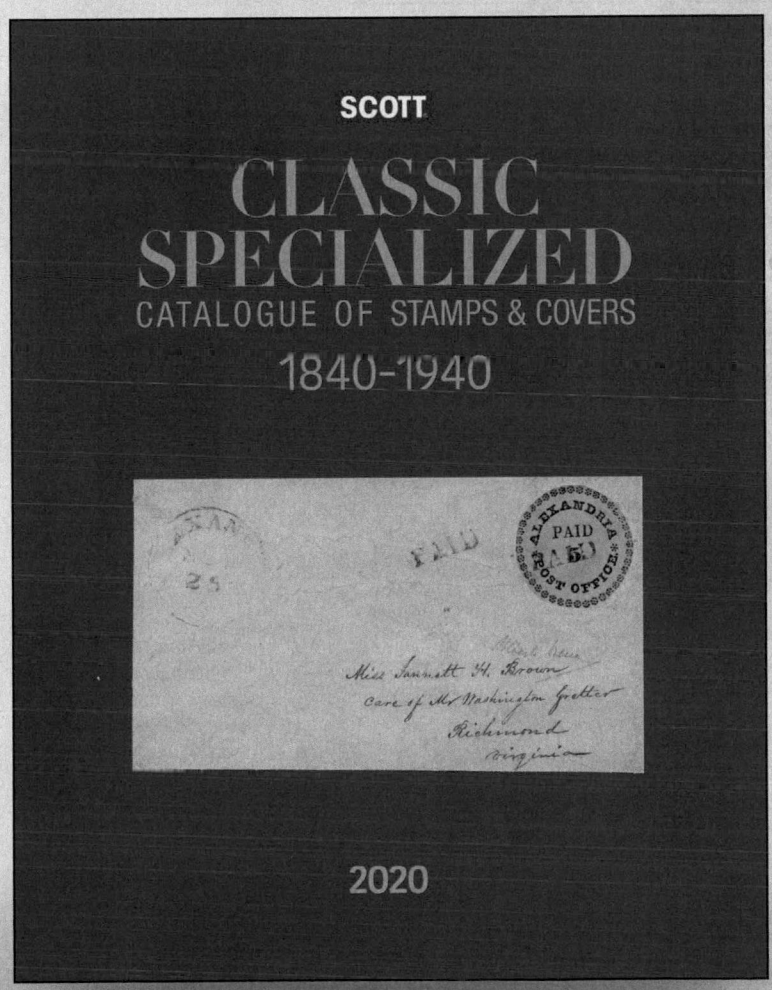

Illustrated Identifier

This section pictures stamps or parts of stamp designs that will help identify postage stamps that do not have English words on them.

Many of the symbols that identify stamps of countries are shown here as well as typical examples of their stamps.

See the Index and Identifier for stamps with inscriptions such as "sen," "posta," "Baja Porto," "Helvetia," "K.S.A.", etc.

1. HEADS, PICTURES AND NUMERALS

GREAT BRITAIN

Great Britain stamps never show the country name, but, except for postage dues, show a picture of the reigning monarch.

Victoria

Edward VII   George V   Edward VIII

George VI

Elizabeth II

Some George VI and Elizabeth II stamps are surcharged in annas, new paisa or rupees. These are listed under Oman.

Silhouette (sometimes facing right, generally at the top of stamp)

The silhouette indicates this is a British stamp. It is not a U.S. stamp.

VICTORIA

Queen Victoria

INDIA

Other stamps of India show this portrait of Queen Victoria and the words "Service" (or "Postage") and "Annas."

AUSTRIA

YUGOSLAVIA

(Also BOSNIA & HERZEGOVINA if imperf.)

BOSNIA & HERZEGOVINA

Denominations also appear in top corners instead of bottom corners.

HUNGARY

Another stamp has posthorn facing left

BRAZIL

AUSTRALIA

Kangaroo and Emu

GERMANY

Mecklenburg-Vorpommern

SWITZERLAND

PALAU

2. ORIENTAL INSCRIPTIONS

CHINA

Any stamp with this one character is from China (Imperial, Republic or People's Republic). This character appears in a four-character overprint on stamps of Manchukuo. These stamps are local provisionals, which are unlisted. Other overprinted Manchukuo stamps show this character, but have more than four characters in the overprints. These are listed in People's Republic of China.

Some Chinese stamps show the Sun.

Most stamps of Republic of China show this series of characters.

Stamps with the China character and this character are from People's Republic of China.

Calligraphic form of People's Republic of China

(一)	(二)	(三)	(四)	(五)	(六)
1	2	3	4	5	6
(七)	(八)	(九)	(十)	(一十)	(二十)
7	8	9	10	11	12

Chinese stamps without China character

REPUBLIC OF CHINA

PEOPLE'S REPUBLIC OF CHINA

Mao Tse-tung

MANCHUKUO

Temple   Emperor Pu-Yi

The first 3 characters are common to
many Manchukuo stamps.

The last 3 characters are common to
other Manchukuo stamps.

Orchid Crest

Manchukuo
stamp
without
these
elements

JAPAN

Chrysanthemum Crest   Country Name

Japanese stamps without these elements

The number of characters in the
center and the design of dragons on
the sides will vary.

RYUKYU ISLANDS

Country Name

PHILIPPINES
(Japanese Occupation)

Country Name

NETHERLANDS INDIES
(Japanese Occupation)

Indicates Japanese Occupation

Java   Sumatra

Country Name   Country Name

Moluccas, Celebes and
South Borneo

Country Name

NORTH BORNEO
(Japanese Occupation)

Indicates Japanese   Country
Occupation   Name

MALAYA
(Japanese Occupation)

Indicates Japanese   Country
Occupation   Name

BURMA
Union of Myanmar

Union of Myanmar
(Japanese Occupation)

Indicates Japanese
Occupation

Country
Name

Other Burma Japanese Occupation stamps
without these elements

Burmese Script

KOREA

These two characters, in any order,
are common to stamps from the
Republic of Korea (South Korea) or of
the People's Democratic Republic of
Korea (North Korea).

This series of four characters can be found
on the stamps of both Koreas.
Most stamps of the Democratic People's
Republic of Korea (North Korea)
have just this inscription.

Indicates Republic of Korea (South Korea)

South Korean postage stamps issed after
1952 do not show currency expressed
in Latin letters. Stamps wiith "
HW," "HWAN," "WON,"
"WN," "W" or "W" with two lines through it,
if not illustrated in listings of stamps
before this date, are revenues.
North Korean postage stamps do not have
currency expressed in Latin letters.

Yin Yang appears on some stamps.

South Korean stamps show Yin Yang and
starting in 1966, 'KOREA' in Latin letters

Example of South Korean stamps lacking
Latin text, Yin Yang and standard Korean
text of country name. North Korean stamps
never show Yin Yang and starting in 1976
are inscribed "DPRK" or "DPR KOREA" in
Latin letters.

THAILAND

Country Name

King Chulalongkorn

King Prajadhipok and
Chao P'ya Chakri

3. CENTRAL AND EASTERN ASIAN INSCRIPTIONS

INDIA - FEUDATORY STATES

Alwar

Bhor

Bundi

Similar stamps come with
different designs in corners
and differently drawn daggers
(at center of circle).

Dhar   Duttia

Faridkot

Hyderabad

Similar stamps exist with
different central design which is
inscribed "Postage"
or "Post & Receipt."

Indore

Jammu & Kashmir

Text varies.

Jasdan

Jhalawar

Kotah

Size and text varies

Nandgaon

Nowanuggur

Poonch

Similar stamps exist
in various sizes with different text

Rajasthan

Rajpeepla

Soruth

Tonk

BANGLADESH

Country Name

NEPAL

Similar stamps are smaller, have squares in
upper corners and have five or nine
characters in central bottom panel.

TANNU TUVA   ISRAEL

GEORGIA

This inscription
is found on other
pictorial stamps.

Country Name

ARMENIA

The four characters are found somewhere
on pictorial stamps. On some stamps only
the middle two are found.

4. AFRICAN INSCRIPTIONS

ETHIOPIA

5. ARABIC INSCRIPTIONS

١٢٣٤٥
1 2 3 4 5

٧٨٩٠
6 7 8 9 0

AFGHANISTAN

Many early Afghanistan stamps show Tiger's head, many of these have ornaments protruding from outer ring, others show inscriptions in black.

Arabic Script

Crest of King Amanullah

Mosque Gate & Crossed Cannons

افغانستان

The four characters are found somewhere on pictorial stamps. On some stamps only the middle two are found.

BAHRAIN

EGYPT

Postage

IRAN

Country Name

Royal Crown

Lion with Sword

Symbol

Emblem

IRAQ

JORDAN

LEBANON

Similar types have
denominations at top
and slightly different
design.

LIBYA

Country Name in various styles

Other Libya stamps show Eagle and
Shield (head facing either direction) or
Red, White and Black Shield (with or with-
out eagle in center).

Without Country Name

SAUDI ARABIA

Tughra (Central design)

← Palm Tree and Swords

SYRIA

Arab Government Issues

THRACE   **YEMEN**

PAKISTAN

PAKISTAN - BAHAWALPUR

Country Name in top panel, star and crescent

TURKEY

Star & Crescent is a device found on many Turkish stamps, but is also found on stamps from other Arabic areas (see Pakistan-Bahawalpur)

Tughra (similar tughras can be found on stamps of Turkey in Asia, Afghanistan and Saudi Arabia)

Mohammed V

Mustafa Kemal

Plane, Star and Crescent

TURKEY IN ASIA

Other Turkey in Asia pictorials show star & crescent. Other stamps show tughra shown under Turkey.

6. GREEK INSCRIPTIONS

GREECE

Country Name in various styles
(Some Crete stamps overprinted with the Greece country name are listed in Crete.)

Lepta

Drachma   Drachmas   Lepton
Abbreviated Country Name
Other forms of Country Name

No country name

CRETE

Country Name

Crete stamps with a surcharge that have the year "1922" are listed under Greece.

EPIRUS

Similar stamps have text above the eagle.

IONIAN IS.

7. CYRILLIC INSCRIPTIONS

RUSSIA

Postage Stamp   Imperial Eagle

Postage in various styles

Abbreviation   Abbreviation   Russia
for Kopeck   for Ruble

Abbreviation for Russian Soviet Federated Socialist Republic RSFSR stamps were overprinted (see below)

Abbreviation for Union of Soviet Socialist Republics

This item is footnoted in Latvia

RUSSIA - Army of the North

"OKCA"

RUSSIA - Wenden

RUSSIAN OFFICES IN THE TURKISH EMPIRE

These letters appear on other stamps of the Russian offices.

The unoverprinted version of this stamp and a similar stamp were overprinted by various countries (see below).

ARMENIA

BELARUS

FAR EASTERN REPUBLIC

Country Name

FINLAND

Circles and Dots
on stamps similar
to Imperial
Russia issues

SOUTH RUSSIA

Country Name

BATUM

Forms of Country Name

TRANSCAUCASIAN FEDERATED REPUBLICS

Abbreviation for
Country Name

KAZAKHSTAN

COUNTRY NAME KYRGYZSTAN

КЫРГЫЗСТАН Country
Name

ROMANIA

TAJIKISTAN

Country Name & Abbreviation

UKRAINE

Country Name in various forms

The trident appears
on many stamps,
usually as
an overprint.

Abbreviation for
Ukrainian
Soviet
Socialist
Republic

WESTERN UKRAINE

Abbreviation for
Country Name

AZERBAIJAN

AZƏRBAYCAN

Country Name

Abbreviation for Azerbaijan
Soviet Socialist Republic

MONTENEGRO

ЦРНА ГОРА

Country Name in various forms

Abbreviation
for country
name

No country name
(A similar Montenegro
stamp without coun-
try name has same
vignette.)

SERBIA

Country Name in various forms

Abbreviation for country name

No country name

MACEDONIA

Country Name

Different form of Country Name

SERBIA & MONTENEGRO

YUGOSLAVIA

Showing country name

No Country Name

BOSNIA & HERZEGOVINA
(Serb Administration)

РЕПУБЛИКА СРПСКА

Country Name

Different form of Country Name

No Country Name

BULGARIA

Country Name   Postage

Stotinka

Stotinki (plural)   Abbreviation for Stotinki

Country Name in various forms and styles

No country name

Abbreviation for Lev, leva

MONGOLIA

Country name in one word   Tugrik in Cyrillic

Country name in two words   Mung in Cyrillic

Mung in Mongolian

Tugrik in Mongolian

Arms

No Country Name

TOOLS OF THE EXPERTS!

6-IN-1 LED POCKET MAGNIFIER/MICROSCOPE (55X)

A powerful LED microscope (up to 55X magnification) teams up with two aspheric Perspex lenses (3X magnification large and 10X magnification small) to examine objects at various levels of detail. Built-in focus wheel ensures clarity. View objects even in low-light conditions with three lighting functions: three LED flashlight, simple UV light, one white LED. Black composite housing.

Item	Retail	AA*
MG61LED	$21.95	$19.95

3.2X LED ILLUMINATED MAGNIFIER

This 7" aluminum 3.2X magnifier is both beautiful and functional. Six LEDs surround the 1.375" lens to provide glare-free illumination. Zippered protective case and 2 AA batteries included.

Item	Retail	AA*
MG32XL	$35.95	$31.95

BLACK TRUE COLOR LIGHT

A versatile, compact light that provides superior image and color rendering while reducing glare and eye strain. Technologically advanced light produces a precise blend of light for contrast and brightness that makes colors vibrant and details incredibly clear. The lamp comes with an "E"(electronic) tube for a quicker starting time. This does plug into an outlet for long uses.

Item	Retail	AA*
ACC191BB	$79.99	$49.99

ZOOM 20X-40X MICROSCOPE WITH LED

This practical zoom microscope provides what collectors have been waiting for – outstanding clarity and resolution. Magnification is continuously adjustable between 20X and 40X. Powerful LED lighting illuminates the stage (3 #LR44 batteries included). Stand, examination slides, and slide covers also included.

Item	Retail	AA*
LHPM3	$29.95	$21.95

10X POCKET MAGNIFIER

This compact, portable and easy-to-use 10x pocket magnifier comes with its own illumination from a brilliant white LED. The glass lens is 18mm (3/4") in diameter.

Item	Retail	AA*
MG10XLED	$12.95	$11.95

PHONESCOPE DIGITAL MICROSCOPE

Clip this compact Lighthouse Phonescope lens on your smartphone or tablet to transform it into a powerful digital microscope. See the smallest details and instantly capture high-quality images and videos. The precision macro glass lens offers up to 60X magnification and requires no batteries. Field of view: 1/2" (13mm). Phonescope works with all popular smartphones without scratching display. Image resolution and zoom function dependent upon your device.

Item	Retail	AA*
LHSCOPE	$25.99	$21.99

SHERLOCK WATERMARK DETECTOR

Reveal every detail of your stamps whether it is watermarks or pape irregularities, quality defects, or repairs. Easy to use: Insert stamp, turn on the light, and you can already see the secrets of your stamps in every detail. The special feature of this watermark detector is the different light colors (white, red, green, and blue), which can be chosen to light up the stamp. The brightness can be infinitely adjusted. Overall size: 35/8" x 51/8" x 57/8"

Item	Retail	AA*
LHWZ2	$325.00	$276.25

13W DUOFLEX MAGNIFIER DESK LAMP

The OttLite DuoFlex has a two-pronged approach to enhance your vision. First, the large 3X-5X magnifier enlarges your subject. Then the energy-efficient 13w "E" bulb spotlights the field. Flexible arms allow nearly infinite positioning. Long-term bulb is rated to last up to 10,000 hours.

Item	Retail	AA*
ACC213W	$109.99	$59.99

DIGITAL MICROSCOPE & 16" STAND

The industry-leading 5.0 megapixel resolution makes the smallest details on coins and stamps visible on your computer screen via the included USB cable. With the magnification range of 10x-300x, makes this microscope a valuable tool. With this exclusive deal from Amos Advantage, you will receive an adjustable 16" stainless-steel stand. This will allow you to get the best photos and videos of your collection.

Item	Retail	AA
LHDMSET	$249.90	$223.16

www.AmosAdvantage.com

Call: 1-800-572-6885

Outside U.S. & Canada Call: 1-937-498-0800

ORDERING INFORMATION: *AA prices apply to paid subscribers of Amos Media titles, or orders placed online. Prices, terms and product availability subject to change. Taxes will apply in CA, OH, & IL. Shipping and handling rates will apply. See below.

SHOWGARD MOUNTS

Showgard mounts are manufactured with the highest archival qualities in mind. The foil used to produce the mounts is acid free and stronger than other mounts for maximum protection and durability. Selecting the right size mount for your stamp is easy. Simply use a millimeter ruler to measure the stamps' width then the height. Showgard incorporates these measurements into their product numbers to insure you get the right size. Mounts available with clear (c) or black (b) backgrounds, with a few exceptions. Please specify background preference when ordering.

Item	Description	Mounts	Retail	AA*
SGC50X31	50/31 U.S. Jumbo Singles - Horizontal	40	$3.95	$2.85
SGCV31X50	31/50 U.S. Jumbo Singles - Vertical	40	$3.95	$2.85
SGJ40X25	40/25 U.S. Commem. - Horizontal	40	$3.95	$2.85
SGJV25X40	25/40 U.S. Commem. - Vertical	40	$3.95	$2.85
SGE22X25	22/25 U.S. Regular Issues - Vertical	40	$3.95	$2.85
SGEH25X22	25/22 U.S. Regular Issues - Horizontal	40	$3.95	$2.85
SGT25X27	25/27 U.S. Famous Americans	40	$3.95	$2.85
SGU33X27	33/27 U.N., Germany	40	$3.95	$2.85
SGN40X27	40/27 United Nations	40	$3.95	$2.85
SGAH41X31	41/31 U.S. Semi Jumbo - Horizontal	40	$3.95	$2.85
SGAV31X41	31/41 U.S. Semi Jumbo - Vertical	40	$3.95	$2.85
SGDH52X36	52/36 U.S. Duck Stamps	30	$3.95	$2.85
SGS31X31	31/31 U.S. Celebrate the Century	30	$3.95	$2.85
SGUS2	Cut Style with Tray-8 Sizes	320	$32.95	$23.50
SGUS3	Strip Style w/Tray-No. 22 thru No. 52	75	$49.95	$35.75
SGUS1	U.S. Strip Sizes No. 22 thru No. 52	50	$24.50	$17.50
SG67X25	67/25 U.S. Coil Strips of 3	40	$8.35	$5.95
SG57X55	57/55 U.S. Regular Issue	25	$8.35	$5.95
SG106X55	106/55 U.S. 3¢, 4¢ Commemoratives	20	$8.35	$5.95
SG105X57	105/57 U.S. Giori Press Issues	20	$8.35	$5.95
SG127X70	127/70 U.S. Jumbo Issues	10	$8.35	$5.95
SG140X89	140/89 Postcards, Souvenir Sheets	10	$8.35	$5.95
SG165X94	165/94 First Day Covers	10	$8.35	$5.95
SG20	215/20 U.S. Mini Stamps, etc.	22	$9.75	$6.95
SG22	215/22 Narrow U.S. Airs	22	$9.75	$6.95
SG24	215/24 U.K. and Canada, early U.S.	22	$9.75	$6.95
SG25	215/25 U.S. Commem. & Regular Issues	22	$9.75	$6.95
SG27	215/27 U.S. Famous Americans, U.N.	22	$9.75	$6.95
SG28	215/28 Switzerland, Liechtenstein	22	$9.75	$6.95
SG30	215/30 U.S. Special Stamps, Jamestown	22	$9.75	$6.95
SG31	315/31 U.S. Squares & Semi Jumbo	22	$9.75	$6.95
SG33	215/33 U.K. Issues, Misc. Foreign	22	$9.75	$6.95
SG36	215/36 Duck Stamps, Misc. Foreign	15	$9.75	$6.95
SG39	215/39 U.S. Magsaysay, Misc. Foreign	15	$9.75	$6.95
SG41	215/41 U.S. Vertical Commem. Israel Tabs	15	$9.75	$6.95
SG44	215/44 Booklet Panes, Hatteras Quartet	15	$9.75	$6.95
SG48	215/48 Canada Reg. Issue & Comm Blocks	15	$9.75	$6.95
SG50	215/50 U.S. Plain Blocks of 4	15	$9.75	$6.95
SG52	215/52 France Paintings, Misc. Foreign	15	$9.75	$6.95
SG57	215/57 U.S. Commem. Plate Blocks	15	$9.75	$6.95
SG61	215/61 Souvenir Sheets, Tab Singles, etc.	15	$9.75	$6.95
SG63	240/63 U.S. Semi Jumbo Blocks	10	$11.95	$8.75
SG66	240/66 U.S. ATM Panes, SA Duck Panes	10	$11.95	$8.75
SG68	240/68 Canadian Plate Blocks, etc.	10	$11.95	$8.75
SG74	240/74 U.N. Inscription Blocks of 4	10	$11.95	$8.75
SG80	240/80 U.S. Commem. Blocks	10	$11.95	$8.75
SG82	240/82 U.N. Chagall SS, Canada Plate Blocks	10	$11.95	$8.75
SG84	240/84 Israel Plate Blocks, etc.	10	$11.95	$8.75
SG89	240/89 U.N. Inscription Blocks of 6	10	$11.95	$8.75
SG100	240/100 U.S. Squares Plate Blocks	7	$11.95	$8.75
SG120	240/120 Miniature Sheets	7	$11.95	$8.75
SG70	264/70 U.S. Jumbo Plate Blocks	10	$16.25	$11.50
SG91	264/91 U.K. Souvenir Sheets	10	$16.25	$11.50
SG105	264/105 U.K. Blocks, Covers, etc.	10	$16.25	$11.50
SG107	264/107 U.S. Plate No. Strip of 20	10	$16.25	$11.50
SG111	264/111 U.S. Floating Plate No. Strips of 20	5	$10.75	$7.75
SG127	264/127 Modern U.S. Definitive Sheets of 20	5	$11.95	$8.50
SG137	264/137 U.N. SS, U.K. Coronation	5	$12.95	$9.50
SG158	264/158 Miniature Sheets, Apollo Soyuz PB	5	$14.50	$10.50
SG175	264/175 U.S. Sheets-Pan American Reissues	5	$15.95	$11.75
SG188	264/188 U.S. Miniature Sheets-Hollywood, etc.	5	$16.95	$11.95
SG198	264/198 U.S. Miniature Sheets	5	$17.25	$12.50
SGMPK	Assortment No. 22 thru No. 41	12	$7.50	$5.50
SGMPK2	Assortment No. 76 thru No. 171	15	$32.75	$23.75
SGAB	U.S. SS to 1975-except White Plains	11	$8.75	$6.50
SGWSE	World Stamp Expo Souvenir Sheets	3	$2.75	$1.95
SGRP94	U.S. 1994 Souvenir Sheets (Black Only)	5	$10.25	$7.50
SGRPAC97	Pacific 97 Issues	7	$5.75	$4.25
SGDC2006	Washington 2006 Souvenir Sheets (Black Only)	4	$7.95	$5.75
SGTM	Trans-Mississippi Issues	11	$5.75	$4.25
SGSPC	Space Exploration Sheets	5	$7.25	$5.25
SGNY2016	New York 2016 WWS Releases		$12.50	$10.00
SG265X231	265/231 U.S. Full Sheets & Souvenir Cards	5	$21.25	$15.25
SG260X25	260/25 U.S. Coil Strips of up to 11 stamps	25	$12.75	$8.95
SG293X30	293/30 U.S. American Eagle Coil Strips of up to 11 stamps	5	$4.25	$3.25

Item	Description	Mounts	Retail	AA*
SG260X40	260/40 U.S. Postal People Full Strip	10	$10.50	$7.50
SG260X46	260/46 U.S. Vending Booklets	10	$10.50	$7.50
SG260X55	260/55 U.S. 13¢ Eagle Full Strip	10	$10.50	$7.50
SG260X59	260/59 U.S. Double Press Reg. Iss. Strips of 20	10	$10.50	$7.50
SG111X91	111/91 U.S. Columbian Souvenir Sheets	6	$5.50	$3.95
SG229X131	229/131 U.S. WWII Sheets, Looney Tunes	5	$10.75	$7.75
SG187X144	187/144 U.N. Flag Sheetlets	10	$18.50	$12.95
SG204X153	204/153 U.S. Commem. Sheets, Bicentennial	5	$11.25	$8.25
SG120X207	120/207 U.S. Ameripex Presidential Sheetlets	4	$7.75	$5.75
SG192X201	192/201 U.S. Classics Mini-Sheets	5	$13.50	$9.75
SG280X228	280/228 U.S. Greetings From America Sheets	5	$20.50	$14.75
SG191X229	191/229 U.S. Celebrate The Century Sheets	5	$15.25	$11.25
SG89X83	89/83 Washington 2006 Souvenir sheet and other miniature panes	3	$2.50	$1.89
SG146X84	146/84 Distinguished Americans, Cycling Souvenir Sheet and other miniature panes	3	$3.75	$2.75
SG203X146	203/146 Hanukkah, Kwanzaa, Eid, Wedding Cake Series, Ronald Reagan, Dogs at Work, Jose Ferrer, Samuel de Champlain SS, etc.	3	$7.50	$5.50
SG178X181	178/181 Butterfly Series, Carmel Mission Express Mail, Celebrate Scouting, Cranes, etc.	3	$7.50	$5.50
SG148X196	148/196 $5.00 Waves of Color, Moon Landing 25th Anniversary, etc.	3	$7.50	$5.50
SG76	264/76 BEP SS, Booklets, Plate Blocks	5	$11.95	$8.75
SG96	264/96 Souvenir Sheets, Panes	5	$11.95	$8.75
SG109	264/109 Foreign Miniature Sheets	5	$11.95	$8.75
SG115	264/115 Foreign Miniature Sheets	5	$11.95	$8.75
SG117	264/117 Foreign Miniature Sheets	5	$11.95	$8.75
SG121	264/121 Foreign Miniature Sheets	5	$11.95	$8.75
SG131	264/131 Looney Toons, Misc. Sheetlets	5	$11.95	$8.75
SG135	264/135 Foreign Miniature Sheets	5	$11.95	$8.75
SG139	264/139 White House Pane, etc.	5	$11.95	$8.75
SG143	264/143 Victorian Love, Misc. Sheets	5	$11.95	$8.75
SG147	264/147 Cinco de Mayo, etc.	5	$14.95	$10.75
SG151	264/151 Antique Auto, Communication, etc.	5	$15.50	$11.08
SG163	264/163 Tropical Flowers, UN Human Rights	5	$14.95	$10.75
SG167	264/167 Misc. U.S. Sheetlets	5	$14.95	$10.75
SG171	264/171 Helping Children Learn, etc.	5	$14.95	$10.75
SG181	264/181 U.S. Sheets—Calder, All Aboard, etc.	5	$18.50	$13.25
SG201	264/201 Dinosaurs, etc.	5	$18.50	$13.25
SG215	264/215 U.S. Sheets—Arctic Animals, Ballet, etc.	5	$18.50	$13.25

7" LIGHTHOUSE STAMP MOUNT CUTTER

This affordable and versatile mount cutter features an attachable measuring scale up to 7" (180mm) with an adjustable stop for accurate and clean cuts every time.

Item	Retail	AA*
LH180MC	$23.99	$19.99

AMOS ADVANTAGE

Call **1-800-572-6885**

Outside U.S. & Canada: (937) 498-0800

Visit www.**AmosAdvantage**.com

Mail orders to: P.O. Box 4129, Sidney, OH 45365

INDEX TO ADVERTISERS
2020 VOLUME 6B

2020
VOLUME 6B
DEALER DIRECTORY
YELLOW PAGE LISTINGS

This section of your Scott Catalogue contains
advertisements to help you conveniently find
what you need, when you need it...!